20 MAY 14
SINCE HE CAME UP FELIX 73 QS
8+ INNINGS / 2 E.
#2 CLIFF LEE 71



# The Bill James Handbook 2014

## Baseball Info Solutions

www.baseballinfosolutions.com

## Published by ACTA Sports

A Division of ACTA Publications

Cover by Tom A. Wright
Cover Photo by Jim Cowsert
Back Cover Photo by Reid Compton



First Edition: November 2013

Published by:
ACTA Sports, a division of ACTA Publications
4848 North Clark Street
Chicago, IL 60640
(800) 397-2282
www.actasports.com www.actapublications.com

ISBN: 978-0879-465131
ISSN: 1940-8668

Printed in the United States of America by McNaughton & Gunn

## Dedication

Producing this book in the time frame that we do is no small accomplishment. For 14 days after the end of the major league baseball season we give up our personal lives to produce this book. It takes a huge toll on us, our families, and our friends. I would like to dedicate this book to my wife, Renee, and my two children, Cierra and Cayden.

I would also like to thank everyone here at BIS that contributed to the creation of this book.

Patrick Coyle

# Table of Contents

# Introduction to the 25th Edition

The Sporting News used to publish an annual summary of player batting records, the *Baseball Register*, and you have to understand, I loved the *Baseball Register*. In the fall of 1988 we still thought of The Sporting News as a national institution, more on the level of Mount Rushmore than The Andy Griffith Show. We didn't really have any intention of competing with the *Baseball Register* or The Sporting News; it was more along the lines of filling a gap in the market. They didn't publish the *Register* until the rosters were finalized at the end of spring training, which meant that the book wasn't available until May of next year. That was kind of ridiculous, and there were problems with the product, which had to do with the fact that the book had been designed in 1940 and had evolved backward. The book didn't publish walks and strikeouts by hitters, or stolen bases. The pitcher's records didn't have a "Save" column.

Our notion was to do the things that they chose not to do. In July or August of 1988 I wrote a memo to John Dewan and Don Zminda of STATS, Inc., proposing that we do a book which summarized each player's record, but which would come out in the fall and would have a more modern composition of statistical categories. I went to Chicago a few weeks later, and was astonished to discover that John, Don, Sue Dewan and the rest of the staff had taken my memo, and had actually produced the book in draft form. Astonished may be an understatement. I had worked with New York publishers for about ten years by then, and my experience with publishing companies of the 1980s was that they were not quick on their feet. It was a revelation to me that somebody could, by determination, hard work and modern technology, take something from a concept to a product in the space of a few weeks.

In those days I used to work in baseball salary negotiations, on behalf of the players, employed by their agents. It was another revelation to me when, weeks later, I went to a baseball salary arbitration case, and the team had two copies of my book—this book—on the table. I wouldn't have thought to use my own book as a source, because the rule is that anything that is privately generated is somewhat suspect. You don't go into a salary arbitration case, as a rule, and say, "Here, I've come up with a new way of rating players." Doesn't work. The next year, there were five copies of the *Handbook* on the arbitration table, and, the year after that, everybody had one. It had become the standard reference.

That was pre-internet, of course; I guess the internet existed then, but the sites and sources we all use now didn't. In ten or twelve years the *Handbook* had driven *The Baseball Register* out of existence, which was never our intention, and about which, in all candor, I've always been disappointed; I loved the old *Registers*, and I wish they could have found a way to keep the ship in the water. They needed to be creative, and they weren't.

We took the book from STATS, Inc. to Baseball Info Solutions. Reagan was President when we started the book. John Dewan and I still work together on this book. I don't see Don Zminda much anymore, although he still works in the business and I still think of him as a friend. Don't see Sue Dewan as much as I used to, every couple of years, maybe. I quit working with the agents when the money got so big it was no longer money, but the concept of money. I went to work for the Red Sox, eleven years ago, and still do. Hundreds and hundreds of people have worked on the book, over the years. We have gone through generations of software engineers and fact checkers and writers and editors. I wish I could remember all of your names; I'd like to thank you all individually. That doesn't seem practical.

And now. . .well, 25 years, hard to believe, and the market is changing on us as it did on the other guys, and we won't be able to keep this one afloat forever, either. We add new features every year, occasionally get rid of an old feature; we try to make space and time to do a little bit of original writing each year. Like everyone in our generation, we are trapped in the difficult transition from the hard copy economic models that had existed for many decades to the electronic market. It is not easy to get young people to buy books.

But this is not a transition to a darker world, but a transition to something better. The essential economic problem that the internet has created for publishers is that the production and distribution costs have all but disappeared, and the profit rode on the back of the production and distribution costs. There was a supply chain: Bookstores, book distributors, printers, publishers, writers. The supply chain has evaporated, leaving the publishers and writers standing naked in the rain. The writer and the reader communicate literally at the speed of light. The invention of the automobile was tough on people who made a living selling buggy whips. We will adapt and survive, and we'll make it to 30 years, looking up.

# 2013 Team Statistics

Curious to know how a specific team stacked up against the competition? This is the section where you will find that info. In addition to the traditional Win-Loss standings, we've got various split types, the number of days each team held down first place during the seaon, and a team-by-team breakdown of head-to-head wins. For instance, after moving into the American League for 2013, the Houston Astros had a 8-12 record against their old National League adversaries. And the team that spent the most time in first place in 2013 without winning its division was the Texas Rangers (92 days).

You will also find batting, pitching, and fielding stats for each team in these pages. This includes a Pitching Staff Summary for each team, as well as a breakdown of the Defensive Runs Saved for each team at each position. You'll see that the Minnesota Twins got the fewest innings out of their starters in 2013, and that the Tampa Bay Rays were the most successful team at implementing defensive shifts.

# 2013 American League Standings

## Overall

| EAST | | | | | | |
|---|---|---|---|---|---|---|
| Team | W-L | Pct | GB | D1 | LD1 | LLd |
| Boston Red Sox | 97-65 | .599 | 0.0 | 158 | 9/30 | 9.5 |
| Tampa Bay Rays | 92-71 | .564 | 5.5 | 8 | 8/24 | 0.5 |
| New York Yankees | 85-77 | .525 | 12.0 | 19 | 5/26 | 2.0 |
| Baltimore Orioles | 85-77 | .525 | 12.0 | 6 | 5/8 | 0.0 |
| Toronto Blue Jays | 74-88 | .457 | 23.0 | 0 | - | 0.0 |

| CENTRAL | | | | | | |
|---|---|---|---|---|---|---|
| Team | W-L | Pct | GB | D1 | LD1 | LLd |
| Detroit Tigers | 93-69 | .574 | 0.0 | 155 | 9/30 | 8.5 |
| Cleveland Indians | 92-70 | .568 | 1.0 | 15 | 7/2 | 2.5 |
| Kansas City Royals | 86-76 | .531 | 7.0 | 20 | 5/2 | 1.5 |
| Minnesota Twins | 66-96 | .407 | 27.0 | 4 | 4/7 | 0.0 |
| Chicago White Sox | 63-99 | .389 | 30.0 | 8 | 4/8 | 0.5 |

| WEST | | | | | | |
|---|---|---|---|---|---|---|
| Team | W-L | Pct | GB | D1 | LD1 | LLd |
| Oakland Athletics | 96-66 | .593 | 0.0 | 93 | 9/30 | 8.5 |
| Texas Rangers | 91-72 | .558 | 5.5 | 92 | 9/5 | 7.0 |
| Los Angeles Angels | 78-84 | .481 | 18.0 | 1 | 4/1 | 0.0 |
| Seattle Mariners | 71-91 | .438 | 25.0 | 3 | 4/3 | 0.5 |
| Houston Astros | 51-111 | .315 | 45.0 | 2 | 4/1 | 1.0 |

**Wild Card Clinch Dates: Cleveland 9/29, Tampa Bay 9/30. Division Clinch Dates:Boston 9/20, Oakland 9/22, Detroit 9/25.**
**D1 = Number of days a team had at least a share of first place of their division; LD1 = Last date the team had at least a share of first place; LLd = The largest number of games that a team led their division by.**

## East Division

| | AT | | VERSUS | | | | | | CONDITIONS | | | | GAME | | | MONTHLY | | | | | | ALL-STAR | |
|---|---|---|---|---|---|---|---|---|---|---|---|---|---|---|---|---|---|---|---|---|---|---|---|
| Tm | Home | Road | East | Cent | West | NL | LHS | RHS | Day | Night | Grass | Turf | 1-Rn | 5+Rn | XInn | April | May | June | July | Aug | Sept | Pre | Post |
| Bos | 53-28 | 44-37 | 44-32 | 19-15 | 20-12 | 14-6 | 32-22 | 65-43 | 28-15 | 69-50 | 86-58 | 11-7 | 21-21 | 33-13 | 10-6 | 18-8 | 15-15 | 17-11 | 15-10 | 16-12 | 16-9 | 58-39 | 39-26 |
| TB | 51-30 | 41-41 | 43-33 | 19-14 | 18-16 | 12-8 | 30-23 | 62-48 | 29-24 | 63-47 | 36-37 | 56-34 | 26-21 | 23-20 | 9-7 | 12-14 | 18-10 | 13-15 | 21-5 | 11-15 | 17-12 | 55-41 | 37-30 |
| NYY | 46-35 | 39-42 | 37-39 | 22-11 | 17-16 | 9-11 | 32-23 | 53-54 | 32-24 | 53-53 | 77-67 | 8-10 | 30-16 | 18-20 | 6-6 | 16-10 | 15-13 | 11-16 | 14-12 | 16-12 | 13-14 | 51-44 | 34-33 |
| Bal | 46-35 | 39-42 | 36-40 | 17-16 | 21-12 | 11-9 | 27-26 | 58-51 | 27-29 | 58-48 | 78-64 | 7-13 | 20-31 | 14-11 | 8-7 | 16-11 | 15-13 | 16-12 | 12-13 | 12-14 | 14-14 | 53-43 | 32-34 |
| Tor | 40-41 | 34-47 | 30-46 | 16-16 | 17-17 | 11-9 | 19-24 | 55-64 | 31-30 | 43-58 | 30-41 | 44-47 | 20-29 | 21-22 | 8-9 | 10-17 | 13-15 | 17-9 | 10-16 | 12-17 | 12-14 | 45-49 | 29-39 |

## Central Division

| | AT | | VERSUS | | | | | | CONDITIONS | | | | GAME | | | MONTHLY | | | | | | ALL-STAR | |
|---|---|---|---|---|---|---|---|---|---|---|---|---|---|---|---|---|---|---|---|---|---|---|---|
| Tm | Home | Road | East | Cent | West | NL | LHS | RHS | Day | Night | Grass | Turf | 1-Rn | 5+Rn | XInn | April | May | June | July | Aug | Sept | Pre | Post |
| Det | 51-30 | 42-39 | 17-15 | 47-29 | 17-17 | 12-8 | 27-23 | 66-46 | 32-29 | 61-40 | 89-66 | 4-3 | 20-26 | 33-15 | 6-13 | 15-10 | 14-14 | 14-13 | 18-8 | 19-11 | 13-13 | 52-42 | 41-27 |
| Cle | 51-30 | 41-40 | 12-21 | 44-32 | 25-8 | 11-9 | 36-20 | 56-50 | 33-20 | 59-50 | 89-67 | 3-3 | 30-17 | 28-21 | 10-2 | 11-13 | 18-12 | 15-13 | 15-10 | 12-16 | 21-6 | 51-44 | 41-26 |
| KC | 44-37 | 42-39 | 19-15 | 44-32 | 14-18 | 9-11 | 24-24 | 62-52 | 34-21 | 52-55 | 82-73 | 4-3 | 31-25 | 20-13 | 11-4 | 14-10 | 8-20 | 16-11 | 15-10 | 16-15 | 17-10 | 43-49 | 43-27 |
| Min | 32-49 | 34-47 | 10-23 | 29-47 | 19-14 | 8-12 | 16-21 | 50-75 | 30-34 | 36-62 | 65-90 | 1-6 | 24-25 | 12-30 | 9-7 | 11-12 | 12-17 | 13-13 | 9-17 | 13-17 | 8-20 | 39-53 | 27-43 |
| CWS | 37-44 | 26-55 | 14-19 | 26-50 | 15-18 | 8-12 | 13-25 | 50-74 | 24-32 | 39-67 | 61-94 | 2-5 | 24-36 | 7-21 | 8-15 | 10-15 | 14-13 | 8-19 | 8-18 | 16-13 | 7-21 | 37-55 | 26-44 |

## West Division

| | AT | | VERSUS | | | | | | CONDITIONS | | | | GAME | | | MONTHLY | | | | | | ALL-STAR | |
|---|---|---|---|---|---|---|---|---|---|---|---|---|---|---|---|---|---|---|---|---|---|---|---|
| Tm | Home | Road | East | Cent | West | NL | LHS | RHS | Day | Night | Grass | Turf | 1-Rn | 5+Rn | XInn | April | May | June | July | Aug | Sept | Pre | Post |
| Oak | 52-29 | 44-37 | 17-15 | 22-12 | 44-32 | 13-7 | 32-22 | 64-44 | 39-29 | 57-37 | 93-62 | 3-4 | 30-20 | 29-16 | 7-6 | 16-12 | 16-12 | 16-11 | 15-10 | 14-13 | 19-8 | 56-39 | 40-27 |
| Tex | 46-36 | 45-36 | 15-20 | 13-19 | 53-23 | 10-10 | 32-19 | 59-53 | 21-25 | 70-47 | 88-68 | 3-4 | 27-20 | 27-17 | 3-9 | 17-9 | 17-11 | 14-14 | 11-15 | 20-7 | 12-16 | 54-41 | 37-31 |
| LAA | 39-42 | 39-42 | 18-16 | 18-14 | 32-44 | 10-10 | 18-26 | 60-58 | 25-22 | 53-62 | 73-83 | 5-1 | 24-28 | 18-23 | 8-8 | 9-17 | 16-13 | 14-13 | 9-15 | 14-14 | 16-12 | 44-49 | 34-35 |
| Sea | 36-45 | 35-46 | 14-18 | 13-21 | 36-40 | 8-12 | 22-29 | 49-62 | 22-32 | 49-59 | 68-88 | 3-3 | 19-29 | 18-36 | 6-15 | 12-17 | 12-14 | 11-16 | 15-10 | 12-16 | 9-18 | 43-52 | 28-39 |
| Hou | 24-57 | 27-54 | 9-24 | 9-24 | 25-51 | 8-12 | 13-33 | 38-78 | 11-35 | 40-76 | 49-106 | 2-5 | 18-36 | 13-34 | 4-8 | 8-19 | 10-18 | 12-15 | 6-18 | 8-21 | 7-20 | 33-61 | 18-50 |

## Team vs. Team Breakdown

| | EAST | | | | | CENTRAL | | | | | WEST | | | | |
|---|---|---|---|---|---|---|---|---|---|---|---|---|---|---|---|
| | Bos | TB | NYY | Bal | Tor | Det | Cle | KC | Min | CWS | Oak | Tex | LAA | Sea | Hou |
| Boston Red Sox | - | 12 | 13 | 8 | 11 | 3 | 6 | 2 | 4 | 4 | 3 | 2 | 3 | 6 | 6 |
| Tampa Bay Rays | 7 | - | 12 | 13 | 11 | 3 | 4 | 1 | 6 | 5 | 3 | 4 | 3 | 3 | 5 |
| New York Yankees | 6 | 7 | - | 10 | 14 | 3 | 6 | 5 | 5 | 3 | 1 | 3 | 4 | 4 | 5 |
| Baltimore Orioles | 11 | 6 | 9 | - | 10 | 4 | 3 | 3 | 3 | 4 | 5 | 5 | 5 | 2 | 4 |
| Toronto Blue Jays | 8 | 8 | 5 | 9 | - | 2 | 2 | 4 | 5 | 3 | 3 | 6 | 1 | 3 | 4 |
| Detroit Tigers | 4 | 3 | 3 | 2 | 5 | - | 15 | 9 | 11 | 12 | 3 | 3 | 0 | 5 | 6 |
| Cleveland Indians | 1 | 2 | 1 | 4 | 4 | 4 | - | 10 | 13 | 17 | 5 | 5 | 4 | 5 | 6 |
| Kansas City Royals | 5 | 6 | 2 | 4 | 2 | 10 | 9 | - | 15 | 10 | 1 | 3 | 2 | 4 | 4 |
| Minnesota Twins | 3 | 1 | 2 | 3 | 1 | 8 | 6 | 4 | - | 11 | 1 | 4 | 5 | 4 | 5 |
| Chicago White Sox | 2 | 2 | 3 | 3 | 4 | 7 | 2 | 9 | 8 | - | 2 | 4 | 3 | 3 | 3 |
| Oakland Athletics | 3 | 3 | 5 | 2 | 4 | 4 | 2 | 5 | 6 | 5 | - | 10 | 11 | 8 | 15 |
| Texas Rangers | 4 | 4 | 4 | 2 | 1 | 4 | 1 | 3 | 3 | 2 | 9 | - | 15 | 12 | 17 |
| Los Angeles Angels | 3 | 4 | 3 | 2 | 6 | 6 | 2 | 5 | 1 | 4 | 8 | 4 | - | 11 | 9 |
| Seattle Mariners | 1 | 3 | 3 | 4 | 3 | 2 | 2 | 3 | 3 | 3 | 11 | 7 | 8 | - | 10 |
| Houston Astros | 1 | 2 | 1 | 2 | 3 | 1 | 1 | 2 | 1 | 4 | 4 | 2 | 10 | 9 | - |

# 2013 National League Standings

## Overall

| EAST | | | | | | | CENTRAL | | | | | | | WEST | | | | | | |
|---|---|---|---|---|---|---|---|---|---|---|---|---|---|---|---|---|---|---|---|---|
| Team | W-L | Pct | GB | D1 | LD1 | LLd | Team | W-L | Pct | GB | D1 | LD1 | LLd | Team | W-L | Pct | GB | D1 | LD1 | LLd |
| Atlanta Braves | 96-66 | .593 | 0.0 | 182 | 9/30 | 16.0 | St Louis Cardinals | 97-65 | .599 | 0.0 | 130 | 9/30 | 4.0 | Los Angeles Dodgers | 92-70 | .568 | 0.0 | 73 | 9/30 | 13.5 |
| Washington Nationals | 86-76 | .531 | 10.0 | 6 | 4/6 | 1.0 | Pittsburgh Pirates | 94-68 | .580 | 3.0 | 55 | 9/16 | 4.0 | Arizona Diamondbacks | 81-81 | .500 | 11.0 | 80 | 7/21 | 4.5 |
| New York Mets | 74-88 | .457 | 22.0 | 3 | 4/3 | 0.0 | Cincinnati Reds | 90-72 | .556 | 7.0 | 11 | 4/22 | 2.0 | San Francisco Giants | 76-86 | .469 | 16.0 | 29 | 5/26 | 2.5 |
| Philadelphia Phillies | 73-89 | .451 | 23.0 | 0 | - | 0.0 | Milwaukee Brewers | 74-88 | .457 | 23.0 | 1 | 4/1 | 0.0 | San Diego Padres | 76-86 | .469 | 16.0 | 0 | - | 0.0 |
| Miami Marlins | 62-100 | .383 | 34.0 | 0 | - | 0.0 | Chicago Cubs | 66-96 | .407 | 31.0 | 4 | 4/4 | 0.5 | Colorado Rockies | 74-88 | .457 | 18.0 | 32 | 5/25 | 2.5 |

**Wild Card Clinch Dates: Pittsburgh 9/28, Cincinnati 9/28. Division Clinch Dates:Los Angeles 9/19, Atlanta 9/22, St Louis 9/27.**
**D1 = Number of days a team had at least a share of first place of their division; LD1 = Last date the team had at least a share of first place; LLd = The largest number of games that a team led their division**

## East Division

| | AT | | VERSUS | | | | | | CONDITIONS | | | | GAME | | | MONTHLY | | | | | | ALL-STAR | |
|---|---|---|---|---|---|---|---|---|---|---|---|---|---|---|---|---|---|---|---|---|---|---|---|
| Tm | Home | Road | East | Cent | West | AL | LHS | RHS | Day | Night | Grass | Turf | 1-Rn | 5+Rn | XInn | April | May | June | July | Aug | Sept | Pre | Post |
| Atl | 56-25 | 40-41 | 47-29 | 19-14 | 19-14 | 11-9 | 25-16 | 71-50 | 28-21 | 68-45 | 95-65 | 1-1 | 27-20 | 28-11 | 12-5 | 17-9 | 15-13 | 16-12 | 15-11 | 20-7 | 13-14 | 54-41 | 42-25 |
| Was | 47-34 | 39-42 | 43-33 | 15-19 | 17-15 | 11-9 | 26-20 | 60-56 | 25-27 | 61-49 | 86-76 | 0-0 | 28-24 | 21-18 | 7-8 | 13-14 | 15-13 | 13-13 | 11-16 | 16-11 | 18-9 | 48-47 | 38-29 |
| NYM | 33-48 | 41-40 | 34-42 | 12-21 | 17-16 | 11-9 | 25-26 | 49-62 | 31-34 | 43-54 | 74-88 | 0-0 | 29-28 | 18-24 | 8-12 | 10-15 | 12-15 | 11-15 | 15-12 | 14-15 | 12-16 | 41-50 | 33-38 |
| Phi | 43-38 | 30-51 | 37-39 | 12-21 | 17-16 | 7-13 | 21-21 | 52-68 | 16-25 | 57-64 | 73-89 | 0-0 | 28-28 | 11-35 | 6-7 | 12-15 | 14-14 | 13-15 | 11-13 | 12-17 | 11-15 | 48-48 | 25-41 |
| Mia | 36-45 | 26-55 | 29-47 | 9-23 | 15-19 | 9-11 | 22-29 | 40-71 | 20-30 | 42-70 | 62-98 | 0-2 | 24-35 | 11-26 | 7-13 | 8-19 | 6-22 | 15-10 | 12-14 | 8-20 | 13-15 | 35-58 | 27-42 |

## Central Division

| | AT | | VERSUS | | | | | | CONDITIONS | | | | GAME | | | MONTHLY | | | | | | ALL-STAR | |
|---|---|---|---|---|---|---|---|---|---|---|---|---|---|---|---|---|---|---|---|---|---|---|---|
| Tm | Home | Road | East | Cent | West | AL | LHS | RHS | Day | Night | Grass | Turf | 1-Rn | 5+Rn | XInn | April | May | June | July | Aug | Sept | Pre | Post |
| StL | 54-27 | 43-38 | 23-10 | 46-30 | 18-15 | 10-10 | 19-23 | 78-42 | 33-16 | 64-49 | 97-65 | 0-0 | 20-16 | 35-17 | 6-6 | 15-11 | 20-7 | 14-14 | 13-12 | 16-13 | 19-8 | 57-36 | 40-29 |
| Pit | 50-31 | 44-37 | 20-14 | 45-31 | 14-18 | 15-5 | 18-13 | 76-55 | 30-28 | 64-40 | 94-68 | 0-0 | 29-23 | 20-15 | 9-9 | 15-12 | 19-9 | 17-9 | 14-12 | 14-14 | 15-12 | 56-37 | 38-31 |
| Cin | 49-31 | 41-41 | 20-13 | 40-36 | 19-14 | 11-9 | 27-25 | 63-47 | 34-27 | 56-45 | 90-72 | 0-0 | 27-22 | 25-15 | 13-9 | 15-13 | 19-8 | 12-15 | 14-13 | 16-11 | 14-12 | 53-42 | 37-30 |
| Mil | 37-44 | 37-44 | 21-12 | 34-42 | 13-20 | 6-14 | 16-28 | 58-60 | 18-35 | 56-53 | 74-88 | 0-0 | 18-25 | 17-20 | 6-7 | 14-11 | 6-22 | 12-15 | 14-14 | 13-14 | 15-12 | 38-56 | 36-32 |
| ChC | 31-50 | 35-46 | 14-18 | 25-51 | 14-20 | 13-7 | 22-22 | 44-74 | 31-49 | 35-47 | 66-96 | 0-0 | 20-33 | 17-19 | 7-6 | 10-16 | 13-14 | 12-15 | 14-13 | 8-20 | 9-18 | 42-51 | 24-45 |

## West Division

| | AT | | VERSUS | | | | | | CONDITIONS | | | | GAME | | | MONTHLY | | | | | | ALL-STAR | |
|---|---|---|---|---|---|---|---|---|---|---|---|---|---|---|---|---|---|---|---|---|---|---|---|
| Tm | Home | Road | East | Cent | West | AL | LHS | RHS | Day | Night | Grass | Turf | 1-Rn | 5+Rn | XInn | April | May | June | July | Aug | Sept | Pre | Post |
| LAD | 47-34 | 45-36 | 22-11 | 21-12 | 37-39 | 12-8 | 26-27 | 66-43 | 26-17 | 66-53 | 89-70 | 3-0 | 25-21 | 24-13 | 10-5 | 13-13 | 10-17 | 15-13 | 19-6 | 23-6 | 12-15 | 47-47 | 45-23 |
| Ari | 45-36 | 36-45 | 14-18 | 20-14 | 36-40 | 11-9 | 25-23 | 56-58 | 23-22 | 58-59 | 80-80 | 1-1 | 34-21 | 22-18 | 17-8 | 15-12 | 15-12 | 12-15 | 13-13 | 14-13 | 12-16 | 50-45 | 31-36 |
| SF | 42-40 | 34-46 | 15-17 | 11-23 | 44-32 | 6-14 | 24-31 | 52-55 | 30-27 | 46-59 | 75-82 | 1-4 | 28-28 | 14-25 | 8-10 | 15-12 | 14-13 | 10-17 | 8-17 | 13-16 | 16-11 | 43-51 | 33-35 |
| SD | 45-36 | 31-50 | 16-17 | 17-16 | 35-41 | 8-12 | 27-27 | 49-59 | 22-27 | 54-59 | 76-83 | 0-3 | 28-24 | 16-23 | 8-7 | 10-16 | 15-13 | 15-13 | 10-17 | 10-16 | 16-11 | 42-54 | 34-32 |
| Col | 45-36 | 29-52 | 13-22 | 18-13 | 38-38 | 5-15 | 20-33 | 54-55 | 27-26 | 47-62 | 74-85 | 0-3 | 25-26 | 21-23 | 6-9 | 16-11 | 12-16 | 13-15 | 10-16 | 13-15 | 10-15 | 46-50 | 28-38 |

## Team vs. Team Breakdown

| | EAST | | | | | CENTRAL | | | | | WEST | | | | |
|---|---|---|---|---|---|---|---|---|---|---|---|---|---|---|---|
| | Atl | Was | NYM | Phi | Mia | StL | Pit | Cin | Mil | ChC | LAD | Ari | SF | SD | Col |
| Atlanta Braves | - | 13 | 10 | 11 | 13 | 4 | 4 | 4 | 2 | 5 | 5 | 4 | 3 | 1 | 6 |
| Washington Nationals | 6 | - | 12 | 11 | 14 | 0 | 3 | 4 | 4 | 4 | 1 | 4 | 3 | 5 | 4 |
| New York Mets | 9 | 7 | - | 10 | 8 | 2 | 2 | 2 | 3 | 3 | 1 | 4 | 4 | 4 | 4 |
| Philadelphia Phillies | 8 | 8 | 9 | - | 12 | 2 | 3 | 2 | 2 | 3 | 2 | 4 | 3 | 4 | 4 |
| Miami Marlins | 6 | 5 | 11 | 7 | - | 2 | 2 | 1 | 1 | 3 | 2 | 2 | 4 | 3 | 4 |
| St Louis Cardinals | 3 | 6 | 5 | 5 | 4 | - | 9 | 11 | 14 | 12 | 3 | 3 | 4 | 4 | 4 |
| Pittsburgh Pirates | 3 | 4 | 5 | 4 | 4 | 10 | - | 11 | 12 | 12 | 2 | 3 | 4 | 3 | 2 |
| Cincinnati Reds | 3 | 3 | 4 | 4 | 6 | 8 | 8 | - | 10 | 14 | 4 | 4 | 6 | 3 | 2 |
| Milwaukee Brewers | 4 | 3 | 4 | 5 | 5 | 5 | 7 | 9 | - | 13 | 2 | 1 | 5 | 3 | 2 |
| Chicago Cubs | 1 | 3 | 3 | 3 | 4 | 7 | 7 | 5 | 6 | - | 1 | 3 | 4 | 3 | 3 |
| Los Angeles Dodgers | 2 | 5 | 5 | 5 | 5 | 4 | 4 | 3 | 4 | 6 | - | 9 | 8 | 11 | 9 |
| Arizona Diamondbacks | 2 | 2 | 3 | 3 | 4 | 4 | 3 | 3 | 6 | 4 | 10 | - | 7 | 7 | 12 |
| San Francisco Giants | 4 | 3 | 2 | 3 | 3 | 2 | 3 | 1 | 2 | 3 | 11 | 12 | - | 11 | 10 |
| San Diego Padres | 5 | 2 | 3 | 2 | 4 | 2 | 4 | 3 | 4 | 4 | 8 | 12 | 8 | - | 7 |
| Colorado Rockies | 1 | 3 | 3 | 3 | 3 | 3 | 4 | 4 | 4 | 3 | 10 | 7 | 9 | 12 | - |

# American League Batting

| BATTING | | | | | | | | | | | | | | | | | | | BASERUNNING | | | | | PERCENTAGES | | |
|---|---|---|---|---|---|---|---|---|---|---|---|---|---|---|---|---|---|---|---|---|---|---|---|---|---|---|
| Tm | G | AB | H | 2B | 3B | HR | (Hm | Rd) | TB | R | RBI | TBB | IBB | SO | HBP | SH | SF | ShO | SB | CS | SB% | GDP | LOB | Avg | OBP | Slg |
| Bos | 162 | 5651 | 1566 | 363 | 29 | 178 | (83 | 95) | 2521 | 853 | 819 | 581 | 51 | 1308 | 72 | 24 | 50 | 11 | 123 | 19 | .87 | 137 | 1816 | .277 | .349 | .446 |
| Det | 162 | 5735 | 1625 | 292 | 23 | 176 | (88 | 88) | 2491 | 796 | 767 | 531 | 40 | 1073 | 43 | 32 | 47 | 12 | 35 | 20 | .64 | 147 | 1862 | .283 | .346 | .434 |
| Oak | 162 | 5521 | 1403 | 301 | 25 | 186 | (83 | 103) | 2312 | 767 | 725 | 573 | 29 | 1178 | 45 | 21 | 49 | 10 | 74 | 28 | .73 | 108 | 1696 | .254 | .327 | .419 |
| Cle | 162 | 5465 | 1391 | 290 | 23 | 171 | (87 | 84) | 2240 | 745 | 711 | 562 | 19 | 1283 | 51 | 31 | 56 | 8 | 117 | 36 | .76 | 106 | 1700 | .255 | .327 | .410 |
| Bal | 162 | 5620 | 1460 | 298 | 14 | 212 | (115 | 97) | 2422 | 745 | 719 | 416 | 36 | 1125 | 36 | 27 | 45 | 6 | 79 | 29 | .73 | 105 | 1595 | .260 | .313 | .431 |
| LAA | 162 | 5588 | 1476 | 270 | 39 | 164 | (77 | 87) | 2316 | 733 | 696 | 523 | 40 | 1221 | 48 | 37 | 64 | 8 | 82 | 34 | .71 | 150 | 1755 | .264 | .329 | .414 |
| Tex | 163 | 5585 | 1465 | 262 | 23 | 176 | (85 | 91) | 2301 | 730 | 691 | 462 | 26 | 1067 | 61 | 45 | 42 | 11 | 149 | 46 | .76 | 125 | 1732 | .262 | .323 | .412 |
| Tor | 162 | 5537 | 1398 | 273 | 24 | 185 | (95 | 90) | 2274 | 712 | 669 | 510 | 19 | 1123 | 38 | 29 | 38 | 8 | 112 | 41 | .73 | 133 | 1610 | .252 | .318 | .411 |
| TB | 163 | 5538 | 1421 | 296 | 23 | 165 | (81 | 84) | 2258 | 700 | 670 | 589 | 31 | 1171 | 36 | 24 | 55 | 8 | 73 | 38 | .66 | 140 | 1738 | .257 | .329 | .408 |
| NYY | 162 | 5449 | 1321 | 247 | 24 | 144 | (75 | 69) | 2048 | 650 | 614 | 466 | 33 | 1214 | 57 | 36 | 36 | 12 | 115 | 31 | .79 | 121 | 1612 | .242 | .307 | .376 |
| KC | 162 | 5549 | 1443 | 254 | 34 | 112 | (55 | 57) | 2101 | 648 | 620 | 422 | 38 | 1048 | 42 | 37 | 42 | 10 | 153 | 32 | .83 | 131 | 1724 | .260 | .315 | .379 |
| Sea | 162 | 5558 | 1318 | 249 | 17 | 188 | (88 | 100) | 2165 | 624 | 597 | 529 | 21 | 1353 | 31 | 26 | 28 | 11 | 49 | 23 | .68 | 122 | 1691 | .237 | .306 | .390 |
| Min | 162 | 5564 | 1346 | 285 | 15 | 151 | (68 | 83) | 2114 | 614 | 590 | 533 | 20 | 1430 | 52 | 29 | 32 | 15 | 52 | 33 | .61 | 104 | 1778 | .242 | .312 | .380 |
| Hou | 162 | 5457 | 1307 | 266 | 16 | 148 | (81 | 67) | 2049 | 610 | 566 | 426 | 17 | 1535 | 52 | 46 | 38 | 14 | 110 | 61 | .64 | 110 | 1506 | .240 | .299 | .375 |
| CWS | 162 | 5563 | 1385 | 237 | 19 | 148 | (81 | 67) | 2104 | 598 | 574 | 411 | 23 | 1207 | 34 | 19 | 48 | 13 | 105 | 42 | .71 | 124 | 1614 | .249 | .302 | .378 |
| AL | 1216 | 83380 | 21325 | 4183 | 348 | 2504 | (1242 | 1262) | 33716 | 10525 | 10028 | 7534 | 443 | 18336 | 698 | 463 | 670 | 157 | 1428 | 513 | .74 | 1863 | 25429 | .256 | .320 | .404 |

# American League Pitching

| HOW MUCH THEY PITCHED | | | | | WHAT THEY GAVE UP | | | | | | | | | | | | THE RESULTS | | | | | | | | | |
|---|---|---|---|---|---|---|---|---|---|---|---|---|---|---|---|---|---|---|---|---|---|---|---|---|---|---|
| Tm | G | CG | Rel | IP | BFP | H | R | ER | HR | SH | SF | HB | TBB | IBB | SO | WP | Bk | W | L | Pct. | ShO | Sv-Op | Hld | OAvg | OOBP | OSlg | ERA |
| KC | 162 | 5 | 427 | 1448.1 | 6049 | 1366 | 601 | 555 | 155 | 25 | 47 | 41 | 469 | 21 | 1208 | 60 | 4 | 86 | 76 | .531 | 12 | 52-73 | 85 | .250 | .311 | .387 | 3.45 |
| Det | 162 | 3 | 428 | 1462.2 | 6119 | 1369 | 624 | 587 | 128 | 33 | 42 | 42 | 462 | 29 | 1428 | 63 | 7 | 93 | 69 | .574 | 12 | 39-55 | 68 | .247 | .308 | .373 | 3.61 |
| Oak | 162 | 6 | 447 | 1452.0 | 6069 | 1339 | 625 | 574 | 163 | 35 | 42 | 35 | 428 | 23 | 1183 | 56 | 1 | 96 | 66 | .593 | 13 | 46-67 | 64 | .242 | .299 | .379 | 3.56 |
| Tex | 163 | 4 | 475 | 1463.1 | 6146 | 1370 | 636 | 589 | 157 | 30 | 44 | 48 | 498 | 35 | 1309 | 68 | 5 | 91 | 72 | .558 | 10 | 46-57 | 74 | .248 | .313 | .387 | 3.62 |
| TB | 163 | 9 | 485 | 1464.0 | 6083 | 1315 | 646 | 608 | 153 | 25 | 42 | 52 | 482 | 38 | 1310 | 69 | 6 | 92 | 71 | .564 | 17 | 42-60 | 85 | .240 | .305 | .381 | 3.74 |
| Bos | 162 | 5 | 450 | 1454.0 | 6143 | 1366 | 656 | 613 | 156 | 21 | 42 | 47 | 524 | 10 | 1294 | 47 | 5 | 97 | 65 | .599 | 8 | 33-57 | 73 | .248 | .316 | .393 | 3.79 |
| Cle | 162 | 3 | 540 | 1441.1 | 6154 | 1359 | 662 | 611 | 147 | 38 | 36 | 58 | 554 | 26 | 1379 | 71 | 3 | 92 | 70 | .568 | 16 | 38-60 | 78 | .249 | .322 | .386 | 3.82 |
| NYY | 162 | 7 | 428 | 1447.1 | 6128 | 1452 | 671 | 633 | 171 | 29 | 46 | 51 | 437 | 34 | 1233 | 57 | 1 | 85 | 77 | .525 | 10 | 49-62 | 67 | .261 | .318 | .413 | 3.94 |
| Bal | 162 | 2 | 473 | 1453.0 | 6144 | 1438 | 709 | 678 | 202 | 33 | 43 | 50 | 473 | 32 | 1169 | 38 | 3 | 85 | 77 | .525 | 6 | 57-84 | 80 | .259 | .321 | .428 | 4.20 |
| CWS | 162 | 5 | 470 | 1455.0 | 6214 | 1424 | 723 | 643 | 182 | 33 | 48 | 60 | 509 | 24 | 1249 | 62 | 4 | 63 | 99 | .389 | 5 | 40-60 | 89 | .256 | .322 | .408 | 3.98 |
| LAA | 162 | 4 | 496 | 1457.2 | 6298 | 1475 | 737 | 685 | 167 | 37 | 35 | 45 | 533 | 36 | 1200 | 74 | 4 | 78 | 84 | .481 | 12 | 41-58 | 79 | .261 | .328 | .408 | 4.23 |
| Sea | 162 | 4 | 448 | 1465.0 | 6257 | 1467 | 754 | 702 | 174 | 31 | 47 | 42 | 478 | 48 | 1297 | 74 | 1 | 71 | 91 | .438 | 14 | 43-66 | 65 | .259 | .319 | .417 | 4.31 |
| Tor | 162 | 4 | 487 | 1452.0 | 6250 | 1451 | 756 | 685 | 195 | 28 | 47 | 65 | 500 | 33 | 1208 | 54 | 7 | 74 | 88 | .457 | 11 | 39-58 | 62 | .259 | .324 | .426 | 4.25 |
| Min | 162 | 1 | 511 | 1450.1 | 6257 | 1591 | 788 | 733 | 168 | 27 | 49 | 44 | 458 | 31 | 985 | 50 | 4 | 66 | 96 | .407 | 7 | 40-58 | 77 | .280 | .336 | .434 | 4.55 |
| Hou | 162 | 2 | 448 | 1440.0 | 6370 | 1530 | 848 | 766 | 191 | 31 | 46 | 56 | 616 | 32 | 1084 | 61 | 6 | 51 | 111 | .315 | 5 | 32-61 | 70 | .272 | .347 | .445 | 4.79 |
| AL | 1216 | 64 | 7013 | 21806.0 | 92681 | 21312 | 10436 | 9662 | 2509 | 456 | 656 | 736 | 7421 | 452 | 18536 | 904 | 61 | 1220 | 1212 | .502 | 158 | 637-936 | 1116 | .256 | .320 | .405 | 3.99 |

# American League Fielding

| Fielding | | | | | | | | | | | | | | | | | | | | |
|---|---|---|---|---|---|---|---|---|---|---|---|---|---|---|---|---|---|---|---|---|
| Team | G | Inn | PO | Ast | OFAst | E | (Throw | Field) | TC | DP | GDP | SB | CS | SB% | CPkof | PPkof | PB | UER | UERA | FPct |
| Baltimore | 162 | 1453.0 | 4359 | 1614 | 26 | 54 | 28 | 26 | 6027 | 165 | 147 | 63 | 32 | .66 | 1 | 1 | 8 | 31 | 0.19 | .991 |
| Tampa Bay | 163 | 1464.0 | 4392 | 1593 | 19 | 59 | 33 | 26 | 6044 | 147 | 121 | 119 | 33 | .78 | 3 | 6 | 10 | 38 | 0.23 | .990 |
| New York | 162 | 1447.1 | 4342 | 1544 | 25 | 69 | 33 | 36 | 5955 | 139 | 117 | 72 | 30 | .71 | 1 | 8 | 16 | 38 | 0.24 | .988 |
| Detroit | 162 | 1462.2 | 4388 | 1507 | 21 | 76 | 41 | 35 | 5971 | 136 | 118 | 128 | 29 | .82 | 0 | 9 | 14 | 37 | 0.23 | .987 |
| Minnesota | 162 | 1450.1 | 4351 | 1723 | 44 | 81 | 37 | 44 | 6155 | 178 | 147 | 73 | 38 | .66 | 0 | 0 | 6 | 55 | 0.34 | .987 |
| Boston | 162 | 1454.0 | 4362 | 1517 | 24 | 80 | 38 | 42 | 5959 | 142 | 118 | 133 | 43 | .76 | 0 | 4 | 15 | 43 | 0.27 | .987 |
| Texas | 163 | 1463.1 | 4390 | 1549 | 33 | 86 | 38 | 48 | 6025 | 147 | 129 | 73 | 34 | .68 | 0 | 4 | 7 | 47 | 0.29 | .986 |
| Kansas City | 162 | 1448.1 | 4345 | 1520 | 40 | 85 | 41 | 44 | 5950 | 136 | 120 | 77 | 36 | .68 | 2 | 6 | 6 | 46 | 0.29 | .986 |
| Seattle | 162 | 1465.0 | 4395 | 1646 | 22 | 88 | 39 | 49 | 6129 | 149 | 128 | 89 | 30 | .75 | 0 | 2 | 11 | 52 | 0.32 | .986 |
| Cleveland | 162 | 1441.1 | 4324 | 1503 | 29 | 98 | 45 | 53 | 5925 | 135 | 118 | 84 | 31 | .73 | 6 | 4 | 10 | 51 | 0.32 | .983 |
| Oakland | 162 | 1452.0 | 4356 | 1377 | 25 | 97 | 48 | 49 | 5830 | 112 | 96 | 87 | 27 | .76 | 1 | 2 | 15 | 51 | 0.32 | .983 |
| Toronto | 162 | 1452.0 | 4356 | 1605 | 21 | 111 | 59 | 52 | 6072 | 145 | 125 | 87 | 29 | .75 | 2 | 5 | 30 | 71 | 0.44 | .982 |
| Los Angeles | 162 | 1457.2 | 4373 | 1500 | 21 | 112 | 42 | 70 | 5985 | 135 | 118 | 131 | 35 | .79 | 5 | 3 | 7 | 52 | 0.32 | .981 |
| Chicago | 162 | 1455.0 | 4365 | 1555 | 28 | 121 | 49 | 72 | 6041 | 155 | 129 | 102 | 35 | .74 | 1 | 5 | 21 | 80 | 0.49 | .980 |
| Houston | 162 | 1440.0 | 4320 | 1635 | 28 | 125 | 58 | 67 | 6080 | 168 | 145 | 98 | 37 | .73 | 1 | 3 | 14 | 82 | 0.51 | .979 |
| American League | 1216 | 21806.0 | 65418 | 23388 | 406 | 1342 | 629 | 713 | 90148 | 2189 | 1876 | 1416 | 499 | .74 | 23 | 62 | 190 | 774 | 0.32 | .985 |

# National League Batting

| BATTING | | | | | | | | | | | | | | | | | | | BASERUNNING | | | | | PERCENTAGES | | |
|---|---|---|---|---|---|---|---|---|---|---|---|---|---|---|---|---|---|---|---|---|---|---|---|---|---|---|
| Tm | G | AB | H | 2B | 3B | HR | (Hm | Rd) | TB | R | RBI | TBB | IBB | SO | HBP | SH | SF | ShO | SB | CS | SB% | GDP | LOB | Avg | OBP | Slg |
| StL | 162 | 5557 | 1494 | 322 | 20 | 125 | (58 | 67) | 2231 | 783 | 745 | 481 | 38 | 1110 | 64 | 56 | 44 | 11 | 45 | 22 | .67 | 155 | 1656 | .269 | .332 | .401 |
| Col | 162 | 5599 | 1511 | 283 | 36 | 159 | (88 | 71) | 2343 | 706 | 673 | 427 | 26 | 1204 | 26 | 65 | 35 | 12 | 112 | 32 | .78 | 111 | 1692 | .270 | .323 | .418 |
| Cin | 162 | 5499 | 1370 | 274 | 20 | 155 | (82 | 73) | 2149 | 698 | 664 | 585 | 65 | 1245 | 76 | 85 | 46 | 11 | 67 | 35 | .66 | 129 | 1783 | .249 | .327 | .391 |
| Atl | 162 | 5441 | 1354 | 247 | 21 | 181 | (90 | 91) | 2186 | 688 | 656 | 542 | 36 | 1384 | 55 | 58 | 35 | 17 | 64 | 31 | .67 | 120 | 1659 | .249 | .321 | .402 |
| Ari | 162 | 5676 | 1468 | 302 | 31 | 130 | (68 | 62) | 2222 | 685 | 647 | 519 | 51 | 1142 | 43 | 50 | 43 | 7 | 62 | 41 | .60 | 160 | 1754 | .259 | .323 | .391 |
| Was | 162 | 5436 | 1365 | 259 | 27 | 161 | (70 | 91) | 2161 | 656 | 621 | 464 | 35 | 1192 | 40 | 68 | 39 | 12 | 88 | 28 | .76 | 115 | 1625 | .251 | .313 | .398 |
| LAD | 162 | 5491 | 1447 | 281 | 17 | 138 | (65 | 73) | 2176 | 649 | 618 | 476 | 45 | 1146 | 57 | 71 | 48 | 9 | 78 | 28 | .74 | 130 | 1761 | .264 | .326 | .396 |
| Mil | 162 | 5474 | 1381 | 238 | 43 | 157 | (82 | 75) | 2176 | 640 | 610 | 407 | 22 | 1183 | 71 | 77 | 35 | 6 | 142 | 50 | .74 | 116 | 1627 | .252 | .311 | .398 |
| Pit | 162 | 5486 | 1346 | 273 | 35 | 161 | (69 | 92) | 2172 | 634 | 603 | 469 | 41 | 1330 | 88 | 62 | 29 | 12 | 94 | 42 | .69 | 120 | 1682 | .245 | .313 | .396 |
| SF | 162 | 5552 | 1446 | 280 | 35 | 107 | (44 | 63) | 2117 | 629 | 596 | 469 | 40 | 1078 | 39 | 66 | 42 | 11 | 67 | 26 | .72 | 131 | 1767 | .260 | .320 | .381 |
| NYM | 162 | 5559 | 1318 | 263 | 32 | 130 | (59 | 71) | 2035 | 619 | 593 | 512 | 40 | 1384 | 51 | 53 | 32 | 8 | 114 | 35 | .77 | 106 | 1698 | .237 | .306 | .366 |
| SD | 162 | 5517 | 1349 | 246 | 26 | 146 | (66 | 80) | 2085 | 618 | 578 | 467 | 36 | 1309 | 52 | 52 | 34 | 9 | 118 | 34 | .78 | 100 | 1663 | .245 | .308 | .378 |
| Phi | 162 | 5456 | 1355 | 255 | 32 | 140 | (84 | 56) | 2094 | 610 | 578 | 417 | 41 | 1205 | 53 | 57 | 31 | 15 | 73 | 29 | .72 | 132 | 1621 | .248 | .306 | .384 |
| ChC | 162 | 5498 | 1307 | 297 | 18 | 172 | (102 | 70) | 2156 | 602 | 576 | 439 | 28 | 1230 | 67 | 43 | 30 | 16 | 63 | 32 | .66 | 120 | 1666 | .238 | .300 | .392 |
| Mia | 162 | 5449 | 1257 | 219 | 31 | 95 | (36 | 59) | 1823 | 513 | 485 | 432 | 31 | 1232 | 56 | 57 | 26 | 18 | 78 | 29 | .73 | 131 | 1627 | .231 | .293 | .335 |
| NL | 1215 | 82690 | 20768 | 4039 | 424 | 2157 | (1063 | 1094) | 32126 | 9730 | 9243 | 7106 | 575 | 18374 | 838 | 920 | 549 | 174 | 1265 | 494 | .72 | 1876 | 25281 | .251 | .315 | .389 |

# National League Pitching

| HOW MUCH THEY PITCHED | | | | | WHAT THEY GAVE UP | | | | | | | | | | | | THE RESULTS | | | | | | | | | |
|---|---|---|---|---|---|---|---|---|---|---|---|---|---|---|---|---|---|---|---|---|---|---|---|---|---|---|
| Tm | G | CG | Rel | IP | BFP | H | R | ER | HR | SH | SF | HB | TBB | IBB | SO | WP | Bk | W | L | Pct. | ShO | Sv-Op | Hld | OAvg | OOBP | OSlg | ERA |
| Atl | 162 | 1 | 466 | 1450.1 | 5989 | 1326 | 548 | 512 | 127 | 57 | 28 | 51 | 409 | 35 | 1232 | 50 | 3 | 96 | 66 | .593 | 12 | 53-69 | 91 | .244 | .301 | .370 | 3.18 |
| Pit | 162 | 3 | 465 | 1470.2 | 6147 | 1299 | 577 | 533 | 101 | 54 | 40 | 70 | 515 | 26 | 1261 | 81 | 6 | 94 | 68 | .580 | 16 | 55-70 | 86 | .238 | .309 | .341 | 3.26 |
| LAD | 162 | 7 | 504 | 1450.1 | 6032 | 1321 | 582 | 524 | 127 | 64 | 29 | 43 | 460 | 44 | 1292 | 66 | 3 | 92 | 70 | .568 | 22 | 46-65 | 83 | .243 | .306 | .365 | 3.25 |
| Cin | 162 | 5 | 461 | 1473.2 | 6077 | 1294 | 589 | 554 | 170 | 62 | 36 | 66 | 435 | 28 | 1296 | 44 | 5 | 90 | 72 | .556 | 17 | 43-59 | 78 | .236 | .298 | .384 | 3.38 |
| StL | 162 | 7 | 483 | 1459.2 | 6104 | 1366 | 596 | 555 | 112 | 63 | 32 | 64 | 451 | 26 | 1254 | 33 | 1 | 97 | 65 | .599 | 15 | 44-64 | 83 | .249 | .311 | .368 | 3.42 |
| Was | 162 | 6 | 440 | 1445.2 | 6038 | 1367 | 626 | 576 | 142 | 61 | 26 | 48 | 405 | 17 | 1236 | 43 | 8 | 86 | 76 | .531 | 13 | 47-68 | 79 | .249 | .305 | .379 | 3.59 |
| Mia | 162 | 2 | 471 | 1460.0 | 6166 | 1376 | 646 | 602 | 121 | 63 | 46 | 47 | 526 | 58 | 1177 | 53 | 2 | 62 | 100 | .383 | 13 | 36-53 | 52 | .251 | .319 | .384 | 3.71 |
| NYM | 162 | 4 | 535 | 1476.2 | 6249 | 1442 | 684 | 618 | 152 | 66 | 48 | 54 | 458 | 38 | 1209 | 47 | 3 | 74 | 88 | .457 | 10 | 40-58 | 68 | .256 | .316 | .393 | 3.77 |
| Mil | 162 | 4 | 501 | 1442.2 | 6100 | 1401 | 687 | 615 | 175 | 64 | 40 | 43 | 466 | 29 | 1125 | 51 | 2 | 74 | 88 | .457 | 15 | 40-63 | 83 | .255 | .317 | .397 | 3.84 |
| ChC | 162 | 3 | 489 | 1448.0 | 6149 | 1332 | 689 | 643 | 160 | 62 | 35 | 62 | 540 | 43 | 1184 | 59 | 4 | 66 | 96 | .407 | 6 | 39-65 | 63 | .244 | .318 | .400 | 4.00 |
| SF | 162 | 2 | 524 | 1447.1 | 6163 | 1380 | 691 | 643 | 145 | 61 | 38 | 50 | 521 | 64 | 1256 | 60 | 4 | 76 | 86 | .469 | 13 | 41-54 | 81 | .251 | .320 | .390 | 4.00 |
| Ari | 162 | 6 | 527 | 1495.0 | 6338 | 1460 | 695 | 651 | 176 | 64 | 37 | 60 | 485 | 42 | 1218 | 84 | 3 | 81 | 81 | .500 | 7 | 38-67 | 64 | .257 | .320 | .411 | 3.92 |
| SD | 162 | 3 | 488 | 1455.0 | 6179 | 1407 | 700 | 643 | 156 | 64 | 39 | 40 | 525 | 31 | 1171 | 51 | 2 | 76 | 86 | .469 | 6 | 40-53 | 75 | .255 | .322 | .403 | 3.98 |
| Phi | 162 | 6 | 466 | 1436.1 | 6213 | 1465 | 749 | 689 | 152 | 63 | 43 | 62 | 506 | 33 | 1199 | 48 | 6 | 73 | 89 | .451 | 3 | 32-48 | 55 | .265 | .331 | .415 | 4.32 |
| Col | 162 | 1 | 503 | 1436.0 | 6248 | 1545 | 760 | 708 | 136 | 59 | 46 | 40 | 517 | 52 | 1064 | 62 | 15 | 74 | 88 | .457 | 5 | 35-53 | 82 | .277 | .340 | .423 | 4.44 |
| NL | 1215 | 60 | 7323 | 21847.1 | 92192 | 20781 | 9819 | 9066 | 2152 | 927 | 563 | 800 | 7219 | 566 | 18174 | 832 | 67 | 1211 | 1219 | .498 | 173 | 629-909 | 1123 | .251 | .316 | .388 | 3.73 |

# National League Fielding

| Fielding | | | | | | | | | | | | | | | | | | | | |
|---|---|---|---|---|---|---|---|---|---|---|---|---|---|---|---|---|---|---|---|---|
| Team | G | Inn | PO | Ast | OFAst | E | (Throw | Field) | TC | DP | GDP | SB | CS | SB% | CPkof | PPkof | PB | UER | UERA | FPct |
| Arizona | 162 | 1495.0 | 4485 | 1733 | 44 | 75 | 34 | 41 | 6293 | 135 | 120 | 48 | 22 | .69 | 4 | 3 | 10 | 44 | 0.26 | .988 |
| St Louis | 162 | 1459.2 | 4379 | 1718 | 12 | 75 | 28 | 47 | 6172 | 177 | 160 | 39 | 26 | .60 | 0 | 2 | 6 | 41 | 0.25 | .988 |
| Cincinnati | 162 | 1473.2 | 4421 | 1643 | 26 | 76 | 38 | 38 | 6140 | 131 | 120 | 70 | 35 | .67 | 1 | 2 | 8 | 35 | 0.21 | .988 |
| San Diego | 162 | 1455.0 | 4365 | 1698 | 27 | 83 | 44 | 39 | 6146 | 140 | 106 | 107 | 43 | .71 | 0 | 5 | 7 | 57 | 0.35 | .986 |
| Atlanta | 162 | 1450.1 | 4351 | 1680 | 18 | 85 | 36 | 49 | 6116 | 141 | 115 | 79 | 32 | .71 | 1 | 14 | 6 | 36 | 0.22 | .986 |
| Miami | 162 | 1460.0 | 4380 | 1687 | 29 | 88 | 38 | 50 | 6155 | 144 | 126 | 90 | 37 | .71 | 1 | 7 | 16 | 44 | 0.27 | .986 |
| Colorado | 162 | 1436.0 | 4308 | 1855 | 22 | 90 | 45 | 45 | 6253 | 162 | 139 | 89 | 33 | .73 | 1 | 2 | 13 | 52 | 0.33 | .986 |
| New York | 162 | 1476.2 | 4430 | 1642 | 39 | 93 | 42 | 51 | 6165 | 127 | 117 | 87 | 29 | .75 | 2 | 5 | 11 | 66 | 0.40 | .985 |
| Philadelphia | 162 | 1436.1 | 4309 | 1614 | 30 | 97 | 42 | 55 | 6020 | 141 | 122 | 114 | 35 | .77 | 3 | 2 | 5 | 60 | 0.38 | .984 |
| Pittsburgh | 162 | 1470.2 | 4412 | 1924 | 29 | 106 | 49 | 57 | 6442 | 154 | 134 | 95 | 43 | .69 | 3 | 2 | 7 | 44 | 0.27 | .984 |
| Chicago | 162 | 1448.0 | 4344 | 1602 | 25 | 100 | 40 | 60 | 6046 | 129 | 107 | 107 | 42 | .72 | 5 | 2 | 13 | 46 | 0.29 | .983 |
| Los Angeles | 162 | 1450.1 | 4351 | 1723 | 24 | 109 | 43 | 66 | 6183 | 160 | 138 | 63 | 40 | .61 | 2 | 8 | 10 | 58 | 0.36 | .982 |
| Washington | 162 | 1445.2 | 4337 | 1549 | 30 | 107 | 61 | 46 | 5993 | 146 | 122 | 95 | 20 | .83 | 0 | 0 | 5 | 50 | 0.31 | .982 |
| San Francisco | 162 | 1447.1 | 4342 | 1536 | 25 | 107 | 53 | 54 | 5985 | 128 | 112 | 95 | 41 | .70 | 1 | 2 | 8 | 48 | 0.30 | .982 |
| Milwaukee | 162 | 1442.2 | 4328 | 1627 | 35 | 114 | 52 | 62 | 6069 | 153 | 125 | 99 | 30 | .77 | 3 | 4 | 10 | 72 | 0.45 | .981 |
| National League | 1215 | 21847.1 | 65542 | 25231 | 415 | 1405 | 645 | 760 | 92178 | 2168 | 1863 | 1277 | 508 | .72 | 27 | 60 | 135 | 753 | 0.31 | .985 |

# Team Pitching Staff Summary

| | Starters | | | | Bullpen | | | | | |
|---|---|---|---|---|---|---|---|---|---|---|
| Team | IP | ERA | ERA Rank | W-L | IP | ERA | ERA Rank | W-L | Sv-Opp | Sv Pct |
| Arizona Diamondbacks | 976.1 | 4.13 | 19 | 46-59 | 518.2 | 3.52 | 15 | 35-22 | 38-67 | 57% |
| Atlanta Braves | 989.2 | 3.51 | 6 | 67-51 | 460.2 | 2.46 | 1 | 29-15 | 53-69 | 77% |
| Baltimore Orioles | 939.0 | 4.57 | 26 | 56-51 | 514.0 | 3.52 | 15 | 29-26 | 57-84 | 68% |
| Boston Red Sox | 984.0 | 3.84 | 11 | 67-42 | 470.0 | 3.70 | 21 | 30-23 | 33-57 | 58% |
| Chicago Cubs | 974.0 | 3.97 | 15 | 45-65 | 474.0 | 4.04 | 25 | 21-31 | 39-65 | 60% |
| Chicago White Sox | 982.2 | 3.99 | 16 | 44-63 | 472.1 | 4.00 | 23 | 19-36 | 40-60 | 67% |
| Cincinnati Reds | 1003.1 | 3.43 | 3 | 66-48 | 470.1 | 3.29 | 7 | 24-24 | 43-59 | 73% |
| Cleveland Indians | 924.2 | 3.92 | 14 | 59-54 | 516.2 | 3.62 | 19 | 33-16 | 38-60 | 63% |
| Colorado Rockies | 880.1 | 4.57 | 26 | 54-60 | 555.2 | 4.23 | 28 | 20-28 | 35-53 | 66% |
| Detroit Tigers | 1023.0 | 3.44 | 4 | 76-44 | 439.2 | 4.01 | 24 | 17-25 | 39-55 | 71% |
| Houston Astros | 906.0 | 4.72 | 28 | 37-71 | 534.0 | 4.92 | 30 | 14-40 | 32-61 | 52% |
| Kansas City Royals | 986.2 | 3.87 | 12 | 53-52 | 461.2 | 2.55 | 2 | 33-24 | 52-73 | 71% |
| Los Angeles Angels | 964.0 | 4.30 | 22 | 58-57 | 493.2 | 4.12 | 26 | 20-27 | 41-58 | 71% |
| Los Angeles Dodgers | 979.0 | 3.13 | 1 | 62-46 | 471.1 | 3.49 | 13 | 30-24 | 46-65 | 71% |
| Miami Marlins | 944.0 | 3.87 | 12 | 38-66 | 516.0 | 3.42 | 11 | 24-34 | 36-53 | 68% |
| Milwaukee Brewers | 918.2 | 4.20 | 21 | 48-60 | 524.0 | 3.19 | 5 | 26-28 | 40-63 | 63% |
| Minnesota Twins | 871.0 | 5.26 | 30 | 39-74 | 579.1 | 3.50 | 14 | 27-22 | 40-58 | 69% |
| New York Mets | 969.2 | 3.68 | 8 | 48-57 | 507.0 | 3.98 | 22 | 26-31 | 40-58 | 69% |
| New York Yankees | 969.2 | 4.08 | 18 | 55-63 | 477.2 | 3.66 | 20 | 30-14 | 49-62 | 79% |
| Oakland Athletics | 976.2 | 3.72 | 9 | 72-48 | 475.1 | 3.22 | 6 | 24-18 | 46-67 | 69% |
| Philadelphia Phillies | 961.2 | 4.41 | 25 | 48-63 | 474.2 | 4.19 | 27 | 25-26 | 32-48 | 67% |
| Pittsburgh Pirates | 925.0 | 3.50 | 5 | 64-48 | 545.2 | 2.89 | 3 | 30-20 | 55-70 | 79% |
| San Diego Padres | 932.1 | 4.31 | 23 | 51-57 | 522.2 | 3.39 | 10 | 25-29 | 40-53 | 75% |
| San Francisco Giants | 946.0 | 4.37 | 24 | 49-56 | 501.1 | 3.30 | 8 | 27-30 | 41-54 | 76% |
| Seattle Mariners | 960.0 | 4.18 | 20 | 55-58 | 505.0 | 4.58 | 29 | 16-33 | 43-66 | 65% |
| St Louis Cardinals | 984.1 | 3.42 | 2 | 77-46 | 475.1 | 3.45 | 12 | 20-19 | 44-64 | 69% |
| Tampa Bay Rays | 965.1 | 3.81 | 10 | 65-47 | 498.2 | 3.59 | 18 | 27-24 | 42-60 | 70% |
| Texas Rangers | 971.2 | 3.99 | 16 | 56-54 | 491.2 | 2.91 | 4 | 35-18 | 46-57 | 81% |
| Toronto Blue Jays | 899.1 | 4.81 | 29 | 46-57 | 552.2 | 3.37 | 9 | 28-31 | 39-58 | 67% |
| Washington Nationals | 968.1 | 3.60 | 7 | 57-54 | 477.1 | 3.56 | 17 | 29-22 | 47-68 | 69% |

## Team Defense

Defensive Runs Saved by Position and Team

| Team | P | C | 1B | 2B | 3B | SS | LF | CF | RF | Shifts | Total |
|---|---|---|---|---|---|---|---|---|---|---|---|
| Kansas City Royals | 2 | 9 | 2 | 18 | -2 | 5 | 21 | 22 | 16 | -1 | 92 |
| Arizona Diamondbacks | 12 | -10 | 14 | 4 | -10 | 4 | 6 | 13 | 53 | 4 | 90 |
| Pittsburgh Pirates | 7 | 10 | -3 | 13 | 5 | 9 | 26 | 8 | -7 | 9 | 77 |
| Milwaukee Brewers | 3 | 4 | -4 | -12 | -5 | 8 | 10 | 41 | 13 | 9 | 67 |
| Los Angeles Dodgers | 3 | 4 | 13 | -2 | 21 | 6 | 6 | -12 | 8 | 0 | 47 |
| Texas Rangers | -2 | -1 | 1 | 5 | -7 | 14 | 11 | 21 | -3 | 8 | 47 |
| Atlanta Braves | 15 | -1 | 8 | -20 | -3 | 42 | -16 | 2 | 19 | 0 | 46 |
| Cincinnati Reds | 9 | 0 | 7 | 5 | 3 | 8 | -4 | -15 | 20 | 11 | 44 |
| Baltimore Orioles | -1 | -11 | -10 | 7 | 35 | 9 | -4 | -1 | -7 | 11 | 28 |
| Chicago Cubs | -3 | 20 | 16 | 9 | 5 | -6 | -3 | -11 | -1 | -1 | 25 |
| New York Yankees | 13 | -1 | 7 | 6 | 3 | -23 | 8 | 9 | -1 | 3 | 24 |
| Boston Red Sox | -13 | -4 | 6 | 15 | -18 | -4 | -5 | 9 | 23 | 15 | 24 |
| Tampa Bay Rays | 3 | -6 | 4 | 8 | 12 | 7 | 2 | -8 | -14 | 16 | 24 |
| Toronto Blue Jays | 12 | -2 | -15 | 10 | -1 | -4 | -1 | 13 | 3 | 5 | 20 |
| San Diego Padres | 10 | 3 | 14 | 1 | 0 | -13 | -8 | -1 | 1 | 3 | 10 |
| San Francisco Giants | 1 | 3 | 4 | -11 | 3 | -2 | 12 | 1 | -7 | 2 | 6 |
| Miami Marlins | -5 | 2 | 3 | 0 | 4 | -5 | 2 | -3 | -3 | 9 | 4 |
| Colorado Rockies | -1 | -2 | -3 | 3 | 23 | 5 | 4 | -13 | -21 | 2 | -3 |
| New York Mets | 0 | -9 | 2 | -16 | 3 | -12 | -6 | 18 | 11 | 5 | -4 |
| Minnesota Twins | -6 | 1 | 8 | 10 | -7 | 19 | -11 | -7 | -17 | 1 | -9 |
| Washington Nationals | -18 | 4 | 0 | 0 | -6 | -4 | -2 | 2 | 8 | 2 | -14 |
| Cleveland Indians | -8 | -1 | -1 | -1 | -12 | -16 | 5 | 0 | -8 | 9 | -33 |
| St Louis Cardinals | -4 | 10 | -5 | -3 | -10 | 0 | -16 | -5 | -6 | 0 | -39 |
| Houston Astros | 3 | 6 | -14 | -4 | 6 | -8 | -10 | 0 | -22 | -1 | -44 |
| Oakland Athletics | -14 | -11 | -15 | -13 | 11 | -21 | 3 | -2 | 6 | 9 | -47 |
| Los Angeles Angels | -13 | -7 | 0 | -9 | -4 | -12 | 1 | -6 | -13 | 6 | -57 |
| Chicago White Sox | -2 | 5 | -16 | -12 | -6 | 5 | -4 | -19 | -6 | -3 | -58 |
| Detroit Tigers | -21 | -8 | -10 | -7 | -15 | 6 | 1 | 0 | -12 | 3 | -63 |
| Seattle Mariners | 0 | -11 | -11 | 0 | -8 | 1 | -19 | -34 | -17 | 2 | -97 |
| Philadelphia Phillies | -5 | -1 | -2 | -6 | -26 | -16 | -7 | -20 | -19 | -1 | -103 |

# Team Efficiency Summary

Sometimes teams surprise us. And sometimes they find a way to surprise us over and over again. Considering how depleted their roster was by injuries in 2013, it was not surprising that the New York Yankees didn't make the playoffs. What was surprising, though, was how long they remained in contention. Despite the absence of many of their star players for long stretches of the season, the Yankees managed to get the most out of those that filled in. They were by far the most efficient team in baseball when it came to winning ballgames.

In the following tables we lay out how efficient each team in the big leagues was in 2013. We measure efficiency in several ways. On offense, we use various components of production (singles, doubles, triples, etc.) to calculate the expected number of runs that a team would score, and then compare that to their actual runs scored. However much that team scored above or below their expected runs we call their Hitting Efficiency. We do the same for pitching, with the difference between their actual runs allowed and their expected runs allowed representing their Pitching Efficiency. Similarly, we can use team runs scored and runs allowed to determine how many games they would be expected to win. Comparing that to their actual wins tells us their Runs Efficiency. And finally, combining all three of these types of efficiency allows us to determine their Overall Efficiency.

## 2013 American League Team Efficiency Summary

| | RC | Runs | Hit Eff | Exp RA | RA | Pit Eff | Exp Wins | Wins | Runs Eff | Eff Wins | Wins | Overall Eff |
|---|---|---|---|---|---|---|---|---|---|---|---|---|
| New York Yankees | 625 | 650 | 104 | 693 | 671 | 103 | 78 | 85 | 108 | 73 | 85 | 117 |
| Cleveland Indians | 737 | 745 | 101 | 682 | 662 | 103 | 91 | 92 | 102 | 87 | 92 | 105 |
| Kansas City Royals | 664 | 648 | 98 | 649 | 601 | 108 | 87 | 86 | 99 | 83 | 86 | 104 |
| Oakland Athletics | 751 | 767 | 102 | 629 | 625 | 101 | 97 | 96 | 99 | 95 | 96 | 101 |
| Baltimore Orioles | 735 | 745 | 101 | 701 | 709 | 99 | 85 | 85 | 100 | 85 | 85 | 100 |
| Texas Rangers | 738 | 730 | 99 | 657 | 636 | 103 | 93 | 91 | 98 | 91 | 91 | 100 |
| Toronto Blue Jays | 706 | 712 | 101 | 762 | 756 | 101 | 76 | 74 | 97 | 75 | 74 | 99 |
| Seattle Mariners | 645 | 624 | 97 | 714 | 754 | 95 | 66 | 71 | 108 | 73 | 71 | 98 |
| Los Angeles Angels | 747 | 733 | 98 | 756 | 737 | 103 | 81 | 78 | 97 | 80 | 78 | 98 |
| Houston Astros | 591 | 610 | 103 | 851 | 848 | 100 | 55 | 51 | 92 | 53 | 51 | 97 |
| Minnesota Twins | 653 | 614 | 94 | 768 | 788 | 98 | 61 | 66 | 108 | 68 | 66 | 97 |
| Tampa Bay Rays | 730 | 700 | 96 | 605 | 646 | 94 | 88 | 92 | 105 | 97 | 92 | 95 |
| Boston Red Sox | 875 | 853 | 98 | 664 | 656 | 101 | 102 | 97 | 95 | 103 | 97 | 94 |
| Chicago White Sox | 622 | 598 | 96 | 738 | 723 | 102 | 66 | 63 | 96 | 67 | 63 | 94 |
| Detroit Tigers | 847 | 796 | 94 | 615 | 624 | 99 | 100 | 93 | 93 | 106 | 93 | 88 |

## 2013 National League Team Efficiency Summary

| | RC | Runs | Hit Eff | Exp RA | RA | Pit Eff | Exp Wins | Wins | Runs Eff | Eff Wins | Wins | Overall Eff |
|---|---|---|---|---|---|---|---|---|---|---|---|---|
| Philadelphia Phillies | 622 | 610 | 98 | 723 | 749 | 97 | 65 | 73 | 113 | 69 | 73 | 106 |
| Pittsburgh Pirates | 665 | 634 | 95 | 591 | 577 | 102 | 89 | 94 | 106 | 90 | 94 | 104 |
| Arizona Diamondbacks | 693 | 685 | 99 | 714 | 695 | 103 | 80 | 81 | 102 | 79 | 81 | 103 |
| Atlanta Braves | 692 | 688 | 99 | 577 | 548 | 105 | 99 | 96 | 97 | 96 | 96 | 100 |
| San Diego Padres | 644 | 618 | 96 | 683 | 700 | 98 | 71 | 76 | 107 | 76 | 76 | 100 |
| New York Mets | 624 | 619 | 99 | 680 | 684 | 100 | 73 | 74 | 102 | 74 | 74 | 100 |
| St Louis Cardinals | 721 | 783 | 109 | 582 | 596 | 98 | 103 | 97 | 95 | 98 | 97 | 99 |
| Washington Nationals | 667 | 656 | 98 | 619 | 626 | 99 | 85 | 86 | 101 | 87 | 86 | 99 |
| Los Angeles Dodgers | 703 | 649 | 92 | 598 | 582 | 103 | 90 | 92 | 103 | 94 | 92 | 98 |
| Cincinnati Reds | 700 | 698 | 100 | 601 | 589 | 102 | 95 | 90 | 95 | 93 | 90 | 97 |
| Milwaukee Brewers | 667 | 640 | 96 | 692 | 687 | 101 | 75 | 74 | 98 | 78 | 74 | 95 |
| Miami Marlins | 528 | 513 | 97 | 636 | 646 | 99 | 63 | 62 | 99 | 66 | 62 | 94 |
| San Francisco Giants | 673 | 629 | 94 | 676 | 691 | 98 | 73 | 76 | 104 | 81 | 76 | 94 |
| Colorado Rockies | 747 | 706 | 95 | 749 | 760 | 99 | 75 | 74 | 99 | 81 | 74 | 92 |
| Chicago Cubs | 622 | 602 | 97 | 672 | 689 | 98 | 70 | 66 | 94 | 75 | 66 | 88 |

Paul Goldschmidt
Dustin Pedroia
Manny Machado
Andrelton Simmons
Alex Gordon
Carlos Gomez
Gerardo Parra
Yadier Molina
R.A. Dickey

**THE FIELDING BIBLE AWARDS 2013**

# The Fielding Bible Awards 2013

John Dewan

It was a historic defensive season in baseball in 2013.

Andrelton Simmons set a single-season record (since we started tracking Defensive Runs Saved in 2003) by saving 41 runs at shortstop for the Atlanta Braves. He broke the mark of 35 runs saved in 2010 by New York Yankee outfielder Brett Gardner. Simmons had company breaking the record. Gerardo Parra saved 36 runs in right field for the Arizona Diamondbacks in 2013. But with four more runs saved in center field and one run saved in left, Parra also had 41 total Defensive Runs Saved and joins Simmons with the highest runs saved performances on record.

On top of that, Carlos Gomez saved 38 runs for the Milwaukee Brewers playing center field. And Manny Machado had 35 runs saved for the Baltimore Orioles at third base.

So, four players set or tied the previous record for most Defensive Runs Saved in a season. Four players who had never received a Fielding Bible Award or Gold Glove in their careers. Until now. All four players were rewarded with their first Fielding Bible Awards.

We expanded the panel this year from ten to an even dozen. Joining the panel are Brian Kenny from MLB Network and Dave Cameron of FanGraphs. The panel is charged with the task of determining the best fielders in baseball, using all the tools at their disposal. It's not just about the numbers; it's about scouting as well. About observing players in action. About understanding what goes into playing good defense. The expertise of The Fielding Bible panel in this area is unparalleled.

This is the eighth year of The Fielding Bible Awards. Two other players join Simmons, Parra, Gomez and Machado as first-year winners making a total of six first timers this year. Parra's teammate, Paul Goldschmidt, wins the Award at first base. R.A. Dickey unseats his Toronto Blue Jays teammate, four-time winner Mark Buehrle, in winning the Award at pitcher. Alex Gordon of the Kansas City Royals repeats as the winner in left field. Dustin Pedroia rounds out the list receiving his second Fielding Bible Award with a superlative defensive season playing second base for the Boston Red Sox.

Here's a short refresher course on how the awards are determined: We asked our panel of twelve experts to rank the top 10 players at each position. We then use a voting technique similar to the Major League Baseball MVP voting. A first place vote gets 10 points, second place 9 points, third place 8 points, etc. Total up the points for each player and the player with the most points wins the award. A perfect score is 120.

One important distinction that differentiates our award from most other baseball awards, including the Gold Gloves, is that we only have one winner for all of Major League Baseball, instead of separate winners for each league. Our intention is to continue to stand up and say, "This is the best fielder at this position in the major leagues last season."

Here are the Fielding Bible Awards for the 2013 season:

**First Base – Paul Goldschmidt, Arizona Diamondbacks**

Paul Goldschmidt had an MVP-worthy season and defense was an important part of the equation. On offense, Goldy led all National leaguers with the highest slugging percentage (.551) and highest OPS (.952). And now, on defense, the Fielding Bible Award panel declares that Goldschmidt is the best defensive first baseman in the game. Baseball Info Solutions Video Scouts cover every pitch and every play of every game and one of the many things they chart are Good Fielding Plays. They've been tracking this for ten years now, and in 2013 Goldschmidt was the first player to record over 100 Good Fielding Plays. He had 113. He saved 13 runs with his defense for the Diamondbacks, finishing second among first basemen to Anthony Rizzo (16) with the Cubs. Goldschmidt tallied 110 points to 98 for Rizzo in the Award voting.

Previous Winners:

| | | | |
|---|---|---|---|
| 2012 | Mark Teixeira | 2008 | Albert Pujols |
| 2011 | Albert Pujols | 2007 | Albert Pujols |
| 2010 | Daric Barton | 2006 | Albert Pujols |
| 2009 | Albert Pujols | | |

**Second Base – Dustin Pedroia, Boston Red Sox**

With the most Defensive Runs Saved at second base in 2013 (15), and the most Defensive Runs Saved at that position over the last three years (44), Dustin Pedroia wins his second Fielding Bible Award in those three years. Pedroia has the highest total of Good Fielding Plays ever by a second baseman, with 89. He is especially adept at making plays going to his left; he has made 32 more plays than an average second baseman to his left over the last three years. His sure-handedness is legendary. He has the fourth-best fielding percentage of all-time at second base at .991 with a minimum of 500 games played. He has never had a single season below .990 playing regularly. Pedroia beat out 2012 award winner Darwin Barney in the voting by garnering 11 out of 12 first-place votes, good for 118 points. Barney finished second in the voting with 98 points.

Previous Winners:

| | | | |
|---|---|---|---|
| 2012 | Darwin Barney | 2008 | Brandon Phillips |
| 2011 | Dustin Pedroia | 2007 | Aaron Hill |
| 2010 | Chase Utley | 2006 | Orlando Hudson |
| 2009 | Aaron Hill | | |

**Third Base – Manny Machado, Baltimore Orioles**

At age 21, Manny Machado is the youngest player ever to win a Fielding Bible Award, and he did it unanimously as the award panelists put him in the top position on each of their ballots. Machado is a shortstop playing third base. He has all the skills to be one of the best at shortstop, the most demanding position in the infield defensively. It comes as no surprise to everyone who has seen him play shortstop that he excels at third base as well. But the level of excellence is off the charts. He saved 35 runs playing third base for the Orioles last year. In this season of many "best defensive seasons" on record, Machado's performance is the best by a third baseman, topping Ryan Zimmerman's total of 25 runs in 2009. His range is tremendous in all directions, whether to his right, to his left, or straight on. Compared to an average third baseman, Machado made 11 more plays to his right, 14 more to his left and 15 more straight on. No other third baseman has had double-digit totals in every direction before. Nolan Arenado came in second in the voting with 100 points and was no slouch himself as he saved 30 runs for the Rockies defensively in 2013.

Previous Winners:

| | | | |
|---|---|---|---|
| 2012 | Adrian Beltre | 2008 | Adrian Beltre |
| 2011 | Adrian Beltre | 2007 | Pedro Feliz |
| 2010 | Evan Longoria | 2006 | Adrian Beltre |
| 2009 | Ryan Zimmerman | | |

**Shortstop – Andrelton Simmons, Atlanta Braves**

Is Andrelton Simmons the second coming of Ozzie Smith? It sure looks like it. He has everything that Ozzie had: soft hands, a quick release, tremendous range, an incredible flair for the shortstop position. And even one skill a little better than The Wizard of Oz: a stronger throwing arm. We won't crown Simmons with the all-time title just yet, but saving 41 runs in one year is the best on record. That's on top of having saved 19 runs for the Braves in about a third of the 2012 season. The competition wasn't even close this past year. The next best runs saved totals at shortstop were 12, 12 and 11 (Pedro Florimon, Clint Barmes and Elvis Andrus). The Awards panel rewarded Simmons with a unanimous vote.

Previous Winners:

| | | | |
|---|---|---|---|
| 2012 | Brendan Ryan | 2008 | Jimmy Rollins |
| 2011 | Troy Tulowitzki | 2007 | Troy Tulowitzki |
| 2010 | Troy Tulowitzki | 2006 | Adam Everett |
| 2009 | Jack Wilson | | |

## Left Field – Alex Gordon, Kansas City Royals

First Carl Crawford. Then Brett Gardner. Now Alex Gordon repeats in consecutive years as The Fielding Bible Award winner in left field. Gordon has great range but it's his throwing arm that sets him apart. He is always aware of how to set himself up to make the best throw possible after fielding the ball. He has 39 baserunner kills in the last three years, the most in baseball. (A baserunner kill is a direct throw to a base or the plate to nab a runner.) Gordon has been consistent about it too, with 12 kills in 2011, 14 in 2012 and 13 in 2013. Overall, Starling Marte of the Pittsburgh Pirates saved a few more runs than Gordon (20 to 17) and actually tied Gordon in the award vote with 112 points. We had to go to the first tie-breaker to determine the winner, with Gordon winning the Fielding Bible Award by a one-vote margin, six first-place votes for Gordon to five for Marte.

Previous Winners:

| | | | |
|---|---|---|---|
| 2012 | Alex Gordon | 2008 | Carl Crawford |
| 2011 | Brett Gardner | 2007 | Eric Byrnes |
| 2010 | Brett Gardner | 2006 | Carl Crawford |
| 2009 | Carl Crawford | | |

## Center Field – Carlos Gomez, Milwaukee Brewers

Carlos Gomez was an All-Star for the Milwaukee Brewers in 2013 as his offensive production took a leap upwards. But defensively, Gomez has always been an All-Star and his leaping ability is no small part of his arsenal of defensive skills. In 2013, Gomez robbed five home runs as they were going over the fence, the highest single-season total since Baseball Info Solutions began tracking this ten years ago. No one else had more than two in 2013. Those home run robberies accounted for eight Defensive Runs Saved. Gomez has tremendous range, and, not only does he prevent home runs, he prevents a ton of doubles and triples by ranging deep into territories where most other center fielders don't venture. His throwing arm is above average as well. His total of 38 runs saved is the third-highest season total on record behind the records set this year by Andrelton Simmons and Gerardo Parra (41 apiece). Gomez received 11 first-place votes out of 12 for 119 points. Juan Lagares of the Mets was placed second on nine ballots and received 100 points overall.

Previous Winners:

| | | | |
|---|---|---|---|
| 2012 | Mike Trout | 2008 | Carlos Beltran |
| 2011 | Austin Jackson | 2007 | Andruw Jones |
| 2010 | Michael Bourn | 2006 | Carlos Beltran |
| 2009 | Franklin Gutierrez | | |

**Right Field – Gerardo Parra, Arizona Diamondbacks**

Andrelton Simmons got all the ink, but Gerardo Parra quietly tied Simmons for the highest single-season runs saved total on record (41) this past season. He did it primarily playing right field (36 runs saved), but his prowess extends to all the outfield positions as he added five more runs saved in limited action playing left and center fields. Parra had the best range of any right fielder in baseball, with 23 of his 36 runs saved making plays that other right fielders don't make. But he also had the best throwing arm of any right fielder, with 10 runs saved throwing out runners and preventing others from advancing. Parra received 11 out of 12 first place votes by the panelists for a total of 117 points overall. Shane Victorino of the Red Sox received the remaining first place vote and was second overall with 106 points.

Previous Winners:

| | | | |
|---|---|---|---|
| 2012 | Jason Heyward | 2008 | Franklin Gutierrez |
| 2011 | Justin Upton | 2007 | Alex Rios |
| 2010 | Ichiro Suzuki | 2006 | Ichiro Suzuki |
| 2009 | Ichiro Suzuki | | |

**Catcher – Yadier Molina, St. Louis Cardinals**

Yadier Molina stands alone. His six Fielding Bible Awards in the eight-year history of the awards are more than anyone else has received (Albert Pujols has five). Yadier, one of the Catching Molina Brothers, also has six seasons with double-digit Defensive Run Saved totals, including 12 in 2013. He threw out over 40 percent of runners trying to steal once again (seventh time in his career). Looking at all the pitches thrown in the dirt while he was behind the plate with runners on base, Molina blocked 97 percent from becoming wild pitches, the highest rate in all of baseball. Molina had some good competition for the award from Russell Martin (Pirates) and Salvador Perez (Royals). Molina had 114 votes to 102 and 101 for Martin and Perez respectively.

Previous Winners:

| | | | |
|---|---|---|---|
| 2012 | Yadier Molina | 2008 | Yadier Molina |
| 2011 | Matt Wieters | 2007 | Yadier Molina |
| 2010 | Yadier Molina | 2006 | Ivan Rodriguez |
| 2009 | Yadier Molina | | |

### Pitcher – R.A. Dickey, Toronto Blue Jays

Mark Buehrle won the previous four Fielding Bible Awards at pitcher. In 2013, Buehrle joined the Blue Jays and teammate R.A. Dickey wins the Award. Did Mr. Buehrle give Mr. Dickey a few pointers? Maybe. But the fact is that Dickey has been a superlative defender for quite some time now. He has been in the top 10 among 175 qualifying pitchers in Defensive Runs Saved in each of that last four years. He excels in all facets of defending his position. As a knuckleballer, Dickey always puts himself in good fielding position after each pitch. He covers bunts very well, and has a tremendous pickoff move. He has picked off 12 runners in the last three years, which is tied for the second-most in baseball behind James Shields (19) among right-handed pitchers. The vote totals: Dickey 105, Zack Greinke (Dodgers) 98, Buehrle 73.

Previous Winners:

| | | | |
|---|---|---|---|
| 2012 | Mark Buehrle | 2008 | Kenny Rodgers |
| 2011 | Mark Buehrle | 2007 | Johan Santana |
| 2010 | Mark Buehrle | 2006 | Greg Maddux |
| 2009 | Mark Buehrle | | |

## Background of the Fielding Bible Awards

While *The Fielding Bible*, *The Fielding Bible-Volume II*, and *The Fielding Bible-Volume III* put a lot of emphasis on the numbers, especially Defensive Runs Saved and the Plus-Minus system, we feel that visual observation and subjective judgment are still very important parts of determining the best defensive players. Also, we believe people have a right to know who is voting and all the players they are voting for. Therefore, in setting up the Fielding Bible Awards, we took the following steps:

1. ***We appointed a panel of experts to vote.*** We have a panel of twelve experts plus three "tie-breaker" ballots. (See below.)

2. ***We rate everybody in one group.*** The Gold Glove vote is divided into National League and American League. We make ours different by putting everybody together. Besides, is playing shortstop in the American League one thing and playing shortstop in the National League a different thing, or are they really very much the same thing? A few years back, we had a great example of this decision. Without the Fielding Bible Award, Jack Wilson wins nada, because he switched

leagues in mid-year. According to our panelists (and unlike the Gold Glove voters), Jack was the best fielding shortstop in baseball in 2009. Period. He deserved to be recognized for that.

3. ***We use a ten-man ballot and a ten-point scale.*** We use a ten-man ballot. We give ten points for first place, nine points for second place, etc, down to one point for tenth place. We feel strongly that a ten-man ballot with weighted positions leads to more accurate outcomes.

4. ***We defined the list of candidates.*** Only players who actually were regulars at the position are candidates. This eliminates the possibility of a vote going to somebody who wasn't really playing the position.

5. ***We are publishing the balloting.*** We summarize the voting at each position, clearly identifying whom everybody voted for. Publishing the actual vote totals encourages the voters to take their votes more seriously. Also, we feel the public will have more respect for the voting if they have more insight into the process.

A perfect score is 120 points. If all 12 voters place one player first on their ballot, he scores 120. Two players had perfect scores of 120 this year, Andrelton Simmons and Manny Machado.

Here are the tie-breaker rules (which came into play in our very first year, and did so again this year, as well as in 2010). They are applied one at a time until we have a winner:

1. Most first-place votes wins.
2. Count the tie-breaker ballots, highest point tally wins.
3. Award goes to player with the higher plus/minus rating.

Ballots were due four days after the end of the regular season. Here is this year's panel:

Since you have this book, you probably know **Bill James**, a baseball writer and analyst published for more than thirty years. Bill is the Senior Baseball Operations Advisor for the Boston Red Sox.

The **BIS Video Scouts** at Baseball Info Solutions (BIS) study every game of the season, multiple times, charting a huge list of valuable game details.

As the MLB Network on-air host of *Clubhouse Confidential* and *MLB Now*, **Brian Kenny** brings an analytical perspective on the game of baseball to a national television audience. He also won a 2003 Sports Emmy Award as host of ESPN's *Baseball Tonight*.

**Dave Cameron** is the Managing Editor of FanGraphs. He resides in Winston-Salem, North Carolina, where the local minor league team once forced him to watch Michael Morse play shortstop for an entire season. He has appreciated defensive value ever since.

**Doug Glanville** played nine seasons in Major League Baseball and was well known for his excellent outfield defense. Currently, he is a baseball analyst at ESPN, primarily on *Baseball Tonight*, ESPN.com and *ESPN The Magazine*.

The man who created Strat-O-Matic Baseball, **Hal Richman**, continues to lead his company's annual in-depth analysis of each player's season. Hal cautions SOM players that his voting on this ballot may or may not reflect the eventual fielding ratings for players in his game. Ballots were due prior to the completion of his annual research effort to evaluate player defense.

Named the best sports columnist in America in 2012 by the National Sportswriters and Sportscasters Hall of Fame, **Joe Posnanski** is the National Columnist at NBC Sports.

For over twenty-five years, BIS owner **John Dewan** has collected, analyzed, and published in-depth baseball statistics and analysis. He authored *The Fielding Bible* in 2006 and *The Fielding Bible-Volume II* in 2009, and co-authored *The Fielding Bible-Volume III* in 2012.

**Mark Simon** has been a researcher for ESPN Stats & Information since 2002 and currently helps oversee the Stats & Information blog and Twitter (@espnstatsinfo). He is a regular contributor on baseball (often writing on defense) for ESPNNY.com and ESPN.com.

**Peter Gammons** serves as on-air and online analyst for MLB Network, MLB.com and NESN (New England Sports Network). He is the 56th recipient of the J. G. Taylor Spink Award for outstanding baseball writing given by the BBWAA (Baseball Writers Association of America).

After nearly fifteen years with ESPN.com, **Rob Neyer** joined SB Nation as National Baseball Editor in 2011. He has written six books about baseball.

The **Tom Tango Fan Poll** represents the results of a poll taken at the website, Tango on Baseball (www.tangotiger.net). Besides hosting the website, Tom writes research articles devoted to sabermetrics and is the co-author of *The Book: Playing the Percentages in Baseball.*

Our three tie-breakers are **Ben Jedlovec**, Vice President of Baseball Info Solutions and co-author of *The Fielding Bible-Volume III*, **Dan Casey**, veteran Video Scout and Senior Operations Analyst at BIS, and **Sean Forman**, the founder of Baseball-Reference.com.

# The Fielding Bible Awards

Below we show the final point tally for The Fielding Bible Awards in the 2013 season. We asked a panel of experts to complete a ten-man ballot ranking players from 1 to 10 based on their defensive abilities. We show the ranks in the tables below. We then awarded points similar to Major League Baseball's MVP voting: ten points for a first place vote, nine for second, etc., down to one point for tenth place. We cover all nine positions, looking at only their fielding work for the 2013 season. Position players are eligible if they played at least 600 innings while catchers require a minimum of 500 innings. Either can qualify with 10 Runs Saved, as well. Pitchers require a minimum of 120 innings pitched or 5 Runs Saved.

## First Basemen

| First Basemen | Bill | BIS Video Scouts | Brian | Dave | Doug | Hal | Joe | John | Mark | Peter | Rob | Tango Fan Poll | Total Points |
|---|---|---|---|---|---|---|---|---|---|---|---|---|---|
| Paul Goldschmidt | 1 | 1 | 1 | 3 | 1 | 4 | 1 | 4 | 2 | 2 | 1 | 1 | 110 |
| Anthony Rizzo | 3 | 2 | 3 | 4 | 3 | 3 | 2 | 2 | 3 | 1 | 2 | 6 | 98 |
| Adrian Gonzalez | 4 | 3 | 2 | 2 | | 5 | 3 | 1 | 1 | 3 | 4 | 4 | 89 |
| Freddie Freeman | 5 | 4 | 7 | | 5 | 7 | 7 | 6 | 4 | 5 | 7 | 5 | 59 |
| Joey Votto | 10 | 5 | 6 | | 2 | 1 | 8 | 3 | 7 | 8 | 6 | | 54 |
| Mike Napoli | 9 | 6 | 4 | 5 | 8 | 10 | 5 | 9 | 5 | 4 | 3 | | 53 |
| Eric Hosmer | 7 | 7 | | 10 | 4 | 8 | 4 | | | 7 | 9 | 2 | 41 |
| Brandon Belt | 2 | 8 | | | | 2 | | 5 | | 6 | 5 | 9 | 40 |
| James Loney | 6 | 9 | 9 | 1 | | 9 | | | 8 | 10 | 10 | 3 | 34 |
| Justin Morneau | 8 | | | 8 | 6 | | 10 | | 6 | | 8 | | 20 |
| Others receiving points: Yonder Alonso 14, Adam LaRoche 14, Mark Trumbo 11, Nick Swisher 10, Todd Helton 5, Lyle Overbay 4, Allen Craig 3, Mitch Moreland 1 | | | | | | | | | | | | | |

## Second Basemen

| Second Basemen | Bill | BIS Video Scouts | Brian | Dave | Doug | Hal | Joe | John | Mark | Peter | Rob | Tango Fan Poll | Total Points |
|---|---|---|---|---|---|---|---|---|---|---|---|---|---|
| Dustin Pedroia | 1 | 1 | 1 | 1 | 1 | 3 | 1 | 1 | 1 | 1 | 1 | 1 | 118 |
| Darwin Barney | 5 | 2 | 2 | 3 | 4 | 2 | 3 | 2 | 3 | 4 | 2 | 2 | 98 |
| Mark Ellis | 3 | 3 | 7 | 4 | 7 | 9 | | 3 | 2 | 2 | 3 | 7 | 71 |
| Ben Zobrist | 6 | 9 | 3 | 2 | | 6 | 6 | | 4 | 6 | 4 | 4 | 60 |
| Brandon Phillips | 9 | 6 | 5 | 5 | 9 | 1 | 4 | 7 | 6 | | 9 | 3 | 57 |
| Ian Kinsler | 4 | 4 | 4 | | 8 | | 2 | 4 | 5 | 7 | 7 | | 54 |
| Robinson Cano | 2 | 7 | 10 | | 5 | 4 | 7 | 6 | 9 | 9 | 6 | 5 | 51 |
| Brian Dozier | 10 | 5 | | | 2 | 8 | 5 | | 8 | 3 | 8 | 8 | 42 |
| D.J. LeMahieu | | 8 | 6 | 7 | 6 | 10 | 10 | 5 | 7 | | 5 | 9 | 37 |
| Neil Walker | | 10 | | | 3 | | 8 | | | 5 | | | 18 |
| Others receiving points: Chase Utley 12, Ryan Goins 8, Omar Infante 8, Dustin Ackley 6, Gordon Beckham 5, Emilio Bonifacio 5, Jason Kipnis 3, Jose Altuve 2, Elliot Johnson 2, Eric Sogard 2, Aaron Hill 1 | | | | | | | | | | | | | |

## Third Basemen

| Third Basemen | Bill | BIS Video Scouts | Brian | Dave | Doug | Hal | Joe | John | Mark | Peter | Rob | Tango Fan Poll | Total Points |
|---|---|---|---|---|---|---|---|---|---|---|---|---|---|
| Manny Machado | 1 | 1 | 1 | 1 | 1 | 1 | 1 | 1 | 1 | 1 | 1 | 1 | 120 |
| Nolan Arenado | 6 | 2 | 2 | 2 | 2 | 2 | 2 | 2 | 2 | 2 | 4 | 4 | 100 |
| Evan Longoria | 2 | 3 | 4 | 3 | 3 | 3 | 3 | 3 | 4 | 3 | 2 | 3 | 96 |
| Josh Donaldson | 4 | 4 | 5 | 5 | 5 | 6 | 4 | 5 | 5 | 4 | 5 | 6 | 74 |
| Juan Uribe | | 5 | 3 | 4 | 4 | 9 | | 4 | 3 | 5 | 3 | 7 | 63 |
| David Wright | 7 | 8 | 7 | 10 | 8 | 8 | 5 | 7 | 9 | 7 | 6 | 9 | 41 |
| Brett Lawrie | 10 | 9 | | 8 | 6 | 5 | 7 | 6 | | | | 2 | 35 |
| Todd Frazier | 5 | 7 | 6 | 7 | | 7 | | 10 | 6 | 9 | 7 | | 35 |
| Matt Dominguez | 3 | 6 | | | 7 | | 8 | | 10 | 6 | 8 | 8 | 32 |
| Adrian Beltre | 8 | | 9 | 6 | | 4 | 6 | | | | | 5 | 28 |
| Others receiving points: Chase Headley 15, Luis Valbuena 9, Martin Prado 4, Jeff Bianchi 3, Trevor Plouffe 3, Ryan Zimmerman 2 | | | | | | | | | | | | | |

## Shortstops

| Shortstops | Bill | BIS Video Scouts | Brian | Dave | Doug | Hal | Joe | John | Mark | Peter | Rob | Tango Fan Poll | Total Points |
|---|---|---|---|---|---|---|---|---|---|---|---|---|---|
| Andrelton Simmons | 1 | 1 | 1 | 1 | 1 | 1 | 1 | 1 | 1 | 1 | 1 | 1 | 120 |
| Elvis Andrus | 7 | 2 | 4 | | 2 | 4 | 3 | 3 | 4 | 5 | 3 | | 73 |
| Pedro Florimon | 3 | 5 | 10 | | 3 | 7 | 4 | 4 | 3 | 2 | 6 | | 63 |
| Clint Barmes | | 3 | 2 | 8 | 9 | | 6 | 2 | 2 | | 2 | 7 | 58 |
| Troy Tulowitzki | 4 | 4 | | | 8 | 3 | 2 | 8 | 9 | 3 | 7 | 4 | 58 |
| Alcides Escobar | 5 | 9 | 3 | 2 | 5 | 2 | 5 | | 5 | | 9 | 8 | 57 |
| J.J. Hardy | 6 | 6 | 6 | 4 | 6 | 6 | | 6 | 8 | 4 | 5 | 10 | 54 |
| Brendan Ryan | 8 | 7 | 5 | 10 | | 9 | 7 | 5 | 7 | | | 3 | 38 |
| Jose Iglesias | 2 | 8 | | 5 | | 5 | | | | 9 | | 2 | 35 |
| Yunel Escobar | | | 7 | 6 | | 8 | | 7 | 6 | 6 | 10 | 5 | 33 |
| Others receiving points: Pete Kozma 19, Zack Cozart 17, Jean Segura 14, Didi Gregorius 5, Stephen Drew 4, Cliff Pennington 4, Alexei Ramirez 4, Ian Desmond 3, Brandon Crawford 1 | | | | | | | | | | | | | |

## Left Fielders

| Left Fielders | Bill | BIS Video Scouts | Brian | Dave | Doug | Hal | Joe | John | Mark | Peter | Rob | Tango Fan Poll | Total Points |
|---|---|---|---|---|---|---|---|---|---|---|---|---|---|
| Alex Gordon | 1 | 2 | 2 | 3 | 1 | 3 | 1 | 1 | 2 | 1 | 2 | 1 | 112 |
| Starling Marte | 3 | 1 | 1 | 1 | 2 | 2 | 2 | 2 | 1 | 2 | 1 | 2 | 112 |
| Carlos Gonzalez | 2 | 3 | 3 | 4 | 3 | 1 | 3 | 5 | 3 | 5 | 3 | 3 | 94 |
| David Murphy | 5 | 4 | 4 | 6 | 6 | 9 | 5 | 3 | 4 | 4 | 5 | | 66 |
| Andy Dirks | 4 | 5 | 5 | 8 | 4 | 7 | 6 | 4 | 5 | | 4 | | 58 |
| Michael Brantley | 7 | 6 | | 9 | 7 | 6 | | 8 | 8 | 3 | 8 | 5 | 43 |
| Yoenis Cespedes | 6 | 8 | 6 | 5 | 9 | 8 | | 10 | 9 | 6 | 6 | 7 | 41 |
| Carl Crawford | | 10 | 9 | 2 | 10 | 10 | 7 | | 7 | | 7 | 9 | 28 |
| Bryce Harper | 9 | 9 | 8 | | | 4 | | 9 | | 9 | 10 | 4 | 26 |
| Vernon Wells | | | 10 | 7 | 5 | | | 7 | | 7 | | | 19 |
| Others receiving points: Logan Schafer 15, Nate McLouth 14, Eric Young 10, Rajai Davis 6, Domonic Brown 5, J.B. Shuck 5, Jonny Gomes 4, Alfonso Soriano 3 | | | | | | | | | | | | | |

## Center Fielders

| Center Fielders | Bill | BIS Video Scouts | Brian | Dave | Doug | Hal | Joe | John | Mark | Peter | Rob | Tango Fan Poll | Total Points |
|---|---|---|---|---|---|---|---|---|---|---|---|---|---|
| Carlos Gomez | 1 | 1 | 1 | 1 | 1 | 2 | 1 | 1 | 1 | 1 | 1 | 1 | 119 |
| Juan Lagares | 6 | 2 | 2 | 2 | 2 | 5 | 3 | 2 | 2 | 2 | 2 | 2 | 110 |
| Jacoby Ellsbury | 2 | 3 | 5 | 4 | 3 | | 4 | 3 | 5 | 3 | 4 | | 74 |
| Lorenzo Cain | 9 | 4 | 3 | 7 | 4 | 10 | 2 | 4 | 3 | | 3 | 5 | 67 |
| A.J. Pollock | 10 | 5 | 4 | 10 | 5 | | 6 | 9 | 4 | 4 | 5 | 4 | 55 |
| Andrew McCutchen | 3 | 6 | 8 | 3 | | 3 | 8 | | 8 | 6 | 8 | 9 | 48 |
| Brandon Barnes | 7 | 8 | | | 7 | 7 | 5 | 10 | 6 | 8 | 9 | | 32 |
| Leonys Martin | | 7 | 6 | | 8 | 8 | 10 | | | 5 | 7 | | 26 |
| Denard Span | | 10 | | 5 | 6 | | | 6 | 7 | | 10 | 8 | 25 |
| Mike Trout | | | 9 | 8 | | 1 | | | | | | 3 | 23 |
| Others receiving points: Craig Gentry 23, Austin Jackson 19, Colby Rasmus 18, Michael Bourn 12, Brett Gardner 8, Adam Jones 6, Coco Crisp 5 | | | | | | | | | | | | | |

## Right Fielders

| Right Fielders | Bill | BIS Video Scouts | Brian | Dave | Doug | Hal | Joe | John | Mark | Peter | Rob | Tango Fan Poll | Total Points |
|---|---|---|---|---|---|---|---|---|---|---|---|---|---|
| Gerardo Parra | 4 | 1 | 1 | 1 | 1 | 1 | 1 | 1 | 1 | 1 | 1 | 1 | 117 |
| Shane Victorino | 1 | 3 | 2 | 2 | 2 | 2 | 2 | 3 | 2 | 2 | 2 | 3 | 106 |
| Jason Heyward | 3 | 2 | 5 | 3 | 4 | 5 | 3 | 2 | 3 | 3 | 3 | 2 | 94 |
| Jay Bruce | 2 | 4 | 3 | | 3 | 4 | 4 | 6 | 4 | 4 | 4 | 7 | 76 |
| Josh Reddick | 6 | 5 | 6 | 4 | 5 | 3 | 5 | 4 | 5 | 5 | 5 | 4 | 75 |
| Norichika Aoki | 7 | 6 | 4 | | 6 | 6 | 10 | 5 | | 6 | 8 | | 41 |
| Ichiro Suzuki | 8 | 8 | 8 | 5 | 7 | 9 | 8 | 9 | 8 | | 6 | 5 | 40 |
| Yasiel Puig | 5 | 7 | 9 | | | 10 | | 7 | | 10 | 7 | 6 | 27 |
| David Lough | | 9 | 7 | 7 | 10 | | 6 | | 6 | | | 10 | 22 |
| Marlon Byrd | | 10 | | | 8 | | 9 | 10 | 7 | 9 | 9 | | 15 |

Others receiving points: Drew Stubbs 12, Chris Denorfia 12, Marcell Ozuna 5, Will Venable 4, Matt Joyce 3, Hunter Pence 3, Nate Schierholtz 3, Wil Myers 2, Cody Ross 2, Jose Bautista 1

## Catchers

| Catchers | Bill | BIS Video Scouts | Brian | Dave | Doug | Hal | Joe | John | Mark | Peter | Rob | Tango Fan Poll | Total Points |
|---|---|---|---|---|---|---|---|---|---|---|---|---|---|
| Yadier Molina | 1 | 1 | 2 | 2 | 4 | 1 | 1 | 1 | 2 | 1 | 1 | 1 | 114 |
| Russell Martin | 6 | 2 | 1 | 1 | 1 | 4 | 4 | 3 | 1 | 2 | 2 | 3 | 102 |
| Salvador Perez | 2 | 3 | 3 | 3 | 3 | 2 | 2 | 2 | 3 | 3 | 3 | 2 | 101 |
| Welington Castillo | 4 | 4 | 7 | 10 | 2 | 7 | 3 | 4 | 4 | 7 | 8 | | 61 |
| Yan Gomes | 7 | 5 | 8 | 5 | 5 | | 5 | 7 | 5 | 4 | | 5 | 54 |
| Jonathan Lucroy | | 7 | 5 | 4 | | | | | 10 | 8 | 5 | 8 | 30 |
| Buster Posey | 5 | 9 | | 7 | 10 | 8 | 8 | 10 | | 5 | 9 | 9 | 30 |
| Joe Mauer | 9 | 8 | | | 7 | 10 | 6 | 8 | 9 | | | 6 | 25 |
| Chris Stewart | | | 9 | | 8 | | | 6 | 7 | 9 | 4 | | 23 |
| A.J. Ellis | | | | | 6 | 5 | | | 6 | 6 | 10 | 10 | 23 |

Others receiving points: Matt Wieters 21, Jose Molina 20, Jeff Mathis 19, Ryan Hanigan 12, Brian McCann 8, Miguel Montero 6, J.P. Arencibia 4, Jarrod Saltalamacchia 3, Wilson Ramos 2, Carlos Ruiz 2

## Pitchers

| Pitchers | Bill | BIS Video Scouts | Brian | Dave | Doug | Hal | Joe | John | Mark | Peter | Rob | Ben | Total Points |
|---|---|---|---|---|---|---|---|---|---|---|---|---|---|
| R.A. Dickey | 2 | 2 | 3 | 4 | 1 | 1 | 2 | 1 | 2 | 4 | 2 | 3 | 105 |
| Zack Greinke | 3 | 1 | | 5 | 2 | 4 | 1 | 2 | 1 | 2 | 1 | 1 | 98 |
| Mark Buehrle | 6 | 3 | 1 | 1 | | 2 | 8 | 5 | 3 | 6 | 5 | 8 | 73 |
| Patrick Corbin | 8 | 4 | 7 | 2 | | 3 | 5 | 3 | 7 | 1 | | 2 | 68 |
| Hiroki Kuroda | 7 | 6 | 2 | | 3 | 8 | | 6 | 9 | 7 | 3 | 7 | 52 |
| Mike Leake | 9 | 5 | 6 | 6 | 5 | 7 | | 4 | 8 | 9 | 6 | 10 | 46 |
| Clayton Kershaw | 5 | | 4 | 8 | | 5 | | 7 | | | | 6 | 31 |
| Julio Teheran | | 8 | | | 6 | | 9 | 10 | 4 | 8 | 4 | 9 | 30 |
| Madison Bumgarner | | | | 3 | 4 | 9 | 7 | | | 5 | | | 27 |
| Adam Wainwright | | 9 | 10 | | 9 | 6 | 3 | | 6 | | | | 23 |

Others receiving points: Andrew Cashner 23, Kyle Kendrick 20, Hisashi Iwakuma 15, David Price 11, James Shields 9, Jorge de la Rosa 6, Hector Santiago 6, Joe Saunders 3, Hyun-Jin Ryu 3, Chris Tillman 3, Mike Minor 2, Andy Pettitte 2, Francisco Liriano 1, Trevor Cahill 1, Cliff Lee 1, Wade Miley 1

# Runs Saved and Plus/Minus Leaders

The Runs Saved and Plus/Minus Leaders showcase baseball's best fielders of 2013 and over the past three years. Take a look at the top 10 at each position on the 2013 Leaderboard to see who excelled on the defensive side of the ball this past season. And if you are interested in who the best defenders have been year after year, the 3-Year Leaderboards will have that information.

The Plus/Minus System is a way to evaluate defensive range by measuring how often defenders turn grounders and fly balls into outs. A number greater than zero (plus "+") is above average. Below zero (minus "-") is below average. In 2013, Elvis Andrus had a Plus/Minus figure of +11, which means he made 11 more plays than an average shortstop would have made on the same types of batted balls. Runs Saved is an estimate of the number of runs each player saves with his defense. It combines Plus/Minus with our analysis of bunts, double plays, outfield arms, catchers' earned runs, catchers stolen bases allowed, pitchers' stolen bases allowed and good plays/misplays to form a complete evaluation of a fielder.

Please see the glossary for a more complete description of Runs Saved and Plus/Minus.

# Infield Runs Saved Leaders

### First Basemen 3-Year Leaders

| | |
|---|---|
| Gonzalez,Adrian | 39 |
| Rizzo,Anthony | 22 |
| Loney,James | 21 |
| Teixeira,Mark | 20 |
| Votto,Joey | 19 |
| Pujols,Albert | 19 |
| LaRoche,Adam | 14 |
| Goldschmidt,Paul | 11 |
| Trumbo,Mark | 11 |
| Belt,Brandon | 11 |

### Second Basemen 3-Year Leaders

| | |
|---|---|
| Pedroia,Dustin | 44 |
| Barney,Darwin | 40 |
| Ellis,Mark | 39 |
| Kinsler,Ian | 30 |
| Zobrist,Ben | 25 |
| Ackley,Dustin | 24 |
| Cano,Robinson | 22 |
| Casilla,Alexi | 20 |
| Phillips,Brandon | 18 |
| LeMahieu,DJ | 18 |

### Third Basemen 3-Year Leaders

| | |
|---|---|
| Machado,Manny | 42 |
| Lawrie,Brett | 38 |
| Longoria,Evan | 35 |
| Arenado,Nolan | 30 |
| Uribe,Juan | 24 |
| Beltre,Adrian | 21 |
| Wright,David | 15 |
| Donaldson,Josh | 15 |
| Polanco,Placido | 14 |
| Cruz,Luis | 14 |

### Shortstops 3-Year Leaders

| | |
|---|---|
| Simmons,Andrelton | 60 |
| Ryan,Brendan | 51 |
| Barmes,Clint | 39 |
| Hardy,J.J. | 34 |
| Andrus,Elvis | 26 |
| Escobar,Yunel | 25 |
| Ramirez,Alexei | 22 |
| Cozart,Zack | 20 |
| Florimon,Pedro | 18 |
| McDonald,John | 18 |

### First Basemen 3-Year Trailers

| | |
|---|---|
| Fielder,Prince | -26 |
| Howard,Ryan | -20 |
| Konerko,Paul | -18 |
| Dunn,Adam | -17 |
| Moss,Brandon | -16 |
| Davis,Chris | -13 |

### Second Basemen 3-Year Trailers

| | |
|---|---|
| Weeks,Rickie | -50 |
| Uggla,Dan | -28 |
| Murphy,Daniel | -26 |
| Keppinger,Jeff | -21 |
| Weeks,Jemile | -21 |
| Schumaker,Skip | -18 |

### Third Basemen 3-Year Trailers

| | |
|---|---|
| Reynolds,Mark | -35 |
| Young,Michael | -29 |
| Johnson,Chris | -29 |
| Ramirez,Aramis | -26 |
| Cabrera,Miguel | -22 |
| Nelson,Chris | -19 |

### Shortstops 3-Year Trailers

| | |
|---|---|
| Nunez,Eduardo | -38 |
| Jeter,Derek | -38 |
| Reyes,Jose | -33 |
| Rollins,Jimmy | -30 |
| Lowrie,Jed | -24 |
| Gordon,Dee | -21 |

### First Basemen 2013 Leaders

| | |
|---|---|
| Rizzo,Anthony | 16 |
| Goldschmidt,Paul | 13 |
| Gonzalez,Adrian | 11 |
| Napoli,Mike | 10 |
| Freeman,Freddie | 7 |
| Alonso,Yonder | 7 |
| Votto,Joey | 6 |
| Swisher,Nick | 6 |
| Morneau,Justin | 5 |
| Overbay,Lyle | 5 |

### Second Basemen 2013 Leaders

| | |
|---|---|
| Pedroia,Dustin | 15 |
| Ellis,Mark | 12 |
| Barney,Darwin | 11 |
| Kinsler,Ian | 11 |
| LeMahieu,DJ | 10 |
| Bonifacio,Emilio | 10 |
| Johnson,Elliot | 10 |
| Dozier,Brian | 9 |
| Walker,Neil | 9 |
| Zobrist,Ben | 7 |

### Third Basemen 2013 Leaders

| | |
|---|---|
| Machado,Manny | 35 |
| Arenado,Nolan | 30 |
| Uribe,Juan | 15 |
| Longoria,Evan | 12 |
| Donaldson,Josh | 11 |
| Dominguez,Matt | 8 |
| Valbuena,Luis | 6 |
| Headley,Chase | 5 |
| Wright,David | 5 |
| Frazier,Todd | 5 |

### Shortstops 2013 Leaders

| | |
|---|---|
| Simmons,Andrelton | 41 |
| Florimon,Pedro | 12 |
| Barmes,Clint | 12 |
| Andrus,Elvis | 11 |
| Kozma,Pete | 8 |
| Hardy,J.J. | 8 |
| Tulowitzki,Troy | 6 |
| Ryan,Brendan | 6 |
| Cozart,Zack | 4 |
| Escobar,Alcides | 4 |

### First Basemen 2013 Trailers

| | |
|---|---|
| Fielder,Prince | -13 |
| Dunn,Adam | -12 |
| Moss,Brandon | -12 |
| Encarnacion,Edwin | -8 |
| Smoak,Justin | -8 |
| Lind,Adam | -7 |

### Second Basemen 2013 Trailers

| | |
|---|---|
| Uggla,Dan | -19 |
| Weeks,Rickie | -15 |
| Murphy,Daniel | -13 |
| Rutledge,Josh | -9 |
| Hill,Aaron | -9 |
| Scutaro,Marco | -7 |

### Third Basemen 2013 Trailers

| | |
|---|---|
| Young,Michael | -20 |
| Cabrera,Miguel | -18 |
| Freese,David | -14 |
| Ramirez,Aramis | -12 |
| Chavez,Eric | -10 |
| Middlebrooks,Will | -8 |

### Shortstops 2013 Trailers

| | |
|---|---|
| Nunez,Eduardo | -28 |
| Lowrie,Jed | -18 |
| Cabrera,Asdrubal | -16 |
| Rollins,Jimmy | -15 |
| Quintanilla,Omar | -8 |
| Castro,Starlin | -8 |

# Outfield Runs Saved Leaders

| Left Fielders 3-Year Leaders | |
|---|---|
| Gordon,Alex | 60 |
| Marte,Starling | 26 |
| Prado,Martin | 19 |
| Murphy,David | 16 |
| Dirks,Andy | 16 |
| Braun,Ryan | 14 |
| Parra,Gerardo | 14 |
| Fuld,Sam | 13 |
| Wells,Casper | 13 |
| Brantley,Michael | 10 |

| Center Fielders 3-Year Leaders | |
|---|---|
| Gomez,Carlos | 56 |
| Jackson,Austin | 37 |
| Span,Denard | 32 |
| Gentry,Craig | 32 |
| Lagares,Juan | 26 |
| Bourn,Michael | 24 |
| Ellsbury,Jacoby | 23 |
| Cain,Lorenzo | 23 |
| Young,Chris | 22 |
| Bourjos,Peter | 20 |

| Right Fielders 3-Year Leaders | |
|---|---|
| Heyward,Jason | 50 |
| Parra,Gerardo | 45 |
| Reddick,Josh | 42 |
| Victorino,Shane | 24 |
| Aoki,Norichika | 21 |
| Suzuki,Ichiro | 15 |
| Hunter,Torii | 14 |
| Bogusevic,Brian | 14 |
| Denorfia,Chris | 13 |
| Bruce,Jay | 12 |

| Left Fielders 3-Year Trailers | |
|---|---|
| Ibanez,Raul | -43 |
| Willingham,Josh | -21 |
| Holliday,Matt | -20 |
| Quentin,Carlos | -15 |
| Duda,Lucas | -13 |
| Ludwick,Ryan | -13 |

| Center Fielders 3-Year Trailers | |
|---|---|
| Saunders,Michael | -24 |
| Kemp,Matt | -24 |
| Pagan,Angel | -23 |
| Jones,Adam | -22 |
| De Aza,Alejandro | -21 |
| Coghlan,Chris | -18 |

| Right Fielders 3-Year Trailers | |
|---|---|
| Cuddyer,Michael | -34 |
| Cruz,Nelson | -21 |
| Morse,Michael | -15 |
| Pence,Hunter | -15 |
| Brown,Domonic | -14 |
| Francoeur,Jeff | -12 |

| Left Fielders 2013 Leaders | |
|---|---|
| Marte,Starling | 20 |
| Gordon,Alex | 16 |
| Gonzalez,Carlos | 10 |
| Murphy,David | 8 |
| Dirks,Andy | 6 |
| Wells,Vernon | 5 |
| Heisey,Chris | 5 |
| Blanco,Gregor | 5 |
| Cespedes,Yoenis | 4 |
| Harper,Bryce | 4 |

| Center Fielders 2013 Leaders | |
|---|---|
| Gomez,Carlos | 38 |
| Lagares,Juan | 26 |
| Cain,Lorenzo | 17 |
| Pollock,A.J. | 15 |
| Martin,Leonys | 14 |
| Ellsbury,Jacoby | 13 |
| Rasmus,Colby | 11 |
| Gentry,Craig | 8 |
| McCutchen,Andrew | 7 |
| Barnes,Brandon | 7 |

| Right Fielders 2013 Leaders | |
|---|---|
| Parra,Gerardo | 36 |
| Victorino,Shane | 24 |
| Bruce,Jay | 18 |
| Heyward,Jason | 15 |
| Aoki,Norichika | 13 |
| Reddick,Josh | 13 |
| Byrd,Marlon | 12 |
| Puig,Yasiel | 10 |
| Lough,David | 10 |
| Denorfia,Chris | 9 |

| Left Fielders 2013 Trailers | |
|---|---|
| Ibanez,Raul | -19 |
| Holliday,Matt | -13 |
| Duda,Lucas | -11 |
| Arcia,Oswaldo | -9 |
| Willingham,Josh | -8 |
| Upton,Justin | -8 |

| Center Fielders 2013 Trailers | |
|---|---|
| De Aza,Alejandro | -18 |
| Choo,Shin-Soo | -17 |
| Saunders,Michael | -14 |
| Jay,Jon | -10 |
| Pagan,Angel | -9 |
| Trout,Mike NB | -9 |

| Right Fielders 2013 Trailers | |
|---|---|
| Cuddyer,Michael | -16 |
| Morse,Michael | -15 |
| Young,Delmon | -10 |
| Hunter,Torii | -10 |
| Hamilton,Josh NB | -8 |
| Joyce,Matt | -7 |

# Pitcher/Catcher Runs Saved Leaders

| Pitchers 3-Year Leaders | |
|---|---|
| Dickey,R.A. | 23 |
| Westbrook,Jake | 23 |
| Buehrle,Mark | 23 |
| Greinke,Zack | 17 |
| Leake,Mike | 16 |
| Kuroda,Hiroki | 15 |
| Kershaw,Clayton | 15 |
| Cueto,Johnny | 13 |
| Saunders,Joe | 12 |
| Corbin,Patrick | 12 |

| Catchers 3-Year Leaders | |
|---|---|
| Molina,Yadier | 24 |
| Perez,Salvador | 21 |
| Castillo,Welington | 21 |
| Mathis,Jeff | 18 |
| Stewart,Chris | 17 |
| Martin,Russell | 17 |
| Quintero,Humberto | 14 |
| Maldonado,Martin | 10 |
| Flowers,Tyler | 10 |
| Gomes,Yan | 10 |

| Pitchers 3-Year Trailers | |
|---|---|
| Volquez,Edinson | -17 |
| Hanson,Tommy | -14 |
| Garza,Matt | -12 |
| Humber,Philip | -11 |
| Lackey,John | -11 |
| Lowe,Derek | -11 |

| Catchers 3-Year Trailers | |
|---|---|
| Torrealba,Yorvit | -18 |
| Pierzynski,A.J. | -17 |
| Saltalamacchia,J | -15 |
| Santana,Carlos | -14 |
| Doumit,Ryan | -14 |
| Buck,John | -13 |

| Pitchers 2013 Leaders | |
|---|---|
| Corbin,Patrick | 8 |
| Dickey,R.A. | 7 |
| Greinke,Zack | 7 |
| Leake,Mike | 6 |
| Kuroda,Hiroki | 6 |
| Teheran,Julio | 6 |
| Santiago,Hector | 6 |
| Cashner,Andrew | 5 |
| Bumgarner,Madison | 5 |
| 2 tied with | 5 |

| Catchers 2013 Leaders | |
|---|---|
| Castillo,Welington | 19 |
| Martin,Russell | 16 |
| Molina,Yadier | 12 |
| Perez,Salvador | 11 |
| Gomes,Yan | 11 |
| Mathis,Jeff | 5 |
| Mauer,Joe | 5 |
| Ramos,Wilson | 5 |
| Posey,Buster | 4 |
| Ruiz,Carlos | 3 |

| Pitchers 2013 Trailers | |
|---|---|
| Lincecum,Tim | -8 |
| Volquez,Edinson | -7 |
| Sanchez,Anibal | -6 |
| Samardzija,Jeff | -6 |
| Johnson,Josh | -5 |
| Lackey,John | -5 |

| Catchers 2013 Trailers | |
|---|---|
| Wieters,Matt | -13 |
| Santana,Carlos | -12 |
| Buck,John | -10 |
| Iannetta,Chris | -7 |
| Saltalamacchia,J | -6 |
| Norris,Derek | -6 |

# Infield Plus/Minus Leaders

| First Basemen 3-Year Leaders | |
|---|---|
| Gonzalez,Adrian | +39 |
| Votto,Joey | +29 |
| Rizzo,Anthony | +27 |
| Teixeira,Mark | +22 |
| Loney,James | +17 |
| Pujols,Albert | +17 |
| Sanchez,Gaby | +17 |
| Belt,Brandon | +14 |
| Trumbo,Mark | +13 |
| Goldschmidt,Paul | +10 |

| Second Basemen 3-Year Leaders | |
|---|---|
| Barney,Darwin | +48 |
| Pedroia,Dustin | +42 |
| Ellis,Mark | +41 |
| Zobrist,Ben | +33 |
| Kinsler,Ian | +31 |
| Cano,Robinson | +30 |
| Phillips,Brandon | +28 |
| Ackley,Dustin | +27 |
| Utley,Chase | +20 |
| LeMahieu,DJ | +19 |

| Third Basemen 3-Year Leaders | |
|---|---|
| Machado,Manny | +55 |
| Lawrie,Brett | +53 |
| Uribe,Juan | +37 |
| Arenado,Nolan | +36 |
| Longoria,Evan | +34 |
| Wright,David | +24 |
| Moustakas,Mike | +21 |
| Beltre,Adrian | +20 |
| Sandoval,Pablo | +20 |
| Donaldson,Josh | +19 |

| Shortstops 3-Year Leaders | |
|---|---|
| Simmons,Andrelton | +69 |
| Ryan,Brendan | +55 |
| Barmes,Clint | +50 |
| Escobar,Yunel | +39 |
| Hardy,J.J. | +33 |
| Andrus,Elvis | +30 |
| Cozart,Zack | +27 |
| Florimon,Pedro | +25 |
| Crawford,Brandon | +23 |
| Ramirez,Alexei | +22 |

| First Basemen 3-Year Trailers | |
|---|---|
| Fielder,Prince | -30 |
| Konerko,Paul | -23 |
| Moss,Brandon | -20 |
| Howard,Ryan | -19 |
| Reynolds,Mark | -17 |
| Hosmer,Eric | -15 |

| Second Basemen 3-Year Trailers | |
|---|---|
| Weeks,Rickie | -56 |
| Uggla,Dan | -29 |
| Altuve,Jose | -27 |
| Weeks,Jemile | -26 |
| Murphy,Daniel | -25 |
| Keppinger,Jeff | -21 |

| Third Basemen 3-Year Trailers | |
|---|---|
| Johnson,Chris | -38 |
| Reynolds,Mark | -36 |
| Cabrera,Miguel | -36 |
| Young,Michael | -32 |
| Ramirez,Aramis | -32 |
| Zimmerman,Ryan | -29 |

| Shortstops 3-Year Trailers | |
|---|---|
| Jeter,Derek | -50 |
| Rollins,Jimmy | -49 |
| Reyes,Jose | -45 |
| Nunez,Eduardo | -43 |
| Lowrie,Jed | -27 |
| Cabrera,Asdrubal | -25 |

| First Basemen 2013 Leaders | |
|---|---|
| Rizzo,Anthony | +22 |
| Goldschmidt,Paul | +15 |
| Gonzalez,Adrian | +15 |
| Napoli,Mike | +12 |
| Alonso,Yonder | +10 |
| Votto,Joey | +9 |
| Belt,Brandon | +9 |
| Freeman,Freddie | +7 |
| Swisher,Nick | +6 |
| Hosmer,Eric | +4 |

| Second Basemen 2013 Leaders | |
|---|---|
| Pedroia,Dustin | +17 |
| Barney,Darwin | +15 |
| Dozier,Brian | +14 |
| Ellis,Mark | +14 |
| Johnson,Elliot | +11 |
| Kinsler,Ian | +10 |
| Walker,Neil | +10 |
| Bonifacio,Emilio | +10 |
| LeMahieu,DJ | +9 |
| Cano,Robinson | +8 |

| Third Basemen 2013 Leaders | |
|---|---|
| Machado,Manny | +47 |
| Arenado,Nolan | +36 |
| Uribe,Juan | +24 |
| Longoria,Evan | +14 |
| Donaldson,Josh | +13 |
| Wright,David | +9 |
| Alvarez,Pedro | +8 |
| Headley,Chase | +8 |
| Dominguez,Matt | +7 |
| Frazier,Todd | +6 |

| Shortstops 2013 Leaders | |
|---|---|
| Simmons,Andrelton | +49 |
| Barmes,Clint | +17 |
| Florimon,Pedro | +15 |
| Andrus,Elvis | +11 |
| Kozma,Pete | +10 |
| Tulowitzki,Troy | +9 |
| Ramirez,Hanley | +8 |
| Escobar,Yunel | +7 |
| Ryan,Brendan | +7 |
| Cozart,Zack | +6 |

| First Basemen 2013 Trailers | |
|---|---|
| Fielder,Prince | -18 |
| Moss,Brandon | -16 |
| Dunn,Adam | -12 |
| Lind,Adam | -11 |
| Encarnacion,Edwin | -9 |
| Davis,Chris | -8 |

| Second Basemen 2013 Trailers | |
|---|---|
| Uggla,Dan | -20 |
| Weeks,Rickie | -18 |
| Murphy,Daniel | -13 |
| Rutledge,Josh | -11 |
| Hill,Aaron | -10 |
| Scutaro,Marco | -9 |

| Third Basemen 2013 Trailers | |
|---|---|
| Cabrera,Miguel | -25 |
| Freese,David | -22 |
| Young,Michael | -21 |
| Seager,Kyle | -13 |
| Ramirez,Aramis | -12 |
| Asche,Cody | -11 |

| Shortstops 2013 Trailers | |
|---|---|
| Nunez,Eduardo | -33 |
| Rollins,Jimmy | -23 |
| Lowrie,Jed | -22 |
| Cabrera,Asdrubal | -21 |
| Tejada,Ruben | -9 |
| Reyes,Jose | -9 |

# Outfield Plus/Minus Leaders

**Left Fielders 3-Year Leaders**

| | |
|---|---|
| Marte,Starling | +42 |
| Murphy,David | +33 |
| Gordon,Alex | +32 |
| Braun,Ryan | +32 |
| Dirks,Andy | +30 |
| Presley,Alex | +24 |
| Parra,Gerardo | +22 |
| Tabata,Jose | +22 |
| Hamilton,Josh | +16 |
| Prado,Martin | +15 |

**Center Fielders 3-Year Leaders**

| | |
|---|---|
| Span,Denard | +63 |
| Gomez,Carlos | +62 |
| Jackson,Austin | +52 |
| Ellsbury,Jacoby | +50 |
| Young,Chris | +48 |
| Bourn,Michael | +47 |
| Gentry,Craig | +44 |
| Maybin,Cameron | +41 |
| Trout,Mike | +31 |
| Cain,Lorenzo | +31 |

**Right Fielders 3-Year Leaders**

| | |
|---|---|
| Heyward,Jason | +104 |
| Parra,Gerardo | +52 |
| Reddick,Josh | +49 |
| Upton,Justin | +47 |
| Victorino,Shane | +33 |
| Aoki,Norichika | +28 |
| Stanton,Giancarlo | +27 |
| Ethier,Andre | +24 |
| DeJesus,David | +23 |
| Venable,Will | +21 |

**Left Fielders 3-Year Trailers**

| | |
|---|---|
| Ibanez,Raul | -49 |
| Willingham,Josh | -29 |
| Duda,Lucas | -26 |
| Brown,Domonic | -26 |
| Kubel,Jason | -24 |
| Viciedo,Dayan | -20 |

**Center Fielders 3-Year Trailers**

| | |
|---|---|
| Kemp,Matt | -68 |
| Jones,Adam | -60 |
| Saunders,Michael | -43 |
| Coghlan,Chris | -32 |
| Granderson,Curtis | -30 |
| Choo,Shin-Soo | -29 |

**Right Fielders 3-Year Trailers**

| | |
|---|---|
| Cuddyer,Michael | -56 |
| Francoeur,Jeff | -54 |
| Markakis,Nick | -44 |
| Bautista,Jose | -40 |
| Cruz,Nelson | -26 |
| Pence,Hunter | -23 |

**Left Fielders 2013 Leaders**

| | |
|---|---|
| Marte,Starling | +34 |
| Pierre,Juan | +17 |
| Crawford,Carl | +11 |
| Heisey,Chris | +11 |
| Murphy,David | +9 |
| Torres,Andres | +9 |
| Gordon,Alex | +8 |
| Dirks,Andy | +8 |
| Cespedes,Yoenis | +8 |
| Blanco,Gregor | +8 |

**Center Fielders 2013 Leaders**

| | |
|---|---|
| Gomez,Carlos | +44 |
| Pollock,A.J. | +26 |
| Ellsbury,Jacoby | +22 |
| Lagares,Juan | +19 |
| Cain,Lorenzo | +18 |
| Crisp,Coco | +17 |
| Martin,Leonys | +16 |
| Gentry,Craig | +14 |
| Rasmus,Colby | +12 |
| Dyson,Jarrod | +12 |

**Right Fielders 2013 Leaders**

| | |
|---|---|
| Parra,Gerardo | +39 |
| Victorino,Shane | +33 |
| Heyward,Jason | +32 |
| Bruce,Jay | +18 |
| Aoki,Norichika | +16 |
| Puig,Yasiel | +13 |
| Reddick,Josh | +12 |
| Byrd,Marlon | +11 |
| Lough,David | +11 |
| Denorfia,Chris | +10 |

**Left Fielders 2013 Trailers**

| | |
|---|---|
| Ibanez,Raul | -22 |
| Brown,Domonic | -22 |
| Viciedo,Dayan | -20 |
| Duda,Lucas | -16 |
| Arcia,Oswaldo | -16 |
| Willingham,Josh | -14 |

**Center Fielders 2013 Trailers**

| | |
|---|---|
| Choo,Shin-Soo | -29 |
| Saunders,Michael | -23 |
| Kemp,Matt | -16 |
| De Aza,Alejandro | -16 |
| Jones,Adam | -16 |
| Pagan,Angel | -13 |

**Right Fielders 2013 Trailers**

| | |
|---|---|
| Markakis,Nick | -21 |
| Cuddyer,Michael | -20 |
| Morse,Michael | -19 |
| Young,Delmon | -19 |
| Hunter,Torii | -15 |
| Rios,Alex | -15 |

# Pitcher Plus/Minus Leaders

| Pitchers 3-Year Leaders | |
|---|---|
| Westbrook,Jake | +19 |
| Dickey,R.A. | +18 |
| Leake,Mike | +15 |
| Buehrle,Mark | +14 |
| Kuroda,Hiroki | +13 |
| Chacin,Jhoulys | +12 |
| Liriano,Francisco | +11 |
| Saunders,Joe | +10 |
| Greinke,Zack | +10 |
| Ziegler,Brad | +10 |

| Pitchers 3-Year Trailers | |
|---|---|
| Scherzer,Max | -13 |
| Volquez,Edinson | -12 |
| Morrow,Brandon | -10 |
| McAllister,Zach | -9 |
| Garza,Matt | -9 |
| Lynn,Lance | -9 |

| Pitchers 2013 Leaders | |
|---|---|
| Leake,Mike | +8 |
| Cashner,Andrew | +7 |
| Liriano,Francisco | +7 |
| Santiago,Hector | +7 |
| Dickey,R.A. | +6 |
| Stults,Eric | +6 |
| Bumgarner,Madison | +6 |
| Iwakuma,Hisashi | +6 |
| Corbin,Patrick | +5 |
| 2 tied with | +5 |

| Pitchers 2013 Trailers | |
|---|---|
| Samardzija,Jeff | -7 |
| Lynn,Lance | -7 |
| Peralta,Wily | -6 |
| Johnson,Josh | -5 |
| Vargas,Jason | -5 |
| Correia,Kevin | -5 |

# 2013 Career Register

This section contains the complete up-to-date career statistics of every major league player in the 2013 season. For players who have appeared in fewer than three major league seasons, we have included their minor league statistics for the last five years. For those players with three or more years in the big leagues who also spent time in the minor league in 2013 (for example, if they had a rehab assignment) we have included only their 2013 minor league statistics—indicated by an asterisk. Those players that split time between the majors and minors last season but have fewer than three years of major league experience will still have their full minor league statistics for the last five years.

If a player led either the American or National League in a particular category, that number will appear in **boldface**.

Age is seasonal as of June 30, 2014.

For pitchers, BFP is Batters Facing Pitcher; TBB is Total Bases on Balls (or Total Walks, intentional and unintentional); Op is Save Opportunities; Hld is Holds.

For the various levels of Class-A ball, we have used "A+" to indicate High-A and "A-" to indicate Low-A. To help readers decode our minor league abbreviations, there is a legend in the back of the book.

Regardless of whether their name at the time was Los Angeles, Anaheim, California, or Los Angeles of Anaheim, the abbreviation LAA denotes a reference to the Angels franchise.

A pronunciation guide is provided underneath the name of select players.

The Register also features Runs Created (RC) for hitters and Component ERA (ERC) for pitchers, in addition to the more traditional statistics. Developed by Bill James, Runs Created is a method of measuring every facet of a hitter's strengths and weaknesses, combining those factors into one number, indicative of a player's production. Component ERA measures what a pitcher's ERA should have been based on his raw pitching statistics and gives us a good indication of whether or not a pitcher actually deserved his ERA. An explanation of Bill's most current formulas for both RC and ERC can be found in the Baseball Glossary at the end of the Handbook.

A player's total career numbers in the postseason appear on one line above his total regular season career numbers. Since we work hard to bring you this publication by November 1, 2013, postseason data from 2013 is not included.

## David Aardsma

: R **Bats:** R **Pos:** RP-43 ARDZ-muh **Ht:** 6'3" **Wt:** 205 **Born:** 12/27/1981 **Age:** 32

| HOW MUCH HE PITCHED | | | | | | | | | WHAT HE GAVE UP | | | | | | | | | | | | THE RESULTS | | | | | | | |
|---|---|---|---|---|---|---|---|---|---|---|---|---|---|---|---|---|---|---|---|---|---|---|---|---|---|---|---|---|
| Year | Team | Lg | G | GS | CG | GF | IP | BFP | H | R | ER | HR | SH | SF | HB | TBB | IBB | SO | WP | Bk | W | L | Pct | Sh | Sv-Op | Hld | ERC | ERA |
| 2013 | NewOr* | AAA | 10 | 0 | 0 | 2 | 14.0 | 58 | 9 | 5 | 4 | 2 | 0 | 0 | 0 | 8 | 2 | 12 | 0 | 1 | 1 | 0 | 1.000 | 0 | 0- - | - | 2.89 | 2.57 |
| 2013 | LsVgs* | AAA | 8 | 0 | 0 | 8 | 8.0 | 35 | 5 | 1 | 1 | 1 | 1 | 0 | 0 | 7 | 1 | 11 | 0 | 0 | 0 | 0 | - | 0 | 3- - | - | 3.83 | 1.13 |
| 2004 | SF | NL | 11 | 0 | 0 | 5 | 10.2 | 61 | 20 | 8 | 8 | 1 | 0 | 1 | 2 | 10 | 0 | 5 | 0 | 0 | 1 | 0 | 1.000 | 0 | 0-1 | 1 | 13.38 | 6.75 |
| 2006 | ChC | NL | 45 | 0 | 0 | 9 | 53.0 | 225 | 41 | 25 | 24 | 9 | 1 | 3 | 1 | 28 | 0 | 49 | 1 | 0 | 3 | 0 | 1.000 | 0 | 0-0 | 5 | 3.88 | 4.08 |
| 2007 | CWS | AL | 25 | 0 | 0 | 7 | 32.1 | 151 | 39 | 24 | 23 | 4 | 2 | 1 | 1 | 17 | 3 | 36 | 2 | 0 | 2 | 1 | .667 | 0 | 0-3 | 3 | 5.93 | 6.40 |
| 2008 | Bos | AL | 47 | 0 | 0 | 7 | 48.2 | 228 | 49 | 32 | 30 | 4 | 3 | 2 | 5 | 35 | 2 | 49 | 3 | 0 | 4 | 2 | .667 | 0 | 0-1 | 4 | 5.63 | 5.55 |
| 2009 | Sea | AL | 73 | 0 | 0 | 53 | 71.1 | 296 | 49 | 23 | 20 | 4 | 2 | 1 | 0 | 34 | 3 | 80 | 2 | 0 | 3 | 6 | .333 | 0 | 38-42 | 6 | 2.34 | 2.52 |
| 2010 | Sea | AL | 53 | 0 | 0 | 43 | 49.2 | 202 | 33 | 19 | 19 | 5 | 7 | 1 | 2 | 25 | 5 | 49 | 2 | 0 | 0 | 6 | .000 | 0 | 31-36 | 0 | 2.74 | 3.44 |
| 2012 | NYY | AL | 1 | 0 | 0 | 1 | 1.0 | 5 | 1 | 1 | 1 | 1 | 0 | 0 | 0 | 1 | 0 | 1 | 0 | 0 | 0 | 0 | - | 0 | 0-0 | 0 | 14.27 | 9.00 |
| 2013 | NYM | NL | 43 | 0 | 0 | 7 | 39.2 | 178 | 39 | 20 | 19 | 7 | 2 | 1 | 4 | 19 | 6 | 36 | 1 | 1 | 2 | 2 | .500 | 0 | 0-2 | 4 | 4.99 | 4.31 |
| 8 ML YEARS | | | 298 | 0 | 0 | 132 | 306.1 | 1346 | 271 | 152 | 144 | 35 | 17 | 10 | 15 | 169 | 19 | 305 | 11 | 1 | 15 | 17 | .469 | 0 | 69-85 | 23 | 4.21 | 4.23 |

## Fernando Abad

**Pitches:** L **Bats:** L **Pos:** RP-39 ah-BAHD **Ht:** 6'1" **Wt:** 220 **Born:** 12/17/1985 **Age:** 28

| HOW MUCH HE PITCHED | | | | | | | | | WHAT HE GAVE UP | | | | | | | | | | | | THE RESULTS | | | | | | | |
|---|---|---|---|---|---|---|---|---|---|---|---|---|---|---|---|---|---|---|---|---|---|---|---|---|---|---|---|---|
| Year | Team | Lg | G | GS | CG | GF | IP | BFP | H | R | ER | HR | SH | SF | HB | TBB | IBB | SO | WP | Bk | W | L | Pct | Sh | Sv-Op | Hld | ERC | ERA |
| 2013 | Syrcse* | AAA | 17 | 0 | 0 | 2 | 17.0 | 69 | 17 | 2 | 2 | 0 | 0 | 0 | 0 | 2 | 0 | 12 | 0 | 0 | 1 | 0 | 1.000 | 0 | 0- - | - | 2.37 | 1.06 |
| 2010 | Hou | NL | 22 | 0 | 0 | 6 | 19.0 | 76 | 14 | 6 | 6 | 3 | 0 | 1 | 0 | 5 | 0 | 12 | 0 | 0 | 0 | 1 | .000 | 0 | 0-0 | 6 | 2.49 | 2.84 |
| 2011 | Hou | NL | 29 | 0 | 0 | 1 | 19.2 | 99 | 28 | 18 | 16 | 5 | 1 | 2 | 1 | 9 | 0 | 15 | 0 | 0 | 1 | 4 | .200 | 0 | 0-2 | 7 | 8.06 | 7.32 |
| 2012 | Hou | NL | 37 | 6 | 0 | 8 | 46.0 | 208 | 57 | 27 | 26 | 6 | 2 | 1 | 3 | 19 | 1 | 38 | 4 | 0 | 0 | 6 | .000 | 0 | 0-0 | 3 | 6.13 | 5.09 |
| 2013 | Was | NL | 39 | 0 | 0 | 17 | 37.2 | 166 | 42 | 14 | 14 | 3 | 0 | 0 | 1 | 10 | 0 | 32 | 0 | 0 | 0 | 3 | .000 | 0 | 0-1 | 2 | 4.05 | 3.35 |
| 4 ML YEARS | | | 127 | 6 | 0 | 32 | 122.1 | 549 | 141 | 65 | 62 | 17 | 3 | 4 | 5 | 43 | 1 | 97 | 4 | 0 | 1 | 14 | .067 | 0 | 0-3 | 18 | 5.15 | 4.56 |

## Tony Abreu

**Bats:** B **Throws:** R **Pos:** 2B-30;PH-23;3B-3;SS-3 **Ht:** 5'9" **Wt:** 200 **Born:** 11/13/1984 **Age:** 29

| BATTING | | | | | | | | | | | | | | | | | | | | | BASERUNNING | | | | AVERAGES | | |
|---|---|---|---|---|---|---|---|---|---|---|---|---|---|---|---|---|---|---|---|---|---|---|---|---|---|---|---|
| Year | Team | Lg | G | AB | H | 2B | 3B | HR | (Hm | Rd) | TB | R | RBI | RC | TBB | IBB | SO | HBP | SH | SF | SB | CS | SB% | GDP | Avg | OBP | Slg |
| 2013 | Fresno* | AAA | 22 | 65 | 22 | 9 | 0 | 1 | (- | -) | 34 | 9 | 9 | 12 | 1 | 0 | 15 | 3 | 0 | 2 | 1 | 1 | .50 | 1 | .338 | .366 | .523 |
| 2007 | LAD | NL | 59 | 166 | 45 | 14 | 1 | 2 | (0 | 2) | 67 | 19 | 17 | 18 | 7 | 1 | 21 | 3 | 0 | 2 | 0 | 0 | - | 5 | .271 | .309 | .404 |
| 2009 | LAD | NL | 6 | 8 | 2 | 0 | 0 | 0 | (0 | 0) | 2 | 0 | 1 | 2 | 3 | 0 | 2 | 0 | 0 | 0 | 0 | 1 | .00 | 0 | .250 | .455 | .250 |
| 2010 | Ari | NL | 81 | 193 | 45 | 11 | 1 | 1 | (1 | 0) | 61 | 16 | 13 | 12 | 4 | 0 | 47 | 0 | 0 | 4 | 2 | 1 | .67 | 8 | .233 | .244 | .316 |
| 2012 | KC | AL | 22 | 70 | 18 | 2 | 1 | 1 | (1 | 0) | 25 | 5 | 15 | 13 | 2 | 0 | 13 | 1 | 0 | 1 | 0 | 0 | - | 1 | .257 | .284 | .357 |
| 2013 | SF | NL | 53 | 138 | 37 | 12 | 3 | 2 | (1 | 1) | 61 | 21 | 14 | 14 | 6 | 1 | 33 | 1 | 1 | 1 | 0 | 2 | .00 | 5 | .268 | .301 | .442 |
| 5 ML YEARS | | | 221 | 575 | 147 | 39 | 6 | 6 | (3 | 3) | 216 | 61 | 60 | 59 | 22 | 2 | 116 | 5 | 1 | 8 | 2 | 4 | .33 | 19 | .256 | .285 | .376 |

## Alfredo Aceves

**Pitches:** R **Bats:** R **Pos:** SP-6; RP-5 ah-SEVV-us **Ht:** 6'2" **Wt:** 205 **Born:** 12/8/1982 **Age:** 31

| HOW MUCH HE PITCHED | | | | | | | | | WHAT HE GAVE UP | | | | | | | | | | | | THE RESULTS | | | | | | | |
|---|---|---|---|---|---|---|---|---|---|---|---|---|---|---|---|---|---|---|---|---|---|---|---|---|---|---|---|---|
| Year | Team | Lg | G | GS | CG | GF | IP | BFP | H | R | ER | HR | SH | SF | HB | TBB | IBB | SO | WP | Bk | W | L | Pct | Sh | Sv-Op | Hld | ERC | ERA |
| 2013 | Pwtckt* | AAA | 8 | 8 | 0 | 0 | 48.2 | 210 | 48 | 25 | 23 | 10 | 1 | 1 | 2 | 17 | 1 | 39 | 0 | 0 | 4 | 2 | .667 | 0 | 0- - | - | 4.64 | 4.25 |
| 2013 | RedSx* | R | 2 | 0 | 0 | 0 | 2.1 | 7 | 0 | 0 | 0 | 0 | 0 | 0 | 0 | 1 | 0 | 1 | 0 | 0 | 0 | 0 | - | 0 | 0- - | - | 0.23 | 0.00 |
| 2008 | NYY | AL | 6 | 4 | 0 | 1 | 30.0 | 120 | 25 | 8 | 8 | 4 | 0 | 0 | 0 | 10 | 0 | 16 | 1 | 0 | 1 | 0 | 1.000 | 0 | 0-0 | 0 | 3.23 | 2.40 |
| 2009 | NYY | AL | 43 | 1 | 0 | 10 | 84.0 | 337 | 69 | 36 | 33 | 10 | 1 | 2 | 5 | 16 | 2 | 69 | 0 | 0 | 10 | 1 | .909 | 0 | 1-2 | 5 | 2.65 | 3.54 |
| 2010 | NYY | AL | 10 | 0 | 0 | 2 | 12.0 | 53 | 10 | 5 | 4 | 1 | 0 | 0 | 1 | 4 | 1 | 2 | 0 | 0 | 3 | 0 | 1.000 | 0 | 1-1 | 1 | 2.80 | 3.00 |
| 2011 | Bos | AL | 55 | 4 | 0 | 15 | 114.0 | 474 | 84 | 37 | 33 | 8 | 3 | 3 | 15 | 42 | 1 | 80 | 1 | **2** | 10 | 2 | .833 | 0 | 2-5 | 11 | 2.84 | 2.61 |
| 2012 | Bos | AL | 69 | 0 | 0 | 55 | 84.0 | 361 | 80 | 51 | 50 | 11 | 2 | 7 | 6 | 31 | 2 | 75 | 3 | 1 | 2 | 10 | .167 | 0 | 25-33 | 0 | 4.16 | 5.36 |
| 2013 | Bos | AL | 11 | 6 | 0 | 3 | 37.0 | 169 | 42 | 21 | 20 | 8 | 0 | 1 | 0 | 22 | 0 | 24 | 0 | **2** | 4 | 1 | .800 | 0 | 0-0 | 0 | 6.70 | 4.86 |
| Postseason | | | 4 | 0 | 0 | 1 | 4.1 | 20 | 5 | 2 | 2 | 0 | 1 | 0 | 0 | 3 | 1 | 2 | 1 | 0 | 0 | 1 | .000 | 0 | 0-0 | 0 | 5.01 | 4.15 |
| 6 ML YEARS | | | 194 | 15 | 0 | 86 | 361.0 | 1514 | 310 | 158 | 148 | 42 | 6 | 13 | 27 | 125 | 6 | 266 | 5 | 5 | 30 | 14 | .682 | 0 | 29-41 | 17 | 3.48 | 3.69 |

## Dustin Ackley

**Bats:** L **Throws:** R **Pos:** 2B-53;CF-50;LF-11;1B-6;PH-6;PR-3;DH-1 **Ht:** 6'1" **Wt:** 195 **Born:** 2/26/1988 **Age:** 26

| BATTING | | | | | | | | | | | | | | | | | | | | | BASERUNNING | | | | AVERAGES | | |
|---|---|---|---|---|---|---|---|---|---|---|---|---|---|---|---|---|---|---|---|---|---|---|---|---|---|---|---|
| Year | Team | Lg | G | AB | H | 2B | 3B | HR | (Hm | Rd) | TB | R | RBI | RC | TBB | IBB | SO | HBP | SH | SF | SB | CS | SB% | GDP | Avg | OBP | Slg |
| 2013 | Tacom* | AAA | 25 | 104 | 38 | 8 | 0 | 2 | (- | -) | 52 | 21 | 14 | 25 | 19 | 2 | 14 | 2 | 1 | 0 | 0 | 0 | - | 1 | .365 | .472 | .500 |
| 2011 | Sea | AL | 90 | 333 | 91 | 16 | 7 | 6 | (3 | 3) | 139 | 39 | 36 | 53 | 40 | 1 | 79 | 0 | 0 | 3 | 6 | 0 | 1.00 | 3 | .273 | .348 | .417 |
| 2012 | Sea | AL | 153 | 607 | 137 | 22 | 2 | 12 | (2 | 10) | 199 | 84 | 50 | 62 | 59 | 7 | 124 | 0 | 1 | 1 | 13 | 3 | .81 | 3 | .226 | .294 | .328 |
| 2013 | Sea | AL | 113 | 384 | 97 | 18 | 2 | 4 | (2 | 2) | 131 | 40 | 31 | 45 | 37 | 1 | 72 | 1 | 4 | 1 | 2 | 3 | .40 | 6 | .253 | .319 | .341 |
| 3 ML YEARS | | | 356 | 1324 | 325 | 56 | 11 | 22 | (7 | 15) | 469 | 163 | 117 | 160 | 136 | 9 | 275 | 1 | 5 | 5 | 21 | 6 | .78 | 12 | .245 | .315 | .354 |

## David Adams

**Bats:** R **Throws:** R **Pos:** 3B-31;2B-9;1B-4;PH-1 **Ht:** 6'1" **Wt:** 205 **Born:** 5/15/1987 **Age:** 27

| BATTING | | | | | | | | | | | | | | | | | | | | | BASERUNNING | | | | AVERAGES | | |
|---|---|---|---|---|---|---|---|---|---|---|---|---|---|---|---|---|---|---|---|---|---|---|---|---|---|---|---|
| Year | Team | Lg | G | AB | H | 2B | 3B | HR | (Hm | Rd) | TB | R | RBI | RC | TBB | IBB | SO | HBP | SH | SF | SB | CS | SB% | GDP | Avg | OBP | Slg |
| 2009 | CtnSC | A | 67 | 259 | 75 | 23 | 2 | 0 | (- | -) | 102 | 32 | 34 | 43 | 35 | 0 | 49 | 7 | 0 | 3 | 8 | 4 | .67 | 7 | .290 | .385 | .394 |
| 2009 | Tampa | A+ | 65 | 231 | 65 | 17 | 6 | 7 | (- | -) | 115 | 37 | 41 | 41 | 26 | 1 | 39 | 4 | 1 | 3 | 3 | 4 | .43 | 9 | .281 | .360 | .498 |
| 2010 | Trntn | AA | 39 | 152 | 47 | 15 | 3 | 3 | (- | -) | 77 | 31 | 32 | 30 | 18 | 0 | 31 | 3 | 0 | 0 | 5 | 2 | .71 | 4 | .309 | .393 | .507 |
| 2011 | Tampa | A+ | 12 | 52 | 16 | 3 | 0 | 0 | (- | -) | 19 | 6 | 4 | 6 | 4 | 0 | 8 | 1 | 0 | 0 | 0 | 2 | .00 | 2 | .308 | .368 | .365 |
| 2011 | Yanks | R | 17 | 56 | 24 | 9 | 0 | 1 | (- | -) | 36 | 13 | 11 | 15 | 5 | 0 | 10 | 1 | 0 | 2 | 2 | 1 | .67 | 1 | .429 | .469 | .643 |
| 2012 | Trntn | AA | 86 | 327 | 100 | 23 | 0 | 8 | (- | -) | 147 | 44 | 48 | 60 | 38 | 0 | 53 | 9 | 1 | 8 | 3 | 1 | .75 | 12 | .306 | .385 | .450 |
| 2013 | S-WB | AAA | 59 | 220 | 59 | 11 | 2 | 5 | (- | -) | 89 | 28 | 21 | 35 | 29 | 0 | 43 | 5 | 1 | 0 | 0 | 0 | - | 5 | .268 | .366 | .405 |
| 2013 | NYY | AL | 43 | 140 | 27 | 5 | 1 | 2 | (0 | 2) | 40 | 10 | 13 | 11 | 9 | 0 | 43 | 2 | 1 | 0 | 0 | 0 | - | 4 | .193 | .252 | .286 |

## Matt Adams

**Bats:** L **Throws:** R **Pos:** 1B-74;PH-39 **Ht:** 6'3" **Wt:** 260 **Born:** 8/31/1988 **Age:** 25

| BATTING | | | | | | | | | | | | | | | | | | | | | BASERUNNING | | | | AVERAGES | | |
|---|---|---|---|---|---|---|---|---|---|---|---|---|---|---|---|---|---|---|---|---|---|---|---|---|---|---|---|
| Year Team | Lg | G | AB | H | 2B | 3B | HR | (Hm | Rd) | TB | R | RBI | RC | TBB | IBB | SO | HBP | SH | SF | SB | CS | SB% | GDP | Avg | OBP | Slg |
| 2009 JhsCty | R | 32 | 115 | 42 | 6 | 0 | 6 | (- | -) | 66 | 15 | 25 | 26 | 9 | 0 | 20 | 1 | 0 | 3 | 0 | 0 | - | 3 | .365 | .406 | .574 |
| 2009 Batvia | A- | 31 | 130 | 45 | 11 | 0 | 4 | (- | -) | 68 | 16 | 27 | 26 | 11 | 3 | 21 | 0 | 0 | 1 | 0 | 0 | - | 4 | .346 | .394 | .523 |
| 2010 QuadC | A | 121 | 464 | 144 | 41 | 0 | 22 | (- | -) | 251 | 71 | 88 | 90 | 33 | 3 | 78 | 4 | 0 | 9 | 5 | 1 | .83 | 11 | .310 | .355 | .541 |
| 2011 Sprgfld | AA | 115 | 463 | 139 | 23 | 2 | 32 | (- | -) | 262 | 80 | 101 | 92 | 40 | 7 | 90 | 4 | 0 | 6 | 0 | 1 | .00 | 12 | .300 | .357 | .566 |
| 2012 Memp | AAA | 67 | 258 | 85 | 22 | 0 | 18 | (- | -) | 161 | 41 | 50 | 56 | 15 | 1 | 57 | 0 | 0 | 3 | 3 | 1 | .75 | 5 | .329 | .362 | .624 |
| 2013 Sprgfld | AA | 3 | 12 | 3 | 1 | 0 | 0 | (- | -) | 4 | 1 | 2 | 0 | 0 | 0 | 4 | 0 | 0 | 0 | 0 | 0 | - | 1 | .250 | .250 | .333 |
| 2012 StL | NL | 27 | 86 | 21 | 6 | 0 | 2 | (1 | 1) | 33 | 8 | 13 | 9 | 5 | 0 | 24 | 0 | 0 | 0 | 0 | 0 | - | 3 | .244 | .286 | .384 |
| 2013 StL | NL | 108 | 296 | 84 | 14 | 0 | 17 | (10 | 7) | 149 | 46 | 51 | 49 | 23 | 0 | 80 | 0 | 0 | 0 | 0 | 1 | .00 | 9 | .284 | .335 | .503 |
| 2 ML YEARS | | 135 | 382 | 105 | 20 | 0 | 19 | (11 | 8) | 182 | 54 | 64 | 58 | 28 | 0 | 104 | 0 | 0 | 0 | 0 | 1 | .00 | 12 | .275 | .324 | .476 |

## Mike Adams

**Pitches:** R **Bats:** R **Pos:** RP-28 **Ht:** 6'5" **Wt:** 195 **Born:** 7/29/1978 **Age:** 35

| HOW MUCH HE PITCHED | | | | | | | | WHAT HE GAVE UP | | | | | | | | | | | | THE RESULTS | | | | | | | |
|---|---|---|---|---|---|---|---|---|---|---|---|---|---|---|---|---|---|---|---|---|---|---|---|---|---|---|---|
| Year Team | Lg | G | GS | CG | GF | IP | BFP | H | R | ER | HR | SH | SF | HB | TBB | IBB | SO | WP | Bk | W | L | Pct | Sh | Sv-Op | Hld | ERC | ERA |
| 2004 Mil | NL | 46 | 0 | 0 | 13 | 53.0 | 225 | 50 | 21 | 20 | 5 | 5 | 2 | 2 | 14 | 2 | 39 | 2 | 0 | 2 | 3 | .400 | 0 | 0-5 | 12 | 3.22 | 3.40 |
| 2005 Mil | NL | 13 | 0 | 0 | 7 | 13.1 | 61 | 12 | 4 | 4 | 2 | 0 | 0 | 0 | 10 | 1 | 14 | 1 | 0 | 0 | 1 | .000 | 0 | 1-2 | 2 | 5.12 | 2.70 |
| 2006 Mil | NL | 2 | 0 | 0 | 0 | 2.1 | 13 | 4 | 3 | 3 | 1 | 0 | 0 | 0 | 2 | 0 | 1 | 0 | 0 | 0 | 0 | - | 0 | 0-0 | 0 | 13.74 | 11.57 |
| 2008 SD | NL | 54 | 0 | 0 | 11 | 65.1 | 259 | 49 | 18 | 18 | 7 | 2 | 3 | 0 | 19 | 2 | 74 | 0 | 0 | 2 | 3 | .400 | 0 | 0-2 | 10 | 2.38 | 2.48 |
| 2009 SD | NL | 37 | 0 | 0 | 5 | 37.0 | 136 | 14 | 9 | 3 | 1 | 2 | 0 | 0 | 8 | 1 | 45 | 1 | 0 | 0 | 0 | - | 0 | 0-1 | 15 | 0.65 | 0.73 |
| 2010 SD | NL | 70 | 0 | 0 | 3 | 66.2 | 268 | 48 | 14 | 13 | 2 | 0 | 0 | 0 | 23 | 2 | 73 | 0 | 0 | 4 | 1 | .800 | 0 | 0-4 | 38 | 1.95 | 1.76 |
| 2011 2 Tms | | 76 | 0 | 0 | 11 | 73.2 | 277 | 44 | 13 | 12 | 5 | 2 | 1 | 0 | 14 | 2 | 74 | 0 | 0 | 5 | 4 | .556 | 0 | 2-5 | 32 | 1.31 | 1.47 |
| 2012 Tex | AL | 61 | 0 | 0 | 7 | 52.1 | 228 | 56 | 21 | 19 | 4 | 0 | 0 | 3 | 17 | 1 | 45 | 2 | 0 | 5 | 3 | .625 | 0 | 1-2 | 27 | 4.20 | 3.27 |
| 2013 Phi | NL | 28 | 0 | 0 | 4 | 25.0 | 107 | 23 | 11 | 11 | 5 | 0 | 0 | 1 | 11 | 0 | 23 | 1 | 0 | 1 | 4 | .200 | 0 | 0-1 | 8 | 4.69 | 3.96 |
| 11 SD | NL | 49 | 0 | 0 | 6 | 48.0 | 179 | 26 | 7 | 6 | 2 | 1 | 1 | 0 | 9 | 1 | 49 | 0 | 0 | 3 | 1 | .750 | 0 | 1-3 | 23 | 1.06 | 1.13 |
| 11 Tex | AL | 27 | 0 | 0 | 5 | 25.2 | 98 | 18 | 6 | 6 | 3 | 1 | 0 | 0 | 5 | 1 | 25 | 0 | 0 | 2 | 3 | .400 | 0 | 1-2 | 9 | 1.88 | 2.10 |
| Postseason | | 11 | 0 | 0 | 2 | 8.1 | 39 | 11 | 3 | 3 | 2 | 0 | 0 | 0 | 6 | 1 | 6 | 0 | 0 | 2 | 0 | 1.000 | 0 | 0-0 | 5 | 8.84 | 3.24 |
| 9 ML YEARS | | 387 | 0 | 0 | 61 | 388.2 | 1574 | 300 | 114 | 103 | 32 | 11 | 6 | 6 | 118 | 11 | 388 | 7 | 0 | 19 | 19 | .500 | 0 | 4-22 | 144 | 2.41 | 2.39 |

## Jim Adduci

**Bats:** L **Throws:** L **Pos:** LF-8;PH-6;1B-4;DH-4;PR-2 ah-DOO-see **Ht:** 6'2" **Wt:** 210 **Born:** 5/15/1985 **Age:** 29

| BATTING | | | | | | | | | | | | | | | | | | | | | BASERUNNING | | | | AVERAGES | | |
|---|---|---|---|---|---|---|---|---|---|---|---|---|---|---|---|---|---|---|---|---|---|---|---|---|---|---|---|
| Year Team | Lg | G | AB | H | 2B | 3B | HR | (Hm | Rd) | TB | R | RBI | RC | TBB | IBB | SO | HBP | SH | SF | SB | CS | SB% | GDP | Avg | OBP | Slg |
| 2009 Tenn | AA | 131 | 467 | 140 | 21 | 4 | 4 | (- | -) | 181 | 63 | 51 | 75 | 58 | 2 | 76 | 0 | 9 | 0 | 35 | 12 | .74 | 8 | .300 | .377 | .388 |
| 2010 Iowa | AAA | 114 | 367 | 91 | 9 | 1 | 3 | (- | -) | 111 | 60 | 33 | 36 | 27 | 2 | 80 | 3 | 6 | 4 | 23 | 9 | .72 | 5 | .248 | .302 | .302 |
| 2011 Tenn | AA | 71 | 237 | 73 | 13 | 2 | 4 | (- | -) | 102 | 44 | 20 | 42 | 26 | 1 | 33 | 1 | 3 | 0 | 21 | 4 | .84 | 3 | .308 | .379 | .430 |
| 2011 Cubs | R | 4 | 17 | 3 | 0 | 0 | 0 | (- | -) | 3 | 0 | 0 | 0 | 0 | 0 | 2 | 0 | 0 | 0 | 2 | 0 | 1.00 | 0 | .176 | .176 | .176 |
| 2012 Tenn | AA | 84 | 252 | 74 | 12 | 1 | 5 | (- | -) | 103 | 40 | 27 | 41 | 31 | 3 | 47 | 0 | 7 | 3 | 11 | 3 | .79 | 2 | .294 | .367 | .409 |
| 2012 Iowa | AAA | 42 | 147 | 45 | 9 | 2 | 2 | (- | -) | 64 | 27 | 17 | 25 | 17 | 2 | 40 | 1 | 3 | 2 | 7 | 4 | .64 | 2 | .306 | .377 | .435 |
| 2013 RdRck | AAA | 127 | 473 | 141 | 24 | 3 | 16 | (- | -) | 219 | 75 | 65 | 90 | 65 | 3 | 107 | 2 | 5 | 6 | 32 | 9 | .78 | 4 | .298 | .381 | .463 |
| 2013 Tex | AL | 17 | 31 | 8 | 1 | 0 | 0 | (0 | 0) | 9 | 2 | 0 | 3 | 3 | 0 | 9 | 0 | 0 | 0 | 2 | 0 | 1.00 | 0 | .258 | .324 | .290 |

## Ehire Adrianza

**Bats:** B **Throws:** R **Pos:** SS-6;PH-2;PR-2 A-ee-ray A-dree-ahn-zuh **Ht:** 6'1" **Wt:** 165 **Born:** 8/21/1989 **Age:** 24

| BATTING | | | | | | | | | | | | | | | | | | | | | BASERUNNING | | | | AVERAGES | | |
|---|---|---|---|---|---|---|---|---|---|---|---|---|---|---|---|---|---|---|---|---|---|---|---|---|---|---|---|
| Year Team | Lg | G | AB | H | 2B | 3B | HR | (Hm | Rd) | TB | R | RBI | RC | TBB | IBB | SO | HBP | SH | SF | SB | CS | SB% | GDP | Avg | OBP | Slg |
| 2009 Augsta | A | 117 | 388 | 100 | 15 | 3 | 2 | (- | -) | 127 | 54 | 46 | 48 | 42 | 0 | 66 | 5 | 6 | 7 | 7 | 1 | .88 | 5 | .258 | .333 | .327 |
| 2010 SnJos | A+ | 124 | 445 | 114 | 22 | 5 | 3 | (- | -) | 155 | 70 | 35 | 56 | 47 | 0 | 87 | 5 | 10 | 1 | 33 | 15 | .69 | 7 | .256 | .333 | .348 |
| 2011 Augsta | A | 38 | 143 | 33 | 10 | 1 | 3 | (- | -) | 54 | 18 | 17 | 18 | 18 | 0 | 32 | 0 | 6 | 1 | 3 | 2 | .60 | 4 | .231 | .315 | .378 |
| 2011 SnJos | A+ | 56 | 230 | 69 | 24 | 3 | 3 | (- | -) | 108 | 34 | 27 | 42 | 23 | 0 | 46 | 6 | 1 | 2 | 5 | 1 | .83 | 3 | .300 | .375 | .470 |
| 2012 Rchmd | AA | 127 | 451 | 99 | 22 | 5 | 3 | (- | -) | 140 | 52 | 32 | 44 | 41 | 2 | 90 | 4 | 13 | 3 | 16 | 4 | .80 | 10 | .220 | .289 | .310 |
| 2013 Rchmd | AA | 73 | 250 | 60 | 12 | 0 | 2 | (- | -) | 78 | 31 | 23 | 29 | 31 | 0 | 45 | 4 | 4 | 2 | 11 | 6 | .65 | 5 | .240 | .331 | .312 |
| 2013 Fresno | AAA | 45 | 145 | 45 | 7 | 6 | 0 | (- | -) | 64 | 23 | 12 | 28 | 23 | 1 | 31 | 2 | 6 | 1 | 6 | 2 | .75 | 1 | .310 | .409 | .441 |
| 2013 SF | NL | 9 | 18 | 4 | 1 | 0 | 1 | (0 | 1) | 8 | 3 | 3 | 1 | 1 | 0 | 5 | 0 | 1 | 0 | 0 | 0 | - | 1 | .222 | .263 | .444 |

## Jeremy Affeldt

**Pitches:** L **Bats:** L **Pos:** RP-39 AFF-felt **Ht:** 6'4" **Wt:** 225 **Born:** 6/6/1979 **Age:** 35

| HOW MUCH HE PITCHED | | | | | | | | WHAT HE GAVE UP | | | | | | | | | | | | THE RESULTS | | | | | | | |
|---|---|---|---|---|---|---|---|---|---|---|---|---|---|---|---|---|---|---|---|---|---|---|---|---|---|---|---|
| Year Team | Lg | G | GS | CG | GF | IP | BFP | H | R | ER | HR | SH | SF | HB | TBB | IBB | SO | WP | Bk | W | L | Pct | Sh | Sv-Op | Hld | ERC | ERA |
| 2002 KC | AL | 34 | 7 | 0 | 4 | 77.2 | 353 | 85 | 41 | 40 | 8 | 2 | 1 | 3 | 37 | 4 | 67 | 5 | 2 | 3 | 4 | .429 | 0 | 0-1 | 1 | 4.97 | 4.64 |
| 2003 KC | AL | 36 | 18 | 0 | 5 | 126.0 | 533 | 126 | 58 | 55 | 12 | 2 | 5 | 5 | 38 | 1 | 98 | 2 | 2 | 7 | 6 | .538 | 0 | 4-4 | 3 | 3.82 | 3.93 |
| 2004 KC | AL | 38 | 8 | 0 | 26 | 76.1 | 344 | 91 | 49 | 42 | 6 | 4 | 4 | 3 | 32 | 2 | 49 | 4 | 3 | 3 | 4 | .429 | 0 | 13-17 | 0 | 5.26 | 4.95 |
| 2005 KC | AL | 49 | 0 | 0 | 13 | 49.2 | 232 | 56 | 35 | 29 | 3 | 0 | 1 | 0 | 29 | 2 | 39 | 5 | 0 | 0 | 2 | .000 | 0 | 0-0 | 12 | 5.08 | 5.26 |
| 2006 2 Tms | | 54 | 9 | 0 | 12 | 97.1 | 448 | 102 | 74 | 67 | 13 | 4 | 4 | 2 | 55 | 3 | 48 | 2 | 0 | 8 | 8 | .500 | 0 | 1-3 | 5 | 5.21 | 6.20 |
| 2007 Col | NL | 75 | 0 | 0 | 11 | 59.0 | 253 | 47 | 26 | 23 | 3 | 3 | 6 | 3 | 33 | 9 | 46 | 6 | 1 | 4 | 3 | .571 | 0 | 0-4 | 9 | 3.19 | 3.51 |
| 2008 Cin | NL | 74 | 0 | 0 | 20 | 78.1 | 335 | 78 | 36 | 29 | 9 | 7 | 0 | 3 | 25 | 0 | 80 | 6 | 0 | 1 | 1 | .500 | 0 | 0-1 | 5 | 3.98 | 3.33 |
| 2009 SF | NL | 74 | 0 | 0 | 8 | 62.1 | 248 | 42 | 14 | 12 | 3 | 0 | 1 | 3 | 31 | 3 | 55 | 5 | 0 | 2 | 2 | .500 | 0 | 0-0 | **33** | 2.61 | 1.73 |
| 2010 SF | NL | 53 | 0 | 0 | 14 | 50.0 | 228 | 56 | 25 | 23 | 4 | 7 | 1 | 3 | 24 | 5 | 44 | 4 | 0 | 4 | 3 | .571 | 0 | 4-7 | 7 | 4.99 | 4.14 |
| 2011 SF | NL | 67 | 0 | 0 | 12 | 61.2 | 259 | 47 | 22 | 18 | 5 | 4 | 0 | 4 | 24 | 3 | 54 | 4 | 0 | 3 | 2 | .600 | 0 | 3-6 | 13 | 2.77 | 2.63 |
| 2012 SF | NL | 67 | 0 | 0 | 10 | 63.1 | 267 | 57 | 23 | 19 | 1 | 4 | 0 | 3 | 23 | 1 | 57 | 5 | 0 | 1 | 2 | .333 | 0 | 3-4 | 16 | 2.98 | 2.70 |
| 2013 SF | NL | 39 | 0 | 0 | 11 | 33.2 | 146 | 27 | 14 | 14 | 2 | 4 | 1 | 4 | 17 | 5 | 21 | 2 | 0 | 1 | 5 | .167 | 0 | 0-4 | 11 | 3.31 | 3.74 |
| 06 KC | AL | 27 | 9 | 0 | 3 | 70.0 | 320 | 71 | 51 | 46 | 9 | 3 | 3 | 1 | 42 | 0 | 28 | 2 | 0 | 4 | 6 | .400 | 0 | 0-0 | 2 | 5.18 | 5.91 |
| 06 Col | NL | 27 | 0 | 0 | 9 | 27.1 | 128 | 31 | 23 | 21 | 4 | 1 | 1 | 1 | 13 | 3 | 20 | 0 | 0 | 4 | 2 | .667 | 0 | 1-3 | 3 | 5.29 | 6.91 |
| Postseason | | 22 | 0 | 0 | 2 | 19.2 | 73 | 9 | 3 | 3 | 1 | 0 | 0 | 1 | 6 | 2 | 18 | 2 | 0 | 0 | 0 | - | 0 | 0-0 | 3 | 1.15 | 1.37 |
| 12 ML YEARS | | 660 | 42 | 0 | 146 | 835.1 | 3646 | 814 | 417 | 371 | 69 | 41 | 24 | 36 | 368 | 38 | 658 | 50 | 8 | 37 | 42 | .468 | 0 | 28-51 | 115 | 4.06 | 4.00 |

# Andrew Albers

**Pitches:** L **Bats:** R **Pos:** SP-10 **Ht:** 6'1" **Wt:** 195 **Born:** 10/6/1985 **Age:** 28

| HOW MUCH HE PITCHED | | | | | | | | | WHAT HE GAVE UP | | | | | | | | | | | | THE RESULTS | | | | | | | |
|---|---|---|---|---|---|---|---|---|---|---|---|---|---|---|---|---|---|---|---|---|---|---|---|---|---|---|---|---|
| Year | Team | Lg | G | GS | CG | GF | IP | BFP | H | R | ER | HR | SH | SF | HB | TBB | IBB | SO | WP | Bk | W | L | Pct | Sh | Sv-Op | Hld | ERC | ERA |
| 2011 | FtMyrs | A+ | 22 | 2 | 0 | 8 | 52.1 | 203 | 48 | 11 | 9 | 2 | 1 | 0 | 1 | 7 | 0 | 46 | 1 | 0 | 4 | 1 | .800 | 0 | 4-- | - | 2.43 | 1.55 |
| 2011 | NwBrit | AA | 13 | 5 | 0 | 2 | 43.1 | 176 | 44 | 15 | 14 | 0 | 1 | 0 | 5 | 7 | 0 | 34 | 2 | 0 | 4 | 1 | .800 | 0 | 0-- | - | 3.13 | 2.91 |
| 2012 | NwBrit | AA | 19 | 17 | 0 | 0 | 98.1 | 395 | 111 | 41 | 41 | 7 | 5 | 2 | 2 | 12 | 0 | 73 | 6 | 3 | 4 | 3 | .571 | 0 | 0-- | - | 3.75 | 3.75 |
| 2012 | Twins | R | 2 | 1 | 0 | 0 | 4.2 | 21 | 4 | 1 | 1 | 0 | 0 | 0 | 0 | 3 | 0 | 3 | 0 | 0 | 1 | 0 | 1.000 | 0 | 0-- | - | 3.39 | 1.93 |
| 2013 | Roch | AAA | 22 | 22 | 3 | 0 | 132.1 | 533 | 124 | 46 | 42 | 14 | 2 | 3 | 0 | 32 | 0 | 116 | 0 | 1 | 11 | 5 | .688 | 1 | 0-- | - | 3.23 | 2.86 |
| 2013 | Min | AL | 10 | 10 | 1 | 0 | 60.0 | 249 | 64 | 34 | 27 | 6 | 2 | 2 | 2 | 7 | 0 | 25 | 0 | 1 | 2 | 5 | .286 | 1 | 0-0 | 0 | 3.45 | 4.05 |

# Matt Albers

**Pitches:** R **Bats:** L **Pos:** RP-56 **Ht:** 6'1" **Wt:** 225 **Born:** 1/20/1983 **Age:** 31

| HOW MUCH HE PITCHED | | | | | | | | | WHAT HE GAVE UP | | | | | | | | | | | | THE RESULTS | | | | | | | |
|---|---|---|---|---|---|---|---|---|---|---|---|---|---|---|---|---|---|---|---|---|---|---|---|---|---|---|---|---|
| Year | Team | Lg | G | GS | CG | GF | IP | BFP | H | R | ER | HR | SH | SF | HB | TBB | IBB | SO | WP | Bk | W | L | Pct | Sh | Sv-Op | Hld | ERC | ERA |
| 2006 | Hou | NL | 4 | 2 | 0 | 0 | 15.0 | 66 | 17 | 10 | 10 | 1 | 2 | 0 | 0 | 7 | 0 | 11 | 0 | 0 | 0 | 2 | .000 | 0 | 0-0 | 0 | 4.97 | 6.00 |
| 2007 | Hou | NL | 31 | 18 | 0 | 2 | 110.2 | 508 | 127 | 77 | 72 | 18 | 6 | 8 | 7 | 50 | 6 | 71 | 7 | 0 | 4 | 11 | .267 | 0 | 0-0 | 0 | 5.76 | 5.86 |
| 2008 | Bal | AL | 28 | 3 | 0 | 5 | 49.0 | 208 | 43 | 21 | 19 | 4 | 1 | 3 | 2 | 22 | 1 | 26 | 1 | 0 | 3 | 3 | .500 | 0 | 0-2 | 6 | 3.62 | 3.49 |
| 2009 | Bal | AL | 56 | 0 | 0 | 13 | 67.0 | 309 | 80 | 43 | 41 | 3 | 5 | 2 | 2 | 36 | 3 | 49 | 3 | 0 | 3 | 6 | .333 | 0 | 0-4 | 10 | 5.41 | 5.51 |
| 2010 | Bal | AL | 62 | 0 | 0 | 19 | 75.2 | 329 | 78 | 41 | 38 | 6 | 3 | 0 | 2 | 34 | 5 | 49 | 2 | 0 | 5 | 3 | .625 | 0 | 0-2 | 7 | 4.35 | 4.52 |
| 2011 | Bos | AL | 56 | 0 | 0 | 10 | 64.2 | 289 | 62 | 35 | 34 | 7 | 4 | 2 | 5 | 31 | 1 | 68 | 2 | 0 | 4 | 4 | .500 | 0 | 0-3 | 10 | 4.44 | 4.73 |
| 2012 | 2 Tms | | 63 | 0 | 0 | 12 | 60.1 | 241 | 46 | 21 | 16 | 9 | 1 | 2 | 2 | 22 | 3 | 44 | 1 | 0 | 3 | 1 | .750 | 0 | 0-6 | 9 | 3.13 | 2.39 |
| 2013 | Cle | AL | 56 | 0 | 0 | 21 | 63.0 | 262 | 57 | 25 | 22 | 2 | 2 | 0 | 1 | 23 | 3 | 35 | 6 | 0 | 3 | 1 | .750 | 0 | 0-0 | 1 | 2.99 | 3.14 |
| 12 | Bos | AL | 40 | 0 | 0 | 8 | 39.1 | 157 | 30 | 14 | 10 | 6 | 0 | 2 | 1 | 15 | 3 | 25 | 0 | 0 | 2 | 0 | 1.000 | 0 | 0-4 | 7 | 3.16 | 2.29 |
| 12 | Ari | NL | 23 | 0 | 0 | 4 | 21.0 | 84 | 16 | 7 | 6 | 3 | 1 | 0 | 1 | 7 | 0 | 19 | 1 | 0 | 1 | 1 | .500 | 0 | 0-2 | 2 | 3.07 | 2.57 |
| 8 ML YEARS | | | 356 | 23 | 0 | 82 | 505.1 | 2212 | 510 | 273 | 252 | 50 | 24 | 17 | 21 | 225 | 22 | 353 | 22 | 0 | 25 | 31 | .446 | 0 | 0-17 | 43 | 4.41 | 4.49 |

# Al Alburquerque

**Pitches:** R **Bats:** R **Pos:** RP-53 AL-buh-kur-kee **Ht:** 6'0" **Wt:** 195 **Born:** 6/10/1986 **Age:** 28

| HOW MUCH HE PITCHED | | | | | | | | | WHAT HE GAVE UP | | | | | | | | | | | | THE RESULTS | | | | | | | |
|---|---|---|---|---|---|---|---|---|---|---|---|---|---|---|---|---|---|---|---|---|---|---|---|---|---|---|---|---|
| Year | Team | Lg | G | GS | CG | GF | IP | BFP | H | R | ER | HR | SH | SF | HB | TBB | IBB | SO | WP | Bk | W | L | Pct | Sh | Sv-Op | Hld | ERC | ERA |
| 2013 | Toledo* | AAA | 10 | 0 | 0 | 1 | 14.1 | 64 | 9 | 5 | 5 | 2 | 0 | 0 | 0 | 13 | 0 | 27 | 1 | 0 | 0 | 1 | .000 | 0 | 1-- | - | 4.24 | 3.14 |
| 2011 | Det | AL | 41 | 0 | 0 | 11 | 43.1 | 182 | 21 | 9 | 9 | 0 | 2 | 1 | 2 | 29 | 4 | 67 | 4 | 0 | 6 | 1 | .857 | 0 | 0-0 | 6 | 1.73 | 1.87 |
| 2012 | Det | AL | 8 | 0 | 0 | 0 | 13.1 | 53 | 6 | 1 | 1 | 0 | 0 | 0 | 0 | 8 | 0 | 18 | 0 | 1 | 0 | 0 | - | 0 | 0-0 | 1 | 1.50 | 0.68 |
| 2013 | Det | AL | 53 | 0 | 0 | 12 | 49.0 | 220 | 39 | 25 | 25 | 5 | 0 | 1 | 2 | 34 | 5 | 70 | 9 | 1 | 4 | 3 | .571 | 0 | 0-0 | 10 | 4.02 | 4.59 |
| Postseason | | | 7 | 0 | 0 | 2 | 5.1 | 22 | 3 | 4 | 4 | 2 | 0 | 0 | 0 | 3 | 0 | 5 | 1 | 1 | 1 | 0 | 1.000 | 0 | 0-0 | 1 | 4.00 | 6.75 |
| 3 ML YEARS | | | 102 | 0 | 0 | 23 | 105.2 | 455 | 66 | 35 | 35 | 5 | 2 | 2 | 4 | 71 | 9 | 155 | 13 | 2 | 10 | 4 | .714 | 0 | 0-0 | 17 | 2.68 | 2.98 |

# Cody Allen

**Pitches:** R **Bats:** R **Pos:** RP-77 **Ht:** 6'1" **Wt:** 210 **Born:** 11/20/1988 **Age:** 25

| HOW MUCH HE PITCHED | | | | | | | | | WHAT HE GAVE UP | | | | | | | | | | | | THE RESULTS | | | | | | | |
|---|---|---|---|---|---|---|---|---|---|---|---|---|---|---|---|---|---|---|---|---|---|---|---|---|---|---|---|---|
| Year | Team | Lg | G | GS | CG | GF | IP | BFP | H | R | ER | HR | SH | SF | HB | TBB | IBB | SO | WP | Bk | W | L | Pct | Sh | Sv-Op | Hld | ERC | ERA |
| 2011 | MhVlly | A- | 14 | 0 | 0 | 3 | 33.2 | 133 | 21 | 9 | 8 | 1 | 3 | 3 | 3 | 9 | 0 | 42 | 1 | 2 | 3 | 1 | .750 | 0 | 0-- | - | 1.62 | 2.14 |
| 2011 | Lk Cty | A | 7 | 0 | 0 | 1 | 17.0 | 66 | 10 | 0 | 0 | 0 | 0 | 0 | 0 | 5 | 0 | 28 | 2 | 0 | 2 | 0 | 1.000 | 0 | 0-- | - | 1.26 | 0.00 |
| 2011 | Akron | AA | 1 | 0 | 0 | 1 | 1.0 | 6 | 3 | 2 | 2 | 0 | 0 | 0 | 0 | 0 | 0 | 2 | 0 | 0 | 0 | 0 | - | 0 | 0-- | - | 14.52 | 18.00 |
| 2011 | Knstn | A+ | 1 | 0 | 0 | 0 | 3.0 | 10 | 1 | 0 | 0 | 0 | 0 | 0 | 0 | 0 | 0 | 3 | 0 | 0 | 0 | 0 | - | 0 | 0-- | - | 0.25 | 0.00 |
| 2012 | Carlina | A+ | 2 | 0 | 0 | 1 | 4.0 | 13 | 1 | 0 | 0 | 0 | 0 | 0 | 0 | 0 | 0 | 8 | 0 | 0 | 0 | 0 | - | 0 | 0-- | - | 0.14 | 0.00 |
| 2012 | Akron | AA | 5 | 0 | 0 | 2 | 7.2 | 25 | 2 | 1 | 1 | 1 | 0 | 0 | 0 | 0 | 0 | 10 | 0 | 0 | 0 | 0 | - | 0 | 1-- | - | 0.33 | 1.17 |
| 2012 | Clmbs | AAA | 24 | 0 | 0 | 10 | 31.2 | 125 | 22 | 8 | 8 | 3 | 3 | 0 | 0 | 9 | 1 | 35 | 0 | 0 | 3 | 2 | .600 | 0 | 2-- | - | 2.00 | 2.27 |
| 2012 | Cle | AL | 27 | 0 | 0 | 9 | 29.0 | 126 | 29 | 12 | 12 | 2 | 1 | 1 | 0 | 15 | 0 | 27 | 0 | 0 | 0 | 1 | .000 | 0 | 0-1 | 1 | 4.39 | 3.72 |
| 2013 | Cle | AL | 77 | 0 | 0 | 12 | 70.1 | 301 | 62 | 22 | 19 | 7 | 4 | 4 | 1 | 26 | 2 | 88 | 9 | 0 | 6 | 1 | .857 | 0 | 2-4 | 11 | 3.24 | 2.43 |
| 2 ML YEARS | | | 104 | 0 | 0 | 21 | 99.1 | 427 | 91 | 34 | 31 | 9 | 5 | 5 | 1 | 41 | 2 | 115 | 9 | 0 | 6 | 2 | .750 | 0 | 2-5 | 12 | 3.56 | 2.81 |

# Abraham Almonte

**Bats:** B **Throws:** R **Pos:** CF-15;RF-7;PR-4;LF-2;DH-1;PH-1 **Ht:** 5'9" **Wt:** 205 **Born:** 6/27/1989 **Age:** 25

| BATTING | | | | | | | | | | | | | | | | | | | | | BASERUNNING | | | | AVERAGES | | |
|---|---|---|---|---|---|---|---|---|---|---|---|---|---|---|---|---|---|---|---|---|---|---|---|---|---|---|---|
| Year | Team | Lg | G | AB | H | 2B | 3B | HR | (Hm | Rd) | TB | R | RBI | RC | TBB | IBB | SO | HBP | SH | SF | SB | CS | SB% | GDP | Avg | OBP | Slg |
| 2009 | CtnSC | A | 115 | 440 | 123 | 14 | 10 | 5 | (- | -) | 172 | 63 | 56 | 65 | 35 | 0 | 81 | 2 | 4 | 3 | 36 | 5 | .88 | 5 | .280 | .333 | .391 |
| 2010 | Tampa | A+ | 15 | 57 | 15 | 3 | 1 | 0 | (- | -) | 20 | 9 | 3 | 6 | 6 | 0 | 16 | 0 | 0 | 0 | 5 | 3 | .63 | 0 | .263 | .333 | .351 |
| 2011 | Tampa | A+ | 131 | 537 | 144 | 27 | 11 | 4 | (- | -) | 205 | 92 | 52 | 73 | 52 | 2 | 100 | 2 | 3 | 4 | 30 | 11 | .73 | 9 | .268 | .333 | .382 |
| 2012 | Trntn | AA | 78 | 319 | 88 | 17 | 4 | 4 | (- | -) | 125 | 47 | 25 | 50 | 37 | 2 | 59 | 0 | 2 | 1 | 30 | 5 | .86 | 1 | .276 | .350 | .392 |
| 2012 | Yanks | R | 7 | 18 | 4 | 2 | 0 | 0 | (- | -) | 6 | 2 | 0 | 2 | 2 | 0 | 4 | 0 | 0 | 0 | 2 | 0 | 1.00 | 0 | .222 | .300 | .333 |
| 2013 | Jacksn | AA | 29 | 102 | 26 | 6 | 1 | 4 | (- | -) | 46 | 18 | 18 | 18 | 18 | 2 | 28 | 0 | 0 | 0 | 6 | 1 | .86 | 3 | .255 | .367 | .451 |
| 2013 | Tacom | AAA | 94 | 338 | 106 | 17 | 5 | 11 | (- | -) | 166 | 63 | 50 | 69 | 49 | 3 | 66 | 2 | 6 | 1 | 20 | 7 | .74 | 2 | .314 | .403 | .491 |
| 2013 | Sea | AL | 25 | 72 | 19 | 4 | 0 | 2 | (1 | 1) | 29 | 10 | 9 | 9 | 6 | 0 | 21 | 0 | 2 | 2 | 1 | 0 | 1.00 | 2 | .264 | .313 | .403 |

# Zoilo Almonte

**Bats:** B **Throws:** R **Pos:** LF-25;PH-4;RF-3;DH-2;PR-2 ZOY-low **Ht:** 6'0" **Wt:** 205 **Born:** 6/10/1989 **Age:** 25

| BATTING | | | | | | | | | | | | | | | | | | | | | BASERUNNING | | | | AVERAGES | | |
|---|---|---|---|---|---|---|---|---|---|---|---|---|---|---|---|---|---|---|---|---|---|---|---|---|---|---|---|
| Year | Team | Lg | G | AB | H | 2B | 3B | HR | (Hm | Rd) | TB | R | RBI | RC | TBB | IBB | SO | HBP | SH | SF | SB | CS | SB% | GDP | Avg | OBP | Slg |
| 2009 | StIsInd | A- | 69 | 259 | 71 | 20 | 1 | 7 | (- | -) | 114 | 43 | 39 | 42 | 31 | 1 | 58 | 2 | 1 | 1 | 15 | 7 | .68 | 8 | .274 | .355 | .440 |
| 2010 | CtnSC | A | 58 | 227 | 63 | 13 | 2 | 10 | (- | -) | 110 | 33 | 35 | 37 | 21 | 1 | 65 | 2 | 3 | 2 | 7 | 6 | .54 | 3 | .278 | .341 | .485 |
| 2010 | Tampa | A+ | 63 | 238 | 62 | 10 | 3 | 3 | (- | -) | 87 | 26 | 26 | 31 | 23 | 3 | 65 | 0 | 0 | 3 | 8 | 1 | .89 | 9 | .261 | .322 | .366 |
| 2011 | Tampa | A+ | 70 | 259 | 76 | 15 | 3 | 12 | (- | -) | 133 | 38 | 54 | 51 | 31 | 2 | 60 | 2 | 0 | 4 | 14 | 4 | .78 | 3 | .293 | .368 | .514 |

| BATTING | | | | | | | | | | | | | | | | | | | | | | BASERUNNING | | | | AVERAGES | | |
|---|---|---|---|---|---|---|---|---|---|---|---|---|---|---|---|---|---|---|---|---|---|---|---|---|---|---|---|---|
| Year | Team | Lg | G | AB | H | 2B | 3B | HR | (Hm | Rd) | TB | R | RBI | RC | TBB | IBB | SO | HBP | SH | SF | SB | CS | SB% | GDP | Avg | OBP | Slg |
| 2011 | Trntn | AA | 46 | 175 | 44 | 11 | 1 | 3 | (- | -) | 66 | 23 | 23 | 21 | 14 | 0 | 45 | 1 | 0 | 1 | 4 | 1 | .80 | 1 | .251 | .309 | .377 |
| 2012 | Trntn | AA | 106 | 419 | 116 | 23 | 1 | 21 | (- | -) | 204 | 64 | 70 | 67 | 25 | 2 | 103 | 4 | 0 | 3 | 15 | 4 | .79 | 11 | .277 | .322 | .487 |
| 2013 | S-WB | AAA | 68 | 259 | 77 | 12 | 1 | 6 | (- | -) | 109 | 30 | 36 | 42 | 30 | 0 | 47 | 1 | 0 | 3 | 4 | 1 | .80 | 12 | .297 | .369 | .421 |
| 2013 | NYY | AL | 34 | 106 | 25 | 4 | 0 | 1 | (1 | 0) | 32 | 9 | 9 | 9 | 6 | 0 | 19 | 0 | 0 | 1 | 3 | 1 | .75 | 2 | .236 | .274 | .302 |

# Yonder Alonso

YONN-dur ah-LONN-zo

**Bats:** L **Throws:** R **Pos:** 1B-92;PH-6;PR-2;2B-1;3B-1;LF-1 **Ht:** 6'2" **Wt:** 250 **Born:** 4/8/1987 **Age:** 27

| BATTING | | | | | | | | | | | | | | | | | | | | | | BASERUNNING | | | | AVERAGES | | |
|---|---|---|---|---|---|---|---|---|---|---|---|---|---|---|---|---|---|---|---|---|---|---|---|---|---|---|---|---|
| Year | Team | Lg | G | AB | H | 2B | 3B | HR | (Hm | Rd) | TB | R | RBI | RC | TBB | IBB | SO | HBP | SH | SF | SB | CS | SB% | GDP | Avg | OBP | Slg |
| 2013 | Tucsn* | AAA | 4 | 14 | 8 | 0 | 0 | 0 | (- | -) | 8 | 1 | 2 | 3 | 0 | 0 | 0 | 0 | 0 | 0 | 0 | 1 | .00 | 0 | .571 | .571 | .571 |
| 2010 | Cin | NL | 22 | 29 | 6 | 2 | 0 | 0 | (0 | 0) | 8 | 2 | 3 | 0 | 0 | 0 | 10 | 0 | 0 | 0 | 0 | 0 | - | 1 | .207 | .207 | .276 |
| 2011 | Cin | NL | 47 | 88 | 29 | 4 | 0 | 5 | (2 | 3) | 48 | 9 | 15 | 16 | 10 | 0 | 21 | 0 | 0 | 0 | 0 | 0 | - | 2 | .330 | .398 | .545 |
| 2012 | SD | NL | 155 | 549 | 150 | 39 | 0 | 9 | (3 | 6) | 216 | 47 | 62 | 71 | 62 | 9 | 101 | 3 | 1 | 4 | 3 | 0 | 1.00 | 14 | .273 | .348 | .393 |
| 2013 | SD | NL | 97 | 334 | 94 | 11 | 0 | 6 | (4 | 2) | 123 | 34 | 45 | 46 | 32 | 5 | 47 | 2 | 0 | 7 | 6 | 0 | 1.00 | 9 | .281 | .341 | .368 |
| 4 ML YEARS | | | 321 | 1000 | 279 | 56 | 0 | 20 | (9 | 11) | 395 | 92 | 125 | 133 | 104 | 14 | 179 | 5 | 1 | 11 | 9 | 0 | 1.00 | 26 | .279 | .346 | .395 |

# Jose Altuve

al-TOO-vay

**Bats:** R **Throws:** R **Pos:** 2B-145;DH-7 **Ht:** 5'5" **Wt:** 175 **Born:** 5/6/1990 **Age:** 24

| BATTING | | | | | | | | | | | | | | | | | | | | | | BASERUNNING | | | | AVERAGES | | |
|---|---|---|---|---|---|---|---|---|---|---|---|---|---|---|---|---|---|---|---|---|---|---|---|---|---|---|---|---|
| Year | Team | Lg | G | AB | H | 2B | 3B | HR | (Hm | Rd) | TB | R | RBI | RC | TBB | IBB | SO | HBP | SH | SF | SB | CS | SB% | GDP | Avg | OBP | Slg |
| 2011 | Hou | NL | 57 | 221 | 61 | 10 | 1 | 2 | (2 | 0) | 79 | 26 | 12 | 18 | 5 | 0 | 29 | 2 | 5 | 1 | 7 | 3 | .70 | 5 | .276 | .297 | .357 |
| 2012 | Hou | NL | 147 | 576 | 167 | 34 | 4 | 7 | (4 | 3) | 230 | 80 | 37 | 76 | 40 | 0 | 74 | 6 | 4 | 4 | 33 | 11 | .75 | 8 | .290 | .340 | .399 |
| 2013 | Hou | AL | 152 | 626 | 177 | 31 | 2 | 5 | (4 | 1) | 227 | 64 | 52 | 67 | 32 | 5 | 85 | 2 | 4 | 8 | 35 | **13** | .73 | 24 | .283 | .316 | .363 |
| 3 ML YEARS | | | 356 | 1423 | 405 | 75 | 7 | 14 | (10 | 4) | 536 | 170 | 101 | 161 | 77 | 5 | 188 | 10 | 13 | 13 | 75 | 27 | .74 | 37 | .285 | .323 | .377 |

# Henderson Alvarez

**Pitches:** R **Bats:** R **Pos:** SP-17 **Ht:** 6'0" **Wt:** 210 **Born:** 4/18/1990 **Age:** 24

| HOW MUCH HE PITCHED | | | | | | | | | WHAT HE GAVE UP | | | | | | | | | | | | THE RESULTS | | | | | | | |
|---|---|---|---|---|---|---|---|---|---|---|---|---|---|---|---|---|---|---|---|---|---|---|---|---|---|---|---|---|
| Year | Team | Lg | G | GS | CG | GF | IP | BFP | H | R | ER | HR | SH | SF | HB | TBB | IBB | SO | WP | Bk | W | L | Pct | Sh | Sv-Op | Hld | ERC | ERA |
| 2013 | Jupiter* | A+ | 2 | 2 | 0 | 0 | 10.0 | 37 | 9 | 3 | 3 | 1 | 0 | 0 | 0 | 1 | 0 | 2 | 0 | 0 | 1 | 0 | 1.000 | 0 | 0-- | - | 2.62 | 2.70 |
| 2013 | Jaxnvl* | AA | 2 | 2 | 0 | 0 | 14.1 | 48 | 5 | 0 | 0 | 0 | 1 | 0 | 0 | 0 | 0 | 13 | 0 | 0 | 1 | 0 | 1.000 | 0 | 0-- | - | 0.27 | 0.00 |
| 2011 | Tor | AL | 10 | 10 | 0 | 0 | 63.2 | 259 | 64 | 26 | 25 | 8 | 1 | 2 | 4 | 8 | 0 | 40 | 2 | 0 | 1 | 3 | .250 | 0 | 0-0 | 0 | 3.49 | 3.53 |
| 2012 | Tor | AL | 31 | 31 | 1 | 0 | 187.1 | 807 | 216 | 110 | 101 | 29 | 2 | 4 | 3 | 54 | 2 | 79 | 3 | 1 | 9 | 14 | .391 | 1 | 0-0 | 0 | 5.01 | 4.85 |
| 2013 | Mia | NL | 17 | 17 | 1 | 0 | 102.2 | 418 | 90 | 42 | 41 | 2 | 0 | 4 | 7 | 27 | 1 | 57 | 4 | 1 | 5 | 6 | .455 | 1 | 0-0 | 0 | 2.66 | 3.59 |
| 3 ML YEARS | | | 58 | 58 | 2 | 0 | 353.2 | 1484 | 370 | 178 | 167 | 39 | 3 | 10 | 14 | 89 | 3 | 176 | 9 | 2 | 15 | 23 | .395 | 2 | 0-0 | 0 | 4.02 | 4.25 |

# Jose Alvarez

**Pitches:** L **Bats:** L **Pos:** RP-8; SP-6 **Ht:** 5'11" **Wt:** 180 **Born:** 5/6/1989 **Age:** 25

| HOW MUCH HE PITCHED | | | | | | | | | WHAT HE GAVE UP | | | | | | | | | | | | THE RESULTS | | | | | | | |
|---|---|---|---|---|---|---|---|---|---|---|---|---|---|---|---|---|---|---|---|---|---|---|---|---|---|---|---|---|
| Year | Team | Lg | G | GS | CG | GF | IP | BFP | H | R | ER | HR | SH | SF | HB | TBB | IBB | SO | WP | Bk | W | L | Pct | Sh | Sv-Op | Hld | ERC | ERA |
| 2009 | Salem | A+ | 12 | 0 | 0 | 8 | 24.2 | 111 | 32 | 15 | 13 | 1 | 1 | 0 | 0 | 6 | 0 | 11 | 1 | 0 | 1 | 1 | .500 | 0 | 0-- | - | 4.63 | 4.74 |
| 2009 | Lowell | A- | 14 | 12 | 2 | 1 | 83.0 | 318 | 60 | 17 | 14 | 4 | 3 | 2 | 8 | 10 | 0 | 63 | 0 | 0 | 8 | 3 | .727 | 2 | 0-- | - | 1.75 | 1.52 |
| 2010 | Grnsbr | A | 26 | 13 | 0 | 3 | 108.0 | 457 | 114 | 52 | 43 | 9 | 1 | 3 | 3 | 32 | 0 | 113 | 6 | 0 | 10 | 3 | .769 | 0 | 0-- | - | 4.03 | 3.58 |
| 2011 | Jupiter | A+ | 15 | 14 | 0 | 1 | 82.0 | 330 | 79 | 32 | 27 | 2 | 0 | 4 | 1 | 19 | 3 | 73 | 2 | 1 | 6 | 5 | .545 | 0 | 0-- | - | 2.82 | 2.96 |
| 2011 | Jaxnvl | AA | 12 | 12 | 0 | 0 | 65.2 | 290 | 80 | 47 | 39 | 9 | 3 | 4 | 1 | 22 | 0 | 45 | 4 | 2 | 2 | 6 | .250 | 0 | 0-- | - | 5.49 | 5.35 |
| 2012 | Jaxnvl | AA | 25 | 24 | 3 | 0 | 136.1 | 560 | 140 | 66 | 64 | 8 | 8 | 6 | 6 | 26 | 1 | 70 | 2 | 0 | 6 | 9 | .400 | 1 | 0-- | - | 3.36 | 4.22 |
| 2013 | Toledo | AAA | 21 | 20 | 1 | 1 | 128.2 | 518 | 114 | 46 | 40 | 11 | 0 | 4 | 3 | 25 | 0 | 115 | 4 | 0 | 8 | 6 | .571 | 0 | 1-- | - | 2.70 | 2.80 |
| 2013 | Det | AL | 14 | 6 | 0 | 0 | 38.2 | 172 | 42 | 26 | 25 | 7 | 2 | 2 | 2 | 16 | 1 | 31 | 0 | 1 | 1 | 5 | .167 | 0 | 0-0 | 2 | 5.41 | 5.82 |

# Pedro Alvarez

**Bats:** L **Throws:** R **Pos:** 3B-150;PH-3;DH-1 **Ht:** 6'3" **Wt:** 235 **Born:** 2/6/1987 **Age:** 27

| BATTING | | | | | | | | | | | | | | | | | | | | | | BASERUNNING | | | | AVERAGES | | |
|---|---|---|---|---|---|---|---|---|---|---|---|---|---|---|---|---|---|---|---|---|---|---|---|---|---|---|---|---|
| Year | Team | Lg | G | AB | H | 2B | 3B | HR | (Hm | Rd) | TB | R | RBI | RC | TBB | IBB | SO | HBP | SH | SF | SB | CS | SB% | GDP | Avg | OBP | Slg |
| 2010 | Pit | NL | 95 | 347 | 89 | 21 | 1 | 16 | (12 | 4) | 160 | 42 | 64 | 50 | 37 | 1 | 119 | 0 | 0 | 2 | 0 | 0 | - | 8 | .256 | .326 | .461 |
| 2011 | Pit | NL | 74 | 235 | 45 | 9 | 1 | 4 | (0 | 4) | 68 | 18 | 19 | 14 | 24 | 1 | 80 | 2 | 1 | 0 | 1 | 0 | 1.00 | 11 | .191 | .272 | .289 |
| 2012 | Pit | NL | 149 | 525 | 128 | 25 | 1 | 30 | (12 | 18) | 245 | 64 | 85 | 77 | 57 | 6 | 180 | 1 | 0 | 3 | 1 | 0 | 1.00 | 10 | .244 | .317 | .467 |
| 2013 | Pit | NL | 152 | 558 | 130 | 22 | 2 | **36** | (16 | **20)** | 264 | 70 | 100 | 66 | 48 | 7 | **186** | 4 | 0 | 4 | 2 | 0 | 1.00 | 16 | .233 | .296 | .473 |
| 4 ML YEARS | | | 470 | 1665 | 392 | 77 | 5 | 86 | (40 | 46) | 737 | 194 | 268 | 207 | 166 | 15 | 565 | 7 | 1 | 9 | 4 | 0 | 1.00 | 45 | .235 | .306 | .443 |

# Alexi Amarista

ah-mah-REE-stah

**Bats:** L **Throws:** R **Pos:** CF-87;PH-30;2B-23;SS-13;LF-11;3B-9;PR-4 **Ht:** 5'8" **Wt:** 150 **Born:** 4/6/1989 **Age:** 25

| BATTING | | | | | | | | | | | | | | | | | | | | | BASERUNNING | | | | AVERAGES | | |
|---|---|---|---|---|---|---|---|---|---|---|---|---|---|---|---|---|---|---|---|---|---|---|---|---|---|---|---|
| Year | Team | Lg | G | AB | H | 2B | 3B | HR | (Hm | Rd) | TB | R | RBI | RC | TBB | IBB | SO | HBP | SH | SF | SB | CS | SB% | GDP | Avg | OBP | Slg |
| 2011 | LAA | AL | 23 | 52 | 8 | 3 | 1 | 0 | (0 | 0) | 13 | 2 | 5 | 1 | 2 | 0 | 8 | 0 | 1 | 1 | 0 | 0 | - | 1 | .154 | .182 | .250 |
| 2012 | 2 Tms | | 106 | 275 | 66 | 15 | 5 | 5 | (0 | 5) | 106 | 36 | 32 | 31 | 17 | 1 | 42 | 0 | 6 | 2 | 8 | 4 | .67 | 2 | .240 | .282 | .385 |
| 2013 | SD | NL | 146 | 368 | 87 | 14 | 4 | 5 | (1 | 4) | 124 | 35 | 32 | 40 | 22 | 1 | 57 | 2 | 3 | 1 | 4 | 2 | .67 | 7 | .236 | .282 | .337 |
| 12 | LAA | AL | 1 | 0 | 0 | 0 | 0 | 0 | (0 | 0) | 0 | 1 | 0 | 0 | 0 | 0 | 0 | 0 | 0 | 0 | 0 | 0 | - | 0 | - | - | - |
| 12 | SD | NL | 105 | 275 | 66 | 15 | 5 | 5 | (0 | 5) | 106 | 35 | 32 | 31 | 17 | 1 | 42 | 0 | 6 | 2 | 8 | 4 | .67 | 2 | .240 | .282 | .385 |
| 3 ML YEARS | | | 275 | 695 | 161 | 32 | 10 | 10 | (1 | 9) | 243 | 73 | 69 | 72 | 41 | 2 | 107 | 2 | 10 | 4 | 12 | 6 | .67 | 10 | .232 | .275 | .350 |

# Hector Ambriz

**Pitches:** R **Bats:** L **Pos:** RP-43 AMM-brizz **Ht:** 6'2" **Wt:** 235 **Born:** 5/24/1984 **Age:** 30

| HOW MUCH HE PITCHED | | | | | | | | | WHAT HE GAVE UP | | | | | | | | | | | | THE RESULTS | | | | | | | |
|---|---|---|---|---|---|---|---|---|---|---|---|---|---|---|---|---|---|---|---|---|---|---|---|---|---|---|---|---|
| Year | Team | Lg | G | GS | CG | GF | IP | BFP | H | R | ER | HR | SH | SF | HB | TBB | IBB | SO | WP | Bk | W | L | Pct | Sh | Sv-Op | Hld | ERC | ERA |
| 2013 | OKCity* | AAA | 14 | 0 | 0 | 10 | 16.2 | 78 | 23 | 12 | 10 | 3 | 1 | 1 | 0 | 3 | 0 | 12 | 3 | 0 | 1 | 2 | .333 | 0 | 3- - | - | 5.69 | 5.40 |
| 2010 | Cle | AL | 34 | 0 | 0 | 20 | 48.1 | 224 | 68 | 31 | 30 | 10 | 2 | 3 | 1 | 17 | 1 | 37 | 4 | 0 | 0 | 2 | .000 | 0 | 0-0 | 0 | 7.30 | 5.59 |
| 2012 | Hou | NL | 18 | 0 | 0 | 2 | 19.1 | 83 | 14 | 9 | 9 | 0 | 2 | 0 | 2 | 11 | 2 | 22 | 4 | 0 | 1 | 1 | .500 | 0 | 0-0 | 3 | 2.74 | 4.19 |
| 2013 | Hou | AL | 43 | 0 | 0 | 10 | 36.1 | 171 | 50 | 28 | 23 | 8 | 0 | 2 | 1 | 14 | 1 | 27 | 4 | 0 | 2 | 4 | .333 | 0 | 2-5 | 13 | 7.28 | 5.70 |
| 3 ML YEARS | | | 95 | 0 | 0 | 32 | 104.0 | 478 | 132 | 68 | 62 | 18 | 4 | 5 | 4 | 42 | 4 | 86 | 12 | 0 | 3 | 7 | .300 | 0 | 2-5 | 16 | 6.37 | 5.37 |

# Steven Ames

**Pitches:** R **Bats:** R **Pos:** RP-4 **Ht:** 6'1" **Wt:** 205 **Born:** 3/15/1988 **Age:** 26

| HOW MUCH HE PITCHED | | | | | | | | | WHAT HE GAVE UP | | | | | | | | | | | | THE RESULTS | | | | | | | |
|---|---|---|---|---|---|---|---|---|---|---|---|---|---|---|---|---|---|---|---|---|---|---|---|---|---|---|---|---|
| Year | Team | Lg | G | GS | CG | GF | IP | BFP | H | R | ER | HR | SH | SF | HB | TBB | IBB | SO | WP | Bk | W | L | Pct | Sh | Sv-Op | Hld | ERC | ERA |
| 2009 | Ogden | R+ | 17 | 0 | 0 | 11 | 30.0 | 112 | 20 | 7 | 7 | 2 | 0 | 2 | 0 | 6 | 0 | 47 | 3 | 0 | 1 | 1 | .500 | 0 | 7- - | - | 1.60 | 2.10 |
| 2010 | Ddgrs | R | 3 | 0 | 0 | 2 | 3.0 | 11 | 2 | 0 | 0 | 0 | 0 | 0 | 0 | 0 | 0 | 4 | 0 | 0 | 0 | 0 | - | 0 | 0- - | - | 0.91 | 0.00 |
| 2010 | Gt Lks | A | 23 | 0 | 0 | 22 | 28.1 | 111 | 21 | 9 | 8 | 0 | 1 | 0 | 0 | 3 | 0 | 44 | 2 | 0 | 0 | 2 | .000 | 0 | 16- - | - | 1.29 | 2.54 |
| 2011 | RCuca | A+ | 15 | 0 | 0 | 15 | 15.1 | 60 | 10 | 3 | 2 | 1 | 1 | 2 | 0 | 2 | 1 | 28 | 1 | 0 | 0 | 0 | - | 0 | 9- - | - | 1.25 | 1.17 |
| 2011 | Chatt | AA | 28 | 0 | 0 | 9 | 32.2 | 138 | 32 | 10 | 9 | 3 | 3 | 1 | 0 | 11 | 4 | 41 | 2 | 2 | 2 | 2 | .500 | 0 | 5- - | - | 3.47 | 2.48 |
| 2012 | Chatt | AA | 54 | 0 | 0 | 32 | 63.1 | 250 | 52 | 11 | 11 | 2 | 3 | 0 | 0 | 13 | 0 | 72 | 1 | 0 | 3 | 3 | .500 | 0 | 18- - | - | 2.04 | 1.56 |
| 2013 | Albq | AAA | 30 | 0 | 0 | 17 | 34.1 | 158 | 45 | 20 | 14 | 4 | 1 | 1 | 1 | 13 | 1 | 29 | 1 | 0 | 2 | 2 | .500 | 0 | 8- - | - | 6.03 | 3.67 |
| 2013 | NewOr | AAA | 9 | 0 | 0 | 2 | 12.0 | 50 | 14 | 5 | 5 | 2 | 0 | 0 | 0 | 4 | 0 | 5 | 0 | 0 | 1 | 0 | 1.000 | 0 | 0- - | - | 5.59 | 3.75 |
| 2013 | Mia | NL | 4 | 0 | 0 | 3 | 4.0 | 19 | 6 | 2 | 2 | 0 | 1 | 0 | 0 | 2 | 1 | 4 | 0 | 0 | 0 | 1 | .000 | 0 | 0-0 | 0 | 6.32 | 4.50 |

# Brett Anderson

**Pitches:** L **Bats:** L **Pos:** RP-11; SP-5 **Ht:** 6'4" **Wt:** 235 **Born:** 2/1/1988 **Age:** 26

| HOW MUCH HE PITCHED | | | | | | | | | WHAT HE GAVE UP | | | | | | | | | | | | THE RESULTS | | | | | | | |
|---|---|---|---|---|---|---|---|---|---|---|---|---|---|---|---|---|---|---|---|---|---|---|---|---|---|---|---|---|
| Year | Team | Lg | G | GS | CG | GF | IP | BFP | H | R | ER | HR | SH | SF | HB | TBB | IBB | SO | WP | Bk | W | L | Pct | Sh | Sv-Op | Hld | ERC | ERA |
| 2013 | Mdlnd* | AA | 1 | 1 | 0 | 0 | 3.2 | 21 | 6 | 6 | 6 | 0 | 0 | 0 | 0 | 4 | 0 | 3 | 1 | 0 | 0 | 1 | .000 | 0 | 0- - | - | 9.89 | 14.73 |
| 2013 | Scrmto* | AAA | 1 | 1 | 0 | 0 | 2.1 | 12 | 3 | 2 | 2 | 0 | 0 | 0 | 0 | 3 | 0 | 2 | 0 | 0 | 0 | 0 | - | 0 | 0- - | - | 9.14 | 7.71 |
| 2013 | Stcktn* | A+ | 1 | 1 | 0 | 0 | 3.1 | 17 | 5 | 5 | 5 | 2 | 0 | 0 | 0 | 2 | 0 | 6 | 0 | 0 | 0 | 1 | .000 | 0 | 0- - | - | 12.33 | 13.50 |
| 2009 | Oak | AL | 30 | 30 | 1 | 0 | 175.1 | 735 | 180 | 94 | 79 | 20 | 4 | 4 | 3 | 45 | 1 | 150 | 0 | 1 | 11 | 11 | .500 | 1 | 0-0 | 0 | 3.84 | 4.06 |
| 2010 | Oak | AL | 19 | 19 | 0 | 0 | 112.1 | 470 | 112 | 41 | 35 | 6 | 3 | 2 | 7 | 22 | 2 | 75 | 4 | 2 | 7 | 6 | .538 | 0 | 0-0 | 0 | 3.16 | 2.80 |
| 2011 | Oak | AL | 13 | 13 | 1 | 0 | 83.1 | 356 | 86 | 40 | 37 | 8 | 4 | 1 | 7 | 25 | 1 | 61 | 0 | 1 | 3 | 6 | .333 | 0 | 0-0 | 0 | 4.20 | 4.00 |
| 2012 | Oak | AL | 6 | 6 | 0 | 0 | 35.0 | 137 | 29 | 11 | 10 | 1 | 0 | 0 | 1 | 7 | 1 | 25 | 1 | 0 | 4 | 2 | .667 | 0 | 0-0 | 0 | 2.13 | 2.57 |
| 2013 | Oak | AL | 16 | 5 | 0 | 4 | 44.2 | 200 | 51 | 32 | 30 | 5 | 1 | 0 | 0 | 21 | 1 | 46 | 0 | 0 | 1 | 4 | .200 | 0 | 3-3 | 1 | 5.27 | 6.04 |
| Postseason | | | 1 | 1 | 0 | 0 | 6.0 | 21 | 2 | 0 | 0 | 0 | 0 | 0 | 0 | 2 | 0 | 6 | 0 | 0 | 1 | 0 | 1.000 | 0 | 0-0 | 0 | 0.72 | 0.00 |
| 5 ML YEARS | | | 84 | 73 | 2 | 4 | 450.2 | 1898 | 458 | 218 | 191 | 40 | 12 | 7 | 18 | 120 | 6 | 357 | 5 | 4 | 26 | 29 | .473 | 1 | 3-3 | 1 | 3.72 | 3.81 |

# Bryan Anderson

**Bats:** L **Throws:** R **Pos:** C-10 **Ht:** 6'1" **Wt:** 200 **Born:** 12/16/1986 **Age:** 27

| BATTING | | | | | | | | | | | | | | | | | | | | | BASERUNNING | | | | AVERAGES | | |
|---|---|---|---|---|---|---|---|---|---|---|---|---|---|---|---|---|---|---|---|---|---|---|---|---|---|---|---|
| Year | Team | Lg | G | AB | H | 2B | 3B | HR | (Hm | Rd) | TB | R | RBI | RC | TBB | IBB | SO | HBP | SH | SF | SB | CS | SB% | GDP | Avg | OBP | Slg |
| 2013 | Charltt* | AAA | 64 | 210 | 47 | 14 | 1 | 7 | (- | -) | 84 | 26 | 26 | 27 | 24 | 0 | 60 | 0 | 0 | 1 | 2 | 0 | 1.00 | 7 | .224 | .302 | .400 |
| 2010 | StL | NL | 15 | 32 | 9 | 2 | 0 | 0 | (0 | 0) | 11 | 1 | 4 | 5 | 1 | 0 | 7 | 1 | 0 | 1 | 0 | 0 | - | 0 | .281 | .314 | .344 |
| 2012 | StL | NL | 10 | 12 | 3 | 1 | 0 | 0 | (0 | 0) | 4 | 2 | 0 | 2 | 1 | 0 | 6 | 1 | 0 | 0 | 1 | 0 | 1.00 | 0 | .250 | .357 | .333 |
| 2013 | CWS | AL | 10 | 18 | 1 | 1 | 0 | 0 | (0 | 0) | 2 | 1 | 2 | 0 | 1 | 0 | 5 | 0 | 0 | 0 | 0 | 0 | - | 0 | .056 | .105 | .111 |
| 3 ML YEARS | | | 35 | 62 | 13 | 4 | 0 | 0 | (0 | 0) | 17 | 4 | 6 | 7 | 3 | 0 | 18 | 2 | 0 | 1 | 1 | 0 | 1.00 | 0 | .210 | .265 | .274 |

# Robert Andino

**Bats:** R **Throws:** R **Pos:** SS-18;2B-8;3B-4;PR-2;PH-1 ann-DEE-no **Ht:** 6'0" **Wt:** 195 **Born:** 4/25/1984 **Age:** 30

| BATTING | | | | | | | | | | | | | | | | | | | | | BASERUNNING | | | | AVERAGES | | |
|---|---|---|---|---|---|---|---|---|---|---|---|---|---|---|---|---|---|---|---|---|---|---|---|---|---|---|---|
| Year | Team | Lg | G | AB | H | 2B | 3B | HR | (Hm | Rd) | TB | R | RBI | RC | TBB | IBB | SO | HBP | SH | SF | SB | CS | SB% | GDP | Avg | OBP | Slg |
| 2013 | Tacom* | AAA | 44 | 153 | 35 | 5 | 1 | 3 | (- | -) | 51 | 17 | 12 | 14 | 12 | 0 | 38 | 0 | 0 | 2 | 2 | 1 | .67 | 5 | .229 | .281 | .333 |
| 2013 | Indy* | AAA | 25 | 96 | 29 | 8 | 0 | 0 | (- | -) | 37 | 7 | 9 | 12 | 5 | 0 | 20 | 0 | 2 | 2 | 0 | 1 | .00 | 1 | .302 | .330 | .385 |
| 2005 | Fla | NL | 17 | 44 | 7 | 4 | 0 | 0 | (0 | 0) | 11 | 4 | 1 | 1 | 5 | 1 | 8 | 0 | 1 | 0 | 1 | 0 | 1.00 | 2 | .159 | .245 | .250 |
| 2006 | Fla | NL | 11 | 24 | 4 | 1 | 0 | 0 | (0 | 0) | 5 | 0 | 2 | 0 | 1 | 0 | 6 | 0 | 1 | 2 | 1 | 0 | 1.00 | 0 | .167 | .185 | .208 |
| 2007 | Fla | NL | 7 | 13 | 5 | 1 | 0 | 0 | (0 | 0) | 6 | 0 | 0 | 1 | 0 | 0 | 2 | 0 | 0 | 0 | 0 | 0 | - | 0 | .385 | .385 | .462 |
| 2008 | Fla | NL | 44 | 63 | 13 | 2 | 0 | 2 | (1 | 1) | 21 | 7 | 9 | 7 | 4 | 0 | 23 | 0 | 1 | 0 | 0 | 0 | - | 1 | .206 | .254 | .333 |
| 2009 | Bal | AL | 78 | 198 | 44 | 7 | 0 | 2 | (1 | 1) | 57 | 31 | 10 | 11 | 15 | 1 | 47 | 0 | 0 | 2 | 3 | 3 | .50 | 6 | .222 | .274 | .288 |
| 2010 | Bal | AL | 16 | 61 | 18 | 4 | 0 | 2 | (2 | 0) | 28 | 6 | 6 | 4 | 3 | 0 | 13 | 1 | 0 | 1 | 1 | 1 | .50 | 3 | .295 | .333 | .459 |
| 2011 | Bal | AL | 139 | 457 | 120 | 22 | 0 | 5 | (2 | 3) | 157 | 63 | 36 | 52 | 41 | 0 | 83 | 3 | 9 | 1 | 13 | 3 | .81 | 14 | .263 | .327 | .344 |

| BATTING | | | | | | | | | | | | | | | | | | | | | | BASERUNNING | | | | AVERAGES | | |
|---|---|---|---|---|---|---|---|---|---|---|---|---|---|---|---|---|---|---|---|---|---|---|---|---|---|---|---|---|
| Year | Team | Lg | G | AB | H | 2B | 3B | HR | (Hm | Rd) | TB | R | RBI | RC | TBB | IBB | SO | HBP | SH | SF | SB | CS | SB% | GDP | Avg | OBP | Slg |
| 2012 | Bal | AL | 127 | 384 | 81 | 13 | 1 | 7 | (4 | 3) | 117 | 41 | 28 | 31 | 37 | 0 | 100 | 2 | 7 | 1 | 5 | 5 | .50 | 13 | .211 | .283 | .305 |
| 2013 | Sea | AL | 29 | 76 | 14 | 4 | 0 | 0 | (0 | 0) | 18 | 5 | 4 | 3 | 7 | 0 | 27 | 0 | 2 | 0 | 0 | 0 | - | 3 | .184 | .253 | .237 |
| Postseason | | | 6 | 12 | 5 | 1 | 0 | 0 | (0 | 0) | 6 | 3 | 0 | 4 | 0 | 0 | 2 | 0 | 1 | 0 | 0 | 0 | - | 0 | .417 | .417 | .500 |
| 9 ML YEARS | | | 468 | 1320 | 306 | 58 | 1 | 18 | (10 | 8) | 420 | 157 | 96 | 110 | 113 | 2 | 309 | 6 | 21 | 7 | 24 | 12 | .67 | 42 | .232 | .294 | .318 |

# Elvis Andrus

**Bats:** R **Throws:** R **Pos:** SS-146;DH-10;PH-1 AHN-drews **Ht:** 6'0" **Wt:** 200 **Born:** 8/26/1988 **Age:** 25

| BATTING | | | | | | | | | | | | | | | | | | | | | | BASERUNNING | | | | AVERAGES | | |
|---|---|---|---|---|---|---|---|---|---|---|---|---|---|---|---|---|---|---|---|---|---|---|---|---|---|---|---|---|
| Year | Team | Lg | G | AB | H | 2B | 3B | HR | (Hm | Rd) | TB | R | RBI | RC | TBB | IBB | SO | HBP | SH | SF | SB | CS | SB% | GDP | Avg | OBP | Slg |
| 2009 | Tex | AL | 145 | 480 | 128 | 17 | 8 | 6 | (3 | 3) | 179 | 72 | 40 | 65 | 40 | 0 | 77 | 6 | 12 | 3 | 33 | 6 | .85 | 4 | .267 | .329 | .373 |
| 2010 | Tex | AL | 148 | 588 | 156 | 15 | 3 | 0 | (0 | 0) | 177 | 88 | 35 | 79 | 64 | 0 | 96 | 5 | **17** | 0 | 32 | 15 | .68 | 6 | .265 | .342 | .301 |
| 2011 | Tex | AL | 150 | 587 | 164 | 27 | 3 | 5 | (2 | 3) | 212 | 96 | 60 | 76 | 56 | 0 | 74 | 5 | 16 | 1 | 37 | 12 | .76 | 17 | .279 | .347 | .361 |
| 2012 | Tex | AL | 158 | 629 | 180 | 31 | 9 | 3 | (1 | 2) | 238 | 85 | 62 | 92 | 57 | 0 | 96 | 5 | **17** | 3 | 21 | 10 | .68 | 15 | .286 | .349 | .378 |
| 2013 | Tex | AL | 156 | 620 | 168 | 17 | 4 | 4 | (0 | 4) | 205 | 91 | 67 | 72 | 52 | 1 | 97 | 4 | **16** | 6 | 42 | 8 | .84 | 19 | .271 | .328 | .331 |
| Postseason | | | 34 | 140 | 38 | 4 | 0 | 0 | (0 | 0) | 42 | 18 | 5 | 13 | 12 | 0 | 20 | 1 | 4 | 1 | 9 | 3 | .75 | 6 | .271 | .331 | .300 |
| 5 ML YEARS | | | 757 | 2904 | 796 | 107 | 27 | 18 | (6 | 12) | 1011 | 432 | 264 | 384 | 269 | 1 | 440 | 25 | 78 | 13 | 165 | 51 | .76 | 61 | .274 | .339 | .348 |

# Rick Ankiel

**Bats:** L **Throws:** L **Pos:** RF-26;CF-17;PH-7 ANN-keel **Ht:** 6'1" **Wt:** 210 **Born:** 7/19/1979 **Age:** 34

| BATTING | | | | | | | | | | | | | | | | | | | | | | BASERUNNING | | | | AVERAGES | | |
|---|---|---|---|---|---|---|---|---|---|---|---|---|---|---|---|---|---|---|---|---|---|---|---|---|---|---|---|---|
| Year | Team | Lg | G | AB | H | 2B | 3B | HR | (Hm | Rd) | TB | R | RBI | RC | TBB | IBB | SO | HBP | SH | SF | SB | CS | SB% | GDP | Avg | OBP | Slg |
| 1999 | StL | NL | 9 | 10 | 1 | 0 | 0 | 0 | (0 | 0) | 1 | 0 | 0 | 0 | 0 | 0 | 3 | 0 | 1 | 0 | 0 | 0 | - | 0 | .100 | .100 | .100 |
| 2000 | StL | NL | 33 | 68 | 17 | 1 | 1 | 2 | (2 | 0) | 26 | 8 | 9 | 0 | 4 | 0 | 20 | 0 | 1 | 0 | 0 | 0 | - | 1 | .250 | .292 | .382 |
| 2001 | StL | NL | 6 | 8 | 0 | 0 | 0 | 0 | (0 | 0) | 0 | 1 | 0 | 0 | 1 | 0 | 5 | 0 | 1 | 0 | 0 | 0 | - | 0 | .000 | .111 | .000 |
| 2004 | StL | NL | 5 | 1 | 0 | 0 | 0 | 0 | (0 | 0) | 0 | 0 | 0 | 0 | 1 | 0 | 1 | 0 | 0 | 0 | 0 | 0 | - | 0 | .000 | .500 | .000 |
| 2007 | StL | NL | 47 | 172 | 49 | 8 | 1 | 11 | (9 | 2) | 92 | 31 | 39 | 32 | 13 | 0 | 41 | 0 | 1 | 4 | 1 | 0 | 1.00 | 3 | .285 | .328 | .535 |
| 2008 | StL | NL | 120 | 413 | 109 | 21 | 2 | 25 | (11 | 14) | 209 | 65 | 71 | 60 | 42 | 3 | 100 | 5 | 0 | 3 | 2 | 1 | .67 | 8 | .264 | .337 | .506 |
| 2009 | StL | NL | 122 | 372 | 86 | 21 | 2 | 11 | (4 | 7) | 144 | 50 | 38 | 32 | 26 | 4 | 99 | 3 | 0 | 3 | 4 | 3 | .57 | 5 | .231 | .285 | .387 |
| 2010 | 2 Tms | | 74 | 211 | 49 | 13 | 1 | 6 | (1 | 5) | 82 | 31 | 24 | 22 | 26 | 2 | 71 | 2 | 0 | 1 | 3 | 1 | .75 | 3 | .232 | .321 | .389 |
| 2011 | Was | NL | 122 | 380 | 91 | 20 | 0 | 9 | (8 | 1) | 138 | 46 | 37 | 35 | 29 | 1 | 96 | 2 | 3 | 1 | 10 | 3 | .77 | 7 | .239 | .296 | .363 |
| 2012 | Was | NL | 68 | 158 | 36 | 10 | 2 | 5 | (2 | 3) | 65 | 15 | 15 | 14 | 12 | 3 | 59 | 0 | 1 | 0 | 1 | 3 | .25 | 3 | .228 | .282 | .411 |
| 2013 | 2 Tms | | 45 | 128 | 24 | 7 | 1 | 7 | (3 | 4) | 54 | 13 | 18 | 14 | 8 | 0 | 60 | 0 | 0 | 0 | 0 | 1 | .00 | 1 | .188 | .235 | .422 |
| 10 | KC | AL | 27 | 92 | 24 | 7 | 0 | 4 | (1 | 3) | 43 | 14 | 15 | 11 | 7 | 0 | 29 | 1 | 0 | 1 | 1 | 0 | 1.00 | 2 | .261 | .317 | .467 |
| 10 | Atl | NL | 47 | 119 | 25 | 6 | 1 | 2 | (0 | 2) | 39 | 17 | 9 | 11 | 19 | 2 | 42 | 1 | 0 | 0 | 2 | 1 | .67 | 1 | .210 | .324 | .328 |
| 13 | Hou | AL | 25 | 62 | 12 | 3 | 0 | 5 | (3 | 2) | 30 | 6 | 11 | 9 | 3 | 0 | 35 | 0 | 0 | 0 | 0 | 0 | - | 0 | .194 | .231 | .484 |
| 13 | NYM | NL | 20 | 66 | 12 | 4 | 1 | 2 | (0 | 2) | 24 | 7 | 7 | 5 | 5 | 0 | 25 | 0 | 0 | 0 | 0 | 1 | .00 | 1 | .182 | .239 | .364 |
| Postseason | | | 9 | 15 | 2 | 0 | 0 | 1 | (0 | 1) | 5 | 1 | 1 | 1 | 2 | 0 | 6 | 0 | 0 | 0 | 0 | 0 | - | 0 | .133 | .235 | .333 |
| 11 ML YEARS | | | 651 | 1921 | 462 | 101 | 10 | 76 | (40 | 36) | 811 | 260 | 251 | 209 | 162 | 13 | 555 | 12 | 8 | 12 | 21 | 12 | .64 | 31 | .240 | .302 | .422 |

# Norichika Aoki

**Bats:** L **Throws:** R **Pos:** RF-149;PH-7;CF-2;PR-1 no-ree-CHEE-kah AH-oh-kee **Ht:** 5'9" **Wt:** 175 **Born:** 1/5/1982 **Age:** 32

| BATTING | | | | | | | | | | | | | | | | | | | | | | BASERUNNING | | | | AVERAGES | | |
|---|---|---|---|---|---|---|---|---|---|---|---|---|---|---|---|---|---|---|---|---|---|---|---|---|---|---|---|---|
| Year | Team | Lg | G | AB | H | 2B | 3B | HR | (Hm | Rd) | TB | R | RBI | RC | TBB | IBB | SO | HBP | SH | SF | SB | CS | SB% | GDP | Avg | OBP | Slg |
| 2009 | | Jap | 142 | 531 | 161 | 23 | 2 | 16 | (- | -) | 236 | 87 | 66 | 100 | 75 | - | 65 | 13 | 1 | 4 | 18 | 10 | .64 | - | .303 | .400 | .444 |
| 2010 | | Jap | 144 | 583 | 209 | 44 | 1 | 14 | (- | -) | 297 | 92 | 63 | 131 | 63 | - | 61 | 18 | 0 | 3 | 19 | 4 | .83 | - | .358 | .435 | .509 |
| 2011 | | Jap | 144 | 583 | 170 | 18 | 5 | 4 | (- | -) | 210 | 73 | 44 | 81 | 51 | - | 55 | 9 | 0 | 0 | 8 | 3 | .73 | - | .292 | .358 | .360 |
| 2012 | Mil | NL | 151 | 520 | 150 | 37 | 4 | 10 | (4 | 6) | 225 | 81 | 50 | 80 | 43 | 1 | 55 | 13 | 7 | 5 | 30 | 8 | .79 | 6 | .288 | .355 | .433 |
| 2013 | Mil | NL | 155 | 597 | 171 | 20 | 3 | 8 | (5 | 3) | 221 | 80 | 37 | 80 | 55 | 1 | 40 | 11 | 8 | 3 | 20 | 12 | .63 | 9 | .286 | .356 | .370 |
| 2 ML YEARS | | | 306 | 1117 | 321 | 57 | 7 | 18 | (9 | 9) | 446 | 161 | 87 | 160 | 98 | 2 | 95 | 24 | 15 | 8 | 50 | 20 | .71 | 15 | .287 | .355 | .399 |

# Chris Archer

**Pitches:** R **Bats:** R **Pos:** SP-23 **Ht:** 6'3" **Wt:** 200 **Born:** 9/26/1988 **Age:** 25

| HOW MUCH HE PITCHED | | | | | | | | | WHAT HE GAVE UP | | | | | | | | | | | | THE RESULTS | | | | | | | |
|---|---|---|---|---|---|---|---|---|---|---|---|---|---|---|---|---|---|---|---|---|---|---|---|---|---|---|---|---|
| Year | Team | Lg | G | GS | CG | GF | IP | BFP | H | R | ER | HR | SH | SF | HB | TBB | IBB | SO | WP | Bk | W | L | Pct | Sh | Sv-Op | Hld | ERC | ERA |
| 2009 | Peoria | A | 27 | 26 | 0 | 0 | 109.0 | 463 | 78 | 41 | 34 | 0 | 2 | 2 | 7 | 66 | 0 | 119 | 10 | 1 | 6 | 4 | .600 | 0 | 0-- | - | 2.89 | 2.81 |
| 2010 | Dytona | A+ | 15 | 14 | 0 | 1 | 72.1 | 299 | 54 | 27 | 23 | 4 | 1 | 2 | 3 | 26 | 1 | 82 | 1 | 0 | 7 | 1 | .875 | 0 | 0-- | - | 2.40 | 2.86 |
| 2010 | Tenn | AA | 13 | 13 | 0 | 0 | 70.0 | 291 | 48 | 19 | 14 | 2 | 4 | 4 | 2 | 39 | 1 | 67 | 5 | 0 | 8 | 2 | .800 | 0 | 0-- | - | 2.62 | 1.80 |
| 2011 | Mont | AA | 25 | 25 | 0 | 0 | 134.1 | 612 | 136 | 76 | 66 | 11 | 7 | 4 | 10 | 80 | 1 | 118 | 18 | 0 | 8 | 7 | .533 | 0 | 0-- | - | 5.10 | 4.42 |
| 2011 | Drham | AAA | 2 | 2 | 0 | 0 | 13.0 | 55 | 11 | 1 | 1 | 0 | 0 | 0 | 0 | 6 | 0 | 12 | 0 | 0 | 1 | 0 | 1.000 | 0 | 0-- | - | 2.79 | 0.69 |
| 2012 | Drham | AAA | 25 | 25 | 0 | 0 | 128.0 | 531 | 99 | 54 | 52 | 6 | 2 | 2 | 7 | 62 | 0 | 139 | 12 | 1 | 7 | 9 | .438 | 0 | 0-- | - | 3.09 | 3.66 |
| 2013 | Drham | AAA | 10 | 10 | 0 | 0 | 50.0 | 224 | 50 | 26 | 22 | 6 | 0 | 0 | 2 | 23 | 0 | 52 | 3 | 1 | 5 | 3 | .625 | 0 | 0-- | - | 4.53 | 3.96 |
| 2012 | TB | AL | 6 | 4 | 0 | 1 | 29.1 | 122 | 23 | 17 | 15 | 3 | 1 | 0 | 1 | 13 | 0 | 36 | 2 | 0 | 1 | 3 | .250 | 0 | 0-0 | 0 | 3.24 | 4.60 |
| 2013 | TB | AL | 23 | 23 | 2 | 0 | 128.2 | 525 | 107 | 49 | 46 | 15 | 1 | 5 | 8 | 38 | 2 | 101 | 7 | 0 | 9 | 7 | .563 | 2 | 0-0 | 0 | 3.13 | 3.22 |
| 2 ML YEARS | | | 29 | 27 | 2 | 1 | 158.0 | 647 | 130 | 66 | 61 | 18 | 2 | 5 | 9 | 51 | 2 | 137 | 9 | 0 | 10 | 10 | .500 | 2 | 0-0 | 0 | 3.15 | 3.47 |

# Oswaldo Arcia

**Bats:** L **Throws:** R **Pos:** LF-56;RF-29;DH-9;PH-6 ARR-see-ya **Ht:** 6'0" **Wt:** 210 **Born:** 5/9/1991 **Age:** 23

| BATTING | | | | | | | | | | | | | | | | | | | | | | BASERUNNING | | | | AVERAGES | | |
|---|---|---|---|---|---|---|---|---|---|---|---|---|---|---|---|---|---|---|---|---|---|---|---|---|---|---|---|---|
| Year | Team | Lg | G | AB | H | 2B | 3B | HR | (Hm | Rd) | TB | R | RBI | RC | TBB | IBB | SO | HBP | SH | SF | SB | CS | SB% | GDP | Avg | OBP | Slg |
| 2009 | Twins | R | 44 | 167 | 46 | 11 | 2 | 5 | (- | -) | 76 | 20 | 24 | 28 | 15 | 0 | 18 | 2 | 0 | 3 | 8 | 0 | 1.00 | 3 | .275 | .337 | .455 |
| 2010 | Elizab | R | 64 | 259 | 97 | 21 | 7 | 14 | (- | -) | 174 | 47 | 51 | 66 | 19 | 3 | 67 | 4 | 0 | 1 | 4 | 4 | .50 | 5 | .375 | .424 | .672 |
| 2011 | Beloit | A | 20 | 71 | 25 | 8 | 1 | 5 | (- | -) | 50 | 18 | 18 | 19 | 9 | 0 | 16 | 0 | 0 | 1 | 2 | 2 | .50 | 1 | .352 | .420 | .704 |
| 2011 | Twins | R | 2 | 8 | 4 | 1 | 1 | 0 | (- | -) | 7 | 1 | 1 | 2 | 0 | 0 | 1 | 0 | 0 | 0 | 0 | 0 | - | 0 | .500 | .500 | .875 |
| 2011 | FtMyrs | A+ | 59 | 213 | 56 | 14 | 2 | 8 | (- | -) | 98 | 27 | 32 | 29 | 9 | 0 | 53 | 3 | 0 | 2 | 1 | 1 | .50 | 3 | .263 | .300 | .460 |

| Year Team | Lg | G | AB | H | 2B | 3B | HR | (Hm | Rd) | TB | R | RBI | RC | TBB | IBB | SO | HBP | SH | SF | SB | CS | SB% | GDP | Avg | OBP | Slg |
|---|---|---|---|---|---|---|---|---|---|---|---|---|---|---|---|---|---|---|---|---|---|---|---|---|---|---|
| 2012 FtMyrs | A+ | 55 | 207 | 64 | 16 | 3 | 7 | (- | -) | 107 | 22 | 31 | 39 | 23 | 2 | 45 | 1 | 1 | 3 | 1 | 3 | .25 | 3 | .309 | .376 | .517 |
| 2012 NwBrit | AA | 69 | 262 | 86 | 20 | 5 | 10 | (- | -) | 146 | 54 | 67 | 57 | 28 | 1 | 62 | 5 | 0 | 4 | 3 | 2 | .60 | 4 | .328 | .398 | .557 |
| 2013 Roch | AAA | 38 | 128 | 40 | 6 | 0 | 10 | (- | -) | 76 | 25 | 30 | 32 | 22 | 0 | 37 | 4 | 0 | 1 | 2 | 1 | .67 | 1 | .313 | .426 | .594 |
| 2013 Min | AL | 97 | 351 | 88 | 17 | 2 | 14 | (6 | 8) | 151 | 34 | 43 | 37 | 23 | 0 | 117 | 4 | 0 | 0 | 1 | 2 | .33 | 4 | .251 | .304 | .430 |

## Nolan Arenado

**Bats:** R **Throws:** R **Pos:** 3B-130;PH-3 ahr-eh-NOD-oh **Ht:** 6'1" **Wt:** 205 **Born:** 4/16/1991 **Age:** 23

| Year Team | Lg | G | AB | H | 2B | 3B | HR | (Hm | Rd) | TB | R | RBI | RC | TBB | IBB | SO | HBP | SH | SF | SB | CS | SB% | GDP | Avg | OBP | Slg |
|---|---|---|---|---|---|---|---|---|---|---|---|---|---|---|---|---|---|---|---|---|---|---|---|---|---|---|
| 2009 Casper | R+ | 54 | 203 | 61 | 15 | 0 | 2 | (- | -) | 82 | 28 | 22 | 30 | 16 | 0 | 18 | 2 | 0 | 4 | 5 | 2 | .71 | 6 | .300 | .351 | .404 |
| 2010 Ashvll | A | 92 | 373 | 115 | 41 | 1 | 12 | (- | -) | 194 | 45 | 65 | 65 | 19 | 0 | 52 | 1 | 0 | 7 | 1 | 3 | .25 | 8 | .308 | .338 | .520 |
| 2011 Mdest | A+ | 134 | 517 | 154 | 32 | 3 | 20 | (- | -) | 252 | 82 | 122 | 91 | 47 | 3 | 53 | 1 | 4 | 14 | 2 | 1 | .67 | 21 | .298 | .349 | .487 |
| 2012 Tulsa | AA | 134 | 516 | 147 | 36 | 1 | 12 | (- | -) | 221 | 55 | 56 | 77 | 39 | 5 | 58 | 7 | 1 | 10 | 0 | 2 | .00 | 18 | .285 | .337 | .428 |
| 2013 ColSpr | AAA | 18 | 66 | 24 | 11 | 0 | 3 | (- | -) | 44 | 14 | 21 | 15 | 5 | 1 | 9 | 0 | 1 | 3 | 0 | 2 | .00 | 0 | .364 | .392 | .667 |
| 2013 Col | NL | 133 | 486 | 130 | 29 | 4 | 10 | (5 | 5) | 197 | 49 | 52 | 48 | 23 | 1 | 72 | 1 | 2 | 2 | 2 | 0 | 1.00 | 16 | .267 | .301 | .405 |

## J.P. Arencibia

**Bats:** R **Throws:** R **Pos:** C-131;PH-16;DH-3 air-en-SEE-bee-uh **Ht:** 6'0" **Wt:** 200 **Born:** 1/5/1986 **Age:** 28

| Year Team | Lg | G | AB | H | 2B | 3B | HR | (Hm | Rd) | TB | R | RBI | RC | TBB | IBB | SO | HBP | SH | SF | SB | CS | SB% | GDP | Avg | OBP | Slg |
|---|---|---|---|---|---|---|---|---|---|---|---|---|---|---|---|---|---|---|---|---|---|---|---|---|---|---|
| 2010 Tor | AL | 11 | 35 | 5 | 1 | 0 | 2 | (2 | 0) | 12 | 3 | 4 | 4 | 2 | 0 | 11 | 0 | 0 | 0 | 0 | 0 | - | 0 | .143 | .189 | .343 |
| 2011 Tor | AL | 129 | 443 | 97 | 20 | 4 | 23 | (13 | 10) | 194 | 47 | 78 | 58 | 36 | 3 | 133 | 4 | 0 | 3 | 1 | 1 | .50 | 6 | .219 | .282 | .438 |
| 2012 Tor | AL | 102 | 347 | 81 | 16 | 0 | 18 | (9 | 9) | 151 | 45 | 56 | 47 | 18 | 1 | 108 | 3 | 1 | 3 | 1 | 0 | 1.00 | 4 | .233 | .275 | .435 |
| 2013 Tor | AL | 138 | 474 | 92 | 18 | 0 | 21 | (13 | 8) | 173 | 45 | 55 | 30 | 18 | 0 | 148 | 3 | 0 | 2 | 0 | 2 | .00 | 8 | .194 | .227 | .365 |
| 4 ML YEARS | | 380 | 1299 | 275 | 55 | 4 | 64 | (37 | 27) | 530 | 140 | 193 | 139 | 74 | 4 | 400 | 10 | 1 | 8 | 2 | 3 | .40 | 18 | .212 | .258 | .408 |

## Joaquin Arias

wah-KEEN AH-ree-us

**Bats:** R **Throws:** R **Pos:** 3B-55;SS-24;PH-24;2B-13;1B-6;PR-3 **Ht:** 6'1" **Wt:** 160 **Born:** 9/21/1984 **Age:** 29

| Year Team | Lg | G | AB | H | 2B | 3B | HR | (Hm | Rd) | TB | R | RBI | RC | TBB | IBB | SO | HBP | SH | SF | SB | CS | SB% | GDP | Avg | OBP | Slg |
|---|---|---|---|---|---|---|---|---|---|---|---|---|---|---|---|---|---|---|---|---|---|---|---|---|---|---|
| 2013 Fresno* | AAA | 2 | 8 | 2 | 0 | 0 | 0 | (- | -) | 2 | 0 | 0 | 0 | 0 | 0 | 3 | 0 | 0 | 0 | 0 | 0 | - | 0 | .250 | .250 | .250 |
| 2006 Tex | AL | 6 | 11 | 6 | 1 | 0 | 0 | (0 | 0) | 7 | 4 | 1 | 3 | 1 | 0 | 0 | 0 | 0 | 0 | 0 | 1 | .00 | 0 | .545 | .583 | .636 |
| 2008 Tex | AL | 32 | 110 | 32 | 7 | 3 | 0 | (0 | 0) | 45 | 15 | 9 | 15 | 7 | 0 | 12 | 2 | 1 | 0 | 4 | 1 | .80 | 4 | .291 | .345 | .409 |
| 2009 Tex | AL | 3 | 8 | 0 | 0 | 0 | 0 | (0 | 0) | 0 | 0 | 0 | 0 | 0 | 0 | 3 | 0 | 1 | 0 | 0 | 0 | - | 0 | .000 | .000 | .000 |
| 2010 2 Tms | | 72 | 128 | 33 | 6 | 1 | 0 | (0 | 0) | 41 | 23 | 13 | 10 | 4 | 0 | 23 | 0 | 2 | 0 | 1 | 0 | 1.00 | 2 | .258 | .280 | .320 |
| 2012 SF | NL | 112 | 319 | 86 | 13 | 5 | 5 | (0 | 5) | 124 | 30 | 34 | 32 | 13 | 4 | 44 | 5 | 2 | 5 | 5 | 1 | .83 | 12 | .270 | .304 | .389 |
| 2013 SF | NL | 102 | 225 | 61 | 9 | 2 | 1 | (1 | 0) | 77 | 17 | 19 | 18 | 4 | 1 | 33 | 1 | 4 | 2 | 1 | 0 | 1.00 | 4 | .271 | .284 | .342 |
| 10 Tex | AL | 50 | 98 | 27 | 5 | 1 | 0 | (0 | 0) | 34 | 18 | 9 | 8 | 2 | 0 | 17 | 0 | 1 | 0 | 1 | 0 | 1.00 | 2 | .276 | .290 | .347 |
| 10 NYM | NL | 22 | 30 | 6 | 1 | 0 | 0 | (0 | 0) | 7 | 5 | 4 | 2 | 2 | 0 | 6 | 0 | 1 | 0 | 0 | 0 | - | 0 | .200 | .250 | .233 |
| Postseason | | 12 | 8 | 3 | 2 | 0 | 0 | (0 | 0) | 5 | 3 | 0 | 1 | 0 | 0 | 1 | 0 | 0 | 0 | 0 | 0 | - | 0 | .375 | .375 | .625 |
| 6 ML YEARS | | 327 | 801 | 218 | 36 | 11 | 6 | (1 | 5) | 294 | 89 | 76 | 78 | 29 | 5 | 115 | 8 | 10 | 7 | 11 | 3 | .79 | 22 | .272 | .302 | .367 |

## Jake Arrieta

**Pitches:** R **Bats:** R **Pos:** SP-14 air-ee-ETT-uh **Ht:** 6'4" **Wt:** 225 **Born:** 3/6/1986 **Age:** 28

| | | HOW MUCH HE PITCHED | | | | | | WHAT HE GAVE UP | | | | | | | | | | | | THE RESULTS | | | | | | | |
|---|---|---|---|---|---|---|---|---|---|---|---|---|---|---|---|---|---|---|---|---|---|---|---|---|---|---|---|
| Year Team | Lg | G | GS | CG | GF | IP | BFP | H | R | ER | HR | SH | SF | HB | TBB | IBB | SO | WP | Bk | W | L | Pct | Sh | Sv-Op | Hld | ERC | ERA |
| 2013 Norfolk* | AAA | 9 | 8 | 1 | 1 | 49.0 | 202 | 45 | 26 | 24 | 4 | 2 | 1 | 1 | 14 | 0 | 38 | 4 | 0 | 5 | 3 | .625 | 1 | 0-- | - | 3.17 | 4.41 |
| 2013 Iowa* | AAA | 7 | 7 | 0 | 0 | 30.1 | 136 | 32 | 16 | 12 | 2 | 0 | 0 | 2 | 16 | 0 | 39 | 5 | 0 | 2 | 2 | .500 | 0 | 0-- | - | 4.97 | 3.56 |
| 2010 Bal | AL | 18 | 18 | 0 | 0 | 100.1 | 449 | 106 | 57 | 52 | 9 | 4 | 2 | 4 | 48 | 3 | 52 | 5 | 0 | 6 | 6 | .500 | 0 | 0-0 | 0 | 4.74 | 4.66 |
| 2011 Bal | AL | 22 | 22 | 0 | 0 | 119.1 | 523 | 115 | 70 | 67 | 21 | 3 | 2 | 4 | 59 | 2 | 93 | 0 | 0 | 10 | 8 | .556 | 0 | 0-0 | 0 | 4.93 | 5.05 |
| 2012 Bal | AL | 24 | 18 | 0 | 1 | 114.2 | 496 | 122 | 82 | 79 | 16 | 3 | 4 | 5 | 35 | 3 | 109 | 4 | 0 | 3 | 9 | .250 | 0 | 0-0 | 1 | 4.47 | 6.20 |
| 2013 2 Tms | | 14 | 14 | 0 | 0 | 75.1 | 324 | 59 | 41 | 40 | 9 | 2 | 3 | 5 | 41 | 1 | 60 | 1 | 0 | 5 | 4 | .556 | 0 | 0-0 | 0 | 3.82 | 4.78 |
| 13 Bal | AL | 5 | 5 | 0 | 0 | 23.2 | 111 | 25 | 19 | 19 | 2 | 0 | 3 | 2 | 17 | 1 | 23 | 1 | 0 | 1 | 2 | .333 | 0 | 0-0 | 0 | 5.91 | 7.23 |
| 13 ChC | NL | 9 | 9 | 0 | 0 | 51.2 | 213 | 34 | 22 | 21 | 7 | 2 | 0 | 3 | 24 | 0 | 37 | 0 | 0 | 4 | 2 | .667 | 0 | 0-0 | 0 | 2.94 | 3.66 |
| 4 ML YEARS | | 78 | 72 | 0 | 1 | 409.2 | 1792 | 402 | 250 | 238 | 55 | 12 | 11 | 18 | 183 | 9 | 314 | 10 | 0 | 24 | 27 | .471 | 0 | 0-0 | 1 | 4.55 | 5.23 |

## Bronson Arroyo

**Pitches:** R **Bats:** R **Pos:** SP-32 uh-ROY-oh **Ht:** 6'4" **Wt:** 195 **Born:** 2/24/1977 **Age:** 37

| | | HOW MUCH HE PITCHED | | | | | | WHAT HE GAVE UP | | | | | | | | | | | | THE RESULTS | | | | | | | |
|---|---|---|---|---|---|---|---|---|---|---|---|---|---|---|---|---|---|---|---|---|---|---|---|---|---|---|---|
| Year Team | Lg | G | GS | CG | GF | IP | BFP | H | R | ER | HR | SH | SF | HB | TBB | IBB | SO | WP | Bk | W | L | Pct | Sh | Sv-Op | Hld | ERC | ERA |
| 2000 Pit | NL | 20 | 12 | 0 | 1 | 71.2 | 338 | 88 | 61 | 51 | 10 | 5 | 2 | 4 | 36 | 6 | 50 | 3 | 1 | 2 | 6 | .250 | 0 | 0-0 | 0 | 6.18 | 6.40 |
| 2001 Pit | NL | 24 | 13 | 1 | 1 | 88.1 | 390 | 99 | 54 | 50 | 12 | 4 | 6 | 4 | 34 | 6 | 39 | 4 | 1 | 5 | 7 | .417 | 0 | 0-0 | 2 | 5.09 | 5.09 |
| 2002 Pit | NL | 9 | 4 | 0 | 1 | 27.0 | 123 | 30 | 14 | 12 | 1 | 1 | 1 | 0 | 15 | 3 | 22 | 0 | 0 | 2 | 1 | .667 | 0 | 0-0 | 1 | 4.64 | 4.00 |
| 2003 Bos | AL | 6 | 0 | 0 | 2 | 17.1 | 66 | 10 | 5 | 4 | 0 | 0 | 0 | 1 | 4 | 2 | 14 | 0 | 0 | 0 | 0 | - | 0 | 1-1 | 0 | 1.14 | 2.08 |
| 2004 Bos | AL | 32 | 29 | 0 | 0 | 178.2 | 764 | 171 | 99 | 80 | 17 | 5 | 4 | **20** | 47 | 3 | 142 | 5 | 0 | 10 | 9 | .526 | 0 | 0-0 | 0 | 3.65 | 4.03 |
| 2005 Bos | AL | 35 | 32 | 0 | 1 | 205.1 | 878 | 213 | 116 | 103 | 22 | 4 | 4 | 14 | 54 | 3 | 100 | 5 | 1 | 14 | 10 | .583 | 0 | 0-0 | 0 | 4.04 | 4.51 |
| 2006 Cin | NL | 35 | **35** | 3 | 0 | **240.2** | 992 | 222 | 98 | 88 | 31 | 9 | 2 | 5 | 64 | 7 | 184 | 6 | 0 | 14 | 11 | .560 | 1 | 0-0 | 0 | 3.37 | 3.29 |
| 2007 Cin | NL | 34 | 34 | 1 | 0 | 210.2 | 921 | 232 | 109 | 99 | 28 | 10 | 7 | 13 | 63 | 6 | 156 | 4 | 0 | 9 | 15 | .375 | 0 | 0-0 | 0 | 4.68 | 4.23 |
| 2008 Cin | NL | 34 | **34** | 1 | 0 | 200.0 | 871 | 219 | **116** | 106 | 29 | 13 | 6 | 6 | 68 | 2 | 163 | 6 | 0 | 15 | 11 | .577 | 0 | 0-0 | 0 | 4.83 | 4.77 |
| 2009 Cin | NL | 33 | 33 | 3 | 0 | 220.1 | 923 | 214 | 101 | 94 | 31 | 9 | 5 | 9 | 65 | 6 | 127 | 1 | 0 | 15 | 13 | .536 | **2** | 0-0 | 0 | 3.94 | 3.84 |
| 2010 Cin | NL | 33 | 33 | 2 | 0 | 215.2 | 880 | 188 | 95 | 93 | 29 | 6 | 5 | 6 | 59 | 5 | 121 | 1 | 1 | 17 | 10 | .630 | 0 | 0-0 | 0 | 3.21 | 3.88 |
| 2011 Cin | NL | 32 | 32 | 1 | 0 | 199.0 | 855 | 227 | **119** | **112** | **46** | 6 | 5 | 6 | 45 | 5 | 108 | 0 | 0 | 9 | 12 | .429 | 1 | 0-0 | 0 | 5.20 | 5.07 |

| | | | HOW MUCH HE PITCHED | | | | | | WHAT HE GAVE UP | | | | | | | | | | | THE RESULTS | | | | | | | |
|---|---|---|---|---|---|---|---|---|---|---|---|---|---|---|---|---|---|---|---|---|---|---|---|---|---|---|---|
| Year | Team | Lg | G | GS | CG | GF | IP | BFP | H | R | ER | HR | SH | SF | HB | TBB | IBB | SO | WP | Bk | W | L | Pct | Sh | Sv-Op | Hld | ERC | ERA |
| 2012 | Cin | NL | 32 | 32 | 1 | 0 | 202.0 | 835 | 209 | 86 | 84 | 26 | 7 | 6 | 5 | 35 | 1 | 129 | 3 | 0 | 12 | 10 | .545 | 1 | 0-0 | 0 | 3.68 | 3.74 |
| 2013 | Cin | NL | 32 | 32 | 2 | 0 | 202.0 | 823 | 199 | 88 | 85 | **32** | 4 | 7 | 7 | 34 | 2 | 124 | 1 | 2 | 14 | 12 | .538 | 1 | 0-0 | 0 | 3.63 | 3.79 |
| Postseason | | | 12 | 4 | 0 | 3 | 29.1 | 127 | 24 | 17 | 15 | 5 | 0 | 0 | 2 | 13 | 0 | 26 | 0 | 0 | 1 | 0 | 1.000 | 0 | 0-0 | 2 | 3.91 | 4.60 |
| 14 ML YEARS | | | 391 | 355 | 15 | 6 | 2278.2 | 9659 | 2321 | 1161 | 1061 | 314 | 83 | 60 | 100 | 623 | 57 | 1479 | 39 | 6 | 138 | 127 | .521 | 6 | 1-1 | 3 | 4.09 | 4.19 |

# Cody Asche

**Bats:** L **Throws:** R **Pos:** 3B-44;PH-6 ASH-ee **Ht:** 6'1" **Wt:** 180 **Born:** 6/30/1990 **Age:** 24

| | | | BATTING | | | | | | | | | | | | | | | | | | BASERUNNING | | | | AVERAGES | | |
|---|---|---|---|---|---|---|---|---|---|---|---|---|---|---|---|---|---|---|---|---|---|---|---|---|---|---|---|
| Year | Team | Lg | G | AB | H | 2B | 3B | HR | (Hm | Rd) | TB | R | RBI | RC | TBB | IBB | SO | HBP | SH | SF | SB | CS | SB% | GDP | Avg | OBP | Slg |
| 2011 | Wmspt | A- | 68 | 239 | 46 | 11 | 0 | 2 | (- | -) | 63 | 14 | 19 | 16 | 24 | 1 | 50 | 3 | 1 | 1 | 0 | 3 | .00 | 2 | .192 | .273 | .264 |
| 2012 | Clrwtr | A+ | 62 | 255 | 89 | 13 | 3 | 2 | (- | -) | 114 | 31 | 25 | 44 | 12 | 1 | 37 | 1 | 0 | 2 | 10 | 2 | .83 | 4 | .349 | .378 | .447 |
| 2012 | Rdng | AA | 68 | 263 | 79 | 20 | 3 | 10 | (- | -) | 135 | 42 | 47 | 48 | 22 | 0 | 56 | 3 | 0 | 1 | 1 | 1 | .50 | 3 | .300 | .360 | .513 |
| 2013 | LV | AAA | 104 | 404 | 119 | 24 | 4 | 15 | (- | -) | 196 | 52 | 68 | 71 | 35 | 1 | 95 | 3 | 0 | 4 | 11 | 3 | .79 | 7 | .295 | .352 | .485 |
| 2013 | Phi | NL | 50 | 162 | 38 | 8 | 1 | 5 | (4 | 1) | 63 | 18 | 22 | 18 | 15 | 3 | 43 | 1 | 0 | 1 | 1 | 0 | 1.00 | 1 | .235 | .302 | .389 |

# Jairo Asencio

**Pitches:** R **Bats:** R **Pos:** RP-4 HIGH-row ahh-SEN-cee-oh **Ht:** 6'2" **Wt:** 180 **Born:** 5/30/1983 **Age:** 31

| | | | HOW MUCH HE PITCHED | | | | | | WHAT HE GAVE UP | | | | | | | | | | | THE RESULTS | | | | | | | |
|---|---|---|---|---|---|---|---|---|---|---|---|---|---|---|---|---|---|---|---|---|---|---|---|---|---|---|---|
| Year | Team | Lg | G | GS | CG | GF | IP | BFP | H | R | ER | HR | SH | SF | HB | TBB | IBB | SO | WP | Bk | W | L | Pct | Sh | Sv-Op | Hld | ERC | ERA |
| 2013 | Norfolk* | AAA | 47 | 0 | 0 | 40 | 50.2 | 202 | 35 | 17 | 15 | 5 | 4 | 0 | 1 | 14 | 4 | 56 | 2 | 0 | 5 | 0 | 1.000 | 0 | 28-- | - | 1.97 | 2.66 |
| 2009 | Atl | NL | 3 | 0 | 0 | 2 | 2.2 | 13 | 3 | 1 | 1 | 0 | 0 | 0 | 0 | 2 | 0 | 0 | 0 | 0 | 0 | 1 | .000 | 0 | 0-0 | 0 | 5.24 | 3.38 |
| 2011 | Atl | NL | 6 | 0 | 0 | 3 | 10.1 | 52 | 16 | 11 | 8 | 1 | 0 | 0 | 0 | 5 | 2 | 8 | 0 | 0 | 0 | 0 | - | 0 | 0-1 | 0 | 7.18 | 6.97 |
| 2012 | 2 Tms | | 30 | 0 | 0 | 13 | 40.1 | 175 | 39 | 23 | 22 | 5 | 0 | 0 | 1 | 19 | 1 | 29 | 3 | 0 | 1 | 1 | .500 | 0 | 0-0 | 0 | 4.44 | 4.91 |
| 2013 | Bal | AL | 4 | 0 | 0 | 1 | 2.1 | 12 | 3 | 2 | 2 | 1 | 0 | 0 | 0 | 2 | 1 | 4 | 0 | 0 | 0 | 0 | - | 0 | 0-0 | 0 | 9.65 | 7.71 |
| 12 | Cle | AL | 18 | 0 | 0 | 9 | 25.2 | 108 | 27 | 17 | 17 | 4 | 0 | 0 | 1 | 8 | 0 | 21 | 3 | 0 | 1 | 1 | .500 | 0 | 0-0 | 0 | 4.70 | 5.96 |
| 12 | ChC | NL | 12 | 0 | 0 | 4 | 14.2 | 67 | 12 | 6 | 5 | 1 | 0 | 0 | 0 | 11 | 1 | 8 | 0 | 0 | 0 | 0 | - | 0 | 0-0 | 0 | 3.96 | 3.07 |
| 4 ML YEARS | | | 43 | 0 | 0 | 19 | 55.2 | 252 | 61 | 37 | 33 | 7 | 0 | 0 | 1 | 28 | 4 | 41 | 3 | 0 | 1 | 2 | .333 | 0 | 0-1 | 0 | 5.17 | 5.34 |

# Scott Atchison

**Pitches:** R **Bats:** R **Pos:** RP-51 **Ht:** 6'2" **Wt:** 200 **Born:** 3/29/1976 **Age:** 38

| | | | HOW MUCH HE PITCHED | | | | | | WHAT HE GAVE UP | | | | | | | | | | | THE RESULTS | | | | | | | |
|---|---|---|---|---|---|---|---|---|---|---|---|---|---|---|---|---|---|---|---|---|---|---|---|---|---|---|---|
| Year | Team | Lg | G | GS | CG | GF | IP | BFP | H | R | ER | HR | SH | SF | HB | TBB | IBB | SO | WP | Bk | W | L | Pct | Sh | Sv-Op | Hld | ERC | ERA |
| 2013 | StLuci* | A+ | 1 | 0 | 0 | 1 | 1.0 | 3 | 0 | 0 | 0 | 0 | 0 | 0 | 0 | 0 | 0 | 1 | 0 | 0 | 0 | 0 | - | 0 | 1-- | - | 0.00 | 0.00 |
| 2013 | Bnghtn* | AA | 4 | 0 | 0 | 1 | 4.0 | 13 | 2 | 0 | 0 | 0 | 0 | 0 | 0 | 0 | 0 | 4 | 0 | 0 | 1 | 0 | 1.000 | 0 | 0-- | - | 0.58 | 0.00 |
| 2013 | Mets* | R | 2 | 2 | 0 | 0 | 2.0 | 9 | 3 | 1 | 1 | 0 | 0 | 0 | 0 | 0 | 0 | 3 | 0 | 0 | 0 | 1 | .000 | 0 | 0-- | - | 4.47 | 4.50 |
| 2004 | Sea | AL | 25 | 0 | 0 | 8 | 30.2 | 133 | 29 | 12 | 12 | 4 | 2 | 1 | 0 | 14 | 2 | 36 | 2 | 0 | 2 | 3 | .400 | 0 | 0-0 | 2 | 4.08 | 3.52 |
| 2005 | Sea | AL | 6 | 0 | 0 | 2 | 6.2 | 27 | 7 | 5 | 5 | 1 | 0 | 0 | 0 | 1 | 0 | 9 | 0 | 0 | 0 | 0 | - | 0 | 0-0 | 0 | 3.77 | 6.75 |
| 2007 | SF | NL | 22 | 0 | 0 | 4 | 30.2 | 131 | 32 | 14 | 14 | 5 | 1 | 2 | 1 | 10 | 0 | 25 | 2 | 0 | 0 | 0 | - | 0 | 0-1 | 5 | 4.65 | 4.11 |
| 2010 | Bos | AL | 43 | 1 | 0 | 8 | 60.0 | 253 | 58 | 37 | 30 | 9 | 1 | 2 | 1 | 19 | 2 | 41 | 4 | 0 | 2 | 3 | .400 | 0 | 0-0 | 7 | 3.92 | 4.50 |
| 2011 | Bos | AL | 17 | 0 | 0 | 4 | 30.1 | 122 | 31 | 11 | 11 | 0 | 1 | 2 | 2 | 6 | 0 | 17 | 2 | 0 | 1 | 0 | 1.000 | 0 | 1-1 | 0 | 3.15 | 3.26 |
| 2012 | Bos | AL | 42 | 0 | 0 | 7 | 51.1 | 200 | 42 | 10 | 9 | 2 | 1 | 2 | 0 | 9 | 3 | 36 | 2 | 0 | 2 | 1 | .667 | 0 | 0-1 | 5 | 1.91 | 1.58 |
| 2013 | NYM | NL | 51 | 0 | 0 | 10 | 45.1 | 194 | 45 | 27 | 22 | 4 | 2 | 3 | 0 | 12 | 0 | 28 | 5 | 0 | 3 | 3 | .500 | 0 | 0-0 | 10 | 3.33 | 4.37 |
| 7 ML YEARS | | | 206 | 1 | 0 | 43 | 255.0 | 1060 | 244 | 116 | 103 | 25 | 8 | 12 | 4 | 71 | 7 | 192 | 17 | 0 | 10 | 10 | .500 | 0 | 1-3 | 29 | 3.39 | 3.64 |

# Phillippe Aumont

**Pitches:** R **Bats:** L **Pos:** RP-22 fih-LEEP ah-MOHNT **Ht:** 6'7" **Wt:** 260 **Born:** 1/7/1989 **Age:** 25

| | | | HOW MUCH HE PITCHED | | | | | | WHAT HE GAVE UP | | | | | | | | | | | THE RESULTS | | | | | | | |
|---|---|---|---|---|---|---|---|---|---|---|---|---|---|---|---|---|---|---|---|---|---|---|---|---|---|---|---|
| Year | Team | Lg | G | GS | CG | GF | IP | BFP | H | R | ER | HR | SH | SF | HB | TBB | IBB | SO | WP | Bk | W | L | Pct | Sh | Sv-Op | Hld | ERC | ERA |
| 2009 | Hi Dsrt | A+ | 29 | 0 | 0 | 21 | 33.1 | 137 | 24 | 14 | 12 | 3 | 0 | 0 | 2 | 12 | 0 | 35 | 5 | 0 | 1 | 2 | .333 | 0 | 12-- | - | 2.58 | 3.24 |
| 2009 | WTenn | AA | 15 | 0 | 0 | 11 | 17.2 | 88 | 21 | 15 | 10 | 1 | 1 | 1 | 3 | 11 | 1 | 24 | 6 | 2 | 1 | 4 | .200 | 0 | 4-- | - | 6.16 | 5.09 |
| 2010 | Rdng | AA | 11 | 11 | 0 | 0 | 49.2 | 240 | 55 | 45 | 41 | 4 | 1 | 1 | 6 | 38 | 0 | 38 | 6 | 1 | 1 | 6 | .143 | 0 | 0-- | - | 6.60 | 7.43 |
| 2010 | Clrwtr | A+ | 16 | 10 | 1 | 2 | 72.1 | 325 | 74 | 41 | 36 | 6 | 0 | 3 | 6 | 42 | 0 | 77 | 11 | 1 | 2 | 5 | .286 | 0 | 1-- | - | 5.24 | 4.48 |
| 2011 | Rdng | AA | 25 | 0 | 0 | 21 | 31.0 | 134 | 23 | 16 | 8 | 2 | 4 | 0 | 1 | 11 | 1 | 41 | 1 | 0 | 1 | 5 | .167 | 0 | 4-- | - | 2.23 | 2.32 |
| 2011 | LV | AAA | 18 | 0 | 0 | 9 | 22.2 | 104 | 21 | 9 | 8 | 0 | 1 | 1 | 2 | 14 | 1 | 37 | 2 | 1 | 1 | 0 | 1.000 | 0 | 3-- | - | 3.94 | 3.18 |
| 2012 | LV | AAA | 41 | 0 | 0 | 26 | 44.1 | 203 | 34 | 23 | 21 | 3 | 1 | 0 | 5 | 34 | 1 | 59 | 15 | 1 | 3 | 1 | .750 | 0 | 15-- | - | 4.30 | 4.26 |
| 2013 | LV | AAA | 32 | 0 | 0 | 12 | 35.2 | 175 | 29 | 16 | 16 | 0 | 2 | 3 | 6 | 38 | 0 | 42 | 13 | 0 | 0 | 2 | .000 | 0 | 2-- | - | 5.44 | 4.04 |
| 2012 | Phi | NL | 18 | 0 | 0 | 3 | 14.2 | 65 | 10 | 6 | 6 | 0 | 2 | 0 | 1 | 9 | 1 | 14 | 2 | 0 | 0 | 1 | .000 | 0 | 2-3 | 5 | 2.50 | 3.68 |
| 2013 | Phi | NL | 22 | 0 | 0 | 8 | 19.1 | 95 | 24 | 11 | 9 | 0 | 0 | 1 | 3 | 13 | 1 | 19 | 2 | 1 | 1 | 3 | .250 | 0 | 0-0 | 1 | 6.34 | 4.19 |
| 2 ML YEARS | | | 40 | 0 | 0 | 11 | 34.0 | 160 | 34 | 17 | 15 | 0 | 2 | 1 | 4 | 22 | 2 | 33 | 4 | 1 | 1 | 4 | .200 | 0 | 2-3 | 6 | 4.54 | 3.97 |

# Alex Avila

**Bats:** L **Throws:** R **Pos:** C-98;PH-4 ah-VEE-lah **Ht:** 5'11" **Wt:** 210 **Born:** 1/29/1987 **Age:** 27

| | | | BATTING | | | | | | | | | | | | | | | | | | BASERUNNING | | | | AVERAGES | | |
|---|---|---|---|---|---|---|---|---|---|---|---|---|---|---|---|---|---|---|---|---|---|---|---|---|---|---|---|
| Year | Team | Lg | G | AB | H | 2B | 3B | HR | (Hm | Rd) | TB | R | RBI | RC | TBB | IBB | SO | HBP | SH | SF | SB | CS | SB% | GDP | Avg | OBP | Slg |
| 2013 | Toledo* | AAA | 12 | 44 | 11 | 3 | 0 | 1 | (- | -) | 17 | 5 | 5 | 6 | 7 | 0 | 12 | 0 | 0 | 0 | 0 | 0 | - | 0 | .250 | .353 | .386 |
| 2009 | Det | AL | 29 | 61 | 17 | 4 | 0 | 5 | (4 | 1) | 36 | 9 | 14 | 12 | 10 | 0 | 18 | 0 | 0 | 1 | 0 | 0 | - | 0 | .279 | .375 | .590 |
| 2010 | Det | AL | 104 | 294 | 67 | 12 | 0 | 7 | (4 | 3) | 100 | 28 | 31 | 26 | 36 | 0 | 71 | 2 | 1 | 0 | 2 | 2 | .50 | 12 | .228 | .316 | .340 |
| 2011 | Det | AL | 141 | 464 | 137 | 33 | 4 | 19 | (10 | 9) | 235 | 63 | 82 | 86 | 73 | 9 | 131 | 3 | 3 | 8 | 3 | 1 | .75 | 8 | .295 | .389 | .506 |
| 2012 | Det | AL | 116 | 367 | 89 | 21 | 2 | 9 | (7 | 2) | 141 | 42 | 48 | 53 | 61 | 2 | 104 | 2 | 2 | 2 | 2 | 0 | 1.00 | 12 | .243 | .352 | .384 |
| 2013 | Det | AL | 102 | 330 | 75 | 14 | 1 | 11 | (7 | 4) | 124 | 39 | 47 | 37 | 44 | 0 | 112 | 1 | 1 | 3 | 0 | 0 | - | 10 | .227 | .317 | .376 |
| Postseason | | | 20 | 70 | 9 | 1 | 0 | 2 | (2 | 0) | 16 | 3 | 3 | 0 | 3 | 0 | 28 | 0 | 1 | 0 | 0 | 0 | - | 1 | .129 | .164 | .229 |
| 5 ML YEARS | | | 492 | 1516 | 385 | 84 | 7 | 51 | (32 | 19) | 636 | 181 | 222 | 214 | 224 | 11 | 436 | 8 | 7 | 14 | 7 | 3 | .70 | 42 | .254 | .350 | .420 |

# Luis Avilan

**Pitches:** L **Bats:** L **Pos:** RP-75 ah-VEE-lan **Ht:** 6'2" **Wt:** 195 **Born:** 7/19/1989 **Age:** 24

| HOW MUCH HE PITCHED | | | | | | | | WHAT HE GAVE UP | | | | | | | | | | | | THE RESULTS | | | | | | | |
|---|---|---|---|---|---|---|---|---|---|---|---|---|---|---|---|---|---|---|---|---|---|---|---|---|---|---|---|
| Year Team | Lg | G | GS | CG | GF | IP | BFP | H | R | ER | HR | SH | SF | HB | TBB | IBB | SO | WP | Bk | W | L | Pct | Sh | Sv-Op | Hld | ERC | ERA |
| 2009 Danvle | R | 14 | 3 | 0 | 7 | 38.1 | 157 | 25 | 14 | 13 | 1 | 1 | 0 | 4 | 17 | 0 | 34 | 0 | 0 | 0 | 2 | .000 | 0 | 2-- | - | 2.34 | 3.05 |
| 2010 Rome | A | 10 | 0 | 0 | 2 | 20.2 | 87 | 15 | 8 | 6 | 1 | 1 | 2 | 1 | 9 | 0 | 21 | 0 | 0 | 2 | 1 | .667 | 0 | 0-- | - | 2.54 | 2.61 |
| 2010 MrtlBh | A+ | 31 | 0 | 0 | 21 | 48.0 | 203 | 42 | 25 | 21 | 5 | 4 | 3 | 3 | 18 | 4 | 37 | 3 | 1 | 4 | 3 | .571 | 0 | 9-- | - | 3.43 | 3.94 |
| 2011 Missi | AA | 36 | 13 | 0 | 5 | 105.1 | 472 | 113 | 66 | 54 | 10 | 4 | 5 | 8 | 36 | 4 | 77 | 5 | 3 | 4 | 8 | .333 | 0 | 1-- | - | 4.36 | 4.61 |
| 2012 Missi | AA | 16 | 12 | 0 | 2 | 61.1 | 260 | 50 | 27 | 22 | 7 | 4 | 1 | 1 | 31 | 0 | 55 | 5 | 0 | 3 | 6 | .333 | 0 | 1-- | - | 3.65 | 3.23 |
| 2012 Atl | NL | 31 | 0 | 0 | 2 | 36.0 | 142 | 27 | 9 | 8 | 1 | 3 | 0 | 1 | 10 | 1 | 33 | 3 | 1 | 1 | 0 | 1.000 | 0 | 0-0 | 5 | 2.00 | 2.00 |
| 2013 Atl | NL | 75 | 0 | 0 | 7 | 65.0 | 256 | 40 | 12 | 11 | 1 | 1 | 1 | 4 | 22 | 2 | 38 | 3 | 1 | 5 | 0 | 1.000 | 0 | 0-2 | 27 | 1.62 | 1.52 |
| 2 ML YEARS | | 106 | 0 | 0 | 9 | 101.0 | 398 | 67 | 21 | 19 | 2 | 4 | 1 | 5 | 32 | 3 | 71 | 6 | 2 | 6 | 0 | 1.000 | 0 | 0-2 | 32 | 1.74 | 1.69 |

# Mike Aviles

uh-VEE-less

**Bats:** R **Throws:** R **Pos:** 3B-56;SS-46;PH-14;2B-12;PR-12;LF-4;DH-2;RF-1 **Ht:** 5'10" **Wt:** 205 **Born:** 3/13/1981 **Age:** 33

| BATTING | | | | | | | | | | | | | | | | | | | | BASERUNNING | | | | AVERAGES | | |
|---|---|---|---|---|---|---|---|---|---|---|---|---|---|---|---|---|---|---|---|---|---|---|---|---|---|---|
| Year Team | Lg | G | AB | H | 2B | 3B | HR | (Hm | Rd) | TB | R | RBI | RC | TBB | IBB | SO | HBP | SH | SF | SB | CS | SB% | GDP | Avg | OBP | Slg |
| 2008 KC | AL | 102 | 419 | 136 | 27 | 4 | 10 | (4 | 6) | 201 | 68 | 51 | 62 | 18 | 4 | 58 | 2 | 0 | 2 | 8 | 3 | .73 | 12 | .325 | .354 | .480 |
| 2009 KC | AL | 36 | 120 | 22 | 3 | 1 | 1 | (1 | 0) | 30 | 10 | 8 | 4 | 4 | 0 | 26 | 0 | 2 | 1 | 1 | 0 | 1.00 | 3 | .183 | .208 | .250 |
| 2010 KC | AL | 110 | 424 | 129 | 16 | 3 | 8 | (4 | 4) | 175 | 63 | 32 | 47 | 20 | 0 | 49 | 1 | 0 | 3 | 14 | 5 | .74 | 13 | .304 | .335 | .413 |
| 2011 2 Tms | AL | 91 | 286 | 73 | 17 | 3 | 7 | (4 | 3) | 117 | 31 | 39 | 31 | 13 | 0 | 44 | 2 | 4 | 4 | 14 | 4 | .78 | 8 | .255 | .289 | .409 |
| 2012 Bos | AL | 136 | 512 | 128 | 28 | 0 | 13 | (7 | 6) | 195 | 57 | 60 | 57 | 23 | 0 | 77 | 2 | 3 | 6 | 14 | 6 | .70 | 6 | .250 | .282 | .381 |
| 2013 Cle | AL | 124 | 361 | 91 | 15 | 0 | 9 | (3 | 6) | 133 | 54 | 46 | 35 | 15 | 0 | 41 | 3 | 7 | 8 | 8 | 5 | .62 | 11 | .252 | .282 | .368 |
| 11 KC | AL | 53 | 185 | 41 | 11 | 3 | 5 | (2 | 3) | 73 | 14 | 31 | 18 | 9 | 0 | 27 | 2 | 3 | 3 | 10 | 2 | .83 | 5 | .222 | .261 | .395 |
| 11 Bos | AL | 38 | 101 | 32 | 6 | 0 | 2 | (2 | 0) | 44 | 17 | 8 | 13 | 4 | 0 | 17 | 0 | 1 | 1 | 4 | 2 | .67 | 3 | .317 | .340 | .436 |
| 6 ML YEARS | | 599 | 2122 | 579 | 106 | 11 | 48 | (23 | 25) | 851 | 283 | 236 | 236 | 93 | 4 | 295 | 10 | 16 | 24 | 59 | 23 | .72 | 53 | .273 | .303 | .401 |

# Dylan Axelrod

**Pitches:** R **Bats:** R **Pos:** SP-20; RP-10 **Ht:** 6'0" **Wt:** 185 **Born:** 7/30/1985 **Age:** 28

| HOW MUCH HE PITCHED | | | | | | | | WHAT HE GAVE UP | | | | | | | | | | | | THE RESULTS | | | | | | | |
|---|---|---|---|---|---|---|---|---|---|---|---|---|---|---|---|---|---|---|---|---|---|---|---|---|---|---|---|
| Year Team | Lg | G | GS | CG | GF | IP | BFP | H | R | ER | HR | SH | SF | HB | TBB | IBB | SO | WP | Bk | W | L | Pct | Sh | Sv-Op | Hld | ERC | ERA |
| 2011 CWS | AL | 4 | 3 | 0 | 1 | 18.2 | 82 | 18 | 6 | 6 | 1 | 0 | 2 | 1 | 9 | 2 | 19 | 0 | 0 | 1 | 0 | 1.000 | 0 | 0-0 | 0 | 3.89 | 2.89 |
| 2012 CWS | AL | 14 | 7 | 0 | 4 | 51.0 | 231 | 56 | 32 | 31 | 8 | 0 | 2 | 4 | 21 | 0 | 40 | 1 | 0 | 2 | 2 | .500 | 0 | 0-0 | 0 | 5.39 | 5.47 |
| 2013 CWS | AL | 30 | 20 | 0 | 8 | 128.1 | 586 | 170 | 89 | 81 | 24 | 2 | 3 | 4 | 43 | 2 | 73 | 5 | 0 | 4 | 11 | .267 | 0 | 0-0 | 0 | 6.55 | 5.68 |
| 3 ML YEARS | | 48 | 30 | 0 | 13 | 198.0 | 899 | 244 | 127 | 118 | 33 | 2 | 7 | 9 | 73 | 4 | 132 | 6 | 0 | 7 | 13 | .350 | 0 | 0-0 | 0 | 5.98 | 5.36 |

# John Axford

**Pitches:** R **Bats:** R **Pos:** RP-75 **Ht:** 6'5" **Wt:** 220 **Born:** 4/1/1983 **Age:** 31

| HOW MUCH HE PITCHED | | | | | | | | WHAT HE GAVE UP | | | | | | | | | | | | THE RESULTS | | | | | | | |
|---|---|---|---|---|---|---|---|---|---|---|---|---|---|---|---|---|---|---|---|---|---|---|---|---|---|---|---|
| Year Team | Lg | G | GS | CG | GF | IP | BFP | H | R | ER | HR | SH | SF | HB | TBB | IBB | SO | WP | Bk | W | L | Pct | Sh | Sv-Op | Hld | ERC | ERA |
| 2009 Mil | NL | 7 | 0 | 0 | 6 | 7.2 | 34 | 5 | 3 | 3 | 0 | 0 | 0 | 0 | 6 | 1 | 9 | 1 | 0 | 0 | 0 | - | 0 | 1-1 | 0 | 2.62 | 3.52 |
| 2010 Mil | NL | 50 | 0 | 0 | 43 | 58.0 | 238 | 42 | 17 | 16 | 1 | 2 | 2 | 1 | 27 | 3 | 76 | 4 | 0 | 8 | 2 | .800 | 0 | 24-27 | 3 | 2.33 | 2.48 |
| 2011 Mil | NL | 74 | 0 | 0 | 63 | 73.2 | 305 | 59 | 19 | 16 | 4 | 1 | 1 | 0 | 25 | 1 | 86 | 8 | 0 | 2 | 2 | .500 | 0 | **46**-48 | 0 | 2.44 | 1.95 |
| 2012 Mil | NL | 75 | 0 | 0 | 54 | 69.1 | 310 | 61 | 42 | 36 | 10 | 1 | 2 | 2 | 39 | 2 | 93 | 10 | 0 | 5 | 8 | .385 | 0 | 35-44 | 3 | 4.33 | 4.67 |
| 2013 2 Tms | NL | 75 | 0 | 0 | 16 | 65.0 | 289 | 73 | 32 | 29 | 10 | 4 | 1 | 2 | 26 | 3 | 65 | 5 | 0 | 7 | 7 | .500 | 0 | 0-7 | 19 | 5.25 | 4.02 |
| 13 Mil | NL | 62 | 0 | 0 | 13 | 54.2 | 245 | 62 | 29 | 27 | 10 | 3 | 1 | 1 | 23 | 3 | 54 | 5 | 0 | 6 | 7 | .462 | 0 | 0-6 | 19 | 5.53 | 4.45 |
| 13 StL | NL | 13 | 0 | 0 | 3 | 10.1 | 44 | 11 | 3 | 2 | 0 | 1 | 0 | 1 | 3 | 0 | 11 | 0 | 0 | 1 | 0 | 1.000 | 0 | 0-1 | 0 | 3.75 | 1.74 |
| Postseason | | 6 | 0 | 0 | 6 | 7.0 | 28 | 5 | 1 | 1 | 0 | 0 | 0 | 0 | 2 | 0 | 9 | 0 | 0 | 1 | 0 | 1.000 | 0 | 3-4 | 0 | 1.62 | 1.29 |
| 5 ML YEARS | | 281 | 0 | 0 | 182 | 273.2 | 1176 | 240 | 113 | 100 | 25 | 8 | 6 | 5 | 123 | 10 | 329 | 28 | 0 | 22 | 19 | .537 | 0 | 106-127 | 25 | 3.51 | 3.29 |

# Luis Ayala

**Pitches:** R **Bats:** R **Pos:** RP-39 eye-YA-lah **Ht:** 6'2" **Wt:** 175 **Born:** 1/12/1978 **Age:** 36

| HOW MUCH HE PITCHED | | | | | | | | WHAT HE GAVE UP | | | | | | | | | | | | THE RESULTS | | | | | | | |
|---|---|---|---|---|---|---|---|---|---|---|---|---|---|---|---|---|---|---|---|---|---|---|---|---|---|---|---|
| Year Team | Lg | G | GS | CG | GF | IP | BFP | H | R | ER | HR | SH | SF | HB | TBB | IBB | SO | WP | Bk | W | L | Pct | Sh | Sv-Op | Hld | ERC | ERA |
| 2013 Gwnntt* | AAA | 8 | 0 | 0 | 0 | 8.1 | 38 | 9 | 6 | 6 | 1 | 0 | 0 | 0 | 5 | 0 | 8 | 0 | 0 | 0 | 1 | .000 | 0 | 0-- | - | 5.53 | 6.48 |
| 2013 Missi* | AA | 3 | 0 | 0 | 0 | 3.0 | 12 | 2 | 0 | 0 | 0 | 0 | 0 | 1 | 0 | 0 | 2 | 0 | 0 | 0 | 0 | - | 0 | 0-- | - | 1.57 | 0.00 |
| 2003 Mon | NL | 65 | 0 | 0 | 24 | 71.0 | 288 | 65 | 27 | 23 | 8 | 3 | 1 | 5 | 13 | 3 | 46 | 1 | 0 | 10 | 3 | .769 | 0 | 5-8 | 19 | 3.11 | 2.92 |
| 2004 Mon | NL | 81 | 0 | 0 | 28 | 90.1 | 367 | 92 | 30 | 27 | 6 | 2 | 2 | 5 | 15 | 2 | 63 | 3 | 1 | 6 | 12 | .333 | 0 | 2-7 | 21 | 3.32 | 2.69 |
| 2005 Was | NL | 68 | 0 | 0 | 18 | 71.0 | 293 | 75 | 23 | 21 | 7 | 8 | 3 | 6 | 14 | 4 | 40 | 0 | 0 | 8 | 7 | .533 | 0 | 1-3 | 22 | 3.95 | 2.66 |
| 2007 Was | NL | 44 | 0 | 0 | 11 | 42.1 | 181 | 43 | 16 | 15 | 5 | 3 | 4 | 1 | 12 | 0 | 28 | 1 | 0 | 2 | 2 | .500 | 0 | 1-2 | 6 | 3.88 | 3.19 |
| 2008 2 Tms | NL | 81 | 0 | 0 | 25 | 75.2 | 335 | 86 | 53 | 48 | 9 | 4 | 3 | 4 | 24 | 4 | 50 | 1 | 0 | 2 | 10 | .167 | 0 | 9-15 | 19 | 4.76 | 5.71 |
| 2009 2 Tms | | 38 | 0 | 0 | 13 | 40.0 | 180 | 50 | 28 | 25 | 5 | 3 | 2 | 4 | 14 | 3 | 28 | 0 | 0 | 1 | 5 | .167 | 0 | 0-4 | 3 | 5.94 | 5.63 |
| 2011 NYY | AL | 52 | 0 | 0 | 20 | 56.0 | 233 | 51 | 17 | 13 | 5 | 4 | 4 | 6 | 20 | 3 | 39 | 2 | 1 | 2 | 2 | .500 | 0 | 0-1 | 4 | 3.80 | 2.09 |
| 2012 Bal | AL | 66 | 0 | 0 | 15 | 75.0 | 320 | 81 | 27 | 22 | 7 | 2 | 2 | 4 | 14 | 3 | 51 | 2 | 0 | 5 | 5 | .500 | 0 | 1-3 | 11 | 3.75 | 2.64 |
| 2013 2 Tms | | 39 | 0 | 0 | 7 | 33.0 | 143 | 38 | 12 | 12 | 2 | 1 | 0 | 0 | 13 | 2 | 22 | 1 | 0 | 2 | 1 | .667 | 0 | 0-3 | 10 | 4.64 | 3.27 |
| 08 Was | NL | 62 | 0 | 0 | 12 | 57.2 | 257 | 63 | 41 | 37 | 6 | 4 | 2 | 4 | 22 | 4 | 36 | 1 | 0 | 1 | 8 | .111 | 0 | 0-4 | 19 | 4.70 | 5.77 |
| 08 NYM | NL | 19 | 0 | 0 | 13 | 18.0 | 78 | 23 | 12 | 11 | 3 | 0 | 1 | 0 | 2 | 0 | 14 | 0 | 0 | 1 | 2 | .333 | 0 | 9-11 | 0 | 4.91 | 5.50 |
| 09 Min | AL | 28 | 0 | 0 | 11 | 32.1 | 138 | 38 | 18 | 15 | 4 | 1 | 2 | 3 | 8 | 0 | 21 | 0 | 0 | 1 | 2 | .333 | 0 | 0-3 | 1 | 5.21 | 4.18 |
| 09 Fla | NL | 10 | 0 | 0 | 2 | 7.2 | 42 | 12 | 10 | 10 | 1 | 2 | 0 | 1 | 6 | 3 | 7 | 0 | 0 | 0 | 3 | .000 | 0 | 0-1 | 2 | 9.04 | 11.74 |
| 13 Bal | AL | 2 | 0 | 0 | 0 | 2.0 | 10 | 4 | 2 | 2 | 1 | 0 | 0 | 0 | 0 | 0 | 2 | 0 | 0 | 1 | 0 | 1.000 | 0 | 0-1 | 0 | 11.88 | 9.00 |
| 13 Atl | NL | 37 | 0 | 0 | 7 | 31.0 | 133 | 34 | 10 | 10 | 1 | 1 | 0 | 0 | 13 | 2 | 20 | 1 | 0 | 1 | 1 | .500 | 0 | 0-2 | 10 | 4.22 | 2.90 |
| Postseason | | 3 | 0 | 0 | 1 | 1.2 | 11 | 5 | 1 | 1 | 0 | 1 | 0 | 1 | 0 | 0 | 1 | 0 | 0 | 0 | 0 | - | 0 | 0-0 | 0 | 17.54 | 5.40 |
| 9 ML YEARS | | 534 | 0 | 0 | 161 | 554.1 | 2340 | 581 | 233 | 206 | 54 | 30 | 21 | 35 | 139 | 24 | 367 | 11 | 2 | 38 | 47 | .447 | 0 | 19-46 | 115 | 3.97 | 3.34 |

# Erick Aybar

**Bats:** B **Throws:** R **Pos:** SS-138 EYE-barr **Ht:** 5'10" **Wt:** 180 **Born:** 1/14/1984 **Age:** 30

| BATTING | | | | | | | | | | | | | | | | | | | | | BASERUNNING | | | | AVERAGES | | |
|---|---|---|---|---|---|---|---|---|---|---|---|---|---|---|---|---|---|---|---|---|---|---|---|---|---|---|---|
| Year Team | Lg | G | AB | H | 2B | 3B | HR | (Hm | Rd) | TB | R | RBI | RC | TBB | IBB | SO | HBP | SH | SF | SB | CS | SB% | GDP | Avg | OBP | Slg |
| 2013 Salt Lk* | AAA | 1 | 5 | 2 | 1 | 0 | 1 | (- | -) | 6 | 1 | 2 | 2 | 0 | 0 | 0 | 0 | 0 | 0 | 0 | 0 | - | 0 | .400 | .400 | 1.200 |
| 2006 LAA | AL | 34 | 40 | 10 | 1 | 1 | 0 | (0 | 0) | 13 | 5 | 2 | 4 | 0 | 0 | 8 | 0 | 0 | 0 | 1 | 0 | 1.00 | 1 | .250 | .250 | .325 |
| 2007 LAA | AL | 79 | 194 | 46 | 5 | 1 | 1 | (0 | 1) | 56 | 18 | 19 | 16 | 10 | 0 | 32 | 2 | 3 | 2 | 4 | 4 | .50 | 8 | .237 | .279 | .289 |
| 2008 LAA | AL | 98 | 346 | 96 | 18 | 5 | 3 | (2 | 1) | 133 | 53 | 39 | 49 | 14 | 0 | 45 | 5 | 9 | 1 | 7 | 2 | .78 | 2 | .277 | .314 | .384 |
| 2009 LAA | AL | 137 | 504 | 157 | 23 | 9 | 5 | (2 | 3) | 213 | 70 | 58 | 73 | 30 | 1 | 54 | 5 | 12 | 5 | 14 | 7 | .67 | 9 | .312 | .353 | .423 |
| 2010 LAA | AL | 138 | 534 | 135 | 18 | 4 | 5 | (3 | 2) | 176 | 69 | 29 | 51 | 35 | 1 | 81 | 7 | 11 | 2 | 22 | 8 | .73 | 7 | .253 | .306 | .330 |
| 2011 LAA | AL | 143 | 556 | 155 | 33 | 8 | 10 | (2 | 8) | 234 | 71 | 59 | 72 | 31 | 1 | 68 | 6 | 9 | 3 | 30 | 6 | .83 | 13 | .279 | .322 | .421 |
| 2012 LAA | AL | 141 | 517 | 150 | 31 | 5 | 8 | (4 | 4) | 215 | 67 | 45 | 63 | 22 | 1 | 61 | 5 | 7 | 2 | 20 | 4 | .83 | 11 | .290 | .324 | .416 |
| 2013 LAA | AL | 138 | 550 | 149 | 33 | 5 | 6 | (4 | 2) | 210 | 68 | 54 | 61 | 23 | 1 | 59 | 3 | 8 | 5 | 12 | 7 | .63 | 14 | .271 | .301 | .382 |
| Postseason | | 14 | 50 | 11 | 2 | 1 | 0 | (0 | 0) | 15 | 4 | 4 | 4 | 1 | 0 | 4 | 0 | 2 | 0 | 3 | 0 | 1.00 | 2 | .220 | .235 | .300 |
| 8 ML YEARS | | 908 | 3241 | 898 | 162 | 38 | 38 | (17 | 21) | 1250 | 421 | 305 | 389 | 165 | 5 | 408 | 33 | 59 | 20 | 110 | 38 | .74 | 65 | .277 | .317 | .386 |

# Burke Badenhop

**Pitches:** R **Bats:** R **Pos:** RP-63 BADE-en-hopp **Ht:** 6'5" **Wt:** 220 **Born:** 2/8/1983 **Age:** 31

| HOW MUCH HE PITCHED | | | | | | | | WHAT HE GAVE UP | | | | | | | | | | | | THE RESULTS | | | | | | | |
|---|---|---|---|---|---|---|---|---|---|---|---|---|---|---|---|---|---|---|---|---|---|---|---|---|---|---|---|
| Year Team | Lg | G | GS | CG | GF | IP | BFP | H | R | ER | HR | SH | SF | HB | TBB | IBB | SO | WP | Bk | W | L | Pct | Sh | Sv-Op | Hld | ERC | ERA |
| 2008 Fla | NL | 13 | 8 | 0 | 2 | 47.1 | 218 | 55 | 34 | 32 | 7 | 2 | 2 | 3 | 21 | 1 | 35 | 2 | 0 | 2 | 3 | .400 | 0 | 0-0 | 0 | 5.74 | 6.08 |
| 2009 Fla | NL | 35 | 2 | 0 | 7 | 72.0 | 303 | 71 | 32 | 30 | 5 | 3 | 2 | 1 | 24 | 4 | 57 | 1 | 0 | 7 | 4 | .636 | 0 | 0-1 | 2 | 3.53 | 3.75 |
| 2010 Fla | NL | 53 | 0 | 0 | 16 | 67.2 | 281 | 62 | 33 | 30 | 5 | 5 | 1 | 2 | 21 | 5 | 47 | 1 | 0 | 2 | 5 | .286 | 0 | 1-3 | 8 | 3.12 | 3.99 |
| 2011 Fla | NL | 50 | 0 | 0 | 15 | 63.2 | 276 | 65 | 29 | 29 | 1 | 1 | 2 | 4 | 24 | 4 | 51 | 4 | 0 | 2 | 3 | .400 | 0 | 1-1 | 5 | 3.65 | 4.10 |
| 2012 TB | AL | 66 | 0 | 0 | 14 | 62.1 | 262 | 63 | 24 | 21 | 6 | 2 | 4 | 1 | 12 | 5 | 42 | 1 | 0 | 3 | 2 | .600 | 0 | 0-0 | 5 | 3.19 | 3.03 |
| 2013 Mil | NL | 63 | 0 | 0 | 23 | 62.1 | 254 | 62 | 32 | 24 | 6 | 7 | 2 | 0 | 12 | 4 | 42 | 2 | 0 | 2 | 3 | .400 | 0 | 1-4 | 5 | 3.16 | 3.47 |
| 6 ML YEARS | | 280 | 10 | 0 | 77 | 375.1 | 1594 | 378 | 184 | 166 | 30 | 20 | 13 | 11 | 114 | 23 | 274 | 11 | 0 | 18 | 20 | .474 | 0 | 3-9 | 25 | 3.62 | 3.98 |

# Andrew Bailey

**Pitches:** R **Bats:** R **Pos:** RP-30 **Ht:** 6'3" **Wt:** 240 **Born:** 5/31/1984 **Age:** 30

| HOW MUCH HE PITCHED | | | | | | | | WHAT HE GAVE UP | | | | | | | | | | | | THE RESULTS | | | | | | | |
|---|---|---|---|---|---|---|---|---|---|---|---|---|---|---|---|---|---|---|---|---|---|---|---|---|---|---|---|
| Year Team | Lg | G | GS | CG | GF | IP | BFP | H | R | ER | HR | SH | SF | HB | TBB | IBB | SO | WP | Bk | W | L | Pct | Sh | Sv-Op | Hld | ERC | ERA |
| 2013 Pwtckt* | AAA | 1 | 0 | 0 | 0 | 1.0 | 5 | 2 | 1 | 1 | 1 | 0 | 0 | 0 | 0 | 0 | 2 | 0 | 0 | 0 | 0 | - | 0 | 0- - | - | 16.28 | 9.00 |
| 2009 Oak | AL | 68 | 0 | 0 | 54 | 83.1 | 323 | 49 | 17 | 17 | 5 | 3 | 2 | 0 | 24 | 3 | 91 | 6 | 0 | 6 | 3 | .667 | 0 | 26-30 | 2 | 1.44 | 1.84 |
| 2010 Oak | AL | 47 | 0 | 0 | 42 | 49.0 | 189 | 34 | 8 | 8 | 3 | 2 | 3 | 0 | 13 | 1 | 42 | 0 | 0 | 1 | 3 | .250 | 0 | 25-28 | 0 | 1.82 | 1.47 |
| 2011 Oak | AL | 42 | 0 | 0 | 37 | 41.2 | 170 | 34 | 18 | 15 | 3 | 1 | 1 | 0 | 12 | 2 | 41 | 0 | 0 | 0 | 4 | .000 | 0 | 24-26 | 1 | 2.42 | 3.24 |
| 2012 Bos | AL | 19 | 0 | 0 | 13 | 15.1 | 74 | 21 | 12 | 12 | 2 | 0 | 0 | 0 | 8 | 2 | 14 | 0 | 1 | 1 | 1 | .500 | 0 | 6-9 | 1 | 6.73 | 7.04 |
| 2013 Bos | AL | 30 | 0 | 0 | 17 | 28.2 | 116 | 23 | 12 | 12 | 7 | 1 | 0 | 0 | 12 | 0 | 39 | 0 | 0 | 3 | 1 | .750 | 0 | 8-13 | 8 | 4.13 | 3.77 |
| 5 ML YEARS | | 206 | 0 | 0 | 163 | 218.0 | 872 | 161 | 67 | 64 | 20 | 7 | 6 | 0 | 69 | 8 | 227 | 6 | 1 | 11 | 12 | .478 | 0 | 89-106 | 12 | 2.30 | 2.64 |

# Homer Bailey

**Pitches:** R **Bats:** R **Pos:** SP-32 **Ht:** 6'4" **Wt:** 230 **Born:** 5/3/1986 **Age:** 28

| HOW MUCH HE PITCHED | | | | | | | | WHAT HE GAVE UP | | | | | | | | | | | | THE RESULTS | | | | | | | |
|---|---|---|---|---|---|---|---|---|---|---|---|---|---|---|---|---|---|---|---|---|---|---|---|---|---|---|---|
| Year Team | Lg | G | GS | CG | GF | IP | BFP | H | R | ER | HR | SH | SF | HB | TBB | IBB | SO | WP | Bk | W | L | Pct | Sh | Sv-Op | Hld | ERC | ERA |
| 2007 Cin | NL | 9 | 9 | 0 | 0 | 45.1 | 205 | 43 | 32 | 29 | 3 | 1 | 6 | 3 | 28 | 1 | 28 | 1 | 1 | 4 | 2 | .667 | 0 | 0-0 | 0 | 4.61 | 5.76 |
| 2008 Cin | NL | 8 | 8 | 0 | 0 | 36.1 | 180 | 59 | 36 | 32 | 8 | 5 | 2 | 0 | 17 | 1 | 18 | 4 | 1 | 0 | 6 | .000 | 0 | 0-0 | 0 | 9.31 | 7.93 |
| 2009 Cin | NL | 20 | 20 | 0 | 0 | 113.1 | 496 | 115 | 61 | 57 | 12 | 4 | 4 | 3 | 52 | 1 | 86 | 6 | 0 | 8 | 5 | .615 | 0 | 0-0 | 0 | 4.56 | 4.53 |
| 2010 Cin | NL | 19 | 19 | 1 | 0 | 109.0 | 465 | 109 | 55 | 54 | 11 | 2 | 1 | 3 | 40 | 6 | 100 | 3 | 1 | 4 | 3 | .571 | 1 | 0-0 | 0 | 4.01 | 4.46 |
| 2011 Cin | NL | 22 | 22 | 0 | 0 | 132.0 | 561 | 136 | 68 | 65 | 18 | 4 | 4 | 5 | 33 | 2 | 106 | 4 | 0 | 9 | 7 | .563 | 0 | 0-0 | 0 | 4.01 | 4.43 |
| 2012 Cin | NL | 33 | **33** | 2 | 0 | 208.0 | 874 | 206 | 97 | 85 | 26 | 5 | 5 | 8 | 52 | 3 | 168 | 3 | 0 | 13 | 10 | .565 | 1 | 0-0 | 0 | 3.73 | 3.68 |
| 2013 Cin | NL | 32 | 32 | 2 | 0 | 209.0 | 849 | 181 | 85 | 81 | 20 | 8 | 4 | 10 | 54 | 2 | 199 | 5 | 2 | 11 | 12 | .478 | 1 | 0-0 | 0 | 2.99 | 3.49 |
| Postseason | | 2 | 1 | 0 | 0 | 9.0 | 32 | 3 | 1 | 1 | 0 | 1 | 1 | 1 | 1 | 0 | 12 | 0 | 0 | 0 | 0 | - | 0 | 0-0 | 0 | 0.52 | 1.00 |
| 7 ML YEARS | | 143 | 143 | 5 | 0 | 853.0 | 3630 | 849 | 434 | 403 | 98 | 29 | 26 | 32 | 276 | 16 | 705 | 26 | 5 | 49 | 45 | .521 | 3 | 0-0 | 0 | 3.98 | 4.25 |

# Jeff Baker

**Bats:** R **Throws:** R **Pos:** PH-26;1B-21;LF-21;DH-11;3B-10;2B-1;RF-1;PR-1 **Ht:** 6'2" **Wt:** 210 **Born:** 6/21/1981 **Age:** 33

| BATTING | | | | | | | | | | | | | | | | | | | | | BASERUNNING | | | | AVERAGES | | |
|---|---|---|---|---|---|---|---|---|---|---|---|---|---|---|---|---|---|---|---|---|---|---|---|---|---|---|---|
| Year Team | Lg | G | AB | H | 2B | 3B | HR | (Hm | Rd) | TB | R | RBI | RC | TBB | IBB | SO | HBP | SH | SF | SB | CS | SB% | GDP | Avg | OBP | Slg |
| 2013 Frisco* | AA | 3 | 11 | 2 | 0 | 0 | 0 | (- | -) | 2 | 0 | 0 | 0 | 0 | 0 | 2 | 0 | 0 | 0 | 0 | 0 | - | 0 | .182 | .182 | .182 |
| 2005 Col | NL | 12 | 38 | 8 | 4 | 0 | 1 | (1 | 0) | 15 | 6 | 4 | 4 | 5 | 0 | 12 | 0 | 0 | 0 | 0 | 0 | - | 1 | .211 | .302 | .395 |
| 2006 Col | NL | 18 | 57 | 21 | 7 | 2 | 5 | (4 | 1) | 47 | 13 | 21 | 17 | 1 | 0 | 14 | 0 | 0 | 0 | 2 | 0 | 1.00 | 0 | .368 | .379 | .825 |
| 2007 Col | NL | 85 | 144 | 32 | 2 | 2 | 4 | (4 | 0) | 50 | 17 | 12 | 8 | 13 | 1 | 40 | 2 | 0 | 0 | 0 | 0 | - | 7 | .222 | .296 | .347 |
| 2008 Col | NL | 104 | 299 | 80 | 22 | 1 | 12 | (8 | 4) | 140 | 55 | 48 | 40 | 26 | 2 | 85 | 1 | 1 | 6 | 4 | 0 | 1.00 | 5 | .268 | .322 | .468 |
| 2009 2 Tms | NL | 81 | 226 | 65 | 15 | 2 | 4 | (3 | 1) | 96 | 27 | 24 | 28 | 18 | 0 | 53 | 2 | 0 | 2 | 1 | 0 | 1.00 | 8 | .288 | .343 | .425 |
| 2010 ChC | NL | 79 | 206 | 56 | 13 | 2 | 4 | (3 | 1) | 85 | 29 | 21 | 21 | 16 | 0 | 50 | 1 | 0 | 1 | 1 | 0 | 1.00 | 6 | .272 | .326 | .413 |
| 2011 ChC | NL | 81 | 201 | 54 | 12 | 1 | 3 | (1 | 2) | 77 | 20 | 23 | 20 | 10 | 0 | 46 | 0 | 0 | 1 | 0 | 0 | - | 8 | .269 | .302 | .383 |
| 2012 3 Tms | | 83 | 188 | 45 | 12 | 1 | 4 | (1 | 3) | 71 | 18 | 25 | 18 | 11 | 1 | 48 | 0 | 0 | 2 | 4 | 1 | .80 | 7 | .239 | .279 | .378 |
| 2013 Tex | AL | 74 | 154 | 43 | 8 | 0 | 11 | (4 | 7) | 84 | 21 | 21 | 26 | 18 | 1 | 48 | 2 | 0 | 1 | 1 | 0 | 1.00 | 5 | .279 | .360 | .545 |
| 09 Col | NL | 12 | 23 | 3 | 0 | 1 | 0 | (0 | 0) | 5 | 0 | 3 | 0 | 1 | 0 | 7 | 0 | 0 | 0 | 1 | 0 | 1.00 | 3 | .130 | .167 | .217 |
| 09 ChC | NL | 69 | 203 | 62 | 15 | 1 | 4 | (3 | 1) | 91 | 27 | 21 | 28 | 17 | 0 | 46 | 2 | 0 | 2 | 0 | 0 | - | 5 | .305 | .362 | .448 |
| 12 ChC | NL | 54 | 134 | 36 | 10 | 1 | 4 | (1 | 3) | 60 | 16 | 20 | 17 | 8 | 0 | 28 | 0 | 0 | 2 | 4 | 1 | .80 | 4 | .269 | .306 | .448 |
| 12 Det | AL | 15 | 35 | 7 | 2 | 0 | 0 | (0 | 0) | 9 | 1 | 4 | 1 | 2 | 0 | 10 | 0 | 0 | 0 | 0 | 0 | - | 3 | .200 | .243 | .257 |
| 12 Atl | NL | 14 | 19 | 2 | 0 | 0 | 0 | (0 | 0) | 2 | 1 | 1 | 0 | 1 | 1 | 10 | 0 | 0 | 0 | 0 | 0 | - | 0 | .105 | .150 | .105 |
| Postseason | | 4 | 4 | 2 | 0 | 0 | 0 | (0 | 0) | 2 | 0 | 1 | 1 | 0 | 0 | 1 | 0 | 0 | 0 | 0 | 0 | - | 0 | .500 | .500 | .500 |
| 9 ML YEARS | | 617 | 1513 | 404 | 95 | 11 | 48 | (29 | 19) | 665 | 206 | 199 | 182 | 118 | 5 | 396 | 8 | 1 | 13 | 13 | 1 | .93 | 47 | .267 | .321 | .440 |

# John Baker

**Bats:** L **Throws:** R **Pos:** C-14;PH-3 **Ht:** 6'1" **Wt:** 215 **Born:** 1/20/1981 **Age:** 33

| BATTING | | | | | | | | | | | | | | | | | | | | | BASERUNNING | | | | AVERAGES | | |
|---|---|---|---|---|---|---|---|---|---|---|---|---|---|---|---|---|---|---|---|---|---|---|---|---|---|---|---|
| Year Team | Lg | G | AB | H | 2B | 3B | HR | (Hm | Rd) | TB | R | RBI | RC | TBB | IBB | SO | HBP | SH | SF | SB | CS | SB% | GDP | Avg | OBP | Slg |
| 2013 Tucsn* | AAA | 4 | 13 | 3 | 0 | 0 | 0 | (- | -) | 3 | 2 | 1 | 1 | 2 | 0 | 5 | 1 | 0 | 0 | 0 | 0 | - | 0 | .231 | .375 | .231 |
| 2013 Albq* | AAA | 40 | 133 | 27 | 1 | 0 | 4 | (- | -) | 40 | 14 | 17 | 12 | 18 | 0 | 33 | 0 | 0 | 2 | 0 | 1 | .00 | 0 | .203 | .294 | .301 |
| 2008 Fla | NL | 61 | 197 | 59 | 14 | 0 | 5 | (3 | 2) | 88 | 32 | 32 | 36 | 30 | 4 | 48 | 2 | 1 | 3 | 0 | 0 | - | 6 | .299 | .392 | .447 |
| 2009 Fla | NL | 112 | 373 | 101 | 25 | 0 | 9 | (3 | 6) | 153 | 59 | 50 | 54 | 41 | 5 | 89 | 5 | 2 | 2 | 0 | 0 | - | 10 | .271 | .349 | .410 |
| 2010 Fla | NL | 23 | 78 | 17 | 3 | 1 | 0 | (0 | 0) | 22 | 7 | 6 | 4 | 9 | 1 | 18 | 1 | 0 | 0 | 0 | 0 | - | 5 | .218 | .307 | .282 |
| 2011 Fla | NL | 16 | 13 | 2 | 0 | 0 | 0 | (0 | 0) | 2 | 0 | 1 | 0 | 2 | 0 | 3 | 0 | 1 | 0 | 0 | 0 | - | 0 | .154 | .267 | .154 |
| 2012 SD | NL | 63 | 193 | 46 | 8 | 0 | 0 | (0 | 0) | 54 | 17 | 14 | 19 | 20 | 2 | 41 | 0 | 1 | 0 | 2 | 1 | .67 | 4 | .238 | .310 | .280 |
| 2013 SD | NL | 16 | 40 | 6 | 0 | 0 | 0 | (0 | 0) | 6 | 0 | 2 | 0 | 6 | 0 | 12 | 0 | 0 | 0 | 0 | 0 | - | 4 | .150 | .261 | .150 |
| 6 ML YEARS | | 291 | 894 | 231 | 50 | 1 | 14 | (6 | 8) | 325 | 115 | 105 | 113 | 108 | 12 | 211 | 8 | 5 | 5 | 2 | 1 | .67 | 29 | .258 | .342 | .364 |

# Scott Baker

**Pitches:** R **Bats:** R **Pos:** SP-3 **Ht:** 6'4" **Wt:** 215 **Born:** 9/19/1981 **Age:** 32

| HOW MUCH HE PITCHED | | | | | | | | WHAT HE GAVE UP | | | | | | | | | | | | THE RESULTS | | | | | | | |
|---|---|---|---|---|---|---|---|---|---|---|---|---|---|---|---|---|---|---|---|---|---|---|---|---|---|---|---|
| Year Team | Lg | G | GS | CG | GF | IP | BFP | H | R | ER | HR | SH | SF | HB | TBB | IBB | SO | WP | Bk | W | L | Pct | Sh | Sv-Op | Hld | ERC | ERA |
| 2013 Kane* | A | 6 | 6 | 0 | 0 | 23.1 | 103 | 29 | 16 | 16 | 4 | 1 | 0 | 0 | 8 | 0 | 14 | 0 | 0 | 1 | 2 | .333 | 0 | 0- - | - | 5.90 | 6.17 |
| 2013 Dytona* | A+ | 2 | 2 | 0 | 0 | 6.1 | 26 | 6 | 3 | 2 | 2 | 0 | 0 | 0 | 2 | 0 | 2 | 0 | 0 | 0 | 1 | .000 | 0 | 0- - | - | 5.00 | 2.84 |
| 2005 Min | AL | 10 | 9 | 0 | 0 | 53.2 | 217 | 48 | 21 | 20 | 5 | 2 | 2 | 0 | 14 | 0 | 32 | 0 | 0 | 3 | 3 | .500 | 0 | 0-0 | 1 | 2.97 | 3.35 |
| 2006 Min | AL | 16 | 16 | 0 | 0 | 83.1 | 377 | 114 | 63 | 59 | 17 | 2 | 4 | 3 | 16 | 1 | 62 | 0 | 0 | 5 | 8 | .385 | 0 | 0-0 | 0 | 6.26 | 6.37 |
| 2007 Min | AL | 24 | 23 | 2 | 0 | 143.2 | 606 | 162 | 70 | 68 | 15 | 6 | 2 | 5 | 29 | 4 | 102 | 0 | 0 | 9 | 9 | .500 | 1 | 0-0 | 1 | 4.19 | 4.26 |
| 2008 Min | AL | 28 | 28 | 0 | 0 | 172.1 | 703 | 161 | 66 | 66 | 20 | 2 | 3 | 3 | 42 | 2 | 141 | 6 | 0 | 11 | 4 | .733 | 0 | 0-0 | 0 | 3.31 | 3.45 |
| 2009 Min | AL | 33 | 33 | 1 | 0 | 200.0 | 828 | 190 | 99 | 97 | 28 | 1 | 6 | 4 | 48 | 1 | 162 | 4 | 0 | 15 | 9 | .625 | 1 | 0-0 | 0 | 3.51 | 4.37 |
| 2010 Min | AL | 29 | 29 | 0 | 0 | 170.1 | 725 | 186 | 87 | 85 | 23 | 1 | 4 | 6 | 43 | 0 | 148 | 7 | 0 | 12 | 9 | .571 | 0 | 0-0 | 0 | 4.43 | 4.49 |
| 2011 Min | AL | 23 | 21 | 1 | 2 | 134.2 | 548 | 126 | 50 | 47 | 15 | 1 | 2 | 4 | 32 | 2 | 123 | 4 | 0 | 8 | 6 | .571 | 0 | 0-0 | 0 | 3.32 | 3.14 |
| 2013 ChC | NL | 3 | 3 | 0 | 0 | 15.0 | 57 | 9 | 6 | 6 | 3 | 1 | 0 | 0 | 4 | 0 | 6 | 0 | 0 | 0 | 0 | - | 0 | 0-0 | 0 | 2.13 | 3.60 |
| Postseason | | 1 | 0 | 0 | 0 | 2.1 | 10 | 3 | 1 | 1 | 1 | 0 | 0 | 0 | 0 | 0 | 2 | 0 | 0 | 0 | 0 | - | 0 | 0-0 | 0 | 6.14 | 3.86 |
| 8 ML YEARS | | 166 | 162 | 4 | 2 | 973.0 | 4061 | 996 | 462 | 448 | 126 | 16 | 23 | 25 | 228 | 10 | 776 | 21 | 0 | 63 | 48 | .568 | 2 | 0-0 | 2 | 3.87 | 4.14 |

# Grant Balfour

**Pitches:** R **Bats:** R **Pos:** RP-65 BAL-fore **Ht:** 6'2" **Wt:** 200 **Born:** 12/30/1977 **Age:** 36

| HOW MUCH HE PITCHED | | | | | | | | WHAT HE GAVE UP | | | | | | | | | | | | THE RESULTS | | | | | | | |
|---|---|---|---|---|---|---|---|---|---|---|---|---|---|---|---|---|---|---|---|---|---|---|---|---|---|---|---|
| Year Team | Lg | G | GS | CG | GF | IP | BFP | H | R | ER | HR | SH | SF | HB | TBB | IBB | SO | WP | Bk | W | L | Pct | Sh | Sv-Op | Hld | ERC | ERA |
| 2001 Min | AL | 2 | 0 | 0 | 1 | 2.2 | 14 | 3 | 4 | 4 | 2 | 1 | 1 | 0 | 3 | 0 | 2 | 0 | 0 | 0 | 0 | - | 0 | 0-0 | 0 | 13.78 | 13.50 |
| 2003 Min | AL | 17 | 1 | 0 | 6 | 26.0 | 115 | 23 | 12 | 12 | 4 | 2 | 1 | 0 | 14 | 2 | 30 | 0 | 0 | 1 | 0 | 1.000 | 0 | 0-1 | 1 | 4.14 | 4.15 |
| 2004 Min | AL | 36 | 0 | 0 | 14 | 39.1 | 172 | 35 | 19 | 19 | 4 | 2 | 0 | 2 | 21 | 1 | 42 | 3 | 0 | 4 | 1 | .800 | 0 | 0-1 | 4 | 4.16 | 4.35 |
| 2007 2 Tms | | 25 | 0 | 0 | 8 | 24.2 | 121 | 30 | 21 | 21 | 2 | 2 | 3 | 1 | 20 | 0 | 30 | 0 | 0 | 1 | 2 | .333 | 0 | 0-0 | 1 | 7.15 | 7.66 |
| 2008 TB | AL | 51 | 0 | 0 | 12 | 58.1 | 224 | 28 | 10 | 10 | 3 | 1 | 3 | 0 | 24 | 1 | 82 | 2 | 0 | 6 | 2 | .750 | 0 | 4-5 | 14 | 1.38 | 1.54 |
| 2009 TB | AL | 73 | 0 | 0 | 15 | 67.1 | 289 | 59 | 38 | 36 | 6 | 1 | 2 | 2 | 33 | 0 | 69 | 1 | 0 | 5 | 4 | .556 | 0 | 4-9 | 18 | 3.79 | 4.81 |
| 2010 TB | AL | 57 | 0 | 0 | 8 | 55.1 | 222 | 43 | 16 | 14 | 3 | 2 | 4 | 0 | 17 | 2 | 56 | 4 | 1 | 2 | 1 | .667 | 0 | 0-1 | 16 | 2.24 | 2.28 |
| 2011 Oak | AL | 62 | 0 | 0 | 15 | 62.0 | 242 | 44 | 17 | 17 | 8 | 1 | 0 | 0 | 20 | 1 | 59 | 0 | 0 | 5 | 2 | .714 | 0 | 2-7 | 26 | 2.49 | 2.47 |
| 2012 Oak | AL | 75 | 0 | 0 | 34 | 74.2 | 289 | 41 | 21 | 21 | 4 | 0 | 3 | 1 | 28 | 2 | 72 | 2 | 0 | 3 | 2 | .600 | 0 | 24-26 | 15 | 1.55 | 2.53 |
| 2013 Oak | AL | 65 | 0 | 0 | 55 | 62.2 | 262 | 48 | 20 | 18 | 7 | 2 | 0 | 0 | 27 | 2 | 72 | 9 | 0 | 1 | 3 | .250 | 0 | 38-41 | 0 | 2.92 | 2.59 |
| 07 Mil | NL | 3 | 0 | 0 | 2 | 2.2 | 18 | 4 | 6 | 6 | 1 | 1 | 0 | 1 | 4 | 0 | 3 | 0 | 0 | 0 | 2 | .000 | 0 | 0-0 | 0 | 15.83 | 20.25 |
| 07 TB | AL | 22 | 0 | 0 | 6 | 22.0 | 103 | 26 | 15 | 15 | 1 | 1 | 3 | 0 | 16 | 0 | 27 | 0 | 0 | 1 | 0 | 1.000 | 0 | 0-0 | 1 | 6.19 | 6.14 |
| Postseason | | 17 | 0 | 0 | 5 | 16.2 | 73 | 16 | 7 | 7 | 2 | 1 | 1 | 1 | 9 | 4 | 12 | 1 | 0 | 0 | 1 | .000 | 0 | 1-1 | 2 | 4.46 | 3.78 |
| 10 ML YEARS | | 463 | 1 | 0 | 168 | 473.0 | 1950 | 354 | 178 | 172 | 43 | 14 | 17 | 6 | 207 | 11 | 514 | 21 | 1 | 28 | 17 | .622 | 0 | 72-91 | 95 | 2.83 | 3.27 |

# Brandon Bantz

**Bats:** R **Throws:** R **Pos:** C-1 BANTS **Ht:** 6'1" **Wt:** 205 **Born:** 1/7/1987 **Age:** 27

| BATTING | | | | | | | | | | | | | | | | | | | | | BASERUNNING | | | | AVERAGES | | |
|---|---|---|---|---|---|---|---|---|---|---|---|---|---|---|---|---|---|---|---|---|---|---|---|---|---|---|---|
| Year Team | Lg | G | AB | H | 2B | 3B | HR | (Hm | Rd) | TB | R | RBI | RC | TBB | IBB | SO | HBP | SH | SF | SB | CS | SB% | GDP | Avg | OBP | Slg |
| 2009 Pulaski | R | 10 | 26 | 6 | 2 | 0 | 0 | (- | -) | 8 | 6 | 1 | 4 | 6 | 0 | 5 | 3 | 0 | 0 | 0 | 0 | - | 1 | .231 | .429 | .308 |
| 2009 Everett | A- | 19 | 62 | 18 | 8 | 1 | 3 | (- | -) | 37 | 16 | 15 | 14 | 5 | 0 | 8 | 6 | 0 | 0 | 0 | 0 | - | 2 | .290 | .397 | .597 |
| 2010 Clinton | A | 32 | 114 | 26 | 6 | 1 | 1 | (- | -) | 37 | 15 | 18 | 11 | 7 | 0 | 27 | 3 | 0 | 2 | 0 | 0 | - | 2 | .228 | .286 | .325 |
| 2010 WTenn | AA | 24 | 79 | 19 | 6 | 1 | 1 | (- | -) | 30 | 9 | 6 | 9 | 4 | 0 | 17 | 2 | 1 | 0 | 0 | 0 | - | 1 | .241 | .294 | .380 |
| 2011 Jacksn | AA | 83 | 236 | 51 | 9 | 0 | 1 | (- | -) | 63 | 27 | 20 | 23 | 32 | 0 | 55 | 5 | 15 | 1 | 0 | 1 | .00 | 3 | .216 | .321 | .267 |
| 2012 Tacom | AAA | 34 | 109 | 25 | 7 | 0 | 2 | (- | -) | 38 | 11 | 14 | 10 | 5 | 0 | 28 | 1 | 4 | 4 | 1 | 1 | .50 | 3 | .229 | .261 | .349 |
| 2012 Hi Dsrt | A+ | 1 | 3 | 0 | 0 | 0 | 0 | (- | -) | 0 | 0 | 0 | 0 | 1 | 0 | 1 | 0 | 0 | 0 | 0 | 0 | - | 0 | .000 | .250 | .000 |
| 2013 Jacksn | AA | 22 | 69 | 11 | 2 | 0 | 1 | (- | -) | 16 | 5 | 4 | 2 | 4 | 0 | 21 | 0 | 1 | 0 | 1 | 0 | 1.00 | 1 | .159 | .205 | .232 |
| 2013 Tacom | AAA | 37 | 123 | 31 | 2 | 2 | 2 | (- | -) | 43 | 8 | 11 | 13 | 11 | 0 | 27 | 2 | 1 | 0 | 0 | 3 | .00 | 6 | .252 | .324 | .350 |
| 2013 Sea | AL | 1 | 2 | 0 | 0 | 0 | 0 | (0 | 0) | 0 | 0 | 0 | 0 | 0 | 0 | 1 | 0 | 0 | 0 | 0 | 0 | - | 0 | .000 | .000 | .000 |

# Daniel Bard

**Pitches:** R **Bats:** R **Pos:** RP-2 **Ht:** 6'4" **Wt:** 215 **Born:** 6/25/1985 **Age:** 29

| HOW MUCH HE PITCHED | | | | | | | | WHAT HE GAVE UP | | | | | | | | | | | | THE RESULTS | | | | | | | |
|---|---|---|---|---|---|---|---|---|---|---|---|---|---|---|---|---|---|---|---|---|---|---|---|---|---|---|---|
| Year Team | Lg | G | GS | CG | GF | IP | BFP | H | R | ER | HR | SH | SF | HB | TBB | IBB | SO | WP | Bk | W | L | Pct | Sh | Sv-Op | Hld | ERC | ERA |
| 2013 Portlnd* | AA | 13 | 0 | 0 | 0 | 12.2 | 64 | 13 | 11 | 9 | 1 | 1 | 0 | 0 | 17 | 0 | 6 | 8 | 0 | 0 | 1 | .000 | 0 | 0- - | - | 8.26 | 6.39 |
| 2013 RedSx* | R | 2 | 0 | 0 | 0 | 1.2 | 11 | 1 | 2 | 2 | 0 | 0 | 0 | 0 | 6 | 0 | 1 | 2 | 0 | 0 | 0 | - | 0 | 0- - | - | 14.82 | 10.80 |
| 2013 Lowell* | A- | 1 | 0 | 0 | 0 | 1.0 | 6 | 0 | 0 | 0 | 0 | 0 | 0 | 0 | 4 | 0 | 2 | 1 | 0 | 0 | 0 | - | 0 | 0- - | - | 12.88 | 0.00 |
| 2009 Bos | AL | 49 | 0 | 0 | 12 | 49.1 | 212 | 41 | 24 | 20 | 5 | 4 | 3 | 3 | 22 | 3 | 63 | 1 | 1 | 2 | 2 | .500 | 0 | 1-4 | 13 | 3.43 | 3.65 |
| 2010 Bos | AL | 73 | 0 | 0 | 12 | 74.2 | 295 | 45 | 18 | 16 | 6 | 2 | 5 | 2 | 30 | 3 | 76 | 2 | 0 | 1 | 2 | .333 | 0 | 3-10 | **32** | 1.99 | 1.93 |
| 2011 Bos | AL | 70 | 0 | 0 | 10 | 73.0 | 288 | 46 | 29 | 27 | 5 | 5 | 0 | 2 | 24 | 3 | 74 | 2 | 1 | 2 | 9 | .182 | 0 | 1-6 | **34** | 1.80 | 3.33 |

| Year | Team | Lg | G | GS | CG | GF | IP | BFP | H | R | ER | HR | SH | SF | HB | TBB | IBB | SO | WP | Bk | W | L | Pct | Sh | Sv-Op | Hld | ERC | ERA |
|---|---|---|---|---|---|---|---|---|---|---|---|---|---|---|---|---|---|---|---|---|---|---|---|---|---|---|---|---|
| HOW MUCH HE PITCHED | | | | | | | | | WHAT HE GAVE UP | | | | | | | | | | | | THE RESULTS | | | | | | | |
| 2012 | Bos | AL | 17 | 10 | 0 | 2 | 59.1 | 277 | 60 | 42 | 41 | 9 | 2 | 3 | 8 | 43 | 1 | 38 | 1 | 2 | 5 | 6 | .455 | 0 | 0-0 | 0 | 6.55 | 6.22 |
| 2013 | Bos | AL | 2 | 0 | 0 | 1 | 1.0 | 6 | 1 | 1 | 1 | 0 | 0 | 0 | 0 | 2 | 0 | 1 | 0 | 0 | 0 | 0 | - | 0 | 0-0 | 0 | 9.51 | 9.00 |
| Postseason | | | 2 | 0 | 0 | 1 | 3.0 | 8 | 0 | 0 | 0 | 0 | 0 | 0 | 0 | 0 | 0 | 4 | 0 | 0 | 0 | 0 | - | 0 | 0-0 | 1 | 0.00 | 0.00 |
| 5 ML YEARS | | | 211 | 10 | 0 | 37 | 257.1 | 1078 | 193 | 114 | 105 | 25 | 13 | 11 | 15 | 121 | 10 | 252 | 6 | 4 | 10 | 19 | .345 | 0 | 5-20 | 79 | 3.15 | 3.67 |

# Clint Barmes

**Bats:** R **Throws:** R **Pos:** SS-106;PH-4 BAR-mess **Ht:** 6'1" **Wt:** 200 **Born:** 3/6/1979 **Age:** 35

| Year | Team | Lg | G | AB | H | 2B | 3B | HR | (Hm | Rd) | TB | R | RBI | RC | TBB | IBB | SO | HBP | SH | SF | SB | CS | SB% | GDP | Avg | OBP | Slg |
|---|---|---|---|---|---|---|---|---|---|---|---|---|---|---|---|---|---|---|---|---|---|---|---|---|---|---|---|
| BATTING | | | | | | | | | | | | | | | | | | | | | BASERUNNING | | | | AVERAGES | | |
| 2003 | Col | NL | 12 | 25 | 8 | 2 | 0 | 0 | (0 | 0) | 10 | 2 | 2 | 3 | 0 | 0 | 10 | 2 | 0 | 1 | 0 | 0 | - | 0 | .320 | .357 | .400 |
| 2004 | Col | NL | 20 | 71 | 20 | 3 | 1 | 2 | (0 | 2) | 31 | 14 | 10 | 12 | 3 | 0 | 10 | 1 | 2 | 0 | 0 | 1 | .00 | 2 | .282 | .320 | .437 |
| 2005 | Col | NL | 81 | 350 | 101 | 19 | 1 | 10 | (7 | 3) | 152 | 55 | 46 | 49 | 16 | 1 | 36 | 6 | 4 | 1 | 6 | 4 | .60 | 4 | .289 | .330 | .434 |
| 2006 | Col | NL | 131 | 478 | 105 | 26 | 4 | 7 | (3 | 4) | 160 | 57 | 56 | 47 | 22 | 6 | 72 | 9 | 19 | 7 | 5 | 4 | .56 | 2 | .220 | .264 | .335 |
| 2007 | Col | NL | 27 | 37 | 8 | 3 | 0 | 0 | (0 | 0) | 11 | 5 | 1 | 1 | 1 | 1 | 13 | 0 | 1 | 0 | 0 | 0 | - | 1 | .216 | .237 | .297 |
| 2008 | Col | NL | 107 | 393 | 114 | 25 | 6 | 11 | (8 | 3) | 184 | 47 | 44 | 54 | 17 | 0 | 69 | 2 | 4 | 1 | 13 | 4 | .76 | 9 | .290 | .322 | .468 |
| 2009 | Col | NL | 154 | 550 | 135 | 32 | 3 | 23 | (13 | 10) | 242 | 69 | 76 | 63 | 31 | 2 | 121 | 10 | 6 | 7 | 12 | 10 | .55 | 6 | .245 | .294 | .440 |
| 2010 | Col | NL | 133 | 387 | 91 | 21 | 0 | 8 | (4 | 4) | 136 | 43 | 50 | 43 | 35 | 10 | 66 | 5 | 2 | 3 | 3 | 2 | .60 | 5 | .235 | .305 | .351 |
| 2011 | Hou | NL | 123 | 446 | 109 | 27 | 0 | 12 | (5 | 7) | 172 | 47 | 39 | 46 | 38 | 2 | 88 | 7 | 2 | 2 | 3 | 1 | .75 | 9 | .244 | .312 | .386 |
| 2012 | Pit | NL | 144 | 455 | 104 | 16 | 1 | 8 | (3 | 5) | 146 | 34 | 45 | 38 | 20 | 3 | 106 | 8 | 8 | 2 | 0 | 2 | .00 | 9 | .229 | .272 | .321 |
| 2013 | Pit | NL | 108 | 304 | 64 | 15 | 0 | 5 | (1 | 4) | 94 | 22 | 23 | 20 | 14 | 3 | 70 | 2 | 9 | 1 | 0 | 0 | - | 5 | .211 | .249 | .309 |
| Postseason | | | 4 | 14 | 0 | 0 | 0 | 0 | (0 | 0) | 0 | 0 | 0 | 0 | 0 | 0 | 2 | 0 | 1 | 0 | 0 | 0 | - | 0 | .000 | .000 | .000 |
| 11 ML YEARS | | | 1040 | 3496 | 859 | 189 | 16 | 86 | (44 | 42) | 1338 | 395 | 392 | 376 | 197 | 28 | 661 | 52 | 57 | 25 | 42 | 28 | .60 | 52 | .246 | .294 | .383 |

# Brandon Barnes

**Bats:** R **Throws:** R **Pos:** CF-116;RF-13;LF-8;PR-6;PH-5 **Ht:** 6'2" **Wt:** 205 **Born:** 5/15/1986 **Age:** 28

| Year | Team | Lg | G | AB | H | 2B | 3B | HR | (Hm | Rd) | TB | R | RBI | RC | TBB | IBB | SO | HBP | SH | SF | SB | CS | SB% | GDP | Avg | OBP | Slg |
|---|---|---|---|---|---|---|---|---|---|---|---|---|---|---|---|---|---|---|---|---|---|---|---|---|---|---|---|
| BATTING | | | | | | | | | | | | | | | | | | | | | BASERUNNING | | | | AVERAGES | | |
| 2009 | Lxngtn | A | 57 | 197 | 52 | 11 | 3 | 5 | (- | -) | 84 | 23 | 25 | 25 | 10 | 1 | 52 | 4 | 2 | 2 | 3 | 6 | .33 | 3 | .264 | .310 | .426 |
| 2009 | Lancst | A+ | 68 | 266 | 78 | 19 | 3 | 12 | (- | -) | 139 | 51 | 52 | 46 | 15 | 0 | 74 | 5 | 3 | 2 | 1 | 2 | .33 | 5 | .293 | .340 | .523 |
| 2009 | CpChr | AA | 7 | 21 | 2 | 0 | 0 | 1 | (- | -) | 5 | 2 | 1 | 0 | 3 | 0 | 7 | 0 | 0 | 0 | 0 | 0 | - | 0 | .095 | .208 | .238 |
| 2010 | Lancst | A+ | 126 | 491 | 132 | 31 | 5 | 27 | (- | -) | 254 | 81 | 80 | 85 | 37 | 1 | 122 | 5 | 4 | 1 | 14 | 3 | .82 | 6 | .269 | .326 | .517 |
| 2010 | RdRck | AAA | 6 | 21 | 6 | 1 | 0 | 1 | (- | -) | 10 | 2 | 1 | 3 | 1 | 0 | 6 | 0 | 0 | 0 | 1 | 0 | 1.00 | 0 | .286 | .318 | .476 |
| 2011 | CpChr | AA | 54 | 203 | 58 | 13 | 0 | 7 | (- | -) | 92 | 25 | 27 | 31 | 14 | 0 | 42 | 2 | 3 | 2 | 6 | 3 | .67 | 4 | .286 | .335 | .453 |
| 2011 | OKCity | AAA | 71 | 229 | 45 | 13 | 5 | 8 | (- | -) | 92 | 34 | 27 | 29 | 29 | 0 | 69 | 3 | 1 | 1 | 5 | 1 | .83 | 6 | .197 | .294 | .402 |
| 2012 | CpChr | AA | 44 | 164 | 52 | 20 | 0 | 7 | (- | -) | 93 | 30 | 31 | 35 | 14 | 0 | 42 | 3 | 0 | 2 | 7 | 2 | .78 | 8 | .317 | .377 | .567 |
| 2012 | OKCity | AAA | 62 | 235 | 76 | 19 | 1 | 5 | (- | -) | 112 | 51 | 38 | 44 | 23 | 0 | 49 | 1 | 2 | 2 | 14 | 4 | .78 | 4 | .323 | .383 | .477 |
| 2012 | Hou | NL | 43 | 98 | 20 | 3 | 0 | 1 | (0 | 1) | 26 | 8 | 7 | 4 | 5 | 0 | 29 | 1 | 1 | 0 | 1 | 1 | .50 | 1 | .204 | .250 | .265 |
| 2013 | Hou | AL | 136 | 408 | 98 | 17 | 1 | 8 | (7 | 1) | 141 | 46 | 41 | 47 | 21 | 0 | 127 | 8 | 6 | 2 | 11 | 11 | .50 | 5 | .240 | .289 | .346 |
| 2 ML YEARS | | | 179 | 506 | 118 | 20 | 1 | 9 | (7 | 2) | 167 | 54 | 48 | 51 | 26 | 0 | 156 | 9 | 7 | 2 | 12 | 12 | .50 | 6 | .233 | .282 | .330 |

# Scott Barnes

**Pitches:** L **Bats:** L **Pos:** RP-6 **Ht:** 6'4" **Wt:** 200 **Born:** 9/5/1987 **Age:** 26

| Year | Team | Lg | G | GS | CG | GF | IP | BFP | H | R | ER | HR | SH | SF | HB | TBB | IBB | SO | WP | Bk | W | L | Pct | Sh | Sv-Op | Hld | ERC | ERA |
|---|---|---|---|---|---|---|---|---|---|---|---|---|---|---|---|---|---|---|---|---|---|---|---|---|---|---|---|---|
| HOW MUCH HE PITCHED | | | | | | | | | WHAT HE GAVE UP | | | | | | | | | | | | THE RESULTS | | | | | | | |
| 2009 | SnJos | A+ | 18 | 18 | 0 | 0 | 98.0 | 401 | 82 | 36 | 31 | 7 | 1 | 1 | 9 | 29 | 0 | 99 | 5 | 0 | 12 | 3 | .800 | 0 | 0- - | - | 3.01 | 2.85 |
| 2009 | Knstn | A+ | 3 | 3 | 0 | 0 | 12.2 | 56 | 14 | 3 | 3 | 1 | 0 | 0 | 0 | 6 | 0 | 10 | 1 | 0 | 0 | 0 | - | 0 | 0- - | - | 4.88 | 2.13 |
| 2009 | Akron | AA | 6 | 6 | 0 | 0 | 31.2 | 140 | 35 | 22 | 20 | 7 | 2 | 2 | 2 | 14 | 0 | 29 | 3 | 0 | 2 | 2 | .500 | 0 | 0- - | - | 6.19 | 5.68 |
| 2010 | Akron | AA | 26 | 26 | 0 | 0 | 138.0 | 599 | 126 | 90 | 80 | 15 | 2 | 8 | 9 | 58 | 0 | 127 | 1 | 1 | 6 | 11 | .353 | 0 | 0- - | - | 3.96 | 5.22 |
| 2011 | Akron | AA | 2 | 2 | 0 | 0 | 11.0 | 39 | 5 | 2 | 2 | 0 | 1 | 0 | 0 | 2 | 0 | 17 | 0 | 0 | 1 | 0 | 1.000 | 0 | 0- - | - | 0.74 | 1.64 |
| 2011 | Clmbs | AAA | 16 | 15 | 0 | 1 | 88.0 | 372 | 80 | 41 | 36 | 12 | 1 | 0 | 3 | 34 | 0 | 90 | 3 | 1 | 7 | 4 | .636 | 0 | 0- - | - | 3.92 | 3.68 |
| 2012 | Clmbs | AAA | 31 | 3 | 0 | 8 | 52.0 | 220 | 37 | 26 | 23 | 1 | 1 | 3 | 4 | 23 | 0 | 67 | 3 | 0 | 2 | 3 | .400 | 0 | 2- - | - | 2.41 | 3.98 |
| 2013 | Clmbs | AAA | 23 | 0 | 0 | 3 | 27.2 | 130 | 30 | 24 | 24 | 4 | 2 | 2 | 1 | 20 | 0 | 35 | 4 | 0 | 3 | 3 | .500 | 0 | 0- - | - | 6.46 | 7.81 |
| 2013 | Indns | R | 1 | 1 | 0 | 0 | 1.0 | 6 | 3 | 3 | 3 | 1 | 0 | 0 | 0 | 0 | 0 | 0 | 0 | 0 | 0 | 0 | - | 0 | 0- - | - | 25.51 | 27.00 |
| 2012 | Cle | AL | 16 | 0 | 0 | 3 | 19.0 | 82 | 17 | 9 | 9 | 1 | 0 | 0 | 3 | 7 | 0 | 16 | 2 | 0 | 0 | 0 | - | 0 | 0-0 | 1 | 3.66 | 4.26 |
| 2013 | Cle | AL | 6 | 0 | 0 | 4 | 8.2 | 38 | 8 | 7 | 7 | 3 | 0 | 0 | 2 | 3 | 0 | 10 | 1 | 0 | 0 | 1 | .000 | 0 | 1-1 | 0 | 6.21 | 7.27 |
| 2 ML YEARS | | | 22 | 0 | 0 | 7 | 27.2 | 120 | 25 | 16 | 16 | 4 | 0 | 0 | 5 | 10 | 0 | 26 | 3 | 0 | 0 | 1 | .000 | 0 | 1-1 | 1 | 4.44 | 5.20 |

# Darwin Barney

**Bats:** R **Throws:** R **Pos:** 2B-141;PH-1 **Ht:** 5'10" **Wt:** 185 **Born:** 11/8/1985 **Age:** 28

| Year | Team | Lg | G | AB | H | 2B | 3B | HR | (Hm | Rd) | TB | R | RBI | RC | TBB | IBB | SO | HBP | SH | SF | SB | CS | SB% | GDP | Avg | OBP | Slg |
|---|---|---|---|---|---|---|---|---|---|---|---|---|---|---|---|---|---|---|---|---|---|---|---|---|---|---|---|
| BATTING | | | | | | | | | | | | | | | | | | | | | BASERUNNING | | | | AVERAGES | | |
| 2013 | Iowa* | AAA | 3 | 10 | 5 | 1 | 0 | 0 | (- | -) | 6 | 4 | 0 | 3 | 3 | 0 | 3 | 0 | 0 | 0 | 1 | 0 | 1.00 | 0 | .500 | .615 | .600 |
| 2010 | ChC | NL | 30 | 79 | 19 | 4 | 0 | 0 | (0 | 0) | 23 | 12 | 2 | 6 | 6 | 0 | 12 | 0 | 0 | 0 | 0 | 0 | - | 0 | .241 | .294 | .291 |
| 2011 | ChC | NL | 143 | 529 | 146 | 23 | 6 | 2 | (2 | 0) | 187 | 66 | 43 | 60 | 22 | 2 | 67 | 8 | 7 | 4 | 9 | 2 | .82 | 14 | .276 | .313 | .353 |
| 2012 | ChC | NL | 156 | 548 | 139 | 26 | 4 | 7 | (7 | 0) | 194 | 73 | 44 | 60 | 33 | 1 | 58 | 3 | 3 | 1 | 6 | 1 | .86 | 11 | .254 | .299 | .354 |
| 2013 | ChC | NL | 141 | 501 | 104 | 25 | 1 | 7 | (4 | 3) | 152 | 49 | 41 | 30 | 36 | 5 | 64 | 6 | 4 | 6 | 4 | 2 | .67 | 22 | .208 | .266 | .303 |
| 4 ML YEARS | | | 470 | 1657 | 408 | 78 | 11 | 16 | (13 | 3) | 556 | 200 | 130 | 156 | 97 | 8 | 201 | 17 | 14 | 11 | 19 | 5 | .79 | 47 | .246 | .293 | .336 |

## Daric Barton

**Bats:** L **Throws:** R **Pos:** 1B-36;PH-2;PR-1 DARE-ick **Ht:** 6'0" **Wt:** 205 **Born:** 8/16/1985 **Age:** 28

| | | | BATTING | | | | | | | | | | | | | | | | | | | BASERUNNING | | | | AVERAGES | | |
|---|---|---|---|---|---|---|---|---|---|---|---|---|---|---|---|---|---|---|---|---|---|---|---|---|---|---|---|---|
| Year | Team | Lg | G | AB | H | 2B | 3B | HR | (Hm | Rd) | TB | R | RBI | RC | TBB | IBB | SO | HBP | SH | SF | SB | CS | SB% | GDP | Avg | OBP | Slg |
| 2013 | Scrmto* | AAA | 110 | 391 | 116 | 29 | 1 | 7 | (- | -) | 168 | 77 | 69 | 79 | 87 | 0 | 57 | 3 | 1 | 6 | 1 | 2 | .33 | 10 | .297 | .423 | .430 |
| 2007 | Oak | AL | 18 | 72 | 25 | 9 | 0 | 4 | (2 | 2) | 46 | 16 | 8 | 14 | 10 | 0 | 11 | 1 | 0 | 1 | 1 | 0 | 1.00 | 2 | .347 | .429 | .639 |
| 2008 | Oak | AL | 140 | 446 | 101 | 17 | 5 | 9 | (1 | 8) | 155 | 59 | 47 | 56 | 65 | 5 | 99 | 3 | 6 | 3 | 2 | 1 | .67 | 6 | .226 | .327 | .348 |
| 2009 | Oak | AL | 54 | 160 | 43 | 12 | 1 | 3 | (2 | 1) | 66 | 31 | 24 | 28 | 26 | 0 | 25 | 2 | 1 | 3 | 0 | 2 | .00 | 1 | .269 | .372 | .413 |
| 2010 | Oak | AL | 159 | 556 | 152 | 33 | 5 | 10 | (1 | 9) | 225 | 79 | 57 | 92 | **110** | 2 | 102 | 3 | 12 | 5 | 7 | 3 | .70 | 8 | .273 | .393 | .405 |
| 2011 | Oak | AL | 67 | 236 | 50 | 13 | 0 | 0 | (0 | 0) | 63 | 27 | 21 | 24 | 39 | 3 | 47 | 2 | 0 | 3 | 2 | 1 | .67 | 6 | .212 | .325 | .267 |
| 2012 | Oak | AL | 46 | 113 | 23 | 7 | 0 | 1 | (0 | 1) | 33 | 8 | 6 | 14 | 22 | 0 | 32 | 1 | 0 | 0 | 1 | 0 | 1.00 | 1 | .204 | .338 | .292 |
| 2013 | Oak | AL | 37 | 104 | 28 | 2 | 0 | 3 | (2 | 1) | 39 | 15 | 16 | 19 | 13 | 0 | 18 | 1 | 0 | 2 | 0 | 0 | - | 1 | .269 | .350 | .375 |
| 7 ML YEARS | | | 521 | 1687 | 422 | 93 | 11 | 30 | (8 | 22) | 627 | 235 | 179 | 247 | 285 | 10 | 334 | 13 | 19 | 17 | 13 | 7 | .65 | 25 | .250 | .360 | .372 |

## Anthony Bass

**Pitches:** R **Bats:** R **Pos:** RP-24 **Ht:** 6'2" **Wt:** 195 **Born:** 11/1/1987 **Age:** 26

| | | | HOW MUCH HE PITCHED | | | | | | WHAT HE GAVE UP | | | | | | | | | | | | THE RESULTS | | | | | | | |
|---|---|---|---|---|---|---|---|---|---|---|---|---|---|---|---|---|---|---|---|---|---|---|---|---|---|---|---|---|
| Year | Team | Lg | G | GS | CG | GF | IP | BFP | H | R | ER | HR | SH | SF | HB | TBB | IBB | SO | WP | Bk | W | L | Pct | Sh | Sv-Op | Hld | ERC | ERA |
| 2013 | Tucsn* | AAA | 15 | 15 | 0 | 0 | 79.1 | 350 | 108 | 51 | 48 | 11 | 1 | 5 | 1 | 17 | 0 | 60 | 2 | 0 | 4 | 6 | .400 | 0 | 0- - | - | 5.88 | 5.45 |
| 2011 | SD | NL | 27 | 3 | 0 | 6 | 48.1 | 198 | 41 | 9 | 9 | 3 | 2 | 0 | 1 | 21 | 1 | 24 | 1 | 0 | 2 | 0 | 1.000 | 0 | 0-0 | 4 | 3.28 | 1.68 |
| 2012 | SD | NL | 24 | 15 | 1 | 3 | 97.0 | 411 | 89 | 59 | 51 | 10 | 2 | 2 | 1 | 39 | 3 | 80 | 5 | 1 | 2 | 8 | .200 | 0 | 1-1 | 1 | 3.65 | 4.73 |
| 2013 | SD | NL | 24 | 0 | 0 | 9 | 42.0 | 193 | 51 | 26 | 25 | 4 | 1 | 0 | 0 | 20 | 4 | 31 | 5 | 0 | 0 | 0 | - | 0 | 0-0 | 0 | 5.41 | 5.36 |
| 3 ML YEARS | | | 75 | 18 | 1 | 18 | 187.1 | 802 | 181 | 94 | 85 | 17 | 5 | 2 | 2 | 80 | 8 | 135 | 11 | 1 | 4 | 8 | .333 | 0 | 1-1 | 5 | 3.93 | 4.08 |

## Antonio Bastardo

**Pitches:** L **Bats:** R **Pos:** RP-48 bah-STAHR-doh **Ht:** 5'11" **Wt:** 200 **Born:** 9/21/1985 **Age:** 28

| | | | HOW MUCH HE PITCHED | | | | | | WHAT HE GAVE UP | | | | | | | | | | | | THE RESULTS | | | | | | | |
|---|---|---|---|---|---|---|---|---|---|---|---|---|---|---|---|---|---|---|---|---|---|---|---|---|---|---|---|---|
| Year | Team | Lg | G | GS | CG | GF | IP | BFP | H | R | ER | HR | SH | SF | HB | TBB | IBB | SO | WP | Bk | W | L | Pct | Sh | Sv-Op | Hld | ERC | ERA |
| 2009 | Phi | NL | 6 | 5 | 0 | 0 | 23.2 | 106 | 26 | 18 | 17 | 4 | 0 | 0 | 2 | 9 | 0 | 19 | 0 | 0 | 2 | 3 | .400 | 0 | 0-0 | 0 | 5.41 | 6.46 |
| 2010 | Phi | NL | 25 | 0 | 0 | 2 | 18.2 | 86 | 19 | 9 | 9 | 1 | 0 | 0 | 2 | 9 | 0 | 26 | 0 | 0 | 2 | 0 | 1.000 | 0 | 0-1 | 2 | 4.46 | 4.34 |
| 2011 | Phi | NL | 64 | 0 | 0 | 15 | 58.0 | 225 | 28 | 17 | 17 | 6 | 2 | 2 | 0 | 26 | 0 | 70 | 4 | 0 | 6 | 1 | .857 | 0 | 8-9 | 17 | 1.69 | 2.64 |
| 2012 | Phi | NL | 65 | 0 | 0 | 10 | 52.0 | 224 | 40 | 26 | 25 | 7 | 1 | 2 | 2 | 26 | 3 | 81 | 5 | 0 | 2 | 5 | .286 | 0 | 1-5 | 26 | 3.42 | 4.33 |
| 2013 | Phi | NL | 48 | 0 | 0 | 15 | 42.2 | 179 | 33 | 12 | 11 | 2 | 4 | 1 | 1 | 21 | 1 | 47 | 4 | 0 | 3 | 2 | .600 | 0 | 2-5 | 14 | 2.91 | 2.32 |
| Postseason | | | 5 | 0 | 0 | 0 | 1.2 | 8 | 2 | 0 | 0 | 0 | 1 | 0 | 0 | 1 | 0 | 2 | 0 | 0 | 0 | 0 | - | 0 | 0-0 | 1 | 5.10 | 0.00 |
| 5 ML YEARS | | | 208 | 5 | 0 | 42 | 195.0 | 820 | 146 | 82 | 79 | 20 | 7 | 5 | 7 | 91 | 4 | 243 | 13 | 0 | 15 | 11 | .577 | 0 | 11-20 | 59 | 3.07 | 3.65 |

## Trevor Bauer

**Pitches:** R **Bats:** R **Pos:** SP-4 **Ht:** 6'1" **Wt:** 190 **Born:** 1/17/1991 **Age:** 23

| | | | HOW MUCH HE PITCHED | | | | | | WHAT HE GAVE UP | | | | | | | | | | | | THE RESULTS | | | | | | | |
|---|---|---|---|---|---|---|---|---|---|---|---|---|---|---|---|---|---|---|---|---|---|---|---|---|---|---|---|---|
| Year | Team | Lg | G | GS | CG | GF | IP | BFP | H | R | ER | HR | SH | SF | HB | TBB | IBB | SO | WP | Bk | W | L | Pct | Sh | Sv-Op | Hld | ERC | ERA |
| 2011 | Visalia | A+ | 3 | 3 | 0 | 0 | 9.0 | 39 | 7 | 3 | 3 | 1 | 0 | 0 | 0 | 4 | 0 | 17 | 1 | 0 | 0 | 1 | .000 | 0 | 0- - | - | 2.97 | 3.00 |
| 2011 | Mobile | AA | 4 | 4 | 0 | 0 | 16.2 | 80 | 20 | 14 | 14 | 2 | 0 | 0 | 2 | 8 | 0 | 26 | 5 | 0 | 1 | 1 | .500 | 0 | 0- - | - | 6.09 | 7.56 |
| 2012 | Mobile | AA | 8 | 8 | 0 | 0 | 48.1 | 201 | 33 | 12 | 9 | 1 | 1 | 0 | 2 | 26 | 0 | 60 | 8 | 0 | 7 | 1 | .875 | 0 | 0- - | - | 2.55 | 1.68 |
| 2012 | Reno | AAA | 14 | 14 | 1 | 0 | 82.0 | 347 | 74 | 28 | 26 | 8 | 3 | 2 | 0 | 35 | 0 | 97 | 12 | 0 | 5 | 1 | .833 | 0 | 0- - | - | 3.64 | 2.85 |
| 2013 | Clmbs | AAA | 22 | 22 | 1 | 0 | 121.1 | 548 | 119 | 64 | 56 | 14 | 8 | 6 | 13 | 73 | 0 | 106 | 5 | 1 | 6 | 7 | .462 | 0 | 0- - | - | 5.41 | 4.15 |
| 2012 | Ari | NL | 4 | 4 | 0 | 0 | 16.1 | 77 | 14 | 13 | 11 | 2 | 1 | 1 | 1 | 13 | 0 | 17 | 2 | 0 | 1 | 2 | .333 | 0 | 0-0 | 0 | 5.12 | 6.06 |
| 2013 | Cle | AL | 4 | 4 | 0 | 0 | 17.0 | 81 | 15 | 11 | 10 | 3 | 0 | 1 | 1 | 16 | 0 | 11 | 1 | 0 | 1 | 2 | .333 | 0 | 0-0 | 0 | 6.47 | 5.29 |
| 2 ML YEARS | | | 8 | 8 | 0 | 0 | 33.1 | 158 | 29 | 24 | 21 | 5 | 1 | 2 | 2 | 29 | 0 | 28 | 3 | 0 | 2 | 4 | .333 | 0 | 0-0 | 0 | 5.79 | 5.67 |

## Jose Bautista

**Bats:** R **Throws:** R **Pos:** RF-109;DH-7;3B-3;1B-1 bah-TEE-stah **Ht:** 6'0" **Wt:** 190 **Born:** 10/19/1980 **Age:** 33

| | | | BATTING | | | | | | | | | | | | | | | | | | | BASERUNNING | | | | AVERAGES | | |
|---|---|---|---|---|---|---|---|---|---|---|---|---|---|---|---|---|---|---|---|---|---|---|---|---|---|---|---|---|
| Year | Team | Lg | G | AB | H | 2B | 3B | HR | (Hm | Rd) | TB | R | RBI | RC | TBB | IBB | SO | HBP | SH | SF | SB | CS | SB% | GDP | Avg | OBP | Slg |
| 2004 | 4 Tms | | 64 | 88 | 18 | 3 | 0 | 0 | (0 | 0) | 21 | 6 | 2 | 2 | 7 | 0 | 40 | 0 | 1 | 0 | 0 | 1 | .00 | 1 | .205 | .263 | .239 |
| 2005 | Pit | NL | 11 | 28 | 4 | 1 | 0 | 0 | (0 | 0) | 5 | 3 | 1 | 0 | 3 | 0 | 7 | 0 | 0 | 0 | 1 | 0 | 1.00 | 2 | .143 | .226 | .179 |
| 2006 | Pit | NL | 117 | 400 | 94 | 20 | 3 | 16 | (11 | 5) | 168 | 58 | 51 | 55 | 46 | 2 | 110 | 16 | 3 | 4 | 2 | 4 | .33 | 12 | .235 | .335 | .420 |
| 2007 | Pit | NL | 142 | 532 | 135 | 36 | 2 | 15 | (8 | 7) | 220 | 75 | 63 | 71 | 68 | 1 | 101 | 4 | 4 | 6 | 6 | 3 | .67 | 16 | .254 | .339 | .414 |
| 2008 | 2 Tms | | 128 | 370 | 88 | 17 | 0 | 15 | (5 | 10) | 150 | 45 | 54 | 43 | 40 | 5 | 91 | 2 | 8 | 4 | 1 | 1 | .50 | 12 | .238 | .313 | .405 |
| 2009 | Tor | AL | 113 | 336 | 79 | 13 | 3 | 13 | (5 | 8) | 137 | 54 | 40 | 42 | 56 | 1 | 85 | 4 | 6 | 2 | 4 | 0 | 1.00 | 9 | .235 | .349 | .408 |
| 2010 | Tor | AL | 161 | 569 | 148 | 35 | 3 | **54** | **(33** | **21)** | **351** | 109 | 124 | **132** | 100 | 2 | 116 | 10 | 0 | 4 | 9 | 2 | .82 | 10 | .260 | .378 | .617 |
| 2011 | Tor | AL | 149 | 513 | 155 | 24 | 2 | **43** | (20 | **23)** | 312 | 105 | 103 | 133 | **132** | **24** | 111 | 6 | 0 | 4 | 9 | 5 | .64 | 8 | .302 | .447 | **.608** |
| 2012 | Tor | AL | 92 | 332 | 80 | 14 | 0 | 27 | (11 | 16) | 175 | 64 | 65 | 58 | 59 | 2 | 63 | 4 | 0 | 4 | 5 | 2 | .71 | 11 | .241 | .358 | .527 |
| 2013 | Tor | AL | 118 | 452 | 117 | 24 | 0 | 28 | (14 | 14) | 225 | 82 | 73 | 81 | 69 | 2 | 84 | 3 | 0 | 4 | 7 | 2 | .78 | 13 | .259 | .358 | .498 |
| 04 | Bal | AL | 16 | 11 | 3 | 0 | 0 | 0 | (0 | 0) | 3 | 3 | 0 | 1 | 1 | 0 | 3 | 0 | 0 | 0 | 0 | 0 | - | 0 | .273 | .333 | .273 |
| 04 | TB | AL | 12 | 12 | 2 | 0 | 0 | 0 | (0 | 0) | 2 | 1 | 1 | 0 | 3 | 0 | 7 | 0 | 0 | 0 | 0 | 1 | .00 | 0 | .167 | .333 | .167 |
| 04 | KC | AL | 13 | 25 | 5 | 1 | 0 | 0 | (0 | 0) | 6 | 1 | 1 | 0 | 1 | 0 | 12 | 0 | 0 | 0 | 0 | 0 | - | 0 | .200 | .231 | .240 |
| 04 | Pit | NL | 23 | 40 | 8 | 2 | 0 | 0 | (0 | 0) | 10 | 1 | 0 | 1 | 2 | 0 | 18 | 0 | 1 | 0 | 0 | 0 | - | 1 | .200 | .238 | .250 |
| 08 | Pit | NL | 107 | 314 | 76 | 15 | 0 | 12 | (3 | 9) | 127 | 38 | 44 | 39 | 38 | 4 | 77 | 2 | 6 | 3 | 1 | 1 | .50 | 10 | .242 | .325 | .404 |
| 08 | Tor | AL | 21 | 56 | 12 | 2 | 0 | 3 | (2 | 1) | 23 | 7 | 10 | 4 | 2 | 1 | 14 | 0 | 2 | 1 | 0 | 0 | - | 2 | .214 | .237 | .411 |
| 10 ML YEARS | | | 1095 | 3620 | 918 | 187 | 13 | 211 | (107 | 104) | 1764 | 601 | 576 | 617 | 580 | 39 | 808 | 49 | 22 | 32 | 44 | 20 | .69 | 94 | .254 | .361 | .487 |

# Mike Baxter

**Bats:** L **Throws:** R **Pos:** PH-36;RF-30;LF-17 **Ht:** 6'0" **Wt:** 195 **Born:** 12/7/1984 **Age:** 29

| BATTING | | | | | | | | | | | | | | | | | | | | | BASERUNNING | | | | AVERAGES | | |
|---|---|---|---|---|---|---|---|---|---|---|---|---|---|---|---|---|---|---|---|---|---|---|---|---|---|---|---|
| Year | Team | Lg | G | AB | H | 2B | 3B | HR | (Hm | Rd) | TB | R | RBI | RC | TBB | IBB | SO | HBP | SH | SF | SB | CS | SB% | GDP | Avg | OBP | Slg |
| 2013 | LsVgs* | AAA | 53 | 187 | 54 | 12 | 5 | 7 | (- | -) | 97 | 38 | 22 | 36 | 24 | 0 | 27 | 4 | 0 | 1 | 4 | 5 | .44 | 6 | .289 | .380 | .519 |
| 2010 | SD | NL | 9 | 8 | 1 | 0 | 0 | 0 | (0 | 0) | 1 | 0 | 1 | 0 | 0 | 0 | 2 | 0 | 0 | 1 | 0 | 0 | - | 1 | .125 | .111 | .125 |
| 2011 | NYM | NL | 22 | 34 | 8 | 2 | 1 | 1 | (1 | 0) | 15 | 6 | 4 | 5 | 5 | 0 | 9 | 1 | 0 | 0 | 0 | 0 | - | 1 | .235 | .350 | .441 |
| 2012 | NYM | NL | 89 | 179 | 47 | 14 | 2 | 3 | (1 | 2) | 74 | 26 | 17 | 30 | 25 | 4 | 45 | 5 | 0 | 2 | 5 | 3 | .63 | 0 | .263 | .365 | .413 |
| 2013 | NYM | NL | 74 | 132 | 25 | 6 | 1 | 0 | (0 | 0) | 33 | 14 | 4 | 11 | 17 | 0 | 28 | 5 | 0 | 1 | 5 | 2 | .71 | 1 | .189 | .303 | .250 |
| 4 ML YEARS | | | 194 | 353 | 81 | 22 | 4 | 4 | (2 | 2) | 123 | 46 | 26 | 46 | 47 | 4 | 84 | 11 | 0 | 4 | 10 | 5 | .67 | 3 | .229 | .335 | .348 |

# Jason Bay

**Bats:** R **Throws:** R **Pos:** LF-38;RF-25;PH-10;PR-4;DH-3;CF-1 **Ht:** 6'2" **Wt:** 210 **Born:** 9/20/1978 **Age:** 35

| BATTING | | | | | | | | | | | | | | | | | | | | | BASERUNNING | | | | AVERAGES | | |
|---|---|---|---|---|---|---|---|---|---|---|---|---|---|---|---|---|---|---|---|---|---|---|---|---|---|---|---|
| Year | Team | Lg | G | AB | H | 2B | 3B | HR | (Hm | Rd) | TB | R | RBI | RC | TBB | IBB | SO | HBP | SH | SF | SB | CS | SB% | GDP | Avg | OBP | Slg |
| 2003 | 2 Tms | NL | 30 | 87 | 25 | 7 | 1 | 4 | (2 | 2) | 46 | 15 | 14 | 19 | 19 | 0 | 29 | 1 | 0 | 0 | 3 | 1 | .75 | 0 | .287 | .421 | .529 |
| 2004 | Pit | NL | 120 | 411 | 116 | 24 | 4 | 26 | (15 | 11) | 226 | 61 | 82 | 75 | 41 | 2 | 129 | 10 | 5 | 5 | 4 | 6 | .40 | 9 | .282 | .358 | .550 |
| 2005 | Pit | NL | **162** | 599 | 183 | 44 | 6 | 32 | (9 | 23) | 335 | 110 | 101 | 128 | 95 | 9 | 142 | 6 | 0 | 7 | 21 | 1 | **.95** | 12 | .306 | .402 | .559 |
| 2006 | Pit | NL | 159 | 570 | 163 | 29 | 3 | 35 | (13 | 22) | 303 | 101 | 109 | 103 | 102 | 9 | 156 | 8 | 0 | 9 | 11 | 2 | .85 | 15 | .286 | .396 | .532 |
| 2007 | Pit | NL | 145 | 538 | 133 | 25 | 2 | 21 | (7 | 14) | 225 | 78 | 84 | 74 | 59 | 3 | 141 | 9 | 0 | 8 | 4 | 1 | .80 | 8 | .247 | .327 | .418 |
| 2008 | 2 Tms | | 155 | 577 | 165 | 35 | 4 | 31 | (18 | 13) | 301 | 111 | 101 | 104 | 81 | 4 | 137 | 4 | 0 | 8 | 10 | 0 | 1.00 | 7 | .286 | .373 | .522 |
| 2009 | Bos | AL | 151 | 531 | 142 | 29 | 3 | 36 | (15 | **21)** | 285 | 103 | 119 | 122 | 94 | 4 | 162 | 9 | 0 | 4 | 13 | 3 | .81 | 9 | .267 | .384 | .537 |
| 2010 | NYM | NL | 95 | 348 | 90 | 20 | 6 | 6 | (3 | 3) | 140 | 48 | 47 | 50 | 44 | 3 | 91 | 5 | 0 | 4 | 10 | 0 | 1.00 | 7 | .259 | .347 | .402 |
| 2011 | NYM | NL | 123 | 444 | 109 | 19 | 1 | 12 | (6 | 6) | 166 | 59 | 57 | 50 | 56 | 3 | 109 | 2 | 1 | 6 | 11 | 1 | .92 | 8 | .245 | .329 | .374 |
| 2012 | NYM | NL | 70 | 194 | 32 | 2 | 0 | 8 | (2 | 6) | 58 | 21 | 20 | 11 | 19 | 0 | 58 | 0 | 0 | 2 | 5 | 1 | .83 | 3 | .165 | .237 | .299 |
| 2013 | Sea | AL | 68 | 206 | 42 | 6 | 0 | 11 | (6 | 5) | 81 | 30 | 20 | 17 | 26 | 1 | 62 | 2 | 1 | 1 | 3 | 1 | .75 | 6 | .204 | .298 | .393 |
| 03 | SD | NL | 3 | 8 | 2 | 1 | 0 | 1 | (0 | 1) | 6 | 2 | 2 | 2 | 1 | 0 | 1 | 1 | 0 | 0 | 0 | 0 | - | 0 | .250 | .400 | .750 |
| 03 | Pit | NL | 27 | 79 | 23 | 6 | 1 | 3 | (2 | 1) | 40 | 13 | 12 | 17 | 18 | 0 | 28 | 0 | 0 | 0 | 3 | 1 | .75 | 0 | .291 | .423 | .506 |
| 08 | Pit | NL | 106 | 393 | 111 | 23 | 2 | 22 | (15 | 7) | 204 | 72 | 64 | 73 | 59 | 2 | 86 | 2 | 0 | 5 | 7 | 0 | 1.00 | 3 | .282 | .375 | .519 |
| 08 | Bos | AL | 49 | 184 | 54 | 12 | 2 | 9 | (3 | 6) | 97 | 39 | 37 | 31 | 22 | 2 | 51 | 2 | 0 | 3 | 3 | 0 | 1.00 | 4 | .293 | .370 | .527 |
| Postseason | | | 14 | 49 | 15 | 3 | 0 | 3 | (0 | 3) | 27 | 6 | 9 | 11 | 12 | 1 | 15 | 1 | 0 | 0 | 0 | 0 | - | 0 | .306 | .452 | .551 |
| 11 ML YEARS | | | 1278 | 4505 | 1200 | 240 | 30 | 222 | (96 | 126) | 2166 | 737 | 754 | 753 | 636 | 38 | 1216 | 56 | 7 | 54 | 95 | 17 | .85 | 84 | .266 | .360 | .481 |

# Brandon Beachy

**Pitches:** R **Bats:** R **Pos:** SP-5 BEE-chee **Ht:** 6'3" **Wt:** 215 **Born:** 9/3/1986 **Age:** 27

| HOW MUCH HE PITCHED | | | | | | | | | WHAT HE GAVE UP | | | | | | | | | | | | THE RESULTS | | | | | | | |
|---|---|---|---|---|---|---|---|---|---|---|---|---|---|---|---|---|---|---|---|---|---|---|---|---|---|---|---|---|
| Year | Team | Lg | G | GS | CG | GF | IP | BFP | H | R | ER | HR | SH | SF | HB | TBB | IBB | SO | WP | Bk | W | L | Pct | Sh | Sv-Op | Hld | ERC | ERA |
| 2013 | Gwnntt* | AAA | 7 | 7 | 0 | 0 | 30.0 | 130 | 23 | 12 | 10 | 3 | 2 | 1 | 0 | 18 | 0 | 26 | 2 | 0 | 1 | 4 | .200 | 0 | 0-- | - | 3.52 | 3.00 |
| 2013 | Rome* | A | 1 | 1 | 0 | 0 | 5.0 | 18 | 3 | 0 | 0 | 0 | 0 | 0 | 0 | 1 | 0 | 3 | 0 | 0 | 1 | 0 | 1.000 | 0 | 0-- | - | 1.17 | 0.00 |
| 2013 | Missi* | AA | 1 | 1 | 0 | 0 | 5.0 | 21 | 6 | 3 | 3 | 1 | 0 | 0 | 0 | 1 | 0 | 4 | 0 | 0 | 1 | 0 | 1.000 | 0 | 0-- | - | 5.26 | 5.40 |
| 2010 | Atl | NL | 3 | 3 | 0 | 0 | 15.0 | 67 | 16 | 9 | 5 | 0 | 0 | 0 | 0 | 7 | 3 | 15 | 1 | 0 | 0 | 2 | .000 | 0 | 0-0 | 0 | 3.58 | 3.00 |
| 2011 | Atl | NL | 25 | 25 | 0 | 0 | 141.2 | 591 | 125 | 62 | 58 | 16 | 6 | 5 | 5 | 46 | **9** | 169 | 11 | 1 | 7 | 3 | .700 | 0 | 0-0 | 0 | 3.27 | 3.68 |
| 2012 | Atl | NL | 13 | 13 | 1 | 0 | 81.0 | 319 | 49 | 24 | 18 | 6 | 1 | 2 | 1 | 29 | 1 | 68 | 4 | 0 | 5 | 5 | .500 | 1 | 0-0 | 0 | 1.80 | 2.00 |
| 2013 | Atl | NL | 5 | 5 | 0 | 0 | 30.0 | 120 | 27 | 17 | 15 | 5 | 2 | 1 | 0 | 4 | 0 | 23 | 2 | 0 | 2 | 1 | .667 | 0 | 0-0 | 0 | 2.90 | 4.50 |
| 4 ML YEARS | | | 46 | 46 | 1 | 0 | 267.2 | 1097 | 217 | 112 | 96 | 27 | 9 | 8 | 6 | 86 | 13 | 275 | 18 | 1 | 14 | 11 | .560 | 1 | 0-0 | 0 | 2.78 | 3.23 |

# Pedro Beato

**Pitches:** R **Bats:** R **Pos:** RP-10 bay-AHH-toe **Ht:** 6'6" **Wt:** 230 **Born:** 10/27/1986 **Age:** 27

| HOW MUCH HE PITCHED | | | | | | | | | WHAT HE GAVE UP | | | | | | | | | | | | THE RESULTS | | | | | | | |
|---|---|---|---|---|---|---|---|---|---|---|---|---|---|---|---|---|---|---|---|---|---|---|---|---|---|---|---|---|
| Year | Team | Lg | G | GS | CG | GF | IP | BFP | H | R | ER | HR | SH | SF | HB | TBB | IBB | SO | WP | Bk | W | L | Pct | Sh | Sv-Op | Hld | ERC | ERA |
| 2013 | Pwtckt* | AAA | 34 | 0 | 0 | 12 | 51.1 | 218 | 46 | 22 | 17 | 7 | 1 | 1 | 4 | 24 | 1 | 45 | 1 | 0 | 5 | 3 | .625 | 0 | 5-- | - | 4.42 | 2.98 |
| 2011 | NYM | NL | 60 | 0 | 0 | 7 | 67.0 | 283 | 59 | 41 | 32 | 5 | 2 | 4 | 4 | 27 | 3 | 39 | 1 | 0 | 2 | 1 | .667 | 0 | 0-1 | 11 | 3.45 | 4.30 |
| 2012 | 2 Tms | | 11 | 0 | 0 | 2 | 12.0 | 51 | 11 | 9 | 9 | 1 | 0 | 0 | 1 | 5 | 0 | 12 | 1 | 0 | 1 | 0 | 1.000 | 0 | 0-0 | 1 | 3.96 | 6.75 |
| 2013 | Bos | AL | 10 | 0 | 0 | 5 | 10.0 | 46 | 12 | 5 | 4 | 1 | 0 | 0 | 1 | 2 | 0 | 5 | 0 | 0 | 1 | 1 | .500 | 0 | 0-0 | 0 | 4.58 | 3.60 |
| 12 | NYM | NL | 7 | 0 | 0 | 2 | 4.1 | 20 | 5 | 5 | 5 | 1 | 0 | 0 | 0 | 2 | 0 | 5 | 1 | 0 | 0 | 0 | - | 0 | 0-0 | 1 | 6.09 | 10.38 |
| 12 | Bos | AL | 4 | 0 | 0 | 0 | 7.2 | 31 | 6 | 4 | 4 | 0 | 0 | 0 | 1 | 3 | 0 | 7 | 0 | 0 | 1 | 0 | 1.000 | 0 | 0-0 | 0 | 2.83 | 4.70 |
| 3 ML YEARS | | | 81 | 0 | 0 | 14 | 89.0 | 380 | 82 | 55 | 45 | 7 | 2 | 4 | 6 | 34 | 3 | 56 | 2 | 0 | 4 | 2 | .667 | 0 | 0-1 | 12 | 3.64 | 4.55 |

# Blake Beavan

**Pitches:** R **Bats:** R **Pos:** RP-10; SP-2 BEV-uhn **Ht:** 6'7" **Wt:** 255 **Born:** 1/17/1989 **Age:** 25

| HOW MUCH HE PITCHED | | | | | | | | | WHAT HE GAVE UP | | | | | | | | | | | | THE RESULTS | | | | | | | |
|---|---|---|---|---|---|---|---|---|---|---|---|---|---|---|---|---|---|---|---|---|---|---|---|---|---|---|---|---|
| Year | Team | Lg | G | GS | CG | GF | IP | BFP | H | R | ER | HR | SH | SF | HB | TBB | IBB | SO | WP | Bk | W | L | Pct | Sh | Sv-Op | Hld | ERC | ERA |
| 2013 | Tacom* | AAA | 16 | 16 | 0 | 0 | 94.0 | 411 | 120 | 61 | 58 | 15 | 3 | 2 | 5 | 23 | 0 | 47 | 0 | 0 | 6 | 6 | .500 | 0 | 0-- | - | 5.87 | 5.55 |
| 2011 | Sea | AL | 15 | 15 | 0 | 0 | 97.0 | 405 | 106 | 46 | 46 | 13 | 1 | 5 | 3 | 15 | 0 | 42 | 4 | 0 | 5 | 6 | .455 | 0 | 0-0 | 0 | 3.99 | 4.27 |
| 2012 | Sea | AL | 26 | 26 | 0 | 0 | 152.1 | 638 | 168 | 76 | 75 | 23 | 1 | 5 | 10 | 24 | 0 | 67 | 3 | 0 | 11 | 11 | .500 | 0 | 0-0 | 0 | 4.36 | 4.43 |
| 2013 | Sea | AL | 12 | 2 | 0 | 4 | 39.2 | 174 | 46 | 27 | 27 | 8 | 1 | 2 | 1 | 8 | 0 | 27 | 0 | 0 | 0 | 2 | .000 | 0 | 0-0 | 0 | 4.89 | 6.13 |
| 3 ML YEARS | | | 53 | 43 | 0 | 4 | 289.0 | 1217 | 320 | 149 | 148 | 44 | 3 | 12 | 14 | 47 | 0 | 136 | 7 | 0 | 16 | 19 | .457 | 0 | 0-0 | 0 | 4.31 | 4.61 |

# Josh Beckett

**Pitches:** R **Bats:** R **Pos:** SP-8 **Ht:** 6'5" **Wt:** 225 **Born:** 5/15/1980 **Age:** 34

| HOW MUCH HE PITCHED | | | | | | | | | WHAT HE GAVE UP | | | | | | | | | | | | THE RESULTS | | | | | | | |
|---|---|---|---|---|---|---|---|---|---|---|---|---|---|---|---|---|---|---|---|---|---|---|---|---|---|---|---|---|
| Year | Team | Lg | G | GS | CG | GF | IP | BFP | H | R | ER | HR | SH | SF | HB | TBB | IBB | SO | WP | Bk | W | L | Pct | Sh | Sv-Op | Hld | ERC | ERA |
| 2001 | Fla | NL | 4 | 4 | 0 | 0 | 24.0 | 99 | 14 | 9 | 4 | 3 | 0 | 0 | 1 | 11 | 0 | 24 | 1 | 0 | 2 | 2 | .500 | 0 | 0-0 | 0 | 2.36 | 1.50 |
| 2002 | Fla | NL | 23 | 21 | 0 | 0 | 107.2 | 454 | 93 | 56 | 49 | 13 | 5 | 3 | 1 | 44 | 2 | 113 | 5 | 0 | 6 | 7 | .462 | 0 | 0-0 | 0 | 3.50 | 4.10 |
| 2003 | Fla | NL | 24 | 23 | 0 | 1 | 142.0 | 601 | 132 | 54 | 48 | 9 | 5 | 1 | 2 | 56 | 4 | 152 | 6 | 1 | 9 | 8 | .529 | 0 | 0-0 | 0 | 3.44 | 3.04 |
| 2004 | Fla | NL | 26 | 26 | 1 | 0 | 156.2 | 654 | 137 | 72 | 66 | 16 | 9 | 3 | 6 | 54 | 3 | 152 | 5 | 0 | 9 | 9 | .500 | 1 | 0-0 | 0 | 3.32 | 3.79 |

| Year | Team | Lg | G | GS | CG | GF | IP | BFP | H | R | ER | HR | SH | SF | HB | TBB | IBB | SO | WP | Bk | W | L | Pct | Sh | Sv-Op | Hld | ERC | ERA |
|---|---|---|---|---|---|---|---|---|---|---|---|---|---|---|---|---|---|---|---|---|---|---|---|---|---|---|---|---|
| | | | HOW MUCH HE PITCHED | | | | | | WHAT HE GAVE UP | | | | | | | | | | | | THE RESULTS | | | | | | | |
| 2005 | Fla | NL | 29 | 29 | 2 | 0 | 178.2 | 728 | 153 | 75 | 67 | 14 | 8 | 2 | 7 | 58 | 2 | 166 | 5 | 0 | 15 | 8 | .652 | 1 | 0-0 | 0 | 3.07 | 3.38 |
| 2006 | Bos | AL | 33 | 33 | 0 | 0 | 204.2 | 869 | 191 | 120 | 114 | 36 | 2 | 3 | 10 | 74 | 1 | 158 | 11 | 1 | 16 | 11 | .593 | 0 | 0-0 | 0 | 4.28 | 5.01 |
| 2007 | Bos | AL | 30 | 30 | 1 | 0 | 200.2 | 822 | 189 | 76 | 73 | 17 | 3 | 2 | 5 | 40 | 0 | 194 | 3 | 0 | **20** | 7 | .741 | 0 | 0-0 | 0 | 2.99 | 3.27 |
| 2008 | Bos | AL | 27 | 27 | 1 | 0 | 174.1 | 725 | 173 | 80 | 78 | 18 | 4 | 3 | 9 | 34 | 1 | 172 | 5 | 0 | 12 | 10 | .545 | 0 | 0-0 | 0 | 3.45 | 4.03 |
| 2009 | Bos | AL | 32 | 32 | 4 | 0 | 212.1 | 883 | 198 | 99 | 91 | 25 | 5 | 5 | 7 | 55 | 1 | 199 | 3 | 1 | 17 | 6 | .739 | 2 | 0-0 | 0 | 3.39 | 3.86 |
| 2010 | Bos | AL | 21 | 21 | 0 | 0 | 127.2 | 577 | 151 | 89 | 82 | 20 | 4 | 2 | 8 | 45 | 3 | 116 | 3 | 0 | 6 | 6 | .500 | 0 | 0-0 | 0 | 5.56 | 5.78 |
| 2011 | Bos | AL | 30 | 30 | 1 | 0 | 193.0 | 767 | 146 | 65 | 62 | 21 | 8 | 5 | 9 | 52 | 1 | 175 | 6 | 0 | 13 | 7 | .650 | 1 | 0-0 | 0 | 2.56 | 2.89 |
| 2012 | 2 Tms | | 28 | 28 | 0 | 0 | 170.1 | 730 | 174 | 91 | 88 | 21 | 5 | 8 | 5 | 52 | 6 | 132 | 5 | 0 | 7 | 14 | .333 | 0 | 0-0 | 0 | 4.02 | 4.65 |
| 2013 | LAD | NL | 8 | 8 | 1 | 0 | 43.1 | 195 | 50 | 30 | 25 | 8 | 5 | 1 | 1 | 15 | 2 | 41 | 0 | 0 | 0 | 5 | .000 | 0 | 0-0 | 0 | 5.29 | 5.19 |
| 12 | Bos | AL | 21 | 21 | 0 | 0 | 127.1 | 547 | 131 | 75 | 74 | 16 | 3 | 8 | 5 | 38 | 2 | 94 | 4 | 0 | 5 | 11 | .313 | 0 | 0-0 | 0 | 4.12 | 5.23 |
| 12 | LAD | NL | 7 | 7 | 0 | 0 | 43.0 | 183 | 43 | 16 | 14 | 5 | 2 | 0 | 0 | 14 | 4 | 38 | 1 | 0 | 2 | 3 | .400 | 0 | 0-0 | 0 | 3.73 | 2.93 |
| Postseason | | | 14 | 13 | 3 | 0 | 93.2 | 366 | 67 | 32 | 32 | 11 | 2 | 1 | 4 | 21 | 1 | 99 | 3 | 0 | 7 | 3 | .700 | 3 | 0-0 | 0 | 2.22 | 3.07 |
| 13 ML YEARS | | | 315 | 312 | 11 | 1 | 1935.1 | 8104 | 1801 | 916 | 847 | 221 | 63 | 38 | 71 | 590 | 26 | 1794 | 58 | 3 | 132 | 100 | .569 | 5 | 0-0 | 0 | 3.55 | 3.94 |

# Gordon Beckham

**Bats:** R **Throws:** R **Pos:** 2B-103;SS-2;PH-1;PR-1 **Ht:** 6'0" **Wt:** 190 **Born:** 9/16/1986 **Age:** 27

| Year | Team | Lg | G | AB | H | 2B | 3B | HR | (Hm | Rd) | TB | R | RBI | RC | TBB | IBB | SO | HBP | SH | SF | SB | CS | SB% | GDP | Avg | OBP | Slg |
|---|---|---|---|---|---|---|---|---|---|---|---|---|---|---|---|---|---|---|---|---|---|---|---|---|---|---|---|
| | | | BATTING | | | | | | | | | | | | | | | | | | BASERUNNING | | | | AVERAGES | | |
| 2013 | Charltt* | AAA | 8 | 36 | 12 | 2 | 0 | 0 | (- | -) | 14 | 7 | 5 | 5 | 2 | 0 | 6 | 0 | 0 | 0 | 0 | 0 | - | 0 | .333 | .368 | .389 |
| 2009 | CWS | AL | 103 | 378 | 102 | 28 | 1 | 14 | (4 | 10) | 174 | 58 | 63 | 60 | 41 | 0 | 65 | 6 | 1 | 4 | 7 | 4 | .64 | 10 | .270 | .347 | .460 |
| 2010 | CWS | AL | 131 | 444 | 112 | 25 | 2 | 9 | (7 | 2) | 168 | 58 | 49 | 52 | 37 | 0 | 92 | 7 | 6 | 4 | 4 | 6 | .40 | 9 | .252 | .317 | .378 |
| 2011 | CWS | AL | 150 | 499 | 115 | 23 | 0 | 10 | (7 | 3) | 168 | 60 | 44 | 48 | 35 | 0 | 111 | 13 | 7 | 3 | 5 | 3 | .63 | 6 | .230 | .296 | .337 |
| 2012 | CWS | AL | 151 | 525 | 123 | 24 | 0 | 16 | (12 | 4) | 195 | 62 | 60 | 58 | 40 | 0 | 89 | 7 | 8 | 2 | 5 | 4 | .56 | 10 | .234 | .296 | .371 |
| 2013 | CWS | AL | 103 | 371 | 99 | 22 | 1 | 5 | (3 | 2) | 138 | 46 | 24 | 36 | 28 | 2 | 56 | 4 | 1 | 4 | 5 | 1 | .83 | 10 | .267 | .322 | .372 |
| 5 ML YEARS | | | 638 | 2217 | 551 | 122 | 4 | 54 | (33 | 21) | 843 | 284 | 240 | 254 | 181 | 2 | 413 | 37 | 23 | 17 | 26 | 18 | .59 | 45 | .249 | .314 | .380 |

# Tim Beckham

**Bats:** R **Throws:** R **Pos:** PH-4;2B-3;SS-1 **Ht:** 6'0" **Wt:** 190 **Born:** 1/27/1990 **Age:** 24

| Year | Team | Lg | G | AB | H | 2B | 3B | HR | (Hm | Rd) | TB | R | RBI | RC | TBB | IBB | SO | HBP | SH | SF | SB | CS | SB% | GDP | Avg | OBP | Slg |
|---|---|---|---|---|---|---|---|---|---|---|---|---|---|---|---|---|---|---|---|---|---|---|---|---|---|---|---|
| | | | BATTING | | | | | | | | | | | | | | | | | | BASERUNNING | | | | AVERAGES | | |
| 2009 | BG | A | 125 | 491 | 135 | 33 | 4 | 5 | (- | -) | 191 | 58 | 63 | 64 | 34 | 0 | 116 | 7 | 0 | 5 | 13 | 10 | .57 | 10 | .275 | .328 | .389 |
| 2010 | Charltt | A+ | 123 | 465 | 119 | 23 | 5 | 5 | (- | -) | 167 | 68 | 57 | 62 | 62 | 2 | 119 | 4 | 7 | 4 | 22 | 14 | .61 | 14 | .256 | .346 | .359 |
| 2011 | Mont | AA | 107 | 418 | 115 | 25 | 2 | 7 | (- | -) | 165 | 82 | 57 | 60 | 39 | 0 | 91 | 3 | 5 | 3 | 15 | 4 | .79 | 7 | .275 | .339 | .395 |
| 2011 | Drham | AAA | 24 | 106 | 27 | 3 | 2 | 5 | (- | -) | 49 | 12 | 13 | 13 | 3 | 0 | 29 | 1 | 1 | 0 | 2 | 1 | .67 | 0 | .255 | .282 | .462 |
| 2012 | Drham | AAA | 72 | 285 | 73 | 10 | 1 | 6 | (- | -) | 103 | 40 | 28 | 37 | 29 | 2 | 71 | 2 | 3 | 4 | 6 | 0 | 1.00 | 8 | .256 | .325 | .361 |
| 2013 | Drham | AAA | 122 | 460 | 127 | 25 | 7 | 4 | (- | -) | 178 | 71 | 51 | 65 | 44 | 0 | 108 | 5 | 8 | 5 | 17 | 7 | .71 | 17 | .276 | .342 | .387 |
| 2013 | TB | AL | 5 | 7 | 3 | 0 | 0 | 0 | (0 | 0) | 3 | 1 | 1 | 1 | 0 | 0 | 0 | 0 | 0 | 1 | 0 | 0 | - | 0 | .429 | .375 | .429 |

# Erik Bedard

**Pitches:** L **Bats:** L **Pos:** SP-26; RP-6 buh-DARD **Ht:** 6'1" **Wt:** 200 **Born:** 3/5/1979 **Age:** 35

| Year | Team | Lg | G | GS | CG | GF | IP | BFP | H | R | ER | HR | SH | SF | HB | TBB | IBB | SO | WP | Bk | W | L | Pct | Sh | Sv-Op | Hld | ERC | ERA |
|---|---|---|---|---|---|---|---|---|---|---|---|---|---|---|---|---|---|---|---|---|---|---|---|---|---|---|---|---|
| | | | HOW MUCH HE PITCHED | | | | | | WHAT HE GAVE UP | | | | | | | | | | | | THE RESULTS | | | | | | | |
| 2002 | Bal | AL | 2 | 0 | 0 | 0 | 0.2 | 4 | 2 | 1 | 1 | 0 | 0 | 0 | 0 | 0 | 0 | 1 | 0 | 0 | 0 | 0 | - | 0 | 0-0 | 0 | 14.52 | 13.50 |
| 2004 | Bal | AL | 27 | 26 | 0 | 0 | 137.1 | 633 | 149 | 83 | 70 | 13 | 0 | 4 | 7 | 71 | 1 | 121 | 7 | 2 | 6 | 10 | .375 | 0 | 0-0 | 0 | 5.11 | 4.59 |
| 2005 | Bal | AL | 24 | 24 | 0 | 0 | 141.2 | 606 | 139 | 66 | 63 | 10 | 3 | 6 | 5 | 57 | 1 | 125 | 4 | 1 | 6 | 8 | .429 | 0 | 0-0 | 0 | 3.95 | 4.00 |
| 2006 | Bal | AL | 33 | 33 | 0 | 0 | 196.1 | 844 | 196 | 92 | 82 | 16 | 6 | 4 | 5 | 69 | 0 | 171 | 6 | 0 | 15 | 11 | .577 | 0 | 0-0 | 0 | 3.83 | 3.76 |
| 2007 | Bal | AL | 28 | 28 | 1 | 0 | 182.0 | 733 | 141 | 66 | 64 | 19 | 2 | 4 | 5 | 57 | 0 | 221 | 3 | 0 | 13 | 5 | .722 | 1 | 0-0 | 0 | **2.71** | 3.16 |
| 2008 | Sea | AL | 15 | 15 | 0 | 0 | 81.0 | 347 | 70 | 38 | 33 | 9 | 1 | 2 | 4 | 37 | 0 | 72 | 3 | 0 | 6 | 4 | .600 | 0 | 0-0 | 0 | 3.82 | 3.67 |
| 2009 | Sea | AL | 15 | 15 | 0 | 0 | 83.0 | 348 | 65 | 29 | 26 | 8 | 2 | 1 | 4 | 34 | 0 | 90 | 2 | 0 | 5 | 3 | .625 | 0 | 0-0 | 0 | 3.08 | 2.82 |
| 2011 | 2 Tms | AL | 24 | 24 | 0 | 0 | 129.1 | 541 | 118 | 63 | 52 | 14 | 1 | 1 | 1 | 48 | 0 | 125 | 5 | 0 | 5 | 9 | .357 | 0 | 0-0 | 0 | 3.60 | 3.62 |
| 2012 | Pit | NL | 24 | 24 | 0 | 0 | 125.2 | 557 | 129 | 76 | 70 | 14 | 5 | 2 | 3 | 56 | 2 | 118 | 1 | 1 | 7 | 14 | .333 | 0 | 0-0 | 0 | 4.52 | 5.01 |
| 2013 | Hou | AL | 32 | 26 | 0 | 3 | 151.0 | 663 | 149 | 83 | 77 | 18 | 2 | 6 | 6 | 75 | 0 | 138 | 1 | 0 | 4 | 12 | .250 | 0 | 1-3 | 0 | 4.73 | 4.59 |
| 11 | Sea | AL | 16 | 16 | 0 | 0 | 91.1 | 373 | 77 | 41 | 35 | 11 | 1 | 0 | 1 | 30 | 0 | 87 | 5 | 0 | 4 | 7 | .364 | 0 | 0-0 | 0 | 3.16 | 3.45 |
| 11 | Bos | AL | 8 | 8 | 0 | 0 | 38.0 | 168 | 41 | 22 | 17 | 3 | 0 | 1 | 0 | 18 | 0 | 38 | 0 | 0 | 1 | 2 | .333 | 0 | 0-0 | 0 | 4.70 | 4.03 |
| 10 ML YEARS | | | 224 | 215 | 1 | 3 | 1228.0 | 5276 | 1158 | 597 | 538 | 121 | 22 | 30 | 40 | 504 | 4 | 1182 | 32 | 4 | 67 | 76 | .469 | 1 | 1-3 | 0 | 3.91 | 3.94 |

# Mike Belfiore

**Pitches:** L **Bats:** R **Pos:** RP-1 bell-FEE-or-ee **Ht:** 6'3" **Wt:** 220 **Born:** 10/3/1988 **Age:** 25

| Year | Team | Lg | G | GS | CG | GF | IP | BFP | H | R | ER | HR | SH | SF | HB | TBB | IBB | SO | WP | Bk | W | L | Pct | Sh | Sv-Op | Hld | ERC | ERA |
|---|---|---|---|---|---|---|---|---|---|---|---|---|---|---|---|---|---|---|---|---|---|---|---|---|---|---|---|---|
| | | | HOW MUCH HE PITCHED | | | | | | WHAT HE GAVE UP | | | | | | | | | | | | THE RESULTS | | | | | | | |
| 2009 | Msoula | R+ | 14 | 11 | 0 | 1 | 58.0 | 245 | 59 | 29 | 14 | 2 | 2 | 1 | 1 | 13 | 0 | 55 | 2 | 0 | 2 | 2 | .500 | 0 | 0- - | - | 3.08 | 2.17 |
| 2010 | Sbend | A | 25 | 25 | 0 | 0 | 126.1 | 552 | 139 | 75 | 56 | 6 | 5 | 3 | 1 | 42 | 0 | 105 | 10 | 0 | 3 | 10 | .231 | 0 | 0- - | - | 4.00 | 3.99 |
| 2011 | Visalia | A+ | 35 | 8 | 0 | 7 | 79.0 | 369 | 86 | 58 | 52 | 17 | 2 | 0 | 1 | 57 | 0 | 79 | 5 | 1 | 4 | 4 | .500 | 0 | 0- - | - | 7.00 | 5.92 |
| 2012 | Visalia | A+ | 12 | 0 | 0 | 4 | 19.0 | 72 | 13 | 5 | 5 | 2 | 1 | 0 | 0 | 5 | 0 | 28 | 1 | 1 | 0 | 0 | - | 0 | 1- - | - | 2.07 | 2.37 |
| 2012 | Bowie | AA | 28 | 0 | 0 | 7 | 47.1 | 209 | 43 | 20 | 15 | 2 | 0 | 1 | 7 | 21 | 1 | 50 | 0 | 0 | 5 | 1 | .833 | 0 | 2- - | - | 3.83 | 2.85 |
| 2013 | Norfolk | AAA | 37 | 0 | 0 | 14 | 76.1 | 328 | 81 | 27 | 27 | 8 | 1 | 2 | 1 | 29 | 0 | 82 | 5 | 0 | 2 | 1 | .667 | 0 | 1- - | - | 4.50 | 3.18 |
| 2013 | Bal | AL | 1 | 0 | 0 | 1 | 1.1 | 7 | 3 | 2 | 2 | 2 | 0 | 0 | 0 | 1 | 0 | 0 | 0 | 0 | 0 | 0 | - | 0 | 0-0 | 0 | 33.37 | 13.50 |

# Ronald Belisario

**Pitches:** R **Bats:** R **Pos:** RP-77 | bell-ih-SAR-ee-oh | **Ht:** 6'3" **Wt:** 240 **Born:** 12/31/1982 **Age:** 31

| | | | HOW MUCH HE PITCHED | | | | | | WHAT HE GAVE UP | | | | | | | | | | | | THE RESULTS | | | | | | | |
|---|---|---|---|---|---|---|---|---|---|---|---|---|---|---|---|---|---|---|---|---|---|---|---|---|---|---|---|---|
| Year | Team | Lg | G | GS | CG | GF | IP | BFP | H | R | ER | HR | SH | SF | HB | TBB | IBB | SO | WP | Bk | W | L | Pct | Sh | Sv-Op | Hld | ERC | ERA |
| 2009 | LAD | NL | 69 | 0 | 0 | 13 | 70.2 | 299 | 52 | 21 | 16 | 4 | 3 | 2 | 6 | 29 | 7 | 64 | 4 | 0 | 4 | 3 | .571 | 0 | 0-7 | 12 | 2.54 | 2.04 |
| 2010 | LAD | NL | 59 | 0 | 0 | 13 | 55.1 | 233 | 52 | 31 | 31 | 6 | 3 | 0 | 3 | 19 | 4 | 38 | 4 | 1 | 3 | 1 | .750 | 0 | 2-4 | 16 | 3.72 | 5.04 |
| 2012 | LAD | NL | 68 | 0 | 0 | 13 | 71.0 | 286 | 47 | 22 | 20 | 3 | 1 | 0 | 4 | 29 | 4 | 69 | 1 | 0 | 8 | 1 | .889 | 0 | 1-5 | 23 | 2.14 | 2.54 |
| 2013 | LAD | NL | 77 | 0 | 0 | 12 | 68.0 | 300 | 72 | 34 | 30 | 3 | 2 | 2 | 5 | 28 | **10** | 49 | 3 | 0 | 5 | 7 | .417 | 0 | 1-5 | 21 | 4.10 | 3.97 |
| Postseason | | | 6 | 0 | 0 | 2 | 4.2 | 20 | 5 | 4 | 4 | 1 | 0 | 0 | 0 | 1 | 0 | 0 | 1 | 0 | 0 | 0 | - | 0 | 0-0 | 2 | 4.41 | 7.71 |
| 4 ML YEARS | | | 273 | 0 | 0 | 51 | 265.0 | 1118 | 223 | 108 | 97 | 16 | 9 | 4 | 18 | 105 | 25 | 220 | 12 | 1 | 20 | 12 | .625 | 0 | 4-21 | 72 | 3.05 | 3.29 |

# Matt Belisle

**Pitches:** R **Bats:** R **Pos:** RP-72 | bell-EYE-el | **Ht:** 6'4" **Wt:** 225 **Born:** 6/6/1980 **Age:** 34

| | | | HOW MUCH HE PITCHED | | | | | | WHAT HE GAVE UP | | | | | | | | | | | | THE RESULTS | | | | | | | |
|---|---|---|---|---|---|---|---|---|---|---|---|---|---|---|---|---|---|---|---|---|---|---|---|---|---|---|---|---|
| Year | Team | Lg | G | GS | CG | GF | IP | BFP | H | R | ER | HR | SH | SF | HB | TBB | IBB | SO | WP | Bk | W | L | Pct | Sh | Sv-Op | Hld | ERC | ERA |
| 2003 | Cin | NL | 6 | 0 | 0 | 2 | 8.2 | 39 | 10 | 5 | 5 | 1 | 2 | 1 | 1 | 2 | 0 | 6 | 0 | 0 | 1 | 1 | .500 | 0 | 0-1 | 0 | 4.73 | 5.19 |
| 2005 | Cin | NL | 60 | 5 | 0 | 17 | 85.2 | 382 | 101 | 49 | 42 | 11 | 4 | 2 | 6 | 26 | 6 | 59 | 3 | 0 | 4 | 8 | .333 | 0 | 1-4 | 8 | 5.08 | 4.41 |
| 2006 | Cin | NL | 30 | 2 | 0 | 5 | 40.0 | 180 | 43 | 18 | 16 | 5 | 1 | 2 | 3 | 19 | 1 | 26 | 3 | 0 | 2 | 0 | 1.000 | 0 | 0-1 | 0 | 5.29 | 3.60 |
| 2007 | Cin | NL | 30 | 30 | 1 | 0 | 177.2 | 771 | 212 | 111 | 105 | 26 | 7 | 9 | 7 | 43 | 4 | 125 | 6 | 1 | 8 | 9 | .471 | 0 | 0-0 | 0 | 5.05 | 5.32 |
| 2008 | Cin | NL | 6 | 6 | 0 | 0 | 29.2 | 142 | 47 | 27 | 24 | 4 | 1 | 2 | 0 | 6 | 0 | 14 | 2 | 0 | 1 | 4 | .200 | 0 | 0-0 | 0 | 6.87 | 7.28 |
| 2009 | Col | NL | 24 | 0 | 0 | 6 | 31.0 | 133 | 35 | 21 | 19 | 6 | 0 | 2 | 1 | 5 | 1 | 22 | 1 | 0 | 3 | 1 | .750 | 0 | 0-0 | 1 | 4.50 | 5.52 |
| 2010 | Col | NL | 76 | 0 | 0 | 11 | 92.0 | 365 | 84 | 34 | 30 | 7 | 4 | 2 | 2 | 16 | 5 | 91 | 3 | 1 | 7 | 5 | .583 | 0 | 1-2 | 21 | 2.67 | 2.93 |
| 2011 | Col | NL | 74 | 0 | 0 | 10 | 72.0 | 301 | 77 | 33 | 26 | 5 | 4 | 0 | 4 | 14 | 3 | 58 | 2 | 0 | 10 | 4 | .714 | 0 | 0-7 | 14 | 3.65 | 3.25 |
| 2012 | Col | NL | **80** | 0 | 0 | 14 | 80.0 | 348 | 91 | 36 | 33 | 5 | 4 | 0 | 3 | 18 | 6 | 69 | 1 | 1 | 3 | 8 | .273 | 0 | 3-10 | 26 | 3.87 | 3.71 |
| 2013 | Col | NL | 72 | 0 | 0 | 16 | 73.0 | 301 | 76 | 37 | 35 | 6 | 2 | 1 | 0 | 15 | 2 | 62 | 3 | 0 | 5 | 7 | .417 | 0 | 0-5 | 24 | 3.42 | 4.32 |
| Postseason | | | 2 | 0 | 0 | 0 | 2.0 | 7 | 0 | 0 | 0 | 0 | 0 | 0 | 0 | 1 | 0 | 2 | 0 | 0 | 0 | 0 | - | 0 | 0-0 | 1 | 0.27 | 0.00 |
| 10 ML YEARS | | | 458 | 43 | 1 | 81 | 689.2 | 2962 | 776 | 371 | 335 | 76 | 29 | 21 | 27 | 164 | 28 | 532 | 24 | 3 | 44 | 47 | .484 | 0 | 5-30 | 94 | 4.31 | 4.37 |

# Jeff Beliveau

**Pitches:** L **Bats:** L **Pos:** RP-1 | bell-eh-VOH | **Ht:** 6'1" **Wt:** 195 **Born:** 1/17/1987 **Age:** 27

| | | | HOW MUCH HE PITCHED | | | | | | WHAT HE GAVE UP | | | | | | | | | | | | THE RESULTS | | | | | | | |
|---|---|---|---|---|---|---|---|---|---|---|---|---|---|---|---|---|---|---|---|---|---|---|---|---|---|---|---|---|
| Year | Team | Lg | G | GS | CG | GF | IP | BFP | H | R | ER | HR | SH | SF | HB | TBB | IBB | SO | WP | Bk | W | L | Pct | Sh | Sv-Op | Hld | ERC | ERA |
| 2009 | Peoria | A | 29 | 7 | 0 | 9 | 96.2 | 414 | 77 | 40 | 38 | 5 | 2 | 4 | 7 | 45 | 1 | 117 | 7 | 1 | 5 | 4 | .556 | 0 | 3-- | - | 3.12 | 3.54 |
| 2010 | Peoria | A | 6 | 0 | 0 | 1 | 11.1 | 44 | 6 | 2 | 2 | 1 | 0 | 0 | 1 | 6 | 0 | 23 | 1 | 0 | 0 | 0 | - | 0 | 0-- | - | 2.51 | 1.59 |
| 2010 | Dytona | A+ | 40 | 0 | 0 | 14 | 53.0 | 225 | 41 | 20 | 17 | 4 | 3 | 0 | 2 | 23 | 3 | 74 | 0 | 0 | 4 | 2 | .667 | 0 | 2-- | - | 2.82 | 2.89 |
| 2011 | Dytona | A+ | 12 | 0 | 0 | 3 | 17.1 | 69 | 13 | 1 | 1 | 0 | 2 | 1 | 2 | 6 | 2 | 20 | 0 | 0 | 0 | 1 | .000 | 0 | 2-- | - | 2.27 | 0.52 |
| 2011 | Tenn | AA | 41 | 0 | 0 | 9 | 57.0 | 220 | 37 | 14 | 12 | 7 | 2 | 2 | 1 | 13 | 3 | 69 | 1 | 0 | 6 | 1 | .857 | 0 | 3-- | - | 1.80 | 1.89 |
| 2012 | Iowa | AAA | 37 | 0 | 0 | 13 | 44.0 | 190 | 44 | 21 | 19 | 4 | 1 | 2 | 0 | 18 | 0 | 52 | 2 | 1 | 4 | 5 | .444 | 0 | 0-- | - | 4.05 | 3.89 |
| 2013 | RdRck | AAA | 1 | 0 | 0 | 0 | 2.0 | 7 | 1 | 0 | 0 | 0 | 0 | 0 | 0 | 0 | 0 | 0 | 0 | 0 | 0 | 0 | - | 0 | 0-- | - | 0.54 | 0.00 |
| 2013 | Drham | AAA | 38 | 0 | 0 | 11 | 44.2 | 199 | 41 | 15 | 13 | 1 | 1 | 2 | 1 | 22 | 2 | 76 | 2 | 0 | 2 | 3 | .400 | 0 | 1-- | - | 3.33 | 2.62 |
| 2013 | Mont | AA | 2 | 0 | 0 | 0 | 2.0 | 7 | 0 | 0 | 0 | 0 | 0 | 0 | 0 | 1 | 0 | 5 | 0 | 0 | 0 | 0 | - | 0 | 0-- | - | 0.27 | 0.00 |
| 2012 | ChC | NL | 22 | 0 | 0 | 4 | 17.2 | 86 | 21 | 9 | 9 | 5 | 1 | 0 | 1 | 12 | 1 | 17 | 1 | 1 | 1 | 0 | 1.000 | 0 | 0-0 | 1 | 7.98 | 4.58 |
| 2013 | TB | AL | 1 | 0 | 0 | 0 | 0.2 | 4 | 1 | 0 | 0 | 0 | 0 | 0 | 0 | 1 | 0 | 0 | 0 | 0 | 0 | 0 | - | 0 | 0-0 | 0 | 10.76 | 0.00 |
| 2 ML YEARS | | | 23 | 0 | 0 | 4 | 18.1 | 90 | 22 | 9 | 9 | 5 | 1 | 0 | 1 | 13 | 1 | 17 | 1 | 1 | 1 | 0 | 1.000 | 0 | 0-0 | 1 | 8.09 | 4.42 |

# Heath Bell

**Pitches:** R **Bats:** R **Pos:** RP-69 | **Ht:** 6'3" **Wt:** 250 **Born:** 9/29/1977 **Age:** 36

| | | | HOW MUCH HE PITCHED | | | | | | WHAT HE GAVE UP | | | | | | | | | | | | THE RESULTS | | | | | | | |
|---|---|---|---|---|---|---|---|---|---|---|---|---|---|---|---|---|---|---|---|---|---|---|---|---|---|---|---|---|
| Year | Team | Lg | G | GS | CG | GF | IP | BFP | H | R | ER | HR | SH | SF | HB | TBB | IBB | SO | WP | Bk | W | L | Pct | Sh | Sv-Op | Hld | ERC | ERA |
| 2004 | NYM | NL | 17 | 0 | 0 | 2 | 24.1 | 94 | 22 | 9 | 9 | 5 | 1 | 0 | 0 | 6 | 0 | 27 | 0 | 0 | 0 | 2 | .000 | 0 | 0-1 | 1 | 3.86 | 3.33 |
| 2005 | NYM | NL | 42 | 0 | 0 | 12 | 46.2 | 206 | 56 | 30 | 29 | 3 | 4 | 0 | 1 | 13 | 3 | 43 | 0 | 1 | 1 | 3 | .250 | 0 | 0-0 | 4 | 4.42 | 5.59 |
| 2006 | NYM | NL | 22 | 0 | 0 | 6 | 37.0 | 166 | 51 | 25 | 21 | 6 | 1 | 0 | 0 | 11 | 2 | 35 | 1 | 0 | 0 | 0 | - | 0 | 0-0 | 0 | 6.40 | 5.11 |
| 2007 | SD | NL | 81 | 0 | 0 | 16 | 93.2 | 363 | 60 | 21 | 21 | 3 | 4 | 1 | 2 | 30 | 1 | 102 | 4 | 0 | 6 | 4 | .600 | 0 | 2-6 | 34 | 1.67 | 2.02 |
| 2008 | SD | NL | 74 | 0 | 0 | 8 | 78.0 | 324 | 66 | 31 | 31 | 5 | 3 | 2 | 3 | 28 | 4 | 71 | 2 | 0 | 6 | 6 | .500 | 0 | 0-7 | 23 | 2.93 | 3.58 |
| 2009 | SD | NL | 68 | 0 | 0 | 59 | 69.2 | 278 | 54 | 21 | 21 | 3 | 0 | 0 | 0 | 24 | 1 | 79 | 4 | 0 | 6 | 4 | .600 | 0 | **42-48** | 0 | 2.36 | 2.71 |
| 2010 | SD | NL | 67 | 0 | 0 | 57 | 70.0 | 287 | 56 | 17 | 15 | 1 | 4 | 1 | 1 | 28 | 3 | 86 | 1 | 0 | 6 | 1 | .857 | 0 | 47-50 | 0 | 2.47 | 1.93 |
| 2011 | SD | NL | 64 | 0 | 0 | 54 | 62.2 | 256 | 51 | 20 | 17 | 4 | 5 | 1 | 0 | 21 | 2 | 51 | 8 | 0 | 3 | 4 | .429 | 0 | 43-48 | 0 | 2.57 | 2.44 |
| 2012 | Mia | NL | 73 | 0 | 0 | 41 | 63.2 | 286 | 70 | 38 | 36 | 5 | 2 | 4 | 2 | 29 | 3 | 59 | 2 | 0 | 4 | 5 | .444 | 0 | 19-27 | 13 | 4.74 | 5.09 |
| 2013 | Ari | NL | 69 | 0 | 0 | 32 | 65.2 | 287 | 74 | 30 | 30 | 12 | 2 | 1 | 3 | 16 | 1 | 72 | 4 | 0 | 5 | 2 | .714 | 0 | 15-22 | 8 | 4.86 | 4.11 |
| 10 ML YEARS | | | 577 | 0 | 0 | 287 | 611.1 | 2547 | 560 | 242 | 230 | 47 | 26 | 10 | 12 | 206 | 20 | 625 | 26 | 1 | 37 | 31 | .544 | 0 | 168-209 | 83 | 3.27 | 3.39 |

# Duane Below

**Pitches:** L **Bats:** L **Pos:** RP-2 | BEE-low | **Ht:** 6'3" **Wt:** 220 **Born:** 11/15/1985 **Age:** 28

| | | | HOW MUCH HE PITCHED | | | | | | WHAT HE GAVE UP | | | | | | | | | | | | THE RESULTS | | | | | | | |
|---|---|---|---|---|---|---|---|---|---|---|---|---|---|---|---|---|---|---|---|---|---|---|---|---|---|---|---|---|
| Year | Team | Lg | G | GS | CG | GF | IP | BFP | H | R | ER | HR | SH | SF | HB | TBB | IBB | SO | WP | Bk | W | L | Pct | Sh | Sv-Op | Hld | ERC | ERA |
| 2013 | Toledo* | AAA | 4 | 4 | 0 | 0 | 25.2 | 96 | 15 | 6 | 6 | 1 | 2 | 0 | 0 | 4 | 0 | 15 | 0 | 0 | 1 | 2 | .333 | 0 | 0-- | - | 1.12 | 2.10 |
| 2013 | NewOr* | AAA | 13 | 13 | 0 | 0 | 74.0 | 310 | 77 | 31 | 21 | 3 | 1 | 2 | 1 | 21 | 2 | 53 | 1 | 1 | 5 | 5 | .500 | 0 | 0-- | - | 3.50 | 2.55 |
| 2011 | Det | AL | 14 | 2 | 0 | 4 | 29.0 | 127 | 28 | 16 | 14 | 2 | 1 | 3 | 1 | 11 | 2 | 14 | 2 | 0 | 0 | 2 | .000 | 0 | 0-0 | 0 | 3.52 | 4.34 |
| 2012 | Det | AL | 27 | 1 | 0 | 7 | 46.1 | 189 | 49 | 25 | 20 | 6 | 2 | 3 | 1 | 8 | 0 | 29 | 1 | 1 | 2 | 1 | .667 | 0 | 0-0 | 0 | 3.88 | 3.88 |
| 2013 | Mia | NL | 2 | 0 | 0 | 0 | 2.2 | 15 | 6 | 3 | 3 | 0 | 0 | 1 | 0 | 2 | 1 | 2 | 0 | 0 | 0 | 1 | .000 | 0 | 0-0 | 0 | 12.51 | 10.13 |
| 3 ML YEARS | | | 43 | 3 | 0 | 11 | 78.0 | 331 | 83 | 44 | 37 | 8 | 3 | 7 | 2 | 21 | 3 | 45 | 3 | 1 | 2 | 4 | .333 | 0 | 0-0 | 0 | 4.00 | 4.27 |

# Brandon Belt

**Bats:** L **Throws:** L **Pos:** 1B-143;PH-12 **Ht:** 6'5" **Wt:** 220 **Born:** 4/20/1988 **Age:** 26

| BATTING | | | | | | | | | | | | | | | | | | | | | | BASERUNNING | | | | AVERAGES | | |
|---|---|---|---|---|---|---|---|---|---|---|---|---|---|---|---|---|---|---|---|---|---|---|---|---|---|---|---|---|
| Year | Team | Lg | G | AB | H | 2B | 3B | HR | (Hm | Rd) | TB | R | RBI | RC | TBB | IBB | SO | HBP | SH | SF | | SB | CS | SB% | GDP | Avg | OBP | Slg |
| 2011 | SF | NL | 63 | 187 | 42 | 6 | 1 | 9 | (2 | 7) | 77 | 21 | 18 | 20 | 20 | 1 | 57 | 2 | 0 | 0 | | 3 | 2 | .60 | 3 | .225 | .306 | .412 |
| 2012 | SF | NL | 145 | 411 | 113 | 27 | 6 | 7 | (5 | 2) | 173 | 47 | 56 | 63 | 54 | 5 | 106 | 3 | 0 | 4 | | 12 | 2 | .86 | 3 | .275 | .360 | .421 |
| 2013 | SF | NL | 150 | 509 | 147 | 39 | 4 | 17 | (6 | 11) | 245 | 76 | 67 | 82 | 52 | 4 | 125 | 6 | 1 | 3 | | 5 | 2 | .71 | 4 | .289 | .360 | .481 |
| Postseason | | | 15 | 49 | 9 | 1 | 2 | 1 | (1 | 0) | 17 | 7 | 3 | 6 | 7 | 0 | 19 | 0 | 0 | 0 | | 1 | 1 | .50 | 0 | .184 | .286 | .347 |
| 3 ML YEARS | | | 358 | 1107 | 302 | 72 | 11 | 33 | (13 | 20) | 495 | 144 | 141 | 165 | 126 | 10 | 288 | 11 | 1 | 7 | | 20 | 6 | .77 | 10 | .273 | .351 | .447 |

# Carlos Beltran

**Bats:** B **Throws:** R **Pos:** RF-137;PH-6;DH-3 BELL-trahn **Ht:** 6'1" **Wt:** 210 **Born:** 4/24/1977 **Age:** 37

| BATTING | | | | | | | | | | | | | | | | | | | | | | BASERUNNING | | | | AVERAGES | | |
|---|---|---|---|---|---|---|---|---|---|---|---|---|---|---|---|---|---|---|---|---|---|---|---|---|---|---|---|---|
| Year | Team | Lg | G | AB | H | 2B | 3B | HR | (Hm | Rd) | TB | R | RBI | RC | TBB | IBB | SO | HBP | SH | SF | | SB | CS | SB% | GDP | Avg | OBP | Slg |
| 1998 | KC | AL | 14 | 58 | 16 | 5 | 3 | 0 | (0 | 0) | 27 | 12 | 7 | 9 | 3 | 0 | 12 | 1 | 0 | 1 | | 3 | 0 | 1.00 | 2 | .276 | .317 | .466 |
| 1999 | KC | AL | 156 | 663 | 194 | 27 | 7 | 22 | (12 | 10) | 301 | 112 | 108 | 100 | 46 | 2 | 123 | 4 | 0 | 10 | | 27 | 8 | .77 | 17 | .293 | .337 | .454 |
| 2000 | KC | AL | 98 | 372 | 92 | 15 | 4 | 7 | (4 | 3) | 136 | 49 | 44 | 43 | 35 | 2 | 69 | 0 | 2 | 4 | | 13 | 0 | 1.00 | 12 | .247 | .309 | .366 |
| 2001 | KC | AL | 155 | 617 | 189 | 32 | 12 | 24 | (7 | 17) | 317 | 106 | 101 | 118 | 52 | 2 | 120 | 5 | 1 | 5 | | 31 | 1 | **.97** | 7 | .306 | .362 | .514 |
| 2002 | KC | AL | **162** | 637 | 174 | 44 | 7 | 29 | (19 | 10) | 319 | 114 | 105 | 117 | 71 | 1 | 135 | 4 | 3 | 7 | | 35 | 7 | .83 | 12 | .273 | .346 | .501 |
| 2003 | KC | AL | 141 | 521 | 160 | 14 | 10 | 26 | (10 | 16) | 272 | 102 | 100 | 117 | 72 | 4 | 81 | 2 | 0 | 7 | | 41 | 4 | **.91** | 8 | .307 | .389 | .522 |
| 2004 | 2 Tms | | 159 | 599 | 160 | 36 | 9 | 38 | (15 | 23) | 328 | 121 | 104 | 124 | 92 | 10 | 101 | 7 | 3 | 7 | | 42 | 3 | .93 | 8 | .267 | .367 | .548 |
| 2005 | NYM | NL | 151 | 582 | 155 | 34 | 2 | 16 | (6 | 10) | 241 | 83 | 78 | 88 | 56 | 5 | 96 | 2 | 4 | 6 | | 17 | 6 | .74 | 9 | .266 | .330 | .414 |
| 2006 | NYM | NL | 140 | 510 | 140 | 38 | 1 | 41 | (15 | 26) | 303 | 127 | 116 | 121 | 95 | 6 | 99 | 4 | 1 | 7 | | 18 | 3 | .86 | 6 | .275 | .388 | .594 |
| 2007 | NYM | NL | 144 | 554 | 153 | 33 | 3 | 33 | (11 | 22) | 291 | 93 | 112 | 97 | 69 | 10 | 111 | 2 | 1 | 10 | | 23 | 2 | .92 | 8 | .276 | .353 | .525 |
| 2008 | NYM | NL | 161 | 606 | 172 | 40 | 5 | 27 | (14 | 13) | 303 | 116 | 112 | 116 | 92 | 13 | 96 | 1 | 1 | 6 | | 25 | 3 | .89 | 11 | .284 | .376 | .500 |
| 2009 | NYM | NL | 81 | 308 | 100 | 22 | 1 | 10 | (3 | 7) | 154 | 50 | 48 | 54 | 47 | 10 | 43 | 1 | 0 | 1 | | 11 | 1 | .92 | 9 | .325 | .415 | .500 |
| 2010 | NYM | NL | 64 | 220 | 56 | 11 | 3 | 7 | (3 | 4) | 94 | 21 | 27 | 31 | 30 | 5 | 39 | 1 | 0 | 4 | | 3 | 1 | .75 | 4 | .255 | .341 | .427 |
| 2011 | 2 Tms | NL | 142 | 520 | 156 | 39 | 6 | 22 | (14 | 8) | 273 | 78 | 84 | 96 | 71 | 7 | 88 | 3 | 0 | 4 | | 4 | 2 | .67 | 18 | .300 | .385 | .525 |
| 2012 | StL | NL | 151 | 547 | 147 | 26 | 1 | 32 | (20 | 12) | 271 | 83 | 97 | 87 | 65 | 15 | 124 | 2 | 1 | 4 | | 13 | 6 | .68 | 9 | .269 | .346 | .495 |
| 2013 | StL | NL | 145 | 554 | 164 | 30 | 3 | 24 | (12 | 12) | 272 | 79 | 84 | 91 | 38 | 1 | 90 | 1 | 1 | 6 | | 2 | 1 | .67 | 12 | .296 | .339 | .491 |
| 04 | KC | AL | 69 | 266 | 74 | 19 | 2 | 15 | (8 | 7) | 142 | 51 | 51 | 57 | 37 | 7 | 44 | 2 | 1 | 3 | | 14 | 3 | .82 | 4 | .278 | .367 | .534 |
| 04 | Hou | NL | 90 | 333 | 86 | 17 | 7 | 23 | (7 | 16) | 186 | 70 | 53 | 67 | 55 | 3 | 57 | 5 | 2 | 4 | | 28 | 0 | 1.00 | 4 | .258 | .368 | .559 |
| 11 | NYM | NL | 98 | 353 | 102 | 30 | 2 | 15 | (9 | 6) | 181 | 61 | 66 | 72 | 60 | 6 | 61 | 2 | 0 | 4 | | 3 | 0 | 1.00 | 9 | .289 | .391 | .513 |
| 11 | SF | NL | 44 | 167 | 54 | 9 | 4 | 7 | (5 | 2) | 92 | 17 | 18 | 24 | 11 | 1 | 27 | 1 | 0 | 0 | | 1 | 2 | .33 | 9 | .323 | .369 | .551 |
| Postseason | | | 34 | 124 | 45 | 10 | 0 | 14 | (6 | 8) | 97 | 39 | 25 | 39 | 25 | 1 | 18 | 1 | 0 | 1 | | 11 | 0 | 1.00 | 2 | .363 | .470 | .782 |
| 16 ML YEARS | | | 2064 | 7868 | 2228 | 446 | 77 | 358 | (165 | 193) | 3902 | 1346 | 1327 | 1409 | 934 | 93 | 1427 | 40 | 18 | 89 | | 308 | 48 | .87 | 152 | .283 | .359 | .496 |

# Adrian Beltre

**Bats:** R **Throws:** R **Pos:** 3B-146;DH-15 **Ht:** 5'11" **Wt:** 220 **Born:** 4/7/1979 **Age:** 35

| BATTING | | | | | | | | | | | | | | | | | | | | | | BASERUNNING | | | | AVERAGES | | |
|---|---|---|---|---|---|---|---|---|---|---|---|---|---|---|---|---|---|---|---|---|---|---|---|---|---|---|---|---|
| Year | Team | Lg | G | AB | H | 2B | 3B | HR | (Hm | Rd) | TB | R | RBI | RC | TBB | IBB | SO | HBP | SH | SF | | SB | CS | SB% | GDP | Avg | OBP | Slg |
| 1998 | LAD | NL | 77 | 195 | 42 | 9 | 0 | 7 | (5 | 2) | 72 | 18 | 22 | 20 | 14 | 0 | 37 | 3 | 2 | 0 | | 3 | 1 | .75 | 4 | .215 | .278 | .369 |
| 1999 | LAD | NL | 152 | 538 | 148 | 27 | 5 | 15 | (6 | 9) | 230 | 84 | 67 | 84 | 61 | 12 | 105 | 6 | 4 | 5 | | 18 | 7 | .72 | 4 | .275 | .352 | .428 |
| 2000 | LAD | NL | 138 | 510 | 148 | 30 | 2 | 20 | (7 | 13) | 242 | 71 | 85 | 85 | 56 | 2 | 80 | 2 | 3 | 4 | | 12 | 5 | .71 | 13 | .290 | .360 | .475 |
| 2001 | LAD | NL | 126 | 475 | 126 | 22 | 4 | 13 | (4 | 9) | 195 | 59 | 60 | 60 | 28 | 1 | 82 | 5 | 2 | 5 | | 13 | 4 | .76 | 9 | .265 | .310 | .411 |
| 2002 | LAD | NL | 159 | 587 | 151 | 26 | 5 | 21 | (7 | 14) | 250 | 70 | 75 | 74 | 37 | 4 | 96 | 4 | 1 | 6 | | 7 | 5 | .58 | 17 | .257 | .303 | .426 |
| 2003 | LAD | NL | 158 | 559 | 134 | 30 | 2 | 23 | (13 | 10) | 237 | 50 | 80 | 66 | 37 | 4 | 103 | 5 | 1 | 6 | | 2 | 2 | .50 | 13 | .240 | .290 | .424 |
| 2004 | LAD | NL | 156 | 598 | 200 | 32 | 0 | **48** | (23 | 25) | 376 | 104 | 121 | 120 | 53 | 9 | 87 | 2 | 0 | 4 | | 7 | 2 | .78 | 15 | .334 | .388 | .629 |
| 2005 | Sea | AL | 156 | 603 | 154 | 36 | 1 | 19 | (7 | 12) | 249 | 69 | 87 | 75 | 38 | 6 | 108 | 5 | 0 | 4 | | 3 | 1 | .75 | 15 | .255 | .303 | .413 |
| 2006 | Sea | AL | 156 | 620 | 166 | 39 | 4 | 25 | (16 | 9) | 288 | 88 | 89 | 85 | 47 | 4 | 118 | 10 | 1 | 3 | | 11 | 5 | .69 | 15 | .268 | .328 | .465 |
| 2007 | Sea | AL | 149 | 595 | 164 | 41 | 2 | 26 | (11 | 15) | 287 | 87 | 99 | 79 | 38 | 2 | 104 | 2 | 0 | 4 | | 14 | 2 | .88 | 18 | .276 | .319 | .482 |
| 2008 | Sea | AL | 143 | 556 | 148 | 29 | 1 | 25 | (10 | 15) | 254 | 74 | 77 | 71 | 50 | 10 | 90 | 2 | 0 | 4 | | 8 | 2 | .80 | 11 | .266 | .327 | .457 |
| 2009 | Sea | AL | 111 | 449 | 119 | 27 | 0 | 8 | (4 | 4) | 170 | 54 | 44 | 48 | 19 | 1 | 74 | 7 | 0 | 2 | | 13 | 2 | .87 | 19 | .265 | .304 | .379 |
| 2010 | Bos | AL | 154 | 589 | 189 | **49** | 2 | 28 | (13 | 15) | 326 | 84 | 102 | 103 | 40 | 10 | 82 | 5 | 0 | 7 | | 2 | 1 | .67 | 25 | .321 | .365 | .553 |
| 2011 | Tex | AL | 124 | 487 | 144 | 33 | 0 | 32 | **(23** | 9) | 273 | 82 | 105 | 80 | 25 | 0 | 53 | 5 | 0 | 8 | | 1 | 1 | .50 | 13 | .296 | .331 | .561 |
| 2012 | Tex | AL | 156 | 604 | 194 | 33 | 2 | 36 | (20 | 16) | 339 | 95 | 102 | 109 | 36 | 8 | 82 | 5 | 0 | 9 | | 1 | 0 | 1.00 | 8 | .321 | .359 | .561 |
| 2013 | Tex | AL | 161 | 631 | **199** | 32 | 0 | 30 | (15 | 15) | 321 | 88 | 92 | 97 | 50 | 12 | 78 | 7 | 0 | 2 | | 1 | 0 | 1.00 | 17 | .315 | .371 | .509 |
| Postseason | | | 22 | 91 | 23 | 5 | 0 | 5 | (1 | 4) | 43 | 15 | 10 | 8 | 2 | 1 | 22 | 2 | 0 | 1 | | 0 | 0 | - | 1 | .253 | .281 | .473 |
| 16 ML YEARS | | | 2276 | 8596 | 2426 | 495 | 30 | 376 | (184 | 192) | 4109 | 1177 | 1307 | 1256 | 629 | 85 | 1379 | 75 | 14 | 73 | | 116 | 40 | .74 | 216 | .282 | .334 | .478 |

# Engel Beltre

**Bats:** L **Throws:** L **Pos:** PR-7;RF-6;LF-5;CF-5;DH-2;PH-2 ahn-HELL **Ht:** 6'2" **Wt:** 180 **Born:** 11/1/1989 **Age:** 24

| BATTING | | | | | | | | | | | | | | | | | | | | | | BASERUNNING | | | | AVERAGES | | |
|---|---|---|---|---|---|---|---|---|---|---|---|---|---|---|---|---|---|---|---|---|---|---|---|---|---|---|---|---|
| Year | Team | Lg | G | AB | H | 2B | 3B | HR | (Hm | Rd) | TB | R | RBI | RC | TBB | IBB | SO | HBP | SH | SF | | SB | CS | SB% | GDP | Avg | OBP | Slg |
| 2009 | Bkrsfld | A+ | 84 | 357 | 81 | 13 | 5 | 3 | (- | -) | 113 | 44 | 23 | 33 | 17 | 1 | 77 | 10 | 5 | 0 | | 17 | 7 | .71 | 6 | .227 | .281 | .317 |
| 2009 | Rngrs | R | 3 | 10 | 3 | 1 | 1 | 0 | (- | -) | 6 | 4 | 0 | 2 | 0 | 0 | 3 | 1 | 0 | 0 | | 2 | 0 | 1.00 | 0 | .300 | .364 | .600 |
| 2009 | Frisco | AA | 4 | 14 | 1 | 1 | 0 | 0 | (- | -) | 2 | 1 | 1 | 0 | 0 | 0 | 2 | 1 | 0 | 0 | | 1 | 0 | 1.00 | 0 | .071 | .133 | .143 |
| 2010 | Bkrsfld | A+ | 68 | 263 | 87 | 11 | 4 | 5 | (- | -) | 121 | 38 | 35 | 45 | 11 | 1 | 34 | 10 | 3 | 3 | | 10 | 7 | .59 | 0 | .331 | .376 | .460 |
| 2010 | Frisco | AA | 47 | 181 | 46 | 4 | 4 | 1 | (- | -) | 61 | 14 | 14 | 20 | 10 | 0 | 24 | 3 | 2 | 2 | | 8 | 2 | .80 | 1 | .254 | .301 | .337 |
| 2011 | Frisco | AA | 118 | 437 | 101 | 15 | 6 | 1 | (- | -) | 131 | 64 | 28 | 39 | 28 | 1 | 103 | 5 | 11 | 1 | | 16 | 6 | .73 | 7 | .231 | .285 | .300 |
| 2012 | Frisco | AA | 133 | 564 | 147 | 17 | 17 | 13 | (- | -) | 237 | 80 | 55 | 78 | 26 | 1 | 118 | 13 | 8 | 3 | | 36 | 10 | .78 | 14 | .261 | .307 | .420 |
| 2013 | RdRck | AAA | 94 | 394 | 115 | 19 | 1 | 7 | (- | -) | 157 | 58 | 34 | 54 | 28 | 2 | 84 | 3 | 9 | 5 | | 15 | 12 | .56 | 8 | .292 | .340 | .398 |
| 2013 | Tex | AL | 22 | 40 | 10 | 1 | 0 | 0 | (0 | 0) | 11 | 7 | 2 | 2 | 0 | 0 | 5 | 1 | 1 | 0 | | 1 | 2 | .33 | 1 | .250 | .268 | .275 |

# Joaquin Benoit

**Pitches:** R **Bats:** R **Pos:** RP-66 ben-WAH **Ht:** 6'3" **Wt:** 220 **Born:** 7/26/1977 **Age:** 36

| | | | HOW MUCH HE PITCHED | | | | | | WHAT HE GAVE UP | | | | | | | | | | | | THE RESULTS | | | | | | | |
|---|---|---|---|---|---|---|---|---|---|---|---|---|---|---|---|---|---|---|---|---|---|---|---|---|---|---|---|---|
| Year | Team | Lg | G | GS | CG | GF | IP | BFP | H | R | ER | HR | SH | SF | HB | TBB | IBB | SO | WP | Bk | W | L | Pct | Sh | Sv-Op | Hld | ERC | ERA |
| 2001 | Tex | AL | 1 | 1 | 0 | 0 | 5.0 | 26 | 8 | 6 | 6 | 3 | 0 | 1 | 0 | 3 | 0 | 4 | 0 | 0 | 0 | 0 | - | 0 | 0-0 | 0 | 13.11 | 10.80 |
| 2002 | Tex | AL | 17 | 13 | 0 | 2 | 84.2 | 405 | 91 | 51 | 50 | 6 | 4 | 3 | 5 | 58 | 2 | 59 | 7 | 0 | 4 | 5 | .444 | 0 | 1-1 | 0 | 5.52 | 5.31 |
| 2003 | Tex | AL | 25 | 17 | 0 | 1 | 105.0 | 462 | 99 | 67 | 64 | 23 | 1 | 4 | 3 | 51 | 0 | 87 | 3 | 1 | 8 | 5 | .615 | 0 | 0-0 | 0 | 5.03 | 5.49 |
| 2004 | Tex | AL | 28 | 15 | 0 | 2 | 103.0 | 456 | 113 | 67 | 65 | 19 | 2 | 10 | 8 | 31 | 0 | 95 | 3 | 0 | 3 | 5 | .375 | 0 | 0-0 | 0 | 5.10 | 5.68 |
| 2005 | Tex | AL | 32 | 9 | 0 | 6 | 87.0 | 369 | 69 | 39 | 36 | 9 | 2 | 1 | 2 | 38 | 0 | 78 | 1 | 0 | 4 | 4 | .500 | 0 | 0-0 | 5 | 3.15 | 3.72 |
| 2006 | Tex | AL | 56 | 0 | 0 | 7 | 79.2 | 347 | 68 | 49 | 43 | 5 | 0 | 3 | 3 | 38 | 4 | 85 | 3 | 0 | 1 | 1 | .500 | 0 | 0-2 | 7 | 3.30 | 4.86 |
| 2007 | Tex | AL | 70 | 0 | 0 | 22 | 82.0 | 337 | 68 | 28 | 26 | 6 | 3 | 2 | 2 | 28 | 2 | 87 | 3 | 0 | 7 | 4 | .636 | 0 | 6-13 | 19 | 2.83 | 2.85 |
| 2008 | Tex | AL | 44 | 0 | 0 | 8 | 45.0 | 209 | 40 | 28 | 25 | 6 | 2 | 0 | 0 | 35 | 2 | 43 | 3 | 0 | 3 | 2 | .600 | 0 | 1-4 | 13 | 5.02 | 5.00 |
| 2010 | TB | AL | 63 | 0 | 0 | 16 | 60.1 | 217 | 30 | 10 | 9 | 6 | 0 | 2 | 0 | 11 | 1 | 75 | 1 | 0 | 1 | 2 | .333 | 0 | 1-4 | 25 | 1.14 | 1.34 |
| 2011 | Det | AL | 66 | 0 | 0 | 13 | 61.0 | 241 | 47 | 22 | 20 | 5 | 1 | 5 | 2 | 17 | 1 | 63 | 3 | 0 | 4 | 3 | .571 | 0 | 2-7 | 29 | 2.46 | 2.95 |
| 2012 | Det | AL | 73 | 0 | 0 | 18 | 71.0 | 288 | 59 | 31 | 29 | 14 | 3 | 3 | 1 | 22 | 2 | 84 | 2 | 0 | 5 | 3 | .625 | 0 | 2-6 | 30 | 3.48 | 3.68 |
| 2013 | Det | AL | 66 | 0 | 0 | 43 | 67.0 | 265 | 47 | 15 | 15 | 5 | 4 | 0 | 1 | 22 | 2 | 73 | 2 | 0 | 4 | 1 | .800 | 0 | 24-26 | 9 | 2.15 | 2.01 |
| Postseason | | | 14 | 0 | 0 | 0 | 16.2 | 62 | 10 | 3 | 3 | 2 | 0 | 0 | 0 | 4 | 0 | 17 | 2 | 0 | 1 | 0 | 1.000 | 0 | 0-1 | 5 | 1.67 | 1.62 |
| 12 ML YEARS | | | 541 | 55 | 0 | 138 | 850.2 | 3622 | 739 | 413 | 388 | 107 | 22 | 34 | 27 | 354 | 16 | 833 | 31 | 1 | 44 | 35 | .557 | 0 | 37-63 | 137 | 3.66 | 4.11 |

# Lance Berkman

**Bats:** B **Throws:** L **Pos:** DH-65;1B-4;PH-4 **Ht:** 6'1" **Wt:** 220 **Born:** 2/10/1976 **Age:** 38

| | | | BATTING | | | | | | | | | | | | | | | | | | BASERUNNING | | | | AVERAGES | | |
|---|---|---|---|---|---|---|---|---|---|---|---|---|---|---|---|---|---|---|---|---|---|---|---|---|---|---|---|
| Year | Team | Lg | G | AB | H | 2B | 3B | HR | (Hm | Rd) | TB | R | RBI | RC | TBB | IBB | SO | HBP | SH | SF | SB | CS | SB% | GDP | Avg | OBP | Slg |
| 2013 | RdRck* | AAA | 2 | 7 | 3 | 0 | 0 | 1 | (- | -) | 6 | 1 | 2 | 2 | 0 | 0 | 1 | 0 | 0 | 0 | 0 | 0 | - | 0 | .429 | .429 | .857 |
| 2013 | Frisco* | AA | 2 | 4 | 1 | 0 | 0 | 0 | (- | -) | 1 | 2 | 1 | 1 | 3 | 0 | 1 | 0 | 0 | 0 | 0 | 0 | - | 0 | .250 | .571 | .250 |
| 1999 | Hou | NL | 34 | 93 | 22 | 2 | 0 | 4 | (2 | 2) | 36 | 10 | 15 | 12 | 12 | 0 | 21 | 0 | 0 | 1 | 5 | 1 | .83 | 2 | .237 | .321 | .387 |
| 2000 | Hou | NL | 114 | 353 | 105 | 28 | 1 | 21 | (10 | 11) | 198 | 76 | 67 | 76 | 56 | 1 | 73 | 1 | 0 | 7 | 6 | 2 | .75 | 6 | .297 | .388 | .561 |
| 2001 | Hou | NL | 156 | 577 | 191 | **55** | 5 | 34 | (13 | 21) | 358 | 110 | 126 | 144 | 92 | 5 | 121 | 13 | 0 | 6 | 7 | 9 | .44 | 8 | .331 | .430 | .620 |
| 2002 | Hou | NL | 158 | 578 | 169 | 35 | 2 | 42 | (20 | 22) | 334 | 106 | **128** | 130 | 107 | 20 | 118 | 4 | 0 | 3 | 8 | 4 | .67 | 10 | .292 | .405 | .578 |
| 2003 | Hou | NL | 153 | 538 | 155 | 35 | 6 | 25 | (11 | 14) | 277 | 110 | 93 | 115 | 107 | 13 | 108 | 9 | 1 | 3 | 5 | 3 | .63 | 10 | .288 | .412 | .515 |
| 2004 | Hou | NL | 160 | 544 | 172 | 40 | 3 | 30 | (8 | 22) | 308 | 104 | 106 | 126 | 127 | 14 | 101 | 10 | 0 | 6 | 9 | 7 | .56 | 10 | .316 | .450 | .566 |
| 2005 | Hou | NL | 132 | 468 | 137 | 34 | 1 | 24 | (13 | 11) | 245 | 76 | 82 | 88 | 91 | 12 | 72 | 4 | 0 | 2 | 4 | 1 | .80 | 18 | .293 | .411 | .524 |
| 2006 | Hou | NL | 152 | 536 | 169 | 29 | 0 | 45 | (24 | 21) | 333 | 95 | 136 | 138 | 98 | 22 | 106 | 4 | 0 | 8 | 3 | 2 | .60 | 11 | .315 | .420 | .621 |
| 2007 | Hou | NL | 153 | 561 | 156 | 24 | 2 | 34 | (13 | 21) | 286 | 95 | 102 | 105 | 94 | 11 | 125 | 8 | 0 | 5 | 7 | 3 | .70 | 11 | .278 | .386 | .510 |
| 2008 | Hou | NL | 159 | 554 | 173 | **46** | 4 | 29 | (16 | 13) | 314 | 114 | 106 | 129 | 99 | 18 | 108 | 7 | 0 | 5 | 18 | 4 | .82 | 13 | .312 | .420 | .567 |
| 2009 | Hou | NL | 136 | 460 | 126 | 31 | 1 | 25 | (14 | 11) | 234 | 73 | 80 | 83 | 97 | 14 | 98 | 1 | 0 | 4 | 7 | 4 | .64 | 13 | .274 | .399 | .509 |
| 2010 | 2 Tms | | 122 | 404 | 100 | 23 | 1 | 14 | (10 | 4) | 167 | 48 | 58 | 61 | 77 | 7 | 85 | 0 | 0 | 0 | 3 | 2 | .60 | 18 | .248 | .368 | .413 |
| 2011 | StL | NL | 145 | 488 | 147 | 23 | 2 | 31 | (9 | **22**) | 267 | 90 | 94 | 107 | 92 | 17 | 93 | 3 | 0 | 4 | 2 | 6 | .25 | 7 | .301 | .412 | .547 |
| 2012 | StL | NL | 32 | 81 | 21 | 7 | 1 | 2 | (0 | 2) | 36 | 12 | 7 | 10 | 14 | 3 | 19 | 2 | 0 | 0 | 2 | 0 | 1.00 | 3 | .259 | .381 | .444 |
| 2013 | Tex | AL | 73 | 256 | 62 | 10 | 1 | 6 | (3 | 3) | 92 | 27 | 34 | 38 | 38 | 3 | 52 | 0 | 0 | 0 | 0 | 0 | - | 7 | .242 | .340 | .359 |
| 10 | Hou | NL | 85 | 298 | 73 | 16 | 1 | 13 | (9 | 4) | 130 | 39 | 49 | 48 | 60 | 4 | 70 | 0 | 0 | 0 | 3 | 2 | .60 | 12 | .245 | .372 | .436 |
| 10 | NYY | AL | 37 | 106 | 27 | 7 | 0 | 1 | (1 | 0) | 37 | 9 | 9 | 13 | 17 | 3 | 15 | 0 | 0 | 0 | 0 | 0 | - | 6 | .255 | .358 | .349 |
| Postseason | | | 52 | 186 | 59 | 11 | 1 | 9 | (5 | 4) | 99 | 38 | 41 | 46 | 31 | 6 | 41 | 3 | 0 | 3 | 4 | 1 | .80 | 4 | .317 | .417 | .532 |
| 15 ML YEARS | | | 1879 | 6491 | 1905 | 422 | 30 | 366 | (166 | 200) | 3485 | 1146 | 1234 | 1362 | 1201 | 160 | 1300 | 66 | 1 | 54 | 86 | 48 | .64 | 147 | .293 | .406 | .537 |

# Roger Bernadina

**Bats:** L **Throws:** L **Pos:** RF-40;PH-30;LF-29;CF-18;PR-7 burn-ah-DEEN-ah **Ht:** 6'2" **Wt:** 200 **Born:** 6/12/1984 **Age:** 30

| | | | BATTING | | | | | | | | | | | | | | | | | | BASERUNNING | | | | AVERAGES | | |
|---|---|---|---|---|---|---|---|---|---|---|---|---|---|---|---|---|---|---|---|---|---|---|---|---|---|---|---|
| Year | Team | Lg | G | AB | H | 2B | 3B | HR | (Hm | Rd) | TB | R | RBI | RC | TBB | IBB | SO | HBP | SH | SF | SB | CS | SB% | GDP | Avg | OBP | Slg |
| 2008 | Was | NL | 26 | 76 | 16 | 1 | 1 | 0 | (0 | 0) | 19 | 10 | 2 | 4 | 9 | 0 | 21 | 0 | 1 | 0 | 4 | 3 | .57 | 3 | .211 | .294 | .250 |
| 2009 | Was | NL | 3 | 4 | 1 | 1 | 0 | 0 | (0 | 0) | 2 | 1 | 0 | 1 | 1 | 0 | 1 | 0 | 0 | 0 | 1 | 0 | 1.00 | 0 | .250 | .400 | .500 |
| 2010 | Was | NL | 134 | 414 | 102 | 18 | 3 | 11 | (3 | 8) | 159 | 52 | 47 | 53 | 35 | 1 | 93 | 4 | 2 | 6 | 16 | 2 | .89 | 3 | .246 | .307 | .384 |
| 2011 | Was | NL | 91 | 309 | 75 | 12 | 2 | 7 | (5 | 2) | 112 | 40 | 27 | 34 | 22 | 1 | 63 | 4 | 2 | 0 | 17 | 3 | .85 | 7 | .243 | .301 | .362 |
| 2012 | Was | NL | 129 | 227 | 66 | 11 | 0 | 5 | (1 | 4) | 92 | 25 | 25 | 40 | 28 | 3 | 53 | 2 | 3 | 1 | 15 | 3 | .83 | 2 | .291 | .372 | .405 |
| 2013 | 2 Tms | NL | 112 | 227 | 41 | 10 | 2 | 4 | (2 | 2) | 67 | 26 | 11 | 15 | 16 | 1 | 65 | 5 | 2 | 0 | 4 | 0 | 1.00 | 4 | .181 | .250 | .295 |
| 13 | Was | NL | 85 | 152 | 27 | 6 | 1 | 2 | (1 | 1) | 41 | 18 | 6 | 8 | 12 | 1 | 44 | 2 | 1 | 0 | 3 | 0 | 1.00 | 4 | .178 | .247 | .270 |
| 13 | Phi | NL | 27 | 75 | 14 | 4 | 1 | 2 | (1 | 1) | 26 | 8 | 5 | 7 | 4 | 0 | 21 | 3 | 1 | 0 | 1 | 0 | 1.00 | 0 | .187 | .256 | .347 |
| Postseason | | | 4 | 2 | 0 | 0 | 0 | 0 | (0 | 0) | 0 | 0 | 0 | 0 | 2 | 0 | 1 | 0 | 0 | 0 | 0 | 0 | - | 0 | .000 | .500 | .000 |
| 6 ML YEARS | | | 495 | 1257 | 301 | 53 | 8 | 27 | (11 | 16) | 451 | 154 | 112 | 147 | 111 | 6 | 296 | 15 | 10 | 7 | 57 | 11 | .84 | 19 | .239 | .307 | .359 |

# Doug Bernier

burr-NEER

**Bats:** R **Throws:** R **Pos:** SS-20;PR-10;3B-7;2B-4;PH-2;DH-1 **Ht:** 6'1" **Wt:** 185 **Born:** 6/24/1980 **Age:** 34

| | | | BATTING | | | | | | | | | | | | | | | | | | BASERUNNING | | | | AVERAGES | | |
|---|---|---|---|---|---|---|---|---|---|---|---|---|---|---|---|---|---|---|---|---|---|---|---|---|---|---|---|
| Year | Team | Lg | G | AB | H | 2B | 3B | HR | (Hm | Rd) | TB | R | RBI | RC | TBB | IBB | SO | HBP | SH | SF | SB | CS | SB% | GDP | Avg | OBP | Slg |
| 2009 | S-WB | AAA | 80 | 227 | 41 | 9 | 2 | 0 | (- | -) | 54 | 33 | 20 | 19 | 34 | 2 | 71 | 7 | 4 | 1 | 1 | 0 | 1.00 | 6 | .181 | .305 | .238 |
| 2010 | Indy | AAA | 69 | 200 | 48 | 14 | 0 | 1 | (- | -) | 65 | 24 | 15 | 21 | 17 | 0 | 48 | 1 | 7 | 1 | 6 | 1 | .86 | 5 | .240 | .301 | .325 |
| 2011 | S-WB | AAA | 96 | 291 | 69 | 13 | 4 | 0 | (- | -) | 90 | 32 | 29 | 33 | 37 | 0 | 78 | 3 | 4 | 1 | 4 | 1 | .80 | 6 | .237 | .328 | .309 |
| 2012 | S-WB | AAA | 58 | 174 | 35 | 9 | 0 | 0 | (- | -) | 44 | 13 | 10 | 15 | 27 | 0 | 49 | 0 | 6 | 1 | 1 | 2 | .33 | 5 | .201 | .307 | .253 |
| 2013 | Roch | AAA | 92 | 302 | 89 | 15 | 5 | 3 | (- | -) | 123 | 47 | 41 | 48 | 31 | 1 | 74 | 7 | 10 | 3 | 4 | 2 | .67 | 8 | .295 | .370 | .407 |
| 2008 | Col | NL | 2 | 4 | 0 | 0 | 0 | 0 | (0 | 0) | 0 | 0 | 0 | 0 | 0 | 0 | 1 | 0 | 0 | 0 | 0 | 0 | - | 0 | .000 | .000 | .000 |
| 2013 | Min | AL | 33 | 53 | 12 | 3 | 0 | 0 | (0 | 0) | 15 | 9 | 5 | 7 | 8 | 1 | 15 | 1 | 2 | 0 | 2 | 1 | .67 | 1 | .226 | .339 | .283 |
| 2 ML YEARS | | | 35 | 57 | 12 | 3 | 0 | 0 | (0 | 0) | 15 | 9 | 5 | 7 | 8 | 1 | 16 | 1 | 2 | 0 | 2 | 1 | .67 | 1 | .211 | .318 | .263 |

# Quintin Berry

**Bats:** L **Throws:** L **Pos:** PR-8;LF-4;RF-4;CF-3;PH-1 **Ht:** 6'0" **Wt:** 175 **Born:** 11/21/1984 **Age:** 29

| BATTING | | | | | | | | | | | | | | | | | | | | | BASERUNNING | | | | AVERAGES | | |
|---|---|---|---|---|---|---|---|---|---|---|---|---|---|---|---|---|---|---|---|---|---|---|---|---|---|---|---|
| Year Team | Lg | G | AB | H | 2B | 3B | HR | (Hm | Rd) | TB | R | RBI | RC | TBB | IBB | SO | HBP | SH | SF | | SB | CS | SB% | GDP | Avg | OBP | Slg |
| 2009 Rdng | AA | 135 | 516 | 137 | 17 | 2 | 5 | (- | -) | 173 | 89 | 28 | 72 | 63 | 2 | 118 | 9 | 10 | 0 | | 48 | 14 | .77 | 10 | .266 | .355 | .335 |
| 2010 Rdng | AA | 66 | 238 | 50 | 10 | 2 | 2 | (- | -) | 70 | 35 | 25 | 27 | 33 | 0 | 50 | 3 | 9 | 2 | | 23 | 6 | .79 | 6 | .210 | .312 | .294 |
| 2010 SnAnt | AA | 33 | 110 | 23 | 1 | 1 | 1 | (- | -) | 29 | 11 | 8 | 9 | 10 | 0 | 28 | 3 | 1 | 0 | | 4 | 2 | .67 | 1 | .209 | .293 | .264 |
| 2011 Carlina | AA | 93 | 320 | 95 | 16 | 1 | 6 | (- | -) | 131 | 64 | 41 | 61 | 52 | 1 | 83 | 3 | 2 | 1 | | 40 | 7 | .85 | 4 | .297 | .399 | .409 |
| 2011 Lsvlle | AAA | 4 | 18 | 1 | 0 | 0 | 0 | (- | -) | 1 | 2 | 0 | 0 | 0 | 0 | 4 | 0 | 1 | 0 | | 2 | 0 | 1.00 | 0 | .056 | .056 | .056 |
| 2012 Toledo | AAA | 39 | 159 | 43 | 8 | 0 | 0 | (- | -) | 51 | 18 | 11 | 24 | 22 | 0 | 46 | 3 | 2 | 1 | | 19 | 3 | .86 | 1 | .270 | .368 | .321 |
| 2013 Toledo | AAA | 49 | 167 | 28 | 8 | 0 | 1 | (- | -) | 39 | 16 | 15 | 14 | 23 | 0 | 45 | 3 | 5 | 1 | | 15 | 2 | .88 | 4 | .168 | .278 | .234 |
| 2013 Omha | AAA | 49 | 144 | 32 | 2 | 1 | 2 | (- | -) | 42 | 18 | 16 | 18 | 26 | 1 | 34 | 1 | 0 | 1 | | 13 | 2 | .87 | 0 | .222 | .343 | .292 |
| 2013 Pwtckt | AAA | 3 | 8 | 1 | 0 | 0 | 0 | (- | -) | 1 | 1 | 0 | 0 | 1 | 0 | 2 | 1 | 0 | 0 | | 2 | 0 | 1.00 | 0 | .125 | .300 | .125 |
| 2012 Det | AL | 94 | 291 | 75 | 10 | 6 | 2 | (1 | 1) | 103 | 44 | 29 | 44 | 25 | 0 | 80 | 7 | 6 | 1 | | 21 | 0 | **1.00** | 4 | .258 | .330 | .354 |
| 2013 Bos | AL | 13 | 8 | 5 | 0 | 0 | 1 | (0 | 1) | 8 | 5 | 4 | 5 | 1 | 0 | 2 | 0 | 0 | 0 | | 3 | 0 | 1.00 | 0 | .625 | .667 | 1.000 |
| Postseason | | 11 | 26 | 5 | 2 | 0 | 0 | (0 | 0) | 7 | 3 | 0 | 3 | 2 | 0 | 6 | 0 | 1 | 0 | | 2 | 0 | 1.00 | 1 | .192 | .250 | .269 |
| 2 ML YEARS | | 107 | 299 | 80 | 10 | 6 | 3 | (1 | 2) | 111 | 49 | 33 | 49 | 26 | 0 | 82 | 7 | 6 | 1 | | 24 | 0 | 1.00 | 4 | .268 | .339 | .371 |

# Dellin Betances

**Pitches:** R **Bats:** R **Pos:** RP-6 DELL-inn buh-TAN-siss **Ht:** 6'8" **Wt:** 260 **Born:** 3/23/1988 **Age:** 26

| HOW MUCH HE PITCHED | | | | | | | | WHAT HE GAVE UP | | | | | | | | | | | | | THE RESULTS | | | | | | | |
|---|---|---|---|---|---|---|---|---|---|---|---|---|---|---|---|---|---|---|---|---|---|---|---|---|---|---|---|---|
| Year Team | Lg | G | GS | CG | GF | IP | BFP | H | R | ER | HR | SH | SF | HB | TBB | IBB | SO | WP | Bk | | W | L | Pct | Sh | Sv-Op | Hld | ERC | ERA |
| 2009 Tampa | A+ | 11 | 11 | 0 | 0 | 44.1 | 206 | 48 | 29 | 27 | 2 | 2 | 2 | 2 | 27 | 0 | 44 | 3 | 0 | | 2 | 5 | .286 | 0 | 0- - | - | 5.11 | 5.48 |
| 2010 Tampa | A+ | 14 | 14 | 0 | 0 | 71.0 | 278 | 43 | 18 | 14 | 1 | 1 | 1 | 3 | 19 | 0 | 88 | 3 | 0 | | 8 | 1 | .889 | 0 | 0- - | - | 1.40 | 1.77 |
| 2010 Trntn | AA | 3 | 3 | 0 | 0 | 14.1 | 55 | 10 | 7 | 6 | 3 | 1 | 0 | 1 | 3 | 0 | 20 | 3 | 0 | | 0 | 0 | - | 0 | 0- - | - | 2.75 | 3.77 |
| 2011 Trntn | AA | 21 | 21 | 0 | 0 | 105.1 | 460 | 86 | 49 | 40 | 7 | 3 | 1 | 9 | 55 | 0 | 115 | 5 | 1 | | 4 | 6 | .400 | 0 | 0- - | - | 3.59 | 3.42 |
| 2011 S-WB | AAA | 4 | 4 | 1 | 0 | 21.0 | 94 | 16 | 12 | 12 | 2 | 1 | 0 | 1 | 15 | 0 | 27 | 2 | 0 | | 0 | 3 | .000 | 0 | 0- - | - | 4.07 | 5.14 |
| 2012 S-WB | AAA | 16 | 16 | 0 | 0 | 74.2 | 363 | 71 | 58 | 53 | 9 | 3 | 1 | 6 | 69 | 0 | 71 | 13 | 3 | | 3 | 5 | .375 | 0 | 0- - | - | 6.39 | 6.39 |
| 2012 Trntn | AA | 11 | 10 | 0 | 1 | 56.2 | 269 | 73 | 49 | 41 | 4 | 2 | 2 | 6 | 30 | 0 | 53 | 7 | 1 | | 3 | 4 | .429 | 0 | 0- - | - | 6.61 | 6.51 |
| 2013 S-WB | AAA | 38 | 6 | 0 | 11 | 84.0 | 345 | 52 | 25 | 25 | 2 | 2 | 2 | 7 | 42 | 0 | 108 | 8 | 0 | | 6 | 4 | .600 | 0 | 5- - | - | 2.28 | 2.68 |
| 2011 NYY | AL | 2 | 1 | 0 | 0 | 2.2 | 16 | 1 | 2 | 2 | 0 | 0 | 1 | 1 | 6 | 0 | 2 | 0 | 0 | | 0 | 0 | - | 0 | 0-0 | 0 | 7.94 | 6.75 |
| 2013 NYY | AL | 6 | 0 | 0 | 3 | 5.0 | 26 | 9 | 6 | 6 | 1 | 0 | 0 | 0 | 2 | 0 | 10 | 0 | 0 | | 0 | 0 | - | 0 | 0-0 | 0 | 9.81 | 10.80 |
| 2 ML YEARS | | 8 | 1 | 0 | 3 | 7.2 | 42 | 10 | 8 | 8 | 1 | 0 | 1 | 1 | 8 | 0 | 12 | 0 | 0 | | 0 | 0 | - | 0 | 0-0 | 0 | 9.35 | 9.39 |

# Rafael Betancourt

**Pitches:** R **Bats:** R **Pos:** RP-32 BETT-an-court **Ht:** 6'2" **Wt:** 220 **Born:** 4/29/1975 **Age:** 39

| HOW MUCH HE PITCHED | | | | | | | | WHAT HE GAVE UP | | | | | | | | | | | | | THE RESULTS | | | | | | | |
|---|---|---|---|---|---|---|---|---|---|---|---|---|---|---|---|---|---|---|---|---|---|---|---|---|---|---|---|---|
| Year Team | Lg | G | GS | CG | GF | IP | BFP | H | R | ER | HR | SH | SF | HB | TBB | IBB | SO | WP | Bk | | W | L | Pct | Sh | Sv-Op | Hld | ERC | ERA |
| 2013 ColSpr* | AAA | 1 | 0 | 0 | 0 | 1.0 | 5 | 2 | 1 | 1 | 0 | 0 | 0 | 0 | 0 | 0 | 1 | 0 | 0 | | 0 | 0 | - | 0 | 0- - | - | 7.48 | 9.00 |
| 2003 Cle | AL | 33 | 0 | 0 | 13 | 38.0 | 154 | 27 | 11 | 9 | 5 | 1 | 1 | 1 | 13 | 2 | 36 | 1 | 0 | | 2 | 2 | .500 | 0 | 1-3 | 4 | 2.54 | 2.13 |
| 2004 Cle | AL | 68 | 0 | 0 | 21 | 66.2 | 286 | 71 | 32 | 29 | 7 | 1 | 2 | 0 | 18 | 6 | 76 | 5 | 1 | | 5 | 6 | .455 | 0 | 4-11 | 12 | 3.77 | 3.92 |
| 2005 Cle | AL | 54 | 0 | 0 | 12 | 67.2 | 272 | 57 | 23 | 21 | 5 | 1 | 0 | 0 | 17 | 2 | 73 | 0 | 0 | | 4 | 3 | .571 | 0 | 1-3 | 10 | 2.49 | 2.79 |
| 2006 Cle | AL | 50 | 0 | 0 | 17 | 56.2 | 231 | 52 | 25 | 24 | 7 | 2 | 2 | 0 | 11 | 5 | 48 | 0 | 0 | | 3 | 4 | .429 | 0 | 3-6 | 7 | 2.84 | 3.81 |
| 2007 Cle | AL | 68 | 0 | 0 | 15 | 79.1 | 289 | 51 | 13 | 13 | 4 | 0 | 2 | 0 | 9 | 3 | 80 | 0 | 0 | | 5 | 1 | .833 | 0 | 3-6 | **31** | 1.24 | 1.47 |
| 2008 Cle | AL | 69 | 0 | 0 | 20 | 71.0 | 309 | 76 | 41 | 40 | 11 | 4 | 5 | 0 | 25 | 5 | 64 | 2 | 0 | | 3 | 4 | .429 | 0 | 4-8 | 12 | 4.53 | 5.07 |
| 2009 2 Tms | | 61 | 0 | 0 | 10 | 56.0 | 227 | 42 | 20 | 17 | 4 | 2 | 4 | 0 | 20 | 5 | 61 | 0 | 0 | | 4 | 3 | .571 | 0 | 2-6 | 20 | 2.30 | 2.73 |
| 2010 Col | NL | 72 | 0 | 0 | 18 | 62.1 | 248 | 52 | 25 | 25 | 9 | 3 | 1 | 0 | 8 | 2 | 89 | 7 | 0 | | 5 | 1 | .833 | 0 | 1-5 | 23 | 2.35 | 3.61 |
| 2011 Col | NL | 68 | 0 | 0 | 24 | 62.1 | 237 | 46 | 21 | 20 | 7 | 0 | 2 | 0 | 8 | 0 | 73 | 1 | 2 | | 2 | 0 | 1.000 | 0 | 8-12 | 22 | 1.84 | 2.89 |
| 2012 Col | NL | 60 | 0 | 0 | 53 | 57.2 | 236 | 53 | 19 | 18 | 6 | 2 | 2 | 0 | 12 | 4 | 57 | 0 | 1 | | 1 | 4 | .200 | 0 | 31-38 | 1 | 2.81 | 2.81 |
| 2013 Col | NL | 32 | 0 | 0 | 29 | 28.2 | 123 | 26 | 15 | 13 | 2 | 3 | 1 | 0 | 11 | 2 | 27 | 1 | 0 | | 2 | 5 | .286 | 0 | 16-19 | 0 | 3.12 | 4.08 |
| 09 Cle | AL | 29 | 0 | 0 | 7 | 30.2 | 129 | 25 | 15 | 12 | 3 | 1 | 2 | 0 | 15 | 4 | 32 | 0 | 0 | | 1 | 2 | .333 | 0 | 1-3 | 8 | 3.21 | 3.52 |
| 09 Col | NL | 32 | 0 | 0 | 3 | 25.1 | 98 | 17 | 5 | 5 | 1 | 1 | 2 | 0 | 5 | 1 | 29 | 0 | 0 | | 3 | 1 | .750 | 0 | 1-3 | 12 | 1.42 | 1.78 |
| Postseason | | 10 | 0 | 0 | 2 | 12.1 | 49 | 9 | 8 | 7 | 2 | 1 | 1 | 0 | 2 | 1 | 12 | 0 | 0 | | 0 | 0 | - | 0 | 0-0 | 3 | 1.98 | 5.11 |
| 11 ML YEARS | | 635 | 0 | 0 | 232 | 646.1 | 2612 | 553 | 245 | 229 | 67 | 19 | 22 | 1 | 152 | 36 | 684 | 17 | 4 | | 36 | 33 | .522 | 0 | 74-117 | 142 | 2.63 | 3.19 |

# Yuniesky Betancourt

yoo-NESS-kee BETT-an-coor

**Bats:** R **Throws:** R **Pos:** 1B-68;3B-59;PH-30;2B-5;SS-3;LF-2 **Ht:** 5'10" **Wt:** 205 **Born:** 1/31/1982 **Age:** 32

| BATTING | | | | | | | | | | | | | | | | | | | | | BASERUNNING | | | | AVERAGES | | |
|---|---|---|---|---|---|---|---|---|---|---|---|---|---|---|---|---|---|---|---|---|---|---|---|---|---|---|---|
| Year Team | Lg | G | AB | H | 2B | 3B | HR | (Hm | Rd) | TB | R | RBI | RC | TBB | IBB | SO | HBP | SH | SF | | SB | CS | SB% | GDP | Avg | OBP | Slg |
| 2005 Sea | AL | 60 | 211 | 54 | 11 | 5 | 1 | (1 | 0) | 78 | 24 | 15 | 21 | 11 | 0 | 24 | 2 | 2 | 2 | | 1 | 3 | .25 | 2 | .256 | .296 | .370 |
| 2006 Sea | AL | 157 | 558 | 161 | 28 | 6 | 8 | (2 | 6) | 225 | 68 | 47 | 60 | 17 | 0 | 54 | 1 | 7 | 1 | | 11 | 8 | .58 | 10 | .289 | .310 | .403 |
| 2007 Sea | AL | 155 | 536 | 155 | 38 | 2 | 9 | (6 | 3) | 224 | 72 | 67 | 73 | 15 | 3 | 48 | 1 | 3 | 4 | | 5 | 4 | .56 | 10 | .289 | .308 | .418 |
| 2008 Sea | AL | 153 | 559 | 156 | 36 | 3 | 7 | (3 | 4) | 219 | 66 | 51 | 53 | 17 | 0 | 42 | 2 | 6 | 6 | | 4 | 4 | .50 | 23 | .279 | .300 | .392 |
| 2009 2 Tms | AL | 134 | 470 | 115 | 20 | 6 | 6 | (2 | 4) | 165 | 40 | 49 | 41 | 21 | 0 | 44 | 0 | 11 | 6 | | 3 | 3 | .50 | 17 | .245 | .274 | .351 |
| 2010 KC | AL | 151 | 556 | 144 | 29 | 2 | 16 | (8 | 8) | 225 | 60 | 78 | 56 | 23 | 1 | 64 | 1 | 4 | 4 | | 2 | 3 | .40 | 13 | .259 | .288 | .405 |
| 2011 Mil | NL | 152 | 556 | 140 | 27 | 3 | 13 | (8 | 5) | 212 | 51 | 68 | 47 | 16 | 3 | 63 | 2 | 0 | **10** | | 4 | 4 | .50 | 16 | .252 | .271 | .381 |
| 2012 KC | AL | 57 | 215 | 49 | 14 | 1 | 7 | (4 | 3) | 86 | 21 | 36 | 19 | 9 | 0 | 25 | 0 | 1 | 3 | | 0 | 1 | .00 | 10 | .228 | .256 | .400 |
| 2013 Mil | NL | 137 | 391 | 83 | 15 | 1 | 13 | (7 | 6) | 139 | 35 | 46 | 30 | 14 | 3 | 71 | 1 | 0 | 3 | | 0 | 0 | - | 9 | .212 | .240 | .355 |
| 09 Sea | AL | 63 | 224 | 56 | 10 | 1 | 2 | (1 | 1) | 74 | 15 | 22 | 19 | 10 | 0 | 18 | 0 | 8 | 3 | | 3 | 1 | .75 | 9 | .250 | .278 | .330 |
| 09 KC | AL | 71 | 246 | 59 | 10 | 5 | 4 | (1 | 3) | 91 | 25 | 27 | 22 | 11 | 0 | 26 | 0 | 3 | 3 | | 0 | 2 | .00 | 8 | .240 | .269 | .370 |
| Postseason | | 11 | 42 | 13 | 3 | 1 | 1 | (1 | 0) | 21 | 7 | 6 | 8 | 1 | 0 | 4 | 0 | 0 | 0 | | 0 | 0 | - | 1 | .310 | .326 | .500 |
| 9 ML YEARS | | 1156 | 4052 | 1057 | 218 | 29 | 80 | (41 | 39) | 1573 | 437 | 457 | 400 | 143 | 10 | 435 | 10 | 34 | 39 | | 30 | 30 | .50 | 110 | .261 | .285 | .388 |

## Wilson Betemit

**Bats:** B **Throws:** R **Pos:** DH-5;PH-2;1B-1 BETT-uh-meet **Ht:** 6'2" **Wt:** 220 **Born:** 11/2/1981 **Age:** 32

| BATTING | | | | | | | | | | | | | | | | | | | | | BASERUNNING | | | | AVERAGES | | |
|---|---|---|---|---|---|---|---|---|---|---|---|---|---|---|---|---|---|---|---|---|---|---|---|---|---|---|---|
| Year Team | Lg | G | AB | H | 2B | 3B | HR | (Hm | Rd) | TB | R | RBI | RC | TBB | IBB | SO | HBP | SH | SF | SB | CS | SB% | GDP | Avg | OBP | Slg |
| 2013 Orioles* | R | 5 | 16 | 6 | 2 | 0 | 0 | (- | -) | 8 | 1 | 3 | 3 | 2 | 0 | 2 | 0 | 0 | 0 | 0 | 0 | - | 2 | .375 | .444 | .500 |
| 2013 Frdrck* | A+ | 4 | 17 | 5 | 0 | 0 | 0 | (- | -) | 5 | 1 | 4 | 1 | 0 | 0 | 4 | 0 | 0 | 0 | 0 | 0 | - | 0 | .294 | .294 | .294 |
| 2013 Bowie* | AA | 5 | 17 | 6 | 0 | 0 | 0 | (- | -) | 6 | 1 | 3 | 3 | 4 | 0 | 4 | 0 | 0 | 0 | 0 | 0 | - | 2 | .353 | .476 | .353 |
| 2013 Norfolk* | AAA | 4 | 12 | 1 | 1 | 0 | 0 | (- | -) | 2 | 1 | 0 | 0 | 1 | 0 | 5 | 0 | 0 | 0 | 0 | 0 | - | 1 | .083 | .154 | .167 |
| 2001 Atl | NL | 8 | 3 | 0 | 0 | 0 | 0 | (0 | 0) | 0 | 1 | 0 | 0 | 2 | 0 | 3 | 0 | 0 | 0 | 1 | 0 | 1.00 | 0 | .000 | .400 | .000 |
| 2004 Atl | NL | 22 | 47 | 8 | 0 | 0 | 0 | (0 | 0) | 8 | 2 | 3 | 0 | 4 | 0 | 16 | 0 | 0 | 1 | 0 | 1 | .00 | 0 | .170 | .231 | .170 |
| 2005 Atl | NL | 115 | 246 | 75 | 12 | 4 | 4 | (0 | 4) | 107 | 36 | 20 | 36 | 22 | 4 | 55 | 0 | 4 | 2 | 1 | 3 | .25 | 5 | .305 | .359 | .435 |
| 2006 2 Tms | NL | 143 | 373 | 98 | 23 | 0 | 18 | (7 | 11) | 175 | 49 | 53 | 52 | 36 | 6 | 102 | 0 | 1 | 2 | 3 | 1 | .75 | 11 | .263 | .326 | .469 |
| 2007 2 Tms | | 121 | 240 | 55 | 12 | 0 | 14 | (8 | 6) | 109 | 33 | 50 | 42 | 38 | 0 | 82 | 1 | 2 | 3 | 0 | 0 | - | 2 | .229 | .333 | .454 |
| 2008 NYY | AL | 87 | 189 | 50 | 13 | 0 | 6 | (5 | 1) | 81 | 24 | 25 | 17 | 6 | 0 | 56 | 1 | 1 | 1 | 0 | 1 | .00 | 7 | .265 | .289 | .429 |
| 2009 CWS | AL | 20 | 45 | 9 | 5 | 0 | 0 | (0 | 0) | 14 | 2 | 3 | 3 | 5 | 0 | 13 | 0 | 0 | 0 | 0 | 0 | - | 2 | .200 | .280 | .311 |
| 2010 KC | AL | 84 | 276 | 82 | 20 | 0 | 13 | (7 | 6) | 141 | 36 | 43 | 48 | 36 | 2 | 74 | 1 | 0 | 2 | 0 | 0 | - | 3 | .297 | .378 | .511 |
| 2011 2 Tms | AL | 97 | 323 | 92 | 22 | 4 | 8 | (6 | 2) | 146 | 40 | 46 | 50 | 31 | 6 | 105 | 0 | 0 | 5 | 4 | 1 | .80 | 7 | .285 | .343 | .452 |
| 2012 Bal | AL | 102 | 341 | 89 | 19 | 0 | 12 | (7 | 5) | 144 | 41 | 40 | 42 | 31 | 0 | 103 | 1 | 0 | 3 | 0 | 1 | .00 | 8 | .261 | .322 | .422 |
| 2013 Bal | AL | 6 | 10 | 0 | 0 | 0 | 0 | (0 | 0) | 0 | 0 | 0 | 0 | 0 | 0 | 3 | 0 | 0 | 0 | 0 | 0 | - | 1 | .000 | .000 | .000 |
| 06 Atl | NL | 88 | 199 | 56 | 16 | 0 | 9 | (3 | 6) | 99 | 30 | 29 | 35 | 19 | 3 | 57 | 0 | 1 | 0 | 2 | 1 | .67 | 4 | .281 | .344 | .497 |
| 06 LAD | NL | 55 | 174 | 42 | 7 | 0 | 9 | (4 | 5) | 76 | 19 | 24 | 17 | 17 | 3 | 45 | 0 | 0 | 2 | 1 | 0 | 1.00 | 7 | .241 | .306 | .437 |
| 07 LAD | NL | 84 | 156 | 36 | 8 | 0 | 10 | (6 | 4) | 74 | 22 | 26 | 26 | 32 | 0 | 49 | 1 | 0 | 3 | 0 | 0 | - | 1 | .231 | .359 | .474 |
| 07 NYY | AL | 37 | 84 | 19 | 4 | 0 | 4 | (2 | 2) | 35 | 11 | 24 | 16 | 6 | 0 | 33 | 0 | 2 | 0 | 0 | 0 | - | 1 | .226 | .278 | .417 |
| 11 KC | AL | 57 | 203 | 57 | 15 | 1 | 3 | (2 | 1) | 83 | 29 | 27 | 30 | 20 | 6 | 58 | 0 | 0 | 3 | 3 | 1 | .75 | 6 | .281 | .341 | .409 |
| 11 Det | AL | 40 | 120 | 35 | 7 | 3 | 5 | (4 | 1) | 63 | 11 | 19 | 20 | 11 | 0 | 47 | 0 | 0 | 2 | 1 | 0 | 1.00 | 1 | .292 | .346 | .525 |
| Postseason | | 10 | 19 | 5 | 1 | 0 | 1 | (0 | 1) | 9 | 3 | 1 | 2 | 2 | 1 | 7 | 0 | 0 | 0 | 0 | 0 | - | 0 | .263 | .333 | .474 |
| 11 ML YEARS | | 805 | 2093 | 558 | 126 | 8 | 75 | (40 | 35) | 925 | 264 | 283 | 290 | 211 | 18 | 612 | 4 | 8 | 19 | 9 | 8 | .53 | 46 | .267 | .332 | .442 |

## Christian Bethancourt

**Bats:** R **Throws:** R **Pos:** PH-1 BETH-an-court **Ht:** 6'2" **Wt:** 215 **Born:** 9/2/1991 **Age:** 22

| BATTING | | | | | | | | | | | | | | | | | | | | | BASERUNNING | | | | AVERAGES | | |
|---|---|---|---|---|---|---|---|---|---|---|---|---|---|---|---|---|---|---|---|---|---|---|---|---|---|---|---|
| Year Team | Lg | G | AB | H | 2B | 3B | HR | (Hm | Rd) | TB | R | RBI | RC | TBB | IBB | SO | HBP | SH | SF | SB | CS | SB% | GDP | Avg | OBP | Slg |
| 2009 Braves | R | 32 | 116 | 33 | 9 | 1 | 2 | (- | -) | 50 | 22 | 19 | 19 | 11 | 0 | 22 | 1 | 0 | 3 | 7 | 0 | 1.00 | 4 | .284 | .344 | .431 |
| 2009 Danvle | R | 14 | 50 | 13 | 5 | 0 | 2 | (- | -) | 24 | 10 | 8 | 8 | 6 | 0 | 16 | 0 | 0 | 0 | 1 | 1 | .50 | 0 | .260 | .339 | .480 |
| 2010 Rome | A | 108 | 399 | 100 | 19 | 2 | 3 | (- | -) | 132 | 31 | 34 | 38 | 14 | 1 | 62 | 2 | 0 | 5 | 11 | 3 | .79 | 6 | .251 | .276 | .331 |
| 2011 Rome | A | 54 | 221 | 67 | 10 | 3 | 4 | (- | -) | 95 | 25 | 33 | 31 | 8 | 0 | 27 | 1 | 0 | 5 | 6 | 3 | .67 | 4 | .303 | .323 | .430 |
| 2011 Lynbrg | A+ | 45 | 166 | 45 | 6 | 0 | 1 | (- | -) | 54 | 11 | 20 | 15 | 3 | 0 | 35 | 0 | 2 | 4 | 3 | 2 | .60 | 5 | .271 | .277 | .325 |
| 2012 Missi | AA | 71 | 268 | 65 | 5 | 1 | 2 | (- | -) | 78 | 30 | 26 | 21 | 11 | 0 | 45 | 2 | 4 | 3 | 8 | 6 | .57 | 3 | .243 | .275 | .291 |
| 2013 Missi | AA | 90 | 358 | 99 | 21 | 0 | 12 | (- | -) | 156 | 42 | 45 | 48 | 16 | 1 | 57 | 2 | 5 | 7 | 11 | 7 | .61 | 8 | .277 | .305 | .436 |
| 2013 Atl | NL | 1 | 1 | 0 | 0 | 0 | 0 | (0 | 0) | 0 | 0 | 0 | 0 | 0 | 0 | 1 | 0 | 0 | 0 | 0 | 0 | - | 0 | .000 | .000 | .000 |

## Chad Bettis

**Pitches:** R **Bats:** R **Pos:** SP-8; RP-8 **Ht:** 6'1" **Wt:** 200 **Born:** 4/26/1989 **Age:** 25

| HOW MUCH HE PITCHED | | | | | | | | WHAT HE GAVE UP | | | | | | | | | | | | THE RESULTS | | | | | | | |
|---|---|---|---|---|---|---|---|---|---|---|---|---|---|---|---|---|---|---|---|---|---|---|---|---|---|---|---|
| Year Team | Lg | G | GS | CG | GF | IP | BFP | H | R | ER | HR | SH | SF | HB | TBB | IBB | SO | WP | Bk | W | L | Pct | Sh | Sv-Op | Hld | ERC | ERA |
| 2010 TriCity | A- | 10 | 9 | 0 | 0 | 48.1 | 205 | 44 | 11 | 6 | 0 | 1 | 0 | 0 | 10 | 0 | 39 | 4 | 0 | 4 | 1 | .800 | 0 | 0-- | - | 2.13 | 1.12 |
| 2010 Ashvll | A | 3 | 3 | 0 | 0 | 18.2 | 71 | 14 | 2 | 2 | 1 | 0 | 1 | 0 | 3 | 0 | 17 | 0 | 0 | 2 | 0 | 1.000 | 0 | 0-- | - | 1.72 | 0.96 |
| 2011 Mdest | A+ | 27 | 27 | 0 | 0 | 169.2 | 690 | 142 | 72 | 63 | 10 | 3 | 4 | 8 | 45 | 0 | 184 | 10 | 1 | 12 | 5 | .706 | 0 | 0-- | - | 2.63 | 3.34 |
| 2013 Tulsa | AA | 12 | 12 | 0 | 0 | 63.0 | 259 | 60 | 28 | 26 | 9 | 6 | 2 | 3 | 13 | 0 | 68 | 1 | 0 | 3 | 4 | .429 | 0 | 0-- | - | 3.55 | 3.71 |
| 2013 Col | NL | 16 | 8 | 0 | 0 | 44.2 | 208 | 55 | 34 | 28 | 6 | 3 | 1 | 2 | 20 | 2 | 30 | 2 | 1 | 1 | 3 | .250 | 0 | 0-1 | 3 | 5.95 | 5.64 |

## Jeff Bianchi

bee-YANK-ee

**Bats:** R **Throws:** R **Pos:** 3B-42;PH-23;SS-20;2B-19;PR-5;LF-3 **Ht:** 5'11" **Wt:** 180 **Born:** 10/5/1986 **Age:** 27

| BATTING | | | | | | | | | | | | | | | | | | | | | BASERUNNING | | | | AVERAGES | | |
|---|---|---|---|---|---|---|---|---|---|---|---|---|---|---|---|---|---|---|---|---|---|---|---|---|---|---|---|
| Year Team | Lg | G | AB | H | 2B | 3B | HR | (Hm | Rd) | TB | R | RBI | RC | TBB | IBB | SO | HBP | SH | SF | SB | CS | SB% | GDP | Avg | OBP | Slg |
| 2009 Wilmg | A+ | 60 | 220 | 66 | 12 | 2 | 4 | (- | -) | 94 | 32 | 28 | 36 | 20 | 3 | 47 | 1 | 3 | 1 | 12 | 2 | .86 | 3 | .300 | .360 | .427 |
| 2009 NWArk | AA | 68 | 270 | 85 | 17 | 1 | 5 | (- | -) | 119 | 42 | 42 | 44 | 19 | 0 | 58 | 1 | 2 | 5 | 10 | 4 | .71 | 2 | .315 | .356 | .441 |
| 2011 NWArk | AA | 119 | 444 | 115 | 23 | 2 | 2 | (- | -) | 148 | 63 | 48 | 53 | 39 | 0 | 85 | 3 | 9 | 4 | 20 | 5 | .80 | 7 | .259 | .320 | .333 |
| 2012 Hntsvl | AA | 19 | 77 | 27 | 4 | 0 | 0 | (- | -) | 31 | 11 | 6 | 12 | 6 | 1 | 11 | 0 | 2 | 0 | 3 | 1 | .75 | 1 | .351 | .398 | .403 |
| 2012 Nashv | AAA | 73 | 249 | 79 | 13 | 1 | 5 | (- | -) | 109 | 33 | 19 | 42 | 22 | 1 | 48 | 1 | 5 | 1 | 11 | 5 | .69 | 3 | .317 | .374 | .438 |
| 2013 Hntsvl | AA | 5 | 15 | 4 | 0 | 0 | 0 | (- | -) | 4 | 0 | 1 | 0 | 1 | 0 | 2 | 0 | 0 | 0 | 0 | 1 | .00 | 1 | .267 | .313 | .267 |
| 2013 Nashv | AAA | 10 | 41 | 10 | 1 | 1 | 1 | (- | -) | 16 | 6 | 6 | 4 | 2 | 0 | 8 | 0 | 0 | 0 | 0 | 0 | - | 4 | .244 | .279 | .390 |
| 2012 Mil | NL | 33 | 69 | 13 | 2 | 0 | 3 | (1 | 2) | 24 | 8 | 9 | 6 | 4 | 0 | 13 | 0 | 2 | 1 | 0 | 0 | - | 1 | .188 | .230 | .348 |
| 2013 Mil | NL | 100 | 236 | 56 | 8 | 1 | 1 | (0 | 1) | 69 | 22 | 25 | 19 | 11 | 0 | 46 | 1 | 2 | 2 | 4 | 4 | .50 | 4 | .237 | .272 | .292 |
| 2 ML YEARS | | 133 | 305 | 69 | 10 | 1 | 4 | (1 | 3) | 93 | 30 | 34 | 25 | 15 | 0 | 59 | 1 | 4 | 3 | 4 | 4 | .50 | 5 | .226 | .262 | .305 |

## Chad Billingsley

**Pitches:** R **Bats:** R **Pos:** SP-2 **Ht:** 6'1" **Wt:** 240 **Born:** 7/29/1984 **Age:** 29

| HOW MUCH HE PITCHED | | | | | | | | WHAT HE GAVE UP | | | | | | | | | | | | THE RESULTS | | | | | | | |
|---|---|---|---|---|---|---|---|---|---|---|---|---|---|---|---|---|---|---|---|---|---|---|---|---|---|---|---|
| Year Team | Lg | G | GS | CG | GF | IP | BFP | H | R | ER | HR | SH | SF | HB | TBB | IBB | SO | WP | Bk | W | L | Pct | Sh | Sv-Op | Hld | ERC | ERA |
| 2013 RCuca* | A+ | 1 | 1 | 0 | 0 | 4.0 | 22 | 7 | 4 | 3 | 0 | 0 | 0 | 1 | 3 | 0 | 2 | 0 | 0 | 0 | 0 | - | 0 | 0-- | - | 10.76 | 6.75 |
| 2006 LAD | NL | 18 | 16 | 0 | 0 | 90.0 | 403 | 92 | 43 | 38 | 7 | 4 | 0 | 3 | 58 | 3 | 59 | 5 | 0 | 7 | 4 | .636 | 0 | 0-0 | 0 | 5.22 | 3.80 |
| 2007 LAD | NL | 43 | 20 | 1 | 6 | 147.0 | 623 | 131 | 56 | 54 | 15 | 9 | 3 | 3 | 64 | 3 | 141 | 5 | 0 | 12 | 5 | .706 | 0 | 0-1 | 3 | 3.70 | 3.31 |
| 2008 LAD | NL | 35 | 32 | 1 | 1 | 200.2 | 859 | 188 | 76 | 70 | 14 | 8 | 5 | 8 | 80 | 6 | 201 | 10 | 0 | 16 | 10 | .615 | 1 | 0-0 | 1 | 3.62 | 3.14 |
| 2009 LAD | NL | 33 | 32 | 0 | 0 | 196.1 | 823 | 173 | 94 | 88 | 17 | 9 | **11** | 7 | 86 | 7 | 179 | **14** | 0 | 12 | 11 | .522 | 0 | 0-0 | 0 | 3.63 | 4.03 |
| 2010 LAD | NL | 31 | 31 | 1 | 0 | 191.2 | 817 | 176 | 82 | 76 | 8 | 7 | **11** | 10 | 69 | 7 | 171 | 4 | 0 | 12 | 11 | .522 | 1 | 0-0 | 0 | 3.20 | 3.57 |

| Year | Team | Lg | G | GS | CG | GF | IP | BFP | H | R | ER | HR | SH | SF | HB | TBB | IBB | SO | WP | Bk | W | L | Pct | Sh | Sv-Op | Hld | ERC | ERA |
|---|---|---|---|---|---|---|---|---|---|---|---|---|---|---|---|---|---|---|---|---|---|---|---|---|---|---|---|---|
| HOW MUCH HE PITCHED | | | | | | | | | WHAT HE GAVE UP | | | | | | | | | | | | THE RESULTS | | | | | | | |
| 2011 | LAD | NL | 32 | 32 | 1 | 0 | 188.0 | 829 | 189 | 98 | 88 | 14 | 13 | 8 | 7 | 84 | 4 | 152 | 5 | 0 | 11 | 11 | .500 | 0 | 0-0 | 0 | 4.19 | 4.21 |
| 2012 | LAD | NL | 25 | 25 | 0 | 0 | 149.2 | 634 | 148 | 66 | 59 | 11 | 6 | 3 | 5 | 45 | 2 | 128 | 5 | 0 | 10 | 9 | .526 | 0 | 0-0 | 0 | 3.55 | 3.55 |
| 2013 | LAD | NL | 2 | 2 | 0 | 0 | 12.0 | 49 | 12 | 4 | 4 | 1 | 2 | 0 | 0 | 5 | 0 | 6 | 0 | 0 | 1 | 0 | 1.000 | 0 | 0-0 | 0 | 4.29 | 3.00 |
| Postseason | | | 6 | 3 | 0 | 0 | 17.0 | 78 | 20 | 14 | 13 | 1 | 0 | 0 | 0 | 10 | 2 | 22 | 2 | 0 | 1 | 2 | .333 | 0 | 0-0 | 0 | 5.40 | 6.88 |
| 8 ML YEARS | | | 219 | 190 | 4 | 7 | 1175.1 | 5037 | 1109 | 519 | 477 | 87 | 58 | 41 | 43 | 491 | 32 | 1037 | 48 | 0 | 81 | 61 | .570 | 2 | 0-1 | 4 | 3.77 | 3.65 |

## Vic Black

**Pitches:** R **Bats:** R **Pos:** RP-18 **Ht:** 6'4" **Wt:** 215 **Born:** 5/23/1988 **Age:** 26

| Year | Team | Lg | G | GS | CG | GF | IP | BFP | H | R | ER | HR | SH | SF | HB | TBB | IBB | SO | WP | Bk | W | L | Pct | Sh | Sv-Op | Hld | ERC | ERA |
|---|---|---|---|---|---|---|---|---|---|---|---|---|---|---|---|---|---|---|---|---|---|---|---|---|---|---|---|---|
| HOW MUCH HE PITCHED | | | | | | | | | WHAT HE GAVE UP | | | | | | | | | | | | THE RESULTS | | | | | | | |
| 2009 | StCol | A- | 13 | 7 | 0 | 2 | 31.1 | 140 | 26 | 17 | 12 | 0 | 1 | 1 | 1 | 15 | 0 | 33 | 4 | 0 | 1 | 2 | .333 | 0 | 1- - | - | 2.71 | 3.45 |
| 2010 | WV | A | 2 | 2 | 0 | 0 | 4.2 | 23 | 3 | 5 | 5 | 1 | 0 | 0 | 1 | 5 | 0 | 8 | 2 | 0 | 0 | 0 | - | 0 | 0- - | - | 6.35 | 9.64 |
| 2011 | WV | A | 22 | 0 | 0 | 5 | 29.0 | 131 | 30 | 21 | 17 | 0 | 0 | 1 | 2 | 16 | 0 | 23 | 5 | 0 | 2 | 1 | .667 | 0 | 1- - | - | 4.40 | 5.28 |
| 2011 | Bradtn | A+ | 5 | 0 | 0 | 1 | 6.2 | 31 | 8 | 4 | 3 | 1 | 2 | 0 | 1 | 4 | 0 | 5 | 0 | 0 | 1 | 0 | 1.000 | 0 | 0- - | - | 7.47 | 4.05 |
| 2012 | Altna | AA | 51 | 0 | 0 | 38 | 60.0 | 249 | 40 | 14 | 11 | 2 | 2 | 2 | 4 | 29 | 0 | 85 | 12 | 1 | 2 | 3 | .400 | 0 | 13- - | - | 2.43 | 1.65 |
| 2013 | Indy | AAA | 38 | 0 | 0 | 30 | 46.2 | 190 | 28 | 15 | 13 | 2 | 2 | 0 | 1 | 21 | 3 | 63 | 3 | 0 | 5 | 3 | .625 | 0 | 17- - | - | 1.82 | 2.51 |
| 2013 | 2 Tms | NL | 18 | 0 | 0 | 6 | 17.0 | 76 | 17 | 7 | 7 | 1 | 0 | 1 | 2 | 6 | 0 | 15 | 4 | 0 | 3 | 0 | 1.000 | 0 | 1-2 | 4 | 3.95 | 3.71 |
| 13 | Pit | NL | 3 | 0 | 0 | 2 | 4.0 | 21 | 6 | 2 | 2 | 0 | 0 | 0 | 1 | 2 | 0 | 3 | 1 | 0 | 0 | 0 | - | 0 | 0-0 | 0 | 7.52 | 4.50 |
| 13 | NYM | NL | 15 | 0 | 0 | 4 | 13.0 | 55 | 11 | 5 | 5 | 1 | 0 | 1 | 1 | 4 | 0 | 12 | 3 | 0 | 3 | 0 | 1.000 | 0 | 1-2 | 4 | 2.97 | 3.46 |

## Travis Blackley

**Pitches:** L **Bats:** L **Pos:** RP-43; SP-3 **Ht:** 6'3" **Wt:** 205 **Born:** 11/4/1982 **Age:** 31

| Year | Team | Lg | G | GS | CG | GF | IP | BFP | H | R | ER | HR | SH | SF | HB | TBB | IBB | SO | WP | Bk | W | L | Pct | Sh | Sv-Op | Hld | ERC | ERA |
|---|---|---|---|---|---|---|---|---|---|---|---|---|---|---|---|---|---|---|---|---|---|---|---|---|---|---|---|---|
| HOW MUCH HE PITCHED | | | | | | | | | WHAT HE GAVE UP | | | | | | | | | | | | THE RESULTS | | | | | | | |
| 2013 | OKCity* | AAA | 1 | 1 | 0 | 0 | 2.0 | 7 | 0 | 1 | 1 | 0 | 0 | 0 | 1 | 0 | 0 | 1 | 0 | 0 | 0 | 0 | - | 0 | 0- - | - | 0.27 | 4.50 |
| 2013 | RdRck* | AAA | 1 | 1 | 0 | 0 | 3.0 | 10 | 1 | 0 | 0 | 0 | 0 | 0 | 0 | 2 | 0 | 2 | 1 | 0 | 0 | 0 | - | 0 | 0- - | - | 1.51 | 0.00 |
| 2004 | Sea | AL | 6 | 6 | 0 | 0 | 26.0 | 134 | 35 | 31 | 29 | 9 | 1 | 1 | 1 | 22 | 0 | 16 | 3 | 1 | 1 | 3 | .250 | 0 | 0-0 | 0 | 10.52 | 10.04 |
| 2007 | SF | NL | 2 | 2 | 0 | 0 | 8.2 | 40 | 10 | 7 | 7 | 2 | 1 | 0 | 0 | 5 | 0 | 5 | 0 | 1 | 0 | 0 | - | 0 | 0-0 | 0 | 6.78 | 7.27 |
| 2012 | 2 Tms | | 28 | 15 | 0 | 6 | 107.2 | 444 | 98 | 53 | 49 | 10 | 3 | 3 | 3 | 32 | 1 | 71 | 7 | 3 | 6 | 4 | .600 | 0 | 0-0 | 0 | 3.27 | 4.10 |
| 2013 | 2 Tms | AL | 46 | 3 | 0 | 5 | 50.1 | 211 | 46 | 27 | 27 | 12 | 1 | 2 | 1 | 22 | 4 | 40 | 7 | 0 | 2 | 2 | .500 | 0 | 0-1 | 13 | 4.78 | 4.83 |
| 12 | SF | NL | 4 | 0 | 0 | 1 | 5.0 | 25 | 7 | 6 | 5 | 0 | 2 | 0 | 0 | 2 | 0 | 2 | 1 | 0 | 0 | 0 | - | 0 | 0-0 | 0 | 5.23 | 9.00 |
| 12 | Oak | AL | 24 | 15 | 0 | 5 | 102.2 | 419 | 91 | 47 | 44 | 10 | 1 | 3 | 3 | 30 | 1 | 69 | 6 | 3 | 6 | 4 | .600 | 0 | 0-0 | 0 | 3.18 | 3.86 |
| 13 | Hou | AL | 42 | 0 | 0 | 5 | 35.0 | 152 | 30 | 19 | 19 | 10 | 1 | 2 | 1 | 20 | 4 | 29 | 4 | 0 | 1 | 1 | .500 | 0 | 0-1 | 13 | 5.26 | 4.89 |
| 13 | Tex | AL | 4 | 3 | 0 | 0 | 15.1 | 59 | 16 | 8 | 8 | 2 | 0 | 0 | 0 | 2 | 0 | 11 | 3 | 0 | 1 | 1 | .500 | 0 | 0-0 | 0 | 3.72 | 4.70 |
| 4 ML YEARS | | | 82 | 26 | 0 | 11 | 192.2 | 829 | 189 | 118 | 112 | 33 | 6 | 6 | 5 | 81 | 5 | 132 | 17 | 5 | 9 | 9 | .500 | 0 | 0-1 | 13 | 4.66 | 5.23 |

## Charlie Blackmon

**Bats:** L **Throws:** L **Pos:** RF-34;CF-25;LF-17;PH-17 **Ht:** 6'3" **Wt:** 210 **Born:** 7/1/1986 **Age:** 27

| Year | Team | Lg | G | AB | H | 2B | 3B | HR | (Hm | Rd) | TB | R | RBI | RC | TBB | IBB | SO | HBP | SH | SF | SB | CS | SB% | GDP | Avg | OBP | Slg |
|---|---|---|---|---|---|---|---|---|---|---|---|---|---|---|---|---|---|---|---|---|---|---|---|---|---|---|---|
| BATTING | | | | | | | | | | | | | | | | | | | | | BASERUNNING | | | | AVERAGES | | |
| 2013 | ColSpr* | AAA | 68 | 257 | 74 | 15 | 6 | 3 | (- | -) | 110 | 56 | 40 | 43 | 35 | 2 | 41 | 3 | 1 | 3 | 7 | 5 | .58 | 6 | .288 | .376 | .428 |
| 2011 | Col | NL | 27 | 98 | 25 | 1 | 0 | 1 | (1 | 0) | 29 | 9 | 8 | 10 | 3 | 1 | 8 | 0 | 1 | 0 | 5 | 1 | .83 | 2 | .255 | .277 | .296 |
| 2012 | Col | NL | 42 | 113 | 32 | 8 | 0 | 2 | (1 | 1) | 46 | 15 | 9 | 11 | 4 | 0 | 17 | 3 | 1 | 0 | 1 | 2 | .33 | 4 | .283 | .325 | .407 |
| 2013 | Col | NL | 82 | 246 | 76 | 17 | 2 | 6 | (3 | 3) | 115 | 35 | 22 | 35 | 7 | 0 | 49 | 3 | 2 | 0 | 7 | 0 | 1.00 | 1 | .309 | .336 | .467 |
| 3 ML YEARS | | | 151 | 457 | 133 | 26 | 2 | 9 | (5 | 4) | 190 | 59 | 39 | 56 | 14 | 1 | 74 | 6 | 4 | 0 | 13 | 3 | .81 | 7 | .291 | .321 | .416 |

## Gregor Blanco

**Bats:** L **Throws:** L **Pos:** CF-76;LF-72;PH-20;RF-1 GREH-gore BLAHN-koh **Ht:** 5'11" **Wt:** 185 **Born:** 12/24/1983 **Age:** 30

| Year | Team | Lg | G | AB | H | 2B | 3B | HR | (Hm | Rd) | TB | R | RBI | RC | TBB | IBB | SO | HBP | SH | SF | SB | CS | SB% | GDP | Avg | OBP | Slg |
|---|---|---|---|---|---|---|---|---|---|---|---|---|---|---|---|---|---|---|---|---|---|---|---|---|---|---|---|
| BATTING | | | | | | | | | | | | | | | | | | | | | BASERUNNING | | | | AVERAGES | | |
| 2008 | Atl | NL | 144 | 430 | 108 | 14 | 4 | 1 | (0 | 1) | 133 | 52 | 38 | 60 | 74 | 2 | 99 | 6 | 6 | 3 | 13 | 5 | .72 | 3 | .251 | .366 | .309 |
| 2009 | Atl | NL | 24 | 43 | 8 | 0 | 1 | 0 | (0 | 0) | 10 | 5 | 1 | 2 | 4 | 0 | 9 | 0 | 1 | 0 | 2 | 0 | 1.00 | 1 | .186 | .255 | .233 |
| 2010 | 2 Tms | | 85 | 237 | 67 | 9 | 4 | 1 | (1 | 0) | 87 | 31 | 14 | 30 | 29 | 1 | 50 | 0 | 2 | 1 | 11 | 4 | .73 | 5 | .283 | .360 | .367 |
| 2012 | SF | NL | 141 | 393 | 96 | 14 | 5 | 5 | (2 | 3) | 135 | 56 | 34 | 50 | 51 | 2 | 104 | 2 | 5 | 2 | 26 | 6 | .81 | 0 | .244 | .333 | .344 |
| 2013 | SF | NL | 141 | 452 | 120 | 17 | 6 | 3 | (0 | 3) | 158 | 50 | 41 | 54 | 52 | 4 | 95 | 1 | 3 | 3 | 14 | 9 | .61 | 10 | .265 | .341 | .350 |
| 10 | Atl | NL | 36 | 58 | 18 | 1 | 1 | 0 | (0 | 0) | 21 | 9 | 3 | 8 | 8 | 1 | 15 | 0 | 0 | 0 | 1 | 2 | .33 | 2 | .310 | .394 | .362 |
| 10 | KC | AL | 49 | 179 | 49 | 8 | 3 | 1 | (1 | 0) | 66 | 22 | 11 | 22 | 21 | 0 | 35 | 0 | 2 | 1 | 10 | 2 | .83 | 3 | .274 | .348 | .369 |
| Postseason | | | 16 | 51 | 12 | 2 | 2 | 1 | (0 | 1) | 21 | 10 | 5 | 10 | 7 | 0 | 14 | 1 | 0 | 0 | 0 | 0 | - | 0 | .235 | .339 | .412 |
| 5 ML YEARS | | | 535 | 1555 | 399 | 54 | 20 | 10 | (3 | 7) | 523 | 194 | 128 | 196 | 210 | 9 | 357 | 9 | 17 | 9 | 66 | 24 | .73 | 19 | .257 | .347 | .336 |

## Henry Blanco

**Bats:** R **Throws:** R **Pos:** C-47;PH-3 BLAHN-koh **Ht:** 5'11" **Wt:** 220 **Born:** 8/29/1971 **Age:** 42

| Year | Team | Lg | G | AB | H | 2B | 3B | HR | (Hm | Rd) | TB | R | RBI | RC | TBB | IBB | SO | HBP | SH | SF | SB | CS | SB% | GDP | Avg | OBP | Slg |
|---|---|---|---|---|---|---|---|---|---|---|---|---|---|---|---|---|---|---|---|---|---|---|---|---|---|---|---|
| BATTING | | | | | | | | | | | | | | | | | | | | | BASERUNNING | | | | AVERAGES | | |
| 1997 | LAD | NL | 3 | 5 | 2 | 0 | 0 | 1 | (0 | 1) | 5 | 1 | 1 | 2 | 0 | 0 | 1 | 0 | 0 | 0 | 0 | 0 | - | 0 | .400 | .400 | 1.000 |
| 1999 | Col | NL | 88 | 263 | 61 | 12 | 3 | 6 | (3 | 3) | 97 | 30 | 28 | 32 | 34 | 1 | 38 | 1 | 3 | 2 | 1 | 1 | .50 | 4 | .232 | .320 | .369 |
| 2000 | Mil | NL | 93 | 284 | 67 | 24 | 0 | 7 | (3 | 4) | 112 | 29 | 31 | 33 | 36 | 6 | 60 | 0 | 0 | 4 | 0 | 3 | .00 | 9 | .236 | .318 | .394 |
| 2001 | Mil | NL | 104 | 314 | 66 | 18 | 3 | 6 | (4 | 2) | 108 | 33 | 31 | 30 | 34 | 6 | 72 | 2 | 5 | 2 | 3 | 1 | .75 | 10 | .210 | .290 | .344 |
| 2002 | Atl | NL | 81 | 221 | 45 | 9 | 1 | 6 | (4 | 2) | 74 | 17 | 22 | 15 | 20 | 5 | 51 | 1 | 2 | 5 | 0 | 2 | .00 | 5 | .204 | .267 | .335 |
| 2003 | Atl | NL | 55 | 151 | 30 | 8 | 0 | 1 | (0 | 1) | 41 | 11 | 13 | 13 | 10 | 2 | 21 | 1 | 3 | 1 | 0 | 0 | - | 3 | .199 | .252 | .272 |
| 2004 | Min | AL | 114 | 315 | 65 | 19 | 1 | 10 | (4 | 6) | 116 | 36 | 37 | 25 | 21 | 0 | 56 | 3 | 11 | 3 | 0 | 3 | .00 | 8 | .206 | .260 | .368 |
| 2005 | ChC | NL | 54 | 161 | 39 | 6 | 0 | 6 | (2 | 4) | 63 | 16 | 25 | 17 | 11 | 1 | 24 | 0 | 4 | 2 | 0 | 0 | - | 6 | .242 | .287 | .391 |
| 2006 | ChC | NL | 74 | 241 | 64 | 15 | 2 | 6 | (2 | 4) | 101 | 23 | 37 | 26 | 14 | 1 | 38 | 0 | 4 | 2 | 0 | 0 | - | 8 | .266 | .304 | .419 |
| 2007 | ChC | NL | 22 | 54 | 9 | 3 | 0 | 0 | (0 | 0) | 12 | 3 | 4 | 2 | 2 | 0 | 12 | 0 | 1 | 1 | 0 | 0 | - | 0 | .167 | .193 | .222 |
| 2008 | ChC | NL | 58 | 120 | 35 | 3 | 0 | 3 | (2 | 1) | 47 | 15 | 12 | 11 | 6 | 1 | 22 | 0 | 2 | 0 | 0 | 0 | - | 4 | .292 | .325 | .392 |

| | | | BATTING | | | | | | | | | | | | | | | | | | BASERUNNING | | | | AVERAGES | | |
|---|---|---|---|---|---|---|---|---|---|---|---|---|---|---|---|---|---|---|---|---|---|---|---|---|---|---|---|
| Year | Team | Lg | G | AB | H | 2B | 3B | HR | (Hm | Rd) | TB | R | RBI | RC | TBB | IBB | SO | HBP | SH | SF | SB | CS | SB% | GDP | Avg | OBP | Slg |
| 2009 | SD | NL | 67 | 204 | 48 | 12 | 0 | 6 | (4 | 2) | 78 | 21 | 16 | 20 | 26 | 2 | 50 | 0 | 1 | 1 | 0 | 0 | - | 5 | .235 | .320 | .382 |
| 2010 | NYM | NL | 50 | 130 | 28 | 5 | 0 | 2 | (2 | 0) | 39 | 10 | 8 | 7 | 11 | 2 | 26 | 0 | 0 | 3 | 1 | 0 | 1.00 | 1 | .215 | .271 | .300 |
| 2011 | Ari | NL | 37 | 100 | 25 | 3 | 1 | 8 | (6 | 2) | 54 | 12 | 12 | 13 | 12 | 1 | 21 | 0 | 0 | 0 | 0 | 1 | .00 | 2 | .250 | .330 | .540 |
| 2012 | Ari | NL | 21 | 64 | 12 | 3 | 0 | 1 | (0 | 1) | 18 | 6 | 7 | 6 | 3 | 0 | 18 | 0 | 0 | 0 | 1 | 0 | 1.00 | 1 | .188 | .224 | .281 |
| 2013 | 2 Tms | AL | 50 | 134 | 19 | 5 | 0 | 3 | (0 | 3) | 33 | 11 | 14 | 7 | 14 | 0 | 36 | 1 | 1 | 0 | 0 | 0 | - | 5 | .142 | .228 | .246 |
| 13 | Tor | AL | 15 | 38 | 7 | 3 | 0 | 0 | (0 | 0) | 10 | 3 | 0 | 1 | 4 | 0 | 10 | 0 | 1 | 0 | 0 | 0 | - | 3 | .184 | .262 | .263 |
| 13 | Sea | AL | 35 | 96 | 12 | 2 | 0 | 3 | (0 | 3) | 23 | 8 | 14 | 6 | 10 | 0 | 26 | 1 | 0 | 0 | 0 | 0 | - | 2 | .125 | .215 | .240 |
| Postseason | | | 7 | 15 | 3 | 0 | 0 | 1 | (1 | 0) | 6 | 1 | 2 | 0 | 0 | 0 | 4 | 0 | 1 | 1 | 0 | 0 | - | 1 | .200 | .188 | .400 |
| 16 ML YEARS | | | 971 | 2761 | 615 | 145 | 11 | 72 | (36 | 36) | 998 | 274 | 298 | 259 | 254 | 28 | 546 | 9 | 37 | 26 | 6 | 11 | .35 | 71 | .223 | .288 | .361 |

## Kyle Blanks

**Bats:** R **Throws:** R **Pos:** RF-37;LF-35;1B-34;PH-8;DH-2;PR-2 **Ht:** 6'6" **Wt:** 265 **Born:** 9/11/1986 **Age:** 27

| | | | BATTING | | | | | | | | | | | | | | | | | | BASERUNNING | | | | AVERAGES | | |
|---|---|---|---|---|---|---|---|---|---|---|---|---|---|---|---|---|---|---|---|---|---|---|---|---|---|---|---|
| Year | Team | Lg | G | AB | H | 2B | 3B | HR | (Hm | Rd) | TB | R | RBI | RC | TBB | IBB | SO | HBP | SH | SF | SB | CS | SB% | GDP | Avg | OBP | Slg |
| 2013 | Tucsn* | AAA | 12 | 38 | 9 | 3 | 0 | 1 | (- | -) | 15 | 8 | 4 | 6 | 6 | 0 | 10 | 2 | 0 | 0 | 0 | 0 | - | 0 | .237 | .370 | .395 |
| 2009 | SD | NL | 54 | 148 | 37 | 9 | 0 | 10 | (6 | 4) | 76 | 24 | 22 | 21 | 18 | 1 | 55 | 6 | 0 | 0 | 1 | 1 | .50 | 4 | .250 | .355 | .514 |
| 2010 | SD | NL | 33 | 102 | 16 | 6 | 1 | 3 | (2 | 1) | 33 | 14 | 15 | 10 | 15 | 0 | 46 | 3 | 0 | 0 | 1 | 0 | 1.00 | 1 | .157 | .283 | .324 |
| 2011 | SD | NL | 55 | 170 | 39 | 7 | 1 | 7 | (2 | 5) | 69 | 21 | 26 | 16 | 16 | 0 | 51 | 2 | 0 | 2 | 2 | 0 | 1.00 | 3 | .229 | .300 | .406 |
| 2012 | SD | NL | 4 | 5 | 1 | 0 | 0 | 0 | (0 | 0) | 1 | 0 | 0 | 0 | 1 | 0 | 2 | 0 | 0 | 0 | 0 | 0 | - | 0 | .200 | .333 | .200 |
| 2013 | SD | NL | 88 | 280 | 68 | 14 | 0 | 8 | (3 | 5) | 106 | 31 | 35 | 39 | 21 | 1 | 85 | 5 | 0 | 2 | 1 | 1 | .50 | 2 | .243 | .305 | .379 |
| 5 ML YEARS | | | 234 | 705 | 161 | 36 | 2 | 28 | (13 | 15) | 285 | 90 | 98 | 86 | 71 | 2 | 239 | 16 | 0 | 4 | 5 | 2 | .71 | 10 | .228 | .312 | .404 |

## Joe Blanton

**Pitches:** R **Bats:** R **Pos:** SP-20; RP-8 **Ht:** 6'2" **Wt:** 220 **Born:** 12/11/1980 **Age:** 33

| | | | HOW MUCH HE PITCHED | | | | | | WHAT HE GAVE UP | | | | | | | | | | | | THE RESULTS | | | | | | | |
|---|---|---|---|---|---|---|---|---|---|---|---|---|---|---|---|---|---|---|---|---|---|---|---|---|---|---|---|---|
| Year | Team | Lg | G | GS | CG | GF | IP | BFP | H | R | ER | HR | SH | SF | HB | TBB | IBB | SO | WP | Bk | W | L | Pct | Sh | Sv-Op | Hld | ERC | ERA |
| 2004 | Oak | AL | 3 | 0 | 0 | 1 | 8.0 | 30 | 6 | 5 | 5 | 1 | 0 | 0 | 0 | 2 | 0 | 6 | 0 | 0 | 0 | 0 | - | 0 | 0-0 | 0 | 2.52 | 5.63 |
| 2005 | Oak | AL | 33 | 33 | 2 | 0 | 201.1 | 835 | 178 | 86 | 79 | 23 | 2 | 7 | 5 | 67 | 3 | 116 | 4 | 2 | 12 | 12 | .500 | 0 | 0-0 | 0 | 3.37 | 3.53 |
| 2006 | Oak | AL | 32 | 31 | 1 | 0 | 194.1 | 856 | 241 | 111 | 104 | 17 | 3 | 9 | 5 | 58 | 4 | 107 | 3 | 0 | 16 | 12 | .571 | 1 | 0-0 | 0 | 5.09 | 4.82 |
| 2007 | Oak | AL | 34 | **34** | 3 | 0 | 230.0 | 950 | **240** | 106 | 101 | 16 | 5 | 8 | 4 | 40 | 4 | 140 | 3 | 1 | 14 | 10 | .583 | 1 | 0-0 | 0 | 3.30 | 3.95 |
| 2008 | 2 Tms | | 33 | 33 | 0 | 0 | 197.2 | 855 | 211 | 110 | 103 | 22 | 2 | 4 | 4 | 66 | 3 | 111 | 2 | 0 | 9 | 12 | .429 | 0 | 0-0 | 0 | 4.33 | 4.69 |
| 2009 | Phi | NL | 31 | 31 | 0 | 0 | 195.1 | 837 | 198 | 89 | 88 | 30 | 11 | 4 | 8 | 59 | 4 | 163 | 7 | 0 | 12 | 8 | .600 | 0 | 0-0 | 0 | 4.25 | 4.05 |
| 2010 | Phi | NL | 29 | 28 | 0 | 0 | 175.2 | 765 | 206 | 104 | 94 | 27 | 5 | 7 | 3 | 43 | 6 | 134 | 2 | 0 | 9 | 6 | .600 | 0 | 0-0 | 0 | 4.81 | 4.82 |
| 2011 | Phi | NL | 11 | 8 | 0 | 1 | 41.1 | 180 | 52 | 23 | 23 | 5 | 5 | 2 | 1 | 9 | 0 | 35 | 0 | 0 | 1 | 2 | .333 | 0 | 0-0 | 0 | 5.13 | 5.01 |
| 2012 | 2 Tms | NL | 31 | 30 | 2 | 1 | 191.0 | 806 | 207 | 106 | 100 | 29 | 8 | 4 | 3 | 34 | 5 | 166 | 5 | 0 | 10 | 13 | .435 | 1 | 0-0 | 0 | 4.00 | 4.71 |
| 2013 | LAA | AL | 28 | 20 | 0 | 7 | 132.2 | 611 | 180 | 96 | 89 | 29 | 1 | 5 | 4 | 34 | 4 | 108 | 9 | 0 | 2 | 14 | .125 | 0 | 0-0 | 0 | 6.48 | 6.04 |
| 08 | Oak | AL | 20 | 20 | 0 | 0 | 127.0 | 550 | 145 | 74 | 70 | 12 | 1 | 2 | 1 | 35 | 3 | 62 | 1 | 0 | 5 | 12 | .294 | 0 | 0-0 | 0 | 4.33 | 4.96 |
| 08 | Phi | NL | 13 | 13 | 0 | 0 | 70.2 | 305 | 66 | 36 | 33 | 10 | 1 | 2 | 3 | 31 | 0 | 49 | 1 | 0 | 4 | 0 | 1.000 | 0 | 0-0 | 0 | 4.33 | 4.20 |
| 12 | Phi | NL | 21 | 20 | 2 | 1 | 133.1 | 560 | 141 | 74 | 68 | 22 | 6 | 3 | 3 | 18 | 2 | 115 | 4 | 0 | 8 | 9 | .471 | 1 | 0-0 | 0 | 3.77 | 4.59 |
| 12 | LAD | NL | 10 | 10 | 0 | 0 | 57.2 | 246 | 66 | 32 | 32 | 7 | 2 | 1 | 0 | 16 | 3 | 51 | 1 | 0 | 2 | 4 | .333 | 0 | 0-0 | 0 | 4.54 | 4.99 |
| Postseason | | | 10 | 6 | 0 | 1 | 40.1 | 172 | 36 | 19 | 18 | 5 | 1 | 1 | 3 | 13 | 2 | 33 | 2 | 0 | 2 | 0 | 1.000 | 0 | 0-0 | 0 | 3.51 | 4.02 |
| 10 ML YEARS | | | 265 | 248 | 8 | 10 | 1567.1 | 6725 | 1719 | 836 | 786 | 199 | 42 | 50 | 37 | 412 | 33 | 1086 | 35 | 3 | 85 | 89 | .489 | 3 | 0-0 | 0 | 4.33 | 4.51 |

## Michael Blazek

**Pitches:** R **Bats:** R **Pos:** RP-18 BLAY-zek **Ht:** 6'0" **Wt:** 200 **Born:** 3/16/1989 **Age:** 25

| | | | HOW MUCH HE PITCHED | | | | | | WHAT HE GAVE UP | | | | | | | | | | | | THE RESULTS | | | | | | | |
|---|---|---|---|---|---|---|---|---|---|---|---|---|---|---|---|---|---|---|---|---|---|---|---|---|---|---|---|---|
| Year | Team | Lg | G | GS | CG | GF | IP | BFP | H | R | ER | HR | SH | SF | HB | TBB | IBB | SO | WP | Bk | W | L | Pct | Sh | Sv-Op | Hld | ERC | ERA |
| 2009 | Batvia | A- | 15 | 12 | 0 | 1 | 64.0 | 292 | 73 | 45 | 32 | 3 | 1 | 5 | 5 | 24 | 1 | 62 | 13 | 0 | 4 | 9 | .308 | 0 | 0-- | - | 4.58 | 4.50 |
| 2010 | QuadC | A | 32 | 11 | 0 | 6 | 103.0 | 412 | 78 | 41 | 31 | 5 | 1 | 5 | 4 | 31 | 0 | 104 | 9 | 2 | 8 | 4 | .667 | 0 | 3-- | - | 2.29 | 2.71 |
| 2010 | PlmBh | A+ | 1 | 1 | 0 | 0 | 4.1 | 27 | 9 | 6 | 6 | 0 | 1 | 1 | 0 | 5 | 0 | 2 | 0 | 0 | 0 | 1 | .000 | 0 | 0-- | - | 13.28 | 12.46 |
| 2011 | Sprgfld | AA | 24 | 24 | 0 | 0 | 133.2 | 612 | 148 | 90 | 81 | 25 | 6 | 5 | 9 | 64 | 2 | 128 | 11 | 5 | 11 | 6 | .647 | 0 | 0-- | - | 5.91 | 5.45 |
| 2011 | Memp | AAA | 1 | 1 | 0 | 0 | 6.0 | 25 | 4 | 1 | 1 | 0 | 1 | 0 | 0 | 4 | 0 | 5 | 1 | 0 | 1 | 0 | 1.000 | 0 | 0-- | - | 2.66 | 1.50 |
| 2012 | Sprgfld | AA | 40 | 7 | 0 | 15 | 80.0 | 328 | 61 | 37 | 37 | 11 | 2 | 2 | 3 | 34 | 1 | 83 | 5 | 0 | 5 | 8 | .385 | 0 | 0-- | - | 3.31 | 4.16 |
| 2012 | Memp | AAA | 2 | 1 | 0 | 1 | 3.1 | 16 | 6 | 4 | 4 | 1 | 0 | 0 | 1 | 2 | 0 | 1 | 0 | 0 | 0 | 1 | .000 | 0 | 0-- | - | 15.88 | 10.80 |
| 2013 | Sprgfld | AA | 17 | 0 | 0 | 12 | 19.2 | 80 | 11 | 4 | 2 | 0 | 0 | 0 | 0 | 10 | 1 | 25 | 0 | 0 | 0 | 0 | - | 0 | 7-- | - | 1.56 | 0.92 |
| 2013 | Memp | AAA | 19 | 0 | 0 | 11 | 26.0 | 109 | 17 | 8 | 8 | 1 | 0 | 1 | 0 | 16 | 0 | 27 | 2 | 0 | 1 | 2 | .333 | 0 | 2-- | - | 2.62 | 2.77 |
| 2013 | 2 Tms | NL | 18 | 0 | 0 | 7 | 17.1 | 84 | 16 | 12 | 11 | 3 | 1 | 1 | 1 | 13 | 0 | 14 | 0 | 0 | 0 | 1 | .000 | 0 | 0-0 | 0 | 5.57 | 5.71 |
| 13 | StL | NL | 11 | 0 | 0 | 3 | 10.1 | 52 | 10 | 8 | 8 | 2 | 0 | 0 | 1 | 10 | 0 | 10 | 0 | 0 | 0 | 0 | - | 0 | 0-0 | 0 | 7.25 | 6.97 |
| 13 | Mil | NL | 7 | 0 | 0 | 4 | 7.0 | 32 | 6 | 4 | 3 | 1 | 1 | 1 | 0 | 3 | 0 | 4 | 0 | 0 | 0 | 1 | .000 | 0 | 0-0 | 0 | 3.35 | 3.86 |

## Jerry Blevins

**Pitches:** L **Bats:** L **Pos:** RP-67 **Ht:** 6'6" **Wt:** 175 **Born:** 9/6/1983 **Age:** 30

| | | | HOW MUCH HE PITCHED | | | | | | WHAT HE GAVE UP | | | | | | | | | | | | THE RESULTS | | | | | | | |
|---|---|---|---|---|---|---|---|---|---|---|---|---|---|---|---|---|---|---|---|---|---|---|---|---|---|---|---|---|
| Year | Team | Lg | G | GS | CG | GF | IP | BFP | H | R | ER | HR | SH | SF | HB | TBB | IBB | SO | WP | Bk | W | L | Pct | Sh | Sv-Op | Hld | ERC | ERA |
| 2007 | Oak | AL | 6 | 0 | 0 | 1 | 4.2 | 25 | 8 | 6 | 5 | 1 | 0 | 0 | 0 | 2 | 0 | 3 | 0 | 0 | 0 | 1 | .000 | 0 | 0-0 | 0 | 9.08 | 9.64 |
| 2008 | Oak | AL | 36 | 0 | 0 | 8 | 37.2 | 156 | 32 | 14 | 13 | 2 | 0 | 1 | 3 | 13 | 2 | 35 | 0 | 0 | 1 | 3 | .250 | 0 | 0-1 | 5 | 3.00 | 3.11 |
| 2009 | Oak | AL | 20 | 0 | 0 | 5 | 22.1 | 90 | 19 | 12 | 12 | 2 | 0 | 1 | 0 | 6 | 1 | 23 | 0 | 0 | 0 | 0 | - | 0 | 0-0 | 0 | 2.68 | 4.84 |
| 2010 | Oak | AL | 63 | 0 | 0 | 9 | 48.2 | 220 | 54 | 20 | 20 | 7 | 3 | 1 | 1 | 18 | 1 | 46 | 0 | 0 | 2 | 1 | .667 | 0 | 1-2 | 11 | 4.81 | 3.70 |
| 2011 | Oak | AL | 26 | 0 | 0 | 11 | 28.1 | 122 | 24 | 14 | 9 | 2 | 2 | 3 | 1 | 14 | 1 | 26 | 0 | 0 | 0 | 0 | - | 0 | 0-0 | 0 | 3.45 | 2.86 |
| 2012 | Oak | AL | 63 | 0 | 0 | 17 | 65.1 | 261 | 45 | 20 | 18 | 7 | 5 | 2 | 5 | 25 | 5 | 54 | 2 | 0 | 5 | 1 | .833 | 0 | 1-1 | 14 | 2.66 | 2.48 |
| 2013 | Oak | AL | 67 | 0 | 0 | 14 | 60.0 | 245 | 47 | 23 | 21 | 7 | 3 | 5 | 4 | 17 | 2 | 52 | 2 | 0 | 5 | 0 | 1.000 | 0 | 0-4 | 4 | 2.78 | 3.15 |
| Postseason | | | 3 | 0 | 0 | 1 | 3.2 | 12 | 1 | 0 | 0 | 0 | 0 | 0 | 0 | 0 | 0 | 0 | 0 | 0 | 0 | 0 | - | 0 | 0-0 | 0 | 0.17 | 0.00 |
| 7 ML YEARS | | | 281 | 0 | 0 | 65 | 267.0 | 1119 | 229 | 109 | 98 | 28 | 13 | 13 | 14 | 95 | 12 | 239 | 4 | 0 | 13 | 6 | .684 | 0 | 2-8 | 34 | 3.29 | 3.30 |

## Willie Bloomquist

**Bats:** R **Throws:** R **Pos:** PH-18;2B-15;SS-9;LF-7;PR-1 **Ht:** 5'11" **Wt:** 190 **Born:** 11/27/1977 **Age:** 36

| BATTING | | | | | | | | | | | | | | | | | | | | | BASERUNNING | | | | AVERAGES | | |
|---|---|---|---|---|---|---|---|---|---|---|---|---|---|---|---|---|---|---|---|---|---|---|---|---|---|---|---|
| Year | Team | Lg | G | AB | H | 2B | 3B | HR | (Hm | Rd) | TB | R | RBI | RC | TBB | IBB | SO | HBP | SH | SF | SB | CS | SB% | GDP | Avg | OBP | Slg |
| 2013 | Reno* | AAA | 6 | 21 | 9 | 0 | 1 | 0 | (- | -) | 11 | 5 | 9 | 5 | 2 | 0 | 2 | 0 | 0 | 0 | 0 | 0 | - | 0 | .429 | .478 | .524 |
| 2013 | DBcks* | R | 4 | 12 | 6 | 1 | 0 | 0 | (- | -) | 7 | 4 | 1 | 3 | 2 | 0 | 1 | 0 | 0 | 0 | 0 | 0 | - | 1 | .500 | .571 | .583 |
| 2002 | Sea | AL | 12 | 33 | 15 | 4 | 0 | 0 | (0 | 0) | 19 | 11 | 7 | 10 | 5 | 0 | 2 | 0 | 0 | 0 | 3 | 1 | .75 | 0 | .455 | .526 | .576 |
| 2003 | Sea | AL | 89 | 196 | 49 | 7 | 2 | 1 | (1 | 0) | 63 | 30 | 14 | 18 | 19 | 1 | 39 | 1 | 2 | 2 | 4 | 1 | .80 | 6 | .250 | .317 | .321 |
| 2004 | Sea | AL | 93 | 188 | 46 | 10 | 0 | 2 | (0 | 2) | 62 | 27 | 18 | 18 | 10 | 0 | 48 | 0 | 3 | 0 | 13 | 2 | .87 | 2 | .245 | .283 | .330 |
| 2005 | Sea | AL | 82 | 249 | 64 | 15 | 2 | 0 | (0 | 0) | 83 | 27 | 22 | 26 | 11 | 0 | 38 | 1 | 4 | 2 | 14 | 1 | .93 | 5 | .257 | .289 | .333 |
| 2006 | Sea | AL | 102 | 251 | 62 | 6 | 2 | 1 | (0 | 1) | 75 | 36 | 15 | 27 | 24 | 0 | 40 | 4 | 2 | 2 | 16 | 3 | .84 | 3 | .247 | .320 | .299 |
| 2007 | Sea | AL | 91 | 173 | 48 | 3 | 0 | 2 | (1 | 1) | 57 | 28 | 13 | 16 | 10 | 0 | 35 | 1 | 4 | 0 | 7 | 5 | .58 | 7 | .277 | .321 | .329 |
| 2008 | Sea | AL | 71 | 165 | 46 | 1 | 0 | 0 | (0 | 0) | 47 | 32 | 9 | 24 | 25 | 1 | 29 | 1 | 1 | 0 | 14 | 3 | .82 | 1 | .279 | .377 | .285 |
| 2009 | KC | AL | 125 | 434 | 115 | 11 | 8 | 4 | (0 | 4) | 154 | 52 | 29 | 45 | 27 | 1 | 73 | 1 | 4 | 2 | 25 | 6 | .81 | 7 | .265 | .308 | .355 |
| 2010 | 2 Tms | | 83 | 187 | 50 | 10 | 1 | 3 | (2 | 1) | 71 | 31 | 17 | 19 | 9 | 0 | 28 | 0 | 2 | 1 | 8 | 5 | .62 | 4 | .267 | .299 | .380 |
| 2011 | Ari | NL | 97 | 350 | 93 | 10 | 2 | 4 | (2 | 2) | 119 | 44 | 26 | 37 | 23 | 3 | 51 | 4 | 2 | 2 | 20 | 10 | .67 | 3 | .266 | .317 | .340 |
| 2012 | Ari | NL | 80 | 324 | 98 | 21 | 5 | 0 | (0 | 0) | 129 | 47 | 23 | 46 | 12 | 0 | 55 | 0 | 0 | 2 | 7 | 10 | .41 | 5 | .302 | .325 | .398 |
| 2013 | Ari | NL | 48 | 139 | 44 | 5 | 1 | 0 | (0 | 0) | 51 | 16 | 14 | 20 | 8 | 0 | 11 | 2 | 0 | 1 | 0 | 2 | .00 | 3 | .317 | .360 | .367 |
| 10 | KC | AL | 72 | 170 | 45 | 10 | 1 | 3 | (2 | 1) | 66 | 31 | 17 | 18 | 8 | 0 | 25 | 0 | 2 | 1 | 8 | 5 | .62 | 4 | .265 | .296 | .388 |
| 10 | Cin | NL | 11 | 17 | 5 | 0 | 0 | 0 | (0 | 0) | 5 | 0 | 0 | 1 | 1 | 0 | 3 | 0 | 0 | 0 | 0 | 0 | - | 0 | .294 | .333 | .294 |
| Postseason | | | 5 | 22 | 7 | 0 | 0 | 0 | (0 | 0) | 7 | 3 | 1 | 3 | 1 | 0 | 3 | 0 | 0 | 0 | 3 | 0 | 1.00 | 2 | .318 | .348 | .318 |
| 12 ML YEARS | | | 973 | 2689 | 730 | 103 | 23 | 17 | (6 | 11) | 930 | 381 | 207 | 306 | 183 | 6 | 449 | 15 | 24 | 14 | 131 | 49 | .73 | 46 | .271 | .320 | .346 |

## Brennan Boesch

**Bats:** L **Throws:** L **Pos:** RF-15;PH-9;DH-3 BOSH **Ht:** 6'4" **Wt:** 235 **Born:** 4/12/1985 **Age:** 29

| BATTING | | | | | | | | | | | | | | | | | | | | | BASERUNNING | | | | AVERAGES | | |
|---|---|---|---|---|---|---|---|---|---|---|---|---|---|---|---|---|---|---|---|---|---|---|---|---|---|---|---|
| Year | Team | Lg | G | AB | H | 2B | 3B | HR | (Hm | Rd) | TB | R | RBI | RC | TBB | IBB | SO | HBP | SH | SF | SB | CS | SB% | GDP | Avg | OBP | Slg |
| 2013 | S-WB* | AAA | 8 | 30 | 6 | 2 | 0 | 0 | (- | -) | 8 | 6 | 2 | 3 | 7 | 0 | 8 | 0 | 0 | 0 | 0 | 0 | - | 0 | .200 | .351 | .267 |
| 2010 | Det | AL | 133 | 464 | 119 | 26 | 3 | 14 | (7 | 7) | 193 | 49 | 67 | 61 | 40 | 5 | 99 | 5 | 0 | 3 | 7 | 1 | .88 | 5 | .256 | .320 | .416 |
| 2011 | Det | AL | 115 | 428 | 121 | 25 | 1 | 16 | (9 | 7) | 196 | 75 | 54 | 56 | 35 | 2 | 83 | 5 | 0 | 4 | 5 | 3 | .63 | 7 | .283 | .341 | .458 |
| 2012 | Det | AL | 132 | 470 | 113 | 22 | 2 | 12 | (9 | 3) | 175 | 52 | 54 | 47 | 26 | 1 | 104 | 5 | 0 | 2 | 6 | 3 | .67 | 11 | .240 | .286 | .372 |
| 2013 | NYY | AL | 23 | 51 | 14 | 2 | 1 | 3 | (2 | 1) | 27 | 6 | 8 | 8 | 2 | 0 | 9 | 0 | 0 | 0 | 0 | 0 | - | 2 | .275 | .302 | .529 |
| 4 ML YEARS | | | 403 | 1413 | 367 | 75 | 7 | 45 | (27 | 18) | 591 | 182 | 183 | 172 | 103 | 8 | 295 | 15 | 0 | 9 | 18 | 7 | .72 | 25 | .260 | .315 | .418 |

## Xander Bogaerts

**Bats:** R **Throws:** R **Pos:** 3B-9;SS-8;PH-2;PR-1 ZAN-derr BO-garts **Ht:** 6'3" **Wt:** 185 **Born:** 10/1/1992 **Age:** 21

| BATTING | | | | | | | | | | | | | | | | | | | | | BASERUNNING | | | | AVERAGES | | |
|---|---|---|---|---|---|---|---|---|---|---|---|---|---|---|---|---|---|---|---|---|---|---|---|---|---|---|---|
| Year | Team | Lg | G | AB | H | 2B | 3B | HR | (Hm | Rd) | TB | R | RBI | RC | TBB | IBB | SO | HBP | SH | SF | SB | CS | SB% | GDP | Avg | OBP | Slg |
| 2011 | Grnvlle | A | 72 | 265 | 69 | 14 | 2 | 16 | (- | -) | 135 | 38 | 45 | 44 | 25 | 0 | 71 | 2 | 0 | 4 | 1 | 3 | .25 | 4 | .260 | .324 | .509 |
| 2012 | Salem | A+ | 104 | 384 | 116 | 27 | 3 | 15 | (- | -) | 194 | 59 | 64 | 73 | 43 | 1 | 85 | 5 | 1 | 2 | 4 | 4 | .50 | 8 | .302 | .378 | .505 |
| 2012 | Portlnd | AA | 23 | 92 | 30 | 10 | 0 | 5 | (- | -) | 55 | 12 | 17 | 18 | 1 | 0 | 21 | 3 | 0 | 1 | 1 | 1 | .50 | 0 | .326 | .351 | .598 |
| 2013 | Portlnd | AA | 56 | 219 | 68 | 12 | 6 | 6 | (- | -) | 110 | 40 | 35 | 46 | 35 | 0 | 51 | 2 | 1 | 2 | 5 | 1 | .83 | 4 | .311 | .407 | .502 |
| 2013 | Pwtckt | AAA | 60 | 225 | 64 | 11 | 0 | 9 | (- | -) | 102 | 32 | 32 | 38 | 28 | 1 | 44 | 2 | 1 | 0 | 2 | 2 | .50 | 8 | .284 | .369 | .453 |
| 2013 | Bos | AL | 18 | 44 | 11 | 2 | 0 | 1 | (0 | 1) | 16 | 7 | 5 | 4 | 5 | 0 | 13 | 0 | 0 | 1 | 1 | 0 | 1.00 | 1 | .250 | .320 | .364 |

## Mitchell Boggs

**Pitches:** R **Bats:** R **Pos:** RP-27 **Ht:** 6'4" **Wt:** 235 **Born:** 2/15/1984 **Age:** 30

| HOW MUCH HE PITCHED | | | | | | | | | WHAT HE GAVE UP | | | | | | | | | | | | THE RESULTS | | | | | | | |
|---|---|---|---|---|---|---|---|---|---|---|---|---|---|---|---|---|---|---|---|---|---|---|---|---|---|---|---|---|
| Year | Team | Lg | G | GS | CG | GF | IP | BFP | H | R | ER | HR | SH | SF | HB | TBB | IBB | SO | WP | Bk | W | L | Pct | Sh | Sv-Op | Hld | ERC | ERA |
| 2013 | Memp* | AAA | 18 | 3 | 0 | 4 | 23.2 | 118 | 30 | 21 | 15 | 2 | 0 | 2 | 4 | 11 | 0 | 14 | 2 | 0 | 0 | 2 | .000 | 0 | 0-- | - | 6.23 | 5.70 |
| 2013 | Tulsa* | AA | 4 | 0 | 0 | 2 | 6.0 | 21 | 2 | 1 | 1 | 1 | 0 | 0 | 0 | 0 | 0 | 3 | 0 | 0 | 0 | 0 | - | 0 | 1-- | - | 0.50 | 1.50 |
| 2013 | ColSpr* | AAA | 12 | 0 | 0 | 6 | 16.1 | 98 | 33 | 26 | 15 | 1 | 3 | 2 | 1 | 11 | 0 | 7 | 2 | 0 | 1 | 4 | .200 | 0 | 0-- | - | 11.08 | 8.27 |
| 2008 | StL | NL | 8 | 6 | 0 | 1 | 34.0 | 164 | 42 | 29 | 28 | 5 | 1 | 1 | 2 | 22 | 0 | 13 | 2 | 0 | 3 | 2 | .600 | 0 | 0-0 | 0 | 7.17 | 7.41 |
| 2009 | StL | NL | 16 | 9 | 0 | 2 | 58.0 | 268 | 71 | 28 | 27 | 3 | 1 | 2 | 4 | 33 | 0 | 46 | 4 | 1 | 2 | 3 | .400 | 0 | 0-0 | 1 | 6.15 | 4.19 |
| 2010 | StL | NL | 61 | 0 | 0 | 22 | 67.1 | 285 | 60 | 29 | 27 | 5 | 4 | 3 | 4 | 27 | 2 | 52 | 5 | 0 | 2 | 3 | .400 | 0 | 0-0 | 6 | 3.51 | 3.61 |
| 2011 | StL | NL | 51 | 0 | 0 | 20 | 60.2 | 260 | 62 | 27 | 24 | 4 | 2 | 2 | 2 | 21 | 2 | 48 | 5 | 0 | 2 | 3 | .400 | 0 | 4-8 | 1 | 3.84 | 3.56 |
| 2012 | StL | NL | 78 | 0 | 0 | 12 | 73.1 | 296 | 56 | 20 | 18 | 5 | 6 | 0 | 4 | 21 | 3 | 58 | 0 | 0 | 4 | 1 | .800 | 0 | 0-3 | **34** | 2.36 | 2.21 |
| 2013 | 2 Tms | NL | 27 | 0 | 0 | 14 | 23.1 | 120 | 28 | 23 | 21 | 5 | 2 | 2 | 3 | 20 | 4 | 16 | 1 | 0 | 0 | 3 | .000 | 0 | 2-5 | 1 | 8.31 | 8.10 |
| 13 | StL | NL | 18 | 0 | 0 | 10 | 14.2 | 82 | 21 | 20 | 18 | 3 | 2 | 1 | 2 | 15 | 4 | 11 | 1 | 0 | 0 | 3 | .000 | 0 | 2-5 | 0 | 10.26 | 11.05 |
| 13 | Col | NL | 9 | 0 | 0 | 4 | 8.2 | 38 | 7 | 3 | 3 | 2 | 0 | 1 | 1 | 5 | 0 | 5 | 0 | 0 | 0 | 0 | - | 0 | 0-0 | 1 | 5.15 | 3.12 |
| Postseason | | | 17 | 0 | 0 | 3 | 16.1 | 74 | 18 | 9 | 7 | 3 | 1 | 1 | 0 | 8 | 0 | 11 | 0 | 0 | 0 | 1 | .000 | 0 | 0-0 | 5 | 5.62 | 3.86 |
| 6 ML YEARS | | | 241 | 15 | 0 | 71 | 316.2 | 1393 | 319 | 156 | 145 | 27 | 16 | 10 | 19 | 144 | 11 | 233 | 17 | 1 | 13 | 15 | .464 | 0 | 6-16 | 43 | 4.43 | 4.12 |

## Brian Bogusevic

**Bats:** L **Throws:** L **Pos:** LF-29;CF-10;PH-10;RF-1 boe-gah-SEVV-ick **Ht:** 6'3" **Wt:** 220 **Born:** 2/18/1984 **Age:** 30

| BATTING | | | | | | | | | | | | | | | | | | | | | BASERUNNING | | | | AVERAGES | | |
|---|---|---|---|---|---|---|---|---|---|---|---|---|---|---|---|---|---|---|---|---|---|---|---|---|---|---|---|
| Year | Team | Lg | G | AB | H | 2B | 3B | HR | (Hm | Rd) | TB | R | RBI | RC | TBB | IBB | SO | HBP | SH | SF | SB | CS | SB% | GDP | Avg | OBP | Slg |
| 2013 | Iowa* | AAA | 79 | 265 | 84 | 14 | 3 | 10 | (- | -) | 134 | 50 | 32 | 59 | 41 | 2 | 58 | 4 | 0 | 0 | 16 | 2 | .89 | 3 | .317 | .416 | .506 |
| 2013 | Cubs* | R | 7 | 25 | 10 | 4 | 1 | 0 | (- | -) | 16 | 7 | 5 | 8 | 7 | 0 | 5 | 0 | 0 | 0 | 3 | 0 | 1.00 | 0 | .400 | .531 | .640 |
| 2010 | Hou | NL | 19 | 28 | 5 | 3 | 0 | 0 | (0 | 0) | 8 | 5 | 3 | 2 | 3 | 0 | 12 | 0 | 0 | 0 | 1 | 1 | .50 | 2 | .179 | .258 | .286 |
| 2011 | Hou | NL | 87 | 164 | 47 | 14 | 1 | 4 | (2 | 2) | 75 | 22 | 15 | 19 | 15 | 1 | 40 | 1 | 1 | 1 | 4 | 2 | .67 | 8 | .287 | .348 | .457 |
| 2012 | Hou | NL | 146 | 355 | 72 | 9 | 2 | 7 | (4 | 3) | 106 | 39 | 28 | 31 | 41 | 1 | 96 | 7 | 0 | 1 | 15 | 4 | .79 | 6 | .203 | .297 | .299 |
| 2013 | ChC | NL | 47 | 143 | 39 | 7 | 1 | 6 | (4 | 2) | 66 | 18 | 16 | 18 | 10 | 1 | 35 | 1 | 0 | 1 | 2 | 0 | 1.00 | 4 | .273 | .323 | .462 |
| 4 ML YEARS | | | 299 | 690 | 163 | 33 | 4 | 17 | (10 | 7) | 255 | 84 | 62 | 70 | 69 | 3 | 183 | 9 | 1 | 3 | 22 | 7 | .76 | 20 | .236 | .313 | .370 |

## Jeremy Bonderman

**Pitches:** R **Bats:** R **Pos:** RP-11; SP-7 **Ht:** 6'0" **Wt:** 220 **Born:** 10/28/1982 **Age:** 31

| HOW MUCH HE PITCHED | | | | | | | | | WHAT HE GAVE UP | | | | | | | | | | | | THE RESULTS | | | | | | | |
|---|---|---|---|---|---|---|---|---|---|---|---|---|---|---|---|---|---|---|---|---|---|---|---|---|---|---|---|---|
| Year | Team | Lg | G | GS | CG | GF | IP | BFP | H | R | ER | HR | SH | SF | HB | TBB | IBB | SO | WP | Bk | W | L | Pct | Sh | Sv-Op | Hld | ERC | ERA |
| 2013 | Tacom* | AAA | 11 | 11 | 0 | 0 | 63.2 | 276 | 77 | 34 | 32 | 7 | 1 | 1 | 1 | 18 | 1 | 33 | 2 | 0 | 2 | 4 | .333 | 0 | 0-- | - | 5.01 | 4.52 |
| 2013 | Toledo* | AAA | 7 | 0 | 0 | 3 | 9.2 | 32 | 3 | 0 | 0 | 0 | 0 | 0 | 0 | 0 | 0 | 5 | 0 | 0 | 0 | 0 | - | 0 | 0-- | - | 0.22 | 0.00 |
| 2003 | Det | AL | 33 | 28 | 0 | 0 | 162.0 | 727 | 193 | 118 | 100 | 23 | 3 | 6 | 4 | 58 | 2 | 108 | 12 | 2 | 6 | 19 | .240 | 0 | 0-0 | 0 | 5.39 | 5.56 |
| 2004 | Det | AL | 33 | 32 | 2 | 0 | 184.0 | 793 | 168 | 101 | 100 | 24 | 10 | 5 | 10 | 73 | 5 | 168 | 7 | 0 | 11 | 13 | .458 | **2** | 0-0 | 0 | 3.93 | 4.89 |
| 2005 | Det | AL | 29 | 29 | 4 | 0 | 189.0 | 801 | 199 | 101 | 96 | 21 | 3 | 3 | 4 | 57 | 0 | 145 | 5 | 1 | 14 | 13 | .519 | 0 | 0-0 | 0 | 4.20 | 4.57 |
| 2006 | Det | AL | 34 | **34** | 0 | 0 | 214.0 | 903 | 214 | 104 | 97 | 18 | 3 | 6 | 3 | 64 | 7 | 202 | 3 | 1 | 14 | 8 | .636 | 0 | 0-0 | 0 | 3.58 | 4.08 |
| 2007 | Det | AL | 28 | 28 | 0 | 0 | 174.1 | 753 | 193 | 105 | 97 | 23 | 2 | 4 | 4 | 48 | 6 | 145 | 12 | 1 | 11 | 9 | .550 | 0 | 0-0 | 0 | 4.44 | 5.01 |
| 2008 | Det | AL | 12 | 12 | 0 | 0 | 71.1 | 319 | 75 | 39 | 34 | 9 | 2 | 3 | 3 | 36 | 2 | 44 | 1 | 0 | 3 | 4 | .429 | 0 | 0-0 | 0 | 5.14 | 4.29 |
| 2009 | Det | AL | 8 | 1 | 0 | 1 | 10.1 | 53 | 16 | 10 | 10 | 4 | 0 | 0 | 1 | 8 | 0 | 5 | 0 | 0 | 0 | 1 | .000 | 0 | 0-0 | 0 | 12.87 | 8.71 |
| 2010 | Det | AL | 30 | 29 | 0 | 0 | 171.0 | 754 | 187 | 113 | 105 | 25 | 3 | 5 | 10 | 60 | 1 | 112 | 8 | 0 | 8 | 10 | .444 | 0 | 0-0 | 1 | 4.98 | 5.53 |
| 2013 | 2 Tms | AL | 18 | 7 | 0 | 4 | 55.0 | 246 | 58 | 36 | 33 | 7 | 1 | 2 | 2 | 27 | 3 | 32 | 3 | 0 | 2 | 4 | .333 | 0 | 0-0 | 0 | 5.02 | 5.40 |
| 13 | Sea | AL | 7 | 7 | 0 | 0 | 38.1 | 170 | 40 | 23 | 21 | 4 | 0 | 1 | 2 | 17 | 2 | 16 | 2 | 0 | 1 | 3 | .250 | 0 | 0-0 | 0 | 4.65 | 4.93 |
| 13 | Det | AL | 11 | 0 | 0 | 4 | 16.2 | 76 | 18 | 13 | 12 | 3 | 1 | 1 | 0 | 10 | 1 | 16 | 1 | 0 | 1 | 1 | .500 | 0 | 0-0 | 0 | 5.90 | 6.48 |
| Postseason | | | 3 | 3 | 0 | 0 | 20.1 | 84 | 17 | 7 | 7 | 1 | 1 | 0 | 0 | 7 | 1 | 11 | 1 | 0 | 1 | 0 | 1.000 | 0 | 0-0 | 0 | 2.58 | 3.10 |
| 9 ML YEARS | | | 225 | 200 | 6 | 5 | 1231.0 | 5349 | 1303 | 727 | 672 | 154 | 27 | 34 | 41 | 431 | 26 | 961 | 51 | 5 | 69 | 81 | .460 | 2 | 0-0 | 1 | 4.49 | 4.91 |

## Emilio Bonifacio

bo-knee-FAH-see-oh

**Bats:** B **Throws:** R **Pos:** 2B-90;LF-20;CF-15;PR-11;PH-8;3B-6;RF-5;SS-1;DH-1 **Ht:** 5'11" **Wt:** 205 **Born:** 4/23/1985 **Age:** 29

| BATTING | | | | | | | | | | | | | | | | | | | | | BASERUNNING | | | | AVERAGES | | |
|---|---|---|---|---|---|---|---|---|---|---|---|---|---|---|---|---|---|---|---|---|---|---|---|---|---|---|---|
| Year | Team | Lg | G | AB | H | 2B | 3B | HR | (Hm | Rd) | TB | R | RBI | RC | TBB | IBB | SO | HBP | SH | SF | SB | CS | SB% | GDP | Avg | OBP | Slg |
| 2007 | Ari | NL | 11 | 23 | 5 | 1 | 0 | 0 | (0 | 0) | 6 | 2 | 2 | 4 | 4 | 0 | 3 | 0 | 0 | 0 | 0 | 1 | .00 | 0 | .217 | .333 | .261 |
| 2008 | 2 Tms | NL | 49 | 169 | 41 | 6 | 5 | 0 | (0 | 0) | 57 | 29 | 14 | 16 | 14 | 0 | 46 | 0 | 0 | 3 | 7 | 4 | .64 | 2 | .243 | .296 | .337 |
| 2009 | Fla | NL | 127 | 461 | 116 | 11 | 6 | 1 | (1 | 0) | 142 | 72 | 27 | 41 | 34 | 0 | 95 | 2 | 8 | 4 | 21 | 9 | .70 | 5 | .252 | .303 | .308 |
| 2010 | Fla | NL | 73 | 180 | 47 | 6 | 3 | 0 | (0 | 0) | 59 | 30 | 10 | 24 | 17 | 0 | 42 | 0 | 1 | 3 | 12 | 0 | 1.00 | 1 | .261 | .320 | .328 |
| 2011 | Fla | NL | 152 | 565 | 167 | 26 | 7 | 5 | (1 | 4) | 222 | 78 | 36 | 83 | 59 | 1 | 129 | 1 | 11 | 5 | 40 | 11 | .78 | 4 | .296 | .360 | .393 |
| 2012 | Mia | NL | 64 | 244 | 63 | 3 | 4 | 1 | (1 | 0) | 77 | 30 | 11 | 30 | 25 | 1 | 52 | 1 | 4 | 0 | 30 | 3 | .91 | 3 | .258 | .330 | .316 |
| 2013 | 2 Tms | AL | 136 | 420 | 102 | 22 | 3 | 3 | (1 | 2) | 139 | 54 | 31 | 39 | 30 | 0 | 103 | 2 | 6 | 3 | 28 | 8 | .78 | 4 | .243 | .295 | .331 |
| 08 | Ari | NL | 8 | 12 | 2 | 1 | 0 | 0 | (0 | 0) | 3 | 3 | 2 | 1 | 0 | 0 | 5 | 0 | 0 | 0 | 1 | 0 | 1.00 | 0 | .167 | .167 | .250 |
| 08 | Was | NL | 41 | 157 | 39 | 5 | 5 | 0 | (0 | 0) | 54 | 26 | 12 | 15 | 14 | 0 | 41 | 0 | 0 | 3 | 6 | 4 | .60 | 2 | .248 | .305 | .344 |
| 13 | Tor | AL | 94 | 262 | 57 | 16 | 1 | 3 | (1 | 2) | 84 | 33 | 20 | 19 | 13 | 0 | 66 | 2 | 3 | 2 | 12 | 6 | .67 | 3 | .218 | .258 | .321 |
| 13 | KC | AL | 42 | 158 | 45 | 6 | 2 | 0 | (0 | 0) | 55 | 21 | 11 | 20 | 17 | 0 | 37 | 0 | 3 | 1 | 16 | 2 | .89 | 1 | .285 | .352 | .348 |
| 7 ML YEARS | | | 612 | 2062 | 541 | 75 | 28 | 10 | (4 | 6) | 702 | 295 | 131 | 237 | 183 | 2 | 470 | 6 | 30 | 18 | 138 | 36 | .79 | 19 | .262 | .322 | .340 |

## Chris Bootcheck

**Pitches:** R **Bats:** R **Pos:** RP-1 **Ht:** 6'5" **Wt:** 210 **Born:** 10/24/1978 **Age:** 35

| HOW MUCH HE PITCHED | | | | | | | | | WHAT HE GAVE UP | | | | | | | | | | | | THE RESULTS | | | | | | | |
|---|---|---|---|---|---|---|---|---|---|---|---|---|---|---|---|---|---|---|---|---|---|---|---|---|---|---|---|---|
| Year | Team | Lg | G | GS | CG | GF | IP | BFP | H | R | ER | HR | SH | SF | HB | TBB | IBB | SO | WP | Bk | W | L | Pct | Sh | Sv-Op | Hld | ERC | ERA |
| 2013 | S-WB* | AAA | 24 | 23 | 2 | 0 | 136.2 | 576 | 135 | 61 | 56 | 15 | 4 | 3 | 4 | 41 | 0 | 97 | 3 | 1 | 10 | 7 | .588 | 0 | 0-- | - | 3.82 | 3.69 |
| 2003 | LAA | AL | 4 | 1 | 0 | 2 | 10.1 | 53 | 16 | 13 | 11 | 5 | 0 | 0 | 0 | 6 | 0 | 7 | 0 | 0 | 0 | 1 | .000 | 0 | 0-0 | 0 | 11.53 | 9.58 |
| 2005 | LAA | AL | 5 | 2 | 0 | 1 | 18.2 | 79 | 19 | 7 | 7 | 1 | 0 | 1 | 0 | 4 | 1 | 8 | 1 | 0 | 0 | 1 | .000 | 0 | 1-1 | 0 | 3.00 | 3.38 |
| 2006 | LAA | AL | 7 | 0 | 0 | 5 | 10.1 | 54 | 16 | 12 | 12 | 3 | 1 | 0 | 0 | 9 | 0 | 7 | 1 | 0 | 0 | 1 | .000 | 0 | 0-0 | 0 | 11.63 | 10.45 |
| 2007 | LAA | AL | 51 | 0 | 0 | 17 | 77.1 | 331 | 81 | 43 | 41 | 7 | 2 | 4 | 5 | 24 | 3 | 56 | 6 | 1 | 3 | 3 | .500 | 0 | 0-1 | 4 | 4.16 | 4.77 |
| 2008 | LAA | AL | 10 | 0 | 0 | 4 | 16.0 | 90 | 30 | 18 | 18 | 2 | 0 | 0 | 0 | 12 | 0 | 14 | 2 | 0 | 0 | 1 | .000 | 0 | 0-0 | 1 | 11.28 | 10.13 |
| 2009 | Pit | NL | 13 | 0 | 0 | 3 | 14.2 | 70 | 16 | 18 | 18 | 1 | 3 | 1 | 1 | 9 | 0 | 13 | 0 | 0 | 0 | 0 | - | 0 | 0-0 | 1 | 5.35 | 11.05 |
| 2013 | NYY | AL | 1 | 0 | 0 | 1 | 1.0 | 7 | 2 | 1 | 1 | 0 | 0 | 0 | 0 | 2 | 0 | 1 | 0 | 0 | 0 | 0 | - | 0 | 0-0 | 0 | 16.69 | 9.00 |
| 7 ML YEARS | | | 91 | 3 | 0 | 33 | 148.1 | 684 | 180 | 112 | 108 | 19 | 6 | 6 | 6 | 66 | 4 | 106 | 10 | 1 | 3 | 7 | .300 | 0 | 1-2 | 6 | 5.82 | 6.55 |

## Julio Borbon

bore-BONE

**Bats:** L **Throws:** L **Pos:** PH-44;CF-12;LF-9;RF-8;PR-4;DH-2 **Ht:** 6'0" **Wt:** 195 **Born:** 2/20/1986 **Age:** 28

| BATTING | | | | | | | | | | | | | | | | | | | | | BASERUNNING | | | | AVERAGES | | |
|---|---|---|---|---|---|---|---|---|---|---|---|---|---|---|---|---|---|---|---|---|---|---|---|---|---|---|---|
| Year | Team | Lg | G | AB | H | 2B | 3B | HR | (Hm | Rd) | TB | R | RBI | RC | TBB | IBB | SO | HBP | SH | SF | SB | CS | SB% | GDP | Avg | OBP | Slg |
| 2013 | Iowa* | AAA | 24 | 73 | 19 | 5 | 0 | 0 | (- | -) | 24 | 10 | 1 | 10 | 12 | 2 | 15 | 0 | 0 | 1 | 5 | 1 | .83 | 0 | .260 | .360 | .329 |
| 2009 | Tex | AL | 46 | 157 | 49 | 4 | 0 | 4 | (2 | 2) | 65 | 30 | 20 | 27 | 15 | 0 | 28 | 1 | 6 | 0 | 19 | 4 | .83 | 3 | .312 | .376 | .414 |
| 2010 | Tex | AL | 137 | 438 | 121 | 11 | 4 | 3 | (2 | 1) | 149 | 60 | 42 | 48 | 19 | 0 | 59 | 2 | 8 | 1 | 15 | 7 | .68 | 5 | .276 | .309 | .340 |
| 2011 | Tex | AL | 32 | 89 | 24 | 1 | 3 | 0 | (0 | 0) | 31 | 10 | 11 | 14 | 3 | 0 | 9 | 2 | 3 | 1 | 6 | 2 | .75 | 2 | .270 | .305 | .348 |
| 2013 | 2 Tms | | 73 | 105 | 21 | 3 | 1 | 1 | (0 | 1) | 29 | 11 | 3 | 9 | 12 | 0 | 22 | 0 | 1 | 0 | 7 | 1 | .88 | 0 | .200 | .282 | .276 |
| 13 | Tex | AL | 1 | 1 | 0 | 0 | 0 | 0 | (0 | 0) | 0 | 1 | 0 | 0 | 0 | 0 | 0 | 0 | 0 | 0 | 0 | 0 | - | 0 | .000 | .000 | .000 |
| 13 | ChC | NL | 72 | 104 | 21 | 3 | 1 | 1 | (0 | 1) | 29 | 10 | 3 | 9 | 12 | 0 | 22 | 0 | 1 | 0 | 7 | 1 | .88 | 0 | .202 | .284 | .279 |
| Postseason | | | 8 | 9 | 1 | 0 | 0 | 0 | (0 | 0) | 1 | 4 | 0 | 1 | 0 | 0 | 3 | 0 | 0 | 0 | 0 | 0 | - | 0 | .111 | .111 | .111 |
| 4 ML YEARS | | | 288 | 789 | 215 | 19 | 8 | 8 | (4 | 4) | 274 | 111 | 76 | 98 | 49 | 0 | 118 | 5 | 18 | 2 | 47 | 14 | .77 | 10 | .272 | .318 | .347 |

## J.C. Boscan

**Bats:** R **Throws:** R **Pos:** C-4;PH-2 BAHS-cann **Ht:** 6'2" **Wt:** 215 **Born:** 12/26/1979 **Age:** 34

| BATTING | | | | | | | | | | | | | | | | | | | | | BASERUNNING | | | | AVERAGES | | |
|---|---|---|---|---|---|---|---|---|---|---|---|---|---|---|---|---|---|---|---|---|---|---|---|---|---|---|---|
| Year | Team | Lg | G | AB | H | 2B | 3B | HR | (Hm | Rd) | TB | R | RBI | RC | TBB | IBB | SO | HBP | SH | SF | SB | CS | SB% | GDP | Avg | OBP | Slg |
| 2013 | Iowa* | AAA | 74 | 233 | 54 | 9 | 0 | 0 | (- | -) | 63 | 17 | 18 | 19 | 21 | 1 | 44 | 1 | 2 | 1 | 1 | 1 | .50 | 5 | .232 | .297 | .270 |
| 2010 | Atl | NL | 1 | 0 | 0 | 0 | 0 | 0 | (0 | 0) | 0 | 1 | 0 | 0 | 1 | 0 | 0 | 0 | 0 | 0 | 0 | 0 | - | 0 | - | 1.000 | - |
| 2011 | Atl | NL | 4 | 9 | 3 | 0 | 0 | 0 | (0 | 0) | 3 | 0 | 0 | 0 | 0 | 0 | 5 | 0 | 0 | 0 | 0 | 0 | - | 0 | .333 | .333 | .333 |
| 2012 | Atl | NL | 6 | 10 | 2 | 0 | 0 | 0 | (0 | 0) | 2 | 0 | 2 | 0 | 0 | 0 | 1 | 0 | 0 | 0 | 0 | 0 | - | 0 | .200 | .200 | .200 |
| 2013 | ChC | NL | 6 | 9 | 2 | 1 | 0 | 0 | (0 | 0) | 3 | 1 | 0 | 1 | 0 | 0 | 2 | 1 | 0 | 0 | 0 | 0 | - | 0 | .222 | .300 | .333 |
| 4 ML YEARS | | | 17 | 28 | 7 | 1 | 0 | 0 | (0 | 0) | 8 | 2 | 2 | 1 | 1 | 0 | 8 | 1 | 0 | 0 | 0 | 0 | - | 0 | .250 | .300 | .286 |

## Buddy Boshers

**Pitches:** L **Bats:** L **Pos:** RP-25 — bo-SHEERS — **Ht:** 6'3" **Wt:** 205 **Born:** 5/9/1988 **Age:** 26

| HOW MUCH HE PITCHED | | | | | | | | WHAT HE GAVE UP | | | | | | | | | | | | THE RESULTS | | | | | | | |
|---|---|---|---|---|---|---|---|---|---|---|---|---|---|---|---|---|---|---|---|---|---|---|---|---|---|---|---|
| Year Team | Lg | G | GS | CG | GF | IP | BFP | H | R | ER | HR | SH | SF | HB | TBB | IBB | SO | WP | Bk | W | L | Pct | Sh | Sv-Op | Hld | ERC | ERA |
| 2009 Salt Lk | AAA | 2 | 0 | 0 | 2 | 1.1 | 5 | 1 | 0 | 0 | 0 | 0 | 0 | 0 | 0 | 0 | 1 | 0 | 0 | 0 | 0 | - | 0 | 0- - | - | 1.13 | 0.00 |
| 2009 Orem | R+ | 5 | 5 | 0 | 0 | 24.2 | 106 | 24 | 11 | 7 | 2 | 1 | 0 | 0 | 8 | 0 | 23 | 0 | 0 | 2 | 1 | .667 | 0 | 0- - | - | 3.42 | 2.55 |
| 2009 CRpds | A | 6 | 6 | 1 | 0 | 31.2 | 132 | 31 | 21 | 21 | 5 | 1 | 1 | 1 | 7 | 0 | 27 | 0 | 0 | 3 | 1 | .750 | 0 | 0- - | - | 3.75 | 5.97 |
| 2010 CRpds | A | 36 | 7 | 1 | 4 | 77.1 | 339 | 84 | 44 | 37 | 5 | 1 | 3 | 3 | 20 | 2 | 75 | 4 | 0 | 3 | 0 | 1.000 | 0 | 0- - | - | 3.77 | 4.31 |
| 2011 InldEm | A+ | 43 | 4 | 0 | 9 | 75.1 | 343 | 88 | 43 | 36 | 7 | 5 | 2 | 1 | 41 | 0 | 61 | 5 | 0 | 2 | 5 | .286 | 0 | 1- - | - | 5.73 | 4.30 |
| 2012 InldEm | A+ | 26 | 0 | 0 | 11 | 39.1 | 167 | 30 | 15 | 11 | 4 | 1 | 1 | 0 | 16 | 1 | 48 | 1 | 0 | 4 | 2 | .667 | 0 | 1- - | - | 2.70 | 2.52 |
| 2012 Ark | AA | 19 | 0 | 0 | 0 | 24.0 | 106 | 28 | 10 | 10 | 3 | 3 | 1 | 1 | 5 | 1 | 27 | 2 | 0 | 1 | 0 | 1.000 | 0 | 0- - | - | 4.42 | 3.75 |
| 2013 Ark | AA | 28 | 0 | 0 | 7 | 28.2 | 117 | 20 | 12 | 10 | 1 | 1 | 1 | 0 | 13 | 0 | 35 | 3 | 1 | 3 | 2 | .600 | 0 | 1- - | - | 2.28 | 3.14 |
| 2013 Salt Lk | AAA | 16 | 0 | 0 | 2 | 19.2 | 88 | 18 | 11 | 8 | 1 | 3 | 0 | 0 | 12 | 1 | 26 | 3 | 1 | 1 | 0 | 1.000 | 0 | 1- - | - | 3.92 | 3.66 |
| 2013 LAA | AL | 25 | 0 | 0 | 1 | 15.1 | 63 | 13 | 8 | 8 | 0 | 0 | 0 | 1 | 8 | 1 | 13 | 0 | 0 | 0 | 0 | - | 0 | 0-0 | 6 | 3.33 | 4.70 |

## Jason Bourgeois

**Bats:** R **Throws:** R **Pos:** LF-6;PH-3;DH-2;PR-2;RF-1 — boosh-WAH — **Ht:** 5'9" **Wt:** 190 **Born:** 1/4/1982 **Age:** 32

| BATTING | | | | | | | | | | | | | | | | | | | | BASERUNNING | | | | AVERAGES | | |
|---|---|---|---|---|---|---|---|---|---|---|---|---|---|---|---|---|---|---|---|---|---|---|---|---|---|---|
| Year Team | Lg | G | AB | H | 2B | 3B | HR | (Hm | Rd) | TB | R | RBI | RC | TBB | IBB | SO | HBP | SH | SF | SB | CS | SB% | GDP | Avg | OBP | Slg |
| 2013 Drham* | AAA | 90 | 348 | 101 | 15 | 3 | 2 | (- | -) | 128 | 52 | 61 | 49 | 31 | 1 | 38 | 0 | 6 | 6 | 22 | 6 | .79 | 11 | .290 | .343 | .368 |
| 2008 CWS | AL | 6 | 3 | 1 | 1 | 0 | 0 | (0 | 0) | 2 | 0 | 0 | 0 | 0 | 0 | 0 | 0 | 0 | 0 | 0 | 0 | - | 0 | .333 | .333 | .667 |
| 2009 Mil | NL | 24 | 37 | 7 | 0 | 0 | 1 | (1 | 0) | 10 | 6 | 3 | 1 | 3 | 0 | 7 | 0 | 0 | 0 | 3 | 0 | 1.00 | 2 | .189 | .250 | .270 |
| 2010 Hou | NL | 69 | 123 | 27 | 4 | 1 | 0 | (0 | 0) | 33 | 16 | 3 | 8 | 13 | 0 | 16 | 0 | 0 | 0 | 12 | 4 | .75 | 5 | .220 | .294 | .268 |
| 2011 Hou | NL | 93 | 238 | 70 | 8 | 2 | 1 | (0 | 1) | 85 | 30 | 16 | 31 | 10 | 0 | 24 | 0 | 4 | 0 | 31 | 6 | .84 | 5 | .294 | .323 | .357 |
| 2012 KC | AL | 30 | 62 | 16 | 2 | 1 | 0 | (0 | 0) | 20 | 10 | 5 | 5 | 4 | 0 | 4 | 0 | 0 | 0 | 5 | 4 | .56 | 1 | .258 | .303 | .323 |
| 2013 TB | AL | 9 | 16 | 3 | 0 | 0 | 1 | (0 | 1) | 6 | 2 | 2 | 1 | 2 | 0 | 4 | 0 | 0 | 0 | 0 | 0 | - | 0 | .188 | .278 | .375 |
| 6 ML YEARS | | 231 | 479 | 124 | 15 | 4 | 3 | (1 | 2) | 156 | 64 | 29 | 46 | 32 | 0 | 55 | 0 | 4 | 0 | 51 | 14 | .78 | 13 | .259 | .305 | .326 |

## Peter Bourjos

**Bats:** R **Throws:** R **Pos:** CF-53;PH-3;PR-2 — BORE-juss — **Ht:** 6'1" **Wt:** 185 **Born:** 3/31/1987 **Age:** 27

| BATTING | | | | | | | | | | | | | | | | | | | | BASERUNNING | | | | AVERAGES | | |
|---|---|---|---|---|---|---|---|---|---|---|---|---|---|---|---|---|---|---|---|---|---|---|---|---|---|---|
| Year Team | Lg | G | AB | H | 2B | 3B | HR | (Hm | Rd) | TB | R | RBI | RC | TBB | IBB | SO | HBP | SH | SF | SB | CS | SB% | GDP | Avg | OBP | Slg |
| 2013 InldEm* | A+ | 3 | 11 | 3 | 0 | 1 | 1 | (- | -) | 8 | 3 | 2 | 2 | 0 | 0 | 2 | 0 | 0 | 0 | 0 | 0 | - | 1 | .273 | .273 | .727 |
| 2013 Salt Lk* | AAA | 12 | 48 | 10 | 4 | 0 | 2 | (- | -) | 20 | 13 | 7 | 6 | 4 | 0 | 19 | 2 | 0 | 1 | 0 | 0 | - | 1 | .208 | .291 | .417 |
| 2010 LAA | AL | 51 | 181 | 37 | 6 | 4 | 6 | (1 | 5) | 69 | 19 | 15 | 13 | 6 | 0 | 40 | 2 | 3 | 1 | 10 | 3 | .77 | 2 | .204 | .237 | .381 |
| 2011 LAA | AL | 147 | 502 | 136 | 26 | **11** | 12 | (7 | 5) | 220 | 72 | 43 | 66 | 32 | 0 | 124 | 10 | 7 | 1 | 22 | 9 | .71 | 7 | .271 | .327 | .438 |
| 2012 LAA | AL | 101 | 168 | 37 | 7 | 0 | 3 | (1 | 2) | 53 | 27 | 19 | 18 | 15 | 0 | 44 | 3 | 6 | 3 | 3 | 1 | .75 | 2 | .220 | .291 | .315 |
| 2013 LAA | AL | 55 | 175 | 48 | 3 | 3 | 3 | (1 | 2) | 66 | 26 | 12 | 19 | 10 | 0 | 43 | 6 | 4 | 1 | 6 | 0 | 1.00 | 8 | .274 | .333 | .377 |
| 4 ML YEARS | | 354 | 1026 | 258 | 42 | 18 | 24 | (10 | 14) | 408 | 144 | 89 | 116 | 63 | 0 | 251 | 21 | 20 | 6 | 41 | 13 | .76 | 19 | .251 | .306 | .398 |

## Michael Bourn

**Bats:** L **Throws:** R **Pos:** CF-128;PH-4;DH-1;PR-1 — BORN — **Ht:** 5'11" **Wt:** 180 **Born:** 12/27/1982 **Age:** 31

| BATTING | | | | | | | | | | | | | | | | | | | | BASERUNNING | | | | AVERAGES | | |
|---|---|---|---|---|---|---|---|---|---|---|---|---|---|---|---|---|---|---|---|---|---|---|---|---|---|---|
| Year Team | Lg | G | AB | H | 2B | 3B | HR | (Hm | Rd) | TB | R | RBI | RC | TBB | IBB | SO | HBP | SH | SF | SB | CS | SB% | GDP | Avg | OBP | Slg |
| 2013 Clmbs* | AAA | 2 | 7 | 1 | 0 | 0 | 0 | (- | -) | 1 | 0 | 0 | 0 | 1 | 0 | 3 | 0 | 0 | 0 | 1 | 0 | 1.00 | 0 | .143 | .250 | .143 |
| 2006 Phi | NL | 17 | 8 | 1 | 0 | 0 | 0 | (0 | 0) | 1 | 2 | 0 | 0 | 1 | 0 | 3 | 0 | 2 | 0 | 1 | 2 | .33 | 0 | .125 | .222 | .125 |
| 2007 Phi | NL | 105 | 119 | 33 | 3 | 3 | 1 | (1 | 0) | 45 | 29 | 6 | 19 | 13 | 2 | 21 | 0 | 1 | 0 | 18 | 1 | .95 | 1 | .277 | .348 | .378 |
| 2008 Hou | NL | 138 | 467 | 107 | 10 | 4 | 5 | (3 | 2) | 140 | 57 | 29 | 43 | 37 | 0 | 111 | 2 | 7 | 1 | 41 | 10 | .80 | 3 | .229 | .288 | .300 |
| 2009 Hou | NL | 157 | 606 | 173 | 27 | 12 | 3 | (2 | 1) | 233 | 97 | 35 | 94 | 63 | 1 | 140 | 2 | 5 | 2 | **61** | 12 | .84 | 1 | .285 | .354 | .384 |
| 2010 Hou | NL | 141 | 535 | 142 | 25 | 6 | 2 | (0 | 2) | 185 | 84 | 38 | 74 | 59 | 5 | 109 | 3 | 6 | 2 | **52** | 12 | .81 | 6 | .265 | .341 | .346 |
| 2011 2 Tms | NL | 158 | 656 | 193 | 34 | 10 | 2 | (2 | 0) | 253 | 94 | 50 | 92 | 53 | 3 | 140 | 4 | 5 | 4 | **61** | **14** | .81 | 6 | .294 | .349 | .386 |
| 2012 Atl | NL | 155 | 624 | 171 | 26 | 10 | 9 | (2 | 7) | 244 | 96 | 57 | 102 | 70 | 1 | 155 | 3 | 2 | 4 | 42 | **13** | .76 | 2 | .274 | .348 | .391 |
| 2013 Cle | AL | 130 | 525 | 138 | 21 | 6 | 6 | (2 | 4) | 189 | 75 | 50 | 65 | 40 | 0 | 132 | 2 | 5 | 3 | 23 | 12 | .66 | 2 | .263 | .316 | .360 |
| 11 Hou | NL | 105 | 429 | 130 | 26 | 7 | 1 | (1 | 0) | 173 | 64 | 32 | 66 | 38 | 2 | 90 | 3 | 2 | 1 | 39 | 7 | .85 | 5 | .303 | .363 | .403 |
| 11 Atl | NL | 53 | 227 | 63 | 8 | 3 | 1 | (1 | 0) | 80 | 30 | 18 | 26 | 15 | 1 | 50 | 1 | 3 | 3 | 22 | 7 | .76 | 1 | .278 | .321 | .352 |
| Postseason | | 3 | 6 | 1 | 0 | 0 | 0 | (0 | 0) | 1 | 0 | 1 | 0 | 0 | 0 | 2 | 0 | 0 | 0 | 0 | 0 | - | 0 | .167 | .167 | .167 |
| 8 ML YEARS | | 1001 | 3540 | 958 | 146 | 51 | 28 | (12 | 16) | 1290 | 534 | 265 | 489 | 336 | 12 | 811 | 16 | 33 | 16 | 299 | 76 | .80 | 21 | .271 | .335 | .364 |

## Michael Bowden

**Pitches:** R **Bats:** R **Pos:** RP-34 — BOE-din — **Ht:** 6'3" **Wt:** 215 **Born:** 9/9/1986 **Age:** 27

| HOW MUCH HE PITCHED | | | | | | | | WHAT HE GAVE UP | | | | | | | | | | | | THE RESULTS | | | | | | | |
|---|---|---|---|---|---|---|---|---|---|---|---|---|---|---|---|---|---|---|---|---|---|---|---|---|---|---|---|
| Year Team | Lg | G | GS | CG | GF | IP | BFP | H | R | ER | HR | SH | SF | HB | TBB | IBB | SO | WP | Bk | W | L | Pct | Sh | Sv-Op | Hld | ERC | ERA |
| 2013 Iowa* | AAA | 13 | 0 | 0 | 5 | 18.2 | 74 | 14 | 5 | 5 | 1 | 0 | 0 | 0 | 3 | 0 | 28 | 0 | 0 | 0 | 0 | - | 0 | 2- - | - | 1.64 | 2.41 |
| 2008 Bos | AL | 1 | 1 | 0 | 0 | 5.0 | 22 | 7 | 2 | 2 | 0 | 0 | 0 | 0 | 1 | 0 | 3 | 0 | 0 | 1 | 0 | 1.000 | 0 | 0-0 | 0 | 4.92 | 3.60 |
| 2009 Bos | AL | 8 | 1 | 0 | 3 | 16.0 | 75 | 23 | 17 | 17 | 3 | 0 | 0 | 0 | 6 | 0 | 12 | 3 | 0 | 1 | 1 | .500 | 0 | 0-0 | 1 | 7.35 | 9.56 |
| 2010 Bos | AL | 14 | 0 | 0 | 7 | 15.1 | 66 | 20 | 8 | 8 | 2 | 0 | 0 | 0 | 4 | 0 | 13 | 2 | 0 | 0 | 1 | .000 | 0 | 0-0 | 0 | 5.73 | 4.70 |
| 2011 Bos | AL | 14 | 0 | 0 | 9 | 20.0 | 90 | 19 | 9 | 9 | 3 | 0 | 0 | 0 | 11 | 0 | 17 | 3 | 0 | 0 | 0 | - | 0 | 0-0 | 0 | 4.65 | 4.05 |
| 2012 2 Tms | | 32 | 0 | 0 | 13 | 39.2 | 165 | 32 | 13 | 13 | 5 | 2 | 2 | 1 | 17 | 1 | 32 | 1 | 0 | 0 | 0 | - | 0 | 0-1 | 2 | 3.39 | 2.95 |
| 2013 ChC | NL | 34 | 0 | 0 | 12 | 37.2 | 158 | 32 | 18 | 18 | 3 | 4 | 2 | 3 | 15 | 2 | 23 | 4 | 1 | 1 | 3 | .250 | 0 | 0-2 | 0 | 3.37 | 4.30 |
| 12 Bos | AL | 2 | 0 | 0 | 2 | 3.0 | 11 | 2 | 1 | 1 | 1 | 0 | 0 | 0 | 1 | 0 | 3 | 0 | 0 | 0 | 0 | - | 0 | 0-0 | 0 | 3.72 | 3.00 |
| 12 ChC | NL | 30 | 0 | 0 | 11 | 36.2 | 154 | 30 | 12 | 12 | 4 | 2 | 2 | 1 | 16 | 1 | 29 | 1 | 0 | 0 | 0 | - | 0 | 0-1 | 2 | 3.35 | 2.95 |
| 6 ML YEARS | | 103 | 2 | 0 | 44 | 133.2 | 576 | 133 | 67 | 67 | 16 | 6 | 4 | 4 | 54 | 3 | 100 | 13 | 1 | 3 | 5 | .375 | 0 | 0-3 | 3 | 4.32 | 4.51 |

# Brad Boxberger

**Pitches:** R **Bats:** R **Pos:** RP-18 **Ht:** 6'2" **Wt:** 220 **Born:** 5/27/1988 **Age:** 26

| HOW MUCH HE PITCHED | | | | | | | | WHAT HE GAVE UP | | | | | | | | | | | | THE RESULTS | | | | | | | |
|---|---|---|---|---|---|---|---|---|---|---|---|---|---|---|---|---|---|---|---|---|---|---|---|---|---|---|---|
| Year Team | Lg | G | GS | CG | GF | IP | BFP | H | R | ER | HR | SH | SF | HB | TBB | IBB | SO | WP | Bk | W | L | Pct | Sh | Sv-Op | Hld | ERC | ERA |
| 2010 Lynbrg | A+ | 14 | 13 | 0 | 0 | 62.0 | 259 | 57 | 30 | 22 | 3 | 3 | 2 | 5 | 20 | 0 | 70 | 1 | 0 | 4 | 6 | .400 | 0 | 0-- | - | 3.35 | 3.19 |
| 2010 Carlina | AA | 22 | 0 | 0 | 6 | 29.2 | 148 | 35 | 28 | 28 | 4 | 2 | 0 | 3 | 22 | 1 | 40 | 5 | 1 | 1 | 4 | .200 | 0 | 0-- | - | 7.10 | 8.49 |
| 2011 Carlina | AA | 30 | 0 | 0 | 22 | 34.1 | 130 | 16 | 5 | 5 | 2 | 2 | 0 | 0 | 13 | 1 | 57 | 1 | 0 | 1 | 2 | .333 | 0 | 4-- | - | 1.29 | 1.31 |
| 2011 Lsvlle | AAA | 25 | 0 | 0 | 12 | 27.2 | 113 | 16 | 10 | 9 | 2 | 1 | 1 | 0 | 15 | 0 | 36 | 0 | 1 | 1 | 2 | .333 | 0 | 7-- | - | 2.22 | 2.93 |
| 2012 Tucsn | AAA | 37 | 0 | 0 | 15 | 43.1 | 183 | 37 | 14 | 13 | 0 | 2 | 1 | 2 | 19 | 0 | 62 | 4 | 0 | 2 | 2 | .500 | 0 | 5-- | - | 2.93 | 2.70 |
| 2013 Tucsn | AAA | 42 | 0 | 0 | 10 | 57.1 | 236 | 50 | 24 | 23 | 3 | 2 | 2 | 0 | 19 | 1 | 89 | 3 | 1 | 2 | 4 | .333 | 0 | 5-- | - | 2.80 | 3.61 |
| 2012 SD | NL | 24 | 0 | 0 | 4 | 27.2 | 120 | 22 | 12 | 8 | 3 | 0 | 1 | 2 | 18 | 1 | 33 | 0 | 0 | 0 | 0 | - | 0 | 0-0 | 1 | 4.28 | 2.60 |
| 2013 SD | NL | 18 | 0 | 0 | 6 | 22.0 | 94 | 19 | 9 | 7 | 3 | 3 | 2 | 0 | 13 | 0 | 24 | 0 | 0 | 0 | 1 | .000 | 0 | 1-1 | 0 | 4.43 | 2.86 |
| 2 ML YEARS | | 42 | 0 | 0 | 10 | 49.2 | 214 | 41 | 21 | 15 | 6 | 3 | 3 | 2 | 31 | 1 | 57 | 0 | 0 | 0 | 1 | .000 | 0 | 1-1 | 1 | 4.35 | 2.72 |

# Brad Brach

BROCK

**Pitches:** R **Bats:** R **Pos:** RP-33 **Ht:** 6'6" **Wt:** 215 **Born:** 4/12/1986 **Age:** 28

| HOW MUCH HE PITCHED | | | | | | | | WHAT HE GAVE UP | | | | | | | | | | | | THE RESULTS | | | | | | | |
|---|---|---|---|---|---|---|---|---|---|---|---|---|---|---|---|---|---|---|---|---|---|---|---|---|---|---|---|
| Year Team | Lg | G | GS | CG | GF | IP | BFP | H | R | ER | HR | SH | SF | HB | TBB | IBB | SO | WP | Bk | W | L | Pct | Sh | Sv-Op | Hld | ERC | ERA |
| 2013 Tucsn* | AAA | 33 | 0 | 0 | 13 | 44.1 | 189 | 43 | 15 | 14 | 5 | 3 | 1 | 2 | 14 | 1 | 44 | 1 | 0 | 4 | 3 | .571 | 0 | 3-- | - | 3.79 | 2.84 |
| 2011 SD | NL | 9 | 0 | 0 | 4 | 7.0 | 38 | 9 | 5 | 4 | 0 | 0 | 0 | 1 | 7 | 4 | 11 | 1 | 0 | 0 | 2 | .000 | 0 | 0-0 | 0 | 6.51 | 5.14 |
| 2012 SD | NL | 67 | 0 | 0 | 13 | 66.2 | 280 | 50 | 28 | 28 | 11 | 1 | 3 | 2 | 33 | 7 | 75 | 4 | 0 | 2 | 4 | .333 | 0 | 0-1 | 15 | 3.47 | 3.78 |
| 2013 SD | NL | 33 | 0 | 0 | 6 | 31.0 | 141 | 36 | 15 | 11 | 3 | 0 | 3 | 0 | 19 | 0 | 31 | 4 | 0 | 1 | 0 | 1.000 | 0 | 0-0 | 2 | 6.03 | 3.19 |
| 3 ML YEARS | | 109 | 0 | 0 | 23 | 104.2 | 459 | 95 | 48 | 43 | 14 | 1 | 6 | 3 | 59 | 11 | 117 | 9 | 0 | 3 | 6 | .333 | 0 | 0-1 | 17 | 4.41 | 3.70 |

# Jackie Bradley Jr.

**Bats:** L **Throws:** R **Pos:** CF-19;LF-14;PR-3;RF-2;PH-2 **Ht:** 5'10" **Wt:** 195 **Born:** 4/19/1990 **Age:** 24

| BATTING | | | | | | | | | | | | | | | | | | | | BASERUNNING | | | | AVERAGES | | |
|---|---|---|---|---|---|---|---|---|---|---|---|---|---|---|---|---|---|---|---|---|---|---|---|---|---|---|
| Year Team | Lg | G | AB | H | 2B | 3B | HR | (Hm | Rd) | TB | R | RBI | RC | TBB | IBB | SO | HBP | SH | SF | SB | CS | SB% | GDP | Avg | OBP | Slg |
| 2011 Lowell | A- | 6 | 21 | 4 | 0 | 0 | 0 | (- | -) | 4 | 5 | 0 | 0 | 4 | 0 | 5 | 0 | 0 | 0 | 0 | 2 | .00 | 0 | .190 | .320 | .190 |
| 2011 Grnvlle | A | 4 | 15 | 5 | 1 | 0 | 1 | (- | -) | 9 | 2 | 3 | 2 | 0 | 0 | 3 | 0 | 0 | 0 | 0 | 0 | - | 0 | .333 | .333 | .600 |
| 2012 Salem | A+ | 67 | 234 | 84 | 26 | 2 | 3 | (- | -) | 123 | 53 | 34 | 64 | 52 | 1 | 40 | 10 | 0 | 8 | 16 | 6 | .73 | 5 | .359 | .480 | .526 |
| 2012 Portlnd | AA | 61 | 229 | 62 | 16 | 2 | 6 | (- | -) | 100 | 37 | 29 | 40 | 35 | 0 | 49 | 4 | 0 | 3 | 8 | 3 | .73 | 3 | .271 | .373 | .437 |
| 2013 Pwtckt | AAA | 80 | 320 | 88 | 26 | 3 | 10 | (- | -) | 150 | 57 | 35 | 57 | 41 | 2 | 75 | 10 | 2 | 1 | 7 | 7 | .50 | 3 | .275 | .374 | .469 |
| 2013 Bos | AL | 37 | 95 | 18 | 5 | 0 | 3 | (2 | 1) | 32 | 18 | 10 | 8 | 10 | 0 | 31 | 2 | 0 | 0 | 2 | 0 | 1.00 | 1 | .189 | .280 | .337 |

# Michael Brantley

**Bats:** L **Throws:** L **Pos:** LF-151;PH-4;CF-1 **Ht:** 6'2" **Wt:** 200 **Born:** 5/15/1987 **Age:** 27

| BATTING | | | | | | | | | | | | | | | | | | | | BASERUNNING | | | | AVERAGES | | |
|---|---|---|---|---|---|---|---|---|---|---|---|---|---|---|---|---|---|---|---|---|---|---|---|---|---|---|
| Year Team | Lg | G | AB | H | 2B | 3B | HR | (Hm | Rd) | TB | R | RBI | RC | TBB | IBB | SO | HBP | SH | SF | SB | CS | SB% | GDP | Avg | OBP | Slg |
| 2009 Cle | AL | 28 | 112 | 35 | 4 | 0 | 0 | (0 | 0) | 39 | 10 | 11 | 16 | 8 | 0 | 19 | 0 | 1 | 0 | 4 | 4 | .50 | 3 | .313 | .358 | .348 |
| 2010 Cle | AL | 72 | 297 | 73 | 9 | 3 | 3 | (2 | 1) | 97 | 38 | 22 | 32 | 22 | 0 | 38 | 0 | 4 | 2 | 10 | 2 | .83 | 6 | .246 | .296 | .327 |
| 2011 Cle | AL | 114 | 451 | 120 | 24 | 4 | 7 | (4 | 3) | 173 | 63 | 46 | 56 | 34 | 2 | 76 | 3 | 3 | 5 | 13 | 5 | .72 | 11 | .266 | .318 | .384 |
| 2012 Cle | AL | 149 | 552 | 159 | 37 | 4 | 6 | (3 | 3) | 222 | 63 | 60 | 76 | 53 | 12 | 56 | 0 | 0 | 4 | 12 | 9 | .57 | 7 | .288 | .348 | .402 |
| 2013 Cle | AL | 151 | 556 | 158 | 26 | 3 | 10 | (9 | 1) | 220 | 66 | 73 | 86 | 40 | 1 | 67 | 4 | 3 | 8 | 17 | 4 | .81 | 11 | .284 | .332 | .396 |
| 5 ML YEARS | | 514 | 1968 | 545 | 100 | 14 | 26 | (18 | 8) | 751 | 240 | 212 | 266 | 157 | 15 | 256 | 7 | 11 | 19 | 56 | 24 | .70 | 38 | .277 | .330 | .382 |

# Rob Brantly

**Bats:** L **Throws:** R **Pos:** C-65;PH-2;PR-1 **Ht:** 6'1" **Wt:** 195 **Born:** 7/14/1989 **Age:** 24

| BATTING | | | | | | | | | | | | | | | | | | | | BASERUNNING | | | | AVERAGES | | |
|---|---|---|---|---|---|---|---|---|---|---|---|---|---|---|---|---|---|---|---|---|---|---|---|---|---|---|
| Year Team | Lg | G | AB | H | 2B | 3B | HR | (Hm | Rd) | TB | R | RBI | RC | TBB | IBB | SO | HBP | SH | SF | SB | CS | SB% | GDP | Avg | OBP | Slg |
| 2010 WMich | A | 52 | 188 | 48 | 10 | 1 | 1 | (- | -) | 63 | 26 | 21 | 24 | 23 | 0 | 22 | 5 | 1 | 0 | 2 | 2 | .50 | 9 | .255 | .352 | .335 |
| 2011 WMich | A | 75 | 284 | 86 | 16 | 1 | 7 | (- | -) | 125 | 42 | 44 | 47 | 24 | 3 | 39 | 5 | 3 | 1 | 2 | 2 | .50 | 12 | .303 | .366 | .440 |
| 2011 Lkland | A+ | 39 | 146 | 32 | 6 | 0 | 3 | (- | -) | 47 | 16 | 18 | 11 | 5 | 0 | 17 | 0 | 0 | 4 | 0 | 0 | - | 4 | .219 | .239 | .322 |
| 2012 Erie | AA | 46 | 180 | 56 | 16 | 1 | 3 | (- | -) | 83 | 16 | 24 | 29 | 12 | 0 | 17 | 2 | 0 | 1 | 0 | 3 | .00 | 4 | .311 | .359 | .461 |
| 2012 Toledo | AAA | 36 | 130 | 33 | 4 | 0 | 0 | (- | -) | 37 | 11 | 6 | 11 | 7 | 0 | 25 | 1 | 0 | 1 | 0 | 0 | - | 5 | .254 | .295 | .285 |
| 2012 NewOr | AAA | 14 | 52 | 19 | 4 | 0 | 2 | (- | -) | 29 | 7 | 11 | 10 | 1 | 0 | 9 | 1 | 0 | 0 | 0 | 0 | - | 0 | .365 | .389 | .558 |
| 2013 NewOr | AAA | 20 | 70 | 13 | 3 | 0 | 1 | (- | -) | 19 | 9 | 3 | 3 | 3 | 0 | 8 | 0 | 1 | 0 | 0 | 0 | - | 4 | .186 | .219 | .271 |
| 2012 Mia | NL | 31 | 100 | 29 | 8 | 0 | 3 | (1 | 2) | 46 | 14 | 8 | 14 | 13 | 2 | 16 | 0 | 0 | 0 | 1 | 1 | .50 | 1 | .290 | .372 | .460 |
| 2013 Mia | NL | 67 | 223 | 47 | 9 | 0 | 1 | (1 | 0) | 59 | 11 | 18 | 14 | 15 | 1 | 53 | 2 | 0 | 3 | 0 | 0 | - | 8 | .211 | .263 | .265 |
| 2 ML YEARS | | 98 | 323 | 76 | 17 | 0 | 4 | (2 | 2) | 105 | 25 | 26 | 28 | 28 | 3 | 69 | 2 | 0 | 3 | 1 | 1 | .50 | 9 | .235 | .298 | .325 |

# Ryan Brasier

BRAY-zhur

**Pitches:** R **Bats:** R **Pos:** RP-7 **Ht:** 6'0" **Wt:** 205 **Born:** 8/26/1987 **Age:** 26

| HOW MUCH HE PITCHED | | | | | | | | WHAT HE GAVE UP | | | | | | | | | | | | THE RESULTS | | | | | | | |
|---|---|---|---|---|---|---|---|---|---|---|---|---|---|---|---|---|---|---|---|---|---|---|---|---|---|---|---|
| Year Team | Lg | G | GS | CG | GF | IP | BFP | H | R | ER | HR | SH | SF | HB | TBB | IBB | SO | WP | Bk | W | L | Pct | Sh | Sv-Op | Hld | ERC | ERA |
| 2009 RCuca | A+ | 27 | 14 | 0 | 6 | 98.0 | 422 | 103 | 63 | 57 | 17 | 3 | 4 | 1 | 32 | 0 | 93 | 8 | 1 | 5 | 4 | .556 | 0 | 0-- | - | 4.62 | 5.23 |
| 2009 Ark | AA | 8 | 0 | 0 | 4 | 11.1 | 55 | 13 | 8 | 7 | 1 | 0 | 1 | 0 | 7 | 1 | 6 | 2 | 1 | 2 | 1 | .667 | 0 | 2-- | - | 5.31 | 5.56 |
| 2010 Ark | AA | 28 | 23 | 1 | 0 | 142.0 | 609 | 127 | 89 | 80 | 28 | 4 | 8 | 4 | 68 | 3 | 94 | 11 | 1 | 7 | 12 | .368 | 1 | 0-- | - | 4.59 | 5.07 |
| 2011 Ark | AA | 25 | 0 | 0 | 24 | 25.1 | 105 | 18 | 3 | 2 | 1 | 0 | 0 | 0 | 14 | 0 | 26 | 3 | 0 | 0 | 1 | .000 | 0 | 16-- | - | 2.73 | 0.71 |
| 2011 Salt Lk | AAA | 25 | 0 | 0 | 18 | 27.0 | 113 | 26 | 16 | 15 | 2 | 0 | 3 | 0 | 9 | 0 | 26 | 1 | 0 | 2 | 1 | .667 | 0 | 3-- | - | 3.46 | 5.00 |
| 2012 Salt Lk | AAA | 55 | 0 | 0 | 48 | 59.2 | 260 | 66 | 30 | 29 | 1 | 3 | 1 | 1 | 24 | 0 | 54 | 2 | 0 | 7 | 3 | .700 | 0 | 13-- | - | 4.20 | 4.37 |
| 2013 Salt Lk | AAA | 38 | 0 | 0 | 22 | 56.2 | 252 | 69 | 31 | 26 | 6 | 1 | 1 | 0 | 16 | 1 | 57 | 3 | 0 | 5 | 2 | .714 | 0 | 10-- | - | 4.80 | 4.13 |
| 2013 LAA | AL | 7 | 0 | 0 | 7 | 9.0 | 35 | 7 | 2 | 2 | 1 | 0 | 1 | 0 | 4 | 0 | 7 | 0 | 0 | 0 | 0 | - | 0 | 0-0 | 0 | 3.37 | 2.00 |

# Ryan Braun

**Bats:** R **Throws:** R **Pos:** LF-59;PH-2 **Ht:** 6'2" **Wt:** 205 **Born:** 11/17/1983 **Age:** 30

| BATTING | | | | | | | | | | | | | | | | | | | | | BASERUNNING | | | | AVERAGES | | |
|---|---|---|---|---|---|---|---|---|---|---|---|---|---|---|---|---|---|---|---|---|---|---|---|---|---|---|---|
| Year Team | Lg | G | AB | H | 2B | 3B | HR | (Hm | Rd) | TB | R | RBI | RC | TBB | IBB | SO | HBP | SH | SF | | SB | CS | SB% | GDP | Avg | OBP | Slg |
| 2007 Mil | NL | 113 | 451 | 146 | 26 | 6 | 34 | (17 | 17) | 286 | 91 | 97 | 94 | 29 | 1 | 112 | 7 | 0 | 5 | | 15 | 5 | .75 | 13 | .324 | .370 | **.634** |
| 2008 Mil | NL | 151 | 611 | 174 | 39 | 7 | 37 | (23 | 14) | 338 | 92 | 106 | 100 | 42 | 4 | 129 | 6 | 0 | 4 | | 14 | 4 | .78 | 13 | .285 | .335 | .553 |
| 2009 Mil | NL | 158 | 635 | **203** | 39 | 6 | 32 | (15 | 17) | 350 | 113 | 114 | 133 | 57 | 1 | 121 | 13 | 0 | 3 | | 20 | 6 | .77 | 7 | .320 | .386 | .551 |
| 2010 Mil | NL | 157 | 619 | 188 | 45 | 1 | 25 | (13 | 12) | 310 | 101 | 103 | 104 | 56 | 1 | 105 | 6 | 0 | 3 | | 14 | 3 | .82 | 17 | .304 | .365 | .501 |
| 2011 Mil | NL | 150 | 563 | 187 | 38 | 6 | 33 | (16 | 17) | 336 | 109 | 111 | 124 | 58 | 2 | 93 | 5 | 0 | 3 | | 33 | 6 | .85 | 9 | .332 | .397 | **.597** |
| 2012 Mil | NL | 154 | 598 | 191 | 36 | 3 | **41** | **(24** | 17) | **356** | **108** | 112 | **125** | 63 | 15 | 128 | 11 | 0 | 5 | | 30 | 7 | .81 | 12 | .319 | .391 | .595 |
| 2013 Mil | NL | 61 | 225 | 67 | 14 | 2 | 9 | (5 | 4) | 112 | 30 | 38 | 39 | 27 | 7 | 56 | 0 | 0 | 1 | | 4 | 5 | .44 | 8 | .298 | .372 | .498 |
| Postseason | | 15 | 58 | 22 | 9 | 0 | 2 | (2 | 0) | 37 | 7 | 12 | 13 | 4 | 0 | 13 | 1 | 0 | 1 | | 1 | 0 | 1.00 | 0 | .379 | .422 | .638 |
| 7 ML YEARS | | 944 | 3702 | 1156 | 237 | 31 | 211 | (113 | 98) | 2088 | 644 | 681 | 719 | 332 | 31 | 744 | 48 | 0 | 24 | | 130 | 36 | .78 | 79 | .312 | .374 | .564 |

# Craig Breslow

**Pitches:** L **Bats:** L **Pos:** RP-61 BREHZ-loh **Ht:** 6'1" **Wt:** 190 **Born:** 8/8/1980 **Age:** 33

| HOW MUCH HE PITCHED | | | | | | | | WHAT HE GAVE UP | | | | | | | | | | | | THE RESULTS | | | | | | | |
|---|---|---|---|---|---|---|---|---|---|---|---|---|---|---|---|---|---|---|---|---|---|---|---|---|---|---|---|
| Year Team | Lg | G | GS | CG | GF | IP | BFP | H | R | ER | HR | SH | SF | HB | TBB | IBB | SO | WP | Bk | W | L | Pct | Sh | Sv-Op | Hld | ERC | ERA |
| 2013 Portlnd* | AA | 1 | 1 | 0 | 0 | 0.0 | 4 | 3 | 3 | 3 | 0 | 0 | 0 | 0 | 1 | 0 | 0 | 0 | 0 | 0 | 0 | - | 0 | 0-- | - | - | - |
| 2013 Pwtckt* | AAA | 4 | 0 | 0 | 0 | 3.2 | 16 | 4 | 1 | 1 | 0 | 0 | 0 | 0 | 3 | 0 | 4 | 0 | 0 | 0 | 0 | - | 0 | 0-- | - | 6.04 | 2.45 |
| 2005 SD | NL | 14 | 0 | 0 | 3 | 16.1 | 78 | 15 | 6 | 4 | 1 | 0 | 1 | 1 | 13 | 0 | 14 | 1 | 0 | 0 | 0 | - | 0 | 0-0 | 1 | 4.98 | 2.20 |
| 2006 Bos | AL | 13 | 0 | 0 | 3 | 12.0 | 55 | 12 | 5 | 5 | 0 | 0 | 2 | 1 | 6 | 1 | 12 | 2 | 1 | 0 | 2 | .000 | 0 | 0-0 | 3 | 3.78 | 3.75 |
| 2008 2 Tms | AL | 49 | 0 | 0 | 13 | 47.0 | 189 | 34 | 12 | 10 | 1 | 2 | 0 | 0 | 19 | 2 | 39 | 4 | 1 | 0 | 2 | .000 | 0 | 1-2 | 5 | 2.12 | 1.91 |
| 2009 2 Tms | AL | 77 | 0 | 0 | 9 | 69.2 | 281 | 48 | 31 | 26 | 8 | 4 | 1 | 3 | 29 | 0 | 55 | 3 | 1 | 8 | 7 | .533 | 0 | 0-2 | 15 | 2.79 | 3.36 |
| 2010 Oak | AL | 75 | 0 | 0 | 23 | 74.2 | 304 | 53 | 26 | 25 | 9 | 2 | 0 | 0 | 29 | 4 | 71 | 0 | 1 | 4 | 4 | .500 | 0 | 5-7 | 16 | 2.53 | 3.01 |
| 2011 Oak | AL | 67 | 0 | 0 | 10 | 59.1 | 261 | 69 | 29 | 25 | 4 | 3 | 2 | 2 | 21 | 1 | 44 | 3 | 0 | 0 | 2 | .000 | 0 | 0-3 | 8 | 4.74 | 3.79 |
| 2012 2 Tms | | 63 | 0 | 0 | 16 | 63.1 | 261 | 52 | 22 | 19 | 5 | 3 | 3 | 2 | 22 | 2 | 61 | 2 | 0 | 3 | 0 | 1.000 | 0 | 0-1 | 9 | 2.86 | 2.70 |
| 2013 Bos | AL | 61 | 0 | 0 | 13 | 59.2 | 237 | 49 | 16 | 12 | 3 | 0 | 2 | 2 | 18 | 0 | 33 | 2 | 0 | 5 | 2 | .714 | 0 | 0-1 | 13 | 2.66 | 1.81 |
| 08 Cle | AL | 7 | 0 | 0 | 3 | 8.1 | 40 | 10 | 3 | 3 | 1 | 0 | 0 | 0 | 5 | 0 | 7 | 0 | 0 | 0 | 0 | - | 0 | 0-0 | 0 | 6.09 | 3.24 |
| 08 Min | AL | 42 | 0 | 0 | 10 | 38.2 | 149 | 24 | 9 | 7 | 0 | 2 | 0 | 0 | 14 | 2 | 32 | 4 | 1 | 0 | 2 | .000 | 0 | 1-2 | 5 | 1.49 | 1.63 |
| 09 Min | AL | 17 | 0 | 0 | 5 | 14.1 | 64 | 11 | 11 | 10 | 3 | 2 | 0 | 1 | 11 | 0 | 11 | 3 | 0 | 1 | 2 | .333 | 0 | 0-0 | 2 | 5.38 | 6.28 |
| 09 Oak | AL | 60 | 0 | 0 | 4 | 55.1 | 217 | 37 | 20 | 16 | 5 | 2 | 1 | 2 | 18 | 0 | 44 | 0 | 1 | 7 | 5 | .583 | 0 | 0-2 | 13 | 2.21 | 2.60 |
| 12 Ari | NL | 40 | 0 | 0 | 12 | 43.1 | 180 | 38 | 15 | 13 | 5 | 2 | 1 | 1 | 13 | 0 | 42 | 1 | 0 | 2 | 0 | 1.000 | 0 | 0-0 | 4 | 3.19 | 2.70 |
| 12 Bos | AL | 23 | 0 | 0 | 4 | 20.0 | 81 | 14 | 7 | 6 | 0 | 1 | 2 | 1 | 9 | 2 | 19 | 1 | 0 | 1 | 0 | 1.000 | 0 | 0-1 | 5 | 2.12 | 2.70 |
| 8 ML YEARS | | 419 | 0 | 0 | 90 | 402.0 | 1666 | 332 | 147 | 126 | 31 | 14 | 11 | 11 | 157 | 10 | 329 | 17 | 4 | 20 | 19 | .513 | 0 | 6-16 | 70 | 3.04 | 2.82 |

# Charles Brewer

**Pitches:** R **Bats:** R **Pos:** RP-4 **Ht:** 6'3" **Wt:** 205 **Born:** 4/7/1988 **Age:** 26

| HOW MUCH HE PITCHED | | | | | | | | WHAT HE GAVE UP | | | | | | | | | | | | THE RESULTS | | | | | | | |
|---|---|---|---|---|---|---|---|---|---|---|---|---|---|---|---|---|---|---|---|---|---|---|---|---|---|---|---|
| Year Team | Lg | G | GS | CG | GF | IP | BFP | H | R | ER | HR | SH | SF | HB | TBB | IBB | SO | WP | Bk | W | L | Pct | Sh | Sv-Op | Hld | ERC | ERA |
| 2009 Msoula | R+ | 17 | 7 | 0 | 1 | 54.2 | 222 | 43 | 24 | 15 | 4 | 3 | 1 | 4 | 15 | 0 | 61 | 2 | 0 | 7 | 2 | .778 | 0 | 0-- | - | 2.59 | 2.47 |
| 2010 Sbend | A | 13 | 13 | 0 | 0 | 69.0 | 280 | 55 | 20 | 14 | 3 | 1 | 2 | 2 | 20 | 0 | 78 | 2 | 1 | 4 | 5 | .444 | 0 | 0-- | - | 2.35 | 1.83 |
| 2010 Visalia | A+ | 14 | 14 | 0 | 0 | 81.2 | 335 | 74 | 29 | 27 | 5 | 3 | 2 | 6 | 15 | 0 | 75 | 5 | 0 | 7 | 3 | .700 | 0 | 0-- | - | 2.77 | 2.98 |
| 2011 Mobile | AA | 11 | 11 | 2 | 0 | 52.1 | 210 | 48 | 16 | 15 | 2 | 0 | 2 | 2 | 19 | 0 | 48 | 0 | 0 | 5 | 1 | .833 | 0 | 0-- | - | 3.41 | 2.58 |
| 2011 DBcks | R | 1 | 1 | 0 | 0 | 3.0 | 12 | 3 | 0 | 0 | 0 | 0 | 0 | 0 | 0 | 0 | 4 | 0 | 0 | 0 | 0 | - | 0 | 0-- | - | 1.95 | 0.00 |
| 2012 Mobile | AA | 3 | 3 | 0 | 0 | 17.1 | 73 | 19 | 9 | 8 | 2 | 0 | 0 | 0 | 2 | 0 | 13 | 3 | 0 | 0 | 0 | - | 0 | 0-- | - | 3.51 | 4.15 |
| 2012 Reno | AAA | 24 | 24 | 2 | 0 | 133.2 | 605 | 177 | 110 | 89 | 26 | 6 | 6 | 3 | 34 | 0 | 104 | 5 | 0 | 11 | 7 | .611 | 0 | 0-- | - | 6.15 | 5.99 |
| 2013 Reno | AAA | 25 | 22 | 0 | 1 | 139.2 | 606 | 158 | 83 | 76 | 13 | 5 | 2 | 9 | 43 | 0 | 107 | 8 | 0 | 5 | 12 | .294 | 0 | 0-- | - | 4.74 | 4.90 |
| 2013 Ari | NL | 4 | 0 | 0 | 2 | 6.0 | 27 | 8 | 2 | 2 | 0 | 0 | 0 | 0 | 2 | 0 | 5 | 0 | 0 | 0 | 0 | - | 0 | 0-0 | 0 | 5.03 | 3.00 |

# Reid Brignac

**Bats:** L **Throws:** R **Pos:** SS-20;PH-16;3B-8;2B-3;LF-1 BRINN-yak **Ht:** 6'3" **Wt:** 190 **Born:** 1/16/1986 **Age:** 28

| BATTING | | | | | | | | | | | | | | | | | | | | | BASERUNNING | | | | AVERAGES | | |
|---|---|---|---|---|---|---|---|---|---|---|---|---|---|---|---|---|---|---|---|---|---|---|---|---|---|---|---|
| Year Team | Lg | G | AB | H | 2B | 3B | HR | (Hm | Rd) | TB | R | RBI | RC | TBB | IBB | SO | HBP | SH | SF | | SB | CS | SB% | GDP | Avg | OBP | Slg |
| 2013 ColSpr* | AAA | 48 | 165 | 38 | 8 | 0 | 2 | (- | -) | 52 | 25 | 11 | 19 | 21 | 0 | 33 | 3 | 2 | 2 | | 2 | 1 | .67 | 3 | .230 | .325 | .315 |
| 2008 TB | AL | 4 | 10 | 0 | 0 | 0 | 0 | (0 | 0) | 0 | 1 | 0 | 0 | 1 | 0 | 5 | 0 | 0 | 0 | | 0 | 0 | - | 0 | .000 | .091 | .000 |
| 2009 TB | AL | 31 | 90 | 25 | 8 | 2 | 1 | (0 | 1) | 40 | 10 | 6 | 10 | 3 | 0 | 20 | 0 | 0 | 0 | | 2 | 2 | .50 | 1 | .278 | .301 | .444 |
| 2010 TB | AL | 113 | 301 | 77 | 13 | 1 | 8 | (3 | 5) | 116 | 39 | 45 | 38 | 20 | 3 | 77 | 3 | 0 | 2 | | 3 | 3 | .50 | 6 | .256 | .307 | .385 |
| 2011 TB | AL | 92 | 249 | 48 | 4 | 0 | 1 | (0 | 1) | 55 | 18 | 15 | 8 | 10 | 1 | 63 | 1 | 4 | 0 | | 3 | 1 | .75 | 2 | .193 | .227 | .221 |
| 2012 TB | AL | 16 | 21 | 2 | 0 | 0 | 0 | (0 | 0) | 2 | 1 | 1 | 0 | 1 | 0 | 5 | 0 | 0 | 0 | | 0 | 0 | - | 0 | .095 | .136 | .095 |
| 2013 2 Tms | | 46 | 92 | 17 | 4 | 0 | 1 | (0 | 1) | 24 | 5 | 6 | 7 | 4 | 1 | 30 | 0 | 2 | 0 | | 0 | 0 | - | 6 | .185 | .219 | .261 |
| 13 Col | NL | 29 | 48 | 12 | 3 | 0 | 1 | (0 | 1) | 18 | 4 | 6 | 7 | 3 | 1 | 13 | 0 | 2 | 0 | | 0 | 0 | - | 3 | .250 | .294 | .375 |
| 13 NYY | AL | 17 | 44 | 5 | 1 | 0 | 0 | (0 | 0) | 6 | 1 | 0 | 0 | 1 | 0 | 17 | 0 | 0 | 0 | | 0 | 0 | - | 3 | .114 | .133 | .136 |
| Postseason | | 5 | 4 | 0 | 0 | 0 | 0 | (0 | 0) | 0 | 0 | 0 | 0 | 1 | 0 | 3 | 0 | 0 | 0 | | 0 | 0 | - | 0 | .000 | .200 | .000 |
| 6 ML YEARS | | 302 | 763 | 169 | 29 | 3 | 11 | (3 | 8) | 237 | 74 | 73 | 63 | 39 | 5 | 200 | 4 | 6 | 2 | | 8 | 6 | .57 | 15 | .221 | .262 | .311 |

# Drake Britton

**Pitches:** L **Bats:** L **Pos:** RP-18 **Ht:** 6'2" **Wt:** 215 **Born:** 5/22/1989 **Age:** 25

| HOW MUCH HE PITCHED | | | | | | | | WHAT HE GAVE UP | | | | | | | | | | | | THE RESULTS | | | | | | | |
|---|---|---|---|---|---|---|---|---|---|---|---|---|---|---|---|---|---|---|---|---|---|---|---|---|---|---|---|
| Year Team | Lg | G | GS | CG | GF | IP | BFP | H | R | ER | HR | SH | SF | HB | TBB | IBB | SO | WP | Bk | W | L | Pct | Sh | Sv-Op | Hld | ERC | ERA |
| 2009 RedSx | R | 4 | 4 | 0 | 0 | 7.0 | 29 | 2 | 0 | 0 | 0 | 0 | 0 | 0 | 4 | 0 | 11 | 0 | 0 | 0 | 0 | - | 0 | 0-- | - | 0.89 | 0.00 |
| 2009 Lowell | A- | 3 | 3 | 0 | 0 | 4.2 | 22 | 4 | 1 | 1 | 0 | 0 | 1 | 1 | 3 | 0 | 8 | 0 | 0 | 0 | 0 | - | 0 | 0-- | - | 4.14 | 1.93 |
| 2010 Grnvlle | A | 21 | 21 | 0 | 0 | 75.2 | 318 | 69 | 32 | 25 | 5 | 3 | 2 | 2 | 23 | 0 | 78 | 7 | 0 | 2 | 3 | .400 | 0 | 0-- | - | 3.07 | 2.97 |
| 2011 Salem | A+ | 26 | 26 | 0 | 0 | 97.2 | 458 | 111 | 81 | 75 | 12 | 3 | 5 | 6 | 55 | 0 | 89 | 16 | 0 | 1 | 13 | .071 | 0 | 0-- | - | 5.93 | 6.91 |
| 2012 Salem | A+ | 10 | 8 | 0 | 0 | 45.0 | 201 | 42 | 35 | 29 | 5 | 5 | 2 | 4 | 19 | 0 | 42 | 2 | 0 | 3 | 5 | .375 | 0 | 0-- | - | 4.10 | 5.80 |

| Year | Team | Lg | HOW MUCH HE PITCHED: G | GS | CG | GF | IP | BFP | WHAT HE GAVE UP: H | R | ER | HR | SH | SF | HB | TBB | IBB | SO | WP | Bk | THE RESULTS: W | L | Pct | Sh | Sv-Op | Hld | ERC | ERA |
|---|---|---|---|---|---|---|---|---|---|---|---|---|---|---|---|---|---|---|---|---|---|---|---|---|---|---|---|---|---|
| 2012 | Portlnd | AA | 16 | 16 | 0 | 0 | 84.2 | 369 | 86 | 41 | 35 | 3 | 5 | 2 | 1 | 38 | 0 | 76 | 2 | 0 | 4 | 7 | .364 | 0 | 0-- | - | 3.95 | 3.72 |
| 2013 | Portlnd | AA | 17 | 16 | 1 | 0 | 97.1 | 410 | 94 | 52 | 38 | 5 | 1 | 1 | 2 | 36 | 0 | 80 | 6 | 0 | 7 | 6 | .538 | 1 | 0-- | - | 3.56 | 3.51 |
| 2013 | Pwtckt | AAA | 1 | 1 | 0 | 0 | 5.1 | 28 | 10 | 5 | 5 | 0 | 1 | 0 | 0 | 1 | 0 | 5 | 0 | 0 | 0 | 1 | .000 | 0 | 0-- | - | 7.22 | 8.44 |
| 2013 | Bos | AL | 18 | 0 | 0 | 7 | 21.0 | 84 | 21 | 9 | 9 | 1 | 0 | 2 | 0 | 7 | 1 | 17 | 0 | 0 | 1 | 1 | .500 | 0 | 0-2 | 1 | 3.62 | 3.86 |

## Zach Britton

**Pitches:** L **Bats:** L **Pos:** SP-7; RP-1 **Ht:** 6'3" **Wt:** 195 **Born:** 12/22/1987 **Age:** 26

| Year | Team | Lg | HOW MUCH HE PITCHED: G | GS | CG | GF | IP | BFP | WHAT HE GAVE UP: H | R | ER | HR | SH | SF | HB | TBB | IBB | SO | WP | Bk | THE RESULTS: W | L | Pct | Sh | Sv-Op | Hld | ERC | ERA |
|---|---|---|---|---|---|---|---|---|---|---|---|---|---|---|---|---|---|---|---|---|---|---|---|---|---|---|---|---|---|
| 2013 | Norfolk* | AAA | 19 | 19 | 0 | 0 | 103.1 | 461 | 112 | 59 | 49 | 5 | 3 | 6 | 5 | 46 | 0 | 75 | 9 | 0 | 6 | 5 | .545 | 0 | 0-- | - | 4.55 | 4.27 |
| 2011 | Bal | AL | 28 | 28 | 0 | 0 | 154.1 | 666 | 162 | 93 | 79 | 12 | 8 | 7 | 1 | 62 | 3 | 97 | 7 | 0 | 11 | 11 | .500 | 0 | 0-0 | 0 | 4.24 | 4.61 |
| 2012 | Bal | AL | 12 | 11 | 0 | 0 | 60.1 | 270 | 61 | 37 | 34 | 6 | 0 | 1 | 2 | 32 | 3 | 53 | 4 | 0 | 5 | 3 | .625 | 0 | 0-0 | 0 | 4.70 | 5.07 |
| 2013 | Bal | AL | 8 | 7 | 0 | 0 | 40.0 | 182 | 52 | 23 | 22 | 4 | 1 | 1 | 1 | 17 | 1 | 18 | 1 | 0 | 2 | 3 | .400 | 0 | 0-0 | 0 | 6.14 | 4.95 |
| 3 ML YEARS | | | 48 | 46 | 0 | 0 | 254.2 | 1118 | 275 | 153 | 135 | 22 | 9 | 9 | 4 | 111 | 7 | 168 | 12 | 0 | 18 | 17 | .514 | 0 | 0-0 | 0 | 4.63 | 4.77 |

## Rex Brothers

**Pitches:** L **Bats:** L **Pos:** RP-72 **Ht:** 6'0" **Wt:** 210 **Born:** 12/18/1987 **Age:** 26

| Year | Team | Lg | HOW MUCH HE PITCHED: G | GS | CG | GF | IP | BFP | WHAT HE GAVE UP: H | R | ER | HR | SH | SF | HB | TBB | IBB | SO | WP | Bk | THE RESULTS: W | L | Pct | Sh | Sv-Op | Hld | ERC | ERA |
|---|---|---|---|---|---|---|---|---|---|---|---|---|---|---|---|---|---|---|---|---|---|---|---|---|---|---|---|---|---|
| 2011 | Col | NL | 48 | 0 | 0 | 6 | 40.2 | 172 | 33 | 14 | 13 | 4 | 0 | 0 | 0 | 20 | 2 | 59 | 2 | 0 | 1 | 2 | .333 | 0 | 1-3 | 16 | 3.31 | 2.88 |
| 2012 | Col | NL | 75 | 0 | 0 | 10 | 67.2 | 295 | 63 | 33 | 29 | 5 | 3 | 3 | 1 | 37 | 7 | 83 | 5 | 1 | 8 | 2 | .800 | 0 | 0-5 | 18 | 3.99 | 3.86 |
| 2013 | Col | NL | 72 | 0 | 0 | 40 | 67.1 | 281 | 51 | 16 | 13 | 5 | 1 | 0 | 0 | 36 | 2 | 76 | 3 | **3** | 2 | 1 | .667 | 0 | 19-21 | 12 | 3.09 | 1.74 |
| 3 ML YEARS | | | 195 | 0 | 0 | 56 | 175.2 | 748 | 147 | 63 | 55 | 14 | 4 | 3 | 1 | 93 | 11 | 218 | 10 | 4 | 11 | 5 | .688 | 0 | 20-29 | 46 | 3.48 | 2.82 |

## Andrew Brown

**Bats:** R **Throws:** R **Pos:** PH-26;RF-25;LF-14;DH-3;PR-2;1B-1 **Ht:** 6'0" **Wt:** 185 **Born:** 9/10/1984 **Age:** 29

| Year | Team | Lg | BATTING: G | AB | H | 2B | 3B | HR | (Hm | Rd) | TB | R | RBI | RC | TBB | IBB | SO | HBP | SH | SF | BASERUNNING: SB | CS | SB% | GDP | AVERAGES: Avg | OBP | Slg |
|---|---|---|---|---|---|---|---|---|---|---|---|---|---|---|---|---|---|---|---|---|---|---|---|---|---|---|---|---|
| 2013 | LsVgs* | AAA | 41 | 153 | 53 | 15 | 6 | 7 | (- | -) | 101 | 39 | 41 | 42 | 23 | 1 | 34 | 4 | 0 | 5 | 0 | 0 | - | 8 | .346 | .432 | .660 |
| 2011 | StL | NL | 11 | 22 | 4 | 1 | 0 | 0 | (0 | 0) | 5 | 1 | 3 | 1 | 0 | 0 | 8 | 0 | 0 | 0 | 0 | 0 | - | 1 | .182 | .182 | .227 |
| 2012 | Col | NL | 46 | 112 | 26 | 7 | 0 | 5 | (3 | 2) | 48 | 14 | 11 | 7 | 12 | 0 | 34 | 0 | 0 | 2 | 2 | 2 | .50 | 3 | .232 | .302 | .429 |
| 2013 | NYM | NL | 68 | 150 | 34 | 5 | 0 | 7 | (3 | 4) | 60 | 16 | 24 | 19 | 13 | 0 | 44 | 0 | 2 | 0 | 1 | 0 | 1.00 | 3 | .227 | .288 | .400 |
| 3 ML YEARS | | | 125 | 284 | 64 | 13 | 0 | 12 | (6 | 6) | 113 | 31 | 38 | 27 | 25 | 0 | 86 | 0 | 2 | 2 | 3 | 2 | .60 | 7 | .225 | .286 | .398 |

## Corey Brown

**Bats:** L **Throws:** L **Pos:** LF-5;PH-5;RF-3;CF-1;PR-1 **Ht:** 6'1" **Wt:** 210 **Born:** 11/26/1985 **Age:** 28

| Year | Team | Lg | BATTING: G | AB | H | 2B | 3B | HR | (Hm | Rd) | TB | R | RBI | RC | TBB | IBB | SO | HBP | SH | SF | BASERUNNING: SB | CS | SB% | GDP | AVERAGES: Avg | OBP | Slg |
|---|---|---|---|---|---|---|---|---|---|---|---|---|---|---|---|---|---|---|---|---|---|---|---|---|---|---|---|---|
| 2013 | Syrcse* | AAA | 107 | 389 | 99 | 26 | 1 | 19 | (- | -) | 184 | 57 | 56 | 62 | 40 | 3 | 132 | 3 | 3 | 3 | 12 | 4 | .75 | 2 | .254 | .326 | .473 |
| 2011 | Was | NL | 3 | 3 | 0 | 0 | 0 | 0 | (0 | 0) | 0 | 0 | 0 | 0 | 0 | 0 | 2 | 0 | 0 | 0 | 0 | 0 | - | 0 | .000 | .000 | .000 |
| 2012 | Was | NL | 19 | 25 | 5 | 2 | 0 | 1 | (0 | 1) | 10 | 4 | 3 | 2 | 1 | 0 | 9 | 0 | 1 | 0 | 0 | 0 | - | 0 | .200 | .231 | .400 |
| 2013 | Was | NL | 14 | 12 | 2 | 1 | 0 | 1 | (0 | 1) | 6 | 2 | 1 | 2 | 3 | 0 | 4 | 0 | 0 | 0 | 1 | 0 | 1.00 | 1 | .167 | .333 | .500 |
| 3 ML YEARS | | | 36 | 40 | 7 | 3 | 0 | 2 | (0 | 2) | 16 | 6 | 4 | 4 | 4 | 0 | 15 | 0 | 1 | 0 | 1 | 0 | 1.00 | 1 | .175 | .250 | .400 |

## Domonic Brown

**Bats:** L **Throws:** L **Pos:** LF-132;PH-7;RF-2 **Ht:** 6'5" **Wt:** 205 **Born:** 9/3/1987 **Age:** 26

| Year | Team | Lg | BATTING: G | AB | H | 2B | 3B | HR | (Hm | Rd) | TB | R | RBI | RC | TBB | IBB | SO | HBP | SH | SF | BASERUNNING: SB | CS | SB% | GDP | AVERAGES: Avg | OBP | Slg |
|---|---|---|---|---|---|---|---|---|---|---|---|---|---|---|---|---|---|---|---|---|---|---|---|---|---|---|---|---|
| 2013 | Lakwd* | A | 1 | 5 | 3 | 0 | 0 | 1 | (- | -) | 6 | 2 | 2 | 2 | 0 | 0 | 0 | 0 | 0 | 0 | 0 | 0 | - | 0 | .600 | .600 | 1.200 |
| 2010 | Phi | NL | 35 | 62 | 13 | 3 | 0 | 2 | (2 | 0) | 22 | 8 | 13 | 5 | 5 | 1 | 24 | 0 | 0 | 3 | 2 | 1 | .67 | 1 | .210 | .257 | .355 |
| 2011 | Phi | NL | 56 | 184 | 45 | 10 | 1 | 5 | (4 | 1) | 72 | 28 | 19 | 21 | 25 | 1 | 35 | 0 | 0 | 1 | 3 | 1 | .75 | 2 | .245 | .333 | .391 |
| 2012 | Phi | NL | 56 | 187 | 44 | 11 | 2 | 5 | (3 | 2) | 74 | 21 | 26 | 25 | 21 | 2 | 34 | 2 | 0 | 2 | 0 | 0 | - | 6 | .235 | .316 | .396 |
| 2013 | Phi | NL | 139 | 496 | 135 | 21 | 4 | 27 | (14 | 13) | 245 | 65 | 83 | 76 | 39 | 5 | 97 | 1 | 0 | 4 | 8 | 3 | .73 | 5 | .272 | .324 | .494 |
| Postseason | | | 3 | 3 | 0 | 0 | 0 | 0 | (0 | 0) | 0 | 1 | 0 | 0 | 0 | 0 | 0 | 0 | 0 | 0 | 0 | 0 | - | 0 | .000 | .000 | .000 |
| 4 ML YEARS | | | 286 | 929 | 237 | 45 | 7 | 39 | (23 | 16) | 413 | 122 | 141 | 127 | 90 | 9 | 190 | 3 | 0 | 10 | 13 | 5 | .72 | 14 | .255 | .320 | .445 |

## Jordan Brown

**Bats:** L **Throws:** L **Pos:** PH-13;DH-1 **Ht:** 6'0" **Wt:** 220 **Born:** 12/18/1983 **Age:** 30

| Year | Team | Lg | BATTING: G | AB | H | 2B | 3B | HR | (Hm | Rd) | TB | R | RBI | RC | TBB | IBB | SO | HBP | SH | SF | BASERUNNING: SB | CS | SB% | GDP | AVERAGES: Avg | OBP | Slg |
|---|---|---|---|---|---|---|---|---|---|---|---|---|---|---|---|---|---|---|---|---|---|---|---|---|---|---|---|---|
| 2009 | Clmbs | AAA | 111 | 417 | 140 | 35 | 1 | 15 | (- | -) | 222 | 65 | 67 | 81 | 30 | 3 | 64 | 2 | 3 | 3 | 2 | 4 | .33 | 7 | .336 | .381 | .532 |
| 2010 | Clmbs | AAA | 83 | 326 | 97 | 28 | 1 | 8 | (- | -) | 151 | 31 | 67 | 53 | 21 | 1 | 48 | 3 | 0 | 5 | 2 | 0 | 1.00 | 9 | .298 | .341 | .463 |
| 2011 | Clmbs | AAA | 20 | 72 | 20 | 3 | 1 | 3 | (- | -) | 34 | 10 | 13 | 13 | 11 | 2 | 15 | 0 | 0 | 0 | 0 | 0 | - | 1 | .278 | .373 | .472 |
| 2011 | Nashv | AAA | 99 | 348 | 110 | 28 | 0 | 7 | (- | -) | 159 | 49 | 49 | 55 | 12 | 1 | 32 | 3 | 3 | 6 | 2 | 0 | 1.00 | 9 | .316 | .339 | .457 |
| 2012 | Nashv | AAA | 104 | 359 | 110 | 22 | 1 | 8 | (- | -) | 158 | 43 | 37 | 55 | 22 | 1 | 49 | 1 | 4 | 2 | 2 | 3 | .40 | 7 | .306 | .346 | .440 |
| 2013 | NewOr | AAA | 97 | 291 | 84 | 22 | 0 | 2 | (- | -) | 112 | 31 | 28 | 40 | 24 | 2 | 34 | 3 | 3 | 3 | 0 | 2 | .00 | 6 | .289 | .346 | .385 |
| 2010 | Cle | AL | 26 | 87 | 20 | 7 | 0 | 0 | (0 | 0) | 27 | 9 | 2 | 1 | 4 | 0 | 10 | 1 | 0 | 0 | 0 | 0 | - | 3 | .230 | .272 | .310 |
| 2013 | Mia | NL | 14 | 15 | 3 | 1 | 0 | 0 | (0 | 0) | 4 | 0 | 5 | 2 | 1 | 0 | 1 | 0 | 0 | 1 | 0 | 0 | - | 0 | .200 | .235 | .267 |
| 2 ML YEARS | | | 40 | 102 | 23 | 8 | 0 | 0 | (0 | 0) | 31 | 9 | 7 | 3 | 5 | 0 | 11 | 1 | 0 | 1 | 0 | 0 | - | 3 | .225 | .266 | .304 |

## Jonathan Broxton

**Pitches:** R **Bats:** R **Pos:** RP-34 **Ht:** 6'4" **Wt:** 310 **Born:** 6/16/1984 **Age:** 30

| | | | HOW MUCH HE PITCHED | | | | | | WHAT HE GAVE UP | | | | | | | | | | | | THE RESULTS | | | | | | | |
|---|---|---|---|---|---|---|---|---|---|---|---|---|---|---|---|---|---|---|---|---|---|---|---|---|---|---|---|---|
| Year | Team | Lg | G | GS | CG | GF | IP | BFP | H | R | ER | HR | SH | SF | HB | TBB | IBB | SO | WP | Bk | W | L | Pct | Sh | Sv-Op | Hld | ERC | ERA |
| 2013 | Lsvlle* | AAA | 2 | 2 | 0 | 0 | 2.0 | 11 | 5 | 0 | 0 | 0 | 0 | 0 | 0 | 0 | 0 | 3 | 0 | 0 | 0 | 0 | - | 0 | 0- - | - | 10.86 | 0.00 |
| 2005 | LAD | NL | 14 | 0 | 0 | 5 | 13.2 | 68 | 13 | 11 | 9 | 0 | 0 | 2 | 1 | 12 | 2 | 22 | 2 | 0 | 1 | 0 | 1.000 | 0 | 0-1 | 1 | 4.65 | 5.93 |
| 2006 | LAD | NL | 68 | 0 | 0 | 20 | 76.1 | 320 | 61 | 25 | 22 | 7 | 3 | 1 | 1 | 33 | 6 | 97 | 7 | 0 | 4 | 1 | .800 | 0 | 3-7 | 12 | 2.97 | 2.59 |
| 2007 | LAD | NL | 83 | 0 | 0 | 18 | 82.0 | 334 | 69 | 30 | 26 | 6 | 0 | 1 | 1 | 25 | 3 | 99 | 4 | 0 | 4 | 4 | .500 | 0 | 2-8 | 32 | 2.71 | 2.85 |
| 2008 | LAD | NL | 70 | 0 | 0 | 32 | 69.0 | 285 | 54 | 29 | 24 | 2 | 3 | 3 | 3 | 27 | 5 | 88 | 3 | 0 | 3 | 5 | .375 | 0 | 14-22 | 13 | 2.48 | 3.13 |
| 2009 | LAD | NL | 73 | 0 | 0 | 58 | 76.0 | 300 | 44 | 24 | 22 | 4 | 0 | 3 | 1 | 29 | 1 | 114 | 2 | 0 | 7 | 2 | .778 | 0 | 36-42 | 1 | 1.65 | 2.61 |
| 2010 | LAD | NL | 64 | 0 | 0 | 46 | 62.1 | 271 | 64 | 30 | 28 | 4 | 3 | 1 | 2 | 28 | 5 | 73 | 1 | 0 | 5 | 6 | .455 | 0 | 22-29 | 3 | 4.21 | 4.04 |
| 2011 | LAD | NL | 14 | 0 | 0 | 12 | 12.2 | 62 | 15 | 10 | 8 | 2 | 0 | 0 | 0 | 9 | 2 | 10 | 0 | 0 | 1 | 2 | .333 | 0 | 7-8 | 0 | 6.47 | 5.68 |
| 2012 | 2 Tms | | 60 | 0 | 0 | 39 | 58.0 | 238 | 56 | 18 | 16 | 2 | 2 | 1 | 3 | 17 | 0 | 45 | 0 | 0 | 4 | 5 | .444 | 0 | 27-33 | 10 | 3.34 | 2.48 |
| 2013 | Cin | NL | 34 | 0 | 0 | 8 | 30.2 | 133 | 27 | 17 | 14 | 4 | 1 | 2 | 4 | 12 | 2 | 25 | 0 | 0 | 2 | 2 | .500 | 0 | 0-3 | 12 | 3.97 | 4.11 |
| 12 | KC | AL | 35 | 0 | 0 | 32 | 35.2 | 151 | 36 | 11 | 9 | 1 | 2 | 1 | 2 | 14 | 0 | 25 | 0 | 0 | 1 | 2 | .333 | 0 | 23-27 | 0 | 3.93 | 2.27 |
| 12 | Cin | NL | 25 | 0 | 0 | 7 | 22.1 | 87 | 20 | 7 | 7 | 1 | 0 | 0 | 1 | 3 | 0 | 20 | 0 | 0 | 3 | 3 | .500 | 0 | 4-6 | 10 | 2.44 | 2.82 |
| Postseason | | | 16 | 0 | 0 | 11 | 17.1 | 79 | 18 | 8 | 7 | 1 | 0 | 0 | 1 | 7 | 0 | 19 | 0 | 0 | 0 | 3 | .000 | 0 | 3-5 | 1 | 4.06 | 3.63 |
| 9 ML YEARS | | | 480 | 0 | 0 | 238 | 480.2 | 2011 | 403 | 194 | 169 | 31 | 12 | 14 | 16 | 192 | 26 | 573 | 19 | 0 | 31 | 27 | .534 | 0 | 111-153 | 84 | 3.01 | 3.16 |

## Jay Bruce

**Bats:** L **Throws:** L **Pos:** RF-160 **Ht:** 6'3" **Wt:** 215 **Born:** 4/3/1987 **Age:** 27

| | | | BATTING | | | | | | | | | | | | | | | | | | BASERUNNING | | | | AVERAGES | | |
|---|---|---|---|---|---|---|---|---|---|---|---|---|---|---|---|---|---|---|---|---|---|---|---|---|---|---|---|
| Year | Team | Lg | G | AB | H | 2B | 3B | HR | (Hm | Rd) | TB | R | RBI | RC | TBB | IBB | SO | HBP | SH | SF | SB | CS | SB% | GDP | Avg | OBP | Slg |
| 2008 | Cin | NL | 108 | 413 | 105 | 17 | 1 | 21 | (13 | 8) | 187 | 63 | 52 | 49 | 33 | 1 | 110 | 4 | 0 | 2 | 4 | 6 | .40 | 8 | .254 | .314 | .453 |
| 2009 | Cin | NL | 101 | 345 | 77 | 15 | 2 | 22 | (13 | 9) | 162 | 47 | 58 | 47 | 38 | 2 | 75 | 2 | 1 | 1 | 3 | 3 | .50 | 5 | .223 | .303 | .470 |
| 2010 | Cin | NL | 148 | 509 | 143 | 23 | 5 | 25 | (19 | 6) | 251 | 80 | 70 | 71 | 58 | 5 | 136 | 1 | 0 | 5 | 5 | 4 | .56 | 12 | .281 | .353 | .493 |
| 2011 | Cin | NL | 157 | 585 | 150 | 27 | 2 | 32 | (16 | 16) | 277 | 84 | 97 | 96 | 71 | 14 | 158 | 5 | 1 | 2 | 8 | 7 | .53 | 8 | .256 | .341 | .474 |
| 2012 | Cin | NL | 155 | 560 | 141 | 35 | 5 | 34 | (21 | 13) | 288 | 89 | 99 | 85 | 62 | 11 | 155 | 4 | 0 | 7 | 9 | 3 | .75 | 5 | .252 | .327 | .514 |
| 2013 | Cin | NL | 160 | 626 | 164 | 43 | 1 | 30 | (16 | 14) | 299 | 89 | 109 | 88 | 63 | 13 | 185 | 2 | 0 | 5 | 7 | 3 | .70 | 9 | .262 | .329 | .478 |
| Postseason | | | 8 | 27 | 7 | 2 | 0 | 2 | (0 | 2) | 15 | 3 | 5 | 4 | 4 | 0 | 2 | 1 | 0 | 0 | 0 | 1 | .00 | 0 | .259 | .375 | .556 |
| 6 ML YEARS | | | 829 | 3038 | 780 | 160 | 16 | 164 | (98 | 66) | 1464 | 452 | 485 | 436 | 325 | 46 | 819 | 18 | 2 | 22 | 36 | 26 | .58 | 47 | .257 | .330 | .482 |

## Clay Buchholz

**Pitches:** R **Bats:** L **Pos:** SP-16 BUCK-holtz **Ht:** 6'3" **Wt:** 190 **Born:** 8/14/1984 **Age:** 29

| | | | HOW MUCH HE PITCHED | | | | | | WHAT HE GAVE UP | | | | | | | | | | | | THE RESULTS | | | | | | | |
|---|---|---|---|---|---|---|---|---|---|---|---|---|---|---|---|---|---|---|---|---|---|---|---|---|---|---|---|---|
| Year | Team | Lg | G | GS | CG | GF | IP | BFP | H | R | ER | HR | SH | SF | HB | TBB | IBB | SO | WP | Bk | W | L | Pct | Sh | Sv-Op | Hld | ERC | ERA |
| 2013 | Lowell* | A- | 1 | 1 | 0 | 0 | 0.2 | 7 | 1 | 3 | 1 | 0 | 0 | 0 | 0 | 3 | 0 | 1 | 0 | 0 | 0 | 0 | - | 0 | 0- - | - | 21.02 | 13.50 |
| 2013 | Pwtckt* | AAA | 1 | 1 | 0 | 0 | 3.1 | 16 | 7 | 1 | 1 | 0 | 0 | 0 | 0 | 0 | 0 | 2 | 0 | 0 | 0 | 0 | - | 0 | 0- - | - | 8.68 | 2.70 |
| 2007 | Bos | AL | 4 | 3 | 1 | 0 | 22.2 | 88 | 14 | 6 | 4 | 0 | 0 | 1 | 1 | 10 | 0 | 22 | 0 | 0 | 3 | 1 | .750 | 1 | 0-0 | 0 | 1.90 | 1.59 |
| 2008 | Bos | AL | 16 | 15 | 1 | 0 | 76.0 | 357 | 93 | 63 | 57 | 11 | 0 | 3 | 2 | 41 | 1 | 72 | 2 | 1 | 2 | 9 | .182 | 0 | 0-0 | 0 | 6.40 | 6.75 |
| 2009 | Bos | AL | 16 | 16 | 0 | 0 | 92.0 | 399 | 91 | 44 | 43 | 13 | 2 | 3 | 2 | 36 | 1 | 68 | 1 | 0 | 7 | 4 | .636 | 0 | 0-0 | 0 | 4.31 | 4.21 |
| 2010 | Bos | AL | 28 | 28 | 1 | 0 | 173.2 | 711 | 142 | 55 | 45 | 9 | 5 | 5 | 5 | 67 | 1 | 120 | 7 | 1 | 17 | 7 | .708 | 1 | 0-0 | 0 | 2.88 | 2.33 |
| 2011 | Bos | AL | 14 | 14 | 0 | 0 | 82.2 | 353 | 76 | 34 | 32 | 10 | 1 | 4 | 2 | 31 | 1 | 60 | 3 | 0 | 6 | 3 | .667 | 0 | 0-0 | 0 | 3.72 | 3.48 |
| 2012 | Bos | AL | 29 | 29 | 2 | 0 | 189.1 | 802 | 187 | 104 | 96 | 25 | 5 | 9 | 12 | 64 | 2 | 129 | 2 | 2 | 11 | 8 | .579 | 1 | 0-0 | 0 | 4.29 | 4.56 |
| 2013 | Bos | AL | 16 | 16 | 1 | 0 | 108.1 | 416 | 75 | 23 | 21 | 4 | 1 | 2 | 1 | 36 | 0 | 96 | 1 | 0 | 12 | 1 | .923 | 1 | 0-0 | 0 | 2.00 | 1.74 |
| Postseason | | | 1 | 1 | 0 | 0 | 5.0 | 23 | 6 | 2 | 2 | 1 | 0 | 0 | 1 | 1 | 0 | 3 | 0 | 1 | 0 | 0 | - | 0 | 0-0 | 0 | 5.87 | 3.60 |
| 7 ML YEARS | | | 123 | 121 | 6 | 0 | 744.2 | 3126 | 678 | 329 | 298 | 72 | 14 | 27 | 25 | 285 | 6 | 567 | 16 | 4 | 58 | 33 | .637 | 4 | 0-0 | 0 | 3.65 | 3.60 |

## John Buck

**Bats:** R **Throws:** R **Pos:** C-104;PH-7;DH-1 **Ht:** 6'3" **Wt:** 245 **Born:** 7/7/1980 **Age:** 33

| | | | BATTING | | | | | | | | | | | | | | | | | | BASERUNNING | | | | AVERAGES | | |
|---|---|---|---|---|---|---|---|---|---|---|---|---|---|---|---|---|---|---|---|---|---|---|---|---|---|---|---|
| Year | Team | Lg | G | AB | H | 2B | 3B | HR | (Hm | Rd) | TB | R | RBI | RC | TBB | IBB | SO | HBP | SH | SF | SB | CS | SB% | GDP | Avg | OBP | Slg |
| 2004 | KC | AL | 71 | 238 | 56 | 9 | 0 | 12 | (6 | 6) | 101 | 36 | 30 | 26 | 15 | 0 | 79 | 0 | 4 | 1 | 1 | 1 | .50 | 6 | .235 | .280 | .424 |
| 2005 | KC | AL | 118 | 401 | 97 | 21 | 1 | 12 | (3 | 9) | 156 | 40 | 47 | 43 | 23 | 2 | 94 | 3 | 1 | 2 | 2 | 2 | .50 | 9 | .242 | .287 | .389 |
| 2006 | KC | AL | 114 | 371 | 91 | 21 | 1 | 11 | (6 | 5) | 147 | 37 | 50 | 43 | 26 | 2 | 84 | 7 | 4 | 1 | 0 | 2 | .00 | 7 | .245 | .306 | .396 |
| 2007 | KC | AL | 113 | 347 | 77 | 18 | 0 | 18 | (6 | 12) | 149 | 41 | 48 | 37 | 36 | 0 | 92 | 10 | 0 | 6 | 0 | 1 | .00 | 11 | .222 | .308 | .429 |
| 2008 | KC | AL | 109 | 370 | 83 | 23 | 1 | 9 | (4 | 5) | 135 | 48 | 48 | 42 | 38 | 2 | 96 | 6 | 0 | 4 | 0 | 3 | .00 | 12 | .224 | .304 | .365 |
| 2009 | KC | AL | 59 | 186 | 46 | 12 | 4 | 8 | (3 | 5) | 90 | 16 | 36 | 30 | 13 | 0 | 55 | 1 | 1 | 1 | 1 | 1 | .50 | 2 | .247 | .299 | .484 |
| 2010 | Tor | AL | 118 | 409 | 115 | 25 | 0 | 20 | (9 | 11) | 200 | 53 | 66 | 61 | 16 | 1 | 111 | 6 | 0 | 6 | 0 | 0 | - | 6 | .281 | .314 | .489 |
| 2011 | Fla | NL | 140 | 466 | 106 | 15 | 1 | 16 | (7 | 9) | 171 | 41 | 57 | 55 | 54 | 7 | 115 | 7 | 2 | 1 | 0 | 1 | .00 | 11 | .227 | .316 | .367 |
| 2012 | Mia | NL | 106 | 343 | 66 | 15 | 1 | 12 | (4 | 8) | 119 | 29 | 41 | 40 | 49 | 5 | 103 | 3 | 1 | 2 | 0 | 0 | - | 8 | .192 | .297 | .347 |
| 2013 | 2 Tms | NL | 110 | 392 | 87 | 11 | 0 | 15 | (6 | 9) | 143 | 39 | 62 | 45 | 29 | 4 | 104 | 8 | 0 | 2 | 2 | 1 | .67 | 13 | .222 | .288 | .365 |
| 13 | NYM | NL | 101 | 368 | 79 | 11 | 0 | 15 | (6 | 9) | 135 | 38 | 60 | 43 | 29 | 4 | 99 | 8 | 0 | 2 | 2 | 1 | .67 | 12 | .215 | .285 | .367 |
| 13 | Pit | NL | 9 | 24 | 8 | 0 | 0 | 0 | (0 | 0) | 8 | 1 | 2 | 2 | 0 | 0 | 5 | 0 | 0 | 0 | 0 | 0 | - | 1 | .333 | .333 | .333 |
| 10 ML YEARS | | | 1058 | 3523 | 824 | 170 | 9 | 133 | (54 | 79) | 1411 | 380 | 485 | 422 | 299 | 23 | 933 | 51 | 13 | 26 | 6 | 12 | .33 | 85 | .234 | .301 | .401 |

## Billy Buckner

**Pitches:** R **Bats:** R **Pos:** RP-5; SP-2 **Ht:** 6'2" **Wt:** 205 **Born:** 8/27/1983 **Age:** 30

| | | | HOW MUCH HE PITCHED | | | | | | WHAT HE GAVE UP | | | | | | | | | | | | THE RESULTS | | | | | | | |
|---|---|---|---|---|---|---|---|---|---|---|---|---|---|---|---|---|---|---|---|---|---|---|---|---|---|---|---|---|
| Year | Team | Lg | G | GS | CG | GF | IP | BFP | H | R | ER | HR | SH | SF | HB | TBB | IBB | SO | WP | Bk | W | L | Pct | Sh | Sv-Op | Hld | ERC | ERA |
| 2013 | Salt Lk* | AAA | 18 | 18 | 0 | 0 | 94.1 | 426 | 101 | 61 | 51 | 7 | 1 | 2 | 2 | 50 | 0 | 77 | 4 | 1 | 7 | 4 | .636 | 0 | 0- - | - | 4.89 | 4.87 |
| 2007 | KC | AL | 7 | 5 | 0 | 1 | 34.0 | 143 | 37 | 20 | 20 | 5 | 0 | 1 | 0 | 16 | 0 | 17 | 0 | 0 | 1 | 2 | .333 | 0 | 0-0 | 0 | 5.57 | 5.29 |
| 2008 | Ari | NL | 10 | 0 | 0 | 5 | 14.0 | 59 | 16 | 5 | 5 | 3 | 0 | 0 | 1 | 4 | 1 | 11 | 2 | 0 | 1 | 0 | 1.000 | 0 | 0-0 | 0 | 5.72 | 3.21 |
| 2009 | Ari | NL | 16 | 13 | 0 | 0 | 77.1 | 342 | 94 | 57 | 55 | 12 | 2 | 1 | 3 | 29 | 0 | 64 | 6 | 0 | 4 | 6 | .400 | 0 | 0-0 | 0 | 5.97 | 6.40 |
| 2010 | Ari | NL | 3 | 3 | 0 | 0 | 13.0 | 72 | 26 | 17 | 16 | 4 | 0 | 1 | 2 | 5 | 0 | 11 | 1 | 0 | 0 | 3 | .000 | 0 | 0-0 | 0 | 13.00 | 11.08 |
| 2013 | LAA | AL | 7 | 2 | 0 | 4 | 17.1 | 73 | 17 | 9 | 9 | 5 | 1 | 1 | 1 | 7 | 0 | 7 | 2 | 0 | 1 | 0 | 1.000 | 0 | 0-0 | 0 | 5.79 | 4.67 |
| 5 ML YEARS | | | 43 | 23 | 0 | 10 | 155.2 | 689 | 190 | 108 | 105 | 29 | 3 | 4 | 7 | 61 | 1 | 110 | 11 | 0 | 7 | 11 | .389 | 0 | 0-0 | 0 | 6.38 | 6.07 |

# Mark Buehrle

**Pitches:** L **Bats:** L **Pos:** SP-33 BURR-lee **Ht:** 6'2" **Wt:** 245 **Born:** 3/23/1979 **Age:** 35

| | | | HOW MUCH HE PITCHED | | | | | | WHAT HE GAVE UP | | | | | | | | | | | | THE RESULTS | | | | | | | |
|---|---|---|---|---|---|---|---|---|---|---|---|---|---|---|---|---|---|---|---|---|---|---|---|---|---|---|---|---|
| Year | Team | Lg | G | GS | CG | GF | IP | BFP | H | R | ER | HR | SH | SF | HB | TBB | IBB | SO | WP | Bk | W | L | Pct | Sh | Sv-Op | Hld | ERC | ERA |
| 2000 | CWS | AL | 28 | 3 | 0 | 6 | 51.1 | 225 | 55 | 27 | 24 | 5 | 1 | 0 | 3 | 19 | 1 | 37 | 0 | 0 | 4 | 1 | .800 | 0 | 0-2 | 3 | 4.56 | 4.21 |
| 2001 | CWS | AL | 32 | 32 | 4 | 0 | 221.1 | 885 | 188 | 89 | 81 | 24 | 9 | 4 | 8 | 48 | 2 | 126 | 1 | 5 | 16 | 8 | .667 | 2 | 0-0 | 0 | 2.79 | 3.29 |
| 2002 | CWS | AL | 34 | 34 | 5 | 0 | 239.0 | 984 | 236 | 102 | 95 | 25 | 9 | 3 | 3 | 61 | 7 | 134 | 6 | 1 | 19 | 12 | .613 | 2 | 0-0 | 0 | 3.53 | 3.58 |
| 2003 | CWS | AL | 35 | 35 | 2 | 0 | 230.1 | 978 | 250 | 124 | 106 | 22 | 7 | 7 | 5 | 61 | 2 | 119 | 1 | 0 | 14 | 14 | .500 | 0 | 0-0 | 0 | 4.10 | 4.14 |
| 2004 | CWS | AL | 35 | **35** | 4 | 0 | **245.1** | **1016** | 257 | 119 | 106 | 33 | 4 | 6 | 8 | 51 | 2 | 165 | 0 | 0 | 16 | 10 | .615 | 1 | 0-0 | 0 | 4.00 | 3.89 |
| 2005 | CWS | AL | 33 | 33 | 3 | 0 | **236.2** | **971** | **240** | 99 | 82 | 20 | 7 | 4 | 4 | 40 | 4 | 149 | 2 | 2 | 16 | 8 | .667 | 1 | 0-0 | 0 | 3.21 | 3.12 |
| 2006 | CWS | AL | 32 | 32 | 1 | 0 | 204.0 | 876 | **247** | 124 | 113 | 36 | 6 | 7 | 6 | 48 | 5 | 98 | 0 | 1 | 12 | 13 | .480 | 0 | 0-0 | 0 | 5.37 | 4.99 |
| 2007 | CWS | AL | 30 | 30 | 3 | 0 | 201.0 | 835 | 208 | 86 | 81 | 22 | 7 | 5 | 5 | 45 | 5 | 115 | 1 | 0 | 10 | 9 | .526 | 1 | 0-0 | 0 | 3.75 | 3.63 |
| 2008 | CWS | AL | 34 | **34** | 1 | 0 | 218.2 | 918 | **240** | 106 | 92 | 22 | 2 | 6 | 5 | 52 | 4 | 140 | 4 | 0 | 15 | 12 | .556 | 0 | 0-0 | 0 | 4.12 | 3.79 |
| 2009 | CWS | AL | 33 | 33 | 1 | 0 | 213.1 | 874 | 222 | 97 | 91 | 27 | **11** | 7 | 5 | 45 | 3 | 105 | 2 | 1 | 13 | 10 | .565 | 1 | 0-0 | 0 | 3.91 | 3.84 |
| 2010 | CWS | AL | 33 | 33 | 3 | 0 | 210.1 | 897 | **246** | 105 | 100 | 17 | 6 | 7 | 1 | 49 | 1 | 99 | 3 | **5** | 13 | 13 | .500 | 0 | 0-0 | 0 | 4.29 | 4.28 |
| 2011 | CWS | AL | 31 | 31 | 0 | 0 | 205.1 | 858 | 221 | 93 | 82 | 21 | 6 | 7 | 2 | 45 | 3 | 109 | 1 | 0 | 13 | 9 | .591 | 0 | 0-0 | 0 | 3.86 | 3.59 |
| 2012 | Mia | NL | 31 | 31 | 1 | 0 | 202.1 | 828 | 197 | 88 | 84 | 26 | 14 | 7 | 4 | 40 | 3 | 125 | 2 | 0 | 13 | 13 | .500 | 0 | 0-0 | 0 | 3.41 | 3.74 |
| 2013 | Tor | AL | 33 | 33 | 1 | 0 | 203.2 | 876 | 223 | 100 | 94 | 24 | 3 | 6 | 9 | 51 | 3 | 139 | 2 | 0 | 12 | 10 | .545 | 1 | 0-0 | 0 | 4.29 | 4.15 |
| Postseason | | | 6 | 4 | 1 | 2 | 30.2 | 124 | 32 | 14 | 14 | 3 | 2 | 1 | 1 | 1 | 1 | 16 | 0 | 0 | 2 | 1 | .667 | 0 | 1-1 | 0 | 2.95 | 4.11 |
| 14 ML YEARS | | | 454 | 429 | 29 | 6 | 2882.2 | 12021 | 3030 | 1359 | 1231 | 324 | 92 | 76 | 68 | 655 | 45 | 1660 | 25 | 15 | 186 | 142 | .567 | 9 | 0-2 | 3 | 3.88 | 3.84 |

# Francisley Bueno

**Pitches:** L **Bats:** L **Pos:** RP-7 fran-SISS-lee BWAY-no **Ht:** 5'10" **Wt:** 215 **Born:** 3/5/1981 **Age:** 33

| | | | HOW MUCH HE PITCHED | | | | | | WHAT HE GAVE UP | | | | | | | | | | | | THE RESULTS | | | | | | | |
|---|---|---|---|---|---|---|---|---|---|---|---|---|---|---|---|---|---|---|---|---|---|---|---|---|---|---|---|---|
| Year | Team | Lg | G | GS | CG | GF | IP | BFP | H | R | ER | HR | SH | SF | HB | TBB | IBB | SO | WP | Bk | W | L | Pct | Sh | Sv-Op | Hld | ERC | ERA |
| 2013 | Omha* | AAA | 36 | 1 | 0 | 9 | 67.2 | 285 | 64 | 27 | 20 | 5 | 2 | 0 | 1 | 24 | 1 | 56 | 8 | 0 | 3 | 3 | .500 | 0 | 1-- | - | 3.47 | 2.66 |
| 2008 | Atl | NL | 1 | 0 | 0 | 0 | 2.1 | 13 | 5 | 2 | 2 | 1 | 0 | 0 | 0 | 1 | 0 | 1 | 0 | 0 | 0 | 0 | - | 0 | 0-0 | 0 | 14.73 | 7.71 |
| 2012 | KC | AL | 18 | 0 | 0 | 6 | 17.1 | 69 | 16 | 4 | 3 | 0 | 0 | 1 | 1 | 2 | 1 | 7 | 0 | 0 | 1 | 1 | .500 | 0 | 0-0 | 4 | 2.16 | 1.56 |
| 2013 | KC | AL | 7 | 0 | 0 | 0 | 8.1 | 31 | 4 | 0 | 0 | 0 | 1 | 0 | 0 | 2 | 1 | 5 | 0 | 0 | 1 | 0 | 1.000 | 0 | 0-0 | 1 | 0.79 | 0.00 |
| 3 ML YEARS | | | 26 | 0 | 0 | 6 | 28.0 | 113 | 25 | 6 | 5 | 1 | 1 | 1 | 1 | 5 | 2 | 13 | 0 | 0 | 2 | 1 | .667 | 0 | 0-0 | 5 | 2.32 | 1.61 |

# Madison Bumgarner

**Pitches:** L **Bats:** R **Pos:** SP-31 **Ht:** 6'5" **Wt:** 235 **Born:** 8/1/1989 **Age:** 24

| | | | HOW MUCH HE PITCHED | | | | | | WHAT HE GAVE UP | | | | | | | | | | | | THE RESULTS | | | | | | | |
|---|---|---|---|---|---|---|---|---|---|---|---|---|---|---|---|---|---|---|---|---|---|---|---|---|---|---|---|---|
| Year | Team | Lg | G | GS | CG | GF | IP | BFP | H | R | ER | HR | SH | SF | HB | TBB | IBB | SO | WP | Bk | W | L | Pct | Sh | Sv-Op | Hld | ERC | ERA |
| 2009 | SF | NL | 4 | 1 | 0 | 1 | 10.0 | 40 | 8 | 2 | 2 | 2 | 1 | 1 | 0 | 3 | 1 | 10 | 0 | 0 | 0 | 0 | - | 0 | 0-0 | 0 | 3.14 | 1.80 |
| 2010 | SF | NL | 18 | 18 | 0 | 0 | 111.0 | 472 | 119 | 40 | 37 | 11 | 0 | 4 | 5 | 26 | 2 | 86 | 1 | 1 | 7 | 6 | .538 | 0 | 0-0 | 0 | 3.98 | 3.00 |
| 2011 | SF | NL | 33 | 33 | 0 | 0 | 204.2 | 844 | 202 | 82 | 73 | 12 | 12 | 4 | 5 | 46 | 5 | 191 | 0 | 1 | 13 | 13 | .500 | 0 | 0-0 | 0 | 3.14 | 3.21 |
| 2012 | SF | NL | 32 | 32 | 2 | 0 | 208.1 | 849 | 183 | 87 | 78 | 23 | 7 | 4 | 7 | 49 | 6 | 191 | 3 | 2 | 16 | 11 | .593 | 1 | 0-0 | 0 | 2.95 | 3.37 |
| 2013 | SF | NL | 31 | 31 | 0 | 0 | 201.1 | 803 | 146 | 68 | 62 | 15 | 10 | 4 | 6 | 62 | 6 | 199 | 6 | 0 | 13 | 9 | .591 | 0 | 0-0 | 0 | 2.23 | 2.77 |
| Postseason | | | 7 | 6 | 0 | 0 | 35.2 | 147 | 35 | 15 | 15 | 4 | 2 | 1 | 2 | 9 | 1 | 32 | 0 | 0 | 3 | 2 | .600 | 0 | 0-0 | 0 | 3.74 | 3.79 |
| 5 ML YEARS | | | 118 | 115 | 2 | 1 | 735.1 | 3008 | 658 | 279 | 252 | 63 | 30 | 17 | 23 | 186 | 20 | 677 | 10 | 4 | 49 | 39 | .557 | 1 | 0-0 | 0 | 2.95 | 3.08 |

# Hiram Burgos

**Pitches:** R **Bats:** R **Pos:** SP-6 HIGH-rum BURR-gohs **Ht:** 5'11" **Wt:** 210 **Born:** 8/4/1987 **Age:** 26

| | | | HOW MUCH HE PITCHED | | | | | | WHAT HE GAVE UP | | | | | | | | | | | | THE RESULTS | | | | | | | |
|---|---|---|---|---|---|---|---|---|---|---|---|---|---|---|---|---|---|---|---|---|---|---|---|---|---|---|---|---|
| Year | Team | Lg | G | GS | CG | GF | IP | BFP | H | R | ER | HR | SH | SF | HB | TBB | IBB | SO | WP | Bk | W | L | Pct | Sh | Sv-Op | Hld | ERC | ERA |
| 2009 | Helena | R+ | 14 | 7 | 0 | 1 | 57.2 | 260 | 75 | 45 | 36 | 7 | 1 | 1 | 1 | 14 | 0 | 53 | 5 | 2 | 3 | 2 | .600 | 0 | 0-- | - | 5.34 | 5.62 |
| 2010 | Wisc | A | 19 | 8 | 0 | 8 | 74.1 | 315 | 77 | 40 | 37 | 5 | 4 | 3 | 3 | 21 | 0 | 62 | 6 | 0 | 5 | 7 | .417 | 0 | 0-- | - | 3.77 | 4.48 |
| 2010 | Helena | R+ | 6 | 6 | 0 | 0 | 38.0 | 152 | 31 | 11 | 10 | 1 | 0 | 0 | 3 | 5 | 0 | 48 | 0 | 0 | 3 | 0 | 1.000 | 0 | 0-- | - | 1.96 | 2.37 |
| 2011 | BrvdCt | A+ | 24 | 22 | 0 | 0 | 119.2 | 527 | 142 | 70 | 65 | 13 | 8 | 7 | 7 | 35 | 0 | 80 | 3 | 0 | 6 | 8 | .429 | 0 | 0-- | - | 5.06 | 4.89 |
| 2012 | BrvdCt | A+ | 7 | 6 | 0 | 0 | 41.1 | 150 | 21 | 5 | 4 | 1 | 3 | 0 | 1 | 6 | 0 | 41 | 0 | 1 | 2 | 1 | .667 | 0 | 0-- | - | 0.91 | 0.87 |
| 2012 | Hntsvl | AA | 13 | 13 | 1 | 0 | 83.1 | 331 | 68 | 21 | 18 | 3 | 2 | 2 | 3 | 28 | 0 | 77 | 2 | 0 | 6 | 1 | .857 | 0 | 0-- | - | 2.69 | 1.94 |
| 2012 | Nashv | AAA | 8 | 8 | 0 | 0 | 46.1 | 191 | 39 | 18 | 15 | 4 | 0 | 1 | 1 | 15 | 1 | 35 | 2 | 1 | 2 | 2 | .500 | 0 | 0-- | - | 2.89 | 2.91 |
| 2013 | Nashv | AAA | 7 | 7 | 0 | 0 | 30.2 | 121 | 25 | 14 | 13 | 6 | 2 | 1 | 1 | 12 | 0 | 24 | 1 | 0 | 1 | 4 | .200 | 0 | 0-- | - | 4.04 | 3.82 |
| 2013 | Wisc | A | 1 | 1 | 0 | 0 | 2.0 | 9 | 2 | 1 | 1 | 0 | 0 | 0 | 0 | 1 | 0 | 3 | 0 | 0 | 0 | 1 | .000 | 0 | 0-- | - | 3.63 | 4.50 |
| 2013 | BrvdCt | A+ | 1 | 1 | 0 | 0 | 4.0 | 16 | 5 | 2 | 2 | 0 | 0 | 0 | 0 | 0 | 0 | 4 | 0 | 0 | 0 | 0 | - | 0 | 0-- | - | 3.37 | 4.50 |
| 2013 | Mil | NL | 6 | 6 | 0 | 0 | 29.1 | 139 | 38 | 23 | 21 | 5 | 1 | 2 | 2 | 11 | 0 | 18 | 0 | 0 | 1 | 2 | .333 | 0 | 0-0 | 0 | 6.41 | 6.44 |

# Greg Burke

**Pitches:** R **Bats:** R **Pos:** RP-32 **Ht:** 6'4" **Wt:** 215 **Born:** 9/21/1982 **Age:** 31

| | | | HOW MUCH HE PITCHED | | | | | | WHAT HE GAVE UP | | | | | | | | | | | | THE RESULTS | | | | | | | |
|---|---|---|---|---|---|---|---|---|---|---|---|---|---|---|---|---|---|---|---|---|---|---|---|---|---|---|---|---|
| Year | Team | Lg | G | GS | CG | GF | IP | BFP | H | R | ER | HR | SH | SF | HB | TBB | IBB | SO | WP | Bk | W | L | Pct | Sh | Sv-Op | Hld | ERC | ERA |
| 2009 | Portlnd | AAA | 13 | 0 | 0 | 13 | 16.0 | 59 | 8 | 4 | 4 | 1 | 1 | 0 | 0 | 4 | 0 | 14 | 2 | 0 | 3 | 0 | 1.000 | 0 | 7-- | - | 1.17 | 2.25 |
| 2010 | Portlnd | AAA | 53 | 0 | 0 | 15 | 58.2 | 256 | 62 | 42 | 37 | 13 | 4 | 1 | 1 | 21 | 3 | 46 | 1 | 0 | 2 | 2 | .500 | 0 | 0-- | - | 5.06 | 5.68 |
| 2011 | Tucsn | AAA | 64 | 0 | 0 | 22 | 79.0 | 375 | 100 | 57 | 50 | 8 | 4 | 10 | 2 | 40 | 0 | 76 | 10 | 1 | 2 | 2 | .500 | 0 | 1-- | - | 6.12 | 5.70 |
| 2012 | Bowie | AA | 23 | 0 | 0 | 20 | 29.1 | 117 | 21 | 6 | 5 | 0 | 1 | 1 | 1 | 4 | 1 | 20 | 0 | 0 | 1 | 0 | 1.000 | 0 | 14-- | - | 1.31 | 1.53 |
| 2012 | Norfolk | AAA | 21 | 0 | 0 | 8 | 35.1 | 142 | 25 | 8 | 6 | 1 | 2 | 0 | 1 | 11 | 1 | 30 | 2 | 0 | 2 | 1 | .667 | 0 | 3-- | - | 1.86 | 1.53 |
| 2013 | LsVgs | AAA | 31 | 0 | 0 | 10 | 31.2 | 137 | 33 | 16 | 16 | 3 | 3 | 2 | 2 | 10 | 0 | 34 | 1 | 0 | 2 | 2 | .500 | 0 | 5-- | - | 4.19 | 4.55 |
| 2009 | SD | NL | 48 | 0 | 0 | 13 | 45.2 | 204 | 48 | 23 | 21 | 4 | 3 | 0 | 1 | 23 | 5 | 33 | 3 | 0 | 3 | 3 | .500 | 0 | 0-2 | 10 | 4.59 | 4.14 |
| 2013 | NYM | NL | 32 | 0 | 0 | 12 | 31.2 | 156 | 43 | 27 | 20 | 3 | 3 | 0 | 0 | 15 | 2 | 28 | 0 | 0 | 0 | 3 | .000 | 0 | 0-0 | 1 | 6.06 | 5.68 |
| 2 ML YEARS | | | 80 | 0 | 0 | 25 | 77.1 | 360 | 91 | 50 | 41 | 7 | 6 | 0 | 1 | 38 | 7 | 61 | 3 | 0 | 3 | 6 | .333 | 0 | 0-2 | 11 | 5.18 | 4.77 |

# A.J. Burnett

**Pitches:** R **Bats:** R **Pos:** SP-30 **Ht:** 6'4" **Wt:** 225 **Born:** 1/3/1977 **Age:** 37

| | | | HOW MUCH HE PITCHED | | | | | | WHAT HE GAVE UP | | | | | | | | | | | | THE RESULTS | | | | | | | |
|---|---|---|---|---|---|---|---|---|---|---|---|---|---|---|---|---|---|---|---|---|---|---|---|---|---|---|---|---|
| Year | Team | Lg | G | GS | CG | GF | IP | BFP | H | R | ER | HR | SH | SF | HB | TBB | IBB | SO | WP | Bk | W | L | Pct | Sh | Sv-Op | Hld | ERC | ERA |
| 1999 | Fla | NL | 7 | 7 | 0 | 0 | 41.1 | 182 | 37 | 23 | 16 | 3 | 1 | 3 | 0 | 25 | 2 | 33 | 0 | 0 | 4 | 2 | .667 | 0 | 0-0 | 0 | 4.00 | 3.48 |
| 2000 | Fla | NL | 13 | 13 | 0 | 0 | 82.2 | 364 | 80 | 46 | 44 | 8 | 6 | 3 | 2 | 44 | 3 | 57 | 2 | 0 | 3 | 7 | .300 | 0 | 0-0 | 0 | 4.45 | 4.79 |
| 2001 | Fla | NL | 27 | 27 | 2 | 0 | 173.1 | 733 | 145 | 82 | 78 | 20 | 6 | 8 | 7 | 83 | 3 | 128 | 7 | 1 | 11 | 12 | .478 | 1 | 0-0 | 0 | 3.76 | 4.05 |
| 2002 | Fla | NL | 31 | 29 | 7 | 0 | 204.1 | 844 | 153 | 84 | 75 | 12 | 9 | 4 | 9 | 90 | 5 | 203 | **14** | 0 | 12 | 9 | .571 | **5** | 0-1 | 0 | 2.77 | 3.30 |
| 2003 | Fla | NL | 4 | 4 | 0 | 0 | 23.0 | 106 | 18 | 13 | 12 | 2 | 2 | 1 | 2 | 18 | 2 | 21 | 2 | 0 | 0 | 2 | .000 | 0 | 0-0 | 0 | 4.36 | 4.70 |
| 2004 | Fla | NL | 20 | 19 | 1 | 0 | 120.0 | 490 | 102 | 50 | 49 | 9 | 3 | 3 | 4 | 38 | 0 | 113 | 7 | 0 | 7 | 6 | .538 | 0 | 0-0 | 0 | 2.95 | 3.68 |
| 2005 | Fla | NL | 32 | 32 | 4 | 0 | 209.0 | 873 | 184 | 97 | 80 | 12 | 7 | 5 | 7 | 79 | 1 | 198 | 12 | 0 | 12 | 12 | .500 | 2 | 0-0 | 0 | 3.20 | 3.44 |
| 2006 | Tor | AL | 21 | 21 | 2 | 0 | 135.2 | 577 | 138 | 67 | 60 | 14 | 4 | 3 | 8 | 39 | 3 | 118 | 6 | 1 | 10 | 8 | .556 | 1 | 0-0 | 0 | 3.97 | 3.98 |
| 2007 | Tor | AL | 25 | 25 | 2 | 0 | 165.2 | 691 | 131 | 74 | 69 | 23 | 0 | 2 | 12 | 66 | 2 | 176 | 5 | 0 | 10 | 8 | .556 | 0 | 0-0 | 0 | 3.47 | 3.75 |
| 2008 | Tor | AL | 35 | **34** | 1 | 1 | 221.1 | 957 | 211 | 109 | 100 | 19 | **8** | 5 | 9 | 86 | 2 | **231** | 11 | 2 | 18 | 10 | .643 | 0 | 0-0 | 0 | 3.78 | 4.07 |
| 2009 | NYY | AL | 33 | 33 | 1 | 0 | 207.0 | 896 | 193 | 99 | 93 | 25 | 2 | 5 | 10 | **97** | 0 | 195 | **17** | 1 | 13 | 9 | .591 | 0 | 0-0 | 0 | 4.34 | 4.04 |
| 2010 | NYY | AL | 33 | 33 | 1 | 0 | 186.2 | 829 | 204 | 118 | 109 | 25 | 7 | 10 | **19** | 78 | 2 | 145 | 16 | 0 | 10 | 15 | .400 | 0 | 0-0 | 0 | 5.43 | 5.26 |
| 2011 | NYY | AL | 33 | 32 | 0 | 0 | 190.1 | 837 | 190 | 115 | 109 | 31 | 4 | **10** | 9 | 83 | 2 | 173 | **25** | 0 | 11 | 11 | .500 | 0 | 0-0 | 0 | 4.83 | 5.15 |
| 2012 | Pit | NL | 31 | 31 | 1 | 0 | 202.1 | 851 | 189 | 86 | 79 | 18 | 5 | 8 | 9 | 62 | 1 | 180 | 10 | 0 | 16 | 10 | .615 | 1 | 0-0 | 0 | 3.44 | 3.51 |
| 2013 | Pit | NL | 30 | 30 | 1 | 0 | 191.0 | 801 | 165 | 79 | 70 | 11 | 8 | 3 | 9 | 67 | 3 | 209 | 12 | 0 | 10 | 11 | .476 | 0 | 0-0 | 0 | 3.01 | 3.30 |
| Postseason | | | 7 | 7 | 0 | 0 | 39.0 | 173 | 32 | 22 | 22 | 3 | 1 | 0 | 6 | 23 | 3 | 31 | 4 | 0 | 2 | 2 | .500 | 0 | 0-0 | 0 | 4.13 | 5.08 |
| 15 ML YEARS | | | 375 | 370 | 23 | 1 | 2353.2 | 10031 | 2140 | 1142 | 1043 | 232 | 72 | 73 | 116 | 955 | 31 | 2180 | 146 | 5 | 147 | 132 | .527 | 10 | 0-1 | 0 | 3.77 | 3.99 |

# Alex Burnett

**Pitches:** R **Bats:** R **Pos:** RP-3 **Ht:** 6'0" **Wt:** 220 **Born:** 7/26/1987 **Age:** 26

| | | | HOW MUCH HE PITCHED | | | | | | WHAT HE GAVE UP | | | | | | | | | | | | THE RESULTS | | | | | | | |
|---|---|---|---|---|---|---|---|---|---|---|---|---|---|---|---|---|---|---|---|---|---|---|---|---|---|---|---|---|
| Year | Team | Lg | G | GS | CG | GF | IP | BFP | H | R | ER | HR | SH | SF | HB | TBB | IBB | SO | WP | Bk | W | L | Pct | Sh | Sv-Op | Hld | ERC | ERA |
| 2013 | Buffalo* | AAA | 2 | 0 | 0 | 0 | 2.1 | 9 | 1 | 0 | 0 | 0 | 0 | 0 | 0 | 1 | 0 | 0 | 0 | 0 | 0 | 0 | - | 0 | 0-- | - | 1.08 | 0.00 |
| 2013 | Norfolk* | AAA | 7 | 0 | 0 | 0 | 9.2 | 41 | 10 | 2 | 2 | 0 | 0 | 0 | 1 | 1 | 0 | 8 | 0 | 0 | 1 | 0 | 1.000 | 0 | 0-- | - | 2.79 | 1.86 |
| 2013 | Iowa* | AAA | 3 | 0 | 0 | 1 | 3.1 | 18 | 5 | 3 | 3 | 0 | 1 | 0 | 0 | 3 | 0 | 1 | 1 | 0 | 1 | 0 | 1.000 | 0 | 0-- | - | 8.16 | 8.10 |
| 2010 | Min | AL | 41 | 0 | 0 | 11 | 47.2 | 211 | 52 | 28 | 28 | 6 | 4 | 1 | 2 | 23 | 3 | 37 | 2 | 2 | 2 | 2 | .500 | 0 | 0-0 | 2 | 5.30 | 5.29 |
| 2011 | Min | AL | 66 | 0 | 0 | 12 | 50.2 | 225 | 50 | 32 | 31 | 4 | 2 | 4 | 8 | 21 | 1 | 33 | 2 | 0 | 2 | 5 | .286 | 0 | 0-2 | 10 | 4.51 | 5.51 |
| 2012 | Min | AL | 67 | 0 | 0 | 18 | 71.2 | 309 | 71 | 33 | 28 | 4 | 2 | 2 | 3 | 26 | 5 | 36 | 6 | 0 | 4 | 4 | .500 | 0 | 0-1 | 10 | 3.61 | 3.52 |
| 2013 | 2 Tms | | 3 | 0 | 0 | 1 | 2.1 | 14 | 5 | 3 | 3 | 0 | 0 | 0 | 0 | 2 | 0 | 2 | 0 | 0 | 0 | 0 | - | 0 | 0-0 | 0 | 12.37 | 11.57 |
| 13 | Bal | AL | 2 | 0 | 0 | 0 | 1.1 | 10 | 4 | 3 | 3 | 0 | 0 | 0 | 0 | 2 | 0 | 2 | 0 | 0 | 0 | 0 | - | 0 | 0-0 | 0 | 22.07 | 20.25 |
| 13 | ChC | NL | 1 | 0 | 0 | 1 | 1.0 | 4 | 1 | 0 | 0 | 0 | 0 | 0 | 0 | 0 | 0 | 0 | 0 | 0 | 0 | 0 | - | 0 | 0-0 | 0 | 1.95 | 0.00 |
| 4 ML YEARS | | | 177 | 0 | 0 | 42 | 172.1 | 759 | 178 | 96 | 90 | 14 | 8 | 7 | 13 | 72 | 9 | 108 | 10 | 2 | 8 | 11 | .421 | 0 | 0-3 | 22 | 4.43 | 4.70 |

# Sean Burnett

**Pitches:** L **Bats:** L **Pos:** RP-13 **Ht:** 6'1" **Wt:** 180 **Born:** 9/17/1982 **Age:** 31

| | | | HOW MUCH HE PITCHED | | | | | | WHAT HE GAVE UP | | | | | | | | | | | | THE RESULTS | | | | | | | |
|---|---|---|---|---|---|---|---|---|---|---|---|---|---|---|---|---|---|---|---|---|---|---|---|---|---|---|---|---|
| Year | Team | Lg | G | GS | CG | GF | IP | BFP | H | R | ER | HR | SH | SF | HB | TBB | IBB | SO | WP | Bk | W | L | Pct | Sh | Sv-Op | Hld | ERC | ERA |
| 2013 | InldEm* | A+ | 1 | 0 | 0 | 0 | 1.0 | 4 | 1 | 1 | 1 | 1 | 0 | 0 | 0 | 0 | 0 | 0 | 0 | 0 | 0 | 0 | - | 0 | 0-- | - | 7.45 | 9.00 |
| 2004 | Pit | NL | 13 | 13 | 1 | 0 | 71.2 | 318 | 86 | 41 | 40 | 9 | 2 | 1 | 1 | 28 | 2 | 30 | 2 | 0 | 5 | 5 | .500 | 1 | 0-0 | 0 | 5.49 | 5.02 |
| 2008 | Pit | NL | 58 | 0 | 0 | 16 | 56.2 | 253 | 57 | 31 | 30 | 7 | 4 | 3 | 2 | 34 | 3 | 42 | 4 | 0 | 1 | 1 | .500 | 0 | 0-0 | 8 | 5.23 | 4.76 |
| 2009 | 2 Tms | NL | 71 | 0 | 0 | 8 | 57.2 | 237 | 36 | 21 | 20 | 6 | 6 | 1 | 3 | 28 | 8 | 43 | 4 | 0 | 2 | 3 | .400 | 0 | 1-3 | 11 | 2.43 | 3.12 |
| 2010 | Was | NL | 73 | 0 | 0 | 10 | 63.0 | 261 | 52 | 17 | 15 | 3 | 4 | 0 | 1 | 20 | 4 | 62 | 2 | 0 | 1 | 7 | .125 | 0 | 3-4 | 20 | 2.43 | 2.14 |
| 2011 | Was | NL | 69 | 0 | 0 | 17 | 56.2 | 242 | 54 | 24 | 24 | 6 | 3 | 2 | 3 | 21 | 4 | 33 | 2 | 0 | 5 | 5 | .500 | 0 | 4-11 | 15 | 3.85 | 3.81 |
| 2012 | Was | NL | 70 | 0 | 0 | 16 | 56.2 | 239 | 58 | 16 | 15 | 4 | 1 | 2 | 3 | 12 | 3 | 57 | 2 | 0 | 1 | 2 | .333 | 0 | 2-5 | 31 | 3.38 | 2.38 |
| 2013 | LAA | AL | 13 | 0 | 0 | 1 | 9.2 | 40 | 9 | 1 | 1 | 1 | 2 | 0 | 0 | 4 | 0 | 7 | 1 | 0 | 0 | 0 | - | 0 | 0-0 | 5 | 3.90 | 0.93 |
| 09 | Pit | NL | 38 | 0 | 0 | 7 | 32.1 | 133 | 22 | 12 | 11 | 3 | 4 | 1 | 3 | 15 | 4 | 23 | 2 | 0 | 1 | 2 | .333 | 0 | 1-2 | 6 | 2.77 | 3.06 |
| 09 | Was | NL | 33 | 0 | 0 | 1 | 25.1 | 104 | 14 | 9 | 9 | 3 | 2 | 0 | 0 | 13 | 4 | 20 | 2 | 0 | 1 | 1 | .500 | 0 | 0-1 | 5 | 2.02 | 3.20 |
| Postseason | | | 2 | 0 | 0 | 0 | 1.0 | 7 | 3 | 4 | 3 | 1 | 0 | 0 | 0 | 1 | 0 | 1 | 0 | 0 | 0 | 0 | - | 0 | 0-0 | 1 | 32.12 | 27.00 |
| 7 ML YEARS | | | 367 | 13 | 1 | 68 | 372.0 | 1590 | 352 | 151 | 145 | 36 | 22 | 9 | 13 | 147 | 24 | 274 | 17 | 0 | 15 | 23 | .395 | 1 | 10-23 | 90 | 3.78 | 3.51 |

# Cory Burns

**Pitches:** R **Bats:** R **Pos:** RP-10 **Ht:** 6'0" **Wt:** 205 **Born:** 10/9/1987 **Age:** 26

| | | | HOW MUCH HE PITCHED | | | | | | WHAT HE GAVE UP | | | | | | | | | | | | THE RESULTS | | | | | | | |
|---|---|---|---|---|---|---|---|---|---|---|---|---|---|---|---|---|---|---|---|---|---|---|---|---|---|---|---|---|
| Year | Team | Lg | G | GS | CG | GF | IP | BFP | H | R | ER | HR | SH | SF | HB | TBB | IBB | SO | WP | Bk | W | L | Pct | Sh | Sv-Op | Hld | ERC | ERA |
| 2009 | MhVlly | A- | 22 | 0 | 0 | 21 | 32.2 | 124 | 18 | 8 | 7 | 2 | 0 | 1 | 2 | 6 | 0 | 37 | 2 | 0 | 3 | 2 | .600 | 0 | 11-- | - | 1.28 | 1.93 |
| 2010 | Lk Cty | A | 14 | 0 | 0 | 14 | 15.2 | 61 | 13 | 4 | 4 | 0 | 0 | 0 | 0 | 1 | 0 | 25 | 1 | 0 | 0 | 0 | - | 0 | 12-- | - | 1.49 | 2.30 |
| 2010 | Knstn | A+ | 40 | 0 | 0 | 39 | 39.1 | 161 | 30 | 13 | 8 | 2 | 2 | 1 | 2 | 13 | 0 | 56 | 1 | 0 | 1 | 2 | .333 | 0 | 30-- | - | 2.43 | 1.83 |
| 2011 | Akron | AA | 54 | 0 | 0 | 52 | 59.2 | 235 | 47 | 15 | 14 | 3 | 5 | 1 | 0 | 15 | 2 | 70 | 7 | 0 | 2 | 5 | .286 | 0 | 35-- | - | 2.11 | 2.11 |
| 2012 | Tucsn | AAA | 54 | 0 | 0 | 15 | 66.0 | 261 | 49 | 25 | 23 | 1 | 1 | 0 | 4 | 17 | 3 | 78 | 8 | 0 | 1 | 2 | .333 | 0 | 3-- | - | 1.90 | 3.14 |
| 2013 | RdRck | AAA | 38 | 0 | 0 | 35 | 37.2 | 166 | 39 | 11 | 9 | 0 | 2 | 0 | 1 | 15 | 2 | 48 | 4 | 1 | 0 | 2 | .000 | 0 | 20-- | - | 3.51 | 2.15 |
| 2012 | SD | NL | 17 | 0 | 0 | 9 | 18.0 | 92 | 26 | 11 | 11 | 1 | 0 | 0 | 1 | 10 | 1 | 18 | 1 | 0 | 0 | 1 | .000 | 0 | 0-0 | 0 | 6.90 | 5.50 |
| 2013 | Tex | AL | 10 | 0 | 0 | 4 | 11.1 | 54 | 12 | 4 | 4 | 1 | 0 | 0 | 1 | 7 | 2 | 5 | 2 | 0 | 1 | 0 | 1.000 | 0 | 0-0 | 0 | 5.09 | 3.18 |
| 2 ML YEARS | | | 27 | 0 | 0 | 13 | 29.1 | 146 | 38 | 15 | 15 | 2 | 0 | 0 | 2 | 17 | 3 | 23 | 3 | 0 | 1 | 1 | .500 | 0 | 0-0 | 0 | 6.18 | 4.60 |

# Jared Burton

**Pitches:** R **Bats:** R **Pos:** RP-71 **Ht:** 6'5" **Wt:** 225 **Born:** 6/2/1981 **Age:** 33

| | | | HOW MUCH HE PITCHED | | | | | | WHAT HE GAVE UP | | | | | | | | | | | | THE RESULTS | | | | | | | |
|---|---|---|---|---|---|---|---|---|---|---|---|---|---|---|---|---|---|---|---|---|---|---|---|---|---|---|---|---|
| Year | Team | Lg | G | GS | CG | GF | IP | BFP | H | R | ER | HR | SH | SF | HB | TBB | IBB | SO | WP | Bk | W | L | Pct | Sh | Sv-Op | Hld | ERC | ERA |
| 2007 | Cin | NL | 47 | 0 | 0 | 12 | 43.0 | 176 | 28 | 15 | 12 | 2 | 1 | 1 | 2 | 22 | 4 | 36 | 3 | 1 | 4 | 2 | .667 | 0 | 0-3 | 11 | 2.37 | 2.51 |
| 2008 | Cin | NL | 54 | 0 | 0 | 12 | 58.2 | 257 | 56 | 24 | 21 | 6 | 2 | 3 | 2 | 25 | 3 | 58 | 2 | 1 | 5 | 1 | .833 | 0 | 0-2 | 11 | 3.93 | 3.22 |
| 2009 | Cin | NL | 53 | 0 | 0 | 13 | 59.1 | 265 | 61 | 30 | 29 | 5 | 3 | 1 | 4 | 23 | 6 | 45 | 2 | 0 | 1 | 0 | 1.000 | 0 | 0-0 | 7 | 4.08 | 4.40 |
| 2010 | Cin | NL | 4 | 0 | 0 | 2 | 3.1 | 10 | 0 | 0 | 0 | 0 | 0 | 0 | 0 | 0 | 0 | 1 | 0 | 0 | 0 | 0 | - | 0 | 0-0 | 1 | 0.00 | 0.00 |

| HOW MUCH HE PITCHED | | | | | | | | WHAT HE GAVE UP | | | | | | | | | | | | THE RESULTS | | | | | | | |
|---|---|---|---|---|---|---|---|---|---|---|---|---|---|---|---|---|---|---|---|---|---|---|---|---|---|---|---|
| Year | Team | Lg | G | GS | CG | GF | IP | BFP | H | R | ER | HR | SH | SF | HB | TBB | IBB | SO | WP | Bk | W | L | Pct | Sh | Sv-Op | Hld | ERC | ERA |
| 2011 | Cin | NL | 6 | 0 | 0 | 1 | 4.2 | 23 | 6 | 2 | 2 | 1 | 1 | 0 | 0 | 3 | 0 | 3 | 0 | 0 | 0 | 0 | - | 0 | 0-0 | 1 | 7.61 | 3.86 |
| 2012 | Min | AL | 64 | 0 | 0 | 12 | 62.0 | 245 | 41 | 21 | 15 | 5 | 2 | 1 | 5 | 16 | 1 | 55 | 0 | 0 | 3 | 2 | .600 | 0 | 5-9 | 18 | 1.98 | 2.18 |
| 2013 | Min | AL | 71 | 0 | 0 | 14 | 66.0 | 281 | 61 | 29 | 28 | 6 | 2 | 0 | 5 | 22 | 5 | 61 | 2 | 0 | 2 | 9 | .182 | 0 | 2-7 | 27 | 3.50 | 3.82 |
| 7 ML YEARS | | | 299 | 0 | 0 | 66 | 297.0 | 1257 | 253 | 121 | 107 | 25 | 11 | 6 | 18 | 111 | 19 | 259 | 9 | 2 | 15 | 14 | .517 | 0 | 7-21 | 76 | 3.17 | 3.24 |

## Dave Bush

**Pitches:** R **Bats:** R **Pos:** RP-1 **Ht:** 6'2" **Wt:** 205 **Born:** 11/9/1979 **Age:** 34

| HOW MUCH HE PITCHED | | | | | | | | | WHAT HE GAVE UP | | | | | | | | | | | | THE RESULTS | | | | | | | |
|---|---|---|---|---|---|---|---|---|---|---|---|---|---|---|---|---|---|---|---|---|---|---|---|---|---|---|---|---|
| Year | Team | Lg | G | GS | CG | GF | IP | BFP | H | R | ER | HR | SH | SF | HB | TBB | IBB | SO | WP | Bk | W | L | Pct | Sh | Sv-Op | Hld | ERC | ERA |
| 2013 | Buffalo* | AAA | 19 | 15 | 1 | 2 | 90.0 | 381 | 95 | 47 | 42 | 16 | 0 | 0 | 4 | 17 | 0 | 69 | 0 | 1 | 8 | 7 | .533 | 0 | 0- - | - | 4.22 | 4.20 |
| 2004 | Tor | AL | 16 | 16 | 1 | 0 | 97.2 | 412 | 95 | 47 | 40 | 11 | 4 | 4 | 6 | 25 | 2 | 64 | 3 | 0 | 5 | 4 | .556 | 1 | 0-0 | 0 | 3.65 | 3.69 |
| 2005 | Tor | AL | 25 | 24 | 2 | 1 | 136.1 | 575 | 142 | 73 | 68 | 20 | 3 | 2 | 13 | 29 | 3 | 75 | 2 | 0 | 5 | 11 | .313 | 0 | 0-0 | 0 | 4.28 | 4.49 |
| 2006 | Mil | NL | 34 | 32 | 3 | 0 | 210.0 | 869 | 201 | 111 | 103 | 26 | 9 | 6 | 18 | 38 | 2 | 166 | 6 | 0 | 12 | 11 | .522 | 2 | 0-0 | 1 | 3.47 | 4.41 |
| 2007 | Mil | NL | 33 | 31 | 0 | 2 | 186.1 | 810 | 217 | 110 | 106 | 27 | 6 | 2 | 11 | 44 | 1 | 134 | 3 | 0 | 12 | 10 | .545 | 0 | 0-0 | 0 | 4.93 | 5.12 |
| 2008 | Mil | NL | 31 | 29 | 0 | 0 | 185.0 | 763 | 163 | 92 | 86 | 29 | 4 | 3 | 10 | 48 | 3 | 109 | 2 | 1 | 9 | 10 | .474 | 0 | 0-0 | 0 | 3.44 | 4.18 |
| 2009 | Mil | NL | 22 | 21 | 0 | 0 | 114.1 | 508 | 131 | 84 | 81 | 19 | 6 | 5 | **15** | 37 | 2 | 89 | 2 | 0 | 5 | 9 | .357 | 0 | 0-0 | 0 | 5.70 | 6.38 |
| 2010 | Mil | NL | 32 | 31 | 0 | 0 | 174.1 | 781 | 198 | 108 | 88 | 28 | 9 | 10 | 4 | 65 | 6 | 107 | 1 | 1 | 8 | 13 | .381 | 0 | 0-0 | 1 | 5.17 | 4.54 |
| 2011 | Tex | AL | 17 | 3 | 0 | 7 | 37.1 | 166 | 47 | 27 | 24 | 6 | 2 | 0 | 3 | 9 | 2 | 23 | 2 | 0 | 0 | 1 | .000 | 0 | 0-0 | 1 | 5.67 | 5.79 |
| 2013 | Tor | AL | 1 | 0 | 0 | 0 | 3.0 | 15 | 5 | 5 | 5 | 4 | 0 | 0 | 0 | 1 | 0 | 1 | 0 | 0 | 0 | 0 | - | 0 | 0-0 | 0 | 18.54 | 15.00 |
| Postseason | | | 1 | 1 | 0 | 0 | 5.1 | 21 | 5 | 1 | 1 | 0 | 0 | 0 | 0 | 0 | 0 | 3 | 0 | 0 | 1 | 0 | 1.000 | 0 | 0-0 | 0 | 1.68 | 1.69 |
| 9 ML YEARS | | | 211 | 187 | 6 | 10 | 1144.1 | 4899 | 1199 | 657 | 601 | 170 | 43 | 32 | 80 | 296 | 21 | 768 | 21 | 2 | 56 | 69 | .448 | 3 | 0-0 | 3 | 4.38 | 4.73 |

## Nick Buss

**Bats:** L **Throws:** R **Pos:** LF-3;RF-3;PH-3;CF-1 **Ht:** 6'2" **Wt:** 195 **Born:** 12/15/1986 **Age:** 27

| BATTING | | | | | | | | | | | | | | | | | | | | | BASERUNNING | | | | AVERAGES | | |
|---|---|---|---|---|---|---|---|---|---|---|---|---|---|---|---|---|---|---|---|---|---|---|---|---|---|---|---|
| Year | Team | Lg | G | AB | H | 2B | 3B | HR | (Hm | Rd) | TB | R | RBI | RC | TBB | IBB | SO | HBP | SH | SF | SB | CS | SB% | GDP | Avg | OBP | Slg |
| 2009 | Gt Lks | A | 110 | 416 | 108 | 15 | 5 | 10 | (- | -) | 163 | 55 | 63 | 52 | 21 | 0 | 75 | 4 | 5 | 6 | 14 | 3 | .82 | 6 | .260 | .298 | .392 |
| 2010 | InldEm | A+ | 65 | 247 | 60 | 10 | 6 | 0 | (- | -) | 82 | 32 | 25 | 24 | 13 | 0 | 33 | 1 | 7 | 3 | 6 | 3 | .67 | 5 | .243 | .280 | .332 |
| 2010 | Gt Lks | A | 61 | 242 | 69 | 9 | 2 | 1 | (- | -) | 85 | 42 | 23 | 35 | 24 | 1 | 30 | 5 | 4 | 3 | 20 | 5 | .80 | 2 | .285 | .358 | .351 |
| 2011 | RCuca | A+ | 115 | 479 | 157 | 30 | 8 | 14 | (- | -) | 245 | 86 | 55 | 91 | 27 | 2 | 63 | 6 | 15 | 3 | 28 | 10 | .74 | 5 | .328 | .369 | .511 |
| 2012 | Chatt | AA | 132 | 492 | 134 | 24 | 10 | 8 | (- | -) | 202 | 70 | 57 | 68 | 38 | 1 | 71 | 5 | 19 | 4 | 19 | 13 | .59 | 4 | .272 | .328 | .411 |
| 2013 | Albq | AAA | 131 | 459 | 139 | 29 | 11 | 17 | (- | -) | 241 | 84 | 100 | 92 | 41 | 1 | 90 | 7 | 3 | 8 | 21 | 2 | .91 | 6 | .303 | .363 | .525 |
| 2013 | LAD | NL | 8 | 19 | 2 | 0 | 0 | 0 | (0 | 0) | 2 | 0 | 0 | 0 | 1 | 0 | 1 | 0 | 0 | 0 | 0 | 0 | - | 0 | .105 | .150 | .105 |

## Drew Butera

**Bats:** R **Throws:** R **Pos:** C-4;1B-2

bue-TARE-ah

**Ht:** 6'1" **Wt:** 200 **Born:** 8/9/1983 **Age:** 30

| BATTING | | | | | | | | | | | | | | | | | | | | | BASERUNNING | | | | AVERAGES | | |
|---|---|---|---|---|---|---|---|---|---|---|---|---|---|---|---|---|---|---|---|---|---|---|---|---|---|---|---|
| Year | Team | Lg | G | AB | H | 2B | 3B | HR | (Hm | Rd) | TB | R | RBI | RC | TBB | IBB | SO | HBP | SH | SF | SB | CS | SB% | GDP | Avg | OBP | Slg |
| 2013 | Roch* | AAA | 27 | 87 | 19 | 2 | 0 | 2 | (- | -) | 27 | 8 | 10 | 6 | 2 | 0 | 15 | 2 | 1 | 2 | 0 | 0 | - | 1 | .218 | .247 | .310 |
| 2013 | Albq* | AAA | 16 | 52 | 7 | 3 | 1 | 0 | (- | -) | 12 | 3 | 3 | 1 | 4 | 0 | 14 | 0 | 1 | 0 | 0 | 0 | - | 2 | .135 | .196 | .231 |
| 2010 | Min | AL | 49 | 142 | 28 | 6 | 1 | 2 | (0 | 2) | 42 | 12 | 13 | 7 | 4 | 0 | 25 | 4 | 3 | 2 | 0 | 0 | - | 5 | .197 | .237 | .296 |
| 2011 | Min | AL | 93 | 234 | 39 | 9 | 1 | 2 | (1 | 1) | 56 | 19 | 23 | 11 | 11 | 0 | 42 | 2 | 6 | 1 | 0 | 0 | - | 7 | .167 | .210 | .239 |
| 2012 | Min | AL | 42 | 111 | 22 | 6 | 0 | 1 | (1 | 0) | 31 | 7 | 5 | 6 | 9 | 0 | 26 | 2 | 0 | 0 | 0 | 0 | - | 3 | .198 | .270 | .279 |
| 2013 | 2 Tms | | 6 | 10 | 1 | 0 | 0 | 0 | (0 | 0) | 1 | 0 | 0 | 0 | 0 | 0 | 5 | 0 | 0 | 0 | 0 | 0 | - | 0 | .100 | .100 | .100 |
| 13 | Min | AL | 2 | 3 | 0 | 0 | 0 | 0 | (0 | 0) | 0 | 0 | 0 | 0 | 0 | 0 | 1 | 0 | 0 | 0 | 0 | 0 | - | 0 | .000 | .000 | .000 |
| 13 | LAD | NL | 4 | 7 | 1 | 0 | 0 | 0 | (0 | 0) | 1 | 0 | 0 | 0 | 0 | 0 | 4 | 0 | 0 | 0 | 0 | 0 | - | 0 | .143 | .143 | .143 |
| 4 ML YEARS | | | 190 | 497 | 90 | 21 | 2 | 5 | (2 | 3) | 130 | 38 | 41 | 24 | 24 | 0 | 98 | 8 | 9 | 3 | 0 | 0 | - | 15 | .181 | .229 | .262 |

## Billy Butler

**Bats:** R **Throws:** R **Pos:** DH-150;1B-7;PH-5 **Ht:** 6'1" **Wt:** 240 **Born:** 4/18/1986 **Age:** 28

| BATTING | | | | | | | | | | | | | | | | | | | | | BASERUNNING | | | | AVERAGES | | |
|---|---|---|---|---|---|---|---|---|---|---|---|---|---|---|---|---|---|---|---|---|---|---|---|---|---|---|---|
| Year | Team | Lg | G | AB | H | 2B | 3B | HR | (Hm | Rd) | TB | R | RBI | RC | TBB | IBB | SO | HBP | SH | SF | SB | CS | SB% | GDP | Avg | OBP | Slg |
| 2007 | KC | AL | 92 | 329 | 96 | 23 | 2 | 8 | (5 | 3) | 147 | 38 | 52 | 50 | 27 | 5 | 55 | 2 | 0 | 2 | 0 | 0 | - | 8 | .292 | .347 | .447 |
| 2008 | KC | AL | 124 | 443 | 122 | 22 | 0 | 11 | (4 | 7) | 177 | 44 | 55 | 57 | 33 | 0 | 57 | 0 | 0 | 2 | 0 | 1 | .00 | 23 | .275 | .324 | .400 |
| 2009 | KC | AL | 159 | 608 | 183 | 51 | 1 | 21 | (16 | 5) | 299 | 78 | 93 | 99 | 58 | 3 | 103 | 2 | 0 | 4 | 1 | 0 | 1.00 | 20 | .301 | .362 | .492 |
| 2010 | KC | AL | 158 | 595 | 189 | 45 | 0 | 15 | (9 | 6) | 279 | 77 | 78 | 91 | 69 | 8 | 78 | 5 | 0 | 9 | 0 | 0 | - | **32** | .318 | .388 | .469 |
| 2011 | KC | AL | 159 | 597 | 174 | 44 | 0 | 19 | (9 | 10) | 275 | 74 | 95 | 94 | 66 | 15 | 95 | 3 | 0 | 7 | 2 | 1 | .67 | 16 | .291 | .361 | .461 |
| 2012 | KC | AL | 161 | 614 | 192 | 32 | 1 | 29 | (11 | 18) | 313 | 72 | 107 | 102 | 54 | 9 | 111 | 7 | 0 | 4 | 2 | 1 | .67 | 20 | .313 | .373 | .510 |
| 2013 | KC | AL | **162** | 582 | 168 | 27 | 0 | 15 | (6 | 9) | 240 | 62 | 82 | 87 | 79 | 11 | 102 | 3 | 0 | 4 | 0 | 0 | - | **28** | .289 | .374 | .412 |
| 7 ML YEARS | | | 1015 | 3768 | 1124 | 244 | 4 | 118 | (60 | 58) | 1730 | 445 | 562 | 580 | 386 | 51 | 601 | 22 | 0 | 32 | 5 | 3 | .63 | 147 | .298 | .364 | .459 |

## Joey Butler

**Bats:** R **Throws:** R **Pos:** LF-3;PH-3;RF-2;DH-2 **Ht:** 6'2" **Wt:** 220 **Born:** 3/12/1986 **Age:** 28

| BATTING | | | | | | | | | | | | | | | | | | | | | BASERUNNING | | | | AVERAGES | | |
|---|---|---|---|---|---|---|---|---|---|---|---|---|---|---|---|---|---|---|---|---|---|---|---|---|---|---|---|
| Year | Team | Lg | G | AB | H | 2B | 3B | HR | (Hm | Rd) | TB | R | RBI | RC | TBB | IBB | SO | HBP | SH | SF | SB | CS | SB% | GDP | Avg | OBP | Slg |
| 2009 | Bkrsfld | A+ | 134 | 522 | 146 | 33 | 1 | 12 | (- | -) | 217 | 82 | 76 | 76 | 46 | 0 | 146 | 5 | 0 | 1 | 6 | 4 | .60 | 14 | .280 | .343 | .416 |
| 2010 | Frisco | AA | 132 | 516 | 143 | 26 | 6 | 10 | (- | -) | 211 | 67 | 58 | 74 | 47 | 3 | 120 | 5 | 0 | 5 | 8 | 6 | .57 | 21 | .277 | .340 | .409 |
| 2011 | Frisco | AA | 13 | 44 | 10 | 1 | 0 | 2 | (- | -) | 17 | 11 | 4 | 7 | 7 | 0 | 16 | 4 | 0 | 0 | 2 | 1 | .67 | 1 | .227 | .382 | .386 |
| 2011 | RdRck | AAA | 113 | 426 | 137 | 27 | 5 | 12 | (- | -) | 210 | 73 | 57 | 82 | 43 | 2 | 138 | 4 | 0 | 1 | 13 | 4 | .76 | 9 | .322 | .388 | .493 |
| 2012 | RdRck | AAA | 137 | 493 | 143 | 28 | 1 | 20 | (- | -) | 233 | 93 | 78 | 95 | 79 | 3 | 128 | 7 | 0 | 5 | 6 | 4 | .60 | 16 | .290 | .392 | .473 |
| 2013 | RdRck | AAA | 119 | 426 | 124 | 26 | 0 | 12 | (- | -) | 186 | 71 | 51 | 78 | 69 | 0 | 119 | 6 | 1 | 3 | 1 | 2 | .33 | 10 | .291 | .395 | .437 |
| 2013 | Tex | AL | 8 | 12 | 4 | 2 | 0 | 0 | (0 | 0) | 6 | 3 | 1 | 2 | 3 | 0 | 6 | 0 | 0 | 0 | 0 | 0 | - | 0 | .333 | .467 | .500 |

# Keith Butler

**Pitches:** R **Bats:** R **Pos:** RP-16 **Ht:** 6'0" **Wt:** 170 **Born:** 1/30/1989 **Age:** 25

| | | | HOW MUCH HE PITCHED | | | | | | WHAT HE GAVE UP | | | | | | | | | | | | THE RESULTS | | | | | | | |
|---|---|---|---|---|---|---|---|---|---|---|---|---|---|---|---|---|---|---|---|---|---|---|---|---|---|---|---|---|
| Year | Team | Lg | G | GS | CG | GF | IP | BFP | H | R | ER | HR | SH | SF | HB | TBB | IBB | SO | WP | Bk | W | L | Pct | Sh | Sv-Op | Hld | ERC | ERA |
| 2009 | Cards | R | 21 | 0 | 0 | 14 | 28.1 | 115 | 18 | 9 | 7 | 0 | 0 | 0 | 4 | 12 | 0 | 34 | 3 | 1 | 1 | 1 | .500 | 0 | 6- - | - | 2.17 | 2.22 |
| 2009 | JhsCty | R | 2 | 0 | 0 | 1 | 2.0 | 7 | 0 | 0 | 0 | 0 | 0 | 0 | 0 | 1 | 0 | 4 | 0 | 0 | 0 | 0 | - | 0 | 0- - | - | 0.27 | 0.00 |
| 2010 | Batvia | A- | 27 | 0 | 0 | 16 | 30.2 | 139 | 29 | 15 | 10 | 1 | 2 | 1 | 1 | 15 | 3 | 50 | 8 | 0 | 0 | 3 | .000 | 0 | 5- - | - | 3.44 | 2.93 |
| 2011 | QuadC | A | 12 | 0 | 0 | 12 | 15.1 | 57 | 7 | 2 | 2 | 0 | 0 | 0 | 0 | 5 | 1 | 16 | 1 | 0 | 0 | 1 | .000 | 0 | 5- - | - | 0.93 | 1.17 |
| 2011 | PlmBh | A+ | 34 | 0 | 0 | 27 | 36.0 | 147 | 19 | 6 | 5 | 1 | 1 | 0 | 2 | 18 | 0 | 52 | 0 | 0 | 1 | 0 | 1.000 | 0 | 12- - | - | 1.75 | 1.25 |
| 2012 | Sprgfld | AA | 54 | 0 | 0 | 43 | 59.1 | 250 | 53 | 22 | 18 | 5 | 3 | 1 | 2 | 23 | 1 | 59 | 2 | 1 | 5 | 1 | .833 | 0 | 25- - | - | 3.46 | 2.73 |
| 2013 | Sprgfld | AA | 13 | 0 | 0 | 13 | 13.2 | 51 | 8 | 1 | 1 | 1 | 0 | 0 | 0 | 2 | 0 | 21 | 0 | 1 | 0 | 0 | - | 0 | 7- - | - | 1.21 | 0.66 |
| 2013 | Memp | AAA | 20 | 1 | 0 | 7 | 27.1 | 111 | 21 | 12 | 11 | 3 | 1 | 1 | 0 | 9 | 2 | 29 | 0 | 0 | 3 | 2 | .600 | 0 | 2- - | - | 2.53 | 3.62 |
| 2013 | StL | NL | 16 | 0 | 0 | 8 | 20.0 | 85 | 13 | 9 | 9 | 0 | 0 | 1 | 1 | 11 | 0 | 16 | 0 | 0 | 0 | 0 | - | 0 | 0-0 | 0 | 2.25 | 4.05 |

# Marlon Byrd

**Bats:** R **Throws:** R **Pos:** RF-138;PH-11;LF-2;CF-2 **Ht:** 6'0" **Wt:** 245 **Born:** 8/30/1977 **Age:** 36

| | | | BATTING | | | | | | | | | | | | | | | | | | BASERUNNING | | | | AVERAGES | | |
|---|---|---|---|---|---|---|---|---|---|---|---|---|---|---|---|---|---|---|---|---|---|---|---|---|---|---|---|
| Year | Team | Lg | G | AB | H | 2B | 3B | HR | (Hm | Rd) | TB | R | RBI | RC | TBB | IBB | SO | HBP | SH | SF | SB | CS | SB% | GDP | Avg | OBP | Slg |
| 2002 | Phi | NL | 10 | 35 | 8 | 2 | 0 | 1 | (1 | 0) | 13 | 2 | 1 | 0 | 1 | 0 | 8 | 0 | 0 | 0 | 0 | 2 | .00 | 0 | .229 | .250 | .371 |
| 2003 | Phi | NL | 135 | 495 | 150 | 28 | 4 | 7 | (3 | 4) | 207 | 86 | 45 | 72 | 44 | 3 | 94 | 7 | 4 | 3 | 11 | 1 | .92 | 8 | .303 | .366 | .418 |
| 2004 | Phi | NL | 106 | 346 | 79 | 13 | 2 | 5 | (3 | 2) | 111 | 48 | 33 | 35 | 22 | 1 | 68 | 7 | 2 | 1 | 2 | 2 | .50 | 10 | .228 | .287 | .321 |
| 2005 | 2 Tms | NL | 79 | 229 | 61 | 15 | 2 | 2 | (0 | 2) | 86 | 20 | 26 | 30 | 19 | 1 | 50 | 2 | 5 | 4 | 5 | 1 | .83 | 5 | .266 | .323 | .376 |
| 2006 | Was | NL | 78 | 197 | 44 | 8 | 1 | 5 | (1 | 4) | 69 | 28 | 18 | 18 | 22 | 1 | 47 | 6 | 1 | 2 | 3 | 3 | .50 | 6 | .223 | .317 | .350 |
| 2007 | Tex | AL | 109 | 414 | 127 | 17 | 8 | 10 | (4 | 6) | 190 | 60 | 70 | 68 | 29 | 3 | 88 | 5 | 0 | 6 | 5 | 3 | .63 | 9 | .307 | .355 | .459 |
| 2008 | Tex | AL | 122 | 403 | 120 | 28 | 4 | 10 | (7 | 3) | 186 | 70 | 53 | 63 | 46 | 3 | 62 | 9 | 2 | 2 | 7 | 2 | .78 | 10 | .298 | .380 | .462 |
| 2009 | Tex | AL | 146 | 547 | 155 | 43 | 2 | 20 | (14 | 6) | 262 | 66 | 89 | 91 | 32 | 2 | 98 | 10 | 0 | **10** | 8 | 4 | .67 | 11 | .283 | .329 | .479 |
| 2010 | ChC | NL | 152 | 580 | 170 | 39 | 2 | 12 | (6 | 6) | 249 | 84 | 66 | 80 | 31 | 1 | 98 | 17 | 0 | 2 | 5 | 1 | .83 | 12 | .293 | .346 | .429 |
| 2011 | ChC | NL | 119 | 446 | 123 | 22 | 2 | 9 | (4 | 5) | 176 | 51 | 35 | 43 | 25 | 2 | 78 | 8 | 1 | 2 | 3 | 2 | .60 | 13 | .276 | .324 | .395 |
| 2012 | 2 Tms | | 48 | 143 | 30 | 2 | 0 | 1 | (0 | 1) | 35 | 10 | 9 | 8 | 5 | 1 | 31 | 2 | 1 | 2 | 0 | 3 | .00 | 3 | .210 | .243 | .245 |
| 2013 | 2 Tms | NL | 147 | 532 | 155 | 35 | 5 | 24 | (9 | 15) | 272 | 75 | 88 | 85 | 31 | 2 | 144 | 8 | 1 | 7 | 2 | 4 | .33 | 11 | .291 | .336 | .511 |
| 05 | Phi | NL | 5 | 13 | 4 | 0 | 0 | 0 | (0 | 0) | 4 | 0 | 0 | 2 | 1 | 0 | 3 | 1 | 0 | 0 | 0 | 0 | - | 0 | .308 | .400 | .308 |
| 05 | Was | NL | 74 | 216 | 57 | 15 | 2 | 2 | (0 | 2) | 82 | 20 | 26 | 28 | 18 | 1 | 47 | 1 | 5 | 4 | 5 | 1 | .83 | 5 | .264 | .318 | .380 |
| 12 | ChC | NL | 13 | 43 | 3 | 0 | 0 | 0 | (0 | 0) | 3 | 1 | 2 | 0 | 3 | 1 | 10 | 1 | 0 | 0 | 0 | 1 | .00 | 2 | .070 | .149 | .070 |
| 12 | Bos | AL | 35 | 100 | 27 | 2 | 0 | 1 | (0 | 1) | 32 | 9 | 7 | 8 | 2 | 0 | 21 | 1 | 1 | 2 | 0 | 2 | .00 | 1 | .270 | .286 | .320 |
| 13 | NYM | NL | 117 | 425 | 121 | 26 | 5 | 21 | (7 | 14) | 220 | 61 | 71 | 68 | 25 | 2 | 124 | 7 | 1 | 6 | 2 | 4 | .33 | 6 | .285 | .330 | .518 |
| 13 | Pit | NL | 30 | 107 | 34 | 9 | 0 | 3 | (2 | 1) | 52 | 14 | 17 | 17 | 6 | 0 | 20 | 1 | 0 | 1 | 0 | 0 | - | 5 | .318 | .357 | .486 |
| 12 ML YEARS | | | 1251 | 4367 | 1222 | 252 | 32 | 106 | (52 | 54) | 1856 | 600 | 533 | 593 | 307 | 20 | 866 | 81 | 17 | 41 | 51 | 28 | .65 | 98 | .280 | .336 | .425 |

# Tim Byrdak

**Pitches:** L **Bats:** L **Pos:** RP-8 BURR-dack **Ht:** 5'11" **Wt:** 190 **Born:** 10/31/1973 **Age:** 40

| | | | HOW MUCH HE PITCHED | | | | | | WHAT HE GAVE UP | | | | | | | | | | | | THE RESULTS | | | | | | | |
|---|---|---|---|---|---|---|---|---|---|---|---|---|---|---|---|---|---|---|---|---|---|---|---|---|---|---|---|---|
| Year | Team | Lg | G | GS | CG | GF | IP | BFP | H | R | ER | HR | SH | SF | HB | TBB | IBB | SO | WP | Bk | W | L | Pct | Sh | Sv-Op | Hld | ERC | ERA |
| 2013 | Mets* | R | 1 | 1 | 0 | 0 | 1.0 | 4 | 0 | 0 | 0 | 0 | 0 | 0 | 0 | 1 | 0 | 1 | 0 | 0 | 0 | 0 | - | 0 | 0- - | - | 0.95 | 0.00 |
| 2013 | StLuci* | A+ | 14 | 0 | 0 | 4 | 12.1 | 49 | 6 | 3 | 3 | 0 | 0 | 1 | 0 | 7 | 0 | 13 | 1 | 0 | 1 | 1 | .500 | 0 | 3- - | - | 1.54 | 2.19 |
| 2013 | LsVgs* | AAA | 11 | 0 | 0 | 2 | 8.0 | 36 | 6 | 0 | 0 | 0 | 0 | 0 | 2 | 5 | 0 | 10 | 0 | 0 | 2 | 0 | 1.000 | 0 | 0- - | - | 3.76 | 0.00 |
| 1998 | KC | AL | 3 | 0 | 0 | 0 | 1.2 | 9 | 5 | 1 | 1 | 1 | 0 | 0 | 0 | 0 | 0 | 1 | 0 | 0 | 0 | 0 | - | 0 | 0-0 | 0 | 23.52 | 5.40 |
| 1999 | KC | AL | 33 | 0 | 0 | 5 | 24.2 | 128 | 32 | 24 | 21 | 5 | 3 | 0 | 1 | 20 | 2 | 17 | 3 | 1 | 0 | 3 | .000 | 0 | 1-4 | 10 | 8.29 | 7.66 |
| 2000 | KC | AL | 12 | 0 | 0 | 1 | 6.1 | 34 | 11 | 8 | 8 | 3 | 0 | 0 | 0 | 4 | 0 | 8 | 1 | 0 | 0 | 1 | .000 | 0 | 0-2 | 3 | 13.14 | 11.37 |
| 2005 | Bal | AL | 41 | 0 | 0 | 3 | 26.2 | 131 | 27 | 14 | 12 | 1 | 2 | 1 | 1 | 21 | 1 | 31 | 5 | 0 | 0 | 1 | .000 | 0 | 1-1 | 11 | 5.04 | 4.05 |
| 2006 | Bal | AL | 16 | 0 | 0 | 2 | 7.0 | 42 | 14 | 10 | 10 | 2 | 2 | 0 | 0 | 8 | 1 | 2 | 1 | 0 | 1 | 0 | 1.000 | 0 | 0-0 | 3 | 15.90 | 12.86 |
| 2007 | Det | AL | 39 | 0 | 0 | 3 | 45.0 | 199 | 38 | 23 | 16 | 3 | 2 | 5 | 1 | 26 | 4 | 49 | 3 | 0 | 3 | 0 | 1.000 | 0 | 1-2 | 8 | 3.53 | 3.20 |
| 2008 | Hou | NL | 59 | 0 | 0 | 9 | 55.1 | 237 | 45 | 24 | 24 | 10 | 2 | 1 | 2 | 29 | 2 | 47 | 0 | 0 | 2 | 1 | .667 | 0 | 0-0 | 8 | 4.18 | 3.90 |
| 2009 | Hou | NL | 76 | 0 | 0 | 8 | 61.1 | 261 | 39 | 23 | 22 | 10 | 0 | 3 | 3 | 36 | 0 | 58 | 2 | 0 | 1 | 2 | .333 | 0 | 0-2 | 9 | 3.38 | 3.23 |
| 2010 | Hou | NL | 64 | 0 | 0 | 9 | 38.2 | 170 | 40 | 15 | 15 | 4 | 0 | 3 | 0 | 20 | 0 | 29 | 2 | 0 | 2 | 2 | .500 | 0 | 0-0 | 11 | 4.83 | 3.49 |
| 2011 | NYM | NL | 72 | 0 | 0 | 10 | 37.2 | 168 | 34 | 20 | 16 | 3 | 4 | 2 | 1 | 19 | 4 | 47 | 1 | 0 | 2 | 1 | .667 | 0 | 1-4 | 8 | 3.61 | 3.82 |
| 2012 | NYM | NL | 56 | 0 | 0 | 4 | 30.2 | 125 | 18 | 16 | 15 | 2 | 4 | 2 | 1 | 18 | 5 | 34 | 0 | 0 | 2 | 2 | .500 | 0 | 0-2 | 17 | 2.29 | 4.40 |
| 2013 | NYM | NL | 8 | 0 | 0 | 2 | 4.2 | 21 | 5 | 4 | 4 | 2 | 0 | 0 | 0 | 2 | 0 | 3 | 0 | 0 | 0 | 0 | - | 0 | 0-0 | 0 | 6.89 | 7.71 |
| 12 ML YEARS | | | 479 | 0 | 0 | 56 | 339.2 | 1525 | 308 | 182 | 164 | 46 | 19 | 17 | 10 | 203 | 19 | 326 | 18 | 1 | 13 | 13 | .500 | 0 | 4-17 | 88 | 4.55 | 4.35 |

# Cesar Cabral

**Pitches:** L **Bats:** L **Pos:** RP-8 kuh-BRAWL **Ht:** 6'3" **Wt:** 250 **Born:** 2/11/1989 **Age:** 25

| | | | HOW MUCH HE PITCHED | | | | | | WHAT HE GAVE UP | | | | | | | | | | | | THE RESULTS | | | | | | | |
|---|---|---|---|---|---|---|---|---|---|---|---|---|---|---|---|---|---|---|---|---|---|---|---|---|---|---|---|---|
| Year | Team | Lg | G | GS | CG | GF | IP | BFP | H | R | ER | HR | SH | SF | HB | TBB | IBB | SO | WP | Bk | W | L | Pct | Sh | Sv-Op | Hld | ERC | ERA |
| 2009 | Lowell | A- | 15 | 9 | 0 | 5 | 60.1 | 273 | 66 | 35 | 27 | 2 | 2 | 2 | 3 | 17 | 0 | 47 | 5 | 0 | 1 | 6 | .143 | 0 | 4- - | - | 3.66 | 4.03 |
| 2010 | Grnvlle | A | 17 | 0 | 0 | 13 | 31.1 | 114 | 16 | 1 | 1 | 0 | 3 | 0 | 3 | 7 | 0 | 35 | 0 | 0 | 2 | 0 | 1.000 | 0 | 5- - | - | 1.15 | 0.29 |
| 2010 | Salem | A+ | 28 | 0 | 0 | 11 | 48.0 | 211 | 60 | 31 | 31 | 1 | 1 | 3 | 2 | 14 | 0 | 45 | 6 | 1 | 2 | 0 | 1.000 | 0 | 4- - | - | 4.74 | 5.81 |
| 2011 | Salem | A+ | 12 | 0 | 0 | 11 | 16.2 | 71 | 15 | 5 | 3 | 0 | 3 | 0 | 0 | 5 | 0 | 24 | 2 | 0 | 1 | 0 | 1.000 | 0 | 8- - | - | 2.41 | 1.62 |
| 2011 | Portlnd | AA | 24 | 0 | 0 | 11 | 38.1 | 169 | 41 | 17 | 15 | 3 | 2 | 1 | 1 | 16 | 0 | 46 | 2 | 2 | 2 | 4 | .333 | 0 | 1- - | - | 4.49 | 3.52 |
| 2013 | Tampa | A+ | 5 | 0 | 0 | 0 | 7.0 | 35 | 6 | 2 | 2 | 0 | 1 | 1 | 1 | 8 | 0 | 5 | 2 | 0 | 0 | 0 | - | 0 | 0- - | - | 5.91 | 2.57 |
| 2013 | Trntn | AA | 15 | 0 | 0 | 6 | 19.2 | 89 | 22 | 12 | 12 | 2 | 1 | 0 | 2 | 9 | 1 | 22 | 2 | 0 | 1 | 0 | 1.000 | 0 | 0- - | - | 5.39 | 5.49 |
| 2013 | S-WB | AAA | 10 | 0 | 0 | 2 | 10.0 | 47 | 12 | 8 | 8 | 0 | 0 | 0 | 1 | 5 | 0 | 16 | 3 | 1 | 0 | 1 | .000 | 0 | 0- - | - | 5.22 | 7.20 |
| 2013 | NYY | AL | 8 | 0 | 0 | 0 | 3.2 | 15 | 3 | 1 | 1 | 0 | 0 | 0 | 1 | 1 | 0 | 6 | 2 | 0 | 0 | 0 | - | 0 | 0-0 | 1 | 3.10 | 2.45 |

## Alberto Cabrera

**Pitches:** R **Bats:** R **Pos:** RP-7 **Ht:** 6'4" **Wt:** 210 **Born:** 10/25/1988 **Age:** 25

| HOW MUCH HE PITCHED | | | | | | | | | WHAT HE GAVE UP | | | | | | | | | | | | THE RESULTS | | | | | | | |
|---|---|---|---|---|---|---|---|---|---|---|---|---|---|---|---|---|---|---|---|---|---|---|---|---|---|---|---|---|
| Year | Team | Lg | G | GS | CG | GF | IP | BFP | H | R | ER | HR | SH | SF | HB | TBB | IBB | SO | WP | Bk | W | L | Pct | Sh | Sv-Op | Hld | ERC | ERA |
| 2009 | Peoria | A | 27 | 8 | 0 | 2 | 96.1 | 434 | 94 | 53 | 48 | 6 | 4 | 3 | 6 | 54 | 2 | 73 | 15 | 3 | 8 | 2 | .800 | 0 | 1-- | - | 4.48 | 4.48 |
| 2010 | Dytona | A+ | 18 | 17 | 1 | 0 | 93.1 | 391 | 92 | 44 | 34 | 6 | 0 | 1 | 1 | 26 | 1 | 90 | 12 | 1 | 7 | 5 | .583 | 1 | 0-- | - | 3.31 | 3.28 |
| 2010 | Tenn | AA | 10 | 9 | 0 | 0 | 42.2 | 213 | 57 | 39 | 30 | 1 | 2 | 3 | 3 | 24 | 0 | 35 | 8 | 1 | 0 | 4 | .000 | 0 | 0-- | - | 6.20 | 6.33 |
| 2011 | Tenn | AA | 9 | 9 | 0 | 0 | 48.2 | 225 | 60 | 36 | 29 | 4 | 4 | 3 | 2 | 21 | 0 | 34 | 4 | 0 | 6 | 2 | .750 | 0 | 0-- | - | 5.56 | 5.36 |
| 2011 | Iowa | AAA | 19 | 17 | 0 | 1 | 88.2 | 421 | 118 | 67 | 65 | 11 | 3 | 4 | 3 | 53 | 0 | 67 | 11 | 0 | 3 | 6 | .333 | 0 | 0-- | - | 7.41 | 6.60 |
| 2012 | Tenn | AA | 23 | 0 | 0 | 13 | 35.2 | 149 | 30 | 15 | 10 | 2 | 0 | 1 | 0 | 10 | 0 | 45 | 1 | 0 | 2 | 1 | .667 | 0 | 5-- | - | 2.42 | 2.52 |
| 2012 | Iowa | AAA | 13 | 0 | 0 | 7 | 19.1 | 93 | 29 | 13 | 9 | 4 | 0 | 0 | 2 | 4 | 0 | 29 | 2 | 0 | 2 | 0 | 1.000 | 0 | 0-- | - | 7.42 | 4.19 |
| 2013 | Tenn | AA | 18 | 18 | 1 | 0 | 112.2 | 465 | 102 | 41 | 40 | 10 | 7 | 6 | 5 | 39 | 1 | 107 | 11 | 3 | 9 | 3 | .750 | 0 | 0-- | - | 3.51 | 3.20 |
| 2013 | Iowa | AAA | 15 | 0 | 0 | 3 | 20.1 | 97 | 26 | 16 | 16 | 4 | 2 | 2 | 0 | 12 | 2 | 19 | 2 | 0 | 1 | 3 | .250 | 0 | 0-- | - | 7.14 | 7.08 |
| 2012 | ChC | NL | 25 | 0 | 0 | 6 | 21.2 | 99 | 16 | 15 | 13 | 1 | 1 | 1 | 1 | 18 | 1 | 27 | 5 | 0 | 1 | 1 | .500 | 0 | 0-0 | 1 | 3.90 | 5.40 |
| 2013 | ChC | NL | 7 | 0 | 0 | 0 | 6.0 | 30 | 7 | 3 | 3 | 0 | 0 | 0 | 1 | 5 | 0 | 4 | 0 | 0 | 0 | 0 | - | 0 | 0-0 | 0 | 6.71 | 4.50 |
| 2 ML YEARS | | | 32 | 0 | 0 | 6 | 27.2 | 129 | 23 | 18 | 16 | 1 | 1 | 1 | 2 | 23 | 1 | 31 | 5 | 0 | 1 | 1 | .500 | 0 | 0-0 | 1 | 4.47 | 5.20 |

## Asdrubal Cabrera

**Bats:** B **Throws:** R **Pos:** SS-129;DH-5;PH-3 azz-DRUE-bull **Ht:** 6'0" **Wt:** 205 **Born:** 11/13/1985 **Age:** 28

| BATTING | | | | | | | | | | | | | | | | | | | | BASERUNNING | | | | AVERAGES | | |
|---|---|---|---|---|---|---|---|---|---|---|---|---|---|---|---|---|---|---|---|---|---|---|---|---|---|---|
| Year | Team | Lg | G | AB | H | 2B | 3B | HR | (Hm | Rd) | TB | R | RBI | RC | TBB | IBB | SO | HBP | SH | SF | SB | CS | SB% | GDP | Avg | OBP | Slg |
| 2007 | Cle | AL | 45 | 159 | 45 | 9 | 2 | 3 | (1 | 2) | 67 | 30 | 22 | 27 | 17 | 0 | 29 | 2 | 5 | 3 | 0 | 0 | - | 7 | .283 | .354 | .421 |
| 2008 | Cle | AL | 114 | 352 | 91 | 20 | 0 | 6 | (5 | 1) | 129 | 48 | 47 | 48 | 46 | 2 | 77 | 4 | 11 | 5 | 4 | 4 | .50 | 8 | .259 | .346 | .366 |
| 2009 | Cle | AL | 131 | 523 | 161 | 42 | 4 | 6 | (4 | 2) | 229 | 81 | 68 | 81 | 44 | 1 | 89 | 1 | 10 | 3 | 17 | 4 | .81 | 13 | .308 | .361 | .438 |
| 2010 | Cle | AL | 97 | 381 | 105 | 16 | 1 | 3 | (2 | 1) | 132 | 39 | 29 | 46 | 25 | 0 | 60 | 5 | 11 | 3 | 6 | 4 | .60 | 10 | .276 | .326 | .346 |
| 2011 | Cle | AL | 151 | 604 | 165 | 32 | 3 | 25 | (13 | 12) | 278 | 87 | 92 | 100 | 44 | 5 | 119 | 11 | 4 | 4 | 17 | 5 | .77 | 10 | .273 | .332 | .460 |
| 2012 | Cle | AL | 143 | 555 | 150 | 35 | 1 | 16 | (10 | 6) | 235 | 70 | 68 | 74 | 52 | 3 | 99 | 6 | 1 | 2 | 9 | 4 | .69 | 18 | .270 | .338 | .423 |
| 2013 | Cle | AL | 136 | 508 | 123 | 35 | 2 | 14 | (8 | 6) | 204 | 66 | 64 | 51 | 35 | 1 | 114 | 8 | 6 | 5 | 9 | 3 | .75 | 10 | .242 | .299 | .402 |
| Postseason | | | 11 | 46 | 10 | 0 | 0 | 1 | (1 | 0) | 13 | 5 | 6 | 5 | 2 | 0 | 12 | 0 | 3 | 1 | 0 | 0 | - | 2 | .217 | .245 | .283 |
| 7 ML YEARS | | | 817 | 3082 | 840 | 189 | 13 | 73 | (43 | 30) | 1274 | 421 | 390 | 427 | 263 | 12 | 587 | 37 | 48 | 25 | 62 | 24 | .72 | 76 | .273 | .335 | .413 |

## Everth Cabrera

**Bats:** B **Throws:** R **Pos:** SS-95 EVV-urth **Ht:** 5'10" **Wt:** 190 **Born:** 11/17/1986 **Age:** 27

| BATTING | | | | | | | | | | | | | | | | | | | | BASERUNNING | | | | AVERAGES | | |
|---|---|---|---|---|---|---|---|---|---|---|---|---|---|---|---|---|---|---|---|---|---|---|---|---|---|---|
| Year | Team | Lg | G | AB | H | 2B | 3B | HR | (Hm | Rd) | TB | R | RBI | RC | TBB | IBB | SO | HBP | SH | SF | SB | CS | SB% | GDP | Avg | OBP | Slg |
| 2013 | FtWyn* | A | 2 | 7 | 0 | 0 | 0 | 0 | (- | -) | 0 | 1 | 0 | 0 | 1 | 0 | 5 | 0 | 0 | 0 | 0 | 0 | - | 0 | .000 | .125 | .000 |
| 2009 | SD | NL | 103 | 377 | 96 | 18 | 8 | 2 | (1 | 1) | 136 | 59 | 31 | 48 | 46 | 5 | 88 | 5 | 8 | 2 | 25 | 8 | .76 | 3 | .255 | .342 | .361 |
| 2010 | SD | NL | 76 | 212 | 44 | 6 | 3 | 1 | (0 | 1) | 59 | 22 | 22 | 15 | 19 | 3 | 54 | 2 | 8 | 0 | 10 | 6 | .63 | 8 | .208 | .279 | .278 |
| 2011 | SD | NL | 2 | 8 | 1 | 0 | 0 | 0 | (0 | 0) | 1 | 1 | 0 | 1 | 1 | 0 | 3 | 0 | 0 | 0 | 2 | 0 | 1.00 | 0 | .125 | .222 | .125 |
| 2012 | SD | NL | 115 | 398 | 98 | 19 | 3 | 2 | (0 | 2) | 129 | 49 | 24 | 43 | 43 | 2 | 110 | 3 | 5 | 0 | **44** | 4 | **.92** | 3 | .246 | .324 | .324 |
| 2013 | SD | NL | 95 | 381 | 108 | 15 | 5 | 4 | (1 | 3) | 145 | 54 | 31 | 59 | 41 | 0 | 69 | 2 | 10 | 1 | 37 | 12 | .76 | 1 | .283 | .355 | .381 |
| 5 ML YEARS | | | 391 | 1376 | 347 | 58 | 19 | 9 | (2 | 7) | 470 | 185 | 108 | 166 | 150 | 10 | 324 | 12 | 31 | 3 | 118 | 30 | .80 | 15 | .252 | .330 | .342 |

## Melky Cabrera

**Bats:** B **Throws:** L **Pos:** LF-77;DH-9;PH-3 **Ht:** 6'0" **Wt:** 200 **Born:** 8/11/1984 **Age:** 29

| BATTING | | | | | | | | | | | | | | | | | | | | BASERUNNING | | | | AVERAGES | | |
|---|---|---|---|---|---|---|---|---|---|---|---|---|---|---|---|---|---|---|---|---|---|---|---|---|---|---|
| Year | Team | Lg | G | AB | H | 2B | 3B | HR | (Hm | Rd) | TB | R | RBI | RC | TBB | IBB | SO | HBP | SH | SF | SB | CS | SB% | GDP | Avg | OBP | Slg |
| 2013 | Dnedin* | A+ | 2 | 6 | 1 | 0 | 0 | 0 | (- | -) | 1 | 0 | 0 | 0 | 0 | 0 | 2 | 0 | 0 | 0 | 0 | 0 | - | 0 | .167 | .167 | .167 |
| 2013 | NHam* | AA | 3 | 11 | 4 | 0 | 0 | 1 | (- | -) | 7 | 1 | 2 | 2 | 0 | 0 | 1 | 0 | 0 | 0 | 1 | 0 | 1.00 | 0 | .364 | .364 | .636 |
| 2013 | Buffalo* | AAA | 2 | 5 | 3 | 0 | 0 | 0 | (- | -) | 3 | 1 | 1 | 1 | 0 | 0 | 0 | 0 | 0 | 1 | 0 | 0 | - | 0 | .600 | .500 | .600 |
| 2005 | NYY | AL | 6 | 19 | 4 | 0 | 0 | 0 | (0 | 0) | 4 | 1 | 0 | 0 | 0 | 0 | 2 | 0 | 0 | 0 | 0 | 0 | - | 0 | .211 | .211 | .211 |
| 2006 | NYY | AL | 130 | 460 | 129 | 26 | 2 | 7 | (3 | 4) | 180 | 75 | 50 | 68 | 56 | 3 | 59 | 2 | 5 | 1 | 12 | 5 | .71 | 9 | .280 | .360 | .391 |
| 2007 | NYY | AL | 150 | 545 | 149 | 24 | 8 | 8 | (4 | 4) | 213 | 66 | 73 | 70 | 43 | 0 | 68 | 5 | 10 | 9 | 13 | 5 | .72 | 14 | .273 | .327 | .391 |
| 2008 | NYY | AL | 129 | 414 | 103 | 12 | 1 | 8 | (4 | 4) | 141 | 42 | 37 | 37 | 29 | 5 | 58 | 3 | 4 | 3 | 9 | 2 | .82 | 11 | .249 | .301 | .341 |
| 2009 | NYY | AL | 154 | 485 | 133 | 28 | 1 | 13 | (9 | 4) | 202 | 66 | 68 | 69 | 43 | 4 | 59 | 4 | 4 | 4 | 10 | 2 | .83 | 15 | .274 | .336 | .416 |
| 2010 | Atl | NL | 147 | 458 | 117 | 27 | 3 | 4 | (1 | 3) | 162 | 50 | 42 | 45 | 42 | 11 | 64 | 1 | 5 | 3 | 7 | 1 | .88 | 8 | .255 | .317 | .354 |
| 2011 | KC | AL | 155 | 658 | 201 | 44 | 5 | 18 | (6 | 12) | 309 | 102 | 87 | 92 | 35 | 3 | 94 | 1 | 7 | 5 | 20 | 10 | .67 | 13 | .305 | .339 | .470 |
| 2012 | SF | NL | 113 | 459 | 159 | 25 | 10 | 11 | (2 | 9) | 237 | 84 | 60 | 83 | 36 | 4 | 63 | 0 | 1 | 5 | 13 | 5 | .72 | 8 | **.346** | .390 | .516 |
| 2013 | Tor | AL | 88 | 344 | 96 | 15 | 2 | 3 | (3 | 0) | 124 | 39 | 30 | 39 | 23 | 0 | 47 | 0 | 2 | 3 | 2 | 2 | .50 | 7 | .279 | .322 | .360 |
| Postseason | | | 22 | 75 | 16 | 2 | 0 | 1 | (0 | 1) | 21 | 8 | 7 | 5 | 3 | 0 | 16 | 0 | 2 | 0 | 0 | 0 | - | 0 | .213 | .244 | .280 |
| 9 ML YEARS | | | 1072 | 3842 | 1091 | 201 | 32 | 72 | (32 | 40) | 1572 | 525 | 447 | 503 | 307 | 30 | 514 | 16 | 38 | 33 | 86 | 32 | .73 | 85 | .284 | .337 | .409 |

## Miguel Cabrera

**Bats:** R **Throws:** R **Pos:** 3B-145;DH-1;PH-1 **Ht:** 6'4" **Wt:** 240 **Born:** 4/18/1983 **Age:** 31

| BATTING | | | | | | | | | | | | | | | | | | | | BASERUNNING | | | | AVERAGES | | |
|---|---|---|---|---|---|---|---|---|---|---|---|---|---|---|---|---|---|---|---|---|---|---|---|---|---|---|
| Year | Team | Lg | G | AB | H | 2B | 3B | HR | (Hm | Rd) | TB | R | RBI | RC | TBB | IBB | SO | HBP | SH | SF | SB | CS | SB% | GDP | Avg | OBP | Slg |
| 2003 | Fla | NL | 87 | 314 | 84 | 21 | 3 | 12 | (7 | 5) | 147 | 39 | 62 | 51 | 25 | 3 | 84 | 2 | 4 | 1 | 0 | 2 | .00 | 12 | .268 | .325 | .468 |
| 2004 | Fla | NL | 160 | 603 | 177 | 31 | 1 | 33 | (14 | 19) | 309 | 101 | 112 | 92 | 68 | 5 | 148 | 6 | 0 | 8 | 5 | 2 | .71 | 20 | .294 | .366 | .512 |
| 2005 | Fla | NL | 158 | 613 | 198 | 43 | 2 | 33 | (11 | 22) | 344 | 106 | 116 | 108 | 64 | 12 | 125 | 2 | 0 | 6 | 1 | 0 | 1.00 | 20 | .323 | .385 | .561 |
| 2006 | Fla | NL | 158 | 576 | 195 | 50 | 2 | 26 | (15 | 11) | 327 | 112 | 114 | 132 | 86 | 27 | 108 | 10 | 0 | 4 | 9 | 6 | .60 | 18 | .339 | .430 | .568 |
| 2007 | Fla | NL | 157 | 588 | 188 | 38 | 2 | 34 | (19 | 15) | 332 | 91 | 119 | 122 | 79 | 23 | 127 | 5 | 1 | 7 | 2 | 1 | .67 | 17 | .320 | .401 | .565 |
| 2008 | Det | AL | 160 | 616 | 180 | 36 | 2 | **37** | (19 | **18)** | **331** | 85 | 127 | 109 | 56 | 6 | 126 | 3 | 0 | 9 | 1 | 0 | 1.00 | 16 | .292 | .349 | .537 |
| 2009 | Det | AL | 160 | 611 | 198 | 34 | 0 | 34 | (19 | 15) | 334 | 96 | 103 | 114 | 68 | 14 | 107 | 5 | 0 | 1 | 6 | 2 | .75 | 22 | .324 | .396 | .547 |
| 2010 | Det | AL | 150 | 548 | 180 | 45 | 1 | 38 | (17 | **21)** | 341 | 111 | **126** | 122 | 89 | **32** | 95 | 3 | 0 | 8 | 3 | 3 | .50 | 17 | .328 | **.420** | .622 |
| 2011 | Det | AL | **161** | 572 | 197 | **48** | 0 | 30 | (15 | 15) | 335 | 111 | 105 | **141** | 108 | 22 | 89 | 3 | 0 | 5 | 2 | 1 | .67 | 24 | **.344** | **.448** | .586 |

| BATTING | | | | | | | | | | | | | | | | | | | | | | BASERUNNING | | | | AVERAGES | | |
|---|---|---|---|---|---|---|---|---|---|---|---|---|---|---|---|---|---|---|---|---|---|---|---|---|---|---|---|---|
| Year | Team | Lg | G | AB | H | 2B | 3B | HR | (Hm | Rd) | TB | R | RBI | RC | TBB | IBB | SO | HBP | SH | SF | SB | CS | SB% | GDP | Avg | OBP | Slg |
| 2012 | Det | AL | 161 | 622 | 205 | 40 | 0 | **44** | (**28** | 16) | **377** | 109 | **139** | 123 | 66 | 17 | 98 | 3 | 0 | 6 | 4 | 1 | .80 | **28** | **.330** | .393 | **.606** |
| 2013 | Det | AL | 148 | 555 | 193 | 26 | 1 | 44 | (17 | **27**) | 353 | 103 | 137 | **146** | 90 | 19 | 94 | 5 | 0 | 2 | 3 | 0 | 1.00 | 19 | **.348** | **.442** | **.636** |
| Postseason | | | 41 | 152 | 42 | 9 | 0 | 10 | (4 | 6) | 81 | 23 | 30 | 26 | 23 | 6 | 37 | 2 | 1 | 0 | 2 | 0 | 1.00 | 5 | .276 | .379 | .533 |
| 11 ML YEARS | | | 1660 | 6218 | 1995 | 412 | 14 | 365 | (181 | 184) | 3530 | 1064 | 1260 | 1260 | 799 | 180 | 1201 | 47 | 5 | 57 | 36 | 18 | .67 | 213 | .321 | .399 | .568 |

## Trevor Cahill

**Pitches:** R **Bats:** R **Pos:** SP-25; RP-1 KAY-hill **Ht:** 6'4" **Wt:** 220 **Born:** 3/1/1988 **Age:** 26

| HOW MUCH HE PITCHED | | | | | | | | | WHAT HE GAVE UP | | | | | | | | | | | | THE RESULTS | | | | | | | |
|---|---|---|---|---|---|---|---|---|---|---|---|---|---|---|---|---|---|---|---|---|---|---|---|---|---|---|---|---|
| Year | Team | Lg | G | GS | CG | GF | IP | BFP | H | R | ER | HR | SH | SF | HB | TBB | IBB | SO | WP | Bk | W | L | Pct | Sh | Sv-Op | Hld | ERC | ERA |
| 2013 | DBcks* | R | 1 | 1 | 0 | 0 | 5.0 | 19 | 1 | 1 | 0 | 0 | 1 | 0 | 0 | 2 | 0 | 9 | 0 | 0 | 0 | 0 | - | 0 | 0-- | - | 0.48 | 0.00 |
| 2013 | Reno* | AAA | 3 | 3 | 0 | 0 | 16.2 | 70 | 16 | 12 | 11 | 3 | 0 | 0 | 0 | 9 | 0 | 13 | 3 | 0 | 0 | 2 | .000 | 0 | 0-- | - | 5.27 | 5.94 |
| 2009 | Oak | AL | 32 | 32 | 0 | 0 | 178.2 | 773 | 185 | 99 | 92 | 27 | 4 | 7 | 4 | 72 | 1 | 90 | 5 | 0 | 10 | 13 | .435 | 0 | 0-0 | 0 | 4.79 | 4.63 |
| 2010 | Oak | AL | 30 | 30 | 1 | 0 | 196.2 | 783 | 155 | 73 | 65 | 19 | 3 | 6 | 6 | 63 | 1 | 118 | 2 | 2 | 18 | 8 | .692 | 1 | 0-0 | 0 | 2.81 | 2.97 |
| 2011 | Oak | AL | 34 | **34** | 0 | 0 | 207.2 | 901 | 214 | 102 | 96 | 19 | 8 | 6 | 8 | 82 | 1 | 147 | 15 | 0 | 12 | 14 | .462 | 0 | 0-0 | 0 | 4.34 | 4.16 |
| 2012 | Ari | NL | 32 | 32 | 2 | 0 | 200.0 | 839 | 184 | 93 | 84 | 16 | 12 | 6 | 11 | 74 | 0 | 156 | 10 | 2 | 13 | 12 | .520 | 1 | 0-0 | 0 | 3.66 | 3.78 |
| 2013 | Ari | NL | 26 | 25 | 0 | 1 | 146.2 | 636 | 143 | 70 | 65 | 13 | 9 | 9 | 6 | 65 | 2 | 102 | **17** | 0 | 8 | 10 | .444 | 0 | 0-0 | 0 | 4.19 | 3.99 |
| 5 ML YEARS | | | 154 | 153 | 3 | 1 | 929.2 | 3932 | 881 | 437 | 402 | 94 | 36 | 34 | 35 | 356 | 5 | 613 | 49 | 4 | 61 | 57 | .517 | 2 | 0-0 | 0 | 3.92 | 3.89 |

## Lorenzo Cain

**Bats:** R **Throws:** R **Pos:** CF-92;RF-32;PH-3;DH-1 **Ht:** 6'2" **Wt:** 205 **Born:** 4/13/1986 **Age:** 28

| BATTING | | | | | | | | | | | | | | | | | | | | | | BASERUNNING | | | | AVERAGES | | |
|---|---|---|---|---|---|---|---|---|---|---|---|---|---|---|---|---|---|---|---|---|---|---|---|---|---|---|---|---|
| Year | Team | Lg | G | AB | H | 2B | 3B | HR | (Hm | Rd) | TB | R | RBI | RC | TBB | IBB | SO | HBP | SH | SF | SB | CS | SB% | GDP | Avg | OBP | Slg |
| 2010 | Mil | NL | 43 | 147 | 45 | 11 | 1 | 1 | (1 | 0) | 61 | 17 | 13 | 23 | 9 | 0 | 28 | 1 | 0 | 1 | 7 | 1 | .88 | 1 | .306 | .348 | .415 |
| 2011 | KC | AL | 6 | 22 | 6 | 1 | 0 | 0 | (0 | 0) | 7 | 4 | 1 | 2 | 1 | 0 | 4 | 0 | 0 | 0 | 0 | 0 | - | 0 | .273 | .304 | .318 |
| 2012 | KC | AL | 61 | 222 | 59 | 9 | 2 | 7 | (3 | 4) | 93 | 27 | 31 | 32 | 15 | 0 | 56 | 3 | 0 | 4 | 10 | 0 | 1.00 | 4 | .266 | .316 | .419 |
| 2013 | KC | AL | 115 | 399 | 100 | 21 | 3 | 4 | (3 | 1) | 139 | 54 | 46 | 46 | 33 | 2 | 90 | 4 | 0 | 6 | 14 | 6 | .70 | 10 | .251 | .310 | .348 |
| 4 ML YEARS | | | 225 | 790 | 210 | 42 | 6 | 12 | (7 | 5) | 300 | 102 | 91 | 103 | 58 | 2 | 178 | 8 | 0 | 11 | 31 | 7 | .82 | 15 | .266 | .318 | .380 |

## Matt Cain

**Pitches:** R **Bats:** R **Pos:** SP-30 **Ht:** 6'3" **Wt:** 230 **Born:** 10/1/1984 **Age:** 29

| HOW MUCH HE PITCHED | | | | | | | | | WHAT HE GAVE UP | | | | | | | | | | | | THE RESULTS | | | | | | | |
|---|---|---|---|---|---|---|---|---|---|---|---|---|---|---|---|---|---|---|---|---|---|---|---|---|---|---|---|---|
| Year | Team | Lg | G | GS | CG | GF | IP | BFP | H | R | ER | HR | SH | SF | HB | TBB | IBB | SO | WP | Bk | W | L | Pct | Sh | Sv-Op | Hld | ERC | ERA |
| 2005 | SF | NL | 7 | 7 | 1 | 0 | 46.1 | 181 | 24 | 12 | 12 | 4 | 2 | 1 | 0 | 19 | 1 | 30 | 1 | 0 | 2 | 1 | .667 | 0 | 0-0 | 0 | 1.61 | 2.33 |
| 2006 | SF | NL | 32 | 31 | 1 | 1 | 190.2 | 818 | 157 | 93 | 88 | 18 | 11 | 6 | 6 | 87 | 1 | 179 | 9 | 2 | 13 | 12 | .520 | 1 | 0-0 | 0 | 3.35 | 4.15 |
| 2007 | SF | NL | 32 | 32 | 1 | 0 | 200.0 | 832 | 173 | 84 | 81 | 14 | 8 | 5 | 5 | 79 | 3 | 163 | **12** | 0 | 7 | 16 | .304 | 0 | 0-0 | 0 | 3.23 | 3.65 |
| 2008 | SF | NL | 34 | **34** | 1 | 0 | 217.2 | 933 | 206 | 95 | 91 | 19 | 7 | 7 | 7 | 91 | 9 | 186 | 7 | 2 | 8 | 14 | .364 | 1 | 0-0 | 0 | 3.84 | 3.76 |
| 2009 | SF | NL | 33 | 33 | **4** | 0 | 217.2 | 886 | 184 | 73 | 70 | 22 | 10 | 6 | 3 | 73 | 6 | 171 | 9 | 0 | 14 | 8 | .636 | 0 | 0-0 | 0 | 3.06 | 2.89 |
| 2010 | SF | NL | 33 | 33 | 4 | 0 | 223.1 | 896 | 181 | 84 | 78 | 22 | 6 | 7 | 4 | 61 | 4 | 177 | 8 | 0 | 13 | 11 | .542 | 2 | 0-0 | 0 | 2.65 | 3.14 |
| 2011 | SF | NL | 33 | 33 | 1 | 0 | 221.2 | 907 | 177 | 82 | 71 | 9 | 11 | 6 | 9 | 63 | 5 | 179 | 4 | 0 | 12 | 11 | .522 | 0 | 0-0 | 0 | 2.31 | 2.88 |
| 2012 | SF | NL | 32 | 32 | 2 | 0 | 219.1 | 876 | 177 | 73 | 68 | 21 | 11 | 9 | 9 | 51 | 1 | 193 | 8 | 0 | 16 | 5 | .762 | 2 | 0-0 | 0 | 2.57 | 2.79 |
| 2013 | SF | NL | 30 | 30 | 0 | 0 | 184.1 | 760 | 158 | 85 | 82 | 23 | 6 | 2 | 5 | 55 | 3 | 158 | 1 | 0 | 8 | 10 | .444 | 0 | 0-0 | 0 | 3.15 | 4.00 |
| Postseason | | | 8 | 8 | 0 | 0 | 51.1 | 210 | 40 | 13 | 12 | 6 | 1 | 0 | 6 | 14 | 2 | 33 | 1 | 0 | 4 | 2 | .667 | 0 | 0-0 | 0 | 2.92 | 2.10 |
| 9 ML YEARS | | | 266 | 265 | 15 | 1 | 1721.0 | 7089 | 1437 | 681 | 641 | 152 | 72 | 49 | 48 | 579 | 33 | 1436 | 59 | 4 | 93 | 88 | .514 | 6 | 0-0 | 0 | 2.96 | 3.35 |

## Kole Calhoun

**Bats:** L **Throws:** L **Pos:** RF-54;1B-6;PH-4;PR-1 **Ht:** 5'10" **Wt:** 190 **Born:** 10/14/1987 **Age:** 26

| BATTING | | | | | | | | | | | | | | | | | | | | | | BASERUNNING | | | | AVERAGES | | |
|---|---|---|---|---|---|---|---|---|---|---|---|---|---|---|---|---|---|---|---|---|---|---|---|---|---|---|---|---|
| Year | Team | Lg | G | AB | H | 2B | 3B | HR | (Hm | Rd) | TB | R | RBI | RC | TBB | IBB | SO | HBP | SH | SF | SB | CS | SB% | GDP | Avg | OBP | Slg |
| 2010 | Orem | R+ | 56 | 202 | 59 | 14 | 4 | 7 | (- | -) | 102 | 43 | 42 | 44 | 39 | 1 | 45 | 3 | 1 | 2 | 3 | 1 | .75 | 3 | .292 | .411 | .505 |
| 2011 | InldEm | A+ | 133 | 512 | 166 | 36 | 6 | 22 | (- | -) | 280 | 94 | 99 | 114 | 73 | 3 | 96 | 4 | 1 | 4 | 20 | 10 | .67 | 10 | .324 | .410 | .547 |
| 2012 | Salt Lk | AAA | 105 | 410 | 122 | 30 | 7 | 14 | (- | -) | 208 | 79 | 73 | 79 | 44 | 0 | 88 | 5 | 0 | 4 | 12 | 3 | .80 | 9 | .298 | .369 | .507 |
| 2013 | Salt Lk | AAA | 59 | 240 | 85 | 15 | 6 | 12 | (- | -) | 148 | 48 | 49 | 61 | 32 | 1 | 32 | 1 | 0 | 1 | 10 | 2 | .83 | 3 | .354 | .431 | .617 |
| 2012 | LAA | AL | 21 | 23 | 4 | 1 | 0 | 0 | (0 | 0) | 5 | 2 | 1 | 0 | 2 | 1 | 6 | 0 | 0 | 0 | 1 | 0 | 1.00 | 0 | .174 | .240 | .217 |
| 2013 | LAA | AL | 58 | 195 | 55 | 7 | 2 | 8 | (5 | 3) | 90 | 29 | 32 | 33 | 21 | 0 | 41 | 1 | 0 | 5 | 2 | 2 | .50 | 6 | .282 | .347 | .462 |
| 2 ML YEARS | | | 79 | 218 | 59 | 8 | 2 | 8 | (5 | 3) | 95 | 31 | 33 | 33 | 23 | 1 | 47 | 1 | 0 | 5 | 3 | 2 | .60 | 6 | .271 | .336 | .436 |

## Alberto Callaspo

**Bats:** B **Throws:** R **Pos:** 3B-93;2B-33;DH-10;PH-9 ky-AHS-po **Ht:** 5'9" **Wt:** 225 **Born:** 4/19/1983 **Age:** 31

| BATTING | | | | | | | | | | | | | | | | | | | | | | BASERUNNING | | | | AVERAGES | | |
|---|---|---|---|---|---|---|---|---|---|---|---|---|---|---|---|---|---|---|---|---|---|---|---|---|---|---|---|---|
| Year | Team | Lg | G | AB | H | 2B | 3B | HR | (Hm | Rd) | TB | R | RBI | RC | TBB | IBB | SO | HBP | SH | SF | SB | CS | SB% | GDP | Avg | OBP | Slg |
| 2013 | InldEm* | A+ | 3 | 7 | 2 | 0 | 0 | 1 | (- | -) | 5 | 1 | 3 | 2 | 2 | 0 | 1 | 0 | 0 | 1 | 0 | 0 | - | 0 | .286 | .400 | .714 |
| 2006 | Ari | NL | 23 | 42 | 10 | 1 | 1 | 0 | (0 | 0) | 13 | 2 | 6 | 5 | 4 | 0 | 6 | 0 | 0 | 1 | 0 | 1 | .00 | 0 | .238 | .298 | .310 |
| 2007 | Ari | NL | 56 | 144 | 31 | 8 | 0 | 0 | (0 | 0) | 39 | 10 | 7 | 7 | 9 | 0 | 14 | 1 | 1 | 1 | 1 | 1 | .50 | 8 | .215 | .265 | .271 |
| 2008 | KC | AL | 74 | 213 | 65 | 8 | 3 | 0 | (0 | 0) | 79 | 21 | 16 | 25 | 19 | 0 | 14 | 0 | 1 | 1 | 2 | 1 | .67 | 6 | .305 | .361 | .371 |
| 2009 | KC | AL | 155 | 576 | 173 | 41 | 8 | 11 | (6 | 5) | 263 | 79 | 73 | 90 | 52 | 4 | 51 | 1 | 0 | 5 | 2 | 1 | .67 | 15 | .300 | .356 | .457 |
| 2010 | 2 Tms | AL | 146 | 562 | 149 | 27 | 2 | 10 | (2 | 8) | 210 | 61 | 56 | 54 | 31 | 3 | 42 | 1 | 1 | 6 | 5 | 3 | .63 | 22 | .265 | .302 | .374 |
| 2011 | LAA | AL | 141 | 475 | 137 | 23 | 0 | 6 | (1 | 5) | 178 | 54 | 46 | 66 | 58 | 8 | 48 | 1 | 0 | 2 | 8 | 1 | .89 | 11 | .288 | .366 | .375 |
| 2012 | LAA | AL | 138 | 457 | 115 | 20 | 0 | 10 | (3 | 7) | 165 | 55 | 53 | 60 | 56 | 1 | 59 | 0 | 3 | 4 | 4 | 3 | .57 | 6 | .252 | .331 | .361 |
| 2013 | 2 Tms | AL | 136 | 453 | 117 | 20 | 0 | 10 | (5 | 5) | 167 | 52 | 58 | 60 | 53 | 2 | 47 | 1 | 3 | 6 | 0 | 2 | .00 | 12 | .258 | .333 | .369 |
| 10 | KC | AL | 88 | 349 | 96 | 19 | 2 | 8 | (2 | 6) | 143 | 40 | 43 | 38 | 19 | 2 | 29 | 0 | 0 | 5 | 3 | 1 | .75 | 14 | .275 | .308 | .410 |
| 10 | LAA | AL | 58 | 213 | 53 | 8 | 0 | 2 | (0 | 2) | 67 | 21 | 13 | 16 | 12 | 1 | 13 | 1 | 1 | 1 | 2 | 2 | .50 | 8 | .249 | .291 | .315 |
| 13 | LAA | AL | 86 | 294 | 74 | 13 | 0 | 5 | (2 | 3) | 102 | 32 | 36 | 37 | 34 | 2 | 22 | 0 | 3 | 5 | 0 | 2 | .00 | 8 | .252 | .324 | .347 |
| 13 | Oak | AL | 50 | 159 | 43 | 7 | 0 | 5 | (3 | 2) | 65 | 20 | 22 | 23 | 19 | 0 | 25 | 1 | 0 | 1 | 0 | 0 | - | 4 | .270 | .350 | .409 |
| Postseason | | | 2 | 2 | 0 | 0 | 0 | 0 | (0 | 0) | 0 | 0 | 0 | 0 | 0 | 0 | 0 | 0 | 0 | 0 | 0 | 0 | - | 0 | .000 | .000 | .000 |
| 8 ML YEARS | | | 869 | 2922 | 797 | 148 | 14 | 47 | (17 | 30) | 1114 | 334 | 315 | 367 | 282 | 18 | 281 | 5 | 9 | 26 | 22 | 13 | .63 | 80 | .273 | .335 | .381 |

# Arquimedes Caminero

**Pitches:** R **Bats:** R **Pos:** RP-13 ahr-keh-MEE-deez **Ht:** 6'4" **Wt:** 255 **Born:** 6/16/1987 **Age:** 27

| | | | HOW MUCH HE PITCHED | | | | | | WHAT HE GAVE UP | | | | | | | | | | | | THE RESULTS | | | | | | | |
|---|---|---|---|---|---|---|---|---|---|---|---|---|---|---|---|---|---|---|---|---|---|---|---|---|---|---|---|---|
| Year | Team | Lg | G | GS | CG | GF | IP | BFP | H | R | ER | HR | SH | SF | HB | TBB | IBB | SO | WP | Bk | W | L | Pct | Sh | Sv-Op | Hld | ERC | ERA |
| 2009 | Jupiter | A+ | 2 | 0 | 0 | 1 | 2.1 | 17 | 7 | 8 | 8 | 3 | 0 | 0 | 1 | 2 | 0 | 2 | 0 | 0 | 0 | 0 | - | 0 | 0-- | - | 37.62 | 30.86 |
| 2009 | Jmstwn | A- | 15 | 0 | 0 | 2 | 24.0 | 108 | 19 | 9 | 8 | 1 | 1 | 1 | 3 | 16 | 3 | 42 | 5 | 1 | 3 | 1 | .750 | 0 | 0-- | - | 3.74 | 3.00 |
| 2009 | Grnsbr | A | 10 | 0 | 0 | 3 | 14.1 | 70 | 16 | 14 | 9 | 1 | 0 | 1 | 3 | 8 | 0 | 17 | 6 | 0 | 0 | 0 | - | 0 | 0-- | - | 5.85 | 5.65 |
| 2010 | Grnsbr | A | 48 | 0 | 0 | 22 | 74.2 | 322 | 55 | 34 | 25 | 4 | 3 | 3 | 7 | 34 | 2 | 97 | 14 | 1 | 5 | 2 | .714 | 0 | 3-- | - | 2.78 | 3.01 |
| 2011 | Mrlns | R | 1 | 0 | 0 | 0 | 1.0 | 6 | 2 | 1 | 1 | 0 | 0 | 0 | 0 | 1 | 0 | 2 | 0 | 0 | 0 | 0 | - | 0 | 0-- | - | 12.01 | 9.00 |
| 2012 | Jupiter | A+ | 19 | 0 | 0 | 5 | 20.2 | 87 | 12 | 2 | 1 | 0 | 0 | 0 | 3 | 9 | 0 | 27 | 1 | 0 | 1 | 0 | 1.000 | 0 | 1-- | - | 1.86 | 0.44 |
| 2012 | Jaxnvl | AA | 12 | 0 | 0 | 5 | 17.2 | 77 | 16 | 6 | 6 | 0 | 1 | 0 | 0 | 10 | 0 | 17 | 3 | 0 | 0 | 0 | - | 0 | 2-- | - | 3.48 | 3.06 |
| 2013 | Jaxnvl | AA | 42 | 0 | 0 | 11 | 52.1 | 211 | 34 | 23 | 21 | 4 | 1 | 0 | 3 | 21 | 0 | 68 | 1 | 0 | 5 | 2 | .714 | 0 | 5-- | - | 2.33 | 3.61 |
| 2013 | NewOr | AAA | 1 | 0 | 0 | 0 | 2.0 | 6 | 0 | 0 | 0 | 0 | 0 | 0 | 0 | 0 | 0 | 1 | 0 | 0 | 1 | 0 | 1.000 | 0 | 0-- | - | 0.00 | 0.00 |
| 2013 | Mia | NL | 13 | 0 | 0 | 6 | 13.0 | 52 | 10 | 4 | 4 | 2 | 0 | 0 | 1 | 3 | 0 | 12 | 1 | 0 | 0 | 0 | - | 0 | 0-1 | 1 | 2.85 | 2.77 |

# Shawn Camp

**Pitches:** R **Bats:** R **Pos:** RP-26 **Ht:** 6'0" **Wt:** 205 **Born:** 11/18/1975 **Age:** 38

| | | | HOW MUCH HE PITCHED | | | | | | WHAT HE GAVE UP | | | | | | | | | | | | THE RESULTS | | | | | | | |
|---|---|---|---|---|---|---|---|---|---|---|---|---|---|---|---|---|---|---|---|---|---|---|---|---|---|---|---|---|
| Year | Team | Lg | G | GS | CG | GF | IP | BFP | H | R | ER | HR | SH | SF | HB | TBB | IBB | SO | WP | Bk | W | L | Pct | Sh | Sv-Op | Hld | ERC | ERA |
| 2013 | Kane* | A | 2 | 0 | 0 | 1 | 3.0 | 13 | 2 | 0 | 0 | 0 | 0 | 0 | 1 | 0 | 0 | 4 | 1 | 0 | 0 | 0 | - | 0 | 0-- | - | 1.45 | 0.00 |
| 2013 | Reno* | AAA | 17 | 0 | 0 | 7 | 22.1 | 91 | 22 | 6 | 6 | 2 | 0 | 1 | 0 | 5 | 0 | 19 | 1 | 0 | 0 | 0 | - | 0 | 0-- | - | 3.30 | 2.42 |
| 2004 | KC | AL | 42 | 0 | 0 | 12 | 66.2 | 286 | 74 | 37 | 29 | 10 | 2 | 3 | 5 | 16 | 1 | 51 | 2 | 1 | 2 | 2 | .500 | 0 | 2-3 | 5 | 4.74 | 3.92 |
| 2005 | KC | AL | 29 | 0 | 0 | 7 | 49.0 | 228 | 69 | 40 | 35 | 4 | 0 | 3 | 4 | 13 | 3 | 28 | 3 | 0 | 1 | 4 | .200 | 0 | 0-2 | 0 | 6.00 | 6.43 |
| 2006 | TB | AL | 75 | 0 | 0 | 15 | 75.0 | 328 | 93 | 43 | 39 | 9 | 2 | 3 | 7 | 19 | 3 | 53 | 4 | 0 | 7 | 4 | .636 | 0 | 4-6 | 12 | 5.48 | 4.68 |
| 2007 | TB | AL | 50 | 0 | 0 | 8 | 40.0 | 198 | 63 | 33 | 32 | 7 | 5 | 1 | 3 | 18 | 6 | 36 | 2 | 0 | 0 | 3 | .000 | 0 | 0-2 | 11 | 8.59 | 7.20 |
| 2008 | Tor | AL | 40 | 0 | 0 | 16 | 39.1 | 166 | 40 | 18 | 18 | 2 | 0 | 1 | 2 | 11 | 3 | 31 | 0 | 0 | 3 | 1 | .750 | 0 | 0-0 | 7 | 3.47 | 4.12 |
| 2009 | Tor | AL | 59 | 0 | 0 | 17 | 79.2 | 333 | 73 | 36 | 31 | 7 | 1 | 1 | 4 | 29 | 4 | 58 | 0 | 0 | 2 | 6 | .250 | 0 | 1-1 | 6 | 3.57 | 3.50 |
| 2010 | Tor | AL | 70 | 0 | 0 | 13 | 72.1 | 298 | 71 | 26 | 24 | 8 | 0 | 2 | 4 | 18 | 5 | 46 | 2 | 0 | 4 | 3 | .571 | 0 | 2-4 | 13 | 3.65 | 2.99 |
| 2011 | Tor | AL | 67 | 0 | 0 | 23 | 66.1 | 292 | 79 | 36 | 31 | 3 | 2 | 1 | 6 | 22 | **9** | 32 | 0 | 0 | 6 | 3 | .667 | 0 | 1-4 | 5 | 4.72 | 4.21 |
| 2012 | ChC | NL | **80** | 0 | 0 | 21 | 77.2 | 327 | 79 | 32 | 31 | 7 | 1 | 2 | 0 | 21 | 4 | 54 | 1 | 0 | 3 | 6 | .333 | 0 | 2-6 | 18 | 3.51 | 3.59 |
| 2013 | ChC | NL | 26 | 0 | 0 | 8 | 23.0 | 108 | 34 | 18 | 18 | 7 | 2 | 3 | 0 | 9 | 2 | 13 | 0 | 2 | 1 | 1 | .500 | 0 | 0-3 | 4 | 8.63 | 7.04 |
| 10 ML YEARS | | | 538 | 0 | 0 | 140 | 589.0 | 2564 | 675 | 319 | 288 | 64 | 15 | 20 | 35 | 176 | 40 | 402 | 14 | 3 | 29 | 33 | .468 | 0 | 12-31 | 81 | 4.75 | 4.40 |

# Tony Campana

**Bats:** L **Throws:** L **Pos:** PH-15;CF-8;PR-7;LF-2 camm-PAH-nah **Ht:** 5'8" **Wt:** 165 **Born:** 5/30/1986 **Age:** 28

| | | | BATTING | | | | | | | | | | | | | | | | | BASERUNNING | | | | AVERAGES | | |
|---|---|---|---|---|---|---|---|---|---|---|---|---|---|---|---|---|---|---|---|---|---|---|---|---|---|---|
| Year | Team | Lg | G | AB | H | 2B | 3B | HR | (Hm | Rd) | TB | R | RBI | RC | TBB | IBB | SO | HBP | SH | SF | SB | CS | SB% | GDP | Avg | OBP | Slg |
| 2013 | Reno* | AAA | 102 | 351 | 103 | 11 | 6 | 1 | (- | -) | 129 | 65 | 29 | 51 | 34 | 1 | 77 | 0 | 4 | 2 | 32 | 8 | .80 | 2 | .293 | .354 | .368 |
| 2011 | ChC | NL | 95 | 143 | 37 | 3 | 0 | 1 | (1 | 0) | 43 | 24 | 6 | 17 | 8 | 1 | 30 | 1 | 3 | 0 | 24 | 2 | **.92** | 1 | .259 | .303 | .301 |
| 2012 | ChC | NL | 89 | 174 | 46 | 6 | 0 | 0 | (0 | 0) | 52 | 26 | 5 | 20 | 11 | 0 | 43 | 0 | 7 | 0 | 30 | 3 | .91 | 0 | .264 | .308 | .299 |
| 2013 | Ari | NL | 29 | 46 | 12 | 0 | 1 | 0 | (0 | 0) | 14 | 10 | 0 | 6 | 8 | 0 | 14 | 0 | 0 | 0 | 8 | 2 | .80 | 0 | .261 | .370 | .304 |
| 3 ML YEARS | | | 213 | 363 | 95 | 9 | 1 | 1 | (1 | 0) | 109 | 60 | 11 | 43 | 27 | 1 | 87 | 1 | 10 | 0 | 62 | 7 | .90 | 1 | .262 | .315 | .300 |

# Robinson Cano

**Bats:** L **Throws:** R **Pos:** 2B-153;DH-6;SS-1 kuh-NOE **Ht:** 6'0" **Wt:** 210 **Born:** 10/22/1982 **Age:** 31

| | | | BATTING | | | | | | | | | | | | | | | | | BASERUNNING | | | | AVERAGES | | |
|---|---|---|---|---|---|---|---|---|---|---|---|---|---|---|---|---|---|---|---|---|---|---|---|---|---|---|
| Year | Team | Lg | G | AB | H | 2B | 3B | HR | (Hm | Rd) | TB | R | RBI | RC | TBB | IBB | SO | HBP | SH | SF | SB | CS | SB% | GDP | Avg | OBP | Slg |
| 2005 | NYY | AL | 132 | 522 | 155 | 34 | 4 | 14 | (5 | 9) | 239 | 78 | 62 | 59 | 16 | 1 | 68 | 3 | 7 | 3 | 1 | 3 | .25 | 16 | .297 | .320 | .458 |
| 2006 | NYY | AL | 122 | 482 | 165 | 41 | 1 | 15 | (9 | 6) | 253 | 62 | 78 | 74 | 18 | 3 | 54 | 2 | 1 | 5 | 5 | 2 | .71 | 19 | .342 | .365 | .525 |
| 2007 | NYY | AL | 160 | 617 | 189 | 41 | 7 | 19 | (10 | 9) | 301 | 93 | 97 | 94 | 39 | 5 | 85 | 8 | 1 | 4 | 4 | 5 | .44 | 19 | .306 | .353 | .488 |
| 2008 | NYY | AL | 159 | 597 | 162 | 35 | 3 | 14 | (7 | 7) | 245 | 70 | 72 | 64 | 26 | 3 | 65 | 5 | 1 | 5 | 2 | 4 | .33 | 18 | .271 | .305 | .410 |
| 2009 | NYY | AL | **161** | 637 | 204 | 48 | 2 | 25 | (14 | 11) | 331 | 103 | 85 | 79 | 30 | 2 | 63 | 3 | 0 | 4 | 5 | 7 | .42 | 22 | .320 | .352 | .520 |
| 2010 | NYY | AL | 160 | 626 | 200 | 41 | 3 | 29 | (16 | 13) | 334 | 103 | 109 | 118 | 57 | 14 | 77 | 8 | 0 | 5 | 3 | 2 | .60 | 19 | .319 | .381 | .534 |
| 2011 | NYY | AL | 159 | 623 | 188 | 46 | 7 | 28 | (16 | 12) | 332 | 104 | 118 | 111 | 38 | 11 | 96 | 12 | 0 | 8 | 8 | 2 | .80 | 18 | .302 | .349 | .533 |
| 2012 | NYY | AL | 161 | 627 | 196 | 48 | 1 | 33 | (22 | 11) | 345 | 105 | 94 | 110 | 61 | 10 | 96 | 7 | 0 | 2 | 3 | 2 | .60 | 22 | .313 | .379 | .550 |
| 2013 | NYY | AL | 160 | 605 | 190 | 41 | 0 | 27 | (11 | 16) | 312 | 81 | 107 | 120 | 65 | 16 | 85 | 6 | 0 | 5 | 7 | 1 | .88 | 18 | .314 | .383 | .516 |
| Postseason | | | 51 | 203 | 45 | 10 | 3 | 8 | (5 | 3) | 85 | 22 | 33 | 23 | 11 | 3 | 28 | 2 | 0 | 1 | 0 | 2 | .00 | 7 | .222 | .267 | .419 |
| 9 ML YEARS | | | 1374 | 5336 | 1649 | 375 | 28 | 204 | (110 | 94) | 2692 | 799 | 822 | 829 | 350 | 65 | 689 | 54 | 10 | 41 | 38 | 28 | .58 | 171 | .309 | .355 | .504 |

# Carter Capps

**Pitches:** R **Bats:** R **Pos:** RP-53 **Ht:** 6'5" **Wt:** 220 **Born:** 8/7/1990 **Age:** 23

| | | | HOW MUCH HE PITCHED | | | | | | WHAT HE GAVE UP | | | | | | | | | | | | THE RESULTS | | | | | | | |
|---|---|---|---|---|---|---|---|---|---|---|---|---|---|---|---|---|---|---|---|---|---|---|---|---|---|---|---|---|
| Year | Team | Lg | G | GS | CG | GF | IP | BFP | H | R | ER | HR | SH | SF | HB | TBB | IBB | SO | WP | Bk | W | L | Pct | Sh | Sv-Op | Hld | ERC | ERA |
| 2011 | Clinton | A | 4 | 4 | 0 | 0 | 18.0 | 81 | 19 | 12 | 12 | 1 | 0 | 2 | 2 | 10 | 0 | 21 | 1 | 0 | 1 | 1 | .500 | 0 | 0-- | - | 5.25 | 6.00 |
| 2012 | Jacksn | AA | 38 | 0 | 0 | 31 | 50.0 | 203 | 40 | 8 | 7 | 2 | 1 | 0 | 1 | 12 | 0 | 72 | 1 | 0 | 2 | 3 | .400 | 0 | 19-- | - | 2.11 | 1.26 |
| 2012 | Tacom | AAA | 1 | 0 | 0 | 0 | 1.1 | 4 | 0 | 0 | 0 | 0 | 0 | 0 | 0 | 0 | 0 | 3 | 0 | 0 | 0 | 0 | - | 0 | 0-- | - | 0.00 | 0.00 |
| 2013 | Tacom | AAA | 7 | 0 | 0 | 3 | 11.0 | 44 | 6 | 3 | 2 | 0 | 0 | 1 | 3 | 4 | 0 | 9 | 1 | 0 | 0 | 0 | - | 0 | 0-- | - | 2.01 | 1.64 |
| 2012 | Sea | AL | 18 | 0 | 0 | 2 | 25.0 | 109 | 25 | 11 | 11 | 0 | 1 | 1 | 0 | 11 | 0 | 28 | 1 | 0 | 0 | 0 | - | 0 | 0-0 | 2 | 3.49 | 3.96 |
| 2013 | Sea | AL | 53 | 0 | 0 | 11 | 59.0 | 270 | 73 | 37 | 36 | 12 | 2 | 1 | 2 | 23 | 4 | 66 | 5 | 0 | 3 | 3 | .500 | 0 | 0-2 | 9 | 6.23 | 5.49 |
| 2 ML YEARS | | | 71 | 0 | 0 | 13 | 84.0 | 379 | 98 | 48 | 47 | 12 | 3 | 2 | 2 | 34 | 4 | 94 | 6 | 0 | 3 | 3 | .500 | 0 | 0-2 | 11 | 5.38 | 5.04 |

# Chris Capuano

**Pitches:** L **Bats:** L **Pos:** SP-20; RP-4 capp-ue-AHH-noe **Ht:** 6'3" **Wt:** 215 **Born:** 8/19/1978 **Age:** 35

| HOW MUCH HE PITCHED | | | | | | | | | WHAT HE GAVE UP | | | | | | | | | | | | THE RESULTS | | | | | | | |
|---|---|---|---|---|---|---|---|---|---|---|---|---|---|---|---|---|---|---|---|---|---|---|---|---|---|---|---|---|
| Year | Team | Lg | G | GS | CG | GF | IP | BFP | H | R | ER | HR | SH | SF | HB | TBB | IBB | SO | WP | Bk | W | L | Pct | Sh | Sv-Op | Hld | ERC | ERA |
| 2013 | Albq* | AAA | 2 | 2 | 0 | 0 | 9.1 | 38 | 8 | 2 | 2 | 0 | 0 | 0 | 0 | 3 | 0 | 9 | 1 | 0 | 0 | 0 | - | 0 | 0- - | - | 2.40 | 1.93 |
| 2003 | Ari | NL | 9 | 5 | 0 | 2 | 33.0 | 139 | 27 | 19 | 17 | 3 | 4 | 1 | 6 | 11 | 1 | 23 | 3 | 0 | 2 | 4 | .333 | 0 | 0-0 | 1 | 3.45 | 4.64 |
| 2004 | Mil | NL | 17 | 17 | 0 | 0 | 88.1 | 385 | 91 | 55 | 49 | 18 | 4 | 1 | 5 | 37 | 1 | 80 | 3 | 1 | 6 | 8 | .429 | 0 | 0-0 | 0 | 5.37 | 4.99 |
| 2005 | Mil | NL | 35 | **35** | 0 | 0 | 219.0 | 949 | 212 | 105 | 97 | 31 | 14 | 5 | 12 | 91 | 6 | 176 | 3 | **4** | 18 | 12 | .600 | 0 | 0-0 | 0 | 4.44 | 3.99 |
| 2006 | Mil | NL | 34 | 34 | 3 | 0 | 221.1 | 936 | 229 | 108 | 99 | 29 | 9 | 8 | 9 | 47 | 4 | 174 | 7 | 0 | 11 | 12 | .478 | 2 | 0-0 | 0 | 3.84 | 4.03 |
| 2007 | Mil | NL | 29 | 25 | 0 | 0 | 150.0 | 669 | 170 | 93 | 85 | 20 | 10 | 3 | 8 | 54 | 2 | 132 | 10 | 0 | 5 | 12 | .294 | 0 | 0-0 | 0 | 5.11 | 5.10 |
| 2010 | Mil | NL | 24 | 9 | 0 | 5 | 66.0 | 278 | 65 | 29 | 29 | 9 | 3 | 2 | 1 | 21 | 1 | 54 | 5 | 0 | 4 | 4 | .500 | 0 | 0-0 | 1 | 3.98 | 3.95 |
| 2011 | NYM | NL | 33 | 31 | 1 | 0 | 186.0 | 802 | 198 | 99 | 94 | 27 | 9 | 1 | 5 | 53 | 5 | 168 | 4 | 0 | 11 | 12 | .478 | 1 | 0-0 | 1 | 4.33 | 4.55 |
| 2012 | LAD | NL | 33 | **33** | 0 | 0 | 198.1 | 817 | 188 | 91 | 82 | 25 | 16 | 4 | 2 | 54 | 4 | 162 | 6 | 0 | 12 | 12 | .500 | 0 | 0-0 | 0 | 3.51 | 3.72 |
| 2013 | LAD | NL | 24 | 20 | 0 | 0 | 105.2 | 457 | 125 | 57 | 50 | 11 | 6 | 3 | 0 | 24 | 5 | 81 | 5 | 0 | 4 | 7 | .364 | 0 | 0-1 | 0 | 4.36 | 4.26 |
| 9 ML YEARS | | | 238 | 209 | 4 | 7 | 1267.2 | 5432 | 1305 | 656 | 602 | 173 | 75 | 28 | 48 | 392 | 29 | 1050 | 46 | 5 | 73 | 83 | .468 | 3 | 0-1 | 3 | 4.25 | 4.27 |

# Mike Carp

**Bats:** L **Throws:** R **Pos:** LF-41;1B-29;PH-25;DH-4;RF-2;PR-1 **Ht:** 6'2" **Wt:** 210 **Born:** 6/30/1986 **Age:** 28

| BATTING | | | | | | | | | | | | | | | | | | | | BASERUNNING | | | | AVERAGES | | |
|---|---|---|---|---|---|---|---|---|---|---|---|---|---|---|---|---|---|---|---|---|---|---|---|---|---|---|
| Year | Team | Lg | G | AB | H | 2B | 3B | HR | (Hm | Rd) | TB | R | RBI | RC | TBB | IBB | SO | HBP | SH | SF | SB | CS | SB% | GDP | Avg | OBP | Slg |
| 2009 | Sea | AL | 21 | 54 | 17 | 3 | 1 | 1 | (1 | 0) | 25 | 7 | 5 | 8 | 8 | 0 | 10 | 2 | 0 | 1 | 0 | 0 | - | 1 | .315 | .415 | .463 |
| 2010 | Sea | AL | 14 | 37 | 7 | 2 | 0 | 0 | (0 | 0) | 9 | 1 | 0 | 2 | 4 | 0 | 8 | 0 | 0 | 0 | 0 | 0 | - | 0 | .189 | .268 | .243 |
| 2011 | Sea | AL | 79 | 290 | 80 | 17 | 1 | 12 | (5 | 7) | 135 | 27 | 46 | 39 | 19 | 0 | 81 | 3 | 0 | 1 | 0 | 2 | .00 | 10 | .276 | .326 | .466 |
| 2012 | Sea | AL | 59 | 164 | 35 | 6 | 0 | 5 | (2 | 3) | 56 | 17 | 20 | 15 | 21 | 1 | 46 | 3 | 0 | 1 | 1 | 0 | 1.00 | 7 | .213 | .312 | .341 |
| 2013 | Bos | AL | 86 | 216 | 64 | 18 | 2 | 9 | (4 | 5) | 113 | 34 | 43 | 40 | 22 | 0 | 67 | 2 | 0 | 3 | 1 | 0 | 1.00 | 3 | .296 | .362 | .523 |
| 5 ML YEARS | | | 259 | 761 | 203 | 46 | 4 | 27 | (12 | 15) | 338 | 86 | 114 | 104 | 74 | 1 | 212 | 10 | 0 | 6 | 2 | 2 | .50 | 21 | .267 | .337 | .444 |

# Chris Carpenter

**Pitches:** R **Bats:** R **Pos:** P **Ht:** 6'6" **Wt:** 230 **Born:** 4/27/1975 **Age:** 39

| HOW MUCH HE PITCHED | | | | | | | | | WHAT HE GAVE UP | | | | | | | | | | | | THE RESULTS | | | | | | | |
|---|---|---|---|---|---|---|---|---|---|---|---|---|---|---|---|---|---|---|---|---|---|---|---|---|---|---|---|---|
| Year | Team | Lg | G | GS | CG | GF | IP | BFP | H | R | ER | HR | SH | SF | HB | TBB | IBB | SO | WP | Bk | W | L | Pct | Sh | Sv-Op | Hld | ERC | ERA |
| 2013 | Sprgfld* | AA | 1 | 1 | 0 | 0 | 2.2 | 17 | 6 | 3 | 2 | 1 | 0 | 0 | 0 | 2 | 0 | 5 | 0 | 0 | 0 | 1 | .000 | 0 | 0- - | - | 15.74 | 6.75 |
| 2013 | Memp* | AAA | 1 | 1 | 0 | 0 | 3.1 | 19 | 9 | 4 | 4 | 0 | 0 | 0 | 0 | 2 | 0 | 2 | 0 | 0 | 0 | 1 | .000 | 0 | 0- - | - | 16.90 | 10.80 |
| 1997 | Tor | AL | 14 | 13 | 1 | 1 | 81.1 | 374 | 108 | 55 | 46 | 7 | 1 | 2 | 2 | 37 | 0 | 55 | 7 | 1 | 3 | 7 | .300 | 1 | 0-0 | 0 | 6.38 | 5.09 |
| 1998 | Tor | AL | 33 | 24 | 1 | 4 | 175.0 | 742 | 177 | 97 | 85 | 18 | 4 | 5 | 5 | 61 | 1 | 136 | 5 | 0 | 12 | 7 | .632 | 1 | 0-0 | 0 | 4.12 | 4.37 |
| 1999 | Tor | AL | 24 | 24 | 4 | 0 | 150.0 | 663 | 177 | 81 | 73 | 16 | 4 | 6 | 3 | 48 | 1 | 106 | 9 | 1 | 9 | 8 | .529 | 1 | 0-0 | 0 | 4.90 | 4.38 |
| 2000 | Tor | AL | 34 | 27 | 2 | 1 | 175.1 | 795 | 204 | **130** | **122** | 30 | 3 | 1 | 5 | 83 | 1 | 113 | 3 | 0 | 10 | 12 | .455 | 0 | 0-0 | 0 | 6.04 | 6.26 |
| 2001 | Tor | AL | 34 | 34 | 3 | 0 | 215.2 | 930 | 229 | 112 | 98 | 29 | 3 | 1 | 16 | 75 | 5 | 157 | 5 | 0 | 11 | 11 | .500 | 2 | 0-0 | 0 | 4.82 | 4.09 |
| 2002 | Tor | AL | 13 | 13 | 1 | 0 | 73.1 | 327 | 89 | 45 | 43 | 11 | 1 | 4 | 4 | 27 | 0 | 45 | 3 | 0 | 4 | 5 | .444 | 0 | 0-0 | 0 | 5.91 | 5.28 |
| 2004 | StL | NL | 28 | 28 | 1 | 0 | 182.0 | 746 | 169 | 75 | 70 | 24 | 6 | 3 | 8 | 38 | 2 | 152 | 4 | 0 | 15 | 5 | .750 | 0 | 0-0 | 0 | 3.32 | 3.46 |
| 2005 | StL | NL | 33 | 33 | **7** | 0 | 241.2 | 953 | 204 | 82 | 76 | 18 | 7 | 7 | 3 | 51 | 0 | 213 | 5 | 0 | 21 | 5 | .808 | 4 | 0-0 | 0 | 2.49 | 2.83 |
| 2006 | StL | NL | 32 | 32 | 5 | 0 | 221.2 | 896 | 194 | 81 | 76 | 21 | 12 | 4 | 10 | 43 | 3 | 184 | 3 | 0 | 15 | 8 | .652 | **3** | 0-0 | 0 | **2.75** | 3.09 |
| 2007 | StL | NL | 1 | 1 | 0 | 0 | 6.0 | 29 | 9 | 5 | 5 | 0 | 1 | 0 | 1 | 1 | 0 | 3 | 0 | 0 | 0 | 1 | .000 | 0 | 0-0 | 0 | 5.80 | 7.50 |
| 2008 | StL | NL | 4 | 3 | 0 | 0 | 15.1 | 63 | 16 | 5 | 3 | 0 | 2 | 1 | 0 | 4 | 0 | 7 | 0 | 0 | 0 | 1 | .000 | 0 | 0-0 | 0 | 3.19 | 1.76 |
| 2009 | StL | NL | 28 | 28 | 3 | 0 | 192.2 | 750 | 156 | 49 | 48 | 7 | 10 | 4 | 7 | 38 | 1 | 144 | 1 | 0 | 17 | 4 | **.810** | 1 | 0-0 | 0 | **2.14** | **2.24** |
| 2010 | StL | NL | 35 | **35** | 1 | 0 | 235.0 | 969 | 214 | 99 | 84 | 21 | 9 | 7 | 13 | 63 | 4 | 179 | 3 | 0 | 16 | 9 | .640 | 0 | 0-0 | 0 | 3.23 | 3.22 |
| 2011 | StL | NL | 34 | **34** | 4 | 0 | **237.1** | **996** | 243 | 98 | 91 | 16 | 11 | 3 | 6 | 55 | 5 | 191 | 3 | 1 | 11 | 9 | .550 | 2 | 0-0 | 0 | 3.40 | 3.45 |
| 2012 | StL | NL | 3 | 3 | 0 | 0 | 17.0 | 72 | 16 | 7 | 7 | 2 | 1 | 0 | 2 | 3 | 0 | 12 | 0 | 0 | 0 | 2 | .000 | 0 | 0-0 | 0 | 3.39 | 3.71 |
| Postseason | | | 18 | 18 | 1 | 0 | 108.0 | 461 | 104 | 43 | 36 | 11 | 12 | 3 | 6 | 36 | 2 | 68 | 1 | 0 | 10 | 4 | .714 | 1 | 0-0 | 0 | 3.81 | 3.00 |
| 15 ML YEARS | | | 350 | 332 | 33 | 6 | 2219.1 | 9305 | 2205 | 1021 | 927 | 220 | 75 | 48 | 85 | 627 | 23 | 1697 | 51 | 3 | 144 | 94 | .605 | 15 | 0-0 | 0 | 3.74 | 3.76 |

# David Carpenter

**Pitches:** R **Bats:** R **Pos:** RP-56 **Ht:** 6'2" **Wt:** 215 **Born:** 7/15/1985 **Age:** 28

| HOW MUCH HE PITCHED | | | | | | | | | WHAT HE GAVE UP | | | | | | | | | | | | THE RESULTS | | | | | | | |
|---|---|---|---|---|---|---|---|---|---|---|---|---|---|---|---|---|---|---|---|---|---|---|---|---|---|---|---|---|
| Year | Team | Lg | G | GS | CG | GF | IP | BFP | H | R | ER | HR | SH | SF | HB | TBB | IBB | SO | WP | Bk | W | L | Pct | Sh | Sv-Op | Hld | ERC | ERA |
| 2013 | Gwnntt* | AAA | 6 | 0 | 0 | 1 | 15.1 | 64 | 17 | 6 | 6 | 1 | 0 | 2 | 1 | 4 | 0 | 11 | 1 | 0 | 1 | 2 | .333 | 0 | 0- - | - | 4.33 | 3.52 |
| 2011 | Hou | NL | 34 | 0 | 0 | 12 | 27.2 | 125 | 28 | 9 | 9 | 3 | 4 | 1 | 4 | 13 | 7 | 29 | 2 | 1 | 1 | 3 | .250 | 0 | 1-2 | 3 | 4.62 | 2.93 |
| 2012 | 2 Tms | | 33 | 0 | 0 | 9 | 32.1 | 163 | 51 | 31 | 29 | 5 | 2 | 0 | 2 | 16 | 4 | 31 | 2 | 0 | 0 | 2 | .000 | 0 | 0-1 | 2 | 8.52 | 8.07 |
| 2013 | Atl | NL | 56 | 0 | 0 | 14 | 65.2 | 256 | 45 | 13 | 13 | 5 | 2 | 4 | 3 | 20 | 3 | 74 | 4 | 0 | 4 | 1 | .800 | 0 | 0-0 | 12 | 2.12 | 1.78 |
| 12 | Hou | NL | 30 | 0 | 0 | 8 | 29.2 | 143 | 43 | 21 | 20 | 4 | 2 | 0 | 1 | 14 | 3 | 27 | 2 | 0 | 0 | 2 | .000 | 0 | 0-1 | 2 | 7.38 | 6.07 |
| 12 | Tor | AL | 3 | 0 | 0 | 1 | 2.2 | 20 | 8 | 10 | 9 | 1 | 0 | 0 | 1 | 2 | 1 | 4 | 0 | 0 | 0 | 0 | - | 0 | 0-0 | 0 | 22.64 | 30.38 |
| 3 ML YEARS | | | 123 | 0 | 0 | 35 | 125.2 | 544 | 124 | 53 | 51 | 13 | 8 | 5 | 9 | 49 | 14 | 134 | 8 | 1 | 5 | 6 | .455 | 0 | 1-3 | 17 | 4.11 | 3.65 |

# David Carpenter

**Pitches:** R **Bats:** R **Pos:** RP-1 **Ht:** 6'3" **Wt:** 180 **Born:** 9/1/1987 **Age:** 26

| HOW MUCH HE PITCHED | | | | | | | | | WHAT HE GAVE UP | | | | | | | | | | | | THE RESULTS | | | | | | | |
|---|---|---|---|---|---|---|---|---|---|---|---|---|---|---|---|---|---|---|---|---|---|---|---|---|---|---|---|---|
| Year | Team | Lg | G | GS | CG | GF | IP | BFP | H | R | ER | HR | SH | SF | HB | TBB | IBB | SO | WP | Bk | W | L | Pct | Sh | Sv-Op | Hld | ERC | ERA |
| 2009 | Orem | R+ | 25 | 0 | 0 | 16 | 34.1 | 142 | 26 | 12 | 9 | 2 | 1 | 0 | 1 | 11 | 1 | 42 | 2 | 1 | 2 | 2 | .500 | 0 | 8- - | - | 2.25 | 2.36 |
| 2010 | CRpds | A | 37 | 0 | 0 | 28 | 45.1 | 193 | 36 | 19 | 13 | 2 | 3 | 4 | 7 | 19 | 2 | 52 | 3 | 0 | 2 | 4 | .333 | 0 | 8- - | - | 3.17 | 2.58 |
| 2011 | InldEm | A+ | 25 | 0 | 0 | 18 | 29.0 | 118 | 23 | 6 | 3 | 1 | 2 | 1 | 1 | 9 | 2 | 36 | 1 | 0 | 0 | 1 | .000 | 0 | 11- - | - | 2.27 | 0.93 |
| 2011 | Ark | AA | 19 | 0 | 0 | 15 | 18.2 | 75 | 12 | 0 | 0 | 0 | 2 | 1 | 1 | 5 | 0 | 16 | 2 | 0 | 1 | 0 | 1.000 | 0 | 5- - | - | 1.45 | 0.00 |
| 2012 | Salt Lk | AAA | 15 | 0 | 0 | 6 | 19.2 | 77 | 10 | 6 | 6 | 2 | 0 | 1 | 1 | 8 | 0 | 14 | 1 | 0 | 0 | 0 | - | 0 | 1- - | - | 1.82 | 2.75 |
| 2013 | Salt Lk | AAA | 24 | 0 | 0 | 5 | 31.1 | 162 | 42 | 35 | 33 | 4 | 2 | 3 | 0 | 27 | 0 | 31 | 4 | 0 | 5 | 1 | .833 | 0 | 2- - | - | 8.22 | 9.48 |
| 2013 | Ark | AA | 29 | 0 | 0 | 14 | 29.1 | 116 | 20 | 13 | 11 | 1 | 2 | 0 | 3 | 8 | 2 | 21 | 0 | 0 | 0 | 2 | .000 | 0 | 5- - | - | 1.89 | 3.38 |
| 2012 | LAA | AL | 28 | 0 | 0 | 12 | 39.2 | 172 | 42 | 21 | 21 | 6 | 1 | 1 | 0 | 17 | 0 | 28 | 2 | 0 | 1 | 2 | .333 | 0 | 0-0 | 2 | 4.97 | 4.76 |
| 2013 | LAA | AL | 1 | 0 | 0 | 0 | 0.1 | 5 | 2 | 4 | 4 | 1 | 0 | 0 | 0 | 2 | 0 | 1 | 1 | 0 | 0 | 0 | - | 0 | 0-0 | 0 | 124.7 | 108.0 |
| 2 ML YEARS | | | 29 | 0 | 0 | 12 | 40.0 | 177 | 44 | 25 | 25 | 7 | 1 | 1 | 0 | 19 | 0 | 29 | 3 | 0 | 1 | 2 | .333 | 0 | 0-0 | 2 | 5.60 | 5.63 |

## Matt Carpenter

**Bats:** L **Throws:** R **Pos:** 2B-132;3B-42;PH-3;1B-2;RF-2 **Ht:** 6'3" **Wt:** 215 **Born:** 11/26/1985 **Age:** 28

| BATTING | | | | | | | | | | | | | | | | | | | | | BASERUNNING | | | | AVERAGES | | |
|---|---|---|---|---|---|---|---|---|---|---|---|---|---|---|---|---|---|---|---|---|---|---|---|---|---|---|---|
| Year | Team | Lg | G | AB | H | 2B | 3B | HR | (Hm | Rd) | TB | R | RBI | RC | TBB | IBB | SO | HBP | SH | SF | SB | CS | SB% | GDP | Avg | OBP | Slg |
| 2011 | StL | NL | 7 | 15 | 1 | 1 | 0 | 0 | (0 | 0) | 2 | 0 | 0 | 0 | 4 | 0 | 4 | 0 | 0 | 0 | 0 | 0 | - | 0 | .067 | .263 | .133 |
| 2012 | StL | NL | 114 | 296 | 87 | 22 | 5 | 6 | (3 | 3) | 137 | 44 | 46 | 46 | 34 | 2 | 63 | 3 | 0 | 7 | 1 | 1 | .50 | 10 | .294 | .365 | .463 |
| 2013 | StL | NL | 157 | 626 | **199** | **55** | 7 | 11 | (6 | 5) | 301 | **126** | 78 | 119 | 72 | 1 | 98 | 9 | 3 | 7 | 3 | 3 | .50 | 4 | .318 | .392 | .481 |
| Postseason | | | 9 | 14 | 4 | 1 | 0 | 1 | (1 | 0) | 8 | 3 | 3 | 4 | 3 | 0 | 5 | 0 | 0 | 0 | 0 | 0 | - | 0 | .286 | .412 | .571 |
| 3 ML YEARS | | | 278 | 937 | 287 | 78 | 12 | 17 | (9 | 8) | 440 | 170 | 124 | 165 | 110 | 3 | 165 | 12 | 3 | 14 | 4 | 4 | .50 | 14 | .306 | .381 | .470 |

## Carlos Carrasco

**Pitches:** R **Bats:** R **Pos:** RP-8; SP-7 **Ht:** 6'3" **Wt:** 210 **Born:** 3/21/1987 **Age:** 27

| HOW MUCH HE PITCHED | | | | | | | | | WHAT HE GAVE UP | | | | | | | | | | | | THE RESULTS | | | | | | | |
|---|---|---|---|---|---|---|---|---|---|---|---|---|---|---|---|---|---|---|---|---|---|---|---|---|---|---|---|---|
| Year | Team | Lg | G | GS | CG | GF | IP | BFP | H | R | ER | HR | SH | SF | HB | TBB | IBB | SO | WP | Bk | W | L | Pct | Sh | Sv-Op | Hld | ERC | ERA |
| 2013 | Clmbs* | AAA | 16 | 14 | 0 | 1 | 71.2 | 298 | 59 | 31 | 25 | 6 | 3 | 1 | 6 | 21 | 0 | 79 | 1 | 0 | 3 | 1 | .750 | 0 | 1-- | - | 2.91 | 3.14 |
| 2009 | Cle | AL | 5 | 5 | 0 | 0 | 22.1 | 112 | 40 | 23 | 22 | 6 | 0 | 1 | 0 | 11 | 1 | 11 | 0 | 1 | 0 | 4 | .000 | 0 | 0-0 | 0 | 11.36 | 8.87 |
| 2010 | Cle | AL | 7 | 7 | 1 | 0 | 44.2 | 188 | 47 | 20 | 19 | 6 | 2 | 1 | 1 | 14 | 1 | 38 | 1 | 0 | 2 | 2 | .500 | 0 | 0-0 | 0 | 4.42 | 3.83 |
| 2011 | Cle | AL | 21 | 21 | 1 | 0 | 124.2 | 536 | 130 | 68 | 64 | 15 | 3 | 7 | 4 | 40 | 3 | 85 | 3 | 0 | 8 | 9 | .471 | 0 | 0-0 | 0 | 4.24 | 4.62 |
| 2013 | Cle | AL | 15 | 7 | 0 | 5 | 46.2 | 218 | 64 | 36 | 35 | 4 | 2 | 3 | 1 | 18 | 2 | 30 | 2 | 0 | 1 | 4 | .200 | 0 | 0-0 | 0 | 6.11 | 6.75 |
| 4 ML YEARS | | | 48 | 40 | 2 | 5 | 238.1 | 1054 | 281 | 147 | 140 | 31 | 7 | 12 | 6 | 83 | 7 | 164 | 6 | 1 | 11 | 19 | .367 | 0 | 0-0 | 0 | 5.21 | 5.29 |

## Ezequiel Carrera

**Bats:** L **Throws:** L **Pos:** PH-7;RF-6;PR-2;LF-1;CF-1 ee-ZEEK-ee-ull **Ht:** 5'10" **Wt:** 185 **Born:** 6/11/1987 **Age:** 27

| BATTING | | | | | | | | | | | | | | | | | | | | | BASERUNNING | | | | AVERAGES | | |
|---|---|---|---|---|---|---|---|---|---|---|---|---|---|---|---|---|---|---|---|---|---|---|---|---|---|---|---|
| Year | Team | Lg | G | AB | H | 2B | 3B | HR | (Hm | Rd) | TB | R | RBI | RC | TBB | IBB | SO | HBP | SH | SF | SB | CS | SB% | GDP | Avg | OBP | Slg |
| 2013 | Clmbs* | AAA | 105 | 416 | 103 | 16 | 5 | 5 | (- | -) | 144 | 57 | 31 | 51 | 38 | 0 | 87 | 2 | 6 | 2 | 43 | 12 | .78 | 4 | .248 | .312 | .346 |
| 2011 | Cle | AL | 68 | 202 | 49 | 8 | 3 | 0 | (0 | 0) | 63 | 27 | 14 | 25 | 16 | 0 | 35 | 1 | 7 | 0 | 10 | 5 | .67 | 4 | .243 | .301 | .312 |
| 2012 | Cle | AL | 48 | 147 | 40 | 6 | 3 | 2 | (0 | 2) | 58 | 20 | 11 | 17 | 8 | 1 | 35 | 1 | 1 | 1 | 8 | 1 | .89 | 3 | .272 | .312 | .395 |
| 2013 | 2 Tms | | 15 | 17 | 3 | 0 | 0 | 0 | (0 | 0) | 3 | 3 | 1 | 1 | 1 | 0 | 5 | 2 | 1 | 0 | 0 | 0 | - | 1 | .176 | .300 | .176 |
| 13 | Phi | NL | 13 | 13 | 1 | 0 | 0 | 0 | (0 | 0) | 1 | 2 | 0 | 0 | 1 | 0 | 4 | 2 | 0 | 0 | 0 | 0 | - | 0 | .077 | .250 | .077 |
| 13 | Cle | AL | 2 | 4 | 2 | 0 | 0 | 0 | (0 | 0) | 2 | 1 | 1 | 1 | 0 | 0 | 1 | 0 | 1 | 0 | 0 | 0 | - | 1 | .500 | .500 | .500 |
| 3 ML YEARS | | | 131 | 366 | 92 | 14 | 6 | 2 | (0 | 2) | 124 | 50 | 26 | 43 | 25 | 1 | 75 | 4 | 9 | 1 | 18 | 6 | .75 | 8 | .251 | .306 | .339 |

## Jamey Carroll

**Bats:** R **Throws:** R **Pos:** 3B-47;2B-18;PR-6;PH-5;SS-3;DH-1 **Ht:** 5'11" **Wt:** 175 **Born:** 2/18/1974 **Age:** 40

| BATTING | | | | | | | | | | | | | | | | | | | | | BASERUNNING | | | | AVERAGES | | |
|---|---|---|---|---|---|---|---|---|---|---|---|---|---|---|---|---|---|---|---|---|---|---|---|---|---|---|---|
| Year | Team | Lg | G | AB | H | 2B | 3B | HR | (Hm | Rd) | TB | R | RBI | RC | TBB | IBB | SO | HBP | SH | SF | SB | CS | SB% | GDP | Avg | OBP | Slg |
| 2002 | Mon | NL | 16 | 71 | 22 | 5 | 3 | 1 | (1 | 0) | 36 | 16 | 6 | 12 | 4 | 0 | 12 | 0 | 4 | 0 | 1 | 0 | 1.00 | 1 | .310 | .347 | .507 |
| 2003 | Mon | NL | 105 | 227 | 59 | 10 | 1 | 1 | (1 | 0) | 74 | 31 | 10 | 18 | 19 | 0 | 39 | 3 | 9 | 2 | 5 | 2 | .71 | 10 | .260 | .323 | .326 |
| 2004 | Mon | NL | 102 | 218 | 63 | 14 | 2 | 0 | (0 | 0) | 81 | 36 | 16 | 28 | 32 | 1 | 21 | 1 | 2 | 3 | 5 | 1 | .83 | 3 | .289 | .378 | .372 |
| 2005 | Was | NL | 113 | 303 | 76 | 8 | 1 | 0 | (0 | 0) | 86 | 44 | 22 | 38 | 34 | 1 | 55 | 5 | 13 | 3 | 3 | 4 | .43 | 2 | .251 | .333 | .284 |
| 2006 | Col | NL | 136 | 463 | 139 | 23 | 5 | 5 | (2 | 3) | 187 | 84 | 36 | 65 | 56 | 1 | 66 | 3 | 9 | 3 | 10 | 12 | .45 | 10 | .300 | .377 | .404 |
| 2007 | Col | NL | 108 | 227 | 51 | 9 | 1 | 2 | (1 | 1) | 68 | 45 | 22 | 24 | 28 | 1 | 34 | 4 | 6 | 3 | 6 | 2 | .75 | 2 | .225 | .317 | .300 |
| 2008 | Cle | AL | 113 | 347 | 96 | 13 | 4 | 1 | (0 | 1) | 120 | 60 | 36 | 48 | 34 | 0 | 65 | 9 | 10 | 2 | 7 | 3 | .70 | 2 | .277 | .355 | .346 |
| 2009 | Cle | AL | 93 | 315 | 87 | 10 | 2 | 2 | (0 | 2) | 107 | 53 | 26 | 43 | 36 | 0 | 63 | 3 | 3 | 1 | 4 | 2 | .67 | 8 | .276 | .355 | .340 |
| 2010 | LAD | NL | 133 | 351 | 102 | 15 | 1 | 0 | (0 | 0) | 119 | 48 | 23 | 48 | 51 | 3 | 64 | 2 | 5 | 5 | 12 | 4 | .75 | 8 | .291 | .379 | .339 |
| 2011 | LAD | NL | 146 | 452 | 131 | 14 | 6 | 0 | (0 | 0) | 157 | 52 | 17 | 55 | 47 | 3 | 58 | 2 | 8 | 1 | 10 | 0 | 1.00 | 3 | .290 | .359 | .347 |
| 2012 | Min | AL | 138 | 470 | 126 | 18 | 1 | 1 | (0 | 1) | 149 | 65 | 40 | 62 | 52 | 0 | 65 | 4 | 7 | 4 | 9 | 5 | .64 | 9 | .268 | .343 | .317 |
| 2013 | 2 Tms | AL | 73 | 227 | 48 | 9 | 0 | 0 | (0 | 0) | 57 | 26 | 11 | 18 | 17 | 0 | 39 | 1 | 2 | 2 | 2 | 1 | .67 | 3 | .211 | .267 | .251 |
| 13 | Min | AL | 59 | 191 | 44 | 6 | 0 | 0 | (0 | 0) | 50 | 21 | 9 | 18 | 13 | 0 | 35 | 1 | 1 | 0 | 2 | 0 | 1.00 | 2 | .230 | .283 | .262 |
| 13 | KC | AL | 14 | 36 | 4 | 3 | 0 | 0 | (0 | 0) | 7 | 5 | 2 | 0 | 4 | 0 | 4 | 0 | 1 | 2 | 0 | 1 | .00 | 1 | .111 | .190 | .194 |
| Postseason | | | 4 | 2 | 0 | 0 | 0 | 0 | (0 | 0) | 0 | 0 | 0 | 0 | 1 | 0 | 0 | 0 | 0 | 0 | 0 | 0 | - | 0 | .000 | .333 | .000 |
| 12 ML YEARS | | | 1276 | 3671 | 1000 | 148 | 27 | 13 | (5 | 8) | 1241 | 560 | 265 | 459 | 410 | 10 | 581 | 37 | 78 | 29 | 74 | 36 | .67 | 61 | .272 | .349 | .338 |

## Matt Carson

**Bats:** R **Throws:** R **Pos:** RF-14;PR-9;LF-4;DH-1;PH-1 **Ht:** 6'2" **Wt:** 200 **Born:** 7/1/1981 **Age:** 32

| BATTING | | | | | | | | | | | | | | | | | | | | | BASERUNNING | | | | AVERAGES | | |
|---|---|---|---|---|---|---|---|---|---|---|---|---|---|---|---|---|---|---|---|---|---|---|---|---|---|---|---|
| Year | Team | Lg | G | AB | H | 2B | 3B | HR | (Hm | Rd) | TB | R | RBI | RC | TBB | IBB | SO | HBP | SH | SF | SB | CS | SB% | GDP | Avg | OBP | Slg |
| 2013 | Clmbs* | AAA | 121 | 436 | 110 | 16 | 2 | 14 | (- | -) | 172 | 57 | 49 | 59 | 39 | 3 | 119 | 7 | 6 | 2 | 14 | 4 | .78 | 11 | .252 | .322 | .394 |
| 2009 | Oak | AL | 10 | 21 | 6 | 0 | 0 | 1 | (1 | 0) | 9 | 1 | 5 | 4 | 0 | 0 | 7 | 0 | 0 | 1 | 0 | 0 | - | 0 | .286 | .273 | .429 |
| 2010 | Oak | AL | 36 | 79 | 14 | 2 | 0 | 4 | (2 | 2) | 28 | 7 | 9 | 3 | 2 | 0 | 23 | 0 | 0 | 2 | 4 | 0 | 1.00 | 0 | .177 | .193 | .354 |
| 2012 | Min | AL | 26 | 66 | 15 | 1 | 0 | 0 | (0 | 0) | 16 | 3 | 4 | 3 | 2 | 0 | 21 | 0 | 0 | 1 | 0 | 0 | - | 0 | .227 | .246 | .242 |
| 2013 | Cle | AL | 20 | 11 | 7 | 0 | 0 | 1 | (0 | 1) | 10 | 5 | 3 | 5 | 1 | 0 | 1 | 1 | 0 | 0 | 3 | 0 | 1.00 | 0 | .636 | .692 | .909 |
| 4 ML YEARS | | | 92 | 177 | 42 | 3 | 0 | 6 | (3 | 3) | 63 | 16 | 21 | 15 | 5 | 0 | 52 | 1 | 0 | 4 | 7 | 0 | 1.00 | 0 | .237 | .257 | .356 |

## Robert Carson

**Pitches:** L **Bats:** L **Pos:** RP-14 **Ht:** 6'4" **Wt:** 240 **Born:** 1/23/1989 **Age:** 25

| HOW MUCH HE PITCHED | | | | | | | | | WHAT HE GAVE UP | | | | | | | | | | | | THE RESULTS | | | | | | | |
|---|---|---|---|---|---|---|---|---|---|---|---|---|---|---|---|---|---|---|---|---|---|---|---|---|---|---|---|---|
| Year | Team | Lg | G | GS | CG | GF | IP | BFP | H | R | ER | HR | SH | SF | HB | TBB | IBB | SO | WP | Bk | W | L | Pct | Sh | Sv-Op | Hld | ERC | ERA |
| 2009 | Savann | A | 25 | 25 | 2 | 0 | 131.2 | 575 | 139 | 68 | 47 | 4 | 4 | 6 | 5 | 45 | 0 | 90 | 14 | 3 | 8 | 10 | .444 | 1 | 0-- | - | 3.78 | 3.21 |
| 2010 | StLuci | A+ | 17 | 16 | 0 | 0 | 86.1 | 385 | 98 | 42 | 40 | 5 | 4 | 2 | 5 | 33 | 0 | 69 | 3 | 1 | 7 | 5 | .583 | 0 | 0-- | - | 4.70 | 4.17 |
| 2010 | Bnghtn | AA | 10 | 10 | 0 | 0 | 48.2 | 228 | 68 | 46 | 45 | 7 | 4 | 1 | 2 | 23 | 0 | 30 | 3 | 0 | 1 | 6 | .143 | 0 | 0-- | - | 7.52 | 8.32 |
| 2011 | Bnghtn | AA | 25 | 24 | 0 | 1 | 128.1 | 583 | 154 | 88 | 72 | 14 | 5 | 5 | 3 | 55 | 1 | 91 | 7 | 2 | 4 | 11 | .267 | 0 | 0-- | - | 5.51 | 5.05 |
| 2012 | Bnghtn | AA | 31 | 0 | 0 | 22 | 35.2 | 168 | 44 | 22 | 18 | 2 | 1 | 2 | 0 | 15 | 1 | 37 | 5 | 1 | 1 | 2 | .333 | 0 | 9-- | - | 4.92 | 4.54 |
| 2012 | Buffalo | AAA | 10 | 0 | 0 | 5 | 15.2 | 65 | 16 | 4 | 3 | 1 | 1 | 0 | 0 | 6 | 1 | 15 | 1 | 0 | 0 | 0 | - | 0 | 1-- | - | 3.93 | 1.72 |

| | | | HOW MUCH HE PITCHED | | | | | | WHAT HE GAVE UP | | | | | | | | | | | | THE RESULTS | | | | | | | |
|---|---|---|---|---|---|---|---|---|---|---|---|---|---|---|---|---|---|---|---|---|---|---|---|---|---|---|---|---|
| Year | Team | Lg | G | GS | CG | GF | IP | BFP | H | R | ER | HR | SH | SF | HB | TBB | IBB | SO | WP | Bk | W | L | Pct | Sh | Sv-Op | Hld | ERC | ERA |
| 2013 | LsVgs | AAA | 43 | 0 | 0 | 26 | 44.1 | 196 | 48 | 25 | 20 | 3 | 2 | 0 | 0 | 19 | 2 | 36 | 4 | 1 | 3 | 3 | .500 | 0 | 11- - | - | 4.33 | 4.06 |
| 2012 | NYM | NL | 17 | 0 | 0 | 2 | 13.1 | 57 | 13 | 7 | 7 | 2 | 1 | 0 | 2 | 4 | 0 | 5 | 0 | 0 | 0 | 0 | - | 0 | 0-0 | 1 | 4.56 | 4.73 |
| 2013 | NYM | NL | 14 | 0 | 0 | 3 | 19.2 | 88 | 21 | 19 | 18 | 9 | 1 | 1 | 1 | 7 | 0 | 8 | 0 | 0 | 0 | 0 | - | 0 | 0-0 | 1 | 6.97 | 8.24 |
| 2 ML YEARS | | | 31 | 0 | 0 | 5 | 33.0 | 145 | 34 | 26 | 25 | 11 | 2 | 1 | 3 | 11 | 0 | 13 | 0 | 0 | 0 | 0 | - | 0 | 0-0 | 2 | 6.00 | 6.82 |

## Chris Carter

**Bats:** R **Throws:** R **Pos:** 1B-61;LF-49;DH-47;PH-5;RF-2 **Ht:** 6'4" **Wt:** 245 **Born:** 12/18/1986 **Age:** 27

| | | | BATTING | | | | | | | | | | | | | | | | | | BASERUNNING | | | | AVERAGES | | |
|---|---|---|---|---|---|---|---|---|---|---|---|---|---|---|---|---|---|---|---|---|---|---|---|---|---|---|---|
| Year | Team | Lg | G | AB | H | 2B | 3B | HR | (Hm | Rd) | TB | R | RBI | RC | TBB | IBB | SO | HBP | SH | SF | SB | CS | SB% | GDP | Avg | OBP | Slg |
| 2010 | Oak | AL | 24 | 70 | 13 | 1 | 0 | 3 | (1 | 2) | 23 | 8 | 7 | 5 | 7 | 0 | 21 | 0 | 0 | 1 | 1 | 0 | 1.00 | 3 | .186 | .256 | .329 |
| 2011 | Oak | AL | 15 | 44 | 6 | 0 | 0 | 0 | (0 | 0) | 6 | 2 | 0 | 0 | 2 | 0 | 20 | 0 | 0 | 0 | 0 | 0 | - | 1 | .136 | .174 | .136 |
| 2012 | Oak | AL | 67 | 218 | 52 | 12 | 0 | 16 | (5 | 11) | 112 | 38 | 39 | 36 | 39 | 1 | 83 | 0 | 0 | 3 | 0 | 0 | - | 4 | .239 | .350 | .514 |
| 2013 | Hou | AL | 148 | 506 | 113 | 24 | 2 | 29 | (10 | 19) | 228 | 64 | 82 | 74 | 70 | 1 | **212** | 4 | 0 | 5 | 2 | 0 | 1.00 | 8 | .223 | .320 | .451 |
| 4 ML YEARS | | | 254 | 838 | 184 | 37 | 2 | 48 | (16 | 32) | 369 | 112 | 128 | 115 | 118 | 2 | 336 | 4 | 0 | 9 | 3 | 0 | 1.00 | 16 | .220 | .316 | .440 |

## Andrew Cashner

**Pitches:** R **Bats:** R **Pos:** SP-26; RP-5 **Ht:** 6'6" **Wt:** 220 **Born:** 9/11/1986 **Age:** 27

| | | | HOW MUCH HE PITCHED | | | | | | WHAT HE GAVE UP | | | | | | | | | | | | THE RESULTS | | | | | | | |
|---|---|---|---|---|---|---|---|---|---|---|---|---|---|---|---|---|---|---|---|---|---|---|---|---|---|---|---|---|
| Year | Team | Lg | G | GS | CG | GF | IP | BFP | H | R | ER | HR | SH | SF | HB | TBB | IBB | SO | WP | Bk | W | L | Pct | Sh | Sv-Op | Hld | ERC | ERA |
| 2010 | ChC | NL | 53 | 0 | 0 | 9 | 54.1 | 248 | 55 | 31 | 29 | 8 | 6 | 2 | 4 | 30 | 5 | 50 | 4 | 1 | 2 | 6 | .250 | 0 | 0-1 | 16 | 5.22 | 4.80 |
| 2011 | ChC | NL | 7 | 1 | 0 | 0 | 10.2 | 39 | 3 | 2 | 2 | 1 | 0 | 0 | 0 | 4 | 0 | 8 | 0 | 0 | 0 | 0 | - | 0 | 0-0 | 1 | 0.91 | 1.69 |
| 2012 | SD | NL | 33 | 5 | 0 | 5 | 46.1 | 196 | 42 | 23 | 22 | 5 | 3 | 1 | 1 | 19 | 1 | 52 | 2 | 0 | 3 | 4 | .429 | 0 | 0-4 | 6 | 3.73 | 4.27 |
| 2013 | SD | NL | 31 | 26 | 1 | 2 | 175.0 | 707 | 151 | 68 | 60 | 12 | 6 | 3 | 4 | 47 | 3 | 128 | 5 | 0 | 10 | 9 | .526 | 1 | 0-0 | 1 | 2.74 | 3.09 |
| 4 ML YEARS | | | 124 | 32 | 1 | 16 | 286.1 | 1190 | 251 | 124 | 113 | 26 | 15 | 6 | 9 | 100 | 9 | 238 | 11 | 1 | 15 | 19 | .441 | 1 | 0-5 | 24 | 3.24 | 3.55 |

## Alexi Casilla

**Bats:** B **Throws:** R **Pos:** 2B-51;PR-11;PH-8;SS-2;DH-2 cuh-SEE-ya **Ht:** 5'9" **Wt:** 170 **Born:** 7/20/1984 **Age:** 29

| | | | BATTING | | | | | | | | | | | | | | | | | | BASERUNNING | | | | AVERAGES | | |
|---|---|---|---|---|---|---|---|---|---|---|---|---|---|---|---|---|---|---|---|---|---|---|---|---|---|---|---|
| Year | Team | Lg | G | AB | H | 2B | 3B | HR | (Hm | Rd) | TB | R | RBI | RC | TBB | IBB | SO | HBP | SH | SF | SB | CS | SB% | GDP | Avg | OBP | Slg |
| 2006 | Min | AL | 9 | 4 | 1 | 0 | 0 | 0 | (0 | 0) | 1 | 1 | 0 | 1 | 2 | 0 | 1 | 0 | 0 | 0 | 0 | 0 | - | 0 | .250 | .500 | .250 |
| 2007 | Min | AL | 56 | 189 | 42 | 5 | 1 | 0 | (0 | 0) | 49 | 15 | 9 | 11 | 9 | 0 | 29 | 0 | 5 | 1 | 11 | 1 | .92 | 5 | .222 | .256 | .259 |
| 2008 | Min | AL | 98 | 385 | 108 | 15 | 0 | 7 | (2 | 5) | 144 | 58 | 50 | 50 | 31 | 0 | 45 | 2 | **13** | 6 | 7 | 2 | .78 | 8 | .281 | .333 | .374 |
| 2009 | Min | AL | 80 | 228 | 46 | 7 | 3 | 0 | (0 | 0) | 59 | 25 | 17 | 20 | 22 | 0 | 36 | 3 | 2 | 1 | 11 | 0 | 1.00 | 6 | .202 | .280 | .259 |
| 2010 | Min | AL | 69 | 152 | 42 | 7 | 4 | 1 | (1 | 0) | 60 | 26 | 20 | 23 | 13 | 0 | 17 | 0 | 4 | 1 | 6 | 1 | .86 | 5 | .276 | .331 | .395 |
| 2011 | Min | AL | 97 | 323 | 84 | 21 | 4 | 2 | (1 | 1) | 119 | 52 | 21 | 33 | 28 | 0 | 45 | 3 | 8 | 3 | 15 | 4 | .79 | 4 | .260 | .322 | .368 |
| 2012 | Min | AL | 106 | 299 | 72 | 17 | 2 | 1 | (0 | 1) | 96 | 33 | 30 | 29 | 16 | 0 | 52 | 3 | 3 | 5 | 21 | 1 | .95 | 6 | .241 | .282 | .321 |
| 2013 | Bal | AL | 62 | 112 | 24 | 4 | 1 | 1 | (1 | 0) | 33 | 15 | 10 | 10 | 9 | 0 | 20 | 0 | 2 | 2 | 9 | 2 | .82 | 1 | .214 | .268 | .295 |
| 8 ML YEARS | | | 577 | 1692 | 419 | 76 | 15 | 12 | (5 | 7) | 561 | 225 | 157 | 177 | 130 | 0 | 245 | 11 | 37 | 19 | 80 | 11 | .88 | 35 | .248 | .302 | .332 |

## Santiago Casilla

**Pitches:** R **Bats:** R **Pos:** RP-57 cuh-SEE-ya **Ht:** 6'0" **Wt:** 210 **Born:** 7/25/1980 **Age:** 33

| | | | HOW MUCH HE PITCHED | | | | | | WHAT HE GAVE UP | | | | | | | | | | | | THE RESULTS | | | | | | | |
|---|---|---|---|---|---|---|---|---|---|---|---|---|---|---|---|---|---|---|---|---|---|---|---|---|---|---|---|---|
| Year | Team | Lg | G | GS | CG | GF | IP | BFP | H | R | ER | HR | SH | SF | HB | TBB | IBB | SO | WP | Bk | W | L | Pct | Sh | Sv-Op | Hld | ERC | ERA |
| 2013 | SnJos* | A+ | 5 | 2 | 0 | 0 | 5.0 | 26 | 7 | 3 | 3 | 0 | 0 | 1 | 0 | 5 | 0 | 2 | 0 | 0 | 0 | 0 | - | 0 | 0- - | - | 8.26 | 5.40 |
| 2004 | Oak | AL | 4 | 0 | 0 | 2 | 5.2 | 32 | 5 | 8 | 8 | 3 | 0 | 0 | 1 | 9 | 0 | 5 | 0 | 0 | 0 | 0 | - | 0 | 0-0 | 0 | 13.22 | 12.71 |
| 2005 | Oak | AL | 3 | 0 | 0 | 3 | 3.0 | 12 | 2 | 1 | 1 | 0 | 0 | 0 | 0 | 1 | 0 | 1 | 1 | 0 | 0 | 0 | - | 0 | 0-0 | 0 | 1.57 | 3.00 |
| 2006 | Oak | AL | 2 | 0 | 0 | 1 | 2.1 | 10 | 2 | 3 | 3 | 0 | 0 | 0 | 0 | 2 | 0 | 2 | 0 | 0 | 0 | 0 | - | 0 | 0-0 | 0 | 4.61 | 11.57 |
| 2007 | Oak | AL | 46 | 0 | 0 | 10 | 50.2 | 219 | 43 | 25 | 25 | 6 | 0 | 3 | 1 | 23 | 6 | 52 | 5 | 0 | 3 | 1 | .750 | 0 | 2-5 | 12 | 3.39 | 4.44 |
| 2008 | Oak | AL | 51 | 0 | 0 | 9 | 50.1 | 229 | 60 | 22 | 22 | 5 | 3 | 2 | 3 | 20 | 2 | 43 | 6 | 0 | 2 | 1 | .667 | 0 | 2-3 | 7 | 5.34 | 3.93 |
| 2009 | Oak | AL | 46 | 0 | 0 | 15 | 48.1 | 233 | 61 | 36 | 32 | 6 | 1 | 3 | 3 | 25 | 3 | 35 | 5 | 0 | 1 | 2 | .333 | 0 | 0-0 | 5 | 6.32 | 5.96 |
| 2010 | SF | NL | 52 | 0 | 0 | 13 | 55.1 | 225 | 40 | 14 | 12 | 2 | 2 | 1 | 4 | 26 | 4 | 56 | 10 | 0 | 7 | 2 | .778 | 0 | 2-3 | 11 | 2.68 | 1.95 |
| 2011 | SF | NL | 49 | 0 | 0 | 20 | 51.2 | 211 | 33 | 11 | 10 | 1 | 4 | 0 | 2 | 25 | 1 | 45 | 5 | 0 | 2 | 2 | .500 | 0 | 6-7 | 6 | 2.11 | 1.74 |
| 2012 | SF | NL | 73 | 0 | 0 | 37 | 63.1 | 272 | 55 | 24 | 20 | 8 | 2 | 1 | 2 | 22 | 4 | 55 | 1 | 0 | 7 | 6 | .538 | 0 | 25-31 | 12 | 3.24 | 2.84 |
| 2013 | SF | NL | 57 | 0 | 0 | 12 | 50.0 | 208 | 39 | 14 | 12 | 2 | 2 | 3 | 2 | 25 | 6 | 38 | 8 | 0 | 7 | 2 | .778 | 0 | 2-3 | 22 | 2.88 | 2.16 |
| Postseason | | | 15 | 0 | 0 | 2 | 11.2 | 52 | 11 | 3 | 2 | 0 | 0 | 0 | 2 | 2 | 1 | 13 | 3 | 0 | 1 | 0 | 1.000 | 0 | 0-0 | 4 | 2.55 | 1.54 |
| 10 ML YEARS | | | 383 | 0 | 0 | 122 | 380.2 | 1651 | 340 | 158 | 145 | 33 | 14 | 13 | 18 | 178 | 26 | 332 | 41 | 0 | 29 | 16 | .644 | 0 | 39-52 | 75 | 3.70 | 3.43 |

## Alex Castellanos

**Bats:** R **Throws:** R **Pos:** RF-6;LF-2;PH-2 kah-stay-AH-nos **Ht:** 6'0" **Wt:** 200 **Born:** 8/4/1986 **Age:** 27

| | | | BATTING | | | | | | | | | | | | | | | | | | BASERUNNING | | | | AVERAGES | | |
|---|---|---|---|---|---|---|---|---|---|---|---|---|---|---|---|---|---|---|---|---|---|---|---|---|---|---|---|
| Year | Team | Lg | G | AB | H | 2B | 3B | HR | (Hm | Rd) | TB | R | RBI | RC | TBB | IBB | SO | HBP | SH | SF | SB | CS | SB% | GDP | Avg | OBP | Slg |
| 2009 | QuadC | A | 82 | 311 | 84 | 21 | 4 | 5 | (- | -) | 128 | 51 | 34 | 47 | 20 | 0 | 89 | 12 | 1 | 2 | 21 | 4 | .84 | 5 | .270 | .336 | .412 |
| 2009 | PlmBh | A+ | 21 | 53 | 10 | 1 | 1 | 1 | (- | -) | 16 | 5 | 2 | 2 | 2 | 0 | 19 | 1 | 0 | 0 | 0 | 2 | .00 | 2 | .189 | .232 | .302 |
| 2010 | PlmBh | A+ | 129 | 459 | 124 | 35 | 7 | 13 | (- | -) | 212 | 62 | 58 | 74 | 38 | 3 | 112 | 12 | 4 | 4 | 19 | 9 | .68 | 11 | .270 | .339 | .462 |
| 2011 | Sprgfld | AA | 93 | 354 | 113 | 21 | 4 | 19 | (- | -) | 199 | 72 | 62 | 75 | 24 | 3 | 94 | 11 | 0 | 2 | 10 | 1 | .91 | 7 | .319 | .379 | .562 |
| 2011 | Chatt | AA | 32 | 121 | 39 | 14 | 4 | 4 | (- | -) | 73 | 30 | 23 | 29 | 15 | 1 | 24 | 4 | 0 | 3 | 4 | 1 | .80 | 3 | .322 | .406 | .603 |
| 2012 | Albq | AAA | 94 | 344 | 113 | 25 | 7 | 17 | (- | -) | 203 | 74 | 52 | 83 | 46 | 2 | 85 | 11 | 2 | 4 | 16 | 8 | .67 | 3 | .328 | .420 | .590 |
| 2013 | Albq | AAA | 105 | 385 | 99 | 14 | 5 | 19 | (- | -) | 180 | 75 | 61 | 66 | 41 | 1 | 112 | 12 | 1 | 0 | 19 | 5 | .79 | 3 | .257 | .347 | .468 |
| 2012 | LAD | NL | 16 | 23 | 4 | 0 | 1 | 1 | (1 | 0) | 9 | 3 | 3 | 2 | 0 | 0 | 8 | 1 | 0 | 1 | 0 | 0 | - | 0 | .174 | .200 | .391 |
| 2013 | LAD | NL | 8 | 18 | 3 | 1 | 0 | 1 | (1 | 0) | 7 | 2 | 1 | 0 | 0 | 0 | 5 | 0 | 0 | 0 | 0 | 0 | - | 0 | .167 | .167 | .389 |
| 2 ML YEARS | | | 24 | 41 | 7 | 1 | 1 | 2 | (2 | 0) | 16 | 5 | 4 | 2 | 0 | 0 | 13 | 1 | 0 | 1 | 0 | 0 | - | 0 | .171 | .186 | .390 |

# Nick Castellanos

**Bats:** R **Throws:** R **Pos:** LF-9;PH-3;DH-1;PR-1 CAHS-tell-ah-noase **Ht:** 6'4" **Wt:** 210 **Born:** 3/4/1992 **Age:** 22

| BATTING | | | | | | | | | | | | | | | | | | | | | BASERUNNING | | | | AVERAGES | | |
|---|---|---|---|---|---|---|---|---|---|---|---|---|---|---|---|---|---|---|---|---|---|---|---|---|---|---|---|
| Year | Team | Lg | G | AB | H | 2B | 3B | HR | (Hm | Rd) | TB | R | RBI | RC | TBB | IBB | SO | HBP | SH | SF | SB | CS | SB% | GDP | Avg | OBP | Slg |
| 2010 | Tigers | R | 7 | 24 | 8 | 2 | 0 | 0 | (- | -) | 10 | 5 | 3 | 4 | 4 | 0 | 5 | 0 | 0 | 1 | 0 | 1 | .00 | 1 | .333 | .414 | .417 |
| 2011 | WMich | A | 135 | 507 | 158 | 36 | 3 | 7 | (- | -) | 221 | 65 | 76 | 83 | 45 | 2 | 130 | 3 | 1 | 6 | 3 | 2 | .60 | 5 | .312 | .367 | .436 |
| 2012 | Lkland | A+ | 55 | 215 | 87 | 17 | 3 | 3 | (- | -) | 119 | 37 | 32 | 52 | 22 | 1 | 42 | 3 | 0 | 3 | 3 | 2 | .60 | 5 | .405 | .461 | .553 |
| 2012 | Erie | AA | 79 | 322 | 84 | 14 | 1 | 7 | (- | -) | 121 | 35 | 25 | 35 | 14 | 1 | 76 | 2 | 0 | 3 | 5 | 4 | .56 | 12 | .261 | .293 | .376 |
| 2013 | Toledo | AAA | 134 | 533 | 147 | 37 | 1 | 18 | (- | -) | 240 | 81 | 76 | 86 | 54 | 2 | 100 | 3 | 0 | 5 | 4 | 1 | .80 | 12 | .276 | .343 | .450 |
| 2013 | Det | AL | 11 | 18 | 5 | 0 | 0 | 0 | (0 | 0) | 5 | 1 | 0 | 1 | 0 | 0 | 1 | 0 | 0 | 0 | 0 | 0 | - | 0 | .278 | .278 | .278 |

# Welington Castillo

**Bats:** R **Throws:** R **Pos:** C-111;PH-2 WELL-ing-tunn **Ht:** 5'10" **Wt:** 210 **Born:** 4/24/1987 **Age:** 27

| BATTING | | | | | | | | | | | | | | | | | | | | | BASERUNNING | | | | AVERAGES | | |
|---|---|---|---|---|---|---|---|---|---|---|---|---|---|---|---|---|---|---|---|---|---|---|---|---|---|---|---|
| Year | Team | Lg | G | AB | H | 2B | 3B | HR | (Hm | Rd) | TB | R | RBI | RC | TBB | IBB | SO | HBP | SH | SF | SB | CS | SB% | GDP | Avg | OBP | Slg |
| 2010 | ChC | NL | 7 | 20 | 6 | 4 | 0 | 1 | (0 | 1) | 13 | 3 | 5 | 3 | 1 | 0 | 7 | 0 | 0 | 0 | 0 | 0 | - | 0 | .300 | .333 | .650 |
| 2011 | ChC | NL | 4 | 13 | 2 | 0 | 0 | 0 | (0 | 0) | 2 | 0 | 0 | 0 | 0 | 0 | 4 | 0 | 0 | 0 | 0 | 0 | - | 1 | .154 | .154 | .154 |
| 2012 | ChC | NL | 52 | 170 | 45 | 11 | 0 | 5 | (4 | 1) | 71 | 16 | 22 | 22 | 17 | 2 | 51 | 2 | 0 | 1 | 0 | 0 | - | 4 | .265 | .337 | .418 |
| 2013 | ChC | NL | 113 | 380 | 104 | 23 | 0 | 8 | (1 | 7) | 151 | 41 | 32 | 44 | 34 | 3 | 97 | 11 | 1 | 2 | 2 | 0 | 1.00 | 13 | .274 | .349 | .397 |
| 4 ML YEARS | | | 176 | 583 | 157 | 38 | 0 | 14 | (5 | 9) | 237 | 60 | 59 | 69 | 52 | 5 | 159 | 13 | 1 | 3 | 2 | 0 | 1.00 | 18 | .269 | .341 | .407 |

# Jason Castro

**Bats:** L **Throws:** R **Pos:** C-98;DH-18;PH-6 **Ht:** 6'3" **Wt:** 215 **Born:** 6/18/1987 **Age:** 27

| BATTING | | | | | | | | | | | | | | | | | | | | | BASERUNNING | | | | AVERAGES | | |
|---|---|---|---|---|---|---|---|---|---|---|---|---|---|---|---|---|---|---|---|---|---|---|---|---|---|---|---|
| Year | Team | Lg | G | AB | H | 2B | 3B | HR | (Hm | Rd) | TB | R | RBI | RC | TBB | IBB | SO | HBP | SH | SF | SB | CS | SB% | GDP | Avg | OBP | Slg |
| 2010 | Hou | NL | 67 | 195 | 40 | 8 | 1 | 2 | (1 | 1) | 56 | 26 | 8 | 12 | 22 | 2 | 41 | 0 | 0 | 0 | 0 | 0 | - | 4 | .205 | .286 | .287 |
| 2012 | Hou | NL | 87 | 257 | 66 | 15 | 2 | 6 | (3 | 3) | 103 | 29 | 29 | 33 | 31 | 2 | 61 | 1 | 2 | 4 | 0 | 0 | - | 8 | .257 | .334 | .401 |
| 2013 | Hou | AL | 120 | 435 | 120 | 35 | 1 | 18 | (13 | 5) | 211 | 63 | 56 | 76 | 50 | 3 | 130 | 2 | 0 | 4 | 2 | 1 | .67 | 4 | .276 | .350 | .485 |
| 3 ML YEARS | | | 274 | 887 | 226 | 58 | 4 | 26 | (17 | 9) | 370 | 118 | 93 | 121 | 103 | 7 | 232 | 3 | 2 | 8 | 2 | 1 | .67 | 16 | .255 | .332 | .417 |

# Simon Castro

**Pitches:** R **Bats:** R **Pos:** RP-4 SEE-moan **Ht:** 6'5" **Wt:** 230 **Born:** 4/9/1988 **Age:** 26

| HOW MUCH HE PITCHED | | | | | | | | | WHAT HE GAVE UP | | | | | | | | | | | | THE RESULTS | | | | | | | |
|---|---|---|---|---|---|---|---|---|---|---|---|---|---|---|---|---|---|---|---|---|---|---|---|---|---|---|---|---|
| Year | Team | Lg | G | GS | CG | GF | IP | BFP | H | R | ER | HR | SH | SF | HB | TBB | IBB | SO | WP | Bk | W | L | Pct | Sh | Sv-Op | Hld | ERC | ERA |
| 2009 | FtWyn | A | 28 | 27 | 1 | 0 | 140.1 | 574 | 118 | 61 | 52 | 9 | 3 | 2 | 10 | 37 | 0 | 157 | 15 | 3 | 10 | 6 | .625 | 1 | 0-- | - | 2.76 | 3.33 |
| 2010 | SnAnt | AA | 24 | 23 | 0 | 0 | 129.2 | 529 | 107 | 55 | 42 | 8 | 4 | 4 | 6 | 36 | 1 | 107 | 2 | 3 | 7 | 6 | .538 | 0 | 0-- | - | 2.61 | 2.92 |
| 2010 | Portlnd | AAA | 2 | 2 | 0 | 0 | 10.1 | 54 | 16 | 10 | 9 | 1 | 0 | 0 | 0 | 6 | 0 | 6 | 0 | 0 | 0 | 1 | .000 | 0 | 0-- | - | 7.84 | 7.84 |
| 2011 | Tucsn | AAA | 6 | 6 | 0 | 0 | 25.2 | 130 | 37 | 30 | 29 | 5 | 0 | 1 | 0 | 18 | 0 | 21 | 6 | 1 | 2 | 2 | .500 | 0 | 0-- | - | 8.88 | 10.17 |
| 2011 | SnAnt | AA | 16 | 16 | 0 | 0 | 89.1 | 375 | 95 | 48 | 43 | 9 | 1 | 2 | 6 | 16 | 0 | 73 | 3 | 1 | 5 | 6 | .455 | 0 | 0-- | - | 3.85 | 4.33 |
| 2012 | Brham | AA | 15 | 15 | 0 | 0 | 90.0 | 380 | 89 | 50 | 37 | 4 | 2 | 4 | 3 | 21 | 0 | 72 | 1 | 0 | 6 | 4 | .600 | 0 | 0-- | - | 3.09 | 3.70 |
| 2012 | Charltt | AAA | 5 | 5 | 0 | 0 | 25.0 | 109 | 32 | 13 | 12 | 2 | 0 | 0 | 2 | 6 | 0 | 16 | 1 | 0 | 1 | 1 | .500 | 0 | 0-- | - | 5.40 | 4.32 |
| 2012 | Bristol | R | 1 | 1 | 0 | 0 | 2.0 | 8 | 3 | 1 | 1 | 0 | 1 | 0 | 0 | 0 | 0 | 0 | 0 | 0 | 0 | 0 | - | 0 | 0-- | - | 5.09 | 4.50 |
| 2013 | Charltt | AAA | 27 | 12 | 0 | 4 | 92.2 | 400 | 98 | 61 | 60 | 14 | 1 | 3 | 3 | 33 | 0 | 82 | 2 | 1 | 3 | 7 | .300 | 0 | 0-- | - | 4.77 | 5.83 |
| 2013 | CWS | AL | 4 | 0 | 0 | 4 | 6.2 | 28 | 5 | 2 | 2 | 1 | 1 | 0 | 1 | 3 | 0 | 6 | 0 | 0 | 0 | 1 | .000 | 0 | 0-0 | 0 | 3.90 | 2.70 |

# Starlin Castro

**Bats:** R **Throws:** R **Pos:** SS-159;PH-2 STARR-linn **Ht:** 5'10" **Wt:** 190 **Born:** 3/24/1990 **Age:** 24

| BATTING | | | | | | | | | | | | | | | | | | | | | BASERUNNING | | | | AVERAGES | | |
|---|---|---|---|---|---|---|---|---|---|---|---|---|---|---|---|---|---|---|---|---|---|---|---|---|---|---|---|
| Year | Team | Lg | G | AB | H | 2B | 3B | HR | (Hm | Rd) | TB | R | RBI | RC | TBB | IBB | SO | HBP | SH | SF | SB | CS | SB% | GDP | Avg | OBP | Slg |
| 2010 | ChC | NL | 125 | 463 | 139 | 31 | 5 | 3 | (1 | 2) | 189 | 53 | 41 | 56 | 29 | 7 | 71 | 6 | 4 | 4 | 10 | 8 | .56 | 14 | .300 | .347 | .408 |
| 2011 | ChC | NL | 158 | **674** | **207** | 36 | 9 | 10 | (4 | 6) | 291 | 91 | 66 | 93 | 35 | 2 | 96 | 2 | 0 | 4 | 22 | 9 | .71 | 20 | .307 | .341 | .432 |
| 2012 | ChC | NL | **162** | **646** | 183 | 29 | 12 | 14 | (7 | 7) | 278 | 78 | 78 | 91 | 36 | 5 | 100 | 4 | 0 | 5 | 25 | **13** | .66 | 15 | .283 | .323 | .430 |
| 2013 | ChC | NL | 161 | **666** | 163 | 34 | 2 | 10 | (9 | 1) | 231 | 59 | 44 | 55 | 30 | 0 | 129 | 7 | 1 | 1 | 9 | 6 | .60 | 21 | .245 | .284 | .347 |
| 4 ML YEARS | | | 606 | 2449 | 692 | 130 | 28 | 37 | (21 | 16) | 989 | 281 | 229 | 295 | 130 | 14 | 396 | 19 | 5 | 14 | 66 | 36 | .65 | 70 | .283 | .322 | .404 |

# Brett Cecil

**Pitches:** L **Bats:** R **Pos:** RP-60 SEE-sill **Ht:** 6'1" **Wt:** 215 **Born:** 7/2/1986 **Age:** 27

| HOW MUCH HE PITCHED | | | | | | | | | WHAT HE GAVE UP | | | | | | | | | | | | THE RESULTS | | | | | | | |
|---|---|---|---|---|---|---|---|---|---|---|---|---|---|---|---|---|---|---|---|---|---|---|---|---|---|---|---|---|
| Year | Team | Lg | G | GS | CG | GF | IP | BFP | H | R | ER | HR | SH | SF | HB | TBB | IBB | SO | WP | Bk | W | L | Pct | Sh | Sv-Op | Hld | ERC | ERA |
| 2009 | Tor | AL | 18 | 17 | 0 | 1 | 93.1 | 422 | 116 | 59 | 55 | 17 | 0 | 2 | 5 | 38 | 0 | 69 | 0 | 0 | 7 | 4 | .636 | 0 | 0-0 | 0 | 6.53 | 5.30 |
| 2010 | Tor | AL | 28 | 28 | 0 | 0 | 172.2 | 726 | 175 | 87 | 81 | 18 | 1 | 6 | 1 | 54 | 2 | 117 | 7 | 1 | 15 | 7 | .682 | 0 | 0-0 | 0 | 3.88 | 4.22 |
| 2011 | Tor | AL | 20 | 20 | 2 | 0 | 123.2 | 532 | 122 | 68 | 65 | 22 | 3 | 5 | 6 | 42 | 1 | 87 | 1 | 0 | 4 | 11 | .267 | 1 | 0-0 | 0 | 4.47 | 4.73 |
| 2012 | Tor | AL | 21 | 9 | 0 | 2 | 61.1 | 270 | 70 | 40 | 39 | 11 | 3 | 3 | 3 | 23 | 0 | 51 | 0 | 0 | 2 | 4 | .333 | 0 | 0-0 | 1 | 5.68 | 5.72 |
| 2013 | Tor | AL | 60 | 0 | 0 | 12 | 60.2 | 250 | 44 | 20 | 19 | 4 | 3 | 2 | 3 | 23 | 3 | 70 | 5 | 1 | 5 | 1 | .833 | 0 | 1-3 | 11 | 2.42 | 2.82 |
| 5 ML YEARS | | | 147 | 74 | 2 | 15 | 511.2 | 2200 | 527 | 274 | 259 | 72 | 10 | 18 | 18 | 180 | 6 | 394 | 13 | 2 | 33 | 27 | .550 | 1 | 1-3 | 12 | 4.49 | 4.56 |

# Ronny Cedeno

**Bats:** R **Throws:** R **Pos:** SS-76;DH-7;PH-6;1B-1;3B-1;PR-1 **Ht:** 6'0" **Wt:** 195 **Born:** 2/2/1983 **Age:** 31

| BATTING | | | | | | | | | | | | | | | | | | | | | BASERUNNING | | | | AVERAGES | | |
|---|---|---|---|---|---|---|---|---|---|---|---|---|---|---|---|---|---|---|---|---|---|---|---|---|---|---|---|
| Year | Team | Lg | G | AB | H | 2B | 3B | HR | (Hm | Rd) | TB | R | RBI | RC | TBB | IBB | SO | HBP | SH | SF | SB | CS | SB% | GDP | Avg | OBP | Slg |
| 2013 | Lk Els* | A+ | 2 | 8 | 1 | 1 | 0 | 0 | (- | -) | 2 | 1 | 0 | 0 | 2 | 0 | 1 | 0 | 0 | 0 | 0 | 0 | - | 0 | .125 | .300 | .250 |
| 2005 | ChC | NL | 41 | 80 | 24 | 3 | 0 | 1 | (0 | 1) | 30 | 13 | 6 | 11 | 5 | 1 | 11 | 2 | 2 | 0 | 1 | 0 | 1.00 | 4 | .300 | .356 | .375 |
| 2006 | ChC | NL | 151 | 534 | 131 | 18 | 7 | 6 | (4 | 2) | 181 | 51 | 41 | 41 | 17 | 4 | 109 | 3 | 15 | 3 | 8 | 8 | .50 | 10 | .245 | .271 | .339 |
| 2007 | ChC | NL | 38 | 74 | 15 | 2 | 0 | 4 | (2 | 2) | 29 | 6 | 13 | 8 | 3 | 0 | 18 | 0 | 2 | 1 | 2 | 1 | .67 | 0 | .203 | .231 | .392 |
| 2008 | ChC | NL | 99 | 216 | 58 | 12 | 0 | 2 | (2 | 0) | 76 | 36 | 28 | 23 | 18 | 2 | 41 | 1 | 1 | 0 | 4 | 1 | .80 | 6 | .269 | .328 | .352 |

| BATTING | | | | | | | | | | | | | | | | | | | | | | BASERUNNING | | | | AVERAGES | | |
|---|---|---|---|---|---|---|---|---|---|---|---|---|---|---|---|---|---|---|---|---|---|---|---|---|---|---|---|---|
| Year Team | Lg | G | AB | H | 2B | 3B | HR | (Hm | Rd) | TB | R | RBI | RC | TBB | IBB | SO | HBP | SH | SF | SB | CS | SB% | GDP | Avg | OBP | Slg |
| 2009 2 Tms | | 105 | 341 | 71 | 8 | 3 | 10 | (7 | 3) | 115 | 32 | 38 | 29 | 19 | 3 | 79 | 3 | 13 | 0 | 5 | 2 | .71 | 9 | .208 | .256 | .337 |
| 2010 Pit | NL | 139 | 468 | 120 | 29 | 3 | 8 | (4 | 4) | 179 | 42 | 38 | 46 | 23 | 4 | 106 | 2 | 7 | 2 | 12 | 3 | .80 | 10 | .256 | .293 | .382 |
| 2011 Pit | NL | 128 | 413 | 103 | 25 | 3 | 2 | (0 | 2) | 140 | 43 | 32 | 36 | 30 | 7 | 93 | 0 | 6 | 5 | 2 | 5 | .29 | 11 | .249 | .297 | .339 |
| 2012 NYM | NL | 78 | 166 | 43 | 11 | 1 | 4 | (3 | 1) | 68 | 18 | 22 | 19 | 17 | 0 | 35 | 1 | 2 | 0 | 0 | 1 | .00 | 10 | .259 | .332 | .410 |
| 2013 2 Tms | | 89 | 264 | 64 | 8 | 3 | 3 | (2 | 1) | 87 | 24 | 21 | 23 | 14 | 1 | 73 | 3 | 6 | 1 | 5 | 4 | .56 | 6 | .242 | .287 | .330 |
| 09 Sea | AL | 59 | 186 | 31 | 4 | 2 | 5 | (2 | 3) | 54 | 15 | 17 | 7 | 10 | 1 | 50 | 1 | 9 | 0 | 3 | 2 | .60 | 6 | .167 | .213 | .290 |
| 09 Pit | NL | 46 | 155 | 40 | 4 | 1 | 5 | (5 | 0) | 61 | 17 | 21 | 22 | 9 | 2 | 29 | 2 | 4 | 0 | 2 | 0 | 1.00 | 3 | .258 | .307 | .394 |
| 13 Hou | AL | 51 | 141 | 31 | 6 | 1 | 1 | (1 | 0) | 42 | 12 | 12 | 10 | 6 | 0 | 42 | 2 | 5 | 1 | 2 | 1 | .67 | 4 | .220 | .260 | .298 |
| 13 SD | NL | 38 | 123 | 33 | 2 | 2 | 2 | (1 | 1) | 45 | 12 | 9 | 13 | 8 | 1 | 31 | 1 | 1 | 0 | 3 | 3 | .50 | 2 | .268 | .318 | .366 |
| Postseason | | 3 | 0 | 0 | 0 | 0 | 0 | (0 | 0) | 0 | 0 | 0 | 0 | 0 | 0 | 0 | 0 | 0 | 0 | 1 | 0 | 1.00 | 0 | - | - | - |
| 9 ML YEARS | | 868 | 2556 | 629 | 116 | 20 | 40 | (24 | 16) | 905 | 265 | 239 | 236 | 146 | 22 | 565 | 15 | 54 | 12 | 39 | 25 | .61 | 66 | .246 | .289 | .354 |

# Xavier Cedeno

**Pitches:** L **Bats:** L **Pos:** RP-16 **Ht:** 6'1" **Wt:** 205 **Born:** 8/26/1986 **Age:** 27

| HOW MUCH HE PITCHED | | | | | | | | WHAT HE GAVE UP | | | | | | | | | | | | THE RESULTS | | | | | | | |
|---|---|---|---|---|---|---|---|---|---|---|---|---|---|---|---|---|---|---|---|---|---|---|---|---|---|---|---|
| Year Team | Lg | G | GS | CG | GF | IP | BFP | H | R | ER | HR | SH | SF | HB | TBB | IBB | SO | WP | Bk | W | L | Pct | Sh | Sv-Op | Hld | ERC | ERA |
| 2013 Syrcse* | AAA | 39 | 0 | 0 | 8 | 34.1 | 140 | 23 | 11 | 5 | 2 | 1 | 0 | 1 | 16 | 3 | 45 | 5 | 0 | 2 | 0 | 1.000 | 0 | 4-- | - | 2.32 | 1.31 |
| 2011 Hou | NL | 3 | 0 | 0 | 0 | 1.2 | 11 | 7 | 5 | 5 | 2 | 0 | 0 | 0 | 0 | 0 | 0 | 0 | 0 | 0 | 0 | - | 0 | 0-0 | 0 | 43.10 | 27.00 |
| 2012 Hou | NL | 44 | 0 | 0 | 12 | 31.0 | 138 | 30 | 15 | 13 | 3 | 2 | 3 | 1 | 14 | 1 | 36 | 3 | 0 | 0 | 1 | .000 | 0 | 1-3 | 6 | 4.05 | 3.77 |
| 2013 2 Tms | | 16 | 0 | 0 | 3 | 12.1 | 60 | 15 | 12 | 9 | 0 | 1 | 0 | 2 | 8 | 0 | 9 | 0 | 0 | 0 | 0 | - | 0 | 0-0 | 2 | 6.24 | 6.57 |
| 13 Hou | AL | 5 | 0 | 0 | 0 | 6.1 | 37 | 10 | 11 | 8 | 0 | 1 | 0 | 2 | 7 | 0 | 3 | 0 | 0 | 0 | 0 | - | 0 | 0-0 | 0 | 11.27 | 11.37 |
| 13 Was | NL | 11 | 0 | 0 | 3 | 6.0 | 23 | 5 | 1 | 1 | 0 | 0 | 0 | 0 | 1 | 0 | 6 | 0 | 0 | 0 | 0 | - | 0 | 0-0 | 2 | 1.84 | 1.50 |
| 3 ML YEARS | | 63 | 0 | 0 | 15 | 45.0 | 209 | 52 | 32 | 27 | 5 | 3 | 3 | 3 | 22 | 1 | 45 | 3 | 0 | 0 | 1 | .000 | 0 | 1-3 | 8 | 5.61 | 5.40 |

# Juan Centeno

**Bats:** L **Throws:** R **Pos:** C-4 sen-TAIN-no **Ht:** 5'10" **Wt:** 170 **Born:** 11/16/1989 **Age:** 24

| BATTING | | | | | | | | | | | | | | | | | | | | BASERUNNING | | | | AVERAGES | | |
|---|---|---|---|---|---|---|---|---|---|---|---|---|---|---|---|---|---|---|---|---|---|---|---|---|---|---|
| Year Team | Lg | G | AB | H | 2B | 3B | HR | (Hm | Rd) | TB | R | RBI | RC | TBB | IBB | SO | HBP | SH | SF | SB | CS | SB% | GDP | Avg | OBP | Slg |
| 2009 Bklyn | A- | 32 | 110 | 18 | 2 | 1 | 0 | (- | -) | 22 | 8 | 9 | 3 | 5 | 0 | 18 | 2 | 2 | 1 | 1 | 1 | .50 | 2 | .164 | .212 | .200 |
| 2010 StLuci | A+ | 11 | 35 | 7 | 0 | 0 | 0 | (- | -) | 7 | 1 | 1 | 2 | 3 | 1 | 7 | 0 | 2 | 1 | 1 | 0 | 1.00 | 4 | .200 | .256 | .200 |
| 2010 Bnghtn | AA | 1 | 1 | 0 | 0 | 0 | 0 | (- | -) | 0 | 0 | 0 | 0 | 0 | 0 | 0 | 0 | 0 | 0 | 0 | 0 | - | 0 | .000 | .000 | .000 |
| 2010 Bklyn | A- | 32 | 89 | 33 | 8 | 1 | 1 | (- | -) | 46 | 17 | 10 | 19 | 6 | 1 | 8 | 1 | 8 | 0 | 1 | 0 | 1.00 | 1 | .371 | .417 | .517 |
| 2011 StLuci | A+ | 52 | 157 | 50 | 5 | 1 | 1 | (- | -) | 60 | 22 | 11 | 23 | 12 | 0 | 22 | 1 | 7 | 1 | 3 | 1 | .75 | 4 | .318 | .368 | .382 |
| 2012 Bnghtn | AA | 79 | 281 | 80 | 12 | 2 | 0 | (- | -) | 96 | 29 | 35 | 34 | 23 | 0 | 43 | 1 | 4 | 4 | 1 | 1 | .50 | 21 | .285 | .337 | .342 |
| 2013 Bnghtn | AA | 6 | 23 | 6 | 1 | 1 | 0 | (- | -) | 9 | 4 | 3 | 2 | 0 | 0 | 5 | 0 | 1 | 0 | 0 | 0 | - | 3 | .261 | .261 | .391 |
| 2013 LsVgs | AAA | 67 | 213 | 65 | 10 | 2 | 0 | (- | -) | 79 | 25 | 28 | 29 | 12 | 0 | 24 | 3 | 6 | 3 | 1 | 1 | .50 | 7 | .305 | .346 | .371 |
| 2013 NYM | NL | 4 | 10 | 3 | 0 | 0 | 0 | (0 | 0) | 3 | 0 | 1 | 1 | 0 | 0 | 1 | 0 | 0 | 0 | 0 | 0 | - | 0 | .300 | .300 | .300 |

# Francisco Cervelli

**Bats:** R **Throws:** R **Pos:** C-17;2B-1 serr-VELL-ee **Ht:** 6'1" **Wt:** 205 **Born:** 3/6/1986 **Age:** 28

| BATTING | | | | | | | | | | | | | | | | | | | | BASERUNNING | | | | AVERAGES | | |
|---|---|---|---|---|---|---|---|---|---|---|---|---|---|---|---|---|---|---|---|---|---|---|---|---|---|---|
| Year Team | Lg | G | AB | H | 2B | 3B | HR | (Hm | Rd) | TB | R | RBI | RC | TBB | IBB | SO | HBP | SH | SF | SB | CS | SB% | GDP | Avg | OBP | Slg |
| 2008 NYY | AL | 3 | 5 | 0 | 0 | 0 | 0 | (0 | 0) | 0 | 0 | 0 | 0 | 0 | 0 | 3 | 0 | 0 | 0 | 0 | 0 | - | 1 | .000 | .000 | .000 |
| 2009 NYY | AL | 42 | 94 | 28 | 4 | 0 | 1 | (0 | 1) | 35 | 13 | 11 | 11 | 2 | 0 | 11 | 0 | 4 | 1 | 0 | 3 | .00 | 1 | .298 | .309 | .372 |
| 2010 NYY | AL | 93 | 266 | 72 | 11 | 3 | 0 | (0 | 0) | 89 | 27 | 38 | 40 | 33 | 1 | 42 | 6 | 8 | 4 | 1 | 1 | .50 | 7 | .271 | .359 | .335 |
| 2011 NYY | AL | 43 | 124 | 33 | 4 | 0 | 4 | (2 | 2) | 49 | 17 | 22 | 17 | 9 | 0 | 29 | 2 | 1 | 1 | 4 | 1 | .80 | 4 | .266 | .324 | .395 |
| 2012 NYY | AL | 3 | 1 | 0 | 0 | 0 | 0 | (0 | 0) | 0 | 1 | 0 | 0 | 1 | 0 | 0 | 0 | 0 | 0 | 0 | 0 | - | 0 | .000 | .500 | .000 |
| 2013 NYY | AL | 17 | 52 | 14 | 3 | 0 | 3 | (3 | 0) | 26 | 12 | 8 | 9 | 8 | 0 | 9 | 1 | 0 | 0 | 0 | 0 | - | 1 | .269 | .377 | .500 |
| Postseason | | 3 | 3 | 0 | 0 | 0 | 0 | (0 | 0) | 0 | 0 | 0 | 0 | 0 | 0 | 2 | 0 | 0 | 0 | 0 | 0 | - | 0 | .000 | .000 | .000 |
| 6 ML YEARS | | 201 | 542 | 147 | 22 | 3 | 8 | (5 | 3) | 199 | 70 | 79 | 77 | 53 | 1 | 94 | 9 | 13 | 6 | 5 | 5 | .50 | 14 | .271 | .343 | .367 |

# Yoenis Cespedes

**Bats:** R **Throws:** R **Pos:** LF-94;DH-27;CF-18;PH-1 yo-EHN-ess SESS-peh-des **Ht:** 5'10" **Wt:** 210 **Born:** 10/18/1985 **Age:** 28

| BATTING | | | | | | | | | | | | | | | | | | | | BASERUNNING | | | | AVERAGES | | |
|---|---|---|---|---|---|---|---|---|---|---|---|---|---|---|---|---|---|---|---|---|---|---|---|---|---|---|
| Year Team | Lg | G | AB | H | 2B | 3B | HR | (Hm | Rd) | TB | R | RBI | RC | TBB | IBB | SO | HBP | SH | SF | SB | CS | SB% | GDP | Avg | OBP | Slg |
| 2012 Scrmto | AAA | 3 | 9 | 3 | 0 | 0 | 0 | (- | -) | 3 | 1 | 0 | 1 | 1 | 0 | 1 | 1 | 0 | 0 | 0 | 0 | - | 0 | .333 | .455 | .333 |
| 2013 Scrmto | AAA | 3 | 9 | 3 | 0 | 0 | 1 | (- | -) | 6 | 5 | 4 | 2 | 2 | 0 | 3 | 0 | 0 | 0 | 1 | 0 | 1.00 | 1 | .333 | .455 | .667 |
| 2012 Oak | AL | 129 | 487 | 142 | 25 | 5 | 23 | (11 | 12) | 246 | 70 | 82 | 90 | 43 | 5 | 102 | 7 | 0 | 3 | 16 | 4 | .80 | 9 | .292 | .356 | .505 |
| 2013 Oak | AL | 135 | 529 | 127 | 21 | 4 | 26 | (14 | 12) | 234 | 74 | 80 | 65 | 37 | 5 | 137 | 5 | 0 | 3 | 7 | 7 | .50 | 8 | .240 | .294 | .442 |
| Postseason | | 5 | 19 | 6 | 1 | 0 | 0 | (0 | 0) | 7 | 1 | 2 | 3 | 2 | 0 | 2 | 0 | 0 | 0 | 2 | 0 | 1.00 | 0 | .316 | .381 | .368 |
| 2 ML YEARS | | 264 | 1016 | 269 | 46 | 9 | 49 | (25 | 24) | 480 | 144 | 162 | 155 | 80 | 10 | 239 | 12 | 0 | 6 | 23 | 11 | .68 | 17 | .265 | .324 | .472 |

# Jhoulys Chacin

**Pitches:** R **Bats:** R **Pos:** SP-31 joo-LEEZ cha-SEEN **Ht:** 6'3" **Wt:** 225 **Born:** 1/7/1988 **Age:** 26

| HOW MUCH HE PITCHED | | | | | | | | WHAT HE GAVE UP | | | | | | | | | | | | THE RESULTS | | | | | | | |
|---|---|---|---|---|---|---|---|---|---|---|---|---|---|---|---|---|---|---|---|---|---|---|---|---|---|---|---|
| Year Team | Lg | G | GS | CG | GF | IP | BFP | H | R | ER | HR | SH | SF | HB | TBB | IBB | SO | WP | Bk | W | L | Pct | Sh | Sv-Op | Hld | ERC | ERA |
| 2009 Col | NL | 9 | 1 | 0 | 3 | 11.0 | 48 | 6 | 6 | 6 | 1 | 1 | 0 | 0 | 11 | 0 | 13 | 2 | 0 | 0 | 1 | .000 | 0 | 0-0 | 0 | 3.87 | 4.91 |
| 2010 Col | NL | 28 | 21 | 0 | 2 | 137.1 | 583 | 114 | 64 | 50 | 10 | 6 | 5 | 9 | 61 | 5 | 138 | 4 | 0 | 9 | 11 | .450 | 0 | 0-0 | 0 | 3.33 | 3.28 |
| 2011 Col | NL | 31 | 31 | 2 | 0 | 194.0 | 827 | 168 | 87 | 78 | 20 | 5 | 3 | 4 | **87** | 1 | 150 | 7 | 0 | 11 | 14 | .440 | 1 | 0-0 | 0 | 3.61 | 3.62 |
| 2012 Col | NL | 14 | 14 | 0 | 0 | 69.0 | 314 | 80 | 35 | 34 | 10 | 1 | 1 | 2 | 32 | 0 | 45 | 3 | 0 | 3 | 5 | .375 | 0 | 0-0 | 0 | 5.73 | 4.43 |
| 2013 Col | NL | 31 | 31 | 0 | 0 | 197.1 | 816 | 188 | 82 | 76 | 11 | 3 | 7 | 3 | 61 | 3 | 126 | 5 | 1 | 14 | 10 | .583 | 0 | 0-0 | 0 | 3.26 | 3.47 |
| 5 ML YEARS | | 113 | 98 | 2 | 5 | 608.2 | 2588 | 556 | 274 | 244 | 52 | 16 | 16 | 18 | 252 | 9 | 472 | 21 | 1 | 37 | 41 | .474 | 1 | 0-0 | 0 | 3.66 | 3.61 |

# Joba Chamberlain

**Pitches:** R **Bats:** R **Pos:** RP-45 JOBB-ah CHAME-berr-linn **Ht:** 6'2" **Wt:** 250 **Born:** 9/23/1985 **Age:** 28

| | | | HOW MUCH HE PITCHED | | | | | | WHAT HE GAVE UP | | | | | | | | | | | | THE RESULTS | | | | | | | |
|---|---|---|---|---|---|---|---|---|---|---|---|---|---|---|---|---|---|---|---|---|---|---|---|---|---|---|---|---|
| Year | Team | Lg | G | GS | CG | GF | IP | BFP | H | R | ER | HR | SH | SF | HB | TBB | IBB | SO | WP | Bk | W | L | Pct | Sh | Sv-Op | Hld | ERC | ERA |
| 2013 | S-WB* | AAA | 1 | 1 | 0 | 0 | 1.0 | 5 | 2 | 0 | 0 | 0 | 0 | 0 | 0 | 0 | 0 | 0 | 0 | 0 | 0 | 0 | - | 0 | 0-- | - | 7.48 | 0.00 |
| 2007 | NYY | AL | 19 | 0 | 0 | 3 | 24.0 | 91 | 12 | 2 | 1 | 1 | 1 | 0 | 1 | 6 | 0 | 34 | 1 | 0 | 2 | 0 | 1.000 | 0 | 1-1 | 8 | 1.16 | 0.38 |
| 2008 | NYY | AL | 42 | 12 | 0 | 5 | 100.1 | 417 | 87 | 32 | 29 | 5 | 2 | 1 | 2 | 39 | 3 | 118 | 4 | 2 | 4 | 3 | .571 | 0 | 0-1 | 19 | 3.04 | 2.60 |
| 2009 | NYY | AL | 32 | 31 | 0 | 0 | 157.1 | 709 | 167 | 94 | 83 | 21 | 6 | 5 | **12** | 76 | 2 | 133 | 5 | 2 | 9 | 6 | .600 | 0 | 0-0 | 0 | 5.32 | 4.75 |
| 2010 | NYY | AL | 73 | 0 | 0 | 18 | 71.2 | 305 | 71 | 37 | 35 | 6 | 0 | 1 | 1 | 22 | 2 | 77 | 5 | 1 | 3 | 4 | .429 | 0 | 3-7 | 26 | 3.53 | 4.40 |
| 2011 | NYY | AL | 27 | 0 | 0 | 3 | 28.2 | 110 | 23 | 10 | 9 | 3 | 0 | 1 | 1 | 7 | 0 | 24 | 1 | 0 | 2 | 0 | 1.000 | 0 | 0-1 | 12 | 2.76 | 2.83 |
| 2012 | NYY | AL | 22 | 0 | 0 | 5 | 20.2 | 95 | 26 | 11 | 10 | 3 | 0 | 1 | 2 | 6 | 2 | 22 | 0 | 0 | 1 | 0 | 1.000 | 0 | 0-0 | 4 | 5.63 | 4.35 |
| 2013 | NYY | AL | 45 | 0 | 0 | 14 | 42.0 | 198 | 47 | 23 | 23 | 8 | 0 | 1 | 1 | 26 | 1 | 38 | 3 | 0 | 2 | 1 | .667 | 0 | 1-1 | 5 | 6.38 | 4.93 |
| Postseason | | | 19 | 0 | 0 | 1 | 15.2 | 73 | 20 | 5 | 5 | 1 | 1 | 1 | 1 | 6 | 0 | 15 | 2 | 0 | 1 | 0 | 1.000 | 0 | 0-2 | 3 | 5.54 | 2.87 |
| 7 ML YEARS | | | 260 | 43 | 0 | 48 | 444.2 | 1925 | 433 | 209 | 190 | 47 | 9 | 10 | 20 | 182 | 10 | 446 | 19 | 5 | 23 | 14 | .622 | 0 | 5-11 | 74 | 4.15 | 3.85 |

# Adron Chambers

**Bats:** L **Throws:** L **Pos:** PH-13;LF-11;RF-6;PR-6 AID-run **Ht:** 5'10" **Wt:** 200 **Born:** 10/8/1986 **Age:** 27

| | | | BATTING | | | | | | | | | | | | | | | | | | BASERUNNING | | | | AVERAGES | | |
|---|---|---|---|---|---|---|---|---|---|---|---|---|---|---|---|---|---|---|---|---|---|---|---|---|---|---|---|
| Year | Team | Lg | G | AB | H | 2B | 3B | HR | (Hm | Rd) | TB | R | RBI | RC | TBB | IBB | SO | HBP | SH | SF | SB | CS | SB% | GDP | Avg | OBP | Slg |
| 2013 | Memp* | AAA | 101 | 333 | 84 | 13 | 4 | 8 | (- | -) | 129 | 51 | 43 | 50 | 39 | 0 | 75 | 7 | 8 | 6 | 16 | 2 | .89 | 7 | .252 | .338 | .387 |
| 2011 | StL | NL | 18 | 8 | 3 | 0 | 1 | 0 | (0 | 0) | 5 | 2 | 4 | 3 | 0 | 0 | 1 | 0 | 0 | 0 | 0 | 0 | - | 0 | .375 | .375 | .625 |
| 2012 | StL | NL | 41 | 54 | 12 | 0 | 2 | 0 | (0 | 0) | 16 | 4 | 4 | 7 | 5 | 2 | 18 | 1 | 2 | 0 | 2 | 1 | .67 | 0 | .222 | .300 | .296 |
| 2013 | StL | NL | 25 | 26 | 4 | 1 | 0 | 0 | (0 | 0) | 5 | 5 | 1 | 1 | 3 | 2 | 11 | 0 | 0 | 0 | 0 | 1 | .00 | 0 | .154 | .241 | .192 |
| Postseason | | | 17 | 7 | 1 | 0 | 0 | 0 | (0 | 0) | 1 | 4 | 2 | 1 | 1 | 0 | 4 | 0 | 0 | 1 | 0 | 0 | - | 0 | .143 | .222 | .143 |
| 3 ML YEARS | | | 84 | 88 | 19 | 1 | 3 | 0 | (0 | 0) | 26 | 11 | 9 | 11 | 8 | 4 | 30 | 1 | 2 | 0 | 2 | 2 | .50 | 0 | .216 | .289 | .295 |

# Aroldis Chapman

**Pitches:** L **Bats:** L **Pos:** RP-68 ah-ROLL-diss **Ht:** 6'4" **Wt:** 205 **Born:** 2/28/1988 **Age:** 26

| | | | HOW MUCH HE PITCHED | | | | | | WHAT HE GAVE UP | | | | | | | | | | | | THE RESULTS | | | | | | | |
|---|---|---|---|---|---|---|---|---|---|---|---|---|---|---|---|---|---|---|---|---|---|---|---|---|---|---|---|---|
| Year | Team | Lg | G | GS | CG | GF | IP | BFP | H | R | ER | HR | SH | SF | HB | TBB | IBB | SO | WP | Bk | W | L | Pct | Sh | Sv-Op | Hld | ERC | ERA |
| 2010 | Cin | NL | 15 | 0 | 0 | 3 | 13.1 | 51 | 9 | 4 | 3 | 0 | 0 | 0 | 0 | 5 | 0 | 19 | 2 | 0 | 2 | 2 | .500 | 0 | 0-1 | 4 | 1.82 | 2.03 |
| 2011 | Cin | NL | 54 | 0 | 0 | 13 | 50.0 | 207 | 24 | 21 | 20 | 2 | 1 | 0 | 2 | 41 | 0 | 71 | 4 | 0 | 4 | 1 | .800 | 0 | 1-3 | 13 | 2.69 | 3.60 |
| 2012 | Cin | NL | 68 | 0 | 0 | 52 | 71.2 | 276 | 35 | 13 | 12 | 4 | 0 | 1 | 4 | 23 | 0 | 122 | 4 | 0 | 5 | 5 | .500 | 0 | 38-43 | 6 | 1.35 | 1.51 |
| 2013 | Cin | NL | 68 | 0 | 0 | 55 | 63.2 | 258 | 37 | 18 | 18 | 7 | 1 | 0 | 3 | 29 | 0 | 112 | 6 | 0 | 4 | 5 | .444 | 0 | 38-43 | 0 | 2.33 | 2.54 |
| Postseason | | | 5 | 0 | 0 | 3 | 4.2 | 24 | 5 | 4 | 1 | 0 | 0 | 0 | 1 | 2 | 0 | 4 | 2 | 0 | 0 | 1 | .000 | 0 | 0-1 | 0 | 4.11 | 1.93 |
| 4 ML YEARS | | | 205 | 0 | 0 | 123 | 198.2 | 792 | 105 | 56 | 53 | 13 | 2 | 1 | 9 | 98 | 0 | 324 | 16 | 0 | 15 | 13 | .536 | 0 | 77-90 | 23 | 1.97 | 2.40 |

# Kevin Chapman

**Pitches:** L **Bats:** L **Pos:** RP-25 **Ht:** 6'3" **Wt:** 220 **Born:** 2/19/1988 **Age:** 26

| | | | HOW MUCH HE PITCHED | | | | | | WHAT HE GAVE UP | | | | | | | | | | | | THE RESULTS | | | | | | | |
|---|---|---|---|---|---|---|---|---|---|---|---|---|---|---|---|---|---|---|---|---|---|---|---|---|---|---|---|---|
| Year | Team | Lg | G | GS | CG | GF | IP | BFP | H | R | ER | HR | SH | SF | HB | TBB | IBB | SO | WP | Bk | W | L | Pct | Sh | Sv-Op | Hld | ERC | ERA |
| 2010 | Wilmg | A+ | 14 | 0 | 0 | 8 | 18.0 | 86 | 20 | 13 | 11 | 1 | 2 | 0 | 1 | 8 | 0 | 20 | 1 | 0 | 1 | 1 | .500 | 0 | 1-- | - | 4.47 | 5.50 |
| 2011 | Wilmg | A+ | 15 | 0 | 0 | 12 | 22.1 | 99 | 24 | 14 | 12 | 1 | 1 | 0 | 0 | 7 | 0 | 40 | 2 | 0 | 0 | 2 | .000 | 0 | 7-- | - | 3.63 | 4.84 |
| 2011 | NWArk | AA | 25 | 0 | 0 | 8 | 39.2 | 173 | 37 | 25 | 22 | 5 | 3 | 2 | 2 | 21 | 0 | 50 | 1 | 0 | 1 | 2 | .333 | 0 | 3-- | - | 4.67 | 4.99 |
| 2012 | CpChr | AA | 49 | 0 | 0 | 11 | 58.0 | 256 | 49 | 19 | 17 | 2 | 3 | 3 | 1 | 32 | 3 | 59 | 2 | 0 | 6 | 3 | .667 | 0 | 2-- | - | 3.24 | 2.64 |
| 2013 | OKCity | AAA | 45 | 0 | 0 | 7 | 50.2 | 229 | 42 | 23 | 18 | 2 | 3 | 1 | 1 | 36 | 0 | 61 | 2 | 0 | 1 | 2 | .333 | 0 | 2-- | - | 3.88 | 3.20 |
| 2013 | Hou | AL | 25 | 0 | 0 | 2 | 20.1 | 87 | 13 | 6 | 4 | 1 | 2 | 0 | 1 | 13 | 2 | 15 | 3 | 0 | 1 | 1 | .500 | 0 | 1-4 | 4 | 2.69 | 1.77 |

# Tyler Chatwood

**Pitches:** R **Bats:** R **Pos:** SP-20 **Ht:** 6'0" **Wt:** 185 **Born:** 12/16/1989 **Age:** 24

| | | | HOW MUCH HE PITCHED | | | | | | WHAT HE GAVE UP | | | | | | | | | | | | THE RESULTS | | | | | | | |
|---|---|---|---|---|---|---|---|---|---|---|---|---|---|---|---|---|---|---|---|---|---|---|---|---|---|---|---|---|
| Year | Team | Lg | G | GS | CG | GF | IP | BFP | H | R | ER | HR | SH | SF | HB | TBB | IBB | SO | WP | Bk | W | L | Pct | Sh | Sv-Op | Hld | ERC | ERA |
| 2013 | ColSpr* | AAA | 6 | 6 | 1 | 0 | 34.0 | 142 | 37 | 11 | 11 | 0 | 1 | 0 | 1 | 7 | 0 | 33 | 3 | 0 | 2 | 1 | .667 | 1 | 0-- | - | 3.28 | 2.91 |
| 2011 | LAA | AL | 27 | 25 | 0 | 0 | 142.0 | 633 | 166 | 81 | 75 | 14 | 6 | 3 | 6 | 71 | 4 | 74 | 3 | 1 | 6 | 11 | .353 | 0 | 0-0 | 0 | 5.78 | 4.75 |
| 2012 | Col | NL | 19 | 12 | 0 | 3 | 64.2 | 294 | 74 | 43 | 39 | 9 | 4 | 2 | 0 | 33 | 2 | 41 | 4 | 0 | 5 | 6 | .455 | 0 | 1-1 | 0 | 5.62 | 5.43 |
| 2013 | Col | NL | 20 | 20 | 1 | 0 | 111.1 | 476 | 118 | 44 | 39 | 5 | 2 | 4 | 4 | 41 | 5 | 66 | 10 | 0 | 8 | 5 | .615 | 0 | 0-0 | 0 | 4.05 | 3.15 |
| 3 ML YEARS | | | 66 | 57 | 1 | 3 | 318.0 | 1403 | 358 | 168 | 153 | 28 | 12 | 9 | 10 | 145 | 11 | 181 | 17 | 1 | 19 | 22 | .463 | 0 | 1-1 | 0 | 5.12 | 4.33 |

# Endy Chavez

EN-dee SHAH-vezz

**Bats:** L **Throws:** L **Pos:** RF-50;CF-24;LF-16;PH-14;PR-9;DH-3 **Ht:** 5'11" **Wt:** 170 **Born:** 2/7/1978 **Age:** 36

| | | | BATTING | | | | | | | | | | | | | | | | | | BASERUNNING | | | | AVERAGES | | |
|---|---|---|---|---|---|---|---|---|---|---|---|---|---|---|---|---|---|---|---|---|---|---|---|---|---|---|---|
| Year | Team | Lg | G | AB | H | 2B | 3B | HR | (Hm | Rd) | TB | R | RBI | RC | TBB | IBB | SO | HBP | SH | SF | SB | CS | SB% | GDP | Avg | OBP | Slg |
| 2013 | Tacom* | AAA | 6 | 28 | 12 | 1 | 0 | 0 | (- | -) | 13 | 8 | 1 | 5 | 3 | 0 | 3 | 0 | 0 | 0 | 0 | 2 | .00 | 0 | .429 | .484 | .464 |
| 2001 | KC | AL | 29 | 77 | 16 | 2 | 0 | 0 | (0 | 0) | 18 | 4 | 5 | 2 | 3 | 0 | 8 | 0 | 0 | 0 | 0 | 2 | .00 | 3 | .208 | .238 | .234 |
| 2002 | Mon | NL | 36 | 125 | 37 | 8 | 5 | 1 | (0 | 1) | 58 | 20 | 9 | 14 | 5 | 0 | 16 | 0 | 7 | 1 | 3 | 5 | .38 | 0 | .296 | .321 | .464 |
| 2003 | Mon | NL | 141 | 483 | 121 | 25 | 5 | 5 | (4 | 1) | 171 | 66 | 47 | 56 | 31 | 3 | 59 | 0 | 9 | 3 | 18 | 7 | .72 | 7 | .251 | .294 | .354 |
| 2004 | Mon | NL | 132 | 502 | 139 | 20 | 6 | 5 | (4 | 1) | 186 | 65 | 34 | 56 | 30 | 0 | 40 | 1 | 12 | 2 | 32 | 7 | .82 | 6 | .277 | .318 | .371 |
| 2005 | 2 Tms | NL | 98 | 116 | 25 | 4 | 3 | 0 | (0 | 0) | 35 | 19 | 11 | 8 | 7 | 0 | 14 | 0 | 7 | 0 | 2 | 2 | .50 | 3 | .216 | .260 | .302 |
| 2006 | NYM | NL | 133 | 353 | 108 | 22 | 5 | 4 | (2 | 2) | 152 | 48 | 42 | 54 | 24 | 3 | 44 | 0 | 11 | 2 | 12 | 3 | .80 | 7 | .306 | .348 | .431 |
| 2007 | NYM | NL | 71 | 150 | 43 | 7 | 2 | 1 | (1 | 0) | 57 | 20 | 17 | 20 | 9 | 0 | 16 | 0 | 5 | 1 | 5 | 2 | .71 | 5 | .287 | .325 | .380 |
| 2008 | NYM | NL | 133 | 270 | 72 | 10 | 2 | 1 | (1 | 0) | 89 | 30 | 12 | 21 | 17 | 3 | 22 | 0 | 9 | 2 | 6 | 1 | .86 | 6 | .267 | .308 | .330 |
| 2009 | Sea | AL | 54 | 161 | 44 | 3 | 1 | 2 | (1 | 1) | 55 | 17 | 13 | 15 | 14 | 1 | 22 | 0 | 5 | 2 | 9 | 1 | .90 | 4 | .273 | .328 | .342 |
| 2011 | Tex | AL | 83 | 256 | 77 | 11 | 3 | 5 | (3 | 2) | 109 | 37 | 27 | 32 | 10 | 0 | 30 | 0 | 5 | 3 | 10 | 5 | .67 | 7 | .301 | .323 | .426 |
| 2012 | Bal | AL | 64 | 158 | 32 | 6 | 0 | 2 | (0 | 2) | 44 | 15 | 12 | 10 | 6 | 1 | 24 | 1 | 4 | 0 | 3 | 2 | .60 | 2 | .203 | .236 | .278 |
| 2013 | Sea | AL | 97 | 266 | 71 | 10 | 0 | 2 | (0 | 2) | 87 | 22 | 14 | 17 | 9 | 1 | 31 | 0 | 3 | 1 | 1 | 3 | .25 | 9 | .267 | .290 | .327 |

| BATTING | | | | | | | | | | | | | | | | | | | | | BASERUNNING | | | | AVERAGES | | |
|---|---|---|---|---|---|---|---|---|---|---|---|---|---|---|---|---|---|---|---|---|---|---|---|---|---|---|---|
| Year | Team | Lg | G | AB | H | 2B | 3B | HR | (Hm | Rd) | TB | R | RBI | RC | TBB | IBB | SO | HBP | SH | SF | SB | CS | SB% | GDP | Avg | OBP | Slg |
| 05 | Was | NL | 7 | 9 | 2 | 1 | 0 | 0 | (0 | 0) | 3 | 2 | 1 | 1 | 3 | 0 | 1 | 0 | 0 | 0 | 0 | 1 | .00 | 1 | .222 | .417 | .333 |
| 05 | Phi | NL | 91 | 107 | 23 | 3 | 3 | 0 | (0 | 0) | 32 | 17 | 10 | 7 | 4 | 0 | 13 | 0 | 7 | 0 | 2 | 1 | .67 | 2 | .215 | .243 | .299 |
| Postseason | | | 19 | 41 | 8 | 2 | 0 | 0 | (0 | 0) | 10 | 2 | 0 | 0 | 0 | 0 | 2 | 0 | 0 | 0 | 0 | 0 | - | 1 | .195 | .195 | .244 |
| 12 ML YEARS | | | 1071 | 2917 | 785 | 128 | 32 | 28 | (16 | 12) | 1061 | 363 | 243 | 305 | 165 | 12 | 326 | 2 | 77 | 17 | 101 | 40 | .72 | 59 | .269 | .307 | .364 |

# Eric Chavez

**Bats:** L **Throws:** R **Pos:** 3B-52;PH-22;1B-6;DH-4 shah-VEZZ **Ht:** 6'1" **Wt:** 215 **Born:** 12/7/1977 **Age:** 36

| BATTING | | | | | | | | | | | | | | | | | | | | | BASERUNNING | | | | AVERAGES | | |
|---|---|---|---|---|---|---|---|---|---|---|---|---|---|---|---|---|---|---|---|---|---|---|---|---|---|---|---|
| Year | Team | Lg | G | AB | H | 2B | 3B | HR | (Hm | Rd) | TB | R | RBI | RC | TBB | IBB | SO | HBP | SH | SF | SB | CS | SB% | GDP | Avg | OBP | Slg |
| 2013 | Reno* | AAA | 3 | 8 | 2 | 0 | 0 | 0 | (- | -) | 2 | 0 | 0 | 1 | 2 | 0 | 1 | 0 | 0 | 0 | 0 | 0 | - | 1 | .250 | .400 | .250 |
| 2013 | DBcks* | R | 3 | 7 | 1 | 0 | 0 | 1 | (- | -) | 4 | 1 | 2 | 0 | 0 | 0 | 0 | 0 | 0 | 1 | 0 | 0 | - | 2 | .143 | .125 | .571 |
| 1998 | Oak | AL | 16 | 45 | 14 | 4 | 1 | 0 | (0 | 0) | 20 | 6 | 6 | 7 | 3 | 1 | 5 | 0 | 0 | 0 | 1 | 1 | .50 | 1 | .311 | .354 | .444 |
| 1999 | Oak | AL | 115 | 356 | 88 | 21 | 2 | 13 | (8 | 5) | 152 | 47 | 50 | 50 | 46 | 4 | 56 | 0 | 0 | 0 | 1 | 1 | .50 | 7 | .247 | .333 | .427 |
| 2000 | Oak | AL | 153 | 501 | 139 | 23 | 4 | 26 | (15 | 11) | 248 | 89 | 86 | 86 | 62 | 8 | 94 | 1 | 0 | 5 | 2 | 2 | .50 | 9 | .277 | .355 | .495 |
| 2001 | Oak | AL | 151 | 552 | 159 | 43 | 0 | 32 | (14 | 18) | 298 | 91 | 114 | 99 | 41 | 9 | 99 | 4 | 0 | 7 | 8 | 2 | .80 | 7 | .288 | .338 | .540 |
| 2002 | Oak | AL | 153 | 585 | 161 | 31 | 3 | 34 | (17 | 17) | 300 | 87 | 109 | 103 | 65 | 13 | 119 | 1 | 0 | 2 | 8 | 3 | .73 | 8 | .275 | .348 | .513 |
| 2003 | Oak | AL | 156 | 588 | 166 | 39 | 5 | 29 | (12 | 17) | 302 | 94 | 101 | 97 | 62 | 10 | 89 | 1 | 0 | 3 | 8 | 3 | .73 | 14 | .282 | .350 | .514 |
| 2004 | Oak | AL | 125 | 475 | 131 | 20 | 0 | 29 | (15 | 14) | 238 | 87 | 77 | 84 | **95** | 10 | 99 | 3 | 0 | 4 | 6 | 3 | .67 | 21 | .276 | .397 | .501 |
| 2005 | Oak | AL | 160 | 625 | 168 | 40 | 1 | 27 | (15 | 12) | 291 | 92 | 101 | 95 | 58 | 4 | 129 | 2 | 0 | 9 | 6 | 0 | 1.00 | 9 | .269 | .329 | .466 |
| 2006 | Oak | AL | 137 | 485 | 117 | 24 | 2 | 22 | (8 | 14) | 211 | 74 | 72 | 70 | 84 | 6 | 100 | 1 | 0 | 6 | 3 | 0 | 1.00 | 19 | .241 | .351 | .435 |
| 2007 | Oak | AL | 90 | 341 | 82 | 21 | 2 | 15 | (10 | 5) | 152 | 43 | 46 | 38 | 34 | 2 | 76 | 0 | 0 | 4 | 4 | 2 | .67 | 9 | .240 | .306 | .446 |
| 2008 | Oak | AL | 23 | 89 | 22 | 7 | 0 | 2 | (1 | 1) | 35 | 10 | 14 | 14 | 6 | 0 | 18 | 0 | 0 | 0 | 0 | 0 | - | 2 | .247 | .295 | .393 |
| 2009 | Oak | AL | 8 | 30 | 3 | 1 | 0 | 0 | (0 | 0) | 4 | 0 | 1 | 0 | 1 | 0 | 7 | 0 | 0 | 0 | 0 | 0 | - | 0 | .100 | .129 | .133 |
| 2010 | Oak | AL | 33 | 111 | 26 | 8 | 0 | 1 | (0 | 1) | 37 | 10 | 10 | 7 | 8 | 0 | 31 | 0 | 0 | 4 | 0 | 0 | - | 3 | .234 | .276 | .333 |
| 2011 | NYY | AL | 58 | 160 | 42 | 7 | 1 | 2 | (0 | 2) | 57 | 16 | 26 | 26 | 14 | 3 | 34 | 0 | 0 | 1 | 0 | 0 | - | 4 | .263 | .320 | .356 |
| 2012 | NYY | AL | 113 | 278 | 78 | 12 | 0 | 16 | (7 | 9) | 138 | 36 | 37 | 39 | 30 | 3 | 59 | 1 | 0 | 4 | 0 | 0 | - | 10 | .281 | .348 | .496 |
| 2013 | Ari | NL | 80 | 228 | 64 | 14 | 2 | 9 | (4 | 5) | 109 | 28 | 44 | 35 | 19 | 4 | 45 | 1 | 0 | 5 | 1 | 0 | 1.00 | 7 | .281 | .332 | .478 |
| Postseason | | | 34 | 125 | 24 | 7 | 0 | 3 | (3 | 0) | 40 | 11 | 12 | 12 | 7 | 2 | 31 | 0 | 0 | 0 | 1 | 0 | 1.00 | 2 | .192 | .235 | .320 |
| 16 ML YEARS | | | 1571 | 5449 | 1460 | 315 | 23 | 257 | (126 | 131) | 2592 | 810 | 894 | 850 | 628 | 77 | 1060 | 15 | 0 | 54 | 48 | 17 | .74 | 130 | .268 | .342 | .476 |

# Jesse Chavez

**Pitches:** R **Bats:** R **Pos:** RP-35 CHAH-vezz **Ht:** 6'2" **Wt:** 160 **Born:** 8/21/1983 **Age:** 30

| HOW MUCH HE PITCHED | | | | | | | | | WHAT HE GAVE UP | | | | | | | | | | | | THE RESULTS | | | | | | | |
|---|---|---|---|---|---|---|---|---|---|---|---|---|---|---|---|---|---|---|---|---|---|---|---|---|---|---|---|---|
| Year | Team | Lg | G | GS | CG | GF | IP | BFP | H | R | ER | HR | SH | SF | HB | TBB | IBB | SO | WP | Bk | W | L | Pct | Sh | Sv-Op | Hld | ERC | ERA |
| 2013 | Scrmto* | AAA | 5 | 5 | 0 | 0 | 30.0 | 130 | 35 | 16 | 9 | 1 | 0 | 1 | 1 | 5 | 0 | 26 | 0 | 0 | 2 | 2 | .500 | 0 | 0- - | - | 3.69 | 2.70 |
| 2008 | Pit | NL | 15 | 0 | 0 | 6 | 15.0 | 74 | 20 | 11 | 11 | 2 | 3 | 1 | 0 | 9 | 2 | 16 | 2 | 0 | 0 | 1 | .000 | 0 | 0-2 | 0 | 6.76 | 6.60 |
| 2009 | Pit | NL | 73 | 0 | 0 | 24 | 67.1 | 286 | 69 | 33 | 30 | 11 | 1 | 1 | 1 | 22 | 3 | 47 | 5 | 0 | 1 | 4 | .200 | 0 | 0-4 | 15 | 4.39 | 4.01 |
| 2010 | 2 Tms | | 51 | 0 | 0 | 26 | 62.2 | 280 | 69 | 44 | 41 | 11 | 5 | 3 | 1 | 23 | 7 | 45 | 2 | 0 | 5 | 5 | .500 | 0 | 0-1 | 6 | 4.85 | 5.89 |
| 2011 | KC | AL | 4 | 0 | 0 | 3 | 7.2 | 39 | 12 | 9 | 9 | 3 | 0 | 0 | 0 | 5 | 0 | 8 | 0 | 0 | 0 | 0 | - | 0 | 0-0 | 0 | 11.48 | 10.57 |
| 2012 | 2 Tms | AL | 13 | 2 | 0 | 3 | 24.2 | 123 | 34 | 29 | 27 | 7 | 0 | 1 | 3 | 11 | 1 | 30 | 1 | 0 | 1 | 1 | .500 | 0 | 0-0 | 0 | 8.32 | 9.85 |
| 2013 | Oak | AL | 35 | 0 | 0 | 16 | 57.1 | 248 | 50 | 27 | 25 | 3 | 6 | 2 | 3 | 20 | 4 | 55 | 5 | 0 | 2 | 4 | .333 | 0 | 1-2 | 1 | 2.85 | 3.92 |
| 10 | Atl | NL | 28 | 0 | 0 | 16 | 36.2 | 162 | 40 | 24 | 24 | 6 | 3 | 2 | 1 | 12 | 3 | 29 | 0 | 0 | 3 | 2 | .600 | 0 | 0-0 | 0 | 4.65 | 5.89 |
| 10 | KC | AL | 23 | 0 | 0 | 10 | 26.0 | 118 | 29 | 20 | 17 | 5 | 2 | 1 | 0 | 11 | 4 | 16 | 2 | 0 | 2 | 3 | .400 | 0 | 0-1 | 6 | 5.13 | 5.88 |
| 12 | Tor | AL | 9 | 2 | 0 | 2 | 21.1 | 102 | 25 | 22 | 20 | 6 | 0 | 1 | 2 | 10 | 1 | 27 | 0 | 0 | 1 | 1 | .500 | 0 | 0-0 | 0 | 6.90 | 8.44 |
| 12 | Oak | AL | 4 | 0 | 0 | 1 | 3.1 | 21 | 9 | 7 | 7 | 1 | 0 | 0 | 1 | 1 | 0 | 3 | 1 | 0 | 0 | 0 | - | 0 | 0-0 | 0 | 18.70 | 18.90 |
| 6 ML YEARS | | | 191 | 2 | 0 | 78 | 234.2 | 1050 | 254 | 153 | 143 | 37 | 15 | 8 | 8 | 90 | 17 | 201 | 15 | 0 | 9 | 15 | .375 | 0 | 1-9 | 22 | 4.83 | 5.48 |

# Bruce Chen

**Pitches:** L **Bats:** L **Pos:** RP-19; SP-15 **Ht:** 6'2" **Wt:** 215 **Born:** 6/19/1977 **Age:** 37

| HOW MUCH HE PITCHED | | | | | | | | | WHAT HE GAVE UP | | | | | | | | | | | | THE RESULTS | | | | | | | |
|---|---|---|---|---|---|---|---|---|---|---|---|---|---|---|---|---|---|---|---|---|---|---|---|---|---|---|---|---|
| Year | Team | Lg | G | GS | CG | GF | IP | BFP | H | R | ER | HR | SH | SF | HB | TBB | IBB | SO | WP | Bk | W | L | Pct | Sh | Sv-Op | Hld | ERC | ERA |
| 1998 | Atl | NL | 4 | 4 | 0 | 0 | 20.1 | 91 | 23 | 9 | 9 | 3 | 1 | 0 | 1 | 9 | 1 | 17 | 0 | 0 | 2 | 0 | 1.000 | 0 | 0-0 | 0 | 5.55 | 3.98 |
| 1999 | Atl | NL | 16 | 7 | 0 | 3 | 51.0 | 214 | 38 | 32 | 31 | 11 | 1 | 1 | 2 | 27 | 3 | 45 | 0 | 0 | 2 | 2 | .500 | 0 | 0-0 | 0 | 4.07 | 5.47 |
| 2000 | 2 Tms | NL | 37 | 15 | 0 | 4 | 134.0 | 559 | 116 | 54 | 49 | 18 | 8 | 3 | 2 | 46 | 4 | 112 | 4 | 1 | 7 | 4 | .636 | 0 | 0-0 | 0 | 3.35 | 3.29 |
| 2001 | 2 Tms | NL | 27 | 27 | 0 | 0 | 146.0 | 634 | 146 | 90 | 79 | 29 | 4 | 7 | 1 | 59 | 4 | 126 | 5 | 0 | 7 | 7 | .500 | 0 | 0-0 | 0 | 4.75 | 4.87 |
| 2002 | 3 Tms | NL | 55 | 6 | 0 | 9 | 77.2 | 360 | 85 | 53 | 48 | 16 | 2 | 3 | 2 | 43 | 5 | 80 | 4 | 0 | 2 | 5 | .286 | 0 | 0-0 | 4 | 5.99 | 5.56 |
| 2003 | 2 Tms | | 16 | 2 | 0 | 4 | 24.1 | 110 | 26 | 16 | 15 | 6 | 3 | 3 | 2 | 10 | 1 | 20 | 0 | 0 | 0 | 1 | .000 | 0 | 0-0 | 1 | 5.81 | 5.55 |
| 2004 | Bal | AL | 8 | 7 | 1 | 0 | 47.2 | 196 | 39 | 19 | 16 | 7 | 2 | 1 | 0 | 16 | 0 | 32 | 0 | 0 | 2 | 1 | .667 | 0 | 0-0 | 0 | 3.13 | 3.02 |
| 2005 | Bal | AL | 34 | 32 | 1 | 0 | 197.1 | 832 | 187 | 94 | 84 | 33 | 3 | 3 | 9 | 63 | 0 | 133 | 2 | 1 | 13 | 10 | .565 | 0 | 0-0 | 0 | 4.12 | 3.83 |
| 2006 | Bal | AL | 40 | 12 | 0 | 16 | 98.2 | 453 | 137 | 81 | 76 | 28 | 3 | 5 | 0 | 35 | 3 | 70 | 1 | 0 | 0 | 7 | .000 | 0 | 0-1 | 1 | 7.73 | 6.93 |
| 2007 | Tex | AL | 5 | 0 | 0 | 3 | 10.0 | 46 | 11 | 11 | 8 | 3 | 0 | 0 | 0 | 6 | 1 | 7 | 0 | 0 | 0 | 0 | - | 0 | 0-0 | 0 | 6.90 | 7.20 |
| 2009 | KC | AL | 17 | 9 | 0 | 4 | 62.1 | 279 | 74 | 42 | 40 | 12 | 2 | 2 | 4 | 25 | 3 | 45 | 4 | 0 | 1 | 6 | .143 | 0 | 0-0 | 0 | 6.18 | 5.78 |
| 2010 | KC | AL | 33 | 23 | 1 | 4 | 140.1 | 608 | 136 | 68 | 65 | 17 | 6 | 7 | 3 | 57 | 4 | 98 | 3 | 0 | 12 | 7 | .632 | 1 | 1-1 | 0 | 4.09 | 4.17 |
| 2011 | KC | AL | 25 | 25 | 1 | 0 | 155.0 | 654 | 152 | 71 | 65 | 18 | 3 | 5 | 7 | 50 | 2 | 97 | 2 | 0 | 12 | 8 | .600 | 0 | 0-0 | 0 | 3.98 | 3.77 |
| 2012 | KC | AL | 34 | **34** | 0 | 0 | 191.2 | 827 | 215 | 114 | 108 | 33 | 3 | 5 | 8 | 47 | 3 | 140 | 5 | 0 | 11 | 14 | .440 | 0 | 0-0 | 0 | 4.80 | 5.07 |
| 2013 | KC | AL | 34 | 15 | 0 | 3 | 121.0 | 498 | 107 | 46 | 44 | 13 | 2 | 5 | 3 | 36 | 4 | 78 | 0 | 1 | 9 | 4 | .692 | 0 | 0-2 | 2 | 3.17 | 3.27 |
| 00 | Atl | NL | 22 | 0 | 0 | 4 | 39.2 | 176 | 35 | 15 | 11 | 4 | 3 | 2 | 1 | 19 | 2 | 32 | 0 | 1 | 4 | 0 | 1.000 | 0 | 0-0 | 0 | 3.62 | 2.50 |
| 00 | Phi | NL | 15 | 15 | 0 | 0 | 94.1 | 383 | 81 | 39 | 38 | 14 | 5 | 1 | 1 | 27 | 2 | 80 | 4 | 0 | 3 | 4 | .429 | 0 | 0-0 | 0 | 3.22 | 3.63 |
| 01 | Phi | NL | 16 | 16 | 0 | 0 | 86.1 | 381 | 90 | 53 | 48 | 19 | 2 | 4 | 1 | 31 | 4 | 79 | 2 | 0 | 4 | 5 | .444 | 0 | 0-0 | 0 | 4.87 | 5.00 |
| 01 | NYM | NL | 11 | 11 | 0 | 0 | 59.2 | 253 | 56 | 37 | 31 | 10 | 2 | 3 | 0 | 28 | 0 | 47 | 3 | 0 | 3 | 2 | .600 | 0 | 0-0 | 0 | 4.58 | 4.68 |
| 02 | NYM | NL | 1 | 0 | 0 | 0 | 0.2 | 3 | 1 | 0 | 0 | 0 | 0 | 0 | 0 | 0 | 0 | 0 | 0 | 0 | 0 | 0 | - | 0 | 0-0 | 0 | 4.47 | 0.00 |
| 02 | Mon | NL | 15 | 5 | 0 | 4 | 37.1 | 179 | 47 | 29 | 29 | 9 | 0 | 0 | 1 | 23 | 3 | 43 | 3 | 0 | 2 | 3 | .400 | 0 | 0-0 | 0 | 7.69 | 6.99 |
| 02 | Cin | NL | 39 | 1 | 0 | 5 | 39.2 | 178 | 37 | 24 | 19 | 7 | 2 | 3 | 1 | 20 | 2 | 37 | 1 | 0 | 0 | 2 | .000 | 0 | 0-0 | 4 | 4.55 | 4.31 |
| 03 | Hou | NL | 11 | 0 | 0 | 2 | 12.0 | 60 | 14 | 8 | 8 | 2 | 3 | 2 | 2 | 8 | 1 | 8 | 0 | 0 | 0 | 0 | - | 0 | 0-0 | 1 | 7.11 | 6.00 |
| 03 | Bos | AL | 5 | 2 | 0 | 2 | 12.1 | 50 | 12 | 8 | 7 | 4 | 0 | 1 | 0 | 2 | 0 | 12 | 0 | 0 | 0 | 1 | .000 | 0 | 0-0 | 0 | 4.40 | 5.11 |
| 15 ML YEARS | | | 385 | 218 | 4 | 50 | 1477.1 | 6361 | 1492 | 800 | 737 | 247 | 43 | 50 | 44 | 529 | 38 | 1100 | 30 | 3 | 80 | 76 | .513 | 1 | 1-3 | 8 | 4.52 | 4.49 |

## Wei-Yin Chen

**Pitches:** L **Bats:** L **Pos:** SP-23 way-ying **Ht:** 6'0" **Wt:** 195 **Born:** 7/21/1985 **Age:** 28

| | | | HOW MUCH HE PITCHED | | | | | | WHAT HE GAVE UP | | | | | | | | | | | | THE RESULTS | | | | | | | |
|---|---|---|---|---|---|---|---|---|---|---|---|---|---|---|---|---|---|---|---|---|---|---|---|---|---|---|---|---|
| Year | Team | Lg | G | GS | CG | GF | IP | BFP | H | R | ER | HR | SH | SF | HB | TBB | IBB | SO | WP | Bk | W | L | Pct | Sh | Sv-Op | Hld | ERC | ERA |
| 2009 | Chnchi | Jap | 24 | 23 | 5 | - | 164.0 | 645 | 113 | 32 | 28 | 10 | - | - | 3 | 40 | 0 | 146 | 2 | 0 | 8 | 4 | .667 | 4 | 0-- | - | 1.76 | 1.54 |
| 2010 | Chnchi | Jap | 29 | 27 | 3 | - | 188.0 | 779 | 166 | 63 | 60 | 21 | - | - | 8 | 49 | 2 | 153 | 5 | 0 | 13 | 10 | .565 | 2 | 0-- | - | 3.11 | 2.87 |
| 2011 | Chnchi | Jap | 25 | 24 | 4 | - | 164.2 | 663 | 138 | 57 | 49 | 9 | - | - | 5 | 31 | 2 | 94 | 2 | 0 | 8 | 10 | .444 | 1 | 0-- | - | 2.24 | 2.68 |
| 2013 | Bowie | AA | 2 | 2 | 0 | 0 | 12.0 | 44 | 9 | 4 | 4 | 0 | 0 | 0 | 0 | 2 | 0 | 8 | 0 | 0 | 1 | 0 | 1.000 | 0 | 0-- | - | 1.57 | 3.00 |
| 2012 | Bal | AL | 32 | 32 | 0 | 0 | 192.2 | 818 | 186 | 97 | 86 | 29 | 5 | 8 | 5 | 57 | 0 | 154 | 2 | 1 | 12 | 11 | .522 | 0 | 0-0 | 0 | 3.88 | 4.02 |
| 2013 | Bal | AL | 23 | 23 | 0 | 0 | 137.0 | 572 | 142 | 62 | 62 | 17 | 2 | 6 | 2 | 39 | 2 | 104 | 3 | 0 | 7 | 7 | .500 | 0 | 0-0 | 0 | 4.11 | 4.07 |
| Postseason | | | 1 | 1 | 0 | 0 | 6.1 | 29 | 8 | 2 | 1 | 0 | 0 | 0 | 0 | 1 | 0 | 3 | 0 | 0 | 1 | 0 | 1.000 | 0 | 0-0 | 0 | 3.63 | 1.42 |
| 2 ML YEARS | | | 55 | 55 | 0 | 0 | 329.2 | 1390 | 328 | 159 | 148 | 46 | 7 | 14 | 7 | 96 | 2 | 258 | 5 | 1 | 19 | 18 | .514 | 0 | 0-0 | 0 | 3.97 | 4.04 |

## Robinson Chirinos

**Bats:** R **Throws:** R **Pos:** 1B-4;C-3;3B-3;PH-3;DH-1 chee-REE-nos **Ht:** 6'1" **Wt:** 205 **Born:** 6/5/1984 **Age:** 30

| | | | BATTING | | | | | | | | | | | | | | | | | BASERUNNING | | | | AVERAGES | | |
|---|---|---|---|---|---|---|---|---|---|---|---|---|---|---|---|---|---|---|---|---|---|---|---|---|---|---|
| Year | Team | Lg | G | AB | H | 2B | 3B | HR | (Hm | Rd) | TB | R | RBI | RC | TBB | IBB | SO | HBP | SH | SF | SB | CS | SB% | GDP | Avg | OBP | Slg |
| 2009 | Dytona | A+ | 69 | 227 | 68 | 13 | 5 | 11 | (- | -) | 124 | 40 | 47 | 50 | 35 | 0 | 40 | 5 | 0 | 3 | 2 | 2 | .50 | 4 | .300 | .400 | .546 |
| 2009 | Tenn | AA | 12 | 35 | 9 | 3 | 0 | 0 | (- | -) | 12 | 4 | 5 | 4 | 7 | 0 | 4 | 0 | 0 | 1 | 0 | 1 | .00 | 1 | .257 | .372 | .343 |
| 2010 | Tenn | AA | 77 | 264 | 84 | 24 | 0 | 15 | (- | -) | 153 | 53 | 64 | 62 | 42 | 4 | 35 | 5 | 0 | 7 | 1 | 5 | .17 | 6 | .318 | .412 | .580 |
| 2010 | Iowa | AAA | 15 | 55 | 20 | 4 | 0 | 3 | (- | -) | 33 | 10 | 10 | 13 | 2 | 0 | 8 | 5 | 0 | 0 | 0 | 0 | - | 3 | .364 | .435 | .600 |
| 2011 | Drham | AAA | 78 | 282 | 73 | 13 | 1 | 6 | (- | -) | 106 | 24 | 24 | 38 | 29 | 0 | 69 | 7 | 1 | 0 | 1 | 1 | .50 | 9 | .259 | .343 | .376 |
| 2013 | RdRck | AAA | 74 | 265 | 68 | 10 | 2 | 8 | (- | -) | 106 | 35 | 40 | 41 | 38 | 1 | 55 | 4 | 2 | 2 | 2 | 0 | 1.00 | 6 | .257 | .356 | .400 |
| 2011 | TB | AL | 20 | 55 | 12 | 2 | 0 | 1 | (1 | 0) | 17 | 4 | 7 | 5 | 5 | 0 | 13 | 0 | 0 | 0 | 0 | 0 | - | 0 | .218 | .283 | .309 |
| 2013 | Tex | AL | 13 | 28 | 5 | 3 | 0 | 0 | (0 | 0) | 8 | 3 | 0 | 0 | 2 | 0 | 6 | 0 | 0 | 0 | 0 | 0 | - | 1 | .179 | .233 | .286 |
| 2 ML YEARS | | | 33 | 83 | 17 | 5 | 0 | 1 | (1 | 0) | 25 | 7 | 7 | 5 | 7 | 0 | 19 | 0 | 0 | 0 | 0 | 0 | - | 1 | .205 | .267 | .301 |

## Lonnie Chisenhall

**Bats:** L **Throws:** R **Pos:** 3B-88;PH-6;DH-1;PR-1 CHIZZ-en-hall **Ht:** 6'2" **Wt:** 190 **Born:** 10/4/1988 **Age:** 25

| | | | BATTING | | | | | | | | | | | | | | | | | BASERUNNING | | | | AVERAGES | | |
|---|---|---|---|---|---|---|---|---|---|---|---|---|---|---|---|---|---|---|---|---|---|---|---|---|---|---|
| Year | Team | Lg | G | AB | H | 2B | 3B | HR | (Hm | Rd) | TB | R | RBI | RC | TBB | IBB | SO | HBP | SH | SF | SB | CS | SB% | GDP | Avg | OBP | Slg |
| 2013 | Clmbs* | AAA | 27 | 105 | 41 | 8 | 2 | 6 | (- | -) | 71 | 21 | 26 | 31 | 12 | 0 | 24 | 4 | 0 | 4 | 2 | 0 | 1.00 | 0 | .390 | .456 | .676 |
| 2011 | Cle | AL | 66 | 212 | 54 | 13 | 0 | 7 | (2 | 5) | 88 | 27 | 22 | 24 | 8 | 1 | 49 | 1 | 1 | 1 | 1 | 0 | 1.00 | 3 | .255 | .284 | .415 |
| 2012 | Cle | AL | 43 | 142 | 38 | 6 | 1 | 5 | (4 | 1) | 61 | 16 | 16 | 18 | 8 | 0 | 27 | 1 | 0 | 0 | 2 | 1 | .67 | 2 | .268 | .311 | .430 |
| 2013 | Cle | AL | 94 | 289 | 65 | 17 | 0 | 11 | (4 | 7) | 115 | 30 | 36 | 31 | 16 | 0 | 56 | 2 | 1 | 0 | 1 | 0 | 1.00 | 8 | .225 | .270 | .398 |
| 3 ML YEARS | | | 203 | 643 | 157 | 36 | 1 | 23 | (10 | 13) | 264 | 73 | 74 | 73 | 32 | 1 | 132 | 4 | 2 | 1 | 4 | 1 | .80 | 13 | .244 | .284 | .411 |

## Randy Choate

**Pitches:** L **Bats:** L **Pos:** RP-64 CHOTE **Ht:** 6'1" **Wt:** 210 **Born:** 9/5/1975 **Age:** 38

| | | | HOW MUCH HE PITCHED | | | | | | WHAT HE GAVE UP | | | | | | | | | | | | THE RESULTS | | | | | | | |
|---|---|---|---|---|---|---|---|---|---|---|---|---|---|---|---|---|---|---|---|---|---|---|---|---|---|---|---|---|
| Year | Team | Lg | G | GS | CG | GF | IP | BFP | H | R | ER | HR | SH | SF | HB | TBB | IBB | SO | WP | Bk | W | L | Pct | Sh | Sv-Op | Hld | ERC | ERA |
| 2000 | NYY | AL | 22 | 0 | 0 | 6 | 17.0 | 75 | 14 | 10 | 9 | 3 | 0 | 1 | 1 | 8 | 0 | 12 | 1 | 0 | 0 | 1 | .000 | 0 | 0-0 | 2 | 3.99 | 4.76 |
| 2001 | NYY | AL | 37 | 0 | 0 | 13 | 48.1 | 207 | 34 | 21 | 18 | 0 | 2 | 1 | 9 | 27 | 2 | 35 | 3 | 0 | 3 | 1 | .750 | 0 | 0-0 | 3 | 3.03 | 3.35 |
| 2002 | NYY | AL | 18 | 0 | 0 | 11 | 22.1 | 101 | 18 | 18 | 15 | 1 | 0 | 0 | 3 | 15 | 0 | 17 | 3 | 0 | 0 | 0 | - | 0 | 0-0 | 0 | 4.13 | 6.04 |
| 2003 | NYY | AL | 5 | 0 | 0 | 2 | 3.2 | 16 | 7 | 3 | 3 | 0 | 0 | 0 | 0 | 1 | 0 | 0 | 0 | 0 | 0 | 0 | - | 0 | 0-0 | 0 | 9.72 | 7.36 |
| 2004 | Ari | NL | 74 | 0 | 0 | 17 | 50.2 | 232 | 52 | 26 | 26 | 1 | 0 | 4 | 5 | 28 | 11 | 49 | 1 | 1 | 2 | 4 | .333 | 0 | 0-2 | 11 | 4.18 | 4.62 |
| 2005 | Ari | NL | 8 | 0 | 0 | 0 | 7.0 | 35 | 8 | 7 | 7 | 0 | 0 | 0 | 1 | 5 | 1 | 4 | 1 | 0 | 0 | 0 | - | 0 | 0-0 | 2 | 5.48 | 9.00 |
| 2006 | Ari | NL | 30 | 0 | 0 | 3 | 16.0 | 75 | 21 | 9 | 7 | 0 | 0 | 0 | 3 | 3 | 0 | 12 | 0 | 0 | 0 | 1 | .000 | 0 | 0-0 | 5 | 4.87 | 3.94 |
| 2007 | Ari | NL | 2 | 0 | 0 | 0 | 0.0 | 3 | 3 | 0 | 0 | 0 | 0 | 0 | 0 | 0 | 0 | 0 | 0 | 0 | 0 | 0 | - | 0 | 0-0 | 0 | - | - |
| 2009 | TB | AL | 61 | 0 | 0 | 13 | 36.1 | 142 | 28 | 15 | 14 | 4 | 0 | 0 | 0 | 11 | 3 | 28 | 0 | 0 | 1 | 0 | 1.000 | 0 | 5-5 | 9 | 2.54 | 3.47 |
| 2010 | TB | AL | **85** | 0 | 0 | 8 | 44.2 | 187 | 41 | 23 | 21 | 3 | 2 | 2 | 3 | 17 | 5 | 40 | 4 | 0 | 4 | 3 | .571 | 0 | 0-2 | 18 | 3.48 | 4.23 |
| 2011 | Fla | NL | 54 | 0 | 0 | 6 | 24.2 | 103 | 13 | 7 | 5 | 3 | 1 | 0 | 2 | 13 | 5 | 31 | 0 | 0 | 1 | 1 | .500 | 0 | 0-0 | 14 | 2.16 | 1.82 |
| 2012 | 2 Tms | NL | **80** | 0 | 0 | 4 | 38.2 | 168 | 29 | 18 | 13 | 1 | 2 | 2 | 5 | 18 | 3 | 38 | 2 | 0 | 0 | 0 | - | 0 | 1-1 | 20 | 2.76 | 3.03 |
| 2013 | StL | NL | 64 | 0 | 0 | 9 | 35.1 | 141 | 26 | 9 | 9 | 0 | 2 | 1 | 2 | 11 | 0 | 28 | 0 | 0 | 2 | 1 | .667 | 0 | 0-1 | 15 | 2.00 | 2.29 |
| 12 | Mia | NL | 44 | 0 | 0 | 4 | 25.1 | 104 | 16 | 11 | 7 | 0 | 1 | 1 | 3 | 9 | 0 | 27 | 2 | 0 | 0 | 0 | - | 0 | 1-1 | 15 | 1.79 | 2.49 |
| 12 | LAD | NL | 36 | 0 | 0 | 0 | 13.1 | 64 | 13 | 7 | 6 | 1 | 1 | 1 | 2 | 9 | 3 | 11 | 0 | 0 | 0 | 0 | - | 0 | 0-0 | 5 | 4.87 | 4.05 |
| Postseason | | | 7 | 0 | 0 | 0 | 6.1 | 30 | 7 | 5 | 2 | 0 | 0 | 0 | 0 | 2 | 1 | 4 | 0 | 0 | 0 | 0 | - | 0 | 0-0 | 0 | 3.01 | 2.84 |
| 13 ML YEARS | | | 540 | 0 | 0 | 92 | 344.2 | 1485 | 294 | 166 | 147 | 16 | 9 | 11 | 34 | 157 | 30 | 294 | 15 | 1 | 13 | 12 | .520 | 0 | 6-11 | 99 | 3.34 | 3.84 |

## Michael Choice

**Bats:** R **Throws:** R **Pos:** RF-4;LF-2;CF-2;DH-2;PH-2 **Ht:** 6'0" **Wt:** 215 **Born:** 11/10/1989 **Age:** 24

| | | | BATTING | | | | | | | | | | | | | | | | | BASERUNNING | | | | AVERAGES | | |
|---|---|---|---|---|---|---|---|---|---|---|---|---|---|---|---|---|---|---|---|---|---|---|---|---|---|---|
| Year | Team | Lg | G | AB | H | 2B | 3B | HR | (Hm | Rd) | TB | R | RBI | RC | TBB | IBB | SO | HBP | SH | SF | SB | CS | SB% | GDP | Avg | OBP | Slg |
| 2010 | As | R | 3 | 7 | 0 | 0 | 0 | 0 | (- | -) | 0 | 1 | 0 | 0 | 2 | 0 | 2 | 0 | 0 | 0 | 0 | 0 | - | 0 | .000 | .222 | .000 |
| 2010 | Vancvr | A- | 27 | 102 | 29 | 10 | 2 | 7 | (- | -) | 64 | 20 | 26 | 25 | 15 | 1 | 43 | 3 | 0 | 1 | 6 | 1 | .86 | 1 | .284 | .388 | .627 |
| 2011 | Stcktn | A+ | 118 | 467 | 133 | 28 | 1 | 30 | (- | -) | 253 | 79 | 82 | 96 | 61 | 2 | 134 | 10 | 0 | 4 | 9 | 5 | .64 | 9 | .285 | .376 | .542 |
| 2012 | Mdlnd | AA | 91 | 359 | 102 | 15 | 2 | 10 | (- | -) | 151 | 59 | 57 | 56 | 33 | 4 | 88 | 7 | 0 | 3 | 5 | 1 | .83 | 6 | .284 | .353 | .421 |
| 2013 | Scrmto | AAA | 132 | 510 | 154 | 29 | 1 | 14 | (- | -) | 227 | 90 | 89 | 94 | 69 | 0 | 115 | 11 | 0 | 10 | 1 | 2 | .33 | 15 | .302 | .390 | .445 |
| 2013 | Oak | AL | 9 | 18 | 5 | 1 | 0 | 0 | (0 | 0) | 6 | 2 | 0 | 2 | 1 | 0 | 6 | 0 | 0 | 0 | 0 | 0 | - | 0 | .278 | .316 | .333 |

# Shin-Soo Choo

**Bats:** L **Throws:** L **Pos:** CF-150;LF-3;PH-1 SHIN-sue CHEW **Ht:** 5'11" **Wt:** 205 **Born:** 7/13/1982 **Age:** 31

| | | | BATTING | | | | | | | | | | | | | | | | | | BASERUNNING | | | | AVERAGES | | |
|---|---|---|---|---|---|---|---|---|---|---|---|---|---|---|---|---|---|---|---|---|---|---|---|---|---|---|---|
| Year | Team | Lg | G | AB | H | 2B | 3B | HR | (Hm | Rd) | TB | R | RBI | RC | TBB | IBB | SO | HBP | SH | SF | SB | CS | SB% | GDP | Avg | OBP | Slg |
| 2005 | Sea | AL | 10 | 18 | 1 | 0 | 0 | 0 | (0 | 0) | 1 | 1 | 1 | 0 | 3 | 0 | 4 | 0 | 0 | 0 | 0 | 0 | - | 0 | .056 | .190 | .056 |
| 2006 | 2 Tms | AL | 49 | 157 | 44 | 12 | 3 | 3 | (2 | 1) | 71 | 23 | 22 | 24 | 18 | 2 | 50 | 2 | 1 | 1 | 5 | 3 | .63 | 3 | .280 | .360 | .452 |
| 2007 | Cle | AL | 6 | 17 | 5 | 0 | 0 | 0 | (0 | 0) | 5 | 5 | 5 | 3 | 2 | 1 | 5 | 0 | 0 | 1 | 0 | 1 | .00 | 0 | .294 | .350 | .294 |
| 2008 | Cle | AL | 94 | 317 | 98 | 28 | 3 | 14 | (10 | 4) | 174 | 68 | 66 | 72 | 44 | 4 | 78 | 5 | 0 | 4 | 4 | 3 | .57 | 5 | .309 | .397 | .549 |
| 2009 | Cle | AL | 156 | 583 | 175 | 38 | 6 | 20 | (11 | 9) | 285 | 87 | 86 | 111 | 78 | 5 | 151 | 17 | 0 | 7 | 21 | 2 | .91 | 9 | .300 | .394 | .489 |
| 2010 | Cle | AL | 144 | 550 | 165 | 31 | 2 | 22 | (8 | 14) | 266 | 81 | 90 | 106 | 83 | 11 | 118 | 11 | 0 | 2 | 22 | 7 | .76 | 11 | .300 | .401 | .484 |
| 2011 | Cle | AL | 85 | 313 | 81 | 11 | 3 | 8 | (7 | 1) | 122 | 37 | 36 | 38 | 36 | 3 | 78 | 6 | 0 | 3 | 12 | 5 | .71 | 7 | .259 | .344 | .390 |
| 2012 | Cle | AL | 155 | 598 | 169 | 43 | 2 | 16 | (8 | 8) | 264 | 88 | 67 | 96 | 73 | 0 | 150 | 14 | 0 | 1 | 21 | 7 | .75 | 11 | .283 | .373 | .441 |
| 2013 | Cin | NL | 154 | 569 | 162 | 34 | 2 | 21 | (10 | 11) | 263 | 107 | 54 | 111 | 112 | 5 | 133 | **26** | 3 | 2 | 20 | 11 | .65 | 3 | .285 | .423 | .462 |
| 06 | Sea | AL | 4 | 11 | 1 | 1 | 0 | 0 | (0 | 0) | 2 | 0 | 0 | 0 | 0 | 0 | 4 | 1 | 0 | 0 | 0 | 0 | - | 1 | .091 | .167 | .182 |
| 06 | Cle | AL | 45 | 146 | 43 | 11 | 3 | 3 | (2 | 1) | 69 | 23 | 22 | 24 | 18 | 2 | 46 | 1 | 1 | 1 | 5 | 3 | .63 | 2 | .295 | .373 | .473 |
| 9 ML YEARS | | | 853 | 3122 | 900 | 197 | 21 | 104 | (56 | 48) | 1451 | 497 | 427 | 561 | 449 | 31 | 767 | 81 | 4 | 21 | 105 | 39 | .73 | 49 | .288 | .389 | .465 |

# Nick Christiani

**Pitches:** R **Bats:** R **Pos:** RP-3 **Ht:** 6'0" **Wt:** 190 **Born:** 7/17/1987 **Age:** 26

| | | | HOW MUCH HE PITCHED | | | | | | WHAT HE GAVE UP | | | | | | | | | | | | | THE RESULTS | | | | | | | |
|---|---|---|---|---|---|---|---|---|---|---|---|---|---|---|---|---|---|---|---|---|---|---|---|---|---|---|---|---|---|
| Year | Team | Lg | G | GS | CG | GF | IP | BFP | H | R | ER | HR | SH | SF | HB | TBB | IBB | SO | WP | Bk | W | L | Pct | Sh | Sv-Op | Hld | ERC | ERA |
| 2010 | Dayton | A | 7 | 0 | 0 | 2 | 14.0 | 55 | 12 | 6 | 6 | 1 | 1 | 1 | 0 | 2 | 0 | 12 | 0 | 0 | 1 | 0 | 1.000 | 0 | 1-- | - | 2.22 | 3.86 |
| 2010 | Lynbrg | A+ | 38 | 0 | 0 | 17 | 52.1 | 219 | 56 | 25 | 20 | 6 | 1 | 0 | 4 | 11 | 1 | 37 | 1 | 0 | 1 | 3 | .250 | 0 | 4-- | - | 4.18 | 3.44 |
| 2010 | Carlina | AA | 2 | 0 | 0 | 2 | 2.0 | 10 | 4 | 1 | 1 | 0 | 1 | 1 | 0 | 0 | 0 | 1 | 0 | 0 | 0 | 0 | - | 0 | 0-- | - | 7.48 | 4.50 |
| 2011 | Carlina | AA | 20 | 0 | 0 | 6 | 25.2 | 96 | 16 | 5 | 5 | 0 | 0 | 2 | 0 | 5 | 0 | 22 | 1 | 0 | 2 | 0 | 1.000 | 0 | 3-- | - | 1.19 | 1.75 |
| 2011 | Lsvlle | AAA | 33 | 0 | 0 | 17 | 35.2 | 170 | 46 | 23 | 21 | 2 | 4 | 0 | 2 | 15 | 2 | 19 | 2 | 0 | 2 | 3 | .400 | 0 | 7-- | - | 5.49 | 5.30 |
| 2012 | Lsvlle | AAA | 54 | 0 | 0 | 11 | 72.2 | 318 | 84 | 34 | 27 | 4 | 4 | 2 | 2 | 29 | 9 | 35 | 1 | 0 | 2 | 5 | .286 | 0 | 1-- | - | 4.63 | 3.34 |
| 2013 | Lsvlle | AAA | 49 | 0 | 0 | 22 | 56.0 | 235 | 49 | 26 | 24 | 6 | 3 | 4 | 3 | 17 | 3 | 49 | 3 | 0 | 6 | 5 | .545 | 0 | 3-- | - | 3.16 | 3.86 |
| 2013 | Cin | NL | 3 | 0 | 0 | 1 | 4.0 | 16 | 2 | 1 | 1 | 1 | 0 | 1 | 1 | 2 | 0 | 1 | 0 | 0 | 0 | 0 | - | 0 | 0-0 | 0 | 3.91 | 2.25 |

# Tony Cingrani

**Pitches:** L **Bats:** L **Pos:** SP-18; RP-5 sin-GRAHN-ee **Ht:** 6'4" **Wt:** 215 **Born:** 7/5/1989 **Age:** 24

| | | | HOW MUCH HE PITCHED | | | | | | WHAT HE GAVE UP | | | | | | | | | | | | | THE RESULTS | | | | | | | |
|---|---|---|---|---|---|---|---|---|---|---|---|---|---|---|---|---|---|---|---|---|---|---|---|---|---|---|---|---|---|
| Year | Team | Lg | G | GS | CG | GF | IP | BFP | H | R | ER | HR | SH | SF | HB | TBB | IBB | SO | WP | Bk | W | L | Pct | Sh | Sv-Op | Hld | ERC | ERA |
| 2011 | Billings | R+ | 13 | 13 | 0 | 0 | 51.1 | 191 | 35 | 11 | 10 | 1 | 0 | 0 | 1 | 6 | 0 | 80 | 1 | 0 | 3 | 2 | .600 | 0 | 0-- | - | 1.31 | 1.75 |
| 2012 | Bkrsfld | A+ | 10 | 10 | 0 | 0 | 56.2 | 220 | 39 | 13 | 7 | 2 | 1 | 0 | 0 | 13 | 0 | 71 | 1 | 0 | 5 | 1 | .833 | 0 | 0-- | - | 1.57 | 1.11 |
| 2012 | Pnscla | AA | 16 | 15 | 1 | 0 | 89.1 | 350 | 59 | 24 | 21 | 7 | 3 | 0 | 1 | 39 | 0 | 101 | 1 | 0 | 5 | 3 | .625 | 0 | 0-- | - | 2.44 | 2.12 |
| 2013 | Lsvlle | AAA | 6 | 6 | 0 | 0 | 31.1 | 117 | 14 | 4 | 4 | 1 | 0 | 0 | 1 | 11 | 0 | 49 | 1 | 1 | 3 | 0 | 1.000 | 0 | 0-- | - | 1.19 | 1.15 |
| 2012 | Cin | NL | 3 | 0 | 0 | 1 | 5.0 | 22 | 4 | 1 | 1 | 1 | 0 | 0 | 0 | 2 | 0 | 9 | 0 | 0 | 0 | 0 | - | 0 | 0-0 | 0 | 3.38 | 1.80 |
| 2013 | Cin | NL | 23 | 18 | 0 | 0 | 104.2 | 420 | 72 | 37 | 34 | 14 | 4 | 4 | 2 | 43 | 1 | 120 | 4 | 0 | 7 | 4 | .636 | 0 | 0-0 | 1 | 2.78 | 2.92 |
| 2 ML YEARS | | | 26 | 18 | 0 | 1 | 109.2 | 442 | 76 | 38 | 35 | 15 | 4 | 4 | 2 | 45 | 1 | 129 | 4 | 0 | 7 | 4 | .636 | 0 | 0-0 | 1 | 2.80 | 2.87 |

# Pedro Ciriaco

see-ree-AH-koe

**Bats:** R **Throws:** R **Pos:** SS-29;3B-10;PR-9;2B-5;DH-5;PH-5;1B-1 **Ht:** 6'0" **Wt:** 180 **Born:** 9/27/1985 **Age:** 28

| | | | BATTING | | | | | | | | | | | | | | | | | | BASERUNNING | | | | AVERAGES | | |
|---|---|---|---|---|---|---|---|---|---|---|---|---|---|---|---|---|---|---|---|---|---|---|---|---|---|---|---|
| Year | Team | Lg | G | AB | H | 2B | 3B | HR | (Hm | Rd) | TB | R | RBI | RC | TBB | IBB | SO | HBP | SH | SF | SB | CS | SB% | GDP | Avg | OBP | Slg |
| 2013 | Omha* | AAA | 43 | 160 | 45 | 8 | 1 | 1 | (- | -) | 58 | 19 | 15 | 18 | 6 | 0 | 22 | 1 | 3 | 1 | 4 | 1 | .80 | 2 | .281 | .310 | .363 |
| 2010 | Pit | NL | 8 | 6 | 3 | 1 | 1 | 0 | (0 | 0) | 6 | 3 | 1 | 3 | 0 | 0 | 3 | 0 | 0 | 0 | 0 | 0 | - | 0 | .500 | .500 | 1.000 |
| 2011 | Pit | NL | 23 | 33 | 10 | 2 | 1 | 0 | (0 | 0) | 14 | 4 | 6 | 5 | 1 | 0 | 6 | 0 | 0 | 0 | 2 | 1 | .67 | 1 | .303 | .324 | .424 |
| 2012 | Bos | AL | 76 | 259 | 76 | 15 | 2 | 2 | (2 | 0) | 101 | 33 | 19 | 32 | 8 | 2 | 47 | 0 | 5 | 0 | 16 | 3 | .84 | 2 | .293 | .315 | .390 |
| 2013 | 3 Tms | | 56 | 125 | 28 | 4 | 2 | 2 | (2 | 0) | 42 | 9 | 8 | 11 | 9 | 2 | 23 | 1 | 1 | 1 | 9 | 1 | .90 | 2 | .224 | .279 | .336 |
| 13 | Bos | AL | 28 | 51 | 11 | 2 | 1 | 1 | (1 | 0) | 18 | 4 | 4 | 5 | 6 | 0 | 12 | 0 | 0 | 1 | 2 | 1 | .67 | 0 | .216 | .293 | .353 |
| 13 | SD | NL | 23 | 63 | 15 | 1 | 1 | 1 | (1 | 0) | 21 | 5 | 4 | 6 | 3 | 2 | 10 | 1 | 1 | 0 | 6 | 0 | 1.00 | 2 | .238 | .284 | .333 |
| 13 | KC | AL | 5 | 11 | 2 | 1 | 0 | 0 | (0 | 0) | 3 | 0 | 0 | 0 | 0 | 0 | 1 | 0 | 0 | 0 | 1 | 0 | 1.00 | 0 | .182 | .182 | .273 |
| 4 ML YEARS | | | 163 | 423 | 117 | 22 | 6 | 4 | (4 | 0) | 163 | 49 | 34 | 51 | 18 | 4 | 79 | 1 | 6 | 1 | 27 | 5 | .84 | 5 | .277 | .307 | .385 |

# Steve Cishek

**Pitches:** R **Bats:** R **Pos:** RP-69 SEE-sheck **Ht:** 6'6" **Wt:** 215 **Born:** 6/18/1986 **Age:** 28

| | | | HOW MUCH HE PITCHED | | | | | | WHAT HE GAVE UP | | | | | | | | | | | | | THE RESULTS | | | | | | | |
|---|---|---|---|---|---|---|---|---|---|---|---|---|---|---|---|---|---|---|---|---|---|---|---|---|---|---|---|---|---|
| Year | Team | Lg | G | GS | CG | GF | IP | BFP | H | R | ER | HR | SH | SF | HB | TBB | IBB | SO | WP | Bk | W | L | Pct | Sh | Sv-Op | Hld | ERC | ERA |
| 2010 | Fla | NL | 3 | 0 | 0 | 2 | 4.1 | 15 | 1 | 0 | 0 | 0 | 0 | 0 | 0 | 1 | 0 | 3 | 0 | 0 | 0 | 0 | - | 0 | 0-0 | 0 | 0.35 | 0.00 |
| 2011 | Fla | NL | 45 | 0 | 0 | 21 | 54.2 | 229 | 45 | 18 | 16 | 1 | 3 | 0 | 3 | 19 | 7 | 55 | 5 | 0 | 2 | 1 | .667 | 0 | 3-3 | 2 | 2.38 | 2.63 |
| 2012 | Mia | NL | 68 | 0 | 0 | 36 | 63.2 | 275 | 54 | 26 | 19 | 3 | 3 | 2 | 6 | 29 | 6 | 68 | 1 | 1 | 5 | 2 | .714 | 0 | 15-19 | 13 | 3.28 | 2.69 |
| 2013 | Mia | NL | 69 | 0 | 0 | 62 | 69.2 | 281 | 53 | 19 | 18 | 3 | 3 | 3 | 2 | 22 | 6 | 74 | 1 | 0 | 4 | 6 | .400 | 0 | 34-36 | 1 | 2.15 | 2.33 |
| 4 ML YEARS | | | 185 | 0 | 0 | 121 | 192.1 | 800 | 153 | 63 | 53 | 7 | 9 | 5 | 11 | 71 | 19 | 200 | 7 | 1 | 11 | 9 | .550 | 0 | 52-58 | 16 | 2.51 | 2.48 |

# Jose Cisnero

**Pitches:** R **Bats:** R **Pos:** RP-28 siss-NEHR-oh **Ht:** 6'3" **Wt:** 230 **Born:** 4/11/1989 **Age:** 25

| | | | HOW MUCH HE PITCHED | | | | | | WHAT HE GAVE UP | | | | | | | | | | | | | THE RESULTS | | | | | | | |
|---|---|---|---|---|---|---|---|---|---|---|---|---|---|---|---|---|---|---|---|---|---|---|---|---|---|---|---|---|---|
| Year | Team | Lg | G | GS | CG | GF | IP | BFP | H | R | ER | HR | SH | SF | HB | TBB | IBB | SO | WP | Bk | W | L | Pct | Sh | Sv-Op | Hld | ERC | ERA |
| 2009 | Grnvlle | R | 13 | 13 | 0 | 0 | 55.2 | 236 | 32 | 25 | 22 | 5 | 3 | 1 | 8 | 30 | 0 | 64 | 7 | 2 | 4 | 2 | .667 | 0 | 0-- | - | 2.76 | 3.56 |
| 2010 | Lxngtn | A | 26 | 26 | 0 | 0 | 133.0 | 572 | 106 | 69 | 54 | 11 | 4 | 7 | 15 | 65 | 0 | 126 | 16 | 2 | 8 | 6 | .571 | 0 | 0-- | - | 3.62 | 3.65 |
| 2011 | Lancst | A+ | 27 | 27 | 0 | 0 | 123.1 | 559 | 115 | 88 | 83 | 13 | 4 | 4 | 8 | 75 | 0 | 152 | 16 | 3 | 8 | 11 | .421 | 0 | 0-- | - | 4.78 | 6.06 |

| | | | HOW MUCH HE PITCHED | | | | | | WHAT HE GAVE UP | | | | | | | | | | | | THE RESULTS | | | | | | | |
|---|---|---|---|---|---|---|---|---|---|---|---|---|---|---|---|---|---|---|---|---|---|---|---|---|---|---|---|---|
| Year | Team | Lg | G | GS | CG | GF | IP | BFP | H | R | ER | HR | SH | SF | HB | TBB | IBB | SO | WP | Bk | W | L | Pct | Sh | Sv-Op | Hld | ERC | ERA |
| 2012 | CpChr | AA | 20 | 20 | 2 | 0 | 108.2 | 464 | 93 | 44 | 41 | 7 | 1 | 4 | 3 | 46 | 2 | 116 | 5 | 1 | 9 | 6 | .600 | 1 | 0- - | - | 3.17 | 3.40 |
| 2012 | OKCity | AAA | 8 | 8 | 0 | 0 | 39.2 | 182 | 52 | 23 | 20 | 1 | 1 | 2 | 3 | 18 | 0 | 32 | 1 | 0 | 4 | 1 | .800 | 0 | 0- - | - | 6.02 | 4.54 |
| 2013 | OKCity | AAA | 12 | 1 | 0 | 2 | 17.2 | 90 | 25 | 18 | 17 | 2 | 0 | 0 | 2 | 13 | 0 | 24 | 3 | 0 | 1 | 1 | .500 | 0 | 0- - | - | 8.77 | 8.66 |
| 2013 | Hou | AL | 28 | 0 | 0 | 11 | 43.2 | 198 | 49 | 23 | 20 | 5 | 0 | 2 | 1 | 22 | 5 | 41 | 1 | 2 | 2 | 2 | .500 | 0 | 0-2 | 5 | 5.21 | 4.12 |

## Preston Claiborne

**Pitches:** R **Bats:** R **Pos:** RP-44 **Ht:** 6'2" **Wt:** 225 **Born:** 1/21/1988 **Age:** 26

| | | | HOW MUCH HE PITCHED | | | | | | WHAT HE GAVE UP | | | | | | | | | | | | THE RESULTS | | | | | | | |
|---|---|---|---|---|---|---|---|---|---|---|---|---|---|---|---|---|---|---|---|---|---|---|---|---|---|---|---|---|
| Year | Team | Lg | G | GS | CG | GF | IP | BFP | H | R | ER | HR | SH | SF | HB | TBB | IBB | SO | WP | Bk | W | L | Pct | Sh | Sv-Op | Hld | ERC | ERA |
| 2010 | StIsInd | A- | 19 | 0 | 0 | 7 | 23.2 | 94 | 20 | 9 | 6 | 0 | 3 | 0 | 0 | 8 | 0 | 30 | 2 | 0 | 1 | 2 | .333 | 0 | 2- - | - | 2.48 | 2.28 |
| 2010 | Tampa | A+ | 5 | 0 | 0 | 0 | 7.1 | 32 | 7 | 3 | 3 | 1 | 0 | 1 | 1 | 4 | 0 | 6 | 1 | 0 | 0 | 1 | .000 | 0 | 0- - | - | 5.45 | 3.68 |
| 2011 | Tampa | A+ | 38 | 0 | 0 | 19 | 81.0 | 347 | 73 | 33 | 28 | 8 | 5 | 4 | 7 | 30 | 4 | 75 | 3 | 0 | 3 | 7 | .300 | 0 | 5- - | - | 3.65 | 3.11 |
| 2012 | Trntn | AA | 30 | 0 | 0 | 10 | 48.2 | 199 | 33 | 17 | 12 | 1 | 3 | 2 | 1 | 24 | 3 | 49 | 1 | 2 | 2 | 2 | .500 | 0 | 5- - | - | 2.22 | 2.22 |
| 2012 | S-WB | AAA | 20 | 0 | 0 | 7 | 33.1 | 138 | 31 | 17 | 15 | 2 | 2 | 2 | 0 | 12 | 1 | 29 | 1 | 0 | 4 | 0 | 1.000 | 0 | 1- - | - | 3.28 | 4.05 |
| 2013 | S-WB | AAA | 8 | 0 | 0 | 7 | 10.1 | 43 | 14 | 5 | 4 | 0 | 0 | 0 | 0 | 1 | 0 | 10 | 1 | 0 | 0 | 0 | - | 0 | 3- - | - | 4.36 | 3.48 |
| 2013 | Tampa | A+ | 1 | 1 | 0 | 0 | 1.0 | 4 | 0 | 0 | 0 | 0 | 0 | 0 | 0 | 1 | 0 | 1 | 0 | 0 | 0 | 0 | - | 0 | 0- - | - | 0.95 | 0.00 |
| 2013 | NYY | AL | 44 | 0 | 0 | 12 | 50.1 | 214 | 51 | 23 | 23 | 7 | 2 | 0 | 2 | 14 | 4 | 42 | 2 | 0 | 0 | 2 | .000 | 0 | 0-0 | 4 | 3.96 | 4.11 |

## Cody Clark

**Bats:** R **Throws:** R **Pos:** C-16;PH-1;PR-1 **Ht:** 6'3" **Wt:** 200 **Born:** 9/14/1981 **Age:** 32

| | | | BATTING | | | | | | | | | | | | | | | | | | BASERUNNING | | | | AVERAGES | | |
|---|---|---|---|---|---|---|---|---|---|---|---|---|---|---|---|---|---|---|---|---|---|---|---|---|---|---|---|
| Year | Team | Lg | G | AB | H | 2B | 3B | HR | (Hm | Rd) | TB | R | RBI | RC | TBB | IBB | SO | HBP | SH | SF | SB | CS | SB% | GDP | Avg | OBP | Slg |
| 2009 | Omha | AAA | 3 | 8 | 4 | 1 | 0 | 0 | (- | -) | 5 | 2 | 0 | 3 | 2 | 0 | 1 | 1 | 0 | 0 | 0 | 0 | - | 0 | .500 | .636 | .625 |
| 2009 | NWArk | AA | 66 | 191 | 58 | 13 | 0 | 8 | (- | -) | 95 | 33 | 32 | 34 | 15 | 1 | 27 | 5 | 2 | 2 | 1 | 2 | .33 | 5 | .304 | .366 | .497 |
| 2010 | Omha | AAA | 72 | 220 | 56 | 13 | 2 | 4 | (- | -) | 85 | 27 | 25 | 29 | 22 | 0 | 35 | 1 | 11 | 3 | 1 | 1 | .50 | 4 | .255 | .321 | .386 |
| 2011 | Omha | AAA | 51 | 159 | 37 | 12 | 0 | 4 | (- | -) | 61 | 18 | 13 | 18 | 12 | 0 | 26 | 2 | 4 | 1 | 0 | 0 | - | 4 | .233 | .293 | .384 |
| 2012 | Omha | AAA | 72 | 205 | 37 | 6 | 0 | 4 | (- | -) | 55 | 23 | 22 | 14 | 17 | 0 | 39 | 2 | 12 | 4 | 0 | 0 | - | 6 | .180 | .246 | .268 |
| 2013 | OKCity | AAA | 44 | 143 | 31 | 5 | 0 | 1 | (- | -) | 39 | 16 | 12 | 9 | 7 | 0 | 32 | 1 | 7 | 0 | 0 | 0 | - | 3 | .217 | .258 | .273 |
| 2013 | CpChr | AA | 2 | 8 | 1 | 0 | 0 | 0 | (- | -) | 1 | 0 | 1 | 0 | 0 | 0 | 0 | 0 | 0 | 1 | 0 | 0 | - | 0 | .125 | .111 | .125 |
| 2013 | Hou | AL | 16 | 38 | 4 | 1 | 0 | 0 | (0 | 0) | 5 | 1 | 0 | 0 | 1 | 0 | 15 | 0 | 1 | 0 | 0 | 0 | - | 0 | .105 | .128 | .132 |

## Zach Clark

**Pitches:** R **Bats:** R **Pos:** RP-1 **Ht:** 6'0" **Wt:** 200 **Born:** 7/11/1983 **Age:** 30

| | | | HOW MUCH HE PITCHED | | | | | | WHAT HE GAVE UP | | | | | | | | | | | | THE RESULTS | | | | | | | |
|---|---|---|---|---|---|---|---|---|---|---|---|---|---|---|---|---|---|---|---|---|---|---|---|---|---|---|---|---|
| Year | Team | Lg | G | GS | CG | GF | IP | BFP | H | R | ER | HR | SH | SF | HB | TBB | IBB | SO | WP | Bk | W | L | Pct | Sh | Sv-Op | Hld | ERC | ERA |
| 2009 | Orioles | R | 4 | 4 | 0 | 0 | 9.0 | 32 | 5 | 1 | 0 | 0 | 0 | 0 | 1 | 0 | 0 | 9 | 0 | 0 | 0 | 0 | - | 0 | 0- - | - | 0.86 | 0.00 |
| 2009 | Bowie | AA | 13 | 0 | 0 | 1 | 26.2 | 118 | 34 | 16 | 15 | 1 | 1 | 0 | 1 | 8 | 0 | 16 | 1 | 0 | 2 | 1 | .667 | 0 | 0- - | - | 5.03 | 5.06 |
| 2009 | Frdrck | A+ | 4 | 0 | 0 | 1 | 8.0 | 30 | 4 | 2 | 1 | 1 | 2 | 1 | 0 | 2 | 1 | 7 | 0 | 0 | 0 | 0 | - | 0 | 0- - | - | 1.26 | 1.13 |
| 2009 | Norfolk | AAA | 2 | 0 | 0 | 1 | 4.2 | 21 | 5 | 2 | 2 | 0 | 0 | 0 | 0 | 3 | 0 | 3 | 0 | 0 | 0 | 0 | - | 0 | 0- - | - | 4.78 | 3.86 |
| 2010 | Bowie | AA | 14 | 2 | 0 | 5 | 37.0 | 151 | 38 | 18 | 14 | 2 | 1 | 4 | 2 | 6 | 0 | 19 | 2 | 0 | 1 | 1 | .500 | 0 | 1- - | - | 3.28 | 3.41 |
| 2010 | Dlmrva | A | 1 | 0 | 0 | 0 | 2.0 | 7 | 1 | 0 | 0 | 0 | 0 | 0 | 0 | 0 | 0 | 1 | 0 | 0 | 0 | 0 | - | 0 | 0- - | - | 0.54 | 0.00 |
| 2010 | Norfolk | AAA | 6 | 4 | 0 | 1 | 28.1 | 125 | 32 | 15 | 13 | 3 | 1 | 1 | 1 | 10 | 1 | 16 | 1 | 0 | 0 | 5 | .000 | 0 | 0- - | - | 4.76 | 4.13 |
| 2010 | Frdrck | A+ | 9 | 9 | 0 | 0 | 48.0 | 209 | 58 | 31 | 28 | 4 | 2 | 3 | 4 | 12 | 0 | 38 | 2 | 2 | 2 | 3 | .400 | 0 | 0- - | - | 4.98 | 5.25 |
| 2011 | Bowie | AA | 24 | 23 | 0 | 0 | 138.2 | 586 | 161 | 79 | 77 | 11 | 3 | 0 | 4 | 42 | 1 | 81 | 3 | 2 | 10 | 9 | .526 | 0 | 0- - | - | 4.76 | 5.00 |
| 2012 | Bowie | AA | 20 | 19 | 1 | 0 | 121.1 | 501 | 112 | 47 | 43 | 8 | 4 | 1 | 7 | 38 | 1 | 66 | 4 | 0 | 10 | 5 | .667 | 0 | 0- - | - | 3.37 | 3.19 |
| 2012 | Norfolk | AAA | 8 | 7 | 1 | 1 | 46.1 | 189 | 38 | 10 | 9 | 1 | 1 | 1 | 4 | 16 | 0 | 32 | 2 | 0 | 5 | 2 | .714 | 1 | 0- - | - | 2.78 | 1.75 |
| 2013 | Norfolk | AAA | 5 | 5 | 0 | 0 | 25.2 | 114 | 30 | 19 | 13 | 1 | 1 | 1 | 1 | 7 | 0 | 20 | 0 | 0 | 1 | 2 | .333 | 0 | 0- - | - | 4.17 | 4.56 |
| 2013 | Bowie | AA | 6 | 5 | 0 | 1 | 24.0 | 121 | 32 | 26 | 23 | 2 | 0 | 3 | 2 | 20 | 0 | 17 | 5 | 3 | 1 | 4 | .200 | 0 | 0- - | - | 8.30 | 8.63 |
| 2013 | Orioles | R | 4 | 4 | 0 | 0 | 17.1 | 81 | 21 | 15 | 13 | 1 | 1 | 0 | 3 | 6 | 0 | 8 | 5 | 0 | 0 | 2 | .000 | 0 | 0- - | - | 5.39 | 6.75 |
| 2013 | Frdrck | A+ | 10 | 10 | 0 | 0 | 44.1 | 230 | 51 | 53 | 48 | 3 | 2 | 3 | 11 | 42 | 0 | 20 | 10 | 1 | 1 | 7 | .125 | 0 | 0- - | - | 8.07 | 9.74 |
| 2013 | Bal | AL | 1 | 0 | 0 | 0 | 1.2 | 10 | 3 | 3 | 3 | 0 | 0 | 1 | 0 | 2 | 0 | 1 | 0 | 0 | 0 | 0 | - | 0 | 0-0 | 0 | 11.51 | 16.20 |

## Paul Clemens

**Pitches:** R **Bats:** R **Pos:** RP-30; SP-5 **Ht:** 6'4" **Wt:** 195 **Born:** 2/14/1988 **Age:** 26

| | | | HOW MUCH HE PITCHED | | | | | | WHAT HE GAVE UP | | | | | | | | | | | | THE RESULTS | | | | | | | |
|---|---|---|---|---|---|---|---|---|---|---|---|---|---|---|---|---|---|---|---|---|---|---|---|---|---|---|---|---|
| Year | Team | Lg | G | GS | CG | GF | IP | BFP | H | R | ER | HR | SH | SF | HB | TBB | IBB | SO | WP | Bk | W | L | Pct | Sh | Sv-Op | Hld | ERC | ERA |
| 2009 | Rome | A | 26 | 11 | 0 | 5 | 85.1 | 413 | 105 | 67 | 56 | 7 | 3 | 2 | 4 | 49 | 0 | 64 | 7 | 1 | 6 | 5 | .545 | 0 | 3- - | - | 6.06 | 5.91 |
| 2010 | Rome | A | 8 | 0 | 0 | 2 | 19.0 | 76 | 11 | 5 | 3 | 1 | 0 | 1 | 0 | 8 | 0 | 16 | 1 | 0 | 2 | 0 | 1.000 | 0 | 1- - | - | 1.71 | 1.42 |
| 2010 | MrtlBh | A+ | 27 | 8 | 0 | 9 | 75.2 | 334 | 83 | 46 | 31 | 5 | 1 | 1 | 2 | 28 | 4 | 65 | 10 | 0 | 0 | 4 | .000 | 0 | 2- - | - | 4.25 | 3.69 |
| 2011 | Missi | AA | 20 | 20 | 0 | 0 | 108.2 | 468 | 103 | 57 | 45 | 8 | 2 | 3 | 5 | 44 | 0 | 93 | 7 | 1 | 6 | 5 | .545 | 0 | 0- - | - | 3.80 | 3.73 |
| 2011 | CpChr | AA | 5 | 5 | 0 | 0 | 30.2 | 127 | 23 | 9 | 8 | 3 | 0 | 0 | 0 | 12 | 1 | 26 | 0 | 1 | 2 | 1 | .667 | 0 | 0- - | - | 2.61 | 2.35 |
| 2011 | OKCity | AAA | 1 | 1 | 0 | 0 | 4.2 | 24 | 4 | 8 | 8 | 1 | 1 | 1 | 0 | 6 | 0 | 6 | 1 | 1 | 0 | 1 | .000 | 0 | 0- - | - | 7.69 | 15.43 |
| 2012 | OKCity | AAA | 20 | 20 | 0 | 0 | 101.2 | 470 | 145 | 82 | 76 | 16 | 7 | 4 | 2 | 32 | 2 | 68 | 4 | 2 | 8 | 8 | .500 | 0 | 0- - | - | 6.82 | 6.73 |
| 2012 | CpChr | AA | 7 | 7 | 0 | 0 | 41.2 | 175 | 41 | 18 | 16 | 7 | 0 | 1 | 2 | 11 | 0 | 37 | 5 | 2 | 3 | 2 | .600 | 0 | 0- - | - | 4.12 | 3.46 |
| 2013 | OKCity | AAA | 6 | 6 | 0 | 0 | 30.0 | 131 | 27 | 19 | 15 | 1 | 1 | 2 | 2 | 11 | 1 | 16 | 2 | 0 | 3 | 2 | .600 | 0 | 0- - | - | 3.04 | 4.50 |
| 2013 | Hou | AL | 35 | 5 | 0 | 8 | 73.1 | 323 | 82 | 48 | 44 | 16 | 0 | 5 | 2 | 26 | 1 | 49 | 2 | 0 | 4 | 7 | .364 | 0 | 0-2 | 7 | 5.53 | 5.40 |

## Maikel Cleto

**Pitches:** R **Bats:** R **Pos:** RP-1 MY-kel CLAY-toe **Ht:** 6'3" **Wt:** 250 **Born:** 5/1/1989 **Age:** 25

| | | | HOW MUCH HE PITCHED | | | | | | WHAT HE GAVE UP | | | | | | | | | | | | THE RESULTS | | | | | | | |
|---|---|---|---|---|---|---|---|---|---|---|---|---|---|---|---|---|---|---|---|---|---|---|---|---|---|---|---|---|
| Year | Team | Lg | G | GS | CG | GF | IP | BFP | H | R | ER | HR | SH | SF | HB | TBB | IBB | SO | WP | Bk | W | L | Pct | Sh | Sv-Op | Hld | ERC | ERA |
| 2013 | Memp* | AAA | 16 | 9 | 0 | 2 | 53.1 | 260 | 49 | 42 | 41 | 4 | 3 | 2 | 3 | 53 | 0 | 53 | 4 | 0 | 2 | 3 | .400 | 0 | 0- - | - | 5.97 | 6.92 |
| 2013 | Omha* | AAA | 19 | 1 | 0 | 8 | 38.0 | 167 | 35 | 16 | 15 | 1 | 1 | 3 | 1 | 21 | 0 | 36 | 5 | 0 | 1 | 2 | .333 | 0 | 1- - | - | 3.79 | 3.55 |

| HOW MUCH HE PITCHED | | | | | | | | | WHAT HE GAVE UP | | | | | | | | | | | | | THE RESULTS | | | | | | | | |
|---|---|---|---|---|---|---|---|---|---|---|---|---|---|---|---|---|---|---|---|---|---|---|---|---|---|---|---|---|---|---|
| Year | Team | Lg | G | GS | CG | GF | IP | BFP | H | R | ER | HR | SH | SF | HB | TBB | IBB | SO | WP | Bk | W | L | Pct | Sh | Sv-Op | Hld | ERC | ERA |
| 2011 | StL | NL | 3 | 0 | 0 | 2 | 4.1 | 25 | 7 | 6 | 6 | 2 | 0 | 0 | 0 | 4 | 0 | 6 | 0 | 0 | 0 | 0 | - | 0 | 0-0 | 0 | 13.10 | 12.46 |
| 2012 | StL | NL | 9 | 0 | 0 | 2 | 9.0 | 41 | 13 | 7 | 7 | 4 | 0 | 0 | 1 | 2 | 0 | 15 | 0 | 0 | 0 | 0 | - | 0 | 0-0 | 1 | 9.58 | 7.00 |
| 2013 | StL | NL | 1 | 0 | 0 | 1 | 2.1 | 15 | 5 | 5 | 5 | 1 | 0 | 0 | 2 | 1 | 0 | 5 | 0 | 0 | 0 | 0 | - | 0 | 0-0 | 0 | 19.41 | 19.29 |
| 3 ML YEARS | | | 13 | 0 | 0 | 5 | 15.2 | 81 | 25 | 18 | 18 | 7 | 0 | 0 | 3 | 7 | 0 | 26 | 0 | 0 | 0 | 0 | - | 0 | 0-0 | 1 | 12.01 | 10.34 |

# Steve Clevenger

**Bats:** L **Throws:** R **Pos:** PH-7;C-4;3B-2 CLEV-en-jer **Ht:** 6'0" **Wt:** 195 **Born:** 4/5/1986 **Age:** 28

| BATTING | | | | | | | | | | | | | | | | | | | | BASERUNNING | | | | AVERAGES | | |
|---|---|---|---|---|---|---|---|---|---|---|---|---|---|---|---|---|---|---|---|---|---|---|---|---|---|---|
| Year Team | Lg | G | AB | H | 2B | 3B | HR | (Hm | Rd) | TB | R | RBI | RC | TBB | IBB | SO | HBP | SH | SF | SB | CS | SB% | GDP | Avg | OBP | Slg |
| 2013 Iowa* | AAA | 15 | 52 | 17 | 5 | 0 | 3 | (- | -) | 31 | 14 | 11 | 12 | 9 | 0 | 7 | 0 | 0 | 0 | 0 | 0 | - | 2 | .327 | .426 | .596 |
| 2013 Orioles* | R | 4 | 13 | 3 | 0 | 0 | 0 | (- | -) | 3 | 0 | 1 | 0 | 0 | 0 | 3 | 0 | 0 | 1 | 0 | 0 | - | 0 | .231 | .214 | .231 |
| 2013 Abrdn* | A- | 5 | 18 | 7 | 0 | 0 | 0 | (- | -) | 7 | 4 | 1 | 3 | 2 | 0 | 0 | 0 | 0 | 0 | 0 | 0 | - | 1 | .389 | .450 | .389 |
| 2013 Norfolk* | AAA | 20 | 71 | 23 | 2 | 0 | 2 | (- | -) | 31 | 12 | 11 | 13 | 10 | 0 | 9 | 0 | 0 | 1 | 0 | 0 | - | 3 | .324 | .402 | .437 |
| 2011 ChC | NL | 2 | 4 | 1 | 1 | 0 | 0 | (0 | 0) | 2 | 1 | 0 | 0 | 0 | 0 | 0 | 1 | 0 | 0 | 0 | 0 | - | 0 | .250 | .400 | .500 |
| 2012 ChC | NL | 69 | 199 | 40 | 12 | 0 | 1 | (1 | 0) | 55 | 16 | 16 | 12 | 16 | 0 | 39 | 0 | 0 | 0 | 0 | 1 | .00 | 10 | .201 | .260 | .276 |
| 2013 2 Tms | | 12 | 23 | 5 | 1 | 0 | 0 | (0 | 0) | 6 | 2 | 2 | 1 | 1 | 0 | 5 | 0 | 0 | 0 | 0 | 0 | - | 1 | .217 | .250 | .261 |
| 13 ChC | NL | 8 | 8 | 1 | 0 | 0 | 0 | (0 | 0) | 1 | 1 | 0 | 0 | 1 | 0 | 3 | 0 | 0 | 0 | 0 | 0 | - | 0 | .125 | .222 | .125 |
| 13 Bal | AL | 4 | 15 | 4 | 1 | 0 | 0 | (0 | 0) | 5 | 1 | 2 | 1 | 0 | 0 | 2 | 0 | 0 | 0 | 0 | 0 | - | 1 | .267 | .267 | .333 |
| 3 ML YEARS | | 83 | 226 | 46 | 14 | 0 | 1 | (1 | 0) | 63 | 19 | 18 | 13 | 17 | 0 | 44 | 1 | 0 | 0 | 0 | 1 | .00 | 11 | .204 | .262 | .279 |

# Tyler Clippard

**Pitches:** R **Bats:** R **Pos:** RP-72 **Ht:** 6'3" **Wt:** 200 **Born:** 2/14/1985 **Age:** 29

| HOW MUCH HE PITCHED | | | | | | | | | WHAT HE GAVE UP | | | | | | | | | | | | | THE RESULTS | | | | | | | | |
|---|---|---|---|---|---|---|---|---|---|---|---|---|---|---|---|---|---|---|---|---|---|---|---|---|---|---|---|---|---|---|
| Year | Team | Lg | G | GS | CG | GF | IP | BFP | H | R | ER | HR | SH | SF | HB | TBB | IBB | SO | WP | Bk | W | L | Pct | Sh | Sv-Op | Hld | ERC | ERA |
| 2007 | NYY | AL | 6 | 6 | 0 | 0 | 27.0 | 124 | 29 | 19 | 19 | 6 | 0 | 0 | 0 | 17 | 1 | 18 | 2 | 1 | 3 | 1 | .750 | 0 | 0-0 | 0 | 6.37 | 6.33 |
| 2008 | Was | NL | 2 | 2 | 0 | 0 | 10.1 | 48 | 12 | 5 | 5 | 2 | 0 | 0 | 0 | 7 | 1 | 8 | 1 | 0 | 1 | 1 | .500 | 0 | 0-0 | 0 | 6.90 | 4.35 |
| 2009 | Was | NL | 41 | 0 | 0 | 8 | 60.1 | 246 | 36 | 20 | 18 | 9 | 3 | 1 | 1 | 32 | 1 | 67 | 1 | 1 | 4 | 2 | .667 | 0 | 0-1 | 3 | 2.79 | 2.69 |
| 2010 | Was | NL | 78 | 0 | 0 | 18 | 91.0 | 378 | 69 | 33 | 31 | 8 | 3 | 7 | 2 | 41 | 4 | 112 | 1 | 1 | 11 | 8 | .579 | 0 | 1-11 | 23 | 2.91 | 3.07 |
| 2011 | Was | NL | 72 | 0 | 0 | 8 | 88.1 | 329 | 48 | 18 | 18 | 11 | 4 | 3 | 0 | 26 | 2 | 104 | 1 | 0 | 3 | 0 | 1.000 | 0 | 0-7 | **38** | 1.61 | 1.83 |
| 2012 | Was | NL | 74 | 0 | 0 | 42 | 72.2 | 307 | 55 | 32 | 30 | 7 | 3 | 4 | 2 | 29 | 2 | 84 | 5 | 0 | 2 | 6 | .250 | 0 | 32-37 | 13 | 2.73 | 3.72 |
| 2013 | Was | NL | 72 | 0 | 0 | 6 | 71.0 | 275 | 37 | 19 | 19 | 9 | 2 | 1 | 4 | 24 | 1 | 73 | 2 | 0 | 6 | 3 | .667 | 0 | 0-3 | **33** | 1.79 | 2.41 |
| Postseason | | | 3 | 0 | 0 | 0 | 3.0 | 12 | 1 | 1 | 1 | 1 | 1 | 0 | 0 | 1 | 0 | 5 | 0 | 0 | 0 | 0 | - | 0 | 0-0 | 2 | 1.55 | 3.00 |
| 7 ML YEARS | | | 345 | 8 | 0 | 82 | 420.2 | 1707 | 286 | 146 | 140 | 52 | 15 | 16 | 9 | 176 | 12 | 466 | 13 | 3 | 30 | 21 | .588 | 0 | 33-59 | 110 | 2.65 | 3.00 |

# Tyler Cloyd

**Pitches:** R **Bats:** R **Pos:** SP-11; RP-2 CLOID **Ht:** 6'3" **Wt:** 210 **Born:** 5/16/1987 **Age:** 27

| HOW MUCH HE PITCHED | | | | | | | | | WHAT HE GAVE UP | | | | | | | | | | | | | THE RESULTS | | | | | | | | |
|---|---|---|---|---|---|---|---|---|---|---|---|---|---|---|---|---|---|---|---|---|---|---|---|---|---|---|---|---|---|---|
| Year | Team | Lg | G | GS | CG | GF | IP | BFP | H | R | ER | HR | SH | SF | HB | TBB | IBB | SO | WP | Bk | W | L | Pct | Sh | Sv-Op | Hld | ERC | ERA |
| 2009 | Lakwd | A | 14 | 14 | 1 | 0 | 88.2 | 362 | 90 | 32 | 30 | 3 | 4 | 1 | 2 | 19 | 2 | 77 | 1 | 0 | 7 | 3 | .700 | 0 | 0- - | - | 3.13 | 3.05 |
| 2009 | Clrwtr | A+ | 13 | 12 | 0 | 0 | 76.2 | 337 | 83 | 43 | 35 | 4 | 0 | 5 | 6 | 23 | 1 | 39 | 1 | 0 | 5 | 6 | .455 | 0 | 0- - | - | 4.05 | 4.11 |
| 2010 | Clrwtr | A+ | 35 | 4 | 0 | 8 | 69.1 | 310 | 85 | 45 | 41 | 8 | 3 | 5 | 2 | 16 | 0 | 67 | 5 | 0 | 4 | 3 | .571 | 0 | 0- - | - | 4.81 | 5.32 |
| 2010 | Rdng | AA | 2 | 1 | 0 | 1 | 9.0 | 34 | 5 | 4 | 4 | 3 | 0 | 0 | 0 | 1 | 0 | 6 | 0 | 0 | 1 | 1 | .500 | 0 | 0- - | - | 1.82 | 4.00 |
| 2011 | Clrwtr | A+ | 13 | 5 | 0 | 3 | 39.1 | 154 | 31 | 12 | 12 | 3 | 0 | 0 | 1 | 7 | 0 | 39 | 2 | 0 | 3 | 1 | .750 | 0 | 0- - | - | 2.13 | 2.75 |
| 2011 | Rdng | AA | 18 | 17 | 0 | 0 | 106.2 | 430 | 101 | 35 | 33 | 7 | 2 | 2 | 7 | 15 | 0 | 99 | 2 | 0 | 6 | 3 | .667 | 0 | 0- - | - | 2.87 | 2.78 |
| 2012 | LV | AAA | 22 | 22 | 1 | 0 | 142.0 | 552 | 105 | 39 | 37 | 14 | 6 | 3 | 4 | 38 | 3 | 93 | 1 | 0 | 12 | 1 | .923 | 1 | 0- - | - | 2.37 | 2.35 |
| 2012 | Rdng | AA | 4 | 4 | 0 | 0 | 25.0 | 97 | 22 | 5 | 5 | 1 | 0 | 1 | 1 | 3 | 0 | 20 | 0 | 0 | 3 | 0 | 1.000 | 0 | 0- - | - | 2.26 | 1.80 |
| 2013 | LV | AAA | 19 | 19 | 2 | 0 | 112.2 | 483 | 125 | 70 | 59 | 21 | 2 | 1 | 1 | 26 | 0 | 93 | 1 | 1 | 5 | 9 | .357 | 0 | 0- - | - | 4.62 | 4.71 |
| 2012 | Phi | NL | 6 | 6 | 0 | 0 | 33.0 | 138 | 33 | 18 | 18 | 8 | 2 | 0 | 2 | 7 | 0 | 30 | 0 | 0 | 2 | 2 | .500 | 0 | 0-0 | 0 | 4.54 | 4.91 |
| 2013 | Phi | NL | 13 | 11 | 0 | 1 | 60.1 | 282 | 83 | 45 | 44 | 7 | 2 | 1 | 1 | 25 | 2 | 41 | 3 | 0 | 2 | 7 | .222 | 0 | 0-0 | 0 | 6.55 | 6.56 |
| 2 ML YEARS | | | 19 | 17 | 0 | 1 | 93.1 | 420 | 116 | 63 | 62 | 15 | 4 | 1 | 3 | 32 | 2 | 71 | 3 | 0 | 4 | 9 | .308 | 0 | 0-0 | 0 | 5.84 | 5.98 |

# Alex Cobb

**Pitches:** R **Bats:** R **Pos:** SP-22 **Ht:** 6'3" **Wt:** 190 **Born:** 10/7/1987 **Age:** 26

| HOW MUCH HE PITCHED | | | | | | | | | WHAT HE GAVE UP | | | | | | | | | | | | | THE RESULTS | | | | | | | | |
|---|---|---|---|---|---|---|---|---|---|---|---|---|---|---|---|---|---|---|---|---|---|---|---|---|---|---|---|---|---|---|
| Year | Team | Lg | G | GS | CG | GF | IP | BFP | H | R | ER | HR | SH | SF | HB | TBB | IBB | SO | WP | Bk | W | L | Pct | Sh | Sv-Op | Hld | ERC | ERA |
| 2013 | Charltt* | A+ | 3 | 3 | 0 | 0 | 8.1 | 36 | 8 | 4 | 4 | 0 | 0 | 0 | 1 | 4 | 0 | 8 | 0 | 0 | 0 | 1 | .000 | 0 | 0- - | - | 4.02 | 4.32 |
| 2011 | TB | AL | 9 | 9 | 0 | 0 | 52.2 | 224 | 49 | 21 | 20 | 3 | 0 | 1 | 1 | 21 | 1 | 37 | 2 | 0 | 3 | 2 | .600 | 0 | 0-0 | 0 | 3.44 | 3.42 |
| 2012 | TB | AL | 23 | 23 | 2 | 0 | 136.1 | 569 | 130 | 67 | 61 | 11 | 3 | 6 | 9 | 40 | 2 | 106 | 8 | 1 | 11 | 9 | .550 | 1 | 0-0 | 0 | 3.56 | 4.03 |
| 2013 | TB | AL | 22 | 22 | 1 | 0 | 143.1 | 578 | 120 | 46 | 44 | 13 | 1 | 2 | 3 | 45 | 4 | 134 | 5 | 1 | 11 | 3 | .786 | 0 | 0-0 | 0 | 2.92 | 2.76 |
| 3 ML YEARS | | | 54 | 54 | 3 | 0 | 332.1 | 1371 | 299 | 134 | 125 | 27 | 4 | 9 | 13 | 106 | 7 | 277 | 15 | 2 | 25 | 14 | .641 | 1 | 0-0 | 0 | 3.26 | 3.39 |

# Robert Coello

**Pitches:** R **Bats:** R **Pos:** RP-16 koe-AY-oh **Ht:** 6'5" **Wt:** 250 **Born:** 11/23/1984 **Age:** 29

| HOW MUCH HE PITCHED | | | | | | | | | WHAT HE GAVE UP | | | | | | | | | | | | | THE RESULTS | | | | | | | | |
|---|---|---|---|---|---|---|---|---|---|---|---|---|---|---|---|---|---|---|---|---|---|---|---|---|---|---|---|---|---|---|
| Year | Team | Lg | G | GS | CG | GF | IP | BFP | H | R | ER | HR | SH | SF | HB | TBB | IBB | SO | WP | Bk | W | L | Pct | Sh | Sv-Op | Hld | ERC | ERA |
| 2013 | Salt Lk* | AAA | 15 | 0 | 0 | 9 | 18.2 | 83 | 15 | 10 | 10 | 1 | 0 | 1 | 1 | 11 | 0 | 29 | 0 | 0 | 1 | 0 | 1.000 | 0 | 4- - | - | 3.50 | 4.82 |
| 2013 | Ark* | AA | 1 | 0 | 0 | 0 | 1.0 | 3 | 0 | 0 | 0 | 0 | 0 | 0 | 0 | 0 | 0 | 2 | 0 | 0 | 0 | 0 | - | 0 | 0- - | - | 0.00 | 0.00 |
| 2010 | Bos | AL | 6 | 0 | 0 | 2 | 5.2 | 26 | 4 | 3 | 3 | 0 | 0 | 0 | 0 | 5 | 0 | 5 | 1 | 0 | 0 | 0 | - | 0 | 0-0 | 0 | 3.44 | 4.76 |
| 2012 | Tor | AL | 6 | 0 | 0 | 1 | 6.1 | 33 | 10 | 9 | 9 | 2 | 0 | 0 | 1 | 4 | 0 | 11 | 0 | 0 | 0 | 1 | .000 | 0 | 0-0 | 1 | 11.62 | 12.79 |
| 2013 | LAA | AL | 16 | 0 | 0 | 8 | 17.0 | 73 | 14 | 7 | 7 | 1 | 1 | 0 | 0 | 8 | 0 | 23 | 0 | 0 | 2 | 2 | .500 | 0 | 1-1 | 0 | 3.04 | 3.71 |
| 3 ML YEARS | | | 28 | 0 | 0 | 11 | 29.0 | 132 | 28 | 19 | 19 | 3 | 1 | 0 | 1 | 17 | 0 | 39 | 1 | 0 | 2 | 3 | .400 | 0 | 1-1 | 1 | 4.71 | 5.90 |

# Chris Coghlan

COGG-lan

**Bats:** L **Throws:** R **Pos:** PH-22;LF-18;CF-17;3B-8;RF-4;2B-1;DH-1 **Ht:** 6'0" **Wt:** 195 **Born:** 6/18/1985 **Age:** 29

| BATTING | | | | | | | | | | | | | | | | | | | | BASERUNNING | | | | AVERAGES | | |
|---|---|---|---|---|---|---|---|---|---|---|---|---|---|---|---|---|---|---|---|---|---|---|---|---|---|---|
| Year Team | Lg | G | AB | H | 2B | 3B | HR | (Hm | Rd) | TB | R | RBI | RC | TBB | IBB | SO | HBP | SH | SF | SB | CS | SB% | GDP | Avg | OBP | Slg |
| 2013 Jupiter* | A+ | 9 | 27 | 5 | 0 | 1 | 0 | (- | -) | 7 | 1 | 2 | 1 | 1 | 0 | 6 | 0 | 0 | 0 | 0 | 0 | - | 2 | .185 | .214 | .259 |
| 2013 NewOr* | AAA | 3 | 12 | 6 | 1 | 0 | 1 | (- | -) | 10 | 1 | 3 | 4 | 2 | 1 | 0 | 0 | 0 | 0 | 1 | 1 | .50 | 0 | .500 | .571 | .833 |
| 2009 Fla | NL | 128 | 504 | 162 | 31 | 6 | 9 | (5 | 4) | 232 | 84 | 47 | 91 | 53 | 2 | 77 | 4 | 3 | 1 | 8 | 5 | .62 | 3 | .321 | .390 | .460 |
| 2010 Fla | NL | 91 | 358 | 96 | 20 | 3 | 5 | (5 | 0) | 137 | 60 | 28 | 43 | 33 | 1 | 84 | 4 | 3 | 2 | 10 | 3 | .77 | 3 | .268 | .335 | .383 |
| 2011 Fla | NL | 65 | 269 | 62 | 20 | 1 | 5 | (4 | 1) | 99 | 33 | 22 | 23 | 22 | 3 | 49 | 4 | 1 | 2 | 7 | 6 | .54 | 3 | .230 | .296 | .368 |
| 2012 Mia | NL | 39 | 93 | 13 | 1 | 0 | 1 | (1 | 0) | 17 | 10 | 10 | 2 | 9 | 1 | 12 | 0 | 1 | 2 | 0 | 2 | .00 | 4 | .140 | .212 | .183 |
| 2013 Mia | NL | 70 | 195 | 50 | 10 | 3 | 1 | (0 | 1) | 69 | 10 | 10 | 20 | 17 | 1 | 43 | 1 | 0 | 1 | 2 | 0 | 1.00 | 2 | .256 | .318 | .354 |
| 5 ML YEARS | | 393 | 1419 | 383 | 82 | 13 | 21 | (15 | 6) | 554 | 197 | 117 | 179 | 134 | 8 | 265 | 13 | 8 | 8 | 27 | 16 | .63 | 15 | .270 | .337 | .390 |

# Phil Coke

**Pitches:** L **Bats:** L **Pos:** RP-49 **Ht:** 6'1" **Wt:** 210 **Born:** 7/19/1982 **Age:** 31

| HOW MUCH HE PITCHED | | | | | | | | WHAT HE GAVE UP | | | | | | | | | | | | THE RESULTS | | | | | | | |
|---|---|---|---|---|---|---|---|---|---|---|---|---|---|---|---|---|---|---|---|---|---|---|---|---|---|---|---|
| Year Team | Lg | G | GS | CG | GF | IP | BFP | H | R | ER | HR | SH | SF | HB | TBB | IBB | SO | WP | Bk | W | L | Pct | Sh | Sv-Op | Hld | ERC | ERA |
| 2013 Toledo* | AAA | 6 | 0 | 0 | 0 | 6.0 | 24 | 5 | 0 | 0 | 0 | 1 | 0 | 0 | 1 | 1 | 9 | 0 | 0 | 1 | 0 | 1.000 | 0 | 0- - | - | 1.57 | 0.00 |
| 2008 NYY | AL | 12 | 0 | 0 | 0 | 14.2 | 52 | 8 | 1 | 1 | 0 | 0 | 0 | 0 | 2 | 0 | 14 | 1 | 0 | 1 | 0 | 1.000 | 0 | 0-0 | 5 | 0.89 | 0.61 |
| 2009 NYY | AL | 72 | 0 | 0 | 13 | 60.0 | 238 | 44 | 34 | 30 | 10 | 1 | 5 | 1 | 20 | 4 | 49 | 7 | 0 | 4 | 3 | .571 | 0 | 2-7 | 21 | 2.84 | 4.50 |
| 2010 Det | AL | 74 | 1 | 0 | 18 | 64.2 | 279 | 67 | 29 | 27 | 2 | 2 | 3 | 4 | 26 | 4 | 53 | 3 | 0 | 7 | 5 | .583 | 0 | 2-4 | 17 | 4.00 | 3.76 |
| 2011 Det | AL | 48 | 14 | 0 | 6 | 108.2 | 474 | 118 | 64 | 54 | 5 | 4 | 3 | 4 | 40 | 5 | 69 | 4 | 0 | 3 | 9 | .250 | 0 | 1-2 | 7 | 4.13 | 4.47 |
| 2012 Det | AL | 66 | 0 | 0 | 11 | 54.0 | 245 | 71 | 28 | 24 | 5 | 5 | 2 | 1 | 18 | 4 | 51 | 3 | 0 | 2 | 3 | .400 | 0 | 1-3 | 20 | 5.56 | 4.00 |
| 2013 Det | AL | 49 | 0 | 0 | 14 | 38.1 | 177 | 43 | 24 | 23 | 3 | 4 | 4 | 0 | 21 | 7 | 30 | 1 | 0 | 0 | 5 | .000 | 0 | 1-3 | 4 | 4.81 | 5.40 |
| Postseason | | 21 | 0 | 0 | 9 | 17.2 | 72 | 16 | 7 | 7 | 2 | 1 | 0 | 0 | 5 | 0 | 19 | 0 | 0 | 0 | 1 | .000 | 0 | 3-3 | 2 | 3.24 | 3.57 |
| 6 ML YEARS | | 321 | 15 | 0 | 62 | 340.1 | 1465 | 351 | 180 | 159 | 25 | 16 | 17 | 10 | 127 | 24 | 266 | 19 | 0 | 17 | 25 | .405 | 0 | 7-19 | 74 | 3.99 | 4.20 |

# Chris Colabello

**Bats:** R **Throws:** R **Pos:** 1B-26;RF-11;DH-11;PH-9 CAHL-uh-bell-oh **Ht:** 6'4" **Wt:** 220 **Born:** 10/24/1983 **Age:** 30

| BATTING | | | | | | | | | | | | | | | | | | | | BASERUNNING | | | | AVERAGES | | |
|---|---|---|---|---|---|---|---|---|---|---|---|---|---|---|---|---|---|---|---|---|---|---|---|---|---|---|
| Year Team | Lg | G | AB | H | 2B | 3B | HR | (Hm | Rd) | TB | R | RBI | RC | TBB | IBB | SO | HBP | SH | SF | SB | CS | SB% | GDP | Avg | OBP | Slg |
| 2009 Wrcstr | IND | 84 | 321 | 97 | 22 | 0 | 9 | (- | -) | 146 | 48 | 55 | 55 | 34 | 2 | 46 | 4 | 0 | 3 | 3 | 5 | .38 | 3 | .302 | .373 | .455 |
| 2010 Wrcstr | IND | 82 | 316 | 95 | 16 | 1 | 13 | (- | -) | 152 | 53 | 59 | 57 | 29 | 1 | 53 | 6 | 1 | 4 | 3 | 2 | .60 | - | .301 | .366 | .481 |
| 2011 Wrcstr | IND | 92 | 365 | 127 | 32 | 0 | 20 | (- | -) | 219 | 75 | 79 | 86 | 39 | 2 | 39 | 3 | 0 | 5 | 1 | 3 | .25 | - | .348 | .410 | .600 |
| 2012 NwBrit | AA | 134 | 496 | 141 | 37 | 1 | 19 | (- | -) | 237 | 78 | 98 | 87 | 47 | 2 | 94 | 13 | 0 | 5 | 0 | 0 | - | 19 | .284 | .358 | .478 |
| 2013 Roch | AAA | 89 | 338 | 119 | 25 | 0 | 24 | (- | -) | 216 | 58 | 76 | 87 | 43 | 3 | 89 | 5 | 0 | 5 | 2 | 1 | .67 | 11 | .352 | .427 | .639 |
| 2013 Min | AL | 55 | 160 | 31 | 3 | 0 | 7 | (1 | 6) | 55 | 14 | 17 | 13 | 20 | 0 | 58 | 1 | 0 | 0 | 0 | 1 | .00 | 5 | .194 | .287 | .344 |

# Gerrit Cole

**Pitches:** R **Bats:** R **Pos:** SP-19 **Ht:** 6'4" **Wt:** 235 **Born:** 9/8/1990 **Age:** 23

| HOW MUCH HE PITCHED | | | | | | | | WHAT HE GAVE UP | | | | | | | | | | | | THE RESULTS | | | | | | | |
|---|---|---|---|---|---|---|---|---|---|---|---|---|---|---|---|---|---|---|---|---|---|---|---|---|---|---|---|
| Year Team | Lg | G | GS | CG | GF | IP | BFP | H | R | ER | HR | SH | SF | HB | TBB | IBB | SO | WP | Bk | W | L | Pct | Sh | Sv-Op | Hld | ERC | ERA |
| 2012 Bradtn | A+ | 13 | 13 | 0 | 0 | 67.0 | 273 | 53 | 24 | 19 | 5 | 0 | 4 | 3 | 21 | 0 | 69 | 3 | 1 | 5 | 1 | .833 | 0 | 0- - | - | 2.65 | 2.55 |
| 2012 Altna | AA | 12 | 12 | 0 | 0 | 59.0 | 252 | 54 | 28 | 19 | 2 | 1 | 0 | 2 | 23 | 0 | 60 | 3 | 1 | 3 | 6 | .333 | 0 | 0- - | - | 3.23 | 2.90 |
| 2012 Indy | AAA | 1 | 1 | 0 | 0 | 6.0 | 24 | 6 | 3 | 3 | 0 | 0 | 1 | 0 | 1 | 0 | 7 | 0 | 0 | 1 | 0 | 1.000 | 0 | 0- - | - | 2.62 | 4.50 |
| 2013 Indy | AAA | 12 | 12 | 0 | 0 | 68.0 | 268 | 44 | 23 | 22 | 4 | 1 | 3 | 4 | 28 | 0 | 47 | 4 | 1 | 5 | 3 | .625 | 0 | 0- - | - | 2.32 | 2.91 |
| 2013 Pit | NL | 19 | 19 | 0 | 0 | 117.1 | 469 | 109 | 43 | 42 | 7 | 5 | 2 | 3 | 28 | 0 | 100 | 4 | 0 | 10 | 7 | .588 | 0 | 0-0 | 0 | 3.02 | 3.22 |

# Louis Coleman

**Pitches:** R **Bats:** R **Pos:** RP-27 **Ht:** 6'4" **Wt:** 205 **Born:** 4/4/1986 **Age:** 28

| HOW MUCH HE PITCHED | | | | | | | | WHAT HE GAVE UP | | | | | | | | | | | | THE RESULTS | | | | | | | |
|---|---|---|---|---|---|---|---|---|---|---|---|---|---|---|---|---|---|---|---|---|---|---|---|---|---|---|---|
| Year Team | Lg | G | GS | CG | GF | IP | BFP | H | R | ER | HR | SH | SF | HB | TBB | IBB | SO | WP | Bk | W | L | Pct | Sh | Sv-Op | Hld | ERC | ERA |
| 2013 Omha* | AAA | 24 | 0 | 0 | 11 | 44.2 | 185 | 36 | 10 | 8 | 1 | 2 | 1 | 0 | 17 | 3 | 52 | 2 | 0 | 3 | 2 | .600 | 0 | 6- - | - | 2.35 | 1.61 |
| 2013 Wilmg* | A+ | 2 | 0 | 0 | 1 | 2.0 | 7 | 0 | 0 | 0 | 0 | 0 | 0 | 0 | 0 | 0 | 4 | 0 | 0 | 0 | 0 | - | 0 | 0- - | - | 0.00 | 0.00 |
| 2011 KC | AL | 48 | 0 | 0 | 11 | 59.2 | 244 | 44 | 20 | 19 | 9 | 1 | 1 | 3 | 26 | 6 | 64 | 4 | 0 | 1 | 4 | .200 | 0 | 1-2 | 11 | 3.23 | 2.87 |
| 2012 KC | AL | 42 | 0 | 0 | 18 | 51.0 | 217 | 41 | 23 | 21 | 10 | 3 | 0 | 1 | 26 | 3 | 65 | 1 | 0 | 0 | 0 | - | 0 | 0-0 | 2 | 4.07 | 3.71 |
| 2013 KC | AL | 27 | 0 | 0 | 8 | 29.2 | 110 | 19 | 2 | 2 | 1 | 1 | 0 | 1 | 6 | 1 | 32 | 1 | 0 | 3 | 0 | 1.000 | 0 | 0-0 | 4 | 1.45 | 0.61 |
| 3 ML YEARS | | 117 | 0 | 0 | 37 | 140.1 | 571 | 104 | 45 | 42 | 20 | 5 | 1 | 5 | 58 | 10 | 161 | 6 | 0 | 4 | 4 | .500 | 0 | 1-2 | 17 | 3.09 | 2.69 |

# Tim Collins

**Pitches:** L **Bats:** L **Pos:** RP-66 **Ht:** 5'7" **Wt:** 165 **Born:** 8/21/1989 **Age:** 24

| HOW MUCH HE PITCHED | | | | | | | | WHAT HE GAVE UP | | | | | | | | | | | | THE RESULTS | | | | | | | |
|---|---|---|---|---|---|---|---|---|---|---|---|---|---|---|---|---|---|---|---|---|---|---|---|---|---|---|---|
| Year Team | Lg | G | GS | CG | GF | IP | BFP | H | R | ER | HR | SH | SF | HB | TBB | IBB | SO | WP | Bk | W | L | Pct | Sh | Sv-Op | Hld | ERC | ERA |
| 2011 KC | AL | 68 | 0 | 0 | 18 | 67.0 | 295 | 52 | 28 | 27 | 5 | 3 | 1 | 2 | 48 | 2 | 60 | 3 | 0 | 4 | 4 | .500 | 0 | 0-1 | 11 | 3.95 | 3.63 |
| 2012 KC | AL | 72 | 0 | 0 | 9 | 69.2 | 295 | 55 | 29 | 26 | 8 | 3 | 1 | 2 | 34 | 8 | 93 | 3 | 0 | 5 | 4 | .556 | 0 | 0-4 | 11 | 3.29 | 3.36 |
| 2013 KC | AL | 66 | 0 | 0 | 8 | 53.1 | 233 | 49 | 26 | 21 | 3 | 2 | 2 | 0 | 28 | 1 | 52 | 0 | 0 | 3 | 6 | .333 | 0 | 0-5 | 21 | 3.74 | 3.54 |
| 3 ML YEARS | | 206 | 0 | 0 | 35 | 190.0 | 823 | 156 | 83 | 74 | 16 | 8 | 4 | 4 | 110 | 11 | 205 | 6 | 0 | 12 | 14 | .462 | 0 | 0-10 | 43 | 3.65 | 3.51 |

# Josh Collmenter

**Pitches:** R **Bats:** R **Pos:** RP-49 COLE-men-ter **Ht:** 6'4" **Wt:** 235 **Born:** 2/7/1986 **Age:** 28

| HOW MUCH HE PITCHED | | | | | | | | | WHAT HE GAVE UP | | | | | | | | | | | | | THE RESULTS | | | | | | | |
|---|---|---|---|---|---|---|---|---|---|---|---|---|---|---|---|---|---|---|---|---|---|---|---|---|---|---|---|---|
| Year | Team | Lg | G | GS | CG | GF | IP | BFP | H | R | ER | HR | SH | SF | HB | TBB | IBB | SO | WP | Bk | W | L | Pct | Sh | Sv-Op | Hld | ERC | ERA |
| 2011 | Ari | NL | 31 | 24 | 0 | 3 | 154.1 | 621 | 137 | 61 | 58 | 17 | 9 | 2 | 5 | 28 | 2 | 100 | 1 | 1 | 10 | 10 | .500 | 0 | 0-0 | 0 | 2.82 | 3.38 |
| 2012 | Ari | NL | 28 | 11 | 0 | 7 | 90.1 | 375 | 92 | 39 | 37 | 13 | 5 | 0 | 0 | 22 | 2 | 80 | 1 | 0 | 5 | 3 | .625 | 0 | 0-0 | 0 | 3.85 | 3.69 |
| 2013 | Ari | NL | 49 | 0 | 0 | 10 | 92.0 | 384 | 79 | 34 | 32 | 8 | 8 | 0 | 2 | 33 | 8 | 85 | 3 | 0 | 5 | 5 | .500 | 0 | 0-1 | 5 | 3.01 | 3.13 |
| Postseason | | | 1 | 1 | 0 | 0 | 7.0 | 26 | 2 | 1 | 1 | 1 | 0 | 0 | 1 | 2 | 0 | 6 | 0 | 0 | 1 | 0 | 1.000 | 0 | 0-0 | 0 | 1.18 | 1.29 |
| 3 ML YEARS | | | 108 | 35 | 0 | 20 | 336.2 | 1380 | 308 | 134 | 127 | 38 | 22 | 2 | 7 | 83 | 12 | 265 | 5 | 1 | 20 | 18 | .526 | 0 | 0-1 | 5 | 3.14 | 3.40 |

# Alex Colome

**Pitches:** R **Bats:** R **Pos:** SP-3 CAHL-ah-may **Ht:** 6'2" **Wt:** 185 **Born:** 12/31/1988 **Age:** 25

| HOW MUCH HE PITCHED | | | | | | | | | WHAT HE GAVE UP | | | | | | | | | | | | | THE RESULTS | | | | | | | |
|---|---|---|---|---|---|---|---|---|---|---|---|---|---|---|---|---|---|---|---|---|---|---|---|---|---|---|---|---|
| Year | Team | Lg | G | GS | CG | GF | IP | BFP | H | R | ER | HR | SH | SF | HB | TBB | IBB | SO | WP | Bk | W | L | Pct | Sh | Sv-Op | Hld | ERC | ERA |
| 2009 | HudVal | A- | 15 | 15 | 2 | 0 | 76.0 | 303 | 46 | 22 | 14 | 0 | 0 | 1 | 5 | 32 | 0 | 94 | 5 | 0 | 7 | 4 | .636 | 1 | 0- - | - | 1.78 | 1.66 |
| 2010 | BG | A | 22 | 22 | 1 | 0 | 114.0 | 475 | 98 | 59 | 50 | 14 | 3 | 3 | 4 | 45 | 0 | 118 | 4 | 2 | 6 | 6 | .500 | 0 | 0- - | - | 3.62 | 3.95 |
| 2010 | Charltt | A+ | 1 | 1 | 0 | 0 | 4.0 | 17 | 5 | 1 | 1 | 0 | 1 | 0 | 1 | 0 | 0 | 8 | 0 | 0 | 0 | 0 | - | 0 | 0- - | - | 4.32 | 2.25 |
| 2011 | Charltt | A+ | 19 | 19 | 1 | 0 | 105.2 | 427 | 78 | 45 | 43 | 8 | 8 | 4 | 6 | 44 | 0 | 92 | 9 | 2 | 9 | 5 | .643 | 0 | 0- - | - | 2.88 | 3.66 |
| 2011 | Mont | AA | 9 | 9 | 1 | 0 | 52.0 | 222 | 41 | 25 | 24 | 5 | 0 | 1 | 6 | 28 | 1 | 31 | 8 | 0 | 3 | 4 | .429 | 1 | 0- - | - | 3.91 | 4.15 |
| 2012 | Mont | AA | 14 | 14 | 1 | 0 | 75.0 | 313 | 69 | 30 | 29 | 2 | 2 | 3 | 0 | 34 | 0 | 75 | 6 | 3 | 8 | 3 | .727 | 0 | 0- - | - | 3.43 | 3.48 |
| 2012 | Drham | AAA | 3 | 3 | 0 | 0 | 16.2 | 68 | 12 | 6 | 6 | 1 | 0 | 0 | 1 | 9 | 0 | 15 | 2 | 0 | 0 | 1 | .000 | 0 | 0- - | - | 3.19 | 3.24 |
| 2013 | Drham | AAA | 14 | 14 | 0 | 0 | 70.1 | 303 | 63 | 30 | 24 | 5 | 0 | 3 | 4 | 29 | 0 | 72 | 5 | 0 | 4 | 6 | .400 | 0 | 0- - | - | 3.54 | 3.07 |
| 2013 | TB | AL | 3 | 3 | 0 | 0 | 16.0 | 71 | 14 | 8 | 4 | 2 | 0 | 0 | 1 | 9 | 0 | 12 | 1 | 0 | 1 | 1 | .500 | 0 | 0-0 | 0 | 4.41 | 2.25 |

# Bartolo Colon

**Pitches:** R **Bats:** R **Pos:** SP-30 co-LONE **Ht:** 5'11" **Wt:** 265 **Born:** 5/24/1973 **Age:** 41

| HOW MUCH HE PITCHED | | | | | | | | | WHAT HE GAVE UP | | | | | | | | | | | | | THE RESULTS | | | | | | | |
|---|---|---|---|---|---|---|---|---|---|---|---|---|---|---|---|---|---|---|---|---|---|---|---|---|---|---|---|---|
| Year | Team | Lg | G | GS | CG | GF | IP | BFP | H | R | ER | HR | SH | SF | HB | TBB | IBB | SO | WP | Bk | W | L | Pct | Sh | Sv-Op | Hld | ERC | ERA |
| 1997 | Cle | AL | 19 | 17 | 1 | 0 | 94.0 | 427 | 107 | 66 | 59 | 12 | 4 | 1 | 3 | 45 | 1 | 66 | 5 | 0 | 4 | 7 | .364 | 0 | 0-0 | 0 | 5.53 | 5.65 |
| 1998 | Cle | AL | 31 | 31 | 6 | 0 | 204.0 | 883 | 205 | 91 | 84 | 15 | **10** | 2 | 3 | 79 | 5 | 158 | 4 | 0 | 14 | 9 | .609 | 2 | 0-0 | 0 | 3.87 | 3.71 |
| 1999 | Cle | AL | 32 | 32 | 1 | 0 | 205.0 | 858 | 185 | 97 | 90 | 24 | 5 | 4 | 7 | 76 | 5 | 161 | 4 | 0 | 18 | 5 | .783 | 1 | 0-0 | 0 | 3.68 | 3.95 |
| 2000 | Cle | AL | 30 | 30 | 2 | 0 | 188.0 | 807 | 163 | 86 | 81 | 21 | 2 | 3 | 4 | 98 | 4 | 212 | 4 | 0 | 15 | 8 | .652 | 1 | 0-0 | 0 | 3.97 | 3.88 |
| 2001 | Cle | AL | 34 | 34 | 1 | 0 | 222.1 | 947 | 220 | 106 | 101 | 26 | 8 | 4 | 2 | 90 | 2 | 201 | 4 | 1 | 14 | 12 | .538 | 0 | 0-0 | 0 | 4.24 | 4.09 |
| 2002 | 2 Tms | | 33 | 33 | 8 | 0 | 233.1 | 966 | 219 | 85 | 76 | 20 | 19 | 6 | 2 | 70 | 5 | 149 | 4 | 0 | 20 | 8 | .714 | 3 | 0-0 | 0 | 3.29 | 2.93 |
| 2003 | CWS | AL | 34 | 34 | **9** | 0 | 242.0 | 984 | 223 | 107 | 104 | 30 | 5 | 8 | 5 | 67 | 3 | 173 | 8 | 3 | 15 | 13 | .536 | 0 | 0-0 | 0 | 3.47 | 3.87 |
| 2004 | LAA | AL | 34 | 34 | 0 | 0 | 208.1 | 897 | 215 | 122 | 116 | 38 | 5 | 8 | 3 | 71 | 1 | 158 | 1 | 0 | 18 | 12 | .600 | 0 | 0-0 | 0 | 4.64 | 5.01 |
| 2005 | LAA | AL | 33 | 33 | 2 | 0 | 222.2 | 906 | 215 | 93 | 86 | 26 | **9** | 4 | 3 | 43 | 0 | 157 | 2 | 1 | **21** | 8 | .724 | 0 | 0-0 | 0 | 3.28 | 3.48 |
| 2006 | LAA | AL | 10 | 10 | 1 | 0 | 56.1 | 251 | 71 | 39 | 32 | 11 | 4 | 1 | 3 | 11 | 0 | 31 | 1 | 0 | 1 | 5 | .167 | 1 | 0-0 | 0 | 5.61 | 5.11 |
| 2007 | LAA | AL | 19 | 18 | 0 | 0 | 99.1 | 453 | 132 | 74 | 70 | 15 | 4 | 3 | 5 | 29 | 1 | 76 | 1 | 0 | 6 | 8 | .429 | 0 | 0-0 | 1 | 6.17 | 6.34 |
| 2008 | Bos | AL | 7 | 7 | 0 | 0 | 39.0 | 173 | 44 | 23 | 17 | 5 | 3 | 2 | 2 | 10 | 0 | 27 | 0 | 0 | 4 | 2 | .667 | 0 | 0-0 | 0 | 4.53 | 3.92 |
| 2009 | CWS | AL | 12 | 12 | 0 | 0 | 62.1 | 276 | 69 | 42 | 29 | 13 | 4 | 3 | 2 | 21 | 3 | 38 | 1 | 0 | 3 | 6 | .333 | 0 | 0-0 | 0 | 5.22 | 4.19 |
| 2011 | NYY | AL | 29 | 26 | 1 | 0 | 164.1 | 694 | 172 | 85 | 73 | 21 | 2 | 6 | 3 | 40 | 3 | 135 | 0 | 0 | 8 | 10 | .444 | 1 | 0-0 | 0 | 3.95 | 4.00 |
| 2012 | Oak | AL | 24 | 24 | 0 | 0 | 152.1 | 636 | 161 | 62 | 58 | 17 | 3 | 4 | 1 | 23 | 3 | 91 | 0 | 0 | 10 | 9 | .526 | 0 | 0-0 | 0 | 3.45 | 3.43 |
| 2013 | Oak | AL | 30 | 30 | 3 | 0 | 190.1 | 769 | 193 | 60 | 56 | 14 | 3 | 6 | 0 | 29 | 0 | 117 | 1 | 0 | 18 | 6 | .750 | **3** | 0-0 | 0 | 3.07 | 2.65 |
| 02 | Cle | AL | 16 | 16 | 4 | 0 | 116.1 | 467 | 104 | 37 | 33 | 11 | 6 | 3 | 2 | 31 | 1 | 75 | 3 | 0 | 10 | 4 | .714 | 2 | 0-0 | 0 | 3.09 | 2.55 |
| 02 | Mon | NL | 17 | 17 | 4 | 0 | 117.0 | 499 | 115 | 48 | 43 | 9 | 13 | 3 | 0 | 39 | 4 | 74 | 1 | 0 | 10 | 4 | .714 | 1 | 0-0 | 0 | 3.48 | 3.31 |
| Postseason | | | 9 | 9 | 1 | 0 | 52.1 | 215 | 49 | 21 | 21 | 5 | 1 | 1 | 1 | 22 | 1 | 41 | 0 | 0 | 2 | 3 | .400 | 0 | 0-0 | 0 | 4.01 | 3.61 |
| 16 ML YEARS | | | 411 | 405 | 35 | 0 | 2583.2 | 10927 | 2594 | 1238 | 1132 | 308 | 90 | 65 | 48 | 802 | 36 | 1950 | 40 | 5 | 189 | 128 | .596 | 12 | 0-0 | 1 | 3.95 | 3.94 |

# Tyler Colvin

**Bats:** L **Throws:** L **Pos:** CF-16;PH-6;LF-4;RF-4;1B-1 **Ht:** 6'3" **Wt:** 210 **Born:** 9/5/1985 **Age:** 28

| BATTING | | | | | | | | | | | | | | | | | | | | | BASERUNNING | | | | AVERAGES | | |
|---|---|---|---|---|---|---|---|---|---|---|---|---|---|---|---|---|---|---|---|---|---|---|---|---|---|---|---|
| Year | Team | Lg | G | AB | H | 2B | 3B | HR | (Hm | Rd) | TB | R | RBI | RC | TBB | IBB | SO | HBP | SH | SF | SB | CS | SB% | GDP | Avg | OBP | Slg |
| 2013 | ColSpr* | AAA | 67 | 229 | 63 | 8 | 6 | 9 | (- | -) | 110 | 47 | 32 | 43 | 36 | 2 | 62 | 2 | 1 | 1 | 6 | 3 | .67 | 4 | .275 | .377 | .480 |
| 2009 | ChC | NL | 6 | 17 | 3 | 0 | 0 | 0 | (0 | 0) | 3 | 1 | 2 | 1 | 2 | 0 | 5 | 0 | 0 | 1 | 0 | 0 | - | 0 | .176 | .250 | .176 |
| 2010 | ChC | NL | 135 | 358 | 91 | 18 | 5 | 20 | (9 | 11) | 179 | 60 | 56 | 46 | 30 | 2 | 100 | 3 | 1 | 2 | 6 | 1 | .86 | 6 | .254 | .316 | .500 |
| 2011 | ChC | NL | 80 | 206 | 31 | 8 | 3 | 6 | (2 | 4) | 63 | 17 | 20 | 9 | 14 | 3 | 58 | 0 | 1 | 1 | 0 | 0 | - | 2 | .150 | .204 | .306 |
| 2012 | Col | NL | 136 | 420 | 122 | 27 | 10 | 18 | (11 | 7) | 223 | 62 | 72 | 73 | 21 | 0 | 117 | 2 | 2 | 1 | 7 | 3 | .70 | 6 | .290 | .327 | .531 |
| 2013 | Col | NL | 27 | 75 | 12 | 0 | 0 | 3 | (3 | 0) | 21 | 8 | 10 | 5 | 3 | 1 | 27 | 0 | 0 | 0 | 0 | 0 | - | 2 | .160 | .192 | .280 |
| 5 ML YEARS | | | 384 | 1076 | 259 | 53 | 18 | 47 | (25 | 22) | 489 | 148 | 160 | 134 | 70 | 6 | 307 | 5 | 4 | 5 | 13 | 4 | .76 | 16 | .241 | .289 | .454 |

# Hank Conger

**Bats:** B **Throws:** R **Pos:** C-71;PH-22;DH-5;PR-2 KONG-gerr **Ht:** 6'1" **Wt:** 220 **Born:** 1/29/1988 **Age:** 26

| BATTING | | | | | | | | | | | | | | | | | | | | | BASERUNNING | | | | AVERAGES | | |
|---|---|---|---|---|---|---|---|---|---|---|---|---|---|---|---|---|---|---|---|---|---|---|---|---|---|---|---|
| Year | Team | Lg | G | AB | H | 2B | 3B | HR | (Hm | Rd) | TB | R | RBI | RC | TBB | IBB | SO | HBP | SH | SF | SB | CS | SB% | GDP | Avg | OBP | Slg |
| 2010 | LAA | AL | 13 | 29 | 5 | 1 | 1 | 0 | (0 | 0) | 8 | 2 | 5 | 3 | 5 | 0 | 9 | 0 | 0 | 0 | 0 | 0 | - | 1 | .172 | .294 | .276 |
| 2011 | LAA | AL | 59 | 177 | 37 | 8 | 0 | 6 | (2 | 4) | 63 | 14 | 19 | 18 | 17 | 2 | 37 | 1 | 2 | 0 | 0 | 0 | - | 2 | .209 | .282 | .356 |
| 2012 | LAA | AL | 7 | 18 | 3 | 0 | 0 | 0 | (0 | 0) | 3 | 0 | 1 | 1 | 1 | 0 | 0 | 1 | 1 | 1 | 0 | 0 | - | 1 | .167 | .238 | .167 |
| 2013 | LAA | AL | 92 | 233 | 58 | 13 | 1 | 7 | (3 | 4) | 94 | 23 | 21 | 24 | 17 | 2 | 61 | 4 | 0 | 1 | 0 | 1 | .00 | 6 | .249 | .310 | .403 |
| 4 ML YEARS | | | 171 | 457 | 103 | 22 | 2 | 13 | (5 | 8) | 168 | 39 | 46 | 46 | 40 | 4 | 107 | 6 | 3 | 2 | 0 | 1 | .00 | 10 | .225 | .295 | .368 |

## Jose Constanza

**Bats:** L **Throws:** L **Pos:** LF-9;PH-9;PR-4;CF-2 cohn-STAHN-zah **Ht:** 5'9" **Wt:** 150 **Born:** 9/1/1983 **Age:** 30

| BATTING | | | | | | | | | | | | | | | | | | | | | BASERUNNING | | | | AVERAGES | | |
|---|---|---|---|---|---|---|---|---|---|---|---|---|---|---|---|---|---|---|---|---|---|---|---|---|---|---|---|
| Year Team | Lg | G | AB | H | 2B | 3B | HR | (Hm | Rd) | TB | R | RBI | RC | TBB | IBB | SO | HBP | SH | SF | SB | CS | SB% | GDP | Avg | OBP | Slg |
| 2013 Gwnntt* | AAA | 83 | 341 | 94 | 7 | 3 | 0 | (- | -) | 107 | 39 | 17 | 38 | 29 | 0 | 49 | 0 | 3 | 0 | 21 | 9 | .70 | 4 | .276 | .332 | .314 |
| 2011 Atl | NL | 42 | 109 | 33 | 1 | 1 | 2 | (1 | 1) | 42 | 21 | 10 | 12 | 6 | 0 | 14 | 0 | 4 | 0 | 7 | 4 | .64 | 1 | .303 | .339 | .385 |
| 2012 Atl | NL | 37 | 76 | 19 | 2 | 0 | 0 | (0 | 0) | 21 | 8 | 4 | 9 | 8 | 2 | 21 | 0 | 2 | 0 | 5 | 2 | .71 | 0 | .250 | .321 | .276 |
| 2013 Atl | NL | 21 | 31 | 8 | 0 | 0 | 0 | (0 | 0) | 8 | 2 | 3 | 3 | 0 | 0 | 5 | 0 | 0 | 0 | 0 | 3 | .00 | 1 | .258 | .258 | .258 |
| Postseason | | 1 | 1 | 1 | 0 | 1 | 0 | (0 | 0) | 3 | 1 | 0 | 1 | 0 | 0 | 0 | 0 | 0 | 0 | 0 | 0 | - | 0 | 1.000 | 1.000 | 3.000 |
| 3 ML YEARS | | 100 | 216 | 60 | 3 | 1 | 2 | (1 | 1) | 71 | 31 | 17 | 24 | 14 | 2 | 40 | 0 | 6 | 0 | 12 | 9 | .57 | 2 | .278 | .322 | .329 |

## Jose Contreras

**Pitches:** R **Bats:** R **Pos:** RP-7 conn-TRAIR-us **Ht:** 6'4" **Wt:** 255 **Born:** 12/6/1971 **Age:** 42

| HOW MUCH HE PITCHED | | | | | | | | WHAT HE GAVE UP | | | | | | | | | | | | THE RESULTS | | | | | | | |
|---|---|---|---|---|---|---|---|---|---|---|---|---|---|---|---|---|---|---|---|---|---|---|---|---|---|---|---|
| Year Team | Lg | G | GS | CG | GF | IP | BFP | H | R | ER | HR | SH | SF | HB | TBB | IBB | SO | WP | Bk | W | L | Pct | Sh | Sv-Op | Hld | ERC | ERA |
| 2013 Bradtn* | A+ | 1 | 0 | 0 | 0 | 2.0 | 10 | 2 | 2 | 2 | 0 | 1 | 0 | 1 | 1 | 0 | 2 | 0 | 0 | 0 | 1 | .000 | 0 | 0-- | - | 5.48 | 9.00 |
| 2013 Altna* | AA | 2 | 0 | 0 | 1 | 2.0 | 6 | 0 | 0 | 0 | 0 | 0 | 0 | 0 | 0 | 0 | 1 | 0 | 0 | 0 | 0 | - | 0 | 0-- | - | 0.00 | 0.00 |
| 2013 Indy* | AAA | 16 | 0 | 0 | 2 | 19.1 | 75 | 13 | 3 | 2 | 1 | 3 | 1 | 2 | 5 | 0 | 24 | 3 | 0 | 2 | 0 | 1.000 | 0 | 1-- | - | 2.03 | 0.93 |
| 2013 Pwtckt* | AAA | 8 | 0 | 0 | 2 | 9.2 | 45 | 9 | 9 | 7 | 2 | 0 | 0 | 0 | 6 | 0 | 15 | 2 | 0 | 0 | 2 | .000 | 0 | 0-- | - | 5.12 | 6.52 |
| 2003 NYY | AL | 18 | 9 | 0 | 2 | 71.0 | 293 | 52 | 27 | 26 | 4 | 0 | 1 | 5 | 30 | 1 | 72 | 2 | 0 | 7 | 2 | .778 | 0 | 0-1 | 1 | 2.71 | 3.30 |
| 2004 2 Tms | AL | 31 | 31 | 0 | 0 | 170.1 | 758 | 166 | 114 | 104 | 31 | 3 | 6 | 8 | 84 | 1 | 150 | **17** | 0 | 13 | 9 | .591 | 0 | 0-0 | 0 | 5.05 | 5.50 |
| 2005 CWS | AL | 32 | 32 | 1 | 0 | 204.2 | 857 | 177 | 91 | 82 | 23 | 7 | 2 | 9 | 75 | 2 | 154 | **20** | 2 | 15 | 7 | .682 | 0 | 0-0 | 0 | 3.46 | 3.61 |
| 2006 CWS | AL | 30 | 30 | 1 | 0 | 196.0 | 833 | 194 | 101 | 93 | 20 | 2 | 8 | 10 | 55 | 4 | 134 | 16 | 0 | 13 | 9 | .591 | 1 | 0-0 | 0 | 3.72 | 4.27 |
| 2007 CWS | AL | 32 | 30 | 2 | 2 | 189.0 | 858 | 232 | **134** | 117 | 21 | 8 | **10** | 15 | 62 | 1 | 113 | 3 | 0 | 10 | 17 | .370 | **2** | 0-0 | 0 | 5.49 | 5.57 |
| 2008 CWS | AL | 20 | 20 | 1 | 0 | 121.0 | 522 | 130 | 64 | 61 | 12 | 4 | 2 | 3 | 35 | 0 | 70 | 6 | 0 | 7 | 6 | .538 | 0 | 0-0 | 0 | 4.13 | 4.54 |
| 2009 2 Tms | | 28 | 23 | 0 | 0 | 131.2 | 589 | 141 | 86 | 72 | 13 | 10 | 2 | 6 | 53 | 4 | 106 | 8 | 0 | 6 | 13 | .316 | 0 | 0-1 | 1 | 4.55 | 4.92 |
| 2010 Phi | NL | 67 | 0 | 0 | 21 | 56.2 | 233 | 53 | 22 | 21 | 5 | 4 | 1 | 4 | 16 | 2 | 57 | 0 | 0 | 6 | 4 | .600 | 0 | 4-5 | 13 | 3.50 | 3.34 |
| 2011 Phi | NL | 17 | 0 | 0 | 8 | 14.0 | 60 | 11 | 6 | 6 | 0 | 1 | 0 | 1 | 8 | 0 | 13 | 0 | 0 | 0 | 0 | - | 0 | 5-5 | 4 | 3.15 | 3.86 |
| 2012 Phi | NL | 17 | 0 | 0 | 3 | 13.2 | 56 | 13 | 10 | 8 | 1 | 0 | 1 | 1 | 3 | 0 | 15 | 0 | 0 | 1 | 0 | 1.000 | 0 | 0-0 | 4 | 3.28 | 5.27 |
| 2013 Pit | NL | 7 | 0 | 0 | 1 | 5.0 | 28 | 7 | 5 | 5 | 1 | 0 | 0 | 0 | 6 | 0 | 5 | 0 | 0 | 0 | 0 | - | 0 | 0-0 | 2 | 10.82 | 9.00 |
| 04 NYY | AL | 18 | 18 | 0 | 0 | 95.2 | 425 | 93 | 66 | 60 | 22 | 1 | 4 | 6 | 42 | 1 | 82 | 10 | 0 | 8 | 5 | .615 | 0 | 0-0 | 0 | 5.18 | 5.64 |
| 04 CWS | AL | 13 | 13 | 0 | 0 | 74.2 | 333 | 73 | 48 | 44 | 9 | 2 | 2 | 2 | 42 | 0 | 68 | 7 | 0 | 5 | 4 | .556 | 0 | 0-0 | 0 | 4.87 | 5.30 |
| 09 CWS | AL | 21 | 21 | 0 | 0 | 114.2 | 513 | 121 | 83 | 69 | 11 | 7 | 2 | 6 | 45 | 3 | 89 | 8 | 0 | 5 | 13 | .278 | 0 | 0-0 | 0 | 4.41 | 5.42 |
| 09 Col | NL | 7 | 2 | 0 | 0 | 17.0 | 76 | 20 | 3 | 3 | 2 | 3 | 0 | 0 | 8 | 1 | 17 | 0 | 0 | 1 | 0 | 1.000 | 0 | 0-1 | 1 | 5.51 | 1.59 |
| Postseason | | 18 | 4 | 1 | 4 | 49.0 | 199 | 41 | 19 | 19 | 2 | 5 | 1 | 3 | 11 | 0 | 38 | 3 | 0 | 4 | 3 | .571 | 0 | 0-1 | 4 | 2.41 | 3.49 |
| 11 ML YEARS | | 299 | 175 | 5 | 37 | 1173.0 | 5087 | 1176 | 660 | 595 | 131 | 39 | 33 | 62 | 427 | 15 | 889 | 72 | 2 | 78 | 67 | .538 | 3 | 9-12 | 25 | 4.21 | 4.57 |

## Ryan Cook

**Pitches:** R **Bats:** R **Pos:** RP-71 **Ht:** 6'2" **Wt:** 215 **Born:** 6/30/1987 **Age:** 27

| HOW MUCH HE PITCHED | | | | | | | | WHAT HE GAVE UP | | | | | | | | | | | | THE RESULTS | | | | | | | |
|---|---|---|---|---|---|---|---|---|---|---|---|---|---|---|---|---|---|---|---|---|---|---|---|---|---|---|---|
| Year Team | Lg | G | GS | CG | GF | IP | BFP | H | R | ER | HR | SH | SF | HB | TBB | IBB | SO | WP | Bk | W | L | Pct | Sh | Sv-Op | Hld | ERC | ERA |
| 2011 Ari | NL | 12 | 0 | 0 | 5 | 7.2 | 41 | 11 | 6 | 6 | 0 | 0 | 0 | 0 | 8 | 0 | 7 | 1 | 1 | 0 | 1 | .000 | 0 | 0-0 | 1 | 8.56 | 7.04 |
| 2012 Oak | AL | 71 | 0 | 0 | 23 | 73.1 | 288 | 42 | 18 | 17 | 4 | 3 | 1 | 4 | 27 | 4 | 80 | 4 | 0 | 6 | 2 | .750 | 0 | 14-21 | 21 | 1.68 | 2.09 |
| 2013 Oak | AL | 71 | 0 | 0 | 13 | 67.1 | 294 | 62 | 22 | 19 | 2 | 0 | 4 | 4 | 25 | 1 | 67 | 7 | 0 | 6 | 4 | .600 | 0 | 2-9 | 23 | 3.16 | 2.54 |
| Postseason | | 4 | 0 | 0 | 1 | 3.1 | 16 | 4 | 3 | 3 | 0 | 1 | 0 | 1 | 1 | 0 | 4 | 1 | 0 | 1 | 0 | 1.000 | 0 | 0-1 | 1 | 5.10 | 8.10 |
| 3 ML YEARS | | 154 | 0 | 0 | 41 | 148.1 | 623 | 115 | 46 | 42 | 6 | 3 | 5 | 8 | 60 | 5 | 154 | 12 | 1 | 12 | 7 | .632 | 0 | 16-30 | 45 | 2.62 | 2.55 |

## Patrick Corbin

**Pitches:** L **Bats:** L **Pos:** SP-32 **Ht:** 6'2" **Wt:** 185 **Born:** 7/19/1989 **Age:** 24

| HOW MUCH HE PITCHED | | | | | | | | WHAT HE GAVE UP | | | | | | | | | | | | THE RESULTS | | | | | | | |
|---|---|---|---|---|---|---|---|---|---|---|---|---|---|---|---|---|---|---|---|---|---|---|---|---|---|---|---|
| Year Team | Lg | G | GS | CG | GF | IP | BFP | H | R | ER | HR | SH | SF | HB | TBB | IBB | SO | WP | Bk | W | L | Pct | Sh | Sv-Op | Hld | ERC | ERA |
| 2009 Orem | R+ | 13 | 12 | 0 | 0 | 46.1 | 214 | 59 | 34 | 26 | 6 | 0 | 0 | 0 | 11 | 0 | 46 | 6 | 1 | 4 | 2 | .667 | 0 | 0-- | - | 4.95 | 5.05 |
| 2010 CRpds | A | 9 | 9 | 0 | 0 | 58.1 | 230 | 52 | 28 | 25 | 2 | 2 | 3 | 3 | 10 | 0 | 42 | 4 | 1 | 8 | 0 | 1.000 | 0 | 0-- | - | 2.50 | 3.86 |
| 2010 RCuca | A+ | 11 | 11 | 0 | 0 | 60.1 | 253 | 57 | 29 | 26 | 7 | 1 | 2 | 1 | 18 | 0 | 64 | 6 | 0 | 5 | 3 | .625 | 0 | 0-- | - | 3.54 | 3.88 |
| 2010 Visalia | A+ | 8 | 8 | 0 | 0 | 26.0 | 99 | 17 | 4 | 4 | 1 | 0 | 0 | 0 | 9 | 0 | 30 | 0 | 0 | 0 | 1 | .000 | 0 | 0-- | - | 1.85 | 1.38 |
| 2011 Mobile | AA | 26 | 26 | 1 | 0 | 160.1 | 688 | 172 | 78 | 75 | 15 | 7 | 3 | 12 | 40 | 0 | 142 | 16 | 1 | 9 | 8 | .529 | 1 | 0-- | - | 4.15 | 4.21 |
| 2012 Mobile | AA | 4 | 4 | 0 | 0 | 27.0 | 106 | 22 | 5 | 5 | 0 | 3 | 0 | 1 | 8 | 0 | 25 | 2 | 0 | 2 | 0 | 1.000 | 0 | 0-- | - | 2.33 | 1.67 |
| 2012 Reno | AAA | 9 | 9 | 0 | 0 | 52.1 | 227 | 57 | 24 | 20 | 4 | 1 | 2 | 1 | 15 | 1 | 55 | 1 | 0 | 3 | 2 | .600 | 0 | 0-- | - | 3.97 | 3.44 |
| 2012 Ari | NL | 22 | 17 | 0 | 3 | 107.0 | 454 | 117 | 56 | 54 | 14 | 2 | 5 | 4 | 25 | 2 | 86 | 1 | 0 | 6 | 8 | .429 | 0 | 1-1 | 0 | 4.31 | 4.54 |
| 2013 Ari | NL | 32 | 32 | 3 | 0 | 208.1 | 860 | 189 | 81 | 79 | 19 | 8 | 1 | 9 | 54 | 1 | 178 | 13 | 0 | 14 | 8 | .636 | 0 | 0-0 | 0 | 3.14 | 3.41 |
| 2 ML YEARS | | 54 | 49 | 3 | 3 | 315.1 | 1314 | 306 | 137 | 133 | 33 | 10 | 6 | 13 | 79 | 3 | 264 | 14 | 0 | 20 | 16 | .556 | 0 | 1-1 | 0 | 3.52 | 3.80 |

## Manny Corpas

**Pitches:** R **Bats:** R **Pos:** RP-31 **Ht:** 6'3" **Wt:** 210 **Born:** 12/3/1982 **Age:** 31

| HOW MUCH HE PITCHED | | | | | | | | WHAT HE GAVE UP | | | | | | | | | | | | THE RESULTS | | | | | | | |
|---|---|---|---|---|---|---|---|---|---|---|---|---|---|---|---|---|---|---|---|---|---|---|---|---|---|---|---|
| Year Team | Lg | G | GS | CG | GF | IP | BFP | H | R | ER | HR | SH | SF | HB | TBB | IBB | SO | WP | Bk | W | L | Pct | Sh | Sv-Op | Hld | ERC | ERA |
| 2013 ColSpr* | AAA | 21 | 0 | 0 | 3 | 41.0 | 179 | 45 | 26 | 25 | 5 | 4 | 0 | 1 | 15 | 0 | 35 | 3 | 0 | 3 | 3 | .500 | 0 | 1-- | - | 4.78 | 5.49 |
| 2006 Col | NL | 35 | 0 | 0 | 3 | 32.1 | 136 | 36 | 13 | 13 | 3 | 0 | 0 | 2 | 8 | 1 | 27 | 2 | 0 | 1 | 2 | .333 | 0 | 0-2 | 7 | 4.39 | 3.62 |
| 2007 Col | NL | 78 | 0 | 0 | 46 | 78.0 | 306 | 63 | 20 | 18 | 6 | 2 | 1 | 2 | 20 | 3 | 58 | 0 | 0 | 4 | 2 | .667 | 0 | 19-22 | 16 | 2.51 | 2.08 |
| 2008 Col | NL | 76 | 0 | 0 | 20 | 79.2 | 346 | 93 | 41 | 40 | 7 | 6 | 1 | 2 | 23 | 4 | 50 | 1 | 0 | 3 | 4 | .429 | 0 | 4-13 | 19 | 4.55 | 4.52 |
| 2009 Col | NL | 35 | 0 | 0 | 16 | 33.2 | 146 | 44 | 22 | 22 | 3 | 2 | 1 | 1 | 7 | 0 | 24 | 0 | 0 | 1 | 3 | .250 | 0 | 1-3 | 7 | 5.24 | 5.88 |
| 2010 Col | NL | 56 | 0 | 0 | 27 | 62.1 | 274 | 66 | 33 | 32 | 7 | 2 | 3 | 2 | 22 | 5 | 47 | 1 | 0 | 3 | 5 | .375 | 0 | 10-14 | 2 | 4.25 | 4.62 |
| 2012 ChC | NL | 48 | 0 | 0 | 11 | 46.2 | 205 | 50 | 27 | 26 | 7 | 1 | 0 | 5 | 16 | 3 | 28 | 1 | 0 | 0 | 2 | .000 | 0 | 0-3 | 6 | 4.99 | 5.01 |
| 2013 Col | NL | 31 | 0 | 0 | 9 | 41.2 | 178 | 40 | 21 | 21 | 5 | 1 | 3 | 1 | 16 | 3 | 30 | 3 | 1 | 1 | 2 | .333 | 0 | 0-0 | 3 | 3.92 | 4.54 |
| Postseason | | 9 | 0 | 0 | 8 | 10.1 | 37 | 6 | 1 | 1 | 0 | 0 | 0 | 1 | 0 | 0 | 7 | 0 | 0 | 1 | 0 | 1.000 | 0 | 5-6 | 0 | 0.90 | 0.87 |
| 7 ML YEARS | | 359 | 0 | 0 | 132 | 374.1 | 1591 | 392 | 177 | 172 | 38 | 14 | 9 | 15 | 112 | 19 | 264 | 8 | 1 | 13 | 20 | .394 | 0 | 34-57 | 60 | 4.08 | 4.14 |

## Carlos Corporan

**Bats:** B **Throws:** R **Pos:** C-57;PH-7;1B-1;DH-1 CORE-poor-run **Ht:** 6'2" **Wt:** 230 **Born:** 1/7/1984 **Age:** 30

| BATTING | | | | | | | | | | | | | | | | | | | | | BASERUNNING | | | | AVERAGES | | |
|---|---|---|---|---|---|---|---|---|---|---|---|---|---|---|---|---|---|---|---|---|---|---|---|---|---|---|---|
| Year | Team | Lg | G | AB | H | 2B | 3B | HR | (Hm | Rd) | TB | R | RBI | RC | TBB | IBB | SO | HBP | SH | SF | SB | CS | SB% | GDP | Avg | OBP | Slg |
| 2009 | Mil | NL | 1 | 1 | 1 | 0 | 0 | 0 | (0 | 0) | 1 | 1 | 0 | 1 | 0 | 0 | 0 | 0 | 0 | 0 | 0 | 0 | - | 0 | 1.000 | 1.000 | 1.000 |
| 2011 | Hou | NL | 52 | 154 | 29 | 8 | 1 | 0 | (0 | 0) | 39 | 9 | 11 | 11 | 10 | 4 | 49 | 4 | 3 | 2 | 0 | 0 | - | 5 | .188 | .253 | .253 |
| 2012 | Hou | NL | 27 | 78 | 21 | 2 | 0 | 4 | (3 | 1) | 35 | 5 | 13 | 7 | 4 | 0 | 19 | 1 | 1 | 1 | 0 | 1 | .00 | 2 | .269 | .310 | .449 |
| 2013 | Hou | AL | 64 | 191 | 43 | 5 | 0 | 7 | (4 | 3) | 69 | 16 | 20 | 15 | 10 | 1 | 60 | 7 | 1 | 1 | 0 | 0 | - | 3 | .225 | .287 | .361 |
| 4 ML YEARS | | | 144 | 424 | 94 | 15 | 1 | 11 | (7 | 4) | 144 | 31 | 44 | 34 | 24 | 5 | 128 | 12 | 5 | 4 | 0 | 1 | .00 | 10 | .222 | .280 | .340 |

## Kevin Correia

**Pitches:** R **Bats:** R **Pos:** SP-31 kore-AY-ah **Ht:** 6'3" **Wt:** 200 **Born:** 8/24/1980 **Age:** 33

| HOW MUCH HE PITCHED | | | | | | | | | WHAT HE GAVE UP | | | | | | | | | | | | THE RESULTS | | | | | | | |
|---|---|---|---|---|---|---|---|---|---|---|---|---|---|---|---|---|---|---|---|---|---|---|---|---|---|---|---|---|
| Year | Team | Lg | G | GS | CG | GF | IP | BFP | H | R | ER | HR | SH | SF | HB | TBB | IBB | SO | WP | Bk | W | L | Pct | Sh | Sv-Op | Hld | ERC | ERA |
| 2003 | SF | NL | 10 | 7 | 0 | 1 | 39.1 | 173 | 41 | 16 | 16 | 6 | 1 | 1 | 4 | 18 | 1 | 28 | 2 | 0 | 3 | 1 | .750 | 0 | 0-0 | 0 | 5.46 | 3.66 |
| 2004 | SF | NL | 12 | 1 | 0 | 5 | 19.0 | 92 | 25 | 20 | 17 | 3 | 3 | 3 | 1 | 10 | 0 | 14 | 0 | 0 | 0 | 1 | .000 | 0 | 0-0 | 0 | 7.12 | 8.05 |
| 2005 | SF | NL | 16 | 11 | 0 | 1 | 58.1 | 264 | 61 | 31 | 30 | 12 | 5 | 1 | 4 | 31 | 2 | 44 | 2 | 0 | 2 | 5 | .286 | 0 | 0-0 | 0 | 5.94 | 4.63 |
| 2006 | SF | NL | 48 | 0 | 0 | 9 | 69.2 | 295 | 64 | 27 | 27 | 5 | 1 | 4 | 3 | 22 | 0 | 57 | 0 | 0 | 2 | 0 | 1.000 | 0 | 0-1 | 10 | 3.25 | 3.49 |
| 2007 | SF | NL | 59 | 8 | 0 | 9 | 101.2 | 437 | 94 | 39 | 39 | 9 | 4 | 3 | 2 | 40 | 7 | 80 | 1 | 1 | 4 | 7 | .364 | 0 | 0-3 | 12 | 3.48 | 3.45 |
| 2008 | SF | NL | 25 | 19 | 0 | 2 | 110.0 | 514 | 141 | 80 | 74 | 15 | 3 | 5 | 4 | 47 | 3 | 66 | 5 | 0 | 3 | 8 | .273 | 0 | 0-0 | 0 | 6.19 | 6.05 |
| 2009 | SD | NL | 33 | 33 | 1 | 0 | 198.0 | 830 | 194 | 92 | 86 | 17 | 9 | 3 | 4 | 64 | 6 | 142 | 5 | 1 | 12 | 11 | .522 | 1 | 0-0 | 0 | 3.64 | 3.91 |
| 2010 | SD | NL | 28 | 26 | 0 | 0 | 145.0 | 641 | 152 | 89 | 87 | 20 | 6 | 5 | 5 | 64 | 6 | 115 | 3 | 0 | 10 | 10 | .500 | 0 | 0-0 | 0 | 4.87 | 5.40 |
| 2011 | Pit | NL | 27 | 26 | 1 | 1 | 154.0 | 660 | 175 | 90 | 82 | 24 | 7 | 2 | 2 | 39 | 0 | 77 | 3 | 1 | 12 | 11 | .522 | 0 | 0-0 | 0 | 4.74 | 4.79 |
| 2012 | Pit | NL | 32 | 28 | 0 | 0 | 171.0 | 728 | 176 | 89 | 80 | 20 | 14 | 7 | 3 | 46 | 2 | 89 | 2 | 0 | 12 | 11 | .522 | 0 | 0-0 | 0 | 3.86 | 4.21 |
| 2013 | Min | AL | 31 | 31 | 0 | 0 | 185.1 | 792 | 218 | 89 | 86 | 24 | 6 | 5 | 2 | 45 | 1 | 101 | 2 | 0 | 9 | 13 | .409 | 0 | 0-0 | 0 | 4.77 | 4.18 |
| 11 ML YEARS | | | 321 | 190 | 2 | 28 | 1251.1 | 5426 | 1341 | 662 | 624 | 155 | 59 | 39 | 34 | 426 | 28 | 813 | 25 | 3 | 69 | 78 | .469 | 1 | 0-4 | 22 | 4.50 | 4.49 |

## Jarred Cosart

**Pitches:** R **Bats:** R **Pos:** SP-10 KOZE-art **Ht:** 6'3" **Wt:** 180 **Born:** 5/25/1990 **Age:** 24

| HOW MUCH HE PITCHED | | | | | | | | | WHAT HE GAVE UP | | | | | | | | | | | | THE RESULTS | | | | | | | |
|---|---|---|---|---|---|---|---|---|---|---|---|---|---|---|---|---|---|---|---|---|---|---|---|---|---|---|---|---|
| Year | Team | Lg | G | GS | CG | GF | IP | BFP | H | R | ER | HR | SH | SF | HB | TBB | IBB | SO | WP | Bk | W | L | Pct | Sh | Sv-Op | Hld | ERC | ERA |
| 2009 | Phillies | R | 7 | 5 | 0 | 1 | 24.1 | 92 | 12 | 8 | 6 | 0 | 0 | 0 | 1 | 7 | 0 | 25 | 1 | 0 | 2 | 2 | .500 | 0 | 0- - | - | 1.08 | 2.22 |
| 2010 | Lakwd | A | 14 | 14 | 1 | 0 | 71.1 | 293 | 60 | 34 | 30 | 3 | 2 | 1 | 5 | 16 | 0 | 77 | 7 | 0 | 7 | 3 | .700 | 1 | 0- - | - | 2.44 | 3.79 |
| 2011 | Clrwtr | A+ | 20 | 19 | 0 | 0 | 108.0 | 461 | 98 | 55 | 47 | 7 | 5 | 2 | 8 | 43 | 1 | 79 | 12 | 1 | 9 | 8 | .529 | 0 | 0- - | - | 3.60 | 3.92 |
| 2011 | CpChr | AA | 7 | 7 | 0 | 0 | 36.1 | 157 | 33 | 20 | 19 | 4 | 2 | 1 | 0 | 13 | 0 | 22 | 2 | 0 | 1 | 2 | .333 | 0 | 0- - | - | 3.35 | 4.71 |
| 2012 | CpChr | AA | 15 | 15 | 0 | 0 | 87.0 | 383 | 83 | 37 | 34 | 3 | 3 | 3 | 7 | 38 | 0 | 68 | 6 | 3 | 5 | 5 | .500 | 0 | 0- - | - | 3.77 | 3.52 |
| 2012 | OKCity | AAA | 6 | 5 | 0 | 0 | 27.2 | 118 | 26 | 10 | 8 | 0 | 0 | 0 | 1 | 13 | 0 | 24 | 3 | 1 | 1 | 2 | .333 | 0 | 0- - | - | 3.51 | 2.60 |
| 2013 | OKCity | AAA | 18 | 17 | 1 | 0 | 93.0 | 401 | 74 | 37 | 34 | 5 | 0 | 1 | 3 | 50 | 1 | 93 | 6 | 0 | 7 | 4 | .636 | 0 | 0- - | - | 3.24 | 3.29 |
| 2013 | Hou | AL | 10 | 10 | 0 | 0 | 60.0 | 246 | 46 | 15 | 13 | 3 | 0 | 2 | 0 | 35 | 0 | 33 | 3 | 0 | 1 | 1 | .500 | 0 | 0-0 | 0 | 3.31 | 1.95 |

## Neal Cotts

**Pitches:** L **Bats:** L **Pos:** RP-58 **Ht:** 6'1" **Wt:** 200 **Born:** 3/25/1980 **Age:** 34

| HOW MUCH HE PITCHED | | | | | | | | | WHAT HE GAVE UP | | | | | | | | | | | | THE RESULTS | | | | | | | |
|---|---|---|---|---|---|---|---|---|---|---|---|---|---|---|---|---|---|---|---|---|---|---|---|---|---|---|---|---|
| Year | Team | Lg | G | GS | CG | GF | IP | BFP | H | R | ER | HR | SH | SF | HB | TBB | IBB | SO | WP | Bk | W | L | Pct | Sh | Sv-Op | Hld | ERC | ERA |
| 2013 | RdRck* | AAA | 15 | 0 | 0 | 2 | 23.0 | 82 | 13 | 3 | 2 | 1 | 0 | 1 | 0 | 5 | 0 | 42 | 0 | 0 | 3 | 1 | .750 | 0 | 2- - | - | 1.27 | 0.78 |
| 2003 | CWS | AL | 4 | 4 | 0 | 0 | 13.1 | 69 | 15 | 12 | 12 | 1 | 1 | 0 | 0 | 17 | 0 | 10 | 0 | 0 | 1 | 1 | .500 | 0 | 0-0 | 0 | 8.43 | 8.10 |
| 2004 | CWS | AL | 56 | 1 | 0 | 12 | 65.1 | 281 | 61 | 45 | 41 | 13 | 0 | 1 | 3 | 30 | 2 | 58 | 8 | 0 | 4 | 4 | .500 | 0 | 0-2 | 4 | 4.84 | 5.65 |
| 2005 | CWS | AL | 69 | 0 | 0 | 10 | 60.1 | 248 | 38 | 15 | 13 | 1 | 0 | 3 | 4 | 29 | 5 | 58 | 3 | 0 | 4 | 0 | 1.000 | 0 | 0-2 | 13 | 2.03 | 1.94 |
| 2006 | CWS | AL | 70 | 0 | 0 | 14 | 54.0 | 251 | 64 | 33 | 31 | 12 | 3 | 1 | 3 | 24 | 6 | 43 | 3 | 0 | 1 | 2 | .333 | 0 | 1-4 | 14 | 6.24 | 5.17 |
| 2007 | ChC | NL | 16 | 0 | 0 | 4 | 16.2 | 76 | 15 | 9 | 9 | 1 | 1 | 2 | 3 | 9 | 0 | 14 | 0 | 0 | 0 | 1 | .000 | 0 | 0-0 | 2 | 4.41 | 4.86 |
| 2008 | ChC | NL | 50 | 0 | 0 | 7 | 35.2 | 160 | 38 | 18 | 17 | 7 | 3 | 0 | 1 | 13 | 2 | 43 | 3 | 0 | 0 | 2 | .000 | 0 | 0-2 | 9 | 4.87 | 4.29 |
| 2009 | ChC | NL | 19 | 0 | 0 | 3 | 11.0 | 55 | 14 | 9 | 9 | 3 | 0 | 0 | 1 | 9 | 0 | 9 | 0 | 0 | 0 | 2 | .000 | 0 | 0-1 | 2 | 9.64 | 7.36 |
| 2013 | Tex | AL | 58 | 0 | 0 | 6 | 57.0 | 223 | 36 | 8 | 7 | 2 | 2 | 3 | 0 | 18 | 1 | 65 | 3 | 0 | 8 | 3 | .727 | 0 | 1-4 | 11 | 1.57 | 1.11 |
| Postseason | | | 8 | 0 | 0 | 3 | 4.0 | 16 | 2 | 0 | 0 | 0 | 0 | 0 | 0 | 2 | 0 | 5 | 0 | 0 | 1 | 0 | 1.000 | 0 | 0-0 | 2 | 1.41 | 0.00 |
| 8 ML YEARS | | | 342 | 5 | 0 | 56 | 313.1 | 1363 | 281 | 149 | 139 | 40 | 10 | 10 | 15 | 149 | 16 | 300 | 20 | 0 | 18 | 15 | .545 | 0 | 2-15 | 55 | 4.08 | 3.99 |

## Scott Cousins

**Bats:** L **Throws:** L **Pos:** PH-4;LF-3;RF-1 **Ht:** 6'1" **Wt:** 200 **Born:** 1/22/1985 **Age:** 29

| BATTING | | | | | | | | | | | | | | | | | | | | | BASERUNNING | | | | AVERAGES | | |
|---|---|---|---|---|---|---|---|---|---|---|---|---|---|---|---|---|---|---|---|---|---|---|---|---|---|---|---|
| Year | Team | Lg | G | AB | H | 2B | 3B | HR | (Hm | Rd) | TB | R | RBI | RC | TBB | IBB | SO | HBP | SH | SF | SB | CS | SB% | GDP | Avg | OBP | Slg |
| 2013 | Salt Lk* | AAA | 52 | 193 | 45 | 3 | 4 | 1 | (- | -) | 59 | 30 | 19 | 20 | 16 | 0 | 46 | 6 | 4 | 1 | 7 | 2 | .78 | 1 | .233 | .310 | .306 |
| 2013 | Angels* | R | 2 | 7 | 2 | 0 | 1 | 0 | (- | -) | 4 | 3 | 0 | 1 | 1 | 0 | 3 | 0 | 0 | 0 | 0 | 0 | - | 0 | .286 | .375 | .571 |
| 2010 | Fla | NL | 27 | 37 | 11 | 2 | 2 | 0 | (0 | 0) | 17 | 2 | 2 | 4 | 1 | 0 | 13 | 0 | 0 | 0 | 0 | 0 | - | 0 | .297 | .316 | .459 |
| 2011 | Fla | NL | 48 | 52 | 7 | 1 | 0 | 1 | (1 | 0) | 11 | 5 | 4 | 2 | 6 | 0 | 21 | 0 | 0 | 0 | 1 | 1 | .50 | 0 | .135 | .224 | .212 |
| 2012 | Mia | NL | 53 | 86 | 14 | 4 | 1 | 1 | (0 | 1) | 23 | 7 | 3 | 1 | 4 | 2 | 24 | 0 | 2 | 0 | 1 | 1 | .50 | 2 | .163 | .200 | .267 |
| 2013 | LAA | AL | 7 | 4 | 0 | 0 | 0 | 0 | (0 | 0) | 0 | 1 | 0 | 0 | 1 | 0 | 3 | 0 | 0 | 0 | 0 | 0 | - | 0 | .000 | .200 | .000 |
| 4 ML YEARS | | | 135 | 179 | 32 | 7 | 3 | 2 | (1 | 1) | 51 | 15 | 9 | 7 | 12 | 2 | 61 | 0 | 2 | 0 | 2 | 2 | .50 | 2 | .179 | .230 | .285 |

## Collin Cowgill

**Bats:** R **Throws:** L **Pos:** LF-32;CF-24;RF-17;PH-9;PR-4 **Ht:** 5'9" **Wt:** 185 **Born:** 5/22/1986 **Age:** 28

| BATTING | | | | | | | | | | | | | | | | | | | | | BASERUNNING | | | | AVERAGES | | |
|---|---|---|---|---|---|---|---|---|---|---|---|---|---|---|---|---|---|---|---|---|---|---|---|---|---|---|---|
| Year | Team | Lg | G | AB | H | 2B | 3B | HR | (Hm | Rd) | TB | R | RBI | RC | TBB | IBB | SO | HBP | SH | SF | SB | CS | SB% | GDP | Avg | OBP | Slg |
| 2013 | LsVgs* | AAA | 33 | 123 | 33 | 6 | 0 | 5 | (- | -) | 54 | 22 | 12 | 21 | 17 | 0 | 25 | 2 | 3 | 0 | 4 | 0 | 1.00 | 3 | .268 | .366 | .439 |
| 2013 | Salt Lk* | AAA | 4 | 15 | 9 | 1 | 0 | 2 | (- | -) | 16 | 4 | 7 | 7 | 1 | 0 | 3 | 1 | 0 | 0 | 1 | 0 | 1.00 | 0 | .600 | .647 | 1.067 |
| 2011 | Ari | NL | 37 | 92 | 22 | 3 | 0 | 1 | (1 | 0) | 28 | 8 | 9 | 8 | 8 | 1 | 28 | 0 | 0 | 0 | 4 | 2 | .67 | 0 | .239 | .300 | .304 |
| 2012 | Oak | AL | 38 | 104 | 28 | 2 | 0 | 1 | (1 | 0) | 33 | 10 | 9 | 14 | 11 | 0 | 27 | 0 | 0 | 1 | 3 | 4 | .43 | 3 | .269 | .336 | .317 |

| Year | Team | Lg | G | AB | H | 2B | 3B | HR | (Hm | Rd) | TB | R | RBI | RC | TBB | IBB | SO | HBP | SH | SF | SB | CS | SB% | GDP | Avg | OBP | Slg |
|---|---|---|---|---|---|---|---|---|---|---|---|---|---|---|---|---|---|---|---|---|---|---|---|---|---|---|---|
| | | | BATTING | | | | | | | | | | | | | | | | | | BASERUNNING | | | | AVERAGES | | |
| 2013 | 2 Tms | | 73 | 152 | 32 | 5 | 2 | 4 | (3 | 1) | 53 | 18 | 16 | 12 | 7 | 0 | 42 | 0 | 3 | 0 | 1 | 0 | 1.00 | 1 | .211 | .245 | .349 |
| 13 | NYM | NL | 23 | 61 | 11 | 2 | 0 | 2 | (2 | 0) | 19 | 7 | 8 | 5 | 2 | 0 | 15 | 0 | 0 | 0 | 0 | 0 | - | 0 | .180 | .206 | .311 |
| 13 | LAA | AL | 50 | 91 | 21 | 3 | 2 | 2 | (1 | 1) | 34 | 11 | 8 | 7 | 5 | 0 | 27 | 0 | 3 | 0 | 1 | 0 | 1.00 | 1 | .231 | .271 | .374 |
| Postseason | | | 2 | 1 | 1 | 0 | 0 | 0 | (0 | 0) | 1 | 0 | 2 | 1 | 0 | 0 | 0 | 0 | 0 | 0 | 0 | 0 | - | 0 | 1.000 | 1.000 | 1.000 |
| 3 ML YEARS | | | 148 | 348 | 82 | 10 | 2 | 6 | (5 | 1) | 114 | 36 | 34 | 34 | 26 | 1 | 97 | 0 | 3 | 1 | 8 | 6 | .57 | 4 | .236 | .288 | .328 |

## Zack Cozart

**Bats:** R **Throws:** R **Pos:** SS-150;PH-4 COE-zart **Ht:** 6'0" **Wt:** 195 **Born:** 8/12/1985 **Age:** 28

| Year | Team | Lg | G | AB | H | 2B | 3B | HR | (Hm | Rd) | TB | R | RBI | RC | TBB | IBB | SO | HBP | SH | SF | SB | CS | SB% | GDP | Avg | OBP | Slg |
|---|---|---|---|---|---|---|---|---|---|---|---|---|---|---|---|---|---|---|---|---|---|---|---|---|---|---|---|
| | | | BATTING | | | | | | | | | | | | | | | | | | BASERUNNING | | | | AVERAGES | | |
| 2011 | Cin | NL | 11 | 37 | 12 | 0 | 0 | 2 | (2 | 0) | 18 | 6 | 3 | 3 | 0 | 0 | 6 | 0 | 1 | 0 | 0 | 0 | - | 2 | .324 | .324 | .486 |
| 2012 | Cin | NL | 138 | 561 | 138 | 33 | 4 | 15 | (6 | 9) | 224 | 72 | 35 | 51 | 31 | 0 | 113 | 3 | 2 | 3 | 4 | 0 | 1.00 | 11 | .246 | .288 | .399 |
| 2013 | Cin | NL | 151 | 567 | 144 | 30 | 3 | 12 | (7 | 5) | 216 | 74 | 63 | 56 | 26 | 2 | 102 | 2 | 13 | **10** | 0 | 0 | - | 18 | .254 | .284 | .381 |
| Postseason | | | 5 | 21 | 5 | 0 | 0 | 0 | (0 | 0) | 5 | 2 | 0 | 1 | 2 | 0 | 5 | 1 | 0 | 0 | 0 | 0 | - | 0 | .238 | .333 | .238 |
| 3 ML YEARS | | | 300 | 1165 | 294 | 63 | 7 | 29 | (15 | 14) | 458 | 152 | 101 | 110 | 57 | 2 | 221 | 5 | 16 | 13 | 4 | 0 | 1.00 | 31 | .252 | .287 | .393 |

## Allen Craig

**Bats:** R **Throws:** R **Pos:** 1B-95;LF-25;RF-22;PH-2;DH-1 **Ht:** 6'2" **Wt:** 215 **Born:** 7/18/1984 **Age:** 29

| Year | Team | Lg | G | AB | H | 2B | 3B | HR | (Hm | Rd) | TB | R | RBI | RC | TBB | IBB | SO | HBP | SH | SF | SB | CS | SB% | GDP | Avg | OBP | Slg |
|---|---|---|---|---|---|---|---|---|---|---|---|---|---|---|---|---|---|---|---|---|---|---|---|---|---|---|---|
| | | | BATTING | | | | | | | | | | | | | | | | | | BASERUNNING | | | | AVERAGES | | |
| 2010 | StL | NL | 44 | 114 | 28 | 7 | 0 | 4 | (3 | 1) | 47 | 12 | 18 | 14 | 9 | 1 | 26 | 0 | 0 | 1 | 0 | 1 | .00 | 1 | .246 | .298 | .412 |
| 2011 | StL | NL | 75 | 200 | 63 | 15 | 0 | 11 | (3 | 8) | 111 | 33 | 40 | 37 | 15 | 0 | 40 | 1 | 1 | 2 | 5 | 0 | 1.00 | 7 | .315 | .362 | .555 |
| 2012 | StL | NL | 119 | 469 | 144 | 35 | 0 | 22 | (11 | 11) | 245 | 76 | 92 | 89 | 37 | 1 | 89 | 1 | 0 | 7 | 2 | 1 | .67 | 15 | .307 | .354 | .522 |
| 2013 | StL | NL | 134 | 508 | 160 | 29 | 2 | 13 | (2 | 11) | 232 | 71 | 97 | 98 | 40 | 2 | 100 | 10 | 0 | 5 | 2 | 0 | 1.00 | 12 | .315 | .373 | .457 |
| Postseason | | | 28 | 84 | 20 | 4 | 1 | 5 | (4 | 1) | 41 | 13 | 14 | 12 | 13 | 1 | 25 | 2 | 1 | 1 | 0 | 2 | .00 | 1 | .238 | .350 | .488 |
| 4 ML YEARS | | | 372 | 1291 | 395 | 86 | 2 | 50 | (19 | 31) | 635 | 192 | 247 | 238 | 101 | 4 | 255 | 12 | 1 | 15 | 9 | 2 | .82 | 35 | .306 | .358 | .492 |

## Jesse Crain

**Pitches:** R **Bats:** R **Pos:** RP-38 **Ht:** 6'1" **Wt:** 215 **Born:** 7/5/1981 **Age:** 32

| Year | Team | Lg | G | GS | CG | GF | IP | BFP | H | R | ER | HR | SH | SF | HB | TBB | IBB | SO | WP | Bk | W | L | Pct | Sh | Sv-Op | Hld | ERC | ERA |
|---|---|---|---|---|---|---|---|---|---|---|---|---|---|---|---|---|---|---|---|---|---|---|---|---|---|---|---|---|
| | | | HOW MUCH HE PITCHED | | | | | | WHAT HE GAVE UP | | | | | | | | | | | | THE RESULTS | | | | | | | |
| 2004 | Min | AL | 22 | 0 | 0 | 3 | 27.0 | 109 | 17 | 6 | 6 | 2 | 1 | 0 | 1 | 12 | 1 | 14 | 1 | 0 | 3 | 0 | 1.000 | 0 | 0-1 | 2 | 2.25 | 2.00 |
| 2005 | Min | AL | 75 | 0 | 0 | 17 | 79.2 | 326 | 61 | 28 | 24 | 6 | **9** | 3 | 5 | 29 | 7 | 25 | 2 | 0 | 12 | 5 | .706 | 0 | 1-4 | 11 | 2.66 | 2.71 |
| 2006 | Min | AL | 68 | 0 | 0 | 24 | 76.2 | 325 | 79 | 31 | 30 | 6 | 1 | 2 | 2 | 18 | 2 | 60 | 1 | 0 | 4 | 5 | .444 | 0 | 1-4 | 10 | 3.48 | 3.52 |
| 2007 | Min | AL | 18 | 0 | 0 | 5 | 16.1 | 71 | 19 | 16 | 10 | 4 | 0 | 1 | 1 | 4 | 0 | 10 | 0 | 1 | 1 | 2 | .333 | 0 | 0-0 | 6 | 5.73 | 5.51 |
| 2008 | Min | AL | 66 | 0 | 0 | 14 | 62.2 | 268 | 62 | 29 | 25 | 6 | 0 | 2 | 1 | 24 | 3 | 50 | 2 | 0 | 5 | 4 | .556 | 0 | 0-3 | 17 | 3.93 | 3.59 |
| 2009 | Min | AL | 56 | 0 | 0 | 15 | 51.2 | 230 | 48 | 28 | 27 | 3 | 3 | 3 | 5 | 27 | 3 | 43 | 1 | 1 | 7 | 4 | .636 | 0 | 0-0 | 4 | 4.12 | 4.70 |
| 2010 | Min | AL | 71 | 0 | 0 | 16 | 68.0 | 278 | 53 | 27 | 23 | 5 | 3 | 0 | 1 | 27 | 4 | 62 | 3 | 0 | 1 | 1 | .500 | 0 | 1-4 | 21 | 2.71 | 3.04 |
| 2011 | CWS | AL | 67 | 0 | 0 | 11 | 65.1 | 268 | 50 | 20 | 19 | 7 | 1 | 3 | 0 | 31 | 5 | 70 | 0 | 1 | 8 | 3 | .727 | 0 | 1-7 | 24 | 3.08 | 2.62 |
| 2012 | CWS | AL | 51 | 0 | 0 | 6 | 48.0 | 194 | 29 | 14 | 13 | 5 | 0 | 0 | 1 | 23 | 1 | 60 | 4 | 0 | 2 | 3 | .400 | 0 | 0-4 | 10 | 2.38 | 2.44 |
| 2013 | CWS | AL | 38 | 0 | 0 | 5 | 36.2 | 152 | 31 | 6 | 3 | 0 | 2 | 0 | 1 | 11 | 1 | 46 | 0 | 0 | 2 | 3 | .400 | 0 | 0-1 | 19 | 2.27 | 0.74 |
| Postseason | | | 4 | 0 | 0 | 0 | 1.2 | 14 | 7 | 5 | 3 | 2 | 0 | 0 | 0 | 1 | 0 | 1 | 0 | 0 | 0 | 1 | .000 | 0 | 0-0 | 0 | 40.37 | 16.20 |
| 10 ML YEARS | | | 532 | 0 | 0 | 116 | 532.0 | 2221 | 449 | 205 | 180 | 44 | 20 | 14 | 18 | 206 | 27 | 440 | 14 | 3 | 45 | 30 | .600 | 0 | 4-28 | 124 | 3.13 | 3.05 |

## Brandon Crawford

**Bats:** L **Throws:** R **Pos:** SS-147;PH-4;PR-1 **Ht:** 6'2" **Wt:** 215 **Born:** 1/21/1987 **Age:** 27

| Year | Team | Lg | G | AB | H | 2B | 3B | HR | (Hm | Rd) | TB | R | RBI | RC | TBB | IBB | SO | HBP | SH | SF | SB | CS | SB% | GDP | Avg | OBP | Slg |
|---|---|---|---|---|---|---|---|---|---|---|---|---|---|---|---|---|---|---|---|---|---|---|---|---|---|---|---|
| | | | BATTING | | | | | | | | | | | | | | | | | | BASERUNNING | | | | AVERAGES | | |
| 2011 | SF | NL | 66 | 196 | 40 | 5 | 2 | 3 | (0 | 3) | 58 | 22 | 21 | 20 | 23 | 1 | 31 | 0 | 1 | 0 | 1 | 3 | .25 | 4 | .204 | .288 | .296 |
| 2012 | SF | NL | 143 | 435 | 108 | 26 | 3 | 4 | (1 | 3) | 152 | 44 | 45 | 40 | 33 | 6 | 95 | 3 | 2 | 3 | 1 | 4 | .20 | 4 | .248 | .304 | .349 |
| 2013 | SF | NL | 149 | 499 | 124 | 24 | 3 | 9 | (2 | 7) | 181 | 52 | 43 | 42 | 42 | 6 | 96 | 5 | 1 | 3 | 1 | 2 | .33 | 10 | .248 | .311 | .363 |
| Postseason | | | 16 | 46 | 10 | 1 | 1 | 0 | (0 | 0) | 13 | 3 | 7 | 6 | 7 | 2 | 12 | 0 | 1 | 0 | 1 | 0 | 1.00 | 1 | .217 | .321 | .283 |
| 3 ML YEARS | | | 358 | 1130 | 272 | 55 | 8 | 16 | (3 | 13) | 391 | 118 | 109 | 102 | 98 | 13 | 222 | 8 | 4 | 6 | 3 | 9 | .25 | 18 | .241 | .304 | .346 |

## Carl Crawford

**Bats:** L **Throws:** L **Pos:** LF-107;PH-13;DH-3;PR-1 **Ht:** 6'2" **Wt:** 215 **Born:** 8/5/1981 **Age:** 32

| Year | Team | Lg | G | AB | H | 2B | 3B | HR | (Hm | Rd) | TB | R | RBI | RC | TBB | IBB | SO | HBP | SH | SF | SB | CS | SB% | GDP | Avg | OBP | Slg |
|---|---|---|---|---|---|---|---|---|---|---|---|---|---|---|---|---|---|---|---|---|---|---|---|---|---|---|---|
| | | | BATTING | | | | | | | | | | | | | | | | | | BASERUNNING | | | | AVERAGES | | |
| 2013 | RCuca* | A+ | 4 | 13 | 5 | 1 | 0 | 0 | (- | -) | 6 | 2 | 3 | 2 | 1 | 0 | 2 | 0 | 0 | 0 | 1 | 0 | 1.00 | 0 | .385 | .429 | .462 |
| 2002 | TB | AL | 63 | 259 | 67 | 11 | 6 | 2 | (1 | 1) | 96 | 23 | 30 | 34 | 9 | 0 | 41 | 3 | 6 | 1 | 9 | 5 | .64 | 0 | .259 | .290 | .371 |
| 2003 | TB | AL | 151 | 630 | 177 | 18 | 9 | 5 | (5 | 0) | 228 | 80 | 54 | 80 | 26 | 4 | 102 | 1 | 1 | 3 | **55** | 10 | .85 | 5 | .281 | .309 | .362 |
| 2004 | TB | AL | 152 | 626 | 185 | 26 | **19** | 11 | (6 | 5) | 282 | 104 | 55 | 96 | 35 | 2 | 81 | 1 | 4 | 6 | **59** | **15** | .80 | 2 | .296 | .331 | .450 |
| 2005 | TB | AL | 156 | 644 | 194 | 33 | **15** | 15 | (5 | 10) | 302 | 101 | 81 | 102 | 27 | 1 | 84 | 5 | 5 | 6 | 46 | 8 | .85 | 11 | .301 | .331 | .469 |
| 2006 | TB | AL | 151 | 600 | 183 | 20 | **16** | 18 | (7 | 11) | 289 | 89 | 77 | 113 | 37 | 3 | 85 | 4 | 9 | 2 | **58** | 9 | .87 | 8 | .305 | .348 | .482 |
| 2007 | TB | AL | 143 | 584 | 184 | 37 | 9 | 11 | (6 | 5) | 272 | 93 | 80 | 97 | 32 | 5 | 112 | 5 | 1 | 2 | **50** | 10 | .83 | 11 | .315 | .355 | .466 |
| 2008 | TB | AL | 109 | 443 | 121 | 12 | 10 | 8 | (3 | 5) | 177 | 69 | 57 | 57 | 30 | 1 | 60 | 2 | 0 | 5 | 25 | 7 | .78 | 10 | .273 | .319 | .400 |
| 2009 | TB | AL | 156 | 606 | 185 | 28 | 8 | 15 | (9 | 6) | 274 | 96 | 68 | 91 | 51 | 1 | 99 | 8 | 2 | 5 | 60 | 16 | .79 | 7 | .305 | .364 | .452 |
| 2010 | TB | AL | 154 | 600 | 184 | 30 | **13** | 19 | (11 | 8) | 297 | 110 | 90 | 120 | 46 | 3 | 104 | 3 | 3 | 5 | 47 | 10 | .82 | 2 | .307 | .356 | .495 |
| 2011 | Bos | AL | 130 | 506 | 129 | 29 | 7 | 11 | (4 | 7) | 205 | 65 | 56 | 54 | 23 | 1 | 104 | 3 | 2 | 4 | 18 | 6 | .75 | 7 | .255 | .289 | .405 |
| 2012 | Bos | AL | 31 | 117 | 33 | 10 | 2 | 3 | (2 | 1) | 56 | 23 | 19 | 17 | 3 | 0 | 22 | 2 | 1 | 2 | 5 | 0 | 1.00 | 1 | .282 | .306 | .479 |
| 2013 | LAD | NL | 116 | 435 | 123 | 30 | 3 | 6 | (5 | 1) | 177 | 62 | 31 | 55 | 28 | 2 | 66 | 3 | 0 | 2 | 15 | 4 | .79 | 4 | .283 | .329 | .407 |
| Postseason | | | 21 | 83 | 21 | 3 | 1 | 3 | (1 | 2) | 35 | 10 | 9 | 11 | 3 | 0 | 14 | 1 | 0 | 0 | 8 | 0 | 1.00 | 1 | .253 | .287 | .422 |
| 12 ML YEARS | | | 1512 | 6050 | 1765 | 284 | 117 | 124 | (64 | 60) | 2655 | 915 | 698 | 916 | 347 | 23 | 960 | 40 | 34 | 43 | 447 | 100 | .82 | 68 | .292 | .332 | .439 |

# Coco Crisp

**Bats:** B **Throws:** R **Pos:** CF-110;DH-20;PH-3;PR-1 **Ht:** 5'10" **Wt:** 185 **Born:** 11/1/1979 **Age:** 34

| | | | BATTING | | | | | | | | | | | | | | | | | | BASERUNNING | | | | AVERAGES | | |
|---|---|---|---|---|---|---|---|---|---|---|---|---|---|---|---|---|---|---|---|---|---|---|---|---|---|---|---|
| Year | Team | Lg | G | AB | H | 2B | 3B | HR | (Hm | Rd) | TB | R | RBI | RC | TBB | IBB | SO | HBP | SH | SF | SB | CS | SB% | GDP | Avg | OBP | Slg |
| 2002 | Cle | AL | 32 | 127 | 33 | 9 | 2 | 1 | (1 | 0) | 49 | 16 | 9 | 19 | 11 | 0 | 19 | 0 | 3 | 2 | 4 | 1 | .80 | 0 | .260 | .314 | .386 |
| 2003 | Cle | AL | 99 | 414 | 110 | 15 | 6 | 3 | (3 | 0) | 146 | 55 | 27 | 48 | 23 | 1 | 51 | 0 | 7 | 3 | 15 | 9 | .63 | 4 | .266 | .302 | .353 |
| 2004 | Cle | AL | 139 | 491 | 146 | 24 | 2 | 15 | (8 | 7) | 219 | 78 | 71 | 72 | 36 | 4 | 69 | 0 | 9 | 2 | 20 | 13 | .61 | 8 | .297 | .344 | .446 |
| 2005 | Cle | AL | 145 | 594 | 178 | 42 | 4 | 16 | (4 | 12) | 276 | 86 | 69 | 92 | 44 | 1 | 81 | 0 | **13** | 5 | 15 | 6 | .71 | 7 | .300 | .345 | .465 |
| 2006 | Bos | AL | 105 | 413 | 109 | 22 | 2 | 8 | (4 | 4) | 159 | 58 | 36 | 51 | 31 | 1 | 67 | 1 | 7 | 0 | 22 | 4 | .85 | 5 | .264 | .317 | .385 |
| 2007 | Bos | AL | 145 | 526 | 141 | 28 | 7 | 6 | (1 | 5) | 201 | 85 | 60 | 68 | 50 | 1 | 84 | 1 | 9 | 5 | 28 | 6 | .82 | 12 | .268 | .330 | .382 |
| 2008 | Bos | AL | 118 | 361 | 102 | 18 | 3 | 7 | (1 | 6) | 147 | 55 | 41 | 49 | 35 | 0 | 59 | 1 | 8 | 4 | 20 | 7 | .74 | 6 | .283 | .344 | .407 |
| 2009 | KC | AL | 49 | 180 | 41 | 8 | 5 | 3 | (0 | 3) | 68 | 30 | 14 | 25 | 29 | 1 | 23 | 1 | 4 | 1 | 13 | 2 | .87 | 4 | .228 | .336 | .378 |
| 2010 | Oak | AL | 75 | 290 | 81 | 14 | 4 | 8 | (6 | 2) | 127 | 51 | 38 | 49 | 30 | 0 | 49 | 0 | 3 | 5 | 32 | 3 | **.91** | 6 | .279 | .342 | .438 |
| 2011 | Oak | AL | 136 | 531 | 140 | 27 | 5 | 8 | (4 | 4) | 201 | 69 | 54 | 69 | 41 | 2 | 65 | 1 | 4 | 6 | **49** | 9 | .84 | 11 | .264 | .314 | .379 |
| 2012 | Oak | AL | 120 | 455 | 118 | 25 | 7 | 11 | (6 | 5) | 190 | 68 | 46 | 71 | 45 | 0 | 64 | 0 | 6 | 2 | 39 | 4 | .91 | 9 | .259 | .325 | .418 |
| 2013 | Oak | AL | 131 | 513 | 134 | 22 | 3 | 22 | (9 | 13) | 228 | 93 | 66 | 78 | 61 | 3 | 65 | 0 | 2 | 8 | 21 | 5 | .81 | 7 | .261 | .335 | .444 |
| Postseason | | | 25 | 79 | 20 | 3 | 0 | 1 | (0 | 1) | 26 | 10 | 5 | 7 | 6 | 0 | 14 | 0 | 0 | 0 | 3 | 0 | 1.00 | 3 | .253 | .306 | .329 |
| 12 ML YEARS | | | 1294 | 4895 | 1333 | 254 | 50 | 108 | (47 | 61) | 2011 | 744 | 531 | 691 | 436 | 14 | 696 | 5 | 75 | 43 | 278 | 69 | .80 | 79 | .272 | .330 | .411 |

# Aaron Crow

**Pitches:** R **Bats:** R **Pos:** RP-57 **Ht:** 6'3" **Wt:** 195 **Born:** 11/10/1986 **Age:** 27

| | | | HOW MUCH HE PITCHED | | | | | | WHAT HE GAVE UP | | | | | | | | | | | | THE RESULTS | | | | | | | |
|---|---|---|---|---|---|---|---|---|---|---|---|---|---|---|---|---|---|---|---|---|---|---|---|---|---|---|---|---|
| Year | Team | Lg | G | GS | CG | GF | IP | BFP | H | R | ER | HR | SH | SF | HB | TBB | IBB | SO | WP | Bk | W | L | Pct | Sh | Sv-Op | Hld | ERC | ERA |
| 2011 | KC | AL | 57 | 0 | 0 | 19 | 62.0 | 266 | 55 | 20 | 19 | 8 | 3 | 0 | 0 | 31 | 2 | 65 | 9 | 1 | 4 | 4 | .500 | 0 | 0-7 | 8 | 4.00 | 2.76 |
| 2012 | KC | AL | 73 | 0 | 0 | 20 | 64.2 | 260 | 54 | 27 | 25 | 4 | 1 | 2 | 1 | 22 | 2 | 65 | 4 | 0 | 3 | 1 | .750 | 0 | 2-8 | 19 | 2.81 | 3.48 |
| 2013 | KC | AL | 57 | 0 | 0 | 14 | 48.0 | 210 | 49 | 19 | 18 | 6 | 2 | 3 | 2 | 22 | 3 | 44 | 5 | 0 | 7 | 5 | .583 | 0 | 1-4 | 19 | 4.73 | 3.38 |
| 3 ML YEARS | | | 187 | 0 | 0 | 53 | 174.2 | 736 | 158 | 66 | 62 | 18 | 6 | 5 | 3 | 75 | 7 | 174 | 18 | 1 | 14 | 10 | .583 | 0 | 3-19 | 46 | 3.74 | 3.19 |

# Trevor Crowe

**Bats:** B **Throws:** R **Pos:** RF-25;LF-24;CF-14;PH-6;PR-5;DH-2 CROW **Ht:** 5'10" **Wt:** 190 **Born:** 11/17/1983 **Age:** 30

| | | | BATTING | | | | | | | | | | | | | | | | | | BASERUNNING | | | | AVERAGES | | |
|---|---|---|---|---|---|---|---|---|---|---|---|---|---|---|---|---|---|---|---|---|---|---|---|---|---|---|---|
| Year | Team | Lg | G | AB | H | 2B | 3B | HR | (Hm | Rd) | TB | R | RBI | RC | TBB | IBB | SO | HBP | SH | SF | SB | CS | SB% | GDP | Avg | OBP | Slg |
| 2013 | OKCity* | AAA | 60 | 237 | 72 | 7 | 2 | 3 | (- | -) | 92 | 40 | 23 | 35 | 22 | 2 | 34 | 1 | 3 | 1 | 16 | 7 | .70 | 7 | .304 | .364 | .388 |
| 2013 | Astros* | R | 2 | 4 | 1 | 0 | 0 | 0 | (- | -) | 1 | 0 | 0 | 0 | 0 | 0 | 0 | 0 | 0 | 0 | 0 | 1 | .00 | 0 | .250 | .250 | .250 |
| 2009 | Cle | AL | 68 | 183 | 43 | 9 | 3 | 1 | (0 | 1) | 61 | 22 | 17 | 18 | 11 | 0 | 39 | 1 | 4 | 3 | 6 | 0 | 1.00 | 7 | .235 | .278 | .333 |
| 2010 | Cle | AL | 122 | 442 | 111 | 24 | 3 | 2 | (1 | 1) | 147 | 48 | 36 | 43 | 29 | 1 | 73 | 3 | 5 | 0 | 20 | 7 | .74 | 13 | .251 | .302 | .333 |
| 2011 | Cle | AL | 15 | 28 | 6 | 1 | 0 | 0 | (0 | 0) | 7 | 6 | 2 | 4 | 4 | 0 | 9 | 0 | 0 | 0 | 3 | 0 | 1.00 | 1 | .214 | .313 | .250 |
| 2013 | Hou | AL | 60 | 165 | 36 | 7 | 1 | 1 | (1 | 0) | 48 | 18 | 13 | 13 | 16 | 0 | 39 | 0 | 0 | 0 | 6 | 1 | .86 | 3 | .218 | .287 | .291 |
| 4 ML YEARS | | | 265 | 818 | 196 | 41 | 7 | 4 | (2 | 2) | 263 | 94 | 68 | 78 | 60 | 1 | 160 | 4 | 9 | 3 | 35 | 8 | .81 | 24 | .240 | .294 | .322 |

# Luis Cruz

**Bats:** R **Throws:** R **Pos:** 3B-41;SS-20;PH-5;1B-1;LF-1;PR-1 **Ht:** 6'1" **Wt:** 210 **Born:** 2/10/1984 **Age:** 30

| | | | BATTING | | | | | | | | | | | | | | | | | | BASERUNNING | | | | AVERAGES | | |
|---|---|---|---|---|---|---|---|---|---|---|---|---|---|---|---|---|---|---|---|---|---|---|---|---|---|---|---|
| Year | Team | Lg | G | AB | H | 2B | 3B | HR | (Hm | Rd) | TB | R | RBI | RC | TBB | IBB | SO | HBP | SH | SF | SB | CS | SB% | GDP | Avg | OBP | Slg |
| 2008 | Pit | NL | 22 | 67 | 15 | 3 | 0 | 0 | (0 | 0) | 18 | 6 | 3 | 4 | 3 | 0 | 2 | 2 | 2 | 0 | 1 | 1 | .50 | 3 | .224 | .278 | .269 |
| 2009 | Pit | NL | 27 | 70 | 15 | 1 | 0 | 0 | (0 | 0) | 16 | 5 | 2 | 3 | 6 | 1 | 7 | 1 | 0 | 1 | 0 | 0 | - | 1 | .214 | .282 | .229 |
| 2010 | Mil | NL | 7 | 17 | 4 | 0 | 1 | 0 | (0 | 0) | 6 | 2 | 1 | 2 | 0 | 0 | 2 | 0 | 0 | 0 | 0 | 0 | - | 1 | .235 | .235 | .353 |
| 2012 | LAD | NL | 78 | 283 | 84 | 20 | 0 | 6 | (2 | 4) | 122 | 26 | 40 | 39 | 9 | 1 | 34 | 2 | 1 | 1 | 2 | 1 | .67 | 7 | .297 | .322 | .431 |
| 2013 | 2 Tms | | 61 | 173 | 25 | 3 | 0 | 1 | (1 | 0) | 31 | 18 | 11 | 4 | 6 | 1 | 33 | 4 | 3 | 1 | 1 | 0 | 1.00 | 6 | .145 | .190 | .179 |
| 13 | LAD | NL | 45 | 118 | 15 | 2 | 0 | 1 | (1 | 0) | 20 | 12 | 6 | 1 | 5 | 1 | 20 | 2 | 2 | 1 | 0 | 0 | - | 3 | .127 | .175 | .169 |
| 13 | NYY | AL | 16 | 55 | 10 | 1 | 0 | 0 | (0 | 0) | 11 | 6 | 5 | 3 | 1 | 0 | 13 | 2 | 1 | 0 | 1 | 0 | 1.00 | 3 | .182 | .224 | .200 |
| 5 ML YEARS | | | 195 | 610 | 143 | 27 | 1 | 7 | (3 | 4) | 193 | 57 | 57 | 52 | 24 | 3 | 78 | 9 | 6 | 3 | 4 | 2 | .67 | 18 | .234 | .272 | .316 |

# Nelson Cruz

**Bats:** R **Throws:** R **Pos:** RF-102;DH-7 **Ht:** 6'2" **Wt:** 230 **Born:** 7/1/1980 **Age:** 33

| | | | BATTING | | | | | | | | | | | | | | | | | | BASERUNNING | | | | AVERAGES | | |
|---|---|---|---|---|---|---|---|---|---|---|---|---|---|---|---|---|---|---|---|---|---|---|---|---|---|---|---|
| Year | Team | Lg | G | AB | H | 2B | 3B | HR | (Hm | Rd) | TB | R | RBI | RC | TBB | IBB | SO | HBP | SH | SF | SB | CS | SB% | GDP | Avg | OBP | Slg |
| 2005 | Mil | NL | 8 | 5 | 1 | 1 | 0 | 0 | (0 | 0) | 2 | 1 | 0 | 1 | 2 | 0 | 0 | 0 | 0 | 0 | 0 | 0 | - | 0 | .200 | .429 | .400 |
| 2006 | Tex | AL | 41 | 130 | 29 | 3 | 0 | 6 | (3 | 3) | 50 | 15 | 22 | 18 | 7 | 0 | 32 | 0 | 0 | 1 | 1 | 0 | 1.00 | 1 | .223 | .261 | .385 |
| 2007 | Tex | AL | 96 | 307 | 72 | 15 | 2 | 9 | (4 | 5) | 118 | 35 | 34 | 32 | 21 | 1 | 87 | 2 | 1 | 1 | 2 | 4 | .33 | 5 | .235 | .287 | .384 |
| 2008 | Tex | AL | 31 | 115 | 38 | 9 | 1 | 7 | (4 | 3) | 70 | 19 | 26 | 30 | 17 | 2 | 28 | 1 | 0 | 0 | 3 | 1 | .75 | 1 | .330 | .421 | .609 |
| 2009 | Tex | AL | 128 | 462 | 120 | 21 | 1 | 33 | (18 | 15) | 242 | 75 | 76 | 72 | 49 | 6 | 118 | 2 | 0 | 2 | 20 | 4 | .83 | 9 | .260 | .332 | .524 |
| 2010 | Tex | AL | 108 | 399 | 127 | 31 | 3 | 22 | (13 | 9) | 230 | 60 | 78 | 77 | 38 | 5 | 81 | 1 | 1 | 6 | 17 | 4 | .81 | 12 | .318 | .374 | .576 |
| 2011 | Tex | AL | 124 | 475 | 125 | 28 | 1 | 29 | (19 | 10) | 242 | 64 | 87 | 79 | 33 | 1 | 116 | 2 | 0 | 3 | 9 | 5 | .64 | 8 | .263 | .312 | .509 |
| 2012 | Tex | AL | 159 | 585 | 152 | 45 | 0 | 24 | (18 | 6) | 269 | 86 | 90 | 80 | 48 | 2 | 140 | 5 | 0 | 4 | 8 | 4 | .67 | 7 | .260 | .319 | .460 |
| 2013 | Tex | AL | 109 | 413 | 110 | 18 | 0 | 27 | (13 | 14) | 209 | 49 | 76 | 69 | 35 | 2 | 109 | 4 | 0 | 4 | 5 | 1 | .83 | 14 | .266 | .327 | .506 |
| Postseason | | | 34 | 126 | 35 | 9 | 0 | 14 | (9 | 5) | 86 | 26 | 27 | 27 | 10 | 2 | 31 | 1 | 0 | 0 | 1 | 1 | .50 | 3 | .278 | .336 | .683 |
| 9 ML YEARS | | | 804 | 2891 | 774 | 171 | 8 | 157 | (92 | 65) | 1432 | 404 | 489 | 458 | 250 | 19 | 711 | 17 | 2 | 21 | 65 | 23 | .74 | 57 | .268 | .327 | .495 |

## Rhiner Cruz

**Pitches:** R **Bats:** R **Pos:** RP-20 RYE-ner **Ht:** 6'2" **Wt:** 215 **Born:** 11/1/1986 **Age:** 27

| HOW MUCH HE PITCHED | | | | | | | | | WHAT HE GAVE UP | | | | | | | | | | | | THE RESULTS | | | | | | | |
|---|---|---|---|---|---|---|---|---|---|---|---|---|---|---|---|---|---|---|---|---|---|---|---|---|---|---|---|---|
| Year | Team | Lg | G | GS | CG | GF | IP | BFP | H | R | ER | HR | SH | SF | HB | TBB | IBB | SO | WP | Bk | W | L | Pct | Sh | Sv-Op | Hld | ERC | ERA |
| 2009 | Savann | A | 50 | 0 | 0 | 37 | 61.0 | 253 | 42 | 14 | 13 | 2 | 1 | 2 | 8 | 31 | 0 | 55 | 8 | 0 | 3 | 3 | .500 | 0 | 22- - | - | 2.92 | 1.92 |
| 2010 | StLuci | A+ | 51 | 0 | 0 | 23 | 75.1 | 341 | 62 | 34 | 29 | 6 | 5 | 3 | 12 | 53 | 3 | 66 | 9 | 0 | 0 | 5 | .000 | 0 | 6- - | - | 4.72 | 3.46 |
| 2011 | StLuci | A+ | 8 | 0 | 0 | 5 | 13.0 | 55 | 9 | 9 | 4 | 1 | 1 | 1 | 2 | 6 | 0 | 18 | 3 | 0 | 2 | 1 | .667 | 0 | 0- - | - | 3.07 | 2.77 |
| 2011 | Bnghtn | AA | 36 | 0 | 0 | 21 | 58.2 | 260 | 43 | 27 | 27 | 4 | 1 | 1 | 5 | 39 | 1 | 51 | 7 | 0 | 3 | 2 | .600 | 0 | 7- - | - | 3.64 | 4.14 |
| 2012 | OKCity | AAA | 2 | 0 | 0 | 1 | 1.2 | 7 | 1 | 2 | 1 | 0 | 0 | 0 | 1 | 1 | 0 | 3 | 0 | 0 | 0 | 0 | - | 0 | 0- - | - | 4.62 | 5.40 |
| 2013 | OKCity | AAA | 37 | 0 | 0 | 15 | 41.2 | 190 | 34 | 25 | 22 | 6 | 1 | 2 | 3 | 32 | 3 | 38 | 6 | 1 | 1 | 2 | .333 | 0 | 2- - | - | 4.97 | 4.75 |
| 2012 | Hou | NL | 52 | 0 | 0 | 26 | 55.0 | 253 | 65 | 38 | 37 | 8 | 1 | 2 | 2 | 29 | 0 | 46 | 3 | 0 | 1 | 1 | .500 | 0 | 0-1 | 0 | 6.24 | 6.05 |
| 2013 | Hou | AL | 20 | 0 | 0 | 11 | 21.1 | 98 | 25 | 9 | 8 | 2 | 0 | 2 | 2 | 11 | 0 | 10 | 1 | 0 | 0 | 2 | .000 | 0 | 0-0 | 1 | 6.00 | 3.38 |
| 2 ML YEARS | | | 72 | 0 | 0 | 37 | 76.1 | 351 | 90 | 47 | 45 | 10 | 1 | 4 | 4 | 40 | 0 | 56 | 4 | 0 | 1 | 3 | .250 | 0 | 0-1 | 1 | 6.17 | 5.31 |

## Tony Cruz

**Bats:** R **Throws:** R **Pos:** C-44;PH-16;3B-3 **Ht:** 5'11" **Wt:** 215 **Born:** 8/18/1986 **Age:** 27

| BATTING | | | | | | | | | | | | | | | | | | | | BASERUNNING | | | | AVERAGES | | |
|---|---|---|---|---|---|---|---|---|---|---|---|---|---|---|---|---|---|---|---|---|---|---|---|---|---|---|
| Year | Team | Lg | G | AB | H | 2B | 3B | HR | (Hm | Rd) | TB | R | RBI | RC | TBB | IBB | SO | HBP | SH | SF | SB | CS | SB% | GDP | Avg | OBP | Slg |
| 2011 | StL | NL | 38 | 65 | 17 | 5 | 0 | 0 | (0 | 0) | 22 | 8 | 6 | 7 | 6 | 1 | 13 | 1 | 0 | 0 | 0 | 1 | .00 | 1 | .262 | .333 | .338 |
| 2012 | StL | NL | 51 | 126 | 32 | 9 | 1 | 1 | (0 | 1) | 46 | 11 | 11 | 9 | 3 | 0 | 19 | 0 | 0 | 2 | 0 | 1 | .00 | 4 | .254 | .267 | .365 |
| 2013 | StL | NL | 51 | 123 | 25 | 6 | 1 | 1 | (0 | 1) | 36 | 13 | 13 | 9 | 4 | 1 | 25 | 2 | 0 | 0 | 0 | 0 | - | 7 | .203 | .240 | .293 |
| Postseason | | | 2 | 1 | 0 | 0 | 0 | 0 | (0 | 0) | 0 | 0 | 0 | 0 | 0 | 0 | 1 | 0 | 0 | 0 | 0 | 0 | - | 0 | .000 | .000 | .000 |
| 3 ML YEARS | | | 140 | 314 | 74 | 20 | 2 | 2 | (0 | 2) | 104 | 32 | 30 | 25 | 13 | 2 | 57 | 3 | 0 | 2 | 0 | 2 | .00 | 12 | .236 | .271 | .331 |

## Michael Cuddyer

**Bats:** R **Throws:** R **Pos:** RF-118;1B-15;PH-3;DH-1 cuh-DYE-err **Ht:** 6'2" **Wt:** 220 **Born:** 3/27/1979 **Age:** 35

| BATTING | | | | | | | | | | | | | | | | | | | | BASERUNNING | | | | AVERAGES | | |
|---|---|---|---|---|---|---|---|---|---|---|---|---|---|---|---|---|---|---|---|---|---|---|---|---|---|---|
| Year | Team | Lg | G | AB | H | 2B | 3B | HR | (Hm | Rd) | TB | R | RBI | RC | TBB | IBB | SO | HBP | SH | SF | SB | CS | SB% | GDP | Avg | OBP | Slg |
| 2001 | Min | AL | 8 | 18 | 4 | 2 | 0 | 0 | (0 | 0) | 6 | 1 | 1 | 2 | 2 | 0 | 6 | 0 | 0 | 0 | 1 | 0 | 1.00 | 1 | .222 | .300 | .333 |
| 2002 | Min | AL | 41 | 112 | 29 | 7 | 0 | 4 | (2 | 2) | 48 | 12 | 13 | 14 | 8 | 0 | 30 | 1 | 1 | 1 | 2 | 0 | 1.00 | 3 | .259 | .311 | .429 |
| 2003 | Min | AL | 35 | 102 | 25 | 1 | 3 | 4 | (1 | 3) | 44 | 14 | 8 | 10 | 12 | 0 | 19 | 0 | 0 | 0 | 1 | 1 | .50 | 6 | .245 | .325 | .431 |
| 2004 | Min | AL | 115 | 339 | 89 | 22 | 1 | 12 | (8 | 4) | 149 | 49 | 45 | 51 | 37 | 2 | 74 | 3 | 2 | 1 | 5 | 5 | .50 | 8 | .263 | .339 | .440 |
| 2005 | Min | AL | 126 | 422 | 111 | 25 | 3 | 12 | (8 | 4) | 178 | 55 | 42 | 43 | 41 | 5 | 93 | 3 | 1 | 3 | 3 | 4 | .43 | 19 | .263 | .330 | .422 |
| 2006 | Min | AL | 150 | 557 | 158 | 41 | 5 | 24 | (15 | 9) | 281 | 102 | 109 | 101 | 62 | 5 | 130 | 10 | 0 | 6 | 6 | 0 | 1.00 | 11 | .284 | .362 | .504 |
| 2007 | Min | AL | 144 | 547 | 151 | 28 | 5 | 16 | (8 | 8) | 237 | 87 | 81 | 82 | 64 | 1 | 107 | 7 | 0 | 5 | 5 | 0 | 1.00 | 19 | .276 | .356 | .433 |
| 2008 | Min | AL | 71 | 249 | 62 | 13 | 4 | 3 | (1 | 2) | 92 | 30 | 36 | 37 | 25 | 4 | 40 | 5 | 0 | 0 | 5 | 1 | .83 | 7 | .249 | .330 | .369 |
| 2009 | Min | AL | 153 | 588 | 162 | 34 | 7 | 32 | (18 | 14) | 306 | 93 | 94 | 89 | 54 | 3 | 118 | 6 | 0 | 2 | 6 | 1 | .86 | 22 | .276 | .342 | .520 |
| 2010 | Min | AL | 157 | 609 | 165 | 37 | 5 | 14 | (7 | 7) | 254 | 93 | 81 | 77 | 58 | 7 | 93 | 4 | 0 | 4 | 7 | 3 | .70 | 26 | .271 | .336 | .417 |
| 2011 | Min | AL | 139 | 529 | 150 | 29 | 2 | 20 | (10 | 10) | 243 | 70 | 70 | 75 | 48 | 3 | 95 | 4 | 0 | 3 | 11 | 1 | .92 | 18 | .284 | .346 | .459 |
| 2012 | Col | NL | 101 | 358 | 93 | 30 | 2 | 16 | (9 | 7) | 175 | 53 | 58 | 46 | 32 | 1 | 78 | 0 | 0 | 4 | 8 | 3 | .73 | 12 | .260 | .317 | .489 |
| 2013 | Col | NL | 130 | 489 | 162 | 31 | 3 | 20 | (11 | 9) | 259 | 74 | 84 | 87 | 46 | 5 | 100 | 2 | 0 | 3 | 10 | 3 | .77 | 13 | **.331** | .389 | .530 |
| Postseason | | | 22 | 74 | 25 | 2 | 1 | 2 | (2 | 0) | 35 | 5 | 8 | 4 | 4 | 1 | 18 | 0 | 0 | 0 | 0 | 2 | .00 | 1 | .338 | .372 | .473 |
| 13 ML YEARS | | | 1370 | 4919 | 1361 | 300 | 40 | 177 | (98 | 79) | 2272 | 733 | 722 | 714 | 489 | 36 | 983 | 45 | 4 | 32 | 70 | 22 | .76 | 165 | .277 | .345 | .462 |

## Johnny Cueto

**Pitches:** R **Bats:** R **Pos:** SP-11 KWAY-toe **Ht:** 5'11" **Wt:** 215 **Born:** 2/15/1986 **Age:** 28

| HOW MUCH HE PITCHED | | | | | | | | | WHAT HE GAVE UP | | | | | | | | | | | | THE RESULTS | | | | | | | |
|---|---|---|---|---|---|---|---|---|---|---|---|---|---|---|---|---|---|---|---|---|---|---|---|---|---|---|---|---|
| Year | Team | Lg | G | GS | CG | GF | IP | BFP | H | R | ER | HR | SH | SF | HB | TBB | IBB | SO | WP | Bk | W | L | Pct | Sh | Sv-Op | Hld | ERC | ERA |
| 2013 | Dayton* | A | 2 | 2 | 0 | 0 | 8.0 | 30 | 7 | 1 | 1 | 0 | 0 | 0 | 0 | 0 | 0 | 8 | 0 | 0 | 1 | 0 | 1.000 | 0 | 0- - | - | 1.54 | 1.13 |
| 2008 | Cin | NL | 31 | 31 | 0 | 0 | 174.0 | 769 | 178 | 101 | 93 | 29 | 9 | 5 | **14** | 68 | 1 | 158 | 6 | 1 | 9 | 14 | .391 | 0 | 0-0 | 0 | 4.95 | 4.81 |
| 2009 | Cin | NL | 30 | 30 | 0 | 0 | 171.1 | 740 | 172 | 90 | 84 | 24 | 5 | 3 | 14 | 61 | 0 | 132 | 4 | 0 | 11 | 11 | .500 | 0 | 0-0 | 0 | 4.57 | 4.41 |
| 2010 | Cin | NL | 31 | 31 | 1 | 0 | 185.2 | 780 | 181 | 79 | 75 | 19 | 9 | 3 | 9 | 56 | 5 | 138 | 5 | 2 | 12 | 7 | .632 | 1 | 0-0 | 0 | 3.75 | 3.64 |
| 2011 | Cin | NL | 24 | 24 | 3 | 0 | 156.0 | 631 | 123 | 51 | 40 | 8 | 10 | 4 | 10 | 47 | 0 | 104 | 5 | 1 | 9 | 5 | .643 | 1 | 0-0 | 0 | 2.55 | 2.31 |
| 2012 | Cin | NL | 33 | **33** | 2 | 0 | 217.0 | 888 | 205 | 73 | 67 | 15 | 6 | 6 | 12 | 49 | 5 | 170 | 1 | 3 | 19 | 9 | .679 | 0 | 0-0 | 0 | 3.13 | 2.78 |
| 2013 | Cin | NL | 11 | 11 | 0 | 0 | 60.2 | 242 | 46 | 20 | 19 | 7 | 2 | 1 | 1 | 18 | 1 | 51 | 1 | 0 | 5 | 2 | .714 | 0 | 0-0 | 0 | 2.57 | 2.82 |
| Postseason | | | 2 | 2 | 0 | 0 | 5.1 | 23 | 5 | 2 | 1 | 1 | 1 | 0 | 0 | 1 | 0 | 3 | 0 | 0 | 0 | 1 | .000 | 0 | 0-0 | 0 | 3.22 | 1.69 |
| 6 ML YEARS | | | 160 | 160 | 6 | 0 | 964.2 | 4050 | 905 | 414 | 378 | 102 | 41 | 22 | 60 | 299 | 12 | 753 | 22 | 7 | 65 | 48 | .575 | 2 | 0-0 | 0 | 3.67 | 3.53 |

## Charlie Culberson

**Bats:** R **Throws:** R **Pos:** LF-27;PH-20;2B-4;PR-1 **Ht:** 6'1" **Wt:** 200 **Born:** 4/10/1989 **Age:** 25

| BATTING | | | | | | | | | | | | | | | | | | | | BASERUNNING | | | | AVERAGES | | |
|---|---|---|---|---|---|---|---|---|---|---|---|---|---|---|---|---|---|---|---|---|---|---|---|---|---|---|
| Year | Team | Lg | G | AB | H | 2B | 3B | HR | (Hm | Rd) | TB | R | RBI | RC | TBB | IBB | SO | HBP | SH | SF | SB | CS | SB% | GDP | Avg | OBP | Slg |
| 2009 | Augsta | A | 132 | 509 | 125 | 19 | 3 | 2 | (- | -) | 156 | 71 | 36 | 51 | 33 | 1 | 110 | 10 | 4 | 2 | 15 | 4 | .79 | 7 | .246 | .303 | .306 |
| 2010 | SnJos | A+ | 128 | 503 | 146 | 28 | 4 | 16 | (- | -) | 230 | 80 | 71 | 82 | 33 | 2 | 99 | 8 | 1 | 6 | 25 | 7 | .78 | 15 | .290 | .340 | .457 |
| 2011 | Rchmd | AA | 137 | 553 | 143 | 34 | 2 | 10 | (- | -) | 211 | 69 | 56 | 64 | 22 | 3 | 129 | 6 | 4 | 2 | 14 | 4 | .78 | 8 | .259 | .293 | .382 |
| 2012 | Fresno | AAA | 91 | 351 | 83 | 14 | 6 | 10 | (- | -) | 139 | 53 | 53 | 41 | 20 | 0 | 76 | 4 | 2 | 3 | 8 | 2 | .80 | 10 | .236 | .283 | .396 |
| 2012 | ColSpr | AAA | 30 | 125 | 42 | 11 | 1 | 2 | (- | -) | 61 | 17 | 12 | 20 | 1 | 0 | 18 | 1 | 0 | 1 | 6 | 2 | .75 | 5 | .336 | .344 | .488 |
| 2013 | ColSpr | AAA | 97 | 397 | 123 | 27 | 8 | 14 | (- | -) | 208 | 63 | 64 | 68 | 17 | 3 | 74 | 1 | 2 | 2 | 13 | 9 | .59 | 11 | .310 | .338 | .524 |
| 2012 | SF | NL | 6 | 22 | 3 | 0 | 0 | 0 | (0 | 0) | 3 | 0 | 1 | 0 | 0 | 0 | 7 | 0 | 1 | 0 | 0 | 0 | - | 0 | .136 | .136 | .136 |
| 2013 | Col | NL | 47 | 99 | 29 | 5 | 0 | 2 | (0 | 2) | 40 | 12 | 12 | 13 | 4 | 1 | 23 | 0 | 0 | 1 | 5 | 1 | .83 | 5 | .293 | .317 | .404 |
| 2 ML YEARS | | | 53 | 121 | 32 | 5 | 0 | 2 | (0 | 2) | 43 | 12 | 13 | 13 | 4 | 1 | 30 | 0 | 1 | 1 | 5 | 1 | .83 | 5 | .264 | .286 | .355 |

## Brandon Cumpton

**Pitches:** R **Bats:** R **Pos:** SP-5; RP-1 **Ht:** 6'2" **Wt:** 220 **Born:** 11/16/1988 **Age:** 25

| HOW MUCH HE PITCHED | | | | | | | | WHAT HE GAVE UP | | | | | | | | | | | | THE RESULTS | | | | | | | |
|---|---|---|---|---|---|---|---|---|---|---|---|---|---|---|---|---|---|---|---|---|---|---|---|---|---|---|---|
| Year Team | Lg | G | GS | CG | GF | IP | BFP | H | R | ER | HR | SH | SF | HB | TBB | IBB | SO | WP | Bk | W | L | Pct | Sh | Sv-Op | Hld | ERC | ERA |
| 2010 StCol | A- | 4 | 3 | 0 | 0 | 10.2 | 45 | 8 | 3 | 3 | 0 | 0 | 0 | 0 | 5 | 0 | 6 | 0 | 0 | 0 | 1 | .000 | 0 | 0- - | - | 2.30 | 2.53 |
| 2011 WV | A | 13 | 12 | 0 | 0 | 67.0 | 280 | 60 | 34 | 32 | 6 | 2 | 1 | 9 | 18 | 0 | 48 | 3 | 0 | 7 | 4 | .636 | 0 | 0- - | - | 3.48 | 4.30 |
| 2011 Bradtn | A+ | 13 | 12 | 0 | 0 | 66.1 | 284 | 73 | 29 | 27 | 6 | 2 | 3 | 6 | 12 | 1 | 42 | 2 | 0 | 3 | 3 | .500 | 0 | 0- - | - | 4.04 | 3.66 |
| 2012 Altna | AA | 27 | 27 | 0 | 0 | 152.1 | 642 | 149 | 72 | 65 | 9 | 6 | 3 | 15 | 46 | 0 | 88 | 7 | 2 | 12 | 11 | .522 | 0 | 0- - | - | 3.74 | 3.84 |
| 2013 Altna | AA | 2 | 2 | 0 | 0 | 9.2 | 46 | 11 | 9 | 8 | 0 | 0 | 0 | 2 | 5 | 0 | 7 | 0 | 0 | 0 | 1 | .000 | 0 | 0- - | - | 5.34 | 7.45 |
| 2013 Indy | AAA | 21 | 19 | 1 | 0 | 122.0 | 514 | 115 | 52 | 45 | 6 | 6 | 1 | 8 | 44 | 1 | 90 | 6 | 0 | 6 | 7 | .462 | 0 | 0- - | - | 3.55 | 3.32 |
| 2013 Pit | NL | 6 | 5 | 0 | 0 | 30.2 | 124 | 26 | 8 | 7 | 1 | 2 | 1 | 1 | 5 | 0 | 22 | 1 | 0 | 2 | 1 | .667 | 0 | 0-0 | 0 | 2.08 | 2.05 |

## Todd Cunningham

**Bats:** B **Throws:** R **Pos:** LF-5;PH-3;RF-2 **Ht:** 6'0" **Wt:** 200 **Born:** 3/20/1989 **Age:** 25

| BATTING | | | | | | | | | | | | | | | | | | | | | BASERUNNING | | | | AVERAGES | | |
|---|---|---|---|---|---|---|---|---|---|---|---|---|---|---|---|---|---|---|---|---|---|---|---|---|---|---|---|
| Year Team | Lg | G | AB | H | 2B | 3B | HR | (Hm | Rd) | TB | R | RBI | RC | TBB | IBB | SO | HBP | SH | SF | SB | CS | SB% | GDP | Avg | OBP | Slg |
| 2010 Rome | A | 65 | 231 | 60 | 9 | 3 | 1 | (- | -) | 78 | 32 | 20 | 29 | 14 | 0 | 30 | 15 | 2 | 1 | 7 | 4 | .64 | 4 | .260 | .341 | .338 |
| 2011 Lynbrg | A+ | 87 | 334 | 86 | 12 | 4 | 4 | (- | -) | 118 | 59 | 20 | 45 | 33 | 0 | 47 | 14 | 4 | 1 | 14 | 6 | .70 | 7 | .257 | .348 | .353 |
| 2011 Braves | R | 4 | 11 | 2 | 0 | 1 | 0 | (- | -) | 4 | 2 | 4 | 1 | 1 | 0 | 5 | 1 | 0 | 1 | 1 | 0 | 1.00 | 0 | .182 | .286 | .364 |
| 2012 Missi | AA | 120 | 466 | 144 | 23 | 6 | 3 | (- | -) | 188 | 77 | 51 | 73 | 38 | 2 | 51 | 4 | 8 | 3 | 24 | 8 | .75 | 8 | .309 | .364 | .403 |
| 2013 Gwnntt | AAA | 116 | 427 | 113 | 13 | 5 | 2 | (- | -) | 142 | 60 | 38 | 54 | 41 | 0 | 62 | 10 | 8 | 1 | 20 | 7 | .74 | 5 | .265 | .342 | .333 |
| 2013 Atl | NL | 8 | 8 | 2 | 0 | 0 | 0 | (0 | 0) | 2 | 2 | 0 | 1 | 0 | 0 | 3 | 0 | 0 | 0 | 0 | 0 | - | 1 | .250 | .250 | .250 |

## Jermaine Curtis

**Bats:** R **Throws:** R **Pos:** PH-5;LF-1 **Ht:** 5'11" **Wt:** 190 **Born:** 7/10/1987 **Age:** 26

| BATTING | | | | | | | | | | | | | | | | | | | | | BASERUNNING | | | | AVERAGES | | |
|---|---|---|---|---|---|---|---|---|---|---|---|---|---|---|---|---|---|---|---|---|---|---|---|---|---|---|---|
| Year Team | Lg | G | AB | H | 2B | 3B | HR | (Hm | Rd) | TB | R | RBI | RC | TBB | IBB | SO | HBP | SH | SF | SB | CS | SB% | GDP | Avg | OBP | Slg |
| 2009 PlmBh | A+ | 90 | 314 | 62 | 7 | 0 | 1 | (- | -) | 72 | 36 | 24 | 25 | 34 | 0 | 52 | 14 | 4 | 3 | 7 | 4 | .64 | 6 | .197 | .301 | .229 |
| 2009 QuadC | A | 30 | 112 | 34 | 12 | 0 | 1 | (- | -) | 49 | 20 | 10 | 24 | 19 | 2 | 21 | 5 | 0 | 0 | 12 | 2 | .86 | 1 | .304 | .426 | .438 |
| 2010 PlmBh | A+ | 56 | 191 | 51 | 10 | 0 | 0 | (- | -) | 61 | 34 | 24 | 30 | 28 | 1 | 25 | 13 | 2 | 4 | 5 | 1 | .83 | 4 | .267 | .390 | .319 |
| 2010 Sprgfld | AA | 23 | 55 | 13 | 3 | 0 | 0 | (- | -) | 16 | 6 | 3 | 6 | 7 | 0 | 10 | 2 | 1 | 0 | 0 | 0 | - | 0 | .236 | .344 | .291 |
| 2011 Sprgfld | AA | 91 | 276 | 87 | 12 | 3 | 5 | (- | -) | 120 | 41 | 32 | 53 | 38 | 3 | 31 | 9 | 5 | 1 | 0 | 0 | - | 11 | .315 | .414 | .435 |
| 2012 Memp | AAA | 17 | 29 | 8 | 1 | 0 | 0 | (- | -) | 9 | 7 | 1 | 5 | 9 | 0 | 4 | 0 | 0 | 0 | 0 | 0 | - | 1 | .276 | .447 | .310 |
| 2012 Sprgfld | AA | 96 | 368 | 115 | 19 | 1 | 1 | (- | -) | 139 | 61 | 24 | 65 | 47 | 2 | 51 | 19 | 5 | 1 | 6 | 1 | .86 | 8 | .313 | .416 | .378 |
| 2013 Memp | AAA | 115 | 370 | 95 | 17 | 1 | 5 | (- | -) | 129 | 45 | 49 | 53 | 52 | 3 | 53 | 7 | 2 | 5 | 10 | 2 | .83 | 9 | .257 | .355 | .349 |
| 2013 StL | NL | 5 | 3 | 0 | 0 | 0 | 0 | (0 | 0) | 0 | 0 | 0 | 0 | 1 | 0 | 1 | 1 | 0 | 0 | 0 | 0 | - | 0 | .000 | .400 | .000 |

## Matt Daley

**Pitches:** R **Bats:** R **Pos:** RP-7 **Ht:** 6'2" **Wt:** 180 **Born:** 6/23/1982 **Age:** 32

| HOW MUCH HE PITCHED | | | | | | | | WHAT HE GAVE UP | | | | | | | | | | | | THE RESULTS | | | | | | | |
|---|---|---|---|---|---|---|---|---|---|---|---|---|---|---|---|---|---|---|---|---|---|---|---|---|---|---|---|
| Year Team | Lg | G | GS | CG | GF | IP | BFP | H | R | ER | HR | SH | SF | HB | TBB | IBB | SO | WP | Bk | W | L | Pct | Sh | Sv-Op | Hld | ERC | ERA |
| 2013 Tampa* | A+ | 4 | 0 | 0 | 3 | 5.1 | 22 | 5 | 0 | 0 | 0 | 0 | 0 | 1 | 0 | 0 | 10 | 0 | 0 | 0 | 0 | - | 0 | 0- - | - | 2.27 | 0.00 |
| 2013 Trntn* | AA | 10 | 0 | 0 | 3 | 9.0 | 35 | 5 | 1 | 1 | 0 | 0 | 0 | 0 | 4 | 1 | 11 | 0 | 0 | 3 | 0 | 1.000 | 0 | 0- - | - | 1.40 | 1.00 |
| 2013 S-WB* | AAA | 30 | 0 | 0 | 18 | 39.0 | 154 | 28 | 12 | 11 | 3 | 2 | 2 | 2 | 6 | 0 | 53 | 0 | 0 | 2 | 3 | .400 | 0 | 1- - | - | 1.76 | 2.54 |
| 2009 Col | NL | 57 | 0 | 0 | 15 | 51.0 | 211 | 43 | 24 | 24 | 6 | 2 | 3 | 2 | 18 | 2 | 55 | 0 | 0 | 1 | 1 | .500 | 0 | 0-3 | 12 | 3.27 | 4.24 |
| 2010 Col | NL | 28 | 0 | 0 | 4 | 23.1 | 108 | 27 | 11 | 11 | 2 | 2 | 1 | 3 | 10 | 1 | 18 | 1 | 0 | 0 | 1 | .000 | 0 | 0-0 | 6 | 5.41 | 4.24 |
| 2011 Col | NL | 7 | 0 | 0 | 0 | 6.0 | 27 | 8 | 7 | 7 | 1 | 0 | 1 | 0 | 2 | 0 | 7 | 0 | 0 | 0 | 0 | - | 0 | 0-0 | 0 | 6.38 | 10.50 |
| 2013 NYY | AL | 7 | 0 | 0 | 4 | 6.0 | 21 | 2 | 0 | 0 | 0 | 0 | 0 | 1 | 0 | 0 | 8 | 0 | 0 | 1 | 0 | 1.000 | 0 | 0-0 | 0 | 0.45 | 0.00 |
| Postseason | | 1 | 0 | 0 | 0 | 1.0 | 5 | 1 | 0 | 0 | 0 | 1 | 0 | 0 | 1 | 0 | 0 | 1 | 0 | 0 | 0 | - | 0 | 0-0 | 0 | 5.48 | 0.00 |
| 4 ML YEARS | | 99 | 0 | 0 | 23 | 86.1 | 367 | 80 | 42 | 42 | 9 | 4 | 5 | 6 | 30 | 3 | 88 | 1 | 0 | 2 | 2 | .500 | 0 | 0-3 | 18 | 3.72 | 4.38 |

## John Danks

**Pitches:** L **Bats:** L **Pos:** SP-22 **Ht:** 6'1" **Wt:** 215 **Born:** 4/15/1985 **Age:** 29

| HOW MUCH HE PITCHED | | | | | | | | WHAT HE GAVE UP | | | | | | | | | | | | THE RESULTS | | | | | | | |
|---|---|---|---|---|---|---|---|---|---|---|---|---|---|---|---|---|---|---|---|---|---|---|---|---|---|---|---|
| Year Team | Lg | G | GS | CG | GF | IP | BFP | H | R | ER | HR | SH | SF | HB | TBB | IBB | SO | WP | Bk | W | L | Pct | Sh | Sv-Op | Hld | ERC | ERA |
| 2013 Brham* | AA | 1 | 1 | 0 | 0 | 7.0 | 26 | 5 | 2 | 2 | 1 | 0 | 0 | 0 | 1 | 0 | 1 | 0 | 0 | 1 | 0 | 1.000 | 0 | 0- - | - | 1.99 | 2.57 |
| 2013 Charltt* | AAA | 3 | 3 | 0 | 0 | 15.2 | 71 | 13 | 8 | 6 | 1 | 1 | 1 | 2 | 12 | 0 | 14 | 0 | 0 | 1 | 0 | 1.000 | 0 | 0- - | - | 4.86 | 3.45 |
| 2007 CWS | AL | 26 | 26 | 0 | 0 | 139.0 | 622 | 160 | 92 | 85 | 28 | 7 | 4 | 4 | 54 | 4 | 109 | 3 | 0 | 6 | 13 | .316 | 0 | 0-0 | 0 | 5.73 | 5.50 |
| 2008 CWS | AL | 33 | 33 | 0 | 0 | 195.0 | 804 | 182 | 74 | 72 | 15 | 2 | 2 | 4 | 57 | 1 | 159 | 7 | 0 | 12 | 9 | .571 | 0 | 0-0 | 0 | 3.26 | 3.32 |
| 2009 CWS | AL | 32 | 32 | 1 | 0 | 200.1 | 839 | 184 | 89 | 84 | 28 | 5 | 6 | 5 | 73 | 1 | 149 | 1 | 0 | 13 | 11 | .542 | 0 | 0-0 | 0 | 3.89 | 3.77 |
| 2010 CWS | AL | 32 | 32 | 1 | 0 | 213.0 | 878 | 189 | 93 | 88 | 18 | 5 | 0 | 4 | 70 | 2 | 162 | 2 | 1 | 15 | 11 | .577 | 1 | 0-0 | 0 | 3.18 | 3.72 |
| 2011 CWS | AL | 27 | 27 | 2 | 0 | 170.1 | 728 | 182 | 89 | 82 | 19 | 4 | 6 | 7 | 46 | 5 | 135 | 6 | 0 | 8 | 12 | .400 | 1 | 0-0 | 0 | 4.16 | 4.33 |
| 2012 CWS | AL | 9 | 9 | 0 | 0 | 53.2 | 238 | 57 | 35 | 34 | 7 | 3 | 2 | 1 | 23 | 0 | 30 | 5 | 0 | 3 | 4 | .429 | 0 | 0-0 | 0 | 4.82 | 5.70 |
| 2013 CWS | AL | 22 | 22 | 0 | 0 | 138.1 | 583 | 151 | 81 | 73 | 28 | 1 | 5 | 4 | 27 | 0 | 89 | 3 | 0 | 4 | 14 | .222 | 0 | 0-0 | 0 | 4.61 | 4.75 |
| Postseason | | 1 | 1 | 0 | 0 | 6.2 | 30 | 7 | 3 | 3 | 1 | 0 | 0 | 0 | 3 | 0 | 7 | 0 | 0 | 1 | 0 | 1.000 | 0 | 0-0 | 0 | 4.81 | 4.05 |
| 7 ML YEARS | | 181 | 181 | 4 | 0 | 1109.2 | 4692 | 1105 | 553 | 518 | 143 | 27 | 25 | 29 | 350 | 13 | 833 | 27 | 1 | 61 | 74 | .452 | 2 | 0-0 | 0 | 4.03 | 4.20 |

## Jordan Danks

**Bats:** L **Throws:** R **Pos:** CF-47;RF-20;PR-13;PH-9;DH-4;LF-2 **Ht:** 6'4" **Wt:** 210 **Born:** 8/7/1986 **Age:** 27

| BATTING | | | | | | | | | | | | | | | | | | | | | BASERUNNING | | | | AVERAGES | | |
|---|---|---|---|---|---|---|---|---|---|---|---|---|---|---|---|---|---|---|---|---|---|---|---|---|---|---|---|
| Year Team | Lg | G | AB | H | 2B | 3B | HR | (Hm | Rd) | TB | R | RBI | RC | TBB | IBB | SO | HBP | SH | SF | SB | CS | SB% | GDP | Avg | OBP | Slg |
| 2009 WinSa | A+ | 30 | 118 | 38 | 11 | 2 | 3 | (- | -) | 62 | 25 | 21 | 26 | 18 | 0 | 32 | 0 | 1 | 1 | 5 | 1 | .83 | 4 | .322 | .409 | .525 |
| 2009 Brham | AA | 73 | 284 | 69 | 12 | 1 | 6 | (- | -) | 101 | 50 | 20 | 37 | 37 | 1 | 73 | 4 | 4 | 1 | 7 | 3 | .70 | 2 | .243 | .337 | .356 |
| 2010 Charltt | AAA | 119 | 445 | 109 | 27 | 3 | 8 | (- | -) | 166 | 62 | 42 | 55 | 41 | 1 | 151 | 4 | 9 | 3 | 15 | 6 | .71 | 6 | .245 | .312 | .373 |
| 2011 Charltt | AAA | 133 | 463 | 119 | 24 | 6 | 14 | (- | -) | 197 | 65 | 65 | 73 | 57 | 1 | 155 | 5 | 9 | 1 | 18 | 4 | .82 | 6 | .257 | .344 | .425 |
| 2012 Charltt | AAA | 64 | 218 | 69 | 17 | 1 | 8 | (- | -) | 112 | 37 | 30 | 49 | 44 | 1 | 66 | 0 | 0 | 2 | 6 | 3 | .67 | 0 | .317 | .428 | .514 |

| Year Team | Lg | G | AB | H | 2B | 3B | HR | (Hm | Rd) | TB | R | RBI | RC | TBB | IBB | SO | HBP | SH | SF | SB | CS | SB% | GDP | Avg | OBP | Slg |
|---|---|---|---|---|---|---|---|---|---|---|---|---|---|---|---|---|---|---|---|---|---|---|---|---|---|---|
| **BATTING** | | | | | | | | | | | | | | | | | | | | **BASERUNNING** | | | | **AVERAGES** | | |
| 2013 Charltt | AAA | 54 | 208 | 58 | 9 | 2 | 6 | (- | -) | 89 | 35 | 28 | 34 | 26 | 0 | 57 | 2 | 1 | 1 | 3 | 1 | .75 | 3 | .279 | .363 | .428 |
| 2012 CWS | AL | 50 | 67 | 15 | 1 | 0 | 1 | (1 | 0) | 19 | 12 | 4 | 3 | 6 | 0 | 16 | 0 | 0 | 2 | 3 | 1 | .75 | 1 | .224 | .280 | .284 |
| 2013 CWS | AL | 79 | 160 | 37 | 7 | 0 | 5 | (4 | 1) | 59 | 15 | 12 | 12 | 18 | 0 | 57 | 1 | 0 | 0 | 7 | 2 | .78 | 5 | .231 | .313 | .369 |
| 2 ML YEARS | | 129 | 227 | 52 | 8 | 0 | 6 | (5 | 1) | 78 | 27 | 16 | 15 | 24 | 0 | 73 | 1 | 0 | 2 | 10 | 3 | .77 | 6 | .229 | .303 | .344 |

## Travis d'Arnaud

**Bats:** R **Throws:** R **Pos:** C-30;PH-1 dar-NO **Ht:** 6'2" **Wt:** 195 **Born:** 2/10/1989 **Age:** 25

| Year Team | Lg | G | AB | H | 2B | 3B | HR | (Hm | Rd) | TB | R | RBI | RC | TBB | IBB | SO | HBP | SH | SF | SB | CS | SB% | GDP | Avg | OBP | Slg |
|---|---|---|---|---|---|---|---|---|---|---|---|---|---|---|---|---|---|---|---|---|---|---|---|---|---|---|
| **BATTING** | | | | | | | | | | | | | | | | | | | | **BASERUNNING** | | | | **AVERAGES** | | |
| 2009 Lakwd | A | 126 | 482 | 123 | 38 | 1 | 13 | (- | -) | 202 | 71 | 71 | 68 | 41 | 1 | 75 | 8 | 0 | 9 | 8 | 4 | .67 | 10 | .255 | .319 | .419 |
| 2010 Dnedin | A+ | 71 | 263 | 68 | 20 | 1 | 6 | (- | -) | 108 | 36 | 38 | 36 | 20 | 1 | 63 | 4 | 0 | 5 | 3 | 1 | .75 | 6 | .259 | .315 | .411 |
| 2011 NHam | AA | 114 | 424 | 132 | 33 | 1 | 21 | (- | -) | 230 | 72 | 78 | 84 | 33 | 1 | 100 | 8 | 0 | 1 | 4 | 2 | .67 | 5 | .311 | .371 | .542 |
| 2012 LsVgs | AAA | 67 | 279 | 93 | 21 | 2 | 16 | (- | -) | 166 | 45 | 52 | 60 | 19 | 1 | 59 | 3 | 0 | 2 | 1 | 1 | .50 | 11 | .333 | .380 | .595 |
| 2013 LsVgs | AAA | 19 | 56 | 17 | 8 | 0 | 2 | (- | -) | 31 | 19 | 12 | 16 | 21 | 2 | 12 | 0 | 0 | 1 | 0 | 0 | - | 2 | .304 | .487 | .554 |
| 2013 Mets | R | 6 | 22 | 7 | 3 | 0 | 0 | (- | -) | 10 | 4 | 5 | 3 | 1 | 0 | 2 | 0 | 0 | 0 | 0 | 0 | - | 0 | .318 | .348 | .455 |
| 2013 Bnghtn | AA | 7 | 27 | 6 | 2 | 1 | 1 | (- | -) | 13 | 2 | 3 | 4 | 3 | 0 | 9 | 0 | 0 | 0 | 0 | 0 | - | 1 | .222 | .300 | .481 |
| 2013 NYM | NL | 31 | 99 | 20 | 3 | 0 | 1 | (1 | 0) | 26 | 4 | 5 | 6 | 12 | 0 | 21 | 0 | 0 | 1 | 0 | 0 | - | 3 | .202 | .286 | .263 |

## Yu Darvish

**Pitches:** R **Bats:** R **Pos:** SP-32 YOO DARR-vish **Ht:** 6'5" **Wt:** 225 **Born:** 8/16/1986 **Age:** 27

| Year Team | Lg | G | GS | CG | GF | IP | BFP | H | R | ER | HR | SH | SF | HB | TBB | IBB | SO | WP | Bk | W | L | Pct | Sh | Sv-Op | Hld | ERC | ERA |
|---|---|---|---|---|---|---|---|---|---|---|---|---|---|---|---|---|---|---|---|---|---|---|---|---|---|---|---|
| **HOW MUCH HE PITCHED** | | | | | | | | **WHAT HE GAVE UP** | | | | | | | | | | | | **THE RESULTS** | | | | | | | |
| 2009 Hokado | Jap | 23 | 23 | 8 | - | 182.0 | 701 | 118 | 36 | 35 | 9 | - | - | 6 | 45 | 0 | 167 | 5 | 0 | 15 | 5 | .750 | 2 | 0-- | - | 1.63 | 1.73 |
| 2010 Hokado | Jap | 26 | 25 | 10 | - | 202.0 | 805 | 158 | 48 | 40 | 5 | - | - | 7 | 47 | 0 | 222 | 6 | 0 | 12 | 8 | .600 | 2 | 0-- | - | 2.01 | 1.78 |
| 2011 Hokado | Jap | 28 | 28 | 10 | - | 232.0 | 885 | 156 | 42 | 37 | 5 | - | - | 6 | 36 | 0 | 276 | 10 | 1 | 18 | 6 | .750 | 6 | 0-- | - | 1.37 | 1.44 |
| 2012 Tex | AL | 29 | 29 | 0 | 0 | 191.1 | 816 | 156 | 89 | 83 | 14 | 2 | 7 | 10 | 89 | 1 | 221 | 8 | 0 | 16 | 9 | .640 | 0 | 0-0 | 0 | 3.31 | 3.90 |
| 2013 Tex | AL | 32 | 32 | 0 | 0 | 209.2 | 841 | 145 | 68 | 66 | 26 | 0 | 5 | 8 | 80 | 1 | **277** | 7 | 1 | 13 | 9 | .591 | 0 | 0-0 | 0 | 2.70 | 2.83 |
| Postseason | | 1 | 1 | 0 | 0 | 6.2 | 27 | 5 | 3 | 2 | 0 | 1 | 1 | 1 | 0 | 0 | 7 | 0 | 0 | 0 | 1 | .000 | 0 | 0-0 | 0 | 1.38 | 2.70 |
| 2 ML YEARS | | 61 | 61 | 0 | 0 | 401.0 | 1657 | 301 | 157 | 149 | 40 | 2 | 12 | 18 | 169 | 2 | 498 | 15 | 1 | 29 | 18 | .617 | 0 | 0-0 | 0 | 2.99 | 3.34 |

## Matt Davidson

**Bats:** R **Throws:** R **Pos:** 3B-20;PH-12 **Ht:** 6'2" **Wt:** 225 **Born:** 3/26/1991 **Age:** 23

| Year Team | Lg | G | AB | H | 2B | 3B | HR | (Hm | Rd) | TB | R | RBI | RC | TBB | IBB | SO | HBP | SH | SF | SB | CS | SB% | GDP | Avg | OBP | Slg |
|---|---|---|---|---|---|---|---|---|---|---|---|---|---|---|---|---|---|---|---|---|---|---|---|---|---|---|
| **BATTING** | | | | | | | | | | | | | | | | | | | | **BASERUNNING** | | | | **AVERAGES** | | |
| 2009 Yakima | A- | 72 | 270 | 65 | 15 | 0 | 2 | (- | -) | 86 | 29 | 28 | 27 | 21 | 0 | 75 | 7 | 1 | 0 | 0 | 2 | .00 | 9 | .241 | .312 | .319 |
| 2010 Sbend | A | 113 | 415 | 120 | 35 | 3 | 16 | (- | -) | 209 | 58 | 79 | 78 | 43 | 2 | 109 | 13 | 0 | 4 | 0 | 2 | .00 | 8 | .289 | .371 | .504 |
| 2010 Visalia | A+ | 21 | 71 | 12 | 1 | 0 | 2 | (- | -) | 19 | 6 | 11 | 6 | 12 | 1 | 25 | 1 | 0 | 0 | 0 | 0 | - | 2 | .169 | .298 | .268 |
| 2011 Visalia | A+ | 135 | 535 | 148 | 39 | 1 | 20 | (- | -) | 249 | 93 | 106 | 89 | 52 | 1 | 147 | 11 | 0 | 8 | 0 | 1 | .00 | 7 | .277 | .348 | .465 |
| 2012 Mobile | AA | 135 | 486 | 127 | 28 | 2 | 23 | (- | -) | 228 | 81 | 77 | 87 | 69 | 5 | 126 | 15 | 0 | 5 | 3 | 4 | .43 | 12 | .261 | .367 | .469 |
| 2013 Reno | AAA | 115 | 443 | 124 | 32 | 3 | 17 | (- | -) | 213 | 55 | 74 | 77 | 46 | 1 | 134 | 5 | 0 | 6 | 1 | 0 | 1.00 | 16 | .280 | .350 | .481 |
| 2013 Ari | NL | 31 | 76 | 18 | 6 | 0 | 3 | (1 | 2) | 33 | 8 | 12 | 12 | 10 | 1 | 24 | 1 | 0 | 0 | 0 | 1 | .00 | 1 | .237 | .333 | .434 |

## Chris Davis

**Bats:** L **Throws:** R **Pos:** 1B-155;DH-5 **Ht:** 6'3" **Wt:** 230 **Born:** 3/17/1986 **Age:** 28

| Year Team | Lg | G | AB | H | 2B | 3B | HR | (Hm | Rd) | TB | R | RBI | RC | TBB | IBB | SO | HBP | SH | SF | SB | CS | SB% | GDP | Avg | OBP | Slg |
|---|---|---|---|---|---|---|---|---|---|---|---|---|---|---|---|---|---|---|---|---|---|---|---|---|---|---|
| **BATTING** | | | | | | | | | | | | | | | | | | | | **BASERUNNING** | | | | **AVERAGES** | | |
| 2008 Tex | AL | 80 | 295 | 84 | 23 | 2 | 17 | (8 | 9) | 162 | 51 | 55 | 44 | 20 | 1 | 88 | 1 | 0 | 1 | 1 | 2 | .33 | 5 | .285 | .331 | .549 |
| 2009 Tex | AL | 113 | 391 | 93 | 15 | 1 | 21 | (11 | 10) | 173 | 48 | 59 | 50 | 24 | 2 | 150 | 2 | 0 | 2 | 0 | 0 | - | 6 | .238 | .284 | .442 |
| 2010 Tex | AL | 45 | 120 | 23 | 9 | 0 | 1 | (0 | 1) | 35 | 7 | 4 | 5 | 15 | 3 | 40 | 0 | 0 | 1 | 3 | 0 | 1.00 | 3 | .192 | .279 | .292 |
| 2011 2 Tms | AL | 59 | 199 | 53 | 12 | 0 | 5 | (2 | 3) | 80 | 25 | 19 | 23 | 11 | 1 | 63 | 0 | 0 | 0 | 1 | 0 | 1.00 | 4 | .266 | .305 | .402 |
| 2012 Bal | AL | 139 | 515 | 139 | 20 | 0 | 33 | (22 | 11) | 258 | 75 | 85 | 85 | 37 | 6 | 169 | 7 | 0 | 3 | 2 | 3 | .40 | 8 | .270 | .326 | .501 |
| 2013 Bal | AL | 160 | 584 | 167 | 42 | 1 | **53** | **(28** | 25) | **370** | 103 | **138** | 134 | 72 | 12 | 199 | 10 | 0 | 7 | 4 | 1 | .80 | 4 | .286 | .370 | .634 |
| 11 Tex | AL | 28 | 76 | 19 | 3 | 0 | 3 | (1 | 2) | 31 | 9 | 6 | 7 | 5 | 0 | 24 | 0 | 0 | 0 | 0 | 0 | - | 2 | .250 | .296 | .408 |
| 11 Bal | AL | 31 | 123 | 34 | 9 | 0 | 2 | (1 | 1) | 49 | 16 | 13 | 16 | 6 | 1 | 39 | 0 | 0 | 0 | 1 | 0 | 1.00 | 2 | .276 | .310 | .398 |
| Postseason | | 6 | 24 | 5 | 0 | 0 | 0 | (0 | 0) | 5 | 1 | 2 | 1 | 1 | 0 | 9 | 1 | 0 | 0 | 0 | 0 | - | 0 | .208 | .269 | .208 |
| 6 ML YEARS | | 596 | 2104 | 559 | 121 | 4 | 130 | (71 | 59) | 1078 | 309 | 360 | 341 | 179 | 25 | 709 | 20 | 0 | 14 | 11 | 6 | .65 | 30 | .266 | .327 | .512 |

## Erik Davis

**Pitches:** R **Bats:** R **Pos:** RP-10 **Ht:** 6'2" **Wt:** 190 **Born:** 10/8/1986 **Age:** 27

| Year Team | Lg | G | GS | CG | GF | IP | BFP | H | R | ER | HR | SH | SF | HB | TBB | IBB | SO | WP | Bk | W | L | Pct | Sh | Sv-Op | Hld | ERC | ERA |
|---|---|---|---|---|---|---|---|---|---|---|---|---|---|---|---|---|---|---|---|---|---|---|---|---|---|---|---|
| **HOW MUCH HE PITCHED** | | | | | | | | **WHAT HE GAVE UP** | | | | | | | | | | | | **THE RESULTS** | | | | | | | |
| 2009 FtWyn | A | 32 | 19 | 0 | 1 | 123.2 | 522 | 111 | 56 | 50 | 5 | 3 | 3 | 8 | 44 | 1 | 106 | 6 | 0 | 16 | 6 | .727 | 0 | 0-- | - | 3.18 | 3.64 |
| 2010 Lk Els | A+ | 19 | 19 | 0 | 0 | 99.0 | 433 | 102 | 49 | 42 | 5 | 4 | 3 | 8 | 34 | 0 | 91 | 7 | 0 | 9 | 3 | .750 | 0 | 0-- | - | 3.96 | 3.82 |
| 2010 Portlnd | AAA | 1 | 1 | 0 | 0 | 5.0 | 19 | 3 | 2 | 2 | 1 | 0 | 0 | 0 | 2 | 0 | 7 | 0 | 0 | 1 | 0 | 1.000 | 0 | 0-- | - | 2.72 | 3.60 |
| 2010 SnAnt | AA | 7 | 7 | 0 | 0 | 39.1 | 154 | 29 | 13 | 12 | 1 | 3 | 0 | 1 | 12 | 1 | 35 | 0 | 0 | 4 | 0 | 1.000 | 0 | 0-- | - | 2.03 | 2.75 |
| 2011 Hrsbrg | AA | 20 | 19 | 1 | 0 | 94.0 | 427 | 110 | 60 | 50 | 9 | 1 | 1 | 3 | 41 | 3 | 93 | 11 | 0 | 5 | 7 | .417 | 0 | 0-- | - | 5.23 | 4.79 |
| 2011 Ptomc | A+ | 6 | 6 | 1 | 0 | 33.1 | 153 | 37 | 26 | 25 | 2 | 3 | 1 | 5 | 16 | 0 | 24 | 0 | 0 | 0 | 5 | .000 | 0 | 0-- | - | 5.37 | 6.75 |
| 2012 Hrsbrg | AA | 40 | 0 | 0 | 17 | 64.1 | 264 | 61 | 18 | 18 | 5 | 3 | 1 | 1 | 18 | 3 | 69 | 4 | 1 | 7 | 3 | .700 | 0 | 5-- | - | 3.23 | 2.52 |
| 2012 Syrcse | AAA | 8 | 0 | 0 | 3 | 8.2 | 38 | 10 | 5 | 4 | 1 | 0 | 0 | 0 | 2 | 0 | 5 | 1 | 0 | 1 | 0 | 1.000 | 0 | 0-- | - | 4.27 | 4.15 |
| 2013 Syrcse | AAA | 45 | 0 | 0 | 32 | 52.1 | 231 | 55 | 25 | 18 | 4 | 4 | 1 | 0 | 20 | 3 | 54 | 2 | 0 | 3 | 7 | .300 | 0 | 15-- | - | 3.95 | 3.10 |
| 2013 Was | NL | 10 | 0 | 0 | 2 | 8.2 | 38 | 10 | 3 | 3 | 0 | 1 | 0 | 0 | 1 | 0 | 12 | 1 | 0 | 1 | 0 | 1.000 | 0 | 0-0 | 0 | 2.97 | 3.12 |

# Ike Davis

**Bats:** L **Throws:** L **Pos:** 1B-96;PH-10 **Ht:** 6'4" **Wt:** 230 **Born:** 3/22/1987 **Age:** 27

| BATTING | | | | | | | | | | | | | | | | | | | | | BASERUNNING | | | | AVERAGES | | |
|---|---|---|---|---|---|---|---|---|---|---|---|---|---|---|---|---|---|---|---|---|---|---|---|---|---|---|---|
| Year | Team | Lg | G | AB | H | 2B | 3B | HR | (Hm | Rd) | TB | R | RBI | RC | TBB | IBB | SO | HBP | SH | SF | SB | CS | SB% | GDP | Avg | OBP | Slg |
| 2013 | LsVgs* | AAA | 21 | 75 | 22 | 7 | 0 | 7 | (- | -) | 50 | 21 | 13 | 20 | 17 | 1 | 18 | 0 | 0 | 0 | 0 | 0 | - | 3 | .293 | .424 | .667 |
| 2010 | NYM | NL | 147 | 523 | 138 | 33 | 1 | 19 | (8 | 11) | 230 | 73 | 71 | 75 | 72 | 6 | 138 | 1 | 0 | 5 | 3 | 2 | .60 | 13 | .264 | .351 | .440 |
| 2011 | NYM | NL | 36 | 129 | 39 | 8 | 1 | 7 | (5 | 2) | 70 | 20 | 25 | 22 | 17 | 3 | 31 | 1 | 0 | 2 | 0 | 0 | - | 5 | .302 | .383 | .543 |
| 2012 | NYM | NL | 156 | 519 | 118 | 26 | 0 | 32 | (11 | **21**) | 240 | 66 | 90 | 68 | 61 | 3 | 141 | 1 | 0 | 3 | 0 | 2 | .00 | 10 | .227 | .308 | .462 |
| 2013 | NYM | NL | 103 | 317 | 65 | 14 | 0 | 9 | (5 | 4) | 106 | 37 | 33 | 36 | 57 | 5 | 101 | 1 | 0 | 2 | 4 | 0 | 1.00 | 9 | .205 | .326 | .334 |
| 4 ML YEARS | | | 442 | 1488 | 360 | 81 | 2 | 67 | (29 | 38) | 646 | 196 | 219 | 201 | 207 | 17 | 411 | 4 | 0 | 12 | 7 | 4 | .64 | 37 | .242 | .334 | .434 |

# Khris Davis

**Bats:** R **Throws:** R **Pos:** LF-34;PH-22;DH-2 **Ht:** 5'11" **Wt:** 200 **Born:** 12/21/1987 **Age:** 26

| BATTING | | | | | | | | | | | | | | | | | | | | | BASERUNNING | | | | AVERAGES | | |
|---|---|---|---|---|---|---|---|---|---|---|---|---|---|---|---|---|---|---|---|---|---|---|---|---|---|---|---|
| Year | Team | Lg | G | AB | H | 2B | 3B | HR | (Hm | Rd) | TB | R | RBI | RC | TBB | IBB | SO | HBP | SH | SF | SB | CS | SB% | GDP | Avg | OBP | Slg |
| 2009 | Helena | R+ | 1 | 1 | 0 | 0 | 0 | 0 | (- | -) | 0 | 0 | 0 | 0 | 0 | 0 | 0 | 0 | 0 | 0 | 0 | 0 | - | 0 | .000 | .000 | .000 |
| 2009 | Brewrs | R | 10 | 37 | 9 | 0 | 2 | 2 | (- | -) | 19 | 7 | 8 | 7 | 6 | 0 | 11 | 1 | 0 | 1 | 4 | 0 | 1.00 | 0 | .243 | .356 | .514 |
| 2010 | Wisc | A | 128 | 457 | 128 | 26 | 4 | 22 | (- | -) | 228 | 86 | 72 | 94 | 77 | 2 | 120 | 15 | 2 | 4 | 17 | 10 | .63 | 11 | .280 | .398 | .499 |
| 2011 | BrvdCt | A+ | 90 | 304 | 94 | 21 | 1 | 15 | (- | -) | 162 | 50 | 68 | 69 | 51 | 1 | 70 | 9 | 0 | 7 | 10 | 5 | .67 | 11 | .309 | .415 | .533 |
| 2011 | Hntsvl | AA | 35 | 124 | 26 | 7 | 1 | 2 | (- | -) | 41 | 10 | 16 | 11 | 10 | 0 | 23 | 1 | 0 | 1 | 0 | 0 | - | 6 | .210 | .272 | .331 |
| 2012 | Hntsvl | AA | 44 | 128 | 49 | 9 | 0 | 8 | (- | -) | 82 | 23 | 23 | 36 | 20 | 0 | 33 | 5 | 1 | 0 | 2 | 2 | .50 | 3 | .383 | .484 | .641 |
| 2012 | Brewrs | R | 6 | 19 | 7 | 0 | 0 | 3 | (- | -) | 16 | 7 | 5 | 6 | 2 | 0 | 7 | 1 | 0 | 0 | 1 | 1 | .50 | 0 | .368 | .455 | .842 |
| 2012 | Nashv | AAA | 32 | 113 | 35 | 12 | 0 | 4 | (- | -) | 59 | 23 | 24 | 26 | 20 | 1 | 27 | 3 | 0 | 4 | 1 | 0 | 1.00 | 4 | .310 | .414 | .522 |
| 2013 | Nashv | AAA | 69 | 243 | 62 | 12 | 1 | 13 | (- | -) | 115 | 35 | 37 | 41 | 31 | 2 | 59 | 5 | 0 | 2 | 6 | 4 | .60 | 10 | .255 | .349 | .473 |
| 2013 | Mil | NL | 56 | 136 | 38 | 10 | 0 | 11 | (5 | 6) | 81 | 27 | 27 | 25 | 11 | 0 | 34 | 5 | 0 | 1 | 3 | 0 | 1.00 | 4 | .279 | .353 | .596 |

# Rajai Davis

RAHJ-ay

**Bats:** R **Throws:** R **Pos:** LF-57;RF-35;CF-16;PR-11;DH-8;PH-5 **Ht:** 5'9" **Wt:** 195 **Born:** 10/19/1980 **Age:** 33

| BATTING | | | | | | | | | | | | | | | | | | | | | BASERUNNING | | | | AVERAGES | | |
|---|---|---|---|---|---|---|---|---|---|---|---|---|---|---|---|---|---|---|---|---|---|---|---|---|---|---|---|
| Year | Team | Lg | G | AB | H | 2B | 3B | HR | (Hm | Rd) | TB | R | RBI | RC | TBB | IBB | SO | HBP | SH | SF | SB | CS | SB% | GDP | Avg | OBP | Slg |
| 2013 | Dnedin* | A+ | 3 | 10 | 3 | 0 | 1 | 0 | (- | -) | 5 | 2 | 0 | 1 | 0 | 0 | 1 | 0 | 0 | 0 | 0 | 0 | - | 1 | .300 | .300 | .500 |
| 2006 | Pit | NL | 20 | 14 | 2 | 1 | 0 | 0 | (0 | 0) | 3 | 1 | 0 | 0 | 2 | 0 | 3 | 0 | 1 | 0 | 1 | 3 | .25 | 0 | .143 | .250 | .214 |
| 2007 | 2 Tms | NL | 75 | 190 | 53 | 11 | 2 | 1 | (0 | 1) | 71 | 32 | 9 | 26 | 21 | 1 | 28 | 4 | 3 | 1 | 22 | 6 | .79 | 1 | .279 | .361 | .374 |
| 2008 | 2 Tms | | 113 | 214 | 52 | 5 | 4 | 3 | (0 | 3) | 74 | 30 | 19 | 24 | 8 | 0 | 40 | 1 | 2 | 1 | 29 | 6 | .83 | 1 | .243 | .272 | .346 |
| 2009 | Oak | AL | 125 | 390 | 119 | 27 | 5 | 3 | (1 | 2) | 165 | 65 | 48 | 63 | 29 | 0 | 70 | 7 | 2 | 4 | 41 | 12 | .77 | 12 | .305 | .360 | .423 |
| 2010 | Oak | AL | 143 | 525 | 149 | 28 | 3 | 5 | (5 | 0) | 198 | 66 | 52 | 62 | 26 | 0 | 78 | 4 | 1 | 5 | 50 | 11 | .82 | 10 | .284 | .320 | .377 |
| 2011 | Tor | AL | 95 | 320 | 76 | 21 | 6 | 1 | (1 | 0) | 112 | 44 | 29 | 32 | 15 | 0 | 63 | 1 | 1 | 1 | 34 | 11 | .76 | 4 | .238 | .273 | .350 |
| 2012 | Tor | AL | 142 | 447 | 115 | 24 | 3 | 8 | (5 | 3) | 169 | 64 | 43 | 59 | 29 | 3 | 102 | 6 | 1 | 4 | 46 | **13** | .78 | 8 | .257 | .309 | .378 |
| 2013 | Tor | AL | 108 | 331 | 86 | 16 | 2 | 6 | (3 | 3) | 124 | 49 | 24 | 36 | 21 | 0 | 67 | 5 | 1 | 2 | 45 | 6 | .88 | 8 | .260 | .312 | .375 |
| 07 | Pit | NL | 24 | 48 | 13 | 2 | 1 | 0 | (0 | 0) | 17 | 6 | 2 | 6 | 7 | 0 | 3 | 0 | 1 | 1 | 5 | 2 | .71 | 1 | .271 | .357 | .354 |
| 07 | SF | NL | 51 | 142 | 40 | 9 | 1 | 1 | (0 | 1) | 54 | 26 | 7 | 20 | 14 | 1 | 25 | 4 | 2 | 0 | 17 | 4 | .81 | 0 | .282 | .363 | .380 |
| 08 | SF | NL | 12 | 18 | 1 | 0 | 0 | 0 | (0 | 0) | 1 | 2 | 0 | 0 | 1 | 0 | 6 | 0 | 0 | 0 | 4 | 0 | 1.00 | 0 | .056 | .105 | .056 |
| 08 | Oak | AL | 101 | 196 | 51 | 5 | 4 | 3 | (0 | 3) | 73 | 28 | 19 | 24 | 7 | 0 | 34 | 1 | 2 | 1 | 25 | 6 | .81 | 1 | .260 | .288 | .372 |
| 8 ML YEARS | | | 821 | 2431 | 652 | 133 | 25 | 27 | (15 | 12) | 916 | 351 | 224 | 302 | 151 | 4 | 451 | 28 | 12 | 18 | 268 | 68 | .80 | 44 | .268 | .316 | .377 |

# Wade Davis

**Pitches:** R **Bats:** R **Pos:** SP-24; RP-7 **Ht:** 6'5" **Wt:** 225 **Born:** 9/7/1985 **Age:** 28

| HOW MUCH HE PITCHED | | | | | | | | | WHAT HE GAVE UP | | | | | | | | | | | | THE RESULTS | | | | | | | |
|---|---|---|---|---|---|---|---|---|---|---|---|---|---|---|---|---|---|---|---|---|---|---|---|---|---|---|---|---|
| Year | Team | Lg | G | GS | CG | GF | IP | BFP | H | R | ER | HR | SH | SF | HB | TBB | IBB | SO | WP | Bk | W | L | Pct | Sh | Sv-Op | Hld | ERC | ERA |
| 2013 | Wilmg* | A+ | 1 | 0 | 0 | 0 | 2.0 | 7 | 1 | 0 | 0 | 0 | 0 | 0 | 0 | 0 | 0 | 5 | 1 | 0 | 0 | 0 | - | 0 | 0-- | - | 0.54 | 0.00 |
| 2009 | TB | AL | 6 | 6 | 1 | 0 | 36.1 | 150 | 33 | 19 | 15 | 2 | 0 | 0 | 0 | 13 | 1 | 36 | 1 | 0 | 2 | 2 | .500 | 1 | 0-0 | 0 | 3.12 | 3.72 |
| 2010 | TB | AL | 29 | 29 | 0 | 0 | 168.0 | 722 | 165 | 77 | 76 | 24 | 3 | 6 | 5 | 62 | 2 | 113 | 4 | 0 | 12 | 10 | .545 | 0 | 0-0 | 0 | 4.25 | 4.07 |
| 2011 | TB | AL | 29 | 29 | 1 | 0 | 184.0 | 795 | 190 | 96 | 91 | 23 | 5 | 7 | 8 | 63 | 1 | 105 | 6 | 0 | 11 | 10 | .524 | 0 | 0-0 | 0 | 4.38 | 4.45 |
| 2012 | TB | AL | 54 | 0 | 0 | 15 | 70.1 | 284 | 48 | 20 | 19 | 5 | 0 | 1 | 0 | 29 | 2 | 87 | 2 | 0 | 3 | 0 | 1.000 | 0 | 0-1 | 6 | 2.25 | 2.43 |
| 2013 | KC | AL | 31 | 24 | 0 | 2 | 135.1 | 618 | 169 | 89 | 80 | 15 | 1 | 5 | 4 | 58 | 2 | 114 | 7 | 0 | 8 | 11 | .421 | 0 | 0-0 | 0 | 5.88 | 5.32 |
| Postseason | | | 3 | 1 | 0 | 2 | 7.1 | 33 | 8 | 2 | 2 | 1 | 0 | 0 | 0 | 4 | 0 | 8 | 0 | 0 | 1 | 0 | 1.000 | 0 | 0-0 | 0 | 5.52 | 2.45 |
| 5 ML YEARS | | | 149 | 88 | 2 | 17 | 594.0 | 2569 | 605 | 301 | 281 | 69 | 9 | 19 | 17 | 225 | 8 | 455 | 20 | 0 | 36 | 33 | .522 | 1 | 0-1 | 6 | 4.31 | 4.26 |

# Alejandro De Aza

**Bats:** L **Throws:** L **Pos:** CF-107;LF-79;PH-4;PR-2 day-AH-zah **Ht:** 6'0" **Wt:** 190 **Born:** 4/11/1984 **Age:** 30

| BATTING | | | | | | | | | | | | | | | | | | | | | BASERUNNING | | | | AVERAGES | | |
|---|---|---|---|---|---|---|---|---|---|---|---|---|---|---|---|---|---|---|---|---|---|---|---|---|---|---|---|
| Year | Team | Lg | G | AB | H | 2B | 3B | HR | (Hm | Rd) | TB | R | RBI | RC | TBB | IBB | SO | HBP | SH | SF | SB | CS | SB% | GDP | Avg | OBP | Slg |
| 2007 | Fla | NL | 45 | 144 | 33 | 8 | 2 | 0 | (0 | 0) | 45 | 14 | 8 | 11 | 6 | 1 | 37 | 1 | 5 | 2 | 2 | 0 | 1.00 | 2 | .229 | .261 | .313 |
| 2009 | Fla | NL | 22 | 20 | 5 | 1 | 0 | 0 | (0 | 0) | 6 | 6 | 3 | 4 | 5 | 0 | 5 | 0 | 1 | 1 | 0 | 0 | - | 0 | .250 | .385 | .300 |
| 2010 | CWS | AL | 19 | 30 | 9 | 3 | 0 | 0 | (0 | 0) | 12 | 7 | 2 | 4 | 1 | 0 | 4 | 0 | 1 | 0 | 2 | 1 | .67 | 0 | .300 | .323 | .400 |
| 2011 | CWS | AL | 54 | 152 | 50 | 11 | 3 | 4 | (2 | 2) | 79 | 29 | 23 | 34 | 17 | 1 | 34 | 1 | 1 | 0 | 12 | 5 | .71 | 2 | .329 | .400 | .520 |
| 2012 | CWS | AL | 131 | 524 | 147 | 29 | 6 | 9 | (2 | 7) | 215 | 81 | 50 | 79 | 47 | 3 | 109 | 9 | 4 | 1 | 26 | 12 | .68 | 1 | .281 | .349 | .410 |
| 2013 | CWS | AL | 153 | 607 | 160 | 27 | 4 | 17 | (4 | 13) | 246 | 84 | 62 | 82 | 50 | 1 | 147 | 6 | 6 | 6 | 20 | 8 | .71 | 8 | .264 | .323 | .405 |
| 6 ML YEARS | | | 424 | 1477 | 404 | 79 | 15 | 30 | (8 | 22) | 603 | 221 | 148 | 214 | 126 | 6 | 336 | 17 | 18 | 10 | 62 | 26 | .70 | 13 | .274 | .336 | .408 |

# Justin De Fratus

**Pitches:** R **Bats:** B **Pos:** RP-58 duh-FRAY-tiss **Ht:** 6'4" **Wt:** 220 **Born:** 10/21/1987 **Age:** 26

| HOW MUCH HE PITCHED | | | | | | | | | WHAT HE GAVE UP | | | | | | | | | | | | THE RESULTS | | | | | | | | |
|---|---|---|---|---|---|---|---|---|---|---|---|---|---|---|---|---|---|---|---|---|---|---|---|---|---|---|---|---|
| Year Team | Lg | G | GS | CG | GF | IP | BFP | H | R | ER | HR | SH | SF | HB | TBB | IBB | SO | WP | Bk | W | L | Pct | Sh | Sv-Op | Hld | ERC | ERA |
| 2013 LV* | AAA | 13 | 0 | 0 | 6 | 19.0 | 81 | 18 | 5 | 4 | 0 | 5 | 1 | 2 | 6 | 0 | 17 | 2 | 0 | 3 | 0 | 1.000 | 0 | 0- - | - | 3.18 | 1.89 |
| 2011 Phi | NL | 5 | 0 | 0 | 2 | 4.0 | 17 | 1 | 2 | 1 | 0 | 1 | 0 | 1 | 3 | 1 | 3 | 1 | 0 | 1 | 0 | 1.000 | 0 | 0-0 | 0 | 1.39 | 2.25 |
| 2012 Phi | NL | 13 | 0 | 0 | 2 | 10.2 | 44 | 7 | 5 | 4 | 0 | 0 | 0 | 0 | 5 | 1 | 8 | 1 | 0 | 0 | 0 | - | 0 | 0-0 | 5 | 1.75 | 3.38 |
| 2013 Phi | NL | 58 | 0 | 0 | 12 | 46.2 | 208 | 45 | 21 | 20 | 3 | 2 | 2 | 5 | 25 | 3 | 42 | 6 | 0 | 3 | 3 | .500 | 0 | 0-1 | 9 | 4.50 | 3.86 |
| 3 ML YEARS | | 76 | 0 | 0 | 16 | 61.1 | 269 | 53 | 28 | 25 | 3 | 3 | 2 | 6 | 33 | 5 | 53 | 8 | 0 | 4 | 3 | .571 | 0 | 0-1 | 14 | 3.73 | 3.67 |

# Dane de la Rosa

**Pitches:** R **Bats:** R **Pos:** RP-75 **Ht:** 6'7" **Wt:** 245 **Born:** 2/1/1983 **Age:** 31

| HOW MUCH HE PITCHED | | | | | | | | | WHAT HE GAVE UP | | | | | | | | | | | | THE RESULTS | | | | | | | | |
|---|---|---|---|---|---|---|---|---|---|---|---|---|---|---|---|---|---|---|---|---|---|---|---|---|---|---|---|---|
| Year Team | Lg | G | GS | CG | GF | IP | BFP | H | R | ER | HR | SH | SF | HB | TBB | IBB | SO | WP | Bk | W | L | Pct | Sh | Sv-Op | Hld | ERC | ERA |
| 2013 Salt Lk* | AAA | 3 | 0 | 0 | 1 | 3.1 | 12 | 1 | 1 | 1 | 0 | 1 | 0 | 0 | 2 | 0 | 1 | 0 | 0 | 1 | 0 | 1.000 | 0 | 1- - | - | 1.13 | 2.70 |
| 2011 TB | AL | 7 | 0 | 0 | 2 | 7.1 | 34 | 10 | 8 | 8 | 1 | 0 | 0 | 0 | 3 | 0 | 8 | 1 | 0 | 0 | 0 | - | 0 | 0-0 | 0 | 6.62 | 9.82 |
| 2012 TB | AL | 5 | 0 | 0 | 5 | 5.0 | 22 | 7 | 7 | 7 | 2 | 0 | 0 | 0 | 2 | 0 | 5 | 0 | 0 | 0 | 0 | - | 0 | 0-0 | 0 | 9.62 | 12.60 |
| 2013 LAA | AL | 75 | 0 | 0 | 20 | 72.1 | 291 | 56 | 25 | 23 | 3 | 2 | 4 | 1 | 28 | 2 | 65 | 6 | 0 | 6 | 1 | .857 | 0 | 2-5 | 20 | 2.53 | 2.86 |
| 3 ML YEARS | | 87 | 0 | 0 | 27 | 84.2 | 347 | 73 | 40 | 38 | 6 | 2 | 4 | 1 | 33 | 2 | 78 | 7 | 0 | 6 | 1 | .857 | 0 | 2-5 | 20 | 3.18 | 4.04 |

# Eury De la Rosa

**Pitches:** L **Bats:** L **Pos:** RP-19 YURR-ee **Ht:** 5'9" **Wt:** 165 **Born:** 2/24/1990 **Age:** 24

| HOW MUCH HE PITCHED | | | | | | | | | WHAT HE GAVE UP | | | | | | | | | | | | THE RESULTS | | | | | | | | |
|---|---|---|---|---|---|---|---|---|---|---|---|---|---|---|---|---|---|---|---|---|---|---|---|---|---|---|---|---|
| Year Team | Lg | G | GS | CG | GF | IP | BFP | H | R | ER | HR | SH | SF | HB | TBB | IBB | SO | WP | Bk | W | L | Pct | Sh | Sv-Op | Hld | ERC | ERA |
| 2009 Msoula | R+ | 14 | 4 | 0 | 2 | 37.0 | 175 | 47 | 28 | 22 | 5 | 0 | 1 | 3 | 16 | 0 | 32 | 3 | 1 | 0 | 2 | .000 | 0 | 0- - | - | 6.35 | 5.35 |
| 2010 Yakima | A- | 27 | 0 | 0 | 12 | 45.0 | 180 | 23 | 10 | 5 | 0 | 2 | 1 | 8 | 14 | 0 | 56 | 1 | 0 | 1 | 1 | .500 | 0 | 9- - | - | 1.43 | 1.00 |
| 2011 Sbend | A | 39 | 0 | 0 | 23 | 53.0 | 206 | 36 | 11 | 8 | 3 | 2 | 3 | 5 | 13 | 1 | 51 | 5 | 1 | 1 | 0 | 1.000 | 0 | 10- - | - | 1.98 | 1.36 |
| 2011 Visalia | A+ | 1 | 0 | 0 | 0 | 1.0 | 5 | 1 | 0 | 0 | 0 | 0 | 0 | 0 | 1 | 0 | 1 | 0 | 0 | 0 | 0 | - | 0 | 0- - | - | 5.48 | 0.00 |
| 2011 Reno | AAA | 1 | 0 | 0 | 0 | 1.0 | 6 | 3 | 2 | 2 | 0 | 0 | 0 | 0 | 1 | 0 | 1 | 1 | 0 | 0 | 0 | - | 0 | 0- - | - | 22.91 | 18.00 |
| 2012 Mobile | AA | 53 | 0 | 0 | 13 | 63.1 | 249 | 47 | 20 | 20 | 3 | 1 | 1 | 2 | 17 | 1 | 68 | 5 | 0 | 4 | 4 | .500 | 0 | 8- - | - | 2.07 | 2.84 |
| 2013 Reno | AAA | 44 | 0 | 0 | 13 | 49.2 | 225 | 52 | 33 | 29 | 6 | 3 | 2 | 2 | 27 | 2 | 49 | 2 | 1 | 3 | 5 | .375 | 0 | 0- - | - | 5.17 | 5.26 |
| 2013 Ari | NL | 19 | 0 | 0 | 6 | 14.2 | 62 | 13 | 13 | 12 | 5 | 1 | 0 | 0 | 5 | 0 | 16 | 1 | 0 | 0 | 1 | .000 | 0 | 0-0 | 2 | 4.70 | 7.36 |

# Jorge de la Rosa

**Pitches:** L **Bats:** L **Pos:** SP-30 **Ht:** 6'1" **Wt:** 220 **Born:** 4/5/1981 **Age:** 33

| HOW MUCH HE PITCHED | | | | | | | | | WHAT HE GAVE UP | | | | | | | | | | | | THE RESULTS | | | | | | | | |
|---|---|---|---|---|---|---|---|---|---|---|---|---|---|---|---|---|---|---|---|---|---|---|---|---|---|---|---|---|
| Year Team | Lg | G | GS | CG | GF | IP | BFP | H | R | ER | HR | SH | SF | HB | TBB | IBB | SO | WP | Bk | W | L | Pct | Sh | Sv-Op | Hld | ERC | ERA |
| 2004 Mil | NL | 5 | 5 | 0 | 0 | 22.2 | 113 | 29 | 20 | 16 | 1 | 1 | 3 | 1 | 14 | 0 | 5 | 3 | 0 | 0 | 3 | .000 | 0 | 0-0 | 0 | 6.12 | 6.35 |
| 2005 Mil | NL | 38 | 0 | 0 | 13 | 42.1 | 208 | 48 | 23 | 21 | 1 | 2 | 2 | 0 | 38 | 4 | 42 | 6 | 0 | 2 | 2 | .500 | 0 | 0-2 | 5 | 6.04 | 4.46 |
| 2006 2 Tms | | 28 | 13 | 0 | 4 | 79.0 | 367 | 81 | 59 | 57 | 14 | 2 | 4 | 2 | 54 | 1 | 67 | 6 | 1 | 5 | 6 | .455 | 0 | 0-0 | 1 | 6.05 | 6.49 |
| 2007 KC | AL | 26 | 23 | 0 | 1 | 130.0 | 589 | 160 | 88 | 84 | 20 | 2 | 4 | 3 | 53 | 6 | 82 | 4 | 1 | 8 | 12 | .400 | 0 | 0-0 | 0 | 5.93 | 5.82 |
| 2008 Col | NL | 28 | 23 | 0 | 0 | 130.0 | 571 | 128 | 77 | 71 | 13 | 6 | 7 | 7 | 62 | 3 | 128 | 14 | 1 | 10 | 8 | .556 | 0 | 0-0 | 0 | 4.50 | 4.92 |
| 2009 Col | NL | 33 | 32 | 0 | 0 | 185.0 | 799 | 172 | 95 | 90 | 20 | 11 | 6 | 9 | 83 | 3 | 193 | 12 | 1 | 16 | 9 | .640 | 0 | 0-0 | 0 | 4.11 | 4.38 |
| 2010 Col | NL | 20 | 20 | 0 | 0 | 121.2 | 512 | 105 | 62 | 57 | 15 | 3 | 3 | 5 | 55 | 4 | 113 | 9 | 1 | 8 | 7 | .533 | 0 | 0-0 | 0 | 3.86 | 4.22 |
| 2011 Col | NL | 10 | 10 | 1 | 0 | 59.0 | 245 | 48 | 25 | 23 | 4 | 4 | 1 | 2 | 22 | 0 | 52 | 6 | 1 | 5 | 2 | .714 | 0 | 0-0 | 0 | 2.88 | 3.51 |
| 2012 Col | NL | 3 | 3 | 0 | 0 | 10.2 | 53 | 17 | 14 | 11 | 5 | 1 | 0 | 0 | 2 | 0 | 6 | 2 | 0 | 0 | 2 | .000 | 0 | 0-0 | 0 | 9.22 | 9.28 |
| 2013 Col | NL | 30 | 30 | 0 | 0 | 167.2 | 714 | 170 | 70 | 65 | 11 | 11 | 5 | 5 | 62 | 5 | 112 | 5 | 0 | 16 | 6 | .727 | 0 | 0-0 | 0 | 3.92 | 3.49 |
| 06 Mil | NL | 18 | 3 | 0 | 4 | 30.1 | 146 | 32 | 30 | 29 | 4 | 1 | 3 | 1 | 22 | 1 | 31 | 4 | 0 | 2 | 2 | .500 | 0 | 0-0 | 1 | 5.90 | 8.60 |
| 06 KC | AL | 10 | 10 | 0 | 0 | 48.2 | 221 | 49 | 29 | 28 | 10 | 1 | 1 | 1 | 32 | 0 | 36 | 2 | 1 | 3 | 4 | .429 | 0 | 0-0 | 0 | 6.14 | 5.18 |
| 10 ML YEARS | | 221 | 159 | 1 | 18 | 948.0 | 4171 | 958 | 533 | 495 | 104 | 43 | 35 | 34 | 445 | 26 | 800 | 67 | 6 | 70 | 57 | .551 | 0 | 0-2 | 6 | 4.60 | 4.70 |

# Rubby de la Rosa

**Pitches:** R **Bats:** R **Pos:** RP-11 ROO-bee **Ht:** 6'1" **Wt:** 205 **Born:** 3/4/1989 **Age:** 25

| HOW MUCH HE PITCHED | | | | | | | | | WHAT HE GAVE UP | | | | | | | | | | | | THE RESULTS | | | | | | | | |
|---|---|---|---|---|---|---|---|---|---|---|---|---|---|---|---|---|---|---|---|---|---|---|---|---|---|---|---|---|
| Year Team | Lg | G | GS | CG | GF | IP | BFP | H | R | ER | HR | SH | SF | HB | TBB | IBB | SO | WP | Bk | W | L | Pct | Sh | Sv-Op | Hld | ERC | ERA |
| 2013 Pwtckt* | AAA | 24 | 20 | 0 | 0 | 80.1 | 351 | 65 | 40 | 38 | 9 | 3 | 3 | 7 | 48 | 0 | 76 | 1 | 0 | 3 | 3 | .500 | 0 | 0- - | - | 4.24 | 4.26 |
| 2011 LAD | NL | 13 | 10 | 0 | 2 | 60.2 | 254 | 54 | 26 | 25 | 6 | 2 | 0 | 0 | 31 | 3 | 60 | 3 | 0 | 4 | 5 | .444 | 0 | 0-1 | 1 | 3.94 | 3.71 |
| 2012 LAD | NL | 1 | 0 | 0 | 0 | 0.2 | 4 | 0 | 2 | 2 | 0 | 0 | 0 | 0 | 2 | 0 | 0 | 0 | 0 | 0 | 0 | - | 0 | 0-0 | 0 | 7.00 | 27.00 |
| 2013 Bos | AL | 11 | 0 | 0 | 7 | 11.1 | 53 | 15 | 7 | 7 | 2 | 0 | 0 | 3 | 2 | 0 | 6 | 1 | 0 | 0 | 2 | .000 | 0 | 0-0 | 0 | 6.76 | 5.56 |
| 3 ML YEARS | | 25 | 10 | 0 | 9 | 72.2 | 311 | 69 | 35 | 34 | 8 | 2 | 0 | 3 | 35 | 3 | 66 | 4 | 0 | 4 | 7 | .364 | 0 | 0-1 | 1 | 4.39 | 4.21 |

# Jose De La Torre

**Pitches:** R **Bats:** R **Pos:** RP-7 **Ht:** 5'10" **Wt:** 185 **Born:** 10/17/1985 **Age:** 28

| HOW MUCH HE PITCHED | | | | | | | | | WHAT HE GAVE UP | | | | | | | | | | | | THE RESULTS | | | | | | | | |
|---|---|---|---|---|---|---|---|---|---|---|---|---|---|---|---|---|---|---|---|---|---|---|---|---|---|---|---|---|
| Year Team | Lg | G | GS | CG | GF | IP | BFP | H | R | ER | HR | SH | SF | HB | TBB | IBB | SO | WP | Bk | W | L | Pct | Sh | Sv-Op | Hld | ERC | ERA |
| 2009 StLuci | A+ | 26 | 0 | 0 | 10 | 39.0 | 170 | 33 | 16 | 12 | 1 | 4 | 2 | 3 | 17 | 2 | 35 | 4 | 1 | 3 | 3 | .500 | 0 | 3- - | - | 2.99 | 2.77 |
| 2009 Bnghtn | AA | 18 | 0 | 0 | 8 | 30.1 | 134 | 23 | 14 | 9 | 1 | 1 | 0 | 1 | 17 | 2 | 37 | 1 | 0 | 3 | 2 | .600 | 0 | 2- - | - | 2.81 | 2.67 |
| 2010 Bnghtn | AA | 15 | 0 | 0 | 6 | 22.0 | 90 | 16 | 5 | 5 | 0 | 1 | 0 | 1 | 12 | 0 | 22 | 1 | 1 | 0 | 0 | - | 0 | 2- - | - | 2.76 | 2.05 |
| 2010 Buffalo | AAA | 36 | 0 | 0 | 13 | 48.1 | 207 | 36 | 21 | 16 | 5 | 4 | 0 | 4 | 22 | 1 | 58 | 2 | 0 | 3 | 2 | .600 | 0 | 1- - | - | 3.14 | 2.98 |
| 2011 Buffalo | AAA | 16 | 0 | 0 | 4 | 20.1 | 87 | 14 | 5 | 2 | 0 | 0 | 2 | 1 | 12 | 2 | 17 | 4 | 0 | 2 | 2 | .500 | 0 | 0- - | - | 2.43 | 0.89 |
| 2011 Mets | R | 5 | 5 | 0 | 0 | 4.0 | 21 | 4 | 3 | 1 | 0 | 0 | 0 | 2 | 3 | 0 | 6 | 0 | 0 | 0 | 0 | - | 0 | 0- - | - | 6.45 | 2.25 |
| 2011 Bklyn | A- | 2 | 0 | 0 | 0 | 3.0 | 12 | 2 | 0 | 0 | 0 | 0 | 0 | 0 | 1 | 0 | 6 | 0 | 0 | 0 | 0 | - | 0 | 0- - | - | 1.57 | 0.00 |
| 2012 Akron | AA | 27 | 1 | 0 | 8 | 45.0 | 179 | 33 | 16 | 14 | 0 | 1 | 2 | 1 | 19 | 0 | 42 | 6 | 1 | 7 | 1 | .875 | 0 | 2- - | - | 2.29 | 2.80 |

| HOW MUCH HE PITCHED | | | | | | | | WHAT HE GAVE UP | | | | | | | | | | | | THE RESULTS | | | | | | | |
|---|---|---|---|---|---|---|---|---|---|---|---|---|---|---|---|---|---|---|---|---|---|---|---|---|---|---|---|
| Year | Team | Lg | G | GS | CG | GF | IP | BFP | H | R | ER | HR | SH | SF | HB | TBB | IBB | SO | WP | Bk | W | L | Pct | Sh | Sv-Op | Hld | ERC | ERA |
| 2012 | Clmbs | AAA | 7 | 0 | 0 | 3 | 10.2 | 42 | 9 | 4 | 4 | 0 | 0 | 1 | 1 | 2 | 0 | 16 | 1 | 0 | 1 | 0 | 1.000 | 0 | 0-- | - | 2.27 | 3.38 |
| 2012 | Pwtckt | AAA | 12 | 0 | 0 | 7 | 18.1 | 70 | 15 | 5 | 5 | 2 | 0 | 1 | 0 | 3 | 0 | 16 | 1 | 0 | 1 | 0 | 1.000 | 0 | 2-- | - | 2.38 | 2.45 |
| 2013 | Pwtckt | AAA | 34 | 0 | 0 | 9 | 52.1 | 216 | 35 | 18 | 16 | 2 | 0 | 2 | 0 | 27 | 1 | 59 | 3 | 0 | 5 | 1 | .833 | 0 | 1-- | - | 2.33 | 2.75 |
| 2013 | Bos | AL | 7 | 0 | 0 | 5 | 11.1 | 53 | 10 | 8 | 8 | 2 | 0 | 1 | 1 | 10 | 0 | 15 | 0 | 0 | 0 | 0 | - | 0 | 0-0 | 0 | 6.43 | 6.35 |

## Jorge De Leon

**Pitches:** R **Bats:** R **Pos:** RP-11 day-lee-OWN **Ht:** 6'0" **Wt:** 185 **Born:** 8/15/1987 **Age:** 26

| HOW MUCH HE PITCHED | | | | | | | | WHAT HE GAVE UP | | | | | | | | | | | | THE RESULTS | | | | | | | |
|---|---|---|---|---|---|---|---|---|---|---|---|---|---|---|---|---|---|---|---|---|---|---|---|---|---|---|---|
| Year | Team | Lg | G | GS | CG | GF | IP | BFP | H | R | ER | HR | SH | SF | HB | TBB | IBB | SO | WP | Bk | W | L | Pct | Sh | Sv-Op | Hld | ERC | ERA |
| 2010 | TriCity | A- | 23 | 0 | 0 | 20 | 28.0 | 121 | 26 | 5 | 2 | 0 | 3 | 0 | 1 | 12 | 2 | 29 | 2 | 0 | 2 | 1 | .667 | 0 | 6-- | - | 3.09 | 0.64 |
| 2011 | Lxngtn | A | 43 | 0 | 0 | 35 | 55.1 | 229 | 48 | 29 | 21 | 5 | 1 | 1 | 1 | 13 | 1 | 51 | 5 | 2 | 6 | 4 | .600 | 0 | 16-- | - | 2.66 | 3.42 |
| 2012 | Lancst | A+ | 40 | 14 | 0 | 16 | 87.2 | 418 | 116 | 88 | 75 | 11 | 3 | 5 | 4 | 44 | 1 | 60 | 9 | 0 | 2 | 9 | .182 | 0 | 6-- | - | 6.80 | 7.70 |
| 2013 | CpChr | AA | 29 | 3 | 0 | 13 | 52.2 | 206 | 42 | 26 | 25 | 7 | 1 | 2 | 2 | 15 | 1 | 36 | 3 | 0 | 0 | 3 | .000 | 0 | 6-- | - | 3.01 | 4.27 |
| 2013 | OKCity | AAA | 12 | 0 | 0 | 8 | 15.0 | 55 | 8 | 1 | 1 | 0 | 0 | 0 | 0 | 2 | 0 | 12 | 0 | 0 | 0 | 0 | - | 0 | 6-- | - | 0.82 | 0.60 |
| 2013 | Hou | AL | 11 | 0 | 0 | 7 | 10.0 | 50 | 12 | 7 | 6 | 1 | 0 | 1 | 1 | 7 | 1 | 6 | 2 | 0 | 0 | 1 | .000 | 0 | 0-0 | 1 | 6.56 | 5.40 |

## Jaff Decker

**Bats:** L **Throws:** L **Pos:** LF-8;PH-4;PR-1 JEFF **Ht:** 5'10" **Wt:** 190 **Born:** 2/23/1990 **Age:** 24

| BATTING | | | | | | | | | | | | | | | | | | | | | BASERUNNING | | | | AVERAGES | | |
|---|---|---|---|---|---|---|---|---|---|---|---|---|---|---|---|---|---|---|---|---|---|---|---|---|---|---|---|
| Year | Team | Lg | G | AB | H | 2B | 3B | HR | (Hm | Rd) | TB | R | RBI | RC | TBB | IBB | SO | HBP | SH | SF | SB | CS | SB% | GDP | Avg | OBP | Slg |
| 2009 | FtWyn | A | 104 | 358 | 107 | 25 | 2 | 16 | (- | -) | 184 | 78 | 64 | 85 | 85 | 5 | 92 | 9 | 0 | 3 | 10 | 6 | .63 | 6 | .299 | .442 | .514 |
| 2010 | Lk Els | A+ | 79 | 290 | 76 | 14 | 2 | 17 | (- | -) | 145 | 53 | 58 | 56 | 47 | 3 | 80 | 7 | 0 | 4 | 5 | 4 | .56 | 3 | .262 | .374 | .500 |
| 2011 | SnAnt | AA | 133 | 496 | 117 | 29 | 2 | 19 | (- | -) | 207 | 90 | 92 | 87 | 103 | 7 | 145 | 8 | 1 | 5 | 15 | 5 | .75 | 11 | .236 | .373 | .417 |
| 2012 | SnAnt | AA | 47 | 147 | 27 | 3 | 2 | 3 | (- | -) | 43 | 30 | 9 | 20 | 40 | 2 | 37 | 2 | 1 | 0 | 6 | 2 | .75 | 2 | .184 | .365 | .293 |
| 2012 | Padres | R | 9 | 27 | 8 | 1 | 2 | 1 | (- | -) | 16 | 5 | 7 | 6 | 4 | 0 | 3 | 1 | 0 | 1 | 0 | 0 | - | 1 | .296 | .394 | .593 |
| 2013 | Tucsn | AAA | 105 | 350 | 100 | 23 | 1 | 10 | (- | -) | 155 | 63 | 40 | 61 | 55 | 1 | 94 | 1 | 6 | 3 | 4 | 6 | .40 | 8 | .286 | .381 | .443 |
| 2013 | SD | NL | 13 | 26 | 4 | 0 | 0 | 1 | (0 | 1) | 7 | 3 | 2 | 0 | 3 | 0 | 4 | 0 | 1 | 1 | 0 | 1 | .00 | 0 | .154 | .233 | .269 |

## Samuel Deduno

**Pitches:** R **Bats:** R **Pos:** SP-18 deh-DUE-noh **Ht:** 6'3" **Wt:** 190 **Born:** 7/2/1983 **Age:** 30

| HOW MUCH HE PITCHED | | | | | | | | WHAT HE GAVE UP | | | | | | | | | | | | THE RESULTS | | | | | | | |
|---|---|---|---|---|---|---|---|---|---|---|---|---|---|---|---|---|---|---|---|---|---|---|---|---|---|---|---|
| Year | Team | Lg | G | GS | CG | GF | IP | BFP | H | R | ER | HR | SH | SF | HB | TBB | IBB | SO | WP | Bk | W | L | Pct | Sh | Sv-Op | Hld | ERC | ERA |
| 2013 | Roch* | AAA | 3 | 3 | 0 | 0 | 16.2 | 69 | 14 | 6 | 5 | 1 | 0 | 0 | 0 | 10 | 0 | 17 | 2 | 0 | 0 | 0 | - | 0 | 0-- | - | 3.89 | 2.70 |
| 2010 | Col | NL | 4 | 0 | 0 | 3 | 2.2 | 12 | 3 | 1 | 1 | 1 | 0 | 0 | 0 | 1 | 0 | 3 | 0 | 0 | 0 | 0 | - | 0 | 0-0 | 1 | 6.59 | 3.38 |
| 2011 | SD | NL | 2 | 0 | 0 | 0 | 3.0 | 17 | 5 | 1 | 1 | 0 | 0 | 0 | 0 | 3 | 1 | 4 | 1 | 0 | 0 | 0 | - | 0 | 0-0 | 0 | 8.91 | 3.00 |
| 2012 | Min | AL | 15 | 15 | 0 | 0 | 79.0 | 347 | 69 | 40 | 39 | 10 | 1 | 2 | 5 | 53 | 0 | 57 | 5 | 0 | 6 | 5 | .545 | 0 | 0-0 | 0 | 5.03 | 4.44 |
| 2013 | Min | AL | 18 | 18 | 0 | 0 | 108.0 | 461 | 105 | 48 | 46 | 7 | 3 | 3 | 9 | 41 | 0 | 67 | 8 | **2** | 8 | 8 | .500 | 0 | 0-0 | 0 | 3.99 | 3.83 |
| 4 ML YEARS | | | 39 | 33 | 0 | 3 | 192.2 | 837 | 182 | 90 | 87 | 18 | 4 | 5 | 14 | 98 | 1 | 131 | 14 | 2 | 14 | 13 | .519 | 0 | 0-0 | 1 | 4.52 | 4.06 |

## David DeJesus

**Bats:** L **Throws:** L **Pos:** CF-81;LF-30;PH-25;RF-6;PR-1 da-HAY-soos **Ht:** 5'11" **Wt:** 190 **Born:** 12/20/1979 **Age:** 34

| BATTING | | | | | | | | | | | | | | | | | | | | | BASERUNNING | | | | AVERAGES | | |
|---|---|---|---|---|---|---|---|---|---|---|---|---|---|---|---|---|---|---|---|---|---|---|---|---|---|---|---|
| Year | Team | Lg | G | AB | H | 2B | 3B | HR | (Hm | Rd) | TB | R | RBI | RC | TBB | IBB | SO | HBP | SH | SF | SB | CS | SB% | GDP | Avg | OBP | Slg |
| 2013 | Cubs* | R | 4 | 12 | 4 | 2 | 0 | 0 | (- | -) | 6 | 4 | 0 | 2 | 2 | 0 | 3 | 0 | 0 | 0 | 1 | 0 | 1.00 | 1 | .333 | .429 | .500 |
| 2003 | KC | AL | 12 | 7 | 2 | 0 | 1 | 0 | (0 | 0) | 4 | 0 | 0 | 2 | 1 | 0 | 2 | 1 | 1 | 0 | 0 | 0 | - | 0 | .286 | .444 | .571 |
| 2004 | KC | AL | 96 | 363 | 104 | 15 | 3 | 7 | (2 | 5) | 146 | 58 | 39 | 53 | 33 | 0 | 53 | 9 | 8 | 0 | 8 | 11 | .42 | 6 | .287 | .360 | .402 |
| 2005 | KC | AL | 122 | 461 | 135 | 31 | 6 | 9 | (6 | 3) | 205 | 69 | 56 | 77 | 42 | 1 | 76 | 9 | 5 | 6 | 5 | 5 | .50 | 6 | .293 | .359 | .445 |
| 2006 | KC | AL | 119 | 491 | 145 | 36 | 7 | 8 | (4 | 4) | 219 | 83 | 56 | 76 | 43 | 4 | 70 | 12 | 2 | 4 | 6 | 3 | .67 | 10 | .295 | .364 | .446 |
| 2007 | KC | AL | 157 | 605 | 157 | 29 | 9 | 7 | (3 | 4) | 225 | 101 | 58 | 87 | 64 | 7 | 83 | **23** | 7 | 4 | 10 | 4 | .71 | 10 | .260 | .351 | .372 |
| 2008 | KC | AL | 135 | 518 | 159 | 25 | 7 | 12 | (6 | 6) | 234 | 70 | 73 | 93 | 46 | 3 | 71 | 5 | 4 | 4 | 11 | 8 | .58 | 10 | .307 | .366 | .452 |
| 2009 | KC | AL | 144 | 558 | 157 | 28 | 9 | 13 | (4 | 9) | 242 | 74 | 71 | 83 | 51 | 0 | 87 | 8 | 5 | 5 | 4 | 9 | .31 | 10 | .281 | .347 | .434 |
| 2010 | KC | AL | 91 | 352 | 112 | 23 | 3 | 5 | (2 | 3) | 156 | 46 | 37 | 50 | 34 | 2 | 47 | 4 | 3 | 1 | 3 | 3 | .50 | 10 | .318 | .384 | .443 |
| 2011 | Oak | AL | 131 | 442 | 106 | 20 | 5 | 10 | (4 | 6) | 166 | 60 | 46 | 49 | 45 | 1 | 86 | 11 | 4 | 4 | 4 | 3 | .57 | 14 | .240 | .323 | .376 |
| 2012 | ChC | NL | 148 | 506 | 133 | 28 | 8 | 9 | (4 | 5) | 204 | 76 | 50 | 73 | 61 | 1 | 89 | 9 | 2 | 4 | 7 | 8 | .47 | 9 | .263 | .350 | .403 |
| 2013 | 3 Tms | | 122 | 391 | 98 | 29 | 3 | 8 | (5 | 3) | 157 | 52 | 38 | 51 | 39 | 0 | 79 | 6 | 2 | 1 | 5 | 3 | .63 | 6 | .251 | .327 | .402 |
| 13 | ChC | NL | 84 | 284 | 71 | 19 | 3 | 6 | (4 | 2) | 114 | 39 | 27 | 40 | 29 | 0 | 55 | 5 | 0 | 0 | 3 | 0 | 1.00 | 3 | .250 | .330 | .401 |
| 13 | Was | NL | 3 | 3 | 0 | 0 | 0 | 0 | (0 | 0) | 0 | 0 | 0 | 0 | 0 | 0 | 1 | 0 | 1 | 0 | 0 | 0 | - | 0 | .000 | .000 | .000 |
| 13 | TB | AL | 35 | 104 | 27 | 10 | 0 | 2 | (1 | 1) | 43 | 13 | 11 | 11 | 10 | 0 | 23 | 1 | 1 | 1 | 2 | 3 | .40 | 3 | .260 | .328 | .413 |
| 11 ML YEARS | | | 1277 | 4694 | 1308 | 264 | 61 | 88 | (40 | 48) | 1958 | 689 | 524 | 694 | 459 | 19 | 743 | 97 | 43 | 33 | 63 | 57 | .53 | 91 | .279 | .353 | .417 |

## Steve Delabar

**Pitches:** R **Bats:** R **Pos:** RP-55 DELL-uh-bar **Ht:** 6'4" **Wt:** 230 **Born:** 7/17/1983 **Age:** 30

| HOW MUCH HE PITCHED | | | | | | | | WHAT HE GAVE UP | | | | | | | | | | | | THE RESULTS | | | | | | | |
|---|---|---|---|---|---|---|---|---|---|---|---|---|---|---|---|---|---|---|---|---|---|---|---|---|---|---|---|
| Year | Team | Lg | G | GS | CG | GF | IP | BFP | H | R | ER | HR | SH | SF | HB | TBB | IBB | SO | WP | Bk | W | L | Pct | Sh | Sv-Op | Hld | ERC | ERA |
| 2013 | B Jays* | R | 1 | 0 | 0 | 0 | 1.0 | 3 | 0 | 0 | 0 | 0 | 0 | 0 | 0 | 0 | 0 | 0 | 0 | 0 | 0 | 0 | - | 0 | 0-- | - | 0.00 | 0.00 |
| 2013 | Dnedin* | A+ | 1 | 0 | 0 | 0 | 1.0 | 3 | 0 | 0 | 0 | 0 | 0 | 0 | 0 | 0 | 0 | 0 | 0 | 0 | 0 | 0 | - | 0 | 0-- | - | 0.00 | 0.00 |
| 2011 | Sea | AL | 6 | 0 | 0 | 4 | 7.0 | 28 | 5 | 2 | 2 | 1 | 0 | 0 | 1 | 4 | 1 | 7 | 0 | 0 | 1 | 1 | .500 | 0 | 0-0 | 0 | 4.15 | 2.57 |
| 2012 | 2 Tms | AL | 61 | 0 | 0 | 12 | 66.0 | 274 | 46 | 29 | 28 | 12 | 3 | 2 | 5 | 26 | 1 | 92 | 6 | 0 | 4 | 3 | .571 | 0 | 0-2 | 12 | 3.18 | 3.82 |
| 2013 | Tor | AL | 55 | 0 | 0 | 14 | 58.2 | 253 | 50 | 25 | 21 | 4 | 3 | 3 | 2 | 29 | 5 | 82 | 4 | 1 | 5 | 5 | .500 | 0 | 1-6 | 6 | 3.38 | 3.22 |
| 12 | Sea | AL | 34 | 0 | 0 | 11 | 36.2 | 148 | 23 | 17 | 17 | 9 | 2 | 0 | 5 | 11 | 1 | 46 | 3 | 0 | 2 | 1 | .667 | 0 | 0-2 | 3 | 3.07 | 4.17 |
| 12 | Tor | AL | 27 | 0 | 0 | 1 | 29.1 | 126 | 23 | 12 | 11 | 3 | 1 | 2 | 0 | 15 | 0 | 46 | 3 | 0 | 2 | 2 | .500 | 0 | 0-0 | 9 | 3.27 | 3.38 |
| 3 ML YEARS | | | 122 | 0 | 0 | 30 | 131.2 | 555 | 101 | 56 | 51 | 17 | 6 | 5 | 8 | 59 | 7 | 181 | 10 | 1 | 10 | 9 | .526 | 0 | 1-8 | 18 | 3.33 | 3.49 |

# Randall Delgado

**Pitches:** R **Bats:** R **Pos:** SP-19; RP-1 **Ht:** 6'3" **Wt:** 200 **Born:** 2/9/1990 **Age:** 24

| HOW MUCH HE PITCHED | | | | | | | | WHAT HE GAVE UP | | | | | | | | | | | | THE RESULTS | | | | | | | |
|---|---|---|---|---|---|---|---|---|---|---|---|---|---|---|---|---|---|---|---|---|---|---|---|---|---|---|---|
| Year Team | Lg | G | GS | CG | GF | IP | BFP | H | R | ER | HR | SH | SF | HB | TBB | IBB | SO | WP | Bk | W | L | Pct | Sh | Sv-Op | Hld | ERC | ERA |
| 2013 Reno* | AAA | 13 | 13 | 0 | 0 | 64.0 | 295 | 69 | 46 | 42 | 9 | 2 | 0 | 4 | 35 | 0 | 57 | 4 | 0 | 2 | 5 | .286 | 0 | 0- - | - | 5.66 | 5.91 |
| 2011 Atl | NL | 7 | 7 | 0 | 0 | 35.0 | 147 | 29 | 12 | 11 | 5 | 0 | 0 | 1 | 14 | 1 | 18 | 2 | 0 | 1 | 1 | .500 | 0 | 0-0 | 0 | 3.48 | 2.83 |
| 2012 Atl | NL | 18 | 17 | 0 | 0 | 92.2 | 401 | 89 | 48 | 45 | 8 | 5 | 3 | 4 | 42 | 4 | 76 | 5 | 1 | 4 | 9 | .308 | 0 | 0-0 | 0 | 4.10 | 4.37 |
| 2013 Ari | NL | 20 | 19 | 1 | 0 | 116.1 | 473 | 116 | 59 | 55 | 24 | 5 | 5 | 1 | 23 | 2 | 79 | 3 | 1 | 5 | 7 | .417 | 1 | 0-0 | 0 | 4.03 | 4.26 |
| 3 ML YEARS | | 45 | 43 | 1 | 0 | 244.0 | 1021 | 234 | 119 | 111 | 37 | 10 | 8 | 6 | 79 | 7 | 173 | 10 | 2 | 10 | 17 | .370 | 1 | 0-0 | 0 | 4.00 | 4.09 |

# Ryan Dempster

**Pitches:** R **Bats:** R **Pos:** SP-29; RP-3 **Ht:** 6'2" **Wt:** 215 **Born:** 5/3/1977 **Age:** 37

| HOW MUCH HE PITCHED | | | | | | | | WHAT HE GAVE UP | | | | | | | | | | | | THE RESULTS | | | | | | | |
|---|---|---|---|---|---|---|---|---|---|---|---|---|---|---|---|---|---|---|---|---|---|---|---|---|---|---|---|
| Year Team | Lg | G | GS | CG | GF | IP | BFP | H | R | ER | HR | SH | SF | HB | TBB | IBB | SO | WP | Bk | W | L | Pct | Sh | Sv-Op | Hld | ERC | ERA |
| 1998 Fla | NL | 14 | 11 | 0 | 1 | 54.2 | 272 | 72 | 47 | 43 | 6 | 5 | 6 | 9 | 38 | 1 | 35 | 5 | 0 | 1 | 5 | .167 | 0 | 0-1 | 0 | 8.14 | 7.08 |
| 1999 Fla | NL | 25 | 25 | 0 | 0 | 147.0 | 666 | 146 | 77 | 77 | 21 | 3 | 6 | 6 | 93 | 2 | 126 | 8 | 0 | 7 | 8 | .467 | 0 | 0-0 | 0 | 5.49 | 4.71 |
| 2000 Fla | NL | 33 | 33 | 2 | 0 | 226.1 | 974 | 210 | 102 | 92 | 30 | 4 | 5 | 5 | 97 | 7 | 209 | 4 | 0 | 14 | 10 | .583 | 1 | 0-0 | 0 | 4.04 | 3.66 |
| 2001 Fla | NL | 34 | 34 | 2 | 0 | 211.1 | 954 | 218 | 123 | 116 | 21 | 15 | 7 | 10 | **112** | 5 | 171 | 5 | 0 | 15 | 12 | .556 | 1 | 0-0 | 0 | 4.91 | 4.94 |
| 2002 2 Tms | NL | 33 | 33 | 4 | 0 | 209.0 | 915 | 228 | 127 | 125 | 28 | 9 | 6 | 10 | 93 | 2 | 153 | 2 | 0 | 10 | 13 | .435 | 0 | 0-0 | 0 | 5.35 | 5.38 |
| 2003 Cin | NL | 22 | 20 | 0 | 1 | 115.2 | 545 | 134 | 89 | 84 | 14 | 9 | 4 | 5 | 70 | 4 | 84 | 3 | 0 | 3 | 7 | .300 | 0 | 0-0 | 0 | 6.11 | 6.54 |
| 2004 ChC | NL | 23 | 0 | 0 | 8 | 20.2 | 93 | 16 | 9 | 9 | 1 | 1 | 0 | 2 | 13 | 0 | 18 | 1 | 0 | 1 | 1 | .500 | 0 | 2-2 | 3 | 3.61 | 3.92 |
| 2005 ChC | NL | 63 | 6 | 0 | 53 | 92.0 | 401 | 83 | 35 | 32 | 4 | 5 | 0 | 4 | 49 | 7 | 89 | 4 | 0 | 5 | 3 | .625 | 0 | 33-35 | 0 | 3.69 | 3.13 |
| 2006 ChC | NL | 74 | 0 | 0 | 64 | 75.0 | 342 | 77 | 47 | 40 | 5 | 5 | 4 | 3 | 36 | 3 | 67 | 6 | 0 | 1 | 9 | .100 | 0 | 24-33 | 2 | 4.26 | 4.80 |
| 2007 ChC | NL | 66 | 0 | 0 | 58 | 66.2 | 282 | 59 | 36 | 35 | 8 | 3 | 2 | 1 | 30 | 4 | 55 | 2 | 1 | 2 | 7 | .222 | 0 | 28-31 | 0 | 3.77 | 4.73 |
| 2008 ChC | NL | 33 | 33 | 1 | 0 | 206.2 | 856 | 174 | 75 | 68 | 14 | 4 | 3 | 7 | 76 | 1 | 187 | 5 | 0 | 17 | 6 | .739 | 0 | 0-0 | 0 | 3.03 | 2.96 |
| 2009 ChC | NL | 31 | 31 | 1 | 0 | 200.0 | 842 | 196 | 94 | 81 | 22 | 10 | 8 | 6 | 65 | 4 | 172 | 11 | 0 | 11 | 9 | .550 | 1 | 0-0 | 0 | 3.87 | 3.65 |
| 2010 ChC | NL | 34 | 34 | 1 | 0 | 215.1 | 918 | 198 | 110 | 92 | 25 | 9 | 2 | 10 | 86 | 4 | 208 | 6 | 0 | 15 | 12 | .556 | 0 | 0-0 | 0 | 3.91 | 3.85 |
| 2011 ChC | NL | 34 | **34** | 0 | 0 | 202.1 | 881 | 211 | 111 | 108 | 23 | 12 | 3 | 5 | 82 | 2 | 191 | 7 | 0 | 10 | 14 | .417 | 0 | 0-0 | 0 | 4.55 | 4.80 |
| 2012 2 Tms | | 28 | 28 | 0 | 0 | 173.0 | 717 | 155 | 71 | 65 | 19 | 5 | 4 | 2 | 52 | 0 | 153 | 2 | 1 | 12 | 8 | .600 | 0 | 0-0 | 0 | 3.23 | 3.38 |
| 2013 Bos | AL | 32 | 29 | 0 | 1 | 171.1 | 754 | 170 | 97 | 87 | 26 | 1 | 4 | 6 | 79 | 1 | 157 | 9 | 1 | 8 | 9 | .471 | 0 | 0-0 | 0 | 4.78 | 4.57 |
| 02 Fla | NL | 18 | 18 | 3 | 0 | 120.1 | 521 | 126 | 66 | 64 | 12 | 7 | 3 | 7 | 55 | 1 | 87 | 0 | 0 | 5 | 8 | .385 | 0 | 0-0 | 0 | 4.95 | 4.79 |
| 02 Cin | NL | 15 | 15 | 1 | 0 | 88.2 | 394 | 102 | 61 | 61 | 16 | 2 | 3 | 3 | 38 | 1 | 66 | 2 | 0 | 5 | 5 | .500 | 0 | 0-0 | 0 | 5.90 | 6.19 |
| 12 ChC | NL | 16 | 16 | 0 | 0 | 104.0 | 417 | 81 | 28 | 26 | 9 | 2 | 1 | 1 | 27 | 0 | 83 | 0 | 1 | 5 | 5 | .500 | 0 | 0-0 | 0 | 2.34 | 2.25 |
| 12 Tex | AL | 12 | 12 | 0 | 0 | 69.0 | 300 | 74 | 43 | 39 | 10 | 3 | 3 | 1 | 25 | 0 | 70 | 2 | 0 | 7 | 3 | .700 | 0 | 0-0 | 0 | 4.73 | 5.09 |
| Postseason | | 2 | 1 | 0 | 1 | 5.2 | 27 | 4 | 4 | 4 | 1 | 0 | 0 | 0 | 7 | 0 | 4 | 0 | 0 | 0 | 1 | .000 | 0 | 0-0 | 0 | 6.45 | 6.35 |
| 16 ML YEARS | | 579 | 351 | 11 | 186 | 2387.0 | 10412 | 2347 | 1250 | 1154 | 267 | 100 | 64 | 91 | 1071 | 47 | 2075 | 80 | 3 | 132 | 133 | .498 | 3 | 87-102 | 5 | 4.39 | 4.35 |

# Matt den Dekker

**Bats:** L **Throws:** L **Pos:** CF-16;RF-7;PH-3;PR-3;LF-1 **Ht:** 6'1" **Wt:** 205 **Born:** 8/10/1987 **Age:** 26

| BATTING | | | | | | | | | | | | | | | | | | | | BASERUNNING | | | | AVERAGES | | |
|---|---|---|---|---|---|---|---|---|---|---|---|---|---|---|---|---|---|---|---|---|---|---|---|---|---|---|
| Year Team | Lg | G | AB | H | 2B | 3B | HR | (Hm | Rd) | TB | R | RBI | RC | TBB | IBB | SO | HBP | SH | SF | SB | CS | SB% | GDP | Avg | OBP | Slg |
| 2010 Mets | R | 5 | 18 | 5 | 2 | 0 | 0 | (- | -) | 7 | 2 | 5 | 2 | 2 | 0 | 5 | 0 | 1 | 0 | 0 | 0 | - | 1 | .278 | .350 | .389 |
| 2010 Savann | A | 27 | 104 | 36 | 13 | 0 | 0 | (- | -) | 49 | 21 | 15 | 20 | 9 | 0 | 28 | 1 | 0 | 0 | 3 | 0 | 1.00 | 0 | .346 | .404 | .471 |
| 2011 StLuci | A+ | 67 | 267 | 79 | 19 | 8 | 6 | (- | -) | 132 | 54 | 36 | 49 | 24 | 0 | 65 | 5 | 4 | 2 | 12 | 5 | .71 | 3 | .296 | .362 | .494 |
| 2011 Bnghtn | AA | 72 | 272 | 64 | 13 | 3 | 11 | (- | -) | 116 | 49 | 32 | 38 | 27 | 0 | 91 | 5 | 6 | 4 | 12 | 5 | .71 | 3 | .235 | .312 | .426 |
| 2012 Bnghtn | AA | 58 | 238 | 81 | 21 | 4 | 8 | (- | -) | 134 | 47 | 29 | 51 | 20 | 0 | 64 | 5 | 1 | 4 | 10 | 7 | .59 | 3 | .340 | .397 | .563 |
| 2012 Buffalo | AAA | 77 | 295 | 65 | 10 | 4 | 9 | (- | -) | 110 | 37 | 47 | 30 | 14 | 1 | 90 | 2 | 1 | 5 | 11 | 2 | .85 | 2 | .220 | .256 | .373 |
| 2013 StLuci | A+ | 14 | 58 | 16 | 2 | 0 | 0 | (- | -) | 18 | 8 | 4 | 6 | 3 | 0 | 6 | 0 | 0 | 1 | 1 | 0 | 1.00 | 1 | .276 | .306 | .310 |
| 2013 LsVgs | AAA | 53 | 179 | 53 | 8 | 4 | 6 | (- | -) | 87 | 34 | 38 | 33 | 20 | 3 | 46 | 1 | 0 | 2 | 8 | 1 | .89 | 2 | .296 | .366 | .486 |
| 2013 NYM | NL | 27 | 58 | 12 | 1 | 0 | 1 | (0 | 1) | 16 | 7 | 6 | 5 | 4 | 0 | 23 | 1 | 0 | 0 | 4 | 1 | .80 | 0 | .207 | .270 | .276 |

# Chris Denorfia

denn-ORE-fee-ah

**Bats:** R **Throws:** R **Pos:** RF-97;LF-58;CF-41;PH-24;DH-1 **Ht:** 6'0" **Wt:** 195 **Born:** 7/15/1980 **Age:** 33

| BATTING | | | | | | | | | | | | | | | | | | | | BASERUNNING | | | | AVERAGES | | |
|---|---|---|---|---|---|---|---|---|---|---|---|---|---|---|---|---|---|---|---|---|---|---|---|---|---|---|
| Year Team | Lg | G | AB | H | 2B | 3B | HR | (Hm | Rd) | TB | R | RBI | RC | TBB | IBB | SO | HBP | SH | SF | SB | CS | SB% | GDP | Avg | OBP | Slg |
| 2005 Cin | NL | 18 | 38 | 10 | 3 | 0 | 1 | (1 | 0) | 16 | 8 | 2 | 3 | 6 | 0 | 9 | 0 | 0 | 0 | 1 | 0 | 1.00 | 1 | .263 | .364 | .421 |
| 2006 Cin | NL | 49 | 106 | 30 | 6 | 0 | 1 | (0 | 1) | 39 | 14 | 7 | 13 | 11 | 1 | 21 | 1 | 2 | 0 | 1 | 1 | .50 | 1 | .283 | .356 | .368 |
| 2008 Oak | AL | 29 | 62 | 18 | 3 | 0 | 1 | (0 | 1) | 24 | 10 | 9 | 9 | 6 | 0 | 16 | 1 | 2 | 0 | 2 | 0 | 1.00 | 3 | .290 | .362 | .387 |
| 2009 Oak | AL | 4 | 2 | 0 | 0 | 0 | 0 | (0 | 0) | 0 | 1 | 1 | 0 | 0 | 0 | 0 | 0 | 0 | 0 | 0 | 0 | - | 0 | .000 | .000 | .000 |
| 2010 SD | NL | 99 | 284 | 77 | 15 | 2 | 9 | (3 | 6) | 123 | 41 | 36 | 37 | 27 | 3 | 51 | 2 | 1 | 3 | 8 | 4 | .67 | 5 | .271 | .335 | .433 |
| 2011 SD | NL | 111 | 307 | 85 | 13 | 2 | 5 | (1 | 4) | 117 | 38 | 19 | 34 | 28 | 1 | 49 | 1 | 2 | 2 | 11 | 6 | .65 | 10 | .277 | .337 | .381 |
| 2012 SD | NL | 130 | 348 | 102 | 19 | 6 | 8 | (3 | 5) | 157 | 56 | 36 | 49 | 27 | 0 | 52 | 2 | 2 | 3 | 13 | 5 | .72 | 9 | .293 | .345 | .451 |
| 2013 SD | NL | 144 | 473 | 132 | 21 | 2 | 10 | (6 | 4) | 187 | 67 | 47 | 63 | 42 | 2 | 84 | 1 | 0 | 4 | 11 | 0 | 1.00 | 14 | .279 | .337 | .395 |
| 8 ML YEARS | | 584 | 1620 | 454 | 80 | 12 | 35 | (14 | 21) | 663 | 235 | 157 | 208 | 147 | 7 | 282 | 8 | 9 | 12 | 47 | 16 | .75 | 43 | .280 | .341 | .409 |

# Mark DeRosa

**Bats:** R **Throws:** R **Pos:** 2B-29;PH-29;3B-25;1B-17;DH-14;LF-1;PR-1 **Ht:** 6'1" **Wt:** 215 **Born:** 2/26/1975 **Age:** 39

| BATTING | | | | | | | | | | | | | | | | | | | | BASERUNNING | | | | AVERAGES | | |
|---|---|---|---|---|---|---|---|---|---|---|---|---|---|---|---|---|---|---|---|---|---|---|---|---|---|---|
| Year Team | Lg | G | AB | H | 2B | 3B | HR | (Hm | Rd) | TB | R | RBI | RC | TBB | IBB | SO | HBP | SH | SF | SB | CS | SB% | GDP | Avg | OBP | Slg |
| 1998 Atl | NL | 5 | 3 | 1 | 0 | 0 | 0 | (0 | 0) | 1 | 2 | 0 | 0 | 0 | 0 | 1 | 0 | 0 | 0 | 0 | 0 | - | 0 | .333 | .333 | .333 |
| 1999 Atl | NL | 7 | 8 | 0 | 0 | 0 | 0 | (0 | 0) | 0 | 0 | 0 | 0 | 0 | 0 | 2 | 0 | 0 | 0 | 0 | 0 | - | 0 | .000 | .000 | .000 |
| 2000 Atl | NL | 22 | 13 | 4 | 1 | 0 | 0 | (0 | 0) | 5 | 9 | 3 | 2 | 2 | 0 | 1 | 0 | 0 | 0 | 0 | 0 | - | 0 | .308 | .400 | .385 |
| 2001 Atl | NL | 66 | 164 | 47 | 8 | 0 | 3 | (3 | 0) | 64 | 27 | 20 | 22 | 12 | 6 | 19 | 5 | 1 | 2 | 2 | 1 | .67 | 3 | .287 | .350 | .390 |
| 2002 Atl | NL | 72 | 212 | 63 | 9 | 2 | 5 | (3 | 2) | 91 | 24 | 23 | 27 | 12 | 3 | 24 | 3 | 2 | 3 | 2 | 3 | .40 | 5 | .297 | .339 | .429 |
| 2003 Atl | NL | 103 | 266 | 70 | 14 | 0 | 6 | (3 | 3) | 102 | 40 | 22 | 28 | 16 | 0 | 49 | 5 | 0 | 1 | 1 | 0 | 1.00 | 6 | .263 | .316 | .383 |
| 2004 Atl | NL | 118 | 309 | 74 | 16 | 0 | 3 | (0 | 3) | 99 | 33 | 31 | 24 | 23 | 3 | 53 | 3 | 4 | 6 | 1 | 3 | .25 | 6 | .239 | .293 | .320 |

| | | | BATTING | | | | | | | | | | | | | | | | | | BASERUNNING | | | | AVERAGES | | |
|---|---|---|---|---|---|---|---|---|---|---|---|---|---|---|---|---|---|---|---|---|---|---|---|---|---|---|---|
| Year | Team | Lg | G | AB | H | 2B | 3B | HR | (Hm | Rd) | TB | R | RBI | RC | TBB | IBB | SO | HBP | SH | SF | SB | CS | SB% | GDP | Avg | OBP | Slg |
| 2005 | Tex | AL | 66 | 148 | 36 | 5 | 0 | 8 | (7 | 1) | 65 | 26 | 20 | 20 | 16 | 0 | 35 | 2 | 0 | 0 | 1 | 0 | 1.00 | 5 | .243 | .325 | .439 |
| 2006 | Tex | AL | 136 | 520 | 154 | 40 | 2 | 13 | (5 | 8) | 237 | 78 | 74 | 78 | 44 | 1 | 102 | 6 | 0 | 2 | 4 | 4 | .50 | 13 | .296 | .357 | .456 |
| 2007 | ChC | NL | 149 | 502 | 147 | 28 | 3 | 10 | (5 | 5) | 211 | 64 | 72 | 76 | 58 | 2 | 93 | 7 | 3 | 4 | 1 | 2 | .33 | 17 | .293 | .371 | .420 |
| 2008 | ChC | NL | 149 | 505 | 144 | 30 | 3 | 21 | (11 | 10) | 243 | 103 | 87 | 95 | 69 | 0 | 106 | 9 | 2 | 8 | 6 | 0 | 1.00 | 9 | .285 | .376 | .481 |
| 2009 | 2 Tms | | 139 | 515 | 129 | 23 | 1 | 23 | (11 | 12) | 223 | 78 | 78 | 68 | 47 | 1 | 121 | 7 | 2 | 5 | 3 | 2 | .60 | 11 | .250 | .319 | .433 |
| 2010 | SF | NL | 26 | 93 | 18 | 3 | 0 | 1 | (0 | 1) | 24 | 9 | 10 | 6 | 9 | 0 | 16 | 2 | 0 | 0 | 0 | 2 | .00 | 6 | .194 | .279 | .258 |
| 2011 | SF | NL | 47 | 86 | 24 | 2 | 0 | 0 | (0 | 0) | 26 | 9 | 12 | 10 | 8 | 0 | 18 | 2 | 0 | 1 | 1 | 1 | .50 | 4 | .279 | .351 | .302 |
| 2012 | Was | NL | 48 | 85 | 16 | 5 | 0 | 0 | (0 | 0) | 21 | 13 | 6 | 5 | 14 | 0 | 18 | 0 | 1 | 1 | 1 | 0 | 1.00 | 3 | .188 | .300 | .247 |
| 2013 | Tor | AL | 88 | 204 | 48 | 12 | 1 | 7 | (5 | 2) | 83 | 23 | 36 | 28 | 28 | 1 | 49 | 1 | 0 | 3 | 0 | 0 | - | 8 | .235 | .326 | .407 |
| 09 | Cle | AL | 71 | 278 | 75 | 13 | 0 | 13 | (8 | 5) | 127 | 47 | 50 | 45 | 29 | 1 | 63 | 3 | 1 | 3 | 1 | 1 | .50 | 6 | .270 | .342 | .457 |
| 09 | StL | NL | 68 | 237 | 54 | 10 | 1 | 10 | (3 | 7) | 96 | 31 | 28 | 23 | 18 | 0 | 58 | 4 | 1 | 2 | 2 | 1 | .67 | 5 | .228 | .291 | .405 |
| Postseason | | | 22 | 53 | 19 | 6 | 1 | 1 | (1 | 0) | 30 | 8 | 10 | 7 | 4 | 0 | 8 | 1 | 0 | 0 | 0 | 0 | - | 2 | .358 | .414 | .566 |
| 16 ML YEARS | | | 1241 | 3633 | 975 | 196 | 12 | 100 | (53 | 47) | 1495 | 538 | 494 | 489 | 358 | 17 | 707 | 52 | 15 | 36 | 23 | 18 | .56 | 96 | .268 | .340 | .412 |

# Daniel Descalso

**Bats:** L **Throws:** R **Pos:** SS-55;2B-39;3B-38;PH-26 dess-CAL-so **Ht:** 5'10" **Wt:** 190 **Born:** 10/19/1986 **Age:** 27

| | | | BATTING | | | | | | | | | | | | | | | | | | BASERUNNING | | | | AVERAGES | | |
|---|---|---|---|---|---|---|---|---|---|---|---|---|---|---|---|---|---|---|---|---|---|---|---|---|---|---|---|
| Year | Team | Lg | G | AB | H | 2B | 3B | HR | (Hm | Rd) | TB | R | RBI | RC | TBB | IBB | SO | HBP | SH | SF | SB | CS | SB% | GDP | Avg | OBP | Slg |
| 2010 | StL | NL | 11 | 34 | 9 | 2 | 0 | 0 | (0 | 0) | 11 | 6 | 4 | 5 | 2 | 0 | 6 | 1 | 0 | 0 | 1 | 0 | 1.00 | 0 | .265 | .324 | .324 |
| 2011 | StL | NL | 148 | 326 | 86 | 20 | 3 | 1 | (1 | 0) | 115 | 35 | 28 | 40 | 33 | 9 | 65 | 3 | 10 | 3 | 2 | 2 | .50 | 3 | .264 | .334 | .353 |
| 2012 | StL | NL | 143 | 374 | 85 | 10 | 7 | 4 | (0 | 4) | 121 | 41 | 26 | 29 | 37 | 3 | 83 | 5 | 7 | 3 | 6 | 3 | .67 | 5 | .227 | .303 | .324 |
| 2013 | StL | NL | 123 | 328 | 78 | 25 | 1 | 5 | (1 | 4) | 120 | 43 | 43 | 40 | 22 | 5 | 56 | 3 | 3 | 2 | 6 | 3 | .67 | 7 | .238 | .290 | .366 |
| Postseason | | | 26 | 56 | 14 | 2 | 0 | 2 | (1 | 1) | 22 | 12 | 6 | 5 | 2 | 1 | 14 | 0 | 4 | 1 | 2 | 0 | 1.00 | 1 | .250 | .271 | .393 |
| 4 ML YEARS | | | 425 | 1062 | 258 | 57 | 11 | 10 | (2 | 8) | 367 | 125 | 101 | 114 | 94 | 17 | 210 | 12 | 20 | 8 | 15 | 8 | .65 | 15 | .243 | .310 | .346 |

# Ian Desmond

**Bats:** R **Throws:** R **Pos:** SS-158 **Ht:** 6'3" **Wt:** 210 **Born:** 9/20/1985 **Age:** 28

| | | | BATTING | | | | | | | | | | | | | | | | | | BASERUNNING | | | | AVERAGES | | |
|---|---|---|---|---|---|---|---|---|---|---|---|---|---|---|---|---|---|---|---|---|---|---|---|---|---|---|---|
| Year | Team | Lg | G | AB | H | 2B | 3B | HR | (Hm | Rd) | TB | R | RBI | RC | TBB | IBB | SO | HBP | SH | SF | SB | CS | SB% | GDP | Avg | OBP | Slg |
| 2009 | Was | NL | 21 | 82 | 23 | 7 | 2 | 4 | (2 | 2) | 46 | 9 | 12 | 10 | 5 | 0 | 14 | 0 | 1 | 1 | 1 | 0 | 1.00 | 2 | .280 | .318 | .561 |
| 2010 | Was | NL | 154 | 525 | 141 | 27 | 4 | 10 | (8 | 2) | 206 | 59 | 65 | 58 | 28 | 3 | 109 | 5 | 9 | 7 | 17 | 5 | .77 | 9 | .269 | .308 | .392 |
| 2011 | Was | NL | 154 | 584 | 148 | 27 | 5 | 8 | (7 | 1) | 209 | 65 | 49 | 65 | 35 | 2 | 139 | 4 | 11 | 5 | 25 | 10 | .71 | 9 | .253 | .298 | .358 |
| 2012 | Was | NL | 130 | 513 | 150 | 33 | 2 | 25 | (16 | 9) | 262 | 72 | 73 | 73 | 30 | 1 | 113 | 3 | 0 | 1 | 21 | 6 | .78 | 17 | .292 | .335 | .511 |
| 2013 | Was | NL | 158 | 600 | 168 | 38 | 3 | 20 | (10 | 10) | 272 | 77 | 80 | 81 | 43 | 3 | 145 | 5 | 2 | 5 | 21 | 6 | .78 | 16 | .280 | .331 | .453 |
| Postseason | | | 5 | 19 | 7 | 1 | 0 | 0 | (0 | 0) | 8 | 2 | 0 | 2 | 0 | 0 | 3 | 0 | 0 | 0 | 0 | 0 | - | 0 | .368 | .368 | .421 |
| 5 ML YEARS | | | 617 | 2304 | 630 | 132 | 16 | 67 | (43 | 24) | 995 | 282 | 279 | 287 | 141 | 9 | 520 | 17 | 23 | 19 | 85 | 27 | .76 | 53 | .273 | .318 | .432 |

# Ross Detwiler

**Pitches:** L **Bats:** R **Pos:** SP-13 DETT-why-lerr **Ht:** 6'5" **Wt:** 200 **Born:** 3/6/1986 **Age:** 28

| | | | HOW MUCH HE PITCHED | | | | | | WHAT HE GAVE UP | | | | | | | | | | | | THE RESULTS | | | | | | | |
|---|---|---|---|---|---|---|---|---|---|---|---|---|---|---|---|---|---|---|---|---|---|---|---|---|---|---|---|---|
| Year | Team | Lg | G | GS | CG | GF | IP | BFP | H | R | ER | HR | SH | SF | HB | TBB | IBB | SO | WP | Bk | W | L | Pct | Sh | Sv-Op | Hld | ERC | ERA |
| 2013 | Ptomc* | A+ | 1 | 1 | 0 | 0 | 3.2 | 18 | 7 | 1 | 1 | 0 | 0 | 0 | 0 | 0 | 0 | 4 | 0 | 0 | 0 | 0 | - | 0 | 0- - | - | 6.90 | 2.45 |
| 2007 | Was | NL | 1 | 0 | 0 | 1 | 1.0 | 4 | 0 | 0 | 0 | 0 | 0 | 0 | 0 | 0 | 0 | 1 | 0 | 0 | 0 | 0 | - | 0 | 0-0 | 0 | 0.00 | 0.00 |
| 2009 | Was | NL | 15 | 14 | 1 | 0 | 75.2 | 341 | 87 | 43 | 42 | 3 | 4 | 1 | 2 | 33 | 3 | 43 | 4 | 0 | 1 | 6 | .143 | 0 | 0-0 | 0 | 4.65 | 5.00 |
| 2010 | Was | NL | 8 | 5 | 0 | 1 | 29.2 | 135 | 34 | 22 | 14 | 5 | 2 | 0 | 1 | 14 | 1 | 17 | 1 | 0 | 1 | 3 | .250 | 0 | 0-0 | 0 | 5.83 | 4.25 |
| 2011 | Was | NL | 15 | 10 | 0 | 0 | 66.0 | 277 | 63 | 26 | 22 | 7 | 7 | 3 | 3 | 20 | 2 | 41 | 2 | 0 | 4 | 5 | .444 | 0 | 0-0 | 1 | 3.64 | 3.00 |
| 2012 | Was | NL | 33 | 27 | 0 | 1 | 164.1 | 686 | 149 | 75 | 62 | 15 | 8 | 3 | 5 | 52 | 0 | 105 | 4 | 1 | 10 | 8 | .556 | 0 | 0-0 | 1 | 3.30 | 3.40 |
| 2013 | Was | NL | 13 | 13 | 0 | 0 | 71.1 | 316 | 92 | 37 | 32 | 5 | 4 | 1 | 5 | 14 | 2 | 39 | 0 | 0 | 2 | 7 | .222 | 0 | 0-0 | 0 | 4.96 | 4.04 |
| Postseason | | | 1 | 1 | 0 | 0 | 6.0 | 25 | 3 | 1 | 0 | 0 | 1 | 1 | 0 | 3 | 1 | 2 | 0 | 0 | 0 | 0 | - | 0 | 0-0 | 0 | 1.21 | 0.00 |
| 6 ML YEARS | | | 85 | 69 | 1 | 3 | 408.0 | 1759 | 425 | 203 | 172 | 35 | 25 | 8 | 16 | 133 | 8 | 246 | 11 | 1 | 18 | 29 | .383 | 0 | 0-0 | 2 | 4.04 | 3.79 |

# Cole DeVries

**Pitches:** R **Bats:** R **Pos:** SP-2; RP-2 **Ht:** 6'1" **Wt:** 180 **Born:** 2/12/1985 **Age:** 29

| | | | HOW MUCH HE PITCHED | | | | | | WHAT HE GAVE UP | | | | | | | | | | | | THE RESULTS | | | | | | | |
|---|---|---|---|---|---|---|---|---|---|---|---|---|---|---|---|---|---|---|---|---|---|---|---|---|---|---|---|---|
| Year | Team | Lg | G | GS | CG | GF | IP | BFP | H | R | ER | HR | SH | SF | HB | TBB | IBB | SO | WP | Bk | W | L | Pct | Sh | Sv-Op | Hld | ERC | ERA |
| 2009 | NwBrit | AA | 26 | 26 | 1 | 0 | 137.2 | 613 | 162 | 88 | 74 | 16 | 1 | 4 | 6 | 46 | 2 | 90 | 7 | 0 | 7 | 14 | .333 | 0 | 0- - | - | 5.10 | 4.84 |
| 2010 | NwBrit | AA | 39 | 2 | 0 | 16 | 68.1 | 314 | 87 | 53 | 44 | 10 | 2 | 2 | 3 | 25 | 0 | 63 | 6 | 0 | 1 | 5 | .167 | 0 | 1- - | - | 6.06 | 5.80 |
| 2010 | Roch | AAA | 9 | 3 | 0 | 3 | 23.1 | 109 | 25 | 17 | 15 | 2 | 1 | 0 | 0 | 14 | 1 | 24 | 3 | 1 | 0 | 3 | .000 | 0 | 0- - | - | 4.97 | 5.79 |
| 2011 | NwBrit | AA | 15 | 0 | 0 | 12 | 27.2 | 105 | 17 | 9 | 7 | 3 | 0 | 0 | 0 | 5 | 0 | 33 | 1 | 0 | 0 | 0 | - | 0 | 9- - | - | 1.49 | 2.28 |
| 2011 | Roch | AAA | 30 | 2 | 0 | 10 | 62.1 | 270 | 74 | 30 | 27 | 4 | 2 | 2 | 0 | 18 | 2 | 42 | 0 | 0 | 4 | 2 | .667 | 0 | 0- - | - | 4.43 | 3.90 |
| 2012 | Roch | AAA | 12 | 12 | 0 | 0 | 70.0 | 290 | 75 | 37 | 34 | 7 | 2 | 2 | 1 | 10 | 0 | 50 | 1 | 1 | 3 | 5 | .375 | 0 | 0- - | - | 3.52 | 4.37 |
| 2013 | FtMyrs | A+ | 2 | 2 | 0 | 0 | 9.0 | 36 | 8 | 2 | 1 | 0 | 1 | 0 | 0 | 0 | 0 | 6 | 0 | 0 | 1 | 0 | 1.000 | 0 | 0- - | - | 1.49 | 1.00 |
| 2013 | NwBrit | AA | 3 | 3 | 0 | 0 | 16.0 | 63 | 12 | 7 | 3 | 3 | 1 | 0 | 1 | 2 | 0 | 11 | 0 | 0 | 0 | 2 | .000 | 0 | 0- - | - | 2.44 | 1.69 |
| 2013 | Roch | AAA | 10 | 10 | 0 | 0 | 50.0 | 237 | 77 | 40 | 39 | 6 | 1 | 7 | 1 | 13 | 1 | 24 | 3 | 1 | 3 | 4 | .429 | 0 | 0- - | - | 6.90 | 7.02 |
| 2013 | Twins | R | 1 | 1 | 0 | 0 | 3.0 | 9 | 0 | 0 | 0 | 0 | 0 | 0 | 0 | 0 | 0 | 4 | 0 | 0 | 0 | 0 | - | 0 | 0- - | - | 0.00 | 0.00 |
| 2012 | Min | AL | 17 | 16 | 0 | 1 | 87.2 | 375 | 88 | 48 | 40 | 16 | 4 | 0 | 4 | 18 | 0 | 58 | 1 | 0 | 5 | 5 | .500 | 0 | 0-0 | 0 | 3.95 | 4.11 |
| 2013 | Min | AL | 4 | 2 | 0 | 0 | 15.0 | 76 | 22 | 18 | 18 | 6 | 0 | 1 | 0 | 9 | 0 | 12 | 0 | 0 | 0 | 2 | .000 | 0 | 0-0 | 0 | 10.27 | 10.80 |
| 2 ML YEARS | | | 21 | 18 | 0 | 1 | 102.2 | 451 | 110 | 66 | 58 | 22 | 4 | 1 | 4 | 27 | 0 | 70 | 1 | 0 | 5 | 7 | .417 | 0 | 0-0 | 0 | 4.76 | 5.08 |

# Blake DeWitt

**Bats:** L **Throws:** R **Pos:** PH-4;3B-1 **Ht:** 5'11" **Wt:** 195 **Born:** 8/20/1985 **Age:** 28

| | | BATTING | | | | | | | | | | | | | | | | | | BASERUNNING | | | | AVERAGES | | |
|---|---|---|---|---|---|---|---|---|---|---|---|---|---|---|---|---|---|---|---|---|---|---|---|---|---|---|
| Year Team | Lg | G | AB | H | 2B | 3B | HR | (Hm | Rd) | TB | R | RBI | RC | TBB | IBB | SO | HBP | SH | SF | SB | CS | SB% | GDP | Avg | OBP | Slg |
| 2013 Gwnntt* | AAA | 2 | 6 | 2 | 0 | 0 | 0 | (- | -) | 2 | 2 | 0 | 0 | 0 | 0 | 1 | 0 | 0 | 0 | 0 | 0 | - | 0 | .333 | .333 | .333 |
| 2008 LAD | NL | 117 | 368 | 97 | 13 | 2 | 9 | (5 | 4) | 141 | 45 | 52 | 51 | 45 | 9 | 68 | 3 | 0 | 5 | 3 | 0 | 1.00 | 6 | .264 | .344 | .383 |
| 2009 LAD | NL | 31 | 49 | 10 | 3 | 0 | 2 | (1 | 1) | 19 | 4 | 4 | 1 | 3 | 0 | 7 | 0 | 0 | 1 | 0 | 0 | - | 2 | .204 | .245 | .388 |
| 2010 2 Tms | NL | 135 | 440 | 115 | 24 | 5 | 5 | (4 | 1) | 164 | 47 | 52 | 62 | 47 | 8 | 86 | 4 | 2 | 3 | 3 | 2 | .60 | 5 | .261 | .336 | .373 |
| 2011 ChC | NL | 121 | 230 | 61 | 11 | 4 | 5 | (2 | 3) | 95 | 21 | 26 | 25 | 12 | 1 | 31 | 1 | 0 | 0 | 1 | 0 | 1.00 | 6 | .265 | .305 | .413 |
| 2012 ChC | NL | 18 | 29 | 4 | 1 | 0 | 0 | (0 | 0) | 5 | 1 | 1 | 0 | 0 | 0 | 2 | 0 | 0 | 1 | 0 | 0 | - | 1 | .138 | .133 | .172 |
| 2013 Atl | NL | 4 | 3 | 1 | 1 | 0 | 0 | (0 | 0) | 2 | 0 | 0 | 0 | 0 | 0 | 0 | 0 | 1 | 0 | 0 | 0 | - | 0 | .333 | .333 | .667 |
| 10 LAD | NL | 82 | 256 | 69 | 15 | 4 | 1 | (1 | 0) | 95 | 29 | 30 | 36 | 30 | 4 | 49 | 3 | 2 | 1 | 2 | 2 | .50 | 4 | .270 | .352 | .371 |
| 10 ChC | NL | 53 | 184 | 46 | 9 | 1 | 4 | (3 | 1) | 69 | 18 | 22 | 26 | 17 | 4 | 37 | 1 | 0 | 2 | 1 | 0 | 1.00 | 1 | .250 | .314 | .375 |
| Postseason | | 8 | 24 | 4 | 2 | 1 | 0 | (0 | 0) | 8 | 2 | 6 | 0 | 1 | 0 | 6 | 0 | 0 | 1 | 0 | 0 | - | 3 | .167 | .192 | .333 |
| 6 ML YEARS | | 426 | 1119 | 288 | 53 | 11 | 21 | (12 | 9) | 426 | 118 | 135 | 139 | 107 | 18 | 194 | 8 | 3 | 10 | 7 | 2 | .78 | 20 | .257 | .324 | .381 |

# Scott Diamond

**Pitches:** L **Bats:** L **Pos:** SP-24 **Ht:** 6'3" **Wt:** 220 **Born:** 7/30/1986 **Age:** 27

| | | HOW MUCH HE PITCHED | | | | | | WHAT HE GAVE UP | | | | | | | | | | | | THE RESULTS | | | | | | | |
|---|---|---|---|---|---|---|---|---|---|---|---|---|---|---|---|---|---|---|---|---|---|---|---|---|---|---|---|
| Year Team | Lg | G | GS | CG | GF | IP | BFP | H | R | ER | HR | SH | SF | HB | TBB | IBB | SO | WP | Bk | W | L | Pct | Sh | Sv-Op | Hld | ERC | ERA |
| 2013 FtMyrs* | A+ | 1 | 1 | 0 | 0 | 5.0 | 21 | 6 | 4 | 4 | 1 | 0 | 0 | 0 | 0 | 0 | 3 | 0 | 0 | 0 | 0 | - | 0 | 0- - | - | 4.14 | 7.20 |
| 2013 Roch* | AAA | 6 | 6 | 1 | 0 | 41.0 | 162 | 33 | 13 | 11 | 4 | 0 | 1 | 0 | 9 | 0 | 19 | 0 | 0 | 4 | 0 | 1.000 | 1 | 0- - | - | 2.38 | 2.41 |
| 2011 Min | AL | 7 | 7 | 0 | 0 | 39.0 | 181 | 51 | 25 | 22 | 3 | 2 | 1 | 0 | 17 | 3 | 19 | 3 | 0 | 1 | 5 | .167 | 0 | 0-0 | 0 | 5.69 | 5.08 |
| 2012 Min | AL | 27 | 27 | 1 | 0 | 173.0 | 714 | 184 | 76 | 68 | 17 | 3 | 5 | 4 | 31 | 2 | 90 | 10 | 0 | 12 | 9 | .571 | 1 | 0-0 | 0 | 3.68 | 3.54 |
| 2013 Min | AL | 24 | 24 | 0 | 0 | 131.0 | 576 | 163 | 88 | 79 | 21 | 1 | 5 | 1 | 36 | 4 | 52 | 5 | 0 | 6 | 13 | .316 | 0 | 0-0 | 0 | 5.45 | 5.43 |
| 3 ML YEARS | | 58 | 58 | 1 | 0 | 343.0 | 1471 | 398 | 189 | 169 | 41 | 6 | 11 | 5 | 84 | 9 | 161 | 18 | 0 | 19 | 27 | .413 | 1 | 0-0 | 0 | 4.56 | 4.43 |

# Jonathan Diaz

**Bats:** R **Throws:** R **Pos:** 3B-3;2B-1;PH-1;PR-1 **Ht:** 5'9" **Wt:** 165 **Born:** 4/10/1985 **Age:** 29

| | | BATTING | | | | | | | | | | | | | | | | | | BASERUNNING | | | | AVERAGES | | |
|---|---|---|---|---|---|---|---|---|---|---|---|---|---|---|---|---|---|---|---|---|---|---|---|---|---|---|
| Year Team | Lg | G | AB | H | 2B | 3B | HR | (Hm | Rd) | TB | R | RBI | RC | TBB | IBB | SO | HBP | SH | SF | SB | CS | SB% | GDP | Avg | OBP | Slg |
| 2009 NHam | AA | 65 | 182 | 39 | 9 | 0 | 1 | (- | -) | 51 | 22 | 14 | 20 | 34 | 0 | 32 | 3 | 4 | 0 | 3 | 4 | .43 | 5 | .214 | .347 | .280 |
| 2009 LsVgs | AAA | 29 | 80 | 12 | 0 | 0 | 0 | (- | -) | 12 | 15 | 4 | 4 | 14 | 0 | 13 | 3 | 7 | 0 | 0 | 0 | - | 0 | .150 | .299 | .150 |
| 2010 NHam | AA | 99 | 312 | 72 | 20 | 1 | 0 | (- | -) | 94 | 48 | 33 | 40 | 53 | 0 | 48 | 9 | 8 | 3 | 5 | 2 | .71 | 7 | .231 | .355 | .301 |
| 2010 LsVgs | AAA | 28 | 94 | 25 | 3 | 0 | 2 | (- | -) | 34 | 20 | 10 | 12 | 8 | 0 | 18 | 0 | 10 | 1 | 1 | 0 | 1.00 | 0 | .266 | .320 | .362 |
| 2011 NHam | AA | 70 | 218 | 55 | 11 | 0 | 1 | (- | -) | 69 | 29 | 19 | 28 | 28 | 0 | 48 | 9 | 6 | 1 | 7 | 5 | .58 | 8 | .252 | .359 | .317 |
| 2011 LsVgs | AAA | 19 | 64 | 19 | 3 | 0 | 1 | (- | -) | 25 | 9 | 10 | 12 | 15 | 0 | 15 | 0 | 0 | 1 | 2 | 1 | .67 | 1 | .297 | .425 | .391 |
| 2011 Dnedin | A+ | 3 | 10 | 4 | 1 | 0 | 0 | (- | -) | 5 | 3 | 1 | 2 | 3 | 0 | 3 | 0 | 0 | 0 | 0 | 0 | - | 0 | .400 | .538 | .500 |
| 2012 NHam | AA | 39 | 145 | 26 | 2 | 0 | 1 | (- | -) | 31 | 18 | 9 | 8 | 13 | 0 | 28 | 2 | 2 | 1 | 6 | 2 | .75 | 4 | .179 | .255 | .214 |
| 2012 LsVgs | AAA | 95 | 312 | 75 | 11 | 2 | 3 | (- | -) | 99 | 58 | 31 | 46 | 62 | 0 | 56 | 7 | 15 | 4 | 12 | 4 | .75 | 7 | .240 | .374 | .317 |
| 2013 Pwtckt | AAA | 103 | 332 | 84 | 11 | 2 | 2 | (- | -) | 105 | 45 | 31 | 44 | 47 | 0 | 67 | 8 | 11 | 1 | 10 | 3 | .77 | 6 | .253 | .358 | .316 |
| 2013 Bos | AL | 5 | 4 | 0 | 0 | 0 | 0 | (0 | 0) | 0 | 2 | 0 | 0 | 0 | 0 | 0 | 0 | 0 | 0 | 0 | 0 | - | 0 | .000 | .000 | .000 |

# Matt Diaz

**Bats:** R **Throws:** R **Pos:** PH-7;LF-4 DYE-azz **Ht:** 6'0" **Wt:** 215 **Born:** 3/3/1978 **Age:** 36

| | | BATTING | | | | | | | | | | | | | | | | | | BASERUNNING | | | | AVERAGES | | |
|---|---|---|---|---|---|---|---|---|---|---|---|---|---|---|---|---|---|---|---|---|---|---|---|---|---|---|
| Year Team | Lg | G | AB | H | 2B | 3B | HR | (Hm | Rd) | TB | R | RBI | RC | TBB | IBB | SO | HBP | SH | SF | SB | CS | SB% | GDP | Avg | OBP | Slg |
| 2013 NewOr* | AAA | 24 | 85 | 29 | 4 | 0 | 2 | (- | -) | 39 | 8 | 10 | 16 | 6 | 3 | 7 | 0 | 0 | 0 | 6 | 0 | 1.00 | 7 | .341 | .385 | .459 |
| 2003 TB | AL | 4 | 9 | 1 | 0 | 0 | 0 | (0 | 0) | 1 | 2 | 0 | 0 | 1 | 0 | 3 | 0 | 0 | 0 | 0 | 0 | - | 0 | .111 | .200 | .111 |
| 2004 TB | AL | 10 | 21 | 4 | 1 | 1 | 1 | (1 | 0) | 10 | 3 | 3 | 2 | 1 | 0 | 6 | 2 | 0 | 0 | 0 | 0 | - | 0 | .190 | .292 | .476 |
| 2005 KC | AL | 34 | 89 | 25 | 4 | 2 | 1 | (0 | 1) | 36 | 7 | 9 | 11 | 4 | 0 | 15 | 2 | 1 | 1 | 0 | 1 | .00 | 3 | .281 | .323 | .404 |
| 2006 Atl | NL | 124 | 297 | 97 | 15 | 4 | 7 | (3 | 4) | 141 | 37 | 32 | 40 | 11 | 3 | 49 | 9 | 1 | 4 | 5 | 5 | .50 | 9 | .327 | .364 | .475 |
| 2007 Atl | NL | 135 | 358 | 121 | 21 | 0 | 12 | (5 | 7) | 178 | 44 | 45 | 53 | 16 | 3 | 63 | 4 | 1 | 5 | 4 | 0 | 1.00 | 8 | .338 | .368 | .497 |
| 2008 Atl | NL | 43 | 135 | 33 | 2 | 0 | 2 | (2 | 0) | 41 | 9 | 14 | 10 | 3 | 0 | 32 | 1 | 0 | 1 | 4 | 2 | .67 | 4 | .244 | .264 | .304 |
| 2009 Atl | NL | 125 | 371 | 116 | 18 | 4 | 13 | (4 | 9) | 181 | 56 | 58 | 67 | 35 | 2 | 90 | 13 | 5 | 1 | 12 | 5 | .71 | 14 | .313 | .390 | .488 |
| 2010 Atl | NL | 84 | 224 | 56 | 17 | 2 | 7 | (5 | 2) | 98 | 27 | 31 | 30 | 13 | 3 | 44 | 4 | 2 | 1 | 3 | 1 | .75 | 6 | .250 | .302 | .438 |
| 2011 2 Tms | NL | 116 | 251 | 66 | 13 | 1 | 0 | (0 | 0) | 81 | 16 | 20 | 20 | 12 | 0 | 52 | 3 | 0 | 2 | 5 | 2 | .71 | 11 | .263 | .302 | .323 |
| 2012 Atl | NL | 51 | 108 | 24 | 6 | 0 | 2 | (1 | 1) | 36 | 10 | 13 | 8 | 9 | 1 | 21 | 0 | 0 | 1 | 0 | 0 | - | 4 | .222 | .280 | .333 |
| 2013 Mia | NL | 10 | 18 | 3 | 1 | 0 | 0 | (0 | 0) | 4 | 1 | 1 | 0 | 1 | 0 | 3 | 0 | 0 | 0 | 0 | 0 | - | 1 | .167 | .211 | .222 |
| 11 Pit | NL | 100 | 216 | 56 | 12 | 1 | 0 | (0 | 0) | 70 | 14 | 19 | 19 | 11 | 0 | 44 | 3 | 0 | 1 | 4 | 2 | .67 | 8 | .259 | .303 | .324 |
| 11 Atl | NL | 16 | 35 | 10 | 1 | 0 | 0 | (0 | 0) | 11 | 2 | 1 | 1 | 1 | 0 | 8 | 0 | 0 | 1 | 1 | 0 | 1.00 | 3 | .286 | .297 | .314 |
| Postseason | | 4 | 10 | 1 | 0 | 0 | 0 | (0 | 0) | 1 | 0 | 0 | 0 | 0 | 0 | 2 | 0 | 0 | 0 | 0 | 0 | - | 0 | .100 | .100 | .100 |
| 11 ML YEARS | | 736 | 1881 | 546 | 98 | 14 | 45 | (21 | 24) | 807 | 212 | 226 | 241 | 106 | 12 | 378 | 38 | 10 | 16 | 33 | 16 | .67 | 60 | .290 | .338 | .429 |

# Chris Dickerson

**Bats:** L **Throws:** L **Pos:** DH-20;LF-17;PH-11;PR-9;RF-6;CF-5 **Ht:** 6'4" **Wt:** 230 **Born:** 4/10/1982 **Age:** 32

| | | BATTING | | | | | | | | | | | | | | | | | | BASERUNNING | | | | AVERAGES | | |
|---|---|---|---|---|---|---|---|---|---|---|---|---|---|---|---|---|---|---|---|---|---|---|---|---|---|---|
| Year Team | Lg | G | AB | H | 2B | 3B | HR | (Hm | Rd) | TB | R | RBI | RC | TBB | IBB | SO | HBP | SH | SF | SB | CS | SB% | GDP | Avg | OBP | Slg |
| 2013 Norfolk* | AAA | 37 | 136 | 33 | 7 | 2 | 2 | (- | -) | 50 | 24 | 8 | 19 | 21 | 1 | 35 | 2 | 0 | 1 | 1 | 1 | .50 | 5 | .243 | .350 | .368 |
| 2008 Cin | NL | 31 | 102 | 31 | 9 | 2 | 6 | (4 | 2) | 62 | 20 | 15 | 22 | 17 | 0 | 35 | 2 | 1 | 0 | 5 | 3 | .63 | 0 | .304 | .413 | .608 |
| 2009 Cin | NL | 97 | 255 | 70 | 13 | 3 | 2 | (0 | 2) | 95 | 31 | 15 | 34 | 39 | 1 | 66 | 1 | 2 | 2 | 11 | 3 | .79 | 3 | .275 | .370 | .373 |
| 2010 2 Tms | NL | 45 | 97 | 20 | 2 | 2 | 0 | (0 | 0) | 26 | 11 | 5 | 6 | 6 | 0 | 34 | 0 | 2 | 1 | 4 | 0 | 1.00 | 1 | .206 | .250 | .268 |
| 2011 NYY | AL | 60 | 50 | 13 | 2 | 0 | 1 | (0 | 1) | 18 | 9 | 7 | 6 | 2 | 0 | 17 | 1 | 1 | 1 | 4 | 0 | 1.00 | 1 | .260 | .296 | .360 |
| 2012 NYY | AL | 25 | 14 | 4 | 0 | 0 | 2 | (1 | 1) | 10 | 5 | 5 | 4 | 3 | 0 | 5 | 0 | 0 | 0 | 3 | 0 | 1.00 | 1 | .286 | .412 | .714 |
| 2013 Bal | AL | 56 | 105 | 25 | 5 | 0 | 4 | (4 | 0) | 42 | 17 | 13 | 12 | 4 | 0 | 36 | 0 | 0 | 0 | 5 | 1 | .83 | 0 | .238 | .266 | .400 |

| Year | Team | Lg | G | AB | H | 2B | 3B | HR | (Hm | Rd) | TB | R | RBI | RC | TBB | IBB | SO | HBP | SH | SF | SB | CS | SB% | GDP | Avg | OBP | Slg |
|---|---|---|---|---|---|---|---|---|---|---|---|---|---|---|---|---|---|---|---|---|---|---|---|---|---|---|---|
| | | | BATTING | | | | | | | | | | | | | | | | | | BASERUNNING | | | | AVERAGES | | |
| 10 | Cin | NL | 20 | 44 | 9 | 1 | 1 | 0 | (0 | 0) | 12 | 9 | 0 | 3 | 1 | 0 | 19 | 0 | 0 | 0 | 3 | 0 | 1.00 | 1 | .205 | .222 | .273 |
| 10 | Mil | NL | 25 | 53 | 11 | 1 | 1 | 0 | (0 | 0) | 14 | 2 | 5 | 3 | 5 | 0 | 15 | 0 | 2 | 1 | 1 | 0 | 1.00 | 0 | .208 | .271 | .264 |
| Postseason | | | 1 | 1 | 0 | 0 | 0 | 0 | (0 | 0) | 0 | 1 | 0 | 0 | 0 | 0 | 0 | 0 | 0 | 0 | 0 | 0 | - | 0 | .000 | .000 | .000 |
| 6 ML YEARS | | | 314 | 623 | 163 | 31 | 7 | 15 | (9 | 6) | 253 | 93 | 60 | 84 | 71 | 1 | 193 | 4 | 6 | 4 | 32 | 7 | .82 | 6 | .262 | .339 | .406 |

## Corey Dickerson

**Bats:** L **Throws:** R **Pos:** LF-36;PH-21;CF-15;RF-4;DH-1 **Ht:** 6'1" **Wt:** 205 **Born:** 5/22/1989 **Age:** 25

| Year | Team | Lg | G | AB | H | 2B | 3B | HR | (Hm | Rd) | TB | R | RBI | RC | TBB | IBB | SO | HBP | SH | SF | SB | CS | SB% | GDP | Avg | OBP | Slg |
|---|---|---|---|---|---|---|---|---|---|---|---|---|---|---|---|---|---|---|---|---|---|---|---|---|---|---|---|
| | | | BATTING | | | | | | | | | | | | | | | | | | BASERUNNING | | | | AVERAGES | | |
| 2010 | Casper | R+ | 69 | 276 | 96 | 22 | 9 | 13 | (- | -) | 175 | 54 | 61 | - | 28 | 5 | 51 | 3 | 0 | 1 | 12 | 6 | .67 | 4 | .348 | .412 | .634 |
| 2011 | Ashvll | A | 106 | 383 | 108 | 27 | 5 | 32 | (- | -) | 241 | 78 | 87 | 84 | 39 | 0 | 99 | 8 | 0 | 5 | 9 | 6 | .60 | 5 | .282 | .356 | .629 |
| 2012 | Mdest | A+ | 60 | 240 | 81 | 24 | 4 | 9 | (- | -) | 140 | 43 | 43 | 54 | 25 | 5 | 42 | 1 | 0 | 4 | 9 | 5 | .64 | 3 | .338 | .396 | .583 |
| 2012 | Tulsa | AA | 67 | 266 | 73 | 16 | 3 | 13 | (- | -) | 134 | 40 | 38 | 44 | 18 | 1 | 51 | 2 | 0 | 3 | 7 | 3 | .70 | 2 | .274 | .322 | .504 |
| 2013 | ColSpr | AAA | 75 | 315 | 117 | 21 | 14 | 11 | (- | -) | 199 | 61 | 50 | 74 | 26 | 2 | 49 | 0 | 0 | 4 | 6 | 10 | .38 | 2 | .371 | .414 | .632 |
| 2013 | Col | NL | 69 | 194 | 51 | 13 | 5 | 5 | (4 | 1) | 89 | 32 | 17 | 23 | 16 | 0 | 41 | 0 | 1 | 2 | 2 | 2 | .50 | 1 | .263 | .316 | .459 |

## R.A. Dickey

**Pitches:** R **Bats:** R **Pos:** SP-34 **Ht:** 6'2" **Wt:** 215 **Born:** 10/29/1974 **Age:** 39

| Year | Team | Lg | G | GS | CG | GF | IP | BFP | H | R | ER | HR | SH | SF | HB | TBB | IBB | SO | WP | Bk | W | L | Pct | Sh | Sv-Op | Hld | ERC | ERA |
|---|---|---|---|---|---|---|---|---|---|---|---|---|---|---|---|---|---|---|---|---|---|---|---|---|---|---|---|---|
| | | | HOW MUCH HE PITCHED | | | | | | WHAT HE GAVE UP | | | | | | | | | | | | THE RESULTS | | | | | | | |
| 2001 | Tex | AL | 4 | 0 | 0 | 1 | 12.0 | 53 | 13 | 9 | 9 | 3 | 0 | 0 | 0 | 7 | 1 | 4 | 1 | 0 | 0 | 1 | .000 | 0 | 0-0 | 0 | 6.57 | 6.75 |
| 2003 | Tex | AL | 38 | 13 | 1 | 6 | 116.2 | 513 | 135 | 68 | 66 | 16 | 4 | 3 | 5 | 38 | 5 | 94 | 5 | 2 | 9 | 8 | .529 | 1 | 1-1 | 3 | 5.09 | 5.09 |
| 2004 | Tex | AL | 25 | 15 | 0 | 2 | 104.1 | 480 | 136 | 77 | 65 | 17 | 3 | 3 | 4 | 33 | 1 | 57 | 5 | 1 | 6 | 7 | .462 | 0 | 1-1 | 0 | 6.08 | 5.61 |
| 2005 | Tex | AL | 9 | 4 | 0 | 2 | 29.2 | 134 | 29 | 23 | 22 | 4 | 0 | 1 | 2 | 17 | 0 | 15 | 2 | 0 | 1 | 2 | .333 | 0 | 0-0 | 0 | 5.18 | 6.67 |
| 2006 | Tex | AL | 1 | 1 | 0 | 0 | 3.1 | 18 | 8 | 7 | 7 | 6 | 0 | 0 | 0 | 1 | 0 | 1 | 0 | 0 | 0 | 1 | .000 | 0 | 0-0 | 0 | 32.05 | 18.90 |
| 2008 | Sea | AL | 32 | 14 | 0 | 9 | 112.1 | 500 | 124 | 65 | 65 | 15 | 4 | 6 | 2 | 51 | 4 | 58 | 11 | 1 | 5 | 8 | .385 | 0 | 0-0 | 0 | 5.19 | 5.21 |
| 2009 | Min | AL | 35 | 1 | 0 | 13 | 64.1 | 293 | 74 | 34 | 33 | 8 | 2 | 2 | 4 | 30 | 1 | 42 | 4 | 0 | 1 | 1 | .500 | 0 | 0-0 | 1 | 5.66 | 4.62 |
| 2010 | NYM | NL | 27 | 26 | 2 | 0 | 174.1 | 713 | 165 | 62 | 55 | 13 | 7 | 3 | 4 | 42 | 3 | 104 | 11 | 0 | 11 | 9 | .550 | 1 | 0-0 | 1 | 3.11 | 2.84 |
| 2011 | NYM | NL | 33 | 32 | 1 | 0 | 208.2 | 876 | 202 | 85 | 76 | 18 | **16** | 7 | 9 | 54 | 2 | 134 | 9 | 1 | 8 | 13 | .381 | 0 | 0-0 | 1 | 3.40 | 3.28 |
| 2012 | NYM | NL | 34 | **33** | **5** | 1 | **233.2** | **927** | 192 | 78 | 71 | 24 | 9 | 7 | 9 | 54 | 2 | **230** | 4 | 1 | 20 | 6 | .769 | **3** | 0-0 | 0 | 2.70 | 2.73 |
| 2013 | Tor | AL | 34 | **34** | 3 | 0 | 224.2 | 943 | 207 | 113 | 105 | 35 | 2 | 6 | 10 | 71 | 0 | 177 | 7 | 1 | 14 | 13 | .519 | 1 | 0-0 | 0 | 3.87 | 4.21 |
| 11 ML YEARS | | | 272 | 173 | 12 | 34 | 1284.0 | 5450 | 1285 | 621 | 574 | 159 | 47 | 38 | 49 | 398 | 19 | 916 | 59 | 7 | 75 | 69 | .521 | 6 | 2-2 | 6 | 4.04 | 4.02 |

## Jake Diekman

**Pitches:** L **Bats:** L **Pos:** RP-45 DEEK-man **Ht:** 6'4" **Wt:** 200 **Born:** 1/21/1987 **Age:** 27

| Year | Team | Lg | G | GS | CG | GF | IP | BFP | H | R | ER | HR | SH | SF | HB | TBB | IBB | SO | WP | Bk | W | L | Pct | Sh | Sv-Op | Hld | ERC | ERA |
|---|---|---|---|---|---|---|---|---|---|---|---|---|---|---|---|---|---|---|---|---|---|---|---|---|---|---|---|---|
| | | | HOW MUCH HE PITCHED | | | | | | WHAT HE GAVE UP | | | | | | | | | | | | THE RESULTS | | | | | | | |
| 2009 | Lakwd | A | 32 | 2 | 0 | 11 | 55.2 | 252 | 59 | 32 | 25 | 3 | 1 | 1 | 0 | 28 | 0 | 52 | 4 | 3 | 2 | 0 | 1.000 | 0 | 2-- | - | 4.40 | 4.04 |
| 2010 | Lakwd | A | 21 | 0 | 0 | 5 | 23.2 | 110 | 16 | 11 | 5 | 0 | 0 | 0 | 5 | 15 | 0 | 30 | 3 | 0 | 2 | 0 | 1.000 | 0 | 0-- | - | 3.06 | 1.90 |
| 2010 | Clrwtr | A+ | 24 | 0 | 0 | 7 | 32.0 | 144 | 22 | 20 | 13 | 2 | 1 | 1 | 6 | 23 | 0 | 26 | 2 | 0 | 0 | 2 | .000 | 0 | 0-- | - | 3.99 | 3.66 |
| 2011 | Rdng | AA | 53 | 0 | 0 | 19 | 65.0 | 288 | 47 | 29 | 22 | 3 | 1 | 2 | 5 | 44 | 2 | 83 | 7 | 0 | 0 | 1 | .000 | 0 | 3-- | - | 3.42 | 3.05 |
| 2012 | LV | AAA | 25 | 0 | 0 | 14 | 26.2 | 114 | 19 | 5 | 5 | 0 | 1 | 1 | 2 | 13 | 1 | 37 | 0 | 0 | 1 | 1 | .500 | 0 | 7-- | - | 2.37 | 1.69 |
| 2013 | LV | AAA | 30 | 0 | 0 | 23 | 30.0 | 142 | 31 | 22 | 19 | 1 | 0 | 2 | 1 | 24 | 1 | 37 | 1 | 0 | 1 | 0 | 1.000 | 0 | 11-- | - | 5.42 | 5.70 |
| 2012 | Phi | NL | 32 | 0 | 0 | 7 | 27.1 | 131 | 25 | 17 | 12 | 1 | 1 | 0 | 3 | 20 | 3 | 35 | 1 | 0 | 1 | 1 | .500 | 0 | 0-1 | 4 | 4.45 | 3.95 |
| 2013 | Phi | NL | 45 | 0 | 0 | 11 | 38.1 | 164 | 34 | 15 | 11 | 1 | 2 | 1 | 0 | 16 | 2 | 41 | 2 | 1 | 1 | 4 | .200 | 0 | 0-1 | 11 | 2.89 | 2.58 |
| 2 ML YEARS | | | 77 | 0 | 0 | 18 | 65.2 | 295 | 59 | 32 | 23 | 2 | 3 | 1 | 3 | 36 | 5 | 76 | 3 | 1 | 2 | 5 | .286 | 0 | 0-2 | 15 | 3.53 | 3.15 |

## Derek Dietrich

**Bats:** L **Throws:** R **Pos:** 2B-57 DEE-trick **Ht:** 6'0" **Wt:** 200 **Born:** 7/18/1989 **Age:** 24

| Year | Team | Lg | G | AB | H | 2B | 3B | HR | (Hm | Rd) | TB | R | RBI | RC | TBB | IBB | SO | HBP | SH | SF | SB | CS | SB% | GDP | Avg | OBP | Slg |
|---|---|---|---|---|---|---|---|---|---|---|---|---|---|---|---|---|---|---|---|---|---|---|---|---|---|---|---|
| | | | BATTING | | | | | | | | | | | | | | | | | | BASERUNNING | | | | AVERAGES | | |
| 2010 | HudVal | A- | 45 | 179 | 50 | 12 | 2 | 3 | (- | -) | 75 | 33 | 20 | 26 | 11 | 2 | 42 | 6 | 1 | 1 | 2 | 2 | .50 | 2 | .279 | .340 | .419 |
| 2011 | BG | A | 127 | 480 | 133 | 34 | 4 | 22 | (- | -) | 241 | 73 | 81 | 83 | 38 | 2 | 128 | 15 | 0 | 5 | 5 | 7 | .42 | 14 | .277 | .346 | .502 |
| 2012 | Charltt | A+ | 98 | 372 | 105 | 21 | 9 | 10 | (- | -) | 174 | 49 | 58 | 61 | 25 | 1 | 78 | 12 | 3 | 5 | 4 | 2 | .67 | 6 | .282 | .343 | .468 |
| 2012 | Mont | AA | 34 | 133 | 36 | 7 | 1 | 4 | (- | -) | 57 | 22 | 17 | 18 | 7 | 0 | 36 | 4 | 1 | 1 | 0 | 1 | .00 | 2 | .271 | .324 | .429 |
| 2013 | Jaxnvl | AA | 63 | 218 | 59 | 13 | 3 | 11 | (- | -) | 111 | 35 | 38 | 44 | 29 | 2 | 60 | 10 | 0 | 0 | 3 | 0 | 1.00 | 1 | .271 | .381 | .509 |
| 2013 | Mia | NL | 57 | 215 | 46 | 10 | 2 | 9 | (3 | 6) | 87 | 32 | 23 | 24 | 11 | 1 | 56 | 7 | 0 | 0 | 1 | 0 | 1.00 | 1 | .214 | .275 | .405 |

## Andy Dirks

**Bats:** L **Throws:** L **Pos:** LF-116;PH-19;RF-15;CF-4;DH-3;PR-3 **Ht:** 6'0" **Wt:** 195 **Born:** 1/24/1986 **Age:** 28

| Year | Team | Lg | G | AB | H | 2B | 3B | HR | (Hm | Rd) | TB | R | RBI | RC | TBB | IBB | SO | HBP | SH | SF | SB | CS | SB% | GDP | Avg | OBP | Slg |
|---|---|---|---|---|---|---|---|---|---|---|---|---|---|---|---|---|---|---|---|---|---|---|---|---|---|---|---|
| | | | BATTING | | | | | | | | | | | | | | | | | | BASERUNNING | | | | AVERAGES | | |
| 2011 | Det | AL | 78 | 219 | 55 | 13 | 0 | 7 | (6 | 1) | 89 | 34 | 28 | 27 | 11 | 1 | 36 | 3 | 2 | 0 | 5 | 2 | .71 | 3 | .251 | .296 | .406 |
| 2012 | Det | AL | 88 | 314 | 101 | 18 | 5 | 8 | (3 | 5) | 153 | 56 | 35 | 50 | 23 | 2 | 53 | 2 | 3 | 2 | 1 | 1 | .50 | 4 | .322 | .370 | .487 |
| 2013 | Det | AL | 131 | 438 | 112 | 16 | 2 | 9 | (5 | 4) | 159 | 60 | 37 | 48 | 42 | 2 | 84 | 2 | 1 | 1 | 7 | 1 | .88 | 6 | .256 | .323 | .363 |
| Postseason | | | 15 | 49 | 11 | 2 | 0 | 0 | (0 | 0) | 13 | 1 | 1 | 3 | 2 | 0 | 8 | 0 | 1 | 0 | 2 | 0 | 1.00 | 0 | .224 | .255 | .265 |
| 3 ML YEARS | | | 297 | 971 | 268 | 47 | 7 | 24 | (14 | 10) | 401 | 150 | 100 | 125 | 76 | 5 | 173 | 7 | 6 | 3 | 13 | 4 | .76 | 13 | .276 | .332 | .413 |

## Greg Dobbs

**Bats:** L **Throws:** R **Pos:** PH-59;1B-51;DH-4;RF-1 **Ht:** 6'1" **Wt:** 210 **Born:** 7/2/1978 **Age:** 35

| BATTING | | | | | | | | | | | | | | | | | | | | | BASERUNNING | | | | AVERAGES | | |
|---|---|---|---|---|---|---|---|---|---|---|---|---|---|---|---|---|---|---|---|---|---|---|---|---|---|---|---|
| Year | Team | Lg | G | AB | H | 2B | 3B | HR | (Hm | Rd) | TB | R | RBI | RC | TBB | IBB | SO | HBP | SH | SF | SB | CS | SB% | GDP | Avg | OBP | Slg |
| 2004 | Sea | AL | 18 | 53 | 12 | 1 | 0 | 1 | (1 | 0) | 16 | 4 | 9 | 5 | 1 | 0 | 14 | 1 | 0 | 1 | 0 | 0 | - | 0 | .226 | .250 | .302 |
| 2005 | Sea | AL | 59 | 142 | 35 | 7 | 1 | 1 | (0 | 1) | 47 | 8 | 20 | 16 | 9 | 3 | 25 | 0 | 1 | 2 | 1 | 0 | 1.00 | 4 | .246 | .288 | .331 |
| 2006 | Sea | AL | 23 | 27 | 10 | 3 | 1 | 0 | (0 | 0) | 15 | 4 | 3 | 5 | 0 | 0 | 4 | 1 | 0 | 0 | 0 | 1 | .00 | 0 | .370 | .393 | .556 |
| 2007 | Phi | NL | 142 | 324 | 88 | 20 | 4 | 10 | (5 | 5) | 146 | 45 | 55 | 42 | 29 | 4 | 67 | 1 | 0 | 4 | 3 | 0 | 1.00 | 7 | .272 | .330 | .451 |
| 2008 | Phi | NL | 128 | 226 | 68 | 14 | 1 | 9 | (3 | 6) | 111 | 30 | 40 | 38 | 11 | 1 | 40 | 1 | 0 | 2 | 3 | 1 | .75 | 4 | .301 | .333 | .491 |
| 2009 | Phi | NL | 97 | 154 | 38 | 6 | 0 | 5 | (3 | 2) | 59 | 15 | 20 | 15 | 11 | 1 | 29 | 1 | 0 | 3 | 1 | 0 | 1.00 | 2 | .247 | .296 | .383 |
| 2010 | Phi | NL | 88 | 163 | 32 | 7 | 0 | 5 | (2 | 3) | 54 | 13 | 15 | 14 | 12 | 1 | 39 | 0 | 1 | 0 | 1 | 1 | .50 | 2 | .196 | .251 | .331 |
| 2011 | Fla | NL | 134 | 411 | 113 | 23 | 0 | 8 | (2 | 6) | 160 | 38 | 49 | 40 | 22 | 3 | 83 | 1 | 2 | 3 | 0 | 0 | - | 12 | .275 | .311 | .389 |
| 2012 | Mia | NL | 120 | 319 | 91 | 13 | 2 | 5 | (3 | 2) | 123 | 26 | 39 | 38 | 14 | 5 | 53 | 2 | 0 | 7 | 4 | 2 | .67 | 8 | .285 | .313 | .386 |
| 2013 | Mia | NL | 114 | 237 | 54 | 11 | 0 | 2 | (1 | 1) | 71 | 21 | 22 | 21 | 22 | 6 | 40 | 5 | 0 | 3 | 1 | 1 | .50 | 5 | .228 | .303 | .300 |
| Postseason | | | 16 | 21 | 7 | 1 | 0 | 0 | (0 | 0) | 8 | 2 | 0 | 2 | 3 | 2 | 6 | 0 | 0 | 0 | 0 | 0 | - | 0 | .333 | .417 | .381 |
| 10 ML YEARS | | | 923 | 2056 | 541 | 105 | 9 | 46 | (20 | 26) | 802 | 204 | 272 | 234 | 131 | 24 | 394 | 13 | 4 | 25 | 14 | 6 | .70 | 44 | .263 | .308 | .390 |

## Rafael Dolis

**Pitches:** R **Bats:** R **Pos:** RP-5 DOE-leese **Ht:** 6'4" **Wt:** 215 **Born:** 1/10/1988 **Age:** 26

| HOW MUCH HE PITCHED | | | | | | | | | WHAT HE GAVE UP | | | | | | | | | | | | THE RESULTS | | | | | | | |
|---|---|---|---|---|---|---|---|---|---|---|---|---|---|---|---|---|---|---|---|---|---|---|---|---|---|---|---|---|
| Year | Team | Lg | G | GS | CG | GF | IP | BFP | H | R | ER | HR | SH | SF | HB | TBB | IBB | SO | WP | Bk | W | L | Pct | Sh | Sv-Op | Hld | ERC | ERA |
| 2013 | Iowa* | AAA | 12 | 0 | 0 | 8 | 11.2 | 53 | 11 | 7 | 7 | 1 | 0 | 0 | 0 | 7 | 0 | 13 | 4 | 0 | 1 | 0 | 1.000 | 0 | 1- - | - | 4.33 | 5.40 |
| 2013 | Cubs* | R | 3 | 2 | 0 | 0 | 3.0 | 10 | 0 | 0 | 0 | 0 | 0 | 0 | 0 | 1 | 0 | 2 | 0 | 0 | 0 | 0 | - | 0 | 0- - | - | 0.13 | 0.00 |
| 2013 | Kane* | A | 1 | 0 | 0 | 0 | 0.0 | 2 | 1 | 0 | 0 | 0 | 0 | 0 | 0 | 1 | 0 | 0 | 0 | 0 | 0 | 0 | - | 0 | 0- - | - | - | - |
| 2011 | ChC | NL | 1 | 0 | 0 | 0 | 1.1 | 4 | 0 | 0 | 0 | 0 | 0 | 0 | 0 | 1 | 0 | 1 | 0 | 0 | 0 | 0 | - | 0 | 0-0 | 0 | 0.71 | 0.00 |
| 2012 | ChC | NL | 34 | 0 | 0 | 15 | 38.0 | 173 | 40 | 29 | 27 | 5 | 2 | 1 | 3 | 23 | 1 | 24 | 1 | 0 | 2 | 4 | .333 | 0 | 4-6 | 3 | 5.85 | 6.39 |
| 2013 | ChC | NL | 5 | 0 | 0 | 2 | 5.0 | 21 | 3 | 2 | 0 | 0 | 0 | 0 | 0 | 2 | 0 | 0 | 0 | 0 | 0 | 0 | - | 0 | 0-0 | 0 | 1.44 | 0.00 |
| 3 ML YEARS | | | 40 | 0 | 0 | 17 | 44.1 | 198 | 43 | 31 | 27 | 5 | 2 | 1 | 3 | 26 | 1 | 25 | 1 | 0 | 2 | 4 | .333 | 0 | 4-6 | 3 | 5.04 | 5.48 |

## Jose Dominguez

**Pitches:** R **Bats:** R **Pos:** RP-9 **Ht:** 6'0" **Wt:** 160 **Born:** 8/7/1990 **Age:** 23

| HOW MUCH HE PITCHED | | | | | | | | | WHAT HE GAVE UP | | | | | | | | | | | | THE RESULTS | | | | | | | |
|---|---|---|---|---|---|---|---|---|---|---|---|---|---|---|---|---|---|---|---|---|---|---|---|---|---|---|---|---|
| Year | Team | Lg | G | GS | CG | GF | IP | BFP | H | R | ER | HR | SH | SF | HB | TBB | IBB | SO | WP | Bk | W | L | Pct | Sh | Sv-Op | Hld | ERC | ERA |
| 2011 | Ddgrs | R | 10 | 10 | 0 | 0 | 43.2 | 182 | 38 | 20 | 17 | 3 | 0 | 0 | 8 | 13 | 0 | 43 | 3 | 0 | 4 | 1 | .800 | 0 | 0- - | - | 3.55 | 3.50 |
| 2011 | Ogden | R+ | 3 | 3 | 0 | 0 | 10.0 | 60 | 26 | 22 | 20 | 2 | 0 | 0 | 1 | 3 | 0 | 9 | 3 | 1 | 0 | 3 | .000 | 0 | 0- - | - | 15.72 | 18.00 |
| 2012 | Gt Lks | A | 33 | 5 | 0 | 7 | 72.0 | 343 | 77 | 51 | 42 | 4 | 2 | 2 | 5 | 47 | 0 | 78 | 5 | 3 | 4 | 3 | .571 | 0 | 4- - | - | 5.31 | 5.25 |
| 2012 | Chatt | AA | 5 | 0 | 0 | 5 | 7.0 | 23 | 2 | 1 | 1 | 0 | 2 | 0 | 0 | 0 | 0 | 9 | 0 | 0 | 0 | 1 | .000 | 0 | 1- - | - | 0.19 | 1.29 |
| 2013 | Chatt | AA | 14 | 0 | 0 | 6 | 17.1 | 68 | 8 | 5 | 5 | 0 | 1 | 0 | 1 | 8 | 1 | 28 | 2 | 0 | 1 | 0 | 1.000 | 0 | 5- - | - | 1.31 | 2.60 |
| 2013 | Albq | AAA | 8 | 0 | 0 | 2 | 8.0 | 30 | 1 | 0 | 0 | 0 | 0 | 0 | 0 | 5 | 0 | 12 | 2 | 0 | 1 | 0 | 1.000 | 0 | 0- - | - | 0.66 | 0.00 |
| 2013 | LAD | NL | 9 | 0 | 0 | 2 | 8.1 | 39 | 11 | 3 | 2 | 0 | 0 | 0 | 1 | 3 | 0 | 4 | 1 | 0 | 0 | 0 | - | 0 | 0-0 | 1 | 5.47 | 2.16 |

## Matt Dominguez

**Bats:** R **Throws:** R **Pos:** 3B-149;PH-2;DH-1 **Ht:** 6'1" **Wt:** 215 **Born:** 8/28/1989 **Age:** 24

| BATTING | | | | | | | | | | | | | | | | | | | | | BASERUNNING | | | | AVERAGES | | |
|---|---|---|---|---|---|---|---|---|---|---|---|---|---|---|---|---|---|---|---|---|---|---|---|---|---|---|---|
| Year | Team | Lg | G | AB | H | 2B | 3B | HR | (Hm | Rd) | TB | R | RBI | RC | TBB | IBB | SO | HBP | SH | SF | SB | CS | SB% | GDP | Avg | OBP | Slg |
| 2011 | Fla | NL | 17 | 45 | 11 | 4 | 0 | 0 | (0 | 0) | 15 | 2 | 2 | 3 | 2 | 0 | 8 | 1 | 0 | 0 | 0 | 0 | - | 2 | .244 | .292 | .333 |
| 2012 | Hou | NL | 31 | 109 | 31 | 2 | 2 | 5 | (2 | 3) | 52 | 14 | 16 | 13 | 4 | 1 | 17 | 0 | 0 | 0 | 0 | 0 | - | 4 | .284 | .310 | .477 |
| 2013 | Hou | AL | 152 | 543 | 131 | 25 | 0 | 21 | (12 | 9) | 219 | 56 | 77 | 59 | 30 | 1 | 96 | 7 | 2 | 7 | 0 | 1 | .00 | 17 | .241 | .286 | .403 |
| 3 ML YEARS | | | 200 | 697 | 173 | 31 | 2 | 26 | (14 | 12) | 286 | 72 | 95 | 75 | 36 | 2 | 121 | 8 | 2 | 7 | 0 | 1 | .00 | 23 | .248 | .290 | .410 |

## Josh Donaldson

**Bats:** R **Throws:** R **Pos:** 3B-155;DH-2;1B-1;SS-1 **Ht:** 6'0" **Wt:** 220 **Born:** 12/8/1985 **Age:** 28

| BATTING | | | | | | | | | | | | | | | | | | | | | BASERUNNING | | | | AVERAGES | | |
|---|---|---|---|---|---|---|---|---|---|---|---|---|---|---|---|---|---|---|---|---|---|---|---|---|---|---|---|
| Year | Team | Lg | G | AB | H | 2B | 3B | HR | (Hm | Rd) | TB | R | RBI | RC | TBB | IBB | SO | HBP | SH | SF | SB | CS | SB% | GDP | Avg | OBP | Slg |
| 2010 | Oak | AL | 14 | 32 | 5 | 1 | 0 | 1 | (0 | 1) | 9 | 1 | 4 | 3 | 2 | 0 | 12 | 0 | 0 | 0 | 0 | 0 | - | 0 | .156 | .206 | .281 |
| 2012 | Oak | AL | 75 | 274 | 66 | 16 | 0 | 9 | (3 | 6) | 109 | 34 | 33 | 33 | 14 | 0 | 61 | 5 | 0 | 1 | 4 | 1 | .80 | 6 | .241 | .289 | .398 |
| 2013 | Oak | AL | 158 | 579 | 174 | 37 | 3 | 24 | (13 | 11) | 289 | 89 | 93 | 112 | 76 | 2 | 110 | 6 | 1 | 6 | 5 | 2 | .71 | 15 | .301 | .384 | .499 |
| Postseason | | | 5 | 17 | 5 | 1 | 0 | 0 | (0 | 0) | 6 | 1 | 0 | 1 | 1 | 0 | 4 | 0 | 0 | 0 | 0 | 0 | - | 1 | .294 | .333 | .353 |
| 3 ML YEARS | | | 247 | 885 | 245 | 54 | 3 | 34 | (16 | 18) | 407 | 124 | 130 | 148 | 92 | 2 | 183 | 11 | 1 | 7 | 9 | 3 | .75 | 21 | .277 | .350 | .460 |

## Sean Doolittle

**Pitches:** L **Bats:** L **Pos:** RP-70 **Ht:** 6'3" **Wt:** 210 **Born:** 9/26/1986 **Age:** 27

| HOW MUCH HE PITCHED | | | | | | | | | WHAT HE GAVE UP | | | | | | | | | | | | THE RESULTS | | | | | | | |
|---|---|---|---|---|---|---|---|---|---|---|---|---|---|---|---|---|---|---|---|---|---|---|---|---|---|---|---|---|
| Year | Team | Lg | G | GS | CG | GF | IP | BFP | H | R | ER | HR | SH | SF | HB | TBB | IBB | SO | WP | Bk | W | L | Pct | Sh | Sv-Op | Hld | ERC | ERA |
| 2011 | As | R | 1 | 0 | 0 | 0 | 1.0 | 4 | 0 | 1 | 1 | 0 | 0 | 0 | 0 | 1 | 0 | 2 | 0 | 0 | 0 | 0 | - | 0 | 0- - | - | 0.95 | 9.00 |
| 2012 | Stcktn | A+ | 6 | 0 | 0 | 0 | 10.1 | 39 | 5 | 2 | 1 | 0 | 0 | 0 | 2 | 2 | 0 | 21 | 0 | 0 | 0 | 0 | - | 0 | 0- - | - | 1.18 | 0.87 |
| 2012 | Mdlnd | AA | 8 | 0 | 0 | 4 | 11.0 | 41 | 2 | 2 | 1 | 0 | 0 | 0 | 1 | 4 | 0 | 19 | 0 | 0 | 0 | 0 | - | 0 | 1- - | - | 0.53 | 0.82 |
| 2012 | Scrmto | AAA | 2 | 0 | 0 | 1 | 3.2 | 13 | 1 | 0 | 0 | 0 | 0 | 0 | 0 | 1 | 0 | 8 | 0 | 0 | 0 | 0 | - | 0 | 0- - | - | 0.47 | 0.00 |
| 2012 | Oak | AL | 44 | 0 | 0 | 7 | 47.1 | 191 | 40 | 18 | 16 | 3 | 2 | 2 | 0 | 11 | 1 | 60 | 0 | 0 | 2 | 1 | .667 | 0 | 1-2 | 18 | 2.36 | 3.04 |
| 2013 | Oak | AL | 70 | 0 | 0 | 11 | 69.0 | 266 | 53 | 24 | 24 | 4 | 3 | 0 | 2 | 13 | 1 | 60 | 2 | 0 | 5 | 5 | .500 | 0 | 2-7 | 26 | 2.00 | 3.13 |
| Postseason | | | 3 | 0 | 0 | 0 | 2.2 | 14 | 5 | 3 | 1 | 0 | 1 | 0 | 0 | 0 | 0 | 5 | 0 | 0 | 0 | 0 | - | 0 | 0-1 | 1 | 6.17 | 3.38 |
| 2 ML YEARS | | | 114 | 0 | 0 | 18 | 116.1 | 457 | 93 | 42 | 40 | 7 | 5 | 2 | 2 | 24 | 2 | 120 | 2 | 0 | 7 | 6 | .538 | 0 | 3-9 | 44 | 2.15 | 3.09 |

# Octavio Dotel

**Pitches:** R **Bats:** R **Pos:** RP-6 OCK-tay-vee-oh dough-TELL **Ht:** 6'0" **Wt:** 230 **Born:** 11/25/1973 **Age:** 40

| HOW MUCH HE PITCHED | | | | | | | | WHAT HE GAVE UP | | | | | | | | | | | | THE RESULTS | | | | | | | |
|---|---|---|---|---|---|---|---|---|---|---|---|---|---|---|---|---|---|---|---|---|---|---|---|---|---|---|---|
| Year Team | Lg | G | GS | CG | GF | IP | BFP | H | R | ER | HR | SH | SF | HB | TBB | IBB | SO | WP | Bk | W | L | Pct | Sh | Sv-Op | Hld | ERC | ERA |
| 2013 Lkland* | A+ | 5 | 2 | 0 | 0 | 4.2 | 22 | 9 | 4 | 4 | 0 | 0 | 1 | 0 | 0 | 0 | 2 | 0 | 0 | 0 | 1 | .000 | 0 | 0- - | - | 7.37 | 7.71 |
| 2013 Tigers* | R | 2 | 2 | 0 | 0 | 2.0 | 6 | 0 | 0 | 0 | 0 | 0 | 0 | 0 | 0 | 0 | 2 | 0 | 0 | 0 | 0 | - | 0 | 0- - | - | 0.00 | 0.00 |
| 2013 Toledo* | AAA | 3 | 0 | 0 | 0 | 1.1 | 9 | 3 | 2 | 2 | 0 | 0 | 0 | 0 | 2 | 0 | 3 | 0 | 0 | 0 | 0 | - | 0 | 0- - | - | 16.21 | 13.50 |
| 1999 NYM | NL | 19 | 14 | 0 | 1 | 85.1 | 368 | 69 | 52 | 51 | 12 | 3 | 5 | 6 | 49 | 1 | 85 | 3 | 2 | 8 | 3 | .727 | 0 | 0-0 | 0 | 4.30 | 5.38 |
| 2000 Hou | NL | 50 | 16 | 0 | 25 | 125.0 | 563 | 127 | 80 | 75 | 26 | 7 | 8 | 7 | 61 | 3 | 142 | 6 | 0 | 3 | 7 | .300 | 0 | 16-23 | 0 | 5.47 | 5.40 |
| 2001 Hou | NL | 61 | 4 | 0 | 20 | 105.0 | 438 | 79 | 35 | 31 | 5 | 2 | 2 | 2 | 47 | 2 | 145 | 4 | 0 | 7 | 5 | .583 | 0 | 2-4 | 14 | 2.62 | 2.66 |
| 2002 Hou | NL | 83 | 0 | 0 | 22 | 97.1 | 376 | 58 | 21 | 20 | 7 | 3 | 7 | 4 | 27 | 2 | 118 | 2 | 0 | 6 | 4 | .600 | 0 | 6-10 | 31 | 1.61 | 1.85 |
| 2003 Hou | NL | 76 | 0 | 0 | 13 | 87.0 | 346 | 53 | 25 | 24 | 9 | 2 | 1 | 3 | 31 | 2 | 97 | 2 | 0 | 6 | 4 | .600 | 0 | 4-6 | **33** | 2.02 | 2.48 |
| 2004 2 Tms | | 77 | 0 | 0 | 70 | 85.1 | 356 | 68 | 38 | 35 | 13 | 4 | 2 | 4 | 33 | 7 | 122 | 4 | 1 | 6 | 6 | .500 | 0 | 36-45 | 0 | 3.31 | 3.69 |
| 2005 Oak | AL | 15 | 0 | 0 | 13 | 15.1 | 65 | 10 | 6 | 6 | 2 | 0 | 0 | 0 | 11 | 2 | 16 | 1 | 0 | 1 | 2 | .333 | 0 | 7-11 | 0 | 3.44 | 3.52 |
| 2006 NYY | AL | 14 | 0 | 0 | 7 | 10.0 | 59 | 18 | 13 | 12 | 2 | 0 | 1 | 0 | 11 | 1 | 7 | 3 | 0 | 0 | 0 | - | 0 | 0-0 | 1 | 12.97 | 10.80 |
| 2007 2 Tms | | 33 | 0 | 0 | 25 | 30.2 | 138 | 29 | 16 | 14 | 4 | 1 | 0 | 4 | 12 | 4 | 41 | 2 | 0 | 2 | 1 | .667 | 0 | 11-15 | 1 | 4.12 | 4.11 |
| 2008 CWS | AL | 72 | 0 | 0 | 10 | 67.0 | 288 | 52 | 34 | 28 | 12 | 4 | 0 | 5 | 29 | 3 | 92 | 4 | 0 | 4 | 4 | .500 | 0 | 1-5 | 21 | 3.64 | 3.76 |
| 2009 CWS | AL | 62 | 0 | 0 | 12 | 62.1 | 268 | 54 | 26 | 23 | 7 | 3 | 3 | 0 | 36 | 1 | 75 | 4 | 1 | 3 | 3 | .500 | 0 | 0-3 | 16 | 4.14 | 3.32 |
| 2010 3 Tms | NL | 68 | 0 | 0 | 50 | 64.0 | 279 | 52 | 32 | 29 | 9 | 2 | 4 | 3 | 32 | 5 | 75 | 8 | 0 | 3 | 4 | .429 | 0 | 22-28 | 4 | 3.69 | 4.08 |
| 2011 2 Tms | | 65 | 0 | 0 | 21 | 54.0 | 218 | 36 | 23 | 21 | 6 | 3 | 1 | 2 | 17 | 2 | 62 | 1 | 0 | 5 | 4 | .556 | 0 | 3-3 | 9 | 2.15 | 3.50 |
| 2012 Det | AL | 57 | 0 | 0 | 15 | 58.0 | 234 | 50 | 23 | 23 | 3 | 2 | 2 | 1 | 12 | 4 | 62 | 2 | 0 | 5 | 3 | .625 | 0 | 1-4 | 11 | 2.29 | 3.57 |
| 2013 Det | AL | 6 | 0 | 0 | 1 | 4.2 | 28 | 10 | 7 | 7 | 0 | 0 | 0 | 0 | 4 | 0 | 4 | 0 | 0 | 0 | 0 | - | 0 | 0-1 | 0 | 12.37 | 13.50 |
| 04 Hou | NL | 32 | 0 | 0 | 29 | 34.2 | 146 | 27 | 15 | 12 | 4 | 2 | 1 | 1 | 15 | 4 | 50 | 3 | 1 | 0 | 4 | .000 | 0 | 14-17 | 0 | 3.01 | 3.12 |
| 04 Oak | AL | 45 | 0 | 0 | 41 | 50.2 | 210 | 41 | 23 | 23 | 9 | 2 | 1 | 3 | 18 | 3 | 72 | 1 | 0 | 6 | 2 | .750 | 0 | 22-28 | 0 | 3.52 | 4.09 |
| 07 KC | AL | 24 | 0 | 0 | 22 | 23.0 | 108 | 24 | 11 | 10 | 3 | 1 | 0 | 4 | 11 | 4 | 29 | 2 | 0 | 2 | 1 | .667 | 0 | 11-14 | 0 | 5.13 | 3.91 |
| 07 Atl | NL | 9 | 0 | 0 | 3 | 7.2 | 30 | 5 | 5 | 4 | 1 | 0 | 0 | 0 | 1 | 0 | 12 | 0 | 0 | 0 | 0 | - | 0 | 0-1 | 1 | 1.51 | 4.70 |
| 10 Pit | NL | 41 | 0 | 0 | 37 | 40.0 | 173 | 35 | 21 | 19 | 5 | 2 | 3 | 3 | 17 | 2 | 48 | 2 | 0 | 2 | 2 | .500 | 0 | 21-26 | 0 | 3.83 | 4.28 |
| 10 LAD | NL | 19 | 0 | 0 | 12 | 18.2 | 78 | 11 | 7 | 7 | 3 | 0 | 1 | 0 | 11 | 3 | 21 | 3 | 0 | 1 | 1 | .500 | 0 | 1-2 | 3 | 2.72 | 3.38 |
| 10 Col | NL | 8 | 0 | 0 | 1 | 5.1 | 28 | 6 | 4 | 3 | 1 | 0 | 0 | 0 | 4 | 0 | 6 | 3 | 0 | 0 | 1 | .000 | 0 | 0-0 | 1 | 6.30 | 5.06 |
| 11 Tor | AL | 36 | 0 | 0 | 11 | 29.1 | 122 | 20 | 13 | 12 | 5 | 1 | 0 | 2 | 12 | 2 | 30 | 0 | 0 | 2 | 1 | .667 | 0 | 1-1 | 4 | 2.97 | 3.68 |
| 11 StL | NL | 29 | 0 | 0 | 10 | 24.2 | 96 | 16 | 10 | 9 | 1 | 2 | 1 | 0 | 5 | 0 | 32 | 1 | 0 | 3 | 3 | .500 | 0 | 2-2 | 5 | 1.38 | 3.28 |
| Postseason | | 26 | 0 | 0 | 2 | 23.1 | 99 | 17 | 11 | 10 | 2 | 0 | 2 | 2 | 11 | 2 | 33 | 2 | 0 | 3 | 1 | .750 | 0 | 0-0 | 5 | 2.95 | 3.86 |
| 15 ML YEARS | | 758 | 34 | 0 | 305 | 951.0 | 4024 | 765 | 431 | 399 | 117 | 36 | 36 | 41 | 412 | 39 | 1143 | 46 | 4 | 59 | 50 | .541 | 0 | 109-158 | 141 | 3.37 | 3.78 |

# Felix Doubront

**Pitches:** L **Bats:** L **Pos:** SP-27; RP-2 due-BRAWNDT **Ht:** 6'2" **Wt:** 225 **Born:** 10/23/1987 **Age:** 26

| HOW MUCH HE PITCHED | | | | | | | | WHAT HE GAVE UP | | | | | | | | | | | | THE RESULTS | | | | | | | |
|---|---|---|---|---|---|---|---|---|---|---|---|---|---|---|---|---|---|---|---|---|---|---|---|---|---|---|---|
| Year Team | Lg | G | GS | CG | GF | IP | BFP | H | R | ER | HR | SH | SF | HB | TBB | IBB | SO | WP | Bk | W | L | Pct | Sh | Sv-Op | Hld | ERC | ERA |
| 2010 Bos | AL | 12 | 3 | 0 | 5 | 25.0 | 113 | 27 | 16 | 12 | 3 | 1 | 1 | 1 | 10 | 0 | 23 | 3 | 0 | 2 | 2 | .500 | 0 | 2-3 | 1 | 4.72 | 4.32 |
| 2011 Bos | AL | 11 | 0 | 0 | 1 | 10.1 | 47 | 12 | 7 | 7 | 1 | 0 | 1 | 0 | 8 | 0 | 6 | 0 | 0 | 0 | 0 | - | 0 | 1-1 | 0 | 6.97 | 6.10 |
| 2012 Bos | AL | 29 | 29 | 0 | 0 | 161.0 | 709 | 162 | 95 | 87 | 24 | 1 | 6 | 5 | 71 | 0 | 167 | 5 | 0 | 11 | 10 | .524 | 0 | 0-0 | 0 | 4.73 | 4.86 |
| 2013 Bos | AL | 29 | 27 | 0 | 0 | 162.1 | 705 | 161 | 84 | 78 | 13 | 3 | 10 | 5 | 71 | 0 | 139 | 8 | 0 | 11 | 6 | .647 | 0 | 0-0 | 0 | 4.18 | 4.32 |
| 4 ML YEARS | | 81 | 59 | 0 | 6 | 358.2 | 1574 | 362 | 202 | 184 | 41 | 5 | 18 | 11 | 160 | 0 | 335 | 16 | 0 | 24 | 18 | .571 | 0 | 3-4 | 1 | 4.54 | 4.62 |

# Ryan Doumit

**Bats:** B **Throws:** R **Pos:** DH-49;C-43;RF-32;PH-16;LF-1 DOE-mitt **Ht:** 6'1" **Wt:** 220 **Born:** 4/3/1981 **Age:** 33

| BATTING | | | | | | | | | | | | | | | | | | | | BASERUNNING | | | | AVERAGES | | |
|---|---|---|---|---|---|---|---|---|---|---|---|---|---|---|---|---|---|---|---|---|---|---|---|---|---|---|
| Year Team | Lg | G | AB | H | 2B | 3B | HR | (Hm | Rd) | TB | R | RBI | RC | TBB | IBB | SO | HBP | SH | SF | SB | CS | SB% | GDP | Avg | OBP | Slg |
| 2005 Pit | NL | 75 | 231 | 59 | 13 | 1 | 6 | (4 | 2) | 92 | 25 | 35 | 32 | 11 | 1 | 48 | 13 | 1 | 1 | 2 | 1 | .67 | 5 | .255 | .324 | .398 |
| 2006 Pit | NL | 61 | 149 | 31 | 9 | 0 | 6 | (3 | 3) | 58 | 15 | 17 | 17 | 15 | 1 | 42 | 11 | 1 | 2 | 0 | 0 | - | 3 | .208 | .322 | .389 |
| 2007 Pit | NL | 83 | 252 | 69 | 19 | 2 | 9 | (7 | 2) | 119 | 33 | 32 | 34 | 22 | 2 | 59 | 4 | 0 | 1 | 1 | 2 | .33 | 5 | .274 | .341 | .472 |
| 2008 Pit | NL | 116 | 431 | 137 | 34 | 0 | 15 | (8 | 7) | 216 | 71 | 69 | 79 | 23 | 4 | 55 | 6 | 0 | 5 | 2 | 2 | .50 | 10 | .318 | .357 | .501 |
| 2009 Pit | NL | 75 | 280 | 70 | 16 | 0 | 10 | (6 | 4) | 116 | 31 | 38 | 26 | 20 | 6 | 49 | 1 | 0 | 3 | 4 | 0 | 1.00 | 12 | .250 | .299 | .414 |
| 2010 Pit | NL | 124 | 406 | 102 | 22 | 1 | 13 | (7 | 6) | 165 | 42 | 45 | 47 | 41 | 4 | 87 | 8 | 0 | 1 | 1 | 0 | 1.00 | 18 | .251 | .331 | .406 |
| 2011 Pit | NL | 77 | 218 | 66 | 12 | 1 | 8 | (6 | 2) | 104 | 17 | 30 | 36 | 16 | 0 | 35 | 1 | 1 | 0 | 0 | 1 | .00 | 5 | .303 | .353 | .477 |
| 2012 Min | AL | 134 | 484 | 133 | 34 | 1 | 18 | (8 | 10) | 223 | 56 | 75 | 61 | 29 | 5 | 98 | 7 | 0 | 8 | 0 | 0 | - | 17 | .275 | .320 | .461 |
| 2013 Min | AL | 135 | 485 | 120 | 28 | 1 | 14 | (6 | 8) | 192 | 49 | 55 | 51 | 48 | 4 | 99 | 1 | 0 | 4 | 1 | 0 | 1.00 | 13 | .247 | .314 | .396 |
| 9 ML YEARS | | 880 | 2936 | 787 | 187 | 7 | 99 | (55 | 44) | 1285 | 339 | 396 | 383 | 225 | 27 | 572 | 52 | 3 | 25 | 11 | 6 | .65 | 88 | .268 | .329 | .438 |

# Darin Downs

**Pitches:** L **Bats:** R **Pos:** RP-29 **Ht:** 6'3" **Wt:** 210 **Born:** 12/26/1984 **Age:** 29

| HOW MUCH HE PITCHED | | | | | | | | WHAT HE GAVE UP | | | | | | | | | | | | THE RESULTS | | | | | | | |
|---|---|---|---|---|---|---|---|---|---|---|---|---|---|---|---|---|---|---|---|---|---|---|---|---|---|---|---|
| Year Team | Lg | G | GS | CG | GF | IP | BFP | H | R | ER | HR | SH | SF | HB | TBB | IBB | SO | WP | Bk | W | L | Pct | Sh | Sv-Op | Hld | ERC | ERA |
| 2009 Charltt | A+ | 20 | 19 | 1 | 0 | 121.2 | 494 | 117 | 35 | 27 | 11 | 4 | 1 | 4 | 23 | 0 | 111 | 4 | 0 | 12 | 4 | .750 | 0 | 0- - | - | 3.16 | 2.00 |
| 2009 Mont | AA | 2 | 2 | 0 | 0 | 11.1 | 49 | 13 | 6 | 6 | 1 | 1 | 0 | 0 | 4 | 1 | 9 | 0 | 0 | 0 | 2 | .000 | 0 | 0- - | - | 4.58 | 4.76 |
| 2010 Mont | AA | 18 | 3 | 0 | 4 | 48.0 | 194 | 40 | 16 | 9 | 2 | 3 | 2 | 1 | 15 | 2 | 57 | 1 | 1 | 6 | 2 | .750 | 0 | 0- - | - | 2.55 | 1.69 |
| 2010 Drham | AAA | 23 | 1 | 0 | 7 | 40.1 | 181 | 44 | 21 | 20 | 4 | 0 | 1 | 4 | 17 | 2 | 45 | 5 | 0 | 6 | 2 | .750 | 0 | 0- - | - | 5.01 | 4.46 |
| 2011 Jaxnvl | AA | 22 | 13 | 0 | 3 | 76.1 | 332 | 87 | 44 | 41 | 7 | 3 | 2 | 3 | 23 | 0 | 48 | 3 | 0 | 2 | 5 | .286 | 0 | 0- - | - | 4.61 | 4.83 |
| 2011 NewOr | AAA | 10 | 5 | 0 | 1 | 35.2 | 147 | 34 | 17 | 17 | 1 | 1 | 2 | 0 | 8 | 0 | 39 | 2 | 0 | 3 | 2 | .600 | 0 | 0- - | - | 2.68 | 4.29 |
| 2012 Toledo | AAA | 25 | 0 | 0 | 8 | 29.1 | 118 | 25 | 8 | 7 | 0 | 2 | 1 | 0 | 8 | 0 | 33 | 3 | 0 | 0 | 2 | .000 | 0 | 0- - | - | 2.22 | 2.15 |
| 2013 WMich | A | 1 | 0 | 0 | 0 | 1.0 | 3 | 0 | 0 | 0 | 0 | 0 | 0 | 0 | 0 | 0 | 1 | 0 | 0 | 0 | 0 | - | 0 | 0- - | - | 0.00 | 0.00 |
| 2013 Toledo | AAA | 12 | 0 | 0 | 1 | 15.2 | 62 | 9 | 5 | 4 | 0 | 1 | 1 | 0 | 6 | 1 | 12 | 3 | 0 | 0 | 1 | .000 | 0 | 0- - | - | 1.34 | 2.30 |
| 2012 Det | AL | 18 | 0 | 0 | 5 | 20.2 | 86 | 18 | 8 | 8 | 1 | 0 | 0 | 1 | 9 | 2 | 20 | 1 | 0 | 2 | 1 | .667 | 0 | 0-0 | 1 | 3.27 | 3.48 |
| 2013 Det | AL | 29 | 0 | 0 | 8 | 35.1 | 151 | 36 | 20 | 19 | 4 | 1 | 1 | 2 | 11 | 2 | 37 | 2 | 0 | 0 | 2 | .000 | 0 | 0-0 | 4 | 4.08 | 4.84 |
| 2 ML YEARS | | 47 | 0 | 0 | 13 | 56.0 | 237 | 54 | 28 | 27 | 5 | 1 | 1 | 3 | 20 | 4 | 57 | 3 | 0 | 2 | 3 | .400 | 0 | 0-0 | 5 | 3.78 | 4.34 |

# Scott Downs

**Pitches:** L **Bats:** L **Pos:** RP-68 **Ht:** 6'2" **Wt:** 220 **Born:** 3/17/1976 **Age:** 38

| | | | HOW MUCH HE PITCHED | | | | | | WHAT HE GAVE UP | | | | | | | | | | | | THE RESULTS | | | | | | | |
|---|---|---|---|---|---|---|---|---|---|---|---|---|---|---|---|---|---|---|---|---|---|---|---|---|---|---|---|---|
| Year | Team | Lg | G | GS | CG | GF | IP | BFP | H | R | ER | HR | SH | SF | HB | TBB | IBB | SO | WP | Bk | W | L | Pct | Sh | Sv-Op | Hld | ERC | ERA |
| 2000 | 2 Tms | NL | 19 | 19 | 0 | 0 | 97.0 | 442 | 122 | 62 | 57 | 13 | 2 | 4 | 5 | 40 | 1 | 63 | 1 | 0 | 4 | 3 | .571 | 0 | 0-0 | 0 | 6.19 | 5.29 |
| 2003 | Mon | NL | 1 | 1 | 0 | 0 | 3.0 | 17 | 5 | 5 | 5 | 2 | 0 | 0 | 0 | 3 | 2 | 4 | 0 | 1 | 0 | 1 | .000 | 0 | 0-0 | 0 | 15.01 | 15.00 |
| 2004 | Mon | NL | 12 | 12 | 1 | 0 | 63.0 | 284 | 79 | 47 | 36 | 9 | 2 | 1 | 3 | 23 | 2 | 38 | 2 | 0 | 3 | 6 | .333 | 1 | 0-0 | 0 | 5.97 | 5.14 |
| 2005 | Tor | AL | 26 | 13 | 0 | 0 | 94.0 | 407 | 93 | 49 | 45 | 12 | 0 | 1 | 5 | 34 | 0 | 75 | 3 | 0 | 4 | 3 | .571 | 0 | 0-0 | 0 | 4.25 | 4.31 |
| 2006 | Tor | AL | 59 | 5 | 0 | 13 | 77.0 | 327 | 73 | 38 | 35 | 9 | 1 | 1 | 2 | 30 | 6 | 61 | 7 | 0 | 6 | 2 | .750 | 0 | 1-4 | 6 | 3.87 | 4.09 |
| 2007 | Tor | AL | **81** | 0 | 0 | 13 | 58.0 | 239 | 47 | 15 | 14 | 3 | 1 | 2 | 1 | 24 | 3 | 57 | 2 | 1 | 4 | 2 | .667 | 0 | 1-4 | 24 | 2.81 | 2.17 |
| 2008 | Tor | AL | 66 | 0 | 0 | 14 | 70.2 | 290 | 54 | 15 | 14 | 3 | 5 | 0 | 4 | 27 | 7 | 57 | 3 | 0 | 0 | 3 | .000 | 0 | 5-9 | 24 | 2.47 | 1.78 |
| 2009 | Tor | AL | 48 | 0 | 0 | 24 | 46.2 | 200 | 46 | 18 | 16 | 4 | 0 | 2 | 2 | 13 | 1 | 43 | 1 | 0 | 1 | 3 | .250 | 0 | 9-13 | 10 | 3.50 | 3.09 |
| 2010 | Tor | AL | 67 | 0 | 0 | 14 | 61.1 | 241 | 47 | 19 | 18 | 3 | 0 | 0 | 4 | 14 | 3 | 48 | 1 | 0 | 5 | 5 | .500 | 0 | 0-2 | 26 | 2.14 | 2.64 |
| 2011 | LAA | AL | 60 | 0 | 0 | 10 | 53.2 | 218 | 39 | 11 | 8 | 3 | 5 | 2 | 0 | 15 | 3 | 35 | 2 | 0 | 6 | 3 | .667 | 0 | 1-4 | 26 | 1.83 | 1.34 |
| 2012 | LAA | AL | 57 | 0 | 0 | 11 | 45.2 | 194 | 43 | 17 | 16 | 3 | 0 | 2 | 0 | 17 | 2 | 32 | 1 | 0 | 1 | 1 | .500 | 0 | 9-12 | 25 | 3.33 | 3.15 |
| 2013 | 2 Tms | | 68 | 0 | 0 | 5 | 43.1 | 189 | 45 | 13 | 12 | 1 | 4 | 1 | 2 | 19 | 2 | 37 | 2 | 0 | 4 | 4 | .500 | 0 | 0-4 | 26 | 4.03 | 2.49 |
| 00 | ChC | NL | 18 | 18 | 0 | 0 | 94.0 | 426 | 117 | 59 | 54 | 13 | 2 | 4 | 5 | 37 | 1 | 63 | 1 | 0 | 4 | 3 | .571 | 0 | 0-0 | 0 | 6.07 | 5.17 |
| 00 | Mon | NL | 1 | 1 | 0 | 0 | 3.0 | 16 | 5 | 3 | 3 | 0 | 0 | 0 | 0 | 3 | 0 | 0 | 0 | 0 | 0 | 0 | - | 0 | 0-0 | 0 | 10.34 | 9.00 |
| 13 | LAA | AL | 43 | 0 | 0 | 3 | 29.1 | 122 | 26 | 7 | 6 | 1 | 2 | 0 | 2 | 11 | 2 | 22 | 1 | 0 | 2 | 3 | .400 | 0 | 0-3 | 18 | 3.13 | 1.84 |
| 13 | Atl | NL | 25 | 0 | 0 | 2 | 14.0 | 67 | 19 | 6 | 6 | 0 | 2 | 1 | 0 | 8 | 0 | 15 | 1 | 0 | 2 | 1 | .667 | 0 | 0-1 | 8 | 6.10 | 3.86 |
| 12 ML YEARS | | | 564 | 50 | 1 | 104 | 713.1 | 3048 | 693 | 309 | 276 | 65 | 20 | 16 | 28 | 259 | 32 | 550 | 25 | 2 | 38 | 36 | .514 | 1 | 26-52 | 167 | 3.80 | 3.48 |

# Brian Dozier

**Bats:** R **Throws:** R **Pos:** 2B-146;PR-2 DOUGH-zher **Ht:** 5'11" **Wt:** 190 **Born:** 5/15/1987 **Age:** 27

| | | | BATTING | | | | | | | | | | | | | | | | | | BASERUNNING | | | | AVERAGES | | |
|---|---|---|---|---|---|---|---|---|---|---|---|---|---|---|---|---|---|---|---|---|---|---|---|---|---|---|---|
| Year | Team | Lg | G | AB | H | 2B | 3B | HR | (Hm | Rd) | TB | R | RBI | RC | TBB | IBB | SO | HBP | SH | SF | SB | CS | SB% | GDP | Avg | OBP | Slg |
| 2009 | Twins | R | 5 | 14 | 4 | 0 | 0 | 0 | (- | -) | 4 | 1 | 0 | 1 | 2 | 0 | 1 | 0 | 0 | 0 | 0 | 0 | - | 0 | .286 | .375 | .286 |
| 2009 | Elizab | R | 53 | 218 | 77 | 17 | 0 | 0 | (- | -) | 94 | 38 | 14 | 41 | 23 | 0 | 26 | 3 | 1 | 3 | 3 | 0 | 1.00 | 4 | .353 | .417 | .431 |
| 2010 | Beloit | A | 39 | 151 | 42 | 7 | 1 | 0 | (- | -) | 51 | 24 | 17 | 20 | 16 | 0 | 16 | 0 | 3 | 0 | 6 | 1 | .86 | 3 | .278 | .347 | .338 |
| 2010 | FtMyrs | A+ | 93 | 350 | 96 | 11 | 1 | 5 | (- | -) | 124 | 44 | 42 | 49 | 44 | 2 | 41 | 1 | 9 | 6 | 10 | 4 | .71 | 9 | .274 | .352 | .354 |
| 2011 | FtMyrs | A+ | 49 | 180 | 58 | 11 | 5 | 2 | (- | -) | 85 | 32 | 22 | 39 | 27 | 2 | 20 | 6 | 3 | 2 | 13 | 4 | .76 | 5 | .322 | .423 | .472 |
| 2011 | NwBrit | AA | 78 | 311 | 99 | 22 | 7 | 7 | (- | -) | 156 | 60 | 34 | 59 | 28 | 0 | 46 | 5 | 7 | 0 | 11 | 7 | .61 | 8 | .318 | .384 | .502 |
| 2012 | Roch | AAA | 48 | 181 | 42 | 11 | 1 | 2 | (- | -) | 61 | 15 | 17 | 18 | 14 | 1 | 34 | 1 | 1 | 3 | 3 | 2 | .60 | 5 | .232 | .286 | .337 |
| 2012 | Min | AL | 84 | 316 | 74 | 11 | 1 | 6 | (4 | 2) | 105 | 33 | 33 | 24 | 16 | 0 | 58 | 1 | 4 | 3 | 9 | 2 | .82 | 10 | .234 | .271 | .332 |
| 2013 | Min | AL | 147 | 558 | 136 | 33 | 4 | 18 | (8 | 10) | 231 | 72 | 66 | 74 | 51 | 0 | 120 | 6 | 3 | 4 | 14 | 7 | .67 | 14 | .244 | .312 | .414 |
| 2 ML YEARS | | | 231 | 874 | 210 | 44 | 5 | 24 | (12 | 12) | 336 | 105 | 99 | 98 | 67 | 0 | 178 | 7 | 7 | 7 | 23 | 9 | .72 | 24 | .240 | .297 | .384 |

# Kyle Drabek

**Pitches:** R **Bats:** R **Pos:** RP-3 DRAY-beck **Ht:** 6'1" **Wt:** 230 **Born:** 12/8/1987 **Age:** 26

| | | | HOW MUCH HE PITCHED | | | | | | WHAT HE GAVE UP | | | | | | | | | | | | THE RESULTS | | | | | | | |
|---|---|---|---|---|---|---|---|---|---|---|---|---|---|---|---|---|---|---|---|---|---|---|---|---|---|---|---|---|
| Year | Team | Lg | G | GS | CG | GF | IP | BFP | H | R | ER | HR | SH | SF | HB | TBB | IBB | SO | WP | Bk | W | L | Pct | Sh | Sv-Op | Hld | ERC | ERA |
| 2013 | Dnedin* | A+ | 8 | 6 | 0 | 0 | 20.2 | 78 | 14 | 6 | 6 | 2 | 0 | 1 | 1 | 3 | 0 | 20 | 4 | 0 | 0 | 1 | .000 | 0 | 0- - | - | 1.73 | 2.61 |
| 2013 | NHam* | AA | 2 | 2 | 0 | 0 | 8.0 | 30 | 4 | 3 | 3 | 2 | 0 | 0 | 0 | 1 | 0 | 3 | 0 | 0 | 0 | 1 | .000 | 0 | 0- - | - | 1.39 | 3.38 |
| 2013 | Buffalo* | AAA | 4 | 3 | 0 | 0 | 14.1 | 58 | 14 | 6 | 6 | 1 | 0 | 0 | 0 | 2 | 0 | 12 | 1 | 0 | 1 | 2 | .333 | 0 | 0- - | - | 2.77 | 3.77 |
| 2010 | Tor | AL | 3 | 3 | 0 | 0 | 17.0 | 69 | 18 | 9 | 9 | 2 | 1 | 2 | 0 | 5 | 0 | 12 | 2 | 0 | 0 | 3 | .000 | 0 | 0-0 | 0 | 4.34 | 4.76 |
| 2011 | Tor | AL | 18 | 14 | 0 | 2 | 78.2 | 365 | 87 | 54 | 53 | 10 | 3 | 5 | 1 | 55 | 0 | 51 | 11 | 0 | 4 | 5 | .444 | 0 | 0-0 | 0 | 6.30 | 6.06 |
| 2012 | Tor | AL | 13 | 13 | 0 | 0 | 71.1 | 317 | 67 | 41 | 37 | 10 | 0 | 1 | 1 | 47 | 0 | 47 | 7 | 0 | 4 | 7 | .364 | 0 | 0-0 | 0 | 5.21 | 4.67 |
| 2013 | Tor | AL | 3 | 0 | 0 | 1 | 2.1 | 14 | 4 | 2 | 2 | 1 | 0 | 0 | 1 | 2 | 0 | 3 | 0 | 0 | 0 | 0 | - | 0 | 0-0 | 0 | 16.01 | 7.71 |
| 4 ML YEARS | | | 37 | 30 | 0 | 3 | 169.1 | 765 | 176 | 106 | 101 | 23 | 4 | 8 | 3 | 109 | 0 | 113 | 20 | 0 | 8 | 15 | .348 | 0 | 0-0 | 0 | 5.75 | 5.37 |

# Stephen Drew

**Bats:** L **Throws:** R **Pos:** SS-124;PH-1 **Ht:** 6'0" **Wt:** 190 **Born:** 3/16/1983 **Age:** 31

| | | | BATTING | | | | | | | | | | | | | | | | | | BASERUNNING | | | | AVERAGES | | |
|---|---|---|---|---|---|---|---|---|---|---|---|---|---|---|---|---|---|---|---|---|---|---|---|---|---|---|---|
| Year | Team | Lg | G | AB | H | 2B | 3B | HR | (Hm | Rd) | TB | R | RBI | RC | TBB | IBB | SO | HBP | SH | SF | SB | CS | SB% | GDP | Avg | OBP | Slg |
| 2013 | PortInd* | AA | 6 | 20 | 4 | 2 | 0 | 1 | (- | -) | 9 | 1 | 4 | 2 | 2 | 0 | 4 | 0 | 0 | 1 | 0 | 0 | - | 0 | .200 | .261 | .450 |
| 2006 | Ari | NL | 59 | 209 | 66 | 13 | 7 | 5 | (3 | 2) | 108 | 27 | 23 | 31 | 14 | 4 | 50 | 0 | 2 | 1 | 2 | 0 | 1.00 | 1 | .316 | .357 | .517 |
| 2007 | Ari | NL | 150 | 543 | 129 | 28 | 4 | 12 | (6 | 6) | 201 | 60 | 60 | 71 | 60 | 5 | 100 | 3 | 5 | 8 | 9 | 0 | 1.00 | 4 | .238 | .313 | .370 |
| 2008 | Ari | NL | 152 | 611 | 178 | 44 | 11 | 21 | (9 | 12) | 307 | 91 | 67 | 97 | 41 | 6 | 109 | 1 | 3 | 7 | 3 | 3 | .50 | 5 | .291 | .333 | .502 |
| 2009 | Ari | NL | 135 | 533 | 139 | 29 | 12 | 12 | (4 | 8) | 228 | 71 | 65 | 76 | 49 | 7 | 87 | 1 | 5 | 7 | 5 | 1 | .83 | 5 | .261 | .320 | .428 |
| 2010 | Ari | NL | 151 | 565 | 157 | 33 | 12 | 15 | (5 | 10) | 259 | 83 | 61 | 84 | 62 | 2 | 108 | 3 | 2 | 1 | 10 | 5 | .67 | 8 | .278 | .352 | .458 |
| 2011 | Ari | NL | 86 | 321 | 81 | 21 | 5 | 5 | (3 | 2) | 127 | 44 | 45 | 41 | 30 | 0 | 74 | 1 | 1 | 1 | 4 | 4 | .50 | 3 | .252 | .317 | .396 |
| 2012 | 2 Tms | | 79 | 287 | 64 | 13 | 1 | 7 | (4 | 3) | 100 | 38 | 28 | 30 | 37 | 2 | 76 | 0 | 0 | 3 | 1 | 2 | .33 | 2 | .223 | .309 | .348 |
| 2013 | Bos | AL | 124 | 442 | 112 | 29 | 8 | 13 | (6 | 7) | 196 | 57 | 67 | 63 | 54 | 3 | 124 | 1 | 0 | 4 | 6 | 0 | 1.00 | 9 | .253 | .333 | .443 |
| 12 | Ari | NL | 40 | 135 | 26 | 8 | 1 | 2 | (0 | 2) | 42 | 17 | 12 | 12 | 19 | 1 | 35 | 0 | 0 | 1 | 0 | 1 | .00 | 1 | .193 | .290 | .311 |
| 12 | Oak | AL | 39 | 152 | 38 | 5 | 0 | 5 | (4 | 1) | 58 | 21 | 16 | 18 | 18 | 1 | 41 | 0 | 0 | 2 | 1 | 1 | .50 | 1 | .250 | .326 | .382 |
| Postseason | | | 12 | 50 | 16 | 3 | 1 | 2 | (1 | 1) | 27 | 6 | 5 | 6 | 3 | 0 | 14 | 0 | 0 | 0 | 1 | 0 | 1.00 | 1 | .320 | .358 | .540 |
| 8 ML YEARS | | | 936 | 3511 | 926 | 210 | 60 | 90 | (40 | 50) | 1526 | 471 | 416 | 493 | 347 | 29 | 728 | 10 | 18 | 32 | 40 | 15 | .73 | 37 | .264 | .329 | .435 |

# Lucas Duda

**Bats:** L **Throws:** R **Pos:** LF-58;1B-34;PH-6;DH-2 DOO-duh **Ht:** 6'4" **Wt:** 255 **Born:** 2/3/1986 **Age:** 28

| | | | BATTING | | | | | | | | | | | | | | | | | | BASERUNNING | | | | AVERAGES | | |
|---|---|---|---|---|---|---|---|---|---|---|---|---|---|---|---|---|---|---|---|---|---|---|---|---|---|---|---|
| Year | Team | Lg | G | AB | H | 2B | 3B | HR | (Hm | Rd) | TB | R | RBI | RC | TBB | IBB | SO | HBP | SH | SF | SB | CS | SB% | GDP | Avg | OBP | Slg |
| 2013 | Mets* | R | 4 | 13 | 0 | 0 | 0 | 0 | (- | -) | 0 | 1 | 1 | 0 | 3 | 0 | 8 | 0 | 0 | 0 | 0 | 0 | - | 1 | .000 | .188 | .000 |
| 2013 | StLuci* | A+ | 7 | 28 | 7 | 2 | 0 | 1 | (- | -) | 12 | 4 | 5 | 3 | 2 | 0 | 7 | 0 | 0 | 0 | 0 | 0 | - | 2 | .250 | .300 | .429 |
| 2013 | LsVgs* | AAA | 18 | 62 | 19 | 3 | 0 | 0 | (- | -) | 22 | 13 | 8 | 11 | 14 | 0 | 15 | 0 | 0 | 2 | 1 | 0 | 1.00 | 0 | .306 | .423 | .355 |
| 2010 | NYM | NL | 29 | 84 | 17 | 6 | 0 | 4 | (3 | 1) | 35 | 11 | 13 | 5 | 6 | 0 | 22 | 1 | 0 | 1 | 0 | 0 | - | 2 | .202 | .261 | .417 |

| BATTING | | | | | | | | | | | | | | | | | | | | | BASERUNNING | | | | AVERAGES | | |
|---|---|---|---|---|---|---|---|---|---|---|---|---|---|---|---|---|---|---|---|---|---|---|---|---|---|---|---|
| Year | Team | Lg | G | AB | H | 2B | 3B | HR | (Hm | Rd) | TB | R | RBI | RC | TBB | IBB | SO | HBP | SH | SF | SB | CS | SB% | GDP | Avg | OBP | Slg |
| 2011 | NYM | NL | 100 | 301 | 88 | 21 | 3 | 10 | (2 | 8) | 145 | 38 | 50 | 44 | 33 | 3 | 57 | 7 | 1 | 5 | 1 | 0 | 1.00 | 5 | .292 | .370 | .482 |
| 2012 | NYM | NL | 121 | 401 | 96 | 15 | 0 | 15 | (9 | 6) | 156 | 43 | 57 | 58 | 51 | 0 | 120 | 4 | 0 | 3 | 1 | 0 | 1.00 | 5 | .239 | .329 | .389 |
| 2013 | NYM | NL | 100 | 318 | 71 | 16 | 0 | 15 | (9 | 6) | 132 | 42 | 33 | 38 | 55 | 4 | 102 | 9 | 0 | 2 | 0 | 3 | .00 | 1 | .223 | .352 | .415 |
| 4 ML YEARS | | | 350 | 1104 | 272 | 58 | 3 | 44 | (23 | 21) | 468 | 134 | 153 | 145 | 145 | 7 | 301 | 21 | 1 | 11 | 2 | 3 | .40 | 13 | .246 | .342 | .424 |

# Brian Duensing

**Pitches:** L **Bats:** L **Pos:** RP-73 DUNN-sing **Ht:** 6'0" **Wt:** 205 **Born:** 2/22/1983 **Age:** 31

| HOW MUCH HE PITCHED | | | | | | | | | WHAT HE GAVE UP | | | | | | | | | | | | THE RESULTS | | | | | | | | |
|---|---|---|---|---|---|---|---|---|---|---|---|---|---|---|---|---|---|---|---|---|---|---|---|---|---|---|---|---|---|
| Year | Team | Lg | G | GS | CG | GF | IP | BFP | H | R | ER | HR | SH | SF | HB | TBB | IBB | SO | WP | Bk | W | L | Pct | Sh | Sv-Op | Hld | ERC | ERA |
| 2009 | Min | AL | 24 | 9 | 0 | 3 | 84.0 | 359 | 84 | 37 | 34 | 7 | 3 | 2 | 3 | 31 | 1 | 53 | 1 | 0 | 5 | 2 | .714 | 0 | 0-0 | 1 | 4.00 | 3.64 |
| 2010 | Min | AL | 53 | 13 | 1 | 11 | 130.2 | 535 | 122 | 42 | 38 | 11 | 4 | 0 | 3 | 35 | 5 | 78 | 1 | 0 | 10 | 3 | .769 | 1 | 0-0 | 9 | 3.18 | 2.62 |
| 2011 | Min | AL | 32 | 28 | 1 | 0 | 161.2 | 711 | 193 | 102 | 94 | 21 | 7 | 6 | 1 | 52 | 3 | 115 | 3 | 0 | 9 | 14 | .391 | 1 | 0-0 | 0 | 5.12 | 5.23 |
| 2012 | Min | AL | 55 | 11 | 0 | 8 | 109.0 | 472 | 126 | 71 | 62 | 10 | 2 | 3 | 2 | 27 | 3 | 69 | 5 | 0 | 4 | 12 | .250 | 0 | 0-1 | 7 | 4.31 | 5.12 |
| 2013 | Min | AL | 73 | 0 | 0 | 9 | 61.0 | 268 | 68 | 28 | 27 | 4 | 2 | 2 | 2 | 22 | 4 | 56 | 6 | 0 | 6 | 2 | .750 | 0 | 1-4 | 15 | 4.35 | 3.98 |
| Postseason | | | 2 | 2 | 0 | 0 | 8.0 | 39 | 14 | 10 | 10 | 2 | 0 | 0 | 0 | 2 | 0 | 4 | 1 | 0 | 0 | 2 | .000 | 0 | 0-0 | 0 | 9.43 | 11.25 |
| 5 ML YEARS | | | 237 | 61 | 2 | 31 | 546.1 | 2345 | 593 | 280 | 255 | 53 | 18 | 13 | 11 | 167 | 16 | 371 | 16 | 0 | 34 | 33 | .507 | 2 | 1-5 | 32 | 4.22 | 4.20 |

# Danny Duffy

**Pitches:** L **Bats:** L **Pos:** SP-5 **Ht:** 6'3" **Wt:** 200 **Born:** 12/21/1988 **Age:** 25

| HOW MUCH HE PITCHED | | | | | | | | | WHAT HE GAVE UP | | | | | | | | | | | | THE RESULTS | | | | | | | | |
|---|---|---|---|---|---|---|---|---|---|---|---|---|---|---|---|---|---|---|---|---|---|---|---|---|---|---|---|---|---|
| Year | Team | Lg | G | GS | CG | GF | IP | BFP | H | R | ER | HR | SH | SF | HB | TBB | IBB | SO | WP | Bk | W | L | Pct | Sh | Sv-Op | Hld | ERC | ERA |
| 2013 | NWArk* | AA | 4 | 4 | 0 | 0 | 16.0 | 68 | 16 | 7 | 7 | 3 | 0 | 0 | 3 | 5 | 0 | 28 | 1 | 1 | 0 | 2 | .000 | 0 | 0- - | - | 5.33 | 3.94 |
| 2013 | Omha* | AAA | 12 | 10 | 0 | 0 | 53.0 | 230 | 50 | 26 | 24 | 4 | 2 | 0 | 2 | 25 | 0 | 59 | 2 | 0 | 3 | 0 | 1.000 | 0 | 0- - | - | 4.03 | 4.08 |
| 2011 | KC | AL | 20 | 20 | 0 | 0 | 105.1 | 474 | 119 | 66 | 66 | 15 | 2 | 2 | 5 | 51 | 1 | 87 | 4 | 1 | 4 | 8 | .333 | 0 | 0-0 | 0 | 5.76 | 5.64 |
| 2012 | KC | AL | 6 | 6 | 0 | 0 | 27.2 | 121 | 26 | 13 | 12 | 2 | 0 | 0 | 0 | 18 | 1 | 28 | 0 | 1 | 2 | 2 | .500 | 0 | 0-0 | 0 | 4.58 | 3.90 |
| 2013 | KC | AL | 5 | 5 | 0 | 0 | 24.1 | 104 | 19 | 5 | 5 | 0 | 0 | 0 | 1 | 14 | 0 | 22 | 2 | 0 | 2 | 0 | 1.000 | 0 | 0-0 | 0 | 3.02 | 1.85 |
| 3 ML YEARS | | | 31 | 31 | 0 | 0 | 157.1 | 699 | 164 | 84 | 83 | 17 | 2 | 2 | 6 | 83 | 2 | 137 | 6 | 2 | 8 | 10 | .444 | 0 | 0-0 | 0 | 5.10 | 4.75 |

# Zach Duke

**Pitches:** L **Bats:** L **Pos:** RP-25; SP-1 **Ht:** 6'2" **Wt:** 210 **Born:** 4/19/1983 **Age:** 31

| HOW MUCH HE PITCHED | | | | | | | | | WHAT HE GAVE UP | | | | | | | | | | | | THE RESULTS | | | | | | | | |
|---|---|---|---|---|---|---|---|---|---|---|---|---|---|---|---|---|---|---|---|---|---|---|---|---|---|---|---|---|---|
| Year | Team | Lg | G | GS | CG | GF | IP | BFP | H | R | ER | HR | SH | SF | HB | TBB | IBB | SO | WP | Bk | W | L | Pct | Sh | Sv-Op | Hld | ERC | ERA |
| 2013 | Lsvlle* | AAA | 26 | 0 | 0 | 4 | 27.2 | 104 | 19 | 4 | 4 | 2 | 0 | 1 | 1 | 5 | 0 | 34 | 0 | 0 | 2 | 0 | 1.000 | 0 | 2- - | - | 1.74 | 1.30 |
| 2005 | Pit | NL | 14 | 14 | 0 | 0 | 84.2 | 341 | 79 | 20 | 17 | 3 | 3 | 1 | 2 | 23 | 2 | 58 | 1 | 0 | 8 | 2 | .800 | 0 | 0-0 | 0 | 2.96 | 1.81 |
| 2006 | Pit | NL | 34 | 34 | 2 | 0 | 215.1 | 935 | **255** | 116 | 107 | 17 | 13 | 4 | 7 | 68 | 6 | 117 | 8 | 1 | 10 | 15 | .400 | 1 | 0-0 | 0 | 4.82 | 4.47 |
| 2007 | Pit | NL | 20 | 19 | 0 | 0 | 107.1 | 482 | 161 | 74 | 66 | 14 | 2 | 4 | 3 | 25 | 2 | 41 | 0 | 1 | 3 | 8 | .273 | 0 | 0-0 | 0 | 6.96 | 5.53 |
| 2008 | Pit | NL | 31 | 31 | 1 | 0 | 185.0 | 829 | 230 | 111 | 99 | 19 | **14** | 4 | 7 | 47 | 1 | 87 | 2 | 2 | 5 | 14 | .263 | 1 | 0-0 | 0 | 4.99 | 4.82 |
| 2009 | Pit | NL | 32 | 32 | 3 | 0 | 213.0 | 891 | 231 | 101 | 96 | 23 | **18** | 10 | 3 | 49 | 0 | 106 | 2 | 1 | 11 | **16** | .407 | 1 | 0-0 | 0 | 4.05 | 4.06 |
| 2010 | Pit | NL | 29 | 29 | 0 | 0 | 159.0 | 730 | 212 | 115 | 101 | 25 | 9 | 6 | 4 | 51 | 2 | 96 | 4 | **3** | 8 | 15 | .348 | 0 | 0-0 | 0 | 6.22 | 5.72 |
| 2011 | Ari | NL | 21 | 9 | 0 | 5 | 76.2 | 338 | 101 | 42 | 42 | 6 | 3 | 3 | 1 | 19 | 0 | 32 | 1 | 0 | 3 | 4 | .429 | 0 | 1-1 | 0 | 5.27 | 4.93 |
| 2012 | Was | NL | 8 | 0 | 0 | 3 | 13.2 | 56 | 11 | 2 | 2 | 0 | 0 | 0 | 0 | 4 | 0 | 10 | 0 | 0 | 1 | 0 | 1.000 | 0 | 0-0 | 0 | 2.00 | 1.32 |
| 2013 | 2 Tms | NL | 26 | 1 | 0 | 3 | 31.1 | 142 | 39 | 23 | 21 | 3 | 2 | 2 | 1 | 10 | 3 | 18 | 2 | 0 | 1 | 2 | .333 | 0 | 0-0 | 1 | 5.04 | 6.03 |
| 13 | Was | NL | 12 | 1 | 0 | 1 | 20.2 | 101 | 31 | 22 | 20 | 2 | 2 | 2 | 1 | 8 | 3 | 11 | 1 | 0 | 1 | 1 | .500 | 0 | 0-0 | 0 | 6.83 | 8.71 |
| 13 | Cin | NL | 14 | 0 | 0 | 2 | 10.2 | 41 | 8 | 1 | 1 | 1 | 0 | 0 | 0 | 2 | 0 | 7 | 1 | 0 | 0 | 1 | .000 | 0 | 0-0 | 1 | 2.01 | 0.84 |
| 9 ML YEARS | | | 215 | 169 | 6 | 11 | 1086.0 | 4744 | 1319 | 604 | 551 | 110 | 64 | 34 | 28 | 296 | 16 | 565 | 20 | 8 | 50 | 76 | .397 | 3 | 1-1 | 1 | 4.93 | 4.57 |

# Shelley Duncan

**Bats:** R **Throws:** R **Pos:** DH-14;PH-5;1B-4 **Ht:** 6'5" **Wt:** 215 **Born:** 9/29/1979 **Age:** 34

| BATTING | | | | | | | | | | | | | | | | | | | | | BASERUNNING | | | | AVERAGES | | |
|---|---|---|---|---|---|---|---|---|---|---|---|---|---|---|---|---|---|---|---|---|---|---|---|---|---|---|---|
| Year | Team | Lg | G | AB | H | 2B | 3B | HR | (Hm | Rd) | TB | R | RBI | RC | TBB | IBB | SO | HBP | SH | SF | SB | CS | SB% | GDP | Avg | OBP | Slg |
| 2013 | Drham* | AAA | 90 | 335 | 72 | 21 | 1 | 11 | (- | -) | 128 | 36 | 54 | 39 | 33 | 1 | 82 | 3 | 0 | 5 | 0 | 0 | - | 7 | .215 | .287 | .382 |
| 2007 | NYY | AL | 34 | 74 | 19 | 1 | 0 | 7 | (6 | 1) | 41 | 16 | 17 | 14 | 8 | 0 | 20 | 0 | 1 | 0 | 0 | 0 | - | 2 | .257 | .329 | .554 |
| 2008 | NYY | AL | 23 | 57 | 10 | 3 | 0 | 1 | (1 | 0) | 16 | 7 | 6 | 4 | 7 | 0 | 13 | 0 | 0 | 1 | 0 | 0 | - | 1 | .175 | .262 | .281 |
| 2009 | NYY | AL | 11 | 15 | 3 | 0 | 0 | 0 | (0 | 0) | 3 | 1 | 1 | 1 | 0 | 0 | 5 | 0 | 0 | 0 | 0 | 0 | - | 1 | .200 | .200 | .200 |
| 2010 | Cle | AL | 85 | 229 | 53 | 10 | 0 | 11 | (9 | 2) | 96 | 29 | 36 | 30 | 26 | 2 | 76 | 3 | 0 | 1 | 1 | 0 | 1.00 | 4 | .231 | .317 | .419 |
| 2011 | Cle | AL | 76 | 223 | 58 | 17 | 0 | 11 | (4 | 7) | 108 | 29 | 47 | 38 | 19 | 1 | 56 | 3 | 0 | 2 | 0 | 1 | .00 | 7 | .260 | .324 | .484 |
| 2012 | Cle | AL | 81 | 232 | 47 | 10 | 0 | 11 | (4 | 7) | 90 | 29 | 31 | 22 | 28 | 1 | 59 | 1 | 0 | 3 | 1 | 2 | .33 | 9 | .203 | .288 | .388 |
| 2013 | TB | AL | 20 | 55 | 10 | 1 | 0 | 2 | (1 | 1) | 17 | 6 | 6 | 5 | 9 | 0 | 14 | 0 | 0 | 0 | 0 | 0 | - | 4 | .182 | .297 | .309 |
| Postseason | | | 3 | 4 | 2 | 0 | 0 | 0 | (0 | 0) | 2 | 1 | 0 | 1 | 0 | 0 | 1 | 0 | 0 | 0 | 0 | 0 | - | 0 | .500 | .500 | .500 |
| 7 ML YEARS | | | 330 | 885 | 200 | 42 | 0 | 43 | (25 | 18) | 371 | 117 | 144 | 114 | 97 | 4 | 243 | 7 | 1 | 7 | 2 | 3 | .40 | 28 | .226 | .305 | .419 |

# Adam Dunn

**Bats:** L **Throws:** R **Pos:** DH-73;1B-71;LF-3;PH-3 **Ht:** 6'6" **Wt:** 285 **Born:** 11/9/1979 **Age:** 34

| BATTING | | | | | | | | | | | | | | | | | | | | | BASERUNNING | | | | AVERAGES | | |
|---|---|---|---|---|---|---|---|---|---|---|---|---|---|---|---|---|---|---|---|---|---|---|---|---|---|---|---|
| Year | Team | Lg | G | AB | H | 2B | 3B | HR | (Hm | Rd) | TB | R | RBI | RC | TBB | IBB | SO | HBP | SH | SF | SB | CS | SB% | GDP | Avg | OBP | Slg |
| 2001 | Cin | NL | 66 | 244 | 64 | 18 | 1 | 19 | (8 | 11) | 141 | 54 | 43 | 51 | 38 | 2 | 74 | 4 | 0 | 0 | 4 | 2 | .67 | 4 | .262 | .371 | .578 |
| 2002 | Cin | NL | 158 | 535 | 133 | 28 | 2 | 26 | (13 | 13) | 243 | 84 | 71 | 96 | 128 | 13 | 170 | 9 | 1 | 3 | 19 | 9 | .68 | 8 | .249 | .400 | .454 |
| 2003 | Cin | NL | 116 | 381 | 82 | 12 | 1 | 27 | (16 | 11) | 177 | 70 | 57 | 61 | 74 | 8 | 126 | 10 | 0 | 4 | 8 | 2 | .80 | 4 | .215 | .354 | .465 |
| 2004 | Cin | NL | 161 | 568 | 151 | 34 | 0 | 46 | (25 | 21) | 323 | 105 | 102 | 108 | 108 | 11 | **195** | 5 | 0 | 0 | 6 | 1 | .86 | 8 | .266 | .388 | .569 |
| 2005 | Cin | NL | 160 | 543 | 134 | 35 | 2 | 40 | **(26** | 14) | 293 | 107 | 101 | 112 | 114 | 14 | **168** | 12 | 0 | 2 | 4 | 2 | .67 | 6 | .247 | .387 | .540 |
| 2006 | Cin | NL | 160 | 561 | 131 | 24 | 0 | 40 | (22 | 18) | 275 | 99 | 92 | 96 | 112 | 12 | **194** | 6 | 1 | 3 | 7 | 0 | 1.00 | 6 | .234 | .365 | .490 |
| 2007 | Cin | NL | 152 | 522 | 138 | 27 | 2 | 40 | (19 | 21) | 289 | 101 | 106 | 103 | 101 | 8 | 165 | 5 | 0 | 4 | 9 | 2 | .82 | 12 | .264 | .386 | .554 |
| 2008 | 2 Tms | NL | 158 | 517 | 122 | 23 | 0 | 40 | (21 | 19) | 265 | 79 | 100 | 101 | **122** | 13 | 164 | 7 | 0 | 5 | 2 | 1 | .67 | 7 | .236 | .386 | .513 |
| 2009 | Was | NL | 159 | 546 | 146 | 29 | 0 | 38 | (19 | 19) | 289 | 81 | 105 | 109 | 116 | 16 | 177 | 4 | 0 | 2 | 0 | 1 | .00 | 8 | .267 | .398 | .529 |
| 2010 | Was | NL | 158 | 558 | 145 | 36 | 2 | 38 | (20 | 18) | 299 | 85 | 103 | 88 | 77 | 10 | 199 | 9 | 0 | 4 | 0 | 1 | .00 | 10 | .260 | .356 | .536 |

| Year | Team | Lg | G | AB | H | 2B | 3B | HR | (Hm | Rd) | TB | R | RBI | RC | TBB | IBB | SO | HBP | SH | SF | SB | CS | SB% | GDP | Avg | OBP | Slg |
|---|---|---|---|---|---|---|---|---|---|---|---|---|---|---|---|---|---|---|---|---|---|---|---|---|---|---|---|
| | | | BATTING | | | | | | | | | | | | | | | | | | BASERUNNING | | | | AVERAGES | | |
| 2011 | CWS | AL | 122 | 415 | 66 | 16 | 0 | 11 | (8 | 3) | 115 | 36 | 42 | 34 | 75 | 0 | 177 | 4 | 0 | 2 | 0 | 1 | .00 | 10 | .159 | .292 | .277 |
| 2012 | CWS | AL | 151 | 539 | 110 | 19 | 0 | 41 | (18 | **23)** | 252 | 87 | 96 | 85 | **105** | 3 | **222** | 1 | 0 | 4 | 2 | 1 | .67 | 8 | .204 | .333 | .468 |
| 2013 | CWS | AL | 149 | 525 | 115 | 15 | 0 | 34 | (21 | 13) | 232 | 60 | 86 | 75 | 76 | 7 | 189 | 3 | 0 | 3 | 1 | 1 | .50 | 2 | .219 | .320 | .442 |
| 08 | Cin | NL | 114 | 373 | 87 | 14 | 0 | 32 | (16 | 16) | 197 | 58 | 74 | 74 | 80 | 6 | 120 | 6 | 0 | 5 | 1 | 1 | .50 | 4 | .233 | .373 | .528 |
| 08 | Ari | NL | 44 | 144 | 35 | 9 | 0 | 8 | (5 | 3) | 68 | 21 | 26 | 27 | 42 | 7 | 44 | 1 | 0 | 0 | 1 | 0 | 1.00 | 3 | .243 | .417 | .472 |
| 13 ML YEARS | | | 1870 | 6454 | 1537 | 316 | 10 | 440 | (236 | 204) | 3193 | 1048 | 1104 | 1119 | 1246 | 117 | 2220 | 79 | 2 | 36 | 62 | 24 | .72 | 95 | .238 | .366 | .495 |

# Mike Dunn

**Pitches:** L **Bats:** L **Pos:** RP-75 **Ht:** 6'0" **Wt:** 205 **Born:** 5/23/1985 **Age:** 29

| Year | Team | Lg | G | GS | CG | GF | IP | BFP | H | R | ER | HR | SH | SF | HB | TBB | IBB | SO | WP | Bk | W | L | Pct | Sh | Sv-Op | Hld | ERC | ERA |
|---|---|---|---|---|---|---|---|---|---|---|---|---|---|---|---|---|---|---|---|---|---|---|---|---|---|---|---|---|
| | | | HOW MUCH HE PITCHED | | | | | | WHAT HE GAVE UP | | | | | | | | | | | | THE RESULTS | | | | | | | |
| 2009 | NYY | AL | 4 | 0 | 0 | 3 | 4.0 | 20 | 3 | 3 | 3 | 1 | 0 | 0 | 0 | 5 | 0 | 5 | 1 | 0 | 0 | 0 | - | 0 | 0-0 | 0 | 7.17 | 6.75 |
| 2010 | Atl | NL | 25 | 0 | 0 | 5 | 19.0 | 88 | 15 | 4 | 4 | 1 | 0 | 0 | 0 | 17 | 2 | 27 | 2 | 0 | 2 | 0 | 1.000 | 0 | 0-0 | 1 | 4.19 | 1.89 |
| 2011 | Fla | NL | 72 | 0 | 0 | 11 | 63.0 | 267 | 51 | 28 | 24 | 9 | 4 | 2 | 2 | 31 | 2 | 68 | 3 | 0 | 5 | 6 | .455 | 0 | 0-4 | 15 | 3.77 | 3.43 |
| 2012 | Mia | NL | 60 | 0 | 0 | 8 | 44.0 | 208 | 49 | 31 | 24 | 3 | 2 | 4 | 0 | 29 | 8 | 47 | 2 | 0 | 0 | 3 | .000 | 0 | 1-6 | 18 | 5.10 | 4.91 |
| 2013 | Mia | NL | 75 | 0 | 0 | 15 | 67.2 | 282 | 53 | 21 | 20 | 5 | 1 | 3 | 0 | 28 | 4 | 72 | 2 | 0 | 3 | 4 | .429 | 0 | 2-5 | 18 | 2.68 | 2.66 |
| Postseason | | | 3 | 0 | 0 | 0 | 1.1 | 6 | 2 | 0 | 0 | 0 | 0 | 0 | 0 | 0 | 0 | 2 | 0 | 0 | 0 | 0 | - | 0 | 0-1 | 0 | 4.47 | 0.00 |
| 5 ML YEARS | | | 236 | 0 | 0 | 42 | 197.2 | 865 | 171 | 87 | 75 | 19 | 7 | 9 | 2 | 110 | 16 | 219 | 10 | 0 | 10 | 13 | .435 | 0 | 3-15 | 52 | 3.78 | 3.41 |

# Jake Dunning

**Pitches:** R **Bats:** R **Pos:** RP-29 **Ht:** 6'4" **Wt:** 190 **Born:** 8/12/1988 **Age:** 25

| Year | Team | Lg | G | GS | CG | GF | IP | BFP | H | R | ER | HR | SH | SF | HB | TBB | IBB | SO | WP | Bk | W | L | Pct | Sh | Sv-Op | Hld | ERC | ERA |
|---|---|---|---|---|---|---|---|---|---|---|---|---|---|---|---|---|---|---|---|---|---|---|---|---|---|---|---|---|
| | | | HOW MUCH HE PITCHED | | | | | | WHAT HE GAVE UP | | | | | | | | | | | | THE RESULTS | | | | | | | |
| 2009 | Giants | R | 1 | 0 | 0 | 0 | 1.0 | 6 | 2 | 1 | 1 | 0 | 1 | 0 | 0 | 1 | 0 | 2 | 0 | 0 | 0 | 0 | - | 0 | 0- - | - | 12.01 | 9.00 |
| 2010 | SlmKzr | A- | 18 | 0 | 0 | 8 | 36.2 | 148 | 30 | 15 | 12 | 2 | 1 | 1 | 2 | 8 | 0 | 46 | 4 | 0 | 1 | 0 | 1.000 | 0 | 2- - | - | 2.36 | 2.95 |
| 2011 | SnJos | A+ | 41 | 7 | 0 | 19 | 76.0 | 328 | 86 | 42 | 40 | 7 | 2 | 3 | 6 | 24 | 0 | 71 | 5 | 0 | 6 | 3 | .667 | 0 | 10- - | - | 4.88 | 4.74 |
| 2012 | Rchmd | AA | 44 | 0 | 0 | 14 | 68.0 | 296 | 74 | 36 | 31 | 2 | 6 | 4 | 4 | 22 | 2 | 53 | 6 | 0 | 5 | 2 | .714 | 0 | 0- - | - | 3.96 | 4.10 |
| 2013 | Fresno | AAA | 34 | 0 | 0 | 5 | 48.1 | 203 | 47 | 14 | 8 | 3 | 2 | 1 | 5 | 14 | 1 | 44 | 4 | 0 | 2 | 2 | .500 | 0 | 1- - | - | 3.67 | 1.49 |
| 2013 | SF | NL | 29 | 0 | 0 | 9 | 25.1 | 104 | 20 | 8 | 8 | 2 | 0 | 1 | 3 | 11 | 1 | 16 | 1 | 0 | 0 | 2 | .000 | 0 | 0-0 | 2 | 3.45 | 2.84 |

# Chad Durbin

**Pitches:** R **Bats:** R **Pos:** RP-16 DURR-binn **Ht:** 6'2" **Wt:** 225 **Born:** 12/3/1977 **Age:** 36

| Year | Team | Lg | G | GS | CG | GF | IP | BFP | H | R | ER | HR | SH | SF | HB | TBB | IBB | SO | WP | Bk | W | L | Pct | Sh | Sv-Op | Hld | ERC | ERA |
|---|---|---|---|---|---|---|---|---|---|---|---|---|---|---|---|---|---|---|---|---|---|---|---|---|---|---|---|---|
| | | | HOW MUCH HE PITCHED | | | | | | WHAT HE GAVE UP | | | | | | | | | | | | THE RESULTS | | | | | | | |
| 1999 | KC | AL | 1 | 0 | 0 | 0 | 2.1 | 9 | 1 | 0 | 0 | 0 | 0 | 0 | 0 | 1 | 0 | 3 | 1 | 0 | 0 | 0 | - | 0 | 0-0 | 0 | 1.08 | 0.00 |
| 2000 | KC | AL | 16 | 16 | 0 | 0 | 72.1 | 349 | 91 | 71 | 66 | 14 | 1 | 3 | 0 | 43 | 1 | 37 | 7 | 0 | 2 | 5 | .286 | 0 | 0-0 | 0 | 7.05 | 8.21 |
| 2001 | KC | AL | 29 | 29 | 2 | 0 | 179.0 | 777 | 201 | 109 | 98 | 26 | 2 | 7 | 11 | 58 | 0 | 95 | 6 | 0 | 9 | 16 | .360 | 0 | 0-0 | 0 | 5.15 | 4.93 |
| 2002 | KC | AL | 2 | 2 | 0 | 0 | 8.1 | 43 | 13 | 11 | 11 | 3 | 0 | 0 | 1 | 4 | 0 | 5 | 0 | 0 | 0 | 1 | .000 | 0 | 0-0 | 0 | 10.58 | 11.88 |
| 2003 | Cle | AL | 3 | 1 | 0 | 0 | 8.2 | 45 | 18 | 12 | 7 | 2 | 0 | 0 | 0 | 3 | 0 | 8 | 2 | 0 | 0 | 1 | .000 | 0 | 0-0 | 0 | 12.37 | 7.27 |
| 2004 | 2 Tms | | 24 | 8 | 1 | 5 | 60.2 | 291 | 72 | 50 | 47 | 11 | 2 | 2 | 5 | 35 | 3 | 48 | 5 | 0 | 6 | 7 | .462 | 0 | 0-0 | 1 | 6.75 | 6.97 |
| 2006 | Det | AL | 3 | 0 | 0 | 1 | 6.0 | 24 | 6 | 1 | 1 | 1 | 0 | 0 | 0 | 0 | 0 | 3 | 0 | 0 | 0 | 0 | - | 0 | 0-0 | 0 | 2.87 | 1.50 |
| 2007 | Det | AL | 36 | 19 | 0 | 7 | 127.2 | 561 | 133 | 71 | 67 | 21 | 1 | 7 | 8 | 49 | 4 | 66 | 2 | 0 | 8 | 7 | .533 | 0 | 1-2 | 3 | 4.92 | 4.72 |
| 2008 | Phi | NL | 71 | 0 | 0 | 12 | 87.2 | 365 | 81 | 33 | 28 | 5 | 4 | 2 | 4 | 35 | 7 | 63 | 3 | 0 | 5 | 4 | .556 | 0 | 1-7 | 17 | 3.51 | 2.87 |
| 2009 | Phi | NL | 59 | 0 | 0 | 15 | 69.2 | 314 | 56 | 38 | 34 | 8 | 3 | 3 | 7 | 47 | 2 | 62 | 2 | 0 | 2 | 2 | .500 | 0 | 2-3 | 8 | 4.47 | 4.39 |
| 2010 | Phi | NL | 64 | 0 | 0 | 9 | 68.2 | 291 | 63 | 29 | 29 | 7 | 1 | 2 | 5 | 27 | 2 | 63 | 0 | 0 | 4 | 1 | .800 | 0 | 0-1 | 15 | 3.90 | 3.80 |
| 2011 | Cle | AL | 56 | 0 | 0 | 11 | 68.1 | 318 | 86 | 45 | 42 | 12 | 1 | 7 | 3 | 26 | 3 | 59 | 6 | 0 | 2 | 2 | .500 | 0 | 0-1 | 3 | 6.11 | 5.53 |
| 2012 | Atl | NL | 76 | 0 | 0 | 19 | 61.0 | 257 | 52 | 25 | 21 | 9 | 2 | 2 | 0 | 28 | 3 | 49 | 1 | 0 | 4 | 1 | .800 | 0 | 1-3 | 15 | 3.76 | 3.10 |
| 2013 | Phi | NL | 16 | 0 | 0 | 3 | 16.0 | 81 | 25 | 17 | 16 | 4 | 0 | 2 | 0 | 9 | 1 | 16 | 0 | 0 | 1 | 0 | 1.000 | 0 | 0-0 | 0 | 9.40 | 9.00 |
| 04 | Cle | AL | 17 | 8 | 1 | 5 | 51.1 | 239 | 63 | 40 | 38 | 10 | 0 | 2 | 4 | 24 | 3 | 38 | 3 | 0 | 5 | 6 | .455 | 0 | 0-0 | 0 | 6.70 | 6.66 |
| 04 | Ari | NL | 7 | 0 | 0 | 0 | 9.1 | 52 | 9 | 10 | 9 | 1 | 2 | 0 | 1 | 11 | 0 | 10 | 2 | 0 | 1 | 1 | .500 | 0 | 0-0 | 1 | 6.92 | 8.68 |
| Postseason | | | 16 | 0 | 0 | 2 | 10.0 | 52 | 12 | 9 | 7 | 1 | 1 | 0 | 2 | 8 | 0 | 7 | 0 | 0 | 2 | 0 | 1.000 | 0 | 0-1 | 3 | 7.61 | 6.30 |
| 14 ML YEARS | | | 456 | 75 | 3 | 82 | 836.1 | 3725 | 898 | 512 | 467 | 123 | 17 | 37 | 44 | 365 | 26 | 577 | 35 | 0 | 43 | 47 | .478 | 0 | 5-17 | 62 | 5.17 | 5.03 |

# Chris Dwyer

**Pitches:** L **Bats:** R **Pos:** RP-2 **Ht:** 6'3" **Wt:** 210 **Born:** 4/10/1988 **Age:** 26

| Year | Team | Lg | G | GS | CG | GF | IP | BFP | H | R | ER | HR | SH | SF | HB | TBB | IBB | SO | WP | Bk | W | L | Pct | Sh | Sv-Op | Hld | ERC | ERA |
|---|---|---|---|---|---|---|---|---|---|---|---|---|---|---|---|---|---|---|---|---|---|---|---|---|---|---|---|---|
| | | | HOW MUCH HE PITCHED | | | | | | WHAT HE GAVE UP | | | | | | | | | | | | THE RESULTS | | | | | | | |
| 2009 | Idaho | R+ | 4 | 4 | 0 | 0 | 8.2 | 45 | 12 | 5 | 4 | 1 | 0 | 0 | 0 | 8 | 0 | 15 | 2 | 0 | 0 | 0 | - | 0 | 0- - | - | 8.82 | 4.15 |
| 2010 | Wilmg | A+ | 15 | 15 | 1 | 0 | 84.1 | 363 | 79 | 36 | 28 | 3 | 4 | 3 | 2 | 33 | 0 | 93 | 6 | 0 | 6 | 3 | .667 | 0 | 0- - | - | 3.30 | 2.99 |
| 2010 | NWArk | AA | 4 | 4 | 0 | 0 | 17.2 | 73 | 11 | 8 | 6 | 2 | 0 | 0 | 0 | 10 | 0 | 20 | 1 | 0 | 2 | 1 | .667 | 0 | 0- - | - | 2.78 | 3.06 |
| 2011 | NWArk | AA | 27 | 27 | 1 | 0 | 140.1 | 610 | 124 | 93 | 88 | 14 | 3 | 5 | 6 | 78 | 1 | 126 | 16 | 2 | 8 | 10 | .444 | 0 | 0- - | - | 4.23 | 5.64 |
| 2012 | NWArk | AA | 17 | 16 | 0 | 0 | 85.2 | 377 | 79 | 57 | 50 | 13 | 0 | 2 | 4 | 44 | 0 | 71 | 1 | 0 | 5 | 8 | .385 | 0 | 0- - | - | 4.64 | 5.25 |
| 2012 | Omha | AAA | 9 | 9 | 1 | 0 | 50.1 | 240 | 73 | 41 | 39 | 10 | 4 | 2 | 1 | 24 | 0 | 33 | 1 | 0 | 3 | 4 | .429 | 0 | 0- - | - | 8.20 | 6.97 |
| 2013 | Omha | AAA | 29 | 28 | 0 | 1 | 159.2 | 680 | 140 | 75 | 63 | 15 | 1 | 4 | 3 | 72 | 0 | 112 | 6 | 0 | 10 | 11 | .476 | 0 | 0- - | - | 3.63 | 3.55 |
| 2013 | KC | AL | 2 | 0 | 0 | 0 | 3.0 | 11 | 2 | 0 | 0 | 0 | 0 | 0 | 0 | 1 | 0 | 2 | 0 | 0 | 0 | 0 | - | 0 | 0-0 | 0 | 1.73 | 0.00 |

# Jarrod Dyson

**Bats:** L **Throws:** R **Pos:** CF-73;PR-14;DH-7;PH-2 juh-ROD **Ht:** 5'9" **Wt:** 160 **Born:** 8/15/1984 **Age:** 29

| Year | Team | Lg | G | AB | H | 2B | 3B | HR | (Hm | Rd) | TB | R | RBI | RC | TBB | IBB | SO | HBP | SH | SF | SB | CS | SB% | GDP | Avg | OBP | Slg |
|---|---|---|---|---|---|---|---|---|---|---|---|---|---|---|---|---|---|---|---|---|---|---|---|---|---|---|---|
| | | | BATTING | | | | | | | | | | | | | | | | | | BASERUNNING | | | | AVERAGES | | |
| 2013 | Omha* | AAA | 15 | 52 | 8 | 2 | 0 | 0 | (- | -) | 10 | 8 | 1 | 2 | 3 | 0 | 12 | 2 | 1 | 0 | 5 | 0 | 1.00 | 0 | .154 | .228 | .192 |
| 2010 | KC | AL | 18 | 57 | 12 | 4 | 2 | 1 | (1 | 0) | 23 | 11 | 5 | 9 | 6 | 0 | 16 | 0 | 2 | 0 | 9 | 1 | .90 | 2 | .211 | .286 | .404 |

| | | | BATTING | | | | | | | | | | | | | | | | | | BASERUNNING | | | | AVERAGES | | |
|---|---|---|---|---|---|---|---|---|---|---|---|---|---|---|---|---|---|---|---|---|---|---|---|---|---|---|---|
| Year | Team | Lg | G | AB | H | 2B | 3B | HR | (Hm | Rd) | TB | R | RBI | RC | TBB | IBB | SO | HBP | SH | SF | SB | CS | SB% | GDP | Avg | OBP | Slg |
| 2011 | KC | AL | 26 | 44 | 9 | 1 | 0 | 0 | (0 | 0) | 10 | 8 | 3 | 7 | 7 | 0 | 14 | 0 | 1 | 1 | 11 | 1 | .92 | 0 | .205 | .308 | .227 |
| 2012 | KC | AL | 102 | 292 | 76 | 8 | 5 | 0 | (0 | 0) | 94 | 52 | 9 | 36 | 30 | 1 | 56 | 1 | 4 | 3 | 30 | 5 | .86 | 5 | .260 | .328 | .322 |
| 2013 | KC | AL | 87 | 213 | 55 | 9 | 4 | 2 | (2 | 0) | 78 | 30 | 17 | 28 | 21 | 1 | 45 | 1 | 3 | 1 | 34 | 6 | .85 | 4 | .258 | .326 | .366 |
| 4 ML YEARS | | | 233 | 606 | 152 | 22 | 11 | 3 | (3 | 0) | 205 | 101 | 34 | 80 | 64 | 2 | 131 | 2 | 10 | 5 | 84 | 13 | .87 | 11 | .251 | .322 | .338 |

# Sam Dyson

**Pitches:** R **Bats:** R **Pos:** RP-4; SP-1 **Ht:** 6'1" **Wt:** 210 **Born:** 5/7/1988 **Age:** 26

| | | | HOW MUCH HE PITCHED | | | | | | WHAT HE GAVE UP | | | | | | | | | | | | THE RESULTS | | | | | | | |
|---|---|---|---|---|---|---|---|---|---|---|---|---|---|---|---|---|---|---|---|---|---|---|---|---|---|---|---|---|
| Year | Team | Lg | G | GS | CG | GF | IP | BFP | H | R | ER | HR | SH | SF | HB | TBB | IBB | SO | WP | Bk | W | L | Pct | Sh | Sv-Op | Hld | ERC | ERA |
| 2012 | Dnedin | A+ | 6 | 6 | 0 | 0 | 28.2 | 124 | 35 | 16 | 13 | 1 | 0 | 0 | 1 | 5 | 0 | 16 | 1 | 0 | 2 | 0 | 1.000 | 0 | 0- | - | 4.10 | 4.08 |
| 2012 | NHam | AA | 33 | 0 | 0 | 20 | 45.1 | 188 | 38 | 20 | 12 | 2 | 4 | 2 | 4 | 15 | 0 | 22 | 3 | 0 | 2 | 2 | .500 | 0 | 9- | - | 2.93 | 2.38 |
| 2013 | Jaxnvl | AA | 16 | 15 | 0 | 0 | 75.1 | 327 | 72 | 36 | 22 | 0 | 7 | 1 | 10 | 23 | 1 | 41 | 1 | 0 | 3 | 7 | .300 | 0 | 0- | - | 3.21 | 2.63 |
| 2013 | Mrlns | R | 1 | 1 | 0 | 0 | 5.0 | 22 | 6 | 3 | 2 | 0 | 1 | 0 | 1 | 1 | 0 | 5 | 1 | 0 | 0 | 1 | .000 | 0 | 0- | - | 4.56 | 3.60 |
| 2013 | NewOr | AAA | 5 | 5 | 0 | 0 | 31.0 | 125 | 23 | 10 | 9 | 1 | 2 | 2 | 1 | 12 | 1 | 16 | 1 | 0 | 1 | 3 | .250 | 0 | 0- | - | 2.35 | 2.61 |
| 2012 | Tor | AL | 2 | 0 | 0 | 0 | 0.2 | 8 | 4 | 3 | 3 | 0 | 0 | 0 | 0 | 2 | 0 | 1 | 0 | 0 | 0 | 0 | - | 0 | 0-0 | 0 | 56.02 | 40.50 |
| 2013 | Mia | NL | 5 | 1 | 0 | 1 | 11.0 | 54 | 16 | 12 | 11 | 2 | 1 | 1 | 1 | 5 | 1 | 5 | 0 | 0 | 0 | 2 | .000 | 0 | 0-0 | 0 | 7.96 | 9.00 |
| 2 ML YEARS | | | 7 | 1 | 0 | 1 | 11.2 | 62 | 20 | 15 | 14 | 2 | 1 | 1 | 1 | 7 | 1 | 6 | 0 | 0 | 0 | 2 | .000 | 0 | 0-0 | 0 | 10.29 | 10.80 |

# Adam Eaton

**Bats:** L **Throws:** L **Pos:** LF-35;CF-30;PH-6;RF-4;PR-3;DH-1 **Ht:** 5'8" **Wt:** 185 **Born:** 12/6/1988 **Age:** 25

| | | | BATTING | | | | | | | | | | | | | | | | | | BASERUNNING | | | | AVERAGES | | |
|---|---|---|---|---|---|---|---|---|---|---|---|---|---|---|---|---|---|---|---|---|---|---|---|---|---|---|---|
| Year | Team | Lg | G | AB | H | 2B | 3B | HR | (Hm | Rd) | TB | R | RBI | RC | TBB | IBB | SO | HBP | SH | SF | SB | CS | SB% | GDP | Avg | OBP | Slg |
| 2010 | Msoula | R+ | 68 | 226 | 87 | 14 | 4 | 7 | (- | -) | 130 | 48 | 37 | 65 | 35 | 4 | 44 | 19 | 0 | 2 | 20 | 8 | .71 | 1 | .385 | .500 | .575 |
| 2011 | Visalia | A+ | 65 | 244 | 81 | 15 | 3 | 6 | (- | -) | 120 | 54 | 39 | 59 | 42 | 0 | 41 | 14 | 0 | 1 | 24 | 8 | .75 | 2 | .332 | .455 | .492 |
| 2011 | Mobile | AA | 56 | 212 | 64 | 7 | 4 | 4 | (- | -) | 91 | 31 | 28 | 40 | 30 | 1 | 35 | 9 | 3 | 1 | 10 | 6 | .63 | 0 | .302 | .409 | .429 |
| 2012 | Mobile | AA | 11 | 40 | 12 | 1 | 0 | 0 | (- | -) | 13 | 11 | 3 | 8 | 6 | 0 | 8 | 5 | 0 | 0 | 6 | 1 | .86 | 0 | .300 | .451 | .325 |
| 2012 | Reno | AAA | 119 | 488 | 186 | 46 | 5 | 7 | (- | -) | 263 | 119 | 45 | 120 | 53 | 3 | 68 | 15 | 5 | 1 | 38 | 10 | .79 | 9 | .381 | .456 | .539 |
| 2013 | Reno | AAA | 10 | 35 | 5 | 2 | 0 | 1 | (- | -) | 10 | 5 | 5 | 2 | 3 | 0 | 8 | 1 | 0 | 1 | 0 | 0 | - | 1 | .143 | .225 | .286 |
| 2013 | Visalia | A+ | 15 | 53 | 17 | 3 | 0 | 1 | (- | -) | 23 | 12 | 6 | 12 | 10 | 0 | 6 | 1 | 0 | 0 | 8 | 1 | .89 | 2 | .321 | .438 | .434 |
| 2013 | DBcks | R | 1 | 2 | 1 | 0 | 0 | 0 | (- | -) | 1 | 1 | 2 | 1 | 1 | 0 | 1 | 1 | 0 | 1 | 0 | 0 | - | 0 | .500 | .600 | .500 |
| 2012 | Ari | NL | 22 | 85 | 22 | 3 | 2 | 2 | (1 | 1) | 35 | 19 | 5 | 13 | 14 | 0 | 15 | 3 | 1 | 0 | 2 | 3 | .40 | 0 | .259 | .382 | .412 |
| 2013 | Ari | NL | 66 | 250 | 63 | 10 | 4 | 3 | (2 | 1) | 90 | 40 | 22 | 27 | 17 | 0 | 44 | 6 | 3 | 1 | 5 | 2 | .71 | 4 | .252 | .314 | .360 |
| 2 ML YEARS | | | 88 | 335 | 85 | 13 | 6 | 5 | (3 | 2) | 125 | 59 | 27 | 40 | 31 | 0 | 59 | 9 | 4 | 1 | 7 | 5 | .58 | 4 | .254 | .332 | .373 |

# Josh Edgin

**Pitches:** L **Bats:** L **Pos:** RP-34 EDGE-inn **Ht:** 6'1" **Wt:** 225 **Born:** 12/17/1986 **Age:** 27

| | | | HOW MUCH HE PITCHED | | | | | | WHAT HE GAVE UP | | | | | | | | | | | | THE RESULTS | | | | | | | |
|---|---|---|---|---|---|---|---|---|---|---|---|---|---|---|---|---|---|---|---|---|---|---|---|---|---|---|---|---|
| Year | Team | Lg | G | GS | CG | GF | IP | BFP | H | R | ER | HR | SH | SF | HB | TBB | IBB | SO | WP | Bk | W | L | Pct | Sh | Sv-Op | Hld | ERC | ERA |
| 2010 | Kngspt | R | 18 | 0 | 0 | 8 | 31.2 | 139 | 28 | 15 | 10 | 2 | 2 | 0 | 4 | 12 | 0 | 41 | 1 | 1 | 0 | 1 | .000 | 0 | 3- | - | 3.50 | 2.84 |
| 2010 | Savann | A | 2 | 0 | 0 | 0 | 3.0 | 11 | 3 | 0 | 0 | 0 | 0 | 0 | 0 | 0 | 0 | 5 | 0 | 0 | 0 | 0 | - | 0 | 0- | - | 2.18 | 0.00 |
| 2011 | Savann | A | 24 | 0 | 0 | 19 | 31.0 | 118 | 14 | 4 | 3 | 0 | 3 | 1 | 0 | 10 | 1 | 41 | 3 | 0 | 1 | 0 | 1.000 | 0 | 16- | - | 0.92 | 0.87 |
| 2011 | StLuci | A+ | 25 | 0 | 0 | 17 | 35.0 | 146 | 30 | 10 | 8 | 2 | 1 | 2 | 1 | 13 | 1 | 35 | 1 | 0 | 2 | 1 | .667 | 0 | 11- | - | 2.98 | 2.06 |
| 2012 | Bnghtn | AA | 6 | 0 | 0 | 6 | 6.1 | 26 | 5 | 1 | 1 | 1 | 0 | 0 | 0 | 2 | 0 | 5 | 0 | 0 | 0 | 0 | - | 0 | 2- | - | 2.94 | 1.42 |
| 2012 | Buffalo | AAA | 35 | 0 | 0 | 6 | 37.0 | 164 | 34 | 19 | 16 | 0 | 3 | 1 | 1 | 18 | 0 | 40 | 0 | 0 | 3 | 2 | .600 | 0 | 1- | - | 3.26 | 3.89 |
| 2013 | Bnghtn | AA | 5 | 0 | 0 | 2 | 8.0 | 38 | 10 | 7 | 7 | 2 | 0 | 1 | 0 | 5 | 0 | 10 | 0 | 0 | 0 | 0 | - | 0 | 0- | - | 7.81 | 7.88 |
| 2013 | LsVgs | AAA | 11 | 0 | 0 | 4 | 10.2 | 48 | 14 | 7 | 7 | 1 | 0 | 1 | 1 | 2 | 0 | 12 | 2 | 0 | 2 | 0 | 1.000 | 0 | 0- | - | 5.34 | 5.91 |
| 2012 | NYM | NL | 34 | 0 | 0 | 6 | 25.2 | 107 | 19 | 14 | 13 | 5 | 2 | 0 | 2 | 10 | 0 | 30 | 0 | 0 | 1 | 2 | .333 | 0 | 0-2 | 5 | 3.52 | 4.56 |
| 2013 | NYM | NL | 34 | 0 | 0 | 5 | 28.2 | 122 | 26 | 12 | 12 | 2 | 1 | 0 | 2 | 12 | 3 | 20 | 0 | 0 | 1 | 1 | .500 | 0 | 1-2 | 3 | 3.57 | 3.77 |
| 2 ML YEARS | | | 68 | 0 | 0 | 11* | 54.1 | 229 | 45 | 26 | 25 | 7 | 3 | 0 | 4 | 22 | 3 | 50 | 0 | 0 | 2 | 3 | .400 | 0 | 1-4 | 8 | 3.56 | 4.14 |

# A.J. Ellis

**Bats:** R **Throws:** R **Pos:** C-113;PH-2 **Ht:** 6'3" **Wt:** 220 **Born:** 4/9/1981 **Age:** 33

| | | | BATTING | | | | | | | | | | | | | | | | | | BASERUNNING | | | | AVERAGES | | |
|---|---|---|---|---|---|---|---|---|---|---|---|---|---|---|---|---|---|---|---|---|---|---|---|---|---|---|---|
| Year | Team | Lg | G | AB | H | 2B | 3B | HR | (Hm | Rd) | TB | R | RBI | RC | TBB | IBB | SO | HBP | SH | SF | SB | CS | SB% | GDP | Avg | OBP | Slg |
| 2013 | RCuca* | A+ | 2 | 7 | 0 | 0 | 0 | 0 | (- | -) | 0 | 0 | 0 | 0 | 0 | 0 | 3 | 0 | 0 | 0 | 0 | 0 | - | 0 | .000 | .000 | .000 |
| 2008 | LAD | NL | 4 | 3 | 0 | 0 | 0 | 0 | (0 | 0) | 0 | 1 | 0 | 0 | 0 | 0 | 2 | 0 | 0 | 0 | 0 | 0 | - | 0 | .000 | .000 | .000 |
| 2009 | LAD | NL | 8 | 10 | 1 | 0 | 0 | 0 | (0 | 0) | 1 | 0 | 1 | 0 | 0 | 0 | 1 | 0 | 0 | 0 | 0 | 0 | - | 0 | .100 | .100 | .100 |
| 2010 | LAD | NL | 44 | 108 | 30 | 5 | 0 | 0 | (0 | 0) | 35 | 6 | 16 | 16 | 14 | 1 | 18 | 1 | 4 | 1 | 0 | 0 | - | 5 | .278 | .363 | .324 |
| 2011 | LAD | NL | 31 | 85 | 23 | 1 | 1 | 2 | (0 | 2) | 32 | 8 | 11 | 11 | 14 | 0 | 16 | 3 | 1 | 0 | 0 | 1 | .00 | 2 | .271 | .392 | .376 |
| 2012 | LAD | NL | 133 | 423 | 114 | 20 | 1 | 13 | (6 | 7) | 175 | 44 | 52 | 61 | 65 | 11 | 107 | 7 | 6 | 4 | 0 | 0 | - | 17 | .270 | .373 | .414 |
| 2013 | LAD | NL | 115 | 390 | 93 | 17 | 1 | 10 | (2 | 8) | 142 | 43 | 52 | 43 | 45 | 1 | 78 | 3 | 4 | 6 | 0 | 2 | .00 | 11 | .238 | .318 | .364 |
| 6 ML YEARS | | | 335 | 1019 | 261 | 43 | 3 | 25 | (8 | 17) | 385 | 102 | 132 | 131 | 138 | 13 | 222 | 14 | 15 | 11 | 0 | 3 | .00 | 35 | .256 | .349 | .378 |

# Mark Ellis

**Bats:** R **Throws:** R **Pos:** 2B-119;PH-14;3B-1 **Ht:** 5'10" **Wt:** 190 **Born:** 6/6/1977 **Age:** 37

| | | | BATTING | | | | | | | | | | | | | | | | | | BASERUNNING | | | | AVERAGES | | |
|---|---|---|---|---|---|---|---|---|---|---|---|---|---|---|---|---|---|---|---|---|---|---|---|---|---|---|---|
| Year | Team | Lg | G | AB | H | 2B | 3B | HR | (Hm | Rd) | TB | R | RBI | RC | TBB | IBB | SO | HBP | SH | SF | SB | CS | SB% | GDP | Avg | OBP | Slg |
| 2013 | Chatt* | AA | 2 | 4 | 0 | 0 | 0 | 0 | (- | -) | 0 | 1 | 0 | 0 | 1 | 0 | 2 | 0 | 0 | 0 | 0 | 0 | - | 0 | .000 | .200 | .000 |
| 2002 | Oak | AL | 98 | 345 | 94 | 16 | 4 | 6 | (6 | 0) | 136 | 58 | 35 | 55 | 44 | 1 | 54 | 4 | 8 | 3 | 4 | 2 | .67 | 3 | .272 | .359 | .394 |
| 2003 | Oak | AL | 154 | 553 | 137 | 31 | 5 | 9 | (7 | 2) | 205 | 78 | 52 | 69 | 48 | 4 | 94 | 7 | 9 | 5 | 6 | 2 | .75 | 7 | .248 | .313 | .371 |
| 2005 | Oak | AL | 122 | 434 | 137 | 21 | 5 | 13 | (5 | 8) | 207 | 76 | 52 | 78 | 44 | 1 | 51 | 4 | 4 | 0 | 1 | 3 | .25 | 10 | .316 | .384 | .477 |
| 2006 | Oak | AL | 124 | 441 | 110 | 25 | 1 | 11 | (7 | 4) | 170 | 64 | 52 | 53 | 40 | 1 | 76 | 8 | 4 | 7 | 4 | 0 | 1.00 | 13 | .249 | .319 | .385 |
| 2007 | Oak | AL | 150 | 583 | 161 | 33 | 3 | 19 | (10 | 9) | 257 | 84 | 76 | 76 | 44 | 1 | 94 | 10 | 2 | 3 | 9 | 4 | .69 | 10 | .276 | .336 | .441 |
| 2008 | Oak | AL | 117 | 442 | 103 | 20 | 3 | 12 | (7 | 5) | 165 | 55 | 41 | 54 | 53 | 2 | 65 | 5 | 5 | 2 | 14 | 2 | .88 | 11 | .233 | .321 | .373 |
| 2009 | Oak | AL | 105 | 377 | 99 | 23 | 0 | 10 | (4 | 6) | 152 | 52 | 61 | 54 | 23 | 1 | 54 | 2 | 3 | 5 | 10 | 3 | .77 | 10 | .263 | .305 | .403 |

| BATTING | | | | | | | | | | | | | | | | | | | | | BASERUNNING | | | | AVERAGES | | |
|---|---|---|---|---|---|---|---|---|---|---|---|---|---|---|---|---|---|---|---|---|---|---|---|---|---|---|---|
| Year Team | Lg | G | AB | H | 2B | 3B | HR | (Hm | Rd) | TB | R | RBI | RC | TBB | IBB | SO | HBP | SH | SF | SB | CS | SB% | GDP | Avg | OBP | Slg |
| 2010 Oak | AL | 124 | 436 | 127 | 24 | 0 | 5 | (0 | 5) | 166 | 45 | 49 | 66 | 40 | 4 | 56 | 8 | 3 | 5 | 7 | 6 | .54 | 7 | .291 | .358 | .381 |
| 2011 2 Tms | | 132 | 480 | 119 | 24 | 1 | 7 | (6 | 1) | 166 | 55 | 41 | 40 | 22 | 0 | 75 | 6 | 9 | 2 | 14 | 5 | .74 | 8 | .248 | .288 | .346 |
| 2012 LAD | NL | 110 | 415 | 107 | 21 | 1 | 7 | (6 | 1) | 151 | 62 | 31 | 44 | 40 | 0 | 70 | 7 | 2 | 0 | 5 | 0 | 1.00 | 5 | .258 | .333 | .364 |
| 2013 LAD | NL | 126 | 433 | 117 | 13 | 2 | 6 | (3 | 3) | 152 | 46 | 48 | 52 | 26 | 2 | 74 | 10 | 6 | 5 | 4 | 1 | .80 | 5 | .270 | .323 | .351 |
| 11 Oak | AL | 62 | 217 | 47 | 11 | 1 | 1 | (1 | 0) | 63 | 21 | 16 | 10 | 8 | 0 | 32 | 3 | 4 | 1 | 7 | 2 | .78 | 3 | .217 | .253 | .290 |
| 11 Col | NL | 70 | 263 | 72 | 13 | 0 | 6 | (5 | 1) | 103 | 34 | 25 | 30 | 14 | 0 | 43 | 3 | 5 | 1 | 7 | 3 | .70 | 5 | .274 | .317 | .392 |
| Postseason | | 12 | 43 | 11 | 2 | 0 | 1 | (1 | 0) | 16 | 3 | 4 | 6 | 5 | 0 | 11 | 1 | 0 | 0 | 0 | 0 | - | 0 | .256 | .347 | .372 |
| 11 ML YEARS | | 1362 | 4939 | 1311 | 251 | 25 | 105 | (61 | 44) | 1927 | 675 | 538 | 641 | 424 | 17 | 763 | 71 | 55 | 37 | 78 | 28 | .74 | 89 | .265 | .330 | .390 |

## Jacoby Ellsbury

**Bats:** L **Throws:** L **Pos:** CF-134 **Ht:** 6'1" **Wt:** 195 **Born:** 9/11/1983 **Age:** 30

| BATTING | | | | | | | | | | | | | | | | | | | | | BASERUNNING | | | | AVERAGES | | |
|---|---|---|---|---|---|---|---|---|---|---|---|---|---|---|---|---|---|---|---|---|---|---|---|---|---|---|---|
| Year Team | Lg | G | AB | H | 2B | 3B | HR | (Hm | Rd) | TB | R | RBI | RC | TBB | IBB | SO | HBP | SH | SF | SB | CS | SB% | GDP | Avg | OBP | Slg |
| 2007 Bos | AL | 33 | 116 | 41 | 7 | 1 | 3 | (3 | 0) | 59 | 20 | 18 | 26 | 8 | 0 | 15 | 1 | 0 | 2 | 9 | 0 | 1.00 | 2 | .353 | .394 | .509 |
| 2008 Bos | AL | 145 | 554 | 155 | 22 | 7 | 9 | (4 | 5) | 218 | 98 | 47 | 71 | 41 | 2 | 80 | 7 | 4 | 3 | **50** | 11 | .82 | 10 | .280 | .336 | .394 |
| 2009 Bos | AL | 153 | 624 | 188 | 27 | **10** | 8 | (4 | 4) | 259 | 94 | 60 | 97 | 49 | 3 | 74 | 6 | 6 | 6 | **70** | 12 | .85 | 13 | .301 | .355 | .415 |
| 2010 Bos | AL | 18 | 78 | 15 | 4 | 0 | 0 | (0 | 0) | 19 | 10 | 5 | 4 | 4 | 0 | 9 | 1 | 0 | 0 | 7 | 1 | .88 | 0 | .192 | .241 | .244 |
| 2011 Bos | AL | 158 | 660 | 212 | 46 | 5 | 32 | (15 | 17) | **364** | 119 | 105 | 134 | 52 | 1 | 98 | 9 | 3 | 5 | 39 | 15 | .72 | 8 | .321 | .376 | .552 |
| 2012 Bos | AL | 74 | 303 | 82 | 18 | 0 | 4 | (3 | 1) | 112 | 43 | 26 | 37 | 19 | 0 | 43 | 0 | 0 | 1 | 14 | 3 | .82 | 5 | .271 | .313 | .370 |
| 2013 Bos | AL | 134 | 577 | 172 | 31 | 8 | 9 | (4 | 5) | 246 | 92 | 53 | 90 | 47 | 3 | 92 | 5 | 1 | 2 | **52** | 4 | .93 | 12 | .298 | .355 | .426 |
| Postseason | | 22 | 69 | 18 | 7 | 1 | 0 | (0 | 0) | 27 | 12 | 11 | 11 | 6 | 1 | 10 | 0 | 0 | 1 | 5 | 1 | .83 | 2 | .261 | .316 | .391 |
| 7 ML YEARS | | 715 | 2912 | 865 | 155 | 31 | 65 | (33 | 32) | 1277 | 476 | 314 | 459 | 220 | 9 | 411 | 29 | 14 | 19 | 241 | 46 | .84 | 50 | .297 | .350 | .439 |

## Jake Elmore

**Bats:** R **Throws:** R **Pos:** SS-20;2B-12;LF-9;PH-9;PR-7;DH-4;CF-2;C-1;1B-1;3B-1;RF-1 **Ht:** 5'9" **Wt:** 185 **Born:** 6/15/1987 **Age:** 27

| BATTING | | | | | | | | | | | | | | | | | | | | | BASERUNNING | | | | AVERAGES | | |
|---|---|---|---|---|---|---|---|---|---|---|---|---|---|---|---|---|---|---|---|---|---|---|---|---|---|---|---|
| Year Team | Lg | G | AB | H | 2B | 3B | HR | (Hm | Rd) | TB | R | RBI | RC | TBB | IBB | SO | HBP | SH | SF | SB | CS | SB% | GDP | Avg | OBP | Slg |
| 2009 Sbend | A | 118 | 387 | 100 | 21 | 3 | 3 | (- | -) | 136 | 62 | 38 | 56 | 61 | 0 | 55 | 5 | 2 | 2 | 13 | 7 | .65 | 11 | .258 | .365 | .351 |
| 2010 Mobile | AA | 124 | 388 | 107 | 17 | 2 | 2 | (- | -) | 134 | 64 | 31 | 57 | 58 | 1 | 57 | 4 | 7 | 5 | 25 | 13 | .66 | 19 | .276 | .371 | .345 |
| 2011 Mobile | AA | 121 | 381 | 103 | 19 | 1 | 3 | (- | -) | 133 | 58 | 41 | 54 | 54 | 1 | 65 | 7 | 5 | 11 | 15 | 11 | .58 | 9 | .270 | .362 | .349 |
| 2012 Reno | AAA | 108 | 419 | 144 | 30 | 9 | 1 | (- | -) | 195 | 95 | 73 | 95 | 74 | 1 | 54 | 5 | 7 | 6 | 32 | 8 | .80 | 12 | .344 | .442 | .465 |
| 2013 OKCity | AAA | 70 | 268 | 80 | 13 | 4 | 5 | (- | -) | 116 | 42 | 30 | 48 | 31 | 0 | 37 | 7 | 1 | 3 | 16 | 6 | .73 | 5 | .299 | .382 | .433 |
| 2012 Ari | NL | 30 | 68 | 13 | 4 | 0 | 0 | (0 | 0) | 17 | 1 | 7 | 3 | 5 | 0 | 6 | 0 | 0 | 0 | 0 | 0 | - | 1 | .191 | .247 | .250 |
| 2013 Hou | AL | 52 | 120 | 29 | 4 | 0 | 2 | (1 | 1) | 39 | 16 | 6 | 13 | 13 | 0 | 20 | 0 | 2 | 1 | 1 | 6 | .14 | 1 | .242 | .313 | .325 |
| 2 ML YEARS | | 82 | 188 | 42 | 8 | 0 | 2 | (1 | 1) | 56 | 17 | 13 | 16 | 18 | 0 | 26 | 0 | 2 | 1 | 1 | 6 | .14 | 2 | .223 | .290 | .298 |

## Edwin Encarnacion

**Bats:** R **Throws:** R **Pos:** 1B-79;DH-55;3B-10 **Ht:** 6'2" **Wt:** 230 **Born:** 1/7/1983 **Age:** 31

| BATTING | | | | | | | | | | | | | | | | | | | | | BASERUNNING | | | | AVERAGES | | |
|---|---|---|---|---|---|---|---|---|---|---|---|---|---|---|---|---|---|---|---|---|---|---|---|---|---|---|---|
| Year Team | Lg | G | AB | H | 2B | 3B | HR | (Hm | Rd) | TB | R | RBI | RC | TBB | IBB | SO | HBP | SH | SF | SB | CS | SB% | GDP | Avg | OBP | Slg |
| 2005 Cin | NL | 69 | 211 | 49 | 16 | 0 | 9 | (3 | 6) | 92 | 25 | 31 | 24 | 20 | 2 | 60 | 3 | 0 | 0 | 3 | 0 | 1.00 | 8 | .232 | .308 | .436 |
| 2006 Cin | NL | 117 | 406 | 112 | 33 | 1 | 15 | (7 | 8) | 192 | 60 | 72 | 66 | 41 | 3 | 78 | 13 | 0 | 3 | 6 | 3 | .67 | 9 | .276 | .359 | .473 |
| 2007 Cin | NL | 139 | 502 | 145 | 25 | 1 | 16 | (10 | 6) | 220 | 66 | 76 | 86 | 39 | 4 | 86 | 14 | 0 | 1 | 8 | 1 | .89 | 5 | .289 | .356 | .438 |
| 2008 Cin | NL | 146 | 506 | 127 | 29 | 1 | 26 | (15 | 11) | 236 | 75 | 68 | 72 | 61 | 1 | 102 | 10 | 0 | 5 | 1 | 0 | 1.00 | 13 | .251 | .340 | .466 |
| 2009 2 Tms | | 85 | 293 | 66 | 11 | 2 | 13 | (5 | 8) | 120 | 35 | 39 | 37 | 37 | 0 | 67 | 5 | 0 | 3 | 2 | 1 | .67 | 5 | .225 | .320 | .410 |
| 2010 Tor | AL | 96 | 332 | 81 | 16 | 0 | 21 | (7 | 14) | 160 | 47 | 51 | 41 | 29 | 1 | 60 | 2 | 0 | 4 | 1 | 0 | 1.00 | 9 | .244 | .305 | .482 |
| 2011 Tor | AL | 134 | 481 | 131 | 36 | 0 | 17 | (14 | 3) | 218 | 70 | 55 | 67 | 43 | 2 | 77 | 3 | 0 | 3 | 8 | 2 | .80 | 17 | .272 | .334 | .453 |
| 2012 Tor | AL | 151 | 542 | 152 | 24 | 0 | 42 | (23 | 19) | 302 | 93 | 110 | 124 | 84 | 12 | 94 | 11 | 0 | 7 | 13 | 3 | .81 | 6 | .280 | .384 | .557 |
| 2013 Tor | AL | 142 | 530 | 144 | 29 | 1 | 36 | (12 | 24) | 283 | 90 | 104 | 102 | 82 | 7 | 62 | 4 | 0 | 5 | 7 | 1 | .88 | 20 | .272 | .370 | .534 |
| 09 Cin | NL | 43 | 139 | 29 | 6 | 1 | 5 | (3 | 2) | 52 | 10 | 16 | 19 | 24 | 0 | 38 | 2 | 0 | 0 | 1 | 1 | .50 | 3 | .209 | .333 | .374 |
| 09 Tor | AL | 42 | 154 | 37 | 5 | 1 | 8 | (2 | 6) | 68 | 25 | 23 | 18 | 13 | 0 | 29 | 3 | 0 | 3 | 1 | 0 | 1.00 | 2 | .240 | .306 | .442 |
| 9 ML YEARS | | 1079 | 3803 | 1007 | 219 | 6 | 195 | (96 | 99) | 1823 | 561 | 606 | 619 | 436 | 32 | 686 | 65 | 0 | 31 | 49 | 11 | .82 | 92 | .265 | .348 | .479 |

## Barry Enright

**Pitches:** R **Bats:** R **Pos:** SP-2; RP-2 **Ht:** 6'3" **Wt:** 220 **Born:** 3/30/1986 **Age:** 28

| HOW MUCH HE PITCHED | | | | | | | | WHAT HE GAVE UP | | | | | | | | | | | | THE RESULTS | | | | | | | |
|---|---|---|---|---|---|---|---|---|---|---|---|---|---|---|---|---|---|---|---|---|---|---|---|---|---|---|---|
| Year Team | Lg | G | GS | CG | GF | IP | BFP | H | R | ER | HR | SH | SF | HB | TBB | IBB | SO | WP | Bk | W | L | Pct | Sh | Sv-Op | Hld | ERC | ERA |
| 2013 Salt Lk* | AAA | 24 | 22 | 0 | 0 | 116.1 | 541 | 153 | 95 | 92 | 30 | 2 | 5 | 3 | 48 | 0 | 78 | 4 | 0 | 7 | 7 | .500 | 0 | 0-- | - | 7.40 | 7.12 |
| 2010 Ari | NL | 17 | 17 | 0 | 0 | 99.0 | 410 | 97 | 43 | 43 | 20 | 8 | 1 | 1 | 29 | 0 | 49 | 0 | 0 | 6 | 7 | .462 | 0 | 0-0 | 0 | 4.34 | 3.91 |
| 2011 Ari | NL | 7 | 7 | 0 | 0 | 37.2 | 175 | 50 | 31 | 31 | 11 | 3 | 2 | 1 | 15 | 1 | 21 | 2 | 0 | 1 | 4 | .200 | 0 | 0-0 | 0 | 7.65 | 7.41 |
| 2012 LAA | AL | 3 | 0 | 0 | 2 | 3.2 | 20 | 7 | 6 | 6 | 1 | 0 | 0 | 0 | 1 | 0 | 0 | 0 | 0 | 0 | 0 | - | 0 | 0-0 | 0 | 10.06 | 14.73 |
| 2013 LAA | AL | 4 | 2 | 0 | 1 | 8.1 | 43 | 12 | 12 | 12 | 2 | 0 | 0 | 0 | 7 | 0 | 6 | 1 | 0 | 0 | 2 | .000 | 0 | 0-0 | 0 | 10.04 | 12.96 |
| 4 ML YEARS | | 31 | 26 | 0 | 3 | 148.2 | 648 | 166 | 92 | 92 | 34 | 11 | 3 | 2 | 52 | 1 | 76 | 3 | 0 | 7 | 13 | .350 | 0 | 0-0 | 0 | 5.57 | 5.57 |

## Nathan Eovaldi

**Pitches:** R **Bats:** R **Pos:** SP-18 eh-VOLL-dee **Ht:** 6'2" **Wt:** 210 **Born:** 2/13/1990 **Age:** 24

| HOW MUCH HE PITCHED | | | | | | | | WHAT HE GAVE UP | | | | | | | | | | | | THE RESULTS | | | | | | | |
|---|---|---|---|---|---|---|---|---|---|---|---|---|---|---|---|---|---|---|---|---|---|---|---|---|---|---|---|
| Year Team | Lg | G | GS | CG | GF | IP | BFP | H | R | ER | HR | SH | SF | HB | TBB | IBB | SO | WP | Bk | W | L | Pct | Sh | Sv-Op | Hld | ERC | ERA |
| 2013 Jupiter* | A+ | 2 | 2 | 0 | 0 | 9.0 | 36 | 9 | 3 | 3 | 1 | 0 | 0 | 0 | 2 | 0 | 6 | 0 | 0 | 0 | 1 | .000 | 0 | 0-- | - | 3.60 | 3.00 |
| 2013 Jaxnvl* | AA | 3 | 3 | 0 | 0 | 11.2 | 51 | 13 | 7 | 7 | 0 | 1 | 1 | 0 | 4 | 0 | 9 | 0 | 0 | 1 | 0 | 1.000 | 0 | 0-- | - | 3.75 | 5.40 |
| 2011 LAD | NL | 10 | 6 | 0 | 1 | 34.2 | 146 | 28 | 14 | 14 | 2 | 2 | 0 | 2 | 20 | 0 | 23 | 0 | 0 | 1 | 2 | .333 | 0 | 0-0 | 1 | 3.75 | 3.63 |
| 2012 2 Tms | NL | 22 | 22 | 0 | 0 | 119.1 | 526 | 133 | 59 | 57 | 10 | 1 | 6 | 3 | 47 | 3 | 78 | 1 | 0 | 4 | 13 | .235 | 0 | 0-0 | 0 | 4.67 | 4.30 |

| HOW MUCH HE PITCHED | | | | | | | | | WHAT HE GAVE UP | | | | | | | | | | | | THE RESULTS | | | | | | | |
|---|---|---|---|---|---|---|---|---|---|---|---|---|---|---|---|---|---|---|---|---|---|---|---|---|---|---|---|
| Year | Team | Lg | G | GS | CG | GF | IP | BFP | H | R | ER | HR | SH | SF | HB | TBB | IBB | SO | WP | Bk | W | L | Pct | Sh | Sv-Op | Hld | ERC | ERA |
| 2013 | Mia | NL | 18 | 18 | 0 | 0 | 106.1 | 451 | 100 | 44 | 40 | 7 | 6 | 1 | 1 | 40 | 3 | 78 | 3 | 0 | 4 | 6 | .400 | 0 | 0-0 | 0 | 3.41 | 3.39 |
| 12 | LAD | NL | 10 | 10 | 0 | 0 | 56.1 | 241 | 63 | 27 | 26 | 5 | 0 | 3 | 0 | 20 | 2 | 34 | 1 | 0 | 1 | 6 | .143 | 0 | 0-0 | 0 | 4.54 | 4.15 |
| 12 | Mia | NL | 12 | 12 | 0 | 0 | 63.0 | 285 | 70 | 32 | 31 | 5 | 1 | 3 | 3 | 27 | 1 | 44 | 0 | 0 | 3 | 7 | .300 | 0 | 0-0 | 0 | 4.79 | 4.43 |
| 3 ML YEARS | | | 50 | 46 | 0 | 1 | 260.1 | 1123 | 261 | 117 | 111 | 19 | 9 | 7 | 6 | 107 | 6 | 179 | 4 | 0 | 9 | 21 | .300 | 0 | 0-0 | 1 | 4.02 | 3.84 |

## Cody Eppley

**Pitches:** R **Bats:** R **Pos:** RP-2 **Ht:** 6'5" **Wt:** 205 **Born:** 10/8/1985 **Age:** 28

| HOW MUCH HE PITCHED | | | | | | | | | WHAT HE GAVE UP | | | | | | | | | | | | THE RESULTS | | | | | | | |
|---|---|---|---|---|---|---|---|---|---|---|---|---|---|---|---|---|---|---|---|---|---|---|---|---|---|---|---|---|
| Year | Team | Lg | G | GS | CG | GF | IP | BFP | H | R | ER | HR | SH | SF | HB | TBB | IBB | SO | WP | Bk | W | L | Pct | Sh | Sv-Op | Hld | ERC | ERA |
| 2013 | S-WB* | AAA | 19 | 0 | 0 | 10 | 19.0 | 101 | 30 | 18 | 18 | 1 | 3 | 1 | 2 | 15 | 2 | 19 | 1 | 0 | 2 | 2 | .500 | 0 | 3-- | - | 9.22 | 8.53 |
| 2013 | Roch* | AAA | 22 | 0 | 0 | 5 | 24.0 | 106 | 23 | 13 | 13 | 0 | 2 | 0 | 0 | 13 | 1 | 20 | 0 | 0 | 2 | 0 | 1.000 | 0 | 0-- | - | 3.57 | 4.88 |
| 2011 | Tex | AL | 10 | 0 | 0 | 1 | 9.0 | 43 | 11 | 8 | 8 | 3 | 1 | 0 | 1 | 5 | 1 | 6 | 1 | 0 | 1 | 1 | .500 | 0 | 0-1 | 2 | 8.30 | 8.00 |
| 2012 | NYY | AL | 59 | 0 | 0 | 14 | 46.0 | 194 | 46 | 19 | 17 | 3 | 4 | 0 | 0 | 17 | 2 | 32 | 2 | 0 | 1 | 2 | .333 | 0 | 0-0 | 9 | 3.70 | 3.33 |
| 2013 | NYY | AL | 2 | 0 | 0 | 1 | 1.2 | 8 | 4 | 4 | 4 | 0 | 0 | 0 | 0 | 0 | 0 | 1 | 2 | 0 | 0 | 0 | - | 0 | 0-0 | 0 | 11.50 | 21.60 |
| Postseason | | | 4 | 0 | 0 | 1 | 3.2 | 17 | 4 | 0 | 0 | 0 | 0 | 0 | 0 | 1 | 0 | 4 | 0 | 0 | 0 | 0 | - | 0 | 0-0 | 0 | 3.07 | 0.00 |
| 3 ML YEARS | | | 71 | 0 | 0 | 16 | 56.2 | 245 | 61 | 31 | 29 | 6 | 5 | 0 | 1 | 22 | 3 | 39 | 5 | 0 | 2 | 3 | .400 | 0 | 0-1 | 11 | 4.56 | 4.61 |

## Robbie Erlin

**Pitches:** L **Bats:** R **Pos:** SP-9; RP-2 **Ht:** 5'11" **Wt:** 190 **Born:** 10/8/1990 **Age:** 23

| HOW MUCH HE PITCHED | | | | | | | | | WHAT HE GAVE UP | | | | | | | | | | | | THE RESULTS | | | | | | | |
|---|---|---|---|---|---|---|---|---|---|---|---|---|---|---|---|---|---|---|---|---|---|---|---|---|---|---|---|---|
| Year | Team | Lg | G | GS | CG | GF | IP | BFP | H | R | ER | HR | SH | SF | HB | TBB | IBB | SO | WP | Bk | W | L | Pct | Sh | Sv-Op | Hld | ERC | ERA |
| 2009 | Rngrs | R | 3 | 0 | 0 | 0 | 4.0 | 18 | 5 | 1 | 1 | 0 | 0 | 0 | 0 | 1 | 0 | 9 | 0 | 0 | 0 | 0 | - | 0 | 0-- | - | 4.05 | 2.25 |
| 2010 | Hkry | A | 28 | 17 | 0 | 2 | 114.2 | 447 | 89 | 37 | 27 | 9 | 6 | 2 | 4 | 17 | 0 | 125 | 4 | 0 | 6 | 3 | .667 | 0 | 1-- | - | 2.01 | 2.12 |
| 2011 | MrtlBh | A+ | 9 | 9 | 0 | 0 | 54.2 | 198 | 25 | 15 | 13 | 7 | 0 | 1 | 3 | 5 | 0 | 62 | 1 | 0 | 3 | 2 | .600 | 0 | 0-- | - | 1.02 | 2.14 |
| 2011 | Frisco | AA | 11 | 10 | 0 | 0 | 66.2 | 274 | 73 | 34 | 32 | 9 | 2 | 3 | 2 | 7 | 0 | 61 | 1 | 2 | 5 | 2 | .714 | 0 | 0-- | - | 3.83 | 4.32 |
| 2011 | SnAnt | AA | 6 | 6 | 0 | 0 | 26.0 | 103 | 26 | 4 | 4 | 2 | 0 | 1 | 0 | 4 | 0 | 31 | 0 | 0 | 1 | 0 | 1.000 | 0 | 0-- | - | 3.09 | 1.38 |
| 2012 | SnAnt | AA | 11 | 11 | 0 | 0 | 52.1 | 228 | 53 | 21 | 17 | 6 | 2 | 1 | 3 | 14 | 1 | 72 | 1 | 0 | 3 | 1 | .750 | 0 | 0-- | - | 3.81 | 2.92 |
| 2012 | Padres | R | 3 | 3 | 0 | 0 | 8.1 | 37 | 7 | 7 | 2 | 0 | 0 | 1 | 0 | 2 | 0 | 8 | 1 | 0 | 0 | 2 | .000 | 0 | 0-- | - | 1.79 | 2.16 |
| 2013 | Tucsn | AAA | 20 | 20 | 0 | 0 | 99.1 | 454 | 125 | 65 | 56 | 11 | 5 | 7 | 1 | 34 | 0 | 84 | 4 | 1 | 8 | 3 | .727 | 0 | 0-- | - | 5.38 | 5.07 |
| 2013 | SD | NL | 11 | 9 | 0 | 2 | 54.2 | 227 | 53 | 26 | 25 | 6 | 3 | 1 | 0 | 15 | 0 | 40 | 3 | 0 | 3 | 3 | .500 | 0 | 0-0 | 0 | 3.50 | 4.12 |

## Edgmer Escalona

**Pitches:** R **Bats:** R **Pos:** RP-37 EGG-merr **Ht:** 6'4" **Wt:** 235 **Born:** 10/6/1986 **Age:** 27

| HOW MUCH HE PITCHED | | | | | | | | | WHAT HE GAVE UP | | | | | | | | | | | | THE RESULTS | | | | | | | |
|---|---|---|---|---|---|---|---|---|---|---|---|---|---|---|---|---|---|---|---|---|---|---|---|---|---|---|---|---|
| Year | Team | Lg | G | GS | CG | GF | IP | BFP | H | R | ER | HR | SH | SF | HB | TBB | IBB | SO | WP | Bk | W | L | Pct | Sh | Sv-Op | Hld | ERC | ERA |
| 2013 | ColSpr* | AAA | 1 | 0 | 0 | 0 | 1.1 | 5 | 1 | 0 | 0 | 0 | 0 | 0 | 0 | 0 | 0 | 2 | 0 | 0 | 0 | 0 | - | 0 | 0-- | - | 1.13 | 0.00 |
| 2010 | Col | NL | 5 | 0 | 0 | 2 | 6.0 | 26 | 4 | 1 | 1 | 0 | 0 | 1 | 0 | 4 | 2 | 2 | 1 | 0 | 0 | 0 | - | 0 | 0-0 | 0 | 2.02 | 1.50 |
| 2011 | Col | NL | 14 | 0 | 0 | 5 | 25.2 | 99 | 17 | 5 | 5 | 3 | 1 | 0 | 0 | 7 | 2 | 14 | 0 | 0 | 0 | 0 | - | 0 | 0-0 | 0 | 1.92 | 1.75 |
| 2012 | Col | NL | 22 | 0 | 0 | 6 | 22.1 | 97 | 23 | 16 | 15 | 5 | 1 | 1 | 1 | 7 | 1 | 21 | 2 | 0 | 0 | 1 | .000 | 0 | 0-0 | 2 | 4.83 | 6.04 |
| 2013 | Col | NL | 37 | 0 | 0 | 7 | 46.0 | 205 | 52 | 32 | 29 | 8 | 2 | 1 | 2 | 14 | 2 | 34 | 2 | **3** | 1 | 4 | .200 | 0 | 0-1 | 7 | 4.99 | 5.67 |
| 4 ML YEARS | | | 78 | 0 | 0 | 20 | 100.0 | 427 | 96 | 54 | 50 | 16 | 4 | 3 | 3 | 32 | 7 | 71 | 5 | 3 | 1 | 5 | .167 | 0 | 0-1 | 9 | 3.91 | 4.50 |

## Alcides Escobar

**Bats:** R **Throws:** R **Pos:** SS-158; PH-1; PR-1 al-SEE-dess **Ht:** 6'1" **Wt:** 195 **Born:** 12/16/1986 **Age:** 27

| BATTING | | | | | | | | | | | | | | | | | | | | | BASERUNNING | | | | AVERAGES | | |
|---|---|---|---|---|---|---|---|---|---|---|---|---|---|---|---|---|---|---|---|---|---|---|---|---|---|---|---|
| Year | Team | Lg | G | AB | H | 2B | 3B | HR | (Hm | Rd) | TB | R | RBI | RC | TBB | IBB | SO | HBP | SH | SF | SB | CS | SB% | GDP | Avg | OBP | Slg |
| 2008 | Mil | NL | 9 | 4 | 2 | 0 | 0 | 0 | (0 | 0) | 2 | 2 | 0 | 0 | 0 | 0 | 1 | 0 | 0 | 0 | 0 | 0 | - | 0 | .500 | .500 | .500 |
| 2009 | Mil | NL | 38 | 125 | 38 | 3 | 1 | 1 | (0 | 1) | 46 | 20 | 11 | 16 | 4 | 0 | 18 | 2 | 2 | 1 | 4 | 2 | .67 | 0 | .304 | .333 | .368 |
| 2010 | Mil | NL | 145 | 506 | 119 | 14 | 10 | 4 | (3 | 1) | 165 | 57 | 41 | 51 | 36 | 7 | 70 | 3 | 4 | 3 | 10 | 4 | .71 | 8 | .235 | .288 | .326 |
| 2011 | KC | AL | 158 | 548 | 139 | 21 | 8 | 4 | (0 | 4) | 188 | 69 | 46 | 46 | 25 | 1 | 73 | 4 | 18 | 3 | 26 | 9 | .74 | 10 | .254 | .290 | .343 |
| 2012 | KC | AL | 155 | 605 | 177 | 30 | 7 | 5 | (5 | 0) | 236 | 68 | 52 | 72 | 27 | 2 | 100 | 8 | 8 | 0 | 35 | 5 | .88 | 14 | .293 | .331 | .390 |
| 2013 | KC | AL | 158 | 607 | 142 | 20 | 4 | 4 | (1 | 3) | 182 | 57 | 52 | 51 | 19 | 1 | 84 | 3 | 9 | 4 | 22 | 0 | **1.00** | 12 | .234 | .259 | .300 |
| 6 ML YEARS | | | 663 | 2395 | 617 | 88 | 30 | 18 | (9 | 9) | 819 | 273 | 202 | 236 | 111 | 11 | 346 | 20 | 41 | 11 | 97 | 20 | .83 | 44 | .258 | .295 | .342 |

## Eduardo Escobar

**Bats:** B **Throws:** R **Pos:** SS-38; 3B-23; PR-10; 2B-7; PH-4; LF-1; DH-1 **Ht:** 5'10" **Wt:** 175 **Born:** 1/5/1989 **Age:** 25

| BATTING | | | | | | | | | | | | | | | | | | | | | BASERUNNING | | | | AVERAGES | | |
|---|---|---|---|---|---|---|---|---|---|---|---|---|---|---|---|---|---|---|---|---|---|---|---|---|---|---|---|
| Year | Team | Lg | G | AB | H | 2B | 3B | HR | (Hm | Rd) | TB | R | RBI | RC | TBB | IBB | SO | HBP | SH | SF | SB | CS | SB% | GDP | Avg | OBP | Slg |
| 2013 | Roch* | AAA | 43 | 166 | 51 | 16 | 2 | 4 | (- | -) | 83 | 22 | 27 | 32 | 17 | 0 | 37 | 3 | 1 | 1 | 6 | 2 | .75 | 0 | .307 | .380 | .500 |
| 2011 | CWS | AL | 9 | 7 | 2 | 0 | 0 | 0 | (0 | 0) | 2 | 0 | 0 | 1 | 0 | 0 | 1 | 0 | 0 | 0 | 0 | 0 | - | 0 | .286 | .286 | .286 |
| 2012 | 2 Tms | AL | 50 | 131 | 28 | 4 | 1 | 0 | (0 | 0) | 34 | 18 | 9 | 12 | 11 | 0 | 31 | 1 | 2 | 1 | 3 | 0 | 1.00 | 0 | .214 | .278 | .260 |
| 2013 | Min | AL | 66 | 165 | 39 | 5 | 2 | 3 | (2 | 1) | 57 | 23 | 10 | 14 | 11 | 0 | 34 | 0 | 2 | 1 | 0 | 2 | .00 | 0 | .236 | .282 | .345 |
| 12 | CWS | AL | 36 | 87 | 18 | 4 | 1 | 0 | (0 | 0) | 24 | 14 | 3 | 7 | 9 | 0 | 23 | 0 | 1 | 0 | 2 | 0 | 1.00 | 0 | .207 | .281 | .276 |
| 12 | Min | AL | 14 | 44 | 10 | 0 | 0 | 0 | (0 | 0) | 10 | 4 | 6 | 5 | 2 | 0 | 8 | 1 | 1 | 1 | 1 | 0 | 1.00 | 0 | .227 | .271 | .227 |
| 3 ML YEARS | | | 125 | 303 | 69 | 9 | 3 | 3 | (2 | 1) | 93 | 41 | 19 | 27 | 22 | 0 | 66 | 1 | 4 | 2 | 3 | 2 | .60 | 0 | .228 | .280 | .307 |

# Yunel Escobar

**Bats:** R **Throws:** R **Pos:** SS-153;PH-1 you-NELL **Ht:** 6'2" **Wt:** 210 **Born:** 11/2/1982 **Age:** 31

| BATTING | | | | | | | | | | | | | | | | | | | | BASERUNNING | | | | AVERAGES | | |
|---|---|---|---|---|---|---|---|---|---|---|---|---|---|---|---|---|---|---|---|---|---|---|---|---|---|---|
| Year Team | Lg | G | AB | H | 2B | 3B | HR | (Hm | Rd) | TB | R | RBI | RC | TBB | IBB | SO | HBP | SH | SF | SB | CS | SB% | GDP | Avg | OBP | Slg |
| 2007 Atl | NL | 94 | 319 | 104 | 25 | 0 | 5 | (3 | 2) | 144 | 54 | 28 | 52 | 27 | 1 | 44 | 5 | 2 | 2 | 5 | 3 | .63 | 6 | .326 | .385 | .451 |
| 2008 Atl | NL | 136 | 514 | 148 | 24 | 2 | 10 | (5 | 5) | 206 | 71 | 60 | 70 | 59 | 4 | 62 | 5 | 7 | 2 | 2 | 5 | .29 | 24 | .288 | .366 | .401 |
| 2009 Atl | NL | 141 | 528 | 158 | 26 | 2 | 14 | (7 | 7) | 230 | 89 | 76 | 90 | 57 | 3 | 62 | 10 | 7 | 2 | 5 | 4 | .56 | 21 | .299 | .377 | .436 |
| 2010 2 Tms | | 135 | 497 | 127 | 19 | 0 | 4 | (2 | 2) | 158 | 60 | 35 | 53 | 56 | 1 | 57 | 5 | 9 | 0 | 6 | 2 | .75 | 18 | .256 | .337 | .318 |
| 2011 Tor | AL | 133 | 513 | 149 | 24 | 3 | 11 | (8 | 3) | 212 | 77 | 48 | 84 | 61 | 1 | 70 | 6 | 5 | 5 | 3 | 3 | .50 | 14 | .290 | .369 | .413 |
| 2012 Tor | AL | 145 | 558 | 141 | 22 | 1 | 9 | (6 | 3) | 192 | 58 | 51 | 51 | 35 | 1 | 70 | 4 | 7 | 4 | 5 | 1 | .83 | 21 | .253 | .300 | .344 |
| 2013 TB | AL | 153 | 508 | 130 | 27 | 1 | 9 | (5 | 4) | 186 | 61 | 56 | 60 | 57 | 2 | 73 | 3 | 6 | 4 | 4 | 4 | .50 | 19 | .256 | .332 | .366 |
| 10 Atl | NL | 75 | 261 | 62 | 12 | 0 | 0 | (0 | 0) | 74 | 28 | 19 | 25 | 37 | 1 | 31 | 1 | 2 | 0 | 5 | 1 | .83 | 9 | .238 | .334 | .284 |
| 10 Tor | AL | 60 | 236 | 65 | 7 | 0 | 4 | (2 | 2) | 84 | 32 | 16 | 28 | 19 | 0 | 26 | 4 | 7 | 0 | 1 | 1 | .50 | 9 | .275 | .340 | .356 |
| 7 ML YEARS | | 937 | 3437 | 957 | 167 | 9 | 62 | (36 | 26) | 1328 | 470 | 354 | 460 | 352 | 13 | 438 | 38 | 43 | 19 | 30 | 22 | .58 | 123 | .278 | .350 | .386 |

# Danny Espinosa

**Bats:** B **Throws:** R **Pos:** 2B-43;SS-1 **Ht:** 6'0" **Wt:** 205 **Born:** 4/25/1987 **Age:** 27

| BATTING | | | | | | | | | | | | | | | | | | | | BASERUNNING | | | | AVERAGES | | |
|---|---|---|---|---|---|---|---|---|---|---|---|---|---|---|---|---|---|---|---|---|---|---|---|---|---|---|
| Year Team | Lg | G | AB | H | 2B | 3B | HR | (Hm | Rd) | TB | R | RBI | RC | TBB | IBB | SO | HBP | SH | SF | SB | CS | SB% | GDP | Avg | OBP | Slg |
| 2013 Syrcse* | AAA | 75 | 283 | 61 | 12 | 1 | 2 | (- | -) | 81 | 32 | 22 | 24 | 19 | 0 | 101 | 7 | 2 | 2 | 7 | 1 | .88 | 5 | .216 | .280 | .286 |
| 2010 Was | NL | 28 | 103 | 22 | 4 | 1 | 6 | (4 | 2) | 46 | 16 | 15 | 15 | 9 | 1 | 30 | 0 | 0 | 0 | 0 | 2 | .00 | 0 | .214 | .277 | .447 |
| 2011 Was | NL | 158 | 573 | 135 | 29 | 5 | 21 | (11 | 10) | 237 | 72 | 66 | 83 | 57 | 4 | 166 | **19** | 5 | 4 | 17 | 6 | .74 | 6 | .236 | .323 | .414 |
| 2012 Was | NL | 160 | 594 | 147 | 37 | 2 | 17 | (7 | 10) | 239 | 82 | 56 | 69 | 46 | 4 | **189** | 13 | 3 | 2 | 20 | 6 | .77 | 11 | .247 | .315 | .402 |
| 2013 Was | NL | 44 | 158 | 25 | 9 | 0 | 3 | (2 | 1) | 43 | 11 | 12 | 8 | 4 | 0 | 47 | 3 | 1 | 1 | 1 | 0 | 1.00 | 1 | .158 | .193 | .272 |
| Postseason | | 5 | 15 | 1 | 0 | 0 | 0 | (0 | 0) | 1 | 0 | 0 | 0 | 2 | 0 | 7 | 0 | 2 | 0 | 0 | 0 | - | 0 | .067 | .176 | .067 |
| 4 ML YEARS | | 390 | 1428 | 329 | 79 | 8 | 47 | (24 | 23) | 565 | 181 | 149 | 175 | 116 | 9 | 432 | 35 | 9 | 7 | 38 | 14 | .73 | 18 | .230 | .303 | .396 |

# Marco Estrada

**Pitches:** R **Bats:** R **Pos:** SP-21 **Ht:** 5'11" **Wt:** 200 **Born:** 7/5/1983 **Age:** 30

| HOW MUCH HE PITCHED | | | | | | | | WHAT HE GAVE UP | | | | | | | | | | | | THE RESULTS | | | | | | | |
|---|---|---|---|---|---|---|---|---|---|---|---|---|---|---|---|---|---|---|---|---|---|---|---|---|---|---|---|
| Year Team | Lg | G | GS | CG | GF | IP | BFP | H | R | ER | HR | SH | SF | HB | TBB | IBB | SO | WP | Bk | W | L | Pct | Sh | Sv-Op | Hld | ERC | ERA |
| 2013 Wisc* | A | 1 | 1 | 0 | 0 | 2.2 | 17 | 8 | 6 | 6 | 1 | 0 | 0 | 0 | 1 | 0 | 5 | 1 | 0 | 0 | 1 | .000 | 0 | 0- - | - | 20.77 | 20.25 |
| 2013 Brewrs* | R | 1 | 1 | 0 | 0 | 2.2 | 11 | 3 | 1 | 1 | 0 | 0 | 0 | 0 | 0 | 0 | 4 | 1 | 0 | 0 | 0 | - | 0 | 0- - | - | 2.52 | 3.38 |
| 2013 Nashv* | AAA | 1 | 1 | 0 | 0 | 2.2 | 13 | 3 | 2 | 2 | 0 | 0 | 0 | 0 | 2 | 0 | 2 | 0 | 0 | 0 | 0 | - | 0 | 0- - | - | 5.24 | 6.75 |
| 2008 Was | NL | 11 | 0 | 0 | 3 | 12.2 | 63 | 17 | 13 | 11 | 4 | 0 | 0 | 2 | 5 | 1 | 10 | 0 | 0 | 0 | 0 | - | 0 | 0-1 | 3 | 8.13 | 7.82 |
| 2009 Was | NL | 4 | 1 | 0 | 1 | 7.1 | 33 | 6 | 6 | 5 | 1 | 1 | 0 | 0 | 4 | 0 | 9 | 1 | 0 | 0 | 1 | .000 | 0 | 0-0 | 0 | 3.67 | 6.14 |
| 2010 Mil | NL | 7 | 1 | 0 | 0 | 11.1 | 58 | 14 | 13 | 12 | 3 | 1 | 0 | 1 | 6 | 0 | 13 | 2 | 0 | 0 | 0 | - | 0 | 0-0 | 0 | 7.17 | 9.53 |
| 2011 Mil | NL | 43 | 7 | 0 | 12 | 92.2 | 381 | 83 | 45 | 42 | 11 | 7 | 1 | 2 | 29 | 2 | 88 | 4 | 2 | 4 | 8 | .333 | 0 | 0-3 | 4 | 3.39 | 4.08 |
| 2012 Mil | NL | 29 | 23 | 0 | 0 | 138.1 | 562 | 129 | 62 | 56 | 18 | 7 | 3 | 0 | 29 | 0 | 143 | 4 | 1 | 5 | 7 | .417 | 0 | 0-0 | 1 | 3.18 | 3.64 |
| 2013 Mil | NL | 21 | 21 | 0 | 0 | 128.0 | 512 | 109 | 56 | 55 | 19 | 3 | 2 | 2 | 29 | 0 | 118 | 3 | 0 | 7 | 4 | .636 | 0 | 0-0 | 0 | 3.01 | 3.87 |
| Postseason | | 4 | 0 | 0 | 2 | 6.0 | 27 | 7 | 4 | 4 | 0 | 0 | 0 | 0 | 2 | 0 | 9 | 1 | 0 | 0 | 0 | - | 0 | 0-0 | 0 | 3.91 | 6.00 |
| 6 ML YEARS | | 115 | 53 | 0 | 16 | 390.1 | 1609 | 358 | 195 | 181 | 56 | 19 | 6 | 7 | 102 | 3 | 381 | 14 | 3 | 16 | 20 | .444 | 0 | 0-4 | 8 | 3.43 | 4.17 |

# Andre Ethier

**Bats:** L **Throws:** L **Pos:** CF-74;RF-54;PH-9;LF-8;DH-2 EE-thee-er **Ht:** 6'2" **Wt:** 205 **Born:** 4/10/1982 **Age:** 32

| BATTING | | | | | | | | | | | | | | | | | | | | BASERUNNING | | | | AVERAGES | | |
|---|---|---|---|---|---|---|---|---|---|---|---|---|---|---|---|---|---|---|---|---|---|---|---|---|---|---|
| Year Team | Lg | G | AB | H | 2B | 3B | HR | (Hm | Rd) | TB | R | RBI | RC | TBB | IBB | SO | HBP | SH | SF | SB | CS | SB% | GDP | Avg | OBP | Slg |
| 2006 LAD | NL | 126 | 396 | 122 | 20 | 7 | 11 | (9 | 2) | 189 | 50 | 55 | 62 | 34 | 2 | 77 | 5 | 0 | 6 | 5 | 5 | .50 | 11 | .308 | .365 | .477 |
| 2007 LAD | NL | 153 | 447 | 127 | 32 | 2 | 13 | (8 | 5) | 202 | 50 | 64 | 65 | 46 | 12 | 68 | 4 | 0 | 8 | 0 | 4 | .00 | 10 | .284 | .350 | .452 |
| 2008 LAD | NL | 141 | 525 | 160 | 38 | 5 | 20 | (10 | 10) | 268 | 90 | 77 | 99 | 59 | 0 | 88 | 4 | 1 | 7 | 6 | 3 | .67 | 6 | .305 | .375 | .510 |
| 2009 LAD | NL | 160 | 596 | 162 | 42 | 3 | 31 | (22 | 9) | 303 | 92 | 106 | 94 | 72 | 10 | 116 | 13 | 0 | 4 | 6 | 4 | .60 | 19 | .272 | .361 | .508 |
| 2010 LAD | NL | 139 | 517 | 151 | 33 | 1 | 23 | (14 | 9) | 255 | 71 | 82 | 89 | 59 | 11 | 102 | 3 | 0 | 6 | 2 | 1 | .67 | 11 | .292 | .364 | .493 |
| 2011 LAD | NL | 135 | 487 | 142 | 30 | 0 | 11 | (8 | 3) | 205 | 67 | 62 | 73 | 58 | 9 | 103 | 3 | 0 | 3 | 0 | 1 | .00 | 8 | .292 | .368 | .421 |
| 2012 LAD | NL | 149 | 556 | 158 | 36 | 1 | 20 | (14 | 6) | 256 | 79 | 89 | 89 | 50 | 6 | 124 | 9 | 0 | 3 | 2 | 2 | .50 | 13 | .284 | .351 | .460 |
| 2013 LAD | NL | 142 | 482 | 131 | 33 | 2 | 12 | (6 | 6) | 204 | 54 | 52 | 62 | 61 | 11 | 95 | 7 | 0 | 3 | 4 | 3 | .57 | 9 | .272 | .360 | .423 |
| Postseason | | 18 | 64 | 17 | 4 | 1 | 3 | (1 | 2) | 32 | 13 | 6 | 8 | 8 | 0 | 16 | 1 | 0 | 0 | 0 | 1 | .00 | 1 | .266 | .356 | .500 |
| 8 ML YEARS | | 1145 | 4006 | 1153 | 264 | 21 | 141 | (91 | 50) | 1882 | 553 | 587 | 633 | 439 | 61 | 773 | 48 | 1 | 40 | 25 | 23 | .52 | 87 | .288 | .362 | .470 |

# Irving Falu

**Bats:** B **Throws:** R **Pos:** 3B-1 **Ht:** 5'10" **Wt:** 185 **Born:** 6/6/1983 **Age:** 31

| BATTING | | | | | | | | | | | | | | | | | | | | BASERUNNING | | | | AVERAGES | | |
|---|---|---|---|---|---|---|---|---|---|---|---|---|---|---|---|---|---|---|---|---|---|---|---|---|---|---|
| Year Team | Lg | G | AB | H | 2B | 3B | HR | (Hm | Rd) | TB | R | RBI | RC | TBB | IBB | SO | HBP | SH | SF | SB | CS | SB% | GDP | Avg | OBP | Slg |
| 2009 Omha | AAA | 122 | 465 | 125 | 19 | 5 | 2 | (- | -) | 160 | 64 | 40 | 61 | 52 | 1 | 35 | 2 | 8 | 5 | 12 | 5 | .71 | 9 | .269 | .342 | .344 |
| 2010 Omha | AAA | 119 | 503 | 137 | 14 | 6 | 1 | (- | -) | 166 | 75 | 46 | 59 | 42 | 2 | 39 | 0 | 5 | 2 | 15 | 4 | .79 | 12 | .272 | .327 | .330 |
| 2011 Omha | AAA | 111 | 385 | 116 | 10 | 9 | 2 | (- | -) | 150 | 50 | 47 | 57 | 35 | 3 | 47 | 1 | 12 | 4 | 21 | 11 | .66 | 11 | .301 | .358 | .390 |
| 2012 Omha | AAA | 88 | 365 | 120 | 22 | 3 | 7 | (- | -) | 169 | 69 | 50 | 66 | 28 | 1 | 41 | 0 | 11 | 2 | 21 | 6 | .78 | 11 | .329 | .375 | .463 |
| 2013 Omha | AAA | 135 | 508 | 130 | 19 | 6 | 2 | (- | -) | 167 | 50 | 31 | 57 | 47 | 1 | 51 | 1 | 11 | 1 | 20 | 10 | .67 | 12 | .256 | .320 | .329 |
| 2012 KC | AL | 24 | 85 | 29 | 6 | 1 | 0 | (0 | 0) | 37 | 14 | 7 | 12 | 4 | 0 | 9 | 0 | 2 | 0 | 0 | 2 | .00 | 2 | .341 | .371 | .435 |
| 2013 KC | AL | 1 | 4 | 1 | 0 | 0 | 0 | (0 | 0) | 1 | 0 | 0 | 0 | 0 | 0 | 0 | 0 | 0 | 0 | 0 | 0 | - | 0 | .250 | .250 | .250 |
| 2 ML YEARS | | 25 | 89 | 30 | 6 | 1 | 0 | (0 | 0) | 38 | 14 | 7 | 12 | 4 | 0 | 9 | 0 | 2 | 0 | 0 | 2 | .00 | 2 | .337 | .366 | .427 |

# Jeurys Familia

**Pitches:** R **Bats:** R **Pos:** RP-9 JAY-your-ees fuh-MEAL-yuh **Ht:** 6'4" **Wt:** 230 **Born:** 10/10/1989 **Age:** 24

| | | HOW MUCH HE PITCHED | | | | | | WHAT HE GAVE UP | | | | | | | | | | | | THE RESULTS | | | | | | | |
|---|---|---|---|---|---|---|---|---|---|---|---|---|---|---|---|---|---|---|---|---|---|---|---|---|---|---|---|
| Year Team | Lg | G | GS | CG | GF | IP | BFP | H | R | ER | HR | SH | SF | HB | TBB | IBB | SO | WP | Bk | W | L | Pct | Sh | Sv-Op | Hld | ERC | ERA |
| 2009 Savann | A | 24 | 23 | 0 | 1 | 134.0 | 558 | 109 | 49 | 40 | 3 | 2 | 5 | 12 | 46 | 0 | 109 | 17 | 5 | 10 | 6 | .625 | 0 | 0-- | - | 2.69 | 2.69 |
| 2010 StLuci | A+ | 24 | 24 | 0 | 0 | 121.0 | 556 | 117 | 87 | 75 | 7 | 7 | 5 | 15 | 74 | 0 | 137 | 25 | 3 | 6 | 9 | .400 | 0 | 0-- | - | 4.89 | 5.58 |
| 2011 StLuci | A+ | 6 | 6 | 0 | 0 | 36.1 | 135 | 21 | 7 | 6 | 1 | 2 | 1 | 1 | 8 | 0 | 36 | 1 | 0 | 1 | 1 | .500 | 0 | 0-- | - | 1.28 | 1.49 |
| 2011 Bnghtn | AA | 17 | 17 | 0 | 0 | 87.2 | 388 | 85 | 43 | 35 | 10 | 3 | 0 | 8 | 35 | 0 | 96 | 10 | 0 | 4 | 4 | .500 | 0 | 0-- | - | 4.30 | 3.59 |
| 2012 Buffalo | AAA | 28 | 28 | 1 | 0 | 137.0 | 625 | 145 | 84 | 72 | 8 | 4 | 1 | 4 | 73 | 0 | 128 | 13 | 2 | 9 | 9 | .500 | 0 | 0-- | - | 4.68 | 4.73 |
| 2013 LsVgs | AAA | 4 | 0 | 0 | 2 | 5.0 | 19 | 5 | 0 | 0 | 0 | 0 | 0 | 0 | 1 | 0 | 4 | 0 | 0 | 0 | 0 | - | 0 | 1-- | - | 2.93 | 0.00 |
| 2013 StLuci | A+ | 3 | 1 | 0 | 0 | 3.0 | 13 | 2 | 1 | 1 | 0 | 0 | 0 | 0 | 2 | 0 | 3 | 2 | 0 | 0 | 1 | .000 | 0 | 0-- | - | 2.54 | 3.00 |
| 2013 Bklyn | A- | 1 | 1 | 0 | 0 | 1.0 | 4 | 1 | 1 | 0 | 0 | 0 | 0 | 0 | 0 | 0 | 0 | 0 | 0 | 0 | 0 | - | 0 | 0-- | - | 1.95 | 0.00 |
| 2012 NYM | NL | 8 | 1 | 0 | 4 | 12.1 | 52 | 10 | 8 | 8 | 0 | 0 | 0 | 0 | 9 | 0 | 10 | 0 | 0 | 0 | 0 | - | 0 | 0-0 | 0 | 3.76 | 5.84 |
| 2013 NYM | NL | 9 | 0 | 0 | 3 | 10.2 | 52 | 12 | 5 | 5 | 2 | 2 | 0 | 0 | 9 | 1 | 8 | 3 | 0 | 0 | 0 | - | 0 | 1-1 | 0 | 7.20 | 4.22 |
| 2 ML YEARS | | 17 | 1 | 0 | 7 | 23.0 | 104 | 22 | 13 | 13 | 2 | 2 | 0 | 0 | 18 | 1 | 18 | 3 | 0 | 0 | 0 | - | 0 | 1-1 | 0 | 5.31 | 5.09 |

# Kyle Farnsworth

**Pitches:** R **Bats:** R **Pos:** RP-48 **Ht:** 6'4" **Wt:** 230 **Born:** 4/14/1976 **Age:** 38

| | | HOW MUCH HE PITCHED | | | | | | WHAT HE GAVE UP | | | | | | | | | | | | THE RESULTS | | | | | | | |
|---|---|---|---|---|---|---|---|---|---|---|---|---|---|---|---|---|---|---|---|---|---|---|---|---|---|---|---|
| Year Team | Lg | G | GS | CG | GF | IP | BFP | H | R | ER | HR | SH | SF | HB | TBB | IBB | SO | WP | Bk | W | L | Pct | Sh | Sv-Op | Hld | ERC | ERA |
| 2013 Indy* | AAA | 6 | 0 | 0 | 2 | 6.2 | 29 | 7 | 3 | 3 | 0 | 1 | 0 | 0 | 4 | 1 | 3 | 0 | 0 | 1 | 1 | .500 | 0 | 0-- | - | 4.30 | 4.05 |
| 1999 ChC | NL | 27 | 21 | 1 | 1 | 130.0 | 579 | 140 | 80 | 73 | 28 | 6 | 2 | 3 | 52 | 1 | 70 | 7 | 1 | 5 | 9 | .357 | 1 | 0-0 | 0 | 5.39 | 5.05 |
| 2000 ChC | NL | 46 | 5 | 0 | 8 | 77.0 | 371 | 90 | 58 | 55 | 14 | 4 | 4 | 4 | 50 | 8 | 74 | 3 | 0 | 2 | 9 | .182 | 0 | 1-6 | 6 | 6.72 | 6.43 |
| 2001 ChC | NL | 76 | 0 | 0 | 24 | 82.0 | 339 | 65 | 26 | 25 | 8 | 2 | 2 | 1 | 29 | 2 | 107 | 2 | 2 | 4 | 6 | .400 | 0 | 2-3 | 24 | 2.76 | 2.74 |
| 2002 ChC | NL | 45 | 0 | 0 | 17 | 46.2 | 213 | 53 | 47 | 38 | 9 | 2 | 5 | 1 | 24 | 7 | 46 | 1 | 0 | 4 | 6 | .400 | 0 | 1-7 | 6 | 5.89 | 7.33 |
| 2003 ChC | NL | 77 | 0 | 0 | 13 | 76.1 | 312 | 53 | 31 | 28 | 6 | 4 | 1 | 0 | 36 | 1 | 92 | 6 | 0 | 3 | 2 | .600 | 0 | 0-3 | 19 | 2.58 | 3.30 |
| 2004 ChC | NL | 72 | 0 | 0 | 25 | 66.2 | 298 | 67 | 39 | 35 | 10 | 5 | 0 | 2 | 33 | 1 | 78 | 1 | 0 | 4 | 5 | .444 | 0 | 0-4 | 18 | 4.91 | 4.73 |
| 2005 2 Tms | | 72 | 0 | 0 | 34 | 70.0 | 277 | 44 | 18 | 17 | 5 | 2 | 1 | 3 | 27 | 0 | 87 | 3 | 1 | 1 | 1 | .500 | 0 | 16-18 | 19 | 2.12 | 2.19 |
| 2006 NYY | AL | 72 | 0 | 0 | 24 | 66.0 | 289 | 62 | 34 | 32 | 8 | 3 | 2 | 1 | 28 | 3 | 75 | 5 | 1 | 3 | 6 | .333 | 0 | 6-10 | 19 | 3.88 | 4.36 |
| 2007 NYY | AL | 64 | 0 | 0 | 11 | 60.0 | 266 | 60 | 35 | 32 | 9 | 1 | 2 | 2 | 27 | 2 | 48 | 4 | 2 | 2 | 1 | .667 | 0 | 0-3 | 15 | 4.67 | 4.80 |
| 2008 2 Tms | AL | 61 | 0 | 0 | 11 | 60.1 | 261 | 70 | 32 | 30 | 15 | 3 | 1 | 1 | 22 | 4 | 61 | 1 | 1 | 2 | 3 | .400 | 0 | 1-4 | 14 | 6.11 | 4.48 |
| 2009 KC | AL | 41 | 0 | 0 | 18 | 37.1 | 168 | 43 | 22 | 19 | 3 | 1 | 2 | 1 | 14 | 2 | 42 | 2 | 1 | 1 | 5 | .167 | 0 | 0-2 | 5 | 4.65 | 4.58 |
| 2010 2 Tms | | 60 | 0 | 0 | 15 | 64.2 | 267 | 55 | 25 | 24 | 4 | 3 | 2 | 4 | 19 | 1 | 61 | 3 | 0 | 3 | 2 | .600 | 0 | 0-3 | 9 | 2.84 | 3.34 |
| 2011 TB | AL | 63 | 0 | 0 | 51 | 57.2 | 231 | 45 | 15 | 14 | 5 | 1 | 2 | 3 | 12 | 1 | 51 | 2 | 0 | 5 | 1 | .833 | 0 | 25-31 | 0 | 2.29 | 2.18 |
| 2012 TB | AL | 34 | 0 | 0 | 8 | 27.0 | 120 | 22 | 13 | 12 | 1 | 2 | 1 | 1 | 14 | 2 | 25 | 2 | 0 | 1 | 6 | .143 | 0 | 0-0 | 7 | 2.96 | 4.00 |
| 2013 2 Tms | | 48 | 0 | 0 | 17 | 38.1 | 162 | 43 | 20 | 20 | 5 | 0 | 0 | 1 | 10 | 0 | 28 | 0 | 1 | 3 | 1 | .750 | 0 | 2-3 | 2 | 4.64 | 4.70 |
| 05 Det | AL | 46 | 0 | 0 | 16 | 42.2 | 174 | 29 | 12 | 11 | 1 | 1 | 1 | 1 | 20 | 0 | 55 | 2 | 0 | 1 | 1 | .500 | 0 | 6-8 | 15 | 2.26 | 2.32 |
| 05 Atl | NL | 26 | 0 | 0 | 18 | 27.1 | 103 | 15 | 6 | 6 | 4 | 1 | 0 | 2 | 7 | 0 | 32 | 1 | 1 | 0 | 0 | - | 0 | 10-10 | 4 | 1.86 | 1.98 |
| 08 NYY | AL | 45 | 0 | 0 | 6 | 44.1 | 185 | 43 | 18 | 18 | 11 | 3 | 1 | 1 | 17 | 3 | 43 | 1 | 1 | 1 | 2 | .333 | 0 | 1-1 | 11 | 5.02 | 3.65 |
| 08 Det | AL | 16 | 0 | 0 | 5 | 16.0 | 76 | 27 | 14 | 12 | 4 | 0 | 0 | 0 | 5 | 1 | 18 | 0 | 0 | 1 | 1 | .500 | 0 | 0-3 | 3 | 9.43 | 6.75 |
| 10 KC | AL | 37 | 0 | 0 | 9 | 44.2 | 185 | 40 | 13 | 12 | 2 | 1 | 1 | 4 | 12 | 0 | 36 | 2 | 0 | 3 | 0 | 1.000 | 0 | 0-2 | 7 | 3.01 | 2.42 |
| 10 Atl | NL | 23 | 0 | 0 | 6 | 20.0 | 82 | 15 | 12 | 12 | 2 | 2 | 1 | 0 | 7 | 1 | 25 | 1 | 0 | 0 | 2 | .000 | 0 | 0-1 | 2 | 2.46 | 5.40 |
| 13 TB | AL | 39 | 0 | 0 | 10 | 29.2 | 129 | 37 | 19 | 19 | 4 | 0 | 0 | 1 | 7 | 0 | 19 | 0 | 1 | 2 | 0 | 1.000 | 0 | 0-1 | 2 | 5.32 | 5.76 |
| 13 Pit | NL | 9 | 0 | 0 | 7 | 8.2 | 33 | 6 | 1 | 1 | 1 | 0 | 0 | 0 | 3 | 0 | 9 | 0 | 0 | 1 | 1 | .500 | 0 | 2-2 | 0 | 2.51 | 1.04 |
| Postseason | | 15 | 0 | 0 | 5 | 16.0 | 66 | 12 | 9 | 9 | 2 | 1 | 1 | 1 | 6 | 2 | 17 | 0 | 0 | 1 | 0 | 1.000 | 0 | 0-0 | 2 | 2.86 | 5.06 |
| 15 ML YEARS | | 858 | 26 | 1 | 277 | 960.0 | 4153 | 912 | 495 | 454 | 130 | 39 | 27 | 28 | 397 | 35 | 945 | 42 | 10 | 43 | 63 | .406 | 1 | 54-97 | 163 | 4.13 | 4.26 |

# Danny Farquhar

**Pitches:** R **Bats:** R **Pos:** RP-46 FARK-war **Ht:** 5'9" **Wt:** 180 **Born:** 2/17/1987 **Age:** 27

| | | HOW MUCH HE PITCHED | | | | | | WHAT HE GAVE UP | | | | | | | | | | | | THE RESULTS | | | | | | | |
|---|---|---|---|---|---|---|---|---|---|---|---|---|---|---|---|---|---|---|---|---|---|---|---|---|---|---|---|
| Year Team | Lg | G | GS | CG | GF | IP | BFP | H | R | ER | HR | SH | SF | HB | TBB | IBB | SO | WP | Bk | W | L | Pct | Sh | Sv-Op | Hld | ERC | ERA |
| 2009 Dnedin | A+ | 17 | 0 | 0 | 15 | 17.0 | 73 | 10 | 4 | 1 | 0 | 0 | 0 | 1 | 11 | 0 | 23 | 2 | 0 | 1 | 0 | 1.000 | 0 | 7-- | - | 2.29 | 0.53 |
| 2009 NHam | AA | 37 | 0 | 0 | 27 | 45.2 | 199 | 31 | 15 | 12 | 1 | 1 | 2 | 5 | 30 | 3 | 51 | 4 | 0 | 1 | 4 | .200 | 0 | 15-- | - | 3.03 | 2.36 |
| 2010 NHam | AA | 53 | 0 | 0 | 35 | 76.2 | 322 | 50 | 32 | 30 | 7 | 5 | 2 | 8 | 42 | 3 | 79 | 3 | 0 | 4 | 3 | .571 | 0 | 17-- | - | 3.06 | 3.52 |
| 2011 Scrmto | AAA | 4 | 0 | 0 | 1 | 8.0 | 36 | 7 | 1 | 0 | 0 | 1 | 0 | 2 | 3 | 1 | 9 | 0 | 0 | 0 | 0 | - | 0 | 1-- | - | 3.21 | 0.00 |
| 2011 LsVgs | AAA | 50 | 0 | 0 | 40 | 51.2 | 234 | 63 | 32 | 27 | 4 | 1 | 1 | 4 | 18 | 0 | 43 | 2 | 0 | 4 | 5 | .444 | 0 | 14-- | - | 5.29 | 4.70 |
| 2012 NHam | AA | 20 | 0 | 0 | 6 | 30.1 | 133 | 28 | 14 | 10 | 2 | 0 | 2 | 3 | 10 | 0 | 33 | 1 | 0 | 0 | 1 | .000 | 0 | 1-- | - | 3.41 | 2.97 |
| 2012 Scrmto | AAA | 5 | 0 | 0 | 3 | 8.0 | 42 | 10 | 9 | 9 | 1 | 2 | 1 | 2 | 6 | 2 | 6 | 0 | 0 | 1 | 2 | .333 | 0 | 0-- | - | 7.62 | 10.13 |
| 2012 Trntn | AA | 6 | 0 | 0 | 5 | 11.0 | 35 | 2 | 0 | 0 | 0 | 0 | 0 | 0 | 0 | 0 | 14 | 0 | 0 | 1 | 0 | 1.000 | 0 | 4-- | - | 0.08 | 0.00 |
| 2012 S-WB | AAA | 1 | 0 | 0 | 1 | 2.0 | 5 | 0 | 0 | 0 | 0 | 0 | 0 | 0 | 0 | 0 | 1 | 0 | 0 | 0 | 0 | - | 0 | 0-- | - | 0.00 | 0.00 |
| 2012 Tacom | AAA | 12 | 0 | 0 | 7 | 16.2 | 64 | 9 | 1 | 1 | 0 | 0 | 1 | 1 | 5 | 0 | 16 | 2 | 0 | 1 | 0 | 1.000 | 0 | 4-- | - | 1.27 | 0.54 |
| 2013 Tacom | AAA | 15 | 0 | 0 | 11 | 20.0 | 82 | 17 | 6 | 5 | 1 | 1 | 0 | 0 | 4 | 0 | 30 | 2 | 1 | 0 | 1 | .000 | 0 | 6-- | - | 2.17 | 2.25 |
| 2011 Tor | AL | 3 | 0 | 0 | 2 | 2.0 | 11 | 4 | 4 | 3 | 0 | 0 | 1 | 0 | 2 | 0 | 1 | 0 | 0 | 0 | 0 | - | 0 | 0-0 | 0 | 13.16 | 13.50 |
| 2013 Sea | AL | 46 | 0 | 0 | 27 | 55.2 | 228 | 44 | 29 | 26 | 2 | 1 | 2 | 0 | 22 | 4 | 79 | 2 | 1 | 0 | 3 | .000 | 0 | 16-20 | 2 | 2.44 | 4.20 |
| 2 ML YEARS | | 49 | 0 | 0 | 29 | 57.2 | 239 | 48 | 33 | 29 | 2 | 1 | 3 | 0 | 24 | 4 | 80 | 2 | 1 | 0 | 3 | .000 | 0 | 16-20 | 2 | 2.72 | 4.53 |

# Tim Federowicz

**Bats:** R **Throws:** R **Pos:** C-45;PH-10;1B-2 fed-ur-OWE-vitch **Ht:** 5'10" **Wt:** 215 **Born:** 8/5/1987 **Age:** 26

| | | BATTING | | | | | | | | | | | | | | | | | | BASERUNNING | | | | AVERAGES | | |
|---|---|---|---|---|---|---|---|---|---|---|---|---|---|---|---|---|---|---|---|---|---|---|---|---|---|---|
| Year Team | Lg | G | AB | H | 2B | 3B | HR | (Hm | Rd) | TB | R | RBI | RC | TBB | IBB | SO | HBP | SH | SF | SB | CS | SB% | GDP | Avg | OBP | Slg |
| 2013 Albq* | AAA | 21 | 79 | 33 | 8 | 1 | 8 | (- | -) | 67 | 20 | 25 | 29 | 14 | 0 | 26 | 1 | 2 | 2 | 0 | 0 | - | 1 | .418 | .500 | .848 |
| 2011 LAD | NL | 7 | 13 | 2 | 0 | 0 | 0 | (0 | 0) | 2 | 0 | 1 | 1 | 2 | 0 | 4 | 1 | 0 | 0 | 0 | 0 | - | 0 | .154 | .313 | .154 |
| 2012 LAD | NL | 3 | 3 | 1 | 0 | 0 | 0 | (0 | 0) | 1 | 0 | 0 | 1 | 1 | 0 | 2 | 0 | 0 | 0 | 0 | 0 | - | 0 | .333 | .500 | .333 |
| 2013 LAD | NL | 56 | 160 | 37 | 8 | 0 | 4 | (1 | 3) | 57 | 12 | 16 | 9 | 10 | 5 | 56 | 0 | 2 | 1 | 0 | 0 | - | 5 | .231 | .275 | .356 |
| 3 ML YEARS | | 66 | 176 | 40 | 8 | 0 | 4 | (1 | 3) | 60 | 12 | 17 | 11 | 13 | 5 | 62 | 1 | 2 | 1 | 0 | 0 | - | 5 | .227 | .283 | .341 |

# Scott Feldman

**Pitches:** R **Bats:** L **Pos:** SP-30 **Ht:** 6'7" **Wt:** 230 **Born:** 2/7/1983 **Age:** 31

| | | | HOW MUCH HE PITCHED | | | | | | WHAT HE GAVE UP | | | | | | | | | | | | THE RESULTS | | | | | | | |
|---|---|---|---|---|---|---|---|---|---|---|---|---|---|---|---|---|---|---|---|---|---|---|---|---|---|---|---|---|
| Year | Team | Lg | G | GS | CG | GF | IP | BFP | H | R | ER | HR | SH | SF | HB | TBB | IBB | SO | WP | Bk | W | L | Pct | Sh | Sv-Op | Hld | ERC | ERA |
| 2005 | Tex | AL | 8 | 0 | 0 | 3 | 9.1 | 37 | 9 | 1 | 1 | 0 | 0 | 0 | 0 | 2 | 1 | 4 | 0 | 0 | 0 | 1 | .000 | 0 | 0-0 | 1 | 2.48 | 0.96 |
| 2006 | Tex | AL | 36 | 0 | 0 | 5 | 41.1 | 175 | 42 | 19 | 18 | 4 | 2 | 1 | 4 | 10 | 0 | 30 | 0 | 0 | 0 | 2 | .000 | 0 | 0-1 | 7 | 3.94 | 3.92 |
| 2007 | Tex | AL | 29 | 0 | 0 | 10 | 39.0 | 192 | 44 | 26 | 25 | 3 | 0 | 2 | 3 | 32 | 5 | 19 | 2 | 2 | 1 | 2 | .333 | 0 | 0-0 | 0 | 6.40 | 5.77 |
| 2008 | Tex | AL | 28 | 25 | 0 | 2 | 151.1 | 651 | 161 | 103 | 89 | 22 | 1 | 9 | 10 | 56 | 2 | 74 | 4 | 2 | 6 | 8 | .429 | 0 | 0-0 | 0 | 5.03 | 5.29 |
| 2009 | Tex | AL | 34 | 31 | 0 | 0 | 189.2 | 791 | 178 | 87 | 86 | 18 | 1 | 3 | 9 | 65 | 0 | 113 | 5 | 2 | 17 | 8 | .680 | 0 | 0-0 | 0 | 3.74 | 4.08 |
| 2010 | Tex | AL | 29 | 22 | 0 | 2 | 141.1 | 641 | 181 | 98 | 86 | 18 | 5 | 8 | 5 | 45 | 2 | 75 | 11 | 0 | 7 | 11 | .389 | 0 | 0-0 | 0 | 5.71 | 5.48 |
| 2011 | Tex | AL | 11 | 2 | 0 | 5 | 32.0 | 129 | 25 | 14 | 14 | 3 | 0 | 1 | 2 | 10 | 0 | 22 | 2 | 0 | 2 | 1 | .667 | 0 | 0-0 | 0 | 2.83 | 3.94 |
| 2012 | Tex | AL | 29 | 21 | 0 | 5 | 123.2 | 536 | 139 | 79 | 70 | 14 | 0 | 5 | 1 | 32 | 2 | 96 | 2 | 1 | 6 | 11 | .353 | 0 | 0-0 | 0 | 4.27 | 5.09 |
| 2013 | 2 Tms | | 30 | 30 | 2 | 0 | 181.2 | 758 | 159 | 87 | 78 | 19 | 7 | 7 | 9 | 56 | 1 | 132 | 7 | 1 | 12 | 12 | .500 | 1 | 0-0 | 0 | 3.24 | 3.86 |
| 13 | ChC | NL | 15 | 15 | 1 | 0 | 91.0 | 376 | 79 | 42 | 35 | 10 | 6 | 4 | 3 | 25 | 0 | 67 | 4 | 0 | 7 | 6 | .538 | 0 | 0-0 | 0 | 3.05 | 3.46 |
| 13 | Bal | AL | 15 | 15 | 1 | 0 | 90.2 | 382 | 80 | 45 | 43 | 9 | 1 | 3 | 6 | 31 | 1 | 65 | 3 | 1 | 5 | 6 | .455 | 1 | 0-0 | 0 | 3.44 | 4.27 |
| Postseason | | | 9 | 0 | 0 | 1 | 13.2 | 56 | 8 | 5 | 5 | 0 | 2 | 0 | 2 | 6 | 2 | 11 | 0 | 0 | 1 | 0 | 1.000 | 0 | 0-1 | 0 | 1.75 | 3.29 |
| 9 ML YEARS | | | 234 | 131 | 2 | 32 | 909.1 | 3910 | 938 | 514 | 467 | 101 | 16 | 36 | 43 | 308 | 13 | 565 | 33 | 8 | 51 | 56 | .477 | 1 | 0-1 | 8 | 4.28 | 4.62 |

# Pedro Feliciano

**Pitches:** L **Bats:** L **Pos:** RP-25 **Ht:** 5'10" **Wt:** 195 **Born:** 8/25/1976 **Age:** 37

| | | | HOW MUCH HE PITCHED | | | | | | WHAT HE GAVE UP | | | | | | | | | | | | THE RESULTS | | | | | | | |
|---|---|---|---|---|---|---|---|---|---|---|---|---|---|---|---|---|---|---|---|---|---|---|---|---|---|---|---|---|
| Year | Team | Lg | G | GS | CG | GF | IP | BFP | H | R | ER | HR | SH | SF | HB | TBB | IBB | SO | WP | Bk | W | L | Pct | Sh | Sv-Op | Hld | ERC | ERA |
| 2013 | StLuci* | A+ | 5 | 0 | 0 | 0 | 4.2 | 21 | 5 | 3 | 1 | 0 | 1 | 2 | 0 | 2 | 0 | 4 | 0 | 0 | 0 | 0 | - | 0 | 0-- | - | 3.75 | 1.93 |
| 2013 | Bnghtn* | AA | 14 | 0 | 0 | 3 | 14.1 | 53 | 9 | 2 | 2 | 0 | 0 | 0 | 1 | 2 | 0 | 14 | 0 | 0 | 0 | 0 | - | 0 | 0-- | - | 1.25 | 1.26 |
| 2013 | LsVgs* | AAA | 3 | 0 | 0 | 2 | 2.0 | 6 | 0 | 0 | 0 | 0 | 0 | 0 | 0 | 0 | 0 | 1 | 0 | 0 | 0 | 0 | - | 0 | 1-- | - | 0.00 | 0.00 |
| 2002 | NYM | NL | 6 | 0 | 0 | 3 | 6.0 | 26 | 9 | 5 | 5 | 0 | 0 | 0 | 0 | 1 | 0 | 4 | 0 | 0 | 0 | 0 | - | 0 | 0-0 | 0 | 5.56 | 7.50 |
| 2003 | NYM | NL | 23 | 0 | 0 | 8 | 48.1 | 218 | 52 | 21 | 18 | 5 | 0 | 1 | 3 | 21 | 3 | 43 | 3 | 1 | 0 | 0 | - | 0 | 0-0 | 0 | 4.77 | 3.35 |
| 2004 | NYM | NL | 22 | 0 | 0 | 3 | 18.1 | 82 | 14 | 12 | 11 | 2 | 1 | 1 | 1 | 12 | 0 | 14 | 1 | 0 | 1 | 1 | .500 | 0 | 0-0 | 2 | 3.93 | 5.40 |
| 2006 | NYM | NL | 64 | 0 | 0 | 10 | 60.1 | 256 | 56 | 15 | 14 | 4 | 4 | 3 | 3 | 20 | 1 | 54 | 1 | 0 | 7 | 2 | .778 | 0 | 0-3 | 10 | 3.34 | 2.09 |
| 2007 | NYM | NL | 78 | 0 | 0 | 12 | 64.0 | 275 | 47 | 26 | 22 | 3 | 2 | 2 | 5 | 31 | 4 | 61 | 1 | 1 | 2 | 2 | .500 | 0 | 2-3 | 18 | 2.74 | 3.09 |
| 2008 | NYM | NL | **86** | 0 | 0 | 14 | 53.1 | 237 | 57 | 24 | 24 | 7 | 2 | 3 | 3 | 26 | 8 | 50 | 2 | 0 | 3 | 4 | .429 | 0 | 2-4 | 21 | 5.11 | 4.05 |
| 2009 | NYM | NL | **88** | 0 | 0 | 11 | 59.1 | 242 | 51 | 25 | 20 | 7 | 2 | 1 | 0 | 18 | 4 | 59 | 2 | 1 | 6 | 4 | .600 | 0 | 0-2 | 24 | 2.98 | 3.03 |
| 2010 | NYM | NL | **92** | 0 | 0 | 16 | 62.2 | 280 | 66 | 24 | 23 | 1 | 2 | 0 | 6 | 30 | 6 | 56 | 1 | 0 | 3 | 6 | .333 | 0 | 0-1 | 23 | 4.30 | 3.30 |
| 2013 | NYM | NL | 25 | 0 | 0 | 3 | 11.1 | 51 | 11 | 5 | 5 | 1 | 1 | 1 | 1 | 6 | 2 | 9 | 1 | 0 | 0 | 2 | .000 | 0 | 0-0 | 5 | 4.35 | 3.97 |
| Postseason | | | 6 | 0 | 0 | 0 | 4.2 | 18 | 2 | 1 | 1 | 1 | 0 | 0 | 0 | 2 | 0 | 3 | 1 | 0 | 1 | 0 | 1.000 | 0 | 0-0 | 1 | 1.92 | 1.93 |
| 9 ML YEARS | | | 484 | 0 | 0 | 80 | 383.2 | 1667 | 363 | 157 | 142 | 30 | 14 | 12 | 22 | 165 | 28 | 350 | 12 | 3 | 22 | 21 | .512 | 0 | 4-13 | 103 | 3.83 | 3.33 |

# Neftali Feliz

neff-TAH-lee

**Pitches:** R **Bats:** R **Pos:** RP-6 **Ht:** 6'3" **Wt:** 225 **Born:** 5/2/1988 **Age:** 26

| | | | HOW MUCH HE PITCHED | | | | | | WHAT HE GAVE UP | | | | | | | | | | | | THE RESULTS | | | | | | | |
|---|---|---|---|---|---|---|---|---|---|---|---|---|---|---|---|---|---|---|---|---|---|---|---|---|---|---|---|---|
| Year | Team | Lg | G | GS | CG | GF | IP | BFP | H | R | ER | HR | SH | SF | HB | TBB | IBB | SO | WP | Bk | W | L | Pct | Sh | Sv-Op | Hld | ERC | ERA |
| 2013 | Rngrs* | R | 2 | 1 | 0 | 0 | 2.0 | 8 | 1 | 0 | 0 | 0 | 0 | 0 | 0 | 2 | 0 | 4 | 0 | 0 | 0 | 0 | - | 0 | 0-- | - | 3.21 | 0.00 |
| 2013 | RdRck* | AAA | 6 | 0 | 0 | 1 | 8.2 | 32 | 4 | 0 | 0 | 0 | 0 | 0 | 0 | 2 | 0 | 9 | 0 | 0 | 0 | 0 | - | 0 | 0-- | - | 0.82 | 0.00 |
| 2009 | Tex | AL | 20 | 0 | 0 | 3 | 31.0 | 117 | 13 | 6 | 6 | 2 | 1 | 0 | 3 | 8 | 0 | 39 | 0 | 0 | 1 | 0 | 1.000 | 0 | 2-3 | 9 | 1.14 | 1.74 |
| 2010 | Tex | AL | 70 | 0 | 0 | 59 | 69.1 | 269 | 43 | 21 | 21 | 5 | 1 | 0 | 5 | 18 | 1 | 71 | 5 | 0 | 4 | 3 | .571 | 0 | 40-43 | 3 | 1.75 | 2.73 |
| 2011 | Tex | AL | 64 | 0 | 0 | 56 | 62.1 | 252 | 42 | 22 | 19 | 4 | 3 | 2 | 0 | 30 | 1 | 54 | 2 | 1 | 2 | 3 | .400 | 0 | 32-38 | 0 | 2.45 | 2.74 |
| 2012 | Tex | AL | 8 | 7 | 1 | 0 | 42.2 | 175 | 28 | 15 | 15 | 5 | 0 | 0 | 2 | 23 | 0 | 37 | 0 | 0 | 3 | 1 | .750 | 0 | 0-0 | 0 | 3.11 | 3.16 |
| 2013 | Tex | AL | 6 | 0 | 0 | 2 | 4.2 | 21 | 5 | 0 | 0 | 0 | 0 | 0 | 1 | 2 | 0 | 4 | 0 | 0 | 0 | 0 | - | 0 | 0-0 | 0 | 4.78 | 0.00 |
| Postseason | | | 18 | 0 | 0 | 15 | 18.2 | 76 | 8 | 4 | 4 | 1 | 1 | 0 | 1 | 13 | 1 | 23 | 1 | 0 | 0 | 0 | - | 0 | 7-8 | 0 | 2.04 | 1.93 |
| 5 ML YEARS | | | 168 | 7 | 1 | 120 | 210.0 | 834 | 131 | 64 | 61 | 16 | 5 | 2 | 11 | 81 | 2 | 205 | 7 | 1 | 10 | 7 | .588 | 0 | 74-84 | 12 | 2.14 | 2.61 |

# Jose Fernandez

**Pitches:** R **Bats:** R **Pos:** SP-28 **Ht:** 6'2" **Wt:** 240 **Born:** 7/31/1992 **Age:** 21

| | | | HOW MUCH HE PITCHED | | | | | | WHAT HE GAVE UP | | | | | | | | | | | | THE RESULTS | | | | | | | |
|---|---|---|---|---|---|---|---|---|---|---|---|---|---|---|---|---|---|---|---|---|---|---|---|---|---|---|---|---|
| Year | Team | Lg | G | GS | CG | GF | IP | BFP | H | R | ER | HR | SH | SF | HB | TBB | IBB | SO | WP | Bk | W | L | Pct | Sh | Sv-Op | Hld | ERC | ERA |
| 2011 | Mrlns | R | 1 | 1 | 0 | 0 | 2.0 | 9 | 1 | 1 | 0 | 0 | 0 | 0 | 0 | 1 | 0 | 3 | 1 | 0 | 0 | 0 | - | 0 | 0-- | - | 1.26 | 0.00 |
| 2011 | Jmstwn | A- | 1 | 1 | 0 | 0 | 2.1 | 14 | 4 | 5 | 5 | 0 | 0 | 0 | 1 | 3 | 0 | 4 | 0 | 0 | 0 | 1 | .000 | 0 | 0-- | - | 14.22 | 19.29 |
| 2012 | Grnsbr | A | 14 | 14 | 0 | 0 | 79.0 | 295 | 51 | 16 | 14 | 2 | 2 | 3 | 2 | 18 | 0 | 99 | 1 | 3 | 7 | 0 | 1.000 | 0 | 0-- | - | 1.50 | 1.59 |
| 2012 | Jupiter | A+ | 11 | 11 | 0 | 0 | 55.0 | 218 | 38 | 12 | 12 | 0 | 0 | 1 | 3 | 17 | 0 | 59 | 4 | 1 | 7 | 1 | .875 | 0 | 0-- | - | 1.78 | 1.96 |
| 2013 | Mia | NL | 28 | 28 | 0 | 0 | 172.2 | 681 | 111 | 47 | 42 | 10 | 3 | 4 | 5 | 58 | 5 | 187 | 3 | 1 | 12 | 6 | .667 | 0 | 0-0 | 0 | 1.85 | 2.19 |

# Tommy Field

**Bats:** R **Throws:** R **Pos:** 2B-9;SS-5;3B-3;PR-1 **Ht:** 5'10" **Wt:** 185 **Born:** 2/22/1987 **Age:** 27

| | | | BATTING | | | | | | | | | | | | | | | | | | BASERUNNING | | | | AVERAGES | | |
|---|---|---|---|---|---|---|---|---|---|---|---|---|---|---|---|---|---|---|---|---|---|---|---|---|---|---|---|
| Year | Team | Lg | G | AB | H | 2B | 3B | HR | (Hm | Rd) | TB | R | RBI | RC | TBB | IBB | SO | HBP | SH | SF | SB | CS | SB% | GDP | Avg | OBP | Slg |
| 2013 | Salt Lk* | AAA | 81 | 314 | 95 | 20 | 2 | 11 | (- | -) | 152 | 56 | 49 | 62 | 44 | 1 | 68 | 5 | 4 | 5 | 6 | 2 | .75 | 7 | .303 | .391 | .484 |
| 2011 | Col | NL | 16 | 48 | 13 | 0 | 0 | 0 | (0 | 0) | 13 | 4 | 3 | 4 | 3 | 0 | 14 | 0 | 0 | 0 | 0 | 0 | - | 1 | .271 | .314 | .271 |
| 2012 | Col | NL | 2 | 2 | 0 | 0 | 0 | 0 | (0 | 0) | 0 | 0 | 0 | 0 | 1 | 0 | 1 | 0 | 0 | 0 | 0 | 0 | - | 0 | .000 | .333 | .000 |
| 2013 | LAA | AL | 15 | 26 | 4 | 0 | 0 | 0 | (0 | 0) | 4 | 4 | 0 | 0 | 1 | 0 | 7 | 0 | 0 | 0 | 0 | 0 | - | 0 | .154 | .185 | .154 |
| 3 ML YEARS | | | 33 | 76 | 17 | 0 | 0 | 0 | (0 | 0) | 17 | 8 | 3 | 4 | 5 | 0 | 22 | 0 | 0 | 0 | 0 | 0 | - | 1 | .224 | .272 | .224 |

# Prince Fielder

**Bats:** L **Throws:** R **Pos:** 1B-151;DH-11 **Ht:** 5'11" **Wt:** 275 **Born:** 5/9/1984 **Age:** 30

| BATTING | | | | | | | | | | | | | | | | | | | | | | BASERUNNING | | | | AVERAGES | | |
|---|---|---|---|---|---|---|---|---|---|---|---|---|---|---|---|---|---|---|---|---|---|---|---|---|---|---|---|---|
| Year | Team | Lg | G | AB | H | 2B | 3B | HR | (Hm | Rd) | TB | R | RBI | RC | TBB | IBB | SO | HBP | SH | SF | | SB | CS | SB% | GDP | Avg | OBP | Slg |
| 2005 | Mil | NL | 39 | 59 | 17 | 4 | 0 | 2 | (2 | 0) | 27 | 2 | 10 | 10 | 2 | 0 | 17 | 0 | 0 | 1 | | 0 | 0 | - | 0 | .288 | .306 | .458 |
| 2006 | Mil | NL | 157 | 569 | 154 | 35 | 1 | 28 | (11 | 17) | 275 | 82 | 81 | 84 | 59 | 5 | 125 | 12 | 0 | 8 | | 7 | 2 | .78 | 17 | .271 | .347 | .483 |
| 2007 | Mil | NL | 158 | 573 | 165 | 35 | 2 | **50** | **(27** | 23) | 354 | 109 | 119 | 125 | 90 | 21 | 121 | 14 | 0 | 4 | | 2 | 2 | .50 | 9 | .288 | .395 | .618 |
| 2008 | Mil | NL | 159 | 588 | 162 | 30 | 2 | 34 | (18 | 16) | 298 | 86 | 102 | 105 | 84 | 19 | 134 | 12 | 0 | 10 | | 3 | 2 | .60 | 12 | .276 | .372 | .507 |
| 2009 | Mil | NL | **162** | 591 | 177 | 35 | 3 | 46 | **(23** | 23) | 356 | 103 | **141** | 134 | 110 | 21 | 138 | 9 | 0 | 9 | | 2 | 3 | .40 | 14 | .299 | .412 | .602 |
| 2010 | Mil | NL | 161 | 578 | 151 | 25 | 0 | 32 | (18 | 14) | 272 | 94 | 83 | 94 | **114** | 17 | 138 | 21 | 0 | 1 | | 1 | 0 | 1.00 | 12 | .261 | .401 | .471 |
| 2011 | Mil | NL | **162** | 569 | 170 | 36 | 1 | 38 | **(24** | 14) | 322 | 95 | 120 | 120 | 107 | **32** | 106 | 10 | 0 | 6 | | 1 | 1 | .50 | 17 | .299 | .415 | .566 |
| 2012 | Det | AL | **162** | 581 | 182 | 33 | 1 | 30 | (18 | 12) | 307 | 83 | 108 | 116 | 85 | **18** | 84 | **17** | 0 | 7 | | 1 | 0 | 1.00 | 19 | .313 | .412 | .528 |
| 2013 | Det | AL | **162** | 624 | 174 | 36 | 0 | 25 | (13 | 12) | 285 | 82 | 106 | 94 | 75 | 5 | 117 | 9 | 0 | 4 | | 1 | 1 | .50 | 20 | .279 | .362 | .457 |
| Postseason | | | 28 | 104 | 19 | 4 | 0 | 5 | (4 | 1) | 38 | 9 | 11 | 9 | 11 | 5 | 25 | 3 | 0 | 1 | | 0 | 0 | - | 6 | .183 | .277 | .365 |
| 9 ML YEARS | | | 1322 | 4732 | 1352 | 269 | 10 | 285 | (154 | 131) | 2496 | 736 | 870 | 882 | 726 | 138 | 980 | 104 | 0 | 50 | | 18 | 11 | .62 | 120 | .286 | .389 | .527 |

# Josh Fields

**Pitches:** R **Bats:** R **Pos:** RP-41 **Ht:** 6'0" **Wt:** 180 **Born:** 8/19/1985 **Age:** 28

| HOW MUCH HE PITCHED | | | | | | | | | WHAT HE GAVE UP | | | | | | | | | | | | THE RESULTS | | | | | | | |
|---|---|---|---|---|---|---|---|---|---|---|---|---|---|---|---|---|---|---|---|---|---|---|---|---|---|---|---|---|
| Year | Team | Lg | G | GS | CG | GF | IP | BFP | H | R | ER | HR | SH | SF | HB | TBB | IBB | SO | WP | Bk | W | L | Pct | Sh | Sv-Op | Hld | ERC | ERA |
| 2009 | WTenn | AA | 31 | 0 | 0 | 15 | 33.1 | 155 | 32 | 33 | 24 | 2 | 1 | 1 | 1 | 22 | 0 | 36 | 3 | 0 | 2 | 2 | .500 | 0 | 1-- | - | 4.57 | 6.48 |
| 2010 | WTenn | AA | 21 | 0 | 0 | 14 | 28.2 | 121 | 19 | 12 | 10 | 0 | 1 | 2 | 0 | 18 | 2 | 28 | 2 | 0 | 1 | 1 | .500 | 0 | 6-- | - | 2.34 | 3.14 |
| 2011 | Jacksn | AA | 20 | 0 | 0 | 11 | 26.0 | 115 | 17 | 11 | 8 | 0 | 0 | 0 | 4 | 19 | 0 | 26 | 2 | 0 | 1 | 2 | .333 | 0 | 3-- | - | 3.28 | 2.77 |
| 2011 | Tacom | AAA | 9 | 0 | 0 | 4 | 13.0 | 63 | 11 | 10 | 9 | 2 | 0 | 2 | 0 | 13 | 0 | 13 | 0 | 1 | 0 | 0 | - | 0 | 0-- | - | 5.89 | 6.23 |
| 2011 | Portlnd | AA | 9 | 0 | 0 | 5 | 17.1 | 69 | 10 | 6 | 6 | 2 | 0 | 2 | 1 | 10 | 0 | 25 | 3 | 1 | 3 | 0 | 1.000 | 0 | 1-- | - | 2.95 | 3.12 |
| 2012 | Portlnd | AA | 32 | 0 | 0 | 28 | 44.2 | 182 | 30 | 14 | 13 | 4 | 1 | 2 | 1 | 16 | 1 | 59 | 2 | 0 | 3 | 3 | .500 | 0 | 8-- | - | 2.16 | 2.62 |
| 2012 | Pwtckt | AAA | 10 | 0 | 0 | 5 | 13.2 | 49 | 8 | 0 | 0 | 0 | 1 | 0 | 0 | 2 | 0 | 19 | 0 | 0 | 1 | 0 | 1.000 | 0 | 4-- | - | 1.01 | 0.00 |
| 2013 | QuadC | A | 2 | 1 | 0 | 0 | 4.0 | 14 | 2 | 0 | 0 | 0 | 0 | 0 | 0 | 0 | 0 | 4 | 0 | 0 | 0 | 0 | - | 0 | 0-- | - | 0.54 | 0.00 |
| 2013 | CpChr | AA | 5 | 0 | 0 | 0 | 6.0 | 24 | 7 | 2 | 2 | 0 | 0 | 0 | 0 | 0 | 0 | 4 | 0 | 0 | 0 | 0 | - | 0 | 0-- | - | 2.86 | 3.00 |
| 2013 | Hou | AL | 41 | 0 | 0 | 16 | 38.0 | 160 | 31 | 21 | 21 | 8 | 1 | 0 | 0 | 18 | 4 | 40 | 0 | 0 | 1 | 3 | .250 | 0 | 5-6 | 6 | 3.94 | 4.97 |

# Casey Fien

**Pitches:** R **Bats:** R **Pos:** RP-73 FEEN **Ht:** 6'2" **Wt:** 205 **Born:** 10/21/1983 **Age:** 30

| HOW MUCH HE PITCHED | | | | | | | | | WHAT HE GAVE UP | | | | | | | | | | | | THE RESULTS | | | | | | | |
|---|---|---|---|---|---|---|---|---|---|---|---|---|---|---|---|---|---|---|---|---|---|---|---|---|---|---|---|---|
| Year | Team | Lg | G | GS | CG | GF | IP | BFP | H | R | ER | HR | SH | SF | HB | TBB | IBB | SO | WP | Bk | W | L | Pct | Sh | Sv-Op | Hld | ERC | ERA |
| 2009 | Det | AL | 9 | 0 | 0 | 5 | 11.1 | 53 | 13 | 11 | 10 | 2 | 0 | 2 | 0 | 6 | 0 | 9 | 0 | 0 | 0 | 1 | .000 | 0 | 0-0 | 0 | 5.92 | 7.94 |
| 2010 | Det | AL | 2 | 0 | 0 | 2 | 2.2 | 12 | 4 | 3 | 3 | 2 | 1 | 0 | 0 | 0 | 0 | 0 | 0 | 0 | 0 | 0 | - | 0 | 0-0 | 0 | 9.96 | 10.13 |
| 2012 | Min | AL | 35 | 0 | 0 | 7 | 35.0 | 141 | 25 | 9 | 8 | 3 | 1 | 2 | 1 | 9 | 4 | 32 | 0 | 0 | 2 | 1 | .667 | 0 | 0-0 | 6 | 1.90 | 2.06 |
| 2013 | Min | AL | 73 | 0 | 0 | 20 | 62.0 | 244 | 51 | 28 | 27 | 9 | 3 | 2 | 0 | 12 | 3 | 73 | 2 | 0 | 5 | 2 | .714 | 0 | 0-2 | 17 | 2.59 | 3.92 |
| 4 ML YEARS | | | 119 | 0 | 0 | 34 | 111.0 | 450 | 93 | 51 | 48 | 16 | 5 | 6 | 1 | 27 | 7 | 114 | 2 | 0 | 7 | 4 | .636 | 0 | 0-2 | 23 | 2.81 | 3.89 |

# Mike Fiers

**Pitches:** R **Bats:** R **Pos:** RP-8; SP-3 FIRES **Ht:** 6'2" **Wt:** 195 **Born:** 6/15/1985 **Age:** 29

| HOW MUCH HE PITCHED | | | | | | | | | WHAT HE GAVE UP | | | | | | | | | | | | THE RESULTS | | | | | | | |
|---|---|---|---|---|---|---|---|---|---|---|---|---|---|---|---|---|---|---|---|---|---|---|---|---|---|---|---|---|
| Year | Team | Lg | G | GS | CG | GF | IP | BFP | H | R | ER | HR | SH | SF | HB | TBB | IBB | SO | WP | Bk | W | L | Pct | Sh | Sv-Op | Hld | ERC | ERA |
| 2013 | Nashv* | AAA | 5 | 5 | 1 | 0 | 28.2 | 120 | 24 | 8 | 7 | 3 | 0 | 0 | 0 | 12 | 0 | 30 | 1 | 0 | 1 | 2 | .333 | 0 | 0-- | - | 3.29 | 2.20 |
| 2013 | BrvdCt* | A+ | 1 | 1 | 0 | 0 | 6.0 | 24 | 6 | 4 | 4 | 1 | 0 | 0 | 0 | 0 | 0 | 8 | 0 | 0 | 0 | 0 | - | 0 | 0-- | - | 2.87 | 6.00 |
| 2011 | Mil | NL | 2 | 0 | 0 | 2 | 2.0 | 10 | 2 | 0 | 0 | 0 | 0 | 0 | 0 | 3 | 0 | 2 | 0 | 0 | 0 | 0 | - | 0 | 0-0 | 0 | 8.25 | 0.00 |
| 2012 | Mil | NL | 23 | 22 | 0 | 1 | 127.2 | 539 | 125 | 56 | 53 | 12 | 4 | 4 | 2 | 36 | 0 | 135 | 4 | 0 | 9 | 10 | .474 | 0 | 0-0 | 0 | 3.50 | 3.74 |
| 2013 | Mil | NL | 11 | 3 | 0 | 4 | 22.1 | 103 | 28 | 20 | 18 | 8 | 1 | 2 | 0 | 6 | 0 | 15 | 1 | 0 | 1 | 4 | .200 | 0 | 0-0 | 0 | 6.65 | 7.25 |
| 3 ML YEARS | | | 36 | 25 | 0 | 7 | 152.0 | 652 | 155 | 76 | 71 | 20 | 5 | 6 | 2 | 45 | 0 | 152 | 5 | 0 | 10 | 14 | .417 | 0 | 0-0 | 0 | 4.00 | 4.20 |

# Stephen Fife

**Pitches:** R **Bats:** R **Pos:** SP-10; RP-2 **Ht:** 6'3" **Wt:** 220 **Born:** 10/4/1986 **Age:** 27

| HOW MUCH HE PITCHED | | | | | | | | | WHAT HE GAVE UP | | | | | | | | | | | | THE RESULTS | | | | | | | |
|---|---|---|---|---|---|---|---|---|---|---|---|---|---|---|---|---|---|---|---|---|---|---|---|---|---|---|---|---|
| Year | Team | Lg | G | GS | CG | GF | IP | BFP | H | R | ER | HR | SH | SF | HB | TBB | IBB | SO | WP | Bk | W | L | Pct | Sh | Sv-Op | Hld | ERC | ERA |
| 2009 | Grnvlle | A | 8 | 8 | 0 | 0 | 36.2 | 146 | 32 | 13 | 11 | 1 | 1 | 1 | 0 | 4 | 0 | 35 | 3 | 0 | 0 | 3 | .000 | 0 | 0-- | - | 1.89 | 2.70 |
| 2009 | Salem | A+ | 10 | 10 | 0 | 0 | 50.2 | 220 | 58 | 28 | 25 | 7 | 2 | 1 | 2 | 10 | 0 | 51 | 1 | 0 | 3 | 2 | .600 | 0 | 0-- | - | 4.45 | 4.44 |
| 2010 | Portlnd | AA | 26 | 26 | 0 | 0 | 136.1 | 592 | 144 | 84 | 72 | 11 | 4 | 7 | 5 | 46 | 0 | 82 | 6 | 4 | 8 | 6 | .571 | 0 | 0-- | - | 4.14 | 4.75 |
| 2011 | Portlnd | AA | 19 | 18 | 0 | 0 | 103.1 | 447 | 107 | 47 | 42 | 7 | 1 | 4 | 6 | 37 | 0 | 70 | 4 | 0 | 11 | 4 | .733 | 0 | 0-- | - | 4.14 | 3.66 |
| 2011 | Chatt | AA | 6 | 6 | 0 | 0 | 33.2 | 152 | 36 | 18 | 15 | 2 | 2 | 1 | 1 | 15 | 0 | 25 | 0 | 0 | 3 | 0 | 1.000 | 0 | 0-- | - | 4.38 | 4.01 |
| 2012 | Albq | AAA | 25 | 24 | 0 | 0 | 135.1 | 607 | 157 | 85 | 70 | 13 | 7 | 3 | 10 | 44 | 1 | 93 | 10 | 1 | 11 | 7 | .611 | 0 | 0-- | - | 4.91 | 4.66 |
| 2013 | Albq | AAA | 10 | 8 | 0 | 0 | 37.1 | 177 | 46 | 31 | 25 | 3 | 1 | 1 | 4 | 21 | 0 | 33 | 4 | 0 | 2 | 4 | .333 | 0 | 0-- | - | 6.47 | 6.03 |
| 2013 | RCuca | A+ | 1 | 1 | 0 | 0 | 4.0 | 19 | 6 | 4 | 3 | 1 | 0 | 0 | 0 | 1 | 0 | 3 | 0 | 0 | 0 | 1 | .000 | 0 | 0-- | - | 7.48 | 6.75 |
| 2012 | LAD | NL | 5 | 5 | 0 | 0 | 26.2 | 115 | 25 | 8 | 8 | 2 | 3 | 0 | 2 | 12 | 0 | 20 | 4 | 0 | 0 | 2 | .000 | 0 | 0-0 | 0 | 4.09 | 2.70 |
| 2013 | LAD | NL | 12 | 10 | 0 | 0 | 58.1 | 258 | 69 | 28 | 24 | 7 | 4 | 2 | 5 | 20 | 2 | 45 | 6 | 0 | 4 | 4 | .500 | 0 | 0-0 | 0 | 5.46 | 3.70 |
| 2 ML YEARS | | | 17 | 15 | 0 | 0 | 85.0 | 373 | 94 | 36 | 32 | 9 | 7 | 2 | 7 | 32 | 2 | 65 | 10 | 0 | 4 | 6 | .400 | 0 | 0-0 | 0 | 5.02 | 3.39 |

# Alfredo Figaro

**Pitches:** R **Bats:** R **Pos:** RP-28; SP-5 FIGG-uh-roe **Ht:** 6'0" **Wt:** 175 **Born:** 7/7/1984 **Age:** 29

| HOW MUCH HE PITCHED | | | | | | | | | WHAT HE GAVE UP | | | | | | | | | | | | THE RESULTS | | | | | | | |
|---|---|---|---|---|---|---|---|---|---|---|---|---|---|---|---|---|---|---|---|---|---|---|---|---|---|---|---|---|
| Year | Team | Lg | G | GS | CG | GF | IP | BFP | H | R | ER | HR | SH | SF | HB | TBB | IBB | SO | WP | Bk | W | L | Pct | Sh | Sv-Op | Hld | ERC | ERA |
| 2013 | Brewrs* | R | 1 | 1 | 0 | 0 | 2.1 | 8 | 1 | 0 | 0 | 0 | 0 | 0 | 0 | 0 | 0 | 4 | 0 | 0 | 0 | 0 | - | 0 | 0-- | - | 0.40 | 0.00 |
| 2013 | Nashv* | AAA | 3 | 3 | 0 | 0 | 13.0 | 59 | 14 | 6 | 4 | 0 | 0 | 1 | 0 | 9 | 0 | 8 | 2 | 0 | 1 | 0 | 1.000 | 0 | 0-- | - | 5.02 | 2.77 |

| HOW MUCH HE PITCHED | | | | | | | | WHAT HE GAVE UP | | | | | | | | | | | | THE RESULTS | | | | | | | |
|---|---|---|---|---|---|---|---|---|---|---|---|---|---|---|---|---|---|---|---|---|---|---|---|---|---|---|---|
| Year Team | Lg | G | GS | CG | GF | IP | BFP | H | R | ER | HR | SH | SF | HB | TBB | IBB | SO | WP | Bk | W | L | Pct | Sh | Sv-Op | Hld | ERC | ERA |
| 2009 Det | AL | 5 | 3 | 0 | 0 | 17.0 | 83 | 23 | 13 | 12 | 3 | 1 | 0 | 1 | 10 | 0 | 16 | 0 | 0 | 2 | 2 | .500 | 0 | 0-0 | 0 | 7.94 | 6.35 |
| 2010 Det | AL | 8 | 1 | 0 | 5 | 14.2 | 69 | 18 | 12 | 11 | 1 | 2 | 1 | 0 | 8 | 2 | 5 | 2 | 0 | 0 | 2 | .000 | 0 | 0-0 | 0 | 5.43 | 6.75 |
| 2013 Mil | NL | 33 | 5 | 0 | 8 | 74.0 | 316 | 77 | 41 | 34 | 15 | 3 | 4 | 1 | 15 | 2 | 54 | 4 | 1 | 3 | 3 | .500 | 0 | 1-1 | 0 | 4.11 | 4.14 |
| 3 ML YEARS | | 46 | 9 | 0 | 13 | 105.2 | 468 | 118 | 66 | 57 | 19 | 6 | 5 | 2 | 33 | 4 | 75 | 6 | 1 | 5 | 7 | .417 | 0 | 1-1 | 0 | 4.89 | 4.85 |

## Pedro Figueroa

**Pitches:** L **Bats:** L **Pos:** RP-5 figg-uh-ROE-ah **Ht:** 6'0" **Wt:** 215 **Born:** 11/23/1985 **Age:** 28

| HOW MUCH HE PITCHED | | | | | | | | WHAT HE GAVE UP | | | | | | | | | | | | THE RESULTS | | | | | | | |
|---|---|---|---|---|---|---|---|---|---|---|---|---|---|---|---|---|---|---|---|---|---|---|---|---|---|---|---|
| Year Team | Lg | G | GS | CG | GF | IP | BFP | H | R | ER | HR | SH | SF | HB | TBB | IBB | SO | WP | Bk | W | L | Pct | Sh | Sv-Op | Hld | ERC | ERA |
| 2009 Kane | A | 16 | 16 | 0 | 0 | 86.1 | 370 | 89 | 37 | 31 | 6 | 2 | 0 | 4 | 31 | 0 | 78 | 6 | 2 | 10 | 2 | .833 | 0 | 0-- | - | 4.11 | 3.23 |
| 2009 Stcktn | A+ | 11 | 11 | 0 | 0 | 65.2 | 285 | 62 | 27 | 26 | 3 | 2 | 0 | 1 | 35 | 1 | 67 | 4 | 0 | 3 | 4 | .429 | 0 | 0-- | - | 3.97 | 3.56 |
| 2010 Mdlnd | AA | 13 | 13 | 0 | 0 | 71.1 | 319 | 83 | 45 | 42 | 6 | 1 | 2 | 2 | 29 | 1 | 57 | 4 | 5 | 1 | 6 | .143 | 0 | 0-- | - | 5.04 | 5.30 |
| 2011 As | R | 2 | 2 | 0 | 0 | 2.0 | 10 | 3 | 1 | 1 | 0 | 0 | 0 | 0 | 0 | 0 | 6 | 0 | 0 | 0 | 0 | - | 0 | 0-- | - | 3.96 | 4.50 |
| 2012 Scrmto | AAA | 32 | 0 | 0 | 7 | 44.2 | 187 | 35 | 17 | 13 | 1 | 1 | 0 | 3 | 18 | 0 | 40 | 0 | 0 | 0 | 2 | .000 | 0 | 1-- | - | 2.66 | 2.62 |
| 2013 Scrmto | AAA | 46 | 1 | 0 | 9 | 59.1 | 263 | 57 | 29 | 27 | 9 | 1 | 1 | 2 | 33 | 1 | 49 | 6 | 2 | 3 | 4 | .429 | 0 | 2-- | - | 5.00 | 4.10 |
| 2012 Oak | AL | 19 | 0 | 0 | 6 | 21.2 | 89 | 16 | 9 | 8 | 2 | 0 | 0 | 0 | 15 | 1 | 14 | 2 | 0 | 0 | 0 | - | 0 | 0-0 | 0 | 3.87 | 3.32 |
| 2013 Oak | AL | 5 | 0 | 0 | 1 | 3.0 | 18 | 6 | 4 | 4 | 2 | 0 | 0 | 0 | 3 | 0 | 3 | 0 | 0 | 0 | 0 | - | 0 | 0-0 | 0 | 19.34 | 12.00 |
| 2 ML YEARS | | 24 | 0 | 0 | 7 | 24.2 | 107 | 22 | 13 | 12 | 4 | 0 | 0 | 0 | 18 | 1 | 17 | 2 | 0 | 0 | 0 | - | 0 | 0-0 | 0 | 5.42 | 4.38 |

## Doug Fister

**Pitches:** R **Bats:** L **Pos:** SP-32; RP-1 **Ht:** 6'8" **Wt:** 210 **Born:** 2/4/1984 **Age:** 30

| HOW MUCH HE PITCHED | | | | | | | | WHAT HE GAVE UP | | | | | | | | | | | | THE RESULTS | | | | | | | |
|---|---|---|---|---|---|---|---|---|---|---|---|---|---|---|---|---|---|---|---|---|---|---|---|---|---|---|---|
| Year Team | Lg | G | GS | CG | GF | IP | BFP | H | R | ER | HR | SH | SF | HB | TBB | IBB | SO | WP | Bk | W | L | Pct | Sh | Sv-Op | Hld | ERC | ERA |
| 2009 Sea | AL | 11 | 10 | 0 | 1 | 61.0 | 256 | 63 | 29 | 28 | 11 | 0 | 0 | 2 | 15 | 0 | 36 | 1 | 0 | 3 | 4 | .429 | 0 | 0-0 | 0 | 4.36 | 4.13 |
| 2010 Sea | AL | 28 | 28 | 0 | 0 | 171.0 | 720 | 187 | 85 | 78 | 13 | 2 | 4 | 6 | 32 | 2 | 93 | 8 | 3 | 6 | 14 | .300 | 0 | 0-0 | 0 | 3.73 | 4.11 |
| 2011 2 Tms | AL | 32 | 31 | 3 | 0 | 216.1 | 875 | 193 | 76 | 68 | 11 | 4 | 9 | 12 | 37 | 2 | 146 | 3 | 1 | 11 | 13 | .458 | 0 | 0-0 | 0 | 2.53 | 2.83 |
| 2012 Det | AL | 26 | 26 | 2 | 0 | 161.2 | 673 | 156 | 73 | 62 | 15 | 3 | 0 | 7 | 37 | 1 | 137 | 1 | 0 | 10 | 10 | .500 | 1 | 0-0 | 0 | 3.33 | 3.45 |
| 2013 Det | AL | 33 | 32 | 1 | 0 | 208.2 | 881 | 229 | 91 | 85 | 14 | 2 | 5 | 16 | 44 | 2 | 159 | 7 | 0 | 14 | 9 | .609 | 0 | 0-0 | 0 | 4.00 | 3.67 |
| 11 Sea | AL | 21 | 21 | 3 | 0 | 146.0 | 602 | 139 | 57 | 54 | 7 | 3 | 7 | 9 | 32 | 2 | 89 | 3 | 1 | 3 | 12 | .200 | 0 | 0-0 | 0 | 3.02 | 3.33 |
| 11 Det | AL | 11 | 10 | 0 | 0 | 70.1 | 273 | 54 | 19 | 14 | 4 | 1 | 2 | 3 | 5 | 0 | 57 | 0 | 0 | 8 | 1 | .889 | 0 | 0-0 | 0 | 1.63 | 1.79 |
| Postseason | | 6 | 5 | 0 | 0 | 36.1 | 153 | 35 | 12 | 12 | 1 | 2 | 0 | 3 | 11 | 0 | 29 | 0 | 1 | 2 | 2 | .500 | 0 | 0-0 | 0 | 3.36 | 2.97 |
| 5 ML YEARS | | 130 | 127 | 6 | 1 | 818.2 | 3405 | 828 | 354 | 321 | 64 | 11 | 18 | 43 | 165 | 7 | 571 | 20 | 4 | 44 | 50 | .468 | 1 | 0-0 | 0 | 3.43 | 3.53 |

## Ryan Flaherty

**Bats:** L **Throws:** R **Pos:** 2B-65;PH-10;SS-9;3B-7;1B-4;DH-3 **Ht:** 6'3" **Wt:** 210 **Born:** 7/27/1986 **Age:** 27

| BATTING | | | | | | | | | | | | | | | | | | | | BASERUNNING | | | | AVERAGES | | |
|---|---|---|---|---|---|---|---|---|---|---|---|---|---|---|---|---|---|---|---|---|---|---|---|---|---|---|
| Year Team | Lg | G | AB | H | 2B | 3B | HR | (Hm | Rd) | TB | R | RBI | RC | TBB | IBB | SO | HBP | SH | SF | SB | CS | SB% | GDP | Avg | OBP | Slg |
| 2009 Peoria | A | 131 | 485 | 134 | 24 | 5 | 20 | (- | -) | 228 | 81 | 81 | 80 | 50 | 0 | 98 | 2 | 2 | 4 | 7 | 6 | .54 | 9 | .276 | .344 | .470 |
| 2010 Tenn | AA | 23 | 71 | 13 | 2 | 0 | 1 | (- | -) | 18 | 10 | 9 | 6 | 10 | 2 | 12 | 1 | 0 | 2 | 1 | 0 | 1.00 | 0 | .183 | .286 | .254 |
| 2010 Dytona | A+ | 108 | 420 | 120 | 34 | 3 | 9 | (- | -) | 187 | 65 | 63 | 68 | 41 | 2 | 74 | 4 | 1 | 9 | 6 | 3 | .67 | 10 | .286 | .348 | .445 |
| 2011 Tenn | AA | 83 | 302 | 92 | 20 | 2 | 14 | (- | -) | 158 | 52 | 66 | 59 | 40 | 2 | 55 | 0 | 0 | 2 | 4 | 6 | .40 | 12 | .305 | .384 | .523 |
| 2011 Iowa | AAA | 49 | 173 | 41 | 11 | 1 | 5 | (- | -) | 69 | 22 | 22 | 19 | 10 | 0 | 44 | 0 | 2 | 1 | 1 | 0 | 1.00 | 8 | .237 | .277 | .399 |
| 2012 Norfolk | AAA | 9 | 38 | 11 | 1 | 1 | 2 | (- | -) | 20 | 5 | 3 | 6 | 2 | 0 | 9 | 1 | 0 | 0 | 0 | 0 | - | 1 | .289 | .341 | .526 |
| 2013 Norfolk | AAA | 8 | 34 | 9 | 1 | 0 | 2 | (- | -) | 16 | 4 | 5 | 4 | 1 | 0 | 8 | 0 | 0 | 0 | 0 | 0 | - | 0 | .265 | .286 | .471 |
| 2013 Dlmrva | A | 2 | 8 | 2 | 1 | 0 | 0 | (- | -) | 3 | 1 | 1 | 0 | 0 | 0 | 3 | 0 | 0 | 0 | 0 | 0 | - | 0 | .250 | .250 | .375 |
| 2013 Frdrck | A+ | 2 | 7 | 2 | 0 | 0 | 1 | (- | -) | 5 | 1 | 2 | 1 | 0 | 0 | 3 | 0 | 0 | 0 | 0 | 0 | - | 0 | .286 | .286 | .714 |
| 2012 Bal | AL | 77 | 153 | 33 | 2 | 1 | 6 | (3 | 3) | 55 | 15 | 19 | 15 | 6 | 0 | 43 | 3 | 3 | 1 | 1 | 0 | 1.00 | 3 | .216 | .258 | .359 |
| 2013 Bal | AL | 85 | 246 | 55 | 11 | 0 | 10 | (6 | 4) | 96 | 28 | 27 | 27 | 19 | 3 | 62 | 5 | 1 | 0 | 2 | 0 | 1.00 | 2 | .224 | .293 | .390 |
| Postseason | | 4 | 11 | 3 | 0 | 0 | 1 | (0 | 1) | 6 | 1 | 1 | 0 | 0 | 0 | 2 | 0 | 0 | 0 | 0 | 0 | - | 0 | .273 | .273 | .545 |
| 2 ML YEARS | | 162 | 399 | 88 | 13 | 1 | 16 | (9 | 7) | 151 | 43 | 46 | 42 | 25 | 3 | 105 | 8 | 4 | 1 | 3 | 0 | 1.00 | 5 | .221 | .279 | .378 |

## Wilmer Flores

**Bats:** R **Throws:** R **Pos:** 3B-26;2B-2;PH-1 **Ht:** 6'3" **Wt:** 190 **Born:** 8/6/1991 **Age:** 22

| BATTING | | | | | | | | | | | | | | | | | | | | BASERUNNING | | | | AVERAGES | | |
|---|---|---|---|---|---|---|---|---|---|---|---|---|---|---|---|---|---|---|---|---|---|---|---|---|---|---|
| Year Team | Lg | G | AB | H | 2B | 3B | HR | (Hm | Rd) | TB | R | RBI | RC | TBB | IBB | SO | HBP | SH | SF | SB | CS | SB% | GDP | Avg | OBP | Slg |
| 2009 Savann | A | 125 | 488 | 129 | 20 | 2 | 3 | (- | -) | 162 | 44 | 36 | 51 | 22 | 1 | 72 | 9 | 3 | 6 | 3 | 3 | .50 | 11 | .264 | .305 | .332 |
| 2010 Savann | A | 66 | 277 | 77 | 18 | 2 | 7 | (- | -) | 120 | 30 | 44 | 42 | 23 | 6 | 37 | 5 | 0 | 2 | 2 | 1 | .67 | 8 | .278 | .342 | .433 |
| 2010 StLuci | A+ | 67 | 277 | 83 | 18 | 1 | 4 | (- | -) | 115 | 32 | 40 | 36 | 9 | 0 | 40 | 2 | 0 | 2 | 2 | 4 | .33 | 10 | .300 | .324 | .415 |
| 2011 StLuci | A+ | 133 | 516 | 139 | 26 | 2 | 9 | (- | -) | 196 | 52 | 81 | 63 | 27 | 3 | 68 | 6 | 2 | 8 | 2 | 2 | .50 | 11 | .269 | .309 | .380 |
| 2012 StLuci | A+ | 64 | 242 | 70 | 12 | 0 | 10 | (- | -) | 112 | 31 | 42 | 39 | 18 | 2 | 30 | 3 | 1 | 8 | 3 | 2 | .60 | 6 | .289 | .336 | .463 |
| 2012 Bnghtn | AA | 66 | 251 | 78 | 18 | 2 | 8 | (- | -) | 124 | 37 | 33 | 45 | 20 | 0 | 30 | 1 | 1 | 2 | 0 | 0 | - | 9 | .311 | .361 | .494 |
| 2013 LsVgs | AAA | 107 | 424 | 136 | 36 | 4 | 15 | (- | -) | 225 | 69 | 86 | 79 | 25 | 2 | 63 | 3 | 3 | 8 | 1 | 3 | .25 | 13 | .321 | .357 | .531 |
| 2013 NYM | NL | 27 | 95 | 20 | 5 | 0 | 1 | (0 | 1) | 28 | 8 | 13 | 7 | 5 | 0 | 23 | 0 | 0 | 1 | 0 | 0 | - | 1 | .211 | .248 | .295 |

## Pedro Florimon

**Bats:** B **Throws:** R **Pos:** SS-133;PR-3 FLOOR-ih-moan **Ht:** 6'2" **Wt:** 180 **Born:** 12/10/1986 **Age:** 27

| BATTING | | | | | | | | | | | | | | | | | | | | BASERUNNING | | | | AVERAGES | | |
|---|---|---|---|---|---|---|---|---|---|---|---|---|---|---|---|---|---|---|---|---|---|---|---|---|---|---|
| Year Team | Lg | G | AB | H | 2B | 3B | HR | (Hm | Rd) | TB | R | RBI | RC | TBB | IBB | SO | HBP | SH | SF | SB | CS | SB% | GDP | Avg | OBP | Slg |
| 2011 Bal | AL | 4 | 8 | 1 | 1 | 0 | 0 | (0 | 0) | 2 | 1 | 2 | 1 | 1 | 0 | 6 | 0 | 1 | 0 | 0 | 0 | - | 0 | .125 | .222 | .250 |
| 2012 Min | AL | 43 | 137 | 30 | 5 | 2 | 1 | (1 | 0) | 42 | 16 | 10 | 8 | 10 | 0 | 30 | 0 | 3 | 0 | 3 | 1 | .75 | 3 | .219 | .272 | .307 |
| 2013 Min | AL | 134 | 403 | 89 | 17 | 0 | 9 | (3 | 6) | 133 | 44 | 44 | 38 | 33 | 1 | 115 | 2 | 5 | 3 | 15 | 6 | .71 | 7 | .221 | .281 | .330 |
| 3 ML YEARS | | 181 | 548 | 120 | 23 | 2 | 10 | (4 | 6) | 177 | 61 | 56 | 47 | 44 | 1 | 151 | 2 | 9 | 3 | 18 | 7 | .72 | 10 | .219 | .278 | .323 |

# Tyler Flowers

**Bats:** R **Throws:** R **Pos:** C-84 **Ht:** 6'4" **Wt:** 245 **Born:** 1/24/1986 **Age:** 28

| BATTING | | | | | | | | | | | | | | | | | | | | | BASERUNNING | | | | AVERAGES | | |
|---|---|---|---|---|---|---|---|---|---|---|---|---|---|---|---|---|---|---|---|---|---|---|---|---|---|---|---|
| Year | Team | Lg | G | AB | H | 2B | 3B | HR | (Hm | Rd) | TB | R | RBI | RC | TBB | IBB | SO | HBP | SH | SF | SB | CS | SB% | GDP | Avg | OBP | Slg |
| 2009 | CWS | AL | 10 | 16 | 3 | 1 | 0 | 0 | (0 | 0) | 4 | 3 | 0 | 2 | 3 | 0 | 8 | 1 | 0 | 0 | 0 | 0 | - | 1 | .188 | .350 | .250 |
| 2010 | CWS | AL | 8 | 11 | 1 | 0 | 0 | 0 | (0 | 0) | 1 | 2 | 0 | 1 | 4 | 0 | 5 | 0 | 0 | 0 | 0 | 0 | - | 0 | .091 | .333 | .091 |
| 2011 | CWS | AL | 38 | 110 | 23 | 5 | 1 | 5 | (3 | 2) | 45 | 13 | 16 | 13 | 14 | 0 | 38 | 3 | 0 | 2 | 0 | 1 | .00 | 2 | .209 | .310 | .409 |
| 2012 | CWS | AL | 52 | 136 | 29 | 6 | 0 | 7 | (5 | 2) | 56 | 19 | 13 | 13 | 12 | 0 | 56 | 4 | 1 | 0 | 2 | 1 | .67 | 2 | .213 | .296 | .412 |
| 2013 | CWS | AL | 84 | 256 | 50 | 11 | 0 | 10 | (7 | 3) | 91 | 24 | 24 | 14 | 14 | 1 | 94 | 4 | 0 | 1 | 0 | 1 | .00 | 9 | .195 | .247 | .355 |
| 5 ML YEARS | | | 192 | 529 | 106 | 23 | 1 | 22 | (15 | 7) | 197 | 61 | 53 | 43 | 47 | 1 | 201 | 12 | 1 | 3 | 2 | 3 | .40 | 14 | .200 | .279 | .372 |

# Gavin Floyd

**Pitches:** R **Bats:** R **Pos:** SP-5 **Ht:** 6'6" **Wt:** 235 **Born:** 1/27/1983 **Age:** 31

| HOW MUCH HE PITCHED | | | | | | | | | WHAT HE GAVE UP | | | | | | | | | | | | THE RESULTS | | | | | | | |
|---|---|---|---|---|---|---|---|---|---|---|---|---|---|---|---|---|---|---|---|---|---|---|---|---|---|---|---|---|
| Year | Team | Lg | G | GS | CG | GF | IP | BFP | H | R | ER | HR | SH | SF | HB | TBB | IBB | SO | WP | Bk | W | L | Pct | Sh | Sv-Op | Hld | ERC | ERA |
| 2004 | Phi | NL | 6 | 4 | 0 | 0 | 28.1 | 126 | 25 | 11 | 11 | 1 | 1 | 0 | 5 | 16 | 0 | 24 | 1 | 1 | 2 | 0 | 1.000 | 0 | 0-0 | 0 | 4.33 | 3.49 |
| 2005 | Phi | NL | 7 | 4 | 0 | 0 | 26.0 | 127 | 30 | 31 | 29 | 5 | 1 | 1 | 3 | 16 | 2 | 17 | 2 | 0 | 1 | 2 | .333 | 0 | 0-0 | 0 | 6.82 | 10.04 |
| 2006 | Phi | NL | 11 | 11 | 1 | 0 | 54.1 | 264 | 70 | 48 | 44 | 14 | 2 | 5 | 3 | 32 | 3 | 34 | 2 | 0 | 4 | 3 | .571 | 1 | 0-0 | 0 | 8.02 | 7.29 |
| 2007 | CWS | AL | 16 | 10 | 0 | 4 | 70.0 | 314 | 85 | 45 | 41 | 17 | 3 | 2 | 6 | 19 | 0 | 49 | 1 | 0 | 1 | 5 | .167 | 0 | 0-0 | 0 | 6.22 | 5.27 |
| 2008 | CWS | AL | 33 | 33 | 1 | 0 | 206.1 | 878 | 190 | 107 | 88 | 30 | 7 | 5 | 9 | 70 | 6 | 145 | 9 | 0 | 17 | 8 | .680 | 0 | 0-0 | 0 | 3.80 | 3.84 |
| 2009 | CWS | AL | 30 | 30 | 1 | 0 | 193.0 | 797 | 178 | 93 | 87 | 21 | 2 | 3 | 2 | 59 | 4 | 163 | 8 | 0 | 11 | 11 | .500 | 0 | 0-0 | 0 | 3.38 | 4.06 |
| 2010 | CWS | AL | 31 | 31 | 1 | 0 | 187.1 | 798 | 199 | 92 | 85 | 14 | 3 | 4 | 6 | 58 | 4 | 151 | 9 | 1 | 10 | 13 | .435 | 0 | 0-0 | 0 | 4.03 | 4.08 |
| 2011 | CWS | AL | 31 | 30 | 1 | 1 | 193.2 | 798 | 180 | 97 | 94 | 22 | 4 | 8 | 11 | 45 | 2 | 151 | 12 | 1 | 12 | 13 | .480 | 0 | 0-0 | 0 | 3.36 | 4.37 |
| 2012 | CWS | AL | 29 | 29 | 0 | 0 | 168.0 | 724 | 166 | 84 | 80 | 22 | 3 | 3 | **14** | 63 | 2 | 144 | 8 | 0 | 12 | 11 | .522 | 0 | 0-0 | 0 | 4.50 | 4.29 |
| 2013 | CWS | AL | 5 | 5 | 0 | 0 | 24.1 | 110 | 27 | 15 | 14 | 4 | 2 | 2 | 0 | 12 | 1 | 25 | 1 | 0 | 0 | 4 | .000 | 0 | 0-0 | 0 | 5.48 | 5.18 |
| Postseason | | | 1 | 1 | 0 | 0 | 3.0 | 16 | 5 | 4 | 4 | 2 | 0 | 0 | 0 | 2 | 0 | 4 | 0 | 0 | 0 | 1 | .000 | 0 | 0-0 | 0 | 14.65 | 12.00 |
| 10 ML YEARS | | | 199 | 187 | 5 | 5 | 1151.1 | 4936 | 1150 | 623 | 573 | 150 | 28 | 33 | 59 | 390 | 24 | 903 | 53 | 3 | 70 | 70 | .500 | 1 | 0-0 | 0 | 4.22 | 4.48 |

# Brian Flynn

**Pitches:** L **Bats:** L **Pos:** SP-4 **Ht:** 6'7" **Wt:** 240 **Born:** 4/19/1990 **Age:** 24

| HOW MUCH HE PITCHED | | | | | | | | | WHAT HE GAVE UP | | | | | | | | | | | | THE RESULTS | | | | | | | |
|---|---|---|---|---|---|---|---|---|---|---|---|---|---|---|---|---|---|---|---|---|---|---|---|---|---|---|---|---|
| Year | Team | Lg | G | GS | CG | GF | IP | BFP | H | R | ER | HR | SH | SF | HB | TBB | IBB | SO | WP | Bk | W | L | Pct | Sh | Sv-Op | Hld | ERC | ERA |
| 2011 | WMich | A | 13 | 13 | 0 | 0 | 67.2 | 280 | 58 | 28 | 26 | 3 | 2 | 4 | 4 | 23 | 0 | 57 | 2 | 0 | 7 | 2 | .778 | 0 | 0- - | - | 2.96 | 3.46 |
| 2012 | Lkland | A+ | 18 | 18 | 0 | 0 | 102.0 | 441 | 113 | 47 | 42 | 5 | 0 | 3 | 3 | 32 | 0 | 84 | 4 | 0 | 8 | 4 | .667 | 0 | 0- - | - | 4.12 | 3.71 |
| 2012 | Erie | AA | 1 | 1 | 0 | 0 | 5.0 | 24 | 8 | 5 | 5 | 1 | 0 | 1 | 0 | 2 | 0 | 3 | 0 | 0 | 0 | 1 | .000 | 0 | 0- - | - | 8.81 | 9.00 |
| 2012 | Jaxnvl | AA | 8 | 8 | 0 | 0 | 45.0 | 195 | 48 | 22 | 19 | 3 | 2 | 0 | 4 | 13 | 0 | 32 | 1 | 0 | 3 | 0 | 1.000 | 0 | 0- - | - | 4.14 | 3.80 |
| 2013 | Jaxnvl | AA | 4 | 4 | 0 | 0 | 23.0 | 87 | 18 | 4 | 4 | 2 | 2 | 0 | 1 | 3 | 0 | 26 | 0 | 0 | 1 | 1 | .500 | 0 | 0- - | - | 2.13 | 1.57 |
| 2013 | NewOr | AAA | 23 | 23 | 0 | 0 | 138.0 | 570 | 127 | 52 | 43 | 7 | 8 | 1 | 4 | 40 | 1 | 122 | 7 | 2 | 6 | 11 | .353 | 0 | 0- - | - | 3.02 | 2.80 |
| 2013 | Mia | NL | 4 | 4 | 0 | 0 | 18.0 | 88 | 27 | 17 | 17 | 4 | 2 | 0 | 0 | 13 | 0 | 15 | 3 | 0 | 0 | 2 | .000 | 0 | 0-0 | 0 | 10.17 | 8.50 |

# Wilmer Font

FAHNT

**Pitches:** R **Bats:** R **Pos:** RP-2 **Ht:** 6'4" **Wt:** 230 **Born:** 5/24/1990 **Age:** 24

| HOW MUCH HE PITCHED | | | | | | | | | WHAT HE GAVE UP | | | | | | | | | | | | THE RESULTS | | | | | | | |
|---|---|---|---|---|---|---|---|---|---|---|---|---|---|---|---|---|---|---|---|---|---|---|---|---|---|---|---|---|
| Year | Team | Lg | G | GS | CG | GF | IP | BFP | H | R | ER | HR | SH | SF | HB | TBB | IBB | SO | WP | Bk | W | L | Pct | Sh | Sv-Op | Hld | ERC | ERA |
| 2009 | Hkry | A | 29 | 24 | 0 | 0 | 108.1 | 481 | 93 | 51 | 42 | 4 | 5 | 5 | 9 | 59 | 1 | 105 | 16 | 2 | 8 | 3 | .727 | 0 | 0- - | - | 3.64 | 3.49 |
| 2010 | Hkry | A | 7 | 7 | 0 | 0 | 29.2 | 136 | 35 | 18 | 17 | 3 | 2 | 1 | 1 | 13 | 0 | 33 | 5 | 0 | 4 | 1 | .800 | 0 | 0- - | - | 5.37 | 5.16 |
| 2010 | Bkrsfld | A+ | 9 | 9 | 0 | 0 | 49.0 | 212 | 38 | 26 | 21 | 5 | 1 | 2 | 2 | 32 | 0 | 52 | 1 | 0 | 1 | 2 | .333 | 0 | 0- - | - | 4.04 | 3.86 |
| 2012 | MrtlBh | A+ | 23 | 19 | 0 | 2 | 83.1 | 337 | 58 | 41 | 39 | 10 | 4 | 0 | 3 | 37 | 0 | 109 | 8 | 1 | 2 | 5 | .286 | 0 | 0- - | - | 2.95 | 4.21 |
| 2012 | Frisco | AA | 10 | 0 | 0 | 3 | 15.0 | 62 | 9 | 5 | 5 | 1 | 1 | 0 | 1 | 7 | 1 | 29 | 1 | 0 | 2 | 0 | 1.000 | 0 | 1- - | - | 2.14 | 3.00 |
| 2013 | Frisco | AA | 26 | 0 | 0 | 19 | 32.0 | 134 | 14 | 8 | 5 | 2 | 2 | 0 | 2 | 24 | 0 | 45 | 4 | 0 | 1 | 2 | .333 | 0 | 10- - | - | 2.39 | 1.41 |
| 2013 | RdRck | AAA | 16 | 0 | 0 | 9 | 20.0 | 79 | 8 | 3 | 1 | 0 | 0 | 0 | 2 | 10 | 0 | 26 | 4 | 0 | 1 | 0 | 1.000 | 0 | 4- - | - | 1.34 | 0.45 |
| 2012 | Tex | AL | 3 | 0 | 0 | 0 | 2.0 | 10 | 0 | 2 | 2 | 0 | 0 | 0 | 0 | 4 | 0 | 1 | 1 | 0 | 0 | 0 | - | 0 | 0-0 | 0 | 3.47 | 9.00 |
| 2013 | Tex | AL | 2 | 0 | 0 | 2 | 1.1 | 7 | 1 | 0 | 0 | 0 | 0 | 0 | 0 | 2 | 0 | 0 | 0 | 0 | 0 | 0 | - | 0 | 0-0 | 0 | 5.91 | 0.00 |
| 2 ML YEARS | | | 5 | 0 | 0 | 2 | 3.1 | 17 | 1 | 2 | 2 | 0 | 0 | 0 | 0 | 6 | 0 | 1 | 1 | 0 | 0 | 0 | - | 0 | 0-0 | 0 | 4.42 | 5.40 |

# Logan Forsythe

FOR-sigh-th

**Bats:** R **Throws:** R **Pos:** 2B-34;PH-12;3B-11;SS-11;LF-11;RF-3 **Ht:** 6'1" **Wt:** 195 **Born:** 1/14/1987 **Age:** 27

| BATTING | | | | | | | | | | | | | | | | | | | | | BASERUNNING | | | | AVERAGES | | |
|---|---|---|---|---|---|---|---|---|---|---|---|---|---|---|---|---|---|---|---|---|---|---|---|---|---|---|---|
| Year | Team | Lg | G | AB | H | 2B | 3B | HR | (Hm | Rd) | TB | R | RBI | RC | TBB | IBB | SO | HBP | SH | SF | SB | CS | SB% | GDP | Avg | OBP | Slg |
| 2013 | Tucsn* | AAA | 8 | 25 | 9 | 2 | 2 | 2 | (- | -) | 21 | 6 | 5 | 9 | 8 | 0 | 7 | 0 | 0 | 0 | 0 | 0 | - | 2 | .360 | .515 | .840 |
| 2011 | SD | NL | 62 | 150 | 32 | 9 | 1 | 0 | (0 | 0) | 43 | 12 | 12 | 15 | 12 | 3 | 33 | 3 | 2 | 2 | 3 | 1 | .75 | 3 | .213 | .281 | .287 |
| 2012 | SD | NL | 91 | 315 | 86 | 13 | 3 | 6 | (5 | 1) | 123 | 45 | 26 | 37 | 28 | 0 | 57 | 6 | 0 | 1 | 8 | 2 | .80 | 6 | .273 | .343 | .390 |
| 2013 | SD | NL | 75 | 220 | 47 | 6 | 1 | 6 | (2 | 4) | 73 | 22 | 19 | 16 | 19 | 2 | 54 | 2 | 1 | 1 | 6 | 1 | .86 | 5 | .214 | .281 | .332 |
| 3 ML YEARS | | | 228 | 685 | 165 | 28 | 5 | 12 | (7 | 5) | 239 | 79 | 57 | 68 | 59 | 5 | 144 | 11 | 3 | 4 | 17 | 4 | .81 | 14 | .241 | .310 | .349 |

# Dexter Fowler

**Bats:** B **Throws:** R **Pos:** CF-110;PH-9;PR-1 **Ht:** 6'4" **Wt:** 190 **Born:** 3/22/1986 **Age:** 28

| BATTING | | | | | | | | | | | | | | | | | | | | | BASERUNNING | | | | AVERAGES | | |
|---|---|---|---|---|---|---|---|---|---|---|---|---|---|---|---|---|---|---|---|---|---|---|---|---|---|---|---|
| Year | Team | Lg | G | AB | H | 2B | 3B | HR | (Hm | Rd) | TB | R | RBI | RC | TBB | IBB | SO | HBP | SH | SF | SB | CS | SB% | GDP | Avg | OBP | Slg |
| 2013 | ColSpr* | AAA | 2 | 6 | 0 | 0 | 0 | 0 | (- | -) | 0 | 0 | 0 | 0 | 3 | 0 | 2 | 0 | 0 | 0 | 1 | 0 | 1.00 | 0 | .000 | .333 | .000 |
| 2008 | Col | NL | 13 | 26 | 4 | 0 | 0 | 0 | (0 | 0) | 4 | 3 | 0 | 0 | 0 | 0 | 5 | 1 | 0 | 0 | 0 | 1 | .00 | 0 | .154 | .185 | .154 |
| 2009 | Col | NL | 135 | 433 | 115 | 29 | 10 | 4 | (2 | 2) | 176 | 73 | 34 | 68 | 67 | 1 | 116 | 1 | 14 | 3 | 27 | 10 | .73 | 4 | .266 | .363 | .406 |
| 2010 | Col | NL | 132 | 439 | 114 | 20 | **14** | 6 | (5 | 1) | 180 | 73 | 36 | 68 | 57 | 0 | 104 | 2 | 7 | 0 | 13 | 8 | .62 | 5 | .260 | .347 | .410 |
| 2011 | Col | NL | 125 | 481 | 128 | 35 | 15 | 5 | (3 | 2) | 208 | 84 | 45 | 79 | 68 | 3 | 130 | 6 | 7 | 1 | 12 | 9 | .57 | 6 | .266 | .363 | .432 |

| BATTING | | | | | | | | | | | | | | | | | | | | BASERUNNING | | | | AVERAGES | | |
|---|---|---|---|---|---|---|---|---|---|---|---|---|---|---|---|---|---|---|---|---|---|---|---|---|---|---|
| Year Team | Lg | G | AB | H | 2B | 3B | HR | (Hm | Rd) | TB | R | RBI | RC | TBB | IBB | SO | HBP | SH | SF | SB | CS | SB% | GDP | Avg | OBP | Slg |
| 2012 Col | NL | 143 | 454 | 136 | 18 | 11 | 13 | (10 | 3) | 215 | 72 | 53 | 81 | 68 | 1 | 128 | 0 | 6 | 2 | 12 | 5 | .71 | 5 | .300 | .389 | .474 |
| 2013 Col | NL | 119 | 415 | 109 | 18 | 3 | 12 | (7 | 5) | 169 | 71 | 42 | 62 | 65 | 1 | 105 | 6 | 4 | 2 | 19 | 9 | .68 | 5 | .263 | .369 | .407 |
| Postseason | | 4 | 14 | 3 | 0 | 0 | 0 | (0 | 0) | 3 | 1 | 2 | 1 | 1 | 0 | 3 | 0 | 1 | 2 | 0 | 0 | - | 1 | .214 | .235 | .214 |
| 6 ML YEARS | | 667 | 2248 | 606 | 120 | 53 | 40 | (27 | 13) | 952 | 376 | 210 | 358 | 325 | 6 | 588 | 16 | 38 | 8 | 83 | 42 | .66 | 25 | .270 | .365 | .423 |

# Jeff Francis

**Pitches:** L **Bats:** L **Pos:** SP-12; RP-11 **Ht:** 6'5" **Wt:** 205 **Born:** 1/8/1981 **Age:** 33

| HOW MUCH HE PITCHED | | | | | | | | WHAT HE GAVE UP | | | | | | | | | | | | THE RESULTS | | | | | | | |
|---|---|---|---|---|---|---|---|---|---|---|---|---|---|---|---|---|---|---|---|---|---|---|---|---|---|---|---|
| Year Team | Lg | G | GS | CG | GF | IP | BFP | H | R | ER | HR | SH | SF | HB | TBB | IBB | SO | WP | Bk | W | L | Pct | Sh | Sv-Op | Hld | ERC | ERA |
| 2013 ColSpr* | AAA | 11 | 6 | 0 | 0 | 37.1 | 167 | 42 | 24 | 18 | 1 | 3 | 3 | 2 | 9 | 0 | 33 | 1 | 0 | 2 | 2 | .500 | 0 | 0- - | - | 3.69 | 4.34 |
| 2004 Col | NL | 7 | 7 | 0 | 0 | 36.2 | 164 | 42 | 22 | 21 | 8 | 2 | 1 | 1 | 13 | 1 | 32 | 2 | 0 | 3 | 2 | .600 | 0 | 0-0 | 0 | 5.62 | 5.15 |
| 2005 Col | NL | 33 | 33 | 0 | 0 | 183.2 | 828 | 228 | 119 | 116 | 26 | 6 | **10** | 8 | 70 | 5 | 128 | 2 | 0 | 14 | 12 | .538 | 0 | 0-0 | 0 | 5.94 | 5.68 |
| 2006 Col | NL | 32 | 32 | 1 | 0 | 199.0 | 843 | 187 | 101 | 92 | 18 | 7 | 7 | 13 | 69 | **15** | 117 | 0 | 0 | 13 | 11 | .542 | 1 | 0-0 | 0 | 3.63 | 4.16 |
| 2007 Col | NL | 34 | 34 | 1 | 0 | 215.1 | 922 | 234 | 103 | 101 | 25 | 7 | 4 | 7 | 63 | 7 | 165 | 1 | 1 | 17 | 9 | .654 | 1 | 0-0 | 0 | 4.37 | 4.22 |
| 2008 Col | NL | 24 | 24 | 0 | 0 | 143.2 | 636 | 164 | 84 | 80 | 21 | 6 | 4 | 3 | 49 | 4 | 94 | 0 | 0 | 4 | 10 | .286 | 0 | 0-0 | 0 | 5.00 | 5.01 |
| 2010 Col | NL | 20 | 19 | 0 | 0 | 104.1 | 441 | 119 | 61 | 58 | 11 | 6 | 4 | 2 | 23 | 3 | 67 | 1 | 0 | 4 | 6 | .400 | 0 | 0-0 | 0 | 4.29 | 5.00 |
| 2011 KC | AL | 31 | 31 | 1 | 0 | 183.0 | 803 | 224 | 102 | 98 | 19 | 7 | 8 | 5 | 39 | 5 | 91 | 5 | 1 | 6 | 16 | .273 | 0 | 0-0 | 0 | 4.67 | 4.82 |
| 2012 Col | NL | 24 | 24 | 0 | 0 | 113.0 | 502 | 145 | 71 | 70 | 15 | 10 | 3 | 8 | 22 | 5 | 76 | 2 | 0 | 6 | 7 | .462 | 0 | 0-0 | 0 | 5.34 | 5.58 |
| 2013 Col | NL | 23 | 12 | 0 | 4 | 70.1 | 324 | 89 | 54 | 49 | 12 | 4 | 4 | 1 | 24 | 2 | 63 | 5 | 0 | 3 | 5 | .375 | 0 | 0-0 | 0 | 5.82 | 6.27 |
| Postseason | | 3 | 3 | 0 | 0 | 16.2 | 75 | 21 | 9 | 9 | 3 | 0 | 0 | 2 | 6 | 2 | 15 | 0 | 0 | 2 | 1 | .667 | 0 | 0-0 | 0 | 6.57 | 4.86 |
| 9 ML YEARS | | 228 | 216 | 3 | 4 | 1249.0 | 5463 | 1432 | 717 | 685 | 155 | 55 | 45 | 48 | 372 | 47 | 833 | 18 | 2 | 70 | 78 | .473 | 2 | 0-0 | 0 | 4.78 | 4.94 |

# Ben Francisco

**Bats:** R **Throws:** R **Pos:** DH-11;RF-5;PH-4;LF-3;PR-1 **Ht:** 6'1" **Wt:** 195 **Born:** 10/23/1981 **Age:** 32

| BATTING | | | | | | | | | | | | | | | | | | | | BASERUNNING | | | | AVERAGES | | |
|---|---|---|---|---|---|---|---|---|---|---|---|---|---|---|---|---|---|---|---|---|---|---|---|---|---|---|
| Year Team | Lg | G | AB | H | 2B | 3B | HR | (Hm | Rd) | TB | R | RBI | RC | TBB | IBB | SO | HBP | SH | SF | SB | CS | SB% | GDP | Avg | OBP | Slg |
| 2013 Tucsn* | AAA | 60 | 187 | 45 | 8 | 1 | 1 | (- | -) | 58 | 20 | 16 | 20 | 18 | 1 | 38 | 1 | 2 | 1 | 6 | 1 | .86 | 3 | .241 | .309 | .310 |
| 2007 Cle | AL | 25 | 62 | 17 | 5 | 0 | 3 | (2 | 1) | 31 | 10 | 12 | 6 | 3 | 0 | 19 | 0 | 0 | 1 | 0 | 2 | .00 | 2 | .274 | .303 | .500 |
| 2008 Cle | AL | 121 | 447 | 119 | 32 | 0 | 15 | (7 | 8) | 196 | 65 | 54 | 57 | 40 | 0 | 86 | 6 | 2 | 4 | 4 | 3 | .57 | 10 | .266 | .332 | .438 |
| 2009 2 Tms | | 126 | 405 | 104 | 30 | 1 | 15 | (6 | 9) | 181 | 58 | 46 | 56 | 38 | 0 | 83 | 9 | 4 | 3 | 14 | 7 | .67 | 12 | .257 | .332 | .447 |
| 2010 Phi | NL | 88 | 179 | 48 | 13 | 0 | 6 | (1 | 5) | 79 | 24 | 28 | 26 | 14 | 1 | 35 | 2 | 1 | 1 | 8 | 0 | 1.00 | 6 | .268 | .327 | .441 |
| 2011 Phi | NL | 100 | 250 | 61 | 10 | 1 | 6 | (4 | 2) | 91 | 24 | 34 | 32 | 33 | 1 | 42 | 5 | 2 | 3 | 4 | 4 | .50 | 5 | .244 | .340 | .364 |
| 2012 3 Tms | | 82 | 192 | 46 | 14 | 1 | 4 | (2 | 2) | 74 | 14 | 15 | 17 | 13 | 0 | 49 | 0 | 0 | 2 | 0 | 1 | .00 | 1 | .240 | .285 | .385 |
| 2013 NYY | AL | 21 | 44 | 5 | 0 | 0 | 1 | (1 | 0) | 8 | 4 | 1 | 0 | 5 | 0 | 11 | 1 | 0 | 0 | 0 | 0 | - | 0 | .114 | .220 | .182 |
| 09 Cle | AL | 89 | 308 | 77 | 21 | 1 | 10 | (4 | 6) | 130 | 48 | 33 | 43 | 33 | 0 | 59 | 8 | 4 | 2 | 13 | 3 | .81 | 11 | .250 | .336 | .422 |
| 09 Phi | NL | 37 | 97 | 27 | 9 | 0 | 5 | (2 | 3) | 51 | 10 | 13 | 13 | 5 | 0 | 24 | 1 | 0 | 1 | 1 | 4 | .20 | 1 | .278 | .317 | .526 |
| 12 Tor | AL | 27 | 50 | 12 | 5 | 1 | 0 | (0 | 0) | 19 | 5 | 2 | 4 | 4 | 0 | 10 | 0 | 0 | 0 | 0 | 1 | .00 | 0 | .240 | .296 | .380 |
| 12 Hou | NL | 31 | 85 | 21 | 4 | 0 | 2 | (2 | 0) | 31 | 5 | 5 | 8 | 5 | 0 | 23 | 0 | 0 | 0 | 0 | 0 | - | 0 | .247 | .289 | .365 |
| 12 TB | AL | 24 | 57 | 13 | 5 | 0 | 2 | (0 | 2) | 24 | 4 | 8 | 5 | 4 | 0 | 16 | 0 | 0 | 2 | 0 | 0 | - | 1 | .228 | .270 | .421 |
| Postseason | | 17 | 19 | 2 | 0 | 0 | 1 | (0 | 1) | 5 | 2 | 3 | 2 | 1 | 0 | 5 | 1 | 0 | 0 | 0 | 0 | - | 1 | .105 | .190 | .263 |
| 7 ML YEARS | | 563 | 1579 | 400 | 104 | 3 | 50 | (23 | 27) | 660 | 199 | 190 | 194 | 146 | 2 | 325 | 23 | 9 | 14 | 30 | 17 | .64 | 36 | .253 | .323 | .418 |

# Frank Francisco

**Pitches:** R **Bats:** R **Pos:** RP-8 **Ht:** 6'2" **Wt:** 250 **Born:** 9/11/1979 **Age:** 34

| HOW MUCH HE PITCHED | | | | | | | | WHAT HE GAVE UP | | | | | | | | | | | | THE RESULTS | | | | | | | |
|---|---|---|---|---|---|---|---|---|---|---|---|---|---|---|---|---|---|---|---|---|---|---|---|---|---|---|---|
| Year Team | Lg | G | GS | CG | GF | IP | BFP | H | R | ER | HR | SH | SF | HB | TBB | IBB | SO | WP | Bk | W | L | Pct | Sh | Sv-Op | Hld | ERC | ERA |
| 2013 StLuci* | A+ | 5 | 0 | 0 | 0 | 5.0 | 18 | 1 | 0 | 0 | 0 | 1 | 0 | 0 | 2 | 0 | 6 | 0 | 0 | 0 | 0 | - | 0 | 0- - | - | 0.50 | 0.00 |
| 2013 Mets* | R | 5 | 4 | 0 | 0 | 5.0 | 20 | 5 | 2 | 1 | 1 | 0 | 0 | 0 | 0 | 0 | 7 | 0 | 0 | 0 | 2 | .000 | 0 | 0- - | - | 3.05 | 1.80 |
| 2013 Bnghtn* | AA | 2 | 0 | 0 | 0 | 2.0 | 8 | 2 | 0 | 0 | 0 | 0 | 0 | 0 | 1 | 0 | 1 | 0 | 0 | 0 | 0 | - | 0 | 0- - | - | 4.15 | 0.00 |
| 2004 Tex | AL | 45 | 0 | 0 | 7 | 51.1 | 216 | 36 | 19 | 19 | 4 | 2 | 1 | 3 | 28 | 2 | 60 | 4 | 1 | 5 | 1 | .833 | 0 | 0-3 | 10 | 3.04 | 3.33 |
| 2006 Tex | AL | 8 | 0 | 0 | 2 | 7.1 | 32 | 8 | 4 | 4 | 2 | 0 | 0 | 0 | 2 | 0 | 6 | 1 | 0 | 0 | 1 | .000 | 0 | 0-0 | 2 | 5.17 | 4.91 |
| 2007 Tex | AL | 59 | 0 | 0 | 16 | 59.1 | 268 | 57 | 33 | 30 | 3 | 6 | 1 | 2 | 38 | 4 | 49 | 8 | 0 | 1 | 1 | .500 | 0 | 0-0 | 21 | 4.44 | 4.55 |
| 2008 Tex | AL | 58 | 0 | 0 | 18 | 63.1 | 264 | 47 | 24 | 22 | 7 | 0 | 3 | 0 | 26 | 2 | 83 | 5 | 0 | 3 | 5 | .375 | 0 | 5-11 | 12 | 2.70 | 3.13 |
| 2009 Tex | AL | 51 | 0 | 0 | 42 | 49.1 | 203 | 40 | 21 | 21 | 6 | 0 | 0 | 1 | 15 | 1 | 57 | 3 | 0 | 2 | 3 | .400 | 0 | 25-29 | 4 | 2.85 | 3.83 |
| 2010 Tex | AL | 56 | 0 | 0 | 20 | 52.2 | 221 | 49 | 23 | 22 | 5 | 3 | 1 | 1 | 18 | 2 | 60 | 2 | 1 | 6 | 4 | .600 | 0 | 2-6 | 15 | 3.46 | 3.76 |
| 2011 Tor | AL | 54 | 0 | 0 | 38 | 50.2 | 218 | 49 | 21 | 20 | 7 | 1 | 0 | 0 | 18 | 2 | 53 | 2 | 0 | 1 | 4 | .200 | 0 | 17-21 | 2 | 3.85 | 3.55 |
| 2012 NYM | NL | 48 | 0 | 0 | 38 | 42.1 | 197 | 47 | 27 | 26 | 5 | 0 | 1 | 0 | 21 | 1 | 47 | 2 | 1 | 1 | 3 | .250 | 0 | 23-26 | 1 | 5.01 | 5.53 |
| 2013 NYM | NL | 8 | 0 | 0 | 3 | 6.1 | 26 | 4 | 3 | 3 | 0 | 0 | 0 | 1 | 3 | 0 | 6 | 0 | 0 | 1 | 0 | 1.000 | 0 | 1-1 | 0 | 2.37 | 4.26 |
| 9 ML YEARS | | 387 | 0 | 0 | 184 | 382.2 | 1645 | 337 | 175 | 167 | 39 | 12 | 7 | 8 | 169 | 14 | 421 | 27 | 3 | 20 | 22 | .476 | 0 | 73-97 | 67 | 3.58 | 3.93 |

# Juan Francisco

**Bats:** L **Throws:** R **Pos:** 1B-67;3B-34;PH-25;DH-2 **Ht:** 6'2" **Wt:** 240 **Born:** 6/24/1987 **Age:** 27

| BATTING | | | | | | | | | | | | | | | | | | | | BASERUNNING | | | | AVERAGES | | |
|---|---|---|---|---|---|---|---|---|---|---|---|---|---|---|---|---|---|---|---|---|---|---|---|---|---|---|
| Year Team | Lg | G | AB | H | 2B | 3B | HR | (Hm | Rd) | TB | R | RBI | RC | TBB | IBB | SO | HBP | SH | SF | SB | CS | SB% | GDP | Avg | OBP | Slg |
| 2009 Cin | NL | 14 | 21 | 9 | 1 | 0 | 1 | (1 | 0) | 13 | 4 | 7 | 6 | 3 | 0 | 7 | 1 | 0 | 0 | 0 | 0 | - | 0 | .429 | .520 | .619 |
| 2010 Cin | NL | 36 | 55 | 15 | 3 | 0 | 1 | (1 | 0) | 21 | 3 | 7 | 3 | 4 | 0 | 20 | 0 | 0 | 0 | 0 | 1 | .00 | 2 | .273 | .322 | .382 |
| 2011 Cin | NL | 31 | 93 | 24 | 7 | 1 | 3 | (1 | 2) | 42 | 10 | 15 | 12 | 4 | 1 | 24 | 0 | 0 | 0 | 1 | 0 | 1.00 | 1 | .258 | .289 | .452 |
| 2012 Atl | NL | 93 | 192 | 45 | 11 | 0 | 9 | (4 | 5) | 83 | 17 | 32 | 20 | 11 | 2 | 70 | 1 | 0 | 1 | 1 | 1 | .50 | 5 | .234 | .278 | .432 |
| 2013 2 Tms | NL | 124 | 348 | 79 | 12 | 1 | 18 | (8 | 10) | 147 | 36 | 48 | 39 | 32 | 3 | 138 | 3 | 0 | 2 | 0 | 2 | .00 | 3 | .227 | .296 | .422 |
| 13 Atl | NL | 35 | 108 | 26 | 2 | 0 | 5 | (2 | 3) | 43 | 10 | 16 | 14 | 7 | 0 | 43 | 0 | 0 | 0 | 0 | 1 | .00 | 0 | .241 | .287 | .398 |
| 13 Mil | NL | 89 | 240 | 53 | 10 | 1 | 13 | (6 | 7) | 104 | 26 | 32 | 25 | 25 | 3 | 95 | 3 | 0 | 2 | 0 | 1 | .00 | 3 | .221 | .300 | .433 |
| Postseason | | 1 | 1 | 0 | 0 | 0 | 0 | (0 | 0) | 0 | 0 | 0 | 0 | 0 | 0 | 0 | 0 | 0 | 0 | 0 | 0 | - | 0 | .000 | .000 | .000 |
| 5 ML YEARS | | 298 | 709 | 172 | 34 | 2 | 32 | (15 | 17) | 306 | 70 | 109 | 80 | 54 | 6 | 259 | 5 | 0 | 3 | 2 | 4 | .33 | 11 | .243 | .300 | .432 |

# Jeff Francoeur

frann-COOR

**Bats:** R **Throws:** R **Pos:** RF-55;LF-16;PH-11;PR-3;CF-2;DH-2 **Ht:** 6'4" **Wt:** 210 **Born:** 1/8/1984 **Age:** 30

| | | | BATTING | | | | | | | | | | | | | | | | | | BASERUNNING | | | | AVERAGES | | |
|---|---|---|---|---|---|---|---|---|---|---|---|---|---|---|---|---|---|---|---|---|---|---|---|---|---|---|---|
| Year | Team | Lg | G | AB | H | 2B | 3B | HR | (Hm | Rd) | TB | R | RBI | RC | TBB | IBB | SO | HBP | SH | SF | SB | CS | SB% | GDP | Avg | OBP | Slg |
| 2013 | Fresno* | AAA | 4 | 18 | 4 | 0 | 0 | 0 | (- | -) | 4 | 0 | 2 | 0 | 0 | 0 | 3 | 0 | 0 | 0 | 0 | 0 | - | 1 | .222 | .222 | .222 |
| 2005 | Atl | NL | 70 | 257 | 77 | 20 | 1 | 14 | (11 | 3) | 141 | 41 | 45 | 50 | 11 | 3 | 58 | 4 | 0 | 2 | 3 | 2 | .60 | 4 | .300 | .336 | .549 |
| 2006 | Atl | NL | **162** | 651 | 169 | 24 | 6 | 29 | (19 | 10) | 292 | 83 | 103 | 91 | 23 | 6 | 132 | 9 | 0 | 3 | 1 | 6 | .14 | 15 | .260 | .293 | .449 |
| 2007 | Atl | NL | **162** | 642 | 188 | 40 | 0 | 19 | (7 | 12) | 285 | 84 | 105 | 97 | 42 | 5 | 129 | 5 | 0 | 7 | 5 | 2 | .71 | 14 | .293 | .338 | .444 |
| 2008 | Atl | NL | 155 | 599 | 143 | 33 | 3 | 11 | (5 | 6) | 215 | 70 | 71 | 49 | 39 | 5 | 111 | 10 | 0 | 4 | 0 | 1 | .00 | 18 | .239 | .294 | .359 |
| 2009 | 2 Tms | NL | 157 | 593 | 166 | 32 | 4 | 15 | (7 | 8) | 251 | 72 | 76 | 59 | 23 | 5 | 92 | 6 | 1 | 9 | 6 | 4 | .60 | 13 | .280 | .309 | .423 |
| 2010 | 2 Tms | | 139 | 454 | 113 | 18 | 2 | 13 | (5 | 8) | 174 | 52 | 65 | 46 | 30 | 8 | 81 | 8 | 0 | 11 | 8 | 3 | .73 | 9 | .249 | .300 | .383 |
| 2011 | KC | AL | 153 | 601 | 171 | 47 | 4 | 20 | (10 | 10) | 286 | 77 | 87 | 83 | 37 | 3 | 123 | 8 | 0 | 10 | 22 | 10 | .69 | 17 | .285 | .329 | .476 |
| 2012 | KC | AL | 148 | 561 | 132 | 26 | 3 | 16 | (7 | 9) | 212 | 58 | 49 | 50 | 34 | 9 | 119 | 7 | 0 | 1 | 4 | 7 | .36 | 14 | .235 | .287 | .378 |
| 2013 | 2 Tms | | 81 | 245 | 50 | 10 | 2 | 3 | (1 | 2) | 73 | 20 | 17 | 11 | 9 | 2 | 61 | 2 | 0 | 0 | 3 | 0 | 1.00 | 7 | .204 | .238 | .298 |
| 09 | Atl | NL | 82 | 304 | 76 | 12 | 2 | 5 | (3 | 2) | 107 | 32 | 35 | 25 | 12 | 2 | 46 | 3 | 1 | 4 | 5 | 1 | .83 | 10 | .250 | .282 | .352 |
| 09 | NYM | NL | 75 | 289 | 90 | 20 | 2 | 10 | (4 | 6) | 144 | 40 | 41 | 34 | 11 | 3 | 46 | 3 | 0 | 5 | 1 | 3 | .25 | 3 | .311 | .338 | .498 |
| 10 | NYM | NL | 124 | 401 | 95 | 16 | 2 | 11 | (5 | 6) | 148 | 43 | 54 | 39 | 29 | 8 | 76 | 7 | 0 | 10 | 8 | 2 | .80 | 7 | .237 | .293 | .369 |
| 10 | Tex | AL | 15 | 53 | 18 | 2 | 0 | 2 | (0 | 2) | 26 | 9 | 11 | 7 | 1 | 0 | 5 | 1 | 0 | 1 | 0 | 1 | .00 | 2 | .340 | .357 | .491 |
| 13 | KC | AL | 59 | 183 | 38 | 8 | 2 | 3 | (1 | 2) | 59 | 19 | 13 | 10 | 8 | 2 | 49 | 2 | 0 | 0 | 2 | 0 | 1.00 | 5 | .208 | .249 | .322 |
| 13 | SF | NL | 22 | 62 | 12 | 2 | 0 | 0 | (0 | 0) | 14 | 1 | 4 | 1 | 1 | 0 | 12 | 0 | 0 | 0 | 1 | 0 | 1.00 | 2 | .194 | .206 | .226 |
| Postseason | | | 13 | 41 | 7 | 2 | 1 | 0 | (0 | 0) | 11 | 3 | 2 | 3 | 3 | 1 | 7 | 1 | 1 | 0 | 0 | 0 | - | 2 | .171 | .244 | .268 |
| 9 ML YEARS | | | 1227 | 4603 | 1209 | 250 | 25 | 140 | (72 | 68) | 1929 | 557 | 618 | 536 | 248 | 46 | 906 | 59 | 1 | 47 | 52 | 35 | .60 | 111 | .263 | .306 | .419 |

# Kevin Frandsen

**Bats:** R **Throws:** R **Pos:** PH-61;1B-40;2B-20;3B-4 FRAND-zen **Ht:** 6'0" **Wt:** 185 **Born:** 5/24/1982 **Age:** 32

| | | | BATTING | | | | | | | | | | | | | | | | | | BASERUNNING | | | | AVERAGES | | |
|---|---|---|---|---|---|---|---|---|---|---|---|---|---|---|---|---|---|---|---|---|---|---|---|---|---|---|---|
| Year | Team | Lg | G | AB | H | 2B | 3B | HR | (Hm | Rd) | TB | R | RBI | RC | TBB | IBB | SO | HBP | SH | SF | SB | CS | SB% | GDP | Avg | OBP | Slg |
| 2006 | SF | NL | 41 | 93 | 20 | 4 | 0 | 2 | (0 | 2) | 30 | 12 | 7 | 7 | 3 | 0 | 14 | 6 | 0 | 0 | 0 | 1 | .00 | 3 | .215 | .284 | .323 |
| 2007 | SF | NL | 109 | 264 | 71 | 12 | 1 | 5 | (1 | 4) | 100 | 26 | 31 | 29 | 21 | 3 | 24 | 5 | 3 | 3 | 4 | 3 | .57 | 17 | .269 | .331 | .379 |
| 2008 | SF | NL | 1 | 1 | 0 | 0 | 0 | 0 | (0 | 0) | 0 | 0 | 0 | 0 | 0 | 0 | 0 | 0 | 0 | 0 | 0 | 0 | - | 0 | .000 | .000 | .000 |
| 2009 | SF | NL | 23 | 50 | 7 | 2 | 0 | 0 | (0 | 0) | 9 | 3 | 1 | 0 | 3 | 0 | 4 | 1 | 0 | 0 | 0 | 0 | - | 2 | .140 | .204 | .180 |
| 2010 | LAA | AL | 54 | 160 | 40 | 11 | 0 | 0 | (0 | 0) | 51 | 24 | 14 | 16 | 9 | 0 | 10 | 1 | 3 | 0 | 2 | 0 | 1.00 | 5 | .250 | .294 | .319 |
| 2012 | Phi | NL | 55 | 195 | 66 | 10 | 3 | 2 | (1 | 1) | 88 | 24 | 14 | 30 | 9 | 2 | 18 | 5 | 1 | 0 | 0 | 1 | .00 | 4 | .338 | .383 | .451 |
| 2013 | Phi | NL | 119 | 252 | 59 | 10 | 1 | 5 | (2 | 3) | 86 | 27 | 26 | 21 | 12 | 0 | 29 | 11 | 1 | 2 | 1 | 0 | 1.00 | 10 | .234 | .296 | .341 |
| 7 ML YEARS | | | 402 | 1015 | 263 | 49 | 5 | 14 | (4 | 10) | 364 | 116 | 93 | 103 | 57 | 5 | 99 | 29 | 8 | 5 | 7 | 5 | .58 | 41 | .259 | .316 | .359 |

# Nick Franklin

**Bats:** B **Throws:** R **Pos:** 2B-96;PH-5;SS-3;PR-3;DH-2 **Ht:** 6'1" **Wt:** 195 **Born:** 3/2/1991 **Age:** 23

| | | | BATTING | | | | | | | | | | | | | | | | | | BASERUNNING | | | | AVERAGES | | |
|---|---|---|---|---|---|---|---|---|---|---|---|---|---|---|---|---|---|---|---|---|---|---|---|---|---|---|---|
| Year | Team | Lg | G | AB | H | 2B | 3B | HR | (Hm | Rd) | TB | R | RBI | RC | TBB | IBB | SO | HBP | SH | SF | SB | CS | SB% | GDP | Avg | OBP | Slg |
| 2009 | Ms | R | 10 | 43 | 13 | 2 | 0 | 1 | (- | -) | 18 | 6 | 4 | 5 | 1 | 0 | 6 | 0 | 0 | 0 | 0 | 0 | - | 0 | .302 | .318 | .419 |
| 2009 | Everett | A- | 6 | 20 | 8 | 2 | 1 | 0 | (- | -) | 12 | 4 | 2 | 4 | 1 | 0 | 2 | 0 | 0 | 0 | 1 | 0 | 1.00 | 0 | .400 | .429 | .600 |
| 2010 | Clinton | A | 129 | 513 | 144 | 22 | 7 | 23 | (- | -) | 249 | 89 | 65 | 90 | 50 | 4 | 123 | 7 | 2 | 2 | 25 | 10 | .71 | 4 | .281 | .351 | .485 |
| 2010 | WTenn | AA | 1 | 3 | 2 | 0 | 0 | 0 | (- | -) | 2 | 3 | 0 | 1 | 1 | 0 | 1 | 0 | 0 | 0 | 0 | 0 | - | 0 | .667 | .750 | .667 |
| 2011 | Hi Dsrt | A+ | 64 | 258 | 71 | 10 | 5 | 5 | (- | -) | 106 | 50 | 20 | 42 | 31 | 0 | 56 | 2 | 5 | 1 | 13 | 1 | .93 | 3 | .275 | .356 | .411 |
| 2011 | Jacksn | AA | 21 | 83 | 27 | 3 | 2 | 2 | (- | -) | 40 | 13 | 6 | 14 | 6 | 0 | 18 | 0 | 3 | 0 | 5 | 3 | .63 | 1 | .325 | .371 | .482 |
| 2011 | Ms | R | 3 | 11 | 1 | 0 | 0 | 0 | (- | -) | 1 | 1 | 0 | 0 | 0 | 0 | 6 | 0 | 1 | 0 | 0 | 0 | - | 0 | .091 | .091 | .091 |
| 2012 | Jacksn | AA | 57 | 205 | 66 | 17 | 4 | 4 | (- | -) | 103 | 25 | 26 | 42 | 24 | 1 | 38 | 1 | 8 | 1 | 9 | 2 | .82 | 5 | .322 | .394 | .502 |
| 2012 | Tacom | AAA | 64 | 267 | 65 | 15 | 5 | 7 | (- | -) | 111 | 39 | 29 | 35 | 24 | 0 | 68 | 2 | 2 | 1 | 3 | 2 | .60 | 6 | .243 | .310 | .416 |
| 2013 | Tacom | AAA | 39 | 142 | 46 | 9 | 0 | 4 | (- | -) | 67 | 28 | 20 | 33 | 30 | 2 | 20 | 1 | 2 | 2 | 7 | 0 | 1.00 | 1 | .324 | .440 | .472 |
| 2013 | Sea | AL | 102 | 369 | 83 | 20 | 1 | 12 | (4 | 8) | 141 | 38 | 45 | 48 | 42 | 1 | 113 | 0 | 0 | 1 | 6 | 1 | .86 | 2 | .225 | .303 | .382 |

# Jason Frasor

**Pitches:** R **Bats:** R **Pos:** RP-61 FRAY-zer **Ht:** 5'9" **Wt:** 180 **Born:** 8/9/1977 **Age:** 36

| | | | HOW MUCH HE PITCHED | | | | | | WHAT HE GAVE UP | | | | | | | | | | | | THE RESULTS | | | | | | | |
|---|---|---|---|---|---|---|---|---|---|---|---|---|---|---|---|---|---|---|---|---|---|---|---|---|---|---|---|---|
| Year | Team | Lg | G | GS | CG | GF | IP | BFP | H | R | ER | HR | SH | SF | HB | TBB | IBB | SO | WP | Bk | W | L | Pct | Sh | Sv-Op | Hld | ERC | ERA |
| 2004 | Tor | AL | 63 | 0 | 0 | 37 | 68.1 | 299 | 64 | 31 | 31 | 4 | 3 | 3 | 2 | 36 | 3 | 54 | 4 | 2 | 4 | 6 | .400 | 0 | 17-19 | 8 | 3.97 | 4.08 |
| 2005 | Tor | AL | 67 | 0 | 0 | 12 | 74.2 | 305 | 67 | 31 | 27 | 8 | 2 | 1 | 3 | 28 | 2 | 62 | 1 | 0 | 3 | 5 | .375 | 0 | 1-3 | 15 | 3.72 | 3.25 |
| 2006 | Tor | AL | 51 | 0 | 0 | 12 | 50.0 | 215 | 47 | 24 | 24 | 8 | 0 | 3 | 2 | 17 | 1 | 51 | 3 | 0 | 3 | 2 | .600 | 0 | 0-1 | 12 | 3.98 | 4.32 |
| 2007 | Tor | AL | 51 | 0 | 0 | 18 | 57.0 | 242 | 47 | 29 | 29 | 3 | 1 | 2 | 2 | 23 | 1 | 59 | 2 | 1 | 1 | 5 | .167 | 0 | 3-6 | 4 | 2.88 | 4.58 |
| 2008 | Tor | AL | 49 | 0 | 0 | 21 | 47.1 | 208 | 36 | 23 | 22 | 4 | 0 | 2 | 1 | 32 | 4 | 42 | 6 | 0 | 1 | 2 | .333 | 0 | 0-1 | 4 | 3.62 | 4.18 |
| 2009 | Tor | AL | 61 | 0 | 0 | 36 | 57.2 | 227 | 43 | 17 | 16 | 4 | 1 | 2 | 2 | 16 | 3 | 56 | 2 | 0 | 7 | 3 | .700 | 0 | 11-14 | 4 | 2.22 | 2.50 |
| 2010 | Tor | AL | 69 | 0 | 0 | 18 | 63.2 | 279 | 61 | 30 | 26 | 4 | 1 | 0 | 4 | 27 | 6 | 65 | 5 | 0 | 3 | 4 | .429 | 0 | 4-8 | 14 | 3.72 | 3.68 |
| 2011 | 2 Tms | AL | 64 | 0 | 0 | 10 | 60.0 | 261 | 58 | 25 | 24 | 7 | 2 | 4 | 3 | 26 | 3 | 57 | 3 | 0 | 3 | 3 | .500 | 0 | 0-2 | 14 | 4.26 | 3.60 |
| 2012 | Tor | AL | 50 | 0 | 0 | 9 | 43.2 | 191 | 42 | 20 | 20 | 6 | 1 | 2 | 2 | 22 | 1 | 53 | 5 | 1 | 1 | 1 | .500 | 0 | 0-3 | 12 | 4.74 | 4.12 |
| 2013 | Tex | AL | 61 | 0 | 0 | 11 | 49.0 | 200 | 36 | 15 | 14 | 4 | 1 | 2 | 0 | 20 | 3 | 48 | 2 | 0 | 4 | 3 | .571 | 0 | 0-1 | 10 | 2.50 | 2.57 |
| 11 | Tor | AL | 44 | 0 | 0 | 6 | 42.1 | 178 | 38 | 15 | 14 | 4 | 2 | 3 | 2 | 15 | 1 | 37 | 2 | 0 | 2 | 1 | .667 | 0 | 0-2 | 10 | 3.46 | 2.98 |
| 11 | CWS | AL | 20 | 0 | 0 | 4 | 17.2 | 83 | 20 | 10 | 10 | 3 | 0 | 1 | 1 | 11 | 2 | 20 | 1 | 0 | 1 | 2 | .333 | 0 | 0-0 | 4 | 6.37 | 5.09 |
| 10 ML YEARS | | | 586 | 0 | 0 | 184 | 571.1 | 2427 | 501 | 245 | 233 | 52 | 12 | 21 | 21 | 247 | 27 | 547 | 33 | 4 | 30 | 34 | .469 | 0 | 36-58 | 97 | 3.54 | 3.67 |

## Todd Frazier

**Bats:** R **Throws:** R **Pos:** 3B-147;PH-6;LF-2 **Ht:** 6'3" **Wt:** 220 **Born:** 2/12/1986 **Age:** 28

| BATTING | | | | | | | | | | | | | | | | | | | | | BASERUNNING | | | | AVERAGES | | |
|---|---|---|---|---|---|---|---|---|---|---|---|---|---|---|---|---|---|---|---|---|---|---|---|---|---|---|---|
| Year Team | Lg | G | AB | H | 2B | 3B | HR | (Hm | Rd) | TB | R | RBI | RC | TBB | IBB | SO | HBP | SH | SF | | SB | CS | SB% | GDP | Avg | OBP | Slg |
| 2011 Cin | NL | 41 | 112 | 26 | 5 | 0 | 6 | (2 | 4) | 49 | 17 | 15 | 13 | 7 | 0 | 27 | 2 | 0 | 0 | | 1 | 0 | 1.00 | 2 | .232 | .289 | .438 |
| 2012 Cin | NL | 128 | 422 | 115 | 26 | 6 | 19 | (10 | 9) | 210 | 55 | 67 | 59 | 36 | 1 | 103 | 3 | 0 | 4 | | 3 | 2 | .60 | 9 | .273 | .331 | .498 |
| 2013 Cin | NL | 150 | 531 | 124 | 29 | 3 | 19 | (12 | 7) | 216 | 63 | 73 | 67 | 50 | 1 | 125 | 14 | 2 | 3 | | 6 | 5 | .55 | 14 | .234 | .314 | .407 |
| Postseason | | 4 | 6 | 1 | 0 | 0 | 0 | (0 | 0) | 1 | 0 | 1 | 0 | 1 | 0 | 2 | 0 | 0 | 0 | | 0 | 0 | - | 0 | .167 | .286 | .167 |
| 3 ML YEARS | | 319 | 1065 | 265 | 60 | 9 | 44 | (24 | 20) | 475 | 135 | 155 | 139 | 93 | 2 | 255 | 19 | 2 | 7 | | 10 | 7 | .59 | 25 | .249 | .318 | .446 |

## Freddie Freeman

**Bats:** L **Throws:** R **Pos:** 1B-147;PR-1 **Ht:** 6'5" **Wt:** 225 **Born:** 9/12/1989 **Age:** 24

| BATTING | | | | | | | | | | | | | | | | | | | | | BASERUNNING | | | | AVERAGES | | |
|---|---|---|---|---|---|---|---|---|---|---|---|---|---|---|---|---|---|---|---|---|---|---|---|---|---|---|---|
| Year Team | Lg | G | AB | H | 2B | 3B | HR | (Hm | Rd) | TB | R | RBI | RC | TBB | IBB | SO | HBP | SH | SF | | SB | CS | SB% | GDP | Avg | OBP | Slg |
| 2013 Gwnntt* | AAA | 3 | 10 | 5 | 2 | 0 | 0 | (- | -) | 7 | 3 | 2 | 3 | 1 | 0 | 3 | 1 | 0 | 0 | | 0 | 0 | - | 0 | .500 | .583 | .700 |
| 2010 Atl | NL | 20 | 24 | 4 | 1 | 0 | 1 | (0 | 1) | 8 | 3 | 1 | 0 | 0 | 0 | 8 | 0 | 0 | 0 | | 0 | 0 | - | 1 | .167 | .167 | .333 |
| 2011 Atl | NL | 157 | 571 | 161 | 32 | 0 | 21 | (9 | 12) | 256 | 67 | 76 | 79 | 53 | 3 | 142 | 6 | 0 | 5 | | 4 | 4 | .50 | 15 | .282 | .346 | .448 |
| 2012 Atl | NL | 147 | 540 | 140 | 33 | 2 | 23 | (12 | 11) | 246 | 91 | 94 | 82 | 64 | 4 | 129 | 7 | 0 | 9 | | 2 | 0 | 1.00 | 10 | .259 | .340 | .456 |
| 2013 Atl | NL | 147 | 551 | 176 | 27 | 2 | 23 | (16 | 7) | 276 | 89 | 109 | 124 | 66 | 10 | 121 | 7 | 0 | 5 | | 1 | 0 | 1.00 | 11 | .319 | .396 | .501 |
| Postseason | | 1 | 4 | 3 | 1 | 0 | 0 | (0 | 0) | 4 | 0 | 0 | 1 | 1 | 0 | 1 | 0 | 0 | 0 | | 0 | 0 | - | 0 | .750 | .800 | 1.000 |
| 4 ML YEARS | | 471 | 1686 | 481 | 93 | 4 | 68 | (37 | 31) | 786 | 250 | 280 | 285 | 183 | 17 | 400 | 20 | 0 | 19 | | 7 | 4 | .64 | 37 | .285 | .358 | .466 |

## Justin Freeman

**Pitches:** R **Bats:** R **Pos:** RP-1 **Ht:** 5'11" **Wt:** 175 **Born:** 10/22/1986 **Age:** 27

| HOW MUCH HE PITCHED | | | | | | | | WHAT HE GAVE UP | | | | | | | | | | | | | THE RESULTS | | | | | | | |
|---|---|---|---|---|---|---|---|---|---|---|---|---|---|---|---|---|---|---|---|---|---|---|---|---|---|---|---|---|
| Year Team | Lg | G | GS | CG | GF | IP | BFP | H | R | ER | HR | SH | SF | HB | TBB | IBB | SO | WP | Bk | | W | L | Pct | Sh | Sv-Op | Hld | ERC | ERA |
| 2009 Srsota | A+ | 37 | 0 | 0 | 11 | 64.2 | 280 | 75 | 34 | 25 | 1 | 6 | 3 | 4 | 10 | 2 | 49 | 4 | 0 | | 2 | 5 | .286 | 0 | 3-- | - | 3.55 | 3.48 |
| 2010 Lynbrg | A+ | 45 | 0 | 0 | 26 | 55.2 | 226 | 49 | 19 | 18 | 4 | 4 | 0 | 4 | 7 | 0 | 53 | 0 | 0 | | 1 | 2 | .333 | 0 | 7-- | - | 2.47 | 2.91 |
| 2010 Carlina | AA | 8 | 0 | 0 | 2 | 11.0 | 42 | 8 | 3 | 3 | 0 | 0 | 1 | 0 | 2 | 0 | 5 | 1 | 0 | | 0 | 0 | - | 0 | 0-- | - | 1.47 | 2.45 |
| 2011 Carlina | AA | 54 | 0 | 0 | 14 | 60.0 | 278 | 74 | 39 | 35 | 10 | 2 | 2 | 6 | 25 | 2 | 56 | 3 | 0 | | 2 | 4 | .333 | 0 | 1-- | - | 6.43 | 5.25 |
| 2012 Pnscla | AA | 57 | 0 | 0 | 29 | 68.0 | 266 | 49 | 22 | 22 | 7 | 2 | 0 | 1 | 16 | 3 | 68 | 3 | 0 | | 4 | 7 | .364 | 0 | 16-- | - | 2.06 | 2.91 |
| 2013 Lsvlle | AAA | 6 | 0 | 0 | 3 | 7.0 | 29 | 5 | 1 | 1 | 1 | 0 | 0 | 1 | 2 | 0 | 8 | 0 | 0 | | 0 | 0 | - | 0 | 1-- | - | 2.88 | 1.29 |
| 2013 Cin | NL | 1 | 0 | 0 | 0 | 1.0 | 5 | 2 | 2 | 2 | 1 | 0 | 0 | 0 | 0 | 0 | 0 | 0 | 0 | | 0 | 0 | - | 0 | 0-0 | 0 | 16.28 | 18.00 |

## Sam Freeman

**Pitches:** L **Bats:** R **Pos:** RP-13 **Ht:** 5'11" **Wt:** 165 **Born:** 6/24/1987 **Age:** 27

| HOW MUCH HE PITCHED | | | | | | | | WHAT HE GAVE UP | | | | | | | | | | | | | THE RESULTS | | | | | | | |
|---|---|---|---|---|---|---|---|---|---|---|---|---|---|---|---|---|---|---|---|---|---|---|---|---|---|---|---|---|
| Year Team | Lg | G | GS | CG | GF | IP | BFP | H | R | ER | HR | SH | SF | HB | TBB | IBB | SO | WP | Bk | | W | L | Pct | Sh | Sv-Op | Hld | ERC | ERA |
| 2009 PlmBh | A+ | 26 | 0 | 0 | 13 | 33.0 | 133 | 18 | 7 | 6 | 0 | 2 | 3 | 0 | 13 | 0 | 30 | 2 | 0 | | 2 | 1 | .667 | 0 | 1-- | - | 1.31 | 1.64 |
| 2009 Sprgfld | AA | 15 | 0 | 0 | 6 | 23.0 | 97 | 19 | 9 | 9 | 6 | 3 | 0 | 1 | 14 | 3 | 17 | 2 | 0 | | 0 | 1 | .000 | 0 | 1-- | - | 5.28 | 3.52 |
| 2011 PlmBh | A+ | 7 | 0 | 0 | 2 | 9.0 | 37 | 8 | 5 | 4 | 0 | 0 | 2 | 0 | 4 | 0 | 7 | 0 | 0 | | 0 | 0 | - | 0 | 0-- | - | 3.06 | 4.00 |
| 2011 Sprgfld | AA | 52 | 0 | 0 | 25 | 59.1 | 255 | 53 | 28 | 20 | 5 | 3 | 1 | 2 | 28 | 0 | 52 | 3 | 1 | | 2 | 2 | .500 | 0 | 3-- | - | 3.80 | 3.03 |
| 2012 Sprgfld | AA | 15 | 0 | 0 | 8 | 17.1 | 69 | 12 | 5 | 3 | 1 | 1 | 0 | 1 | 4 | 1 | 12 | 2 | 0 | | 1 | 3 | .250 | 0 | 1-- | - | 1.75 | 1.56 |
| 2012 Memp | AAA | 27 | 0 | 0 | 6 | 30.1 | 123 | 25 | 7 | 7 | 3 | 0 | 1 | 0 | 12 | 2 | 27 | 2 | 0 | | 2 | 2 | .500 | 0 | 0-- | - | 3.09 | 2.08 |
| 2013 Memp | AAA | 49 | 0 | 0 | 17 | 69.2 | 294 | 57 | 25 | 23 | 4 | 1 | 1 | 3 | 27 | 1 | 66 | 3 | 0 | | 7 | 2 | .778 | 0 | 2-- | - | 2.87 | 2.97 |
| 2012 StL | NL | 24 | 0 | 0 | 7 | 20.0 | 86 | 17 | 13 | 12 | 2 | 1 | 0 | 1 | 10 | 0 | 18 | 0 | 0 | | 0 | 2 | .000 | 0 | 0-0 | 2 | 3.84 | 5.40 |
| 2013 StL | NL | 13 | 0 | 0 | 2 | 12.1 | 50 | 8 | 3 | 3 | 0 | 1 | 0 | 0 | 5 | 0 | 8 | 2 | 0 | | 1 | 0 | 1.000 | 0 | 0-0 | 1 | 1.67 | 2.19 |
| 2 ML YEARS | | 37 | 0 | 0 | 9 | 32.1 | 136 | 25 | 16 | 15 | 2 | 2 | 0 | 1 | 15 | 0 | 26 | 2 | 0 | | 1 | 2 | .333 | 0 | 0-0 | 3 | 2.95 | 4.18 |

## David Freese

**Bats:** R **Throws:** R **Pos:** 3B-132;PH-4;DH-2 FREEZE **Ht:** 6'2" **Wt:** 225 **Born:** 4/28/1983 **Age:** 31

| BATTING | | | | | | | | | | | | | | | | | | | | | BASERUNNING | | | | AVERAGES | | |
|---|---|---|---|---|---|---|---|---|---|---|---|---|---|---|---|---|---|---|---|---|---|---|---|---|---|---|---|
| Year Team | Lg | G | AB | H | 2B | 3B | HR | (Hm | Rd) | TB | R | RBI | RC | TBB | IBB | SO | HBP | SH | SF | | SB | CS | SB% | GDP | Avg | OBP | Slg |
| 2013 Memp* | AAA | 3 | 12 | 4 | 2 | 0 | 0 | (- | -) | 6 | 2 | 4 | 2 | 1 | 0 | 2 | 0 | 0 | 0 | | 0 | 0 | - | 0 | .333 | .385 | .500 |
| 2009 StL | NL | 17 | 31 | 10 | 2 | 0 | 1 | (0 | 1) | 15 | 3 | 7 | 4 | 2 | 0 | 7 | 0 | 0 | 1 | | 0 | 0 | - | 1 | .323 | .353 | .484 |
| 2010 StL | NL | 70 | 240 | 71 | 12 | 1 | 4 | (3 | 1) | 97 | 28 | 36 | 36 | 21 | 0 | 59 | 4 | 4 | 1 | | 1 | 1 | .50 | 7 | .296 | .361 | .404 |
| 2011 StL | NL | 97 | 333 | 99 | 16 | 1 | 10 | (6 | 4) | 147 | 41 | 55 | 50 | 24 | 0 | 75 | 4 | 0 | 2 | | 1 | 0 | 1.00 | 18 | .297 | .350 | .441 |
| 2012 StL | NL | 144 | 501 | 147 | 25 | 1 | 20 | (8 | 12) | 234 | 70 | 79 | 79 | 57 | 2 | 122 | 7 | 0 | 2 | | 3 | 3 | .50 | 19 | .293 | .372 | .467 |
| 2013 StL | NL | 138 | 462 | 121 | 26 | 1 | 9 | (4 | 5) | 176 | 53 | 60 | 48 | 47 | 1 | 106 | 9 | 0 | 3 | | 1 | 2 | .33 | 26 | .262 | .340 | .381 |
| Postseason | | 31 | 110 | 38 | 13 | 1 | 6 | (2 | 4) | 71 | 17 | 25 | 28 | 11 | 2 | 27 | 1 | 0 | 1 | | 0 | 1 | .00 | 4 | .345 | .407 | .645 |
| 5 ML YEARS | | 466 | 1567 | 448 | 81 | 4 | 44 | (21 | 23) | 669 | 195 | 237 | 217 | 151 | 3 | 369 | 24 | 4 | 9 | | 6 | 6 | .50 | 71 | .286 | .356 | .427 |

## Nate Freiman

**Bats:** R **Throws:** R **Pos:** 1B-59;PH-23;DH-12 FRY-men **Ht:** 6'8" **Wt:** 250 **Born:** 12/31/1986 **Age:** 27

| BATTING | | | | | | | | | | | | | | | | | | | | | BASERUNNING | | | | AVERAGES | | |
|---|---|---|---|---|---|---|---|---|---|---|---|---|---|---|---|---|---|---|---|---|---|---|---|---|---|---|---|
| Year Team | Lg | G | AB | H | 2B | 3B | HR | (Hm | Rd) | TB | R | RBI | RC | TBB | IBB | SO | HBP | SH | SF | | SB | CS | SB% | GDP | Avg | OBP | Slg |
| 2009 Eugene | A- | 72 | 289 | 85 | 22 | 0 | 11 | (- | -) | 140 | 36 | 68 | 52 | 30 | 1 | 55 | 3 | 0 | 2 | | 2 | 0 | 1.00 | 13 | .294 | .364 | .484 |
| 2010 FtWyn | A | 136 | 523 | 154 | 43 | 0 | 14 | (- | -) | 239 | 83 | 84 | 91 | 58 | 5 | 117 | 7 | 0 | 6 | | 0 | 0 | - | 21 | .294 | .369 | .457 |
| 2011 Lk Els | A+ | 138 | 548 | 158 | 35 | 4 | 22 | (- | -) | 267 | 81 | 111 | 98 | 50 | 4 | 93 | 11 | 0 | 9 | | 6 | 1 | .86 | 15 | .288 | .354 | .487 |
| 2012 SnAnt | AA | 137 | 516 | 154 | 31 | 1 | 24 | (- | -) | 259 | 80 | 105 | 96 | 49 | 1 | 95 | 12 | 0 | 4 | | 0 | 2 | .00 | 11 | .298 | .370 | .502 |
| 2013 Oak | AL | 80 | 190 | 52 | 8 | 1 | 4 | (3 | 1) | 74 | 10 | 24 | 23 | 14 | 0 | 31 | 2 | 0 | 2 | | 0 | 0 | - | 8 | .274 | .327 | .389 |

# Ernesto Frieri

**Pitches:** R **Bats:** R **Pos:** RP-67 free-AIR-ee **Ht:** 6'2" **Wt:** 205 **Born:** 7/19/1985 **Age:** 28

| HOW MUCH HE PITCHED | | | | | | | | WHAT HE GAVE UP | | | | | | | | | | | | THE RESULTS | | | | | | | |
|---|---|---|---|---|---|---|---|---|---|---|---|---|---|---|---|---|---|---|---|---|---|---|---|---|---|---|---|
| Year Team | Lg | G | GS | CG | GF | IP | BFP | H | R | ER | HR | SH | SF | HB | TBB | IBB | SO | WP | Bk | W | L | Pct | Sh | Sv-Op | Hld | ERC | ERA |
| 2009 SD | NL | 2 | 0 | 0 | 2 | 2.0 | 7 | 0 | 0 | 0 | 0 | 0 | 0 | 0 | 1 | 0 | 2 | 0 | 0 | 0 | 0 | - | 0 | 0-0 | 0 | 0.27 | 0.00 |
| 2010 SD | NL | 33 | 0 | 0 | 12 | 31.2 | 128 | 18 | 7 | 6 | 2 | 0 | 0 | 0 | 17 | 3 | 41 | 2 | 0 | 1 | 1 | .500 | 0 | 0-0 | 7 | 1.99 | 1.71 |
| 2011 SD | NL | 59 | 0 | 0 | 19 | 63.0 | 276 | 51 | 21 | 19 | 3 | 1 | 1 | 9 | 34 | 5 | 76 | 1 | 1 | 1 | 2 | .333 | 0 | 0-0 | 4 | 3.60 | 2.71 |
| 2012 2 Tms | | 67 | 0 | 0 | 51 | 66.0 | 269 | 35 | 20 | 17 | 9 | 1 | 1 | 7 | 30 | 0 | 98 | 1 | 0 | 5 | 2 | .714 | 0 | 23-26 | 7 | 2.43 | 2.32 |
| 2013 LAA | AL | 67 | 0 | 0 | 51 | 68.2 | 292 | 55 | 29 | 29 | 11 | 2 | 2 | 3 | 30 | 1 | 98 | 1 | 0 | 2 | 4 | .333 | 0 | 37-41 | 2 | 3.64 | 3.80 |
| 12 SD | NL | 11 | 0 | 0 | 5 | 11.2 | 50 | 9 | 5 | 3 | 2 | 0 | 0 | 2 | 4 | 0 | 18 | 0 | 0 | 1 | 0 | 1.000 | 0 | 0-0 | 1 | 3.67 | 2.31 |
| 12 LAA | AL | 56 | 0 | 0 | 46 | 54.1 | 219 | 26 | 15 | 14 | 7 | 1 | 1 | 5 | 26 | 0 | 80 | 1 | 0 | 4 | 2 | .667 | 0 | 23-26 | 6 | 2.18 | 2.32 |
| 5 ML YEARS | | 228 | 0 | 0 | 135 | 231.1 | 972 | 159 | 77 | 71 | 25 | 4 | 4 | 19 | 112 | 9 | 315 | 5 | 1 | 9 | 9 | .500 | 0 | 60-67 | 20 | 3.00 | 2.76 |

# Eric Fryer

**Bats:** R **Throws:** R **Pos:** C-5;DH-1;PH-1 **Ht:** 6'2" **Wt:** 215 **Born:** 8/26/1985 **Age:** 28

| BATTING | | | | | | | | | | | | | | | | | | | | BASERUNNING | | | | AVERAGES | | |
|---|---|---|---|---|---|---|---|---|---|---|---|---|---|---|---|---|---|---|---|---|---|---|---|---|---|---|
| Year Team | Lg | G | AB | H | 2B | 3B | HR | (Hm | Rd) | TB | R | RBI | RC | TBB | IBB | SO | HBP | SH | SF | SB | CS | SB% | GDP | Avg | OBP | Slg |
| 2013 Roch* | AAA | 65 | 200 | 43 | 11 | 2 | 5 | (- | -) | 73 | 32 | 31 | 29 | 35 | 0 | 47 | 4 | 1 | 3 | 8 | 0 | 1.00 | 4 | .215 | .339 | .365 |
| 2011 Pit | NL | 10 | 26 | 7 | 0 | 0 | 0 | (0 | 0) | 7 | 5 | 0 | 2 | 3 | 1 | 7 | 0 | 0 | 0 | 1 | 1 | .50 | 0 | .269 | .345 | .269 |
| 2012 Pit | NL | 6 | 4 | 1 | 0 | 0 | 0 | (0 | 0) | 1 | 0 | 0 | 1 | 1 | 0 | 1 | 0 | 0 | 0 | 0 | 0 | - | 0 | .250 | .400 | .250 |
| 2013 Min | AL | 6 | 13 | 5 | 1 | 0 | 1 | (1 | 0) | 9 | 2 | 4 | 5 | 3 | 0 | 3 | 0 | 0 | 0 | 0 | 0 | - | 1 | .385 | .500 | .692 |
| 3 ML YEARS | | 22 | 43 | 13 | 1 | 0 | 1 | (1 | 0) | 17 | 7 | 4 | 8 | 7 | 1 | 11 | 0 | 0 | 0 | 1 | 1 | .50 | 1 | .302 | .400 | .395 |

# Reymond Fuentes

**Bats:** L **Throws:** L **Pos:** CF-15;PH-6;PR-4;LF-2 foo-WHEN-tayz **Ht:** 6'0" **Wt:** 160 **Born:** 2/12/1991 **Age:** 23

| BATTING | | | | | | | | | | | | | | | | | | | | BASERUNNING | | | | AVERAGES | | |
|---|---|---|---|---|---|---|---|---|---|---|---|---|---|---|---|---|---|---|---|---|---|---|---|---|---|---|
| Year Team | Lg | G | AB | H | 2B | 3B | HR | (Hm | Rd) | TB | R | RBI | RC | TBB | IBB | SO | HBP | SH | SF | SB | CS | SB% | GDP | Avg | OBP | Slg |
| 2009 RedSx | R | 40 | 145 | 42 | 6 | 2 | 1 | (- | -) | 55 | 16 | 14 | 19 | 7 | 1 | 24 | 3 | 2 | 2 | 9 | 5 | .64 | 3 | .290 | .331 | .379 |
| 2010 Grnvlle | A | 104 | 374 | 101 | 15 | 5 | 5 | (- | -) | 141 | 59 | 41 | 54 | 25 | 1 | 87 | 8 | 5 | 2 | 42 | 5 | .89 | 3 | .270 | .328 | .377 |
| 2011 Lk Els | A+ | 124 | 510 | 140 | 15 | 9 | 5 | (- | -) | 188 | 84 | 45 | 70 | 44 | 2 | 117 | 9 | 9 | 1 | 41 | 14 | .75 | 1 | .275 | .342 | .369 |
| 2012 SnAnt | AA | 136 | 473 | 103 | 20 | 4 | 4 | (- | -) | 143 | 53 | 34 | 50 | 52 | 1 | 133 | 6 | 7 | 3 | 35 | 9 | .80 | 2 | .218 | .301 | .302 |
| 2013 SnAnt | AA | 93 | 345 | 109 | 21 | 2 | 6 | (- | -) | 152 | 56 | 35 | 65 | 41 | 2 | 71 | 6 | 9 | 2 | 29 | 10 | .74 | 2 | .316 | .396 | .441 |
| 2013 Tucsn | AAA | 14 | 55 | 23 | 4 | 0 | 0 | (- | -) | 27 | 17 | 8 | 15 | 10 | 0 | 10 | 1 | 1 | 0 | 6 | 1 | .86 | 1 | .418 | .515 | .491 |
| 2013 SD | NL | 23 | 33 | 5 | 0 | 0 | 0 | (0 | 0) | 5 | 4 | 1 | 1 | 3 | 0 | 16 | 0 | 0 | 0 | 3 | 0 | 1.00 | 0 | .152 | .222 | .152 |

# Kyuji Fujikawa

**Pitches:** R **Bats:** L **Pos:** RP-12 CUE-jee foo-jee-KOW-uh **Ht:** 6'0" **Wt:** 190 **Born:** 7/21/1980 **Age:** 33

| HOW MUCH HE PITCHED | | | | | | | | WHAT HE GAVE UP | | | | | | | | | | | | THE RESULTS | | | | | | | |
|---|---|---|---|---|---|---|---|---|---|---|---|---|---|---|---|---|---|---|---|---|---|---|---|---|---|---|---|
| Year Team | Lg | G | GS | CG | GF | IP | BFP | H | R | ER | HR | SH | SF | HB | TBB | IBB | SO | WP | Bk | W | L | Pct | Sh | Sv-Op | Hld | ERC | ERA |
| 2009 Hnshn | Jap | 49 | 0 | 0 | - | 57.2 | 217 | 32 | 9 | 8 | 4 | - | - | 1 | 15 | 2 | 86 | 0 | 0 | 5 | 3 | .625 | 0 | 25-- | - | 1.38 | 1.25 |
| 2010 Hnshn | Jap | 58 | 0 | 0 | 49 | 62.2 | 257 | 47 | 14 | 14 | 7 | - | - | 5 | 20 | 2 | 81 | 1 | 0 | 3 | 4 | .429 | 0 | 28-- | - | 2.76 | 2.01 |
| 2011 Hnshn | Jap | 56 | 0 | 0 | 49 | 51.0 | 193 | 25 | 9 | 7 | 2 | - | - | 1 | 13 | 1 | 80 | 3 | 0 | 3 | 3 | .500 | 0 | 41-- | - | 1.07 | 1.24 |
| 2012 Hnshn | Jap | 48 | 0 | 0 | 45 | 47.2 | 189 | 34 | 7 | 7 | 1 | - | - | 1 | 15 | 2 | 58 | 2 | 0 | 2 | 2 | .500 | 0 | 24-- | - | 1.85 | 1.32 |
| 2013 Iowa | AAA | 1 | 0 | 0 | 0 | 1.0 | 4 | 0 | 0 | 0 | 0 | 0 | 0 | 0 | 1 | 0 | 2 | 0 | 0 | 0 | 0 | - | 0 | 0-- | - | 0.95 | 0.00 |
| 2013 Tenn | AA | 1 | 0 | 0 | 0 | 2.0 | 6 | 1 | 0 | 0 | 0 | 0 | 0 | 0 | 0 | 0 | 0 | 0 | 0 | 0 | 0 | - | 0 | 0-- | - | 0.63 | 0.00 |
| 2013 ChC | NL | 12 | 0 | 0 | 5 | 12.0 | 50 | 11 | 7 | 7 | 1 | 0 | 0 | 2 | 2 | 0 | 14 | 2 | 0 | 1 | 1 | .500 | 0 | 2-3 | 1 | 3.26 | 5.25 |

# Sam Fuld

**Bats:** L **Throws:** L **Pos:** LF-55;CF-29;RF-28;PR-13;PH-12;DH-3 **Ht:** 5'10" **Wt:** 175 **Born:** 11/20/1981 **Age:** 32

| BATTING | | | | | | | | | | | | | | | | | | | | BASERUNNING | | | | AVERAGES | | |
|---|---|---|---|---|---|---|---|---|---|---|---|---|---|---|---|---|---|---|---|---|---|---|---|---|---|---|
| Year Team | Lg | G | AB | H | 2B | 3B | HR | (Hm | Rd) | TB | R | RBI | RC | TBB | IBB | SO | HBP | SH | SF | SB | CS | SB% | GDP | Avg | OBP | Slg |
| 2007 ChC | NL | 14 | 6 | 0 | 0 | 0 | 0 | (0 | 0) | 0 | 3 | 0 | 0 | 3 | 0 | 3 | 0 | 0 | 0 | 0 | 0 | - | 0 | .000 | .333 | .000 |
| 2009 ChC | NL | 65 | 97 | 29 | 6 | 1 | 1 | (1 | 0) | 40 | 17 | 2 | 15 | 17 | 1 | 10 | 1 | 0 | 0 | 2 | 1 | .67 | 1 | .299 | .409 | .412 |
| 2010 ChC | NL | 19 | 28 | 4 | 1 | 0 | 0 | (0 | 0) | 5 | 3 | 3 | 1 | 3 | 0 | 5 | 0 | 0 | 0 | 0 | 0 | - | 2 | .143 | .226 | .179 |
| 2011 TB | AL | 105 | 308 | 74 | 18 | 5 | 3 | (2 | 1) | 111 | 41 | 27 | 37 | 32 | 0 | 49 | 1 | 4 | 1 | 20 | 8 | .71 | 3 | .240 | .313 | .360 |
| 2012 TB | AL | 44 | 98 | 25 | 3 | 2 | 0 | (0 | 0) | 32 | 14 | 5 | 13 | 8 | 0 | 14 | 1 | 0 | 0 | 7 | 2 | .78 | 0 | .255 | .318 | .327 |
| 2013 TB | AL | 119 | 176 | 35 | 0 | 3 | 2 | (2 | 0) | 47 | 25 | 17 | 14 | 17 | 0 | 28 | 1 | 4 | 2 | 8 | 2 | .80 | 6 | .199 | .270 | .267 |
| Postseason | | 3 | 3 | 0 | 0 | 0 | 0 | (0 | 0) | 0 | 0 | 0 | 0 | 0 | 0 | 1 | 0 | 0 | 0 | 0 | 0 | - | 0 | .000 | .000 | .000 |
| 6 ML YEARS | | 366 | 713 | 167 | 28 | 11 | 6 | (5 | 1) | 235 | 103 | 54 | 80 | 80 | 1 | 109 | 4 | 8 | 3 | 37 | 13 | .74 | 12 | .234 | .314 | .330 |

# Charlie Furbush

**Pitches:** L **Bats:** L **Pos:** RP-71 FUR-bush **Ht:** 6'5" **Wt:** 215 **Born:** 4/11/1986 **Age:** 28

| HOW MUCH HE PITCHED | | | | | | | | WHAT HE GAVE UP | | | | | | | | | | | | THE RESULTS | | | | | | | |
|---|---|---|---|---|---|---|---|---|---|---|---|---|---|---|---|---|---|---|---|---|---|---|---|---|---|---|---|
| Year Team | Lg | G | GS | CG | GF | IP | BFP | H | R | ER | HR | SH | SF | HB | TBB | IBB | SO | WP | Bk | W | L | Pct | Sh | Sv-Op | Hld | ERC | ERA |
| 2011 2 Tms | AL | 28 | 12 | 0 | 1 | 85.1 | 372 | 97 | 59 | 52 | 16 | 2 | 4 | 6 | 30 | 2 | 67 | 2 | 1 | 4 | 10 | .286 | 0 | 0-0 | 1 | 5.72 | 5.48 |
| 2012 Sea | AL | 48 | 0 | 0 | 8 | 46.1 | 182 | 28 | 15 | 14 | 3 | 2 | 1 | 2 | 16 | 4 | 53 | 5 | 0 | 5 | 2 | .714 | 0 | 0-0 | 6 | 1.72 | 2.72 |
| 2013 Sea | AL | 71 | 0 | 0 | 5 | 65.0 | 280 | 48 | 33 | 27 | 5 | 2 | 5 | 3 | 29 | 2 | 80 | 3 | 0 | 2 | 6 | .250 | 0 | 0-6 | 20 | 2.71 | 3.74 |
| 11 Det | AL | 17 | 2 | 0 | 1 | 32.1 | 139 | 36 | 18 | 13 | 5 | 2 | 1 | 3 | 14 | 1 | 26 | 0 | 1 | 1 | 3 | .250 | 0 | 0-0 | 1 | 5.96 | 3.62 |
| 11 Sea | AL | 11 | 10 | 0 | 0 | 53.0 | 233 | 61 | 41 | 39 | 11 | 0 | 3 | 3 | 16 | 1 | 41 | 2 | 0 | 3 | 7 | .300 | 0 | 0-0 | 0 | 5.57 | 6.62 |
| 3 ML YEARS | | 147 | 12 | 0 | 14 | 196.2 | 834 | 173 | 107 | 93 | 24 | 6 | 10 | 11 | 75 | 8 | 200 | 10 | 1 | 11 | 18 | .379 | 0 | 0-6 | 27 | 3.64 | 4.26 |

# Rafael Furcal

**Bats:** B **Throws:** R **Pos:** SS **Ht:** 5'8" **Wt:** 195 **Born:** 10/24/1977 **Age:** 36

| BATTING | | | | | | | | | | | | | | | | | | | | | BASERUNNING | | | | AVERAGES | | |
|---|---|---|---|---|---|---|---|---|---|---|---|---|---|---|---|---|---|---|---|---|---|---|---|---|---|---|---|
| Year | Team | Lg | G | AB | H | 2B | 3B | HR | (Hm | Rd) | TB | R | RBI | RC | TBB | IBB | SO | HBP | SH | SF | SB | CS | SB% | GDP | Avg | OBP | Slg |
| 2000 | Atl | NL | 131 | 455 | 134 | 20 | 4 | 4 | (1 | 3) | 174 | 87 | 37 | 78 | 73 | 0 | 80 | 3 | 9 | 2 | 40 | 14 | .74 | 2 | .295 | .394 | .382 |
| 2001 | Atl | NL | 79 | 324 | 89 | 19 | 0 | 4 | (3 | 1) | 120 | 39 | 30 | 41 | 24 | 1 | 56 | 1 | 4 | 6 | 22 | 6 | .79 | 5 | .275 | .321 | .370 |
| 2002 | Atl | NL | 154 | 636 | 175 | 31 | 8 | 8 | (4 | 4) | 246 | 95 | 47 | 80 | 43 | 0 | 114 | 3 | 9 | 2 | 27 | 15 | .64 | 8 | .275 | .323 | .387 |
| 2003 | Atl | NL | 156 | 664 | 194 | 35 | **10** | 15 | (4 | 11) | 294 | 130 | 61 | 107 | 60 | 2 | 76 | 3 | 3 | 4 | 25 | 2 | **.93** | 1 | .292 | .352 | .443 |
| 2004 | Atl | NL | 143 | 563 | 157 | 24 | 5 | 14 | (5 | 9) | 233 | 103 | 59 | 82 | 58 | 4 | 71 | 1 | 5 | 5 | 29 | 6 | .83 | 9 | .279 | .344 | .414 |
| 2005 | Atl | NL | 154 | 616 | 175 | 31 | 11 | 12 | (9 | 3) | 264 | 100 | 58 | 98 | 62 | 3 | 78 | 1 | 5 | 5 | 46 | 10 | .82 | 11 | .284 | .348 | .429 |
| 2006 | LAD | NL | 159 | 654 | 196 | 32 | 9 | 15 | (12 | 3) | 291 | 113 | 63 | 110 | 73 | 3 | 98 | 1 | 5 | 3 | 37 | 13 | .74 | 7 | .300 | .369 | .445 |
| 2007 | LAD | NL | 138 | 581 | 157 | 23 | 4 | 6 | (4 | 2) | 206 | 87 | 47 | 65 | 55 | 3 | 68 | 1 | 2 | 3 | 25 | 6 | .81 | 11 | .270 | .333 | .355 |
| 2008 | LAD | NL | 36 | 143 | 51 | 12 | 2 | 5 | (3 | 2) | 82 | 34 | 16 | 33 | 20 | 0 | 17 | 1 | 0 | 0 | 8 | 3 | .73 | 3 | .357 | .439 | .573 |
| 2009 | LAD | NL | 150 | 613 | 165 | 28 | 5 | 9 | (5 | 4) | 230 | 92 | 47 | 73 | 61 | 2 | 89 | 1 | 3 | 2 | 12 | 6 | .67 | 11 | .269 | .335 | .375 |
| 2010 | LAD | NL | 97 | 383 | 115 | 23 | 7 | 8 | (5 | 3) | 176 | 66 | 43 | 66 | 40 | 5 | 60 | 1 | 2 | 2 | 22 | 4 | .85 | 5 | .300 | .366 | .460 |
| 2011 | 2 Tms | NL | 87 | 333 | 77 | 15 | 0 | 8 | (5 | 3) | 116 | 44 | 28 | 31 | 28 | 0 | 39 | 4 | 3 | 1 | 9 | 5 | .64 | 3 | .231 | .298 | .348 |
| 2012 | StL | NL | 121 | 477 | 126 | 18 | 3 | 5 | (2 | 3) | 165 | 69 | 49 | 57 | 44 | 1 | 57 | 1 | 5 | 4 | 12 | 4 | .75 | 7 | .264 | .325 | .346 |
| 11 | LAD | NL | 37 | 137 | 27 | 4 | 0 | 1 | (1 | 0) | 34 | 15 | 12 | 12 | 11 | 0 | 21 | 3 | 1 | 0 | 5 | 3 | .63 | 0 | .197 | .272 | .248 |
| 11 | StL | NL | 50 | 196 | 50 | 11 | 0 | 7 | (4 | 3) | 82 | 29 | 16 | 19 | 17 | 0 | 18 | 1 | 2 | 1 | 4 | 2 | .67 | 3 | .255 | .316 | .418 |
| Postseason | | | 59 | 247 | 56 | 5 | 5 | 4 | (3 | 1) | 83 | 33 | 16 | 25 | 27 | 1 | 34 | 2 | 7 | 2 | 13 | 2 | .87 | 2 | .227 | .306 | .336 |
| 13 ML YEARS | | | 1605 | 6442 | 1811 | 311 | 68 | 113 | (62 | 51) | 2597 | 1059 | 585 | 921 | 641 | 24 | 903 | 22 | 55 | 39 | 314 | 94 | .77 | 83 | .281 | .346 | .403 |

# Yovani Gallardo

**Pitches:** R **Bats:** R **Pos:** SP-31 guy-YARR-doe **Ht:** 6'2" **Wt:** 215 **Born:** 2/27/1986 **Age:** 28

| HOW MUCH HE PITCHED | | | | | | | | | WHAT HE GAVE UP | | | | | | | | | | | | THE RESULTS | | | | | | | |
|---|---|---|---|---|---|---|---|---|---|---|---|---|---|---|---|---|---|---|---|---|---|---|---|---|---|---|---|---|
| Year | Team | Lg | G | GS | CG | GF | IP | BFP | H | R | ER | HR | SH | SF | HB | TBB | IBB | SO | WP | Bk | W | L | Pct | Sh | Sv-Op | Hld | ERC | ERA |
| 2007 | Mil | NL | 20 | 17 | 0 | 1 | 110.1 | 466 | 103 | 48 | 45 | 8 | 4 | 3 | 2 | 37 | 2 | 101 | 3 | 0 | 9 | 5 | .643 | 0 | 0-0 | 0 | 3.30 | 3.67 |
| 2008 | Mil | NL | 4 | 4 | 0 | 0 | 24.0 | 97 | 22 | 5 | 5 | 3 | 2 | 1 | 0 | 8 | 0 | 20 | 0 | 0 | 0 | 0 | - | 0 | 0-0 | 0 | 3.66 | 1.88 |
| 2009 | Mil | NL | 30 | 30 | 1 | 0 | 185.2 | 793 | 150 | 78 | 77 | 21 | 5 | 3 | 5 | 94 | 5 | 204 | 9 | 0 | 13 | 12 | .520 | 0 | 0-0 | 0 | 3.57 | 3.73 |
| 2010 | Mil | NL | 31 | 31 | 2 | 0 | 185.0 | 803 | 178 | 89 | 79 | 12 | 11 | 4 | 3 | 75 | 5 | 200 | 7 | 1 | 14 | 7 | .667 | 2 | 0-0 | 0 | 3.61 | 3.84 |
| 2011 | Mil | NL | 33 | 33 | 1 | 0 | 207.1 | 865 | 193 | 92 | 81 | 27 | 10 | 7 | 1 | 59 | 1 | 207 | 12 | 0 | 17 | 10 | .630 | 1 | 0-0 | 0 | 3.43 | 3.52 |
| 2012 | Mil | NL | 33 | **33** | 0 | 0 | 204.0 | 860 | 185 | 86 | 83 | 26 | 11 | 6 | 0 | 81 | 3 | 204 | 5 | 0 | 16 | 9 | .640 | 0 | 0-0 | 0 | 3.72 | 3.66 |
| 2013 | Mil | NL | 31 | 31 | 0 | 0 | 180.2 | 773 | 180 | 92 | 84 | 18 | 8 | 7 | 3 | 66 | 1 | 144 | 5 | 0 | 12 | 10 | .545 | 0 | 0-0 | 0 | 3.98 | 4.18 |
| Postseason | | | 5 | 4 | 0 | 0 | 26.0 | 109 | 22 | 9 | 6 | 2 | 1 | 0 | 0 | 13 | 3 | 20 | 4 | 0 | 1 | 2 | .333 | 0 | 0-0 | 0 | 3.34 | 2.08 |
| 7 ML YEARS | | | 182 | 179 | 4 | 1 | 1097.0 | 4657 | 1011 | 490 | 454 | 115 | 51 | 31 | 14 | 420 | 17 | 1080 | 41 | 1 | 81 | 53 | .604 | 3 | 0-0 | 0 | 3.62 | 3.72 |

# Freddy Galvis

**Bats:** B **Throws:** R **Pos:** 2B-23;3B-16;PH-14;SS-11;LF-10 GAL-viss **Ht:** 5'10" **Wt:** 170 **Born:** 11/14/1989 **Age:** 24

| BATTING | | | | | | | | | | | | | | | | | | | | | BASERUNNING | | | | AVERAGES | | |
|---|---|---|---|---|---|---|---|---|---|---|---|---|---|---|---|---|---|---|---|---|---|---|---|---|---|---|---|
| Year | Team | Lg | G | AB | H | 2B | 3B | HR | (Hm | Rd) | TB | R | RBI | RC | TBB | IBB | SO | HBP | SH | SF | SB | CS | SB% | GDP | Avg | OBP | Slg |
| 2009 | Clrwtr | A+ | 63 | 251 | 62 | 8 | 2 | 1 | (- | -) | 77 | 29 | 15 | 22 | 10 | 0 | 43 | 2 | 8 | 1 | 6 | 3 | .67 | 4 | .247 | .280 | .307 |
| 2009 | Phillies | R | 7 | 29 | 8 | 1 | 0 | 0 | (- | -) | 9 | 6 | 0 | 2 | 1 | 0 | 4 | 0 | 0 | 0 | 1 | 1 | .50 | 3 | .276 | .300 | .310 |
| 2009 | Rdng | AA | 16 | 61 | 12 | 0 | 0 | 1 | (- | -) | 15 | 6 | 5 | 2 | 2 | 0 | 7 | 0 | 0 | 0 | 0 | 1 | .00 | 0 | .197 | .222 | .246 |
| 2010 | Rdng | AA | 138 | 501 | 117 | 16 | 4 | 5 | (- | -) | 156 | 58 | 48 | 45 | 30 | 2 | 89 | 1 | 8 | 4 | 15 | 4 | .79 | 8 | .234 | .276 | .311 |
| 2011 | Rdng | AA | 104 | 422 | 115 | 22 | 4 | 8 | (- | -) | 169 | 63 | 35 | 56 | 28 | 0 | 68 | 6 | 7 | 1 | 19 | 11 | .63 | 3 | .273 | .326 | .400 |
| 2011 | LV | AAA | 33 | 121 | 36 | 6 | 1 | 0 | (- | -) | 44 | 15 | 8 | 13 | 3 | 1 | 18 | 0 | 2 | 0 | 4 | 2 | .67 | 2 | .298 | .315 | .364 |
| 2013 | LV | AAA | 62 | 241 | 59 | 14 | 2 | 3 | (- | -) | 86 | 26 | 25 | 25 | 11 | 0 | 51 | 1 | 7 | 6 | 3 | 1 | .75 | 7 | .245 | .274 | .357 |
| 2012 | Phi | NL | 58 | 190 | 43 | 15 | 1 | 3 | (3 | 0) | 69 | 14 | 24 | 14 | 7 | 0 | 29 | 0 | 3 | 0 | 0 | 0 | - | 6 | .226 | .254 | .363 |
| 2013 | Phi | NL | 70 | 205 | 48 | 5 | 4 | 6 | (4 | 2) | 79 | 13 | 19 | 20 | 13 | 2 | 45 | 1 | 3 | 0 | 1 | 0 | 1.00 | 5 | .234 | .283 | .385 |
| 2 ML YEARS | | | 128 | 395 | 91 | 20 | 5 | 9 | (7 | 2) | 148 | 27 | 43 | 34 | 20 | 2 | 74 | 1 | 6 | 0 | 1 | 0 | 1.00 | 11 | .230 | .269 | .375 |

# Mat Gamel

**Bats:** L **Throws:** R **Pos:** 1B GAMM-ell **Ht:** 6'1" **Wt:** 220 **Born:** 7/26/1985 **Age:** 28

| BATTING | | | | | | | | | | | | | | | | | | | | | BASERUNNING | | | | AVERAGES | | |
|---|---|---|---|---|---|---|---|---|---|---|---|---|---|---|---|---|---|---|---|---|---|---|---|---|---|---|---|
| Year | Team | Lg | G | AB | H | 2B | 3B | HR | (Hm | Rd) | TB | R | RBI | RC | TBB | IBB | SO | HBP | SH | SF | SB | CS | SB% | GDP | Avg | OBP | Slg |
| 2008 | Mil | NL | 2 | 2 | 1 | 1 | 0 | 0 | (0 | 0) | 2 | 0 | 0 | 1 | 0 | 0 | 1 | 0 | 0 | 0 | 0 | 0 | - | 0 | .500 | .500 | 1.000 |
| 2009 | Mil | NL | 61 | 128 | 31 | 6 | 1 | 5 | (4 | 1) | 54 | 11 | 20 | 20 | 18 | 2 | 54 | 1 | 0 | 1 | 1 | 0 | 1.00 | 1 | .242 | .338 | .422 |
| 2010 | Mil | NL | 12 | 15 | 3 | 1 | 0 | 0 | (0 | 0) | 4 | 1 | 1 | 1 | 1 | 0 | 8 | 1 | 0 | 0 | 0 | 0 | - | 1 | .200 | .294 | .267 |
| 2011 | Mil | NL | 10 | 26 | 3 | 1 | 0 | 0 | (0 | 0) | 4 | 1 | 2 | 2 | 1 | 0 | 4 | 0 | 0 | 0 | 0 | 0 | - | 1 | .115 | .148 | .154 |
| 2012 | Mil | NL | 21 | 69 | 17 | 2 | 1 | 1 | (1 | 0) | 24 | 10 | 6 | 8 | 4 | 0 | 15 | 1 | 0 | 1 | 3 | 0 | 1.00 | 0 | .246 | .293 | .348 |
| 5 ML YEARS | | | 106 | 240 | 55 | 11 | 2 | 6 | (5 | 1) | 88 | 23 | 29 | 32 | 24 | 2 | 82 | 3 | 0 | 2 | 4 | 0 | 1.00 | 3 | .229 | .305 | .367 |

# Avisail Garcia

**Bats:** R **Throws:** R **Pos:** RF-41;CF-31;PH-10;LF-3 ah-vee-sigh-EEL **Ht:** 6'4" **Wt:** 240 **Born:** 6/12/1991 **Age:** 23

| BATTING | | | | | | | | | | | | | | | | | | | | | BASERUNNING | | | | AVERAGES | | |
|---|---|---|---|---|---|---|---|---|---|---|---|---|---|---|---|---|---|---|---|---|---|---|---|---|---|---|---|
| Year | Team | Lg | G | AB | H | 2B | 3B | HR | (Hm | Rd) | TB | R | RBI | RC | TBB | IBB | SO | HBP | SH | SF | SB | CS | SB% | GDP | Avg | OBP | Slg |
| 2009 | Lkland | A+ | 3 | 8 | 2 | 0 | 0 | 0 | (- | -) | 2 | 1 | 0 | 0 | 0 | 0 | 2 | 0 | 0 | 0 | 0 | 0 | - | 0 | .250 | .250 | .250 |
| 2009 | WMich | A | 81 | 299 | 79 | 11 | 2 | 1 | (- | -) | 97 | 36 | 31 | 27 | 8 | 0 | 70 | 4 | 0 | 4 | 8 | 7 | .53 | 13 | .264 | .289 | .324 |
| 2010 | WMich | A | 125 | 494 | 139 | 17 | 4 | 4 | (- | -) | 176 | 58 | 63 | 59 | 20 | 1 | 113 | 5 | 0 | 5 | 20 | 4 | .83 | 14 | .281 | .313 | .356 |
| 2011 | Lkland | A+ | 129 | 488 | 129 | 16 | 6 | 11 | (- | -) | 190 | 53 | 56 | 58 | 18 | 1 | 132 | 6 | 0 | 3 | 14 | 5 | .74 | 17 | .264 | .297 | .389 |
| 2012 | Lkland | A+ | 67 | 266 | 77 | 8 | 5 | 8 | (- | -) | 119 | 47 | 36 | 40 | 11 | 1 | 57 | 5 | 0 | 5 | 14 | 4 | .78 | 8 | .289 | .324 | .447 |
| 2012 | Erie | AA | 55 | 215 | 67 | 9 | 3 | 6 | (- | -) | 100 | 31 | 22 | 34 | 7 | 0 | 38 | 4 | 0 | 0 | 9 | 4 | .69 | 9 | .312 | .345 | .465 |
| 2013 | Lkland | A+ | 6 | 24 | 10 | 0 | 2 | 1 | (- | -) | 17 | 9 | 4 | 8 | 4 | 0 | 1 | 0 | 0 | 0 | 2 | 0 | 1.00 | 1 | .417 | .500 | .708 |
| 2013 | Toledo | AAA | 33 | 147 | 55 | 7 | 1 | 5 | (- | -) | 79 | 23 | 23 | 30 | 8 | 0 | 32 | 1 | 0 | 0 | 4 | 2 | .67 | 1 | .374 | .410 | .537 |
| 2013 | Charltt | AAA | 8 | 27 | 10 | 0 | 1 | 1 | (- | -) | 15 | 6 | 9 | 6 | 4 | 0 | 4 | 1 | 0 | 0 | 0 | 0 | - | 2 | .370 | .469 | .556 |
| 2012 | Det | AL | 23 | 47 | 15 | 0 | 0 | 0 | (0 | 0) | 15 | 7 | 3 | 5 | 3 | 1 | 10 | 1 | 0 | 0 | 0 | 2 | .00 | 1 | .319 | .373 | .319 |
| 2013 | 2 Tms | AL | 72 | 244 | 69 | 7 | 3 | 7 | (3 | 4) | 103 | 31 | 31 | 30 | 9 | 0 | 59 | 1 | 0 | 2 | 3 | 3 | .50 | 8 | .283 | .309 | .422 |

| | | | BATTING | | | | | | | | | | | | | | | | | | BASERUNNING | | | | AVERAGES | | |
|---|---|---|---|---|---|---|---|---|---|---|---|---|---|---|---|---|---|---|---|---|---|---|---|---|---|---|---|
| Year | Team | Lg | G | AB | H | 2B | 3B | HR | (Hm | Rd) | TB | R | RBI | RC | TBB | IBB | SO | HBP | SH | SF | SB | CS | SB% | GDP | Avg | OBP | Slg |
| 13 | Det | AL | 30 | 83 | 20 | 3 | 1 | 2 | (1 | 1) | 31 | 12 | 10 | 7 | 4 | 0 | 21 | 0 | 0 | 1 | 0 | 1 | .00 | 3 | .241 | .273 | .373 |
| 13 | CWS | AL | 42 | 161 | 49 | 4 | 2 | 5 | (2 | 3) | 72 | 19 | 21 | 23 | 5 | 0 | 38 | 1 | 0 | 1 | 3 | 2 | .60 | 5 | .304 | .327 | .447 |
| Postseason | | | 12 | 23 | 6 | 1 | 0 | 0 | (0 | 0) | 7 | 0 | 4 | 4 | 2 | 0 | 5 | 0 | 0 | 0 | 1 | 0 | 1.00 | 0 | .261 | .320 | .304 |
| 2 ML YEARS | | | 95 | 291 | 84 | 7 | 3 | 7 | (3 | 4) | 118 | 38 | 34 | 35 | 12 | 1 | 69 | 2 | 0 | 2 | 3 | 5 | .38 | 9 | .289 | .319 | .405 |

# Freddy Garcia

**Pitches:** R **Bats:** R **Pos:** SP-13; RP-4 **Ht:** 6'4" **Wt:** 255 **Born:** 10/6/1976 **Age:** 37

| | | | HOW MUCH HE PITCHED | | | | | | WHAT HE GAVE UP | | | | | | | | | | | | THE RESULTS | | | | | | | |
|---|---|---|---|---|---|---|---|---|---|---|---|---|---|---|---|---|---|---|---|---|---|---|---|---|---|---|---|---|
| Year | Team | Lg | G | GS | CG | GF | IP | BFP | H | R | ER | HR | SH | SF | HB | TBB | IBB | SO | WP | Bk | W | L | Pct | Sh | Sv-Op | Hld | ERC | ERA |
| 2013 | Norfolk* | AAA | 13 | 13 | 0 | 0 | 82.1 | 326 | 73 | 28 | 26 | 10 | 2 | 4 | 0 | 15 | 0 | 61 | 5 | 0 | 8 | 3 | .727 | 0 | 0-- | - | 2.81 | 2.84 |
| 2013 | Gwnntt* | AAA | 1 | 1 | 0 | 0 | 3.2 | 23 | 7 | 8 | 8 | 1 | 0 | 0 | 0 | 5 | 0 | 1 | 2 | 0 | 0 | 1 | .000 | 0 | 0-- | - | 16.17 | 19.64 |
| 1999 | Sea | AL | 33 | 33 | 2 | 0 | 201.1 | 888 | 205 | 96 | 91 | 18 | 3 | 6 | 10 | 90 | 4 | 170 | 12 | **3** | 17 | 8 | .680 | 1 | 0-0 | 0 | 4.46 | 4.07 |
| 2000 | Sea | AL | 21 | 20 | 0 | 0 | 124.1 | 538 | 112 | 62 | 54 | 16 | 6 | 1 | 2 | 64 | 4 | 79 | 4 | 2 | 9 | 5 | .643 | 0 | 0-0 | 0 | 4.20 | 3.91 |
| 2001 | Sea | AL | 34 | 34 | 4 | 0 | **238.2** | 971 | 199 | 88 | 81 | 16 | 8 | 5 | 5 | 69 | 6 | 163 | 3 | 1 | 18 | 6 | .750 | 3 | 0-0 | 0 | **2.61** | **3.05** |
| 2002 | Sea | AL | 34 | 34 | 1 | 0 | 223.2 | 955 | 227 | 110 | 109 | 30 | 4 | 8 | 6 | 63 | 3 | 181 | 7 | 1 | 16 | 10 | .615 | 0 | 0-0 | 0 | 3.98 | 4.39 |
| 2003 | Sea | AL | 33 | 33 | 1 | 0 | 201.1 | 862 | 196 | 109 | 101 | 31 | 2 | 8 | 11 | 71 | 2 | 144 | 11 | 0 | 12 | 14 | .462 | 0 | 0-0 | 0 | 4.33 | 4.51 |
| 2004 | 2 Tms | AL | 31 | 31 | 1 | 0 | 210.0 | 878 | 192 | 92 | 89 | 22 | 8 | 3 | 7 | 64 | 3 | 184 | 8 | 0 | 13 | 11 | .542 | 0 | 0-0 | 0 | 3.37 | 3.81 |
| 2005 | CWS | AL | 33 | 33 | 2 | 0 | 228.0 | 943 | 225 | 102 | 98 | 26 | 5 | 5 | 3 | 60 | 2 | 146 | **20** | 1 | 14 | 8 | .636 | 0 | 0-0 | 0 | 3.65 | 3.87 |
| 2006 | CWS | AL | 33 | 33 | 1 | 0 | 216.1 | 917 | 228 | 116 | 109 | 32 | 1 | 6 | 7 | 48 | 3 | 135 | 4 | 0 | 17 | 9 | .654 | 0 | 0-0 | 0 | 4.09 | 4.53 |
| 2007 | Phi | NL | 11 | 11 | 0 | 0 | 58.0 | 264 | 74 | 39 | 38 | 12 | 4 | 3 | 5 | 19 | 3 | 50 | 5 | 0 | 1 | 5 | .167 | 0 | 0-0 | 0 | 6.57 | 5.90 |
| 2008 | Det | AL | 3 | 3 | 0 | 0 | 15.0 | 61 | 11 | 8 | 7 | 3 | 0 | 0 | 1 | 6 | 0 | 12 | 0 | 0 | 1 | 1 | .500 | 0 | 0-0 | 0 | 3.61 | 4.20 |
| 2009 | CWS | AL | 9 | 9 | 0 | 0 | 56.0 | 229 | 56 | 27 | 27 | 4 | 0 | 1 | 0 | 12 | 0 | 37 | 2 | 0 | 3 | 4 | .429 | 0 | 0-0 | 0 | 3.21 | 4.34 |
| 2010 | CWS | AL | 28 | 28 | 0 | 0 | 157.0 | 671 | 171 | 85 | 81 | 23 | 5 | 4 | 3 | 45 | 5 | 89 | 4 | 0 | 12 | 6 | .667 | 0 | 0-0 | 0 | 4.52 | 4.64 |
| 2011 | NYY | AL | 26 | 25 | 0 | 1 | 146.2 | 626 | 152 | 63 | 59 | 16 | 4 | 7 | 3 | 45 | 5 | 96 | 4 | 0 | 12 | 8 | .600 | 0 | 0-0 | 0 | 4.01 | 3.62 |
| 2012 | NYY | AL | 30 | 17 | 0 | 10 | 107.1 | 461 | 112 | 64 | 62 | 18 | 4 | 4 | 3 | 35 | 2 | 89 | 10 | 1 | 7 | 6 | .538 | 0 | 0-0 | 0 | 4.60 | 5.20 |
| 2013 | 2 Tms | | 17 | 13 | 0 | 2 | 80.1 | 331 | 83 | 40 | 39 | 18 | 5 | 1 | 1 | 17 | 0 | 46 | 1 | 0 | 4 | 7 | .364 | 0 | 0-0 | 0 | 4.46 | 4.37 |
| 04 | Sea | AL | 15 | 15 | 1 | 0 | 107.0 | 446 | 96 | 39 | 38 | 8 | 4 | 1 | 2 | 32 | 1 | 82 | 5 | 0 | 4 | 7 | .364 | 0 | 0-0 | 0 | 3.00 | 3.20 |
| 04 | CWS | AL | 16 | 16 | 0 | 0 | 103.0 | 432 | 96 | 53 | 51 | 14 | 4 | 2 | 5 | 32 | 2 | 102 | 3 | 0 | 9 | 4 | .692 | 0 | 0-0 | 0 | 3.77 | 4.46 |
| 13 | Bal | AL | 11 | 10 | 0 | 1 | 53.0 | 225 | 60 | 35 | 34 | 16 | 2 | 1 | 1 | 12 | 0 | 26 | 0 | 0 | 3 | 5 | .375 | 0 | 0-0 | 0 | 5.69 | 5.77 |
| 13 | Atl | NL | 6 | 3 | 0 | 1 | 27.1 | 106 | 23 | 5 | 5 | 2 | 3 | 0 | 0 | 5 | 0 | 20 | 1 | 0 | 1 | 2 | .333 | 0 | 0-0 | 0 | 2.34 | 1.65 |
| Postseason | | | 10 | 10 | 1 | 0 | 60.1 | 253 | 57 | 24 | 22 | 6 | 2 | 0 | 2 | 22 | 1 | 51 | 1 | 0 | 6 | 3 | .667 | 0 | 0-0 | 0 | 3.80 | 3.28 |
| 15 ML YEARS | | | 376 | 357 | 12 | 13 | 2264.0 | 9595 | 2243 | 1101 | 1045 | 285 | 59 | 62 | 67 | 708 | 42 | 1621 | 95 | 9 | 156 | 108 | .591 | 4 | 0-0 | 0 | 3.96 | 4.15 |

# Jaime Garcia

HY-may

**Pitches:** L **Bats:** L **Pos:** SP-9 **Ht:** 6'2" **Wt:** 215 **Born:** 7/8/1986 **Age:** 27

| | | | HOW MUCH HE PITCHED | | | | | | WHAT HE GAVE UP | | | | | | | | | | | | THE RESULTS | | | | | | | |
|---|---|---|---|---|---|---|---|---|---|---|---|---|---|---|---|---|---|---|---|---|---|---|---|---|---|---|---|---|
| Year | Team | Lg | G | GS | CG | GF | IP | BFP | H | R | ER | HR | SH | SF | HB | TBB | IBB | SO | WP | Bk | W | L | Pct | Sh | Sv-Op | Hld | ERC | ERA |
| 2008 | StL | NL | 10 | 1 | 0 | 4 | 16.0 | 69 | 14 | 10 | 10 | 4 | 0 | 0 | 1 | 8 | 0 | 8 | 3 | 0 | 1 | 1 | .500 | 0 | 0-0 | 3 | 5.15 | 5.63 |
| 2010 | StL | NL | 28 | 28 | 1 | 0 | 163.1 | 695 | 151 | 64 | 49 | 9 | 3 | 3 | 3 | 64 | 4 | 132 | 4 | 1 | 13 | 8 | .619 | 1 | 0-0 | 0 | 3.34 | 2.70 |
| 2011 | StL | NL | 32 | 32 | 2 | 0 | 194.2 | 826 | 207 | 100 | 77 | 15 | 10 | 5 | 2 | 50 | 2 | 156 | 12 | 1 | 13 | 7 | .650 | 2 | 0-0 | 0 | 3.73 | 3.56 |
| 2012 | StL | NL | 20 | 20 | 0 | 0 | 121.2 | 515 | 136 | 58 | 53 | 7 | 8 | 7 | 0 | 30 | 1 | 98 | 12 | 1 | 7 | 7 | .500 | 0 | 0-0 | 0 | 3.86 | 3.92 |
| 2013 | StL | NL | 9 | 9 | 0 | 0 | 55.1 | 234 | 57 | 26 | 22 | 6 | 2 | 0 | 0 | 15 | 0 | 43 | 3 | 0 | 5 | 2 | .714 | 0 | 0-0 | 0 | 3.78 | 3.58 |
| Postseason | | | 6 | 6 | 0 | 0 | 27.2 | 120 | 29 | 13 | 13 | 3 | 1 | 0 | 1 | 11 | 2 | 24 | 1 | 0 | 0 | 2 | .000 | 0 | 0-0 | 0 | 4.48 | 4.23 |
| 5 ML YEARS | | | 99 | 90 | 3 | 4 | 551.0 | 2339 | 565 | 258 | 211 | 41 | 23 | 15 | 6 | 167 | 7 | 437 | 34 | 3 | 39 | 25 | .609 | 3 | 0-0 | 3 | 3.69 | 3.45 |

# Leury Garcia

lay-OOH-ree

**Bats:** B **Throws:** R **Pos:** 2B-21;PH-9;SS-7;3B-6;CF-6;PR-4;DH-3 **Ht:** 5'7" **Wt:** 160 **Born:** 3/18/1991 **Age:** 23

| | | | BATTING | | | | | | | | | | | | | | | | | | BASERUNNING | | | | AVERAGES | | |
|---|---|---|---|---|---|---|---|---|---|---|---|---|---|---|---|---|---|---|---|---|---|---|---|---|---|---|---|
| Year | Team | Lg | G | AB | H | 2B | 3B | HR | (Hm | Rd) | TB | R | RBI | RC | TBB | IBB | SO | HBP | SH | SF | SB | CS | SB% | GDP | Avg | OBP | Slg |
| 2009 | Hkry | A | 83 | 276 | 64 | 6 | 3 | 1 | (- | -) | 79 | 28 | 18 | 25 | 18 | 0 | 64 | 4 | 9 | 1 | 19 | 6 | .76 | 2 | .232 | .288 | .286 |
| 2010 | Hkry | A | 89 | 359 | 94 | 5 | 4 | 3 | (- | -) | 116 | 57 | 22 | 42 | 23 | 0 | 57 | 1 | 8 | 1 | 47 | 9 | .84 | 4 | .262 | .307 | .323 |
| 2010 | Rngrs | R | 6 | 18 | 9 | 2 | 0 | 0 | (- | -) | 11 | 5 | 2 | 6 | 4 | 0 | 4 | 0 | 0 | 0 | 4 | 2 | .67 | 0 | .500 | .591 | .611 |
| 2011 | MrtlBh | A+ | 109 | 442 | 113 | 19 | 5 | 3 | (- | -) | 151 | 65 | 38 | 49 | 28 | 1 | 100 | 4 | 8 | 0 | 30 | 12 | .71 | 7 | .256 | .306 | .342 |
| 2012 | Frisco | AA | 100 | 377 | 110 | 12 | 11 | 2 | (- | -) | 150 | 55 | 30 | 55 | 22 | 2 | 79 | 5 | 9 | 3 | 31 | 7 | .82 | 3 | .292 | .337 | .398 |
| 2013 | RdRck | AAA | 47 | 193 | 51 | 8 | 4 | 4 | (- | -) | 79 | 31 | 19 | 26 | 14 | 0 | 53 | 0 | 1 | 0 | 12 | 4 | .75 | 5 | .264 | .314 | .409 |
| 2013 | Charltt | AAA | 8 | 30 | 8 | 1 | 0 | 0 | (- | -) | 9 | 3 | 1 | 3 | 1 | 0 | 8 | 1 | 0 | 0 | 3 | 0 | 1.00 | 0 | .267 | .313 | .300 |
| 2013 | 2 Tms | AL | 45 | 101 | 20 | 1 | 1 | 0 | (0 | 0) | 23 | 10 | 2 | 4 | 7 | 0 | 34 | 0 | 2 | 1 | 7 | 2 | .78 | 0 | .198 | .248 | .228 |
| 13 | Tex | AL | 25 | 52 | 10 | 0 | 1 | 0 | (0 | 0) | 12 | 8 | 1 | 2 | 3 | 0 | 16 | 0 | 2 | 0 | 1 | 0 | 1.00 | 0 | .192 | .236 | .231 |
| 13 | CWS | AL | 20 | 49 | 10 | 1 | 0 | 0 | (0 | 0) | 11 | 2 | 1 | 2 | 4 | 0 | 18 | 0 | 0 | 1 | 6 | 2 | .75 | 0 | .204 | .259 | .224 |

# Luis Garcia

**Pitches:** R **Bats:** R **Pos:** RP-24 **Ht:** 6'2" **Wt:** 215 **Born:** 1/30/1987 **Age:** 27

| | | | HOW MUCH HE PITCHED | | | | | | WHAT HE GAVE UP | | | | | | | | | | | | THE RESULTS | | | | | | | |
|---|---|---|---|---|---|---|---|---|---|---|---|---|---|---|---|---|---|---|---|---|---|---|---|---|---|---|---|---|
| Year | Team | Lg | G | GS | CG | GF | IP | BFP | H | R | ER | HR | SH | SF | HB | TBB | IBB | SO | WP | Bk | W | L | Pct | Sh | Sv-Op | Hld | ERC | ERA |
| 2009 | Gt Lks | A | 34 | 0 | 0 | 15 | 71.0 | 296 | 68 | 27 | 23 | 5 | 1 | 2 | 1 | 15 | 1 | 55 | 7 | 0 | 5 | 3 | .625 | 0 | 5-- | - | 2.91 | 2.92 |
| 2009 | Ptomc | A+ | 2 | 0 | 0 | 0 | 4.0 | 13 | 0 | 0 | 0 | 0 | 0 | 0 | 0 | 1 | 0 | 7 | 0 | 0 | 1 | 0 | 1.000 | 0 | 0-- | - | 0.07 | 0.00 |
| 2010 | Ptomc | A+ | 6 | 0 | 0 | 1 | 8.2 | 57 | 21 | 17 | 10 | 0 | 3 | 1 | 0 | 10 | 0 | 3 | 2 | 0 | 0 | 0 | - | 0 | 0-- | - | 15.85 | 10.38 |
| 2010 | Hgrstn | A | 26 | 0 | 0 | 5 | 51.0 | 221 | 48 | 25 | 22 | 3 | 6 | 0 | 5 | 17 | 1 | 43 | 10 | 0 | 4 | 4 | .500 | 0 | 0-- | - | 3.50 | 3.88 |
| 2013 | LV | AAA | 8 | 0 | 0 | 6 | 11.0 | 42 | 5 | 1 | 1 | 0 | 0 | 0 | 0 | 4 | 0 | 8 | 2 | 0 | 0 | 0 | - | 0 | 3-- | - | 1.03 | 0.82 |
| 2013 | Clrwtr | A+ | 14 | 0 | 0 | 10 | 19.2 | 78 | 15 | 3 | 3 | 2 | 0 | 0 | 1 | 5 | 0 | 20 | 0 | 0 | 0 | 1 | .000 | 0 | 7-- | - | 2.52 | 1.37 |
| 2013 | Rdng | AA | 11 | 0 | 0 | 8 | 11.0 | 43 | 10 | 3 | 3 | 1 | 0 | 0 | 0 | 3 | 0 | 13 | 2 | 0 | 2 | 1 | .667 | 0 | 1-- | - | 3.22 | 2.45 |
| 2013 | Phi | NL | 24 | 0 | 0 | 6 | 31.1 | 138 | 27 | 15 | 13 | 3 | 0 | 0 | 1 | 23 | 0 | 23 | 3 | 0 | 1 | 1 | .500 | 0 | 0-0 | 1 | 4.85 | 3.73 |

# Onelki Garcia

**Pitches:** L **Bats:** L **Pos:** RP-3 oh-NELL-key **Ht:** 6'3" **Wt:** 220 **Born:** 8/2/1989 **Age:** 24

| HOW MUCH HE PITCHED | | | | | | | | | WHAT HE GAVE UP | | | | | | | | | | | | THE RESULTS | | | | | | | |
|---|---|---|---|---|---|---|---|---|---|---|---|---|---|---|---|---|---|---|---|---|---|---|---|---|---|---|---|---|
| Year | Team | Lg | G | GS | CG | GF | IP | BFP | H | R | ER | HR | SH | SF | HB | TBB | IBB | SO | WP | Bk | W | L | Pct | Sh | Sv-Op | Hld | ERC | ERA |
| 2012 | RCuca | A+ | 1 | 1 | 0 | 0 | 2.0 | 6 | 0 | 0 | 0 | 0 | 0 | 0 | 0 | 0 | 0 | 4 | 0 | 0 | 0 | 0 | - | 0 | 0- - | - | 0.00 | 0.00 |
| 2013 | Chatt | AA | 25 | 6 | 0 | 6 | 52.1 | 227 | 41 | 19 | 16 | 3 | 1 | 1 | 2 | 32 | 0 | 53 | 6 | 4 | 2 | 3 | .400 | 0 | 1- - | - | 3.54 | 2.75 |
| 2013 | Albq | AAA | 10 | 0 | 0 | 1 | 9.2 | 37 | 5 | 4 | 4 | 0 | 0 | 0 | 1 | 3 | 0 | 14 | 1 | 0 | 0 | 1 | .000 | 0 | 0- - | - | 1.33 | 3.72 |
| 2013 | LAD | NL | 3 | 0 | 0 | 1 | 1.1 | 9 | 1 | 2 | 2 | 1 | 0 | 0 | 0 | 4 | 0 | 1 | 0 | 0 | 0 | 0 | - | 0 | 0-0 | 0 | 21.19 | 13.50 |

# Brett Gardner

**Bats:** L **Throws:** L **Pos:** CF-138;PH-9;DH-2 **Ht:** 5'10" **Wt:** 185 **Born:** 8/24/1983 **Age:** 30

| BATTING | | | | | | | | | | | | | | | | | | | | | | BASERUNNING | | | | AVERAGES | | |
|---|---|---|---|---|---|---|---|---|---|---|---|---|---|---|---|---|---|---|---|---|---|---|---|---|---|---|---|---|
| Year | Team | Lg | G | AB | H | 2B | 3B | HR | (Hm | Rd) | TB | R | RBI | RC | TBB | IBB | SO | HBP | SH | SF | SB | CS | SB% | GDP | Avg | OBP | Slg |
| 2008 | NYY | AL | 42 | 127 | 29 | 5 | 2 | 0 | (0 | 0) | 38 | 18 | 16 | 17 | 8 | 0 | 30 | 2 | 3 | 1 | 13 | 1 | .93 | 0 | .228 | .283 | .299 |
| 2009 | NYY | AL | 108 | 248 | 67 | 6 | 6 | 3 | (1 | 2) | 94 | 48 | 23 | 38 | 26 | 0 | 40 | 3 | 6 | 1 | 26 | 5 | .84 | 3 | .270 | .345 | .379 |
| 2010 | NYY | AL | 150 | 477 | 132 | 20 | 7 | 5 | (5 | 0) | 181 | 97 | 47 | 77 | 79 | 1 | 101 | 5 | 5 | 3 | 47 | 9 | .84 | 6 | .277 | .383 | .379 |
| 2011 | NYY | AL | 159 | 510 | 132 | 19 | 8 | 7 | (4 | 3) | 188 | 87 | 36 | 77 | 60 | 1 | 93 | 8 | 8 | 2 | **49** | 13 | .79 | 5 | .259 | .345 | .369 |
| 2012 | NYY | AL | 16 | 31 | 10 | 2 | 0 | 0 | (0 | 0) | 12 | 7 | 3 | 7 | 5 | 0 | 7 | 0 | 1 | 0 | 2 | 2 | .50 | 0 | .323 | .417 | .387 |
| 2013 | NYY | AL | 145 | 539 | 147 | 33 | **10** | 8 | (6 | 2) | 224 | 81 | 52 | 88 | 52 | 1 | 127 | 8 | 7 | 3 | 24 | 8 | .75 | 8 | .273 | .344 | .416 |
| Postseason | | | 33 | 65 | 14 | 1 | 0 | 0 | (0 | 0) | 15 | 8 | 7 | 5 | 4 | 0 | 17 | 0 | 2 | 1 | 5 | 2 | .71 | 0 | .215 | .257 | .231 |
| 6 ML YEARS | | | 620 | 1932 | 517 | 85 | 33 | 23 | (16 | 7) | 737 | 338 | 177 | 304 | 230 | 3 | 398 | 26 | 30 | 10 | 161 | 38 | .81 | 22 | .268 | .352 | .381 |

# Jon Garland

**Pitches:** R **Bats:** R **Pos:** SP-12 **Ht:** 6'6" **Wt:** 210 **Born:** 9/27/1979 **Age:** 34

| HOW MUCH HE PITCHED | | | | | | | | | WHAT HE GAVE UP | | | | | | | | | | | | THE RESULTS | | | | | | | |
|---|---|---|---|---|---|---|---|---|---|---|---|---|---|---|---|---|---|---|---|---|---|---|---|---|---|---|---|---|
| Year | Team | Lg | G | GS | CG | GF | IP | BFP | H | R | ER | HR | SH | SF | HB | TBB | IBB | SO | WP | Bk | W | L | Pct | Sh | Sv-Op | Hld | ERC | ERA |
| 2000 | CWS | AL | 15 | 13 | 0 | 1 | 69.2 | 324 | 82 | 55 | 50 | 10 | 0 | 2 | 1 | 40 | 0 | 42 | 4 | 0 | 4 | 8 | .333 | 0 | 0-0 | 1 | 6.26 | 6.46 |
| 2001 | CWS | AL | 35 | 16 | 0 | 8 | 117.0 | 510 | 123 | 59 | 48 | 16 | 2 | 5 | 4 | 55 | 2 | 61 | 3 | 0 | 6 | 7 | .462 | 0 | 1-1 | 2 | 5.16 | 3.69 |
| 2002 | CWS | AL | 33 | 33 | 1 | 0 | 192.2 | 827 | 188 | 109 | 98 | 23 | 3 | 4 | 9 | 83 | 1 | 112 | 5 | 0 | 12 | 12 | .500 | 1 | 0-0 | 0 | 4.46 | 4.58 |
| 2003 | CWS | AL | 32 | 32 | 0 | 0 | 191.2 | 813 | 188 | 103 | 96 | 28 | 4 | 8 | 4 | 74 | 1 | 108 | 8 | 0 | 12 | 13 | .480 | 0 | 0-0 | 0 | 4.38 | 4.51 |
| 2004 | CWS | AL | 34 | 33 | 1 | 0 | 217.0 | 923 | 223 | 125 | 118 | 34 | 9 | 5 | 4 | 76 | 2 | 113 | 3 | 0 | 12 | 11 | .522 | 0 | 0-0 | 0 | 4.56 | 4.89 |
| 2005 | CWS | AL | 32 | 32 | 3 | 0 | 221.0 | 901 | 212 | 93 | 86 | 26 | **9** | 8 | 7 | 47 | 3 | 115 | 2 | 0 | 18 | 10 | .643 | **3** | 0-0 | 0 | 3.39 | 3.50 |
| 2006 | CWS | AL | 33 | 32 | 1 | 0 | 211.1 | 900 | **247** | 112 | 106 | 26 | 5 | 8 | 6 | 41 | 4 | 112 | 4 | 0 | 18 | 7 | .720 | 1 | 0-0 | 0 | 4.50 | 4.51 |
| 2007 | CWS | AL | 32 | 32 | 2 | 0 | 208.1 | 883 | 219 | 114 | 98 | 19 | 3 | 7 | 4 | 57 | 3 | 98 | 1 | 0 | 10 | 13 | .435 | 1 | 0-0 | 0 | 3.87 | 4.23 |
| 2008 | LAA | AL | 32 | 32 | 1 | 0 | 196.2 | 864 | 237 | 116 | 107 | 23 | **8** | 8 | 8 | 59 | 4 | 90 | 4 | 0 | 14 | 8 | .636 | 0 | 0-0 | 0 | 5.18 | 4.90 |
| 2009 | 2 Tms | NL | 33 | 33 | 1 | 0 | 204.0 | 882 | 225 | 106 | 91 | 23 | 11 | 6 | 6 | 61 | 7 | 109 | 6 | 0 | 11 | 13 | .458 | 0 | 0-0 | 0 | 4.42 | 4.01 |
| 2010 | SD | NL | 33 | 33 | 0 | 0 | 200.0 | 837 | 176 | 86 | 77 | 20 | 5 | 5 | 6 | 87 | 9 | 136 | 6 | 0 | 14 | 12 | .538 | 0 | 0-0 | 0 | 3.67 | 3.47 |
| 2011 | LAD | NL | 9 | 9 | 1 | 0 | 54.0 | 230 | 55 | 26 | 26 | 6 | 5 | 4 | 2 | 20 | 0 | 28 | 0 | 1 | 1 | 5 | .167 | 0 | 0-0 | 0 | 4.37 | 4.33 |
| 2013 | Col | NL | 12 | 12 | 0 | 0 | 68.0 | 303 | 85 | 45 | 44 | 9 | 6 | 2 | 2 | 23 | 3 | 32 | 4 | 0 | 4 | 6 | .400 | 0 | 0-0 | 0 | 5.65 | 5.82 |
| 09 | Ari | NL | 27 | 27 | 1 | 0 | 167.2 | 728 | 188 | 90 | 80 | 19 | 9 | 4 | 6 | 52 | 5 | 83 | 5 | 0 | 8 | 11 | .421 | 0 | 0-0 | 0 | 4.63 | 4.29 |
| 09 | LAD | NL | 6 | 6 | 0 | 0 | 36.1 | 154 | 37 | 16 | 11 | 4 | 2 | 2 | 0 | 9 | 2 | 26 | 1 | 0 | 3 | 2 | .600 | 0 | 0-0 | 0 | 3.51 | 2.72 |
| Postseason | | | 2 | 2 | 1 | 0 | 16.0 | 58 | 11 | 6 | 4 | 2 | 2 | 0 | 0 | 3 | 0 | 11 | 0 | 0 | 1 | 0 | 1.000 | 0 | 0-0 | 0 | 2.00 | 2.25 |
| 13 ML YEARS | | | 365 | 342 | 11 | 9 | 2151.1 | 9197 | 2260 | 1149 | 1045 | 263 | 70 | 72 | 63 | 723 | 39 | 1156 | 50 | 1 | 136 | 125 | .521 | 6 | 1-1 | 3 | 4.41 | 4.37 |

# Matt Garza

**Pitches:** R **Bats:** R **Pos:** SP-24 **Ht:** 6'4" **Wt:** 215 **Born:** 11/26/1983 **Age:** 30

| HOW MUCH HE PITCHED | | | | | | | | | WHAT HE GAVE UP | | | | | | | | | | | | THE RESULTS | | | | | | | |
|---|---|---|---|---|---|---|---|---|---|---|---|---|---|---|---|---|---|---|---|---|---|---|---|---|---|---|---|---|
| Year | Team | Lg | G | GS | CG | GF | IP | BFP | H | R | ER | HR | SH | SF | HB | TBB | IBB | SO | WP | Bk | W | L | Pct | Sh | Sv-Op | Hld | ERC | ERA |
| 2013 | Tenn* | AA | 2 | 2 | 0 | 0 | 6.0 | 26 | 4 | 1 | 1 | 0 | 0 | 0 | 0 | 4 | 0 | 2 | 0 | 0 | 0 | 1 | .000 | 0 | 0- - | - | 2.54 | 1.50 |
| 2013 | Iowa* | AAA | 2 | 2 | 0 | 0 | 9.1 | 34 | 6 | 1 | 1 | 0 | 0 | 0 | 1 | 0 | 0 | 9 | 0 | 0 | 1 | 0 | 1.000 | 0 | 0- - | - | 1.08 | 0.96 |
| 2006 | Min | AL | 10 | 9 | 0 | 0 | 50.0 | 232 | 62 | 33 | 32 | 6 | 0 | 3 | 0 | 23 | 0 | 38 | 1 | 0 | 3 | 6 | .333 | 0 | 0-0 | 0 | 5.82 | 5.76 |
| 2007 | Min | AL | 16 | 15 | 0 | 1 | 83.0 | 367 | 96 | 44 | 34 | 8 | 1 | 4 | 4 | 32 | 4 | 67 | 4 | 0 | 5 | 7 | .417 | 0 | 0-0 | 0 | 5.08 | 3.69 |
| 2008 | TB | AL | 30 | 30 | 3 | 0 | 184.2 | 772 | 170 | 83 | 76 | 19 | 3 | 9 | 6 | 59 | 2 | 128 | 3 | 2 | 11 | 9 | .550 | **2** | 0-0 | 0 | 3.47 | 3.70 |
| 2009 | TB | AL | 32 | 32 | 0 | 0 | 203.0 | 861 | 177 | 93 | 89 | 25 | 2 | 8 | 11 | 79 | 0 | 189 | 3 | 0 | 8 | 12 | .400 | 0 | 0-0 | 0 | 3.69 | 3.95 |
| 2010 | TB | AL | 33 | 32 | 3 | 1 | 204.2 | 855 | 193 | 94 | 89 | 28 | 1 | 6 | 7 | 63 | 2 | 150 | 12 | 2 | 15 | 10 | .600 | 1 | 1-1 | 0 | 3.80 | 3.91 |
| 2011 | ChC | NL | 31 | 31 | 2 | 0 | 198.0 | 839 | 186 | 90 | 73 | 14 | 11 | 2 | 3 | 63 | 5 | 197 | 6 | 0 | 10 | 10 | .500 | 0 | 0-0 | 0 | 3.21 | 3.32 |
| 2012 | ChC | NL | 18 | 18 | 0 | 0 | 103.2 | 424 | 90 | 48 | 45 | 15 | 5 | 1 | 4 | 32 | 0 | 96 | 1 | 0 | 5 | 7 | .417 | 0 | 0-0 | 0 | 3.50 | 3.91 |
| 2013 | 2 Tms | | 24 | 24 | 1 | 0 | 155.1 | 652 | 150 | 73 | 66 | 20 | 8 | 3 | 5 | 42 | 3 | 136 | 6 | 0 | 10 | 6 | .625 | 0 | 0-0 | 0 | 3.66 | 3.82 |
| 13 | ChC | NL | 11 | 11 | 0 | 0 | 71.0 | 293 | 61 | 26 | 25 | 8 | 2 | 1 | 4 | 20 | 2 | 62 | 2 | 0 | 6 | 1 | .857 | 0 | 0-0 | 0 | 3.12 | 3.17 |
| 13 | Tex | AL | 13 | 13 | 1 | 0 | 84.1 | 359 | 89 | 47 | 41 | 12 | 6 | 2 | 1 | 22 | 1 | 74 | 4 | 0 | 4 | 5 | .444 | 0 | 0-0 | 0 | 4.14 | 4.38 |
| Postseason | | | 5 | 5 | 0 | 0 | 31.0 | 131 | 26 | 13 | 12 | 5 | 0 | 1 | 1 | 14 | 0 | 29 | 2 | 0 | 2 | 1 | .667 | 0 | 0-0 | 0 | 3.95 | 3.48 |
| 8 ML YEARS | | | 194 | 191 | 9 | 2 | 1182.1 | 5002 | 1124 | 558 | 504 | 135 | 31 | 36 | 40 | 393 | 16 | 1001 | 36 | 4 | 67 | 67 | .500 | 3 | 1-1 | 0 | 3.75 | 3.84 |

# John Gast

**Pitches:** L **Bats:** L **Pos:** SP-3 **Ht:** 6'1" **Wt:** 195 **Born:** 2/16/1989 **Age:** 25

| HOW MUCH HE PITCHED | | | | | | | | | WHAT HE GAVE UP | | | | | | | | | | | | THE RESULTS | | | | | | | |
|---|---|---|---|---|---|---|---|---|---|---|---|---|---|---|---|---|---|---|---|---|---|---|---|---|---|---|---|---|
| Year | Team | Lg | G | GS | CG | GF | IP | BFP | H | R | ER | HR | SH | SF | HB | TBB | IBB | SO | WP | Bk | W | L | Pct | Sh | Sv-Op | Hld | ERC | ERA |
| 2010 | Batvia | A- | 8 | 6 | 0 | 0 | 35.0 | 129 | 27 | 6 | 6 | 1 | 0 | 1 | 1 | 8 | 0 | 36 | 3 | 0 | 6 | 0 | 1.000 | 0 | 0- - | - | 2.14 | 1.54 |
| 2011 | PlmBh | A+ | 13 | 12 | 1 | 0 | 82.0 | 356 | 85 | 40 | 36 | 7 | 5 | 1 | 8 | 28 | 1 | 59 | 5 | 0 | 5 | 4 | .556 | 0 | 0- - | - | 4.35 | 3.95 |
| 2011 | Sprgfld | AA | 13 | 13 | 1 | 0 | 79.1 | 345 | 80 | 42 | 36 | 9 | 4 | 3 | 4 | 33 | 0 | 54 | 4 | 0 | 4 | 4 | .500 | 0 | 0- - | - | 4.52 | 4.08 |
| 2012 | Sprgfld | AA | 8 | 8 | 0 | 0 | 51.1 | 196 | 38 | 13 | 11 | 5 | 2 | 0 | 1 | 13 | 0 | 41 | 0 | 0 | 4 | 2 | .667 | 0 | 0- - | - | 2.35 | 1.93 |
| 2012 | Memp | AAA | 20 | 20 | 0 | 0 | 109.1 | 484 | 124 | 69 | 62 | 10 | 5 | 2 | 2 | 42 | 3 | 86 | 7 | 0 | 9 | 5 | .643 | 0 | 0- - | - | 4.75 | 5.10 |
| 2013 | Memp | AAA | 7 | 7 | 0 | 0 | 38.2 | 152 | 28 | 6 | 5 | 0 | 4 | 1 | 3 | 13 | 0 | 35 | 0 | 0 | 3 | 1 | .750 | 0 | 0- - | - | 2.15 | 1.16 |
| 2013 | StL | NL | 3 | 3 | 0 | 0 | 12.1 | 52 | 11 | 7 | 7 | 1 | 0 | 0 | 0 | 5 | 0 | 8 | 0 | 0 | 2 | 0 | 1.000 | 0 | 0-0 | 0 | 3.38 | 5.11 |

# Evan Gattis

**Bats:** R **Throws:** R **Pos:** LF-48;C-42;PH-13;1B-4;DH-2 GAT-iss **Ht:** 6'4" **Wt:** 230 **Born:** 8/18/1986 **Age:** 27

| BATTING | | | | | | | | | | | | | | | | | | | | | BASERUNNING | | | | AVERAGES | | |
|---|---|---|---|---|---|---|---|---|---|---|---|---|---|---|---|---|---|---|---|---|---|---|---|---|---|---|---|
| Year | Team | Lg | G | AB | H | 2B | 3B | HR | (Hm | Rd) | TB | R | RBI | RC | TBB | IBB | SO | HBP | SH | SF | SB | CS | SB% | GDP | Avg | OBP | Slg |
| 2010 | Danvle | R | 60 | 222 | 64 | 10 | 0 | 4 | (- | -) | 86 | 33 | 29 | 30 | 6 | 0 | 44 | 12 | 0 | 2 | 0 | 0 | - | 4 | .288 | .339 | .387 |
| 2011 | Rome | A | 88 | 338 | 109 | 24 | 2 | 22 | (- | -) | 203 | 58 | 71 | 74 | 25 | 1 | 53 | 11 | 1 | 2 | 2 | 4 | .33 | 9 | .322 | .386 | .601 |
| 2012 | Lynbrg | A+ | 21 | 78 | 30 | 7 | 0 | 9 | (- | -) | 64 | 14 | 29 | 26 | 10 | 2 | 12 | 4 | 0 | 2 | 1 | 1 | .50 | 0 | .385 | .468 | .821 |
| 2012 | Missi | AA | 49 | 182 | 47 | 13 | 4 | 9 | (- | -) | 95 | 24 | 37 | 33 | 20 | 1 | 29 | 4 | 0 | 1 | 1 | 1 | .50 | 14 | .258 | .343 | .522 |
| 2012 | Braves | R | 4 | 12 | 6 | 0 | 0 | 0 | (- | -) | 6 | 2 | 1 | 3 | 1 | 0 | 2 | 0 | 0 | 0 | 0 | 0 | - | 0 | .500 | .538 | .500 |
| 2013 | Gwnntt | AAA | 5 | 21 | 7 | 4 | 0 | 1 | (- | -) | 14 | 1 | 1 | 4 | 0 | 0 | 4 | 1 | 0 | 0 | 0 | 0 | - | 1 | .333 | .364 | .667 |
| 2013 | Atl | NL | 105 | 354 | 86 | 21 | 0 | 21 | (8 | 13) | 170 | 44 | 65 | 43 | 21 | 4 | 81 | 4 | 0 | 3 | 0 | 0 | - | 10 | .243 | .291 | .480 |

# Chad Gaudin

**Pitches:** R **Bats:** R **Pos:** RP-18; SP-12 goe-DANN **Ht:** 5'10" **Wt:** 185 **Born:** 3/24/1983 **Age:** 31

| HOW MUCH HE PITCHED | | | | | | | | | WHAT HE GAVE UP | | | | | | | | | | | | THE RESULTS | | | | | | | |
|---|---|---|---|---|---|---|---|---|---|---|---|---|---|---|---|---|---|---|---|---|---|---|---|---|---|---|---|---|
| Year | Team | Lg | G | GS | CG | GF | IP | BFP | H | R | ER | HR | SH | SF | HB | TBB | IBB | SO | WP | Bk | W | L | Pct | Sh | Sv-Op | Hld | ERC | ERA |
| 2003 | TB | AL | 15 | 3 | 0 | 5 | 40.0 | 173 | 37 | 18 | 16 | 4 | 0 | 2 | 1 | 16 | 0 | 23 | 1 | 0 | 2 | 0 | 1.000 | 0 | 0-0 | 0 | 3.70 | 3.60 |
| 2004 | TB | AL | 26 | 4 | 0 | 5 | 42.2 | 201 | 59 | 27 | 23 | 4 | 2 | 4 | 4 | 16 | 4 | 30 | 0 | 0 | 1 | 2 | .333 | 0 | 0-1 | 5 | 6.46 | 4.85 |
| 2005 | Tor | AL | 5 | 3 | 0 | 0 | 13.0 | 74 | 31 | 19 | 19 | 6 | 0 | 1 | 1 | 6 | 0 | 12 | 0 | 0 | 1 | 3 | .250 | 0 | 0-0 | 0 | 18.35 | 13.15 |
| 2006 | Oak | AL | 55 | 0 | 0 | 13 | 64.0 | 276 | 51 | 24 | 22 | 3 | 0 | 3 | 1 | 42 | 2 | 36 | 2 | 2 | 4 | 2 | .667 | 0 | 2-3 | 11 | 3.62 | 3.09 |
| 2007 | Oak | AL | 34 | **34** | 1 | 0 | 199.1 | 886 | 205 | 108 | 98 | 21 | 3 | 6 | 8 | 100 | 8 | 154 | 3 | 1 | 11 | 13 | .458 | 0 | 0-0 | 0 | 4.80 | 4.42 |
| 2008 | 2 Tms | | 50 | 6 | 0 | 14 | 90.0 | 382 | 92 | 50 | 44 | 11 | 2 | 2 | 3 | 27 | 3 | 71 | 2 | 2 | 9 | 5 | .643 | 0 | 0-1 | 4 | 4.06 | 4.40 |
| 2009 | 2 Tms | | 31 | 25 | 0 | 4 | 147.1 | 664 | 146 | 85 | 76 | 14 | 7 | 8 | 8 | 76 | 4 | 139 | 7 | 1 | 6 | 10 | .375 | 0 | 0-0 | 0 | 4.56 | 4.64 |
| 2010 | 2 Tms | AL | 42 | 0 | 0 | 23 | 65.1 | 295 | 73 | 45 | 41 | 16 | 4 | 2 | 8 | 25 | 0 | 53 | 3 | 0 | 1 | 4 | .200 | 0 | 0-1 | 1 | 6.33 | 5.65 |
| 2011 | Was | NL | 10 | 0 | 0 | 1 | 8.1 | 45 | 12 | 10 | 6 | 1 | 1 | 0 | 0 | 8 | 0 | 10 | 0 | 0 | 1 | 1 | .500 | 0 | 0-0 | 2 | 9.20 | 6.48 |
| 2012 | Mia | NL | 46 | 0 | 0 | 11 | 69.1 | 302 | 72 | 39 | 35 | 6 | 8 | 2 | 3 | 26 | 5 | 57 | 3 | 1 | 4 | 2 | .667 | 0 | 0-0 | 1 | 4.15 | 4.54 |
| 2013 | SF | NL | 30 | 12 | 0 | 4 | 97.0 | 406 | 81 | 34 | 33 | 6 | 3 | 4 | 2 | 40 | 3 | 88 | 5 | 1 | 5 | 2 | .714 | 0 | 0-0 | 2 | 3.01 | 3.06 |
| 08 | Oak | AL | 26 | 6 | 0 | 9 | 62.2 | 263 | 63 | 29 | 25 | 6 | 2 | 1 | 3 | 17 | 1 | 44 | 2 | 1 | 5 | 3 | .625 | 0 | 0-0 | 2 | 3.78 | 3.59 |
| 08 | ChC | NL | 24 | 0 | 0 | 5 | 27.1 | 119 | 29 | 21 | 19 | 5 | 0 | 1 | 0 | 10 | 2 | 27 | 0 | 1 | 4 | 2 | .667 | 0 | 0-1 | 2 | 4.74 | 6.26 |
| 09 | SD | NL | 20 | 19 | 0 | 0 | 105.1 | 476 | 105 | 69 | 60 | 7 | 7 | 6 | 5 | 56 | 3 | 105 | 4 | 1 | 4 | 10 | .286 | 0 | 0-0 | 0 | 4.41 | 5.13 |
| 09 | NYY | AL | 11 | 6 | 0 | 4 | 42.0 | 188 | 41 | 16 | 16 | 7 | 0 | 2 | 3 | 20 | 1 | 34 | 3 | 0 | 2 | 0 | 1.000 | 0 | 0-0 | 0 | 4.93 | 3.43 |
| 10 | Oak | AL | 12 | 0 | 0 | 6 | 17.1 | 86 | 27 | 18 | 17 | 5 | 2 | 1 | 3 | 5 | 0 | 20 | 0 | 0 | 0 | 2 | .000 | 0 | 0-0 | 1 | 9.34 | 8.83 |
| 10 | NYY | AL | 30 | 0 | 0 | 17 | 48.0 | 209 | 46 | 27 | 24 | 11 | 2 | 1 | 5 | 20 | 0 | 33 | 3 | 0 | 1 | 2 | .333 | 0 | 0-1 | 0 | 5.32 | 4.50 |
| Postseason | | | 4 | 0 | 0 | 1 | 4.1 | 18 | 2 | 0 | 0 | 0 | 1 | 0 | 0 | 3 | 1 | 1 | 0 | 0 | 0 | 0 | - | 0 | 0-0 | 0 | 1.45 | 0.00 |
| 11 ML YEARS | | | 344 | 87 | 1 | 80 | 836.1 | 3704 | 859 | 459 | 413 | 92 | 30 | 34 | 39 | 382 | 29 | 673 | 26 | 8 | 45 | 44 | .506 | 0 | 2-6 | 26 | 4.66 | 4.44 |

# Kevin Gausman

**Pitches:** R **Bats:** R **Pos:** RP-15; SP-5 GAHZ-man **Ht:** 6'3" **Wt:** 190 **Born:** 1/6/1991 **Age:** 23

| HOW MUCH HE PITCHED | | | | | | | | | WHAT HE GAVE UP | | | | | | | | | | | | THE RESULTS | | | | | | | |
|---|---|---|---|---|---|---|---|---|---|---|---|---|---|---|---|---|---|---|---|---|---|---|---|---|---|---|---|---|
| Year | Team | Lg | G | GS | CG | GF | IP | BFP | H | R | ER | HR | SH | SF | HB | TBB | IBB | SO | WP | Bk | W | L | Pct | Sh | Sv-Op | Hld | ERC | ERA |
| 2012 | Abrdn | A- | 2 | 2 | 0 | 0 | 6.0 | 19 | 1 | 0 | 0 | 0 | 0 | 0 | 0 | 0 | 0 | 5 | 0 | 0 | 0 | 0 | - | 0 | 0- - | - | 0.07 | 0.00 |
| 2012 | Frdrck | A+ | 3 | 3 | 0 | 0 | 9.0 | 38 | 10 | 6 | 6 | 3 | 1 | 0 | 0 | 1 | 0 | 8 | 0 | 1 | 0 | 1 | .000 | 0 | 0- - | - | 4.96 | 6.00 |
| 2013 | Bowie | AA | 8 | 8 | 0 | 0 | 46.1 | 191 | 44 | 21 | 16 | 3 | 2 | 2 | 3 | 5 | 0 | 49 | 7 | 0 | 2 | 4 | .333 | 0 | 0- - | - | 2.66 | 3.11 |
| 2013 | Norfolk | AAA | 8 | 7 | 0 | 1 | 35.2 | 143 | 36 | 16 | 16 | 1 | 0 | 0 | 1 | 9 | 0 | 33 | 2 | 0 | 1 | 2 | .333 | 0 | 0- - | - | 3.36 | 4.04 |
| 2013 | Bal | AL | 20 | 5 | 0 | 3 | 47.2 | 201 | 51 | 30 | 30 | 8 | 2 | 1 | 0 | 13 | 2 | 49 | 4 | 0 | 3 | 5 | .375 | 0 | 0-2 | 2 | 4.41 | 5.66 |

# Cory Gearrin

**Pitches:** R **Bats:** R **Pos:** RP-37 GARE-inn **Ht:** 6'3" **Wt:** 200 **Born:** 4/14/1986 **Age:** 28

| HOW MUCH HE PITCHED | | | | | | | | | WHAT HE GAVE UP | | | | | | | | | | | | THE RESULTS | | | | | | | |
|---|---|---|---|---|---|---|---|---|---|---|---|---|---|---|---|---|---|---|---|---|---|---|---|---|---|---|---|---|
| Year | Team | Lg | G | GS | CG | GF | IP | BFP | H | R | ER | HR | SH | SF | HB | TBB | IBB | SO | WP | Bk | W | L | Pct | Sh | Sv-Op | Hld | ERC | ERA |
| 2011 | Atl | NL | 18 | 0 | 0 | 4 | 18.1 | 85 | 17 | 16 | 16 | 0 | 0 | 1 | 2 | 12 | 4 | 25 | 1 | 0 | 1 | 1 | .500 | 0 | 0-1 | 3 | 3.84 | 7.85 |
| 2012 | Atl | NL | 22 | 0 | 0 | 7 | 20.0 | 80 | 17 | 4 | 4 | 1 | 0 | 0 | 2 | 5 | 0 | 20 | 2 | 0 | 0 | 1 | .000 | 0 | 0-1 | 4 | 2.86 | 1.80 |
| 2013 | Atl | NL | 37 | 0 | 0 | 12 | 31.0 | 133 | 30 | 13 | 13 | 2 | 1 | 0 | 4 | 16 | 2 | 23 | 3 | 0 | 2 | 1 | .667 | 0 | 1-3 | 1 | 4.73 | 3.77 |
| 3 ML YEARS | | | 77 | 0 | 0 | 23 | 69.1 | 298 | 64 | 33 | 33 | 3 | 1 | 1 | 8 | 33 | 6 | 68 | 6 | 0 | 3 | 3 | .500 | 0 | 1-5 | 8 | 3.94 | 4.28 |

# Dillon Gee

**Pitches:** R **Bats:** R **Pos:** SP-32 JEE **Ht:** 6'1" **Wt:** 205 **Born:** 4/28/1986 **Age:** 28

| HOW MUCH HE PITCHED | | | | | | | | | WHAT HE GAVE UP | | | | | | | | | | | | THE RESULTS | | | | | | | |
|---|---|---|---|---|---|---|---|---|---|---|---|---|---|---|---|---|---|---|---|---|---|---|---|---|---|---|---|---|
| Year | Team | Lg | G | GS | CG | GF | IP | BFP | H | R | ER | HR | SH | SF | HB | TBB | IBB | SO | WP | Bk | W | L | Pct | Sh | Sv-Op | Hld | ERC | ERA |
| 2010 | NYM | NL | 5 | 5 | 0 | 0 | 33.0 | 136 | 25 | 10 | 8 | 2 | 3 | 0 | 0 | 15 | 2 | 17 | 0 | 0 | 2 | 2 | .500 | 0 | 0-0 | 0 | 2.66 | 2.18 |
| 2011 | NYM | NL | 30 | 27 | 1 | 1 | 160.2 | 706 | 150 | 85 | 79 | 18 | 10 | 5 | 14 | 71 | 4 | 114 | 6 | 1 | 13 | 6 | .684 | 0 | 0-0 | 0 | 4.23 | 4.43 |
| 2012 | NYM | NL | 17 | 17 | 0 | 0 | 109.2 | 463 | 108 | 56 | 50 | 12 | 2 | 3 | 6 | 29 | 0 | 97 | 0 | 1 | 6 | 7 | .462 | 0 | 0-0 | 0 | 3.74 | 4.10 |
| 2013 | NYM | NL | 32 | 32 | 2 | 0 | 199.0 | 841 | 208 | 84 | 80 | 24 | 9 | 3 | 7 | 47 | 0 | 142 | 4 | 0 | 12 | 11 | .522 | 0 | 0-0 | 0 | 3.97 | 3.62 |
| 4 ML YEARS | | | 84 | 81 | 3 | 1 | 502.1 | 2146 | 491 | 235 | 217 | 56 | 24 | 11 | 27 | 162 | 6 | 370 | 10 | 2 | 33 | 26 | .559 | 0 | 0-0 | 0 | 3.91 | 3.89 |

# Scooter Gennett

**Bats:** L **Throws:** R **Pos:** 2B-59;PH-12 jen-ETT **Ht:** 5'10" **Wt:** 180 **Born:** 5/1/1990 **Age:** 24

| BATTING | | | | | | | | | | | | | | | | | | | | | BASERUNNING | | | | AVERAGES | | |
|---|---|---|---|---|---|---|---|---|---|---|---|---|---|---|---|---|---|---|---|---|---|---|---|---|---|---|---|
| Year | Team | Lg | G | AB | H | 2B | 3B | HR | (Hm | Rd) | TB | R | RBI | RC | TBB | IBB | SO | HBP | SH | SF | SB | CS | SB% | GDP | Avg | OBP | Slg |
| 2010 | Wisc | A | 118 | 482 | 149 | 39 | 4 | 9 | (- | -) | 223 | 87 | 55 | 81 | 31 | 2 | 91 | 5 | 3 | 4 | 14 | 4 | .78 | 6 | .309 | .354 | .463 |
| 2011 | BrvdCt | A+ | 134 | 556 | 167 | 20 | 6 | 9 | (- | -) | 226 | 74 | 51 | 76 | 27 | 0 | 69 | 4 | 8 | 6 | 11 | 10 | .52 | 9 | .300 | .334 | .406 |
| 2012 | Hntsvl | AA | 133 | 533 | 156 | 30 | 2 | 5 | (- | -) | 205 | 66 | 44 | 70 | 28 | 2 | 71 | 3 | 6 | 3 | 11 | 5 | .69 | 15 | .293 | .330 | .385 |
| 2013 | Nashv | AAA | 79 | 321 | 90 | 10 | 5 | 3 | (- | -) | 119 | 44 | 22 | 40 | 21 | 1 | 59 | 2 | 3 | 2 | 10 | 5 | .67 | 4 | .280 | .327 | .371 |
| 2013 | Mil | NL | 69 | 213 | 69 | 11 | 2 | 6 | (0 | 6) | 102 | 29 | 21 | 35 | 10 | 0 | 42 | 1 | 5 | 1 | 2 | 1 | .67 | 0 | .324 | .356 | .479 |

# Craig Gentry

**Bats:** R **Throws:** R **Pos:** CF-71;LF-34;PH-28;DH-2;PR-1 JEN-tree **Ht:** 6'2" **Wt:** 190 **Born:** 11/29/1983 **Age:** 30

| BATTING | | | | | | | | | | | | | | | | | | | | BASERUNNING | | | | AVERAGES | | |
|---|---|---|---|---|---|---|---|---|---|---|---|---|---|---|---|---|---|---|---|---|---|---|---|---|---|---|
| Year | Team | Lg | G | AB | H | 2B | 3B | HR | (Hm | Rd) | TB | R | RBI | RC | TBB | IBB | SO | HBP | SH | SF | SB | CS | SB% | GDP | Avg | OBP | Slg |
| 2013 | Frisco* | AA | 4 | 13 | 3 | 1 | 0 | 0 | (- | -) | 4 | 2 | 1 | 1 | 1 | 0 | 3 | 0 | 0 | 1 | 0 | 0 | - | 0 | .231 | .267 | .308 |
| 2009 | Tex | AL | 11 | 17 | 2 | 1 | 0 | 0 | (0 | 0) | 3 | 4 | 1 | 1 | 2 | 0 | 5 | 0 | 0 | 0 | 0 | 0 | - | 0 | .118 | .211 | .176 |
| 2010 | Tex | AL | 20 | 33 | 7 | 0 | 0 | 0 | (0 | 0) | 7 | 4 | 3 | 1 | 1 | 0 | 11 | 0 | 0 | 1 | 1 | 0 | 1.00 | 1 | .212 | .229 | .212 |
| 2011 | Tex | AL | 64 | 133 | 36 | 5 | 1 | 1 | (1 | 0) | 46 | 26 | 13 | 21 | 10 | 1 | 27 | 6 | 3 | 1 | 18 | 0 | 1.00 | 2 | .271 | .347 | .346 |
| 2012 | Tex | AL | 122 | 240 | 73 | 12 | 3 | 1 | (0 | 1) | 94 | 31 | 26 | 33 | 14 | 1 | 41 | 10 | 5 | 0 | 13 | 7 | .65 | 4 | .304 | .367 | .392 |
| 2013 | Tex | AL | 106 | 246 | 69 | 12 | 4 | 2 | (2 | 0) | 95 | 39 | 22 | 42 | 29 | 2 | 46 | 8 | 3 | 1 | 24 | 3 | .89 | 5 | .280 | .373 | .386 |
| | Postseason | | 14 | 17 | 5 | 0 | 0 | 0 | (0 | 0) | 5 | 2 | 1 | 3 | 1 | 0 | 4 | 1 | 1 | 0 | 2 | 1 | .67 | 0 | .294 | .368 | .294 |
| | 5 ML YEARS | | 323 | 669 | 187 | 30 | 8 | 4 | (3 | 1) | 245 | 104 | 65 | 98 | 56 | 4 | 130 | 24 | 11 | 3 | 56 | 10 | .85 | 12 | .280 | .355 | .366 |

# Justin Germano

**Pitches:** R **Bats:** R **Pos:** RP-1 jerr-MAHN-oh **Ht:** 6'2" **Wt:** 210 **Born:** 8/6/1982 **Age:** 31

| HOW MUCH HE PITCHED | | | | | | | | | WHAT HE GAVE UP | | | | | | | | | | | | THE RESULTS | | | | | | | |
|---|---|---|---|---|---|---|---|---|---|---|---|---|---|---|---|---|---|---|---|---|---|---|---|---|---|---|---|---|
| Year | Team | Lg | G | GS | CG | GF | IP | BFP | H | R | ER | HR | SH | SF | HB | TBB | IBB | SO | WP | Bk | W | L | Pct | Sh | Sv-Op | Hld | ERC | ERA |
| 2013 | Buffalo* | AAA | 25 | 24 | 2 | 1 | 151.0 | 652 | 184 | 84 | 75 | 12 | 6 | 2 | 7 | 27 | 1 | 103 | 6 | 0 | 8 | 9 | .471 | 0 | 0-- | - | 4.49 | 4.47 |
| 2004 | SD | NL | 7 | 5 | 0 | 0 | 21.1 | 109 | 31 | 24 | 21 | 2 | 3 | 1 | 0 | 14 | 0 | 16 | 0 | 0 | 1 | 2 | .333 | 0 | 0-0 | 0 | 7.69 | 8.86 |
| 2006 | Cin | NL | 2 | 1 | 0 | 0 | 6.2 | 31 | 8 | 4 | 4 | 1 | 0 | 0 | 1 | 3 | 1 | 8 | 0 | 0 | 0 | 1 | .000 | 0 | 0-0 | 0 | 6.26 | 5.40 |
| 2007 | SD | NL | 26 | 23 | 0 | 3 | 133.1 | 566 | 133 | 72 | 66 | 14 | 4 | 0 | 8 | 40 | 3 | 78 | 1 | 0 | 7 | 10 | .412 | 0 | 0-0 | 0 | 3.93 | 4.46 |
| 2008 | SD | NL | 12 | 6 | 0 | 4 | 43.2 | 194 | 54 | 31 | 29 | 8 | 2 | 1 | 1 | 13 | 2 | 17 | 4 | 0 | 0 | 3 | .000 | 0 | 0-0 | 0 | 5.69 | 5.98 |
| 2010 | Cle | AL | 23 | 1 | 0 | 4 | 35.1 | 146 | 27 | 15 | 13 | 6 | 1 | 0 | 6 | 8 | 1 | 29 | 0 | 0 | 0 | 3 | .000 | 0 | 0-1 | 2 | 3.17 | 3.31 |
| 2011 | Cle | AL | 9 | 0 | 0 | 5 | 12.2 | 60 | 15 | 8 | 8 | 1 | 1 | 0 | 2 | 5 | 0 | 5 | 0 | 0 | 0 | 1 | .000 | 0 | 0-0 | 0 | 5.46 | 5.68 |
| 2012 | 2 Tms | | 14 | 12 | 0 | 1 | 69.2 | 320 | 86 | 52 | 48 | 7 | 5 | 3 | 7 | 21 | 2 | 52 | 5 | 0 | 2 | 10 | .167 | 0 | 0-0 | 0 | 5.32 | 6.20 |
| 2013 | Tor | AL | 1 | 0 | 0 | 1 | 2.0 | 12 | 6 | 2 | 2 | 1 | 0 | 0 | 0 | 0 | 0 | 1 | 0 | 0 | 0 | 0 | - | 0 | 0-0 | 0 | 20.02 | 9.00 |
| 12 | Bos | AL | 1 | 0 | 0 | 1 | 5.2 | 24 | 5 | 0 | 0 | 0 | 0 | 0 | 0 | 2 | 0 | 7 | 1 | 0 | 0 | 0 | - | 0 | 0-0 | 0 | 2.55 | 0.00 |
| 12 | ChC | NL | 13 | 12 | 0 | 0 | 64.0 | 296 | 81 | 52 | 48 | 7 | 5 | 3 | 7 | 19 | 2 | 45 | 4 | 0 | 2 | 10 | .167 | 0 | 0-0 | 0 | 5.59 | 6.75 |
| | 8 ML YEARS | | 94 | 48 | 0 | 18 | 324.2 | 1438 | 360 | 208 | 191 | 40 | 16 | 5 | 25 | 104 | 9 | 206 | 10 | 0 | 10 | 30 | .250 | 0 | 0-1 | 2 | 4.79 | 5.29 |

# Gonzalez Germen

**Pitches:** R **Bats:** R **Pos:** RP-29 hare-MEN **Ht:** 6'2" **Wt:** 200 **Born:** 9/23/1987 **Age:** 26

| HOW MUCH HE PITCHED | | | | | | | | | WHAT HE GAVE UP | | | | | | | | | | | | THE RESULTS | | | | | | | |
|---|---|---|---|---|---|---|---|---|---|---|---|---|---|---|---|---|---|---|---|---|---|---|---|---|---|---|---|---|
| Year | Team | Lg | G | GS | CG | GF | IP | BFP | H | R | ER | HR | SH | SF | HB | TBB | IBB | SO | WP | Bk | W | L | Pct | Sh | Sv-Op | Hld | ERC | ERA |
| 2009 | Mets | R | 2 | 1 | 0 | 0 | 6.0 | 25 | 6 | 5 | 4 | 1 | 0 | 0 | 1 | 0 | 0 | 7 | 0 | 0 | 0 | 1 | .000 | 0 | 0-- | - | 3.52 | 6.00 |
| 2010 | Kngspt | R | 10 | 10 | 0 | 0 | 61.0 | 256 | 64 | 33 | 25 | 3 | 4 | 3 | 4 | 11 | 0 | 54 | 2 | 1 | 2 | 5 | .286 | 0 | 0-- | - | 3.41 | 3.69 |
| 2010 | Savann | A | 2 | 2 | 1 | 0 | 13.0 | 51 | 11 | 4 | 4 | 1 | 0 | 0 | 0 | 1 | 0 | 10 | 0 | 0 | 1 | 0 | 1.000 | 0 | 0-- | - | 1.93 | 2.77 |
| 2011 | Savann | A | 26 | 21 | 0 | 3 | 119.0 | 511 | 126 | 56 | 52 | 9 | 2 | 2 | 7 | 35 | 0 | 111 | 5 | 2 | 7 | 7 | .500 | 0 | 0-- | - | 4.07 | 3.93 |
| 2012 | StLuci | A+ | 5 | 4 | 0 | 0 | 26.2 | 108 | 25 | 10 | 9 | 3 | 0 | 2 | 0 | 8 | 0 | 21 | 1 | 0 | 3 | 0 | 1.000 | 0 | 0-- | - | 3.54 | 3.04 |
| 2012 | Bnghtn | AA | 20 | 19 | 0 | 1 | 119.2 | 514 | 127 | 72 | 61 | 11 | 5 | 5 | 4 | 33 | 0 | 97 | 9 | 0 | 8 | 12 | .400 | 0 | 0-- | - | 3.99 | 4.59 |
| 2012 | Buffalo | AAA | 1 | 1 | 0 | 0 | 7.0 | 30 | 7 | 4 | 4 | 0 | 0 | 0 | 1 | 2 | 0 | 3 | 1 | 0 | 1 | 0 | 1.000 | 0 | 0-- | - | 3.51 | 5.14 |
| 2013 | LsVgs | AAA | 35 | 0 | 0 | 8 | 44.0 | 188 | 47 | 29 | 27 | 7 | 2 | 1 | 0 | 11 | 0 | 51 | 1 | 0 | 3 | 3 | .500 | 0 | 4-- | - | 4.22 | 5.52 |
| 2013 | NYM | NL | 29 | 0 | 0 | 8 | 34.1 | 149 | 32 | 15 | 15 | 1 | 0 | 0 | 0 | 16 | 1 | 33 | 2 | 0 | 1 | 2 | .333 | 0 | 1-3 | 1 | 3.37 | 3.93 |

# Chris Getz

**Bats:** L **Throws:** R **Pos:** 2B-68;PR-9;DH-4;PH-3 GETS **Ht:** 5'11" **Wt:** 185 **Born:** 8/30/1983 **Age:** 30

| BATTING | | | | | | | | | | | | | | | | | | | | BASERUNNING | | | | AVERAGES | | |
|---|---|---|---|---|---|---|---|---|---|---|---|---|---|---|---|---|---|---|---|---|---|---|---|---|---|---|
| Year | Team | Lg | G | AB | H | 2B | 3B | HR | (Hm | Rd) | TB | R | RBI | RC | TBB | IBB | SO | HBP | SH | SF | SB | CS | SB% | GDP | Avg | OBP | Slg |
| 2013 | Omha* | AAA | 19 | 84 | 26 | 5 | 1 | 1 | (- | -) | 36 | 7 | 10 | 11 | 1 | 0 | 5 | 1 | 0 | 2 | 3 | 1 | .75 | 1 | .310 | .318 | .429 |
| 2008 | CWS | AL | 10 | 7 | 2 | 0 | 0 | 0 | (0 | 0) | 2 | 2 | 1 | 1 | 0 | 0 | 1 | 0 | 0 | 0 | 1 | 1 | .50 | 0 | .286 | .286 | .286 |
| 2009 | CWS | AL | 107 | 375 | 98 | 18 | 4 | 2 | (1 | 1) | 130 | 49 | 31 | 47 | 30 | 1 | 54 | 6 | 1 | 3 | 25 | 2 | **.93** | 4 | .261 | .324 | .347 |
| 2010 | KC | AL | 72 | 224 | 53 | 9 | 0 | 0 | (0 | 0) | 62 | 23 | 18 | 21 | 19 | 1 | 28 | 2 | 3 | 0 | 15 | 2 | .88 | 3 | .237 | .302 | .277 |
| 2011 | KC | AL | 118 | 380 | 97 | 6 | 3 | 0 | (0 | 0) | 109 | 50 | 26 | 43 | 30 | 0 | 45 | 3 | 14 | 2 | 21 | 7 | .75 | 5 | .255 | .313 | .287 |
| 2012 | KC | AL | 64 | 189 | 52 | 10 | 3 | 0 | (0 | 0) | 68 | 22 | 17 | 23 | 11 | 0 | 17 | 0 | 8 | 2 | 9 | 3 | .75 | 3 | .275 | .312 | .360 |
| 2013 | KC | AL | 78 | 209 | 46 | 6 | 1 | 1 | (0 | 1) | 57 | 29 | 18 | 16 | 20 | 3 | 24 | 0 | 8 | 0 | 16 | 3 | .84 | 9 | .220 | .288 | .273 |
| | 6 ML YEARS | | 449 | 1384 | 348 | 49 | 11 | 3 | (1 | 2) | 428 | 175 | 111 | 151 | 110 | 5 | 169 | 11 | 34 | 7 | 87 | 18 | .83 | 24 | .251 | .310 | .309 |

# Jason Giambi

**Bats:** L **Throws:** R **Pos:** DH-56;PH-17 jee-AHM-bee **Ht:** 6'3" **Wt:** 250 **Born:** 1/8/1971 **Age:** 43

| BATTING | | | | | | | | | | | | | | | | | | | | BASERUNNING | | | | AVERAGES | | |
|---|---|---|---|---|---|---|---|---|---|---|---|---|---|---|---|---|---|---|---|---|---|---|---|---|---|---|
| Year | Team | Lg | G | AB | H | 2B | 3B | HR | (Hm | Rd) | TB | R | RBI | RC | TBB | IBB | SO | HBP | SH | SF | SB | CS | SB% | GDP | Avg | OBP | Slg |
| 1995 | Oak | AL | 54 | 176 | 45 | 7 | 0 | 6 | (3 | 3) | 70 | 27 | 25 | 27 | 28 | 0 | 31 | 3 | 1 | 2 | 2 | 1 | .67 | 4 | .256 | .364 | .398 |
| 1996 | Oak | AL | 140 | 536 | 156 | 40 | 1 | 20 | (6 | 14) | 258 | 84 | 79 | 88 | 51 | 3 | 95 | 5 | 1 | 5 | 0 | 1 | .00 | 15 | .291 | .355 | .481 |
| 1997 | Oak | AL | 142 | 519 | 152 | 41 | 2 | 20 | (14 | 6) | 257 | 66 | 81 | 91 | 55 | 3 | 89 | 6 | 0 | 8 | 0 | 1 | .00 | 11 | .293 | .362 | .495 |
| 1998 | Oak | AL | 153 | 562 | 166 | 28 | 0 | 27 | (12 | 15) | 275 | 92 | 110 | 103 | 81 | 7 | 102 | 5 | 0 | 9 | 2 | 2 | .50 | 16 | .295 | .384 | .489 |
| 1999 | Oak | AL | 158 | 575 | 181 | 36 | 1 | 33 | (17 | 16) | 318 | 115 | 123 | 132 | 105 | 6 | 106 | 7 | 0 | 8 | 1 | 1 | .50 | 11 | .315 | .422 | .553 |
| 2000 | Oak | AL | 152 | 510 | 170 | 29 | 1 | 43 | (23 | 20) | 330 | 108 | 137 | 152 | **137** | 6 | 96 | 9 | 0 | 8 | 2 | 0 | 1.00 | 9 | .333 | **.476** | .647 |
| 2001 | Oak | AL | 154 | 520 | 178 | **47** | 2 | 38 | (27 | 11) | 343 | 109 | 120 | **153** | **129** | 24 | 83 | 13 | 0 | 9 | 2 | 0 | 1.00 | 17 | .342 | **.477** | **.660** |
| 2002 | NYY | AL | 155 | 560 | 176 | 34 | 1 | 41 | (19 | 22) | 335 | 120 | 122 | 139 | 109 | 4 | 112 | 15 | 0 | 5 | 2 | 2 | .50 | 18 | .314 | .435 | .598 |
| 2003 | NYY | AL | 156 | 535 | 134 | 25 | 0 | 41 | (12 | **29)** | 282 | 97 | 107 | 120 | **129** | 9 | **140** | **21** | 0 | 5 | 2 | 1 | .67 | 9 | .250 | .412 | .527 |
| 2004 | NYY | AL | 80 | 264 | 55 | 9 | 0 | 12 | (5 | 7) | 100 | 33 | 40 | 42 | 47 | 1 | 62 | 8 | 0 | 3 | 0 | 1 | .00 | 5 | .208 | .342 | .379 |
| 2005 | NYY | AL | 139 | 417 | 113 | 14 | 0 | 32 | (16 | 16) | 223 | 74 | 87 | 102 | **108** | 5 | 109 | 19 | 0 | 1 | 0 | 0 | - | 7 | .271 | **.440** | .535 |
| 2006 | NYY | AL | 139 | 446 | 113 | 25 | 0 | 37 | (20 | 17) | 249 | 92 | 113 | 106 | 110 | 12 | 106 | 16 | 0 | 7 | 2 | 0 | 1.00 | 10 | .253 | .413 | .558 |
| 2007 | NYY | AL | 83 | 254 | 60 | 8 | 0 | 14 | (6 | 8) | 110 | 31 | 39 | 41 | 40 | 2 | 66 | 8 | 0 | 1 | 1 | 0 | 1.00 | 5 | .236 | .356 | .433 |
| 2008 | NYY | AL | 145 | 458 | 113 | 19 | 1 | 32 | (16 | 16) | 230 | 68 | 96 | 79 | 76 | 5 | 111 | **22** | 0 | 9 | 2 | 1 | .67 | 6 | .247 | .373 | .502 |
| 2009 | 2 Tms | | 102 | 293 | 59 | 14 | 0 | 13 | (7 | 6) | 112 | 43 | 51 | 44 | 57 | 1 | 80 | 7 | 0 | 2 | 0 | 0 | - | 6 | .201 | .343 | .382 |
| 2010 | Col | NL | 87 | 176 | 43 | 9 | 0 | 6 | (4 | 2) | 70 | 17 | 35 | 35 | 35 | 5 | 47 | 6 | 0 | 5 | 2 | 0 | 1.00 | 5 | .244 | .378 | .398 |
| 2011 | Col | NL | 64 | 131 | 34 | 6 | 0 | 13 | (6 | 7) | 79 | 20 | 32 | 26 | 17 | 0 | 45 | 3 | 0 | 1 | 0 | 0 | - | 1 | .260 | .355 | .603 |

| BATTING | | | | | | | | | | | | | | | | | | | | | BASERUNNING | | | | AVERAGES | | |
|---|---|---|---|---|---|---|---|---|---|---|---|---|---|---|---|---|---|---|---|---|---|---|---|---|---|---|---|
| Year Team | Lg | G | AB | H | 2B | 3B | HR | (Hm | Rd) | TB | R | RBI | RC | TBB | IBB | SO | HBP | SH | SF | | SB | CS | SB% | GDP | Avg | OBP | Slg |
| 2012 Col | NL | 60 | 89 | 20 | 4 | 0 | 1 | (1 | 0) | 27 | 7 | 8 | 14 | 20 | 2 | 24 | 2 | 0 | 2 | | 0 | 0 | - | 4 | .225 | .372 | .303 |
| 2013 Cle | AL | 71 | 186 | 34 | 8 | 0 | 9 | (5 | 4) | 69 | 21 | 31 | 22 | 23 | 0 | 56 | 4 | 0 | 3 | | 0 | 1 | .00 | 8 | .183 | .282 | .371 |
| 09 Oak | AL | 83 | 269 | 52 | 13 | 0 | 11 | (7 | 4) | 98 | 39 | 40 | 36 | 50 | 1 | 72 | 7 | 0 | 2 | | 0 | 0 | - | 6 | .193 | .332 | .364 |
| 09 Col | NL | 19 | 24 | 7 | 1 | 0 | 2 | (0 | 2) | 14 | 4 | 11 | 8 | 7 | 0 | 8 | 0 | 0 | 0 | | 0 | 0 | - | 0 | .292 | .452 | .583 |
| Postseason | | 45 | 138 | 40 | 6 | 0 | 7 | (5 | 2) | 67 | 19 | 19 | 25 | 30 | 2 | 30 | 4 | 0 | 2 | | 2 | 0 | 1.00 | 3 | .290 | .425 | .486 |
| 19 ML YEARS | | 2234 | 7207 | 2002 | 403 | 9 | 438 | (219 | 219) | 3737 | 1224 | 1436 | 1516 | 1357 | 95 | 1560 | 179 | 2 | 93 | | 20 | 12 | .63 | 163 | .278 | .400 | .519 |

# Johnny Giavotella

**Bats:** R **Throws:** R **Pos:** 2B-13;DH-1;PH-1 gee-uh-vo-TELL-uh **Ht:** 5'8" **Wt:** 180 **Born:** 7/10/1987 **Age:** 26

| BATTING | | | | | | | | | | | | | | | | | | | | BASERUNNING | | | | AVERAGES | | |
|---|---|---|---|---|---|---|---|---|---|---|---|---|---|---|---|---|---|---|---|---|---|---|---|---|---|---|
| Year Team | Lg | G | AB | H | 2B | 3B | HR | (Hm | Rd) | TB | R | RBI | RC | TBB | IBB | SO | HBP | SH | SF | SB | CS | SB% | GDP | Avg | OBP | Slg |
| 2013 Omha* | AAA | 100 | 370 | 106 | 24 | 0 | 7 | (- | -) | 151 | 48 | 46 | 60 | 51 | 6 | 59 | 0 | 0 | 5 | 8 | 4 | .67 | 12 | .286 | .369 | .408 |
| 2011 KC | AL | 46 | 178 | 44 | 9 | 4 | 2 | (2 | 0) | 67 | 20 | 21 | 15 | 6 | 0 | 32 | 1 | 0 | 2 | 5 | 2 | .71 | 4 | .247 | .273 | .376 |
| 2012 KC | AL | 53 | 181 | 43 | 7 | 1 | 1 | (1 | 0) | 55 | 21 | 15 | 14 | 8 | 0 | 35 | 0 | 0 | 0 | 3 | 0 | 1.00 | 4 | .238 | .270 | .304 |
| 2013 KC | AL | 14 | 41 | 9 | 3 | 0 | 0 | (0 | 0) | 12 | 4 | 4 | 5 | 5 | 0 | 4 | 2 | 0 | 0 | 0 | 0 | - | 0 | .220 | .333 | .293 |
| 3 ML YEARS | | 113 | 400 | 96 | 19 | 5 | 3 | (3 | 0) | 134 | 45 | 40 | 34 | 19 | 0 | 71 | 3 | 0 | 2 | 8 | 2 | .80 | 8 | .240 | .278 | .335 |

# Kyle Gibson

**Pitches:** R **Bats:** R **Pos:** SP-10 **Ht:** 6'6" **Wt:** 210 **Born:** 10/23/1987 **Age:** 26

| HOW MUCH HE PITCHED | | | | | | | | WHAT HE GAVE UP | | | | | | | | | | | | | THE RESULTS | | | | | | | |
|---|---|---|---|---|---|---|---|---|---|---|---|---|---|---|---|---|---|---|---|---|---|---|---|---|---|---|---|---|
| Year Team | Lg | G | GS | CG | GF | IP | BFP | H | R | ER | HR | SH | SF | HB | TBB | IBB | SO | WP | Bk | W | L | Pct | Sh | Sv-Op | Hld | ERC | ERA |
| 2010 FtMyrs | A+ | 7 | 7 | 1 | 0 | 43.1 | 169 | 33 | 11 | 9 | 2 | 0 | 0 | 2 | 12 | 0 | 40 | 2 | 0 | 4 | 1 | .800 | 1 | 0- - | - | 2.30 | 1.87 |
| 2010 NwBrit | AA | 16 | 16 | 1 | 0 | 93.0 | 388 | 91 | 39 | 38 | 5 | 3 | 6 | 4 | 22 | 0 | 77 | 3 | 0 | 7 | 5 | .583 | 0 | 0- - | - | 3.19 | 3.68 |
| 2010 Roch | AAA | 3 | 3 | 0 | 0 | 15.2 | 64 | 12 | 5 | 3 | 0 | 0 | 2 | 1 | 5 | 0 | 9 | 1 | 0 | 0 | 0 | - | 0 | 0- - | - | 2.15 | 1.72 |
| 2011 Roch | AAA | 18 | 18 | 0 | 0 | 95.1 | 419 | 109 | 57 | 51 | 11 | 2 | 3 | 1 | 27 | 1 | 91 | 5 | 0 | 3 | 8 | .273 | 0 | 0- - | - | 4.49 | 4.81 |
| 2012 Twins | R | 9 | 7 | 0 | 0 | 14.2 | 55 | 9 | 4 | 4 | 1 | 0 | 0 | 0 | 4 | 0 | 16 | 1 | 0 | 0 | 0 | - | 0 | 0- - | - | 1.60 | 2.45 |
| 2012 FtMyrs | A+ | 2 | 2 | 0 | 0 | 7.0 | 29 | 6 | 2 | 2 | 1 | 1 | 0 | 1 | 1 | 0 | 7 | 0 | 0 | 0 | 0 | - | 0 | 0- - | - | 3.08 | 2.57 |
| 2012 Roch | AAA | 2 | 2 | 0 | 0 | 6.2 | 31 | 11 | 7 | 7 | 1 | 0 | 0 | 0 | 1 | 0 | 10 | 0 | 0 | 0 | 2 | .000 | 0 | 0- - | - | 7.43 | 9.45 |
| 2013 Roch | AAA | 17 | 17 | 2 | 0 | 101.2 | 412 | 85 | 36 | 33 | 5 | 4 | 0 | 0 | 33 | 0 | 87 | 3 | 0 | 7 | 5 | .583 | 2 | 0- - | - | 2.63 | 2.92 |
| 2013 Min | AL | 10 | 10 | 0 | 0 | 51.0 | 238 | 69 | 38 | 37 | 7 | 0 | 2 | 5 | 20 | 0 | 29 | 4 | 0 | 2 | 4 | .333 | 0 | 0-0 | 0 | 6.98 | 6.53 |

# Conor Gillaspie

**Bats:** L **Throws:** R **Pos:** 3B-113;PH-15;1B-12;PR-2;DH-1 gah-LESS-pee **Ht:** 6'1" **Wt:** 205 **Born:** 7/18/1987 **Age:** 26

| BATTING | | | | | | | | | | | | | | | | | | | | BASERUNNING | | | | AVERAGES | | |
|---|---|---|---|---|---|---|---|---|---|---|---|---|---|---|---|---|---|---|---|---|---|---|---|---|---|---|
| Year Team | Lg | G | AB | H | 2B | 3B | HR | (Hm | Rd) | TB | R | RBI | RC | TBB | IBB | SO | HBP | SH | SF | SB | CS | SB% | GDP | Avg | OBP | Slg |
| 2008 SF | NL | 8 | 5 | 1 | 0 | 0 | 0 | (0 | 0) | 1 | 1 | 0 | 1 | 2 | 0 | 0 | 0 | 0 | 0 | 0 | 0 | - | 0 | .200 | .429 | .200 |
| 2011 SF | NL | 15 | 19 | 5 | 0 | 0 | 1 | (1 | 0) | 8 | 2 | 2 | 4 | 2 | 0 | 1 | 0 | 0 | 0 | 0 | 0 | - | 0 | .263 | .333 | .421 |
| 2012 SF | NL | 6 | 20 | 3 | 1 | 0 | 0 | (0 | 0) | 4 | 2 | 2 | 0 | 0 | 0 | 2 | 0 | 0 | 0 | 0 | 0 | - | 0 | .150 | .150 | .200 |
| 2013 CWS | AL | 134 | 408 | 100 | 14 | 3 | 13 | (8 | 5) | 159 | 46 | 40 | 46 | 37 | 4 | 79 | 1 | 0 | 6 | 0 | 1 | .00 | 7 | .245 | .305 | .390 |
| 4 ML YEARS | | 163 | 452 | 109 | 15 | 3 | 14 | (9 | 5) | 172 | 51 | 44 | 51 | 41 | 4 | 82 | 1 | 0 | 6 | 0 | 1 | .00 | 7 | .241 | .302 | .381 |

# Cole Gillespie

**Bats:** R **Throws:** R **Pos:** RF-13;PH-11;LF-6;CF-1 gil-EH-spee **Ht:** 6'1" **Wt:** 215 **Born:** 6/20/1984 **Age:** 30

| BATTING | | | | | | | | | | | | | | | | | | | | BASERUNNING | | | | AVERAGES | | |
|---|---|---|---|---|---|---|---|---|---|---|---|---|---|---|---|---|---|---|---|---|---|---|---|---|---|---|
| Year Team | Lg | G | AB | H | 2B | 3B | HR | (Hm | Rd) | TB | R | RBI | RC | TBB | IBB | SO | HBP | SH | SF | SB | CS | SB% | GDP | Avg | OBP | Slg |
| 2013 Fresno* | AAA | 74 | 235 | 65 | 11 | 2 | 9 | (- | -) | 107 | 35 | 31 | 41 | 32 | 0 | 52 | 0 | 0 | 2 | 7 | 0 | 1.00 | 3 | .277 | .361 | .455 |
| 2010 Ari | NL | 45 | 104 | 24 | 8 | 0 | 2 | (2 | 0) | 38 | 11 | 12 | 10 | 7 | 1 | 29 | 1 | 0 | 1 | 1 | 1 | .50 | 2 | .231 | .283 | .365 |
| 2011 Ari | NL | 5 | 6 | 2 | 0 | 0 | 1 | (1 | 0) | 5 | 2 | 4 | 3 | 1 | 0 | 1 | 0 | 0 | 0 | 0 | 0 | - | 0 | .333 | .429 | .833 |
| 2013 2 Tms | NL | 28 | 59 | 12 | 2 | 0 | 0 | (0 | 0) | 14 | 6 | 4 | 5 | 7 | 1 | 13 | 1 | 1 | 1 | 0 | 0 | - | 2 | .203 | .294 | .237 |
| 13 SF | NL | 3 | 9 | 0 | 0 | 0 | 0 | (0 | 0) | 0 | 0 | 0 | 0 | 1 | 1 | 0 | 0 | 0 | 0 | 0 | 0 | - | 0 | .000 | .100 | .000 |
| 13 ChC | NL | 25 | 50 | 12 | 2 | 0 | 0 | (0 | 0) | 14 | 6 | 4 | 5 | 6 | 0 | 13 | 1 | 1 | 1 | 0 | 0 | - | 2 | .240 | .328 | .280 |
| 3 ML YEARS | | 78 | 169 | 38 | 10 | 0 | 3 | (3 | 0) | 57 | 19 | 20 | 18 | 15 | 2 | 43 | 2 | 1 | 2 | 1 | 1 | .50 | 4 | .225 | .293 | .337 |

# Chris Gimenez

**Bats:** R **Throws:** R **Pos:** PH-2;C-1;1B-1;3B-1 JIMM-inn-ezz **Ht:** 6'2" **Wt:** 220 **Born:** 12/27/1982 **Age:** 31

| BATTING | | | | | | | | | | | | | | | | | | | | BASERUNNING | | | | AVERAGES | | |
|---|---|---|---|---|---|---|---|---|---|---|---|---|---|---|---|---|---|---|---|---|---|---|---|---|---|---|
| Year Team | Lg | G | AB | H | 2B | 3B | HR | (Hm | Rd) | TB | R | RBI | RC | TBB | IBB | SO | HBP | SH | SF | SB | CS | SB% | GDP | Avg | OBP | Slg |
| 2013 Drham* | AAA | 95 | 308 | 69 | 16 | 0 | 3 | (- | -) | 94 | 43 | 22 | 39 | 57 | 0 | 63 | 4 | 4 | 2 | 1 | 1 | .50 | 11 | .224 | .350 | .305 |
| 2009 Cle | AL | 45 | 111 | 16 | 2 | 0 | 3 | (0 | 3) | 27 | 12 | 7 | 3 | 17 | 0 | 36 | 0 | 1 | 1 | 1 | 1 | .50 | 3 | .144 | .256 | .243 |
| 2010 Cle | AL | 28 | 58 | 11 | 5 | 0 | 1 | (1 | 0) | 19 | 6 | 8 | 5 | 8 | 0 | 22 | 0 | 1 | 0 | 0 | 0 | - | 1 | .190 | .288 | .328 |
| 2011 Sea | AL | 24 | 59 | 12 | 1 | 0 | 1 | (0 | 1) | 16 | 6 | 6 | 5 | 10 | 0 | 13 | 0 | 0 | 1 | 0 | 1 | .00 | 1 | .203 | .314 | .271 |
| 2012 TB | AL | 42 | 100 | 26 | 4 | 0 | 1 | (0 | 1) | 33 | 10 | 9 | 10 | 8 | 0 | 24 | 0 | 1 | 0 | 0 | 0 | - | 4 | .260 | .315 | .330 |
| 2013 TB | AL | 4 | 3 | 1 | 1 | 0 | 0 | (0 | 0) | 2 | 0 | 0 | 0 | 1 | 0 | 1 | 0 | 0 | 0 | 0 | 0 | - | 1 | .333 | .500 | .667 |
| 5 ML YEARS | | 143 | 331 | 66 | 13 | 0 | 6 | (1 | 5) | 97 | 34 | 30 | 23 | 44 | 0 | 96 | 0 | 3 | 2 | 1 | 2 | .33 | 10 | .199 | .292 | .293 |

# Hector Gimenez

**Bats:** B **Throws:** R **Pos:** C-23;PH-3 hee-MEN-ezz **Ht:** 5'10" **Wt:** 230 **Born:** 9/28/1982 **Age:** 31

| BATTING | | | | | | | | | | | | | | | | | | | | BASERUNNING | | | | AVERAGES | | |
|---|---|---|---|---|---|---|---|---|---|---|---|---|---|---|---|---|---|---|---|---|---|---|---|---|---|---|
| Year Team | Lg | G | AB | H | 2B | 3B | HR | (Hm | Rd) | TB | R | RBI | RC | TBB | IBB | SO | HBP | SH | SF | SB | CS | SB% | GDP | Avg | OBP | Slg |
| 2013 Charltt* | AAA | 5 | 17 | 5 | 1 | 1 | 0 | (- | -) | 8 | 4 | 2 | 3 | 4 | 0 | 5 | 0 | 1 | 0 | 0 | 0 | - | 0 | .294 | .429 | .471 |
| 2006 Hou | NL | 2 | 2 | 0 | 0 | 0 | 0 | (0 | 0) | 0 | 0 | 0 | 0 | 0 | 0 | 1 | 0 | 0 | 0 | 0 | 0 | - | 0 | .000 | .000 | .000 |

| BATTING | | | | | | | | | | | | | | | | | | | | | BASERUNNING | | | | AVERAGES | | |
|---|---|---|---|---|---|---|---|---|---|---|---|---|---|---|---|---|---|---|---|---|---|---|---|---|---|---|---|
| Year Team | Lg | G | AB | H | 2B | 3B | HR | (Hm | Rd) | TB | R | RBI | RC | TBB | IBB | SO | HBP | SH | SF | SB | CS | SB% | GDP | Avg | OBP | Slg |
| 2011 LAD | NL | 4 | 7 | 1 | 0 | 0 | 0 | (0 | 0) | 1 | 0 | 0 | 0 | 0 | 0 | 3 | 0 | 0 | 0 | 0 | 0 | - | 0 | .143 | .143 | .143 |
| 2012 CWS | AL | 5 | 11 | 5 | 0 | 0 | 0 | (0 | 0) | 5 | 1 | 1 | 3 | 0 | 0 | 3 | 0 | 0 | 0 | 0 | 0 | - | 0 | .455 | .455 | .455 |
| 2013 CWS | AL | 26 | 68 | 13 | 4 | 0 | 2 | (1 | 1) | 23 | 8 | 10 | 6 | 7 | 1 | 22 | 2 | 0 | 3 | 0 | 0 | - | 1 | .191 | .275 | .338 |
| 4 ML YEARS | | 37 | 88 | 19 | 4 | 0 | 2 | (1 | 1) | 29 | 9 | 11 | 9 | 7 | 1 | 29 | 2 | 0 | 3 | 0 | 0 | - | 1 | .216 | .280 | .330 |

## Caleb Gindl

**Bats:** L **Throws:** L **Pos:** LF-30;PH-23;RF-5 GINN-dul **Ht:** 5'7" **Wt:** 205 **Born:** 8/31/1988 **Age:** 25

| BATTING | | | | | | | | | | | | | | | | | | | | BASERUNNING | | | | AVERAGES | | |
|---|---|---|---|---|---|---|---|---|---|---|---|---|---|---|---|---|---|---|---|---|---|---|---|---|---|---|
| Year Team | Lg | G | AB | H | 2B | 3B | HR | (Hm | Rd) | TB | R | RBI | RC | TBB | IBB | SO | HBP | SH | SF | SB | CS | SB% | GDP | Avg | OBP | Slg |
| 2009 BrvdCt | A+ | 112 | 394 | 109 | 15 | 3 | 17 | (- | -) | 181 | 61 | 71 | 71 | 57 | 5 | 92 | 1 | 2 | 8 | 18 | 4 | .82 | 7 | .277 | .363 | .459 |
| 2010 Hntsvl | AA | 128 | 463 | 126 | 33 | 1 | 9 | (- | -) | 188 | 61 | 60 | 71 | 55 | 0 | 78 | 5 | 6 | 5 | 10 | 5 | .67 | 3 | .272 | .352 | .406 |
| 2011 Nashv | AAA | 125 | 468 | 145 | 23 | 5 | 15 | (- | -) | 223 | 84 | 60 | 88 | 62 | 2 | 93 | 1 | 2 | 0 | 6 | 5 | .55 | 10 | .310 | .392 | .476 |
| 2012 Nashv | AAA | 127 | 452 | 118 | 27 | 5 | 12 | (- | -) | 191 | 54 | 50 | 63 | 37 | 1 | 98 | 2 | 2 | 4 | 4 | 1 | .80 | 9 | .261 | .317 | .423 |
| 2013 Nashv | AAA | 83 | 312 | 92 | 21 | 3 | 11 | (- | -) | 152 | 33 | 51 | 54 | 30 | 1 | 72 | 2 | 1 | 2 | 1 | 2 | .33 | 10 | .295 | .358 | .487 |
| 2013 Mil | NL | 57 | 132 | 32 | 7 | 2 | 5 | (3 | 2) | 58 | 17 | 14 | 20 | 20 | 1 | 25 | 0 | 2 | 1 | 2 | 1 | .67 | 0 | .242 | .340 | .439 |

## Ryan Goins

**Bats:** L **Throws:** R **Pos:** 2B-32;SS-2;PH-1 GO-inns **Ht:** 5'10" **Wt:** 170 **Born:** 2/13/1988 **Age:** 26

| BATTING | | | | | | | | | | | | | | | | | | | | BASERUNNING | | | | AVERAGES | | |
|---|---|---|---|---|---|---|---|---|---|---|---|---|---|---|---|---|---|---|---|---|---|---|---|---|---|---|
| Year Team | Lg | G | AB | H | 2B | 3B | HR | (Hm | Rd) | TB | R | RBI | RC | TBB | IBB | SO | HBP | SH | SF | SB | CS | SB% | GDP | Avg | OBP | Slg |
| 2009 B Jays | R | 3 | 9 | 1 | 0 | 0 | 0 | (- | -) | 1 | 1 | 0 | 0 | 0 | 0 | 2 | 0 | 0 | 0 | 0 | 0 | - | 1 | .111 | .111 | .111 |
| 2009 Auburn | A- | 24 | 101 | 30 | 5 | 1 | 0 | (- | -) | 37 | 15 | 8 | 13 | 8 | 0 | 23 | 0 | 1 | 0 | 2 | 2 | .50 | 1 | .297 | .349 | .366 |
| 2009 Lnsng | A | 19 | 81 | 16 | 4 | 0 | 0 | (- | -) | 20 | 6 | 9 | 4 | 7 | 0 | 23 | 0 | 0 | 1 | 1 | 2 | .33 | 1 | .198 | .258 | .247 |
| 2010 Lnsng | A | 77 | 295 | 91 | 19 | 2 | 3 | (- | -) | 123 | 49 | 35 | 48 | 35 | 0 | 60 | 1 | 4 | 3 | 6 | 7 | .46 | 4 | .308 | .380 | .417 |
| 2010 Dnedin | A+ | 47 | 166 | 34 | 9 | 0 | 0 | (- | -) | 43 | 8 | 18 | 10 | 11 | 0 | 33 | 0 | 3 | 2 | 1 | 1 | .50 | 1 | .205 | .251 | .259 |
| 2011 Dnedin | A+ | 101 | 353 | 101 | 24 | 5 | 3 | (- | -) | 144 | 50 | 52 | 51 | 32 | 0 | 67 | 0 | 10 | 3 | 2 | 2 | .50 | 4 | .286 | .343 | .408 |
| 2011 B Jays | R | 1 | 3 | 0 | 0 | 0 | 0 | (- | -) | 0 | 0 | 0 | 0 | 0 | 0 | 1 | 0 | 0 | 0 | 0 | 0 | - | 1 | .000 | .000 | .000 |
| 2012 NHam | AA | 136 | 546 | 158 | 33 | 4 | 7 | (- | -) | 220 | 66 | 61 | 79 | 47 | 3 | 78 | 0 | 19 | 6 | 15 | 9 | .63 | 8 | .289 | .342 | .403 |
| 2013 Buffalo | AAA | 111 | 377 | 97 | 22 | 1 | 6 | (- | -) | 139 | 42 | 46 | 44 | 29 | 0 | 85 | 1 | 9 | 2 | 3 | 5 | .38 | 9 | .257 | .311 | .369 |
| 2013 Tor | AL | 34 | 119 | 30 | 5 | 0 | 2 | (2 | 0) | 41 | 11 | 8 | 11 | 2 | 0 | 28 | 0 | 0 | 0 | 0 | 0 | - | 1 | .252 | .264 | .345 |

## Paul Goldschmidt

**Bats:** R **Throws:** R **Pos:** 1B-159;PH-2 **Ht:** 6'3" **Wt:** 245 **Born:** 9/10/1987 **Age:** 26

| BATTING | | | | | | | | | | | | | | | | | | | | BASERUNNING | | | | AVERAGES | | |
|---|---|---|---|---|---|---|---|---|---|---|---|---|---|---|---|---|---|---|---|---|---|---|---|---|---|---|
| Year Team | Lg | G | AB | H | 2B | 3B | HR | (Hm | Rd) | TB | R | RBI | RC | TBB | IBB | SO | HBP | SH | SF | SB | CS | SB% | GDP | Avg | OBP | Slg |
| 2011 Ari | NL | 48 | 156 | 39 | 9 | 1 | 8 | (2 | 6) | 74 | 28 | 26 | 26 | 20 | 0 | 53 | 0 | 0 | 1 | 4 | 0 | 1.00 | 4 | .250 | .333 | .474 |
| 2012 Ari | NL | 145 | 514 | 147 | 43 | 1 | 20 | (10 | 10) | 252 | 82 | 82 | 86 | 60 | 4 | 130 | 4 | 0 | **9** | 18 | 3 | .86 | 9 | .286 | .359 | .490 |
| 2013 Ari | NL | 160 | 602 | 182 | 36 | 3 | **36** | **(17** | 19) | **332** | 103 | **125** | **131** | 99 | **19** | 145 | 3 | 0 | 5 | 15 | 7 | .68 | 25 | .302 | .401 | **.551** |
| Postseason | | 4 | 16 | 7 | 0 | 0 | 2 | (1 | 1) | 13 | 4 | 6 | 5 | 2 | 0 | 5 | 1 | 0 | 0 | 1 | 0 | 1.00 | 0 | .438 | .526 | .813 |
| 3 ML YEARS | | 353 | 1272 | 368 | 88 | 5 | 64 | (29 | 35) | 658 | 213 | 233 | 243 | 179 | 23 | 328 | 7 | 0 | 15 | 37 | 10 | .79 | 38 | .289 | .376 | .517 |

## Brandon Gomes

**Pitches:** R **Bats:** R **Pos:** RP-26 GOHMS **Ht:** 5'11" **Wt:** 185 **Born:** 7/15/1984 **Age:** 29

| HOW MUCH HE PITCHED | | | | | | | | WHAT HE GAVE UP | | | | | | | | | | | | THE RESULTS | | | | | | | |
|---|---|---|---|---|---|---|---|---|---|---|---|---|---|---|---|---|---|---|---|---|---|---|---|---|---|---|---|
| Year Team | Lg | G | GS | CG | GF | IP | BFP | H | R | ER | HR | SH | SF | HB | TBB | IBB | SO | WP | Bk | W | L | Pct | Sh | Sv-Op | Hld | ERC | ERA |
| 2013 Charltt* | A+ | 5 | 4 | 0 | 0 | 6.0 | 26 | 9 | 5 | 5 | 3 | 0 | 0 | 0 | 0 | 0 | 5 | 0 | 0 | 0 | 0 | - | 0 | 0-- | - | 8.47 | 7.50 |
| 2013 Rays* | R | 1 | 1 | 0 | 0 | 1.0 | 4 | 0 | 0 | 0 | 0 | 0 | 0 | 1 | 0 | 0 | 1 | 0 | 0 | 0 | 0 | - | 0 | 0-- | - | 0.95 | 0.00 |
| 2013 Drham* | AAA | 9 | 0 | 0 | 0 | 10.1 | 40 | 7 | 3 | 3 | 1 | 0 | 1 | 1 | 1 | 0 | 14 | 3 | 0 | 0 | 0 | - | 0 | 0-- | - | 1.67 | 2.61 |
| 2011 TB | AL | 40 | 0 | 0 | 17 | 37.0 | 160 | 34 | 15 | 12 | 3 | 1 | 3 | 1 | 16 | 0 | 32 | 1 | 0 | 2 | 1 | .667 | 0 | 0-0 | 5 | 3.69 | 2.92 |
| 2012 TB | AL | 15 | 0 | 0 | 4 | 17.2 | 83 | 16 | 12 | 10 | 2 | 0 | 1 | 2 | 12 | 3 | 15 | 1 | 0 | 2 | 2 | .500 | 0 | 0-0 | 0 | 4.76 | 5.09 |
| 2013 TB | AL | 26 | 0 | 0 | 9 | 19.1 | 83 | 18 | 15 | 14 | 4 | 1 | 2 | 0 | 7 | 3 | 29 | 1 | 0 | 3 | 1 | .750 | 0 | 0-0 | 0 | 3.94 | 6.52 |
| Postseason | | 3 | 0 | 0 | 0 | 2.1 | 10 | 1 | 2 | 2 | 1 | 0 | 0 | 0 | 2 | 0 | 3 | 0 | 0 | 0 | 0 | - | 0 | 0-0 | 0 | 4.86 | 7.71 |
| 3 ML YEARS | | 81 | 0 | 0 | 30 | 74.0 | 326 | 68 | 42 | 36 | 9 | 2 | 6 | 3 | 35 | 6 | 76 | 3 | 0 | 7 | 4 | .636 | 0 | 0-0 | 5 | 4.02 | 4.38 |

## Jonny Gomes

**Bats:** R **Throws:** R **Pos:** LF-98;PH-30;DH-10;RF-4;PR-1 GOHMS **Ht:** 6'1" **Wt:** 230 **Born:** 11/22/1980 **Age:** 33

| BATTING | | | | | | | | | | | | | | | | | | | | BASERUNNING | | | | AVERAGES | | |
|---|---|---|---|---|---|---|---|---|---|---|---|---|---|---|---|---|---|---|---|---|---|---|---|---|---|---|
| Year Team | Lg | G | AB | H | 2B | 3B | HR | (Hm | Rd) | TB | R | RBI | RC | TBB | IBB | SO | HBP | SH | SF | SB | CS | SB% | GDP | Avg | OBP | Slg |
| 2003 TB | AL | 8 | 15 | 2 | 1 | 0 | 0 | (0 | 0) | 3 | 1 | 0 | 0 | 0 | 0 | 6 | 1 | 0 | 0 | 0 | 0 | - | 0 | .133 | .188 | .200 |
| 2004 TB | AL | 5 | 14 | 1 | 0 | 0 | 0 | (0 | 0) | 1 | 0 | 1 | 0 | 1 | 0 | 6 | 0 | 0 | 0 | 0 | 0 | - | 0 | .071 | .133 | .071 |
| 2005 TB | AL | 101 | 348 | 98 | 13 | 6 | 21 | (11 | 10) | 186 | 61 | 54 | 62 | 39 | 1 | 113 | 14 | 1 | 5 | 9 | 5 | .64 | 6 | .282 | .372 | .534 |
| 2006 TB | AL | 117 | 385 | 83 | 21 | 1 | 20 | (7 | 13) | 166 | 53 | 59 | 53 | 61 | 2 | 116 | 6 | 0 | 9 | 1 | 5 | .17 | 10 | .216 | .325 | .431 |
| 2007 TB | AL | 107 | 348 | 85 | 20 | 2 | 17 | (10 | 7) | 160 | 48 | 49 | 47 | 35 | 1 | 126 | 7 | 0 | 4 | 12 | 4 | .75 | 1 | .244 | .322 | .460 |
| 2008 TB | AL | 77 | 154 | 28 | 5 | 1 | 8 | (2 | 6) | 59 | 23 | 21 | 18 | 15 | 1 | 46 | 7 | 0 | 1 | 8 | 1 | .89 | 1 | .182 | .282 | .383 |
| 2009 Cin | NL | 98 | 281 | 75 | 17 | 0 | 20 | (11 | 9) | 152 | 39 | 51 | 46 | 26 | 2 | 85 | 5 | 0 | 2 | 3 | 1 | .75 | 8 | .267 | .338 | .541 |
| 2010 Cin | NL | 148 | 511 | 136 | 24 | 3 | 18 | (11 | 7) | 220 | 77 | 86 | 83 | 39 | 3 | 123 | 12 | 0 | 9 | 5 | 3 | .63 | 4 | .266 | .327 | .431 |
| 2011 2 Tms | NL | 120 | 311 | 65 | 12 | 1 | 14 | (8 | 6) | 121 | 41 | 43 | 36 | 48 | 1 | 105 | 8 | 0 | 5 | 7 | 3 | .70 | 2 | .209 | .325 | .389 |
| 2012 Oak | AL | 99 | 279 | 73 | 10 | 0 | 18 | (7 | 11) | 137 | 46 | 47 | 54 | 44 | 2 | 104 | 8 | 1 | 1 | 3 | 1 | .75 | 2 | .262 | .377 | .491 |
| 2013 Bos | AL | 116 | 312 | 77 | 17 | 0 | 13 | (5 | 8) | 133 | 49 | 52 | 54 | 43 | 3 | 89 | 6 | 0 | 5 | 1 | 0 | 1.00 | 6 | .247 | .344 | .426 |
| 11 Cin | NL | 77 | 218 | 46 | 8 | 0 | 11 | (7 | 4) | 87 | 30 | 31 | 28 | 38 | 1 | 74 | 5 | 0 | 4 | 5 | 3 | .63 | 1 | .211 | .336 | .399 |
| 11 Was | NL | 43 | 93 | 19 | 4 | 1 | 3 | (1 | 2) | 34 | 11 | 12 | 8 | 10 | 0 | 31 | 3 | 0 | 1 | 2 | 0 | 1.00 | 1 | .204 | .299 | .366 |
| Postseason | | 3 | 7 | 0 | 0 | 0 | 0 | (0 | 0) | 0 | 0 | 0 | 0 | 0 | 0 | 3 | 0 | 0 | 0 | 0 | 0 | - | 0 | .000 | .000 | .000 |
| 11 ML YEARS | | 996 | 2958 | 723 | 140 | 14 | 149 | (72 | 77) | 1338 | 438 | 463 | 453 | 351 | 16 | 919 | 74 | 2 | 41 | 49 | 23 | .68 | 40 | .244 | .335 | .452 |

## Yan Gomes

**Bats:** R **Throws:** R **Pos:** C-85;DH-3;PH-3;1B-1 YAHN GOHMS **Ht:** 6'2" **Wt:** 215 **Born:** 7/19/1987 **Age:** 26

| BATTING | | | | | | | | | | | | | | | | | | | | BASERUNNING | | | | AVERAGES | | |
|---|---|---|---|---|---|---|---|---|---|---|---|---|---|---|---|---|---|---|---|---|---|---|---|---|---|---|
| Year Team | Lg | G | AB | H | 2B | 3B | HR | (Hm | Rd) | TB | R | RBI | RC | TBB | IBB | SO | HBP | SH | SF | SB | CS | SB% | GDP | Avg | OBP | Slg |
| 2009 B Jays | R | 4 | 14 | 5 | 0 | 0 | 0 | (- | -) | 5 | 1 | 2 | 2 | 3 | 0 | 2 | 0 | 0 | 0 | 0 | 0 | - | 0 | .357 | .471 | .357 |
| 2009 Auburn | A- | 60 | 223 | 66 | 23 | 2 | 2 | (- | -) | 99 | 22 | 44 | 36 | 22 | 1 | 37 | 2 | 0 | 1 | 0 | 2 | .00 | 9 | .296 | .363 | .444 |
| 2010 Dnedin | A+ | 68 | 233 | 64 | 21 | 1 | 9 | (- | -) | 114 | 37 | 40 | 35 | 9 | 0 | 64 | 4 | 0 | 1 | 0 | 0 | - | 6 | .275 | .312 | .489 |
| 2010 Lnsng | A | 7 | 26 | 6 | 2 | 0 | 0 | (- | -) | 8 | 2 | 8 | 2 | 3 | 0 | 11 | 0 | 0 | 2 | 0 | 0 | - | 1 | .231 | .290 | .308 |
| 2011 NHam | AA | 79 | 276 | 69 | 18 | 1 | 13 | (- | -) | 128 | 34 | 51 | 42 | 25 | 1 | 75 | 4 | 0 | 4 | 0 | 0 | - | 7 | .250 | .317 | .464 |
| 2011 LsVgs | AAA | 4 | 14 | 3 | 1 | 0 | 0 | (- | -) | 4 | 1 | 1 | 1 | 1 | 0 | 4 | 0 | 0 | 0 | 0 | 0 | - | 1 | .214 | .267 | .286 |
| 2012 LsVgs | AAA | 79 | 305 | 100 | 29 | 1 | 13 | (- | -) | 170 | 44 | 58 | 63 | 25 | 0 | 72 | 2 | 0 | 2 | 4 | 0 | 1.00 | 4 | .328 | .380 | .557 |
| 2013 Clmbs | AAA | 6 | 20 | 6 | 4 | 0 | 0 | (- | -) | 10 | 2 | 3 | 4 | 4 | 0 | 4 | 0 | 0 | 0 | 0 | 0 | - | 1 | .300 | .417 | .500 |
| 2012 Tor | AL | 43 | 98 | 20 | 4 | 0 | 4 | (3 | 1) | 36 | 9 | 13 | 11 | 6 | 0 | 32 | 3 | 1 | 3 | 0 | 0 | - | 3 | .204 | .264 | .367 |
| 2013 Cle | AL | 88 | 293 | 86 | 18 | 2 | 11 | (6 | 5) | 141 | 45 | 38 | 42 | 18 | 0 | 67 | 7 | 0 | 4 | 2 | 0 | 1.00 | 12 | .294 | .345 | .481 |
| 2 ML YEARS | | 131 | 391 | 106 | 22 | 2 | 15 | (9 | 6) | 177 | 54 | 51 | 53 | 24 | 0 | 99 | 10 | 1 | 7 | 2 | 0 | 1.00 | 15 | .271 | .324 | .453 |

## Carlos Gomez

**Bats:** R **Throws:** R **Pos:** CF-145;PH-3 **Ht:** 6'3" **Wt:** 215 **Born:** 12/4/1985 **Age:** 28

| BATTING | | | | | | | | | | | | | | | | | | | | BASERUNNING | | | | AVERAGES | | |
|---|---|---|---|---|---|---|---|---|---|---|---|---|---|---|---|---|---|---|---|---|---|---|---|---|---|---|
| Year Team | Lg | G | AB | H | 2B | 3B | HR | (Hm | Rd) | TB | R | RBI | RC | TBB | IBB | SO | HBP | SH | SF | SB | CS | SB% | GDP | Avg | OBP | Slg |
| 2007 NYM | NL | 58 | 125 | 29 | 3 | 0 | 2 | (1 | 1) | 38 | 14 | 12 | 11 | 8 | 2 | 27 | 3 | 0 | 3 | 12 | 3 | .80 | 0 | .232 | .288 | .304 |
| 2008 Min | AL | 153 | 577 | 149 | 24 | 7 | 7 | (3 | 4) | 208 | 79 | 59 | 66 | 25 | 0 | 142 | 7 | 3 | 2 | 33 | 11 | .75 | 7 | .258 | .296 | .360 |
| 2009 Min | AL | 137 | 315 | 72 | 15 | 5 | 3 | (1 | 2) | 106 | 51 | 28 | 33 | 22 | 0 | 72 | 4 | 7 | 1 | 14 | 7 | .67 | 1 | .229 | .287 | .337 |
| 2010 Mil | NL | 97 | 291 | 72 | 11 | 3 | 5 | (3 | 2) | 104 | 38 | 24 | 28 | 17 | 1 | 72 | 4 | 6 | 0 | 18 | 3 | **.86** | 10 | .247 | .298 | .357 |
| 2011 Mil | NL | 94 | 231 | 52 | 11 | 3 | 8 | (4 | 4) | 93 | 37 | 24 | 25 | 15 | 0 | 64 | 2 | 8 | 2 | 16 | 2 | .89 | 2 | .225 | .276 | .403 |
| 2012 Mil | NL | 137 | 415 | 108 | 19 | 4 | 19 | (11 | 8) | 192 | 72 | 51 | 59 | 20 | 1 | 98 | 8 | 6 | 3 | 37 | 6 | .86 | 6 | .260 | .305 | .463 |
| 2013 Mil | NL | 147 | 536 | 152 | 27 | 10 | 24 | (15 | 9) | 271 | 80 | 73 | 81 | 37 | 2 | 146 | 10 | 1 | 6 | 40 | 7 | .85 | 11 | .284 | .338 | .506 |
| Postseason | | 9 | 18 | 5 | 0 | 0 | 1 | (0 | 1) | 8 | 4 | 2 | 2 | 1 | 0 | 4 | 2 | 2 | 0 | 2 | 1 | .67 | 0 | .278 | .381 | .444 |
| 7 ML YEARS | | 823 | 2490 | 634 | 110 | 32 | 68 | (38 | 30) | 1012 | 371 | 271 | 303 | 144 | 6 | 621 | 38 | 31 | 17 | 170 | 39 | .81 | 37 | .255 | .303 | .406 |

## Jeanmar Gomez

**Pitches:** R **Bats:** R **Pos:** RP-26; SP-8 JENN-marr **Ht:** 6'3" **Wt:** 220 **Born:** 2/10/1988 **Age:** 26

| HOW MUCH HE PITCHED | | | | | | | | WHAT HE GAVE UP | | | | | | | | | | | | | THE RESULTS | | | | | | | | |
|---|---|---|---|---|---|---|---|---|---|---|---|---|---|---|---|---|---|---|---|---|---|---|---|---|---|---|---|---|---|
| Year Team | Lg | G | GS | CG | GF | IP | BFP | H | R | ER | HR | SH | SF | HB | TBB | IBB | SO | WP | Bk | W | L | Pct | Sh | Sv-Op | Hld | ERC | ERA |
| 2013 Indy* | AAA | 2 | 2 | 0 | 0 | 8.0 | 32 | 3 | 2 | 1 | 0 | 0 | 0 | 1 | 4 | 0 | 7 | 2 | 0 | 1 | 0 | 1.000 | 0 | 0-- | - | 1.30 | 1.13 |
| 2010 Cle | AL | 11 | 11 | 0 | 0 | 57.2 | 265 | 73 | 36 | 30 | 7 | 0 | 3 | 2 | 22 | 3 | 34 | 1 | 0 | 4 | 5 | .444 | 0 | 0-0 | 0 | 5.75 | 4.68 |
| 2011 Cle | AL | 11 | 10 | 0 | 0 | 58.1 | 259 | 73 | 31 | 29 | 6 | 0 | 2 | 1 | 15 | 1 | 31 | 2 | 0 | 5 | 3 | .625 | 0 | 0-0 | 0 | 4.99 | 4.47 |
| 2012 Cle | AL | 20 | 17 | 0 | 1 | 90.2 | 395 | 95 | 66 | 60 | 15 | 2 | 7 | 4 | 34 | 5 | 47 | 2 | 0 | 5 | 8 | .385 | 0 | 0-0 | 0 | 4.83 | 5.96 |
| 2013 Pit | NL | 34 | 8 | 0 | 6 | 80.2 | 333 | 65 | 35 | 30 | 6 | 4 | 6 | 3 | 28 | 3 | 53 | 6 | 0 | 3 | 0 | 1.000 | 0 | 0-0 | 3 | 2.75 | 3.35 |
| 4 ML YEARS | | 76 | 46 | 0 | 7 | 287.1 | 1252 | 306 | 168 | 149 | 34 | 6 | 18 | 10 | 99 | 12 | 165 | 11 | 0 | 17 | 16 | .515 | 0 | 0-0 | 3 | 4.41 | 4.67 |

## Adrian Gonzalez

**Bats:** L **Throws:** L **Pos:** 1B-151;PH-6;DH-1 **Ht:** 6'2" **Wt:** 225 **Born:** 5/8/1982 **Age:** 32

| BATTING | | | | | | | | | | | | | | | | | | | | BASERUNNING | | | | AVERAGES | | |
|---|---|---|---|---|---|---|---|---|---|---|---|---|---|---|---|---|---|---|---|---|---|---|---|---|---|---|
| Year Team | Lg | G | AB | H | 2B | 3B | HR | (Hm | Rd) | TB | R | RBI | RC | TBB | IBB | SO | HBP | SH | SF | SB | CS | SB% | GDP | Avg | OBP | Slg |
| 2004 Tex | AL | 16 | 42 | 10 | 3 | 0 | 1 | (1 | 0) | 16 | 7 | 7 | 7 | 2 | 0 | 6 | 0 | 0 | 0 | 0 | 0 | - | 0 | .238 | .273 | .381 |
| 2005 Tex | AL | 43 | 150 | 34 | 7 | 1 | 6 | (3 | 3) | 61 | 17 | 17 | 13 | 10 | 2 | 37 | 0 | 0 | 2 | 0 | 0 | - | 3 | .227 | .272 | .407 |
| 2006 SD | NL | 156 | 570 | 173 | 38 | 1 | 24 | (10 | 14) | 285 | 83 | 82 | 82 | 52 | 9 | 113 | 3 | 1 | 5 | 0 | 1 | .00 | **24** | .304 | .362 | .500 |
| 2007 SD | NL | 161 | 646 | 182 | 46 | 3 | 30 | (10 | 20) | 324 | 101 | 100 | 108 | 65 | 9 | 140 | 3 | 0 | 6 | 0 | 0 | - | 6 | .282 | .347 | .502 |
| 2008 SD | NL | **162** | 616 | 172 | 32 | 1 | 36 | (14 | **22)** | 314 | 103 | 119 | 107 | 74 | 18 | 142 | 7 | 0 | 3 | 0 | 0 | - | 24 | .279 | .361 | .510 |
| 2009 SD | NL | 160 | 552 | 153 | 27 | 2 | 40 | (12 | **28)** | 304 | 90 | 99 | 109 | **119** | 22 | 109 | 5 | 1 | 4 | 1 | 1 | .50 | 23 | .277 | .407 | .551 |
| 2010 SD | NL | 160 | 591 | 176 | 33 | 0 | 31 | (11 | 20) | 302 | 87 | 101 | 122 | 93 | 35 | 114 | 2 | 2 | 4 | 0 | 0 | - | 15 | .298 | .393 | .511 |
| 2011 Bos | AL | 159 | 630 | **213** | 45 | 3 | 27 | (10 | 17) | 345 | 108 | 117 | 121 | 74 | 20 | 119 | 6 | 0 | 5 | 1 | 0 | 1.00 | **28** | .338 | .410 | .548 |
| 2012 2 Tms | | 159 | 629 | 188 | 47 | 1 | 18 | (9 | 9) | 291 | 75 | 108 | 113 | 42 | 5 | 110 | 5 | 0 | 8 | 2 | 0 | 1.00 | 10 | .299 | .344 | .463 |
| 2013 LAD | NL | 157 | 583 | 171 | 32 | 0 | 22 | (11 | 11) | 269 | 69 | 100 | 89 | 47 | 6 | 98 | 1 | 0 | **10** | 1 | 0 | 1.00 | 12 | .293 | .342 | .461 |
| 12 Bos | AL | 123 | 484 | 145 | 37 | 0 | 15 | (8 | 7) | 227 | 63 | 86 | 89 | 31 | 4 | 81 | 5 | 0 | 7 | 0 | 0 | - | 9 | .300 | .343 | .469 |
| 12 LAD | NL | 36 | 145 | 43 | 10 | 1 | 3 | (1 | 2) | 64 | 12 | 22 | 24 | 11 | 1 | 29 | 0 | 0 | 1 | 2 | 0 | 1.00 | 1 | .297 | .344 | .441 |
| Postseason | | 4 | 14 | 5 | 0 | 0 | 0 | (0 | 0) | 5 | 2 | 0 | 1 | 3 | 0 | 3 | 0 | 0 | 0 | 0 | 0 | - | 0 | .357 | .471 | .357 |
| 10 ML YEARS | | 1333 | 5009 | 1472 | 310 | 12 | 235 | (91 | 144) | 2511 | 740 | 850 | 871 | 578 | 126 | 988 | 32 | 4 | 47 | 5 | 2 | .71 | 145 | .294 | .367 | .501 |

## Alberto Gonzalez

**Bats:** R **Throws:** R **Pos:** 2B-10;3B-7;SS-5;LF-1;RF-1;PR-1 **Ht:** 5'10" **Wt:** 195 **Born:** 4/18/1983 **Age:** 31

| BATTING | | | | | | | | | | | | | | | | | | | | BASERUNNING | | | | AVERAGES | | |
|---|---|---|---|---|---|---|---|---|---|---|---|---|---|---|---|---|---|---|---|---|---|---|---|---|---|---|
| Year Team | Lg | G | AB | H | 2B | 3B | HR | (Hm | Rd) | TB | R | RBI | RC | TBB | IBB | SO | HBP | SH | SF | SB | CS | SB% | GDP | Avg | OBP | Slg |
| 2013 Iowa* | AAA | 10 | 33 | 10 | 1 | 0 | 0 | (- | -) | 11 | 4 | 3 | 4 | 5 | 0 | 4 | 0 | 0 | 0 | 0 | 0 | - | 2 | .303 | .395 | .333 |
| 2013 S-WB* | AAA | 55 | 191 | 35 | 4 | 0 | 1 | (- | -) | 42 | 10 | 12 | 8 | 14 | 0 | 33 | 1 | 3 | 2 | 0 | 2 | .00 | 6 | .183 | .240 | .220 |
| 2007 NYY | AL | 12 | 14 | 1 | 0 | 0 | 0 | (0 | 0) | 1 | 3 | 1 | 0 | 1 | 0 | 1 | 0 | 0 | 0 | 0 | 1 | .00 | 1 | .071 | .133 | .071 |
| 2008 2 Tms | | 45 | 101 | 26 | 8 | 0 | 1 | (0 | 1) | 37 | 13 | 10 | 11 | 8 | 0 | 14 | 1 | 2 | 0 | 0 | 1 | .00 | 6 | .257 | .318 | .366 |
| 2009 Was | NL | 105 | 291 | 77 | 16 | 3 | 1 | (1 | 0) | 102 | 31 | 33 | 30 | 14 | 1 | 27 | 3 | 2 | 6 | 1 | 1 | .50 | 8 | .265 | .299 | .351 |
| 2010 Was | NL | 115 | 186 | 46 | 8 | 1 | 0 | (0 | 0) | 56 | 19 | 5 | 9 | 7 | 0 | 30 | 1 | 3 | 1 | 0 | 0 | - | 8 | .247 | .277 | .301 |
| 2011 SD | NL | 102 | 247 | 53 | 10 | 2 | 1 | (1 | 0) | 70 | 18 | 32 | 20 | 13 | 3 | 37 | 2 | 1 | 4 | 1 | 2 | .33 | 5 | .215 | .256 | .283 |
| 2012 Tex | AL | 24 | 54 | 13 | 2 | 1 | 0 | (0 | 0) | 17 | 7 | 4 | 3 | 0 | 0 | 9 | 0 | 1 | 0 | 0 | 0 | - | 0 | .241 | .241 | .315 |
| 2013 2 Tms | | 24 | 57 | 11 | 2 | 0 | 1 | (1 | 0) | 16 | 6 | 6 | 3 | 2 | 1 | 12 | 0 | 0 | 1 | 0 | 0 | - | 2 | .193 | .217 | .281 |
| 08 NYY | AL | 28 | 52 | 9 | 2 | 0 | 0 | (0 | 0) | 11 | 4 | 1 | 0 | 4 | 0 | 8 | 0 | 2 | 0 | 0 | 0 | - | 4 | .173 | .232 | .212 |
| 08 Was | NL | 17 | 49 | 17 | 6 | 0 | 1 | (0 | 1) | 26 | 9 | 9 | 11 | 4 | 0 | 6 | 1 | 0 | 0 | 0 | 1 | .00 | 2 | .347 | .407 | .531 |
| 13 ChC | NL | 11 | 23 | 5 | 1 | 0 | 1 | (1 | 0) | 9 | 3 | 2 | 1 | 2 | 1 | 6 | 0 | 0 | 1 | 0 | 0 | - | 1 | .217 | .269 | .391 |
| 13 NYY | AL | 13 | 34 | 6 | 1 | 0 | 0 | (0 | 0) | 7 | 3 | 4 | 2 | 0 | 0 | 6 | 0 | 0 | 0 | 0 | 0 | - | 1 | .176 | .176 | .206 |
| 7 ML YEARS | | 427 | 950 | 227 | 46 | 7 | 4 | (3 | 1) | 299 | 97 | 91 | 76 | 45 | 5 | 130 | 7 | 9 | 12 | 2 | 5 | .29 | 30 | .239 | .275 | .315 |

# Alex Gonzalez

**Bats:** R **Throws:** R **Pos:** 1B-22;3B-11;PH-9;SS-3;PR-2 **Ht:** 6'1" **Wt:** 210 **Born:** 2/15/1977 **Age:** 37

| | | | BATTING | | | | | | | | | | | | | | | | | | BASERUNNING | | | | AVERAGES | | |
|---|---|---|---|---|---|---|---|---|---|---|---|---|---|---|---|---|---|---|---|---|---|---|---|---|---|---|---|
| Year | Team | Lg | G | AB | H | 2B | 3B | HR | (Hm | Rd) | TB | R | RBI | RC | TBB | IBB | SO | HBP | SH | SF | SB | CS | SB% | GDP | Avg | OBP | Slg |
| 1998 | Fla | NL | 25 | 86 | 13 | 2 | 0 | 3 | (1 | 2) | 24 | 11 | 7 | 5 | 9 | 0 | 30 | 1 | 2 | 0 | 0 | 0 | - | 2 | .151 | .240 | .279 |
| 1999 | Fla | NL | 136 | 560 | 155 | 28 | 8 | 14 | (7 | 7) | 241 | 81 | 59 | 69 | 15 | 0 | 113 | 12 | 1 | 3 | 3 | 5 | .38 | 13 | .277 | .308 | .430 |
| 2000 | Fla | NL | 109 | 385 | 77 | 17 | 4 | 7 | (5 | 2) | 123 | 35 | 42 | 26 | 13 | 0 | 77 | 2 | 5 | 2 | 7 | 1 | .88 | 7 | .200 | .229 | .319 |
| 2001 | Fla | NL | 145 | 515 | 129 | 36 | 1 | 9 | (5 | 4) | 194 | 57 | 48 | 56 | 30 | 6 | 107 | 10 | 3 | 3 | 2 | 2 | .50 | 13 | .250 | .303 | .377 |
| 2002 | Fla | NL | 42 | 151 | 34 | 7 | 1 | 2 | (1 | 1) | 49 | 15 | 18 | 14 | 12 | 1 | 32 | 4 | 3 | 2 | 3 | 1 | .75 | 2 | .225 | .296 | .325 |
| 2003 | Fla | NL | 150 | 528 | 135 | 33 | 6 | 18 | (7 | 11) | 234 | 52 | 77 | 67 | 33 | 13 | 106 | 13 | 3 | 5 | 0 | 4 | .00 | 8 | .256 | .313 | .443 |
| 2004 | Fla | NL | 159 | 561 | 130 | 30 | 3 | 23 | (13 | 10) | 235 | 67 | 79 | 58 | 27 | 9 | 126 | 4 | 3 | 4 | 3 | 1 | .75 | 17 | .232 | .270 | .419 |
| 2005 | Fla | NL | 130 | 435 | 115 | 30 | 0 | 5 | (2 | 3) | 160 | 45 | 45 | 47 | 31 | 10 | 81 | 5 | 4 | 3 | 5 | 3 | .63 | 11 | .264 | .319 | .368 |
| 2006 | Bos | AL | 111 | 388 | 99 | 24 | 2 | 9 | (4 | 5) | 154 | 48 | 50 | 40 | 22 | 1 | 67 | 5 | 7 | 7 | 1 | 0 | 1.00 | 6 | .255 | .299 | .397 |
| 2007 | Cin | NL | 110 | 393 | 107 | 27 | 1 | 16 | (8 | 8) | 184 | 55 | 55 | 51 | 24 | 1 | 75 | 8 | 2 | 3 | 0 | 1 | .00 | 13 | .272 | .325 | .468 |
| 2009 | 2 Tms | | 112 | 391 | 93 | 22 | 0 | 8 | (7 | 1) | 139 | 42 | 41 | 40 | 20 | 4 | 65 | 4 | 10 | 4 | 2 | 1 | .67 | 7 | .238 | .279 | .355 |
| 2010 | 2 Tms | | 157 | 595 | 149 | 42 | 3 | 23 | (11 | 12) | 266 | 74 | 88 | 75 | 31 | 2 | 118 | 7 | 3 | 4 | 1 | 2 | .33 | 16 | .250 | .294 | .447 |
| 2011 | Atl | NL | 149 | 564 | 136 | 27 | 1 | 15 | (7 | 8) | 210 | 59 | 56 | 50 | 22 | 1 | 126 | 1 | 4 | 2 | 2 | 0 | 1.00 | 19 | .241 | .270 | .372 |
| 2012 | Mil | NL | 24 | 81 | 21 | 4 | 0 | 4 | (1 | 3) | 37 | 8 | 15 | 12 | 6 | 0 | 15 | 2 | 0 | 0 | 1 | 1 | .50 | 1 | .259 | .326 | .457 |
| 2013 | Mil | NL | 41 | 113 | 20 | 3 | 0 | 1 | (1 | 0) | 26 | 14 | 8 | 2 | 3 | 0 | 26 | 1 | 0 | 1 | 0 | 0 | - | 1 | .177 | .203 | .230 |
| 09 | Cin | NL | 68 | 243 | 51 | 12 | 0 | 3 | (2 | 1) | 72 | 16 | 26 | 25 | 15 | 4 | 36 | 2 | 6 | 4 | 0 | 1 | .00 | 3 | .210 | .258 | .296 |
| 09 | Bos | AL | 44 | 148 | 42 | 10 | 0 | 5 | (5 | 0) | 67 | 26 | 15 | 15 | 5 | 0 | 29 | 2 | 4 | 0 | 2 | 0 | 1.00 | 4 | .284 | .316 | .453 |
| 10 | Tor | AL | 85 | 328 | 85 | 25 | 1 | 17 | (8 | 9) | 163 | 47 | 50 | 47 | 17 | 0 | 65 | 1 | 0 | 2 | 1 | 0 | 1.00 | 9 | .259 | .296 | .497 |
| 10 | Atl | NL | 72 | 267 | 64 | 17 | 2 | 6 | (3 | 3) | 103 | 27 | 38 | 28 | 14 | 2 | 53 | 6 | 3 | 2 | 0 | 2 | .00 | 7 | .240 | .291 | .386 |
| Postseason | | | 24 | 83 | 14 | 5 | 0 | 1 | (1 | 0) | 22 | 8 | 8 | 3 | 2 | 0 | 22 | 0 | 1 | 0 | 0 | 1 | .00 | 2 | .169 | .188 | .265 |
| 15 ML YEARS | | | 1600 | 5746 | 1413 | 332 | 30 | 157 | (80 | 77) | 2276 | 663 | 688 | 612 | 298 | 48 | 1164 | 79 | 50 | 43 | 30 | 22 | .58 | 136 | .246 | .290 | .396 |

# Carlos Gonzalez

**Bats:** L **Throws:** L **Pos:** LF-106;PH-2;DH-1;PR-1 **Ht:** 6'1" **Wt:** 220 **Born:** 10/17/1985 **Age:** 28

| | | | BATTING | | | | | | | | | | | | | | | | | | BASERUNNING | | | | AVERAGES | | |
|---|---|---|---|---|---|---|---|---|---|---|---|---|---|---|---|---|---|---|---|---|---|---|---|---|---|---|---|
| Year | Team | Lg | G | AB | H | 2B | 3B | HR | (Hm | Rd) | TB | R | RBI | RC | TBB | IBB | SO | HBP | SH | SF | SB | CS | SB% | GDP | Avg | OBP | Slg |
| 2013 | ColSpr* | AAA | 2 | 6 | 1 | 0 | 0 | 0 | (- | -) | 1 | 0 | 0 | 0 | 1 | 0 | 1 | 0 | 0 | 0 | 0 | 0 | - | 1 | .167 | .286 | .167 |
| 2008 | Oak | AL | 85 | 302 | 73 | 22 | 1 | 4 | (3 | 1) | 109 | 31 | 26 | 30 | 13 | 1 | 81 | 0 | 1 | 0 | 4 | 1 | .80 | 7 | .242 | .273 | .361 |
| 2009 | Col | NL | 89 | 278 | 79 | 14 | 7 | 13 | (7 | 6) | 146 | 53 | 29 | 42 | 28 | 3 | 70 | 3 | 5 | 3 | 16 | 4 | .80 | 3 | .284 | .353 | .525 |
| 2010 | Col | NL | 145 | 587 | **197** | 34 | 9 | 34 | **(26** | 8) | **351** | 111 | 117 | 118 | 40 | 8 | 135 | 2 | 0 | 7 | 26 | 8 | .76 | 9 | **.336** | .376 | .598 |
| 2011 | Col | NL | 127 | 481 | 142 | 27 | 3 | 26 | (16 | 10) | 253 | 92 | 92 | 95 | 48 | 8 | 105 | 7 | 0 | 6 | 20 | 5 | .80 | 11 | .295 | .363 | .526 |
| 2012 | Col | NL | 135 | 518 | 157 | 31 | 5 | 22 | (13 | 9) | 264 | 89 | 85 | 88 | 56 | 11 | 115 | 2 | 0 | 3 | 20 | 5 | .80 | 11 | .303 | .371 | .510 |
| 2013 | Col | NL | 110 | 391 | 118 | 23 | 6 | 26 | (12 | 14) | 231 | 72 | 70 | 69 | 41 | 2 | 118 | 1 | 0 | 3 | 21 | 3 | .88 | 7 | .302 | .367 | .591 |
| Postseason | | | 4 | 17 | 10 | 2 | 0 | 1 | (1 | 0) | 15 | 5 | 1 | 5 | 2 | 0 | 1 | 0 | 0 | 0 | 2 | 1 | .67 | 0 | .588 | .632 | .882 |
| 6 ML YEARS | | | 691 | 2557 | 766 | 151 | 31 | 125 | (77 | 48) | 1354 | 448 | 419 | 442 | 226 | 33 | 624 | 15 | 6 | 22 | 107 | 26 | .80 | 48 | .300 | .357 | .530 |

# Edgar Gonzalez

**Pitches:** R **Bats:** R **Pos:** RP-8 **Ht:** 6'2" **Wt:** 210 **Born:** 2/23/1983 **Age:** 31

| | | | HOW MUCH HE PITCHED | | | | | | WHAT HE GAVE UP | | | | | | | | | | | | THE RESULTS | | | | | | | |
|---|---|---|---|---|---|---|---|---|---|---|---|---|---|---|---|---|---|---|---|---|---|---|---|---|---|---|---|---|
| Year | Team | Lg | G | GS | CG | GF | IP | BFP | H | R | ER | HR | SH | SF | HB | TBB | IBB | SO | WP | Bk | W | L | Pct | Sh | Sv-Op | Hld | ERC | ERA |
| 2013 | Buffalo* | AAA | 4 | 4 | 0 | 0 | 19.2 | 86 | 26 | 12 | 12 | 2 | 0 | 1 | 2 | 2 | 0 | 15 | 0 | 1 | 1 | 0 | 1.000 | 0 | 0-- | - | 5.21 | 5.49 |
| 2013 | TriCity* | A- | 1 | 1 | 0 | 0 | 1.0 | 3 | 0 | 0 | 0 | 0 | 0 | 0 | 0 | 0 | 0 | 1 | 0 | 0 | 0 | 0 | - | 0 | 0-- | - | 0.00 | 0.00 |
| 2003 | Ari | NL | 9 | 2 | 0 | 1 | 18.1 | 85 | 28 | 10 | 10 | 3 | 1 | 1 | 0 | 7 | 2 | 14 | 2 | 0 | 2 | 1 | .667 | 0 | 0-1 | 0 | 7.81 | 4.91 |
| 2004 | Ari | NL | 10 | 10 | 0 | 0 | 46.1 | 228 | 72 | 49 | 48 | 15 | 5 | 1 | 5 | 18 | 4 | 31 | 3 | 1 | 0 | 9 | .000 | 0 | 0-0 | 0 | 9.78 | 9.32 |
| 2005 | Ari | NL | 1 | 0 | 0 | 0 | 0.1 | 5 | 2 | 4 | 4 | 1 | 0 | 0 | 0 | 2 | 0 | 1 | 1 | 0 | 0 | 0 | - | 0 | 0-0 | 0 | 124.7 | 108.0 |
| 2006 | Ari | NL | 11 | 5 | 0 | 1 | 42.2 | 182 | 45 | 20 | 20 | 7 | 4 | 1 | 3 | 9 | 0 | 28 | 2 | 0 | 3 | 4 | .429 | 0 | 0-0 | 1 | 4.33 | 4.22 |
| 2007 | Ari | NL | 32 | 12 | 0 | 5 | 102.0 | 437 | 110 | 61 | 57 | 18 | 2 | 3 | 4 | 28 | 4 | 62 | 5 | 1 | 8 | 4 | .667 | 0 | 0-0 | 0 | 4.67 | 5.03 |
| 2008 | Ari | NL | 17 | 6 | 0 | 3 | 48.0 | 221 | 58 | 34 | 32 | 8 | 4 | 1 | 3 | 21 | 2 | 32 | 4 | 0 | 1 | 3 | .250 | 0 | 0-0 | 0 | 6.16 | 6.00 |
| 2009 | Oak | AL | 26 | 6 | 0 | 10 | 65.1 | 299 | 76 | 41 | 40 | 4 | 2 | 3 | 6 | 28 | 4 | 39 | 4 | 0 | 0 | 4 | .000 | 0 | 0-0 | 0 | 5.09 | 5.51 |
| 2011 | Col | NL | 1 | 0 | 0 | 1 | 2.0 | 11 | 5 | 2 | 2 | 0 | 0 | 0 | 0 | 1 | 0 | 1 | 0 | 0 | 0 | 0 | - | 0 | 0-0 | 0 | 14.52 | 9.00 |
| 2012 | Hou | NL | 6 | 6 | 0 | 0 | 25.0 | 105 | 23 | 14 | 14 | 3 | 1 | 0 | 0 | 8 | 0 | 18 | 1 | 0 | 3 | 1 | .750 | 0 | 0-0 | 0 | 3.43 | 5.04 |
| 2013 | 2 Tms | AL | 8 | 0 | 0 | 2 | 18.0 | 87 | 26 | 16 | 15 | 6 | 0 | 0 | 1 | 8 | 0 | 11 | 0 | 0 | 0 | 1 | .000 | 0 | 0-0 | 0 | 9.24 | 7.50 |
| 13 | Tor | AL | 3 | 0 | 0 | 1 | 8.0 | 38 | 9 | 7 | 7 | 2 | 0 | 0 | 1 | 5 | 0 | 3 | 0 | 0 | 0 | 0 | - | 0 | 0-0 | 0 | 7.57 | 7.88 |
| 13 | Hou | AL | 5 | 0 | 0 | 1 | 10.0 | 49 | 17 | 9 | 8 | 4 | 0 | 0 | 0 | 3 | 0 | 8 | 0 | 0 | 0 | 1 | .000 | 0 | 0-0 | 0 | 10.62 | 7.20 |
| 10 ML YEARS | | | 121 | 47 | 0 | 23 | 368.0 | 1660 | 445 | 251 | 242 | 65 | 19 | 10 | 22 | 130 | 16 | 237 | 22 | 2 | 17 | 27 | .386 | 0 | 0-1 | 1 | 5.88 | 5.92 |

# Gio Gonzalez

**Pitches:** L **Bats:** R **Pos:** SP-32 JEE-oh **Ht:** 6'0" **Wt:** 200 **Born:** 9/19/1985 **Age:** 28

| | | | HOW MUCH HE PITCHED | | | | | | WHAT HE GAVE UP | | | | | | | | | | | | THE RESULTS | | | | | | | |
|---|---|---|---|---|---|---|---|---|---|---|---|---|---|---|---|---|---|---|---|---|---|---|---|---|---|---|---|---|
| Year | Team | Lg | G | GS | CG | GF | IP | BFP | H | R | ER | HR | SH | SF | HB | TBB | IBB | SO | WP | Bk | W | L | Pct | Sh | Sv-Op | Hld | ERC | ERA |
| 2008 | Oak | AL | 10 | 7 | 0 | 3 | 34.0 | 163 | 32 | 34 | 29 | 9 | 2 | 1 | 3 | 25 | 1 | 34 | 1 | 0 | 1 | 4 | .200 | 0 | 0-0 | 0 | 6.54 | 7.68 |
| 2009 | Oak | AL | 20 | 17 | 0 | 0 | 98.2 | 455 | 113 | 68 | 63 | 14 | 2 | 3 | 1 | 56 | 2 | 109 | 2 | 0 | 6 | 7 | .462 | 0 | 0-0 | 0 | 5.96 | 5.75 |
| 2010 | Oak | AL | 33 | 33 | 1 | 0 | 200.2 | 851 | 171 | 75 | 72 | 15 | 5 | 2 | 4 | 92 | 1 | 171 | 4 | 1 | 15 | 9 | .625 | 0 | 0-0 | 0 | 3.39 | 3.23 |
| 2011 | Oak | AL | 32 | 32 | 0 | 0 | 202.0 | 864 | 175 | 81 | 70 | 17 | 3 | 2 | 8 | **91** | 1 | 197 | 6 | 1 | 16 | 12 | .571 | 0 | 0-0 | 0 | 3.56 | 3.12 |
| 2012 | Was | NL | 32 | 32 | 2 | 0 | 199.1 | 822 | 149 | 69 | 64 | 9 | 9 | 7 | 5 | 76 | 3 | 207 | 10 | 1 | **21** | 8 | .724 | 1 | 0-0 | 0 | 2.37 | 2.89 |
| 2013 | Was | NL | 32 | 32 | 1 | 0 | 195.2 | 819 | 169 | 79 | 73 | 17 | 7 | 1 | 2 | 76 | 1 | 192 | 4 | 1 | 11 | 8 | .579 | 1 | 0-0 | 0 | 3.23 | 3.36 |
| Postseason | | | 2 | 2 | 0 | 0 | 10.0 | 45 | 6 | 5 | 5 | 0 | 0 | 1 | 0 | 11 | 0 | 10 | 2 | 0 | 0 | 0 | - | 0 | 0-0 | 0 | 3.81 | 4.50 |
| 6 ML YEARS | | | 159 | 153 | 4 | 3 | 930.1 | 3974 | 809 | 406 | 371 | 81 | 28 | 16 | 23 | 416 | 9 | 910 | 27 | 4 | 70 | 48 | .593 | 2 | 0-0 | 0 | 3.52 | 3.59 |

# Marwin Gonzalez

**Bats:** B **Throws:** R **Pos:** SS-53;2B-10;PR-9;3B-4 MARR-win **Ht:** 6'1" **Wt:** 210 **Born:** 3/14/1989 **Age:** 25

| BATTING | | | | | | | | | | | | | | | | | | | | | BASERUNNING | | | | AVERAGES | | |
|---|---|---|---|---|---|---|---|---|---|---|---|---|---|---|---|---|---|---|---|---|---|---|---|---|---|---|---|
| Year | Team | Lg | G | AB | H | 2B | 3B | HR | (Hm | Rd) | TB | R | RBI | RC | TBB | IBB | SO | HBP | SH | SF | SB | CS | SB% | GDP | Avg | OBP | Slg |
| 2009 | Dytona | A+ | 120 | 424 | 102 | 15 | 4 | 2 | (- | -) | 131 | 43 | 34 | 37 | 26 | 0 | 77 | 2 | 8 | 1 | 9 | 8 | .53 | 11 | .241 | .287 | .309 |
| 2010 | Dytona | A+ | 23 | 85 | 23 | 3 | 0 | 0 | (- | -) | 26 | 7 | 5 | 10 | 7 | 0 | 13 | 1 | 2 | 1 | 7 | 1 | .88 | 1 | .271 | .330 | .306 |
| 2010 | Tenn | AA | 86 | 305 | 75 | 11 | 3 | 4 | (- | -) | 104 | 24 | 41 | 30 | 17 | 3 | 41 | 1 | 3 | 4 | 6 | 4 | .60 | 7 | .246 | .284 | .341 |
| 2011 | Tenn | AA | 64 | 216 | 65 | 18 | 1 | 2 | (- | -) | 91 | 29 | 20 | 33 | 17 | 2 | 27 | 3 | 2 | 1 | 4 | 2 | .67 | 5 | .301 | .359 | .421 |
| 2011 | Iowa | AAA | 60 | 197 | 54 | 12 | 1 | 2 | (- | -) | 74 | 24 | 19 | 26 | 16 | 2 | 21 | 1 | 8 | 4 | 3 | 1 | .75 | 2 | .274 | .326 | .376 |
| 2012 | OKCity | AAA | 13 | 39 | 13 | 4 | 0 | 1 | (- | -) | 20 | 2 | 10 | 7 | 3 | 1 | 7 | 1 | 0 | 0 | 0 | 0 | - | 1 | .333 | .395 | .513 |
| 2013 | OKCity | AAA | 44 | 172 | 45 | 10 | 1 | 1 | (- | -) | 60 | 16 | 15 | 18 | 8 | 1 | 23 | 0 | 2 | 1 | 4 | 1 | .80 | 3 | .262 | .293 | .349 |
| 2012 | Hou | NL | 80 | 205 | 48 | 13 | 0 | 2 | (1 | 1) | 67 | 21 | 12 | 12 | 13 | 0 | 29 | 0 | 1 | 0 | 3 | 3 | .50 | 9 | .234 | .280 | .327 |
| 2013 | Hou | AL | 72 | 204 | 45 | 8 | 0 | 4 | (2 | 2) | 65 | 22 | 14 | 10 | 9 | 0 | 37 | 0 | 8 | 1 | 6 | 2 | .75 | 5 | .221 | .252 | .319 |
| 2 ML YEARS | | | 152 | 409 | 93 | 21 | 0 | 6 | (3 | 3) | 132 | 43 | 26 | 22 | 22 | 0 | 66 | 0 | 9 | 1 | 9 | 5 | .64 | 14 | .227 | .266 | .323 |

# Michael Gonzalez

**Pitches:** L **Bats:** R **Pos:** RP-75 **Ht:** 6'2" **Wt:** 200 **Born:** 5/23/1978 **Age:** 36

| HOW MUCH HE PITCHED | | | | | | | | | WHAT HE GAVE UP | | | | | | | | | | | THE RESULTS | | | | | | | |
|---|---|---|---|---|---|---|---|---|---|---|---|---|---|---|---|---|---|---|---|---|---|---|---|---|---|---|---|
| Year | Team | Lg | G | GS | CG | GF | IP | BFP | H | R | ER | HR | SH | SF | HB | TBB | IBB | SO | WP | Bk | W | L | Pct | Sh | Sv-Op | Hld | ERC | ERA |
| 2003 | Pit | NL | 16 | 0 | 0 | 2 | 8.1 | 38 | 7 | 7 | 7 | 4 | 1 | 1 | 0 | 6 | 0 | 6 | 1 | 0 | 0 | 1 | .000 | 0 | 0-0 | 3 | 7.18 | 7.56 |
| 2004 | Pit | NL | 47 | 0 | 0 | 12 | 43.1 | 169 | 32 | 7 | 6 | 2 | 3 | 0 | 1 | 6 | 0 | 55 | 4 | 0 | 3 | 1 | .750 | 0 | 1-4 | 13 | 1.60 | 1.25 |
| 2005 | Pit | NL | 51 | 0 | 0 | 15 | 50.0 | 212 | 35 | 15 | 15 | 2 | 0 | 2 | 1 | 31 | 2 | 58 | 3 | 0 | 1 | 3 | .250 | 0 | 3-3 | 15 | 2.90 | 2.70 |
| 2006 | Pit | NL | 54 | 0 | 0 | 47 | 54.0 | 234 | 42 | 13 | 13 | 1 | 3 | 1 | 2 | 31 | 2 | 64 | 0 | 0 | 3 | 4 | .429 | 0 | 24-24 | 3 | 3.00 | 2.17 |
| 2007 | Atl | NL | 18 | 0 | 0 | 5 | 17.0 | 70 | 15 | 3 | 3 | 0 | 0 | 1 | 0 | 8 | 0 | 13 | 0 | 0 | 2 | 0 | 1.000 | 0 | 2-2 | 5 | 3.13 | 1.59 |
| 2008 | Atl | NL | 36 | 0 | 0 | 29 | 33.2 | 142 | 26 | 21 | 16 | 6 | 1 | 2 | 1 | 14 | 3 | 44 | 0 | 0 | 0 | 3 | .000 | 0 | 14-16 | 0 | 3.33 | 4.28 |
| 2009 | Atl | NL | 80 | 0 | 0 | 29 | 74.1 | 315 | 56 | 28 | 20 | 7 | 6 | 1 | 7 | 33 | 8 | 90 | 5 | 0 | 5 | 4 | .556 | 0 | 10-17 | 17 | 3.04 | 2.42 |
| 2010 | Bal | AL | 29 | 0 | 0 | 7 | 24.2 | 106 | 18 | 11 | 11 | 1 | 3 | 1 | 0 | 14 | 4 | 31 | 3 | 0 | 1 | 3 | .250 | 0 | 1-3 | 10 | 2.54 | 4.01 |
| 2011 | 2 Tms | AL | 56 | 0 | 0 | 15 | 53.1 | 230 | 51 | 30 | 26 | 7 | 0 | 3 | 2 | 21 | 1 | 51 | 5 | 0 | 2 | 2 | .500 | 0 | 1-2 | 8 | 4.13 | 4.39 |
| 2012 | Was | NL | 47 | 0 | 0 | 13 | 35.2 | 151 | 31 | 14 | 12 | 2 | 3 | 1 | 0 | 16 | 0 | 39 | 2 | 1 | 0 | 0 | - | 0 | 0-2 | 7 | 3.25 | 3.03 |
| 2013 | Mil | NL | 75 | 0 | 0 | 11 | 50.0 | 235 | 58 | 28 | 26 | 10 | 1 | 1 | 2 | 25 | 2 | 60 | 4 | 0 | 0 | 3 | .000 | 0 | 0-3 | 11 | 6.16 | 4.68 |
| 11 | Bal | AL | 49 | 0 | 0 | 14 | 46.1 | 202 | 46 | 26 | 22 | 7 | 0 | 2 | 2 | 18 | 1 | 46 | 4 | 0 | 2 | 2 | .500 | 0 | 1-2 | 6 | 4.46 | 4.27 |
| 11 | Tex | AL | 7 | 0 | 0 | 1 | 7.0 | 28 | 5 | 4 | 4 | 0 | 0 | 1 | 0 | 3 | 0 | 5 | 1 | 0 | 0 | 0 | - | 0 | 0-0 | 2 | 2.11 | 5.14 |
| Postseason | | | 9 | 0 | 0 | 1 | 5.1 | 21 | 4 | 3 | 3 | 2 | 0 | 1 | 0 | 1 | 0 | 5 | 0 | 0 | 0 | 0 | - | 0 | 0-0 | 1 | 3.42 | 5.06 |
| 11 ML YEARS | | | 509 | 0 | 0 | 185 | 444.1 | 1902 | 371 | 177 | 155 | 42 | 21 | 14 | 16 | 205 | 22 | 511 | 27 | 1 | 17 | 24 | .415 | 0 | 56-76 | 92 | 3.40 | 3.14 |

# Miguel Gonzalez

**Pitches:** R **Bats:** R **Pos:** SP-28; RP-2 **Ht:** 6'1" **Wt:** 170 **Born:** 5/27/1984 **Age:** 30

| HOW MUCH HE PITCHED | | | | | | | | | WHAT HE GAVE UP | | | | | | | | | | | THE RESULTS | | | | | | | |
|---|---|---|---|---|---|---|---|---|---|---|---|---|---|---|---|---|---|---|---|---|---|---|---|---|---|---|---|
| Year | Team | Lg | G | GS | CG | GF | IP | BFP | H | R | ER | HR | SH | SF | HB | TBB | IBB | SO | WP | Bk | W | L | Pct | Sh | Sv-Op | Hld | ERC | ERA |
| 2010 | Salem | A+ | 17 | 16 | 0 | 1 | 73.1 | 318 | 82 | 42 | 37 | 5 | 2 | 4 | 8 | 18 | 0 | 47 | 8 | 0 | 6 | 4 | .600 | 0 | 0-- | - | 4.37 | 4.54 |
| 2011 | Salem | A+ | 2 | 2 | 0 | 0 | 5.0 | 22 | 5 | 1 | 1 | 0 | 0 | 0 | 1 | 2 | 0 | 4 | 0 | 0 | 0 | 1 | .000 | 0 | 0-- | - | 4.20 | 1.80 |
| 2011 | Portlnd | AA | 15 | 6 | 0 | 2 | 46.2 | 222 | 55 | 41 | 32 | 4 | 0 | 4 | 7 | 19 | 0 | 45 | 3 | 1 | 0 | 5 | .000 | 0 | 0-- | - | 5.47 | 6.17 |
| 2011 | Pwtckt | AAA | 1 | 1 | 0 | 0 | 5.0 | 18 | 2 | 1 | 1 | 1 | 0 | 0 | 0 | 2 | 0 | 5 | 0 | 0 | 0 | 1 | .000 | 0 | 0-- | - | 1.76 | 1.80 |
| 2012 | Norfolk | AAA | 14 | 6 | 0 | 1 | 44.2 | 165 | 22 | 12 | 8 | 1 | 1 | 0 | 0 | 10 | 0 | 53 | 1 | 0 | 3 | 2 | .600 | 0 | 1-- | - | 0.96 | 1.61 |
| 2012 | Bal | AL | 18 | 15 | 0 | 0 | 105.1 | 434 | 92 | 38 | 38 | 13 | 1 | 2 | 5 | 35 | 2 | 77 | 3 | 2 | 9 | 4 | .692 | 0 | 0-0 | 0 | 3.49 | 3.25 |
| 2013 | Bal | AL | 30 | 28 | 0 | 1 | 171.1 | 712 | 157 | 81 | 72 | 24 | 3 | 6 | 3 | 53 | 3 | 120 | 4 | 0 | 11 | 8 | .579 | 0 | 0-0 | 0 | 3.58 | 3.78 |
| Postseason | | | 1 | 1 | 0 | 0 | 7.0 | 25 | 5 | 1 | 1 | 0 | 0 | 0 | 0 | 0 | 0 | 8 | 0 | 0 | 0 | 0 | - | 0 | 0-0 | 0 | 1.08 | 1.29 |
| 2 ML YEARS | | | 48 | 43 | 0 | 1 | 276.2 | 1146 | 249 | 119 | 110 | 37 | 4 | 8 | 8 | 88 | 5 | 197 | 7 | 2 | 20 | 12 | .625 | 0 | 0-0 | 0 | 3.55 | 3.58 |

# Miguel Gonzalez

**Bats:** R **Throws:** R **Pos:** C-4;DH-1;PH-1 **Ht:** 5'11" **Wt:** 180 **Born:** 12/3/1990 **Age:** 23

| BATTING | | | | | | | | | | | | | | | | | | | | | BASERUNNING | | | | AVERAGES | | |
|---|---|---|---|---|---|---|---|---|---|---|---|---|---|---|---|---|---|---|---|---|---|---|---|---|---|---|---|
| Year | Team | Lg | G | AB | H | 2B | 3B | HR | (Hm | Rd) | TB | R | RBI | RC | TBB | IBB | SO | HBP | SH | SF | SB | CS | SB% | GDP | Avg | OBP | Slg |
| 2009 | Bristol | R | 45 | 151 | 47 | 15 | 1 | 4 | (- | -) | 76 | 24 | 19 | 29 | 16 | 0 | 25 | 2 | 4 | 0 | 2 | 1 | .67 | 2 | .311 | .385 | .503 |
| 2009 | Charltt | AAA | 3 | 11 | 2 | 0 | 0 | 0 | (- | -) | 2 | 1 | 1 | 0 | 0 | 0 | 2 | 0 | 0 | 0 | 0 | 0 | - | 0 | .182 | .182 | .182 |
| 2010 | Knapol | A | 92 | 326 | 71 | 9 | 2 | 2 | (- | -) | 90 | 35 | 19 | 23 | 16 | 0 | 63 | 4 | 4 | 4 | 2 | 1 | .67 | 7 | .218 | .260 | .276 |
| 2011 | Knapol | A | 55 | 184 | 47 | 7 | 0 | 2 | (- | -) | 60 | 17 | 21 | 21 | 16 | 1 | 34 | 3 | 4 | 1 | 5 | 1 | .83 | 5 | .255 | .324 | .326 |
| 2012 | WinSa | A+ | 50 | 162 | 40 | 9 | 0 | 1 | (- | -) | 52 | 20 | 16 | 16 | 12 | 1 | 24 | 2 | 6 | 2 | 0 | 1 | .00 | 5 | .247 | .303 | .321 |
| 2012 | Brham | AA | 22 | 70 | 15 | 1 | 0 | 0 | (- | -) | 16 | 5 | 7 | 5 | 7 | 0 | 16 | 1 | 2 | 0 | 0 | 0 | - | 3 | .214 | .295 | .229 |
| 2013 | Brham | AA | 37 | 119 | 29 | 5 | 1 | 2 | (- | -) | 42 | 12 | 16 | 14 | 10 | 0 | 25 | 3 | 0 | 0 | 3 | 1 | .75 | 8 | .244 | .318 | .353 |
| 2013 | Charltt | AAA | 16 | 50 | 14 | 3 | 0 | 0 | (- | -) | 17 | 5 | 4 | 6 | 6 | 0 | 11 | 0 | 0 | 2 | 0 | 0 | - | 1 | .280 | .345 | .340 |
| 2013 | CWS | AL | 5 | 9 | 2 | 0 | 0 | 0 | (0 | 0) | 2 | 0 | 0 | 0 | 0 | 0 | 3 | 0 | 0 | 0 | 0 | 0 | - | 0 | .222 | .222 | .222 |

# Alex Gordon

**Bats:** L **Throws:** R **Pos:** LF-155;PH-1 **Ht:** 6'1" **Wt:** 220 **Born:** 2/10/1984 **Age:** 30

| BATTING | | | | | | | | | | | | | | | | | | | | | BASERUNNING | | | | AVERAGES | | |
|---|---|---|---|---|---|---|---|---|---|---|---|---|---|---|---|---|---|---|---|---|---|---|---|---|---|---|---|
| Year | Team | Lg | G | AB | H | 2B | 3B | HR | (Hm | Rd) | TB | R | RBI | RC | TBB | IBB | SO | HBP | SH | SF | SB | CS | SB% | GDP | Avg | OBP | Slg |
| 2007 | KC | AL | 151 | 543 | 134 | 36 | 4 | 15 | (8 | 7) | 223 | 60 | 60 | 69 | 41 | 4 | 137 | 13 | 1 | 2 | 14 | 4 | .78 | 12 | .247 | .314 | .411 |
| 2008 | KC | AL | 134 | 493 | 128 | 35 | 1 | 16 | (9 | 7) | 213 | 72 | 59 | 71 | 66 | 5 | 120 | 6 | 1 | 5 | 9 | 2 | .82 | 8 | .260 | .351 | .432 |
| 2009 | KC | AL | 49 | 164 | 38 | 6 | 0 | 6 | (2 | 4) | 62 | 28 | 22 | 16 | 21 | 0 | 43 | 2 | 1 | 1 | 5 | 0 | 1.00 | 5 | .232 | .324 | .378 |
| 2010 | KC | AL | 74 | 242 | 52 | 10 | 0 | 8 | (5 | 3) | 86 | 34 | 20 | 23 | 34 | 1 | 62 | 2 | 2 | 1 | 1 | 5 | .17 | 9 | .215 | .315 | .355 |
| 2011 | KC | AL | 151 | 611 | 185 | 45 | 4 | 23 | (12 | 11) | 307 | 101 | 87 | 103 | 67 | 2 | 139 | 7 | 0 | 3 | 17 | 8 | .68 | 9 | .303 | .376 | .502 |
| 2012 | KC | AL | 161 | 642 | 189 | **51** | 5 | 14 | (6 | 8) | 292 | 93 | 72 | 94 | 73 | 3 | 140 | 3 | 0 | 3 | 10 | 5 | .67 | 14 | .294 | .368 | .455 |
| 2013 | KC | AL | 156 | 633 | 168 | 27 | 6 | 20 | (10 | 10) | 267 | 90 | 81 | 90 | 52 | 7 | 141 | 9 | 0 | 6 | 11 | 3 | .79 | 4 | .265 | .327 | .422 |
| 7 ML YEARS | | | 876 | 3328 | 894 | 210 | 20 | 102 | (52 | 50) | 1450 | 478 | 401 | 466 | 354 | 22 | 782 | 42 | 5 | 21 | 67 | 27 | .71 | 61 | .269 | .344 | .436 |

## Dee Gordon

**Bats:** L **Throws:** R **Pos:** SS-27;PH-5;PR-5;2B-3 **Ht:** 5'11" **Wt:** 160 **Born:** 4/22/1988 **Age:** 26

| BATTING | | | | | | | | | | | | | | | | | | | | | BASERUNNING | | | | AVERAGES | | |
|---|---|---|---|---|---|---|---|---|---|---|---|---|---|---|---|---|---|---|---|---|---|---|---|---|---|---|---|
| Year Team | Lg | G | AB | H | 2B | 3B | HR | (Hm | Rd) | TB | R | RBI | RC | TBB | IBB | SO | HBP | SH | SF | SB | CS | SB% | GDP | Avg | OBP | Slg |
| 2013 Albq* | AAA | 92 | 374 | 111 | 17 | 9 | 0 | (- | -) | 146 | 65 | 33 | 66 | 51 | 1 | 70 | 3 | 4 | 1 | 49 | 11 | .82 | 2 | .297 | .385 | .390 |
| 2011 LAD | NL | 56 | 224 | 68 | 9 | 2 | 0 | (0 | 0) | 81 | 34 | 11 | 25 | 7 | 0 | 27 | 0 | 2 | 0 | 24 | 7 | .77 | 1 | .304 | .325 | .362 |
| 2012 LAD | NL | 87 | 303 | 69 | 9 | 2 | 1 | (0 | 1) | 85 | 38 | 17 | 22 | 20 | 0 | 62 | 3 | 2 | 2 | 32 | 10 | .76 | 5 | .228 | .280 | .281 |
| 2013 LAD | NL | 38 | 94 | 22 | 1 | 1 | 1 | (1 | 0) | 28 | 9 | 6 | 9 | 10 | 2 | 21 | 1 | 1 | 0 | 10 | 2 | .83 | 0 | .234 | .314 | .298 |
| 3 ML YEARS | | 181 | 621 | 159 | 19 | 5 | 2 | (1 | 1) | 194 | 81 | 34 | 56 | 37 | 2 | 110 | 4 | 5 | 2 | 66 | 19 | .78 | 6 | .256 | .301 | .312 |

## Tom Gorzelanny

**Pitches:** L **Bats:** R **Pos:** RP-33; SP-10 gore-zah-LAWN-ee **Ht:** 6'2" **Wt:** 210 **Born:** 7/12/1982 **Age:** 31

| HOW MUCH HE PITCHED | | | | | | | | WHAT HE GAVE UP | | | | | | | | | | | | THE RESULTS | | | | | | | |
|---|---|---|---|---|---|---|---|---|---|---|---|---|---|---|---|---|---|---|---|---|---|---|---|---|---|---|---|
| Year Team | Lg | G | GS | CG | GF | IP | BFP | H | R | ER | HR | SH | SF | HB | TBB | IBB | SO | WP | Bk | W | L | Pct | Sh | Sv-Op | Hld | ERC | ERA |
| 2005 Pit | NL | 3 | 1 | 0 | 0 | 6.0 | 32 | 10 | 8 | 8 | 1 | 1 | 0 | 0 | 3 | 0 | 3 | 0 | 0 | 0 | 1 | .000 | 0 | 0-0 | 0 | 8.76 | 12.00 |
| 2006 Pit | NL | 11 | 11 | 0 | 0 | 61.2 | 267 | 50 | 29 | 26 | 3 | 7 | 4 | 4 | 31 | 2 | 40 | 3 | 0 | 2 | 5 | .286 | 0 | 0-0 | 0 | 3.23 | 3.79 |
| 2007 Pit | NL | 32 | 32 | 1 | 0 | 201.2 | 874 | 214 | 90 | 87 | 18 | 3 | 9 | 11 | 68 | 3 | 135 | 5 | 1 | 14 | 10 | .583 | 1 | 0-0 | 0 | 4.31 | 3.88 |
| 2008 Pit | NL | 21 | 21 | 0 | 0 | 105.1 | 490 | 120 | 79 | 78 | 20 | 3 | 6 | 1 | 70 | 0 | 67 | 5 | 1 | 6 | 9 | .400 | 0 | 0-0 | 0 | 6.86 | 6.66 |
| 2009 2 Tms | NL | 22 | 7 | 0 | 2 | 47.0 | 204 | 45 | 30 | 29 | 6 | 3 | 3 | 1 | 17 | 0 | 47 | 1 | 0 | 7 | 3 | .700 | 0 | 0-1 | 2 | 3.88 | 5.55 |
| 2010 ChC | NL | 29 | 23 | 0 | 3 | 136.1 | 604 | 136 | 70 | 62 | 11 | 4 | 6 | 2 | 68 | 4 | 119 | 0 | 0 | 7 | 9 | .438 | 0 | 1-1 | 1 | 4.30 | 4.09 |
| 2011 Was | NL | 30 | 15 | 0 | 1 | 105.0 | 447 | 102 | 50 | 47 | 15 | 8 | 4 | 6 | 33 | 5 | 95 | 5 | 1 | 4 | 6 | .400 | 0 | 0-1 | 4 | 4.03 | 4.03 |
| 2012 Was | NL | 45 | 1 | 0 | 11 | 72.0 | 306 | 65 | 27 | 23 | 7 | 3 | 2 | 2 | 30 | 1 | 62 | 4 | 0 | 4 | 2 | .667 | 0 | 1-1 | 9 | 3.68 | 2.88 |
| 2013 Mil | NL | 43 | 10 | 0 | 4 | 85.1 | 356 | 77 | 41 | 37 | 11 | 1 | 2 | 2 | 31 | 1 | 83 | 2 | 0 | 3 | 6 | .333 | 0 | 0-1 | 6 | 3.70 | 3.90 |
| 09 Pit | NL | 9 | 0 | 0 | 2 | 8.2 | 36 | 6 | 5 | 5 | 0 | 1 | 0 | 0 | 4 | 0 | 7 | 0 | 0 | 3 | 1 | .750 | 0 | 0-1 | 1 | 2.02 | 5.19 |
| 09 ChC | NL | 13 | 7 | 0 | 0 | 38.1 | 168 | 39 | 25 | 24 | 6 | 2 | 3 | 1 | 13 | 0 | 40 | 1 | 0 | 4 | 2 | .667 | 0 | 0-0 | 1 | 4.33 | 5.63 |
| Postseason | | 1 | 0 | 0 | 1 | 0.1 | 2 | 1 | 0 | 0 | 0 | 0 | 0 | 0 | 0 | 0 | 0 | 0 | 0 | 0 | 0 | - | 0 | 0-0 | 0 | 14.52 | 0.00 |
| 9 ML YEARS | | 236 | 121 | 1 | 21 | 820.1 | 3580 | 819 | 424 | 397 | 92 | 33 | 36 | 29 | 351 | 16 | 651 | 25 | 3 | 47 | 51 | .480 | 1 | 2-5 | 22 | 4.38 | 4.36 |

## Anthony Gose

**Bats:** L **Throws:** L **Pos:** CF-34;LF-15;PH-6;PR-3;RF-2;DH-1 GOASE **Ht:** 6'1" **Wt:** 195 **Born:** 8/10/1990 **Age:** 23

| BATTING | | | | | | | | | | | | | | | | | | | | | BASERUNNING | | | | AVERAGES | | |
|---|---|---|---|---|---|---|---|---|---|---|---|---|---|---|---|---|---|---|---|---|---|---|---|---|---|---|---|
| Year Team | Lg | G | AB | H | 2B | 3B | HR | (Hm | Rd) | TB | R | RBI | RC | TBB | IBB | SO | HBP | SH | SF | SB | CS | SB% | GDP | Avg | OBP | Slg |
| 2009 Lakwd | A | 131 | 510 | 132 | 24 | 9 | 2 | (- | -) | 180 | 72 | 52 | 68 | 35 | 2 | 110 | 15 | 9 | 3 | 76 | 20 | .79 | 9 | .259 | .323 | .353 |
| 2010 Clrwtr | A+ | 103 | 418 | 110 | 17 | 11 | 4 | (- | -) | 161 | 67 | 21 | 50 | 32 | 4 | 103 | 6 | 5 | 0 | 36 | 27 | .57 | 6 | .263 | .325 | .385 |
| 2010 Dnedin | A+ | 27 | 94 | 24 | 3 | 2 | 3 | (- | -) | 40 | 21 | 6 | 15 | 13 | 0 | 29 | 3 | 2 | 1 | 9 | 5 | .64 | 0 | .255 | .360 | .426 |
| 2011 NHam | AA | 137 | 509 | 129 | 20 | 7 | 16 | (- | -) | 211 | 87 | 59 | 85 | 62 | 0 | 154 | 13 | 2 | 1 | 70 | 15 | .82 | 3 | .253 | .349 | .415 |
| 2012 LsVgs | AAA | 102 | 420 | 120 | 21 | 10 | 5 | (- | -) | 176 | 87 | 43 | 69 | 49 | 1 | 101 | 5 | 4 | 1 | 34 | 12 | .74 | 3 | .286 | .366 | .419 |
| 2013 Buffalo | AAA | 106 | 393 | 94 | 17 | 6 | 3 | (- | -) | 132 | 64 | 27 | 44 | 38 | 0 | 121 | 7 | 3 | 2 | 22 | 13 | .63 | 7 | .239 | .316 | .336 |
| 2012 Tor | AL | 56 | 166 | 37 | 7 | 3 | 1 | (0 | 1) | 53 | 25 | 11 | 21 | 17 | 0 | 59 | 2 | 4 | 0 | 15 | 3 | .83 | 1 | .223 | .303 | .319 |
| 2013 Tor | AL | 52 | 147 | 38 | 6 | 5 | 2 | (2 | 0) | 60 | 15 | 12 | 13 | 5 | 0 | 37 | 0 | 1 | 0 | 4 | 3 | .57 | 5 | .259 | .283 | .408 |
| 2 ML YEARS | | 108 | 313 | 75 | 13 | 8 | 3 | (2 | 1) | 113 | 40 | 23 | 34 | 22 | 0 | 96 | 2 | 5 | 0 | 19 | 6 | .76 | 6 | .240 | .294 | .361 |

## Tuffy Gosewisch

**Bats:** R **Throws:** R **Pos:** C-13;PH-1 GOES-uh-wish **Ht:** 5'11" **Wt:** 180 **Born:** 8/17/1983 **Age:** 30

| BATTING | | | | | | | | | | | | | | | | | | | | | BASERUNNING | | | | AVERAGES | | |
|---|---|---|---|---|---|---|---|---|---|---|---|---|---|---|---|---|---|---|---|---|---|---|---|---|---|---|---|
| Year Team | Lg | G | AB | H | 2B | 3B | HR | (Hm | Rd) | TB | R | RBI | RC | TBB | IBB | SO | HBP | SH | SF | SB | CS | SB% | GDP | Avg | OBP | Slg |
| 2009 Rdng | AA | 60 | 205 | 50 | 17 | 0 | 1 | (- | -) | 70 | 16 | 20 | 23 | 14 | 1 | 34 | 7 | 3 | 0 | 0 | 1 | .00 | 9 | .244 | .314 | .341 |
| 2009 LV | AAA | 16 | 55 | 11 | 3 | 0 | 0 | (- | -) | 14 | 6 | 1 | 2 | 2 | 0 | 13 | 0 | 0 | 0 | 0 | 0 | - | 3 | .200 | .228 | .255 |
| 2010 Rdng | AA | 98 | 312 | 75 | 22 | 1 | 9 | (- | -) | 126 | 46 | 32 | 48 | 49 | 0 | 67 | 5 | 5 | 0 | 0 | 0 | - | 2 | .240 | .352 | .404 |
| 2011 Rdng | AA | 109 | 369 | 91 | 19 | 0 | 13 | (- | -) | 149 | 41 | 66 | 44 | 20 | 2 | 61 | 8 | 3 | 6 | 4 | 6 | .40 | 11 | .247 | .295 | .404 |
| 2012 LV | AAA | 65 | 213 | 41 | 13 | 0 | 4 | (- | -) | 66 | 22 | 20 | 15 | 9 | 0 | 42 | 5 | 0 | 1 | 0 | 0 | - | 4 | .192 | .241 | .310 |
| 2012 LsVgs | AAA | 24 | 83 | 23 | 8 | 1 | 1 | (- | -) | 36 | 9 | 8 | 13 | 9 | 0 | 17 | 3 | 1 | 1 | 0 | 1 | .00 | 3 | .277 | .365 | .434 |
| 2013 Reno | AAA | 72 | 250 | 71 | 20 | 1 | 7 | (- | -) | 114 | 30 | 33 | 38 | 17 | 0 | 40 | 1 | 0 | 4 | 1 | 1 | .50 | 5 | .284 | .327 | .456 |
| 2013 Ari | NL | 14 | 45 | 8 | 2 | 0 | 0 | (0 | 0) | 10 | 1 | 3 | 0 | 0 | 0 | 8 | 0 | 1 | 1 | 0 | 0 | - | 3 | .178 | .174 | .222 |

## Phil Gosselin

**Bats:** R **Throws:** R **Pos:** 2B-3;PH-1;PR-1 GAHSS-eh-lin **Ht:** 6'1" **Wt:** 190 **Born:** 10/3/1988 **Age:** 25

| BATTING | | | | | | | | | | | | | | | | | | | | | BASERUNNING | | | | AVERAGES | | |
|---|---|---|---|---|---|---|---|---|---|---|---|---|---|---|---|---|---|---|---|---|---|---|---|---|---|---|---|
| Year Team | Lg | G | AB | H | 2B | 3B | HR | (Hm | Rd) | TB | R | RBI | RC | TBB | IBB | SO | HBP | SH | SF | SB | CS | SB% | GDP | Avg | OBP | Slg |
| 2010 Rome | A | 57 | 214 | 63 | 9 | 3 | 2 | (- | -) | 84 | 26 | 24 | 33 | 25 | 0 | 51 | 3 | 1 | 1 | 7 | 3 | .70 | 2 | .294 | .374 | .393 |
| 2010 MrtlBh | A+ | 6 | 26 | 4 | 1 | 1 | 0 | (- | -) | 7 | 2 | 0 | 0 | 0 | 0 | 7 | 0 | 0 | 0 | 0 | 0 | - | 0 | .154 | .154 | .269 |
| 2011 Lynbrg | A+ | 115 | 424 | 112 | 24 | 6 | 6 | (- | -) | 166 | 60 | 63 | 58 | 37 | 1 | 76 | 5 | 9 | 9 | 6 | 2 | .75 | 6 | .264 | .324 | .392 |
| 2012 Missi | AA | 128 | 484 | 117 | 23 | 3 | 3 | (- | -) | 155 | 55 | 46 | 54 | 46 | 1 | 90 | 9 | 4 | 4 | 12 | 4 | .75 | 9 | .242 | .317 | .320 |
| 2013 Missi | AA | 59 | 218 | 53 | 10 | 1 | 1 | (- | -) | 68 | 27 | 23 | 21 | 12 | 0 | 31 | 4 | 4 | 3 | 5 | 1 | .83 | 3 | .243 | .291 | .312 |
| 2013 Gwnntt | AAA | 58 | 207 | 55 | 4 | 1 | 2 | (- | -) | 67 | 17 | 15 | 21 | 12 | 0 | 38 | 1 | 7 | 1 | 1 | 0 | 1.00 | 1 | .266 | .308 | .324 |
| 2013 Atl | NL | 4 | 6 | 2 | 0 | 0 | 0 | (0 | 0) | 2 | 2 | 0 | 1 | 1 | 1 | 2 | 0 | 0 | 0 | 0 | 0 | - | 0 | .333 | .429 | .333 |

## Yasmani Grandal

**Bats:** B **Throws:** R **Pos:** C-26;PH-2;1B-1 yaz-MON-ee gran-DAHL **Ht:** 6'2" **Wt:** 215 **Born:** 11/8/1988 **Age:** 25

| BATTING | | | | | | | | | | | | | | | | | | | | | BASERUNNING | | | | AVERAGES | | |
|---|---|---|---|---|---|---|---|---|---|---|---|---|---|---|---|---|---|---|---|---|---|---|---|---|---|---|---|
| Year Team | Lg | G | AB | H | 2B | 3B | HR | (Hm | Rd) | TB | R | RBI | RC | TBB | IBB | SO | HBP | SH | SF | SB | CS | SB% | GDP | Avg | OBP | Slg |
| 2010 Reds | R | 8 | 28 | 8 | 1 | 0 | 0 | (- | -) | 9 | 4 | 1 | 3 | 4 | 0 | 4 | 1 | 0 | 0 | 0 | 1 | .00 | 0 | .286 | .394 | .321 |
| 2011 Bkrsfld | A+ | 56 | 206 | 61 | 14 | 0 | 10 | (- | -) | 105 | 47 | 40 | 45 | 41 | 0 | 57 | 1 | 0 | 3 | 0 | 0 | - | 6 | .296 | .410 | .510 |
| 2011 Carlina | AA | 45 | 156 | 47 | 15 | 0 | 4 | (- | -) | 74 | 20 | 26 | 26 | 13 | 1 | 39 | 2 | 0 | 1 | 0 | 1 | .00 | 0 | .301 | .360 | .474 |
| 2011 Lsvlle | AAA | 4 | 12 | 6 | 2 | 0 | 0 | (- | -) | 8 | 2 | 2 | 5 | 5 | 0 | 1 | 1 | 0 | 0 | 0 | 0 | - | 0 | .500 | .667 | .667 |
| 2012 Tucsn | AAA | 56 | 194 | 65 | 18 | 0 | 6 | (- | -) | 101 | 40 | 35 | 46 | 37 | 4 | 35 | 2 | 0 | 2 | 0 | 0 | - | 7 | .335 | .443 | .521 |

| BATTING | | | | | | | | | | | | | | | | | | | | BASERUNNING | | | | AVERAGES | | |
|---|---|---|---|---|---|---|---|---|---|---|---|---|---|---|---|---|---|---|---|---|---|---|---|---|---|---|
| Year Team | Lg | G | AB | H | 2B | 3B | HR | (Hm | Rd) | TB | R | RBI | RC | TBB | IBB | SO | HBP | SH | SF | SB | CS | SB% | GDP | Avg | OBP | Slg |
| 2012 Lk Els | A+ | 2 | 7 | 0 | 0 | 0 | 0 | (- | -) | 0 | 0 | 0 | 0 | 1 | 0 | 3 | 0 | 0 | 0 | 0 | 0 | - | 0 | .000 | .125 | .000 |
| 2013 Tucsn | AAA | 9 | 36 | 11 | 3 | 0 | 0 | (- | -) | 14 | 3 | 2 | 4 | 2 | 0 | 8 | 0 | 0 | 0 | 0 | 0 | - | 0 | .306 | .342 | .389 |
| 2012 SD | NL | 60 | 192 | 57 | 7 | 1 | 8 | (3 | 5) | 90 | 28 | 36 | 37 | 31 | 1 | 39 | 1 | 0 | 2 | 0 | 0 | - | 8 | .297 | .394 | .469 |
| 2013 SD | NL | 28 | 88 | 19 | 8 | 0 | 1 | (1 | 0) | 30 | 13 | 9 | 12 | 18 | 2 | 18 | 1 | 0 | 1 | 0 | 0 | - | 1 | .216 | .352 | .341 |
| 2 ML YEARS | | 88 | 280 | 76 | 15 | 1 | 9 | (4 | 5) | 120 | 41 | 45 | 49 | 49 | 3 | 57 | 2 | 0 | 3 | 0 | 0 | - | 9 | .271 | .380 | .429 |

# Curtis Granderson

**Bats:** L **Throws:** R **Pos:** CF-25;DH-15;RF-14;LF-13;PH-5 **Ht:** 6'1" **Wt:** 195 **Born:** 3/16/1981 **Age:** 33

| BATTING | | | | | | | | | | | | | | | | | | | | BASERUNNING | | | | AVERAGES | | |
|---|---|---|---|---|---|---|---|---|---|---|---|---|---|---|---|---|---|---|---|---|---|---|---|---|---|---|
| Year Team | Lg | G | AB | H | 2B | 3B | HR | (Hm | Rd) | TB | R | RBI | RC | TBB | IBB | SO | HBP | SH | SF | SB | CS | SB% | GDP | Avg | OBP | Slg |
| 2013 S-WB* | AAA | 5 | 20 | 8 | 0 | 0 | 1 | (- | -) | 11 | 2 | 3 | 4 | 1 | 0 | 4 | 0 | 0 | 0 | 0 | 0 | - | 1 | .400 | .429 | .550 |
| 2013 Tampa* | A+ | 4 | 13 | 2 | 0 | 0 | 0 | (- | -) | 2 | 2 | 1 | 0 | 1 | 0 | 4 | 0 | 0 | 0 | 0 | 0 | - | 0 | .154 | .214 | .154 |
| 2013 Trntn* | AA | 2 | 6 | 2 | 0 | 1 | 0 | (- | -) | 4 | 1 | 0 | 2 | 3 | 0 | 1 | 0 | 0 | 0 | 0 | 0 | - | 0 | .333 | .556 | .667 |
| 2004 Det | AL | 9 | 25 | 6 | 1 | 1 | 0 | (0 | 0) | 9 | 2 | 0 | 2 | 3 | 0 | 8 | 0 | 0 | 0 | 0 | 0 | - | 1 | .240 | .321 | .360 |
| 2005 Det | AL | 47 | 162 | 44 | 6 | 3 | 8 | (5 | 3) | 80 | 18 | 20 | 26 | 10 | 0 | 43 | 0 | 2 | 0 | 1 | 1 | .50 | 2 | .272 | .314 | .494 |
| 2006 Det | AL | 159 | 596 | 155 | 31 | 9 | 19 | (7 | 12) | 261 | 90 | 68 | 89 | 66 | 0 | **174** | 4 | 7 | 6 | 8 | 5 | .62 | 4 | .260 | .335 | .438 |
| 2007 Det | AL | 158 | 612 | 185 | 38 | **23** | 23 | (10 | 13) | 338 | 122 | 74 | 106 | 52 | 3 | 141 | 5 | 5 | 2 | 26 | 1 | **.96** | 3 | .302 | .361 | .552 |
| 2008 Det | AL | 141 | 553 | 155 | 26 | **13** | 22 | (11 | 11) | 273 | 112 | 66 | 100 | 71 | 1 | 111 | 3 | 1 | 1 | 12 | 4 | .75 | 7 | .280 | .365 | .494 |
| 2009 Det | AL | 160 | 631 | 157 | 23 | 8 | 30 | (10 | 20) | 286 | 91 | 71 | 92 | 72 | 4 | 141 | 2 | 3 | 2 | 20 | 6 | .77 | 1 | .249 | .327 | .453 |
| 2010 NYY | AL | 136 | 466 | 115 | 17 | 7 | 24 | (14 | 10) | 218 | 76 | 67 | 71 | 53 | 3 | 116 | 2 | 4 | 3 | 12 | 2 | .86 | 3 | .247 | .324 | .468 |
| 2011 NYY | AL | 156 | 583 | 153 | 26 | 10 | 41 | (21 | 20) | 322 | **136** | **119** | 113 | 85 | 0 | 169 | 12 | 4 | 7 | 25 | 10 | .71 | 12 | .262 | .364 | .552 |
| 2012 NYY | AL | 160 | 596 | 138 | 18 | 4 | 43 | (26 | 17) | 293 | 102 | 106 | 92 | 75 | 4 | 195 | 5 | 1 | 7 | 10 | 3 | .77 | 5 | .232 | .319 | .492 |
| 2013 NYY | AL | 61 | 214 | 49 | 13 | 2 | 7 | (2 | 5) | 87 | 31 | 15 | 23 | 27 | 1 | 69 | 1 | 2 | 1 | 8 | 2 | .80 | 1 | .229 | .317 | .407 |
| Postseason | | 36 | 131 | 30 | 6 | 3 | 6 | (4 | 2) | 60 | 16 | 17 | 22 | 20 | 1 | 38 | 1 | 1 | 1 | 5 | 1 | .83 | 2 | .229 | .333 | .458 |
| 10 ML YEARS | | 1187 | 4438 | 1157 | 199 | 80 | 217 | (106 | 111) | 2167 | 780 | 606 | 714 | 514 | 16 | 1167 | 34 | 29 | 29 | 122 | 34 | .78 | 39 | .261 | .340 | .488 |

# Sonny Gray

**Pitches:** R **Bats:** R **Pos:** SP-10; RP-2 **Ht:** 5'11" **Wt:** 200 **Born:** 11/7/1989 **Age:** 24

| HOW MUCH HE PITCHED | | | | | | | | WHAT HE GAVE UP | | | | | | | | | | | | THE RESULTS | | | | | | | |
|---|---|---|---|---|---|---|---|---|---|---|---|---|---|---|---|---|---|---|---|---|---|---|---|---|---|---|---|
| Year Team | Lg | G | GS | CG | GF | IP | BFP | H | R | ER | HR | SH | SF | HB | TBB | IBB | SO | WP | Bk | W | L | Pct | Sh | Sv-Op | Hld | ERC | ERA |
| 2011 As | R | 1 | 1 | 0 | 0 | 2.0 | 9 | 4 | 1 | 1 | 0 | 0 | 0 | 0 | 0 | 0 | 2 | 0 | 0 | 0 | 1 | .000 | 0 | 0-- | - | 8.38 | 4.50 |
| 2011 Mdlnd | AA | 5 | 5 | 0 | 0 | 20.0 | 78 | 15 | 1 | 1 | 0 | 2 | 0 | 0 | 6 | 0 | 18 | 2 | 0 | 1 | 0 | 1.000 | 0 | 0-- | - | 1.88 | 0.45 |
| 2012 Mdlnd | AA | 26 | 26 | 1 | 0 | 148.0 | 629 | 148 | 73 | 68 | 8 | 0 | 6 | 4 | 57 | 0 | 97 | 16 | 1 | 6 | 9 | .400 | 1 | 0-- | - | 3.87 | 4.14 |
| 2012 Scrmto | AAA | 1 | 1 | 0 | 0 | 4.0 | 24 | 10 | 4 | 4 | 0 | 0 | 2 | 1 | 1 | 0 | 2 | 1 | 0 | 0 | 0 | - | 0 | 0-- | - | 13.27 | 9.00 |
| 2013 Scrmto | AAA | 20 | 20 | 1 | 0 | 118.1 | 494 | 117 | 51 | 45 | 5 | 1 | 3 | 0 | 39 | 0 | 118 | 10 | 0 | 10 | 7 | .588 | 0 | 0-- | - | 3.40 | 3.42 |
| 2013 Oak | AL | 12 | 10 | 0 | 0 | 64.0 | 261 | 51 | 22 | 19 | 4 | 0 | 3 | 0 | 20 | 0 | 67 | 2 | 1 | 5 | 3 | .625 | 0 | 0-0 | 0 | 2.42 | 2.67 |

# Grant Green

**Bats:** R **Throws:** R **Pos:** 2B-45;PH-2 **Ht:** 6'3" **Wt:** 180 **Born:** 9/27/1987 **Age:** 26

| BATTING | | | | | | | | | | | | | | | | | | | | BASERUNNING | | | | AVERAGES | | |
|---|---|---|---|---|---|---|---|---|---|---|---|---|---|---|---|---|---|---|---|---|---|---|---|---|---|---|
| Year Team | Lg | G | AB | H | 2B | 3B | HR | (Hm | Rd) | TB | R | RBI | RC | TBB | IBB | SO | HBP | SH | SF | SB | CS | SB% | GDP | Avg | OBP | Slg |
| 2009 Stcktn | A+ | 5 | 19 | 6 | 1 | 0 | 0 | (- | -) | 7 | 2 | 3 | 2 | 1 | 0 | 5 | 0 | 0 | 0 | 1 | 0 | 1.00 | 1 | .316 | .350 | .368 |
| 2010 Stcktn | A+ | 131 | 548 | 174 | 39 | 6 | 20 | (- | -) | 285 | 107 | 87 | 103 | 38 | 2 | 117 | 7 | 3 | 10 | 9 | 5 | .64 | 14 | .318 | .363 | .520 |
| 2011 Mdlnd | AA | 127 | 530 | 154 | 33 | 1 | 9 | (- | -) | 216 | 76 | 62 | 75 | 39 | 2 | 119 | 6 | 6 | 6 | 6 | 8 | .43 | 14 | .291 | .343 | .408 |
| 2012 Scrmto | AAA | 125 | 524 | 155 | 28 | 6 | 15 | (- | -) | 240 | 73 | 75 | 81 | 33 | 1 | 75 | 2 | 0 | 3 | 13 | 9 | .59 | 13 | .296 | .338 | .458 |
| 2013 Scrmto | AAA | 87 | 378 | 123 | 27 | 3 | 11 | (- | -) | 189 | 66 | 50 | 71 | 27 | 1 | 70 | 6 | 3 | 1 | 4 | 1 | .80 | 11 | .325 | .379 | .500 |
| 2013 Salt Lk | AAA | 6 | 24 | 8 | 1 | 0 | 0 | (- | -) | 9 | 2 | 3 | 3 | 3 | 1 | 7 | 0 | 0 | 1 | 0 | 1 | .00 | 0 | .333 | .393 | .375 |
| 2013 2 Tms | AL | 45 | 140 | 35 | 8 | 1 | 1 | (1 | 0) | 48 | 16 | 17 | 16 | 10 | 0 | 44 | 1 | 0 | 2 | 0 | 0 | - | 3 | .250 | .301 | .343 |
| 13 Oak | AL | 5 | 15 | 0 | 0 | 0 | 0 | (0 | 0) | 0 | 0 | 1 | 0 | 0 | 0 | 6 | 0 | 0 | 1 | 0 | 0 | - | 0 | .000 | .000 | .000 |
| 13 LAA | AL | 40 | 125 | 35 | 8 | 1 | 1 | (1 | 0) | 48 | 16 | 16 | 16 | 10 | 0 | 38 | 1 | 0 | 1 | 0 | 0 | - | 3 | .280 | .336 | .384 |

# Nick Green

**Bats:** R **Throws:** R **Pos:** SS-8;1B-6;2B-2;3B-2;PH-1 **Ht:** 5'11" **Wt:** 190 **Born:** 9/10/1978 **Age:** 35

| BATTING | | | | | | | | | | | | | | | | | | | | BASERUNNING | | | | AVERAGES | | |
|---|---|---|---|---|---|---|---|---|---|---|---|---|---|---|---|---|---|---|---|---|---|---|---|---|---|---|
| Year Team | Lg | G | AB | H | 2B | 3B | HR | (Hm | Rd) | TB | R | RBI | RC | TBB | IBB | SO | HBP | SH | SF | SB | CS | SB% | GDP | Avg | OBP | Slg |
| 2013 NewOr* | AAA | 90 | 318 | 68 | 11 | 1 | 12 | (- | -) | 117 | 39 | 34 | 31 | 18 | 0 | 82 | 4 | 2 | 1 | 1 | 2 | .33 | 6 | .214 | .264 | .368 |
| 2004 Atl | NL | 95 | 264 | 72 | 15 | 3 | 3 | (3 | 0) | 102 | 40 | 26 | 36 | 12 | 1 | 63 | 4 | 8 | 2 | 1 | 2 | .33 | 0 | .273 | .312 | .386 |
| 2005 TB | AL | 111 | 318 | 76 | 15 | 2 | 5 | (2 | 3) | 110 | 53 | 29 | 38 | 33 | 0 | 86 | 11 | 10 | 3 | 3 | 1 | .75 | 5 | .239 | .329 | .346 |
| 2006 2 Tms | AL | 63 | 114 | 21 | 5 | 0 | 2 | (1 | 1) | 32 | 12 | 4 | 10 | 11 | 0 | 40 | 1 | 1 | 0 | 1 | 4 | .20 | 2 | .184 | .262 | .281 |
| 2007 Sea | AL | 6 | 7 | 0 | 0 | 0 | 0 | (0 | 0) | 0 | 0 | 0 | 0 | 0 | 0 | 3 | 0 | 0 | 0 | 0 | 0 | - | 0 | .000 | .000 | .000 |
| 2009 Bos | AL | 104 | 276 | 65 | 18 | 0 | 6 | (4 | 2) | 101 | 35 | 35 | 28 | 20 | 1 | 69 | 8 | 2 | 3 | 1 | 4 | .20 | 10 | .236 | .303 | .366 |
| 2010 2 Tms | | 14 | 21 | 3 | 0 | 0 | 0 | (0 | 0) | 3 | 2 | 2 | 1 | 1 | 0 | 5 | 1 | 0 | 0 | 0 | 0 | - | 0 | .143 | .217 | .143 |
| 2012 Mia | NL | 7 | 23 | 4 | 3 | 0 | 0 | (0 | 0) | 7 | 1 | 1 | 1 | 0 | 0 | 6 | 1 | 0 | 0 | 0 | 0 | - | 0 | .174 | .208 | .304 |
| 2013 Mia | NL | 18 | 55 | 13 | 2 | 0 | 1 | (1 | 0) | 18 | 4 | 6 | 6 | 3 | 0 | 14 | 3 | 2 | 2 | 0 | 0 | - | 1 | .236 | .302 | .327 |
| 06 TB | AL | 17 | 39 | 3 | 0 | 0 | 0 | (0 | 0) | 3 | 4 | 0 | 0 | 6 | 0 | 11 | 0 | 0 | 0 | 0 | 3 | .00 | 2 | .077 | .200 | .077 |
| 06 NYY | AL | 46 | 75 | 18 | 5 | 0 | 2 | (1 | 1) | 29 | 8 | 4 | 10 | 5 | 0 | 29 | 1 | 1 | 0 | 1 | 1 | .50 | 0 | .240 | .296 | .387 |
| 10 LAD | NL | 5 | 8 | 1 | 0 | 0 | 0 | (0 | 0) | 1 | 0 | 1 | 0 | 0 | 0 | 2 | 1 | 0 | 0 | 0 | 0 | - | 0 | .125 | .222 | .125 |
| 10 Tor | AL | 9 | 13 | 2 | 0 | 0 | 0 | (0 | 0) | 2 | 2 | 1 | 1 | 1 | 0 | 3 | 0 | 0 | 0 | 0 | 0 | - | 0 | .154 | .214 | .154 |
| Postseason | | 2 | 0 | 0 | 0 | 0 | 0 | (0 | 0) | 0 | 0 | 0 | 0 | 0 | 0 | 0 | 0 | 0 | 0 | 0 | 0 | - | 0 | - | - | - |
| 8 ML YEARS | | 418 | 1078 | 254 | 58 | 5 | 17 | (11 | 6) | 373 | 147 | 103 | 120 | 80 | 2 | 286 | 29 | 23 | 10 | 6 | 11 | .35 | 18 | .236 | .303 | .346 |

## Tyler Greene

**Bats:** R **Throws:** R **Pos:** 2B-19;PR-6;PH-2 **Ht:** 6'2" **Wt:** 190 **Born:** 8/17/1983 **Age:** 30

| BATTING | | | | | | | | | | | | | | | | | | | | | BASERUNNING | | | | AVERAGES | | |
|---|---|---|---|---|---|---|---|---|---|---|---|---|---|---|---|---|---|---|---|---|---|---|---|---|---|---|---|
| Year Team | Lg | G | AB | H | 2B | 3B | HR | (Hm | Rd) | TB | R | RBI | RC | TBB | IBB | SO | HBP | SH | SF | SB | CS | SB% | GDP | Avg | OBP | Slg |
| 2013 Charltt* | AAA | 56 | 208 | 50 | 10 | 2 | 3 | (- | -) | 73 | 26 | 27 | 22 | 15 | 1 | 66 | 1 | 2 | 0 | 10 | 4 | .71 | 4 | .240 | .295 | .351 |
| 2013 Gwnntt* | AAA | 13 | 42 | 14 | 4 | 0 | 1 | (- | -) | 21 | 8 | 4 | 8 | 3 | 1 | 7 | 3 | 0 | 0 | 0 | 0 | - | 0 | .333 | .417 | .500 |
| 2009 StL | NL | 48 | 108 | 24 | 5 | 0 | 2 | (1 | 1) | 35 | 9 | 7 | 6 | 4 | 0 | 32 | 3 | 1 | 0 | 3 | 0 | 1.00 | 2 | .222 | .270 | .324 |
| 2010 StL | NL | 44 | 104 | 23 | 3 | 1 | 2 | (2 | 0) | 34 | 14 | 10 | 10 | 13 | 4 | 24 | 4 | 0 | 1 | 2 | 0 | 1.00 | 1 | .221 | .328 | .327 |
| 2011 StL | NL | 58 | 104 | 22 | 5 | 0 | 1 | (0 | 1) | 30 | 22 | 11 | 12 | 13 | 2 | 31 | 4 | 0 | 0 | 11 | 0 | 1.00 | 3 | .212 | .322 | .288 |
| 2012 2 Tms | NL | 116 | 305 | 70 | 15 | 2 | 11 | (6 | 5) | 122 | 34 | 30 | 27 | 19 | 1 | 95 | 1 | 2 | 3 | 12 | 4 | .75 | 7 | .230 | .274 | .400 |
| 2013 CWS | AL | 22 | 54 | 12 | 2 | 1 | 1 | (1 | 0) | 19 | 7 | 3 | 4 | 3 | 0 | 19 | 0 | 0 | 0 | 0 | 0 | - | 1 | .222 | .263 | .352 |
| 12 StL | NL | 77 | 179 | 39 | 9 | 2 | 4 | (2 | 2) | 64 | 16 | 19 | 16 | 13 | 1 | 56 | 1 | 2 | 2 | 9 | 2 | .82 | 4 | .218 | .272 | .358 |
| 12 Hou | NL | 39 | 126 | 31 | 6 | 0 | 7 | (4 | 3) | 58 | 18 | 11 | 11 | 6 | 0 | 39 | 0 | 0 | 1 | 3 | 2 | .60 | 3 | .246 | .278 | .460 |
| 5 ML YEARS | | 288 | 675 | 151 | 30 | 4 | 17 | (10 | 7) | 240 | 86 | 61 | 59 | 52 | 7 | 201 | 12 | 3 | 4 | 28 | 4 | .88 | 14 | .224 | .289 | .356 |

## Luke Gregerson

**Pitches:** R **Bats:** L **Pos:** RP-73 **Ht:** 6'3" **Wt:** 200 **Born:** 5/14/1984 **Age:** 30

| HOW MUCH HE PITCHED | | | | | | | | WHAT HE GAVE UP | | | | | | | | | | | | THE RESULTS | | | | | | | |
|---|---|---|---|---|---|---|---|---|---|---|---|---|---|---|---|---|---|---|---|---|---|---|---|---|---|---|---|
| Year Team | Lg | G | GS | CG | GF | IP | BFP | H | R | ER | HR | SH | SF | HB | TBB | IBB | SO | WP | Bk | W | L | Pct | Sh | Sv-Op | Hld | ERC | ERA |
| 2009 SD | NL | 72 | 0 | 0 | 7 | 75.0 | 318 | 62 | 29 | 27 | 3 | 3 | 1 | 3 | 31 | 9 | 93 | 4 | 0 | 2 | 4 | .333 | 0 | 1-7 | 27 | 2.72 | 3.24 |
| 2010 SD | NL | 80 | 0 | 0 | 9 | 78.1 | 297 | 47 | 30 | 28 | 8 | 1 | 1 | 1 | 18 | 2 | 89 | 0 | 0 | 4 | 7 | .364 | 0 | 2-7 | **40** | 1.56 | 3.22 |
| 2011 SD | NL | 61 | 0 | 0 | 11 | 55.2 | 241 | 57 | 23 | 17 | 2 | 5 | 1 | 2 | 19 | 3 | 34 | 2 | 0 | 3 | 3 | .500 | 0 | 0-4 | 16 | 3.55 | 2.75 |
| 2012 SD | NL | 77 | 0 | 0 | 15 | 71.2 | 294 | 57 | 19 | 19 | 7 | 5 | 0 | 3 | 21 | 3 | 72 | 3 | 0 | 2 | 0 | 1.000 | 0 | 9-13 | 24 | 2.64 | 2.39 |
| 2013 SD | NL | 73 | 0 | 0 | 17 | 66.1 | 268 | 49 | 24 | 20 | 3 | 4 | 1 | 4 | 18 | 2 | 64 | 1 | 0 | 6 | 8 | .429 | 0 | 4-9 | 25 | 2.07 | 2.71 |
| 5 ML YEARS | | 363 | 0 | 0 | 59 | 347.0 | 1418 | 272 | 125 | 111 | 23 | 18 | 4 | 13 | 107 | 19 | 352 | 10 | 0 | 17 | 22 | .436 | 0 | 16-40 | 132 | 2.43 | 2.88 |

## Kevin Gregg

**Pitches:** R **Bats:** R **Pos:** RP-62 **Ht:** 6'6" **Wt:** 245 **Born:** 6/20/1978 **Age:** 36

| HOW MUCH HE PITCHED | | | | | | | | WHAT HE GAVE UP | | | | | | | | | | | | THE RESULTS | | | | | | | |
|---|---|---|---|---|---|---|---|---|---|---|---|---|---|---|---|---|---|---|---|---|---|---|---|---|---|---|---|
| Year Team | Lg | G | GS | CG | GF | IP | BFP | H | R | ER | HR | SH | SF | HB | TBB | IBB | SO | WP | Bk | W | L | Pct | Sh | Sv-Op | Hld | ERC | ERA |
| 2003 LAA | AL | 5 | 3 | 0 | 0 | 24.2 | 97 | 18 | 9 | 9 | 3 | 0 | 0 | 1 | 8 | 0 | 14 | 0 | 0 | 2 | 0 | 1.000 | 0 | 0-0 | 0 | 2.74 | 3.28 |
| 2004 LAA | AL | 55 | 0 | 0 | 23 | 87.2 | 377 | 86 | 43 | 41 | 6 | 4 | 5 | 3 | 28 | 3 | 84 | 13 | 1 | 5 | 2 | .714 | 0 | 1-2 | 3 | 3.47 | 4.21 |
| 2005 LAA | AL | 33 | 2 | 0 | 9 | 64.1 | 290 | 70 | 37 | 36 | 8 | 1 | 1 | 3 | 29 | 2 | 52 | 5 | 0 | 1 | 2 | .333 | 0 | 0-1 | 1 | 5.08 | 5.04 |
| 2006 LAA | AL | 32 | 3 | 0 | 12 | 78.1 | 341 | 88 | 41 | 36 | 10 | 0 | 3 | 2 | 21 | 0 | 71 | 6 | 0 | 3 | 4 | .429 | 0 | 0-0 | 0 | 4.51 | 4.14 |
| 2007 Fla | NL | 74 | 0 | 0 | 55 | 84.0 | 355 | 63 | 34 | 33 | 7 | 3 | 0 | 6 | 40 | 1 | 87 | 6 | 0 | 0 | 5 | .000 | 0 | 32-36 | 6 | 3.15 | 3.54 |
| 2008 Fla | NL | 72 | 0 | 0 | 59 | 68.2 | 296 | 51 | 30 | 26 | 3 | 3 | 1 | 4 | 37 | 4 | 58 | 7 | 0 | 7 | 8 | .467 | 0 | 29-38 | 3 | 2.90 | 3.41 |
| 2009 ChC | NL | 72 | 0 | 0 | 51 | 68.2 | 298 | 60 | 38 | 36 | 13 | 0 | 3 | 3 | 30 | 2 | 71 | 7 | 0 | 5 | 6 | .455 | 0 | 23-30 | 1 | 4.19 | 4.72 |
| 2010 Tor | AL | 63 | 0 | 0 | 56 | 59.0 | 254 | 52 | 24 | 23 | 4 | 1 | 3 | 1 | 30 | 1 | 58 | 3 | 0 | 2 | 6 | .250 | 0 | 37-43 | 3 | 3.66 | 3.51 |
| 2011 Bal | AL | 63 | 0 | 0 | 48 | 59.2 | 275 | 58 | 35 | 29 | 7 | 4 | 1 | 2 | 40 | 4 | 53 | 2 | 0 | 0 | 3 | .000 | 0 | 22-29 | 0 | 5.10 | 4.37 |
| 2012 Bal | AL | 40 | 0 | 0 | 13 | 43.2 | 200 | 50 | 26 | 24 | 6 | 0 | 1 | 3 | 24 | 2 | 37 | 0 | 0 | 3 | 2 | .600 | 0 | 0-0 | 0 | 6.15 | 4.95 |
| 2013 ChC | NL | 62 | 0 | 0 | 52 | 62.0 | 269 | 53 | 26 | 24 | 6 | 4 | 1 | 1 | 32 | 2 | 56 | 1 | 0 | 2 | 6 | .250 | 0 | 33-38 | 0 | 3.67 | 3.48 |
| Postseason | | 2 | 0 | 0 | 0 | 4.0 | 18 | 4 | 0 | 0 | 0 | 0 | 0 | 0 | 2 | 0 | 3 | 1 | 0 | 0 | 0 | - | 0 | 0-0 | 0 | 3.63 | 0.00 |
| 11 ML YEARS | | 571 | 8 | 0 | 378 | 700.2 | 3052 | 649 | 343 | 317 | 73 | 20 | 19 | 29 | 319 | 21 | 641 | 50 | 1 | 30 | 44 | .405 | 0 | 177-217 | 17 | 4.00 | 4.07 |

## Didi Gregorius

**Bats:** L **Throws:** R **Pos:** SS-100;PH-4 dee-dee greh-GORE-ee-us **Ht:** 6'1" **Wt:** 185 **Born:** 2/18/1990 **Age:** 24

| BATTING | | | | | | | | | | | | | | | | | | | | | BASERUNNING | | | | AVERAGES | | |
|---|---|---|---|---|---|---|---|---|---|---|---|---|---|---|---|---|---|---|---|---|---|---|---|---|---|---|---|
| Year Team | Lg | G | AB | H | 2B | 3B | HR | (Hm | Rd) | TB | R | RBI | RC | TBB | IBB | SO | HBP | SH | SF | SB | CS | SB% | GDP | Avg | OBP | Slg |
| 2009 Srsota | A+ | 22 | 71 | 18 | 4 | 0 | 0 | (- | -) | 22 | 8 | 2 | 6 | 1 | 0 | 9 | 1 | 1 | 0 | 0 | 0 | - | 0 | .254 | .274 | .310 |
| 2009 Billings | R+ | 50 | 204 | 64 | 10 | 1 | 1 | (- | -) | 79 | 28 | 16 | 29 | 12 | 1 | 27 | 5 | 2 | 2 | 8 | 6 | .57 | 6 | .314 | .363 | .387 |
| 2010 Dayton | A | 120 | 501 | 137 | 16 | 11 | 5 | (- | -) | 190 | 65 | 41 | 65 | 33 | 1 | 62 | 7 | 6 | 1 | 16 | 7 | .70 | 3 | .273 | .327 | .379 |
| 2010 Lynbrg | A+ | 7 | 25 | 6 | 0 | 0 | 0 | (- | -) | 6 | 4 | 0 | 2 | 2 | 0 | 6 | 1 | 1 | 0 | 0 | 0 | - | 0 | .240 | .321 | .240 |
| 2011 Bkrsfld | A+ | 46 | 188 | 57 | 12 | 1 | 5 | (- | -) | 86 | 30 | 28 | 27 | 10 | 1 | 25 | 0 | 2 | 3 | 8 | 8 | .50 | 2 | .303 | .333 | .457 |
| 2011 Carlina | AA | 38 | 148 | 40 | 6 | 3 | 2 | (- | -) | 58 | 18 | 16 | 18 | 9 | 0 | 25 | 0 | 3 | 0 | 3 | 2 | .60 | 1 | .270 | .312 | .392 |
| 2012 Pnscla | AA | 81 | 316 | 88 | 11 | 8 | 1 | (- | -) | 118 | 45 | 31 | 42 | 29 | 0 | 49 | 4 | 7 | 3 | 3 | 4 | .43 | 4 | .278 | .344 | .373 |
| 2012 Lsvlle | AAA | 48 | 185 | 45 | 10 | 3 | 6 | (- | -) | 79 | 25 | 23 | 22 | 12 | 2 | 31 | 0 | 4 | 1 | 0 | 2 | .00 | 1 | .243 | .288 | .427 |
| 2013 Reno | AAA | 7 | 31 | 12 | 2 | 0 | 2 | (- | -) | 20 | 7 | 2 | 7 | 2 | 0 | 1 | 0 | 0 | 0 | 1 | 0 | 1.00 | 0 | .387 | .424 | .645 |
| 2012 Cin | NL | 8 | 20 | 6 | 0 | 0 | 0 | (0 | 0) | 6 | 1 | 2 | 2 | 0 | 0 | 5 | 0 | 1 | 0 | 0 | 0 | - | 0 | .300 | .300 | .300 |
| 2013 Ari | NL | 103 | 357 | 90 | 16 | 3 | 7 | (3 | 4) | 133 | 47 | 28 | 42 | 37 | 5 | 65 | 6 | 2 | 1 | 0 | 2 | .00 | 4 | .252 | .332 | .373 |
| 2 ML YEARS | | 111 | 377 | 96 | 16 | 3 | 7 | (3 | 4) | 139 | 48 | 30 | 44 | 37 | 5 | 70 | 6 | 3 | 1 | 0 | 2 | .00 | 4 | .255 | .330 | .369 |

## Zack Greinke

**Pitches:** R **Bats:** R **Pos:** SP-28 GRAIN-key **Ht:** 6'2" **Wt:** 195 **Born:** 10/21/1983 **Age:** 30

| HOW MUCH HE PITCHED | | | | | | | | WHAT HE GAVE UP | | | | | | | | | | | | THE RESULTS | | | | | | | |
|---|---|---|---|---|---|---|---|---|---|---|---|---|---|---|---|---|---|---|---|---|---|---|---|---|---|---|---|
| Year Team | Lg | G | GS | CG | GF | IP | BFP | H | R | ER | HR | SH | SF | HB | TBB | IBB | SO | WP | Bk | W | L | Pct | Sh | Sv-Op | Hld | ERC | ERA |
| 2013 RCuca* | A+ | 1 | 1 | 0 | 0 | 4.1 | 21 | 6 | 8 | 3 | 1 | 0 | 0 | 0 | 0 | 0 | 4 | 0 | 0 | 0 | 0 | - | 0 | 0- - | - | 4.87 | 6.23 |
| 2004 KC | AL | 24 | 24 | 0 | 0 | 145.0 | 599 | 143 | 64 | 64 | 26 | 3 | 2 | 8 | 26 | 3 | 100 | 1 | 1 | 8 | 11 | .421 | 0 | 0-0 | 0 | 3.85 | 3.97 |
| 2005 KC | AL | 33 | 33 | 2 | 0 | 183.0 | 829 | 233 | 125 | 118 | 23 | 4 | 4 | 13 | 53 | 0 | 114 | 4 | 2 | 5 | **17** | .227 | 0 | 0-0 | 0 | 5.71 | 5.80 |
| 2006 KC | AL | 3 | 0 | 0 | 1 | 6.1 | 28 | 7 | 3 | 3 | 1 | 0 | 0 | 0 | 3 | 2 | 5 | 0 | 0 | 1 | 0 | 1.000 | 0 | 0-0 | 0 | 4.93 | 4.26 |
| 2007 KC | AL | 52 | 14 | 0 | 7 | 122.0 | 507 | 122 | 52 | 50 | 12 | 3 | 4 | 3 | 36 | 5 | 106 | 3 | 1 | 7 | 7 | .500 | 0 | 1-1 | 12 | 3.77 | 3.69 |
| 2008 KC | AL | 32 | 32 | 1 | 0 | 202.1 | 851 | 202 | 87 | 78 | 21 | 2 | 4 | 4 | 56 | 1 | 183 | 8 | 1 | 13 | 10 | .565 | 0 | 0-0 | 0 | 3.68 | 3.47 |
| 2009 KC | AL | 33 | 33 | 6 | 0 | 229.1 | 915 | 195 | 64 | 55 | 11 | 8 | 3 | 4 | 51 | 0 | 242 | 5 | 0 | 16 | 8 | .667 | 3 | 0-0 | 0 | **2.39** | **2.16** |
| 2010 KC | AL | 33 | 33 | 3 | 0 | 220.0 | 919 | 219 | 114 | 102 | 18 | 6 | 7 | 7 | 55 | 1 | 181 | 4 | 0 | 10 | 14 | .417 | 0 | 0-0 | 0 | 3.48 | 4.17 |
| 2011 Mil | NL | 28 | 28 | 0 | 0 | 171.2 | 715 | 161 | 82 | 73 | 19 | 6 | 1 | 4 | 45 | 0 | 201 | 10 | 0 | 16 | 6 | .727 | 0 | 0-0 | 0 | 3.35 | 3.83 |
| 2012 2 Tms | | 34 | 34 | 0 | 0 | 212.1 | 868 | 200 | 84 | 82 | 18 | 7 | 2 | 2 | 54 | 0 | 200 | 8 | 0 | 15 | 5 | .750 | 0 | 0-0 | 0 | 3.17 | 3.48 |
| 2013 LAD | NL | 28 | 28 | 1 | 0 | 177.2 | 717 | 152 | 54 | 52 | 13 | **13** | 1 | 7 | 46 | 1 | 148 | 5 | 0 | 15 | 4 | **.789** | 1 | 0-0 | 0 | 2.78 | 2.63 |

| HOW MUCH HE PITCHED | | | | | | | | | WHAT HE GAVE UP | | | | | | | | | | | | THE RESULTS | | | | | | | |
|---|---|---|---|---|---|---|---|---|---|---|---|---|---|---|---|---|---|---|---|---|---|---|---|---|---|---|---|---|
| Year | Team | Lg | G | GS | CG | GF | IP | BFP | H | R | ER | HR | SH | SF | HB | TBB | IBB | SO | WP | Bk | W | L | Pct | Sh | Sv-Op | Hld | ERC | ERA |
| 12 | Mil | NL | 21 | 21 | 0 | 0 | 123.0 | 504 | 120 | 49 | 47 | 7 | 3 | 0 | 0 | 28 | 0 | 122 | 4 | 0 | 9 | 3 | .750 | 0 | 0-0 | 0 | 3.02 | 3.44 |
| 12 | LAA | AL | 13 | 13 | 0 | 0 | 89.1 | 364 | 80 | 35 | 35 | 11 | 4 | 2 | 2 | 26 | 0 | 78 | 4 | 0 | 6 | 2 | .750 | 0 | 0-0 | 0 | 3.38 | 3.53 |
| Postseason | | | 3 | 3 | 0 | 0 | 16.2 | 80 | 23 | 15 | 12 | 4 | 1 | 0 | 1 | 4 | 0 | 13 | 0 | 0 | 1 | 1 | .500 | 0 | 0-0 | 0 | 6.67 | 6.48 |
| 10 ML YEARS | | | 300 | 259 | 13 | 8 | 1669.2 | 6948 | 1634 | 729 | 677 | 162 | 52 | 28 | 52 | 425 | 13 | 1480 | 48 | 5 | 106 | 82 | .564 | 4 | 1-1 | 12 | 3.50 | 3.65 |

## A.J. Griffin

**Pitches:** R **Bats:** R **Pos:** SP-32 **Ht:** 6'5" **Wt:** 230 **Born:** 1/28/1988 **Age:** 26

| HOW MUCH HE PITCHED | | | | | | | | | WHAT HE GAVE UP | | | | | | | | | | | | THE RESULTS | | | | | | | |
|---|---|---|---|---|---|---|---|---|---|---|---|---|---|---|---|---|---|---|---|---|---|---|---|---|---|---|---|---|
| Year | Team | Lg | G | GS | CG | GF | IP | BFP | H | R | ER | HR | SH | SF | HB | TBB | IBB | SO | WP | Bk | W | L | Pct | Sh | Sv-Op | Hld | ERC | ERA |
| 2010 | As | R | 4 | 0 | 0 | 1 | 5.0 | 16 | 1 | 0 | 0 | 0 | 0 | 0 | 0 | 0 | 0 | 6 | 0 | 0 | 0 | 0 | - | 0 | 0-- | - | 0.09 | 0.00 |
| 2010 | Vancvr | A- | 20 | 0 | 0 | 18 | 21.1 | 86 | 14 | 9 | 7 | 0 | 0 | 0 | 3 | 7 | 1 | 27 | 2 | 0 | 1 | 1 | .500 | 0 | 15-- | - | 1.87 | 2.95 |
| 2011 | Burlgtn | A | 8 | 8 | 0 | 0 | 52.0 | 202 | 36 | 10 | 9 | 2 | 1 | 1 | 2 | 5 | 0 | 46 | 0 | 0 | 4 | 0 | 1.000 | 0 | 0-- | - | 1.35 | 1.56 |
| 2011 | Stcktn | A+ | 12 | 12 | 0 | 0 | 70.2 | 283 | 64 | 31 | 28 | 8 | 4 | 3 | 2 | 14 | 0 | 82 | 3 | 1 | 5 | 3 | .625 | 0 | 0-- | - | 3.04 | 3.57 |
| 2011 | Scrmto | AAA | 1 | 1 | 0 | 0 | 6.0 | 24 | 6 | 3 | 2 | 1 | 0 | 0 | 0 | 2 | 0 | 8 | 0 | 0 | 0 | 1 | .000 | 0 | 0-- | - | 4.57 | 3.00 |
| 2011 | Mdlnd | AA | 6 | 6 | 0 | 0 | 32.0 | 146 | 39 | 24 | 23 | 6 | 0 | 0 | 2 | 11 | 0 | 20 | 0 | 0 | 2 | 3 | .400 | 0 | 0-- | - | 6.00 | 6.47 |
| 2012 | Mdlnd | AA | 7 | 7 | 0 | 0 | 43.1 | 164 | 31 | 12 | 12 | 4 | 1 | 1 | 1 | 7 | 0 | 44 | 1 | 0 | 3 | 1 | .750 | 0 | 0-- | - | 1.85 | 2.49 |
| 2012 | Scrmto | AAA | 10 | 10 | 2 | 0 | 58.2 | 238 | 48 | 27 | 20 | 3 | 0 | 2 | 4 | 11 | 1 | 47 | 2 | 0 | 4 | 2 | .667 | 0 | 0-- | - | 2.23 | 3.07 |
| 2012 | Oak | AL | 15 | 15 | 0 | 0 | 82.1 | 336 | 74 | 29 | 28 | 10 | 0 | 2 | 1 | 19 | 0 | 64 | 0 | 0 | 7 | 1 | .875 | 0 | 0-0 | 0 | 3.06 | 3.06 |
| 2013 | Oak | AL | 32 | 32 | 1 | 0 | 200.0 | 823 | 171 | 91 | 85 | **36** | 4 | 4 | 4 | 54 | 2 | 171 | 7 | 0 | 14 | 10 | .583 | 1 | 0-0 | 0 | 3.33 | 3.83 |
| Postseason | | | 1 | 1 | 0 | 0 | 5.0 | 21 | 7 | 2 | 2 | 1 | 1 | 0 | 0 | 0 | 0 | 1 | 0 | 0 | 0 | 0 | - | 0 | 0-0 | 0 | 5.60 | 3.60 |
| 2 ML YEARS | | | 47 | 47 | 1 | 0 | 282.1 | 1159 | 245 | 120 | 113 | 46 | 4 | 6 | 5 | 73 | 2 | 235 | 7 | 0 | 21 | 11 | .656 | 1 | 0-0 | 0 | 3.25 | 3.60 |

## Jason Grilli

**Pitches:** R **Bats:** R **Pos:** RP-54 GRILL-ee **Ht:** 6'4" **Wt:** 235 **Born:** 11/11/1976 **Age:** 37

| HOW MUCH HE PITCHED | | | | | | | | | WHAT HE GAVE UP | | | | | | | | | | | | THE RESULTS | | | | | | | |
|---|---|---|---|---|---|---|---|---|---|---|---|---|---|---|---|---|---|---|---|---|---|---|---|---|---|---|---|---|
| Year | Team | Lg | G | GS | CG | GF | IP | BFP | H | R | ER | HR | SH | SF | HB | TBB | IBB | SO | WP | Bk | W | L | Pct | Sh | Sv-Op | Hld | ERC | ERA |
| 2013 | Altna* | AA | 2 | 2 | 0 | 0 | 2.0 | 9 | 2 | 0 | 0 | 0 | 0 | 0 | 0 | 0 | 0 | 4 | 1 | 0 | 0 | 0 | - | 0 | 0-- | - | 1.68 | 0.00 |
| 2000 | Fla | NL | 1 | 1 | 0 | 0 | 6.2 | 35 | 11 | 4 | 4 | 0 | 2 | 0 | 2 | 2 | 0 | 3 | 0 | 0 | 1 | 0 | 1.000 | 0 | 0-0 | 0 | 7.84 | 5.40 |
| 2001 | Fla | NL | 6 | 5 | 0 | 1 | 26.2 | 115 | 30 | 18 | 18 | 6 | 1 | 0 | 2 | 11 | 0 | 17 | 0 | 0 | 2 | 2 | .500 | 0 | 0-0 | 0 | 6.44 | 6.08 |
| 2004 | CWS | AL | 8 | 8 | 1 | 0 | 45.0 | 203 | 52 | 38 | 37 | 11 | 2 | 1 | 3 | 20 | 0 | 26 | 2 | 0 | 2 | 3 | .400 | 0 | 0-0 | 0 | 6.67 | 7.40 |
| 2005 | Det | AL | 3 | 2 | 0 | 0 | 16.0 | 63 | 14 | 6 | 6 | 1 | 1 | 1 | 0 | 6 | 0 | 5 | 0 | 0 | 1 | 1 | .500 | 0 | 0-0 | 0 | 3.27 | 3.38 |
| 2006 | Det | AL | 51 | 0 | 0 | 18 | 62.0 | 270 | 61 | 31 | 29 | 6 | 2 | 4 | 5 | 25 | 3 | 31 | 5 | 0 | 2 | 3 | .400 | 0 | 0-0 | 9 | 4.23 | 4.21 |
| 2007 | Det | AL | 57 | 0 | 0 | 13 | 79.2 | 352 | 81 | 46 | 42 | 5 | 1 | 5 | 5 | 32 | 1 | 62 | 5 | 0 | 5 | 3 | .625 | 0 | 0-2 | 11 | 4.09 | 4.74 |
| 2008 | 2 Tms | | 60 | 0 | 0 | 16 | 75.0 | 323 | 67 | 27 | 25 | 2 | 1 | 3 | 2 | 38 | 7 | 69 | 4 | 0 | 3 | 3 | .500 | 0 | 1-2 | 4 | 3.34 | 3.00 |
| 2009 | 2 Tms | | 52 | 0 | 0 | 11 | 45.2 | 212 | 50 | 27 | 27 | 4 | 2 | 1 | 1 | 27 | 2 | 49 | 2 | 0 | 2 | 3 | .400 | 0 | 1-1 | 7 | 5.25 | 5.32 |
| 2011 | Pit | NL | 28 | 0 | 0 | 4 | 32.2 | 140 | 24 | 10 | 9 | 2 | 1 | 0 | 4 | 15 | 5 | 37 | 3 | 0 | 2 | 1 | .667 | 0 | 1-1 | 9 | 2.79 | 2.48 |
| 2012 | Pit | NL | 64 | 0 | 0 | 11 | 58.2 | 244 | 45 | 20 | 19 | 7 | 2 | 1 | 2 | 22 | 4 | 90 | 0 | 0 | 1 | 6 | .143 | 0 | 2-5 | 32 | 2.85 | 2.91 |
| 2013 | Pit | NL | 54 | 0 | 0 | 41 | 50.0 | 202 | 40 | 15 | 15 | 4 | 1 | 0 | 1 | 13 | 0 | 74 | 1 | 0 | 0 | 2 | .000 | 0 | 33-35 | 2 | 2.44 | 2.70 |
| 08 | Det | AL | 9 | 0 | 0 | 4 | 13.2 | 59 | 12 | 5 | 5 | 1 | 0 | 0 | 1 | 7 | 1 | 10 | 1 | 0 | 0 | 1 | .000 | 0 | 0-1 | 0 | 3.85 | 3.29 |
| 08 | Col | NL | 51 | 0 | 0 | 12 | 61.1 | 264 | 55 | 22 | 20 | 1 | 1 | 3 | 1 | 31 | 6 | 59 | 3 | 0 | 3 | 2 | .600 | 0 | 1-1 | 4 | 3.23 | 2.93 |
| 09 | Col | NL | 22 | 0 | 0 | 6 | 19.1 | 99 | 29 | 13 | 13 | 2 | 1 | 1 | 0 | 13 | 2 | 22 | 2 | 0 | 0 | 1 | .000 | 0 | 1-1 | 3 | 8.02 | 6.05 |
| 09 | Tex | AL | 30 | 0 | 0 | 5 | 26.1 | 113 | 21 | 14 | 14 | 2 | 1 | 0 | 1 | 14 | 0 | 27 | 0 | 0 | 2 | 2 | .500 | 0 | 0-0 | 4 | 3.44 | 4.78 |
| Postseason | | | 5 | 0 | 0 | 0 | 3.0 | 14 | 1 | 0 | 0 | 0 | 0 | 0 | 0 | 4 | 1 | 1 | 0 | 0 | 0 | 0 | - | 0 | 0-0 | 1 | 2.44 | 0.00 |
| 11 ML YEARS | | | 384 | 16 | 1 | 115 | 498.0 | 2159 | 475 | 242 | 231 | 48 | 16 | 16 | 27 | 211 | 22 | 463 | 22 | 0 | 21 | 27 | .438 | 0 | 38-46 | 74 | 4.03 | 4.17 |

## Justin Grimm

**Pitches:** R **Bats:** R **Pos:** SP-17; RP-10 **Ht:** 6'3" **Wt:** 200 **Born:** 8/16/1988 **Age:** 25

| HOW MUCH HE PITCHED | | | | | | | | | WHAT HE GAVE UP | | | | | | | | | | | | THE RESULTS | | | | | | | |
|---|---|---|---|---|---|---|---|---|---|---|---|---|---|---|---|---|---|---|---|---|---|---|---|---|---|---|---|---|
| Year | Team | Lg | G | GS | CG | GF | IP | BFP | H | R | ER | HR | SH | SF | HB | TBB | IBB | SO | WP | Bk | W | L | Pct | Sh | Sv-Op | Hld | ERC | ERA |
| 2011 | Hkry | A | 9 | 9 | 0 | 0 | 50.1 | 209 | 45 | 23 | 19 | 5 | 2 | 4 | 3 | 18 | 0 | 54 | 4 | 1 | 2 | 1 | .667 | 0 | 0-- | - | 3.63 | 3.40 |
| 2011 | MrtlBh | A+ | 16 | 16 | 0 | 0 | 90.1 | 386 | 84 | 40 | 34 | 2 | 6 | 4 | 6 | 30 | 0 | 73 | 4 | 0 | 5 | 2 | .714 | 0 | 0-- | - | 3.12 | 3.39 |
| 2012 | Frisco | AA | 16 | 14 | 0 | 0 | 83.2 | 324 | 70 | 21 | 16 | 3 | 1 | 0 | 1 | 14 | 0 | 73 | 2 | 0 | 9 | 3 | .750 | 0 | 0-- | - | 2.09 | 1.72 |
| 2012 | RdRck | AAA | 9 | 8 | 0 | 0 | 51.0 | 218 | 53 | 27 | 26 | 2 | 2 | 2 | 4 | 16 | 0 | 30 | 4 | 0 | 2 | 3 | .400 | 0 | 0-- | - | 3.89 | 4.59 |
| 2013 | RdRck | AAA | 1 | 1 | 0 | 0 | 5.2 | 22 | 4 | 1 | 1 | 0 | 0 | 0 | 0 | 2 | 0 | 4 | 0 | 0 | 1 | 0 | 1.000 | 0 | 0-- | - | 1.86 | 1.59 |
| 2013 | Iowa | AAA | 8 | 8 | 0 | 0 | 42.1 | 186 | 46 | 23 | 22 | 1 | 2 | 2 | 0 | 17 | 0 | 41 | 6 | 0 | 2 | 3 | .400 | 0 | 0-- | - | 4.00 | 4.68 |
| 2012 | Tex | AL | 5 | 2 | 0 | 3 | 14.0 | 65 | 22 | 14 | 14 | 1 | 0 | 2 | 0 | 3 | 0 | 13 | 3 | 0 | 1 | 1 | .500 | 0 | 0-0 | 0 | 6.54 | 9.00 |
| 2013 | 2 Tms | | 27 | 17 | 0 | 3 | 98.0 | 442 | 120 | 70 | 65 | 15 | 4 | 2 | 2 | 34 | 1 | 76 | 4 | 0 | 7 | 9 | .438 | 0 | 0-0 | 3 | 5.61 | 5.97 |
| 13 | Tex | AL | 17 | 17 | 0 | 0 | 89.0 | 406 | 116 | 67 | 63 | 15 | 2 | 2 | 1 | 31 | 1 | 68 | 4 | 0 | 7 | 7 | .500 | 0 | 0-0 | 0 | 6.21 | 6.37 |
| 13 | ChC | NL | 10 | 0 | 0 | 3 | 9.0 | 36 | 4 | 3 | 2 | 0 | 2 | 0 | 1 | 3 | 0 | 8 | 0 | 0 | 0 | 2 | .000 | 0 | 0-0 | 3 | 1.12 | 2.00 |
| 2 ML YEARS | | | 32 | 19 | 0 | 6 | 112.0 | 507 | 142 | 84 | 79 | 16 | 4 | 4 | 2 | 37 | 1 | 89 | 7 | 0 | 8 | 10 | .444 | 0 | 0-0 | 3 | 5.72 | 6.35 |

## Robbie Grossman

**Bats:** B **Throws:** L **Pos:** LF-45;CF-29;RF-2;DH-1 **Ht:** 6'0" **Wt:** 205 **Born:** 9/16/1989 **Age:** 24

| BATTING | | | | | | | | | | | | | | | | | | | | BASERUNNING | | | | AVERAGES | | |
|---|---|---|---|---|---|---|---|---|---|---|---|---|---|---|---|---|---|---|---|---|---|---|---|---|---|---|
| Year | Team | Lg | G | AB | H | 2B | 3B | HR | (Hm | Rd) | TB | R | RBI | RC | TBB | IBB | SO | HBP | SH | SF | SB | CS | SB% | GDP | Avg | OBP | Slg |
| 2009 | WV | A | 116 | 451 | 120 | 21 | 2 | 5 | (- | -) | 160 | 83 | 42 | 68 | 75 | 2 | 164 | 2 | 7 | 0 | 35 | 12 | .74 | 7 | .266 | .373 | .355 |
| 2010 | Bradtn | A+ | 125 | 470 | 115 | 29 | 3 | 4 | (- | -) | 162 | 84 | 50 | 62 | 66 | 1 | 118 | 8 | 12 | 6 | 15 | 8 | .65 | 8 | .245 | .344 | .345 |
| 2011 | Bradtn | A+ | 134 | 490 | 144 | 34 | 2 | 13 | (- | -) | 221 | 127 | 56 | 102 | 104 | 0 | 111 | 6 | 9 | 7 | 24 | 10 | .71 | 8 | .294 | .418 | .451 |
| 2012 | Altna | AA | 95 | 350 | 93 | 20 | 4 | 7 | (- | -) | 142 | 59 | 36 | 56 | 59 | 1 | 78 | 4 | 4 | 0 | 9 | 10 | .47 | 3 | .266 | .378 | .406 |
| 2012 | CpChr | AA | 36 | 135 | 36 | 8 | 2 | 3 | (- | -) | 57 | 22 | 11 | 23 | 18 | 0 | 43 | 5 | 1 | 1 | 4 | 1 | .80 | 0 | .267 | .371 | .422 |
| 2013 | OKCity | AAA | 70 | 253 | 71 | 11 | 2 | 2 | (- | -) | 92 | 42 | 20 | 41 | 48 | 2 | 66 | 1 | 7 | 1 | 15 | 8 | .65 | 6 | .281 | .396 | .364 |
| 2013 | Hou | AL | 63 | 257 | 69 | 14 | 0 | 4 | (3 | 1) | 95 | 29 | 21 | 37 | 23 | 0 | 70 | 2 | 5 | 1 | 6 | 7 | .46 | 2 | .268 | .332 | .370 |

# Javy Guerra

**Pitches:** R **Bats:** R **Pos:** RP-9 GEHR-uh **Ht:** 6'1" **Wt:** 190 **Born:** 10/31/1985 **Age:** 28

| HOW MUCH HE PITCHED | | | | | | | | | WHAT HE GAVE UP | | | | | | | | | | | | THE RESULTS | | | | | | | |
|---|---|---|---|---|---|---|---|---|---|---|---|---|---|---|---|---|---|---|---|---|---|---|---|---|---|---|---|---|
| Year | Team | Lg | G | GS | CG | GF | IP | BFP | H | R | ER | HR | SH | SF | HB | TBB | IBB | SO | WP | Bk | W | L | Pct | Sh | Sv-Op | Hld | ERC | ERA |
| 2013 | Albq* | AAA | 27 | 4 | 0 | 22 | 39.1 | 174 | 46 | 18 | 16 | 6 | 4 | 1 | 2 | 14 | 0 | 36 | 3 | 0 | 0 | 4 | .000 | 0 | 12- - | - | 5.55 | 3.66 |
| 2013 | Ddgrs* | R | 1 | 1 | 0 | 0 | 3.0 | 10 | 1 | 0 | 0 | 0 | 0 | 0 | 0 | 0 | 0 | 2 | 0 | 0 | 0 | 0 | - | 0 | 0- - | - | 0.25 | 0.00 |
| 2011 | LAD | NL | 47 | 0 | 0 | 38 | 46.2 | 195 | 37 | 12 | 12 | 2 | 3 | 1 | 3 | 18 | 1 | 38 | 2 | 0 | 2 | 2 | .500 | 0 | 21-23 | 0 | 2.73 | 2.31 |
| 2012 | LAD | NL | 45 | 0 | 0 | 17 | 45.0 | 196 | 44 | 13 | 13 | 1 | 4 | 2 | 1 | 23 | 5 | 37 | 1 | 0 | 2 | 3 | .400 | 0 | 8-13 | 4 | 3.76 | 2.60 |
| 2013 | LAD | NL | 9 | 0 | 0 | 5 | 10.2 | 55 | 15 | 9 | 8 | 1 | 0 | 1 | 1 | 6 | 0 | 12 | 0 | 0 | 0 | 0 | - | 0 | 0-0 | 0 | 7.24 | 6.75 |
| 3 ML YEARS | | | 101 | 0 | 0 | 60 | 102.1 | 446 | 96 | 34 | 33 | 4 | 7 | 4 | 5 | 47 | 6 | 87 | 3 | 0 | 4 | 5 | .444 | 0 | 29-36 | 4 | 3.61 | 2.90 |

# Matt Guerrier

**Pitches:** R **Bats:** R **Pos:** RP-49 gurr-REAR **Ht:** 6'3" **Wt:** 195 **Born:** 8/2/1978 **Age:** 35

| HOW MUCH HE PITCHED | | | | | | | | | WHAT HE GAVE UP | | | | | | | | | | | | THE RESULTS | | | | | | | |
|---|---|---|---|---|---|---|---|---|---|---|---|---|---|---|---|---|---|---|---|---|---|---|---|---|---|---|---|---|
| Year | Team | Lg | G | GS | CG | GF | IP | BFP | H | R | ER | HR | SH | SF | HB | TBB | IBB | SO | WP | Bk | W | L | Pct | Sh | Sv-Op | Hld | ERC | ERA |
| 2004 | Min | AL | 9 | 2 | 0 | 5 | 19.0 | 84 | 22 | 13 | 12 | 5 | 2 | 0 | 1 | 6 | 0 | 11 | 0 | 0 | 0 | 1 | .000 | 0 | 0-0 | 0 | 6.10 | 5.68 |
| 2005 | Min | AL | 43 | 0 | 0 | 14 | 71.2 | 306 | 71 | 29 | 27 | 6 | 4 | 1 | 3 | 24 | 5 | 46 | 3 | 0 | 0 | 3 | .000 | 0 | 0-0 | 1 | 3.71 | 3.39 |
| 2006 | Min | AL | 39 | 1 | 0 | 13 | 69.2 | 300 | 78 | 29 | 26 | 9 | 3 | 4 | 0 | 21 | 0 | 37 | 6 | 0 | 1 | 0 | 1.000 | 0 | 1-1 | 2 | 4.59 | 3.36 |
| 2007 | Min | AL | 73 | 0 | 0 | 16 | 88.0 | 351 | 71 | 23 | 23 | 9 | 0 | 3 | 5 | 21 | 1 | 68 | 6 | 0 | 2 | 4 | .333 | 0 | 1-4 | 14 | 2.70 | 2.35 |
| 2008 | Min | AL | **76** | 0 | 0 | 15 | 76.1 | 344 | 84 | 47 | 44 | 12 | 1 | 1 | 0 | 37 | **9** | 59 | 2 | 0 | 6 | 9 | .400 | 0 | 1-5 | 20 | 5.20 | 5.19 |
| 2009 | Min | AL | **79** | 0 | 0 | 15 | 76.1 | 304 | 58 | 23 | 20 | 10 | 3 | 1 | 4 | 16 | 2 | 47 | 6 | 0 | 5 | 1 | .833 | 0 | 1-4 | **33** | 2.44 | 2.36 |
| 2010 | Min | AL | 74 | 0 | 0 | 13 | 71.0 | 286 | 56 | 28 | 25 | 7 | 2 | 3 | 3 | 22 | 1 | 42 | 2 | 0 | 5 | 7 | .417 | 0 | 1-7 | 23 | 2.78 | 3.17 |
| 2011 | LAD | NL | 70 | 0 | 0 | 12 | 66.1 | 282 | 59 | 31 | 30 | 4 | 3 | 1 | 0 | 25 | 5 | 50 | 2 | 0 | 4 | 3 | .571 | 0 | 1-4 | 13 | 2.95 | 4.07 |
| 2012 | LAD | NL | 16 | 0 | 0 | 2 | 14.0 | 56 | 8 | 6 | 6 | 3 | 1 | 1 | 1 | 7 | 1 | 9 | 0 | 0 | 0 | 2 | .000 | 0 | 0-1 | 3 | 3.15 | 3.86 |
| 2013 | 2 Tms | NL | 49 | 0 | 0 | 7 | 42.2 | 181 | 43 | 22 | 19 | 3 | 2 | 2 | 1 | 17 | 2 | 30 | 0 | 0 | 4 | 4 | .500 | 0 | 0-3 | 8 | 4.01 | 4.01 |
| 13 | LAD | NL | 34 | 0 | 0 | 5 | 30.0 | 130 | 32 | 18 | 16 | 3 | 2 | 2 | 1 | 12 | 2 | 21 | 0 | 0 | 2 | 3 | .400 | 0 | 0-1 | 3 | 4.55 | 4.80 |
| 13 | ChC | NL | 15 | 0 | 0 | 2 | 12.2 | 51 | 11 | 4 | 3 | 0 | 0 | 0 | 0 | 5 | 0 | 9 | 0 | 0 | 2 | 1 | .667 | 0 | 0-2 | 5 | 2.80 | 2.13 |
| Postseason | | | 5 | 0 | 0 | 1 | 4.2 | 16 | 1 | 0 | 0 | 0 | 0 | 1 | 0 | 1 | 0 | 4 | 0 | 0 | 0 | 0 | - | 0 | 0-0 | 1 | 0.30 | 0.00 |
| 10 ML YEARS | | | 528 | 3 | 0 | 112 | 595.0 | 2494 | 550 | 251 | 232 | 68 | 21 | 17 | 18 | 196 | 26 | 399 | 27 | 0 | 27 | 34 | .443 | 0 | 6-29 | 117 | 3.54 | 3.51 |

# Preston Guilmet

**Pitches:** R **Bats:** R **Pos:** RP-4 GILL-met **Ht:** 6'2" **Wt:** 200 **Born:** 7/27/1987 **Age:** 26

| HOW MUCH HE PITCHED | | | | | | | | | WHAT HE GAVE UP | | | | | | | | | | | | THE RESULTS | | | | | | | |
|---|---|---|---|---|---|---|---|---|---|---|---|---|---|---|---|---|---|---|---|---|---|---|---|---|---|---|---|---|
| Year | Team | Lg | G | GS | CG | GF | IP | BFP | H | R | ER | HR | SH | SF | HB | TBB | IBB | SO | WP | Bk | W | L | Pct | Sh | Sv-Op | Hld | ERC | ERA |
| 2009 | MhVlly | A- | 15 | 15 | 0 | 0 | 70.1 | 297 | 70 | 41 | 32 | 8 | 2 | 2 | 2 | 16 | 0 | 62 | 5 | 0 | 6 | 6 | .500 | 0 | 0- - | - | 3.53 | 4.09 |
| 2010 | Lk Cty | A | 30 | 0 | 0 | 21 | 52.0 | 200 | 35 | 13 | 13 | 3 | 2 | 0 | 2 | 10 | 1 | 79 | 3 | 0 | 4 | 1 | .800 | 0 | 11- - | - | 1.60 | 2.25 |
| 2011 | Knstn | A+ | 52 | 0 | 0 | 48 | 58.1 | 226 | 43 | 14 | 14 | 4 | 2 | 0 | 0 | 11 | 1 | 60 | 3 | 0 | 1 | 1 | .500 | 0 | 35- - | - | 1.78 | 2.16 |
| 2012 | Akron | AA | 50 | 0 | 0 | 39 | 52.2 | 209 | 41 | 14 | 14 | 4 | 1 | 1 | 0 | 13 | 0 | 51 | 4 | 0 | 2 | 2 | .500 | 0 | 24- - | - | 2.21 | 2.39 |
| 2013 | Clmbs | AAA | 49 | 0 | 0 | 34 | 64.1 | 251 | 43 | 19 | 12 | 4 | 0 | 1 | 0 | 14 | 2 | 72 | 2 | 0 | 5 | 4 | .556 | 0 | 20- - | - | 1.54 | 1.68 |
| 2013 | Cle | AL | 4 | 0 | 0 | 1 | 5.1 | 28 | 8 | 6 | 6 | 0 | 0 | 0 | 0 | 3 | 0 | 1 | 0 | 0 | 0 | 0 | - | 0 | 0-0 | 0 | 6.48 | 10.13 |

# Jeremy Guthrie

**Pitches:** R **Bats:** R **Pos:** SP-33 **Ht:** 6'1" **Wt:** 205 **Born:** 4/8/1979 **Age:** 35

| HOW MUCH HE PITCHED | | | | | | | | | WHAT HE GAVE UP | | | | | | | | | | | | THE RESULTS | | | | | | | |
|---|---|---|---|---|---|---|---|---|---|---|---|---|---|---|---|---|---|---|---|---|---|---|---|---|---|---|---|---|
| Year | Team | Lg | G | GS | CG | GF | IP | BFP | H | R | ER | HR | SH | SF | HB | TBB | IBB | SO | WP | Bk | W | L | Pct | Sh | Sv-Op | Hld | ERC | ERA |
| 2004 | Cle | AL | 6 | 0 | 0 | 2 | 11.2 | 49 | 9 | 6 | 6 | 1 | 0 | 0 | 1 | 6 | 0 | 7 | 1 | 0 | 0 | 0 | - | 0 | 0-0 | 0 | 3.58 | 4.63 |
| 2005 | Cle | AL | 1 | 0 | 0 | 1 | 6.0 | 29 | 9 | 4 | 4 | 2 | 1 | 1 | 0 | 2 | 0 | 3 | 0 | 0 | 0 | 0 | - | 0 | 0-0 | 0 | 8.58 | 6.00 |
| 2006 | Cle | AL | 9 | 1 | 0 | 1 | 19.1 | 93 | 24 | 15 | 15 | 2 | 0 | 0 | 2 | 15 | 1 | 14 | 3 | 0 | 0 | 0 | - | 0 | 0-0 | 0 | 7.78 | 6.98 |
| 2007 | Bal | AL | 32 | 26 | 0 | 3 | 175.1 | 723 | 165 | 78 | 72 | 23 | 4 | 6 | 4 | 47 | 2 | 123 | 8 | 1 | 7 | 5 | .583 | 0 | 0-1 | 0 | 3.55 | 3.70 |
| 2008 | Bal | AL | 30 | 30 | 1 | 0 | 190.2 | 796 | 176 | 82 | 77 | 24 | 2 | 2 | 7 | 58 | 2 | 120 | 3 | 0 | 10 | 12 | .455 | 0 | 0-0 | 0 | 3.59 | 3.63 |
| 2009 | Bal | AL | 33 | 33 | 1 | 0 | 200.0 | 874 | 224 | **120** | 112 | **35** | 1 | 8 | 9 | 60 | 1 | 110 | 1 | 1 | 10 | **17** | .370 | 0 | 0-0 | 0 | 5.08 | 5.04 |
| 2010 | Bal | AL | 32 | 32 | 1 | 0 | 209.1 | 872 | 193 | 93 | 89 | 25 | 3 | 9 | 16 | 50 | 1 | 119 | 1 | 1 | 11 | 14 | .440 | 0 | 0-0 | 0 | 3.44 | 3.83 |
| 2011 | Bal | AL | 34 | 32 | 2 | 1 | 208.0 | 889 | 213 | 113 | 100 | 26 | 5 | **10** | 9 | 66 | 5 | 130 | 0 | 0 | 9 | **17** | .346 | 0 | 0-0 | 0 | 4.21 | 4.33 |
| 2012 | 2 Tms | | 33 | 29 | 0 | 0 | 181.2 | 788 | 206 | 109 | 96 | 30 | 8 | 6 | 9 | 50 | 2 | 101 | 2 | 2 | 8 | 12 | .400 | 0 | 0-1 | 0 | 5.03 | 4.76 |
| 2013 | KC | AL | 33 | 33 | 3 | 0 | 211.2 | 905 | **236** | 99 | 95 | 30 | 2 | 8 | 8 | 59 | 1 | 111 | 7 | 0 | 15 | 12 | .556 | 2 | 0-0 | 0 | 4.76 | 4.04 |
| 12 | Col | NL | 19 | 15 | 0 | 0 | 90.2 | 422 | 122 | 72 | 64 | 21 | 5 | 3 | 7 | 31 | 2 | 45 | 1 | 1 | 3 | 9 | .250 | 0 | 0-1 | 0 | 7.26 | 6.35 |
| 12 | KC | AL | 14 | 14 | 0 | 0 | 91.0 | 366 | 84 | 37 | 32 | 9 | 3 | 3 | 2 | 19 | 0 | 56 | 1 | 1 | 5 | 3 | .625 | 0 | 0-0 | 0 | 3.06 | 3.16 |
| 10 ML YEARS | | | 243 | 216 | 7 | 8 | 1413.2 | 6018 | 1455 | 719 | 666 | 198 | 26 | 50 | 65 | 413 | 15 | 838 | 26 | 5 | 70 | 89 | .440 | 2 | 0-2 | 0 | 4.28 | 4.24 |

# Franklin Gutierrez

**Bats:** R **Throws:** R **Pos:** RF-21;CF-17;PH-4 **Ht:** 6'2" **Wt:** 195 **Born:** 2/21/1983 **Age:** 31

| BATTING | | | | | | | | | | | | | | | | | | | | | BASERUNNING | | | | AVERAGES | | |
|---|---|---|---|---|---|---|---|---|---|---|---|---|---|---|---|---|---|---|---|---|---|---|---|---|---|---|---|
| Year | Team | Lg | G | AB | H | 2B | 3B | HR | (Hm | Rd) | TB | R | RBI | RC | TBB | IBB | SO | HBP | SH | SF | SB | CS | SB% | GDP | Avg | OBP | Slg |
| 2013 | Tacom* | AAA | 47 | 194 | 41 | 16 | 0 | 3 | (- | -) | 66 | 27 | 25 | 18 | 15 | 0 | 60 | 2 | 0 | 2 | 4 | 2 | .67 | 6 | .211 | .272 | .340 |
| 2005 | Cle | AL | 7 | 1 | 0 | 0 | 0 | 0 | (0 | 0) | 0 | 2 | 0 | 0 | 1 | 0 | 0 | 0 | 0 | 0 | 0 | 0 | - | 0 | .000 | .500 | .000 |
| 2006 | Cle | AL | 43 | 136 | 37 | 9 | 0 | 1 | (1 | 0) | 49 | 21 | 8 | 12 | 3 | 0 | 28 | 0 | 2 | 0 | 0 | 0 | - | 4 | .272 | .288 | .360 |
| 2007 | Cle | AL | 100 | 271 | 72 | 13 | 2 | 13 | (10 | 3) | 128 | 41 | 36 | 36 | 21 | 1 | 77 | 1 | 5 | 3 | 8 | 3 | .73 | 7 | .266 | .318 | .472 |
| 2008 | Cle | AL | 134 | 399 | 99 | 26 | 2 | 8 | (6 | 2) | 153 | 54 | 41 | 37 | 27 | 1 | 87 | 8 | 4 | 2 | 9 | 3 | .75 | 10 | .248 | .307 | .383 |
| 2009 | Sea | AL | 153 | 565 | 160 | 24 | 1 | 18 | (7 | 11) | 240 | 85 | 70 | 80 | 46 | 3 | 122 | 3 | 13 | 2 | 16 | 5 | .76 | 14 | .283 | .339 | .425 |
| 2010 | Sea | AL | 152 | 568 | 139 | 25 | 3 | 12 | (6 | 6) | 206 | 61 | 64 | 61 | 50 | 5 | 137 | 1 | 2 | 8 | 25 | 3 | .89 | 10 | .245 | .303 | .363 |
| 2011 | Sea | AL | 92 | 322 | 72 | 13 | 0 | 1 | (0 | 1) | 88 | 26 | 19 | 25 | 16 | 1 | 56 | 1 | 3 | 2 | 13 | 2 | .87 | 6 | .224 | .261 | .273 |
| 2012 | Sea | AL | 40 | 150 | 39 | 10 | 1 | 4 | (2 | 2) | 63 | 18 | 17 | 19 | 9 | 0 | 31 | 2 | 1 | 1 | 3 | 1 | .75 | 5 | .260 | .309 | .420 |
| 2013 | Sea | AL | 41 | 145 | 36 | 7 | 0 | 10 | (6 | 4) | 73 | 18 | 24 | 16 | 5 | 0 | 43 | 0 | 1 | 0 | 3 | 1 | .75 | 2 | .248 | .273 | .503 |
| Postseason | | | 10 | 29 | 6 | 0 | 0 | 1 | (0 | 1) | 9 | 5 | 4 | 3 | 5 | 0 | 11 | 0 | 0 | 0 | 0 | 0 | - | 1 | .207 | .324 | .310 |
| 9 ML YEARS | | | 762 | 2557 | 654 | 127 | 9 | 67 | (38 | 29) | 1000 | 326 | 279 | 286 | 178 | 11 | 581 | 16 | 31 | 18 | 77 | 18 | .81 | 58 | .256 | .306 | .391 |

## J.C. Gutierrez

**Pitches:** R **Bats:** R **Pos:** RP-53 **Ht:** 6'3" **Wt:** 245 **Born:** 7/14/1983 **Age:** 30

| HOW MUCH HE PITCHED | | | | | | | | | WHAT HE GAVE UP | | | | | | | | | | | | THE RESULTS | | | | | | | |
|---|---|---|---|---|---|---|---|---|---|---|---|---|---|---|---|---|---|---|---|---|---|---|---|---|---|---|---|---|
| Year | Team | Lg | G | GS | CG | GF | IP | BFP | H | R | ER | HR | SH | SF | HB | TBB | IBB | SO | WP | Bk | W | L | Pct | Sh | Sv-Op | Hld | ERC | ERA |
| 2007 | Hou | NL | 7 | 3 | 0 | 1 | 21.1 | 93 | 25 | 14 | 14 | 3 | 0 | 3 | 0 | 6 | 2 | 16 | 1 | 0 | 1 | 1 | .500 | 0 | 0-0 | 0 | 4.71 | 5.91 |
| 2009 | Ari | NL | 65 | 0 | 0 | 21 | 71.0 | 307 | 67 | 33 | 32 | 2 | 2 | 4 | 3 | 30 | 5 | 66 | 5 | 0 | 4 | 3 | .571 | 0 | 9-10 | 7 | 3.38 | 4.06 |
| 2010 | Ari | NL | 58 | 0 | 0 | 35 | 56.2 | 247 | 55 | 33 | 32 | 13 | 1 | 1 | 4 | 23 | 5 | 47 | 1 | 0 | 0 | 6 | .000 | 0 | 15-17 | 8 | 5.00 | 5.08 |
| 2011 | Ari | NL | 20 | 0 | 0 | 3 | 18.1 | 90 | 22 | 16 | 11 | 3 | 0 | 0 | 1 | 9 | 0 | 23 | 0 | 0 | 0 | 0 | - | 0 | 0-1 | 2 | 5.99 | 5.40 |
| 2013 | 2 Tms | AL | 53 | 0 | 0 | 17 | 55.1 | 236 | 56 | 29 | 26 | 5 | 1 | 3 | 1 | 20 | 2 | 45 | 3 | 0 | 1 | 5 | .167 | 0 | 0-1 | 4 | 3.97 | 4.23 |
| 13 | KC | AL | 25 | 0 | 0 | 13 | 29.1 | 120 | 30 | 13 | 11 | 2 | 0 | 2 | 1 | 8 | 1 | 17 | 1 | 0 | 0 | 1 | .000 | 0 | 0-0 | 2 | 3.72 | 3.38 |
| 13 | LAA | AL | 28 | 0 | 0 | 4 | 26.0 | 116 | 26 | 16 | 15 | 3 | 1 | 1 | 0 | 12 | 1 | 28 | 2 | 0 | 1 | 4 | .200 | 0 | 0-1 | 2 | 4.26 | 5.19 |
| 5 ML YEARS | | | 203 | 3 | 0 | 77 | 222.2 | 973 | 225 | 125 | 115 | 26 | 4 | 11 | 9 | 88 | 14 | 197 | 10 | 0 | 6 | 15 | .286 | 0 | 24-29 | 21 | 4.27 | 4.65 |

## Freddy Guzman

**Bats:** B **Throws:** R **Pos:** DH-1;PR-1 **Ht:** 5'10" **Wt:** 165 **Born:** 1/20/1981 **Age:** 33

| BATTING | | | | | | | | | | | | | | | | | | | | BASERUNNING | | | | AVERAGES | | |
|---|---|---|---|---|---|---|---|---|---|---|---|---|---|---|---|---|---|---|---|---|---|---|---|---|---|---|
| Year | Team | Lg | G | AB | H | 2B | 3B | HR | (Hm | Rd) | TB | R | RBI | RC | TBB | IBB | SO | HBP | SH | SF | SB | CS | SB% | GDP | Avg | OBP | Slg |
| 2004 | SD | NL | 20 | 76 | 16 | 3 | 0 | 0 | (0 | 0) | 19 | 8 | 5 | 4 | 3 | 0 | 13 | 1 | 0 | 0 | 5 | 2 | .71 | 0 | .211 | .250 | .250 |
| 2006 | Tex | AL | 9 | 7 | 2 | 0 | 0 | 0 | (0 | 0) | 2 | 1 | 0 | 1 | 1 | 0 | 1 | 1 | 0 | 0 | 0 | 0 | - | 0 | .286 | .444 | .286 |
| 2007 | Tex | AL | 8 | 6 | 1 | 0 | 0 | 1 | (0 | 1) | 4 | 2 | 1 | 0 | 0 | 0 | 2 | 0 | 0 | 0 | 0 | 1 | .00 | 0 | .167 | .167 | .667 |
| 2009 | NYY | AL | 10 | 6 | 1 | 0 | 0 | 0 | (0 | 0) | 1 | 2 | 1 | 0 | 0 | 0 | 1 | 0 | 0 | 1 | 4 | 1 | .80 | 0 | .167 | .143 | .167 |
| 2013 | TB | AL | 1 | 0 | 0 | 0 | 0 | 0 | (0 | 0) | 0 | 1 | 0 | 0 | 0 | 0 | 0 | 0 | 0 | 0 | 1 | 0 | 1.00 | 0 | - | - | - |
| Postseason | | | 2 | 1 | 0 | 0 | 0 | 0 | (0 | 0) | 0 | 0 | 0 | 0 | 0 | 0 | 1 | 0 | 0 | 0 | 0 | 0 | - | 0 | .000 | .000 | .000 |
| 5 ML YEARS | | | 48 | 95 | 20 | 3 | 0 | 1 | (0 | 1) | 26 | 14 | 7 | 5 | 4 | 0 | 17 | 2 | 0 | 1 | 10 | 4 | .71 | 0 | .211 | .255 | .274 |

## Jesus Guzman

**Bats:** R **Throws:** R **Pos:** PH-53;1B-38;LF-35;RF-5;3B-3;2B-1 **Ht:** 6'1" **Wt:** 200 **Born:** 6/14/1984 **Age:** 30

| BATTING | | | | | | | | | | | | | | | | | | | | BASERUNNING | | | | AVERAGES | | |
|---|---|---|---|---|---|---|---|---|---|---|---|---|---|---|---|---|---|---|---|---|---|---|---|---|---|---|
| Year | Team | Lg | G | AB | H | 2B | 3B | HR | (Hm | Rd) | TB | R | RBI | RC | TBB | IBB | SO | HBP | SH | SF | SB | CS | SB% | GDP | Avg | OBP | Slg |
| 2009 | SF | NL | 12 | 20 | 5 | 0 | 0 | 0 | (0 | 0) | 5 | 0 | 0 | 0 | 0 | 0 | 3 | 0 | 0 | 0 | 0 | 0 | - | 2 | .250 | .250 | .250 |
| 2011 | SD | NL | 76 | 247 | 77 | 22 | 2 | 5 | (4 | 1) | 118 | 33 | 44 | 49 | 22 | 2 | 43 | 1 | 0 | 1 | 9 | 2 | .82 | 6 | .312 | .369 | .478 |
| 2012 | SD | NL | 120 | 287 | 71 | 18 | 2 | 9 | (4 | 5) | 120 | 32 | 48 | 40 | 29 | 3 | 71 | 2 | 1 | 2 | 3 | 3 | .50 | 2 | .247 | .319 | .418 |
| 2013 | SD | NL | 126 | 288 | 65 | 17 | 0 | 9 | (0 | 9) | 109 | 33 | 35 | 35 | 27 | 1 | 79 | 2 | 1 | 0 | 3 | 0 | 1.00 | 4 | .226 | .297 | .378 |
| 4 ML YEARS | | | 334 | 842 | 218 | 57 | 4 | 23 | (8 | 15) | 352 | 98 | 127 | 124 | 78 | 6 | 196 | 5 | 2 | 3 | 15 | 5 | .75 | 14 | .259 | .324 | .418 |

## Jedd Gyorko

**Bats:** R **Throws:** R **Pos:** 2B-117;3B-13;PH-2 JERK-oh **Ht:** 5'10" **Wt:** 210 **Born:** 9/23/1988 **Age:** 25

| BATTING | | | | | | | | | | | | | | | | | | | | BASERUNNING | | | | AVERAGES | | |
|---|---|---|---|---|---|---|---|---|---|---|---|---|---|---|---|---|---|---|---|---|---|---|---|---|---|---|
| Year | Team | Lg | G | AB | H | 2B | 3B | HR | (Hm | Rd) | TB | R | RBI | RC | TBB | IBB | SO | HBP | SH | SF | SB | CS | SB% | GDP | Avg | OBP | Slg |
| 2010 | Eugene | A- | 26 | 106 | 35 | 6 | 0 | 5 | (- | -) | 56 | 16 | 18 | 20 | 9 | 0 | 26 | 0 | 0 | 0 | 1 | 1 | .50 | 3 | .330 | .383 | .528 |
| 2010 | FtWyn | A | 42 | 162 | 46 | 11 | 0 | 2 | (- | -) | 63 | 19 | 23 | 24 | 19 | 0 | 31 | 2 | 0 | 0 | 1 | 0 | 1.00 | 3 | .284 | .366 | .389 |
| 2011 | Lk Els | A+ | 81 | 340 | 124 | 35 | 2 | 18 | (- | -) | 217 | 78 | 74 | 88 | 38 | 4 | 64 | 2 | 0 | 2 | 11 | 3 | .79 | 6 | .365 | .429 | .638 |
| 2011 | SnAnt | AA | 59 | 236 | 68 | 12 | 0 | 7 | (- | -) | 101 | 41 | 40 | 38 | 26 | 1 | 50 | 1 | 0 | 2 | 1 | 0 | 1.00 | 5 | .288 | .358 | .428 |
| 2012 | SnAnt | AA | 34 | 130 | 34 | 4 | 0 | 6 | (- | -) | 56 | 18 | 17 | 20 | 17 | 2 | 27 | 2 | 0 | 0 | 1 | 1 | .50 | 3 | .262 | .356 | .431 |
| 2012 | Tucsn | AAA | 92 | 369 | 121 | 24 | 0 | 24 | (- | -) | 217 | 62 | 83 | 80 | 34 | 0 | 68 | 0 | 0 | 5 | 4 | 3 | .57 | 10 | .328 | .380 | .588 |
| 2013 | SnAnt | AA | 1 | 1 | 1 | 0 | 0 | 0 | (- | -) | 1 | 0 | 0 | 0 | 0 | 0 | 0 | 0 | 0 | 0 | 0 | 0 | - | 0 | 1.000 | 1.000 | 1.000 |
| 2013 | Lk Els | A+ | 2 | 7 | 4 | 1 | 0 | 0 | (- | -) | 5 | 2 | 1 | 2 | 0 | 0 | 1 | 0 | 0 | 0 | 0 | 0 | - | 0 | .571 | .571 | .714 |
| 2013 | SD | NL | 125 | 486 | 121 | 26 | 0 | 23 | (13 | 10) | 216 | 62 | 63 | 48 | 33 | 1 | 123 | 4 | 0 | 2 | 1 | 1 | .50 | 14 | .249 | .301 | .444 |

## Travis Hafner

**Bats:** L **Throws:** R **Pos:** DH-72;PH-15 HAFF-nerr **Ht:** 6'3" **Wt:** 240 **Born:** 6/3/1977 **Age:** 37

| BATTING | | | | | | | | | | | | | | | | | | | | BASERUNNING | | | | AVERAGES | | |
|---|---|---|---|---|---|---|---|---|---|---|---|---|---|---|---|---|---|---|---|---|---|---|---|---|---|---|
| Year | Team | Lg | G | AB | H | 2B | 3B | HR | (Hm | Rd) | TB | R | RBI | RC | TBB | IBB | SO | HBP | SH | SF | SB | CS | SB% | GDP | Avg | OBP | Slg |
| 2002 | Tex | AL | 23 | 62 | 15 | 4 | 1 | 1 | (0 | 1) | 24 | 6 | 6 | 7 | 8 | 1 | 15 | 0 | 0 | 0 | 0 | 1 | .00 | 0 | .242 | .329 | .387 |
| 2003 | Cle | AL | 91 | 291 | 74 | 19 | 3 | 14 | (7 | 7) | 141 | 35 | 40 | 42 | 22 | 2 | 81 | 10 | 0 | 1 | 2 | 1 | .67 | 7 | .254 | .327 | .485 |
| 2004 | Cle | AL | 140 | 482 | 150 | 41 | 3 | 28 | (7 | 21) | 281 | 96 | 109 | 103 | 68 | 7 | 111 | **17** | 0 | 6 | 3 | 2 | .60 | 11 | .311 | .410 | .583 |
| 2005 | Cle | AL | 137 | 486 | 148 | 42 | 0 | 33 | (14 | 19) | 289 | 94 | 108 | 115 | 79 | 7 | 123 | 9 | 0 | 4 | 0 | 0 | - | 9 | .305 | .408 | .595 |
| 2006 | Cle | AL | 129 | 454 | 140 | 31 | 1 | 42 | (21 | 21) | 299 | 100 | 117 | 118 | 100 | 16 | 111 | 7 | 0 | 2 | 0 | 0 | - | 10 | .308 | **.439** | **.659** |
| 2007 | Cle | AL | 152 | 545 | 145 | 25 | 2 | 24 | (12 | 12) | 246 | 80 | 100 | 94 | 102 | 17 | 115 | 7 | 0 | 5 | 1 | 1 | .50 | 15 | .266 | .385 | .451 |
| 2008 | Cle | AL | 57 | 198 | 39 | 10 | 0 | 5 | (2 | 3) | 64 | 21 | 24 | 21 | 27 | 6 | 55 | 5 | 0 | 3 | 1 | 1 | .50 | 4 | .197 | .305 | .323 |
| 2009 | Cle | AL | 94 | 338 | 92 | 19 | 0 | 16 | (9 | 7) | 159 | 46 | 49 | 49 | 41 | 6 | 67 | 3 | 0 | 1 | 0 | 0 | - | 7 | .272 | .355 | .470 |
| 2010 | Cle | AL | 118 | 396 | 110 | 29 | 0 | 13 | (10 | 3) | 178 | 46 | 50 | 57 | 51 | 10 | 94 | 12 | 0 | 3 | 2 | 1 | .67 | 2 | .278 | .374 | .449 |
| 2011 | Cle | AL | 94 | 325 | 91 | 16 | 0 | 13 | (9 | 4) | 146 | 41 | 57 | 61 | 36 | 5 | 78 | 6 | 0 | 1 | 0 | 0 | - | 7 | .280 | .361 | .449 |
| 2012 | Cle | AL | 66 | 219 | 50 | 6 | 2 | 12 | (8 | 4) | 96 | 23 | 34 | 22 | 32 | 2 | 47 | 9 | 0 | 3 | 0 | 0 | - | 9 | .228 | .346 | .438 |
| 2013 | NYY | AL | 82 | 262 | 53 | 8 | 1 | 12 | (8 | 4) | 99 | 31 | 37 | 34 | 32 | 2 | 79 | 5 | 0 | 0 | 2 | 0 | 1.00 | 5 | .202 | .301 | .378 |
| Postseason | | | 11 | 43 | 8 | 1 | 0 | 2 | (1 | 1) | 15 | 6 | 4 | 3 | 7 | 1 | 15 | 0 | 0 | 0 | 0 | 0 | - | 1 | .186 | .300 | .349 |
| 12 ML YEARS | | | 1183 | 4058 | 1107 | 250 | 13 | 213 | (107 | 106) | 2022 | 619 | 731 | 723 | 598 | 81 | 976 | 90 | 0 | 29 | 11 | 7 | .61 | 86 | .273 | .376 | .498 |

## Nick Hagadone

**Pitches:** L **Bats:** L **Pos:** RP-36 HAGG-uh-donn **Ht:** 6'5" **Wt:** 230 **Born:** 1/1/1986 **Age:** 28

| HOW MUCH HE PITCHED | | | | | | | | | WHAT HE GAVE UP | | | | | | | | | | | | THE RESULTS | | | | | | | |
|---|---|---|---|---|---|---|---|---|---|---|---|---|---|---|---|---|---|---|---|---|---|---|---|---|---|---|---|---|
| Year | Team | Lg | G | GS | CG | GF | IP | BFP | H | R | ER | HR | SH | SF | HB | TBB | IBB | SO | WP | Bk | W | L | Pct | Sh | Sv-Op | Hld | ERC | ERA |
| 2013 | Clmbs* | AAA | 27 | 0 | 0 | 15 | 32.1 | 137 | 24 | 9 | 9 | 1 | 1 | 1 | 0 | 17 | 0 | 46 | 0 | 0 | 2 | 3 | .400 | 0 | 7- - | - | 2.67 | 2.51 |

| Year | Team | Lg | G | GS | CG | GF | IP | BFP | H | R | ER | HR | SH | SF | HB | TBB | IBB | SO | WP | Bk | W | L | Pct | Sh | Sv-Op | Hld | ERC | ERA |
|---|---|---|---|---|---|---|---|---|---|---|---|---|---|---|---|---|---|---|---|---|---|---|---|---|---|---|---|---|
| | | | HOW MUCH HE PITCHED | | | | | | WHAT HE GAVE UP | | | | | | | | | | | | THE RESULTS | | | | | | | |
| 2011 | Cle | AL | 9 | 0 | 0 | 3 | 11.0 | 42 | 4 | 6 | 5 | 0 | 0 | 1 | 1 | 6 | 0 | 11 | 2 | 0 | 1 | 0 | 1.000 | 0 | 0-0 | 0 | 1.35 | 4.09 |
| 2012 | Cle | AL | 27 | 0 | 0 | 10 | 25.1 | 116 | 26 | 18 | 18 | 4 | 0 | 2 | 0 | 15 | 0 | 26 | 2 | 0 | 1 | 0 | 1.000 | 0 | 1-2 | 2 | 5.37 | 6.39 |
| 2013 | Cle | AL | 36 | 0 | 0 | 1 | 31.1 | 133 | 24 | 21 | 19 | 4 | 2 | 1 | 0 | 21 | 1 | 30 | 3 | 0 | 0 | 1 | .000 | 0 | 0-1 | 2 | 4.08 | 5.46 |
| 3 ML YEARS | | | 72 | 0 | 0 | 14 | 67.2 | 291 | 54 | 45 | 42 | 8 | 2 | 4 | 1 | 42 | 1 | 67 | 7 | 0 | 2 | 1 | .667 | 0 | 1-3 | 4 | 4.02 | 5.59 |

## Jerry Hairston

**Bats:** R **Throws:** R **Pos:** PH-39;3B-28;LF-23;1B-13;RF-4;2B-1;PR-1 **Ht:** 5'10" **Wt:** 195 **Born:** 5/29/1976 **Age:** 38

| Year | Team | Lg | G | AB | H | 2B | 3B | HR | (Hm | Rd) | TB | R | RBI | RC | TBB | IBB | SO | HBP | SH | SF | SB | CS | SB% | GDP | Avg | OBP | Slg |
|---|---|---|---|---|---|---|---|---|---|---|---|---|---|---|---|---|---|---|---|---|---|---|---|---|---|---|---|
| | | | BATTING | | | | | | | | | | | | | | | | | | BASERUNNING | | | | AVERAGES | | |
| 2013 | RCuca* | A+ | 2 | 5 | 0 | 0 | 0 | 0 | (- | -) | 0 | 0 | 0 | 0 | 0 | 0 | 0 | 0 | 0 | 0 | 0 | 0 | - | 1 | .000 | .000 | .000 |
| 1998 | Bal | AL | 6 | 7 | 0 | 0 | 0 | 0 | (0 | 0) | 0 | 2 | 0 | 0 | 0 | 0 | 1 | 0 | 0 | 0 | 0 | 0 | - | 0 | .000 | .000 | .000 |
| 1999 | Bal | AL | 50 | 175 | 47 | 12 | 1 | 4 | (1 | 3) | 73 | 26 | 17 | 24 | 11 | 0 | 24 | 3 | 4 | 0 | 9 | 4 | .69 | 2 | .269 | .323 | .417 |
| 2000 | Bal | AL | 49 | 180 | 46 | 5 | 0 | 5 | (2 | 3) | 66 | 27 | 19 | 22 | 21 | 0 | 22 | 6 | 5 | 0 | 8 | 5 | .62 | 8 | .256 | .353 | .367 |
| 2001 | Bal | AL | 159 | 532 | 124 | 25 | 5 | 8 | (5 | 3) | 183 | 63 | 47 | 57 | 44 | 0 | 73 | 13 | 9 | 4 | 29 | 11 | .73 | 12 | .233 | .305 | .344 |
| 2002 | Bal | AL | 122 | 426 | 114 | 25 | 3 | 5 | (2 | 3) | 160 | 55 | 32 | 55 | 34 | 0 | 55 | 7 | 8 | 4 | 21 | 6 | .78 | 5 | .268 | .329 | .376 |
| 2003 | Bal | AL | 58 | 218 | 59 | 12 | 2 | 2 | (1 | 1) | 81 | 25 | 21 | 32 | 23 | 0 | 25 | 6 | 10 | 2 | 14 | 5 | .74 | 8 | .271 | .353 | .372 |
| 2004 | Bal | AL | 86 | 287 | 87 | 19 | 1 | 2 | (0 | 2) | 114 | 43 | 24 | 45 | 29 | 1 | 29 | 8 | 6 | 4 | 13 | 8 | .62 | 3 | .303 | .378 | .397 |
| 2005 | ChC | NL | 114 | 380 | 99 | 25 | 2 | 4 | (3 | 1) | 140 | 51 | 30 | 46 | 31 | 0 | 46 | 12 | 7 | 0 | 8 | 9 | .47 | 5 | .261 | .336 | .368 |
| 2006 | 2 Tms | | 101 | 170 | 35 | 6 | 1 | 0 | (0 | 0) | 43 | 25 | 10 | 9 | 13 | 2 | 34 | 2 | 7 | 0 | 5 | 2 | .71 | 5 | .206 | .270 | .253 |
| 2007 | Tex | AL | 73 | 159 | 30 | 7 | 0 | 3 | (1 | 2) | 46 | 22 | 16 | 12 | 11 | 0 | 24 | 3 | 7 | 4 | 5 | 1 | .83 | 5 | .189 | .249 | .289 |
| 2008 | Cin | NL | 80 | 261 | 85 | 20 | 2 | 6 | (3 | 3) | 127 | 47 | 36 | 52 | 23 | 0 | 36 | 3 | 8 | 2 | 15 | 3 | .83 | 0 | .326 | .384 | .487 |
| 2009 | 2 Tms | | 131 | 383 | 96 | 23 | 1 | 10 | (8 | 2) | 151 | 62 | 39 | 42 | 32 | 0 | 54 | 6 | 8 | 4 | 7 | 4 | .64 | 3 | .251 | .315 | .394 |
| 2010 | SD | NL | 119 | 430 | 105 | 13 | 2 | 10 | (7 | 3) | 152 | 53 | 50 | 47 | 31 | 2 | 54 | 5 | 4 | 6 | 9 | 6 | .60 | 5 | .244 | .299 | .353 |
| 2011 | 2 Tms | NL | 120 | 337 | 91 | 21 | 1 | 5 | (2 | 3) | 129 | 43 | 31 | 41 | 33 | 1 | 46 | 5 | 1 | 0 | 3 | 2 | .60 | 7 | .270 | .344 | .383 |
| 2012 | LAD | NL | 78 | 238 | 65 | 13 | 1 | 4 | (1 | 3) | 92 | 19 | 26 | 31 | 23 | 2 | 27 | 3 | 1 | 2 | 1 | 2 | .33 | 7 | .273 | .342 | .387 |
| 2013 | LAD | NL | 96 | 204 | 43 | 7 | 0 | 2 | (1 | 1) | 56 | 17 | 22 | 14 | 14 | 0 | 22 | 2 | 3 | 3 | 0 | 0 | - | 7 | .211 | .265 | .275 |
| 06 | ChC | NL | 38 | 82 | 17 | 3 | 0 | 0 | (0 | 0) | 20 | 8 | 4 | 5 | 4 | 2 | 14 | 1 | 5 | 0 | 3 | 0 | 1.00 | 1 | .207 | .253 | .244 |
| 06 | Tex | AL | 63 | 88 | 18 | 3 | 1 | 0 | (0 | 0) | 23 | 17 | 6 | 4 | 9 | 0 | 20 | 1 | 2 | 0 | 2 | 2 | .50 | 4 | .205 | .286 | .261 |
| 09 | Cin | NL | 86 | 307 | 78 | 18 | 1 | 8 | (6 | 2) | 122 | 47 | 27 | 30 | 21 | 0 | 46 | 3 | 6 | 3 | 7 | 3 | .70 | 2 | .254 | .305 | .397 |
| 09 | NYY | AL | 45 | 76 | 18 | 5 | 0 | 2 | (2 | 0) | 29 | 15 | 12 | 12 | 11 | 0 | 8 | 3 | 2 | 1 | 0 | 1 | .00 | 1 | .237 | .352 | .382 |
| 11 | Was | NL | 75 | 213 | 57 | 11 | 1 | 4 | (2 | 2) | 82 | 25 | 24 | 28 | 22 | 1 | 30 | 2 | 1 | 0 | 2 | 2 | .50 | 3 | .268 | .342 | .385 |
| 11 | Mil | NL | 45 | 124 | 34 | 10 | 0 | 1 | (0 | 1) | 47 | 18 | 7 | 13 | 11 | 0 | 16 | 3 | 0 | 0 | 1 | 0 | 1.00 | 4 | .274 | .348 | .379 |
| Postseason | | | 17 | 47 | 17 | 6 | 0 | 0 | (0 | 0) | 23 | 9 | 4 | 7 | 4 | 0 | 6 | 0 | 1 | 2 | 0 | 0 | - | 0 | .362 | .396 | .489 |
| 16 ML YEARS | | | 1442 | 4387 | 1126 | 233 | 22 | 70 | (37 | 33) | 1613 | 580 | 420 | 529 | 373 | 8 | 572 | 84 | 88 | 35 | 147 | 68 | .68 | 82 | .257 | .324 | .368 |

## Scott Hairston

**Bats:** R **Throws:** R **Pos:** PH-46;RF-31;LF-16;DH-1;PR-1 **Ht:** 6'0" **Wt:** 205 **Born:** 5/25/1980 **Age:** 34

| Year | Team | Lg | G | AB | H | 2B | 3B | HR | (Hm | Rd) | TB | R | RBI | RC | TBB | IBB | SO | HBP | SH | SF | SB | CS | SB% | GDP | Avg | OBP | Slg |
|---|---|---|---|---|---|---|---|---|---|---|---|---|---|---|---|---|---|---|---|---|---|---|---|---|---|---|---|
| | | | BATTING | | | | | | | | | | | | | | | | | | BASERUNNING | | | | AVERAGES | | |
| 2004 | Ari | NL | 101 | 339 | 84 | 15 | 6 | 13 | (6 | 7) | 150 | 39 | 29 | 32 | 21 | 0 | 88 | 1 | 2 | 1 | 3 | 3 | .50 | 4 | .248 | .293 | .442 |
| 2005 | Ari | NL | 15 | 20 | 2 | 1 | 0 | 0 | (0 | 0) | 3 | 0 | 0 | 0 | 0 | 0 | 6 | 0 | 0 | 0 | 0 | 0 | - | 1 | .100 | .100 | .150 |
| 2006 | Ari | NL | 9 | 15 | 6 | 2 | 0 | 0 | (0 | 0) | 8 | 2 | 2 | 2 | 1 | 0 | 5 | 0 | 0 | 0 | 0 | 0 | - | 1 | .400 | .438 | .533 |
| 2007 | 2 Tms | NL | 107 | 263 | 64 | 18 | 2 | 11 | (6 | 5) | 119 | 37 | 36 | 36 | 26 | 0 | 55 | 1 | 3 | 1 | 2 | 0 | 1.00 | 4 | .243 | .313 | .452 |
| 2008 | SD | NL | 112 | 326 | 81 | 18 | 3 | 17 | (9 | 8) | 156 | 42 | 31 | 43 | 28 | 2 | 84 | 3 | 3 | 2 | 3 | 1 | .75 | 2 | .248 | .312 | .479 |
| 2009 | 2 Tms | | 116 | 430 | 114 | 27 | 2 | 17 | (9 | 8) | 196 | 50 | 64 | 60 | 25 | 0 | 83 | 3 | 1 | 5 | 11 | 3 | .79 | 9 | .265 | .307 | .456 |
| 2010 | SD | NL | 104 | 295 | 62 | 10 | 0 | 10 | (5 | 5) | 102 | 34 | 36 | 28 | 31 | 1 | 69 | 6 | 0 | 4 | 6 | 1 | .86 | 3 | .210 | .295 | .346 |
| 2011 | NYM | NL | 79 | 132 | 31 | 8 | 1 | 7 | (2 | 5) | 62 | 20 | 24 | 16 | 11 | 2 | 34 | 2 | 0 | 0 | 1 | 1 | .50 | 2 | .235 | .303 | .470 |
| 2012 | NYM | NL | 134 | 377 | 99 | 25 | 3 | 20 | (11 | 9) | 190 | 52 | 57 | 53 | 19 | 0 | 83 | 1 | 0 | 1 | 8 | 2 | .80 | 10 | .263 | .299 | .504 |
| 2013 | 2 Tms | NL | 85 | 157 | 30 | 5 | 0 | 10 | (7 | 3) | 65 | 18 | 26 | 14 | 9 | 0 | 44 | 2 | 1 | 5 | 2 | 0 | 1.00 | 3 | .191 | .237 | .414 |
| 07 | Ari | NL | 76 | 176 | 39 | 13 | 1 | 3 | (1 | 2) | 63 | 21 | 16 | 19 | 19 | 0 | 37 | 1 | 3 | 0 | 2 | 0 | 1.00 | 4 | .222 | .301 | .358 |
| 07 | SD | NL | 31 | 87 | 25 | 5 | 1 | 8 | (5 | 3) | 56 | 16 | 20 | 17 | 7 | 0 | 18 | 0 | 0 | 1 | 0 | 0 | - | 0 | .287 | .337 | .644 |
| 09 | SD | NL | 56 | 197 | 59 | 14 | 1 | 10 | (5 | 5) | 105 | 26 | 29 | 35 | 17 | 0 | 45 | 1 | 1 | 0 | 8 | 1 | .89 | 4 | .299 | .358 | .533 |
| 09 | Oak | AL | 60 | 233 | 55 | 13 | 1 | 7 | (4 | 3) | 91 | 24 | 35 | 25 | 8 | 0 | 38 | 2 | 0 | 5 | 3 | 2 | .60 | 5 | .236 | .262 | .391 |
| 13 | ChC | NL | 52 | 99 | 17 | 2 | 0 | 8 | (7 | 1) | 43 | 13 | 19 | 9 | 7 | 0 | 25 | 2 | 0 | 4 | 2 | 0 | 1.00 | 3 | .172 | .232 | .434 |
| 13 | Was | NL | 33 | 58 | 13 | 3 | 0 | 2 | (0 | 2) | 22 | 5 | 7 | 5 | 2 | 0 | 19 | 0 | 1 | 1 | 0 | 0 | - | 0 | .224 | .246 | .379 |
| 10 ML YEARS | | | 862 | 2354 | 573 | 129 | 17 | 105 | (55 | 50) | 1051 | 294 | 305 | 284 | 171 | 5 | 551 | 19 | 10 | 19 | 36 | 11 | .77 | 39 | .243 | .298 | .446 |

## David Hale

**Pitches:** R **Bats:** R **Pos:** SP-2 **Ht:** 6'2" **Wt:** 205 **Born:** 9/27/1987 **Age:** 26

| Year | Team | Lg | G | GS | CG | GF | IP | BFP | H | R | ER | HR | SH | SF | HB | TBB | IBB | SO | WP | Bk | W | L | Pct | Sh | Sv-Op | Hld | ERC | ERA |
|---|---|---|---|---|---|---|---|---|---|---|---|---|---|---|---|---|---|---|---|---|---|---|---|---|---|---|---|---|
| | | | HOW MUCH HE PITCHED | | | | | | WHAT HE GAVE UP | | | | | | | | | | | | THE RESULTS | | | | | | | |
| 2009 | Danvle | R | 7 | 1 | 0 | 2 | 16.0 | 63 | 7 | 4 | 2 | 0 | 0 | 2 | 2 | 5 | 0 | 12 | 2 | 0 | 2 | 1 | .667 | 0 | 1-- | - | 1.10 | 1.13 |
| 2010 | Rome | A | 28 | 7 | 0 | 12 | 93.2 | 420 | 97 | 52 | 43 | 1 | 6 | 3 | 4 | 44 | 0 | 69 | 11 | 0 | 5 | 8 | .385 | 0 | 5-- | - | 4.01 | 4.13 |
| 2011 | Lynbrg | A+ | 28 | 13 | 1 | 3 | 101.0 | 432 | 106 | 52 | 46 | 9 | 3 | 4 | 10 | 30 | 1 | 86 | 7 | 0 | 4 | 6 | .400 | 0 | 0-- | - | 4.33 | 4.10 |
| 2012 | Missi | AA | 27 | 27 | 0 | 0 | 145.2 | 618 | 121 | 66 | 61 | 11 | 7 | 3 | 10 | 67 | 2 | 124 | 9 | 0 | 8 | 4 | .667 | 0 | 0-- | - | 3.48 | 3.77 |
| 2013 | Gwnntt | AAA | 22 | 20 | 0 | 1 | 114.2 | 495 | 123 | 50 | 41 | 8 | 5 | 6 | 7 | 36 | 3 | 77 | 2 | 1 | 6 | 9 | .400 | 0 | 0-- | - | 4.16 | 3.22 |
| 2013 | Atl | NL | 2 | 2 | 0 | 0 | 11.0 | 46 | 11 | 1 | 1 | 0 | 0 | 0 | 0 | 1 | 0 | 14 | 0 | 0 | 1 | 0 | 1.000 | 0 | 0-0 | 0 | 2.18 | 0.82 |

## Roy Halladay

**Pitches:** R **Bats:** R **Pos:** SP-13 HAL-ah-day **Ht:** 6'6" **Wt:** 225 **Born:** 5/14/1977 **Age:** 37

| Year | Team | Lg | G | GS | CG | GF | IP | BFP | H | R | ER | HR | SH | SF | HB | TBB | IBB | SO | WP | Bk | W | L | Pct | Sh | Sv-Op | Hld | ERC | ERA |
|---|---|---|---|---|---|---|---|---|---|---|---|---|---|---|---|---|---|---|---|---|---|---|---|---|---|---|---|---|
| | | | HOW MUCH HE PITCHED | | | | | | WHAT HE GAVE UP | | | | | | | | | | | | THE RESULTS | | | | | | | |
| 2013 | Phillies* | R | 1 | 1 | 0 | 0 | 6.0 | 26 | 6 | 3 | 3 | 1 | 0 | 0 | 0 | 3 | 0 | 4 | 0 | 0 | 0 | 0 | - | 0 | 0-- | - | 5.06 | 4.50 |
| 2013 | Lakwd* | A | 1 | 1 | 0 | 0 | 6.0 | 25 | 7 | 2 | 1 | 0 | 1 | 0 | 0 | 3 | 0 | 4 | 0 | 0 | 0 | 0 | - | 0 | 0-- | - | 5.14 | 1.50 |
| 1998 | Tor | AL | 2 | 2 | 1 | 0 | 14.0 | 53 | 9 | 4 | 3 | 2 | 0 | 0 | 0 | 2 | 0 | 13 | 0 | 0 | 1 | 0 | 1.000 | 0 | 0-0 | 0 | 1.61 | 1.93 |
| 1999 | Tor | AL | 36 | 18 | 1 | 2 | 149.1 | 668 | 156 | 76 | 65 | 19 | 3 | 4 | 4 | 79 | 1 | 82 | 6 | 0 | 8 | 7 | .533 | 1 | 1-1 | 2 | 5.19 | 3.92 |
| 2000 | Tor | AL | 19 | 13 | 0 | 4 | 67.2 | 349 | 107 | 87 | 80 | 14 | 2 | 3 | 2 | 42 | 0 | 44 | 6 | 1 | 4 | 7 | .364 | 0 | 0-0 | 0 | 9.70 | 10.64 |

| Year | Team | Lg | G | GS | CG | GF | IP | BFP | H | R | ER | HR | SH | SF | HB | TBB | IBB | SO | WP | Bk | W | L | Pct | Sh | Sv-Op | Hld | ERC | ERA |
|---|---|---|---|---|---|---|---|---|---|---|---|---|---|---|---|---|---|---|---|---|---|---|---|---|---|---|---|---|
| | | | **HOW MUCH HE PITCHED** | | | | | | **WHAT HE GAVE UP** | | | | | | | | | | | | **THE RESULTS** | | | | | | | |
| 2001 | Tor | AL | 17 | 16 | 1 | 0 | 105.1 | 432 | 97 | 41 | 37 | 3 | 3 | 1 | 1 | 25 | 0 | 96 | 4 | 1 | 5 | 3 | .625 | 1 | 0-0 | 0 | 2.61 | 3.16 |
| 2002 | Tor | AL | 34 | 34 | 2 | 0 | **239.1** | 993 | 223 | 93 | 78 | 10 | 9 | 2 | 7 | 62 | 6 | 168 | 4 | 1 | 19 | 7 | .731 | 1 | 0-0 | 0 | 2.85 | 2.93 |
| 2003 | Tor | AL | 36 | **36** | **9** | 0 | **266.0** | **1071** | **253** | 111 | 96 | 26 | 3 | 2 | 9 | 32 | 1 | 204 | 6 | 1 | **22** | 7 | .759 | **2** | 0-0 | 0 | 2.86 | 3.25 |
| 2004 | Tor | AL | 21 | 21 | 1 | 0 | 133.0 | 561 | 140 | 66 | 62 | 13 | 4 | 3 | 1 | 39 | 1 | 95 | 2 | 2 | 8 | 8 | .500 | 1 | 0-0 | 0 | 4.00 | 4.20 |
| 2005 | Tor | AL | 19 | 19 | **5** | 0 | 141.2 | 553 | 118 | 39 | 38 | 11 | 2 | 1 | 7 | 18 | 2 | 108 | 2 | 1 | 12 | 4 | .750 | 2 | 0-0 | 0 | 2.26 | 2.41 |
| 2006 | Tor | AL | 32 | 32 | 4 | 0 | 220.0 | 876 | 208 | 82 | 78 | 19 | 3 | 5 | 5 | 34 | 5 | 132 | 3 | 0 | 16 | 5 | .762 | 0 | 0-0 | 0 | 2.87 | 3.19 |
| 2007 | Tor | AL | 31 | 31 | **7** | 0 | 225.1 | 927 | 232 | 101 | 93 | 15 | 2 | 7 | 3 | 48 | 3 | 139 | 4 | 0 | 16 | 7 | .696 | 1 | 0-0 | 0 | 3.37 | 3.71 |
| 2008 | Tor | AL | 34 | 33 | **9** | 0 | **246.0** | **987** | 220 | 88 | 76 | 18 | 5 | 4 | 12 | 39 | 3 | 206 | 4 | 0 | 20 | 11 | .645 | **2** | 0-0 | 1 | **2.62** | 2.78 |
| 2009 | Tor | AL | 32 | 32 | **9** | 0 | 239.0 | 963 | 234 | 82 | 74 | 22 | 1 | 9 | 5 | 35 | 0 | 208 | 2 | 0 | 17 | 10 | .630 | **4** | 0-0 | 0 | 3.06 | 2.79 |
| 2010 | Phi | NL | 33 | 33 | **9** | 0 | **250.2** | **993** | **231** | 74 | 68 | 24 | 9 | 5 | 6 | 30 | 1 | 219 | 5 | 1 | **21** | 10 | .677 | **4** | 0-0 | 0 | 2.69 | 2.44 |
| 2011 | Phi | NL | 32 | 32 | **8** | 0 | 233.2 | 933 | 208 | 65 | 61 | 10 | 15 | 7 | 4 | 35 | 4 | 220 | 2 | 1 | 19 | 6 | .760 | 1 | 0-0 | 0 | 2.26 | 2.35 |
| 2012 | Phi | NL | 25 | 25 | 0 | 0 | 156.1 | 646 | 155 | 78 | 78 | 18 | 5 | 6 | 5 | 36 | 0 | 132 | 2 | 0 | 11 | 8 | .579 | 0 | 0-0 | 0 | 3.63 | 4.49 |
| 2013 | Phi | NL | 13 | 13 | 1 | 0 | 62.0 | 282 | 55 | 48 | 47 | 12 | 3 | 2 | 10 | 36 | 1 | 51 | 4 | 0 | 4 | 5 | .444 | 0 | 0-0 | 0 | 5.47 | 6.82 |
| Postseason | | | 5 | 5 | 1 | 0 | 38.0 | 143 | 23 | 10 | 10 | 3 | 1 | 0 | 0 | 5 | 1 | 35 | 1 | 0 | 3 | 2 | .600 | 1 | 0-0 | 0 | 1.23 | 2.37 |
| 16 ML YEARS | | | 416 | 390 | 67 | 6 | 2749.1 | 11287 | 2646 | 1135 | 1034 | 236 | 69 | 61 | 81 | 592 | 28 | 2117 | 56 | 9 | 203 | 105 | .659 | 20 | 1-1 | 3 | 3.19 | 3.38 |

# Sean Halton

**Bats:** R **Throws:** R **Pos:** 1B-25;PH-16;LF-3;RF-3;3B-1 HALL-ton **Ht:** 6'4" **Wt:** 260 **Born:** 6/7/1987 **Age:** 27

| Year | Team | Lg | G | AB | H | 2B | 3B | HR | (Hm | Rd) | TB | R | RBI | RC | TBB | IBB | SO | HBP | SH | SF | SB | CS | SB% | GDP | Avg | OBP | Slg |
|---|---|---|---|---|---|---|---|---|---|---|---|---|---|---|---|---|---|---|---|---|---|---|---|---|---|---|---|
| | | | **BATTING** | | | | | | | | | | | | | | | | | | **BASERUNNING** | | | | **AVERAGES** | | |
| 2009 | Brewrs | R | 25 | 94 | 31 | 7 | 1 | 3 | (- | -) | 49 | 13 | 17 | 20 | 8 | 0 | 18 | 3 | 0 | 1 | 3 | 0 | 1.00 | 2 | .330 | .396 | .521 |
| 2009 | Helena | R+ | 44 | 161 | 57 | 14 | 0 | 3 | (- | -) | 80 | 27 | 28 | 30 | 9 | 0 | 38 | 4 | 0 | 2 | 4 | 4 | .50 | 2 | .354 | .398 | .497 |
| 2010 | Wisc | A | 23 | 86 | 19 | 4 | 0 | 0 | (- | -) | 23 | 11 | 11 | 5 | 5 | 0 | 14 | 1 | 0 | 1 | 0 | 1 | .00 | 1 | .221 | .269 | .267 |
| 2010 | BrvdCt | A+ | 104 | 397 | 116 | 17 | 1 | 10 | (- | -) | 165 | 42 | 77 | 59 | 28 | 2 | 88 | 9 | 2 | 9 | 2 | 2 | .50 | 10 | .292 | .345 | .416 |
| 2011 | Hntsvl | AA | 116 | 439 | 131 | 39 | 1 | 7 | (- | -) | 193 | 49 | 65 | 70 | 32 | 2 | 83 | 4 | 0 | 7 | 6 | 1 | .86 | 10 | .298 | .346 | .440 |
| 2012 | Nashv | AAA | 119 | 358 | 98 | 23 | 3 | 17 | (- | -) | 178 | 48 | 57 | 64 | 43 | 3 | 81 | 5 | 0 | 6 | 0 | 2 | .00 | 9 | .274 | .354 | .497 |
| 2013 | Nashv | AAA | 96 | 352 | 96 | 29 | 2 | 11 | (- | -) | 162 | 51 | 51 | 59 | 35 | 0 | 92 | 8 | 0 | 4 | 6 | 2 | .75 | 5 | .273 | .348 | .460 |
| 2013 | Mil | NL | 42 | 101 | 24 | 4 | 0 | 4 | (3 | 1) | 40 | 9 | 17 | 10 | 5 | 0 | 31 | 3 | 1 | 1 | 0 | 0 | - | 2 | .238 | .291 | .396 |

# Cole Hamels

**Pitches:** L **Bats:** L **Pos:** SP-33 **Ht:** 6'3" **Wt:** 195 **Born:** 12/27/1983 **Age:** 30

| Year | Team | Lg | G | GS | CG | GF | IP | BFP | H | R | ER | HR | SH | SF | HB | TBB | IBB | SO | WP | Bk | W | L | Pct | Sh | Sv-Op | Hld | ERC | ERA |
|---|---|---|---|---|---|---|---|---|---|---|---|---|---|---|---|---|---|---|---|---|---|---|---|---|---|---|---|---|
| | | | **HOW MUCH HE PITCHED** | | | | | | **WHAT HE GAVE UP** | | | | | | | | | | | | **THE RESULTS** | | | | | | | |
| 2006 | Phi | NL | 23 | 23 | 0 | 0 | 132.1 | 558 | 117 | 66 | 60 | 19 | 6 | 8 | 3 | 48 | 4 | 145 | 5 | 0 | 9 | 8 | .529 | 0 | 0-0 | 0 | 3.61 | 4.08 |
| 2007 | Phi | NL | 28 | 28 | 2 | 0 | 183.1 | 743 | 163 | 72 | 69 | 25 | 5 | 5 | 3 | 43 | 4 | 177 | 5 | 0 | 15 | 5 | .750 | 0 | 0-0 | 0 | 3.12 | 3.39 |
| 2008 | Phi | NL | 33 | 33 | 2 | 0 | 227.1 | 914 | 193 | 89 | 78 | 28 | 6 | 2 | 1 | 53 | 7 | 196 | 0 | 0 | 14 | 10 | .583 | 2 | 0-0 | 0 | 2.76 | 3.09 |
| 2009 | Phi | NL | 32 | 32 | 2 | 0 | 193.2 | 814 | 206 | 95 | 93 | 24 | 7 | 5 | 5 | 43 | 4 | 168 | 1 | 0 | 10 | 11 | .476 | **2** | 0-0 | 0 | 3.98 | 4.32 |
| 2010 | Phi | NL | 33 | 33 | 1 | 0 | 208.2 | 856 | 185 | 74 | 71 | 26 | 7 | 0 | 8 | 61 | 5 | 211 | 3 | 0 | 12 | 11 | .522 | 0 | 0-0 | 0 | 3.36 | 3.06 |
| 2011 | Phi | NL | 32 | 31 | 3 | 0 | 216.0 | 850 | 169 | 68 | 67 | 19 | 9 | 3 | 5 | 44 | 2 | 194 | 3 | 3 | 14 | 9 | .609 | 0 | 0-0 | 0 | 2.23 | 2.79 |
| 2012 | Phi | NL | 31 | 31 | 2 | 0 | 215.1 | 867 | 190 | 80 | 73 | 24 | 6 | 4 | 3 | 52 | 3 | 216 | 3 | 2 | 17 | 6 | .739 | 2 | 0-0 | 0 | 2.98 | 3.05 |
| 2013 | Phi | NL | 33 | 33 | 1 | 0 | 220.0 | 905 | 205 | 94 | 88 | 21 | 11 | 3 | 9 | 50 | 5 | 202 | 4 | 0 | 8 | 14 | .364 | 0 | 0-0 | 0 | 3.15 | 3.60 |
| Postseason | | | 13 | 13 | 1 | 0 | 81.2 | 326 | 65 | 29 | 28 | 9 | 3 | 2 | 2 | 21 | 1 | 77 | 0 | 0 | 7 | 4 | .636 | 1 | 0-0 | 0 | 2.62 | 3.09 |
| 8 ML YEARS | | | 245 | 244 | 13 | 0 | 1596.2 | 6507 | 1428 | 638 | 599 | 186 | 57 | 30 | 37 | 394 | 34 | 1509 | 24 | 5 | 99 | 74 | .572 | 6 | 0-0 | 0 | 3.10 | 3.38 |

# Billy Hamilton

**Bats:** B **Throws:** R **Pos:** CF-7;PR-7 **Ht:** 6'0" **Wt:** 160 **Born:** 9/9/1990 **Age:** 23

| Year | Team | Lg | G | AB | H | 2B | 3B | HR | (Hm | Rd) | TB | R | RBI | RC | TBB | IBB | SO | HBP | SH | SF | SB | CS | SB% | GDP | Avg | OBP | Slg |
|---|---|---|---|---|---|---|---|---|---|---|---|---|---|---|---|---|---|---|---|---|---|---|---|---|---|---|---|
| | | | **BATTING** | | | | | | | | | | | | | | | | | | **BASERUNNING** | | | | **AVERAGES** | | |
| 2009 | Reds | R | 43 | 166 | 34 | 6 | 3 | 0 | (- | -) | 46 | 19 | 11 | 12 | 11 | 0 | 47 | 0 | 2 | 1 | 14 | 3 | .82 | 0 | .205 | .253 | .277 |
| 2010 | Billings | R+ | 69 | 283 | 90 | 13 | 10 | 2 | (- | -) | 129 | 61 | 24 | 56 | 28 | 0 | 56 | 3 | 0 | 2 | 48 | 9 | .84 | 2 | .318 | .383 | .456 |
| 2011 | Dayton | A | 135 | 550 | 153 | 18 | 9 | 3 | (- | -) | 198 | 99 | 50 | 83 | 52 | 0 | 133 | 1 | 4 | 3 | 103 | 20 | .84 | 5 | .278 | .340 | .360 |
| 2012 | Bkrsfld | A+ | 82 | 337 | 109 | 18 | 9 | 1 | (- | -) | 148 | 79 | 30 | 76 | 50 | 1 | 70 | 2 | 2 | 1 | 104 | 21 | .83 | 2 | .323 | .413 | .439 |
| 2012 | Pnscla | AA | 50 | 175 | 50 | 4 | 5 | 1 | (- | -) | 67 | 33 | 15 | 34 | 36 | 1 | 43 | 0 | 1 | 1 | 51 | 16 | .76 | 0 | .286 | .406 | .383 |
| 2013 | Lsvlle | AAA | 123 | 504 | 129 | 18 | 4 | 6 | (- | -) | 173 | 75 | 41 | 63 | 38 | 0 | 102 | 0 | 4 | 1 | 75 | 15 | .83 | 4 | .256 | .308 | .343 |
| 2013 | Cin | NL | 13 | 19 | 7 | 2 | 0 | 0 | (0 | 0) | 9 | 9 | 1 | 5 | 2 | 0 | 4 | 0 | 1 | 0 | 13 | 1 | .93 | 0 | .368 | .429 | .474 |

# Josh Hamilton

**Bats:** L **Throws:** L **Pos:** RF-83;DH-37;LF-19;CF-6;PH-6 **Ht:** 6'4" **Wt:** 225 **Born:** 5/21/1981 **Age:** 33

| Year | Team | Lg | G | AB | H | 2B | 3B | HR | (Hm | Rd) | TB | R | RBI | RC | TBB | IBB | SO | HBP | SH | SF | SB | CS | SB% | GDP | Avg | OBP | Slg |
|---|---|---|---|---|---|---|---|---|---|---|---|---|---|---|---|---|---|---|---|---|---|---|---|---|---|---|---|
| | | | **BATTING** | | | | | | | | | | | | | | | | | | **BASERUNNING** | | | | **AVERAGES** | | |
| 2007 | Cin | NL | 90 | 298 | 87 | 17 | 2 | 19 | (11 | 8) | 165 | 52 | 47 | 58 | 33 | 4 | 65 | 4 | 0 | 2 | 3 | 3 | .50 | 6 | .292 | .368 | .554 |
| 2008 | Tex | AL | 156 | 624 | 190 | 35 | 5 | 32 | (19 | 13) | **331** | 98 | **130** | 119 | 64 | 9 | 126 | 7 | 0 | 9 | 9 | 1 | .90 | 8 | .304 | .371 | .530 |
| 2009 | Tex | AL | 89 | 336 | 90 | 19 | 2 | 10 | (6 | 4) | 143 | 43 | 54 | 51 | 24 | 2 | 79 | 1 | 0 | 4 | 8 | 3 | .73 | 5 | .268 | .315 | .426 |
| 2010 | Tex | AL | 133 | 518 | 186 | 40 | 3 | 32 | (22 | 10) | 328 | 95 | 100 | 121 | 43 | 5 | 95 | 5 | 1 | 4 | 8 | 1 | .89 | 11 | **.359** | .411 | **.633** |
| 2011 | Tex | AL | 121 | 487 | 145 | 31 | 5 | 25 | (14 | 11) | 261 | 80 | 94 | 78 | 39 | 13 | 93 | 2 | 0 | 10 | 8 | 1 | .89 | 8 | .298 | .346 | .536 |
| 2012 | Tex | AL | 148 | 562 | 160 | 31 | 2 | 43 | (22 | 21) | 324 | 103 | 128 | 108 | 60 | 13 | 162 | 5 | 0 | 9 | 7 | 4 | .64 | 9 | .285 | .354 | .577 |
| 2013 | LAA | AL | 151 | 576 | 144 | 32 | 5 | 21 | (9 | 12) | 249 | 73 | 79 | 67 | 47 | 4 | 158 | 4 | 0 | 9 | 4 | 0 | 1.00 | 16 | .250 | .307 | .432 |
| Postseason | | | 34 | 132 | 30 | 8 | 0 | 6 | (2 | 4) | 56 | 18 | 22 | 17 | 14 | 7 | 23 | 0 | 0 | 3 | 4 | 1 | .80 | 4 | .227 | .295 | .424 |
| 7 ML YEARS | | | 888 | 3401 | 1002 | 205 | 24 | 182 | (103 | 79) | 1801 | 544 | 632 | 602 | 310 | 50 | 778 | 28 | 1 | 47 | 47 | 13 | .78 | 63 | .295 | .354 | .530 |

## Jason Hammel

**Pitches:** R **Bats:** R **Pos:** SP-23; RP-3 **Ht:** 6'6" **Wt:** 225 **Born:** 9/2/1982 **Age:** 31

| HOW MUCH HE PITCHED | | | | | | | | | WHAT HE GAVE UP | | | | | | | | | | | | THE RESULTS | | | | | | | |
|---|---|---|---|---|---|---|---|---|---|---|---|---|---|---|---|---|---|---|---|---|---|---|---|---|---|---|---|---|
| Year | Team | Lg | G | GS | CG | GF | IP | BFP | H | R | ER | HR | SH | SF | HB | TBB | IBB | SO | WP | Bk | W | L | Pct | Sh | Sv-Op | Hld | ERC | ERA |
| 2013 | Bowie* | AA | 1 | 1 | 0 | 0 | 2.2 | 13 | 3 | 0 | 0 | 0 | 0 | 0 | 2 | 0 | 0 | 3 | 0 | 0 | 0 | 0 | - | 0 | 0-- | - | 5.24 | 0.00 |
| 2013 | Abrdn* | A- | 1 | 1 | 0 | 0 | 4.0 | 16 | 3 | 1 | 1 | 0 | 0 | 0 | 0 | 1 | 0 | 2 | 0 | 0 | 0 | 0 | - | 0 | 0-- | - | 1.65 | 2.25 |
| 2006 | TB | AL | 9 | 9 | 0 | 0 | 44.0 | 208 | 61 | 38 | 38 | 7 | 0 | 3 | 1 | 21 | 0 | 32 | 3 | 2 | 0 | 6 | .000 | 0 | 0-0 | 0 | 7.40 | 7.77 |
| 2007 | TB | AL | 24 | 14 | 0 | 2 | 85.0 | 384 | 100 | 58 | 58 | 12 | 2 | 0 | 2 | 40 | 1 | 64 | 3 | 0 | 3 | 5 | .375 | 0 | 0-0 | 0 | 5.86 | 6.14 |
| 2008 | TB | AL | 40 | 5 | 0 | 21 | 78.1 | 346 | 83 | 45 | 40 | 11 | 2 | 2 | 2 | 35 | 4 | 44 | 7 | 0 | 4 | 4 | .500 | 0 | 2-2 | 1 | 4.94 | 4.60 |
| 2009 | Col | NL | 34 | 30 | 1 | 0 | 176.2 | 771 | 203 | 94 | 85 | 17 | 10 | 9 | 9 | 42 | 6 | 133 | 4 | 0 | 10 | 8 | .556 | 0 | 0-0 | 0 | 4.37 | 4.33 |
| 2010 | Col | NL | 30 | 30 | 0 | 0 | 177.2 | 770 | 201 | 97 | 95 | 18 | 11 | 6 | 6 | 47 | 1 | 141 | 13 | 2 | 10 | 9 | .526 | 0 | 0-0 | 0 | 4.41 | 4.81 |
| 2011 | Col | NL | 32 | 27 | 0 | 2 | 170.1 | 739 | 175 | 100 | 90 | 21 | 11 | 6 | 6 | 68 | 3 | 94 | 8 | 1 | 7 | 13 | .350 | 0 | 1-1 | 0 | 4.54 | 4.76 |
| 2012 | Bal | AL | 20 | 20 | 1 | 0 | 118.0 | 493 | 104 | 48 | 45 | 9 | 3 | 1 | 2 | 42 | 2 | 113 | 3 | 0 | 8 | 6 | .571 | 1 | 0-0 | 0 | 3.14 | 3.43 |
| 2013 | Bal | AL | 26 | 23 | 0 | 1 | 139.1 | 611 | 155 | 81 | 77 | 22 | 2 | 8 | 8 | 48 | 1 | 96 | 1 | 0 | 7 | 8 | .467 | 0 | 1-1 | 1 | 5.19 | 4.97 |
| Postseason | | | 3 | 3 | 0 | 0 | 15.0 | 62 | 12 | 8 | 8 | 1 | 0 | 0 | 0 | 9 | 2 | 16 | 0 | 0 | 0 | 1 | .000 | 0 | 0-0 | 0 | 3.46 | 4.80 |
| 8 ML YEARS | | | 215 | 158 | 2 | 26 | 989.1 | 4322 | 1082 | 561 | 528 | 117 | 41 | 35 | 36 | 343 | 18 | 717 | 42 | 5 | 49 | 59 | .454 | 1 | 4-4 | 2 | 4.66 | 4.80 |

## Brad Hand

**Pitches:** L **Bats:** L **Pos:** RP-5; SP-2 **Ht:** 6'3" **Wt:** 215 **Born:** 3/20/1990 **Age:** 24

| HOW MUCH HE PITCHED | | | | | | | | | WHAT HE GAVE UP | | | | | | | | | | | | THE RESULTS | | | | | | | |
|---|---|---|---|---|---|---|---|---|---|---|---|---|---|---|---|---|---|---|---|---|---|---|---|---|---|---|---|---|
| Year | Team | Lg | G | GS | CG | GF | IP | BFP | H | R | ER | HR | SH | SF | HB | TBB | IBB | SO | WP | Bk | W | L | Pct | Sh | Sv-Op | Hld | ERC | ERA |
| 2013 | NewOr* | AAA | 15 | 15 | 0 | 0 | 81.2 | 351 | 69 | 33 | 31 | 7 | 4 | 2 | 2 | 45 | 0 | 81 | 6 | 0 | 3 | 5 | .375 | 0 | 0-- | - | 3.83 | 3.42 |
| 2013 | Mrlns* | R | 2 | 2 | 0 | 0 | 8.0 | 30 | 5 | 2 | 1 | 0 | 0 | 0 | 0 | 2 | 0 | 11 | 1 | 0 | 0 | 1 | .000 | 0 | 0-- | - | 1.32 | 1.13 |
| 2011 | Fla | NL | 12 | 12 | 0 | 0 | 60.0 | 263 | 53 | 32 | 28 | 10 | 4 | 3 | 1 | 35 | 1 | 38 | 0 | 1 | 1 | 8 | .111 | 0 | 0-0 | 0 | 4.68 | 4.20 |
| 2012 | Mia | NL | 1 | 1 | 0 | 0 | 3.2 | 23 | 6 | 7 | 7 | 1 | 0 | 0 | 0 | 6 | 1 | 3 | 0 | 0 | 0 | 1 | .000 | 0 | 0-0 | 0 | 14.74 | 17.18 |
| 2013 | Mia | NL | 7 | 2 | 0 | 2 | 20.2 | 82 | 13 | 7 | 7 | 2 | 0 | 0 | 0 | 8 | 0 | 15 | 1 | 0 | 1 | 1 | .500 | 0 | 0-0 | 0 | 2.10 | 3.05 |
| 3 ML YEARS | | | 20 | 15 | 0 | 2 | 84.1 | 368 | 72 | 46 | 42 | 13 | 4 | 3 | 1 | 49 | 2 | 56 | 1 | 1 | 2 | 10 | .167 | 0 | 0-0 | 0 | 4.36 | 4.48 |

## Donovan Hand

**Pitches:** R **Bats:** R **Pos:** RP-24; SP-7 **Ht:** 6'3" **Wt:** 210 **Born:** 4/20/1986 **Age:** 28

| HOW MUCH HE PITCHED | | | | | | | | | WHAT HE GAVE UP | | | | | | | | | | | | THE RESULTS | | | | | | | |
|---|---|---|---|---|---|---|---|---|---|---|---|---|---|---|---|---|---|---|---|---|---|---|---|---|---|---|---|---|
| Year | Team | Lg | G | GS | CG | GF | IP | BFP | H | R | ER | HR | SH | SF | HB | TBB | IBB | SO | WP | Bk | W | L | Pct | Sh | Sv-Op | Hld | ERC | ERA |
| 2009 | Hntsvl | AA | 27 | 12 | 0 | 2 | 98.2 | 409 | 102 | 44 | 39 | 12 | 3 | 2 | 2 | 21 | 2 | 51 | 2 | 1 | 8 | 5 | .615 | 0 | 1-- | - | 3.76 | 3.56 |
| 2010 | Hntsvl | AA | 27 | 1 | 0 | 9 | 50.1 | 213 | 57 | 25 | 16 | 3 | 2 | 0 | 3 | 8 | 1 | 38 | 2 | 0 | 2 | 1 | .667 | 0 | 2-- | - | 3.81 | 2.86 |
| 2010 | Nashv | AAA | 21 | 0 | 0 | 7 | 25.1 | 107 | 29 | 16 | 13 | 1 | 0 | 1 | 0 | 5 | 0 | 11 | 0 | 0 | 2 | 0 | 1.000 | 0 | 0-- | - | 3.69 | 4.62 |
| 2011 | Hntsvl | AA | 9 | 0 | 0 | 2 | 11.1 | 48 | 16 | 3 | 3 | 0 | 1 | 0 | 0 | 1 | 0 | 12 | 0 | 0 | 0 | 0 | - | 0 | 1-- | - | 4.62 | 2.38 |
| 2011 | Nashv | AAA | 38 | 0 | 0 | 11 | 53.0 | 234 | 65 | 24 | 22 | 6 | 6 | 1 | 0 | 20 | 1 | 32 | 2 | 0 | 2 | 6 | .250 | 0 | 1-- | - | 5.48 | 3.74 |
| 2012 | Nashv | AAA | 44 | 3 | 0 | 6 | 79.2 | 332 | 90 | 35 | 34 | 7 | 4 | 1 | 1 | 18 | 2 | 54 | 2 | 0 | 3 | 3 | .500 | 0 | 0-- | - | 4.16 | 3.84 |
| 2013 | Nashv | AAA | 20 | 0 | 0 | 5 | 35.2 | 152 | 34 | 15 | 13 | 4 | 1 | 0 | 0 | 11 | 1 | 38 | 2 | 0 | 3 | 1 | .750 | 0 | 0-- | - | 3.43 | 3.28 |
| 2013 | Mil | NL | 31 | 7 | 0 | 5 | 68.1 | 286 | 71 | 29 | 28 | 10 | 1 | 5 | 5 | 21 | 1 | 37 | 3 | 0 | 1 | 5 | .167 | 0 | 0-1 | 2 | 4.70 | 3.69 |

## Ryan Hanigan

**Bats:** R **Throws:** R **Pos:** C-72;PH-4 HANN-eh-gann **Ht:** 6'0" **Wt:** 210 **Born:** 8/16/1980 **Age:** 33

| BATTING | | | | | | | | | | | | | | | | | | | | | BASERUNNING | | | | AVERAGES | | |
|---|---|---|---|---|---|---|---|---|---|---|---|---|---|---|---|---|---|---|---|---|---|---|---|---|---|---|---|
| Year | Team | Lg | G | AB | H | 2B | 3B | HR | (Hm | Rd) | TB | R | RBI | RC | TBB | IBB | SO | HBP | SH | SF | SB | CS | SB% | GDP | Avg | OBP | Slg |
| 2013 | Lsvlle* | AAA | 3 | 8 | 3 | 0 | 0 | 0 | (- | -) | 3 | 2 | 2 | 1 | 1 | 0 | 1 | 0 | 0 | 0 | 0 | 0 | - | 0 | .375 | .444 | .375 |
| 2007 | Cin | NL | 5 | 10 | 3 | 1 | 0 | 0 | (0 | 0) | 4 | 3 | 2 | 2 | 1 | 1 | 2 | 0 | 0 | 0 | 0 | 0 | - | 0 | .300 | .364 | .400 |
| 2008 | Cin | NL | 31 | 85 | 23 | 2 | 0 | 2 | (1 | 1) | 31 | 9 | 9 | 12 | 10 | 1 | 9 | 3 | 0 | 0 | 0 | 0 | - | 2 | .271 | .367 | .365 |
| 2009 | Cin | NL | 90 | 251 | 66 | 6 | 1 | 3 | (3 | 0) | 83 | 22 | 11 | 25 | 37 | 7 | 31 | 2 | 2 | 1 | 0 | 0 | - | 9 | .263 | .361 | .331 |
| 2010 | Cin | NL | 70 | 203 | 61 | 11 | 0 | 5 | (2 | 3) | 87 | 25 | 40 | 41 | 33 | 4 | 21 | 4 | 1 | 2 | 0 | 0 | - | 6 | .300 | .405 | .429 |
| 2011 | Cin | NL | 91 | 266 | 71 | 6 | 0 | 6 | (4 | 2) | 95 | 27 | 31 | 38 | 35 | 3 | 32 | 2 | 1 | 0 | 0 | 0 | - | 3 | .267 | .356 | .357 |
| 2012 | Cin | NL | 112 | 317 | 87 | 14 | 0 | 2 | (0 | 2) | 107 | 25 | 24 | 40 | 44 | 13 | 37 | 3 | 4 | 3 | 0 | 0 | - | 6 | .274 | .365 | .338 |
| 2013 | Cin | NL | 75 | 222 | 44 | 8 | 0 | 2 | (1 | 1) | 58 | 17 | 21 | 18 | 29 | 9 | 27 | 6 | 2 | 1 | 0 | 1 | .00 | 7 | .198 | .306 | .261 |
| Postseason | | | 6 | 19 | 3 | 0 | 0 | 0 | (0 | 0) | 3 | 3 | 3 | 1 | 0 | 0 | 3 | 1 | 0 | 0 | 0 | 0 | - | 1 | .158 | .200 | .158 |
| 7 ML YEARS | | | 474 | 1354 | 355 | 48 | 1 | 20 | (11 | 9) | 465 | 128 | 138 | 176 | 189 | 38 | 159 | 20 | 10 | 7 | 0 | 1 | .00 | 33 | .262 | .359 | .343 |

## Jack Hannahan

**Bats:** L **Throws:** R **Pos:** PH-46;3B-37;1B-10;2B-1;DH-1 **Ht:** 6'2" **Wt:** 210 **Born:** 3/4/1980 **Age:** 34

| BATTING | | | | | | | | | | | | | | | | | | | | | BASERUNNING | | | | AVERAGES | | |
|---|---|---|---|---|---|---|---|---|---|---|---|---|---|---|---|---|---|---|---|---|---|---|---|---|---|---|---|
| Year | Team | Lg | G | AB | H | 2B | 3B | HR | (Hm | Rd) | TB | R | RBI | RC | TBB | IBB | SO | HBP | SH | SF | SB | CS | SB% | GDP | Avg | OBP | Slg |
| 2006 | Det | AL | 3 | 9 | 0 | 0 | 0 | 0 | (0 | 0) | 0 | 0 | 0 | 0 | 1 | 0 | 1 | 0 | 0 | 0 | 0 | 0 | - | 0 | .000 | .100 | .000 |
| 2007 | Oak | AL | 41 | 144 | 40 | 12 | 0 | 3 | (1 | 2) | 61 | 16 | 24 | 23 | 21 | 0 | 39 | 1 | 1 | 2 | 1 | 0 | 1.00 | 6 | .278 | .369 | .424 |
| 2008 | Oak | AL | 143 | 436 | 95 | 27 | 0 | 9 | (4 | 5) | 149 | 48 | 47 | 38 | 55 | 4 | 131 | 2 | 3 | 5 | 2 | 0 | 1.00 | 5 | .218 | .305 | .342 |
| 2009 | 2 Tms | AL | 103 | 267 | 57 | 14 | 2 | 4 | (2 | 2) | 87 | 27 | 19 | 20 | 30 | 0 | 71 | 2 | 1 | 1 | 1 | 1 | .50 | 4 | .213 | .297 | .326 |
| 2011 | Cle | AL | 110 | 320 | 80 | 16 | 2 | 8 | (7 | 1) | 124 | 38 | 40 | 47 | 38 | 0 | 80 | 2 | 4 | 2 | 2 | 1 | .67 | 7 | .250 | .331 | .388 |
| 2012 | Cle | AL | 105 | 287 | 70 | 16 | 0 | 4 | (3 | 1) | 98 | 23 | 29 | 31 | 27 | 0 | 63 | 2 | 1 | 1 | 0 | 2 | .00 | 9 | .244 | .312 | .341 |
| 2013 | Cin | NL | 83 | 139 | 30 | 5 | 1 | 1 | (1 | 0) | 40 | 12 | 14 | 15 | 19 | 1 | 38 | 2 | 0 | 1 | 0 | 0 | - | 6 | .216 | .317 | .288 |
| 09 | Oak | AL | 52 | 119 | 23 | 6 | 2 | 1 | (1 | 0) | 36 | 12 | 8 | 7 | 13 | 0 | 36 | 1 | 1 | 0 | 0 | 0 | - | 2 | .193 | .278 | .303 |
| 09 | Sea | AL | 51 | 148 | 34 | 8 | 0 | 3 | (1 | 2) | 51 | 15 | 11 | 13 | 17 | 0 | 35 | 1 | 0 | 1 | 1 | 1 | .50 | 2 | .230 | .311 | .345 |
| 7 ML YEARS | | | 588 | 1602 | 372 | 90 | 5 | 29 | (18 | 11) | 559 | 164 | 173 | 174 | 191 | 5 | 423 | 11 | 10 | 12 | 6 | 4 | .60 | 37 | .232 | .316 | .349 |

## Joel Hanrahan

**Pitches:** R **Bats:** R **Pos:** RP-9 **Ht:** 6'4" **Wt:** 250 **Born:** 10/6/1981 **Age:** 32

| HOW MUCH HE PITCHED | | | | | | | | | WHAT HE GAVE UP | | | | | | | | | | | | THE RESULTS | | | | | | | |
|---|---|---|---|---|---|---|---|---|---|---|---|---|---|---|---|---|---|---|---|---|---|---|---|---|---|---|---|---|
| Year | Team | Lg | G | GS | CG | GF | IP | BFP | H | R | ER | HR | SH | SF | HB | TBB | IBB | SO | WP | Bk | W | L | Pct | Sh | Sv-Op | Hld | ERC | ERA |
| 2013 | Pwtckt* | AAA | 2 | 0 | 0 | 1 | 2.0 | 9 | 2 | 2 | 2 | 1 | 0 | 0 | 0 | 1 | 0 | 1 | 0 | 0 | 0 | 0 | - | 0 | 0- - | - | 7.30 | 9.00 |
| 2007 | Was | NL | 12 | 11 | 0 | 0 | 51.0 | 247 | 59 | 35 | 34 | 9 | 2 | 1 | 0 | 38 | 0 | 43 | 3 | 0 | 5 | 3 | .625 | 0 | 0-0 | 0 | 7.01 | 6.00 |
| 2008 | Was | NL | 69 | 0 | 0 | 34 | 84.1 | 364 | 73 | 40 | 37 | 9 | 2 | 6 | 1 | 42 | 7 | 93 | 6 | 0 | 6 | 3 | .667 | 0 | 9-13 | 3 | 3.65 | 3.95 |
| 2009 | 2 Tms | NL | 67 | 0 | 0 | 30 | 64.0 | 297 | 73 | 40 | 34 | 3 | 0 | 1 | 3 | 34 | 1 | 72 | 11 | 1 | 1 | 4 | .200 | 0 | 5-10 | 9 | 5.12 | 4.78 |
| 2010 | Pit | NL | 72 | 0 | 0 | 27 | 69.2 | 294 | 58 | 28 | 28 | 6 | 0 | 1 | 4 | 26 | 0 | 100 | 5 | 0 | 4 | 1 | .800 | 0 | 6-10 | 18 | 3.16 | 3.62 |
| 2011 | Pit | NL | 70 | 0 | 0 | 59 | 68.2 | 274 | 56 | 17 | 14 | 1 | 1 | 2 | 1 | 16 | 2 | 61 | 6 | 0 | 1 | 4 | .200 | 0 | 40-44 | 0 | 2.00 | 1.83 |
| 2012 | Pit | NL | 63 | 0 | 0 | 57 | 59.2 | 254 | 40 | 18 | 18 | 8 | 3 | 0 | 1 | 36 | 0 | 67 | 6 | 0 | 5 | 2 | .714 | 0 | 36-40 | 0 | 3.32 | 2.72 |
| 2013 | Bos | AL | 9 | 0 | 0 | 6 | 7.1 | 37 | 10 | 8 | 8 | 4 | 1 | 0 | 0 | 6 | 0 | 5 | 1 | 0 | 0 | 1 | .000 | 0 | 4-6 | 0 | 12.34 | 9.82 |
| 09 | Was | NL | 34 | 0 | 0 | 23 | 32.2 | 163 | 50 | 28 | 28 | 3 | 0 | 1 | 2 | 14 | 0 | 35 | 6 | 1 | 1 | 3 | .250 | 0 | 5-10 | 2 | 7.49 | 7.71 |
| 09 | Pit | NL | 33 | 0 | 0 | 7 | 31.1 | 134 | 23 | 12 | 6 | 0 | 0 | 0 | 1 | 20 | 1 | 37 | 5 | 0 | 0 | 1 | .000 | 0 | 0-0 | 7 | 2.92 | 1.72 |
| 7 ML YEARS | | | 362 | 11 | 0 | 213 | 404.2 | 1767 | 369 | 186 | 173 | 40 | 9 | 11 | 10 | 198 | 10 | 441 | 38 | 1 | 22 | 18 | .550 | 0 | 100-123 | 30 | 3.95 | 3.85 |

## Tommy Hanson

**Pitches:** R **Bats:** R **Pos:** SP-13; RP-2 **Ht:** 6'6" **Wt:** 220 **Born:** 8/28/1986 **Age:** 27

| HOW MUCH HE PITCHED | | | | | | | | | WHAT HE GAVE UP | | | | | | | | | | | | THE RESULTS | | | | | | | |
|---|---|---|---|---|---|---|---|---|---|---|---|---|---|---|---|---|---|---|---|---|---|---|---|---|---|---|---|---|
| Year | Team | Lg | G | GS | CG | GF | IP | BFP | H | R | ER | HR | SH | SF | HB | TBB | IBB | SO | WP | Bk | W | L | Pct | Sh | Sv-Op | Hld | ERC | ERA |
| 2013 | InldEm* | A+ | 1 | 1 | 0 | 0 | 3.1 | 14 | 3 | 2 | 2 | 0 | 1 | 0 | 0 | 1 | 0 | 6 | 0 | 0 | 0 | 1 | .000 | 0 | 0- - | - | 2.46 | 5.40 |
| 2013 | Salt Lk* | AAA | 4 | 4 | 0 | 0 | 19.2 | 91 | 23 | 14 | 12 | 5 | 1 | 0 | 1 | 6 | 0 | 15 | 0 | 0 | 0 | 2 | .000 | 0 | 0- - | - | 5.75 | 5.49 |
| 2009 | Atl | NL | 21 | 21 | 0 | 0 | 127.2 | 522 | 105 | 42 | 41 | 10 | 4 | 1 | 5 | 46 | 1 | 116 | 2 | 0 | 11 | 4 | .733 | 0 | 0-0 | 0 | 3.02 | 2.89 |
| 2010 | Atl | NL | 34 | 34 | 1 | 0 | 202.2 | 845 | 182 | 86 | 75 | 14 | 9 | 5 | **14** | 56 | 3 | 173 | 3 | 0 | 10 | 11 | .476 | 0 | 0-0 | 0 | 3.08 | 3.33 |
| 2011 | Atl | NL | 22 | 22 | 0 | 0 | 130.0 | 540 | 106 | 55 | 52 | 17 | 4 | 3 | 3 | 46 | 3 | 142 | 5 | 0 | 11 | 7 | .611 | 0 | 0-0 | 0 | 3.13 | 3.60 |
| 2012 | Atl | NL | 31 | 31 | 0 | 0 | 174.2 | 761 | 183 | 95 | 87 | 27 | 8 | 2 | 5 | 71 | 5 | 161 | 6 | 0 | 13 | 10 | .565 | 0 | 0-0 | 0 | 4.88 | 4.48 |
| 2013 | LAA | AL | 15 | 13 | 0 | 1 | 73.0 | 327 | 83 | 47 | 44 | 10 | 0 | 4 | 3 | 30 | 3 | 56 | 6 | 0 | 4 | 3 | .571 | 0 | 0-0 | 0 | 5.30 | 5.42 |
| Postseason | | | 1 | 1 | 0 | 0 | 4.0 | 17 | 5 | 4 | 4 | 1 | 0 | 0 | 0 | 1 | 0 | 5 | 0 | 0 | 0 | 0 | - | 0 | 0-0 | 0 | 6.26 | 9.00 |
| 5 ML YEARS | | | 123 | 121 | 1 | 1 | 708.0 | 2995 | 659 | 325 | 299 | 78 | 25 | 15 | 30 | 249 | 15 | 648 | 22 | 0 | 49 | 35 | .583 | 0 | 0-0 | 0 | 3.72 | 3.80 |

## J.A. Happ

**Pitches:** L **Bats:** L **Pos:** SP-18 JAY **Ht:** 6'6" **Wt:** 195 **Born:** 10/19/1982 **Age:** 31

| HOW MUCH HE PITCHED | | | | | | | | | WHAT HE GAVE UP | | | | | | | | | | | | THE RESULTS | | | | | | | |
|---|---|---|---|---|---|---|---|---|---|---|---|---|---|---|---|---|---|---|---|---|---|---|---|---|---|---|---|---|
| Year | Team | Lg | G | GS | CG | GF | IP | BFP | H | R | ER | HR | SH | SF | HB | TBB | IBB | SO | WP | Bk | W | L | Pct | Sh | Sv-Op | Hld | ERC | ERA |
| 2013 | B Jays* | R | 1 | 1 | 0 | 0 | 3.0 | 14 | 4 | 2 | 0 | 0 | 0 | 0 | 0 | 0 | 0 | 0 | 0 | 0 | 0 | 0 | - | 0 | 0- - | - | 3.27 | 0.00 |
| 2013 | Dnedin* | A+ | 1 | 1 | 0 | 0 | 5.0 | 17 | 3 | 0 | 0 | 0 | 0 | 0 | 0 | 0 | 0 | 7 | 0 | 0 | 0 | 0 | - | 0 | 0- - | - | 0.80 | 0.00 |
| 2013 | Buffalo* | AAA | 3 | 3 | 0 | 0 | 13.1 | 62 | 17 | 10 | 10 | 2 | 1 | 0 | 0 | 8 | 0 | 13 | 1 | 0 | 0 | 2 | .000 | 0 | 0- - | - | 7.16 | 6.75 |
| 2007 | Phi | NL | 1 | 1 | 0 | 0 | 4.0 | 21 | 7 | 5 | 5 | 3 | 0 | 0 | 0 | 2 | 0 | 5 | 0 | 0 | 0 | 1 | .000 | 0 | 0-0 | 0 | 15.13 | 11.25 |
| 2008 | Phi | NL | 8 | 4 | 0 | 1 | 31.2 | 138 | 28 | 13 | 13 | 3 | 2 | 1 | 1 | 14 | 1 | 26 | 1 | 0 | 1 | 0 | 1.000 | 0 | 0-0 | 1 | 3.55 | 3.69 |
| 2009 | Phi | NL | 35 | 23 | 3 | 4 | 166.0 | 685 | 149 | 55 | 54 | 20 | 7 | 6 | 5 | 56 | 2 | 119 | 2 | 0 | 12 | 4 | .750 | **2** | 0-0 | 0 | 3.57 | 2.93 |
| 2010 | 2 Tms | NL | 16 | 16 | 1 | 0 | 87.1 | 374 | 73 | 37 | 33 | 8 | 5 | 4 | 1 | 47 | 1 | 70 | 4 | 0 | 6 | 4 | .600 | 1 | 0-0 | 0 | 3.69 | 3.40 |
| 2011 | Hou | NL | 28 | 28 | 0 | 0 | 156.1 | 698 | 157 | 103 | 93 | 21 | 12 | 8 | 2 | 83 | 5 | 134 | 3 | 2 | 6 | 15 | .286 | 0 | 0-0 | 0 | 4.86 | 5.35 |
| 2012 | 2 Tms | | 28 | 24 | 0 | 3 | 144.2 | 627 | 147 | 79 | 77 | 19 | 9 | 4 | 2 | 56 | 1 | 144 | 7 | 0 | 10 | 11 | .476 | 0 | 0-0 | 1 | 4.37 | 4.79 |
| 2013 | Tor | AL | 18 | 18 | 0 | 0 | 92.2 | 415 | 91 | 53 | 47 | 10 | 1 | 3 | 2 | 45 | 0 | 77 | 5 | 0 | 5 | 7 | .417 | 0 | 0-0 | 0 | 4.36 | 4.56 |
| 10 | Phi | NL | 3 | 3 | 0 | 0 | 15.1 | 70 | 13 | 4 | 3 | 1 | 1 | 1 | 0 | 12 | 0 | 9 | 1 | 0 | 1 | 0 | 1.000 | 0 | 0-0 | 0 | 4.40 | 1.76 |
| 10 | Hou | NL | 13 | 13 | 1 | 0 | 72.0 | 304 | 60 | 33 | 30 | 7 | 4 | 3 | 1 | 35 | 1 | 61 | 3 | 0 | 5 | 4 | .556 | 1 | 0-0 | 0 | 3.53 | 3.75 |
| 12 | Hou | NL | 18 | 18 | 0 | 0 | 104.1 | 457 | 112 | 58 | 56 | 17 | 7 | 2 | 1 | 39 | 0 | 98 | 5 | 0 | 7 | 9 | .438 | 0 | 0-0 | 0 | 4.86 | 4.83 |
| 12 | Tor | AL | 10 | 6 | 0 | 3 | 40.1 | 170 | 35 | 21 | 21 | 2 | 2 | 2 | 1 | 17 | 1 | 46 | 2 | 0 | 3 | 2 | .600 | 0 | 0-0 | 1 | 3.16 | 4.69 |
| Postseason | | | 8 | 1 | 0 | 0 | 9.1 | 46 | 12 | 5 | 5 | 1 | 0 | 0 | 0 | 8 | 0 | 10 | 0 | 0 | 0 | 0 | - | 0 | 0-0 | 1 | 7.96 | 4.82 |
| 7 ML YEARS | | | 134 | 114 | 4 | 8 | 682.2 | 2958 | 652 | 345 | 322 | 84 | 36 | 26 | 13 | 303 | 10 | 575 | 22 | 2 | 40 | 42 | .488 | 3 | 0-0 | 2 | 4.21 | 4.25 |

## Aaron Harang

**Pitches:** R **Bats:** R **Pos:** SP-26 huh-RANG **Ht:** 6'7" **Wt:** 260 **Born:** 5/9/1978 **Age:** 36

| HOW MUCH HE PITCHED | | | | | | | | | WHAT HE GAVE UP | | | | | | | | | | | | THE RESULTS | | | | | | | |
|---|---|---|---|---|---|---|---|---|---|---|---|---|---|---|---|---|---|---|---|---|---|---|---|---|---|---|---|---|
| Year | Team | Lg | G | GS | CG | GF | IP | BFP | H | R | ER | HR | SH | SF | HB | TBB | IBB | SO | WP | Bk | W | L | Pct | Sh | Sv-Op | Hld | ERC | ERA |
| 2013 | LsVgs* | AAA | 1 | 0 | 0 | 0 | 4.0 | 19 | 7 | 2 | 2 | 1 | 0 | 0 | 0 | 1 | 0 | 5 | 1 | 0 | 0 | 0 | - | 0 | 0- - | - | 9.69 | 4.50 |
| 2002 | Oak | AL | 16 | 15 | 0 | 0 | 78.1 | 354 | 78 | 44 | 42 | 7 | 3 | 4 | 3 | 45 | 2 | 64 | 1 | 0 | 5 | 4 | .556 | 0 | 0-0 | 0 | 4.76 | 4.83 |
| 2003 | 2 Tms | | 16 | 15 | 0 | 1 | 76.1 | 327 | 89 | 47 | 45 | 11 | 5 | 1 | 1 | 19 | 0 | 42 | 3 | 1 | 5 | 6 | .455 | 0 | 0-0 | 0 | 4.84 | 5.31 |
| 2004 | Cin | NL | 28 | 28 | 1 | 0 | 161.0 | 711 | 177 | 90 | 87 | 26 | 13 | 6 | 5 | 53 | 5 | 125 | 7 | 0 | 10 | 9 | .526 | 1 | 0-0 | 0 | 4.81 | 4.86 |
| 2005 | Cin | NL | 32 | 32 | 1 | 0 | 211.2 | 887 | 217 | 93 | 90 | 22 | 11 | 5 | 8 | 51 | 3 | 163 | 6 | 0 | 11 | 13 | .458 | 0 | 0-0 | 0 | 3.77 | 3.83 |
| 2006 | Cin | NL | 36 | **35** | **6** | 0 | 234.1 | **993** | 242 | 109 | 98 | 28 | **21** | 8 | 8 | 56 | 8 | **216** | 6 | 1 | **16** | 11 | .593 | 2 | 0-0 | 0 | 3.82 | 3.76 |
| 2007 | Cin | NL | 34 | 34 | 2 | 0 | 231.2 | 948 | 213 | 100 | 96 | 28 | 4 | 5 | 8 | 52 | 3 | 218 | **12** | 1 | 16 | 6 | .727 | 1 | 0-0 | 0 | 3.22 | 3.73 |
| 2008 | Cin | NL | 30 | 29 | 1 | 0 | 184.1 | 793 | 205 | 104 | 98 | 35 | 11 | 7 | 2 | 50 | 5 | 153 | 2 | 0 | 6 | **17** | .261 | 1 | 0-0 | 0 | 4.83 | 4.78 |
| 2009 | Cin | NL | 26 | 26 | 2 | 0 | 162.1 | 703 | 186 | 82 | 76 | 24 | 6 | 2 | 4 | 43 | 6 | 142 | 6 | 0 | 6 | 14 | .300 | 1 | 0-0 | 0 | 4.76 | 4.21 |
| 2010 | Cin | NL | 22 | 20 | 0 | 1 | 111.2 | 504 | 139 | 71 | 66 | 16 | 4 | 3 | 4 | 38 | 0 | 82 | 9 | 0 | 6 | 7 | .462 | 0 | 0-0 | 0 | 5.75 | 5.32 |
| 2011 | SD | NL | 28 | 28 | 0 | 0 | 170.2 | 719 | 175 | 73 | 69 | 20 | 5 | 2 | 3 | 58 | 4 | 124 | 3 | 0 | 14 | 7 | .667 | 0 | 0-0 | 0 | 4.22 | 3.64 |
| 2012 | LAD | NL | 31 | 31 | 0 | 0 | 179.2 | 786 | 167 | 85 | 72 | 14 | 9 | **10** | 4 | 85 | **10** | 131 | 4 | 0 | 10 | 10 | .500 | 0 | 0-0 | 0 | 3.76 | 3.61 |
| 2013 | 2 Tms | | 26 | 26 | 2 | 0 | 143.1 | 626 | 153 | 91 | 86 | 26 | 1 | 6 | 6 | 40 | 1 | 113 | 4 | 0 | 5 | 12 | .294 | 2 | 0-0 | 0 | 4.62 | 5.40 |
| 03 | Oak | AL | 7 | 6 | 0 | 1 | 30.1 | 136 | 41 | 19 | 18 | 5 | 2 | 1 | 0 | 9 | 0 | 16 | 0 | 1 | 1 | 3 | .250 | 0 | 0-0 | 0 | 6.32 | 5.34 |
| 03 | Cin | NL | 9 | 9 | 0 | 0 | 46.0 | 191 | 48 | 28 | 27 | 6 | 3 | 0 | 1 | 10 | 0 | 26 | 3 | 0 | 4 | 3 | .571 | 0 | 0-0 | 0 | 3.94 | 5.28 |
| 13 | Sea | AL | 22 | 22 | 2 | 0 | 120.1 | 526 | 133 | 81 | 77 | 21 | 1 | 6 | 5 | 28 | 1 | 87 | 3 | 0 | 5 | 11 | .313 | 2 | 0-0 | 0 | 4.58 | 5.76 |
| 13 | NYM | NL | 4 | 4 | 0 | 0 | 23.0 | 100 | 20 | 10 | 9 | 5 | 0 | 0 | 1 | 12 | 0 | 26 | 1 | 0 | 0 | 1 | .000 | 0 | 0-0 | 0 | 4.84 | 3.52 |
| 12 ML YEARS | | | 325 | 319 | 15 | 2 | 1945.1 | 8351 | 2041 | 989 | 925 | 257 | 93 | 59 | 56 | 590 | 47 | 1573 | 63 | 3 | 110 | 116 | .487 | 8 | 0-0 | 0 | 4.27 | 4.28 |

## J.J. Hardy

**Bats:** R **Throws:** R **Pos:** SS-159 **Ht:** 6'1" **Wt:** 190 **Born:** 8/19/1982 **Age:** 31

| BATTING | | | | | | | | | | | | | | | | | | | | | BASERUNNING | | | | AVERAGES | | |
|---|---|---|---|---|---|---|---|---|---|---|---|---|---|---|---|---|---|---|---|---|---|---|---|---|---|---|---|
| Year Team | Lg | G | AB | H | 2B | 3B | HR | (Hm | Rd) | TB | R | RBI | RC | TBB | IBB | SO | HBP | SH | SF | | SB | CS | SB% | GDP | Avg | OBP | Slg |
| 2005 Mil | NL | 124 | 372 | 92 | 22 | 1 | 9 | (6 | 3) | 143 | 46 | 50 | 49 | 44 | 7 | 48 | 1 | 8 | 2 | | 0 | 0 | - | 10 | .247 | .327 | .384 |
| 2006 Mil | NL | 35 | 128 | 31 | 5 | 0 | 5 | (4 | 1) | 51 | 13 | 14 | 13 | 10 | 0 | 23 | 0 | 0 | 1 | | 1 | 1 | .50 | 4 | .242 | .295 | .398 |
| 2007 Mil | NL | 151 | 592 | 164 | 30 | 1 | 26 | (15 | 11) | 274 | 89 | 80 | 84 | 40 | 1 | 73 | 1 | 4 | 1 | | 2 | 3 | .40 | 13 | .277 | .323 | .463 |
| 2008 Mil | NL | 146 | 569 | 161 | 31 | 4 | 24 | (14 | 10) | 272 | 78 | 74 | 78 | 52 | 3 | 98 | 1 | 5 | 2 | | 2 | 1 | .67 | 18 | .283 | .343 | .478 |
| 2009 Mil | NL | 115 | 414 | 95 | 16 | 2 | 11 | (6 | 5) | 148 | 53 | 47 | 32 | 43 | 0 | 85 | 2 | 1 | 5 | | 0 | 1 | .00 | 14 | .229 | .302 | .357 |
| 2010 Min | AL | 101 | 340 | 91 | 19 | 3 | 6 | (1 | 5) | 134 | 44 | 38 | 41 | 28 | 1 | 54 | 0 | 3 | 4 | | 1 | 1 | .50 | 8 | .268 | .320 | .394 |
| 2011 Bal | AL | 129 | 527 | 142 | 27 | 0 | 30 | (15 | 15) | 259 | 76 | 80 | 78 | 31 | 3 | 92 | 2 | 2 | 5 | | 0 | 0 | - | 10 | .269 | .310 | .491 |
| 2012 Bal | AL | 158 | 663 | 158 | 30 | 2 | 22 | (15 | 7) | 258 | 85 | 68 | 71 | 38 | 4 | 106 | 3 | 7 | 2 | | 0 | 0 | - | 21 | .238 | .282 | .389 |
| 2013 Bal | AL | 159 | 601 | 158 | 27 | 0 | 25 | (11 | 14) | 260 | 66 | 76 | 71 | 38 | 3 | 73 | 0 | 3 | 2 | | 2 | 1 | .67 | 14 | .263 | .306 | .433 |
| Postseason | | 13 | 51 | 12 | 4 | 0 | 0 | (0 | 0) | 16 | 3 | 4 | 4 | 3 | 0 | 7 | 0 | 0 | 0 | | 0 | 0 | - | 1 | .235 | .278 | .314 |
| 9 ML YEARS | | 1118 | 4206 | 1092 | 207 | 13 | 158 | (87 | 71) | 1799 | 550 | 527 | 517 | 324 | 22 | 652 | 10 | 33 | 24 | | 8 | 8 | .50 | 112 | .260 | .312 | .428 |

## Dan Haren

**Pitches:** R **Bats:** R **Pos:** SP-30; RP-1 **Ht:** 6'5" **Wt:** 215 **Born:** 9/17/1980 **Age:** 33

| HOW MUCH HE PITCHED | | | | | | | | WHAT HE GAVE UP | | | | | | | | | | | | THE RESULTS | | | | | | | |
|---|---|---|---|---|---|---|---|---|---|---|---|---|---|---|---|---|---|---|---|---|---|---|---|---|---|---|---|
| Year Team | Lg | G | GS | CG | GF | IP | BFP | H | R | ER | HR | SH | SF | HB | TBB | IBB | SO | WP | Bk | W | L | Pct | Sh | Sv-Op | Hld | ERC | ERA |
| 2003 StL | NL | 14 | 14 | 0 | 0 | 72.2 | 320 | 84 | 44 | 41 | 9 | 4 | 2 | 5 | 22 | 0 | 43 | 3 | 0 | 3 | 7 | .300 | 0 | 0-0 | 0 | 5.07 | 5.08 |
| 2004 StL | NL | 14 | 5 | 0 | 2 | 46.0 | 195 | 45 | 23 | 23 | 4 | 4 | 2 | 2 | 17 | 2 | 32 | 1 | 0 | 3 | 3 | .500 | 0 | 0-0 | 0 | 3.91 | 4.50 |
| 2005 Oak | AL | 34 | 34 | 3 | 0 | 217.0 | 897 | 212 | 101 | 90 | 26 | 3 | 5 | 6 | 53 | 5 | 163 | 6 | 0 | 14 | 12 | .538 | 0 | 0-0 | 0 | 3.58 | 3.73 |
| 2006 Oak | AL | 34 | **34** | 2 | 0 | 223.0 | 930 | 224 | 109 | 102 | 31 | 3 | 3 | 10 | 45 | 6 | 176 | 10 | 0 | 14 | 13 | .519 | 0 | 0-0 | 0 | 3.72 | 4.12 |
| 2007 Oak | AL | 34 | **34** | 0 | 0 | 222.2 | 935 | 214 | 91 | 76 | 24 | 2 | 8 | 3 | 55 | 1 | 192 | 10 | 0 | 15 | 9 | .625 | 0 | 0-0 | 0 | 3.32 | 3.07 |
| 2008 Ari | NL | 33 | 33 | 1 | 0 | 216.0 | 881 | 204 | 86 | 80 | 19 | 7 | 3 | 6 | 40 | 4 | 206 | 11 | 0 | 16 | 8 | .667 | 1 | 0-0 | 0 | 2.96 | 3.33 |
| 2009 Ari | NL | 33 | 33 | 3 | 0 | 229.1 | 909 | 192 | 83 | 80 | 27 | 8 | 3 | 4 | 38 | 2 | 223 | 13 | 0 | 14 | 10 | .583 | 1 | 0-0 | 0 | 2.50 | 3.14 |
| 2010 2 Tms | | 35 | 35 | 2 | 0 | 235.0 | 994 | 245 | 110 | 102 | 31 | 6 | 10 | 5 | 54 | 6 | 216 | 12 | 2 | 12 | 12 | .500 | 0 | 0-0 | 0 | 3.88 | 3.91 |
| 2011 LAA | AL | 35 | **34** | 4 | 1 | 238.1 | 953 | 211 | 91 | 84 | 20 | **12** | 5 | 5 | 33 | 1 | 192 | 6 | 0 | 16 | 10 | .615 | 3 | 0-0 | 0 | 2.45 | 3.17 |
| 2012 LAA | AL | 30 | 30 | 1 | 0 | 176.2 | 747 | 190 | 95 | 85 | 28 | **7** | 8 | 3 | 38 | 3 | 142 | 5 | 1 | 12 | 13 | .480 | 1 | 0-0 | 0 | 4.20 | 4.33 |
| 2013 Was | NL | 31 | 30 | 0 | 1 | 169.2 | 717 | 179 | 92 | 88 | 28 | 8 | 4 | 7 | 31 | 0 | 151 | 8 | 1 | 10 | 14 | .417 | 0 | 1-1 | 0 | 4.09 | 4.67 |
| 10 Ari | NL | 21 | 21 | 1 | 0 | 141.0 | 607 | 161 | 79 | 72 | 23 | 6 | 4 | 3 | 29 | 4 | 141 | 8 | 1 | 7 | 8 | .467 | 0 | 0-0 | 0 | 4.55 | 4.60 |
| 10 LAA | AL | 14 | 14 | 1 | 0 | 94.0 | 387 | 84 | 31 | 30 | 8 | 0 | 6 | 2 | 25 | 2 | 75 | 4 | 1 | 5 | 4 | .556 | 0 | 0-0 | 0 | 2.94 | 2.87 |
| Postseason | | 7 | 2 | 0 | 0 | 19.1 | 86 | 24 | 7 | 7 | 3 | 1 | 0 | 0 | 7 | 0 | 16 | 2 | 0 | 2 | 0 | 1.000 | 0 | 0-0 | 0 | 5.83 | 3.26 |
| 11 ML YEARS | | 327 | 316 | 16 | 4 | 2046.1 | 8478 | 2000 | 925 | 851 | 247 | 64 | 53 | 56 | 426 | 30 | 1736 | 85 | 4 | 129 | 111 | .538 | 6 | 1-1 | 0 | 3.42 | 3.74 |

## Bryce Harper

**Bats:** L **Throws:** R **Pos:** LF-97;RF-16;CF-9;PH-3 **Ht:** 6'2" **Wt:** 230 **Born:** 10/16/1992 **Age:** 21

| BATTING | | | | | | | | | | | | | | | | | | | | | BASERUNNING | | | | AVERAGES | | |
|---|---|---|---|---|---|---|---|---|---|---|---|---|---|---|---|---|---|---|---|---|---|---|---|---|---|---|---|
| Year Team | Lg | G | AB | H | 2B | 3B | HR | (Hm | Rd) | TB | R | RBI | RC | TBB | IBB | SO | HBP | SH | SF | | SB | CS | SB% | GDP | Avg | OBP | Slg |
| 2011 Hgrstn | A | 72 | 258 | 82 | 17 | 1 | 14 | (- | -) | 143 | 49 | 46 | 62 | 44 | 7 | 61 | 3 | 0 | 0 | | 19 | 5 | .79 | 5 | .318 | .423 | .554 |
| 2011 Hrsbrg | AA | 37 | 129 | 33 | 7 | 1 | 3 | (- | -) | 51 | 14 | 12 | 18 | 15 | 0 | 26 | 0 | 1 | 2 | | 7 | 2 | .78 | 4 | .256 | .329 | .395 |
| 2012 Syrcse | AAA | 21 | 74 | 18 | 4 | 1 | 1 | (- | -) | 27 | 8 | 3 | 9 | 9 | 0 | 14 | 0 | 1 | 0 | | 1 | 1 | .50 | 0 | .243 | .325 | .365 |
| 2013 Ptomc | A+ | 2 | 4 | 2 | 1 | 0 | 1 | (- | -) | 6 | 2 | 1 | 2 | 1 | 0 | 1 | 0 | 0 | 0 | | 0 | 0 | - | 0 | .500 | .600 | 1.500 |
| 2013 Hrsbrg | AA | 2 | 7 | 2 | 0 | 1 | 0 | (- | -) | 4 | 3 | 2 | 1 | 2 | 0 | 3 | 0 | 0 | 0 | | 0 | 0 | - | 0 | .286 | .444 | .571 |
| 2012 Was | NL | 139 | 533 | 144 | 26 | 9 | 22 | (10 | 12) | 254 | 98 | 59 | 82 | 56 | 0 | 120 | 2 | 3 | 3 | | 18 | 6 | .75 | 8 | .270 | .340 | .477 |
| 2013 Was | NL | 118 | 424 | 116 | 24 | 3 | 20 | (13 | 7) | 206 | 71 | 58 | 73 | 61 | 4 | 94 | 5 | 3 | 4 | | 11 | 4 | .73 | 4 | .274 | .368 | .486 |
| Postseason | | 5 | 23 | 3 | 1 | 1 | 1 | (1 | 0) | 9 | 2 | 2 | 1 | 0 | 0 | 8 | 0 | 0 | 0 | | 0 | 0 | - | 0 | .130 | .130 | .391 |
| 2 ML YEARS | | 257 | 957 | 260 | 50 | 12 | 42 | (23 | 19) | 460 | 169 | 117 | 155 | 117 | 4 | 214 | 7 | 6 | 7 | | 29 | 10 | .74 | 12 | .272 | .353 | .481 |

2014 106 352 96 10 2 13 149 41 32 38 104 2 273 341 423

## Lucas Harrell

**Pitches:** R **Bats:** B **Pos:** SP-22; RP-14 HAH-rell **Ht:** 6'2" **Wt:** 210 **Born:** 6/3/1985 **Age:** 29

| HOW MUCH HE PITCHED | | | | | | | | WHAT HE GAVE UP | | | | | | | | | | | | THE RESULTS | | | | | | | |
|---|---|---|---|---|---|---|---|---|---|---|---|---|---|---|---|---|---|---|---|---|---|---|---|---|---|---|---|
| Year Team | Lg | G | GS | CG | GF | IP | BFP | H | R | ER | HR | SH | SF | HB | TBB | IBB | SO | WP | Bk | W | L | Pct | Sh | Sv-Op | Hld | ERC | ERA |
| 2010 CWS | AL | 8 | 3 | 0 | 3 | 24.0 | 119 | 34 | 18 | 13 | 2 | 1 | 0 | 0 | 17 | 1 | 15 | 1 | 0 | 1 | 0 | 1.000 | 0 | 0-0 | 0 | 7.77 | 4.88 |
| 2011 2 Tms | | 9 | 2 | 0 | 2 | 18.0 | 86 | 23 | 12 | 9 | 0 | 1 | 1 | 1 | 8 | 0 | 15 | 1 | 1 | 0 | 2 | .000 | 0 | 0-0 | 0 | 5.16 | 4.50 |
| 2012 Hou | NL | 32 | 32 | 1 | 0 | 193.2 | 827 | 185 | 90 | 81 | 13 | 8 | **10** | 1 | 78 | 5 | 140 | 10 | 3 | 11 | 11 | .500 | 1 | 0-0 | 0 | 3.59 | 3.76 |
| 2013 Hou | AL | 36 | 22 | 0 | 8 | 153.2 | 707 | 174 | 111 | 100 | 20 | 6 | 5 | 6 | **88** | 5 | 89 | 8 | 0 | 6 | **17** | .261 | 0 | 0-1 | 0 | 5.95 | 5.86 |
| 11 CWS | AL | 3 | 0 | 0 | 2 | 5.0 | 26 | 11 | 4 | 4 | 0 | 0 | 0 | 0 | 1 | 0 | 5 | 0 | 0 | 0 | 0 | - | 0 | 0-0 | 0 | 10.11 | 7.20 |
| 11 Hou | NL | 6 | 2 | 0 | 0 | 13.0 | 60 | 12 | 8 | 5 | 0 | 1 | 1 | 1 | 7 | 0 | 10 | 1 | 1 | 0 | 2 | .000 | 0 | 0-0 | 0 | 3.57 | 3.46 |
| 4 ML YEARS | | 85 | 59 | 1 | 13 | 389.1 | 1739 | 416 | 231 | 203 | 35 | 16 | 16 | 8 | 191 | 11 | 259 | 20 | 4 | 18 | 30 | .375 | 1 | 0-1 | 0 | 4.80 | 4.69 |

## Brendan Harris

**Bats:** R **Throws:** R **Pos:** SS-21;PH-8;3B-7;1B-6;2B-6;PR-3;LF-1;DH-1 **Ht:** 6'1" **Wt:** 200 **Born:** 8/26/1980 **Age:** 33

| BATTING | | | | | | | | | | | | | | | | | | | | | BASERUNNING | | | | AVERAGES | | |
|---|---|---|---|---|---|---|---|---|---|---|---|---|---|---|---|---|---|---|---|---|---|---|---|---|---|---|---|
| Year Team | Lg | G | AB | H | 2B | 3B | HR | (Hm | Rd) | TB | R | RBI | RC | TBB | IBB | SO | HBP | SH | SF | | SB | CS | SB% | GDP | Avg | OBP | Slg |
| 2013 S-WB* | AAA | 22 | 73 | 17 | 3 | 0 | 1 | (- | -) | 23 | 9 | 4 | 9 | 13 | 0 | 12 | 1 | 0 | 0 | | 0 | 0 | - | 2 | .233 | .356 | .315 |
| 2013 RdRck* | AAA | 12 | 41 | 10 | 0 | 0 | 2 | (- | -) | 16 | 7 | 5 | 6 | 7 | 0 | 7 | 1 | 0 | 0 | | 0 | 0 | - | 3 | .244 | .367 | .390 |
| 2004 2 Tms | NL | 23 | 59 | 10 | 3 | 0 | 1 | (0 | 1) | 16 | 4 | 3 | 2 | 3 | 0 | 12 | 1 | 0 | 0 | | 0 | 0 | - | 0 | .169 | .222 | .271 |
| 2005 Was | NL | 4 | 9 | 3 | 1 | 0 | 1 | (0 | 1) | 7 | 1 | 3 | 3 | 0 | 0 | 0 | 1 | 0 | 0 | | 0 | 0 | - | 2 | .333 | .400 | .778 |
| 2006 2 Tms | NL | 25 | 42 | 10 | 2 | 0 | 1 | (1 | 0) | 15 | 5 | 3 | 4 | 4 | 0 | 7 | 1 | 0 | 0 | | 0 | 0 | - | 2 | .238 | .319 | .357 |
| 2007 TB | AL | 137 | 521 | 149 | 35 | 3 | 12 | (5 | 7) | 226 | 72 | 59 | 70 | 42 | 1 | 96 | 4 | 8 | 1 | | 4 | 1 | .80 | 19 | .286 | .343 | .434 |
| 2008 Min | AL | 130 | 434 | 115 | 29 | 3 | 7 | (3 | 4) | 171 | 57 | 49 | 52 | 39 | 0 | 98 | 4 | 7 | 6 | | 1 | 1 | .50 | 13 | .265 | .327 | .394 |
| 2009 Min | AL | 123 | 414 | 108 | 22 | 1 | 6 | (5 | 1) | 150 | 44 | 37 | 43 | 29 | 0 | 78 | 3 | 1 | 6 | | 0 | 2 | .00 | 16 | .261 | .310 | .362 |
| 2010 Min | AL | 43 | 108 | 17 | 3 | 0 | 1 | (0 | 1) | 23 | 11 | 4 | 4 | 9 | 0 | 23 | 2 | 0 | 1 | | 0 | 0 | - | 2 | .157 | .233 | .213 |
| 2013 LAA | AL | 44 | 107 | 22 | 4 | 0 | 4 | (0 | 4) | 38 | 14 | 9 | 8 | 6 | 0 | 29 | 1 | 2 | 1 | | 0 | 1 | .00 | 2 | .206 | .252 | .355 |
| 04 ChC | NL | 3 | 9 | 2 | 1 | 0 | 0 | (0 | 0) | 3 | 0 | 1 | 1 | 1 | 0 | 1 | 0 | 0 | 0 | | 0 | 0 | - | 0 | .222 | .300 | .333 |
| 04 Mon | NL | 20 | 50 | 8 | 2 | 0 | 1 | (0 | 1) | 13 | 4 | 2 | 1 | 2 | 0 | 11 | 1 | 0 | 0 | | 0 | 0 | - | 0 | .160 | .208 | .260 |

| BATTING | | | | | | | | | | | | | | | | | | | | BASERUNNING | | | | AVERAGES | | |
|---|---|---|---|---|---|---|---|---|---|---|---|---|---|---|---|---|---|---|---|---|---|---|---|---|---|---|
| Year Team Lg | G | AB | H | 2B | 3B | HR | (Hm | Rd) | TB | R | RBI | RC | TBB | IBB | SO | HBP | SH | SF | SB | CS | SB% | GDP | Avg | OBP | Slg |
| 06 Was NL | 17 | 32 | 8 | 2 | 0 | 0 | (0 | 0) | 10 | 3 | 2 | 3 | 3 | 0 | 3 | 1 | 0 | 0 | 0 | 0 | - | 1 | .250 | .333 | .313 |
| 06 Cin NL | 8 | 10 | 2 | 0 | 0 | 1 | (1 | 0) | 5 | 2 | 1 | 1 | 1 | 0 | 4 | 0 | 0 | 0 | 0 | 0 | - | 1 | .200 | .273 | .500 |
| Postseason | 3 | 12 | 3 | 0 | 1 | 0 | (0 | 0) | 5 | 1 | 1 | 1 | 0 | 0 | 3 | 0 | 0 | 0 | 0 | 0 | - | 0 | .250 | .250 | .417 |
| 8 ML YEARS | 529 | 1694 | 434 | 99 | 7 | 33 | (14 | 19) | 646 | 208 | 167 | 186 | 132 | 1 | 343 | 17 | 18 | 15 | 5 | 5 | .50 | 56 | .256 | .314 | .381 |

## Will Harris

**Pitches:** R **Bats:** R **Pos:** RP-61 **Ht:** 6'4" **Wt:** 225 **Born:** 8/28/1984 **Age:** 29

| HOW MUCH HE PITCHED | | | | | | | WHAT HE GAVE UP | | | | | | | | | | | | THE RESULTS | | | | | | | |
|---|---|---|---|---|---|---|---|---|---|---|---|---|---|---|---|---|---|---|---|---|---|---|---|---|---|---|
| Year Team Lg | G | GS | CG | GF | IP | BFP | H | R | ER | HR | SH | SF | HB | TBB | IBB | SO | WP | Bk | W | L | Pct | Sh | Sv-Op | Hld | ERC | ERA |
| 2009 TriCity A- | 1 | 0 | 0 | 0 | 1.0 | 4 | 1 | 0 | 0 | 0 | 0 | 0 | 0 | 0 | 0 | 2 | 0 | 0 | 0 | 0 | - | 0 | 0-- | - | 1.95 | 0.00 |
| 2011 Mdest A+ | 33 | 0 | 0 | 15 | 47.0 | 202 | 45 | 29 | 29 | 4 | 4 | 0 | 0 | 21 | 1 | 55 | 4 | 0 | 3 | 2 | .600 | 0 | 0-- | - | 3.90 | 5.55 |
| 2012 Tulsa AA | 31 | 0 | 0 | 6 | 34.1 | 140 | 26 | 12 | 10 | 2 | 0 | 0 | 1 | 12 | 0 | 46 | 1 | 0 | 2 | 1 | .667 | 0 | 1-- | - | 2.45 | 2.62 |
| 2012 ColSpr AAA | 13 | 0 | 0 | 5 | 17.2 | 63 | 9 | 2 | 2 | 0 | 0 | 0 | 0 | 1 | 0 | 20 | 1 | 0 | 2 | 0 | 1.000 | 0 | 0-- | - | 0.64 | 1.02 |
| 2013 Reno AAA | 12 | 0 | 0 | 11 | 11.2 | 55 | 12 | 7 | 6 | 1 | 0 | 0 | 0 | 6 | 0 | 23 | 0 | 0 | 0 | 0 | - | 0 | 2-- | - | 4.29 | 4.63 |
| 2012 Col NL | 20 | 0 | 0 | 10 | 17.2 | 89 | 27 | 18 | 16 | 3 | 2 | 1 | 1 | 6 | 1 | 19 | 4 | 0 | 1 | 1 | .500 | 0 | 0-0 | 3 | 7.39 | 8.15 |
| 2013 Ari NL | 61 | 0 | 0 | 11 | 52.2 | 217 | 50 | 17 | 17 | 3 | 0 | 4 | 2 | 15 | 1 | 53 | 4 | 0 | 4 | 1 | .800 | 0 | 0-1 | 4 | 3.25 | 2.91 |
| 2 ML YEARS | 81 | 0 | 0 | 21 | 70.1 | 306 | 77 | 35 | 33 | 6 | 2 | 5 | 3 | 21 | 2 | 72 | 8 | 0 | 5 | 2 | .714 | 0 | 0-1 | 7 | 4.21 | 4.22 |

## Josh Harrison

**Bats:** R **Throws:** R **Pos:** PH-30;RF-14;2B-11;3B-7;PR-7;SS-4;LF-1;DH-1 **Ht:** 5'8" **Wt:** 200 **Born:** 7/8/1987 **Age:** 26

| BATTING | | | | | | | | | | | | | | | | | | | | BASERUNNING | | | | AVERAGES | | |
|---|---|---|---|---|---|---|---|---|---|---|---|---|---|---|---|---|---|---|---|---|---|---|---|---|---|---|
| Year Team Lg | G | AB | H | 2B | 3B | HR | (Hm | Rd) | TB | R | RBI | RC | TBB | IBB | SO | HBP | SH | SF | SB | CS | SB% | GDP | Avg | OBP | Slg |
| 2013 Indy* AAA | 64 | 268 | 85 | 29 | 5 | 4 | (- | -) | 136 | 50 | 34 | 51 | 20 | 0 | 39 | 4 | 4 | 0 | 19 | 7 | .73 | 9 | .317 | .373 | .507 |
| 2011 Pit NL | 65 | 195 | 53 | 13 | 2 | 1 | (1 | 0) | 73 | 21 | 16 | 19 | 3 | 0 | 24 | 0 | 5 | 1 | 4 | 1 | .80 | 6 | .272 | .281 | .374 |
| 2012 Pit NL | 104 | 249 | 58 | 9 | 5 | 3 | (1 | 2) | 86 | 34 | 16 | 22 | 10 | 0 | 37 | 7 | 7 | 3 | 7 | 3 | .70 | 3 | .233 | .279 | .345 |
| 2013 Pit NL | 60 | 88 | 22 | 1 | 2 | 3 | (1 | 2) | 36 | 10 | 14 | 11 | 2 | 0 | 10 | 3 | 2 | 0 | 2 | 0 | 1.00 | 4 | .250 | .290 | .409 |
| 3 ML YEARS | 229 | 532 | 133 | 23 | 9 | 7 | (3 | 4) | 195 | 65 | 46 | 52 | 15 | 0 | 71 | 10 | 14 | 4 | 13 | 4 | .76 | 13 | .250 | .282 | .367 |

## Matt Harrison

**Pitches:** L **Bats:** L **Pos:** SP-2 **Ht:** 6'4" **Wt:** 250 **Born:** 9/16/1985 **Age:** 28

| HOW MUCH HE PITCHED | | | | | | | WHAT HE GAVE UP | | | | | | | | | | | | THE RESULTS | | | | | | | |
|---|---|---|---|---|---|---|---|---|---|---|---|---|---|---|---|---|---|---|---|---|---|---|---|---|---|---|
| Year Team Lg | G | GS | CG | GF | IP | BFP | H | R | ER | HR | SH | SF | HB | TBB | IBB | SO | WP | Bk | W | L | Pct | Sh | Sv-Op | Hld | ERC | ERA |
| 2013 Frisco* AA | 2 | 2 | 0 | 0 | 5.0 | 21 | 5 | 1 | 1 | 0 | 0 | 0 | 0 | 2 | 0 | 5 | 0 | 0 | 0 | 1 | .000 | 0 | 0-- | - | 3.46 | 1.80 |
| 2013 RdRck* AAA | 1 | 1 | 0 | 0 | 3.0 | 15 | 3 | 4 | 3 | 1 | 0 | 0 | 0 | 2 | 0 | 0 | 0 | 0 | 0 | 1 | .000 | 0 | 0-- | - | 6.35 | 9.00 |
| 2008 Tex AL | 15 | 15 | 1 | 0 | 83.2 | 372 | 100 | 57 | 51 | 12 | 1 | 5 | 2 | 31 | 2 | 42 | 2 | 2 | 9 | 3 | .750 | 1 | 0-0 | 0 | 5.53 | 5.49 |
| 2009 Tex AL | 11 | 11 | 2 | 0 | 63.1 | 283 | 81 | 43 | 43 | 9 | 1 | 1 | 2 | 23 | 0 | 34 | 0 | 0 | 4 | 5 | .444 | 1 | 0-0 | 0 | 6.17 | 6.11 |
| 2010 Tex AL | 37 | 6 | 0 | 9 | 78.1 | 356 | 80 | 45 | 41 | 10 | 2 | 8 | 2 | 39 | 3 | 46 | 4 | 0 | 3 | 2 | .600 | 0 | 2-3 | 3 | 4.71 | 4.71 |
| 2011 Tex AL | 31 | 30 | 0 | 0 | 185.2 | 772 | 180 | 79 | 70 | 13 | 8 | 5 | 1 | 57 | 1 | 126 | 6 | 1 | 14 | 9 | .609 | 0 | 0-0 | 0 | 3.40 | 3.39 |
| 2012 Tex AL | 32 | 32 | 4 | 0 | 213.1 | 876 | 210 | 82 | 78 | 22 | 1 | 2 | 1 | 59 | 0 | 133 | 2 | 0 | 18 | 11 | .621 | 2 | 0-0 | 0 | 3.63 | 3.29 |
| 2013 Tex AL | 2 | 2 | 0 | 0 | 10.2 | 51 | 14 | 11 | 10 | 2 | 0 | 1 | 0 | 7 | 2 | 12 | 0 | 0 | 0 | 2 | .000 | 0 | 0-0 | 0 | 7.54 | 8.44 |
| Postseason | 5 | 4 | 0 | 0 | 18.1 | 83 | 20 | 13 | 11 | 2 | 0 | 0 | 0 | 9 | 1 | 16 | 1 | 0 | 1 | 2 | .333 | 0 | 0-0 | 0 | 4.88 | 5.40 |
| 6 ML YEARS | 128 | 96 | 7 | 9 | 635.0 | 2710 | 665 | 317 | 293 | 68 | 13 | 22 | 8 | 216 | 8 | 393 | 14 | 3 | 48 | 32 | .600 | 4 | 2-3 | 3 | 4.23 | 4.15 |

## Corey Hart

**Bats:** R **Throws:** R **Pos:** 1B **Ht:** 6'6" **Wt:** 235 **Born:** 3/24/1982 **Age:** 32

| BATTING | | | | | | | | | | | | | | | | | | | | BASERUNNING | | | | AVERAGES | | |
|---|---|---|---|---|---|---|---|---|---|---|---|---|---|---|---|---|---|---|---|---|---|---|---|---|---|---|
| Year Team Lg | G | AB | H | 2B | 3B | HR | (Hm | Rd) | TB | R | RBI | RC | TBB | IBB | SO | HBP | SH | SF | SB | CS | SB% | GDP | Avg | OBP | Slg |
| 2004 Mil NL | 1 | 1 | 0 | 0 | 0 | 0 | (0 | 0) | 0 | 0 | 0 | 0 | 0 | 0 | 1 | 0 | 0 | 0 | 0 | 0 | - | 0 | .000 | .000 | .000 |
| 2005 Mil NL | 21 | 57 | 11 | 2 | 1 | 2 | (2 | 0) | 21 | 9 | 7 | 4 | 6 | 0 | 11 | 0 | 0 | 0 | 2 | 0 | 1.00 | 6 | .193 | .270 | .368 |
| 2006 Mil NL | 87 | 237 | 67 | 13 | 2 | 9 | (6 | 3) | 111 | 32 | 33 | 30 | 17 | 1 | 58 | 0 | 0 | 2 | 5 | 8 | .38 | 7 | .283 | .328 | .468 |
| 2007 Mil NL | 140 | 505 | 149 | 33 | 9 | 24 | (15 | 9) | 272 | 86 | 81 | 94 | 36 | 3 | 99 | 13 | 5 | 7 | 23 | 7 | .77 | 6 | .295 | .353 | .539 |
| 2008 Mil NL | 157 | 612 | 164 | 45 | 6 | 20 | (7 | 13) | 281 | 76 | 91 | 81 | 27 | 2 | 109 | 5 | 4 | 9 | 23 | 7 | .77 | 17 | .268 | .300 | .459 |
| 2009 Mil NL | 115 | 419 | 109 | 24 | 3 | 12 | (9 | 3) | 175 | 64 | 48 | 51 | 43 | 0 | 92 | 6 | 1 | 3 | 11 | 6 | .65 | 9 | .260 | .335 | .418 |
| 2010 Mil NL | 145 | 558 | 158 | 34 | 4 | 31 | (16 | 15) | 293 | 91 | 102 | 83 | 45 | 2 | 140 | 6 | 0 | 5 | 7 | 6 | .54 | 14 | .283 | .340 | .525 |
| 2011 Mil NL | 130 | 492 | 140 | 25 | 4 | 26 | (17 | 9) | 251 | 80 | 63 | 79 | 51 | 1 | 114 | 4 | 3 | 1 | 7 | 6 | .54 | 12 | .285 | .356 | .510 |
| 2012 Mil NL | 149 | 562 | 152 | 35 | 4 | 30 | (22 | 8) | 285 | 91 | 83 | 87 | 44 | 5 | 151 | 11 | 2 | 3 | 5 | 0 | 1.00 | 13 | .270 | .334 | .507 |
| Postseason | 14 | 54 | 13 | 0 | 0 | 2 | (1 | 1) | 19 | 6 | 5 | 4 | 3 | 0 | 11 | 1 | 1 | 1 | 0 | 0 | - | 1 | .241 | .288 | .352 |
| 9 ML YEARS | 945 | 3443 | 950 | 211 | 33 | 154 | (94 | 60) | 1689 | 529 | 508 | 509 | 269 | 14 | 775 | 45 | 15 | 30 | 83 | 40 | .67 | 84 | .276 | .334 | .491 |

## Matt Harvey

**Pitches:** R **Bats:** R **Pos:** SP-26 **Ht:** 6'4" **Wt:** 225 **Born:** 3/27/1989 **Age:** 25

| HOW MUCH HE PITCHED | | | | | | | WHAT HE GAVE UP | | | | | | | | | | | | THE RESULTS | | | | | | | |
|---|---|---|---|---|---|---|---|---|---|---|---|---|---|---|---|---|---|---|---|---|---|---|---|---|---|---|
| Year Team Lg | G | GS | CG | GF | IP | BFP | H | R | ER | HR | SH | SF | HB | TBB | IBB | SO | WP | Bk | W | L | Pct | Sh | Sv-Op | Hld | ERC | ERA |
| 2011 StLuci A+ | 14 | 14 | 0 | 0 | 76.0 | 308 | 67 | 24 | 20 | 5 | 1 | 0 | 2 | 24 | 0 | 92 | 1 | 0 | 8 | 2 | .800 | 0 | 0-- | - | 3.07 | 2.37 |
| 2011 Bnghtn AA | 12 | 12 | 0 | 0 | 59.2 | 259 | 59 | 32 | 31 | 4 | 3 | 2 | 3 | 23 | 0 | 64 | 5 | 0 | 5 | 3 | .625 | 0 | 0-- | - | 3.91 | 4.68 |
| 2012 Buffalo AAA | 20 | 20 | 0 | 0 | 110.0 | 473 | 97 | 46 | 45 | 9 | 2 | 1 | 6 | 48 | 1 | 112 | 9 | 0 | 7 | 5 | .583 | 0 | 0-- | - | 3.62 | 3.68 |
| 2012 NYM NL | 10 | 10 | 0 | 0 | 59.1 | 245 | 42 | 19 | 18 | 5 | 3 | 3 | 3 | 26 | 0 | 70 | 3 | 0 | 3 | 5 | .375 | 0 | 0-0 | 0 | 2.75 | 2.73 |
| 2013 NYM NL | 26 | 26 | 1 | 0 | 178.1 | 690 | 135 | 46 | 45 | 7 | 5 | 4 | 4 | 31 | 1 | 191 | 2 | 0 | 9 | 5 | .643 | 1 | 0-0 | 0 | 1.76 | 2.27 |
| 2 ML YEARS | 36 | 36 | 1 | 0 | 237.2 | 935 | 177 | 65 | 63 | 12 | 8 | 7 | 7 | 57 | 1 | 261 | 5 | 0 | 12 | 10 | .545 | 1 | 0-0 | 0 | 2.00 | 2.39 |

## Chris Hatcher

**Pitches:** R **Bats:** B **Pos:** RP-7 **Ht:** 6'1" **Wt:** 205 **Born:** 1/12/1985 **Age:** 29

| HOW MUCH HE PITCHED | | | | | | | | | WHAT HE GAVE UP | | | | | | | | | | | | THE RESULTS | | | | | | | |
|---|---|---|---|---|---|---|---|---|---|---|---|---|---|---|---|---|---|---|---|---|---|---|---|---|---|---|---|---|
| Year | Team | Lg | G | GS | CG | GF | IP | BFP | H | R | ER | HR | SH | SF | HB | TBB | IBB | SO | WP | Bk | W | L | Pct | Sh | Sv-Op | Hld | ERC | ERA |
| 2013 | NewOr* | AAA | 60 | 0 | 0 | 55 | 67.1 | 296 | 69 | 27 | 27 | 8 | 3 | 1 | 1 | 28 | 5 | 65 | 3 | 0 | 4 | 3 | .571 | 0 | 33- - | - | 4.31 | 3.61 |
| 2011 | Fla | NL | 11 | 0 | 0 | 4 | 10.1 | 48 | 14 | 8 | 8 | 2 | 0 | 3 | 0 | 4 | 1 | 8 | 2 | 0 | 0 | 0 | - | 0 | 0-0 | 0 | 6.69 | 6.97 |
| 2012 | Mia | NL | 11 | 0 | 0 | 7 | 14.2 | 66 | 17 | 9 | 7 | 3 | 0 | 0 | 1 | 6 | 0 | 10 | 1 | 0 | 0 | 0 | - | 0 | 0-0 | 0 | 6.19 | 4.30 |
| 2013 | Mia | NL | 7 | 0 | 0 | 2 | 8.2 | 44 | 13 | 13 | 12 | 1 | 0 | 0 | 0 | 4 | 1 | 7 | 0 | 0 | 0 | 1 | .000 | 0 | 0-0 | 0 | 6.92 | 12.46 |
| 3 ML YEARS | | | 29 | 0 | 0 | 13 | 33.2 | 158 | 44 | 30 | 27 | 6 | 0 | 3 | 1 | 14 | 2 | 25 | 3 | 0 | 0 | 1 | .000 | 0 | 0-0 | 0 | 6.54 | 7.22 |

## LaTroy Hawkins

**Pitches:** R **Bats:** R **Pos:** RP-72 **Ht:** 6'5" **Wt:** 220 **Born:** 12/21/1972 **Age:** 41

| HOW MUCH HE PITCHED | | | | | | | | | WHAT HE GAVE UP | | | | | | | | | | | | THE RESULTS | | | | | | | |
|---|---|---|---|---|---|---|---|---|---|---|---|---|---|---|---|---|---|---|---|---|---|---|---|---|---|---|---|---|
| Year | Team | Lg | G | GS | CG | GF | IP | BFP | H | R | ER | HR | SH | SF | HB | TBB | IBB | SO | WP | Bk | W | L | Pct | Sh | Sv-Op | Hld | ERC | ERA |
| 1995 | Min | AL | 6 | 6 | 1 | 0 | 27.0 | 131 | 39 | 29 | 26 | 3 | 0 | 3 | 1 | 12 | 0 | 9 | 1 | 1 | 2 | 3 | .400 | 0 | 0-0 | 0 | 7.14 | 8.67 |
| 1996 | Min | AL | 7 | 6 | 0 | 1 | 26.1 | 124 | 42 | 24 | 24 | 8 | 1 | 1 | 0 | 9 | 0 | 24 | 1 | 1 | 1 | 1 | .500 | 0 | 0-0 | 0 | 9.49 | 8.20 |
| 1997 | Min | AL | 20 | 20 | 0 | 0 | 103.1 | 478 | 134 | 71 | 67 | 19 | 2 | 2 | 4 | 47 | 0 | 58 | 6 | 3 | 6 | 12 | .333 | 0 | 0-0 | 0 | 7.01 | 5.84 |
| 1998 | Min | AL | 33 | 33 | 0 | 0 | 190.1 | 840 | 227 | 126 | 111 | 27 | 4 | 10 | 5 | 61 | 1 | 105 | 10 | 2 | 7 | 14 | .333 | 0 | 0-0 | 0 | 5.31 | 5.25 |
| 1999 | Min | AL | 33 | 33 | 1 | 0 | 174.1 | 803 | 238 | **136** | **129** | 29 | 1 | 5 | 1 | 60 | 2 | 103 | 9 | 0 | 10 | 14 | .417 | 0 | 0-0 | 0 | 6.55 | 6.66 |
| 2000 | Min | AL | 66 | 0 | 0 | 38 | 87.2 | 370 | 85 | 34 | 33 | 7 | 4 | 1 | 1 | 32 | 1 | 59 | 6 | 0 | 2 | 5 | .286 | 0 | 14-14 | 7 | 3.70 | 3.39 |
| 2001 | Min | AL | 62 | 0 | 0 | 51 | 51.1 | 248 | 59 | 34 | 34 | 3 | 1 | 4 | 1 | 39 | 3 | 36 | 7 | 0 | 1 | 5 | .167 | 0 | 28-37 | 1 | 6.02 | 5.96 |
| 2002 | Min | AL | 65 | 0 | 0 | 15 | 80.1 | 310 | 63 | 23 | 19 | 5 | 2 | 3 | 0 | 15 | 1 | 63 | 5 | 0 | 6 | 0 | 1.000 | 0 | 0-3 | 13 | 1.99 | 2.13 |
| 2003 | Min | AL | 74 | 0 | 0 | 12 | 77.1 | 310 | 69 | 20 | 16 | 4 | 4 | 1 | 1 | 15 | 1 | 75 | 5 | 0 | 9 | 3 | .750 | 0 | 2-8 | 28 | 2.48 | 1.86 |
| 2004 | ChC | NL | 77 | 0 | 0 | 50 | 82.0 | 333 | 72 | 27 | 24 | 10 | 6 | 2 | 2 | 14 | 5 | 69 | 2 | 0 | 5 | 4 | .556 | 0 | 25-34 | 4 | 2.66 | 2.63 |
| 2005 | 2 Tms | NL | 66 | 0 | 0 | 21 | 56.1 | 247 | 58 | 27 | 24 | 7 | 3 | 1 | 0 | 24 | 3 | 43 | 1 | 0 | 2 | 8 | .200 | 0 | 6-15 | 15 | 4.41 | 3.83 |
| 2006 | Bal | AL | 60 | 0 | 0 | 12 | 60.1 | 261 | 73 | 30 | 30 | 4 | 1 | 2 | 0 | 15 | 3 | 27 | 2 | 0 | 3 | 2 | .600 | 0 | 0-4 | 16 | 4.37 | 4.48 |
| 2007 | Col | NL | 62 | 0 | 0 | 10 | 55.1 | 225 | 52 | 21 | 21 | 6 | 2 | 1 | 0 | 16 | 1 | 29 | 2 | 0 | 2 | 5 | .286 | 0 | 0-5 | 18 | 3.43 | 3.42 |
| 2008 | 2 Tms | | 57 | 0 | 0 | 15 | 62.0 | 252 | 53 | 29 | 27 | 3 | 1 | 3 | 0 | 22 | 4 | 48 | 3 | 0 | 3 | 1 | .750 | 0 | 1-2 | 13 | 2.75 | 3.92 |
| 2009 | Hou | NL | 65 | 0 | 0 | 34 | 63.1 | 259 | 60 | 16 | 15 | 7 | 2 | 2 | 2 | 16 | 2 | 45 | 2 | 0 | 1 | 4 | .200 | 0 | 11-15 | 19 | 3.42 | 2.13 |
| 2010 | Mil | NL | 18 | 0 | 0 | 5 | 16.0 | 74 | 21 | 15 | 15 | 2 | 1 | 0 | 2 | 6 | 1 | 18 | 1 | 0 | 0 | 3 | .000 | 0 | 0-2 | 6 | 6.55 | 8.44 |
| 2011 | Mil | NL | 52 | 0 | 0 | 10 | 48.1 | 204 | 50 | 15 | 13 | 1 | 1 | 1 | 0 | 10 | 1 | 28 | 2 | 0 | 3 | 1 | .750 | 0 | 0-0 | 20 | 2.91 | 2.42 |
| 2012 | LAA | AL | 48 | 0 | 0 | 7 | 42.0 | 178 | 45 | 20 | 17 | 5 | 3 | 1 | 0 | 13 | 1 | 23 | 0 | 0 | 2 | 3 | .400 | 0 | 1-4 | 6 | 4.27 | 3.64 |
| 2013 | NYM | NL | 72 | 0 | 0 | 28 | 70.2 | 288 | 71 | 27 | 23 | 6 | 3 | 5 | 1 | 10 | 2 | 55 | 1 | 0 | 3 | 2 | .600 | 0 | 13-16 | 12 | 3.03 | 2.93 |
| 05 | ChC | NL | 21 | 0 | 0 | 12 | 19.0 | 80 | 18 | 9 | 7 | 4 | 1 | 0 | 0 | 7 | 0 | 13 | 0 | 0 | 1 | 4 | .200 | 0 | 4-8 | 0 | 4.44 | 3.32 |
| 05 | SF | NL | 45 | 0 | 0 | 9 | 37.1 | 167 | 40 | 18 | 17 | 3 | 2 | 1 | 0 | 17 | 3 | 30 | 1 | 0 | 1 | 4 | .200 | 0 | 2-7 | 15 | 4.36 | 4.10 |
| 08 | NYY | AL | 33 | 0 | 0 | 11 | 41.0 | 173 | 42 | 26 | 26 | 3 | 1 | 2 | 0 | 17 | 3 | 23 | 2 | 0 | 1 | 1 | .500 | 0 | 0-1 | 1 | 4.09 | 5.71 |
| 08 | Hou | NL | 24 | 0 | 0 | 4 | 21.0 | 79 | 11 | 3 | 1 | 0 | 0 | 1 | 0 | 5 | 1 | 25 | 1 | 0 | 2 | 0 | 1.000 | 0 | 1-1 | 12 | 0.95 | 0.43 |
| Postseason | | | 19 | 0 | 0 | 4 | 15.2 | 65 | 13 | 7 | 6 | 0 | 3 | 1 | 0 | 6 | 1 | 17 | 0 | 0 | 1 | 0 | 1.000 | 0 | 0-0 | 4 | 2.35 | 3.45 |
| 19 ML YEARS | | | 943 | 98 | 2 | 309 | 1374.1 | 5935 | 1511 | 724 | 668 | 156 | 42 | 48 | 21 | 436 | 32 | 917 | 66 | 7 | 68 | 90 | .430 | 0 | 101-159 | 178 | 4.45 | 4.37 |

## Brad Hawpe

**Bats:** L **Throws:** L **Pos:** 1B-7;RF-5;PH-3;PR-2;LF-1;DH-1 HOP **Ht:** 6'2" **Wt:** 190 **Born:** 6/22/1979 **Age:** 35

| BATTING | | | | | | | | | | | | | | | | | | | | | BASERUNNING | | | | AVERAGES | | |
|---|---|---|---|---|---|---|---|---|---|---|---|---|---|---|---|---|---|---|---|---|---|---|---|---|---|---|---|
| Year | Team | Lg | G | AB | H | 2B | 3B | HR | (Hm | Rd) | TB | R | RBI | RC | TBB | IBB | SO | HBP | SH | SF | SB | CS | SB% | GDP | Avg | OBP | Slg |
| 2013 | Salt Lk* | AAA | 37 | 131 | 40 | 8 | 0 | 6 | (- | -) | 66 | 21 | 28 | 27 | 21 | 0 | 40 | 1 | 0 | 0 | 1 | 1 | .50 | 2 | .305 | .405 | .504 |
| 2004 | Col | NL | 42 | 105 | 26 | 3 | 2 | 3 | (1 | 2) | 42 | 12 | 9 | 11 | 11 | 3 | 34 | 1 | 0 | 1 | 1 | 1 | .50 | 4 | .248 | .322 | .400 |
| 2005 | Col | NL | 101 | 305 | 80 | 10 | 3 | 9 | (5 | 4) | 123 | 38 | 47 | 44 | 43 | 3 | 70 | 0 | 0 | 3 | 2 | 2 | .50 | 5 | .262 | .350 | .403 |
| 2006 | Col | NL | 150 | 499 | 146 | 33 | 6 | 22 | (6 | 16) | 257 | 67 | 84 | 85 | 74 | 11 | 123 | 0 | 0 | 2 | 5 | 5 | .50 | 8 | .293 | .383 | .515 |
| 2007 | Col | NL | 152 | 516 | 150 | 33 | 4 | 29 | (19 | 10) | 278 | 80 | 116 | 103 | 81 | 11 | 137 | 3 | 1 | 5 | 0 | 2 | .00 | 13 | .291 | .387 | .539 |
| 2008 | Col | NL | 138 | 488 | 138 | 24 | 3 | 25 | (14 | 11) | 243 | 69 | 85 | 86 | 76 | 6 | 134 | 3 | 0 | 2 | 2 | 2 | .50 | 7 | .283 | .381 | .498 |
| 2009 | Col | NL | 145 | 501 | 143 | 42 | 3 | 23 | (9 | 14) | 260 | 82 | 86 | 91 | 79 | 7 | 145 | 4 | 0 | 4 | 1 | 3 | .25 | 18 | .285 | .384 | .519 |
| 2010 | 2 Tms | | 103 | 298 | 73 | 21 | 2 | 9 | (6 | 3) | 125 | 31 | 44 | 35 | 42 | 4 | 85 | 2 | 0 | 4 | 2 | 1 | .67 | 5 | .245 | .338 | .419 |
| 2011 | SD | NL | 62 | 195 | 45 | 10 | 0 | 4 | (3 | 1) | 67 | 19 | 19 | 16 | 19 | 2 | 68 | 1 | 0 | 1 | 0 | 0 | - | 7 | .231 | .301 | .344 |
| 2013 | LAA | AL | 17 | 27 | 5 | 0 | 0 | 0 | (0 | 0) | 5 | 2 | 2 | 4 | 5 | 0 | 14 | 0 | 0 | 0 | 0 | 0 | - | 0 | .185 | .313 | .185 |
| 10 | Col | NL | 88 | 259 | 66 | 21 | 2 | 7 | (6 | 1) | 112 | 24 | 37 | 30 | 36 | 4 | 68 | 1 | 0 | 4 | 2 | 1 | .67 | 4 | .255 | .343 | .432 |
| 10 | TB | AL | 15 | 39 | 7 | 0 | 0 | 2 | (0 | 2) | 13 | 7 | 7 | 5 | 6 | 0 | 17 | 1 | 0 | 0 | 0 | 0 | - | 1 | .179 | .304 | .333 |
| Postseason | | | 13 | 43 | 11 | 0 | 1 | 1 | (1 | 0) | 16 | 4 | 4 | 6 | 8 | 0 | 17 | 0 | 0 | 0 | 0 | 0 | - | 0 | .256 | .373 | .372 |
| 9 ML YEARS | | | 910 | 2934 | 806 | 176 | 23 | 124 | (63 | 61) | 1400 | 400 | 492 | 475 | 430 | 47 | 810 | 14 | 1 | 22 | 13 | 16 | .45 | 67 | .275 | .368 | .477 |

## Brett Hayes

**Bats:** R **Throws:** R **Pos:** C-5;PR-1 **Ht:** 6'0" **Wt:** 200 **Born:** 2/13/1984 **Age:** 30

| BATTING | | | | | | | | | | | | | | | | | | | | | BASERUNNING | | | | AVERAGES | | |
|---|---|---|---|---|---|---|---|---|---|---|---|---|---|---|---|---|---|---|---|---|---|---|---|---|---|---|---|
| Year | Team | Lg | G | AB | H | 2B | 3B | HR | (Hm | Rd) | TB | R | RBI | RC | TBB | IBB | SO | HBP | SH | SF | SB | CS | SB% | GDP | Avg | OBP | Slg |
| 2013 | Omha* | AAA | 78 | 275 | 64 | 15 | 1 | 17 | (- | -) | 132 | 39 | 44 | 38 | 17 | 0 | 64 | 2 | 1 | 3 | 2 | 0 | 1.00 | 5 | .233 | .279 | .480 |
| 2009 | Fla | NL | 14 | 11 | 3 | 1 | 0 | 1 | (0 | 1) | 7 | 5 | 2 | 1 | 0 | 0 | 4 | 1 | 0 | 0 | 0 | 0 | - | 1 | .273 | .333 | .636 |
| 2010 | Fla | NL | 26 | 77 | 16 | 6 | 1 | 2 | (1 | 1) | 30 | 6 | 6 | 7 | 6 | 1 | 26 | 0 | 0 | 0 | 0 | 0 | - | 1 | .208 | .265 | .390 |
| 2011 | Fla | NL | 64 | 130 | 30 | 9 | 0 | 5 | (3 | 2) | 54 | 19 | 16 | 13 | 11 | 2 | 39 | 0 | 3 | 0 | 0 | 0 | - | 2 | .231 | .291 | .415 |
| 2012 | Mia | NL | 39 | 114 | 23 | 6 | 0 | 0 | (0 | 0) | 29 | 7 | 3 | 2 | 4 | 3 | 49 | 0 | 0 | 0 | 1 | 0 | 1.00 | 1 | .202 | .229 | .254 |
| 2013 | KC | AL | 5 | 18 | 5 | 3 | 0 | 1 | (0 | 1) | 11 | 2 | 2 | 3 | 0 | 0 | 3 | 0 | 0 | 0 | 0 | 0 | - | 0 | .278 | .278 | .611 |
| 5 ML YEARS | | | 148 | 350 | 77 | 25 | 1 | 9 | (4 | 5) | 131 | 39 | 29 | 26 | 21 | 6 | 121 | 1 | 3 | 0 | 1 | 0 | 1.00 | 5 | .220 | .266 | .374 |

## Chase Headley

**Bats:** B **Throws:** R **Pos:** 3B-140;PH-1 HEDD-lee **Ht:** 6'2" **Wt:** 220 **Born:** 5/9/1984 **Age:** 30

| BATTING | | | | | | | | | | | | | | | | | | | | | BASERUNNING | | | | AVERAGES | | |
|---|---|---|---|---|---|---|---|---|---|---|---|---|---|---|---|---|---|---|---|---|---|---|---|---|---|---|---|
| Year Team | Lg | G | AB | H | 2B | 3B | HR | (Hm | Rd) | TB | R | RBI | RC | TBB | IBB | SO | HBP | SH | SF | | SB | CS | SB% | GDP | Avg | OBP | Slg |
| 2013 Lk Els* | A+ | 4 | 12 | 3 | 1 | 0 | 0 | (- | -) | 4 | 0 | 0 | 0 | 0 | 0 | 2 | 0 | 0 | 0 | | 0 | 0 | - | 0 | .250 | .250 | .333 |
| 2007 SD | NL | 8 | 18 | 4 | 1 | 0 | 0 | (0 | 0) | 5 | 1 | 0 | 1 | 2 | 0 | 4 | 1 | 0 | 0 | | 0 | 0 | - | 2 | .222 | .333 | .278 |
| 2008 SD | NL | 91 | 331 | 89 | 19 | 2 | 9 | (4 | 5) | 139 | 34 | 38 | 42 | 30 | 1 | 104 | 5 | 0 | 2 | | 4 | 1 | .80 | 5 | .269 | .337 | .420 |
| 2009 SD | NL | 156 | 543 | 142 | 31 | 2 | 12 | (7 | 5) | 213 | 62 | 64 | 68 | 62 | 3 | 133 | 5 | 0 | 2 | | 10 | 2 | .83 | 19 | .262 | .342 | .392 |
| 2010 SD | NL | 161 | 610 | 161 | 29 | 3 | 11 | (3 | 8) | 229 | 77 | 58 | 70 | 56 | 3 | 139 | 3 | 1 | 4 | | 17 | 5 | .77 | 11 | .264 | .327 | .375 |
| 2011 SD | NL | 113 | 381 | 110 | 28 | 1 | 4 | (1 | 3) | 152 | 43 | 44 | 61 | 52 | 8 | 92 | 2 | 1 | 3 | | 13 | 2 | .87 | 6 | .289 | .374 | .399 |
| 2012 SD | NL | 161 | 604 | 173 | 31 | 2 | 31 | (13 | 18) | 301 | 95 | **115** | 112 | 86 | 2 | 157 | 4 | 0 | 5 | | 17 | 6 | .74 | 7 | .286 | .376 | .498 |
| 2013 SD | NL | 141 | 520 | 130 | 35 | 2 | 13 | (5 | 8) | 208 | 59 | 50 | 64 | 67 | 7 | 142 | 11 | 0 | 2 | | 8 | 4 | .67 | 9 | .250 | .347 | .400 |
| 7 ML YEARS | | 831 | 3007 | 809 | 174 | 12 | 80 | (33 | 47) | 1247 | 371 | 369 | 418 | 355 | 24 | 771 | 31 | 2 | 18 | | 69 | 20 | .78 | 59 | .269 | .350 | .415 |

## Deunte Heath

**Pitches:** R **Bats:** R **Pos:** RP-5 dee-UN-tay **Ht:** 6'4" **Wt:** 240 **Born:** 8/8/1985 **Age:** 28

| HOW MUCH HE PITCHED | | | | | | | | WHAT HE GAVE UP | | | | | | | | | | | | THE RESULTS | | | | | | | |
|---|---|---|---|---|---|---|---|---|---|---|---|---|---|---|---|---|---|---|---|---|---|---|---|---|---|---|---|
| Year Team | Lg | G | GS | CG | GF | IP | BFP | H | R | ER | HR | SH | SF | HB | TBB | IBB | SO | WP | Bk | W | L | Pct | Sh | Sv-Op | Hld | ERC | ERA |
| 2009 Missi | AA | 25 | 12 | 0 | 4 | 80.0 | 355 | 80 | 43 | 37 | 4 | 3 | 1 | 5 | 38 | 0 | 70 | 5 | 4 | 2 | 5 | .286 | 0 | 1-- | - | 4.24 | 4.16 |
| 2009 Gwnntt | AAA | 7 | 2 | 0 | 1 | 18.2 | 95 | 27 | 21 | 20 | 2 | 0 | 0 | 0 | 12 | 0 | 18 | 2 | 0 | 0 | 1 | .000 | 0 | 0-- | - | 7.71 | 9.64 |
| 2010 Brham | AA | 39 | 0 | 0 | 13 | 57.2 | 250 | 49 | 22 | 20 | 4 | 2 | 0 | 4 | 32 | 2 | 84 | 2 | 3 | 2 | 4 | .333 | 0 | 2-- | - | 3.87 | 3.12 |
| 2011 Charltt | AAA | 30 | 16 | 0 | 1 | 102.2 | 465 | 98 | 62 | 51 | 12 | 1 | 4 | 4 | 62 | 0 | 117 | 8 | 1 | 4 | 7 | .364 | 0 | 1-- | - | 4.87 | 4.47 |
| 2012 Charltt | AAA | 36 | 4 | 0 | 11 | 67.0 | 272 | 47 | 13 | 11 | 4 | 0 | 1 | 4 | 20 | 0 | 74 | 2 | 0 | 4 | 3 | .571 | 0 | 3-- | - | 2.09 | 1.48 |
| 2013 Charltt | AAA | 30 | 1 | 0 | 19 | 45.0 | 185 | 36 | 12 | 11 | 1 | 0 | 3 | 2 | 14 | 0 | 36 | 0 | 0 | 2 | 1 | .667 | 0 | 4-- | - | 2.34 | 2.20 |
| 2012 CWS | AL | 3 | 0 | 0 | 2 | 2.0 | 7 | 1 | 1 | 1 | 1 | 0 | 0 | 0 | 1 | 0 | 1 | 0 | 0 | 0 | 0 | - | 0 | 0-0 | 0 | 4.74 | 4.50 |
| 2013 CWS | AL | 5 | 0 | 0 | 3 | 7.2 | 41 | 8 | 10 | 10 | 2 | 0 | 0 | 0 | 12 | 1 | 3 | 1 | 0 | 0 | 0 | - | 0 | 0-0 | 0 | 10.88 | 11.74 |
| 2 ML YEARS | | 8 | 0 | 0 | 5 | 9.2 | 48 | 9 | 11 | 11 | 3 | 0 | 0 | 0 | 13 | 1 | 4 | 1 | 0 | 0 | 0 | - | 0 | 0-0 | 0 | 9.72 | 10.24 |

## Adeiny Hechavarria

**Bats:** R **Throws:** R **Pos:** SS-148;PR-1 a-DAY-nee hetch-a-VA-ree-a **Ht:** 6'0" **Wt:** 185 **Born:** 4/15/1989 **Age:** 25

| BATTING | | | | | | | | | | | | | | | | | | | | | BASERUNNING | | | | AVERAGES | | |
|---|---|---|---|---|---|---|---|---|---|---|---|---|---|---|---|---|---|---|---|---|---|---|---|---|---|---|---|
| Year Team | Lg | G | AB | H | 2B | 3B | HR | (Hm | Rd) | TB | R | RBI | RC | TBB | IBB | SO | HBP | SH | SF | | SB | CS | SB% | GDP | Avg | OBP | Slg |
| 2010 Dnedin | A+ | 41 | 161 | 31 | 7 | 3 | 1 | (- | -) | 47 | 21 | 7 | 10 | 5 | 0 | 25 | 0 | 1 | 0 | | 7 | 0 | 1.00 | 4 | .193 | .217 | .292 |
| 2010 NHam | AA | 61 | 253 | 69 | 11 | 1 | 3 | (- | -) | 91 | 36 | 34 | 29 | 12 | 0 | 40 | 2 | 1 | 5 | | 6 | 3 | .67 | 9 | .273 | .305 | .360 |
| 2011 NHam | AA | 111 | 464 | 109 | 22 | 6 | 6 | (- | -) | 161 | 58 | 46 | 44 | 25 | 2 | 78 | 3 | 4 | 6 | | 19 | 13 | .59 | 9 | .235 | .275 | .347 |
| 2011 LsVgs | AAA | 25 | 108 | 42 | 6 | 2 | 2 | (- | -) | 58 | 16 | 11 | 23 | 8 | 0 | 21 | 0 | 0 | 0 | | 1 | 2 | .33 | 3 | .389 | .431 | .537 |
| 2012 LsVgs | AAA | 102 | 443 | 138 | 20 | 6 | 6 | (- | -) | 188 | 78 | 63 | 71 | 38 | 0 | 86 | 1 | 3 | 5 | | 8 | 2 | .80 | 14 | .312 | .363 | .424 |
| 2013 Jupiter | A+ | 2 | 7 | 3 | 1 | 0 | 0 | (- | -) | 4 | 0 | 1 | 2 | 2 | 0 | 1 | 0 | 0 | 0 | | 1 | 0 | 1.00 | 0 | .429 | .556 | .571 |
| 2012 Tor | AL | 41 | 126 | 32 | 8 | 0 | 2 | (1 | 1) | 46 | 10 | 15 | 15 | 4 | 0 | 32 | 1 | 5 | 1 | | 0 | 0 | - | 2 | .254 | .280 | .365 |
| 2013 Mia | NL | 148 | 543 | 123 | 14 | 8 | 3 | (1 | 2) | 162 | 30 | 42 | 37 | 30 | 1 | 96 | 0 | 4 | 1 | | 11 | 10 | .52 | 19 | .227 | .267 | .298 |
| 2 ML YEARS | | 189 | 669 | 155 | 22 | 8 | 5 | (2 | 3) | 208 | 40 | 57 | 52 | 34 | 1 | 128 | 1 | 9 | 2 | | 11 | 10 | .52 | 21 | .232 | .269 | .311 |

## Jeremy Hefner

**Pitches:** R **Bats:** R **Pos:** SP-23; RP-1 HEFF-ner **Ht:** 6'4" **Wt:** 215 **Born:** 3/11/1986 **Age:** 28

| HOW MUCH HE PITCHED | | | | | | | | WHAT HE GAVE UP | | | | | | | | | | | | THE RESULTS | | | | | | | |
|---|---|---|---|---|---|---|---|---|---|---|---|---|---|---|---|---|---|---|---|---|---|---|---|---|---|---|---|
| Year Team | Lg | G | GS | CG | GF | IP | BFP | H | R | ER | HR | SH | SF | HB | TBB | IBB | SO | WP | Bk | W | L | Pct | Sh | Sv-Op | Hld | ERC | ERA |
| 2009 Lk Els | A+ | 27 | 27 | 0 | 0 | 150.2 | 635 | 165 | 81 | 69 | 13 | 3 | 1 | 11 | 38 | 0 | 142 | 9 | 0 | 14 | 9 | .609 | 0 | 0-- | - | 4.34 | 4.12 |
| 2009 Portlnd | AAA | 1 | 1 | 0 | 0 | 5.1 | 24 | 7 | 2 | 2 | 0 | 0 | 0 | 0 | 2 | 0 | 5 | 0 | 0 | 0 | 0 | - | 0 | 0-- | - | 5.10 | 3.38 |
| 2010 SnAnt | AA | 28 | 28 | 2 | 0 | 167.2 | 687 | 156 | 63 | 55 | 11 | 10 | 7 | 5 | 51 | 3 | 115 | 7 | 0 | 11 | 8 | .579 | 0 | 0-- | - | 3.26 | 2.95 |
| 2011 Tucsn | AAA | 28 | 28 | 0 | 0 | 157.1 | 704 | 178 | 101 | 87 | 21 | 6 | 4 | 3 | 61 | 1 | 120 | 7 | 0 | 9 | 7 | .563 | 0 | 0-- | - | 5.05 | 4.98 |
| 2012 Buffalo | AAA | 10 | 9 | 0 | 1 | 61.2 | 243 | 55 | 25 | 19 | 4 | 2 | 1 | 0 | 10 | 1 | 37 | 1 | 0 | 5 | 2 | .714 | 0 | 0-- | - | 2.42 | 2.77 |
| 2012 NYM | NL | 26 | 13 | 0 | 5 | 93.2 | 408 | 110 | 55 | 53 | 9 | 4 | 1 | 2 | 18 | 1 | 62 | 7 | 0 | 4 | 7 | .364 | 0 | 0-0 | 0 | 4.20 | 5.09 |
| 2013 NYM | NL | 24 | 23 | 0 | 1 | 130.2 | 556 | 132 | 75 | 63 | 20 | 3 | 4 | 5 | 37 | 4 | 99 | 1 | 0 | 4 | 8 | .333 | 0 | 0-0 | 0 | 4.13 | 4.34 |
| 2 ML YEARS | | 50 | 36 | 0 | 6 | 224.1 | 964 | 242 | 130 | 116 | 29 | 7 | 5 | 7 | 55 | 5 | 161 | 8 | 0 | 8 | 15 | .348 | 0 | 0-0 | 0 | 4.16 | 4.65 |

## Chris Heisey

**Bats:** R **Throws:** R **Pos:** LF-69;PH-21;RF-6;DH-4;PR-2;CF-1 HY-zee **Ht:** 6'1" **Wt:** 210 **Born:** 12/14/1984 **Age:** 29

| BATTING | | | | | | | | | | | | | | | | | | | | | BASERUNNING | | | | AVERAGES | | |
|---|---|---|---|---|---|---|---|---|---|---|---|---|---|---|---|---|---|---|---|---|---|---|---|---|---|---|---|
| Year Team | Lg | G | AB | H | 2B | 3B | HR | (Hm | Rd) | TB | R | RBI | RC | TBB | IBB | SO | HBP | SH | SF | | SB | CS | SB% | GDP | Avg | OBP | Slg |
| 2013 Pnscla* | AA | 1 | 0 | 0 | 0 | 0 | 0 | (- | -) | 0 | 0 | 0 | 0 | 0 | 0 | 0 | 0 | 0 | 0 | | 0 | 0 | - | 0 | - | - | - |
| 2013 Lsvlle* | AAA | 6 | 20 | 4 | 1 | 0 | 0 | (- | -) | 5 | 1 | 1 | 1 | 1 | 0 | 6 | 0 | 0 | 1 | | 0 | 0 | - | 0 | .200 | .227 | .250 |
| 2010 Cin | NL | 97 | 201 | 51 | 10 | 1 | 8 | (2 | 6) | 87 | 33 | 21 | 22 | 16 | 1 | 57 | 6 | 1 | 2 | | 1 | 2 | .33 | 3 | .254 | .324 | .433 |
| 2011 Cin | NL | 120 | 279 | 71 | 9 | 1 | 18 | (11 | 7) | 136 | 44 | 50 | 40 | 19 | 3 | 78 | 5 | 1 | 4 | | 6 | 1 | .86 | 1 | .254 | .309 | .487 |
| 2012 Cin | NL | 120 | 347 | 92 | 16 | 5 | 7 | (4 | 3) | 139 | 44 | 31 | 42 | 18 | 0 | 81 | 7 | 3 | 0 | | 6 | 3 | .67 | 8 | .265 | .315 | .401 |
| 2013 Cin | NL | 87 | 224 | 53 | 11 | 1 | 9 | (6 | 3) | 93 | 29 | 23 | 26 | 9 | 0 | 51 | 5 | 4 | 2 | | 3 | 0 | 1.00 | 4 | .237 | .279 | .415 |
| Postseason | | 5 | 5 | 0 | 0 | 0 | 0 | (0 | 0) | 0 | 1 | 0 | 0 | 0 | 0 | 2 | 0 | 0 | 0 | | 0 | 0 | - | 0 | .000 | .000 | .000 |
| 4 ML YEARS | | 424 | 1051 | 267 | 46 | 8 | 42 | (23 | 19) | 455 | 150 | 125 | 130 | 62 | 4 | 267 | 23 | 9 | 8 | | 16 | 6 | .73 | 16 | .254 | .308 | .433 |

## Jeremy Hellickson

**Pitches:** R **Bats:** R **Pos:** SP-31; RP-1 **Ht:** 6'1" **Wt:** 190 **Born:** 4/8/1987 **Age:** 27

| HOW MUCH HE PITCHED | | | | | | | | WHAT HE GAVE UP | | | | | | | | | | | | THE RESULTS | | | | | | | |
|---|---|---|---|---|---|---|---|---|---|---|---|---|---|---|---|---|---|---|---|---|---|---|---|---|---|---|---|
| Year Team | Lg | G | GS | CG | GF | IP | BFP | H | R | ER | HR | SH | SF | HB | TBB | IBB | SO | WP | Bk | W | L | Pct | Sh | Sv-Op | Hld | ERC | ERA |
| 2010 TB | AL | 10 | 4 | 0 | 0 | 36.1 | 149 | 32 | 14 | 14 | 5 | 0 | 1 | 2 | 8 | 2 | 33 | 2 | 0 | 4 | 0 | 1.000 | 0 | 0-1 | 0 | 3.10 | 3.47 |
| 2011 TB | AL | 29 | 29 | 2 | 0 | 189.0 | 774 | 146 | 64 | 62 | 21 | 1 | 2 | 4 | 72 | 8 | 117 | 8 | 1 | 13 | 10 | .565 | 1 | 0-0 | 0 | 2.89 | 2.95 |

| | | | HOW MUCH HE PITCHED | | | | | | WHAT HE GAVE UP | | | | | | | | | | | | THE RESULTS | | | | | | | |
|---|---|---|---|---|---|---|---|---|---|---|---|---|---|---|---|---|---|---|---|---|---|---|---|---|---|---|---|---|
| Year | Team | Lg | G | GS | CG | GF | IP | BFP | H | R | ER | HR | SH | SF | HB | TBB | IBB | SO | WP | Bk | W | L | Pct | Sh | Sv-Op | Hld | ERC | ERA |
| 2012 | TB | AL | 31 | 31 | 0 | 0 | 177.0 | 741 | 163 | 68 | 61 | 25 | 4 | 3 | 4 | 59 | 3 | 124 | 5 | 0 | 10 | 11 | .476 | 0 | 0-0 | 0 | 3.73 | 3.10 |
| 2013 | TB | AL | 32 | 31 | 0 | 1 | 174.0 | 737 | 185 | 103 | 100 | 24 | 2 | 5 | 4 | 50 | 0 | 135 | 7 | **2** | 12 | 10 | .545 | 0 | 0-0 | 0 | 4.40 | 5.17 |
| Postseason | | | 1 | 1 | 0 | 0 | 4.0 | 16 | 4 | 3 | 3 | 3 | 0 | 0 | 0 | 1 | 0 | 1 | 0 | 0 | 0 | 1 | .000 | 0 | 0-0 | 0 | 8.13 | 6.75 |
| 4 ML YEARS | | | 102 | 95 | 2 | 1 | 576.1 | 2401 | 526 | 249 | 237 | 75 | 7 | 11 | 14 | 189 | 13 | 409 | 22 | 3 | 39 | 31 | .557 | 1 | 0-1 | 0 | 3.60 | 3.70 |

# Johnny Hellweg

**Pitches:** R **Bats:** R **Pos:** SP-7; RP-1 **Ht:** 6'9" **Wt:** 205 **Born:** 10/29/1988 **Age:** 25

| | | | HOW MUCH HE PITCHED | | | | | | WHAT HE GAVE UP | | | | | | | | | | | | THE RESULTS | | | | | | | |
|---|---|---|---|---|---|---|---|---|---|---|---|---|---|---|---|---|---|---|---|---|---|---|---|---|---|---|---|---|
| Year | Team | Lg | G | GS | CG | GF | IP | BFP | H | R | ER | HR | SH | SF | HB | TBB | IBB | SO | WP | Bk | W | L | Pct | Sh | Sv-Op | Hld | ERC | ERA |
| 2009 | Angels | R | 18 | 0 | 0 | 14 | 24.1 | 100 | 16 | 8 | 8 | 0 | 2 | 0 | 4 | 8 | 0 | 25 | 7 | 1 | 2 | 1 | .667 | 0 | 6-- | - | 1.99 | 2.96 |
| 2009 | CRpds | A | 5 | 0 | 0 | 3 | 6.2 | 34 | 4 | 3 | 1 | 0 | 0 | 0 | 2 | 7 | 0 | 7 | 2 | 0 | 0 | 0 | - | 0 | 2-- | - | 4.35 | 1.35 |
| 2010 | CRpds | A | 41 | 0 | 0 | 36 | 43.2 | 201 | 20 | 21 | 21 | 2 | 0 | 2 | 4 | 45 | 0 | 66 | 9 | 0 | 2 | 4 | .333 | 0 | 16-- | - | 3.31 | 4.33 |
| 2011 | InldEm | A+ | 28 | 14 | 0 | 5 | 89.1 | 404 | 75 | 43 | 37 | 2 | 3 | 0 | 15 | 59 | 0 | 113 | 12 | 1 | 6 | 4 | .600 | 0 | 0-- | - | 4.27 | 3.73 |
| 2012 | Ark | AA | 21 | 21 | 1 | 0 | 119.2 | 508 | 105 | 52 | 45 | 8 | 4 | 2 | 13 | 60 | 2 | 88 | 14 | 2 | 5 | 10 | .333 | 0 | 0-- | - | 4.09 | 3.38 |
| 2012 | Hntsvl | AA | 7 | 2 | 0 | 0 | 20.0 | 88 | 16 | 7 | 6 | 0 | 0 | 0 | 1 | 15 | 0 | 17 | 3 | 1 | 2 | 1 | .667 | 0 | 0-- | - | 3.83 | 2.70 |
| 2013 | Nashv | AAA | 23 | 23 | 0 | 0 | 125.2 | 549 | 103 | 55 | 44 | 6 | 0 | 2 | 14 | 81 | 0 | 89 | 13 | 1 | 12 | 5 | .706 | 0 | 0-- | - | 4.16 | 3.15 |
| 2013 | Wisc | A | 1 | 1 | 0 | 0 | 6.0 | 26 | 5 | 2 | 2 | 0 | 0 | 0 | 1 | 2 | 0 | 4 | 0 | 0 | 1 | 0 | 1.000 | 0 | 0-- | - | 2.79 | 3.00 |
| 2013 | Mil | NL | 8 | 7 | 0 | 1 | 30.2 | 162 | 40 | 30 | 23 | 3 | 3 | 2 | 8 | 26 | 0 | 9 | 4 | 0 | 1 | 4 | .200 | 0 | 0-0 | 0 | 8.96 | 6.75 |

# Todd Helton

**Bats:** L **Throws:** L **Pos:** 1B-110;PH-14;DH-1 **Ht:** 6'2" **Wt:** 220 **Born:** 8/20/1973 **Age:** 40

| | | | BATTING | | | | | | | | | | | | | | | | | | BASERUNNING | | | | AVERAGES | | |
|---|---|---|---|---|---|---|---|---|---|---|---|---|---|---|---|---|---|---|---|---|---|---|---|---|---|---|---|
| Year | Team | Lg | G | AB | H | 2B | 3B | HR | (Hm | Rd) | TB | R | RBI | RC | TBB | IBB | SO | HBP | SH | SF | SB | CS | SB% | GDP | Avg | OBP | Slg |
| 1997 | Col | NL | 35 | 93 | 26 | 2 | 1 | 5 | (3 | 2) | 45 | 13 | 11 | 15 | 8 | 0 | 11 | 0 | 0 | 0 | 0 | 1 | .00 | 1 | .280 | .337 | .484 |
| 1998 | Col | NL | 152 | 530 | 167 | 37 | 1 | 25 | (13 | 12) | 281 | 78 | 97 | 101 | 53 | 5 | 54 | 6 | 1 | 5 | 3 | 3 | .50 | 15 | .315 | .380 | .530 |
| 1999 | Col | NL | 159 | 578 | 185 | 39 | 5 | 35 | (23 | 12) | 339 | 114 | 113 | 124 | 68 | 6 | 77 | 6 | 0 | 4 | 7 | 6 | .54 | 14 | .320 | .395 | .587 |
| 2000 | Col | NL | 160 | 580 | **216** | **59** | 2 | 42 | (27 | 15) | **405** | 138 | **147** | **169** | 103 | 22 | 61 | 4 | 0 | 10 | 5 | 3 | .63 | 12 | **.372** | **.463** | **.698** |
| 2001 | Col | NL | 159 | 587 | 197 | 54 | 2 | 49 | (27 | 22) | 402 | 132 | 146 | 157 | 98 | 15 | 104 | 5 | 1 | 5 | 7 | 5 | .58 | 14 | .336 | .432 | .685 |
| 2002 | Col | NL | 156 | 553 | 182 | 39 | 4 | 30 | (18 | 12) | 319 | 107 | 109 | 127 | 99 | 21 | 91 | 5 | 0 | 10 | 5 | 1 | .83 | 10 | .329 | .429 | .577 |
| 2003 | Col | NL | 160 | 583 | 209 | 49 | 5 | 33 | (23 | 10) | 367 | 135 | 117 | 160 | 111 | 21 | 72 | 2 | 0 | 7 | 0 | 4 | .00 | 19 | .358 | .458 | .630 |
| 2004 | Col | NL | 154 | 547 | 190 | 49 | 2 | 32 | (21 | 11) | 339 | 115 | 96 | 143 | 127 | 19 | 72 | 3 | 0 | 6 | 3 | 0 | 1.00 | 12 | .347 | .469 | .620 |
| 2005 | Col | NL | 144 | 509 | 163 | 45 | 2 | 20 | (13 | 7) | 272 | 92 | 79 | 114 | 106 | 22 | 80 | 9 | 1 | 1 | 3 | 0 | 1.00 | 14 | .320 | **.445** | .534 |
| 2006 | Col | NL | 145 | 546 | 165 | 40 | 5 | 15 | (8 | 7) | 260 | 94 | 81 | 118 | 91 | 15 | 64 | 6 | 0 | 6 | 3 | 2 | .60 | 10 | .302 | .404 | .476 |
| 2007 | Col | NL | 154 | 557 | 178 | 42 | 2 | 17 | (9 | 8) | 275 | 86 | 91 | 115 | 116 | 16 | 74 | 2 | 0 | 7 | 0 | 1 | .00 | 15 | .320 | .434 | .494 |
| 2008 | Col | NL | 83 | 299 | 79 | 16 | 0 | 7 | (5 | 2) | 116 | 39 | 29 | 45 | 61 | 8 | 50 | 1 | 0 | 0 | 0 | 0 | - | 9 | .264 | .391 | .388 |
| 2009 | Col | NL | 151 | 544 | 177 | 38 | 3 | 15 | (10 | 5) | 266 | 79 | 86 | 108 | 89 | 5 | 73 | 2 | 0 | 10 | 0 | 1 | .00 | 15 | .325 | .416 | .489 |
| 2010 | Col | NL | 118 | 398 | 102 | 18 | 1 | 8 | (4 | 4) | 146 | 48 | 37 | 51 | 67 | 3 | 90 | 2 | 0 | 6 | 0 | 0 | - | 10 | .256 | .362 | .367 |
| 2011 | Col | NL | 124 | 421 | 127 | 27 | 0 | 14 | (8 | 6) | 196 | 59 | 69 | 68 | 59 | 5 | 71 | 3 | 0 | 8 | 0 | 1 | .00 | 6 | .302 | .385 | .466 |
| 2012 | Col | NL | 69 | 240 | 57 | 16 | 1 | 7 | (4 | 3) | 96 | 31 | 37 | 36 | 39 | 1 | 44 | 1 | 0 | 3 | 1 | 1 | .50 | 6 | .238 | .343 | .400 |
| 2013 | Col | NL | 124 | 397 | 99 | 22 | 1 | 15 | (11 | 4) | 168 | 41 | 61 | 51 | 40 | 1 | 87 | 0 | 0 | 5 | 0 | 0 | - | 4 | .249 | .314 | .423 |
| Postseason | | | 15 | 57 | 12 | 2 | 1 | 0 | (0 | 0) | 16 | 11 | 4 | 2 | 8 | 0 | 11 | 0 | 0 | 1 | 0 | 0 | - | 0 | .211 | .303 | .281 |
| 17 ML YEARS | | | 2247 | 7962 | 2519 | 592 | 37 | 369 | (227 | 142) | 4292 | 1401 | 1406 | 1702 | 1335 | 185 | 1175 | 57 | 3 | 93 | 37 | 29 | .56 | 186 | .316 | .414 | .539 |

# Heath Hembree

**Pitches:** R **Bats:** R **Pos:** RP-9 HEHM-bree **Ht:** 6'4" **Wt:** 210 **Born:** 1/13/1989 **Age:** 25

| | | | HOW MUCH HE PITCHED | | | | | | WHAT HE GAVE UP | | | | | | | | | | | | THE RESULTS | | | | | | | |
|---|---|---|---|---|---|---|---|---|---|---|---|---|---|---|---|---|---|---|---|---|---|---|---|---|---|---|---|---|
| Year | Team | Lg | G | GS | CG | GF | IP | BFP | H | R | ER | HR | SH | SF | HB | TBB | IBB | SO | WP | Bk | W | L | Pct | Sh | Sv-Op | Hld | ERC | ERA |
| 2010 | Giants | R | 12 | 0 | 0 | 10 | 11.0 | 41 | 9 | 1 | 1 | 0 | 0 | 0 | 0 | 0 | 0 | 22 | 0 | 0 | 0 | 0 | - | 0 | 3-- | - | 1.35 | 0.82 |
| 2011 | SnJos | A+ | 26 | 0 | 0 | 24 | 24.2 | 101 | 16 | 2 | 2 | 1 | 0 | 0 | 1 | 12 | 0 | 44 | 2 | 0 | 0 | 0 | - | 0 | 21-- | - | 2.33 | 0.73 |
| 2011 | Rchmd | AA | 28 | 0 | 0 | 25 | 28.2 | 118 | 20 | 11 | 9 | 1 | 0 | 2 | 0 | 13 | 1 | 34 | 1 | 0 | 1 | 1 | .500 | 0 | 17-- | - | 2.21 | 2.83 |
| 2012 | Fresno | AAA | 39 | 0 | 0 | 31 | 38.0 | 167 | 29 | 24 | 20 | 2 | 1 | 2 | 4 | 20 | 0 | 36 | 2 | 0 | 1 | 1 | .500 | 0 | 15-- | - | 3.25 | 4.74 |
| 2012 | SnJos | A+ | 5 | 0 | 0 | 3 | 5.0 | 17 | 0 | 0 | 0 | 0 | 0 | 0 | 0 | 1 | 0 | 7 | 0 | 0 | 0 | 0 | - | 0 | 0-- | - | 0.04 | 0.00 |
| 2013 | Fresno | AAA | 54 | 0 | 0 | 48 | 55.1 | 236 | 54 | 26 | 25 | 7 | 0 | 1 | 1 | 16 | 0 | 63 | 3 | 1 | 1 | 4 | .200 | 0 | 31-- | - | 3.69 | 4.07 |
| 2013 | SF | NL | 9 | 0 | 0 | 2 | 7.2 | 29 | 4 | 0 | 0 | 0 | 0 | 0 | 0 | 2 | 0 | 12 | 0 | 0 | 0 | 0 | - | 0 | 0-0 | 0 | 1.02 | 0.00 |

# Jim Henderson

**Pitches:** R **Bats:** L **Pos:** RP-61 **Ht:** 6'5" **Wt:** 220 **Born:** 10/21/1982 **Age:** 31

| | | | HOW MUCH HE PITCHED | | | | | | WHAT HE GAVE UP | | | | | | | | | | | | THE RESULTS | | | | | | | |
|---|---|---|---|---|---|---|---|---|---|---|---|---|---|---|---|---|---|---|---|---|---|---|---|---|---|---|---|---|
| Year | Team | Lg | G | GS | CG | GF | IP | BFP | H | R | ER | HR | SH | SF | HB | TBB | IBB | SO | WP | Bk | W | L | Pct | Sh | Sv-Op | Hld | ERC | ERA |
| 2009 | Wisc | A | 26 | 0 | 0 | 25 | 25.1 | 102 | 19 | 4 | 3 | 0 | 1 | 0 | 1 | 8 | 0 | 26 | 0 | 0 | 0 | 0 | - | 0 | 17-- | - | 2.00 | 1.07 |
| 2009 | BrvdCt | A+ | 15 | 0 | 0 | 5 | 29.1 | 117 | 16 | 11 | 9 | 2 | 1 | 1 | 1 | 14 | 1 | 20 | 1 | 0 | 3 | 0 | 1.000 | 0 | 4-- | - | 1.93 | 2.76 |
| 2009 | Hntsvl | AA | 5 | 0 | 0 | 3 | 7.0 | 35 | 8 | 3 | 2 | 0 | 1 | 1 | 0 | 4 | 0 | 5 | 2 | 0 | 1 | 0 | 1.000 | 0 | 0-- | - | 4.37 | 2.57 |
| 2010 | Hntsvl | AA | 45 | 0 | 0 | 17 | 61.0 | 267 | 49 | 44 | 37 | 8 | 2 | 3 | 3 | 35 | 3 | 61 | 2 | 0 | 4 | 5 | .444 | 0 | 7-- | - | 3.95 | 5.46 |
| 2011 | Nashv | AAA | 20 | 0 | 0 | 8 | 30.1 | 137 | 23 | 20 | 20 | 4 | 3 | 2 | 1 | 23 | 1 | 30 | 0 | 0 | 3 | 1 | .750 | 0 | 0-- | - | 4.36 | 5.93 |
| 2011 | Hntsvl | AA | 22 | 0 | 0 | 11 | 30.2 | 124 | 22 | 9 | 9 | 4 | 2 | 0 | 3 | 8 | 0 | 39 | 2 | 0 | 4 | 1 | .800 | 0 | 5-- | - | 2.60 | 2.64 |
| 2012 | Nashv | AAA | 35 | 0 | 0 | 29 | 48.0 | 195 | 36 | 10 | 9 | 2 | 2 | 1 | 2 | 22 | 2 | 56 | 0 | 0 | 4 | 3 | .571 | 0 | 15-- | - | 2.75 | 1.69 |
| 2013 | Wisc | A | 1 | 0 | 0 | 1 | 1.0 | 4 | 1 | 0 | 0 | 0 | 0 | 0 | 0 | 0 | 0 | 3 | 0 | 0 | 0 | 0 | - | 0 | 0-- | - | 1.95 | 0.00 |
| 2012 | Mil | NL | 36 | 0 | 0 | 6 | 30.2 | 131 | 26 | 12 | 12 | 1 | 1 | 3 | 1 | 13 | 0 | 45 | 1 | 0 | 1 | 3 | .250 | 0 | 3-7 | 14 | 2.96 | 3.52 |
| 2013 | Mil | NL | 61 | 0 | 0 | 45 | 60.0 | 247 | 44 | 18 | 18 | 8 | 1 | 0 | 2 | 24 | 2 | 75 | 0 | 0 | 5 | 5 | .500 | 0 | 28-32 | 5 | 2.93 | 2.70 |
| 2 ML YEARS | | | 97 | 0 | 0 | 51 | 90.2 | 378 | 70 | 30 | 30 | 9 | 2 | 3 | 3 | 37 | 2 | 120 | 1 | 0 | 6 | 8 | .429 | 0 | 31-39 | 19 | 2.95 | 2.98 |

# Liam Hendriks

**Pitches:** R **Bats:** R **Pos:** SP-8; RP-2 **Ht:** 6'1" **Wt:** 205 **Born:** 2/10/1989 **Age:** 25

| HOW MUCH HE PITCHED | | | | | | | | | WHAT HE GAVE UP | | | | | | | | | | | | THE RESULTS | | | | | | | |
|---|---|---|---|---|---|---|---|---|---|---|---|---|---|---|---|---|---|---|---|---|---|---|---|---|---|---|---|---|
| Year | Team | Lg | G | GS | CG | GF | IP | BFP | H | R | ER | HR | SH | SF | HB | TBB | IBB | SO | WP | Bk | W | L | Pct | Sh | Sv-Op | Hld | ERC | ERA |
| 2013 | Roch* | AAA | 16 | 16 | 1 | 0 | 98.1 | 416 | 115 | 56 | 51 | 9 | 3 | 4 | 3 | 15 | 0 | 62 | 2 | 0 | 4 | 8 | .333 | 0 | 0- - | - | 4.14 | 4.67 |
| 2011 | Min | AL | 4 | 4 | 0 | 0 | 23.1 | 100 | 29 | 16 | 16 | 3 | 0 | 1 | 0 | 6 | 0 | 16 | 1 | 0 | 0 | 2 | .000 | 0 | 0-0 | 0 | 5.26 | 6.17 |
| 2012 | Min | AL | 16 | 16 | 1 | 0 | 85.1 | 381 | 106 | 61 | 53 | 17 | 3 | 1 | 4 | 26 | 3 | 50 | 4 | 0 | 1 | 8 | .111 | 0 | 0-0 | 0 | 6.03 | 5.59 |
| 2013 | Min | AL | 10 | 8 | 0 | 1 | 47.1 | 224 | 67 | 39 | 36 | 10 | 0 | 2 | 3 | 14 | 1 | 34 | 1 | 0 | 1 | 3 | .250 | 0 | 0-0 | 0 | 7.16 | 6.85 |
| 3 ML YEARS | | | 30 | 28 | 1 | 1 | 156.0 | 705 | 202 | 116 | 105 | 30 | 3 | 4 | 7 | 46 | 4 | 100 | 6 | 0 | 2 | 13 | .133 | 0 | 0-0 | 0 | 6.25 | 6.06 |

# Sean Henn

**Pitches:** L **Bats:** R **Pos:** RP-4 **Ht:** 6'3" **Wt:** 235 **Born:** 4/23/1981 **Age:** 33

| HOW MUCH HE PITCHED | | | | | | | | | WHAT HE GAVE UP | | | | | | | | | | | | THE RESULTS | | | | | | | |
|---|---|---|---|---|---|---|---|---|---|---|---|---|---|---|---|---|---|---|---|---|---|---|---|---|---|---|---|---|
| Year | Team | Lg | G | GS | CG | GF | IP | BFP | H | R | ER | HR | SH | SF | HB | TBB | IBB | SO | WP | Bk | W | L | Pct | Sh | Sv-Op | Hld | ERC | ERA |
| 2013 | LsVgs* | AAA | 52 | 0 | 0 | 15 | 57.2 | 253 | 60 | 25 | 18 | 0 | 1 | 2 | 0 | 32 | 4 | 49 | 6 | 0 | 3 | 5 | .375 | 0 | 2- - | - | 4.13 | 2.81 |
| 2005 | NYY | AL | 3 | 3 | 0 | 0 | 11.1 | 61 | 18 | 16 | 14 | 3 | 0 | 0 | 0 | 11 | 0 | 3 | 0 | 0 | 0 | 3 | .000 | 0 | 0-0 | 0 | 12.12 | 11.12 |
| 2006 | NYY | AL | 4 | 1 | 0 | 0 | 9.1 | 44 | 11 | 5 | 5 | 2 | 0 | 1 | 1 | 5 | 0 | 7 | 0 | 0 | 0 | 1 | .000 | 0 | 0-0 | 0 | 7.09 | 4.82 |
| 2007 | NYY | AL | 29 | 1 | 0 | 8 | 36.2 | 181 | 44 | 32 | 29 | 6 | 1 | 0 | 3 | 27 | 1 | 28 | 1 | 0 | 2 | 2 | .500 | 0 | 0-0 | 2 | 7.47 | 7.12 |
| 2008 | SD | NL | 4 | 0 | 0 | 2 | 9.1 | 47 | 11 | 8 | 8 | 1 | 1 | 0 | 0 | 9 | 1 | 9 | 1 | 0 | 0 | 0 | - | 0 | 0-0 | 0 | 7.32 | 7.71 |
| 2009 | 2 Tms | AL | 20 | 0 | 0 | 3 | 14.1 | 69 | 15 | 12 | 12 | 2 | 0 | 1 | 1 | 12 | 1 | 15 | 1 | 0 | 0 | 3 | .000 | 0 | 0-2 | 2 | 6.67 | 7.53 |
| 2013 | NYM | NL | 4 | 0 | 0 | 2 | 2.2 | 13 | 3 | 1 | 1 | 1 | 0 | 0 | 0 | 3 | 0 | 1 | 0 | 0 | 0 | 1 | .000 | 0 | 0-0 | 0 | 11.08 | 3.38 |
| 09 | Min | AL | 14 | 0 | 0 | 3 | 11.1 | 50 | 9 | 9 | 9 | 2 | 0 | 1 | 1 | 8 | 1 | 9 | 0 | 0 | 0 | 3 | .000 | 0 | 0-1 | 2 | 4.99 | 7.15 |
| 09 | Bal | AL | 6 | 0 | 0 | 0 | 3.0 | 19 | 6 | 3 | 3 | 0 | 0 | 0 | 0 | 4 | 0 | 6 | 1 | 0 | 0 | 0 | - | 0 | 0-1 | 0 | 13.56 | 9.00 |
| 6 ML YEARS | | | 64 | 5 | 0 | 15 | 83.2 | 415 | 102 | 74 | 69 | 15 | 2 | 2 | 5 | 67 | 3 | 63 | 3 | 0 | 2 | 10 | .167 | 0 | 0-2 | 4 | 7.97 | 7.42 |

# Cesar Hernandez

**Bats:** B **Throws:** R **Pos:** CF-22;2B-10;PH-3;PR-1 **Ht:** 5'10" **Wt:** 175 **Born:** 5/23/1990 **Age:** 24

| BATTING | | | | | | | | | | | | | | | | | | | | | | BASERUNNING | | | | AVERAGES | | |
|---|---|---|---|---|---|---|---|---|---|---|---|---|---|---|---|---|---|---|---|---|---|---|---|---|---|---|---|---|
| Year | Team | Lg | G | AB | H | 2B | 3B | HR | (Hm | Rd) | TB | R | RBI | RC | TBB | IBB | SO | HBP | SH | SF | SB | CS | SB% | GDP | Avg | OBP | Slg |
| 2009 | Phillies | R | 41 | 150 | 40 | 5 | 1 | 0 | (- | -) | 47 | 21 | 18 | 19 | 17 | 0 | 20 | 4 | 1 | 3 | 13 | 5 | .72 | 1 | .267 | .351 | .313 |
| 2010 | Wmspt | A- | 65 | 255 | 83 | 13 | 2 | 0 | (- | -) | 100 | 36 | 23 | 45 | 26 | 1 | 27 | 3 | 0 | 3 | 32 | 6 | .84 | 0 | .325 | .390 | .392 |
| 2011 | Clrwtr | A+ | 119 | 421 | 113 | 7 | 4 | 4 | (- | -) | 140 | 47 | 37 | 45 | 23 | 1 | 80 | 1 | 5 | 2 | 23 | 10 | .70 | 12 | .268 | .306 | .333 |
| 2012 | Rdng | AA | 103 | 411 | 125 | 26 | 11 | 2 | (- | -) | 179 | 50 | 51 | 61 | 27 | 0 | 67 | 0 | 10 | 2 | 17 | 12 | .59 | 11 | .304 | .345 | .436 |
| 2012 | LV | AAA | 30 | 121 | 30 | 4 | 1 | 0 | (- | -) | 36 | 13 | 6 | 9 | 4 | 0 | 11 | 0 | 3 | 1 | 5 | 3 | .63 | 1 | .248 | .270 | .298 |
| 2013 | LV | AAA | 104 | 391 | 121 | 12 | 9 | 2 | (- | -) | 157 | 59 | 34 | 65 | 41 | 0 | 81 | 1 | 5 | 2 | 32 | 8 | .80 | 4 | .309 | .375 | .402 |
| 2013 | Rdng | AA | 3 | 10 | 5 | 1 | 0 | 0 | (- | -) | 6 | 2 | 3 | 3 | 1 | 0 | 1 | 0 | 1 | 1 | 1 | 0 | 1.00 | 0 | .500 | .500 | .600 |
| 2013 | Phi | NL | 34 | 121 | 35 | 5 | 0 | 0 | (0 | 0) | 40 | 17 | 10 | 13 | 9 | 0 | 26 | 1 | 0 | 0 | 0 | 3 | .00 | 2 | .289 | .344 | .331 |

# David Hernandez

**Pitches:** R **Bats:** R **Pos:** RP-62 **Ht:** 6'3" **Wt:** 230 **Born:** 5/13/1985 **Age:** 29

| HOW MUCH HE PITCHED | | | | | | | | | WHAT HE GAVE UP | | | | | | | | | | | | THE RESULTS | | | | | | | |
|---|---|---|---|---|---|---|---|---|---|---|---|---|---|---|---|---|---|---|---|---|---|---|---|---|---|---|---|---|
| Year | Team | Lg | G | GS | CG | GF | IP | BFP | H | R | ER | HR | SH | SF | HB | TBB | IBB | SO | WP | Bk | W | L | Pct | Sh | Sv-Op | Hld | ERC | ERA |
| 2013 | Reno* | AAA | 9 | 0 | 0 | 6 | 9.2 | 43 | 6 | 1 | 1 | 0 | 1 | 1 | 2 | 5 | 0 | 12 | 0 | 0 | 0 | 0 | - | 0 | 2- - | - | 2.43 | 0.93 |
| 2009 | Bal | AL | 20 | 19 | 0 | 0 | 101.1 | 462 | 118 | 62 | 61 | 27 | 2 | 3 | 1 | 46 | 0 | 68 | 3 | 0 | 4 | 10 | .286 | 0 | 0-0 | 0 | 6.55 | 5.42 |
| 2010 | Bal | AL | 41 | 8 | 0 | 16 | 79.1 | 348 | 72 | 40 | 38 | 9 | 1 | 3 | 4 | 42 | 4 | 72 | 9 | 0 | 8 | 8 | .500 | 0 | 2-6 | 2 | 4.28 | 4.31 |
| 2011 | Ari | NL | 74 | 0 | 0 | 28 | 69.1 | 291 | 49 | 27 | 26 | 4 | 3 | 2 | 2 | 30 | 1 | 77 | 7 | 1 | 5 | 3 | .625 | 0 | 11-14 | 23 | 2.40 | 3.38 |
| 2012 | Ari | NL | 72 | 0 | 0 | 21 | 68.1 | 278 | 48 | 21 | 19 | 4 | 0 | 1 | 3 | 22 | 1 | 98 | 4 | 1 | 2 | 3 | .400 | 0 | 4-10 | 25 | 2.10 | 2.50 |
| 2013 | Ari | NL | 62 | 0 | 0 | 12 | 62.1 | 263 | 50 | 33 | 31 | 10 | 2 | 0 | 4 | 24 | 4 | 66 | 6 | 0 | 5 | 6 | .455 | 0 | 2-8 | 15 | 3.45 | 4.48 |
| Postseason | | | 4 | 0 | 0 | 1 | 5.0 | 17 | 2 | 2 | 2 | 1 | 0 | 0 | 0 | 0 | 0 | 5 | 0 | 0 | 0 | 0 | - | 0 | 0-0 | 0 | 0.74 | 3.60 |
| 5 ML YEARS | | | 269 | 27 | 0 | 77 | 380.2 | 1642 | 337 | 183 | 175 | 54 | 8 | 9 | 14 | 164 | 10 | 381 | 29 | 2 | 24 | 30 | .444 | 0 | 19-38 | 65 | 3.91 | 4.14 |

# Felix Hernandez

**Pitches:** R **Bats:** R **Pos:** SP-31 **Ht:** 6'3" **Wt:** 230 **Born:** 4/8/1986 **Age:** 28

| HOW MUCH HE PITCHED | | | | | | | | | WHAT HE GAVE UP | | | | | | | | | | | | THE RESULTS | | | | | | | |
|---|---|---|---|---|---|---|---|---|---|---|---|---|---|---|---|---|---|---|---|---|---|---|---|---|---|---|---|---|
| Year | Team | Lg | G | GS | CG | GF | IP | BFP | H | R | ER | HR | SH | SF | HB | TBB | IBB | SO | WP | Bk | W | L | Pct | Sh | Sv-Op | Hld | ERC | ERA |
| 2005 | Sea | AL | 12 | 12 | 0 | 0 | 84.1 | 328 | 61 | 26 | 25 | 5 | 1 | 2 | 2 | 23 | 0 | 77 | 3 | 0 | 4 | 4 | .500 | 0 | 0-0 | 0 | 2.08 | 2.67 |
| 2006 | Sea | AL | 31 | 31 | 2 | 0 | 191.0 | 816 | 195 | 105 | 96 | 23 | 2 | 3 | 6 | 60 | 2 | 176 | 11 | 0 | 12 | 14 | .462 | 1 | 0-0 | 0 | 4.11 | 4.52 |
| 2007 | Sea | AL | 30 | 30 | 1 | 0 | 190.1 | 808 | 209 | 88 | 83 | 20 | 6 | 1 | 3 | 53 | 4 | 165 | 7 | 1 | 14 | 7 | .667 | 1 | 0-0 | 0 | 4.27 | 3.92 |
| 2008 | Sea | AL | 31 | 31 | 2 | 0 | 200.2 | 857 | 198 | 85 | 77 | 17 | 4 | 6 | 8 | 80 | 7 | 175 | 8 | 1 | 9 | 11 | .450 | 0 | 0-0 | 0 | 4.05 | 3.45 |
| 2009 | Sea | AL | 34 | 34 | 2 | 0 | 238.2 | 977 | 200 | 81 | 66 | 15 | 6 | **11** | 8 | 71 | 0 | 217 | **17** | 1 | **19** | 5 | **.792** | 1 | 0-0 | 0 | 2.72 | 2.49 |
| 2010 | Sea | AL | 34 | **34** | 6 | 0 | **249.2** | **1001** | 194 | 80 | 63 | 17 | 6 | 3 | 8 | 70 | 1 | 232 | 14 | 1 | 13 | 12 | .520 | 1 | 0-0 | 0 | 2.39 | **2.27** |
| 2011 | Sea | AL | 33 | 33 | 5 | 0 | 233.2 | 964 | 218 | 99 | 90 | 19 | 3 | 7 | 7 | 67 | 0 | 222 | 12 | 1 | 14 | 14 | .500 | 0 | 0-0 | 0 | 3.31 | 3.47 |
| 2012 | Sea | AL | 33 | 33 | 5 | 0 | 232.0 | 939 | 209 | 84 | 79 | 14 | 2 | 2 | 12 | 56 | 0 | 223 | 13 | 2 | 13 | 9 | .591 | **5** | 0-0 | 0 | 2.94 | 3.06 |
| 2013 | Sea | AL | 31 | 31 | 0 | 0 | 204.1 | 822 | 185 | 74 | 69 | 15 | 4 | 6 | 3 | 46 | 1 | 216 | 13 | 0 | 12 | 10 | .545 | 0 | 0-0 | 0 | 2.83 | 3.04 |
| 9 ML YEARS | | | 269 | 269 | 23 | 0 | 1824.2 | 7512 | 1669 | 722 | 648 | 145 | 34 | 41 | 57 | 526 | 15 | 1703 | 98 | 7 | 110 | 86 | .561 | 9 | 0-0 | 0 | 3.19 | 3.20 |

# Pedro Hernandez

**Pitches:** L **Bats:** L **Pos:** SP-12; RP-2 **Ht:** 5'10" **Wt:** 210 **Born:** 4/12/1989 **Age:** 25

| HOW MUCH HE PITCHED | | | | | | | | | WHAT HE GAVE UP | | | | | | | | | | | | THE RESULTS | | | | | | | |
|---|---|---|---|---|---|---|---|---|---|---|---|---|---|---|---|---|---|---|---|---|---|---|---|---|---|---|---|---|
| Year | Team | Lg | G | GS | CG | GF | IP | BFP | H | R | ER | HR | SH | SF | HB | TBB | IBB | SO | WP | Bk | W | L | Pct | Sh | Sv-Op | Hld | ERC | ERA |
| 2009 | Eugene | A- | 6 | 4 | 0 | 0 | 16.1 | 85 | 31 | 21 | 18 | 4 | 1 | 1 | 2 | 4 | 0 | 15 | 3 | 2 | 0 | 2 | .000 | 0 | 0- - | - | 10.89 | 9.92 |
| 2009 | Padres | R | 7 | 5 | 0 | 0 | 33.1 | 134 | 33 | 15 | 14 | 2 | 0 | 2 | 1 | 4 | 0 | 31 | 1 | 2 | 4 | 0 | 1.000 | 0 | 0- - | - | 2.85 | 3.78 |
| 2010 | FtWyn | A | 29 | 13 | 0 | 3 | 100.1 | 445 | 122 | 62 | 45 | 6 | 2 | 5 | 7 | 17 | 0 | 79 | 2 | 1 | 4 | 3 | .571 | 0 | 0- - | - | 4.28 | 4.04 |
| 2011 | Lk Els | A+ | 15 | 6 | 0 | 2 | 56.2 | 226 | 52 | 19 | 17 | 3 | 1 | 1 | 0 | 6 | 2 | 44 | 0 | 0 | 5 | 0 | 1.000 | 0 | 0- - | - | 2.20 | 2.70 |
| 2011 | Tucsn | AAA | 4 | 4 | 0 | 0 | 18.0 | 85 | 28 | 17 | 12 | 3 | 1 | 1 | 0 | 6 | 0 | 7 | 0 | 0 | 2 | 1 | .667 | 0 | 0- - | - | 7.83 | 6.00 |
| 2011 | SnAnt | AA | 9 | 8 | 0 | 0 | 41.1 | 171 | 39 | 17 | 16 | 4 | 1 | 1 | 0 | 10 | 0 | 43 | 0 | 0 | 3 | 2 | .600 | 0 | 0- - | - | 3.12 | 3.48 |

| HOW MUCH HE PITCHED | | | | | | | | | WHAT HE GAVE UP | | | | | | | | | | | | THE RESULTS | | | | | | | |
|---|---|---|---|---|---|---|---|---|---|---|---|---|---|---|---|---|---|---|---|---|---|---|---|---|---|---|---|---|
| Year | Team | Lg | G | GS | CG | GF | IP | BFP | H | R | ER | HR | SH | SF | HB | TBB | IBB | SO | WP | Bk | W | L | Pct | Sh | Sv-Op | Hld | ERC | ERA |
| 2012 | Brham | AA | 12 | 12 | 0 | 0 | 68.2 | 284 | 68 | 21 | 21 | 6 | 2 | 2 | 0 | 18 | 0 | 37 | 0 | 1 | 7 | 2 | .778 | 0 | 0- - | - | 3.44 | 2.75 |
| 2012 | Charltt | AAA | 3 | 2 | 0 | 1 | 17.0 | 71 | 18 | 8 | 7 | 1 | 2 | 2 | 0 | 3 | 0 | 17 | 0 | 0 | 1 | 0 | 1.000 | 0 | 0- - | - | 3.23 | 3.71 |
| 2012 | Roch | AAA | 4 | 4 | 0 | 0 | 17.1 | 75 | 25 | 10 | 10 | 1 | 0 | 1 | 0 | 1 | 0 | 11 | 1 | 0 | 0 | 2 | .000 | 0 | 0- - | - | 5.01 | 5.19 |
| 2013 | Roch | AAA | 8 | 7 | 1 | 1 | 46.0 | 201 | 53 | 28 | 23 | 8 | 2 | 3 | 1 | 12 | 0 | 33 | 0 | 0 | 2 | 2 | .500 | 0 | 0- - | - | 4.97 | 4.50 |
| 2013 | Twins | R | 2 | 1 | 0 | 0 | 7.0 | 27 | 8 | 2 | 2 | 0 | 1 | 0 | 0 | 0 | 0 | 6 | 1 | 0 | 0 | 1 | .000 | 0 | 0- - | - | 2.84 | 2.57 |
| 2013 | NwBrit | AA | 2 | 2 | 0 | 0 | 11.0 | 46 | 9 | 1 | 1 | 0 | 0 | 0 | 0 | 3 | 0 | 6 | 0 | 0 | 1 | 0 | 1.000 | 0 | 0- - | - | 1.94 | 0.82 |
| 2012 | CWS | AL | 1 | 1 | 0 | 0 | 4.0 | 25 | 12 | 8 | 8 | 3 | 0 | 0 | 0 | 1 | 0 | 2 | 0 | 0 | 0 | 1 | .000 | 0 | 0-0 | 0 | 24.35 | 18.00 |
| 2013 | Min | AL | 14 | 12 | 0 | 1 | 56.2 | 263 | 80 | 43 | 43 | 10 | 0 | 3 | 0 | 23 | 1 | 29 | 1 | 1 | 3 | 3 | .500 | 0 | 0-0 | 0 | 7.28 | 6.83 |
| 2 ML YEARS | | | 15 | 13 | 0 | 1 | 60.2 | 288 | 92 | 51 | 51 | 13 | 0 | 3 | 0 | 24 | 1 | 31 | 1 | 1 | 3 | 4 | .429 | 0 | 0-0 | 0 | 8.25 | 7.57 |

# Ramon Hernandez

**Bats:** R **Throws:** R **Pos:** C-11;PH-3;1B-2;DH-2 **Ht:** 6'0" **Wt:** 220 **Born:** 5/20/1976 **Age:** 38

| BATTING | | | | | | | | | | | | | | | | | | | | | BASERUNNING | | | | AVERAGES | | |
|---|---|---|---|---|---|---|---|---|---|---|---|---|---|---|---|---|---|---|---|---|---|---|---|---|---|---|---|
| Year | Team | Lg | G | AB | H | 2B | 3B | HR | (Hm | Rd) | TB | R | RBI | RC | TBB | IBB | SO | HBP | SH | SF | SB | CS | SB% | GDP | Avg | OBP | Slg |
| 2013 | Buffalo* | AAA | 5 | 19 | 2 | 0 | 0 | 0 | (- | -) | 2 | 0 | 2 | 0 | 0 | 0 | 3 | 0 | 0 | 0 | 0 | 0 | - | 2 | .105 | .105 | .105 |
| 1999 | Oak | AL | 40 | 136 | 38 | 7 | 0 | 3 | (1 | 2) | 54 | 13 | 21 | 20 | 18 | 0 | 11 | 1 | 1 | 2 | 1 | 0 | 1.00 | 5 | .279 | .363 | .397 |
| 2000 | Oak | AL | 143 | 419 | 101 | 19 | 0 | 14 | (7 | 7) | 162 | 52 | 62 | 49 | 38 | 1 | 64 | 7 | 10 | 5 | 1 | 0 | 1.00 | 14 | .241 | .311 | .387 |
| 2001 | Oak | AL | 136 | 453 | 115 | 25 | 0 | 15 | (5 | 10) | 185 | 55 | 60 | 58 | 37 | 3 | 68 | 6 | 9 | 4 | 1 | 1 | .50 | 10 | .254 | .316 | .408 |
| 2002 | Oak | AL | 136 | 403 | 94 | 20 | 0 | 7 | (3 | 4) | 135 | 51 | 42 | 41 | 43 | 1 | 64 | 5 | 3 | 3 | 0 | 0 | - | 11 | .233 | .313 | .335 |
| 2003 | Oak | AL | 140 | 483 | 132 | 24 | 1 | 21 | (9 | 12) | 221 | 70 | 78 | 69 | 33 | 2 | 79 | 12 | 2 | 6 | 0 | 0 | - | 14 | .273 | .331 | .458 |
| 2004 | SD | NL | 111 | 384 | 106 | 23 | 0 | 18 | (10 | 8) | 183 | 45 | 63 | 50 | 35 | 0 | 45 | 5 | 4 | 4 | 1 | 0 | 1.00 | 16 | .276 | .341 | .477 |
| 2005 | SD | NL | 99 | 369 | 107 | 19 | 2 | 12 | (5 | 7) | 166 | 36 | 58 | 44 | 18 | 0 | 40 | 1 | 1 | 3 | 1 | 0 | 1.00 | 14 | .290 | .322 | .450 |
| 2006 | Bal | AL | 144 | 501 | 138 | 29 | 2 | 23 | (17 | 6) | 240 | 66 | 91 | 82 | 43 | 2 | 79 | 11 | 0 | 5 | 1 | 0 | 1.00 | 13 | .275 | .343 | .479 |
| 2007 | Bal | AL | 106 | 364 | 94 | 18 | 0 | 9 | (4 | 5) | 139 | 40 | 62 | 56 | 36 | 1 | 59 | 6 | 0 | 3 | 1 | 3 | .25 | 9 | .258 | .333 | .382 |
| 2008 | Bal | AL | 133 | 463 | 119 | 22 | 1 | 15 | (10 | 5) | 188 | 49 | 65 | 59 | 32 | 3 | 62 | 5 | 1 | 6 | 0 | 0 | - | 9 | .257 | .308 | .406 |
| 2009 | Cin | NL | 81 | 287 | 74 | 13 | 1 | 5 | (2 | 3) | 104 | 25 | 37 | 42 | 33 | 2 | 34 | 3 | 4 | 4 | 1 | 0 | 1.00 | 7 | .258 | .336 | .362 |
| 2010 | Cin | NL | 97 | 313 | 93 | 18 | 1 | 7 | (3 | 4) | 134 | 30 | 48 | 49 | 29 | 1 | 49 | 5 | 3 | 2 | 0 | 0 | - | 8 | .297 | .364 | .428 |
| 2011 | Cin | NL | 91 | 298 | 84 | 13 | 0 | 12 | (6 | 6) | 133 | 28 | 36 | 36 | 23 | 6 | 41 | 5 | 0 | 2 | 0 | 0 | - | 11 | .282 | .341 | .446 |
| 2012 | Col | NL | 52 | 184 | 40 | 10 | 0 | 5 | (4 | 1) | 65 | 16 | 28 | 16 | 6 | 1 | 32 | 2 | 2 | 2 | 0 | 1 | .00 | 4 | .217 | .247 | .353 |
| 2013 | LAD | NL | 17 | 48 | 10 | 2 | 0 | 3 | (1 | 2) | 21 | 4 | 6 | 1 | 6 | 0 | 7 | 0 | 0 | 1 | 1 | 0 | 1.00 | 6 | .208 | .291 | .438 |
| Postseason | | | 25 | 76 | 16 | 3 | 0 | 1 | (1 | 0) | 22 | 6 | 6 | 7 | 5 | 0 | 13 | 3 | 2 | 0 | 0 | 0 | - | 2 | .211 | .286 | .289 |
| 15 ML YEARS | | | 1526 | 5105 | 1345 | 262 | 8 | 169 | (87 | 82) | 2130 | 580 | 757 | 672 | 430 | 23 | 734 | 74 | 40 | 52 | 9 | 5 | .64 | 151 | .263 | .327 | .417 |

# Roberto Hernandez

**Pitches:** R **Bats:** R **Pos:** SP-24; RP-8 **Ht:** 6'4" **Wt:** 230 **Born:** 8/30/1980 **Age:** 33

| HOW MUCH HE PITCHED | | | | | | | | | WHAT HE GAVE UP | | | | | | | | | | | | THE RESULTS | | | | | | | |
|---|---|---|---|---|---|---|---|---|---|---|---|---|---|---|---|---|---|---|---|---|---|---|---|---|---|---|---|---|
| Year | Team | Lg | G | GS | CG | GF | IP | BFP | H | R | ER | HR | SH | SF | HB | TBB | IBB | SO | WP | Bk | W | L | Pct | Sh | Sv-Op | Hld | ERC | ERA |
| 2006 | Cle | AL | 38 | 7 | 0 | 12 | 74.2 | 340 | 88 | 46 | 45 | 9 | 2 | 4 | 7 | 31 | 3 | 58 | 3 | 1 | 1 | 10 | .091 | 0 | 0-3 | 10 | 5.69 | 5.42 |
| 2007 | Cle | AL | 32 | 32 | 2 | 0 | 215.0 | 879 | 199 | 78 | 73 | 16 | 2 | 4 | 11 | 61 | 2 | 137 | 5 | 1 | 19 | 8 | .704 | 1 | 0-0 | 0 | 3.32 | 3.06 |
| 2008 | Cle | AL | 22 | 22 | 1 | 0 | 120.2 | 549 | 126 | 80 | 73 | 7 | 1 | 4 | 9 | 70 | 0 | 58 | 8 | 1 | 8 | 7 | .533 | 1 | 0-0 | 0 | 5.07 | 5.44 |
| 2009 | Cle | AL | 24 | 24 | 0 | 0 | 125.1 | 596 | 151 | 97 | 88 | 16 | 4 | 2 | 8 | 70 | 0 | 79 | 5 | 1 | 5 | 12 | .294 | 0 | 0-0 | 0 | 6.38 | 6.32 |
| 2010 | Cle | AL | 33 | 33 | 4 | 0 | 210.1 | 880 | 203 | 98 | 88 | 17 | 2 | 10 | 9 | 72 | 0 | 124 | 3 | 0 | 13 | 14 | .481 | 1 | 0-0 | 0 | 3.77 | 3.77 |
| 2011 | Cle | AL | 32 | 32 | 0 | 0 | 188.2 | 833 | 205 | **125** | 110 | 22 | 9 | 7 | 14 | 60 | 3 | 109 | 3 | 1 | 7 | 15 | .318 | 0 | 0-0 | 0 | 4.59 | 5.25 |
| 2012 | Cle | AL | 3 | 3 | 0 | 0 | 14.1 | 62 | 17 | 15 | 12 | 4 | 0 | 2 | 1 | 3 | 0 | 2 | 1 | 0 | 0 | 3 | .000 | 0 | 0-0 | 0 | 6.03 | 7.53 |
| 2013 | TB | AL | 32 | 24 | 1 | 3 | 151.0 | 643 | 164 | 87 | 82 | 24 | 3 | 5 | 13 | 38 | **8** | 113 | 3 | 0 | 6 | 13 | .316 | 0 | 1-1 | 0 | 4.74 | 4.89 |
| Postseason | | | 3 | 3 | 0 | 0 | 15.0 | 66 | 13 | 12 | 12 | 2 | 0 | 0 | 0 | 11 | 0 | 12 | 0 | 0 | 0 | 1 | .000 | 0 | 0-0 | 0 | 5.02 | 7.20 |
| 8 ML YEARS | | | 216 | 177 | 8 | 15 | 1100.0 | 4782 | 1153 | 626 | 571 | 115 | 23 | 38 | 72 | 405 | 16 | 680 | 31 | 5 | 59 | 82 | .418 | 3 | 1-4 | 10 | 4.54 | 4.67 |

# Elian Herrera

**Bats:** B **Throws:** R **Pos:** LF-2;PH-2 EH-lee-ahn **Ht:** 5'10" **Wt:** 190 **Born:** 2/1/1985 **Age:** 29

| BATTING | | | | | | | | | | | | | | | | | | | | | BASERUNNING | | | | AVERAGES | | |
|---|---|---|---|---|---|---|---|---|---|---|---|---|---|---|---|---|---|---|---|---|---|---|---|---|---|---|---|
| Year | Team | Lg | G | AB | H | 2B | 3B | HR | (Hm | Rd) | TB | R | RBI | RC | TBB | IBB | SO | HBP | SH | SF | SB | CS | SB% | GDP | Avg | OBP | Slg |
| 2009 | Gt Lks | A | 13 | 40 | 10 | 0 | 0 | 0 | (- | -) | 10 | 6 | 2 | 2 | 1 | 0 | 9 | 0 | 0 | 1 | 1 | 2 | .33 | 1 | .250 | .262 | .250 |
| 2009 | InldEm | A+ | 99 | 389 | 113 | 18 | 5 | 4 | (- | -) | 153 | 64 | 35 | 62 | 35 | 0 | 95 | 3 | 2 | 2 | 42 | 5 | .89 | 6 | .290 | .352 | .393 |
| 2010 | Chatt | AA | 97 | 299 | 77 | 11 | 4 | 2 | (- | -) | 102 | 44 | 38 | 44 | 47 | 1 | 71 | 4 | 12 | 3 | 31 | 10 | .76 | 6 | .258 | .363 | .341 |
| 2010 | Albq | AAA | 25 | 48 | 11 | 0 | 1 | 0 | (- | -) | 13 | 8 | 8 | 5 | 10 | 0 | 9 | 0 | 0 | 1 | 1 | 1 | .50 | 2 | .229 | .356 | .271 |
| 2011 | Chatt | AA | 116 | 378 | 105 | 17 | 6 | 3 | (- | -) | 143 | 69 | 35 | 60 | 58 | 0 | 103 | 1 | 6 | 6 | 32 | 11 | .74 | 7 | .278 | .370 | .378 |
| 2012 | Albq | AAA | 64 | 273 | 93 | 20 | 10 | 3 | (- | -) | 142 | 50 | 40 | 52 | 17 | 2 | 47 | 2 | 3 | 2 | 11 | 7 | .61 | 3 | .341 | .381 | .520 |
| 2013 | Albq | AAA | 108 | 408 | 115 | 13 | 1 | 7 | (- | -) | 151 | 69 | 43 | 62 | 48 | 1 | 76 | 8 | 10 | 2 | 16 | 3 | .84 | 13 | .282 | .367 | .370 |
| 2012 | LAD | NL | 67 | 187 | 47 | 10 | 1 | 1 | (0 | 1) | 62 | 26 | 17 | 20 | 23 | 0 | 50 | 2 | 2 | 0 | 4 | 2 | .67 | 5 | .251 | .340 | .332 |
| 2013 | LAD | NL | 4 | 8 | 2 | 0 | 0 | 0 | (0 | 0) | 2 | 0 | 0 | 0 | 0 | 0 | 2 | 0 | 0 | 0 | 0 | 0 | - | 0 | .250 | .250 | .250 |
| 2 ML YEARS | | | 71 | 195 | 49 | 10 | 1 | 1 | (0 | 1) | 64 | 26 | 17 | 20 | 23 | 0 | 52 | 2 | 2 | 0 | 4 | 2 | .67 | 5 | .251 | .336 | .328 |

# Jonathan Herrera

**Bats:** B **Throws:** R **Pos:** SS-42;2B-22;PH-17;3B-5;PR-3;LF-2 **Ht:** 5'9" **Wt:** 180 **Born:** 11/3/1984 **Age:** 29

| BATTING | | | | | | | | | | | | | | | | | | | | | BASERUNNING | | | | AVERAGES | | |
|---|---|---|---|---|---|---|---|---|---|---|---|---|---|---|---|---|---|---|---|---|---|---|---|---|---|---|---|
| Year | Team | Lg | G | AB | H | 2B | 3B | HR | (Hm | Rd) | TB | R | RBI | RC | TBB | IBB | SO | HBP | SH | SF | SB | CS | SB% | GDP | Avg | OBP | Slg |
| 2008 | Col | NL | 28 | 61 | 14 | 1 | 1 | 0 | (0 | 0) | 17 | 5 | 3 | 6 | 4 | 0 | 10 | 0 | 1 | 0 | 1 | 1 | .50 | 0 | .230 | .277 | .279 |
| 2010 | Col | NL | 76 | 222 | 63 | 6 | 2 | 1 | (0 | 1) | 76 | 34 | 21 | 29 | 25 | 1 | 36 | 0 | 7 | 3 | 2 | 2 | .50 | 2 | .284 | .352 | .342 |
| 2011 | Col | NL | 104 | 281 | 68 | 5 | 1 | 3 | (2 | 1) | 84 | 28 | 14 | 24 | 28 | 0 | 40 | 1 | 10 | 0 | 4 | 4 | .50 | 7 | .242 | .313 | .299 |
| 2012 | Col | NL | 86 | 225 | 59 | 9 | 1 | 3 | (3 | 0) | 79 | 29 | 12 | 22 | 16 | 3 | 39 | 2 | 7 | 0 | 4 | 1 | .80 | 5 | .262 | .317 | .351 |
| 2013 | Col | NL | 81 | 195 | 57 | 7 | 2 | 1 | (0 | 1) | 71 | 16 | 16 | 22 | 14 | 3 | 24 | 0 | 4 | 2 | 3 | 2 | .60 | 6 | .292 | .336 | .364 |
| 5 ML YEARS | | | 375 | 984 | 261 | 28 | 7 | 8 | (5 | 3) | 327 | 112 | 66 | 103 | 87 | 7 | 149 | 3 | 29 | 5 | 14 | 10 | .58 | 20 | .265 | .325 | .332 |

# Kelvin Herrera

**Pitches:** R **Bats:** R **Pos:** RP-59 **Ht:** 5'10" **Wt:** 200 **Born:** 12/31/1989 **Age:** 24

| HOW MUCH HE PITCHED | | | | | | | | WHAT HE GAVE UP | | | | | | | | | | | | THE RESULTS | | | | | | | |
|---|---|---|---|---|---|---|---|---|---|---|---|---|---|---|---|---|---|---|---|---|---|---|---|---|---|---|---|
| Year | Team | Lg | G | GS | CG | GF | IP | BFP | H | R | ER | HR | SH | SF | HB | TBB | IBB | SO | WP | Bk | W | L | Pct | Sh | Sv-Op | Hld | ERC | ERA |
| 2013 | Omha* | AAA | 10 | 3 | 0 | 7 | 16.0 | 62 | 6 | 2 | 2 | 1 | 0 | 0 | 2 | 6 | 1 | 22 | 0 | 0 | 0 | 1 | .000 | 0 | 2-- | - | 1.24 | 1.13 |
| 2013 | NWArk* | AA | 2 | 0 | 0 | 0 | 2.0 | 7 | 1 | 0 | 0 | 0 | 0 | 0 | 0 | 0 | 0 | 5 | 0 | 0 | 0 | 0 | - | 0 | 0-- | - | 0.54 | 0.00 |
| 2011 | KC | AL | 2 | 0 | 0 | 0 | 2.0 | 9 | 2 | 3 | 3 | 1 | 1 | 0 | 1 | 0 | 0 | 0 | 0 | 0 | 0 | 1 | .000 | 0 | 0-0 | 1 | 7.30 | 13.50 |
| 2012 | KC | AL | 76 | 0 | 0 | 10 | 84.1 | 344 | 79 | 24 | 22 | 4 | 5 | 0 | 2 | 21 | 6 | 77 | 3 | 1 | 4 | 3 | .571 | 0 | 3-4 | 19 | 2.84 | 2.35 |
| 2013 | KC | AL | 59 | 0 | 0 | 16 | 58.1 | 245 | 48 | 27 | 25 | 9 | 0 | 3 | 2 | 21 | 2 | 74 | 5 | 0 | 5 | 7 | .417 | 0 | 2-4 | 20 | 3.35 | 3.86 |
| 3 ML YEARS | | | 137 | 0 | 0 | 26 | 144.2 | 598 | 129 | 54 | 50 | 14 | 6 | 3 | 5 | 42 | 8 | 151 | 8 | 1 | 9 | 11 | .450 | 0 | 5-8 | 40 | 3.10 | 3.11 |

# Chris Herrmann

HERR-men

**Bats:** L **Throws:** R **Pos:** C-27;RF-21;PH-13;LF-3;DH-1;PR-1 **Ht:** 6'0" **Wt:** 200 **Born:** 11/24/1987 **Age:** 26

| BATTING | | | | | | | | | | | | | | | | | | | | | BASERUNNING | | | | AVERAGES | | |
|---|---|---|---|---|---|---|---|---|---|---|---|---|---|---|---|---|---|---|---|---|---|---|---|---|---|---|---|
| Year | Team | Lg | G | AB | H | 2B | 3B | HR | (Hm | Rd) | TB | R | RBI | RC | TBB | IBB | SO | HBP | SH | SF | SB | CS | SB% | GDP | Avg | OBP | Slg |
| 2009 | Elizab | R | 59 | 236 | 70 | 14 | 1 | 7 | (- | -) | 107 | 45 | 30 | 44 | 33 | 1 | 40 | 5 | 1 | 2 | 2 | 2 | .50 | 4 | .297 | .391 | .453 |
| 2010 | FtMyrs | A+ | 107 | 356 | 78 | 17 | 3 | 2 | (- | -) | 107 | 34 | 30 | 36 | 41 | 0 | 74 | 7 | 2 | 2 | 3 | 2 | .60 | 7 | .219 | .310 | .301 |
| 2011 | FtMyrs | A+ | 24 | 87 | 27 | 5 | 1 | 1 | (- | -) | 37 | 14 | 16 | 16 | 15 | 1 | 6 | 0 | 2 | 2 | 1 | 0 | 1.00 | 4 | .310 | .404 | .425 |
| 2011 | NwBrit | AA | 97 | 337 | 87 | 14 | 5 | 7 | (- | -) | 132 | 53 | 46 | 56 | 64 | 3 | 68 | 2 | 3 | 0 | 9 | 3 | .75 | 4 | .258 | .380 | .392 |
| 2012 | NwBrit | AA | 127 | 490 | 135 | 25 | 1 | 10 | (- | -) | 192 | 91 | 61 | 72 | 58 | 2 | 89 | 1 | 1 | 6 | 2 | 1 | .67 | 14 | .276 | .350 | .392 |
| 2013 | Roch | AAA | 69 | 247 | 56 | 9 | 3 | 2 | (- | -) | 77 | 31 | 22 | 24 | 24 | 1 | 61 | 1 | 2 | 1 | 3 | 2 | .60 | 1 | .227 | .297 | .312 |
| 2012 | Min | AL | 7 | 18 | 1 | 0 | 0 | 0 | (0 | 0) | 1 | 0 | 1 | 0 | 1 | 0 | 5 | 0 | 0 | 0 | 0 | 0 | - | 0 | .056 | .105 | .056 |
| 2013 | Min | AL | 57 | 157 | 32 | 7 | 0 | 4 | (1 | 3) | 51 | 16 | 18 | 15 | 18 | 0 | 49 | 0 | 3 | 0 | 0 | 1 | .00 | 3 | .204 | .286 | .325 |
| 2 ML YEARS | | | 64 | 175 | 33 | 7 | 0 | 4 | (1 | 3) | 52 | 16 | 19 | 15 | 19 | 0 | 54 | 0 | 3 | 0 | 0 | 1 | .00 | 3 | .189 | .268 | .297 |

# John Hester

**Bats:** R **Throws:** R **Pos:** C-1;DH-1;PH-1 **Ht:** 6'4" **Wt:** 230 **Born:** 9/14/1983 **Age:** 30

| BATTING | | | | | | | | | | | | | | | | | | | | | BASERUNNING | | | | AVERAGES | | |
|---|---|---|---|---|---|---|---|---|---|---|---|---|---|---|---|---|---|---|---|---|---|---|---|---|---|---|---|
| Year | Team | Lg | G | AB | H | 2B | 3B | HR | (Hm | Rd) | TB | R | RBI | RC | TBB | IBB | SO | HBP | SH | SF | SB | CS | SB% | GDP | Avg | OBP | Slg |
| 2013 | Salt Lk* | AAA | 74 | 253 | 60 | 13 | 1 | 8 | (- | -) | 99 | 40 | 29 | 32 | 27 | 0 | 75 | 0 | 1 | 3 | 3 | 1 | .75 | 11 | .237 | .307 | .391 |
| 2009 | Ari | NL | 15 | 28 | 7 | 2 | 0 | 1 | (1 | 0) | 12 | 4 | 4 | 5 | 2 | 0 | 7 | 0 | 0 | 0 | 0 | 0 | - | 0 | .250 | .300 | .429 |
| 2010 | Ari | NL | 38 | 95 | 20 | 7 | 0 | 2 | (1 | 1) | 33 | 9 | 7 | 9 | 11 | 1 | 32 | 0 | 0 | 0 | 1 | 0 | 1.00 | 2 | .211 | .292 | .347 |
| 2012 | LAA | AL | 39 | 85 | 18 | 1 | 0 | 3 | (1 | 2) | 28 | 14 | 4 | 4 | 8 | 0 | 25 | 1 | 1 | 0 | 0 | 0 | - | 1 | .212 | .287 | .329 |
| 2013 | LAA | AL | 1 | 0 | 0 | 0 | 0 | 0 | (0 | 0) | 0 | 1 | 0 | 0 | 1 | 0 | 0 | 0 | 0 | 0 | 0 | 0 | - | 0 | - | 1.000 | - |
| 4 ML YEARS | | | 93 | 208 | 45 | 10 | 0 | 6 | (3 | 3) | 73 | 28 | 15 | 18 | 22 | 1 | 64 | 1 | 1 | 0 | 1 | 0 | 1.00 | 3 | .216 | .294 | .351 |

# Jason Heyward

**Bats:** L **Throws:** L **Pos:** RF-86;CF-20;PH-3 **Ht:** 6'5" **Wt:** 240 **Born:** 8/9/1989 **Age:** 24

| BATTING | | | | | | | | | | | | | | | | | | | | | BASERUNNING | | | | AVERAGES | | |
|---|---|---|---|---|---|---|---|---|---|---|---|---|---|---|---|---|---|---|---|---|---|---|---|---|---|---|---|
| Year | Team | Lg | G | AB | H | 2B | 3B | HR | (Hm | Rd) | TB | R | RBI | RC | TBB | IBB | SO | HBP | SH | SF | SB | CS | SB% | GDP | Avg | OBP | Slg |
| 2013 | Gwnntt* | AAA | 6 | 20 | 6 | 1 | 0 | 0 | (- | -) | 7 | 1 | 6 | 3 | 4 | 0 | 7 | 1 | 0 | 1 | 1 | 0 | 1.00 | 0 | .300 | .423 | .350 |
| 2010 | Atl | NL | 142 | 520 | 144 | 29 | 5 | 18 | (9 | 9) | 237 | 83 | 72 | 96 | 91 | 2 | 128 | 10 | 0 | 2 | 11 | 6 | .65 | 13 | .277 | .393 | .456 |
| 2011 | Atl | NL | 128 | 396 | 90 | 18 | 2 | 14 | (5 | 9) | 154 | 50 | 42 | 49 | 51 | 4 | 93 | 4 | 0 | 3 | 9 | 2 | .82 | 7 | .227 | .319 | .389 |
| 2012 | Atl | NL | 158 | 587 | 158 | 30 | 6 | 27 | (9 | 18) | 281 | 93 | 82 | 87 | 58 | 1 | 152 | 2 | 0 | 3 | 21 | 8 | .72 | 5 | .269 | .335 | .479 |
| 2013 | Atl | NL | 104 | 382 | 97 | 22 | 1 | 14 | (10 | 4) | 163 | 67 | 38 | 55 | 48 | 1 | 73 | 8 | 1 | 0 | 2 | 4 | .33 | 7 | .254 | .349 | .427 |
| Postseason | | | 5 | 21 | 3 | 1 | 0 | 0 | (0 | 0) | 4 | 0 | 0 | 0 | 1 | 0 | 9 | 0 | 0 | 0 | 0 | 0 | - | 1 | .143 | .182 | .190 |
| 4 ML YEARS | | | 532 | 1885 | 489 | 99 | 14 | 73 | (33 | 40) | 835 | 293 | 234 | 287 | 248 | 8 | 446 | 24 | 1 | 8 | 43 | 20 | .68 | 32 | .259 | .352 | .443 |

# Aaron Hicks

**Bats:** B **Throws:** R **Pos:** CF-81 **Ht:** 6'2" **Wt:** 190 **Born:** 10/2/1989 **Age:** 24

| BATTING | | | | | | | | | | | | | | | | | | | | | BASERUNNING | | | | AVERAGES | | |
|---|---|---|---|---|---|---|---|---|---|---|---|---|---|---|---|---|---|---|---|---|---|---|---|---|---|---|---|
| Year | Team | Lg | G | AB | H | 2B | 3B | HR | (Hm | Rd) | TB | R | RBI | RC | TBB | IBB | SO | HBP | SH | SF | SB | CS | SB% | GDP | Avg | OBP | Slg |
| 2009 | Beloit | A | 67 | 251 | 63 | 15 | 3 | 4 | (- | -) | 96 | 43 | 29 | 36 | 40 | 1 | 55 | 1 | 2 | 3 | 10 | 8 | .56 | 3 | .251 | .353 | .382 |
| 2010 | Beloit | A | 115 | 423 | 118 | 27 | 6 | 8 | (- | -) | 181 | 86 | 49 | 79 | 88 | 2 | 112 | 0 | 4 | 3 | 21 | 10 | .68 | 4 | .279 | .401 | .428 |
| 2011 | FtMyrs | A+ | 122 | 443 | 107 | 31 | 5 | 5 | (- | -) | 163 | 79 | 38 | 64 | 78 | 5 | 110 | 1 | 3 | 3 | 17 | 8 | .68 | 6 | .242 | .354 | .368 |
| 2012 | NwBrit | AA | 129 | 472 | 135 | 21 | 11 | 13 | (- | -) | 217 | 100 | 61 | 90 | 79 | 2 | 116 | 1 | 3 | 8 | 32 | 11 | .74 | 8 | .286 | .384 | .460 |
| 2013 | Roch | AAA | 22 | 72 | 16 | 4 | 2 | 0 | (- | -) | 24 | 7 | 5 | 8 | 10 | 1 | 21 | 0 | 0 | 0 | 1 | 0 | 1.00 | 2 | .222 | .317 | .333 |
| 2013 | Min | AL | 81 | 281 | 54 | 11 | 3 | 8 | (3 | 5) | 95 | 37 | 27 | 25 | 24 | 0 | 84 | 2 | 4 | 2 | 9 | 3 | .75 | 0 | .192 | .259 | .338 |

# Aaron Hill

**Bats:** R **Throws:** R **Pos:** 2B-84;PH-5 **Ht:** 5'11" **Wt:** 205 **Born:** 3/21/1982 **Age:** 32

| BATTING | | | | | | | | | | | | | | | | | | | | | BASERUNNING | | | | AVERAGES | | |
|---|---|---|---|---|---|---|---|---|---|---|---|---|---|---|---|---|---|---|---|---|---|---|---|---|---|---|---|
| Year | Team | Lg | G | AB | H | 2B | 3B | HR | (Hm | Rd) | TB | R | RBI | RC | TBB | IBB | SO | HBP | SH | SF | SB | CS | SB% | GDP | Avg | OBP | Slg |
| 2013 | Reno* | AAA | 6 | 24 | 9 | 1 | 1 | 0 | (- | -) | 12 | 8 | 6 | 4 | 1 | 0 | 3 | 0 | 0 | 1 | 0 | 0 | - | 0 | .375 | .385 | .500 |
| 2005 | Tor | AL | 105 | 361 | 99 | 25 | 3 | 3 | (3 | 0) | 139 | 49 | 40 | 50 | 34 | 0 | 41 | 5 | 3 | 4 | 2 | 1 | .67 | 5 | .274 | .342 | .385 |
| 2006 | Tor | AL | 155 | 546 | 159 | 28 | 3 | 6 | (4 | 2) | 211 | 70 | 50 | 68 | 42 | 5 | 66 | 9 | 4 | 5 | 5 | 2 | .71 | 15 | .291 | .349 | .386 |
| 2007 | Tor | AL | 160 | 608 | 177 | 47 | 2 | 17 | (8 | 9) | 279 | 87 | 78 | 88 | 41 | 1 | 102 | 0 | 3 | 5 | 4 | 3 | .57 | 21 | .291 | .333 | .459 |
| 2008 | Tor | AL | 55 | 205 | 54 | 14 | 0 | 2 | (1 | 1) | 74 | 19 | 20 | 24 | 16 | 0 | 31 | 3 | 4 | 1 | 4 | 2 | .67 | 4 | .263 | .324 | .361 |
| 2009 | Tor | AL | 158 | **682** | 195 | 37 | 0 | 36 | (21 | 15) | 340 | 103 | 108 | 110 | 42 | 1 | 98 | 5 | 1 | 4 | 6 | 2 | .75 | 17 | .286 | .330 | .499 |
| 2010 | Tor | AL | 138 | 528 | 108 | 22 | 0 | 26 | (15 | 11) | 208 | 70 | 68 | 57 | 41 | 2 | 85 | 8 | 1 | 2 | 2 | 2 | .50 | 8 | .205 | .271 | .394 |
| 2011 | 2 Tms | | 137 | 520 | 128 | 27 | 3 | 8 | (4 | 4) | 185 | 61 | 61 | 61 | 35 | 1 | 72 | 7 | 2 | 7 | 21 | 7 | .75 | 10 | .246 | .299 | .356 |
| 2012 | Ari | NL | 156 | 609 | 184 | 44 | 6 | 26 | (14 | 12) | 318 | 93 | 85 | 101 | 52 | 7 | 86 | 4 | 1 | 2 | 14 | 5 | .74 | 15 | .302 | .360 | .522 |
| 2013 | Ari | NL | 87 | 327 | 95 | 21 | 1 | 11 | (7 | 4) | 151 | 45 | 41 | 45 | 29 | 2 | 48 | 5 | 0 | 1 | 1 | 4 | .20 | 6 | .291 | .356 | .462 |

| Year | Team | Lg | G | AB | H | 2B | 3B | HR | (Hm | Rd) | TB | R | RBI | RC | TBB | IBB | SO | HBP | SH | SF | SB | CS | SB% | GDP | Avg | OBP | Slg |
|---|---|---|---|---|---|---|---|---|---|---|---|---|---|---|---|---|---|---|---|---|---|---|---|---|---|---|---|
| | | | BATTING | | | | | | | | | | | | | | | | | | BASERUNNING | | | | AVERAGES | | |
| 11 | Tor | AL | 104 | 396 | 89 | 15 | 1 | 6 | (3 | 3) | 124 | 38 | 45 | 38 | 23 | 1 | 53 | 4 | 0 | 6 | 16 | 3 | .84 | 8 | .225 | .270 | .313 |
| 11 | Ari | NL | 33 | 124 | 39 | 12 | 2 | 2 | (1 | 1) | 61 | 23 | 16 | 23 | 12 | 0 | 19 | 3 | 2 | 1 | 5 | 4 | .56 | 2 | .315 | .386 | .492 |
| Postseason | | | 5 | 18 | 5 | 0 | 0 | 1 | (1 | 0) | 8 | 3 | 1 | 2 | 5 | 0 | 3 | 0 | 0 | 0 | 0 | 0 | - | 1 | .278 | .435 | .444 |
| 9 ML YEARS | | | 1151 | 4386 | 1199 | 265 | 18 | 135 | (77 | 58) | 1905 | 597 | 551 | 604 | 332 | 19 | 629 | 46 | 19 | 31 | 59 | 28 | .68 | 101 | .273 | .329 | .434 |

## Koyie Hill

**Bats:** B **Throws:** R **Pos:** C-18 COY **Ht:** 6'1" **Wt:** 210 **Born:** 3/9/1979 **Age:** 35

| Year | Team | Lg | G | AB | H | 2B | 3B | HR | (Hm | Rd) | TB | R | RBI | RC | TBB | IBB | SO | HBP | SH | SF | SB | CS | SB% | GDP | Avg | OBP | Slg |
|---|---|---|---|---|---|---|---|---|---|---|---|---|---|---|---|---|---|---|---|---|---|---|---|---|---|---|---|
| | | | BATTING | | | | | | | | | | | | | | | | | | BASERUNNING | | | | AVERAGES | | |
| 2013 | NewOr* | AAA | 60 | 190 | 45 | 14 | 0 | 1 | (- | -) | 62 | 18 | 14 | 18 | 15 | 1 | 38 | 0 | 0 | 1 | 0 | 0 | - | 7 | .237 | .291 | .326 |
| 2003 | LAD | NL | 3 | 3 | 1 | 1 | 0 | 0 | (0 | 0) | 2 | 0 | 0 | 0 | 0 | 0 | 2 | 0 | 0 | 0 | 0 | 0 | - | 0 | .333 | .333 | .667 |
| 2004 | Ari | NL | 13 | 36 | 9 | 1 | 0 | 1 | (1 | 0) | 13 | 3 | 6 | 5 | 2 | 1 | 6 | 0 | 0 | 0 | 1 | 0 | 1.00 | 1 | .250 | .289 | .361 |
| 2005 | Ari | NL | 34 | 78 | 17 | 5 | 0 | 0 | (0 | 0) | 22 | 6 | 6 | 6 | 11 | 0 | 27 | 0 | 0 | 2 | 0 | 1 | .00 | 0 | .218 | .308 | .282 |
| 2007 | ChC | NL | 36 | 93 | 15 | 4 | 0 | 2 | (1 | 1) | 25 | 7 | 12 | 3 | 8 | 0 | 18 | 1 | 1 | 2 | 0 | 0 | - | 4 | .161 | .231 | .269 |
| 2008 | ChC | NL | 10 | 21 | 2 | 1 | 0 | 0 | (0 | 0) | 3 | 0 | 1 | 0 | 0 | 0 | 12 | 0 | 1 | 0 | 0 | 0 | - | 0 | .095 | .095 | .143 |
| 2009 | ChC | NL | 83 | 253 | 60 | 12 | 2 | 2 | (1 | 1) | 82 | 26 | 24 | 23 | 27 | 6 | 78 | 1 | 2 | 1 | 0 | 0 | - | 9 | .237 | .312 | .324 |
| 2010 | ChC | NL | 77 | 215 | 46 | 13 | 1 | 1 | (1 | 0) | 64 | 18 | 17 | 17 | 12 | 3 | 61 | 0 | 3 | 1 | 1 | 0 | 1.00 | 5 | .214 | .254 | .298 |
| 2011 | ChC | NL | 46 | 134 | 26 | 3 | 1 | 2 | (1 | 1) | 37 | 15 | 9 | 2 | 14 | 3 | 40 | 0 | 4 | 1 | 1 | 0 | 1.00 | 3 | .194 | .268 | .276 |
| 2012 | ChC | NL | 11 | 39 | 7 | 1 | 0 | 0 | (0 | 0) | 8 | 3 | 1 | 1 | 0 | 0 | 7 | 0 | 0 | 0 | 0 | 0 | - | 0 | .179 | .179 | .205 |
| 2013 | Mia | NL | 18 | 58 | 9 | 2 | 0 | 0 | (0 | 0) | 11 | 3 | 0 | 0 | 2 | 0 | 18 | 0 | 1 | 0 | 0 | 0 | - | 1 | .155 | .183 | .190 |
| 10 ML YEARS | | | 331 | 930 | 192 | 43 | 4 | 8 | (5 | 3) | 267 | 81 | 76 | 57 | 76 | 13 | 269 | 2 | 12 | 7 | 3 | 1 | .75 | 23 | .206 | .266 | .287 |

## Rich Hill

**Pitches:** L **Bats:** L **Pos:** RP-63 **Ht:** 6'5" **Wt:** 220 **Born:** 3/11/1980 **Age:** 34

| Year | Team | Lg | G | GS | CG | GF | IP | BFP | H | R | ER | HR | SH | SF | HB | TBB | IBB | SO | WP | Bk | W | L | Pct | Sh | Sv-Op | Hld | ERC | ERA |
|---|---|---|---|---|---|---|---|---|---|---|---|---|---|---|---|---|---|---|---|---|---|---|---|---|---|---|---|---|
| | | | HOW MUCH HE PITCHED | | | | | | WHAT HE GAVE UP | | | | | | | | | | | | THE RESULTS | | | | | | | |
| 2005 | ChC | NL | 10 | 4 | 0 | 1 | 23.2 | 115 | 25 | 24 | 24 | 3 | 1 | 0 | 1 | 17 | 1 | 21 | 0 | 0 | 0 | 2 | .000 | 0 | 0-0 | 0 | 5.81 | 9.13 |
| 2006 | ChC | NL | 17 | 16 | 2 | 1 | 99.1 | 417 | 83 | 51 | 46 | 16 | 8 | 3 | 2 | 39 | 1 | 90 | 3 | 0 | 6 | 7 | .462 | 1 | 0-0 | 0 | 3.59 | 4.17 |
| 2007 | ChC | NL | 32 | 32 | 0 | 0 | 195.0 | 812 | 170 | 89 | 85 | 27 | 9 | 4 | 12 | 63 | 3 | 183 | 1 | 1 | 11 | 8 | .579 | 0 | 0-0 | 0 | 3.56 | 3.92 |
| 2008 | ChC | NL | 5 | 5 | 0 | 0 | 19.2 | 89 | 13 | 9 | 9 | 2 | 0 | 2 | 1 | 18 | 0 | 15 | 1 | 0 | 1 | 0 | 1.000 | 0 | 0-0 | 0 | 4.38 | 4.12 |
| 2009 | Bal | AL | 14 | 13 | 0 | 0 | 57.2 | 275 | 68 | 53 | 50 | 7 | 2 | 2 | 1 | 40 | 2 | 46 | 1 | 1 | 3 | 3 | .500 | 0 | 0-0 | 0 | 6.55 | 7.80 |
| 2010 | Bos | AL | 6 | 0 | 0 | 0 | 4.0 | 18 | 5 | 0 | 0 | 0 | 0 | 0 | 0 | 1 | 0 | 3 | 0 | 0 | 1 | 0 | 1.000 | 0 | 0-0 | 1 | 4.05 | 0.00 |
| 2011 | Bos | AL | 9 | 0 | 0 | 3 | 8.0 | 30 | 3 | 0 | 0 | 0 | 0 | 0 | 1 | 3 | 0 | 12 | 1 | 0 | 0 | 0 | - | 0 | 0-0 | 3 | 1.10 | 0.00 |
| 2012 | Bos | AL | 25 | 0 | 0 | 3 | 19.2 | 83 | 17 | 4 | 4 | 0 | 0 | 0 | 0 | 11 | 1 | 21 | 0 | 0 | 1 | 0 | 1.000 | 0 | 0-0 | 6 | 3.24 | 1.83 |
| 2013 | Cle | AL | 63 | 0 | 0 | 3 | 38.2 | 182 | 38 | 30 | 27 | 3 | 1 | 2 | 2 | 29 | 6 | 51 | 6 | 1 | 1 | 2 | .333 | 0 | 0-2 | 13 | 5.07 | 6.28 |
| Postseason | | | 1 | 1 | 0 | 0 | 3.0 | 18 | 6 | 3 | 3 | 1 | 0 | 0 | 1 | 2 | 0 | 3 | 0 | 0 | 0 | 1 | .000 | 0 | 0-0 | 0 | 15.68 | 9.00 |
| 9 ML YEARS | | | 181 | 70 | 2 | 11 | 465.2 | 2021 | 422 | 260 | 245 | 58 | 21 | 13 | 20 | 221 | 14 | 442 | 13 | 3 | 24 | 22 | .522 | 1 | 0-2 | 23 | 4.13 | 4.74 |

## Eric Hinske

**Bats:** L **Throws:** R **Pos:** PH-48;1B-6;DH-1 HIN-skee **Ht:** 6'2" **Wt:** 235 **Born:** 8/5/1977 **Age:** 36

| Year | Team | Lg | G | AB | H | 2B | 3B | HR | (Hm | Rd) | TB | R | RBI | RC | TBB | IBB | SO | HBP | SH | SF | SB | CS | SB% | GDP | Avg | OBP | Slg |
|---|---|---|---|---|---|---|---|---|---|---|---|---|---|---|---|---|---|---|---|---|---|---|---|---|---|---|---|
| | | | BATTING | | | | | | | | | | | | | | | | | | BASERUNNING | | | | AVERAGES | | |
| 2013 | Reno* | AAA | 5 | 18 | 1 | 0 | 0 | 0 | (- | -) | 1 | 0 | 0 | 0 | 1 | 0 | 5 | 0 | 0 | 0 | 0 | 0 | - | 0 | .056 | .105 | .056 |
| 2002 | Tor | AL | 151 | 566 | 158 | 38 | 2 | 24 | (15 | 9) | 272 | 99 | 84 | 103 | 77 | 5 | 138 | 2 | 0 | 5 | 13 | 1 | .93 | 12 | .279 | .365 | .481 |
| 2003 | Tor | AL | 124 | 449 | 109 | 45 | 3 | 12 | (4 | 8) | 196 | 74 | 63 | 66 | 59 | 1 | 104 | 1 | 0 | 5 | 12 | 2 | .86 | 11 | .243 | .329 | .437 |
| 2004 | Tor | AL | 155 | 570 | 140 | 23 | 3 | 15 | (6 | 9) | 214 | 66 | 69 | 60 | 54 | 2 | 109 | 4 | 0 | 6 | 12 | 8 | .60 | 14 | .246 | .312 | .375 |
| 2005 | Tor | AL | 147 | 477 | 125 | 31 | 2 | 15 | (7 | 8) | 205 | 79 | 68 | 71 | 46 | 4 | 121 | 8 | 0 | 6 | 8 | 4 | .67 | 8 | .262 | .333 | .430 |
| 2006 | 2 Tms | AL | 109 | 277 | 75 | 17 | 2 | 13 | (7 | 6) | 135 | 43 | 34 | 39 | 35 | 2 | 79 | 0 | 0 | 0 | 2 | 2 | .50 | 8 | .271 | .353 | .487 |
| 2007 | Bos | AL | 84 | 186 | 38 | 12 | 3 | 6 | (4 | 2) | 74 | 25 | 21 | 22 | 28 | 2 | 54 | 3 | 0 | 1 | 3 | 0 | 1.00 | 7 | .204 | .317 | .398 |
| 2008 | TB | AL | 133 | 381 | 94 | 21 | 1 | 20 | (8 | 12) | 177 | 59 | 60 | 53 | 47 | 4 | 88 | 3 | 0 | 1 | 10 | 3 | .77 | 13 | .247 | .333 | .465 |
| 2009 | 2 Tms | | 93 | 190 | 46 | 12 | 0 | 8 | (2 | 6) | 82 | 31 | 25 | 27 | 27 | 1 | 52 | 5 | 0 | 2 | 1 | 0 | 1.00 | 2 | .242 | .348 | .432 |
| 2010 | Atl | NL | 131 | 281 | 72 | 21 | 1 | 11 | (7 | 4) | 128 | 38 | 51 | 40 | 33 | 5 | 75 | 3 | 0 | 3 | 0 | 0 | - | 4 | .256 | .338 | .456 |
| 2011 | Atl | NL | 117 | 236 | 55 | 10 | 0 | 10 | (3 | 7) | 95 | 24 | 28 | 26 | 26 | 1 | 71 | 1 | 0 | 1 | 0 | 1 | .00 | 5 | .233 | .311 | .403 |
| 2012 | Atl | NL | 91 | 132 | 26 | 7 | 1 | 2 | (0 | 2) | 41 | 9 | 13 | 9 | 14 | 2 | 41 | 0 | 0 | 1 | 0 | 0 | - | 5 | .197 | .272 | .311 |
| 2013 | Ari | NL | 52 | 52 | 9 | 3 | 0 | 1 | (0 | 1) | 15 | 2 | 6 | 4 | 6 | 0 | 17 | 0 | 0 | 0 | 0 | 0 | - | 2 | .173 | .259 | .288 |
| 06 | Tor | AL | 78 | 197 | 52 | 9 | 2 | 12 | (6 | 6) | 101 | 35 | 29 | 29 | 27 | 2 | 49 | 0 | 0 | 0 | 1 | 1 | .50 | 6 | .264 | .353 | .513 |
| 06 | Bos | AL | 31 | 80 | 23 | 8 | 0 | 1 | (1 | 0) | 34 | 8 | 5 | 10 | 8 | 0 | 30 | 0 | 0 | 0 | 1 | 1 | .50 | 2 | .288 | .352 | .425 |
| 09 | Pit | NL | 54 | 106 | 27 | 9 | 0 | 1 | (0 | 1) | 39 | 18 | 11 | 16 | 17 | 0 | 27 | 3 | 0 | 0 | 0 | 0 | - | 0 | .255 | .373 | .368 |
| 09 | NYY | AL | 39 | 84 | 19 | 3 | 0 | 7 | (2 | 5) | 43 | 13 | 14 | 11 | 10 | 1 | 25 | 2 | 0 | 2 | 1 | 0 | 1.00 | 2 | .226 | .316 | .512 |
| Postseason | | | 10 | 7 | 2 | 0 | 0 | 2 | (1 | 1) | 8 | 4 | 3 | 2 | 2 | 0 | 4 | 0 | 0 | 0 | 0 | 0 | - | 0 | .286 | .444 | 1.143 |
| 12 ML YEARS | | | 1387 | 3797 | 947 | 240 | 18 | 137 | (63 | 74) | 1634 | 549 | 522 | 520 | 452 | 29 | 949 | 30 | 0 | 31 | 61 | 21 | .74 | 91 | .249 | .332 | .430 |

## Luke Hochevar

**Pitches:** R **Bats:** R **Pos:** RP-58 HOE-chay-vur **Ht:** 6'5" **Wt:** 215 **Born:** 9/15/1983 **Age:** 30

| Year | Team | Lg | G | GS | CG | GF | IP | BFP | H | R | ER | HR | SH | SF | HB | TBB | IBB | SO | WP | Bk | W | L | Pct | Sh | Sv-Op | Hld | ERC | ERA |
|---|---|---|---|---|---|---|---|---|---|---|---|---|---|---|---|---|---|---|---|---|---|---|---|---|---|---|---|---|
| | | | HOW MUCH HE PITCHED | | | | | | WHAT HE GAVE UP | | | | | | | | | | | | THE RESULTS | | | | | | | |
| 2007 | KC | AL | 4 | 1 | 0 | 1 | 12.2 | 54 | 11 | 4 | 3 | 1 | 1 | 0 | 3 | 4 | 0 | 5 | 1 | 0 | 0 | 1 | .000 | 0 | 0-0 | 0 | 3.86 | 2.13 |
| 2008 | KC | AL | 22 | 22 | 0 | 0 | 129.0 | 566 | 143 | 84 | 79 | 12 | 1 | 2 | 5 | 47 | 1 | 72 | 7 | 0 | 6 | 12 | .333 | 0 | 0-0 | 0 | 4.67 | 5.51 |
| 2009 | KC | AL | 25 | 25 | 2 | 0 | 143.0 | 631 | 167 | 109 | 104 | 23 | 2 | 0 | 8 | 46 | 0 | 106 | 9 | 0 | 7 | 13 | .350 | 1 | 0-0 | 0 | 5.46 | 6.55 |
| 2010 | KC | AL | 18 | 17 | 1 | 0 | 103.0 | 450 | 110 | 61 | 55 | 9 | 2 | 2 | 4 | 37 | 1 | 76 | 2 | 1 | 6 | 6 | .500 | 0 | 0-0 | 0 | 4.34 | 4.81 |
| 2011 | KC | AL | 31 | 31 | 0 | 0 | 198.0 | 835 | 192 | 110 | 103 | 23 | 2 | 2 | 7 | 62 | 4 | 128 | 7 | **2** | 11 | 11 | .500 | 0 | 0-0 | 0 | 3.80 | 4.68 |
| 2012 | KC | AL | 32 | 32 | 2 | 0 | 185.1 | 800 | 202 | **127** | **118** | 27 | 4 | 3 | 13 | 61 | 3 | 144 | 8 | 0 | 8 | 16 | .333 | 1 | 0-0 | 0 | 4.99 | 5.73 |
| 2013 | KC | AL | 58 | 0 | 0 | 22 | 70.1 | 262 | 41 | 15 | 15 | 8 | 2 | 0 | 1 | 17 | 1 | 82 | 2 | 0 | 5 | 2 | .714 | 0 | 2-5 | 9 | 1.62 | 1.92 |
| 7 ML YEARS | | | 190 | 128 | 5 | 23 | 841.1 | 3598 | 866 | 510 | 477 | 103 | 14 | 9 | 41 | 274 | 10 | 613 | 36 | 3 | 43 | 61 | .413 | 2 | 2-5 | 9 | 4.32 | 5.10 |

# L.J. Hoes

**Bats:** R **Throws:** R **Pos:** RF-44;LF-3;PH-3;CF-2;DH-1 HOSE **Ht:** 6'0" **Wt:** 190 **Born:** 3/5/1990 **Age:** 24

| BATTING | | | | | | | | | | | | | | | | | | | | | BASERUNNING | | | | AVERAGES | | |
|---|---|---|---|---|---|---|---|---|---|---|---|---|---|---|---|---|---|---|---|---|---|---|---|---|---|---|---|
| Year | Team | Lg | G | AB | H | 2B | 3B | HR | (Hm | Rd) | TB | R | RBI | RC | TBB | IBB | SO | HBP | SH | SF | SB | CS | SB% | GDP | Avg | OBP | Slg |
| 2009 | Dlmrva | A | 119 | 431 | 112 | 19 | 0 | 2 | (- | -) | 137 | 42 | 47 | 44 | 23 | 1 | 80 | 3 | 4 | 4 | 20 | 5 | .80 | 10 | .260 | .299 | .318 |
| 2010 | Frdrck | A+ | 97 | 353 | 98 | 19 | 2 | 3 | (- | -) | 130 | 52 | 44 | 53 | 53 | 1 | 70 | 3 | 2 | 2 | 10 | 8 | .56 | 17 | .278 | .375 | .368 |
| 2010 | Abrdn | A- | 8 | 28 | 13 | 5 | 1 | 1 | (- | -) | 23 | 8 | 5 | 10 | 2 | 0 | 1 | 2 | 0 | 0 | 1 | 1 | .50 | 1 | .464 | .531 | .821 |
| 2010 | Bowie | AA | 3 | 9 | 2 | 0 | 0 | 0 | (- | -) | 2 | 1 | 1 | 0 | 0 | 0 | 1 | 0 | 0 | 0 | 0 | 0 | - | 1 | .222 | .222 | .222 |
| 2011 | Frdrck | A+ | 41 | 158 | 38 | 7 | 0 | 3 | (- | -) | 54 | 23 | 17 | 16 | 10 | 0 | 25 | 3 | 1 | 1 | 4 | 2 | .67 | 7 | .241 | .297 | .342 |
| 2011 | Bowie | AA | 95 | 344 | 105 | 17 | 1 | 6 | (- | -) | 142 | 47 | 54 | 57 | 43 | 0 | 56 | 0 | 3 | 3 | 16 | 7 | .70 | 15 | .305 | .379 | .413 |
| 2012 | Bowie | AA | 51 | 196 | 52 | 9 | 3 | 2 | (- | -) | 73 | 25 | 15 | 30 | 31 | 1 | 33 | 1 | 1 | 0 | 12 | 5 | .71 | 9 | .265 | .368 | .372 |
| 2012 | Norfolk | AAA | 82 | 317 | 95 | 14 | 4 | 3 | (- | -) | 126 | 54 | 38 | 49 | 34 | 0 | 43 | 4 | 1 | 1 | 8 | 7 | .53 | 11 | .300 | .374 | .397 |
| 2013 | Norfolk | AAA | 99 | 365 | 111 | 25 | 1 | 3 | (- | -) | 147 | 62 | 40 | 64 | 58 | 0 | 56 | 5 | 1 | 1 | 7 | 7 | .50 | 13 | .304 | .406 | .403 |
| 2012 | Bal | AL | 2 | 1 | 0 | 0 | 0 | 0 | (0 | 0) | 0 | 0 | 0 | 0 | 0 | 0 | 0 | 0 | 0 | 0 | 0 | 0 | - | 0 | .000 | .000 | .000 |
| 2013 | 2 Tms | AL | 47 | 170 | 48 | 7 | 2 | 1 | (0 | 1) | 62 | 24 | 10 | 21 | 12 | 0 | 35 | 1 | 0 | 1 | 7 | 1 | .88 | 4 | .282 | .332 | .365 |
| 13 | Bal | AL | 1 | 3 | 0 | 0 | 0 | 0 | (0 | 0) | 0 | 0 | 0 | 0 | 0 | 0 | 1 | 0 | 0 | 0 | 0 | 0 | - | 0 | .000 | .000 | .000 |
| 13 | Hou | AL | 46 | 167 | 48 | 7 | 2 | 1 | (0 | 1) | 62 | 24 | 10 | 21 | 12 | 0 | 34 | 1 | 0 | 1 | 7 | 1 | .88 | 4 | .287 | .337 | .371 |
| 2 ML YEARS | | | 49 | 171 | 48 | 7 | 2 | 1 | (0 | 1) | 62 | 24 | 10 | 21 | 12 | 0 | 35 | 1 | 0 | 1 | 7 | 1 | .88 | 4 | .281 | .330 | .363 |

# Bryan Holaday

**Bats:** R **Throws:** R **Pos:** C-14;PR-3;DH-1;PH-1 HAHL-ih-daye **Ht:** 6'0" **Wt:** 205 **Born:** 11/19/1987 **Age:** 26

| BATTING | | | | | | | | | | | | | | | | | | | | | BASERUNNING | | | | AVERAGES | | |
|---|---|---|---|---|---|---|---|---|---|---|---|---|---|---|---|---|---|---|---|---|---|---|---|---|---|---|---|
| Year | Team | Lg | G | AB | H | 2B | 3B | HR | (Hm | Rd) | TB | R | RBI | RC | TBB | IBB | SO | HBP | SH | SF | SB | CS | SB% | GDP | Avg | OBP | Slg |
| 2010 | Lkland | A+ | 44 | 159 | 35 | 8 | 0 | 3 | (- | -) | 52 | 14 | 12 | 19 | 21 | 2 | 43 | 7 | 0 | 1 | 0 | 0 | - | 2 | .220 | .335 | .327 |
| 2011 | Erie | AA | 95 | 330 | 80 | 18 | 0 | 7 | (- | -) | 119 | 35 | 42 | 39 | 27 | 1 | 76 | 4 | 6 | 4 | 6 | 1 | .86 | 7 | .242 | .304 | .361 |
| 2012 | Toledo | AAA | 75 | 250 | 60 | 12 | 1 | 2 | (- | -) | 80 | 18 | 25 | 27 | 22 | 0 | 43 | 5 | 3 | 2 | 2 | 0 | 1.00 | 7 | .240 | .312 | .320 |
| 2013 | Toledo | AAA | 80 | 288 | 75 | 18 | 1 | 4 | (- | -) | 107 | 28 | 24 | 34 | 18 | 0 | 57 | 5 | 6 | 3 | 0 | 1 | .00 | 5 | .260 | .312 | .372 |
| 2012 | Det | AL | 6 | 12 | 3 | 1 | 0 | 0 | (0 | 0) | 4 | 3 | 0 | 1 | 0 | 0 | 2 | 0 | 1 | 0 | 0 | 0 | - | 0 | .250 | .250 | .333 |
| 2013 | Det | AL | 16 | 27 | 8 | 1 | 0 | 1 | (1 | 0) | 12 | 8 | 2 | 3 | 2 | 0 | 3 | 1 | 3 | 0 | 0 | 0 | - | 0 | .296 | .367 | .444 |
| 2 ML YEARS | | | 22 | 39 | 11 | 2 | 0 | 1 | (1 | 0) | 16 | 11 | 2 | 4 | 2 | 0 | 5 | 1 | 4 | 0 | 0 | 0 | - | 0 | .282 | .333 | .410 |

# Derek Holland

**Pitches:** L **Bats:** B **Pos:** SP-33 **Ht:** 6'2" **Wt:** 210 **Born:** 10/9/1986 **Age:** 27

| HOW MUCH HE PITCHED | | | | | | | | WHAT HE GAVE UP | | | | | | | | | | | | THE RESULTS | | | | | | | |
|---|---|---|---|---|---|---|---|---|---|---|---|---|---|---|---|---|---|---|---|---|---|---|---|---|---|---|---|
| Year | Team | Lg | G | GS | CG | GF | IP | BFP | H | R | ER | HR | SH | SF | HB | TBB | IBB | SO | WP | Bk | W | L | Pct | Sh | Sv-Op | Hld | ERC | ERA |
| 2009 | Tex | AL | 33 | 21 | 1 | 0 | 138.1 | 611 | 160 | 98 | 94 | 26 | 2 | 3 | 4 | 47 | 0 | 107 | 3 | 3 | 8 | 13 | .381 | 1 | 0-1 | 2 | 5.52 | 6.12 |
| 2010 | Tex | AL | 14 | 10 | 0 | 2 | 57.1 | 253 | 55 | 30 | 26 | 6 | 0 | 2 | 4 | 24 | 0 | 54 | 0 | 1 | 3 | 4 | .429 | 0 | 0-0 | 1 | 4.17 | 4.08 |
| 2011 | Tex | AL | 32 | 32 | 4 | 0 | 198.0 | 843 | 201 | 97 | 87 | 22 | 1 | 3 | 6 | 67 | 1 | 162 | 2 | 1 | 16 | 5 | .762 | **4** | 0-0 | 0 | 4.15 | 3.95 |
| 2012 | Tex | AL | 29 | 27 | 0 | 1 | 175.1 | 730 | 162 | 100 | 91 | 32 | 5 | 4 | 3 | 52 | 0 | 145 | 1 | 0 | 12 | 7 | .632 | 0 | 0-0 | 0 | 3.86 | 4.67 |
| 2013 | Tex | AL | 33 | 33 | 2 | 0 | 213.0 | 894 | 210 | 90 | 81 | 20 | 8 | 9 | 3 | 64 | 0 | 189 | 9 | 1 | 10 | 9 | .526 | 2 | 0-0 | 0 | 3.64 | 3.42 |
| Postseason | | | 13 | 4 | 0 | 2 | 35.2 | 149 | 32 | 17 | 15 | 7 | 0 | 0 | 1 | 15 | 0 | 24 | 2 | 0 | 3 | 0 | 1.000 | 0 | 0-0 | 2 | 4.46 | 3.79 |
| 5 ML YEARS | | | 141 | 123 | 7 | 3 | 782.0 | 3331 | 788 | 415 | 379 | 106 | 16 | 21 | 20 | 254 | 1 | 657 | 15 | 6 | 49 | 38 | .563 | 7 | 0-1 | 3 | 4.18 | 4.36 |

# Greg Holland

**Pitches:** R **Bats:** R **Pos:** RP-68 **Ht:** 5'10" **Wt:** 200 **Born:** 11/20/1985 **Age:** 28

| HOW MUCH HE PITCHED | | | | | | | | WHAT HE GAVE UP | | | | | | | | | | | | THE RESULTS | | | | | | | |
|---|---|---|---|---|---|---|---|---|---|---|---|---|---|---|---|---|---|---|---|---|---|---|---|---|---|---|---|
| Year | Team | Lg | G | GS | CG | GF | IP | BFP | H | R | ER | HR | SH | SF | HB | TBB | IBB | SO | WP | Bk | W | L | Pct | Sh | Sv-Op | Hld | ERC | ERA |
| 2010 | KC | AL | 15 | 0 | 0 | 10 | 18.2 | 87 | 23 | 15 | 14 | 3 | 1 | 0 | 0 | 8 | 0 | 23 | 2 | 0 | 0 | 1 | .000 | 0 | 0-0 | 0 | 5.88 | 6.75 |
| 2011 | KC | AL | 46 | 0 | 0 | 15 | 60.0 | 233 | 37 | 13 | 12 | 3 | 1 | 1 | 1 | 19 | 3 | 74 | 7 | 0 | 5 | 1 | .833 | 0 | 4-6 | 18 | 1.60 | 1.80 |
| 2012 | KC | AL | 67 | 0 | 0 | 36 | 67.0 | 289 | 58 | 22 | 22 | 2 | 4 | 3 | 0 | 34 | 7 | 91 | 3 | 1 | 7 | 4 | .636 | 0 | 16-20 | 9 | 3.07 | 2.96 |
| 2013 | KC | AL | 68 | 0 | 0 | 61 | 67.0 | 255 | 40 | 11 | 9 | 3 | 1 | 1 | 0 | 18 | 1 | 103 | 2 | 0 | 2 | 1 | .667 | 0 | 47-50 | 1 | 1.41 | 1.21 |
| 4 ML YEARS | | | 196 | 0 | 0 | 122 | 212.2 | 864 | 158 | 61 | 57 | 11 | 7 | 5 | 1 | 79 | 11 | 291 | 14 | 1 | 14 | 7 | .667 | 0 | 67-76 | 28 | 2.26 | 2.41 |

# Matt Holliday

**Bats:** R **Throws:** R **Pos:** LF-136;DH-4;PH-1 **Ht:** 6'4" **Wt:** 250 **Born:** 1/15/1980 **Age:** 34

| BATTING | | | | | | | | | | | | | | | | | | | | | BASERUNNING | | | | AVERAGES | | |
|---|---|---|---|---|---|---|---|---|---|---|---|---|---|---|---|---|---|---|---|---|---|---|---|---|---|---|---|
| Year | Team | Lg | G | AB | H | 2B | 3B | HR | (Hm | Rd) | TB | R | RBI | RC | TBB | IBB | SO | HBP | SH | SF | SB | CS | SB% | GDP | Avg | OBP | Slg |
| 2004 | Col | NL | 121 | 400 | 116 | 31 | 3 | 14 | (10 | 4) | 195 | 65 | 57 | 61 | 31 | 0 | 86 | 6 | 1 | 1 | 3 | 3 | .50 | 9 | .290 | .349 | .488 |
| 2005 | Col | NL | 125 | 479 | 147 | 24 | 7 | 19 | (12 | 7) | 242 | 68 | 87 | 88 | 36 | 1 | 79 | 7 | 0 | 4 | 14 | 3 | .82 | 11 | .307 | .361 | .505 |
| 2006 | Col | NL | 155 | 602 | 196 | 45 | 5 | 34 | (22 | 12) | 353 | 119 | 114 | 112 | 47 | 3 | 110 | 15 | 0 | 3 | 10 | 5 | .67 | 22 | .326 | .387 | .586 |
| 2007 | Col | NL | 158 | 636 | **216** | **50** | 6 | 36 | (25 | 11) | **386** | 120 | **137** | **134** | 63 | 7 | 126 | 10 | 0 | 4 | 11 | 4 | .73 | 23 | **.340** | .405 | .607 |
| 2008 | Col | NL | 139 | 539 | 173 | 38 | 2 | 25 | (15 | 10) | 290 | 107 | 88 | 104 | 74 | 6 | 104 | 8 | 0 | 2 | 28 | 2 | .93 | 9 | .321 | .409 | .538 |
| 2009 | 2 Tms | | 156 | 581 | 182 | 39 | 3 | 24 | (16 | 8) | 299 | 94 | 109 | 112 | 72 | 8 | 101 | 10 | 0 | 7 | 14 | 7 | .67 | 13 | .313 | .394 | .515 |
| 2010 | StL | NL | 158 | 596 | 186 | 45 | 1 | 28 | (13 | 15) | 317 | 95 | 103 | 107 | 69 | 10 | 93 | 8 | 0 | 2 | 9 | 5 | .64 | 13 | .312 | .390 | .532 |
| 2011 | StL | NL | 124 | 446 | 132 | 36 | 0 | 22 | (12 | 10) | 234 | 83 | 75 | 81 | 60 | 4 | 93 | 8 | 0 | 2 | 2 | 1 | .67 | 21 | .296 | .388 | .525 |
| 2012 | StL | NL | 157 | 599 | 177 | 36 | 2 | 27 | (13 | 14) | 298 | 95 | 102 | 99 | 75 | 3 | 132 | 9 | 0 | 5 | 4 | 4 | .50 | 16 | .295 | .379 | .497 |
| 2013 | StL | NL | 141 | 520 | 156 | 31 | 1 | 22 | (14 | 8) | 255 | 103 | 94 | 99 | 69 | 5 | 86 | 9 | 0 | 4 | 6 | 1 | .86 | **31** | .300 | .389 | .490 |
| 09 | Oak | AL | 93 | 346 | 99 | 23 | 1 | 11 | (7 | 4) | 157 | 52 | 54 | 62 | 46 | 3 | 58 | 6 | 0 | 2 | 12 | 3 | .80 | 8 | .286 | .378 | .454 |
| 09 | StL | NL | 63 | 235 | 83 | 16 | 2 | 13 | (9 | 4) | 142 | 42 | 55 | 50 | 26 | 5 | 43 | 4 | 0 | 5 | 2 | 4 | .33 | 5 | .353 | .419 | .604 |
| Postseason | | | 42 | 157 | 41 | 4 | 0 | 8 | (4 | 4) | 69 | 25 | 23 | 18 | 13 | 0 | 38 | 6 | 0 | 0 | 1 | 1 | .50 | 4 | .261 | .341 | .439 |
| 10 ML YEARS | | | 1434 | 5398 | 1681 | 375 | 30 | 251 | (152 | 99) | 2869 | 949 | 966 | 997 | 596 | 47 | 1010 | 90 | 1 | 34 | 101 | 35 | .74 | 168 | .311 | .387 | .531 |

# David Holmberg

**Pitches:** L **Bats:** R **Pos:** SP-1 **Ht:** 6'3" **Wt:** 225 **Born:** 7/19/1991 **Age:** 22

| HOW MUCH HE PITCHED | | | | | | | | | WHAT HE GAVE UP | | | | | | | | | | | | THE RESULTS | | | | | | | |
|---|---|---|---|---|---|---|---|---|---|---|---|---|---|---|---|---|---|---|---|---|---|---|---|---|---|---|---|---|
| Year | Team | Lg | G | GS | CG | GF | IP | BFP | H | R | ER | HR | SH | SF | HB | TBB | IBB | SO | WP | Bk | W | L | Pct | Sh | Sv-Op | Hld | ERC | ERA |
| 2009 | Bristol | R | 14 | 7 | 0 | 0 | 40.0 | 176 | 40 | 26 | 21 | 5 | 0 | 0 | 2 | 18 | 0 | 37 | 4 | 0 | 2 | 2 | .500 | 0 | 0-- | - | 4.66 | 4.73 |
| 2010 | Gr Falls | R+ | 8 | 8 | 0 | 0 | 40.1 | 178 | 52 | 23 | 20 | 2 | 2 | 0 | 2 | 9 | 0 | 29 | 0 | 0 | 1 | 1 | .500 | 0 | 0-- | - | 4.90 | 4.46 |
| 2010 | Msoula | R+ | 7 | 7 | 0 | 0 | 37.1 | 173 | 47 | 26 | 16 | 2 | 0 | 2 | 4 | 7 | 0 | 47 | 3 | 1 | 1 | 4 | .200 | 0 | 0-- | - | 4.58 | 3.86 |
| 2011 | Sbend | A | 14 | 14 | 1 | 0 | 83.0 | 327 | 65 | 27 | 22 | 3 | 0 | 1 | 7 | 13 | 0 | 81 | 3 | 0 | 8 | 3 | .727 | 1 | 0-- | - | 2.01 | 2.39 |
| 2011 | Visalia | A+ | 13 | 13 | 0 | 0 | 71.1 | 321 | 73 | 44 | 37 | 5 | 3 | 2 | 3 | 35 | 0 | 76 | 3 | 0 | 4 | 6 | .400 | 0 | 0-- | - | 4.46 | 4.67 |
| 2012 | Visalia | A+ | 12 | 12 | 0 | 0 | 78.1 | 305 | 62 | 31 | 26 | 6 | 0 | 1 | 0 | 14 | 0 | 86 | 0 | 0 | 6 | 3 | .667 | 0 | 0-- | - | 2.07 | 2.99 |
| 2012 | Mobile | AA | 15 | 15 | 0 | 0 | 95.0 | 401 | 104 | 45 | 38 | 8 | 5 | 1 | 2 | 23 | 0 | 67 | 4 | 1 | 5 | 5 | .500 | 0 | 0-- | - | 4.00 | 3.60 |
| 2013 | Mobile | AA | 26 | 26 | 1 | 0 | 157.1 | 651 | 138 | 59 | 48 | 12 | 9 | 7 | 7 | 50 | 2 | 116 | 3 | 0 | 5 | 8 | .385 | 0 | 0-- | - | 3.11 | 2.75 |
| 2013 | Ari | NL | 1 | 1 | 0 | 0 | 3.2 | 20 | 6 | 3 | 3 | 0 | 0 | 1 | 0 | 3 | 0 | 0 | 0 | 0 | 0 | 0 | - | 0 | 0-0 | 0 | 8.70 | 7.36 |

# Brock Holt

**Bats:** L **Throws:** R **Pos:** 3B-20;2B-5;PR-4;DH-1;PH-1 **Ht:** 5'10" **Wt:** 180 **Born:** 6/11/1988 **Age:** 26

| BATTING | | | | | | | | | | | | | | | | | | | | | BASERUNNING | | | | AVERAGES | | |
|---|---|---|---|---|---|---|---|---|---|---|---|---|---|---|---|---|---|---|---|---|---|---|---|---|---|---|---|
| Year | Team | Lg | G | AB | H | 2B | 3B | HR | (Hm | Rd) | TB | R | RBI | RC | TBB | IBB | SO | HBP | SH | SF | SB | CS | SB% | GDP | Avg | OBP | Slg |
| 2009 | StCol | A- | 66 | 254 | 76 | 14 | 3 | 6 | (- | -) | 114 | 45 | 33 | 44 | 26 | 0 | 31 | 1 | 0 | 4 | 9 | 0 | 1.00 | 2 | .299 | .361 | .449 |
| 2010 | Bradtn | A+ | 47 | 194 | 68 | 12 | 1 | 1 | (- | -) | 85 | 31 | 27 | 35 | 19 | 3 | 30 | 2 | 1 | 2 | 6 | 6 | .50 | 3 | .351 | .410 | .438 |
| 2011 | Altna | AA | 132 | 511 | 147 | 30 | 9 | 1 | (- | -) | 198 | 62 | 40 | 75 | 50 | 1 | 85 | 7 | 6 | 5 | 18 | 10 | .64 | 8 | .288 | .356 | .387 |
| 2012 | Altna | AA | 102 | 382 | 123 | 24 | 6 | 2 | (- | -) | 165 | 52 | 43 | 65 | 40 | 0 | 51 | 4 | 3 | 3 | 11 | 11 | .50 | 8 | .322 | .389 | .432 |
| 2012 | Indy | AAA | 24 | 95 | 41 | 7 | 0 | 1 | (- | -) | 51 | 13 | 7 | 23 | 9 | 1 | 9 | 0 | 1 | 1 | 5 | 2 | .71 | 2 | .432 | .476 | .537 |
| 2013 | Pwtckt | AAA | 83 | 291 | 75 | 6 | 0 | 3 | (- | -) | 90 | 35 | 24 | 33 | 30 | 1 | 54 | 2 | 2 | 4 | 8 | 3 | .73 | 3 | .258 | .327 | .309 |
| 2012 | Pit | NL | 24 | 65 | 19 | 2 | 1 | 0 | (0 | 0) | 23 | 6 | 3 | 10 | 4 | 0 | 14 | 0 | 2 | 1 | 0 | 0 | - | 1 | .292 | .329 | .354 |
| 2013 | Bos | AL | 26 | 59 | 12 | 2 | 0 | 0 | (0 | 0) | 14 | 9 | 11 | 7 | 7 | 0 | 4 | 0 | 3 | 3 | 1 | 0 | 1.00 | 0 | .203 | .275 | .237 |
| 2 ML YEARS | | | 50 | 124 | 31 | 4 | 1 | 0 | (0 | 0) | 37 | 15 | 14 | 17 | 11 | 0 | 18 | 0 | 5 | 4 | 1 | 0 | 1.00 | 1 | .250 | .302 | .298 |

# J.J. Hoover

**Pitches:** R **Bats:** R **Pos:** RP-69 **Ht:** 6'3" **Wt:** 225 **Born:** 8/13/1987 **Age:** 26

| HOW MUCH HE PITCHED | | | | | | | | | WHAT HE GAVE UP | | | | | | | | | | | | THE RESULTS | | | | | | | |
|---|---|---|---|---|---|---|---|---|---|---|---|---|---|---|---|---|---|---|---|---|---|---|---|---|---|---|---|---|
| Year | Team | Lg | G | GS | CG | GF | IP | BFP | H | R | ER | HR | SH | SF | HB | TBB | IBB | SO | WP | Bk | W | L | Pct | Sh | Sv-Op | Hld | ERC | ERA |
| 2009 | Rome | A | 25 | 18 | 0 | 3 | 134.1 | 559 | 135 | 58 | 50 | 9 | 1 | 4 | 7 | 25 | 0 | 148 | 3 | 0 | 7 | 6 | .538 | 0 | 1-- | - | 3.26 | 3.35 |
| 2009 | MrtlBh | A+ | 1 | 1 | 0 | 0 | 3.0 | 17 | 3 | 3 | 3 | 1 | 0 | 0 | 0 | 5 | 1 | 2 | 1 | 0 | 0 | 0 | - | 0 | 0-- | - | 10.78 | 9.00 |
| 2010 | MrtlBh | A+ | 24 | 24 | 0 | 0 | 132.2 | 564 | 126 | 56 | 48 | 7 | 3 | 5 | 6 | 35 | 1 | 118 | 6 | 0 | 11 | 6 | .647 | 0 | 0-- | - | 3.06 | 3.26 |
| 2010 | Missi | AA | 4 | 4 | 0 | 0 | 20.2 | 90 | 15 | 8 | 8 | 1 | 1 | 0 | 0 | 15 | 1 | 34 | 0 | 0 | 3 | 1 | .750 | 0 | 0-- | - | 3.36 | 3.48 |
| 2011 | Missi | AA | 31 | 12 | 0 | 5 | 87.0 | 352 | 65 | 30 | 24 | 5 | 3 | 1 | 4 | 28 | 0 | 86 | 4 | 1 | 2 | 5 | .286 | 0 | 1-- | - | 2.37 | 2.48 |
| 2011 | Gwnntt | AAA | 12 | 2 | 0 | 3 | 18.2 | 82 | 12 | 8 | 7 | 0 | 1 | 0 | 0 | 12 | 0 | 31 | 0 | 0 | 1 | 1 | .500 | 0 | 1-- | - | 2.28 | 3.38 |
| 2012 | Lsvlle | AAA | 30 | 0 | 0 | 21 | 37.0 | 138 | 15 | 9 | 5 | 1 | 0 | 1 | 1 | 12 | 0 | 55 | 3 | 0 | 4 | 0 | 1.000 | 0 | 13-- | - | 0.98 | 1.22 |
| 2012 | Cin | NL | 28 | 0 | 0 | 6 | 30.2 | 123 | 17 | 7 | 7 | 2 | 2 | 2 | 0 | 13 | 1 | 31 | 0 | 0 | 1 | 0 | 1.000 | 0 | 1-2 | 1 | 1.64 | 2.05 |
| 2013 | Cin | NL | 69 | 0 | 0 | 23 | 66.0 | 269 | 47 | 21 | 21 | 6 | 3 | 3 | 2 | 26 | 6 | 67 | 1 | 0 | 5 | 5 | .500 | 0 | 3-5 | 13 | 2.46 | 2.86 |
| Postseason | | | 2 | 0 | 0 | 0 | 2.2 | 8 | 0 | 0 | 0 | 0 | 0 | 0 | 0 | 2 | 0 | 2 | 0 | 0 | 0 | 0 | - | 0 | 0-0 | 0 | 0.71 | 0.00 |
| 2 ML YEARS | | | 97 | 0 | 0 | 29 | 96.2 | 392 | 64 | 28 | 28 | 8 | 5 | 5 | 2 | 39 | 7 | 98 | 1 | 0 | 6 | 5 | .545 | 0 | 4-7 | 14 | 2.18 | 2.61 |

# Jeremy Horst

**Pitches:** L **Bats:** L **Pos:** RP-28 HOARST **Ht:** 6'3" **Wt:** 215 **Born:** 10/1/1985 **Age:** 28

| HOW MUCH HE PITCHED | | | | | | | | | WHAT HE GAVE UP | | | | | | | | | | | | THE RESULTS | | | | | | | |
|---|---|---|---|---|---|---|---|---|---|---|---|---|---|---|---|---|---|---|---|---|---|---|---|---|---|---|---|---|
| Year | Team | Lg | G | GS | CG | GF | IP | BFP | H | R | ER | HR | SH | SF | HB | TBB | IBB | SO | WP | Bk | W | L | Pct | Sh | Sv-Op | Hld | ERC | ERA |
| 2013 | Clrwtr* | A+ | 1 | 1 | 0 | 0 | 1.0 | 4 | 1 | 0 | 0 | 0 | 0 | 0 | 0 | 0 | 0 | 0 | 0 | 0 | 0 | 0 | - | 0 | 0-- | - | 1.95 | 0.00 |
| 2013 | LV* | AAA | 2 | 0 | 0 | 1 | 2.0 | 7 | 1 | 1 | 1 | 0 | 0 | 1 | 0 | 0 | 0 | 3 | 1 | 0 | 0 | 0 | - | 0 | 0-- | - | 0.54 | 4.50 |
| 2011 | Cin | NL | 12 | 0 | 0 | 4 | 15.1 | 69 | 18 | 6 | 5 | 2 | 0 | 1 | 0 | 6 | 1 | 9 | 0 | 1 | 0 | 0 | - | 0 | 0-0 | 0 | 5.11 | 2.93 |
| 2012 | Phi | NL | 32 | 0 | 0 | 9 | 31.1 | 125 | 21 | 8 | 4 | 1 | 1 | 0 | 1 | 14 | 1 | 40 | 1 | 0 | 2 | 0 | 1.000 | 0 | 0-0 | 6 | 2.23 | 1.15 |
| 2013 | Phi | NL | 28 | 0 | 0 | 8 | 26.0 | 123 | 35 | 19 | 18 | 4 | 2 | 1 | 2 | 12 | 1 | 21 | 0 | 0 | 0 | 2 | .000 | 0 | 0-1 | 2 | 7.18 | 6.23 |
| 3 ML YEARS | | | 72 | 0 | 0 | 21 | 72.2 | 317 | 74 | 33 | 27 | 7 | 3 | 2 | 3 | 32 | 3 | 70 | 1 | 1 | 2 | 2 | .500 | 0 | 0-1 | 8 | 4.45 | 3.34 |

# Eric Hosmer

**Bats:** L **Throws:** L **Pos:** 1B-158;PH-2;RF-1;DH-1 HOZZ-mer **Ht:** 6'4" **Wt:** 220 **Born:** 10/24/1989 **Age:** 24

| BATTING | | | | | | | | | | | | | | | | | | | | | BASERUNNING | | | | AVERAGES | | |
|---|---|---|---|---|---|---|---|---|---|---|---|---|---|---|---|---|---|---|---|---|---|---|---|---|---|---|---|
| Year | Team | Lg | G | AB | H | 2B | 3B | HR | (Hm | Rd) | TB | R | RBI | RC | TBB | IBB | SO | HBP | SH | SF | SB | CS | SB% | GDP | Avg | OBP | Slg |
| 2011 | KC | AL | 128 | 523 | 153 | 27 | 3 | 19 | (3 | 16) | 243 | 66 | 78 | 71 | 34 | 7 | 82 | 1 | 0 | 5 | 11 | 5 | .69 | 13 | .293 | .334 | .465 |
| 2012 | KC | AL | 152 | 535 | 124 | 22 | 2 | 14 | (8 | 6) | 192 | 65 | 60 | 61 | 56 | 4 | 95 | 2 | 0 | 5 | 16 | 1 | .94 | 10 | .232 | .304 | .359 |
| 2013 | KC | AL | 159 | 623 | 188 | 34 | 3 | 17 | (10 | 7) | 279 | 86 | 79 | 88 | 51 | 4 | 100 | 1 | 1 | 4 | 11 | 4 | .73 | 15 | .302 | .353 | .448 |
| 3 ML YEARS | | | 439 | 1681 | 465 | 83 | 8 | 50 | (21 | 29) | 714 | 217 | 217 | 220 | 141 | 15 | 277 | 4 | 1 | 14 | 38 | 10 | .79 | 38 | .277 | .332 | .425 |

# Ryan Howard

**Bats:** L **Throws:** L **Pos:** 1B-76;PH-6 **Ht:** 6'4" **Wt:** 240 **Born:** 11/19/1979 **Age:** 34

| BATTING | | | | | | | | | | | | | | | | | | | | | BASERUNNING | | | | AVERAGES | | |
|---|---|---|---|---|---|---|---|---|---|---|---|---|---|---|---|---|---|---|---|---|---|---|---|---|---|---|---|
| Year | Team | Lg | G | AB | H | 2B | 3B | HR | (Hm | Rd) | TB | R | RBI | RC | TBB | IBB | SO | HBP | SH | SF | SB | CS | SB% | GDP | Avg | OBP | Slg |
| 2004 | Phi | NL | 19 | 39 | 11 | 5 | 0 | 2 | (1 | 1) | 22 | 5 | 5 | 7 | 2 | 0 | 13 | 1 | 0 | 0 | 0 | 0 | - | 2 | .282 | .333 | .564 |
| 2005 | Phi | NL | 88 | 312 | 90 | 17 | 2 | 22 | (11 | 11) | 177 | 52 | 63 | 50 | 33 | 8 | 100 | 1 | 0 | 2 | 0 | 1 | .00 | 6 | .288 | .356 | .567 |
| 2006 | Phi | NL | 159 | 581 | 182 | 25 | 1 | **58** | **(29** | **29)** | **383** | 104 | **149** | 138 | 108 | 37 | 181 | 9 | 0 | 6 | 0 | 0 | - | 7 | .313 | .425 | .659 |
| 2007 | Phi | NL | 144 | 529 | 142 | 26 | 0 | 47 | (23 | **24)** | 309 | 94 | 136 | 119 | 107 | 35 | **199** | 5 | 0 | 7 | 1 | 0 | 1.00 | 13 | .268 | .392 | .584 |
| 2008 | Phi | NL | **162** | 610 | 153 | 26 | 4 | **48** | **(26** | **22)** | 331 | 105 | **146** | 117 | 81 | 17 | 199 | 3 | 0 | 6 | 1 | 1 | .50 | 11 | .251 | .339 | .543 |
| 2009 | Phi | NL | 160 | 616 | 172 | 37 | 4 | 45 | (18 | 27) | 352 | 105 | **141** | 117 | 75 | 8 | 186 | 6 | 0 | 6 | 8 | 1 | .89 | 11 | .279 | .360 | .571 |
| 2010 | Phi | NL | 143 | 550 | 152 | 23 | 5 | 31 | (16 | 15) | 278 | 87 | 108 | 94 | 59 | 11 | 157 | 8 | 0 | 3 | 1 | 1 | .50 | 14 | .276 | .353 | .505 |
| 2011 | Phi | NL | 152 | 557 | 141 | 30 | 1 | 33 | (17 | 16) | 272 | 81 | 116 | 91 | 75 | 16 | 172 | 7 | 0 | 5 | 1 | 0 | 1.00 | 10 | .253 | .346 | .488 |

| BATTING | | | | | | | | | | | | | | | | | | | | | | BASERUNNING | | | | AVERAGES | | |
|---|---|---|---|---|---|---|---|---|---|---|---|---|---|---|---|---|---|---|---|---|---|---|---|---|---|---|---|---|
| Year | Team | Lg | G | AB | H | 2B | 3B | HR | (Hm | Rd) | TB | R | RBI | RC | TBB | IBB | SO | HBP | SH | SF | SB | CS | SB% | GDP | Avg | OBP | Slg |
| 2012 | Phi | NL | 71 | 260 | 57 | 11 | 0 | 14 | (10 | 4) | 110 | 28 | 56 | 35 | 25 | 7 | 99 | 4 | 0 | 3 | 0 | 0 | - | 8 | .219 | .295 | .423 |
| 2013 | Phi | NL | 80 | 286 | 76 | 20 | 2 | 11 | (9 | 2) | 133 | 34 | 43 | 36 | 23 | 4 | 95 | 2 | 0 | 6 | 0 | 0 | - | 6 | .266 | .319 | .465 |
| Postseason | | | 46 | 170 | 44 | 13 | 1 | 8 | (6 | 2) | 83 | 22 | 33 | 28 | 26 | 7 | 67 | 1 | 0 | 2 | 1 | 1 | .50 | 1 | .259 | .357 | .488 |
| 10 ML YEARS | | | 1178 | 4340 | 1176 | 220 | 19 | 311 | (160 | 151) | 2367 | 695 | 963 | 804 | 588 | 143 | 1401 | 46 | 0 | 44 | 12 | 4 | .75 | 88 | .271 | .361 | .545 |

# J.P. Howell

**Pitches:** L **Bats:** L **Pos:** RP-67 **Ht:** 6'0" **Wt:** 185 **Born:** 4/25/1983 **Age:** 31

| HOW MUCH HE PITCHED | | | | | | | | | WHAT HE GAVE UP | | | | | | | | | | | | THE RESULTS | | | | | | | |
|---|---|---|---|---|---|---|---|---|---|---|---|---|---|---|---|---|---|---|---|---|---|---|---|---|---|---|---|---|
| Year | Team | Lg | G | GS | CG | GF | IP | BFP | H | R | ER | HR | SH | SF | HB | TBB | IBB | SO | WP | Bk | W | L | Pct | Sh | Sv-Op | Hld | ERC | ERA |
| 2005 | KC | AL | 15 | 15 | 0 | 0 | 72.2 | 328 | 73 | 55 | 50 | 9 | 3 | 3 | 6 | 39 | 0 | 54 | 7 | 0 | 3 | 5 | .375 | 0 | 0-0 | 0 | 5.18 | 6.19 |
| 2006 | TB | AL | 8 | 8 | 0 | 0 | 42.1 | 187 | 52 | 25 | 24 | 4 | 0 | 2 | 3 | 14 | 0 | 33 | 1 | 0 | 1 | 3 | .250 | 0 | 0-0 | 0 | 5.51 | 5.10 |
| 2007 | TB | AL | 10 | 10 | 0 | 0 | 51.0 | 244 | 69 | 45 | 43 | 8 | 2 | 1 | 3 | 21 | 0 | 49 | 3 | 0 | 1 | 6 | .143 | 0 | 0-0 | 0 | 6.84 | 7.59 |
| 2008 | TB | AL | 64 | 0 | 0 | 9 | 89.1 | 370 | 62 | 29 | 22 | 6 | 6 | 1 | 4 | 39 | 1 | 92 | 5 | 0 | 6 | 1 | .857 | 0 | 3-5 | 14 | 2.51 | 2.22 |
| 2009 | TB | AL | 69 | 0 | 0 | 41 | 66.2 | 278 | 47 | 22 | 21 | 7 | 2 | 1 | 3 | 33 | 3 | 79 | 3 | 1 | 7 | 5 | .583 | 0 | 17-25 | 4 | 2.99 | 2.84 |
| 2011 | TB | AL | 46 | 0 | 0 | 5 | 30.2 | 138 | 30 | 24 | 21 | 5 | 1 | 1 | 2 | 18 | 1 | 26 | 2 | **2** | 2 | 3 | .400 | 0 | 1-2 | 10 | 5.43 | 6.16 |
| 2012 | TB | AL | 55 | 0 | 0 | 10 | 50.1 | 203 | 39 | 17 | 17 | 7 | 2 | 0 | 4 | 22 | 2 | 42 | 1 | 0 | 1 | 0 | 1.000 | 0 | 0-0 | 3 | 3.68 | 3.04 |
| 2013 | LAD | NL | 67 | 0 | 0 | 6 | 62.0 | 246 | 42 | 15 | 15 | 2 | 1 | 3 | 1 | 23 | 3 | 54 | 3 | 0 | 4 | 1 | .800 | 0 | 0-0 | 11 | 1.92 | 2.18 |
| Postseason | | | 13 | 0 | 0 | 1 | 12.0 | 51 | 10 | 4 | 4 | 0 | 0 | 1 | 2 | 4 | 1 | 17 | 1 | 0 | 0 | 3 | .000 | 0 | 0-0 | 4 | 2.73 | 3.00 |
| 8 ML YEARS | | | 334 | 33 | 0 | 71 | 465.0 | 1994 | 414 | 232 | 213 | 48 | 17 | 12 | 26 | 209 | 10 | 429 | 25 | 3 | 25 | 24 | .510 | 0 | 21-32 | 42 | 3.89 | 4.12 |

# Daniel Hudson

**Pitches:** R **Bats:** R **Pos:** P **Ht:** 6'3" **Wt:** 225 **Born:** 3/9/1987 **Age:** 27

| HOW MUCH HE PITCHED | | | | | | | | | WHAT HE GAVE UP | | | | | | | | | | | | THE RESULTS | | | | | | | |
|---|---|---|---|---|---|---|---|---|---|---|---|---|---|---|---|---|---|---|---|---|---|---|---|---|---|---|---|---|
| Year | Team | Lg | G | GS | CG | GF | IP | BFP | H | R | ER | HR | SH | SF | HB | TBB | IBB | SO | WP | Bk | W | L | Pct | Sh | Sv-Op | Hld | ERC | ERA |
| 2013 | Mobile* | AA | 1 | 1 | 0 | 0 | 2.0 | 9 | 2 | 1 | 1 | 0 | 0 | 0 | 0 | 1 | 0 | 1 | 0 | 0 | 0 | 0 | - | 0 | 0- - | - | 3.63 | 4.50 |
| 2009 | CWS | AL | 6 | 2 | 0 | 1 | 18.2 | 82 | 16 | 9 | 7 | 3 | 0 | 1 | 1 | 9 | 0 | 14 | 1 | 0 | 1 | 1 | .500 | 0 | 0-0 | 0 | 4.15 | 3.38 |
| 2010 | 2 Tms | | 14 | 14 | 0 | 0 | 95.1 | 372 | 68 | 26 | 26 | 8 | 2 | 2 | 4 | 27 | 1 | 84 | 5 | 0 | 8 | 2 | .800 | 0 | 0-0 | 0 | 2.26 | 2.45 |
| 2011 | Ari | NL | 33 | 33 | 3 | 0 | 222.0 | 921 | 217 | 98 | 86 | 17 | 6 | 6 | 8 | 50 | 1 | 169 | 4 | 1 | 16 | 12 | .571 | 0 | 0-0 | 0 | 3.26 | 3.49 |
| 2012 | Ari | NL | 9 | 9 | 0 | 0 | 45.1 | 202 | 62 | 37 | 37 | 9 | 2 | 1 | 0 | 12 | 0 | 37 | 2 | 0 | 3 | 2 | .600 | 0 | 0-0 | 0 | 6.56 | 7.35 |
| 10 | CWS | AL | 3 | 3 | 0 | 0 | 15.2 | 71 | 17 | 11 | 11 | 1 | 1 | 1 | 0 | 11 | 0 | 14 | 2 | 0 | 1 | 1 | .500 | 0 | 0-0 | 0 | 5.69 | 6.32 |
| 10 | Ari | NL | 11 | 11 | 0 | 0 | 79.2 | 301 | 51 | 15 | 15 | 7 | 1 | 1 | 4 | 16 | 1 | 70 | 3 | 0 | 7 | 1 | .875 | 0 | 0-0 | 0 | 1.70 | 1.69 |
| Postseason | | | 1 | 1 | 0 | 0 | 5.1 | 24 | 9 | 5 | 5 | 1 | 0 | 0 | 0 | 0 | 0 | 6 | 0 | 0 | 0 | 1 | .000 | 0 | 0-0 | 0 | 7.35 | 8.44 |
| 4 ML YEARS | | | 62 | 58 | 3 | 1 | 381.1 | 1577 | 363 | 170 | 156 | 37 | 10 | 10 | 13 | 98 | 2 | 304 | 12 | 1 | 28 | 17 | .622 | 0 | 0-0 | 0 | 3.39 | 3.68 |

# Tim Hudson

**Pitches:** R **Bats:** R **Pos:** SP-21 **Ht:** 6'1" **Wt:** 175 **Born:** 7/14/1975 **Age:** 38

| HOW MUCH HE PITCHED | | | | | | | | | WHAT HE GAVE UP | | | | | | | | | | | | THE RESULTS | | | | | | | |
|---|---|---|---|---|---|---|---|---|---|---|---|---|---|---|---|---|---|---|---|---|---|---|---|---|---|---|---|---|
| Year | Team | Lg | G | GS | CG | GF | IP | BFP | H | R | ER | HR | SH | SF | HB | TBB | IBB | SO | WP | Bk | W | L | Pct | Sh | Sv-Op | Hld | ERC | ERA |
| 1999 | Oak | AL | 21 | 21 | 1 | 0 | 136.1 | 580 | 121 | 56 | 49 | 8 | 1 | 2 | 4 | 62 | 2 | 132 | 6 | 0 | 11 | 2 | .846 | 0 | 0-0 | 0 | 3.50 | 3.23 |
| 2000 | Oak | AL | 32 | 32 | 2 | 0 | 202.1 | 847 | 169 | 100 | 93 | 24 | 5 | 7 | 7 | 82 | 5 | 169 | 7 | 0 | **20** | 6 | **.769** | 2 | 0-0 | 0 | 3.43 | 4.14 |
| 2001 | Oak | AL | 35 | **35** | 3 | 0 | 235.0 | 980 | 216 | 100 | 88 | 20 | **12** | 8 | 6 | 71 | 5 | 181 | 9 | 1 | 18 | 9 | .667 | 0 | 0-0 | 0 | 3.22 | 3.37 |
| 2002 | Oak | AL | 34 | 34 | 4 | 0 | 238.1 | 983 | 237 | 87 | 79 | 19 | 6 | 5 | 8 | 62 | 9 | 152 | 7 | 1 | 15 | 9 | .625 | 2 | 0-0 | 0 | 3.51 | 2.98 |
| 2003 | Oak | AL | 34 | 34 | 3 | 0 | 240.0 | 967 | 197 | 84 | 72 | 15 | 11 | 2 | 10 | 61 | **9** | 162 | 6 | 0 | 16 | 7 | .696 | **2** | 0-0 | 0 | 2.47 | 2.70 |
| 2004 | Oak | AL | 27 | 27 | 3 | 0 | 188.2 | 793 | 194 | 82 | 74 | 8 | 7 | 4 | 12 | 44 | 3 | 103 | 4 | 1 | 12 | 6 | .667 | **2** | 0-0 | 0 | 3.44 | 3.53 |
| 2005 | Atl | NL | 29 | 29 | 2 | 0 | 192.0 | 817 | 194 | 79 | 75 | 20 | 9 | 1 | 9 | 65 | 5 | 115 | 4 | 0 | 14 | 9 | .609 | 0 | 0-0 | 0 | 4.12 | 3.52 |
| 2006 | Atl | NL | 35 | **35** | 2 | 0 | 218.1 | 959 | 235 | 129 | 118 | 25 | 8 | 3 | 9 | 79 | 10 | 141 | 7 | 0 | 13 | 12 | .520 | 1 | 0-0 | 0 | 4.54 | 4.86 |
| 2007 | Atl | NL | 34 | 34 | 1 | 0 | 224.1 | 925 | 221 | 87 | 83 | 10 | 11 | 6 | 8 | 53 | 8 | 132 | 5 | 2 | 16 | 10 | .615 | 1 | 0-0 | 0 | 3.12 | 3.33 |
| 2008 | Atl | NL | 23 | 22 | 1 | 0 | 142.0 | 573 | 125 | 53 | 50 | 11 | 5 | 4 | 2 | 40 | 5 | 85 | 3 | 1 | 11 | 7 | .611 | 1 | 0-0 | 0 | 2.90 | 3.17 |
| 2009 | Atl | NL | 7 | 7 | 0 | 0 | 42.1 | 180 | 49 | 17 | 17 | 4 | 1 | 0 | 0 | 13 | 0 | 30 | 0 | 0 | 2 | 1 | .667 | 0 | 0-0 | 0 | 4.70 | 3.61 |
| 2010 | Atl | NL | 34 | 34 | 1 | 0 | 228.2 | 920 | 189 | 74 | 72 | 20 | 9 | 2 | 9 | 74 | 8 | 139 | 5 | 0 | 17 | 9 | .654 | 0 | 0-0 | 0 | 2.95 | 2.83 |
| 2011 | Atl | NL | 33 | 33 | 1 | 0 | 215.0 | 884 | 189 | 86 | 77 | 14 | 6 | 7 | **15** | 56 | 6 | 158 | 10 | 0 | 16 | 10 | .615 | 1 | 0-0 | 0 | 2.91 | 3.22 |
| 2012 | Atl | NL | 28 | 28 | 1 | 0 | 179.0 | 749 | 168 | 77 | 72 | 12 | 10 | 4 | 9 | 48 | 2 | 102 | 3 | 0 | 16 | 7 | .696 | 1 | 0-0 | 0 | 3.18 | 3.62 |
| 2013 | Atl | NL | 21 | 21 | 0 | 0 | 131.1 | 534 | 120 | 60 | 58 | 10 | 5 | 1 | 2 | 36 | 3 | 95 | 2 | 0 | 8 | 7 | .533 | 0 | 0-0 | 0 | 3.05 | 3.97 |
| Postseason | | | 10 | 9 | 1 | 0 | 54.2 | 236 | 54 | 28 | 21 | 5 | 4 | 2 | 2 | 20 | 1 | 37 | 1 | 0 | 1 | 3 | .250 | 0 | 0-0 | 0 | 3.91 | 3.46 |
| 15 ML YEARS | | | 427 | 426 | 25 | 0 | 2813.2 | 11691 | 2624 | 1171 | 1077 | 220 | 106 | 56 | 110 | 846 | 80 | 1896 | 78 | 6 | 205 | 111 | .649 | 13 | 0-0 | 0 | 3.32 | 3.44 |

# David Huff

**Pitches:** L **Bats:** B **Pos:** RP-12; SP-2 **Ht:** 6'2" **Wt:** 215 **Born:** 8/22/1984 **Age:** 29

| HOW MUCH HE PITCHED | | | | | | | | | WHAT HE GAVE UP | | | | | | | | | | | | THE RESULTS | | | | | | | |
|---|---|---|---|---|---|---|---|---|---|---|---|---|---|---|---|---|---|---|---|---|---|---|---|---|---|---|---|---|
| Year | Team | Lg | G | GS | CG | GF | IP | BFP | H | R | ER | HR | SH | SF | HB | TBB | IBB | SO | WP | Bk | W | L | Pct | Sh | Sv-Op | Hld | ERC | ERA |
| 2013 | Clmbs* | AAA | 9 | 2 | 0 | 0 | 24.1 | 103 | 21 | 13 | 11 | 4 | 0 | 0 | 0 | 9 | 1 | 28 | 0 | 1 | 3 | 1 | .750 | 0 | 0- - | - | 3.50 | 4.07 |
| 2013 | S-WB* | AAA | 13 | 12 | 0 | 1 | 68.0 | 292 | 76 | 31 | 29 | 4 | 1 | 3 | 3 | 13 | 0 | 64 | 1 | 1 | 1 | 6 | .143 | 0 | 1- - | - | 3.76 | 3.84 |
| 2009 | Cle | AL | 23 | 23 | 0 | 0 | 128.1 | 574 | 159 | 82 | 80 | 16 | 2 | 2 | 1 | 41 | 1 | 65 | 1 | 0 | 11 | 8 | .579 | 0 | 0-0 | 0 | 5.33 | 5.61 |
| 2010 | Cle | AL | 15 | 15 | 1 | 0 | 79.2 | 369 | 101 | 61 | 55 | 14 | 3 | 3 | 3 | 34 | 1 | 37 | 2 | 0 | 2 | 11 | .154 | 0 | 0-0 | 0 | 6.50 | 6.21 |
| 2011 | Cle | AL | 11 | 10 | 0 | 1 | 50.2 | 227 | 55 | 35 | 23 | 6 | 0 | 3 | 0 | 17 | 1 | 36 | 4 | 0 | 2 | 6 | .250 | 0 | 0-0 | 0 | 4.23 | 4.09 |
| 2012 | Cle | AL | 6 | 4 | 0 | 0 | 26.2 | 114 | 30 | 14 | 10 | 5 | 0 | 1 | 1 | 5 | 0 | 19 | 0 | 0 | 3 | 1 | .750 | 0 | 0-0 | 0 | 4.67 | 3.38 |
| 2013 | 2 Tms | AL | 14 | 2 | 0 | 4 | 37.2 | 151 | 33 | 23 | 23 | 7 | 1 | 1 | 1 | 9 | 1 | 31 | 1 | 0 | 3 | 1 | .750 | 0 | 0-0 | 0 | 3.45 | 5.50 |
| 13 | Cle | AL | 3 | 0 | 0 | 1 | 3.0 | 15 | 7 | 5 | 5 | 0 | 0 | 0 | 0 | 1 | 0 | 5 | 0 | 0 | 0 | 0 | - | 0 | 0-0 | 0 | 12.85 | 15.00 |
| 13 | NYY | AL | 11 | 2 | 0 | 3 | 34.2 | 136 | 26 | 18 | 18 | 7 | 1 | 1 | 1 | 8 | 1 | 26 | 1 | 0 | 3 | 1 | .750 | 0 | 0-0 | 0 | 2.82 | 4.67 |
| 5 ML YEARS | | | 69 | 54 | 1 | 5 | 323.0 | 1435 | 378 | 215 | 191 | 48 | 6 | 10 | 6 | 106 | 4 | 188 | 8 | 0 | 21 | 27 | .438 | 0 | 0-0 | 0 | 5.15 | 5.32 |

# Jared Hughes

**Pitches:** R **Bats:** R **Pos:** RP-29 **Ht:** 6'7" **Wt:** 240 **Born:** 7/4/1985 **Age:** 28

| HOW MUCH HE PITCHED | | | | | | | | | WHAT HE GAVE UP | | | | | | | | | | | | THE RESULTS | | | | | | | |
|---|---|---|---|---|---|---|---|---|---|---|---|---|---|---|---|---|---|---|---|---|---|---|---|---|---|---|---|---|
| Year | Team | Lg | G | GS | CG | GF | IP | BFP | H | R | ER | HR | SH | SF | HB | TBB | IBB | SO | WP | Bk | W | L | Pct | Sh | Sv-Op | Hld | ERC | ERA |
| 2013 | Indy* | AAA | 18 | 1 | 0 | 10 | 21.0 | 84 | 17 | 1 | 1 | 0 | 1 | 0 | 1 | 7 | 0 | 18 | 1 | 0 | 1 | 0 | 1.000 | 0 | 2-- | - | 2.43 | 0.43 |
| 2013 | Altna* | AA | 1 | 1 | 0 | 0 | 2.0 | 7 | 1 | 0 | 0 | 0 | 0 | 0 | 0 | 0 | 0 | 4 | 0 | 0 | 0 | 0 | - | 0 | 0-- | - | 0.54 | 0.00 |
| 2011 | Pit | NL | 12 | 0 | 0 | 1 | 11.0 | 46 | 9 | 5 | 5 | 1 | 1 | 0 | 0 | 4 | 0 | 10 | 0 | 0 | 0 | 1 | .000 | 0 | 0-0 | 2 | 2.85 | 4.09 |
| 2012 | Pit | NL | 66 | 0 | 0 | 20 | 75.2 | 316 | 65 | 30 | 24 | 7 | 1 | 0 | 5 | 22 | 4 | 50 | 5 | 0 | 2 | 2 | .500 | 0 | 2-4 | 11 | 2.99 | 2.85 |
| 2013 | Pit | NL | 29 | 0 | 0 | 8 | 32.0 | 148 | 37 | 17 | 17 | 2 | 2 | 1 | 2 | 16 | 1 | 23 | 2 | 0 | 2 | 3 | .400 | 0 | 0-0 | 3 | 5.27 | 4.78 |
| 3 ML YEARS | | | 107 | 0 | 0 | 29 | 118.2 | 510 | 111 | 52 | 46 | 10 | 4 | 1 | 7 | 42 | 5 | 83 | 7 | 0 | 4 | 6 | .400 | 0 | 2-4 | 16 | 3.56 | 3.49 |

# Phil Hughes

**Pitches:** R **Bats:** R **Pos:** SP-29; RP-1 **Ht:** 6'5" **Wt:** 240 **Born:** 6/24/1986 **Age:** 28

| HOW MUCH HE PITCHED | | | | | | | | | WHAT HE GAVE UP | | | | | | | | | | | | THE RESULTS | | | | | | | |
|---|---|---|---|---|---|---|---|---|---|---|---|---|---|---|---|---|---|---|---|---|---|---|---|---|---|---|---|---|
| Year | Team | Lg | G | GS | CG | GF | IP | BFP | H | R | ER | HR | SH | SF | HB | TBB | IBB | SO | WP | Bk | W | L | Pct | Sh | Sv-Op | Hld | ERC | ERA |
| 2007 | NYY | AL | 13 | 13 | 0 | 0 | 72.2 | 306 | 64 | 39 | 36 | 8 | 2 | 1 | 2 | 29 | 0 | 58 | 4 | 0 | 5 | 3 | .625 | 0 | 0-0 | 0 | 3.61 | 4.46 |
| 2008 | NYY | AL | 8 | 8 | 0 | 0 | 34.0 | 157 | 43 | 26 | 25 | 3 | 1 | 3 | 1 | 15 | 0 | 23 | 2 | 0 | 0 | 4 | .000 | 0 | 0-0 | 0 | 5.84 | 6.62 |
| 2009 | NYY | AL | 51 | 7 | 0 | 6 | 86.0 | 351 | 68 | 31 | 29 | 8 | 0 | 4 | 5 | 28 | 1 | 96 | 4 | 2 | 8 | 3 | .727 | 0 | 3-6 | 18 | 2.86 | 3.03 |
| 2010 | NYY | AL | 31 | 29 | 0 | 0 | 176.1 | 730 | 162 | 83 | 82 | 25 | 2 | 5 | 0 | 58 | 1 | 146 | 9 | 1 | 18 | 8 | .692 | 0 | 0-0 | 0 | 3.65 | 4.19 |
| 2011 | NYY | AL | 17 | 14 | 1 | 1 | 74.2 | 334 | 84 | 48 | 48 | 9 | 3 | 3 | 4 | 27 | 2 | 47 | 3 | 0 | 5 | 5 | .500 | 1 | 0-0 | 0 | 4.92 | 5.79 |
| 2012 | NYY | AL | 32 | 32 | 1 | 0 | 191.1 | 815 | 196 | 101 | 90 | 35 | 1 | 4 | 6 | 46 | 0 | 165 | 3 | 0 | 16 | 13 | .552 | 0 | 0-0 | 0 | 4.21 | 4.23 |
| 2013 | NYY | AL | 30 | 29 | 0 | 0 | 145.2 | 642 | 170 | 91 | 84 | 24 | 3 | **11** | 5 | 42 | 4 | 121 | 6 | 0 | 4 | 14 | .222 | 0 | 0-0 | 0 | 5.13 | 5.19 |
| Postseason | | | 18 | 5 | 0 | 2 | 39.2 | 176 | 41 | 20 | 20 | 5 | 1 | 0 | 0 | 18 | 3 | 38 | 3 | 0 | 2 | 4 | .333 | 0 | 0-1 | 2 | 4.49 | 4.54 |
| 7 ML YEARS | | | 182 | 132 | 2 | 7 | 780.2 | 3335 | 787 | 419 | 394 | 112 | 12 | 31 | 23 | 245 | 8 | 656 | 31 | 3 | 56 | 50 | .528 | 1 | 3-6 | 18 | 4.17 | 4.54 |

# Philip Humber

UMM-burr

**Pitches:** R **Bats:** R **Pos:** RP-10; SP-7 **Ht:** 6'3" **Wt:** 210 **Born:** 12/21/1982 **Age:** 31

| HOW MUCH HE PITCHED | | | | | | | | | WHAT HE GAVE UP | | | | | | | | | | | | THE RESULTS | | | | | | | |
|---|---|---|---|---|---|---|---|---|---|---|---|---|---|---|---|---|---|---|---|---|---|---|---|---|---|---|---|---|
| Year | Team | Lg | G | GS | CG | GF | IP | BFP | H | R | ER | HR | SH | SF | HB | TBB | IBB | SO | WP | Bk | W | L | Pct | Sh | Sv-Op | Hld | ERC | ERA |
| 2013 | OKCity* | AAA | 20 | 7 | 0 | 2 | 50.0 | 232 | 57 | 32 | 26 | 7 | 2 | 0 | 12 | 18 | 1 | 38 | 6 | 1 | 2 | 4 | .333 | 0 | 0-- | - | 5.99 | 4.68 |
| 2006 | NYM | NL | 2 | 0 | 0 | 1 | 2.0 | 7 | 0 | 0 | 0 | 0 | 0 | 0 | 0 | 1 | 0 | 2 | 0 | 0 | 0 | 0 | - | 0 | 0-0 | 0 | 0.27 | 0.00 |
| 2007 | NYM | NL | 3 | 1 | 0 | 2 | 7.0 | 32 | 9 | 6 | 6 | 1 | 0 | 0 | 0 | 2 | 0 | 2 | 0 | 0 | 0 | 0 | - | 0 | 0-0 | 0 | 5.46 | 7.71 |
| 2008 | Min | AL | 5 | 0 | 0 | 2 | 11.2 | 50 | 11 | 6 | 6 | 4 | 0 | 0 | 1 | 5 | 0 | 6 | 0 | 0 | 0 | 0 | - | 0 | 0-0 | 0 | 6.11 | 4.63 |
| 2009 | Min | AL | 8 | 0 | 0 | 3 | 9.0 | 50 | 17 | 8 | 8 | 1 | 0 | 0 | 0 | 9 | 2 | 9 | 1 | 0 | 0 | 0 | - | 0 | 0-0 | 0 | 12.62 | 8.00 |
| 2010 | KC | AL | 8 | 1 | 0 | 1 | 21.2 | 94 | 22 | 10 | 10 | 1 | 0 | 1 | 1 | 7 | 2 | 16 | 2 | 0 | 2 | 1 | .667 | 0 | 0-0 | 1 | 3.47 | 4.15 |
| 2011 | CWS | AL | 28 | 26 | 0 | 0 | 163.0 | 676 | 151 | 71 | 68 | 14 | 2 | 5 | 6 | 41 | 2 | 116 | 9 | 1 | 9 | 9 | .500 | 0 | 0-0 | 0 | 3.13 | 3.75 |
| 2012 | CWS | AL | 26 | 16 | 1 | 6 | 102.0 | 462 | 113 | 74 | 73 | 23 | 1 | 4 | 4 | 44 | 1 | 85 | 9 | 0 | 5 | 5 | .500 | 1 | 0-0 | 0 | 5.86 | 6.44 |
| 2013 | Hou | AL | 17 | 7 | 0 | 2 | 54.2 | 259 | 75 | 48 | 48 | 9 | 3 | 2 | 1 | 20 | 1 | 36 | 5 | 1 | 0 | 8 | .000 | 0 | 0-2 | 0 | 6.58 | 7.90 |
| 8 ML YEARS | | | 97 | 51 | 1 | 17 | 371.0 | 1630 | 398 | 223 | 219 | 53 | 6 | 12 | 13 | 129 | 8 | 272 | 26 | 2 | 16 | 23 | .410 | 1 | 0-2 | 1 | 4.66 | 5.31 |

# Nick Hundley

**Bats:** R **Throws:** R **Pos:** C-112;PH-6 **Ht:** 6'1" **Wt:** 195 **Born:** 9/8/1983 **Age:** 30

| BATTING | | | | | | | | | | | | | | | | | | | | | BASERUNNING | | | | AVERAGES | | |
|---|---|---|---|---|---|---|---|---|---|---|---|---|---|---|---|---|---|---|---|---|---|---|---|---|---|---|---|
| Year | Team | Lg | G | AB | H | 2B | 3B | HR | (Hm | Rd) | TB | R | RBI | RC | TBB | IBB | SO | HBP | SH | SF | SB | CS | SB% | GDP | Avg | OBP | Slg |
| 2008 | SD | NL | 60 | 198 | 47 | 7 | 1 | 5 | (4 | 1) | 71 | 21 | 24 | 17 | 11 | 0 | 52 | 2 | 0 | 5 | 0 | 0 | - | 1 | .237 | .278 | .359 |
| 2009 | SD | NL | 78 | 256 | 61 | 15 | 2 | 8 | (4 | 4) | 104 | 23 | 30 | 33 | 28 | 1 | 76 | 1 | 1 | 3 | 5 | 1 | .83 | 2 | .238 | .313 | .406 |
| 2010 | SD | NL | 85 | 273 | 68 | 18 | 2 | 8 | (7 | 1) | 114 | 33 | 43 | 37 | 25 | 0 | 66 | 1 | 2 | 6 | 0 | 5 | .00 | 8 | .249 | .308 | .418 |
| 2011 | SD | NL | 82 | 281 | 81 | 16 | 5 | 9 | (6 | 3) | 134 | 34 | 29 | 40 | 22 | 3 | 74 | 4 | 0 | 1 | 1 | 1 | .50 | 3 | .288 | .347 | .477 |
| 2012 | SD | NL | 58 | 204 | 32 | 7 | 1 | 3 | (1 | 2) | 50 | 14 | 22 | 6 | 15 | 2 | 56 | 2 | 1 | 3 | 0 | 3 | .00 | 4 | .157 | .219 | .245 |
| 2013 | SD | NL | 114 | 373 | 87 | 19 | 0 | 13 | (6 | 7) | 145 | 35 | 44 | 36 | 26 | 5 | 98 | 5 | 1 | 3 | 1 | 0 | 1.00 | 7 | .233 | .290 | .389 |
| 6 ML YEARS | | | 477 | 1585 | 376 | 82 | 11 | 46 | (28 | 18) | 618 | 160 | 192 | 169 | 127 | 11 | 422 | 15 | 5 | 21 | 7 | 10 | .41 | 25 | .237 | .296 | .390 |

# Tommy Hunter

**Pitches:** R **Bats:** R **Pos:** RP-68 **Ht:** 6'3" **Wt:** 250 **Born:** 7/3/1986 **Age:** 27

| HOW MUCH HE PITCHED | | | | | | | | | WHAT HE GAVE UP | | | | | | | | | | | | THE RESULTS | | | | | | | |
|---|---|---|---|---|---|---|---|---|---|---|---|---|---|---|---|---|---|---|---|---|---|---|---|---|---|---|---|---|
| Year | Team | Lg | G | GS | CG | GF | IP | BFP | H | R | ER | HR | SH | SF | HB | TBB | IBB | SO | WP | Bk | W | L | Pct | Sh | Sv-Op | Hld | ERC | ERA |
| 2008 | Tex | AL | 3 | 3 | 0 | 0 | 11.0 | 63 | 23 | 20 | 20 | 4 | 0 | 0 | 1 | 3 | 0 | 9 | 0 | 0 | 0 | 2 | .000 | 0 | 0-0 | 0 | 12.66 | 16.36 |
| 2009 | Tex | AL | 19 | 19 | 1 | 0 | 112.0 | 475 | 113 | 55 | 51 | 13 | 2 | 1 | 2 | 33 | 2 | 64 | 6 | 1 | 9 | 6 | .600 | 0 | 0-0 | 0 | 3.86 | 4.10 |
| 2010 | Tex | AL | 23 | 22 | 1 | 0 | 128.0 | 536 | 126 | 55 | 53 | 21 | 3 | 2 | 3 | 33 | 0 | 68 | 1 | 0 | 13 | 4 | **.765** | 0 | 0-0 | 0 | 3.95 | 3.73 |
| 2011 | 2 Tms | AL | 20 | 11 | 0 | 2 | 84.2 | 367 | 100 | 50 | 44 | 12 | 2 | 2 | 4 | 15 | 1 | 45 | 0 | 0 | 4 | 4 | .500 | 0 | 0-1 | 1 | 4.65 | 4.68 |
| 2012 | Bal | AL | 33 | 20 | 0 | 5 | 133.2 | 573 | 161 | 85 | 81 | 32 | 3 | 6 | 4 | 27 | 2 | 77 | 0 | 1 | 7 | 8 | .467 | 0 | 0-1 | 0 | 5.63 | 5.45 |
| 2013 | Bal | AL | 68 | 0 | 0 | 20 | 86.1 | 336 | 71 | 28 | 27 | 11 | 1 | 0 | 2 | 14 | 1 | 68 | 0 | 0 | 6 | 5 | .545 | 0 | 4-6 | 21 | 2.53 | 2.81 |
| 11 | Tex | AL | 8 | 0 | 0 | 2 | 15.1 | 62 | 12 | 6 | 5 | 1 | 1 | 1 | 0 | 5 | 0 | 10 | 0 | 0 | 1 | 1 | .500 | 0 | 0-1 | 0 | 2.44 | 2.93 |
| 11 | Bal | AL | 12 | 11 | 0 | 0 | 69.1 | 305 | 88 | 44 | 39 | 11 | 1 | 1 | 4 | 10 | 1 | 35 | 0 | 0 | 3 | 3 | .500 | 0 | 0-0 | 1 | 5.19 | 5.06 |
| Postseason | | | 5 | 3 | 0 | 1 | 12.2 | 57 | 16 | 8 | 7 | 2 | 0 | 1 | 1 | 1 | 0 | 14 | 0 | 1 | 0 | 2 | .000 | 0 | 0-0 | 0 | 4.80 | 4.97 |
| 6 ML YEARS | | | 166 | 75 | 2 | 27 | 555.2 | 2350 | 594 | 293 | 276 | 93 | 11 | 11 | 16 | 125 | 6 | 331 | 7 | 2 | 39 | 29 | .574 | 0 | 4-8 | 22 | 4.33 | 4.47 |

# Torii Hunter

**Bats:** R **Throws:** R **Pos:** RF-143;PH-6 **Ht:** 6'2" **Wt:** 225 **Born:** 7/18/1975 **Age:** 38

| BATTING | | | | | | | | | | | | | | | | | | | | | BASERUNNING | | | | AVERAGES | | |
|---|---|---|---|---|---|---|---|---|---|---|---|---|---|---|---|---|---|---|---|---|---|---|---|---|---|---|---|
| Year | Team | Lg | G | AB | H | 2B | 3B | HR | (Hm | Rd) | TB | R | RBI | RC | TBB | IBB | SO | HBP | SH | SF | SB | CS | SB% | GDP | Avg | OBP | Slg |
| 1997 | Min | AL | 1 | 0 | 0 | 0 | 0 | 0 | (0 | 0) | 0 | 0 | 0 | 0 | 0 | 0 | 0 | 0 | 0 | 0 | 0 | 0 | - | 0 | - | - | - |
| 1998 | Min | AL | 6 | 17 | 4 | 1 | 0 | 0 | (0 | 0) | 5 | 0 | 2 | 1 | 2 | 0 | 6 | 0 | 0 | 0 | 0 | 1 | .00 | 1 | .235 | .316 | .294 |
| 1999 | Min | AL | 135 | 384 | 98 | 17 | 2 | 9 | (2 | 7) | 146 | 52 | 35 | 44 | 26 | 1 | 72 | 6 | 1 | 5 | 10 | 6 | .63 | 9 | .255 | .309 | .380 |
| 2000 | Min | AL | 99 | 336 | 94 | 14 | 7 | 5 | (4 | 1) | 137 | 44 | 44 | 39 | 18 | 2 | 68 | 2 | 0 | 2 | 4 | 3 | .57 | 13 | .280 | .318 | .408 |
| 2001 | Min | AL | 148 | 564 | 147 | 32 | 5 | 27 | (13 | 14) | 270 | 82 | 92 | 79 | 29 | 0 | 125 | 8 | 1 | 1 | 9 | 6 | .60 | 12 | .261 | .306 | .479 |

| Year Team | Lg | G | AB | H | 2B | 3B | HR | (Hm | Rd) | TB | R | RBI | RC | TBB | IBB | SO | HBP | SH | SF | SB | CS | SB% | GDP | Avg | OBP | Slg |
|---|---|---|---|---|---|---|---|---|---|---|---|---|---|---|---|---|---|---|---|---|---|---|---|---|---|---|
| | | BATTING | | | | | | | | | | | | | | | | | | BASERUNNING | | | | AVERAGES | | |
| 2002 Min | AL | 148 | 561 | 162 | 37 | 4 | 29 | (13 | 16) | 294 | 89 | 94 | 85 | 35 | 3 | 118 | 5 | 0 | 3 | 23 | 8 | .74 | 17 | .289 | .334 | .524 |
| 2003 Min | AL | 154 | 581 | 145 | 31 | 4 | 26 | (12 | 14) | 262 | 83 | 102 | 76 | 50 | 7 | 106 | 5 | 0 | 6 | 6 | 7 | .46 | 15 | .250 | .312 | .451 |
| 2004 Min | AL | 138 | 520 | 141 | 37 | 0 | 23 | (9 | 14) | 247 | 79 | 81 | 69 | 40 | 4 | 101 | 7 | 0 | 2 | 21 | 7 | .75 | 23 | .271 | .330 | .475 |
| 2005 Min | AL | 98 | 372 | 100 | 24 | 1 | 14 | (6 | 8) | 168 | 63 | 56 | 53 | 34 | 3 | 65 | 6 | 0 | 4 | 23 | 7 | .77 | 8 | .269 | .337 | .452 |
| 2006 Min | AL | 147 | 557 | 155 | 21 | 2 | 31 | (15 | 16) | 273 | 86 | 98 | 81 | 45 | 2 | 108 | 5 | 0 | 4 | 12 | 6 | .67 | 19 | .278 | .336 | .490 |
| 2007 Min | AL | 160 | 600 | 172 | 45 | 1 | 28 | (11 | 17) | 303 | 94 | 107 | 99 | 40 | 10 | 101 | 5 | 0 | 5 | 18 | 9 | .67 | 17 | .287 | .334 | .505 |
| 2008 LAA | AL | 146 | 551 | 153 | 37 | 2 | 21 | (10 | 11) | 257 | 85 | 78 | 80 | 50 | 6 | 108 | 6 | 0 | 1 | 19 | 5 | .79 | 15 | .278 | .344 | .466 |
| 2009 LAA | AL | 119 | 451 | 135 | 26 | 1 | 22 | (15 | 7) | 229 | 74 | 90 | 84 | 47 | 4 | 92 | 3 | 0 | 5 | 18 | 4 | .82 | 9 | .299 | .366 | .508 |
| 2010 LAA | AL | 152 | 573 | 161 | 36 | 0 | 23 | (8 | 15) | 266 | 76 | 90 | 93 | 61 | 6 | 106 | 7 | 0 | 5 | 9 | 12 | .43 | 22 | .281 | .354 | .464 |
| 2011 LAA | AL | 156 | 580 | 152 | 24 | 2 | 23 | (15 | 8) | 249 | 80 | 82 | 79 | 62 | 2 | 125 | 4 | 0 | 3 | 5 | 7 | .42 | 24 | .262 | .336 | .429 |
| 2012 LAA | AL | 140 | 534 | 167 | 24 | 1 | 16 | (7 | 9) | 241 | 81 | 92 | 89 | 38 | 1 | 133 | 8 | 1 | 3 | 9 | 1 | .90 | 15 | .313 | .365 | .451 |
| 2013 Det | AL | 144 | 606 | 184 | 37 | 5 | 17 | (8 | 9) | 282 | 90 | 84 | 81 | 26 | 0 | 113 | 7 | 3 | 10 | 3 | 2 | .60 | 11 | .304 | .334 | .465 |
| Postseason | | 34 | 131 | 40 | 10 | 1 | 4 | (1 | 3) | 64 | 19 | 18 | 18 | 13 | 2 | 19 | 1 | 2 | 1 | 3 | 1 | .75 | 4 | .305 | .370 | .489 |
| 17 ML YEARS | | 2091 | 7787 | 2170 | 443 | 37 | 314 | (148 | 166) | 3629 | 1158 | 1227 | 1132 | 603 | 51 | 1547 | 84 | 6 | 59 | 189 | 91 | .68 | 230 | .279 | .335 | .466 |

## Colt Hynes

**Pitches:** L **Bats:** L **Pos:** RP-22 **Ht:** 5'11" **Wt:** 200 **Born:** 6/28/1985 **Age:** 29

| Year Team | Lg | G | GS | CG | GF | IP | BFP | H | R | ER | HR | SH | SF | HB | TBB | IBB | SO | WP | Bk | W | L | Pct | Sh | Sv-Op | Hld | ERC | ERA |
|---|---|---|---|---|---|---|---|---|---|---|---|---|---|---|---|---|---|---|---|---|---|---|---|---|---|---|---|
| | | HOW MUCH HE PITCHED | | | | | | WHAT HE GAVE UP | | | | | | | | | | | | THE RESULTS | | | | | | | |
| 2009 FtWyn | A | 13 | 0 | 0 | 2 | 16.2 | 68 | 13 | 4 | 3 | 0 | 0 | 1 | 0 | 7 | 0 | 17 | 0 | 0 | 2 | 0 | 1.000 | 0 | 0- - | - | 2.37 | 1.62 |
| 2009 Lk Els | A+ | 49 | 0 | 0 | 11 | 59.0 | 252 | 60 | 25 | 19 | 0 | 3 | 2 | 3 | 17 | 1 | 44 | 3 | 0 | 3 | 3 | .500 | 0 | 2- - | - | 3.20 | 2.90 |
| 2010 Lk Els | A+ | 37 | 0 | 0 | 10 | 51.0 | 210 | 55 | 16 | 15 | 2 | 4 | 0 | 3 | 7 | 2 | 38 | 1 | 0 | 3 | 1 | .750 | 0 | 2- - | - | 3.31 | 2.65 |
| 2010 SnAnt | AA | 24 | 0 | 0 | 10 | 30.1 | 142 | 33 | 10 | 4 | 0 | 4 | 2 | 4 | 10 | 3 | 24 | 3 | 0 | 0 | 1 | .000 | 0 | 0- - | - | 3.66 | 1.19 |
| 2011 SnAnt | AA | 45 | 0 | 0 | 17 | 58.0 | 250 | 64 | 29 | 24 | 1 | 2 | 2 | 2 | 20 | 2 | 41 | 3 | 0 | 0 | 6 | .000 | 0 | 1- - | - | 3.98 | 3.72 |
| 2011 Tucsn | AAA | 22 | 0 | 0 | 5 | 26.1 | 116 | 35 | 16 | 16 | 1 | 0 | 2 | 2 | 9 | 0 | 12 | 3 | 0 | 2 | 1 | .667 | 0 | 0- - | - | 5.90 | 5.47 |
| 2012 Tucsn | AAA | 30 | 21 | 0 | 4 | 126.2 | 582 | 190 | 93 | 81 | 11 | 7 | 3 | 3 | 29 | 0 | 74 | 8 | 0 | 6 | 9 | .400 | 0 | 0- - | - | 6.41 | 5.76 |
| 2013 SnAnt | AA | 10 | 0 | 0 | 0 | 12.1 | 44 | 10 | 1 | 1 | 0 | 1 | 0 | 0 | 0 | 0 | 16 | 1 | 0 | 1 | 0 | 1.000 | 0 | 0- - | - | 1.39 | 0.73 |
| 2013 Tucsn | AAA | 31 | 0 | 0 | 9 | 35.0 | 139 | 33 | 10 | 7 | 1 | 2 | 1 | 1 | 2 | 0 | 42 | 4 | 0 | 1 | 0 | 1.000 | 0 | 4- - | - | 2.17 | 1.80 |
| 2013 SD | NL | 22 | 0 | 0 | 6 | 17.0 | 84 | 25 | 17 | 17 | 3 | 0 | 0 | 1 | 9 | 2 | 13 | 1 | 0 | 0 | 0 | - | 0 | 0-0 | 1 | 8.20 | 9.00 |

## Chris Iannetta

**Bats:** R **Throws:** R **Pos:** C-113;PH-9 eye-ah-NETT-ah **Ht:** 6'0" **Wt:** 230 **Born:** 4/8/1983 **Age:** 31

| Year Team | Lg | G | AB | H | 2B | 3B | HR | (Hm | Rd) | TB | R | RBI | RC | TBB | IBB | SO | HBP | SH | SF | SB | CS | SB% | GDP | Avg | OBP | Slg |
|---|---|---|---|---|---|---|---|---|---|---|---|---|---|---|---|---|---|---|---|---|---|---|---|---|---|---|
| | | BATTING | | | | | | | | | | | | | | | | | | BASERUNNING | | | | AVERAGES | | |
| 2006 Col | NL | 21 | 77 | 20 | 4 | 0 | 2 | (0 | 2) | 30 | 12 | 10 | 9 | 13 | 2 | 17 | 1 | 1 | 1 | 0 | 1 | .00 | 1 | .260 | .370 | .390 |
| 2007 Col | NL | 67 | 197 | 43 | 8 | 3 | 4 | (1 | 3) | 69 | 22 | 27 | 27 | 29 | 3 | 58 | 5 | 1 | 2 | 0 | 0 | - | 3 | .218 | .330 | .350 |
| 2008 Col | NL | 104 | 333 | 88 | 22 | 2 | 18 | (11 | 7) | 168 | 50 | 65 | 65 | 56 | 0 | 92 | 14 | 2 | 2 | 0 | 0 | - | 6 | .264 | .390 | .505 |
| 2009 Col | NL | 93 | 289 | 66 | 15 | 2 | 16 | (8 | 8) | 133 | 41 | 52 | 47 | 43 | 3 | 75 | 11 | 1 | 6 | 0 | 1 | .00 | 4 | .228 | .344 | .460 |
| 2010 Col | NL | 61 | 188 | 37 | 6 | 1 | 9 | (7 | 2) | 72 | 20 | 27 | 21 | 30 | 2 | 48 | 4 | 0 | 1 | 1 | 0 | 1.00 | 4 | .197 | .318 | .383 |
| 2011 Col | NL | 112 | 345 | 82 | 17 | 1 | 14 | (10 | 4) | 143 | 51 | 55 | 62 | 70 | 5 | 89 | 5 | 2 | 4 | 6 | 3 | .67 | 10 | .238 | .370 | .414 |
| 2012 LAA | AL | 79 | 221 | 53 | 6 | 1 | 9 | (3 | 6) | 88 | 27 | 26 | 27 | 29 | 0 | 60 | 2 | 0 | 1 | 1 | 3 | .25 | 4 | .240 | .332 | .398 |
| 2013 LAA | AL | 115 | 325 | 73 | 15 | 0 | 11 | (1 | 10) | 121 | 40 | 39 | 44 | 68 | 2 | 100 | 2 | 0 | 4 | 0 | 1 | .00 | 8 | .225 | .358 | .372 |
| 8 ML YEARS | | 652 | 1975 | 462 | 93 | 10 | 83 | (41 | 42) | 824 | 263 | 301 | 302 | 338 | 17 | 539 | 44 | 7 | 21 | 8 | 9 | .47 | 40 | .234 | .355 | .417 |

## Raul Ibanez

**Bats:** L **Throws:** R **Pos:** LF-99;DH-21;PH-5;RF-1 ee-BAHN-yezz **Ht:** 6'2" **Wt:** 225 **Born:** 6/2/1972 **Age:** 42

| Year Team | Lg | G | AB | H | 2B | 3B | HR | (Hm | Rd) | TB | R | RBI | RC | TBB | IBB | SO | HBP | SH | SF | SB | CS | SB% | GDP | Avg | OBP | Slg |
|---|---|---|---|---|---|---|---|---|---|---|---|---|---|---|---|---|---|---|---|---|---|---|---|---|---|---|
| | | BATTING | | | | | | | | | | | | | | | | | | BASERUNNING | | | | AVERAGES | | |
| 1996 Sea | AL | 4 | 5 | 0 | 0 | 0 | 0 | (0 | 0) | 0 | 0 | 0 | 0 | 0 | 0 | 1 | 1 | 0 | 0 | 0 | 0 | - | 0 | .000 | .167 | .000 |
| 1997 Sea | AL | 11 | 26 | 4 | 0 | 1 | 1 | (1 | 0) | 9 | 3 | 4 | 1 | 0 | 0 | 6 | 0 | 0 | 0 | 0 | 0 | - | 0 | .154 | .154 | .346 |
| 1998 Sea | AL | 37 | 98 | 25 | 7 | 1 | 2 | (1 | 1) | 40 | 12 | 12 | 10 | 5 | 0 | 22 | 0 | 0 | 0 | 0 | 0 | - | 4 | .255 | .291 | .408 |
| 1999 Sea | AL | 87 | 209 | 54 | 7 | 0 | 9 | (3 | 6) | 88 | 23 | 27 | 28 | 17 | 1 | 32 | 0 | 0 | 1 | 5 | 1 | .83 | 4 | .258 | .313 | .421 |
| 2000 Sea | AL | 92 | 140 | 32 | 8 | 0 | 2 | (2 | 0) | 46 | 21 | 15 | 15 | 14 | 1 | 25 | 1 | 0 | 1 | 2 | 0 | 1.00 | 1 | .229 | .301 | .329 |
| 2001 KC | AL | 104 | 279 | 78 | 11 | 5 | 13 | (5 | 8) | 138 | 44 | 54 | 46 | 32 | 2 | 51 | 0 | 0 | 1 | 0 | 2 | .00 | 6 | .280 | .353 | .495 |
| 2002 KC | AL | 137 | 497 | 146 | 37 | 6 | 24 | (14 | 10) | 267 | 70 | 103 | 89 | 40 | 5 | 76 | 2 | 1 | 4 | 5 | 3 | .63 | 11 | .294 | .346 | .537 |
| 2003 KC | AL | 157 | 608 | 179 | 33 | 5 | 18 | (8 | 10) | 276 | 95 | 90 | 91 | 49 | 5 | 81 | 3 | 1 | 10 | 8 | 4 | .67 | 10 | .294 | .345 | .454 |
| 2004 Sea | AL | 123 | 481 | 146 | 31 | 1 | 16 | (9 | 7) | 227 | 67 | 62 | 67 | 36 | 5 | 72 | 3 | 0 | 4 | 1 | 2 | .33 | 10 | .304 | .353 | .472 |
| 2005 Sea | AL | **162** | 614 | 172 | 32 | 2 | 20 | (9 | 11) | 268 | 92 | 89 | 99 | 71 | 6 | 99 | 2 | 0 | 3 | 9 | 4 | .69 | 12 | .280 | .355 | .436 |
| 2006 Sea | AL | 159 | 626 | 181 | 33 | 5 | 33 | (17 | 16) | 323 | 103 | 123 | 114 | 65 | 15 | 115 | 1 | 0 | 7 | 2 | 4 | .33 | 13 | .289 | .353 | .516 |
| 2007 Sea | AL | 149 | 573 | 167 | 35 | 5 | 21 | (7 | 14) | 275 | 80 | 105 | 101 | 53 | 4 | 97 | 3 | 0 | 7 | 0 | 0 | - | 14 | .291 | .351 | .480 |
| 2008 Sea | AL | 162 | 635 | 186 | 43 | 3 | 23 | (14 | 9) | 304 | 85 | 110 | 107 | 64 | 11 | 110 | 3 | 0 | 5 | 2 | 4 | .33 | 13 | .293 | .358 | .479 |
| 2009 Phi | NL | 134 | 500 | 136 | 32 | 3 | 34 | (13 | 21) | 276 | 93 | 93 | 80 | 56 | 8 | 119 | 4 | 0 | 5 | 4 | 0 | 1.00 | 16 | .272 | .347 | .552 |
| 2010 Phi | NL | 155 | 561 | 154 | 37 | 5 | 16 | (9 | 7) | 249 | 75 | 83 | 86 | 68 | 11 | 108 | 0 | 0 | 7 | 4 | 3 | .57 | 15 | .275 | .349 | .444 |
| 2011 Phi | NL | 144 | 535 | 131 | 31 | 1 | 20 | (15 | 5) | 224 | 65 | 84 | 64 | 33 | 3 | 106 | 2 | 0 | 5 | 2 | 0 | 1.00 | 13 | .245 | .289 | .419 |
| 2012 NYY | AL | 130 | 384 | 92 | 19 | 3 | 19 | (14 | 5) | 174 | 50 | 62 | 50 | 35 | 5 | 67 | 4 | 0 | 2 | 3 | 0 | 1.00 | 14 | .240 | .308 | .453 |
| 2013 Sea | AL | 124 | 454 | 110 | 20 | 2 | 29 | (17 | 12) | 221 | 54 | 65 | 65 | 42 | 1 | 128 | 0 | 0 | 0 | 0 | 0 | - | 8 | .242 | .306 | .487 |
| Postseason | | 44 | 139 | 34 | 9 | 0 | 6 | (5 | 1) | 61 | 15 | 22 | 18 | 12 | 2 | 38 | 0 | 0 | 0 | 0 | 1 | .00 | 2 | .245 | .305 | .439 |
| 18 ML YEARS | | 2071 | 7225 | 1993 | 416 | 48 | 300 | (158 | 142) | 3405 | 1032 | 1181 | 1113 | 680 | 83 | 1315 | 29 | 2 | 62 | 47 | 27 | .64 | 164 | .276 | .338 | .471 |

## Jose Iglesias

**Bats:** R **Throws:** R **Pos:** SS-71;3B-37;2B-3;PR-3;DH-1 ee-GLAY-see-us **Ht:** 5'11" **Wt:** 185 **Born:** 1/5/1990 **Age:** 24

| Year Team | Lg | G | AB | H | 2B | 3B | HR | (Hm | Rd) | TB | R | RBI | RC | TBB | IBB | SO | HBP | SH | SF | SB | CS | SB% | GDP | Avg | OBP | Slg |
|---|---|---|---|---|---|---|---|---|---|---|---|---|---|---|---|---|---|---|---|---|---|---|---|---|---|---|
| | | BATTING | | | | | | | | | | | | | | | | | | BASERUNNING | | | | AVERAGES | | |
| 2013 Pwtckt* | AAA | 33 | 119 | 24 | 2 | 0 | 4 | (- | -) | 38 | 17 | 15 | 10 | 9 | 0 | 18 | 1 | 3 | 1 | 5 | 3 | .63 | 6 | .202 | .262 | .319 |
| 2011 Bos | AL | 10 | 6 | 2 | 0 | 0 | 0 | (0 | 0) | 2 | 3 | 0 | 0 | 0 | 0 | 2 | 0 | 0 | 0 | 0 | 0 | - | 0 | .333 | .333 | .333 |
| 2012 Bos | AL | 25 | 68 | 8 | 2 | 0 | 1 | (0 | 1) | 13 | 5 | 2 | 0 | 4 | 0 | 16 | 3 | 2 | 0 | 1 | 0 | 1.00 | 2 | .118 | .200 | .191 |

| | | | | | | | | | BATTING | | | | | | | | | | | BASERUNNING | | | | AVERAGES | | |
|---|---|---|---|---|---|---|---|---|---|---|---|---|---|---|---|---|---|---|---|---|---|---|---|---|---|---|
| Year | Team | Lg | G | AB | H | 2B | 3B | HR | (Hm | Rd) | TB | R | RBI | RC | TBB | IBB | SO | HBP | SH | SF | SB | CS | SB% | GDP | Avg | OBP | Slg |
| 2013 | 2 Tms | AL | 109 | 350 | 106 | 16 | 2 | 3 | (1 | 2) | 135 | 39 | 29 | 45 | 15 | 0 | 60 | 11 | 4 | 2 | 5 | 2 | .71 | 7 | .303 | .349 | .386 |
| 13 | Bos | AL | 63 | 215 | 71 | 10 | 2 | 1 | (0 | 1) | 88 | 27 | 19 | 34 | 11 | 0 | 30 | 6 | 0 | 2 | 3 | 1 | .75 | 4 | .330 | .376 | .409 |
| 13 | Det | AL | 46 | 135 | 35 | 6 | 0 | 2 | (1 | 1) | 47 | 12 | 10 | 11 | 4 | 0 | 30 | 5 | 4 | 0 | 2 | 1 | .67 | 3 | .259 | .306 | .348 |
| 3 ML YEARS | | | 144 | 424 | 116 | 18 | 2 | 4 | (1 | 3) | 150 | 47 | 31 | 45 | 19 | 0 | 78 | 14 | 6 | 2 | 6 | 2 | .75 | 9 | .274 | .325 | .354 |

## Omar Infante

**Bats:** R **Throws:** R **Pos:** 2B-118;PH-1;PR-1 in-FAHN-tay **Ht:** 5'11" **Wt:** 195 **Born:** 12/26/1981 **Age:** 32

| | | | | | | | | | BATTING | | | | | | | | | | | BASERUNNING | | | | AVERAGES | | |
|---|---|---|---|---|---|---|---|---|---|---|---|---|---|---|---|---|---|---|---|---|---|---|---|---|---|---|
| Year | Team | Lg | G | AB | H | 2B | 3B | HR | (Hm | Rd) | TB | R | RBI | RC | TBB | IBB | SO | HBP | SH | SF | SB | CS | SB% | GDP | Avg | OBP | Slg |
| 2013 | WMich* | A | 2 | 5 | 2 | 0 | 0 | 0 | (- | -) | 2 | 0 | 0 | 1 | 0 | 0 | 1 | 1 | 0 | 0 | 0 | 0 | - | 0 | .400 | .500 | .400 |
| 2013 | Toledo* | AAA | 5 | 19 | 4 | 0 | 0 | 0 | (- | -) | 4 | 1 | 1 | 1 | 2 | 0 | 2 | 0 | 0 | 0 | 0 | 0 | - | 1 | .211 | .286 | .211 |
| 2002 | Det | AL | 18 | 72 | 24 | 3 | 0 | 1 | (0 | 1) | 30 | 4 | 6 | 12 | 3 | 0 | 10 | 0 | 0 | 0 | 0 | 1 | .00 | 0 | .333 | .360 | .417 |
| 2003 | Det | AL | 69 | 221 | 49 | 6 | 1 | 0 | (0 | 0) | 57 | 24 | 8 | 16 | 18 | 0 | 37 | 0 | 3 | 2 | 6 | 3 | .67 | 1 | .222 | .278 | .258 |
| 2004 | Det | AL | 142 | 503 | 133 | 27 | 9 | 16 | (7 | 9) | 226 | 69 | 55 | 69 | 40 | 3 | 112 | 1 | 7 | 5 | 13 | 7 | .65 | 4 | .264 | .317 | .449 |
| 2005 | Det | AL | 121 | 406 | 90 | 28 | 2 | 9 | (3 | 6) | 149 | 36 | 43 | 38 | 16 | 0 | 73 | 2 | 8 | 2 | 8 | 0 | 1.00 | 5 | .222 | .254 | .367 |
| 2006 | Det | AL | 78 | 224 | 62 | 11 | 4 | 4 | (0 | 4) | 93 | 35 | 25 | 26 | 14 | 0 | 45 | 3 | 2 | 2 | 3 | 2 | .60 | 5 | .277 | .325 | .415 |
| 2007 | Det | AL | 66 | 166 | 45 | 6 | 1 | 2 | (0 | 2) | 59 | 24 | 17 | 23 | 9 | 0 | 29 | 0 | 2 | 1 | 4 | 1 | .80 | 4 | .271 | .307 | .355 |
| 2008 | Atl | NL | 96 | 317 | 93 | 24 | 3 | 3 | (1 | 2) | 132 | 45 | 40 | 45 | 22 | 2 | 44 | 2 | 2 | 5 | 0 | 1 | .00 | 4 | .293 | .338 | .416 |
| 2009 | Atl | NL | 70 | 203 | 62 | 9 | 1 | 2 | (1 | 1) | 79 | 24 | 27 | 29 | 19 | 0 | 28 | 1 | 2 | 4 | 2 | 0 | 1.00 | 5 | .305 | .361 | .389 |
| 2010 | Atl | NL | 134 | 471 | 151 | 15 | 3 | 8 | (1 | 7) | 196 | 65 | 47 | 70 | 29 | 1 | 62 | 0 | 4 | 2 | 7 | 6 | .54 | 14 | .321 | .359 | .416 |
| 2011 | Fla | NL | 148 | 579 | 160 | 24 | 8 | 7 | (2 | 5) | 221 | 55 | 49 | 66 | 34 | 1 | 67 | 2 | **17** | 8 | 4 | 2 | .67 | 12 | .276 | .315 | .382 |
| 2012 | 2 Tms | | 149 | 554 | 152 | 30 | 7 | 12 | (5 | 7) | 232 | 69 | 53 | 58 | 21 | 0 | 65 | 1 | 8 | 4 | 17 | 3 | .85 | 9 | .274 | .300 | .419 |
| 2013 | Det | AL | 118 | 453 | 144 | 24 | 3 | 10 | (7 | 3) | 204 | 54 | 51 | 64 | 20 | 1 | 44 | 0 | 0 | 3 | 5 | 2 | .71 | 11 | .318 | .345 | .450 |
| 12 | Mia | NL | 85 | 328 | 94 | 23 | 2 | 8 | (2 | 6) | 145 | 42 | 33 | 36 | 12 | 0 | 42 | 1 | 4 | 2 | 10 | 1 | .91 | 7 | .287 | .312 | .442 |
| 12 | Det | AL | 64 | 226 | 58 | 7 | 5 | 4 | (3 | 1) | 87 | 27 | 20 | 22 | 9 | 0 | 23 | 0 | 4 | 2 | 7 | 2 | .78 | 2 | .257 | .283 | .385 |
| Postseason | | | 19 | 71 | 20 | 2 | 0 | 0 | (0 | 0) | 22 | 10 | 0 | 6 | 4 | 0 | 19 | 1 | 1 | 0 | 3 | 1 | .75 | 1 | .282 | .329 | .310 |
| 12 ML YEARS | | | 1209 | 4169 | 1165 | 207 | 42 | 74 | (27 | 47) | 1678 | 504 | 421 | 516 | 245 | 8 | 616 | 12 | 55 | 38 | 69 | 28 | .71 | 74 | .279 | .319 | .402 |

## Brandon Inge

**Bats:** R **Throws:** R **Pos:** PH-21;2B-13;3B-10;RF-6;1B-4;SS-1 **Ht:** 5'11" **Wt:** 190 **Born:** 5/19/1977 **Age:** 37

| | | | | | | | | | BATTING | | | | | | | | | | | BASERUNNING | | | | AVERAGES | | |
|---|---|---|---|---|---|---|---|---|---|---|---|---|---|---|---|---|---|---|---|---|---|---|---|---|---|---|
| Year | Team | Lg | G | AB | H | 2B | 3B | HR | (Hm | Rd) | TB | R | RBI | RC | TBB | IBB | SO | HBP | SH | SF | SB | CS | SB% | GDP | Avg | OBP | Slg |
| 2013 | Indy* | AAA | 18 | 60 | 9 | 2 | 0 | 2 | (- | -) | 17 | 4 | 6 | 6 | 12 | 0 | 17 | 3 | 0 | 0 | 1 | 0 | 1.00 | 4 | .150 | .320 | .283 |
| 2001 | Det | AL | 79 | 189 | 34 | 11 | 0 | 0 | (0 | 0) | 45 | 13 | 15 | 6 | 9 | 0 | 41 | 0 | 2 | 2 | 1 | 4 | .20 | 2 | .180 | .215 | .238 |
| 2002 | Det | AL | 95 | 321 | 65 | 15 | 3 | 7 | (3 | 4) | 107 | 27 | 24 | 24 | 24 | 0 | 101 | 4 | 1 | 1 | 1 | 3 | .25 | 7 | .202 | .266 | .333 |
| 2003 | Det | AL | 104 | 330 | 67 | 15 | 3 | 8 | (4 | 4) | 112 | 32 | 30 | 23 | 24 | 0 | 79 | 5 | 4 | 3 | 4 | 4 | .50 | 8 | .203 | .265 | .339 |
| 2004 | Det | AL | 131 | 408 | 117 | 15 | 7 | 13 | (9 | 4) | 185 | 43 | 64 | 63 | 32 | 0 | 72 | 4 | 8 | 6 | 5 | 4 | .56 | 4 | .287 | .340 | .453 |
| 2005 | Det | AL | 160 | 616 | 161 | 31 | 9 | 16 | (10 | 6) | 258 | 75 | 72 | 82 | 63 | 1 | 140 | 3 | 6 | 6 | 7 | 6 | .54 | 14 | .261 | .330 | .419 |
| 2006 | Det | AL | 159 | 542 | 137 | 29 | 2 | 27 | (12 | 15) | 251 | 83 | 83 | 79 | 43 | 2 | 128 | 7 | 4 | 5 | 7 | 4 | .64 | 12 | .253 | .313 | .463 |
| 2007 | Det | AL | 151 | 508 | 120 | 25 | 2 | 14 | (9 | 5) | 191 | 64 | 71 | 65 | 47 | 5 | 150 | 11 | 7 | 4 | 9 | 2 | .82 | 8 | .236 | .312 | .376 |
| 2008 | Det | AL | 113 | 347 | 71 | 16 | 4 | 11 | (8 | 3) | 128 | 41 | 51 | 44 | 43 | 2 | 94 | 8 | 5 | 4 | 4 | 3 | .57 | 4 | .205 | .303 | .369 |
| 2009 | Det | AL | **161** | 562 | 129 | 16 | 1 | 27 | (14 | 13) | 228 | 71 | 84 | 70 | 54 | 1 | 170 | 17 | 1 | 3 | 2 | 5 | .29 | 12 | .230 | .314 | .406 |
| 2010 | Det | AL | 144 | 514 | 127 | 28 | 5 | 13 | (4 | 9) | 204 | 47 | 70 | 64 | 54 | 4 | 134 | 5 | 0 | 7 | 4 | 3 | .57 | 12 | .247 | .321 | .397 |
| 2011 | Det | AL | 102 | 269 | 53 | 10 | 2 | 3 | (3 | 0) | 76 | 29 | 23 | 12 | 24 | 0 | 74 | 2 | 5 | 3 | 1 | 1 | .50 | 9 | .197 | .265 | .283 |
| 2012 | 2 Tms | AL | 83 | 303 | 66 | 14 | 0 | 12 | (8 | 4) | 116 | 33 | 54 | 41 | 24 | 1 | 91 | 1 | 0 | 3 | 0 | 1 | .00 | 8 | .218 | .275 | .383 |
| 2013 | Pit | NL | 50 | 105 | 19 | 3 | 0 | 1 | (0 | 1) | 25 | 5 | 7 | 3 | 2 | 0 | 32 | 1 | 2 | 0 | 0 | 0 | - | 2 | .181 | .204 | .238 |
| 12 | Det | AL | 9 | 20 | 2 | 1 | 0 | 1 | (0 | 1) | 6 | 2 | 2 | 1 | 0 | 0 | 6 | 0 | 0 | 0 | 0 | 0 | - | 0 | .100 | .100 | .300 |
| 12 | Oak | AL | 74 | 283 | 64 | 13 | 0 | 11 | (8 | 3) | 110 | 31 | 52 | 40 | 24 | 1 | 85 | 1 | 0 | 3 | 0 | 1 | .00 | 8 | .226 | .286 | .389 |
| Postseason | | | 23 | 66 | 19 | 4 | 0 | 2 | (1 | 1) | 29 | 10 | 5 | 7 | 7 | 2 | 18 | 1 | 2 | 1 | 0 | 0 | - | 1 | .288 | .360 | .439 |
| 13 ML YEARS | | | 1532 | 5014 | 1166 | 228 | 38 | 152 | (84 | 68) | 1926 | 563 | 648 | 576 | 443 | 16 | 1306 | 68 | 45 | 47 | 45 | 40 | .53 | 102 | .233 | .301 | .384 |

## Phil Irwin

**Pitches:** R **Bats:** R **Pos:** SP-1 **Ht:** 6'3" **Wt:** 210 **Born:** 2/25/1987 **Age:** 27

| | | | HOW MUCH HE PITCHED | | | | | | WHAT HE GAVE UP | | | | | | | | | | | | THE RESULTS | | | | | | | |
|---|---|---|---|---|---|---|---|---|---|---|---|---|---|---|---|---|---|---|---|---|---|---|---|---|---|---|---|---|
| Year | Team | Lg | G | GS | CG | GF | IP | BFP | H | R | ER | HR | SH | SF | HB | TBB | IBB | SO | WP | Bk | W | L | Pct | Sh | Sv-Op | Hld | ERC | ERA |
| 2009 | StCol | A- | 10 | 7 | 0 | 0 | 29.2 | 122 | 27 | 8 | 7 | 1 | 1 | 2 | 2 | 6 | 0 | 32 | 0 | 1 | 1 | 2 | .333 | 0 | 0- - | - | 2.67 | 2.12 |
| 2010 | WV | A | 23 | 20 | 0 | 0 | 113.0 | 455 | 99 | 46 | 42 | 9 | 0 | 6 | 7 | 20 | 0 | 111 | 6 | 1 | 6 | 3 | .667 | 0 | 0- - | - | 2.70 | 3.35 |
| 2011 | Bradtn | A+ | 10 | 10 | 0 | 0 | 53.1 | 217 | 47 | 15 | 12 | 3 | 1 | 0 | 3 | 12 | 0 | 40 | 0 | 0 | 5 | 0 | 1.000 | 0 | 0- - | - | 2.73 | 2.03 |
| 2011 | Altna | AA | 15 | 14 | 0 | 0 | 87.1 | 366 | 91 | 42 | 37 | 9 | 2 | 1 | 8 | 10 | 0 | 69 | 6 | 0 | 8 | 4 | .667 | 0 | 0- - | - | 3.54 | 3.81 |
| 2012 | Bradtn | A+ | 1 | 1 | 0 | 0 | 5.0 | 17 | 2 | 1 | 1 | 0 | 0 | 0 | 0 | 0 | 0 | 6 | 0 | 0 | 1 | 0 | 1.000 | 0 | 0- - | - | 0.35 | 1.80 |
| 2012 | Altna | AA | 18 | 16 | 3 | 1 | 104.1 | 426 | 97 | 39 | 34 | 7 | 4 | 6 | 15 | 17 | 0 | 83 | 4 | 0 | 4 | 7 | .364 | 1 | 0- - | - | 3.18 | 2.93 |
| 2012 | Indy | AAA | 4 | 4 | 0 | 0 | 21.0 | 89 | 20 | 8 | 6 | 1 | 2 | 2 | 1 | 7 | 0 | 28 | 1 | 0 | 3 | 0 | 1.000 | 0 | 0- - | - | 3.39 | 2.57 |
| 2013 | Indy | AAA | 2 | 2 | 0 | 0 | 10.0 | 40 | 5 | 1 | 1 | 0 | 0 | 1 | 2 | 3 | 0 | 8 | 1 | 0 | 1 | 0 | 1.000 | 0 | 0- - | - | 1.41 | 0.90 |
| 2013 | Pit | NL | 1 | 1 | 0 | 0 | 4.2 | 23 | 6 | 5 | 4 | 0 | 0 | 0 | 0 | 4 | 0 | 4 | 0 | 0 | 0 | 0 | - | 0 | 0-0 | 0 | 6.94 | 7.71 |

## Travis Ishikawa

**Bats:** L **Throws:** L **Pos:** 1B-5;DH-2 ee-shee-KAU-wuh **Ht:** 6'3" **Wt:** 220 **Born:** 9/24/1983 **Age:** 30

| | | | | | | | | | BATTING | | | | | | | | | | | BASERUNNING | | | | AVERAGES | | |
|---|---|---|---|---|---|---|---|---|---|---|---|---|---|---|---|---|---|---|---|---|---|---|---|---|---|---|
| Year | Team | Lg | G | AB | H | 2B | 3B | HR | (Hm | Rd) | TB | R | RBI | RC | TBB | IBB | SO | HBP | SH | SF | SB | CS | SB% | GDP | Avg | OBP | Slg |
| 2013 | Norfolk* | AAA | 49 | 177 | 56 | 16 | 0 | 7 | (- | -) | 93 | 29 | 31 | 39 | 29 | 3 | 43 | 1 | 0 | 1 | 1 | 0 | 1.00 | 1 | .316 | .413 | .525 |
| 2013 | Charltt* | AAA | 34 | 120 | 30 | 5 | 2 | 2 | (- | -) | 45 | 17 | 23 | 17 | 15 | 0 | 31 | 4 | 1 | 0 | 0 | 0 | - | 3 | .250 | .353 | .375 |
| 2006 | SF | NL | 12 | 24 | 7 | 3 | 1 | 0 | (0 | 0) | 12 | 1 | 4 | 4 | 1 | 0 | 6 | 0 | 0 | 0 | 0 | 0 | - | 1 | .292 | .320 | .500 |
| 2008 | SF | NL | 33 | 95 | 26 | 6 | 0 | 3 | (1 | 2) | 41 | 12 | 15 | 17 | 9 | 1 | 27 | 0 | 0 | 0 | 1 | 0 | 1.00 | 1 | .274 | .337 | .432 |
| 2009 | SF | NL | 120 | 326 | 85 | 10 | 2 | 9 | (7 | 2) | 126 | 49 | 39 | 44 | 30 | 3 | 89 | 4 | 1 | 2 | 2 | 2 | .50 | 7 | .261 | .329 | .387 |
| 2010 | SF | NL | 116 | 158 | 42 | 11 | 0 | 3 | (0 | 3) | 62 | 18 | 22 | 19 | 13 | 2 | 29 | 0 | 1 | 1 | 0 | 0 | - | 3 | .266 | .320 | .392 |
| 2012 | Mil | NL | 94 | 152 | 39 | 12 | 1 | 4 | (2 | 2) | 65 | 19 | 30 | 24 | 13 | 3 | 42 | 4 | 4 | 1 | 0 | 0 | - | 4 | .257 | .329 | .428 |
| 2013 | 2 Tms | AL | 7 | 19 | 2 | 0 | 0 | 0 | (0 | 0) | 2 | 0 | 1 | 0 | 1 | 0 | 10 | 0 | 0 | 0 | 0 | 0 | - | 0 | .105 | .150 | .105 |

| Year | Team | Lg | BATTING G | AB | H | 2B | 3B | HR | (Hm | Rd) | TB | R | RBI | RC | TBB | IBB | SO | HBP | SH | SF | BASERUNNING SB | CS | SB% | GDP | AVERAGES Avg | OBP | Slg |
|---|---|---|---|---|---|---|---|---|---|---|---|---|---|---|---|---|---|---|---|---|---|---|---|---|---|---|---|
| 13 | Bal | AL | 6 | 17 | 2 | 0 | 0 | 0 | (0 | 0) | 2 | 0 | 1 | 0 | 1 | 0 | 8 | 0 | 0 | 0 | 0 | 0 | - | 0 | .118 | .167 | .118 |
| 13 | NYY | AL | 1 | 2 | 0 | 0 | 0 | 0 | (0 | 0) | 0 | 0 | 0 | 0 | 0 | 0 | 2 | 0 | 0 | 0 | 0 | 0 | - | 0 | .000 | .000 | .000 |
| Postseason | | | 10 | 10 | 2 | 1 | 0 | 0 | (0 | 0) | 3 | 2 | 1 | 1 | 2 | 0 | 4 | 1 | 0 | 0 | 0 | 0 | - | 1 | .200 | .385 | .300 |
| 6 ML YEARS | | | 382 | 774 | 201 | 42 | 4 | 19 | (10 | 9) | 308 | 99 | 111 | 108 | 67 | 9 | 203 | 8 | 6 | 4 | 3 | 2 | .60 | 16 | .260 | .324 | .398 |

# Yoshio Itoi

**Bats:** L **Throws:** R **Pos:** OF yo-SHEE-oh ee-TOY **Ht:** 6'2" **Wt:** 194 **Born:** 7/31/1981 **Age:** 32

| Year | Team | Lg | BATTING G | AB | H | 2B | 3B | HR | (Hm | Rd) | TB | R | RBI | RC | TBB | IBB | SO | HBP | SH | SF | BASERUNNING SB | CS | SB% | GDP | AVERAGES Avg | OBP | Slg |
|---|---|---|---|---|---|---|---|---|---|---|---|---|---|---|---|---|---|---|---|---|---|---|---|---|---|---|---|
| 2009 | Hokado | Jap | 131 | 425 | 130 | 40 | 3 | 15 | (- | -) | 221 | 74 | 58 | 87 | 46 | 8 | 93 | 6 | 18 | 1 | 24 | 6 | .80 | 6 | .306 | .381 | .520 |
| 2010 | Hokado | Jap | 138 | 488 | 151 | 33 | 3 | 15 | (- | -) | 235 | 86 | 64 | 90 | 71 | 2 | 94 | 10 | 13 | 1 | 26 | 8 | .76 | 7 | .309 | .407 | .482 |
| 2011 | Hokado | Jap | 137 | 489 | 156 | 30 | 0 | 11 | (- | -) | 219 | 72 | 54 | 88 | 59 | 2 | 91 | 19 | 9 | 2 | 31 | 6 | .84 | 5 | .319 | .411 | .448 |
| 2012 | Hokado | Jap | 134 | 510 | 155 | 21 | 3 | 9 | (- | -) | 209 | 72 | 48 | 82 | 75 | 2 | 86 | 11 | 0 | 1 | 22 | 9 | .71 | 9 | .304 | .404 | .410 |
| 2013 | Orix | Jap | 134 | 500 | 153 | 32 | 2 | 17 | (- | -) | 240 | 73 | 61 | 89 | 61 | 1 | 89 | 7 | 0 | 3 | 31 | 9 | .78 | 6 | .306 | .387 | .480 |

# Hisashi Iwakuma

**Pitches:** R **Bats:** R **Pos:** SP-33 he-SAH-shee ee-wuh-KOO-muh **Ht:** 6'3" **Wt:** 210 **Born:** 4/12/1981 **Age:** 33

| Year | Team | Lg | HOW MUCH HE PITCHED G | GS | CG | GF | IP | BFP | WHAT HE GAVE UP H | R | ER | HR | SH | SF | HB | TBB | IBB | SO | WP | Bk | THE RESULTS W | L | Pct | Sh | Sv-Op | Hld | ERC | ERA |
|---|---|---|---|---|---|---|---|---|---|---|---|---|---|---|---|---|---|---|---|---|---|---|---|---|---|---|---|---|
| 2009 | Tohoku | Jap | 24 | 24 | 5 | 0 | 169.0 | 729 | 179 | 62 | 61 | 15 | - | - | 6 | 43 | 1 | 121 | 3 | 0 | 13 | 6 | .684 | 0 | 0-- | - | 3.83 | 3.25 |
| 2010 | Tohoku | Jap | 28 | 28 | 4 | 0 | 201.0 | 823 | 184 | 68 | 63 | 11 | - | - | 12 | 36 | 1 | 153 | 1 | 1 | 10 | 9 | .526 | 1 | 0-- | - | 2.71 | 2.82 |
| 2011 | Tohoku | Jap | 17 | 17 | 2 | 0 | 119.0 | 482 | 106 | 34 | 32 | 6 | - | - | 5 | 19 | 0 | 90 | 1 | 0 | 6 | 7 | .462 | 1 | 0-- | - | 2.43 | 2.42 |
| 2012 | Sea | AL | 30 | 16 | 0 | 6 | 125.1 | 519 | 117 | 49 | 44 | 17 | 1 | 1 | 3 | 43 | 3 | 101 | 5 | 0 | 9 | 5 | .643 | 0 | 2-2 | 0 | 3.87 | 3.16 |
| 2013 | Sea | AL | 33 | 33 | 0 | 0 | 219.2 | 866 | 179 | 69 | 65 | 25 | 3 | 6 | 2 | 42 | 4 | 185 | 10 | 0 | 14 | 6 | .700 | 0 | 0-0 | 0 | 2.43 | 2.66 |
| 2 ML YEARS | | | 63 | 49 | 0 | 6 | 345.0 | 1385 | 296 | 118 | 109 | 42 | 4 | 7 | 5 | 85 | 7 | 286 | 15 | 0 | 23 | 11 | .676 | 0 | 2-2 | 0 | 2.93 | 2.84 |

# Cesar Izturis

**Bats:** B **Throws:** R **Pos:** SS-29;PH-24;2B-21;3B-1;PR-1 izz-TOUR-iss **Ht:** 5'9" **Wt:** 180 **Born:** 2/10/1980 **Age:** 34

| Year | Team | Lg | BATTING G | AB | H | 2B | 3B | HR | (Hm | Rd) | TB | R | RBI | RC | TBB | IBB | SO | HBP | SH | SF | BASERUNNING SB | CS | SB% | GDP | AVERAGES Avg | OBP | Slg |
|---|---|---|---|---|---|---|---|---|---|---|---|---|---|---|---|---|---|---|---|---|---|---|---|---|---|---|---|
| 2001 | Tor | AL | 46 | 134 | 36 | 6 | 2 | 2 | (1 | 1) | 52 | 19 | 9 | 16 | 2 | 0 | 15 | 0 | 4 | 0 | 8 | 1 | .89 | 0 | .269 | .279 | .388 |
| 2002 | LAD | NL | 135 | 439 | 102 | 24 | 2 | 1 | (0 | 1) | 133 | 43 | 31 | 26 | 14 | 1 | 39 | 0 | 10 | 5 | 7 | 7 | .50 | 12 | .232 | .253 | .303 |
| 2003 | LAD | NL | 158 | 558 | 140 | 21 | 6 | 1 | (0 | 1) | 176 | 47 | 40 | 42 | 25 | 8 | 70 | 0 | 7 | 3 | 10 | 5 | .67 | 8 | .251 | .282 | .315 |
| 2004 | LAD | NL | 159 | 670 | 193 | 32 | 9 | 4 | (1 | 3) | 255 | 90 | 62 | 95 | 43 | 2 | 70 | 0 | 12 | 3 | 25 | 9 | .74 | 6 | .288 | .330 | .381 |
| 2005 | LAD | NL | 106 | 444 | 114 | 19 | 2 | 2 | (1 | 1) | 143 | 48 | 31 | 37 | 25 | 1 | 51 | 4 | 4 | 1 | 8 | 8 | .50 | 11 | .257 | .302 | .322 |
| 2006 | 2 Tms | NL | 54 | 192 | 47 | 9 | 1 | 1 | (1 | 0) | 61 | 14 | 18 | 14 | 12 | 3 | 14 | 2 | 1 | 1 | 1 | 4 | .20 | 4 | .245 | .295 | .318 |
| 2007 | 2 Tms | NL | 110 | 314 | 81 | 14 | 2 | 0 | (0 | 0) | 99 | 31 | 16 | 27 | 19 | 2 | 19 | 1 | 3 | 0 | 3 | 3 | .50 | 7 | .258 | .302 | .315 |
| 2008 | StL | NL | 135 | 414 | 109 | 10 | 3 | 1 | (0 | 1) | 128 | 50 | 24 | 39 | 29 | 1 | 26 | 6 | 3 | 2 | 24 | 6 | .80 | 6 | .263 | .319 | .309 |
| 2009 | Bal | AL | 114 | 387 | 99 | 14 | 4 | 2 | (1 | 1) | 127 | 34 | 30 | 37 | 18 | 0 | 38 | 3 | 4 | 0 | 12 | 4 | .75 | 11 | .256 | .294 | .328 |
| 2010 | Bal | AL | 150 | 473 | 109 | 13 | 1 | 1 | (0 | 1) | 127 | 42 | 28 | 32 | 25 | 1 | 53 | 6 | 7 | 2 | 11 | 5 | .69 | 11 | .230 | .277 | .268 |
| 2011 | Bal | AL | 18 | 30 | 6 | 0 | 0 | 0 | (0 | 0) | 6 | 4 | 1 | 2 | 2 | 0 | 10 | 0 | 1 | 0 | 0 | 0 | - | 0 | .200 | .250 | .200 |
| 2012 | 2 Tms | NL | 62 | 166 | 40 | 7 | 2 | 2 | (2 | 0) | 57 | 13 | 11 | 12 | 3 | 0 | 13 | 0 | 4 | 0 | 1 | 1 | .50 | 7 | .241 | .254 | .343 |
| 2013 | Cin | NL | 63 | 129 | 27 | 8 | 0 | 0 | (0 | 0) | 35 | 6 | 11 | 9 | 9 | 2 | 13 | 0 | 3 | 1 | 0 | 0 | - | 5 | .209 | .259 | .271 |
| 06 | LAD | NL | 32 | 119 | 30 | 7 | 1 | 1 | (1 | 0) | 42 | 10 | 12 | 10 | 7 | 3 | 6 | 2 | 0 | 1 | 1 | 3 | .25 | 1 | .252 | .302 | .353 |
| 06 | ChC | NL | 22 | 73 | 17 | 2 | 0 | 0 | (0 | 0) | 19 | 4 | 6 | 4 | 5 | 0 | 8 | 0 | 1 | 0 | 0 | 1 | .00 | 3 | .233 | .282 | .260 |
| 07 | ChC | NL | 65 | 191 | 47 | 11 | 0 | 0 | (0 | 0) | 58 | 15 | 8 | 13 | 13 | 2 | 16 | 1 | 2 | 0 | 3 | 0 | 1.00 | 6 | .246 | .298 | .304 |
| 07 | Pit | NL | 45 | 123 | 34 | 3 | 2 | 0 | (0 | 0) | 41 | 16 | 8 | 14 | 6 | 0 | 3 | 0 | 1 | 0 | 0 | 3 | .00 | 1 | .276 | .310 | .333 |
| 12 | Mil | NL | 57 | 162 | 38 | 6 | 2 | 2 | (2 | 0) | 54 | 9 | 11 | 11 | 3 | 0 | 13 | 0 | 4 | 0 | 1 | 1 | .50 | 7 | .235 | .248 | .333 |
| 12 | Was | NL | 5 | 4 | 2 | 1 | 0 | 0 | (0 | 0) | 3 | 4 | 0 | 1 | 0 | 0 | 0 | 0 | 0 | 0 | 0 | 0 | - | 0 | .500 | .500 | .750 |
| Postseason | | | 4 | 17 | 3 | 1 | 0 | 0 | (0 | 0) | 4 | 1 | 0 | 0 | 1 | 0 | 2 | 0 | 0 | 0 | 0 | 0 | - | 0 | .176 | .222 | .235 |
| 13 ML YEARS | | | 1310 | 4350 | 1103 | 177 | 34 | 17 | (7 | 10) | 1399 | 441 | 312 | 388 | 226 | 21 | 431 | 22 | 63 | 18 | 110 | 53 | .67 | 88 | .254 | .293 | .322 |

# Maicer Izturis

**Bats:** B **Throws:** R **Pos:** 2B-59;3B-36;SS-28;PH-7 MY-sare izz-TOUR-iss **Ht:** 5'8" **Wt:** 170 **Born:** 9/12/1980 **Age:** 33

| Year | Team | Lg | BATTING G | AB | H | 2B | 3B | HR | (Hm | Rd) | TB | R | RBI | RC | TBB | IBB | SO | HBP | SH | SF | BASERUNNING SB | CS | SB% | GDP | AVERAGES Avg | OBP | Slg |
|---|---|---|---|---|---|---|---|---|---|---|---|---|---|---|---|---|---|---|---|---|---|---|---|---|---|---|---|
| 2004 | Mon | NL | 32 | 107 | 22 | 5 | 2 | 1 | (1 | 0) | 34 | 10 | 4 | 8 | 10 | 1 | 20 | 2 | 2 | 0 | 4 | 0 | 1.00 | 1 | .206 | .286 | .318 |
| 2005 | LAA | AL | 77 | 191 | 47 | 8 | 4 | 1 | (0 | 1) | 66 | 18 | 15 | 25 | 17 | 2 | 21 | 0 | 1 | 1 | 9 | 3 | .75 | 5 | .246 | .306 | .346 |
| 2006 | LAA | AL | 104 | 352 | 103 | 21 | 3 | 5 | (1 | 4) | 145 | 64 | 44 | 56 | 38 | 1 | 35 | 3 | 5 | 1 | 14 | 6 | .70 | 7 | .293 | .365 | .412 |
| 2007 | LAA | AL | 102 | 336 | 97 | 17 | 2 | 6 | (4 | 2) | 136 | 47 | 51 | 65 | 33 | 2 | 39 | 0 | 1 | 4 | 7 | 1 | .88 | 4 | .289 | .349 | .405 |
| 2008 | LAA | AL | 79 | 290 | 78 | 14 | 2 | 3 | (1 | 2) | 105 | 44 | 37 | 39 | 26 | 0 | 27 | 1 | 2 | 2 | 11 | 2 | .85 | 9 | .269 | .329 | .362 |
| 2009 | LAA | AL | 114 | 387 | 116 | 22 | 3 | 8 | (3 | 5) | 168 | 74 | 65 | 66 | 35 | 2 | 41 | 5 | 3 | 7 | 13 | 5 | .72 | 7 | .300 | .359 | .434 |
| 2010 | LAA | AL | 61 | 212 | 53 | 13 | 1 | 3 | (0 | 3) | 77 | 27 | 27 | 30 | 21 | 0 | 27 | 2 | 1 | 2 | 7 | 3 | .70 | 1 | .250 | .321 | .363 |
| 2011 | LAA | AL | 122 | 449 | 124 | 35 | 0 | 5 | (1 | 4) | 174 | 51 | 38 | 53 | 33 | 3 | 65 | 8 | 0 | 4 | 9 | 6 | .60 | 6 | .276 | .334 | .388 |
| 2012 | LAA | AL | 100 | 289 | 74 | 11 | 0 | 2 | (0 | 2) | 91 | 35 | 20 | 28 | 25 | 0 | 38 | 2 | 3 | 0 | 17 | 2 | .89 | 10 | .256 | .320 | .315 |
| 2013 | Tor | AL | 107 | 365 | 86 | 12 | 0 | 5 | (4 | 1) | 113 | 33 | 32 | 26 | 27 | 0 | 38 | 1 | 3 | 3 | 1 | 5 | .17 | 11 | .236 | .288 | .310 |
| Postseason | | | 10 | 29 | 6 | 3 | 0 | 0 | (0 | 0) | 9 | 3 | 2 | 2 | 1 | 1 | 5 | 0 | 0 | 1 | 3 | 0 | 1.00 | 0 | .207 | .226 | .310 |
| 10 ML YEARS | | | 898 | 2978 | 800 | 158 | 17 | 39 | (15 | 24) | 1109 | 403 | 333 | 396 | 265 | 11 | 351 | 24 | 21 | 24 | 92 | 33 | .74 | 61 | .269 | .331 | .372 |

## Austin Jackson

**Bats:** R **Throws:** R **Pos:** CF-129 **Ht:** 6'1" **Wt:** 185 **Born:** 2/1/1987 **Age:** 27

| BATTING | | | | | | | | | | | | | | | | | | | | BASERUNNING | | | | AVERAGES | | |
|---|---|---|---|---|---|---|---|---|---|---|---|---|---|---|---|---|---|---|---|---|---|---|---|---|---|---|
| Year Team | Lg | G | AB | H | 2B | 3B | HR | (Hm | Rd) | TB | R | RBI | RC | TBB | IBB | SO | HBP | SH | SF | SB | CS | SB% | GDP | Avg | OBP | Slg |
| 2013 Toledo* | AAA | 3 | 13 | 3 | 0 | 0 | 0 | (- | -) | 3 | 1 | 1 | 0 | 1 | 0 | 5 | 0 | 0 | 0 | 0 | 0 | - | 0 | .231 | .286 | .231 |
| 2010 Det | AL | 151 | 618 | 181 | 34 | 10 | 4 | (0 | 4) | 247 | 103 | 41 | 84 | 47 | 4 | **170** | 4 | 3 | 3 | 27 | 6 | .82 | 5 | .293 | .345 | .400 |
| 2011 Det | AL | 153 | 591 | 147 | 22 | **11** | 10 | (5 | 5) | 221 | 90 | 45 | 67 | 56 | 3 | 181 | 4 | 14 | 3 | 22 | 5 | .81 | 11 | .249 | .317 | .374 |
| 2012 Det | AL | 137 | 543 | 163 | 29 | **10** | 16 | (6 | 10) | 260 | 103 | 66 | 90 | 67 | 0 | 134 | 2 | 2 | 3 | 12 | 9 | .57 | 9 | .300 | .377 | .479 |
| 2013 Det | AL | 129 | 552 | 150 | 30 | 7 | 12 | (3 | 9) | 230 | 99 | 49 | 73 | 52 | 0 | 129 | 4 | 3 | 3 | 8 | 4 | .67 | 12 | .272 | .337 | .417 |
| Postseason | | 24 | 91 | 22 | 6 | 1 | 2 | (1 | 1) | 36 | 15 | 8 | 12 | 14 | 0 | 35 | 1 | 2 | 0 | 1 | 1 | .50 | 1 | .242 | .349 | .396 |
| 4 ML YEARS | | 570 | 2304 | 641 | 115 | 38 | 42 | (14 | 28) | 958 | 395 | 201 | 314 | 222 | 7 | 614 | 14 | 22 | 12 | 69 | 24 | .74 | 37 | .278 | .344 | .416 |

## Edwin Jackson

**Pitches:** R **Bats:** R **Pos:** SP-31 **Ht:** 6'3" **Wt:** 210 **Born:** 9/9/1983 **Age:** 30

| HOW MUCH HE PITCHED | | | | | | | | WHAT HE GAVE UP | | | | | | | | | | | | THE RESULTS | | | | | | | |
|---|---|---|---|---|---|---|---|---|---|---|---|---|---|---|---|---|---|---|---|---|---|---|---|---|---|---|---|
| Year Team | Lg | G | GS | CG | GF | IP | BFP | H | R | ER | HR | SH | SF | HB | TBB | IBB | SO | WP | Bk | W | L | Pct | Sh | Sv-Op | Hld | ERC | ERA |
| 2003 LAD | NL | 4 | 3 | 0 | 0 | 22.0 | 91 | 17 | 6 | 6 | 2 | 1 | 1 | 1 | 11 | 1 | 19 | 3 | 0 | 2 | 1 | .667 | 0 | 0-0 | 0 | 3.36 | 2.45 |
| 2004 LAD | NL | 8 | 5 | 0 | 1 | 24.2 | 113 | 31 | 20 | 20 | 7 | 1 | 0 | 0 | 11 | 1 | 16 | 0 | 0 | 2 | 1 | .667 | 0 | 0-0 | 0 | 7.21 | 7.30 |
| 2005 LAD | NL | 7 | 6 | 0 | 0 | 28.2 | 134 | 31 | 22 | 20 | 2 | 0 | 2 | 1 | 17 | 0 | 13 | 2 | 1 | 2 | 2 | .500 | 0 | 0-0 | 0 | 5.13 | 6.28 |
| 2006 TB | AL | 23 | 1 | 0 | 7 | 36.1 | 174 | 42 | 27 | 22 | 2 | 2 | 2 | 1 | 25 | 0 | 27 | 3 | 1 | 0 | 0 | - | 0 | 0-0 | 0 | 5.86 | 5.45 |
| 2007 TB | AL | 32 | 31 | 1 | 0 | 161.0 | 755 | 195 | 116 | 103 | 19 | 5 | 6 | 4 | 88 | 3 | 128 | 7 | 1 | 5 | 15 | .250 | 1 | 0-0 | 0 | 6.11 | 5.76 |
| 2008 TB | AL | 32 | 31 | 0 | 0 | 183.1 | 792 | 199 | 91 | 90 | 23 | 3 | 3 | 2 | 77 | 1 | 108 | 7 | 1 | 14 | 11 | .560 | 0 | 0-1 | 0 | 4.99 | 4.42 |
| 2009 Det | AL | 33 | 33 | 1 | 0 | 214.0 | 890 | 200 | 93 | 86 | 27 | 4 | 2 | 5 | 70 | 3 | 161 | 6 | 0 | 13 | 9 | .591 | 0 | 0-0 | 0 | 3.72 | 3.62 |
| 2010 2 Tms | | 32 | 32 | 1 | 0 | 209.1 | 902 | 214 | 111 | 104 | 21 | 6 | 4 | 6 | 78 | 4 | 181 | 20 | 0 | 10 | 12 | .455 | 1 | 0-0 | 0 | 4.20 | 4.47 |
| 2011 2 Tms | | 32 | 31 | 1 | 1 | 199.2 | 861 | 225 | 92 | 84 | 16 | 15 | 6 | 2 | 62 | 4 | 148 | 9 | 2 | 12 | 9 | .571 | 1 | 0-0 | 0 | 4.34 | 3.79 |
| 2012 Was | NL | 31 | 31 | 1 | 0 | 189.2 | 790 | 173 | 90 | 85 | 23 | 9 | 8 | 2 | 58 | 5 | 168 | 3 | 0 | 10 | 11 | .476 | 0 | 0-0 | 0 | 3.36 | 4.03 |
| 2013 ChC | NL | 31 | 31 | 0 | 0 | 175.1 | 777 | 197 | 110 | 97 | 16 | 8 | 3 | 5 | 59 | 7 | 135 | 14 | 0 | 8 | **18** | .308 | 0 | 0-0 | 0 | 4.46 | 4.98 |
| 10 Ari | NL | 21 | 21 | 1 | 0 | 134.1 | 587 | 141 | 80 | 77 | 13 | 6 | 2 | 5 | 60 | 2 | 104 | 13 | 0 | 6 | 10 | .375 | 1 | 0-0 | 0 | 4.72 | 5.16 |
| 10 CWS | AL | 11 | 11 | 0 | 0 | 75.0 | 315 | 73 | 31 | 27 | 8 | 0 | 2 | 1 | 18 | 2 | 77 | 7 | 0 | 4 | 2 | .667 | 0 | 0-0 | 0 | 3.32 | 3.24 |
| 11 CWS | AL | 19 | 19 | 1 | 0 | 121.2 | 522 | 134 | 55 | 53 | 8 | 6 | 4 | 0 | 39 | 2 | 97 | 7 | 1 | 7 | 7 | .500 | 1 | 0-0 | 0 | 4.10 | 3.92 |
| 11 StL | NL | 13 | 12 | 0 | 1 | 78.0 | 339 | 91 | 37 | 31 | 8 | 9 | 2 | 2 | 23 | 2 | 51 | 2 | 1 | 5 | 2 | .714 | 0 | 0-0 | 0 | 4.73 | 3.58 |
| Postseason | | 9 | 5 | 0 | 2 | 28.0 | 124 | 30 | 17 | 17 | 6 | 2 | 0 | 0 | 15 | 1 | 23 | 0 | 0 | 1 | 2 | .333 | 0 | 0-0 | 1 | 5.97 | 5.46 |
| 11 ML YEARS | | 265 | 235 | 5 | 9 | 1444.0 | 6279 | 1524 | 778 | 717 | 158 | 54 | 37 | 29 | 556 | 29 | 1104 | 74 | 6 | 78 | 89 | .467 | 3 | 0-1 | 0 | 4.46 | 4.47 |

## Ryan Jackson

**Bats:** R **Throws:** R **Pos:** 3B-3;PH-3;2B-2;SS-1;PR-1 **Ht:** 6'3" **Wt:** 180 **Born:** 5/10/1988 **Age:** 26

| BATTING | | | | | | | | | | | | | | | | | | | | BASERUNNING | | | | AVERAGES | | |
|---|---|---|---|---|---|---|---|---|---|---|---|---|---|---|---|---|---|---|---|---|---|---|---|---|---|---|
| Year Team | Lg | G | AB | H | 2B | 3B | HR | (Hm | Rd) | TB | R | RBI | RC | TBB | IBB | SO | HBP | SH | SF | SB | CS | SB% | GDP | Avg | OBP | Slg |
| 2009 Batvia | A- | 67 | 245 | 53 | 4 | 1 | 0 | (- | -) | 59 | 29 | 14 | 19 | 29 | 1 | 37 | 0 | 7 | 2 | 4 | 3 | .57 | 6 | .216 | .297 | .241 |
| 2010 QuadC | A | 84 | 302 | 82 | 13 | 2 | 2 | (- | -) | 105 | 47 | 27 | 42 | 48 | 0 | 63 | 0 | 0 | 5 | 6 | 7 | .46 | 8 | .272 | .366 | .348 |
| 2010 PlmBh | A+ | 41 | 148 | 43 | 10 | 1 | 1 | (- | -) | 58 | 14 | 8 | 20 | 11 | 0 | 21 | 1 | 6 | 1 | 3 | 2 | .60 | 2 | .291 | .342 | .392 |
| 2011 Sprgfld | AA | 135 | 533 | 148 | 34 | 3 | 11 | (- | -) | 221 | 65 | 73 | 78 | 44 | 2 | 91 | 4 | 12 | 6 | 2 | 0 | 1.00 | 17 | .278 | .334 | .415 |
| 2012 Memp | AAA | 117 | 445 | 121 | 23 | 1 | 10 | (- | -) | 176 | 60 | 47 | 62 | 43 | 2 | 75 | 0 | 12 | 3 | 2 | 0 | 1.00 | 18 | .272 | .334 | .396 |
| 2013 Memp | AAA | 121 | 442 | 123 | 19 | 1 | 3 | (- | -) | 153 | 49 | 34 | 61 | 52 | 0 | 91 | 2 | 7 | 7 | 9 | 0 | 1.00 | 13 | .278 | .352 | .346 |
| 2012 StL | NL | 13 | 17 | 2 | 0 | 0 | 0 | (0 | 0) | 2 | 2 | 0 | 0 | 1 | 0 | 3 | 0 | 0 | 0 | 0 | 0 | - | 1 | .118 | .167 | .118 |
| 2013 StL | NL | 7 | 7 | 0 | 0 | 0 | 0 | (0 | 0) | 0 | 0 | 0 | 0 | 0 | 0 | 2 | 0 | 0 | 0 | 0 | 0 | - | 0 | .000 | .000 | .000 |
| 2 ML YEARS | | 20 | 24 | 2 | 0 | 0 | 0 | (0 | 0) | 2 | 2 | 0 | 0 | 1 | 0 | 5 | 0 | 0 | 0 | 0 | 0 | - | 1 | .083 | .120 | .083 |

## Paul Janish

**Bats:** R **Throws:** R **Pos:** 3B-36;PR-10;2B-9;SS-6;PH-4 YONN-ish **Ht:** 6'2" **Wt:** 200 **Born:** 10/12/1982 **Age:** 31

| BATTING | | | | | | | | | | | | | | | | | | | | BASERUNNING | | | | AVERAGES | | |
|---|---|---|---|---|---|---|---|---|---|---|---|---|---|---|---|---|---|---|---|---|---|---|---|---|---|---|
| Year Team | Lg | G | AB | H | 2B | 3B | HR | (Hm | Rd) | TB | R | RBI | RC | TBB | IBB | SO | HBP | SH | SF | SB | CS | SB% | GDP | Avg | OBP | Slg |
| 2013 Gwnntt* | AAA | 41 | 135 | 28 | 5 | 0 | 0 | (- | -) | 33 | 11 | 12 | 10 | 13 | 0 | 32 | 2 | 1 | 1 | 0 | 0 | - | 4 | .207 | .285 | .244 |
| 2008 Cin | NL | 38 | 80 | 15 | 2 | 0 | 1 | (1 | 0) | 20 | 5 | 6 | 5 | 7 | 0 | 18 | 2 | 0 | 0 | 0 | 0 | - | 2 | .188 | .270 | .250 |
| 2009 Cin | NL | 90 | 256 | 54 | 21 | 0 | 1 | (1 | 0) | 78 | 36 | 16 | 18 | 26 | 1 | 40 | 5 | 5 | 0 | 2 | 0 | 1.00 | 8 | .211 | .296 | .305 |
| 2010 Cin | NL | 82 | 200 | 52 | 10 | 0 | 5 | (0 | 5) | 77 | 23 | 25 | 31 | 22 | 2 | 30 | 2 | 3 | 1 | 1 | 3 | .25 | 4 | .260 | .338 | .385 |
| 2011 Cin | NL | 114 | 336 | 72 | 14 | 1 | 0 | (0 | 0) | 88 | 27 | 23 | 21 | 18 | 1 | 46 | 4 | 3 | 5 | 3 | 2 | .60 | 7 | .214 | .259 | .262 |
| 2012 Atl | NL | 55 | 167 | 31 | 6 | 1 | 0 | (0 | 0) | 39 | 18 | 9 | 13 | 17 | 0 | 30 | 2 | 0 | 0 | 1 | 0 | 1.00 | 1 | .186 | .269 | .234 |
| 2013 Atl | NL | 52 | 41 | 7 | 2 | 0 | 0 | (0 | 0) | 9 | 7 | 2 | 1 | 3 | 0 | 11 | 0 | 0 | 1 | 0 | 0 | - | 3 | .171 | .222 | .220 |
| Postseason | | 1 | 1 | 0 | 0 | 0 | 0 | (0 | 0) | 0 | 0 | 0 | 0 | 0 | 0 | 0 | 0 | 1 | 0 | 0 | 0 | - | 0 | .000 | .000 | .000 |
| 6 ML YEARS | | 431 | 1080 | 231 | 55 | 2 | 7 | (2 | 5) | 311 | 116 | 81 | 89 | 93 | 4 | 175 | 15 | 11 | 7 | 7 | 5 | .58 | 25 | .214 | .284 | .288 |

## Kenley Jansen

**Pitches:** R **Bats:** B **Pos:** RP-75 KEN-lee JANN-sen **Ht:** 6'5" **Wt:** 260 **Born:** 9/30/1987 **Age:** 26

| HOW MUCH HE PITCHED | | | | | | | | WHAT HE GAVE UP | | | | | | | | | | | | THE RESULTS | | | | | | | |
|---|---|---|---|---|---|---|---|---|---|---|---|---|---|---|---|---|---|---|---|---|---|---|---|---|---|---|---|
| Year Team | Lg | G | GS | CG | GF | IP | BFP | H | R | ER | HR | SH | SF | HB | TBB | IBB | SO | WP | Bk | W | L | Pct | Sh | Sv-Op | Hld | ERC | ERA |
| 2010 LAD | NL | 25 | 0 | 0 | 8 | 27.0 | 109 | 12 | 2 | 2 | 0 | 1 | 0 | 1 | 15 | 1 | 41 | 1 | 0 | 1 | 0 | 1.000 | 0 | 4-4 | 4 | 1.40 | 0.67 |
| 2011 LAD | NL | 51 | 0 | 0 | 13 | 53.2 | 218 | 30 | 17 | 17 | 3 | 0 | 1 | 2 | 26 | 0 | 96 | 0 | 2 | 2 | 1 | .667 | 0 | 5-6 | 9 | 1.96 | 2.85 |
| 2012 LAD | NL | 65 | 0 | 0 | 40 | 65.0 | 252 | 33 | 18 | 17 | 6 | 0 | 1 | 3 | 22 | 1 | 99 | 3 | 0 | 5 | 3 | .625 | 0 | 25-32 | 8 | 1.55 | 2.35 |
| 2013 LAD | NL | 75 | 0 | 0 | 45 | 76.2 | 292 | 48 | 16 | 16 | 6 | 0 | 0 | 3 | 18 | 1 | 111 | 2 | 0 | 4 | 3 | .571 | 0 | 28-32 | 16 | 1.65 | 1.88 |
| 4 ML YEARS | | 216 | 0 | 0 | 106 | 222.1 | 871 | 123 | 53 | 52 | 15 | 1 | 2 | 9 | 81 | 3 | 347 | 6 | 2 | 12 | 7 | .632 | 0 | 62-74 | 37 | 1.65 | 2.10 |

## Casey Janssen

**Pitches:** R **Bats:** R **Pos:** RP-56 JANN-sen **Ht:** 6'3" **Wt:** 225 **Born:** 9/17/1981 **Age:** 32

| HOW MUCH HE PITCHED | | | | | | | | | WHAT HE GAVE UP | | | | | | | | | | | | THE RESULTS | | | | | | | |
|---|---|---|---|---|---|---|---|---|---|---|---|---|---|---|---|---|---|---|---|---|---|---|---|---|---|---|---|---|
| Year | Team | Lg | G | GS | CG | GF | IP | BFP | H | R | ER | HR | SH | SF | HB | TBB | IBB | SO | WP | Bk | W | L | Pct | Sh | Sv-Op | Hld | ERC | ERA |
| 2006 | Tor | AL | 19 | 17 | 0 | 1 | 94.0 | 407 | 103 | 58 | 53 | 12 | 2 | 2 | 7 | 21 | 3 | 44 | 3 | 2 | 6 | 10 | .375 | 0 | 0-0 | 0 | 4.32 | 5.07 |
| 2007 | Tor | AL | 70 | 0 | 0 | 21 | 72.2 | 297 | 67 | 22 | 19 | 4 | 0 | 3 | 3 | 20 | 2 | 39 | 4 | 0 | 2 | 3 | .400 | 0 | 6-11 | 24 | 3.06 | 2.35 |
| 2009 | Tor | AL | 21 | 5 | 0 | 5 | 40.0 | 192 | 59 | 29 | 26 | 5 | 1 | 2 | 2 | 14 | 1 | 24 | 1 | 0 | 2 | 4 | .333 | 0 | 1-1 | 2 | 7.04 | 5.85 |
| 2010 | Tor | AL | 56 | 0 | 0 | 16 | 68.2 | 298 | 74 | 29 | 28 | 8 | 0 | 1 | 4 | 21 | 1 | 63 | 3 | 0 | 5 | 2 | .714 | 0 | 0-0 | 2 | 4.48 | 3.67 |
| 2011 | Tor | AL | 55 | 0 | 0 | 11 | 55.2 | 223 | 47 | 14 | 14 | 2 | 1 | 0 | 2 | 14 | 1 | 53 | 2 | 0 | 6 | 0 | 1.000 | 0 | 2-4 | 7 | 2.44 | 2.26 |
| 2012 | Tor | AL | 62 | 0 | 0 | 47 | 63.2 | 242 | 44 | 18 | 18 | 7 | 1 | 1 | 3 | 11 | 1 | 67 | 2 | 1 | 1 | 1 | .500 | 0 | 22-25 | 1 | 1.93 | 2.54 |
| 2013 | Tor | AL | 56 | 0 | 0 | 44 | 52.2 | 210 | 39 | 17 | 15 | 3 | 0 | 2 | 2 | 13 | 1 | 50 | 0 | 0 | 4 | 1 | .800 | 0 | 34-36 | 1 | 2.02 | 2.56 |
| 7 ML YEARS | | | 339 | 22 | 0 | 145 | 447.1 | 1869 | 433 | 187 | 173 | 41 | 5 | 11 | 23 | 114 | 10 | 340 | 15 | 3 | 26 | 21 | .553 | 0 | 65-77 | 37 | 3.46 | 3.48 |

## John Jaso

**Bats:** L **Throws:** R **Pos:** C-48;DH-17;PH-14;1B-1 JAY-soe **Ht:** 6'2" **Wt:** 205 **Born:** 9/19/1983 **Age:** 30

| BATTING | | | | | | | | | | | | | | | | | | | | | | BASERUNNING | | | | AVERAGES | | |
|---|---|---|---|---|---|---|---|---|---|---|---|---|---|---|---|---|---|---|---|---|---|---|---|---|---|---|---|---|
| Year | Team | Lg | G | AB | H | 2B | 3B | HR | (Hm | Rd) | TB | R | RBI | RC | TBB | IBB | SO | HBP | SH | SF | SB | CS | SB% | GDP | Avg | OBP | Slg |
| 2008 | TB | AL | 5 | 10 | 2 | 0 | 0 | 0 | (0 | 0) | 2 | 2 | 0 | 0 | 0 | 0 | 2 | 0 | 0 | 0 | 0 | 0 | - | 1 | .200 | .200 | .200 |
| 2010 | TB | AL | 109 | 339 | 89 | 18 | 3 | 5 | (1 | 4) | 128 | 57 | 44 | 57 | 59 | 1 | 39 | 2 | 1 | 3 | 4 | 0 | 1.00 | 8 | .263 | .372 | .378 |
| 2011 | TB | AL | 89 | 246 | 55 | 15 | 1 | 5 | (3 | 2) | 87 | 26 | 27 | 20 | 25 | 0 | 36 | 1 | 1 | 0 | 1 | 2 | .33 | 9 | .224 | .298 | .354 |
| 2012 | Sea | AL | 108 | 294 | 81 | 19 | 2 | 10 | (6 | 4) | 134 | 41 | 50 | 68 | 56 | 1 | 51 | 5 | 1 | 5 | 5 | 0 | 1.00 | 6 | .276 | .394 | .456 |
| 2013 | Oak | AL | 70 | 207 | 56 | 12 | 0 | 3 | (0 | 3) | 77 | 31 | 21 | 36 | 38 | 0 | 45 | 2 | 1 | 1 | 2 | 1 | .67 | 5 | .271 | .387 | .372 |
| Postseason | | | 5 | 14 | 3 | 0 | 0 | 0 | (0 | 0) | 3 | 0 | 1 | 1 | 1 | 0 | 3 | 0 | 0 | 0 | 0 | 0 | - | 0 | .214 | .267 | .214 |
| 5 ML YEARS | | | 381 | 1096 | 283 | 64 | 6 | 23 | (10 | 13) | 428 | 157 | 142 | 181 | 178 | 2 | 173 | 10 | 4 | 9 | 12 | 3 | .80 | 29 | .258 | .364 | .391 |

## Jon Jay

**Bats:** L **Throws:** L **Pos:** CF-152;PH-8;PR-1 **Ht:** 5'11" **Wt:** 195 **Born:** 3/15/1985 **Age:** 29

| BATTING | | | | | | | | | | | | | | | | | | | | | | BASERUNNING | | | | AVERAGES | | |
|---|---|---|---|---|---|---|---|---|---|---|---|---|---|---|---|---|---|---|---|---|---|---|---|---|---|---|---|---|
| Year | Team | Lg | G | AB | H | 2B | 3B | HR | (Hm | Rd) | TB | R | RBI | RC | TBB | IBB | SO | HBP | SH | SF | SB | CS | SB% | GDP | Avg | OBP | Slg |
| 2010 | StL | NL | 105 | 287 | 86 | 19 | 2 | 4 | (2 | 2) | 121 | 47 | 27 | 40 | 24 | 0 | 50 | 3 | 8 | 1 | 2 | 4 | .33 | 5 | .300 | .359 | .422 |
| 2011 | StL | NL | 159 | 455 | 135 | 24 | 2 | 10 | (5 | 5) | 193 | 56 | 37 | 56 | 28 | 1 | 81 | 7 | 9 | 4 | 6 | 7 | .46 | 11 | .297 | .344 | .424 |
| 2012 | StL | NL | 117 | 443 | 135 | 22 | 4 | 4 | (3 | 1) | 177 | 70 | 40 | 65 | 34 | 3 | 71 | 15 | 9 | 1 | 19 | 7 | .73 | 9 | .305 | .373 | .400 |
| 2013 | StL | NL | 157 | 548 | 151 | 27 | 2 | 7 | (2 | 5) | 203 | 75 | 67 | 74 | 52 | 7 | 103 | 14 | 9 | 5 | 10 | 5 | .67 | 13 | .276 | .351 | .370 |
| Postseason | | | 31 | 108 | 20 | 3 | 1 | 0 | (0 | 0) | 25 | 15 | 10 | 9 | 9 | 1 | 17 | 1 | 3 | 1 | 3 | 1 | .75 | 4 | .185 | .252 | .231 |
| 4 ML YEARS | | | 538 | 1733 | 507 | 92 | 10 | 25 | (12 | 13) | 694 | 248 | 171 | 235 | 138 | 11 | 305 | 39 | 35 | 11 | 37 | 23 | .62 | 38 | .293 | .356 | .400 |

## Jeremy Jeffress

**Pitches:** R **Bats:** R **Pos:** RP-10 JEFF-ress **Ht:** 6'0" **Wt:** 195 **Born:** 9/21/1987 **Age:** 26

| HOW MUCH HE PITCHED | | | | | | | | | WHAT HE GAVE UP | | | | | | | | | | | | THE RESULTS | | | | | | | |
|---|---|---|---|---|---|---|---|---|---|---|---|---|---|---|---|---|---|---|---|---|---|---|---|---|---|---|---|---|
| Year | Team | Lg | G | GS | CG | GF | IP | BFP | H | R | ER | HR | SH | SF | HB | TBB | IBB | SO | WP | Bk | W | L | Pct | Sh | Sv-Op | Hld | ERC | ERA |
| 2013 | Dnedin* | A+ | 3 | 0 | 0 | 1 | 5.0 | 17 | 1 | 0 | 0 | 0 | 0 | 0 | 0 | 0 | 0 | 2 | 0 | 0 | 0 | 0 | - | 0 | 0- - | - | 0.09 | 0.00 |
| 2013 | Buffalo* | AAA | 25 | 0 | 0 | 15 | 27.1 | 109 | 22 | 6 | 5 | 0 | 0 | 0 | 0 | 13 | 0 | 28 | 0 | 0 | 1 | 0 | 1.000 | 0 | 7- - | - | 2.81 | 1.65 |
| 2010 | Mil | NL | 10 | 0 | 0 | 5 | 10.0 | 42 | 8 | 4 | 3 | 0 | 0 | 1 | 0 | 6 | 1 | 8 | 1 | 0 | 1 | 0 | 1.000 | 0 | 0-0 | 0 | 2.96 | 2.70 |
| 2011 | KC | AL | 14 | 0 | 0 | 6 | 15.1 | 67 | 12 | 8 | 8 | 1 | 2 | 0 | 0 | 11 | 0 | 13 | 1 | 0 | 1 | 1 | .500 | 0 | 1-2 | 0 | 3.87 | 4.70 |
| 2012 | KC | AL | 13 | 0 | 0 | 6 | 13.1 | 73 | 19 | 14 | 10 | 0 | 0 | 0 | 0 | 13 | 0 | 13 | 1 | 0 | 0 | 0 | - | 0 | 0-0 | 0 | 7.87 | 6.75 |
| 2013 | Tor | AL | 10 | 0 | 0 | 3 | 10.1 | 43 | 8 | 1 | 1 | 1 | 0 | 0 | 0 | 5 | 0 | 12 | 0 | 0 | 1 | 0 | 1.000 | 0 | 0-0 | 0 | 3.17 | 0.87 |
| 4 ML YEARS | | | 47 | 0 | 0 | 20 | 49.0 | 225 | 47 | 27 | 22 | 2 | 2 | 1 | 0 | 35 | 1 | 46 | 3 | 0 | 3 | 1 | .750 | 0 | 1-2 | 0 | 4.56 | 4.04 |

## Chad Jenkins

**Pitches:** R **Bats:** R **Pos:** RP-7; SP-3 **Ht:** 6'3" **Wt:** 225 **Born:** 12/22/1987 **Age:** 26

| HOW MUCH HE PITCHED | | | | | | | | | WHAT HE GAVE UP | | | | | | | | | | | | THE RESULTS | | | | | | | |
|---|---|---|---|---|---|---|---|---|---|---|---|---|---|---|---|---|---|---|---|---|---|---|---|---|---|---|---|---|
| Year | Team | Lg | G | GS | CG | GF | IP | BFP | H | R | ER | HR | SH | SF | HB | TBB | IBB | SO | WP | Bk | W | L | Pct | Sh | Sv-Op | Hld | ERC | ERA |
| 2010 | Lnsng | A | 13 | 13 | 1 | 0 | 79.1 | 332 | 87 | 35 | 32 | 5 | 2 | 2 | 1 | 13 | 0 | 64 | 3 | 0 | 5 | 4 | .556 | 0 | 0- - | - | 3.49 | 3.63 |
| 2010 | Dnedin | A+ | 13 | 13 | 1 | 0 | 62.1 | 280 | 73 | 37 | 30 | 6 | 1 | 1 | 0 | 18 | 1 | 42 | 1 | 0 | 2 | 6 | .250 | 0 | 0- - | - | 4.40 | 4.33 |
| 2011 | Dnedin | A+ | 11 | 11 | 0 | 0 | 67.1 | 284 | 71 | 33 | 23 | 3 | 1 | 3 | 0 | 14 | 1 | 44 | 2 | 0 | 4 | 5 | .444 | 0 | 0- - | - | 3.20 | 3.07 |
| 2011 | NHam | AA | 16 | 16 | 1 | 0 | 100.1 | 410 | 93 | 48 | 47 | 8 | 0 | 5 | 2 | 27 | 0 | 74 | 9 | 0 | 5 | 7 | .417 | 0 | 0- - | - | 3.17 | 4.22 |
| 2012 | NHam | AA | 20 | 20 | 0 | 0 | 114.1 | 507 | 145 | 67 | 63 | 17 | 0 | 3 | 5 | 31 | 0 | 57 | 5 | 0 | 5 | 9 | .357 | 0 | 0- - | - | 5.73 | 4.96 |
| 2013 | NHam | AA | 4 | 3 | 0 | 0 | 15.0 | 60 | 11 | 4 | 2 | 0 | 0 | 0 | 0 | 2 | 0 | 9 | 1 | 0 | 0 | 0 | - | 0 | 0- - | - | 1.31 | 1.20 |
| 2013 | Buffalo | AAA | 5 | 5 | 0 | 0 | 21.2 | 100 | 33 | 20 | 18 | 6 | 0 | 0 | 0 | 4 | 0 | 8 | 0 | 0 | 0 | 3 | .000 | 0 | 0- - | - | 7.70 | 7.48 |
| 2013 | B Jays | R | 2 | 2 | 0 | 0 | 3.0 | 9 | 0 | 0 | 0 | 0 | 0 | 0 | 0 | 0 | 0 | 2 | 0 | 0 | 0 | 0 | - | 0 | 0- - | - | 0.00 | 0.00 |
| 2012 | Tor | AL | 13 | 3 | 0 | 6 | 32.0 | 136 | 32 | 16 | 16 | 5 | 1 | 0 | 1 | 11 | 1 | 16 | 0 | 0 | 1 | 3 | .250 | 0 | 0-0 | 0 | 4.36 | 4.50 |
| 2013 | Tor | AL | 10 | 3 | 0 | 0 | 33.1 | 132 | 31 | 13 | 10 | 3 | 1 | 0 | 1 | 6 | 2 | 15 | 0 | 0 | 1 | 0 | 1.000 | 0 | 0-0 | 0 | 2.92 | 2.70 |
| 2 ML YEARS | | | 23 | 6 | 0 | 6 | 65.1 | 268 | 63 | 29 | 26 | 8 | 2 | 0 | 2 | 17 | 3 | 31 | 0 | 0 | 2 | 3 | .400 | 0 | 0-0 | 0 | 3.61 | 3.58 |

## Dan Jennings

**Pitches:** L **Bats:** L **Pos:** RP-47 **Ht:** 6'3" **Wt:** 210 **Born:** 4/17/1987 **Age:** 27

| HOW MUCH HE PITCHED | | | | | | | | | WHAT HE GAVE UP | | | | | | | | | | | | THE RESULTS | | | | | | | |
|---|---|---|---|---|---|---|---|---|---|---|---|---|---|---|---|---|---|---|---|---|---|---|---|---|---|---|---|---|
| Year | Team | Lg | G | GS | CG | GF | IP | BFP | H | R | ER | HR | SH | SF | HB | TBB | IBB | SO | WP | Bk | W | L | Pct | Sh | Sv-Op | Hld | ERC | ERA |
| 2009 | Grnsbr | A | 34 | 0 | 0 | 12 | 49.1 | 206 | 42 | 21 | 15 | 1 | 5 | 3 | 0 | 21 | 3 | 54 | 8 | 0 | 1 | 2 | .333 | 0 | 0- - | - | 2.76 | 2.74 |
| 2009 | Jupiter | A+ | 8 | 0 | 0 | 6 | 11.2 | 42 | 5 | 0 | 0 | 0 | 0 | 0 | 0 | 4 | 0 | 13 | 1 | 0 | 0 | 0 | - | 0 | 6- - | - | 0.97 | 0.00 |
| 2009 | Jaxnvl | AA | 3 | 0 | 0 | 1 | 1.2 | 8 | 2 | 0 | 0 | 0 | 0 | 0 | 0 | 1 | 0 | 2 | 0 | 0 | 0 | 0 | - | 0 | 0- - | - | 5.10 | 0.00 |
| 2010 | Jaxnvl | AA | 37 | 0 | 0 | 4 | 52.2 | 223 | 49 | 18 | 15 | 0 | 4 | 2 | 0 | 26 | 1 | 44 | 9 | 0 | 4 | 2 | .667 | 0 | 0- - | - | 3.39 | 2.56 |
| 2011 | Jaxnvl | AA | 21 | 0 | 0 | 7 | 25.2 | 112 | 26 | 11 | 9 | 1 | 2 | 1 | 0 | 11 | 0 | 29 | 6 | 0 | 4 | 1 | .800 | 0 | 2- - | - | 3.80 | 3.16 |
| 2011 | NewOr | AAA | 24 | 0 | 0 | 8 | 30.2 | 137 | 34 | 24 | 24 | 3 | 3 | 4 | 0 | 17 | 2 | 27 | 1 | 0 | 1 | 3 | .250 | 0 | 2- - | - | 5.31 | 7.04 |
| 2012 | NewOr | AAA | 42 | 0 | 0 | 10 | 51.2 | 212 | 48 | 19 | 18 | 2 | 5 | 1 | 0 | 16 | 0 | 48 | 6 | 0 | 1 | 3 | .250 | 0 | 2- - | - | 2.99 | 3.14 |

| HOW MUCH HE PITCHED | | | | | | | | | WHAT HE GAVE UP | | | | | | | | | | | | THE RESULTS | | | | | | | |
|---|---|---|---|---|---|---|---|---|---|---|---|---|---|---|---|---|---|---|---|---|---|---|---|---|---|---|---|---|
| Year | Team | Lg | G | GS | CG | GF | IP | BFP | H | R | ER | HR | SH | SF | HB | TBB | IBB | SO | WP | Bk | W | L | Pct | Sh | Sv-Op | Hld | ERC | ERA |
| 2013 | NewOr | AAA | 18 | 0 | 0 | 4 | 25.0 | 105 | 19 | 8 | 5 | 1 | 3 | 0 | 0 | 11 | 1 | 25 | 3 | 0 | 4 | 2 | .667 | 0 | 1-- | - | 2.45 | 1.80 |
| 2012 | Mia | NL | 22 | 0 | 0 | 4 | 19.0 | 86 | 18 | 5 | 4 | 2 | 0 | 0 | 2 | 11 | 1 | 8 | 0 | 0 | 1 | 0 | 1.000 | 0 | 0-0 | 2 | 4.85 | 1.89 |
| 2013 | Mia | NL | 47 | 0 | 0 | 6 | 40.2 | 171 | 39 | 17 | 17 | 1 | 0 | 2 | 0 | 16 | 2 | 38 | 3 | 0 | 2 | 4 | .333 | 0 | 0-2 | 1 | 3.27 | 3.76 |
| 2 ML YEARS | | | 69 | 0 | 0 | 10 | 59.2 | 257 | 57 | 22 | 21 | 3 | 0 | 2 | 2 | 27 | 3 | 46 | 3 | 0 | 3 | 4 | .429 | 0 | 0-2 | 3 | 3.76 | 3.17 |

## Desmond Jennings

**Bats:** R **Throws:** R **Pos:** CF-136;PH-4;PR-2 **Ht:** 6'2" **Wt:** 200 **Born:** 10/30/1986 **Age:** 27

| BATTING | | | | | | | | | | | | | | | | | | | | | BASERUNNING | | | | AVERAGES | | |
|---|---|---|---|---|---|---|---|---|---|---|---|---|---|---|---|---|---|---|---|---|---|---|---|---|---|---|---|
| Year | Team | Lg | G | AB | H | 2B | 3B | HR | (Hm | Rd) | TB | R | RBI | RC | TBB | IBB | SO | HBP | SH | SF | SB | CS | SB% | GDP | Avg | OBP | Slg |
| 2013 | Charltt* | A+ | 1 | 3 | 1 | 0 | 0 | 0 | (- | -) | 1 | 1 | 0 | 0 | 0 | 0 | 1 | 0 | 0 | 0 | 1 | 0 | 1.00 | 0 | .333 | .333 | .333 |
| 2010 | TB | AL | 17 | 21 | 4 | 1 | 1 | 0 | (0 | 0) | 7 | 5 | 2 | 2 | 2 | 0 | 4 | 1 | 0 | 0 | 2 | 2 | .50 | 0 | .190 | .292 | .333 |
| 2011 | TB | AL | 63 | 247 | 64 | 9 | 4 | 10 | (3 | 7) | 111 | 44 | 25 | 45 | 31 | 1 | 59 | 6 | 3 | 0 | 20 | 6 | .77 | 1 | .259 | .356 | .449 |
| 2012 | TB | AL | 132 | 505 | 124 | 19 | 7 | 13 | (9 | 4) | 196 | 85 | 47 | 62 | 46 | 1 | 120 | 5 | 6 | 1 | 31 | 2 | .94 | 7 | .246 | .314 | .388 |
| 2013 | TB | AL | 139 | 527 | 133 | 31 | 6 | 14 | (6 | 8) | 218 | 82 | 54 | 74 | 64 | 0 | 115 | 3 | 3 | 5 | 20 | 8 | .71 | 6 | .252 | .334 | .414 |
| Postseason | | | 6 | 17 | 5 | 1 | 0 | 2 | (2 | 0) | 12 | 4 | 2 | 3 | 3 | 0 | 2 | 0 | 0 | 0 | 0 | 0 | - | 0 | .294 | .400 | .706 |
| 4 ML YEARS | | | 351 | 1300 | 325 | 60 | 18 | 37 | (18 | 19) | 532 | 216 | 128 | 183 | 143 | 2 | 298 | 15 | 12 | 6 | 73 | 18 | .80 | 14 | .250 | .330 | .409 |

## Kevin Jepsen

**Pitches:** R **Bats:** R **Pos:** RP-45 **Ht:** 6'3" **Wt:** 235 **Born:** 7/26/1984 **Age:** 29

| HOW MUCH HE PITCHED | | | | | | | | | WHAT HE GAVE UP | | | | | | | | | | | | THE RESULTS | | | | | | | |
|---|---|---|---|---|---|---|---|---|---|---|---|---|---|---|---|---|---|---|---|---|---|---|---|---|---|---|---|---|
| Year | Team | Lg | G | GS | CG | GF | IP | BFP | H | R | ER | HR | SH | SF | HB | TBB | IBB | SO | WP | Bk | W | L | Pct | Sh | Sv-Op | Hld | ERC | ERA |
| 2013 | InldEm* | A+ | 1 | 0 | 0 | 0 | 1.0 | 3 | 0 | 0 | 0 | 0 | 0 | 0 | 0 | 0 | 0 | 0 | 0 | 0 | 0 | 0 | - | 0 | 0-- | - | 0.00 | 0.00 |
| 2013 | Salt Lk* | AAA | 2 | 0 | 0 | 0 | 2.0 | 10 | 2 | 3 | 3 | 2 | 0 | 0 | 0 | 2 | 0 | 1 | 0 | 0 | 0 | 0 | - | 0 | 0-- | - | 14.27 | 13.50 |
| 2008 | LAA | AL | 9 | 0 | 0 | 0 | 8.1 | 36 | 8 | 5 | 4 | 0 | 0 | 0 | 0 | 4 | 0 | 7 | 1 | 0 | 0 | 1 | .000 | 0 | 0-0 | 3 | 3.46 | 4.32 |
| 2009 | LAA | AL | 54 | 0 | 0 | 13 | 54.2 | 237 | 63 | 33 | 30 | 2 | 0 | 2 | 0 | 19 | 2 | 48 | 6 | 0 | 6 | 4 | .600 | 0 | 1-2 | 17 | 4.27 | 4.94 |
| 2010 | LAA | AL | 68 | 0 | 0 | 4 | 59.0 | 253 | 54 | 26 | 26 | 2 | 4 | 2 | 2 | 29 | 5 | 61 | 8 | 0 | 2 | 4 | .333 | 0 | 0-4 | 27 | 3.53 | 3.97 |
| 2011 | LAA | AL | 16 | 0 | 0 | 5 | 13.0 | 68 | 21 | 11 | 11 | 2 | 1 | 1 | 1 | 9 | 4 | 6 | 5 | 0 | 1 | 2 | .333 | 0 | 0-1 | 2 | 9.45 | 7.62 |
| 2012 | LAA | AL | 49 | 0 | 0 | 11 | 44.2 | 178 | 39 | 17 | 15 | 3 | 3 | 1 | 2 | 12 | 1 | 38 | 1 | 0 | 3 | 2 | .600 | 0 | 2-4 | 18 | 2.93 | 3.02 |
| 2013 | LAA | AL | 45 | 0 | 0 | 7 | 36.0 | 164 | 41 | 21 | 18 | 3 | 3 | 1 | 1 | 14 | 4 | 36 | 2 | 0 | 1 | 3 | .250 | 0 | 0-2 | 8 | 4.50 | 4.50 |
| Postseason | | | 5 | 0 | 0 | 0 | 5.0 | 24 | 8 | 2 | 2 | 1 | 0 | 0 | 0 | 2 | 0 | 3 | 0 | 0 | 1 | 0 | 1.000 | 0 | 0-0 | 1 | 8.81 | 3.60 |
| 6 ML YEARS | | | 241 | 0 | 0 | 40 | 215.2 | 936 | 226 | 113 | 104 | 12 | 11 | 7 | 6 | 87 | 16 | 196 | 23 | 0 | 13 | 16 | .448 | 0 | 3-13 | 75 | 4.06 | 4.34 |

## Derek Jeter

**Bats:** R **Throws:** R **Pos:** SS-13;DH-4 **Ht:** 6'3" **Wt:** 195 **Born:** 6/26/1974 **Age:** 40

| BATTING | | | | | | | | | | | | | | | | | | | | | BASERUNNING | | | | AVERAGES | | |
|---|---|---|---|---|---|---|---|---|---|---|---|---|---|---|---|---|---|---|---|---|---|---|---|---|---|---|---|
| Year | Team | Lg | G | AB | H | 2B | 3B | HR | (Hm | Rd) | TB | R | RBI | RC | TBB | IBB | SO | HBP | SH | SF | SB | CS | SB% | GDP | Avg | OBP | Slg |
| 2013 | S-WB* | AAA | 7 | 18 | 4 | 1 | 0 | 0 | (- | -) | 5 | 4 | 1 | 2 | 5 | 0 | 3 | 0 | 0 | 0 | 0 | 0 | - | 1 | .222 | .391 | .278 |
| 1995 | NYY | AL | 15 | 48 | 12 | 4 | 1 | 0 | (0 | 0) | 18 | 5 | 7 | 5 | 3 | 0 | 11 | 0 | 0 | 0 | 0 | 0 | - | 0 | .250 | .294 | .375 |
| 1996 | NYY | AL | 157 | 582 | 183 | 25 | 6 | 10 | (3 | 7) | 250 | 104 | 78 | 92 | 48 | 1 | 102 | 9 | 6 | 9 | 14 | 7 | .67 | 13 | .314 | .370 | .430 |
| 1997 | NYY | AL | 159 | 654 | 190 | 31 | 7 | 10 | (5 | 5) | 265 | 116 | 70 | 99 | 74 | 0 | 125 | 10 | 8 | 2 | 23 | 12 | .66 | 14 | .291 | .370 | .405 |
| 1998 | NYY | AL | 149 | 626 | 203 | 25 | 8 | 19 | (9 | 10) | 301 | **127** | 84 | 115 | 57 | 1 | 119 | 5 | 3 | 3 | 30 | 6 | .83 | 13 | .324 | .384 | .481 |
| 1999 | NYY | AL | 158 | 627 | **219** | 37 | 9 | 24 | (15 | 9) | 346 | 134 | 102 | 146 | 91 | 5 | 116 | 12 | 3 | 6 | 19 | 8 | .70 | 12 | .349 | .438 | .552 |
| 2000 | NYY | AL | 148 | 593 | 201 | 31 | 4 | 15 | (8 | 7) | 285 | 119 | 73 | 118 | 68 | 4 | 99 | 12 | 3 | 3 | 22 | 4 | .85 | 14 | .339 | .416 | .481 |
| 2001 | NYY | AL | 150 | 614 | 191 | 35 | 3 | 21 | (13 | 8) | 295 | 110 | 74 | 112 | 56 | 3 | 99 | 10 | 5 | 1 | 27 | 3 | .90 | 13 | .311 | .377 | .480 |
| 2002 | NYY | AL | 157 | 644 | 191 | 26 | 0 | 18 | (8 | 10) | 271 | 124 | 75 | 108 | 73 | 2 | 114 | 7 | 3 | 3 | 32 | 3 | .91 | 14 | .297 | .373 | .421 |
| 2003 | NYY | AL | 119 | 482 | 156 | 25 | 3 | 10 | (7 | 3) | 217 | 87 | 52 | 86 | 43 | 2 | 88 | 13 | 3 | 1 | 11 | 5 | .69 | 10 | .324 | .393 | .450 |
| 2004 | NYY | AL | 154 | 643 | 188 | 44 | 1 | 23 | (11 | 12) | 303 | 111 | 78 | 100 | 46 | 1 | 99 | 14 | 16 | 2 | 23 | 4 | .85 | 19 | .292 | .352 | .471 |
| 2005 | NYY | AL | 159 | 654 | 202 | 25 | 5 | 19 | (12 | 7) | 294 | 122 | 70 | 105 | 77 | 3 | 117 | 11 | 7 | 3 | 14 | 5 | .74 | 15 | .309 | .389 | .450 |
| 2006 | NYY | AL | 154 | 623 | 214 | 39 | 3 | 14 | (8 | 6) | 301 | 118 | 97 | **132** | 69 | 4 | 102 | 12 | 7 | 4 | 34 | 5 | .87 | 13 | .343 | .417 | .483 |
| 2007 | NYY | AL | 156 | 639 | 206 | 39 | 4 | 12 | (4 | 8) | 289 | 102 | 73 | 112 | 56 | 3 | 100 | 14 | 3 | 2 | 15 | 8 | .65 | 21 | .322 | .388 | .452 |
| 2008 | NYY | AL | 150 | 596 | 179 | 25 | 3 | 11 | (3 | 8) | 243 | 88 | 69 | 88 | 52 | 0 | 85 | 9 | 7 | 4 | 11 | 5 | .69 | 24 | .300 | .363 | .408 |
| 2009 | NYY | AL | 153 | 634 | 212 | 27 | 1 | 18 | (13 | 5) | 295 | 107 | 66 | 109 | 72 | 4 | 90 | 5 | 4 | 1 | 30 | 5 | .86 | 18 | .334 | .406 | .465 |
| 2010 | NYY | AL | 157 | 663 | 179 | 30 | 3 | 10 | (7 | 3) | 245 | 111 | 67 | 86 | 63 | 4 | 106 | 9 | 1 | 3 | 18 | 5 | .78 | 22 | .270 | .340 | .370 |
| 2011 | NYY | AL | 131 | 546 | 162 | 24 | 4 | 6 | (4 | 2) | 212 | 84 | 61 | 75 | 46 | 0 | 81 | 6 | 4 | 5 | 16 | 6 | .73 | 10 | .297 | .355 | .388 |
| 2012 | NYY | AL | 159 | **683** | **216** | 32 | 0 | 15 | (6 | 9) | 293 | 99 | 58 | 98 | 45 | 1 | 90 | 5 | 6 | 1 | 9 | 4 | .69 | 24 | .316 | .362 | .429 |
| 2013 | NYY | AL | 17 | 63 | 12 | 1 | 0 | 1 | (1 | 0) | 16 | 8 | 7 | 4 | 8 | 1 | 10 | 1 | 0 | 1 | 0 | 0 | - | 3 | .190 | .288 | .254 |
| Postseason | | | 158 | 650 | 200 | 32 | 5 | 20 | (12 | 8) | 302 | 111 | 61 | 99 | 66 | 3 | 135 | 5 | 9 | 4 | 18 | 5 | .78 | 14 | .308 | .374 | .465 |
| 19 ML YEARS | | | 2602 | 10614 | 3316 | 525 | 65 | 256 | (137 | 119) | 4739 | 1876 | 1261 | 1790 | 1047 | 39 | 1753 | 164 | 89 | 54 | 348 | 95 | .79 | 272 | .312 | .381 | .446 |

## Cesar Jimenez

**Pitches:** L **Bats:** L **Pos:** RP-19 hee-MEN-ehs **Ht:** 5'11" **Wt:** 220 **Born:** 11/12/1984 **Age:** 29

| HOW MUCH HE PITCHED | | | | | | | | | WHAT HE GAVE UP | | | | | | | | | | | | THE RESULTS | | | | | | | |
|---|---|---|---|---|---|---|---|---|---|---|---|---|---|---|---|---|---|---|---|---|---|---|---|---|---|---|---|---|
| Year | Team | Lg | G | GS | CG | GF | IP | BFP | H | R | ER | HR | SH | SF | HB | TBB | IBB | SO | WP | Bk | W | L | Pct | Sh | Sv-Op | Hld | ERC | ERA |
| 2013 | LV* | AAA | 36 | 3 | 0 | 10 | 66.1 | 278 | 61 | 24 | 23 | 3 | 1 | 4 | 0 | 26 | 2 | 64 | 2 | 2 | 4 | 2 | .667 | 0 | 3-- | - | 3.21 | 3.12 |
| 2006 | Sea | AL | 4 | 1 | 0 | 1 | 7.1 | 38 | 13 | 12 | 12 | 4 | 0 | 0 | 0 | 4 | 0 | 3 | 2 | 0 | 0 | 0 | - | 0 | 0-0 | 0 | 14.01 | 14.73 |
| 2008 | Sea | AL | 31 | 2 | 0 | 8 | 34.1 | 141 | 32 | 13 | 13 | 2 | 2 | 1 | 1 | 13 | 0 | 26 | 2 | 0 | 0 | 2 | .000 | 0 | 0-4 | 4 | 3.59 | 3.41 |
| 2011 | Sea | AL | 8 | 0 | 0 | 1 | 6.2 | 30 | 6 | 4 | 4 | 0 | 0 | 0 | 0 | 3 | 0 | 7 | 2 | 0 | 1 | 0 | 1.000 | 0 | 0-0 | 0 | 2.83 | 5.40 |
| 2013 | Phi | NL | 19 | 0 | 0 | 5 | 17.0 | 76 | 14 | 7 | 7 | 1 | 1 | 2 | 1 | 10 | 0 | 11 | 2 | 1 | 1 | 1 | .500 | 0 | 0-0 | 0 | 3.66 | 3.71 |
| 4 ML YEARS | | | 62 | 3 | 0 | 15 | 65.1 | 285 | 65 | 36 | 36 | 7 | 3 | 3 | 2 | 30 | 0 | 47 | 8 | 1 | 2 | 3 | .400 | 0 | 0-4 | 4 | 4.49 | 4.96 |

# Luis Jimenez

**Bats:** R **Throws:** R **Pos:** 3B-29;1B-2;SS-1;DH-1;PH-1;PR-1 **Ht:** 6'1" **Wt:** 205 **Born:** 1/18/1988 **Age:** 26

| BATTING | | | | | | | | | | | | | | | | | | | | | BASERUNNING | | | | AVERAGES | | |
|---|---|---|---|---|---|---|---|---|---|---|---|---|---|---|---|---|---|---|---|---|---|---|---|---|---|---|---|
| Year Team | Lg | G | AB | H | 2B | 3B | HR | (Hm | Rd) | TB | R | RBI | RC | TBB | IBB | SO | HBP | SH | SF | | SB | CS | SB% | GDP | Avg | OBP | Slg |
| 2010 CRpds | A | 43 | 168 | 49 | 15 | 5 | 2 | (- | -) | 80 | 32 | 38 | 27 | 11 | 0 | 27 | 1 | 0 | 4 | | 6 | 2 | .75 | 3 | .292 | .332 | .476 |
| 2010 RCuca | A+ | 81 | 318 | 91 | 31 | 4 | 12 | (- | -) | 166 | 52 | 43 | 54 | 13 | 0 | 43 | 6 | 4 | 3 | | 15 | 8 | .65 | 8 | .286 | .324 | .522 |
| 2011 Ark | AA | 125 | 490 | 142 | 40 | 1 | 18 | (- | -) | 238 | 62 | 94 | 82 | 27 | 2 | 72 | 11 | 4 | 9 | | 14 | 6 | .70 | 13 | .290 | .335 | .486 |
| 2012 Salt Lk | AAA | 122 | 485 | 150 | 38 | 2 | 16 | (- | -) | 240 | 78 | 86 | 81 | 19 | 1 | 70 | 2 | 5 | 6 | | 17 | 7 | .71 | 10 | .309 | .334 | .495 |
| 2013 Salt Lk | AAA | 48 | 197 | 56 | 9 | 2 | 4 | (- | -) | 81 | 28 | 42 | 29 | 12 | 2 | 26 | 3 | 0 | 6 | | 11 | 3 | .79 | 1 | .284 | .326 | .411 |
| 2013 Angels | R | 3 | 13 | 6 | 0 | 0 | 1 | (- | -) | 9 | 3 | 4 | 3 | 0 | 0 | 2 | 0 | 0 | 0 | | 0 | 0 | - | 0 | .462 | .462 | .692 |
| 2013 LAA | AL | 34 | 104 | 27 | 6 | 0 | 0 | (0 | 0) | 33 | 15 | 5 | 9 | 2 | 0 | 28 | 3 | 0 | 1 | | 0 | 2 | .00 | 2 | .260 | .291 | .317 |

# Ubaldo Jimenez

**Pitches:** R **Bats:** R **Pos:** SP-32 ooh-BALL-doh **Ht:** 6'5" **Wt:** 210 **Born:** 1/22/1984 **Age:** 30

| HOW MUCH HE PITCHED | | | | | | | | WHAT HE GAVE UP | | | | | | | | | | | | THE RESULTS | | | | | | | |
|---|---|---|---|---|---|---|---|---|---|---|---|---|---|---|---|---|---|---|---|---|---|---|---|---|---|---|---|
| Year Team | Lg | G | GS | CG | GF | IP | BFP | H | R | ER | HR | SH | SF | HB | TBB | IBB | SO | WP | Bk | W | L | Pct | Sh | Sv-Op | Hld | ERC | ERA |
| 2006 Col | NL | 2 | 1 | 0 | 0 | 7.2 | 30 | 5 | 4 | 3 | 1 | 0 | 0 | 0 | 3 | 0 | 3 | 0 | 0 | 0 | 0 | - | 0 | 0-0 | 0 | 2.48 | 3.52 |
| 2007 Col | NL | 15 | 15 | 0 | 0 | 82.0 | 354 | 70 | 46 | 39 | 10 | 3 | 1 | 6 | 37 | 4 | 68 | 3 | 0 | 4 | 4 | .500 | 0 | 0-0 | 0 | 3.80 | 4.28 |
| 2008 Col | NL | 34 | **34** | 1 | 0 | 198.2 | 868 | 182 | 97 | 88 | 11 | 7 | 4 | 10 | 103 | 4 | 172 | 16 | 0 | 12 | 12 | .500 | 0 | 0-0 | 0 | 3.92 | 3.99 |
| 2009 Col | NL | 33 | 33 | 1 | 0 | 218.0 | 914 | 183 | 87 | 84 | 13 | 15 | 6 | 10 | 85 | 6 | 198 | 8 | 3 | 15 | 12 | .556 | 0 | 0-0 | 0 | 3.03 | 3.47 |
| 2010 Col | NL | 33 | 33 | 4 | 0 | 221.2 | 894 | 164 | 73 | 71 | 10 | 7 | 1 | 9 | 92 | 7 | 214 | **16** | 1 | 19 | 8 | **.704** | 2 | 0-0 | 0 | 2.57 | 2.88 |
| 2011 2 Tms | | 32 | 32 | 2 | 0 | 188.1 | 822 | 186 | 111 | 98 | 17 | 2 | 2 | 9 | 78 | 5 | 180 | 8 | 0 | 10 | 13 | .435 | 1 | 0-0 | 0 | 4.13 | 4.68 |
| 2012 Cle | AL | 31 | 31 | 0 | 0 | 176.2 | 805 | 190 | 116 | 106 | 25 | 2 | 3 | 8 | 95 | 3 | 143 | **16** | 1 | 9 | **17** | .346 | 0 | 0-0 | 0 | 5.55 | 5.40 |
| 2013 Cle | AL | 32 | 32 | 0 | 0 | 182.2 | 777 | 163 | 75 | 67 | 16 | 1 | **11** | 3 | 80 | 0 | 194 | 8 | 0 | 13 | 9 | .591 | 0 | 0-0 | 0 | 3.61 | 3.30 |
| 11 Col | NL | 21 | 21 | 2 | 0 | 123.0 | 532 | 118 | 68 | 61 | 10 | 2 | 2 | 7 | 51 | 5 | 118 | 6 | 0 | 6 | 9 | .400 | 1 | 0-0 | 0 | 3.94 | 4.46 |
| 11 Cle | AL | 11 | 11 | 0 | 0 | 65.1 | 290 | 68 | 43 | 37 | 7 | 0 | 0 | 2 | 27 | 0 | 62 | 2 | 0 | 4 | 4 | .500 | 0 | 0-0 | 0 | 4.48 | 5.10 |
| Postseason | | 5 | 5 | 0 | 0 | 28.0 | 123 | 26 | 11 | 11 | 3 | 0 | 1 | 1 | 16 | 2 | 24 | 1 | 0 | 0 | 2 | .000 | 0 | 0-0 | 0 | 4.47 | 3.54 |
| 8 ML YEARS | | 212 | 211 | 8 | 0 | 1275.2 | 5464 | 1143 | 609 | 556 | 103 | 37 | 28 | 55 | 573 | 29 | 1172 | 75 | 5 | 82 | 75 | .522 | 3 | 0-0 | 0 | 3.70 | 3.92 |

# Chris Johnson

**Bats:** R **Throws:** R **Pos:** 3B-125;1B-12;PH-7 **Ht:** 6'3" **Wt:** 220 **Born:** 10/1/1984 **Age:** 29

| BATTING | | | | | | | | | | | | | | | | | | | | BASERUNNING | | | | AVERAGES | | |
|---|---|---|---|---|---|---|---|---|---|---|---|---|---|---|---|---|---|---|---|---|---|---|---|---|---|---|
| Year Team | Lg | G | AB | H | 2B | 3B | HR | (Hm | Rd) | TB | R | RBI | RC | TBB | IBB | SO | HBP | SH | SF | SB | CS | SB% | GDP | Avg | OBP | Slg |
| 2009 Hou | NL | 11 | 22 | 2 | 0 | 0 | 0 | (0 | 0) | 2 | 1 | 1 | 0 | 1 | 0 | 6 | 0 | 0 | 0 | 0 | 0 | - | 0 | .091 | .130 | .091 |
| 2010 Hou | NL | 94 | 341 | 105 | 22 | 2 | 11 | (6 | 5) | 164 | 40 | 52 | 55 | 15 | 2 | 91 | 2 | 0 | 4 | 3 | 0 | 1.00 | 8 | .308 | .337 | .481 |
| 2011 Hou | NL | 107 | 378 | 95 | 21 | 3 | 7 | (2 | 5) | 143 | 32 | 42 | 42 | 16 | 3 | 97 | 7 | 0 | 4 | 2 | 2 | .50 | 2 | .251 | .291 | .378 |
| 2012 2 Tms | NL | 136 | 488 | 137 | 28 | 5 | 15 | (8 | 7) | 220 | 48 | 76 | 75 | 31 | 2 | 132 | 4 | 1 | 4 | 5 | 1 | .83 | 18 | .281 | .326 | .451 |
| 2013 Atl | NL | 142 | 514 | 165 | 34 | 0 | 12 | (4 | 8) | 235 | 54 | 68 | 77 | 29 | 5 | 116 | 2 | 0 | 2 | 0 | 0 | - | 20 | .321 | .358 | .457 |
| 12 Hou | NL | 92 | 341 | 95 | 21 | 3 | 8 | (8 | 0) | 146 | 36 | 41 | 47 | 23 | 1 | 92 | 3 | 0 | 1 | 4 | 1 | .80 | 12 | .279 | .329 | .428 |
| 12 Ari | NL | 44 | 147 | 42 | 7 | 2 | 7 | (0 | 7) | 74 | 12 | 35 | 28 | 8 | 1 | 40 | 1 | 1 | 3 | 1 | 0 | 1.00 | 6 | .286 | .321 | .503 |
| 5 ML YEARS | | 490 | 1743 | 504 | 105 | 10 | 45 | (20 | 25) | 764 | 175 | 239 | 249 | 92 | 12 | 442 | 15 | 1 | 14 | 10 | 3 | .77 | 48 | .289 | .328 | .438 |

# Dan Johnson

**Bats:** L **Throws:** R **Pos:** DH-2;1B-1;PH-1 **Ht:** 6'2" **Wt:** 210 **Born:** 8/10/1979 **Age:** 34

| BATTING | | | | | | | | | | | | | | | | | | | | BASERUNNING | | | | AVERAGES | | |
|---|---|---|---|---|---|---|---|---|---|---|---|---|---|---|---|---|---|---|---|---|---|---|---|---|---|---|
| Year Team | Lg | G | AB | H | 2B | 3B | HR | (Hm | Rd) | TB | R | RBI | RC | TBB | IBB | SO | HBP | SH | SF | SB | CS | SB% | GDP | Avg | OBP | Slg |
| 2013 S-WB* | AAA | 133 | 459 | 116 | 26 | 0 | 21 | (- | -) | 205 | 57 | 69 | 85 | 93 | 4 | 82 | 3 | 0 | 4 | 1 | 0 | 1.00 | 8 | .253 | .379 | .447 |
| 2013 Norfolk* | AAA | 5 | 13 | 2 | 0 | 0 | 0 | (- | -) | 2 | 2 | 1 | 1 | 3 | 0 | 3 | 1 | 0 | 1 | 0 | 0 | - | 1 | .154 | .333 | .154 |
| 2005 Oak | AL | 109 | 375 | 103 | 21 | 0 | 15 | (2 | 13) | 169 | 54 | 58 | 56 | 50 | 1 | 52 | 1 | 0 | 8 | 0 | 1 | .00 | 11 | .275 | .355 | .451 |
| 2006 Oak | AL | 91 | 286 | 67 | 13 | 1 | 9 | (4 | 5) | 109 | 30 | 37 | 33 | 40 | 2 | 45 | 0 | 0 | 5 | 0 | 0 | - | 6 | .234 | .323 | .381 |
| 2007 Oak | AL | 117 | 416 | 98 | 20 | 1 | 18 | (9 | 9) | 174 | 53 | 62 | 58 | 72 | 4 | 77 | 3 | 0 | 4 | 0 | 0 | - | 12 | .236 | .349 | .418 |
| 2008 2 Tms | AL | 11 | 26 | 5 | 0 | 0 | 2 | (1 | 1) | 11 | 3 | 4 | 3 | 3 | 0 | 7 | 0 | 0 | 0 | 0 | 0 | - | 0 | .192 | .276 | .423 |
| 2010 TB | AL | 40 | 111 | 22 | 3 | 0 | 7 | (4 | 3) | 46 | 15 | 23 | 20 | 25 | 0 | 27 | 1 | 0 | 3 | 1 | 0 | 1.00 | 1 | .198 | .343 | .414 |
| 2011 TB | AL | 31 | 84 | 10 | 1 | 0 | 2 | (1 | 1) | 17 | 7 | 4 | 0 | 6 | 0 | 18 | 1 | 0 | 0 | 0 | 0 | - | 3 | .119 | .187 | .202 |
| 2012 CWS | AL | 14 | 22 | 8 | 1 | 0 | 3 | (0 | 3) | 18 | 8 | 6 | 9 | 9 | 1 | 3 | 0 | 0 | 0 | 0 | 0 | - | 0 | .364 | .548 | .818 |
| 2013 Bal | AL | 3 | 5 | 0 | 0 | 0 | 0 | (0 | 0) | 0 | 0 | 0 | 0 | 0 | 0 | 1 | 0 | 0 | 0 | 0 | 0 | - | 0 | .000 | .000 | .000 |
| 08 Oak | AL | 1 | 1 | 0 | 0 | 0 | 0 | (0 | 0) | 0 | 0 | 0 | 0 | 0 | 0 | 0 | 0 | 0 | 0 | 0 | 0 | - | 0 | .000 | .000 | .000 |
| 08 TB | AL | 10 | 25 | 5 | 0 | 0 | 2 | (1 | 1) | 11 | 3 | 4 | 3 | 3 | 0 | 7 | 0 | 0 | 0 | 0 | 0 | - | 0 | .200 | .286 | .440 |
| Postseason | | 5 | 9 | 2 | 1 | 0 | 0 | (0 | 0) | 3 | 1 | 0 | 0 | 3 | 0 | 4 | 0 | 0 | 0 | 0 | 0 | - | 1 | .222 | .417 | .333 |
| 8 ML YEARS | | 416 | 1325 | 313 | 59 | 2 | 56 | (21 | 35) | 544 | 170 | 194 | 179 | 205 | 8 | 230 | 6 | 0 | 20 | 1 | 1 | .50 | 33 | .236 | .337 | .411 |

# Elliot Johnson

**Bats:** B **Throws:** R **Pos:** 2B-74;PR-14;SS-10;PH-9;3B-8;LF-8;DH-4;RF-3 **Ht:** 6'1" **Wt:** 190 **Born:** 3/9/1984 **Age:** 30

| BATTING | | | | | | | | | | | | | | | | | | | | BASERUNNING | | | | AVERAGES | | |
|---|---|---|---|---|---|---|---|---|---|---|---|---|---|---|---|---|---|---|---|---|---|---|---|---|---|---|
| Year Team | Lg | G | AB | H | 2B | 3B | HR | (Hm | Rd) | TB | R | RBI | RC | TBB | IBB | SO | HBP | SH | SF | SB | CS | SB% | GDP | Avg | OBP | Slg |
| 2008 TB | AL | 7 | 19 | 3 | 0 | 0 | 0 | (0 | 0) | 3 | 0 | 0 | 0 | 0 | 0 | 7 | 0 | 0 | 0 | 0 | 1 | .00 | 0 | .158 | .158 | .158 |
| 2011 TB | AL | 70 | 160 | 31 | 7 | 2 | 4 | (2 | 2) | 54 | 20 | 17 | 10 | 14 | 0 | 53 | 0 | 6 | 1 | 6 | 7 | .46 | 3 | .194 | .257 | .338 |
| 2012 TB | AL | 123 | 297 | 72 | 10 | 2 | 6 | (1 | 5) | 104 | 32 | 33 | 39 | 24 | 0 | 84 | 3 | 5 | 2 | 18 | 6 | .75 | 3 | .242 | .304 | .350 |
| 2013 2 Tms | | 111 | 254 | 53 | 7 | 3 | 2 | (1 | 1) | 72 | 27 | 19 | 19 | 16 | 1 | 67 | 0 | 4 | 1 | 22 | 2 | .92 | 4 | .209 | .255 | .283 |
| 13 KC | AL | 79 | 162 | 29 | 2 | 1 | 2 | (1 | 1) | 39 | 19 | 9 | 8 | 8 | 1 | 49 | 0 | 3 | 0 | 14 | 0 | 1.00 | 2 | .179 | .218 | .241 |
| 13 Atl | NL | 32 | 92 | 24 | 5 | 2 | 0 | (0 | 0) | 33 | 8 | 10 | 11 | 8 | 0 | 18 | 0 | 1 | 1 | 8 | 2 | .80 | 2 | .261 | .317 | .359 |
| Postseason | | 1 | 0 | 0 | 0 | 0 | 0 | (0 | 0) | 0 | 0 | 0 | 0 | 0 | 0 | 0 | 0 | 0 | 0 | 0 | 0 | - | 0 | - | - | - |
| 4 ML YEARS | | 311 | 730 | 159 | 24 | 7 | 12 | (4 | 8) | 233 | 79 | 69 | 68 | 54 | 1 | 211 | 3 | 15 | 4 | 46 | 16 | .74 | 10 | .218 | .273 | .319 |

# Erik Johnson

**Pitches:** R **Bats:** R **Pos:** SP-5 **Ht:** 6'3" **Wt:** 235 **Born:** 12/30/1989 **Age:** 24

| | | | HOW MUCH HE PITCHED | | | | | | WHAT HE GAVE UP | | | | | | | | | | | | THE RESULTS | | | | | | | |
|---|---|---|---|---|---|---|---|---|---|---|---|---|---|---|---|---|---|---|---|---|---|---|---|---|---|---|---|---|
| Year | Team | Lg | G | GS | CG | GF | IP | BFP | H | R | ER | HR | SH | SF | HB | TBB | IBB | SO | WP | Bk | W | L | Pct | Sh | Sv-Op | Hld | ERC | ERA |
| 2011 | Gr Falls | R+ | 2 | 0 | 0 | 1 | 2.0 | 11 | 4 | 1 | 1 | 0 | 0 | 0 | 1 | 1 | 0 | 2 | 0 | 0 | 0 | 0 | - | 0 | 0- - | - | 13.16 | 4.50 |
| 2012 | Knapol | A | 9 | 9 | 0 | 0 | 43.0 | 187 | 39 | 15 | 11 | 3 | 0 | 0 | 2 | 19 | 0 | 39 | 1 | 0 | 2 | 2 | .500 | 0 | 0- - | - | 3.65 | 2.30 |
| 2012 | WinSa | A+ | 8 | 8 | 0 | 0 | 49.1 | 200 | 43 | 19 | 15 | 0 | 1 | 1 | 1 | 10 | 0 | 48 | 2 | 0 | 4 | 3 | .571 | 0 | 0- - | - | 2.11 | 2.74 |
| 2013 | Brham | AA | 14 | 14 | 3 | 0 | 84.2 | 327 | 57 | 22 | 21 | 6 | 2 | 1 | 2 | 21 | 0 | 74 | 1 | 0 | 8 | 2 | .800 | 1 | 0- - | - | 1.81 | 2.23 |
| 2013 | Charltt | AAA | 10 | 10 | 0 | 0 | 57.1 | 228 | 43 | 13 | 10 | 1 | 0 | 0 | 3 | 19 | 0 | 57 | 0 | 0 | 4 | 1 | .800 | 0 | 0- - | - | 2.25 | 1.57 |
| 2013 | CWS | AL | 5 | 5 | 0 | 0 | 27.2 | 128 | 32 | 16 | 10 | 5 | 0 | 2 | 1 | 11 | 0 | 18 | 2 | 0 | 3 | 2 | .600 | 0 | 0-0 | 0 | 5.55 | 3.25 |

# Jim Johnson

**Pitches:** R **Bats:** R **Pos:** RP-74 **Ht:** 6'6" **Wt:** 240 **Born:** 6/27/1983 **Age:** 31

| | | | HOW MUCH HE PITCHED | | | | | | WHAT HE GAVE UP | | | | | | | | | | | | THE RESULTS | | | | | | | |
|---|---|---|---|---|---|---|---|---|---|---|---|---|---|---|---|---|---|---|---|---|---|---|---|---|---|---|---|---|
| Year | Team | Lg | G | GS | CG | GF | IP | BFP | H | R | ER | HR | SH | SF | HB | TBB | IBB | SO | WP | Bk | W | L | Pct | Sh | Sv-Op | Hld | ERC | ERA |
| 2006 | Bal | AL | 1 | 1 | 0 | 0 | 3.0 | 21 | 9 | 8 | 8 | 1 | 0 | 1 | 1 | 3 | 0 | 0 | 0 | 0 | 0 | 1 | .000 | 0 | 0-0 | 0 | 26.81 | 24.00 |
| 2007 | Bal | AL | 1 | 0 | 0 | 1 | 2.0 | 11 | 3 | 2 | 2 | 0 | 0 | 1 | 0 | 2 | 0 | 1 | 0 | 0 | 0 | 0 | - | 0 | 0-0 | 0 | 8.58 | 9.00 |
| 2008 | Bal | AL | 54 | 0 | 0 | 18 | 68.2 | 281 | 54 | 18 | 17 | 0 | 2 | 1 | 3 | 28 | 3 | 38 | 1 | 1 | 2 | 4 | .333 | 0 | 1-1 | 19 | 2.45 | 2.23 |
| 2009 | Bal | AL | 64 | 0 | 0 | 29 | 70.0 | 300 | 73 | 32 | 32 | 8 | 2 | 2 | 3 | 23 | 3 | 49 | 2 | 1 | 4 | 6 | .400 | 0 | 10-16 | 14 | 4.28 | 4.11 |
| 2010 | Bal | AL | 26 | 0 | 0 | 6 | 26.1 | 117 | 32 | 11 | 10 | 2 | 3 | 0 | 1 | 5 | 1 | 22 | 4 | 0 | 1 | 1 | .500 | 0 | 1-6 | 11 | 4.26 | 3.42 |
| 2011 | Bal | AL | 69 | 0 | 0 | 20 | 91.0 | 366 | 80 | 30 | 27 | 5 | 4 | 2 | 2 | 21 | 3 | 58 | 2 | 1 | 6 | 5 | .545 | 0 | 9-14 | 18 | 2.58 | 2.67 |
| 2012 | Bal | AL | 71 | 0 | 0 | 63 | 68.2 | 269 | 55 | 21 | 19 | 3 | 1 | 0 | 3 | 15 | 1 | 41 | 1 | 0 | 2 | 1 | .667 | 0 | **51-54** | 0 | 2.22 | 2.49 |
| 2013 | Bal | AL | 74 | 0 | 0 | 63 | 70.1 | 291 | 72 | 26 | 23 | 5 | 2 | 0 | 7 | 18 | 4 | 56 | 2 | 0 | 3 | 8 | .273 | 0 | **50-59** | 0 | 3.89 | 2.94 |
| Postseason | | | 5 | 0 | 0 | 3 | 5.1 | 25 | 8 | 6 | 5 | 2 | 0 | 0 | 0 | 1 | 0 | 4 | 0 | 0 | 0 | 1 | .000 | 0 | 2-3 | 0 | 8.18 | 8.44 |
| 8 ML YEARS | | | 360 | 1 | 0 | 200 | 400.0 | 1656 | 378 | 148 | 138 | 24 | 14 | 7 | 20 | 115 | 15 | 265 | 12 | 3 | 18 | 26 | .409 | 0 | 122-150 | 62 | 3.26 | 3.11 |

# Josh Johnson

**Pitches:** R **Bats:** L **Pos:** SP-16 **Ht:** 6'7" **Wt:** 250 **Born:** 1/31/1984 **Age:** 30

| | | | HOW MUCH HE PITCHED | | | | | | WHAT HE GAVE UP | | | | | | | | | | | | THE RESULTS | | | | | | | |
|---|---|---|---|---|---|---|---|---|---|---|---|---|---|---|---|---|---|---|---|---|---|---|---|---|---|---|---|---|
| Year | Team | Lg | G | GS | CG | GF | IP | BFP | H | R | ER | HR | SH | SF | HB | TBB | IBB | SO | WP | Bk | W | L | Pct | Sh | Sv-Op | Hld | ERC | ERA |
| 2013 | Dnedin* | A+ | 1 | 1 | 0 | 0 | 3.0 | 12 | 3 | 1 | 1 | 0 | 0 | 0 | 0 | 0 | 0 | 5 | 0 | 0 | 0 | 0 | - | 0 | 0- - | - | 1.95 | 3.00 |
| 2013 | Buffalo* | AAA | 2 | 2 | 0 | 0 | 8.2 | 39 | 9 | 6 | 6 | 0 | 0 | 0 | 2 | 4 | 0 | 6 | 0 | 0 | 0 | 1 | .000 | 0 | 0- - | - | 4.80 | 6.23 |
| 2005 | Fla | NL | 4 | 1 | 0 | 0 | 12.1 | 55 | 11 | 5 | 5 | 0 | 1 | 0 | 1 | 10 | 0 | 10 | 0 | 0 | 0 | 0 | - | 0 | 0-0 | 0 | 4.82 | 3.65 |
| 2006 | Fla | NL | 31 | 24 | 0 | 1 | 157.0 | 659 | 136 | 63 | 54 | 14 | 11 | 0 | 4 | 68 | 6 | 133 | 3 | 1 | 12 | 7 | .632 | 0 | 0-1 | 0 | 3.48 | 3.10 |
| 2007 | Fla | NL | 4 | 4 | 0 | 0 | 15.2 | 82 | 26 | 17 | 13 | 1 | 2 | 1 | 0 | 12 | 3 | 14 | 1 | 0 | 0 | 3 | .000 | 0 | 0-0 | 0 | 9.16 | 7.47 |
| 2008 | Fla | NL | 14 | 14 | 1 | 0 | 87.1 | 365 | 91 | 36 | 35 | 7 | 5 | 1 | 1 | 27 | 1 | 77 | 4 | 0 | 7 | 1 | .875 | 0 | 0-0 | 0 | 3.94 | 3.61 |
| 2009 | Fla | NL | 33 | 33 | 2 | 0 | 209.0 | 855 | 184 | 77 | 75 | 14 | 11 | 4 | 6 | 58 | 6 | 191 | 10 | 0 | 15 | 5 | .750 | 0 | 0-0 | 0 | 2.84 | 3.23 |
| 2010 | Fla | NL | 28 | 28 | 1 | 0 | 183.2 | 744 | 155 | 51 | 47 | 7 | 5 | 8 | 5 | 48 | 2 | 186 | 4 | 0 | 11 | 6 | .647 | 0 | 0-0 | 0 | 2.44 | **2.30** |
| 2011 | Fla | NL | 9 | 9 | 0 | 0 | 60.1 | 234 | 39 | 13 | 11 | 2 | 1 | 1 | 1 | 20 | 2 | 56 | 2 | 1 | 3 | 1 | .750 | 0 | 0-0 | 0 | 1.70 | 1.64 |
| 2012 | Mia | NL | 31 | 31 | 0 | 0 | 191.1 | 798 | 180 | 84 | 81 | 14 | 8 | 8 | 4 | 65 | 7 | 165 | 5 | 0 | 8 | 14 | .364 | 0 | 0-0 | 0 | 3.40 | 3.81 |
| 2013 | Tor | AL | 16 | 16 | 0 | 0 | 81.1 | 384 | 105 | 64 | 56 | 15 | 3 | 3 | 3 | 30 | 3 | 83 | 4 | 0 | 2 | 8 | .200 | 0 | 0-0 | 0 | 6.23 | 6.20 |
| 9 ML YEARS | | | 170 | 160 | 4 | 1 | 998.0 | 4176 | 927 | 410 | 377 | 74 | 47 | 26 | 25 | 338 | 30 | 915 | 33 | 2 | 58 | 45 | .563 | 0 | 0-1 | 0 | 3.35 | 3.40 |

# Kelly Johnson

**Bats:** L **Throws:** R **Pos:** LF-53;2B-22;DH-18;PH-17;3B-16;1B-3;PR-1 **Ht:** 6'1" **Wt:** 200 **Born:** 2/22/1982 **Age:** 32

| | | | BATTING | | | | | | | | | | | | | | | | | BASERUNNING | | | | AVERAGES | | |
|---|---|---|---|---|---|---|---|---|---|---|---|---|---|---|---|---|---|---|---|---|---|---|---|---|---|---|
| Year | Team | Lg | G | AB | H | 2B | 3B | HR | (Hm | Rd) | TB | R | RBI | RC | TBB | IBB | SO | HBP | SH | SF | SB | CS | SB% | GDP | Avg | OBP | Slg |
| 2005 | Atl | NL | 87 | 290 | 70 | 12 | 3 | 9 | (2 | 7) | 115 | 46 | 40 | 41 | 40 | 1 | 75 | 1 | 2 | 1 | 2 | 1 | .67 | 11 | .241 | .334 | .397 |
| 2007 | Atl | NL | 147 | 521 | 144 | 26 | 10 | 16 | (5 | 11) | 238 | 91 | 68 | 87 | 79 | 3 | 117 | 4 | 2 | 2 | 9 | 5 | .64 | 8 | .276 | .375 | .457 |
| 2008 | Atl | NL | 150 | 547 | 157 | 39 | 6 | 12 | (5 | 7) | 244 | 86 | 69 | 87 | 52 | 2 | 113 | 2 | 9 | 4 | 11 | 6 | .65 | 3 | .287 | .349 | .446 |
| 2009 | Atl | NL | 106 | 303 | 68 | 20 | 3 | 8 | (4 | 4) | 118 | 47 | 29 | 31 | 32 | 1 | 54 | 3 | 6 | 2 | 7 | 2 | .78 | 4 | .224 | .303 | .389 |
| 2010 | Ari | NL | 154 | 585 | 166 | 36 | 5 | 26 | (16 | 10) | 290 | 93 | 71 | 92 | 79 | 1 | 148 | 2 | 3 | 2 | 13 | 7 | .65 | 12 | .284 | .370 | .496 |
| 2011 | 2 Tms | | 147 | 545 | 121 | 27 | 7 | 21 | (10 | 11) | 225 | 75 | 58 | 70 | 60 | 2 | 163 | 4 | 4 | 0 | 16 | 6 | .73 | 3 | .222 | .304 | .413 |
| 2012 | Tor | AL | 142 | 507 | 114 | 19 | 2 | 16 | (10 | 6) | 185 | 61 | 55 | 63 | 62 | 4 | 159 | 5 | 2 | 4 | 14 | 2 | .88 | 8 | .225 | .313 | .365 |
| 2013 | TB | AL | 118 | 366 | 86 | 12 | 2 | 16 | (6 | 10) | 150 | 41 | 52 | 49 | 35 | 1 | 99 | 3 | 0 | 3 | 7 | 4 | .64 | 4 | .235 | .305 | .410 |
| 11 | Ari | NL | 114 | 430 | 90 | 23 | 5 | 18 | (10 | 8) | 177 | 59 | 49 | 53 | 44 | 2 | 132 | 3 | 4 | 0 | 13 | 3 | .81 | 3 | .209 | .287 | .412 |
| 11 | Tor | AL | 33 | 115 | 31 | 4 | 2 | 3 | (0 | 3) | 48 | 16 | 9 | 17 | 16 | 0 | 31 | 1 | 0 | 0 | 3 | 3 | .50 | 0 | .270 | .364 | .417 |
| Postseason | | | 4 | 2 | 0 | 0 | 0 | 0 | (0 | 0) | 0 | 0 | 0 | 0 | 1 | 0 | 0 | 0 | 0 | 0 | 0 | 0 | - | 0 | .000 | .333 | .000 |
| 8 ML YEARS | | | 1051 | 3664 | 926 | 191 | 38 | 124 | (58 | 66) | 1565 | 540 | 442 | 520 | 439 | 15 | 928 | 24 | 28 | 18 | 79 | 33 | .71 | 53 | .253 | .335 | .427 |

# Kris Johnson

**Pitches:** L **Bats:** L **Pos:** RP-3; SP-1 **Ht:** 6'4" **Wt:** 195 **Born:** 10/14/1984 **Age:** 29

| | | | HOW MUCH HE PITCHED | | | | | | WHAT HE GAVE UP | | | | | | | | | | | | THE RESULTS | | | | | | | |
|---|---|---|---|---|---|---|---|---|---|---|---|---|---|---|---|---|---|---|---|---|---|---|---|---|---|---|---|---|
| Year | Team | Lg | G | GS | CG | GF | IP | BFP | H | R | ER | HR | SH | SF | HB | TBB | IBB | SO | WP | Bk | W | L | Pct | Sh | Sv-Op | Hld | ERC | ERA |
| 2009 | Pwtckt | AAA | 22 | 22 | 0 | 0 | 96.1 | 457 | 128 | 77 | 68 | 8 | 3 | 6 | 4 | 44 | 0 | 65 | 7 | 0 | 3 | 13 | .188 | 0 | 0- - | - | 6.25 | 6.35 |
| 2009 | Portlnd | AA | 3 | 3 | 0 | 0 | 17.0 | 79 | 22 | 14 | 12 | 1 | 0 | 2 | 1 | 5 | 0 | 12 | 1 | 0 | 0 | 3 | .000 | 0 | 0- - | - | 5.14 | 6.35 |
| 2010 | Pwtckt | AAA | 28 | 24 | 0 | 2 | 132.2 | 594 | 152 | 81 | 72 | 15 | 3 | 9 | 5 | 52 | 1 | 79 | 9 | 0 | 6 | 13 | .316 | 0 | 0- - | - | 5.12 | 4.88 |
| 2011 | Pwtckt | AAA | 8 | 3 | 0 | 0 | 20.2 | 109 | 41 | 31 | 29 | 7 | 0 | 2 | 1 | 6 | 0 | 12 | 1 | 0 | 2 | 2 | .500 | 0 | 0- - | - | 12.25 | 12.63 |
| 2012 | Altna | AA | 15 | 9 | 0 | 3 | 56.0 | 242 | 50 | 19 | 13 | 3 | 0 | 1 | 3 | 24 | 0 | 42 | 4 | 0 | 3 | 2 | .600 | 0 | 1- - | - | 3.44 | 2.09 |
| 2012 | Indy | AAA | 20 | 4 | 0 | 5 | 45.2 | 194 | 42 | 25 | 23 | 7 | 1 | 0 | 1 | 18 | 3 | 33 | 2 | 0 | 5 | 2 | .714 | 0 | 0- - | - | 3.96 | 4.53 |
| 2013 | Indy | AAA | 26 | 21 | 1 | 2 | 135.2 | 550 | 116 | 37 | 36 | 6 | 7 | 1 | 4 | 43 | 0 | 94 | 8 | 0 | 10 | 4 | .714 | 0 | 2- - | - | 2.79 | 2.39 |
| 2013 | Pit | NL | 4 | 1 | 0 | 2 | 10.1 | 46 | 12 | 7 | 7 | 0 | 0 | 1 | 1 | 4 | 1 | 9 | 2 | 0 | 0 | 2 | .000 | 0 | 0-0 | 0 | 4.48 | 6.10 |

# Reed Johnson

**Bats:** R **Throws:** R **Pos:** PH-44;RF-15;CF-12;LF-10;PR-2 **Ht:** 5'10" **Wt:** 180 **Born:** 12/8/1976 **Age:** 37

| BATTING | | | | | | | | | | | | | | | | | | | | BASERUNNING | | | | AVERAGES | | |
|---|---|---|---|---|---|---|---|---|---|---|---|---|---|---|---|---|---|---|---|---|---|---|---|---|---|---|
| Year Team | Lg | G | AB | H | 2B | 3B | HR | (Hm | Rd) | TB | R | RBI | RC | TBB | IBB | SO | HBP | SH | SF | SB | CS | SB% | GDP | Avg | OBP | Slg |
| 2003 Tor | AL | 114 | 412 | 121 | 21 | 2 | 10 | (6 | 4) | 176 | 79 | 52 | 64 | 20 | 1 | 67 | 20 | 1 | 4 | 5 | 3 | .63 | 10 | .294 | .353 | .427 |
| 2004 Tor | AL | 141 | 537 | 145 | 25 | 2 | 10 | (8 | 2) | 204 | 68 | 61 | 65 | 28 | 2 | 98 | 12 | 3 | 2 | 6 | 3 | .67 | 17 | .270 | .320 | .380 |
| 2005 Tor | AL | 142 | 398 | 107 | 21 | 6 | 8 | (4 | 4) | 164 | 55 | 58 | 57 | 22 | 1 | 82 | 16 | 2 | 1 | 5 | 6 | .45 | 8 | .269 | .332 | .412 |
| 2006 Tor | AL | 134 | 461 | 147 | 34 | 2 | 12 | (4 | 8) | 221 | 86 | 49 | 76 | 33 | 4 | 81 | **21** | 1 | 1 | 8 | 2 | .80 | 9 | .319 | .390 | .479 |
| 2007 Tor | AL | 79 | 275 | 65 | 13 | 2 | 2 | (1 | 1) | 88 | 31 | 14 | 24 | 16 | 0 | 56 | 11 | 5 | 0 | 4 | 2 | .67 | 7 | .236 | .305 | .320 |
| 2008 ChC | NL | 109 | 333 | 101 | 21 | 0 | 6 | (3 | 3) | 140 | 52 | 50 | 57 | 19 | 1 | 68 | 12 | 5 | 5 | 5 | 6 | .45 | 3 | .303 | .358 | .420 |
| 2009 ChC | NL | 65 | 165 | 42 | 10 | 2 | 4 | (3 | 1) | 68 | 23 | 22 | 19 | 13 | 0 | 27 | 6 | 1 | 1 | 2 | 1 | .67 | 5 | .255 | .330 | .412 |
| 2010 LAD | NL | 102 | 202 | 53 | 11 | 2 | 2 | (1 | 1) | 74 | 24 | 15 | 18 | 5 | 0 | 50 | 4 | 2 | 2 | 2 | 2 | .50 | 3 | .262 | .291 | .366 |
| 2011 ChC | NL | 111 | 246 | 76 | 22 | 1 | 5 | (4 | 1) | 115 | 33 | 28 | 35 | 5 | 1 | 63 | 11 | 2 | 2 | 2 | 1 | .67 | 4 | .309 | .348 | .467 |
| 2012 2 Tms | NL | 119 | 269 | 78 | 14 | 3 | 3 | (0 | 3) | 107 | 30 | 20 | 37 | 13 | 1 | 61 | 6 | 0 | 0 | 2 | 2 | .50 | 4 | .290 | .337 | .398 |
| 2013 Atl | NL | 74 | 123 | 30 | 7 | 1 | 1 | (1 | 0) | 42 | 13 | 11 | 15 | 6 | 0 | 32 | 6 | 1 | 0 | 0 | 0 | - | 3 | .244 | .311 | .341 |
| 12 ChC | NL | 76 | 169 | 51 | 9 | 3 | 3 | (0 | 3) | 75 | 23 | 16 | 26 | 10 | 1 | 43 | 4 | 0 | 0 | 2 | 1 | .67 | 3 | .302 | .355 | .444 |
| 12 Atl | NL | 43 | 100 | 27 | 5 | 0 | 0 | (0 | 0) | 32 | 7 | 4 | 11 | 3 | 0 | 18 | 2 | 0 | 0 | 0 | 1 | .00 | 1 | .270 | .305 | .320 |
| 11 ML YEARS | | 1190 | 3421 | 965 | 199 | 23 | 63 | (35 | 28) | 1399 | 494 | 380 | 467 | 180 | 11 | 685 | 125 | 23 | 18 | 41 | 28 | .59 | 73 | .282 | .339 | .409 |

# Rob Johnson

**Bats:** R **Throws:** R **Pos:** C-15;PH-5 **Ht:** 6'1" **Wt:** 220 **Born:** 7/22/1982 **Age:** 31

| BATTING | | | | | | | | | | | | | | | | | | | | BASERUNNING | | | | AVERAGES | | |
|---|---|---|---|---|---|---|---|---|---|---|---|---|---|---|---|---|---|---|---|---|---|---|---|---|---|---|
| Year Team | Lg | G | AB | H | 2B | 3B | HR | (Hm | Rd) | TB | R | RBI | RC | TBB | IBB | SO | HBP | SH | SF | SB | CS | SB% | GDP | Avg | OBP | Slg |
| 2013 Memp* | AAA | 59 | 195 | 46 | 8 | 1 | 7 | (- | -) | 77 | 27 | 32 | 25 | 24 | 1 | 42 | 0 | 0 | 2 | 0 | 2 | .00 | 4 | .236 | .317 | .395 |
| 2007 Sea | AL | 6 | 3 | 1 | 0 | 0 | 0 | (0 | 0) | 1 | 1 | 0 | 0 | 0 | 0 | 0 | 0 | 0 | 0 | 1 | 0 | 1.00 | 0 | .333 | .333 | .333 |
| 2008 Sea | AL | 14 | 31 | 4 | 0 | 0 | 1 | (1 | 0) | 7 | 2 | 2 | 0 | 0 | 0 | 6 | 0 | 1 | 0 | 0 | 0 | - | 1 | .129 | .129 | .226 |
| 2009 Sea | AL | 80 | 258 | 55 | 19 | 2 | 2 | (2 | 0) | 84 | 21 | 27 | 22 | 26 | 1 | 60 | 2 | 3 | 1 | 1 | 1 | .50 | 11 | .213 | .289 | .326 |
| 2010 Sea | AL | 61 | 178 | 34 | 10 | 0 | 2 | (0 | 2) | 50 | 24 | 13 | 12 | 25 | 2 | 46 | 2 | 1 | 3 | 1 | 1 | .50 | 5 | .191 | .293 | .281 |
| 2011 SD | NL | 67 | 179 | 34 | 6 | 1 | 3 | (1 | 2) | 51 | 9 | 16 | 12 | 14 | 1 | 58 | 3 | 2 | 1 | 3 | 0 | 1.00 | 3 | .190 | .259 | .285 |
| 2012 NYM | NL | 17 | 52 | 13 | 2 | 0 | 0 | (0 | 0) | 15 | 3 | 4 | 2 | 4 | 2 | 10 | 0 | 1 | 1 | 0 | 0 | - | 2 | .250 | .298 | .288 |
| 2013 StL | NL | 20 | 35 | 6 | 1 | 1 | 0 | (0 | 0) | 9 | 2 | 2 | 2 | 3 | 0 | 6 | 0 | 0 | 0 | 0 | 0 | - | 2 | .171 | .237 | .257 |
| 7 ML YEARS | | 265 | 736 | 147 | 38 | 4 | 8 | (4 | 4) | 217 | 62 | 64 | 50 | 72 | 6 | 186 | 7 | 8 | 6 | 6 | 2 | .75 | 24 | .200 | .275 | .295 |

# Steve Johnson

**Pitches:** R **Bats:** R **Pos:** RP-8; SP-1 **Ht:** 6'1" **Wt:** 220 **Born:** 8/31/1987 **Age:** 26

| | | HOW MUCH HE PITCHED | | | | | | WHAT HE GAVE UP | | | | | | | | | | | | THE RESULTS | | | | | | | |
|---|---|---|---|---|---|---|---|---|---|---|---|---|---|---|---|---|---|---|---|---|---|---|---|---|---|---|---|
| Year Team | Lg | G | GS | CG | GF | IP | BFP | H | R | ER | HR | SH | SF | HB | TBB | IBB | SO | WP | Bk | W | L | Pct | Sh | Sv-Op | Hld | ERC | ERA |
| 2009 InldEm | A+ | 18 | 16 | 0 | 1 | 96.2 | 414 | 94 | 50 | 41 | 14 | 3 | 1 | 6 | 42 | 0 | 102 | 2 | 0 | 8 | 4 | .667 | 0 | 1-- | - | 4.74 | 3.82 |
| 2009 Chatt | AA | 2 | 2 | 0 | 0 | 10.2 | 45 | 8 | 5 | 2 | 1 | 1 | 1 | 1 | 3 | 0 | 15 | 0 | 0 | 1 | 1 | .500 | 0 | 0-- | - | 2.50 | 1.69 |
| 2009 Bowie | AA | 7 | 7 | 0 | 0 | 38.0 | 156 | 24 | 13 | 12 | 3 | 0 | 2 | 3 | 17 | 0 | 37 | 2 | 0 | 3 | 2 | .600 | 0 | 0-- | - | 2.47 | 2.84 |
| 2010 Bowie | AA | 28 | 28 | 0 | 0 | 145.0 | 652 | 144 | 87 | 83 | 24 | 4 | 2 | 11 | 78 | 1 | 128 | 13 | 0 | 7 | 8 | .467 | 0 | 0-- | - | 5.40 | 5.15 |
| 2011 Bowie | AA | 10 | 10 | 0 | 0 | 58.1 | 226 | 40 | 14 | 14 | 7 | 1 | 1 | 2 | 15 | 0 | 59 | 0 | 0 | 5 | 1 | .833 | 0 | 0-- | - | 2.21 | 2.16 |
| 2011 Norfolk | AAA | 17 | 17 | 0 | 0 | 87.1 | 404 | 101 | 56 | 54 | 7 | 4 | 4 | 4 | 47 | 0 | 63 | 5 | 0 | 2 | 7 | .222 | 0 | 0-- | - | 5.58 | 5.56 |
| 2012 Norfolk | AAA | 19 | 14 | 1 | 0 | 91.1 | 372 | 66 | 38 | 29 | 7 | 3 | 5 | 6 | 31 | 0 | 86 | 3 | 0 | 4 | 8 | .333 | 0 | 0-- | - | 2.48 | 2.86 |
| 2013 Norfolk | AAA | 10 | 8 | 0 | 0 | 46.0 | 190 | 40 | 22 | 21 | 4 | 1 | 0 | 0 | 17 | 0 | 52 | 5 | 0 | 2 | 3 | .400 | 0 | 0-- | - | 3.19 | 4.11 |
| 2013 Orioles | R | 1 | 1 | 0 | 0 | 2.0 | 6 | 0 | 0 | 0 | 0 | 0 | 0 | 0 | 1 | 0 | 3 | 0 | 0 | 0 | 0 | - | 0 | 0-- | - | 0.32 | 0.00 |
| 2013 Abrdn | A- | 2 | 2 | 0 | 0 | 6.0 | 26 | 5 | 2 | 2 | 1 | 0 | 0 | 2 | 2 | 0 | 6 | 0 | 0 | 0 | 0 | - | 0 | 0-- | - | 4.77 | 3.00 |
| 2012 Bal | AL | 12 | 4 | 0 | 3 | 38.1 | 151 | 23 | 9 | 9 | 4 | 1 | 0 | 0 | 18 | 1 | 46 | 1 | 0 | 4 | 0 | 1.000 | 0 | 0-0 | 0 | 2.31 | 2.11 |
| 2013 Bal | AL | 9 | 1 | 0 | 2 | 15.2 | 73 | 14 | 13 | 13 | 2 | 0 | 0 | 0 | 13 | 1 | 20 | 1 | 0 | 1 | 1 | .500 | 0 | 0-0 | 1 | 5.23 | 7.47 |
| 2 ML YEARS | | 21 | 5 | 0 | 5 | 54.0 | 224 | 37 | 22 | 22 | 6 | 1 | 0 | 0 | 31 | 2 | 66 | 2 | 0 | 5 | 1 | .833 | 0 | 0-0 | 1 | 3.09 | 3.67 |

# Adam Jones

**Bats:** R **Throws:** R **Pos:** CF-156;DH-4 **Ht:** 6'3" **Wt:** 225 **Born:** 8/1/1985 **Age:** 28

| BATTING | | | | | | | | | | | | | | | | | | | | BASERUNNING | | | | AVERAGES | | |
|---|---|---|---|---|---|---|---|---|---|---|---|---|---|---|---|---|---|---|---|---|---|---|---|---|---|---|
| Year Team | Lg | G | AB | H | 2B | 3B | HR | (Hm | Rd) | TB | R | RBI | RC | TBB | IBB | SO | HBP | SH | SF | SB | CS | SB% | GDP | Avg | OBP | Slg |
| 2006 Sea | AL | 32 | 74 | 16 | 4 | 0 | 1 | (0 | 1) | 23 | 6 | 8 | 4 | 2 | 0 | 22 | 0 | 0 | 0 | 3 | 1 | .75 | 3 | .216 | .237 | .311 |
| 2007 Sea | AL | 41 | 65 | 16 | 2 | 1 | 2 | (1 | 1) | 26 | 16 | 4 | 5 | 4 | 0 | 21 | 1 | 1 | 0 | 2 | 1 | .67 | 0 | .246 | .300 | .400 |
| 2008 Bal | AL | 132 | 477 | 129 | 21 | 7 | 9 | (4 | 5) | 191 | 61 | 57 | 56 | 23 | 0 | 108 | 7 | 2 | 5 | 10 | 3 | .77 | 12 | .270 | .311 | .400 |
| 2009 Bal | AL | 119 | 473 | 131 | 22 | 3 | 19 | (11 | 8) | 216 | 83 | 70 | 71 | 36 | 3 | 93 | 7 | 0 | 3 | 10 | 4 | .71 | 13 | .277 | .335 | .457 |
| 2010 Bal | AL | 149 | 581 | 165 | 25 | 5 | 19 | (9 | 10) | 257 | 76 | 69 | 72 | 23 | 1 | 119 | 13 | 2 | 2 | 7 | 7 | .50 | 17 | .284 | .325 | .442 |
| 2011 Bal | AL | 151 | 567 | 159 | 26 | 2 | 25 | (19 | 6) | 264 | 68 | 83 | 77 | 29 | 2 | 113 | 9 | 1 | **12** | 12 | 4 | .75 | 16 | .280 | .319 | .466 |
| 2012 Bal | AL | **162** | 648 | 186 | 39 | 3 | 32 | (15 | 17) | 327 | 103 | 82 | 101 | 34 | 0 | 126 | 13 | 0 | 2 | 16 | 7 | .70 | 15 | .287 | .334 | .505 |
| 2013 Bal | AL | 160 | 653 | 186 | 35 | 1 | 33 | (17 | 16) | 322 | 100 | 108 | 101 | 25 | 4 | 136 | 8 | 0 | 3 | 14 | 3 | .82 | 15 | .285 | .318 | .493 |
| Postseason | | 6 | 26 | 2 | 0 | 0 | 0 | (0 | 0) | 2 | 0 | 1 | 0 | 0 | 0 | 7 | 0 | 0 | 1 | 0 | 0 | - | 0 | .077 | .074 | .077 |
| 8 ML YEARS | | 946 | 3538 | 988 | 174 | 22 | 140 | (76 | 64) | 1626 | 513 | 481 | 487 | 176 | 10 | 738 | 58 | 6 | 27 | 74 | 30 | .71 | 91 | .279 | .322 | .460 |

# Garrett Jones

**Bats:** L **Throws:** L **Pos:** 1B-83;PH-33;RF-32;DH-6 **Ht:** 6'4" **Wt:** 230 **Born:** 6/21/1981 **Age:** 33

| BATTING | | | | | | | | | | | | | | | | | | | | BASERUNNING | | | | AVERAGES | | |
|---|---|---|---|---|---|---|---|---|---|---|---|---|---|---|---|---|---|---|---|---|---|---|---|---|---|---|
| Year Team | Lg | G | AB | H | 2B | 3B | HR | (Hm | Rd) | TB | R | RBI | RC | TBB | IBB | SO | HBP | SH | SF | SB | CS | SB% | GDP | Avg | OBP | Slg |
| 2007 Min | AL | 31 | 77 | 16 | 2 | 1 | 2 | (1 | 1) | 26 | 7 | 5 | 3 | 6 | 0 | 20 | 0 | 0 | 1 | 1 | 1 | .50 | 2 | .208 | .262 | .338 |
| 2009 Pit | NL | 82 | 314 | 92 | 21 | 1 | 21 | (13 | 8) | 178 | 45 | 44 | 47 | 40 | 8 | 76 | 1 | 0 | 3 | 10 | 2 | .83 | 6 | .293 | .372 | .567 |
| 2010 Pit | NL | 158 | 592 | 146 | 34 | 1 | 21 | (11 | 10) | 245 | 64 | 86 | 69 | 53 | 2 | 123 | 1 | 0 | 8 | 7 | 3 | .70 | 18 | .247 | .306 | .414 |
| 2011 Pit | NL | 148 | 423 | 103 | 30 | 1 | 16 | (8 | 8) | 183 | 51 | 58 | 57 | 48 | 2 | 104 | 2 | 0 | 4 | 6 | 3 | .67 | 7 | .243 | .321 | .433 |
| 2012 Pit | NL | 145 | 475 | 130 | 28 | 3 | 27 | (13 | 14) | 245 | 68 | 86 | 84 | 33 | 2 | 103 | 0 | 0 | 7 | 2 | 0 | 1.00 | 3 | .274 | .317 | .516 |
| 2013 Pit | NL | 144 | 403 | 94 | 26 | 2 | 15 | (6 | 9) | 169 | 41 | 51 | 39 | 31 | 0 | 101 | 2 | 0 | 4 | 2 | 0 | 1.00 | 10 | .233 | .289 | .419 |
| 6 ML YEARS | | 708 | 2284 | 581 | 141 | 9 | 102 | (52 | 50) | 1046 | 276 | 330 | 299 | 211 | 14 | 527 | 6 | 0 | 27 | 28 | 9 | .76 | 46 | .254 | .316 | .458 |

# Nate Jones

**Pitches:** R **Bats:** R **Pos:** RP-70 **Ht:** 6'5" **Wt:** 210 **Born:** 1/28/1986 **Age:** 28

| | | | HOW MUCH HE PITCHED | | | | | | WHAT HE GAVE UP | | | | | | | | | | | | THE RESULTS | | | | | | | |
|---|---|---|---|---|---|---|---|---|---|---|---|---|---|---|---|---|---|---|---|---|---|---|---|---|---|---|---|---|
| Year | Team | Lg | G | GS | CG | GF | IP | BFP | H | R | ER | HR | SH | SF | HB | TBB | IBB | SO | WP | Bk | W | L | Pct | Sh | Sv-Op | Hld | ERC | ERA |
| 2009 | Knapol | A | 13 | 0 | 0 | 5 | 18.2 | 72 | 8 | 5 | 5 | 0 | 0 | 0 | 1 | 9 | 0 | 25 | 1 | 0 | 2 | 0 | 1.000 | 0 | 1-- | - | 1.31 | 2.41 |
| 2009 | WinSa | A+ | 32 | 0 | 0 | 16 | 49.1 | 201 | 44 | 20 | 20 | 4 | 4 | 3 | 1 | 13 | 0 | 43 | 4 | 0 | 2 | 1 | .667 | 0 | 0-- | - | 2.95 | 3.65 |
| 2010 | WinSa | A+ | 28 | 28 | 1 | 0 | 152.1 | 671 | 176 | 77 | 69 | 10 | 2 | 7 | 12 | 56 | 0 | 109 | 7 | 1 | 11 | 6 | .647 | 0 | 0-- | - | 5.01 | 4.08 |
| 2011 | Brham | AA | 42 | 0 | 0 | 26 | 63.1 | 272 | 58 | 27 | 23 | 3 | 0 | 4 | 2 | 27 | 1 | 67 | 8 | 0 | 2 | 3 | .400 | 0 | 12-- | - | 3.43 | 3.27 |
| 2012 | CWS | AL | 65 | 0 | 0 | 11 | 71.2 | 301 | 67 | 19 | 19 | 4 | 2 | 4 | 1 | 32 | 3 | 65 | 5 | 0 | 8 | 0 | 1.000 | 0 | 0-3 | 7 | 3.67 | 2.39 |
| 2013 | CWS | AL | 70 | 0 | 0 | 17 | 78.0 | 315 | 69 | 40 | 36 | 5 | 3 | 6 | 1 | 26 | 1 | 89 | 8 | 1 | 4 | 5 | .444 | 0 | 0-4 | 16 | 3.09 | 4.15 |
| 2 ML YEARS | | | 135 | 0 | 0 | 28 | 149.2 | 616 | 136 | 59 | 55 | 9 | 5 | 10 | 2 | 58 | 4 | 154 | 13 | 1 | 12 | 5 | .706 | 0 | 0-7 | 23 | 3.37 | 3.31 |

# Taylor Jordan

**Pitches:** R **Bats:** R **Pos:** SP-9 **Ht:** 6'3" **Wt:** 190 **Born:** 1/17/1989 **Age:** 25

| | | | HOW MUCH HE PITCHED | | | | | | WHAT HE GAVE UP | | | | | | | | | | | | THE RESULTS | | | | | | | |
|---|---|---|---|---|---|---|---|---|---|---|---|---|---|---|---|---|---|---|---|---|---|---|---|---|---|---|---|---|
| Year | Team | Lg | G | GS | CG | GF | IP | BFP | H | R | ER | HR | SH | SF | HB | TBB | IBB | SO | WP | Bk | W | L | Pct | Sh | Sv-Op | Hld | ERC | ERA |
| 2009 | Nats | R | 10 | 6 | 0 | 1 | 34.2 | 141 | 25 | 18 | 14 | 4 | 0 | 0 | 3 | 9 | 0 | 33 | 1 | 0 | 2 | 0 | 1.000 | 0 | 0-- | - | 2.47 | 3.63 |
| 2010 | Hgrstn | A | 1 | 0 | 0 | 0 | 3.1 | 18 | 4 | 5 | 5 | 0 | 0 | 1 | 1 | 3 | 0 | 5 | 0 | 0 | 0 | 1 | .000 | 0 | 0-- | - | 7.49 | 13.50 |
| 2010 | Vrmnt | A- | 13 | 13 | 0 | 0 | 62.0 | 275 | 73 | 40 | 34 | 6 | 4 | 2 | 5 | 17 | 0 | 54 | 3 | 1 | 2 | 3 | .400 | 0 | 0-- | - | 4.88 | 4.94 |
| 2011 | Hgrstn | A | 18 | 17 | 1 | 0 | 94.1 | 399 | 90 | 38 | 26 | 1 | 1 | 5 | 6 | 23 | 0 | 63 | 4 | 0 | 9 | 4 | .692 | 1 | 0-- | - | 2.83 | 2.48 |
| 2012 | Auburn | A- | 6 | 6 | 0 | 0 | 14.1 | 70 | 19 | 15 | 13 | 0 | 1 | 0 | 4 | 2 | 0 | 17 | 0 | 0 | 0 | 3 | .000 | 0 | 0-- | - | 4.95 | 8.16 |
| 2012 | Hgrstn | A | 9 | 9 | 0 | 0 | 40.0 | 178 | 52 | 22 | 18 | 2 | 0 | 0 | 6 | 9 | 0 | 28 | 0 | 3 | 3 | 4 | .429 | 0 | 0-- | - | 5.48 | 4.05 |
| 2013 | Ptomc | A+ | 6 | 6 | 0 | 0 | 36.1 | 143 | 31 | 9 | 5 | 1 | 1 | 0 | 0 | 6 | 0 | 29 | 1 | 0 | 2 | 1 | .667 | 0 | 0-- | - | 2.03 | 1.24 |
| 2013 | Hrsbrg | AA | 9 | 8 | 2 | 0 | 54.0 | 209 | 37 | 6 | 5 | 0 | 3 | 1 | 5 | 9 | 0 | 43 | 0 | 0 | 7 | 0 | 1.000 | 2 | 0-- | - | 1.50 | 0.83 |
| 2013 | Was | NL | 9 | 9 | 0 | 0 | 51.2 | 220 | 59 | 27 | 21 | 3 | 2 | 1 | 3 | 11 | 0 | 29 | 1 | 0 | 1 | 3 | .250 | 0 | 0-0 | 0 | 4.13 | 3.66 |

# Corban Joseph

**Bats:** L **Throws:** R **Pos:** 1B-1;2B-1 **Ht:** 6'0" **Wt:** 180 **Born:** 10/28/1988 **Age:** 25

| | | | BATTING | | | | | | | | | | | | | | | | | | BASERUNNING | | | | AVERAGES | | |
|---|---|---|---|---|---|---|---|---|---|---|---|---|---|---|---|---|---|---|---|---|---|---|---|---|---|---|---|
| Year | Team | Lg | G | AB | H | 2B | 3B | HR | (Hm | Rd) | TB | R | RBI | RC | TBB | IBB | SO | HBP | SH | SF | SB | CS | SB% | GDP | Avg | OBP | Slg |
| 2009 | CtnSC | A | 100 | 380 | 114 | 17 | 8 | 4 | (- | -) | 159 | 39 | 57 | 64 | 49 | 1 | 61 | 3 | 0 | 4 | 8 | 5 | .62 | 5 | .300 | .381 | .418 |
| 2010 | Tampa | A+ | 98 | 381 | 115 | 27 | 3 | 6 | (- | -) | 166 | 52 | 52 | 64 | 43 | 5 | 74 | 7 | 1 | 5 | 5 | 8 | .38 | 6 | .302 | .378 | .436 |
| 2010 | Trntn | AA | 31 | 111 | 24 | 6 | 4 | 0 | (- | -) | 38 | 11 | 13 | 12 | 15 | 0 | 33 | 0 | 2 | 2 | 1 | 0 | 1.00 | 0 | .216 | .305 | .342 |
| 2011 | Trntn | AA | 131 | 499 | 138 | 38 | 8 | 5 | (- | -) | 207 | 75 | 58 | 76 | 59 | 0 | 105 | 1 | 3 | 2 | 4 | 3 | .57 | 11 | .277 | .353 | .415 |
| 2012 | S-WB | AAA | 84 | 327 | 87 | 25 | 2 | 13 | (- | -) | 155 | 50 | 56 | 59 | 53 | 1 | 57 | 0 | 3 | 3 | 0 | 1 | .00 | 7 | .266 | .366 | .474 |
| 2012 | Trntn | AA | 23 | 86 | 27 | 4 | 0 | 2 | (- | -) | 37 | 9 | 6 | 16 | 15 | 0 | 13 | 0 | 0 | 1 | 0 | 0 | - | 0 | .314 | .412 | .430 |
| 2013 | S-WB | AAA | 47 | 188 | 45 | 9 | 0 | 6 | (- | -) | 72 | 30 | 19 | 25 | 21 | 1 | 39 | 4 | 0 | 0 | 2 | 0 | 1.00 | 4 | .239 | .329 | .383 |
| 2013 | NYY | AL | 2 | 6 | 1 | 1 | 0 | 0 | (0 | 0) | 2 | 1 | 0 | 1 | 1 | 0 | 1 | 0 | 0 | 0 | 0 | 0 | - | 0 | .167 | .286 | .333 |

# Donnie Joseph

**Pitches:** L **Bats:** L **Pos:** RP-6 **Ht:** 6'3" **Wt:** 190 **Born:** 11/1/1987 **Age:** 26

| | | | HOW MUCH HE PITCHED | | | | | | WHAT HE GAVE UP | | | | | | | | | | | | THE RESULTS | | | | | | | |
|---|---|---|---|---|---|---|---|---|---|---|---|---|---|---|---|---|---|---|---|---|---|---|---|---|---|---|---|---|
| Year | Team | Lg | G | GS | CG | GF | IP | BFP | H | R | ER | HR | SH | SF | HB | TBB | IBB | SO | WP | Bk | W | L | Pct | Sh | Sv-Op | Hld | ERC | ERA |
| 2009 | Billings | R+ | 8 | 0 | 0 | 2 | 11.2 | 48 | 6 | 6 | 1 | 0 | 2 | 1 | 0 | 4 | 0 | 11 | 4 | 0 | 2 | 1 | .667 | 0 | 0-- | - | 1.08 | 0.77 |
| 2009 | Dayton | A | 16 | 0 | 0 | 13 | 20.2 | 87 | 13 | 10 | 10 | 0 | 1 | 1 | 1 | 10 | 0 | 31 | 2 | 0 | 2 | 2 | .500 | 0 | 4-- | - | 1.92 | 4.35 |
| 2010 | Dayton | A | 19 | 0 | 0 | 16 | 23.0 | 88 | 13 | 3 | 2 | 0 | 0 | 0 | 0 | 7 | 0 | 40 | 3 | 0 | 2 | 1 | .667 | 0 | 6-- | - | 1.23 | 0.78 |
| 2010 | Lynbrg | A+ | 31 | 0 | 0 | 27 | 35.0 | 146 | 23 | 11 | 9 | 2 | 1 | 1 | 1 | 16 | 1 | 56 | 2 | 0 | 0 | 4 | .000 | 0 | 17-- | - | 2.23 | 2.31 |
| 2010 | Carlina | AA | 7 | 0 | 0 | 4 | 7.0 | 30 | 7 | 6 | 4 | 0 | 0 | 0 | 0 | 2 | 0 | 7 | 0 | 1 | 1 | 0 | 1.000 | 0 | 1-- | - | 2.89 | 5.14 |
| 2011 | Carlina | AA | 57 | 0 | 0 | 32 | 58.1 | 272 | 67 | 45 | 45 | 8 | 2 | 1 | 5 | 30 | 3 | 66 | 4 | 0 | 1 | 3 | .250 | 0 | 8-- | - | 5.94 | 6.94 |
| 2012 | Pnscla | AA | 26 | 0 | 0 | 20 | 30.1 | 112 | 13 | 4 | 3 | 1 | 1 | 1 | 1 | 8 | 2 | 46 | 2 | 0 | 4 | 2 | .667 | 0 | 13-- | - | 0.91 | 0.89 |
| 2012 | Lsvlle | AAA | 18 | 0 | 0 | 10 | 22.0 | 95 | 22 | 8 | 7 | 0 | 0 | 1 | 0 | 9 | 1 | 22 | 0 | 0 | 4 | 1 | .800 | 0 | 5-- | - | 3.32 | 2.86 |
| 2012 | Omha | AAA | 11 | 0 | 0 | 7 | 17.1 | 86 | 21 | 9 | 8 | 1 | 2 | 0 | 0 | 13 | 2 | 19 | 5 | 0 | 1 | 0 | 1.000 | 0 | 2-- | - | 6.02 | 4.15 |
| 2013 | Omha | AAA | 47 | 0 | 0 | 21 | 54.2 | 241 | 39 | 25 | 24 | 5 | 2 | 0 | 3 | 40 | 1 | 84 | 6 | 0 | 4 | 3 | .571 | 0 | 6-- | - | 3.88 | 3.95 |
| 2013 | KC | AL | 6 | 0 | 0 | 2 | 5.2 | 25 | 4 | 0 | 0 | 0 | 1 | 0 | 0 | 4 | 0 | 7 | 0 | 0 | 0 | 0 | - | 0 | 0-0 | 0 | 2.85 | 0.00 |

# Matt Joyce

**Bats:** L **Throws:** R **Pos:** LF-58;RF-58;PH-31;DH-20 **Ht:** 6'2" **Wt:** 205 **Born:** 8/3/1984 **Age:** 29

| | | | BATTING | | | | | | | | | | | | | | | | | | BASERUNNING | | | | AVERAGES | | |
|---|---|---|---|---|---|---|---|---|---|---|---|---|---|---|---|---|---|---|---|---|---|---|---|---|---|---|---|
| Year | Team | Lg | G | AB | H | 2B | 3B | HR | (Hm | Rd) | TB | R | RBI | RC | TBB | IBB | SO | HBP | SH | SF | SB | CS | SB% | GDP | Avg | OBP | Slg |
| 2008 | Det | AL | 92 | 242 | 61 | 16 | 3 | 12 | (6 | 6) | 119 | 40 | 33 | 36 | 31 | 0 | 65 | 2 | 0 | 2 | 0 | 2 | .00 | 3 | .252 | .339 | .492 |
| 2009 | TB | AL | 11 | 32 | 6 | 1 | 0 | 3 | (2 | 1) | 16 | 3 | 7 | 5 | 3 | 0 | 7 | 1 | 0 | 1 | 1 | 0 | 1.00 | 0 | .188 | .270 | .500 |
| 2010 | TB | AL | 77 | 216 | 52 | 15 | 3 | 10 | (4 | 6) | 103 | 30 | 40 | 41 | 40 | 2 | 55 | 2 | 0 | 3 | 2 | 2 | .50 | 2 | .241 | .360 | .477 |
| 2011 | TB | AL | 141 | 462 | 128 | 32 | 2 | 19 | (11 | 8) | 221 | 69 | 75 | 77 | 49 | 9 | 106 | 4 | 0 | 7 | 13 | 1 | .93 | 7 | .277 | .347 | .478 |
| 2012 | TB | AL | 124 | 399 | 96 | 18 | 3 | 17 | (4 | 13) | 171 | 55 | 59 | 59 | 55 | 4 | 102 | 6 | 1 | 1 | 4 | 3 | .57 | 10 | .241 | .341 | .429 |
| 2013 | TB | AL | 140 | 413 | 97 | 22 | 0 | 18 | (8 | 10) | 173 | 61 | 47 | 51 | 59 | 0 | 87 | 2 | 0 | 7 | 7 | 3 | .70 | 8 | .235 | .328 | .419 |
| Postseason | | | 8 | 24 | 5 | 1 | 0 | 1 | (0 | 1) | 9 | 1 | 4 | 3 | 1 | 0 | 9 | 0 | 0 | 0 | 1 | 0 | 1.00 | 0 | .208 | .240 | .375 |
| 6 ML YEARS | | | 585 | 1764 | 440 | 104 | 11 | 79 | (35 | 44) | 803 | 258 | 261 | 269 | 237 | 15 | 422 | 17 | 1 | 21 | 27 | 11 | .71 | 30 | .249 | .340 | .455 |

# Jair Jurrjens

**Pitches:** R **Bats:** R **Pos:** SP-1; RP-1 jye-AIR JURR-jens **Ht:** 6'1" **Wt:** 200 **Born:** 1/29/1986 **Age:** 28

| | | | HOW MUCH HE PITCHED | | | | | | WHAT HE GAVE UP | | | | | | | | | | | | THE RESULTS | | | | | | | |
|---|---|---|---|---|---|---|---|---|---|---|---|---|---|---|---|---|---|---|---|---|---|---|---|---|---|---|---|---|
| Year | Team | Lg | G | GS | CG | GF | IP | BFP | H | R | ER | HR | SH | SF | HB | TBB | IBB | SO | WP | Bk | W | L | Pct | Sh | Sv-Op | Hld | ERC | ERA |
| 2013 | Norfolk* | AAA | 16 | 16 | 1 | 0 | 94.2 | 405 | 102 | 48 | 44 | 5 | 4 | 10 | 3 | 24 | 0 | 52 | 2 | 0 | 6 | 6 | .500 | 0 | 0-- | - | 3.72 | 4.18 |
| 2013 | Toledo* | AAA | 7 | 7 | 0 | 0 | 39.1 | 171 | 45 | 24 | 24 | 3 | 2 | 2 | 1 | 14 | 0 | 24 | 1 | 0 | 1 | 4 | .200 | 0 | 0-- | - | 4.74 | 5.49 |
| 2007 | Det | AL | 7 | 7 | 0 | 0 | 30.2 | 122 | 24 | 16 | 16 | 4 | 0 | 1 | 1 | 11 | 0 | 13 | 2 | 0 | 3 | 1 | .750 | 0 | 0-0 | 0 | 3.19 | 4.70 |
| 2008 | Atl | NL | 31 | 31 | 0 | 0 | 188.1 | 813 | 188 | 87 | 77 | 11 | 12 | 5 | 4 | 70 | 9 | 139 | 3 | 0 | 13 | 10 | .565 | 0 | 0-0 | 0 | 3.65 | 3.68 |

| | | | HOW MUCH HE PITCHED | | | | | | WHAT HE GAVE UP | | | | | | | | | | | | THE RESULTS | | | | | | | | |
|---|---|---|---|---|---|---|---|---|---|---|---|---|---|---|---|---|---|---|---|---|---|---|---|---|---|---|---|---|
| Year | Team | Lg | G | GS | CG | GF | IP | BFP | H | R | ER | HR | SH | SF | HB | TBB | IBB | SO | WP | Bk | W | L | Pct | Sh | Sv-Op | Hld | ERC | ERA |
| 2009 | Atl | NL | 34 | **34** | 0 | 0 | 215.0 | 884 | 186 | 71 | 62 | 15 | 16 | 4 | 3 | 75 | 1 | 152 | 3 | 2 | 14 | 10 | .583 | 0 | 0-0 | 0 | 3.03 | 2.60 |
| 2010 | Atl | NL | 20 | 20 | 0 | 0 | 116.1 | 500 | 120 | 63 | 60 | 13 | 7 | 4 | 2 | 42 | 5 | 86 | 2 | 0 | 7 | 6 | .538 | 0 | 0-0 | 0 | 4.20 | 4.64 |
| 2011 | Atl | NL | 23 | 23 | 2 | 0 | 152.0 | 627 | 142 | 52 | 50 | 14 | 6 | 3 | 4 | 44 | 5 | 90 | 4 | 2 | 13 | 6 | .684 | 1 | 0-0 | 0 | 3.33 | 2.96 |
| 2012 | Atl | NL | 11 | 10 | 0 | 1 | 48.1 | 227 | 72 | 40 | 37 | 8 | 2 | 0 | 1 | 18 | 0 | 19 | 1 | 0 | 3 | 4 | .429 | 0 | 0-0 | 0 | 7.70 | 6.89 |
| 2013 | Bal | AL | 2 | 1 | 0 | 0 | 7.1 | 31 | 9 | 4 | 4 | 1 | 0 | 0 | 0 | 1 | 0 | 6 | 1 | 0 | 0 | 0 | - | 0 | 0-0 | 0 | 4.61 | 4.91 |
| 7 ML YEARS | | | 128 | 126 | 2 | 1 | 758.0 | 3204 | 741 | 333 | 306 | 66 | 43 | 17 | 15 | 261 | 20 | 505 | 16 | 4 | 53 | 37 | .589 | 1 | 0-0 | 0 | 3.71 | 3.63 |

## Ryan Kalish

**Bats:** L **Throws:** L **Pos:** OF

KAY-lish

**Ht:** 6'0" **Wt:** 215 **Born:** 3/28/1988 **Age:** 26

| | | | BATTING | | | | | | | | | | | | | | | | | | | BASERUNNING | | | | AVERAGES | | |
|---|---|---|---|---|---|---|---|---|---|---|---|---|---|---|---|---|---|---|---|---|---|---|---|---|---|---|---|---|
| Year | Team | Lg | G | AB | H | 2B | 3B | HR | (Hm | Rd) | TB | R | RBI | RC | TBB | IBB | SO | HBP | SH | SF | SB | CS | SB% | GDP | Avg | OBP | Slg |
| 2009 | Salem | A+ | 32 | 115 | 35 | 5 | 2 | 5 | (- | -) | 59 | 21 | 21 | 27 | 26 | 1 | 20 | 1 | 0 | 1 | 7 | 3 | .70 | 2 | .304 | .434 | .513 |
| 2009 | Portlnd | AA | 103 | 391 | 106 | 19 | 4 | 13 | (- | -) | 172 | 63 | 56 | 62 | 42 | 0 | 87 | 1 | 0 | 3 | 14 | 3 | .82 | 9 | .271 | .341 | .440 |
| 2010 | Portlnd | AA | 41 | 150 | 44 | 9 | 1 | 8 | (- | -) | 79 | 35 | 29 | 35 | 28 | 2 | 21 | 2 | 0 | 3 | 13 | 1 | .93 | 1 | .293 | .404 | .527 |
| 2010 | Pwtckt | AAA | 37 | 143 | 42 | 9 | 1 | 5 | (- | -) | 68 | 22 | 18 | 26 | 14 | 0 | 32 | 1 | 0 | 2 | 12 | 2 | .86 | 3 | .294 | .356 | .476 |
| 2011 | Pwtckt | AAA | 22 | 86 | 18 | 6 | 0 | 0 | (- | -) | 24 | 9 | 9 | 6 | 8 | 0 | 20 | 0 | 0 | 2 | 4 | 3 | .57 | 4 | .209 | .271 | .279 |
| 2011 | Lowell | A- | 2 | 6 | 3 | 0 | 0 | 0 | (- | -) | 3 | 2 | 2 | 1 | 1 | 0 | 1 | 0 | 0 | 0 | 0 | 0 | - | 0 | .500 | .571 | .500 |
| 2012 | Salem | A+ | 3 | 12 | 4 | 0 | 0 | 1 | (- | -) | 7 | 3 | 1 | 2 | 0 | 0 | 3 | 0 | 0 | 0 | 1 | 1 | .50 | 0 | .333 | .333 | .583 |
| 2012 | Portlnd | AA | 3 | 9 | 2 | 1 | 0 | 0 | (- | -) | 3 | 0 | 0 | 1 | 4 | 0 | 1 | 0 | 0 | 0 | 0 | 0 | - | 0 | .222 | .462 | .333 |
| 2012 | Pwtckt | AAA | 27 | 111 | 29 | 5 | 0 | 4 | (- | -) | 46 | 18 | 14 | 16 | 13 | 0 | 30 | 0 | 1 | 1 | 7 | 2 | .78 | 3 | .261 | .336 | .414 |
| 2010 | Bos | AL | 53 | 163 | 41 | 11 | 1 | 4 | (2 | 2) | 66 | 26 | 24 | 23 | 12 | 0 | 38 | 1 | 2 | 1 | 10 | 1 | .91 | 5 | .252 | .305 | .405 |
| 2012 | Bos | AL | 36 | 96 | 22 | 3 | 0 | 0 | (0 | 0) | 25 | 12 | 5 | 3 | 6 | 0 | 26 | 0 | 0 | 1 | 3 | 2 | .60 | 4 | .229 | .272 | .260 |
| 2 ML YEARS | | | 89 | 259 | 63 | 14 | 1 | 4 | (2 | 2) | 91 | 38 | 29 | 26 | 18 | 0 | 64 | 1 | 2 | 2 | 13 | 3 | .81 | 9 | .243 | .293 | .351 |

## Nate Karns

**Pitches:** R **Bats:** R **Pos:** SP-3

**Ht:** 6'3" **Wt:** 230 **Born:** 11/25/1987 **Age:** 26

| | | | HOW MUCH HE PITCHED | | | | | | WHAT HE GAVE UP | | | | | | | | | | | | THE RESULTS | | | | | | | | |
|---|---|---|---|---|---|---|---|---|---|---|---|---|---|---|---|---|---|---|---|---|---|---|---|---|---|---|---|---|
| Year | Team | Lg | G | GS | CG | GF | IP | BFP | H | R | ER | HR | SH | SF | HB | TBB | IBB | SO | WP | Bk | W | L | Pct | Sh | Sv-Op | Hld | ERC | ERA |
| 2011 | Nats | R | 5 | 5 | 0 | 0 | 18.2 | 65 | 2 | 0 | 0 | 0 | 0 | 0 | 2 | 6 | 0 | 26 | 3 | 0 | 0 | 0 | - | 0 | 0-- | - | 0.37 | 0.00 |
| 2011 | Auburn | A- | 8 | 8 | 0 | 0 | 36.2 | 159 | 27 | 14 | 14 | 1 | 0 | 0 | 4 | 27 | 0 | 33 | 7 | 0 | 3 | 2 | .600 | 0 | 0-- | - | 3.91 | 3.44 |
| 2012 | Hgrstn | A | 11 | 5 | 1 | 5 | 44.1 | 179 | 23 | 11 | 10 | 1 | 0 | 0 | 3 | 21 | 0 | 61 | 5 | 0 | 3 | 0 | 1.000 | 0 | 2-- | - | 1.66 | 2.03 |
| 2012 | Ptomc | A+ | 13 | 13 | 1 | 0 | 71.2 | 278 | 47 | 23 | 18 | 1 | 0 | 0 | 4 | 26 | 0 | 87 | 4 | 0 | 8 | 4 | .667 | 0 | 0-- | - | 1.94 | 2.26 |
| 2013 | Hrsbrg | AA | 23 | 23 | 3 | 0 | 132.2 | 553 | 109 | 54 | 48 | 14 | 7 | 5 | 7 | 48 | 1 | 155 | 13 | 1 | 10 | 6 | .625 | 0 | 0-- | - | 3.19 | 3.26 |
| 2013 | Was | NL | 3 | 3 | 0 | 0 | 12.0 | 61 | 17 | 11 | 10 | 5 | 1 | 0 | 1 | 6 | 0 | 11 | 0 | 0 | 0 | 1 | .000 | 0 | 0-0 | 0 | 9.80 | 7.50 |

## Munenori Kawasaki

moo-neh-NO-ree kah-wah-SAH-kee

**Bats:** L **Throws:** R **Pos:** SS-60;2B-18;PH-12;DH-8;PR-4

**Ht:** 5'10" **Wt:** 165 **Born:** 6/3/1981 **Age:** 33

| | | | BATTING | | | | | | | | | | | | | | | | | | | BASERUNNING | | | | AVERAGES | | |
|---|---|---|---|---|---|---|---|---|---|---|---|---|---|---|---|---|---|---|---|---|---|---|---|---|---|---|---|---|
| Year | Team | Lg | G | AB | H | 2B | 3B | HR | (Hm | Rd) | TB | R | RBI | RC | TBB | IBB | SO | HBP | SH | SF | SB | CS | SB% | GDP | Avg | OBP | Slg |
| 2009 | Fkuoka | Jap | 143 | 540 | 140 | 26 | 8 | 4 | (- | -) | 194 | 73 | 34 | 70 | 47 | 1 | 90 | 7 | 43 | 3 | 44 | 17 | .72 | 8 | .259 | .325 | .359 |
| 2010 | Fkuoka | Jap | 144 | 602 | 190 | 27 | 5 | 4 | (- | -) | 239 | 74 | 53 | 93 | 43 | 1 | 86 | 7 | 10 | 0 | 30 | 11 | .73 | 6 | .316 | .368 | .397 |
| 2011 | Fkuoka | Jap | 144 | 603 | 161 | 19 | 7 | 1 | (- | -) | 197 | 71 | 37 | 66 | 36 | 0 | 84 | 3 | 9 | 4 | 31 | 10 | .76 | 5 | .267 | .310 | .327 |
| 2013 | Buffalo | AAA | 25 | 60 | 15 | 0 | 0 | 0 | (- | -) | 15 | 9 | 3 | 9 | 14 | 0 | 12 | 1 | 6 | 0 | 3 | 0 | 1.00 | 2 | .250 | .400 | .250 |
| 2012 | Sea | AL | 61 | 104 | 20 | 1 | 0 | 0 | (0 | 0) | 21 | 13 | 7 | 7 | 8 | 0 | 18 | 1 | 2 | 0 | 2 | 2 | .50 | 2 | .192 | .257 | .202 |
| 2013 | Tor | AL | 96 | 240 | 55 | 6 | 5 | 1 | (1 | 0) | 74 | 27 | 24 | 28 | 32 | 0 | 41 | 4 | 10 | 3 | 7 | 1 | .88 | 5 | .229 | .326 | .308 |
| 2 ML YEARS | | | 157 | 344 | 75 | 7 | 5 | 1 | (1 | 0) | 95 | 40 | 31 | 35 | 40 | 0 | 59 | 5 | 12 | 3 | 9 | 3 | .75 | 7 | .218 | .306 | .276 |

## Scott Kazmir

**Pitches:** L **Bats:** L **Pos:** SP-29

KAZ-meer

**Ht:** 6'0" **Wt:** 185 **Born:** 1/24/1984 **Age:** 30

| | | | HOW MUCH HE PITCHED | | | | | | WHAT HE GAVE UP | | | | | | | | | | | | THE RESULTS | | | | | | | | |
|---|---|---|---|---|---|---|---|---|---|---|---|---|---|---|---|---|---|---|---|---|---|---|---|---|---|---|---|---|
| Year | Team | Lg | G | GS | CG | GF | IP | BFP | H | R | ER | HR | SH | SF | HB | TBB | IBB | SO | WP | Bk | W | L | Pct | Sh | Sv-Op | Hld | ERC | ERA |
| 2013 | Clmbs* | AAA | 1 | 1 | 0 | 0 | 5.0 | 18 | 5 | 1 | 0 | 0 | 0 | 0 | 0 | 0 | 0 | 5 | 0 | 0 | 1 | 0 | 1.000 | 0 | 0-- | - | 2.23 | 0.00 |
| 2004 | TB | AL | 8 | 7 | 0 | 0 | 33.1 | 152 | 33 | 22 | 21 | 4 | 0 | 0 | 2 | 21 | 0 | 41 | 3 | 0 | 2 | 3 | .400 | 0 | 0-0 | 0 | 5.36 | 5.67 |
| 2005 | TB | AL | 32 | 32 | 0 | 0 | 186.0 | 818 | 172 | 90 | 78 | 12 | 6 | 9 | 10 | **100** | 3 | 174 | 7 | 1 | 10 | 9 | .526 | 0 | 0-0 | 0 | 4.13 | 3.77 |
| 2006 | TB | AL | 24 | 24 | 1 | 0 | 144.2 | 610 | 132 | 59 | 52 | 15 | 0 | 5 | 2 | 52 | 3 | 163 | 6 | 0 | 10 | 8 | .556 | 1 | 0-0 | 0 | 3.47 | 3.24 |
| 2007 | TB | AL | 34 | **34** | 0 | 0 | 206.2 | 887 | 196 | 91 | 80 | 18 | 6 | 3 | 7 | 89 | 1 | **239** | 10 | 0 | 13 | 9 | .591 | 0 | 0-0 | 0 | 3.97 | 3.48 |
| 2008 | TB | AL | 27 | 27 | 0 | 0 | 152.1 | 641 | 123 | 61 | 59 | 23 | 4 | 5 | 4 | 70 | 2 | 166 | 5 | 0 | 12 | 8 | .600 | 0 | 0-0 | 0 | 3.69 | 3.49 |
| 2009 | 2 Tms | AL | 26 | 26 | 0 | 0 | 147.1 | 647 | 149 | 85 | 80 | 16 | 1 | 4 | 6 | 60 | 0 | 117 | 13 | 0 | 10 | 9 | .526 | 0 | 0-0 | 0 | 4.36 | 4.89 |
| 2010 | LAA | AL | 28 | 28 | 0 | 0 | 150.0 | 682 | 158 | 103 | 99 | 25 | 3 | 6 | 12 | 79 | 2 | 93 | 6 | 0 | 9 | 15 | .375 | 0 | 0-0 | 0 | 5.74 | 5.94 |
| 2011 | LAA | AL | 1 | 1 | 0 | 0 | 1.2 | 14 | 5 | 5 | 5 | 1 | 0 | 0 | 2 | 2 | 0 | 0 | 0 | 1 | 0 | 0 | - | 0 | 0-0 | 0 | 35.08 | 27.00 |
| 2013 | Cle | AL | 29 | 29 | 0 | 0 | 158.0 | 672 | 162 | 76 | 71 | 19 | 2 | 1 | 3 | 47 | 1 | 162 | 5 | 1 | 10 | 9 | .526 | 0 | 0-0 | 0 | 4.02 | 4.04 |
| 09 | TB | AL | 20 | 20 | 0 | 0 | 111.0 | 504 | 121 | 77 | 73 | 15 | 1 | 4 | 5 | 50 | 0 | 91 | 10 | 0 | 8 | 7 | .533 | 0 | 0-0 | 0 | 5.18 | 5.92 |
| 09 | LAA | AL | 6 | 6 | 0 | 0 | 36.1 | 143 | 28 | 8 | 7 | 1 | 0 | 0 | 1 | 10 | 0 | 26 | 3 | 0 | 2 | 2 | .500 | 0 | 0-0 | 0 | 2.13 | 1.73 |
| Postseason | | | 8 | 7 | 0 | 0 | 36.1 | 176 | 37 | 22 | 21 | 5 | 3 | 2 | 3 | 26 | 0 | 26 | 2 | 0 | 1 | 2 | .333 | 0 | 0-0 | 0 | 5.92 | 5.20 |
| 9 ML YEARS | | | 209 | 208 | 1 | 0 | 1180.0 | 5123 | 1130 | 592 | 545 | 133 | 22 | 33 | 48 | 520 | 12 | 1155 | 55 | 3 | 76 | 70 | .521 | 1 | 0-0 | 0 | 4.24 | 4.16 |

## Austin Kearns

**Bats:** R **Throws:** R **Pos:** PH-15;RF-3;LF-1 KURNS **Ht:** 6'3" **Wt:** 240 **Born:** 5/20/1980 **Age:** 34

| BATTING | | | | | | | | | | | | | | | | | | | | | BASERUNNING | | | | AVERAGES | | |
|---|---|---|---|---|---|---|---|---|---|---|---|---|---|---|---|---|---|---|---|---|---|---|---|---|---|---|---|
| Year Team | Lg | G | AB | H | 2B | 3B | HR | (Hm | Rd) | TB | R | RBI | RC | TBB | IBB | SO | HBP | SH | SF | SB | CS | SB% | GDP | Avg | OBP | Slg | |
| 2002 Cin | NL | 107 | 372 | 117 | 24 | 3 | 13 | (7 | 6) | 186 | 66 | 56 | 70 | 54 | 3 | 81 | 6 | 0 | 3 | 6 | 3 | .67 | 11 | .315 | .407 | .500 | |
| 2003 Cin | NL | 82 | 292 | 77 | 11 | 0 | 15 | (8 | 7) | 133 | 39 | 58 | 52 | 41 | 1 | 68 | 5 | 0 | 0 | 5 | 2 | .71 | 7 | .264 | .364 | .455 | |
| 2004 Cin | NL | 64 | 217 | 50 | 10 | 2 | 9 | (3 | 6) | 91 | 28 | 32 | 26 | 28 | 0 | 71 | 1 | 0 | 0 | 2 | 1 | .67 | 8 | .230 | .321 | .419 | |
| 2005 Cin | NL | 112 | 387 | 93 | 26 | 1 | 18 | (9 | 9) | 175 | 62 | 67 | 55 | 48 | 2 | 107 | 8 | 0 | 5 | 0 | 0 | - | 8 | .240 | .333 | .452 | |
| 2006 2 Tms | NL | 150 | 537 | 142 | 33 | 2 | 24 | (12 | 12) | 251 | 86 | 86 | 81 | 76 | 4 | 135 | 10 | 1 | 5 | 9 | 4 | .69 | 18 | .264 | .363 | .467 | |
| 2007 Was | NL | 161 | 587 | 156 | 35 | 1 | 16 | (8 | 8) | 241 | 84 | 74 | 87 | 71 | 5 | 106 | 12 | 0 | 4 | 2 | 2 | .50 | 13 | .266 | .355 | .411 | |
| 2008 Was | NL | 86 | 313 | 68 | 10 | 0 | 7 | (1 | 6) | 99 | 40 | 32 | 28 | 35 | 0 | 63 | 8 | 0 | 1 | 2 | 2 | .50 | 11 | .217 | .311 | .316 | |
| 2009 Was | NL | 80 | 174 | 34 | 6 | 2 | 3 | (1 | 2) | 53 | 20 | 17 | 17 | 32 | 1 | 51 | 5 | 0 | 0 | 1 | 1 | .50 | 12 | .195 | .336 | .305 | |
| 2010 2 Tms | AL | 120 | 403 | 106 | 21 | 1 | 10 | (5 | 5) | 159 | 55 | 49 | 51 | 46 | 2 | 116 | 10 | 0 | 2 | 4 | 1 | .80 | 16 | .263 | .351 | .395 | |
| 2011 Cle | AL | 57 | 150 | 30 | 5 | 1 | 2 | (1 | 1) | 43 | 18 | 7 | 11 | 18 | 0 | 48 | 4 | 2 | 0 | 0 | 4 | .00 | 2 | .200 | .302 | .287 | |
| 2012 Mia | NL | 87 | 147 | 36 | 6 | 0 | 4 | (2 | 2) | 54 | 21 | 16 | 21 | 22 | 1 | 44 | 6 | 0 | 0 | 2 | 1 | .67 | 8 | .245 | .366 | .367 | |
| 2013 Mia | NL | 19 | 27 | 5 | 0 | 0 | 0 | (0 | 0) | 5 | 3 | 0 | 0 | 4 | 0 | 8 | 0 | 0 | 0 | 0 | 0 | - | 1 | .185 | .290 | .185 | |
| 06 Cin | NL | 87 | 325 | 89 | 21 | 1 | 16 | (8 | 8) | 160 | 53 | 50 | 46 | 35 | 2 | 85 | 5 | 0 | 3 | 7 | 1 | .88 | 14 | .274 | .351 | .492 | |
| 06 Was | NL | 63 | 212 | 53 | 12 | 1 | 8 | (4 | 4) | 91 | 33 | 36 | 35 | 41 | 2 | 50 | 5 | 1 | 2 | 2 | 3 | .40 | 4 | .250 | .381 | .429 | |
| 10 Cle | AL | 84 | 301 | 82 | 18 | 1 | 8 | (4 | 4) | 126 | 42 | 42 | 43 | 34 | 2 | 78 | 5 | 0 | 2 | 4 | 1 | .80 | 12 | .272 | .354 | .419 | |
| 10 NYY | AL | 36 | 102 | 24 | 3 | 0 | 2 | (1 | 1) | 33 | 13 | 7 | 8 | 12 | 0 | 38 | 5 | 0 | 0 | 0 | 0 | - | 4 | .235 | .345 | .324 | |
| 12 ML YEARS | | 1125 | 3606 | 914 | 187 | 13 | 121 | (57 | 64) | 1490 | 522 | 494 | 499 | 475 | 19 | 898 | 75 | 3 | 20 | 33 | 21 | .61 | 115 | .253 | .351 | .413 | |

## Shawn Kelley

**Pitches:** R **Bats:** R **Pos:** RP-57 **Ht:** 6'2" **Wt:** 220 **Born:** 4/26/1984 **Age:** 30

| HOW MUCH HE PITCHED | | | | | | | | WHAT HE GAVE UP | | | | | | | | | | | | THE RESULTS | | | | | | | |
|---|---|---|---|---|---|---|---|---|---|---|---|---|---|---|---|---|---|---|---|---|---|---|---|---|---|---|---|
| Year Team | Lg | G | GS | CG | GF | IP | BFP | H | R | ER | HR | SH | SF | HB | TBB | IBB | SO | WP | Bk | W | L | Pct | Sh | Sv-Op | Hld | ERC | ERA |
| 2009 Sea | AL | 41 | 0 | 0 | 12 | 46.0 | 191 | 45 | 23 | 23 | 9 | 2 | 2 | 3 | 9 | 1 | 41 | 2 | 1 | 5 | 4 | .556 | 0 | 0-4 | 9 | 4.02 | 4.50 |
| 2010 Sea | AL | 22 | 0 | 0 | 7 | 25.0 | 112 | 26 | 11 | 11 | 5 | 0 | 0 | 1 | 12 | 2 | 26 | 0 | 0 | 3 | 1 | .750 | 0 | 0-0 | 3 | 5.38 | 3.96 |
| 2011 Sea | AL | 10 | 0 | 0 | 2 | 12.2 | 47 | 7 | 0 | 0 | 0 | 0 | 0 | 0 | 3 | 1 | 10 | 0 | 0 | 0 | 0 | - | 0 | 0-0 | 1 | 1.01 | 0.00 |
| 2012 Sea | AL | 47 | 0 | 0 | 10 | 44.1 | 190 | 43 | 20 | 16 | 5 | 4 | 3 | 0 | 15 | 6 | 45 | 2 | 1 | 2 | 4 | .333 | 0 | 0-2 | 6 | 3.49 | 3.25 |
| 2013 NYY | AL | 57 | 0 | 0 | 13 | 53.1 | 227 | 47 | 28 | 26 | 8 | 0 | 2 | 0 | 23 | 2 | 71 | 8 | 0 | 4 | 2 | .667 | 0 | 0-1 | 11 | 3.80 | 4.39 |
| 5 ML YEARS | | 177 | 0 | 0 | 44 | 181.1 | 767 | 168 | 82 | 76 | 27 | 6 | 7 | 4 | 62 | 12 | 193 | 12 | 2 | 14 | 11 | .560 | 0 | 0-7 | 30 | 3.74 | 3.77 |

## Don Kelly

**Bats:** L **Throws:** R **Pos:** LF-38;CF-25;3B-22;RF-22;PH-16;PR-15;DH-6;1B-4;2B-3 **Ht:** 6'4" **Wt:** 190 **Born:** 2/15/1980 **Age:** 34

| BATTING | | | | | | | | | | | | | | | | | | | | | BASERUNNING | | | | AVERAGES | | |
|---|---|---|---|---|---|---|---|---|---|---|---|---|---|---|---|---|---|---|---|---|---|---|---|---|---|---|---|
| Year Team | Lg | G | AB | H | 2B | 3B | HR | (Hm | Rd) | TB | R | RBI | RC | TBB | IBB | SO | HBP | SH | SF | SB | CS | SB% | GDP | Avg | OBP | Slg | |
| 2007 Pit | NL | 25 | 27 | 4 | 0 | 0 | 0 | (0 | 0) | 4 | 2 | 0 | 1 | 3 | 0 | 3 | 2 | 0 | 0 | 0 | 0 | - | 1 | .148 | .281 | .148 | |
| 2009 Det | AL | 31 | 56 | 14 | 3 | 1 | 0 | (0 | 0) | 19 | 8 | 3 | 7 | 4 | 0 | 10 | 1 | 1 | 0 | 1 | 0 | 1.00 | 0 | .250 | .311 | .339 | |
| 2010 Det | AL | 119 | 238 | 58 | 4 | 0 | 9 | (4 | 5) | 89 | 30 | 27 | 26 | 8 | 0 | 42 | 2 | 1 | 2 | 3 | 0 | 1.00 | 1 | .244 | .272 | .374 | |
| 2011 Det | AL | 113 | 257 | 63 | 8 | 3 | 7 | (1 | 6) | 98 | 35 | 28 | 27 | 14 | 0 | 32 | 3 | 6 | 1 | 2 | 1 | .67 | 8 | .245 | .291 | .381 | |
| 2012 Det | AL | 75 | 113 | 21 | 2 | 1 | 1 | (1 | 0) | 28 | 14 | 7 | 6 | 14 | 0 | 22 | 0 | 0 | 0 | 2 | 0 | 1.00 | 2 | .186 | .276 | .248 | |
| 2013 Det | AL | 112 | 216 | 48 | 6 | 1 | 6 | (4 | 2) | 74 | 33 | 23 | 27 | 27 | 1 | 28 | 2 | 2 | 4 | 2 | 0 | 1.00 | 4 | .222 | .309 | .343 | |
| Postseason | | 13 | 21 | 6 | 1 | 0 | 1 | (0 | 1) | 10 | 5 | 3 | 1 | 0 | 0 | 5 | 0 | 0 | 1 | 0 | 0 | - | 0 | .286 | .273 | .476 | |
| 6 ML YEARS | | 475 | 907 | 208 | 23 | 6 | 23 | (10 | 13) | 312 | 122 | 88 | 94 | 70 | 1 | 137 | 10 | 10 | 7 | 10 | 1 | .91 | 16 | .229 | .290 | .344 | |

## Joe Kelly

**Pitches:** R **Bats:** R **Pos:** RP-22; SP-15 **Ht:** 6'1" **Wt:** 175 **Born:** 6/9/1988 **Age:** 26

| HOW MUCH HE PITCHED | | | | | | | | WHAT HE GAVE UP | | | | | | | | | | | | THE RESULTS | | | | | | | |
|---|---|---|---|---|---|---|---|---|---|---|---|---|---|---|---|---|---|---|---|---|---|---|---|---|---|---|---|
| Year Team | Lg | G | GS | CG | GF | IP | BFP | H | R | ER | HR | SH | SF | HB | TBB | IBB | SO | WP | Bk | W | L | Pct | Sh | Sv-Op | Hld | ERC | ERA |
| 2009 Batvia | A- | 16 | 2 | 0 | 6 | 30.1 | 138 | 33 | 23 | 16 | 0 | 2 | 1 | 3 | 11 | 0 | 30 | 3 | 0 | 2 | 3 | .400 | 0 | 1- - | - | 3.96 | 4.75 |
| 2010 QuadC | A | 26 | 18 | 0 | 3 | 103.1 | 444 | 103 | 66 | 53 | 3 | 2 | 2 | 7 | 45 | 0 | 92 | 12 | 2 | 6 | 8 | .429 | 0 | 1- - | - | 4.05 | 4.62 |
| 2011 PlmBh | A+ | 12 | 11 | 0 | 0 | 72.2 | 305 | 56 | 26 | 21 | 1 | 2 | 1 | 8 | 34 | 0 | 62 | 5 | 0 | 5 | 2 | .714 | 0 | 0- - | - | 2.96 | 2.60 |
| 2011 Sprgfld | AA | 11 | 11 | 0 | 0 | 59.1 | 264 | 70 | 40 | 33 | 7 | 3 | 2 | 5 | 25 | 2 | 51 | 2 | 1 | 6 | 4 | .600 | 0 | 0- - | - | 5.82 | 5.01 |
| 2012 Memp | AAA | 12 | 12 | 0 | 0 | 72.1 | 299 | 75 | 29 | 23 | 2 | 1 | 3 | 4 | 21 | 1 | 45 | 2 | 0 | 2 | 5 | .286 | 0 | 0- - | - | 3.69 | 2.86 |
| 2012 StL | NL | 24 | 16 | 0 | 4 | 107.0 | 457 | 112 | 50 | 42 | 10 | 4 | 1 | 3 | 36 | 2 | 75 | 4 | 0 | 5 | 7 | .417 | 0 | 0-0 | 0 | 4.17 | 3.53 |
| 2013 StL | NL | 37 | 15 | 0 | 8 | 124.0 | 532 | 124 | 42 | 37 | 10 | 2 | 2 | 5 | 44 | 4 | 79 | 3 | 0 | 10 | 5 | .667 | 0 | 0-1 | 2 | 3.88 | 2.69 |
| Postseason | | 7 | 0 | 0 | 1 | 7.2 | 34 | 6 | 2 | 2 | 0 | 0 | 0 | 0 | 4 | 0 | 5 | 0 | 0 | 0 | 0 | - | 0 | 0-0 | 0 | 2.53 | 2.35 |
| 2 ML YEARS | | 61 | 31 | 0 | 12 | 231.0 | 989 | 236 | 92 | 79 | 20 | 6 | 3 | 8 | 80 | 6 | 154 | 7 | 0 | 15 | 12 | .556 | 0 | 0-1 | 2 | 4.01 | 3.08 |

## Matt Kemp

**Bats:** R **Throws:** R **Pos:** CF-70;PH-4 **Ht:** 6'4" **Wt:** 215 **Born:** 9/23/1984 **Age:** 29

| BATTING | | | | | | | | | | | | | | | | | | | | | BASERUNNING | | | | AVERAGES | | |
|---|---|---|---|---|---|---|---|---|---|---|---|---|---|---|---|---|---|---|---|---|---|---|---|---|---|---|---|
| Year Team | Lg | G | AB | H | 2B | 3B | HR | (Hm | Rd) | TB | R | RBI | RC | TBB | IBB | SO | HBP | SH | SF | SB | CS | SB% | GDP | Avg | OBP | Slg | |
| 2013 Albq* | AAA | 3 | 11 | 2 | 2 | 0 | 0 | (- | -) | 4 | 3 | 0 | 1 | 1 | 0 | 6 | 0 | 0 | 0 | 1 | 0 | 1.00 | 0 | .182 | .250 | .364 | |
| 2013 RCuca* | A+ | 5 | 18 | 0 | 0 | 0 | 0 | (- | -) | 0 | 0 | 0 | 0 | 1 | 0 | 7 | 0 | 0 | 0 | 0 | 1 | .00 | 2 | .000 | .053 | .000 | |
| 2006 LAD | NL | 52 | 154 | 39 | 7 | 1 | 7 | (4 | 3) | 69 | 30 | 23 | 20 | 9 | 1 | 53 | 0 | 0 | 3 | 6 | 0 | 1.00 | 1 | .253 | .289 | .448 | |
| 2007 LAD | NL | 98 | 292 | 100 | 12 | 5 | 10 | (9 | 1) | 152 | 47 | 42 | 49 | 16 | 0 | 66 | 0 | 0 | 3 | 10 | 5 | .67 | 6 | .342 | .373 | .521 | |
| 2008 LAD | NL | 155 | 606 | 176 | 38 | 5 | 18 | (14 | 4) | 278 | 93 | 76 | 86 | 46 | 6 | 153 | 1 | 1 | 3 | 35 | 11 | .76 | 11 | .290 | .340 | .459 | |
| 2009 LAD | NL | 159 | 606 | 180 | 25 | 7 | 26 | (13 | 13) | 297 | 97 | 101 | 100 | 52 | 6 | 139 | 3 | 0 | 6 | 34 | 8 | .81 | 14 | .297 | .352 | .490 | |
| 2010 LAD | NL | **162** | 602 | 150 | 25 | 6 | 28 | (15 | 13) | 271 | 82 | 89 | 74 | 53 | 4 | 170 | 4 | 0 | 9 | 19 | 15 | .56 | 14 | .249 | .310 | .450 | |
| 2011 LAD | NL | 161 | 602 | 195 | 33 | 4 | **39** | (19 | 20) | **353** | **115** | **126** | 129 | 74 | 24 | 159 | 6 | 0 | 7 | 40 | 11 | .78 | 16 | .324 | .399 | .586 | |
| 2012 LAD | NL | 106 | 403 | 122 | 22 | 2 | 23 | (13 | 10) | 217 | 74 | 69 | 75 | 40 | 8 | 103 | 3 | 0 | 3 | 9 | 4 | .69 | 10 | .303 | .367 | .538 | |
| 2013 LAD | NL | 73 | 263 | 71 | 15 | 0 | 6 | (0 | 6) | 104 | 35 | 33 | 27 | 22 | 3 | 76 | 2 | 0 | 3 | 9 | 0 | 1.00 | 11 | .270 | .328 | .395 | |
| Postseason | | 16 | 62 | 14 | 3 | 0 | 2 | (1 | 1) | 23 | 5 | 5 | 1 | 5 | 0 | 25 | 0 | 0 | 0 | 0 | 2 | .00 | 2 | .226 | .284 | .371 | |
| 8 ML YEARS | | 966 | 3528 | 1033 | 177 | 30 | 157 | (87 | 70) | 1741 | 573 | 559 | 560 | 312 | 52 | 919 | 19 | 1 | 37 | 162 | 54 | .75 | 83 | .293 | .350 | .493 | |

## Howie Kendrick

**Bats:** R **Throws:** R **Pos:** 2B-118;DH-4;LF-1 **Ht:** 5'10" **Wt:** 205 **Born:** 7/12/1983 **Age:** 30

| BATTING | | | | | | | | | | | | | | | | | | | | | BASERUNNING | | | | AVERAGES | | |
|---|---|---|---|---|---|---|---|---|---|---|---|---|---|---|---|---|---|---|---|---|---|---|---|---|---|---|---|
| Year | Team | Lg | G | AB | H | 2B | 3B | HR | (Hm | Rd) | TB | R | RBI | RC | TBB | IBB | SO | HBP | SH | SF | SB | CS | SB% | GDP | Avg | OBP | Slg |
| 2006 | LAA | AL | 72 | 267 | 76 | 21 | 1 | 4 | (2 | 2) | 111 | 25 | 30 | 32 | 9 | 2 | 44 | 4 | 0 | 3 | 6 | 0 | 1.00 | 5 | .285 | .314 | .416 |
| 2007 | LAA | AL | 88 | 338 | 109 | 24 | 2 | 5 | (3 | 2) | 152 | 55 | 39 | 41 | 9 | 2 | 61 | 4 | 1 | 1 | 5 | 4 | .56 | 15 | .322 | .347 | .450 |
| 2008 | LAA | AL | 92 | 340 | 104 | 26 | 2 | 3 | (1 | 2) | 143 | 43 | 37 | 50 | 12 | 3 | 58 | 4 | 1 | 4 | 11 | 4 | .73 | 8 | .306 | .333 | .421 |
| 2009 | LAA | AL | 105 | 374 | 109 | 21 | 3 | 10 | (5 | 5) | 166 | 61 | 61 | 58 | 20 | 1 | 71 | 4 | 2 | 0 | 11 | 4 | .73 | 8 | .291 | .334 | .444 |
| 2010 | LAA | AL | 158 | 616 | 172 | 41 | 4 | 10 | (4 | 6) | 251 | 67 | 75 | 81 | 28 | 2 | 94 | 5 | 4 | 5 | 14 | 4 | .78 | 16 | .279 | .313 | .407 |
| 2011 | LAA | AL | 140 | 537 | 153 | 30 | 6 | 18 | (5 | 13) | 249 | 86 | 63 | 69 | 33 | 3 | 119 | 10 | 3 | 0 | 14 | 6 | .70 | 18 | .285 | .338 | .464 |
| 2012 | LAA | AL | 147 | 550 | 158 | 32 | 3 | 8 | (4 | 4) | 220 | 57 | 67 | 65 | 29 | 1 | 115 | 4 | 6 | 5 | 14 | 6 | .70 | 26 | .287 | .325 | .400 |
| 2013 | LAA | AL | 122 | 478 | 142 | 21 | 4 | 13 | (9 | 4) | 210 | 55 | 54 | 57 | 23 | 5 | 89 | 6 | 3 | 3 | 6 | 3 | .67 | 16 | .297 | .335 | .439 |
| Postseason | | | 13 | 46 | 9 | 0 | 1 | 1 | (1 | 0) | 14 | 4 | 2 | 3 | 1 | 0 | 11 | 0 | 2 | 1 | 3 | 0 | 1.00 | 1 | .196 | .208 | .304 |
| 8 ML YEARS | | | 924 | 3500 | 1023 | 216 | 25 | 71 | (33 | 38) | 1502 | 449 | 426 | 453 | 163 | 19 | 651 | 41 | 20 | 21 | 81 | 31 | .72 | 112 | .292 | .329 | .429 |

## Kyle Kendrick

**Pitches:** R **Bats:** R **Pos:** SP-30 **Ht:** 6'3" **Wt:** 210 **Born:** 8/26/1984 **Age:** 29

| HOW MUCH HE PITCHED | | | | | | | | | WHAT HE GAVE UP | | | | | | | | | | | | | THE RESULTS | | | | | | | | |
|---|---|---|---|---|---|---|---|---|---|---|---|---|---|---|---|---|---|---|---|---|---|---|---|---|---|---|---|---|---|---|
| Year | Team | Lg | G | GS | CG | GF | IP | BFP | H | R | ER | HR | SH | SF | HB | TBB | IBB | SO | WP | Bk | W | L | Pct | Sh | Sv-Op | Hld | ERC | ERA |
| 2007 | Phi | NL | 20 | 20 | 0 | 0 | 121.0 | 499 | 129 | 53 | 52 | 16 | 4 | 2 | 7 | 25 | 3 | 49 | 0 | 0 | 10 | 4 | .714 | 0 | 0-0 | 0 | 4.23 | 3.87 |
| 2008 | Phi | NL | 31 | 30 | 0 | 1 | 155.2 | 722 | 194 | 103 | 95 | 23 | 8 | 4 | **14** | 57 | 2 | 68 | 4 | 1 | 11 | 9 | .550 | 0 | 0-0 | 0 | 6.05 | 5.49 |
| 2009 | Phi | NL | 9 | 2 | 0 | 2 | 26.1 | 112 | 27 | 11 | 10 | 1 | 1 | 2 | 1 | 9 | 0 | 15 | 0 | 1 | 3 | 1 | .750 | 0 | 0-0 | 0 | 3.75 | 3.42 |
| 2010 | Phi | NL | 33 | 31 | 1 | 1 | 180.2 | 771 | 199 | 103 | 95 | 26 | 9 | 6 | 3 | 49 | 4 | 84 | 1 | 2 | 11 | 10 | .524 | 0 | 0-0 | 0 | 4.51 | 4.73 |
| 2011 | Phi | NL | 34 | 15 | 0 | 5 | 114.2 | 478 | 110 | 50 | 41 | 14 | 6 | 3 | 7 | 30 | 5 | 59 | 1 | 1 | 8 | 6 | .571 | 0 | 0-1 | 0 | 3.66 | 3.22 |
| 2012 | Phi | NL | 37 | 25 | 1 | 2 | 159.1 | 674 | 154 | 76 | 69 | 20 | 8 | 4 | 7 | 49 | 4 | 116 | 1 | 0 | 11 | 12 | .478 | 1 | 0-1 | 2 | 3.84 | 3.90 |
| 2013 | Phi | NL | 30 | 30 | 2 | 0 | 182.0 | 800 | 207 | 104 | 95 | 18 | 11 | 7 | 7 | 47 | 4 | 110 | 3 | 1 | 10 | 13 | .435 | 1 | 0-0 | 0 | 4.33 | 4.70 |
| Postseason | | | 1 | 1 | 0 | 0 | 3.2 | 18 | 5 | 5 | 5 | 2 | 0 | 0 | 0 | 2 | 1 | 2 | 0 | 0 | 0 | 1 | .000 | 0 | 0-0 | 0 | 9.97 | 12.27 |
| 7 ML YEARS | | | 194 | 153 | 4 | 11 | 939.2 | 4056 | 1020 | 500 | 457 | 118 | 47 | 28 | 46 | 266 | 22 | 501 | 10 | 6 | 64 | 55 | .538 | 2 | 0-2 | 2 | 4.44 | 4.38 |

## Ian Kennedy

**Pitches:** R **Bats:** R **Pos:** SP-31 **Ht:** 6'0" **Wt:** 190 **Born:** 12/19/1984 **Age:** 29

| HOW MUCH HE PITCHED | | | | | | | | | WHAT HE GAVE UP | | | | | | | | | | | | | THE RESULTS | | | | | | | | |
|---|---|---|---|---|---|---|---|---|---|---|---|---|---|---|---|---|---|---|---|---|---|---|---|---|---|---|---|---|---|---|
| Year | Team | Lg | G | GS | CG | GF | IP | BFP | H | R | ER | HR | SH | SF | HB | TBB | IBB | SO | WP | Bk | W | L | Pct | Sh | Sv-Op | Hld | ERC | ERA |
| 2007 | NYY | AL | 3 | 3 | 0 | 0 | 19.0 | 77 | 13 | 6 | 4 | 1 | 0 | 0 | 0 | 9 | 0 | 15 | 0 | 0 | 1 | 0 | 1.000 | 0 | 0-0 | 0 | 2.42 | 1.89 |
| 2008 | NYY | AL | 10 | 9 | 0 | 1 | 39.2 | 194 | 50 | 37 | 36 | 5 | 1 | 4 | 1 | 26 | 0 | 27 | 3 | 0 | 0 | 4 | .000 | 0 | 0-0 | 0 | 6.93 | 8.17 |
| 2009 | NYY | AL | 1 | 0 | 0 | 0 | 1.0 | 6 | 0 | 0 | 0 | 0 | 0 | 0 | 1 | 2 | 0 | 1 | 0 | 0 | 0 | 0 | - | 0 | 0-0 | 1 | 7.00 | 0.00 |
| 2010 | Ari | NL | 32 | 32 | 0 | 0 | 194.0 | 810 | 163 | 87 | 82 | 26 | 11 | 5 | 10 | 70 | 2 | 168 | **16** | 0 | 9 | 10 | .474 | 0 | 0-0 | 0 | 3.47 | 3.80 |
| 2011 | Ari | NL | 33 | 33 | 1 | 0 | 222.0 | 900 | 186 | 73 | 71 | 19 | 9 | 9 | 9 | 55 | 0 | 198 | 11 | 1 | **21** | 4 | **.840** | 1 | 0-0 | 0 | 2.71 | 2.88 |
| 2012 | Ari | NL | 33 | **33** | 1 | 0 | 208.1 | 899 | 216 | 101 | 93 | 28 | 13 | 5 | **14** | 55 | 4 | 187 | 5 | **4** | 15 | 12 | .556 | 0 | 0-0 | 0 | 4.18 | 4.02 |
| 2013 | 2 Tms | NL | 31 | 31 | 0 | 0 | 181.1 | 794 | 180 | 108 | 99 | 27 | 8 | 5 | 12 | 73 | 1 | 163 | 10 | 1 | 7 | 10 | .412 | 0 | 0-0 | 0 | 4.64 | 4.91 |
| 13 | Ari | NL | 21 | 21 | 0 | 0 | 124.0 | 549 | 128 | 79 | 72 | 18 | 8 | 5 | 10 | 48 | 1 | 108 | 9 | 0 | 3 | 8 | .273 | 0 | 0-0 | 0 | 4.82 | 5.23 |
| 13 | SD | NL | 10 | 10 | 0 | 0 | 57.1 | 245 | 52 | 29 | 27 | 9 | 0 | 0 | 2 | 25 | 0 | 55 | 1 | 1 | 4 | 2 | .667 | 0 | 0-0 | 0 | 4.26 | 4.24 |
| Postseason | | | 2 | 2 | 0 | 0 | 12.2 | 57 | 13 | 6 | 6 | 1 | 0 | 2 | 3 | 3 | 0 | 8 | 1 | 0 | 0 | 1 | .000 | 0 | 0-0 | 0 | 4.25 | 4.26 |
| 7 ML YEARS | | | 143 | 141 | 2 | 1 | 865.1 | 3680 | 808 | 412 | 385 | 106 | 42 | 28 | 47 | 290 | 7 | 759 | 45 | 6 | 53 | 40 | .570 | 1 | 0-0 | 1 | 3.80 | 4.00 |

## Logan Kensing

**Pitches:** R **Bats:** R **Pos:** RP-1 **Ht:** 6'1" **Wt:** 190 **Born:** 7/3/1982 **Age:** 31

| HOW MUCH HE PITCHED | | | | | | | | | WHAT HE GAVE UP | | | | | | | | | | | | | THE RESULTS | | | | | | | | |
|---|---|---|---|---|---|---|---|---|---|---|---|---|---|---|---|---|---|---|---|---|---|---|---|---|---|---|---|---|---|---|
| Year | Team | Lg | G | GS | CG | GF | IP | BFP | H | R | ER | HR | SH | SF | HB | TBB | IBB | SO | WP | Bk | W | L | Pct | Sh | Sv-Op | Hld | ERC | ERA |
| 2013 | ColSpr* | AAA | 44 | 0 | 0 | 38 | 44.1 | 194 | 37 | 22 | 15 | 5 | 2 | 2 | 3 | 22 | 0 | 41 | 6 | 0 | 2 | 5 | .286 | 0 | 15-- | - | 3.82 | 3.05 |
| 2004 | Fla | NL | 5 | 3 | 0 | 2 | 13.2 | 66 | 19 | 15 | 15 | 5 | 0 | 1 | 1 | 9 | 0 | 7 | 2 | 0 | 0 | 3 | .000 | 0 | 0-0 | 0 | 10.74 | 9.88 |
| 2005 | Fla | NL | 3 | 0 | 0 | 0 | 5.2 | 31 | 11 | 7 | 7 | 2 | 0 | 1 | 0 | 3 | 0 | 4 | 0 | 0 | 0 | 0 | - | 0 | 0-0 | 1 | 12.96 | 11.12 |
| 2006 | Fla | NL | 37 | 0 | 0 | 10 | 37.2 | 161 | 30 | 19 | 19 | 6 | 3 | 0 | 3 | 19 | 2 | 45 | 0 | 0 | 1 | 3 | .250 | 0 | 1-7 | 14 | 4.02 | 4.54 |
| 2007 | Fla | NL | 9 | 0 | 0 | 0 | 13.1 | 59 | 11 | 2 | 2 | 0 | 1 | 0 | 2 | 7 | 2 | 13 | 0 | 0 | 3 | 0 | 1.000 | 0 | 0-0 | 0 | 3.15 | 1.35 |
| 2008 | Fla | NL | 48 | 0 | 0 | 7 | 55.1 | 254 | 50 | 26 | 26 | 7 | 1 | 2 | 4 | 33 | 5 | 55 | 7 | 0 | 3 | 1 | .750 | 0 | 0-3 | 5 | 4.50 | 4.23 |
| 2009 | 2 Tms | NL | 32 | 0 | 0 | 12 | 35.1 | 172 | 54 | 35 | 35 | 8 | 3 | 1 | 0 | 17 | 1 | 19 | 4 | 1 | 1 | 2 | .333 | 0 | 1-3 | 1 | 8.78 | 8.92 |
| 2013 | Col | NL | 1 | 0 | 0 | 1 | 0.2 | 2 | 0 | 0 | 0 | 0 | 0 | 0 | 0 | 1 | 0 | 1 | 0 | 0 | 0 | 0 | - | 0 | 0-0 | 0 | 3.22 | 0.00 |
| 09 | Fla | NL | 6 | 0 | 0 | 2 | 7.1 | 40 | 14 | 8 | 8 | 1 | 1 | 0 | 0 | 5 | 0 | 7 | 2 | 1 | 0 | 1 | .000 | 0 | 0-0 | 0 | 11.61 | 9.82 |
| 09 | Was | NL | 26 | 0 | 0 | 10 | 28.0 | 132 | 40 | 27 | 27 | 7 | 2 | 1 | 0 | 12 | 1 | 12 | 2 | 0 | 1 | 1 | .500 | 0 | 1-3 | 1 | 8.04 | 8.68 |
| 7 ML YEARS | | | 135 | 3 | 0 | 32 | 161.2 | 745 | 175 | 104 | 104 | 28 | 8 | 5 | 10 | 89 | 10 | 144 | 13 | 1 | 8 | 9 | .471 | 0 | 2-13 | 21 | 5.86 | 5.79 |

## Jeff Keppinger

**Bats:** R **Throws:** R **Pos:** 2B-45;3B-41;1B-20;DH-16;PH-10 **Ht:** 6'0" **Wt:** 185 **Born:** 4/21/1980 **Age:** 34

| BATTING | | | | | | | | | | | | | | | | | | | | | BASERUNNING | | | | AVERAGES | | |
|---|---|---|---|---|---|---|---|---|---|---|---|---|---|---|---|---|---|---|---|---|---|---|---|---|---|---|---|
| Year | Team | Lg | G | AB | H | 2B | 3B | HR | (Hm | Rd) | TB | R | RBI | RC | TBB | IBB | SO | HBP | SH | SF | SB | CS | SB% | GDP | Avg | OBP | Slg |
| 2004 | NYM | NL | 33 | 116 | 33 | 2 | 0 | 3 | (3 | 0) | 44 | 9 | 9 | 12 | 6 | 0 | 7 | 0 | 0 | 1 | 2 | 1 | .67 | 6 | .284 | .317 | .379 |
| 2006 | KC | AL | 22 | 60 | 16 | 2 | 0 | 2 | (0 | 2) | 24 | 11 | 8 | 8 | 5 | 1 | 6 | 0 | 2 | 0 | 0 | 0 | - | 2 | .267 | .323 | .400 |
| 2007 | Cin | NL | 67 | 241 | 80 | 16 | 2 | 5 | (2 | 3) | 115 | 39 | 32 | 42 | 24 | 0 | 12 | 4 | 6 | 1 | 2 | 1 | .67 | 11 | .332 | .400 | .477 |
| 2008 | Cin | NL | 121 | 459 | 122 | 24 | 2 | 3 | (3 | 0) | 159 | 45 | 43 | 52 | 30 | 3 | 24 | 2 | 6 | 5 | 3 | 1 | .75 | 14 | .266 | .310 | .346 |
| 2009 | Hou | NL | 107 | 305 | 78 | 13 | 3 | 7 | (1 | 6) | 118 | 35 | 29 | 28 | 27 | 3 | 33 | 3 | 7 | 2 | 0 | 2 | .00 | 13 | .256 | .320 | .387 |
| 2010 | Hou | NL | 137 | 514 | 148 | 34 | 1 | 6 | (4 | 2) | 202 | 62 | 59 | 72 | 51 | 1 | 36 | 1 | 5 | 4 | 4 | 1 | .80 | 15 | .288 | .351 | .393 |
| 2011 | 2 Tms | NL | 99 | 379 | 105 | 20 | 0 | 6 | (4 | 2) | 143 | 39 | 35 | 38 | 12 | 0 | 24 | 2 | 2 | 4 | 0 | 1 | .00 | 11 | .277 | .300 | .377 |
| 2012 | TB | AL | 115 | 385 | 125 | 15 | 1 | 9 | (5 | 4) | 169 | 46 | 40 | 59 | 24 | 0 | 31 | 4 | 1 | 4 | 1 | 0 | 1.00 | 14 | .325 | .367 | .439 |
| 2013 | CWS | AL | 117 | 423 | 107 | 13 | 1 | 4 | (3 | 1) | 134 | 38 | 40 | 37 | 20 | 1 | 41 | 0 | 2 | 5 | 0 | 1 | .00 | 14 | .253 | .283 | .317 |
| 11 | Hou | NL | 43 | 163 | 50 | 9 | 0 | 4 | (3 | 1) | 71 | 22 | 20 | 18 | 4 | 0 | 7 | 0 | 0 | 2 | 0 | 1 | .00 | 5 | .307 | .320 | .436 |
| 11 | SF | NL | 56 | 216 | 55 | 11 | 0 | 2 | (1 | 1) | 72 | 17 | 15 | 20 | 8 | 0 | 17 | 2 | 2 | 2 | 0 | 0 | - | 6 | .255 | .285 | .333 |
| 9 ML YEARS | | | 818 | 2882 | 814 | 139 | 10 | 45 | (25 | 20) | 1108 | 324 | 295 | 348 | 199 | 9 | 214 | 16 | 31 | 26 | 12 | 8 | .60 | 100 | .282 | .329 | .384 |

# Clayton Kershaw

**Pitches:** L **Bats:** L **Pos:** SP-33 **Ht:** 6'3" **Wt:** 220 **Born:** 3/19/1988 **Age:** 26

| HOW MUCH HE PITCHED | | | | | | | | | WHAT HE GAVE UP | | | | | | | | | | | | THE RESULTS | | | | | | | |
|---|---|---|---|---|---|---|---|---|---|---|---|---|---|---|---|---|---|---|---|---|---|---|---|---|---|---|---|---|
| Year | Team | Lg | G | GS | CG | GF | IP | BFP | H | R | ER | HR | SH | SF | HB | TBB | IBB | SO | WP | Bk | W | L | Pct | Sh | Sv-Op | Hld | ERC | ERA |
| 2008 | LAD | NL | 22 | 21 | 0 | 0 | 107.2 | 470 | 109 | 51 | 51 | 11 | 3 | 3 | 1 | 52 | 3 | 100 | 7 | 0 | 5 | 5 | .500 | 0 | 0-0 | 1 | 4.53 | 4.26 |
| 2009 | LAD | NL | 31 | 30 | 0 | 1 | 171.0 | 701 | 119 | 55 | 53 | 7 | 11 | 2 | 1 | 91 | 4 | 185 | 11 | 2 | 8 | 8 | .500 | 0 | 0-0 | 0 | 2.60 | 2.79 |
| 2010 | LAD | NL | 32 | 32 | 1 | 0 | 204.1 | 848 | 160 | 73 | 66 | 13 | 8 | 4 | 7 | 81 | 9 | 212 | 5 | 2 | 13 | 10 | .565 | 1 | 0-0 | 0 | 2.72 | 2.91 |
| 2011 | LAD | NL | 33 | 33 | 5 | 0 | 233.1 | 912 | 174 | 66 | 59 | 15 | 11 | 2 | 3 | 54 | 2 | **248** | 5 | 1 | **21** | 5 | .808 | 2 | 0-0 | 0 | **2.00** | **2.28** |
| 2012 | LAD | NL | 33 | **33** | 2 | 0 | 227.2 | 901 | 170 | 70 | 64 | 16 | 18 | 4 | 5 | 63 | 5 | 229 | 6 | 2 | 14 | 9 | .609 | 2 | 0-0 | 0 | **2.20** | **2.53** |
| 2013 | LAD | NL | 33 | 33 | 3 | 0 | 236.0 | 908 | 164 | 55 | 48 | 11 | 8 | 3 | 3 | 52 | 2 | **232** | 12 | 2 | 16 | 9 | .640 | **2** | 0-0 | 0 | **1.65** | **1.83** |
| Postseason | | | 5 | 2 | 0 | 0 | 15.1 | 68 | 15 | 10 | 10 | 3 | 3 | 0 | 1 | 9 | 1 | 11 | 4 | 0 | 0 | 1 | .000 | 0 | 0-0 | 1 | 5.72 | 5.87 |
| 6 ML YEARS | | | 184 | 182 | 11 | 1 | 1180.0 | 4740 | 896 | 370 | 341 | 73 | 59 | 18 | 20 | 393 | 25 | 1206 | 46 | 9 | 77 | 46 | .626 | 7 | 0-0 | 1 | 2.38 | 2.60 |

# Dallas Keuchel

**Pitches:** L **Bats:** L **Pos:** SP-22; RP-9 KYE-kull **Ht:** 6'3" **Wt:** 200 **Born:** 1/1/1988 **Age:** 26

| HOW MUCH HE PITCHED | | | | | | | | | WHAT HE GAVE UP | | | | | | | | | | | | THE RESULTS | | | | | | | |
|---|---|---|---|---|---|---|---|---|---|---|---|---|---|---|---|---|---|---|---|---|---|---|---|---|---|---|---|---|
| Year | Team | Lg | G | GS | CG | GF | IP | BFP | H | R | ER | HR | SH | SF | HB | TBB | IBB | SO | WP | Bk | W | L | Pct | Sh | Sv-Op | Hld | ERC | ERA |
| 2009 | TriCity | A- | 11 | 10 | 0 | 0 | 56.2 | 231 | 52 | 18 | 17 | 2 | 3 | 0 | 2 | 9 | 0 | 44 | 2 | 0 | 2 | 3 | .400 | 0 | 0-- | - | 2.43 | 2.70 |
| 2010 | Lancst | A+ | 19 | 18 | 3 | 0 | 120.2 | 505 | 129 | 58 | 45 | 10 | 5 | 1 | 2 | 25 | 1 | 97 | 3 | 0 | 5 | 8 | .385 | 0 | 0-- | - | 3.66 | 3.36 |
| 2010 | CpChr | AA | 9 | 9 | 0 | 0 | 53.2 | 224 | 59 | 32 | 28 | 2 | 2 | 3 | 1 | 11 | 2 | 36 | 0 | 0 | 2 | 6 | .250 | 0 | 0-- | - | 3.50 | 4.70 |
| 2011 | CpChr | AA | 20 | 20 | 1 | 0 | 127.2 | 513 | 116 | 49 | 45 | 9 | 6 | 1 | 4 | 27 | 0 | 76 | 6 | 0 | 9 | 6 | .600 | 1 | 0-- | - | 2.85 | 3.17 |
| 2011 | OKCity | AAA | 7 | 7 | 0 | 0 | 36.0 | 165 | 52 | 30 | 30 | 5 | 2 | 4 | 0 | 12 | 1 | 15 | 0 | 1 | 1 | 1 | .500 | 0 | 0-- | - | 6.85 | 7.50 |
| 2012 | OKCity | AAA | 16 | 16 | 2 | 0 | 92.1 | 375 | 92 | 46 | 40 | 5 | 3 | 3 | 0 | 20 | 3 | 50 | 1 | 1 | 6 | 4 | .600 | 1 | 0-- | - | 3.06 | 3.90 |
| 2013 | OKCity | AAA | 1 | 1 | 1 | 0 | 6.0 | 21 | 3 | 0 | 0 | 0 | 1 | 0 | 0 | 0 | 0 | 5 | 0 | 0 | 1 | 0 | 1.000 | 1 | 0-- | - | 0.54 | 0.00 |
| 2012 | Hou | NL | 16 | 16 | 1 | 0 | 85.1 | 377 | 93 | 56 | 50 | 14 | 9 | 3 | 1 | 39 | 1 | 38 | 2 | 0 | 3 | 8 | .273 | 0 | 0-0 | 0 | 5.39 | 5.27 |
| 2013 | Hou | AL | 31 | 22 | 0 | 2 | 153.2 | 682 | 184 | 96 | 88 | 20 | 2 | 3 | 5 | 52 | 3 | 123 | 7 | 0 | 6 | 10 | .375 | 0 | 0-0 | 2 | 5.33 | 5.15 |
| 2 ML YEARS | | | 47 | 38 | 1 | 2 | 239.0 | 1059 | 277 | 152 | 138 | 34 | 11 | 6 | 6 | 91 | 4 | 161 | 9 | 0 | 9 | 18 | .333 | 0 | 0-0 | 2 | 5.35 | 5.20 |

# Mike Kickham

**Pitches:** L **Bats:** L **Pos:** RP-9; SP-3 KICK-em **Ht:** 6'4" **Wt:** 220 **Born:** 12/12/1988 **Age:** 25

| HOW MUCH HE PITCHED | | | | | | | | | WHAT HE GAVE UP | | | | | | | | | | | | THE RESULTS | | | | | | | |
|---|---|---|---|---|---|---|---|---|---|---|---|---|---|---|---|---|---|---|---|---|---|---|---|---|---|---|---|---|
| Year | Team | Lg | G | GS | CG | GF | IP | BFP | H | R | ER | HR | SH | SF | HB | TBB | IBB | SO | WP | Bk | W | L | Pct | Sh | Sv-Op | Hld | ERC | ERA |
| 2010 | Giants | R | 3 | 0 | 0 | 0 | 2.1 | 12 | 4 | 3 | 3 | 0 | 0 | 0 | 0 | 2 | 0 | 3 | 0 | 0 | 0 | 0 | - | 0 | 0-- | - | 10.22 | 11.57 |
| 2011 | Augsta | A | 21 | 21 | 0 | 0 | 111.2 | 476 | 112 | 58 | 51 | 9 | 3 | 4 | 3 | 37 | 0 | 103 | 8 | 1 | 5 | 10 | .333 | 0 | 0-- | - | 3.80 | 4.11 |
| 2012 | Rchmd | AA | 28 | 27 | 1 | 0 | 150.2 | 630 | 119 | 57 | 51 | 8 | 8 | 2 | 2 | 75 | 0 | 137 | 9 | 3 | 11 | 10 | .524 | 1 | 0-- | - | 3.07 | 3.05 |
| 2013 | Fresno | AAA | 20 | 20 | 0 | 0 | 110.2 | 476 | 105 | 60 | 53 | 9 | 5 | 2 | 0 | 49 | 0 | 90 | 1 | 0 | 7 | 7 | .500 | 0 | 0-- | - | 3.83 | 4.31 |
| 2013 | SF | NL | 12 | 3 | 0 | 5 | 28.1 | 144 | 46 | 34 | 32 | 8 | 2 | 1 | 0 | 10 | 2 | 29 | 2 | 0 | 0 | 3 | .000 | 0 | 0-0 | 0 | 8.75 | 10.16 |

# Kevin Kiermaier

**Bats:** L **Throws:** R **Pos:** CF-1 KEER-my-urr **Ht:** 6'1" **Wt:** 200 **Born:** 4/22/1990 **Age:** 24

| BATTING | | | | | | | | | | | | | | | | | | | | | BASERUNNING | | | | AVERAGES | | |
|---|---|---|---|---|---|---|---|---|---|---|---|---|---|---|---|---|---|---|---|---|---|---|---|---|---|---|---|
| Year | Team | Lg | G | AB | H | 2B | 3B | HR | (Hm | Rd) | TB | R | RBI | RC | TBB | IBB | SO | HBP | SH | SF | SB | CS | SB% | GDP | Avg | OBP | Slg |
| 2010 | Princtn | R | 57 | 218 | 66 | 8 | 7 | 2 | (- | -) | 94 | 44 | 16 | 38 | 24 | 2 | 54 | 3 | 1 | 0 | 17 | 5 | .77 | 4 | .303 | .380 | .431 |
| 2011 | BG | A | 120 | 402 | 97 | 11 | 8 | 4 | (- | -) | 136 | 54 | 39 | 47 | 37 | 0 | 99 | 8 | 9 | 3 | 27 | 10 | .73 | 3 | .241 | .316 | .338 |
| 2012 | Charltt | A+ | 57 | 177 | 46 | 7 | 6 | 0 | (- | -) | 65 | 16 | 12 | 26 | 26 | 0 | 38 | 2 | 7 | 0 | 10 | 4 | .71 | 1 | .260 | .361 | .367 |
| 2012 | Rays | R | 2 | 6 | 1 | 0 | 0 | 0 | (- | -) | 1 | 0 | 0 | 0 | 0 | 0 | 2 | 0 | 0 | 0 | 0 | 0 | - | 0 | .167 | .167 | .167 |
| 2012 | Drham | AAA | 4 | 9 | 3 | 0 | 0 | 0 | (- | -) | 3 | 2 | 1 | 1 | 3 | 0 | 1 | 0 | 0 | 0 | 0 | 0 | - | 0 | .333 | .500 | .333 |
| 2013 | Mont | AA | 97 | 371 | 114 | 14 | 9 | 5 | (- | -) | 161 | 65 | 28 | 60 | 31 | 3 | 61 | 8 | 4 | 3 | 14 | 11 | .56 | 3 | .307 | .370 | .434 |
| 2013 | Drham | AAA | 39 | 137 | 36 | 7 | 6 | 1 | (- | -) | 58 | 24 | 13 | 21 | 14 | 0 | 26 | 2 | 0 | 1 | 7 | 1 | .88 | 0 | .263 | .338 | .423 |
| 2013 | TB | AL | 1 | 0 | 0 | 0 | 0 | 0 | (0 | 0) | 0 | 0 | 0 | 0 | 0 | 0 | 0 | 0 | 0 | 0 | 0 | 0 | - | 0 | - | - | - |

# Roger Kieschnick

**Bats:** L **Throws:** R **Pos:** LF-25;PH-14 KEESH-nick **Ht:** 6'3" **Wt:** 220 **Born:** 1/21/1987 **Age:** 27

| BATTING | | | | | | | | | | | | | | | | | | | | | BASERUNNING | | | | AVERAGES | | |
|---|---|---|---|---|---|---|---|---|---|---|---|---|---|---|---|---|---|---|---|---|---|---|---|---|---|---|---|
| Year | Team | Lg | G | AB | H | 2B | 3B | HR | (Hm | Rd) | TB | R | RBI | RC | TBB | IBB | SO | HBP | SH | SF | SB | CS | SB% | GDP | Avg | OBP | Slg |
| 2009 | SnJos | A+ | 131 | 517 | 153 | 37 | 8 | 23 | (- | -) | 275 | 86 | 110 | 96 | 36 | 2 | 130 | 5 | 0 | 5 | 9 | 1 | .90 | 6 | .296 | .345 | .532 |
| 2010 | Rchmd | AA | 60 | 223 | 56 | 8 | 3 | 4 | (- | -) | 82 | 21 | 23 | 25 | 18 | 1 | 55 | 1 | 0 | 4 | 2 | 3 | .40 | 3 | .251 | .305 | .368 |
| 2011 | Rchmd | AA | 126 | 459 | 117 | 22 | 5 | 16 | (- | -) | 197 | 71 | 65 | 62 | 34 | 1 | 121 | 3 | 0 | 5 | 13 | 7 | .65 | 6 | .255 | .307 | .429 |
| 2012 | Fresno | AAA | 55 | 222 | 68 | 13 | 4 | 15 | (- | -) | 134 | 49 | 40 | 48 | 24 | 1 | 68 | 2 | 0 | 2 | 0 | 2 | .00 | 4 | .306 | .376 | .604 |
| 2012 | Giants | R | 3 | 12 | 1 | 1 | 0 | 0 | (- | -) | 2 | 0 | 4 | 0 | 0 | 0 | 5 | 0 | 0 | 1 | 0 | 0 | - | 0 | .083 | .077 | .167 |
| 2013 | Fresno | AAA | 101 | 374 | 102 | 27 | 9 | 13 | (- | -) | 186 | 50 | 56 | 65 | 40 | 2 | 102 | 1 | 0 | 7 | 4 | 1 | .80 | 4 | .273 | .339 | .497 |
| 2013 | SF | NL | 38 | 84 | 17 | 0 | 1 | 0 | (0 | 0) | 19 | 6 | 5 | 6 | 11 | 2 | 29 | 0 | 0 | 0 | 0 | 0 | - | 3 | .202 | .295 | .226 |

# Craig Kimbrel

**Pitches:** R **Bats:** R **Pos:** RP-68 KIM-brull **Ht:** 5'11" **Wt:** 205 **Born:** 5/28/1988 **Age:** 26

| HOW MUCH HE PITCHED | | | | | | | | | WHAT HE GAVE UP | | | | | | | | | | | | THE RESULTS | | | | | | | |
|---|---|---|---|---|---|---|---|---|---|---|---|---|---|---|---|---|---|---|---|---|---|---|---|---|---|---|---|---|
| Year | Team | Lg | G | GS | CG | GF | IP | BFP | H | R | ER | HR | SH | SF | HB | TBB | IBB | SO | WP | Bk | W | L | Pct | Sh | Sv-Op | Hld | ERC | ERA |
| 2010 | Atl | NL | 21 | 0 | 0 | 7 | 20.2 | 88 | 9 | 2 | 1 | 0 | 0 | 0 | 0 | 16 | 1 | 40 | 4 | 0 | 4 | 0 | 1.000 | 0 | 1-1 | 2 | 1.72 | 0.44 |
| 2011 | Atl | NL | 79 | 0 | 0 | 64 | 77.0 | 306 | 48 | 19 | 18 | 3 | 1 | 2 | 1 | 32 | 1 | 127 | 4 | 0 | 4 | 3 | .571 | 0 | **46**-54 | 0 | 1.88 | 2.10 |
| 2012 | Atl | NL | 63 | 0 | 0 | 56 | 62.2 | 231 | 27 | 7 | 7 | 3 | 0 | 0 | 2 | 14 | 0 | 116 | 5 | 0 | 3 | 1 | .750 | 0 | **42**-45 | 0 | 0.93 | 1.01 |
| 2013 | Atl | NL | 68 | 0 | 0 | 60 | 67.0 | 258 | 39 | 10 | 9 | 4 | 0 | 0 | 3 | 20 | 2 | 98 | 3 | 0 | 4 | 3 | .571 | 0 | **50**-54 | 0 | 1.58 | 1.21 |
| Postseason | | | 5 | 0 | 0 | 3 | 5.1 | 16 | 1 | 2 | 1 | 0 | 0 | 0 | 0 | 1 | 0 | 8 | 0 | 0 | 0 | 1 | .000 | 0 | 0-0 | 1 | 0.27 | 1.69 |
| 4 ML YEARS | | | 231 | 0 | 0 | 187 | 227.1 | 883 | 123 | 38 | 35 | 10 | 1 | 2 | 6 | 82 | 4 | 381 | 16 | 0 | 15 | 7 | .682 | 0 | 139-154 | 2 | 1.48 | 1.39 |

# Ian Kinsler

**Bats:** R **Throws:** R **Pos:** 2B-124;DH-11;PR-1 **Ht:** 6'0" **Wt:** 200 **Born:** 6/22/1982 **Age:** 32

| BATTING | | | | | | | | | | | | | | | | | | | | | | BASERUNNING | | | | AVERAGES | | |
|---|---|---|---|---|---|---|---|---|---|---|---|---|---|---|---|---|---|---|---|---|---|---|---|---|---|---|---|---|
| Year Team | Lg | G | AB | H | 2B | 3B | HR | (Hm | Rd) | TB | R | RBI | RC | TBB | IBB | SO | HBP | SH | SF | | | SB | CS | SB% | GDP | Avg | OBP | Slg |
| 2013 Frisco* | AA | 2 | 8 | 0 | 0 | 0 | 0 | (- | -) | 0 | 0 | 0 | 0 | 1 | 0 | 3 | 0 | 0 | 0 | | | 0 | 0 | - | 0 | .000 | .111 | .000 |
| 2006 Tex | AL | 120 | 423 | 121 | 27 | 1 | 14 | (10 | 4) | 192 | 65 | 55 | 65 | 40 | 1 | 64 | 3 | 1 | 7 | | | 11 | 4 | .73 | 12 | .286 | .347 | .454 |
| 2007 Tex | AL | 130 | 483 | 127 | 22 | 2 | 20 | (12 | 8) | 213 | 96 | 61 | 79 | 62 | 2 | 83 | 9 | 8 | 4 | | | 23 | 2 | .92 | 14 | .263 | .355 | .441 |
| 2008 Tex | AL | 121 | 518 | 165 | 41 | 4 | 18 | (4 | 14) | 268 | 102 | 71 | 106 | 45 | 1 | 67 | 6 | 7 | 7 | | | 26 | 2 | .93 | 12 | .319 | .375 | .517 |
| 2009 Tex | AL | 144 | 566 | 143 | 32 | 4 | 31 | (20 | 11) | 276 | 101 | 86 | 99 | 59 | 0 | 77 | 6 | 3 | 6 | | | 31 | 5 | .86 | 9 | .253 | .327 | .488 |
| 2010 Tex | AL | 103 | 391 | 112 | 20 | 1 | 9 | (4 | 5) | 161 | 73 | 45 | 59 | 56 | 2 | 57 | 7 | 2 | 4 | | | 15 | 5 | .75 | 11 | .286 | .382 | .412 |
| 2011 Tex | AL | 155 | 620 | 158 | 34 | 4 | 32 | (16 | 16) | 296 | 121 | 77 | 100 | 89 | 2 | 71 | 8 | 4 | 2 | | | 30 | 4 | **.88** | 17 | .255 | .355 | .477 |
| 2012 Tex | AL | 157 | 655 | 168 | 42 | 5 | 19 | (14 | 5) | 277 | 105 | 72 | 83 | 60 | 0 | 90 | 10 | 1 | 5 | | | 21 | 9 | .70 | 14 | .256 | .326 | .423 |
| 2013 Tex | AL | 136 | 545 | 151 | 31 | 2 | 13 | (5 | 8) | 225 | 85 | 72 | 84 | 51 | 0 | 59 | 8 | 3 | 7 | | | 15 | 11 | .58 | 5 | .277 | .344 | .413 |
| Postseason | | 34 | 122 | 38 | 7 | 1 | 4 | (1 | 3) | 59 | 18 | 20 | 24 | 23 | 1 | 16 | 1 | 1 | 1 | | | 6 | 5 | .55 | 3 | .311 | .422 | .484 |
| 8 ML YEARS | | 1066 | 4201 | 1145 | 249 | 23 | 156 | (85 | 71) | 1908 | 748 | 539 | 675 | 462 | 8 | 568 | 57 | 29 | 42 | | | 172 | 42 | .80 | 94 | .273 | .349 | .454 |

# Brandon Kintzler

**Pitches:** R **Bats:** R **Pos:** RP-71 **Ht:** 5'10" **Wt:** 185 **Born:** 8/1/1984 **Age:** 29

| HOW MUCH HE PITCHED | | | | | | | | WHAT HE GAVE UP | | | | | | | | | | | | THE RESULTS | | | | | | | |
|---|---|---|---|---|---|---|---|---|---|---|---|---|---|---|---|---|---|---|---|---|---|---|---|---|---|---|---|
| Year Team | Lg | G | GS | CG | GF | IP | BFP | H | R | ER | HR | SH | SF | HB | TBB | IBB | SO | WP | Bk | W | L | Pct | Sh | Sv-Op | Hld | ERC | ERA |
| 2010 Mil | NL | 7 | 0 | 0 | 2 | 7.1 | 33 | 10 | 6 | 6 | 2 | 1 | 0 | 0 | 4 | 1 | 9 | 1 | 0 | 0 | 1 | .000 | 0 | 0-0 | 0 | 8.67 | 7.36 |
| 2011 Mil | NL | 9 | 0 | 0 | 3 | 14.2 | 61 | 14 | 9 | 6 | 3 | 0 | 2 | 0 | 3 | 0 | 15 | 0 | 1 | 1 | 1 | .500 | 0 | 0-0 | 0 | 3.65 | 3.68 |
| 2012 Mil | NL | 14 | 0 | 0 | 1 | 16.2 | 72 | 18 | 7 | 7 | 1 | 0 | 0 | 0 | 7 | 1 | 14 | 1 | 0 | 3 | 0 | 1.000 | 0 | 0-0 | 2 | 4.30 | 3.78 |
| 2013 Mil | NL | 71 | 0 | 0 | 11 | 77.0 | 305 | 66 | 26 | 23 | 2 | 4 | 2 | 1 | 16 | 2 | 58 | 1 | 0 | 3 | 3 | .500 | 0 | 0-4 | 26 | 2.21 | 2.69 |
| 4 ML YEARS | | 101 | 0 | 0 | 17 | 115.2 | 471 | 108 | 48 | 42 | 8 | 5 | 4 | 1 | 30 | 4 | 96 | 3 | 1 | 7 | 5 | .583 | 0 | 0-4 | 28 | 3.01 | 3.27 |

# Jason Kipnis

**Bats:** L **Throws:** R **Pos:** 2B-147;DH-1;PH-1 KIP-niss **Ht:** 5'11" **Wt:** 190 **Born:** 4/3/1987 **Age:** 27

| BATTING | | | | | | | | | | | | | | | | | | | | BASERUNNING | | | | AVERAGES | | |
|---|---|---|---|---|---|---|---|---|---|---|---|---|---|---|---|---|---|---|---|---|---|---|---|---|---|---|
| Year Team | Lg | G | AB | H | 2B | 3B | HR | (Hm | Rd) | TB | R | RBI | RC | TBB | IBB | SO | HBP | SH | SF | SB | CS | SB% | GDP | Avg | OBP | Slg |
| 2011 Cle | AL | 36 | 136 | 37 | 9 | 1 | 7 | (3 | 4) | 69 | 24 | 19 | 22 | 11 | 0 | 34 | 2 | 0 | 1 | 5 | 0 | 1.00 | 0 | .272 | .333 | .507 |
| 2012 Cle | AL | 152 | 591 | 152 | 22 | 4 | 14 | (5 | 9) | 224 | 86 | 76 | 88 | 67 | 2 | 109 | 5 | 3 | 6 | 31 | 7 | .82 | 12 | .257 | .335 | .379 |
| 2013 Cle | AL | 149 | 564 | 160 | 36 | 4 | 17 | (7 | 10) | 255 | 86 | 84 | 99 | 76 | 3 | 143 | 3 | 5 | 10 | 30 | 7 | .81 | 10 | .284 | .366 | .452 |
| 3 ML YEARS | | 337 | 1291 | 349 | 67 | 9 | 38 | (15 | 23) | 548 | 196 | 179 | 209 | 154 | 5 | 286 | 10 | 8 | 17 | 66 | 14 | .83 | 22 | .270 | .349 | .424 |

# Michael Kirkman

**Pitches:** L **Bats:** L **Pos:** RP-25 **Ht:** 6'4" **Wt:** 220 **Born:** 9/18/1986 **Age:** 27

| HOW MUCH HE PITCHED | | | | | | | | WHAT HE GAVE UP | | | | | | | | | | | | THE RESULTS | | | | | | | |
|---|---|---|---|---|---|---|---|---|---|---|---|---|---|---|---|---|---|---|---|---|---|---|---|---|---|---|---|
| Year Team | Lg | G | GS | CG | GF | IP | BFP | H | R | ER | HR | SH | SF | HB | TBB | IBB | SO | WP | Bk | W | L | Pct | Sh | Sv-Op | Hld | ERC | ERA |
| 2013 RdRck* | AAA | 6 | 5 | 0 | 1 | 29.2 | 133 | 31 | 23 | 23 | 3 | 1 | 2 | 1 | 19 | 0 | 23 | 6 | 0 | 2 | 3 | .400 | 0 | 0-- | - | 5.62 | 6.98 |
| 2010 Tex | AL | 14 | 0 | 0 | 2 | 16.1 | 68 | 9 | 3 | 3 | 0 | 0 | 2 | 0 | 10 | 1 | 16 | 0 | 0 | 0 | 0 | - | 0 | 0-1 | 2 | 1.76 | 1.65 |
| 2011 Tex | AL | 15 | 0 | 0 | 7 | 27.1 | 122 | 26 | 22 | 20 | 5 | 1 | 2 | 3 | 12 | 2 | 21 | 2 | 0 | 1 | 1 | .500 | 0 | 0-0 | 1 | 4.81 | 6.59 |
| 2012 Tex | AL | 28 | 0 | 0 | 9 | 35.1 | 151 | 24 | 16 | 15 | 5 | 0 | 1 | 1 | 17 | 1 | 38 | 2 | 0 | 1 | 2 | .333 | 0 | 0-2 | 1 | 2.88 | 3.82 |
| 2013 Tex | AL | 25 | 0 | 0 | 7 | 22.0 | 115 | 36 | 20 | 20 | 2 | 0 | 1 | 0 | 15 | 4 | 25 | 2 | 0 | 0 | 2 | .000 | 0 | 1-2 | 0 | 8.74 | 8.18 |
| Postseason | | 3 | 0 | 0 | 2 | 2.2 | 13 | 4 | 1 | 1 | 0 | 1 | 0 | 0 | 2 | 0 | 2 | 0 | 0 | 0 | 0 | - | 0 | 0-0 | 0 | 8.14 | 3.38 |
| 4 ML YEARS | | 82 | 0 | 0 | 25 | 101.0 | 456 | 95 | 61 | 58 | 12 | 1 | 6 | 4 | 54 | 8 | 100 | 6 | 0 | 2 | 5 | .286 | 0 | 1-5 | 4 | 4.33 | 5.17 |

# Corey Kluber

**Pitches:** R **Bats:** R **Pos:** SP-24; RP-2 CLUE-burr **Ht:** 6'4" **Wt:** 215 **Born:** 4/10/1986 **Age:** 28

| HOW MUCH HE PITCHED | | | | | | | | WHAT HE GAVE UP | | | | | | | | | | | | THE RESULTS | | | | | | | |
|---|---|---|---|---|---|---|---|---|---|---|---|---|---|---|---|---|---|---|---|---|---|---|---|---|---|---|---|
| Year Team | Lg | G | GS | CG | GF | IP | BFP | H | R | ER | HR | SH | SF | HB | TBB | IBB | SO | WP | Bk | W | L | Pct | Sh | Sv-Op | Hld | ERC | ERA |
| 2013 Clmbs* | AAA | 2 | 2 | 0 | 0 | 12.1 | 52 | 14 | 9 | 9 | 2 | 0 | 0 | 0 | 3 | 0 | 12 | 0 | 0 | 1 | 1 | .500 | 0 | 0-- | - | 4.74 | 6.57 |
| 2011 Cle | AL | 3 | 0 | 0 | 2 | 4.1 | 25 | 6 | 4 | 4 | 0 | 0 | 0 | 2 | 3 | 0 | 5 | 1 | 0 | 0 | 0 | - | 0 | 0-0 | 0 | 8.12 | 8.31 |
| 2012 Cle | AL | 12 | 12 | 0 | 0 | 63.0 | 281 | 76 | 44 | 36 | 9 | 1 | 0 | 4 | 18 | 0 | 54 | 2 | 0 | 2 | 5 | .286 | 0 | 0-0 | 0 | 5.38 | 5.14 |
| 2013 Cle | AL | 26 | 24 | 0 | 1 | 147.1 | 608 | 153 | 67 | 63 | 15 | 4 | 2 | 5 | 33 | 0 | 136 | 1 | 0 | 11 | 5 | .688 | 0 | 0-0 | 0 | 3.83 | 3.85 |
| 3 ML YEARS | | 41 | 36 | 0 | 3 | 214.2 | 914 | 235 | 115 | 103 | 24 | 5 | 2 | 11 | 54 | 0 | 195 | 4 | 0 | 13 | 10 | .565 | 0 | 0-0 | 0 | 4.36 | 4.32 |

# Jeff Kobernus

**Bats:** R **Throws:** R **Pos:** PR-8;PH-7;LF-6;CF-3;RF-2 CO-burr-ness **Ht:** 6'2" **Wt:** 210 **Born:** 6/30/1988 **Age:** 26

| BATTING | | | | | | | | | | | | | | | | | | | | BASERUNNING | | | | AVERAGES | | |
|---|---|---|---|---|---|---|---|---|---|---|---|---|---|---|---|---|---|---|---|---|---|---|---|---|---|---|
| Year Team | Lg | G | AB | H | 2B | 3B | HR | (Hm | Rd) | TB | R | RBI | RC | TBB | IBB | SO | HBP | SH | SF | SB | CS | SB% | GDP | Avg | OBP | Slg |
| 2009 Vrmnt | A- | 10 | 41 | 9 | 1 | 0 | 0 | (- | -) | 10 | 8 | 2 | 3 | 2 | 0 | 5 | 1 | 0 | 0 | 4 | 0 | 1.00 | 0 | .220 | .273 | .244 |
| 2010 Hgrstn | A | 74 | 312 | 87 | 18 | 0 | 1 | (- | -) | 108 | 40 | 42 | 36 | 17 | 1 | 58 | 3 | 4 | 7 | 21 | 10 | .68 | 2 | .279 | .316 | .346 |
| 2011 Ptomc | A+ | 124 | 489 | 138 | 22 | 4 | 7 | (- | -) | 189 | 67 | 52 | 67 | 21 | 0 | 87 | 2 | 8 | 2 | 53 | 8 | .87 | 10 | .282 | .313 | .387 |
| 2012 Hrsbrg | AA | 82 | 330 | 93 | 10 | 2 | 1 | (- | -) | 110 | 41 | 19 | 41 | 19 | 0 | 57 | 4 | 9 | 4 | 41 | 11 | .79 | 1 | .282 | .325 | .333 |
| 2013 Syrcse | AAA | 95 | 371 | 118 | 19 | 2 | 1 | (- | -) | 144 | 59 | 36 | 60 | 28 | 2 | 59 | 2 | 8 | 3 | 42 | 9 | .82 | 1 | .318 | .366 | .388 |
| 2013 Was | NL | 24 | 30 | 5 | 0 | 0 | 1 | (0 | 1) | 8 | 8 | 1 | 2 | 5 | 0 | 6 | 1 | 0 | 0 | 3 | 2 | .60 | 0 | .167 | .306 | .267 |

# Tom Koehler

**Pitches:** R **Bats:** R **Pos:** SP-23; RP-6 COLE-err **Ht:** 6'3" **Wt:** 235 **Born:** 6/29/1986 **Age:** 28

| HOW MUCH HE PITCHED | | | | | | | | | WHAT HE GAVE UP | | | | | | | | | | | | THE RESULTS | | | | | | | |
|---|---|---|---|---|---|---|---|---|---|---|---|---|---|---|---|---|---|---|---|---|---|---|---|---|---|---|---|---|
| Year | Team | Lg | G | GS | CG | GF | IP | BFP | H | R | ER | HR | SH | SF | HB | TBB | IBB | SO | WP | Bk | W | L | Pct | Sh | Sv-Op | Hld | ERC | ERA |
| 2009 | Grnsbr | A | 18 | 18 | 0 | 0 | 98.1 | 423 | 88 | 37 | 35 | 9 | 2 | 1 | 11 | 39 | 0 | 82 | 6 | 1 | 5 | 5 | .500 | 0 | 0-- | - | 3.87 | 3.20 |
| 2009 | Jupiter | A+ | 6 | 6 | 0 | 0 | 34.2 | 141 | 35 | 15 | 13 | 0 | 0 | 1 | 2 | 9 | 0 | 25 | 3 | 0 | 4 | 1 | .800 | 0 | 0-- | - | 3.27 | 3.38 |
| 2010 | Jaxnvl | AA | 28 | 28 | 0 | 0 | 158.2 | 650 | 140 | 57 | 46 | 11 | 10 | 5 | 8 | 46 | 1 | 145 | 4 | 0 | 16 | 2 | .889 | 0 | 0-- | - | 3.04 | 2.61 |
| 2011 | NewOr | AAA | 27 | 27 | 0 | 0 | 143.1 | 635 | 140 | 89 | 82 | 18 | 5 | 7 | 5 | 75 | 1 | 108 | 4 | 1 | 11 | 7 | .611 | 0 | 0-- | - | 4.76 | 5.15 |
| 2012 | NewOr | AAA | 29 | 27 | 0 | 0 | 151.0 | 658 | 154 | 80 | 70 | 15 | 8 | 8 | 6 | 61 | 3 | 138 | 2 | 2 | 12 | 11 | .522 | 0 | 0-- | - | 4.33 | 4.17 |
| 2013 | NewOr | AAA | 4 | 4 | 0 | 0 | 23.0 | 94 | 16 | 8 | 7 | 2 | 1 | 0 | 0 | 12 | 0 | 18 | 0 | 0 | 0 | 2 | .000 | 0 | 0-- | - | 2.88 | 2.74 |
| 2012 | Mia | NL | 8 | 1 | 0 | 0 | 13.1 | 56 | 15 | 8 | 8 | 4 | 0 | 0 | 0 | 2 | 1 | 13 | 0 | 0 | 0 | 1 | .000 | 0 | 0-0 | 0 | 4.99 | 5.40 |
| 2013 | Mia | NL | 29 | 23 | 0 | 2 | 143.0 | 601 | 140 | 72 | 70 | 14 | 3 | 2 | 5 | 54 | 2 | 92 | 7 | 0 | 5 | 10 | .333 | 0 | 0-0 | 0 | 4.08 | 4.41 |
| 2 ML YEARS | | | 37 | 24 | 0 | 2 | 156.1 | 657 | 155 | 80 | 78 | 18 | 3 | 2 | 5 | 56 | 3 | 105 | 7 | 0 | 5 | 11 | .313 | 0 | 0-0 | 0 | 4.16 | 4.49 |

# Michael Kohn

**Pitches:** R **Bats:** R **Pos:** RP-63 KAHN **Ht:** 6'2" **Wt:** 200 **Born:** 6/26/1986 **Age:** 28

| HOW MUCH HE PITCHED | | | | | | | | | WHAT HE GAVE UP | | | | | | | | | | | | THE RESULTS | | | | | | | |
|---|---|---|---|---|---|---|---|---|---|---|---|---|---|---|---|---|---|---|---|---|---|---|---|---|---|---|---|---|
| Year | Team | Lg | G | GS | CG | GF | IP | BFP | H | R | ER | HR | SH | SF | HB | TBB | IBB | SO | WP | Bk | W | L | Pct | Sh | Sv-Op | Hld | ERC | ERA |
| 2013 | Salt Lk* | AAA | 5 | 0 | 0 | 3 | 4.1 | 14 | 2 | 0 | 0 | 0 | 0 | 0 | 0 | 0 | 0 | 7 | 0 | 0 | 0 | 0 | - | 0 | 1-- | - | 0.50 | 0.00 |
| 2010 | LAA | AL | 24 | 0 | 0 | 8 | 21.1 | 95 | 17 | 5 | 5 | 0 | 4 | 0 | 0 | 16 | 1 | 20 | 0 | 0 | 2 | 0 | 1.000 | 0 | 1-1 | 1 | 3.45 | 2.11 |
| 2011 | LAA | AL | 14 | 0 | 0 | 7 | 12.1 | 60 | 14 | 10 | 10 | 6 | 0 | 0 | 1 | 9 | 0 | 9 | 1 | 0 | 0 | 1 | .000 | 0 | 1-2 | 1 | 9.92 | 7.30 |
| 2013 | LAA | AL | 63 | 0 | 0 | 13 | 53.0 | 231 | 42 | 22 | 22 | 7 | 1 | 1 | 3 | 28 | 3 | 52 | 4 | 0 | 1 | 4 | .200 | 0 | 0-2 | 8 | 3.72 | 3.74 |
| 3 ML YEARS | | | 101 | 0 | 0 | 28 | 86.2 | 386 | 73 | 37 | 37 | 13 | 5 | 1 | 4 | 53 | 4 | 81 | 5 | 0 | 3 | 5 | .375 | 0 | 2-5 | 10 | 4.44 | 3.84 |

# Paul Konerko

**Bats:** R **Throws:** R **Pos:** 1B-76;DH-50 kun-ER-ko **Ht:** 6'2" **Wt:** 220 **Born:** 3/5/1976 **Age:** 38

| BATTING | | | | | | | | | | | | | | | | | | | | | BASERUNNING | | | | AVERAGES | | |
|---|---|---|---|---|---|---|---|---|---|---|---|---|---|---|---|---|---|---|---|---|---|---|---|---|---|---|---|
| Year | Team | Lg | G | AB | H | 2B | 3B | HR | (Hm | Rd) | TB | R | RBI | RC | TBB | IBB | SO | HBP | SH | SF | SB | CS | SB% | GDP | Avg | OBP | Slg |
| 2013 | Brham* | AA | 3 | 10 | 4 | 0 | 0 | 0 | (- | -) | 4 | 1 | 1 | 1 | 1 | 0 | 1 | 0 | 0 | 0 | 0 | 0 | - | 0 | .400 | .455 | .400 |
| 1997 | LAD | NL | 6 | 7 | 1 | 0 | 0 | 0 | (0 | 0) | 1 | 0 | 0 | 0 | 1 | 0 | 2 | 0 | 0 | 0 | 0 | 0 | - | 1 | .143 | .250 | .143 |
| 1998 | 2 Tms | NL | 75 | 217 | 47 | 4 | 0 | 7 | (2 | 5) | 72 | 21 | 29 | 17 | 16 | 0 | 40 | 3 | 0 | 3 | 0 | 1 | .00 | 10 | .217 | .276 | .332 |
| 1999 | CWS | AL | 142 | 513 | 151 | 31 | 4 | 24 | (16 | 8) | 262 | 71 | 81 | 86 | 45 | 0 | 68 | 2 | 1 | 3 | 1 | 0 | 1.00 | 19 | .294 | .352 | .511 |
| 2000 | CWS | AL | 143 | 524 | 156 | 31 | 1 | 21 | (10 | 11) | 252 | 84 | 97 | 86 | 47 | 0 | 72 | 10 | 0 | 5 | 1 | 0 | 1.00 | 22 | .298 | .363 | .481 |
| 2001 | CWS | AL | 156 | 582 | 164 | 35 | 0 | 32 | (19 | 13) | 295 | 92 | 99 | 99 | 54 | 6 | 89 | 9 | 0 | 5 | 1 | 0 | 1.00 | 17 | .282 | .349 | .507 |
| 2002 | CWS | AL | 151 | 570 | 173 | 30 | 0 | 27 | (13 | 14) | 284 | 81 | 104 | 96 | 44 | 2 | 72 | 9 | 0 | 7 | 0 | 0 | - | 17 | .304 | .359 | .498 |
| 2003 | CWS | AL | 137 | 444 | 104 | 19 | 0 | 18 | (9 | 9) | 177 | 49 | 65 | 42 | 43 | 7 | 50 | 4 | 0 | 4 | 0 | 0 | - | **28** | .234 | .305 | .399 |
| 2004 | CWS | AL | 155 | 563 | 156 | 22 | 0 | 41 | **(29** | 12) | 301 | 84 | 117 | 106 | 69 | 5 | 107 | 6 | 0 | 5 | 1 | 0 | 1.00 | 23 | .277 | .359 | .535 |
| 2005 | CWS | AL | 158 | 575 | 163 | 24 | 0 | 40 | (23 | 17) | 307 | 98 | 100 | 106 | 81 | 10 | 109 | 5 | 0 | 3 | 0 | 0 | - | 9 | .283 | .375 | .534 |
| 2006 | CWS | AL | 152 | 566 | 177 | 30 | 0 | 35 | (21 | 14) | 312 | 97 | 113 | 110 | 60 | 3 | 104 | 8 | 0 | 9 | 1 | 0 | 1.00 | 25 | .313 | .381 | .551 |
| 2007 | CWS | AL | 151 | 549 | 142 | 34 | 0 | 31 | (17 | 14) | 269 | 71 | 90 | 88 | 78 | 9 | 102 | 3 | 0 | 6 | 0 | 1 | .00 | 21 | .259 | .351 | .490 |
| 2008 | CWS | AL | 122 | 438 | 105 | 19 | 1 | 22 | (15 | 7) | 192 | 59 | 62 | 60 | 65 | 4 | 80 | 7 | 0 | 4 | 2 | 0 | 1.00 | 17 | .240 | .344 | .438 |
| 2009 | CWS | AL | 152 | 546 | 151 | 30 | 1 | 28 | (18 | 10) | 267 | 75 | 88 | 91 | 58 | 4 | 89 | 10 | 0 | 7 | 1 | 0 | 1.00 | 15 | .277 | .353 | .489 |
| 2010 | CWS | AL | 149 | 548 | 171 | 30 | 1 | 39 | (26 | 13) | 320 | 89 | 111 | 118 | 72 | 7 | 110 | 5 | 0 | 6 | 0 | 1 | .00 | 9 | .312 | .393 | .584 |
| 2011 | CWS | AL | 149 | 543 | 163 | 25 | 0 | 31 | (19 | 12) | 281 | 69 | 105 | 100 | 77 | 17 | 89 | 8 | 0 | 11 | 1 | 1 | .50 | 14 | .300 | .388 | .517 |
| 2012 | CWS | AL | 144 | 533 | 159 | 22 | 0 | 26 | (14 | 12) | 259 | 66 | 75 | 86 | 56 | 4 | 83 | 7 | 0 | 2 | 0 | 0 | - | 16 | .298 | .371 | .486 |
| 2013 | CWS | AL | 126 | 467 | 114 | 16 | 0 | 12 | (6 | 6) | 166 | 41 | 54 | 58 | 45 | 2 | 74 | 4 | 0 | 4 | 0 | 0 | - | 12 | .244 | .313 | .355 |
| 98 | LAD | NL | 49 | 144 | 31 | 1 | 0 | 4 | (2 | 2) | 44 | 14 | 16 | 10 | 10 | 0 | 30 | 2 | 0 | 2 | 0 | 1 | .00 | 5 | .215 | .272 | .306 |
| 98 | Cin | NL | 26 | 73 | 16 | 3 | 0 | 3 | (0 | 3) | 28 | 7 | 13 | 7 | 6 | 0 | 10 | 1 | 0 | 1 | 0 | 0 | - | 5 | .219 | .284 | .384 |
| Postseason | | | 19 | 74 | 18 | 2 | 0 | 7 | (3 | 4) | 41 | 10 | 17 | 12 | 5 | 2 | 10 | 1 | 0 | 0 | 0 | 0 | - | 4 | .243 | .300 | .554 |
| 17 ML YEARS | | | 2268 | 8185 | 2297 | 402 | 8 | 434 | (257 | 177) | 4017 | 1147 | 1390 | 1349 | 911 | 80 | 1340 | 100 | 1 | 84 | 9 | 4 | .69 | 275 | .281 | .356 | .491 |

# George Kontos

**Pitches:** R **Bats:** R **Pos:** RP-52 CON-toes **Ht:** 6'3" **Wt:** 215 **Born:** 6/12/1985 **Age:** 29

| HOW MUCH HE PITCHED | | | | | | | | | WHAT HE GAVE UP | | | | | | | | | | | | THE RESULTS | | | | | | | |
|---|---|---|---|---|---|---|---|---|---|---|---|---|---|---|---|---|---|---|---|---|---|---|---|---|---|---|---|---|
| Year | Team | Lg | G | GS | CG | GF | IP | BFP | H | R | ER | HR | SH | SF | HB | TBB | IBB | SO | WP | Bk | W | L | Pct | Sh | Sv-Op | Hld | ERC | ERA |
| 2013 | Fresno* | AAA | 18 | 0 | 0 | 9 | 23.2 | 96 | 19 | 11 | 11 | 3 | 0 | 2 | 0 | 3 | 0 | 26 | 1 | 0 | 3 | 2 | .600 | 0 | 4-- | - | 2.07 | 4.18 |
| 2011 | NYY | AL | 7 | 0 | 0 | 4 | 6.0 | 24 | 4 | 2 | 2 | 1 | 0 | 0 | 0 | 3 | 0 | 6 | 0 | 0 | 0 | 0 | - | 0 | 0-0 | 0 | 3.20 | 3.00 |
| 2012 | SF | NL | 44 | 0 | 0 | 9 | 43.2 | 177 | 34 | 15 | 12 | 3 | 0 | 2 | 0 | 12 | 0 | 44 | 1 | 0 | 2 | 1 | .667 | 0 | 0-1 | 5 | 2.23 | 2.47 |
| 2013 | SF | NL | 52 | 0 | 0 | 9 | 55.1 | 238 | 60 | 30 | 27 | 7 | 1 | 4 | 2 | 18 | 2 | 47 | 1 | 0 | 2 | 2 | .500 | 0 | 0-1 | 5 | 4.59 | 4.39 |
| Postseason | | | 8 | 0 | 0 | 1 | 5.1 | 22 | 6 | 4 | 4 | 1 | 1 | 0 | 0 | 1 | 0 | 2 | 0 | 0 | 0 | 0 | - | 0 | 0-0 | 1 | 4.65 | 6.75 |
| 3 ML YEARS | | | 103 | 0 | 0 | 22 | 105.0 | 439 | 98 | 47 | 41 | 11 | 1 | 6 | 2 | 33 | 2 | 97 | 2 | 0 | 4 | 3 | .571 | 0 | 0-2 | 10 | 3.46 | 3.51 |

# Casey Kotchman

**Bats:** L **Throws:** L **Pos:** 1B-6 **Ht:** 6'3" **Wt:** 220 **Born:** 2/22/1983 **Age:** 31

| BATTING | | | | | | | | | | | | | | | | | | | | | BASERUNNING | | | | AVERAGES | | |
|---|---|---|---|---|---|---|---|---|---|---|---|---|---|---|---|---|---|---|---|---|---|---|---|---|---|---|---|
| Year | Team | Lg | G | AB | H | 2B | 3B | HR | (Hm | Rd) | TB | R | RBI | RC | TBB | IBB | SO | HBP | SH | SF | SB | CS | SB% | GDP | Avg | OBP | Slg |
| 2013 | Jupiter* | A+ | 18 | 61 | 18 | 4 | 0 | 0 | (- | -) | 22 | 7 | 8 | 9 | 7 | 1 | 7 | 1 | 0 | 0 | 0 | 0 | - | 2 | .295 | .377 | .361 |
| 2004 | LAA | AL | 38 | 116 | 26 | 6 | 0 | 0 | (0 | 0) | 32 | 7 | 15 | 14 | 7 | 3 | 11 | 4 | 0 | 1 | 3 | 0 | 1.00 | 3 | .224 | .289 | .276 |
| 2005 | LAA | AL | 47 | 126 | 35 | 5 | 0 | 7 | (5 | 2) | 61 | 16 | 22 | 21 | 15 | 0 | 18 | 0 | 1 | 1 | 1 | 1 | .50 | 3 | .278 | .352 | .484 |
| 2006 | LAA | AL | 29 | 79 | 12 | 2 | 0 | 1 | (0 | 1) | 17 | 6 | 6 | 1 | 7 | 0 | 13 | 0 | 2 | 0 | 0 | 1 | .00 | 2 | .152 | .221 | .215 |
| 2007 | LAA | AL | 137 | 443 | 131 | 37 | 3 | 11 | (5 | 6) | 207 | 64 | 68 | 74 | 53 | 1 | 43 | 4 | 3 | 5 | 2 | 4 | .33 | 17 | .296 | .372 | .467 |
| 2008 | 2 Tms | | 143 | 525 | 143 | 28 | 1 | 14 | (3 | 11) | 215 | 65 | 74 | 70 | 36 | 5 | 39 | 9 | 0 | 3 | 2 | 1 | .67 | 18 | .272 | .328 | .410 |
| 2009 | 2 Tms | | 126 | 385 | 103 | 23 | 0 | 7 | (1 | 6) | 147 | 37 | 48 | 49 | 39 | 6 | 42 | 4 | 0 | 3 | 1 | 0 | 1.00 | 11 | .268 | .339 | .382 |
| 2010 | Sea | AL | 125 | 414 | 90 | 20 | 1 | 9 | (5 | 4) | 139 | 37 | 51 | 40 | 35 | 6 | 57 | 3 | 0 | 5 | 0 | 0 | - | 15 | .217 | .280 | .336 |
| 2011 | TB | AL | 146 | 500 | 153 | 24 | 2 | 10 | (7 | 3) | 211 | 44 | 48 | 74 | 48 | 5 | 66 | 12 | 0 | 3 | 2 | 2 | .50 | 13 | .306 | .378 | .422 |
| 2012 | Cle | AL | 142 | 463 | 106 | 12 | 0 | 12 | (6 | 6) | 154 | 46 | 55 | 44 | 26 | 1 | 49 | 7 | 3 | 1 | 3 | 0 | 1.00 | 15 | .229 | .280 | .333 |
| 2013 | Mia | NL | 6 | 20 | 0 | 0 | 0 | 0 | (0 | 0) | 0 | 0 | 1 | 0 | 1 | 0 | 1 | 0 | 0 | 0 | 0 | 0 | - | 1 | .000 | .048 | .000 |
| 08 | LAA | AL | 100 | 373 | 107 | 24 | 0 | 12 | (2 | 10) | 167 | 47 | 54 | 53 | 18 | 3 | 23 | 5 | 0 | 2 | 2 | 1 | .67 | 14 | .287 | .327 | .448 |

| Year | Team | Lg | G | AB | H | 2B | 3B | HR | (Hm | Rd) | TB | R | RBI | RC | TBB | IBB | SO | HBP | SH | SF | SB | CS | SB% | GDP | Avg | OBP | Slg |
|---|---|---|---|---|---|---|---|---|---|---|---|---|---|---|---|---|---|---|---|---|---|---|---|---|---|---|---|
| BATTING | | | | | | | | | | | | | | | | | | | | | BASERUNNING | | | | AVERAGES | | |
| 08 | Atl | NL | 43 | 152 | 36 | 4 | 1 | 2 | (1 | 1) | 48 | 18 | 20 | 17 | 18 | 2 | 16 | 4 | 0 | 1 | 0 | 0 | - | 4 | .237 | .331 | .316 |
| 09 | Atl | NL | 87 | 298 | 84 | 20 | 0 | 6 | (1 | 5) | 122 | 28 | 41 | 43 | 32 | 6 | 28 | 3 | 0 | 3 | 0 | 0 | - | 7 | .282 | .354 | .409 |
| 09 | Bos | AL | 39 | 87 | 19 | 3 | 0 | 1 | (0 | 1) | 25 | 9 | 7 | 6 | 7 | 0 | 14 | 1 | 0 | 0 | 1 | 0 | 1.00 | 4 | .218 | .284 | .287 |
| Postseason | | | 15 | 32 | 6 | 2 | 0 | 0 | (0 | 0) | 8 | 2 | 3 | 4 | 3 | 0 | 3 | 0 | 0 | 0 | 0 | 0 | - | 0 | .188 | .257 | .250 |
| 10 ML YEARS | | | 939 | 3071 | 799 | 157 | 7 | 71 | (32 | 39) | 1183 | 322 | 388 | 387 | 267 | 27 | 339 | 43 | 9 | 22 | 14 | 9 | .61 | 98 | .260 | .326 | .385 |

# Mark Kotsay

**Bats:** L **Throws:** L **Pos:** PH-75;LF-19;RF-6;1B-5;DH-3 **Ht:** 6'0" **Wt:** 220 **Born:** 12/2/1975 **Age:** 38

| Year | Team | Lg | G | AB | H | 2B | 3B | HR | (Hm | Rd) | TB | R | RBI | RC | TBB | IBB | SO | HBP | SH | SF | SB | CS | SB% | GDP | Avg | OBP | Slg |
|---|---|---|---|---|---|---|---|---|---|---|---|---|---|---|---|---|---|---|---|---|---|---|---|---|---|---|---|
| BATTING | | | | | | | | | | | | | | | | | | | | | BASERUNNING | | | | AVERAGES | | |
| 1997 | Fla | NL | 14 | 52 | 10 | 1 | 1 | 0 | (0 | 0) | 13 | 5 | 4 | 3 | 4 | 0 | 7 | 0 | 1 | 0 | 3 | 0 | 1.00 | 1 | .192 | .250 | .250 |
| 1998 | Fla | NL | 154 | 578 | 161 | 25 | 7 | 11 | (5 | 6) | 233 | 72 | 68 | 70 | 34 | 2 | 61 | 1 | 7 | 3 | 10 | 5 | .67 | 17 | .279 | .318 | .403 |
| 1999 | Fla | NL | 148 | 495 | 134 | 23 | 9 | 8 | (5 | 3) | 199 | 57 | 50 | 58 | 29 | 5 | 50 | 0 | 2 | 9 | 7 | 6 | .54 | 11 | .271 | .306 | .402 |
| 2000 | Fla | NL | 152 | 530 | 158 | 31 | 5 | 12 | (5 | 7) | 235 | 87 | 57 | 78 | 42 | 2 | 46 | 0 | 2 | 4 | 19 | 9 | .68 | 17 | .298 | .347 | .443 |
| 2001 | SD | NL | 119 | 406 | 118 | 29 | 1 | 10 | (3 | 7) | 179 | 67 | 58 | 65 | 48 | 1 | 58 | 2 | 1 | 3 | 13 | 5 | .72 | 11 | .291 | .366 | .441 |
| 2002 | SD | NL | 153 | 578 | 169 | 27 | 7 | 17 | (11 | 6) | 261 | 82 | 61 | 92 | 59 | 0 | 89 | 3 | 2 | 4 | 11 | 9 | .55 | 10 | .292 | .359 | .452 |
| 2003 | SD | NL | 128 | 482 | 128 | 28 | 4 | 7 | (1 | 6) | 185 | 64 | 38 | 59 | 56 | 3 | 82 | 1 | 1 | 1 | 6 | 3 | .67 | 8 | .266 | .343 | .384 |
| 2004 | Oak | AL | 148 | 606 | 190 | 37 | 3 | 15 | (9 | 6) | 278 | 78 | 63 | 94 | 55 | 5 | 70 | 2 | 5 | 5 | 8 | 5 | .62 | 6 | .314 | .370 | .459 |
| 2005 | Oak | AL | 139 | 582 | 163 | 35 | 1 | 15 | (4 | 11) | 245 | 75 | 82 | 86 | 40 | 3 | 51 | 1 | 2 | 4 | 5 | 5 | .50 | 13 | .280 | .325 | .421 |
| 2006 | Oak | AL | 129 | 502 | 138 | 29 | 3 | 7 | (1 | 6) | 194 | 57 | 59 | 63 | 44 | 1 | 55 | 2 | 4 | 6 | 6 | 3 | .67 | 18 | .275 | .332 | .386 |
| 2007 | Oak | AL | 56 | 206 | 44 | 14 | 0 | 1 | (0 | 1) | 61 | 20 | 20 | 19 | 19 | 3 | 20 | 0 | 0 | 1 | 1 | 1 | .50 | 4 | .214 | .279 | .296 |
| 2008 | 2 Tms | | 110 | 402 | 111 | 25 | 4 | 6 | (4 | 2) | 162 | 45 | 49 | 49 | 32 | 3 | 45 | 0 | 1 | 1 | 2 | 4 | .33 | 14 | .276 | .329 | .403 |
| 2009 | 2 Tms | AL | 67 | 187 | 52 | 9 | 0 | 4 | (4 | 0) | 73 | 16 | 23 | 22 | 15 | 3 | 21 | 0 | 1 | 3 | 3 | 2 | .60 | 6 | .278 | .327 | .390 |
| 2010 | CWS | AL | 107 | 327 | 78 | 17 | 2 | 8 | (4 | 4) | 123 | 30 | 31 | 33 | 32 | 3 | 36 | 0 | 0 | 0 | 1 | 3 | .25 | 9 | .239 | .306 | .376 |
| 2011 | Mil | NL | 104 | 233 | 63 | 13 | 1 | 3 | (1 | 2) | 87 | 18 | 31 | 31 | 21 | 3 | 27 | 0 | 0 | 1 | 3 | 0 | 1.00 | 4 | .270 | .329 | .373 |
| 2012 | SD | NL | 82 | 143 | 37 | 8 | 0 | 2 | (1 | 1) | 51 | 9 | 14 | 14 | 11 | 1 | 14 | 1 | 0 | 1 | 0 | 2 | .00 | 2 | .259 | .314 | .357 |
| 2013 | SD | NL | 104 | 155 | 30 | 2 | 0 | 1 | (0 | 1) | 35 | 8 | 12 | 6 | 13 | 0 | 25 | 0 | 1 | 2 | 0 | 2 | .00 | 1 | .194 | .253 | .226 |
| 08 | Atl | NL | 88 | 318 | 92 | 17 | 3 | 6 | (4 | 2) | 133 | 39 | 37 | 37 | 25 | 2 | 34 | 0 | 1 | 1 | 2 | 3 | .40 | 13 | .289 | .340 | .418 |
| 08 | Bos | AL | 22 | 84 | 19 | 8 | 1 | 0 | (0 | 0) | 29 | 6 | 12 | 12 | 7 | 1 | 11 | 0 | 0 | 0 | 0 | 1 | .00 | 1 | .226 | .286 | .345 |
| 09 | Bos | AL | 27 | 74 | 19 | 2 | 0 | 1 | (1 | 0) | 24 | 4 | 5 | 6 | 4 | 1 | 12 | 0 | 0 | 1 | 2 | 1 | .67 | 1 | .257 | .291 | .324 |
| 09 | CWS | AL | 40 | 113 | 33 | 7 | 0 | 3 | (3 | 0) | 49 | 12 | 18 | 16 | 11 | 2 | 9 | 0 | 1 | 2 | 1 | 1 | .50 | 5 | .292 | .349 | .434 |
| Postseason | | | 26 | 82 | 17 | 5 | 0 | 2 | (0 | 2) | 28 | 9 | 3 | 3 | 5 | 1 | 12 | 0 | 0 | 0 | 0 | 0 | - | 4 | .207 | .253 | .341 |
| 17 ML YEARS | | | 1914 | 6464 | 1784 | 353 | 48 | 127 | (58 | 69) | 2614 | 790 | 720 | 842 | 554 | 38 | 757 | 13 | 30 | 48 | 98 | 64 | .60 | 152 | .276 | .332 | .404 |

# George Kottaras

**Bats:** L **Throws:** R **Pos:** C-39;PH-12 kah-TARR-iss **Ht:** 6'0" **Wt:** 200 **Born:** 5/10/1983 **Age:** 31

| Year | Team | Lg | G | AB | H | 2B | 3B | HR | (Hm | Rd) | TB | R | RBI | RC | TBB | IBB | SO | HBP | SH | SF | SB | CS | SB% | GDP | Avg | OBP | Slg |
|---|---|---|---|---|---|---|---|---|---|---|---|---|---|---|---|---|---|---|---|---|---|---|---|---|---|---|---|
| BATTING | | | | | | | | | | | | | | | | | | | | | BASERUNNING | | | | AVERAGES | | |
| 2008 | Bos | AL | 3 | 5 | 1 | 1 | 0 | 0 | (0 | 0) | 2 | 1 | 0 | 0 | 0 | 0 | 2 | 0 | 0 | 0 | 0 | 0 | - | 0 | .200 | .200 | .400 |
| 2009 | Bos | AL | 45 | 93 | 22 | 11 | 0 | 1 | (1 | 0) | 36 | 15 | 10 | 10 | 11 | 0 | 25 | 0 | 0 | 3 | 0 | 0 | - | 1 | .237 | .308 | .387 |
| 2010 | Mil | NL | 67 | 212 | 43 | 12 | 1 | 9 | (5 | 4) | 84 | 24 | 26 | 22 | 33 | 1 | 44 | 0 | 1 | 4 | 2 | 0 | 1.00 | 5 | .203 | .305 | .396 |
| 2011 | Mil | NL | 49 | 111 | 28 | 6 | 1 | 5 | (1 | 4) | 51 | 15 | 17 | 15 | 10 | 0 | 26 | 0 | 1 | 1 | 0 | 1 | .00 | 2 | .252 | .311 | .459 |
| 2012 | 2 Tms | | 85 | 171 | 36 | 6 | 1 | 9 | (4 | 5) | 71 | 20 | 31 | 30 | 37 | 1 | 48 | 0 | 1 | 0 | 0 | 0 | - | 4 | .211 | .351 | .415 |
| 2013 | KC | AL | 46 | 100 | 18 | 4 | 0 | 5 | (3 | 2) | 37 | 13 | 12 | 11 | 24 | 2 | 42 | 2 | 0 | 0 | 1 | 0 | 1.00 | 2 | .180 | .349 | .370 |
| 12 | Mil | NL | 58 | 86 | 18 | 4 | 0 | 3 | (1 | 2) | 31 | 10 | 12 | 15 | 29 | 1 | 24 | 0 | 1 | 0 | 0 | 0 | - | 2 | .209 | .409 | .360 |
| 12 | Oak | AL | 27 | 85 | 18 | 2 | 1 | 6 | (3 | 3) | 40 | 10 | 19 | 15 | 8 | 0 | 24 | 0 | 0 | 0 | 0 | 0 | - | 2 | .212 | .280 | .471 |
| Postseason | | | 7 | 12 | 0 | 0 | 0 | 0 | (0 | 0) | 0 | 0 | 2 | 0 | 1 | 0 | 4 | 0 | 1 | 0 | 0 | 0 | - | 0 | .000 | .077 | .000 |
| 6 ML YEARS | | | 295 | 692 | 148 | 40 | 3 | 29 | (14 | 15) | 281 | 88 | 96 | 88 | 115 | 4 | 187 | 2 | 3 | 8 | 3 | 1 | .75 | 14 | .214 | .324 | .406 |

# Pete Kozma

**Bats:** R **Throws:** R **Pos:** SS-139;PR-8;PH-5;LF-1 KAHZ-muh **Ht:** 6'0" **Wt:** 190 **Born:** 4/11/1988 **Age:** 26

| Year | Team | Lg | G | AB | H | 2B | 3B | HR | (Hm | Rd) | TB | R | RBI | RC | TBB | IBB | SO | HBP | SH | SF | SB | CS | SB% | GDP | Avg | OBP | Slg |
|---|---|---|---|---|---|---|---|---|---|---|---|---|---|---|---|---|---|---|---|---|---|---|---|---|---|---|---|
| BATTING | | | | | | | | | | | | | | | | | | | | | BASERUNNING | | | | AVERAGES | | |
| 2011 | StL | NL | 16 | 17 | 3 | 1 | 0 | 0 | (0 | 0) | 4 | 2 | 1 | 2 | 4 | 0 | 4 | 0 | 1 | 0 | 0 | 0 | - | 0 | .176 | .333 | .235 |
| 2012 | StL | NL | 26 | 72 | 24 | 5 | 3 | 2 | (0 | 2) | 41 | 11 | 14 | 13 | 7 | 1 | 19 | 0 | 1 | 2 | 2 | 0 | 1.00 | 4 | .333 | .383 | .569 |
| 2013 | StL | NL | 143 | 410 | 89 | 20 | 0 | 1 | (0 | 1) | 112 | 44 | 35 | 39 | 34 | 8 | 91 | 0 | 1 | 3 | 3 | 1 | .75 | 6 | .217 | .275 | .273 |
| Postseason | | | 13 | 42 | 9 | 2 | 0 | 1 | (0 | 1) | 14 | 8 | 7 | 9 | 8 | 1 | 14 | 1 | 0 | 0 | 1 | 1 | .50 | 1 | .214 | .353 | .333 |
| 3 ML YEARS | | | 185 | 499 | 116 | 26 | 3 | 3 | (0 | 3) | 157 | 57 | 50 | 54 | 45 | 9 | 114 | 0 | 3 | 5 | 5 | 1 | .83 | 10 | .232 | .293 | .315 |

# Erik Kratz

**Bats:** R **Throws:** R **Pos:** C-60;PH-11 **Ht:** 6'4" **Wt:** 255 **Born:** 6/15/1980 **Age:** 34

| Year | Team | Lg | G | AB | H | 2B | 3B | HR | (Hm | Rd) | TB | R | RBI | RC | TBB | IBB | SO | HBP | SH | SF | SB | CS | SB% | GDP | Avg | OBP | Slg |
|---|---|---|---|---|---|---|---|---|---|---|---|---|---|---|---|---|---|---|---|---|---|---|---|---|---|---|---|
| BATTING | | | | | | | | | | | | | | | | | | | | | BASERUNNING | | | | AVERAGES | | |
| 2013 | LV* | AAA | 3 | 12 | 2 | 1 | 0 | 0 | (- | -) | 3 | 0 | 1 | 0 | 0 | 0 | 1 | 0 | 0 | 0 | 0 | 0 | - | 0 | .167 | .167 | .250 |
| 2013 | Rdng* | AA | 1 | 4 | 0 | 0 | 0 | 0 | (- | -) | 0 | 0 | 0 | 0 | 0 | 0 | 1 | 0 | 0 | 0 | 0 | 0 | - | 0 | .000 | .000 | .000 |
| 2010 | Pit | NL | 9 | 34 | 4 | 0 | 0 | 0 | (0 | 0) | 4 | 2 | 1 | 0 | 2 | 0 | 9 | 0 | 0 | 0 | 0 | 0 | - | 0 | .118 | .167 | .118 |
| 2011 | Phi | NL | 2 | 6 | 2 | 1 | 0 | 0 | (0 | 0) | 3 | 0 | 0 | 1 | 0 | 0 | 1 | 0 | 0 | 0 | 0 | 0 | - | 0 | .333 | .333 | .500 |
| 2012 | Phi | NL | 50 | 141 | 35 | 9 | 0 | 9 | (6 | 3) | 71 | 14 | 26 | 20 | 11 | 2 | 34 | 2 | 0 | 3 | 0 | 0 | - | 2 | .248 | .306 | .504 |
| 2013 | Phi | NL | 68 | 197 | 42 | 7 | 0 | 9 | (5 | 4) | 76 | 21 | 26 | 15 | 18 | 4 | 45 | 1 | 0 | 2 | 0 | 0 | - | 11 | .213 | .280 | .386 |
| 4 ML YEARS | | | 129 | 378 | 83 | 17 | 0 | 18 | (11 | 7) | 154 | 37 | 53 | 36 | 31 | 6 | 89 | 3 | 0 | 5 | 0 | 0 | - | 13 | .220 | .281 | .407 |

# Marc Krauss

**Bats:** L **Throws:** R **Pos:** LF-18;PH-16;DH-14;RF-9;1B-2 **Ht:** 6'2" **Wt:** 235 **Born:** 10/5/1987 **Age:** 26

| BATTING | | | | | | | | | | | | | | | | | | | | | BASERUNNING | | | | AVERAGES | | |
|---|---|---|---|---|---|---|---|---|---|---|---|---|---|---|---|---|---|---|---|---|---|---|---|---|---|---|---|
| Year | Team | Lg | G | AB | H | 2B | 3B | HR | (Hm | Rd) | TB | R | RBI | RC | TBB | IBB | SO | HBP | SH | SF | SB | CS | SB% | GDP | Avg | OBP | Slg |
| 2009 | Sbend | A | 32 | 115 | 35 | 12 | 1 | 2 | (- | -) | 55 | 14 | 17 | 20 | 14 | 0 | 21 | 0 | 0 | 1 | 0 | 1 | .00 | 2 | .304 | .377 | .478 |
| 2010 | Visalia | A+ | 138 | 530 | 160 | 27 | 4 | 25 | (- | -) | 270 | 107 | 87 | 100 | 57 | 0 | 141 | 4 | 0 | 5 | 1 | 3 | .25 | 11 | .302 | .371 | .509 |
| 2011 | Mobile | AA | 125 | 433 | 105 | 25 | 6 | 16 | (- | -) | 190 | 69 | 65 | 68 | 64 | 1 | 123 | 2 | 1 | 4 | 2 | 3 | .40 | 9 | .242 | .340 | .439 |
| 2012 | Mobile | AA | 104 | 346 | 97 | 29 | 2 | 15 | (- | -) | 175 | 75 | 61 | 76 | 73 | 1 | 91 | 9 | 0 | 5 | 6 | 4 | .60 | 4 | .280 | .413 | .506 |
| 2012 | CpChr | AA | 7 | 29 | 12 | 2 | 0 | 5 | (- | -) | 29 | 11 | 16 | 12 | 6 | 0 | 5 | 0 | 0 | 0 | 1 | 0 | 1.00 | 0 | .414 | .514 | 1.000 |
| 2012 | OKCity | AAA | 22 | 57 | 7 | 0 | 0 | 0 | (- | -) | 7 | 3 | 2 | 0 | 6 | 0 | 20 | 0 | 2 | 1 | 1 | 1 | .50 | 2 | .123 | .203 | .123 |
| 2013 | OKCity | AAA | 78 | 253 | 71 | 16 | 2 | 10 | (- | -) | 121 | 38 | 39 | 52 | 53 | 6 | 52 | 2 | 0 | 6 | 3 | 3 | .50 | 4 | .281 | .401 | .478 |
| 2013 | Hou | AL | 52 | 134 | 28 | 9 | 0 | 4 | (1 | 3) | 49 | 11 | 13 | 12 | 10 | 0 | 45 | 1 | 0 | 1 | 2 | 0 | 1.00 | 2 | .209 | .267 | .366 |

# Ian Krol

**Pitches:** L **Bats:** L **Pos:** RP-32 KROHL **Ht:** 6'1" **Wt:** 210 **Born:** 5/9/1991 **Age:** 23

| | | | HOW MUCH HE PITCHED | | | | | | WHAT HE GAVE UP | | | | | | | | | | | | THE RESULTS | | | | | | | |
|---|---|---|---|---|---|---|---|---|---|---|---|---|---|---|---|---|---|---|---|---|---|---|---|---|---|---|---|---|
| Year | Team | Lg | G | GS | CG | GF | IP | BFP | H | R | ER | HR | SH | SF | HB | TBB | IBB | SO | WP | Bk | W | L | Pct | Sh | Sv-Op | Hld | ERC | ERA |
| 2009 | As | R | 1 | 1 | 0 | 0 | 1.0 | 3 | 0 | 0 | 0 | 0 | 0 | 0 | 0 | 0 | 0 | 0 | 0 | 0 | 0 | 0 | - | 0 | 0-- | - | 0.00 | 0.00 |
| 2009 | Vancvr | A- | 3 | 1 | 0 | 0 | 3.1 | 18 | 6 | 5 | 3 | 0 | 0 | 1 | 0 | 1 | 0 | 4 | 0 | 0 | 0 | 1 | .000 | 0 | 0-- | - | 7.06 | 8.10 |
| 2010 | Kane | A | 24 | 23 | 0 | 1 | 118.2 | 476 | 98 | 42 | 35 | 5 | 5 | 5 | 7 | 19 | 1 | 91 | 2 | 3 | 9 | 4 | .692 | 0 | 0-- | - | 2.12 | 2.65 |
| 2010 | Stcktn | A+ | 4 | 4 | 0 | 0 | 19.2 | 84 | 18 | 9 | 8 | 3 | 1 | 0 | 1 | 9 | 0 | 20 | 0 | 0 | 1 | 0 | 1.000 | 0 | 0-- | - | 4.48 | 3.66 |
| 2011 | As | R | 3 | 3 | 0 | 0 | 5.0 | 15 | 0 | 0 | 0 | 0 | 0 | 0 | 0 | 0 | 0 | 6 | 0 | 0 | 0 | 0 | - | 0 | 0-- | - | 0.00 | 0.00 |
| 2012 | Stcktn | A+ | 21 | 15 | 0 | 2 | 86.1 | 379 | 95 | 64 | 50 | 13 | 1 | 6 | 3 | 24 | 0 | 79 | 1 | 1 | 1 | 7 | .125 | 0 | 0-- | - | 4.57 | 5.21 |
| 2012 | Mdlnd | AA | 8 | 0 | 0 | 3 | 10.2 | 41 | 11 | 6 | 6 | 0 | 1 | 0 | 0 | 2 | 1 | 10 | 2 | 0 | 1 | 2 | .333 | 0 | 0-- | - | 2.88 | 5.06 |
| 2013 | Hrsbrg | AA | 21 | 0 | 0 | 6 | 26.0 | 101 | 14 | 4 | 2 | 1 | 2 | 1 | 2 | 7 | 0 | 29 | 0 | 0 | 0 | 0 | - | 0 | 1-- | - | 1.37 | 0.69 |
| 2013 | Syrcse | AAA | 5 | 0 | 0 | 1 | 3.2 | 14 | 2 | 2 | 2 | 0 | 0 | 0 | 0 | 1 | 0 | 7 | 0 | 0 | 1 | 1 | .500 | 0 | 0-- | - | 1.10 | 4.91 |
| 2013 | Was | NL | 32 | 0 | 0 | 10 | 27.1 | 117 | 28 | 12 | 12 | 5 | 2 | 1 | 0 | 8 | 1 | 22 | 2 | 0 | 2 | 1 | .667 | 0 | 0-1 | 2 | 4.24 | 3.95 |

# Jason Kubel

**Bats:** L **Throws:** R **Pos:** LF-56;PH-31;RF-8;DH-5 KOO-bull **Ht:** 6'0" **Wt:** 220 **Born:** 5/25/1982 **Age:** 32

| BATTING | | | | | | | | | | | | | | | | | | | | | BASERUNNING | | | | AVERAGES | | |
|---|---|---|---|---|---|---|---|---|---|---|---|---|---|---|---|---|---|---|---|---|---|---|---|---|---|---|---|
| Year | Team | Lg | G | AB | H | 2B | 3B | HR | (Hm | Rd) | TB | R | RBI | RC | TBB | IBB | SO | HBP | SH | SF | SB | CS | SB% | GDP | Avg | OBP | Slg |
| 2004 | Min | AL | 23 | 60 | 18 | 2 | 0 | 2 | (0 | 2) | 26 | 10 | 7 | 13 | 6 | 0 | 9 | 0 | 0 | 1 | 1 | 1 | .50 | 0 | .300 | .358 | .433 |
| 2006 | Min | AL | 73 | 220 | 53 | 8 | 0 | 8 | (3 | 5) | 85 | 23 | 26 | 20 | 12 | 0 | 45 | 0 | 2 | 1 | 2 | 0 | 1.00 | 13 | .241 | .279 | .386 |
| 2007 | Min | AL | 128 | 418 | 114 | 31 | 2 | 13 | (6 | 7) | 188 | 49 | 65 | 64 | 41 | 2 | 79 | 1 | 1 | 5 | 5 | 0 | 1.00 | 9 | .273 | .335 | .450 |
| 2008 | Min | AL | 141 | 463 | 126 | 22 | 5 | 20 | (9 | 11) | 218 | 74 | 78 | 66 | 47 | 2 | 91 | 0 | 0 | 7 | 0 | 1 | .00 | 12 | .272 | .335 | .471 |
| 2009 | Min | AL | 146 | 514 | 154 | 35 | 2 | 28 | (15 | 13) | 277 | 73 | 103 | 95 | 56 | 9 | 106 | 3 | 0 | 5 | 1 | 1 | .50 | 13 | .300 | .369 | .539 |
| 2010 | Min | AL | 143 | 518 | 129 | 23 | 3 | 21 | (8 | 13) | 221 | 68 | 92 | 65 | 56 | 5 | 116 | 3 | 0 | 5 | 0 | 1 | .00 | 16 | .249 | .323 | .427 |
| 2011 | Min | AL | 99 | 366 | 100 | 21 | 1 | 12 | (4 | 8) | 159 | 37 | 58 | 59 | 32 | 2 | 86 | 1 | 0 | 2 | 1 | 1 | .50 | 8 | .273 | .332 | .434 |
| 2012 | Ari | NL | 141 | 506 | 128 | 30 | 4 | 30 | (18 | 12) | 256 | 75 | 90 | 71 | 57 | 7 | 151 | 2 | 0 | 6 | 1 | 1 | .50 | 11 | .253 | .327 | .506 |
| 2013 | 2 Tms | | 97 | 259 | 56 | 9 | 1 | 5 | (3 | 2) | 82 | 21 | 32 | 29 | 29 | 6 | 92 | 0 | 0 | 2 | 0 | 1 | .00 | 6 | .216 | .293 | .317 |
| 13 | Ari | NL | 89 | 241 | 53 | 8 | 1 | 5 | (3 | 2) | 78 | 21 | 32 | 27 | 24 | 3 | 82 | 0 | 0 | 2 | 0 | 1 | .00 | 6 | .220 | .288 | .324 |
| 13 | Cle | AL | 8 | 18 | 3 | 1 | 0 | 0 | (0 | 0) | 4 | 0 | 0 | 2 | 5 | 3 | 10 | 0 | 0 | 0 | 0 | 0 | - | 0 | .167 | .348 | .222 |
| Postseason | | | 8 | 29 | 2 | 1 | 0 | 0 | (0 | 0) | 3 | 0 | 0 | 0 | 3 | 0 | 13 | 0 | 0 | 0 | 0 | 0 | - | 0 | .069 | .156 | .103 |
| 9 ML YEARS | | | 991 | 3324 | 878 | 181 | 18 | 139 | (66 | 73) | 1512 | 430 | 551 | 482 | 336 | 33 | 775 | 10 | 3 | 34 | 11 | 7 | .61 | 88 | .264 | .330 | .455 |

# Hiroki Kuroda

**Pitches:** R **Bats:** R **Pos:** SP-32 hih-ROE-kee kuh-ROE-duh **Ht:** 6'1" **Wt:** 205 **Born:** 2/10/1975 **Age:** 39

| | | | HOW MUCH HE PITCHED | | | | | | WHAT HE GAVE UP | | | | | | | | | | | | THE RESULTS | | | | | | | |
|---|---|---|---|---|---|---|---|---|---|---|---|---|---|---|---|---|---|---|---|---|---|---|---|---|---|---|---|---|
| Year | Team | Lg | G | GS | CG | GF | IP | BFP | H | R | ER | HR | SH | SF | HB | TBB | IBB | SO | WP | Bk | W | L | Pct | Sh | Sv-Op | Hld | ERC | ERA |
| 2008 | LAD | NL | 31 | 31 | 2 | 0 | 183.1 | 776 | 181 | 85 | 76 | 13 | 7 | 5 | 7 | 42 | 8 | 116 | 5 | 0 | 9 | 10 | .474 | 2 | 0-0 | 0 | 3.18 | 3.73 |
| 2009 | LAD | NL | 21 | 20 | 0 | 0 | 117.1 | 485 | 110 | 59 | 49 | 12 | 7 | 1 | 1 | 24 | 1 | 87 | 5 | 0 | 8 | 7 | .533 | 0 | 0-0 | 0 | 2.98 | 3.76 |
| 2010 | LAD | NL | 31 | 31 | 0 | 0 | 196.1 | 810 | 180 | 87 | 74 | 15 | 9 | 7 | 5 | 48 | **13** | 159 | 12 | 0 | 11 | 13 | .458 | 0 | 0-0 | 0 | 2.87 | 3.39 |
| 2011 | LAD | NL | 32 | 32 | 0 | 0 | 202.0 | 838 | 196 | 77 | 69 | 24 | 6 | 5 | 5 | 49 | 6 | 161 | 12 | 1 | 13 | 16 | .448 | 0 | 0-0 | 0 | 3.49 | 3.07 |
| 2012 | NYY | AL | 33 | 33 | 3 | 0 | 219.2 | 891 | 205 | 86 | 81 | 25 | **7** | 3 | 8 | 51 | 2 | 167 | 13 | 0 | 16 | 11 | .593 | 2 | 0-0 | 0 | 3.35 | 3.32 |
| 2013 | NYY | AL | 32 | 32 | 1 | 0 | 201.1 | 824 | 191 | 79 | 74 | 20 | 2 | 7 | 5 | 43 | 2 | 150 | 6 | 0 | 11 | 13 | .458 | 1 | 0-0 | 0 | 3.17 | 3.31 |
| Postseason | | | 5 | 5 | 0 | 0 | 29.2 | 120 | 27 | 13 | 13 | 3 | 1 | 0 | 2 | 4 | 1 | 22 | 0 | 0 | 2 | 2 | .500 | 0 | 0-0 | 0 | 2.80 | 3.94 |
| 6 ML YEARS | | | 180 | 179 | 6 | 0 | 1120.0 | 4624 | 1063 | 473 | 423 | 109 | 38 | 28 | 31 | 257 | 32 | 840 | 53 | 1 | 68 | 70 | .493 | 5 | 0-0 | 0 | 3.19 | 3.40 |

# John Lackey

**Pitches:** R **Bats:** R **Pos:** SP-29 **Ht:** 6'6" **Wt:** 235 **Born:** 10/23/1978 **Age:** 35

| | | | HOW MUCH HE PITCHED | | | | | | WHAT HE GAVE UP | | | | | | | | | | | | THE RESULTS | | | | | | | |
|---|---|---|---|---|---|---|---|---|---|---|---|---|---|---|---|---|---|---|---|---|---|---|---|---|---|---|---|---|
| Year | Team | Lg | G | GS | CG | GF | IP | BFP | H | R | ER | HR | SH | SF | HB | TBB | IBB | SO | WP | Bk | W | L | Pct | Sh | Sv-Op | Hld | ERC | ERA |
| 2013 | Portlnd* | AA | 1 | 1 | 0 | 0 | 3.2 | 15 | 3 | 0 | 0 | 0 | 0 | 0 | 0 | 2 | 0 | 5 | 0 | 0 | 0 | 0 | - | 0 | 0-- | - | 3.10 | 0.00 |
| 2002 | LAA | AL | 18 | 18 | 1 | 0 | 108.1 | 465 | 113 | 52 | 44 | 10 | 0 | 4 | 4 | 33 | 0 | 69 | 7 | 2 | 9 | 4 | .692 | 0 | 0-0 | 0 | 4.03 | 3.66 |
| 2003 | LAA | AL | 33 | 33 | 2 | 0 | 204.0 | 885 | 223 | 117 | 105 | 31 | 2 | 6 | 10 | 66 | 4 | 151 | 11 | 1 | 10 | 16 | .385 | **2** | 0-0 | 0 | 4.88 | 4.63 |
| 2004 | LAA | AL | 33 | 32 | 1 | 0 | 198.1 | 855 | 215 | 108 | 103 | 22 | 9 | 4 | 8 | 60 | 4 | 144 | 11 | 1 | 14 | 13 | .519 | 1 | 0-0 | 0 | 4.39 | 4.67 |
| 2005 | LAA | AL | 33 | 33 | 1 | 0 | 209.0 | 892 | 208 | 85 | 80 | 13 | 1 | 2 | 11 | 71 | 3 | 199 | 18 | 0 | 14 | 5 | .737 | 0 | 0-0 | 0 | 3.76 | 3.44 |
| 2006 | LAA | AL | 33 | 33 | 3 | 0 | 217.2 | 922 | 203 | 98 | 86 | 14 | 8 | 6 | 9 | 72 | 4 | 190 | 16 | 0 | 13 | 11 | .542 | **2** | 0-0 | 0 | 3.31 | 3.56 |
| 2007 | LAA | AL | 33 | 33 | 2 | 0 | 224.0 | 929 | 219 | 87 | 75 | 18 | 1 | 1 | 12 | 52 | 2 | 179 | 9 | 1 | 19 | 9 | .679 | **2** | 0-0 | 0 | 3.40 | **3.01** |
| 2008 | LAA | AL | 24 | 24 | 3 | 0 | 163.1 | 675 | 161 | 71 | 68 | 26 | 5 | 1 | 10 | 40 | 1 | 130 | 5 | 0 | 12 | 5 | .706 | 0 | 0-0 | 0 | 4.10 | 3.75 |
| 2009 | LAA | AL | 27 | 27 | 1 | 0 | 176.1 | 748 | 177 | 84 | 75 | 17 | 9 | 10 | 9 | 47 | 1 | 139 | 6 | 0 | 11 | 8 | .579 | 1 | 0-0 | 0 | 3.73 | 3.83 |
| 2010 | Bos | AL | 33 | 33 | 0 | 0 | 215.0 | 930 | 233 | 114 | 105 | 18 | 4 | 5 | 9 | 72 | 2 | 156 | 3 | 0 | 14 | 11 | .560 | 0 | 0-0 | 0 | 4.37 | 4.40 |
| 2011 | Bos | AL | 28 | 28 | 0 | 0 | 160.0 | 743 | 203 | 119 | **114** | 20 | 2 | 6 | **19** | 56 | 1 | 108 | 11 | 0 | 12 | 12 | .500 | 0 | 0-0 | 0 | 6.11 | 6.41 |
| 2013 | Bos | AL | 29 | 29 | 2 | 0 | 189.1 | 778 | 179 | 80 | 74 | 26 | 3 | 3 | 6 | 40 | 0 | 161 | 4 | 0 | 10 | 13 | .435 | 0 | 0-0 | 0 | 3.42 | 3.52 |
| Postseason | | | 14 | 12 | 0 | 0 | 78.0 | 328 | 75 | 29 | 27 | 4 | 2 | 3 | 1 | 29 | 4 | 53 | 4 | 0 | 3 | 4 | .429 | 0 | 0-0 | 0 | 3.43 | 3.12 |
| 11 ML YEARS | | | 324 | 323 | 16 | 0 | 2065.1 | 8822 | 2134 | 1015 | 929 | 215 | 44 | 48 | 107 | 609 | 22 | 1626 | 101 | 5 | 138 | 107 | .563 | 8 | 0-0 | 0 | 4.08 | 4.05 |

# Aaron Laffey

**Pitches:** L **Bats:** L **Pos:** SP-3; RP-2 LAFF-ee **Ht:** 6'0" **Wt:** 200 **Born:** 4/15/1985 **Age:** 29

| | | | HOW MUCH HE PITCHED | | | | | | WHAT HE GAVE UP | | | | | | | | | | | | THE RESULTS | | | | | | | |
|---|---|---|---|---|---|---|---|---|---|---|---|---|---|---|---|---|---|---|---|---|---|---|---|---|---|---|---|---|
| Year | Team | Lg | G | GS | CG | GF | IP | BFP | H | R | ER | HR | SH | SF | HB | TBB | IBB | SO | WP | Bk | W | L | Pct | Sh | Sv-Op | Hld | ERC | ERA |
| 2013 | Albq* | AAA | 12 | 11 | 0 | 0 | 61.0 | 274 | 72 | 40 | 38 | 12 | 5 | 3 | 3 | 22 | 0 | 29 | 0 | 0 | 4 | 3 | .571 | 0 | 0-- | - | 5.90 | 5.61 |
| 2013 | Nashv* | AAA | 11 | 11 | 0 | 0 | 49.2 | 240 | 68 | 45 | 40 | 5 | 1 | 4 | 7 | 19 | 0 | 26 | 5 | 0 | 2 | 5 | .286 | 0 | 0-- | - | 6.73 | 7.25 |
| 2007 | Cle | AL | 9 | 9 | 0 | 0 | 49.1 | 207 | 54 | 26 | 25 | 2 | 1 | 2 | 4 | 12 | 0 | 25 | 2 | 1 | 4 | 2 | .667 | 0 | 0-0 | 0 | 4.02 | 4.56 |
| 2008 | Cle | AL | 16 | 16 | 0 | 0 | 93.2 | 409 | 103 | 52 | 44 | 10 | 2 | 0 | 9 | 31 | 1 | 43 | 5 | 1 | 5 | 7 | .417 | 0 | 0-0 | 0 | 4.86 | 4.23 |
| 2009 | Cle | AL | 25 | 19 | 0 | 3 | 121.2 | 539 | 140 | 69 | 60 | 9 | 0 | 4 | 2 | 57 | 1 | 59 | 1 | 1 | 7 | 9 | .438 | 0 | 1-1 | 0 | 5.20 | 4.44 |
| 2010 | Cle | AL | 29 | 5 | 0 | 1 | 55.2 | 253 | 62 | 30 | 28 | 1 | 0 | 3 | 2 | 28 | 1 | 28 | 1 | 0 | 2 | 3 | .400 | 0 | 0-0 | 5 | 4.61 | 4.53 |
| 2011 | 2 Tms | AL | 47 | 0 | 0 | 7 | 53.1 | 247 | 67 | 24 | 23 | 7 | 2 | 2 | 3 | 21 | 3 | 30 | 2 | 1 | 3 | 2 | .600 | 0 | 0-1 | 5 | 5.89 | 3.88 |
| 2012 | Tor | AL | 22 | 16 | 0 | 1 | 100.2 | 429 | 100 | 56 | 51 | 17 | 2 | 0 | 5 | 37 | 1 | 48 | 2 | 0 | 4 | 6 | .400 | 0 | 0-0 | 0 | 4.65 | 4.56 |
| 2013 | 2 Tms | | 5 | 3 | 0 | 1 | 12.2 | 64 | 18 | 10 | 10 | 1 | 2 | 2 | 2 | 10 | 0 | 9 | 0 | 0 | 0 | 0 | - | 0 | 0-0 | 0 | 9.19 | 7.11 |
| 11 | Sea | AL | 36 | 0 | 0 | 7 | 42.2 | 197 | 54 | 20 | 19 | 7 | 2 | 1 | 1 | 16 | 3 | 24 | 2 | 1 | 1 | 1 | .500 | 0 | 0-1 | 5 | 5.92 | 4.01 |
| 11 | NYY | AL | 11 | 0 | 0 | 0 | 10.2 | 50 | 13 | 4 | 4 | 0 | 0 | 1 | 2 | 5 | 0 | 6 | 0 | 0 | 2 | 1 | .667 | 0 | 0-0 | 0 | 5.66 | 3.38 |
| 13 | NYM | NL | 4 | 2 | 0 | 1 | 10.0 | 50 | 16 | 8 | 8 | 1 | 1 | 1 | 2 | 5 | 0 | 9 | 0 | 0 | 0 | 0 | - | 0 | 0-0 | 0 | 9.47 | 7.20 |
| 13 | Tor | AL | 1 | 1 | 0 | 0 | 2.2 | 14 | 2 | 2 | 2 | 0 | 1 | 1 | 0 | 5 | 0 | 0 | 0 | 0 | 0 | 0 | - | 0 | 0-0 | 0 | 7.93 | 6.75 |
| Postseason | | | 1 | 0 | 0 | 0 | 4.2 | 16 | 1 | 0 | 0 | 0 | 0 | 0 | 0 | 1 | 0 | 3 | 0 | 0 | 0 | 0 | - | 0 | 0-0 | 0 | 0.30 | 0.00 |
| 7 ML YEARS | | | 153 | 68 | 0 | 13 | 487.0 | 2148 | 544 | 267 | 241 | 47 | 9 | 13 | 27 | 196 | 7 | 242 | 13 | 4 | 25 | 29 | .463 | 0 | 1-2 | 10 | 5.01 | 4.45 |

# Bobby LaFromboise

**Pitches:** L **Bats:** L **Pos:** RP-10 lah-frahm-BOYCE **Ht:** 6'4" **Wt:** 215 **Born:** 6/25/1986 **Age:** 28

| | | | HOW MUCH HE PITCHED | | | | | | WHAT HE GAVE UP | | | | | | | | | | | | THE RESULTS | | | | | | | |
|---|---|---|---|---|---|---|---|---|---|---|---|---|---|---|---|---|---|---|---|---|---|---|---|---|---|---|---|---|
| Year | Team | Lg | G | GS | CG | GF | IP | BFP | H | R | ER | HR | SH | SF | HB | TBB | IBB | SO | WP | Bk | W | L | Pct | Sh | Sv-Op | Hld | ERC | ERA |
| 2009 | Clinton | A | 33 | 19 | 0 | 3 | 138.1 | 575 | 146 | 66 | 62 | 11 | 5 | 7 | 1 | 31 | 0 | 119 | 7 | 0 | 8 | 9 | .471 | 0 | 0-- | - | 3.63 | 4.03 |
| 2010 | Hi Dsrt | A+ | 33 | 14 | 0 | 9 | 113.2 | 506 | 138 | 63 | 57 | 15 | 5 | 4 | 1 | 38 | 0 | 92 | 6 | 1 | 10 | 5 | .667 | 0 | 1-- | - | 5.33 | 4.51 |
| 2011 | Jacksn | AA | 49 | 0 | 0 | 16 | 61.0 | 261 | 62 | 23 | 21 | 6 | 2 | 1 | 3 | 24 | 4 | 53 | 1 | 0 | 3 | 4 | .429 | 0 | 0-- | - | 4.31 | 3.10 |
| 2012 | Jacksn | AA | 20 | 0 | 0 | 7 | 26.2 | 102 | 15 | 4 | 3 | 0 | 2 | 0 | 0 | 5 | 0 | 32 | 1 | 0 | 1 | 0 | 1.000 | 0 | 2-- | - | 0.97 | 1.01 |
| 2012 | Tacom | AAA | 27 | 0 | 0 | 12 | 39.2 | 158 | 30 | 7 | 7 | 1 | 2 | 0 | 0 | 16 | 3 | 38 | 1 | 0 | 5 | 2 | .714 | 0 | 4-- | - | 2.30 | 1.59 |
| 2013 | Tacom | AAA | 45 | 0 | 0 | 14 | 61.0 | 262 | 66 | 29 | 23 | 5 | 1 | 4 | 1 | 18 | 3 | 63 | 6 | 0 | 6 | 0 | 1.000 | 0 | 5-- | - | 3.98 | 3.39 |
| 2013 | Sea | AL | 10 | 0 | 0 | 4 | 10.2 | 47 | 12 | 8 | 7 | 0 | 1 | 0 | 0 | 4 | 1 | 11 | 0 | 0 | 0 | 1 | .000 | 0 | 0-0 | 1 | 3.77 | 5.91 |

# Juan Lagares

**Bats:** R **Throws:** R **Pos:** CF-108;RF-14;PH-10 luh-GAR-ess **Ht:** 6'1" **Wt:** 175 **Born:** 3/17/1989 **Age:** 25

| | | | BATTING | | | | | | | | | | | | | | | | | | BASERUNNING | | | | AVERAGES | | |
|---|---|---|---|---|---|---|---|---|---|---|---|---|---|---|---|---|---|---|---|---|---|---|---|---|---|---|---|
| Year | Team | Lg | G | AB | H | 2B | 3B | HR | (Hm | Rd) | TB | R | RBI | RC | TBB | IBB | SO | HBP | SH | SF | SB | CS | SB% | GDP | Avg | OBP | Slg |
| 2009 | Savann | A | 47 | 168 | 46 | 6 | 2 | 0 | (- | -) | 56 | 23 | 13 | 17 | 6 | 0 | 42 | 2 | 0 | 1 | 9 | 4 | .69 | 4 | .274 | .305 | .333 |
| 2009 | Mets | R | 6 | 24 | 5 | 1 | 0 | 0 | (- | -) | 6 | 1 | 1 | 1 | 1 | 0 | 4 | 0 | 0 | 0 | 1 | 0 | 1.00 | 1 | .208 | .240 | .250 |
| 2010 | Savann | A | 67 | 290 | 87 | 13 | 9 | 5 | (- | -) | 133 | 42 | 39 | 45 | 7 | 0 | 44 | 3 | 2 | 5 | 18 | 2 | .90 | 5 | .300 | .318 | .459 |
| 2010 | StLuci | A+ | 33 | 133 | 31 | 5 | 0 | 2 | (- | -) | 42 | 16 | 16 | 10 | 2 | 0 | 18 | 1 | 0 | 1 | 7 | 3 | .70 | 2 | .233 | .248 | .316 |
| 2011 | StLuci | A+ | 82 | 308 | 104 | 15 | 6 | 7 | (- | -) | 152 | 51 | 49 | 55 | 21 | 1 | 47 | 1 | 3 | 2 | 5 | 6 | .45 | 5 | .338 | .380 | .494 |
| 2011 | Bnghtn | AA | 38 | 162 | 60 | 11 | 3 | 2 | (- | -) | 83 | 21 | 22 | 32 | 5 | 0 | 29 | 1 | 1 | 1 | 10 | 2 | .83 | 2 | .370 | .391 | .512 |
| 2012 | Bnghtn | AA | 130 | 499 | 141 | 29 | 6 | 4 | (- | -) | 194 | 69 | 48 | 68 | 37 | 0 | 93 | 4 | 2 | 5 | 21 | 10 | .68 | 12 | .283 | .334 | .389 |
| 2013 | LsVgs | AAA | 17 | 78 | 27 | 3 | 2 | 3 | (- | -) | 43 | 13 | 9 | 14 | 4 | 0 | 14 | 0 | 0 | 0 | 2 | 3 | .40 | 0 | .346 | .378 | .551 |
| 2013 | NYM | NL | 121 | 392 | 95 | 21 | 5 | 4 | (1 | 3) | 138 | 35 | 34 | 36 | 20 | 4 | 96 | 2 | 5 | 2 | 6 | 3 | .67 | 6 | .242 | .281 | .352 |

# Brandon Laird

**Bats:** R **Throws:** R **Pos:** 1B-13;PH-8;DH-6;3B-4 **Ht:** 6'1" **Wt:** 215 **Born:** 9/11/1987 **Age:** 26

| | | | BATTING | | | | | | | | | | | | | | | | | | BASERUNNING | | | | AVERAGES | | |
|---|---|---|---|---|---|---|---|---|---|---|---|---|---|---|---|---|---|---|---|---|---|---|---|---|---|---|---|
| Year | Team | Lg | G | AB | H | 2B | 3B | HR | (Hm | Rd) | TB | R | RBI | RC | TBB | IBB | SO | HBP | SH | SF | SB | CS | SB% | GDP | Avg | OBP | Slg |
| 2013 | OKCity* | AAA | 119 | 470 | 130 | 33 | 0 | 16 | (- | -) | 211 | 75 | 79 | 70 | 29 | 1 | 87 | 7 | 0 | 7 | 1 | 0 | 1.00 | 11 | .277 | .324 | .449 |
| 2011 | NYY | AL | 11 | 21 | 4 | 0 | 0 | 0 | (0 | 0) | 4 | 3 | 1 | 2 | 3 | 0 | 4 | 0 | 1 | 0 | 0 | 0 | - | 1 | .190 | .292 | .190 |
| 2012 | Hou | NL | 17 | 35 | 9 | 1 | 0 | 1 | (0 | 1) | 13 | 2 | 4 | 5 | 2 | 0 | 8 | 0 | 0 | 0 | 0 | 0 | - | 1 | .257 | .297 | .371 |
| 2013 | Hou | AL | 25 | 71 | 12 | 3 | 0 | 5 | (2 | 3) | 30 | 7 | 11 | 7 | 3 | 0 | 26 | 2 | 0 | 0 | 0 | 0 | - | 2 | .169 | .224 | .423 |
| 3 ML YEARS | | | 53 | 127 | 25 | 4 | 0 | 6 | (2 | 4) | 47 | 12 | 16 | 14 | 8 | 0 | 38 | 2 | 1 | 0 | 0 | 0 | - | 4 | .197 | .255 | .370 |

# Gerald Laird

**Bats:** R **Throws:** R **Pos:** C-40;PH-10 **Ht:** 6'1" **Wt:** 225 **Born:** 11/13/1979 **Age:** 34

| | | | BATTING | | | | | | | | | | | | | | | | | | BASERUNNING | | | | AVERAGES | | |
|---|---|---|---|---|---|---|---|---|---|---|---|---|---|---|---|---|---|---|---|---|---|---|---|---|---|---|---|
| Year | Team | Lg | G | AB | H | 2B | 3B | HR | (Hm | Rd) | TB | R | RBI | RC | TBB | IBB | SO | HBP | SH | SF | SB | CS | SB% | GDP | Avg | OBP | Slg |
| 2013 | Gwnntt* | AAA | 2 | 6 | 0 | 0 | 0 | 0 | (- | -) | 0 | 0 | 0 | 0 | 0 | 0 | 0 | 0 | 0 | 0 | 0 | 0 | - | 0 | .000 | .000 | .000 |
| 2003 | Tex | AL | 19 | 44 | 12 | 2 | 1 | 1 | (0 | 1) | 19 | 9 | 4 | 5 | 5 | 0 | 11 | 1 | 0 | 0 | 0 | 0 | - | 2 | .273 | .360 | .432 |
| 2004 | Tex | AL | 49 | 147 | 33 | 6 | 0 | 1 | (1 | 0) | 42 | 20 | 16 | 11 | 12 | 0 | 35 | 2 | 4 | 3 | 0 | 1 | .00 | 5 | .224 | .287 | .286 |
| 2005 | Tex | AL | 13 | 40 | 9 | 2 | 0 | 1 | (0 | 1) | 14 | 7 | 4 | 4 | 2 | 0 | 7 | 0 | 0 | 0 | 0 | 0 | - | 1 | .225 | .262 | .350 |
| 2006 | Tex | AL | 78 | 243 | 72 | 20 | 1 | 7 | (3 | 4) | 115 | 46 | 22 | 24 | 12 | 0 | 54 | 2 | 1 | 2 | 3 | 1 | .75 | 7 | .296 | .332 | .473 |
| 2007 | Tex | AL | 120 | 407 | 91 | 18 | 3 | 9 | (6 | 3) | 142 | 48 | 47 | 45 | 30 | 1 | 103 | 2 | 5 | 4 | 6 | 2 | .75 | 3 | .224 | .278 | .349 |
| 2008 | Tex | AL | 95 | 344 | 95 | 24 | 0 | 6 | (3 | 3) | 137 | 54 | 41 | 46 | 23 | 2 | 63 | 6 | 4 | 4 | 2 | 4 | .33 | 5 | .276 | .329 | .398 |
| 2009 | Det | AL | 135 | 413 | 93 | 23 | 2 | 4 | (1 | 3) | 132 | 49 | 33 | 41 | 40 | 0 | 68 | 10 | 10 | 4 | 5 | 0 | 1.00 | 11 | .225 | .306 | .320 |
| 2010 | Det | AL | 89 | 270 | 56 | 11 | 0 | 5 | (2 | 3) | 82 | 22 | 25 | 22 | 18 | 0 | 57 | 3 | 6 | 2 | 3 | 1 | .75 | 7 | .207 | .263 | .304 |
| 2011 | StL | NL | 37 | 95 | 22 | 7 | 1 | 1 | (1 | 0) | 34 | 11 | 12 | 10 | 9 | 3 | 19 | 1 | 2 | 1 | 1 | 1 | .50 | 3 | .232 | .302 | .358 |
| 2012 | Det | AL | 63 | 174 | 49 | 8 | 1 | 2 | (0 | 2) | 65 | 24 | 11 | 19 | 14 | 0 | 21 | 1 | 1 | 1 | 0 | 0 | - | 4 | .282 | .337 | .374 |
| 2013 | Atl | NL | 47 | 121 | 34 | 8 | 0 | 1 | (1 | 0) | 45 | 12 | 13 | 18 | 14 | 0 | 23 | 3 | 2 | 1 | 1 | 1 | .50 | 4 | .281 | .367 | .372 |
| Postseason | | | 10 | 21 | 1 | 0 | 0 | 0 | (0 | 0) | 1 | 0 | 0 | 0 | 0 | 0 | 6 | 1 | 0 | 0 | 0 | 0 | - | 0 | .048 | .091 | .048 |
| 11 ML YEARS | | | 745 | 2298 | 566 | 129 | 9 | 38 | (18 | 20) | 827 | 302 | 228 | 245 | 179 | 6 | 461 | 31 | 35 | 22 | 21 | 11 | .66 | 52 | .246 | .307 | .360 |

# Junior Lake

**Bats:** R **Throws:** R **Pos:** LF-32;CF-27;PH-8 **Ht:** 6'3" **Wt:** 215 **Born:** 3/27/1990 **Age:** 24

| BATTING | | | | | | | | | | | | | | | | | | | | BASERUNNING | | | | AVERAGES | | |
|---|---|---|---|---|---|---|---|---|---|---|---|---|---|---|---|---|---|---|---|---|---|---|---|---|---|---|
| Year Team | Lg | G | AB | H | 2B | 3B | HR | (Hm | Rd) | TB | R | RBI | RC | TBB | IBB | SO | HBP | SH | SF | SB | CS | SB% | GDP | Avg | OBP | Slg |
| 2009 Peoria | A | 131 | 463 | 115 | 19 | 7 | 7 | (- | -) | 169 | 71 | 42 | 46 | 18 | 0 | 138 | 2 | 4 | 4 | 10 | 7 | .59 | 11 | .248 | .277 | .365 |
| 2010 Dytona | A+ | 120 | 394 | 104 | 18 | 4 | 9 | (- | -) | 157 | 56 | 46 | 54 | 35 | 0 | 99 | 7 | 8 | 3 | 13 | 9 | .59 | 6 | .264 | .333 | .398 |
| 2011 Dytona | A+ | 49 | 203 | 64 | 11 | 4 | 6 | (- | -) | 101 | 39 | 34 | 35 | 6 | 0 | 49 | 2 | 2 | 3 | 19 | 4 | .83 | 3 | .315 | .336 | .498 |
| 2011 Tenn | AA | 67 | 242 | 60 | 10 | 2 | 6 | (- | -) | 92 | 41 | 17 | 31 | 13 | 0 | 60 | 5 | 2 | 0 | 19 | 2 | .90 | 3 | .248 | .300 | .380 |
| 2012 Tenn | AA | 103 | 405 | 113 | 26 | 3 | 10 | (- | -) | 175 | 56 | 50 | 61 | 35 | 0 | 105 | 4 | 2 | 2 | 21 | 12 | .64 | 5 | .279 | .341 | .432 |
| 2013 Iowa | AAA | 40 | 156 | 46 | 10 | 2 | 4 | (- | -) | 72 | 30 | 18 | 25 | 10 | 0 | 33 | 2 | 0 | 2 | 14 | 5 | .74 | 0 | .295 | .341 | .462 |
| 2013 ChC | NL | 64 | 236 | 67 | 16 | 0 | 6 | (4 | 2) | 101 | 26 | 16 | 26 | 13 | 0 | 68 | 4 | 1 | 0 | 4 | 4 | .50 | 2 | .284 | .332 | .428 |

# Blake Lalli

**Bats:** L **Throws:** R **Pos:** PH-10;1B-5;C-1 LAHL-ee **Ht:** 6'1" **Wt:** 210 **Born:** 5/12/1983 **Age:** 31

| BATTING | | | | | | | | | | | | | | | | | | | | BASERUNNING | | | | AVERAGES | | |
|---|---|---|---|---|---|---|---|---|---|---|---|---|---|---|---|---|---|---|---|---|---|---|---|---|---|---|
| Year Team | Lg | G | AB | H | 2B | 3B | HR | (Hm | Rd) | TB | R | RBI | RC | TBB | IBB | SO | HBP | SH | SF | SB | CS | SB% | GDP | Avg | OBP | Slg |
| 2009 Tenn | AA | 118 | 373 | 117 | 25 | 0 | 5 | (- | -) | 157 | 49 | 51 | 60 | 32 | 6 | 50 | 4 | 1 | 2 | 0 | 2 | .00 | 12 | .314 | .372 | .421 |
| 2010 Tenn | AA | 130 | 453 | 141 | 23 | 0 | 4 | (- | -) | 176 | 63 | 52 | 76 | 68 | 9 | 53 | 2 | 0 | 1 | 0 | 2 | .00 | 10 | .311 | .403 | .389 |
| 2011 Tenn | AA | 108 | 349 | 100 | 22 | 1 | 9 | (- | -) | 151 | 40 | 52 | 57 | 39 | 3 | 59 | 2 | 0 | 3 | 1 | 0 | 1.00 | 14 | .287 | .359 | .433 |
| 2012 Iowa | AAA | 93 | 301 | 78 | 20 | 0 | 7 | (- | -) | 119 | 33 | 40 | 36 | 17 | 1 | 54 | 0 | 0 | 6 | 0 | 1 | .00 | 7 | .259 | .293 | .395 |
| 2012 Scrmto | AAA | 4 | 15 | 3 | 0 | 0 | 1 | (- | -) | 6 | 1 | 1 | 1 | 1 | 0 | 1 | 0 | 0 | 0 | 0 | 1 | .00 | 1 | .200 | .250 | .400 |
| 2013 Nashv | AAA | 82 | 284 | 80 | 14 | 0 | 11 | (- | -) | 127 | 36 | 35 | 43 | 22 | 3 | 68 | 1 | 3 | 1 | 0 | 0 | - | 8 | .282 | .334 | .447 |
| 2012 ChC | NL | 6 | 15 | 2 | 0 | 0 | 0 | (0 | 0) | 2 | 1 | 2 | 1 | 1 | 0 | 3 | 0 | 0 | 0 | 0 | 0 | - | 0 | .133 | .188 | .133 |
| 2013 Mil | NL | 16 | 24 | 3 | 0 | 0 | 0 | (0 | 0) | 3 | 1 | 2 | 0 | 0 | 0 | 7 | 0 | 0 | 0 | 0 | 0 | - | 0 | .125 | .125 | .125 |
| 2 ML YEARS | | 22 | 39 | 5 | 0 | 0 | 0 | (0 | 0) | 5 | 2 | 4 | 1 | 1 | 0 | 10 | 0 | 0 | 0 | 0 | 0 | - | 0 | .128 | .150 | .128 |

# Andrew Lambo

**Bats:** L **Throws:** L **Pos:** PH-10;RF-6;LF-2 **Ht:** 6'3" **Wt:** 210 **Born:** 8/11/1988 **Age:** 25

| BATTING | | | | | | | | | | | | | | | | | | | | BASERUNNING | | | | AVERAGES | | |
|---|---|---|---|---|---|---|---|---|---|---|---|---|---|---|---|---|---|---|---|---|---|---|---|---|---|---|
| Year Team | Lg | G | AB | H | 2B | 3B | HR | (Hm | Rd) | TB | R | RBI | RC | TBB | IBB | SO | HBP | SH | SF | SB | CS | SB% | GDP | Avg | OBP | Slg |
| 2009 Chatt | AA | 130 | 492 | 126 | 39 | 1 | 11 | (- | -) | 200 | 70 | 61 | 64 | 39 | 1 | 95 | 3 | 0 | 7 | 4 | 3 | .57 | 9 | .256 | .311 | .407 |
| 2010 Chatt | AA | 47 | 181 | 49 | 11 | 2 | 4 | (- | -) | 76 | 26 | 25 | 25 | 15 | 1 | 39 | 0 | 1 | 1 | 1 | 1 | .50 | 6 | .271 | .325 | .420 |
| 2010 Altna | AA | 26 | 91 | 25 | 1 | 0 | 2 | (- | -) | 32 | 12 | 10 | 12 | 9 | 1 | 30 | 2 | 0 | 0 | 0 | 0 | - | 0 | .275 | .353 | .352 |
| 2011 Indy | AAA | 60 | 185 | 34 | 11 | 0 | 3 | (- | -) | 54 | 19 | 17 | 14 | 17 | 2 | 48 | 2 | 1 | 2 | 1 | 0 | 1.00 | 2 | .184 | .257 | .292 |
| 2011 Altna | AA | 69 | 252 | 69 | 17 | 0 | 8 | (- | -) | 110 | 35 | 41 | 39 | 26 | 3 | 59 | 3 | 2 | 3 | 4 | 3 | .57 | 2 | .274 | .345 | .437 |
| 2012 Altna | AA | 26 | 92 | 23 | 3 | 1 | 4 | (- | -) | 40 | 13 | 16 | 14 | 14 | 0 | 19 | 0 | 1 | 1 | 0 | 1 | .00 | 0 | .250 | .346 | .435 |
| 2012 Pirates | R | 9 | 33 | 16 | 4 | 0 | 1 | (- | -) | 23 | 10 | 6 | 11 | 5 | 0 | 5 | 1 | 0 | 1 | 1 | 0 | 1.00 | 0 | .485 | .550 | .697 |
| 2013 Altna | AA | 58 | 220 | 64 | 9 | 4 | 14 | (- | -) | 123 | 35 | 46 | 44 | 19 | 1 | 60 | 3 | 2 | 3 | 6 | 1 | .86 | 4 | .291 | .351 | .559 |
| 2013 Indy | AAA | 62 | 224 | 61 | 15 | 1 | 18 | (- | -) | 132 | 32 | 53 | 45 | 24 | 4 | 67 | 2 | 1 | 3 | 1 | 0 | 1.00 | 4 | .272 | .344 | .589 |
| 2013 Pit | NL | 18 | 30 | 7 | 2 | 0 | 1 | (0 | 1) | 12 | 4 | 2 | 1 | 3 | 0 | 11 | 0 | 0 | 0 | 0 | 1 | .00 | 0 | .233 | .303 | .400 |

# Ryan Langerhans

**Bats:** L **Throws:** L **Pos:** 1B-4 LANG-err-hanns **Ht:** 6'3" **Wt:** 220 **Born:** 2/20/1980 **Age:** 34

| BATTING | | | | | | | | | | | | | | | | | | | | BASERUNNING | | | | AVERAGES | | |
|---|---|---|---|---|---|---|---|---|---|---|---|---|---|---|---|---|---|---|---|---|---|---|---|---|---|---|
| Year Team | Lg | G | AB | H | 2B | 3B | HR | (Hm | Rd) | TB | R | RBI | RC | TBB | IBB | SO | HBP | SH | SF | SB | CS | SB% | GDP | Avg | OBP | Slg |
| 2013 Buffalo* | AAA | 64 | 208 | 46 | 7 | 2 | 9 | (- | -) | 84 | 27 | 26 | 30 | 38 | 2 | 69 | 1 | 1 | 0 | 1 | 2 | .33 | 2 | .221 | .344 | .404 |
| 2002 Atl | NL | 1 | 1 | 0 | 0 | 0 | 0 | (0 | 0) | 0 | 0 | 0 | 0 | 0 | 0 | 0 | 0 | 0 | 0 | 0 | 0 | - | 0 | .000 | .000 | .000 |
| 2003 Atl | NL | 16 | 15 | 4 | 0 | 0 | 0 | (0 | 0) | 4 | 2 | 0 | 1 | 0 | 0 | 6 | 0 | 0 | 0 | 0 | 0 | - | 1 | .267 | .267 | .267 |
| 2005 Atl | NL | 128 | 326 | 87 | 22 | 3 | 8 | (3 | 5) | 139 | 48 | 42 | 53 | 37 | 3 | 75 | 5 | 2 | 3 | 0 | 2 | .00 | 2 | .267 | .348 | .426 |
| 2006 Atl | NL | 131 | 315 | 76 | 16 | 3 | 7 | (3 | 4) | 119 | 46 | 28 | 45 | 50 | 8 | 91 | 3 | 0 | 1 | 1 | 2 | .33 | 9 | .241 | .350 | .378 |
| 2007 3 Tms | | 125 | 210 | 35 | 7 | 2 | 6 | (1 | 5) | 64 | 27 | 23 | 22 | 29 | 2 | 81 | 2 | 1 | 2 | 3 | 1 | .75 | 4 | .167 | .272 | .305 |
| 2008 Was | NL | 73 | 111 | 26 | 5 | 2 | 3 | (1 | 2) | 44 | 17 | 12 | 18 | 25 | 1 | 31 | 1 | 2 | 0 | 2 | 0 | 1.00 | 1 | .234 | .380 | .396 |
| 2009 Sea | AL | 38 | 101 | 22 | 6 | 1 | 3 | (2 | 1) | 39 | 12 | 10 | 11 | 14 | 1 | 28 | 1 | 3 | 3 | 0 | 1 | .00 | 0 | .218 | .311 | .386 |
| 2010 Sea | AL | 60 | 107 | 21 | 2 | 1 | 3 | (1 | 2) | 34 | 16 | 4 | 11 | 24 | 1 | 51 | 0 | 1 | 0 | 4 | 1 | .80 | 0 | .196 | .344 | .318 |
| 2011 Sea | AL | 19 | 52 | 9 | 0 | 0 | 3 | (2 | 1) | 18 | 6 | 6 | 5 | 11 | 0 | 22 | 0 | 1 | 0 | 0 | 1 | .00 | 0 | .173 | .317 | .346 |
| 2012 LAA | AL | 2 | 1 | 0 | 0 | 0 | 0 | (0 | 0) | 0 | 0 | 0 | 0 | 0 | 0 | 1 | 0 | 1 | 0 | 0 | 0 | - | 0 | .000 | .000 | .000 |
| 2013 Tor | AL | 4 | 11 | 3 | 0 | 0 | 0 | (0 | 0) | 3 | 3 | 0 | 2 | 2 | 0 | 2 | 0 | 0 | 0 | 1 | 0 | 1.00 | 0 | .273 | .385 | .273 |
| 07 Atl | NL | 20 | 44 | 3 | 1 | 0 | 0 | (0 | 0) | 4 | 3 | 1 | 0 | 6 | 1 | 16 | 1 | 0 | 1 | 0 | 1 | .00 | 3 | .068 | .192 | .091 |
| 07 Oak | AL | 2 | 4 | 0 | 0 | 0 | 0 | (0 | 0) | 0 | 0 | 0 | 0 | 1 | 0 | 2 | 0 | 0 | 0 | 0 | 0 | - | 0 | .000 | .200 | .000 |
| 07 Was | NL | 103 | 162 | 32 | 6 | 2 | 6 | (1 | 5) | 60 | 24 | 22 | 22 | 22 | 1 | 63 | 1 | 1 | 1 | 3 | 0 | 1.00 | 1 | .198 | .296 | .370 |
| Postseason | | 4 | 12 | 4 | 1 | 0 | 0 | (0 | 0) | 5 | 1 | 0 | 2 | 3 | 1 | 3 | 1 | 0 | 0 | 1 | 0 | 1.00 | 0 | .333 | .500 | .417 |
| 11 ML YEARS | | 597 | 1250 | 283 | 58 | 12 | 33 | (13 | 20) | 464 | 177 | 125 | 168 | 192 | 16 | 388 | 12 | 11 | 9 | 11 | 8 | .58 | 17 | .226 | .333 | .371 |

# Matt Langwell

**Pitches:** R **Bats:** R **Pos:** RP-13 **Ht:** 6'2" **Wt:** 220 **Born:** 5/6/1986 **Age:** 28

| HOW MUCH HE PITCHED | | | | | | | | WHAT HE GAVE UP | | | | | | | | | | | | THE RESULTS | | | | | | | |
|---|---|---|---|---|---|---|---|---|---|---|---|---|---|---|---|---|---|---|---|---|---|---|---|---|---|---|---|
| Year Team | Lg | G | GS | CG | GF | IP | BFP | H | R | ER | HR | SH | SF | HB | TBB | IBB | SO | WP | Bk | W | L | Pct | Sh | Sv-Op | Hld | ERC | ERA |
| 2009 Lk Cty | A | 45 | 0 | 0 | 19 | 68.2 | 280 | 54 | 21 | 15 | 4 | 6 | 1 | 2 | 22 | 1 | 68 | 2 | 0 | 1 | 4 | .200 | 0 | 4- | - | 2.47 | 1.97 |
| 2010 Knstn | A+ | 45 | 0 | 0 | 21 | 56.0 | 221 | 44 | 16 | 15 | 4 | 4 | 1 | 1 | 14 | 0 | 58 | 2 | 0 | 4 | 2 | .667 | 0 | 5- | - | 2.33 | 2.41 |
| 2011 Akron | AA | 36 | 1 | 0 | 15 | 50.2 | 215 | 43 | 17 | 15 | 4 | 2 | 1 | 2 | 20 | 2 | 54 | 2 | 0 | 4 | 1 | .800 | 0 | 3- | - | 3.15 | 2.66 |
| 2011 Clmbs | AAA | 12 | 0 | 0 | 5 | 18.0 | 82 | 19 | 9 | 8 | 1 | 0 | 0 | 2 | 8 | 0 | 17 | 1 | 0 | 1 | 0 | 1.000 | 0 | 0- | - | 4.61 | 4.00 |
| 2012 Akron | AA | 10 | 0 | 0 | 6 | 14.1 | 53 | 10 | 2 | 1 | 0 | 2 | 0 | 0 | 5 | 0 | 18 | 0 | 0 | 0 | 0 | - | 0 | 3- | - | 1.92 | 0.63 |
| 2012 Clmbs | AAA | 32 | 0 | 0 | 8 | 54.2 | 236 | 49 | 21 | 20 | 0 | 0 | 1 | 7 | 22 | 1 | 63 | 2 | 0 | 4 | 0 | 1.000 | 0 | 0- | - | 3.27 | 3.29 |
| 2013 Clmbs | AAA | 42 | 1 | 0 | 11 | 60.1 | 253 | 54 | 15 | 15 | 1 | 3 | 1 | 5 | 19 | 1 | 52 | 0 | 0 | 3 | 4 | .429 | 0 | 2- | - | 2.92 | 2.24 |
| 2013 2 Tms | | 13 | 0 | 0 | 5 | 14.0 | 62 | 13 | 8 | 8 | 2 | 0 | 0 | 1 | 7 | 0 | 12 | 0 | 0 | 1 | 0 | 1.000 | 0 | 0-0 | 0 | 4.64 | 5.14 |
| 13 Cle | AL | 5 | 0 | 0 | 2 | 5.1 | 23 | 5 | 3 | 3 | 1 | 0 | 0 | 0 | 2 | 0 | 6 | 0 | 0 | 1 | 0 | 1.000 | 0 | 0-0 | 0 | 4.14 | 5.06 |
| 13 Ari | NL | 8 | 0 | 0 | 3 | 8.2 | 39 | 8 | 5 | 5 | 1 | 0 | 0 | 1 | 5 | 0 | 6 | 0 | 0 | 0 | 0 | - | 0 | 0-0 | 0 | 4.93 | 5.19 |

## John Lannan

**Pitches:** L **Bats:** L **Pos:** SP-14 **Ht:** 6'4" **Wt:** 235 **Born:** 9/27/1984 **Age:** 29

| HOW MUCH HE PITCHED | | | | | | | | | WHAT HE GAVE UP | | | | | | | | | | | | THE RESULTS | | | | | | | |
|---|---|---|---|---|---|---|---|---|---|---|---|---|---|---|---|---|---|---|---|---|---|---|---|---|---|---|---|---|
| Year | Team | Lg | G | GS | CG | GF | IP | BFP | H | R | ER | HR | SH | SF | HB | TBB | IBB | SO | WP | Bk | W | L | Pct | Sh | Sv-Op | Hld | ERC | ERA |
| 2013 | Clrwtr* | A+ | 1 | 1 | 0 | 0 | 4.0 | 20 | 6 | 2 | 1 | 0 | 0 | 0 | 1 | 1 | 0 | 5 | 0 | 0 | 0 | 1 | .000 | 0 | 0-- | - | 6.48 | 2.25 |
| 2013 | Rdng* | AA | 1 | 1 | 0 | 0 | 7.0 | 26 | 7 | 2 | 2 | 0 | 0 | 0 | 0 | 1 | 0 | 1 | 0 | 0 | 0 | 1 | .000 | 0 | 0-- | - | 2.75 | 2.57 |
| 2007 | Was | NL | 6 | 6 | 0 | 0 | 34.2 | 153 | 36 | 17 | 16 | 3 | 2 | 0 | 2 | 17 | 1 | 10 | 1 | 0 | 2 | 2 | .500 | 0 | 0-0 | 0 | 4.82 | 4.15 |
| 2008 | Was | NL | 31 | 31 | 0 | 0 | 182.0 | 779 | 172 | 89 | 79 | 23 | 13 | 5 | 7 | 72 | 1 | 117 | 6 | 2 | 9 | 15 | .375 | 0 | 0-0 | 0 | 4.09 | 3.91 |
| 2009 | Was | NL | 33 | 33 | 2 | 0 | 206.1 | 875 | 210 | 100 | 89 | 22 | 12 | 1 | 6 | 68 | 5 | 89 | 3 | 0 | 9 | 13 | .409 | 1 | 0-0 | 0 | 4.07 | 3.88 |
| 2010 | Was | NL | 25 | 25 | 0 | 0 | 143.1 | 643 | 175 | 82 | 74 | 14 | 5 | 5 | 4 | 49 | 3 | 71 | 1 | 0 | 8 | 8 | .500 | 0 | 0-0 | 0 | 5.18 | 4.65 |
| 2011 | Was | NL | 33 | 33 | 0 | 0 | 184.2 | 808 | 194 | 90 | 76 | 15 | 10 | 1 | 7 | 76 | 3 | 106 | 4 | 0 | 10 | 13 | .435 | 0 | 0-0 | 0 | 4.42 | 3.70 |
| 2012 | Was | NL | 6 | 6 | 0 | 0 | 32.2 | 144 | 33 | 15 | 15 | 0 | 4 | 0 | 4 | 14 | 1 | 17 | 1 | 0 | 4 | 1 | .800 | 0 | 0-0 | 0 | 3.97 | 4.13 |
| 2013 | Phi | NL | 14 | 14 | 0 | 0 | 74.1 | 332 | 86 | 48 | 44 | 6 | 5 | 4 | 5 | 27 | 1 | 38 | 2 | 0 | 3 | 6 | .333 | 0 | 0-0 | 0 | 4.95 | 5.33 |
| 7 ML YEARS | | | 148 | 148 | 2 | 0 | 858.0 | 3734 | 906 | 441 | 393 | 83 | 51 | 16 | 35 | 323 | 15 | 448 | 18 | 2 | 45 | 58 | .437 | 1 | 0-0 | 0 | 4.44 | 4.12 |

## Adam LaRoche

**Bats:** L **Throws:** L **Pos:** 1B-149;PH-4;DH-1 luh-ROASH **Ht:** 6'2" **Wt:** 200 **Born:** 11/6/1979 **Age:** 34

| BATTING | | | | | | | | | | | | | | | | | | | | | BASERUNNING | | | | AVERAGES | | |
|---|---|---|---|---|---|---|---|---|---|---|---|---|---|---|---|---|---|---|---|---|---|---|---|---|---|---|---|
| Year | Team | Lg | G | AB | H | 2B | 3B | HR | (Hm | Rd) | TB | R | RBI | RC | TBB | IBB | SO | HBP | SH | SF | SB | CS | SB% | GDP | Avg | OBP | Slg |
| 2004 | Atl | NL | 110 | 324 | 90 | 27 | 1 | 13 | (7 | 6) | 158 | 45 | 45 | 43 | 27 | 1 | 78 | 1 | 2 | 2 | 0 | 0 | - | 10 | .278 | .333 | .488 |
| 2005 | Atl | NL | 141 | 451 | 117 | 28 | 0 | 20 | (11 | 9) | 205 | 53 | 78 | 63 | 39 | 7 | 87 | 4 | 2 | 6 | 0 | 2 | .00 | 15 | .259 | .320 | .455 |
| 2006 | Atl | NL | 149 | 492 | 140 | 38 | 1 | 32 | (11 | 21) | 276 | 89 | 90 | 83 | 55 | 5 | 128 | 2 | 1 | 7 | 0 | 2 | .00 | 9 | .285 | .354 | .561 |
| 2007 | Pit | NL | 152 | 563 | 153 | 42 | 0 | 21 | (10 | 11) | 258 | 71 | 88 | 84 | 62 | 5 | 131 | 3 | 0 | 4 | 1 | 1 | .50 | 18 | .272 | .345 | .458 |
| 2008 | Pit | NL | 136 | 492 | 133 | 32 | 3 | 25 | (14 | 11) | 246 | 66 | 85 | 76 | 54 | 7 | 122 | 2 | 0 | 6 | 1 | 1 | .50 | 9 | .270 | .341 | .500 |
| 2009 | 3 Tms | | 150 | 555 | 154 | 38 | 2 | 25 | (15 | 10) | 271 | 78 | 83 | 84 | 69 | 12 | 142 | 0 | 0 | 5 | 2 | 2 | .50 | 11 | .277 | .355 | .488 |
| 2010 | Ari | NL | 151 | 560 | 146 | 37 | 2 | 25 | (13 | 12) | 262 | 75 | 100 | 84 | 48 | 4 | 172 | 3 | 0 | 4 | 0 | 1 | .00 | 8 | .261 | .320 | .468 |
| 2011 | Was | NL | 43 | 151 | 26 | 4 | 0 | 3 | (1 | 2) | 39 | 15 | 15 | 11 | 25 | 0 | 37 | 0 | 0 | 1 | 1 | 0 | 1.00 | 2 | .172 | .288 | .258 |
| 2012 | Was | NL | 154 | 571 | 155 | 35 | 1 | 33 | (17 | 16) | 291 | 76 | 100 | 92 | 67 | 7 | 138 | 0 | 0 | **9** | 1 | 1 | .50 | 10 | .271 | .343 | .510 |
| 2013 | Was | NL | 152 | 511 | 121 | 19 | 3 | 20 | (9 | 11) | 206 | 70 | 62 | 68 | 72 | 10 | 131 | 3 | 0 | 4 | 4 | 1 | .80 | 13 | .237 | .332 | .403 |
| 09 | Pit | NL | 87 | 324 | 80 | 25 | 1 | 12 | (7 | 5) | 143 | 46 | 40 | 38 | 41 | 6 | 81 | 0 | 0 | 3 | 2 | 2 | .50 | 9 | .247 | .329 | .441 |
| 09 | Bos | AL | 6 | 19 | 5 | 2 | 0 | 1 | (1 | 0) | 10 | 2 | 3 | 3 | 0 | 0 | 2 | 0 | 0 | 0 | 0 | 0 | - | 1 | .263 | .263 | .526 |
| 09 | Atl | NL | 57 | 212 | 69 | 11 | 1 | 12 | (7 | 5) | 118 | 30 | 40 | 43 | 28 | 6 | 59 | 0 | 0 | 2 | 0 | 0 | - | 1 | .325 | .401 | .557 |
| Postseason | | | 13 | 42 | 11 | 2 | 0 | 4 | (1 | 3) | 25 | 7 | 12 | 7 | 9 | 1 | 9 | 0 | 1 | 0 | 0 | 0 | - | 1 | .262 | .392 | .595 |
| 10 ML YEARS | | | 1338 | 4670 | 1235 | 300 | 13 | 217 | (108 | 109) | 2212 | 638 | 746 | 688 | 518 | 58 | 1166 | 18 | 5 | 48 | 10 | 11 | .48 | 105 | .264 | .337 | .474 |

## Andy LaRoche

**Bats:** R **Throws:** R **Pos:** 3B-1 luh-ROASH **Ht:** 6'0" **Wt:** 205 **Born:** 9/13/1983 **Age:** 30

| BATTING | | | | | | | | | | | | | | | | | | | | | BASERUNNING | | | | AVERAGES | | |
|---|---|---|---|---|---|---|---|---|---|---|---|---|---|---|---|---|---|---|---|---|---|---|---|---|---|---|---|
| Year | Team | Lg | G | AB | H | 2B | 3B | HR | (Hm | Rd) | TB | R | RBI | RC | TBB | IBB | SO | HBP | SH | SF | SB | CS | SB% | GDP | Avg | OBP | Slg |
| 2013 | Buffalo* | AAA | 104 | 365 | 99 | 21 | 1 | 12 | (- | -) | 158 | 45 | 51 | 56 | 37 | 1 | 55 | 4 | 0 | 7 | 4 | 4 | .50 | 13 | .271 | .339 | .433 |
| 2007 | LAD | NL | 35 | 93 | 21 | 5 | 0 | 1 | (0 | 1) | 29 | 16 | 10 | 12 | 20 | 5 | 24 | 1 | 0 | 1 | 2 | 1 | .67 | 1 | .226 | .365 | .312 |
| 2008 | 2 Tms | NL | 76 | 223 | 37 | 5 | 0 | 5 | (1 | 4) | 57 | 17 | 18 | 10 | 24 | 1 | 37 | 2 | 2 | 1 | 2 | 0 | 1.00 | 8 | .166 | .252 | .256 |
| 2009 | Pit | NL | 150 | 524 | 135 | 29 | 5 | 12 | (7 | 5) | 210 | 64 | 64 | 64 | 50 | 1 | 84 | 8 | 6 | 2 | 3 | 1 | .75 | 16 | .258 | .330 | .401 |
| 2010 | Pit | NL | 102 | 247 | 51 | 8 | 0 | 4 | (2 | 2) | 71 | 26 | 16 | 17 | 19 | 0 | 43 | 2 | 2 | 1 | 1 | 1 | .50 | 7 | .206 | .268 | .287 |
| 2011 | Oak | AL | 40 | 93 | 23 | 6 | 1 | 0 | (0 | 0) | 31 | 10 | 5 | 8 | 8 | 1 | 19 | 2 | 1 | 0 | 0 | 0 | - | 6 | .247 | .320 | .333 |
| 2013 | Tor | AL | 1 | 4 | 0 | 0 | 0 | 0 | (0 | 0) | 0 | 0 | 0 | 0 | 0 | 0 | 1 | 0 | 0 | 0 | 0 | 0 | - | 0 | .000 | .000 | .000 |
| 08 | LAD | NL | 27 | 59 | 12 | 1 | 0 | 2 | (0 | 2) | 19 | 6 | 6 | 3 | 10 | 0 | 7 | 0 | 0 | 0 | 0 | 0 | - | 5 | .203 | .319 | .322 |
| 08 | Pit | NL | 49 | 164 | 25 | 4 | 0 | 3 | (1 | 2) | 38 | 11 | 12 | 7 | 14 | 1 | 30 | 2 | 2 | 1 | 2 | 0 | 1.00 | 3 | .152 | .227 | .232 |
| 6 ML YEARS | | | 404 | 1184 | 267 | 53 | 6 | 22 | (10 | 12) | 398 | 133 | 113 | 111 | 121 | 8 | 208 | 15 | 11 | 5 | 8 | 3 | .73 | 38 | .226 | .304 | .336 |

## Mat Latos

**Pitches:** R **Bats:** R **Pos:** SP-32 LAY-tos **Ht:** 6'6" **Wt:** 245 **Born:** 12/9/1987 **Age:** 26

| HOW MUCH HE PITCHED | | | | | | | | | WHAT HE GAVE UP | | | | | | | | | | | | THE RESULTS | | | | | | | |
|---|---|---|---|---|---|---|---|---|---|---|---|---|---|---|---|---|---|---|---|---|---|---|---|---|---|---|---|---|
| Year | Team | Lg | G | GS | CG | GF | IP | BFP | H | R | ER | HR | SH | SF | HB | TBB | IBB | SO | WP | Bk | W | L | Pct | Sh | Sv-Op | Hld | ERC | ERA |
| 2009 | SD | NL | 10 | 10 | 0 | 0 | 50.2 | 212 | 43 | 29 | 26 | 7 | 3 | 1 | 0 | 23 | 1 | 39 | 0 | 2 | 4 | 5 | .444 | 0 | 0-0 | 0 | 3.72 | 4.62 |
| 2010 | SD | NL | 31 | 31 | 1 | 0 | 184.2 | 748 | 150 | 63 | 60 | 16 | 4 | 1 | 2 | 50 | 3 | 189 | 5 | 1 | 14 | 10 | .583 | 1 | 0-0 | 0 | 2.52 | 2.92 |
| 2011 | SD | NL | 31 | 31 | 0 | 0 | 194.1 | 799 | 168 | 82 | 75 | 16 | 8 | 7 | 1 | 62 | 3 | 185 | 5 | 0 | 9 | 14 | .391 | 0 | 0-0 | 0 | 2.93 | 3.47 |
| 2012 | Cin | NL | 33 | **33** | 2 | 0 | 209.1 | 858 | 179 | 87 | 81 | 25 | 9 | 3 | 4 | 64 | 9 | 185 | 3 | 1 | 14 | 4 | .778 | 0 | 0-0 | 0 | 3.08 | 3.48 |
| 2013 | Cin | NL | 32 | 32 | 1 | 0 | 210.2 | 881 | 197 | 82 | 74 | 14 | 12 | 3 | 10 | 58 | 5 | 187 | 8 | 0 | 14 | 7 | .667 | 0 | 0-0 | 0 | 3.16 | 3.16 |
| Postseason | | | 2 | 1 | 0 | 0 | 8.1 | 39 | 11 | 7 | 6 | 2 | 0 | 0 | 0 | 2 | 0 | 5 | 0 | 0 | 0 | 1 | .000 | 0 | 0-0 | 0 | 6.03 | 6.48 |
| 5 ML YEARS | | | 137 | 137 | 4 | 0 | 849.2 | 3498 | 737 | 343 | 316 | 78 | 36 | 15 | 17 | 257 | 21 | 785 | 21 | 4 | 55 | 40 | .579 | 1 | 0-0 | 0 | 2.98 | 3.35 |

## Ryan Lavarnway

**Bats:** R **Throws:** R **Pos:** C-22;PH-5;DH-3 luh-VARN-way **Ht:** 6'4" **Wt:** 240 **Born:** 8/7/1987 **Age:** 26

| BATTING | | | | | | | | | | | | | | | | | | | | | BASERUNNING | | | | AVERAGES | | |
|---|---|---|---|---|---|---|---|---|---|---|---|---|---|---|---|---|---|---|---|---|---|---|---|---|---|---|---|
| Year | Team | Lg | G | AB | H | 2B | 3B | HR | (Hm | Rd) | TB | R | RBI | RC | TBB | IBB | SO | HBP | SH | SF | SB | CS | SB% | GDP | Avg | OBP | Slg |
| 2013 | Pwtckt* | AAA | 50 | 180 | 45 | 9 | 0 | 3 | (- | -) | 63 | 23 | 24 | 25 | 25 | 1 | 25 | 4 | 0 | 5 | 0 | 0 | - | 13 | .250 | .346 | .350 |
| 2011 | Bos | AL | 17 | 39 | 9 | 2 | 0 | 2 | (0 | 2) | 17 | 5 | 8 | 4 | 4 | 0 | 10 | 0 | 0 | 0 | 0 | 0 | - | 1 | .231 | .302 | .436 |
| 2012 | Bos | AL | 46 | 153 | 24 | 8 | 0 | 2 | (0 | 2) | 38 | 11 | 12 | 4 | 11 | 0 | 41 | 0 | 0 | 2 | 0 | 0 | - | 4 | .157 | .211 | .248 |
| 2013 | Bos | AL | 25 | 77 | 23 | 7 | 0 | 1 | (1 | 0) | 33 | 8 | 14 | 11 | 2 | 0 | 17 | 2 | 0 | 1 | 0 | 0 | - | 3 | .299 | .329 | .429 |
| 3 ML YEARS | | | 88 | 269 | 56 | 17 | 0 | 5 | (1 | 4) | 88 | 24 | 34 | 19 | 17 | 0 | 68 | 2 | 0 | 3 | 0 | 0 | - | 8 | .208 | .258 | .327 |

# Brett Lawrie

**Bats:** R **Throws:** R **Pos:** 3B-103;2B-6 LORI **Ht:** 6'0" **Wt:** 225 **Born:** 1/18/1990 **Age:** 24

| BATTING | | | | | | | | | | | | | | | | | | | | | BASERUNNING | | | | AVERAGES | | |
|---|---|---|---|---|---|---|---|---|---|---|---|---|---|---|---|---|---|---|---|---|---|---|---|---|---|---|---|
| Year | Team | Lg | G | AB | H | 2B | 3B | HR | (Hm | Rd) | TB | R | RBI | RC | TBB | IBB | SO | HBP | SH | SF | SB | CS | SB% | GDP | Avg | OBP | Slg |
| 2013 | Dnedin* | A+ | 4 | 12 | 6 | 1 | 1 | 0 | (- | -) | 9 | 1 | 2 | 4 | 1 | 0 | 0 | 0 | 0 | 0 | 0 | 0 | - | 0 | .500 | .538 | .750 |
| 2013 | Lnsng* | A | 2 | 6 | 0 | 0 | 0 | 0 | (- | -) | 0 | 1 | 0 | 0 | 2 | 0 | 1 | 0 | 0 | 0 | 0 | 0 | - | 0 | .000 | .250 | .000 |
| 2013 | NHam* | AA | 3 | 9 | 3 | 0 | 0 | 0 | (- | -) | 3 | 3 | 0 | 2 | 4 | 0 | 2 | 0 | 0 | 0 | 0 | 0 | - | 0 | .333 | .538 | .333 |
| 2013 | Buffalo* | AAA | 3 | 12 | 2 | 0 | 0 | 1 | (- | -) | 5 | 2 | 3 | 1 | 1 | 0 | 7 | 0 | 0 | 0 | 1 | 0 | 1.00 | 0 | .167 | .231 | .417 |
| 2011 | Tor | AL | 43 | 150 | 44 | 8 | 4 | 9 | (5 | 4) | 87 | 26 | 25 | 33 | 16 | 1 | 31 | 3 | 2 | 0 | 7 | 1 | .88 | 0 | .293 | .373 | .580 |
| 2012 | Tor | AL | 125 | 494 | 135 | 26 | 3 | 11 | (7 | 4) | 200 | 73 | 48 | 65 | 33 | 0 | 86 | 5 | 2 | 2 | 13 | 8 | .62 | 9 | .273 | .324 | .405 |
| 2013 | Tor | AL | 107 | 401 | 102 | 18 | 3 | 11 | (4 | 7) | 159 | 41 | 46 | 45 | 30 | 1 | 68 | 7 | 1 | 3 | 9 | 5 | .64 | 8 | .254 | .315 | .397 |
| 3 ML YEARS | | | 275 | 1045 | 281 | 52 | 10 | 31 | (16 | 15) | 446 | 140 | 119 | 143 | 79 | 2 | 185 | 15 | 5 | 5 | 29 | 14 | .67 | 17 | .269 | .328 | .427 |

# Tom Layne

**Pitches:** L **Bats:** L **Pos:** RP-14 **Ht:** 6'2" **Wt:** 190 **Born:** 11/2/1984 **Age:** 29

| HOW MUCH HE PITCHED | | | | | | | | | WHAT HE GAVE UP | | | | | | | | | | | | THE RESULTS | | | | | | | |
|---|---|---|---|---|---|---|---|---|---|---|---|---|---|---|---|---|---|---|---|---|---|---|---|---|---|---|---|---|
| Year | Team | Lg | G | GS | CG | GF | IP | BFP | H | R | ER | HR | SH | SF | HB | TBB | IBB | SO | WP | Bk | W | L | Pct | Sh | Sv-Op | Hld | ERC | ERA |
| 2009 | Visalia | A+ | 29 | 4 | 0 | 9 | 66.0 | 278 | 63 | 27 | 21 | 1 | 1 | 1 | 3 | 25 | 0 | 43 | 7 | 0 | 4 | 2 | .667 | 0 | 0-- | - | 3.39 | 2.86 |
| 2009 | Mobile | AA | 6 | 6 | 0 | 0 | 31.0 | 140 | 27 | 21 | 17 | 0 | 0 | 0 | 3 | 19 | 0 | 24 | 2 | 0 | 0 | 3 | .000 | 0 | 0-- | - | 3.76 | 4.94 |
| 2010 | Mobile | AA | 26 | 26 | 3 | 0 | 149.1 | 641 | 146 | 75 | 62 | 9 | 8 | 2 | 6 | 57 | 0 | 91 | 10 | 1 | 12 | 7 | .632 | 1 | 0-- | - | 3.77 | 3.74 |
| 2011 | Reno | AAA | 32 | 15 | 0 | 7 | 121.2 | 558 | 148 | 95 | 84 | 14 | 5 | 2 | 6 | 57 | 0 | 56 | 6 | 0 | 10 | 7 | .588 | 0 | 0-- | - | 6.01 | 6.21 |
| 2011 | Mobile | AA | 3 | 3 | 0 | 0 | 17.2 | 71 | 16 | 5 | 5 | 1 | 0 | 0 | 1 | 6 | 0 | 14 | 4 | 0 | 2 | 0 | 1.000 | 0 | 0-- | - | 3.44 | 2.55 |
| 2012 | Reno | AAA | 5 | 4 | 0 | 0 | 20.0 | 100 | 30 | 24 | 23 | 4 | 0 | 0 | 2 | 9 | 0 | 14 | 1 | 0 | 0 | 2 | .000 | 0 | 0-- | - | 8.56 | 10.35 |
| 2012 | Tucsn | AAA | 5 | 5 | 0 | 0 | 22.0 | 110 | 28 | 20 | 19 | 4 | 2 | 0 | 3 | 15 | 0 | 19 | 0 | 0 | 0 | 3 | .000 | 0 | 0-- | - | 8.19 | 7.77 |
| 2012 | SnAnt | AA | 32 | 2 | 0 | 3 | 35.2 | 149 | 31 | 15 | 13 | 2 | 1 | 0 | 0 | 16 | 3 | 36 | 1 | 0 | 0 | 5 | .000 | 0 | 1-- | - | 3.16 | 3.28 |
| 2013 | Tucsn | AAA | 49 | 0 | 0 | 9 | 46.0 | 215 | 49 | 29 | 23 | 1 | 3 | 3 | 4 | 27 | 2 | 41 | 5 | 0 | 2 | 4 | .333 | 0 | 0-- | - | 4.78 | 4.50 |
| 2012 | SD | NL | 26 | 0 | 0 | 5 | 16.2 | 68 | 9 | 6 | 6 | 0 | 1 | 0 | 3 | 3 | 0 | 25 | 0 | 0 | 2 | 0 | 1.000 | 0 | 2-3 | 7 | 1.20 | 3.24 |
| 2013 | SD | NL | 14 | 0 | 0 | 2 | 8.2 | 39 | 10 | 4 | 2 | 1 | 1 | 0 | 2 | 5 | 0 | 6 | 1 | 0 | 0 | 2 | .000 | 0 | 0-0 | 0 | 7.38 | 2.08 |
| 2 ML YEARS | | | 40 | 0 | 0 | 7 | 25.1 | 107 | 19 | 10 | 8 | 1 | 2 | 0 | 5 | 8 | 0 | 31 | 1 | 0 | 2 | 2 | .500 | 0 | 2-3 | 7 | 2.73 | 2.84 |

# Brandon League

**Pitches:** R **Bats:** R **Pos:** RP-58 **Ht:** 6'2" **Wt:** 215 **Born:** 3/16/1983 **Age:** 31

| HOW MUCH HE PITCHED | | | | | | | | | WHAT HE GAVE UP | | | | | | | | | | | | THE RESULTS | | | | | | | |
|---|---|---|---|---|---|---|---|---|---|---|---|---|---|---|---|---|---|---|---|---|---|---|---|---|---|---|---|---|
| Year | Team | Lg | G | GS | CG | GF | IP | BFP | H | R | ER | HR | SH | SF | HB | TBB | IBB | SO | WP | Bk | W | L | Pct | Sh | Sv-Op | Hld | ERC | ERA |
| 2004 | Tor | AL | 3 | 0 | 0 | 0 | 4.2 | 18 | 3 | 0 | 0 | 0 | 0 | 0 | 0 | 1 | 0 | 2 | 0 | 0 | 1 | 0 | 1.000 | 0 | 0-0 | 1 | 1.26 | 0.00 |
| 2005 | Tor | AL | 20 | 0 | 0 | 4 | 35.2 | 162 | 42 | 27 | 26 | 8 | 0 | 1 | 2 | 20 | 1 | 17 | 5 | 0 | 1 | 0 | 1.000 | 0 | 0-0 | 1 | 7.24 | 6.56 |
| 2006 | Tor | AL | 33 | 0 | 0 | 8 | 42.2 | 173 | 34 | 17 | 12 | 3 | 2 | 0 | 3 | 9 | 2 | 29 | 0 | 0 | 1 | 2 | .333 | 0 | 1-4 | 12 | 2.30 | 2.53 |
| 2007 | Tor | AL | 14 | 0 | 0 | 2 | 11.2 | 58 | 19 | 8 | 8 | 1 | 0 | 1 | 0 | 7 | 0 | 7 | 3 | 0 | 0 | 0 | - | 0 | 0-1 | 0 | 8.98 | 6.17 |
| 2008 | Tor | AL | 31 | 0 | 0 | 8 | 33.0 | 141 | 28 | 9 | 8 | 2 | 1 | 0 | 3 | 15 | 2 | 23 | 2 | 0 | 1 | 2 | .333 | 0 | 1-1 | 5 | 3.45 | 2.18 |
| 2009 | Tor | AL | 67 | 0 | 0 | 18 | 74.2 | 313 | 72 | 40 | 38 | 8 | 5 | 0 | 7 | 21 | 2 | 76 | 9 | 0 | 3 | 6 | .333 | 0 | 0-3 | 9 | 3.85 | 4.58 |
| 2010 | Sea | AL | 70 | 0 | 0 | 30 | 79.0 | 326 | 67 | 38 | 30 | 7 | 4 | 1 | 2 | 27 | 6 | 56 | 7 | 0 | 9 | 7 | .563 | 0 | 6-12 | 13 | 2.96 | 3.42 |
| 2011 | Sea | AL | 65 | 0 | 0 | 60 | 61.1 | 250 | 56 | 25 | 19 | 3 | 4 | 0 | 2 | 10 | 2 | 45 | 4 | 0 | 1 | 5 | .167 | 0 | 37-42 | 0 | 2.45 | 2.79 |
| 2012 | 2 Tms | | 74 | 0 | 0 | 39 | 72.0 | 301 | 65 | 27 | 25 | 1 | 3 | 0 | 1 | 33 | 7 | 54 | 4 | 0 | 2 | 6 | .250 | 0 | 15-21 | 8 | 3.15 | 3.13 |
| 2013 | LAD | NL | 58 | 0 | 0 | 35 | 54.1 | 249 | 69 | 37 | 32 | 8 | 3 | 2 | 3 | 15 | 1 | 28 | 9 | 0 | 6 | 4 | .600 | 0 | 14-19 | 2 | 5.58 | 5.30 |
| 12 | Sea | AL | 46 | 0 | 0 | 24 | 44.2 | 193 | 48 | 20 | 18 | 1 | 3 | 0 | 0 | 19 | 3 | 27 | 3 | 0 | 0 | 5 | .000 | 0 | 9-15 | 6 | 3.99 | 3.63 |
| 12 | LAD | NL | 28 | 0 | 0 | 15 | 27.1 | 108 | 17 | 7 | 7 | 0 | 0 | 0 | 1 | 14 | 4 | 27 | 1 | 0 | 2 | 1 | .667 | 0 | 6-6 | 2 | 1.89 | 2.30 |
| 10 ML YEARS | | | 435 | 0 | 0 | 204 | 469.0 | 1991 | 455 | 228 | 198 | 41 | 22 | 5 | 23 | 158 | 23 | 337 | 43 | 0 | 25 | 32 | .439 | 0 | 74-103 | 51 | 3.71 | 3.80 |

# Mike Leake

**Pitches:** R **Bats:** R **Pos:** SP-31 LEEK **Ht:** 5'10" **Wt:** 185 **Born:** 11/12/1987 **Age:** 26

| HOW MUCH HE PITCHED | | | | | | | | | WHAT HE GAVE UP | | | | | | | | | | | | THE RESULTS | | | | | | | |
|---|---|---|---|---|---|---|---|---|---|---|---|---|---|---|---|---|---|---|---|---|---|---|---|---|---|---|---|---|
| Year | Team | Lg | G | GS | CG | GF | IP | BFP | H | R | ER | HR | SH | SF | HB | TBB | IBB | SO | WP | Bk | W | L | Pct | Sh | Sv-Op | Hld | ERC | ERA |
| 2010 | Cin | NL | 24 | 22 | 0 | 0 | 138.1 | 604 | 158 | 77 | 65 | 19 | 7 | 3 | 3 | 49 | 2 | 91 | 2 | 0 | 8 | 4 | .667 | 0 | 0-0 | 0 | 5.12 | 4.23 |
| 2011 | Cin | NL | 29 | 26 | 0 | 2 | 167.2 | 693 | 159 | 74 | 72 | 23 | 3 | 6 | 8 | 38 | 3 | 118 | 2 | 1 | 12 | 9 | .571 | 0 | 0-0 | 0 | 3.53 | 3.86 |
| 2012 | Cin | NL | 30 | 30 | 2 | 0 | 179.0 | 757 | 201 | 97 | 91 | 26 | 6 | 7 | 3 | 41 | 3 | 116 | 3 | 0 | 8 | 9 | .471 | 0 | 0-0 | 0 | 4.50 | 4.58 |
| 2013 | Cin | NL | 31 | 31 | 0 | 0 | 192.1 | 801 | 193 | 78 | 72 | 21 | 8 | 5 | 6 | 48 | 4 | 122 | 2 | 0 | 14 | 7 | .667 | 0 | 0-0 | 0 | 3.69 | 3.37 |
| Postseason | | | 1 | 1 | 0 | 0 | 4.1 | 20 | 6 | 5 | 5 | 2 | 1 | 0 | 0 | 2 | 0 | 1 | 0 | 0 | 0 | 1 | .000 | 0 | 0-0 | 0 | 10.00 | 10.38 |
| 4 ML YEARS | | | 114 | 109 | 2 | 2 | 677.1 | 2855 | 711 | 326 | 300 | 89 | 24 | 21 | 20 | 176 | 12 | 447 | 9 | 1 | 42 | 29 | .592 | 0 | 0-0 | 0 | 4.15 | 3.99 |

# Wade LeBlanc

**Pitches:** L **Bats:** L **Pos:** RP-10; SP-7 lah-BLAHNK **Ht:** 6'3" **Wt:** 215 **Born:** 8/7/1984 **Age:** 29

| HOW MUCH HE PITCHED | | | | | | | | | WHAT HE GAVE UP | | | | | | | | | | | | THE RESULTS | | | | | | | |
|---|---|---|---|---|---|---|---|---|---|---|---|---|---|---|---|---|---|---|---|---|---|---|---|---|---|---|---|---|
| Year | Team | Lg | G | GS | CG | GF | IP | BFP | H | R | ER | HR | SH | SF | HB | TBB | IBB | SO | WP | Bk | W | L | Pct | Sh | Sv-Op | Hld | ERC | ERA |
| 2013 | OKCity* | AAA | 19 | 7 | 0 | 4 | 49.2 | 215 | 55 | 26 | 26 | 5 | 2 | 2 | 0 | 16 | 0 | 47 | 5 | 0 | 3 | 1 | .750 | 0 | 1-- | - | 4.38 | 4.71 |
| 2008 | SD | NL | 5 | 4 | 0 | 0 | 21.1 | 104 | 29 | 19 | 19 | 7 | 1 | 0 | 0 | 15 | 2 | 14 | 0 | 0 | 1 | 3 | .250 | 0 | 0-0 | 0 | 9.57 | 8.02 |
| 2009 | SD | NL | 9 | 9 | 0 | 0 | 46.1 | 194 | 35 | 19 | 19 | 6 | 3 | 1 | 4 | 19 | 1 | 30 | 0 | 0 | 3 | 1 | .750 | 0 | 0-0 | 0 | 3.28 | 3.69 |
| 2010 | SD | NL | 26 | 25 | 0 | 0 | 146.0 | 625 | 157 | 69 | 69 | 24 | 7 | 2 | 2 | 51 | 5 | 110 | 2 | 0 | 8 | 12 | .400 | 0 | 0-0 | 0 | 4.84 | 4.25 |
| 2011 | SD | NL | 14 | 14 | 0 | 0 | 79.2 | 339 | 84 | 42 | 41 | 7 | 3 | 3 | 1 | 28 | 1 | 51 | 1 | 1 | 5 | 6 | .455 | 0 | 0-0 | 0 | 4.21 | 4.63 |
| 2012 | Mia | NL | 25 | 9 | 0 | 1 | 68.2 | 284 | 71 | 30 | 28 | 7 | 5 | 1 | 1 | 19 | 1 | 43 | 1 | 0 | 2 | 5 | .286 | 0 | 0-0 | 1 | 3.94 | 3.67 |
| 2013 | 2 Tms | | 17 | 7 | 0 | 1 | 55.0 | 259 | 72 | 40 | 33 | 7 | 2 | 1 | 3 | 20 | 3 | 33 | 0 | 0 | 1 | 5 | .167 | 0 | 0-0 | 0 | 5.97 | 5.40 |
| 13 | Mia | NL | 13 | 7 | 0 | 0 | 48.2 | 222 | 63 | 30 | 28 | 6 | 2 | 1 | 2 | 15 | 2 | 31 | 0 | 0 | 1 | 5 | .167 | 0 | 0-0 | 0 | 5.67 | 5.18 |
| 13 | Hou | AL | 4 | 0 | 0 | 1 | 6.1 | 37 | 9 | 10 | 5 | 1 | 0 | 0 | 1 | 5 | 1 | 2 | 0 | 0 | 0 | 0 | - | 0 | 0-0 | 0 | 8.25 | 7.11 |
| 6 ML YEARS | | | 96 | 68 | 0 | 2 | 417.0 | 1805 | 448 | 219 | 209 | 58 | 21 | 8 | 11 | 152 | 13 | 281 | 4 | 1 | 20 | 32 | .385 | 0 | 0-0 | 1 | 4.74 | 4.51 |

# Sam LeCure

**Pitches:** R **Bats:** R **Pos:** RP-63 leh-CURE **Ht:** 6'0" **Wt:** 205 **Born:** 5/4/1984 **Age:** 30

| HOW MUCH HE PITCHED | | | | | | | | | WHAT HE GAVE UP | | | | | | | | | | | | THE RESULTS | | | | | | | |
|---|---|---|---|---|---|---|---|---|---|---|---|---|---|---|---|---|---|---|---|---|---|---|---|---|---|---|---|---|
| Year | Team | Lg | G | GS | CG | GF | IP | BFP | H | R | ER | HR | SH | SF | HB | TBB | IBB | SO | WP | Bk | W | L | Pct | Sh | Sv-Op | Hld | ERC | ERA |
| 2010 | Cin | NL | 15 | 6 | 0 | 4 | 48.0 | 217 | 50 | 24 | 24 | 6 | 1 | 2 | 5 | 25 | 3 | 37 | 1 | 0 | 2 | 5 | .286 | 0 | 0-0 | 0 | 5.36 | 4.50 |
| 2011 | Cin | NL | 43 | 4 | 0 | 7 | 77.2 | 307 | 57 | 33 | 32 | 10 | 4 | 0 | 4 | 21 | 3 | 73 | 0 | 0 | 2 | 1 | .667 | 0 | 0-0 | 5 | 2.55 | 3.71 |
| 2012 | Cin | NL | 48 | 0 | 0 | 12 | 57.1 | 237 | 46 | 22 | 20 | 3 | 4 | 1 | 1 | 23 | 2 | 61 | 2 | 0 | 3 | 3 | .500 | 0 | 0-1 | 7 | 2.73 | 3.14 |
| 2013 | Cin | NL | 63 | 0 | 0 | 15 | 61.0 | 251 | 50 | 18 | 18 | 4 | 1 | 0 | 1 | 24 | 0 | 66 | 0 | 0 | 2 | 1 | .667 | 0 | 1-3 | 17 | 2.95 | 2.66 |
| Postseason | | | 3 | 0 | 0 | 0 | 4.0 | 16 | 2 | 0 | 0 | 0 | 0 | 1 | 0 | 2 | 1 | 5 | 0 | 0 | 1 | 0 | 1.000 | 0 | 0-0 | 0 | 1.18 | 0.00 |
| 4 ML YEARS | | | 169 | 10 | 0 | 38 | 244.0 | 1012 | 203 | 97 | 94 | 23 | 10 | 3 | 11 | 93 | 8 | 237 | 3 | 0 | 9 | 10 | .474 | 0 | 1-4 | 29 | 3.21 | 3.47 |

# C.C. Lee

**Pitches:** R **Bats:** R **Pos:** RP-8 **Ht:** 5'11" **Wt:** 190 **Born:** 10/21/1986 **Age:** 27

| HOW MUCH HE PITCHED | | | | | | | | | WHAT HE GAVE UP | | | | | | | | | | | | THE RESULTS | | | | | | | |
|---|---|---|---|---|---|---|---|---|---|---|---|---|---|---|---|---|---|---|---|---|---|---|---|---|---|---|---|---|
| Year | Team | Lg | G | GS | CG | GF | IP | BFP | H | R | ER | HR | SH | SF | HB | TBB | IBB | SO | WP | Bk | W | L | Pct | Sh | Sv-Op | Hld | ERC | ERA |
| 2009 | Knstn | A+ | 45 | 0 | 0 | 10 | 83.1 | 350 | 67 | 33 | 31 | 5 | 4 | 5 | 9 | 28 | 1 | 97 | 4 | 0 | 4 | 6 | .400 | 0 | 2-- | - | 2.88 | 3.35 |
| 2010 | Akron | AA | 44 | 0 | 0 | 12 | 72.2 | 300 | 59 | 30 | 26 | 6 | 1 | 3 | 4 | 22 | 0 | 82 | 6 | 0 | 5 | 4 | .556 | 0 | 0-- | - | 2.78 | 3.22 |
| 2011 | Akron | AA | 23 | 0 | 0 | 9 | 39.2 | 162 | 27 | 16 | 11 | 1 | 4 | 3 | 6 | 11 | 1 | 56 | 3 | 0 | 2 | 1 | .667 | 0 | 0-- | - | 2.00 | 2.50 |
| 2011 | Clmbs | AAA | 21 | 0 | 0 | 9 | 31.2 | 128 | 26 | 9 | 8 | 2 | 0 | 1 | 1 | 12 | 1 | 43 | 3 | 0 | 4 | 0 | 1.000 | 0 | 1-- | - | 2.96 | 2.27 |
| 2012 | Clmbs | AAA | 5 | 0 | 0 | 1 | 7.0 | 27 | 5 | 2 | 2 | 1 | 2 | 0 | 0 | 1 | 0 | 8 | 1 | 0 | 2 | 0 | 1.000 | 0 | 0-- | - | 1.89 | 2.57 |
| 2013 | Lk Cty | A | 2 | 0 | 0 | 2 | 2.0 | 7 | 1 | 0 | 0 | 0 | 0 | 0 | 0 | 1 | 0 | 4 | 0 | 0 | 0 | 0 | - | 0 | 0-- | - | 1.62 | 0.00 |
| 2013 | Akron | AA | 8 | 0 | 0 | 0 | 8.0 | 33 | 3 | 3 | 3 | 0 | 0 | 1 | 1 | 4 | 0 | 9 | 0 | 0 | 0 | 0 | - | 0 | 0-- | - | 1.26 | 3.38 |
| 2013 | Clmbs | AAA | 19 | 0 | 0 | 4 | 19.0 | 73 | 14 | 5 | 5 | 1 | 1 | 0 | 1 | 5 | 0 | 24 | 0 | 1 | 1 | 0 | 1.000 | 0 | 0-- | - | 2.22 | 2.37 |
| 2013 | Cle | AL | 8 | 0 | 0 | 1 | 4.1 | 22 | 4 | 3 | 2 | 0 | 0 | 2 | 1 | 3 | 0 | 4 | 0 | 0 | 0 | 0 | - | 0 | 0-0 | 1 | 4.51 | 4.15 |

# Cliff Lee

**Pitches:** L **Bats:** L **Pos:** SP-31 **Ht:** 6'3" **Wt:** 205 **Born:** 8/30/1978 **Age:** 35

| HOW MUCH HE PITCHED | | | | | | | | | WHAT HE GAVE UP | | | | | | | | | | | | THE RESULTS | | | | | | | |
|---|---|---|---|---|---|---|---|---|---|---|---|---|---|---|---|---|---|---|---|---|---|---|---|---|---|---|---|---|
| Year | Team | Lg | G | GS | CG | GF | IP | BFP | H | R | ER | HR | SH | SF | HB | TBB | IBB | SO | WP | Bk | W | L | Pct | Sh | Sv-Op | Hld | ERC | ERA |
| 2002 | Cle | AL | 2 | 2 | 0 | 0 | 10.1 | 44 | 6 | 2 | 2 | 0 | 1 | 0 | 0 | 8 | 1 | 6 | 0 | 1 | 0 | 1 | .000 | 0 | 0-0 | 0 | 2.38 | 1.74 |
| 2003 | Cle | AL | 9 | 9 | 0 | 0 | 52.1 | 210 | 41 | 28 | 21 | 7 | 1 | 1 | 2 | 20 | 1 | 44 | 3 | 0 | 3 | 3 | .500 | 0 | 0-0 | 0 | 3.29 | 3.61 |
| 2004 | Cle | AL | 33 | 33 | 0 | 0 | 179.0 | 802 | 188 | 113 | 108 | 30 | 2 | 6 | 11 | 81 | 1 | 161 | 6 | 0 | 14 | 8 | .636 | 0 | 0-0 | 0 | 5.31 | 5.43 |
| 2005 | Cle | AL | 32 | 32 | 1 | 0 | 202.0 | 838 | 194 | 91 | 85 | 22 | 5 | 7 | 0 | 52 | 1 | 143 | 4 | 0 | 18 | 5 | **.783** | 0 | 0-0 | 0 | 3.35 | 3.79 |
| 2006 | Cle | AL | 33 | 33 | 1 | 0 | 200.2 | 882 | 224 | 114 | 98 | 29 | 3 | 6 | 8 | 58 | 3 | 129 | 3 | 0 | 14 | 11 | .560 | 0 | 0-0 | 0 | 4.69 | 4.40 |
| 2007 | Cle | AL | 20 | 16 | 1 | 1 | 97.1 | 443 | 112 | 73 | 68 | 17 | 3 | 2 | 7 | 36 | 1 | 66 | 5 | 0 | 5 | 8 | .385 | 0 | 0-0 | 0 | 5.59 | 6.29 |
| 2008 | Cle | AL | 31 | 31 | 4 | 0 | 223.1 | 891 | 214 | 68 | 63 | 12 | 2 | 3 | 5 | 34 | 1 | 170 | 4 | 0 | **22** | 3 | **.880** | **2** | 0-0 | 0 | 2.75 | **2.54** |
| 2009 | 2 Tms | | 34 | 34 | 6 | 0 | 231.2 | 969 | 245 | 88 | 83 | 17 | 11 | 9 | 5 | 43 | 1 | 181 | 7 | 0 | 14 | 13 | .519 | 2 | 0-0 | 0 | 3.45 | 3.22 |
| 2010 | 2 Tms | AL | 28 | 28 | **7** | 0 | 212.1 | 843 | 195 | 84 | 75 | 16 | 4 | 6 | 1 | 18 | 2 | 185 | 3 | 1 | 12 | 9 | .571 | 1 | 0-0 | 0 | **2.31** | 3.18 |
| 2011 | Phi | NL | 32 | 32 | 6 | 0 | 232.2 | 920 | 197 | 66 | 62 | 18 | 6 | 4 | 6 | 42 | 0 | 238 | 0 | 0 | 17 | 8 | .680 | **6** | 0-0 | 0 | 2.44 | 2.40 |
| 2012 | Phi | NL | 30 | 30 | 0 | 0 | 211.0 | 847 | 207 | 79 | 74 | 26 | 3 | 4 | 0 | 28 | 0 | 207 | 4 | 0 | 6 | 9 | .400 | 0 | 0-0 | 0 | 3.11 | 3.16 |
| 2013 | Phi | NL | 31 | 31 | 2 | 0 | 222.2 | 876 | 193 | 77 | 71 | 22 | 5 | 3 | 4 | 32 | 0 | 222 | 1 | 0 | 14 | 8 | .636 | 1 | 0-0 | 0 | 2.50 | 2.87 |
| 09 | Cle | AL | 22 | 22 | 3 | 0 | 152.0 | 641 | 165 | 53 | 53 | 10 | 6 | 5 | 3 | 33 | 1 | 107 | 6 | 0 | 7 | 9 | .438 | 1 | 0-0 | 0 | 3.68 | 3.14 |
| 09 | Phi | NL | 12 | 12 | 3 | 0 | 79.2 | 328 | 80 | 35 | 30 | 7 | 5 | 4 | 2 | 10 | 0 | 74 | 1 | 0 | 7 | 4 | .636 | 1 | 0-0 | 0 | 3.03 | 3.39 |
| 10 | Sea | AL | 13 | 13 | 5 | 0 | 103.2 | 408 | 92 | 31 | 27 | 5 | 0 | 3 | 0 | 6 | 0 | 89 | 2 | 1 | 8 | 3 | .727 | 1 | 0-0 | 0 | 1.91 | 2.34 |
| 10 | Tex | AL | 15 | 15 | 2 | 0 | 108.2 | 435 | 103 | 53 | 48 | 11 | 4 | 3 | 1 | 12 | 2 | 96 | 1 | 0 | 4 | 6 | .400 | 0 | 0-0 | 0 | 2.71 | 3.98 |
| Postseason | | | 11 | 11 | 3 | 0 | 82.0 | 320 | 66 | 27 | 23 | 2 | 1 | 0 | 1 | 10 | 0 | 89 | 2 | 0 | 7 | 3 | .700 | 0 | 0-0 | 0 | 1.68 | 2.52 |
| 12 ML YEARS | | | 315 | 311 | 28 | 1 | 2075.1 | 8565 | 2016 | 883 | 810 | 216 | 46 | 51 | 49 | 452 | 12 | 1752 | 40 | 2 | 139 | 86 | .618 | 12 | 0-0 | 0 | 3.33 | 3.51 |

# Charlie Leesman

**Pitches:** L **Bats:** L **Pos:** RP-7; SP-1 LEES-min **Ht:** 6'4" **Wt:** 210 **Born:** 3/10/1987 **Age:** 27

| HOW MUCH HE PITCHED | | | | | | | | | WHAT HE GAVE UP | | | | | | | | | | | | THE RESULTS | | | | | | | |
|---|---|---|---|---|---|---|---|---|---|---|---|---|---|---|---|---|---|---|---|---|---|---|---|---|---|---|---|---|
| Year | Team | Lg | G | GS | CG | GF | IP | BFP | H | R | ER | HR | SH | SF | HB | TBB | IBB | SO | WP | Bk | W | L | Pct | Sh | Sv-Op | Hld | ERC | ERA |
| 2009 | Knapol | A | 27 | 27 | 1 | 0 | 157.2 | 676 | 165 | 66 | 54 | 4 | 3 | 6 | 10 | 58 | 0 | 117 | 10 | 0 | 13 | 5 | .722 | 0 | 0-- | - | 4.01 | 3.08 |
| 2010 | WinSa | A+ | 17 | 17 | 0 | 0 | 84.2 | 393 | 98 | 51 | 48 | 6 | 2 | 3 | 11 | 44 | 0 | 39 | 5 | 0 | 9 | 4 | .692 | 0 | 0-- | - | 5.85 | 5.10 |
| 2010 | Brham | AA | 11 | 11 | 0 | 0 | 63.2 | 251 | 47 | 20 | 19 | 1 | 2 | 2 | 3 | 20 | 0 | 51 | 1 | 0 | 5 | 2 | .714 | 0 | 0-- | - | 2.11 | 2.69 |
| 2011 | Brham | AA | 27 | 27 | 0 | 0 | 152.0 | 678 | 150 | 79 | 68 | 4 | 3 | 9 | 13 | 83 | 0 | 113 | 16 | 2 | 10 | 7 | .588 | 0 | 0-- | - | 4.40 | 4.03 |
| 2012 | Charltt | AAA | 26 | 26 | 0 | 0 | 135.0 | 570 | 129 | 54 | 37 | 8 | 5 | 3 | 5 | 52 | 0 | 103 | 5 | 0 | 12 | 10 | .545 | 0 | 0-- | - | 3.69 | 2.47 |
| 2013 | Charltt | AAA | 16 | 16 | 0 | 0 | 88.1 | 394 | 90 | 50 | 38 | 11 | 4 | 3 | 4 | 41 | 0 | 78 | 5 | 0 | 4 | 3 | .571 | 0 | 0-- | - | 4.77 | 3.87 |
| 2013 | CWS | AL | 8 | 1 | 0 | 1 | 15.1 | 77 | 16 | 14 | 12 | 2 | 0 | 0 | 1 | 16 | 0 | 13 | 2 | 0 | 0 | 0 | - | 0 | 0-0 | 1 | 7.56 | 7.04 |

# DJ LeMahieu

la-MAY-hugh

**Bats:** R **Throws:** R **Pos:** 2B-90;3B-14;PH-9;PR-2;1B-1;SS-1 **Ht:** 6'4" **Wt:** 205 **Born:** 7/13/1988 **Age:** 25

| BATTING | | | | | | | | | | | | | | | | | | | | | | BASERUNNING | | | | AVERAGES | | |
|---|---|---|---|---|---|---|---|---|---|---|---|---|---|---|---|---|---|---|---|---|---|---|---|---|---|---|---|---|
| Year | Team | Lg | G | AB | H | 2B | 3B | HR | (Hm | Rd) | TB | R | RBI | RC | TBB | IBB | SO | HBP | SH | SF | SB | CS | SB% | GDP | Avg | OBP | Slg |
| 2013 | ColSpr* | AAA | 33 | 143 | 52 | 8 | 5 | 1 | (- | -) | 73 | 34 | 22 | 30 | 10 | 0 | 19 | 2 | 0 | 3 | 8 | 2 | .80 | 6 | .364 | .405 | .510 |
| 2011 | ChC | NL | 37 | 60 | 15 | 2 | 0 | 0 | (0 | 0) | 17 | 3 | 4 | 3 | 1 | 0 | 12 | 0 | 1 | 0 | 0 | 0 | - | 2 | .250 | .262 | .283 |
| 2012 | Col | NL | 81 | 229 | 68 | 12 | 4 | 2 | (1 | 1) | 94 | 26 | 22 | 28 | 13 | 4 | 42 | 0 | 3 | 2 | 1 | 2 | .33 | 8 | .297 | .332 | .410 |
| 2013 | Col | NL | 109 | 404 | 113 | 21 | 3 | 2 | (1 | 1) | 146 | 39 | 28 | 42 | 19 | 2 | 67 | 1 | 7 | 3 | 18 | 7 | .72 | 13 | .280 | .311 | .361 |
| 3 ML YEARS | | | 227 | 693 | 196 | 35 | 7 | 4 | (2 | 2) | 257 | 68 | 54 | 73 | 33 | 6 | 121 | 1 | 11 | 5 | 19 | 9 | .68 | 23 | .283 | .314 | .371 |

## Sandy Leon

**Bats:** B **Throws:** R **Pos:** C-1;PH-1 lee-OWN **Ht:** 5'11" **Wt:** 215 **Born:** 3/13/1989 **Age:** 25

| | | | BATTING | | | | | | | | | | | | | | | | | | BASERUNNING | | | | AVERAGES | | |
|---|---|---|---|---|---|---|---|---|---|---|---|---|---|---|---|---|---|---|---|---|---|---|---|---|---|---|---|
| Year | Team | Lg | G | AB | H | 2B | 3B | HR | (Hm | Rd) | TB | R | RBI | RC | TBB | IBB | SO | HBP | SH | SF | SB | CS | SB% | GDP | Avg | OBP | Slg |
| 2009 | Hgrstn | A | 23 | 78 | 17 | 3 | 0 | 0 | (- | -) | 20 | 7 | 6 | 5 | 5 | 0 | 21 | 0 | 0 | 0 | 0 | 0 | - | 0 | .218 | .265 | .256 |
| 2009 | Vrmnt | A- | 50 | 166 | 41 | 10 | 1 | 2 | (- | -) | 59 | 16 | 18 | 22 | 24 | 0 | 29 | 2 | 1 | 2 | 1 | 1 | .50 | 0 | .247 | .345 | .355 |
| 2010 | Hgrstn | A | 98 | 325 | 81 | 10 | 6 | 2 | (- | -) | 109 | 48 | 36 | 41 | 50 | 0 | 79 | 0 | 5 | 5 | 3 | 5 | .38 | 12 | .249 | .345 | .335 |
| 2011 | Ptomc | A+ | 109 | 370 | 93 | 21 | 1 | 6 | (- | -) | 134 | 36 | 43 | 43 | 33 | 2 | 69 | 1 | 9 | 3 | 1 | 3 | .25 | 5 | .251 | .312 | .362 |
| 2012 | Hrsbrg | AA | 40 | 135 | 42 | 12 | 0 | 1 | (- | -) | 57 | 15 | 19 | 21 | 9 | 0 | 16 | 2 | 1 | 2 | 1 | 0 | 1.00 | 3 | .311 | .358 | .422 |
| 2012 | Auburn | A- | 5 | 15 | 5 | 2 | 0 | 0 | (- | -) | 7 | 3 | 3 | 3 | 3 | 0 | 2 | 0 | 0 | 0 | 0 | 0 | - | 0 | .333 | .444 | .467 |
| 2012 | Syrcse | AAA | 19 | 52 | 18 | 5 | 0 | 2 | (- | -) | 29 | 8 | 4 | 13 | 12 | 1 | 12 | 0 | 0 | 0 | 0 | 0 | - | 0 | .346 | .469 | .558 |
| 2013 | Hrsbrg | AA | 95 | 310 | 55 | 12 | 1 | 3 | (- | -) | 78 | 35 | 26 | 25 | 47 | 3 | 57 | 3 | 0 | 1 | 0 | 0 | - | 9 | .177 | .291 | .252 |
| 2013 | Auburn | A- | 3 | 13 | 1 | 0 | 0 | 0 | (- | -) | 1 | 0 | 0 | 0 | 0 | 0 | 3 | 0 | 0 | 0 | 0 | 0 | - | 0 | .077 | .077 | .077 |
| 2012 | Was | NL | 12 | 30 | 8 | 2 | 0 | 0 | (0 | 0) | 10 | 2 | 2 | 2 | 4 | 0 | 11 | 2 | 0 | 0 | 0 | 0 | - | 1 | .267 | .389 | .333 |
| 2013 | Was | NL | 2 | 1 | 0 | 0 | 0 | 0 | (0 | 0) | 0 | 0 | 0 | 0 | 0 | 0 | 1 | 0 | 0 | 0 | 0 | 0 | - | 0 | .000 | .000 | .000 |
| 2 ML YEARS | | | 14 | 31 | 8 | 2 | 0 | 0 | (0 | 0) | 10 | 2 | 2 | 2 | 4 | 0 | 12 | 2 | 0 | 0 | 0 | 0 | - | 1 | .258 | .378 | .323 |

## Chris Leroux

**Pitches:** R **Bats:** L **Pos:** RP-2 leh-RUE **Ht:** 6'6" **Wt:** 225 **Born:** 4/14/1984 **Age:** 30

| | | | HOW MUCH HE PITCHED | | | | | | WHAT HE GAVE UP | | | | | | | | | | | | THE RESULTS | | | | | | | |
|---|---|---|---|---|---|---|---|---|---|---|---|---|---|---|---|---|---|---|---|---|---|---|---|---|---|---|---|---|
| Year | Team | Lg | G | GS | CG | GF | IP | BFP | H | R | ER | HR | SH | SF | HB | TBB | IBB | SO | WP | Bk | W | L | Pct | Sh | Sv-Op | Hld | ERC | ERA |
| 2013 * | | Jap | 5 | 5 | 0 | 0 | 22.0 | 115 | 37 | 26 | 22 | 1 | - | - | 1 | 11 | 0 | 14 | 0 | 3 | 0 | 2 | .000 | 0 | 0- - | - | 8.24 | 9.00 |
| 2009 | Fla | NL | 5 | 0 | 0 | 3 | 6.2 | 35 | 11 | 8 | 8 | 1 | 0 | 0 | 0 | 4 | 0 | 2 | 0 | 0 | 0 | 0 | - | 0 | 0-0 | 0 | 7.84 | 10.80 |
| 2010 | 2 Tms | NL | 23 | 0 | 0 | 7 | 22.2 | 105 | 28 | 18 | 17 | 1 | 0 | 3 | 0 | 14 | 2 | 22 | 1 | 0 | 0 | 1 | .000 | 0 | 0-2 | 3 | 5.86 | 6.75 |
| 2011 | Pit | NL | 23 | 0 | 0 | 5 | 25.0 | 110 | 26 | 9 | 8 | 0 | 1 | 0 | 1 | 7 | 2 | 24 | 2 | 0 | 1 | 1 | .500 | 0 | 0-1 | 2 | 3.05 | 2.88 |
| 2012 | Pit | NL | 10 | 0 | 0 | 3 | 11.1 | 48 | 11 | 9 | 7 | 1 | 1 | 0 | 1 | 2 | 0 | 12 | 1 | 0 | 0 | 0 | - | 0 | 0-0 | 0 | 3.24 | 5.56 |
| 2013 | Pit | NL | 2 | 0 | 0 | 0 | 4.0 | 21 | 4 | 3 | 3 | 1 | 0 | 0 | 0 | 6 | 0 | 3 | 0 | 0 | 0 | 0 | - | 0 | 0-0 | 0 | 10.44 | 6.75 |
| 10 | Fla | NL | 17 | 0 | 0 | 5 | 18.0 | 84 | 24 | 15 | 14 | 1 | 0 | 3 | 0 | 11 | 2 | 18 | 0 | 0 | 0 | 0 | - | 0 | 0-1 | 3 | 6.58 | 7.00 |
| 10 | Pit | NL | 6 | 0 | 0 | 2 | 4.2 | 21 | 4 | 3 | 3 | 0 | 0 | 0 | 0 | 3 | 0 | 4 | 1 | 0 | 0 | 1 | .000 | 0 | 0-1 | 0 | 3.39 | 5.79 |
| 5 ML YEARS | | | 63 | 0 | 0 | 18 | 69.2 | 319 | 80 | 47 | 43 | 3 | 2 | 3 | 2 | 33 | 4 | 63 | 4 | 0 | 1 | 2 | .333 | 0 | 0-3 | 5 | 4.75 | 5.56 |

## Steven Lerud

**Bats:** L **Throws:** R **Pos:** C-5;PH-1 leh-ROOD **Ht:** 6'1" **Wt:** 215 **Born:** 10/13/1984 **Age:** 29

| | | | BATTING | | | | | | | | | | | | | | | | | | BASERUNNING | | | | AVERAGES | | |
|---|---|---|---|---|---|---|---|---|---|---|---|---|---|---|---|---|---|---|---|---|---|---|---|---|---|---|---|
| Year | Team | Lg | G | AB | H | 2B | 3B | HR | (Hm | Rd) | TB | R | RBI | RC | TBB | IBB | SO | HBP | SH | SF | SB | CS | SB% | GDP | Avg | OBP | Slg |
| 2009 | Altna | AA | 95 | 304 | 73 | 17 | 0 | 4 | (- | -) | 102 | 31 | 26 | 39 | 38 | 2 | 53 | 10 | 6 | 5 | 2 | 1 | .67 | 6 | .240 | .339 | .336 |
| 2010 | Norfolk | AAA | 9 | 21 | 2 | 1 | 0 | 0 | (- | -) | 3 | 2 | 2 | 1 | 7 | 0 | 6 | 0 | 0 | 0 | 0 | 0 | - | 0 | .095 | .321 | .143 |
| 2010 | Bowie | AA | 49 | 153 | 31 | 7 | 1 | 6 | (- | -) | 58 | 18 | 14 | 19 | 18 | 1 | 47 | 7 | 1 | 0 | 0 | 0 | - | 2 | .203 | .315 | .379 |
| 2011 | Bowie | AA | 73 | 228 | 44 | 8 | 1 | 5 | (- | -) | 69 | 25 | 30 | 19 | 20 | 1 | 86 | 5 | 5 | 4 | 0 | 1 | .00 | 2 | .193 | .268 | .303 |
| 2012 | Rdng | AA | 36 | 102 | 24 | 7 | 0 | 0 | (- | -) | 31 | 7 | 7 | 12 | 13 | 1 | 35 | 5 | 0 | 0 | 0 | 1 | .00 | 2 | .235 | .350 | .304 |
| 2013 | LV | AAA | 61 | 180 | 39 | 8 | 0 | 3 | (- | -) | 56 | 20 | 21 | 23 | 35 | 1 | 50 | 3 | 1 | 0 | 1 | 0 | 1.00 | 7 | .217 | .353 | .311 |
| 2012 | Phi | NL | 3 | 10 | 2 | 0 | 0 | 0 | (0 | 0) | 2 | 1 | 0 | 1 | 0 | 0 | 2 | 0 | 0 | 0 | 0 | 0 | - | 1 | .200 | .200 | .200 |
| 2013 | Phi | NL | 6 | 5 | 0 | 0 | 0 | 0 | (0 | 0) | 0 | 0 | 0 | 0 | 0 | 0 | 4 | 0 | 0 | 0 | 0 | 0 | - | 0 | .000 | .000 | .000 |
| 2 ML YEARS | | | 9 | 15 | 2 | 0 | 0 | 0 | (0 | 0) | 2 | 1 | 0 | 1 | 0 | 0 | 6 | 0 | 0 | 0 | 0 | 0 | - | 1 | .133 | .133 | .133 |

## Jon Lester

**Pitches:** L **Bats:** L **Pos:** SP-33 **Ht:** 6'4" **Wt:** 240 **Born:** 1/7/1984 **Age:** 30

| | | | HOW MUCH HE PITCHED | | | | | | WHAT HE GAVE UP | | | | | | | | | | | | THE RESULTS | | | | | | | |
|---|---|---|---|---|---|---|---|---|---|---|---|---|---|---|---|---|---|---|---|---|---|---|---|---|---|---|---|---|
| Year | Team | Lg | G | GS | CG | GF | IP | BFP | H | R | ER | HR | SH | SF | HB | TBB | IBB | SO | WP | Bk | W | L | Pct | Sh | Sv-Op | Hld | ERC | ERA |
| 2006 | Bos | AL | 15 | 15 | 0 | 0 | 81.1 | 367 | 91 | 43 | 43 | 7 | 2 | 8 | 5 | 43 | 1 | 60 | 5 | 0 | 7 | 2 | .778 | 0 | 0-0 | 0 | 5.52 | 4.76 |
| 2007 | Bos | AL | 12 | 11 | 0 | 0 | 63.0 | 275 | 61 | 33 | 32 | 10 | 1 | 5 | 1 | 31 | 0 | 50 | 1 | 0 | 4 | 0 | 1.000 | 0 | 0-0 | 0 | 4.78 | 4.57 |
| 2008 | Bos | AL | 33 | 33 | 2 | 0 | 210.1 | 874 | 202 | 78 | 75 | 14 | 6 | 3 | 10 | 66 | 1 | 152 | 3 | 1 | 16 | 6 | .727 | **2** | 0-0 | 0 | 3.55 | 3.21 |
| 2009 | Bos | AL | 32 | 32 | 2 | 0 | 203.1 | 843 | 186 | 80 | 77 | 20 | 2 | 6 | 3 | 64 | 0 | 225 | 6 | 0 | 15 | 8 | .652 | 0 | 0-0 | 0 | 3.35 | 3.41 |
| 2010 | Bos | AL | 32 | 32 | 2 | 0 | 208.0 | 861 | 167 | 81 | 75 | 14 | 4 | 6 | 10 | 83 | 0 | 225 | 6 | 0 | 19 | 9 | .679 | 0 | 0-0 | 0 | 3.00 | 3.25 |
| 2011 | Bos | AL | 31 | 31 | 0 | 0 | 191.2 | 799 | 166 | 77 | 74 | 20 | 2 | 2 | 11 | 75 | 0 | 182 | 4 | 0 | 15 | 9 | .625 | 0 | 0-0 | 0 | 3.62 | 3.47 |
| 2012 | Bos | AL | 33 | 33 | 3 | 0 | 205.1 | 876 | 216 | 117 | 110 | 25 | 5 | 7 | 4 | 68 | 2 | 166 | 6 | 0 | 9 | 14 | .391 | 0 | 0-0 | 0 | 4.36 | 4.82 |
| 2013 | Bos | AL | 33 | 33 | 1 | 0 | 213.1 | 903 | 209 | 94 | 89 | 19 | 1 | 1 | 7 | 67 | 0 | 177 | 5 | 0 | 15 | 8 | .652 | 1 | 0-0 | 0 | 3.69 | 3.75 |
| Postseason | | | 8 | 6 | 0 | 2 | 42.0 | 175 | 34 | 14 | 12 | 5 | 2 | 0 | 0 | 13 | 0 | 39 | 0 | 0 | 2 | 3 | .400 | 0 | 0-0 | 0 | 2.75 | 2.57 |
| 8 ML YEARS | | | 221 | 220 | 10 | 0 | 1376.1 | 5798 | 1298 | 603 | 575 | 129 | 23 | 38 | 51 | 497 | 4 | 1237 | 36 | 1 | 100 | 56 | .641 | 3 | 0-0 | 0 | 3.75 | 3.76 |

## Colby Lewis

**Pitches:** R **Bats:** R **Pos:** P **Ht:** 6'4" **Wt:** 240 **Born:** 8/2/1979 **Age:** 34

| | | | HOW MUCH HE PITCHED | | | | | | WHAT HE GAVE UP | | | | | | | | | | | | THE RESULTS | | | | | | | |
|---|---|---|---|---|---|---|---|---|---|---|---|---|---|---|---|---|---|---|---|---|---|---|---|---|---|---|---|---|
| Year | Team | Lg | G | GS | CG | GF | IP | BFP | H | R | ER | HR | SH | SF | HB | TBB | IBB | SO | WP | Bk | W | L | Pct | Sh | Sv-Op | Hld | ERC | ERA |
| 2013 | RdRck* | AAA | 2 | 2 | 0 | 0 | 6.0 | 30 | 10 | 6 | 6 | 1 | 0 | 0 | 0 | 4 | 0 | 4 | 1 | 0 | 0 | 1 | .000 | 0 | 0- - | - | 10.54 | 9.00 |
| 2013 | Frisco* | AA | 5 | 5 | 0 | 0 | 18.0 | 81 | 23 | 14 | 14 | 4 | 0 | 0 | 0 | 4 | 0 | 15 | 0 | 0 | 0 | 1 | .000 | 0 | 0- - | - | 5.72 | 7.00 |
| 2002 | Tex | AL | 15 | 4 | 0 | 4 | 34.1 | 168 | 42 | 26 | 24 | 4 | 2 | 0 | 2 | 26 | 2 | 28 | 3 | 1 | 1 | 3 | .250 | 0 | 0-2 | 1 | 7.22 | 6.29 |
| 2003 | Tex | AL | 26 | 26 | 0 | 0 | 127.0 | 594 | 163 | 104 | 103 | 23 | 2 | 2 | 5 | 70 | 1 | 88 | 5 | 0 | 10 | 9 | .526 | 0 | 0-0 | 0 | 7.38 | 7.30 |
| 2004 | Tex | AL | 3 | 3 | 0 | 0 | 15.1 | 71 | 13 | 7 | 7 | 1 | 0 | 0 | 1 | 13 | 0 | 11 | 0 | 0 | 1 | 1 | .500 | 0 | 0-0 | 0 | 4.98 | 4.11 |
| 2006 | Det | AL | 2 | 0 | 0 | 1 | 3.0 | 18 | 8 | 1 | 1 | 1 | 0 | 0 | 0 | 1 | 0 | 5 | 0 | 0 | 0 | 0 | - | 0 | 0-0 | 0 | 17.35 | 3.00 |
| 2007 | Oak | AL | 26 | 1 | 0 | 8 | 37.2 | 170 | 44 | 28 | 27 | 7 | 1 | 2 | 3 | 14 | 3 | 23 | 1 | 1 | 0 | 2 | .000 | 0 | 0-1 | 3 | 5.79 | 6.45 |
| 2010 | Tex | AL | 32 | 32 | 1 | 0 | 201.0 | 844 | 174 | 90 | 83 | 21 | 4 | 4 | 6 | 65 | 0 | 196 | 9 | 0 | 12 | 13 | .480 | 0 | 0-0 | 0 | 3.15 | 3.72 |
| 2011 | Tex | AL | 32 | 32 | 2 | 0 | 200.1 | 839 | 187 | 103 | 98 | **35** | 4 | 5 | 6 | 56 | 1 | 169 | 4 | 0 | 14 | 10 | .583 | 1 | 0-0 | 0 | 3.82 | 4.40 |
| 2012 | Tex | AL | 16 | 16 | 2 | 0 | 105.0 | 427 | 99 | 48 | 40 | 16 | 1 | 2 | 6 | 14 | 0 | 93 | 2 | 0 | 6 | 6 | .500 | 0 | 0-0 | 0 | 3.28 | 3.43 |
| Postseason | | | 8 | 8 | 0 | 0 | 50.0 | 204 | 32 | 15 | 13 | 7 | 0 | 0 | 2 | 22 | 0 | 44 | 3 | 0 | 4 | 1 | .800 | 0 | 0-0 | 0 | 2.72 | 2.34 |
| 8 ML YEARS | | | 152 | 114 | 5 | 13 | 723.2 | 3131 | 730 | 407 | 383 | 108 | 14 | 15 | 29 | 259 | 7 | 613 | 24 | 2 | 44 | 44 | .500 | 1 | 0-3 | 4 | 4.44 | 4.76 |

# Alex Liddi

**Bats:** R **Throws:** R **Pos:** 1B-6;PH-2 LID-ee **Ht:** 6'4" **Wt:** 225 **Born:** 8/14/1988 **Age:** 25

| | | | BATTING | | | | | | | | | | | | | | | | | | BASERUNNING | | | | AVERAGES | | |
|---|---|---|---|---|---|---|---|---|---|---|---|---|---|---|---|---|---|---|---|---|---|---|---|---|---|---|---|
| Year | Team | Lg | G | AB | H | 2B | 3B | HR | (Hm | Rd) | TB | R | RBI | RC | TBB | IBB | SO | HBP | SH | SF | SB | CS | SB% | GDP | Avg | OBP | Slg |
| 2013 | Tacom* | AAA | 59 | 240 | 63 | 9 | 2 | 11 | (- | -) | 109 | 46 | 43 | 36 | 20 | 1 | 86 | 1 | 1 | 0 | 7 | 1 | .88 | 6 | .263 | .322 | .454 |
| 2013 | Norfolk* | AAA | 49 | 185 | 41 | 11 | 3 | 4 | (- | -) | 70 | 20 | 22 | 19 | 11 | 0 | 58 | 1 | 1 | 0 | 4 | 1 | .80 | 6 | .222 | .269 | .378 |
| 2011 | Sea | AL | 15 | 40 | 9 | 3 | 0 | 3 | (0 | 3) | 21 | 7 | 6 | 8 | 3 | 0 | 17 | 1 | 0 | 0 | 1 | 0 | 1.00 | 1 | .225 | .295 | .525 |
| 2012 | Sea | AL | 38 | 116 | 26 | 4 | 1 | 3 | (1 | 2) | 41 | 8 | 10 | 14 | 9 | 0 | 49 | 0 | 0 | 1 | 2 | 1 | .67 | 0 | .224 | .278 | .353 |
| 2013 | Sea | AL | 8 | 17 | 1 | 1 | 0 | 0 | (0 | 0) | 2 | 0 | 0 | 0 | 1 | 0 | 7 | 0 | 0 | 0 | 0 | 0 | - | 0 | .059 | .111 | .118 |
| 3 ML YEARS | | | 61 | 173 | 36 | 8 | 1 | 6 | (1 | 5) | 64 | 15 | 16 | 22 | 13 | 0 | 73 | 1 | 0 | 1 | 3 | 1 | .75 | 1 | .208 | .266 | .370 |

# Brent Lillibridge

**Bats:** R **Throws:** R **Pos:** 3B-12;2B-5;PH-2;1B-1;RF-1;DH-1 **Ht:** 5'11" **Wt:** 185 **Born:** 9/18/1983 **Age:** 30

| | | | BATTING | | | | | | | | | | | | | | | | | | BASERUNNING | | | | AVERAGES | | |
|---|---|---|---|---|---|---|---|---|---|---|---|---|---|---|---|---|---|---|---|---|---|---|---|---|---|---|---|
| Year | Team | Lg | G | AB | H | 2B | 3B | HR | (Hm | Rd) | TB | R | RBI | RC | TBB | IBB | SO | HBP | SH | SF | SB | CS | SB% | GDP | Avg | OBP | Slg |
| 2013 | Iowa* | AAA | 48 | 160 | 45 | 8 | 0 | 5 | (- | -) | 68 | 19 | 13 | 22 | 9 | 0 | 45 | 3 | 1 | 0 | 6 | 3 | .67 | 2 | .281 | .331 | .425 |
| 2013 | S-WB* | AAA | 41 | 150 | 41 | 8 | 1 | 7 | (- | -) | 72 | 24 | 18 | 26 | 13 | 0 | 36 | 3 | 0 | 2 | 12 | 2 | .86 | 0 | .273 | .339 | .480 |
| 2008 | Atl | NL | 29 | 80 | 16 | 6 | 1 | 1 | (0 | 1) | 27 | 9 | 8 | 6 | 3 | 0 | 23 | 1 | 1 | 0 | 2 | 0 | 1.00 | 0 | .200 | .238 | .338 |
| 2009 | CWS | AL | 46 | 95 | 15 | 2 | 0 | 0 | (0 | 0) | 17 | 9 | 3 | 5 | 14 | 0 | 26 | 1 | 2 | 0 | 6 | 3 | .67 | 2 | .158 | .273 | .179 |
| 2010 | CWS | AL | 64 | 98 | 22 | 5 | 2 | 2 | (1 | 1) | 37 | 19 | 16 | 11 | 3 | 0 | 36 | 0 | 0 | 0 | 5 | 3 | .63 | 2 | .224 | .248 | .378 |
| 2011 | CWS | AL | 97 | 186 | 48 | 5 | 1 | 13 | (8 | 5) | 94 | 38 | 29 | 30 | 17 | 1 | 62 | 7 | 4 | 2 | 10 | 6 | .63 | 2 | .258 | .340 | .505 |
| 2012 | 3 Tms | AL | 102 | 190 | 37 | 6 | 0 | 3 | (1 | 2) | 52 | 25 | 10 | 9 | 11 | 0 | 71 | 4 | 1 | 3 | 13 | 2 | .87 | 2 | .195 | .250 | .274 |
| 2013 | 2 Tms | | 20 | 59 | 7 | 1 | 0 | 0 | (0 | 0) | 8 | 2 | 5 | 2 | 1 | 0 | 17 | 0 | 1 | 0 | 1 | 0 | 1.00 | 1 | .119 | .133 | .136 |
| 12 | CWS | AL | 49 | 63 | 11 | 1 | 0 | 0 | (0 | 0) | 12 | 10 | 2 | 1 | 4 | 0 | 26 | 1 | 1 | 1 | 7 | 2 | .78 | 0 | .175 | .232 | .190 |
| 12 | Bos | AL | 10 | 16 | 2 | 0 | 0 | 0 | (0 | 0) | 2 | 0 | 0 | 0 | 0 | 0 | 5 | 0 | 0 | 0 | 0 | 0 | - | 0 | .125 | .125 | .125 |
| 12 | Cle | AL | 43 | 111 | 24 | 5 | 0 | 3 | (1 | 2) | 38 | 15 | 8 | 8 | 7 | 0 | 40 | 3 | 0 | 2 | 6 | 0 | 1.00 | 2 | .216 | .276 | .342 |
| 13 | ChC | NL | 9 | 24 | 1 | 0 | 0 | 0 | (0 | 0) | 1 | 0 | 2 | 0 | 0 | 0 | 9 | 0 | 0 | 0 | 0 | 0 | - | 1 | .042 | .042 | .042 |
| 13 | NYY | AL | 11 | 35 | 6 | 1 | 0 | 0 | (0 | 0) | 7 | 2 | 3 | 2 | 1 | 0 | 8 | 0 | 1 | 0 | 1 | 0 | 1.00 | 0 | .171 | .194 | .200 |
| 6 ML YEARS | | | 358 | 708 | 145 | 25 | 4 | 19 | (10 | 9) | 235 | 102 | 71 | 63 | 49 | 1 | 235 | 13 | 9 | 5 | 37 | 14 | .73 | 9 | .205 | .267 | .332 |

# Ted Lilly

**Pitches:** L **Bats:** L **Pos:** SP-5 **Ht:** 6'0" **Wt:** 195 **Born:** 1/4/1976 **Age:** 38

| | | | HOW MUCH HE PITCHED | | | | | | WHAT HE GAVE UP | | | | | | | | | | | | THE RESULTS | | | | | | | |
|---|---|---|---|---|---|---|---|---|---|---|---|---|---|---|---|---|---|---|---|---|---|---|---|---|---|---|---|---|
| Year | Team | Lg | G | GS | CG | GF | IP | BFP | H | R | ER | HR | SH | SF | HB | TBB | IBB | SO | WP | Bk | W | L | Pct | Sh | Sv-Op | Hld | ERC | ERA |
| 2013 | RCuca* | A+ | 5 | 5 | 0 | 0 | 24.1 | 116 | 35 | 23 | 22 | 5 | 1 | 2 | 3 | 7 | 0 | 24 | 0 | 0 | 1 | 4 | .200 | 0 | 0-- | - | 7.61 | 8.14 |
| 2013 | Albq* | AAA | 1 | 1 | 0 | 0 | 6.0 | 27 | 8 | 6 | 5 | 1 | 0 | 0 | 0 | 1 | 0 | 5 | 0 | 0 | 0 | 1 | .000 | 0 | 0-- | - | 5.41 | 7.50 |
| 1999 | Mon | NL | 9 | 3 | 0 | 1 | 23.2 | 110 | 30 | 20 | 20 | 7 | 0 | 1 | 3 | 9 | 0 | 28 | 1 | 0 | 0 | 1 | .000 | 0 | 0-0 | 0 | 7.76 | 7.61 |
| 2000 | NYY | AL | 7 | 0 | 0 | 1 | 8.0 | 39 | 8 | 6 | 5 | 1 | 0 | 0 | 0 | 5 | 0 | 11 | 1 | 1 | 0 | 0 | - | 0 | 0-0 | 0 | 4.76 | 5.63 |
| 2001 | NYY | AL | 26 | 21 | 0 | 2 | 120.2 | 537 | 126 | 81 | 72 | 20 | 2 | 5 | 7 | 51 | 1 | 112 | 9 | 2 | 5 | 6 | .455 | 0 | 0-0 | 0 | 5.10 | 5.37 |
| 2002 | 2 Tms | AL | 22 | 16 | 2 | 1 | 100.0 | 413 | 80 | 43 | 41 | 15 | 0 | 3 | 6 | 31 | 3 | 77 | 6 | 1 | 5 | 7 | .417 | 1 | 0-0 | 0 | 3.14 | 3.69 |
| 2003 | Oak | AL | 32 | 31 | 0 | 0 | 178.1 | 773 | 179 | 92 | 86 | 24 | 3 | 4 | 5 | 58 | 3 | 147 | 5 | **4** | 12 | 10 | .545 | 0 | 0-0 | 0 | 4.06 | 4.34 |
| 2004 | Tor | AL | 32 | 32 | 2 | 0 | 197.1 | 845 | 171 | 92 | 89 | 26 | 3 | 3 | 6 | 89 | 2 | 168 | 6 | **4** | 12 | 10 | .545 | 1 | 0-0 | 0 | 3.84 | 4.06 |
| 2005 | Tor | AL | 25 | 25 | 0 | 0 | 126.1 | 566 | 135 | 79 | 78 | 23 | 3 | 5 | 3 | 58 | 1 | 96 | 2 | 2 | 10 | 11 | .476 | 0 | 0-0 | 0 | 5.38 | 5.56 |
| 2006 | Tor | AL | 32 | 32 | 0 | 0 | 181.2 | 797 | 179 | 98 | 87 | 28 | 4 | 2 | 4 | 81 | 6 | 160 | 7 | **4** | 15 | 13 | .536 | 0 | 0-0 | 0 | 4.57 | 4.31 |
| 2007 | ChC | NL | 34 | 34 | 0 | 0 | 207.0 | 847 | 181 | 91 | 88 | 28 | 11 | 9 | 3 | 55 | 2 | 174 | 7 | 0 | 15 | 8 | .652 | 0 | 0-0 | 0 | 3.14 | 3.83 |
| 2008 | ChC | NL | 34 | **34** | 0 | 0 | 204.2 | 861 | 187 | 96 | 93 | 32 | 5 | 3 | 7 | 64 | 2 | 184 | 4 | **4** | 17 | 9 | .654 | 0 | 0-0 | 0 | 3.73 | 4.09 |
| 2009 | ChC | NL | 27 | 27 | 0 | 0 | 177.0 | 706 | 151 | 66 | 61 | 22 | 9 | 3 | 2 | 36 | 2 | 151 | 3 | 3 | 12 | 9 | .571 | 0 | 0-0 | 0 | 2.74 | 3.10 |
| 2010 | 2 Tms | NL | 30 | 30 | 1 | 0 | 193.2 | 785 | 165 | 83 | 78 | 32 | 14 | 2 | 5 | 44 | 4 | 166 | 2 | 2 | 10 | 12 | .455 | 1 | 0-0 | 0 | 3.08 | 3.62 |
| 2011 | LAD | NL | 33 | 33 | 0 | 0 | 192.2 | 800 | 172 | 88 | 85 | 28 | 12 | 5 | 9 | 51 | 8 | 158 | 2 | 2 | 12 | 14 | .462 | 0 | 0-0 | 0 | 3.36 | 3.97 |
| 2012 | LAD | NL | 8 | 8 | 0 | 0 | 48.2 | 202 | 36 | 23 | 17 | 3 | 2 | 2 | 2 | 19 | 1 | 31 | 3 | 0 | 5 | 1 | .833 | 0 | 0-0 | 0 | 2.51 | 3.14 |
| 2013 | LAD | NL | 5 | 5 | 0 | 0 | 23.0 | 109 | 27 | 16 | 13 | 4 | 0 | 0 | 1 | 10 | 0 | 18 | 0 | 0 | 0 | 2 | .000 | 0 | 0-0 | 0 | 5.73 | 5.09 |
| 02 | NYY | AL | 16 | 11 | 2 | 1 | 76.2 | 314 | 57 | 31 | 29 | 10 | 0 | 3 | 5 | 24 | 3 | 59 | 6 | 0 | 3 | 6 | .333 | 1 | 0-0 | 0 | 2.74 | 3.40 |
| 02 | Oak | AL | 6 | 5 | 0 | 0 | 23.1 | 99 | 23 | 12 | 12 | 5 | 0 | 0 | 1 | 7 | 0 | 18 | 0 | 1 | 2 | 1 | .667 | 0 | 0-0 | 0 | 4.56 | 4.63 |
| 10 | ChC | NL | 18 | 18 | 0 | 0 | 117.0 | 480 | 104 | 53 | 48 | 19 | 8 | 1 | 2 | 29 | 3 | 89 | 2 | 2 | 3 | 8 | .273 | 0 | 0-0 | 0 | 3.30 | 3.69 |
| 10 | LAD | NL | 12 | 12 | 1 | 0 | 76.2 | 305 | 61 | 30 | 30 | 13 | 6 | 1 | 3 | 15 | 1 | 77 | 0 | 0 | 7 | 4 | .636 | 1 | 0-0 | 0 | 2.77 | 3.52 |
| Postseason | | | 5 | 2 | 0 | 0 | 16.1 | 76 | 19 | 13 | 12 | 2 | 1 | 0 | 1 | 7 | 0 | 14 | 1 | 0 | 0 | 2 | .000 | 0 | 0-1 | 0 | 5.43 | 6.61 |
| 15 ML YEARS | | | 356 | 331 | 5 | 5 | 1982.2 | 8390 | 1827 | 974 | 913 | 293 | 68 | 47 | 63 | 661 | 35 | 1681 | 58 | 29 | 130 | 113 | .535 | 3 | 0-0 | 0 | 3.78 | 4.14 |

# Chang-Yong Lim

**Pitches:** R **Bats:** R **Pos:** RP-6 YOHNG LIMM **Ht:** 5'11" **Wt:** 175 **Born:** 6/4/1976 **Age:** 38

| | | | HOW MUCH HE PITCHED | | | | | | WHAT HE GAVE UP | | | | | | | | | | | | THE RESULTS | | | | | | | |
|---|---|---|---|---|---|---|---|---|---|---|---|---|---|---|---|---|---|---|---|---|---|---|---|---|---|---|---|---|
| Year | Team | Lg | G | GS | CG | GF | IP | BFP | H | R | ER | HR | SH | SF | HB | TBB | IBB | SO | WP | Bk | W | L | Pct | Sh | Sv-Op | Hld | ERC | ERA |
| 2013 | Cubs | R | 5 | 5 | 0 | 0 | 5.0 | 19 | 5 | 2 | 2 | 0 | 0 | 1 | 0 | 0 | 0 | 4 | 0 | 0 | 0 | 0 | - | 0 | 0-- | - | 2.09 | 3.60 |
| 2013 | Dytona | A+ | 4 | 0 | 0 | 1 | 5.0 | 19 | 2 | 1 | 1 | 0 | 0 | 0 | 0 | 3 | 0 | 6 | 0 | 0 | 0 | 0 | - | 0 | 0-- | - | 1.39 | 1.80 |
| 2013 | Tenn | AA | 1 | 0 | 0 | 0 | 1.0 | 4 | 1 | 0 | 0 | 0 | 0 | 0 | 0 | 0 | 0 | 2 | 0 | 0 | 0 | 0 | - | 0 | 0-- | - | 1.95 | 0.00 |
| 2013 | Iowa | AAA | 11 | 0 | 0 | 1 | 11.1 | 41 | 5 | 1 | 1 | 0 | 0 | 0 | 0 | 4 | 0 | 12 | 0 | 0 | 0 | 0 | - | 0 | 0-- | - | 1.02 | 0.79 |
| 2013 | ChC | NL | 6 | 0 | 0 | 1 | 5.0 | 27 | 6 | 3 | 3 | 0 | 0 | 0 | 1 | 7 | 1 | 5 | 1 | 0 | 0 | 0 | - | 0 | 0-0 | 0 | 9.35 | 5.40 |

# Tim Lincecum

**Pitches:** R **Bats:** L **Pos:** SP-32 LIN-suh-come **Ht:** 5'11" **Wt:** 170 **Born:** 6/15/1984 **Age:** 30

| | | | HOW MUCH HE PITCHED | | | | | | WHAT HE GAVE UP | | | | | | | | | | | | THE RESULTS | | | | | | | |
|---|---|---|---|---|---|---|---|---|---|---|---|---|---|---|---|---|---|---|---|---|---|---|---|---|---|---|---|---|
| Year | Team | Lg | G | GS | CG | GF | IP | BFP | H | R | ER | HR | SH | SF | HB | TBB | IBB | SO | WP | Bk | W | L | Pct | Sh | Sv-Op | Hld | ERC | ERA |
| 2007 | SF | NL | 24 | 24 | 0 | 0 | 146.1 | 618 | 122 | 70 | 65 | 12 | 5 | 7 | 2 | 65 | 5 | 150 | 10 | 0 | 7 | 5 | .583 | 0 | 0-0 | 0 | 3.21 | 4.00 |
| 2008 | SF | NL | 34 | 33 | 2 | 0 | 227.0 | 928 | 182 | 72 | 66 | 11 | 11 | 3 | 6 | 84 | 1 | **265** | **17** | 2 | 18 | 5 | **.783** | 1 | 0-0 | 0 | **2.69** | 2.62 |
| 2009 | SF | NL | 32 | 32 | **4** | 0 | 225.1 | 905 | 168 | 69 | 62 | 10 | 12 | 5 | 6 | 68 | 2 | **261** | 11 | 0 | 15 | 7 | .682 | **2** | 0-0 | 0 | **2.14** | 2.48 |
| 2010 | SF | NL | 33 | 33 | 1 | 0 | 212.1 | 897 | 194 | 84 | 81 | 18 | 9 | 5 | 5 | 76 | 7 | **231** | 9 | 0 | 16 | 10 | .615 | 1 | 0-0 | 0 | 3.37 | 3.43 |
| 2011 | SF | NL | 33 | 33 | 1 | 0 | 217.0 | 900 | 176 | 74 | 66 | 15 | 13 | 1 | 6 | 86 | 5 | 220 | 9 | 0 | 13 | 14 | .481 | 1 | 0-0 | 0 | 2.92 | 2.74 |

| Year | Team | Lg | G | GS | CG | GF | IP | BFP | H | R | ER | HR | SH | SF | HB | TBB | IBB | SO | WP | Bk | W | L | Pct | Sh | Sv-Op | Hld | ERC | ERA |
|---|---|---|---|---|---|---|---|---|---|---|---|---|---|---|---|---|---|---|---|---|---|---|---|---|---|---|---|---|
| | | | HOW MUCH HE PITCHED | | | | | | WHAT HE GAVE UP | | | | | | | | | | | | THE RESULTS | | | | | | | |
| 2012 | SF | NL | 33 | **33** | 0 | 0 | 186.0 | 825 | 183 | **111** | **107** | 23 | 11 | 6 | 4 | 90 | 3 | 190 | **17** | 2 | 10 | **15** | .400 | 0 | 0-0 | 0 | 4.50 | 5.18 |
| 2013 | SF | NL | 32 | 32 | 1 | 0 | 197.2 | 841 | 184 | 102 | 96 | 21 | 10 | 4 | 7 | 76 | 8 | 193 | 11 | 2 | 10 | 14 | .417 | 1 | 0-0 | 0 | 3.76 | 4.37 |
| Postseason | | | 12 | 6 | 1 | 0 | 54.2 | 212 | 34 | 16 | 15 | 3 | 1 | 3 | 1 | 14 | 0 | 63 | 0 | 0 | 5 | 2 | .714 | 1 | 0-0 | 2 | 1.53 | 2.47 |
| 7 ML YEARS | | | 221 | 220 | 9 | 0 | 1411.2 | 5914 | 1209 | 582 | 543 | 110 | 71 | 31 | 36 | 545 | 31 | 1510 | 84 | 6 | 89 | 70 | .560 | 6 | 0-0 | 0 | 3.16 | 3.46 |

## Brad Lincoln

**Pitches:** R **Bats:** L **Pos:** RP-22 **Ht:** 6'0" **Wt:** 225 **Born:** 5/25/1985 **Age:** 29

| Year | Team | Lg | G | GS | CG | GF | IP | BFP | H | R | ER | HR | SH | SF | HB | TBB | IBB | SO | WP | Bk | W | L | Pct | Sh | Sv-Op | Hld | ERC | ERA |
|---|---|---|---|---|---|---|---|---|---|---|---|---|---|---|---|---|---|---|---|---|---|---|---|---|---|---|---|---|
| | | | HOW MUCH HE PITCHED | | | | | | WHAT HE GAVE UP | | | | | | | | | | | | THE RESULTS | | | | | | | |
| 2013 | Buffalo* | AAA | 23 | 0 | 0 | 15 | 26.1 | 105 | 22 | 7 | 6 | 2 | 2 | 3 | 2 | 8 | 0 | 29 | 0 | 0 | 3 | 2 | .600 | 0 | 5- - | - | 3.09 | 2.05 |
| 2010 | Pit | NL | 11 | 9 | 0 | 0 | 52.2 | 240 | 66 | 42 | 39 | 9 | 3 | 4 | 5 | 15 | 0 | 25 | 1 | 0 | 1 | 4 | .200 | 0 | 0-0 | 0 | 5.99 | 6.66 |
| 2011 | Pit | NL | 12 | 8 | 0 | 0 | 47.2 | 211 | 54 | 27 | 25 | 4 | 2 | 2 | 2 | 16 | 4 | 29 | 0 | 0 | 2 | 3 | .400 | 0 | 0-0 | 0 | 4.46 | 4.72 |
| 2012 | 2 Tms | | 52 | 5 | 0 | 10 | 88.0 | 362 | 80 | 37 | 36 | 14 | 4 | 1 | 1 | 24 | 2 | 88 | 1 | 0 | 5 | 2 | .714 | 0 | 1-2 | 9 | 3.49 | 3.68 |
| 2013 | Tor | AL | 22 | 0 | 0 | 7 | 31.2 | 148 | 28 | 17 | 14 | 4 | 2 | 0 | 3 | 22 | 0 | 25 | 2 | 0 | 1 | 2 | .333 | 0 | 0-0 | 0 | 5.04 | 3.98 |
| 12 | Pit | NL | 28 | 5 | 0 | 6 | 59.1 | 239 | 51 | 19 | 18 | 8 | 2 | 0 | 1 | 14 | 1 | 60 | 0 | 0 | 4 | 2 | .667 | 0 | 1-2 | 5 | 2.97 | 2.73 |
| 12 | Tor | AL | 24 | 0 | 0 | 4 | 28.2 | 123 | 29 | 18 | 18 | 6 | 2 | 1 | 0 | 10 | 1 | 28 | 1 | 0 | 1 | 0 | 1.000 | 0 | 0-0 | 4 | 4.63 | 5.65 |
| 4 ML YEARS | | | 97 | 22 | 0 | 17 | 220.0 | 961 | 228 | 123 | 114 | 31 | 11 | 7 | 11 | 77 | 6 | 167 | 4 | 0 | 9 | 11 | .450 | 0 | 1-2 | 9 | 4.50 | 4.66 |

## Adam Lind

**Bats:** L **Throws:** L **Pos:** 1B-76;DH-58;PH-22 **Ht:** 6'2" **Wt:** 220 **Born:** 7/17/1983 **Age:** 30

| Year | Team | Lg | G | AB | H | 2B | 3B | HR | (Hm | Rd) | TB | R | RBI | RC | TBB | IBB | SO | HBP | SH | SF | SB | CS | SB% | GDP | Avg | OBP | Slg |
|---|---|---|---|---|---|---|---|---|---|---|---|---|---|---|---|---|---|---|---|---|---|---|---|---|---|---|---|
| | | | BATTING | | | | | | | | | | | | | | | | | | BASERUNNING | | | | AVERAGES | | |
| 2006 | Tor | AL | 18 | 60 | 22 | 8 | 0 | 2 | (0 | 2) | 36 | 8 | 8 | 13 | 5 | 0 | 12 | 0 | 0 | 0 | 0 | 0 | - | 0 | .367 | .415 | .600 |
| 2007 | Tor | AL | 89 | 290 | 69 | 14 | 0 | 11 | (10 | 1) | 116 | 34 | 46 | 38 | 16 | 0 | 65 | 1 | 2 | 2 | 1 | 2 | .33 | 7 | .238 | .278 | .400 |
| 2008 | Tor | AL | 88 | 326 | 92 | 16 | 4 | 9 | (2 | 7) | 143 | 48 | 40 | 39 | 16 | 3 | 59 | 2 | 1 | 4 | 2 | 0 | 1.00 | 8 | .282 | .316 | .439 |
| 2009 | Tor | AL | 151 | 587 | 179 | 46 | 0 | 35 | (14 | **21**) | 330 | 93 | 114 | 114 | 58 | 7 | 110 | 5 | 0 | 4 | 1 | 1 | .50 | 15 | .305 | .370 | .562 |
| 2010 | Tor | AL | 150 | 569 | 135 | 32 | 3 | 23 | (15 | 8) | 242 | 57 | 72 | 65 | 38 | 3 | 144 | 3 | 0 | 3 | 0 | 0 | - | 10 | .237 | .287 | .425 |
| 2011 | Tor | AL | 125 | 499 | 125 | 16 | 0 | 26 | (12 | 14) | 219 | 56 | 87 | 67 | 32 | 4 | 107 | 3 | 0 | 8 | 1 | 1 | .50 | 12 | .251 | .295 | .439 |
| 2012 | Tor | AL | 93 | 321 | 82 | 14 | 2 | 11 | (6 | 5) | 133 | 28 | 45 | 47 | 29 | 1 | 61 | 0 | 0 | 3 | 0 | 0 | - | 10 | .255 | .314 | .414 |
| 2013 | Tor | AL | 143 | 465 | 134 | 26 | 1 | 23 | (9 | 14) | 231 | 67 | 67 | 76 | 51 | 5 | 103 | 1 | 0 | 4 | 1 | 0 | 1.00 | 20 | .288 | .357 | .497 |
| 8 ML YEARS | | | 857 | 3117 | 838 | 172 | 10 | 140 | (68 | 72) | 1450 | 391 | 479 | 459 | 245 | 23 | 661 | 15 | 3 | 28 | 6 | 4 | .60 | 82 | .269 | .322 | .465 |

## Josh Lindblom

**Pitches:** R **Bats:** R **Pos:** SP-5; RP-3 LIN-bloom **Ht:** 6'4" **Wt:** 240 **Born:** 6/15/1987 **Age:** 27

| Year | Team | Lg | G | GS | CG | GF | IP | BFP | H | R | ER | HR | SH | SF | HB | TBB | IBB | SO | WP | Bk | W | L | Pct | Sh | Sv-Op | Hld | ERC | ERA |
|---|---|---|---|---|---|---|---|---|---|---|---|---|---|---|---|---|---|---|---|---|---|---|---|---|---|---|---|---|
| | | | HOW MUCH HE PITCHED | | | | | | WHAT HE GAVE UP | | | | | | | | | | | | THE RESULTS | | | | | | | |
| 2013 | RdRck* | AAA | 20 | 18 | 0 | 1 | 108.0 | 442 | 86 | 39 | 37 | 12 | 1 | 0 | 7 | 31 | 0 | 79 | 2 | 0 | 8 | 4 | .667 | 0 | 0- - | - | 2.87 | 3.08 |
| 2011 | LAD | NL | 27 | 0 | 0 | 8 | 29.2 | 116 | 21 | 9 | 9 | 0 | 2 | 3 | 2 | 10 | 3 | 28 | 3 | 0 | 1 | 0 | 1.000 | 0 | 0-1 | 3 | 1.90 | 2.73 |
| 2012 | 2 Tms | NL | 74 | 0 | 0 | 18 | 71.0 | 304 | 61 | 31 | 28 | 13 | 2 | 0 | 4 | 35 | 2 | 70 | 2 | 0 | 3 | 5 | .375 | 0 | 1-4 | 22 | 4.47 | 3.55 |
| 2013 | Tex | AL | 8 | 5 | 0 | 2 | 31.1 | 137 | 35 | 19 | 19 | 4 | 0 | 0 | 0 | 11 | 2 | 21 | 2 | 0 | 1 | 3 | .250 | 0 | 0-0 | 0 | 4.64 | 5.46 |
| 12 | LAD | NL | 48 | 0 | 0 | 12 | 47.2 | 197 | 42 | 16 | 16 | 9 | 2 | 0 | 3 | 18 | 0 | 43 | 1 | 0 | 2 | 2 | .500 | 0 | 0-2 | 15 | 4.31 | 3.02 |
| 12 | Phi | NL | 26 | 0 | 0 | 6 | 23.1 | 107 | 19 | 15 | 12 | 4 | 0 | 0 | 1 | 17 | 2 | 27 | 1 | 0 | 1 | 3 | .250 | 0 | 1-2 | 7 | 4.77 | 4.63 |
| 3 ML YEARS | | | 109 | 5 | 0 | 28 | 132.0 | 557 | 117 | 59 | 56 | 17 | 4 | 3 | 6 | 56 | 7 | 119 | 7 | 0 | 5 | 8 | .385 | 0 | 1-5 | 25 | 3.89 | 3.82 |

## Matt Lindstrom

**Pitches:** R **Bats:** R **Pos:** RP-76 **Ht:** 6'3" **Wt:** 220 **Born:** 2/11/1980 **Age:** 34

| Year | Team | Lg | G | GS | CG | GF | IP | BFP | H | R | ER | HR | SH | SF | HB | TBB | IBB | SO | WP | Bk | W | L | Pct | Sh | Sv-Op | Hld | ERC | ERA |
|---|---|---|---|---|---|---|---|---|---|---|---|---|---|---|---|---|---|---|---|---|---|---|---|---|---|---|---|---|
| | | | HOW MUCH HE PITCHED | | | | | | WHAT HE GAVE UP | | | | | | | | | | | | THE RESULTS | | | | | | | |
| 2007 | Fla | NL | 71 | 0 | 0 | 11 | 67.0 | 284 | 66 | 27 | 23 | 2 | 3 | 1 | 3 | 21 | 4 | 62 | 5 | 0 | 3 | 4 | .429 | 0 | 0-2 | 19 | 3.26 | 3.09 |
| 2008 | Fla | NL | 66 | 0 | 0 | 27 | 57.1 | 245 | 57 | 21 | 20 | 1 | 6 | 1 | 1 | 26 | 4 | 43 | 4 | 0 | 3 | 3 | .500 | 0 | 5-6 | 14 | 3.69 | 3.14 |
| 2009 | Fla | NL | 54 | 0 | 0 | 32 | 47.1 | 219 | 54 | 35 | 31 | 5 | 1 | 0 | 2 | 24 | 2 | 39 | 0 | 1 | 2 | 1 | .667 | 0 | 15-17 | 8 | 5.41 | 5.89 |
| 2010 | Hou | NL | 58 | 0 | 0 | 41 | 53.1 | 244 | 68 | 26 | 26 | 5 | 2 | 0 | 0 | 20 | 1 | 43 | 8 | 0 | 2 | 5 | .286 | 0 | 23-29 | 4 | 5.45 | 4.39 |
| 2011 | Col | NL | 63 | 0 | 0 | 16 | 54.0 | 226 | 52 | 21 | 18 | 3 | 3 | 3 | 2 | 14 | 4 | 36 | 2 | 0 | 2 | 2 | .500 | 0 | 2-5 | 15 | 3.06 | 3.00 |
| 2012 | 2 Tms | | 46 | 0 | 0 | 6 | 47.0 | 200 | 45 | 17 | 14 | 2 | 0 | 1 | 5 | 14 | 2 | 40 | 1 | 1 | 1 | 0 | 1.000 | 0 | 0-1 | 5 | 3.40 | 2.68 |
| 2013 | CWS | AL | 76 | 0 | 0 | 12 | 60.2 | 260 | 64 | 23 | 21 | 2 | 2 | 3 | 1 | 23 | 1 | 46 | 6 | 0 | 2 | 4 | .333 | 0 | 0-4 | 20 | 3.92 | 3.12 |
| 12 | Bal | AL | 34 | 0 | 0 | 3 | 36.1 | 155 | 35 | 14 | 11 | 2 | 0 | 1 | 4 | 12 | 2 | 30 | 1 | 1 | 1 | 0 | 1.000 | 0 | 0-1 | 2 | 3.66 | 2.72 |
| 12 | Ari | NL | 12 | 0 | 0 | 3 | 10.2 | 45 | 10 | 3 | 3 | 0 | 0 | 0 | 1 | 2 | 0 | 10 | 0 | 0 | 0 | 0 | - | 0 | 0-0 | 3 | 2.57 | 2.53 |
| 7 ML YEARS | | | 434 | 0 | 0 | 145 | 386.2 | 1678 | 406 | 170 | 153 | 20 | 17 | 9 | 14 | 142 | 18 | 309 | 26 | 2 | 15 | 19 | .441 | 0 | 45-64 | 85 | 3.96 | 3.56 |

## Francisco Liriano

**Pitches:** L **Bats:** L **Pos:** SP-26 **Ht:** 6'2" **Wt:** 220 **Born:** 10/26/1983 **Age:** 30

| Year | Team | Lg | G | GS | CG | GF | IP | BFP | H | R | ER | HR | SH | SF | HB | TBB | IBB | SO | WP | Bk | W | L | Pct | Sh | Sv-Op | Hld | ERC | ERA |
|---|---|---|---|---|---|---|---|---|---|---|---|---|---|---|---|---|---|---|---|---|---|---|---|---|---|---|---|---|
| | | | HOW MUCH HE PITCHED | | | | | | WHAT HE GAVE UP | | | | | | | | | | | | THE RESULTS | | | | | | | |
| 2013 | Bradtn* | A+ | 1 | 1 | 0 | 0 | 3.0 | 9 | 0 | 0 | 0 | 0 | 0 | 0 | 0 | 0 | 0 | 6 | 0 | 0 | 0 | 0 | - | 0 | 0- - | - | 0.00 | 0.00 |
| 2013 | Altna* | AA | 1 | 1 | 0 | 0 | 2.2 | 15 | 4 | 4 | 4 | 1 | 0 | 0 | 0 | 3 | 0 | 4 | 0 | 0 | 0 | 1 | .000 | 0 | 0- - | - | 12.97 | 13.50 |
| 2013 | Indy* | AAA | 3 | 3 | 0 | 0 | 16.0 | 66 | 15 | 6 | 6 | 1 | 0 | 1 | 1 | 1 | 0 | 23 | 1 | 0 | 2 | 0 | 1.000 | 0 | 0- - | - | 2.38 | 3.38 |
| 2005 | Min | AL | 6 | 4 | 0 | 2 | 23.2 | 93 | 19 | 15 | 15 | 4 | 0 | 0 | 0 | 7 | 0 | 33 | 0 | 0 | 1 | 2 | .333 | 0 | 0-0 | 0 | 3.15 | 5.70 |
| 2006 | Min | AL | 28 | 16 | 0 | 2 | 121.0 | 473 | 89 | 31 | 29 | 9 | 4 | 2 | 1 | 32 | 0 | 144 | 9 | 1 | 12 | 3 | **.800** | 0 | 1-1 | 1 | 2.12 | 2.16 |
| 2008 | Min | AL | 14 | 14 | 0 | 0 | 76.0 | 329 | 74 | 40 | 33 | 7 | 2 | 3 | 1 | 32 | 1 | 67 | 3 | 0 | 6 | 4 | .600 | 0 | 0-0 | 0 | 3.97 | 3.91 |
| 2009 | Min | AL | 29 | 24 | 0 | 2 | 136.2 | 609 | 147 | 93 | 88 | 21 | 5 | 6 | 6 | 65 | 0 | 122 | 5 | 1 | 5 | 13 | .278 | 0 | 0-0 | 0 | 5.46 | 5.80 |
| 2010 | Min | AL | 31 | 31 | 0 | 0 | 191.2 | 806 | 184 | 77 | 77 | 9 | 6 | 2 | 10 | 58 | 0 | 201 | 10 | 1 | 14 | 10 | .583 | 0 | 0-0 | 0 | 3.34 | 3.62 |
| 2011 | Min | AL | 26 | 24 | 1 | 0 | 134.1 | 591 | 125 | 81 | 76 | 14 | 0 | 6 | 7 | 75 | 1 | 112 | 9 | 0 | 9 | 10 | .474 | 1 | 0-0 | 0 | 4.58 | 5.09 |
| 2012 | 2 Tms | AL | 34 | 28 | 0 | 2 | 156.2 | 693 | 143 | 97 | 93 | 19 | 4 | 8 | 7 | 87 | 5 | 167 | 11 | 1 | 6 | 12 | .333 | 0 | 0-0 | 1 | 4.47 | 5.34 |
| 2013 | Pit | NL | 26 | 26 | 2 | 0 | 161.0 | 666 | 134 | 54 | 54 | 9 | 3 | 1 | 0 | 63 | 0 | 163 | 7 | 2 | 16 | 8 | .667 | 0 | 0-0 | 0 | 2.86 | 3.02 |

| Year Team | Lg | G | GS | CG | GF | IP | BFP | H | R | ER | HR | SH | SF | HB | TBB | IBB | SO | WP | Bk | W | L | Pct | Sh | Sv-Op | Hld | ERC | ERA |
|---|---|---|---|---|---|---|---|---|---|---|---|---|---|---|---|---|---|---|---|---|---|---|---|---|---|---|---|
| | | HOW MUCH HE PITCHED | | | | | | WHAT HE GAVE UP | | | | | | | | | | | | THE RESULTS | | | | | | | |
| 12 Min | AL | 22 | 17 | 0 | 2 | 100.0 | 440 | 89 | 63 | 59 | 12 | 2 | 7 | 4 | 55 | 4 | 109 | 6 | 1 | 3 | 10 | .231 | 0 | 0-0 | 1 | 4.27 | 5.31 |
| 12 CWS | AL | 12 | 11 | 0 | 0 | 56.2 | 253 | 54 | 34 | 34 | 7 | 2 | 1 | 3 | 32 | 1 | 58 | 5 | 0 | 3 | 2 | .600 | 0 | 0-0 | 0 | 4.83 | 5.40 |
| Postseason | | 2 | 1 | 0 | 0 | 7.2 | 34 | 7 | 6 | 5 | 1 | 0 | 0 | 0 | 4 | 0 | 8 | 1 | 0 | 0 | 0 | - | 0 | 0-0 | 0 | 4.19 | 5.87 |
| 8 ML YEARS | | 194 | 167 | 3 | 8 | 1001.0 | 4260 | 915 | 488 | 465 | 92 | 24 | 28 | 32 | 419 | 7 | 1009 | 54 | 6 | 69 | 62 | .527 | 1 | 1-1 | 2 | 3.75 | 4.18 |

## Chia-Jen Lo

**Pitches:** R **Bats:** R **Pos:** RP-19 CHI JENN LOW **Ht:** 5'11" **Wt:** 190 **Born:** 4/7/1986 **Age:** 28

| | | HOW MUCH HE PITCHED | | | | | | WHAT HE GAVE UP | | | | | | | | | | | | THE RESULTS | | | | | | | |
|---|---|---|---|---|---|---|---|---|---|---|---|---|---|---|---|---|---|---|---|---|---|---|---|---|---|---|---|
| Year Team | Lg | G | GS | CG | GF | IP | BFP | H | R | ER | HR | SH | SF | HB | TBB | IBB | SO | WP | Bk | W | L | Pct | Sh | Sv-Op | Hld | ERC | ERA |
| 2009 Lancst | A+ | 12 | 0 | 0 | 1 | 25.1 | 96 | 10 | 6 | 5 | 1 | 0 | 0 | 0 | 13 | 2 | 36 | 2 | 0 | 1 | 0 | 1.000 | 0 | 1-- | - | 1.26 | 1.78 |
| 2009 CpChr | AA | 30 | 0 | 0 | 9 | 39.0 | 170 | 30 | 12 | 10 | 1 | 4 | 1 | 4 | 20 | 1 | 39 | 3 | 0 | 0 | 2 | .000 | 0 | 2-- | - | 3.02 | 2.31 |
| 2010 CpChr | AA | 7 | 0 | 0 | 0 | 15.0 | 65 | 9 | 3 | 3 | 0 | 1 | 2 | 1 | 10 | 0 | 13 | 4 | 0 | 0 | 1 | .000 | 0 | 0-- | - | 2.43 | 1.80 |
| 2011 Lxngtn | A | 2 | 0 | 0 | 0 | 2.0 | 10 | 2 | 3 | 3 | 1 | 0 | 0 | 0 | 2 | 0 | 3 | 0 | 0 | 0 | 0 | - | 0 | 0-- | - | 9.87 | 13.50 |
| 2012 Astros | R | 8 | 5 | 0 | 0 | 11.0 | 42 | 5 | 2 | 0 | 0 | 0 | 0 | 1 | 2 | 0 | 11 | 0 | 0 | 0 | 1 | .000 | 0 | 0-- | - | 0.85 | 0.00 |
| 2012 Lancst | A+ | 11 | 0 | 0 | 2 | 19.0 | 68 | 14 | 3 | 3 | 1 | 0 | 0 | 1 | 4 | 0 | 20 | 3 | 0 | 0 | 0 | - | 0 | 0-- | - | 2.20 | 1.42 |
| 2013 TriCity | A- | 6 | 0 | 0 | 6 | 6.0 | 24 | 5 | 3 | 3 | 1 | 0 | 0 | 0 | 1 | 0 | 12 | 0 | 0 | 0 | 0 | - | 0 | 4-- | - | 2.66 | 4.50 |
| 2013 QuadC | A | 3 | 0 | 0 | 3 | 3.0 | 11 | 1 | 0 | 0 | 0 | 0 | 0 | 0 | 1 | 0 | 2 | 0 | 0 | 0 | 0 | - | 0 | 1-- | - | 0.69 | 0.00 |
| 2013 CpChr | AA | 8 | 0 | 0 | 2 | 7.2 | 31 | 9 | 3 | 3 | 1 | 0 | 0 | 0 | 0 | 0 | 6 | 2 | 0 | 0 | 0 | - | 0 | 1-- | - | 3.70 | 3.52 |
| 2013 Hou | AL | 19 | 0 | 0 | 11 | 19.1 | 84 | 14 | 9 | 9 | 2 | 1 | 1 | 0 | 13 | 0 | 16 | 1 | 0 | 0 | 3 | .000 | 0 | 2-5 | 1 | 3.60 | 4.19 |

## Jose Lobaton

**Bats:** B **Throws:** R **Pos:** C-96;PH-9;PR-2 LOE-bah-tone **Ht:** 6'0" **Wt:** 210 **Born:** 10/21/1984 **Age:** 29

| | | BATTING | | | | | | | | | | | | | | | | | | | BASERUNNING | | | | AVERAGES | | |
|---|---|---|---|---|---|---|---|---|---|---|---|---|---|---|---|---|---|---|---|---|---|---|---|---|---|---|---|
| Year Team | Lg | G | AB | H | 2B | 3B | HR | (Hm | Rd) | TB | R | RBI | RC | TBB | IBB | SO | HBP | SH | SF | SB | CS | SB% | GDP | Avg | OBP | Slg |
| 2009 SD | NL | 7 | 17 | 3 | 0 | 0 | 0 | (0 | 0) | 3 | 0 | 0 | 0 | 0 | 0 | 5 | 0 | 0 | 0 | 0 | 0 | - | 1 | .176 | .176 | .176 |
| 2011 TB | AL | 15 | 34 | 4 | 1 | 0 | 0 | (0 | 0) | 5 | 2 | 0 | 0 | 4 | 0 | 8 | 1 | 0 | 0 | 0 | 0 | - | 2 | .118 | .231 | .147 |
| 2012 TB | AL | 69 | 167 | 37 | 10 | 0 | 2 | (1 | 1) | 53 | 16 | 20 | 19 | 24 | 1 | 46 | 2 | 2 | 2 | 0 | 1 | .00 | 6 | .222 | .323 | .317 |
| 2013 TB | AL | 100 | 277 | 69 | 15 | 2 | 7 | (5 | 2) | 109 | 38 | 32 | 32 | 30 | 0 | 65 | 0 | 2 | 2 | 0 | 1 | .00 | 5 | .249 | .320 | .394 |
| 4 ML YEARS | | 191 | 495 | 113 | 26 | 2 | 9 | (6 | 3) | 170 | 56 | 52 | 51 | 58 | 1 | 124 | 3 | 4 | 4 | 0 | 2 | .00 | 14 | .228 | .311 | .343 |

## Jeff Locke

**Pitches:** L **Bats:** L **Pos:** SP-30 LOCK **Ht:** 6'0" **Wt:** 190 **Born:** 11/20/1987 **Age:** 26

| | | HOW MUCH HE PITCHED | | | | | | WHAT HE GAVE UP | | | | | | | | | | | | THE RESULTS | | | | | | | |
|---|---|---|---|---|---|---|---|---|---|---|---|---|---|---|---|---|---|---|---|---|---|---|---|---|---|---|---|
| Year Team | Lg | G | GS | CG | GF | IP | BFP | H | R | ER | HR | SH | SF | HB | TBB | IBB | SO | WP | Bk | W | L | Pct | Sh | Sv-Op | Hld | ERC | ERA |
| 2011 Pit | NL | 4 | 4 | 0 | 0 | 16.2 | 78 | 21 | 12 | 12 | 3 | 1 | 1 | 1 | 10 | 0 | 5 | 0 | 0 | 0 | 3 | .000 | 0 | 0-0 | 0 | 7.62 | 6.48 |
| 2012 Pit | NL | 8 | 6 | 0 | 1 | 34.1 | 148 | 36 | 21 | 21 | 6 | 1 | 0 | 1 | 11 | 0 | 34 | 0 | 0 | 1 | 3 | .250 | 0 | 0-0 | 0 | 4.68 | 5.50 |
| 2013 Pit | NL | 30 | 30 | 0 | 0 | 166.1 | 711 | 146 | 69 | 65 | 11 | 8 | **10** | 6 | **84** | 4 | 125 | 8 | 2 | 10 | 7 | .588 | 0 | 0-0 | 0 | 3.72 | 3.52 |
| 3 ML YEARS | | 42 | 40 | 0 | 1 | 217.1 | 937 | 203 | 102 | 98 | 20 | 10 | 11 | 8 | 105 | 4 | 164 | 8 | 2 | 11 | 13 | .458 | 0 | 0-0 | 0 | 4.14 | 4.06 |

## Kameron Loe

**Pitches:** R **Bats:** R **Pos:** RP-19; SP-1 LOW **Ht:** 6'8" **Wt:** 245 **Born:** 9/10/1981 **Age:** 32

| | | HOW MUCH HE PITCHED | | | | | | WHAT HE GAVE UP | | | | | | | | | | | | THE RESULTS | | | | | | | |
|---|---|---|---|---|---|---|---|---|---|---|---|---|---|---|---|---|---|---|---|---|---|---|---|---|---|---|---|
| Year Team | Lg | G | GS | CG | GF | IP | BFP | H | R | ER | HR | SH | SF | HB | TBB | IBB | SO | WP | Bk | W | L | Pct | Sh | Sv-Op | Hld | ERC | ERA |
| 2013 Gwnntt* | AAA | 27 | 10 | 0 | 4 | 76.1 | 319 | 76 | 32 | 26 | 3 | 3 | 0 | 2 | 17 | 0 | 37 | 3 | 0 | 4 | 4 | .500 | 0 | 2-- | - | 3.05 | 3.07 |
| 2004 Tex | AL | 2 | 1 | 0 | 0 | 6.2 | 29 | 6 | 5 | 4 | 0 | 0 | 0 | 1 | 6 | 0 | 3 | 0 | 0 | 0 | 0 | - | 0 | 0-0 | 0 | 5.87 | 5.40 |
| 2005 Tex | AL | 48 | 8 | 0 | 13 | 92.0 | 392 | 89 | 43 | 35 | 7 | 5 | 1 | 2 | 31 | 6 | 45 | 2 | 0 | 9 | 6 | .600 | 0 | 1-4 | 4 | 3.45 | 3.42 |
| 2006 Tex | AL | 15 | 15 | 1 | 0 | 78.1 | 358 | 105 | 54 | 51 | 10 | 1 | 3 | 1 | 22 | 0 | 34 | 3 | 0 | 3 | 6 | .333 | 1 | 0-0 | 0 | 5.79 | 5.86 |
| 2007 Tex | AL | 28 | 23 | 0 | 0 | 136.0 | 615 | 162 | 96 | 81 | 13 | 1 | 5 | 4 | 56 | 6 | 78 | 6 | 0 | 6 | 11 | .353 | 0 | 0-0 | 0 | 5.24 | 5.36 |
| 2008 Tex | AL | 14 | 0 | 0 | 4 | 30.2 | 134 | 36 | 18 | 11 | 3 | 0 | 1 | 0 | 8 | 1 | 20 | 0 | 0 | 1 | 0 | 1.000 | 0 | 0-1 | 2 | 4.40 | 3.23 |
| 2010 Mil | NL | 53 | 0 | 0 | 9 | 58.1 | 240 | 54 | 23 | 18 | 6 | 1 | 2 | 2 | 15 | 1 | 46 | 4 | 0 | 3 | 5 | .375 | 0 | 0-2 | 22 | 3.27 | 2.78 |
| 2011 Mil | NL | 72 | 0 | 0 | 19 | 72.0 | 291 | 65 | 30 | 28 | 4 | 2 | 0 | 2 | 16 | 2 | 61 | 5 | 0 | 4 | 7 | .364 | 0 | 1-8 | 16 | 2.70 | 3.50 |
| 2012 Mil | NL | 70 | 0 | 0 | 20 | 68.1 | 303 | 78 | 41 | 35 | 9 | 5 | 0 | 3 | 20 | 3 | 55 | 4 | 0 | 6 | 5 | .545 | 0 | 2-7 | 7 | 4.72 | 4.61 |
| 2013 3 Tms | | 20 | 1 | 0 | 9 | 26.2 | 127 | 40 | 21 | 21 | 11 | 1 | 0 | 0 | 10 | 2 | 15 | 1 | 0 | 2 | 3 | .400 | 0 | 0-0 | 1 | 9.54 | 7.09 |
| 13 Sea | AL | 4 | 0 | 0 | 1 | 6.2 | 31 | 11 | 8 | 8 | 6 | 0 | 0 | 0 | 1 | 0 | 3 | 0 | 0 | 1 | 1 | .500 | 0 | 0-0 | 0 | 13.81 | 10.80 |
| 13 ChC | NL | 7 | 0 | 0 | 3 | 8.1 | 39 | 12 | 5 | 5 | 3 | 0 | 0 | 0 | 4 | 0 | 4 | 0 | 0 | 0 | 0 | - | 0 | 0-0 | 1 | 9.62 | 5.40 |
| 13 Atl | NL | 9 | 1 | 0 | 5 | 11.2 | 57 | 17 | 8 | 8 | 2 | 1 | 0 | 0 | 5 | 2 | 8 | 1 | 0 | 1 | 2 | .333 | 0 | 0-0 | 0 | 7.05 | 6.17 |
| Postseason | | 5 | 0 | 0 | 0 | 4.1 | 26 | 13 | 7 | 4 | 0 | 0 | 1 | 0 | 1 | 0 | 3 | 0 | 0 | 0 | 0 | - | 0 | 0-0 | 0 | 16.31 | 8.31 |
| 9 ML YEARS | | 322 | 48 | 1 | 74 | 569.0 | 2489 | 635 | 331 | 284 | 63 | 16 | 12 | 15 | 184 | 21 | 357 | 25 | 0 | 34 | 43 | .442 | 1 | 4-22 | 52 | 4.54 | 4.49 |

## Boone Logan

**Pitches:** L **Bats:** R **Pos:** RP-61 **Ht:** 6'5" **Wt:** 215 **Born:** 8/13/1984 **Age:** 29

| | | HOW MUCH HE PITCHED | | | | | | WHAT HE GAVE UP | | | | | | | | | | | | THE RESULTS | | | | | | | |
|---|---|---|---|---|---|---|---|---|---|---|---|---|---|---|---|---|---|---|---|---|---|---|---|---|---|---|---|
| Year Team | Lg | G | GS | CG | GF | IP | BFP | H | R | ER | HR | SH | SF | HB | TBB | IBB | SO | WP | Bk | W | L | Pct | Sh | Sv-Op | Hld | ERC | ERA |
| 2006 CWS | AL | 21 | 0 | 0 | 4 | 17.1 | 93 | 21 | 18 | 16 | 2 | 1 | 1 | 3 | 15 | 2 | 15 | 1 | 0 | 0 | 0 | - | 0 | 1-2 | 2 | 7.56 | 8.31 |
| 2007 CWS | AL | 68 | 0 | 0 | 13 | 50.2 | 226 | 59 | 30 | 28 | 7 | 2 | 6 | 0 | 20 | 3 | 35 | 2 | 0 | 2 | 1 | .667 | 0 | 0-2 | 11 | 5.18 | 4.97 |
| 2008 CWS | AL | 55 | 0 | 0 | 12 | 42.1 | 197 | 57 | 31 | 28 | 7 | 2 | 0 | 1 | 14 | 3 | 42 | 1 | 0 | 2 | 3 | .400 | 0 | 0-1 | 3 | 6.24 | 5.95 |
| 2009 Atl | NL | 20 | 0 | 0 | 7 | 17.1 | 82 | 21 | 12 | 10 | 1 | 0 | 0 | 1 | 9 | 3 | 10 | 0 | 0 | 1 | 1 | .500 | 0 | 0-0 | 1 | 5.29 | 5.19 |
| 2010 NYY | AL | 51 | 0 | 0 | 8 | 40.0 | 169 | 34 | 13 | 13 | 3 | 0 | 1 | 1 | 20 | 3 | 38 | 1 | 0 | 2 | 0 | 1.000 | 0 | 0-0 | 13 | 3.50 | 2.93 |
| 2011 NYY | AL | 64 | 0 | 0 | 6 | 41.2 | 185 | 43 | 20 | 16 | 4 | 2 | 1 | 4 | 13 | 3 | 46 | 1 | 0 | 5 | 3 | .625 | 0 | 0-2 | 10 | 4.04 | 3.46 |
| 2012 NYY | AL | **80** | 0 | 0 | 8 | 55.1 | 239 | 48 | 23 | 23 | 6 | 1 | 3 | 2 | 28 | 6 | 68 | 3 | 0 | 7 | 2 | .778 | 0 | 1-4 | 23 | 3.78 | 3.74 |
| 2013 NYY | AL | 61 | 0 | 0 | 9 | 39.0 | 159 | 33 | 15 | 14 | 7 | 3 | 3 | 0 | 13 | 4 | 50 | 3 | 0 | 5 | 2 | .714 | 0 | 0-2 | 11 | 3.38 | 3.23 |
| Postseason | | 13 | 0 | 0 | 1 | 7.2 | 30 | 7 | 2 | 2 | 1 | 0 | 0 | 0 | 1 | 0 | 9 | 0 | 1 | 0 | 0 | - | 0 | 0-0 | 2 | 2.83 | 2.35 |
| 8 ML YEARS | | 420 | 0 | 0 | 67 | 303.2 | 1350 | 316 | 162 | 148 | 37 | 11 | 15 | 12 | 132 | 27 | 304 | 12 | 0 | 24 | 12 | .667 | 0 | 2-13 | 74 | 4.58 | 4.39 |

# Kyle Lohse

**Pitches:** R **Bats:** R **Pos:** SP-32 LOESH **Ht:** 6'2" **Wt:** 210 **Born:** 10/4/1978 **Age:** 35

| HOW MUCH HE PITCHED | | | | | | | | | WHAT HE GAVE UP | | | | | | | | | | | | THE RESULTS | | | | | | | |
|---|---|---|---|---|---|---|---|---|---|---|---|---|---|---|---|---|---|---|---|---|---|---|---|---|---|---|---|---|
| Year | Team | Lg | G | GS | CG | GF | IP | BFP | H | R | ER | HR | SH | SF | HB | TBB | IBB | SO | WP | Bk | W | L | Pct | Sh | Sv-Op | Hld | ERC | ERA |
| 2001 | Min | AL | 19 | 16 | 0 | 2 | 90.1 | 402 | 102 | 60 | 57 | 16 | 1 | 5 | 8 | 29 | 0 | 64 | 5 | 0 | 4 | 7 | .364 | 0 | 0-0 | 0 | 5.43 | 5.68 |
| 2002 | Min | AL | 32 | 31 | 1 | 0 | 180.2 | 783 | 181 | 92 | 85 | 26 | 3 | 3 | 9 | 70 | 2 | 124 | 8 | 0 | 13 | 8 | .619 | 1 | 0-1 | 0 | 4.55 | 4.23 |
| 2003 | Min | AL | 33 | 33 | 2 | 0 | 201.0 | 850 | 211 | 107 | 103 | 28 | 8 | 5 | 5 | 45 | 1 | 130 | 10 | 1 | 14 | 11 | .560 | 1 | 0-0 | 0 | 4.00 | 4.61 |
| 2004 | Min | AL | 35 | 34 | 1 | 1 | 194.0 | 883 | 240 | 128 | 115 | 28 | 5 | 7 | 7 | 76 | 5 | 111 | 6 | 0 | 9 | 13 | .409 | 1 | 0-0 | 0 | 5.89 | 5.34 |
| 2005 | Min | AL | 31 | 30 | 0 | 1 | 178.2 | 769 | 211 | 85 | 83 | 22 | 3 | 7 | 9 | 44 | 5 | 86 | 4 | 1 | 9 | 13 | .409 | 0 | 0-0 | 0 | 4.91 | 4.18 |
| 2006 | 2 Tms | | 34 | 19 | 0 | 6 | 126.2 | 566 | 150 | 83 | 82 | 15 | 8 | 5 | 6 | 44 | 4 | 97 | 3 | 1 | 5 | 10 | .333 | 0 | 0-0 | 0 | 5.21 | 5.83 |
| 2007 | 2 Tms | NL | 34 | 32 | 2 | 0 | 192.2 | 829 | 207 | 109 | 99 | 22 | 14 | 4 | 12 | 57 | 3 | 122 | 3 | 0 | 9 | 12 | .429 | 1 | 0-0 | 0 | 4.45 | 4.62 |
| 2008 | StL | NL | 33 | 33 | 0 | 0 | 200.0 | 839 | 211 | 88 | 84 | 18 | 6 | 4 | 3 | 49 | 3 | 119 | 5 | 0 | 15 | 6 | .714 | 0 | 0-0 | 0 | 3.77 | 3.78 |
| 2009 | StL | NL | 23 | 22 | 1 | 0 | 117.2 | 512 | 125 | 69 | 62 | 16 | 3 | 5 | 3 | 36 | 2 | 77 | 3 | 1 | 6 | 10 | .375 | 1 | 0-0 | 0 | 4.33 | 4.74 |
| 2010 | StL | NL | 18 | 18 | 0 | 0 | 92.0 | 431 | 129 | 75 | 67 | 9 | 5 | 4 | 3 | 35 | 2 | 54 | 1 | 0 | 4 | 8 | .333 | 0 | 0-0 | 0 | 6.50 | 6.55 |
| 2011 | StL | NL | 30 | 30 | 1 | 0 | 188.1 | 775 | 178 | 80 | 71 | 16 | 8 | 6 | 3 | 42 | 1 | 111 | 1 | 0 | 14 | 8 | .636 | 1 | 0-0 | 0 | 3.05 | 3.39 |
| 2012 | StL | NL | 33 | **33** | 0 | 0 | 211.0 | 864 | 192 | 74 | 67 | 19 | 11 | 7 | 4 | 38 | 1 | 143 | 1 | 0 | 16 | 3 | **.842** | 0 | 0-0 | 0 | 2.72 | 2.86 |
| 2013 | Mil | NL | 32 | 32 | 2 | 0 | 198.2 | 806 | 196 | 78 | 74 | 26 | 8 | 2 | 3 | 36 | 1 | 125 | 1 | 0 | 11 | 10 | .524 | 1 | 0-0 | 0 | 3.45 | 3.35 |
| 06 | Min | AL | 22 | 8 | 0 | 5 | 63.2 | 295 | 80 | 50 | 50 | 8 | 1 | 3 | 6 | 25 | 2 | 46 | 1 | 1 | 2 | 5 | .286 | 0 | 0-0 | 0 | 6.10 | 7.07 |
| 06 | Cin | NL | 12 | 11 | 0 | 1 | 63.0 | 271 | 70 | 33 | 32 | 7 | 7 | 2 | 0 | 19 | 2 | 51 | 2 | 0 | 3 | 5 | .375 | 0 | 0-0 | 0 | 4.36 | 4.57 |
| 07 | Cin | NL | 21 | 21 | 2 | 0 | 131.2 | 561 | 143 | 76 | 67 | 16 | 8 | 4 | 6 | 33 | 1 | 80 | 3 | 0 | 6 | 12 | .333 | 1 | 0-0 | 0 | 4.32 | 4.58 |
| 07 | Phi | NL | 13 | 11 | 0 | 0 | 61.0 | 268 | 64 | 33 | 32 | 6 | 6 | 0 | 6 | 24 | 2 | 42 | 0 | 0 | 3 | 0 | 1.000 | 0 | 0-0 | 0 | 4.71 | 4.72 |
| Postseason | | | 13 | 8 | 0 | 3 | 46.1 | 199 | 49 | 26 | 25 | 8 | 1 | 0 | 1 | 13 | 1 | 39 | 1 | 0 | 2 | 5 | .286 | 0 | 0-0 | 0 | 4.46 | 4.86 |
| 13 ML YEARS | | | 387 | 363 | 10 | 10 | 2171.2 | 9309 | 2333 | 1128 | 1049 | 261 | 83 | 64 | 75 | 601 | 30 | 1363 | 51 | 4 | 129 | 119 | .520 | 7 | 0-1 | 0 | 4.27 | 4.35 |

# Steve Lombardozzi

**Bats:** B **Throws:** R **Pos:** PH-50;2B-48;LF-23;3B-4 lahm-bar-DOZE-ee **Ht:** 6'0" **Wt:** 200 **Born:** 9/20/1988 **Age:** 25

| BATTING | | | | | | | | | | | | | | | | | | | | | BASERUNNING | | | | AVERAGES | | |
|---|---|---|---|---|---|---|---|---|---|---|---|---|---|---|---|---|---|---|---|---|---|---|---|---|---|---|---|
| Year | Team | Lg | G | AB | H | 2B | 3B | HR | (Hm | Rd) | TB | R | RBI | RC | TBB | IBB | SO | HBP | SH | SF | SB | CS | SB% | GDP | Avg | OBP | Slg |
| 2011 | Was | NL | 13 | 31 | 6 | 1 | 0 | 0 | (0 | 0) | 7 | 3 | 1 | 2 | 1 | 0 | 4 | 0 | 0 | 0 | 0 | 0 | - | 0 | .194 | .219 | .226 |
| 2012 | Was | NL | 126 | 384 | 105 | 16 | 3 | 3 | (2 | 1) | 136 | 40 | 27 | 46 | 19 | 1 | 46 | 6 | 6 | 1 | 5 | 3 | .63 | 1 | .273 | .317 | .354 |
| 2013 | Was | NL | 118 | 290 | 75 | 15 | 1 | 2 | (1 | 1) | 98 | 25 | 22 | 24 | 8 | 1 | 34 | 1 | 5 | 3 | 4 | 3 | .57 | 6 | .259 | .278 | .338 |
| Postseason | | | 3 | 3 | 1 | 0 | 0 | 0 | (0 | 0) | 1 | 0 | 0 | 0 | 0 | 0 | 0 | 0 | 0 | 0 | 0 | 0 | - | 0 | .333 | .333 | .333 |
| 3 ML YEARS | | | 257 | 705 | 186 | 32 | 4 | 5 | (3 | 2) | 241 | 68 | 50 | 72 | 28 | 2 | 84 | 7 | 11 | 4 | 9 | 6 | .60 | 7 | .264 | .297 | .342 |

# James Loney

**Bats:** L **Throws:** L **Pos:** 1B-154;PH-9;DH-1 **Ht:** 6'3" **Wt:** 220 **Born:** 5/7/1984 **Age:** 30

| BATTING | | | | | | | | | | | | | | | | | | | | | BASERUNNING | | | | AVERAGES | | |
|---|---|---|---|---|---|---|---|---|---|---|---|---|---|---|---|---|---|---|---|---|---|---|---|---|---|---|---|
| Year | Team | Lg | G | AB | H | 2B | 3B | HR | (Hm | Rd) | TB | R | RBI | RC | TBB | IBB | SO | HBP | SH | SF | SB | CS | SB% | GDP | Avg | OBP | Slg |
| 2006 | LAD | NL | 48 | 102 | 29 | 6 | 5 | 4 | (1 | 3) | 57 | 20 | 18 | 17 | 8 | 1 | 10 | 1 | 0 | 0 | 1 | 0 | 1.00 | 8 | .284 | .342 | .559 |
| 2007 | LAD | NL | 96 | 344 | 114 | 18 | 4 | 15 | (5 | 10) | 185 | 41 | 67 | 71 | 28 | 5 | 48 | 1 | 0 | 2 | 0 | 1 | .00 | 6 | .331 | .381 | .538 |
| 2008 | LAD | NL | 161 | 595 | 172 | 35 | 6 | 13 | (5 | 8) | 258 | 66 | 90 | 79 | 45 | 6 | 85 | 3 | 1 | 7 | 7 | 4 | .64 | 25 | .289 | .338 | .434 |
| 2009 | LAD | NL | 158 | 576 | 162 | 25 | 2 | 13 | (1 | 12) | 230 | 73 | 90 | 84 | 70 | 10 | 68 | 0 | 1 | 4 | 7 | 3 | .70 | 16 | .281 | .357 | .399 |
| 2010 | LAD | NL | 161 | 588 | 157 | 41 | 2 | 10 | (6 | 4) | 232 | 67 | 88 | 81 | 52 | 9 | 95 | 4 | 0 | 4 | 10 | 5 | .67 | 14 | .267 | .329 | .395 |
| 2011 | LAD | NL | 158 | 531 | 153 | 30 | 1 | 12 | (7 | 5) | 221 | 56 | 65 | 71 | 42 | 7 | 67 | 1 | 3 | 5 | 4 | 0 | 1.00 | 8 | .288 | .339 | .416 |
| 2012 | 2 Tms | | 144 | 434 | 108 | 20 | 0 | 6 | (0 | 6) | 146 | 37 | 41 | 34 | 28 | 7 | 51 | 0 | 1 | 2 | 0 | 3 | .00 | 21 | .249 | .293 | .336 |
| 2013 | TB | AL | 158 | 549 | 164 | 33 | 0 | 13 | (7 | 6) | 236 | 54 | 75 | 75 | 44 | 6 | 77 | 0 | 1 | 4 | 3 | 1 | .75 | 16 | .299 | .348 | .430 |
| 12 | LAD | NL | 114 | 334 | 85 | 18 | 0 | 4 | (0 | 4) | 115 | 32 | 33 | 28 | 23 | 7 | 39 | 0 | 1 | 1 | 0 | 3 | .00 | 16 | .254 | .302 | .344 |
| 12 | Bos | AL | 30 | 100 | 23 | 2 | 0 | 2 | (0 | 2) | 31 | 5 | 8 | 6 | 5 | 0 | 12 | 0 | 0 | 1 | 0 | 0 | - | 5 | .230 | .264 | .310 |
| Postseason | | | 17 | 63 | 22 | 3 | 0 | 3 | (1 | 2) | 34 | 5 | 14 | 13 | 7 | 1 | 10 | 0 | 0 | 0 | 0 | 0 | - | 2 | .349 | .414 | .540 |
| 8 ML YEARS | | | 1084 | 3719 | 1059 | 208 | 20 | 86 | (32 | 54) | 1565 | 414 | 534 | 512 | 317 | 51 | 501 | 10 | 7 | 28 | 32 | 17 | .65 | 114 | .285 | .340 | .421 |

# Evan Longoria

**Bats:** R **Throws:** R **Pos:** 3B-147;DH-14 **Ht:** 6'2" **Wt:** 210 **Born:** 10/7/1985 **Age:** 28

| BATTING | | | | | | | | | | | | | | | | | | | | | BASERUNNING | | | | AVERAGES | | |
|---|---|---|---|---|---|---|---|---|---|---|---|---|---|---|---|---|---|---|---|---|---|---|---|---|---|---|---|
| Year | Team | Lg | G | AB | H | 2B | 3B | HR | (Hm | Rd) | TB | R | RBI | RC | TBB | IBB | SO | HBP | SH | SF | SB | CS | SB% | GDP | Avg | OBP | Slg |
| 2008 | TB | AL | 122 | 448 | 122 | 31 | 2 | 27 | (18 | 9) | 238 | 67 | 85 | 72 | 46 | 4 | 122 | 6 | 0 | 8 | 7 | 0 | 1.00 | 8 | .272 | .343 | .531 |
| 2009 | TB | AL | 157 | 584 | 164 | 44 | 0 | 33 | (16 | 17) | 307 | 100 | 113 | 102 | 72 | 11 | 140 | 8 | 0 | 7 | 9 | 0 | 1.00 | **27** | .281 | .364 | .526 |
| 2010 | TB | AL | 151 | 574 | 169 | 46 | 5 | 22 | (10 | 12) | 291 | 96 | 104 | 99 | 72 | 12 | 124 | 5 | 0 | 10 | 15 | 5 | .75 | 15 | .294 | .372 | .507 |
| 2011 | TB | AL | 133 | 483 | 118 | 26 | 1 | 31 | (14 | 17) | 239 | 78 | 99 | 91 | 80 | 6 | 93 | 6 | 0 | 5 | 3 | 2 | .60 | 11 | .244 | .355 | .495 |
| 2012 | TB | AL | 74 | 273 | 79 | 14 | 0 | 17 | (8 | 9) | 144 | 39 | 55 | 55 | 33 | 6 | 61 | 3 | 0 | 3 | 2 | 3 | .40 | 14 | .289 | .369 | .527 |
| 2013 | TB | AL | 160 | 614 | 165 | 39 | 3 | 32 | (15 | 17) | 306 | 91 | 88 | 90 | 70 | 10 | 162 | 3 | 0 | 6 | 1 | 0 | 1.00 | 16 | .269 | .343 | .498 |
| Postseason | | | 25 | 98 | 19 | 5 | 0 | 8 | (3 | 5) | 48 | 14 | 18 | 11 | 8 | 0 | 32 | 0 | 0 | 0 | 1 | 0 | 1.00 | 3 | .194 | .255 | .490 |
| 6 ML YEARS | | | 797 | 2976 | 817 | 200 | 11 | 162 | (81 | 81) | 1525 | 471 | 544 | 509 | 373 | 49 | 702 | 31 | 0 | 39 | 37 | 10 | .79 | 91 | .275 | .357 | .512 |

# Javier Lopez

**Pitches:** L **Bats:** L **Pos:** RP-69 **Ht:** 6'5" **Wt:** 220 **Born:** 7/11/1977 **Age:** 36

| HOW MUCH HE PITCHED | | | | | | | | | WHAT HE GAVE UP | | | | | | | | | | | | THE RESULTS | | | | | | | |
|---|---|---|---|---|---|---|---|---|---|---|---|---|---|---|---|---|---|---|---|---|---|---|---|---|---|---|---|---|
| Year | Team | Lg | G | GS | CG | GF | IP | BFP | H | R | ER | HR | SH | SF | HB | TBB | IBB | SO | WP | Bk | W | L | Pct | Sh | Sv-Op | Hld | ERC | ERA |
| 2003 | Col | NL | 75 | 0 | 0 | 11 | 58.1 | 242 | 58 | 25 | 24 | 5 | 1 | 0 | 4 | 12 | 2 | 40 | 1 | 3 | 4 | 1 | .800 | 0 | 1-2 | 15 | 3.44 | 3.70 |
| 2004 | Col | NL | 64 | 0 | 0 | 10 | 40.2 | 187 | 45 | 34 | 34 | 1 | 1 | 0 | 3 | 26 | 4 | 20 | 3 | 0 | 1 | 2 | .333 | 0 | 0-1 | 12 | 5.28 | 7.52 |
| 2005 | 2 Tms | NL | 32 | 0 | 0 | 6 | 16.1 | 87 | 26 | 20 | 20 | 2 | 1 | 0 | 1 | 11 | 3 | 12 | 0 | 0 | 1 | 1 | .500 | 0 | 2-4 | 6 | 8.82 | 11.02 |
| 2006 | Bos | AL | 27 | 0 | 0 | 8 | 16.2 | 69 | 13 | 10 | 5 | 1 | 0 | 1 | 2 | 10 | 1 | 11 | 0 | 0 | 1 | 0 | 1.000 | 0 | 1-1 | 6 | 3.96 | 2.70 |
| 2007 | Bos | AL | 61 | 0 | 0 | 11 | 40.2 | 174 | 36 | 16 | 14 | 2 | 1 | 1 | 4 | 18 | 2 | 26 | 1 | 0 | 2 | 1 | .667 | 0 | 0-2 | 13 | 3.59 | 3.10 |
| 2008 | Bos | AL | 70 | 0 | 0 | 10 | 59.1 | 247 | 53 | 18 | 16 | 4 | 1 | 1 | 2 | 27 | 0 | 38 | 1 | 0 | 2 | 0 | 1.000 | 0 | 0-1 | 10 | 3.73 | 2.43 |
| 2009 | Bos | AL | 14 | 0 | 0 | 5 | 11.2 | 64 | 20 | 13 | 12 | 1 | 1 | 1 | 2 | 9 | 0 | 5 | 1 | 0 | 0 | 2 | .000 | 0 | 0-0 | 0 | 11.00 | 9.26 |
| 2010 | 2 Tms | NL | 77 | 0 | 0 | 18 | 57.2 | 235 | 50 | 17 | 15 | 2 | 1 | 2 | 2 | 20 | 3 | 38 | 3 | 0 | 4 | 2 | .667 | 0 | 0-0 | 11 | 2.85 | 2.34 |
| 2011 | SF | NL | 70 | 0 | 0 | 17 | 53.0 | 222 | 42 | 16 | 16 | 0 | 3 | 0 | 3 | 26 | 6 | 40 | 1 | 0 | 5 | 2 | .714 | 0 | 1-3 | 20 | 2.69 | 2.72 |
| 2012 | SF | NL | 70 | 0 | 0 | 19 | 36.0 | 153 | 37 | 13 | 10 | 1 | 1 | 1 | 0 | 14 | 3 | 28 | 2 | 0 | 3 | 0 | 1.000 | 0 | 7-9 | 18 | 3.60 | 2.50 |

| Year Team | Lg | G | GS | CG | GF | IP | BFP | H | R | ER | HR | SH | SF | HB | TBB | IBB | SO | WP | Bk | W | L | Pct | Sh | Sv-Op | Hld | ERC | ERA |
|---|---|---|---|---|---|---|---|---|---|---|---|---|---|---|---|---|---|---|---|---|---|---|---|---|---|---|---|
| | | HOW MUCH HE PITCHED | | | | | | WHAT HE GAVE UP | | | | | | | | | | | | THE RESULTS | | | | | | | |
| 2013 SF | NL | 69 | 0 | 0 | 14 | 39.1 | 161 | 30 | 10 | 8 | 1 | 4 | 1 | 0 | 12 | 5 | 37 | 1 | 0 | 4 | 2 | .667 | 0 | 1-1 | 15 | 1.82 | 1.83 |
| 05 Col | NL | 3 | 0 | 0 | 1 | 2.0 | 13 | 7 | 5 | 5 | 0 | 0 | 0 | 0 | 0 | 0 | 1 | 0 | 0 | 0 | 0 | - | 0 | 0-1 | 0 | 18.39 | 22.50 |
| 05 Ari | NL | 29 | 0 | 0 | 5 | 14.1 | 74 | 19 | 15 | 15 | 2 | 1 | 0 | 1 | 11 | 3 | 11 | 0 | 0 | 1 | 1 | .500 | 0 | 2-3 | 6 | 7.63 | 9.42 |
| 10 Pit | NL | 50 | 0 | 0 | 14 | 38.2 | 166 | 39 | 14 | 12 | 2 | 1 | 2 | 2 | 18 | 3 | 22 | 3 | 0 | 2 | 2 | .500 | 0 | 0-0 | 6 | 4.24 | 2.79 |
| 10 SF | NL | 27 | 0 | 0 | 4 | 19.0 | 69 | 11 | 3 | 3 | 0 | 0 | 0 | 0 | 2 | 0 | 16 | 0 | 0 | 2 | 0 | 1.000 | 0 | 0-0 | 5 | 0.90 | 1.42 |
| Postseason | | 22 | 0 | 0 | 2 | 13.2 | 57 | 12 | 6 | 6 | 0 | 1 | 1 | 0 | 5 | 1 | 11 | 1 | 0 | 1 | 1 | .500 | 0 | 0-0 | 7 | 2.51 | 3.95 |
| 11 ML YEARS | | 629 | 0 | 0 | 129 | 429.2 | 1841 | 410 | 192 | 174 | 20 | 15 | 8 | 23 | 185 | 29 | 295 | 14 | 3 | 27 | 13 | .675 | 0 | 13-24 | 126 | 3.71 | 3.64 |

# Wilton Lopez

**Pitches:** R **Bats:** R **Pos:** RP-75 **Ht:** 6'0" **Wt:** 205 **Born:** 7/19/1983 **Age:** 30

| Year Team | Lg | G | GS | CG | GF | IP | BFP | H | R | ER | HR | SH | SF | HB | TBB | IBB | SO | WP | Bk | W | L | Pct | Sh | Sv-Op | Hld | ERC | ERA |
|---|---|---|---|---|---|---|---|---|---|---|---|---|---|---|---|---|---|---|---|---|---|---|---|---|---|---|---|
| | | HOW MUCH HE PITCHED | | | | | | WHAT HE GAVE UP | | | | | | | | | | | | THE RESULTS | | | | | | | |
| 2009 Hou | NL | 8 | 2 | 0 | 0 | 19.1 | 97 | 32 | 21 | 18 | 4 | 3 | 2 | 1 | 8 | 0 | 9 | 1 | 0 | 0 | 2 | .000 | 0 | 0-1 | 0 | 9.39 | 8.38 |
| 2010 Hou | NL | 68 | 0 | 0 | 14 | 67.0 | 262 | 66 | 23 | 22 | 4 | 2 | 2 | 0 | 5 | 1 | 50 | 2 | 2 | 5 | 2 | .714 | 0 | 1-3 | 14 | 2.56 | 2.96 |
| 2011 Hou | NL | 73 | 0 | 0 | 13 | 71.0 | 298 | 72 | 26 | 22 | 6 | 4 | 0 | 3 | 18 | 3 | 56 | 1 | 1 | 2 | 6 | .250 | 0 | 0-6 | 14 | 3.60 | 2.79 |
| 2012 Hou | NL | 64 | 0 | 0 | 28 | 66.1 | 260 | 61 | 18 | 16 | 4 | 4 | 2 | 2 | 8 | 2 | 54 | 1 | 0 | 6 | 3 | .667 | 0 | 10-13 | 9 | 2.49 | 2.17 |
| 2013 Col | NL | 75 | 0 | 0 | 28 | 75.1 | 321 | 88 | 35 | 34 | 6 | 1 | 1 | 1 | 18 | 4 | 48 | 0 | **3** | 3 | 4 | .429 | 0 | 0-5 | 8 | 4.27 | 4.06 |
| 5 ML YEARS | | 288 | 2 | 0 | 83 | 299.0 | 1238 | 319 | 123 | 112 | 24 | 14 | 7 | 7 | 57 | 10 | 217 | 5 | 6 | 16 | 17 | .485 | 0 | 11-28 | 45 | 3.59 | 3.37 |

# David Lough

**Bats:** L **Throws:** L **Pos:** RF-74;LF-15;PH-12;CF-7;PR-1 LOW **Ht:** 5'11" **Wt:** 180 **Born:** 1/20/1986 **Age:** 28

| Year Team | Lg | G | AB | H | 2B | 3B | HR | (Hm | Rd) | TB | R | RBI | RC | TBB | IBB | SO | HBP | SH | SF | SB | CS | SB% | GDP | Avg | OBP | Slg |
|---|---|---|---|---|---|---|---|---|---|---|---|---|---|---|---|---|---|---|---|---|---|---|---|---|---|---|
| | | BATTING | | | | | | | | | | | | | | | | | | BASERUNNING | | | | AVERAGES | | |
| 2009 Wilmg | A+ | 65 | 222 | 71 | 15 | 2 | 5 | (- | -) | 105 | 28 | 30 | 39 | 12 | 0 | 34 | 7 | 7 | 2 | 6 | 4 | .60 | 4 | .320 | .370 | .473 |
| 2009 NWArk | AA | 61 | 236 | 78 | 13 | 2 | 9 | (- | -) | 122 | 41 | 31 | 45 | 12 | 0 | 30 | 3 | 2 | 0 | 13 | 4 | .76 | 2 | .331 | .371 | .517 |
| 2010 Omha | AAA | 120 | 460 | 129 | 15 | 12 | 11 | (- | -) | 201 | 65 | 58 | 74 | 40 | 2 | 72 | 8 | 19 | 4 | 14 | 5 | .74 | 7 | .280 | .346 | .437 |
| 2011 Omha | AAA | 114 | 456 | 145 | 26 | 11 | 9 | (- | -) | 220 | 87 | 65 | 82 | 36 | 3 | 49 | 4 | 12 | 8 | 14 | 8 | .64 | 10 | .318 | .367 | .482 |
| 2012 Omha | AAA | 130 | 491 | 135 | 19 | 11 | 10 | (- | -) | 206 | 69 | 69 | 71 | 25 | 5 | 65 | 8 | 14 | 6 | 26 | 4 | .87 | 12 | .275 | .317 | .420 |
| 2013 Omha | AAA | 37 | 154 | 52 | 6 | 3 | 3 | (- | -) | 73 | 29 | 17 | 27 | 11 | 1 | 21 | 3 | 3 | 1 | 5 | 5 | .50 | 3 | .338 | .391 | .474 |
| 2012 KC | AL | 20 | 59 | 14 | 2 | 1 | 0 | (0 | 0) | 18 | 9 | 2 | 5 | 4 | 0 | 9 | 1 | 0 | 1 | 1 | 0 | 1.00 | 2 | .237 | .292 | .305 |
| 2013 KC | AL | 96 | 315 | 90 | 17 | 4 | 5 | (1 | 4) | 130 | 35 | 33 | 38 | 10 | 0 | 52 | 3 | 4 | 3 | 5 | 2 | .71 | 3 | .286 | .311 | .413 |
| 2 ML YEARS | | 116 | 374 | 104 | 19 | 5 | 5 | (1 | 4) | 148 | 44 | 35 | 43 | 14 | 0 | 61 | 4 | 4 | 4 | 6 | 2 | .75 | 5 | .278 | .308 | .396 |

# Aaron Loup

**Pitches:** L **Bats:** L **Pos:** RP-64 LOOP **Ht:** 6'0" **Wt:** 210 **Born:** 12/19/1987 **Age:** 26

| Year Team | Lg | G | GS | CG | GF | IP | BFP | H | R | ER | HR | SH | SF | HB | TBB | IBB | SO | WP | Bk | W | L | Pct | Sh | Sv-Op | Hld | ERC | ERA |
|---|---|---|---|---|---|---|---|---|---|---|---|---|---|---|---|---|---|---|---|---|---|---|---|---|---|---|---|
| | | HOW MUCH HE PITCHED | | | | | | WHAT HE GAVE UP | | | | | | | | | | | | THE RESULTS | | | | | | | |
| 2009 B Jays | R | 13 | 0 | 0 | 8 | 16.1 | 71 | 17 | 9 | 7 | 0 | 0 | 2 | 3 | 3 | 0 | 19 | 1 | 0 | 2 | 1 | .667 | 0 | 3- - | - | 3.43 | 3.86 |
| 2010 Lnsng | A | 35 | 5 | 0 | 9 | 73.1 | 309 | 79 | 37 | 37 | 4 | 3 | 0 | 5 | 22 | 1 | 73 | 3 | 0 | 3 | 2 | .600 | 0 | 2- - | - | 4.18 | 4.54 |
| 2011 Dnedin | A+ | 48 | 0 | 0 | 16 | 65.2 | 286 | 67 | 38 | 34 | 6 | 3 | 1 | 6 | 27 | 2 | 56 | 6 | 1 | 4 | 3 | .571 | 0 | 5- - | - | 4.56 | 4.66 |
| 2012 NHam | AA | 37 | 0 | 0 | 16 | 45.1 | 198 | 46 | 19 | 14 | 4 | 3 | 1 | 5 | 14 | 1 | 43 | 3 | 1 | 0 | 3 | .000 | 0 | 3- - | - | 4.08 | 2.78 |
| 2012 Tor | AL | 33 | 0 | 0 | 3 | 30.2 | 117 | 26 | 10 | 9 | 0 | 2 | 1 | 0 | 2 | 0 | 21 | 1 | 1 | 0 | 2 | .000 | 0 | 0-1 | 6 | 1.59 | 2.64 |
| 2013 Tor | AL | 64 | 0 | 0 | 12 | 69.1 | 282 | 66 | 23 | 19 | 5 | 2 | 4 | 7 | 13 | 4 | 53 | 2 | 0 | 4 | 6 | .400 | 0 | 2-3 | 8 | 3.20 | 2.47 |
| 2 ML YEARS | | 97 | 0 | 0 | 15 | 100.0 | 399 | 92 | 33 | 28 | 5 | 4 | 5 | 7 | 15 | 4 | 74 | 3 | 1 | 4 | 8 | .333 | 0 | 2-4 | 14 | 2.66 | 2.52 |

# Derek Lowe

**Pitches:** R **Bats:** R **Pos:** RP-9 **Ht:** 6'6" **Wt:** 230 **Born:** 6/1/1973 **Age:** 41

| Year Team | Lg | G | GS | CG | GF | IP | BFP | H | R | ER | HR | SH | SF | HB | TBB | IBB | SO | WP | Bk | W | L | Pct | Sh | Sv-Op | Hld | ERC | ERA |
|---|---|---|---|---|---|---|---|---|---|---|---|---|---|---|---|---|---|---|---|---|---|---|---|---|---|---|---|
| | | HOW MUCH HE PITCHED | | | | | | WHAT HE GAVE UP | | | | | | | | | | | | THE RESULTS | | | | | | | |
| 1997 2 Tms | AL | 20 | 9 | 0 | 1 | 69.0 | 298 | 74 | 49 | 47 | 11 | 4 | 2 | 4 | 23 | 3 | 52 | 2 | 0 | 2 | 6 | .250 | 0 | 0-2 | 1 | 4.88 | 6.13 |
| 1998 Bos | AL | 63 | 10 | 0 | 8 | 123.0 | 527 | 126 | 65 | 55 | 5 | 4 | 5 | 4 | 42 | 5 | 77 | 8 | 0 | 3 | 9 | .250 | 0 | 4-9 | 12 | 3.64 | 4.02 |
| 1999 Bos | AL | 74 | 0 | 0 | 32 | 109.1 | 436 | 84 | 35 | 32 | 7 | 1 | 2 | 4 | 25 | 1 | 80 | 1 | 0 | 6 | 3 | .667 | 0 | 15-20 | 22 | 2.14 | 2.63 |
| 2000 Bos | AL | 74 | 0 | 0 | **64** | 91.1 | 379 | 90 | 27 | 26 | 6 | 4 | 1 | 2 | 22 | 5 | 79 | 2 | 1 | 4 | 4 | .500 | 0 | **42-47** | 0 | 3.17 | 2.56 |
| 2001 Bos | AL | 67 | 3 | 0 | 50 | 91.2 | 404 | 103 | 39 | 36 | 7 | 5 | 1 | 5 | 29 | **9** | 82 | 4 | 0 | 5 | 10 | .333 | 0 | 24-30 | 4 | 4.31 | 3.53 |
| 2002 Bos | AL | 32 | 32 | 1 | 0 | 219.2 | 854 | 166 | 65 | 63 | 12 | 5 | 2 | 12 | 48 | 0 | 127 | 5 | 0 | 21 | 8 | .724 | 1 | 0-0 | 0 | 2.13 | 2.58 |
| 2003 Bos | AL | 33 | 33 | 1 | 0 | 203.1 | 886 | 216 | 113 | 101 | 17 | 3 | 5 | 11 | 72 | 4 | 110 | 3 | 0 | 17 | 7 | .708 | 0 | 0-0 | 0 | 4.32 | 4.47 |
| 2004 Bos | AL | 33 | 33 | 0 | 0 | 182.2 | 839 | 224 | **138** | 110 | 15 | 8 | 4 | 8 | 71 | 2 | 105 | 3 | 0 | 14 | 12 | .538 | 0 | 0-0 | 0 | 5.31 | 5.42 |
| 2005 LAD | NL | 35 | **35** | 2 | 0 | 222.0 | 934 | 223 | 113 | 89 | 28 | 12 | 5 | 5 | 55 | 1 | 146 | 3 | 2 | 12 | 15 | .444 | 2 | 0-0 | 0 | 3.75 | 3.61 |
| 2006 LAD | NL | 35 | 34 | 1 | 1 | 218.0 | 913 | 221 | 97 | 88 | 14 | 7 | 2 | 5 | 55 | 2 | 123 | 3 | 2 | **16** | 8 | .667 | 0 | 0-0 | 0 | 3.42 | 3.63 |
| 2007 LAD | NL | 33 | 32 | 3 | 0 | 199.1 | 831 | 194 | 100 | 86 | 20 | 6 | 2 | 1 | 59 | 2 | 147 | 3 | 1 | 12 | 14 | .462 | 0 | 0-0 | 1 | 3.55 | 3.88 |
| 2008 LAD | NL | 34 | **34** | 1 | 0 | 211.0 | 851 | 194 | 84 | 76 | 14 | 8 | 7 | 1 | 45 | 7 | 147 | 2 | 0 | 14 | 11 | .560 | 0 | 0-0 | 0 | 2.72 | 3.24 |
| 2009 Atl | NL | 34 | **34** | 0 | 0 | 194.2 | 855 | **232** | 109 | 101 | 16 | 11 | 6 | 4 | 63 | 7 | 111 | 4 | 2 | 15 | 10 | .600 | 0 | 0-0 | 0 | 4.80 | 4.67 |
| 2010 Atl | NL | 33 | 33 | 0 | 0 | 193.2 | 824 | 204 | 88 | 86 | 18 | 10 | 2 | 4 | 61 | 10 | 136 | 4 | 2 | 16 | 12 | .571 | 0 | 0-0 | 0 | 4.03 | 4.00 |
| 2011 Atl | NL | 34 | **34** | 0 | 0 | 187.0 | 830 | 212 | 110 | 105 | 14 | 9 | 5 | 3 | 70 | 4 | 137 | 1 | 2 | 9 | **17** | .346 | 0 | 0-0 | 0 | 4.56 | 5.05 |
| 2012 2 Tms | AL | 38 | 21 | 1 | 10 | 142.2 | 640 | 180 | 88 | 81 | 10 | 3 | 5 | 3 | 51 | 5 | 55 | 7 | 1 | 9 | 11 | .450 | 1 | 1-1 | 1 | 5.27 | 5.11 |
| 2013 Tex | AL | 9 | 0 | 0 | 2 | 13.0 | 57 | 16 | 13 | 13 | 3 | 0 | 0 | 2 | 3 | 0 | 8 | 0 | 0 | 1 | 0 | 1.000 | 0 | 0-0 | 1 | 6.58 | 9.00 |
| 97 Sea | AL | 12 | 9 | 0 | 1 | 53.0 | 234 | 59 | 43 | 41 | 11 | 2 | 1 | 2 | 20 | 2 | 39 | 2 | 0 | 2 | 4 | .333 | 0 | 0-0 | 0 | 5.55 | 6.96 |
| 97 Bos | AL | 8 | 0 | 0 | 0 | 16.0 | 64 | 15 | 6 | 6 | 0 | 2 | 1 | 2 | 3 | 1 | 13 | 0 | 0 | 0 | 2 | .000 | 0 | 0-2 | 1 | 2.78 | 3.38 |
| 12 Cle | AL | 21 | 21 | 1 | 0 | 119.0 | 542 | 156 | 79 | 73 | 8 | 3 | 5 | 3 | 45 | 3 | 41 | 5 | 1 | 8 | 10 | .444 | 1 | 0-0 | 0 | 5.67 | 5.52 |
| 12 NYY | AL | 17 | 0 | 0 | 10 | 23.2 | 98 | 24 | 9 | 8 | 2 | 0 | 0 | 0 | 6 | 2 | 14 | 2 | 0 | 1 | 1 | .500 | 0 | 1-1 | 1 | 3.39 | 3.04 |
| Postseason | | 26 | 12 | 0 | 4 | 97.1 | 408 | 81 | 45 | 37 | 12 | 6 | 0 | 4 | 32 | 6 | 70 | 1 | 0 | 5 | 7 | .417 | 0 | 1-2 | 1 | 3.06 | 3.42 |
| 17 ML YEARS | | 681 | 377 | 10 | 168 | 2671.1 | 11358 | 2759 | 1333 | 1195 | 217 | 100 | 56 | 78 | 794 | 67 | 1722 | 55 | 13 | 176 | 157 | .529 | 4 | 86-109 | 42 | 3.82 | 4.03 |

# Mark Lowe

**Pitches:** R **Bats:** L **Pos:** RP-11 **Ht:** 6'3" **Wt:** 210 **Born:** 6/7/1983 **Age:** 31

| HOW MUCH HE PITCHED | | | | | | | | | WHAT HE GAVE UP | | | | | | | | | | | | THE RESULTS | | | | | | | |
|---|---|---|---|---|---|---|---|---|---|---|---|---|---|---|---|---|---|---|---|---|---|---|---|---|---|---|---|---|
| Year | Team | Lg | G | GS | CG | GF | IP | BFP | H | R | ER | HR | SH | SF | HB | TBB | IBB | SO | WP | Bk | W | L | Pct | Sh | Sv-Op | Hld | ERC | ERA |
| 2013 | InldEm* | A+ | 3 | 0 | 0 | 1 | 5.0 | 17 | 1 | 1 | 1 | 0 | 0 | 0 | 0 | 0 | 0 | 6 | 1 | 0 | 0 | 0 | - | 0 | 1-- | - | 0.09 | 1.80 |
| 2013 | Syrcse* | AAA | 24 | 0 | 0 | 5 | 28.2 | 125 | 31 | 11 | 10 | 3 | 0 | 1 | 0 | 10 | 0 | 37 | 0 | 0 | 3 | 1 | .750 | 0 | 1-- | - | 4.34 | 3.14 |
| 2006 | Sea | AL | 15 | 0 | 0 | 3 | 18.2 | 75 | 12 | 4 | 4 | 1 | 1 | 0 | 2 | 9 | 1 | 20 | 1 | 0 | 1 | 0 | 1.000 | 0 | 0-0 | 6 | 2.61 | 1.93 |
| 2007 | Sea | AL | 4 | 0 | 0 | 1 | 2.2 | 13 | 2 | 2 | 2 | 1 | 0 | 0 | 0 | 3 | 0 | 3 | 0 | 0 | 0 | 0 | - | 0 | 0-0 | 2 | 7.69 | 6.75 |
| 2008 | Sea | AL | 57 | 0 | 0 | 19 | 63.2 | 303 | 78 | 44 | 38 | 6 | 3 | 3 | 4 | 34 | 0 | 55 | 2 | 0 | 1 | 5 | .167 | 0 | 1-5 | 1 | 6.10 | 5.37 |
| 2009 | Sea | AL | 75 | 0 | 0 | 18 | 80.0 | 339 | 71 | 39 | 29 | 7 | 0 | 4 | 0 | 29 | 1 | 69 | 4 | 0 | 2 | 7 | .222 | 0 | 3-13 | 26 | 3.16 | 3.26 |
| 2010 | 2 Tms | AL | 14 | 0 | 0 | 5 | 13.1 | 61 | 18 | 9 | 8 | 2 | 0 | 1 | 0 | 6 | 1 | 12 | 1 | 0 | 1 | 3 | .250 | 0 | 0-0 | 4 | 6.82 | 5.40 |
| 2011 | Tex | AL | 52 | 0 | 0 | 10 | 45.0 | 196 | 46 | 26 | 19 | 6 | 1 | 1 | 0 | 19 | 4 | 42 | 3 | 0 | 2 | 3 | .400 | 0 | 1-3 | 11 | 4.38 | 3.80 |
| 2012 | Tex | AL | 36 | 0 | 0 | 12 | 39.1 | 162 | 35 | 15 | 15 | 5 | 0 | 3 | 0 | 13 | 0 | 28 | 4 | 2 | 0 | 2 | .000 | 0 | 0-0 | 1 | 3.41 | 3.43 |
| 2013 | LAA | AL | 11 | 0 | 0 | 2 | 11.2 | 56 | 11 | 12 | 12 | 1 | 2 | 0 | 0 | 11 | 1 | 7 | 2 | 0 | 1 | 0 | 1.000 | 0 | 0-0 | 1 | 5.60 | 9.26 |
| 10 | Sea | AL | 11 | 0 | 0 | 4 | 10.1 | 45 | 11 | 5 | 4 | 1 | 0 | 1 | 0 | 5 | 1 | 7 | 1 | 0 | 1 | 3 | .250 | 0 | 0-0 | 4 | 4.70 | 3.48 |
| 10 | Tex | AL | 3 | 0 | 0 | 1 | 3.0 | 16 | 7 | 4 | 4 | 1 | 0 | 0 | 0 | 1 | 0 | 5 | 0 | 0 | 0 | 0 | - | 0 | 0-0 | 0 | 15.67 | 12.00 |
| Postseason | | | 4 | 0 | 0 | 1 | 1.2 | 13 | 7 | 7 | 7 | 1 | 0 | 0 | 0 | 1 | 0 | 1 | 0 | 0 | 0 | 1 | .000 | 0 | 0-0 | 0 | 35.40 | 37.80 |
| 8 ML YEARS | | | 264 | 0 | 0 | 70 | 274.1 | 1205 | 273 | 151 | 127 | 29 | 7 | 12 | 6 | 124 | 8 | 236 | 17 | 2 | 8 | 20 | .286 | 0 | 5-21 | 52 | 4.31 | 4.17 |

# Jed Lowrie

**Bats:** B **Throws:** R **Pos:** SS-119;2B-24;DH-12;PH-4 LAU-ree **Ht:** 6'0" **Wt:** 190 **Born:** 4/17/1984 **Age:** 30

| BATTING | | | | | | | | | | | | | | | | | | | | BASERUNNING | | | | AVERAGES | | |
|---|---|---|---|---|---|---|---|---|---|---|---|---|---|---|---|---|---|---|---|---|---|---|---|---|---|---|
| Year | Team | Lg | G | AB | H | 2B | 3B | HR | (Hm | Rd) | TB | R | RBI | RC | TBB | IBB | SO | HBP | SH | SF | SB | CS | SB% | GDP | Avg | OBP | Slg |
| 2008 | Bos | AL | 81 | 260 | 67 | 25 | 3 | 2 | (0 | 2) | 104 | 34 | 46 | 35 | 35 | 0 | 68 | 1 | 2 | 8 | 1 | 0 | 1.00 | 8 | .258 | .339 | .400 |
| 2009 | Bos | AL | 32 | 68 | 10 | 2 | 0 | 2 | (1 | 1) | 18 | 5 | 11 | 5 | 6 | 0 | 20 | 0 | 0 | 2 | 0 | 0 | - | 0 | .147 | .211 | .265 |
| 2010 | Bos | AL | 55 | 171 | 49 | 14 | 0 | 9 | (3 | 6) | 90 | 31 | 24 | 32 | 25 | 0 | 25 | 1 | 0 | 0 | 1 | 1 | .50 | 2 | .287 | .381 | .526 |
| 2011 | Bos | AL | 88 | 309 | 78 | 14 | 4 | 6 | (3 | 3) | 118 | 40 | 36 | 33 | 23 | 2 | 60 | 2 | 1 | 6 | 1 | 1 | .50 | 6 | .252 | .303 | .382 |
| 2012 | Hou | NL | 97 | 340 | 83 | 18 | 0 | 16 | (9 | 7) | 149 | 43 | 42 | 45 | 43 | 0 | 65 | 2 | 0 | 2 | 2 | 0 | 1.00 | 3 | .244 | .331 | .438 |
| 2013 | Oak | AL | 154 | 603 | 175 | 45 | 2 | 15 | (7 | 8) | 269 | 80 | 75 | 88 | 50 | 3 | 91 | 2 | 3 | 4 | 1 | 0 | 1.00 | 17 | .290 | .344 | .446 |
| Postseason | | | 12 | 31 | 6 | 1 | 0 | 0 | (0 | 0) | 7 | 4 | 2 | 2 | 5 | 0 | 8 | 1 | 0 | 1 | 0 | 0 | - | 0 | .194 | .316 | .226 |
| 6 ML YEARS | | | 507 | 1751 | 462 | 118 | 9 | 50 | (23 | 27) | 748 | 233 | 234 | 238 | 182 | 5 | 329 | 8 | 6 | 22 | 6 | 2 | .75 | 36 | .264 | .332 | .427 |

# Ed Lucas

**Bats:** R **Throws:** R **Pos:** 3B-61;1B-25;2B-20;SS-6;PH-2;LF-1;PR-1 **Ht:** 6'3" **Wt:** 210 **Born:** 5/21/1982 **Age:** 32

| BATTING | | | | | | | | | | | | | | | | | | | | BASERUNNING | | | | AVERAGES | | |
|---|---|---|---|---|---|---|---|---|---|---|---|---|---|---|---|---|---|---|---|---|---|---|---|---|---|---|
| Year | Team | Lg | G | AB | H | 2B | 3B | HR | (Hm | Rd) | TB | R | RBI | RC | TBB | IBB | SO | HBP | SH | SF | SB | CS | SB% | GDP | Avg | OBP | Slg |
| 2009 | Omha | AAA | 5 | 8 | 1 | 0 | 0 | 0 | (- | -) | 1 | 1 | 1 | 0 | 2 | 0 | 4 | 0 | 1 | 0 | 0 | 1 | .00 | 0 | .125 | .300 | .125 |
| 2009 | NWArk | AA | 103 | 355 | 103 | 22 | 2 | 10 | (- | -) | 159 | 61 | 58 | 68 | 53 | 1 | 75 | 7 | 4 | 5 | 18 | 2 | .90 | 6 | .290 | .388 | .448 |
| 2010 | Omha | AAA | 99 | 352 | 108 | 20 | 1 | 13 | (- | -) | 169 | 52 | 50 | 70 | 52 | 3 | 68 | 3 | 5 | 3 | 7 | 1 | .88 | 8 | .307 | .398 | .480 |
| 2011 | Gwnntt | AAA | 81 | 262 | 57 | 14 | 1 | 3 | (- | -) | 82 | 25 | 29 | 26 | 28 | 2 | 74 | 1 | 2 | 2 | 4 | 0 | 1.00 | 4 | .218 | .294 | .313 |
| 2011 | Missi | AA | 42 | 159 | 43 | 6 | 0 | 7 | (- | -) | 70 | 32 | 26 | 25 | 15 | 1 | 38 | 4 | 1 | 2 | 0 | 0 | - | 2 | .270 | .344 | .440 |
| 2012 | Salt Lk | AAA | 118 | 412 | 108 | 20 | 2 | 12 | (- | -) | 168 | 61 | 52 | 54 | 28 | 0 | 82 | 6 | 4 | 3 | 5 | 4 | .56 | 12 | .262 | .316 | .408 |
| 2013 | NewOr | AAA | 46 | 181 | 55 | 12 | 0 | 5 | (- | -) | 82 | 26 | 14 | 29 | 12 | 0 | 37 | 2 | 1 | 0 | 2 | 1 | .67 | 2 | .304 | .354 | .453 |
| 2013 | Mia | NL | 94 | 351 | 90 | 14 | 1 | 4 | (1 | 3) | 118 | 43 | 28 | 34 | 26 | 1 | 78 | 2 | 4 | 1 | 1 | 1 | .50 | 6 | .256 | .311 | .336 |

# Jonathan Lucroy

**Bats:** R **Throws:** R **Pos:** C-126;1B-14;PH-12;DH-3 LOO-croy **Ht:** 6'0" **Wt:** 195 **Born:** 6/13/1986 **Age:** 28

| BATTING | | | | | | | | | | | | | | | | | | | | BASERUNNING | | | | AVERAGES | | |
|---|---|---|---|---|---|---|---|---|---|---|---|---|---|---|---|---|---|---|---|---|---|---|---|---|---|---|
| Year | Team | Lg | G | AB | H | 2B | 3B | HR | (Hm | Rd) | TB | R | RBI | RC | TBB | IBB | SO | HBP | SH | SF | SB | CS | SB% | GDP | Avg | OBP | Slg |
| 2010 | Mil | NL | 75 | 277 | 70 | 9 | 0 | 4 | (4 | 0) | 91 | 24 | 26 | 23 | 18 | 1 | 44 | 1 | 0 | 1 | 4 | 2 | .67 | 9 | .253 | .300 | .329 |
| 2011 | Mil | NL | 136 | 430 | 114 | 16 | 1 | 12 | (8 | 4) | 168 | 45 | 59 | 50 | 29 | 0 | 99 | 2 | 4 | 3 | 2 | 1 | .67 | 7 | .265 | .313 | .391 |
| 2012 | Mil | NL | 96 | 316 | 101 | 17 | 4 | 12 | (7 | 5) | 162 | 46 | 58 | 61 | 22 | 1 | 44 | 4 | 1 | 3 | 4 | 1 | .80 | 12 | .320 | .368 | .513 |
| 2013 | Mil | NL | 147 | 521 | 146 | 25 | 6 | 18 | (9 | 9) | 237 | 59 | 82 | 78 | 46 | 2 | 69 | 5 | 0 | 8 | 9 | 1 | .90 | 16 | .280 | .340 | .455 |
| Postseason | | | 10 | 32 | 8 | 1 | 0 | 1 | (1 | 0) | 12 | 3 | 5 | 4 | 0 | 0 | 8 | 0 | 0 | 0 | 0 | 0 | - | 0 | .250 | .250 | .375 |
| 4 ML YEARS | | | 454 | 1544 | 431 | 67 | 11 | 46 | (28 | 18) | 658 | 174 | 225 | 212 | 115 | 4 | 256 | 12 | 5 | 15 | 19 | 5 | .79 | 44 | .279 | .331 | .426 |

# Ryan Ludwick

**Bats:** R **Throws:** L **Pos:** LF-32;PH-4;DH-2 **Ht:** 6'2" **Wt:** 215 **Born:** 7/13/1978 **Age:** 35

| BATTING | | | | | | | | | | | | | | | | | | | | BASERUNNING | | | | AVERAGES | | |
|---|---|---|---|---|---|---|---|---|---|---|---|---|---|---|---|---|---|---|---|---|---|---|---|---|---|---|
| Year | Team | Lg | G | AB | H | 2B | 3B | HR | (Hm | Rd) | TB | R | RBI | RC | TBB | IBB | SO | HBP | SH | SF | SB | CS | SB% | GDP | Avg | OBP | Slg |
| 2013 | Dayton* | A | 3 | 6 | 1 | 0 | 0 | 0 | (- | -) | 1 | 2 | 0 | 0 | 3 | 0 | 2 | 0 | 0 | 0 | 0 | 0 | - | 0 | .167 | .444 | .167 |
| 2013 | Lsvlle* | AAA | 10 | 38 | 5 | 1 | 0 | 1 | (- | -) | 9 | 2 | 4 | 0 | 0 | 0 | 9 | 1 | 0 | 0 | 0 | 0 | - | 1 | .132 | .154 | .237 |
| 2002 | Tex | AL | 23 | 81 | 19 | 6 | 0 | 1 | (1 | 0) | 28 | 10 | 9 | 6 | 7 | 0 | 24 | 0 | 0 | 0 | 2 | 1 | .67 | 4 | .235 | .295 | .346 |
| 2003 | 2 Tms | AL | 47 | 162 | 40 | 8 | 1 | 7 | (2 | 5) | 71 | 17 | 26 | 28 | 12 | 1 | 48 | 0 | 1 | 0 | 2 | 0 | 1.00 | 1 | .247 | .299 | .438 |
| 2004 | Cle | AL | 15 | 50 | 11 | 2 | 0 | 2 | (0 | 2) | 19 | 3 | 4 | 4 | 2 | 0 | 14 | 2 | 0 | 0 | 0 | 0 | - | 0 | .220 | .278 | .380 |
| 2005 | Cle | AL | 19 | 41 | 9 | 0 | 0 | 4 | (3 | 1) | 21 | 8 | 5 | 3 | 7 | 0 | 13 | 0 | 0 | 0 | 0 | 1 | .00 | 1 | .220 | .333 | .512 |
| 2007 | StL | NL | 120 | 303 | 81 | 22 | 0 | 14 | (7 | 7) | 145 | 42 | 52 | 45 | 26 | 1 | 72 | 7 | 3 | 0 | 4 | 4 | .50 | 1 | .267 | .339 | .479 |
| 2008 | StL | NL | 152 | 538 | 161 | 40 | 3 | 37 | (18 | 19) | 318 | 104 | 113 | 100 | 62 | 3 | 146 | 8 | 1 | 8 | 4 | 4 | .50 | 9 | .299 | .375 | .591 |
| 2009 | StL | NL | 139 | 486 | 129 | 20 | 1 | 22 | (4 | 18) | 217 | 63 | 97 | 82 | 41 | 3 | 106 | 7 | 1 | 4 | 4 | 2 | .67 | 6 | .265 | .329 | .447 |
| 2010 | 2 Tms | NL | 136 | 490 | 123 | 27 | 2 | 17 | (8 | 9) | 205 | 63 | 69 | 76 | 48 | 0 | 121 | 8 | 0 | 5 | 0 | 4 | .00 | 13 | .251 | .325 | .418 |
| 2011 | 2 Tms | NL | 139 | 490 | 116 | 23 | 0 | 13 | (6 | 7) | 178 | 56 | 75 | 59 | 51 | 4 | 124 | 4 | 2 | 6 | 1 | 1 | .50 | 9 | .237 | .310 | .363 |
| 2012 | Cin | NL | 125 | 422 | 116 | 28 | 1 | 26 | (16 | 10) | 224 | 53 | 80 | 70 | 42 | 3 | 97 | 5 | 1 | 2 | 0 | 1 | .00 | 9 | .275 | .346 | .531 |
| 2013 | Cin | NL | 38 | 129 | 31 | 5 | 0 | 2 | (1 | 1) | 42 | 7 | 12 | 8 | 10 | 0 | 29 | 0 | 0 | 1 | 0 | 0 | - | 7 | .240 | .293 | .326 |
| 03 | Tex | AL | 8 | 26 | 4 | 1 | 0 | 0 | (0 | 0) | 5 | 3 | 0 | 1 | 4 | 0 | 9 | 0 | 0 | 0 | 0 | 0 | - | 0 | .154 | .267 | .192 |
| 03 | Cle | AL | 39 | 136 | 36 | 7 | 1 | 7 | (2 | 5) | 66 | 14 | 26 | 27 | 8 | 1 | 39 | 0 | 1 | 0 | 2 | 0 | 1.00 | 1 | .265 | .306 | .485 |
| 10 | StL | NL | 77 | 281 | 79 | 20 | 2 | 11 | (4 | 7) | 136 | 44 | 43 | 55 | 24 | 0 | 64 | 4 | 0 | 3 | 0 | 3 | .00 | 4 | .281 | .343 | .484 |
| 10 | SD | NL | 59 | 209 | 44 | 7 | 0 | 6 | (4 | 2) | 69 | 19 | 26 | 21 | 24 | 0 | 57 | 4 | 0 | 2 | 0 | 1 | .00 | 9 | .211 | .301 | .330 |

| BATTING | | | | | | | | | | | | | | | | | | | | | | BASERUNNING | | | | AVERAGES | | |
|---|---|---|---|---|---|---|---|---|---|---|---|---|---|---|---|---|---|---|---|---|---|---|---|---|---|---|---|---|
| Year | Team | Lg | G | AB | H | 2B | 3B | HR | (Hm | Rd) | TB | R | RBI | RC | TBB | IBB | SO | HBP | SH | SF | SB | CS | SB% | GDP | Avg | OBP | Slg |
| 11 | SD | NL | 101 | 378 | 90 | 18 | 0 | 11 | (5 | 6) | 141 | 42 | 64 | 44 | 32 | 1 | 87 | 4 | 1 | 5 | 1 | 1 | .50 | 8 | .238 | .301 | .373 |
| 11 | Pit | NL | 38 | 112 | 26 | 5 | 0 | 2 | (1 | 1) | 37 | 14 | 11 | 15 | 19 | 3 | 37 | 0 | 1 | 1 | 0 | 0 | - | 1 | .232 | .341 | .330 |
| Postseason | | | 8 | 30 | 10 | 0 | 0 | 3 | (2 | 1) | 19 | 5 | 5 | 3 | 5 | 1 | 5 | 0 | 0 | 0 | 0 | 0 | - | 2 | .333 | .429 | .633 |
| 11 ML YEARS | | | 953 | 3192 | 836 | 181 | 8 | 145 | (66 | 79) | 1468 | 426 | 542 | 481 | 308 | 15 | 794 | 41 | 9 | 26 | 17 | 18 | .49 | 60 | .262 | .332 | .460 |

# Cory Luebke

**Pitches:** L **Bats:** R **Pos:** P LUBE-kee **Ht:** 6'4" **Wt:** 200 **Born:** 3/4/1985 **Age:** 29

| HOW MUCH HE PITCHED | | | | | | | | | WHAT HE GAVE UP | | | | | | | | | | | | THE RESULTS | | | | | | | |
|---|---|---|---|---|---|---|---|---|---|---|---|---|---|---|---|---|---|---|---|---|---|---|---|---|---|---|---|---|
| Year | Team | Lg | G | GS | CG | GF | IP | BFP | H | R | ER | HR | SH | SF | HB | TBB | IBB | SO | WP | Bk | W | L | Pct | Sh | Sv-Op | Hld | ERC | ERA |
| 2010 | SD | NL | 4 | 3 | 0 | 1 | 17.2 | 76 | 17 | 8 | 8 | 3 | 0 | 0 | 1 | 6 | 0 | 18 | 0 | 0 | 1 | 1 | .500 | 0 | 0-0 | 0 | 4.30 | 4.08 |
| 2011 | SD | NL | 46 | 17 | 0 | 3 | 139.2 | 555 | 105 | 54 | 51 | 12 | 3 | 4 | 2 | 44 | 3 | 154 | 5 | 2 | 6 | 10 | .375 | 0 | 0-0 | 3 | 2.43 | 3.29 |
| 2012 | SD | NL | 5 | 5 | 0 | 0 | 31.0 | 130 | 28 | 10 | 9 | 1 | 2 | 0 | 0 | 8 | 0 | 23 | 0 | 0 | 3 | 1 | .750 | 0 | 0-0 | 0 | 2.51 | 2.61 |
| 3 ML YEARS | | | 55 | 25 | 0 | 4 | 188.1 | 761 | 150 | 72 | 68 | 16 | 5 | 4 | 3 | 58 | 3 | 195 | 5 | 2 | 10 | 12 | .455 | 0 | 0-0 | 3 | 2.61 | 3.25 |

# Josh Lueke

**Pitches:** R **Bats:** R **Pos:** RP-19 LOO-kee **Ht:** 6'5" **Wt:** 220 **Born:** 12/5/1984 **Age:** 29

| HOW MUCH HE PITCHED | | | | | | | | | WHAT HE GAVE UP | | | | | | | | | | | | THE RESULTS | | | | | | | |
|---|---|---|---|---|---|---|---|---|---|---|---|---|---|---|---|---|---|---|---|---|---|---|---|---|---|---|---|---|
| Year | Team | Lg | G | GS | CG | GF | IP | BFP | H | R | ER | HR | SH | SF | HB | TBB | IBB | SO | WP | Bk | W | L | Pct | Sh | Sv-Op | Hld | ERC | ERA |
| 2013 | Drham* | AAA | 40 | 0 | 0 | 27 | 57.1 | 228 | 41 | 6 | 4 | 1 | 2 | 0 | 2 | 15 | 1 | 81 | 5 | 0 | 3 | 1 | .750 | 0 | 17-- | - | 1.72 | 0.63 |
| 2011 | Sea | AL | 25 | 0 | 0 | 8 | 32.2 | 142 | 34 | 22 | 22 | 2 | 2 | 1 | 0 | 13 | 1 | 29 | 5 | 0 | 1 | 1 | .500 | 0 | 0-0 | 2 | 3.96 | 6.06 |
| 2012 | TB | AL | 3 | 0 | 0 | 2 | 3.1 | 21 | 9 | 7 | 7 | 0 | 0 | 2 | 0 | 3 | 0 | 2 | 0 | 0 | 0 | 0 | - | 0 | 0-0 | 0 | 17.54 | 18.90 |
| 2013 | TB | AL | 19 | 0 | 0 | 6 | 21.1 | 99 | 23 | 12 | 12 | 3 | 1 | 2 | 1 | 12 | 1 | 25 | 3 | 0 | 0 | 2 | .000 | 0 | 0-0 | 2 | 5.54 | 5.06 |
| 3 ML YEARS | | | 47 | 0 | 0 | 16 | 57.1 | 262 | 66 | 41 | 41 | 5 | 3 | 5 | 1 | 28 | 2 | 56 | 8 | 0 | 1 | 3 | .250 | 0 | 0-0 | 4 | 5.19 | 6.44 |

# Lucas Luetge

**Pitches:** L **Bats:** L **Pos:** RP-35 LOOT-key **Ht:** 6'4" **Wt:** 205 **Born:** 3/24/1987 **Age:** 27

| HOW MUCH HE PITCHED | | | | | | | | | WHAT HE GAVE UP | | | | | | | | | | | | THE RESULTS | | | | | | | |
|---|---|---|---|---|---|---|---|---|---|---|---|---|---|---|---|---|---|---|---|---|---|---|---|---|---|---|---|---|
| Year | Team | Lg | G | GS | CG | GF | IP | BFP | H | R | ER | HR | SH | SF | HB | TBB | IBB | SO | WP | Bk | W | L | Pct | Sh | Sv-Op | Hld | ERC | ERA |
| 2009 | BrvdCt | A+ | 27 | 7 | 0 | 4 | 92.1 | 405 | 93 | 55 | 46 | 6 | 4 | 4 | 9 | 38 | 0 | 75 | 5 | 0 | 6 | 7 | .462 | 0 | 2-- | - | 4.32 | 4.48 |
| 2010 | BrvdCt | A+ | 16 | 1 | 0 | 2 | 35.1 | 145 | 36 | 10 | 9 | 1 | 1 | 1 | 1 | 10 | 1 | 21 | 6 | 0 | 1 | 1 | .500 | 0 | 0-- | - | 3.42 | 2.29 |
| 2010 | Hntsvl | AA | 23 | 2 | 0 | 3 | 44.0 | 203 | 52 | 25 | 17 | 4 | 1 | 1 | 2 | 17 | 1 | 47 | 6 | 0 | 3 | 2 | .600 | 0 | 0-- | - | 5.02 | 3.48 |
| 2011 | Hntsvl | AA | 46 | 1 | 0 | 6 | 69.0 | 286 | 63 | 29 | 24 | 3 | 4 | 3 | 1 | 23 | 4 | 69 | 6 | 0 | 1 | 3 | .250 | 0 | 3-- | - | 2.97 | 3.13 |
| 2013 | Tacom | AAA | 22 | 0 | 0 | 11 | 31.0 | 134 | 28 | 16 | 15 | 4 | 2 | 0 | 0 | 16 | 0 | 45 | 2 | 0 | 0 | 0 | - | 0 | 1-- | - | 4.21 | 4.35 |
| 2012 | Sea | AL | 63 | 0 | 0 | 16 | 40.2 | 178 | 37 | 20 | 18 | 3 | 1 | 3 | 1 | 24 | 6 | 38 | 5 | 0 | 2 | 2 | .500 | 0 | 2-3 | 12 | 4.01 | 3.98 |
| 2013 | Sea | AL | 35 | 0 | 0 | 15 | 37.0 | 165 | 42 | 22 | 20 | 2 | 2 | 3 | 2 | 16 | 2 | 27 | 4 | 0 | 1 | 3 | .250 | 0 | 0-0 | 1 | 4.81 | 4.86 |
| 2 ML YEARS | | | 98 | 0 | 0 | 31 | 77.2 | 343 | 79 | 42 | 38 | 5 | 3 | 6 | 3 | 40 | 8 | 65 | 9 | 0 | 3 | 5 | .375 | 0 | 2-3 | 13 | 4.39 | 4.40 |

# Donald Lutz

**Bats:** L **Throws:** R **Pos:** PH-24;LF-17;RF-1 **Ht:** 6'3" **Wt:** 250 **Born:** 2/6/1989 **Age:** 25

| BATTING | | | | | | | | | | | | | | | | | | | | | | BASERUNNING | | | | AVERAGES | | |
|---|---|---|---|---|---|---|---|---|---|---|---|---|---|---|---|---|---|---|---|---|---|---|---|---|---|---|---|---|
| Year | Team | Lg | G | AB | H | 2B | 3B | HR | (Hm | Rd) | TB | R | RBI | RC | TBB | IBB | SO | HBP | SH | SF | SB | CS | SB% | GDP | Avg | OBP | Slg |
| 2009 | Reds | R | 16 | 59 | 10 | 1 | 2 | 1 | (- | -) | 18 | 9 | 10 | 4 | 5 | 0 | 14 | 1 | 0 | 0 | 2 | 1 | .67 | 3 | .169 | .246 | .305 |
| 2010 | Billings | R+ | 55 | 203 | 58 | 10 | 4 | 7 | (- | -) | 97 | 36 | 28 | 36 | 21 | 1 | 45 | 4 | 0 | 5 | 6 | 2 | .75 | 4 | .286 | .356 | .478 |
| 2011 | Dayton | A | 123 | 465 | 140 | 23 | 3 | 20 | (- | -) | 229 | 85 | 75 | 81 | 34 | 4 | 125 | 7 | 0 | 0 | 5 | 4 | .56 | 8 | .301 | .358 | .492 |
| 2012 | Bkrsfld | A+ | 63 | 253 | 67 | 18 | 3 | 17 | (- | -) | 142 | 42 | 51 | 46 | 19 | 5 | 71 | 4 | 0 | 1 | 7 | 2 | .78 | 4 | .265 | .325 | .561 |
| 2012 | Reds | R | 4 | 14 | 9 | 2 | 2 | 0 | (- | -) | 15 | 3 | 5 | 7 | 3 | 0 | 4 | 0 | 0 | 0 | 0 | 0 | - | 0 | .643 | .706 | 1.071 |
| 2012 | Pnscla | AA | 40 | 149 | 36 | 5 | 1 | 5 | (- | -) | 58 | 17 | 15 | 18 | 13 | 0 | 32 | 3 | 0 | 0 | 1 | 3 | .25 | 2 | .242 | .315 | .389 |
| 2013 | Pnscla | AA | 65 | 229 | 56 | 12 | 4 | 7 | (- | -) | 97 | 35 | 30 | 32 | 19 | 4 | 56 | 6 | 0 | 1 | 4 | 1 | .80 | 4 | .245 | .318 | .424 |
| 2013 | Cin | NL | 34 | 58 | 14 | 1 | 0 | 1 | (1 | 0) | 18 | 5 | 8 | 5 | 1 | 0 | 14 | 0 | 0 | 0 | 2 | 0 | 1.00 | 0 | .241 | .254 | .310 |

# Zach Lutz

**Bats:** R **Throws:** R **Pos:** PH-11;3B-3;1B-1;DH-1 **Ht:** 6'1" **Wt:** 220 **Born:** 6/3/1986 **Age:** 28

| BATTING | | | | | | | | | | | | | | | | | | | | | | BASERUNNING | | | | AVERAGES | | |
|---|---|---|---|---|---|---|---|---|---|---|---|---|---|---|---|---|---|---|---|---|---|---|---|---|---|---|---|---|
| Year | Team | Lg | G | AB | H | 2B | 3B | HR | (Hm | Rd) | TB | R | RBI | RC | TBB | IBB | SO | HBP | SH | SF | SB | CS | SB% | GDP | Avg | OBP | Slg |
| 2009 | StLuci | A+ | 99 | 356 | 101 | 19 | 2 | 11 | (- | -) | 157 | 46 | 62 | 63 | 50 | 1 | 72 | 7 | 0 | 2 | 1 | 1 | .50 | 10 | .284 | .381 | .441 |
| 2009 | Bnghtn | AA | 8 | 29 | 6 | 1 | 0 | 0 | (- | -) | 7 | 0 | 2 | 2 | 5 | 0 | 7 | 0 | 0 | 0 | 0 | 0 | - | 1 | .207 | .324 | .241 |
| 2010 | Bnghtn | AA | 61 | 225 | 65 | 14 | 0 | 17 | (- | -) | 130 | 42 | 42 | 49 | 33 | 0 | 63 | 4 | 1 | 0 | 0 | 2 | .00 | 9 | .289 | .389 | .578 |
| 2010 | Mets | R | 5 | 19 | 6 | 1 | 0 | 1 | (- | -) | 10 | 2 | 4 | 3 | 1 | 0 | 4 | 0 | 0 | 0 | 0 | 0 | - | 0 | .316 | .350 | .526 |
| 2010 | StLuci | A+ | 1 | 4 | 0 | 0 | 0 | 0 | (- | -) | 0 | 0 | 0 | 0 | 0 | 0 | 2 | 0 | 0 | 0 | 0 | 0 | - | 1 | .000 | .000 | .000 |
| 2010 | Buffalo | AAA | 5 | 20 | 6 | 4 | 0 | 1 | (- | -) | 13 | 3 | 9 | 4 | 2 | 0 | 3 | 0 | 0 | 0 | 0 | 0 | - | 0 | .300 | .364 | .650 |
| 2011 | Buffalo | AAA | 61 | 220 | 65 | 12 | 0 | 11 | (- | -) | 110 | 38 | 31 | 42 | 27 | 0 | 70 | 3 | 0 | 0 | 0 | 0 | - | 2 | .295 | .380 | .500 |
| 2011 | StLuci | A+ | 2 | 8 | 0 | 0 | 0 | 0 | (- | -) | 0 | 0 | 1 | 0 | 1 | 0 | 2 | 0 | 0 | 0 | 0 | 0 | - | 1 | .000 | .111 | .000 |
| 2012 | Buffalo | AAA | 72 | 244 | 73 | 16 | 1 | 10 | (- | -) | 121 | 34 | 35 | 51 | 42 | 1 | 75 | 5 | 1 | 2 | 0 | 0 | - | 7 | .299 | .410 | .496 |
| 2012 | StLuci | A+ | 6 | 20 | 5 | 2 | 0 | 1 | (- | -) | 10 | 2 | 8 | 4 | 4 | 0 | 5 | 0 | 0 | 2 | 0 | 0 | - | 1 | .250 | .346 | .500 |
| 2013 | LsVgs | AAA | 111 | 399 | 117 | 27 | 4 | 13 | (- | -) | 191 | 62 | 80 | 74 | 54 | 1 | 102 | 4 | 2 | 7 | 0 | 2 | .00 | 12 | .293 | .377 | .479 |
| 2012 | NYM | NL | 7 | 11 | 1 | 0 | 0 | 0 | (0 | 0) | 1 | 1 | 0 | 0 | 0 | 0 | 5 | 0 | 0 | 0 | 0 | 0 | - | 0 | .091 | .091 | .091 |
| 2013 | NYM | NL | 15 | 20 | 6 | 2 | 0 | 0 | (0 | 0) | 8 | 2 | 2 | 4 | 6 | 0 | 6 | 0 | 0 | 0 | 0 | 0 | - | 1 | .300 | .462 | .400 |
| 2 ML YEARS | | | 22 | 31 | 7 | 2 | 0 | 0 | (0 | 0) | 9 | 3 | 2 | 4 | 6 | 0 | 11 | 0 | 0 | 0 | 0 | 0 | - | 1 | .226 | .351 | .290 |

# Jordan Lyles

**Pitches:** R **Bats:** R **Pos:** SP-25; RP-2 **Ht:** 6'4" **Wt:** 215 **Born:** 10/19/1990 **Age:** 23

| | | | HOW MUCH HE PITCHED | | | | | | WHAT HE GAVE UP | | | | | | | | | | | | THE RESULTS | | | | | | | |
|---|---|---|---|---|---|---|---|---|---|---|---|---|---|---|---|---|---|---|---|---|---|---|---|---|---|---|---|---|
| Year | Team | Lg | G | GS | CG | GF | IP | BFP | H | R | ER | HR | SH | SF | HB | TBB | IBB | SO | WP | Bk | W | L | Pct | Sh | Sv-Op | Hld | ERC | ERA |
| 2013 | OKCity* | AAA | 6 | 5 | 0 | 0 | 23.2 | 102 | 30 | 15 | 14 | 1 | 0 | 0 | 0 | 6 | 0 | 11 | 0 | 0 | 2 | 2 | .500 | 0 | 0-- | - | 4.72 | 5.32 |
| 2011 | Hou | NL | 20 | 15 | 0 | 2 | 94.0 | 415 | 107 | 61 | 56 | 14 | 7 | 1 | 5 | 26 | 1 | 67 | 0 | 0 | 2 | 8 | .200 | 0 | 0-0 | 0 | 4.87 | 5.36 |
| 2012 | Hou | NL | 25 | 25 | 1 | 0 | 141.1 | 628 | 159 | 97 | 80 | 20 | 6 | 4 | 5 | 42 | 4 | 99 | 2 | 0 | 5 | 12 | .294 | 1 | 0-0 | 0 | 4.67 | 5.09 |
| 2013 | Hou | AL | 27 | 25 | 0 | 1 | 141.2 | 642 | 165 | 98 | 88 | 17 | 0 | 3 | 11 | 49 | 1 | 93 | 5 | **2** | 7 | 9 | .438 | 0 | 1-1 | 1 | 5.20 | 5.59 |
| 3 ML YEARS | | | 72 | 65 | 1 | 3 | 377.0 | 1685 | 431 | 256 | 224 | 51 | 13 | 8 | 21 | 117 | 6 | 259 | 7 | 2 | 14 | 29 | .326 | 1 | 1-1 | 1 | 4.92 | 5.35 |

# Lance Lynn

**Pitches:** R **Bats:** R **Pos:** SP-33 **Ht:** 6'5" **Wt:** 240 **Born:** 5/12/1987 **Age:** 27

| | | | HOW MUCH HE PITCHED | | | | | | WHAT HE GAVE UP | | | | | | | | | | | | THE RESULTS | | | | | | | |
|---|---|---|---|---|---|---|---|---|---|---|---|---|---|---|---|---|---|---|---|---|---|---|---|---|---|---|---|---|
| Year | Team | Lg | G | GS | CG | GF | IP | BFP | H | R | ER | HR | SH | SF | HB | TBB | IBB | SO | WP | Bk | W | L | Pct | Sh | Sv-Op | Hld | ERC | ERA |
| 2011 | StL | NL | 18 | 2 | 0 | 2 | 34.2 | 136 | 25 | 12 | 12 | 3 | 1 | 0 | 1 | 11 | 1 | 40 | 1 | 0 | 1 | 1 | .500 | 0 | 1-2 | 3 | 2.37 | 3.12 |
| 2012 | StL | NL | 35 | 29 | 0 | 2 | 176.0 | 744 | 168 | 76 | 74 | 16 | 4 | 3 | 10 | 64 | 3 | 180 | 3 | 0 | 18 | 7 | .720 | 0 | 0-0 | 1 | 3.87 | 3.78 |
| 2013 | StL | NL | 33 | 33 | 0 | 0 | 201.2 | 856 | 189 | 92 | 89 | 14 | 11 | 8 | 11 | 76 | 0 | 198 | 6 | 0 | 15 | 10 | .600 | 0 | 0-0 | 0 | 3.67 | 3.97 |
| Postseason | | | 16 | 2 | 0 | 2 | 22.0 | 97 | 23 | 15 | 11 | 5 | 1 | 2 | 0 | 11 | 2 | 20 | 0 | 0 | 3 | 2 | .600 | 0 | 0-0 | 3 | 5.60 | 4.50 |
| 3 ML YEARS | | | 86 | 64 | 0 | 4 | 412.1 | 1736 | 382 | 180 | 175 | 33 | 16 | 11 | 22 | 151 | 4 | 418 | 10 | 0 | 34 | 18 | .654 | 0 | 1-2 | 4 | 3.64 | 3.82 |

# Brandon Lyon

**Pitches:** R **Bats:** R **Pos:** RP-37 **Ht:** 6'1" **Wt:** 200 **Born:** 8/10/1979 **Age:** 34

| | | | HOW MUCH HE PITCHED | | | | | | WHAT HE GAVE UP | | | | | | | | | | | | THE RESULTS | | | | | | | |
|---|---|---|---|---|---|---|---|---|---|---|---|---|---|---|---|---|---|---|---|---|---|---|---|---|---|---|---|---|
| Year | Team | Lg | G | GS | CG | GF | IP | BFP | H | R | ER | HR | SH | SF | HB | TBB | IBB | SO | WP | Bk | W | L | Pct | Sh | Sv-Op | Hld | ERC | ERA |
| 2013 | Pwtckt* | AAA | 4 | 0 | 0 | 3 | 5.1 | 22 | 5 | 2 | 1 | 0 | 0 | 1 | 0 | 1 | 0 | 3 | 0 | 0 | 0 | 0 | - | 0 | 2-- | - | 2.27 | 1.69 |
| 2001 | Tor | AL | 11 | 11 | 0 | 0 | 63.0 | 261 | 63 | 31 | 30 | 6 | 2 | 6 | 1 | 15 | 0 | 35 | 0 | 1 | 5 | 4 | .556 | 0 | 0-0 | 0 | 3.50 | 4.29 |
| 2002 | Tor | AL | 15 | 10 | 0 | 0 | 62.0 | 279 | 78 | 47 | 45 | 14 | 3 | 2 | 2 | 19 | 2 | 30 | 2 | 0 | 1 | 4 | .200 | 0 | 0-1 | 0 | 6.24 | 6.53 |
| 2003 | Bos | AL | 49 | 0 | 0 | 31 | 59.0 | 273 | 73 | 33 | 27 | 6 | 1 | 4 | 2 | 19 | 5 | 50 | 0 | 0 | 4 | 6 | .400 | 0 | 9-12 | 2 | 4.96 | 4.12 |
| 2005 | Ari | NL | 32 | 0 | 0 | 22 | 29.1 | 144 | 44 | 25 | 21 | 6 | 2 | 1 | 2 | 10 | 2 | 17 | 1 | 1 | 0 | 2 | .000 | 0 | 14-15 | 1 | 7.72 | 6.44 |
| 2006 | Ari | NL | 68 | 0 | 0 | 22 | 69.1 | 293 | 68 | 32 | 30 | 7 | 3 | 4 | 0 | 22 | 7 | 46 | 1 | 0 | 2 | 4 | .333 | 0 | 0-7 | 23 | 3.49 | 3.89 |
| 2007 | Ari | NL | 73 | 0 | 0 | 20 | 74.0 | 307 | 70 | 25 | 22 | 2 | 3 | 2 | 1 | 22 | 2 | 40 | 3 | 1 | 6 | 4 | .600 | 0 | 2-5 | **35** | 2.93 | 2.68 |
| 2008 | Ari | NL | 61 | 0 | 0 | 50 | 59.1 | 265 | 75 | 34 | 31 | 7 | 2 | 1 | 0 | 13 | 1 | 44 | 1 | 0 | 3 | 5 | .375 | 0 | 26-31 | 3 | 4.86 | 4.70 |
| 2009 | Det | AL | 65 | 0 | 0 | 27 | 78.2 | 314 | 56 | 25 | 25 | 7 | 5 | 3 | 2 | 31 | **9** | 57 | 3 | 0 | 6 | 5 | .545 | 0 | 3-6 | 15 | 2.46 | 2.86 |
| 2010 | Hou | NL | 79 | 0 | 0 | 28 | 78.0 | 333 | 68 | 28 | 27 | 2 | 4 | 0 | 3 | 31 | 12 | 54 | 3 | 0 | 6 | 6 | .500 | 0 | 20-22 | 19 | 2.73 | 3.12 |
| 2011 | Hou | NL | 15 | 0 | 0 | 13 | 13.1 | 71 | 27 | 17 | 17 | 4 | 0 | 0 | 0 | 5 | 1 | 6 | 1 | 0 | 3 | 3 | .500 | 0 | 4-8 | 0 | 12.27 | 11.48 |
| 2012 | 2 Tms | | 67 | 0 | 0 | 21 | 61.0 | 258 | 56 | 21 | 21 | 5 | 1 | 1 | 3 | 20 | 3 | 63 | 6 | 0 | 4 | 2 | .667 | 0 | 1-3 | 12 | 3.32 | 3.10 |
| 2013 | NYM | NL | 37 | 0 | 0 | 7 | 34.1 | 153 | 43 | 20 | 19 | 3 | 5 | 2 | 0 | 13 | 3 | 23 | 1 | 0 | 2 | 2 | .500 | 0 | 0-3 | 7 | 5.29 | 4.98 |
| 12 | Hou | NL | 37 | 0 | 0 | 11 | 36.0 | 154 | 37 | 13 | 13 | 3 | 0 | 0 | 2 | 11 | 2 | 35 | 5 | 0 | 0 | 2 | .000 | 0 | 0-2 | 5 | 3.89 | 3.25 |
| 12 | Tor | AL | 30 | 0 | 0 | 10 | 25.0 | 104 | 19 | 8 | 8 | 2 | 1 | 1 | 1 | 9 | 1 | 28 | 1 | 0 | 4 | 0 | 1.000 | 0 | 1-1 | 7 | 2.57 | 2.88 |
| Postseason | | | 5 | 0 | 0 | 1 | 6.0 | 20 | 1 | 0 | 0 | 0 | 0 | 0 | 0 | 1 | 0 | 5 | 0 | 0 | 0 | 0 | - | 0 | 0-0 | 2 | 0.19 | 0.00 |
| 12 ML YEARS | | | 572 | 21 | 0 | 241 | 681.1 | 2951 | 721 | 338 | 315 | 69 | 31 | 26 | 16 | 220 | 47 | 465 | 22 | 3 | 42 | 47 | .472 | 0 | 79-113 | 117 | 4.07 | 4.16 |

# Tyler Lyons

**Pitches:** L **Bats:** B **Pos:** SP-8; RP-4 **Ht:** 6'4" **Wt:** 200 **Born:** 2/21/1988 **Age:** 26

| | | | HOW MUCH HE PITCHED | | | | | | WHAT HE GAVE UP | | | | | | | | | | | | THE RESULTS | | | | | | | |
|---|---|---|---|---|---|---|---|---|---|---|---|---|---|---|---|---|---|---|---|---|---|---|---|---|---|---|---|---|
| Year | Team | Lg | G | GS | CG | GF | IP | BFP | H | R | ER | HR | SH | SF | HB | TBB | IBB | SO | WP | Bk | W | L | Pct | Sh | Sv-Op | Hld | ERC | ERA |
| 2011 | PlmBh | A+ | 33 | 12 | 1 | 4 | 94.0 | 402 | 93 | 51 | 47 | 8 | 3 | 1 | 4 | 29 | 2 | 79 | 4 | 1 | 9 | 4 | .692 | 1 | 1-- | - | 3.66 | 4.50 |
| 2012 | Sprgfld | AA | 12 | 12 | 0 | 0 | 64.1 | 274 | 70 | 33 | 28 | 6 | 2 | 2 | 1 | 19 | 0 | 54 | 2 | 0 | 5 | 4 | .556 | 0 | 0-- | - | 4.22 | 3.92 |
| 2012 | Memp | AAA | 15 | 15 | 3 | 0 | 88.1 | 366 | 87 | 42 | 42 | 9 | 4 | 5 | 2 | 18 | 0 | 89 | 0 | 0 | 4 | 9 | .308 | 0 | 0-- | - | 3.32 | 4.28 |
| 2013 | Memp | AAA | 17 | 16 | 0 | 0 | 100.1 | 399 | 85 | 40 | 37 | 6 | 4 | 1 | 6 | 19 | 0 | 86 | 0 | 0 | 7 | 2 | .778 | 0 | 0-- | - | 2.50 | 3.32 |
| 2013 | StL | NL | 12 | 8 | 0 | 1 | 53.0 | 223 | 49 | 29 | 28 | 5 | 1 | 0 | 3 | 16 | 0 | 43 | 0 | 0 | 2 | 4 | .333 | 0 | 0-0 | 0 | 3.46 | 4.75 |

# Manny Machado

**Bats:** R **Throws:** R **Pos:** 3B-156 muh-CHAH-doe **Ht:** 6'2" **Wt:** 180 **Born:** 7/6/1992 **Age:** 21

| | | | BATTING | | | | | | | | | | | | | | | | | | BASERUNNING | | | | AVERAGES | | |
|---|---|---|---|---|---|---|---|---|---|---|---|---|---|---|---|---|---|---|---|---|---|---|---|---|---|---|---|
| Year | Team | Lg | G | AB | H | 2B | 3B | HR | (Hm | Rd) | TB | R | RBI | RC | TBB | IBB | SO | HBP | SH | SF | SB | CS | SB% | GDP | Avg | OBP | Slg |
| 2010 | Orioles | R | 2 | 7 | 1 | 0 | 0 | 1 | (- | -) | 4 | 1 | 2 | 0 | 0 | 0 | 1 | 0 | 0 | 0 | 0 | 0 | - | 0 | .143 | .143 | .571 |
| 2010 | Abrdn | A- | 7 | 29 | 10 | 1 | 1 | 0 | (- | -) | 13 | 2 | 3 | 5 | 3 | 0 | 2 | 0 | 0 | 0 | 0 | 0 | - | 0 | .345 | .406 | .448 |
| 2011 | Dlmrva | A | 38 | 145 | 40 | 8 | 2 | 6 | (- | -) | 70 | 24 | 24 | 27 | 23 | 4 | 25 | 1 | 0 | 1 | 3 | 1 | .75 | 8 | .276 | .376 | .483 |
| 2011 | Frdrck | A+ | 63 | 237 | 58 | 12 | 3 | 5 | (- | -) | 91 | 24 | 26 | 28 | 22 | 0 | 48 | 0 | 0 | 1 | 8 | 5 | .62 | 8 | .245 | .308 | .384 |
| 2012 | Bowie | AA | 109 | 402 | 107 | 26 | 5 | 11 | (- | -) | 176 | 60 | 59 | 66 | 48 | 0 | 70 | 6 | 1 | 2 | 13 | 4 | .76 | 15 | .266 | .352 | .438 |
| 2012 | Bal | AL | 51 | 191 | 50 | 8 | 3 | 7 | (7 | 0) | 85 | 24 | 26 | 29 | 9 | 0 | 38 | 0 | 1 | 1 | 2 | 0 | 1.00 | 6 | .262 | .294 | .445 |
| 2013 | Bal | AL | 156 | **667** | 189 | **51** | 3 | 14 | (5 | 9) | 288 | 88 | 71 | 87 | 29 | 0 | 113 | 2 | 9 | 3 | 6 | 7 | .46 | 15 | .283 | .314 | .432 |
| Postseason | | | 6 | 19 | 3 | 1 | 0 | 1 | (0 | 1) | 7 | 2 | 2 | 1 | 2 | 0 | 6 | 0 | 2 | 0 | 0 | 0 | - | 1 | .158 | .238 | .368 |
| 2 ML YEARS | | | 207 | 858 | 239 | 59 | 6 | 21 | (12 | 9) | 373 | 112 | 97 | 116 | 38 | 0 | 151 | 2 | 10 | 4 | 8 | 7 | .53 | 21 | .279 | .309 | .435 |

# Jean Machi

**Pitches:** R **Bats:** R **Pos:** RP-51 GENE ma-CHEE **Ht:** 6'0" **Wt:** 260 **Born:** 2/1/1982 **Age:** 32

| | | | HOW MUCH HE PITCHED | | | | | | WHAT HE GAVE UP | | | | | | | | | | | | THE RESULTS | | | | | | | |
|---|---|---|---|---|---|---|---|---|---|---|---|---|---|---|---|---|---|---|---|---|---|---|---|---|---|---|---|---|
| Year | Team | Lg | G | GS | CG | GF | IP | BFP | H | R | ER | HR | SH | SF | HB | TBB | IBB | SO | WP | Bk | W | L | Pct | Sh | Sv-Op | Hld | ERC | ERA |
| 2009 | Altna | AA | 28 | 0 | 0 | 22 | 34.2 | 142 | 28 | 12 | 8 | 2 | 4 | 1 | 0 | 13 | 2 | 25 | 5 | 0 | 2 | 3 | .400 | 0 | 6-- | - | 2.61 | 2.08 |
| 2009 | Indy | AAA | 13 | 0 | 0 | 11 | 17.0 | 62 | 8 | 4 | 4 | 1 | 0 | 2 | 0 | 6 | 0 | 12 | 0 | 0 | 1 | 1 | .500 | 0 | 6-- | - | 1.32 | 2.12 |
| 2010 | Indy | AAA | 58 | 0 | 0 | 53 | 59.2 | 260 | 51 | 29 | 26 | 6 | 2 | 3 | 2 | 32 | 2 | 58 | 5 | 0 | 5 | 5 | .500 | 0 | 23-- | - | 3.86 | 3.92 |
| 2011 | Fresno | AAA | 3 | 0 | 0 | 0 | 4.0 | 17 | 5 | 4 | 4 | 0 | 0 | 0 | 0 | 0 | 0 | 6 | 0 | 0 | 1 | 1 | .500 | 0 | 0-- | - | 3.14 | 9.00 |
| 2012 | Fresno | AAA | 53 | 0 | 0 | 34 | 56.2 | 257 | 67 | 29 | 25 | 7 | 3 | 1 | 3 | 17 | 1 | 44 | 0 | 0 | 2 | 1 | .667 | 0 | 15-- | - | 4.96 | 3.97 |

| HOW MUCH HE PITCHED | | | | | | | | | WHAT HE GAVE UP | | | | | | | | | | | | THE RESULTS | | | | | | | |
|---|---|---|---|---|---|---|---|---|---|---|---|---|---|---|---|---|---|---|---|---|---|---|---|---|---|---|---|---|
| Year | Team | Lg | G | GS | CG | GF | IP | BFP | H | R | ER | HR | SH | SF | HB | TBB | IBB | SO | WP | Bk | W | L | Pct | Sh | Sv-Op | Hld | ERC | ERA |
| 2013 | Fresno | AAA | 16 | 0 | 0 | 4 | 18.1 | 68 | 13 | 4 | 2 | 0 | 1 | 0 | 1 | 3 | 0 | 19 | 2 | 0 | 3 | 1 | .750 | 0 | 2-- | - | 1.54 | 0.98 |
| 2012 | SF | NL | 8 | 0 | 0 | 5 | 6.2 | 28 | 7 | 5 | 5 | 2 | 0 | 0 | 0 | 1 | 0 | 4 | 0 | 0 | 0 | 0 | - | 0 | 0-0 | 0 | 4.56 | 6.75 |
| 2013 | SF | NL | 51 | 0 | 0 | 9 | 53.0 | 211 | 46 | 15 | 14 | 2 | 1 | 1 | 0 | 12 | 3 | 51 | 2 | 0 | 3 | 1 | .750 | 0 | 0-2 | 11 | 2.30 | 2.38 |
| 2 ML YEARS | | | 59 | 0 | 0 | 14 | 59.2 | 239 | 53 | 20 | 19 | 4 | 1 | 1 | 0 | 13 | 3 | 55 | 2 | 0 | 3 | 1 | .750 | 0 | 0-2 | 11 | 2.55 | 2.87 |

## Ryan Madson

**Pitches:** R **Bats:** L **Pos:** P **Ht:** 6'6" **Wt:** 210 **Born:** 8/28/1980 **Age:** 33

| HOW MUCH HE PITCHED | | | | | | | | | WHAT HE GAVE UP | | | | | | | | | | | | THE RESULTS | | | | | | | |
|---|---|---|---|---|---|---|---|---|---|---|---|---|---|---|---|---|---|---|---|---|---|---|---|---|---|---|---|---|
| Year | Team | Lg | G | GS | CG | GF | IP | BFP | H | R | ER | HR | SH | SF | HB | TBB | IBB | SO | WP | Bk | W | L | Pct | Sh | Sv-Op | Hld | ERC | ERA |
| 2013 | InldEm* | A+ | 1 | 0 | 0 | 1 | 1.0 | 3 | 0 | 0 | 0 | 0 | 0 | 0 | 0 | 0 | 0 | 1 | 0 | 0 | 0 | 0 | - | 0 | 1-- | - | 0.00 | 0.00 |
| 2003 | Phi | NL | 1 | 0 | 0 | 0 | 2.0 | 6 | 0 | 0 | 0 | 0 | 0 | 0 | 0 | 0 | 0 | 0 | 0 | 0 | 0 | 0 | - | 0 | 0-0 | 0 | 0.00 | 0.00 |
| 2004 | Phi | NL | 52 | 1 | 0 | 14 | 77.0 | 312 | 68 | 23 | 20 | 6 | 1 | 1 | 5 | 19 | 4 | 55 | 7 | 0 | 9 | 3 | .750 | 0 | 1-2 | 7 | 2.95 | 2.34 |
| 2005 | Phi | NL | 78 | 0 | 0 | 10 | 87.0 | 365 | 84 | 44 | 40 | 11 | 5 | 5 | 6 | 25 | 6 | 79 | 6 | 1 | 6 | 5 | .545 | 0 | 0-7 | **32** | 3.83 | 4.14 |
| 2006 | Phi | NL | 50 | 17 | 0 | 8 | 134.1 | 620 | 176 | 92 | 85 | 20 | 9 | 3 | 10 | 50 | 4 | 99 | 12 | 0 | 11 | 9 | .550 | 0 | 2-4 | 6 | 6.50 | 5.69 |
| 2007 | Phi | NL | 38 | 0 | 0 | 9 | 56.0 | 237 | 48 | 19 | 19 | 5 | 2 | 2 | 2 | 23 | 4 | 43 | 2 | 2 | 2 | 2 | .500 | 0 | 1-2 | 7 | 3.28 | 3.05 |
| 2008 | Phi | NL | 76 | 0 | 0 | 14 | 82.2 | 340 | 79 | 29 | 28 | 6 | 3 | 2 | 1 | 23 | 4 | 67 | 2 | 1 | 4 | 2 | .667 | 0 | 1-3 | 17 | 3.20 | 3.05 |
| 2009 | Phi | NL | 79 | 0 | 0 | 28 | 77.1 | 320 | 73 | 29 | 28 | 7 | 3 | 1 | 3 | 22 | 3 | 78 | 1 | 0 | 5 | 5 | .500 | 0 | 10-16 | 26 | 3.39 | 3.26 |
| 2010 | Phi | NL | 55 | 0 | 0 | 21 | 53.0 | 217 | 42 | 16 | 15 | 4 | 2 | 0 | 4 | 13 | 3 | 64 | 2 | 0 | 6 | 2 | .750 | 0 | 5-10 | 15 | 2.42 | 2.55 |
| 2011 | Phi | NL | 62 | 0 | 0 | 46 | 60.2 | 246 | 54 | 16 | 16 | 2 | 6 | 1 | 1 | 16 | 8 | 62 | 0 | 0 | 4 | 2 | .667 | 0 | 32-34 | 3 | 2.45 | 2.37 |
| Postseason | | | 33 | 0 | 0 | 11 | 35.0 | 145 | 33 | 9 | 9 | 2 | 2 | 2 | 1 | 10 | 2 | 43 | 2 | 0 | 2 | 1 | .667 | 0 | 2-6 | 7 | 3.09 | 2.31 |
| 9 ML YEARS | | | 491 | 18 | 0 | 150 | 630.0 | 2663 | 624 | 268 | 251 | 61 | 31 | 15 | 32 | 191 | 36 | 547 | 32 | 4 | 47 | 30 | .610 | 0 | 52-78 | 113 | 3.76 | 3.59 |

## Kenta Maeda

**Pitches:** R **Bats:** R **Pos:** P KEN-tah my-YAY-duh **Ht:** 6'0" **Wt:** 154 **Born:** 4/11/1988 **Age:** 26

| HOW MUCH HE PITCHED | | | | | | | | | WHAT HE GAVE UP | | | | | | | | | | | | THE RESULTS | | | | | | | |
|---|---|---|---|---|---|---|---|---|---|---|---|---|---|---|---|---|---|---|---|---|---|---|---|---|---|---|---|---|
| Year | Team | Lg | G | GS | CG | GF | IP | BFP | H | R | ER | HR | SH | SF | HB | TBB | IBB | SO | WP | Bk | W | L | Pct | Sh | Sv-Op | Hld | ERC | ERA |
| 2009 | Hrshma | Jap | 29 | 29 | 3 | 0 | 193.0 | 795 | 194 | 82 | 72 | 22 | - | - | 3 | 29 | 1 | 147 | 2 | 0 | 8 | 14 | .364 | 1 | 0-- | - | 3.26 | 3.36 |
| 2010 | Hrshma | Jap | 28 | 28 | 6 | 0 | 215.2 | 848 | 166 | 55 | 53 | 15 | - | - | 7 | 46 | 3 | 174 | 2 | 0 | 15 | 8 | .652 | 2 | 0-- | - | 2.13 | 2.21 |
| 2011 | Hrshma | Jap | 31 | 31 | 4 | 0 | 216.0 | 864 | 178 | 61 | 59 | 14 | - | - | 6 | 43 | 0 | 192 | 4 | 0 | 10 | 12 | .455 | 2 | 0-- | - | 2.29 | 2.46 |
| 2012 | Hrshma | Jap | 29 | 29 | 5 | 0 | 206.1 | 820 | 161 | 46 | 35 | 6 | - | - | 9 | 44 | 1 | 171 | 2 | 0 | 14 | 7 | .667 | 2 | 0-- | - | 1.99 | 1.53 |
| 2013 | Hrshma | Jap | 25 | 25 | 3 | 0 | 169.2 | 661 | 120 | 41 | 37 | 12 | - | - | 2 | 38 | 1 | 154 | 1 | 0 | 15 | 6 | .714 | 1 | 0-- | - | 1.82 | 1.96 |

## Matt Magill

**Pitches:** R **Bats:** R **Pos:** SP-6 **Ht:** 6'3" **Wt:** 210 **Born:** 11/10/1989 **Age:** 24

| HOW MUCH HE PITCHED | | | | | | | | | WHAT HE GAVE UP | | | | | | | | | | | | THE RESULTS | | | | | | | |
|---|---|---|---|---|---|---|---|---|---|---|---|---|---|---|---|---|---|---|---|---|---|---|---|---|---|---|---|---|
| Year | Team | Lg | G | GS | CG | GF | IP | BFP | H | R | ER | HR | SH | SF | HB | TBB | IBB | SO | WP | Bk | W | L | Pct | Sh | Sv-Op | Hld | ERC | ERA |
| 2009 | Ogden | R+ | 15 | 15 | 0 | 0 | 72.0 | 305 | 59 | 43 | 32 | 7 | 1 | 4 | 7 | 30 | 0 | 55 | 4 | 1 | 6 | 3 | .667 | 0 | 0-- | - | 3.52 | 4.00 |
| 2010 | Gt Lks | A | 24 | 20 | 1 | 3 | 126.1 | 510 | 87 | 50 | 46 | 13 | 1 | 4 | 5 | 52 | 0 | 135 | 10 | 1 | 7 | 4 | .636 | 0 | 2-- | - | 2.68 | 3.28 |
| 2011 | RCuca | A+ | 26 | 21 | 0 | 1 | 139.1 | 617 | 156 | 78 | 67 | 15 | 3 | 3 | 2 | 52 | 1 | 126 | 9 | 2 | 11 | 5 | .688 | 0 | 0-- | - | 4.73 | 4.33 |
| 2012 | Chatt | AA | 26 | 26 | 0 | 0 | 146.1 | 623 | 127 | 71 | 61 | 8 | 7 | 4 | 3 | 61 | 1 | 168 | 10 | 0 | 11 | 8 | .579 | 0 | 0-- | - | 3.15 | 3.75 |
| 2013 | Albq | AAA | 18 | 16 | 0 | 1 | 85.2 | 362 | 72 | 34 | 33 | 7 | 5 | 4 | 1 | 50 | 0 | 101 | 5 | 2 | 6 | 2 | .750 | 0 | 0-- | - | 3.94 | 3.47 |
| 2013 | Ddgrs | R | 1 | 1 | 0 | 0 | 3.0 | 10 | 1 | 0 | 0 | 0 | 0 | 0 | 0 | 0 | 0 | 3 | 0 | 0 | 0 | 0 | - | 0 | 0-- | - | 0.25 | 0.00 |
| 2013 | LAD | NL | 6 | 6 | 0 | 0 | 27.2 | 137 | 27 | 25 | 20 | 6 | 1 | 2 | 1 | 28 | 1 | 26 | 1 | 0 | 0 | 2 | .000 | 0 | 0-0 | 0 | 7.48 | 6.51 |

## Paul Maholm

**Pitches:** L **Bats:** L **Pos:** SP-26 mah-HALL-uhm **Ht:** 6'2" **Wt:** 220 **Born:** 6/25/1982 **Age:** 32

| HOW MUCH HE PITCHED | | | | | | | | | WHAT HE GAVE UP | | | | | | | | | | | | THE RESULTS | | | | | | | |
|---|---|---|---|---|---|---|---|---|---|---|---|---|---|---|---|---|---|---|---|---|---|---|---|---|---|---|---|---|
| Year | Team | Lg | G | GS | CG | GF | IP | BFP | H | R | ER | HR | SH | SF | HB | TBB | IBB | SO | WP | Bk | W | L | Pct | Sh | Sv-Op | Hld | ERC | ERA |
| 2013 | Rome* | A | 1 | 1 | 0 | 0 | 5.2 | 22 | 4 | 1 | 1 | 0 | 0 | 0 | 1 | 0 | 0 | 6 | 0 | 0 | 1 | 0 | 1.000 | 0 | 0-- | - | 1.36 | 1.59 |
| 2005 | Pit | NL | 6 | 6 | 0 | 0 | 41.1 | 168 | 31 | 10 | 10 | 2 | 0 | 0 | 3 | 17 | 0 | 26 | 0 | 0 | 3 | 1 | .750 | 0 | 0-0 | 0 | 2.79 | 2.18 |
| 2006 | Pit | NL | 30 | 30 | 0 | 0 | 176.0 | 788 | 202 | 98 | 93 | 19 | 7 | 4 | 12 | 81 | 6 | 117 | 3 | 1 | 8 | 10 | .444 | 0 | 0-0 | 0 | 5.58 | 4.76 |
| 2007 | Pit | NL | 29 | 29 | 2 | 0 | 177.2 | 765 | 204 | 110 | 99 | 22 | 13 | 6 | 6 | 49 | 3 | 105 | 5 | 0 | 10 | 15 | .400 | 1 | 0-0 | 0 | 4.77 | 5.02 |
| 2008 | Pit | NL | 31 | 31 | 1 | 0 | 206.1 | 853 | 201 | 89 | 85 | 21 | 8 | 8 | 9 | 63 | 2 | 139 | 2 | 1 | 9 | 9 | .500 | 0 | 0-0 | 0 | 3.84 | 3.71 |
| 2009 | Pit | NL | 31 | 31 | 0 | 0 | 194.2 | 836 | 221 | 102 | 96 | 14 | 7 | 1 | 6 | 60 | 4 | 119 | 11 | 1 | 8 | 9 | .471 | 0 | 0-0 | 0 | 4.45 | 4.44 |
| 2010 | Pit | NL | 32 | 32 | 1 | 0 | 185.1 | 840 | 228 | 119 | 105 | 15 | 10 | 6 | 9 | 62 | 2 | 102 | 2 | 0 | 9 | 15 | .375 | 1 | 0-0 | 0 | 5.14 | 5.10 |
| 2011 | Pit | NL | 26 | 26 | 1 | 0 | 162.1 | 687 | 160 | 72 | 66 | 11 | 8 | **10** | 8 | 50 | 6 | 97 | 3 | 0 | 6 | 14 | .300 | 1 | 0-0 | 0 | 3.57 | 3.66 |
| 2012 | 2 Tms | NL | 32 | 31 | 1 | 0 | 189.0 | 786 | 178 | 80 | 77 | 20 | 7 | 4 | 11 | 53 | 3 | 140 | 5 | 0 | 13 | 11 | .542 | 1 | 0-0 | 0 | 3.57 | 3.67 |
| 2013 | Atl | NL | 26 | 26 | 0 | 0 | 153.0 | 670 | 169 | 82 | 75 | 17 | 8 | 2 | 10 | 47 | 3 | 105 | 3 | 0 | 10 | 11 | .476 | 0 | 0-0 | 0 | 4.61 | 4.41 |
| 12 | ChC | NL | 21 | 20 | 0 | 0 | 120.1 | 503 | 115 | 51 | 50 | 12 | 5 | 4 | 10 | 34 | 2 | 81 | 4 | 0 | 9 | 6 | .600 | 0 | 0-0 | 0 | 3.73 | 3.74 |
| 12 | Atl | NL | 11 | 11 | 1 | 0 | 68.2 | 283 | 63 | 29 | 27 | 8 | 2 | 0 | 1 | 19 | 1 | 59 | 1 | 0 | 4 | 5 | .444 | 1 | 0-0 | 0 | 3.31 | 3.54 |
| 9 ML YEARS | | | 243 | 242 | 6 | 0 | 1485.2 | 6393 | 1594 | 762 | 706 | 141 | 68 | 41 | 74 | 482 | 29 | 950 | 34 | 3 | 76 | 95 | .444 | 4 | 0-0 | 0 | 4.37 | 4.28 |

## Joe Mahoney

**Bats:** L **Throws:** L **Pos:** 1B-7;PH-2 **Ht:** 6'6" **Wt:** 245 **Born:** 2/1/1987 **Age:** 27

| BATTING | | | | | | | | | | | | | | | | | | | | BASERUNNING | | | | AVERAGES | | |
|---|---|---|---|---|---|---|---|---|---|---|---|---|---|---|---|---|---|---|---|---|---|---|---|---|---|---|
| Year | Team | Lg | G | AB | H | 2B | 3B | HR | (Hm | Rd) | TB | R | RBI | RC | TBB | IBB | SO | HBP | SH | SF | SB | CS | SB% | GDP | Avg | OBP | Slg |
| 2009 | Dlmrva | A | 108 | 395 | 110 | 16 | 7 | 7 | (- | -) | 161 | 61 | 53 | 60 | 30 | 2 | 93 | 3 | 0 | 4 | 29 | 1 | .97 | 7 | .278 | .331 | .408 |
| 2009 | Frdrck | A+ | 7 | 30 | 8 | 4 | 0 | 1 | (- | -) | 15 | 2 | 5 | 3 | 0 | 0 | 10 | 0 | 0 | 1 | 0 | 1 | .00 | 0 | .267 | .258 | .500 |
| 2010 | Frdrck | A+ | 72 | 271 | 81 | 18 | 0 | 9 | (- | -) | 126 | 37 | 49 | 45 | 22 | 5 | 56 | 4 | 0 | 2 | 5 | 3 | .63 | 4 | .299 | .358 | .465 |
| 2010 | Bowie | AA | 52 | 191 | 61 | 12 | 2 | 9 | (- | -) | 104 | 30 | 29 | 39 | 17 | 2 | 39 | 1 | 0 | 0 | 9 | 1 | .90 | 2 | .319 | .378 | .545 |
| 2011 | Bowie | AA | 85 | 315 | 91 | 24 | 5 | 11 | (- | -) | 158 | 43 | 67 | 56 | 25 | 1 | 84 | 6 | 0 | 9 | 7 | 2 | .78 | 2 | .289 | .344 | .502 |
| 2011 | Frdrck | A+ | 3 | 8 | 4 | 2 | 0 | 0 | (- | -) | 6 | 0 | 2 | 3 | 4 | 0 | 1 | 0 | 0 | 0 | 0 | 0 | - | 0 | .500 | .667 | .750 |
| 2012 | Norfolk | AAA | 132 | 491 | 130 | 29 | 1 | 10 | (- | -) | 191 | 54 | 56 | 63 | 34 | 6 | 95 | 6 | 0 | 4 | 4 | 2 | .67 | 8 | .265 | .318 | .389 |
| 2013 | Jupiter | A+ | 9 | 33 | 10 | 1 | 0 | 2 | (- | -) | 17 | 4 | 2 | 5 | 1 | 0 | 9 | 0 | 0 | 0 | 0 | 0 | - | 1 | .303 | .324 | .515 |

| | | | BATTING | | | | | | | | | | | | | | | | | | BASERUNNING | | | | AVERAGES | | |
|---|---|---|---|---|---|---|---|---|---|---|---|---|---|---|---|---|---|---|---|---|---|---|---|---|---|---|---|
| Year | Team | Lg | G | AB | H | 2B | 3B | HR | (Hm | Rd) | TB | R | RBI | RC | TBB | IBB | SO | HBP | SH | SF | SB | CS | SB% | GDP | Avg | OBP | Slg |
| 2013 | NewOr | AAA | 55 | 195 | 37 | 8 | 0 | 2 | (- | -) | 51 | 9 | 16 | 8 | 3 | 1 | 66 | 0 | 0 | 2 | 1 | 0 | 1.00 | 3 | .190 | .200 | .262 |
| 2012 | Bal | AL | 2 | 4 | 0 | 0 | 0 | 0 | (0 | 0) | 0 | 0 | 0 | 0 | 0 | 0 | 0 | 0 | 0 | 0 | 0 | 0 | - | 0 | .000 | .000 | .000 |
| 2013 | Mia | NL | 9 | 29 | 8 | 1 | 0 | 1 | (1 | 0) | 12 | 2 | 4 | 4 | 0 | 0 | 4 | 0 | 0 | 0 | 0 | 0 | - | 0 | .276 | .276 | .414 |
| 2 ML YEARS | | | 11 | 33 | 8 | 1 | 0 | 1 | (1 | 0) | 12 | 2 | 4 | 4 | 0 | 0 | 4 | 0 | 0 | 0 | 0 | 0 | - | 0 | .242 | .242 | .364 |

# John Maine

**Pitches:** R **Bats:** R **Pos:** RP-4 **Ht:** 6'4" **Wt:** 220 **Born:** 5/8/1981 **Age:** 33

| | | | HOW MUCH HE PITCHED | | | | | | WHAT HE GAVE UP | | | | | | | | | | | | THE RESULTS | | | | | | | |
|---|---|---|---|---|---|---|---|---|---|---|---|---|---|---|---|---|---|---|---|---|---|---|---|---|---|---|---|---|
| Year | Team | Lg | G | GS | CG | GF | IP | BFP | H | R | ER | HR | SH | SF | HB | TBB | IBB | SO | WP | Bk | W | L | Pct | Sh | Sv-Op | Hld | ERC | ERA |
| 2004 | Bal | AL | 1 | 1 | 0 | 0 | 3.2 | 19 | 7 | 4 | 4 | 1 | 0 | 0 | 0 | 3 | 0 | 1 | 1 | 0 | 0 | 1 | .000 | 0 | 0-0 | 0 | 14.87 | 9.82 |
| 2005 | Bal | AL | 10 | 8 | 0 | 1 | 40.0 | 184 | 39 | 30 | 28 | 8 | 0 | 2 | 1 | 24 | 0 | 24 | 0 | 1 | 2 | 3 | .400 | 0 | 0-0 | 0 | 5.47 | 6.30 |
| 2006 | NYM | NL | 16 | 15 | 1 | 1 | 90.0 | 365 | 69 | 40 | 36 | 15 | 3 | 1 | 2 | 33 | 1 | 71 | 3 | 0 | 6 | 5 | .545 | 1 | 0-0 | 0 | 3.22 | 3.60 |
| 2007 | NYM | NL | 32 | 32 | 1 | 0 | 191.0 | 810 | 168 | 90 | 83 | 23 | 11 | 4 | 5 | 75 | 3 | 180 | 2 | 0 | 15 | 10 | .600 | 1 | 0-0 | 0 | 3.58 | 3.91 |
| 2008 | NYM | NL | 25 | 25 | 0 | 0 | 140.0 | 608 | 122 | 70 | 65 | 16 | 10 | 5 | 4 | 67 | 2 | 122 | 10 | 0 | 10 | 8 | .556 | 0 | 0-0 | 0 | 3.81 | 4.18 |
| 2009 | NYM | NL | 15 | 15 | 0 | 0 | 81.1 | 349 | 67 | 42 | 40 | 8 | 6 | 2 | 4 | 38 | 2 | 55 | 5 | 0 | 7 | 6 | .538 | 0 | 0-0 | 0 | 3.48 | 4.43 |
| 2010 | NYM | NL | 9 | 9 | 0 | 0 | 39.2 | 190 | 47 | 29 | 27 | 8 | 4 | 1 | 2 | 25 | 1 | 39 | 3 | 0 | 1 | 3 | .250 | 0 | 0-0 | 0 | 7.09 | 6.13 |
| 2013 | Mia | NL | 4 | 0 | 0 | 2 | 7.1 | 40 | 15 | 10 | 10 | 2 | 1 | 0 | 0 | 5 | 1 | 7 | 1 | 0 | 0 | 0 | - | 0 | 0-0 | 0 | 14.09 | 12.27 |
| Postseason | | | 3 | 3 | 0 | 0 | 13.2 | 62 | 10 | 5 | 4 | 1 | 1 | 0 | 1 | 11 | 2 | 13 | 0 | 0 | 1 | 0 | 1.000 | 0 | 0-0 | 0 | 3.93 | 2.63 |
| 8 ML YEARS | | | 112 | 105 | 2 | 4 | 593.0 | 2565 | 534 | 315 | 293 | 81 | 35 | 15 | 18 | 270 | 10 | 499 | 25 | 1 | 41 | 36 | .532 | 2 | 0-0 | 0 | 4.06 | 4.45 |

# Martin Maldonado

**Bats:** R **Throws:** R **Pos:** C-47;PH-13;1B-10 **Ht:** 6'0" **Wt:** 235 **Born:** 8/16/1986 **Age:** 27

| | | | BATTING | | | | | | | | | | | | | | | | | | BASERUNNING | | | | AVERAGES | | |
|---|---|---|---|---|---|---|---|---|---|---|---|---|---|---|---|---|---|---|---|---|---|---|---|---|---|---|---|
| Year | Team | Lg | G | AB | H | 2B | 3B | HR | (Hm | Rd) | TB | R | RBI | RC | TBB | IBB | SO | HBP | SH | SF | SB | CS | SB% | GDP | Avg | OBP | Slg |
| 2011 | Mil | NL | 3 | 1 | 0 | 0 | 0 | 0 | (0 | 0) | 0 | 0 | 0 | 0 | 0 | 0 | 1 | 0 | 0 | 0 | 0 | 0 | - | 0 | .000 | .000 | .000 |
| 2012 | Mil | NL | 78 | 233 | 62 | 9 | 0 | 8 | (6 | 2) | 95 | 22 | 30 | 28 | 17 | 0 | 56 | 2 | 4 | 0 | 1 | 1 | .50 | 5 | .266 | .321 | .408 |
| 2013 | Mil | NL | 67 | 183 | 31 | 7 | 1 | 4 | (1 | 3) | 52 | 13 | 22 | 14 | 13 | 1 | 53 | 3 | 3 | 0 | 0 | 0 | - | 2 | .169 | .236 | .284 |
| 3 ML YEARS | | | 148 | 417 | 93 | 16 | 1 | 12 | (7 | 5) | 147 | 35 | 52 | 42 | 30 | 1 | 110 | 5 | 7 | 0 | 1 | 1 | .50 | 7 | .223 | .283 | .353 |

# Seth Maness

**Pitches:** R **Bats:** R **Pos:** RP-66 MAY-ness **Ht:** 6'0" **Wt:** 190 **Born:** 10/14/1988 **Age:** 25

| | | | HOW MUCH HE PITCHED | | | | | | WHAT HE GAVE UP | | | | | | | | | | | | THE RESULTS | | | | | | | |
|---|---|---|---|---|---|---|---|---|---|---|---|---|---|---|---|---|---|---|---|---|---|---|---|---|---|---|---|---|
| Year | Team | Lg | G | GS | CG | GF | IP | BFP | H | R | ER | HR | SH | SF | HB | TBB | IBB | SO | WP | Bk | W | L | Pct | Sh | Sv-Op | Hld | ERC | ERA |
| 2011 | Batvia | A- | 10 | 7 | 0 | 0 | 39.2 | 151 | 27 | 11 | 4 | 0 | 0 | 1 | 1 | 3 | 0 | 31 | 0 | 0 | 0 | 1 | .000 | 0 | 0- - | - | 1.13 | 0.91 |
| 2011 | PlmBh | A+ | 3 | 0 | 0 | 0 | 8.1 | 35 | 7 | 4 | 4 | 0 | 0 | 0 | 1 | 2 | 0 | 8 | 0 | 0 | 1 | 0 | 1.000 | 0 | 0- - | - | 2.37 | 4.32 |
| 2011 | QuadC | A | 2 | 0 | 0 | 0 | 5.0 | 18 | 4 | 1 | 1 | 0 | 0 | 0 | 0 | 0 | 0 | 3 | 0 | 0 | 1 | 0 | 1.000 | 0 | 0- - | - | 1.34 | 1.80 |
| 2012 | PlmBh | A+ | 7 | 7 | 0 | 0 | 46.0 | 177 | 45 | 13 | 11 | 5 | 0 | 0 | 0 | 1 | 0 | 29 | 0 | 0 | 3 | 1 | .750 | 0 | 0- - | - | 2.65 | 2.15 |
| 2012 | Sprgfld | AA | 20 | 20 | 1 | 0 | 123.2 | 503 | 122 | 50 | 45 | 13 | 3 | 2 | 6 | 9 | 0 | 83 | 2 | 0 | 11 | 3 | .786 | 0 | 0- - | - | 2.94 | 3.27 |
| 2013 | Memp | AAA | 4 | 4 | 0 | 0 | 25.0 | 109 | 34 | 12 | 12 | 2 | 1 | 2 | 1 | 3 | 0 | 18 | 0 | 0 | 2 | 2 | .500 | 0 | 0- - | - | 5.10 | 4.32 |
| 2013 | StL | NL | 66 | 0 | 0 | 4 | 62.0 | 249 | 65 | 17 | 16 | 4 | 4 | 0 | 1 | 13 | 7 | 35 | 2 | 0 | 5 | 2 | .714 | 0 | 1-3 | 15 | 3.41 | 2.32 |

# Jeff Manship

**Pitches:** R **Bats:** R **Pos:** RP-7; SP-4 **Ht:** 6'2" **Wt:** 210 **Born:** 1/16/1985 **Age:** 29

| | | | HOW MUCH HE PITCHED | | | | | | WHAT HE GAVE UP | | | | | | | | | | | | THE RESULTS | | | | | | | |
|---|---|---|---|---|---|---|---|---|---|---|---|---|---|---|---|---|---|---|---|---|---|---|---|---|---|---|---|---|
| Year | Team | Lg | G | GS | CG | GF | IP | BFP | H | R | ER | HR | SH | SF | HB | TBB | IBB | SO | WP | Bk | W | L | Pct | Sh | Sv-Op | Hld | ERC | ERA |
| 2013 | ColSpr* | AAA | 24 | 17 | 0 | 4 | 104.0 | 450 | 114 | 66 | 56 | 8 | 6 | 4 | 1 | 32 | 0 | 71 | 7 | 0 | 6 | 8 | .429 | 0 | 0- - | - | 4.11 | 4.85 |
| 2009 | Min | AL | 11 | 5 | 0 | 1 | 31.2 | 146 | 39 | 21 | 20 | 4 | 1 | 3 | 1 | 15 | 0 | 21 | 2 | 0 | 1 | 1 | .500 | 0 | 0-0 | 0 | 6.11 | 5.68 |
| 2010 | Min | AL | 13 | 1 | 0 | 1 | 29.0 | 124 | 34 | 20 | 17 | 3 | 1 | 1 | 0 | 6 | 0 | 21 | 0 | 0 | 2 | 1 | .667 | 0 | 0-0 | 0 | 4.31 | 5.28 |
| 2011 | Min | AL | 5 | 0 | 0 | 1 | 3.1 | 19 | 5 | 3 | 3 | 0 | 0 | 2 | 0 | 4 | 1 | 2 | 0 | 0 | 0 | 0 | - | 0 | 0-0 | 0 | 8.73 | 8.10 |
| 2012 | Min | AL | 12 | 0 | 0 | 2 | 21.2 | 98 | 29 | 19 | 19 | 4 | 1 | 0 | 1 | 7 | 1 | 12 | 0 | 0 | 0 | 0 | - | 0 | 0-0 | 1 | 6.67 | 7.89 |
| 2013 | Col | NL | 11 | 4 | 0 | 3 | 30.2 | 139 | 37 | 25 | 24 | 6 | 0 | 3 | 0 | 12 | 1 | 18 | 0 | 0 | 0 | 5 | .000 | 0 | 0-0 | 0 | 5.87 | 7.04 |
| 5 ML YEARS | | | 52 | 10 | 0 | 8 | 116.1 | 526 | 144 | 88 | 83 | 17 | 3 | 9 | 2 | 44 | 3 | 74 | 2 | 0 | 3 | 7 | .300 | 0 | 0-0 | 1 | 5.77 | 6.42 |

# Shaun Marcum

**Pitches:** R **Bats:** R **Pos:** SP-12; RP-2 **Ht:** 6'0" **Wt:** 195 **Born:** 12/14/1981 **Age:** 32

| | | | HOW MUCH HE PITCHED | | | | | | WHAT HE GAVE UP | | | | | | | | | | | | THE RESULTS | | | | | | | |
|---|---|---|---|---|---|---|---|---|---|---|---|---|---|---|---|---|---|---|---|---|---|---|---|---|---|---|---|---|
| Year | Team | Lg | G | GS | CG | GF | IP | BFP | H | R | ER | HR | SH | SF | HB | TBB | IBB | SO | WP | Bk | W | L | Pct | Sh | Sv-Op | Hld | ERC | ERA |
| 2005 | Tor | AL | 5 | 0 | 0 | 3 | 8.0 | 32 | 6 | 0 | 0 | 0 | 0 | 0 | 0 | 4 | 0 | 4 | 0 | 0 | 0 | 0 | - | 0 | 0-0 | 0 | 2.58 | 0.00 |
| 2006 | Tor | AL | 21 | 14 | 0 | 3 | 78.1 | 357 | 87 | 44 | 44 | 14 | 1 | 2 | 4 | 38 | 3 | 65 | 1 | 0 | 3 | 4 | .429 | 0 | 0-0 | 0 | 5.80 | 5.06 |
| 2007 | Tor | AL | 38 | 25 | 0 | 6 | 159.0 | 660 | 149 | 76 | 73 | 27 | 3 | 3 | 5 | 49 | 1 | 122 | 1 | 0 | 12 | 6 | .667 | 0 | 1-2 | 1 | 4.00 | 4.13 |
| 2008 | Tor | AL | 25 | 25 | 0 | 0 | 151.1 | 630 | 126 | 60 | 57 | 21 | 1 | 3 | 8 | 50 | 2 | 123 | 3 | 0 | 9 | 7 | .563 | 0 | 0-0 | 0 | 3.32 | 3.39 |
| 2010 | Tor | AL | 31 | 31 | 1 | 0 | 195.1 | 800 | 181 | 84 | 79 | 24 | 1 | 3 | 6 | 43 | 3 | 165 | 3 | 0 | 13 | 8 | .619 | 0 | 0-0 | 0 | 3.24 | 3.64 |
| 2011 | Mil | NL | 33 | 33 | 0 | 0 | 200.2 | 823 | 175 | 84 | 79 | 22 | 6 | 6 | 0 | 57 | 3 | 158 | 6 | 0 | 13 | 7 | .650 | 0 | 0-0 | 0 | 2.97 | 3.54 |
| 2012 | Mil | NL | 21 | 21 | 0 | 0 | 124.0 | 527 | 116 | 57 | 51 | 16 | 6 | 2 | 4 | 41 | 2 | 109 | 3 | 2 | 7 | 4 | .636 | 0 | 0-0 | 0 | 3.71 | 3.70 |
| 2013 | NYM | NL | 14 | 12 | 0 | 2 | 78.1 | 334 | 85 | 48 | 46 | 7 | 6 | 4 | 4 | 21 | 2 | 60 | 2 | 0 | 1 | 10 | .091 | 0 | 0-0 | 0 | 4.17 | 5.29 |
| Postseason | | | 3 | 3 | 0 | 0 | 9.2 | 49 | 17 | 16 | 16 | 3 | 1 | 0 | 0 | 5 | 1 | 5 | 0 | 0 | 0 | 3 | .000 | 0 | 0-0 | 0 | 11.38 | 14.90 |
| 8 ML YEARS | | | 188 | 161 | 1 | 14 | 995.0 | 4163 | 925 | 453 | 429 | 131 | 24 | 23 | 31 | 303 | 16 | 806 | 19 | 2 | 58 | 46 | .558 | 0 | 1-2 | 1 | 3.63 | 3.88 |

# Jake Marisnick

**Bats:** R **Throws:** R **Pos:** CF-32;PH-6;PR-2 mah-RIZ-nick **Ht:** 6'3" **Wt:** 225 **Born:** 3/30/1991 **Age:** 23

| BATTING | | | | | | | | | | | | | | | | | | | | | | BASERUNNING | | | | AVERAGES | | |
|---|---|---|---|---|---|---|---|---|---|---|---|---|---|---|---|---|---|---|---|---|---|---|---|---|---|---|---|---|
| Year | Team | Lg | G | AB | H | 2B | 3B | HR | (Hm | Rd) | TB | R | RBI | RC | TBB | IBB | SO | HBP | SH | SF | | SB | CS | SB% | GDP | Avg | OBP | Slg |
| 2010 | B Jays | R | 35 | 122 | 35 | 12 | 0 | 3 | (- | -) | 56 | 17 | 14 | 24 | 13 | 0 | 18 | 5 | 0 | 2 | | 14 | 1 | .93 | 2 | .287 | .373 | .459 |
| 2010 | Lnsng | A | 34 | 127 | 28 | 8 | 2 | 1 | (- | -) | 43 | 16 | 12 | 14 | 9 | 0 | 37 | 5 | 2 | 0 | | 9 | 2 | .82 | 3 | .220 | .298 | .339 |
| 2011 | Lnsng | A | 118 | 462 | 148 | 27 | 6 | 14 | (- | -) | 229 | 68 | 77 | 95 | 43 | 4 | 91 | 14 | 0 | 4 | | 37 | 8 | .82 | 9 | .320 | .392 | .496 |
| 2012 | Dnedin | A+ | 65 | 266 | 70 | 18 | 7 | 6 | (- | -) | 120 | 41 | 35 | 44 | 26 | 0 | 55 | 10 | 2 | 2 | | 10 | 5 | .67 | 1 | .263 | .349 | .451 |
| 2012 | NHam | AA | 55 | 223 | 52 | 11 | 3 | 2 | (- | -) | 75 | 25 | 15 | 23 | 11 | 0 | 45 | 7 | 2 | 4 | | 14 | 4 | .78 | 6 | .233 | .286 | .336 |
| 2013 | Jupiter | A+ | 3 | 15 | 3 | 1 | 0 | 0 | (- | -) | 4 | 2 | 0 | 0 | 0 | 0 | 1 | 0 | 0 | 0 | | 0 | 0 | - | 0 | .200 | .200 | .267 |
| 2013 | Jaxnvl | AA | 67 | 265 | 78 | 13 | 3 | 12 | (- | -) | 133 | 43 | 46 | 48 | 17 | 0 | 68 | 11 | 2 | 3 | | 11 | 6 | .65 | 4 | .294 | .358 | .502 |
| 2013 | Mia | NL | 40 | 109 | 20 | 2 | 1 | 1 | (1 | 0) | 27 | 6 | 5 | 7 | 6 | 0 | 27 | 1 | 1 | 1 | | 3 | 1 | .75 | 1 | .183 | .231 | .248 |

# Nick Markakis

**Bats:** L **Throws:** L **Pos:** RF-155;DH-4;PH-1 mar-KAY-kiss **Ht:** 6'1" **Wt:** 190 **Born:** 11/17/1983 **Age:** 30

| BATTING | | | | | | | | | | | | | | | | | | | | | | BASERUNNING | | | | AVERAGES | | |
|---|---|---|---|---|---|---|---|---|---|---|---|---|---|---|---|---|---|---|---|---|---|---|---|---|---|---|---|---|
| Year | Team | Lg | G | AB | H | 2B | 3B | HR | (Hm | Rd) | TB | R | RBI | RC | TBB | IBB | SO | HBP | SH | SF | | SB | CS | SB% | GDP | Avg | OBP | Slg |
| 2006 | Bal | AL | 147 | 491 | 143 | 25 | 2 | 16 | (9 | 7) | 220 | 72 | 62 | 67 | 43 | 3 | 72 | 3 | 3 | 2 | | 2 | 0 | 1.00 | 15 | .291 | .351 | .448 |
| 2007 | Bal | AL | 161 | 637 | 191 | 43 | 3 | 23 | (15 | 8) | 309 | 97 | 112 | 103 | 61 | 5 | 112 | 5 | 1 | 6 | | 18 | 6 | .75 | 22 | .300 | .362 | .485 |
| 2008 | Bal | AL | 157 | 595 | 182 | 48 | 1 | 20 | (11 | 9) | 292 | 106 | 87 | 113 | 99 | 7 | 113 | 2 | 0 | 1 | | 10 | 7 | .59 | 10 | .306 | .406 | .491 |
| 2009 | Bal | AL | **161** | 642 | 188 | 45 | 2 | 18 | (8 | 10) | 291 | 94 | 101 | 97 | 56 | 0 | 98 | 3 | 0 | **10** | | 6 | 2 | .75 | 12 | .293 | .347 | .453 |
| 2010 | Bal | AL | 160 | 629 | 187 | 45 | 3 | 12 | (8 | 4) | 274 | 79 | 60 | 99 | 73 | 9 | 93 | 2 | 0 | 5 | | 7 | 2 | .78 | 18 | .297 | .370 | .436 |
| 2011 | Bal | AL | 160 | 641 | 182 | 31 | 1 | 15 | (8 | 7) | 260 | 72 | 73 | 90 | 62 | 6 | 75 | 7 | 0 | 6 | | 12 | 3 | .80 | 16 | .284 | .351 | .406 |
| 2012 | Bal | AL | 104 | 420 | 125 | 28 | 3 | 13 | (9 | 4) | 198 | 59 | 54 | 69 | 42 | 3 | 51 | 4 | 0 | 5 | | 1 | 1 | .50 | 11 | .298 | .363 | .471 |
| 2013 | Bal | AL | 160 | 634 | 172 | 24 | 0 | 10 | (6 | 4) | 226 | 89 | 59 | 66 | 55 | 3 | 76 | 3 | 0 | 8 | | 1 | 2 | .33 | 17 | .271 | .329 | .356 |
| 8 ML YEARS | | | 1210 | 4689 | 1370 | 289 | 15 | 127 | (74 | 53) | 2070 | 668 | 608 | 704 | 491 | 36 | 690 | 29 | 4 | 43 | | 57 | 23 | .71 | 121 | .292 | .360 | .441 |

# Carlos Marmol

**Pitches:** R **Bats:** R **Pos:** RP-52 mar-MOLE **Ht:** 6'2" **Wt:** 215 **Born:** 10/14/1982 **Age:** 31

| HOW MUCH HE PITCHED | | | | | | | | | WHAT HE GAVE UP | | | | | | | | | | | | THE RESULTS | | | | | | | |
|---|---|---|---|---|---|---|---|---|---|---|---|---|---|---|---|---|---|---|---|---|---|---|---|---|---|---|---|---|
| Year | Team | Lg | G | GS | CG | GF | IP | BFP | H | R | ER | HR | SH | SF | HB | TBB | IBB | SO | WP | Bk | W | L | Pct | Sh | Sv-Op | Hld | ERC | ERA |
| 2013 | RCuca* | A+ | 3 | 0 | 0 | 1 | 3.0 | 14 | 4 | 2 | 2 | 2 | 0 | 0 | 0 | 1 | 0 | 4 | 1 | 0 | 0 | 0 | - | 0 | 1- - | - | 10.06 | 6.00 |
| 2013 | Chatt* | AA | 2 | 0 | 0 | 1 | 2.0 | 8 | 0 | 0 | 0 | 0 | 0 | 0 | 1 | 1 | 0 | 2 | 0 | 0 | 0 | 0 | - | 0 | 0- - | - | 0.95 | 0.00 |
| 2006 | ChC | NL | 19 | 13 | 0 | 1 | 77.0 | 356 | 71 | 54 | 52 | 14 | 6 | 2 | 5 | 59 | 2 | 59 | 3 | 1 | 5 | 7 | .417 | 0 | 0-0 | 0 | 6.01 | 6.08 |
| 2007 | ChC | NL | 59 | 0 | 0 | 6 | 69.1 | 285 | 41 | 11 | 11 | 3 | 1 | 2 | 4 | 35 | 3 | 96 | 5 | 1 | 5 | 1 | .833 | 0 | 1-2 | 16 | 2.11 | 1.43 |
| 2008 | ChC | NL | 82 | 0 | 0 | 22 | 87.1 | 348 | 40 | 30 | 26 | 10 | 2 | 3 | 6 | 41 | 3 | 114 | 6 | 1 | 2 | 4 | .333 | 0 | 7-9 | **30** | 1.86 | 2.68 |
| 2009 | ChC | NL | 79 | 0 | 0 | 29 | 74.0 | 335 | 43 | 29 | 28 | 2 | 4 | 1 | 12 | 65 | 3 | 93 | 6 | 1 | 2 | 4 | .333 | 0 | 15-19 | 27 | 3.55 | 3.41 |
| 2010 | ChC | NL | 77 | 0 | 0 | 70 | 77.2 | 332 | 40 | 23 | 22 | 1 | 0 | 0 | 8 | 52 | 4 | 138 | 2 | 2 | 2 | 3 | .400 | 0 | 38-43 | 0 | 2.18 | 2.55 |
| 2011 | ChC | NL | 75 | 0 | 0 | 61 | 74.0 | 327 | 54 | 33 | 33 | 5 | 4 | 2 | 9 | 48 | 2 | 99 | 4 | 0 | 2 | 6 | .250 | 0 | 34-44 | 2 | 3.71 | 4.01 |
| 2012 | ChC | NL | 61 | 0 | 0 | 47 | 55.1 | 247 | 40 | 24 | 21 | 4 | 0 | 0 | 2 | 45 | 0 | 72 | 2 | 0 | 3 | 3 | .500 | 0 | 20-23 | 2 | 4.07 | 3.42 |
| 2013 | 2 Tms | NL | 52 | 0 | 0 | 17 | 49.0 | 225 | 40 | 26 | 24 | 7 | 1 | 2 | 4 | 40 | 3 | 59 | 5 | 1 | 2 | 4 | .333 | 0 | 2-5 | 6 | 5.25 | 4.41 |
| 13 | ChC | NL | 31 | 0 | 0 | 9 | 27.2 | 129 | 26 | 19 | 18 | 6 | 1 | 1 | 3 | 21 | 1 | 32 | 2 | 0 | 2 | 4 | .333 | 0 | 2-5 | 5 | 6.57 | 5.86 |
| 13 | LAD | NL | 21 | 0 | 0 | 8 | 21.1 | 96 | 14 | 7 | 6 | 1 | 0 | 1 | 1 | 19 | 2 | 27 | 3 | 1 | 0 | 0 | - | 0 | 0-0 | 1 | 3.65 | 2.53 |
| Postseason | | | 4 | 0 | 0 | 0 | 5.2 | 26 | 6 | 5 | 5 | 2 | 1 | 1 | 0 | 3 | 0 | 9 | 0 | 0 | 0 | 1 | .000 | 0 | 0-0 | 0 | 6.73 | 7.94 |
| 8 ML YEARS | | | 504 | 13 | 0 | 253 | 563.2 | 2455 | 369 | 230 | 217 | 46 | 18 | 12 | 50 | 385 | 20 | 730 | 33 | 7 | 23 | 32 | .418 | 0 | 117-145 | 83 | 3.40 | 3.46 |

# Nick Maronde

**Pitches:** L **Bats:** B **Pos:** RP-10 ma-RON-day **Ht:** 6'3" **Wt:** 205 **Born:** 9/5/1989 **Age:** 24

| HOW MUCH HE PITCHED | | | | | | | | | WHAT HE GAVE UP | | | | | | | | | | | | THE RESULTS | | | | | | | |
|---|---|---|---|---|---|---|---|---|---|---|---|---|---|---|---|---|---|---|---|---|---|---|---|---|---|---|---|---|
| Year | Team | Lg | G | GS | CG | GF | IP | BFP | H | R | ER | HR | SH | SF | HB | TBB | IBB | SO | WP | Bk | W | L | Pct | Sh | Sv-Op | Hld | ERC | ERA |
| 2011 | Orem | R+ | 11 | 11 | 0 | 0 | 46.1 | 185 | 36 | 12 | 11 | 5 | 1 | 0 | 2 | 15 | 0 | 50 | 0 | 0 | 5 | 0 | 1.000 | 0 | 0- - | - | 2.89 | 2.14 |
| 2012 | InldEm | A+ | 10 | 10 | 0 | 0 | 59.1 | 228 | 40 | 13 | 12 | 4 | 0 | 0 | 0 | 14 | 0 | 60 | 1 | 0 | 3 | 1 | .750 | 0 | 0- - | - | 1.68 | 1.82 |
| 2012 | Angels | R | 3 | 3 | 0 | 0 | 8.0 | 32 | 3 | 4 | 1 | 0 | 0 | 1 | 1 | 2 | 0 | 9 | 0 | 0 | 0 | 1 | .000 | 0 | 0- - | - | 0.80 | 1.13 |
| 2012 | Ark | AA | 7 | 5 | 0 | 0 | 32.1 | 135 | 39 | 13 | 12 | 1 | 0 | 1 | 1 | 3 | 0 | 21 | 0 | 0 | 3 | 2 | .600 | 0 | 0- - | - | 3.72 | 3.34 |
| 2013 | Ark | AA | 41 | 0 | 0 | 9 | 56.1 | 245 | 41 | 25 | 22 | 4 | 3 | 1 | 2 | 37 | 2 | 63 | 2 | 0 | 2 | 4 | .333 | 0 | 0- - | - | 3.42 | 3.51 |
| 2012 | LAA | AL | 12 | 0 | 0 | 1 | 6.0 | 27 | 6 | 1 | 1 | 0 | 0 | 1 | 0 | 3 | 0 | 7 | 0 | 0 | 0 | 0 | - | 0 | 0-0 | 3 | 3.63 | 1.50 |
| 2013 | LAA | AL | 10 | 0 | 0 | 2 | 5.1 | 28 | 4 | 6 | 4 | 1 | 0 | 0 | 0 | 8 | 1 | 5 | 1 | 0 | 0 | 0 | - | 0 | 0-0 | 2 | 7.27 | 6.75 |
| 2 ML YEARS | | | 22 | 0 | 0 | 3 | 11.1 | 55 | 10 | 7 | 5 | 1 | 0 | 1 | 0 | 11 | 1 | 12 | 1 | 0 | 0 | 0 | - | 0 | 0-0 | 5 | 5.27 | 3.97 |

# Jason Marquis

**Pitches:** R **Bats:** L **Pos:** SP-20 marr-KEE **Ht:** 6'1" **Wt:** 220 **Born:** 8/21/1978 **Age:** 35

| HOW MUCH HE PITCHED | | | | | | | | | WHAT HE GAVE UP | | | | | | | | | | | | THE RESULTS | | | | | | | |
|---|---|---|---|---|---|---|---|---|---|---|---|---|---|---|---|---|---|---|---|---|---|---|---|---|---|---|---|---|
| Year | Team | Lg | G | GS | CG | GF | IP | BFP | H | R | ER | HR | SH | SF | HB | TBB | IBB | SO | WP | Bk | W | L | Pct | Sh | Sv-Op | Hld | ERC | ERA |
| 2000 | Atl | NL | 15 | 0 | 0 | 7 | 23.1 | 103 | 23 | 16 | 13 | 4 | 1 | 1 | 1 | 12 | 1 | 17 | 1 | 0 | 1 | 0 | 1.000 | 0 | 0-1 | 1 | 5.13 | 5.01 |
| 2001 | Atl | NL | 38 | 16 | 0 | 9 | 129.1 | 556 | 113 | 62 | 50 | 14 | 6 | 5 | 4 | 59 | 4 | 98 | 1 | 2 | 5 | 6 | .455 | 0 | 0-2 | 2 | 3.70 | 3.48 |
| 2002 | Atl | NL | 22 | 22 | 0 | 0 | 114.1 | 507 | 127 | 66 | 64 | 19 | 4 | 3 | 3 | 49 | 3 | 84 | 4 | 0 | 8 | 9 | .471 | 0 | 0-0 | 0 | 5.43 | 5.04 |
| 2003 | Atl | NL | 21 | 2 | 0 | 10 | 40.2 | 182 | 43 | 27 | 25 | 3 | 3 | 0 | 3 | 18 | 2 | 19 | 2 | 0 | 0 | 0 | - | 0 | 1-1 | 0 | 4.45 | 5.53 |
| 2004 | StL | NL | 32 | 32 | 0 | 0 | 201.1 | 874 | 215 | 90 | 83 | 26 | 5 | 6 | 10 | 70 | 1 | 138 | 6 | 0 | 15 | 7 | .682 | 0 | 0-0 | 0 | 4.69 | 3.71 |
| 2005 | StL | NL | 33 | 32 | 3 | 0 | 207.0 | 868 | 206 | 110 | 95 | 29 | 4 | 3 | 5 | 69 | 2 | 100 | 10 | 3 | 13 | 14 | .481 | 1 | 0-0 | 0 | 4.23 | 4.13 |
| 2006 | StL | NL | 33 | 33 | 0 | 0 | 194.1 | 870 | 221 | **136** | **130** | **35** | 12 | 3 | 16 | 75 | 2 | 96 | 2 | 1 | 14 | **16** | .467 | 0 | 0-0 | 0 | 5.79 | 6.02 |
| 2007 | ChC | NL | 34 | 33 | 1 | 0 | 191.2 | 846 | 190 | 111 | 98 | 22 | 13 | 1 | 13 | 76 | 6 | 109 | 3 | 0 | 12 | 9 | .571 | 1 | 0-0 | 0 | 4.28 | 4.60 |
| 2008 | ChC | NL | 29 | 28 | 0 | 0 | 167.0 | 738 | 172 | 87 | 84 | 15 | 10 | 7 | 8 | 70 | 6 | 91 | 8 | 1 | 11 | 9 | .550 | 0 | 0-0 | 1 | 4.35 | 4.53 |
| 2009 | Col | NL | 33 | 33 | 2 | 0 | 216.0 | 921 | 218 | 104 | 97 | 15 | 10 | 10 | 4 | 80 | 6 | 115 | 6 | 1 | 15 | 13 | .536 | 1 | 0-0 | 0 | 3.86 | 4.04 |
| 2010 | Was | NL | 13 | 13 | 0 | 0 | 58.2 | 276 | 76 | 47 | 43 | 9 | 3 | 0 | 8 | 24 | 0 | 31 | 1 | 1 | 2 | 9 | .182 | 0 | 0-0 | 0 | 6.93 | 6.60 |
| 2011 | 2 Tms | NL | 23 | 23 | 1 | 0 | 132.0 | 587 | 154 | 74 | 65 | 11 | 9 | 5 | 5 | 43 | 1 | 76 | 1 | 0 | 8 | 6 | .571 | 1 | 0-0 | 0 | 4.72 | 4.43 |
| 2012 | 2 Tms | | 22 | 22 | 1 | 0 | 127.2 | 561 | 146 | 86 | 74 | 23 | 6 | 4 | 4 | 42 | 3 | 91 | 6 | 0 | 8 | 11 | .421 | 1 | 0-0 | 0 | 5.31 | 5.22 |
| 2013 | SD | NL | 20 | 20 | 0 | 0 | 117.2 | 518 | 111 | 61 | 53 | 18 | 8 | 6 | 4 | 68 | 2 | 72 | 2 | 0 | 9 | 5 | .643 | 0 | 0-0 | 0 | 5.04 | 4.05 |
| 11 | Was | NL | 20 | 20 | 1 | 0 | 120.2 | 524 | 132 | 58 | 53 | 8 | 8 | 5 | 4 | 39 | 1 | 71 | 1 | 0 | 8 | 5 | .615 | 1 | 0-0 | 0 | 4.19 | 3.95 |

| | | | HOW MUCH HE PITCHED | | | | | | WHAT HE GAVE UP | | | | | | | | | | | | THE RESULTS | | | | | | | |
|---|---|---|---|---|---|---|---|---|---|---|---|---|---|---|---|---|---|---|---|---|---|---|---|---|---|---|---|
| Year | Team | Lg | G | GS | CG | GF | IP | BFP | H | R | ER | HR | SH | SF | HB | TBB | IBB | SO | WP | Bk | W | L | Pct | Sh | Sv-Op | Hld | ERC | ERA |
| 11 | Ari | NL | 3 | 3 | 0 | 0 | 11.1 | 63 | 22 | 16 | 12 | 3 | 1 | 0 | 1 | 4 | 0 | 5 | 0 | 0 | 0 | 1 | .000 | 0 | 0-0 | 0 | 11.25 | 9.53 |
| 12 | Min | AL | 7 | 7 | 0 | 0 | 34.0 | 160 | 52 | 33 | 32 | 9 | 1 | 2 | 3 | 14 | 0 | 12 | 1 | 0 | 2 | 4 | .333 | 0 | 0-0 | 0 | 9.67 | 8.47 |
| 12 | SD | NL | 15 | 15 | 1 | 0 | 93.2 | 401 | 94 | 53 | 42 | 14 | 5 | 2 | 1 | 28 | 3 | 79 | 5 | 0 | 6 | 7 | .462 | 1 | 0-0 | 0 | 3.97 | 4.04 |
| Postseason | | | 11 | 3 | 0 | 6 | 23.2 | 115 | 25 | 17 | 12 | 6 | 4 | 1 | 0 | 18 | 1 | 14 | 0 | 0 | 0 | 2 | .000 | 0 | 0-0 | 0 | 6.85 | 4.56 |
| 14 ML YEARS | | | 368 | 309 | 8 | 26 | 1921.0 | 8407 | 2015 | 1077 | 974 | 243 | 91 | 57 | 87 | 755 | 39 | 1137 | 53 | 9 | 121 | 114 | .515 | 5 | 1-4 | 4 | 4.68 | 4.56 |

## Chris Marrero

**Bats:** R **Throws:** R **Pos:** PH-5;1B-3;DH-1 **Ht:** 6'3" **Wt:** 230 **Born:** 7/2/1988 **Age:** 25

| | | | BATTING | | | | | | | | | | | | | | | | | BASERUNNING | | | | AVERAGES | | |
|---|---|---|---|---|---|---|---|---|---|---|---|---|---|---|---|---|---|---|---|---|---|---|---|---|---|---|
| Year | Team | Lg | G | AB | H | 2B | 3B | HR | (Hm | Rd) | TB | R | RBI | RC | TBB | IBB | SO | HBP | SH | SF | SB | CS | SB% | GDP | Avg | OBP | Slg |
| 2009 | Ptomc | A+ | 112 | 414 | 119 | 21 | 2 | 16 | (- | -) | 192 | 58 | 65 | 71 | 42 | 0 | 97 | 8 | 0 | 5 | 2 | 3 | .40 | 7 | .287 | .360 | .464 |
| 2009 | Hrsbrg | AA | 23 | 75 | 20 | 6 | 0 | 1 | (- | -) | 29 | 9 | 11 | 10 | 8 | 0 | 18 | 1 | 0 | 0 | 0 | 1 | .00 | 2 | .267 | .345 | .387 |
| 2010 | Hrsbrg | AA | 141 | 524 | 154 | 28 | 0 | 18 | (- | -) | 236 | 73 | 82 | 84 | 43 | 2 | 102 | 5 | 0 | 5 | 1 | 3 | .25 | 16 | .294 | .350 | .450 |
| 2011 | Syrcse | AAA | 127 | 483 | 145 | 30 | 0 | 14 | (- | -) | 217 | 59 | 69 | 84 | 58 | 2 | 97 | 2 | 0 | 3 | 3 | 2 | .60 | 14 | .300 | .375 | .449 |
| 2012 | Syrcse | AAA | 37 | 127 | 31 | 6 | 1 | 0 | (- | -) | 39 | 13 | 12 | 14 | 16 | 0 | 28 | 1 | 0 | 0 | 0 | 0 | - | 6 | .244 | .333 | .307 |
| 2012 | Hgrstn | A | 2 | 4 | 1 | 1 | 0 | 0 | (- | -) | 2 | 1 | 0 | 1 | 1 | 0 | 2 | 1 | 0 | 0 | 0 | 0 | - | 0 | .250 | .500 | .500 |
| 2012 | Ptomc | A+ | 4 | 13 | 6 | 1 | 0 | 1 | (- | -) | 10 | 1 | 4 | 3 | 0 | 0 | 2 | 0 | 0 | 0 | 0 | 0 | - | 0 | .462 | .462 | .769 |
| 2012 | Hrsbrg | AA | 5 | 22 | 6 | 2 | 0 | 1 | (- | -) | 11 | 2 | 3 | 3 | 0 | 0 | 3 | 1 | 0 | 0 | 0 | 0 | - | 0 | .273 | .304 | .500 |
| 2012 | Auburn | A- | 5 | 14 | 5 | 1 | 0 | 1 | (- | -) | 9 | 4 | 3 | 3 | 2 | 0 | 6 | 0 | 0 | 0 | 0 | 0 | - | 0 | .357 | .438 | .643 |
| 2013 | Syrcse | AAA | 111 | 408 | 110 | 17 | 2 | 11 | (- | -) | 164 | 48 | 59 | 56 | 36 | 2 | 67 | 3 | 0 | 3 | 0 | 1 | .00 | 15 | .270 | .331 | .402 |
| 2011 | Was | NL | 31 | 109 | 27 | 5 | 0 | 0 | (0 | 0) | 32 | 6 | 10 | 7 | 4 | 0 | 27 | 1 | 0 | 3 | 0 | 0 | - | 1 | .248 | .274 | .294 |
| 2013 | Was | NL | 8 | 16 | 2 | 0 | 0 | 0 | (0 | 0) | 2 | 0 | 1 | 0 | 0 | 0 | 4 | 0 | 0 | 0 | 0 | 0 | - | 0 | .125 | .125 | .125 |
| 2 ML YEARS | | | 39 | 125 | 29 | 5 | 0 | 0 | (0 | 0) | 34 | 6 | 11 | 7 | 4 | 0 | 31 | 1 | 0 | 3 | 0 | 0 | - | 1 | .232 | .256 | .272 |

## Brett Marshall

**Pitches:** R **Bats:** R **Pos:** RP-3 **Ht:** 6'1" **Wt:** 195 **Born:** 3/22/1990 **Age:** 24

| | | | HOW MUCH HE PITCHED | | | | | | WHAT HE GAVE UP | | | | | | | | | | | | THE RESULTS | | | | | | | |
|---|---|---|---|---|---|---|---|---|---|---|---|---|---|---|---|---|---|---|---|---|---|---|---|---|---|---|---|---|
| Year | Team | Lg | G | GS | CG | GF | IP | BFP | H | R | ER | HR | SH | SF | HB | TBB | IBB | SO | WP | Bk | W | L | Pct | Sh | Sv-Op | Hld | ERC | ERA |
| 2009 | CtnSC | A | 17 | 17 | 0 | 0 | 87.1 | 393 | 98 | 67 | 54 | 7 | 4 | 5 | 9 | 37 | 0 | 60 | 8 | 0 | 3 | 6 | .333 | 0 | 0- - | - | 5.19 | 5.56 |
| 2010 | Yanks | R | 2 | 1 | 0 | 0 | 8.0 | 36 | 6 | 5 | 2 | 0 | 0 | 0 | 1 | 4 | 0 | 8 | 0 | 0 | 0 | 0 | - | 0 | 0- - | - | 2.71 | 2.25 |
| 2010 | CtnSC | A | 13 | 13 | 1 | 0 | 72.0 | 289 | 52 | 26 | 20 | 2 | 2 | 3 | 1 | 22 | 0 | 56 | 5 | 0 | 4 | 2 | .667 | 1 | 0- - | - | 1.90 | 2.50 |
| 2010 | Tampa | A+ | 1 | 1 | 0 | 0 | 4.0 | 17 | 5 | 3 | 2 | 0 | 0 | 0 | 0 | 0 | 0 | 6 | 0 | 0 | 0 | 0 | - | 0 | 0- - | - | 3.14 | 4.50 |
| 2011 | Tampa | A+ | 27 | 26 | 0 | 0 | 140.1 | 587 | 142 | 67 | 59 | 6 | 7 | 4 | 4 | 48 | 0 | 114 | 5 | 0 | 9 | 7 | .563 | 0 | 0- - | - | 3.73 | 3.78 |
| 2012 | Trntn | AA | 27 | 27 | 0 | 0 | 158.1 | 663 | 151 | 68 | 62 | 15 | 4 | 5 | 9 | 53 | 1 | 120 | 12 | 2 | 13 | 7 | .650 | 0 | 0- - | - | 3.81 | 3.52 |
| 2013 | S-WB | AAA | 25 | 25 | 0 | 0 | 138.2 | 616 | 144 | 88 | 79 | 17 | 4 | 9 | 4 | 68 | 1 | 120 | 12 | 0 | 7 | 10 | .412 | 0 | 0- - | - | 4.95 | 5.13 |
| 2013 | NYY | AL | 3 | 0 | 0 | 1 | 12.0 | 54 | 13 | 6 | 6 | 3 | 0 | 0 | 1 | 7 | 0 | 7 | 2 | 0 | 0 | 0 | - | 0 | 0-0 | 0 | 7.12 | 4.50 |

## Sean Marshall

**Pitches:** L **Bats:** L **Pos:** RP-16 **Ht:** 6'7" **Wt:** 225 **Born:** 8/30/1982 **Age:** 31

| | | | HOW MUCH HE PITCHED | | | | | | WHAT HE GAVE UP | | | | | | | | | | | | THE RESULTS | | | | | | | |
|---|---|---|---|---|---|---|---|---|---|---|---|---|---|---|---|---|---|---|---|---|---|---|---|---|---|---|---|---|
| Year | Team | Lg | G | GS | CG | GF | IP | BFP | H | R | ER | HR | SH | SF | HB | TBB | IBB | SO | WP | Bk | W | L | Pct | Sh | Sv-Op | Hld | ERC | ERA |
| 2013 | Lsvlle* | AAA | 2 | 2 | 0 | 0 | 2.0 | 8 | 2 | 0 | 0 | 0 | 0 | 0 | 0 | 0 | 0 | 4 | 0 | 0 | 0 | 0 | - | 0 | 0- - | - | 1.95 | 0.00 |
| 2006 | ChC | NL | 24 | 24 | 0 | 0 | 125.2 | 563 | 132 | 85 | 78 | 20 | 7 | 1 | 7 | 59 | 3 | 77 | 6 | 0 | 6 | 9 | .400 | 0 | 0-0 | 0 | 5.27 | 5.59 |
| 2007 | ChC | NL | 21 | 19 | 0 | 0 | 103.1 | 446 | 107 | 52 | 45 | 13 | 7 | 2 | 1 | 35 | 3 | 67 | 4 | 0 | 7 | 8 | .467 | 0 | 0-0 | 0 | 4.18 | 3.92 |
| 2008 | ChC | NL | 34 | 7 | 0 | 6 | 65.1 | 279 | 60 | 28 | 28 | 9 | 4 | 3 | 4 | 23 | 4 | 58 | 3 | 0 | 3 | 5 | .375 | 0 | 1-2 | 3 | 3.82 | 3.86 |
| 2009 | ChC | NL | 55 | 9 | 1 | 10 | 85.1 | 373 | 91 | 43 | 41 | 10 | 7 | 1 | 1 | 32 | 4 | 68 | 2 | 0 | 3 | 7 | .300 | 0 | 0-0 | 7 | 4.43 | 4.32 |
| 2010 | ChC | NL | 80 | 0 | 0 | 16 | 74.2 | 307 | 58 | 25 | 22 | 3 | 2 | 2 | 2 | 25 | 5 | 90 | 1 | 0 | 7 | 5 | .583 | 0 | 1-3 | 22 | 2.26 | 2.65 |
| 2011 | ChC | NL | 78 | 0 | 0 | 18 | 75.2 | 307 | 66 | 21 | 19 | 1 | 6 | 0 | 2 | 17 | 4 | 79 | 0 | 1 | 6 | 6 | .500 | 0 | 5-9 | 34 | 2.22 | 2.26 |
| 2012 | Cin | NL | 73 | 0 | 0 | 22 | 61.0 | 256 | 55 | 18 | 17 | 3 | 0 | 0 | 3 | 16 | 2 | 74 | 1 | 1 | 5 | 5 | .500 | 0 | 9-13 | 22 | 2.78 | 2.51 |
| 2013 | Cin | NL | 16 | 0 | 0 | 3 | 10.1 | 37 | 4 | 3 | 2 | 0 | 0 | 0 | 1 | 2 | 0 | 10 | 2 | 0 | 0 | 1 | .000 | 0 | 0-0 | 7 | 0.76 | 1.74 |
| Postseason | | | 5 | 0 | 0 | 0 | 7.1 | 25 | 2 | 1 | 1 | 1 | 0 | 0 | 0 | 1 | 0 | 8 | 0 | 0 | 0 | 0 | - | 0 | 0-0 | 1 | 0.58 | 1.23 |
| 8 ML YEARS | | | 381 | 59 | 1 | 75 | 601.1 | 2568 | 573 | 275 | 252 | 59 | 33 | 9 | 21 | 209 | 25 | 523 | 19 | 2 | 37 | 46 | .446 | 0 | 16-27 | 95 | 3.65 | 3.77 |

## Lou Marson

**Bats:** R **Throws:** R **Pos:** C-3 MARR-son **Ht:** 6'1" **Wt:** 205 **Born:** 6/26/1986 **Age:** 28

| | | | BATTING | | | | | | | | | | | | | | | | | BASERUNNING | | | | AVERAGES | | |
|---|---|---|---|---|---|---|---|---|---|---|---|---|---|---|---|---|---|---|---|---|---|---|---|---|---|---|
| Year | Team | Lg | G | AB | H | 2B | 3B | HR | (Hm | Rd) | TB | R | RBI | RC | TBB | IBB | SO | HBP | SH | SF | SB | CS | SB% | GDP | Avg | OBP | Slg |
| 2013 | Clmbs* | AAA | 8 | 20 | 2 | 0 | 0 | 0 | (- | -) | 2 | 0 | 1 | 0 | 3 | 0 | 8 | 0 | 0 | 0 | 0 | 0 | - | 1 | .100 | .217 | .100 |
| 2013 | Akron* | AA | 1 | 3 | 1 | 0 | 0 | 0 | (- | -) | 1 | 0 | 0 | 0 | 0 | 0 | 1 | 0 | 0 | 0 | 0 | 0 | - | 0 | .333 | .333 | .333 |
| 2008 | Phi | NL | 1 | 4 | 2 | 0 | 0 | 1 | (1 | 0) | 5 | 2 | 2 | 2 | 0 | 0 | 2 | 0 | 0 | 0 | 0 | 0 | - | 0 | .500 | .500 | 1.250 |
| 2009 | 2 Tms | | 21 | 61 | 15 | 7 | 0 | 0 | (0 | 0) | 22 | 9 | 4 | 7 | 10 | 0 | 21 | 0 | 0 | 1 | 0 | 0 | - | 3 | .246 | .347 | .361 |
| 2010 | Cle | AL | 87 | 262 | 51 | 15 | 0 | 3 | (0 | 3) | 75 | 29 | 22 | 17 | 26 | 0 | 55 | 3 | 2 | 1 | 8 | 1 | .89 | 7 | .195 | .274 | .286 |
| 2011 | Cle | AL | 79 | 243 | 56 | 9 | 2 | 1 | (0 | 1) | 72 | 26 | 19 | 19 | 24 | 0 | 68 | 1 | 2 | 2 | 4 | 2 | .67 | 7 | .230 | .300 | .296 |
| 2012 | Cle | AL | 70 | 195 | 44 | 8 | 2 | 0 | (0 | 0) | 56 | 27 | 13 | 18 | 36 | 0 | 44 | 1 | 2 | 1 | 4 | 2 | .67 | 10 | .226 | .348 | .287 |
| 2013 | Cle | AL | 3 | 3 | 0 | 0 | 0 | 0 | (0 | 0) | 0 | 0 | 0 | 0 | 2 | 0 | 0 | 0 | 0 | 0 | 0 | 0 | - | 0 | .000 | .400 | .000 |
| 09 | Phi | NL | 7 | 17 | 4 | 1 | 0 | 0 | (0 | 0) | 5 | 3 | 0 | 1 | 3 | 0 | 7 | 0 | 0 | 0 | 0 | 0 | - | 1 | .235 | .350 | .294 |
| 09 | Cle | AL | 14 | 44 | 11 | 6 | 0 | 0 | (0 | 0) | 17 | 6 | 4 | 6 | 7 | 0 | 14 | 0 | 0 | 1 | 0 | 0 | - | 2 | .250 | .346 | .386 |
| 6 ML YEARS | | | 261 | 768 | 168 | 39 | 4 | 5 | (1 | 4) | 230 | 93 | 60 | 63 | 98 | 0 | 190 | 5 | 6 | 5 | 16 | 5 | .76 | 27 | .219 | .309 | .299 |

## Alfredo Marte

**Bats:** R **Throws:** R **Pos:** PH-12;LF-9;RF-1;DH-1 marr-TAY **Ht:** 5'11" **Wt:** 195 **Born:** 3/31/1989 **Age:** 25

| BATTING | | | | | | | | | | | | | | | | | | | | BASERUNNING | | | | AVERAGES | | |
|---|---|---|---|---|---|---|---|---|---|---|---|---|---|---|---|---|---|---|---|---|---|---|---|---|---|---|
| Year Team | Lg | G | AB | H | 2B | 3B | HR | (Hm | Rd) | TB | R | RBI | RC | TBB | IBB | SO | HBP | SH | SF | SB | CS | SB% | GDP | Avg | OBP | Slg |
| 2009 Sbend | A | 120 | 475 | 119 | 27 | 3 | 7 | (- | -) | 173 | 49 | 71 | 52 | 25 | 0 | 78 | 4 | 2 | 0 | 5 | 2 | .71 | 15 | .251 | .294 | .364 |
| 2010 Visalia | A+ | 130 | 516 | 134 | 26 | 3 | 9 | (- | -) | 193 | 76 | 61 | 63 | 34 | 1 | 107 | 8 | 4 | 3 | 9 | 5 | .64 | 14 | .260 | .314 | .374 |
| 2011 Mobile | AA | 17 | 43 | 10 | 1 | 0 | 1 | (- | -) | 14 | 4 | 6 | 4 | 4 | 0 | 10 | 1 | 0 | 1 | 1 | 0 | 1.00 | 0 | .233 | .306 | .326 |
| 2011 Visalia | A+ | 59 | 234 | 70 | 15 | 3 | 7 | (- | -) | 112 | 35 | 33 | 39 | 14 | 0 | 43 | 2 | 0 | 0 | 5 | 0 | 1.00 | 7 | .299 | .344 | .479 |
| 2012 Mobile | AA | 113 | 398 | 117 | 25 | 3 | 20 | (- | -) | 208 | 68 | 75 | 75 | 34 | 1 | 72 | 11 | 0 | 3 | 6 | 6 | .50 | 12 | .294 | .363 | .523 |
| 2013 Reno | AAA | 86 | 311 | 87 | 24 | 1 | 7 | (- | -) | 134 | 37 | 48 | 46 | 22 | 1 | 63 | 6 | 0 | 4 | 2 | 1 | .67 | 10 | .280 | .335 | .431 |
| 2013 Ari | NL | 22 | 43 | 8 | 3 | 0 | 0 | (0 | 0) | 11 | 4 | 4 | 4 | 4 | 0 | 12 | 1 | 0 | 0 | 0 | 0 | - | 0 | .186 | .271 | .256 |

## Starling Marte

**Bats:** R **Throws:** R **Pos:** LF-124;CF-13;PR-8;PH-2 marr-TAY **Ht:** 6'1" **Wt:** 185 **Born:** 10/9/1988 **Age:** 25

| BATTING | | | | | | | | | | | | | | | | | | | | BASERUNNING | | | | AVERAGES | | |
|---|---|---|---|---|---|---|---|---|---|---|---|---|---|---|---|---|---|---|---|---|---|---|---|---|---|---|
| Year Team | Lg | G | AB | H | 2B | 3B | HR | (Hm | Rd) | TB | R | RBI | RC | TBB | IBB | SO | HBP | SH | SF | SB | CS | SB% | GDP | Avg | OBP | Slg |
| 2009 Pirates | R | 2 | 7 | 0 | 0 | 0 | 0 | (- | -) | 0 | 1 | 0 | 0 | 0 | 0 | 1 | 0 | 0 | 0 | 0 | 0 | - | 0 | .000 | .000 | .000 |
| 2009 WV | A | 54 | 221 | 69 | 9 | 5 | 3 | (- | -) | 97 | 41 | 34 | 39 | 12 | 0 | 55 | 12 | 0 | 2 | 24 | 7 | .77 | 2 | .312 | .377 | .439 |
| 2009 Lynbrg | A+ | 1 | 2 | 2 | 0 | 0 | 0 | (- | -) | 2 | 0 | 1 | 1 | 0 | 0 | 0 | 0 | 0 | 0 | 0 | 0 | - | 0 | 1.000 | 1.000 | 1.000 |
| 2010 Bradtn | A+ | 60 | 222 | 70 | 16 | 5 | 0 | (- | -) | 96 | 41 | 33 | 39 | 12 | 0 | 59 | 15 | 2 | 2 | 22 | 8 | .73 | 5 | .315 | .386 | .432 |
| 2010 Pirates | R | 8 | 26 | 9 | 3 | 0 | 2 | (- | -) | 18 | 6 | 5 | 6 | 1 | 0 | 6 | 1 | 0 | 0 | 4 | 1 | .80 | 0 | .346 | .393 | .692 |
| 2011 Altna | AA | 129 | 536 | 178 | 38 | 8 | 12 | (- | -) | 268 | 91 | 50 | 97 | 22 | 3 | 100 | 11 | 1 | 2 | 24 | 12 | .67 | 9 | .332 | .370 | .500 |
| 2012 Indy | AAA | 99 | 388 | 111 | 21 | 13 | 12 | (- | -) | 194 | 64 | 62 | 67 | 28 | 5 | 91 | 10 | 2 | 3 | 21 | 12 | .64 | 3 | .286 | .347 | .500 |
| 2012 StCol | A- | 1 | 5 | 0 | 0 | 0 | 0 | (- | -) | 0 | 0 | 0 | 0 | 0 | 0 | 3 | 0 | 0 | 0 | 0 | 0 | - | 0 | .000 | .000 | .000 |
| 2012 Pit | NL | 47 | 167 | 43 | 3 | 6 | 5 | (3 | 2) | 73 | 18 | 17 | 21 | 8 | 0 | 50 | 3 | 2 | 2 | 12 | 5 | .71 | 5 | .257 | .300 | .437 |
| 2013 Pit | NL | 135 | 510 | 143 | 26 | 10 | 12 | (5 | 7) | 225 | 83 | 35 | 74 | 25 | 2 | 138 | 24 | 6 | 1 | 41 | **15** | .73 | 6 | .280 | .343 | .441 |
| 2 ML YEARS | | 182 | 677 | 186 | 29 | 16 | 17 | (8 | 9) | 298 | 101 | 52 | 95 | 33 | 2 | 188 | 27 | 8 | 3 | 53 | 20 | .73 | 11 | .275 | .332 | .440 |

## Victor Marte

**Pitches:** R **Bats:** R **Pos:** RP-4 marr-TAY **Ht:** 6'2" **Wt:** 260 **Born:** 11/8/1980 **Age:** 33

| HOW MUCH HE PITCHED | | | | | | | | WHAT HE GAVE UP | | | | | | | | | | | | THE RESULTS | | | | | | | |
|---|---|---|---|---|---|---|---|---|---|---|---|---|---|---|---|---|---|---|---|---|---|---|---|---|---|---|---|
| Year Team | Lg | G | GS | CG | GF | IP | BFP | H | R | ER | HR | SH | SF | HB | TBB | IBB | SO | WP | Bk | W | L | Pct | Sh | Sv-Op | Hld | ERC | ERA |
| 2013 Memp* | AAA | 45 | 0 | 0 | 32 | 54.2 | 253 | 62 | 31 | 30 | 2 | 3 | 2 | 2 | 27 | 5 | 55 | 8 | 0 | 2 | 3 | .400 | 0 | 11- - | - | 4.63 | 4.94 |
| 2009 KC | AL | 8 | 0 | 0 | 4 | 12.0 | 58 | 13 | 12 | 11 | 2 | 0 | 0 | 0 | 12 | 1 | 7 | 1 | 0 | 0 | 0 | - | 0 | 0-0 | 0 | 7.71 | 8.25 |
| 2010 KC | AL | 22 | 0 | 0 | 4 | 27.2 | 137 | 38 | 30 | 30 | 8 | 1 | 0 | 2 | 15 | 1 | 19 | 1 | 0 | 3 | 0 | 1.000 | 0 | 0-0 | 1 | 8.71 | 9.76 |
| 2012 StL | NL | 48 | 0 | 0 | 5 | 40.1 | 185 | 51 | 22 | 22 | 6 | 1 | 1 | 2 | 14 | 2 | 36 | 1 | 0 | 3 | 2 | .600 | 0 | 0-2 | 9 | 5.86 | 4.91 |
| 2013 StL | NL | 4 | 0 | 0 | 1 | 3.0 | 17 | 4 | 2 | 2 | 0 | 0 | 0 | 1 | 3 | 1 | 2 | 0 | 0 | 0 | 1 | .000 | 0 | 0-0 | 0 | 8.12 | 6.00 |
| 4 ML YEARS | | 82 | 0 | 0 | 14 | 83.0 | 397 | 106 | 66 | 65 | 16 | 2 | 1 | 5 | 44 | 5 | 64 | 3 | 0 | 6 | 3 | .667 | 0 | 0-2 | 10 | 7.15 | 7.05 |

## Ethan Martin

**Pitches:** R **Bats:** R **Pos:** SP-8; RP-7 **Ht:** 6'2" **Wt:** 195 **Born:** 6/6/1989 **Age:** 25

| HOW MUCH HE PITCHED | | | | | | | | WHAT HE GAVE UP | | | | | | | | | | | | THE RESULTS | | | | | | | |
|---|---|---|---|---|---|---|---|---|---|---|---|---|---|---|---|---|---|---|---|---|---|---|---|---|---|---|---|
| Year Team | Lg | G | GS | CG | GF | IP | BFP | H | R | ER | HR | SH | SF | HB | TBB | IBB | SO | WP | Bk | W | L | Pct | Sh | Sv-Op | Hld | ERC | ERA |
| 2009 Gt Lks | A | 27 | 19 | 0 | 1 | 100.0 | 447 | 85 | 55 | 43 | 4 | 2 | 8 | 10 | 61 | 0 | 120 | 13 | 1 | 6 | 8 | .429 | 0 | 1- - | - | 3.98 | 3.87 |
| 2010 InldEm | A+ | 25 | 22 | 1 | 0 | 113.1 | 528 | 120 | 84 | 80 | 10 | 3 | 7 | 7 | 81 | 0 | 105 | 14 | 1 | 9 | 14 | .391 | 1 | 0- - | - | 5.94 | 6.35 |
| 2011 RCuca | A+ | 16 | 9 | 0 | 1 | 55.0 | 267 | 65 | 48 | 45 | 8 | 1 | 1 | 5 | 37 | 0 | 61 | 5 | 1 | 4 | 4 | .500 | 0 | 0- - | - | 7.03 | 7.36 |
| 2011 Chatt | AA | 21 | 3 | 0 | 7 | 40.1 | 176 | 31 | 21 | 18 | 3 | 1 | 2 | 0 | 29 | 0 | 43 | 5 | 1 | 5 | 3 | .625 | 0 | 2- - | - | 3.87 | 4.02 |
| 2012 Chatt | AA | 20 | 20 | 0 | 0 | 118.0 | 489 | 89 | 48 | 47 | 5 | 4 | 5 | 3 | 61 | 1 | 112 | 7 | 2 | 8 | 6 | .571 | 0 | 0- - | - | 2.95 | 3.58 |
| 2012 Rdng | AA | 7 | 7 | 0 | 0 | 39.2 | 164 | 29 | 15 | 14 | 3 | 3 | 2 | 0 | 18 | 0 | 35 | 4 | 0 | 5 | 0 | 1.000 | 0 | 0- - | - | 2.68 | 3.18 |
| 2013 LV | AAA | 21 | 21 | 1 | 0 | 115.2 | 494 | 94 | 56 | 53 | 11 | 5 | 4 | 8 | 67 | 4 | 107 | 9 | 2 | 11 | 5 | .688 | 0 | 0- - | - | 4.01 | 4.12 |
| 2013 Phi | NL | 15 | 8 | 0 | 2 | 40.0 | 190 | 42 | 27 | 27 | 9 | 1 | 1 | 1 | 26 | 2 | 47 | 1 | 1 | 2 | 5 | .286 | 0 | 0-1 | 0 | 6.21 | 6.08 |

## Leonys Martin

lay-OH-niece mar-TEEN

**Bats:** L **Throws:** R **Pos:** CF-127;RF-21;PH-18;LF-6;DH-1;PR-1 **Ht:** 6'2" **Wt:** 190 **Born:** 3/6/1988 **Age:** 26

| BATTING | | | | | | | | | | | | | | | | | | | | BASERUNNING | | | | AVERAGES | | |
|---|---|---|---|---|---|---|---|---|---|---|---|---|---|---|---|---|---|---|---|---|---|---|---|---|---|---|
| Year Team | Lg | G | AB | H | 2B | 3B | HR | (Hm | Rd) | TB | R | RBI | RC | TBB | IBB | SO | HBP | SH | SF | SB | CS | SB% | GDP | Avg | OBP | Slg |
| 2011 Tex | AL | 8 | 8 | 3 | 1 | 0 | 0 | (0 | 0) | 4 | 2 | 0 | 1 | 0 | 0 | 1 | 0 | 0 | 0 | 0 | 0 | - | 0 | .375 | .375 | .500 |
| 2012 Tex | AL | 24 | 46 | 8 | 5 | 2 | 0 | (0 | 0) | 17 | 6 | 6 | 4 | 4 | 0 | 12 | 0 | 1 | 1 | 3 | 0 | 1.00 | 2 | .174 | .235 | .370 |
| 2013 Tex | AL | 147 | 457 | 119 | 21 | 6 | 8 | (3 | 5) | 176 | 66 | 49 | 58 | 28 | 0 | 104 | 8 | 12 | 3 | 36 | 9 | .80 | 6 | .260 | .313 | .385 |
| 3 ML YEARS | | 179 | 511 | 130 | 27 | 8 | 8 | (3 | 5) | 197 | 74 | 55 | 63 | 32 | 0 | 117 | 8 | 13 | 4 | 39 | 9 | .81 | 8 | .254 | .306 | .386 |

## Russell Martin

**Bats:** R **Throws:** R **Pos:** C-120;PH-6;3B-3;RF-1;DH-1 **Ht:** 5'10" **Wt:** 215 **Born:** 2/15/1983 **Age:** 31

| BATTING | | | | | | | | | | | | | | | | | | | | BASERUNNING | | | | AVERAGES | | |
|---|---|---|---|---|---|---|---|---|---|---|---|---|---|---|---|---|---|---|---|---|---|---|---|---|---|---|
| Year Team | Lg | G | AB | H | 2B | 3B | HR | (Hm | Rd) | TB | R | RBI | RC | TBB | IBB | SO | HBP | SH | SF | SB | CS | SB% | GDP | Avg | OBP | Slg |
| 2006 LAD | NL | 121 | 415 | 117 | 26 | 4 | 10 | (8 | 2) | 181 | 65 | 65 | 58 | 45 | 8 | 57 | 4 | 1 | 3 | 10 | 5 | .67 | 17 | .282 | .355 | .436 |
| 2007 LAD | NL | 151 | 540 | 158 | 32 | 3 | 19 | (8 | 11) | 253 | 87 | 87 | 84 | 67 | 1 | 89 | 7 | 0 | 6 | 21 | 9 | .70 | 16 | .293 | .374 | .469 |
| 2008 LAD | NL | 155 | 553 | 155 | 25 | 0 | 13 | (6 | 7) | 219 | 87 | 69 | 89 | 90 | 8 | 83 | 5 | 0 | 2 | 18 | 6 | .75 | 16 | .280 | .385 | .396 |
| 2009 LAD | NL | 143 | 505 | 126 | 19 | 0 | 7 | (3 | 4) | 166 | 63 | 53 | 62 | 69 | 9 | 80 | 11 | 2 | 1 | 11 | 6 | .65 | 18 | .250 | .352 | .329 |
| 2010 LAD | NL | 97 | 331 | 82 | 13 | 0 | 5 | (2 | 3) | 110 | 45 | 26 | 40 | 48 | 7 | 61 | 4 | 1 | 3 | 6 | 2 | .75 | 7 | .248 | .347 | .332 |
| 2011 NYY | AL | 125 | 417 | 99 | 17 | 0 | 18 | (8 | 10) | 170 | 57 | 65 | 56 | 50 | 1 | 81 | 5 | 1 | 3 | 8 | 2 | .80 | 19 | .237 | .324 | .408 |
| 2012 NYY | AL | 133 | 422 | 89 | 18 | 0 | 21 | (13 | 8) | 170 | 50 | 53 | 50 | 53 | 0 | 95 | 8 | 2 | 0 | 6 | 1 | .86 | 13 | .211 | .311 | .403 |
| 2013 Pit | NL | 127 | 438 | 99 | 21 | 0 | 15 | (6 | 9) | 165 | 51 | 55 | 47 | 58 | 2 | 108 | 8 | 1 | 1 | 9 | 5 | .64 | 13 | .226 | .327 | .377 |
| Postseason | | 33 | 115 | 23 | 6 | 0 | 2 | (0 | 2) | 35 | 15 | 10 | 8 | 14 | 0 | 25 | 6 | 0 | 0 | 1 | 0 | 1.00 | 3 | .200 | .319 | .304 |
| 8 ML YEARS | | 1052 | 3621 | 925 | 171 | 7 | 108 | (54 | 54) | 1434 | 505 | 473 | 486 | 480 | 36 | 654 | 52 | 8 | 19 | 89 | 36 | .71 | 119 | .255 | .349 | .396 |

# Carlos Martinez

**Pitches:** R **Bats:** R **Pos:** RP-20; SP-1 **Ht:** 6'0" **Wt:** 185 **Born:** 9/21/1991 **Age:** 22

| HOW MUCH HE PITCHED | | | | | | | | | WHAT HE GAVE UP | | | | | | | | | | | | THE RESULTS | | | | | | | |
|---|---|---|---|---|---|---|---|---|---|---|---|---|---|---|---|---|---|---|---|---|---|---|---|---|---|---|---|---|
| Year | Team | Lg | G | GS | CG | GF | IP | BFP | H | R | ER | HR | SH | SF | HB | TBB | IBB | SO | WP | Bk | W | L | Pct | Sh | Sv-Op | Hld | ERC | ERA |
| 2011 | QuadC | A | 8 | 8 | 0 | 0 | 38.2 | 156 | 27 | 10 | 10 | 1 | 0 | 0 | 4 | 14 | 0 | 50 | 3 | 0 | 3 | 2 | .600 | 0 | 0-- | - | 2.31 | 2.33 |
| 2011 | PlmBh | A+ | 10 | 10 | 0 | 0 | 46.0 | 220 | 49 | 31 | 27 | 2 | 1 | 1 | 6 | 30 | 0 | 48 | 7 | 0 | 3 | 3 | .500 | 0 | 0-- | - | 5.47 | 5.28 |
| 2012 | PlmBh | A+ | 7 | 7 | 0 | 0 | 33.0 | 141 | 29 | 12 | 11 | 0 | 1 | 1 | 6 | 10 | 0 | 34 | 1 | 0 | 2 | 2 | .500 | 0 | 0-- | - | 3.04 | 3.00 |
| 2012 | Sprgfld | AA | 15 | 14 | 0 | 0 | 71.1 | 295 | 62 | 27 | 23 | 6 | 3 | 2 | 6 | 22 | 0 | 58 | 1 | 2 | 4 | 3 | .571 | 0 | 0-- | - | 3.27 | 2.90 |
| 2013 | Sprgfld | AA | 3 | 3 | 0 | 0 | 11.2 | 48 | 11 | 3 | 3 | 1 | 0 | 0 | 1 | 1 | 0 | 9 | 0 | 0 | 1 | 0 | 1.000 | 0 | 0-- | - | 2.75 | 2.31 |
| 2013 | Memp | AAA | 13 | 13 | 0 | 0 | 68.0 | 289 | 54 | 22 | 19 | 3 | 2 | 1 | 6 | 27 | 1 | 63 | 6 | 1 | 5 | 3 | .625 | 0 | 0-- | - | 2.85 | 2.51 |
| 2013 | StL | NL | 21 | 1 | 0 | 5 | 28.1 | 124 | 31 | 16 | 16 | 1 | 1 | 1 | 3 | 9 | 1 | 24 | 0 | 0 | 2 | 1 | .667 | 0 | 1-1 | 3 | 4.20 | 5.08 |

# Cristhian Martinez

**Pitches:** R **Bats:** R **Pos:** RP-2 cris-tee-YAN **Ht:** 6'1" **Wt:** 185 **Born:** 3/6/1982 **Age:** 32

| HOW MUCH HE PITCHED | | | | | | | | | WHAT HE GAVE UP | | | | | | | | | | | | THE RESULTS | | | | | | | |
|---|---|---|---|---|---|---|---|---|---|---|---|---|---|---|---|---|---|---|---|---|---|---|---|---|---|---|---|---|
| Year | Team | Lg | G | GS | CG | GF | IP | BFP | H | R | ER | HR | SH | SF | HB | TBB | IBB | SO | WP | Bk | W | L | Pct | Sh | Sv-Op | Hld | ERC | ERA |
| 2013 | Braves* | R | 1 | 1 | 0 | 0 | 2.0 | 7 | 1 | 0 | 0 | 0 | 0 | 0 | 0 | 0 | 0 | 4 | 0 | 0 | 0 | 0 | - | 0 | 0-- | - | 0.54 | 0.00 |
| 2013 | Missi* | AA | 2 | 0 | 0 | 0 | 2.0 | 11 | 2 | 2 | 2 | 0 | 0 | 0 | 0 | 2 | 0 | 2 | 0 | 1 | 0 | 0 | - | 0 | 0-- | - | 4.93 | 9.00 |
| 2009 | Fla | NL | 15 | 0 | 0 | 4 | 26.1 | 112 | 27 | 16 | 15 | 2 | 1 | 0 | 0 | 8 | 1 | 18 | 1 | 0 | 1 | 1 | .500 | 0 | 0-1 | 0 | 3.60 | 5.13 |
| 2010 | Atl | NL | 18 | 0 | 0 | 8 | 26.0 | 110 | 28 | 14 | 14 | 3 | 0 | 1 | 0 | 6 | 1 | 22 | 1 | 0 | 0 | 0 | - | 0 | 0-0 | 0 | 3.87 | 4.85 |
| 2011 | Atl | NL | 46 | 0 | 0 | 12 | 77.2 | 308 | 56 | 30 | 29 | 8 | 2 | 0 | 3 | 19 | 2 | 58 | 3 | 0 | 1 | 3 | .250 | 0 | 0-0 | 3 | 2.18 | 3.36 |
| 2012 | Atl | NL | 54 | 0 | 0 | 26 | 73.2 | 313 | 80 | 33 | 32 | 6 | 3 | 2 | 0 | 19 | 4 | 65 | 2 | 1 | 5 | 4 | .556 | 0 | 1-1 | 3 | 3.78 | 3.91 |
| 2013 | Atl | NL | 2 | 0 | 0 | 0 | 2.1 | 12 | 5 | 2 | 2 | 0 | 0 | 0 | 0 | 0 | 0 | 0 | 0 | 0 | 0 | 0 | - | 0 | 0-0 | 0 | 8.42 | 7.71 |
| 5 ML YEARS | | | 135 | 0 | 0 | 50 | 206.0 | 855 | 196 | 95 | 92 | 19 | 6 | 3 | 3 | 52 | 8 | 163 | 7 | 1 | 7 | 8 | .467 | 0 | 1-2 | 4 | 3.18 | 4.02 |

# David Martinez

**Pitches:** R **Bats:** R **Pos:** RP-4 **Ht:** 6'2" **Wt:** 180 **Born:** 8/4/1987 **Age:** 26

| HOW MUCH HE PITCHED | | | | | | | | | WHAT HE GAVE UP | | | | | | | | | | | | THE RESULTS | | | | | | | |
|---|---|---|---|---|---|---|---|---|---|---|---|---|---|---|---|---|---|---|---|---|---|---|---|---|---|---|---|---|
| Year | Team | Lg | G | GS | CG | GF | IP | BFP | H | R | ER | HR | SH | SF | HB | TBB | IBB | SO | WP | Bk | W | L | Pct | Sh | Sv-Op | Hld | ERC | ERA |
| 2009 | Grnvlle | R | 22 | 0 | 0 | 8 | 40.0 | 184 | 46 | 24 | 20 | 3 | 1 | 3 | 3 | 14 | 0 | 25 | 3 | 0 | 1 | 4 | .200 | 0 | 1-- | - | 4.70 | 4.50 |
| 2010 | TriCity | A- | 17 | 10 | 0 | 0 | 65.2 | 271 | 72 | 29 | 22 | 5 | 2 | 1 | 0 | 11 | 0 | 57 | 3 | 1 | 5 | 2 | .714 | 0 | 0-- | - | 3.59 | 3.02 |
| 2011 | Lxngtn | A | 37 | 5 | 0 | 17 | 66.2 | 297 | 77 | 44 | 31 | 7 | 2 | 2 | 3 | 17 | 0 | 44 | 9 | 1 | 5 | 7 | .417 | 0 | 2-- | - | 4.48 | 4.19 |
| 2012 | Lancst | A+ | 27 | 26 | 0 | 1 | 160.1 | 677 | 181 | 90 | 78 | 19 | 1 | 2 | 5 | 33 | 0 | 114 | 14 | 1 | 9 | 5 | .643 | 0 | 0-- | - | 4.34 | 4.38 |
| 2013 | CpChr | AA | 26 | 18 | 2 | 3 | 129.1 | 501 | 109 | 34 | 29 | 10 | 5 | 6 | 3 | 20 | 1 | 86 | 1 | 1 | 14 | 2 | .875 | 0 | 1-- | - | 2.35 | 2.02 |
| 2013 | OKCity | AAA | 3 | 3 | 0 | 0 | 11.0 | 59 | 15 | 12 | 11 | 1 | 1 | 1 | 0 | 11 | 1 | 10 | 1 | 0 | 0 | 2 | .000 | 0 | 0-- | - | 8.38 | 9.00 |
| 2013 | Hou | AL | 4 | 0 | 0 | 1 | 11.1 | 52 | 16 | 11 | 9 | 1 | 4 | 3 | 0 | 3 | 0 | 6 | 1 | 1 | 1 | 0 | 1.000 | 0 | 0-1 | 0 | 5.82 | 7.15 |

# Fernando Martinez

**Bats:** L **Throws:** R **Pos:** LF-8;RF-2;PH-2;DH-1 **Ht:** 6'1" **Wt:** 210 **Born:** 10/10/1988 **Age:** 25

| BATTING | | | | | | | | | | | | | | | | | | | | | BASERUNNING | | | | AVERAGES | | |
|---|---|---|---|---|---|---|---|---|---|---|---|---|---|---|---|---|---|---|---|---|---|---|---|---|---|---|---|
| Year | Team | Lg | G | AB | H | 2B | 3B | HR | (Hm | Rd) | TB | R | RBI | RC | TBB | IBB | SO | HBP | SH | SF | SB | CS | SB% | GDP | Avg | OBP | Slg |
| 2013 | OKCity* | AAA | 29 | 105 | 23 | 5 | 1 | 3 | (- | -) | 39 | 12 | 21 | 11 | 11 | 0 | 31 | 0 | 0 | 1 | 0 | 0 | - | 3 | .219 | .291 | .371 |
| 2013 | S-WB* | AAA | 22 | 83 | 27 | 7 | 0 | 4 | (- | -) | 46 | 9 | 18 | 18 | 6 | 1 | 12 | 4 | 0 | 1 | 1 | 0 | 1.00 | 1 | .325 | .394 | .554 |
| 2009 | NYM | NL | 29 | 91 | 16 | 6 | 0 | 1 | (0 | 1) | 25 | 11 | 8 | 5 | 5 | 0 | 14 | 3 | 1 | 0 | 2 | 0 | 1.00 | 0 | .176 | .242 | .275 |
| 2010 | NYM | NL | 7 | 18 | 3 | 0 | 0 | 0 | (0 | 0) | 3 | 1 | 2 | 1 | 1 | 0 | 5 | 2 | 0 | 1 | 0 | 1 | .00 | 0 | .167 | .273 | .167 |
| 2011 | NYM | NL | 11 | 22 | 5 | 2 | 0 | 1 | (0 | 1) | 10 | 3 | 2 | 1 | 1 | 0 | 7 | 0 | 0 | 0 | 0 | 0 | - | 0 | .227 | .261 | .455 |
| 2012 | Hou | NL | 41 | 118 | 28 | 7 | 1 | 6 | (2 | 4) | 55 | 12 | 14 | 13 | 6 | 0 | 34 | 5 | 0 | 1 | 0 | 1 | .00 | 1 | .237 | .300 | .466 |
| 2013 | Hou | AL | 11 | 33 | 6 | 0 | 0 | 1 | (1 | 0) | 9 | 1 | 3 | 2 | 1 | 0 | 12 | 1 | 0 | 0 | 0 | 0 | - | 0 | .182 | .229 | .273 |
| 5 ML YEARS | | | 99 | 282 | 58 | 15 | 1 | 9 | (3 | 6) | 102 | 28 | 29 | 22 | 14 | 0 | 72 | 11 | 1 | 2 | 2 | 2 | .50 | 1 | .206 | .269 | .362 |

# J.D. Martinez

**Bats:** R **Throws:** R **Pos:** LF-50;RF-25;DH-12;PH-8 **Ht:** 6'3" **Wt:** 220 **Born:** 8/21/1987 **Age:** 26

| BATTING | | | | | | | | | | | | | | | | | | | | | BASERUNNING | | | | AVERAGES | | |
|---|---|---|---|---|---|---|---|---|---|---|---|---|---|---|---|---|---|---|---|---|---|---|---|---|---|---|---|
| Year | Team | Lg | G | AB | H | 2B | 3B | HR | (Hm | Rd) | TB | R | RBI | RC | TBB | IBB | SO | HBP | SH | SF | SB | CS | SB% | GDP | Avg | OBP | Slg |
| 2013 | CpChr* | AA | 5 | 20 | 6 | 2 | 0 | 1 | (- | -) | 11 | 1 | 5 | 3 | 0 | 0 | 1 | 0 | 0 | 0 | 0 | 0 | - | 0 | .300 | .300 | .550 |
| 2011 | Hou | NL | 53 | 208 | 57 | 13 | 0 | 6 | (3 | 3) | 88 | 29 | 35 | 30 | 13 | 1 | 48 | 2 | 0 | 3 | 0 | 1 | .00 | 4 | .274 | .319 | .423 |
| 2012 | Hou | NL | 113 | 395 | 95 | 14 | 3 | 11 | (5 | 6) | 148 | 34 | 55 | 45 | 40 | 0 | 96 | 1 | 0 | 2 | 0 | 2 | .00 | 18 | .241 | .311 | .375 |
| 2013 | Hou | AL | 86 | 296 | 74 | 17 | 0 | 7 | (4 | 3) | 112 | 24 | 36 | 29 | 10 | 0 | 82 | 0 | 0 | 3 | 2 | 0 | 1.00 | 8 | .250 | .272 | .378 |
| 3 ML YEARS | | | 252 | 899 | 226 | 44 | 3 | 24 | (12 | 12) | 348 | 87 | 126 | 104 | 63 | 1 | 226 | 3 | 0 | 8 | 2 | 3 | .40 | 30 | .251 | .300 | .387 |

# Joe Martinez

**Pitches:** R **Bats:** L **Pos:** RP-2 **Ht:** 6'2" **Wt:** 190 **Born:** 2/26/1983 **Age:** 31

| HOW MUCH HE PITCHED | | | | | | | | | WHAT HE GAVE UP | | | | | | | | | | | | THE RESULTS | | | | | | | |
|---|---|---|---|---|---|---|---|---|---|---|---|---|---|---|---|---|---|---|---|---|---|---|---|---|---|---|---|---|
| Year | Team | Lg | G | GS | CG | GF | IP | BFP | H | R | ER | HR | SH | SF | HB | TBB | IBB | SO | WP | Bk | W | L | Pct | Sh | Sv-Op | Hld | ERC | ERA |
| 2013 | Clmbs* | AAA | 24 | 21 | 0 | 2 | 130.0 | 574 | 163 | 80 | 76 | 19 | 4 | 4 | 4 | 27 | 0 | 90 | 4 | 1 | 3 | 7 | .300 | 0 | 0-- | - | 5.19 | 5.26 |
| 2009 | SF | NL | 9 | 5 | 0 | 1 | 30.0 | 148 | 46 | 27 | 25 | 4 | 2 | 2 | 1 | 12 | 2 | 19 | 0 | 0 | 3 | 2 | .600 | 0 | 0-0 | 0 | 7.49 | 7.50 |
| 2010 | 2 Tms | NL | 9 | 1 | 0 | 0 | 19.2 | 94 | 26 | 11 | 9 | 1 | 0 | 1 | 2 | 9 | 2 | 9 | 1 | 1 | 0 | 1 | .000 | 0 | 0-0 | 0 | 6.02 | 4.12 |
| 2012 | Ari | NL | 1 | 0 | 0 | 1 | 1.0 | 5 | 2 | 1 | 1 | 0 | 0 | 0 | 0 | 0 | 0 | 1 | 0 | 0 | 0 | 0 | - | 0 | 0-0 | 0 | 7.48 | 9.00 |
| 2013 | Cle | AL | 2 | 0 | 0 | 1 | 5.0 | 19 | 4 | 1 | 1 | 0 | 0 | 0 | 0 | 0 | 0 | 3 | 0 | 0 | 1 | 0 | 1.000 | 0 | 0-0 | 0 | 1.27 | 1.80 |
| 10 | SF | NL | 4 | 1 | 0 | 0 | 11.0 | 53 | 15 | 6 | 6 | 1 | 0 | 1 | 1 | 6 | 2 | 3 | 0 | 0 | 0 | 1 | .000 | 0 | 0-0 | 0 | 6.91 | 4.91 |
| 10 | Pit | NL | 5 | 0 | 0 | 0 | 8.2 | 41 | 11 | 5 | 3 | 0 | 0 | 0 | 1 | 3 | 0 | 6 | 1 | 1 | 0 | 0 | - | 0 | 0-0 | 0 | 4.96 | 3.12 |
| 4 ML YEARS | | | 21 | 6 | 0 | 3 | 55.2 | 266 | 78 | 40 | 36 | 5 | 2 | 3 | 3 | 21 | 4 | 32 | 1 | 1 | 4 | 3 | .571 | 0 | 0-0 | 0 | 6.29 | 5.82 |

# Michael Martinez

**Bats:** B **Throws:** R **Pos:** CF-13;PH-8;PR-6;SS-3;3B-2;LF-2;RF-1 **Ht:** 5'9" **Wt:** 175 **Born:** 9/16/1982 **Age:** 31

| BATTING | | | | | | | | | | | | | | | | | | | | BASERUNNING | | | | AVERAGES | | |
|---|---|---|---|---|---|---|---|---|---|---|---|---|---|---|---|---|---|---|---|---|---|---|---|---|---|---|
| Year Team | Lg | G | AB | H | 2B | 3B | HR | (Hm | Rd) | TB | R | RBI | RC | TBB | IBB | SO | HBP | SH | SF | SB | CS | SB% | GDP | Avg | OBP | Slg |
| 2013 LV* | AAA | 71 | 243 | 73 | 11 | 3 | 3 | (- | -) | 99 | 35 | 28 | 35 | 18 | 1 | 37 | 2 | 2 | 1 | 6 | 5 | .55 | 8 | .300 | .352 | .407 |
| 2011 Phi | NL | 88 | 209 | 41 | 5 | 2 | 3 | (1 | 2) | 59 | 25 | 24 | 20 | 18 | 0 | 35 | 0 | 5 | 2 | 3 | 0 | 1.00 | 2 | .196 | .258 | .282 |
| 2012 Phi | NL | 45 | 115 | 20 | 3 | 0 | 2 | (1 | 1) | 29 | 10 | 7 | 5 | 5 | 2 | 21 | 0 | 2 | 0 | 0 | 0 | - | 4 | .174 | .208 | .252 |
| 2013 Phi | NL | 29 | 40 | 7 | 0 | 0 | 0 | (0 | 0) | 7 | 5 | 3 | 3 | 0 | 0 | 12 | 0 | 0 | 0 | 1 | 0 | 1.00 | 1 | .175 | .175 | .175 |
| Postseason | | 2 | 0 | 0 | 0 | 0 | 0 | (0 | 0) | 0 | 1 | 0 | 0 | 0 | 0 | 0 | 0 | 0 | 0 | 0 | 0 | - | 0 | - | - | - |
| 3 ML YEARS | | 162 | 364 | 68 | 8 | 2 | 5 | (2 | 3) | 95 | 40 | 34 | 28 | 23 | 2 | 68 | 0 | 7 | 2 | 4 | 0 | 1.00 | 7 | .187 | .234 | .261 |

# Victor Martinez

**Bats:** B **Throws:** R **Pos:** DH-139;1B-11;PH-6;C-3 **Ht:** 6'2" **Wt:** 210 **Born:** 12/23/1978 **Age:** 35

| BATTING | | | | | | | | | | | | | | | | | | | | BASERUNNING | | | | AVERAGES | | |
|---|---|---|---|---|---|---|---|---|---|---|---|---|---|---|---|---|---|---|---|---|---|---|---|---|---|---|
| Year Team | Lg | G | AB | H | 2B | 3B | HR | (Hm | Rd) | TB | R | RBI | RC | TBB | IBB | SO | HBP | SH | SF | SB | CS | SB% | GDP | Avg | OBP | Slg |
| 2002 Cle | AL | 12 | 32 | 9 | 1 | 0 | 1 | (1 | 0) | 13 | 2 | 5 | 5 | 3 | 0 | 2 | 0 | 0 | 1 | 0 | 0 | - | 1 | .281 | .333 | .406 |
| 2003 Cle | AL | 49 | 159 | 46 | 4 | 0 | 1 | (0 | 1) | 53 | 15 | 16 | 17 | 13 | 0 | 21 | 1 | 0 | 1 | 1 | 1 | .50 | 8 | .289 | .345 | .333 |
| 2004 Cle | AL | 141 | 520 | 147 | 38 | 1 | 23 | (8 | 15) | 256 | 77 | 108 | 90 | 60 | 11 | 69 | 5 | 0 | 6 | 0 | 1 | .00 | 16 | .283 | .359 | .492 |
| 2005 Cle | AL | 147 | 547 | 167 | 33 | 0 | 20 | (10 | 10) | 260 | 73 | 80 | 90 | 63 | 9 | 78 | 5 | 0 | 7 | 0 | 1 | .00 | 16 | .305 | .378 | .475 |
| 2006 Cle | AL | 153 | 572 | 181 | 37 | 0 | 16 | (4 | 12) | 266 | 82 | 93 | 96 | 71 | 8 | 78 | 3 | 0 | 6 | 0 | 0 | - | 27 | .316 | .391 | .465 |
| 2007 Cle | AL | 147 | 562 | 169 | 40 | 0 | 25 | (12 | 13) | 284 | 78 | 114 | 108 | 62 | 12 | 76 | 10 | 0 | **11** | 0 | 0 | - | 19 | .301 | .374 | .505 |
| 2008 Cle | AL | 73 | 266 | 74 | 17 | 0 | 2 | (2 | 0) | 97 | 30 | 35 | 36 | 24 | 4 | 32 | 1 | 0 | 3 | 0 | 0 | - | 12 | .278 | .337 | .365 |
| 2009 2 Tms | AL | 155 | 588 | 178 | 33 | 1 | 23 | (7 | 16) | 282 | 88 | 108 | 101 | 75 | 3 | 74 | 3 | 0 | 6 | 1 | 0 | 1.00 | 17 | .303 | .381 | .480 |
| 2010 Bos | AL | 127 | 493 | 149 | 32 | 1 | 20 | (10 | 10) | 243 | 64 | 79 | 74 | 40 | 5 | 52 | 0 | 0 | 5 | 1 | 0 | 1.00 | 17 | .302 | .351 | .493 |
| 2011 Det | AL | 145 | 540 | 178 | 40 | 0 | 12 | (5 | 7) | 254 | 76 | 103 | 103 | 46 | 6 | 51 | 2 | 0 | 7 | 1 | 0 | 1.00 | 20 | .330 | .380 | .470 |
| 2013 Det | AL | 159 | 605 | 182 | 36 | 0 | 14 | (7 | 7) | 260 | 68 | 83 | 75 | 54 | 10 | 62 | 1 | 0 | 8 | 0 | 2 | .00 | 23 | .301 | .355 | .430 |
| 09 Cle | AL | 99 | 377 | 107 | 21 | 1 | 15 | (6 | 9) | 175 | 56 | 67 | 64 | 51 | 3 | 51 | 2 | 0 | 5 | 0 | 0 | - | 11 | .284 | .368 | .464 |
| 09 Bos | AL | 56 | 211 | 71 | 12 | 0 | 8 | (1 | 7) | 107 | 32 | 41 | 37 | 24 | 0 | 23 | 1 | 0 | 1 | 1 | 0 | 1.00 | 6 | .336 | .405 | .507 |
| Postseason | | 25 | 95 | 26 | 2 | 1 | 4 | (3 | 1) | 42 | 10 | 14 | 15 | 10 | 3 | 16 | 2 | 0 | 0 | 0 | 0 | - | 2 | .274 | .355 | .442 |
| 11 ML YEARS | | 1308 | 4884 | 1480 | 311 | 3 | 157 | (66 | 91) | 2268 | 653 | 824 | 795 | 511 | 68 | 595 | 31 | 0 | 61 | 4 | 5 | .44 | 176 | .303 | .369 | .464 |

# Shairon Martis

SHY-ron MAR-tiss

**Pitches:** R **Bats:** R **Pos:** RP-6 **Ht:** 6'1" **Wt:** 225 **Born:** 3/30/1987 **Age:** 27

| HOW MUCH HE PITCHED | | | | | | | | WHAT HE GAVE UP | | | | | | | | | | | | THE RESULTS | | | | | | | |
|---|---|---|---|---|---|---|---|---|---|---|---|---|---|---|---|---|---|---|---|---|---|---|---|---|---|---|---|
| Year Team | Lg | G | GS | CG | GF | IP | BFP | H | R | ER | HR | SH | SF | HB | TBB | IBB | SO | WP | Bk | W | L | Pct | Sh | Sv-Op | Hld | ERC | ERA |
| 2013 Roch* | AAA | 42 | 3 | 0 | 21 | 80.1 | 337 | 68 | 39 | 38 | 8 | 2 | 5 | 0 | 31 | 1 | 65 | 6 | 0 | 2 | 4 | .333 | 0 | 11-- | - | 3.14 | 4.26 |
| 2008 Was | NL | 5 | 4 | 0 | 0 | 20.2 | 92 | 18 | 14 | 13 | 5 | 0 | 1 | 0 | 12 | 0 | 23 | 1 | 0 | 1 | 3 | .250 | 0 | 0-0 | 0 | 4.98 | 5.66 |
| 2009 Was | NL | 15 | 15 | 1 | 0 | 85.2 | 377 | 83 | 52 | 50 | 11 | 5 | 3 | 4 | 39 | 3 | 34 | 3 | 0 | 5 | 3 | .625 | 0 | 0-0 | 0 | 4.43 | 5.25 |
| 2013 Min | AL | 6 | 0 | 0 | 1 | 9.2 | 39 | 6 | 6 | 6 | 3 | 0 | 0 | 0 | 4 | 0 | 7 | 0 | 0 | 0 | 1 | .000 | 0 | 0-0 | 0 | 3.32 | 5.59 |
| 3 ML YEARS | | 26 | 19 | 1 | 1 | 116.0 | 508 | 107 | 72 | 69 | 19 | 5 | 4 | 4 | 55 | 3 | 64 | 4 | 0 | 6 | 7 | .462 | 0 | 0-0 | 0 | 4.44 | 5.35 |

# Justin Masterson

**Pitches:** R **Bats:** R **Pos:** SP-29; RP-3 **Ht:** 6'6" **Wt:** 250 **Born:** 3/22/1985 **Age:** 29

| HOW MUCH HE PITCHED | | | | | | | | WHAT HE GAVE UP | | | | | | | | | | | | THE RESULTS | | | | | | | |
|---|---|---|---|---|---|---|---|---|---|---|---|---|---|---|---|---|---|---|---|---|---|---|---|---|---|---|---|
| Year Team | Lg | G | GS | CG | GF | IP | BFP | H | R | ER | HR | SH | SF | HB | TBB | IBB | SO | WP | Bk | W | L | Pct | Sh | Sv-Op | Hld | ERC | ERA |
| 2008 Bos | AL | 36 | 9 | 0 | 6 | 88.1 | 365 | 68 | 31 | 31 | 10 | 1 | 1 | 8 | 40 | 3 | 68 | 1 | 0 | 6 | 5 | .545 | 0 | 0-1 | 3 | 3.51 | 3.16 |
| 2009 2 Tms | AL | 42 | 16 | 1 | 4 | 129.1 | 568 | 128 | 73 | 65 | 12 | 10 | 7 | 8 | 60 | 3 | 119 | 5 | 0 | 4 | 10 | .286 | 0 | 0-1 | 6 | 4.45 | 4.52 |
| 2010 Cle | AL | 34 | 29 | 1 | 0 | 180.0 | 802 | 197 | 107 | 94 | 14 | 5 | 4 | 11 | 73 | 4 | 140 | 12 | 0 | 6 | 13 | .316 | 1 | 0-0 | 2 | 4.68 | 4.70 |
| 2011 Cle | AL | 34 | 33 | 1 | 0 | 216.0 | 908 | 211 | 89 | 77 | 11 | 5 | 5 | 11 | 65 | 4 | 158 | 5 | 0 | 12 | 10 | .545 | 0 | 0-0 | 0 | 3.43 | 3.21 |
| 2012 Cle | AL | 34 | **34** | 1 | 0 | 206.1 | 906 | 212 | 122 | 113 | 18 | 6 | **11** | 13 | 88 | 1 | 159 | 14 | 0 | 11 | 15 | .423 | 0 | 0-0 | 0 | 4.51 | 4.93 |
| 2013 Cle | AL | 32 | 29 | 3 | 2 | 193.0 | 803 | 156 | 75 | 74 | 13 | 5 | 2 | **17** | 76 | 0 | 195 | 8 | 0 | 14 | 10 | .583 | **3** | 0-0 | 0 | 3.17 | 3.45 |
| 09 Bos | AL | 31 | 6 | 0 | 4 | 72.0 | 312 | 72 | 38 | 36 | 7 | 9 | 6 | 6 | 25 | 2 | 67 | 3 | 0 | 3 | 3 | .500 | 0 | 0-1 | 6 | 4.13 | 4.50 |
| 09 Cle | AL | 11 | 10 | 1 | 0 | 57.1 | 256 | 56 | 35 | 29 | 5 | 1 | 1 | 2 | 35 | 1 | 52 | 2 | 0 | 1 | 7 | .125 | 0 | 0-0 | 0 | 4.85 | 4.55 |
| Postseason | | 9 | 0 | 0 | 1 | 9.2 | 40 | 10 | 3 | 2 | 0 | 1 | 0 | 1 | 5 | 0 | 9 | 0 | 0 | 1 | 0 | 1.000 | 0 | 0-1 | 4 | 4.85 | 1.86 |
| 6 ML YEARS | | 212 | 150 | 7 | 12 | 1013.0 | 4352 | 972 | 497 | 454 | 78 | 32 | 30 | 68 | 402 | 15 | 839 | 45 | 0 | 53 | 63 | .457 | 4 | 0-2 | 11 | 3.95 | 4.03 |

# Darin Mastroianni

mass-tree-AH-nee

**Bats:** R **Throws:** R **Pos:** LF-19;RF-9;PR-4;CF-3;PH-2;2B-1 **Ht:** 5'11" **Wt:** 190 **Born:** 8/26/1985 **Age:** 28

| BATTING | | | | | | | | | | | | | | | | | | | | BASERUNNING | | | | AVERAGES | | |
|---|---|---|---|---|---|---|---|---|---|---|---|---|---|---|---|---|---|---|---|---|---|---|---|---|---|---|
| Year Team | Lg | G | AB | H | 2B | 3B | HR | (Hm | Rd) | TB | R | RBI | RC | TBB | IBB | SO | HBP | SH | SF | SB | CS | SB% | GDP | Avg | OBP | Slg |
| 2013 Twins* | R | 3 | 7 | 1 | 0 | 0 | 0 | (- | -) | 1 | 1 | 2 | 1 | 2 | 0 | 1 | 1 | 0 | 1 | 2 | 0 | 1.00 | 0 | .143 | .364 | .143 |
| 2013 FtMyrs* | A+ | 3 | 10 | 4 | 2 | 0 | 0 | (- | -) | 6 | 4 | 0 | 3 | 2 | 0 | 1 | 0 | 0 | 0 | 2 | 0 | 1.00 | 0 | .400 | .500 | .600 |
| 2013 Roch* | AAA | 15 | 50 | 12 | 1 | 0 | 0 | (- | -) | 13 | 9 | 5 | 7 | 10 | 0 | 11 | 3 | 0 | 0 | 4 | 0 | 1.00 | 0 | .240 | .397 | .260 |
| 2011 Tor | AL | 1 | 2 | 0 | 0 | 0 | 0 | (0 | 0) | 0 | 0 | 0 | 0 | 0 | 0 | 1 | 0 | 1 | 0 | 0 | 0 | - | 0 | .000 | .000 | .000 |
| 2012 Min | AL | 77 | 163 | 41 | 3 | 2 | 3 | (2 | 1) | 57 | 22 | 17 | 24 | 18 | 0 | 45 | 1 | 3 | 1 | 21 | 3 | .88 | 4 | .252 | .328 | .350 |
| 2013 Min | AL | 30 | 65 | 12 | 2 | 0 | 0 | (0 | 0) | 14 | 5 | 5 | 1 | 3 | 0 | 23 | 1 | 3 | 1 | 2 | 1 | .67 | 2 | .185 | .229 | .215 |
| 3 ML YEARS | | 108 | 230 | 53 | 5 | 2 | 3 | (2 | 1) | 71 | 27 | 22 | 25 | 21 | 0 | 69 | 2 | 7 | 2 | 23 | 4 | .85 | 6 | .230 | .298 | .309 |

## Jeff Mathis

**Bats:** R **Throws:** R **Pos:** C-73;PH-1 **Ht:** 6'0" **Wt:** 205 **Born:** 3/31/1983 **Age:** 31

| BATTING | | | | | | | | | | | | | | | | | | | | BASERUNNING | | | | AVERAGES | | |
|---|---|---|---|---|---|---|---|---|---|---|---|---|---|---|---|---|---|---|---|---|---|---|---|---|---|---|
| Year Team | Lg | G | AB | H | 2B | 3B | HR | (Hm | Rd) | TB | R | RBI | RC | TBB | IBB | SO | HBP | SH | SF | SB | CS | SB% | GDP | Avg | OBP | Slg |
| 2013 Jupiter* | A+ | 4 | 14 | 4 | 2 | 0 | 0 | (- | -) | 6 | 1 | 4 | 2 | 1 | 0 | 4 | 1 | 0 | 0 | 0 | 0 | - | 1 | .286 | .375 | .429 |
| 2013 Jaxnvl* | AA | 3 | 11 | 3 | 1 | 0 | 1 | (- | -) | 7 | 1 | 6 | 2 | 1 | 0 | 6 | 0 | 1 | 0 | 0 | 0 | - | 0 | .273 | .333 | .636 |
| 2013 NewOr* | AAA | 2 | 9 | 2 | 1 | 0 | 1 | (- | -) | 6 | 1 | 2 | 1 | 1 | 0 | 5 | 0 | 0 | 0 | 0 | 0 | - | 0 | .222 | .300 | .667 |
| 2005 LAA | AL | 5 | 3 | 1 | 0 | 0 | 0 | (0 | 0) | 1 | 1 | 0 | 0 | 0 | 0 | 1 | 0 | 0 | 0 | 0 | 0 | - | 0 | .333 | .333 | .333 |
| 2006 LAA | AL | 23 | 55 | 8 | 2 | 0 | 2 | (1 | 1) | 16 | 9 | 6 | 4 | 7 | 1 | 14 | 0 | 0 | 1 | 0 | 0 | - | 0 | .145 | .238 | .291 |
| 2007 LAA | AL | 59 | 171 | 36 | 12 | 0 | 4 | (3 | 1) | 60 | 24 | 23 | 13 | 15 | 0 | 49 | 2 | 3 | 4 | 0 | 1 | .00 | 3 | .211 | .276 | .351 |
| 2008 LAA | AL | 94 | 283 | 55 | 8 | 0 | 9 | (4 | 5) | 90 | 35 | 42 | 33 | 30 | 4 | 90 | 3 | 8 | 4 | 2 | 2 | .50 | 1 | .194 | .275 | .318 |
| 2009 LAA | AL | 84 | 237 | 50 | 8 | 0 | 5 | (3 | 2) | 73 | 26 | 28 | 24 | 22 | 0 | 73 | 4 | 8 | 1 | 2 | 3 | .40 | 2 | .211 | .288 | .308 |
| 2010 LAA | AL | 68 | 205 | 40 | 6 | 1 | 3 | (2 | 1) | 57 | 19 | 18 | 10 | 6 | 0 | 59 | 1 | 3 | 3 | 3 | 0 | 1.00 | 3 | .195 | .219 | .278 |
| 2011 LAA | AL | 93 | 247 | 43 | 12 | 0 | 3 | (1 | 2) | 64 | 18 | 22 | 12 | 15 | 2 | 75 | 2 | 14 | 3 | 1 | 2 | .33 | 3 | .174 | .225 | .259 |
| 2012 Tor | AL | 71 | 211 | 46 | 13 | 0 | 8 | (5 | 3) | 83 | 25 | 27 | 18 | 9 | 0 | 68 | 0 | 6 | 1 | 1 | 0 | 1.00 | 2 | .218 | .249 | .393 |
| 2013 Mia | NL | 73 | 232 | 42 | 7 | 1 | 5 | (3 | 2) | 66 | 14 | 29 | 15 | 21 | 4 | 76 | 1 | 1 | 1 | 0 | 0 | - | 5 | .181 | .251 | .284 |
| Postseason | | 10 | 20 | 9 | 5 | 0 | 0 | (0 | 0) | 14 | 2 | 2 | 3 | 0 | 0 | 5 | 0 | 1 | 0 | 0 | 0 | - | 0 | .450 | .450 | .700 |
| 9 ML YEARS | | 570 | 1644 | 321 | 68 | 2 | 39 | (22 | 17) | 510 | 171 | 195 | 129 | 125 | 11 | 505 | 13 | 43 | 18 | 9 | 8 | .53 | 19 | .195 | .255 | .310 |

## Daisuke Matsuzaka

**Pitches:** R **Bats:** R **Pos:** SP-7 DICE-kay maht-soo-ZAH-kah **Ht:** 6'0" **Wt:** 185 **Born:** 9/13/1980 **Age:** 33

| HOW MUCH HE PITCHED | | | | | | | | WHAT HE GAVE UP | | | | | | | | | | | | THE RESULTS | | | | | | | |
|---|---|---|---|---|---|---|---|---|---|---|---|---|---|---|---|---|---|---|---|---|---|---|---|---|---|---|---|
| Year Team | Lg | G | GS | CG | GF | IP | BFP | H | R | ER | HR | SH | SF | HB | TBB | IBB | SO | WP | Bk | W | L | Pct | Sh | Sv-Op | Hld | ERC | ERA |
| 2013 Clmbs* | AAA | 19 | 19 | 0 | 0 | 103.1 | 431 | 93 | 47 | 45 | 11 | 7 | 2 | 3 | 39 | 0 | 95 | 5 | 0 | 5 | 8 | .385 | 0 | 0-- | - | 3.65 | 3.92 |
| 2007 Bos | AL | 32 | 32 | 1 | 0 | 204.2 | 874 | 191 | 100 | 100 | 25 | 3 | 2 | 13 | 80 | 1 | 201 | 5 | 0 | 15 | 12 | .556 | 0 | 0-0 | 0 | 4.10 | 4.40 |
| 2008 Bos | AL | 29 | 29 | 0 | 0 | 167.2 | 716 | 128 | 58 | 54 | 12 | 3 | 4 | 7 | **94** | 1 | 154 | 5 | 0 | 18 | 3 | .857 | 0 | 0-0 | 0 | 3.36 | 2.90 |
| 2009 Bos | AL | 12 | 12 | 0 | 0 | 59.1 | 283 | 81 | 38 | 38 | 10 | 1 | 1 | 2 | 30 | 1 | 54 | 8 | 0 | 4 | 6 | .400 | 0 | 0-0 | 0 | 7.45 | 5.76 |
| 2010 Bos | AL | 25 | 25 | 0 | 0 | 153.2 | 664 | 137 | 84 | 80 | 13 | 3 | 8 | 8 | 74 | 1 | 133 | 4 | 0 | 9 | 6 | .600 | 0 | 0-0 | 0 | 3.89 | 4.69 |
| 2011 Bos | AL | 8 | 7 | 0 | 1 | 37.1 | 167 | 32 | 24 | 22 | 4 | 0 | 0 | 1 | 23 | 0 | 26 | 0 | 0 | 3 | 3 | .500 | 0 | 0-0 | 0 | 4.21 | 5.30 |
| 2012 Bos | AL | 11 | 11 | 0 | 0 | 45.2 | 215 | 58 | 43 | 42 | 11 | 0 | 3 | 3 | 20 | 0 | 41 | 3 | 0 | 1 | 7 | .125 | 0 | 0-0 | 0 | 7.20 | 8.28 |
| 2013 NYM | NL | 7 | 7 | 0 | 0 | 38.2 | 166 | 32 | 21 | 19 | 4 | 4 | 0 | 5 | 16 | 0 | 33 | 0 | 0 | 3 | 3 | .500 | 0 | 0-0 | 0 | 3.70 | 4.42 |
| Postseason | | 7 | 7 | 0 | 0 | 35.2 | 163 | 39 | 19 | 19 | 4 | 0 | 1 | 1 | 17 | 0 | 33 | 4 | 0 | 3 | 1 | .750 | 0 | 0-0 | 0 | 5.04 | 4.79 |
| 7 ML YEARS | | 124 | 123 | 1 | 1 | 707.0 | 3085 | 659 | 368 | 355 | 79 | 14 | 18 | 39 | 337 | 4 | 642 | 25 | 0 | 53 | 40 | .570 | 0 | 0-0 | 0 | 4.30 | 4.52 |

## Ryan Mattheus

**Pitches:** R **Bats:** R **Pos:** RP-37 MATH-yooz **Ht:** 6'3" **Wt:** 215 **Born:** 11/10/1983 **Age:** 30

| HOW MUCH HE PITCHED | | | | | | | | WHAT HE GAVE UP | | | | | | | | | | | | THE RESULTS | | | | | | | |
|---|---|---|---|---|---|---|---|---|---|---|---|---|---|---|---|---|---|---|---|---|---|---|---|---|---|---|---|
| Year Team | Lg | G | GS | CG | GF | IP | BFP | H | R | ER | HR | SH | SF | HB | TBB | IBB | SO | WP | Bk | W | L | Pct | Sh | Sv-Op | Hld | ERC | ERA |
| 2013 Nats* | R | 1 | 1 | 0 | 0 | 1.0 | 4 | 1 | 0 | 0 | 0 | 0 | 0 | 0 | 0 | 0 | 3 | 1 | 0 | 0 | 0 | - | 0 | 0-- | - | 1.95 | 0.00 |
| 2013 Hgrstn* | A | 1 | 1 | 0 | 0 | 1.0 | 5 | 1 | 1 | 1 | 0 | 0 | 0 | 0 | 0 | 0 | 0 | 1 | 0 | 0 | 0 | - | 0 | 0-- | - | 1.51 | 9.00 |
| 2013 Hrsbrg* | AA | 3 | 0 | 0 | 0 | 4.0 | 17 | 5 | 1 | 1 | 0 | 1 | 0 | 0 | 2 | 0 | 0 | 0 | 1 | 0 | 0 | - | 0 | 0-- | - | 5.65 | 2.25 |
| 2013 Syrcse* | AAA | 6 | 0 | 0 | 2 | 7.1 | 29 | 6 | 1 | 1 | 1 | 0 | 0 | 0 | 1 | 0 | 4 | 1 | 0 | 0 | 0 | - | 0 | 0-- | - | 2.31 | 1.23 |
| 2011 Was | NL | 35 | 0 | 0 | 12 | 32.0 | 136 | 26 | 11 | 10 | 1 | 4 | 1 | 2 | 15 | 3 | 12 | 1 | 1 | 2 | 2 | .500 | 0 | 0-0 | 8 | 2.94 | 2.81 |
| 2012 Was | NL | 66 | 0 | 0 | 11 | 66.1 | 265 | 57 | 22 | 21 | 8 | 2 | 4 | 3 | 19 | 5 | 41 | 3 | 0 | 5 | 3 | .625 | 0 | 0-0 | 18 | 3.19 | 2.85 |
| 2013 Was | NL | 37 | 0 | 0 | 13 | 35.1 | 166 | 52 | 26 | 25 | 1 | 0 | 3 | 0 | 15 | 0 | 22 | 4 | 1 | 0 | 2 | .000 | 0 | 0-3 | 6 | 6.53 | 6.37 |
| Postseason | | 3 | 0 | 0 | 0 | 3.0 | 12 | 3 | 2 | 2 | 0 | 0 | 0 | 0 | 1 | 0 | 0 | 0 | 0 | 1 | 0 | 1.000 | 0 | 0-0 | 0 | 3.35 | 6.00 |
| 3 ML YEARS | | 138 | 0 | 0 | 36 | 133.2 | 567 | 135 | 59 | 56 | 10 | 6 | 8 | 5 | 49 | 8 | 75 | 8 | 2 | 7 | 7 | .500 | 0 | 0-3 | 32 | 3.95 | 3.77 |

## Brian Matusz

**Pitches:** L **Bats:** L **Pos:** RP-65 MATT-uss **Ht:** 6'4" **Wt:** 200 **Born:** 2/11/1987 **Age:** 27

| HOW MUCH HE PITCHED | | | | | | | | WHAT HE GAVE UP | | | | | | | | | | | | THE RESULTS | | | | | | | |
|---|---|---|---|---|---|---|---|---|---|---|---|---|---|---|---|---|---|---|---|---|---|---|---|---|---|---|---|
| Year Team | Lg | G | GS | CG | GF | IP | BFP | H | R | ER | HR | SH | SF | HB | TBB | IBB | SO | WP | Bk | W | L | Pct | Sh | Sv-Op | Hld | ERC | ERA |
| 2009 Bal | AL | 8 | 8 | 0 | 0 | 44.2 | 196 | 52 | 24 | 23 | 6 | 2 | 2 | 0 | 14 | 0 | 38 | 0 | 0 | 5 | 2 | .714 | 0 | 0-0 | 0 | 4.91 | 4.63 |
| 2010 Bal | AL | 32 | 32 | 0 | 0 | 175.2 | 760 | 173 | 88 | 84 | 19 | 6 | 6 | 7 | 63 | 3 | 143 | 1 | 0 | 10 | 12 | .455 | 0 | 0-0 | 0 | 3.98 | 4.30 |
| 2011 Bal | AL | 12 | 12 | 0 | 0 | 49.2 | 245 | 81 | 60 | 59 | 18 | 1 | 2 | 0 | 24 | 1 | 38 | 0 | 0 | 1 | 9 | .100 | 0 | 0-0 | 0 | 10.88 | 10.69 |
| 2012 Bal | AL | 34 | 16 | 0 | 2 | 98.0 | 441 | 112 | 61 | 53 | 15 | 2 | 3 | 0 | 41 | 4 | 81 | 0 | 0 | 6 | 10 | .375 | 0 | 0-0 | 4 | 5.25 | 4.87 |
| 2013 Bal | AL | 65 | 0 | 0 | 9 | 51.0 | 208 | 43 | 21 | 20 | 3 | 1 | 2 | 2 | 16 | 2 | 50 | 0 | 0 | 2 | 1 | .667 | 0 | 0-4 | 18 | 2.77 | 3.53 |
| Postseason | | 6 | 0 | 0 | 2 | 4.2 | 17 | 2 | 1 | 1 | 1 | 0 | 0 | 0 | 2 | 1 | 6 | 1 | 0 | 0 | 1 | .000 | 0 | 0-0 | 2 | 1.82 | 1.93 |
| 5 ML YEARS | | 151 | 68 | 0 | 11 | 419.0 | 1850 | 461 | 254 | 239 | 61 | 12 | 15 | 9 | 158 | 10 | 350 | 1 | 0 | 24 | 34 | .414 | 0 | 0-4 | 22 | 4.92 | 5.13 |

## Joe Mauer

**Bats:** L **Throws:** R **Pos:** C-75;DH-29;1B-8;PH-3 **Ht:** 6'5" **Wt:** 230 **Born:** 4/19/1983 **Age:** 31

| BATTING | | | | | | | | | | | | | | | | | | | | BASERUNNING | | | | AVERAGES | | |
|---|---|---|---|---|---|---|---|---|---|---|---|---|---|---|---|---|---|---|---|---|---|---|---|---|---|---|
| Year Team | Lg | G | AB | H | 2B | 3B | HR | (Hm | Rd) | TB | R | RBI | RC | TBB | IBB | SO | HBP | SH | SF | SB | CS | SB% | GDP | Avg | OBP | Slg |
| 2004 Min | AL | 35 | 107 | 33 | 8 | 1 | 6 | (4 | 2) | 61 | 18 | 17 | 21 | 11 | 0 | 14 | 1 | 0 | 3 | 1 | 0 | 1.00 | 1 | .308 | .369 | .570 |
| 2005 Min | AL | 131 | 489 | 144 | 26 | 2 | 9 | (4 | 5) | 201 | 61 | 55 | 78 | 61 | 12 | 64 | 1 | 0 | 3 | 13 | 1 | .93 | 9 | .294 | .372 | .411 |
| 2006 Min | AL | 140 | 521 | 181 | 36 | 4 | 13 | (3 | 10) | 264 | 86 | 84 | 103 | 79 | 21 | 54 | 1 | 0 | 7 | 8 | 3 | .73 | 24 | **.347** | .429 | .507 |
| 2007 Min | AL | 109 | 406 | 119 | 27 | 3 | 7 | (2 | 5) | 173 | 62 | 60 | 69 | 57 | 10 | 51 | 3 | 2 | 3 | 7 | 1 | .88 | 11 | .293 | .382 | .426 |
| 2008 Min | AL | 146 | 536 | 176 | 31 | 4 | 9 | (7 | 2) | 242 | 98 | 85 | 103 | 84 | 8 | 50 | 1 | 1 | **11** | 1 | 1 | .50 | 21 | **.328** | .413 | .451 |
| 2009 Min | AL | 138 | 523 | 191 | 30 | 1 | 28 | (16 | 12) | 307 | 94 | 96 | **123** | 76 | 14 | 63 | 2 | 0 | 5 | 4 | 1 | .80 | 13 | **.365** | **.444** | **.587** |
| 2010 Min | AL | 137 | 510 | 167 | 43 | 1 | 9 | (1 | 8) | 239 | 88 | 75 | 91 | 65 | 14 | 53 | 3 | 0 | 6 | 1 | 4 | .20 | 19 | .327 | .402 | .469 |
| 2011 Min | AL | 82 | 296 | 85 | 15 | 0 | 3 | (0 | 3) | 109 | 38 | 30 | 39 | 32 | 7 | 38 | 3 | 0 | 2 | 0 | 0 | - | 9 | .287 | .360 | .368 |
| 2012 Min | AL | 147 | 545 | 174 | 31 | 4 | 10 | (4 | 6) | 243 | 81 | 85 | 108 | 90 | 10 | 88 | 2 | 1 | 3 | 8 | 4 | .67 | 23 | .319 | **.416** | .446 |
| 2013 Min | AL | 113 | 445 | 144 | 35 | 0 | 11 | (5 | 6) | 212 | 62 | 47 | 74 | 61 | 7 | 89 | 0 | 0 | 2 | 0 | 1 | .00 | 7 | .324 | .404 | .476 |
| Postseason | | 9 | 35 | 10 | 1 | 0 | 0 | (0 | 0) | 11 | 1 | 1 | 2 | 4 | 0 | 7 | 0 | 0 | 0 | 0 | 0 | - | 0 | .286 | .359 | .314 |
| 10 ML YEARS | | 1178 | 4378 | 1414 | 282 | 20 | 105 | (46 | 59) | 2051 | 688 | 634 | 809 | 616 | 103 | 564 | 17 | 4 | 45 | 43 | 16 | .73 | 137 | .323 | .405 | .468 |

## Brandon Maurer

**Pitches:** R **Bats:** R **Pos:** SP-14; RP-8 **Ht:** 6'5" **Wt:** 215 **Born:** 7/3/1990 **Age:** 23

| | | | HOW MUCH HE PITCHED | | | | | | WHAT HE GAVE UP | | | | | | | | | | | | THE RESULTS | | | | | | | |
|---|---|---|---|---|---|---|---|---|---|---|---|---|---|---|---|---|---|---|---|---|---|---|---|---|---|---|---|---|
| Year | Team | Lg | G | GS | CG | GF | IP | BFP | H | R | ER | HR | SH | SF | HB | TBB | IBB | SO | WP | Bk | W | L | Pct | Sh | Sv-Op | Hld | ERC | ERA |
| 2009 | Pulaski | R | 13 | 12 | 1 | 1 | 67.1 | 280 | 67 | 36 | 27 | 4 | 1 | 2 | 7 | 18 | 0 | 51 | 5 | 1 | 3 | 4 | .429 | 0 | 0-- | - | 3.77 | 3.61 |
| 2010 | Ms | R | 4 | 4 | 0 | 0 | 11.0 | 43 | 8 | 4 | 2 | 0 | 0 | 0 | 2 | 2 | 0 | 14 | 1 | 1 | 0 | 1 | .000 | 0 | 0-- | - | 1.99 | 1.64 |
| 2010 | Clinton | A | 2 | 0 | 0 | 1 | 4.1 | 17 | 5 | 2 | 1 | 1 | 0 | 0 | 0 | 0 | 0 | 6 | 0 | 0 | 0 | 1 | .000 | 0 | 0-- | - | 4.34 | 2.08 |
| 2011 | Clinton | A | 7 | 6 | 0 | 1 | 37.0 | 151 | 28 | 16 | 14 | 2 | 0 | 2 | 2 | 14 | 0 | 44 | 3 | 4 | 1 | 3 | .250 | 0 | 0-- | - | 2.64 | 3.41 |
| 2011 | Hi Dsrt | A+ | 9 | 7 | 0 | 1 | 42.1 | 185 | 47 | 32 | 30 | 8 | 0 | 0 | 3 | 11 | 0 | 37 | 6 | 0 | 2 | 4 | .333 | 0 | 0-- | - | 5.04 | 6.38 |
| 2012 | Jacksn | AA | 24 | 24 | 1 | 0 | 137.2 | 575 | 133 | 54 | 49 | 4 | 6 | 3 | 6 | 48 | 0 | 117 | 7 | 2 | 9 | 2 | .818 | 0 | 0-- | - | 3.45 | 3.20 |
| 2013 | Tacom | AAA | 10 | 10 | 0 | 0 | 46.2 | 215 | 48 | 29 | 27 | 2 | 1 | 0 | 5 | 26 | 0 | 47 | 3 | 2 | 3 | 4 | .429 | 0 | 0-- | - | 4.82 | 5.21 |
| 2013 | Sea | AL | 22 | 14 | 0 | 3 | 90.0 | 402 | 114 | 66 | 63 | 16 | 1 | 2 | 6 | 27 | 0 | 70 | 9 | 0 | 5 | 8 | .385 | 0 | 0-0 | 0 | 6.20 | 6.30 |

## Justin Maxwell

**Bats:** R **Throws:** R **Pos:** RF-47;CF-27;PH-6;PR-3;DH-1 **Ht:** 6'5" **Wt:** 220 **Born:** 11/6/1983 **Age:** 30

| | | | BATTING | | | | | | | | | | | | | | | | | | BASERUNNING | | | | AVERAGES | | |
|---|---|---|---|---|---|---|---|---|---|---|---|---|---|---|---|---|---|---|---|---|---|---|---|---|---|---|---|
| Year | Team | Lg | G | AB | H | 2B | 3B | HR | (Hm | Rd) | TB | R | RBI | RC | TBB | IBB | SO | HBP | SH | SF | SB | CS | SB% | GDP | Avg | OBP | Slg |
| 2013 | CpChr* | AA | 6 | 21 | 1 | 0 | 0 | 0 | (- | -) | 1 | 1 | 2 | 0 | 1 | 0 | 8 | 0 | 0 | 1 | 1 | 0 | 1.00 | 0 | .048 | .087 | .048 |
| 2013 | OKCity* | AAA | 8 | 28 | 5 | 0 | 0 | 1 | (- | -) | 8 | 5 | 3 | 2 | 3 | 0 | 6 | 0 | 0 | 1 | 0 | 0 | - | 2 | .179 | .250 | .286 |
| 2007 | Was | NL | 15 | 26 | 7 | 0 | 0 | 2 | (0 | 2) | 13 | 5 | 5 | 4 | 1 | 0 | 8 | 0 | 0 | 0 | 0 | 0 | - | 0 | .269 | .296 | .500 |
| 2009 | Was | NL | 40 | 89 | 22 | 4 | 1 | 4 | (1 | 3) | 40 | 13 | 9 | 15 | 12 | 0 | 32 | 1 | 0 | 0 | 6 | 1 | .86 | 1 | .247 | .343 | .449 |
| 2010 | Was | NL | 67 | 104 | 15 | 6 | 0 | 3 | (1 | 2) | 30 | 16 | 12 | 11 | 25 | 2 | 43 | 0 | 0 | 2 | 5 | 1 | .83 | 3 | .144 | .305 | .288 |
| 2012 | Hou | NL | 124 | 315 | 72 | 13 | 3 | 18 | (10 | 8) | 145 | 46 | 53 | 52 | 32 | 0 | 114 | 3 | 0 | 2 | 9 | 4 | .69 | 6 | .229 | .304 | .460 |
| 2013 | 2 Tms | AL | 75 | 234 | 59 | 16 | 3 | 7 | (4 | 3) | 102 | 35 | 25 | 28 | 23 | 0 | 78 | 4 | 0 | 1 | 6 | 2 | .75 | 4 | .252 | .328 | .436 |
| 13 | Hou | AL | 40 | 137 | 33 | 10 | 2 | 2 | (0 | 2) | 53 | 21 | 8 | 13 | 12 | 0 | 43 | 2 | 0 | 0 | 4 | 1 | .80 | 1 | .241 | .311 | .387 |
| 13 | KC | AL | 35 | 97 | 26 | 6 | 1 | 5 | (4 | 1) | 49 | 14 | 17 | 15 | 11 | 0 | 35 | 2 | 0 | 1 | 2 | 1 | .67 | 3 | .268 | .351 | .505 |
| 5 ML YEARS | | | 321 | 768 | 175 | 39 | 7 | 34 | (16 | 18) | 330 | 115 | 104 | 110 | 93 | 2 | 275 | 8 | 0 | 5 | 26 | 8 | .76 | 14 | .228 | .316 | .430 |

## Yunesky Maya

**Pitches:** R **Bats:** R **Pos:** RP-1 yoo-NESS-key MY-uh **Ht:** 5'11" **Wt:** 205 **Born:** 8/28/1981 **Age:** 32

| | | | HOW MUCH HE PITCHED | | | | | | WHAT HE GAVE UP | | | | | | | | | | | | THE RESULTS | | | | | | | |
|---|---|---|---|---|---|---|---|---|---|---|---|---|---|---|---|---|---|---|---|---|---|---|---|---|---|---|---|---|
| Year | Team | Lg | G | GS | CG | GF | IP | BFP | H | R | ER | HR | SH | SF | HB | TBB | IBB | SO | WP | Bk | W | L | Pct | Sh | Sv-Op | Hld | ERC | ERA |
| 2013 | Syrcse* | AAA | 24 | 24 | 2 | 0 | 146.1 | 618 | 157 | 73 | 63 | 10 | 5 | 8 | 3 | 31 | 3 | 99 | 2 | 3 | 8 | 8 | .500 | 0 | 0-- | - | 3.57 | 3.87 |
| 2010 | Was | NL | 5 | 5 | 0 | 0 | 26.0 | 118 | 30 | 18 | 17 | 3 | 2 | 1 | 2 | 11 | 1 | 12 | 2 | 3 | 0 | 3 | .000 | 0 | 0-0 | 0 | 5.44 | 5.88 |
| 2011 | Was | NL | 10 | 5 | 0 | 2 | 32.2 | 142 | 40 | 19 | 19 | 3 | 5 | 1 | 2 | 10 | 2 | 15 | 1 | 0 | 1 | 1 | .500 | 0 | 0-0 | 0 | 5.25 | 5.23 |
| 2013 | Was | NL | 1 | 0 | 0 | 1 | 0.1 | 3 | 2 | 2 | 2 | 1 | 0 | 0 | 0 | 0 | 0 | 0 | 0 | 0 | 0 | 1 | .000 | 0 | 0-0 | 0 | 83.63 | 54.00 |
| 3 ML YEARS | | | 16 | 10 | 0 | 3 | 59.0 | 263 | 72 | 39 | 38 | 7 | 7 | 2 | 4 | 21 | 3 | 27 | 3 | 3 | 1 | 5 | .167 | 0 | 0-0 | 0 | 5.62 | 5.80 |

## John Mayberry

**Bats:** R **Throws:** R **Pos:** RF-79;CF-46;PH-15;LF-9;PR-8;1B-7 **Ht:** 6'6" **Wt:** 225 **Born:** 12/21/1983 **Age:** 30

| | | | BATTING | | | | | | | | | | | | | | | | | | BASERUNNING | | | | AVERAGES | | |
|---|---|---|---|---|---|---|---|---|---|---|---|---|---|---|---|---|---|---|---|---|---|---|---|---|---|---|---|
| Year | Team | Lg | G | AB | H | 2B | 3B | HR | (Hm | Rd) | TB | R | RBI | RC | TBB | IBB | SO | HBP | SH | SF | SB | CS | SB% | GDP | Avg | OBP | Slg |
| 2009 | Phi | NL | 39 | 57 | 12 | 3 | 0 | 4 | (1 | 3) | 27 | 8 | 8 | 5 | 2 | 0 | 23 | 1 | 0 | 0 | 0 | 0 | - | 2 | .211 | .250 | .474 |
| 2010 | Phi | NL | 11 | 12 | 4 | 0 | 0 | 2 | (0 | 2) | 10 | 4 | 6 | 4 | 1 | 0 | 4 | 0 | 0 | 0 | 0 | 1 | .00 | 0 | .333 | .385 | .833 |
| 2011 | Phi | NL | 104 | 267 | 73 | 17 | 1 | 15 | (7 | 8) | 137 | 37 | 49 | 44 | 26 | 2 | 55 | 2 | 0 | 1 | 8 | 3 | .73 | 6 | .273 | .341 | .513 |
| 2012 | Phi | NL | 149 | 441 | 108 | 24 | 0 | 14 | (7 | 7) | 174 | 53 | 46 | 47 | 34 | 2 | 111 | 2 | 0 | 2 | 1 | 0 | 1.00 | 17 | .245 | .301 | .395 |
| 2013 | Phi | NL | 134 | 353 | 80 | 23 | 1 | 11 | (7 | 4) | 138 | 47 | 39 | 36 | 27 | 1 | 90 | 3 | 0 | 1 | 5 | 3 | .63 | 6 | .227 | .286 | .391 |
| Postseason | | | 2 | 4 | 0 | 0 | 0 | 0 | (0 | 0) | 0 | 0 | 0 | 0 | 0 | 0 | 1 | 0 | 0 | 0 | 0 | 0 | - | 0 | .000 | .000 | .000 |
| 5 ML YEARS | | | 437 | 1130 | 277 | 67 | 2 | 46 | (22 | 24) | 486 | 149 | 148 | 136 | 90 | 5 | 283 | 8 | 0 | 4 | 14 | 7 | .67 | 31 | .245 | .304 | .430 |

## Cameron Maybin

**Bats:** R **Throws:** R **Pos:** CF-14 **Ht:** 6'3" **Wt:** 205 **Born:** 4/4/1987 **Age:** 27

| | | | BATTING | | | | | | | | | | | | | | | | | | BASERUNNING | | | | AVERAGES | | |
|---|---|---|---|---|---|---|---|---|---|---|---|---|---|---|---|---|---|---|---|---|---|---|---|---|---|---|---|
| Year | Team | Lg | G | AB | H | 2B | 3B | HR | (Hm | Rd) | TB | R | RBI | RC | TBB | IBB | SO | HBP | SH | SF | SB | CS | SB% | GDP | Avg | OBP | Slg |
| 2013 | Tucsn* | AAA | 15 | 46 | 12 | 1 | 0 | 4 | (- | -) | 25 | 7 | 5 | 9 | 10 | 0 | 9 | 0 | 0 | 0 | 1 | 1 | .50 | 1 | .261 | .393 | .543 |
| 2007 | Det | AL | 24 | 49 | 7 | 3 | 0 | 1 | (0 | 1) | 13 | 8 | 2 | 2 | 3 | 0 | 21 | 1 | 0 | 0 | 5 | 0 | 1.00 | 0 | .143 | .208 | .265 |
| 2008 | Fla | NL | 8 | 32 | 16 | 2 | 0 | 0 | (0 | 0) | 18 | 9 | 2 | 8 | 3 | 0 | 8 | 0 | 1 | 0 | 4 | 0 | 1.00 | 0 | .500 | .543 | .563 |
| 2009 | Fla | NL | 54 | 176 | 44 | 12 | 2 | 4 | (1 | 3) | 72 | 30 | 13 | 15 | 17 | 1 | 51 | 1 | 4 | 1 | 1 | 3 | .25 | 2 | .250 | .318 | .409 |
| 2010 | Fla | NL | 82 | 291 | 68 | 7 | 3 | 8 | (5 | 3) | 105 | 46 | 28 | 37 | 24 | 1 | 92 | 5 | 1 | 1 | 9 | 2 | .82 | 4 | .234 | .302 | .361 |
| 2011 | SD | NL | 137 | 516 | 136 | 24 | 8 | 9 | (2 | 7) | 203 | 82 | 40 | 69 | 44 | 2 | 125 | 2 | 4 | 2 | 40 | 8 | .83 | 6 | .264 | .323 | .393 |
| 2012 | SD | NL | 147 | 507 | 123 | 20 | 5 | 8 | (3 | 5) | 177 | 67 | 45 | 52 | 44 | 1 | 110 | 4 | 3 | 3 | 26 | 7 | .79 | 12 | .243 | .306 | .349 |
| 2013 | SD | NL | 14 | 51 | 8 | 1 | 0 | 1 | (0 | 1) | 12 | 7 | 5 | 0 | 4 | 1 | 9 | 1 | 1 | 0 | 4 | 1 | .80 | 3 | .157 | .232 | .235 |
| 7 ML YEARS | | | 466 | 1622 | 402 | 69 | 18 | 31 | (11 | 20) | 600 | 249 | 135 | 183 | 139 | 6 | 416 | 14 | 14 | 7 | 89 | 21 | .81 | 27 | .248 | .311 | .370 |

## Vin Mazzaro

**Pitches:** R **Bats:** R **Pos:** RP-57 muh-ZA-roh **Ht:** 6'2" **Wt:** 220 **Born:** 9/27/1986 **Age:** 27

| | | | HOW MUCH HE PITCHED | | | | | | WHAT HE GAVE UP | | | | | | | | | | | | THE RESULTS | | | | | | | |
|---|---|---|---|---|---|---|---|---|---|---|---|---|---|---|---|---|---|---|---|---|---|---|---|---|---|---|---|---|
| Year | Team | Lg | G | GS | CG | GF | IP | BFP | H | R | ER | HR | SH | SF | HB | TBB | IBB | SO | WP | Bk | W | L | Pct | Sh | Sv-Op | Hld | ERC | ERA |
| 2013 | Indy* | AAA | 3 | 0 | 0 | 1 | 7.0 | 25 | 3 | 0 | 0 | 0 | 0 | 0 | 1 | 1 | 0 | 9 | 0 | 0 | 1 | 0 | 1.000 | 0 | 0-- | - | 0.86 | 0.00 |
| 2009 | Oak | AL | 17 | 17 | 0 | 0 | 91.1 | 423 | 120 | 61 | 54 | 12 | 1 | 3 | 4 | 39 | 3 | 59 | 5 | 0 | 4 | 9 | .308 | 0 | 0-0 | 0 | 6.49 | 5.32 |
| 2010 | Oak | AL | 24 | 18 | 0 | 4 | 122.1 | 537 | 127 | 70 | 58 | 19 | 4 | 4 | 4 | 50 | 0 | 79 | 5 | 0 | 6 | 8 | .429 | 0 | 0-0 | 0 | 4.86 | 4.27 |
| 2011 | KC | AL | 7 | 4 | 0 | 2 | 28.1 | 131 | 39 | 26 | 26 | 4 | 3 | 3 | 1 | 15 | 1 | 10 | 2 | 0 | 1 | 1 | .500 | 0 | 0-0 | 0 | 7.67 | 8.26 |
| 2012 | KC | AL | 18 | 6 | 0 | 4 | 44.0 | 198 | 55 | 29 | 28 | 3 | 1 | 2 | 3 | 19 | 2 | 26 | 1 | 0 | 4 | 3 | .571 | 0 | 0-0 | 0 | 5.80 | 5.73 |
| 2013 | Pit | NL | 57 | 0 | 0 | 17 | 73.2 | 304 | 68 | 23 | 23 | 3 | 3 | 1 | 3 | 21 | 3 | 46 | 5 | 1 | 8 | 2 | .800 | 0 | 1-3 | 6 | 2.95 | 2.81 |
| 5 ML YEARS | | | 123 | 45 | 0 | 27 | 359.2 | 1593 | 409 | 209 | 189 | 41 | 12 | 13 | 15 | 144 | 9 | 220 | 18 | 1 | 23 | 23 | .500 | 0 | 1-3 | 6 | 5.16 | 4.73 |

## Zach McAllister

**Pitches:** R **Bats:** R **Pos:** SP-24 **Ht:** 6'6" **Wt:** 240 **Born:** 12/8/1987 **Age:** 26

| HOW MUCH HE PITCHED | | | | | | | | WHAT HE GAVE UP | | | | | | | | | | | | THE RESULTS | | | | | | | |
|---|---|---|---|---|---|---|---|---|---|---|---|---|---|---|---|---|---|---|---|---|---|---|---|---|---|---|---|
| Year | Team | Lg | G | GS | CG | GF | IP | BFP | H | R | ER | HR | SH | SF | HB | TBB | IBB | SO | WP | Bk | W | L | Pct | Sh | Sv-Op | Hld | ERC | ERA |
| 2013 | Akron* | AA | 1 | 1 | 0 | 0 | 3.1 | 15 | 4 | 2 | 2 | 0 | 0 | 0 | 0 | 1 | 0 | 5 | 0 | 0 | 0 | 0 | - | 0 | 0-- | - | 3.97 | 5.40 |
| 2013 | Clmbs* | AAA | 1 | 1 | 0 | 0 | 6.0 | 20 | 2 | 0 | 0 | 0 | 0 | 0 | 0 | 2 | 0 | 2 | 0 | 0 | 1 | 0 | 1.000 | 0 | 0-- | - | 0.75 | 0.00 |
| 2011 | Cle | AL | 4 | 4 | 0 | 0 | 17.2 | 84 | 26 | 16 | 12 | 1 | 0 | 0 | 0 | 7 | 1 | 14 | 0 | 0 | 0 | 1 | .000 | 0 | 0-0 | 0 | 6.41 | 6.11 |
| 2012 | Cle | AL | 22 | 22 | 0 | 0 | 125.1 | 543 | 133 | 78 | 59 | 19 | 2 | 5 | 1 | 38 | 0 | 110 | 0 | 2 | 6 | 8 | .429 | 0 | 0-0 | 0 | 4.37 | 4.24 |
| 2013 | Cle | AL | 24 | 24 | 0 | 0 | 134.1 | 579 | 134 | 65 | 56 | 13 | 0 | 3 | 6 | 49 | 2 | 101 | 7 | 1 | 9 | 9 | .500 | 0 | 0-0 | 0 | 4.06 | 3.75 |
| 3 ML YEARS | | | 50 | 50 | 0 | 0 | 277.1 | 1206 | 293 | 159 | 127 | 33 | 2 | 8 | 7 | 94 | 3 | 225 | 7 | 3 | 15 | 18 | .455 | 0 | 0-0 | 0 | 4.35 | 4.12 |

## Brian McCann

**Bats:** L **Throws:** R **Pos:** C-92;PH-7;DH-3 **Ht:** 6'3" **Wt:** 230 **Born:** 2/20/1984 **Age:** 30

| BATTING | | | | | | | | | | | | | | | | | | | | | BASERUNNING | | | | AVERAGES | | |
|---|---|---|---|---|---|---|---|---|---|---|---|---|---|---|---|---|---|---|---|---|---|---|---|---|---|---|---|
| Year | Team | Lg | G | AB | H | 2B | 3B | HR | (Hm | Rd) | TB | R | RBI | RC | TBB | IBB | SO | HBP | SH | SF | SB | CS | SB% | GDP | Avg | OBP | Slg |
| 2013 | Rome* | A | 4 | 14 | 5 | 1 | 0 | 3 | (- | -) | 15 | 4 | 7 | 5 | 2 | 0 | 2 | 0 | 0 | 0 | 0 | 0 | - | 1 | .357 | .438 | 1.071 |
| 2013 | Gwnntt* | AAA | 3 | 9 | 3 | 0 | 0 | 1 | (- | -) | 6 | 1 | 2 | 2 | 1 | 0 | 1 | 0 | 0 | 0 | 0 | 0 | - | 2 | .333 | .400 | .667 |
| 2005 | Atl | NL | 59 | 180 | 50 | 7 | 0 | 5 | (2 | 3) | 72 | 20 | 23 | 25 | 18 | 5 | 26 | 1 | 4 | 1 | 1 | 1 | .50 | 5 | .278 | .345 | .400 |
| 2006 | Atl | NL | 130 | 442 | 147 | 34 | 0 | 24 | (10 | 14) | 253 | 61 | 93 | 94 | 41 | 8 | 54 | 3 | 0 | 6 | 2 | 0 | 1.00 | 12 | .333 | .388 | .572 |
| 2007 | Atl | NL | 139 | 504 | 136 | 38 | 0 | 18 | (6 | 12) | 228 | 51 | 92 | 68 | 35 | 7 | 74 | 5 | 2 | 6 | 0 | 1 | .00 | 19 | .270 | .320 | .452 |
| 2008 | Atl | NL | 145 | 509 | 153 | 42 | 1 | 23 | (10 | 13) | 266 | 68 | 87 | 84 | 57 | 4 | 64 | 4 | 0 | 3 | 5 | 0 | 1.00 | 17 | .301 | .373 | .523 |
| 2009 | Atl | NL | 138 | 488 | 137 | 35 | 1 | 21 | (12 | 9) | 237 | 63 | 94 | 83 | 49 | 3 | 83 | 5 | 3 | 6 | 4 | 1 | .80 | 17 | .281 | .349 | .486 |
| 2010 | Atl | NL | 143 | 479 | 129 | 25 | 0 | 21 | (13 | 8) | 217 | 63 | 77 | 76 | 74 | 10 | 98 | 9 | 0 | 4 | 5 | 2 | .71 | 12 | .269 | .375 | .453 |
| 2011 | Atl | NL | 128 | 466 | 126 | 19 | 0 | 24 | (15 | 9) | 217 | 51 | 71 | 76 | 57 | 14 | 89 | 2 | 0 | 2 | 3 | 2 | .60 | 10 | .270 | .351 | .466 |
| 2012 | Atl | NL | 121 | 439 | 101 | 14 | 0 | 20 | (11 | 9) | 175 | 44 | 67 | 45 | 44 | 7 | 76 | 1 | 0 | 3 | 3 | 0 | 1.00 | 15 | .230 | .300 | .399 |
| 2013 | Atl | NL | 102 | 356 | 91 | 13 | 0 | 20 | (12 | 8) | 164 | 43 | 57 | 51 | 39 | 3 | 66 | 5 | 0 | 2 | 0 | 1 | .00 | 9 | .256 | .336 | .461 |
| Postseason | | | 8 | 30 | 9 | 1 | 0 | 3 | (2 | 1) | 19 | 4 | 8 | 5 | 2 | 0 | 10 | 0 | 0 | 1 | 0 | 0 | - | 0 | .300 | .333 | .633 |
| 9 ML YEARS | | | 1105 | 3863 | 1070 | 227 | 2 | 176 | (91 | 85) | 1829 | 464 | 661 | 602 | 414 | 61 | 630 | 35 | 9 | 33 | 23 | 8 | .74 | 116 | .277 | .350 | .473 |

## Brandon McCarthy

**Pitches:** R **Bats:** R **Pos:** SP-22 **Ht:** 6'7" **Wt:** 200 **Born:** 7/7/1983 **Age:** 30

| HOW MUCH HE PITCHED | | | | | | | | WHAT HE GAVE UP | | | | | | | | | | | | THE RESULTS | | | | | | | |
|---|---|---|---|---|---|---|---|---|---|---|---|---|---|---|---|---|---|---|---|---|---|---|---|---|---|---|---|
| Year | Team | Lg | G | GS | CG | GF | IP | BFP | H | R | ER | HR | SH | SF | HB | TBB | IBB | SO | WP | Bk | W | L | Pct | Sh | Sv-Op | Hld | ERC | ERA |
| 2013 | Reno* | AAA | 2 | 2 | 0 | 0 | 10.1 | 50 | 15 | 9 | 8 | 2 | 0 | 1 | 1 | 3 | 0 | 4 | 0 | 0 | 0 | 0 | - | 0 | 0-- | - | 7.34 | 6.97 |
| 2005 | CWS | AL | 12 | 10 | 0 | 0 | 67.0 | 277 | 62 | 30 | 30 | 13 | 1 | 1 | 2 | 17 | 0 | 48 | 1 | 1 | 3 | 2 | .600 | 0 | 0-0 | 0 | 3.83 | 4.03 |
| 2006 | CWS | AL | 53 | 2 | 0 | 13 | 84.2 | 354 | 77 | 44 | 44 | 17 | 3 | 1 | 0 | 33 | 9 | 69 | 5 | 0 | 4 | 7 | .364 | 0 | 0-1 | 11 | 4.10 | 4.68 |
| 2007 | Tex | AL | 23 | 22 | 0 | 0 | 101.2 | 459 | 111 | 62 | 55 | 9 | 3 | 5 | 3 | 48 | 0 | 59 | 4 | 1 | 5 | 10 | .333 | 0 | 0-0 | 0 | 4.89 | 4.87 |
| 2008 | Tex | AL | 5 | 5 | 0 | 0 | 22.0 | 93 | 20 | 11 | 10 | 3 | 0 | 2 | 1 | 8 | 0 | 10 | 0 | 0 | 1 | 1 | .500 | 0 | 0-0 | 0 | 3.87 | 4.09 |
| 2009 | Tex | AL | 17 | 17 | 1 | 0 | 97.1 | 420 | 96 | 55 | 50 | 13 | 0 | 5 | 3 | 36 | 0 | 65 | 0 | 0 | 7 | 4 | .636 | 1 | 0-0 | 0 | 4.22 | 4.62 |
| 2011 | Oak | AL | 25 | 25 | 5 | 0 | 170.2 | 690 | 168 | 73 | 63 | 11 | 4 | 9 | 0 | 25 | 1 | 123 | 3 | 0 | 9 | 9 | .500 | 1 | 0-0 | 0 | 2.80 | 3.32 |
| 2012 | Oak | AL | 18 | 18 | 0 | 0 | 111.0 | 469 | 115 | 44 | 40 | 10 | 5 | 4 | 6 | 24 | 2 | 73 | 0 | 0 | 8 | 6 | .571 | 0 | 0-0 | 0 | 3.67 | 3.24 |
| 2013 | Ari | NL | 22 | 22 | 2 | 0 | 135.0 | 577 | 161 | 71 | 68 | 13 | 6 | 1 | 5 | 21 | 3 | 76 | 1 | 1 | 5 | 11 | .313 | 1 | 0-0 | 0 | 4.29 | 4.53 |
| 8 ML YEARS | | | 175 | 121 | 8 | 13 | 789.1 | 3339 | 810 | 390 | 360 | 89 | 22 | 28 | 20 | 212 | 15 | 523 | 14 | 3 | 42 | 50 | .457 | 3 | 0-1 | 11 | 3.87 | 4.10 |

## Kyle McClellan

**Pitches:** R **Bats:** R **Pos:** RP-7 **Ht:** 6'2" **Wt:** 215 **Born:** 6/12/1984 **Age:** 30

| HOW MUCH HE PITCHED | | | | | | | | WHAT HE GAVE UP | | | | | | | | | | | | THE RESULTS | | | | | | | |
|---|---|---|---|---|---|---|---|---|---|---|---|---|---|---|---|---|---|---|---|---|---|---|---|---|---|---|---|
| Year | Team | Lg | G | GS | CG | GF | IP | BFP | H | R | ER | HR | SH | SF | HB | TBB | IBB | SO | WP | Bk | W | L | Pct | Sh | Sv-Op | Hld | ERC | ERA |
| 2013 | Frisco* | AA | 19 | 0 | 0 | 6 | 27.0 | 112 | 29 | 11 | 10 | 2 | 2 | 0 | 1 | 6 | 0 | 27 | 5 | 0 | 2 | 0 | 1.000 | 0 | 0-- | - | 3.85 | 3.33 |
| 2013 | RdRck* | AAA | 6 | 0 | 0 | 2 | 7.0 | 33 | 8 | 3 | 2 | 1 | 0 | 0 | 2 | 2 | 0 | 9 | 1 | 0 | 1 | 0 | 1.000 | 0 | 2-- | - | 5.81 | 2.57 |
| 2008 | StL | NL | 68 | 0 | 0 | 7 | 75.2 | 327 | 79 | 37 | 34 | 7 | 2 | 1 | 4 | 26 | 2 | 59 | 6 | 0 | 2 | 7 | .222 | 0 | 1-6 | **30** | 4.24 | 4.04 |
| 2009 | StL | NL | 66 | 0 | 0 | 14 | 66.2 | 288 | 56 | 27 | 25 | 4 | 5 | 2 | 2 | 34 | 2 | 51 | 4 | 0 | 4 | 4 | .500 | 0 | 3-6 | 15 | 3.38 | 3.38 |
| 2010 | StL | NL | 68 | 0 | 0 | 18 | 75.1 | 307 | 58 | 20 | 19 | 9 | 4 | 1 | 3 | 23 | 3 | 60 | 2 | 0 | 1 | 4 | .200 | 0 | 2-3 | 19 | 2.70 | 2.27 |
| 2011 | StL | NL | 43 | 17 | 0 | 5 | 141.2 | 607 | 143 | 71 | 66 | 21 | 6 | 2 | 6 | 43 | 3 | 76 | 6 | 0 | 12 | 7 | .632 | 0 | 0-1 | 4 | 4.20 | 4.19 |
| 2012 | StL | NL | 16 | 0 | 0 | 6 | 18.2 | 83 | 16 | 11 | 11 | 2 | 0 | 0 | 2 | 9 | 0 | 11 | 1 | 0 | 0 | 1 | .000 | 0 | 0-0 | 1 | 3.98 | 5.30 |
| 2013 | Tex | AL | 7 | 0 | 0 | 4 | 9.1 | 40 | 7 | 8 | 8 | 2 | 0 | 1 | 1 | 5 | 0 | 3 | 1 | 0 | 0 | 1 | .000 | 0 | 0-0 | 1 | 4.47 | 7.71 |
| Postseason | | | 2 | 0 | 0 | 0 | 1.0 | 8 | 3 | 1 | 1 | 0 | 1 | 0 | 1 | 1 | 0 | 0 | 0 | 0 | 0 | 0 | - | 0 | 0-0 | 0 | 24.59 | 9.00 |
| 6 ML YEARS | | | 268 | 17 | 0 | 54 | 387.1 | 1652 | 359 | 174 | 163 | 45 | 17 | 7 | 18 | 140 | 10 | 260 | 20 | 0 | 19 | 24 | .442 | 0 | 6-16 | 70 | 3.76 | 3.79 |

## Andrew McCutchen

**Bats:** R **Throws:** R **Pos:** CF-155;PH-3 **Ht:** 5'10" **Wt:** 190 **Born:** 10/10/1986 **Age:** 27

| BATTING | | | | | | | | | | | | | | | | | | | | | BASERUNNING | | | | AVERAGES | | |
|---|---|---|---|---|---|---|---|---|---|---|---|---|---|---|---|---|---|---|---|---|---|---|---|---|---|---|---|
| Year | Team | Lg | G | AB | H | 2B | 3B | HR | (Hm | Rd) | TB | R | RBI | RC | TBB | IBB | SO | HBP | SH | SF | SB | CS | SB% | GDP | Avg | OBP | Slg |
| 2009 | Pit | NL | 108 | 433 | 124 | 26 | 9 | 12 | (8 | 4) | 204 | 74 | 54 | 78 | 54 | 2 | 83 | 2 | 0 | 4 | 22 | 5 | .81 | 3 | .286 | .365 | .471 |
| 2010 | Pit | NL | 154 | 570 | 163 | 35 | 5 | 16 | (8 | 8) | 256 | 94 | 56 | 86 | 70 | 1 | 89 | 5 | 1 | 7 | 33 | 10 | .77 | 6 | .286 | .365 | .449 |
| 2011 | Pit | NL | 158 | 572 | 148 | 34 | 5 | 23 | (10 | 13) | 261 | 87 | 89 | 102 | 89 | 3 | 126 | 9 | 2 | 6 | 23 | 10 | .70 | 7 | .259 | .364 | .456 |
| 2012 | Pit | NL | 157 | 593 | **194** | 29 | 6 | 31 | (15 | 16) | 328 | 107 | 96 | **125** | 70 | 13 | 132 | 5 | 0 | 5 | 20 | 12 | .63 | 9 | .327 | .400 | .553 |
| 2013 | Pit | NL | 157 | 583 | 185 | 38 | 5 | 21 | (9 | 12) | 296 | 97 | 84 | 105 | 78 | 12 | 101 | 9 | 0 | 4 | 27 | 10 | .73 | 13 | .317 | .404 | .508 |
| 5 ML YEARS | | | 734 | 2751 | 814 | 162 | 30 | 103 | (50 | 53) | 1345 | 459 | 379 | 496 | 361 | 31 | 531 | 30 | 3 | 26 | 125 | 47 | .73 | 38 | .296 | .380 | .489 |

## Darnell McDonald

**Bats:** R **Throws:** R **Pos:** PH-13;RF-8;LF-7 **Ht:** 5'11" **Wt:** 205 **Born:** 11/17/1978 **Age:** 35

| | | BATTING | | | | | | | | | | | | | | | | | | BASERUNNING | | | | AVERAGES | | |
|---|---|---|---|---|---|---|---|---|---|---|---|---|---|---|---|---|---|---|---|---|---|---|---|---|---|---|
| Year Team | Lg | G | AB | H | 2B | 3B | HR | (Hm | Rd) | TB | R | RBI | RC | TBB | IBB | SO | HBP | SH | SF | SB | CS | SB% | GDP | Avg | OBP | Slg |
| 2013 Iowa* | AAA | 92 | 263 | 62 | 13 | 2 | 4 | (- | -) | 91 | 31 | 26 | 30 | 27 | 1 | 50 | 1 | 1 | 2 | 8 | 2 | .80 | 2 | .236 | .307 | .346 |
| 2004 Bal | AL | 17 | 32 | 5 | 1 | 0 | 0 | (0 | 0) | 6 | 3 | 1 | 2 | 2 | 0 | 6 | 0 | 0 | 0 | 1 | 0 | 1.00 | 0 | .156 | .206 | .188 |
| 2007 Min | AL | 4 | 10 | 1 | 0 | 0 | 0 | (0 | 0) | 1 | 0 | 0 | 0 | 1 | 0 | 3 | 0 | 0 | 0 | 0 | 0 | - | 0 | .100 | .182 | .100 |
| 2009 Cin | NL | 47 | 105 | 28 | 6 | 1 | 2 | (2 | 0) | 42 | 12 | 10 | 10 | 5 | 0 | 31 | 1 | 0 | 0 | 1 | 0 | 1.00 | 4 | .267 | .306 | .400 |
| 2010 Bos | AL | 117 | 319 | 86 | 18 | 3 | 9 | (5 | 4) | 137 | 40 | 34 | 46 | 30 | 1 | 85 | 2 | 12 | 0 | 9 | 1 | .90 | 5 | .270 | .336 | .429 |
| 2011 Bos | AL | 79 | 157 | 37 | 6 | 1 | 6 | (2 | 4) | 63 | 26 | 24 | 19 | 14 | 0 | 33 | 2 | 0 | 2 | 2 | 3 | .40 | 3 | .236 | .303 | .401 |
| 2012 2 Tms | AL | 42 | 88 | 18 | 7 | 0 | 2 | (1 | 1) | 31 | 17 | 9 | 8 | 12 | 0 | 19 | 0 | 2 | 1 | 1 | 1 | .50 | 1 | .205 | .297 | .352 |
| 2013 ChC | NL | 25 | 53 | 16 | 4 | 0 | 1 | (1 | 0) | 23 | 4 | 5 | 9 | 4 | 0 | 8 | 0 | 0 | 0 | 0 | 0 | - | 4 | .302 | .351 | .434 |
| 12 Bos | AL | 38 | 84 | 18 | 7 | 0 | 2 | (1 | 1) | 31 | 17 | 9 | 8 | 12 | 0 | 17 | 0 | 2 | 1 | 1 | 1 | .50 | 1 | .214 | .309 | .369 |
| 12 NYY | AL | 4 | 4 | 0 | 0 | 0 | 0 | (0 | 0) | 0 | 0 | 0 | 0 | 0 | 0 | 2 | 0 | 0 | 0 | 0 | 0 | - | 0 | .000 | .000 | .000 |
| 7 ML YEARS | | 331 | 764 | 191 | 42 | 5 | 20 | (11 | 9) | 303 | 102 | 83 | 94 | 68 | 1 | 185 | 5 | 14 | 3 | 14 | 5 | .74 | 17 | .250 | .314 | .397 |

## James McDonald

**Pitches:** R **Bats:** L **Pos:** SP-6 **Ht:** 6'4" **Wt:** 205 **Born:** 10/19/1984 **Age:** 29

| | | HOW MUCH HE PITCHED | | | | | | WHAT HE GAVE UP | | | | | | | | | | | | THE RESULTS | | | | | | | |
|---|---|---|---|---|---|---|---|---|---|---|---|---|---|---|---|---|---|---|---|---|---|---|---|---|---|---|---|
| Year Team | Lg | G | GS | CG | GF | IP | BFP | H | R | ER | HR | SH | SF | HB | TBB | IBB | SO | WP | Bk | W | L | Pct | Sh | Sv-Op | Hld | ERC | ERA |
| 2013 Altna* | AA | 2 | 2 | 0 | 0 | 4.2 | 21 | 4 | 3 | 3 | 1 | 0 | 0 | 0 | 5 | 0 | 2 | 0 | 0 | 0 | 1 | .000 | 0 | 0-- | - | 7.47 | 5.79 |
| 2013 Indy* | AAA | 4 | 4 | 0 | 0 | 20.2 | 94 | 26 | 16 | 15 | 2 | 0 | 2 | 2 | 9 | 0 | 12 | 1 | 0 | 1 | 3 | .250 | 0 | 0-- | - | 6.31 | 6.53 |
| 2013 Pirates* | R | 3 | 3 | 0 | 0 | 5.2 | 24 | 5 | 4 | 4 | 0 | 0 | 1 | 1 | 1 | 0 | 5 | 1 | 0 | 0 | 0 | - | 0 | 0-- | - | 2.55 | 6.35 |
| 2013 Bradtn* | A+ | 1 | 0 | 0 | 0 | 2.0 | 10 | 4 | 2 | 2 | 1 | 0 | 0 | 0 | 0 | 0 | 1 | 0 | 0 | 0 | 0 | - | 0 | 0-- | - | 11.88 | 9.00 |
| 2008 LAD | NL | 4 | 0 | 0 | 1 | 6.0 | 24 | 5 | 0 | 0 | 0 | 1 | 0 | 0 | 1 | 0 | 2 | 0 | 0 | 0 | 0 | - | 0 | 0-0 | 0 | 1.74 | 0.00 |
| 2009 LAD | NL | 45 | 4 | 0 | 10 | 63.0 | 280 | 60 | 34 | 28 | 6 | 2 | 3 | 5 | 34 | 5 | 54 | 4 | 0 | 5 | 5 | .500 | 0 | 0-0 | 5 | 4.53 | 4.00 |
| 2010 2 Tms | NL | 15 | 12 | 0 | 0 | 71.2 | 306 | 70 | 32 | 32 | 4 | 5 | 3 | 0 | 29 | 5 | 68 | 5 | 0 | 4 | 6 | .400 | 0 | 0-0 | 1 | 3.56 | 4.02 |
| 2011 Pit | NL | 31 | 31 | 0 | 0 | 171.0 | 754 | 176 | 86 | 80 | 24 | 6 | 5 | 7 | 78 | 4 | 142 | 5 | 1 | 9 | 9 | .500 | 0 | 0-0 | 0 | 4.92 | 4.21 |
| 2012 Pit | NL | 30 | 29 | 1 | 0 | 171.0 | 713 | 147 | 85 | 80 | 21 | 5 | 4 | 4 | 69 | 6 | 151 | 3 | 0 | 12 | 8 | .600 | 0 | 0-0 | 0 | 3.55 | 4.21 |
| 2013 Pit | NL | 6 | 6 | 0 | 0 | 29.2 | 138 | 29 | 24 | 19 | 1 | 0 | 0 | 3 | 20 | 1 | 25 | 2 | 0 | 2 | 2 | .500 | 0 | 0-0 | 0 | 4.83 | 5.76 |
| 10 LAD | NL | 4 | 1 | 0 | 0 | 7.2 | 38 | 11 | 7 | 7 | 1 | 0 | 1 | 0 | 5 | 1 | 7 | 0 | 0 | 0 | 1 | .000 | 0 | 0-0 | 1 | 7.83 | 8.22 |
| 10 Pit | NL | 11 | 11 | 0 | 0 | 64.0 | 268 | 59 | 25 | 25 | 3 | 5 | 2 | 0 | 24 | 4 | 61 | 5 | 0 | 4 | 5 | .444 | 0 | 0-0 | 0 | 3.12 | 3.52 |
| Postseason | | 2 | 0 | 0 | 0 | 5.1 | 21 | 3 | 0 | 0 | 0 | 0 | 0 | 0 | 2 | 0 | 7 | 0 | 0 | 0 | 0 | - | 0 | 0-0 | 0 | 1.35 | 0.00 |
| 6 ML YEARS | | 131 | 82 | 1 | 11 | 512.1 | 2215 | 487 | 261 | 239 | 56 | 19 | 15 | 19 | 231 | 21 | 442 | 19 | 1 | 32 | 30 | .516 | 0 | 0-0 | 6 | 4.17 | 4.20 |

## John McDonald

**Bats:** R **Throws:** R **Pos:** SS-19;3B-16;2B-11;PH-7;PR-7;LF-1 **Ht:** 5'9" **Wt:** 180 **Born:** 9/24/1974 **Age:** 39

| | | BATTING | | | | | | | | | | | | | | | | | | BASERUNNING | | | | AVERAGES | | |
|---|---|---|---|---|---|---|---|---|---|---|---|---|---|---|---|---|---|---|---|---|---|---|---|---|---|---|
| Year Team | Lg | G | AB | H | 2B | 3B | HR | (Hm | Rd) | TB | R | RBI | RC | TBB | IBB | SO | HBP | SH | SF | SB | CS | SB% | GDP | Avg | OBP | Slg |
| 2013 Indy* | AAA | 10 | 34 | 9 | 1 | 0 | 0 | (- | -) | 10 | 5 | 1 | 3 | 2 | 0 | 3 | 1 | 0 | 0 | 1 | 0 | 1.00 | 2 | .265 | .324 | .294 |
| 1999 Cle | AL | 18 | 21 | 7 | 0 | 0 | 0 | (0 | 0) | 7 | 2 | 0 | 1 | 0 | 0 | 3 | 0 | 0 | 0 | 0 | 1 | .00 | 2 | .333 | .333 | .333 |
| 2000 Cle | AL | 9 | 9 | 4 | 0 | 0 | 0 | (0 | 0) | 4 | 0 | 0 | 2 | 0 | 0 | 1 | 0 | 0 | 0 | 0 | 0 | - | 0 | .444 | .444 | .444 |
| 2001 Cle | AL | 17 | 22 | 2 | 1 | 0 | 0 | (0 | 0) | 3 | 1 | 0 | 0 | 1 | 0 | 7 | 1 | 1 | 0 | 0 | 0 | - | 0 | .091 | .167 | .136 |
| 2002 Cle | AL | 93 | 264 | 66 | 11 | 3 | 1 | (0 | 1) | 86 | 35 | 12 | 24 | 10 | 0 | 50 | 5 | 7 | 2 | 3 | 0 | 1.00 | 4 | .250 | .288 | .326 |
| 2003 Cle | AL | 82 | 214 | 46 | 9 | 1 | 1 | (0 | 1) | 60 | 21 | 14 | 18 | 11 | 0 | 31 | 2 | 4 | 2 | 3 | 3 | .50 | 4 | .215 | .258 | .280 |
| 2004 Cle | AL | 66 | 93 | 19 | 5 | 1 | 2 | (0 | 2) | 32 | 17 | 7 | 6 | 4 | 0 | 11 | 0 | 3 | 0 | 0 | 0 | - | 2 | .204 | .237 | .344 |
| 2005 2 Tms | AL | 68 | 166 | 46 | 6 | 1 | 0 | (0 | 0) | 54 | 18 | 16 | 19 | 11 | 0 | 24 | 2 | 3 | 2 | 6 | 1 | .86 | 6 | .277 | .326 | .325 |
| 2006 Tor | AL | 104 | 260 | 58 | 7 | 3 | 3 | (1 | 2) | 80 | 35 | 23 | 20 | 16 | 0 | 41 | 2 | 6 | 2 | 7 | 2 | .78 | 8 | .223 | .271 | .308 |
| 2007 Tor | AL | 123 | 327 | 82 | 20 | 2 | 1 | (1 | 0) | 109 | 32 | 31 | 35 | 11 | 0 | 48 | 2 | 12 | 1 | 7 | 2 | .78 | 4 | .251 | .279 | .333 |
| 2008 Tor | AL | 84 | 186 | 39 | 8 | 0 | 1 | (1 | 0) | 50 | 21 | 18 | 11 | 10 | 0 | 25 | 2 | 7 | 2 | 3 | 1 | .75 | 3 | .210 | .255 | .269 |
| 2009 Tor | AL | 73 | 151 | 39 | 7 | 0 | 4 | (2 | 2) | 58 | 18 | 13 | 16 | 1 | 0 | 18 | 2 | 1 | 1 | 0 | 2 | .00 | 1 | .258 | .271 | .384 |
| 2010 Tor | AL | 63 | 152 | 38 | 9 | 2 | 6 | (3 | 3) | 69 | 27 | 23 | 20 | 6 | 0 | 26 | 0 | 2 | 3 | 2 | 1 | .67 | 5 | .250 | .273 | .454 |
| 2011 2 Tms | | 84 | 227 | 52 | 10 | 1 | 2 | (2 | 0) | 70 | 21 | 22 | 23 | 12 | 0 | 27 | 1 | 3 | 2 | 2 | 4 | .33 | 1 | .229 | .269 | .308 |
| 2012 Ari | NL | 70 | 197 | 49 | 9 | 0 | 6 | (4 | 2) | 76 | 16 | 22 | 21 | 12 | 5 | 33 | 1 | 2 | 0 | 0 | 1 | .00 | 3 | .249 | .295 | .386 |
| 2013 4 Tms | | 51 | 69 | 8 | 1 | 0 | 1 | (1 | 0) | 12 | 8 | 4 | 2 | 6 | 0 | 16 | 1 | 1 | 0 | 0 | 0 | - | 4 | .116 | .197 | .174 |
| 05 Tor | AL | 37 | 93 | 27 | 3 | 0 | 0 | (0 | 0) | 30 | 8 | 12 | 13 | 6 | 0 | 12 | 2 | 3 | 2 | 5 | 0 | 1.00 | 3 | .290 | .340 | .323 |
| 05 Det | AL | 31 | 73 | 19 | 3 | 1 | 0 | (0 | 0) | 24 | 10 | 4 | 6 | 5 | 0 | 12 | 0 | 0 | 0 | 1 | 1 | .50 | 3 | .260 | .308 | .329 |
| 11 Tor | AL | 65 | 168 | 42 | 8 | 1 | 2 | (2 | 0) | 58 | 19 | 20 | 21 | 8 | 0 | 18 | 1 | 3 | 2 | 2 | 4 | .33 | 1 | .250 | .285 | .345 |
| 11 Ari | NL | 19 | 59 | 10 | 2 | 0 | 0 | (0 | 0) | 12 | 2 | 2 | 2 | 4 | 0 | 9 | 0 | 0 | 0 | 0 | 0 | - | 0 | .169 | .222 | .203 |
| 13 Pit | NL | 16 | 31 | 2 | 1 | 0 | 0 | (0 | 0) | 3 | 0 | 1 | 0 | 3 | 0 | 8 | 1 | 0 | 0 | 0 | 0 | - | 1 | .065 | .171 | .097 |
| 13 Cle | AL | 8 | 7 | 0 | 0 | 0 | 0 | (0 | 0) | 0 | 2 | 0 | 0 | 1 | 0 | 1 | 0 | 0 | 0 | 0 | 0 | - | 0 | .000 | .125 | .000 |
| 13 Phi | NL | 21 | 23 | 4 | 0 | 0 | 1 | (1 | 0) | 7 | 5 | 3 | 1 | 1 | 0 | 4 | 0 | 1 | 0 | 0 | 0 | - | 3 | .174 | .208 | .304 |
| 13 Bos | AL | 6 | 8 | 2 | 0 | 0 | 0 | (0 | 0) | 2 | 1 | 0 | 1 | 1 | 0 | 3 | 0 | 0 | 0 | 0 | 0 | - | 0 | .250 | .333 | .250 |
| Postseason | | 2 | 2 | 0 | 0 | 0 | 0 | (0 | 0) | 0 | 0 | 0 | 0 | 0 | 0 | 0 | 0 | 0 | 0 | 0 | 0 | - | 0 | .000 | .000 | .000 |
| 15 ML YEARS | | 1005 | 2358 | 555 | 103 | 14 | 28 | (15 | 13) | 770 | 272 | 205 | 218 | 111 | 5 | 361 | 21 | 52 | 17 | 33 | 18 | .65 | 47 | .235 | .274 | .327 |

## T.J. McFarland

**Pitches:** L **Bats:** L **Pos:** RP-37; SP-1 **Ht:** 6'3" **Wt:** 220 **Born:** 6/8/1989 **Age:** 25

| | | HOW MUCH HE PITCHED | | | | | | WHAT HE GAVE UP | | | | | | | | | | | | THE RESULTS | | | | | | | |
|---|---|---|---|---|---|---|---|---|---|---|---|---|---|---|---|---|---|---|---|---|---|---|---|---|---|---|---|
| Year Team | Lg | G | GS | CG | GF | IP | BFP | H | R | ER | HR | SH | SF | HB | TBB | IBB | SO | WP | Bk | W | L | Pct | Sh | Sv-Op | Hld | ERC | ERA |
| 2009 Lk Cty | A | 25 | 23 | 0 | 1 | 120.2 | 516 | 128 | 58 | 48 | 6 | 4 | 2 | 3 | 42 | 0 | 85 | 10 | 1 | 9 | 4 | .692 | 0 | 1-- | - | 4.01 | 3.58 |
| 2010 Knstn | A+ | 24 | 19 | 1 | 3 | 126.2 | 537 | 121 | 50 | 44 | 9 | 1 | 0 | 4 | 40 | 0 | 92 | 6 | 1 | 11 | 5 | .688 | 0 | 0-- | - | 3.41 | 3.13 |
| 2010 Akron | AA | 1 | 1 | 0 | 0 | 4.0 | 23 | 9 | 6 | 5 | 1 | 0 | 0 | 0 | 2 | 0 | 5 | 0 | 0 | 0 | 0 | - | 0 | 0-- | - | 14.09 | 11.25 |
| 2011 Knstn | A+ | 2 | 2 | 0 | 0 | 12.0 | 48 | 9 | 5 | 3 | 2 | 0 | 0 | 0 | 1 | 0 | 12 | 0 | 0 | 0 | 1 | .000 | 0 | 0-- | - | 1.86 | 2.25 |
| 2011 Akron | AA | 25 | 25 | 2 | 0 | 137.1 | 590 | 140 | 73 | 59 | 9 | 1 | 4 | 7 | 50 | 0 | 103 | 12 | 3 | 9 | 9 | .500 | 0 | 0-- | - | 4.04 | 3.87 |
| 2012 Akron | AA | 10 | 10 | 1 | 0 | 60.1 | 240 | 61 | 18 | 18 | 1 | 0 | 1 | 3 | 12 | 0 | 41 | 1 | 0 | 8 | 2 | .800 | 0 | 0-- | - | 3.17 | 2.69 |
| 2012 Clmbs | AAA | 17 | 17 | 1 | 0 | 102.2 | 435 | 112 | 55 | 55 | 9 | 0 | 0 | 1 | 33 | 0 | 55 | 5 | 0 | 8 | 6 | .571 | 1 | 0-- | - | 4.33 | 4.82 |
| 2013 Bal | AL | 38 | 1 | 0 | 8 | 74.2 | 331 | 83 | 37 | 35 | 7 | 2 | 1 | 0 | 28 | 5 | 58 | 2 | 0 | 4 | 1 | .800 | 0 | 0-0 | 0 | 4.40 | 4.22 |

## Jake McGee

**Pitches:** L **Bats:** L **Pos:** RP-71 **Ht:** 6'3" **Wt:** 230 **Born:** 8/6/1986 **Age:** 27

| HOW MUCH HE PITCHED | | | | | | | | | WHAT HE GAVE UP | | | | | | | | | | | | THE RESULTS | | | | | | | |
|---|---|---|---|---|---|---|---|---|---|---|---|---|---|---|---|---|---|---|---|---|---|---|---|---|---|---|---|---|
| Year | Team | Lg | G | GS | CG | GF | IP | BFP | H | R | ER | HR | SH | SF | HB | TBB | IBB | SO | WP | Bk | W | L | Pct | Sh | Sv-Op | Hld | ERC | ERA |
| 2010 | TB | AL | 8 | 0 | 0 | 3 | 5.0 | 20 | 2 | 1 | 1 | 0 | 0 | 0 | 0 | 3 | 0 | 6 | 0 | 0 | 0 | 0 | - | 0 | 0-0 | 0 | 1.32 | 1.80 |
| 2011 | TB | AL | 37 | 0 | 0 | 9 | 28.0 | 124 | 30 | 14 | 14 | 5 | 1 | 0 | 0 | 12 | 1 | 27 | 0 | 0 | 5 | 2 | .714 | 0 | 0-0 | 4 | 5.09 | 4.50 |
| 2012 | TB | AL | 69 | 0 | 0 | 13 | 55.1 | 212 | 33 | 13 | 12 | 3 | 0 | 2 | 1 | 11 | 4 | 73 | 3 | 0 | 5 | 2 | .714 | 0 | 0-2 | 19 | 1.26 | 1.95 |
| 2013 | TB | AL | 71 | 0 | 0 | 6 | 62.2 | 260 | 52 | 28 | 28 | 8 | 1 | 3 | 1 | 22 | 5 | 75 | 4 | 0 | 5 | 3 | .625 | 0 | 1-5 | 27 | 3.07 | 4.02 |
| Postseason | | | 1 | 0 | 0 | 0 | 0.1 | 2 | 0 | 0 | 0 | 0 | 1 | 0 | 1 | 0 | 0 | 0 | 0 | 0 | 0 | 0 | - | 0 | 0-0 | 0 | 7.00 | 0.00 |
| 4 ML YEARS | | | 185 | 0 | 0 | 31 | 151.0 | 616 | 117 | 56 | 55 | 16 | 2 | 5 | 2 | 48 | 10 | 181 | 7 | 0 | 15 | 7 | .682 | 0 | 1-7 | 50 | 2.55 | 3.28 |

## Dustin McGowan

**Pitches:** R **Bats:** R **Pos:** RP-25 **Ht:** 6'3" **Wt:** 230 **Born:** 3/24/1982 **Age:** 32

| HOW MUCH HE PITCHED | | | | | | | | | WHAT HE GAVE UP | | | | | | | | | | | | THE RESULTS | | | | | | | |
|---|---|---|---|---|---|---|---|---|---|---|---|---|---|---|---|---|---|---|---|---|---|---|---|---|---|---|---|---|
| Year | Team | Lg | G | GS | CG | GF | IP | BFP | H | R | ER | HR | SH | SF | HB | TBB | IBB | SO | WP | Bk | W | L | Pct | Sh | Sv-Op | Hld | ERC | ERA |
| 2013 | Dnedin* | A+ | 3 | 0 | 0 | 0 | 3.0 | 11 | 1 | 0 | 0 | 0 | 0 | 0 | 0 | 1 | 0 | 5 | 0 | 0 | 0 | 0 | - | 0 | 0- - | - | 0.69 | 0.00 |
| 2013 | Buffalo* | AAA | 8 | 0 | 0 | 1 | 9.0 | 43 | 10 | 7 | 7 | 1 | 0 | 1 | 0 | 6 | 0 | 12 | 0 | 0 | 0 | 0 | - | 0 | 0- - | - | 5.76 | 7.00 |
| 2005 | Tor | AL | 13 | 7 | 0 | 2 | 45.1 | 205 | 49 | 34 | 32 | 7 | 0 | 4 | 7 | 17 | 0 | 34 | 7 | 0 | 1 | 3 | .250 | 0 | 0-0 | 1 | 5.47 | 6.35 |
| 2006 | Tor | AL | 16 | 3 | 0 | 3 | 27.1 | 143 | 35 | 27 | 22 | 2 | 0 | 1 | 2 | 25 | 2 | 22 | 3 | 1 | 1 | 2 | .333 | 0 | 0-1 | 1 | 7.72 | 7.24 |
| 2007 | Tor | AL | 27 | 27 | 2 | 0 | 169.2 | 705 | 146 | 80 | 77 | 14 | 0 | 6 | 2 | 61 | 3 | 144 | 13 | 0 | 12 | 10 | .545 | 1 | 0-0 | 0 | 3.07 | 4.08 |
| 2008 | Tor | AL | 19 | 19 | 1 | 0 | 111.1 | 474 | 115 | 60 | 54 | 9 | 2 | 8 | 5 | 38 | 1 | 85 | 5 | 0 | 6 | 7 | .462 | 0 | 0-0 | 0 | 4.13 | 4.37 |
| 2011 | Tor | AL | 5 | 4 | 0 | 0 | 21.0 | 96 | 20 | 15 | 15 | 4 | 0 | 1 | 1 | 13 | 0 | 20 | 3 | 0 | 0 | 2 | .000 | 0 | 0-0 | 0 | 5.50 | 6.43 |
| 2013 | Tor | AL | 25 | 0 | 0 | 8 | 25.2 | 114 | 19 | 11 | 7 | 2 | 0 | 0 | 2 | 12 | 1 | 26 | 3 | 0 | 0 | 0 | - | 0 | 0-1 | 6 | 2.83 | 2.45 |
| 6 ML YEARS | | | 105 | 60 | 3 | 13 | 400.1 | 1737 | 384 | 227 | 207 | 38 | 2 | 20 | 19 | 166 | 7 | 331 | 34 | 1 | 20 | 24 | .455 | 1 | 0-2 | 8 | 4.02 | 4.65 |

## Chris McGuiness

**Bats:** L **Throws:** L **Pos:** 1B-10 **Ht:** 6'1" **Wt:** 210 **Born:** 4/11/1988 **Age:** 26

| BATTING | | | | | | | | | | | | | | | | | | | | | BASERUNNING | | | | AVERAGES | | |
|---|---|---|---|---|---|---|---|---|---|---|---|---|---|---|---|---|---|---|---|---|---|---|---|---|---|---|---|
| Year | Team | Lg | G | AB | H | 2B | 3B | HR | (Hm | Rd) | TB | R | RBI | RC | TBB | IBB | SO | HBP | SH | SF | SB | CS | SB% | GDP | Avg | OBP | Slg |
| 2009 | Lowell | A- | 54 | 196 | 50 | 17 | 0 | 6 | (- | -) | 85 | 26 | 38 | 34 | 36 | 2 | 40 | 2 | 0 | 1 | 0 | 1 | .00 | 5 | .255 | .374 | .434 |
| 2009 | Grnvlle | A | 6 | 20 | 3 | 1 | 0 | 0 | (- | -) | 4 | 2 | 1 | 1 | 3 | 0 | 5 | 2 | 0 | 0 | 0 | 0 | - | 0 | .150 | .320 | .200 |
| 2010 | Grnvlle | A | 78 | 282 | 84 | 20 | 1 | 12 | (- | -) | 142 | 41 | 46 | 60 | 53 | 3 | 59 | 5 | 0 | 1 | 2 | 3 | .40 | 11 | .298 | .416 | .504 |
| 2010 | Bkrsfld | A+ | 34 | 120 | 30 | 3 | 0 | 7 | (- | -) | 54 | 19 | 22 | 22 | 24 | 0 | 32 | 2 | 0 | 1 | 1 | 1 | .50 | 1 | .250 | .381 | .450 |
| 2011 | MrtlBh | A+ | 53 | 196 | 42 | 10 | 0 | 2 | (- | -) | 58 | 19 | 26 | 21 | 30 | 1 | 51 | 1 | 0 | 1 | 1 | 0 | 1.00 | 1 | .214 | .320 | .296 |
| 2011 | Rngrs | R | 2 | 5 | 1 | 0 | 0 | 1 | (- | -) | 4 | 3 | 2 | 1 | 1 | 0 | 1 | 1 | 0 | 0 | 0 | 0 | - | 1 | .200 | .429 | .800 |
| 2012 | Frisco | AA | 123 | 456 | 122 | 25 | 0 | 23 | (- | -) | 216 | 65 | 77 | 82 | 69 | 4 | 107 | 3 | 0 | 2 | 0 | 1 | .00 | 9 | .268 | .366 | .474 |
| 2013 | RdRck | AAA | 104 | 362 | 89 | 29 | 1 | 11 | (- | -) | 153 | 52 | 63 | 62 | 68 | 1 | 86 | 4 | 0 | 2 | 1 | 0 | 1.00 | 9 | .246 | .369 | .423 |
| 2013 | Tex | AL | 10 | 34 | 6 | 1 | 0 | 0 | (0 | 0) | 7 | 0 | 1 | 0 | 0 | 0 | 13 | 0 | 0 | 0 | 0 | 0 | - | 1 | .176 | .176 | .206 |

## Collin McHugh

**Pitches:** R **Bats:** R **Pos:** SP-5; RP-2 **Ht:** 6'2" **Wt:** 195 **Born:** 6/19/1987 **Age:** 27

| HOW MUCH HE PITCHED | | | | | | | | | WHAT HE GAVE UP | | | | | | | | | | | | THE RESULTS | | | | | | | |
|---|---|---|---|---|---|---|---|---|---|---|---|---|---|---|---|---|---|---|---|---|---|---|---|---|---|---|---|---|
| Year | Team | Lg | G | GS | CG | GF | IP | BFP | H | R | ER | HR | SH | SF | HB | TBB | IBB | SO | WP | Bk | W | L | Pct | Sh | Sv-Op | Hld | ERC | ERA |
| 2009 | Bklyn | A- | 14 | 14 | 1 | 0 | 75.0 | 305 | 61 | 25 | 23 | 1 | 0 | 0 | 5 | 21 | 0 | 79 | 3 | 0 | 8 | 2 | .800 | 1 | 0- - | - | 2.35 | 2.76 |
| 2010 | Savann | A | 28 | 20 | 0 | 6 | 132.1 | 575 | 139 | 65 | 49 | 7 | 2 | 4 | 12 | 38 | 0 | 129 | 5 | 2 | 7 | 8 | .467 | 0 | 1- - | - | 3.92 | 3.33 |
| 2011 | StLuci | A+ | 9 | 6 | 0 | 3 | 35.2 | 164 | 47 | 27 | 25 | 3 | 0 | 1 | 1 | 14 | 0 | 39 | 2 | 2 | 1 | 2 | .333 | 0 | 1- - | - | 5.95 | 6.31 |
| 2011 | Bnghtn | AA | 18 | 16 | 1 | 2 | 93.1 | 394 | 78 | 32 | 30 | 2 | 3 | 2 | 8 | 32 | 3 | 100 | 7 | 0 | 8 | 2 | .800 | 0 | 2- - | - | 2.70 | 2.89 |
| 2012 | Bnghtn | AA | 12 | 12 | 0 | 0 | 74.2 | 303 | 63 | 21 | 20 | 4 | 3 | 2 | 5 | 17 | 0 | 65 | 6 | 0 | 5 | 5 | .500 | 0 | 0- - | - | 2.57 | 2.41 |
| 2012 | Buffalo | AAA | 13 | 13 | 0 | 0 | 73.2 | 312 | 60 | 32 | 28 | 8 | 0 | 3 | 2 | 29 | 0 | 70 | 2 | 0 | 2 | 4 | .333 | 0 | 0- - | - | 3.14 | 3.42 |
| 2013 | LsVgs | AAA | 9 | 9 | 0 | 0 | 53.1 | 225 | 57 | 21 | 17 | 3 | 1 | 1 | 4 | 13 | 0 | 41 | 3 | 1 | 3 | 2 | .600 | 0 | 0- - | - | 3.91 | 2.87 |
| 2013 | Tulsa | AA | 2 | 2 | 0 | 0 | 13.0 | 45 | 9 | 2 | 2 | 1 | 1 | 0 | 0 | 0 | 0 | 12 | 0 | 0 | 1 | 1 | .500 | 0 | 0- - | - | 1.30 | 1.38 |
| 2013 | ColSpr | AAA | 9 | 9 | 0 | 0 | 46.2 | 207 | 52 | 25 | 24 | 2 | 1 | 1 | 3 | 14 | 0 | 47 | 1 | 0 | 2 | 2 | .500 | 0 | 0- - | - | 4.10 | 4.63 |
| 2012 | NYM | NL | 8 | 4 | 0 | 1 | 21.1 | 99 | 27 | 21 | 18 | 5 | 2 | 1 | 2 | 8 | 2 | 17 | 0 | 0 | 0 | 4 | .000 | 0 | 0-0 | 0 | 6.83 | 7.59 |
| 2013 | 2 Tms | NL | 7 | 5 | 0 | 2 | 26.0 | 125 | 45 | 29 | 29 | 6 | 2 | 2 | 0 | 5 | 0 | 11 | 0 | 0 | 0 | 4 | .000 | 0 | 0-0 | 0 | 8.82 | 10.04 |
| 13 | NYM | NL | 3 | 1 | 0 | 2 | 7.0 | 34 | 12 | 8 | 8 | 2 | 0 | 1 | 0 | 3 | 0 | 3 | 0 | 0 | 0 | 1 | .000 | 0 | 0-0 | 0 | 10.77 | 10.29 |
| 13 | Col | NL | 4 | 4 | 0 | 0 | 19.0 | 91 | 33 | 21 | 21 | 4 | 2 | 1 | 0 | 2 | 0 | 8 | 0 | 0 | 0 | 3 | .000 | 0 | 0-0 | 0 | 8.14 | 9.95 |
| 2 ML YEARS | | | 15 | 9 | 0 | 3 | 47.1 | 224 | 72 | 50 | 47 | 11 | 4 | 3 | 2 | 13 | 2 | 28 | 0 | 0 | 0 | 8 | .000 | 0 | 0-0 | 0 | 7.90 | 8.94 |

## Michael McKenry

**Bats:** R **Throws:** R **Pos:** C-31;PH-10 **Ht:** 5'10" **Wt:** 210 **Born:** 3/4/1985 **Age:** 29

| BATTING | | | | | | | | | | | | | | | | | | | | | BASERUNNING | | | | AVERAGES | | |
|---|---|---|---|---|---|---|---|---|---|---|---|---|---|---|---|---|---|---|---|---|---|---|---|---|---|---|---|
| Year | Team | Lg | G | AB | H | 2B | 3B | HR | (Hm | Rd) | TB | R | RBI | RC | TBB | IBB | SO | HBP | SH | SF | SB | CS | SB% | GDP | Avg | OBP | Slg |
| 2010 | Col | NL | 6 | 8 | 0 | 0 | 0 | 0 | (0 | 0) | 0 | 0 | 0 | 0 | 1 | 0 | 5 | 0 | 0 | 0 | 0 | 0 | - | 0 | .000 | .111 | .000 |
| 2011 | Pit | NL | 58 | 180 | 40 | 12 | 0 | 2 | (1 | 1) | 58 | 17 | 11 | 12 | 14 | 2 | 49 | 0 | 5 | 2 | 0 | 1 | .00 | 3 | .222 | .276 | .322 |
| 2012 | Pit | NL | 88 | 240 | 56 | 14 | 0 | 12 | (3 | 9) | 106 | 25 | 39 | 32 | 29 | 1 | 73 | 3 | 0 | 3 | 0 | 0 | - | 7 | .233 | .320 | .442 |
| 2013 | Pit | NL | 41 | 115 | 25 | 6 | 0 | 3 | (2 | 1) | 40 | 9 | 14 | 11 | 5 | 0 | 24 | 2 | 0 | 0 | 0 | 0 | - | 2 | .217 | .262 | .348 |
| 4 ML YEARS | | | 193 | 543 | 121 | 32 | 0 | 17 | (6 | 11) | 204 | 51 | 64 | 55 | 49 | 3 | 151 | 5 | 5 | 5 | 0 | 1 | .00 | 12 | .223 | .291 | .376 |

## Nate McLouth

**Bats:** L **Throws:** R **Pos:** LF-136;PH-10;CF-3;DH-3;PR-2 mc-CLOWTH **Ht:** 5'11" **Wt:** 180 **Born:** 10/28/1981 **Age:** 32

| BATTING | | | | | | | | | | | | | | | | | | | | | BASERUNNING | | | | AVERAGES | | |
|---|---|---|---|---|---|---|---|---|---|---|---|---|---|---|---|---|---|---|---|---|---|---|---|---|---|---|---|
| Year | Team | Lg | G | AB | H | 2B | 3B | HR | (Hm | Rd) | TB | R | RBI | RC | TBB | IBB | SO | HBP | SH | SF | SB | CS | SB% | GDP | Avg | OBP | Slg |
| 2005 | Pit | NL | 41 | 109 | 28 | 6 | 0 | 5 | (2 | 3) | 49 | 20 | 12 | 9 | 3 | 0 | 20 | 5 | 2 | 1 | 2 | 0 | 1.00 | 3 | .257 | .305 | .450 |
| 2006 | Pit | NL | 106 | 270 | 63 | 16 | 2 | 7 | (3 | 4) | 104 | 50 | 16 | 25 | 18 | 0 | 59 | 5 | 3 | 1 | 10 | 1 | .91 | 7 | .233 | .293 | .385 |
| 2007 | Pit | NL | 137 | 329 | 85 | 21 | 3 | 13 | (5 | 8) | 151 | 62 | 38 | 52 | 39 | 2 | 77 | 9 | 3 | 2 | 22 | 1 | **.96** | 2 | .258 | .351 | .459 |
| 2008 | Pit | NL | 152 | 597 | 165 | **46** | 4 | 26 | (15 | 11) | 297 | 113 | 94 | 105 | 65 | 11 | 93 | 12 | 5 | 6 | 23 | 3 | .88 | 5 | .276 | .356 | .497 |

| BATTING | | | | | | | | | | | | | | | | | | | | | | BASERUNNING | | | | AVERAGES | | |
|---|---|---|---|---|---|---|---|---|---|---|---|---|---|---|---|---|---|---|---|---|---|---|---|---|---|---|---|---|
| Year | Team | Lg | G | AB | H | 2B | 3B | HR | (Hm | Rd) | TB | R | RBI | RC | TBB | IBB | SO | HBP | SH | SF | SB | CS | SB% | GDP | Avg | OBP | Slg |
| 2009 | 2 Tms | NL | 129 | 507 | 130 | 27 | 2 | 20 | (9 | 11) | 221 | 86 | 70 | 85 | 68 | 1 | 99 | 9 | 3 | 4 | 19 | 6 | .76 | 8 | .256 | .352 | .436 |
| 2010 | Atl | NL | 85 | 242 | 46 | 12 | 1 | 6 | (5 | 1) | 78 | 30 | 24 | 23 | 33 | 2 | 57 | 5 | 6 | 2 | 7 | 2 | .78 | 3 | .190 | .298 | .322 |
| 2011 | Atl | NL | 81 | 267 | 61 | 12 | 2 | 4 | (4 | 0) | 89 | 35 | 16 | 36 | 44 | 4 | 52 | 3 | 7 | 0 | 4 | 2 | .67 | 4 | .228 | .344 | .333 |
| 2012 | 2 Tms | | 89 | 266 | 64 | 14 | 1 | 7 | (4 | 3) | 101 | 39 | 20 | 30 | 27 | 1 | 61 | 2 | 2 | 1 | 12 | 1 | .92 | 2 | .241 | .314 | .380 |
| 2013 | Bal | AL | 146 | 531 | 137 | 31 | 4 | 12 | (7 | 5) | 212 | 76 | 36 | 71 | 53 | 1 | 86 | 4 | 4 | 1 | 30 | 7 | .81 | 7 | .258 | .329 | .399 |
| 09 | Pit | NL | 45 | 168 | 43 | 7 | 1 | 9 | (5 | 4) | 79 | 27 | 34 | 33 | 21 | 0 | 29 | 4 | 0 | 2 | 7 | 0 | 1.00 | 2 | .256 | .349 | .470 |
| 09 | Atl | NL | 84 | 339 | 87 | 20 | 1 | 11 | (4 | 7) | 142 | 59 | 36 | 52 | 47 | 1 | 70 | 5 | 3 | 2 | 12 | 6 | .67 | 6 | .257 | .354 | .419 |
| 12 | Pit | NL | 34 | 57 | 8 | 2 | 0 | 0 | (0 | 0) | 10 | 4 | 2 | 1 | 5 | 0 | 18 | 0 | 0 | 0 | 0 | 0 | - | 0 | .140 | .210 | .175 |
| 12 | Bal | AL | 55 | 209 | 56 | 12 | 1 | 7 | (4 | 3) | 91 | 35 | 18 | 29 | 22 | 1 | 43 | 2 | 2 | 1 | 12 | 1 | .92 | 2 | .268 | .342 | .435 |
| Postseason | | | 9 | 28 | 9 | 1 | 0 | 1 | (0 | 1) | 13 | 3 | 5 | 4 | 1 | 0 | 3 | 0 | 0 | 1 | 3 | 1 | .75 | 0 | .321 | .333 | .464 |
| 9 ML YEARS | | | 966 | 3118 | 779 | 185 | 19 | 100 | (54 | 46) | 1302 | 511 | 326 | 436 | 350 | 22 | 604 | 54 | 35 | 18 | 129 | 23 | .85 | 41 | .250 | .334 | .418 |

## Tommy Medica

**Bats:** R **Throws:** R **Pos:** 1B-19 MEDD-ih-kah **Ht:** 6'1" **Wt:** 190 **Born:** 4/9/1988 **Age:** 26

| BATTING | | | | | | | | | | | | | | | | | | | | | | BASERUNNING | | | | AVERAGES | | |
|---|---|---|---|---|---|---|---|---|---|---|---|---|---|---|---|---|---|---|---|---|---|---|---|---|---|---|---|---|
| Year | Team | Lg | G | AB | H | 2B | 3B | HR | (Hm | Rd) | TB | R | RBI | RC | TBB | IBB | SO | HBP | SH | SF | SB | CS | SB% | GDP | Avg | OBP | Slg |
| 2010 | Eugene | A- | 34 | 102 | 18 | 4 | 0 | 0 | (- | -) | 22 | 7 | 9 | 8 | 18 | 0 | 18 | 5 | 2 | 4 | 0 | 2 | .00 | 2 | .176 | .318 | .216 |
| 2011 | FtWyn | A | 44 | 142 | 38 | 19 | 0 | 3 | (- | -) | 66 | 22 | 21 | 24 | 17 | 0 | 33 | 5 | 1 | 0 | 0 | 1 | .00 | 2 | .268 | .366 | .465 |
| 2011 | Padres | R | 6 | 23 | 9 | 2 | 0 | 1 | (- | -) | 14 | 8 | 6 | 6 | 4 | 0 | 3 | 0 | 0 | 1 | 0 | 0 | - | 0 | .391 | .464 | .609 |
| 2011 | Lk Els | A+ | 42 | 139 | 42 | 10 | 0 | 6 | (- | -) | 70 | 21 | 17 | 32 | 25 | 1 | 32 | 10 | 0 | 1 | 0 | 1 | .00 | 4 | .302 | .440 | .504 |
| 2012 | Lk Els | A+ | 93 | 355 | 117 | 37 | 5 | 19 | (- | -) | 221 | 65 | 87 | 86 | 41 | 1 | 86 | 7 | 0 | 3 | 1 | 1 | .50 | 8 | .330 | .406 | .623 |
| 2013 | SnAnt | AA | 76 | 280 | 83 | 20 | 3 | 18 | (- | -) | 163 | 48 | 57 | 60 | 28 | 1 | 67 | 8 | 0 | 4 | 4 | 2 | .67 | 8 | .296 | .372 | .582 |
| 2013 | Padres | R | 5 | 17 | 5 | 2 | 0 | 2 | (- | -) | 13 | 6 | 8 | 4 | 1 | 0 | 7 | 0 | 0 | 0 | 0 | 0 | - | 0 | .294 | .333 | .765 |
| 2013 | SD | NL | 19 | 69 | 20 | 2 | 0 | 3 | (1 | 2) | 31 | 9 | 10 | 12 | 10 | 0 | 23 | 0 | 0 | 0 | 0 | 0 | - | 0 | .290 | .380 | .449 |

## Yoervis Medina

**Pitches:** R **Bats:** R **Pos:** RP-63 yo-EHR-viss meh-DEE-nah **Ht:** 6'3" **Wt:** 245 **Born:** 7/27/1988 **Age:** 25

| HOW MUCH HE PITCHED | | | | | | | | | WHAT HE GAVE UP | | | | | | | | | | | | THE RESULTS | | | | | | | |
|---|---|---|---|---|---|---|---|---|---|---|---|---|---|---|---|---|---|---|---|---|---|---|---|---|---|---|---|---|
| Year | Team | Lg | G | GS | CG | GF | IP | BFP | H | R | ER | HR | SH | SF | HB | TBB | IBB | SO | WP | Bk | W | L | Pct | Sh | Sv-Op | Hld | ERC | ERA |
| 2010 | Everett | A- | 8 | 8 | 0 | 0 | 40.2 | 187 | 49 | 30 | 19 | 4 | 3 | 2 | 2 | 15 | 0 | 48 | 3 | 0 | 3 | 2 | .600 | 0 | 0- - | - | 5.22 | 4.20 |
| 2010 | Tacom | AAA | 1 | 1 | 0 | 0 | 5.2 | 23 | 3 | 0 | 0 | 0 | 0 | 0 | 0 | 4 | 0 | 4 | 0 | 0 | 1 | 0 | 1.000 | 0 | 0- - | - | 2.14 | 0.00 |
| 2010 | Clinton | A | 6 | 6 | 0 | 0 | 36.0 | 151 | 30 | 10 | 10 | 3 | 0 | 1 | 2 | 12 | 0 | 42 | 3 | 0 | 5 | 0 | 1.000 | 0 | 0- - | - | 2.99 | 2.50 |
| 2011 | Hi Dsrt | A+ | 20 | 19 | 1 | 0 | 101.0 | 474 | 139 | 90 | 73 | 19 | 6 | 6 | 5 | 38 | 1 | 73 | 5 | 0 | 1 | 13 | .071 | 0 | 0- - | - | 7.14 | 6.50 |
| 2011 | Ms | R | 1 | 1 | 0 | 0 | 5.0 | 22 | 7 | 4 | 4 | 1 | 0 | 0 | 0 | 1 | 0 | 9 | 1 | 0 | 0 | 0 | - | 0 | 0- - | - | 6.52 | 7.20 |
| 2011 | Jacksn | AA | 4 | 4 | 0 | 0 | 25.0 | 106 | 23 | 13 | 13 | 5 | 2 | 1 | 2 | 9 | 0 | 17 | 2 | 1 | 0 | 1 | .000 | 0 | 0- - | - | 4.53 | 4.68 |
| 2012 | Jacksn | AA | 46 | 1 | 0 | 13 | 69.1 | 303 | 63 | 25 | 25 | 5 | 6 | 0 | 5 | 35 | 3 | 77 | 2 | 1 | 5 | 5 | .500 | 0 | 5- - | - | 4.00 | 3.25 |
| 2013 | Tacom | AAA | 4 | 0 | 0 | 1 | 6.0 | 21 | 2 | 1 | 1 | 0 | 0 | 0 | 0 | 3 | 0 | 7 | 2 | 0 | 0 | 1 | .000 | 0 | 0- - | - | 1.05 | 1.50 |
| 2013 | Sea | AL | 63 | 0 | 0 | 19 | 68.0 | 291 | 49 | 22 | 22 | 5 | 2 | 1 | 4 | 40 | 7 | 71 | 8 | 0 | 4 | 6 | .400 | 0 | 1-4 | 19 | 3.15 | 2.91 |

## Kris Medlen

**Pitches:** R **Bats:** B **Pos:** SP-31; RP-1 MEDD-linn **Ht:** 5'10" **Wt:** 190 **Born:** 10/7/1985 **Age:** 28

| HOW MUCH HE PITCHED | | | | | | | | | WHAT HE GAVE UP | | | | | | | | | | | | THE RESULTS | | | | | | | |
|---|---|---|---|---|---|---|---|---|---|---|---|---|---|---|---|---|---|---|---|---|---|---|---|---|---|---|---|---|
| Year | Team | Lg | G | GS | CG | GF | IP | BFP | H | R | ER | HR | SH | SF | HB | TBB | IBB | SO | WP | Bk | W | L | Pct | Sh | Sv-Op | Hld | ERC | ERA |
| 2009 | Atl | NL | 37 | 4 | 0 | 10 | 67.2 | 294 | 65 | 34 | 32 | 5 | 6 | 2 | 2 | 30 | 2 | 72 | 3 | 1 | 3 | 5 | .375 | 0 | 0-2 | 1 | 3.90 | 4.26 |
| 2010 | Atl | NL | 31 | 14 | 0 | 5 | 107.2 | 438 | 108 | 48 | 44 | 13 | 7 | 3 | 3 | 21 | 1 | 83 | 1 | 1 | 6 | 2 | .750 | 0 | 0-0 | 1 | 3.60 | 3.68 |
| 2011 | Atl | NL | 2 | 0 | 0 | 1 | 2.1 | 8 | 1 | 0 | 0 | 0 | 0 | 0 | 0 | 0 | 0 | 2 | 0 | 0 | 0 | 0 | - | 0 | 0-0 | 0 | 0.40 | 0.00 |
| 2012 | Atl | NL | 50 | 12 | 2 | 7 | 138.0 | 520 | 103 | 26 | 24 | 6 | 1 | 0 | 0 | 23 | 0 | 120 | 3 | 0 | 10 | 1 | .909 | 1 | 1-2 | 7 | 1.69 | 1.57 |
| 2013 | Atl | NL | 32 | 31 | 0 | 1 | 197.0 | 820 | 194 | 77 | 68 | 18 | 9 | 2 | 8 | 47 | 1 | 157 | 2 | 0 | 15 | 12 | .556 | 0 | 0-0 | 0 | 3.48 | 3.11 |
| Postseason | | | 1 | 1 | 0 | 0 | 6.1 | 25 | 3 | 5 | 2 | 1 | 1 | 1 | 1 | 0 | 0 | 4 | 0 | 0 | 0 | 1 | .000 | 0 | 0-0 | 0 | 1.08 | 2.84 |
| 5 ML YEARS | | | 152 | 61 | 2 | 24 | 512.2 | 2080 | 471 | 185 | 168 | 42 | 23 | 7 | 13 | 121 | 4 | 434 | 9 | 2 | 34 | 20 | .630 | 1 | 1-4 | 9 | 3.02 | 2.95 |

## Jenrry Mejia

**Pitches:** R **Bats:** R **Pos:** SP-5 HENN-ree mah-HEE-ah **Ht:** 6'0" **Wt:** 205 **Born:** 10/11/1989 **Age:** 24

| HOW MUCH HE PITCHED | | | | | | | | | WHAT HE GAVE UP | | | | | | | | | | | | THE RESULTS | | | | | | | |
|---|---|---|---|---|---|---|---|---|---|---|---|---|---|---|---|---|---|---|---|---|---|---|---|---|---|---|---|---|
| Year | Team | Lg | G | GS | CG | GF | IP | BFP | H | R | ER | HR | SH | SF | HB | TBB | IBB | SO | WP | Bk | W | L | Pct | Sh | Sv-Op | Hld | ERC | ERA |
| 2013 | StLuci* | A+ | 2 | 2 | 0 | 0 | 8.0 | 37 | 10 | 4 | 4 | 0 | 0 | 0 | 0 | 4 | 0 | 14 | 1 | 0 | 0 | 0 | - | 0 | 0- - | - | 5.15 | 4.50 |
| 2013 | Mets* | R | 2 | 2 | 0 | 0 | 5.2 | 27 | 8 | 4 | 2 | 0 | 0 | 0 | 0 | 2 | 0 | 3 | 2 | 0 | 0 | 0 | - | 0 | 0- - | - | 5.36 | 3.18 |
| 2013 | Bnghtn* | AA | 2 | 2 | 0 | 0 | 11.0 | 40 | 6 | 1 | 1 | 1 | 0 | 0 | 0 | 4 | 0 | 9 | 0 | 0 | 2 | 0 | 1.000 | 0 | 0- - | - | 1.77 | 0.82 |
| 2010 | NYM | NL | 33 | 3 | 0 | 8 | 39.0 | 183 | 46 | 21 | 20 | 3 | 0 | 1 | 3 | 20 | 2 | 22 | 7 | 0 | 0 | 4 | .000 | 0 | 0-1 | 2 | 5.57 | 4.62 |
| 2012 | NYM | NL | 5 | 3 | 0 | 1 | 16.0 | 74 | 20 | 10 | 10 | 2 | 1 | 0 | 0 | 9 | 0 | 8 | 1 | 0 | 1 | 2 | .333 | 0 | 0-0 | 0 | 6.55 | 5.63 |
| 2013 | NYM | NL | 5 | 5 | 0 | 0 | 27.1 | 112 | 28 | 9 | 7 | 2 | 0 | 4 | 0 | 4 | 0 | 27 | 1 | 0 | 1 | 2 | .333 | 0 | 0-0 | 0 | 3.05 | 2.30 |
| 3 ML YEARS | | | 43 | 11 | 0 | 9 | 82.1 | 369 | 94 | 40 | 37 | 7 | 1 | 5 | 3 | 33 | 2 | 57 | 9 | 0 | 2 | 8 | .200 | 0 | 0-1 | 2 | 4.88 | 4.04 |

## Mark Melancon

**Pitches:** R **Bats:** R **Pos:** RP-72 muh-LANN-sun **Ht:** 6'2" **Wt:** 215 **Born:** 3/28/1985 **Age:** 29

| HOW MUCH HE PITCHED | | | | | | | | | WHAT HE GAVE UP | | | | | | | | | | | | THE RESULTS | | | | | | | |
|---|---|---|---|---|---|---|---|---|---|---|---|---|---|---|---|---|---|---|---|---|---|---|---|---|---|---|---|---|
| Year | Team | Lg | G | GS | CG | GF | IP | BFP | H | R | ER | HR | SH | SF | HB | TBB | IBB | SO | WP | Bk | W | L | Pct | Sh | Sv-Op | Hld | ERC | ERA |
| 2009 | NYY | AL | 13 | 0 | 0 | 4 | 16.1 | 74 | 13 | 8 | 7 | 0 | 0 | 0 | 4 | 10 | 0 | 10 | 3 | 0 | 0 | 1 | .000 | 0 | 0-1 | 0 | 3.94 | 3.86 |
| 2010 | 2 Tms | | 22 | 0 | 0 | 4 | 21.1 | 90 | 19 | 13 | 10 | 2 | 0 | 1 | 1 | 8 | 0 | 22 | 2 | 0 | 2 | 0 | 1.000 | 0 | 0-1 | 8 | 3.53 | 4.22 |
| 2011 | Hou | NL | 71 | 0 | 0 | 47 | 74.1 | 309 | 65 | 28 | 23 | 5 | 2 | 0 | 2 | 26 | 6 | 66 | 1 | 0 | 8 | 4 | .667 | 0 | 20-25 | 3 | 2.98 | 2.78 |
| 2012 | Bos | AL | 41 | 0 | 0 | 17 | 45.0 | 194 | 45 | 31 | 31 | 8 | 1 | 2 | 3 | 12 | 1 | 41 | 2 | 0 | 0 | 2 | .000 | 0 | 1-2 | 2 | 4.24 | 6.20 |
| 2013 | Pit | NL | 72 | 0 | 0 | 24 | 71.0 | 279 | 60 | 15 | 11 | 1 | 0 | 1 | 1 | 8 | 0 | 70 | 6 | 0 | 3 | 2 | .600 | 0 | 16-21 | 26 | 1.78 | 1.39 |
| 10 | NYY | AL | 2 | 0 | 0 | 2 | 4.0 | 19 | 7 | 5 | 4 | 1 | 0 | 1 | 0 | 0 | 0 | 3 | 0 | 0 | 0 | 0 | - | 0 | 0-0 | 0 | 7.95 | 9.00 |
| 10 | Hou | NL | 20 | 0 | 0 | 2 | 17.1 | 71 | 12 | 8 | 6 | 1 | 0 | 0 | 1 | 8 | 0 | 19 | 2 | 0 | 2 | 0 | 1.000 | 0 | 0-1 | 8 | 2.65 | 3.12 |
| 5 ML YEARS | | | 219 | 0 | 0 | 96 | 228.0 | 946 | 202 | 95 | 82 | 16 | 3 | 4 | 11 | 64 | 7 | 209 | 14 | 0 | 13 | 9 | .591 | 0 | 37-50 | 39 | 2.94 | 3.24 |

## Luis Mendoza

**Pitches:** R **Bats:** R **Pos:** SP-15; RP-7 **Ht:** 6'3" **Wt:** 245 **Born:** 10/31/1983 **Age:** 30

| | | | HOW MUCH HE PITCHED | | | | | | WHAT HE GAVE UP | | | | | | | | | | | | THE RESULTS | | | | | | | |
|---|---|---|---|---|---|---|---|---|---|---|---|---|---|---|---|---|---|---|---|---|---|---|---|---|---|---|---|---|
| Year | Team | Lg | G | GS | CG | GF | IP | BFP | H | R | ER | HR | SH | SF | HB | TBB | IBB | SO | WP | Bk | W | L | Pct | Sh | Sv-Op | Hld | ERC | ERA |
| 2007 | Tex | AL | 6 | 3 | 0 | 2 | 16.0 | 64 | 13 | 4 | 4 | 1 | 0 | 2 | 2 | 4 | 0 | 7 | 0 | 0 | 1 | 0 | 1.000 | 0 | 0-0 | 0 | 2.83 | 2.25 |
| 2008 | Tex | AL | 25 | 11 | 0 | 6 | 63.1 | 316 | 97 | 74 | 61 | 7 | 0 | 2 | 6 | 25 | 4 | 35 | 5 | 0 | 3 | 8 | .273 | 0 | 1-2 | 0 | 7.53 | 8.67 |
| 2009 | Tex | AL | 1 | 0 | 0 | 0 | 1.0 | 7 | 2 | 4 | 4 | 1 | 0 | 0 | 1 | 1 | 0 | 0 | 0 | 0 | 0 | 0 | - | 0 | 0-0 | 0 | 29.25 | 36.00 |
| 2010 | KC | AL | 4 | 0 | 0 | 1 | 4.0 | 25 | 10 | 10 | 10 | 4 | 0 | 0 | 0 | 3 | 0 | 1 | 0 | 0 | 0 | 1 | .000 | 0 | 0-1 | 0 | 25.91 | 22.50 |
| 2011 | KC | AL | 2 | 2 | 0 | 0 | 14.2 | 60 | 11 | 3 | 2 | 0 | 0 | 1 | 2 | 5 | 0 | 7 | 0 | 0 | 2 | 0 | 1.000 | 0 | 0-0 | 0 | 2.42 | 1.23 |
| 2012 | KC | AL | 30 | 25 | 0 | 0 | 166.0 | 709 | 176 | 84 | 78 | 15 | 2 | 5 | 11 | 59 | 3 | 104 | 6 | 2 | 8 | 10 | .444 | 0 | 0-0 | 0 | 4.53 | 4.23 |
| 2013 | KC | AL | 22 | 15 | 0 | 4 | 94.0 | 419 | 106 | 60 | 56 | 10 | 2 | 4 | 3 | 43 | 0 | 54 | 10 | 1 | 2 | 6 | .250 | 0 | 0-0 | 0 | 5.30 | 5.36 |
| 7 ML YEARS | | | 90 | 56 | 0 | 13 | 359.0 | 1600 | 415 | 239 | 215 | 38 | 4 | 14 | 25 | 140 | 7 | 208 | 21 | 3 | 16 | 25 | .390 | 0 | 1-3 | 0 | 5.30 | 5.39 |

## Jordy Mercer

**Bats:** R **Throws:** R **Pos:** SS-78;2B-26;PH-9;PR-2;1B-1;3B-1 **Ht:** 6'3" **Wt:** 205 **Born:** 8/27/1986 **Age:** 27

| | | | BATTING | | | | | | | | | | | | | | | | | | BASERUNNING | | | | AVERAGES | | |
|---|---|---|---|---|---|---|---|---|---|---|---|---|---|---|---|---|---|---|---|---|---|---|---|---|---|---|---|
| Year | Team | Lg | G | AB | H | 2B | 3B | HR | (Hm | Rd) | TB | R | RBI | RC | TBB | IBB | SO | HBP | SH | SF | SB | CS | SB% | GDP | Avg | OBP | Slg |
| 2009 | Lynbrg | A+ | 131 | 513 | 131 | 36 | 4 | 10 | (- | -) | 205 | 64 | 83 | 69 | 41 | 0 | 93 | 9 | 3 | 14 | 10 | 6 | .63 | 11 | .255 | .314 | .400 |
| 2010 | Altna | AA | 126 | 485 | 137 | 31 | 2 | 3 | (- | -) | 181 | 67 | 65 | 64 | 31 | 1 | 69 | 7 | 6 | 9 | 7 | 1 | .88 | 10 | .282 | .329 | .373 |
| 2011 | Altna | AA | 72 | 265 | 71 | 17 | 1 | 13 | (- | -) | 129 | 40 | 48 | 44 | 23 | 0 | 35 | 4 | 3 | 6 | 6 | 3 | .67 | 3 | .268 | .329 | .487 |
| 2011 | Indy | AAA | 60 | 226 | 54 | 13 | 1 | 6 | (- | -) | 87 | 39 | 21 | 27 | 13 | 0 | 43 | 8 | 3 | 0 | 3 | 3 | .50 | 2 | .239 | .304 | .385 |
| 2012 | Indy | AAA | 56 | 209 | 60 | 14 | 1 | 4 | (- | -) | 88 | 28 | 27 | 31 | 20 | 2 | 45 | 4 | 1 | 2 | 3 | 5 | .38 | 3 | .287 | .357 | .421 |
| 2013 | Indy | AAA | 26 | 96 | 32 | 6 | 1 | 1 | (- | -) | 43 | 11 | 19 | 18 | 12 | 0 | 17 | 0 | 0 | 1 | 3 | 1 | .75 | 7 | .333 | .404 | .448 |
| 2012 | Pit | NL | 42 | 62 | 13 | 5 | 1 | 1 | (1 | 0) | 23 | 7 | 5 | 6 | 4 | 0 | 14 | 1 | 0 | 1 | 0 | 1 | .00 | 0 | .210 | .265 | .371 |
| 2013 | Pit | NL | 103 | 333 | 95 | 22 | 2 | 8 | (1 | 7) | 145 | 33 | 27 | 46 | 22 | 6 | 62 | 4 | 5 | 1 | 3 | 2 | .60 | 7 | .285 | .336 | .435 |
| 2 ML YEARS | | | 145 | 395 | 108 | 27 | 3 | 9 | (2 | 7) | 168 | 40 | 32 | 52 | 26 | 6 | 76 | 5 | 5 | 2 | 3 | 3 | .50 | 7 | .273 | .325 | .425 |

## Melky Mesa

**Bats:** R **Throws:** R **Pos:** LF-3;CF-1;RF-1;PH-1 **Ht:** 6'1" **Wt:** 190 **Born:** 1/31/1987 **Age:** 27

| | | | BATTING | | | | | | | | | | | | | | | | | | BASERUNNING | | | | AVERAGES | | |
|---|---|---|---|---|---|---|---|---|---|---|---|---|---|---|---|---|---|---|---|---|---|---|---|---|---|---|---|
| Year | Team | Lg | G | AB | H | 2B | 3B | HR | (Hm | Rd) | TB | R | RBI | RC | TBB | IBB | SO | HBP | SH | SF | SB | CS | SB% | GDP | Avg | OBP | Slg |
| 2009 | CtnSC | A | 133 | 497 | 112 | 24 | 7 | 20 | (- | -) | 210 | 76 | 74 | 69 | 51 | 3 | 168 | 11 | 0 | 5 | 18 | 6 | .75 | 5 | .225 | .309 | .423 |
| 2010 | Tampa | A+ | 121 | 446 | 116 | 21 | 9 | 19 | (- | -) | 212 | 81 | 74 | 76 | 44 | 0 | 129 | 11 | 1 | 5 | 31 | 9 | .78 | 5 | .260 | .338 | .475 |
| 2011 | Trntn | AA | 105 | 386 | 97 | 24 | 4 | 9 | (- | -) | 156 | 58 | 46 | 52 | 36 | 1 | 129 | 9 | 1 | 1 | 18 | 13 | .58 | 5 | .251 | .329 | .404 |
| 2011 | Tampa | A+ | 4 | 12 | 2 | 1 | 0 | 0 | (- | -) | 3 | 1 | 1 | 2 | 3 | 0 | 4 | 2 | 0 | 0 | 1 | 0 | 1.00 | 0 | .167 | .412 | .250 |
| 2012 | Trntn | AA | 88 | 332 | 92 | 18 | 1 | 14 | (- | -) | 154 | 60 | 46 | 56 | 29 | 1 | 75 | 6 | 0 | 2 | 17 | 3 | .85 | 7 | .277 | .344 | .464 |
| 2012 | S-WB | AAA | 33 | 126 | 29 | 8 | 1 | 9 | (- | -) | 66 | 19 | 21 | 18 | 7 | 0 | 43 | 0 | 0 | 0 | 5 | 1 | .83 | 0 | .230 | .271 | .524 |
| 2013 | S-WB | AAA | 84 | 314 | 82 | 15 | 3 | 13 | (- | -) | 142 | 40 | 39 | 44 | 11 | 0 | 112 | 5 | 0 | 2 | 13 | 2 | .87 | 7 | .261 | .295 | .452 |
| 2012 | NYY | AL | 3 | 2 | 1 | 0 | 0 | 0 | (0 | 0) | 1 | 0 | 1 | 0 | 0 | 0 | 0 | 0 | 0 | 0 | 0 | 0 | - | 0 | .500 | .500 | .500 |
| 2013 | NYY | AL | 5 | 13 | 5 | 2 | 0 | 0 | (0 | 0) | 7 | 2 | 1 | 2 | 1 | 0 | 2 | 0 | 0 | 0 | 0 | 1 | .00 | 0 | .385 | .429 | .538 |
| 2 ML YEARS | | | 8 | 15 | 6 | 2 | 0 | 0 | (0 | 0) | 8 | 2 | 2 | 2 | 1 | 0 | 2 | 0 | 0 | 0 | 0 | 1 | .00 | 0 | .400 | .438 | .533 |

## Devin Mesoraco

**Bats:** R **Throws:** R **Pos:** C-97;PH-10;PR-2;DH-1 mezz-er-OCK-oh **Ht:** 6'1" **Wt:** 230 **Born:** 6/19/1988 **Age:** 26

| | | | BATTING | | | | | | | | | | | | | | | | | | BASERUNNING | | | | AVERAGES | | |
|---|---|---|---|---|---|---|---|---|---|---|---|---|---|---|---|---|---|---|---|---|---|---|---|---|---|---|---|
| Year | Team | Lg | G | AB | H | 2B | 3B | HR | (Hm | Rd) | TB | R | RBI | RC | TBB | IBB | SO | HBP | SH | SF | SB | CS | SB% | GDP | Avg | OBP | Slg |
| 2011 | Cin | NL | 18 | 50 | 9 | 3 | 0 | 2 | (2 | 0) | 18 | 5 | 6 | 5 | 3 | 1 | 10 | 0 | 0 | 0 | 0 | 0 | - | 1 | .180 | .226 | .360 |
| 2012 | Cin | NL | 54 | 165 | 35 | 8 | 0 | 5 | (4 | 1) | 58 | 17 | 14 | 10 | 17 | 4 | 33 | 1 | 0 | 1 | 1 | 1 | .50 | 2 | .212 | .288 | .352 |
| 2013 | Cin | NL | 103 | 323 | 77 | 13 | 0 | 9 | (5 | 4) | 117 | 31 | 42 | 30 | 24 | 4 | 61 | 0 | 0 | 5 | 0 | 2 | .00 | 9 | .238 | .287 | .362 |
| 3 ML YEARS | | | 175 | 538 | 121 | 24 | 0 | 16 | (11 | 5) | 193 | 53 | 62 | 45 | 44 | 9 | 104 | 1 | 0 | 6 | 1 | 3 | .25 | 12 | .225 | .282 | .359 |

## Will Middlebrooks

**Bats:** R **Throws:** R **Pos:** 3B-92;2B-2;1B-1;PH-1;PR-1 **Ht:** 6'3" **Wt:** 220 **Born:** 9/9/1988 **Age:** 25

| | | | BATTING | | | | | | | | | | | | | | | | | | BASERUNNING | | | | AVERAGES | | |
|---|---|---|---|---|---|---|---|---|---|---|---|---|---|---|---|---|---|---|---|---|---|---|---|---|---|---|---|
| Year | Team | Lg | G | AB | H | 2B | 3B | HR | (Hm | Rd) | TB | R | RBI | RC | TBB | IBB | SO | HBP | SH | SF | SB | CS | SB% | GDP | Avg | OBP | Slg |
| 2009 | Grnvlle | A | 103 | 374 | 99 | 25 | 3 | 7 | (- | -) | 151 | 53 | 57 | 55 | 48 | 0 | 123 | 2 | 0 | 3 | 7 | 4 | .64 | 7 | .265 | .349 | .404 |
| 2010 | Salem | A+ | 114 | 435 | 120 | 31 | 2 | 12 | (- | -) | 191 | 69 | 70 | 65 | 35 | 2 | 121 | 4 | 0 | 7 | 5 | 3 | .63 | 6 | .276 | .331 | .439 |
| 2011 | Portlnd | AA | 96 | 371 | 112 | 25 | 1 | 18 | (- | -) | 193 | 54 | 80 | 67 | 21 | 0 | 95 | 4 | 0 | 1 | 6 | 0 | 1.00 | 12 | .302 | .345 | .520 |
| 2011 | Lowell | A- | 4 | 12 | 4 | 1 | 0 | 3 | (- | -) | 14 | 4 | 6 | 5 | 2 | 0 | 1 | 0 | 0 | 1 | 1 | 0 | 1.00 | 0 | .333 | .400 | 1.167 |
| 2011 | Pwtckt | AAA | 16 | 56 | 9 | 0 | 0 | 2 | (- | -) | 15 | 4 | 8 | 2 | 3 | 0 | 18 | 0 | 0 | 1 | 3 | 1 | .75 | 0 | .161 | .200 | .268 |
| 2012 | Pwtckt | AAA | 24 | 93 | 31 | 3 | 1 | 9 | (- | -) | 63 | 18 | 27 | 22 | 7 | 0 | 18 | 0 | 0 | 0 | 3 | 1 | .75 | 1 | .333 | .380 | .677 |
| 2013 | Pwtckt | AAA | 45 | 179 | 48 | 5 | 0 | 10 | (- | -) | 83 | 25 | 35 | 28 | 16 | 0 | 38 | 0 | 0 | 1 | 1 | 0 | 1.00 | 5 | .268 | .327 | .464 |
| 2012 | Bos | AL | 75 | 267 | 77 | 14 | 0 | 15 | (9 | 6) | 136 | 34 | 54 | 46 | 13 | 0 | 70 | 3 | 0 | 3 | 4 | 1 | .80 | 8 | .288 | .325 | .509 |
| 2013 | Bos | AL | 94 | 348 | 79 | 18 | 0 | 17 | (4 | 13) | 148 | 41 | 49 | 29 | 20 | 3 | 98 | 2 | 1 | 3 | 3 | 1 | .75 | 13 | .227 | .271 | .425 |
| 2 ML YEARS | | | 169 | 615 | 156 | 32 | 0 | 32 | (13 | 19) | 284 | 75 | 103 | 75 | 33 | 3 | 168 | 5 | 1 | 6 | 7 | 2 | .78 | 21 | .254 | .294 | .462 |

## Jose Mijares

**Pitches:** L **Bats:** L **Pos:** RP-60 mee-HAHR-ess **Ht:** 5'11" **Wt:** 265 **Born:** 10/29/1984 **Age:** 29

| | | | HOW MUCH HE PITCHED | | | | | | WHAT HE GAVE UP | | | | | | | | | | | | THE RESULTS | | | | | | | |
|---|---|---|---|---|---|---|---|---|---|---|---|---|---|---|---|---|---|---|---|---|---|---|---|---|---|---|---|---|
| Year | Team | Lg | G | GS | CG | GF | IP | BFP | H | R | ER | HR | SH | SF | HB | TBB | IBB | SO | WP | Bk | W | L | Pct | Sh | Sv-Op | Hld | ERC | ERA |
| 2008 | Min | AL | 10 | 0 | 0 | 3 | 10.1 | 34 | 3 | 1 | 1 | 0 | 0 | 0 | 0 | 0 | 0 | 5 | 1 | 0 | 0 | 1 | .000 | 0 | 0-0 | 2 | 0.19 | 0.87 |
| 2009 | Min | AL | 71 | 0 | 0 | 12 | 61.2 | 253 | 50 | 17 | 16 | 7 | 2 | 3 | 2 | 23 | 1 | 55 | 0 | 0 | 2 | 2 | .500 | 0 | 0-1 | 27 | 3.18 | 2.34 |
| 2010 | Min | AL | 47 | 0 | 0 | 10 | 32.2 | 139 | 34 | 14 | 12 | 4 | 1 | 1 | 1 | 9 | 1 | 28 | 1 | 0 | 1 | 1 | .500 | 0 | 0-0 | 9 | 4.04 | 3.31 |
| 2011 | Min | AL | 58 | 0 | 0 | 13 | 49.0 | 228 | 53 | 31 | 25 | 4 | 0 | 2 | 3 | 30 | 2 | 30 | 1 | 0 | 0 | 2 | .000 | 0 | 0-2 | 10 | 5.42 | 4.59 |
| 2012 | 2 Tms | | 78 | 0 | 0 | 11 | 56.1 | 242 | 50 | 18 | 16 | 3 | 4 | 3 | 4 | 21 | 3 | 57 | 3 | 0 | 3 | 2 | .600 | 0 | 0-1 | 18 | 3.18 | 2.56 |
| 2013 | SF | NL | 60 | 0 | 0 | 14 | 49.0 | 236 | 67 | 24 | 23 | 3 | 2 | 2 | 3 | 20 | 4 | 54 | 3 | 0 | 0 | 3 | .000 | 0 | 0-0 | 6 | 5.94 | 4.22 |

| HOW MUCH HE PITCHED | | | | | | | | | WHAT HE GAVE UP | | | | | | | | | | | | | THE RESULTS | | | | | | | | |
|---|---|---|---|---|---|---|---|---|---|---|---|---|---|---|---|---|---|---|---|---|---|---|---|---|---|---|---|---|---|---|
| Year | Team | Lg | G | GS | CG | GF | IP | BFP | H | R | ER | HR | SH | SF | HB | TBB | IBB | SO | WP | Bk | W | L | Pct | Sh | Sv-Op | Hld | ERC | ERA |
| 12 | KC | AL | 51 | 0 | 0 | 8 | 38.2 | 168 | 36 | 13 | 11 | 3 | 3 | 3 | 4 | 13 | 1 | 37 | 1 | 0 | 2 | 2 | .500 | 0 | 0-1 | 11 | 3.59 | 2.56 |
| 12 | SF | NL | 27 | 0 | 0 | 3 | 17.2 | 74 | 14 | 5 | 5 | 0 | 1 | 0 | 0 | 8 | 2 | 20 | 2 | 0 | 1 | 0 | 1.000 | 0 | 0-0 | 7 | 2.32 | 2.55 |
| Postseason | | | 11 | 0 | 0 | 2 | 4.2 | 20 | 4 | 4 | 4 | 1 | 1 | 0 | 0 | 4 | 1 | 4 | 0 | 0 | 0 | 1 | .000 | 0 | 0-0 | 0 | 6.07 | 7.71 |
| 6 ML YEARS | | | 324 | 0 | 0 | 63 | 259.0 | 1132 | 257 | 105 | 93 | 21 | 9 | 11 | 13 | 103 | 11 | 229 | 9 | 0 | 6 | 11 | .353 | 0 | 0-4 | 72 | 3.99 | 3.23 |

# Miles Mikolas

**Pitches:** R **Bats:** R **Pos:** RP-2

MIKE-uh-liss

**Ht:** 6'5" **Wt:** 215 **Born:** 8/23/1988 **Age:** 25

| HOW MUCH HE PITCHED | | | | | | | | | WHAT HE GAVE UP | | | | | | | | | | | | | THE RESULTS | | | | | | | | |
|---|---|---|---|---|---|---|---|---|---|---|---|---|---|---|---|---|---|---|---|---|---|---|---|---|---|---|---|---|---|---|
| Year | Team | Lg | G | GS | CG | GF | IP | BFP | H | R | ER | HR | SH | SF | HB | TBB | IBB | SO | WP | Bk | W | L | Pct | Sh | Sv-Op | Hld | ERC | ERA |
| 2009 | Eugene | A- | 15 | 11 | 0 | 0 | 53.0 | 250 | 77 | 47 | 35 | 1 | 3 | 1 | 5 | 9 | 0 | 39 | 3 | 0 | 1 | 8 | .111 | 0 | 0- - | - | 5.39 | 5.94 |
| 2010 | FtWyn | A | 60 | 0 | 0 | 30 | 81.2 | 335 | 76 | 27 | 20 | 3 | 0 | 3 | 0 | 15 | 2 | 78 | 6 | 0 | 6 | 3 | .667 | 0 | 13- - | - | 2.42 | 2.20 |
| 2011 | Lk Els | A+ | 34 | 0 | 0 | 30 | 39.2 | 159 | 31 | 5 | 5 | 1 | 2 | 0 | 3 | 9 | 2 | 42 | 0 | 0 | 3 | 0 | 1.000 | 0 | 12- - | - | 2.06 | 1.13 |
| 2011 | SnAnt | AA | 28 | 0 | 0 | 20 | 32.1 | 130 | 29 | 6 | 6 | 0 | 3 | 0 | 0 | 6 | 0 | 27 | 1 | 0 | 1 | 0 | 1.000 | 0 | 9- - | - | 2.12 | 1.67 |
| 2012 | SnAnt | AA | 12 | 0 | 0 | 10 | 12.1 | 53 | 16 | 6 | 4 | 0 | 0 | 0 | 0 | 3 | 0 | 11 | 1 | 0 | 1 | 1 | .500 | 0 | 4- - | - | 4.55 | 2.92 |
| 2012 | Tucsn | AAA | 17 | 0 | 0 | 6 | 19.2 | 87 | 20 | 8 | 7 | 1 | 1 | 1 | 0 | 8 | 0 | 17 | 1 | 0 | 2 | 1 | .667 | 0 | 0- - | - | 3.75 | 3.20 |
| 2013 | Tucsn | AAA | 54 | 0 | 0 | 50 | 61.0 | 258 | 62 | 25 | 22 | 6 | 1 | 6 | 0 | 17 | 1 | 40 | 3 | 1 | 4 | 2 | .667 | 0 | 26- - | - | 3.64 | 3.25 |
| 2012 | SD | NL | 25 | 0 | 0 | 9 | 32.1 | 144 | 32 | 15 | 13 | 4 | 2 | 0 | 2 | 15 | 0 | 23 | 2 | 0 | 2 | 1 | .667 | 0 | 0-1 | 1 | 4.65 | 3.62 |
| 2013 | SD | NL | 2 | 0 | 0 | 1 | 1.2 | 7 | 0 | 0 | 0 | 0 | 0 | 0 | 1 | 1 | 0 | 1 | 0 | 0 | 0 | 0 | - | 0 | 0-0 | 0 | 1.30 | 0.00 |
| 2 ML YEARS | | | 27 | 0 | 0 | 10 | 34.0 | 151 | 32 | 15 | 13 | 4 | 2 | 0 | 3 | 16 | 0 | 24 | 2 | 0 | 2 | 1 | .667 | 0 | 0-1 | 1 | 4.46 | 3.44 |

# Wade Miley

**Pitches:** L **Bats:** L **Pos:** SP-33

MY-lee

**Ht:** 6'0" **Wt:** 220 **Born:** 11/13/1986 **Age:** 27

| HOW MUCH HE PITCHED | | | | | | | | | WHAT HE GAVE UP | | | | | | | | | | | | | THE RESULTS | | | | | | | | |
|---|---|---|---|---|---|---|---|---|---|---|---|---|---|---|---|---|---|---|---|---|---|---|---|---|---|---|---|---|---|---|
| Year | Team | Lg | G | GS | CG | GF | IP | BFP | H | R | ER | HR | SH | SF | HB | TBB | IBB | SO | WP | Bk | W | L | Pct | Sh | Sv-Op | Hld | ERC | ERA |
| 2011 | Ari | NL | 8 | 7 | 0 | 0 | 40.0 | 180 | 48 | 20 | 20 | 6 | 3 | 1 | 0 | 18 | 0 | 25 | 1 | 0 | 4 | 2 | .667 | 0 | 0-0 | 0 | 5.90 | 4.50 |
| 2012 | Ari | NL | 32 | 29 | 0 | 0 | 194.2 | 807 | 193 | 79 | 72 | 14 | 8 | 3 | 2 | 37 | 0 | 144 | 6 | 1 | 16 | 11 | .593 | 0 | 0-0 | 0 | 3.05 | 3.33 |
| 2013 | Ari | NL | 33 | 33 | 0 | 0 | 202.2 | 847 | 201 | 88 | 80 | 21 | 6 | 2 | 4 | 66 | 4 | 147 | 13 | 0 | 10 | 10 | .500 | 0 | 0-0 | 0 | 3.88 | 3.55 |
| 3 ML YEARS | | | 73 | 69 | 0 | 0 | 437.1 | 1834 | 442 | 187 | 172 | 41 | 17 | 6 | 6 | 121 | 4 | 316 | 20 | 1 | 30 | 23 | .566 | 0 | 0-0 | 0 | 3.67 | 3.54 |

# Andrew Miller

**Pitches:** L **Bats:** L **Pos:** RP-37

**Ht:** 6'7" **Wt:** 210 **Born:** 5/21/1985 **Age:** 29

| HOW MUCH HE PITCHED | | | | | | | | | WHAT HE GAVE UP | | | | | | | | | | | | | THE RESULTS | | | | | | | | |
|---|---|---|---|---|---|---|---|---|---|---|---|---|---|---|---|---|---|---|---|---|---|---|---|---|---|---|---|---|---|---|
| Year | Team | Lg | G | GS | CG | GF | IP | BFP | H | R | ER | HR | SH | SF | HB | TBB | IBB | SO | WP | Bk | W | L | Pct | Sh | Sv-Op | Hld | ERC | ERA |
| 2006 | Det | AL | 8 | 0 | 0 | 3 | 10.1 | 51 | 8 | 9 | 7 | 0 | 0 | 0 | 2 | 10 | 0 | 6 | 1 | 0 | 0 | 1 | .000 | 0 | 0-0 | 1 | 4.79 | 6.10 |
| 2007 | Det | AL | 13 | 13 | 0 | 0 | 64.0 | 309 | 73 | 43 | 40 | 8 | 3 | 1 | 7 | 39 | 0 | 56 | 4 | 1 | 5 | 5 | .500 | 0 | 0-0 | 0 | 6.31 | 5.63 |
| 2008 | Fla | NL | 29 | 20 | 0 | 1 | 107.1 | 492 | 120 | 78 | 70 | 7 | 10 | 7 | 4 | 56 | 4 | 89 | 4 | 0 | 6 | 10 | .375 | 0 | 0-0 | 2 | 5.04 | 5.87 |
| 2009 | Fla | NL | 20 | 14 | 0 | 1 | 80.0 | 366 | 85 | 52 | 43 | 7 | 6 | 4 | 2 | 43 | 1 | 59 | 10 | 0 | 3 | 5 | .375 | 0 | 0-0 | 1 | 4.90 | 4.84 |
| 2010 | Fla | NL | 9 | 7 | 0 | 1 | 32.2 | 171 | 51 | 34 | 31 | 6 | 5 | 2 | 1 | 26 | 2 | 28 | 5 | 0 | 1 | 5 | .167 | 0 | 0-0 | 0 | 10.20 | 8.54 |
| 2011 | Bos | AL | 17 | 12 | 0 | 2 | 65.0 | 310 | 77 | 43 | 40 | 8 | 6 | 5 | 3 | 41 | 0 | 50 | 2 | 1 | 6 | 3 | .667 | 0 | 0-0 | 0 | 6.48 | 5.54 |
| 2012 | Bos | AL | 53 | 0 | 0 | 4 | 40.1 | 169 | 28 | 15 | 15 | 3 | 0 | 3 | 2 | 20 | 1 | 51 | 1 | 0 | 3 | 2 | .600 | 0 | 0-0 | 13 | 2.76 | 3.35 |
| 2013 | Bos | AL | 37 | 0 | 0 | 11 | 30.2 | 135 | 25 | 12 | 9 | 3 | 1 | 0 | 2 | 17 | 0 | 48 | 2 | 0 | 1 | 2 | .333 | 0 | 0-1 | 6 | 3.83 | 2.64 |
| 8 ML YEARS | | | 186 | 66 | 0 | 23 | 430.1 | 2003 | 467 | 286 | 255 | 42 | 31 | 22 | 23 | 252 | 8 | 387 | 29 | 2 | 25 | 33 | .431 | 0 | 0-1 | 23 | 5.43 | 5.33 |

# Brad Miller

**Bats:** L **Throws:** R **Pos:** SS-68;2B-13;3B-3;PH-3

**Ht:** 6'2" **Wt:** 185 **Born:** 10/18/1989 **Age:** 24

| BATTING | | | | | | | | | | | | | | | | | | | | | | BASERUNNING | | | | AVERAGES | | |
|---|---|---|---|---|---|---|---|---|---|---|---|---|---|---|---|---|---|---|---|---|---|---|---|---|---|---|---|---|
| Year | Team | Lg | G | AB | H | 2B | 3B | HR | (Hm | Rd) | TB | R | RBI | RC | TBB | IBB | SO | HBP | SH | SF | SB | CS | SB% | GDP | Avg | OBP | Slg |
| 2011 | Clinton | A | 14 | 53 | 22 | 4 | 1 | 0 | (- | -) | 28 | 9 | 7 | 12 | 4 | 0 | 9 | 1 | 0 | 1 | 1 | 0 | 1.00 | 1 | .415 | .458 | .528 |
| 2012 | Hi Dsrt | A+ | 97 | 410 | 139 | 33 | 5 | 11 | (- | -) | 215 | 89 | 56 | 90 | 52 | 2 | 79 | 2 | 4 | 5 | 19 | 6 | .76 | 5 | .339 | .412 | .524 |
| 2012 | Jacksn | AA | 40 | 147 | 47 | 7 | 2 | 4 | (- | -) | 70 | 21 | 12 | 29 | 22 | 0 | 26 | 0 | 0 | 1 | 4 | 1 | .80 | 4 | .320 | .406 | .476 |
| 2013 | Jacksn | AA | 42 | 153 | 45 | 7 | 1 | 6 | (- | -) | 72 | 27 | 25 | 27 | 20 | 2 | 30 | 1 | 1 | 0 | 4 | 3 | .57 | 1 | .294 | .379 | .471 |
| 2013 | Tacom | AAA | 26 | 104 | 37 | 5 | 1 | 6 | (- | -) | 62 | 26 | 28 | 26 | 15 | 0 | 18 | 0 | 0 | 3 | 2 | 1 | .67 | 0 | .356 | .426 | .596 |
| 2013 | Sea | AL | 76 | 306 | 81 | 11 | 6 | 8 | (3 | 5) | 128 | 41 | 36 | 41 | 24 | 0 | 52 | 1 | 2 | 2 | 5 | 3 | .63 | 2 | .265 | .318 | .418 |

# Corky Miller

**Bats:** R **Throws:** R **Pos:** C-16;PH-3

**Ht:** 6'1" **Wt:** 250 **Born:** 3/18/1976 **Age:** 38

| BATTING | | | | | | | | | | | | | | | | | | | | | | BASERUNNING | | | | AVERAGES | | |
|---|---|---|---|---|---|---|---|---|---|---|---|---|---|---|---|---|---|---|---|---|---|---|---|---|---|---|---|---|
| Year | Team | Lg | G | AB | H | 2B | 3B | HR | (Hm | Rd) | TB | R | RBI | RC | TBB | IBB | SO | HBP | SH | SF | SB | CS | SB% | GDP | Avg | OBP | Slg |
| 2013 | Lsvlle* | AAA | 45 | 135 | 27 | 6 | 0 | 4 | (- | -) | 45 | 8 | 19 | 14 | 16 | 0 | 23 | 3 | 1 | 2 | 0 | 0 | - | 4 | .200 | .295 | .333 |
| 2001 | Cin | NL | 17 | 49 | 9 | 2 | 0 | 3 | (1 | 2) | 20 | 5 | 7 | 6 | 4 | 0 | 16 | 2 | 0 | 2 | 1 | 0 | 1.00 | 1 | .184 | .263 | .408 |
| 2002 | Cin | NL | 39 | 114 | 29 | 10 | 0 | 3 | (2 | 1) | 48 | 9 | 15 | 15 | 9 | 2 | 20 | 4 | 1 | 1 | 0 | 0 | - | 7 | .254 | .328 | .421 |
| 2003 | Cin | NL | 14 | 30 | 8 | 0 | 0 | 0 | (0 | 0) | 8 | 4 | 1 | 5 | 5 | 0 | 7 | 2 | 0 | 1 | 0 | 0 | - | 1 | .267 | .395 | .267 |
| 2004 | Cin | NL | 13 | 39 | 1 | 0 | 0 | 0 | (0 | 0) | 1 | 2 | 3 | 0 | 6 | 0 | 12 | 3 | 0 | 1 | 0 | 0 | - | 3 | .026 | .204 | .026 |
| 2005 | Min | AL | 5 | 12 | 0 | 0 | 0 | 0 | (0 | 0) | 0 | 0 | 0 | 0 | 0 | 0 | 2 | 0 | 0 | 0 | 0 | 0 | - | 0 | .000 | .000 | .000 |
| 2006 | Bos | AL | 1 | 4 | 0 | 0 | 0 | 0 | (0 | 0) | 0 | 0 | 0 | 0 | 0 | 0 | 1 | 0 | 0 | 0 | 0 | 0 | - | 0 | .000 | .000 | .000 |
| 2007 | Atl | NL | 12 | 27 | 7 | 2 | 0 | 1 | (0 | 1) | 12 | 3 | 4 | 4 | 1 | 0 | 5 | 1 | 0 | 0 | 0 | 0 | - | 1 | .259 | .310 | .444 |
| 2008 | Atl | NL | 31 | 60 | 5 | 0 | 0 | 1 | (0 | 1) | 8 | 4 | 5 | 0 | 5 | 0 | 15 | 0 | 1 | 1 | 0 | 0 | - | 2 | .083 | .152 | .133 |
| 2009 | 2 Tms | | 35 | 95 | 18 | 4 | 0 | 1 | (1 | 0) | 25 | 9 | 15 | 11 | 12 | 0 | 23 | 1 | 2 | 1 | 0 | 0 | - | 2 | .189 | .284 | .263 |
| 2010 | Cin | NL | 32 | 74 | 18 | 5 | 0 | 2 | (1 | 1) | 29 | 5 | 9 | 9 | 2 | 0 | 16 | 2 | 1 | 0 | 0 | 0 | - | 2 | .243 | .282 | .392 |
| 2013 | Cin | NL | 17 | 35 | 9 | 5 | 0 | 0 | (0 | 0) | 14 | 2 | 8 | 6 | 5 | 0 | 6 | 1 | 0 | 0 | 0 | 0 | - | 1 | .257 | .366 | .400 |
| 09 | CWS | AL | 14 | 39 | 8 | 3 | 0 | 0 | (0 | 0) | 11 | 5 | 5 | 3 | 3 | 0 | 9 | 0 | 0 | 0 | 0 | 0 | - | 1 | .205 | .262 | .282 |
| 09 | Cin | NL | 21 | 56 | 10 | 1 | 0 | 1 | (1 | 0) | 14 | 4 | 10 | 8 | 9 | 0 | 14 | 1 | 2 | 1 | 0 | 0 | - | 1 | .179 | .299 | .250 |
| 11 ML YEARS | | | 216 | 539 | 104 | 28 | 0 | 11 | (5 | 6) | 165 | 43 | 67 | 56 | 49 | 2 | 123 | 16 | 5 | 7 | 1 | 0 | 1.00 | 20 | .193 | .277 | .306 |

## Jim Miller

**Pitches:** R **Bats:** R **Pos:** RP-1 **Ht:** 6'1" **Wt:** 200 **Born:** 4/28/1982 **Age:** 32

| HOW MUCH HE PITCHED | | | | | | | | WHAT HE GAVE UP | | | | | | | | | | | | THE RESULTS | | | | | | | |
|---|---|---|---|---|---|---|---|---|---|---|---|---|---|---|---|---|---|---|---|---|---|---|---|---|---|---|---|
| Year Team | Lg | G | GS | CG | GF | IP | BFP | H | R | ER | HR | SH | SF | HB | TBB | IBB | SO | WP | Bk | W | L | Pct | Sh | Sv-Op | Hld | ERC | ERA |
| 2013 S-WB* | AAA | 43 | 1 | 0 | 21 | 63.1 | 274 | 55 | 27 | 25 | 8 | 2 | 4 | 2 | 25 | 0 | 92 | 1 | 0 | 3 | 5 | .375 | 0 | 6- - | - | 3.53 | 3.55 |
| 2008 Bal | AL | 8 | 0 | 0 | 5 | 7.2 | 39 | 9 | 3 | 1 | 0 | 1 | 1 | 1 | 5 | 2 | 8 | 1 | 0 | 0 | 2 | .000 | 0 | 1-2 | 0 | 4.99 | 1.17 |
| 2011 Col | NL | 6 | 0 | 0 | 4 | 7.0 | 29 | 3 | 2 | 2 | 0 | 0 | 2 | 0 | 4 | 0 | 5 | 0 | 0 | 0 | 0 | - | 0 | 0-0 | 0 | 1.30 | 2.57 |
| 2012 Oak | AL | 33 | 0 | 0 | 18 | 48.2 | 211 | 39 | 15 | 14 | 6 | 0 | 1 | 3 | 27 | 2 | 44 | 1 | 0 | 2 | 1 | .667 | 0 | 0-0 | 0 | 3.91 | 2.59 |
| 2013 NYY | AL | 1 | 0 | 0 | 0 | 1.1 | 8 | 3 | 3 | 3 | 1 | 0 | 1 | 0 | 1 | 0 | 0 | 0 | 0 | 0 | 0 | - | 0 | 0-0 | 0 | 20.88 | 20.25 |
| 4 ML YEARS | | 48 | 0 | 0 | 27 | 64.2 | 287 | 54 | 23 | 20 | 7 | 1 | 5 | 4 | 37 | 4 | 57 | 2 | 0 | 2 | 3 | .400 | 0 | 1-2 | 0 | 3.96 | 2.78 |

## Shelby Miller

**Pitches:** R **Bats:** R **Pos:** SP-31 **Ht:** 6'3" **Wt:** 215 **Born:** 10/10/1990 **Age:** 23

| HOW MUCH HE PITCHED | | | | | | | | WHAT HE GAVE UP | | | | | | | | | | | | THE RESULTS | | | | | | | |
|---|---|---|---|---|---|---|---|---|---|---|---|---|---|---|---|---|---|---|---|---|---|---|---|---|---|---|---|
| Year Team | Lg | G | GS | CG | GF | IP | BFP | H | R | ER | HR | SH | SF | HB | TBB | IBB | SO | WP | Bk | W | L | Pct | Sh | Sv-Op | Hld | ERC | ERA |
| 2009 QuadC | A | 2 | 2 | 0 | 0 | 3.0 | 16 | 5 | 3 | 2 | 0 | 0 | 0 | 0 | 2 | 0 | 2 | 0 | 0 | 0 | 0 | - | 0 | 0- - | - | 8.24 | 6.00 |
| 2010 QuadC | A | 24 | 24 | 0 | 0 | 104.1 | 439 | 97 | 51 | 42 | 7 | 2 | 2 | 3 | 33 | 0 | 140 | 2 | 1 | 7 | 5 | .583 | 0 | 0- - | - | 3.25 | 3.62 |
| 2011 PlmBh | A+ | 9 | 9 | 0 | 0 | 53.0 | 219 | 40 | 20 | 17 | 2 | 0 | 1 | 1 | 20 | 0 | 81 | 6 | 0 | 2 | 3 | .400 | 0 | 0- - | - | 2.34 | 2.89 |
| 2011 Sprgfld | AA | 16 | 16 | 0 | 0 | 86.2 | 355 | 72 | 28 | 26 | 2 | 3 | 0 | 4 | 33 | 0 | 89 | 3 | 2 | 9 | 3 | .750 | 0 | 0- - | - | 2.82 | 2.70 |
| 2012 Memp | AAA | 27 | 27 | 0 | 0 | 136.2 | 599 | 138 | 78 | 72 | 24 | 5 | 3 | 11 | 50 | 0 | 160 | 0 | 0 | 11 | 10 | .524 | 0 | 0- - | - | 4.84 | 4.74 |
| 2012 StL | NL | 6 | 1 | 0 | 1 | 13.2 | 54 | 9 | 2 | 2 | 0 | 0 | 0 | 1 | 4 | 0 | 16 | 0 | 0 | 1 | 0 | 1.000 | 0 | 0-0 | 1 | 1.65 | 1.32 |
| 2013 StL | NL | 31 | 31 | 1 | 0 | 173.1 | 722 | 152 | 65 | 59 | 20 | 7 | 3 | 5 | 57 | 0 | 169 | 2 | 0 | 15 | 9 | .625 | 1 | 0-0 | 0 | 3.34 | 3.06 |
| Postseason | | 2 | 0 | 0 | 0 | 3.1 | 15 | 4 | 2 | 2 | 0 | 0 | 0 | 0 | 1 | 0 | 4 | 0 | 0 | 0 | 0 | - | 0 | 0-0 | 0 | 3.97 | 5.40 |
| 2 ML YEARS | | 37 | 32 | 1 | 1 | 187.0 | 776 | 161 | 67 | 61 | 20 | 7 | 3 | 6 | 61 | 0 | 185 | 2 | 0 | 16 | 9 | .640 | 1 | 0-0 | 1 | 3.20 | 2.94 |

## Tommy Milone

**Pitches:** L **Bats:** L **Pos:** SP-26; RP-2 mah-LONE **Ht:** 6'0" **Wt:** 205 **Born:** 2/16/1987 **Age:** 27

| HOW MUCH HE PITCHED | | | | | | | | WHAT HE GAVE UP | | | | | | | | | | | | THE RESULTS | | | | | | | |
|---|---|---|---|---|---|---|---|---|---|---|---|---|---|---|---|---|---|---|---|---|---|---|---|---|---|---|---|
| Year Team | Lg | G | GS | CG | GF | IP | BFP | H | R | ER | HR | SH | SF | HB | TBB | IBB | SO | WP | Bk | W | L | Pct | Sh | Sv-Op | Hld | ERC | ERA |
| 2013 Scrmto* | AAA | 2 | 2 | 0 | 0 | 10.1 | 47 | 16 | 5 | 2 | 0 | 0 | 0 | 0 | 1 | 0 | 15 | 0 | 0 | 0 | 0 | - | 0 | 0- - | - | 5.25 | 1.74 |
| 2011 Was | NL | 5 | 5 | 0 | 0 | 26.0 | 110 | 28 | 11 | 11 | 2 | 3 | 2 | 2 | 4 | 2 | 15 | 0 | 0 | 1 | 0 | 1.000 | 0 | 0-0 | 0 | 3.55 | 3.81 |
| 2012 Oak | AL | 31 | 31 | 1 | 0 | 190.0 | 791 | 207 | 90 | 79 | 24 | 3 | 3 | 4 | 36 | 2 | 137 | 2 | 0 | 13 | 10 | .565 | 0 | 0-0 | 0 | 4.04 | 3.74 |
| 2013 Oak | AL | 28 | 26 | 1 | 0 | 156.1 | 667 | 160 | 83 | 72 | 25 | 0 | 6 | 2 | 39 | 2 | 126 | 1 | 0 | 12 | 9 | .571 | 0 | 0-0 | 0 | 3.98 | 4.14 |
| Postseason | | 1 | 1 | 0 | 0 | 6.0 | 25 | 5 | 1 | 1 | 0 | 0 | 0 | 1 | 1 | 0 | 6 | 1 | 0 | 0 | 0 | - | 0 | 0-0 | 0 | 2.26 | 1.50 |
| 3 ML YEARS | | 64 | 62 | 2 | 0 | 372.1 | 1568 | 395 | 184 | 162 | 51 | 6 | 11 | 8 | 79 | 6 | 278 | 3 | 0 | 26 | 19 | .578 | 0 | 0-0 | 0 | 3.98 | 3.92 |

## Zach Miner

**Pitches:** R **Bats:** R **Pos:** RP-13; SP-3 **Ht:** 6'4" **Wt:** 225 **Born:** 3/12/1982 **Age:** 32

| HOW MUCH HE PITCHED | | | | | | | | WHAT HE GAVE UP | | | | | | | | | | | | THE RESULTS | | | | | | | |
|---|---|---|---|---|---|---|---|---|---|---|---|---|---|---|---|---|---|---|---|---|---|---|---|---|---|---|---|
| Year Team | Lg | G | GS | CG | GF | IP | BFP | H | R | ER | HR | SH | SF | HB | TBB | IBB | SO | WP | Bk | W | L | Pct | Sh | Sv-Op | Hld | ERC | ERA |
| 2013 LV* | AAA | 27 | 12 | 0 | 5 | 85.1 | 368 | 90 | 43 | 37 | 5 | 6 | 3 | 4 | 28 | 1 | 54 | 2 | 0 | 5 | 6 | .455 | 0 | 2- - | - | 3.99 | 3.90 |
| 2006 Det | AL | 27 | 16 | 1 | 4 | 93.0 | 398 | 100 | 53 | 50 | 11 | 2 | 2 | 0 | 32 | 1 | 59 | 1 | 0 | 7 | 6 | .538 | 0 | 0-0 | 1 | 4.44 | 4.84 |
| 2007 Det | AL | 34 | 1 | 0 | 8 | 53.2 | 232 | 56 | 22 | 18 | 3 | 4 | 1 | 0 | 22 | 4 | 34 | 1 | 0 | 3 | 4 | .429 | 0 | 0-2 | 9 | 3.95 | 3.02 |
| 2008 Det | AL | 45 | 13 | 0 | 3 | 118.0 | 509 | 118 | 60 | 56 | 10 | 4 | 3 | 6 | 46 | 3 | 62 | 4 | 0 | 8 | 5 | .615 | 0 | 0-3 | 6 | 4.12 | 4.27 |
| 2009 Det | AL | 51 | 5 | 0 | 9 | 92.1 | 409 | 101 | 49 | 44 | 11 | 2 | 1 | 2 | 45 | 1 | 62 | 2 | 0 | 7 | 5 | .583 | 0 | 1-5 | 8 | 5.28 | 4.29 |
| 2013 Phi | NL | 16 | 3 | 0 | 0 | 28.2 | 133 | 33 | 14 | 14 | 4 | 2 | 1 | 2 | 17 | 1 | 20 | 1 | 0 | 0 | 2 | .000 | 0 | 0-1 | 0 | 6.40 | 4.40 |
| Postseason | | 1 | 0 | 0 | 1 | 0.2 | 2 | 0 | 0 | 0 | 0 | 0 | 0 | 1 | 0 | 0 | 0 | 1 | 0 | 0 | 0 | - | 0 | 0-0 | 0 | 3.22 | 0.00 |
| 5 ML YEARS | | 173 | 38 | 1 | 24 | 385.2 | 1681 | 408 | 198 | 182 | 39 | 14 | 8 | 10 | 162 | 10 | 237 | 9 | 0 | 25 | 22 | .532 | 0 | 1-11 | 24 | 4.61 | 4.25 |

## Mike Minor

**Pitches:** L **Bats:** R **Pos:** SP-32 **Ht:** 6'4" **Wt:** 205 **Born:** 12/26/1987 **Age:** 26

| HOW MUCH HE PITCHED | | | | | | | | WHAT HE GAVE UP | | | | | | | | | | | | THE RESULTS | | | | | | | |
|---|---|---|---|---|---|---|---|---|---|---|---|---|---|---|---|---|---|---|---|---|---|---|---|---|---|---|---|
| Year Team | Lg | G | GS | CG | GF | IP | BFP | H | R | ER | HR | SH | SF | HB | TBB | IBB | SO | WP | Bk | W | L | Pct | Sh | Sv-Op | Hld | ERC | ERA |
| 2010 Atl | NL | 9 | 8 | 0 | 1 | 40.2 | 185 | 53 | 28 | 27 | 6 | 1 | 3 | 1 | 11 | 0 | 43 | 0 | 0 | 3 | 2 | .600 | 0 | 0-0 | 0 | 5.71 | 5.98 |
| 2011 Atl | NL | 15 | 15 | 0 | 0 | 82.2 | 361 | 93 | 39 | 38 | 7 | 3 | 1 | 1 | 30 | 5 | 77 | 2 | 0 | 5 | 3 | .625 | 0 | 0-0 | 0 | 4.51 | 4.14 |
| 2012 Atl | NL | 30 | 30 | 0 | 0 | 179.1 | 728 | 151 | 88 | 82 | 26 | 8 | 8 | 5 | 56 | 7 | 145 | 3 | 0 | 11 | 10 | .524 | 0 | 0-0 | 0 | 3.28 | 4.12 |
| 2013 Atl | NL | 32 | 32 | 1 | 0 | 204.2 | 820 | 177 | 79 | 73 | 22 | 5 | 6 | 1 | 46 | 2 | 181 | 5 | 0 | 13 | 9 | .591 | 0 | 0-0 | 0 | 2.76 | 3.21 |
| 4 ML YEARS | | 86 | 85 | 1 | 1 | 507.1 | 2094 | 474 | 234 | 220 | 61 | 17 | 18 | 8 | 143 | 14 | 446 | 10 | 0 | 32 | 24 | .571 | 0 | 0-0 | 0 | 3.44 | 3.90 |

## Jose Molina

**Bats:** R **Throws:** R **Pos:** C-96;PH-3;DH-1 **Ht:** 6'2" **Wt:** 250 **Born:** 6/3/1975 **Age:** 39

| BATTING | | | | | | | | | | | | | | | | | | | | BASERUNNING | | | | AVERAGES | | |
|---|---|---|---|---|---|---|---|---|---|---|---|---|---|---|---|---|---|---|---|---|---|---|---|---|---|---|
| Year Team | Lg | G | AB | H | 2B | 3B | HR | (Hm | Rd) | TB | R | RBI | RC | TBB | IBB | SO | HBP | SH | SF | SB | CS | SB% | GDP | Avg | OBP | Slg |
| 1999 ChC | NL | 10 | 19 | 5 | 1 | 0 | 0 | (0 | 0) | 6 | 3 | 1 | 2 | 2 | 1 | 4 | 0 | 0 | 0 | 0 | 0 | - | 0 | .263 | .333 | .316 |
| 2001 LAA | AL | 15 | 37 | 10 | 3 | 0 | 2 | (0 | 2) | 19 | 8 | 4 | 6 | 3 | 0 | 8 | 0 | 2 | 0 | 0 | 0 | - | 2 | .270 | .325 | .514 |
| 2002 LAA | AL | 29 | 70 | 19 | 3 | 0 | 0 | (0 | 0) | 22 | 5 | 5 | 4 | 5 | 0 | 15 | 0 | 4 | 2 | 0 | 2 | .00 | 2 | .271 | .312 | .314 |
| 2003 LAA | AL | 53 | 114 | 21 | 4 | 0 | 0 | (0 | 0) | 25 | 12 | 6 | 5 | 1 | 0 | 26 | 3 | 4 | 1 | 0 | 0 | - | 1 | .184 | .210 | .219 |
| 2004 LAA | AL | 73 | 203 | 53 | 10 | 2 | 3 | (1 | 2) | 76 | 26 | 25 | 19 | 10 | 0 | 52 | 0 | 5 | 0 | 4 | 1 | .80 | 6 | .261 | .296 | .374 |
| 2005 LAA | AL | 75 | 184 | 42 | 4 | 0 | 6 | (2 | 4) | 64 | 14 | 25 | 19 | 13 | 0 | 41 | 2 | 4 | 0 | 2 | 0 | 1.00 | 5 | .228 | .286 | .348 |
| 2006 LAA | AL | 78 | 225 | 54 | 17 | 0 | 4 | (0 | 4) | 83 | 18 | 22 | 21 | 9 | 0 | 49 | 2 | 7 | 2 | 1 | 0 | 1.00 | 6 | .240 | .273 | .369 |
| 2007 2 Tms | AL | 69 | 191 | 49 | 13 | 0 | 1 | (1 | 0) | 65 | 18 | 19 | 20 | 5 | 0 | 43 | 0 | 5 | 1 | 2 | 1 | .67 | 4 | .257 | .274 | .340 |
| 2008 NYY | AL | 100 | 268 | 58 | 17 | 0 | 3 | (2 | 1) | 84 | 32 | 18 | 15 | 12 | 0 | 52 | 6 | 8 | 3 | 0 | 0 | - | 9 | .216 | .263 | .313 |
| 2009 NYY | AL | 52 | 138 | 30 | 4 | 0 | 1 | (0 | 1) | 37 | 15 | 11 | 12 | 14 | 0 | 28 | 1 | 1 | 1 | 0 | 0 | - | 6 | .217 | .292 | .268 |
| 2010 Tor | AL | 57 | 167 | 41 | 4 | 0 | 6 | (4 | 2) | 63 | 13 | 12 | 12 | 9 | 1 | 36 | 5 | 2 | 0 | 1 | 0 | 1.00 | 7 | .246 | .304 | .377 |
| 2011 Tor | AL | 55 | 171 | 48 | 12 | 1 | 3 | (1 | 2) | 71 | 19 | 15 | 25 | 15 | 0 | 44 | 1 | 4 | 0 | 2 | 1 | .67 | 2 | .281 | .342 | .415 |
| 2012 TB | AL | 102 | 251 | 56 | 9 | 0 | 8 | (5 | 3) | 89 | 27 | 32 | 23 | 20 | 0 | 60 | 2 | 1 | 0 | 3 | 1 | .75 | 9 | .223 | .286 | .355 |

| Year | Team | Lg | G | AB | H | 2B | 3B | HR | (Hm | Rd) | TB | R | RBI | RC | TBB | IBB | SO | HBP | SH | SF | SB | CS | SB% | GDP | Avg | OBP | Slg |
|---|---|---|---|---|---|---|---|---|---|---|---|---|---|---|---|---|---|---|---|---|---|---|---|---|---|---|---|
| BATTING | | | | | | | | | | | | | | | | | | | | | BASERUNNING | | | | AVERAGES | | |
| 2013 | TB | AL | 99 | 283 | 66 | 14 | 0 | 2 | (1 | 1) | 86 | 26 | 18 | 18 | 22 | 1 | 63 | 2 | 3 | 3 | 2 | 1 | .67 | 11 | .233 | .290 | .304 |
| 07 | LAA | AL | 40 | 125 | 28 | 8 | 0 | 0 | (0 | 0) | 36 | 9 | 10 | 9 | 3 | 0 | 30 | 0 | 3 | 0 | 2 | 1 | .67 | 3 | .224 | .242 | .288 |
| 07 | NYY | AL | 29 | 66 | 21 | 5 | 0 | 1 | (1 | 0) | 29 | 9 | 9 | 11 | 2 | 0 | 13 | 0 | 2 | 1 | 0 | 0 | - | 1 | .318 | .333 | .439 |
| Postseason | | | 15 | 14 | 4 | 0 | 0 | 0 | (0 | 0) | 4 | 3 | 1 | 2 | 3 | 0 | 1 | 0 | 1 | 0 | 0 | 0 | - | 0 | .286 | .412 | .286 |
| 14 ML YEARS | | | 867 | 2321 | 552 | 115 | 3 | 39 | (17 | 22) | 790 | 236 | 213 | 201 | 140 | 3 | 521 | 24 | 50 | 13 | 17 | 7 | .71 | 70 | .238 | .287 | .340 |

## Yadier Molina

**Bats:** R **Throws:** R **Pos:** C-132;1B-5;PH-5 YAH-dee-air **Ht:** 5'11" **Wt:** 220 **Born:** 7/13/1982 **Age:** 31

| Year | Team | Lg | G | AB | H | 2B | 3B | HR | (Hm | Rd) | TB | R | RBI | RC | TBB | IBB | SO | HBP | SH | SF | SB | CS | SB% | GDP | Avg | OBP | Slg |
|---|---|---|---|---|---|---|---|---|---|---|---|---|---|---|---|---|---|---|---|---|---|---|---|---|---|---|---|
| BATTING | | | | | | | | | | | | | | | | | | | | | BASERUNNING | | | | AVERAGES | | |
| 2004 | StL | NL | 51 | 135 | 36 | 6 | 0 | 2 | (1 | 1) | 48 | 12 | 15 | 15 | 13 | 3 | 20 | 0 | 2 | 1 | 0 | 1 | .00 | 4 | .267 | .329 | .356 |
| 2005 | StL | NL | 114 | 385 | 97 | 15 | 1 | 8 | (6 | 2) | 138 | 36 | 49 | 46 | 23 | 3 | 30 | 2 | 8 | 3 | 2 | 3 | .40 | 10 | .252 | .295 | .358 |
| 2006 | StL | NL | 129 | 417 | 90 | 26 | 0 | 6 | (2 | 4) | 134 | 29 | 49 | 35 | 26 | 2 | 41 | 8 | 8 | 2 | 1 | 2 | .33 | 15 | .216 | .274 | .321 |
| 2007 | StL | NL | 111 | 353 | 97 | 15 | 0 | 6 | (4 | 2) | 130 | 30 | 40 | 38 | 34 | 5 | 43 | 3 | 2 | 4 | 1 | 1 | .50 | 18 | .275 | .340 | .368 |
| 2008 | StL | NL | 124 | 444 | 135 | 18 | 0 | 7 | (2 | 5) | 174 | 37 | 56 | 57 | 32 | 4 | 29 | 1 | 3 | 5 | 0 | 2 | .00 | 21 | .304 | .349 | .392 |
| 2009 | StL | NL | 140 | 481 | 141 | 23 | 1 | 6 | (5 | 1) | 184 | 45 | 54 | 64 | 50 | 2 | 39 | 6 | 6 | 1 | 9 | 3 | .75 | 27 | .293 | .366 | .383 |
| 2010 | StL | NL | 136 | 465 | 122 | 19 | 0 | 6 | (1 | 5) | 159 | 34 | 62 | 55 | 42 | 6 | 51 | 7 | 2 | 5 | 8 | 4 | .67 | 19 | .262 | .329 | .342 |
| 2011 | StL | NL | 139 | 475 | 145 | 32 | 1 | 14 | (5 | 9) | 221 | 55 | 65 | 64 | 33 | 4 | 44 | 1 | 5 | 4 | 4 | 5 | .44 | 21 | .305 | .349 | .465 |
| 2012 | StL | NL | 138 | 505 | 159 | 28 | 0 | 22 | (9 | 13) | 253 | 65 | 76 | 91 | 45 | 4 | 55 | 5 | 3 | 5 | 12 | 3 | .80 | 10 | .315 | .373 | .501 |
| 2013 | StL | NL | 136 | 505 | 161 | 44 | 0 | 12 | (5 | 7) | 241 | 68 | 80 | 84 | 30 | 4 | 55 | 3 | 0 | 3 | 3 | 2 | .60 | 14 | .319 | .359 | .477 |
| Postseason | | | 63 | 224 | 67 | 14 | 0 | 2 | (1 | 1) | 87 | 19 | 27 | 24 | 18 | 4 | 23 | 1 | 0 | 1 | 1 | 1 | .50 | 8 | .299 | .352 | .388 |
| 10 ML YEARS | | | 1218 | 4165 | 1183 | 226 | 3 | 89 | (40 | 49) | 1682 | 411 | 546 | 549 | 328 | 37 | 407 | 36 | 39 | 33 | 40 | 26 | .61 | 159 | .284 | .339 | .404 |

## Johnny Monell

**Bats:** L **Throws:** R **Pos:** PH-7;C-1 MO-nell **Ht:** 6'0" **Wt:** 210 **Born:** 3/27/1986 **Age:** 28

| Year | Team | Lg | G | AB | H | 2B | 3B | HR | (Hm | Rd) | TB | R | RBI | RC | TBB | IBB | SO | HBP | SH | SF | SB | CS | SB% | GDP | Avg | OBP | Slg |
|---|---|---|---|---|---|---|---|---|---|---|---|---|---|---|---|---|---|---|---|---|---|---|---|---|---|---|---|
| BATTING | | | | | | | | | | | | | | | | | | | | | BASERUNNING | | | | AVERAGES | | |
| 2009 | Augsta | A | 91 | 293 | 80 | 21 | 0 | 8 | (- | -) | 125 | 46 | 44 | 47 | 33 | 0 | 45 | 5 | 1 | 1 | 4 | 1 | .80 | 14 | .273 | .355 | .427 |
| 2010 | SnJos | A+ | 115 | 421 | 115 | 25 | 4 | 19 | (- | -) | 205 | 66 | 70 | 74 | 48 | 1 | 105 | 2 | 0 | 1 | 12 | 3 | .80 | 12 | .273 | .350 | .487 |
| 2010 | Fresno | AAA | 5 | 15 | 3 | 1 | 1 | 0 | (- | -) | 6 | 0 | 1 | 1 | 2 | 0 | 4 | 0 | 0 | 0 | 0 | 0 | - | 1 | .200 | .294 | .400 |
| 2011 | Rchmd | AA | 119 | 385 | 96 | 24 | 1 | 10 | (- | -) | 152 | 46 | 49 | 53 | 48 | 2 | 93 | 3 | 1 | 3 | 0 | 3 | .00 | 14 | .249 | .335 | .395 |
| 2012 | Rchmd | AA | 108 | 323 | 83 | 27 | 1 | 11 | (- | -) | 145 | 38 | 50 | 52 | 41 | 1 | 84 | 5 | 0 | 5 | 2 | 2 | .50 | 10 | .257 | .345 | .449 |
| 2013 | Fresno | AAA | 121 | 415 | 114 | 27 | 2 | 20 | (- | -) | 205 | 71 | 64 | 77 | 59 | 2 | 105 | 2 | 0 | 5 | 6 | 3 | .67 | 11 | .275 | .364 | .494 |
| 2013 | SF | NL | 8 | 8 | 1 | 0 | 0 | 0 | (0 | 0) | 1 | 2 | 1 | 0 | 0 | 0 | 3 | 1 | 0 | 0 | 0 | 0 | - | 0 | .125 | .222 | .125 |

## Jesus Montero

**Bats:** R **Throws:** R **Pos:** C-26;PH-2;DH-1 **Ht:** 6'3" **Wt:** 230 **Born:** 11/28/1989 **Age:** 24

| Year | Team | Lg | G | AB | H | 2B | 3B | HR | (Hm | Rd) | TB | R | RBI | RC | TBB | IBB | SO | HBP | SH | SF | SB | CS | SB% | GDP | Avg | OBP | Slg |
|---|---|---|---|---|---|---|---|---|---|---|---|---|---|---|---|---|---|---|---|---|---|---|---|---|---|---|---|
| BATTING | | | | | | | | | | | | | | | | | | | | | BASERUNNING | | | | AVERAGES | | |
| 2013 | Tacom* | AAA | 19 | 73 | 18 | 6 | 2 | 1 | (- | -) | 31 | 12 | 9 | 10 | 8 | 0 | 24 | 0 | 0 | 1 | 0 | 0 | - | 1 | .247 | .317 | .425 |
| 2013 | Ms* | R | 8 | 23 | 6 | 1 | 0 | 0 | (- | -) | 7 | 3 | 2 | 3 | 3 | 0 | 5 | 1 | 0 | 1 | 0 | 0 | - | 1 | .261 | .357 | .304 |
| 2011 | NYY | AL | 18 | 61 | 20 | 4 | 0 | 4 | (3 | 1) | 36 | 9 | 12 | 12 | 7 | 2 | 17 | 1 | 0 | 0 | 0 | 0 | - | 2 | .328 | .406 | .590 |
| 2012 | Sea | AL | 135 | 515 | 134 | 20 | 0 | 15 | (6 | 9) | 199 | 46 | 62 | 52 | 29 | 4 | 99 | 2 | 0 | 7 | 0 | 2 | .00 | 15 | .260 | .298 | .386 |
| 2013 | Sea | AL | 29 | 101 | 21 | 1 | 1 | 3 | (1 | 2) | 33 | 6 | 9 | 9 | 8 | 0 | 21 | 0 | 0 | 1 | 0 | 1 | .00 | 2 | .208 | .264 | .327 |
| Postseason | | | 1 | 2 | 2 | 0 | 0 | 0 | (0 | 0) | 2 | 1 | 1 | 2 | 0 | 0 | 0 | 0 | 0 | 0 | 0 | 0 | - | 0 | 1.000 | 1.000 | 1.000 |
| 3 ML YEARS | | | 182 | 677 | 175 | 25 | 1 | 22 | (10 | 12) | 268 | 61 | 83 | 73 | 44 | 6 | 137 | 3 | 0 | 8 | 0 | 3 | .00 | 19 | .258 | .303 | .396 |

## Miguel Montero

**Bats:** L **Throws:** R **Pos:** C-112;PH-4 **Ht:** 5'11" **Wt:** 210 **Born:** 7/9/1983 **Age:** 30

| Year | Team | Lg | G | AB | H | 2B | 3B | HR | (Hm | Rd) | TB | R | RBI | RC | TBB | IBB | SO | HBP | SH | SF | SB | CS | SB% | GDP | Avg | OBP | Slg |
|---|---|---|---|---|---|---|---|---|---|---|---|---|---|---|---|---|---|---|---|---|---|---|---|---|---|---|---|
| BATTING | | | | | | | | | | | | | | | | | | | | | BASERUNNING | | | | AVERAGES | | |
| 2013 | DBcks* | R | 6 | 19 | 5 | 2 | 0 | 0 | (- | -) | 7 | 2 | 4 | 3 | 4 | 0 | 4 | 0 | 0 | 0 | 0 | 0 | - | 2 | .263 | .391 | .368 |
| 2006 | Ari | NL | 6 | 16 | 4 | 1 | 0 | 0 | (0 | 0) | 5 | 0 | 3 | 2 | 1 | 0 | 3 | 0 | 0 | 0 | 0 | 0 | - | 0 | .250 | .294 | .313 |
| 2007 | Ari | NL | 84 | 214 | 48 | 7 | 0 | 10 | (7 | 3) | 85 | 30 | 37 | 19 | 20 | 2 | 35 | 3 | 1 | 6 | 0 | 0 | - | 7 | .224 | .292 | .397 |
| 2008 | Ari | NL | 70 | 184 | 47 | 16 | 1 | 5 | (1 | 4) | 80 | 24 | 18 | 21 | 19 | 3 | 49 | 2 | 1 | 1 | 0 | 0 | - | 1 | .255 | .330 | .435 |
| 2009 | Ari | NL | 128 | 425 | 125 | 30 | 0 | 16 | (5 | 11) | 203 | 61 | 59 | 65 | 38 | 5 | 78 | 3 | 2 | 2 | 1 | 2 | .33 | 6 | .294 | .355 | .478 |
| 2010 | Ari | NL | 85 | 297 | 79 | 20 | 2 | 9 | (0 | 9) | 130 | 36 | 43 | 38 | 29 | 3 | 71 | 2 | 0 | 3 | 0 | 1 | .00 | 10 | .266 | .332 | .438 |
| 2011 | Ari | NL | 140 | 493 | 139 | 36 | 1 | 18 | (8 | 10) | 231 | 65 | 86 | 84 | 47 | 10 | 97 | 8 | 1 | 4 | 1 | 1 | .50 | 14 | .282 | .351 | .469 |
| 2012 | Ari | NL | 141 | 486 | 139 | 25 | 2 | 15 | (4 | 11) | 213 | 65 | 88 | 92 | 73 | 6 | 130 | 12 | 0 | 2 | 0 | 0 | - | 15 | .286 | .391 | .438 |
| 2013 | Ari | NL | 116 | 413 | 95 | 14 | 0 | 11 | (8 | 3) | 142 | 44 | 42 | 42 | 51 | 4 | 110 | 5 | 0 | 6 | 0 | 0 | - | 18 | .230 | .318 | .344 |
| Postseason | | | 9 | 27 | 8 | 2 | 0 | 0 | (0 | 0) | 10 | 4 | 2 | 3 | 3 | 1 | 6 | 0 | 0 | 0 | 0 | 0 | - | 0 | .296 | .367 | .370 |
| 8 ML YEARS | | | 770 | 2528 | 676 | 149 | 6 | 84 | (33 | 51) | 1089 | 325 | 376 | 363 | 278 | 33 | 573 | 35 | 5 | 24 | 2 | 4 | .33 | 71 | .267 | .345 | .431 |

## Luke Montz

**Bats:** R **Throws:** R **Pos:** DH-11;PH-5;1B-1 **Ht:** 6'1" **Wt:** 230 **Born:** 7/7/1983 **Age:** 30

| Year | Team | Lg | G | AB | H | 2B | 3B | HR | (Hm | Rd) | TB | R | RBI | RC | TBB | IBB | SO | HBP | SH | SF | SB | CS | SB% | GDP | Avg | OBP | Slg |
|---|---|---|---|---|---|---|---|---|---|---|---|---|---|---|---|---|---|---|---|---|---|---|---|---|---|---|---|
| BATTING | | | | | | | | | | | | | | | | | | | | | BASERUNNING | | | | AVERAGES | | |
| 2009 | Syrcse | AAA | 12 | 29 | 5 | 1 | 0 | 0 | (- | -) | 6 | 1 | 1 | 1 | 6 | 0 | 7 | 0 | 0 | 0 | 0 | 1 | .00 | 1 | .172 | .314 | .207 |
| 2009 | Hrsbrg | AA | 91 | 291 | 53 | 14 | 0 | 9 | (- | -) | 94 | 32 | 35 | 27 | 41 | 2 | 62 | 1 | 1 | 0 | 1 | 3 | .25 | 5 | .182 | .285 | .323 |
| 2010 | Bnghtn | AA | 33 | 110 | 20 | 3 | 0 | 2 | (- | -) | 29 | 10 | 15 | 7 | 12 | 0 | 32 | 0 | 0 | 3 | 0 | 2 | .00 | 1 | .182 | .256 | .264 |
| 2010 | Mets | R | 5 | 17 | 5 | 0 | 0 | 1 | (- | -) | 8 | 2 | 2 | 3 | 3 | 0 | 3 | 0 | 0 | 0 | 1 | 0 | 1.00 | 0 | .294 | .400 | .471 |
| 2010 | StLuci | A+ | 6 | 16 | 4 | 0 | 0 | 1 | (- | -) | 7 | 3 | 2 | 3 | 5 | 0 | 4 | 0 | 0 | 0 | 0 | 0 | - | 1 | .250 | .429 | .438 |
| 2011 | Jaxnvl | AA | 118 | 395 | 108 | 27 | 0 | 22 | (- | -) | 201 | 66 | 78 | 84 | 74 | 6 | 95 | 7 | 0 | 7 | 8 | 0 | 1.00 | 8 | .273 | .391 | .509 |
| 2012 | NewOr | AAA | 123 | 370 | 82 | 14 | 0 | 29 | (- | -) | 183 | 55 | 74 | 58 | 45 | 4 | 101 | 3 | 0 | 2 | 1 | 3 | .25 | 8 | .222 | .310 | .495 |

| | | | BATTING | | | | | | | | | | | | | | | | | | BASERUNNING | | | | AVERAGES | | |
|---|---|---|---|---|---|---|---|---|---|---|---|---|---|---|---|---|---|---|---|---|---|---|---|---|---|---|---|
| Year | Team | Lg | G | AB | H | 2B | 3B | HR | (Hm | Rd) | TB | R | RBI | RC | TBB | IBB | SO | HBP | SH | SF | SB | CS | SB% | GDP | Avg | OBP | Slg |
| 2013 | Scrmto | AAA | 33 | 122 | 30 | 9 | 0 | 9 | (- | -) | 66 | 17 | 29 | 23 | 19 | 0 | 45 | 2 | 0 | 2 | 0 | 1 | .00 | 5 | .246 | .352 | .541 |
| 2008 | Was | NL | 10 | 21 | 3 | 0 | 0 | 1 | (0 | 1) | 6 | 2 | 3 | 3 | 5 | 0 | 9 | 0 | 0 | 0 | 0 | 0 | - | 0 | .143 | .308 | .286 |
| 2013 | Oak | AL | 13 | 28 | 5 | 3 | 0 | 1 | (0 | 1) | 11 | 2 | 5 | 0 | 1 | 0 | 8 | 0 | 0 | 1 | 0 | 0 | - | 0 | .179 | .200 | .393 |
| 2 ML YEARS | | | 23 | 49 | 8 | 3 | 0 | 2 | (0 | 2) | 17 | 4 | 8 | 3 | 6 | 0 | 17 | 0 | 0 | 1 | 0 | 0 | - | 0 | .163 | .250 | .347 |

# Adam Moore

**Bats:** R **Throws:** R **Pos:** C-5;PH-1 **Ht:** 6'3" **Wt:** 215 **Born:** 5/8/1984 **Age:** 30

| | | | BATTING | | | | | | | | | | | | | | | | | | BASERUNNING | | | | AVERAGES | | |
|---|---|---|---|---|---|---|---|---|---|---|---|---|---|---|---|---|---|---|---|---|---|---|---|---|---|---|---|
| Year | Team | Lg | G | AB | H | 2B | 3B | HR | (Hm | Rd) | TB | R | RBI | RC | TBB | IBB | SO | HBP | SH | SF | SB | CS | SB% | GDP | Avg | OBP | Slg |
| 2013 | Omha* | AAA | 41 | 131 | 25 | 4 | 0 | 8 | (- | -) | 53 | 20 | 23 | 15 | 17 | 0 | 52 | 0 | 0 | 0 | 0 | 0 | - | 4 | .191 | .284 | .405 |
| 2009 | Sea | AL | 6 | 23 | 5 | 1 | 0 | 1 | (1 | 0) | 9 | 4 | 2 | 2 | 0 | 0 | 7 | 1 | 0 | 0 | 1 | 0 | 1.00 | 1 | .217 | .250 | .391 |
| 2010 | Sea | AL | 60 | 205 | 40 | 6 | 0 | 4 | (1 | 3) | 58 | 12 | 15 | 9 | 8 | 1 | 63 | 2 | 1 | 2 | 0 | 1 | .00 | 3 | .195 | .230 | .283 |
| 2011 | Sea | AL | 2 | 6 | 1 | 1 | 0 | 0 | (0 | 0) | 2 | 0 | 0 | 0 | 0 | 0 | 2 | 0 | 0 | 0 | 0 | 0 | - | 0 | .167 | .167 | .333 |
| 2012 | KC | AL | 4 | 11 | 2 | 1 | 0 | 1 | (1 | 0) | 6 | 1 | 2 | 2 | 1 | 0 | 3 | 0 | 0 | 0 | 0 | 0 | - | 0 | .182 | .250 | .545 |
| 2013 | KC | AL | 5 | 10 | 3 | 1 | 0 | 0 | (0 | 0) | 4 | 1 | 0 | 1 | 1 | 0 | 2 | 0 | 0 | 0 | 1 | 0 | 1.00 | 0 | .300 | .364 | .400 |
| 5 ML YEARS | | | 77 | 255 | 51 | 10 | 0 | 6 | (3 | 3) | 79 | 18 | 19 | 14 | 10 | 1 | 77 | 3 | 1 | 2 | 2 | 1 | .67 | 4 | .200 | .237 | .310 |

# Matt Moore

**Pitches:** L **Bats:** L **Pos:** SP-27 **Ht:** 6'3" **Wt:** 210 **Born:** 6/18/1989 **Age:** 25

| | | | HOW MUCH HE PITCHED | | | | | | WHAT HE GAVE UP | | | | | | | | | | | | THE RESULTS | | | | | | | |
|---|---|---|---|---|---|---|---|---|---|---|---|---|---|---|---|---|---|---|---|---|---|---|---|---|---|---|---|---|
| Year | Team | Lg | G | GS | CG | GF | IP | BFP | H | R | ER | HR | SH | SF | HB | TBB | IBB | SO | WP | Bk | W | L | Pct | Sh | Sv-Op | Hld | ERC | ERA |
| 2013 | Drham* | AAA | 1 | 1 | 0 | 0 | 4.0 | 21 | 8 | 4 | 4 | 0 | 1 | 0 | 0 | 2 | 0 | 2 | 0 | 0 | 0 | 0 | - | 0 | 0- - | - | 10.21 | 9.00 |
| 2011 | TB | AL | 3 | 1 | 0 | 0 | 9.1 | 40 | 9 | 3 | 3 | 1 | 0 | 0 | 0 | 3 | 0 | 15 | 2 | 0 | 1 | 0 | 1.000 | 0 | 0-0 | 1 | 3.54 | 2.89 |
| 2012 | TB | AL | 31 | 31 | 0 | 0 | 177.1 | 759 | 158 | 85 | 75 | 18 | 3 | 4 | 7 | 81 | 5 | 175 | 8 | 1 | 11 | 11 | .500 | 0 | 0-0 | 0 | 3.83 | 3.81 |
| 2013 | TB | AL | 27 | 27 | 1 | 0 | 150.1 | 642 | 119 | 58 | 55 | 14 | 5 | 6 | 4 | 76 | 1 | 143 | **17** | 1 | 17 | 4 | .810 | 1 | 0-0 | 0 | 3.36 | 3.29 |
| Postseason | | | 2 | 1 | 0 | 0 | 10.0 | 37 | 3 | 1 | 1 | 1 | 0 | 0 | 1 | 3 | 0 | 8 | 1 | 0 | 1 | 0 | 1.000 | 0 | 0-0 | 0 | 1.03 | 0.90 |
| 3 ML YEARS | | | 61 | 59 | 1 | 0 | 337.0 | 1441 | 286 | 146 | 133 | 33 | 8 | 10 | 11 | 160 | 6 | 333 | 27 | 2 | 29 | 15 | .659 | 1 | 0-0 | 1 | 3.61 | 3.55 |

# Tyler Moore

**Bats:** R **Throws:** R **Pos:** LF-29;PH-18;1B-14;RF-6 **Ht:** 6'2" **Wt:** 220 **Born:** 1/30/1987 **Age:** 27

| | | | BATTING | | | | | | | | | | | | | | | | | | BASERUNNING | | | | AVERAGES | | |
|---|---|---|---|---|---|---|---|---|---|---|---|---|---|---|---|---|---|---|---|---|---|---|---|---|---|---|---|
| Year | Team | Lg | G | AB | H | 2B | 3B | HR | (Hm | Rd) | TB | R | RBI | RC | TBB | IBB | SO | HBP | SH | SF | SB | CS | SB% | GDP | Avg | OBP | Slg |
| 2009 | Hgrstn | A | 111 | 421 | 125 | 30 | 3 | 9 | (- | -) | 188 | 38 | 87 | 71 | 40 | 1 | 111 | 8 | 0 | 8 | 2 | 2 | .50 | 6 | .297 | .363 | .447 |
| 2010 | Ptomc | A+ | 129 | 502 | 135 | 43 | 3 | 31 | (- | -) | 277 | 78 | 111 | 90 | 40 | 1 | 125 | 2 | 2 | 7 | 0 | 0 | - | 5 | .269 | .321 | .552 |
| 2011 | Hrsbrg | AA | 137 | 519 | 140 | 36 | 4 | 31 | (- | -) | 277 | 70 | 90 | 88 | 30 | 2 | 139 | 6 | 0 | 6 | 2 | 0 | 1.00 | 6 | .270 | .314 | .534 |
| 2012 | Syrcse | AAA | 29 | 101 | 31 | 6 | 1 | 9 | (- | -) | 66 | 15 | 26 | 24 | 12 | 0 | 26 | 0 | 0 | 2 | 1 | 0 | 1.00 | 2 | .307 | .374 | .653 |
| 2013 | Syrcse | AAA | 45 | 173 | 55 | 14 | 1 | 10 | (- | -) | 101 | 26 | 46 | 39 | 23 | 0 | 39 | 1 | 0 | 3 | 1 | 0 | 1.00 | 5 | .318 | .395 | .584 |
| 2012 | Was | NL | 75 | 156 | 41 | 9 | 0 | 10 | (3 | 7) | 80 | 20 | 29 | 26 | 14 | 0 | 46 | 1 | 0 | 0 | 3 | 0 | 1.00 | 3 | .263 | .327 | .513 |
| 2013 | Was | NL | 63 | 167 | 37 | 9 | 0 | 4 | (2 | 2) | 58 | 16 | 21 | 17 | 8 | 1 | 58 | 1 | 1 | 1 | 0 | 0 | - | 1 | .222 | .260 | .347 |
| Postseason | | | 1 | 1 | 1 | 0 | 0 | 0 | (0 | 0) | 1 | 0 | 2 | 1 | 0 | 0 | 0 | 0 | 0 | 0 | 0 | 0 | - | 0 | 1.000 | 1.000 | 1.000 |
| 2 ML YEARS | | | 138 | 323 | 78 | 18 | 0 | 14 | (5 | 9) | 138 | 36 | 50 | 43 | 22 | 1 | 104 | 2 | 1 | 1 | 3 | 0 | 1.00 | 4 | .241 | .293 | .427 |

# Franklin Morales

**Pitches:** L **Bats:** L **Pos:** RP-19; SP-1 **Ht:** 6'1" **Wt:** 210 **Born:** 1/24/1986 **Age:** 28

| | | | HOW MUCH HE PITCHED | | | | | | WHAT HE GAVE UP | | | | | | | | | | | | THE RESULTS | | | | | | | |
|---|---|---|---|---|---|---|---|---|---|---|---|---|---|---|---|---|---|---|---|---|---|---|---|---|---|---|---|---|
| Year | Team | Lg | G | GS | CG | GF | IP | BFP | H | R | ER | HR | SH | SF | HB | TBB | IBB | SO | WP | Bk | W | L | Pct | Sh | Sv-Op | Hld | ERC | ERA |
| 2013 | Grnvlle* | A | 1 | 1 | 0 | 0 | 3.0 | 11 | 1 | 0 | 0 | 0 | 0 | 0 | 0 | 2 | 0 | 1 | 0 | 0 | 0 | 0 | - | 0 | 0- - | - | 1.37 | 0.00 |
| 2013 | Portlnd* | AA | 3 | 2 | 0 | 0 | 8.0 | 34 | 10 | 2 | 1 | 0 | 1 | 0 | 0 | 2 | 0 | 7 | 0 | 0 | 1 | 0 | 1.000 | 0 | 0- - | - | 4.32 | 1.13 |
| 2013 | Pwtckt* | AAA | 5 | 2 | 0 | 0 | 11.1 | 41 | 5 | 6 | 6 | 3 | 0 | 0 | 0 | 3 | 0 | 12 | 0 | 0 | 0 | 1 | .000 | 0 | 0- - | - | 1.70 | 4.76 |
| 2007 | Col | NL | 8 | 8 | 0 | 0 | 39.1 | 163 | 34 | 15 | 15 | 2 | 4 | 2 | 2 | 14 | 1 | 26 | 0 | 0 | 3 | 2 | .600 | 0 | 0-0 | 0 | 3.04 | 3.43 |
| 2008 | Col | NL | 5 | 5 | 0 | 0 | 25.1 | 120 | 28 | 18 | 18 | 2 | 2 | 2 | 1 | 17 | 2 | 9 | 1 | 3 | 1 | 2 | .333 | 0 | 0-0 | 0 | 5.58 | 6.39 |
| 2009 | Col | NL | 40 | 2 | 0 | 14 | 40.0 | 179 | 38 | 22 | 20 | 4 | 3 | 0 | 1 | 23 | 4 | 41 | 2 | 0 | 3 | 2 | .600 | 0 | 7-8 | 7 | 4.38 | 4.50 |
| 2010 | Col | NL | 35 | 0 | 0 | 15 | 28.2 | 140 | 28 | 22 | 20 | 5 | 1 | 2 | 3 | 24 | 2 | 27 | 3 | 2 | 0 | 4 | .000 | 0 | 3-6 | 1 | 6.53 | 6.28 |
| 2011 | 2 Tms | | 50 | 0 | 0 | 13 | 46.1 | 193 | 40 | 21 | 19 | 6 | 2 | 1 | 2 | 19 | 1 | 42 | 2 | 1 | 1 | 2 | .333 | 0 | 0-0 | 10 | 3.77 | 3.69 |
| 2012 | Bos | AL | 37 | 9 | 0 | 5 | 76.1 | 325 | 64 | 38 | 32 | 11 | 0 | 3 | 6 | 30 | 3 | 76 | 3 | **5** | 3 | 4 | .429 | 0 | 1-1 | 8 | 3.68 | 3.77 |
| 2013 | Bos | AL | 20 | 1 | 0 | 3 | 25.1 | 112 | 24 | 13 | 13 | 2 | 0 | 0 | 3 | 15 | 2 | 21 | 3 | 0 | 2 | 2 | .500 | 0 | 0-1 | 4 | 4.86 | 4.62 |
| 11 | Col | NL | 14 | 0 | 0 | 4 | 14.0 | 59 | 10 | 6 | 6 | 2 | 1 | 1 | 0 | 8 | 1 | 11 | 1 | 0 | 0 | 1 | .000 | 0 | 0-0 | 2 | 3.36 | 3.86 |
| 11 | Bos | AL | 36 | 0 | 0 | 9 | 32.1 | 134 | 30 | 15 | 13 | 4 | 1 | 0 | 2 | 11 | 0 | 31 | 1 | 1 | 1 | 1 | .500 | 0 | 0-0 | 8 | 3.96 | 3.62 |
| Postseason | | | 8 | 2 | 0 | 0 | 12.2 | 59 | 15 | 11 | 11 | 1 | 0 | 0 | 2 | 7 | 1 | 7 | 0 | 1 | 0 | 0 | - | 0 | 0-0 | 1 | 6.28 | 7.82 |
| 7 ML YEARS | | | 195 | 25 | 0 | 50 | 281.1 | 1232 | 256 | 149 | 137 | 32 | 12 | 10 | 18 | 142 | 15 | 242 | 14 | 11 | 13 | 18 | .419 | 0 | 11-16 | 30 | 4.25 | 4.38 |

# Kendrys Morales

**Bats:** B **Throws:** R **Pos:** DH-122;1B-31;PH-4 KEN-dreez **Ht:** 6'1" **Wt:** 225 **Born:** 6/20/1983 **Age:** 31

| | | | BATTING | | | | | | | | | | | | | | | | | | BASERUNNING | | | | AVERAGES | | |
|---|---|---|---|---|---|---|---|---|---|---|---|---|---|---|---|---|---|---|---|---|---|---|---|---|---|---|---|
| Year | Team | Lg | G | AB | H | 2B | 3B | HR | (Hm | Rd) | TB | R | RBI | RC | TBB | IBB | SO | HBP | SH | SF | SB | CS | SB% | GDP | Avg | OBP | Slg |
| 2006 | LAA | AL | 57 | 197 | 46 | 10 | 1 | 5 | (1 | 4) | 73 | 21 | 22 | 19 | 17 | 1 | 28 | 0 | 0 | 1 | 1 | 1 | .50 | 11 | .234 | .293 | .371 |
| 2007 | LAA | AL | 43 | 119 | 35 | 10 | 0 | 4 | (2 | 2) | 57 | 12 | 15 | 15 | 6 | 2 | 21 | 1 | 0 | 0 | 0 | 1 | .00 | 5 | .294 | .333 | .479 |
| 2008 | LAA | AL | 27 | 61 | 13 | 2 | 0 | 3 | (0 | 3) | 24 | 7 | 8 | 3 | 4 | 0 | 7 | 1 | 0 | 0 | 0 | 1 | .00 | 3 | .213 | .273 | .393 |
| 2009 | LAA | AL | 152 | 566 | 173 | 43 | 2 | 34 | (21 | 13) | 322 | 86 | 108 | 105 | 46 | 10 | 117 | 2 | 0 | 8 | 3 | 7 | .30 | 15 | .306 | .355 | .569 |
| 2010 | LAA | AL | 51 | 193 | 56 | 5 | 0 | 11 | (7 | 4) | 94 | 29 | 39 | 34 | 12 | 3 | 31 | 5 | 0 | 1 | 0 | 1 | .00 | 5 | .290 | .346 | .487 |
| 2012 | LAA | AL | 134 | 484 | 132 | 26 | 1 | 22 | (10 | 12) | 226 | 61 | 73 | 68 | 31 | 1 | 116 | 4 | 0 | 3 | 0 | 1 | .00 | 11 | .273 | .320 | .467 |
| 2013 | Sea | AL | 156 | 602 | 167 | 34 | 0 | 23 | (12 | 11) | 270 | 64 | 80 | 85 | 49 | 6 | 114 | 5 | 0 | 1 | 0 | 0 | - | 21 | .277 | .336 | .449 |
| Postseason | | | 16 | 47 | 9 | 1 | 0 | 2 | (1 | 1) | 16 | 3 | 7 | 3 | 2 | 0 | 8 | 1 | 0 | 1 | 0 | 0 | - | 1 | .191 | .235 | .340 |
| 7 ML YEARS | | | 620 | 2222 | 622 | 130 | 4 | 102 | (53 | 49) | 1066 | 280 | 345 | 329 | 165 | 23 | 434 | 18 | 0 | 14 | 4 | 12 | .25 | 71 | .280 | .333 | .480 |

## Brent Morel

**Bats:** R **Throws:** R **Pos:** 3B-9;1B-3;PH-2;PR-2 more-ELL **Ht:** 6'2" **Wt:** 225 **Born:** 4/21/1987 **Age:** 27

| BATTING | | | | | | | | | | | | | | | | | | | | | BASERUNNING | | | | AVERAGES | | |
|---|---|---|---|---|---|---|---|---|---|---|---|---|---|---|---|---|---|---|---|---|---|---|---|---|---|---|---|
| Year Team | Lg | G | AB | H | 2B | 3B | HR | (Hm | Rd) | TB | R | RBI | RC | TBB | IBB | SO | HBP | SH | SF | SB | CS | SB% | GDP | Avg | OBP | Slg |
| 2013 Charltt* | AAA | 106 | 395 | 105 | 30 | 3 | 6 | (- | -) | 159 | 55 | 54 | 60 | 47 | 1 | 104 | 5 | 2 | 3 | 14 | 3 | .82 | 10 | .266 | .349 | .403 |
| 2010 CWS | AL | 21 | 65 | 15 | 3 | 0 | 3 | (3 | 0) | 27 | 9 | 7 | 4 | 4 | 0 | 17 | 0 | 0 | 1 | 2 | 0 | 1.00 | 2 | .231 | .271 | .415 |
| 2011 CWS | AL | 126 | 413 | 101 | 18 | 1 | 10 | (6 | 4) | 151 | 44 | 41 | 36 | 22 | 0 | 57 | 3 | 5 | 1 | 5 | 4 | .56 | 8 | .245 | .287 | .366 |
| 2012 CWS | AL | 35 | 113 | 20 | 2 | 0 | 0 | (0 | 0) | 22 | 14 | 5 | 4 | 7 | 0 | 39 | 0 | 5 | 0 | 4 | 1 | .80 | 3 | .177 | .225 | .195 |
| 2013 CWS | AL | 12 | 25 | 5 | 0 | 0 | 0 | (0 | 0) | 5 | 3 | 1 | 3 | 5 | 0 | 7 | 0 | 0 | 0 | 1 | 1 | .50 | 1 | .200 | .333 | .200 |
| 4 ML YEARS | | 194 | 616 | 141 | 23 | 1 | 13 | (9 | 4) | 205 | 70 | 54 | 47 | 38 | 0 | 120 | 3 | 10 | 2 | 12 | 6 | .67 | 14 | .229 | .276 | .333 |

## Mitch Moreland

**Bats:** L **Throws:** L **Pos:** 1B-146;PH-7;RF-1;PR-1 **Ht:** 6'2" **Wt:** 240 **Born:** 9/6/1985 **Age:** 28

| BATTING | | | | | | | | | | | | | | | | | | | | | BASERUNNING | | | | AVERAGES | | |
|---|---|---|---|---|---|---|---|---|---|---|---|---|---|---|---|---|---|---|---|---|---|---|---|---|---|---|---|
| Year Team | Lg | G | AB | H | 2B | 3B | HR | (Hm | Rd) | TB | R | RBI | RC | TBB | IBB | SO | HBP | SH | SF | SB | CS | SB% | GDP | Avg | OBP | Slg |
| 2013 Frisco* | AA | 3 | 12 | 6 | 3 | 0 | 1 | (- | -) | 12 | 3 | 3 | 4 | 0 | 0 | 1 | 0 | 0 | 0 | 0 | 0 | - | 1 | .500 | .500 | 1.000 |
| 2010 Tex | AL | 47 | 145 | 37 | 4 | 0 | 9 | (3 | 6) | 68 | 20 | 25 | 27 | 25 | 5 | 36 | 1 | 0 | 2 | 3 | 1 | .75 | 3 | .255 | .364 | .469 |
| 2011 Tex | AL | 134 | 464 | 120 | 22 | 1 | 16 | (7 | 9) | 192 | 60 | 51 | 56 | 39 | 6 | 92 | 4 | 2 | 3 | 2 | 2 | .50 | 9 | .259 | .320 | .414 |
| 2012 Tex | AL | 114 | 327 | 90 | 18 | 0 | 15 | (10 | 5) | 153 | 41 | 50 | 46 | 23 | 5 | 71 | 1 | 2 | 4 | 1 | 1 | .50 | 8 | .275 | .321 | .468 |
| 2013 Tex | AL | 147 | 462 | 107 | 24 | 1 | 23 | (10 | 13) | 202 | 60 | 60 | 55 | 45 | 1 | 117 | 3 | 0 | 8 | 0 | 0 | - | 11 | .232 | .299 | .437 |
| Postseason | | 25 | 76 | 19 | 4 | 0 | 3 | (3 | 0) | 32 | 7 | 10 | 12 | 6 | 1 | 18 | 1 | 1 | 0 | 0 | 0 | - | 3 | .250 | .313 | .421 |
| 4 ML YEARS | | 442 | 1398 | 354 | 68 | 2 | 63 | (30 | 33) | 615 | 181 | 186 | 184 | 132 | 17 | 316 | 9 | 4 | 17 | 6 | 4 | .60 | 31 | .253 | .318 | .440 |

## Justin Morneau

**Bats:** L **Throws:** R **Pos:** 1B-137;DH-12;PH-7 MORE-no **Ht:** 6'4" **Wt:** 215 **Born:** 5/15/1981 **Age:** 33

| BATTING | | | | | | | | | | | | | | | | | | | | | BASERUNNING | | | | AVERAGES | | |
|---|---|---|---|---|---|---|---|---|---|---|---|---|---|---|---|---|---|---|---|---|---|---|---|---|---|---|---|
| Year Team | Lg | G | AB | H | 2B | 3B | HR | (Hm | Rd) | TB | R | RBI | RC | TBB | IBB | SO | HBP | SH | SF | SB | CS | SB% | GDP | Avg | OBP | Slg |
| 2003 Min | AL | 40 | 106 | 24 | 4 | 0 | 4 | (1 | 3) | 40 | 14 | 16 | 11 | 9 | 1 | 30 | 0 | 0 | 0 | 0 | 0 | - | 4 | .226 | .287 | .377 |
| 2004 Min | AL | 74 | 280 | 76 | 17 | 0 | 19 | (9 | 10) | 150 | 39 | 58 | 48 | 28 | 8 | 54 | 2 | 0 | 2 | 0 | 0 | - | 4 | .271 | .340 | .536 |
| 2005 Min | AL | 141 | 490 | 117 | 23 | 4 | 22 | (9 | 13) | 214 | 62 | 79 | 58 | 44 | 8 | 94 | 4 | 0 | 5 | 0 | 2 | .00 | 12 | .239 | .304 | .437 |
| 2006 Min | AL | 157 | 592 | 190 | 37 | 1 | 34 | (17 | 17) | 331 | 97 | 130 | 118 | 53 | 9 | 93 | 5 | 0 | **11** | 3 | 3 | .50 | 10 | .321 | .375 | .559 |
| 2007 Min | AL | 157 | 590 | 160 | 31 | 3 | 31 | (15 | 16) | 290 | 84 | 111 | 95 | 64 | 11 | 91 | 5 | 0 | 9 | 1 | 1 | .50 | 17 | .271 | .343 | .492 |
| 2008 Min | AL | **163** | 623 | 187 | 47 | 4 | 23 | (12 | 11) | 311 | 97 | 129 | **122** | 76 | **16** | 85 | 3 | 0 | 10 | 0 | 1 | .00 | 20 | .300 | .374 | .499 |
| 2009 Min | AL | 135 | 508 | 139 | 31 | 1 | 30 | (14 | 16) | 262 | 85 | 100 | 91 | 72 | 12 | 86 | 3 | 0 | 7 | 0 | 0 | - | 12 | .274 | .363 | .516 |
| 2010 Min | AL | 81 | 296 | 102 | 25 | 1 | 18 | (4 | 14) | 183 | 53 | 56 | 65 | 50 | 7 | 62 | 0 | 0 | 2 | 0 | 0 | - | 6 | .345 | .437 | .618 |
| 2011 Min | AL | 69 | 264 | 60 | 16 | 0 | 4 | (0 | 4) | 88 | 19 | 30 | 28 | 19 | 1 | 44 | 3 | 0 | 2 | 0 | 0 | - | 8 | .227 | .285 | .333 |
| 2012 Min | AL | 134 | 505 | 135 | 26 | 2 | 19 | (7 | 12) | 222 | 63 | 77 | 63 | 49 | 8 | 102 | 6 | 0 | 10 | 1 | 0 | 1.00 | 19 | .267 | .333 | .440 |
| 2013 2 Tms | | 152 | 572 | 148 | 36 | 0 | 17 | (9 | 8) | 235 | 62 | 77 | 71 | 50 | 4 | 110 | 7 | 0 | 6 | 0 | 0 | - | 13 | .259 | .323 | .411 |
| 13 Min | AL | 127 | 495 | 128 | 32 | 0 | 17 | (9 | 8) | 211 | 56 | 74 | 64 | 37 | 3 | 98 | 6 | 0 | 5 | 0 | 0 | - | 10 | .259 | .315 | .426 |
| 13 Pit | NL | 25 | 77 | 20 | 4 | 0 | 0 | (0 | 0) | 24 | 6 | 3 | 7 | 13 | 1 | 12 | 1 | 0 | 1 | 0 | 0 | - | 3 | .260 | .370 | .312 |
| Postseason | | 7 | 29 | 9 | 3 | 0 | 2 | (1 | 1) | 18 | 4 | 4 | 3 | 0 | 0 | 3 | 0 | 0 | 0 | 0 | 0 | - | 0 | .310 | .310 | .621 |
| 11 ML YEARS | | 1303 | 4826 | 1338 | 293 | 16 | 221 | (97 | 124) | 2326 | 675 | 863 | 770 | 514 | 85 | 851 | 38 | 0 | 64 | 5 | 7 | .42 | 125 | .277 | .347 | .482 |

## Bryan Morris

**Pitches:** R **Bats:** L **Pos:** RP-55 **Ht:** 6'3" **Wt:** 225 **Born:** 3/28/1987 **Age:** 27

| HOW MUCH HE PITCHED | | | | | | | | WHAT HE GAVE UP | | | | | | | | | | | | THE RESULTS | | | | | | | |
|---|---|---|---|---|---|---|---|---|---|---|---|---|---|---|---|---|---|---|---|---|---|---|---|---|---|---|---|
| Year Team | Lg | G | GS | CG | GF | IP | BFP | H | R | ER | HR | SH | SF | HB | TBB | IBB | SO | WP | Bk | W | L | Pct | Sh | Sv-Op | Hld | ERC | ERA |
| 2009 Lynbrg | A+ | 15 | 15 | 0 | 0 | 72.2 | 334 | 87 | 58 | 45 | 2 | 4 | 1 | 0 | 34 | 0 | 32 | 10 | 0 | 4 | 9 | .308 | 0 | 0- - | - | 4.87 | 5.57 |
| 2010 Bradtn | A+ | 8 | 8 | 0 | 0 | 44.2 | 180 | 37 | 8 | 3 | 0 | 1 | 2 | 2 | 7 | 0 | 40 | 2 | 1 | 3 | 0 | 1.000 | 0 | 0- - | - | 1.83 | 0.60 |
| 2010 Altna | AA | 19 | 16 | 0 | 1 | 89.0 | 383 | 87 | 45 | 42 | 9 | 7 | 2 | 6 | 31 | 0 | 84 | 8 | 0 | 6 | 4 | .600 | 0 | 0- - | - | 4.02 | 4.25 |
| 2011 Altna | AA | 35 | 6 | 0 | 7 | 78.0 | 326 | 72 | 34 | 29 | 2 | 5 | 1 | 1 | 33 | 0 | 64 | 4 | 1 | 3 | 4 | .429 | 0 | 3- - | - | 3.35 | 3.35 |
| 2012 Indy | AAA | 46 | 0 | 0 | 14 | 81.0 | 335 | 76 | 32 | 24 | 8 | 0 | 1 | 0 | 17 | 0 | 79 | 9 | 1 | 2 | 2 | .500 | 0 | 5- - | - | 2.95 | 2.67 |
| 2013 Indy | AAA | 5 | 0 | 0 | 5 | 6.1 | 24 | 5 | 1 | 1 | 0 | 0 | 0 | 0 | 1 | 0 | 4 | 1 | 0 | 2 | 0 | - | 0 | 5- - | - | 1.64 | 1.42 |
| 2012 Pit | NL | 5 | 0 | 0 | 2 | 5.0 | 20 | 2 | 2 | 1 | 0 | 0 | 1 | 1 | 2 | 0 | 6 | 1 | 0 | 0 | 0 | - | 0 | 0-0 | 0 | 1.32 | 1.80 |
| 2013 Pit | NL | 55 | 0 | 0 | 21 | 65.0 | 270 | 57 | 25 | 25 | 8 | 0 | 5 | 2 | 28 | 5 | 37 | 6 | 0 | 5 | 7 | .417 | 0 | 0-0 | 7 | 3.78 | 3.46 |
| 2 ML YEARS | | 60 | 0 | 0 | 23 | 70.0 | 290 | 59 | 27 | 26 | 8 | 0 | 6 | 3 | 30 | 5 | 43 | 7 | 0 | 5 | 7 | .417 | 0 | 0-0 | 7 | 3.56 | 3.34 |

## Logan Morrison

**Bats:** L **Throws:** L **Pos:** 1B-79;PH-5;DH-1 **Ht:** 6'3" **Wt:** 245 **Born:** 8/25/1987 **Age:** 26

| BATTING | | | | | | | | | | | | | | | | | | | | | BASERUNNING | | | | AVERAGES | | |
|---|---|---|---|---|---|---|---|---|---|---|---|---|---|---|---|---|---|---|---|---|---|---|---|---|---|---|---|
| Year Team | Lg | G | AB | H | 2B | 3B | HR | (Hm | Rd) | TB | R | RBI | RC | TBB | IBB | SO | HBP | SH | SF | SB | CS | SB% | GDP | Avg | OBP | Slg |
| 2013 Jupiter* | A+ | 6 | 23 | 4 | 0 | 0 | 0 | (- | -) | 4 | 0 | 3 | 1 | 4 | 0 | 0 | 0 | 0 | 0 | 0 | 1 | .00 | 1 | .174 | .296 | .174 |
| 2013 Jaxnvl* | AA | 10 | 33 | 6 | 0 | 0 | 2 | (- | -) | 12 | 5 | 7 | 2 | 2 | 0 | 4 | 0 | 0 | 0 | 0 | 0 | - | 2 | .182 | .229 | .364 |
| 2010 Fla | NL | 62 | 244 | 69 | 20 | 7 | 2 | (1 | 1) | 109 | 43 | 18 | 41 | 41 | 0 | 51 | 2 | 0 | 0 | 0 | 1 | .00 | 4 | .283 | .390 | .447 |
| 2011 Fla | NL | 123 | 462 | 114 | 25 | 4 | 23 | (12 | 11) | 216 | 54 | 72 | 55 | 54 | 3 | 99 | 5 | 0 | 4 | 2 | 1 | .67 | 9 | .247 | .330 | .468 |
| 2012 Mia | NL | 93 | 296 | 68 | 15 | 1 | 11 | (4 | 7) | 118 | 30 | 36 | 27 | 31 | 2 | 58 | 4 | 0 | 3 | 1 | 0 | 1.00 | 9 | .230 | .308 | .399 |
| 2013 Mia | NL | 85 | 293 | 71 | 13 | 4 | 6 | (1 | 5) | 110 | 32 | 36 | 37 | 38 | 5 | 56 | 2 | 0 | 0 | 0 | 0 | - | 10 | .242 | .333 | .375 |
| 4 ML YEARS | | 363 | 1295 | 322 | 73 | 16 | 42 | (18 | 24) | 553 | 159 | 162 | 160 | 164 | 10 | 264 | 13 | 0 | 7 | 3 | 2 | .60 | 32 | .249 | .337 | .427 |

## Brandon Morrow

**Pitches:** R **Bats:** R **Pos:** SP-10 **Ht:** 6'3" **Wt:** 200 **Born:** 7/26/1984 **Age:** 29

| HOW MUCH HE PITCHED | | | | | | | | WHAT HE GAVE UP | | | | | | | | | | | | THE RESULTS | | | | | | | |
|---|---|---|---|---|---|---|---|---|---|---|---|---|---|---|---|---|---|---|---|---|---|---|---|---|---|---|---|
| Year | Team | Lg | G | GS | CG | GF | IP | BFP | H | R | ER | HR | SH | SF | HB | TBB | IBB | SO | WP | Bk | W | L | Pct | Sh | Sv-Op | Hld | ERC | ERA |
| 2013 | Dnedin* | A+ | 1 | 1 | 0 | 0 | 2.0 | 11 | 5 | 3 | 3 | 1 | 1 | 0 | 0 | 1 | 0 | 0 | 0 | 0 | 0 | 0 | - | 0 | 0- - | - | 20.52 | 13.50 |
| 2007 | Sea | AL | 60 | 0 | 0 | 18 | 63.1 | 289 | 56 | 29 | 29 | 3 | 4 | 4 | 1 | 50 | 5 | 66 | 4 | 0 | 3 | 4 | .429 | 0 | 0-2 | 18 | 4.47 | 4.12 |
| 2008 | Sea | AL | 45 | 5 | 0 | 24 | 64.2 | 265 | 40 | 26 | 24 | 10 | 1 | 0 | 0 | 34 | 1 | 75 | 5 | 0 | 3 | 4 | .429 | 0 | 10-12 | 3 | 2.84 | 3.34 |
| 2009 | Sea | AL | 26 | 10 | 0 | 9 | 69.2 | 313 | 66 | 38 | 34 | 10 | 1 | 2 | 0 | 44 | 1 | 63 | 3 | 0 | 2 | 4 | .333 | 0 | 6-8 | 1 | 4.99 | 4.39 |
| 2010 | Tor | AL | 26 | 26 | 1 | 0 | 146.1 | 629 | 136 | 76 | 73 | 11 | 2 | 4 | 9 | 66 | 0 | 178 | 8 | 0 | 10 | 7 | .588 | 1 | 0-0 | 0 | 3.99 | 4.49 |
| 2011 | Tor | AL | 30 | 30 | 0 | 0 | 179.1 | 777 | 162 | 103 | 94 | 21 | 4 | 9 | 12 | 69 | 1 | 203 | 12 | 1 | 11 | 11 | .500 | 0 | 0-0 | 0 | 3.79 | 4.72 |
| 2012 | Tor | AL | 21 | 21 | 3 | 0 | 124.2 | 504 | 98 | 45 | 41 | 12 | 1 | 3 | 2 | 41 | 0 | 108 | 3 | 0 | 10 | 7 | .588 | 3 | 0-0 | 0 | 2.73 | 2.96 |
| 2013 | Tor | AL | 10 | 10 | 0 | 0 | 54.1 | 242 | 63 | 39 | 34 | 12 | 0 | 3 | 1 | 18 | 1 | 42 | 1 | 0 | 2 | 3 | .400 | 0 | 0-0 | 0 | 5.60 | 5.63 |
| 7 ML YEARS | | | 218 | 102 | 4 | 51 | 702.1 | 3019 | 621 | 356 | 329 | 79 | 13 | 25 | 25 | 322 | 9 | 735 | 36 | 1 | 41 | 40 | .506 | 4 | 16-22 | 22 | 3.86 | 4.22 |

## Michael Morse

**Bats:** R **Throws:** R **Pos:** RF-55;LF-19;DH-8;1B-7;PH-3 **Ht:** 6'5" **Wt:** 245 **Born:** 3/22/1982 **Age:** 32

| BATTING | | | | | | | | | | | | | | | | | | | | | BASERUNNING | | | | AVERAGES | | |
|---|---|---|---|---|---|---|---|---|---|---|---|---|---|---|---|---|---|---|---|---|---|---|---|---|---|---|---|
| Year | Team | Lg | G | AB | H | 2B | 3B | HR | (Hm | Rd) | TB | R | RBI | RC | TBB | IBB | SO | HBP | SH | SF | SB | CS | SB% | GDP | Avg | OBP | Slg |
| 2013 | Tacom* | AAA | 6 | 24 | 6 | 1 | 0 | 1 | (- | -) | 10 | 3 | 2 | 3 | 2 | 1 | 6 | 0 | 0 | 0 | 0 | 0 | - | 0 | .250 | .308 | .417 |
| 2005 | Sea | AL | 72 | 230 | 64 | 10 | 1 | 3 | (3 | 0) | 85 | 27 | 23 | 28 | 18 | 0 | 50 | 8 | 0 | 2 | 3 | 1 | .75 | 9 | .278 | .349 | .370 |
| 2006 | Sea | AL | 21 | 43 | 16 | 5 | 0 | 0 | (0 | 0) | 21 | 5 | 11 | 9 | 3 | 0 | 7 | 0 | 0 | 2 | 1 | 0 | 1.00 | 2 | .372 | .396 | .488 |
| 2007 | Sea | AL | 9 | 18 | 8 | 2 | 0 | 0 | (0 | 0) | 10 | 1 | 3 | 6 | 1 | 0 | 4 | 1 | 0 | 0 | 0 | 0 | - | 0 | .444 | .500 | .556 |
| 2008 | Sea | AL | 5 | 9 | 2 | 1 | 0 | 0 | (0 | 0) | 3 | 0 | 0 | 1 | 1 | 0 | 4 | 1 | 0 | 0 | 0 | 0 | - | 0 | .222 | .364 | .333 |
| 2009 | Was | NL | 32 | 52 | 13 | 3 | 0 | 3 | (3 | 0) | 25 | 4 | 10 | 8 | 3 | 0 | 16 | 0 | 0 | 0 | 0 | 0 | - | 1 | .250 | .291 | .481 |
| 2010 | Was | NL | 98 | 266 | 77 | 12 | 2 | 15 | (6 | 9) | 138 | 36 | 41 | 42 | 22 | 1 | 64 | 4 | 0 | 1 | 0 | 1 | .00 | 6 | .289 | .352 | .519 |
| 2011 | Was | NL | 146 | 522 | 158 | 36 | 0 | 31 | (11 | 20) | 287 | 73 | 95 | 96 | 36 | 5 | 126 | 13 | 0 | 4 | 2 | 3 | .40 | 9 | .303 | .360 | .550 |
| 2012 | Was | NL | 102 | 406 | 118 | 17 | 1 | 18 | (7 | 11) | 191 | 53 | 62 | 57 | 16 | 0 | 97 | 4 | 0 | 4 | 0 | 1 | .00 | 14 | .291 | .321 | .470 |
| 2013 | 2 Tms | AL | 88 | 312 | 67 | 13 | 0 | 13 | (5 | 8) | 119 | 34 | 27 | 24 | 21 | 1 | 87 | 3 | 0 | 1 | 0 | 0 | - | 12 | .215 | .270 | .381 |
| 13 | Sea | AL | 76 | 283 | 64 | 13 | 0 | 13 | (5 | 8) | 116 | 31 | 27 | 24 | 20 | 1 | 80 | 3 | 0 | 1 | 0 | 0 | - | 10 | .226 | .283 | .410 |
| 13 | Bal | AL | 12 | 29 | 3 | 0 | 0 | 0 | (0 | 0) | 3 | 3 | 0 | 0 | 1 | 0 | 7 | 0 | 0 | 0 | 0 | 0 | - | 2 | .103 | .133 | .103 |
| Postseason | | | 5 | 19 | 5 | 0 | 0 | 1 | (1 | 0) | 8 | 2 | 2 | 2 | 0 | 0 | 4 | 0 | 0 | 0 | 0 | 0 | - | 1 | .263 | .263 | .421 |
| 9 ML YEARS | | | 573 | 1858 | 523 | 99 | 4 | 83 | (35 | 48) | 879 | 233 | 272 | 271 | 121 | 7 | 455 | 34 | 0 | 14 | 6 | 6 | .50 | 53 | .281 | .334 | .473 |

## Clayton Mortensen

**Pitches:** R **Bats:** R **Pos:** RP-24 **Ht:** 6'4" **Wt:** 185 **Born:** 4/10/1985 **Age:** 29

| HOW MUCH HE PITCHED | | | | | | | | WHAT HE GAVE UP | | | | | | | | | | | | THE RESULTS | | | | | | | |
|---|---|---|---|---|---|---|---|---|---|---|---|---|---|---|---|---|---|---|---|---|---|---|---|---|---|---|---|
| Year | Team | Lg | G | GS | CG | GF | IP | BFP | H | R | ER | HR | SH | SF | HB | TBB | IBB | SO | WP | Bk | W | L | Pct | Sh | Sv-Op | Hld | ERC | ERA |
| 2013 | Pwtckt* | AAA | 14 | 6 | 0 | 1 | 43.2 | 178 | 34 | 14 | 12 | 4 | 2 | 1 | 2 | 20 | 0 | 39 | 3 | 0 | 3 | 0 | 1.000 | 0 | 0- - | - | 3.33 | 2.47 |
| 2013 | Omha* | AAA | 1 | 1 | 0 | 0 | 6.0 | 24 | 6 | 3 | 3 | 1 | 0 | 1 | 0 | 3 | 0 | 2 | 0 | 0 | 1 | 0 | 1.000 | 0 | 0- - | - | 5.53 | 4.50 |
| 2009 | 2 Tms | | 7 | 6 | 0 | 1 | 30.2 | 149 | 42 | 34 | 26 | 6 | 1 | 4 | 3 | 13 | 0 | 13 | 1 | 0 | 2 | 4 | .333 | 0 | 0-0 | 0 | 7.50 | 7.63 |
| 2010 | Oak | AL | 1 | 1 | 0 | 0 | 6.0 | 26 | 6 | 4 | 3 | 1 | 0 | 0 | 0 | 2 | 0 | 7 | 0 | 0 | 0 | 0 | - | 0 | 0-0 | 0 | 4.18 | 4.50 |
| 2011 | Col | NL | 16 | 6 | 0 | 6 | 58.1 | 244 | 55 | 30 | 25 | 9 | 4 | 0 | 2 | 24 | 2 | 30 | 3 | 0 | 2 | 4 | .333 | 0 | 0-0 | 0 | 4.40 | 3.86 |
| 2012 | Bos | AL | 26 | 0 | 0 | 8 | 42.0 | 173 | 32 | 15 | 15 | 7 | 0 | 2 | 1 | 19 | 2 | 41 | 3 | 0 | 1 | 1 | .500 | 0 | 0-0 | 1 | 3.49 | 3.21 |
| 2013 | Bos | AL | 24 | 0 | 0 | 7 | 30.1 | 141 | 32 | 19 | 18 | 3 | 1 | 1 | 3 | 16 | 1 | 21 | 1 | 0 | 1 | 2 | .333 | 0 | 0-0 | 0 | 5.14 | 5.34 |
| 09 | StL | NL | 1 | 0 | 0 | 1 | 3.0 | 16 | 5 | 6 | 2 | 1 | 1 | 1 | 1 | 1 | 0 | 2 | 0 | 0 | 0 | 0 | - | 0 | 0-0 | 0 | 11.45 | 6.00 |
| 09 | Oak | AL | 6 | 6 | 0 | 0 | 27.2 | 133 | 37 | 28 | 24 | 5 | 0 | 3 | 2 | 12 | 0 | 11 | 1 | 0 | 2 | 4 | .333 | 0 | 0-0 | 0 | 7.10 | 7.81 |
| 5 ML YEARS | | | 74 | 13 | 0 | 22 | 167.1 | 733 | 167 | 102 | 87 | 26 | 6 | 7 | 9 | 74 | 5 | 112 | 8 | 0 | 6 | 11 | .353 | 0 | 0-0 | 1 | 4.83 | 4.68 |

## Charlie Morton

**Pitches:** R **Bats:** R **Pos:** SP-20 **Ht:** 6'5" **Wt:** 245 **Born:** 11/12/1983 **Age:** 30

| HOW MUCH HE PITCHED | | | | | | | | WHAT HE GAVE UP | | | | | | | | | | | | THE RESULTS | | | | | | | |
|---|---|---|---|---|---|---|---|---|---|---|---|---|---|---|---|---|---|---|---|---|---|---|---|---|---|---|---|
| Year | Team | Lg | G | GS | CG | GF | IP | BFP | H | R | ER | HR | SH | SF | HB | TBB | IBB | SO | WP | Bk | W | L | Pct | Sh | Sv-Op | Hld | ERC | ERA |
| 2013 | Bradtn* | A+ | 1 | 1 | 0 | 0 | 3.0 | 13 | 3 | 2 | 2 | 1 | 0 | 0 | 1 | 0 | 0 | 2 | 0 | 0 | 0 | 0 | - | 0 | 0- - | - | 5.31 | 6.00 |
| 2013 | Altna* | AA | 4 | 4 | 0 | 0 | 18.2 | 71 | 10 | 5 | 5 | 2 | 0 | 0 | 0 | 6 | 0 | 11 | 1 | 0 | 1 | 1 | .500 | 0 | 0- - | - | 1.58 | 2.41 |
| 2013 | Indy* | AAA | 4 | 4 | 0 | 0 | 19.0 | 84 | 16 | 10 | 8 | 1 | 2 | 1 | 1 | 10 | 0 | 12 | 0 | 0 | 0 | 1 | .000 | 0 | 0- - | - | 3.47 | 3.79 |
| 2008 | Atl | NL | 16 | 15 | 0 | 0 | 74.2 | 345 | 80 | 56 | 51 | 9 | 5 | 4 | 2 | 41 | 2 | 48 | 2 | 0 | 4 | 8 | .333 | 0 | 0-0 | 0 | 5.21 | 6.15 |
| 2009 | Pit | NL | 18 | 18 | 1 | 0 | 97.0 | 416 | 102 | 49 | 49 | 7 | 1 | 1 | 5 | 40 | 0 | 62 | 4 | 0 | 5 | 9 | .357 | 1 | 0-0 | 0 | 4.56 | 4.55 |
| 2010 | Pit | NL | 17 | 17 | 0 | 0 | 79.2 | 382 | 112 | 79 | 67 | 15 | 6 | 6 | 7 | 26 | 3 | 59 | 5 | 1 | 2 | 12 | .143 | 0 | 0-0 | 0 | 7.10 | 7.57 |
| 2011 | Pit | NL | 29 | 29 | 2 | 0 | 171.2 | 769 | 186 | 82 | 73 | 6 | 12 | 6 | 13 | 77 | 5 | 110 | 9 | 1 | 10 | 10 | .500 | 1 | 0-0 | 0 | 4.52 | 3.83 |
| 2012 | Pit | NL | 9 | 9 | 0 | 0 | 50.1 | 223 | 62 | 30 | 26 | 5 | 5 | 2 | 2 | 11 | 1 | 25 | 4 | 0 | 2 | 6 | .250 | 0 | 0-0 | 0 | 4.74 | 4.65 |
| 2013 | Pit | NL | 20 | 20 | 0 | 0 | 116.0 | 493 | 113 | 51 | 42 | 6 | 6 | 2 | **16** | 36 | 1 | 85 | 5 | 0 | 7 | 4 | .636 | 0 | 0-0 | 0 | 3.84 | 3.26 |
| 6 ML YEARS | | | 109 | 108 | 3 | 0 | 589.1 | 2628 | 655 | 347 | 308 | 48 | 35 | 21 | 45 | 231 | 12 | 389 | 29 | 2 | 30 | 49 | .380 | 2 | 0-0 | 0 | 4.83 | 4.70 |

## Guillermo Moscoso

**Pitches:** R **Bats:** R **Pos:** RP-11; SP-2 mahs-KOE-soe **Ht:** 6'1" **Wt:** 200 **Born:** 11/14/1983 **Age:** 30

| HOW MUCH HE PITCHED | | | | | | | | WHAT HE GAVE UP | | | | | | | | | | | | THE RESULTS | | | | | | | |
|---|---|---|---|---|---|---|---|---|---|---|---|---|---|---|---|---|---|---|---|---|---|---|---|---|---|---|---|
| Year | Team | Lg | G | GS | CG | GF | IP | BFP | H | R | ER | HR | SH | SF | HB | TBB | IBB | SO | WP | Bk | W | L | Pct | Sh | Sv-Op | Hld | ERC | ERA |
| 2013 | Iowa* | AAA | 17 | 17 | 0 | 0 | 94.0 | 402 | 75 | 46 | 41 | 14 | 8 | 2 | 2 | 47 | 0 | 94 | 1 | 0 | 7 | 5 | .583 | 0 | 0- - | - | 3.73 | 3.93 |
| 2009 | Tex | AL | 10 | 0 | 0 | 6 | 14.0 | 64 | 15 | 7 | 5 | 1 | 0 | 1 | 1 | 6 | 0 | 12 | 4 | 0 | 0 | 0 | - | 0 | 0-0 | 0 | 4.55 | 3.21 |
| 2010 | Tex | AL | 1 | 0 | 0 | 0 | 0.2 | 7 | 2 | 2 | 2 | 0 | 0 | 0 | 1 | 2 | 0 | 2 | 0 | 0 | 0 | 0 | - | 0 | 0-0 | 0 | 37.18 | 27.00 |
| 2011 | Oak | AL | 23 | 21 | 0 | 1 | 128.0 | 526 | 102 | 59 | 48 | 14 | 1 | 3 | 2 | 38 | 1 | 74 | 0 | 1 | 8 | 10 | .444 | 0 | 0-0 | 0 | 2.67 | 3.38 |
| 2012 | Col | NL | 23 | 3 | 0 | 4 | 50.0 | 231 | 67 | 34 | 34 | 8 | 1 | 1 | 1 | 19 | 0 | 47 | 5 | 0 | 3 | 2 | .600 | 0 | 0-1 | 1 | 6.60 | 6.12 |
| 2013 | SF | NL | 13 | 2 | 0 | 0 | 30.0 | 128 | 20 | 17 | 17 | 5 | 0 | 0 | 3 | 21 | 3 | 31 | 5 | 0 | 2 | 2 | .500 | 0 | 0-0 | 0 | 4.22 | 5.10 |
| 5 ML YEARS | | | 70 | 26 | 0 | 11 | 222.2 | 956 | 206 | 119 | 106 | 28 | 2 | 5 | 8 | 86 | 4 | 166 | 14 | 1 | 13 | 14 | .481 | 0 | 0-1 | 1 | 3.87 | 4.28 |

## Brandon Moss

**Bats:** L **Throws:** R **Pos:** 1B-111;RF-27;PH-19;LF-8;DH-3;PR-3;3B-2;CF-2 **Ht:** 6'0" **Wt:** 210 **Born:** 9/16/1983 **Age:** 30

| BATTING | | | | | | | | | | | | | | | | | | | | | BASERUNNING | | | | AVERAGES | | |
|---|---|---|---|---|---|---|---|---|---|---|---|---|---|---|---|---|---|---|---|---|---|---|---|---|---|---|---|
| Year Team | Lg | G | AB | H | 2B | 3B | HR | (Hm | Rd) | TB | R | RBI | RC | TBB | IBB | SO | HBP | SH | SF | | SB | CS | SB% | GDP | Avg | OBP | Slg |
| 2007 Bos | AL | 15 | 25 | 7 | 2 | 1 | 0 | (0 | 0) | 11 | 6 | 1 | 3 | 4 | 0 | 6 | 0 | 0 | 0 | | 0 | 0 | - | 1 | .280 | .379 | .440 |
| 2008 2 Tms | | 79 | 236 | 58 | 15 | 3 | 8 | (4 | 4) | 103 | 19 | 34 | 30 | 21 | 1 | 70 | 1 | 0 | 5 | | 1 | 2 | .33 | 2 | .246 | .304 | .436 |
| 2009 Pit | NL | 133 | 385 | 91 | 20 | 4 | 7 | (4 | 3) | 140 | 47 | 41 | 37 | 34 | 3 | 84 | 4 | 0 | 1 | | 1 | 5 | .17 | 7 | .236 | .304 | .364 |
| 2010 Pit | NL | 17 | 26 | 4 | 1 | 0 | 0 | (0 | 0) | 5 | 2 | 2 | 2 | 1 | 0 | 6 | 0 | 0 | 0 | | 0 | 0 | - | 1 | .154 | .185 | .192 |
| 2011 Phi | NL | 5 | 6 | 0 | 0 | 0 | 0 | (0 | 0) | 0 | 0 | 0 | 0 | 0 | 0 | 2 | 0 | 0 | 0 | | 0 | 0 | - | 1 | .000 | .000 | .000 |
| 2012 Oak | AL | 84 | 265 | 77 | 18 | 0 | 21 | (9 | 12) | 158 | 48 | 52 | 50 | 26 | 2 | 90 | 3 | 0 | 2 | | 1 | 1 | .50 | 5 | .291 | .358 | .596 |
| 2013 Oak | AL | 145 | 446 | 114 | 23 | 3 | 30 | (10 | 20) | 233 | 73 | 87 | 79 | 50 | 3 | 140 | 6 | 0 | 3 | | 4 | 2 | .67 | 4 | .256 | .337 | .522 |
| 08 Bos | AL | 34 | 78 | 23 | 5 | 1 | 2 | (1 | 1) | 36 | 7 | 11 | 11 | 6 | 0 | 25 | 0 | 0 | 2 | | 1 | 1 | .50 | 0 | .295 | .337 | .462 |
| 08 Pit | NL | 45 | 158 | 35 | 10 | 2 | 6 | (3 | 3) | 67 | 12 | 23 | 19 | 15 | 1 | 45 | 1 | 0 | 3 | | 0 | 1 | .00 | 2 | .222 | .288 | .424 |
| Postseason | | 5 | 15 | 2 | 0 | 0 | 0 | (0 | 0) | 2 | 0 | 0 | 1 | 2 | 0 | 7 | 1 | 0 | 0 | | 0 | 0 | - | 0 | .133 | .278 | .133 |
| 7 ML YEARS | | 478 | 1389 | 351 | 79 | 11 | 66 | (27 | 39) | 650 | 195 | 217 | 201 | 136 | 9 | 398 | 14 | 0 | 11 | | 7 | 10 | .41 | 21 | .253 | .323 | .468 |

## Jason Motte

**Pitches:** R **Bats:** R **Pos:** P **Ht:** 6'0" **Wt:** 205 **Born:** 6/22/1982 **Age:** 32

| HOW MUCH HE PITCHED | | | | | | | | WHAT HE GAVE UP | | | | | | | | | | | | THE RESULTS | | | | | | | |
|---|---|---|---|---|---|---|---|---|---|---|---|---|---|---|---|---|---|---|---|---|---|---|---|---|---|---|---|
| Year Team | Lg | G | GS | CG | GF | IP | BFP | H | R | ER | HR | SH | SF | HB | TBB | IBB | SO | WP | Bk | W | L | Pct | Sh | Sv-Op | Hld | ERC | ERA |
| 2008 StL | NL | 12 | 0 | 0 | 4 | 11.0 | 40 | 5 | 2 | 1 | 0 | 1 | 0 | 0 | 3 | 0 | 16 | 0 | 0 | 0 | 0 | - | 0 | 1-1 | 4 | 0.89 | 0.82 |
| 2009 StL | NL | 69 | 0 | 0 | 14 | 56.2 | 244 | 57 | 32 | 30 | 10 | 0 | 3 | 2 | 23 | 1 | 54 | 2 | 1 | 4 | 4 | .500 | 0 | 0-3 | 15 | 4.86 | 4.76 |
| 2010 StL | NL | 56 | 0 | 0 | 13 | 52.1 | 208 | 41 | 13 | 13 | 5 | 1 | 3 | 0 | 18 | 3 | 54 | 1 | 0 | 4 | 2 | .667 | 0 | 2-3 | 12 | 2.68 | 2.24 |
| 2011 StL | NL | 78 | 0 | 0 | 27 | 68.0 | 268 | 49 | 22 | 17 | 2 | 1 | 3 | 5 | 16 | 2 | 63 | 1 | 0 | 5 | 2 | .714 | 0 | 9-13 | 18 | 1.87 | 2.25 |
| 2012 StL | NL | 67 | 0 | 0 | 58 | 72.0 | 279 | 49 | 23 | 22 | 9 | 2 | 1 | 2 | 17 | 1 | 86 | 0 | 0 | 4 | 5 | .444 | 0 | **42-49** | 0 | 2.08 | 2.75 |
| Postseason | | 19 | 0 | 0 | 16 | 21.2 | 79 | 12 | 6 | 5 | 2 | 0 | 0 | 0 | 2 | 0 | 10 | 0 | 0 | 1 | 1 | .500 | 0 | 8-8 | 0 | 1.07 | 2.08 |
| 5 ML YEARS | | 282 | 0 | 0 | 116 | 260.0 | 1039 | 201 | 92 | 83 | 26 | 5 | 10 | 9 | 77 | 7 | 273 | 4 | 1 | 17 | 13 | .567 | 0 | 54-69 | 49 | 2.62 | 2.87 |

## Mike Moustakas

**Bats:** L **Throws:** R **Pos:** 3B-134;PH-3 moo-STOCK-us **Ht:** 6'0" **Wt:** 210 **Born:** 9/11/1988 **Age:** 25

| BATTING | | | | | | | | | | | | | | | | | | | | | BASERUNNING | | | | AVERAGES | | |
|---|---|---|---|---|---|---|---|---|---|---|---|---|---|---|---|---|---|---|---|---|---|---|---|---|---|---|---|
| Year Team | Lg | G | AB | H | 2B | 3B | HR | (Hm | Rd) | TB | R | RBI | RC | TBB | IBB | SO | HBP | SH | SF | | SB | CS | SB% | GDP | Avg | OBP | Slg |
| 2011 KC | AL | 89 | 338 | 89 | 18 | 1 | 5 | (3 | 2) | 124 | 26 | 30 | 31 | 22 | 0 | 51 | 1 | 2 | 2 | | 2 | 0 | 1.00 | 5 | .263 | .309 | .367 |
| 2012 KC | AL | 149 | 563 | 136 | 34 | 1 | 20 | (10 | 10) | 232 | 69 | 73 | 64 | 39 | 4 | 124 | 7 | 0 | 5 | | 5 | 2 | .71 | 4 | .242 | .296 | .412 |
| 2013 KC | AL | 136 | 472 | 110 | 26 | 0 | 12 | (5 | 7) | 172 | 42 | 42 | 35 | 32 | 1 | 83 | 5 | 1 | 4 | | 2 | 4 | .33 | 13 | .233 | .287 | .364 |
| 3 ML YEARS | | 374 | 1373 | 335 | 78 | 2 | 37 | (18 | 19) | 528 | 137 | 145 | 130 | 93 | 5 | 258 | 13 | 3 | 11 | | 9 | 6 | .60 | 22 | .244 | .296 | .385 |

## Peter Moylan

**Pitches:** R **Bats:** R **Pos:** RP-14 **Ht:** 6'2" **Wt:** 225 **Born:** 12/2/1978 **Age:** 35

| HOW MUCH HE PITCHED | | | | | | | | WHAT HE GAVE UP | | | | | | | | | | | | THE RESULTS | | | | | | | |
|---|---|---|---|---|---|---|---|---|---|---|---|---|---|---|---|---|---|---|---|---|---|---|---|---|---|---|---|
| Year Team | Lg | G | GS | CG | GF | IP | BFP | H | R | ER | HR | SH | SF | HB | TBB | IBB | SO | WP | Bk | W | L | Pct | Sh | Sv-Op | Hld | ERC | ERA |
| 2013 Albq* | AAA | 38 | 0 | 0 | 21 | 46.0 | 190 | 38 | 14 | 14 | 1 | 5 | 2 | 2 | 20 | 3 | 45 | 0 | 1 | 4 | 1 | .800 | 0 | 4- - | - | 2.87 | 2.74 |
| 2006 Atl | NL | 15 | 0 | 0 | 5 | 15.0 | 68 | 18 | 8 | 8 | 1 | 1 | 0 | 0 | 5 | 1 | 14 | 0 | 0 | 0 | 0 | - | 0 | 0-0 | 0 | 4.47 | 4.80 |
| 2007 Atl | NL | 80 | 0 | 0 | 16 | 90.0 | 359 | 65 | 27 | 18 | 6 | 4 | 4 | 7 | 31 | **12** | 63 | 2 | 0 | 5 | 3 | .625 | 0 | 1-2 | 8 | 2.36 | 1.80 |
| 2008 Atl | NL | 7 | 0 | 0 | 2 | 5.2 | 25 | 5 | 1 | 1 | 1 | 0 | 0 | 1 | 1 | 0 | 5 | 0 | 0 | 0 | 1 | .000 | 0 | 1-2 | 4 | 3.51 | 1.59 |
| 2009 Atl | NL | 87 | 0 | 0 | 6 | 73.0 | 309 | 65 | 29 | 23 | 0 | 4 | 3 | 2 | 35 | 8 | 61 | 1 | 0 | 6 | 2 | .750 | 0 | 0-5 | 25 | 3.06 | 2.84 |
| 2010 Atl | NL | 85 | 0 | 0 | 7 | 63.2 | 271 | 53 | 24 | 21 | 5 | 5 | 2 | 2 | 37 | 6 | 52 | 3 | 0 | 6 | 2 | .750 | 0 | 1-4 | 21 | 3.75 | 2.97 |
| 2011 Atl | NL | 13 | 0 | 0 | 2 | 8.1 | 38 | 12 | 3 | 3 | 0 | 0 | 0 | 0 | 3 | 0 | 10 | 0 | 0 | 2 | 1 | .667 | 0 | 0-0 | 2 | 5.87 | 3.24 |
| 2012 Atl | NL | 8 | 0 | 0 | 3 | 5.0 | 21 | 3 | 3 | 1 | 1 | 1 | 0 | 0 | 2 | 0 | 2 | 1 | 0 | 1 | 0 | 1.000 | 0 | 1-1 | 1 | 2.40 | 1.80 |
| 2013 LAD | NL | 14 | 0 | 0 | 7 | 15.1 | 70 | 23 | 11 | 11 | 3 | 0 | 0 | 0 | 7 | 1 | 6 | 0 | 0 | 1 | 0 | 1.000 | 0 | 0-0 | 1 | 8.59 | 6.46 |
| Postseason | | 4 | 0 | 0 | 0 | 1.0 | 6 | 1 | 0 | 0 | 0 | 0 | 0 | 0 | 0 | 0 | 1 | 0 | 0 | 0 | 0 | - | 0 | 0-1 | 0 | 1.26 | 0.00 |
| 8 ML YEARS | | 309 | 0 | 0 | 48 | 276.0 | 1161 | 244 | 106 | 86 | 17 | 15 | 9 | 12 | 121 | 28 | 213 | 7 | 0 | 21 | 9 | .700 | 0 | 4-14 | 62 | 3.39 | 2.80 |

## Edward Mujica

**Pitches:** R **Bats:** R **Pos:** RP-65 moo-HEE-kah **Ht:** 6'3" **Wt:** 225 **Born:** 5/10/1984 **Age:** 30

| HOW MUCH HE PITCHED | | | | | | | | WHAT HE GAVE UP | | | | | | | | | | | | THE RESULTS | | | | | | | |
|---|---|---|---|---|---|---|---|---|---|---|---|---|---|---|---|---|---|---|---|---|---|---|---|---|---|---|---|
| Year Team | Lg | G | GS | CG | GF | IP | BFP | H | R | ER | HR | SH | SF | HB | TBB | IBB | SO | WP | Bk | W | L | Pct | Sh | Sv-Op | Hld | ERC | ERA |
| 2006 Cle | AL | 10 | 0 | 0 | 2 | 18.1 | 78 | 25 | 6 | 6 | 1 | 0 | 2 | 1 | 0 | 0 | 12 | 0 | 0 | 0 | 1 | .000 | 0 | 0-0 | 0 | 4.50 | 2.95 |
| 2007 Cle | AL | 10 | 0 | 0 | 5 | 13.0 | 60 | 19 | 12 | 12 | 3 | 0 | 1 | 0 | 2 | 0 | 7 | 0 | 0 | 0 | 0 | - | 0 | 0-0 | 0 | 6.63 | 8.31 |
| 2008 Cle | AL | 33 | 0 | 0 | 13 | 38.2 | 168 | 46 | 29 | 29 | 5 | 0 | 4 | 1 | 10 | 3 | 27 | 1 | 0 | 3 | 2 | .600 | 0 | 0-2 | 1 | 4.82 | 6.75 |
| 2009 SD | NL | 67 | 4 | 0 | 15 | 93.2 | 393 | 101 | 47 | 41 | 14 | 1 | 3 | 0 | 19 | 4 | 76 | 3 | 1 | 3 | 5 | .375 | 0 | 2-3 | 11 | 4.00 | 3.94 |
| 2010 SD | NL | 59 | 0 | 0 | 24 | 69.2 | 268 | 59 | 29 | 28 | 14 | 1 | 0 | 0 | 6 | 0 | 72 | 1 | 0 | 2 | 1 | .667 | 0 | 0-1 | 4 | 2.68 | 3.62 |
| 2011 Fla | NL | 67 | 0 | 0 | 11 | 76.0 | 297 | 64 | 27 | 25 | 7 | 5 | 1 | 2 | 14 | 5 | 63 | 1 | 0 | 9 | 6 | .600 | 0 | 0-3 | 17 | 2.46 | 2.96 |
| 2012 2 Tms | NL | 70 | 0 | 0 | 16 | 65.1 | 258 | 56 | 24 | 22 | 7 | 1 | 1 | 1 | 12 | 3 | 47 | 1 | 0 | 0 | 3 | .000 | 0 | 2-8 | 30 | 2.58 | 3.03 |
| 2013 StL | NL | 65 | 0 | 0 | 49 | 64.2 | 255 | 60 | 20 | 20 | 9 | 3 | 1 | 1 | 5 | 1 | 46 | 0 | 1 | 2 | 1 | .667 | 0 | 37-41 | 5 | 2.75 | 2.78 |
| 12 Mia | NL | 41 | 0 | 0 | 14 | 39.0 | 161 | 36 | 21 | 19 | 6 | 0 | 1 | 1 | 9 | 2 | 26 | 0 | 0 | 0 | 3 | .000 | 0 | 2-6 | 12 | 3.35 | 4.38 |
| 12 StL | NL | 29 | 0 | 0 | 2 | 26.1 | 97 | 20 | 3 | 3 | 1 | 1 | 0 | 0 | 3 | 1 | 21 | 1 | 0 | 0 | 0 | - | 0 | 0-2 | 18 | 1.57 | 1.03 |
| Postseason | | 9 | 0 | 0 | 2 | 7.2 | 32 | 9 | 2 | 2 | 0 | 0 | 1 | 0 | 1 | 0 | 4 | 0 | 0 | 1 | 0 | 1.000 | 0 | 0-0 | 2 | 3.33 | 2.35 |
| 8 ML YEARS | | 381 | 4 | 0 | 135 | 439.1 | 1777 | 430 | 194 | 183 | 60 | 11 | 13 | 6 | 68 | 16 | 350 | 7 | 2 | 19 | 19 | .500 | 0 | 41-58 | 68 | 3.27 | 3.75 |

# Daniel Murphy

**Bats:** L **Throws:** R **Pos:** 2B-150;1B-7;PH-6 **Ht:** 6'2" **Wt:** 205 **Born:** 4/1/1985 **Age:** 29

| BATTING | | | | | | | | | | | | | | | | | | | | | BASERUNNING | | | | AVERAGES | | |
|---|---|---|---|---|---|---|---|---|---|---|---|---|---|---|---|---|---|---|---|---|---|---|---|---|---|---|---|
| Year | Team | Lg | G | AB | H | 2B | 3B | HR | (Hm | Rd) | TB | R | RBI | RC | TBB | IBB | SO | HBP | SH | SF | SB | CS | SB% | GDP | Avg | OBP | Slg |
| 2008 | NYM | NL | 49 | 131 | 41 | 9 | 3 | 2 | (1 | 1) | 62 | 24 | 17 | 26 | 18 | 1 | 28 | 1 | 0 | 1 | 0 | 2 | .00 | 4 | .313 | .397 | .473 |
| 2009 | NYM | NL | 155 | 508 | 135 | 38 | 4 | 12 | (7 | 5) | 217 | 60 | 63 | 60 | 38 | 4 | 69 | 0 | 4 | 6 | 4 | 2 | .67 | 13 | .266 | .313 | .427 |
| 2011 | NYM | NL | 109 | 391 | 125 | 28 | 2 | 6 | (2 | 4) | 175 | 49 | 49 | 57 | 24 | 2 | 42 | 3 | 3 | 2 | 5 | 5 | .50 | 14 | .320 | .362 | .448 |
| 2012 | NYM | NL | 156 | 571 | 166 | 40 | 3 | 6 | (1 | 5) | 230 | 62 | 65 | 78 | 36 | 5 | 82 | 1 | 0 | 4 | 10 | 2 | .83 | 12 | .291 | .332 | .403 |
| 2013 | NYM | NL | 161 | 658 | 188 | 38 | 4 | 13 | (6 | 7) | 273 | 92 | 78 | 86 | 32 | 2 | 95 | 2 | 0 | 5 | 23 | 3 | **.88** | 13 | .286 | .319 | .415 |
| 5 ML YEARS | | | 630 | 2259 | 655 | 153 | 16 | 39 | (17 | 22) | 957 | 287 | 272 | 307 | 148 | 14 | 316 | 7 | 7 | 18 | 42 | 14 | .75 | 56 | .290 | .333 | .424 |

# David Murphy

**Bats:** L **Throws:** L **Pos:** LF-128;PH-15;DH-10;RF-1;PR-1 **Ht:** 6'4" **Wt:** 210 **Born:** 10/18/1981 **Age:** 32

| BATTING | | | | | | | | | | | | | | | | | | | | | BASERUNNING | | | | AVERAGES | | |
|---|---|---|---|---|---|---|---|---|---|---|---|---|---|---|---|---|---|---|---|---|---|---|---|---|---|---|---|
| Year | Team | Lg | G | AB | H | 2B | 3B | HR | (Hm | Rd) | TB | R | RBI | RC | TBB | IBB | SO | HBP | SH | SF | SB | CS | SB% | GDP | Avg | OBP | Slg |
| 2006 | Bos | AL | 20 | 22 | 5 | 1 | 0 | 1 | (0 | 1) | 9 | 4 | 2 | 2 | 4 | 0 | 4 | 0 | 0 | 0 | 0 | 0 | - | 1 | .227 | .346 | .409 |
| 2007 | 2 Tms | AL | 46 | 105 | 36 | 12 | 2 | 2 | (1 | 1) | 58 | 17 | 14 | 23 | 7 | 0 | 20 | 0 | 0 | 0 | 0 | 0 | - | 1 | .343 | .384 | .552 |
| 2008 | Tex | AL | 108 | 415 | 114 | 28 | 3 | 15 | (8 | 7) | 193 | 64 | 74 | 62 | 31 | 3 | 70 | 0 | 2 | 6 | 7 | 2 | .78 | 7 | .275 | .321 | .465 |
| 2009 | Tex | AL | 128 | 432 | 116 | 24 | 1 | 17 | (8 | 9) | 193 | 61 | 57 | 60 | 49 | 3 | 106 | 1 | 2 | 9 | 9 | 4 | .69 | 5 | .269 | .338 | .447 |
| 2010 | Tex | AL | 138 | 419 | 122 | 26 | 2 | 12 | (7 | 5) | 188 | 54 | 65 | 68 | 45 | 2 | 71 | 0 | 0 | 3 | 14 | 2 | .88 | 6 | .291 | .358 | .449 |
| 2011 | Tex | AL | 120 | 404 | 111 | 14 | 2 | 11 | (8 | 3) | 162 | 46 | 46 | 52 | 33 | 3 | 61 | 0 | 1 | 2 | 11 | 6 | .65 | 11 | .275 | .328 | .401 |
| 2012 | Tex | AL | 147 | 457 | 139 | 29 | 3 | 15 | (7 | 8) | 219 | 65 | 61 | 84 | 54 | 7 | 74 | 4 | 0 | 4 | 10 | 5 | .67 | 7 | .304 | .380 | .479 |
| 2013 | Tex | AL | 142 | 436 | 96 | 26 | 1 | 13 | (9 | 4) | 163 | 51 | 45 | 37 | 37 | 2 | 59 | 1 | 0 | 1 | 1 | 4 | .20 | 11 | .220 | .282 | .374 |
| 07 | Bos | AL | 3 | 2 | 1 | 0 | 1 | 0 | (0 | 0) | 3 | 1 | 0 | 1 | 0 | 0 | 1 | 0 | 0 | 0 | 0 | 0 | - | 0 | .500 | .500 | 1.500 |
| 07 | Tex | AL | 43 | 103 | 35 | 12 | 1 | 2 | (1 | 1) | 55 | 16 | 14 | 22 | 7 | 0 | 19 | 0 | 0 | 0 | 0 | 0 | - | 1 | .340 | .382 | .534 |
| Postseason | | | 27 | 70 | 18 | 4 | 1 | 1 | (1 | 0) | 27 | 11 | 6 | 12 | 13 | 3 | 14 | 0 | 0 | 0 | 1 | 0 | 1.00 | 0 | .257 | .373 | .386 |
| 8 ML YEARS | | | 849 | 2690 | 739 | 160 | 14 | 86 | (48 | 38) | 1185 | 362 | 364 | 388 | 260 | 20 | 465 | 6 | 5 | 25 | 52 | 23 | .69 | 49 | .275 | .337 | .441 |

# Donnie Murphy

**Bats:** R **Throws:** R **Pos:** 3B-40;PH-8;SS-3;2B-2 **Ht:** 5'10" **Wt:** 190 **Born:** 3/10/1983 **Age:** 31

| BATTING | | | | | | | | | | | | | | | | | | | | | BASERUNNING | | | | AVERAGES | | |
|---|---|---|---|---|---|---|---|---|---|---|---|---|---|---|---|---|---|---|---|---|---|---|---|---|---|---|---|
| Year | Team | Lg | G | AB | H | 2B | 3B | HR | (Hm | Rd) | TB | R | RBI | RC | TBB | IBB | SO | HBP | SH | SF | SB | CS | SB% | GDP | Avg | OBP | Slg |
| 2013 | Iowa* | AAA | 89 | 302 | 80 | 18 | 2 | 12 | (- | -) | 138 | 32 | 41 | 48 | 27 | 0 | 75 | 8 | 0 | 3 | 5 | 3 | .63 | 5 | .265 | .338 | .457 |
| 2004 | KC | AL | 7 | 27 | 5 | 3 | 0 | 0 | (0 | 0) | 8 | 1 | 3 | 2 | 0 | 0 | 7 | 0 | 0 | 0 | 1 | 0 | 1.00 | 1 | .185 | .185 | .296 |
| 2005 | KC | AL | 32 | 77 | 12 | 5 | 0 | 1 | (0 | 1) | 20 | 4 | 8 | 1 | 9 | 0 | 23 | 0 | 1 | 1 | 0 | 1 | .00 | 3 | .156 | .241 | .260 |
| 2007 | Oak | AL | 42 | 118 | 26 | 8 | 0 | 6 | (2 | 4) | 52 | 21 | 21 | 16 | 10 | 0 | 35 | 2 | 1 | 1 | 1 | 0 | 1.00 | 3 | .220 | .290 | .441 |
| 2008 | Oak | AL | 46 | 103 | 19 | 3 | 0 | 3 | (2 | 1) | 31 | 10 | 13 | 6 | 11 | 0 | 38 | 2 | 0 | 1 | 2 | 1 | .67 | 1 | .184 | .274 | .301 |
| 2010 | Fla | NL | 29 | 44 | 14 | 6 | 1 | 3 | (2 | 1) | 31 | 9 | 16 | 12 | 2 | 0 | 19 | 0 | 1 | 0 | 0 | 0 | - | 0 | .318 | .348 | .705 |
| 2011 | Fla | NL | 36 | 92 | 17 | 4 | 1 | 2 | (0 | 2) | 29 | 10 | 9 | 5 | 4 | 1 | 21 | 3 | 0 | 1 | 0 | 0 | - | 0 | .185 | .240 | .315 |
| 2012 | Mia | NL | 52 | 116 | 25 | 6 | 2 | 3 | (2 | 1) | 44 | 13 | 12 | 12 | 9 | 1 | 35 | 2 | 1 | 1 | 1 | 1 | .50 | 4 | .216 | .281 | .379 |
| 2013 | ChC | NL | 46 | 149 | 38 | 8 | 0 | 11 | (7 | 4) | 79 | 23 | 23 | 22 | 8 | 1 | 48 | 6 | 0 | 0 | 2 | 0 | 1.00 | 1 | .255 | .319 | .530 |
| 8 ML YEARS | | | 290 | 726 | 156 | 43 | 4 | 29 | (15 | 14) | 294 | 91 | 105 | 76 | 53 | 3 | 226 | 15 | 4 | 5 | 7 | 3 | .70 | 13 | .215 | .280 | .405 |

# J.R. Murphy

**Bats:** R **Throws:** R **Pos:** C-15;PH-2 **Ht:** 5'11" **Wt:** 195 **Born:** 5/13/1991 **Age:** 23

| BATTING | | | | | | | | | | | | | | | | | | | | | BASERUNNING | | | | AVERAGES | | |
|---|---|---|---|---|---|---|---|---|---|---|---|---|---|---|---|---|---|---|---|---|---|---|---|---|---|---|---|
| Year | Team | Lg | G | AB | H | 2B | 3B | HR | (Hm | Rd) | TB | R | RBI | RC | TBB | IBB | SO | HBP | SH | SF | SB | CS | SB% | GDP | Avg | OBP | Slg |
| 2009 | Yanks | R | 9 | 33 | 11 | 2 | 0 | 1 | (- | -) | 16 | 4 | 7 | 6 | 3 | 0 | 8 | 1 | 0 | 0 | 0 | 0 | - | 1 | .333 | .405 | .485 |
| 2010 | CtnSC | A | 87 | 330 | 84 | 15 | 2 | 7 | (- | -) | 124 | 46 | 54 | 42 | 36 | 0 | 64 | 2 | 1 | 5 | 4 | 5 | .44 | 8 | .255 | .327 | .376 |
| 2011 | CtnSC | A | 63 | 256 | 76 | 23 | 0 | 6 | (- | -) | 117 | 31 | 32 | 41 | 19 | 1 | 38 | 0 | 0 | 2 | 2 | 0 | 1.00 | 7 | .297 | .343 | .457 |
| 2011 | Tampa | A+ | 23 | 85 | 22 | 6 | 0 | 1 | (- | -) | 31 | 8 | 14 | 8 | 2 | 0 | 9 | 0 | 0 | 2 | 0 | 0 | - | 2 | .259 | .270 | .365 |
| 2012 | Tampa | A+ | 67 | 265 | 68 | 14 | 1 | 5 | (- | -) | 99 | 39 | 28 | 33 | 26 | 0 | 41 | 0 | 2 | 1 | 4 | 3 | .57 | 12 | .257 | .322 | .374 |
| 2012 | Trntn | AA | 43 | 147 | 34 | 12 | 1 | 4 | (- | -) | 60 | 23 | 16 | 20 | 16 | 0 | 32 | 2 | 0 | 5 | 0 | 0 | - | 1 | .231 | .306 | .408 |
| 2013 | Trntn | AA | 49 | 183 | 49 | 10 | 0 | 6 | (- | -) | 77 | 34 | 25 | 29 | 24 | 0 | 32 | 1 | 1 | 2 | 1 | 0 | 1.00 | 4 | .268 | .352 | .421 |
| 2013 | S-WB | AAA | 59 | 230 | 62 | 19 | 0 | 6 | (- | -) | 99 | 26 | 21 | 35 | 23 | 1 | 41 | 3 | 0 | 1 | 0 | 1 | .00 | 8 | .270 | .342 | .430 |
| 2013 | NYY | AL | 16 | 26 | 4 | 1 | 0 | 0 | (0 | 0) | 5 | 3 | 1 | 0 | 1 | 0 | 9 | 0 | 0 | 0 | 0 | 0 | - | 0 | .154 | .185 | .192 |

# Brett Myers

**Pitches:** R **Bats:** R **Pos:** SP-3; RP-1 **Ht:** 6'4" **Wt:** 240 **Born:** 8/17/1980 **Age:** 33

| HOW MUCH HE PITCHED | | | | | | | | | WHAT HE GAVE UP | | | | | | | | | | | | THE RESULTS | | | | | | | | |
|---|---|---|---|---|---|---|---|---|---|---|---|---|---|---|---|---|---|---|---|---|---|---|---|---|---|---|---|---|---|
| Year | Team | Lg | G | GS | CG | GF | IP | BFP | H | R | ER | HR | SH | SF | HB | TBB | IBB | SO | WP | Bk | W | L | Pct | Sh | Sv-Op | Hld | ERC | ERA |
| 2013 | Akron* | AA | 6 | 3 | 0 | 0 | 10.2 | 47 | 7 | 6 | 4 | 1 | 0 | 0 | 1 | 6 | 0 | 6 | 2 | 0 | 1 | 2 | .333 | 0 | 0-- | - | 3.00 | 3.38 |
| 2013 | MhVlly* | A- | 1 | 0 | 0 | 0 | 1.0 | 3 | 0 | 0 | 0 | 0 | 0 | 0 | 0 | 0 | 0 | 1 | 0 | 0 | 0 | 0 | - | 0 | 0-- | - | 0.00 | 0.00 |
| 2002 | Phi | NL | 12 | 12 | 1 | 0 | 72.0 | 307 | 73 | 38 | 34 | 11 | 6 | 2 | 6 | 29 | 1 | 34 | 2 | 1 | 4 | 5 | .444 | 0 | 0-0 | 0 | 5.04 | 4.25 |
| 2003 | Phi | NL | 32 | 32 | 1 | 0 | 193.0 | 848 | 205 | 99 | 95 | 20 | 6 | 3 | 9 | 76 | 8 | 143 | 9 | 0 | 14 | 9 | .609 | 1 | 0-0 | 0 | 4.56 | 4.43 |
| 2004 | Phi | NL | 32 | 31 | 1 | 1 | 176.0 | 778 | 196 | 113 | 108 | 31 | 9 | 3 | 6 | 62 | 4 | 116 | 5 | 0 | 11 | 11 | .500 | 1 | 0-0 | 0 | 5.17 | 5.52 |
| 2005 | Phi | NL | 34 | 34 | 2 | 0 | 215.1 | 905 | 193 | 94 | 89 | 31 | 9 | 3 | 11 | 68 | 2 | 208 | 4 | **4** | 13 | 8 | .619 | 0 | 0-0 | 0 | 3.64 | 3.72 |
| 2006 | Phi | NL | 31 | 31 | 1 | 0 | 198.0 | 833 | 194 | 93 | 86 | 29 | 7 | 4 | 3 | 63 | 3 | 189 | 3 | 0 | 12 | 7 | .632 | 0 | 0-0 | 0 | 4.02 | 3.91 |
| 2007 | Phi | NL | 51 | 3 | 0 | 37 | 68.2 | 293 | 61 | 33 | 33 | 9 | 3 | 1 | 1 | 27 | 1 | 83 | 5 | 0 | 5 | 7 | .417 | 0 | 21-24 | 3 | 3.63 | 4.33 |
| 2008 | Phi | NL | 30 | 30 | 2 | 0 | 190.0 | 817 | 197 | 103 | 96 | 29 | 4 | 3 | 6 | 65 | 6 | 163 | 2 | 0 | 10 | 13 | .435 | 1 | 0-0 | 0 | 4.53 | 4.55 |
| 2009 | Phi | NL | 18 | 10 | 0 | 1 | 70.2 | 304 | 74 | 38 | 38 | 18 | 3 | 2 | 4 | 23 | 1 | 50 | 1 | 0 | 4 | 3 | .571 | 0 | 0-0 | 3 | 5.41 | 4.84 |
| 2010 | Hou | NL | 33 | 33 | 2 | 0 | 223.2 | 936 | 212 | 88 | 78 | 20 | 9 | 4 | 3 | 66 | 3 | 180 | 2 | 0 | 14 | 8 | .636 | 0 | 0-0 | 0 | 3.34 | 3.14 |
| 2011 | Hou | NL | 34 | 33 | 2 | 1 | 216.0 | 917 | 226 | 116 | 107 | 31 | 5 | 6 | 4 | 57 | 5 | 160 | 7 | 0 | 7 | 14 | .333 | 0 | 0-0 | 0 | 4.13 | 4.46 |
| 2012 | 2 Tms | | 70 | 0 | 0 | 41 | 65.1 | 272 | 65 | 30 | 24 | 8 | 2 | 3 | 3 | 15 | 2 | 41 | 2 | 0 | 3 | 8 | .273 | 0 | 19-21 | 8 | 3.69 | 3.31 |
| 2013 | Cle | AL | 4 | 3 | 0 | 1 | 21.1 | 97 | 29 | 19 | 19 | 10 | 1 | 0 | 0 | 5 | 0 | 12 | 0 | 0 | 0 | 3 | .000 | 0 | 0-0 | 0 | 8.26 | 8.02 |

| Year | Team | Lg | G | GS | CG | GF | IP | BFP | H | R | ER | HR | SH | SF | HB | TBB | IBB | SO | WP | Bk | W | L | Pct | Sh | Sv-Op | Hld | ERC | ERA |
|---|---|---|---|---|---|---|---|---|---|---|---|---|---|---|---|---|---|---|---|---|---|---|---|---|---|---|---|---|
| | | | HOW MUCH HE PITCHED | | | | | | WHAT HE GAVE UP | | | | | | | | | | | | THE RESULTS | | | | | | | |
| 12 | Hou | NL | 35 | 0 | 0 | 29 | 30.2 | 134 | 35 | 17 | 12 | 4 | 1 | 2 | 2 | 6 | 1 | 20 | 1 | 0 | 0 | 4 | .000 | 0 | 19-21 | 0 | 4.41 | 3.52 |
| 12 | CWS | AL | 35 | 0 | 0 | 12 | 34.2 | 138 | 30 | 13 | 12 | 4 | 1 | 1 | 1 | 9 | 1 | 21 | 1 | 0 | 3 | 4 | .429 | 0 | 0-0 | 8 | 3.08 | 3.12 |
| Postseason | | | 7 | 3 | 0 | 2 | 22.0 | 96 | 18 | 12 | 11 | 2 | 2 | 0 | 2 | 12 | 3 | 17 | 1 | 0 | 2 | 1 | .667 | 0 | 0-0 | 0 | 3.69 | 4.50 |
| 12 ML YEARS | | | 381 | 252 | 12 | 82 | 1710.0 | 7307 | 1725 | 864 | 807 | 247 | 64 | 34 | 56 | 556 | 36 | 1379 | 42 | 5 | 97 | 96 | .503 | 3 | 40-45 | 14 | 4.24 | 4.25 |

## Wil Myers

**Bats:** R **Throws:** R **Pos:** RF-72;DH-11;CF-8;PH-3 **Ht:** 6'3" **Wt:** 205 **Born:** 12/10/1990 **Age:** 23

| Year | Team | Lg | G | AB | H | 2B | 3B | HR | (Hm | Rd) | TB | R | RBI | RC | TBB | IBB | SO | HBP | SH | SF | SB | CS | SB% | GDP | Avg | OBP | Slg |
|---|---|---|---|---|---|---|---|---|---|---|---|---|---|---|---|---|---|---|---|---|---|---|---|---|---|---|---|
| | | | BATTING | | | | | | | | | | | | | | | | | | BASERUNNING | | | | AVERAGES | | |
| 2009 | Burlgtn | R | 4 | 16 | 2 | 0 | 1 | 1 | (- | -) | 7 | 1 | 4 | 1 | 0 | 0 | 3 | 0 | 0 | 0 | 0 | 0 | - | 2 | .125 | .125 | .438 |
| 2009 | Idaho | R+ | 18 | 68 | 29 | 7 | 1 | 4 | (- | -) | 50 | 18 | 14 | 22 | 9 | 1 | 15 | 1 | 0 | 2 | 2 | 0 | 1.00 | 3 | .426 | .488 | .735 |
| 2010 | Burlgtn | A | 68 | 242 | 70 | 19 | 1 | 10 | (- | -) | 121 | 42 | 45 | 52 | 48 | 0 | 55 | 2 | 0 | 2 | 10 | 3 | .77 | 4 | .289 | .408 | .500 |
| 2010 | Wilmg | A+ | 58 | 205 | 71 | 18 | 2 | 4 | (- | -) | 105 | 28 | 38 | 48 | 37 | 1 | 39 | 4 | 0 | 1 | 2 | 3 | .40 | 5 | .346 | .453 | .512 |
| 2011 | NWArk | AA | 99 | 354 | 90 | 23 | 1 | 8 | (- | -) | 139 | 50 | 49 | 54 | 52 | 1 | 87 | 4 | 2 | 4 | 9 | 2 | .82 | 16 | .254 | .353 | .393 |
| 2012 | NWArk | AA | 35 | 134 | 46 | 11 | 1 | 13 | (- | -) | 98 | 32 | 30 | 37 | 16 | 0 | 42 | 1 | 0 | 1 | 4 | 1 | .80 | 4 | .343 | .414 | .731 |
| 2012 | Omha | AAA | 99 | 388 | 118 | 15 | 5 | 24 | (- | -) | 215 | 66 | 79 | 80 | 45 | 2 | 98 | 3 | 0 | 3 | 2 | 2 | .50 | 7 | .304 | .378 | .554 |
| 2013 | Drham | AAA | 64 | 252 | 72 | 13 | 2 | 14 | (- | -) | 131 | 44 | 57 | 49 | 29 | 1 | 71 | 2 | 0 | 6 | 7 | 1 | .88 | 6 | .286 | .356 | .520 |
| 2013 | TB | AL | 88 | 335 | 98 | 23 | 0 | 13 | (5 | 8) | 160 | 50 | 53 | 52 | 33 | 6 | 91 | 1 | 0 | 4 | 5 | 2 | .71 | 10 | .293 | .354 | .478 |

## Mike Napoli

**Bats:** R **Throws:** R **Pos:** 1B-131;DH-8;PH-3 NAPP-uh-lee **Ht:** 6'0" **Wt:** 220 **Born:** 10/31/1981 **Age:** 32

| Year | Team | Lg | G | AB | H | 2B | 3B | HR | (Hm | Rd) | TB | R | RBI | RC | TBB | IBB | SO | HBP | SH | SF | SB | CS | SB% | GDP | Avg | OBP | Slg |
|---|---|---|---|---|---|---|---|---|---|---|---|---|---|---|---|---|---|---|---|---|---|---|---|---|---|---|---|
| | | | BATTING | | | | | | | | | | | | | | | | | | BASERUNNING | | | | AVERAGES | | |
| 2006 | LAA | AL | 99 | 268 | 61 | 13 | 0 | 16 | (10 | 6) | 122 | 47 | 42 | 40 | 51 | 0 | 90 | 5 | 0 | 1 | 2 | 3 | .40 | 2 | .228 | .360 | .455 |
| 2007 | LAA | AL | 75 | 219 | 54 | 11 | 1 | 10 | (5 | 5) | 97 | 40 | 34 | 35 | 33 | 2 | 63 | 5 | 1 | 5 | 5 | 2 | .71 | 5 | .247 | .351 | .443 |
| 2008 | LAA | AL | 78 | 227 | 62 | 9 | 1 | 20 | (10 | 10) | 133 | 39 | 49 | 46 | 35 | 5 | 70 | 5 | 1 | 6 | 7 | 3 | .70 | 3 | .273 | .374 | .586 |
| 2009 | LAA | AL | 114 | 382 | 104 | 22 | 1 | 20 | (10 | 10) | 188 | 60 | 56 | 52 | 40 | 1 | 103 | 7 | 0 | 3 | 3 | 3 | .50 | 6 | .272 | .350 | .492 |
| 2010 | LAA | AL | 140 | 453 | 108 | 24 | 1 | 26 | (13 | 13) | 212 | 60 | 68 | 60 | 42 | 2 | 137 | 11 | 0 | 4 | 4 | 2 | .67 | 15 | .238 | .316 | .468 |
| 2011 | Tex | AL | 113 | 369 | 118 | 25 | 0 | 30 | (13 | 17) | 233 | 72 | 75 | 90 | 58 | 2 | 85 | 3 | 0 | 2 | 4 | 2 | .67 | 10 | .320 | .414 | .631 |
| 2012 | Tex | AL | 108 | 352 | 80 | 9 | 2 | 24 | (11 | 13) | 165 | 53 | 56 | 54 | 56 | 5 | 125 | 7 | 0 | 2 | 1 | 0 | 1.00 | 9 | .227 | .343 | .469 |
| 2013 | Bos | AL | 139 | 498 | 129 | 38 | 2 | 23 | (11 | 12) | 240 | 79 | 92 | 79 | 73 | 3 | 187 | 6 | 0 | 1 | 1 | 1 | .50 | 15 | .259 | .360 | .482 |
| Postseason | | | 32 | 92 | 25 | 2 | 0 | 5 | (1 | 4) | 42 | 15 | 19 | 20 | 13 | 2 | 25 | 3 | 0 | 2 | 1 | 0 | 1.00 | 1 | .272 | .373 | .457 |
| 8 ML YEARS | | | 866 | 2768 | 716 | 151 | 8 | 169 | (83 | 86) | 1390 | 450 | 472 | 456 | 388 | 20 | 860 | 49 | 2 | 24 | 27 | 16 | .63 | 65 | .259 | .357 | .502 |

## Chris Narveson

**Pitches:** L **Bats:** L **Pos:** RP-2 NARR-vih-son **Ht:** 6'3" **Wt:** 205 **Born:** 12/20/1981 **Age:** 32

| Year | Team | Lg | G | GS | CG | GF | IP | BFP | H | R | ER | HR | SH | SF | HB | TBB | IBB | SO | WP | Bk | W | L | Pct | Sh | Sv-Op | Hld | ERC | ERA |
|---|---|---|---|---|---|---|---|---|---|---|---|---|---|---|---|---|---|---|---|---|---|---|---|---|---|---|---|---|
| | | | HOW MUCH HE PITCHED | | | | | | WHAT HE GAVE UP | | | | | | | | | | | | THE RESULTS | | | | | | | |
| 2013 | Nashv* | AAA | 15 | 15 | 0 | 0 | 77.0 | 339 | 85 | 54 | 44 | 9 | 3 | 2 | 2 | 24 | 0 | 59 | 5 | 1 | 4 | 7 | .364 | 0 | 0- - | - | 4.47 | 5.14 |
| 2006 | StL | NL | 5 | 1 | 0 | 1 | 9.1 | 40 | 6 | 5 | 5 | 1 | 0 | 0 | 1 | 5 | 0 | 12 | 1 | 1 | 0 | 0 | - | 0 | 0-0 | 0 | 3.06 | 4.82 |
| 2009 | Mil | NL | 21 | 4 | 0 | 5 | 47.0 | 205 | 45 | 22 | 20 | 7 | 2 | 3 | 2 | 16 | 1 | 46 | 4 | 0 | 2 | 0 | 1.000 | 0 | 0-0 | 0 | 3.96 | 3.83 |
| 2010 | Mil | NL | 37 | 28 | 0 | 2 | 167.2 | 724 | 172 | 96 | 93 | 21 | 8 | 5 | 5 | 59 | 3 | 137 | 6 | 0 | 12 | 9 | .571 | 0 | 0-1 | 3 | 4.30 | 4.99 |
| 2011 | Mil | NL | 30 | 28 | 0 | 0 | 161.2 | 699 | 160 | 82 | 80 | 17 | 6 | 4 | 1 | 65 | 1 | 126 | 4 | 1 | 11 | 8 | .579 | 0 | 0-0 | 0 | 4.06 | 4.45 |
| 2012 | Mil | NL | 2 | 2 | 0 | 0 | 9.0 | 41 | 10 | 8 | 7 | 2 | 1 | 2 | 0 | 4 | 0 | 5 | 0 | 0 | 1 | 1 | .500 | 0 | 0-0 | 0 | 5.69 | 7.00 |
| 2013 | Mil | NL | 2 | 0 | 0 | 1 | 2.0 | 8 | 1 | 0 | 0 | 0 | 0 | 0 | 0 | 1 | 0 | 0 | 1 | 0 | 0 | 0 | - | 0 | 0-0 | 0 | 1.41 | 0.00 |
| Postseason | | | 6 | 0 | 0 | 2 | 7.1 | 33 | 7 | 9 | 9 | 5 | 0 | 1 | 0 | 2 | 1 | 13 | 0 | 0 | 0 | 0 | - | 0 | 0-0 | 0 | 6.33 | 11.05 |
| 6 ML YEARS | | | 97 | 63 | 0 | 9 | 396.2 | 1717 | 394 | 213 | 205 | 48 | 17 | 14 | 9 | 150 | 5 | 326 | 16 | 2 | 26 | 18 | .591 | 0 | 0-1 | 3 | 4.14 | 4.65 |

## Joe Nathan

**Pitches:** R **Bats:** R **Pos:** RP-67 **Ht:** 6'4" **Wt:** 230 **Born:** 11/22/1974 **Age:** 39

| Year | Team | Lg | G | GS | CG | GF | IP | BFP | H | R | ER | HR | SH | SF | HB | TBB | IBB | SO | WP | Bk | W | L | Pct | Sh | Sv-Op | Hld | ERC | ERA |
|---|---|---|---|---|---|---|---|---|---|---|---|---|---|---|---|---|---|---|---|---|---|---|---|---|---|---|---|---|
| | | | HOW MUCH HE PITCHED | | | | | | WHAT HE GAVE UP | | | | | | | | | | | | THE RESULTS | | | | | | | |
| 1999 | SF | NL | 19 | 14 | 0 | 2 | 90.1 | 395 | 84 | 45 | 42 | 17 | 2 | 0 | 1 | 46 | 0 | 54 | 2 | 0 | 7 | 4 | .636 | 0 | 1-1 | 0 | 4.78 | 4.18 |
| 2000 | SF | NL | 20 | 15 | 0 | 0 | 93.1 | 426 | 89 | 63 | 54 | 12 | 5 | 5 | 4 | 63 | 4 | 61 | 5 | 0 | 5 | 2 | .714 | 0 | 0-1 | 0 | 5.23 | 5.21 |
| 2002 | SF | NL | 4 | 0 | 0 | 3 | 3.2 | 12 | 1 | 0 | 0 | 0 | 0 | 0 | 0 | 0 | 0 | 2 | 0 | 0 | 0 | 0 | - | 0 | 0-0 | 0 | 0.17 | 0.00 |
| 2003 | SF | NL | 78 | 0 | 0 | 9 | 79.0 | 316 | 51 | 26 | 26 | 7 | 2 | 4 | 3 | 33 | 3 | 83 | 4 | 1 | 12 | 4 | .750 | 0 | 0-3 | 20 | 2.34 | 2.96 |
| 2004 | Min | AL | 73 | 0 | 0 | 63 | 72.1 | 284 | 48 | 14 | 13 | 3 | 2 | 0 | 2 | 23 | 3 | 89 | 5 | 0 | 1 | 2 | .333 | 0 | 44-47 | 0 | 1.78 | 1.62 |
| 2005 | Min | AL | 69 | 0 | 0 | 58 | 70.0 | 276 | 46 | 22 | 21 | 5 | 1 | 2 | 0 | 22 | 1 | 94 | 2 | 0 | 7 | 4 | .636 | 0 | 43-48 | 0 | 1.83 | 2.70 |
| 2006 | Min | AL | 64 | 0 | 0 | 61 | 68.1 | 262 | 38 | 12 | 12 | 3 | 3 | 2 | 1 | 16 | 4 | 95 | 3 | 0 | 7 | 0 | 1.000 | 0 | 36-38 | 0 | 1.18 | 1.58 |
| 2007 | Min | AL | 68 | 0 | 0 | 60 | 71.2 | 282 | 54 | 15 | 15 | 4 | 2 | 2 | 1 | 19 | 2 | 77 | 3 | 0 | 4 | 2 | .667 | 0 | 37-41 | 0 | 2.08 | 1.88 |
| 2008 | Min | AL | 68 | 0 | 0 | 57 | 67.2 | 261 | 43 | 13 | 10 | 5 | 1 | 0 | 2 | 18 | 4 | 74 | 2 | 0 | 1 | 2 | .333 | 0 | 39-45 | 0 | 1.67 | 1.33 |
| 2009 | Min | AL | 70 | 0 | 0 | 62 | 68.2 | 271 | 42 | 16 | 16 | 7 | 1 | 0 | 2 | 22 | 1 | 89 | 4 | 0 | 2 | 2 | .500 | 0 | 47-52 | 0 | 1.89 | 2.10 |
| 2011 | Min | AL | 48 | 0 | 0 | 33 | 44.2 | 191 | 38 | 26 | 24 | 7 | 1 | 2 | 3 | 14 | 2 | 43 | 3 | 0 | 2 | 1 | .667 | 0 | 14-17 | 8 | 3.38 | 4.84 |
| 2012 | Tex | AL | 66 | 0 | 0 | 62 | 64.1 | 257 | 55 | 23 | 20 | 7 | 1 | 3 | 2 | 13 | 1 | 78 | 5 | 0 | 3 | 5 | .375 | 0 | 37-40 | 0 | 2.73 | 2.80 |
| 2013 | Tex | AL | 67 | 0 | 0 | 61 | 64.2 | 250 | 36 | 10 | 10 | 2 | 3 | 2 | 1 | 22 | 3 | 73 | 4 | 0 | 6 | 2 | .750 | 0 | 43-46 | 0 | 1.39 | 1.39 |
| Postseason | | | 9 | 0 | 0 | 4 | 9.0 | 49 | 14 | 9 | 9 | 2 | 0 | 1 | 0 | 8 | 3 | 11 | 1 | 0 | 0 | 2 | .000 | 0 | 1-3 | 0 | 9.91 | 9.00 |
| 13 ML YEARS | | | 714 | 29 | 0 | 531 | 858.2 | 3483 | 625 | 285 | 263 | 79 | 24 | 22 | 22 | 311 | 28 | 912 | 42 | 1 | 57 | 30 | .655 | 0 | 341-379 | 28 | 2.50 | 2.76 |

## Daniel Nava

NAH-vah

**Bats:** B **Throws:** L **Pos:** RF-69;LF-63;1B-19;DH-5;PH-4;PR-3;CF-1 **Ht:** 5'11" **Wt:** 200 **Born:** 2/22/1983 **Age:** 31

| | | | | | | BATTING | | | | | | | | | | | | | | | BASERUNNING | | | | AVERAGES | | |
|---|---|---|---|---|---|---|---|---|---|---|---|---|---|---|---|---|---|---|---|---|---|---|---|---|---|---|---|
| Year | Team | Lg | G | AB | H | 2B | 3B | HR | (Hm | Rd) | TB | R | RBI | RC | TBB | IBB | SO | HBP | SH | SF | SB | CS | SB% | GDP | Avg | OBP | Slg |
| 2010 | Bos | AL | 60 | 161 | 39 | 14 | 1 | 1 | (1 | 0) | 58 | 23 | 26 | 26 | 19 | 1 | 46 | 8 | 0 | 0 | 1 | 1 | .50 | 5 | .242 | .351 | .360 |
| 2012 | Bos | AL | 88 | 267 | 65 | 21 | 0 | 6 | (1 | 5) | 104 | 38 | 33 | 33 | 37 | 1 | 63 | 9 | 2 | 2 | 3 | 0 | 1.00 | 5 | .243 | .352 | .390 |
| 2013 | Bos | AL | 134 | 458 | 139 | 29 | 0 | 12 | (5 | 7) | 204 | 77 | 66 | 79 | 51 | 2 | 93 | 15 | 4 | 8 | 0 | 2 | .00 | 10 | .303 | .385 | .445 |
| 3 ML YEARS | | | 282 | 886 | 243 | 64 | 1 | 19 | (7 | 12) | 366 | 138 | 125 | 138 | 107 | 4 | 202 | 32 | 6 | 10 | 4 | 3 | .57 | 20 | .274 | .369 | .413 |

## Dioner Navarro

dee-AHN-err

**Bats:** B **Throws:** R **Pos:** C-55;PH-32;DH-4 **Ht:** 5'9" **Wt:** 205 **Born:** 2/9/1984 **Age:** 30

| | | | | | | BATTING | | | | | | | | | | | | | | | BASERUNNING | | | | AVERAGES | | |
|---|---|---|---|---|---|---|---|---|---|---|---|---|---|---|---|---|---|---|---|---|---|---|---|---|---|---|---|
| Year | Team | Lg | G | AB | H | 2B | 3B | HR | (Hm | Rd) | TB | R | RBI | RC | TBB | IBB | SO | HBP | SH | SF | SB | CS | SB% | GDP | Avg | OBP | Slg |
| 2004 | NYY | AL | 5 | 7 | 3 | 0 | 0 | 0 | (0 | 0) | 3 | 2 | 1 | 1 | 0 | 0 | 0 | 0 | 0 | 0 | 0 | 0 | - | 1 | .429 | .429 | .429 |
| 2005 | LAD | NL | 50 | 176 | 48 | 9 | 0 | 3 | (3 | 0) | 66 | 21 | 14 | 18 | 20 | 1 | 21 | 2 | 1 | 0 | 0 | 0 | - | 3 | .273 | .354 | .375 |
| 2006 | 2 Tms | | 81 | 268 | 68 | 9 | 0 | 6 | (4 | 2) | 95 | 28 | 28 | 27 | 31 | 6 | 51 | 1 | 1 | 1 | 2 | 1 | .67 | 7 | .254 | .332 | .354 |
| 2007 | TB | AL | 119 | 388 | 88 | 19 | 2 | 9 | (5 | 4) | 138 | 46 | 44 | 35 | 33 | 3 | 67 | 1 | 7 | 5 | 3 | 1 | .75 | 11 | .227 | .286 | .356 |
| 2008 | TB | AL | 120 | 427 | 126 | 27 | 0 | 7 | (4 | 3) | 174 | 43 | 54 | 59 | 34 | 1 | 49 | 3 | 3 | 3 | 0 | 4 | .00 | 16 | .295 | .349 | .407 |
| 2009 | TB | AL | 115 | 376 | 82 | 15 | 0 | 8 | (4 | 4) | 121 | 38 | 32 | 22 | 18 | 1 | 51 | 5 | 8 | 3 | 5 | 2 | .71 | 14 | .218 | .261 | .322 |
| 2010 | TB | AL | 48 | 124 | 24 | 5 | 0 | 1 | (1 | 0) | 32 | 11 | 7 | 4 | 12 | 0 | 20 | 1 | 5 | 0 | 0 | 1 | .00 | 3 | .194 | .270 | .258 |
| 2011 | LAD | NL | 64 | 176 | 34 | 6 | 1 | 5 | (3 | 2) | 57 | 13 | 17 | 14 | 20 | 4 | 35 | 1 | 3 | 2 | 0 | 0 | - | 3 | .193 | .276 | .324 |
| 2012 | Cin | NL | 24 | 69 | 20 | 3 | 1 | 2 | (0 | 2) | 31 | 6 | 12 | 10 | 2 | 1 | 12 | 0 | 1 | 1 | 0 | 0 | - | 1 | .290 | .306 | .449 |
| 2013 | ChC | NL | 89 | 240 | 72 | 7 | 0 | 13 | (9 | 4) | 118 | 31 | 34 | 43 | 23 | 1 | 36 | 2 | 0 | 1 | 0 | 1 | .00 | 4 | .300 | .365 | .492 |
| 06 | LAD | NL | 25 | 75 | 21 | 2 | 0 | 2 | (1 | 1) | 29 | 5 | 8 | 8 | 11 | 4 | 18 | 0 | 0 | 0 | 1 | 0 | 1.00 | 1 | .280 | .372 | .387 |
| 06 | TB | AL | 56 | 193 | 47 | 7 | 0 | 4 | (3 | 1) | 66 | 23 | 20 | 19 | 20 | 2 | 33 | 1 | 1 | 1 | 1 | 1 | .50 | 6 | .244 | .316 | .342 |
| Postseason | | | 18 | 62 | 18 | 4 | 0 | 0 | (0 | 0) | 22 | 4 | 5 | 6 | 5 | 0 | 13 | 0 | 0 | 0 | 0 | 1 | .00 | 2 | .290 | .343 | .355 |
| 10 ML YEARS | | | 715 | 2251 | 565 | 100 | 4 | 54 | (33 | 21) | 835 | 239 | 243 | 233 | 193 | 18 | 342 | 16 | 29 | 16 | 10 | 10 | .50 | 63 | .251 | .313 | .371 |

## Efren Navarro

**Bats:** L **Throws:** L **Pos:** 1B-2;PH-2 **Ht:** 6'0" **Wt:** 200 **Born:** 5/14/1986 **Age:** 28

| | | | | | | BATTING | | | | | | | | | | | | | | | BASERUNNING | | | | AVERAGES | | |
|---|---|---|---|---|---|---|---|---|---|---|---|---|---|---|---|---|---|---|---|---|---|---|---|---|---|---|---|
| Year | Team | Lg | G | AB | H | 2B | 3B | HR | (Hm | Rd) | TB | R | RBI | RC | TBB | IBB | SO | HBP | SH | SF | SB | CS | SB% | GDP | Avg | OBP | Slg |
| 2009 | RCuca | A+ | 130 | 481 | 138 | 32 | 3 | 5 | (- | -) | 191 | 64 | 61 | 72 | 53 | 2 | 72 | 3 | 1 | 2 | 3 | 2 | .60 | 13 | .287 | .360 | .397 |
| 2010 | Ark | AA | 128 | 453 | 121 | 25 | 2 | 6 | (- | -) | 168 | 46 | 50 | 55 | 31 | 2 | 47 | 3 | 4 | 3 | 6 | 4 | .60 | 10 | .267 | .316 | .371 |
| 2011 | Salt Lk | AAA | 133 | 492 | 156 | 36 | 6 | 12 | (- | -) | 240 | 76 | 73 | 88 | 42 | 1 | 78 | 2 | 4 | 7 | 5 | 5 | .50 | 10 | .317 | .368 | .488 |
| 2012 | Salt Lk | AAA | 141 | 528 | 155 | 35 | 1 | 7 | (- | -) | 213 | 79 | 74 | 75 | 36 | 1 | 70 | 3 | 0 | 10 | 3 | 2 | .60 | 5 | .294 | .336 | .403 |
| 2013 | Salt Lk | AAA | 134 | 513 | 167 | 39 | 3 | 7 | (- | -) | 233 | 83 | 81 | 97 | 68 | 1 | 99 | 2 | 0 | 3 | 8 | 5 | .62 | 19 | .326 | .404 | .454 |
| 2011 | LAA | AL | 8 | 10 | 2 | 1 | 0 | 0 | (0 | 0) | 3 | 1 | 0 | 0 | 1 | 0 | 1 | 0 | 1 | 0 | 0 | 0 | - | 1 | .200 | .273 | .300 |
| 2013 | LAA | AL | 4 | 4 | 1 | 0 | 0 | 0 | (0 | 0) | 1 | 0 | 1 | 1 | 2 | 0 | 1 | 0 | 0 | 0 | 1 | 0 | 1.00 | 0 | .250 | .500 | .250 |
| 2 ML YEARS | | | 12 | 14 | 3 | 1 | 0 | 0 | (0 | 0) | 4 | 1 | 1 | 1 | 3 | 0 | 2 | 0 | 1 | 0 | 1 | 0 | 1.00 | 1 | .214 | .353 | .286 |

## Yamaico Navarro

ya-MIKE-oh

**Bats:** R **Throws:** R **Pos:** 2B-8 **Ht:** 5'11" **Wt:** 215 **Born:** 10/31/1987 **Age:** 26

| | | | | | | BATTING | | | | | | | | | | | | | | | BASERUNNING | | | | AVERAGES | | |
|---|---|---|---|---|---|---|---|---|---|---|---|---|---|---|---|---|---|---|---|---|---|---|---|---|---|---|---|
| Year | Team | Lg | G | AB | H | 2B | 3B | HR | (Hm | Rd) | TB | R | RBI | RC | TBB | IBB | SO | HBP | SH | SF | SB | CS | SB% | GDP | Avg | OBP | Slg |
| 2013 | Norfolk* | AAA | 108 | 390 | 104 | 21 | 1 | 12 | (- | -) | 163 | 59 | 53 | 63 | 53 | 0 | 73 | 3 | 0 | 6 | 9 | 2 | .82 | 7 | .267 | .354 | .418 |
| 2010 | Bos | AL | 20 | 42 | 6 | 0 | 0 | 0 | (0 | 0) | 6 | 4 | 5 | 1 | 2 | 1 | 17 | 0 | 0 | 2 | 0 | 0 | - | 0 | .143 | .174 | .143 |
| 2011 | 2 Tms | AL | 22 | 60 | 15 | 3 | 0 | 1 | (0 | 1) | 21 | 8 | 9 | 8 | 5 | 0 | 14 | 0 | 0 | 1 | 0 | 0 | - | 0 | .250 | .303 | .350 |
| 2012 | Pit | NL | 29 | 50 | 8 | 0 | 0 | 1 | (0 | 1) | 11 | 4 | 4 | 1 | 5 | 0 | 13 | 0 | 0 | 1 | 0 | 2 | .00 | 2 | .160 | .232 | .220 |
| 2013 | Bal | AL | 8 | 28 | 8 | 0 | 1 | 0 | (0 | 0) | 10 | 3 | 2 | 5 | 2 | 0 | 8 | 0 | 1 | 0 | 0 | 0 | - | 1 | .286 | .333 | .357 |
| 11 | Bos | AL | 16 | 37 | 8 | 2 | 0 | 1 | (0 | 1) | 13 | 6 | 3 | 4 | 3 | 0 | 9 | 0 | 0 | 0 | 0 | 0 | - | 0 | .216 | .275 | .351 |
| 11 | KC | AL | 6 | 23 | 7 | 1 | 0 | 0 | (0 | 0) | 8 | 2 | 6 | 4 | 2 | 0 | 5 | 0 | 0 | 1 | 0 | 0 | - | 0 | .304 | .346 | .348 |
| 4 ML YEARS | | | 79 | 180 | 37 | 3 | 1 | 2 | (0 | 2) | 48 | 19 | 20 | 15 | 14 | 1 | 52 | 0 | 1 | 4 | 0 | 2 | .00 | 3 | .206 | .258 | .267 |

## Thomas Neal

**Bats:** R **Throws:** R **Pos:** LF-2;RF-2;DH-1;PH-1 **Ht:** 6'2" **Wt:** 220 **Born:** 8/17/1987 **Age:** 26

| | | | | | | BATTING | | | | | | | | | | | | | | | BASERUNNING | | | | AVERAGES | | |
|---|---|---|---|---|---|---|---|---|---|---|---|---|---|---|---|---|---|---|---|---|---|---|---|---|---|---|---|
| Year | Team | Lg | G | AB | H | 2B | 3B | HR | (Hm | Rd) | TB | R | RBI | RC | TBB | IBB | SO | HBP | SH | SF | SB | CS | SB% | GDP | Avg | OBP | Slg |
| 2009 | SnJos | A+ | 129 | 475 | 160 | 41 | 4 | 22 | (- | -) | 275 | 102 | 90 | 117 | 65 | 1 | 98 | 16 | 0 | 3 | 3 | 0 | 1.00 | 12 | .337 | .431 | .579 |
| 2010 | Rchmd | AA | 136 | 525 | 154 | 40 | 1 | 12 | (- | -) | 232 | 69 | 69 | 86 | 46 | 3 | 94 | 11 | 0 | 3 | 11 | 5 | .69 | 19 | .293 | .361 | .442 |
| 2011 | Fresno | AAA | 60 | 220 | 65 | 13 | 3 | 2 | (- | -) | 90 | 35 | 25 | 31 | 13 | 0 | 50 | 6 | 0 | 0 | 7 | 6 | .54 | 6 | .295 | .351 | .409 |
| 2011 | Clmbs | AAA | 10 | 36 | 9 | 1 | 0 | 0 | (- | -) | 10 | 5 | 1 | 3 | 1 | 0 | 7 | 1 | 0 | 0 | 1 | 0 | 1.00 | 0 | .250 | .289 | .278 |
| 2012 | Akron | AA | 117 | 405 | 127 | 24 | 1 | 12 | (- | -) | 189 | 77 | 51 | 77 | 46 | 1 | 71 | 14 | 3 | 2 | 12 | 8 | .60 | 16 | .314 | .400 | .467 |
| 2013 | S-WB | AAA | 72 | 265 | 86 | 17 | 0 | 2 | (- | -) | 109 | 36 | 29 | 44 | 23 | 0 | 53 | 7 | 0 | 2 | 2 | 1 | .67 | 9 | .325 | .391 | .411 |
| 2012 | Cle | AL | 9 | 23 | 5 | 1 | 0 | 0 | (0 | 0) | 6 | 2 | 2 | 1 | 0 | 0 | 6 | 1 | 0 | 0 | 0 | 0 | - | 1 | .217 | .250 | .261 |
| 2013 | 2 Tms | | 6 | 15 | 2 | 0 | 0 | 0 | (0 | 0) | 2 | 1 | 0 | 0 | 1 | 0 | 4 | 1 | 0 | 0 | 0 | 0 | - | 0 | .133 | .235 | .133 |
| 13 | NYY | AL | 4 | 11 | 2 | 0 | 0 | 0 | (0 | 0) | 2 | 1 | 0 | 0 | 1 | 0 | 4 | 1 | 0 | 0 | 0 | 0 | - | 0 | .182 | .308 | .182 |
| 13 | ChC | NL | 2 | 4 | 0 | 0 | 0 | 0 | (0 | 0) | 0 | 0 | 0 | 0 | 0 | 0 | 0 | 0 | 0 | 0 | 0 | 0 | - | 0 | .000 | .000 | .000 |
| 2 ML YEARS | | | 15 | 38 | 7 | 1 | 0 | 0 | (0 | 0) | 8 | 3 | 2 | 1 | 1 | 0 | 10 | 2 | 0 | 0 | 0 | 0 | - | 1 | .184 | .244 | .211 |

# Chris Nelson

**Bats:** R **Throws:** R **Pos:** 3B-57;PH-4;PR-3;2B-2;DH-1 **Ht:** 5'11" **Wt:** 205 **Born:** 9/3/1985 **Age:** 28

| BATTING | | | | | | | | | | | | | | | | | | | | | | BASERUNNING | | | | AVERAGES | | |
|---|---|---|---|---|---|---|---|---|---|---|---|---|---|---|---|---|---|---|---|---|---|---|---|---|---|---|---|---|
| Year | Team | Lg | G | AB | H | 2B | 3B | HR | (Hm | Rd) | TB | R | RBI | RC | TBB | IBB | SO | HBP | SH | SF | SB | CS | SB% | GDP | Avg | OBP | Slg |
| 2013 | Salt Lk* | AAA | 34 | 134 | 44 | 11 | 0 | 6 | (- | -) | 73 | 20 | 24 | 26 | 8 | 0 | 23 | 0 | 0 | 2 | 4 | 0 | 1.00 | 3 | .328 | .361 | .545 |
| 2010 | Col | NL | 17 | 25 | 7 | 1 | 0 | 0 | (0 | 0) | 8 | 7 | 0 | 1 | 1 | 0 | 4 | 0 | 1 | 0 | 1 | 0 | 1.00 | 1 | .280 | .308 | .320 |
| 2011 | Col | NL | 63 | 180 | 45 | 10 | 1 | 4 | (3 | 1) | 69 | 20 | 16 | 15 | 7 | 1 | 35 | 1 | 0 | 1 | 3 | 1 | .75 | 5 | .250 | .280 | .383 |
| 2012 | Col | NL | 111 | 345 | 104 | 21 | 3 | 9 | (3 | 6) | 158 | 45 | 53 | 56 | 27 | 4 | 84 | 1 | 2 | 2 | 2 | 1 | .67 | 9 | .301 | .352 | .458 |
| 2013 | 3 Tms | | 64 | 211 | 48 | 4 | 4 | 3 | (0 | 3) | 69 | 19 | 24 | 18 | 13 | 0 | 66 | 1 | 0 | 2 | 2 | 1 | .67 | 8 | .227 | .273 | .327 |
| 13 | Col | NL | 21 | 66 | 16 | 1 | 2 | 0 | (0 | 0) | 21 | 6 | 4 | 5 | 4 | 0 | 19 | 0 | 0 | 1 | 0 | 0 | - | 1 | .242 | .282 | .318 |
| 13 | NYY | AL | 10 | 36 | 8 | 2 | 0 | 0 | (0 | 0) | 10 | 3 | 2 | 1 | 1 | 0 | 11 | 0 | 0 | 0 | 0 | 0 | - | 3 | .222 | .243 | .278 |
| 13 | LAA | AL | 33 | 109 | 24 | 1 | 2 | 3 | (0 | 3) | 38 | 10 | 18 | 12 | 8 | 0 | 36 | 1 | 0 | 1 | 2 | 1 | .67 | 4 | .220 | .277 | .349 |
| 4 ML YEARS | | | 255 | 761 | 204 | 36 | 8 | 16 | (6 | 10) | 304 | 91 | 93 | 90 | 48 | 5 | 189 | 3 | 3 | 5 | 8 | 3 | .73 | 23 | .268 | .312 | .399 |

# Jimmy Nelson

**Pitches:** R **Bats:** R **Pos:** RP-3; SP-1 **Ht:** 6'5" **Wt:** 245 **Born:** 6/5/1989 **Age:** 25

| HOW MUCH HE PITCHED | | | | | | | | | WHAT HE GAVE UP | | | | | | | | | | | | THE RESULTS | | | | | | | |
|---|---|---|---|---|---|---|---|---|---|---|---|---|---|---|---|---|---|---|---|---|---|---|---|---|---|---|---|---|
| Year | Team | Lg | G | GS | CG | GF | IP | BFP | H | R | ER | HR | SH | SF | HB | TBB | IBB | SO | WP | Bk | W | L | Pct | Sh | Sv-Op | Hld | ERC | ERA |
| 2010 | Helena | R+ | 12 | 0 | 0 | 5 | 26.2 | 127 | 30 | 21 | 11 | 2 | 2 | 0 | 0 | 13 | 0 | 33 | 3 | 0 | 2 | 0 | 1.000 | 0 | 3- - | - | 4.66 | 3.71 |
| 2011 | Wisc | A | 26 | 25 | 1 | 0 | 146.0 | 630 | 146 | 81 | 71 | 9 | 3 | 7 | 6 | 65 | 0 | 120 | 13 | 1 | 8 | 9 | .471 | 0 | 0- - | - | 4.21 | 4.38 |
| 2012 | BrvdCt | A+ | 13 | 13 | 1 | 0 | 81.1 | 330 | 63 | 24 | 20 | 3 | 7 | 2 | 5 | 25 | 0 | 77 | 5 | 0 | 4 | 4 | .500 | 0 | 0- - | - | 2.39 | 2.21 |
| 2012 | Hntsvl | AA | 10 | 10 | 0 | 0 | 46.0 | 209 | 34 | 25 | 20 | 2 | 1 | 3 | 3 | 37 | 0 | 42 | 4 | 0 | 2 | 4 | .333 | 0 | 0- - | - | 3.96 | 3.91 |
| 2013 | Hntsvl | AA | 12 | 12 | 1 | 0 | 69.0 | 289 | 63 | 34 | 21 | 5 | 0 | 4 | 9 | 15 | 0 | 72 | 4 | 0 | 5 | 4 | .556 | 0 | 0- - | - | 3.21 | 2.74 |
| 2013 | Nashv | AAA | 15 | 15 | 1 | 0 | 83.1 | 367 | 74 | 39 | 34 | 2 | 4 | 1 | 4 | 50 | 0 | 91 | 6 | 2 | 5 | 6 | .455 | 0 | 0- - | - | 3.88 | 3.67 |
| 2013 | Mil | NL | 4 | 1 | 0 | 0 | 10.0 | 37 | 2 | 1 | 1 | 0 | 0 | 1 | 0 | 5 | 0 | 8 | 1 | 0 | 0 | 0 | - | 0 | 0-0 | 0 | 0.64 | 0.90 |

# Pat Neshek

**Pitches:** R **Bats:** B **Pos:** RP-45 NEE-sheck **Ht:** 6'3" **Wt:** 210 **Born:** 9/4/1980 **Age:** 33

| HOW MUCH HE PITCHED | | | | | | | | | WHAT HE GAVE UP | | | | | | | | | | | | THE RESULTS | | | | | | | |
|---|---|---|---|---|---|---|---|---|---|---|---|---|---|---|---|---|---|---|---|---|---|---|---|---|---|---|---|---|
| Year | Team | Lg | G | GS | CG | GF | IP | BFP | H | R | ER | HR | SH | SF | HB | TBB | IBB | SO | WP | Bk | W | L | Pct | Sh | Sv-Op | Hld | ERC | ERA |
| 2013 | Scrmto* | AAA | 2 | 0 | 0 | 1 | 2.0 | 8 | 2 | 2 | 0 | 1 | 0 | 0 | 0 | 0 | 0 | 2 | 0 | 0 | 0 | 0 | - | 0 | 0- - | - | 4.70 | 0.00 |
| 2006 | Min | AL | 32 | 0 | 0 | 3 | 37.0 | 138 | 23 | 9 | 9 | 6 | 0 | 1 | 0 | 6 | 0 | 53 | 0 | 0 | 4 | 2 | .667 | 0 | 0-2 | 10 | 1.68 | 2.19 |
| 2007 | Min | AL | 74 | 0 | 0 | 20 | 70.1 | 278 | 44 | 25 | 23 | 7 | 4 | 5 | 2 | 27 | 5 | 74 | 2 | 0 | 7 | 2 | .778 | 0 | 0-3 | 15 | 2.12 | 2.94 |
| 2008 | Min | AL | 15 | 0 | 0 | 3 | 13.1 | 56 | 12 | 7 | 7 | 2 | 1 | 1 | 0 | 4 | 1 | 15 | 0 | 0 | 0 | 1 | .000 | 0 | 0-2 | 6 | 3.29 | 4.73 |
| 2010 | Min | AL | 11 | 0 | 0 | 3 | 9.0 | 43 | 7 | 5 | 5 | 1 | 0 | 0 | 1 | 8 | 0 | 9 | 0 | 0 | 0 | 1 | .000 | 0 | 0-1 | 1 | 5.13 | 5.00 |
| 2011 | SD | NL | 25 | 0 | 0 | 13 | 24.2 | 112 | 19 | 12 | 11 | 4 | 1 | 0 | 1 | 22 | 1 | 20 | 1 | 0 | 1 | 1 | .500 | 0 | 0-0 | 0 | 5.37 | 4.01 |
| 2012 | Oak | AL | 24 | 0 | 0 | 5 | 19.2 | 77 | 10 | 3 | 3 | 3 | 0 | 2 | 1 | 6 | 1 | 16 | 1 | 0 | 2 | 1 | .667 | 0 | 0-2 | 4 | 1.66 | 1.37 |
| 2013 | Oak | AL | 45 | 0 | 0 | 17 | 40.1 | 177 | 40 | 17 | 15 | 6 | 0 | 3 | 0 | 15 | 2 | 29 | 1 | 0 | 2 | 1 | .667 | 0 | 0-0 | 1 | 4.06 | 3.35 |
| Postseason | | | 3 | 0 | 0 | 1 | 1.2 | 6 | 1 | 1 | 1 | 0 | 0 | 0 | 0 | 0 | 0 | 2 | 0 | 0 | 0 | 1 | .000 | 0 | 0-0 | 0 | 0.75 | 5.40 |
| 7 ML YEARS | | | 226 | 0 | 0 | 64 | 214.1 | 881 | 155 | 78 | 73 | 29 | 6 | 12 | 5 | 88 | 10 | 216 | 5 | 0 | 16 | 9 | .640 | 0 | 0-10 | 37 | 2.87 | 3.07 |

# Juan Nicasio

**Pitches:** R **Bats:** R **Pos:** SP-31 nih-COSS-ee-oh **Ht:** 6'3" **Wt:** 230 **Born:** 8/31/1986 **Age:** 27

| HOW MUCH HE PITCHED | | | | | | | | | WHAT HE GAVE UP | | | | | | | | | | | | THE RESULTS | | | | | | | |
|---|---|---|---|---|---|---|---|---|---|---|---|---|---|---|---|---|---|---|---|---|---|---|---|---|---|---|---|---|
| Year | Team | Lg | G | GS | CG | GF | IP | BFP | H | R | ER | HR | SH | SF | HB | TBB | IBB | SO | WP | Bk | W | L | Pct | Sh | Sv-Op | Hld | ERC | ERA |
| 2013 | ColSpr* | AAA | 2 | 2 | 0 | 0 | 11.0 | 41 | 8 | 1 | 1 | 0 | 0 | 0 | 0 | 1 | 0 | 8 | 1 | 1 | 1 | 0 | 1.000 | 0 | 0- - | - | 1.28 | 0.82 |
| 2011 | Col | NL | 13 | 13 | 0 | 0 | 71.2 | 299 | 73 | 35 | 33 | 8 | 1 | 0 | 1 | 18 | 3 | 58 | 1 | 0 | 4 | 4 | .500 | 0 | 0-0 | 0 | 3.69 | 4.14 |
| 2012 | Col | NL | 11 | 11 | 0 | 0 | 58.0 | 257 | 72 | 37 | 34 | 7 | 3 | 1 | 1 | 22 | 1 | 54 | 4 | 0 | 2 | 3 | .400 | 0 | 0-0 | 0 | 5.74 | 5.28 |
| 2013 | Col | NL | 31 | 31 | 0 | 0 | 157.2 | 703 | 168 | 97 | 90 | 17 | 6 | 1 | 5 | 64 | 7 | 119 | 6 | 2 | 9 | 9 | .500 | 0 | 0-0 | 0 | 4.52 | 5.14 |
| 3 ML YEARS | | | 55 | 55 | 0 | 0 | 287.1 | 1259 | 313 | 169 | 157 | 32 | 10 | 2 | 7 | 104 | 11 | 231 | 11 | 2 | 15 | 16 | .484 | 0 | 0-0 | 0 | 4.54 | 4.92 |

# Mike Nickeas

**Bats:** R **Throws:** R **Pos:** C-1 NICK-ee-us **Ht:** 6'0" **Wt:** 215 **Born:** 2/13/1983 **Age:** 31

| BATTING | | | | | | | | | | | | | | | | | | | | | | BASERUNNING | | | | AVERAGES | | |
|---|---|---|---|---|---|---|---|---|---|---|---|---|---|---|---|---|---|---|---|---|---|---|---|---|---|---|---|---|
| Year | Team | Lg | G | AB | H | 2B | 3B | HR | (Hm | Rd) | TB | R | RBI | RC | TBB | IBB | SO | HBP | SH | SF | SB | CS | SB% | GDP | Avg | OBP | Slg |
| 2013 | Buffalo* | AAA | 58 | 175 | 29 | 12 | 0 | 1 | (- | -) | 44 | 16 | 11 | 11 | 17 | 0 | 40 | 4 | 4 | 0 | 0 | 0 | - | 8 | .166 | .255 | .251 |
| 2010 | NYM | NL | 5 | 10 | 2 | 0 | 0 | 0 | (0 | 0) | 2 | 0 | 0 | 0 | 0 | 0 | 5 | 0 | 0 | 0 | 0 | 0 | - | 1 | .200 | .200 | .200 |
| 2011 | NYM | NL | 21 | 53 | 10 | 1 | 0 | 1 | (1 | 0) | 14 | 4 | 6 | 3 | 4 | 0 | 11 | 0 | 2 | 0 | 0 | 1 | .00 | 1 | .189 | .246 | .264 |
| 2012 | NYM | NL | 47 | 109 | 19 | 3 | 0 | 1 | (1 | 0) | 25 | 8 | 13 | 10 | 8 | 0 | 27 | 2 | 2 | 1 | 0 | 0 | - | 1 | .174 | .242 | .229 |
| 2013 | Tor | AL | 1 | 0 | 0 | 0 | 0 | 0 | (0 | 0) | 0 | 0 | 0 | 0 | 0 | 0 | 0 | 0 | 0 | 0 | 0 | 0 | - | 0 | - | - | - |
| 4 ML YEARS | | | 74 | 172 | 31 | 4 | 0 | 2 | (2 | 0) | 41 | 12 | 19 | 13 | 12 | 0 | 43 | 2 | 4 | 1 | 0 | 1 | .00 | 3 | .180 | .241 | .238 |

# Jeff Niemann

**Pitches:** R **Bats:** R **Pos:** P NEE-min **Ht:** 6'9" **Wt:** 285 **Born:** 2/28/1983 **Age:** 31

| HOW MUCH HE PITCHED | | | | | | | | | WHAT HE GAVE UP | | | | | | | | | | | | THE RESULTS | | | | | | | |
|---|---|---|---|---|---|---|---|---|---|---|---|---|---|---|---|---|---|---|---|---|---|---|---|---|---|---|---|---|
| Year | Team | Lg | G | GS | CG | GF | IP | BFP | H | R | ER | HR | SH | SF | HB | TBB | IBB | SO | WP | Bk | W | L | Pct | Sh | Sv-Op | Hld | ERC | ERA |
| 2008 | TB | AL | 5 | 2 | 0 | 2 | 16.0 | 76 | 18 | 12 | 9 | 3 | 2 | 0 | 1 | 8 | 0 | 14 | 0 | 0 | 2 | 2 | .500 | 0 | 0-0 | 0 | 5.93 | 5.06 |
| 2009 | TB | AL | 31 | 30 | 2 | 1 | 180.2 | 769 | 185 | 84 | 79 | 17 | 2 | 4 | 9 | 59 | 1 | 125 | 6 | 0 | 13 | 6 | .684 | 2 | 0-0 | 0 | 4.12 | 3.94 |
| 2010 | TB | AL | 30 | 29 | 1 | 0 | 174.1 | 733 | 159 | 86 | 85 | 25 | 5 | 2 | 7 | 61 | 6 | 131 | 4 | 0 | 12 | 8 | .600 | 1 | 0-0 | 0 | 3.81 | 4.39 |
| 2011 | TB | AL | 23 | 23 | 1 | 0 | 135.1 | 572 | 131 | 65 | 61 | 18 | 2 | 4 | 5 | 37 | 1 | 105 | 7 | 0 | 11 | 7 | .611 | 0 | 0-0 | 0 | 3.73 | 4.06 |
| 2012 | TB | AL | 8 | 8 | 0 | 0 | 38.0 | 156 | 30 | 17 | 13 | 2 | 0 | 1 | 2 | 12 | 0 | 34 | 2 | 0 | 2 | 3 | .400 | 0 | 0-0 | 0 | 2.53 | 3.08 |
| Postseason | | | 1 | 0 | 0 | 1 | 3.0 | 9 | 1 | 0 | 0 | 0 | 0 | 0 | 0 | 1 | 0 | 4 | 0 | 0 | 0 | 0 | - | 0 | 0-0 | 0 | 0.84 | 0.00 |
| 5 ML YEARS | | | 97 | 92 | 4 | 3 | 544.1 | 2306 | 523 | 264 | 247 | 65 | 11 | 11 | 24 | 177 | 8 | 409 | 19 | 0 | 40 | 26 | .606 | 3 | 0-0 | 0 | 3.86 | 4.08 |

## Jon Niese

**Pitches:** L **Bats:** L **Pos:** SP-24 NIECE **Ht:** 6'4" **Wt:** 215 **Born:** 10/27/1986 **Age:** 27

| | | | HOW MUCH HE PITCHED | | | | | | WHAT HE GAVE UP | | | | | | | | | | | | THE RESULTS | | | | | | | |
|---|---|---|---|---|---|---|---|---|---|---|---|---|---|---|---|---|---|---|---|---|---|---|---|---|---|---|---|---|
| Year | Team | Lg | G | GS | CG | GF | IP | BFP | H | R | ER | HR | SH | SF | HB | TBB | IBB | SO | WP | Bk | W | L | Pct | Sh | Sv-Op | Hld | ERC | ERA |
| 2013 | Mets* | R | 1 | 1 | 0 | 0 | 2.0 | 10 | 3 | 4 | 1 | 0 | 0 | 0 | 0 | 0 | 0 | 1 | 0 | 0 | 0 | 0 | - | 0 | 0- - | - | 3.96 | 4.50 |
| 2013 | StLuci* | A+ | 1 | 1 | 0 | 0 | 4.0 | 13 | 2 | 0 | 0 | 0 | 0 | 0 | 0 | 1 | 0 | 4 | 0 | 0 | 0 | 0 | - | 0 | 0- - | - | 1.09 | 0.00 |
| 2013 | Bnghtn* | AA | 1 | 1 | 0 | 0 | 5.0 | 20 | 4 | 2 | 2 | 0 | 0 | 0 | 0 | 3 | 0 | 6 | 1 | 0 | 1 | 0 | 1.000 | 0 | 0- - | - | 3.31 | 3.60 |
| 2008 | NYM | NL | 3 | 3 | 0 | 0 | 14.0 | 69 | 20 | 11 | 11 | 2 | 1 | 0 | 0 | 8 | 0 | 11 | 0 | 0 | 1 | 1 | .500 | 0 | 0-0 | 0 | 7.71 | 7.07 |
| 2009 | NYM | NL | 5 | 5 | 0 | 0 | 25.2 | 110 | 27 | 12 | 12 | 1 | 2 | 1 | 0 | 9 | 0 | 18 | 1 | 0 | 1 | 1 | .500 | 0 | 0-0 | 0 | 3.76 | 4.21 |
| 2010 | NYM | NL | 30 | 30 | 2 | 0 | 173.2 | 770 | 192 | 97 | 81 | 20 | 9 | 4 | 9 | 62 | 3 | 148 | 5 | 0 | 9 | 10 | .474 | 1 | 0-0 | 0 | 4.77 | 4.20 |
| 2011 | NYM | NL | 27 | 26 | 0 | 0 | 157.1 | 694 | 178 | 88 | 77 | 14 | **16** | 2 | 5 | 44 | 4 | 138 | 3 | 0 | 11 | 11 | .500 | 0 | 0-0 | 0 | 4.27 | 4.40 |
| 2012 | NYM | NL | 30 | 30 | 0 | 0 | 190.1 | 788 | 174 | 77 | 72 | 22 | 8 | 4 | 4 | 49 | 2 | 155 | 6 | 0 | 13 | 9 | .591 | 0 | 0-0 | 0 | 3.21 | 3.40 |
| 2013 | NYM | NL | 24 | 24 | 1 | 0 | 143.0 | 621 | 158 | 68 | 59 | 10 | 6 | 0 | 4 | 48 | 1 | 105 | 5 | 0 | 8 | 8 | .500 | 1 | 0-0 | 0 | 4.32 | 3.71 |
| 6 ML YEARS | | | 119 | 118 | 3 | 0 | 704.0 | 3052 | 749 | 353 | 312 | 69 | 42 | 11 | 22 | 220 | 10 | 575 | 20 | 0 | 43 | 40 | .518 | 2 | 0-0 | 0 | 4.15 | 3.99 |

## Kirk Nieuwenhuis

**Bats:** L **Throws:** R **Pos:** CF-25;PH-16;LF-9;RF-2;PR-1 NEW-enn-hice **Ht:** 6'3" **Wt:** 215 **Born:** 8/7/1987 **Age:** 26

| | | | BATTING | | | | | | | | | | | | | | | | | | BASERUNNING | | | | AVERAGES | | |
|---|---|---|---|---|---|---|---|---|---|---|---|---|---|---|---|---|---|---|---|---|---|---|---|---|---|---|---|
| Year | Team | Lg | G | AB | H | 2B | 3B | HR | (Hm | Rd) | TB | R | RBI | RC | TBB | IBB | SO | HBP | SH | SF | SB | CS | SB% | GDP | Avg | OBP | Slg |
| 2009 | StLuci | A+ | 123 | 482 | 132 | 35 | 5 | 16 | (- | -) | 225 | 91 | 71 | 84 | 53 | 0 | 118 | 10 | 1 | 1 | 16 | 4 | .80 | 8 | .274 | .357 | .467 |
| 2009 | Bnghtn | AA | 8 | 32 | 13 | 3 | 1 | 1 | (- | -) | 21 | 8 | 2 | 8 | 4 | 0 | 9 | 0 | 0 | 0 | 1 | 1 | .50 | 1 | .406 | .472 | .656 |
| 2010 | Bnghtn | AA | 94 | 394 | 114 | 35 | 2 | 16 | (- | -) | 201 | 81 | 60 | 68 | 30 | 0 | 93 | 1 | 3 | 5 | 13 | 7 | .65 | 5 | .289 | .337 | .510 |
| 2010 | Buffalo | AAA | 30 | 120 | 27 | 8 | 1 | 2 | (- | -) | 43 | 10 | 17 | 13 | 11 | 3 | 39 | 1 | 1 | 0 | 0 | 0 | - | 1 | .225 | .295 | .358 |
| 2011 | Buffalo | AAA | 53 | 188 | 56 | 17 | 2 | 6 | (- | -) | 95 | 33 | 14 | 39 | 32 | 0 | 59 | 1 | 0 | 0 | 5 | 2 | .71 | 2 | .298 | .403 | .505 |
| 2012 | Buffalo | AAA | 5 | 11 | 2 | 1 | 0 | 0 | (- | -) | 3 | 0 | 1 | 1 | 2 | 0 | 4 | 0 | 0 | 0 | 1 | 0 | 1.00 | 0 | .182 | .308 | .273 |
| 2013 | LsVgs | AAA | 74 | 282 | 70 | 15 | 2 | 14 | (- | -) | 131 | 60 | 37 | 47 | 40 | 1 | 78 | 2 | 5 | 1 | 6 | 2 | .75 | 5 | .248 | .345 | .465 |
| 2012 | NYM | NL | 91 | 282 | 71 | 12 | 1 | 7 | (5 | 2) | 106 | 40 | 28 | 28 | 25 | 0 | 98 | 2 | 3 | 2 | 4 | 4 | .50 | 2 | .252 | .315 | .376 |
| 2013 | NYM | NL | 47 | 95 | 18 | 3 | 1 | 3 | (2 | 1) | 32 | 10 | 14 | 8 | 12 | 1 | 32 | 0 | 0 | 1 | 2 | 0 | 1.00 | 1 | .189 | .278 | .337 |
| 2 ML YEARS | | | 138 | 377 | 89 | 15 | 2 | 10 | (7 | 3) | 138 | 50 | 42 | 36 | 37 | 1 | 130 | 2 | 3 | 3 | 6 | 4 | .60 | 3 | .236 | .305 | .366 |

## Wil Nieves

**Bats:** R **Throws:** R **Pos:** C-47;PH-25;DH-1 **Ht:** 5'11" **Wt:** 190 **Born:** 9/25/1977 **Age:** 36

| | | | BATTING | | | | | | | | | | | | | | | | | | BASERUNNING | | | | AVERAGES | | |
|---|---|---|---|---|---|---|---|---|---|---|---|---|---|---|---|---|---|---|---|---|---|---|---|---|---|---|---|
| Year | Team | Lg | G | AB | H | 2B | 3B | HR | (Hm | Rd) | TB | R | RBI | RC | TBB | IBB | SO | HBP | SH | SF | SB | CS | SB% | GDP | Avg | OBP | Slg |
| 2002 | SD | NL | 28 | 72 | 13 | 3 | 1 | 0 | (0 | 0) | 18 | 2 | 3 | 4 | 4 | 4 | 15 | 0 | 0 | 0 | 1 | 0 | 1.00 | 1 | .181 | .224 | .250 |
| 2005 | NYY | AL | 3 | 4 | 0 | 0 | 0 | 0 | (0 | 0) | 0 | 0 | 0 | 0 | 0 | 0 | 1 | 0 | 0 | 0 | 0 | 0 | - | 0 | .000 | .000 | .000 |
| 2006 | NYY | AL | 6 | 6 | 0 | 0 | 0 | 0 | (0 | 0) | 0 | 0 | 0 | 0 | 0 | 0 | 1 | 0 | 0 | 0 | 0 | 0 | - | 0 | .000 | .000 | .000 |
| 2007 | NYY | AL | 26 | 61 | 10 | 4 | 0 | 0 | (0 | 0) | 14 | 6 | 8 | 4 | 2 | 0 | 9 | 0 | 3 | 0 | 0 | 0 | - | 3 | .164 | .190 | .230 |
| 2008 | Was | NL | 68 | 176 | 46 | 9 | 1 | 1 | (1 | 0) | 60 | 15 | 20 | 20 | 13 | 1 | 29 | 0 | 5 | 2 | 0 | 1 | .00 | 7 | .261 | .309 | .341 |
| 2009 | Was | NL | 72 | 224 | 58 | 6 | 0 | 1 | (0 | 1) | 67 | 20 | 26 | 21 | 17 | 1 | 45 | 3 | 0 | 5 | 1 | 0 | 1.00 | 7 | .259 | .313 | .299 |
| 2010 | Was | NL | 59 | 158 | 32 | 8 | 0 | 3 | (1 | 2) | 49 | 10 | 16 | 9 | 8 | 2 | 29 | 1 | 4 | 1 | 0 | 0 | - | 6 | .203 | .244 | .310 |
| 2011 | Mil | NL | 20 | 50 | 7 | 2 | 0 | 0 | (0 | 0) | 9 | 2 | 0 | 0 | 3 | 1 | 12 | 0 | 1 | 0 | 0 | 0 | - | 3 | .140 | .189 | .180 |
| 2012 | 2 Tms | NL | 32 | 83 | 25 | 3 | 0 | 2 | (0 | 2) | 34 | 7 | 8 | 9 | 4 | 2 | 17 | 0 | 1 | 1 | 0 | 1 | .00 | 3 | .301 | .330 | .410 |
| 2013 | Ari | NL | 71 | 195 | 58 | 11 | 0 | 1 | (1 | 0) | 72 | 16 | 22 | 21 | 8 | 0 | 32 | 0 | 0 | 3 | 0 | 0 | - | 7 | .297 | .320 | .369 |
| 12 | Col | NL | 16 | 47 | 14 | 2 | 0 | 1 | (0 | 1) | 19 | 3 | 5 | 6 | 3 | 1 | 9 | 0 | 0 | 1 | 0 | 0 | - | 3 | .298 | .333 | .404 |
| 12 | Ari | NL | 16 | 36 | 11 | 1 | 0 | 1 | (0 | 1) | 15 | 4 | 3 | 3 | 1 | 1 | 8 | 0 | 1 | 0 | 0 | 1 | .00 | 0 | .306 | .324 | .417 |
| 10 ML YEARS | | | 385 | 1029 | 249 | 46 | 2 | 8 | (3 | 5) | 323 | 78 | 103 | 88 | 59 | 11 | 190 | 4 | 14 | 12 | 2 | 2 | .50 | 37 | .242 | .283 | .314 |

## Jayson Nix

**Bats:** R **Throws:** R **Pos:** SS-48;3B-41;2B-4;PR-4;PH-2 **Ht:** 5'11" **Wt:** 195 **Born:** 8/26/1982 **Age:** 31

| | | | BATTING | | | | | | | | | | | | | | | | | | BASERUNNING | | | | AVERAGES | | |
|---|---|---|---|---|---|---|---|---|---|---|---|---|---|---|---|---|---|---|---|---|---|---|---|---|---|---|---|
| Year | Team | Lg | G | AB | H | 2B | 3B | HR | (Hm | Rd) | TB | R | RBI | RC | TBB | IBB | SO | HBP | SH | SF | SB | CS | SB% | GDP | Avg | OBP | Slg |
| 2013 | Yanks* | R | 1 | 2 | 0 | 0 | 0 | 0 | (- | -) | 0 | 0 | 0 | 0 | 0 | 0 | 1 | 1 | 0 | 0 | 0 | 0 | - | 0 | .000 | .333 | .000 |
| 2013 | Tampa* | A+ | 3 | 10 | 1 | 1 | 0 | 0 | (- | -) | 2 | 1 | 1 | 0 | 1 | 0 | 1 | 0 | 0 | 0 | 0 | 0 | - | 0 | .100 | .182 | .200 |
| 2008 | Col | NL | 22 | 56 | 7 | 2 | 0 | 0 | (0 | 0) | 9 | 2 | 2 | 0 | 7 | 2 | 17 | 1 | 1 | 0 | 1 | 0 | 1.00 | 1 | .125 | .234 | .161 |
| 2009 | CWS | AL | 94 | 255 | 57 | 11 | 0 | 12 | (4 | 8) | 104 | 36 | 32 | 31 | 28 | 1 | 64 | 4 | 1 | 2 | 10 | 2 | .83 | 5 | .224 | .308 | .408 |
| 2010 | 2 Tms | AL | 102 | 331 | 74 | 15 | 0 | 14 | (7 | 7) | 131 | 32 | 34 | 35 | 20 | 2 | 87 | 7 | 3 | 2 | 1 | 2 | .33 | 6 | .224 | .281 | .396 |
| 2011 | Tor | AL | 46 | 136 | 23 | 5 | 1 | 4 | (2 | 2) | 42 | 15 | 16 | 12 | 12 | 1 | 42 | 2 | 0 | 1 | 4 | 1 | .80 | 2 | .169 | .245 | .309 |
| 2012 | NYY | AL | 74 | 177 | 43 | 13 | 0 | 4 | (3 | 1) | 68 | 24 | 18 | 23 | 14 | 0 | 53 | 2 | 9 | 0 | 6 | 3 | .67 | 4 | .243 | .306 | .384 |
| 2013 | NYY | AL | 87 | 267 | 63 | 9 | 1 | 3 | (2 | 1) | 83 | 32 | 24 | 27 | 24 | 1 | 80 | 5 | 4 | 3 | 13 | 1 | .93 | 4 | .236 | .308 | .311 |
| 10 | CWS | AL | 24 | 49 | 8 | 1 | 0 | 1 | (0 | 1) | 12 | 3 | 5 | 4 | 7 | 2 | 12 | 0 | 1 | 0 | 0 | 0 | - | 1 | .163 | .268 | .245 |
| 10 | Cle | AL | 78 | 282 | 66 | 14 | 0 | 13 | (7 | 6) | 119 | 29 | 29 | 31 | 13 | 0 | 75 | 7 | 2 | 2 | 1 | 2 | .33 | 5 | .234 | .283 | .422 |
| Postseason | | | 6 | 8 | 2 | 1 | 0 | 0 | (0 | 0) | 3 | 0 | 0 | 1 | 1 | 0 | 1 | 0 | 0 | 0 | 0 | 0 | - | 0 | .250 | .333 | .375 |
| 6 ML YEARS | | | 425 | 1222 | 267 | 55 | 2 | 37 | (18 | 19) | 437 | 141 | 126 | 128 | 105 | 7 | 343 | 21 | 18 | 8 | 35 | 9 | .80 | 22 | .218 | .290 | .358 |

## Layne Nix

**Bats:** L **Throws:** L **Pos:** PH-53;RF-25;1B-8;LF-2;CF-1;PR-1 LANCE **Ht:** 6'1" **Wt:** 220 **Born:** 10/30/1980 **Age:** 33

| | | | BATTING | | | | | | | | | | | | | | | | | | BASERUNNING | | | | AVERAGES | | |
|---|---|---|---|---|---|---|---|---|---|---|---|---|---|---|---|---|---|---|---|---|---|---|---|---|---|---|---|
| Year | Team | Lg | G | AB | H | 2B | 3B | HR | (Hm | Rd) | TB | R | RBI | RC | TBB | IBB | SO | HBP | SH | SF | SB | CS | SB% | GDP | Avg | OBP | Slg |
| 2003 | Tex | AL | 53 | 184 | 47 | 10 | 0 | 8 | (7 | 1) | 81 | 25 | 30 | 25 | 9 | 0 | 53 | 0 | 1 | 1 | 3 | 0 | 1.00 | 1 | .255 | .289 | .440 |
| 2004 | Tex | AL | 115 | 371 | 92 | 20 | 4 | 14 | (9 | 5) | 162 | 58 | 46 | 44 | 23 | 4 | 113 | 2 | 1 | 3 | 1 | 1 | .50 | 6 | .248 | .293 | .437 |
| 2005 | Tex | AL | 63 | 229 | 55 | 12 | 3 | 6 | (3 | 3) | 91 | 28 | 32 | 26 | 9 | 3 | 45 | 0 | 0 | 2 | 2 | 0 | 1.00 | 3 | .240 | .267 | .397 |
| 2006 | 2 Tms | | 19 | 67 | 11 | 2 | 0 | 1 | (1 | 0) | 16 | 3 | 10 | 3 | 0 | 0 | 28 | 2 | 0 | 1 | 0 | 0 | - | 1 | .164 | .186 | .239 |
| 2007 | Mil | NL | 10 | 12 | 0 | 0 | 0 | 0 | (0 | 0) | 0 | 0 | 0 | 0 | 0 | 0 | 4 | 0 | 0 | 0 | 0 | 0 | - | 0 | .000 | .000 | .000 |
| 2008 | Mil | NL | 10 | 12 | 1 | 0 | 0 | 0 | (0 | 0) | 1 | 1 | 0 | 0 | 1 | 0 | 3 | 0 | 0 | 0 | 0 | 0 | - | 0 | .083 | .154 | .083 |
| 2009 | Cin | NL | 116 | 309 | 74 | 26 | 1 | 15 | (5 | 10) | 147 | 42 | 46 | 35 | 22 | 3 | 81 | 2 | 0 | 4 | 0 | 1 | .00 | 5 | .239 | .291 | .476 |
| 2010 | Cin | NL | 97 | 165 | 48 | 11 | 2 | 4 | (1 | 3) | 75 | 16 | 18 | 21 | 15 | 4 | 39 | 0 | 2 | 0 | 0 | 1 | .00 | 5 | .291 | .350 | .455 |
| 2011 | Was | NL | 124 | 324 | 81 | 15 | 1 | 16 | (9 | 7) | 146 | 38 | 44 | 37 | 23 | 2 | 82 | 1 | 0 | 3 | 2 | 2 | .50 | 1 | .250 | .299 | .451 |

| BATTING | | | | | | | | | | | | | | | | | | | | | | BASERUNNING | | | | AVERAGES | | |
|---|---|---|---|---|---|---|---|---|---|---|---|---|---|---|---|---|---|---|---|---|---|---|---|---|---|---|---|---|
| Year | Team | Lg | G | AB | H | 2B | 3B | HR | (Hm | Rd) | TB | R | RBI | RC | TBB | IBB | SO | HBP | SH | SF | SB | CS | SB% | GDP | Avg | OBP | Slg |
| 2012 | Phi | NL | 70 | 114 | 28 | 10 | 0 | 3 | (1 | 2) | 47 | 13 | 16 | 16 | 12 | 0 | 42 | 0 | 0 | 1 | 0 | 0 | - | 1 | .246 | .315 | .412 |
| 2013 | Phi | NL | 81 | 128 | 23 | 4 | 0 | 2 | (1 | 1) | 33 | 11 | 7 | 4 | 8 | 2 | 44 | 0 | 0 | 0 | 1 | 0 | 1.00 | 2 | .180 | .228 | .258 |
| 06 | Tex | AL | 9 | 32 | 3 | 1 | 0 | 0 | (0 | 0) | 4 | 1 | 4 | 0 | 0 | 0 | 17 | 1 | 0 | 1 | 0 | 0 | - | 0 | .094 | .118 | .125 |
| 06 | Mil | NL | 10 | 35 | 8 | 1 | 0 | 1 | (1 | 0) | 12 | 2 | 6 | 3 | 0 | 0 | 11 | 1 | 0 | 0 | 0 | 0 | - | 1 | .229 | .250 | .343 |
| Postseason | | | 1 | 3 | 0 | 0 | 0 | 0 | (0 | 0) | 0 | 1 | 0 | 0 | 0 | 0 | 1 | 0 | 0 | 0 | 0 | 0 | - | 0 | .000 | .000 | .000 |
| 11 ML YEARS | | | 758 | 1915 | 460 | 110 | 11 | 69 | (37 | 32) | 799 | 235 | 249 | 211 | 122 | 18 | 534 | 7 | 4 | 15 | 9 | 5 | .64 | 25 | .240 | .286 | .417 |

# Hector Noesi

**Pitches:** R **Bats:** R **Pos:** RP-11; SP-1 NO-ess-ee **Ht:** 6'3" **Wt:** 205 **Born:** 1/26/1987 **Age:** 27

| HOW MUCH HE PITCHED | | | | | | | | | WHAT HE GAVE UP | | | | | | | | | | | | THE RESULTS | | | | | | | |
|---|---|---|---|---|---|---|---|---|---|---|---|---|---|---|---|---|---|---|---|---|---|---|---|---|---|---|---|---|
| Year | Team | Lg | G | GS | CG | GF | IP | BFP | H | R | ER | HR | SH | SF | HB | TBB | IBB | SO | WP | Bk | W | L | Pct | Sh | Sv-Op | Hld | ERC | ERA |
| 2013 | Jacksn* | AA | 2 | 2 | 0 | 0 | 11.0 | 41 | 5 | 0 | 0 | 0 | 0 | 0 | 1 | 3 | 0 | 12 | 0 | 0 | 1 | 0 | 1.000 | 0 | 0- - | - | 1.05 | 0.00 |
| 2013 | Tacom* | AAA | 15 | 11 | 0 | 0 | 66.1 | 293 | 80 | 45 | 43 | 12 | 1 | 2 | 1 | 14 | 0 | 49 | 4 | 1 | 3 | 3 | .500 | 0 | 0- - | - | 5.03 | 5.83 |
| 2011 | NYY | AL | 30 | 2 | 0 | 14 | 56.1 | 247 | 63 | 29 | 28 | 6 | 1 | 2 | 2 | 22 | 4 | 45 | 4 | 0 | 2 | 2 | .500 | 0 | 0-0 | 4 | 4.85 | 4.47 |
| 2012 | Sea | AL | 22 | 18 | 0 | 4 | 106.2 | 453 | 107 | 71 | 69 | 21 | 3 | 7 | 2 | 39 | 1 | 68 | 1 | 2 | 2 | 12 | .143 | 0 | 0-0 | 0 | 4.77 | 5.82 |
| 2013 | Sea | AL | 12 | 1 | 0 | 4 | 27.1 | 134 | 42 | 21 | 20 | 3 | 1 | 1 | 1 | 12 | 4 | 21 | 2 | 0 | 0 | 1 | .000 | 0 | 0-0 | 0 | 7.45 | 6.59 |
| 3 ML YEARS | | | 64 | 21 | 0 | 22 | 190.1 | 834 | 212 | 121 | 117 | 30 | 5 | 10 | 5 | 73 | 9 | 134 | 7 | 2 | 4 | 15 | .211 | 0 | 0-0 | 4 | 5.17 | 5.53 |

# Ricky Nolasco

**Pitches:** R **Bats:** R **Pos:** SP-33; RP-1 **Ht:** 6'2" **Wt:** 235 **Born:** 12/13/1982 **Age:** 31

| HOW MUCH HE PITCHED | | | | | | | | | WHAT HE GAVE UP | | | | | | | | | | | | THE RESULTS | | | | | | | |
|---|---|---|---|---|---|---|---|---|---|---|---|---|---|---|---|---|---|---|---|---|---|---|---|---|---|---|---|---|
| Year | Team | Lg | G | GS | CG | GF | IP | BFP | H | R | ER | HR | SH | SF | HB | TBB | IBB | SO | WP | Bk | W | L | Pct | Sh | Sv-Op | Hld | ERC | ERA |
| 2006 | Fla | NL | 35 | 22 | 0 | 0 | 140.0 | 613 | 157 | 86 | 75 | 20 | 8 | 6 | 10 | 41 | 5 | 99 | 7 | 0 | 11 | 11 | .500 | 0 | 0-0 | 2 | 4.89 | 4.82 |
| 2007 | Fla | NL | 5 | 4 | 0 | 0 | 21.1 | 99 | 26 | 16 | 13 | 3 | 3 | 5 | 1 | 9 | 2 | 11 | 1 | 0 | 1 | 2 | .333 | 0 | 0-0 | 0 | 5.71 | 5.48 |
| 2008 | Fla | NL | 34 | 32 | 1 | 0 | 212.1 | 868 | 192 | 88 | 83 | 28 | 6 | 9 | 6 | 42 | 6 | 186 | 1 | 3 | 15 | 8 | .652 | 1 | 0-0 | 0 | 3.03 | 3.52 |
| 2009 | Fla | NL | 31 | 31 | 2 | 0 | 185.0 | 785 | 188 | 111 | 104 | 23 | 8 | 5 | 2 | 44 | 7 | 195 | 2 | 0 | 13 | 9 | .591 | 0 | 0-0 | 0 | 3.62 | 5.06 |
| 2010 | Fla | NL | 26 | 26 | 1 | 0 | 157.2 | 665 | 169 | 82 | 79 | 24 | 5 | 5 | 2 | 33 | 1 | 147 | 5 | 0 | 14 | 9 | .609 | 0 | 0-0 | 0 | 4.11 | 4.51 |
| 2011 | Fla | NL | 33 | 33 | 2 | 0 | 206.0 | 891 | **244** | 117 | 107 | 20 | 11 | 5 | 3 | 44 | 8 | 148 | 6 | 0 | 10 | 12 | .455 | 1 | 0-0 | 0 | 4.34 | 4.67 |
| 2012 | Mia | NL | 31 | 31 | 3 | 0 | 191.0 | 832 | 214 | 100 | 95 | 18 | **19** | 6 | 8 | 47 | 9 | 125 | 8 | 1 | 12 | 13 | .480 | 2 | 0-0 | 0 | 4.14 | 4.48 |
| 2013 | 2 Tms | NL | 34 | 33 | 0 | 0 | 199.1 | 834 | 195 | 90 | 82 | 17 | 10 | 3 | 10 | 46 | 1 | 165 | 5 | 0 | 13 | 11 | .542 | 0 | 0-0 | 0 | 3.38 | 3.70 |
| 13 | Mia | NL | 18 | 18 | 0 | 0 | 112.1 | 468 | 112 | 50 | 48 | 11 | 7 | 3 | 4 | 25 | 1 | 90 | 4 | 0 | 5 | 8 | .385 | 0 | 0-0 | 0 | 3.49 | 3.85 |
| 13 | LAD | NL | 16 | 15 | 0 | 0 | 87.0 | 366 | 83 | 40 | 34 | 6 | 3 | 0 | 6 | 21 | 0 | 75 | 1 | 0 | 8 | 3 | .727 | 0 | 0-0 | 0 | 3.25 | 3.52 |
| 8 ML YEARS | | | 229 | 212 | 9 | 0 | 1312.2 | 5587 | 1385 | 690 | 638 | 153 | 70 | 44 | 42 | 306 | 39 | 1076 | 35 | 4 | 89 | 75 | .543 | 4 | 0-0 | 2 | 3.89 | 4.37 |

# Sean Nolin

**Pitches:** L **Bats:** L **Pos:** SP-1 **Ht:** 6'5" **Wt:** 235 **Born:** 12/26/1989 **Age:** 24

| HOW MUCH HE PITCHED | | | | | | | | | WHAT HE GAVE UP | | | | | | | | | | | | THE RESULTS | | | | | | | |
|---|---|---|---|---|---|---|---|---|---|---|---|---|---|---|---|---|---|---|---|---|---|---|---|---|---|---|---|---|
| Year | Team | Lg | G | GS | CG | GF | IP | BFP | H | R | ER | HR | SH | SF | HB | TBB | IBB | SO | WP | Bk | W | L | Pct | Sh | Sv-Op | Hld | ERC | ERA |
| 2010 | B Jays | R | 1 | 1 | 0 | 0 | 2.0 | 7 | 1 | 0 | 0 | 0 | 0 | 0 | 0 | 1 | 0 | 4 | 0 | 0 | 0 | 0 | - | 0 | 0- - | - | 1.62 | 0.00 |
| 2010 | Auburn | A- | 6 | 6 | 0 | 0 | 19.1 | 92 | 25 | 13 | 13 | 0 | 0 | 1 | 2 | 9 | 0 | 22 | 2 | 0 | 0 | 2 | .000 | 0 | 0- - | - | 5.65 | 6.05 |
| 2011 | Lnsng | A | 25 | 21 | 0 | 3 | 108.1 | 447 | 102 | 56 | 42 | 9 | 4 | 5 | 4 | 31 | 0 | 113 | 4 | 1 | 4 | 4 | .500 | 0 | 1- - | - | 3.40 | 3.49 |
| 2012 | Dnedin | A+ | 17 | 15 | 0 | 0 | 86.1 | 344 | 72 | 26 | 21 | 7 | 0 | 1 | 4 | 21 | 0 | 90 | 0 | 0 | 9 | 0 | 1.000 | 0 | 0- - | - | 2.72 | 2.19 |
| 2012 | NHam | AA | 3 | 3 | 0 | 0 | 15.0 | 60 | 9 | 3 | 2 | 0 | 0 | 0 | 1 | 6 | 0 | 18 | 0 | 0 | 1 | 0 | 1.000 | 0 | 0- - | - | 1.68 | 1.20 |
| 2013 | NHam | AA | 17 | 17 | 1 | 0 | 92.2 | 385 | 89 | 33 | 31 | 6 | 2 | 1 | 2 | 25 | 1 | 103 | 4 | 0 | 8 | 3 | .727 | 0 | 0- - | - | 3.20 | 3.01 |
| 2013 | Buffalo | AAA | 3 | 3 | 0 | 0 | 17.2 | 70 | 13 | 3 | 3 | 1 | 3 | 0 | 1 | 10 | 0 | 13 | 0 | 0 | 1 | 1 | .500 | 0 | 0- - | - | 3.48 | 1.53 |
| 2013 | Tor | AL | 1 | 1 | 0 | 0 | 1.1 | 11 | 7 | 6 | 6 | 1 | 0 | 0 | 0 | 1 | 0 | 0 | 0 | 0 | 0 | 1 | .000 | 0 | 0-0 | 0 | 52.56 | 40.50 |

# Nick Noonan

**Bats:** L **Throws:** R **Pos:** PH-33;2B-22;3B-15;SS-1;PR-1 **Ht:** 6'1" **Wt:** 170 **Born:** 5/4/1989 **Age:** 25

| BATTING | | | | | | | | | | | | | | | | | | | | | | BASERUNNING | | | | AVERAGES | | |
|---|---|---|---|---|---|---|---|---|---|---|---|---|---|---|---|---|---|---|---|---|---|---|---|---|---|---|---|---|
| Year | Team | Lg | G | AB | H | 2B | 3B | HR | (Hm | Rd) | TB | R | RBI | RC | TBB | IBB | SO | HBP | SH | SF | SB | CS | SB% | GDP | Avg | OBP | Slg |
| 2009 | SnJos | A+ | 124 | 459 | 119 | 26 | 8 | 7 | (- | -) | 182 | 82 | 64 | 64 | 48 | 1 | 97 | 5 | 9 | 9 | 9 | 5 | .64 | 5 | .259 | .330 | .397 |
| 2010 | Rchmd | AA | 101 | 372 | 88 | 12 | 2 | 3 | (- | -) | 113 | 43 | 26 | 33 | 22 | 2 | 74 | 2 | 6 | 4 | 7 | 3 | .70 | 3 | .237 | .280 | .304 |
| 2011 | Rchmd | AA | 71 | 260 | 55 | 11 | 0 | 3 | (- | -) | 75 | 28 | 25 | 24 | 33 | 5 | 60 | 2 | 2 | 2 | 2 | 2 | .50 | 6 | .212 | .303 | .288 |
| 2011 | Fresno | AAA | 13 | 37 | 11 | 0 | 0 | 1 | (- | -) | 14 | 6 | 4 | 5 | 4 | 0 | 2 | 0 | 0 | 0 | 1 | 0 | 1.00 | 1 | .297 | .366 | .378 |
| 2011 | SnJos | A+ | 28 | 122 | 30 | 6 | 1 | 1 | (- | -) | 41 | 14 | 16 | 13 | 12 | 0 | 18 | 0 | 0 | 1 | 1 | 2 | .33 | 3 | .246 | .311 | .336 |
| 2012 | Fresno | AAA | 129 | 490 | 145 | 26 | 3 | 9 | (- | -) | 204 | 65 | 62 | 74 | 40 | 2 | 84 | 1 | 5 | 5 | 7 | 3 | .70 | 10 | .296 | .347 | .416 |
| 2013 | Fresno | AAA | 48 | 165 | 42 | 13 | 1 | 0 | (- | -) | 57 | 20 | 20 | 19 | 17 | 0 | 44 | 1 | 2 | 3 | 1 | 2 | .33 | 2 | .255 | .323 | .345 |
| 2013 | SF | NL | 62 | 105 | 23 | 2 | 0 | 0 | (0 | 0) | 25 | 12 | 5 | 5 | 6 | 3 | 24 | 0 | 0 | 0 | 0 | 0 | - | 1 | .219 | .261 | .238 |

# Bud Norris

**Pitches:** R **Bats:** R **Pos:** SP-30; RP-2 **Ht:** 6'0" **Wt:** 220 **Born:** 3/2/1985 **Age:** 29

| HOW MUCH HE PITCHED | | | | | | | | | WHAT HE GAVE UP | | | | | | | | | | | | THE RESULTS | | | | | | | |
|---|---|---|---|---|---|---|---|---|---|---|---|---|---|---|---|---|---|---|---|---|---|---|---|---|---|---|---|---|
| Year | Team | Lg | G | GS | CG | GF | IP | BFP | H | R | ER | HR | SH | SF | HB | TBB | IBB | SO | WP | Bk | W | L | Pct | Sh | Sv-Op | Hld | ERC | ERA |
| 2009 | Hou | NL | 11 | 10 | 0 | 0 | 55.2 | 249 | 59 | 29 | 28 | 9 | 1 | 3 | 3 | 25 | 1 | 54 | 3 | 0 | 6 | 3 | .667 | 0 | 0-0 | 0 | 5.26 | 4.53 |
| 2010 | Hou | NL | 27 | 27 | 0 | 0 | 153.2 | 683 | 151 | 94 | 84 | 18 | 6 | 4 | 6 | 77 | 3 | 158 | 5 | 2 | 9 | 10 | .474 | 0 | 0-0 | 0 | 4.61 | 4.92 |
| 2011 | Hou | NL | 31 | 31 | 0 | 0 | 186.0 | 795 | 177 | 93 | 78 | 24 | 9 | 4 | 5 | 70 | 7 | 176 | 3 | 2 | 6 | 11 | .353 | 0 | 0-0 | 0 | 3.96 | 3.77 |
| 2012 | Hou | NL | 29 | 29 | 0 | 0 | 168.1 | 733 | 165 | 90 | 87 | 23 | 7 | 2 | 8 | 66 | 2 | 165 | 8 | 0 | 7 | 13 | .350 | 0 | 0-0 | 0 | 4.34 | 4.65 |
| 2013 | 2 Tms | AL | 32 | 30 | 0 | 2 | 176.2 | 773 | 196 | 89 | 82 | 17 | 6 | 3 | 5 | 67 | 0 | 147 | 4 | 0 | 10 | 12 | .455 | 0 | 0-0 | 0 | 4.75 | 4.18 |
| 13 | Hou | AL | 21 | 21 | 0 | 0 | 126.0 | 541 | 135 | 62 | 55 | 11 | 4 | 3 | 4 | 43 | 0 | 90 | 3 | 0 | 6 | 9 | .400 | 0 | 0-0 | 0 | 4.34 | 3.93 |
| 13 | Bal | AL | 11 | 9 | 0 | 2 | 50.2 | 232 | 61 | 27 | 27 | 6 | 2 | 0 | 1 | 24 | 0 | 57 | 1 | 0 | 4 | 3 | .571 | 0 | 0-0 | 0 | 5.81 | 4.80 |
| 5 ML YEARS | | | 130 | 127 | 0 | 2 | 740.1 | 3233 | 748 | 395 | 359 | 91 | 29 | 16 | 27 | 305 | 13 | 700 | 23 | 4 | 38 | 49 | .437 | 0 | 0-0 | 0 | 4.46 | 4.36 |

## Derek Norris

**Bats:** R **Throws:** R **Pos:** C-91;PH-18;DH-2;1B-1 **Ht:** 6'0" **Wt:** 210 **Born:** 2/14/1989 **Age:** 25

| BATTING | | | | | | | | | | | | | | | | | | | | BASERUNNING | | | | AVERAGES | | |
|---|---|---|---|---|---|---|---|---|---|---|---|---|---|---|---|---|---|---|---|---|---|---|---|---|---|---|
| Year Team | Lg | G | AB | H | 2B | 3B | HR | (Hm | Rd) | TB | R | RBI | RC | TBB | IBB | SO | HBP | SH | SF | SB | CS | SB% | GDP | Avg | OBP | Slg |
| 2009 Hgrstn | A | 126 | 437 | 125 | 30 | 0 | 23 | (- | -) | 224 | 78 | 84 | 97 | 90 | 9 | 116 | 8 | 0 | 5 | 6 | 3 | .67 | 6 | .286 | .413 | .513 |
| 2010 Ptomc | A+ | 94 | 298 | 70 | 19 | 0 | 12 | (- | -) | 125 | 67 | 49 | 61 | 89 | 2 | 94 | 8 | 0 | 4 | 6 | 3 | .67 | 3 | .235 | .419 | .419 |
| 2011 Hrsbrg | AA | 104 | 334 | 70 | 17 | 1 | 20 | (- | -) | 149 | 75 | 46 | 61 | 77 | 1 | 117 | 7 | 3 | 2 | 13 | 4 | .76 | 2 | .210 | .367 | .446 |
| 2012 Scrmto | AAA | 58 | 218 | 59 | 14 | 2 | 9 | (- | -) | 104 | 39 | 38 | 36 | 21 | 0 | 41 | 1 | 0 | 6 | 5 | 1 | .83 | 7 | .271 | .329 | .477 |
| 2013 Scrmto | AAA | 3 | 14 | 6 | 0 | 0 | 2 | (- | -) | 12 | 3 | 4 | 4 | 0 | 0 | 3 | 0 | 0 | 0 | 0 | 0 | - | 0 | .429 | .429 | .857 |
| 2012 Oak | AL | 60 | 209 | 42 | 8 | 1 | 7 | (3 | 4) | 73 | 19 | 34 | 27 | 21 | 1 | 66 | 1 | 0 | 1 | 5 | 1 | .83 | 6 | .201 | .276 | .349 |
| 2013 Oak | AL | 98 | 264 | 65 | 16 | 0 | 9 | (6 | 3) | 108 | 41 | 30 | 40 | 37 | 1 | 71 | 4 | 1 | 2 | 5 | 0 | 1.00 | 5 | .246 | .345 | .409 |
| Postseason | | 5 | 12 | 1 | 0 | 0 | 0 | (0 | 0) | 1 | 0 | 0 | 0 | 0 | 0 | 6 | 0 | 0 | 0 | 0 | 1 | .00 | 0 | .083 | .083 | .083 |
| 2 ML YEARS | | 158 | 473 | 107 | 24 | 1 | 16 | (9 | 7) | 181 | 60 | 64 | 67 | 58 | 2 | 137 | 5 | 1 | 3 | 10 | 1 | .91 | 11 | .226 | .315 | .383 |

## Ivan Nova

**Pitches:** R **Bats:** R **Pos:** SP-20; RP-3 ee-VAHN **Ht:** 6'4" **Wt:** 225 **Born:** 1/12/1987 **Age:** 27

| HOW MUCH HE PITCHED | | | | | | | | WHAT HE GAVE UP | | | | | | | | | | | | THE RESULTS | | | | | | | |
|---|---|---|---|---|---|---|---|---|---|---|---|---|---|---|---|---|---|---|---|---|---|---|---|---|---|---|---|
| Year Team | Lg | G | GS | CG | GF | IP | BFP | H | R | ER | HR | SH | SF | HB | TBB | IBB | SO | WP | Bk | W | L | Pct | Sh | Sv-Op | Hld | ERC | ERA |
| 2013 S-WB* | AAA | 3 | 3 | 0 | 0 | 17.2 | 69 | 15 | 6 | 4 | 1 | 0 | 1 | 0 | 4 | 0 | 17 | 0 | 0 | 2 | 0 | 1.000 | 0 | 0- - | - | 2.45 | 2.04 |
| 2010 NYY | AL | 10 | 7 | 0 | 3 | 42.0 | 185 | 44 | 22 | 21 | 4 | 1 | 1 | 1 | 17 | 2 | 26 | 2 | 0 | 1 | 2 | .333 | 0 | 0-1 | 0 | 4.31 | 4.50 |
| 2011 NYY | AL | 28 | 27 | 0 | 1 | 165.1 | 704 | 163 | 74 | 68 | 13 | 2 | 6 | 6 | 57 | 3 | 98 | 11 | 0 | 16 | 4 | .800 | 0 | 0-0 | 0 | 3.76 | 3.70 |
| 2012 NYY | AL | 28 | 28 | 0 | 0 | 170.1 | 748 | 194 | 100 | 95 | 28 | 3 | 6 | 10 | 56 | 3 | 153 | 6 | 2 | 12 | 8 | .600 | 0 | 0-0 | 0 | 5.32 | 5.02 |
| 2013 NYY | AL | 23 | 20 | 3 | 2 | 139.1 | 586 | 135 | 49 | 48 | 9 | 2 | 3 | 14 | 44 | 3 | 116 | 3 | 0 | 9 | 6 | .600 | 2 | 0-0 | 0 | 3.77 | 3.10 |
| Postseason | | 2 | 1 | 0 | 0 | 8.1 | 34 | 7 | 4 | 4 | 2 | 0 | 0 | 0 | 4 | 0 | 8 | 0 | 0 | 1 | 1 | .500 | 0 | 0-0 | 0 | 4.66 | 4.32 |
| 4 ML YEARS | | 89 | 82 | 3 | 6 | 517.0 | 2223 | 536 | 245 | 232 | 54 | 8 | 16 | 31 | 174 | 11 | 393 | 22 | 2 | 38 | 20 | .655 | 2 | 0-1 | 0 | 4.31 | 4.04 |

## Eduardo Nunez

**Bats:** R **Throws:** R **Pos:** SS-75;3B-14;PR-3;2B-2;PH-2;DH-1 **Ht:** 6'0" **Wt:** 185 **Born:** 6/15/1987 **Age:** 27

| BATTING | | | | | | | | | | | | | | | | | | | | BASERUNNING | | | | AVERAGES | | |
|---|---|---|---|---|---|---|---|---|---|---|---|---|---|---|---|---|---|---|---|---|---|---|---|---|---|---|
| Year Team | Lg | G | AB | H | 2B | 3B | HR | (Hm | Rd) | TB | R | RBI | RC | TBB | IBB | SO | HBP | SH | SF | SB | CS | SB% | GDP | Avg | OBP | Slg |
| 2013 Tampa* | A+ | 3 | 3 | 1 | 0 | 0 | 0 | (- | -) | 1 | 2 | 0 | 1 | 2 | 0 | 0 | 0 | 0 | 0 | 2 | 0 | 1.00 | 0 | .333 | .600 | .333 |
| 2013 CtnSC* | A | 2 | 5 | 2 | 0 | 0 | 0 | (- | -) | 2 | 1 | 0 | 1 | 1 | 0 | 0 | 0 | 0 | 0 | 1 | 0 | 1.00 | 0 | .400 | .500 | .400 |
| 2013 Trntn* | AA | 2 | 8 | 3 | 0 | 0 | 0 | (- | -) | 3 | 1 | 1 | 1 | 1 | 0 | 2 | 0 | 0 | 0 | 0 | 0 | - | 1 | .375 | .444 | .375 |
| 2010 NYY | AL | 30 | 50 | 14 | 1 | 0 | 1 | (0 | 1) | 18 | 12 | 7 | 8 | 3 | 0 | 2 | 0 | 0 | 0 | 5 | 0 | 1.00 | 4 | .280 | .321 | .360 |
| 2011 NYY | AL | 112 | 309 | 82 | 18 | 2 | 5 | (2 | 3) | 119 | 38 | 30 | 42 | 22 | 2 | 37 | 0 | 6 | 1 | 22 | 6 | .79 | 6 | .265 | .313 | .385 |
| 2012 NYY | AL | 38 | 89 | 26 | 4 | 1 | 1 | (1 | 0) | 35 | 14 | 11 | 15 | 6 | 0 | 12 | 1 | 0 | 4 | 11 | 2 | .85 | 1 | .292 | .330 | .393 |
| 2013 NYY | AL | 90 | 304 | 79 | 17 | 4 | 3 | (2 | 1) | 113 | 38 | 28 | 31 | 20 | 1 | 51 | 3 | 4 | 5 | 10 | 3 | .77 | 3 | .260 | .307 | .372 |
| Postseason | | 6 | 11 | 3 | 1 | 1 | 1 | (0 | 1) | 9 | 4 | 1 | 1 | 0 | 0 | 0 | 0 | 0 | 0 | 2 | 0 | 1.00 | 0 | .273 | .273 | .818 |
| 4 ML YEARS | | 270 | 752 | 201 | 40 | 7 | 10 | (5 | 5) | 285 | 102 | 76 | 96 | 51 | 3 | 102 | 4 | 10 | 10 | 48 | 11 | .81 | 14 | .267 | .313 | .379 |

## Vidal Nuno

**Pitches:** L **Bats:** L **Pos:** SP-3; RP-2 vee-DOLL NOON-yo **Ht:** 5'11" **Wt:** 195 **Born:** 7/26/1987 **Age:** 26

| HOW MUCH HE PITCHED | | | | | | | | WHAT HE GAVE UP | | | | | | | | | | | | THE RESULTS | | | | | | | |
|---|---|---|---|---|---|---|---|---|---|---|---|---|---|---|---|---|---|---|---|---|---|---|---|---|---|---|---|
| Year Team | Lg | G | GS | CG | GF | IP | BFP | H | R | ER | HR | SH | SF | HB | TBB | IBB | SO | WP | Bk | W | L | Pct | Sh | Sv-Op | Hld | ERC | ERA |
| 2009 Indns | R | 4 | 0 | 0 | 2 | 7.0 | 34 | 10 | 4 | 4 | 0 | 0 | 0 | 3 | 1 | 0 | 11 | 0 | 1 | 0 | 0 | - | 0 | 1- - | - | 6.54 | 5.14 |
| 2009 MhVlly | A- | 13 | 8 | 0 | 2 | 57.0 | 228 | 43 | 16 | 13 | 3 | 1 | 3 | 2 | 14 | 1 | 48 | 1 | 3 | 5 | 0 | 1.000 | 0 | 0- - | - | 2.05 | 2.05 |
| 2010 Lk Cty | A | 21 | 16 | 0 | 1 | 94.1 | 394 | 104 | 54 | 52 | 13 | 1 | 5 | 7 | 14 | 0 | 94 | 1 | 2 | 6 | 8 | .429 | 0 | 0- - | - | 4.27 | 4.96 |
| 2011 StIsInd | A- | 8 | 0 | 0 | 2 | 25.0 | 91 | 14 | 3 | 2 | 0 | 1 | 0 | 0 | 3 | 0 | 29 | 1 | 0 | 5 | 0 | 1.000 | 0 | 1- - | - | 0.87 | 0.72 |
| 2011 CtnSC | A | 7 | 7 | 0 | 0 | 40.0 | 151 | 37 | 9 | 8 | 4 | 0 | 0 | 0 | 2 | 0 | 37 | 1 | 1 | 2 | 1 | .667 | 0 | 0- - | - | 2.47 | 1.80 |
| 2012 Tampa | A+ | 11 | 1 | 0 | 1 | 24.1 | 102 | 22 | 11 | 8 | 2 | 0 | 0 | 1 | 6 | 0 | 26 | 0 | 0 | 1 | 1 | .500 | 0 | 0- - | - | 2.95 | 2.96 |
| 2012 Trntn | AA | 20 | 20 | 0 | 0 | 114.0 | 465 | 109 | 40 | 31 | 10 | 0 | 4 | 2 | 27 | 0 | 100 | 1 | 1 | 9 | 5 | .643 | 0 | 0- - | - | 3.25 | 2.45 |
| 2013 S-WB | AAA | 5 | 5 | 0 | 0 | 25.0 | 91 | 14 | 4 | 4 | 2 | 0 | 0 | 0 | 2 | 0 | 30 | 0 | 0 | 2 | 0 | 1.000 | 0 | 0- - | - | 1.03 | 1.44 |
| 2013 NYY | AL | 5 | 3 | 0 | 2 | 20.0 | 82 | 16 | 5 | 5 | 2 | 0 | 0 | 1 | 6 | 0 | 9 | 0 | 0 | 1 | 2 | .333 | 0 | 0-0 | 0 | 2.81 | 2.25 |

## Brett Oberholtzer

**Pitches:** L **Bats:** L **Pos:** SP-10; RP-3 **Ht:** 6'1" **Wt:** 235 **Born:** 7/1/1989 **Age:** 24

| HOW MUCH HE PITCHED | | | | | | | | WHAT HE GAVE UP | | | | | | | | | | | | THE RESULTS | | | | | | | |
|---|---|---|---|---|---|---|---|---|---|---|---|---|---|---|---|---|---|---|---|---|---|---|---|---|---|---|---|
| Year Team | Lg | G | GS | CG | GF | IP | BFP | H | R | ER | HR | SH | SF | HB | TBB | IBB | SO | WP | Bk | W | L | Pct | Sh | Sv-Op | Hld | ERC | ERA |
| 2009 Danvle | R | 12 | 12 | 1 | 0 | 67.0 | 251 | 46 | 17 | 15 | 1 | 1 | 1 | 2 | 6 | 0 | 56 | 6 | 1 | 6 | 2 | .750 | 0 | 0- - | - | 1.26 | 2.01 |
| 2010 Rome | A | 4 | 4 | 0 | 0 | 23.0 | 91 | 22 | 7 | 5 | 1 | 1 | 0 | 1 | 5 | 0 | 19 | 2 | 0 | 0 | 2 | .000 | 0 | 0- - | - | 3.10 | 1.96 |
| 2010 MrtlBh | A+ | 22 | 18 | 0 | 3 | 112.2 | 474 | 123 | 59 | 52 | 7 | 6 | 4 | 4 | 18 | 0 | 107 | 6 | 0 | 6 | 6 | .500 | 0 | 2- - | - | 3.52 | 4.15 |
| 2011 Missi | AA | 21 | 21 | 1 | 0 | 127.2 | 533 | 119 | 65 | 53 | 6 | 5 | 8 | 1 | 42 | 4 | 93 | 5 | 0 | 9 | 9 | .500 | 0 | 0- - | - | 3.07 | 3.74 |
| 2011 CpChr | AA | 6 | 6 | 0 | 0 | 27.1 | 117 | 28 | 16 | 16 | 3 | 1 | 0 | 1 | 10 | 0 | 28 | 2 | 0 | 2 | 3 | .400 | 0 | 0- - | - | 4.35 | 5.27 |
| 2012 CpChr | AA | 13 | 13 | 0 | 0 | 77.0 | 332 | 82 | 41 | 36 | 11 | 5 | 1 | 1 | 21 | 1 | 68 | 4 | 0 | 5 | 3 | .625 | 0 | 0- - | - | 4.21 | 4.21 |
| 2012 OKCity | AAA | 15 | 15 | 0 | 0 | 89.2 | 388 | 105 | 48 | 45 | 13 | 3 | 4 | 2 | 19 | 3 | 69 | 3 | 0 | 5 | 7 | .417 | 0 | 0- - | - | 4.63 | 4.52 |
| 2013 OKCity | AAA | 16 | 16 | 0 | 0 | 80.1 | 338 | 77 | 48 | 39 | 9 | 2 | 3 | 2 | 25 | 0 | 72 | 4 | 0 | 6 | 6 | .500 | 0 | 0- - | - | 3.68 | 4.37 |
| 2013 Hou | AL | 13 | 10 | 2 | 1 | 71.2 | 293 | 66 | 26 | 22 | 7 | 0 | 1 | 1 | 13 | 0 | 45 | 0 | 0 | 4 | 5 | .444 | 1 | 0-0 | 0 | 2.82 | 2.76 |

## Darren O'Day

**Pitches:** R **Bats:** R **Pos:** RP-68 **Ht:** 6'4" **Wt:** 220 **Born:** 10/22/1982 **Age:** 31

| HOW MUCH HE PITCHED | | | | | | | | WHAT HE GAVE UP | | | | | | | | | | | | THE RESULTS | | | | | | | |
|---|---|---|---|---|---|---|---|---|---|---|---|---|---|---|---|---|---|---|---|---|---|---|---|---|---|---|---|
| Year Team | Lg | G | GS | CG | GF | IP | BFP | H | R | ER | HR | SH | SF | HB | TBB | IBB | SO | WP | Bk | W | L | Pct | Sh | Sv-Op | Hld | ERC | ERA |
| 2008 LAA | AL | 30 | 0 | 0 | 17 | 43.1 | 194 | 49 | 24 | 22 | 2 | 2 | 1 | 4 | 14 | 6 | 29 | 1 | 0 | 0 | 1 | .000 | 0 | 0-0 | 1 | 4.20 | 4.57 |
| 2009 2 Tms | | 68 | 0 | 0 | 15 | 58.2 | 233 | 41 | 14 | 12 | 3 | 1 | 3 | 5 | 18 | 1 | 56 | 1 | 0 | 2 | 1 | .667 | 0 | 2-2 | 20 | 2.20 | 1.84 |
| 2010 Tex | AL | 72 | 0 | 0 | 14 | 62.0 | 240 | 43 | 15 | 14 | 5 | 1 | 3 | 5 | 12 | 2 | 45 | 0 | 0 | 6 | 2 | .750 | 0 | 0-2 | 22 | 1.93 | 2.03 |
| 2011 Tex | AL | 16 | 0 | 0 | 7 | 16.2 | 74 | 17 | 10 | 10 | 7 | 1 | 1 | 2 | 5 | 0 | 18 | 0 | 0 | 0 | 1 | .000 | 0 | 0-0 | 3 | 6.45 | 5.40 |

| HOW MUCH HE PITCHED | | | | | | | | | WHAT HE GAVE UP | | | | | | | | | | | | THE RESULTS | | | | | | | |
|---|---|---|---|---|---|---|---|---|---|---|---|---|---|---|---|---|---|---|---|---|---|---|---|---|---|---|---|---|
| Year | Team | Lg | G | GS | CG | GF | IP | BFP | H | R | ER | HR | SH | SF | HB | TBB | IBB | SO | WP | Bk | W | L | Pct | Sh | Sv-Op | Hld | ERC | ERA |
| 2012 | Bal | AL | 69 | 0 | 0 | 10 | 67.0 | 263 | 49 | 17 | 17 | 6 | 3 | 1 | 3 | 14 | 2 | 69 | 0 | 0 | 7 | 1 | .875 | 0 | 0-2 | 15 | 2.06 | 2.28 |
| 2013 | Bal | AL | 68 | 0 | 0 | 18 | 62.0 | 247 | 47 | 16 | 15 | 7 | 1 | 1 | 5 | 15 | 1 | 59 | 1 | 0 | 5 | 3 | .625 | 0 | 2-6 | 20 | 2.60 | 2.18 |
| 09 | NYM | NL | 4 | 0 | 0 | 1 | 3.0 | 17 | 5 | 2 | 0 | 0 | 0 | 1 | 1 | 1 | 0 | 2 | 0 | 0 | 0 | 0 | - | 0 | 0-0 | 0 | 7.72 | 0.00 |
| 09 | Tex | AL | 64 | 0 | 0 | 14 | 55.2 | 216 | 36 | 12 | 12 | 3 | 1 | 2 | 4 | 17 | 1 | 54 | 1 | 0 | 2 | 1 | .667 | 0 | 2-2 | 20 | 1.95 | 1.94 |
| Postseason | | | 16 | 0 | 0 | 1 | 11.2 | 46 | 7 | 4 | 4 | 2 | 1 | 0 | 1 | 2 | 0 | 13 | 0 | 0 | 0 | 1 | .000 | 0 | 0-0 | 4 | 1.85 | 3.09 |
| 6 ML YEARS | | | 323 | 0 | 0 | 81 | 309.2 | 1251 | 246 | 96 | 90 | 30 | 9 | 10 | 24 | 78 | 12 | 276 | 3 | 0 | 20 | 9 | .690 | 0 | 4-12 | 81 | 2.66 | 2.62 |

# Jake Odorizzi

**Pitches:** R **Bats:** R **Pos:** SP-4; RP-3 oh-duh-RIZZ-ee **Ht:** 6'2" **Wt:** 185 **Born:** 3/27/1990 **Age:** 24

| HOW MUCH HE PITCHED | | | | | | | | | WHAT HE GAVE UP | | | | | | | | | | | | THE RESULTS | | | | | | | |
|---|---|---|---|---|---|---|---|---|---|---|---|---|---|---|---|---|---|---|---|---|---|---|---|---|---|---|---|---|
| Year | Team | Lg | G | GS | CG | GF | IP | BFP | H | R | ER | HR | SH | SF | HB | TBB | IBB | SO | WP | Bk | W | L | Pct | Sh | Sv-Op | Hld | ERC | ERA |
| 2009 | Helena | R+ | 12 | 10 | 0 | 0 | 47.0 | 203 | 55 | 27 | 23 | 3 | 2 | 4 | 2 | 9 | 0 | 43 | 5 | 0 | 1 | 4 | .200 | 0 | 0- - | - | 4.10 | 4.40 |
| 2010 | Wisc | A | 23 | 20 | 0 | 1 | 120.2 | 505 | 99 | 52 | 46 | 7 | 2 | 4 | 9 | 40 | 0 | 135 | 5 | 0 | 7 | 3 | .700 | 0 | 1- - | - | 2.83 | 3.43 |
| 2011 | Wilmg | A+ | 15 | 15 | 0 | 0 | 78.1 | 317 | 68 | 30 | 25 | 4 | 3 | 1 | 2 | 22 | 0 | 103 | 6 | 0 | 5 | 4 | .556 | 0 | 0- - | - | 2.75 | 2.87 |
| 2011 | NWArk | AA | 12 | 12 | 0 | 0 | 68.2 | 284 | 66 | 38 | 36 | 13 | 1 | 0 | 1 | 22 | 0 | 54 | 1 | 0 | 5 | 3 | .625 | 0 | 0- - | - | 4.30 | 4.72 |
| 2012 | NWArk | AA | 7 | 7 | 0 | 0 | 38.0 | 152 | 27 | 15 | 14 | 2 | 0 | 1 | 0 | 10 | 0 | 47 | 4 | 0 | 4 | 2 | .667 | 0 | 0- - | - | 1.78 | 3.32 |
| 2012 | Omha | AAA | 19 | 18 | 0 | 0 | 107.1 | 460 | 105 | 41 | 35 | 12 | 1 | 4 | 2 | 40 | 0 | 88 | 3 | 0 | 11 | 3 | .786 | 0 | 0- - | - | 4.00 | 2.93 |
| 2013 | Drham | AAA | 22 | 22 | 0 | 0 | 124.1 | 493 | 101 | 49 | 46 | 12 | 2 | 2 | 1 | 40 | 1 | 124 | 5 | 0 | 9 | 6 | .600 | 0 | 0- - | - | 2.87 | 3.33 |
| 2012 | KC | AL | 2 | 2 | 0 | 0 | 7.1 | 34 | 8 | 4 | 4 | 1 | 0 | 0 | 0 | 4 | 0 | 4 | 0 | 0 | 0 | 1 | .000 | 0 | 0-0 | 0 | 5.34 | 4.91 |
| 2013 | TB | AL | 7 | 4 | 0 | 2 | 29.2 | 122 | 28 | 13 | 13 | 3 | 0 | 1 | 2 | 8 | 0 | 22 | 1 | 0 | 0 | 1 | .000 | 0 | 1-1 | 0 | 3.62 | 3.94 |
| 2 ML YEARS | | | 9 | 6 | 0 | 2 | 37.0 | 156 | 36 | 17 | 17 | 4 | 0 | 1 | 2 | 12 | 0 | 26 | 1 | 0 | 0 | 2 | .000 | 0 | 1-1 | 0 | 3.95 | 4.14 |

# Eric O'Flaherty

**Pitches:** L **Bats:** L **Pos:** RP-19 **Ht:** 6'2" **Wt:** 220 **Born:** 2/5/1985 **Age:** 29

| HOW MUCH HE PITCHED | | | | | | | | | WHAT HE GAVE UP | | | | | | | | | | | | THE RESULTS | | | | | | | |
|---|---|---|---|---|---|---|---|---|---|---|---|---|---|---|---|---|---|---|---|---|---|---|---|---|---|---|---|---|
| Year | Team | Lg | G | GS | CG | GF | IP | BFP | H | R | ER | HR | SH | SF | HB | TBB | IBB | SO | WP | Bk | W | L | Pct | Sh | Sv-Op | Hld | ERC | ERA |
| 2006 | Sea | AL | 15 | 0 | 0 | 5 | 11.0 | 57 | 18 | 9 | 5 | 2 | 1 | 0 | 0 | 6 | 3 | 6 | 2 | 0 | 0 | 0 | - | 0 | 0-0 | 1 | 8.63 | 4.09 |
| 2007 | Sea | AL | 56 | 0 | 0 | 9 | 52.1 | 221 | 45 | 26 | 26 | 1 | 0 | 2 | 5 | 20 | 1 | 36 | 4 | 1 | 7 | 1 | .875 | 0 | 0-1 | 4 | 3.04 | 4.47 |
| 2008 | Sea | AL | 7 | 0 | 0 | 1 | 6.2 | 42 | 16 | 15 | 15 | 2 | 0 | 1 | 2 | 4 | 2 | 4 | 0 | 0 | 0 | 1 | .000 | 0 | 0-0 | 2 | 17.12 | 20.25 |
| 2009 | Atl | NL | 78 | 0 | 0 | 8 | 56.1 | 236 | 52 | 23 | 19 | 2 | 1 | 1 | 6 | 18 | 4 | 39 | 2 | 0 | 2 | 1 | .667 | 0 | 0-2 | 15 | 3.26 | 3.04 |
| 2010 | Atl | NL | 56 | 0 | 0 | 7 | 44.0 | 181 | 37 | 14 | 12 | 2 | 1 | 0 | 1 | 18 | 2 | 36 | 3 | 0 | 3 | 2 | .600 | 0 | 0-1 | 9 | 2.97 | 2.45 |
| 2011 | Atl | NL | 78 | 0 | 0 | 5 | 73.2 | 301 | 59 | 9 | 8 | 2 | 7 | 2 | 3 | 21 | 8 | 67 | 1 | 0 | 2 | 4 | .333 | 0 | 0-4 | 32 | 2.13 | 0.98 |
| 2012 | Atl | NL | 64 | 0 | 0 | 7 | 57.1 | 230 | 47 | 14 | 11 | 3 | 3 | 1 | 2 | 19 | 2 | 46 | 1 | 0 | 3 | 0 | 1.000 | 0 | 0-3 | 28 | 2.71 | 1.73 |
| 2013 | Atl | NL | 19 | 0 | 0 | 2 | 18.0 | 70 | 12 | 5 | 5 | 2 | 0 | 1 | 0 | 5 | 1 | 11 | 0 | 0 | 3 | 0 | 1.000 | 0 | 0-1 | 12 | 1.93 | 2.50 |
| Postseason | | | 1 | 0 | 0 | 0 | 1.0 | 4 | 2 | 0 | 0 | 0 | 0 | 0 | 0 | 0 | 0 | 0 | 0 | 0 | 0 | 0 | - | 0 | 0-0 | 0 | 9.49 | 0.00 |
| 8 ML YEARS | | | 373 | 0 | 0 | 44 | 319.1 | 1338 | 286 | 115 | 101 | 16 | 13 | 8 | 19 | 111 | 23 | 245 | 13 | 1 | 20 | 9 | .690 | 0 | 0-12 | 103 | 3.11 | 2.85 |

# Alexi Ogando

**Pitches:** R **Bats:** R **Pos:** SP-18; RP-5 oh-GONE-doh **Ht:** 6'4" **Wt:** 200 **Born:** 10/5/1983 **Age:** 30

| HOW MUCH HE PITCHED | | | | | | | | | WHAT HE GAVE UP | | | | | | | | | | | | THE RESULTS | | | | | | | |
|---|---|---|---|---|---|---|---|---|---|---|---|---|---|---|---|---|---|---|---|---|---|---|---|---|---|---|---|---|
| Year | Team | Lg | G | GS | CG | GF | IP | BFP | H | R | ER | HR | SH | SF | HB | TBB | IBB | SO | WP | Bk | W | L | Pct | Sh | Sv-Op | Hld | ERC | ERA |
| 2013 | Frisco* | AA | 1 | 1 | 0 | 0 | 6.0 | 22 | 4 | 2 | 0 | 1 | 1 | 0 | 0 | 0 | 0 | 4 | 0 | 0 | 1 | 0 | 1.000 | 0 | 0- - | - | 1.41 | 0.00 |
| 2013 | RdRck* | AAA | 3 | 3 | 0 | 0 | 13.0 | 55 | 12 | 9 | 9 | 4 | 0 | 1 | 0 | 4 | 0 | 4 | 1 | 0 | 0 | 1 | .000 | 0 | 0- - | - | 4.56 | 6.23 |
| 2010 | Tex | AL | 44 | 0 | 0 | 12 | 41.2 | 171 | 31 | 6 | 6 | 2 | 3 | 2 | 1 | 16 | 2 | 39 | 3 | 0 | 4 | 1 | .800 | 0 | 0-2 | 7 | 2.34 | 1.30 |
| 2011 | Tex | AL | 31 | 29 | 1 | 2 | 169.0 | 693 | 149 | 73 | 66 | 16 | 2 | 3 | 7 | 43 | 0 | 126 | 5 | 0 | 13 | 8 | .619 | 1 | 0-0 | 0 | 3.01 | 3.51 |
| 2012 | Tex | AL | 58 | 1 | 0 | 11 | 66.0 | 263 | 49 | 26 | 24 | 9 | 0 | 3 | 2 | 17 | 1 | 66 | 5 | 0 | 2 | 0 | 1.000 | 0 | 3-6 | 12 | 2.50 | 3.27 |
| 2013 | Tex | AL | 23 | 18 | 0 | 0 | 104.1 | 428 | 87 | 38 | 36 | 11 | 2 | 3 | 5 | 41 | 1 | 72 | 6 | 1 | 7 | 4 | .636 | 0 | 0-0 | 0 | 3.44 | 3.11 |
| Postseason | | | 18 | 0 | 0 | 2 | 19.0 | 81 | 16 | 6 | 5 | 3 | 0 | 0 | 0 | 10 | 2 | 23 | 1 | 0 | 2 | 0 | 1.000 | 0 | 0-3 | 4 | 3.95 | 2.37 |
| 4 ML YEARS | | | 156 | 48 | 1 | 25 | 381.0 | 1555 | 316 | 143 | 132 | 38 | 7 | 11 | 15 | 117 | 4 | 303 | 19 | 1 | 26 | 13 | .667 | 1 | 3-8 | 19 | 2.96 | 3.12 |

# Ross Ohlendorf

**Pitches:** R **Bats:** R **Pos:** RP-9; SP-7 OH-lenn-dorf **Ht:** 6'4" **Wt:** 240 **Born:** 8/8/1982 **Age:** 31

| HOW MUCH HE PITCHED | | | | | | | | | WHAT HE GAVE UP | | | | | | | | | | | | THE RESULTS | | | | | | | |
|---|---|---|---|---|---|---|---|---|---|---|---|---|---|---|---|---|---|---|---|---|---|---|---|---|---|---|---|---|
| Year | Team | Lg | G | GS | CG | GF | IP | BFP | H | R | ER | HR | SH | SF | HB | TBB | IBB | SO | WP | Bk | W | L | Pct | Sh | Sv-Op | Hld | ERC | ERA |
| 2013 | Syrcse* | AAA | 14 | 13 | 2 | 1 | 74.2 | 320 | 65 | 36 | 35 | 5 | 1 | 3 | 3 | 30 | 2 | 71 | 2 | 0 | 4 | 6 | .400 | 0 | 0- - | - | 3.21 | 4.22 |
| 2013 | Ptomc* | A+ | 1 | 1 | 0 | 0 | 4.0 | 21 | 8 | 3 | 3 | 0 | 0 | 2 | 0 | 1 | 0 | 2 | 0 | 0 | 0 | 0 | - | 0 | 0- - | - | 8.60 | 6.75 |
| 2007 | NYY | AL | 6 | 0 | 0 | 3 | 6.1 | 26 | 5 | 2 | 2 | 1 | 0 | 0 | 0 | 2 | 0 | 9 | 0 | 0 | 0 | 0 | - | 0 | 0-0 | 1 | 2.94 | 2.84 |
| 2008 | 2 Tms | | 30 | 5 | 0 | 3 | 62.2 | 300 | 86 | 49 | 45 | 10 | 1 | 1 | 1 | 31 | 3 | 49 | 10 | 1 | 1 | 4 | .200 | 0 | 0-0 | 4 | 7.16 | 6.46 |
| 2009 | Pit | NL | 29 | 29 | 0 | 0 | 176.2 | 725 | 165 | 80 | 77 | 25 | 11 | 8 | 7 | 53 | 1 | 109 | 2 | 1 | 11 | 10 | .524 | 0 | 0-0 | 0 | 3.84 | 3.92 |
| 2010 | Pit | NL | 21 | 21 | 0 | 0 | 108.1 | 475 | 106 | 54 | 49 | 12 | 9 | 8 | 6 | 44 | 2 | 79 | 5 | 0 | 1 | 11 | .083 | 0 | 0-0 | 0 | 4.20 | 4.07 |
| 2011 | Pit | NL | 9 | 9 | 0 | 0 | 38.2 | 194 | 60 | 38 | 35 | 9 | 5 | 3 | 6 | 15 | 2 | 27 | 2 | 0 | 1 | 3 | .250 | 0 | 0-0 | 0 | 9.12 | 8.15 |
| 2012 | SD | NL | 13 | 9 | 0 | 2 | 48.2 | 233 | 62 | 44 | 42 | 7 | 4 | 0 | 1 | 24 | 0 | 39 | 2 | 1 | 4 | 4 | .500 | 0 | 0-0 | 0 | 6.37 | 7.77 |
| 2013 | Was | NL | 16 | 7 | 0 | 1 | 60.1 | 247 | 56 | 22 | 22 | 8 | 3 | 0 | 1 | 14 | 1 | 45 | 1 | 0 | 4 | 1 | .800 | 0 | 0-1 | 1 | 3.30 | 3.28 |
| 08 | NYY | AL | 25 | 0 | 0 | 3 | 40.0 | 187 | 50 | 31 | 29 | 7 | 0 | 0 | 1 | 19 | 3 | 36 | 6 | 0 | 1 | 1 | .500 | 0 | 0-0 | 4 | 6.39 | 6.53 |
| 08 | Pit | NL | 5 | 5 | 0 | 0 | 22.2 | 113 | 36 | 18 | 16 | 3 | 1 | 1 | 0 | 12 | 0 | 13 | 4 | 1 | 0 | 3 | .000 | 0 | 0-0 | 0 | 8.59 | 6.35 |
| Postseason | | | 1 | 0 | 0 | 0 | 1.0 | 9 | 4 | 3 | 3 | 1 | 0 | 0 | 1 | 1 | 0 | 0 | 0 | 0 | 0 | 0 | - | 0 | 0-0 | 0 | 47.63 | 27.00 |
| 7 ML YEARS | | | 124 | 80 | 0 | 9 | 501.2 | 2200 | 540 | 289 | 272 | 72 | 33 | 20 | 22 | 183 | 9 | 357 | 22 | 3 | 22 | 33 | .400 | 0 | 0-1 | 6 | 4.84 | 4.88 |

# Hideki Okajima

**Pitches:** L **Bats:** L **Pos:** RP-5 oh-kuh-JEE-muh **Ht:** 6'1" **Wt:** 195 **Born:** 12/25/1975 **Age:** 38

| | | | HOW MUCH HE PITCHED | | | | | | WHAT HE GAVE UP | | | | | | | | | | | | THE RESULTS | | | | | | | |
|---|---|---|---|---|---|---|---|---|---|---|---|---|---|---|---|---|---|---|---|---|---|---|---|---|---|---|---|---|
| Year | Team | Lg | G | GS | CG | GF | IP | BFP | H | R | ER | HR | SH | SF | HB | TBB | IBB | SO | WP | Bk | W | L | Pct | Sh | Sv-Op | Hld | ERC | ERA |
| 2013 | Scrmto* | AAA | 37 | 0 | 0 | 11 | 42.2 | 176 | 40 | 21 | 20 | 5 | 2 | 1 | 0 | 9 | 1 | 45 | 2 | 0 | 1 | 3 | .250 | 0 | 1-- | - | 3.04 | 4.22 |
| 2007 | Bos | AL | 66 | 0 | 0 | 13 | 69.0 | 272 | 50 | 17 | 17 | 6 | 5 | 1 | 1 | 17 | 2 | 63 | 0 | 0 | 3 | 2 | .600 | 0 | 5-7 | 27 | 2.03 | 2.22 |
| 2008 | Bos | AL | 64 | 0 | 0 | 11 | 62.0 | 258 | 49 | 18 | 18 | 6 | 0 | 3 | 1 | 23 | 1 | 60 | 2 | 0 | 3 | 2 | .600 | 0 | 1-9 | 23 | 2.82 | 2.61 |
| 2009 | Bos | AL | 68 | 0 | 0 | 6 | 61.0 | 258 | 56 | 23 | 23 | 8 | 3 | 1 | 2 | 21 | 3 | 53 | 0 | 0 | 6 | 0 | 1.000 | 0 | 0-2 | 23 | 3.65 | 3.39 |
| 2010 | Bos | AL | 56 | 0 | 0 | 12 | 46.0 | 213 | 59 | 24 | 23 | 6 | 4 | 1 | 0 | 20 | 5 | 33 | 2 | 0 | 4 | 4 | .500 | 0 | 0-4 | 11 | 5.90 | 4.50 |
| 2011 | Bos | AL | 7 | 0 | 0 | 2 | 8.1 | 36 | 7 | 4 | 4 | 0 | 1 | 0 | 0 | 5 | 0 | 6 | 0 | 0 | 1 | 0 | 1.000 | 0 | 0-0 | 0 | 3.26 | 4.32 |
| 2013 | Oak | AL | 5 | 0 | 0 | 0 | 4.0 | 21 | 7 | 1 | 1 | 1 | 0 | 0 | 0 | 2 | 2 | 1 | 1 | 0 | 0 | 0 | - | 0 | 0-0 | 0 | 9.34 | 2.25 |
| Postseason | | | 17 | 0 | 0 | 2 | 21.1 | 82 | 13 | 5 | 5 | 2 | 0 | 0 | 0 | 5 | 1 | 16 | 0 | 0 | 0 | 0 | - | 0 | 0-0 | 8 | 1.50 | 2.11 |
| 6 ML YEARS | | | 266 | 0 | 0 | 44 | 250.1 | 1058 | 228 | 87 | 86 | 27 | 13 | 6 | 4 | 88 | 13 | 216 | 5 | 0 | 17 | 8 | .680 | 0 | 6-22 | 84 | 3.41 | 3.09 |

# Darren Oliver

**Pitches:** L **Bats:** R **Pos:** RP-50 **Ht:** 6'3" **Wt:** 250 **Born:** 10/6/1970 **Age:** 43

| | | | HOW MUCH HE PITCHED | | | | | | WHAT HE GAVE UP | | | | | | | | | | | | THE RESULTS | | | | | | | |
|---|---|---|---|---|---|---|---|---|---|---|---|---|---|---|---|---|---|---|---|---|---|---|---|---|---|---|---|---|
| Year | Team | Lg | G | GS | CG | GF | IP | BFP | H | R | ER | HR | SH | SF | HB | TBB | IBB | SO | WP | Bk | W | L | Pct | Sh | Sv-Op | Hld | ERC | ERA |
| 2013 | Dnedin* | A+ | 2 | 2 | 0 | 0 | 2.0 | 6 | 0 | 0 | 0 | 0 | 0 | 0 | 0 | 0 | 0 | 4 | 0 | 0 | 0 | 0 | - | 0 | 0-- | - | 0.00 | 0.00 |
| 1993 | Tex | AL | 2 | 0 | 0 | 0 | 3.1 | 14 | 2 | 1 | 1 | 1 | 0 | 0 | 0 | 1 | 1 | 4 | 0 | 0 | 0 | 0 | - | 0 | 0-0 | 0 | 2.15 | 2.70 |
| 1994 | Tex | AL | 43 | 0 | 0 | 10 | 50.0 | 226 | 40 | 24 | 19 | 4 | 6 | 0 | 6 | 35 | 4 | 50 | 2 | 2 | 4 | 0 | 1.000 | 0 | 2-3 | 9 | 4.29 | 3.42 |
| 1995 | Tex | AL | 17 | 7 | 0 | 2 | 49.0 | 222 | 47 | 25 | 23 | 3 | 5 | 1 | 1 | 32 | 1 | 39 | 4 | 0 | 4 | 2 | .667 | 0 | 0-0 | 0 | 4.59 | 4.22 |
| 1996 | Tex | AL | 30 | 30 | 1 | 0 | 173.2 | 777 | 190 | 97 | 90 | 20 | 2 | 7 | 10 | 76 | 3 | 112 | 5 | 1 | 14 | 6 | .700 | 1 | 0-0 | 0 | 5.10 | 4.66 |
| 1997 | Tex | AL | 32 | 32 | 3 | 0 | 201.1 | 887 | 213 | 111 | 94 | 29 | 2 | 5 | 11 | 82 | 3 | 104 | 7 | 0 | 13 | 12 | .520 | 1 | 0-0 | 0 | 4.98 | 4.20 |
| 1998 | 2 Tms | | 29 | 29 | 2 | 0 | 160.1 | 749 | 204 | 115 | 102 | 18 | 8 | 8 | 10 | 66 | 2 | 87 | 7 | 4 | 10 | 11 | .476 | 0 | 0-0 | 0 | 6.01 | 5.73 |
| 1999 | StL | NL | 30 | 30 | 2 | 0 | 196.1 | 842 | 197 | 96 | 93 | 16 | 11 | 4 | 11 | 74 | 4 | 119 | 6 | 2 | 9 | 9 | .500 | 1 | 0-0 | 0 | 4.11 | 4.26 |
| 2000 | Tex | AL | 21 | 21 | 0 | 0 | 108.0 | 501 | 151 | 95 | 89 | 16 | 5 | 4 | 4 | 42 | 3 | 49 | 4 | 1 | 2 | 9 | .182 | 0 | 0-0 | 0 | 7.04 | 7.42 |
| 2001 | Tex | AL | 28 | 28 | 1 | 0 | 154.0 | 696 | 189 | 109 | 103 | 23 | 1 | 5 | 6 | 65 | 0 | 104 | 8 | 2 | 11 | 11 | .500 | 0 | 0-0 | 0 | 6.14 | 6.02 |
| 2002 | Bos | AL | 14 | 9 | 1 | 0 | 58.0 | 258 | 70 | 30 | 30 | 7 | 1 | 3 | 6 | 27 | 0 | 32 | 1 | 0 | 4 | 5 | .444 | 1 | 0-0 | 0 | 6.49 | 4.66 |
| 2003 | Col | NL | 33 | 32 | 1 | 0 | 180.1 | 786 | 201 | 108 | 101 | 21 | 4 | 5 | 8 | 61 | 3 | 88 | 0 | 0 | 13 | 11 | .542 | 0 | 0-0 | 0 | 4.80 | 5.04 |
| 2004 | 2 Tms | NL | 27 | 10 | 0 | 5 | 72.2 | 314 | 87 | 50 | 48 | 14 | 4 | 3 | 1 | 21 | 1 | 46 | 1 | 0 | 3 | 3 | .500 | 0 | 0-0 | 0 | 5.59 | 5.94 |
| 2006 | NYM | NL | 45 | 0 | 0 | 10 | 81.0 | 333 | 70 | 33 | 31 | 13 | 2 | 4 | 3 | 21 | 2 | 60 | 1 | 0 | 4 | 1 | .800 | 0 | 0-0 | 3 | 3.27 | 3.44 |
| 2007 | LAA | AL | 61 | 0 | 0 | 20 | 64.1 | 273 | 58 | 31 | 27 | 5 | 2 | 4 | 1 | 23 | 2 | 51 | 1 | 1 | 3 | 1 | .750 | 0 | 0-0 | 8 | 3.19 | 3.78 |
| 2008 | LAA | AL | 54 | 0 | 0 | 9 | 72.0 | 291 | 67 | 24 | 23 | 5 | 4 | 3 | 4 | 16 | 2 | 48 | 3 | 0 | 7 | 1 | .875 | 0 | 0-2 | 12 | 3.07 | 2.88 |
| 2009 | LAA | AL | 63 | 1 | 0 | 9 | 73.0 | 293 | 61 | 22 | 22 | 5 | 4 | 5 | 5 | 22 | 8 | 65 | 7 | 0 | 5 | 1 | .833 | 0 | 0-1 | 20 | 2.81 | 2.71 |
| 2010 | Tex | AL | 64 | 0 | 0 | 7 | 61.2 | 244 | 53 | 20 | 17 | 4 | 5 | 3 | 2 | 15 | 4 | 65 | 0 | 0 | 1 | 2 | .333 | 0 | 1-4 | 14 | 2.63 | 2.48 |
| 2011 | Tex | AL | 61 | 0 | 0 | 17 | 51.0 | 215 | 47 | 17 | 13 | 3 | 4 | 0 | 1 | 11 | 1 | 44 | 0 | 1 | 5 | 5 | .500 | 0 | 2-6 | 16 | 2.64 | 2.29 |
| 2012 | Tor | AL | 62 | 0 | 0 | 11 | 56.2 | 221 | 43 | 13 | 13 | 3 | 1 | 0 | 4 | 15 | 0 | 52 | 3 | 0 | 3 | 4 | .429 | 0 | 2-4 | 16 | 2.38 | 2.06 |
| 2013 | Tor | AL | 50 | 0 | 0 | 21 | 49.0 | 204 | 47 | 24 | 21 | 6 | 3 | 1 | 2 | 15 | 1 | 40 | 0 | 1 | 3 | 4 | .429 | 0 | 0-3 | 8 | 3.83 | 3.86 |
| 98 | Tex | AL | 19 | 19 | 2 | 0 | 103.1 | 493 | 140 | 84 | 75 | 11 | 3 | 6 | 10 | 43 | 1 | 58 | 6 | 1 | 6 | 7 | .462 | 0 | 0-0 | 0 | 6.68 | 6.53 |
| 98 | StL | NL | 10 | 10 | 0 | 0 | 57.0 | 256 | 64 | 31 | 27 | 7 | 5 | 2 | 0 | 23 | 1 | 29 | 1 | 3 | 4 | 4 | .500 | 0 | 0-0 | 0 | 4.85 | 4.26 |
| 04 | Fla | NL | 18 | 8 | 0 | 3 | 58.2 | 260 | 75 | 44 | 42 | 13 | 4 | 3 | 1 | 17 | 1 | 33 | 1 | 0 | 2 | 3 | .400 | 0 | 0-0 | 0 | 6.30 | 6.44 |
| 04 | Hou | NL | 9 | 2 | 0 | 2 | 14.0 | 54 | 12 | 6 | 6 | 1 | 0 | 0 | 0 | 4 | 0 | 13 | 0 | 0 | 1 | 0 | 1.000 | 0 | 0-0 | 0 | 2.89 | 3.86 |
| Postseason | | | 30 | 1 | 0 | 4 | 41.2 | 165 | 34 | 20 | 20 | 3 | 4 | 0 | 1 | 12 | 2 | 31 | 1 | 0 | 2 | 2 | .500 | 0 | 1-2 | 5 | 2.61 | 4.32 |
| 20 ML YEARS | | | 766 | 229 | 11 | 121 | 1915.2 | 8346 | 2037 | 1045 | 960 | 216 | 74 | 65 | 96 | 720 | 45 | 1259 | 60 | 15 | 118 | 98 | .546 | 4 | 7-23 | 106 | 4.63 | 4.51 |

# Miguel Olivo

**Bats:** R **Throws:** R **Pos:** C-21;PH-11;1B-1;DH-1 oh-LEEV-oh **Ht:** 6'0" **Wt:** 230 **Born:** 7/15/1978 **Age:** 35

| | | | BATTING | | | | | | | | | | | | | | | | | | BASERUNNING | | | | AVERAGES | | |
|---|---|---|---|---|---|---|---|---|---|---|---|---|---|---|---|---|---|---|---|---|---|---|---|---|---|---|---|
| Year | Team | Lg | G | AB | H | 2B | 3B | HR | (Hm | Rd) | TB | R | RBI | RC | TBB | IBB | SO | HBP | SH | SF | SB | CS | SB% | GDP | Avg | OBP | Slg |
| 2002 | CWS | AL | 6 | 19 | 4 | 1 | 0 | 1 | (0 | 1) | 8 | 2 | 5 | 4 | 2 | 0 | 5 | 0 | 0 | 0 | 0 | 0 | - | 1 | .211 | .286 | .421 |
| 2003 | CWS | AL | 114 | 317 | 75 | 19 | 1 | 6 | (4 | 2) | 114 | 37 | 27 | 32 | 19 | 0 | 80 | 4 | 4 | 2 | 6 | 4 | .60 | 3 | .237 | .287 | .360 |
| 2004 | 2 Tms | AL | 96 | 301 | 70 | 15 | 4 | 13 | (8 | 5) | 132 | 46 | 40 | 33 | 20 | 2 | 84 | 3 | 4 | 1 | 7 | 6 | .54 | 4 | .233 | .286 | .439 |
| 2005 | 2 Tms | | 91 | 267 | 58 | 11 | 1 | 9 | (5 | 4) | 98 | 30 | 34 | 23 | 8 | 2 | 80 | 3 | 1 | 2 | 7 | 2 | .78 | 7 | .217 | .246 | .367 |
| 2006 | Fla | NL | 127 | 430 | 113 | 22 | 3 | 16 | (7 | 9) | 189 | 52 | 58 | 49 | 9 | 4 | 103 | 7 | 3 | 3 | 2 | 3 | .40 | 9 | .263 | .287 | .440 |
| 2007 | Fla | NL | 122 | 452 | 107 | 20 | 4 | 16 | (11 | 5) | 183 | 43 | 60 | 43 | 14 | 2 | 123 | 2 | 0 | 1 | 3 | 2 | .60 | 13 | .237 | .262 | .405 |
| 2008 | KC | AL | 84 | 306 | 78 | 22 | 0 | 12 | (3 | 9) | 136 | 29 | 41 | 35 | 7 | 2 | 82 | 3 | 0 | 1 | 7 | 0 | 1.00 | 6 | .255 | .278 | .444 |
| 2009 | KC | AL | 114 | 390 | 97 | 15 | 5 | 23 | (10 | 13) | 191 | 51 | 65 | 47 | 19 | 0 | 126 | 5 | 1 | 1 | 5 | 2 | .71 | 10 | .249 | .292 | .490 |
| 2010 | Col | NL | 112 | 394 | 106 | 17 | 6 | 14 | (10 | 4) | 177 | 55 | 58 | 49 | 27 | 5 | 117 | 1 | 2 | 3 | 7 | 4 | .64 | 6 | .269 | .315 | .449 |
| 2011 | Sea | AL | 130 | 477 | 107 | 19 | 1 | 19 | (10 | 9) | 185 | 54 | 62 | 44 | 20 | 2 | 140 | 1 | 1 | 8 | 6 | 5 | .55 | 7 | .224 | .253 | .388 |
| 2012 | Sea | AL | 87 | 315 | 70 | 14 | 0 | 12 | (5 | 7) | 120 | 27 | 29 | 21 | 7 | 0 | 85 | 0 | 1 | 0 | 3 | 6 | .33 | 8 | .222 | .239 | .381 |
| 2013 | Mia | NL | 33 | 74 | 15 | 2 | 0 | 4 | (1 | 3) | 29 | 5 | 9 | 6 | 5 | 0 | 23 | 0 | 0 | 1 | 0 | 0 | - | 2 | .203 | .250 | .392 |
| 04 | CWS | AL | 46 | 141 | 38 | 7 | 2 | 7 | (4 | 3) | 70 | 21 | 26 | 21 | 10 | 1 | 29 | 0 | 4 | 1 | 5 | 4 | .56 | 2 | .270 | .316 | .496 |
| 04 | Sea | AL | 50 | 160 | 32 | 8 | 2 | 6 | (4 | 2) | 62 | 25 | 14 | 12 | 10 | 1 | 55 | 3 | 0 | 0 | 2 | 2 | .50 | 2 | .200 | .260 | .388 |
| 05 | Sea | AL | 54 | 152 | 23 | 4 | 0 | 5 | (4 | 1) | 42 | 14 | 18 | 6 | 4 | 0 | 49 | 0 | 0 | 1 | 1 | 1 | .50 | 3 | .151 | .172 | .276 |
| 05 | SD | NL | 37 | 115 | 35 | 7 | 1 | 4 | (1 | 3) | 56 | 16 | 16 | 17 | 4 | 2 | 31 | 3 | 1 | 1 | 6 | 1 | .86 | 4 | .304 | .341 | .487 |
| Postseason | | | 1 | 1 | 0 | 0 | 0 | 0 | (0 | 0) | 0 | 0 | 0 | 0 | 0 | 0 | 0 | 0 | 0 | 0 | 0 | 0 | - | 1 | .000 | .000 | .000 |
| 12 ML YEARS | | | 1116 | 3742 | 900 | 177 | 25 | 145 | (74 | 71) | 1562 | 431 | 488 | 386 | 157 | 19 | 1048 | 29 | 17 | 23 | 53 | 34 | .61 | 76 | .241 | .275 | .417 |

# Edgar Olmos

**Pitches:** L **Bats:** L **Pos:** RP-5 OAL-moase **Ht:** 6'4" **Wt:** 215 **Born:** 4/12/1990 **Age:** 24

| | | | HOW MUCH HE PITCHED | | | | | | WHAT HE GAVE UP | | | | | | | | | | | | THE RESULTS | | | | | | | |
|---|---|---|---|---|---|---|---|---|---|---|---|---|---|---|---|---|---|---|---|---|---|---|---|---|---|---|---|---|
| Year | Team | Lg | G | GS | CG | GF | IP | BFP | H | R | ER | HR | SH | SF | HB | TBB | IBB | SO | WP | Bk | W | L | Pct | Sh | Sv-Op | Hld | ERC | ERA |
| 2009 | Mrlns | R | 2 | 2 | 0 | 0 | 5.0 | 15 | 1 | 0 | 0 | 0 | 0 | 0 | 0 | 2 | 0 | 5 | 0 | 0 | 0 | 0 | - | 0 | 0-- | - | 0.60 | 0.00 |
| 2009 | Jmstwn | A- | 1 | 1 | 0 | 0 | 4.0 | 17 | 3 | 1 | 1 | 0 | 0 | 1 | 0 | 2 | 0 | 4 | 1 | 0 | 0 | 0 | - | 0 | 0-- | - | 2.40 | 2.25 |
| 2010 | Grnsbr | A | 25 | 25 | 0 | 0 | 117.1 | 533 | 122 | 68 | 57 | 9 | 5 | 2 | 16 | 59 | 0 | 108 | 7 | 2 | 3 | 9 | .250 | 0 | 0-- | - | 5.12 | 4.37 |
| 2011 | Jupiter | A+ | 28 | 28 | 0 | 0 | 127.2 | 627 | 167 | 110 | 94 | 13 | 3 | 8 | 10 | 81 | 2 | 101 | 16 | 2 | 4 | 17 | .190 | 0 | 0-- | - | 7.22 | 6.63 |

| HOW MUCH HE PITCHED | | | | | | | | | WHAT HE GAVE UP | | | | | | | | | | | | THE RESULTS | | | | | | | |
|---|---|---|---|---|---|---|---|---|---|---|---|---|---|---|---|---|---|---|---|---|---|---|---|---|---|---|---|---|
| Year | Team | Lg | G | GS | CG | GF | IP | BFP | H | R | ER | HR | SH | SF | HB | TBB | IBB | SO | WP | Bk | W | L | Pct | Sh | Sv-Op | Hld | ERC | ERA |
| 2012 | Jupiter | A+ | 24 | 13 | 0 | 0 | 89.1 | 394 | 83 | 50 | 43 | 5 | 0 | 4 | 7 | 48 | 0 | 78 | 10 | 0 | 1 | 5 | .167 | 0 | 0- - | - | 4.23 | 4.33 |
| 2012 | Jaxnvl | AA | 9 | 1 | 0 | 3 | 16.2 | 72 | 8 | 1 | 1 | 0 | 1 | 0 | 0 | 16 | 0 | 13 | 2 | 0 | 0 | 1 | .000 | 0 | 0- - | - | 2.66 | 0.54 |
| 2013 | Jaxnvl | AA | 38 | 0 | 0 | 8 | 50.1 | 222 | 47 | 20 | 14 | 1 | 1 | 0 | 1 | 27 | 0 | 41 | 6 | 0 | 4 | 2 | .667 | 0 | 1- - | - | 3.71 | 2.50 |
| 2013 | Mia | NL | 5 | 0 | 0 | 2 | 5.0 | 24 | 7 | 9 | 4 | 2 | 1 | 0 | 0 | 3 | 1 | 2 | 0 | 0 | 0 | 1 | .000 | 0 | 0-0 | 0 | 9.81 | 7.20 |

# Brian Omogrosso

**Pitches:** R **Bats:** R **Pos:** RP-12 oh-muh-GRAH-so **Ht:** 6'4" **Wt:** 240 **Born:** 4/26/1984 **Age:** 30

| HOW MUCH HE PITCHED | | | | | | | | | WHAT HE GAVE UP | | | | | | | | | | | | THE RESULTS | | | | | | | |
|---|---|---|---|---|---|---|---|---|---|---|---|---|---|---|---|---|---|---|---|---|---|---|---|---|---|---|---|---|
| Year | Team | Lg | G | GS | CG | GF | IP | BFP | H | R | ER | HR | SH | SF | HB | TBB | IBB | SO | WP | Bk | W | L | Pct | Sh | Sv-Op | Hld | ERC | ERA |
| 2009 | Brham | AA | 13 | 13 | 0 | 0 | 73.0 | 320 | 67 | 40 | 34 | 4 | 0 | 1 | 6 | 40 | 0 | 64 | 4 | 1 | 7 | 2 | .778 | 0 | 0- - | - | 4.24 | 4.19 |
| 2009 | Charltt | AAA | 4 | 0 | 0 | 1 | 5.2 | 32 | 12 | 10 | 10 | 2 | 0 | 1 | 0 | 3 | 1 | 6 | 2 | 0 | 0 | 0 | - | 0 | 0- - | - | 13.89 | 15.88 |
| 2010 | Bristol | R | 2 | 0 | 0 | 0 | 2.0 | 8 | 1 | 0 | 0 | 0 | 0 | 0 | 0 | 2 | 0 | 2 | 0 | 0 | 0 | 0 | - | 0 | 0- - | - | 3.21 | 0.00 |
| 2010 | Brham | AA | 3 | 0 | 0 | 0 | 3.0 | 12 | 2 | 1 | 1 | 0 | 0 | 0 | 0 | 1 | 0 | 3 | 0 | 0 | 0 | 1 | .000 | 0 | 0- - | - | 1.57 | 3.00 |
| 2011 | Brham | AA | 31 | 0 | 0 | 15 | 43.0 | 184 | 36 | 18 | 12 | 2 | 4 | 1 | 3 | 16 | 1 | 53 | 7 | 0 | 0 | 2 | .000 | 0 | 2- - | - | 2.89 | 2.51 |
| 2011 | Charltt | AAA | 11 | 1 | 0 | 0 | 22.1 | 97 | 24 | 11 | 10 | 1 | 2 | 2 | 0 | 8 | 0 | 19 | 0 | 0 | 1 | 1 | .500 | 0 | 0- - | - | 3.92 | 4.03 |
| 2012 | Charltt | AAA | 33 | 0 | 0 | 21 | 47.1 | 196 | 43 | 25 | 24 | 3 | 2 | 1 | 2 | 12 | 0 | 59 | 3 | 0 | 0 | 2 | .000 | 0 | 9- - | - | 2.93 | 4.56 |
| 2013 | Charltt | AAA | 10 | 0 | 0 | 6 | 14.2 | 67 | 20 | 8 | 8 | 2 | 2 | 2 | 0 | 4 | 1 | 14 | 0 | 0 | 0 | 1 | .000 | 0 | 2- - | - | 5.79 | 4.91 |
| 2012 | CWS | AL | 17 | 0 | 0 | 1 | 21.0 | 90 | 20 | 6 | 6 | 3 | 0 | 0 | 0 | 9 | 0 | 18 | 0 | 0 | 0 | 0 | - | 0 | 0-1 | 1 | 4.23 | 2.57 |
| 2013 | CWS | AL | 12 | 0 | 0 | 6 | 16.1 | 84 | 28 | 18 | 17 | 2 | 0 | 0 | 1 | 9 | 1 | 16 | 0 | 0 | 0 | 2 | .000 | 0 | 0-0 | 0 | 9.71 | 9.37 |
| 2 ML YEARS | | | 29 | 0 | 0 | 7 | 37.1 | 174 | 48 | 24 | 23 | 5 | 0 | 0 | 1 | 18 | 1 | 34 | 0 | 0 | 0 | 2 | .000 | 0 | 0-1 | 1 | 6.49 | 5.54 |

# Logan Ondrusek

**Pitches:** R **Bats:** R **Pos:** RP-52 ahn-DREW-seck **Ht:** 6'8" **Wt:** 230 **Born:** 2/13/1985 **Age:** 29

| HOW MUCH HE PITCHED | | | | | | | | | WHAT HE GAVE UP | | | | | | | | | | | | THE RESULTS | | | | | | | |
|---|---|---|---|---|---|---|---|---|---|---|---|---|---|---|---|---|---|---|---|---|---|---|---|---|---|---|---|---|
| Year | Team | Lg | G | GS | CG | GF | IP | BFP | H | R | ER | HR | SH | SF | HB | TBB | IBB | SO | WP | Bk | W | L | Pct | Sh | Sv-Op | Hld | ERC | ERA |
| 2013 | Pnscla* | AA | 3 | 0 | 0 | 2 | 2.1 | 8 | 1 | 0 | 0 | 0 | 0 | 0 | 0 | 0 | 0 | 1 | 0 | 0 | 0 | 0 | - | 0 | 0- - | - | 0.40 | 0.00 |
| 2013 | Lsvlle* | AAA | 6 | 0 | 0 | 5 | 8.0 | 29 | 4 | 0 | 0 | 0 | 0 | 0 | 0 | 2 | 0 | 6 | 0 | 0 | 0 | 0 | - | 0 | 1- - | - | 0.98 | 0.00 |
| 2010 | Cin | NL | 60 | 0 | 0 | 11 | 58.2 | 240 | 49 | 25 | 24 | 7 | 1 | 1 | 0 | 20 | 1 | 39 | 2 | 0 | 5 | 0 | 1.000 | 0 | 0-2 | 6 | 3.08 | 3.68 |
| 2011 | Cin | NL | 66 | 0 | 0 | 14 | 61.1 | 268 | 55 | 25 | 22 | 6 | 3 | 4 | 2 | 28 | 7 | 41 | 6 | 0 | 5 | 5 | .500 | 0 | 0-3 | 14 | 3.58 | 3.23 |
| 2012 | Cin | NL | 63 | 0 | 0 | 20 | 54.2 | 243 | 51 | 23 | 21 | 8 | 1 | 1 | 3 | 31 | 4 | 39 | 5 | 0 | 5 | 2 | .714 | 0 | 2-4 | 13 | 4.81 | 3.46 |
| 2013 | Cin | NL | 52 | 0 | 0 | 18 | 55.0 | 233 | 53 | 26 | 25 | 8 | 4 | 0 | 1 | 16 | 1 | 53 | 5 | 1 | 3 | 1 | .750 | 0 | 0-1 | 5 | 3.75 | 4.09 |
| Postseason | | | 2 | 0 | 0 | 0 | 2.0 | 9 | 0 | 0 | 0 | 0 | 0 | 0 | 1 | 1 | 0 | 0 | 0 | 0 | 0 | 0 | - | 0 | 0-0 | 1 | 0.84 | 0.00 |
| 4 ML YEARS | | | 241 | 0 | 0 | 63 | 229.2 | 984 | 208 | 99 | 92 | 29 | 9 | 6 | 6 | 95 | 13 | 172 | 18 | 1 | 18 | 8 | .692 | 0 | 2-10 | 38 | 3.78 | 3.61 |

# Pete Orr

**Bats:** L **Throws:** R **Pos:** PH-11;3B-2;LF-2 **Ht:** 6'1" **Wt:** 195 **Born:** 6/8/1979 **Age:** 35

| BATTING | | | | | | | | | | | | | | | | | | | | | BASERUNNING | | | | AVERAGES | | |
|---|---|---|---|---|---|---|---|---|---|---|---|---|---|---|---|---|---|---|---|---|---|---|---|---|---|---|---|
| Year | Team | Lg | G | AB | H | 2B | 3B | HR | (Hm | Rd) | TB | R | RBI | RC | TBB | IBB | SO | HBP | SH | SF | SB | CS | SB% | GDP | Avg | OBP | Slg |
| 2013 | LV* | AAA | 95 | 325 | 84 | 17 | 6 | 4 | (- | -) | 125 | 40 | 31 | 37 | 17 | 1 | 61 | 3 | 5 | 2 | 9 | 7 | .56 | 3 | .258 | .300 | .385 |
| 2005 | Atl | NL | 112 | 150 | 45 | 8 | 1 | 1 | (0 | 1) | 58 | 32 | 8 | 18 | 6 | 0 | 23 | 1 | 5 | 0 | 7 | 1 | .88 | 2 | .300 | .331 | .387 |
| 2006 | Atl | NL | 102 | 154 | 39 | 3 | 4 | 1 | (1 | 0) | 53 | 22 | 8 | 16 | 5 | 1 | 30 | 0 | 5 | 0 | 2 | 4 | .33 | 1 | .253 | .277 | .344 |
| 2007 | Atl | NL | 57 | 65 | 13 | 1 | 0 | 0 | (0 | 0) | 14 | 11 | 2 | 3 | 3 | 0 | 14 | 0 | 1 | 0 | 1 | 0 | 1.00 | 1 | .200 | .235 | .215 |
| 2008 | Was | NL | 49 | 75 | 19 | 2 | 1 | 0 | (0 | 0) | 23 | 10 | 7 | 6 | 2 | 0 | 16 | 1 | 1 | 0 | 1 | 0 | 1.00 | 0 | .253 | .282 | .307 |
| 2009 | Was | NL | 27 | 75 | 19 | 2 | 1 | 1 | (0 | 1) | 26 | 5 | 10 | 8 | 3 | 0 | 15 | 0 | 0 | 3 | 2 | 1 | .67 | 0 | .253 | .272 | .347 |
| 2011 | Phi | NL | 46 | 96 | 21 | 3 | 0 | 0 | (0 | 0) | 24 | 7 | 4 | 8 | 6 | 2 | 19 | 2 | 0 | 0 | 3 | 0 | 1.00 | 0 | .219 | .279 | .250 |
| 2012 | Phi | NL | 35 | 54 | 17 | 5 | 1 | 0 | (0 | 0) | 24 | 6 | 7 | 9 | 1 | 0 | 18 | 0 | 2 | 0 | 3 | 1 | .75 | 0 | .315 | .327 | .444 |
| 2013 | Phi | NL | 15 | 20 | 4 | 0 | 0 | 0 | (0 | 0) | 4 | 1 | 0 | 1 | 2 | 0 | 8 | 0 | 0 | 0 | 0 | 0 | - | 0 | .200 | .273 | .200 |
| Postseason | | | 3 | 2 | 0 | 0 | 0 | 0 | (0 | 0) | 0 | 0 | 0 | 0 | 0 | 0 | 0 | 0 | 0 | 0 | 0 | 0 | - | 0 | .000 | .000 | .000 |
| 8 ML YEARS | | | 443 | 689 | 177 | 24 | 8 | 3 | (1 | 2) | 226 | 94 | 46 | 69 | 28 | 3 | 143 | 4 | 14 | 3 | 19 | 7 | .73 | 4 | .257 | .289 | .328 |

# Jose Ortega

**Pitches:** R **Bats:** R **Pos:** RP-11 **Ht:** 5'11" **Wt:** 185 **Born:** 10/12/1988 **Age:** 25

| HOW MUCH HE PITCHED | | | | | | | | | WHAT HE GAVE UP | | | | | | | | | | | | THE RESULTS | | | | | | | |
|---|---|---|---|---|---|---|---|---|---|---|---|---|---|---|---|---|---|---|---|---|---|---|---|---|---|---|---|---|
| Year | Team | Lg | G | GS | CG | GF | IP | BFP | H | R | ER | HR | SH | SF | HB | TBB | IBB | SO | WP | Bk | W | L | Pct | Sh | Sv-Op | Hld | ERC | ERA |
| 2009 | Oneont | A- | 25 | 0 | 0 | 13 | 34.0 | 152 | 28 | 19 | 15 | 2 | 1 | 0 | 1 | 23 | 2 | 32 | 3 | 0 | 2 | 2 | .500 | 0 | 1- - | - | 3.83 | 3.97 |
| 2010 | WMich | A | 18 | 0 | 0 | 11 | 25.2 | 120 | 28 | 14 | 13 | 1 | 1 | 0 | 0 | 17 | 1 | 22 | 2 | 0 | 0 | 3 | .000 | 0 | 1- - | - | 5.05 | 4.56 |
| 2010 | Lkland | A+ | 10 | 0 | 0 | 6 | 19.0 | 74 | 14 | 2 | 2 | 0 | 0 | 0 | 1 | 7 | 1 | 20 | 1 | 0 | 2 | 1 | .667 | 0 | 0- - | - | 2.19 | 0.95 |
| 2010 | Erie | AA | 15 | 1 | 0 | 4 | 23.2 | 100 | 22 | 8 | 8 | 2 | 0 | 1 | 1 | 7 | 1 | 19 | 1 | 0 | 1 | 0 | 1.000 | 0 | 0- - | - | 3.25 | 3.04 |
| 2011 | Toledo | AAA | 33 | 0 | 0 | 11 | 50.0 | 233 | 61 | 41 | 35 | 7 | 1 | 5 | 3 | 27 | 1 | 44 | 2 | 0 | 1 | 3 | .250 | 0 | 0- - | - | 6.57 | 6.30 |
| 2012 | Toledo | AAA | 45 | 0 | 0 | 13 | 62.2 | 308 | 76 | 44 | 40 | 4 | 8 | 3 | 2 | 51 | 4 | 68 | 12 | 0 | 5 | 8 | .385 | 0 | 1- - | - | 6.78 | 5.74 |
| 2013 | Toledo | AAA | 40 | 0 | 0 | 14 | 48.1 | 203 | 28 | 13 | 10 | 2 | 1 | 2 | 1 | 33 | 2 | 56 | 3 | 0 | 4 | 3 | .571 | 0 | 4- - | - | 2.52 | 1.86 |
| 2012 | Det | AL | 2 | 0 | 0 | 0 | 2.2 | 13 | 3 | 1 | 1 | 1 | 0 | 0 | 0 | 1 | 0 | 4 | 0 | 0 | 0 | 0 | - | 0 | 0-1 | 0 | 6.04 | 3.38 |
| 2013 | Det | AL | 11 | 0 | 0 | 5 | 11.2 | 52 | 10 | 5 | 5 | 2 | 1 | 0 | 1 | 6 | 1 | 10 | 0 | 0 | 0 | 2 | .000 | 0 | 0-1 | 2 | 4.34 | 3.86 |
| 2 ML YEARS | | | 13 | 0 | 0 | 5 | 14.1 | 65 | 13 | 6 | 6 | 3 | 1 | 0 | 1 | 7 | 1 | 14 | 0 | 0 | 0 | 2 | .000 | 0 | 0-2 | 2 | 4.67 | 3.77 |

# David Ortiz

**Bats:** L **Throws:** L **Pos:** DH-129;1B-6;PH-2 **Ht:** 6'4" **Wt:** 250 **Born:** 11/18/1975 **Age:** 38

| BATTING | | | | | | | | | | | | | | | | | | | | | BASERUNNING | | | | AVERAGES | | |
|---|---|---|---|---|---|---|---|---|---|---|---|---|---|---|---|---|---|---|---|---|---|---|---|---|---|---|---|
| Year | Team | Lg | G | AB | H | 2B | 3B | HR | (Hm | Rd) | TB | R | RBI | RC | TBB | IBB | SO | HBP | SH | SF | SB | CS | SB% | GDP | Avg | OBP | Slg |
| 2013 | Pwtckt* | AAA | 6 | 18 | 4 | 0 | 0 | 1 | (- | -) | 7 | 3 | 4 | 1 | 0 | 0 | 6 | 0 | 0 | 0 | 0 | 0 | - | 2 | .222 | .222 | .389 |
| 1997 | Min | AL | 15 | 49 | 16 | 3 | 0 | 1 | (0 | 1) | 22 | 10 | 6 | 7 | 2 | 0 | 19 | 0 | 0 | 0 | 0 | 0 | - | 1 | .327 | .353 | .449 |
| 1998 | Min | AL | 86 | 278 | 77 | 20 | 0 | 9 | (2 | 7) | 124 | 47 | 46 | 46 | 39 | 3 | 72 | 5 | 0 | 4 | 1 | 0 | 1.00 | 8 | .277 | .371 | .446 |
| 1999 | Min | AL | 10 | 20 | 0 | 0 | 0 | 0 | (0 | 0) | 0 | 1 | 0 | 0 | 5 | 0 | 12 | 0 | 0 | 0 | 0 | 0 | - | 2 | .000 | .200 | .000 |
| 2000 | Min | AL | 130 | 415 | 117 | 36 | 1 | 10 | (7 | 3) | 185 | 59 | 63 | 66 | 57 | 2 | 81 | 0 | 0 | 6 | 1 | 0 | 1.00 | 13 | .282 | .364 | .446 |
| 2001 | Min | AL | 89 | 303 | 71 | 17 | 1 | 18 | (6 | 12) | 144 | 46 | 48 | 46 | 40 | 8 | 68 | 1 | 1 | 2 | 1 | 0 | 1.00 | 6 | .234 | .324 | .475 |

| Year | Team | Lg | G | AB | H | 2B | 3B | HR | (Hm | Rd) | TB | R | RBI | RC | TBB | IBB | SO | HBP | SH | SF | SB | CS | SB% | GDP | Avg | OBP | Slg |
|---|---|---|---|---|---|---|---|---|---|---|---|---|---|---|---|---|---|---|---|---|---|---|---|---|---|---|---|
| | | | BATTING | | | | | | | | | | | | | | | | | | BASERUNNING | | | | AVERAGES | | |
| 2002 | Min | AL | 125 | 412 | 112 | 32 | 1 | 20 | (5 | 15) | 206 | 52 | 75 | 62 | 43 | 0 | 87 | 3 | 0 | 8 | 1 | 2 | .33 | 5 | .272 | .339 | .500 |
| 2003 | Bos | AL | 128 | 448 | 129 | 39 | 2 | 31 | (17 | 14) | 265 | 79 | 101 | 80 | 58 | 8 | 83 | 1 | 0 | 2 | 0 | 0 | - | 9 | .288 | .369 | .592 |
| 2004 | Bos | AL | 150 | 582 | 175 | 47 | 3 | 41 | (17 | **24)** | 351 | 94 | 139 | **127** | 75 | 8 | 133 | 4 | 0 | 8 | 0 | 0 | - | 12 | .301 | .380 | .603 |
| 2005 | Bos | AL | 159 | 601 | 180 | 40 | 1 | 47 | (20 | **27)** | 363 | 119 | **148** | 137 | 102 | 9 | 124 | 1 | 0 | 9 | 1 | 0 | 1.00 | 13 | .300 | .397 | .604 |
| 2006 | Bos | AL | 151 | 558 | 160 | 29 | 2 | **54** | (22 | **32)** | **355** | 115 | **137** | 129 | **119** | 23 | 117 | 4 | 0 | 5 | 1 | 0 | 1.00 | 12 | .287 | .413 | .636 |
| 2007 | Bos | AL | 149 | 549 | 182 | 52 | 1 | 35 | (16 | 19) | 341 | 116 | 117 | 138 | **111** | 12 | 103 | 4 | 0 | 3 | 3 | 1 | .75 | 16 | .332 | **.445** | .621 |
| 2008 | Bos | AL | 109 | 416 | 110 | 30 | 1 | 23 | (12 | 11) | 211 | 74 | 89 | 82 | 70 | 12 | 74 | 1 | 1 | 3 | 1 | 0 | 1.00 | 11 | .264 | .369 | .507 |
| 2009 | Bos | AL | 150 | 541 | 129 | 35 | 1 | 28 | (18 | 10) | 250 | 77 | 99 | 79 | 74 | 5 | 134 | 5 | 0 | 7 | 0 | 2 | .00 | 9 | .238 | .332 | .462 |
| 2010 | Bos | AL | 145 | 518 | 140 | 36 | 1 | 32 | (15 | 17) | 274 | 86 | 102 | 94 | 82 | 14 | 145 | 2 | 0 | 4 | 0 | 1 | .00 | 12 | .270 | .370 | .529 |
| 2011 | Bos | AL | 146 | 525 | 162 | 40 | 1 | 29 | (13 | 16) | 291 | 84 | 96 | 97 | 78 | 12 | 83 | 1 | 0 | 1 | 1 | 1 | .50 | 24 | .309 | .398 | .554 |
| 2012 | Bos | AL | 90 | 324 | 103 | 26 | 0 | 23 | (13 | 10) | 198 | 65 | 60 | 75 | 56 | 13 | 51 | 0 | 0 | 3 | 0 | 1 | .00 | 6 | .318 | .415 | .611 |
| 2013 | Bos | AL | 137 | 518 | 160 | 38 | 2 | 30 | (12 | 18) | 292 | 84 | 103 | 102 | 76 | **27** | 88 | 1 | 0 | 5 | 4 | 0 | 1.00 | 21 | .309 | .395 | .564 |
| Postseason | | | 66 | 244 | 69 | 18 | 2 | 12 | (7 | 5) | 127 | 39 | 47 | 51 | 41 | 7 | 64 | 2 | 0 | 2 | 0 | 1 | .00 | 3 | .283 | .388 | .520 |
| 17 ML YEARS | | | 1969 | 7057 | 2023 | 520 | 18 | 431 | (195 | 236) | 3872 | 1208 | 1429 | 1367 | 1087 | 156 | 1474 | 33 | 2 | 70 | 15 | 8 | .65 | 180 | .287 | .381 | .549 |

## Joe Ortiz

**Pitches:** L **Bats:** L **Pos:** RP-32 **Ht:** 5'7" **Wt:** 175 **Born:** 8/13/1990 **Age:** 23

| Year | Team | Lg | G | GS | CG | GF | IP | BFP | H | R | ER | HR | SH | SF | HB | TBB | IBB | SO | WP | Bk | W | L | Pct | Sh | Sv-Op | Hld | ERC | ERA |
|---|---|---|---|---|---|---|---|---|---|---|---|---|---|---|---|---|---|---|---|---|---|---|---|---|---|---|---|---|
| | | | HOW MUCH HE PITCHED | | | | | | WHAT HE GAVE UP | | | | | | | | | | | | THE RESULTS | | | | | | | |
| 2009 | Hkry | A | 4 | 0 | 0 | 2 | 6.0 | 36 | 11 | 5 | 4 | 1 | 0 | 0 | 0 | 4 | 0 | 6 | 1 | 0 | 0 | 1 | .000 | 0 | 0- - | - | 10.05 | 6.00 |
| 2009 | Spkane | A- | 18 | 0 | 0 | 4 | 36.2 | 144 | 32 | 12 | 12 | 4 | 1 | 2 | 1 | 5 | 0 | 38 | 0 | 2 | 2 | 0 | 1.000 | 0 | 0- - | - | 2.61 | 2.95 |
| 2010 | Hkry | A | 26 | 0 | 0 | 13 | 42.0 | 163 | 30 | 9 | 7 | 2 | 0 | 0 | 0 | 5 | 0 | 59 | 4 | 0 | 4 | 1 | .800 | 0 | 5- - | - | 1.42 | 1.50 |
| 2010 | Bkrsfld | A+ | 2 | 0 | 0 | 1 | 2.1 | 11 | 3 | 1 | 1 | 0 | 1 | 0 | 0 | 1 | 1 | 4 | 0 | 0 | 0 | 0 | - | 0 | 0- - | - | 4.14 | 3.86 |
| 2011 | MrtlBh | A+ | 40 | 0 | 0 | 15 | 67.0 | 270 | 54 | 18 | 16 | 4 | 5 | 1 | 0 | 14 | 1 | 55 | 3 | 0 | 5 | 5 | .500 | 0 | 5- - | - | 2.06 | 2.15 |
| 2012 | Frisco | AA | 27 | 0 | 0 | 14 | 30.2 | 123 | 26 | 10 | 8 | 2 | 0 | 2 | 0 | 6 | 1 | 29 | 1 | 2 | 1 | 2 | .333 | 0 | 4- - | - | 2.24 | 2.35 |
| 2012 | RdRck | AAA | 24 | 0 | 0 | 9 | 32.0 | 126 | 31 | 7 | 7 | 6 | 1 | 0 | 0 | 3 | 0 | 23 | 0 | 0 | 1 | 1 | .500 | 0 | 2- - | - | 3.31 | 1.97 |
| 2013 | RdRck | AAA | 19 | 0 | 0 | 7 | 26.1 | 108 | 24 | 9 | 9 | 2 | 1 | 1 | 0 | 8 | 1 | 29 | 4 | 1 | 2 | 1 | .667 | 0 | 2- - | - | 3.05 | 3.08 |
| 2013 | Tex | AL | 32 | 0 | 0 | 10 | 44.2 | 187 | 46 | 26 | 21 | 5 | 2 | 4 | 0 | 10 | 2 | 27 | 0 | 0 | 2 | 2 | .500 | 0 | 0-0 | 2 | 3.55 | 4.23 |

## Ramon Ortiz

**Pitches:** R **Bats:** R **Pos:** SP-4; RP-3 **Ht:** 6'0" **Wt:** 175 **Born:** 5/23/1973 **Age:** 41

| Year | Team | Lg | G | GS | CG | GF | IP | BFP | H | R | ER | HR | SH | SF | HB | TBB | IBB | SO | WP | Bk | W | L | Pct | Sh | Sv-Op | Hld | ERC | ERA |
|---|---|---|---|---|---|---|---|---|---|---|---|---|---|---|---|---|---|---|---|---|---|---|---|---|---|---|---|---|
| | | | HOW MUCH HE PITCHED | | | | | | WHAT HE GAVE UP | | | | | | | | | | | | THE RESULTS | | | | | | | |
| 2013 | Buffalo* | AAA | 4 | 3 | 0 | 0 | 20.2 | 85 | 15 | 5 | 5 | 4 | 0 | 0 | 4 | 7 | 0 | 13 | 1 | 0 | 2 | 0 | 1.000 | 0 | 0- - | - | 3.79 | 2.18 |
| 1999 | LAA | AL | 9 | 9 | 0 | 0 | 48.1 | 218 | 50 | 35 | 35 | 7 | 0 | 2 | 2 | 25 | 0 | 44 | 2 | 2 | 2 | 3 | .400 | 0 | 0-0 | 0 | 5.23 | 6.52 |
| 2000 | LAA | AL | 18 | 18 | 2 | 0 | 111.1 | 472 | 96 | 69 | 63 | 18 | 4 | 4 | 2 | 55 | 0 | 73 | 7 | 4 | 8 | 6 | .571 | 0 | 0-0 | 0 | 4.24 | 5.09 |
| 2001 | LAA | AL | 32 | 32 | 2 | 0 | 208.2 | 916 | 223 | 114 | 101 | 25 | 9 | 6 | 12 | 76 | 6 | 135 | 7 | 0 | 13 | 11 | .542 | 0 | 0-0 | 0 | 4.65 | 4.36 |
| 2002 | LAA | AL | 32 | 32 | 4 | 0 | 217.1 | 896 | 188 | 97 | 91 | **40** | 2 | 5 | 5 | 68 | 0 | 162 | 7 | **3** | 15 | 9 | .625 | 1 | 0-0 | 0 | 3.64 | 3.77 |
| 2003 | LAA | AL | 32 | 32 | 1 | 0 | 180.0 | 814 | 209 | 121 | 104 | 28 | 3 | 7 | 12 | 63 | 0 | 94 | 4 | 0 | 16 | 13 | .552 | 0 | 0-0 | 0 | 5.44 | 5.20 |
| 2004 | LAA | AL | 34 | 14 | 0 | 13 | 128.0 | 543 | 139 | 64 | 63 | 18 | 2 | 3 | 4 | 38 | 4 | 82 | 5 | 3 | 5 | 7 | .417 | 0 | 0-0 | 0 | 4.61 | 4.43 |
| 2005 | Cin | NL | 30 | 30 | 1 | 0 | 171.1 | 755 | 206 | 110 | 102 | 34 | 7 | 8 | 7 | 51 | 1 | 96 | 4 | 1 | 9 | 11 | .450 | 0 | 0-0 | 0 | 5.78 | 5.36 |
| 2006 | Was | NL | 33 | 33 | 0 | 0 | 190.2 | 871 | 230 | 127 | 118 | 31 | 10 | 4 | 18 | 64 | 14 | 104 | 4 | **3** | 11 | **16** | .407 | 0 | 0-0 | 0 | 5.71 | 5.57 |
| 2007 | 2 Tms | | 38 | 10 | 0 | 15 | 104.0 | 459 | 127 | 65 | 63 | 16 | 1 | 5 | 6 | 22 | 1 | 51 | 2 | 1 | 5 | 4 | .556 | 0 | 0-0 | 0 | 5.17 | 5.45 |
| 2010 | LAD | NL | 16 | 2 | 0 | 3 | 30.0 | 135 | 33 | 22 | 21 | 5 | 3 | 1 | 0 | 16 | 2 | 21 | 1 | 1 | 1 | 2 | .333 | 0 | 0-0 | 1 | 5.64 | 6.30 |
| 2011 | ChC | NL | 22 | 2 | 0 | 5 | 33.1 | 141 | 31 | 20 | 18 | 6 | 1 | 2 | 0 | 11 | 2 | 25 | 1 | 0 | 1 | 2 | .333 | 0 | 0-0 | 1 | 3.81 | 4.86 |
| 2013 | Tor | AL | 7 | 4 | 0 | 1 | 25.1 | 117 | 34 | 17 | 17 | 7 | 1 | 3 | 1 | 11 | 2 | 8 | 2 | 0 | 1 | 2 | .333 | 0 | 0-0 | 0 | 7.92 | 6.04 |
| 07 | Min | AL | 28 | 10 | 0 | 11 | 91.0 | 400 | 112 | 54 | 52 | 12 | 0 | 4 | 5 | 15 | 1 | 44 | 2 | 1 | 4 | 4 | .500 | 0 | 0-0 | 0 | 4.83 | 5.14 |
| 07 | Col | NL | 10 | 0 | 0 | 4 | 13.0 | 59 | 15 | 11 | 11 | 4 | 1 | 1 | 1 | 7 | 0 | 7 | 0 | 0 | 1 | 0 | 1.000 | 0 | 0-0 | 0 | 7.81 | 7.62 |
| Postseason | | | 4 | 3 | 0 | 1 | 15.0 | 73 | 20 | 14 | 14 | 2 | 1 | 2 | 1 | 10 | 2 | 7 | 1 | 0 | 2 | 0 | 1.000 | 0 | 0-0 | 0 | 7.66 | 8.40 |
| 12 ML YEARS | | | 303 | 218 | 10 | 37 | 1448.1 | 6337 | 1566 | 861 | 796 | 235 | 43 | 50 | 69 | 500 | 32 | 895 | 46 | 18 | 87 | 86 | .503 | 1 | 0-0 | 2 | 4.93 | 4.95 |

## Sean O'Sullivan

**Pitches:** R **Bats:** R **Pos:** RP-4; SP-3 **Ht:** 6'1" **Wt:** 240 **Born:** 9/1/1987 **Age:** 26

| Year | Team | Lg | G | GS | CG | GF | IP | BFP | H | R | ER | HR | SH | SF | HB | TBB | IBB | SO | WP | Bk | W | L | Pct | Sh | Sv-Op | Hld | ERC | ERA |
|---|---|---|---|---|---|---|---|---|---|---|---|---|---|---|---|---|---|---|---|---|---|---|---|---|---|---|---|---|
| | | | HOW MUCH HE PITCHED | | | | | | WHAT HE GAVE UP | | | | | | | | | | | | THE RESULTS | | | | | | | |
| 2013 | Tucsn* | AAA | 20 | 20 | 0 | 0 | 115.0 | 501 | 130 | 55 | 49 | 7 | 5 | 0 | 5 | 31 | 0 | 99 | 2 | 0 | 8 | 5 | .615 | 0 | 0- - | - | 4.17 | 3.83 |
| 2009 | LAA | AL | 12 | 10 | 0 | 1 | 51.2 | 227 | 60 | 34 | 34 | 12 | 2 | 4 | 1 | 16 | 1 | 29 | 1 | 0 | 4 | 2 | .667 | 0 | 0-0 | 0 | 5.66 | 5.92 |
| 2010 | 2 Tms | AL | 19 | 14 | 0 | 3 | 83.2 | 368 | 90 | 53 | 51 | 15 | 0 | 3 | 1 | 31 | 2 | 43 | 4 | 2 | 4 | 6 | .400 | 0 | 0-0 | 0 | 4.93 | 5.49 |
| 2011 | KC | AL | 12 | 10 | 0 | 1 | 58.1 | 273 | 78 | 52 | 47 | 10 | 3 | 4 | 2 | 26 | 1 | 19 | 3 | 0 | 2 | 6 | .250 | 0 | 0-1 | 0 | 7.03 | 7.25 |
| 2013 | SD | NL | 7 | 3 | 0 | 2 | 25.0 | 118 | 31 | 12 | 11 | 0 | 1 | 2 | 1 | 14 | 1 | 12 | 0 | 0 | 0 | 2 | .000 | 0 | 0-0 | 0 | 5.40 | 3.96 |
| 10 | LAA | AL | 5 | 1 | 0 | 2 | 13.0 | 49 | 7 | 3 | 3 | 1 | 0 | 0 | 0 | 4 | 2 | 6 | 0 | 0 | 1 | 0 | 1.000 | 0 | 0-0 | 0 | 1.33 | 2.08 |
| 10 | KC | AL | 14 | 13 | 0 | 1 | 70.2 | 319 | 83 | 50 | 48 | 14 | 0 | 3 | 1 | 27 | 0 | 37 | 4 | 2 | 3 | 6 | .333 | 0 | 0-0 | 0 | 5.76 | 6.11 |
| 4 ML YEARS | | | 50 | 37 | 0 | 7 | 218.2 | 986 | 259 | 151 | 143 | 37 | 6 | 13 | 5 | 87 | 5 | 103 | 8 | 2 | 10 | 16 | .385 | 0 | 0-1 | 0 | 5.72 | 5.89 |

## Roy Oswalt

**Pitches:** R **Bats:** R **Pos:** SP-6; RP-3 OWES-walt **Ht:** 6'0" **Wt:** 190 **Born:** 8/29/1977 **Age:** 36

| Year | Team | Lg | G | GS | CG | GF | IP | BFP | H | R | ER | HR | SH | SF | HB | TBB | IBB | SO | WP | Bk | W | L | Pct | Sh | Sv-Op | Hld | ERC | ERA |
|---|---|---|---|---|---|---|---|---|---|---|---|---|---|---|---|---|---|---|---|---|---|---|---|---|---|---|---|---|
| | | | HOW MUCH HE PITCHED | | | | | | WHAT HE GAVE UP | | | | | | | | | | | | THE RESULTS | | | | | | | |
| 2013 | Tulsa* | AA | 5 | 5 | 0 | 0 | 33.1 | 124 | 24 | 10 | 8 | 5 | 1 | 2 | 0 | 7 | 0 | 25 | 0 | 0 | 3 | 2 | .600 | 0 | 0- - | - | 2.34 | 2.16 |
| 2013 | GdJunc* | R+ | 1 | 1 | 0 | 0 | 5.2 | 21 | 3 | 0 | 0 | 0 | 0 | 0 | 0 | 1 | 0 | 2 | 0 | 0 | 1 | 0 | 1.000 | 0 | 0- - | - | 0.89 | 0.00 |
| 2001 | Hou | NL | 28 | 20 | 3 | 4 | 141.2 | 575 | 126 | 48 | 43 | 13 | 4 | 4 | 6 | 24 | 2 | 144 | 0 | 0 | 14 | 3 | **.824** | 1 | 0-0 | 0 | 2.68 | 2.73 |
| 2002 | Hou | NL | 35 | 34 | 0 | 1 | 233.0 | 956 | 215 | 86 | 78 | 17 | 12 | 7 | 5 | 62 | 4 | 208 | 3 | 0 | 19 | 9 | .679 | 0 | 0-0 | 0 | 3.05 | 3.01 |
| 2003 | Hou | NL | 21 | 21 | 0 | 0 | 127.1 | 514 | 116 | 48 | 42 | 15 | 7 | 1 | 5 | 29 | 0 | 108 | 1 | 0 | 10 | 5 | .667 | 0 | 0-0 | 0 | 3.26 | 2.97 |
| 2004 | Hou | NL | 36 | **35** | 2 | 0 | 237.0 | 983 | 233 | 100 | 92 | 17 | 11 | 4 | 11 | 62 | 5 | 206 | 5 | 1 | **20** | 10 | .667 | 2 | 0-0 | 0 | 3.46 | 3.49 |
| 2005 | Hou | NL | 35 | **35** | 4 | 0 | 241.2 | 1002 | 243 | 85 | 79 | 18 | 12 | 7 | 8 | 48 | 3 | 184 | 5 | 1 | 20 | 12 | .625 | 1 | 0-0 | 0 | 3.27 | 2.94 |
| 2006 | Hou | NL | 33 | 32 | 2 | 1 | 220.2 | 896 | 220 | 76 | 73 | 18 | 12 | 4 | 6 | 38 | 4 | 166 | 1 | 1 | 15 | 8 | .652 | 0 | 0-0 | 0 | 3.19 | **2.98** |
| 2007 | Hou | NL | 33 | 32 | 1 | 0 | 212.0 | 910 | 221 | 80 | 75 | 14 | 6 | 4 | 7 | 60 | 6 | 154 | 1 | 1 | 14 | 7 | .667 | 0 | 0-1 | 1 | 3.68 | 3.18 |

| | | | HOW MUCH HE PITCHED | | | | | | WHAT HE GAVE UP | | | | | | | | | | | | THE RESULTS | | | | | | | |
|---|---|---|---|---|---|---|---|---|---|---|---|---|---|---|---|---|---|---|---|---|---|---|---|---|---|---|---|
| Year | Team | Lg | G | GS | CG | GF | IP | BFP | H | R | ER | HR | SH | SF | HB | TBB | IBB | SO | WP | Bk | W | L | Pct | Sh | Sv-Op | Hld | ERC | ERA |
| 2008 | Hou | NL | 32 | 32 | 3 | 0 | 208.2 | 862 | 199 | 89 | 82 | 23 | 8 | 9 | 10 | 47 | 2 | 165 | 1 | 0 | 17 | 10 | .630 | 2 | 0-0 | 0 | 3.40 | 3.54 |
| 2009 | Hou | NL | 30 | 30 | 3 | 0 | 181.1 | 757 | 183 | 83 | 83 | 19 | 12 | 5 | 8 | 42 | 4 | 138 | 4 | 0 | 8 | 6 | .571 | 0 | 0-0 | 0 | 3.67 | 4.12 |
| 2010 | 2 Tms | NL | 33 | 32 | 2 | 0 | 211.2 | 837 | 162 | 70 | 65 | 19 | 10 | 6 | 5 | 55 | 2 | 193 | 2 | 1 | 13 | 13 | .500 | 2 | 0-0 | 0 | 2.37 | 2.76 |
| 2011 | Phi | NL | 23 | 23 | 0 | 0 | 139.0 | 594 | 153 | 60 | 57 | 10 | 7 | 3 | 5 | 33 | 2 | 93 | 3 | 0 | 9 | 10 | .474 | 0 | 0-0 | 0 | 3.93 | 3.69 |
| 2012 | Tex | AL | 17 | 9 | 0 | 2 | 59.0 | 264 | 79 | 41 | 38 | 11 | 3 | 0 | 3 | 11 | 0 | 59 | 3 | 2 | 4 | 3 | .571 | 0 | 0-0 | 0 | 6.05 | 5.80 |
| 2013 | Col | NL | 9 | 6 | 0 | 0 | 32.1 | 151 | 49 | 31 | 31 | 3 | 1 | 3 | 1 | 9 | 0 | 34 | 1 | 0 | 0 | 6 | .000 | 0 | 0-0 | 1 | 6.80 | 8.63 |
| 10 | Hou | NL | 20 | 20 | 1 | 0 | 129.0 | 521 | 109 | 52 | 49 | 13 | 4 | 5 | 2 | 34 | 2 | 120 | 2 | 1 | 6 | 12 | .333 | 1 | 0-0 | 0 | 2.79 | 3.42 |
| 10 | Phi | NL | 13 | 12 | 1 | 0 | 82.2 | 316 | 53 | 18 | 16 | 6 | 6 | 1 | 3 | 21 | 0 | 73 | 0 | 0 | 7 | 1 | .875 | 1 | 0-0 | 0 | 1.76 | 1.74 |
| Postseason | | | 13 | 11 | 0 | 2 | 72.1 | 314 | 73 | 32 | 30 | 9 | 4 | 4 | 6 | 24 | 0 | 56 | 1 | 0 | 5 | 2 | .714 | 0 | 0-0 | 0 | 4.35 | 3.73 |
| 13 ML YEARS | | | 365 | 341 | 20 | 7 | 2245.1 | 9301 | 2199 | 897 | 838 | 197 | 105 | 57 | 80 | 520 | 34 | 1852 | 30 | 7 | 163 | 102 | .615 | 8 | 0-0 | 2 | 3.37 | 3.36 |

# Dan Otero

**Pitches:** R **Bats:** R **Pos:** RP-33 oh-TEHR-oh **Ht:** 6'3" **Wt:** 215 **Born:** 2/19/1985 **Age:** 29

| | | | HOW MUCH HE PITCHED | | | | | | WHAT HE GAVE UP | | | | | | | | | | | | THE RESULTS | | | | | | | |
|---|---|---|---|---|---|---|---|---|---|---|---|---|---|---|---|---|---|---|---|---|---|---|---|---|---|---|---|---|
| Year | Team | Lg | G | GS | CG | GF | IP | BFP | H | R | ER | HR | SH | SF | HB | TBB | IBB | SO | WP | Bk | W | L | Pct | Sh | Sv-Op | Hld | ERC | ERA |
| 2009 | Conn | AA | 39 | 0 | 0 | 32 | 39.0 | 163 | 40 | 6 | 5 | 0 | 2 | 1 | 2 | 10 | 4 | 31 | 2 | 0 | 0 | 3 | .000 | 0 | 19- - | - | 3.06 | 1.15 |
| 2010 | Giants | R | 9 | 0 | 0 | 1 | 10.2 | 40 | 7 | 4 | 0 | 0 | 0 | 0 | 0 | 1 | 0 | 7 | 2 | 0 | 2 | 0 | 1.000 | 0 | 1- - | - | 1.06 | 0.00 |
| 2010 | SnJos | A+ | 10 | 0 | 0 | 4 | 13.1 | 50 | 11 | 6 | 6 | 2 | 0 | 0 | 0 | 1 | 0 | 11 | 0 | 0 | 3 | 0 | 1.000 | 0 | 0- - | - | 2.31 | 4.05 |
| 2011 | Rchmd | AA | 23 | 0 | 0 | 8 | 38.0 | 153 | 34 | 8 | 6 | 0 | 4 | 0 | 2 | 4 | 1 | 40 | 2 | 0 | 2 | 1 | .667 | 0 | 1- - | - | 1.96 | 1.42 |
| 2011 | Fresno | AAA | 33 | 0 | 0 | 23 | 36.0 | 154 | 38 | 15 | 13 | 4 | 2 | 1 | 0 | 7 | 0 | 36 | 1 | 0 | 2 | 3 | .400 | 0 | 12- - | - | 3.54 | 3.25 |
| 2012 | Fresno | AAA | 48 | 0 | 0 | 14 | 62.0 | 258 | 70 | 26 | 20 | 4 | 5 | 3 | 3 | 8 | 1 | 45 | 1 | 0 | 5 | 5 | .500 | 0 | 0- - | - | 3.70 | 2.90 |
| 2013 | Scrmto | AAA | 23 | 0 | 0 | 20 | 27.1 | 99 | 14 | 4 | 3 | 0 | 0 | 2 | 1 | 1 | 0 | 22 | 0 | 0 | 1 | 0 | 1.000 | 0 | 15- - | - | 0.67 | 0.99 |
| 2012 | SF | NL | 12 | 0 | 0 | 4 | 12.1 | 57 | 19 | 11 | 8 | 0 | 0 | 0 | 2 | 2 | 1 | 8 | 1 | 0 | 0 | 0 | - | 0 | 0-0 | 0 | 6.18 | 5.84 |
| 2013 | Oak | AL | 33 | 0 | 0 | 8 | 39.0 | 159 | 42 | 7 | 6 | 0 | 1 | 0 | 0 | 6 | 1 | 27 | 0 | 0 | 2 | 0 | 1.000 | 0 | 0-1 | 8 | 2.90 | 1.38 |
| 2 ML YEARS | | | 45 | 0 | 0 | 12 | 51.1 | 216 | 61 | 18 | 14 | 0 | 1 | 0 | 2 | 8 | 2 | 35 | 1 | 0 | 2 | 0 | 1.000 | 0 | 0-1 | 8 | 3.62 | 2.45 |

# Adam Ottavino

**Pitches:** R **Bats:** B **Pos:** RP-51 ott-tah-VEE-no **Ht:** 6'5" **Wt:** 230 **Born:** 11/22/1985 **Age:** 28

| | | | HOW MUCH HE PITCHED | | | | | | WHAT HE GAVE UP | | | | | | | | | | | | THE RESULTS | | | | | | | |
|---|---|---|---|---|---|---|---|---|---|---|---|---|---|---|---|---|---|---|---|---|---|---|---|---|---|---|---|---|
| Year | Team | Lg | G | GS | CG | GF | IP | BFP | H | R | ER | HR | SH | SF | HB | TBB | IBB | SO | WP | Bk | W | L | Pct | Sh | Sv-Op | Hld | ERC | ERA |
| 2010 | StL | NL | 5 | 3 | 0 | 0 | 22.1 | 110 | 37 | 21 | 21 | 5 | 1 | 0 | 0 | 9 | 1 | 12 | 1 | 0 | 0 | 2 | .000 | 0 | 0-0 | 0 | 9.22 | 8.46 |
| 2012 | Col | NL | 53 | 0 | 0 | 6 | 79.0 | 339 | 76 | 42 | 40 | 9 | 3 | 1 | 1 | 34 | 7 | 81 | 8 | 0 | 5 | 1 | .833 | 0 | 0-2 | 6 | 4.01 | 4.56 |
| 2013 | Col | NL | 51 | 0 | 0 | 5 | 78.1 | 335 | 73 | 27 | 23 | 5 | 6 | 4 | 2 | 31 | 5 | 78 | 9 | 1 | 1 | 3 | .250 | 0 | 0-0 | 8 | 3.42 | 2.64 |
| 3 ML YEARS | | | 109 | 3 | 0 | 11 | 179.2 | 784 | 186 | 90 | 84 | 19 | 10 | 5 | 3 | 74 | 13 | 171 | 18 | 1 | 6 | 6 | .500 | 0 | 0-2 | 14 | 4.31 | 4.21 |

# Josh Outman

**Pitches:** L **Bats:** L **Pos:** RP-61 **Ht:** 6'1" **Wt:** 205 **Born:** 9/14/1984 **Age:** 29

| | | | HOW MUCH HE PITCHED | | | | | | WHAT HE GAVE UP | | | | | | | | | | | | THE RESULTS | | | | | | | |
|---|---|---|---|---|---|---|---|---|---|---|---|---|---|---|---|---|---|---|---|---|---|---|---|---|---|---|---|---|
| Year | Team | Lg | G | GS | CG | GF | IP | BFP | H | R | ER | HR | SH | SF | HB | TBB | IBB | SO | WP | Bk | W | L | Pct | Sh | Sv-Op | Hld | ERC | ERA |
| 2013 | ColSpr* | AAA | 5 | 0 | 0 | 1 | 10.2 | 44 | 8 | 2 | 1 | 1 | 1 | 0 | 0 | 4 | 0 | 14 | 0 | 0 | 1 | 0 | 1.000 | 0 | 0- - | - | 2.57 | 0.84 |
| 2008 | Oak | AL | 6 | 4 | 0 | 0 | 25.2 | 116 | 34 | 14 | 13 | 1 | 0 | 2 | 2 | 8 | 1 | 19 | 1 | 0 | 1 | 2 | .333 | 0 | 0-0 | 0 | 5.49 | 4.56 |
| 2009 | Oak | AL | 14 | 12 | 0 | 1 | 67.1 | 276 | 53 | 30 | 26 | 9 | 1 | 0 | 0 | 25 | 0 | 53 | 1 | 0 | 4 | 1 | .800 | 0 | 0-0 | 0 | 3.04 | 3.48 |
| 2011 | Oak | AL | 13 | 9 | 0 | 2 | 58.1 | 254 | 62 | 27 | 24 | 4 | 4 | 3 | 0 | 23 | 0 | 35 | 3 | 0 | 3 | 5 | .375 | 0 | 0-0 | 1 | 4.19 | 3.70 |
| 2012 | Col | NL | 27 | 7 | 0 | 3 | 40.2 | 185 | 47 | 37 | 37 | 7 | 2 | 1 | 0 | 20 | 0 | 40 | 5 | 0 | 1 | 3 | .250 | 0 | 0-0 | 3 | 5.92 | 8.19 |
| 2013 | Col | NL | 61 | 0 | 0 | 8 | 54.0 | 238 | 56 | 27 | 26 | 3 | 1 | 2 | 3 | 23 | 2 | 53 | 2 | 0 | 3 | 0 | 1.000 | 0 | 0-1 | 13 | 4.22 | 4.33 |
| 5 ML YEARS | | | 121 | 32 | 0 | 14 | 246.0 | 1069 | 252 | 135 | 126 | 24 | 8 | 8 | 5 | 99 | 3 | 200 | 12 | 0 | 12 | 11 | .522 | 0 | 0-1 | 17 | 4.27 | 4.61 |

# Lyle Overbay

**Bats:** L **Throws:** L **Pos:** 1B-130;PH-17;RF-4;DH-2;PR-2 **Ht:** 6'2" **Wt:** 235 **Born:** 1/28/1977 **Age:** 37

| | | | BATTING | | | | | | | | | | | | | | | | | | BASERUNNING | | | | AVERAGES | | |
|---|---|---|---|---|---|---|---|---|---|---|---|---|---|---|---|---|---|---|---|---|---|---|---|---|---|---|---|
| Year | Team | Lg | G | AB | H | 2B | 3B | HR | (Hm | Rd) | TB | R | RBI | RC | TBB | IBB | SO | HBP | SH | SF | SB | CS | SB% | GDP | Avg | OBP | Slg |
| 2001 | Ari | NL | 2 | 2 | 1 | 0 | 0 | 0 | (0 | 0) | 1 | 0 | 0 | 0 | 0 | 0 | 1 | 0 | 0 | 0 | 0 | 0 | - | 0 | .500 | .500 | .500 |
| 2002 | Ari | NL | 10 | 10 | 1 | 0 | 0 | 0 | (0 | 0) | 1 | 0 | 1 | 0 | 0 | 0 | 5 | 0 | 0 | 0 | 0 | 0 | - | 0 | .100 | .100 | .100 |
| 2003 | Ari | NL | 86 | 254 | 70 | 20 | 0 | 4 | (2 | 2) | 102 | 23 | 28 | 34 | 35 | 7 | 67 | 2 | 0 | 2 | 1 | 0 | 1.00 | 8 | .276 | .365 | .402 |
| 2004 | Mil | NL | 159 | 579 | 174 | **53** | 1 | 16 | (6 | 10) | 277 | 83 | 87 | 94 | 81 | 9 | 128 | 2 | 0 | 6 | 2 | 1 | .67 | 11 | .301 | .385 | .478 |
| 2005 | Mil | NL | 158 | 537 | 148 | 34 | 1 | 19 | (10 | 9) | 241 | 80 | 72 | 84 | 78 | 8 | 98 | 2 | 1 | 4 | 1 | 0 | 1.00 | 17 | .276 | .367 | .449 |
| 2006 | Tor | AL | 157 | 581 | 181 | 46 | 1 | 22 | (17 | 5) | 295 | 82 | 92 | 89 | 55 | 7 | 96 | 2 | 0 | 2 | 5 | 3 | .63 | 19 | .312 | .372 | .508 |
| 2007 | Tor | AL | 122 | 425 | 102 | 30 | 2 | 10 | (6 | 4) | 166 | 49 | 44 | 45 | 47 | 4 | 78 | 1 | 0 | 3 | 2 | 0 | 1.00 | 12 | .240 | .315 | .391 |
| 2008 | Tor | AL | 158 | 544 | 147 | 32 | 2 | 15 | (7 | 8) | 228 | 74 | 69 | 73 | 74 | 3 | 116 | 3 | 1 | 5 | 1 | 2 | .33 | 24 | .270 | .358 | .419 |
| 2009 | Tor | AL | 132 | 423 | 112 | 35 | 1 | 16 | (6 | 10) | 197 | 57 | 64 | 64 | 74 | 6 | 95 | 0 | 0 | 3 | 0 | 0 | - | 8 | .265 | .372 | .466 |
| 2010 | Tor | AL | 154 | 534 | 130 | 37 | 2 | 20 | (13 | 7) | 231 | 75 | 67 | 75 | 67 | 7 | 131 | 3 | 0 | 3 | 1 | 0 | 1.00 | 9 | .243 | .329 | .433 |
| 2011 | 2 Tms | NL | 121 | 394 | 92 | 21 | 1 | 9 | (4 | 5) | 142 | 43 | 47 | 41 | 42 | 2 | 88 | 2 | 1 | 1 | 2 | 1 | .67 | 13 | .234 | .310 | .360 |
| 2012 | 2 Tms | NL | 65 | 116 | 30 | 10 | 0 | 2 | (2 | 0) | 46 | 12 | 10 | 11 | 13 | 2 | 34 | 0 | 0 | 1 | 0 | 0 | - | 4 | .259 | .331 | .397 |
| 2013 | NYY | AL | 142 | 445 | 107 | 24 | 1 | 14 | (7 | 7) | 175 | 43 | 59 | 47 | 36 | 0 | 111 | 0 | 0 | 4 | 2 | 0 | 1.00 | 16 | .240 | .295 | .393 |
| 11 | Pit | NL | 103 | 352 | 80 | 17 | 1 | 8 | (3 | 5) | 123 | 40 | 37 | 33 | 36 | 1 | 77 | 1 | 1 | 1 | 1 | 1 | .50 | 12 | .227 | .300 | .349 |
| 11 | Ari | NL | 18 | 42 | 12 | 4 | 0 | 1 | (1 | 0) | 19 | 3 | 10 | 8 | 6 | 1 | 11 | 1 | 0 | 0 | 1 | 0 | 1.00 | 1 | .286 | .388 | .452 |
| 12 | Ari | NL | 45 | 96 | 28 | 9 | 0 | 2 | (2 | 0) | 43 | 11 | 10 | 11 | 12 | 2 | 26 | 0 | 0 | 1 | 0 | 0 | - | 3 | .292 | .367 | .448 |
| 12 | Atl | NL | 20 | 20 | 2 | 1 | 0 | 0 | (0 | 0) | 3 | 1 | 0 | 0 | 1 | 0 | 8 | 0 | 0 | 0 | 0 | 0 | - | 1 | .100 | .143 | .150 |
| Postseason | | | 2 | 4 | 0 | 0 | 0 | 0 | (0 | 0) | 0 | 0 | 0 | 0 | 0 | 0 | 2 | 0 | 0 | 0 | 0 | 0 | - | 0 | .000 | .000 | .000 |
| 13 ML YEARS | | | 1466 | 4844 | 1295 | 342 | 12 | 147 | (80 | 67) | 2102 | 621 | 640 | 657 | 602 | 55 | 1048 | 17 | 3 | 34 | 17 | 7 | .71 | 141 | .267 | .348 | .434 |

## Chris Owings

**Bats:** R **Throws:** R **Pos:** SS-13;PH-5;2B-3 **Ht:** 5'10" **Wt:** 180 **Born:** 8/12/1991 **Age:** 22

| BATTING | | | | | | | | | | | | | | | | | | | | | BASERUNNING | | | | AVERAGES | | |
|---|---|---|---|---|---|---|---|---|---|---|---|---|---|---|---|---|---|---|---|---|---|---|---|---|---|---|---|
| Year Team | Lg | G | AB | H | 2B | 3B | HR | (Hm | Rd) | TB | R | RBI | RC | TBB | IBB | SO | HBP | SH | SF | | SB | CS | SB% | GDP | Avg | OBP | Slg |
| 2009 Msoula | R+ | 24 | 108 | 33 | 5 | 1 | 2 | (- | -) | 46 | 20 | 10 | 15 | 3 | 0 | 25 | 0 | 0 | 0 | | 3 | 0 | 1.00 | 0 | .306 | .324 | .426 |
| 2010 Sbend | A | 62 | 255 | 76 | 19 | 2 | 5 | (- | -) | 114 | 39 | 28 | 36 | 9 | 0 | 50 | 2 | 2 | 3 | | 1 | 3 | .25 | 7 | .298 | .323 | .447 |
| 2011 Visalia | A+ | 121 | 521 | 128 | 29 | 6 | 11 | (- | -) | 202 | 67 | 50 | 56 | 15 | 0 | 130 | 7 | 8 | 4 | | 10 | 4 | .71 | 5 | .246 | .274 | .388 |
| 2012 Visalia | A+ | 59 | 241 | 78 | 16 | 2 | 11 | (- | -) | 131 | 51 | 24 | 46 | 13 | 0 | 63 | 2 | 0 | 1 | | 8 | 3 | .73 | 3 | .324 | .362 | .544 |
| 2012 Mobile | AA | 69 | 297 | 78 | 10 | 3 | 6 | (- | -) | 112 | 35 | 28 | 32 | 11 | 0 | 69 | 1 | 1 | 0 | | 4 | 3 | .57 | 5 | .263 | .291 | .377 |
| 2013 Reno | AAA | 125 | 546 | 180 | 31 | 8 | 12 | (- | -) | 263 | 104 | 81 | 94 | 22 | 2 | 99 | 3 | 4 | 0 | | 20 | 7 | .74 | 14 | .330 | .359 | .482 |
| 2013 Ari | NL | 20 | 55 | 16 | 5 | 0 | 0 | (0 | 0) | 21 | 5 | 5 | 7 | 6 | 1 | 10 | 0 | 0 | 0 | | 2 | 0 | 1.00 | 0 | .291 | .361 | .382 |

## Marcell Ozuna

**Bats:** R **Throws:** R **Pos:** RF-36;CF-33;PH-1 **Ht:** 6'1" **Wt:** 220 **Born:** 11/12/1990 **Age:** 23

| BATTING | | | | | | | | | | | | | | | | | | | | | BASERUNNING | | | | AVERAGES | | |
|---|---|---|---|---|---|---|---|---|---|---|---|---|---|---|---|---|---|---|---|---|---|---|---|---|---|---|---|
| Year Team | Lg | G | AB | H | 2B | 3B | HR | (Hm | Rd) | TB | R | RBI | RC | TBB | IBB | SO | HBP | SH | SF | | SB | CS | SB% | GDP | Avg | OBP | Slg |
| 2009 Mrlns | R | 55 | 214 | 67 | 22 | 0 | 5 | (- | -) | 104 | 32 | 39 | 40 | 22 | 1 | 52 | 3 | 0 | 5 | | 4 | 2 | .67 | 3 | .313 | .377 | .486 |
| 2010 Grnsbr | A | 6 | 25 | 4 | 0 | 0 | 1 | (- | -) | 7 | 3 | 2 | 1 | 2 | 0 | 10 | 0 | 0 | 0 | | 0 | 0 | - | 0 | .160 | .222 | .280 |
| 2010 Jmstwn | A- | 68 | 270 | 72 | 11 | 2 | 21 | (- | -) | 150 | 53 | 60 | 47 | 17 | 2 | 94 | 3 | 0 | 3 | | 3 | 1 | .75 | 7 | .267 | .314 | .556 |
| 2011 Grnsbr | A | 131 | 496 | 132 | 28 | 5 | 23 | (- | -) | 239 | 87 | 71 | 83 | 46 | 2 | 121 | 2 | 6 | 2 | | 17 | 2 | .89 | 7 | .266 | .330 | .482 |
| 2012 Jupiter | A+ | 129 | 489 | 130 | 27 | 2 | 24 | (- | -) | 233 | 89 | 95 | 78 | 44 | 0 | 116 | 3 | 0 | 3 | | 8 | 3 | .73 | 10 | .266 | .328 | .476 |
| 2013 Jupiter | A+ | 4 | 15 | 4 | 1 | 0 | 0 | (- | -) | 5 | 1 | 1 | 1 | 0 | 0 | 4 | 0 | 0 | 0 | | 1 | 0 | 1.00 | 0 | .267 | .267 | .333 |
| 2013 Jaxnvl | AA | 10 | 42 | 14 | 3 | 1 | 5 | (- | -) | 34 | 6 | 15 | 12 | 3 | 1 | 9 | 1 | 0 | 1 | | 1 | 0 | 1.00 | 0 | .333 | .383 | .810 |
| 2013 Mia | NL | 70 | 275 | 73 | 17 | 4 | 3 | (0 | 3) | 107 | 31 | 32 | 35 | 13 | 0 | 57 | 2 | 1 | 0 | | 5 | 1 | .83 | 6 | .265 | .303 | .389 |

## Jordan Pacheco

**Bats:** R **Throws:** R **Pos:** 1B-43;PH-40;C-15;LF-1;DH-1 puh-CHECK-oh **Ht:** 6'1" **Wt:** 200 **Born:** 1/30/1986 **Age:** 28

| BATTING | | | | | | | | | | | | | | | | | | | | | BASERUNNING | | | | AVERAGES | | |
|---|---|---|---|---|---|---|---|---|---|---|---|---|---|---|---|---|---|---|---|---|---|---|---|---|---|---|---|
| Year Team | Lg | G | AB | H | 2B | 3B | HR | (Hm | Rd) | TB | R | RBI | RC | TBB | IBB | SO | HBP | SH | SF | | SB | CS | SB% | GDP | Avg | OBP | Slg |
| 2013 ColSpr* | AAA | 18 | 54 | 17 | 5 | 1 | 1 | (- | -) | 27 | 8 | 6 | 11 | 8 | 0 | 3 | 0 | 1 | 0 | | 3 | 0 | 1.00 | 0 | .315 | .403 | .500 |
| 2011 Col | NL | 21 | 84 | 24 | 1 | 0 | 2 | (2 | 0) | 31 | 5 | 14 | 12 | 3 | 0 | 9 | 1 | 0 | 0 | | 0 | 0 | - | 2 | .286 | .318 | .369 |
| 2012 Col | NL | 132 | 475 | 147 | 32 | 3 | 5 | (4 | 1) | 200 | 51 | 54 | 64 | 22 | 2 | 61 | 3 | 1 | 4 | | 7 | 2 | .78 | 13 | .309 | .341 | .421 |
| 2013 Col | NL | 95 | 247 | 59 | 15 | 0 | 1 | (1 | 0) | 77 | 23 | 22 | 21 | 10 | 0 | 38 | 3 | 1 | 1 | | 0 | 0 | - | 4 | .239 | .276 | .312 |
| 3 ML YEARS | | 248 | 806 | 230 | 48 | 3 | 8 | (7 | 1) | 308 | 79 | 90 | 97 | 35 | 2 | 108 | 7 | 2 | 5 | | 7 | 2 | .78 | 19 | .285 | .319 | .382 |

## Angel Pagan

**Bats:** B **Throws:** R **Pos:** CF-71;PH-4 ANE-gell pah-GONN **Ht:** 6'2" **Wt:** 200 **Born:** 7/2/1981 **Age:** 32

| BATTING | | | | | | | | | | | | | | | | | | | | | BASERUNNING | | | | AVERAGES | | |
|---|---|---|---|---|---|---|---|---|---|---|---|---|---|---|---|---|---|---|---|---|---|---|---|---|---|---|---|
| Year Team | Lg | G | AB | H | 2B | 3B | HR | (Hm | Rd) | TB | R | RBI | RC | TBB | IBB | SO | HBP | SH | SF | | SB | CS | SB% | GDP | Avg | OBP | Slg |
| 2013 SnJos* | A+ | 1 | 2 | 0 | 0 | 0 | 0 | (- | -) | 0 | 0 | 0 | 0 | 1 | 0 | 0 | 0 | 0 | 0 | | 0 | 0 | - | 0 | .000 | .333 | .000 |
| 2013 Giants* | R | 4 | 11 | 2 | 0 | 1 | 0 | (- | -) | 4 | 3 | 0 | 1 | 2 | 0 | 0 | 0 | 0 | 0 | | 0 | 0 | - | 0 | .182 | .308 | .364 |
| 2013 Fresno* | AAA | 5 | 18 | 5 | 0 | 0 | 0 | (- | -) | 5 | 1 | 3 | 2 | 2 | 1 | 2 | 1 | 0 | 1 | | 0 | 0 | - | 1 | .278 | .364 | .278 |
| 2006 ChC | NL | 77 | 170 | 42 | 6 | 2 | 5 | (4 | 1) | 67 | 28 | 18 | 21 | 15 | 0 | 28 | 0 | 1 | 1 | | 4 | 2 | .67 | 3 | .247 | .306 | .394 |
| 2007 ChC | NL | 71 | 148 | 39 | 10 | 2 | 4 | (3 | 1) | 65 | 21 | 21 | 23 | 10 | 0 | 32 | 0 | 1 | 2 | | 4 | 1 | .80 | 0 | .264 | .306 | .439 |
| 2008 NYM | NL | 31 | 91 | 25 | 7 | 1 | 0 | (0 | 0) | 34 | 12 | 13 | 15 | 11 | 0 | 18 | 0 | 1 | 2 | | 4 | 0 | 1.00 | 0 | .275 | .346 | .374 |
| 2009 NYM | NL | 88 | 343 | 105 | 22 | 11 | 6 | (5 | 1) | 167 | 54 | 32 | 53 | 25 | 2 | 56 | 0 | 5 | 3 | | 14 | 7 | .67 | 3 | .306 | .350 | .487 |
| 2010 NYM | NL | 151 | 579 | 168 | 31 | 7 | 11 | (6 | 5) | 246 | 80 | 69 | 90 | 44 | 5 | 97 | 1 | 6 | 3 | | 37 | 9 | .80 | 9 | .290 | .340 | .425 |
| 2011 NYM | NL | 123 | 478 | 125 | 24 | 4 | 7 | (4 | 3) | 178 | 68 | 56 | 64 | 44 | 4 | 62 | 1 | 4 | 5 | | 32 | 7 | .82 | 4 | .262 | .322 | .372 |
| 2012 SF | NL | 154 | 605 | 174 | 38 | **15** | 8 | (1 | 7) | 266 | 95 | 56 | 91 | 48 | 5 | 97 | 0 | 2 | 4 | | 29 | 7 | .81 | 6 | .288 | .338 | .440 |
| 2013 SF | NL | 71 | 280 | 79 | 16 | 3 | 5 | (3 | 2) | 116 | 44 | 30 | 41 | 23 | 0 | 36 | 0 | 0 | 2 | | 9 | 4 | .69 | 1 | .282 | .334 | .414 |
| Postseason | | 16 | 69 | 13 | 3 | 1 | 2 | (1 | 1) | 24 | 10 | 6 | 3 | 4 | 0 | 12 | 0 | 0 | 1 | | 1 | 1 | .50 | 0 | .188 | .230 | .348 |
| 8 ML YEARS | | 766 | 2694 | 757 | 154 | 45 | 46 | (26 | 20) | 1139 | 402 | 295 | 398 | 220 | 16 | 426 | 2 | 20 | 22 | | 133 | 37 | .78 | 26 | .281 | .333 | .423 |

## Matt Pagnozzi

**Bats:** R **Throws:** R **Pos:** C-7;PH-2 **Ht:** 6'2" **Wt:** 215 **Born:** 11/10/1982 **Age:** 31

| BATTING | | | | | | | | | | | | | | | | | | | | | BASERUNNING | | | | AVERAGES | | |
|---|---|---|---|---|---|---|---|---|---|---|---|---|---|---|---|---|---|---|---|---|---|---|---|---|---|---|---|
| Year Team | Lg | G | AB | H | 2B | 3B | HR | (Hm | Rd) | TB | R | RBI | RC | TBB | IBB | SO | HBP | SH | SF | | SB | CS | SB% | GDP | Avg | OBP | Slg |
| 2013 Gwnntt* | AAA | 90 | 290 | 61 | 10 | 1 | 6 | (- | -) | 91 | 31 | 31 | 25 | 21 | 0 | 64 | 5 | 4 | 1 | | 0 | 0 | - | 5 | .210 | .274 | .314 |
| 2009 StL | NL | 6 | 3 | 0 | 0 | 0 | 0 | (0 | 0) | 0 | 1 | 0 | 0 | 1 | 0 | 0 | 0 | 1 | 0 | | 0 | 0 | - | 0 | .000 | .250 | .000 |
| 2010 StL | NL | 15 | 39 | 14 | 2 | 0 | 1 | (1 | 0) | 19 | 4 | 10 | 7 | 2 | 0 | 8 | 1 | 2 | 0 | | 0 | 0 | - | 1 | .359 | .405 | .487 |
| 2011 2 Tms | NL | 12 | 29 | 8 | 0 | 0 | 0 | (0 | 0) | 8 | 2 | 3 | 4 | 1 | 0 | 10 | 1 | 3 | 0 | | 0 | 0 | - | 1 | .276 | .323 | .276 |
| 2013 Hou | AL | 9 | 21 | 3 | 0 | 0 | 0 | (0 | 0) | 3 | 1 | 0 | 0 | 1 | 0 | 3 | 0 | 0 | 0 | | 0 | 0 | - | 0 | .143 | .182 | .143 |
| 11 Col | NL | 7 | 21 | 6 | 0 | 0 | 0 | (0 | 0) | 6 | 2 | 2 | 3 | 1 | 0 | 8 | 1 | 2 | 0 | | 0 | 0 | - | 0 | .286 | .348 | .286 |
| 11 Pit | NL | 5 | 8 | 2 | 0 | 0 | 0 | (0 | 0) | 2 | 0 | 1 | 1 | 0 | 0 | 2 | 0 | 1 | 0 | | 0 | 0 | - | 1 | .250 | .250 | .250 |
| 4 ML YEARS | | 42 | 92 | 25 | 2 | 0 | 1 | (1 | 0) | 30 | 8 | 13 | 11 | 5 | 0 | 21 | 2 | 6 | 0 | | 0 | 0 | - | 2 | .272 | .323 | .326 |

## Jonathan Papelbon

**Pitches:** R **Bats:** R **Pos:** RP-61 PAHP-ill-bonn **Ht:** 6'4" **Wt:** 225 **Born:** 11/23/1980 **Age:** 33

| HOW MUCH HE PITCHED | | | | | | | | WHAT HE GAVE UP | | | | | | | | | | | | THE RESULTS | | | | | | | |
|---|---|---|---|---|---|---|---|---|---|---|---|---|---|---|---|---|---|---|---|---|---|---|---|---|---|---|---|
| Year Team | Lg | G | GS | CG | GF | IP | BFP | H | R | ER | HR | SH | SF | HB | TBB | IBB | SO | WP | Bk | W | L | Pct | Sh | Sv-Op | Hld | ERC | ERA |
| 2005 Bos | AL | 17 | 3 | 0 | 4 | 34.0 | 148 | 33 | 11 | 10 | 4 | 1 | 0 | 3 | 17 | 2 | 34 | 1 | 0 | 3 | 1 | .750 | 0 | 0-1 | 4 | 4.82 | 2.65 |
| 2006 Bos | AL | 59 | 0 | 0 | 49 | 68.1 | 257 | 40 | 8 | 7 | 3 | 1 | 2 | 1 | 13 | 2 | 75 | 2 | 0 | 4 | 2 | .667 | 0 | 35-41 | 1 | 1.22 | 0.92 |
| 2007 Bos | AL | 59 | 0 | 0 | 53 | 58.1 | 224 | 30 | 12 | 12 | 5 | 0 | 0 | 4 | 15 | 0 | 84 | 0 | 0 | 1 | 3 | .250 | 0 | 37-40 | 2 | 1.43 | 1.85 |
| 2008 Bos | AL | 67 | 0 | 0 | 62 | 69.1 | 273 | 58 | 24 | 18 | 4 | 4 | 1 | 0 | 8 | 0 | 77 | 2 | 0 | 5 | 4 | .556 | 0 | 41-46 | 0 | 1.92 | 2.34 |
| 2009 Bos | AL | 66 | 0 | 0 | 59 | 68.0 | 285 | 54 | 15 | 14 | 5 | 1 | 2 | 4 | 24 | 1 | 76 | 0 | 0 | 1 | 1 | .500 | 0 | 38-41 | 0 | 2.78 | 1.85 |
| 2010 Bos | AL | 65 | 0 | 0 | 53 | 67.0 | 287 | 57 | 34 | 29 | 7 | 5 | 0 | 2 | 28 | 4 | 76 | 4 | 0 | 5 | 7 | .417 | 0 | 37-45 | 0 | 3.32 | 3.90 |

| | | | HOW MUCH HE PITCHED | | | | | | WHAT HE GAVE UP | | | | | | | | | | | | THE RESULTS | | | | | | | |
|---|---|---|---|---|---|---|---|---|---|---|---|---|---|---|---|---|---|---|---|---|---|---|---|---|---|---|---|
| Year | Team | Lg | G | GS | CG | GF | IP | BFP | H | R | ER | HR | SH | SF | HB | TBB | IBB | SO | WP | Bk | W | L | Pct | Sh | Sv-Op | Hld | ERC | ERA |
| 2011 | Bos | AL | 63 | 0 | 0 | 54 | 64.1 | 255 | 50 | 22 | 21 | 3 | 0 | 1 | 3 | 10 | 1 | 87 | 1 | 0 | 4 | 1 | .800 | 0 | 31-34 | 0 | 1.86 | 2.94 |
| 2012 | Phi | NL | 70 | 0 | 0 | 64 | 70.0 | 284 | 56 | 22 | 19 | 8 | 3 | 0 | 4 | 18 | 1 | 92 | 0 | 0 | 5 | 6 | .455 | 0 | 38-42 | 0 | 2.75 | 2.44 |
| 2013 | Phi | NL | 61 | 0 | 0 | 54 | 61.2 | 254 | 59 | 23 | 20 | 6 | 0 | 3 | 1 | 11 | 1 | 57 | 2 | 0 | 5 | 1 | .833 | 0 | 29-36 | 0 | 2.98 | 2.92 |
| Postseason | | | 18 | 0 | 0 | 12 | 27.0 | 100 | 14 | 3 | 3 | 0 | 0 | 1 | 0 | 8 | 3 | 23 | 0 | 0 | 2 | 1 | .667 | 0 | 7-9 | 0 | 1.01 | 1.00 |
| 9 ML YEARS | | | 527 | 3 | 0 | 452 | 561.0 | 2267 | 437 | 171 | 150 | 45 | 15 | 9 | 22 | 144 | 12 | 658 | 12 | 0 | 33 | 26 | .559 | 0 | 286-326 | 7 | 2.36 | 2.41 |

## Jimmy Paredes

**Bats:** B **Throws:** R **Pos:** RF-39;PR-6;2B-3;PH-3;3B-1 pah-REY-dez **Ht:** 6'3" **Wt:** 200 **Born:** 11/25/1988 **Age:** 25

| | | | BATTING | | | | | | | | | | | | | | | | | BASERUNNING | | | | AVERAGES | | |
|---|---|---|---|---|---|---|---|---|---|---|---|---|---|---|---|---|---|---|---|---|---|---|---|---|---|---|
| Year | Team | Lg | G | AB | H | 2B | 3B | HR | (Hm | Rd) | TB | R | RBI | RC | TBB | IBB | SO | HBP | SH | SF | SB | CS | SB% | GDP | Avg | OBP | Slg |
| 2013 | OKCity* | AAA | 86 | 327 | 94 | 21 | 6 | 8 | (- | -) | 151 | 50 | 37 | 53 | 28 | 6 | 67 | 1 | 1 | 1 | 16 | 7 | .70 | 4 | .287 | .345 | .462 |
| 2011 | Hou | NL | 46 | 168 | 48 | 8 | 2 | 2 | (0 | 2) | 66 | 16 | 18 | 23 | 9 | 0 | 47 | 0 | 1 | 1 | 5 | 4 | .56 | 3 | .286 | .320 | .393 |
| 2012 | Hou | NL | 24 | 74 | 14 | 1 | 1 | 0 | (0 | 0) | 17 | 7 | 3 | 3 | 6 | 0 | 21 | 0 | 0 | 2 | 2 | 1 | .67 | 0 | .189 | .244 | .230 |
| 2013 | Hou | AL | 48 | 125 | 24 | 4 | 0 | 1 | (1 | 0) | 31 | 8 | 10 | 8 | 6 | 0 | 44 | 1 | 1 | 2 | 4 | 4 | .50 | 1 | .192 | .231 | .248 |
| 3 ML YEARS | | | 118 | 367 | 86 | 13 | 3 | 3 | (1 | 2) | 114 | 31 | 31 | 34 | 21 | 0 | 112 | 1 | 2 | 5 | 11 | 9 | .55 | 4 | .234 | .274 | .311 |

## Blake Parker

**Pitches:** R **Bats:** R **Pos:** RP-49 **Ht:** 6'3" **Wt:** 225 **Born:** 6/19/1985 **Age:** 29

| | | | HOW MUCH HE PITCHED | | | | | | WHAT HE GAVE UP | | | | | | | | | | | | THE RESULTS | | | | | | | |
|---|---|---|---|---|---|---|---|---|---|---|---|---|---|---|---|---|---|---|---|---|---|---|---|---|---|---|---|---|
| Year | Team | Lg | G | GS | CG | GF | IP | BFP | H | R | ER | HR | SH | SF | HB | TBB | IBB | SO | WP | Bk | W | L | Pct | Sh | Sv-Op | Hld | ERC | ERA |
| 2009 | Tenn | AA | 10 | 0 | 0 | 8 | 12.1 | 50 | 8 | 2 | 2 | 0 | 1 | 0 | 0 | 8 | 0 | 19 | 1 | 0 | 0 | 0 | - | 0 | 3-- | - | 2.57 | 1.46 |
| 2009 | Iowa | AAA | 45 | 0 | 0 | 38 | 51.0 | 218 | 36 | 20 | 17 | 3 | 4 | 0 | 3 | 27 | 1 | 58 | 3 | 1 | 2 | 3 | .400 | 0 | 22-- | - | 2.85 | 3.00 |
| 2010 | Iowa | AAA | 35 | 0 | 0 | 21 | 49.1 | 218 | 52 | 30 | 26 | 9 | 1 | 2 | 1 | 28 | 1 | 42 | 1 | 0 | 1 | 4 | .200 | 0 | 2-- | - | 5.93 | 4.74 |
| 2010 | Tenn | AA | 13 | 0 | 0 | 10 | 17.0 | 66 | 11 | 5 | 5 | 0 | 0 | 0 | 0 | 6 | 1 | 25 | 0 | 0 | 0 | 1 | .000 | 0 | 5-- | - | 1.54 | 2.65 |
| 2011 | Tenn | AA | 16 | 0 | 0 | 12 | 24.0 | 105 | 20 | 14 | 11 | 1 | 1 | 2 | 1 | 13 | 2 | 20 | 1 | 0 | 1 | 2 | .333 | 0 | 3-- | - | 3.27 | 4.13 |
| 2011 | Iowa | AAA | 37 | 0 | 0 | 17 | 51.1 | 214 | 37 | 16 | 16 | 5 | 1 | 0 | 2 | 27 | 0 | 60 | 2 | 0 | 3 | 3 | .500 | 0 | 4-- | - | 3.21 | 2.81 |
| 2012 | Iowa | AAA | 21 | 0 | 0 | 15 | 23.2 | 92 | 16 | 9 | 9 | 3 | 0 | 2 | 0 | 6 | 0 | 22 | 0 | 0 | 1 | 1 | .500 | 0 | 6-- | - | 2.04 | 3.42 |
| 2013 | Iowa | AAA | 16 | 0 | 0 | 15 | 17.2 | 73 | 8 | 4 | 4 | 1 | 1 | 1 | 1 | 10 | 0 | 26 | 1 | 1 | 0 | 1 | .000 | 0 | 7-- | - | 1.77 | 2.04 |
| 2012 | ChC | NL | 7 | 0 | 0 | 0 | 6.0 | 32 | 10 | 7 | 4 | 3 | 0 | 0 | 0 | 5 | 1 | 6 | 0 | 0 | 0 | 0 | - | 0 | 0-0 | 0 | 14.02 | 6.00 |
| 2013 | ChC | NL | 49 | 0 | 0 | 18 | 46.1 | 195 | 39 | 17 | 14 | 4 | 0 | 1 | 2 | 15 | 1 | 55 | 2 | 0 | 1 | 2 | .333 | 0 | 1-1 | 7 | 2.91 | 2.72 |
| 2 ML YEARS | | | 56 | 0 | 0 | 18 | 52.1 | 227 | 49 | 24 | 18 | 7 | 0 | 1 | 2 | 20 | 2 | 61 | 2 | 0 | 1 | 2 | .333 | 0 | 1-1 | 7 | 3.91 | 3.10 |

## Jarrod Parker

**Pitches:** R **Bats:** R **Pos:** SP-32 **Ht:** 6'1" **Wt:** 195 **Born:** 11/24/1988 **Age:** 25

| | | | HOW MUCH HE PITCHED | | | | | | WHAT HE GAVE UP | | | | | | | | | | | | THE RESULTS | | | | | | | |
|---|---|---|---|---|---|---|---|---|---|---|---|---|---|---|---|---|---|---|---|---|---|---|---|---|---|---|---|---|
| Year | Team | Lg | G | GS | CG | GF | IP | BFP | H | R | ER | HR | SH | SF | HB | TBB | IBB | SO | WP | Bk | W | L | Pct | Sh | Sv-Op | Hld | ERC | ERA |
| 2011 | Ari | NL | 1 | 1 | 0 | 0 | 5.2 | 22 | 4 | 0 | 0 | 0 | 2 | 0 | 0 | 1 | 0 | 1 | 0 | 0 | 0 | 0 | - | 0 | 0-0 | 0 | 1.36 | 0.00 |
| 2012 | Oak | AL | 29 | 29 | 0 | 0 | 181.1 | 751 | 166 | 71 | 70 | 11 | 7 | 8 | 3 | 63 | 3 | 140 | 10 | 0 | 13 | 8 | .619 | 0 | 0-0 | 0 | 3.24 | 3.47 |
| 2013 | Oak | AL | 32 | 32 | 1 | 0 | 197.0 | 818 | 178 | 92 | 87 | 25 | 8 | 4 | 7 | 63 | 2 | 134 | 7 | 0 | 12 | 8 | .600 | 0 | 0-0 | 0 | 3.57 | 3.97 |
| Postseason | | | 3 | 2 | 0 | 0 | 13.0 | 57 | 16 | 8 | 7 | 1 | 2 | 0 | 1 | 3 | 0 | 11 | 2 | 0 | 0 | 2 | .000 | 0 | 0-0 | 0 | 4.92 | 4.85 |
| 3 ML YEARS | | | 62 | 62 | 1 | 0 | 384.0 | 1591 | 348 | 163 | 157 | 36 | 17 | 12 | 10 | 127 | 5 | 275 | 17 | 0 | 25 | 16 | .610 | 0 | 0-0 | 0 | 3.37 | 3.68 |

## Chris Parmelee

**Bats:** L **Throws:** L **Pos:** RF-68;1B-23;PH-14;CF-1 PAR-muh-lee **Ht:** 6'1" **Wt:** 220 **Born:** 2/24/1988 **Age:** 26

| | | | BATTING | | | | | | | | | | | | | | | | | BASERUNNING | | | | AVERAGES | | |
|---|---|---|---|---|---|---|---|---|---|---|---|---|---|---|---|---|---|---|---|---|---|---|---|---|---|---|
| Year | Team | Lg | G | AB | H | 2B | 3B | HR | (Hm | Rd) | TB | R | RBI | RC | TBB | IBB | SO | HBP | SH | SF | SB | CS | SB% | GDP | Avg | OBP | Slg |
| 2013 | Roch* | AAA | 45 | 173 | 40 | 13 | 1 | 3 | (- | -) | 64 | 23 | 22 | 22 | 22 | 2 | 32 | 1 | 0 | 2 | 1 | 0 | 1.00 | 2 | .231 | .318 | .370 |
| 2011 | Min | AL | 21 | 76 | 27 | 6 | 0 | 4 | (2 | 2) | 45 | 8 | 14 | 19 | 12 | 0 | 13 | 0 | 0 | 0 | 0 | 0 | - | 3 | .355 | .443 | .592 |
| 2012 | Min | AL | 64 | 192 | 44 | 10 | 2 | 5 | (1 | 4) | 73 | 18 | 20 | 18 | 13 | 1 | 52 | 4 | 0 | 1 | 0 | 0 | - | 4 | .229 | .290 | .380 |
| 2013 | Min | AL | 101 | 294 | 67 | 13 | 0 | 8 | (2 | 6) | 104 | 21 | 24 | 27 | 33 | 0 | 81 | 3 | 0 | 3 | 1 | 1 | .50 | 6 | .228 | .309 | .354 |
| 3 ML YEARS | | | 186 | 562 | 138 | 29 | 2 | 17 | (5 | 12) | 222 | 47 | 58 | 64 | 58 | 1 | 146 | 7 | 0 | 4 | 1 | 1 | .50 | 13 | .246 | .322 | .395 |

## Bobby Parnell

**Pitches:** R **Bats:** R **Pos:** RP-49 **Ht:** 6'4" **Wt:** 200 **Born:** 9/8/1984 **Age:** 29

| | | | HOW MUCH HE PITCHED | | | | | | WHAT HE GAVE UP | | | | | | | | | | | | THE RESULTS | | | | | | | |
|---|---|---|---|---|---|---|---|---|---|---|---|---|---|---|---|---|---|---|---|---|---|---|---|---|---|---|---|---|
| Year | Team | Lg | G | GS | CG | GF | IP | BFP | H | R | ER | HR | SH | SF | HB | TBB | IBB | SO | WP | Bk | W | L | Pct | Sh | Sv-Op | Hld | ERC | ERA |
| 2008 | NYM | NL | 6 | 0 | 0 | 3 | 5.0 | 19 | 3 | 3 | 3 | 0 | 0 | 0 | 0 | 2 | 0 | 3 | 1 | 0 | 0 | 0 | - | 0 | 0-0 | 0 | 1.59 | 5.40 |
| 2009 | NYM | NL | 68 | 8 | 0 | 14 | 88.1 | 413 | 101 | 56 | 52 | 8 | 3 | 1 | 4 | 46 | 2 | 74 | 6 | 1 | 4 | 8 | .333 | 0 | 1-5 | 16 | 5.37 | 5.30 |
| 2010 | NYM | NL | 41 | 0 | 0 | 10 | 35.0 | 149 | 41 | 13 | 11 | 1 | 2 | 0 | 0 | 8 | 2 | 33 | 0 | 0 | 0 | 1 | .000 | 0 | 0-2 | 9 | 3.80 | 2.83 |
| 2011 | NYM | NL | 60 | 0 | 0 | 23 | 59.1 | 268 | 60 | 29 | 24 | 4 | 6 | 0 | 2 | 27 | 4 | 64 | 8 | 1 | 4 | 6 | .400 | 0 | 6-12 | 11 | 4.01 | 3.64 |
| 2012 | NYM | NL | 74 | 0 | 0 | 23 | 68.2 | 288 | 65 | 24 | 19 | 4 | 4 | 2 | 1 | 20 | 2 | 61 | 1 | 0 | 5 | 4 | .556 | 0 | 7-12 | 18 | 3.08 | 2.49 |
| 2013 | NYM | NL | 49 | 0 | 0 | 41 | 50.0 | 198 | 38 | 17 | 12 | 1 | 2 | 3 | 1 | 12 | 3 | 44 | 1 | 0 | 5 | 5 | .500 | 0 | 22-26 | 0 | 1.78 | 2.16 |
| 6 ML YEARS | | | 298 | 8 | 0 | 114 | 306.1 | 1335 | 308 | 142 | 121 | 18 | 17 | 6 | 8 | 115 | 13 | 279 | 17 | 2 | 18 | 24 | .429 | 0 | 36-57 | 54 | 3.70 | 3.55 |

## Gerardo Parra

jer-AHR-doh PAH-ruh

**Bats:** L **Throws:** L **Pos:** RF-123;CF-33;LF-6;PH-4;PR-1 **Ht:** 5'11" **Wt:** 200 **Born:** 5/6/1987 **Age:** 27

| | | | BATTING | | | | | | | | | | | | | | | | | BASERUNNING | | | | AVERAGES | | |
|---|---|---|---|---|---|---|---|---|---|---|---|---|---|---|---|---|---|---|---|---|---|---|---|---|---|---|
| Year | Team | Lg | G | AB | H | 2B | 3B | HR | (Hm | Rd) | TB | R | RBI | RC | TBB | IBB | SO | HBP | SH | SF | SB | CS | SB% | GDP | Avg | OBP | Slg |
| 2009 | Ari | NL | 120 | 455 | 132 | 21 | 8 | 5 | (4 | 1) | 184 | 59 | 60 | 58 | 25 | 1 | 89 | 1 | 4 | 6 | 5 | 7 | .42 | 18 | .290 | .324 | .404 |
| 2010 | Ari | NL | 133 | 364 | 95 | 19 | 6 | 3 | (1 | 2) | 135 | 31 | 30 | 38 | 23 | 10 | 76 | 2 | 3 | 1 | 1 | 0 | 1.00 | 8 | .261 | .308 | .371 |
| 2011 | Ari | NL | 141 | 445 | 130 | 20 | 8 | 8 | (3 | 5) | 190 | 55 | 46 | 71 | 43 | 16 | 82 | 3 | 0 | 2 | 15 | 1 | .94 | 8 | .292 | .357 | .427 |

| BATTING | | | | | | | | | | | | | | | | | | | | | | BASERUNNING | | | | AVERAGES | | |
|---|---|---|---|---|---|---|---|---|---|---|---|---|---|---|---|---|---|---|---|---|---|---|---|---|---|---|---|---|
| Year | Team | Lg | G | AB | H | 2B | 3B | HR | (Hm | Rd) | TB | R | RBI | RC | TBB | IBB | SO | HBP | SH | SF | SB | CS | SB% | GDP | Avg | OBP | Slg |
| 2012 | Ari | NL | 133 | 385 | 105 | 21 | 2 | 7 | (5 | 2) | 151 | 58 | 36 | 50 | 33 | 4 | 77 | 4 | 6 | 2 | 15 | 9 | .63 | 4 | .273 | .335 | .392 |
| 2013 | Ari | NL | 156 | 601 | 161 | 43 | 4 | 10 | (6 | 4) | 242 | 79 | 48 | 69 | 48 | 3 | 100 | 3 | 7 | 4 | 10 | 10 | .50 | 12 | .268 | .323 | .403 |
| Postseason | | | 5 | 18 | 1 | 1 | 0 | 0 | (0 | 0) | 2 | 1 | 0 | 0 | 1 | 0 | 7 | 0 | 0 | 0 | 0 | 0 | - | 0 | .056 | .105 | .111 |
| 5 ML YEARS | | | 683 | 2250 | 623 | 124 | 28 | 33 | (19 | 14) | 902 | 282 | 220 | 286 | 172 | 34 | 424 | 13 | 20 | 15 | 46 | 27 | .63 | 50 | .277 | .330 | .401 |

## Manny Parra

**Pitches:** L **Bats:** L **Pos:** RP-57 **Ht:** 6'3" **Wt:** 205 **Born:** 10/30/1982 **Age:** 31

| HOW MUCH HE PITCHED | | | | | | | | | WHAT HE GAVE UP | | | | | | | | | | | | THE RESULTS | | | | | | | |
|---|---|---|---|---|---|---|---|---|---|---|---|---|---|---|---|---|---|---|---|---|---|---|---|---|---|---|---|---|
| Year | Team | Lg | G | GS | CG | GF | IP | BFP | H | R | ER | HR | SH | SF | HB | TBB | IBB | SO | WP | Bk | W | L | Pct | Sh | Sv-Op | Hld | ERC | ERA |
| 2013 | Pnscla* | AA | 3 | 3 | 0 | 0 | 5.0 | 18 | 3 | 0 | 0 | 0 | 0 | 0 | 0 | 1 | 0 | 5 | 0 | 0 | 0 | 0 | - | 0 | 0- - | - | 1.17 | 0.00 |
| 2007 | Mil | NL | 9 | 2 | 0 | 3 | 26.1 | 116 | 25 | 13 | 11 | 1 | 1 | 3 | 2 | 12 | 0 | 26 | 1 | 0 | 0 | 1 | .000 | 0 | 0-0 | 1 | 3.83 | 3.76 |
| 2008 | Mil | NL | 32 | 29 | 0 | 0 | 166.0 | 741 | 181 | 91 | 81 | 18 | 10 | 2 | 2 | 75 | 1 | 147 | **17** | 2 | 10 | 8 | .556 | 0 | 0-0 | 0 | 4.89 | 4.39 |
| 2009 | Mil | NL | 27 | 27 | 0 | 0 | 140.0 | 671 | 179 | 108 | 99 | 19 | 5 | 3 | 1 | 77 | 5 | 116 | 4 | 1 | 11 | 11 | .500 | 0 | 0-0 | 0 | 6.51 | 6.36 |
| 2010 | Mil | NL | 42 | 16 | 0 | 9 | 122.0 | 560 | 135 | 76 | 68 | 18 | 6 | 7 | 3 | 63 | 3 | 129 | 14 | 1 | 3 | 10 | .231 | 0 | 0-0 | 0 | 5.53 | 5.02 |
| 2012 | Mil | NL | 62 | 0 | 0 | 8 | 58.2 | 273 | 62 | 39 | 33 | 3 | 0 | 1 | 3 | 35 | 2 | 61 | 6 | 0 | 2 | 3 | .400 | 0 | 0-2 | 9 | 4.88 | 5.06 |
| 2013 | Cin | NL | 57 | 0 | 0 | 8 | 46.0 | 188 | 40 | 18 | 17 | 5 | 3 | 1 | 1 | 15 | 0 | 56 | 4 | 0 | 2 | 3 | .400 | 0 | 0-1 | 16 | 3.28 | 3.33 |
| Postseason | | | 2 | 0 | 0 | 0 | 2.1 | 9 | 2 | 0 | 0 | 0 | 0 | 0 | 0 | 1 | 0 | 3 | 0 | 0 | 0 | 0 | - | 0 | 0-0 | 0 | 3.03 | 0.00 |
| 6 ML YEARS | | | 229 | 74 | 0 | 28 | 559.0 | 2549 | 622 | 345 | 309 | 64 | 25 | 17 | 12 | 277 | 11 | 535 | 46 | 4 | 28 | 36 | .438 | 0 | 0-3 | 26 | 5.23 | 4.97 |

## Andy Parrino

**Bats:** B **Throws:** R **Pos:** SS-7;2B-5;PH-3;3B-2;PR-1 **Ht:** 6'0" **Wt:** 190 **Born:** 10/31/1985 **Age:** 28

| BATTING | | | | | | | | | | | | | | | | | | | | | | BASERUNNING | | | | AVERAGES | | |
|---|---|---|---|---|---|---|---|---|---|---|---|---|---|---|---|---|---|---|---|---|---|---|---|---|---|---|---|---|
| Year | Team | Lg | G | AB | H | 2B | 3B | HR | (Hm | Rd) | TB | R | RBI | RC | TBB | IBB | SO | HBP | SH | SF | SB | CS | SB% | GDP | Avg | OBP | Slg |
| 2013 | Scrmto* | AAA | 108 | 367 | 77 | 16 | 3 | 4 | (- | -) | 111 | 43 | 36 | 36 | 43 | 0 | 102 | 5 | 3 | 2 | 3 | 1 | .75 | 4 | .210 | .300 | .302 |
| 2011 | SD | NL | 24 | 44 | 8 | 1 | 0 | 0 | (0 | 0) | 9 | 3 | 4 | 4 | 9 | 1 | 17 | 1 | 0 | 1 | 1 | 0 | 1.00 | 1 | .182 | .327 | .205 |
| 2012 | SD | NL | 55 | 116 | 24 | 5 | 0 | 1 | (1 | 0) | 32 | 9 | 6 | 9 | 17 | 7 | 35 | 2 | 2 | 1 | 1 | 0 | 1.00 | 2 | .207 | .316 | .276 |
| 2013 | Oak | AL | 14 | 34 | 4 | 2 | 0 | 0 | (0 | 0) | 6 | 2 | 1 | 0 | 2 | 0 | 12 | 0 | 0 | 0 | 0 | 0 | - | 1 | .118 | .167 | .176 |
| 3 ML YEARS | | | 93 | 194 | 36 | 8 | 0 | 1 | (1 | 0) | 47 | 14 | 11 | 13 | 28 | 8 | 64 | 3 | 2 | 2 | 2 | 0 | 1.00 | 4 | .186 | .295 | .242 |

## Curtis Partch

**Pitches:** R **Bats:** R **Pos:** RP-14 **Ht:** 6'5" **Wt:** 240 **Born:** 2/13/1987 **Age:** 27

| HOW MUCH HE PITCHED | | | | | | | | | WHAT HE GAVE UP | | | | | | | | | | | | THE RESULTS | | | | | | | |
|---|---|---|---|---|---|---|---|---|---|---|---|---|---|---|---|---|---|---|---|---|---|---|---|---|---|---|---|---|
| Year | Team | Lg | G | GS | CG | GF | IP | BFP | H | R | ER | HR | SH | SF | HB | TBB | IBB | SO | WP | Bk | W | L | Pct | Sh | Sv-Op | Hld | ERC | ERA |
| 2009 | Dayton | A | 19 | 19 | 0 | 0 | 104.0 | 456 | 107 | 62 | 54 | 11 | 3 | 6 | 10 | 39 | 0 | 77 | 6 | 4 | 8 | 7 | .533 | 0 | 0- - | - | 4.59 | 4.67 |
| 2009 | Carlina | AA | 1 | 1 | 0 | 0 | 5.0 | 23 | 5 | 1 | 1 | 0 | 0 | 0 | 0 | 2 | 0 | 2 | 0 | 0 | 1 | 0 | 1.000 | 0 | 0- - | - | 3.11 | 1.80 |
| 2009 | Srsota | A+ | 7 | 7 | 0 | 0 | 39.1 | 173 | 38 | 22 | 19 | 0 | 0 | 3 | 4 | 18 | 0 | 25 | 4 | 0 | 3 | 2 | .600 | 0 | 0- - | - | 3.79 | 4.35 |
| 2010 | Lynbrg | A+ | 28 | 24 | 0 | 1 | 132.0 | 599 | 165 | 93 | 73 | 11 | 6 | 5 | 7 | 45 | 2 | 96 | 14 | 2 | 7 | 11 | .389 | 0 | 0- - | - | 5.35 | 4.98 |
| 2010 | Carlina | AA | 1 | 1 | 0 | 0 | 3.0 | 18 | 7 | 7 | 7 | 2 | 0 | 0 | 1 | 2 | 0 | 1 | 0 | 0 | 0 | 1 | .000 | 0 | 0- - | - | 23.41 | 21.00 |
| 2011 | Bkrsfld | A+ | 21 | 21 | 2 | 0 | 121.2 | 561 | 161 | 92 | 71 | 14 | 5 | 8 | 12 | 28 | 0 | 93 | 7 | 1 | 6 | 11 | .353 | 0 | 0- - | - | 5.71 | 5.25 |
| 2011 | Carlina | AA | 7 | 7 | 0 | 0 | 39.0 | 183 | 55 | 32 | 30 | 3 | 2 | 2 | 3 | 13 | 1 | 33 | 1 | 0 | 2 | 2 | .500 | 0 | 0- - | - | 6.35 | 6.92 |
| 2012 | Pnscla | AA | 45 | 4 | 0 | 17 | 70.1 | 314 | 75 | 38 | 37 | 7 | 2 | 0 | 4 | 33 | 3 | 64 | 7 | 1 | 7 | 4 | .636 | 0 | 6- - | - | 4.91 | 4.73 |
| 2012 | Bkrsfld | A+ | 7 | 0 | 0 | 3 | 12.0 | 46 | 7 | 2 | 2 | 1 | 0 | 1 | 0 | 3 | 1 | 15 | 0 | 0 | 0 | 0 | - | 0 | 2- - | - | 1.39 | 1.50 |
| 2013 | Pnscla | AA | 8 | 0 | 0 | 5 | 8.1 | 32 | 6 | 2 | 2 | 0 | 0 | 0 | 0 | 2 | 0 | 14 | 0 | 0 | 0 | 0 | - | 0 | 4- - | - | 1.58 | 2.16 |
| 2013 | Lsvlle | AAA | 24 | 0 | 0 | 7 | 28.1 | 124 | 27 | 13 | 13 | 2 | 1 | 1 | 2 | 12 | 2 | 31 | 1 | 1 | 1 | 2 | .333 | 0 | 2- - | - | 3.83 | 4.13 |
| 2013 | Cin | NL | 14 | 0 | 0 | 4 | 23.1 | 106 | 17 | 16 | 16 | 8 | 3 | 1 | 4 | 17 | 1 | 16 | 0 | 0 | 0 | 1 | .000 | 0 | 0-0 | 0 | 6.32 | 6.17 |

## Tyler Pastornicky

**Bats:** R **Throws:** R **Pos:** PH-12;2B-6;SS-1;CF-1 pas-tor-NICK-ee **Ht:** 5'11" **Wt:** 190 **Born:** 12/13/1989 **Age:** 24

| BATTING | | | | | | | | | | | | | | | | | | | | | | BASERUNNING | | | | AVERAGES | | |
|---|---|---|---|---|---|---|---|---|---|---|---|---|---|---|---|---|---|---|---|---|---|---|---|---|---|---|---|---|
| Year | Team | Lg | G | AB | H | 2B | 3B | HR | (Hm | Rd) | TB | R | RBI | RC | TBB | IBB | SO | HBP | SH | SF | SB | CS | SB% | GDP | Avg | OBP | Slg |
| 2009 | Lnsng | A | 109 | 413 | 111 | 11 | 9 | 1 | (- | -) | 143 | 63 | 31 | 55 | 39 | 0 | 50 | 3 | 3 | 1 | 51 | 15 | .77 | 10 | .269 | .336 | .346 |
| 2009 | Dnedin | A+ | 15 | 63 | 17 | 3 | 0 | 0 | (- | -) | 20 | 9 | 3 | 6 | 3 | 0 | 7 | 0 | 0 | 0 | 6 | 3 | .67 | 1 | .270 | .303 | .317 |
| 2010 | Dnedin | A+ | 77 | 287 | 74 | 16 | 0 | 6 | (- | -) | 108 | 50 | 35 | 42 | 39 | 2 | 49 | 1 | 3 | 1 | 24 | 7 | .77 | 5 | .258 | .348 | .376 |
| 2010 | Missi | AA | 38 | 134 | 34 | 5 | 2 | 2 | (- | -) | 49 | 22 | 15 | 19 | 16 | 0 | 22 | 1 | 7 | 2 | 11 | 2 | .85 | 4 | .254 | .333 | .366 |
| 2011 | Missi | AA | 90 | 355 | 106 | 13 | 5 | 6 | (- | -) | 147 | 50 | 36 | 53 | 24 | 1 | 34 | 2 | 12 | 2 | 20 | 8 | .71 | 4 | .299 | .345 | .414 |
| 2011 | Gwnntt | AAA | 27 | 104 | 38 | 2 | 0 | 1 | (- | -) | 43 | 15 | 9 | 18 | 8 | 0 | 11 | 0 | 4 | 1 | 7 | 3 | .70 | 3 | .365 | .407 | .413 |
| 2012 | Gwnntt | AAA | 38 | 153 | 41 | 15 | 1 | 1 | (- | -) | 61 | 15 | 20 | 19 | 11 | 0 | 21 | 1 | 0 | 2 | 3 | 3 | .50 | 1 | .268 | .317 | .399 |
| 2013 | Gwnntt | AAA | 74 | 288 | 84 | 13 | 2 | 4 | (- | -) | 113 | 42 | 27 | 43 | 27 | 1 | 47 | 2 | 1 | 2 | 9 | 2 | .82 | 11 | .292 | .354 | .392 |
| 2012 | Atl | NL | 76 | 169 | 41 | 6 | 1 | 2 | (1 | 1) | 55 | 21 | 13 | 15 | 10 | 1 | 32 | 1 | 7 | 1 | 2 | 0 | 1.00 | 5 | .243 | .287 | .325 |
| 2013 | Atl | NL | 20 | 30 | 9 | 1 | 0 | 0 | (0 | 0) | 10 | 5 | 0 | 3 | 1 | 0 | 5 | 0 | 2 | 0 | 0 | 0 | - | 0 | .300 | .323 | .333 |
| Postseason | | | 1 | 0 | 0 | 0 | 0 | 0 | (0 | 0) | 0 | 0 | 0 | 0 | 0 | 0 | 0 | 0 | 0 | 0 | 0 | 0 | - | 0 | - | - | - |
| 2 ML YEARS | | | 96 | 199 | 50 | 7 | 1 | 2 | (1 | 1) | 65 | 26 | 13 | 18 | 11 | 1 | 37 | 1 | 9 | 1 | 2 | 0 | 1.00 | 5 | .251 | .292 | .327 |

## Joe Paterson

**Pitches:** L **Bats:** R **Pos:** RP-2 **Ht:** 6'1" **Wt:** 210 **Born:** 5/19/1986 **Age:** 28

| HOW MUCH HE PITCHED | | | | | | | | | WHAT HE GAVE UP | | | | | | | | | | | | THE RESULTS | | | | | | | |
|---|---|---|---|---|---|---|---|---|---|---|---|---|---|---|---|---|---|---|---|---|---|---|---|---|---|---|---|---|
| Year | Team | Lg | G | GS | CG | GF | IP | BFP | H | R | ER | HR | SH | SF | HB | TBB | IBB | SO | WP | Bk | W | L | Pct | Sh | Sv-Op | Hld | ERC | ERA |
| 2013 | Reno* | AAA | 48 | 1 | 0 | 8 | 52.1 | 207 | 40 | 14 | 11 | 2 | 2 | 5 | 4 | 15 | 2 | 53 | 4 | 0 | 3 | 1 | .750 | 0 | 1- - | - | 2.34 | 1.89 |
| 2011 | Ari | NL | 62 | 0 | 0 | 17 | 34.0 | 150 | 28 | 11 | 11 | 1 | 4 | 2 | 4 | 15 | 0 | 28 | 1 | 0 | 0 | 3 | .000 | 0 | 1-1 | 10 | 3.12 | 2.91 |
| 2012 | Ari | NL | 6 | 0 | 0 | 0 | 2.2 | 26 | 15 | 11 | 11 | 2 | 0 | 0 | 0 | 3 | 0 | 0 | 0 | 0 | 0 | 0 | - | 0 | 0-0 | 1 | 53.93 | 37.13 |
| 2013 | Ari | NL | 2 | 0 | 0 | 2 | 2.1 | 11 | 2 | 1 | 1 | 0 | 0 | 0 | 3 | 0 | 0 | 2 | 0 | 0 | 0 | 0 | - | 0 | 0-0 | 0 | 6.30 | 3.86 |
| Postseason | | | 1 | 0 | 0 | 0 | 0.1 | 1 | 0 | 0 | 0 | 0 | 0 | 0 | 0 | 0 | 0 | 1 | 0 | 0 | 0 | 0 | - | 0 | 0-0 | 0 | 0.00 | 0.00 |
| 3 ML YEARS | | | 70 | 0 | 0 | 19 | 39.0 | 187 | 45 | 23 | 23 | 3 | 4 | 2 | 7 | 18 | 0 | 30 | 1 | 0 | 0 | 3 | .000 | 0 | 1-1 | 11 | 5.62 | 5.31 |

## Troy Patton

**Pitches:** L **Bats:** B **Pos:** RP-56 — **Ht:** 6'1" **Wt:** 180 **Born:** 9/3/1985 **Age:** 28

| | | | HOW MUCH HE PITCHED | | | | | | WHAT HE GAVE UP | | | | | | | | | | | | THE RESULTS | | | | | | | |
|---|---|---|---|---|---|---|---|---|---|---|---|---|---|---|---|---|---|---|---|---|---|---|---|---|---|---|---|---|
| Year | Team | Lg | G | GS | CG | GF | IP | BFP | H | R | ER | HR | SH | SF | HB | TBB | IBB | SO | WP | Bk | W | L | Pct | Sh | Sv-Op | Hld | ERC | ERA |
| 2007 | Hou | NL | 3 | 2 | 0 | 1 | 12.2 | 54 | 10 | 6 | 5 | 3 | 1 | 0 | 2 | 4 | 0 | 8 | 0 | 0 | 0 | 2 | .000 | 0 | 0-0 | 0 | 4.04 | 3.55 |
| 2010 | Bal | AL | 1 | 0 | 0 | 0 | 0.2 | 4 | 1 | 0 | 0 | 0 | 0 | 0 | 0 | 1 | 0 | 1 | 0 | 0 | 0 | 0 | - | 0 | 0-0 | 0 | 10.76 | 0.00 |
| 2011 | Bal | AL | 20 | 0 | 0 | 4 | 30.0 | 119 | 25 | 10 | 10 | 2 | 1 | 1 | 0 | 5 | 1 | 22 | 0 | 0 | 2 | 1 | .667 | 0 | 0-0 | 2 | 2.09 | 3.00 |
| 2012 | Bal | AL | 54 | 0 | 0 | 12 | 55.2 | 224 | 45 | 15 | 15 | 5 | 0 | 1 | 2 | 12 | 2 | 49 | 1 | 0 | 1 | 0 | 1.000 | 0 | 0-1 | 9 | 2.39 | 2.43 |
| 2013 | Bal | AL | 56 | 0 | 0 | 8 | 56.0 | 235 | 57 | 25 | 23 | 8 | 2 | 3 | 3 | 16 | 1 | 42 | 0 | 0 | 2 | 0 | 1.000 | 0 | 0-1 | 8 | 4.29 | 3.70 |
| Postseason | | | 3 | 0 | 0 | 0 | 2.0 | 11 | 3 | 1 | 1 | 1 | 0 | 0 | 0 | 2 | 0 | 3 | 0 | 0 | 0 | 0 | - | 0 | 0-0 | 0 | 13.58 | 4.50 |
| 5 ML YEARS | | | 134 | 2 | 0 | 25 | 155.0 | 636 | 138 | 56 | 53 | 18 | 4 | 5 | 7 | 38 | 4 | 122 | 1 | 0 | 5 | 3 | .625 | 0 | 0-2 | 19 | 3.13 | 3.08 |

## Xavier Paul

**Bats:** L **Throws:** R **Pos:** LF-59;PH-37;DH-4 — **Ht:** 5'9" **Wt:** 205 **Born:** 2/25/1985 **Age:** 29

| | | | BATTING | | | | | | | | | | | | | | | | | BASERUNNING | | | | AVERAGES | | |
|---|---|---|---|---|---|---|---|---|---|---|---|---|---|---|---|---|---|---|---|---|---|---|---|---|---|---|
| Year | Team | Lg | G | AB | H | 2B | 3B | HR | (Hm | Rd) | TB | R | RBI | RC | TBB | IBB | SO | HBP | SH | SF | SB | CS | SB% | GDP | Avg | OBP | Slg |
| 2009 | LAD | NL | 11 | 14 | 3 | 1 | 0 | 1 | (0 | 1) | 7 | 3 | 1 | 0 | 2 | 0 | 4 | 0 | 0 | 0 | 0 | 1 | .00 | 1 | .214 | .313 | .500 |
| 2010 | LAD | NL | 44 | 121 | 28 | 8 | 1 | 0 | (0 | 0) | 38 | 16 | 11 | 8 | 8 | 0 | 24 | 0 | 3 | 1 | 3 | 1 | .75 | 3 | .231 | .277 | .314 |
| 2011 | 2 Tms | NL | 128 | 243 | 62 | 6 | 5 | 2 | (1 | 1) | 84 | 30 | 20 | 24 | 13 | 1 | 62 | 0 | 5 | 1 | 16 | 6 | .73 | 2 | .255 | .292 | .346 |
| 2012 | Cin | NL | 55 | 86 | 27 | 5 | 1 | 2 | (1 | 1) | 40 | 8 | 7 | 12 | 9 | 1 | 18 | 0 | 1 | 0 | 4 | 2 | .67 | 2 | .314 | .379 | .465 |
| 2013 | Cin | NL | 97 | 209 | 51 | 12 | 0 | 7 | (4 | 3) | 84 | 24 | 32 | 27 | 27 | 3 | 53 | 3 | 0 | 0 | 0 | 1 | .00 | 6 | .244 | .339 | .402 |
| 11 | LAD | NL | 7 | 11 | 3 | 0 | 0 | 0 | (0 | 0) | 3 | 0 | 0 | 1 | 0 | 0 | 5 | 0 | 0 | 0 | 0 | 0 | - | 0 | .273 | .273 | .273 |
| 11 | Pit | NL | 121 | 232 | 59 | 6 | 5 | 2 | (1 | 1) | 81 | 30 | 20 | 23 | 13 | 1 | 57 | 0 | 5 | 1 | 16 | 6 | .73 | 2 | .254 | .293 | .349 |
| Postseason | | | 3 | 3 | 1 | 0 | 0 | 0 | (0 | 0) | 1 | 1 | 0 | 0 | 0 | 0 | 1 | 0 | 0 | 0 | 0 | 0 | - | 0 | .333 | .333 | .333 |
| 5 ML YEARS | | | 335 | 673 | 171 | 32 | 7 | 12 | (6 | 6) | 253 | 81 | 71 | 71 | 59 | 5 | 161 | 3 | 9 | 2 | 23 | 11 | .68 | 14 | .254 | .316 | .376 |

## James Paxton

**Pitches:** L **Bats:** L **Pos:** SP-4 — **Ht:** 6'4" **Wt:** 220 **Born:** 11/6/1988 **Age:** 25

| | | | HOW MUCH HE PITCHED | | | | | | WHAT HE GAVE UP | | | | | | | | | | | | THE RESULTS | | | | | | | |
|---|---|---|---|---|---|---|---|---|---|---|---|---|---|---|---|---|---|---|---|---|---|---|---|---|---|---|---|---|
| Year | Team | Lg | G | GS | CG | GF | IP | BFP | H | R | ER | HR | SH | SF | HB | TBB | IBB | SO | WP | Bk | W | L | Pct | Sh | Sv-Op | Hld | ERC | ERA |
| 2011 | Clinton | A | 10 | 10 | 0 | 0 | 56.0 | 235 | 45 | 21 | 17 | 1 | 3 | 1 | 1 | 30 | 0 | 80 | 6 | 0 | 3 | 3 | .500 | 0 | 0- - | - | 3.08 | 2.73 |
| 2011 | Jacksn | AA | 7 | 7 | 0 | 0 | 39.0 | 153 | 28 | 10 | 8 | 2 | 0 | 0 | 1 | 13 | 0 | 51 | 3 | 1 | 3 | 0 | 1.000 | 0 | 0- - | - | 2.23 | 1.85 |
| 2012 | Jacksn | AA | 21 | 21 | 0 | 0 | 106.1 | 453 | 96 | 43 | 36 | 5 | 1 | 4 | 1 | 54 | 0 | 110 | 13 | 1 | 9 | 4 | .692 | 0 | 0- - | - | 3.68 | 3.05 |
| 2013 | Tacom | AAA | 28 | 26 | 2 | 0 | 145.2 | 640 | 158 | 84 | 72 | 10 | 3 | 5 | 3 | 58 | 0 | 131 | 14 | 0 | 8 | 11 | .421 | 1 | 0- - | - | 4.41 | 4.45 |
| 2013 | Sea | AL | 4 | 4 | 0 | 0 | 24.0 | 94 | 15 | 5 | 4 | 2 | 0 | 0 | 0 | 7 | 2 | 21 | 0 | 0 | 3 | 0 | 1.000 | 0 | 0-0 | 0 | 1.61 | 1.50 |

## Brad Peacock

**Pitches:** R **Bats:** R **Pos:** SP-14; RP-4 — **Ht:** 6'1" **Wt:** 175 **Born:** 2/2/1988 **Age:** 26

| | | | HOW MUCH HE PITCHED | | | | | | WHAT HE GAVE UP | | | | | | | | | | | | THE RESULTS | | | | | | | |
|---|---|---|---|---|---|---|---|---|---|---|---|---|---|---|---|---|---|---|---|---|---|---|---|---|---|---|---|---|
| Year | Team | Lg | G | GS | CG | GF | IP | BFP | H | R | ER | HR | SH | SF | HB | TBB | IBB | SO | WP | Bk | W | L | Pct | Sh | Sv-Op | Hld | ERC | ERA |
| 2009 | Hgrstn | A | 19 | 17 | 0 | 1 | 100.0 | 429 | 104 | 49 | 45 | 10 | 4 | 2 | 8 | 32 | 0 | 77 | 5 | 0 | 5 | 8 | .385 | 0 | 0- - | - | 4.36 | 4.05 |
| 2009 | Ptomc | A+ | 8 | 7 | 0 | 0 | 47.2 | 199 | 46 | 26 | 23 | 4 | 3 | 1 | 3 | 10 | 0 | 27 | 1 | 0 | 3 | 3 | .500 | 0 | 0- - | - | 3.27 | 4.34 |
| 2010 | Ptomc | A+ | 19 | 18 | 1 | 1 | 103.1 | 444 | 109 | 59 | 51 | 11 | 5 | 3 | 4 | 25 | 0 | 118 | 10 | 2 | 4 | 9 | .308 | 1 | 0- - | - | 3.90 | 4.44 |
| 2010 | Hrsbrg | AA | 7 | 7 | 0 | 0 | 38.2 | 166 | 33 | 21 | 20 | 5 | 2 | 1 | 0 | 22 | 1 | 30 | 0 | 0 | 2 | 2 | .500 | 0 | 0- - | - | 4.13 | 4.66 |
| 2011 | Hrsbrg | AA | 16 | 13 | 1 | 0 | 98.2 | 376 | 62 | 25 | 22 | 4 | 2 | 3 | 2 | 23 | 1 | 129 | 4 | 0 | 10 | 2 | .833 | 0 | 0- - | - | 1.46 | 2.01 |
| 2011 | Syrcse | AAA | 9 | 9 | 0 | 0 | 48.0 | 204 | 36 | 18 | 17 | 5 | 1 | 1 | 2 | 24 | 0 | 48 | 4 | 0 | 5 | 1 | .833 | 0 | 0- - | - | 3.26 | 3.19 |
| 2012 | Scrmto | AAA | 28 | 25 | 0 | 2 | 134.2 | 611 | 147 | 99 | 90 | 16 | 1 | 5 | 5 | 66 | 0 | 139 | 14 | 0 | 12 | 9 | .571 | 0 | 0- - | - | 5.24 | 6.01 |
| 2013 | OKCity | AAA | 14 | 13 | 0 | 0 | 79.0 | 313 | 65 | 29 | 24 | 9 | 1 | 1 | 1 | 22 | 3 | 76 | 3 | 0 | 6 | 2 | .750 | 0 | 0- - | - | 2.83 | 2.73 |
| 2011 | Was | NL | 3 | 2 | 0 | 0 | 12.0 | 48 | 7 | 1 | 1 | 0 | 0 | 0 | 0 | 6 | 0 | 4 | 1 | 0 | 2 | 0 | 1.000 | 0 | 0-1 | 0 | 1.71 | 0.75 |
| 2013 | Hou | AL | 18 | 14 | 0 | 1 | 83.1 | 365 | 78 | 51 | 48 | 15 | 1 | 1 | 3 | 37 | 0 | 77 | 4 | 0 | 5 | 6 | .455 | 0 | 0-0 | 2 | 4.54 | 5.18 |
| 2 ML YEARS | | | 21 | 16 | 0 | 1 | 95.1 | 413 | 85 | 52 | 49 | 15 | 1 | 1 | 3 | 43 | 0 | 81 | 5 | 0 | 7 | 6 | .538 | 0 | 0-1 | 2 | 4.15 | 4.63 |

## Steve Pearce

**Bats:** R **Throws:** R **Pos:** DH-18;LF-15;PH-6;1B-3;RF-3 — **Ht:** 5'11" **Wt:** 210 **Born:** 4/13/1983 **Age:** 31

| | | | BATTING | | | | | | | | | | | | | | | | | BASERUNNING | | | | AVERAGES | | |
|---|---|---|---|---|---|---|---|---|---|---|---|---|---|---|---|---|---|---|---|---|---|---|---|---|---|---|
| Year | Team | Lg | G | AB | H | 2B | 3B | HR | (Hm | Rd) | TB | R | RBI | RC | TBB | IBB | SO | HBP | SH | SF | SB | CS | SB% | GDP | Avg | OBP | Slg |
| 2013 | Orioles* | R | 2 | 5 | 2 | 0 | 0 | 0 | (- | -) | 2 | 0 | 1 | 0 | 0 | 0 | 0 | 0 | 0 | 0 | 0 | 0 | - | 0 | .400 | .400 | .400 |
| 2013 | Frdrck* | A+ | 2 | 6 | 1 | 0 | 0 | 0 | (- | -) | 1 | 0 | 0 | 0 | 1 | 0 | 1 | 1 | 0 | 0 | 0 | 0 | - | 1 | .167 | .375 | .167 |
| 2007 | Pit | NL | 23 | 68 | 20 | 5 | 1 | 0 | (0 | 0) | 27 | 13 | 6 | 9 | 5 | 0 | 12 | 0 | 0 | 0 | 2 | 1 | .67 | 2 | .294 | .342 | .397 |
| 2008 | Pit | NL | 37 | 109 | 27 | 7 | 0 | 4 | (0 | 4) | 46 | 6 | 15 | 13 | 5 | 0 | 22 | 3 | 0 | 2 | 2 | 0 | 1.00 | 1 | .248 | .294 | .422 |
| 2009 | Pit | NL | 60 | 165 | 34 | 13 | 1 | 4 | (3 | 1) | 61 | 19 | 16 | 17 | 21 | 0 | 43 | 0 | 0 | 0 | 1 | 0 | 1.00 | 2 | .206 | .296 | .370 |
| 2010 | Pit | NL | 15 | 29 | 8 | 2 | 1 | 0 | (0 | 0) | 12 | 4 | 5 | 5 | 7 | 0 | 6 | 0 | 0 | 2 | 0 | 0 | - | 0 | .276 | .395 | .414 |
| 2011 | Pit | NL | 50 | 94 | 19 | 2 | 0 | 1 | (1 | 0) | 24 | 8 | 10 | 5 | 7 | 0 | 21 | 1 | 1 | 2 | 0 | 0 | - | 6 | .202 | .260 | .255 |
| 2012 | 3 Tms | | 61 | 159 | 38 | 8 | 1 | 4 | (2 | 2) | 60 | 16 | 26 | 24 | 20 | 1 | 41 | 3 | 2 | 4 | 1 | 2 | .33 | 4 | .239 | .328 | .377 |
| 2013 | Bal | AL | 44 | 119 | 31 | 7 | 0 | 4 | (3 | 1) | 50 | 14 | 13 | 20 | 15 | 2 | 25 | 4 | 0 | 0 | 1 | 0 | 1.00 | 0 | .261 | .362 | .420 |
| 12 | Bal | AL | 28 | 71 | 18 | 4 | 0 | 3 | (2 | 1) | 31 | 8 | 14 | 12 | 8 | 0 | 17 | 0 | 2 | 2 | 0 | 1 | .00 | 1 | .254 | .321 | .437 |
| 12 | Hou | NL | 21 | 63 | 16 | 4 | 1 | 0 | (0 | 0) | 22 | 2 | 8 | 9 | 7 | 1 | 16 | 3 | 0 | 2 | 1 | 1 | .50 | 3 | .254 | .347 | .349 |
| 12 | NYY | AL | 12 | 25 | 4 | 0 | 0 | 1 | (0 | 1) | 7 | 6 | 4 | 3 | 5 | 0 | 8 | 0 | 0 | 0 | 0 | 0 | - | 0 | .160 | .300 | .280 |
| 7 ML YEARS | | | 290 | 743 | 177 | 44 | 4 | 17 | (9 | 8) | 280 | 80 | 91 | 93 | 80 | 3 | 170 | 11 | 3 | 10 | 7 | 3 | .70 | 15 | .238 | .318 | .377 |

## Jake Peavy

**Pitches:** R **Bats:** R **Pos:** SP-23 **Ht:** 6'1" **Wt:** 195 **Born:** 5/31/1981 **Age:** 33

| HOW MUCH HE PITCHED | | | | | | | | | WHAT HE GAVE UP | | | | | | | | | | | | THE RESULTS | | | | | | | |
|---|---|---|---|---|---|---|---|---|---|---|---|---|---|---|---|---|---|---|---|---|---|---|---|---|---|---|---|---|
| Year | Team | Lg | G | GS | CG | GF | IP | BFP | H | R | ER | HR | SH | SF | HB | TBB | IBB | SO | WP | Bk | W | L | Pct | Sh | Sv-Op | Hld | ERC | ERA |
| 2013 | Brham* | AA | 1 | 1 | 0 | 0 | 5.0 | 22 | 5 | 1 | 1 | 0 | 0 | 0 | 0 | 2 | 0 | 4 | 0 | 0 | 1 | 0 | 1.000 | 0 | 0-- | - | 3.28 | 1.80 |
| 2002 | SD | NL | 17 | 17 | 0 | 0 | 97.2 | 430 | 106 | 54 | 49 | 11 | 5 | 2 | 3 | 33 | 4 | 90 | 4 | 1 | 6 | 7 | .462 | 0 | 0-0 | 0 | 4.41 | 4.52 |
| 2003 | SD | NL | 32 | 32 | 0 | 0 | 194.2 | 827 | 173 | 94 | 89 | 33 | 7 | 5 | 6 | 82 | 3 | 156 | 2 | 0 | 12 | 11 | .522 | 0 | 0-0 | 0 | 4.13 | 4.11 |
| 2004 | SD | NL | 27 | 27 | 0 | 0 | 166.1 | 694 | 146 | 49 | 42 | 13 | 5 | 6 | 11 | 53 | 4 | 173 | 1 | 1 | 15 | 6 | .714 | 0 | 0-0 | 0 | 3.18 | **2.27** |
| 2005 | SD | NL | 30 | 30 | 3 | 0 | 203.0 | 812 | 162 | 70 | 65 | 18 | 4 | 5 | 7 | 50 | 3 | **216** | 3 | 1 | 13 | 7 | .650 | 3 | 0-0 | 0 | 2.49 | 2.88 |
| 2006 | SD | NL | 32 | 32 | 2 | 0 | 202.1 | 846 | 187 | 93 | 92 | 23 | 5 | 1 | 6 | 62 | 11 | 215 | 4 | 0 | 11 | 14 | .440 | 0 | 0-0 | 0 | 3.42 | 4.09 |
| 2007 | SD | NL | 34 | 34 | 0 | 0 | 223.1 | 898 | 169 | 67 | 63 | 13 | 5 | 7 | 6 | 68 | 5 | **240** | 4 | 0 | **19** | 6 | .760 | 0 | 0-0 | 0 | **2.27** | **2.54** |
| 2008 | SD | NL | 27 | 27 | 1 | 0 | 173.2 | 709 | 146 | 57 | 55 | 17 | 7 | 1 | 5 | 59 | 1 | 166 | 6 | 0 | 10 | 11 | .476 | 0 | 0-0 | 0 | 3.12 | 2.85 |
| 2009 | 2 Tms | | 16 | 16 | 1 | 0 | 101.2 | 410 | 80 | 41 | 39 | 8 | 3 | 2 | 1 | 34 | 0 | 110 | 2 | 2 | 9 | 6 | .600 | 0 | 0-0 | 0 | 2.63 | 3.45 |
| 2010 | CWS | AL | 17 | 17 | 1 | 0 | 107.0 | 450 | 98 | 55 | 55 | 13 | 1 | 5 | 5 | 34 | 2 | 93 | 2 | 1 | 7 | 6 | .538 | 1 | 0-0 | 0 | 3.59 | 4.63 |
| 2011 | CWS | AL | 19 | 18 | 1 | 0 | 111.2 | 470 | 117 | 61 | 61 | 10 | 1 | 5 | 3 | 24 | 4 | 95 | 4 | 0 | 7 | 7 | .500 | 1 | 0-0 | 0 | 3.59 | 4.92 |
| 2012 | CWS | AL | 32 | 32 | 4 | 0 | 219.0 | 882 | 191 | 88 | 82 | 27 | 1 | 6 | 10 | 49 | 1 | 194 | 3 | 2 | 11 | 12 | .478 | 1 | 0-0 | 0 | 3.07 | 3.37 |
| 2013 | 2 Tms | AL | 23 | 23 | 2 | 0 | 144.2 | 590 | 130 | 70 | 67 | 20 | 2 | 3 | 2 | 36 | 0 | 121 | 0 | **2** | 12 | 5 | .706 | 0 | 0-0 | 0 | 3.25 | 4.17 |
| 09 | SD | NL | 13 | 13 | 1 | 0 | 81.2 | 335 | 69 | 38 | 36 | 7 | 2 | 2 | 1 | 28 | 0 | 92 | 2 | 1 | 6 | 6 | .500 | 0 | 0-0 | 0 | 3.00 | 3.97 |
| 09 | CWS | AL | 3 | 3 | 0 | 0 | 20.0 | 75 | 11 | 3 | 3 | 1 | 1 | 0 | 0 | 6 | 0 | 18 | 0 | 1 | 3 | 0 | 1.000 | 0 | 0-0 | 0 | 1.38 | 1.35 |
| 13 | CWS | AL | 13 | 13 | 1 | 0 | 80.0 | 324 | 74 | 41 | 38 | 14 | 1 | 2 | 1 | 17 | 0 | 76 | 0 | 1 | 8 | 4 | .667 | 0 | 0-0 | 0 | 3.49 | 4.28 |
| 13 | Bos | AL | 10 | 10 | 1 | 0 | 64.2 | 266 | 56 | 29 | 29 | 6 | 1 | 1 | 1 | 19 | 0 | 45 | 0 | 1 | 4 | 1 | .800 | 0 | 0-0 | 0 | 2.96 | 4.04 |
| Postseason | | | 2 | 2 | 0 | 0 | 9.2 | 49 | 19 | 13 | 13 | 3 | 1 | 1 | 0 | 4 | 3 | 5 | 1 | 0 | 0 | 2 | .000 | 0 | 0-0 | 0 | 12.16 | 12.10 |
| 12 ML YEARS | | | 306 | 305 | 15 | 0 | 1945.0 | 8018 | 1705 | 799 | 759 | 206 | 46 | 48 | 65 | 584 | 38 | 1869 | 35 | 10 | 132 | 98 | .574 | 6 | 0-0 | 0 | 3.18 | 3.51 |

## Dustin Pedroia

**Bats:** R **Throws:** R **Pos:** 2B-160;PH-1 peh-DROY-uh **Ht:** 5'8" **Wt:** 165 **Born:** 8/17/1983 **Age:** 30

| BATTING | | | | | | | | | | | | | | | | | | | | BASERUNNING | | | | AVERAGES | | |
|---|---|---|---|---|---|---|---|---|---|---|---|---|---|---|---|---|---|---|---|---|---|---|---|---|---|---|
| Year | Team | Lg | G | AB | H | 2B | 3B | HR | (Hm | Rd) | TB | R | RBI | RC | TBB | IBB | SO | HBP | SH | SF | SB | CS | SB% | GDP | Avg | OBP | Slg |
| 2006 | Bos | AL | 31 | 89 | 17 | 4 | 0 | 2 | (1 | 1) | 27 | 5 | 7 | 3 | 7 | 0 | 7 | 1 | 1 | 0 | 0 | 1 | .00 | 1 | .191 | .258 | .303 |
| 2007 | Bos | AL | 139 | 520 | 165 | 39 | 1 | 8 | (5 | 3) | 230 | 86 | 50 | 79 | 47 | 1 | 42 | 7 | 5 | 2 | 7 | 1 | .88 | 8 | .317 | .380 | .442 |
| 2008 | Bos | AL | 157 | 653 | **213** | **54** | 2 | 17 | (7 | 10) | 322 | **118** | 83 | 107 | 50 | 1 | 52 | 7 | 7 | 9 | 20 | 1 | **.95** | 17 | .326 | .376 | .493 |
| 2009 | Bos | AL | 154 | 626 | 185 | 48 | 1 | 15 | (10 | 5) | 280 | **115** | 72 | 104 | 74 | 3 | 45 | 5 | 3 | 6 | 20 | 8 | .71 | 19 | .296 | .371 | .447 |
| 2010 | Bos | AL | 75 | 302 | 87 | 24 | 1 | 12 | (4 | 8) | 149 | 53 | 41 | 52 | 37 | 1 | 38 | 4 | 2 | 6 | 9 | 1 | .90 | 7 | .288 | .367 | .493 |
| 2011 | Bos | AL | 159 | 635 | 195 | 37 | 3 | 21 | (13 | 8) | 301 | 102 | 91 | 114 | 86 | 6 | 85 | 1 | 2 | 7 | 26 | 8 | .76 | 12 | .307 | .387 | .474 |
| 2012 | Bos | AL | 141 | 563 | 163 | 39 | 3 | 15 | (9 | 6) | 253 | 81 | 65 | 84 | 48 | 3 | 60 | 5 | 1 | 6 | 20 | 6 | .77 | 9 | .290 | .347 | .449 |
| 2013 | Bos | AL | 160 | 641 | 193 | 42 | 2 | 9 | (7 | 2) | 266 | 91 | 84 | 99 | 73 | 4 | 75 | 3 | 0 | 7 | 17 | 5 | .77 | 24 | .301 | .372 | .415 |
| Postseason | | | 28 | 115 | 29 | 9 | 0 | 5 | (2 | 3) | 53 | 22 | 18 | 18 | 14 | 0 | 12 | 2 | 1 | 0 | 2 | 1 | .67 | 3 | .252 | .344 | .461 |
| 8 ML YEARS | | | 1016 | 4029 | 1218 | 287 | 13 | 99 | (56 | 43) | 1828 | 651 | 493 | 642 | 422 | 19 | 404 | 33 | 21 | 43 | 119 | 31 | .79 | 97 | .302 | .370 | .454 |

## Carlos Peguero

**Bats:** L **Throws:** L **Pos:** RF-2 peh-GEHR-oh **Ht:** 6'5" **Wt:** 260 **Born:** 2/22/1987 **Age:** 27

| BATTING | | | | | | | | | | | | | | | | | | | | BASERUNNING | | | | AVERAGES | | |
|---|---|---|---|---|---|---|---|---|---|---|---|---|---|---|---|---|---|---|---|---|---|---|---|---|---|---|
| Year | Team | Lg | G | AB | H | 2B | 3B | HR | (Hm | Rd) | TB | R | RBI | RC | TBB | IBB | SO | HBP | SH | SF | SB | CS | SB% | GDP | Avg | OBP | Slg |
| 2013 | Tacom* | AAA | 118 | 454 | 118 | 28 | 3 | 19 | (- | -) | 209 | 60 | 83 | 68 | 42 | 3 | 156 | 2 | 0 | 7 | 11 | 8 | .58 | 6 | .260 | .321 | .460 |
| 2011 | Sea | AL | 46 | 143 | 28 | 3 | 2 | 6 | (4 | 2) | 53 | 14 | 19 | 12 | 8 | 2 | 54 | 3 | 0 | 1 | 0 | 1 | .00 | 0 | .196 | .252 | .371 |
| 2012 | Sea | AL | 17 | 56 | 10 | 2 | 1 | 2 | (1 | 1) | 20 | 2 | 7 | 5 | 1 | 0 | 28 | 0 | 0 | 0 | 0 | 0 | - | 0 | .179 | .193 | .357 |
| 2013 | Sea | AL | 2 | 6 | 2 | 0 | 0 | 1 | (1 | 0) | 5 | 1 | 1 | 1 | 1 | 1 | 2 | 0 | 0 | 0 | 1 | 0 | 1.00 | 0 | .333 | .429 | .833 |
| 3 ML YEARS | | | 65 | 205 | 40 | 5 | 3 | 9 | (6 | 3) | 78 | 17 | 27 | 18 | 10 | 3 | 84 | 3 | 0 | 1 | 1 | 1 | .50 | 0 | .195 | .242 | .380 |

## Francisco Peguero

**Bats:** R **Throws:** R **Pos:** LF-13;PR-4;PH-3;RF-2 peh-GEHR-oh **Ht:** 6'0" **Wt:** 190 **Born:** 6/1/1988 **Age:** 26

| BATTING | | | | | | | | | | | | | | | | | | | | BASERUNNING | | | | AVERAGES | | |
|---|---|---|---|---|---|---|---|---|---|---|---|---|---|---|---|---|---|---|---|---|---|---|---|---|---|---|
| Year | Team | Lg | G | AB | H | 2B | 3B | HR | (Hm | Rd) | TB | R | RBI | RC | TBB | IBB | SO | HBP | SH | SF | SB | CS | SB% | GDP | Avg | OBP | Slg |
| 2009 | Augsta | A | 58 | 238 | 81 | 12 | 4 | 1 | (- | -) | 104 | 28 | 34 | 38 | 5 | 0 | 39 | 4 | 1 | 4 | 15 | 5 | .75 | 6 | .340 | .359 | .437 |
| 2009 | SlmKzr | A- | 17 | 71 | 28 | 3 | 1 | 0 | (- | -) | 33 | 14 | 12 | 15 | 3 | 0 | 9 | 1 | 0 | 1 | 7 | 0 | 1.00 | 4 | .394 | .421 | .465 |
| 2010 | SnJos | A+ | 122 | 510 | 168 | 19 | 16 | 10 | (- | -) | 249 | 78 | 77 | 87 | 18 | 3 | 88 | 6 | 2 | 2 | 40 | 22 | .65 | 14 | .329 | .358 | .488 |
| 2011 | SnJos | A+ | 16 | 68 | 22 | 2 | 0 | 2 | (- | -) | 30 | 12 | 9 | 12 | 7 | 0 | 8 | 0 | 1 | 0 | 4 | 0 | 1.00 | 2 | .324 | .387 | .441 |
| 2011 | Rchmd | AA | 71 | 285 | 88 | 12 | 6 | 5 | (- | -) | 127 | 34 | 37 | 41 | 5 | 0 | 45 | 1 | 0 | 5 | 8 | 1 | .89 | 6 | .309 | .318 | .446 |
| 2012 | Fresno | AAA | 105 | 449 | 122 | 20 | 10 | 5 | (- | -) | 177 | 46 | 68 | 54 | 15 | 1 | 82 | 3 | 4 | 5 | 1 | 0 | 1.00 | 20 | .272 | .297 | .394 |
| 2013 | Fresno | AAA | 70 | 272 | 86 | 12 | 2 | 3 | (- | -) | 111 | 38 | 31 | 40 | 13 | 1 | 51 | 3 | 0 | 0 | 3 | 0 | 1.00 | 9 | .316 | .354 | .408 |
| 2013 | Giants | R | 6 | 26 | 8 | 0 | 1 | 1 | (- | -) | 13 | 5 | 7 | 3 | 0 | 0 | 2 | 0 | 0 | 0 | 0 | 0 | - | 1 | .308 | .308 | .500 |
| 2012 | SF | NL | 17 | 16 | 3 | 0 | 0 | 0 | (0 | 0) | 3 | 6 | 0 | 1 | 0 | 0 | 7 | 0 | 0 | 0 | 3 | 0 | 1.00 | 0 | .188 | .188 | .188 |
| 2013 | SF | NL | 18 | 29 | 6 | 1 | 0 | 1 | (1 | 0) | 10 | 4 | 1 | 1 | 1 | 0 | 2 | 0 | 0 | 0 | 2 | 0 | 1.00 | 2 | .207 | .233 | .345 |
| 2 ML YEARS | | | 35 | 45 | 9 | 1 | 0 | 1 | (1 | 0) | 13 | 10 | 1 | 2 | 1 | 0 | 9 | 0 | 0 | 0 | 5 | 0 | 1.00 | 2 | .200 | .217 | .289 |

## Mike Pelfrey

**Pitches:** R **Bats:** R **Pos:** SP-29 PELL-free **Ht:** 6'7" **Wt:** 250 **Born:** 1/14/1984 **Age:** 30

| HOW MUCH HE PITCHED | | | | | | | | | WHAT HE GAVE UP | | | | | | | | | | | | THE RESULTS | | | | | | | |
|---|---|---|---|---|---|---|---|---|---|---|---|---|---|---|---|---|---|---|---|---|---|---|---|---|---|---|---|---|
| Year | Team | Lg | G | GS | CG | GF | IP | BFP | H | R | ER | HR | SH | SF | HB | TBB | IBB | SO | WP | Bk | W | L | Pct | Sh | Sv-Op | Hld | ERC | ERA |
| 2013 | CRpds* | A | 1 | 1 | 0 | 0 | 6.0 | 21 | 2 | 2 | 2 | 1 | 0 | 0 | 1 | 0 | 0 | 6 | 0 | 0 | 1 | 0 | 1.000 | 0 | 0-- | - | 0.84 | 3.00 |
| 2006 | NYM | NL | 4 | 4 | 0 | 0 | 21.1 | 99 | 25 | 14 | 13 | 1 | 1 | 1 | 3 | 12 | 0 | 13 | 2 | 0 | 2 | 1 | .667 | 0 | 0-0 | 0 | 6.05 | 5.48 |
| 2007 | NYM | NL | 15 | 13 | 0 | 0 | 72.2 | 342 | 85 | 47 | 45 | 6 | 6 | 3 | 9 | 39 | 1 | 45 | 3 | 0 | 3 | 8 | .273 | 0 | 0-0 | 0 | 5.99 | 5.57 |
| 2008 | NYM | NL | 32 | 32 | 2 | 0 | 200.2 | 851 | 209 | 86 | 83 | 12 | 11 | 5 | 13 | 64 | 1 | 110 | 2 | 0 | 13 | 11 | .542 | 0 | 0-0 | 0 | 4.04 | 3.72 |
| 2009 | NYM | NL | 31 | 31 | 0 | 0 | 184.1 | 824 | 213 | 112 | 103 | 18 | 8 | 5 | 7 | 66 | 8 | 107 | 1 | **6** | 10 | 12 | .455 | 0 | 0-0 | 0 | 4.83 | 5.03 |
| 2010 | NYM | NL | 34 | 33 | 0 | 1 | 204.0 | 870 | 213 | 88 | 83 | 12 | **17** | 4 | 6 | 68 | 5 | 113 | 1 | 1 | 15 | 9 | .625 | 0 | 1-1 | 0 | 3.89 | 3.66 |

| | | | HOW MUCH HE PITCHED | | | | | | WHAT HE GAVE UP | | | | | | | | | | | | THE RESULTS | | | | | | | |
|---|---|---|---|---|---|---|---|---|---|---|---|---|---|---|---|---|---|---|---|---|---|---|---|---|---|---|---|---|
| Year | Team | Lg | G | GS | CG | GF | IP | BFP | H | R | ER | HR | SH | SF | HB | TBB | IBB | SO | WP | Bk | W | L | Pct | Sh | Sv-Op | Hld | ERC | ERA |
| 2011 | NYM | NL | 34 | 33 | 2 | 0 | 193.2 | 860 | 220 | 111 | 102 | 21 | 10 | 8 | 7 | 65 | 7 | 105 | 2 | 2 | 7 | 13 | .350 | 0 | 0-0 | 0 | 4.70 | 4.74 |
| 2012 | NYM | NL | 3 | 3 | 0 | 0 | 19.2 | 85 | 24 | 5 | 5 | 0 | 1 | 0 | 0 | 4 | 0 | 13 | 1 | 0 | 0 | 0 | - | 0 | 0-0 | 0 | 3.82 | 2.29 |
| 2013 | Min | AL | 29 | 29 | 0 | 0 | 152.2 | 680 | 184 | 92 | 88 | 13 | 1 | 7 | 6 | 53 | 0 | 101 | 1 | 0 | 5 | 13 | .278 | 0 | 0-0 | 0 | 5.13 | 5.19 |
| 8 ML YEARS | | | 182 | 178 | 4 | 1 | 1049.0 | 4611 | 1173 | 555 | 522 | 83 | 55 | 33 | 51 | 371 | 22 | 607 | 13 | 9 | 55 | 67 | .451 | 0 | 1-1 | 0 | 4.59 | 4.48 |

## Brayan Pena

**Bats:** B **Throws:** R **Pos:** C-64;PH-13;1B-1;PR-1 BRIAN **Ht:** 5'9" **Wt:** 230 **Born:** 1/7/1982 **Age:** 32

| | | | BATTING | | | | | | | | | | | | | | | | | | BASERUNNING | | | | AVERAGES | | |
|---|---|---|---|---|---|---|---|---|---|---|---|---|---|---|---|---|---|---|---|---|---|---|---|---|---|---|---|
| Year | Team | Lg | G | AB | H | 2B | 3B | HR | (Hm | Rd) | TB | R | RBI | RC | TBB | IBB | SO | HBP | SH | SF | SB | CS | SB% | GDP | Avg | OBP | Slg |
| 2005 | Atl | NL | 18 | 39 | 7 | 2 | 0 | 0 | (0 | 0) | 9 | 2 | 4 | 0 | 1 | 1 | 7 | 0 | 0 | 0 | 0 | 0 | - | 1 | .179 | .200 | .231 |
| 2006 | Atl | NL | 23 | 41 | 11 | 2 | 0 | 1 | (0 | 1) | 16 | 9 | 5 | 4 | 2 | 0 | 5 | 0 | 0 | 0 | 0 | 0 | - | 2 | .268 | .302 | .390 |
| 2007 | Atl | NL | 16 | 33 | 7 | 0 | 0 | 1 | (1 | 0) | 10 | 2 | 3 | 0 | 0 | 0 | 3 | 0 | 0 | 0 | 0 | 1 | .00 | 2 | .212 | .212 | .303 |
| 2008 | Atl | NL | 14 | 14 | 4 | 1 | 0 | 0 | (0 | 0) | 5 | 3 | 0 | 0 | 1 | 0 | 2 | 0 | 0 | 0 | 0 | 0 | - | 0 | .286 | .333 | .357 |
| 2009 | KC | AL | 64 | 165 | 45 | 10 | 0 | 6 | (3 | 3) | 73 | 17 | 18 | 18 | 12 | 2 | 18 | 0 | 4 | 2 | 0 | 0 | - | 5 | .273 | .318 | .442 |
| 2010 | KC | AL | 60 | 158 | 40 | 10 | 0 | 1 | (0 | 1) | 53 | 11 | 19 | 16 | 12 | 0 | 27 | 1 | 1 | 2 | 2 | 0 | 1.00 | 8 | .253 | .306 | .335 |
| 2011 | KC | AL | 72 | 222 | 55 | 11 | 0 | 3 | (0 | 3) | 75 | 17 | 24 | 23 | 12 | 0 | 24 | 2 | 0 | 4 | 0 | 0 | - | 6 | .248 | .288 | .338 |
| 2012 | KC | AL | 68 | 212 | 50 | 10 | 1 | 2 | (1 | 1) | 68 | 16 | 25 | 19 | 9 | 0 | 24 | 0 | 1 | 4 | 0 | 1 | .00 | 7 | .236 | .262 | .321 |
| 2013 | Det | AL | 71 | 229 | 68 | 11 | 0 | 4 | (1 | 3) | 91 | 19 | 22 | 19 | 6 | 0 | 26 | 2 | 2 | 4 | 0 | 2 | .00 | 7 | .297 | .315 | .397 |
| 9 ML YEARS | | | 406 | 1113 | 287 | 57 | 1 | 18 | (6 | 12) | 400 | 96 | 120 | 99 | 55 | 3 | 136 | 5 | 8 | 16 | 2 | 4 | .33 | 38 | .258 | .292 | .359 |

## Carlos Pena

**Bats:** L **Throws:** L **Pos:** 1B-46;DH-38;PH-7 **Ht:** 6'2" **Wt:** 225 **Born:** 5/17/1978 **Age:** 36

| | | | BATTING | | | | | | | | | | | | | | | | | | BASERUNNING | | | | AVERAGES | | |
|---|---|---|---|---|---|---|---|---|---|---|---|---|---|---|---|---|---|---|---|---|---|---|---|---|---|---|---|
| Year | Team | Lg | G | AB | H | 2B | 3B | HR | (Hm | Rd) | TB | R | RBI | RC | TBB | IBB | SO | HBP | SH | SF | SB | CS | SB% | GDP | Avg | OBP | Slg |
| 2013 | Omha* | AAA | 5 | 18 | 6 | 0 | 1 | 2 | (- | -) | 14 | 5 | 6 | 5 | 4 | 0 | 3 | 0 | 0 | 0 | 0 | 0 | - | 0 | .333 | .455 | .778 |
| 2001 | Tex | AL | 22 | 62 | 16 | 4 | 1 | 3 | (2 | 1) | 31 | 6 | 12 | 11 | 10 | 0 | 17 | 0 | 0 | 0 | 0 | 0 | - | 1 | .258 | .361 | .500 |
| 2002 | 2 Tms | AL | 115 | 397 | 96 | 17 | 4 | 19 | (10 | 9) | 178 | 43 | 52 | 56 | 41 | 0 | 111 | 3 | 0 | 2 | 2 | 2 | .50 | 7 | .242 | .316 | .448 |
| 2003 | Det | AL | 131 | 452 | 112 | 21 | 6 | 18 | (8 | 10) | 199 | 51 | 50 | 61 | 53 | 1 | 123 | 6 | 1 | 4 | 4 | 5 | .44 | 6 | .248 | .332 | .440 |
| 2004 | Det | AL | 142 | 481 | 116 | 22 | 4 | 27 | (10 | 17) | 227 | 89 | 82 | 73 | 70 | 2 | 146 | 3 | 2 | 5 | 7 | 1 | .88 | 11 | .241 | .338 | .472 |
| 2005 | Det | AL | 79 | 260 | 61 | 9 | 0 | 18 | (14 | 4) | 124 | 37 | 44 | 40 | 31 | 2 | 95 | 4 | 0 | 0 | 0 | 1 | .00 | 3 | .235 | .325 | .477 |
| 2006 | Bos | AL | 18 | 33 | 9 | 2 | 0 | 1 | (1 | 0) | 14 | 3 | 3 | 3 | 4 | 0 | 10 | 0 | 0 | 0 | 0 | 0 | - | 1 | .273 | .351 | .424 |
| 2007 | TB | AL | 148 | 490 | 138 | 29 | 1 | 46 | (23 | 23) | 307 | 99 | 121 | 114 | 103 | 10 | 142 | 10 | 1 | 8 | 1 | 0 | 1.00 | 7 | .282 | .411 | .627 |
| 2008 | TB | AL | 139 | 490 | 121 | 24 | 2 | 31 | (14 | 17) | 242 | 76 | 102 | 92 | 96 | 7 | 166 | 12 | 0 | 9 | 1 | 1 | .50 | 6 | .247 | .377 | .494 |
| 2009 | TB | AL | 135 | 471 | 107 | 25 | 2 | **39** | (19 | 20) | 253 | 91 | 100 | 88 | 87 | 11 | 163 | 9 | 0 | 3 | 3 | 3 | .50 | 5 | .227 | .356 | .537 |
| 2010 | TB | AL | 144 | 484 | 95 | 18 | 0 | 28 | (18 | 10) | 197 | 64 | 84 | 73 | 87 | 4 | 158 | 7 | 0 | 4 | 5 | 1 | .83 | 2 | .196 | .325 | .407 |
| 2011 | ChC | NL | 153 | 493 | 111 | 27 | 3 | 28 | (12 | 16) | 228 | 72 | 80 | 79 | 101 | 7 | 161 | 4 | 1 | 7 | 2 | 2 | .50 | 6 | .225 | .357 | .462 |
| 2012 | TB | AL | 160 | 497 | 98 | 17 | 2 | 19 | (11 | 8) | 176 | 72 | 61 | 60 | 87 | 2 | 182 | 13 | 0 | 3 | 2 | 3 | .40 | 10 | .197 | .330 | .354 |
| 2013 | 2 Tms | AL | 89 | 280 | 58 | 13 | 1 | 8 | (4 | 4) | 97 | 38 | 25 | 32 | 43 | 5 | 92 | 4 | 1 | 0 | 1 | 3 | .25 | 5 | .207 | .321 | .346 |
| 02 | Oak | AL | 40 | 124 | 27 | 4 | 0 | 7 | (5 | 2) | 52 | 12 | 16 | 17 | 15 | 0 | 38 | 1 | 0 | 1 | 0 | 0 | - | 2 | .218 | .305 | .419 |
| 02 | Det | AL | 75 | 273 | 69 | 13 | 4 | 12 | (5 | 7) | 126 | 31 | 36 | 39 | 26 | 0 | 73 | 2 | 0 | 1 | 2 | 2 | .50 | 5 | .253 | .321 | .462 |
| 13 | Hou | AL | 85 | 277 | 58 | 13 | 1 | 8 | (4 | 4) | 97 | 38 | 25 | 32 | 43 | 5 | 89 | 4 | 1 | 0 | 1 | 3 | .25 | 5 | .209 | .324 | .350 |
| 13 | KC | AL | 4 | 3 | 0 | 0 | 0 | 0 | (0 | 0) | 0 | 0 | 0 | 0 | 0 | 0 | 3 | 0 | 0 | 0 | 0 | 0 | - | 0 | .000 | .000 | .000 |
| Postseason | | | 19 | 67 | 18 | 3 | 1 | 4 | (0 | 4) | 35 | 13 | 14 | 14 | 13 | 2 | 24 | 0 | 0 | 0 | 3 | 2 | .60 | 1 | .269 | .388 | .522 |
| 13 ML YEARS | | | 1475 | 4890 | 1138 | 228 | 26 | 285 | (146 | 139) | 2273 | 741 | 816 | 782 | 813 | 51 | 1566 | 75 | 6 | 45 | 28 | 22 | .56 | 70 | .233 | .348 | .465 |

## Ramiro Pena

**Bats:** B **Throws:** R **Pos:** 3B-32;PH-11;2B-10;SS-7;PR-5 **Ht:** 5'11" **Wt:** 185 **Born:** 7/18/1985 **Age:** 28

| | | | BATTING | | | | | | | | | | | | | | | | | | BASERUNNING | | | | AVERAGES | | |
|---|---|---|---|---|---|---|---|---|---|---|---|---|---|---|---|---|---|---|---|---|---|---|---|---|---|---|---|
| Year | Team | Lg | G | AB | H | 2B | 3B | HR | (Hm | Rd) | TB | R | RBI | RC | TBB | IBB | SO | HBP | SH | SF | SB | CS | SB% | GDP | Avg | OBP | Slg |
| 2009 | NYY | AL | 69 | 115 | 33 | 6 | 1 | 1 | (1 | 0) | 44 | 17 | 10 | 15 | 5 | 0 | 20 | 0 | 1 | 0 | 4 | 1 | .80 | 2 | .287 | .317 | .383 |
| 2010 | NYY | AL | 85 | 154 | 35 | 1 | 1 | 0 | (0 | 0) | 38 | 18 | 18 | 10 | 6 | 0 | 27 | 1 | 4 | 2 | 7 | 1 | .88 | 4 | .227 | .258 | .247 |
| 2011 | NYY | AL | 23 | 40 | 4 | 0 | 0 | 1 | (1 | 0) | 7 | 5 | 4 | 0 | 2 | 0 | 11 | 1 | 2 | 1 | 0 | 0 | - | 1 | .100 | .159 | .175 |
| 2012 | NYY | AL | 3 | 4 | 1 | 0 | 0 | 0 | (0 | 0) | 1 | 0 | 0 | 0 | 0 | 0 | 0 | 0 | 0 | 0 | 0 | 0 | - | 0 | .250 | .250 | .250 |
| 2013 | Atl | NL | 50 | 97 | 27 | 5 | 1 | 3 | (2 | 1) | 43 | 14 | 12 | 12 | 8 | 0 | 18 | 0 | 1 | 1 | 0 | 2 | .00 | 1 | .278 | .330 | .443 |
| 5 ML YEARS | | | 230 | 410 | 100 | 12 | 3 | 5 | (4 | 1) | 133 | 54 | 44 | 37 | 21 | 0 | 76 | 2 | 8 | 4 | 11 | 4 | .73 | 8 | .244 | .281 | .324 |

## Hunter Pence

**Bats:** R **Throws:** R **Pos:** RF-162 **Ht:** 6'4" **Wt:** 220 **Born:** 4/13/1983 **Age:** 31

| | | | BATTING | | | | | | | | | | | | | | | | | | BASERUNNING | | | | AVERAGES | | |
|---|---|---|---|---|---|---|---|---|---|---|---|---|---|---|---|---|---|---|---|---|---|---|---|---|---|---|---|
| Year | Team | Lg | G | AB | H | 2B | 3B | HR | (Hm | Rd) | TB | R | RBI | RC | TBB | IBB | SO | HBP | SH | SF | SB | CS | SB% | GDP | Avg | OBP | Slg |
| 2007 | Hou | NL | 108 | 456 | 147 | 30 | 9 | 17 | (7 | 10) | 246 | 57 | 69 | 77 | 26 | 0 | 95 | 1 | 0 | 1 | 11 | 5 | .69 | 10 | .322 | .360 | .539 |
| 2008 | Hou | NL | 157 | 595 | 160 | 34 | 4 | 25 | (14 | 11) | 277 | 78 | 83 | 82 | 40 | 2 | 124 | 4 | 0 | 3 | 11 | 10 | .52 | 14 | .269 | .318 | .466 |
| 2009 | Hou | NL | 159 | 585 | 165 | 26 | 5 | 25 | (14 | 11) | 276 | 76 | 72 | 80 | 58 | 1 | 109 | 1 | 0 | 3 | 14 | 11 | .56 | 25 | .282 | .346 | .472 |
| 2010 | Hou | NL | 156 | 614 | 173 | 29 | 3 | 25 | (14 | 11) | 283 | 93 | 91 | 89 | 41 | 2 | 105 | 0 | 0 | 3 | 18 | 9 | .67 | 11 | .282 | .325 | .461 |
| 2011 | 2 Tms | NL | 154 | 606 | 190 | 38 | 5 | 22 | (5 | 17) | 304 | 84 | 97 | 102 | 56 | 3 | 124 | 1 | 0 | 5 | 8 | 2 | .80 | 15 | .314 | .370 | .502 |
| 2012 | 2 Tms | NL | 160 | 617 | 156 | 26 | 4 | 24 | (9 | 15) | 262 | 87 | 104 | 81 | 56 | 2 | 145 | 7 | 1 | 7 | 5 | 2 | .71 | 15 | .253 | .319 | .425 |
| 2013 | SF | NL | **162** | 629 | 178 | 35 | 5 | 27 | (10 | 17) | 304 | 91 | 99 | 91 | 52 | 3 | 115 | 3 | 0 | 3 | 22 | 3 | .88 | 17 | .283 | .339 | .483 |
| 11 | Hou | NL | 100 | 399 | 123 | 26 | 3 | 11 | (4 | 7) | 188 | 49 | 62 | 63 | 30 | 1 | 86 | 1 | 0 | 2 | 7 | 1 | .88 | 7 | .308 | .356 | .471 |
| 11 | Phi | NL | 54 | 207 | 67 | 12 | 2 | 11 | (1 | 10) | 116 | 35 | 35 | 39 | 26 | 2 | 38 | 0 | 0 | 3 | 1 | 1 | .50 | 8 | .324 | .394 | .560 |
| 12 | Phi | NL | 101 | 398 | 108 | 15 | 2 | 17 | (7 | 10) | 178 | 59 | 59 | 50 | 37 | 1 | 85 | 3 | 0 | 2 | 4 | 2 | .67 | 14 | .271 | .336 | .447 |
| 12 | SF | NL | 59 | 219 | 48 | 11 | 2 | 7 | (2 | 5) | 84 | 28 | 45 | 31 | 19 | 1 | 60 | 4 | 1 | 5 | 1 | 0 | 1.00 | 1 | .219 | .287 | .384 |
| Postseason | | | 21 | 81 | 17 | 2 | 0 | 1 | (0 | 1) | 22 | 10 | 8 | 3 | 4 | 1 | 19 | 0 | 0 | 1 | 2 | 1 | .67 | 2 | .210 | .244 | .272 |
| 7 ML YEARS | | | 1056 | 4102 | 1169 | 218 | 35 | 165 | (73 | 92) | 1952 | 566 | 615 | 602 | 329 | 13 | 817 | 17 | 1 | 25 | 89 | 42 | .68 | 107 | .285 | .339 | .476 |

## Cliff Pennington

**Bats:** B **Throws:** R **Pos:** SS-51;2B-29;PH-19;PR-5;3B-2 **Ht:** 5'10" **Wt:** 195 **Born:** 6/15/1984 **Age:** 30

| BATTING | | | | | | | | | | | | | | | | | | | | BASERUNNING | | | | AVERAGES | | |
|---|---|---|---|---|---|---|---|---|---|---|---|---|---|---|---|---|---|---|---|---|---|---|---|---|---|---|
| Year Team | Lg | G | AB | H | 2B | 3B | HR | (Hm | Rd) | TB | R | RBI | RC | TBB | IBB | SO | HBP | SH | SF | SB | CS | SB% | GDP | Avg | OBP | Slg |
| 2008 Oak | AL | 36 | 99 | 24 | 5 | 0 | 0 | (0 | 0) | 29 | 14 | 9 | 12 | 13 | 0 | 18 | 2 | 2 | 1 | 4 | 1 | .80 | 1 | .242 | .339 | .293 |
| 2009 Oak | AL | 60 | 208 | 58 | 11 | 3 | 4 | (3 | 1) | 87 | 27 | 21 | 29 | 19 | 0 | 46 | 1 | 1 | 0 | 7 | 5 | .58 | 5 | .279 | .342 | .418 |
| 2010 Oak | AL | 156 | 508 | 127 | 26 | 8 | 6 | (2 | 4) | 187 | 64 | 46 | 66 | 50 | 0 | 96 | 3 | 12 | 3 | 29 | 5 | .85 | 7 | .250 | .319 | .368 |
| 2011 Oak | AL | 148 | 515 | 136 | 26 | 2 | 8 | (3 | 5) | 190 | 57 | 58 | 73 | 42 | 1 | 104 | 1 | 8 | 4 | 14 | 9 | .61 | 5 | .264 | .319 | .369 |
| 2012 Oak | AL | 125 | 418 | 90 | 18 | 2 | 6 | (0 | 6) | 130 | 50 | 28 | 37 | 35 | 0 | 90 | 2 | 5 | 2 | 15 | 6 | .71 | 1 | .215 | .278 | .311 |
| 2013 Ari | NL | 96 | 269 | 65 | 13 | 1 | 1 | (1 | 0) | 83 | 25 | 18 | 23 | 26 | 5 | 54 | 1 | 2 | 1 | 2 | 0 | 1.00 | 7 | .242 | .310 | .309 |
| Postseason | | 5 | 14 | 4 | 0 | 0 | 0 | (0 | 0) | 4 | 1 | 1 | 2 | 3 | 0 | 4 | 0 | 0 | 0 | 0 | 0 | - | 0 | .286 | .412 | .286 |
| 6 ML YEARS | | 621 | 2017 | 500 | 99 | 16 | 25 | (9 | 16) | 706 | 237 | 180 | 240 | 185 | 6 | 408 | 10 | 30 | 11 | 71 | 26 | .73 | 26 | .248 | .313 | .350 |

## Jhonny Peralta

**Bats:** R **Throws:** R **Pos:** SS-106;LF-3;PH-1 pah-RALL-tah **Ht:** 6'2" **Wt:** 215 **Born:** 5/28/1982 **Age:** 32

| BATTING | | | | | | | | | | | | | | | | | | | | BASERUNNING | | | | AVERAGES | | |
|---|---|---|---|---|---|---|---|---|---|---|---|---|---|---|---|---|---|---|---|---|---|---|---|---|---|---|
| Year Team | Lg | G | AB | H | 2B | 3B | HR | (Hm | Rd) | TB | R | RBI | RC | TBB | IBB | SO | HBP | SH | SF | SB | CS | SB% | GDP | Avg | OBP | Slg |
| 2003 Cle | AL | 77 | 242 | 55 | 10 | 1 | 4 | (3 | 1) | 79 | 24 | 21 | 24 | 20 | 0 | 65 | 4 | 2 | 2 | 1 | 3 | .25 | 5 | .227 | .295 | .326 |
| 2004 Cle | AL | 8 | 25 | 6 | 1 | 0 | 0 | (0 | 0) | 7 | 2 | 2 | 2 | 3 | 0 | 6 | 0 | 0 | 0 | 0 | 1 | .00 | 0 | .240 | .321 | .280 |
| 2005 Cle | AL | 141 | 504 | 147 | 35 | 4 | 24 | (14 | 10) | 262 | 82 | 78 | 87 | 58 | 3 | 128 | 3 | 1 | 4 | 0 | 2 | .00 | 12 | .292 | .366 | .520 |
| 2006 Cle | AL | 149 | 569 | 146 | 28 | 3 | 13 | (7 | 6) | 219 | 84 | 68 | 66 | 56 | 0 | 152 | 1 | 3 | 3 | 0 | 1 | .00 | 19 | .257 | .323 | .385 |
| 2007 Cle | AL | 152 | 574 | 155 | 27 | 1 | 21 | (16 | 5) | 247 | 87 | 72 | 85 | 61 | 2 | 146 | 4 | 1 | 7 | 4 | 4 | .50 | 12 | .270 | .341 | .430 |
| 2008 Cle | AL | 154 | 605 | 167 | 42 | 4 | 23 | (11 | 12) | 286 | 104 | 89 | 84 | 48 | 2 | 126 | 4 | 2 | 5 | 3 | 1 | .75 | 26 | .276 | .331 | .473 |
| 2009 Cle | AL | 151 | 582 | 148 | 35 | 1 | 11 | (2 | 9) | 218 | 57 | 83 | 63 | 51 | 0 | 134 | 4 | 2 | 6 | 0 | 2 | .00 | 20 | .254 | .316 | .375 |
| 2010 2 Tms | AL | 148 | 551 | 137 | 30 | 2 | 15 | (4 | 11) | 216 | 60 | 81 | 71 | 53 | 2 | 103 | 1 | 0 | 10 | 1 | 0 | 1.00 | 11 | .249 | .311 | .392 |
| 2011 Det | AL | 146 | 525 | 157 | 25 | 3 | 21 | (13 | 8) | 251 | 68 | 86 | 77 | 40 | 2 | 95 | 2 | 0 | 9 | 0 | 2 | .00 | 17 | .299 | .345 | .478 |
| 2012 Det | AL | 150 | 531 | 127 | 32 | 3 | 13 | (6 | 7) | 204 | 58 | 63 | 53 | 49 | 3 | 105 | 2 | 1 | 2 | 1 | 2 | .33 | 20 | .239 | .305 | .384 |
| 2013 Det | AL | 107 | 409 | 124 | 30 | 0 | 11 | (7 | 4) | 187 | 50 | 55 | 62 | 35 | 2 | 98 | 1 | 1 | 2 | 3 | 3 | .50 | 9 | .303 | .358 | .457 |
| 10 Cle | AL | 91 | 334 | 82 | 23 | 2 | 7 | (3 | 4) | 130 | 37 | 43 | 41 | 32 | 1 | 69 | 1 | 0 | 6 | 1 | 0 | 1.00 | 7 | .246 | .308 | .389 |
| 10 Det | AL | 57 | 217 | 55 | 7 | 0 | 8 | (1 | 7) | 86 | 23 | 38 | 30 | 21 | 1 | 34 | 0 | 0 | 4 | 0 | 0 | - | 4 | .253 | .314 | .396 |
| Postseason | | 35 | 133 | 36 | 9 | 0 | 7 | (4 | 3) | 66 | 13 | 18 | 18 | 9 | 0 | 28 | 1 | 1 | 1 | 2 | 0 | 1.00 | 4 | .271 | .319 | .496 |
| 11 ML YEARS | | 1383 | 5117 | 1369 | 295 | 22 | 156 | (83 | 73) | 2176 | 676 | 698 | 674 | 474 | 16 | 1158 | 26 | 13 | 50 | 13 | 21 | .38 | 151 | .268 | .330 | .425 |

## Joel Peralta

**Pitches:** R **Bats:** R **Pos:** RP-80 joe-ELL pah-RALL-tah **Ht:** 5'11" **Wt:** 205 **Born:** 3/23/1976 **Age:** 38

| HOW MUCH HE PITCHED | | | | | | | | WHAT HE GAVE UP | | | | | | | | | | | | | THE RESULTS | | | | | | | |
|---|---|---|---|---|---|---|---|---|---|---|---|---|---|---|---|---|---|---|---|---|---|---|---|---|---|---|---|---|
| Year Team | Lg | G | GS | CG | GF | IP | BFP | H | R | ER | HR | SH | SF | HB | TBB | IBB | SO | WP | Bk | W | L | Pct | Sh | Sv-Op | Hld | ERC | ERA |
| 2005 LAA | AL | 28 | 0 | 0 | 10 | 34.2 | 145 | 28 | 15 | 15 | 6 | 2 | 1 | 0 | 14 | 2 | 30 | 2 | 0 | 1 | 0 | 1.000 | 0 | 0-0 | 0 | 3.40 | 3.89 |
| 2006 KC | AL | 64 | 0 | 0 | 21 | 73.2 | 304 | 74 | 37 | 36 | 10 | 1 | 3 | 2 | 17 | 2 | 57 | 5 | 0 | 1 | 3 | .250 | 0 | 1-3 | 17 | 3.80 | 4.40 |
| 2007 KC | AL | 62 | 0 | 0 | 18 | 87.2 | 366 | 93 | 39 | 37 | 9 | 2 | 4 | 2 | 19 | 5 | 66 | 2 | 0 | 1 | 3 | .250 | 0 | 1-5 | 7 | 3.75 | 3.80 |
| 2008 KC | AL | 40 | 0 | 0 | 12 | 52.2 | 224 | 56 | 37 | 35 | 15 | 1 | 3 | 2 | 14 | 0 | 38 | 1 | 0 | 1 | 2 | .333 | 0 | 0-1 | 1 | 5.38 | 5.98 |
| 2009 Col | NL | 27 | 0 | 0 | 6 | 24.2 | 113 | 27 | 17 | 17 | 3 | 0 | 1 | 3 | 12 | 2 | 22 | 0 | 0 | 0 | 3 | .000 | 0 | 0-1 | 6 | 5.51 | 6.20 |
| 2010 Was | NL | 39 | 0 | 0 | 10 | 49.0 | 189 | 30 | 12 | 11 | 5 | 2 | 1 | 1 | 9 | 4 | 49 | 0 | 0 | 1 | 0 | 1.000 | 0 | 0-2 | 9 | 1.43 | 2.02 |
| 2011 TB | AL | 71 | 0 | 0 | 18 | 67.2 | 256 | 44 | 23 | 22 | 7 | 2 | 2 | 0 | 18 | 3 | 61 | 3 | 0 | 3 | 4 | .429 | 0 | 6-8 | 19 | 1.84 | 2.93 |
| 2012 TB | AL | 77 | 0 | 0 | 9 | 67.0 | 264 | 49 | 28 | 27 | 9 | 0 | 1 | 1 | 17 | 2 | 84 | 5 | 0 | 2 | 6 | .250 | 0 | 2-5 | **37** | 2.36 | 3.63 |
| 2013 TB | AL | **80** | 0 | 0 | 12 | 71.1 | 291 | 47 | 31 | 27 | 7 | 2 | 0 | 0 | 34 | 1 | 74 | 1 | 0 | 3 | 8 | .273 | 0 | 1-4 | **41** | 2.53 | 3.41 |
| Postseason | | 3 | 0 | 0 | 2 | 2.1 | 10 | 1 | 0 | 0 | 0 | 0 | 0 | 0 | 2 | 0 | 0 | 0 | 0 | 0 | 0 | - | 0 | 0-0 | 0 | 2.03 | 0.00 |
| 9 ML YEARS | | 488 | 0 | 0 | 116 | 528.1 | 2152 | 448 | 239 | 227 | 71 | 12 | 16 | 11 | 154 | 21 | 481 | 19 | 0 | 13 | 29 | .310 | 0 | 11-29 | 137 | 3.10 | 3.87 |

## Wily Peralta

**Pitches:** R **Bats:** R **Pos:** SP-32 **Ht:** 6'1" **Wt:** 245 **Born:** 5/8/1989 **Age:** 25

| HOW MUCH HE PITCHED | | | | | | | | WHAT HE GAVE UP | | | | | | | | | | | | | THE RESULTS | | | | | | | |
|---|---|---|---|---|---|---|---|---|---|---|---|---|---|---|---|---|---|---|---|---|---|---|---|---|---|---|---|---|
| Year Team | Lg | G | GS | CG | GF | IP | BFP | H | R | ER | HR | SH | SF | HB | TBB | IBB | SO | WP | Bk | W | L | Pct | Sh | Sv-Op | Hld | ERC | ERA |
| 2009 Wisc | A | 27 | 15 | 0 | 4 | 103.2 | 446 | 91 | 45 | 40 | 5 | 4 | 4 | 4 | 46 | 0 | 118 | 8 | 0 | 4 | 4 | .500 | 0 | 1-- | - | 3.33 | 3.47 |
| 2010 BrvdCt | A+ | 19 | 17 | 0 | 0 | 105.0 | 454 | 102 | 50 | 45 | 5 | 3 | 2 | 6 | 40 | 0 | 75 | 3 | 1 | 6 | 3 | .667 | 0 | 0-- | - | 3.68 | 3.86 |
| 2010 Hntsvl | AA | 8 | 8 | 0 | 0 | 42.1 | 190 | 43 | 22 | 17 | 5 | 1 | 1 | 4 | 24 | 0 | 29 | 4 | 0 | 2 | 3 | .400 | 0 | 0-- | - | 5.47 | 3.61 |
| 2011 Hntsvl | AA | 21 | 21 | 1 | 0 | 119.2 | 496 | 106 | 57 | 46 | 9 | 3 | 5 | 4 | 48 | 0 | 117 | 8 | 0 | 9 | 7 | .563 | 0 | 0-- | - | 3.50 | 3.46 |
| 2011 Nashv | AAA | 5 | 5 | 0 | 0 | 31.0 | 122 | 21 | 7 | 7 | 0 | 0 | 1 | 1 | 11 | 0 | 40 | 1 | 0 | 2 | 0 | 1.000 | 0 | 0-- | - | 1.81 | 2.03 |
| 2012 Nashv | AAA | 28 | 28 | 1 | 0 | 146.2 | 652 | 154 | 79 | 76 | 9 | 2 | 2 | 9 | 78 | 1 | 141 | 9 | 1 | 7 | 11 | .389 | 0 | 0-- | - | 4.93 | 4.66 |
| 2012 Mil | NL | 6 | 5 | 0 | 1 | 29.0 | 113 | 24 | 8 | 8 | 0 | 3 | 0 | 0 | 11 | 0 | 23 | 1 | 0 | 2 | 1 | .667 | 0 | 0-0 | 0 | 2.61 | 2.48 |
| 2013 Mil | NL | 32 | 32 | 2 | 0 | 183.1 | 802 | 187 | 107 | 89 | 19 | 11 | 3 | 7 | 73 | 3 | 129 | 12 | 0 | 11 | 15 | .423 | 1 | 0-0 | 0 | 4.32 | 4.37 |
| 2 ML YEARS | | 38 | 37 | 2 | 1 | 212.1 | 915 | 211 | 115 | 97 | 19 | 14 | 3 | 7 | 84 | 3 | 152 | 13 | 0 | 13 | 16 | .448 | 1 | 0-0 | 0 | 4.08 | 4.11 |

## Audry Perez

**Bats:** R **Throws:** R **Pos:** C-1;PH-1 AWE-dree **Ht:** 5'9" **Wt:** 230 **Born:** 12/23/1988 **Age:** 25

| BATTING | | | | | | | | | | | | | | | | | | | | BASERUNNING | | | | AVERAGES | | |
|---|---|---|---|---|---|---|---|---|---|---|---|---|---|---|---|---|---|---|---|---|---|---|---|---|---|---|
| Year Team | Lg | G | AB | H | 2B | 3B | HR | (Hm | Rd) | TB | R | RBI | RC | TBB | IBB | SO | HBP | SH | SF | SB | CS | SB% | GDP | Avg | OBP | Slg |
| 2009 JhsCty | R | 40 | 128 | 33 | 7 | 1 | 9 | (- | -) | 69 | 22 | 23 | 21 | 8 | 0 | 28 | 0 | 0 | 0 | 1 | 0 | 1.00 | 5 | .258 | .301 | .539 |
| 2010 Batvia | A- | 45 | 165 | 52 | 11 | 0 | 4 | (- | -) | 75 | 25 | 47 | 27 | 11 | 0 | 33 | 5 | 0 | 4 | 2 | 3 | .40 | 3 | .315 | .368 | .455 |
| 2011 PlmBh | A+ | 22 | 86 | 25 | 4 | 0 | 3 | (- | -) | 38 | 7 | 10 | 11 | 2 | 0 | 13 | 0 | 0 | 0 | 0 | 0 | - | 2 | .291 | .307 | .442 |
| 2011 Sprgfld | AA | 59 | 230 | 60 | 15 | 0 | 8 | (- | -) | 99 | 28 | 37 | 28 | 5 | 0 | 29 | 2 | 3 | 3 | 0 | 0 | - | 6 | .261 | .279 | .430 |
| 2012 Sprgfld | AA | 81 | 312 | 82 | 12 | 1 | 4 | (- | -) | 108 | 28 | 42 | 30 | 6 | 0 | 58 | 3 | 1 | 3 | 0 | 0 | - | 11 | .263 | .281 | .346 |
| 2013 Sprgfld | AA | 57 | 215 | 45 | 12 | 0 | 6 | (- | -) | 75 | 16 | 26 | 16 | 3 | 1 | 39 | 4 | 0 | 0 | 0 | 1 | .00 | 13 | .209 | .234 | .349 |
| 2013 Memp | AAA | 25 | 90 | 19 | 3 | 0 | 0 | (- | -) | 22 | 7 | 7 | 4 | 2 | 0 | 10 | 0 | 1 | 0 | 0 | 0 | - | 5 | .211 | .228 | .244 |
| 2013 StL | NL | 2 | 1 | 0 | 0 | 0 | 0 | (0 | 0) | 0 | 0 | 0 | 0 | 0 | 0 | 1 | 0 | 0 | 0 | 0 | 0 | - | 0 | .000 | .000 | .000 |

# Chris Perez

**Pitches:** R **Bats:** R **Pos:** RP-54 **Ht:** 6'4" **Wt:** 230 **Born:** 7/1/1985 **Age:** 28

| HOW MUCH HE PITCHED | | | | | | | | | WHAT HE GAVE UP | | | | | | | | | | | | THE RESULTS | | | | | | | |
|---|---|---|---|---|---|---|---|---|---|---|---|---|---|---|---|---|---|---|---|---|---|---|---|---|---|---|---|---|
| Year | Team | Lg | G | GS | CG | GF | IP | BFP | H | R | ER | HR | SH | SF | HB | TBB | IBB | SO | WP | Bk | W | L | Pct | Sh | Sv-Op | Hld | ERC | ERA |
| 2013 | Lk Cty* | A | 1 | 1 | 0 | 0 | 1.0 | 3 | 2 | 0 | 0 | 0 | 0 | 0 | 0 | 0 | 0 | 1 | 0 | 0 | 0 | 0 | - | 0 | 0-- | - | 12.84 | 0.00 |
| 2013 | Akron* | AA | 1 | 0 | 0 | 0 | 1.0 | 8 | 5 | 5 | 5 | 3 | 0 | 0 | 1 | 0 | 0 | 2 | 0 | 0 | 0 | 1 | .000 | 0 | 0-- | - | 90.39 | 45.00 |
| 2013 | MhVlly* | A- | 1 | 0 | 0 | 0 | 1.0 | 3 | 0 | 0 | 0 | 0 | 0 | 0 | 0 | 0 | 0 | 1 | 0 | 0 | 0 | 0 | - | 0 | 0-- | - | 0.00 | 0.00 |
| 2008 | StL | NL | 41 | 0 | 0 | 23 | 41.2 | 177 | 34 | 18 | 16 | 5 | 1 | 3 | 1 | 22 | 0 | 42 | 2 | 0 | 3 | 3 | .500 | 0 | 7-11 | 6 | 3.83 | 3.46 |
| 2009 | 2 Tms | | 61 | 0 | 0 | 16 | 57.0 | 239 | 41 | 28 | 27 | 8 | 0 | 2 | 6 | 27 | 0 | 68 | 8 | 0 | 1 | 2 | .333 | 0 | 2-5 | 7 | 3.54 | 4.26 |
| 2010 | Cle | AL | 63 | 0 | 0 | 37 | 63.0 | 260 | 40 | 15 | 12 | 4 | 6 | 1 | 5 | 28 | 3 | 61 | 4 | 0 | 2 | 2 | .500 | 0 | 23-27 | 9 | 2.30 | 1.71 |
| 2011 | Cle | AL | 64 | 0 | 0 | 57 | 59.2 | 248 | 46 | 24 | 22 | 5 | 4 | 1 | 3 | 26 | 4 | 39 | 1 | 0 | 4 | 7 | .364 | 0 | 36-40 | 0 | 2.98 | 3.32 |
| 2012 | Cle | AL | 61 | 0 | 0 | 53 | 57.2 | 242 | 49 | 25 | 23 | 6 | 0 | 3 | 2 | 16 | 1 | 59 | 0 | 0 | 0 | 4 | .000 | 0 | 39-43 | 0 | 2.85 | 3.59 |
| 2013 | Cle | AL | 54 | 0 | 0 | 41 | 54.0 | 243 | 56 | 27 | 26 | 11 | 5 | 0 | 4 | 21 | 2 | 54 | 1 | 0 | 5 | 3 | .625 | 0 | 25-30 | 1 | 5.12 | 4.33 |
| 09 | StL | NL | 29 | 0 | 0 | 8 | 23.2 | 106 | 17 | 12 | 11 | 3 | 0 | 1 | 3 | 15 | 0 | 30 | 4 | 0 | 1 | 1 | .500 | 0 | 1-2 | 3 | 4.01 | 4.18 |
| 09 | Cle | AL | 32 | 0 | 0 | 8 | 33.1 | 133 | 24 | 16 | 16 | 5 | 0 | 1 | 3 | 12 | 0 | 38 | 4 | 0 | 0 | 1 | .000 | 0 | 1-3 | 4 | 3.19 | 4.32 |
| 6 ML YEARS | | | 344 | 0 | 0 | 227 | 333.0 | 1409 | 266 | 137 | 126 | 39 | 16 | 10 | 21 | 140 | 10 | 323 | 16 | 0 | 15 | 21 | .417 | 0 | 132-156 | 23 | 3.35 | 3.41 |

# Eury Perez

**Bats:** R **Throws:** R **Pos:** CF-4;LF-3;PR-2;RF-1;PH-1 YERR-ee **Ht:** 6'0" **Wt:** 180 **Born:** 5/30/1990 **Age:** 24

| BATTING | | | | | | | | | | | | | | | | | | | | BASERUNNING | | | | AVERAGES | | |
|---|---|---|---|---|---|---|---|---|---|---|---|---|---|---|---|---|---|---|---|---|---|---|---|---|---|---|
| Year | Team | Lg | G | AB | H | 2B | 3B | HR | (Hm | Rd) | TB | R | RBI | RC | TBB | IBB | SO | HBP | SH | SF | SB | CS | SB% | GDP | Avg | OBP | Slg |
| 2009 | Nats | R | 47 | 181 | 69 | 3 | 5 | 3 | (- | -) | 91 | 38 | 24 | 39 | 15 | 0 | 20 | 5 | 4 | 0 | 16 | 8 | .67 | 3 | .381 | .443 | .503 |
| 2010 | Hgrstn | A | 131 | 438 | 131 | 17 | 5 | 3 | (- | -) | 167 | 88 | 42 | 67 | 23 | 0 | 74 | 8 | 21 | 1 | 64 | 13 | .83 | 11 | .299 | .345 | .381 |
| 2011 | Ptomc | A+ | 119 | 424 | 120 | 9 | 2 | 1 | (- | -) | 136 | 54 | 41 | 49 | 22 | 1 | 63 | 3 | 11 | 5 | 45 | 15 | .75 | 4 | .283 | .319 | .321 |
| 2012 | Hrsbrg | AA | 82 | 351 | 105 | 11 | 2 | 0 | (- | -) | 120 | 34 | 30 | 41 | 7 | 0 | 53 | 7 | 7 | 1 | 26 | 10 | .72 | 0 | .299 | .325 | .342 |
| 2012 | Nats | R | 5 | 22 | 9 | 1 | 0 | 0 | (- | -) | 10 | 4 | 2 | 5 | 1 | 0 | 0 | 0 | 0 | 0 | 5 | 0 | 1.00 | 1 | .409 | .435 | .455 |
| 2012 | Syrcse | AAA | 40 | 159 | 53 | 7 | 1 | 0 | (- | -) | 62 | 21 | 10 | 25 | 8 | 0 | 26 | 2 | 4 | 0 | 20 | 5 | .80 | 3 | .333 | .373 | .390 |
| 2013 | Syrcse | AAA | 96 | 403 | 121 | 18 | 5 | 7 | (- | -) | 170 | 55 | 28 | 59 | 13 | 0 | 64 | 9 | 8 | 0 | 23 | 8 | .74 | 7 | .300 | .336 | .422 |
| 2012 | Was | NL | 13 | 5 | 1 | 0 | 0 | 0 | (0 | 0) | 1 | 3 | 0 | 0 | 0 | 0 | 0 | 0 | 0 | 0 | 3 | 0 | 1.00 | 0 | .200 | .200 | .200 |
| 2013 | Was | NL | 9 | 8 | 1 | 0 | 0 | 0 | (0 | 0) | 1 | 1 | 0 | 0 | 0 | 0 | 3 | 0 | 0 | 0 | 1 | 0 | 1.00 | 0 | .125 | .125 | .125 |
| 2 ML YEARS | | | 22 | 13 | 2 | 0 | 0 | 0 | (0 | 0) | 2 | 4 | 0 | 0 | 0 | 0 | 3 | 0 | 0 | 0 | 4 | 0 | 1.00 | 0 | .154 | .154 | .154 |

# Hernan Perez

**Bats:** R **Throws:** R **Pos:** 2B-25;PR-8;DH-3;3B-2;SS-2;PH-1 HURR-nen **Ht:** 6'1" **Wt:** 185 **Born:** 3/26/1991 **Age:** 23

| BATTING | | | | | | | | | | | | | | | | | | | | BASERUNNING | | | | AVERAGES | | |
|---|---|---|---|---|---|---|---|---|---|---|---|---|---|---|---|---|---|---|---|---|---|---|---|---|---|---|
| Year | Team | Lg | G | AB | H | 2B | 3B | HR | (Hm | Rd) | TB | R | RBI | RC | TBB | IBB | SO | HBP | SH | SF | SB | CS | SB% | GDP | Avg | OBP | Slg |
| 2009 | Tigers | R | 21 | 81 | 18 | 9 | 1 | 1 | (- | -) | 32 | 9 | 9 | 8 | 3 | 0 | 14 | 1 | 1 | 0 | 2 | 0 | 1.00 | 1 | .222 | .259 | .395 |
| 2009 | Lkland | A+ | 21 | 72 | 19 | 4 | 1 | 0 | (- | -) | 25 | 7 | 10 | 7 | 3 | 0 | 21 | 0 | 1 | 1 | 0 | 0 | - | 2 | .264 | .289 | .347 |
| 2009 | WMich | A | 12 | 44 | 10 | 0 | 1 | 0 | (- | -) | 12 | 0 | 5 | 2 | 0 | 0 | 8 | 0 | 1 | 0 | 2 | 1 | .67 | 1 | .227 | .227 | .273 |
| 2010 | WMich | A | 124 | 473 | 111 | 15 | 0 | 5 | (- | -) | 141 | 45 | 50 | 39 | 25 | 0 | 98 | 2 | 2 | 5 | 5 | 1 | .83 | 19 | .235 | .273 | .298 |
| 2011 | WMich | A | 129 | 503 | 130 | 23 | 3 | 8 | (- | -) | 183 | 69 | 42 | 63 | 38 | 1 | 87 | 6 | 11 | 8 | 23 | 6 | .79 | 9 | .258 | .314 | .364 |
| 2012 | Lkland | A+ | 124 | 441 | 115 | 11 | 4 | 5 | (- | -) | 149 | 50 | 44 | 50 | 24 | 0 | 70 | 2 | 6 | 6 | 27 | 4 | .87 | 7 | .261 | .298 | .338 |
| 2013 | Erie | AA | 87 | 362 | 109 | 28 | 2 | 4 | (- | -) | 153 | 45 | 35 | 52 | 12 | 0 | 48 | 2 | 5 | 3 | 25 | 7 | .78 | 13 | .301 | .325 | .423 |
| 2013 | Toledo | AAA | 16 | 67 | 20 | 3 | 0 | 0 | (- | -) | 23 | 3 | 4 | 9 | 5 | 0 | 7 | 1 | 1 | 0 | 4 | 0 | 1.00 | 1 | .299 | .356 | .343 |
| 2012 | Det | AL | 2 | 2 | 1 | 0 | 0 | 0 | (0 | 0) | 1 | 1 | 0 | 0 | 0 | 0 | 0 | 0 | 0 | 0 | 0 | 0 | - | 0 | .500 | .500 | .500 |
| 2013 | Det | AL | 34 | 66 | 13 | 0 | 1 | 0 | (0 | 0) | 15 | 13 | 5 | 4 | 2 | 0 | 15 | 0 | 2 | 1 | 1 | 0 | 1.00 | 2 | .197 | .217 | .227 |
| 2 ML YEARS | | | 36 | 68 | 14 | 0 | 1 | 0 | (0 | 0) | 16 | 14 | 5 | 4 | 2 | 0 | 15 | 0 | 2 | 1 | 1 | 0 | 1.00 | 2 | .206 | .225 | .235 |

# Juan Perez

**Bats:** R **Throws:** R **Pos:** CF-20;LF-11;PH-4;PR-2;RF-1 **Ht:** 5'11" **Wt:** 185 **Born:** 11/13/1986 **Age:** 27

| BATTING | | | | | | | | | | | | | | | | | | | | BASERUNNING | | | | AVERAGES | | |
|---|---|---|---|---|---|---|---|---|---|---|---|---|---|---|---|---|---|---|---|---|---|---|---|---|---|---|
| Year | Team | Lg | G | AB | H | 2B | 3B | HR | (Hm | Rd) | TB | R | RBI | RC | TBB | IBB | SO | HBP | SH | SF | SB | CS | SB% | GDP | Avg | OBP | Slg |
| 2009 | Augsta | A | 123 | 447 | 109 | 29 | 3 | 9 | (- | -) | 171 | 56 | 54 | 52 | 23 | 0 | 101 | 4 | 3 | 7 | 18 | 4 | .82 | 3 | .244 | .283 | .383 |
| 2010 | SnJos | A+ | 131 | 551 | 164 | 37 | 10 | 13 | (- | -) | 260 | 83 | 63 | 86 | 31 | 2 | 116 | 5 | 3 | 6 | 17 | 15 | .53 | 9 | .298 | .337 | .472 |
| 2011 | Rchmd | AA | 131 | 457 | 117 | 25 | 10 | 4 | (- | -) | 174 | 58 | 40 | 56 | 28 | 0 | 95 | 4 | 5 | 3 | 22 | 6 | .79 | 10 | .256 | .303 | .381 |
| 2012 | Rchmd | AA | 126 | 483 | 146 | 26 | 4 | 11 | (- | -) | 213 | 65 | 53 | 70 | 22 | 0 | 85 | 6 | 2 | 0 | 18 | 15 | .55 | 6 | .302 | .341 | .441 |
| 2013 | Fresno | AAA | 101 | 382 | 111 | 27 | 5 | 10 | (- | -) | 178 | 52 | 50 | 59 | 15 | 0 | 75 | 5 | 4 | 3 | 18 | 6 | .75 | 5 | .291 | .323 | .466 |
| 2013 | SF | NL | 34 | 89 | 23 | 5 | 0 | 1 | (1 | 0) | 31 | 8 | 8 | 10 | 6 | 0 | 21 | 0 | 1 | 1 | 2 | 0 | 1.00 | 3 | .258 | .302 | .348 |

# Juan Perez

**Pitches:** L **Bats:** R **Pos:** RP-19 **Ht:** 6'0" **Wt:** 170 **Born:** 9/3/1978 **Age:** 35

| HOW MUCH HE PITCHED | | | | | | | | | WHAT HE GAVE UP | | | | | | | | | | | | THE RESULTS | | | | | | | |
|---|---|---|---|---|---|---|---|---|---|---|---|---|---|---|---|---|---|---|---|---|---|---|---|---|---|---|---|---|
| Year | Team | Lg | G | GS | CG | GF | IP | BFP | H | R | ER | HR | SH | SF | HB | TBB | IBB | SO | WP | Bk | W | L | Pct | Sh | Sv-Op | Hld | ERC | ERA |
| 2013 | Buffalo* | AAA | 17 | 0 | 0 | 12 | 21.0 | 85 | 12 | 2 | 2 | 0 | 0 | 0 | 0 | 11 | 1 | 25 | 1 | 0 | 2 | 1 | .667 | 0 | 3-- | - | 1.65 | 0.86 |
| 2006 | Pit | NL | 7 | 0 | 0 | 0 | 3.1 | 17 | 5 | 3 | 3 | 1 | 0 | 1 | 2 | 1 | 0 | 3 | 0 | 0 | 0 | 1 | .000 | 0 | 0-0 | 0 | 11.77 | 8.10 |
| 2007 | Pit | NL | 17 | 0 | 0 | 4 | 12.1 | 57 | 14 | 7 | 6 | 2 | 0 | 0 | 0 | 8 | 0 | 10 | 1 | 0 | 0 | 0 | - | 0 | 0-0 | 0 | 6.48 | 4.38 |
| 2011 | Phi | NL | 8 | 0 | 0 | 1 | 5.0 | 21 | 1 | 2 | 2 | 0 | 0 | 0 | 0 | 5 | 0 | 8 | 1 | 0 | 1 | 0 | 1.000 | 0 | 0-0 | 1 | 1.51 | 3.60 |
| 2012 | Mil | NL | 10 | 0 | 0 | 5 | 7.0 | 35 | 6 | 4 | 4 | 2 | 0 | 0 | 1 | 8 | 1 | 10 | 0 | 0 | 0 | 1 | .000 | 0 | 0-0 | 0 | 8.29 | 5.14 |
| 2013 | Tor | AL | 19 | 0 | 0 | 3 | 31.2 | 131 | 23 | 17 | 13 | 3 | 0 | 0 | 1 | 15 | 0 | 33 | 2 | 0 | 1 | 2 | .333 | 0 | 0-1 | 0 | 2.99 | 3.69 |
| 5 ML YEARS | | | 61 | 0 | 0 | 13 | 59.1 | 261 | 49 | 33 | 28 | 8 | 0 | 1 | 4 | 37 | 1 | 64 | 4 | 0 | 2 | 4 | .333 | 0 | 0-1 | 1 | 4.50 | 4.25 |

# Luis Perez

**Pitches:** L **Bats:** L **Pos:** RP-6 **Ht:** 6'0" **Wt:** 210 **Born:** 1/20/1985 **Age:** 29

| | | | HOW MUCH HE PITCHED | | | | | | WHAT HE GAVE UP | | | | | | | | | | | | THE RESULTS | | | | | | | |
|---|---|---|---|---|---|---|---|---|---|---|---|---|---|---|---|---|---|---|---|---|---|---|---|---|---|---|---|---|
| Year | Team | Lg | G | GS | CG | GF | IP | BFP | H | R | ER | HR | SH | SF | HB | TBB | IBB | SO | WP | Bk | W | L | Pct | Sh | Sv-Op | Hld | ERC | ERA |
| 2013 | Dnedin* | A+ | 4 | 2 | 0 | 1 | 6.0 | 23 | 4 | 1 | 1 | 0 | 0 | 0 | 1 | 2 | 0 | 5 | 1 | 0 | 0 | 0 | - | 0 | 0- - | - | 2.25 | 1.50 |
| 2013 | Buffalo* | AAA | 2 | 0 | 0 | 0 | 3.2 | 15 | 3 | 1 | 1 | 0 | 0 | 0 | 0 | 2 | 0 | 1 | 0 | 0 | 0 | 0 | - | 0 | 0- - | - | 3.10 | 2.45 |
| 2011 | Tor | AL | 37 | 4 | 0 | 7 | 65.0 | 294 | 74 | 40 | 37 | 9 | 1 | 3 | 5 | 27 | 1 | 54 | 4 | 0 | 3 | 3 | .500 | 0 | 0-2 | 4 | 5.53 | 5.12 |
| 2012 | Tor | AL | 35 | 0 | 0 | 6 | 42.0 | 175 | 38 | 16 | 16 | 3 | 0 | 0 | 3 | 16 | 0 | 39 | 0 | 0 | 2 | 2 | .500 | 0 | 0-0 | 4 | 3.66 | 3.43 |
| 2013 | Tor | AL | 6 | 0 | 0 | 1 | 5.0 | 21 | 4 | 3 | 3 | 0 | 0 | 0 | 0 | 2 | 0 | 6 | 0 | 0 | 0 | 1 | .000 | 0 | 0-0 | 0 | 2.31 | 5.40 |
| 3 ML YEARS | | | 78 | 4 | 0 | 14 | 112.0 | 490 | 116 | 59 | 56 | 12 | 1 | 3 | 8 | 45 | 1 | 99 | 4 | 0 | 5 | 6 | .455 | 0 | 0-2 | 8 | 4.65 | 4.50 |

# Martin Perez

**Pitches:** L **Bats:** L **Pos:** SP-20 mar-TEEN **Ht:** 6'0" **Wt:** 190 **Born:** 4/4/1991 **Age:** 23

| | | | HOW MUCH HE PITCHED | | | | | | WHAT HE GAVE UP | | | | | | | | | | | | THE RESULTS | | | | | | | |
|---|---|---|---|---|---|---|---|---|---|---|---|---|---|---|---|---|---|---|---|---|---|---|---|---|---|---|---|---|
| Year | Team | Lg | G | GS | CG | GF | IP | BFP | H | R | ER | HR | SH | SF | HB | TBB | IBB | SO | WP | Bk | W | L | Pct | Sh | Sv-Op | Hld | ERC | ERA |
| 2009 | Hkry | A | 22 | 14 | 0 | 3 | 93.2 | 391 | 82 | 35 | 24 | 3 | 5 | 4 | 1 | 33 | 0 | 105 | 5 | 5 | 5 | 5 | .500 | 0 | 1- - | - | 2.80 | 2.31 |
| 2009 | Frisco | AA | 5 | 5 | 0 | 0 | 21.0 | 95 | 29 | 16 | 13 | 2 | 0 | 1 | 0 | 5 | 0 | 14 | 1 | 0 | 1 | 3 | .250 | 0 | 0- - | - | 5.59 | 5.57 |
| 2010 | Frisco | AA | 24 | 23 | 0 | 0 | 99.2 | 461 | 117 | 73 | 66 | 12 | 4 | 3 | 0 | 50 | 1 | 101 | 6 | 2 | 5 | 8 | .385 | 0 | 0- - | - | 5.57 | 5.96 |
| 2011 | Frisco | AA | 17 | 16 | 1 | 0 | 88.1 | 368 | 80 | 35 | 31 | 6 | 3 | 2 | 1 | 36 | 0 | 83 | 4 | 2 | 4 | 2 | .667 | 1 | 0- - | - | 3.48 | 3.16 |
| 2011 | RdRck | AAA | 10 | 10 | 0 | 0 | 49.0 | 237 | 72 | 38 | 35 | 4 | 3 | 4 | 0 | 20 | 0 | 37 | 6 | 4 | 4 | 4 | .500 | 0 | 0- - | - | 6.67 | 6.43 |
| 2012 | RdRck | AAA | 22 | 21 | 2 | 0 | 127.0 | 544 | 122 | 70 | 60 | 10 | 6 | 5 | 4 | 56 | 0 | 69 | 3 | 0 | 7 | 6 | .538 | 0 | 0- - | - | 4.05 | 4.25 |
| 2013 | Frisco | AA | 2 | 2 | 0 | 0 | 7.1 | 37 | 14 | 9 | 9 | 1 | 0 | 0 | 0 | 2 | 1 | 2 | 1 | 0 | 0 | 1 | .000 | 0 | 0- - | - | 9.33 | 11.05 |
| 2013 | RdRck | AAA | 6 | 6 | 0 | 0 | 36.0 | 139 | 29 | 8 | 7 | 1 | 0 | 0 | 2 | 8 | 0 | 28 | 3 | 0 | 5 | 1 | .833 | 0 | 0- - | - | 2.28 | 1.75 |
| 2012 | Tex | AL | 12 | 6 | 0 | 2 | 38.0 | 177 | 47 | 26 | 23 | 3 | 1 | 1 | 2 | 15 | 1 | 25 | 5 | 2 | 1 | 4 | .200 | 0 | 0-0 | 0 | 5.33 | 5.45 |
| 2013 | Tex | AL | 20 | 20 | 1 | 0 | 124.1 | 529 | 129 | 55 | 50 | 15 | 2 | 3 | 3 | 37 | 0 | 84 | 9 | **2** | 10 | 6 | .625 | 0 | 0-0 | 0 | 4.14 | 3.62 |
| 2 ML YEARS | | | 32 | 26 | 1 | 2 | 162.1 | 706 | 176 | 81 | 73 | 18 | 3 | 4 | 5 | 52 | 1 | 109 | 14 | 4 | 11 | 10 | .524 | 0 | 0-0 | 0 | 4.42 | 4.05 |

# Oliver Perez

**Pitches:** L **Bats:** L **Pos:** RP-61 **Ht:** 6'3" **Wt:** 220 **Born:** 8/15/1981 **Age:** 32

| | | | HOW MUCH HE PITCHED | | | | | | WHAT HE GAVE UP | | | | | | | | | | | | THE RESULTS | | | | | | | |
|---|---|---|---|---|---|---|---|---|---|---|---|---|---|---|---|---|---|---|---|---|---|---|---|---|---|---|---|---|
| Year | Team | Lg | G | GS | CG | GF | IP | BFP | H | R | ER | HR | SH | SF | HB | TBB | IBB | SO | WP | Bk | W | L | Pct | Sh | Sv-Op | Hld | ERC | ERA |
| 2002 | SD | NL | 16 | 15 | 0 | 0 | 90.0 | 387 | 71 | 37 | 35 | 13 | 5 | 3 | 5 | 48 | 1 | 94 | 3 | 0 | 4 | 5 | .444 | 0 | 0-0 | 0 | 3.93 | 3.50 |
| 2003 | 2 Tms | NL | 24 | 24 | 0 | 0 | 126.2 | 579 | 129 | 80 | 77 | 22 | 5 | 2 | 4 | 77 | 3 | 141 | 7 | 1 | 4 | 10 | .286 | 0 | 0-0 | 0 | 5.66 | 5.47 |
| 2004 | Pit | NL | 30 | 30 | 2 | 0 | 196.0 | 805 | 145 | 71 | 65 | 22 | 9 | 5 | 9 | 81 | 2 | 239 | 2 | 1 | 12 | 10 | .545 | 1 | 0-0 | 0 | 2.99 | 2.98 |
| 2005 | Pit | NL | 20 | 20 | 0 | 0 | 103.0 | 471 | 102 | 68 | 67 | 23 | 5 | 4 | 6 | 70 | 1 | 97 | 3 | 0 | 7 | 5 | .583 | 0 | 0-0 | 0 | 6.44 | 5.85 |
| 2006 | 2 Tms | NL | 22 | 22 | 1 | 0 | 112.2 | 529 | 129 | 90 | 82 | 20 | 5 | **10** | 6 | 68 | 0 | 102 | 5 | 1 | 3 | 13 | .188 | 1 | 0-0 | 0 | 6.62 | 6.55 |
| 2007 | NYM | NL | 29 | 29 | 0 | 0 | 177.0 | 765 | 153 | 90 | 70 | 22 | 4 | 7 | 7 | 79 | 1 | 174 | 6 | 0 | 15 | 10 | .600 | 0 | 0-0 | 0 | 3.76 | 3.56 |
| 2008 | NYM | NL | 34 | **34** | 0 | 0 | 194.0 | 847 | 167 | 100 | 91 | 24 | 9 | 7 | 11 | **105** | 4 | 180 | 9 | 1 | 10 | 7 | .588 | 0 | 0-0 | 0 | 4.21 | 4.22 |
| 2009 | NYM | NL | 14 | 14 | 0 | 0 | 66.0 | 324 | 69 | 51 | 50 | 12 | 5 | 4 | 4 | 58 | 2 | 62 | 2 | 0 | 3 | 4 | .429 | 0 | 0-0 | 0 | 7.16 | 6.82 |
| 2010 | NYM | NL | 17 | 7 | 0 | 4 | 46.1 | 234 | 54 | 37 | 35 | 9 | 1 | 3 | 4 | 42 | 3 | 37 | 4 | 0 | 0 | 5 | .000 | 0 | 0-0 | 0 | 8.27 | 6.80 |
| 2012 | Sea | AL | 33 | 0 | 0 | 6 | 29.2 | 123 | 27 | 7 | 7 | 1 | 1 | 1 | 0 | 10 | 2 | 24 | 2 | 0 | 1 | 3 | .250 | 0 | 0-2 | 5 | 2.82 | 2.12 |
| 2013 | Sea | AL | 61 | 0 | 0 | 22 | 53.0 | 229 | 50 | 23 | 22 | 6 | 1 | 0 | 1 | 26 | 3 | 74 | 1 | 0 | 3 | 3 | .500 | 0 | 2-3 | 8 | 4.23 | 3.74 |
| 03 | SD | NL | 19 | 19 | 0 | 0 | 103.2 | 473 | 103 | 65 | 62 | 20 | 4 | 2 | 3 | 65 | 2 | 117 | 6 | 1 | 4 | 7 | .364 | 0 | 0-0 | 0 | 5.74 | 5.38 |
| 03 | Pit | NL | 5 | 5 | 0 | 0 | 23.0 | 106 | 26 | 15 | 15 | 2 | 1 | 0 | 1 | 12 | 1 | 24 | 1 | 0 | 0 | 3 | .000 | 0 | 0-0 | 0 | 5.29 | 5.87 |
| 06 | Pit | NL | 15 | 15 | 0 | 0 | 76.0 | 364 | 88 | 64 | 56 | 13 | 5 | 8 | 3 | 51 | 0 | 61 | 4 | 1 | 2 | 10 | .167 | 0 | 0-0 | 0 | 6.85 | 6.63 |
| 06 | NYM | NL | 7 | 7 | 1 | 0 | 36.2 | 165 | 41 | 26 | 26 | 7 | 0 | 2 | 3 | 17 | 0 | 41 | 1 | 0 | 1 | 3 | .250 | 1 | 0-0 | 0 | 6.16 | 6.38 |
| Postseason | | | 2 | 2 | 0 | 0 | 11.2 | 50 | 13 | 6 | 6 | 3 | 2 | 0 | 1 | 3 | 1 | 7 | 0 | 0 | 1 | 0 | 1.000 | 0 | 0-0 | 0 | 5.61 | 4.63 |
| 11 ML YEARS | | | 300 | 195 | 3 | 32 | 1194.1 | 5293 | 1096 | 654 | 601 | 174 | 50 | 46 | 57 | 664 | 22 | 1224 | 44 | 4 | 62 | 75 | .453 | 2 | 2-5 | 13 | 4.72 | 4.53 |

# Salvador Perez

**Bats:** R **Throws:** R **Pos:** C-137;PH-4;1B-1 **Ht:** 6'3" **Wt:** 245 **Born:** 5/10/1990 **Age:** 24

| | | | BATTING | | | | | | | | | | | | | | | | | | BASERUNNING | | | | AVERAGES | | |
|---|---|---|---|---|---|---|---|---|---|---|---|---|---|---|---|---|---|---|---|---|---|---|---|---|---|---|---|
| Year | Team | Lg | G | AB | H | 2B | 3B | HR | (Hm | Rd) | TB | R | RBI | RC | TBB | IBB | SO | HBP | SH | SF | SB | CS | SB% | GDP | Avg | OBP | Slg |
| 2011 | KC | AL | 39 | 148 | 49 | 8 | 2 | 3 | (1 | 2) | 70 | 20 | 21 | 26 | 7 | 0 | 20 | 1 | 0 | 2 | 0 | 0 | - | 5 | .331 | .361 | .473 |
| 2012 | KC | AL | 76 | 289 | 87 | 16 | 0 | 11 | (3 | 8) | 136 | 38 | 39 | 36 | 12 | 3 | 27 | 1 | 0 | 3 | 0 | 0 | - | 14 | .301 | .328 | .471 |
| 2013 | KC | AL | 138 | 496 | 145 | 25 | 3 | 13 | (6 | 7) | 215 | 48 | 79 | 77 | 21 | 2 | 63 | 4 | 0 | 5 | 0 | 0 | - | 13 | .292 | .323 | .433 |
| 3 ML YEARS | | | 253 | 933 | 281 | 49 | 5 | 27 | (10 | 17) | 421 | 106 | 139 | 139 | 40 | 5 | 110 | 6 | 0 | 10 | 0 | 0 | - | 32 | .301 | .331 | .451 |

# Glen Perkins

**Pitches:** L **Bats:** L **Pos:** RP-61 **Ht:** 6'0" **Wt:** 205 **Born:** 3/2/1983 **Age:** 31

| | | | HOW MUCH HE PITCHED | | | | | | WHAT HE GAVE UP | | | | | | | | | | | | THE RESULTS | | | | | | | |
|---|---|---|---|---|---|---|---|---|---|---|---|---|---|---|---|---|---|---|---|---|---|---|---|---|---|---|---|---|
| Year | Team | Lg | G | GS | CG | GF | IP | BFP | H | R | ER | HR | SH | SF | HB | TBB | IBB | SO | WP | Bk | W | L | Pct | Sh | Sv-Op | Hld | ERC | ERA |
| 2006 | Min | AL | 4 | 0 | 0 | 1 | 5.2 | 20 | 3 | 1 | 1 | 0 | 0 | 0 | 0 | 0 | 0 | 6 | 0 | 0 | 0 | 0 | - | 0 | 0-0 | 1 | 0.60 | 1.59 |
| 2007 | Min | AL | 19 | 0 | 0 | 3 | 28.2 | 115 | 23 | 10 | 10 | 2 | 1 | 1 | 2 | 12 | 0 | 20 | 2 | 0 | 0 | 0 | - | 0 | 0-0 | 3 | 3.32 | 3.14 |
| 2008 | Min | AL | 26 | 26 | 0 | 0 | 151.0 | 661 | 183 | 81 | 74 | 25 | 7 | 4 | 3 | 39 | 0 | 74 | 2 | 1 | 12 | 4 | .750 | 0 | 0-0 | 0 | 5.30 | 4.41 |
| 2009 | Min | AL | 18 | 17 | 0 | 1 | 96.1 | 423 | 120 | 64 | 63 | 13 | 1 | 3 | 1 | 23 | 0 | 45 | 2 | 1 | 6 | 7 | .462 | 0 | 0-0 | 0 | 5.14 | 5.89 |
| 2010 | Min | AL | 13 | 1 | 0 | 5 | 21.2 | 98 | 29 | 16 | 14 | 3 | 1 | 2 | 4 | 5 | 1 | 14 | 0 | 0 | 1 | 1 | .500 | 0 | 0-0 | 0 | 6.56 | 5.82 |
| 2011 | Min | AL | 65 | 0 | 0 | 17 | 61.2 | 253 | 55 | 19 | 17 | 2 | 5 | 1 | 1 | 21 | 5 | 65 | 3 | 0 | 4 | 4 | .500 | 0 | 2-5 | 17 | 2.81 | 2.48 |
| 2012 | Min | AL | 70 | 0 | 0 | 43 | 70.1 | 281 | 57 | 25 | 20 | 8 | 3 | 2 | 3 | 16 | 3 | 78 | 3 | 0 | 3 | 1 | .750 | 0 | 16-20 | 11 | 2.63 | 2.56 |
| 2013 | Min | AL | 61 | 0 | 0 | 53 | 62.2 | 240 | 43 | 16 | 16 | 5 | 2 | 1 | 3 | 15 | 0 | 77 | 0 | 0 | 2 | 0 | 1.000 | 0 | 36-40 | 0 | 2.01 | 2.30 |
| Postseason | | | 1 | 0 | 0 | 0 | 0.1 | 3 | 2 | 0 | 0 | 0 | 0 | 0 | 0 | 0 | 0 | 0 | 0 | 0 | 0 | 0 | - | 0 | 0-0 | 0 | 39.65 | 0.00 |
| 8 ML YEARS | | | 276 | 44 | 0 | 123 | 498.0 | 2091 | 513 | 232 | 215 | 58 | 20 | 14 | 17 | 131 | 9 | 379 | 12 | 2 | 28 | 17 | .622 | 0 | 54-65 | 32 | 3.97 | 3.89 |

# Vinnie Pestano

**Pitches:** R **Bats:** R **Pos:** RP-37 peh-STAH-no **Ht:** 6'0" **Wt:** 200 **Born:** 2/20/1985 **Age:** 29

| HOW MUCH HE PITCHED | | | | | | | | WHAT HE GAVE UP | | | | | | | | | | | | THE RESULTS | | | | | | | |
|---|---|---|---|---|---|---|---|---|---|---|---|---|---|---|---|---|---|---|---|---|---|---|---|---|---|---|---|
| Year Team | Lg | G | GS | CG | GF | IP | BFP | H | R | ER | HR | SH | SF | HB | TBB | IBB | SO | WP | Bk | W | L | Pct | Sh | Sv-Op | Hld | ERC | ERA |
| 2013 Lk Cty* | A | 1 | 0 | 0 | 0 | 1.0 | 3 | 0 | 0 | 0 | 0 | 0 | 0 | 0 | 0 | 0 | 1 | 0 | 0 | 0 | 0 | - | 0 | 0-- | - | 0.00 | 0.00 |
| 2013 Clmbs* | AAA | 14 | 0 | 0 | 3 | 13.2 | 55 | 13 | 5 | 5 | 0 | 0 | 1 | 1 | 4 | 0 | 13 | 1 | 0 | 0 | 0 | - | 0 | 0-- | - | 3.17 | 3.29 |
| 2010 Cle | AL | 5 | 0 | 0 | 5 | 5.0 | 23 | 4 | 2 | 2 | 0 | 0 | 0 | 0 | 5 | 0 | 8 | 0 | 0 | 0 | 0 | - | 0 | 1-1 | 0 | 4.56 | 3.60 |
| 2011 Cle | AL | 68 | 0 | 0 | 20 | 62.0 | 250 | 41 | 16 | 16 | 5 | 0 | 0 | 3 | 24 | 3 | 84 | 0 | 0 | 1 | 2 | .333 | 0 | 2-6 | 23 | 2.26 | 2.32 |
| 2012 Cle | AL | 70 | 0 | 0 | 13 | 70.0 | 286 | 53 | 20 | 20 | 7 | 0 | 2 | 4 | 24 | 1 | 76 | 1 | 0 | 3 | 3 | .500 | 0 | 2-5 | 36 | 2.77 | 2.57 |
| 2013 Cle | AL | 37 | 0 | 0 | 21 | 35.1 | 159 | 37 | 18 | 16 | 6 | 0 | 2 | 1 | 21 | 1 | 37 | 2 | 0 | 1 | 2 | .333 | 0 | 6-9 | 6 | 5.84 | 4.08 |
| 4 ML YEARS | | 180 | 0 | 0 | 59 | 172.1 | 718 | 135 | 56 | 54 | 18 | 0 | 4 | 8 | 74 | 5 | 205 | 3 | 0 | 5 | 7 | .417 | 0 | 11-21 | 65 | 3.19 | 2.82 |

# Brock Peterson

**Bats:** R **Throws:** R **Pos:** PH-18;LF-5;1B-4 **Ht:** 6'3" **Wt:** 215 **Born:** 11/20/1983 **Age:** 30

| BATTING | | | | | | | | | | | | | | | | | | | | BASERUNNING | | | | AVERAGES | | |
|---|---|---|---|---|---|---|---|---|---|---|---|---|---|---|---|---|---|---|---|---|---|---|---|---|---|---|
| Year Team | Lg | G | AB | H | 2B | 3B | HR | (Hm | Rd) | TB | R | RBI | RC | TBB | IBB | SO | HBP | SH | SF | SB | CS | SB% | GDP | Avg | OBP | Slg |
| 2009 Roch | AAA | 99 | 316 | 96 | 18 | 2 | 10 | (- | -) | 148 | 47 | 43 | 57 | 34 | 3 | 77 | 4 | 0 | 2 | 0 | 0 | - | 5 | .304 | .376 | .468 |
| 2010 Roch | AAA | 128 | 437 | 108 | 21 | 3 | 19 | (- | -) | 192 | 63 | 57 | 67 | 51 | 1 | 131 | 9 | 1 | 4 | 0 | 2 | .00 | 11 | .247 | .335 | .439 |
| 2012 Memp | AAA | 21 | 72 | 18 | 3 | 1 | 5 | (- | -) | 38 | 10 | 16 | 12 | 8 | 0 | 17 | 0 | 0 | 0 | 0 | 1 | .00 | 3 | .250 | .325 | .528 |
| 2013 Memp | AAA | 122 | 456 | 135 | 30 | 1 | 25 | (- | -) | 242 | 69 | 86 | 87 | 44 | 1 | 114 | 6 | 0 | 2 | 1 | 1 | .50 | 12 | .296 | .364 | .531 |
| 2013 StL | NL | 23 | 26 | 2 | 0 | 0 | 0 | (0 | 0) | 2 | 0 | 2 | 0 | 2 | 0 | 11 | 0 | 0 | 0 | 0 | 0 | - | 0 | .077 | .143 | .077 |

# Shane Peterson

**Bats:** L **Throws:** L **Pos:** 1B-2 **Ht:** 6'0" **Wt:** 210 **Born:** 2/11/1988 **Age:** 26

| BATTING | | | | | | | | | | | | | | | | | | | | BASERUNNING | | | | AVERAGES | | |
|---|---|---|---|---|---|---|---|---|---|---|---|---|---|---|---|---|---|---|---|---|---|---|---|---|---|---|
| Year Team | Lg | G | AB | H | 2B | 3B | HR | (Hm | Rd) | TB | R | RBI | RC | TBB | IBB | SO | HBP | SH | SF | SB | CS | SB% | GDP | Avg | OBP | Slg |
| 2009 PlmBh | A+ | 76 | 285 | 85 | 11 | 4 | 6 | (- | -) | 122 | 32 | 39 | 48 | 21 | 4 | 52 | 11 | 0 | 2 | 10 | 1 | .91 | 5 | .298 | .367 | .428 |
| 2009 Sprgfld | AA | 18 | 74 | 21 | 4 | 1 | 1 | (- | -) | 30 | 10 | 7 | 10 | 5 | 0 | 10 | 1 | 0 | 0 | 2 | 0 | 1.00 | 0 | .284 | .338 | .405 |
| 2009 Mdlnd | AA | 39 | 154 | 42 | 10 | 0 | 3 | (- | -) | 61 | 16 | 17 | 22 | 13 | 0 | 32 | 2 | 1 | 2 | 4 | 0 | 1.00 | 5 | .273 | .333 | .396 |
| 2010 Mdlnd | AA | 128 | 460 | 122 | 24 | 4 | 5 | (- | -) | 169 | 61 | 59 | 68 | 57 | 1 | 108 | 11 | 0 | 8 | 12 | 2 | .86 | 9 | .265 | .354 | .367 |
| 2011 Mdlnd | AA | 59 | 227 | 59 | 16 | 1 | 3 | (- | -) | 86 | 33 | 27 | 35 | 30 | 1 | 38 | 5 | 0 | 1 | 11 | 1 | .92 | 6 | .260 | .357 | .379 |
| 2011 Scrmto | AAA | 46 | 167 | 49 | 7 | 3 | 6 | (- | -) | 80 | 31 | 32 | 31 | 23 | 0 | 37 | 0 | 0 | 1 | 2 | 1 | .67 | 6 | .293 | .377 | .479 |
| 2012 Mdlnd | AA | 48 | 157 | 43 | 11 | 3 | 2 | (- | -) | 66 | 27 | 23 | 34 | 44 | 3 | 47 | 3 | 1 | 0 | 9 | 3 | .75 | 1 | .274 | .441 | .420 |
| 2012 Scrmto | AAA | 39 | 131 | 51 | 7 | 1 | 7 | (- | -) | 81 | 36 | 23 | 36 | 23 | 1 | 31 | 1 | 2 | 0 | 4 | 3 | .57 | 0 | .389 | .484 | .618 |
| 2013 Scrmto | AAA | 126 | 463 | 116 | 25 | 1 | 12 | (- | -) | 179 | 70 | 79 | 73 | 77 | 1 | 127 | 4 | 3 | 6 | 17 | 2 | .89 | 10 | .251 | .358 | .387 |
| 2013 Oak | AL | 2 | 7 | 1 | 0 | 0 | 0 | (0 | 0) | 1 | 1 | 1 | 0 | 1 | 0 | 3 | 0 | 0 | 0 | 0 | 0 | - | 0 | .143 | .250 | .143 |

# Yusmeiro Petit

**Pitches:** R **Bats:** R **Pos:** SP-7; RP-1 USE-mere-oh pa-TEET **Ht:** 6'1" **Wt:** 255 **Born:** 11/22/1984 **Age:** 29

| HOW MUCH HE PITCHED | | | | | | | | WHAT HE GAVE UP | | | | | | | | | | | | THE RESULTS | | | | | | | |
|---|---|---|---|---|---|---|---|---|---|---|---|---|---|---|---|---|---|---|---|---|---|---|---|---|---|---|---|
| Year Team | Lg | G | GS | CG | GF | IP | BFP | H | R | ER | HR | SH | SF | HB | TBB | IBB | SO | WP | Bk | W | L | Pct | Sh | Sv-Op | Hld | ERC | ERA |
| 2013 Fresno* | AAA | 15 | 15 | 1 | 0 | 87.2 | 361 | 92 | 45 | 44 | 16 | 3 | 2 | 0 | 13 | 0 | 91 | 1 | 0 | 5 | 6 | .455 | 0 | 0-- | - | 3.89 | 4.52 |
| 2013 Giants* | R | 1 | 1 | 0 | 0 | 5.0 | 20 | 3 | 1 | 1 | 0 | 0 | 0 | 0 | 0 | 0 | 8 | 0 | 0 | 1 | 0 | 1.000 | 0 | 0-- | - | 0.68 | 1.80 |
| 2006 Fla | NL | 15 | 1 | 0 | 5 | 26.1 | 129 | 46 | 28 | 28 | 7 | 1 | 1 | 0 | 9 | 1 | 20 | 0 | 0 | 1 | 1 | .500 | 0 | 0-0 | 0 | 10.07 | 9.57 |
| 2007 Ari | NL | 14 | 10 | 0 | 2 | 57.0 | 243 | 58 | 30 | 29 | 12 | 1 | 1 | 0 | 18 | 1 | 40 | 0 | 1 | 3 | 4 | .429 | 0 | 0-0 | 0 | 4.56 | 4.58 |
| 2008 Ari | NL | 19 | 8 | 0 | 6 | 56.1 | 229 | 45 | 29 | 27 | 12 | 4 | 2 | 1 | 14 | 2 | 42 | 3 | 1 | 3 | 5 | .375 | 0 | 0-0 | 0 | 3.08 | 4.31 |
| 2009 Ari | NL | 23 | 17 | 0 | 2 | 89.2 | 407 | 102 | 62 | 58 | 19 | 3 | 0 | 0 | 34 | 1 | 74 | 3 | 0 | 3 | 10 | .231 | 0 | 0-0 | 0 | 5.44 | 5.82 |
| 2012 SF | NL | 1 | 1 | 0 | 0 | 4.2 | 22 | 7 | 2 | 2 | 0 | 1 | 0 | 0 | 4 | 0 | 1 | 1 | 0 | 0 | 0 | - | 0 | 0-0 | 0 | 9.14 | 3.86 |
| 2013 SF | NL | 8 | 7 | 1 | 0 | 48.0 | 196 | 46 | 19 | 19 | 4 | 2 | 0 | 0 | 11 | 1 | 47 | 0 | 0 | 4 | 1 | .800 | 1 | 0-0 | 0 | 3.08 | 3.56 |
| 6 ML YEARS | | 80 | 44 | 1 | 15 | 282.0 | 1226 | 304 | 170 | 163 | 54 | 12 | 4 | 1 | 90 | 6 | 224 | 7 | 2 | 14 | 21 | .400 | 1 | 0-0 | 0 | 4.78 | 5.20 |

# Jake Petricka

**Pitches:** R **Bats:** R **Pos:** RP-16 pet-RICH-kah **Ht:** 6'5" **Wt:** 200 **Born:** 6/5/1988 **Age:** 26

| HOW MUCH HE PITCHED | | | | | | | | WHAT HE GAVE UP | | | | | | | | | | | | THE RESULTS | | | | | | | |
|---|---|---|---|---|---|---|---|---|---|---|---|---|---|---|---|---|---|---|---|---|---|---|---|---|---|---|---|
| Year Team | Lg | G | GS | CG | GF | IP | BFP | H | R | ER | HR | SH | SF | HB | TBB | IBB | SO | WP | Bk | W | L | Pct | Sh | Sv-Op | Hld | ERC | ERA |
| 2010 Bristol | R | 8 | 8 | 0 | 0 | 34.2 | 136 | 25 | 12 | 11 | 1 | 0 | 0 | 2 | 7 | 0 | 38 | 4 | 1 | 2 | 4 | .333 | 0 | 0-- | - | 1.74 | 2.86 |
| 2010 Knapol | A | 9 | 0 | 0 | 1 | 9.2 | 55 | 13 | 11 | 4 | 0 | 1 | 0 | 1 | 8 | 0 | 10 | 4 | 0 | 0 | 1 | .000 | 0 | 0-- | - | 6.72 | 3.72 |
| 2011 Knapol | A | 8 | 8 | 0 | 0 | 41.2 | 169 | 39 | 14 | 13 | 0 | 0 | 3 | 0 | 13 | 0 | 48 | 4 | 0 | 3 | 1 | .750 | 0 | 0-- | - | 2.82 | 2.81 |
| 2011 Bristol | R | 2 | 1 | 0 | 0 | 4.0 | 14 | 4 | 0 | 0 | 0 | 0 | 0 | 0 | 0 | 0 | 5 | 0 | 0 | 0 | 0 | - | 0 | 0-- | - | 2.31 | 0.00 |
| 2011 WinSa | A+ | 13 | 13 | 0 | 0 | 67.2 | 303 | 71 | 39 | 33 | 3 | 4 | 1 | 3 | 26 | 0 | 46 | 5 | 0 | 4 | 7 | .364 | 0 | 0-- | - | 3.96 | 4.39 |
| 2012 WinSa | A+ | 19 | 19 | 0 | 0 | 82.2 | 378 | 93 | 58 | 49 | 2 | 2 | 0 | 3 | 46 | 0 | 84 | 9 | 1 | 5 | 5 | .500 | 0 | 0-- | - | 5.01 | 5.33 |
| 2012 Brham | AA | 10 | 10 | 0 | 0 | 57.2 | 257 | 63 | 35 | 35 | 7 | 2 | 3 | 0 | 35 | 0 | 27 | 5 | 0 | 3 | 3 | .500 | 0 | 0-- | - | 5.81 | 5.46 |
| 2013 Brham | AA | 21 | 1 | 0 | 3 | 39.1 | 161 | 36 | 11 | 9 | 1 | 1 | 0 | 1 | 18 | 0 | 41 | 4 | 0 | 3 | 0 | 1.000 | 0 | 0-- | - | 3.61 | 2.06 |
| 2013 Charltt | AAA | 10 | 0 | 0 | 4 | 15.1 | 62 | 9 | 2 | 2 | 0 | 0 | 1 | 0 | 7 | 0 | 17 | 1 | 0 | 2 | 0 | 1.000 | 0 | 1-- | - | 1.59 | 1.17 |
| 2013 CWS | AL | 16 | 0 | 0 | 3 | 19.1 | 85 | 20 | 7 | 7 | 0 | 1 | 1 | 1 | 10 | 1 | 10 | 4 | 0 | 1 | 1 | .500 | 0 | 0-1 | 0 | 4.18 | 3.26 |

# Jonathan Pettibone

**Pitches:** R **Bats:** L **Pos:** SP-18 **Ht:** 6'6" **Wt:** 225 **Born:** 7/19/1990 **Age:** 23

| HOW MUCH HE PITCHED | | | | | | | | WHAT HE GAVE UP | | | | | | | | | | | | THE RESULTS | | | | | | | |
|---|---|---|---|---|---|---|---|---|---|---|---|---|---|---|---|---|---|---|---|---|---|---|---|---|---|---|---|
| Year Team | Lg | G | GS | CG | GF | IP | BFP | H | R | ER | HR | SH | SF | HB | TBB | IBB | SO | WP | Bk | W | L | Pct | Sh | Sv-Op | Hld | ERC | ERA |
| 2009 Wmspt | A- | 9 | 8 | 0 | 0 | 35.1 | 162 | 37 | 28 | 21 | 0 | 1 | 2 | 1 | 16 | 0 | 36 | 1 | 0 | 2 | 4 | .333 | 0 | 0-- | - | 3.76 | 5.35 |
| 2010 Lakwd | A | 24 | 23 | 1 | 0 | 131.1 | 543 | 114 | 63 | 51 | 10 | 8 | 5 | 8 | 41 | 0 | 84 | 9 | 0 | 8 | 6 | .571 | 0 | 0-- | - | 3.13 | 3.49 |
| 2011 Clrwtr | A+ | 27 | 27 | 0 | 0 | 161.0 | 654 | 149 | 62 | 53 | 5 | 7 | 7 | 6 | 34 | 1 | 115 | 7 | 2 | 10 | 11 | .476 | 0 | 0-- | - | 2.68 | 2.96 |
| 2012 Rdng | AA | 19 | 19 | 1 | 0 | 117.1 | 488 | 115 | 52 | 43 | 9 | 7 | 2 | 5 | 27 | 0 | 81 | 4 | 0 | 9 | 7 | .563 | 0 | 0-- | - | 3.33 | 3.30 |

| Year | Team | Lg | G | GS | CG | GF | IP | BFP | H | R | ER | HR | SH | SF | HB | TBB | IBB | SO | WP | Bk | W | L | Pct | Sh | Sv-Op | Hld | ERC | ERA |
|---|---|---|---|---|---|---|---|---|---|---|---|---|---|---|---|---|---|---|---|---|---|---|---|---|---|---|---|---|
| | | | HOW MUCH HE PITCHED | | | | | | WHAT HE GAVE UP | | | | | | | | | | | | THE RESULTS | | | | | | | |
| 2012 | LV | AAA | 7 | 7 | 1 | 0 | 42.1 | 176 | 31 | 12 | 12 | 0 | 2 | 0 | 0 | 22 | 0 | 32 | 2 | 0 | 4 | 1 | .800 | 1 | 0- - | - | 2.45 | 2.55 |
| 2013 | LV | AAA | 4 | 4 | 0 | 0 | 17.1 | 81 | 26 | 15 | 13 | 1 | 2 | 2 | 2 | 5 | 0 | 10 | 1 | 0 | 0 | 2 | .000 | 0 | 0- - | - | 6.93 | 6.75 |
| 2013 | Rdng | AA | 1 | 1 | 0 | 0 | 5.0 | 20 | 5 | 3 | 3 | 0 | 1 | 1 | 0 | 1 | 0 | 4 | 0 | 0 | 0 | 0 | - | 0 | 0- - | - | 2.76 | 5.40 |
| 2013 | Phi | NL | 18 | 18 | 0 | 0 | 100.1 | 437 | 109 | 50 | 45 | 9 | 8 | 2 | 5 | 38 | 3 | 66 | 1 | 0 | 5 | 4 | .556 | 0 | 0-0 | 0 | 4.62 | 4.04 |

# Andy Pettitte

**Pitches:** L **Bats:** L **Pos:** SP-30 PETT-it **Ht:** 6'5" **Wt:** 225 **Born:** 6/15/1972 **Age:** 42

| Year | Team | Lg | G | GS | CG | GF | IP | BFP | H | R | ER | HR | SH | SF | HB | TBB | IBB | SO | WP | Bk | W | L | Pct | Sh | Sv-Op | Hld | ERC | ERA |
|---|---|---|---|---|---|---|---|---|---|---|---|---|---|---|---|---|---|---|---|---|---|---|---|---|---|---|---|---|
| | | | HOW MUCH HE PITCHED | | | | | | WHAT HE GAVE UP | | | | | | | | | | | | THE RESULTS | | | | | | | |
| 1995 | NYY | AL | 31 | 26 | 3 | 1 | 175.0 | 745 | 183 | 86 | 81 | 15 | 4 | 5 | 1 | 63 | 3 | 114 | 8 | 1 | 12 | 9 | .571 | 0 | 0-0 | 0 | 4.13 | 4.17 |
| 1996 | NYY | AL | 35 | 34 | 2 | 1 | 221.0 | 929 | 229 | 105 | 95 | 23 | 7 | 3 | 3 | 72 | 2 | 162 | 6 | 1 | **21** | 8 | .724 | 0 | 0-0 | 0 | 4.14 | 3.87 |
| 1997 | NYY | AL | 35 | **35** | 4 | 0 | 240.1 | 986 | 233 | 86 | 77 | 7 | 6 | 2 | 3 | 65 | 0 | 166 | 7 | 0 | 18 | 7 | .720 | 1 | 0-0 | 0 | 3.05 | 2.88 |
| 1998 | NYY | AL | 33 | 32 | 5 | 0 | 216.1 | 932 | 226 | 110 | 102 | 20 | 6 | 7 | 6 | 87 | 1 | 146 | 5 | 0 | 16 | 11 | .593 | 0 | 0-0 | 0 | 4.46 | 4.24 |
| 1999 | NYY | AL | 31 | 31 | 0 | 0 | 191.2 | 851 | 216 | 105 | 100 | 20 | 6 | 6 | 3 | 89 | 3 | 121 | 3 | 1 | 14 | 11 | .560 | 0 | 0-0 | 0 | 5.22 | 4.70 |
| 2000 | NYY | AL | 32 | 32 | 3 | 0 | 204.2 | 903 | 219 | 111 | 99 | 17 | 7 | 4 | 4 | 80 | 4 | 125 | 2 | 3 | 19 | 9 | .679 | 1 | 0-0 | 0 | 4.32 | 4.35 |
| 2001 | NYY | AL | 31 | 31 | 2 | 0 | 200.2 | 858 | 224 | 103 | 89 | 14 | 8 | 7 | 6 | 41 | 3 | 164 | 2 | 2 | 15 | 10 | .600 | 0 | 0-0 | 0 | 3.82 | 3.99 |
| 2002 | NYY | AL | 22 | 22 | 3 | 0 | 134.2 | 570 | 144 | 58 | 49 | 6 | 3 | 2 | 4 | 32 | 2 | 97 | 2 | 1 | 13 | 5 | .722 | 1 | 0-0 | 0 | 3.55 | 3.27 |
| 2003 | NYY | AL | 33 | 33 | 1 | 0 | 208.1 | 896 | 227 | 109 | 93 | 21 | 5 | 5 | 1 | 50 | 3 | 180 | 5 | 0 | 21 | 8 | .724 | 0 | 0-0 | 0 | 3.89 | 4.02 |
| 2004 | Hou | NL | 15 | 15 | 0 | 0 | 83.0 | 346 | 71 | 37 | 36 | 8 | 1 | 0 | 0 | 31 | 2 | 79 | 4 | 0 | 6 | 4 | .600 | 0 | 0-0 | 0 | 3.12 | 3.90 |
| 2005 | Hou | NL | 33 | 33 | 0 | 0 | 222.1 | 875 | 188 | 66 | 59 | 17 | 10 | 4 | 3 | 41 | 0 | 171 | 2 | 0 | 17 | 9 | .654 | 0 | 0-0 | 0 | 2.40 | 2.39 |
| 2006 | Hou | NL | 36 | **35** | 2 | 1 | 214.1 | 929 | 238 | 114 | 100 | 27 | 14 | 5 | 2 | 70 | 9 | 178 | 2 | 1 | 14 | 13 | .519 | 1 | 0-0 | 0 | 4.58 | 4.20 |
| 2007 | NYY | AL | 36 | **34** | 0 | 0 | 215.1 | 916 | 238 | 106 | 97 | 16 | 5 | 9 | 1 | 69 | 1 | 141 | 3 | 0 | 15 | 9 | .625 | 0 | 0-0 | 1 | 4.27 | 4.05 |
| 2008 | NYY | AL | 33 | 33 | 0 | 0 | 204.0 | 881 | 233 | 112 | 103 | 19 | **8** | 7 | 7 | 55 | 4 | 158 | 6 | 1 | 14 | 14 | .500 | 0 | 0-0 | 0 | 4.45 | 4.54 |
| 2009 | NYY | AL | 32 | 32 | 0 | 0 | 194.2 | 834 | 193 | 101 | 90 | 20 | 4 | 4 | 4 | 76 | 1 | 148 | 3 | 0 | 14 | 8 | .636 | 0 | 0-0 | 0 | 4.11 | 4.16 |
| 2010 | NYY | AL | 21 | 21 | 0 | 0 | 129.0 | 536 | 123 | 52 | 47 | 13 | 8 | 5 | 3 | 41 | 3 | 101 | 2 | 0 | 11 | 3 | .786 | 0 | 0-0 | 0 | 3.62 | 3.28 |
| 2012 | NYY | AL | 12 | 12 | 0 | 0 | 75.1 | 303 | 65 | 26 | 24 | 8 | 2 | 0 | 0 | 21 | 0 | 69 | 1 | 0 | 5 | 4 | .556 | 0 | 0-0 | 0 | 2.96 | 2.87 |
| 2013 | NYY | AL | 30 | 30 | 1 | 0 | 185.1 | 784 | 198 | 85 | 77 | 17 | 4 | 7 | 4 | 48 | 1 | 128 | 6 | 0 | 11 | 11 | .500 | 0 | 0-0 | 0 | 3.95 | 3.74 |
| Postseason | | | 44 | 44 | 0 | 0 | 276.2 | 1157 | 285 | 121 | 117 | 31 | 12 | 9 | 3 | 76 | 4 | 183 | 4 | 1 | 19 | 11 | .633 | 0 | 0-0 | 0 | 3.90 | 3.81 |
| 18 ML YEARS | | | 531 | 521 | 26 | 3 | 3316.0 | 14074 | 3448 | 1572 | 1418 | 288 | 108 | 82 | 55 | 1031 | 42 | 2448 | 69 | 11 | 256 | 153 | .626 | 4 | 0-0 | 1 | 3.93 | 3.85 |

# Josh Phegley

**Bats:** R **Throws:** R **Pos:** C-64;PH-2;2B-1 FEG-lee **Ht:** 5'10" **Wt:** 220 **Born:** 2/12/1988 **Age:** 26

| Year | Team | Lg | G | AB | H | 2B | 3B | HR | (Hm | Rd) | TB | R | RBI | RC | TBB | IBB | SO | HBP | SH | SF | SB | CS | SB% | GDP | Avg | OBP | Slg |
|---|---|---|---|---|---|---|---|---|---|---|---|---|---|---|---|---|---|---|---|---|---|---|---|---|---|---|---|
| | | | BATTING | | | | | | | | | | | | | | | | | | BASERUNNING | | | | AVERAGES | | |
| 2009 | Knapol | A | 52 | 196 | 44 | 9 | 0 | 9 | (- | -) | 80 | 27 | 33 | 23 | 11 | 0 | 40 | 4 | 1 | 2 | 1 | 1 | .50 | 6 | .224 | .277 | .408 |
| 2010 | WinSa | A+ | 25 | 89 | 26 | 3 | 0 | 3 | (- | -) | 38 | 16 | 12 | 13 | 7 | 0 | 22 | 0 | 1 | 2 | 0 | 0 | - | 3 | .292 | .337 | .427 |
| 2010 | Bristol | R | 5 | 15 | 3 | 1 | 0 | 0 | (- | -) | 4 | 1 | 1 | 1 | 2 | 0 | 4 | 1 | 0 | 0 | 0 | 0 | - | 1 | .200 | .333 | .267 |
| 2010 | Brham | AA | 18 | 72 | 21 | 4 | 0 | 2 | (- | -) | 31 | 7 | 13 | 10 | 2 | 1 | 22 | 1 | 3 | 1 | 0 | 0 | - | 4 | .292 | .316 | .431 |
| 2011 | Brham | AA | 94 | 364 | 88 | 21 | 2 | 7 | (- | -) | 134 | 43 | 50 | 40 | 23 | 1 | 61 | 4 | 0 | 3 | 1 | 2 | .33 | 8 | .242 | .292 | .368 |
| 2011 | Charltt | AAA | 22 | 79 | 19 | 4 | 0 | 2 | (- | -) | 29 | 9 | 6 | 10 | 8 | 0 | 18 | 2 | 1 | 0 | 0 | 0 | - | 3 | .241 | .326 | .367 |
| 2012 | Charltt | AAA | 102 | 394 | 105 | 22 | 1 | 6 | (- | -) | 147 | 40 | 48 | 47 | 20 | 1 | 60 | 4 | 0 | 3 | 3 | 0 | 1.00 | 10 | .266 | .306 | .373 |
| 2013 | Charltt | AAA | 61 | 231 | 73 | 18 | 1 | 15 | (- | -) | 138 | 39 | 41 | 50 | 15 | 0 | 38 | 7 | 0 | 5 | 1 | 1 | .50 | 5 | .316 | .368 | .597 |
| 2013 | CWS | AL | 65 | 204 | 42 | 7 | 0 | 4 | (2 | 2) | 61 | 14 | 22 | 12 | 5 | 0 | 41 | 0 | 2 | 2 | 2 | 0 | 1.00 | 6 | .206 | .223 | .299 |

# Cord Phelps

**Bats:** B **Throws:** R **Pos:** 2B-3;PH-1 **Ht:** 6'1" **Wt:** 210 **Born:** 1/23/1987 **Age:** 27

| Year | Team | Lg | G | AB | H | 2B | 3B | HR | (Hm | Rd) | TB | R | RBI | RC | TBB | IBB | SO | HBP | SH | SF | SB | CS | SB% | GDP | Avg | OBP | Slg |
|---|---|---|---|---|---|---|---|---|---|---|---|---|---|---|---|---|---|---|---|---|---|---|---|---|---|---|---|
| | | | BATTING | | | | | | | | | | | | | | | | | | BASERUNNING | | | | AVERAGES | | |
| 2013 | Clmbs* | AAA | 65 | 255 | 68 | 16 | 1 | 9 | (- | -) | 113 | 29 | 46 | 39 | 27 | 0 | 49 | 0 | 2 | 3 | 4 | 3 | .57 | 7 | .267 | .333 | .443 |
| 2011 | Cle | AL | 35 | 71 | 11 | 2 | 1 | 1 | (1 | 0) | 18 | 10 | 6 | 3 | 8 | 0 | 17 | 0 | 1 | 0 | 1 | 0 | 1.00 | 2 | .155 | .241 | .254 |
| 2012 | Cle | AL | 14 | 33 | 7 | 0 | 0 | 1 | (0 | 1) | 10 | 2 | 5 | 5 | 1 | 0 | 10 | 0 | 0 | 0 | 0 | 0 | - | 0 | .212 | .235 | .303 |
| 2013 | Cle | AL | 4 | 9 | 0 | 0 | 0 | 0 | (0 | 0) | 0 | 0 | 0 | 0 | 0 | 0 | 2 | 0 | 0 | 0 | 0 | 0 | - | 0 | .000 | .000 | .000 |
| 3 ML YEARS | | | 53 | 113 | 18 | 2 | 1 | 2 | (1 | 1) | 28 | 12 | 11 | 8 | 9 | 0 | 29 | 0 | 1 | 0 | 1 | 0 | 1.00 | 2 | .159 | .221 | .248 |

# David Phelps

**Pitches:** R **Bats:** R **Pos:** SP-12; RP-10 **Ht:** 6'2" **Wt:** 200 **Born:** 10/9/1986 **Age:** 27

| Year | Team | Lg | G | GS | CG | GF | IP | BFP | H | R | ER | HR | SH | SF | HB | TBB | IBB | SO | WP | Bk | W | L | Pct | Sh | Sv-Op | Hld | ERC | ERA |
|---|---|---|---|---|---|---|---|---|---|---|---|---|---|---|---|---|---|---|---|---|---|---|---|---|---|---|---|---|
| | | | HOW MUCH HE PITCHED | | | | | | WHAT HE GAVE UP | | | | | | | | | | | | THE RESULTS | | | | | | | |
| 2009 | CtnSC | A | 19 | 19 | 0 | 0 | 112.2 | 465 | 117 | 48 | 35 | 9 | 2 | 4 | 4 | 25 | 0 | 90 | 5 | 2 | 10 | 3 | .769 | 0 | 0- - | - | 3.68 | 2.80 |
| 2009 | Tampa | A+ | 7 | 7 | 0 | 0 | 38.1 | 151 | 34 | 9 | 5 | 1 | 0 | 0 | 0 | 6 | 0 | 32 | 2 | 0 | 3 | 1 | .750 | 0 | 0- - | - | 2.16 | 1.17 |
| 2010 | Trntn | AA | 14 | 14 | 0 | 0 | 88.1 | 342 | 63 | 21 | 20 | 2 | 1 | 0 | 2 | 23 | 0 | 85 | 2 | 3 | 6 | 0 | 1.000 | 0 | 0- - | - | 1.78 | 2.04 |
| 2010 | S-WB | AAA | 12 | 11 | 0 | 0 | 70.1 | 297 | 76 | 31 | 24 | 4 | 2 | 4 | 1 | 13 | 0 | 57 | 1 | 1 | 4 | 2 | .667 | 0 | 0- - | - | 3.41 | 3.07 |
| 2011 | S-WB | AAA | 18 | 18 | 1 | 0 | 107.1 | 449 | 115 | 42 | 38 | 11 | 4 | 1 | 4 | 26 | 0 | 90 | 0 | 0 | 6 | 6 | .500 | 1 | 0- - | - | 4.10 | 3.19 |
| 2011 | Yanks | R | 2 | 2 | 0 | 0 | 7.0 | 28 | 4 | 2 | 0 | 0 | 0 | 0 | 0 | 1 | 0 | 5 | 0 | 0 | 1 | 1 | .500 | 0 | 0- - | - | 0.87 | 0.00 |
| 2012 | Tampa | A+ | 2 | 2 | 0 | 0 | 5.1 | 21 | 7 | 0 | 0 | 0 | 0 | 0 | 0 | 1 | 0 | 5 | 0 | 0 | 0 | 0 | - | 0 | 0- - | - | 4.83 | 0.00 |
| 2012 | Trntn | AA | 1 | 1 | 0 | 0 | 6.2 | 22 | 1 | 0 | 0 | 0 | 0 | 0 | 0 | 1 | 0 | 11 | 0 | 0 | 1 | 0 | 1.000 | 0 | 0- - | - | 0.15 | 0.00 |
| 2012 | S-WB | AAA | 1 | 1 | 0 | 0 | 6.2 | 27 | 4 | 0 | 0 | 0 | 0 | 0 | 0 | 3 | 0 | 7 | 0 | 0 | 1 | 0 | 1.000 | 0 | 0- - | - | 1.61 | 0.00 |
| 2013 | Trntn | AA | 2 | 2 | 0 | 0 | 7.2 | 32 | 5 | 3 | 3 | 2 | 0 | 0 | 0 | 5 | 0 | 12 | 0 | 0 | 0 | 0 | - | 0 | 0- - | - | 4.31 | 3.52 |
| 2012 | NYY | AL | 33 | 11 | 0 | 5 | 99.2 | 414 | 81 | 38 | 37 | 14 | 4 | 3 | 6 | 38 | 2 | 96 | 2 | 2 | 4 | 4 | .500 | 0 | 0-0 | 2 | 3.48 | 3.34 |
| 2013 | NYY | AL | 22 | 12 | 0 | 3 | 86.2 | 376 | 88 | 50 | 48 | 8 | 1 | 2 | 5 | 35 | 1 | 79 | 2 | 0 | 6 | 5 | .545 | 0 | 0-1 | 1 | 4.38 | 4.98 |
| Postseason | | | 3 | 0 | 0 | 1 | 3.1 | 19 | 7 | 4 | 3 | 0 | 0 | 0 | 0 | 1 | 0 | 2 | 0 | 0 | 0 | 2 | .000 | 0 | 0-0 | 0 | 8.97 | 8.10 |
| 2 ML YEARS | | | 55 | 23 | 0 | 8 | 186.1 | 790 | 169 | 88 | 85 | 22 | 5 | 5 | 11 | 73 | 3 | 175 | 4 | 2 | 10 | 9 | .526 | 0 | 0-1 | 3 | 3.89 | 4.11 |

## Brandon Phillips

**Bats:** R **Throws:** R **Pos:** 2B-151 **Ht:** 6'0" **Wt:** 200 **Born:** 6/28/1981 **Age:** 33

| BATTING | | | | | | | | | | | | | | | | | | | | | BASERUNNING | | | | AVERAGES | | |
|---|---|---|---|---|---|---|---|---|---|---|---|---|---|---|---|---|---|---|---|---|---|---|---|---|---|---|---|
| Year Team | Lg | G | AB | H | 2B | 3B | HR | (Hm | Rd) | TB | R | RBI | RC | TBB | IBB | SO | HBP | SH | SF | | SB | CS | SB% | GDP | Avg | OBP | Slg |
| 2002 Cle | AL | 11 | 31 | 8 | 3 | 1 | 0 | (0 | 0) | 13 | 5 | 4 | 5 | 3 | 0 | 6 | 1 | 1 | 0 | | 0 | 0 | - | 0 | .258 | .343 | .419 |
| 2003 Cle | AL | 112 | 370 | 77 | 18 | 1 | 6 | (3 | 3) | 115 | 36 | 33 | 22 | 14 | 0 | 77 | 3 | 5 | 1 | | 4 | 5 | .44 | 12 | .208 | .242 | .311 |
| 2004 Cle | AL | 6 | 22 | 4 | 2 | 0 | 0 | (0 | 0) | 6 | 1 | 1 | 0 | 2 | 0 | 5 | 0 | 0 | 0 | | 0 | 2 | .00 | 1 | .182 | .250 | .273 |
| 2005 Cle | AL | 6 | 9 | 0 | 0 | 0 | 0 | (0 | 0) | 0 | 1 | 0 | 0 | 0 | 0 | 4 | 0 | 0 | 0 | | 0 | 0 | - | 0 | .000 | .000 | .000 |
| 2006 Cin | NL | 149 | 536 | 148 | 28 | 1 | 17 | (9 | 8) | 229 | 65 | 75 | 74 | 35 | 3 | 88 | 6 | 4 | 6 | | 25 | 2 | .93 | 19 | .276 | .324 | .427 |
| 2007 Cin | NL | 158 | 650 | 187 | 26 | 6 | 30 | (17 | 13) | 315 | 107 | 94 | 88 | 33 | 4 | 109 | 12 | 2 | 5 | | 32 | 8 | .80 | 26 | .288 | .331 | .485 |
| 2008 Cin | NL | 141 | 559 | 146 | 24 | 7 | 21 | (13 | 8) | 247 | 80 | 78 | 74 | 39 | 6 | 93 | 5 | 0 | 6 | | 23 | 10 | .70 | 13 | .261 | .312 | .442 |
| 2009 Cin | NL | 153 | 584 | 161 | 30 | 5 | 20 | (10 | 10) | 261 | 78 | 98 | 80 | 44 | 3 | 75 | 6 | 2 | 8 | | 25 | 9 | .74 | 21 | .276 | .329 | .447 |
| 2010 Cin | NL | 155 | 626 | 172 | 33 | 5 | 18 | (10 | 8) | 269 | 100 | 59 | 77 | 46 | 1 | 83 | 8 | 6 | 1 | | 16 | 12 | .57 | 14 | .275 | .332 | .430 |
| 2011 Cin | NL | 150 | 610 | 183 | 38 | 2 | 18 | (14 | 4) | 279 | 94 | 82 | 92 | 44 | 3 | 85 | 9 | 5 | 6 | | 14 | 9 | .61 | 15 | .300 | .353 | .457 |
| 2012 Cin | NL | 147 | 580 | 163 | 30 | 1 | 18 | (15 | 3) | 249 | 86 | 77 | 78 | 28 | 2 | 79 | 8 | 3 | 4 | | 15 | 2 | .88 | 19 | .281 | .321 | .429 |
| 2013 Cin | NL | 151 | 606 | 158 | 24 | 2 | 18 | (7 | 11) | 240 | 80 | 103 | 82 | 39 | 6 | 98 | 8 | 4 | 9 | | 5 | 3 | .63 | 19 | .261 | .310 | .396 |
| Postseason | | 8 | 36 | 13 | 4 | 0 | 2 | (0 | 2) | 23 | 3 | 8 | 10 | 0 | 0 | 5 | 0 | 0 | 1 | | 1 | 0 | 1.00 | 0 | .361 | .351 | .639 |
| 12 ML YEARS | | 1339 | 5183 | 1407 | 256 | 31 | 166 | (98 | 68) | 2223 | 733 | 704 | 672 | 327 | 28 | 802 | 66 | 32 | 46 | | 159 | 62 | .72 | 159 | .271 | .320 | .429 |

## Zach Phillips

**Pitches:** L **Bats:** L **Pos:** RP-3 **Ht:** 6'0" **Wt:** 190 **Born:** 9/21/1986 **Age:** 27

| HOW MUCH HE PITCHED | | | | | | | | WHAT HE GAVE UP | | | | | | | | | | | | THE RESULTS | | | | | | | |
|---|---|---|---|---|---|---|---|---|---|---|---|---|---|---|---|---|---|---|---|---|---|---|---|---|---|---|---|
| Year Team | Lg | G | GS | CG | GF | IP | BFP | H | R | ER | HR | SH | SF | HB | TBB | IBB | SO | WP | Bk | W | L | Pct | Sh | Sv-Op | Hld | ERC | ERA |
| 2013 NewOr* | AAA | 50 | 0 | 0 | 11 | 59.0 | 245 | 49 | 19 | 16 | 3 | 1 | 0 | 1 | 24 | 4 | 74 | 2 | 0 | 4 | 2 | .667 | 0 | 1-- | - | 2.84 | 2.44 |
| 2011 Bal | AL | 10 | 0 | 0 | 2 | 8.0 | 33 | 6 | 1 | 1 | 1 | 0 | 0 | 0 | 2 | 0 | 8 | 0 | 0 | 0 | 0 | - | 0 | 0-0 | 0 | 2.24 | 1.13 |
| 2012 Bal | AL | 6 | 0 | 0 | 3 | 6.0 | 28 | 7 | 4 | 4 | 2 | 0 | 0 | 0 | 3 | 1 | 5 | 0 | 0 | 0 | 0 | - | 0 | 0-0 | 0 | 6.85 | 6.00 |
| 2013 Mia | NL | 3 | 0 | 0 | 0 | 1.2 | 11 | 3 | 1 | 1 | 0 | 1 | 0 | 0 | 3 | 0 | 1 | 0 | 0 | 0 | 1 | .000 | 0 | 0-0 | 0 | 14.26 | 5.40 |
| 3 ML YEARS | | 19 | 0 | 0 | 5 | 15.2 | 72 | 16 | 6 | 6 | 3 | 1 | 0 | 0 | 8 | 1 | 14 | 0 | 0 | 0 | 1 | .000 | 0 | 0-0 | 0 | 5.02 | 3.45 |

## Felix Pie

**Bats:** L **Throws:** L **Pos:** LF-13;PH-9;CF-5;PR-3;RF-1 pee-YAY **Ht:** 6'2" **Wt:** 185 **Born:** 2/8/1985 **Age:** 29

| BATTING | | | | | | | | | | | | | | | | | | | | | BASERUNNING | | | | AVERAGES | | |
|---|---|---|---|---|---|---|---|---|---|---|---|---|---|---|---|---|---|---|---|---|---|---|---|---|---|---|---|
| Year Team | Lg | G | AB | H | 2B | 3B | HR | (Hm | Rd) | TB | R | RBI | RC | TBB | IBB | SO | HBP | SH | SF | | SB | CS | SB% | GDP | Avg | OBP | Slg |
| 2013 Indy* | AAA | 105 | 354 | 89 | 17 | 4 | 8 | (- | -) | 138 | 53 | 40 | 51 | 37 | 2 | 83 | 2 | 2 | 1 | | 38 | 9 | .81 | 7 | .251 | .325 | .390 |
| 2007 ChC | NL | 87 | 177 | 38 | 9 | 3 | 2 | (0 | 2) | 59 | 26 | 20 | 21 | 14 | 0 | 43 | 0 | 2 | 1 | | 8 | 1 | .89 | 0 | .215 | .271 | .333 |
| 2008 ChC | NL | 43 | 83 | 20 | 2 | 1 | 1 | (1 | 0) | 27 | 9 | 10 | 9 | 7 | 0 | 29 | 2 | 0 | 1 | | 3 | 0 | 1.00 | 3 | .241 | .312 | .325 |
| 2009 Bal | AL | 101 | 252 | 67 | 10 | 3 | 9 | (6 | 3) | 110 | 38 | 29 | 30 | 24 | 1 | 58 | 0 | 2 | 3 | | 1 | 3 | .25 | 6 | .266 | .326 | .437 |
| 2010 Bal | AL | 82 | 288 | 79 | 15 | 5 | 5 | (3 | 2) | 119 | 39 | 31 | 34 | 13 | 0 | 52 | 1 | 3 | 3 | | 5 | 2 | .71 | 10 | .274 | .305 | .413 |
| 2011 Bal | AL | 85 | 164 | 36 | 8 | 1 | 0 | (0 | 0) | 46 | 15 | 7 | 14 | 10 | 0 | 32 | 0 | 1 | 0 | | 3 | 2 | .60 | 0 | .220 | .264 | .280 |
| 2013 Pit | NL | 27 | 29 | 4 | 1 | 0 | 0 | (0 | 0) | 5 | 5 | 2 | 0 | 2 | 0 | 13 | 0 | 0 | 0 | | 1 | 2 | .33 | 0 | .138 | .194 | .172 |
| Postseason | | 2 | 1 | 0 | 0 | 0 | 0 | (0 | 0) | 0 | 0 | 0 | 0 | 1 | 0 | 1 | 0 | 0 | 0 | | 0 | 0 | - | 0 | .000 | .500 | .000 |
| 6 ML YEARS | | 425 | 993 | 244 | 45 | 13 | 17 | (10 | 7) | 366 | 132 | 99 | 108 | 70 | 1 | 227 | 3 | 8 | 8 | | 21 | 10 | .68 | 19 | .246 | .295 | .369 |

## Juan Pierre

**Bats:** L **Throws:** L **Pos:** LF-64;PH-47;DH-1;PR-1 **Ht:** 5'11" **Wt:** 180 **Born:** 8/14/1977 **Age:** 36

| BATTING | | | | | | | | | | | | | | | | | | | | | BASERUNNING | | | | AVERAGES | | |
|---|---|---|---|---|---|---|---|---|---|---|---|---|---|---|---|---|---|---|---|---|---|---|---|---|---|---|---|
| Year Team | Lg | G | AB | H | 2B | 3B | HR | (Hm | Rd) | TB | R | RBI | RC | TBB | IBB | SO | HBP | SH | SF | | SB | CS | SB% | GDP | Avg | OBP | Slg |
| 2000 Col | NL | 51 | 200 | 62 | 2 | 0 | 0 | (0 | 0) | 64 | 26 | 20 | 23 | 13 | 0 | 15 | 1 | 4 | 1 | | 7 | 6 | .54 | 2 | .310 | .353 | .320 |
| 2001 Col | NL | 156 | 617 | 202 | 26 | 11 | 2 | (0 | 2) | 256 | 108 | 55 | 101 | 41 | 1 | 29 | 10 | 14 | 1 | | **46** | **17** | .73 | 6 | .327 | .378 | .415 |
| 2002 Col | NL | 152 | 592 | 170 | 20 | 5 | 1 | (0 | 1) | 203 | 90 | 35 | 79 | 31 | 0 | 52 | 9 | 8 | 0 | | 47 | 12 | .80 | 7 | .287 | .332 | .343 |
| 2003 Fla | NL | **162** | **668** | 204 | 28 | 7 | 1 | (1 | 0) | 249 | 100 | 41 | 92 | 55 | 1 | 35 | 5 | **15** | 3 | | **65** | **20** | .76 | 9 | .305 | .361 | .373 |
| 2004 Fla | NL | **162** | **678** | **221** | 22 | **12** | 3 | (1 | 2) | 276 | 100 | 49 | 101 | 45 | 1 | 35 | 8 | 15 | 2 | | 45 | **24** | .65 | 9 | .326 | .374 | .407 |
| 2005 Fla | NL | **162** | 656 | 181 | 19 | 13 | 2 | (1 | 1) | 232 | 96 | 47 | 76 | 41 | 1 | 45 | 9 | 10 | 2 | | 57 | **17** | .77 | 10 | .276 | .326 | .354 |
| 2006 ChC | NL | **162** | **699** | **204** | 32 | 13 | 3 | (1 | 2) | 271 | 87 | 40 | 84 | 32 | 0 | 38 | 8 | 10 | 1 | | 58 | **20** | .74 | 6 | .292 | .330 | .388 |
| 2007 LAD | NL | **162** | 668 | 196 | 24 | 8 | 0 | (0 | 0) | 236 | 96 | 41 | 75 | 33 | 0 | 37 | 6 | **20** | 2 | | 64 | 15 | .81 | 10 | .293 | .331 | .353 |
| 2008 LAD | NL | 119 | 375 | 106 | 10 | 2 | 1 | (0 | 1) | 123 | 44 | 28 | 48 | 22 | 1 | 24 | 3 | 5 | 1 | | 40 | 12 | .77 | 3 | .283 | .327 | .328 |
| 2009 LAD | NL | 145 | 380 | 117 | 16 | 8 | 0 | (0 | 0) | 149 | 57 | 31 | 58 | 27 | 3 | 27 | 8 | 9 | 1 | | 30 | 12 | .71 | 7 | .308 | .365 | .392 |
| 2010 CWS | AL | 160 | 651 | 179 | 18 | 3 | 1 | (0 | 1) | 206 | 96 | 47 | 84 | 45 | 0 | 47 | **21** | 15 | 2 | | **68** | **18** | .79 | 8 | .275 | .341 | .316 |
| 2011 CWS | AL | 158 | 639 | 178 | 17 | 4 | 2 | (2 | 0) | 209 | 80 | 50 | 80 | 43 | 0 | 41 | 7 | **19** | 3 | | 27 | **17** | .61 | 7 | .279 | .329 | .327 |
| 2012 Phi | NL | 130 | 394 | 121 | 10 | 6 | 1 | (1 | 0) | 146 | 59 | 25 | 55 | 23 | 0 | 27 | 4 | **17** | 1 | | 37 | 7 | .84 | 4 | .307 | .351 | .371 |
| 2013 Mia | NL | 113 | 308 | 76 | 11 | 2 | 1 | (1 | 0) | 94 | 36 | 8 | 25 | 13 | 0 | 27 | 3 | 6 | 0 | | 23 | 6 | .79 | 4 | .247 | .284 | .305 |
| Postseason | | 26 | 79 | 24 | 5 | 2 | 0 | (0 | 0) | 33 | 16 | 7 | 14 | 8 | 2 | 4 | 1 | 2 | 0 | | 3 | 5 | .38 | 0 | .304 | .375 | .418 |
| 14 ML YEARS | | 1994 | 7525 | 2217 | 255 | 94 | 18 | (8 | 10) | 2714 | 1075 | 517 | 981 | 464 | 8 | 479 | 102 | 167 | 20 | | 614 | 203 | .75 | 92 | .295 | .343 | .361 |

## A.J. Pierzynski

**Bats:** L **Throws:** R **Pos:** C-119;DH-12;PH-11 perr-ZINN-ski **Ht:** 6'3" **Wt:** 235 **Born:** 12/30/1976 **Age:** 37

| BATTING | | | | | | | | | | | | | | | | | | | | | BASERUNNING | | | | AVERAGES | | |
|---|---|---|---|---|---|---|---|---|---|---|---|---|---|---|---|---|---|---|---|---|---|---|---|---|---|---|---|
| Year Team | Lg | G | AB | H | 2B | 3B | HR | (Hm | Rd) | TB | R | RBI | RC | TBB | IBB | SO | HBP | SH | SF | | SB | CS | SB% | GDP | Avg | OBP | Slg |
| 2013 Frisco* | AA | 2 | 6 | 1 | 0 | 0 | 0 | (- | -) | 1 | 0 | 0 | 0 | 0 | 0 | 1 | 0 | 0 | 0 | | 0 | 0 | - | 0 | .167 | .167 | .167 |
| 1998 Min | AL | 7 | 10 | 3 | 0 | 0 | 0 | (0 | 0) | 3 | 1 | 1 | 2 | 1 | 0 | 2 | 1 | 0 | 1 | | 0 | 0 | - | 0 | .300 | .385 | .300 |
| 1999 Min | AL | 9 | 22 | 6 | 2 | 0 | 0 | (0 | 0) | 8 | 3 | 3 | 3 | 1 | 0 | 4 | 1 | 0 | 0 | | 0 | 0 | - | 0 | .273 | .333 | .364 |
| 2000 Min | AL | 33 | 88 | 27 | 5 | 1 | 2 | (1 | 1) | 40 | 12 | 11 | 14 | 5 | 0 | 14 | 2 | 0 | 1 | | 1 | 0 | 1.00 | 1 | .307 | .354 | .455 |
| 2001 Min | AL | 114 | 381 | 110 | 33 | 2 | 7 | (3 | 4) | 168 | 51 | 55 | 50 | 16 | 4 | 57 | 4 | 1 | 3 | | 1 | 7 | .13 | 7 | .289 | .322 | .441 |
| 2002 Min | AL | 130 | 440 | 132 | 31 | 6 | 6 | (2 | 4) | 193 | 54 | 49 | 60 | 13 | 1 | 61 | 11 | 2 | 3 | | 1 | 2 | .33 | 14 | .300 | .334 | .439 |
| 2003 Min | AL | 137 | 487 | 152 | 35 | 3 | 11 | (6 | 5) | 226 | 63 | 74 | 80 | 24 | 12 | 55 | 15 | 2 | 5 | | 3 | 1 | .75 | 13 | .312 | .360 | .464 |
| 2004 SF | NL | 131 | 471 | 128 | 28 | 2 | 11 | (3 | 8) | 193 | 45 | 77 | 58 | 19 | 4 | 27 | 15 | 2 | 3 | | 0 | 1 | .00 | **27** | .272 | .319 | .410 |
| 2005 CWS | AL | 128 | 460 | 118 | 21 | 0 | 18 | (12 | 6) | 193 | 61 | 56 | 55 | 23 | 5 | 68 | 12 | 1 | 1 | | 0 | 2 | .00 | 13 | .257 | .308 | .420 |
| 2006 CWS | AL | 140 | 509 | 150 | 24 | 0 | 16 | (9 | 7) | 222 | 65 | 64 | 68 | 22 | 6 | 72 | 8 | 3 | 1 | | 1 | 0 | 1.00 | 10 | .295 | .333 | .436 |

| BATTING | | | | | | | | | | | | | | | | | | | | | BASERUNNING | | | | AVERAGES | | |
|---|---|---|---|---|---|---|---|---|---|---|---|---|---|---|---|---|---|---|---|---|---|---|---|---|---|---|---|
| Year Team | Lg | G | AB | H | 2B | 3B | HR | (Hm | Rd) | TB | R | RBI | RC | TBB | IBB | SO | HBP | SH | SF | SB | CS | SB% | GDP | Avg | OBP | Slg |
| 2007 CWS | AL | 136 | 472 | 124 | 24 | 0 | 14 | (8 | 6) | 190 | 54 | 50 | 49 | 25 | 5 | 66 | 8 | 1 | 3 | 1 | 1 | .50 | 21 | .263 | .309 | .403 |
| 2008 CWS | AL | 134 | 534 | 150 | 31 | 1 | 13 | (7 | 6) | 222 | 66 | 60 | 64 | 19 | 5 | 71 | 8 | 3 | 6 | 1 | 0 | 1.00 | 14 | .281 | .312 | .416 |
| 2009 CWS | AL | 138 | 504 | 151 | 22 | 1 | 13 | (8 | 5) | 214 | 57 | 49 | 59 | 24 | 6 | 52 | 1 | 3 | 3 | 1 | 1 | .50 | 18 | .300 | .331 | .425 |
| 2010 CWS | AL | 128 | 474 | 128 | 29 | 0 | 9 | (7 | 2) | 184 | 43 | 56 | 51 | 15 | 2 | 39 | 6 | 6 | 2 | 3 | 4 | .43 | 17 | .270 | .300 | .388 |
| 2011 CWS | AL | 129 | 464 | 133 | 29 | 1 | 8 | (5 | 3) | 188 | 38 | 48 | 53 | 23 | 6 | 33 | 5 | 2 | 6 | 0 | 0 | - | 19 | .287 | .323 | .405 |
| 2012 CWS | AL | 135 | 479 | 133 | 18 | 4 | 27 | (18 | 9) | 240 | 68 | 77 | 79 | 28 | 5 | 78 | 8 | 1 | 4 | 0 | 0 | - | 8 | .278 | .326 | .501 |
| 2013 Tex | AL | 134 | 503 | 137 | 24 | 1 | 17 | (10 | 7) | 214 | 48 | 70 | 61 | 11 | 2 | 76 | 9 | 0 | 6 | 1 | 1 | .50 | 14 | .272 | .297 | .425 |
| Postseason | | 30 | 100 | 30 | 5 | 1 | 5 | (3 | 2) | 52 | 16 | 17 | 19 | 10 | 1 | 13 | 2 | 1 | 1 | 2 | 3 | .40 | 2 | .300 | .372 | .520 |
| 16 ML YEARS | | 1763 | 6298 | 1782 | 356 | 22 | 172 | (99 | 73) | 2698 | 729 | 800 | 806 | 269 | 63 | 775 | 114 | 27 | 48 | 14 | 20 | .41 | 196 | .283 | .322 | .428 |

# Brett Pill

**Bats:** R **Throws:** R **Pos:** PH-28;1B-13;LF-8;PR-1 **Ht:** 6'4" **Wt:** 225 **Born:** 9/9/1984 **Age:** 29

| BATTING | | | | | | | | | | | | | | | | | | | | | BASERUNNING | | | | AVERAGES | | |
|---|---|---|---|---|---|---|---|---|---|---|---|---|---|---|---|---|---|---|---|---|---|---|---|---|---|---|---|
| Year Team | Lg | G | AB | H | 2B | 3B | HR | (Hm | Rd) | TB | R | RBI | RC | TBB | IBB | SO | HBP | SH | SF | SB | CS | SB% | GDP | Avg | OBP | Slg |
| 2013 Fresno* | AAA | 68 | 276 | 95 | 21 | 2 | 18 | (- | -) | 174 | 48 | 79 | 63 | 15 | 2 | 40 | 3 | 0 | 4 | 1 | 0 | 1.00 | 2 | .344 | .379 | .630 |
| 2011 SF | NL | 15 | 50 | 15 | 3 | 2 | 2 | (0 | 2) | 28 | 7 | 9 | 6 | 2 | 0 | 8 | 0 | 0 | 1 | 0 | 1 | .00 | 2 | .300 | .321 | .560 |
| 2012 SF | NL | 48 | 105 | 22 | 3 | 0 | 4 | (0 | 4) | 37 | 10 | 11 | 7 | 6 | 1 | 19 | 2 | 1 | 0 | 1 | 0 | 1.00 | 5 | .210 | .265 | .352 |
| 2013 SF | NL | 48 | 85 | 19 | 4 | 0 | 3 | (1 | 2) | 32 | 11 | 12 | 4 | 5 | 0 | 17 | 1 | 0 | 1 | 0 | 0 | - | 5 | .224 | .272 | .376 |
| 3 ML YEARS | | 111 | 240 | 56 | 10 | 2 | 9 | (1 | 8) | 97 | 28 | 32 | 17 | 13 | 1 | 44 | 3 | 1 | 2 | 1 | 1 | .50 | 12 | .233 | .279 | .404 |

# Kevin Pillar

**Bats:** R **Throws:** R **Pos:** LF-33;RF-1;DH-1;PR-1 pih-LAHR **Ht:** 6'0" **Wt:** 200 **Born:** 1/4/1989 **Age:** 25

| BATTING | | | | | | | | | | | | | | | | | | | | | BASERUNNING | | | | AVERAGES | | |
|---|---|---|---|---|---|---|---|---|---|---|---|---|---|---|---|---|---|---|---|---|---|---|---|---|---|---|---|
| Year Team | Lg | G | AB | H | 2B | 3B | HR | (Hm | Rd) | TB | R | RBI | RC | TBB | IBB | SO | HBP | SH | SF | SB | CS | SB% | GDP | Avg | OBP | Slg |
| 2011 Bluefld | R | 60 | 236 | 82 | 17 | 3 | 7 | (- | -) | 126 | 44 | 37 | 46 | 10 | 0 | 36 | 3 | 4 | 3 | 8 | 4 | .67 | 4 | .347 | .377 | .534 |
| 2012 Lnsng | A | 86 | 335 | 108 | 20 | 4 | 5 | (- | -) | 151 | 49 | 57 | 65 | 35 | 1 | 53 | 3 | 1 | 1 | 35 | 6 | .85 | 10 | .322 | .390 | .451 |
| 2012 Dnedin | A+ | 42 | 164 | 53 | 8 | 2 | 1 | (- | -) | 68 | 16 | 34 | 26 | 5 | 0 | 17 | 2 | 1 | 6 | 16 | 3 | .84 | 0 | .323 | .339 | .415 |
| 2013 NHam | AA | 71 | 304 | 95 | 20 | 2 | 5 | (- | -) | 134 | 44 | 30 | 48 | 19 | 0 | 31 | 4 | 0 | 0 | 15 | 8 | .65 | 6 | .313 | .361 | .441 |
| 2013 Buffalo | AAA | 52 | 201 | 60 | 19 | 4 | 4 | (- | -) | 99 | 30 | 27 | 33 | 12 | 0 | 39 | 2 | 1 | 2 | 8 | 5 | .62 | 4 | .299 | .341 | .493 |
| 2013 Tor | AL | 36 | 102 | 21 | 4 | 0 | 3 | (1 | 2) | 34 | 11 | 13 | 9 | 4 | 0 | 29 | 2 | 2 | 0 | 0 | 1 | .00 | 0 | .206 | .250 | .333 |

# Stolmy Pimentel

**Pitches:** R **Bats:** R **Pos:** RP-5 STOLE-mee PIM-en-tell **Ht:** 6'3" **Wt:** 235 **Born:** 2/1/1990 **Age:** 24

| HOW MUCH HE PITCHED | | | | | | | | WHAT HE GAVE UP | | | | | | | | | | | | THE RESULTS | | | | | | | |
|---|---|---|---|---|---|---|---|---|---|---|---|---|---|---|---|---|---|---|---|---|---|---|---|---|---|---|---|
| Year Team | Lg | G | GS | CG | GF | IP | BFP | H | R | ER | HR | SH | SF | HB | TBB | IBB | SO | WP | Bk | W | L | Pct | Sh | Sv-Op | Hld | ERC | ERA |
| 2009 Grnvlle | A | 24 | 23 | 1 | 0 | 117.2 | 505 | 135 | 62 | 50 | 12 | 3 | 4 | 4 | 29 | 0 | 103 | 6 | 1 | 10 | 7 | .588 | 0 | 0- - | - | 4.49 | 3.82 |
| 2010 Salem | A+ | 26 | 26 | 0 | 0 | 128.2 | 535 | 120 | 65 | 58 | 11 | 1 | 3 | 5 | 42 | 1 | 102 | 11 | 2 | 9 | 11 | .450 | 0 | 0- - | - | 3.52 | 4.06 |
| 2011 Portlnd | AA | 15 | 15 | 0 | 0 | 50.1 | 250 | 75 | 57 | 51 | 8 | 1 | 5 | 8 | 23 | 0 | 30 | 6 | 1 | 0 | 9 | .000 | 0 | 0- - | - | 8.59 | 9.12 |
| 2011 Salem | A+ | 11 | 10 | 0 | 0 | 51.2 | 221 | 50 | 29 | 26 | 8 | 2 | 2 | 8 | 16 | 0 | 35 | 5 | 0 | 6 | 4 | .600 | 0 | 0- - | - | 4.62 | 4.53 |
| 2012 Portlnd | AA | 22 | 22 | 1 | 0 | 115.2 | 495 | 115 | 66 | 59 | 9 | 6 | 1 | 2 | 42 | 0 | 86 | 8 | 0 | 6 | 7 | .462 | 0 | 0- - | - | 3.82 | 4.59 |
| 2013 Altna | AA | 13 | 13 | 1 | 0 | 77.1 | 340 | 74 | 36 | 31 | 8 | 2 | 4 | 5 | 35 | 0 | 61 | 4 | 0 | 4 | 3 | .571 | 0 | 0- - | - | 4.30 | 3.61 |
| 2013 Indy | AAA | 14 | 14 | 1 | 0 | 92.0 | 371 | 76 | 38 | 32 | 6 | 3 | 6 | 2 | 21 | 1 | 62 | 5 | 0 | 2 | 6 | .250 | 0 | 0- - | - | 2.36 | 3.13 |
| 2013 Pit | NL | 5 | 0 | 0 | 1 | 9.1 | 38 | 6 | 4 | 2 | 0 | 0 | 1 | 0 | 2 | 0 | 9 | 2 | 0 | 0 | 0 | - | 0 | 0-0 | 1 | 1.19 | 1.93 |

# Michael Pineda

**Pitches:** R **Bats:** R **Pos:** P pih-NAY-duh **Ht:** 6'8" **Wt:** 260 **Born:** 1/18/1989 **Age:** 25

| HOW MUCH HE PITCHED | | | | | | | | WHAT HE GAVE UP | | | | | | | | | | | | THE RESULTS | | | | | | | |
|---|---|---|---|---|---|---|---|---|---|---|---|---|---|---|---|---|---|---|---|---|---|---|---|---|---|---|---|
| Year Team | Lg | G | GS | CG | GF | IP | BFP | H | R | ER | HR | SH | SF | HB | TBB | IBB | SO | WP | Bk | W | L | Pct | Sh | Sv-Op | Hld | ERC | ERA |
| 2009 Hi Dsrt | A+ | 10 | 8 | 0 | 0 | 44.1 | 168 | 29 | 16 | 14 | 3 | 1 | 2 | 6 | 6 | 0 | 48 | 2 | 0 | 4 | 2 | .667 | 0 | 0- - | - | 1.74 | 2.84 |
| 2009 Ms | R | 2 | 2 | 0 | 0 | 3.0 | 10 | 2 | 0 | 0 | 0 | 0 | 0 | 0 | 0 | 0 | 4 | 0 | 0 | 0 | 0 | - | 0 | 0- - | - | 1.01 | 0.00 |
| 2010 WTenn | AA | 13 | 13 | 0 | 0 | 77.0 | 316 | 67 | 23 | 19 | 1 | 1 | 0 | 4 | 17 | 1 | 78 | 2 | 0 | 8 | 1 | .889 | 0 | 0- - | - | 2.32 | 2.22 |
| 2010 Tacom | AAA | 12 | 12 | 0 | 0 | 62.1 | 260 | 54 | 33 | 33 | 9 | 2 | 0 | 3 | 17 | 0 | 76 | 0 | 0 | 3 | 3 | .500 | 0 | 0- - | - | 3.28 | 4.76 |
| 2013 Tampa | A+ | 2 | 2 | 0 | 0 | 8.1 | 36 | 7 | 3 | 1 | 0 | 0 | 0 | 0 | 2 | 0 | 7 | 0 | 0 | 1 | 0 | - | 0 | 0- - | - | 1.85 | 1.08 |
| 2013 Trntn | AA | 2 | 2 | 0 | 0 | 9.0 | 40 | 6 | 4 | 4 | 2 | 0 | 0 | 1 | 6 | 0 | 8 | 0 | 0 | 1 | 0 | 1.000 | 0 | 0- - | - | 4.48 | 4.00 |
| 2013 S-WB | AAA | 6 | 6 | 0 | 0 | 23.1 | 96 | 18 | 10 | 10 | 2 | 0 | 0 | 2 | 6 | 0 | 26 | 1 | 0 | 1 | 1 | .500 | 0 | 0- - | - | 2.52 | 3.86 |
| 2011 Sea | AL | 28 | 28 | 0 | 0 | 171.0 | 696 | 133 | 76 | 71 | 18 | 4 | 3 | 5 | 55 | 1 | 173 | 9 | 0 | 9 | 10 | .474 | 0 | 0-0 | 0 | 2.73 | 3.74 |

# Josmil Pinto

**Bats:** R **Throws:** R **Pos:** C-20;PH-2;DH-1 HOSE-meel PEEN-toe **Ht:** 5'11" **Wt:** 210 **Born:** 3/31/1989 **Age:** 25

| BATTING | | | | | | | | | | | | | | | | | | | | | BASERUNNING | | | | AVERAGES | | |
|---|---|---|---|---|---|---|---|---|---|---|---|---|---|---|---|---|---|---|---|---|---|---|---|---|---|---|---|
| Year Team | Lg | G | AB | H | 2B | 3B | HR | (Hm | Rd) | TB | R | RBI | RC | TBB | IBB | SO | HBP | SH | SF | SB | CS | SB% | GDP | Avg | OBP | Slg |
| 2009 Elizab | R | 53 | 205 | 68 | 14 | 2 | 13 | (- | -) | 125 | 34 | 55 | 46 | 19 | 2 | 39 | 2 | 0 | 4 | 0 | 1 | .00 | 6 | .332 | .387 | .610 |
| 2010 Beloit | A | 100 | 347 | 78 | 21 | 1 | 10 | (- | -) | 131 | 60 | 54 | 40 | 32 | 3 | 67 | 5 | 2 | 6 | 2 | 3 | .40 | 7 | .225 | .295 | .378 |
| 2011 Beloit | A | 9 | 32 | 8 | 3 | 0 | 1 | (- | -) | 14 | 4 | 9 | 4 | 2 | 0 | 10 | 0 | 0 | 2 | 0 | 0 | - | 1 | .250 | .278 | .438 |
| 2011 FtMyrs | A+ | 64 | 221 | 58 | 11 | 1 | 5 | (- | -) | 86 | 21 | 32 | 27 | 12 | 1 | 36 | 2 | 0 | 1 | 1 | 0 | 1.00 | 7 | .262 | .305 | .389 |
| 2012 FtMyrs | A+ | 93 | 349 | 103 | 22 | 2 | 12 | (- | -) | 165 | 45 | 51 | 61 | 39 | 0 | 63 | 0 | 0 | 5 | 0 | 0 | - | 11 | .295 | .361 | .473 |
| 2012 NwBrit | AA | 12 | 47 | 14 | 4 | 1 | 2 | (- | -) | 26 | 8 | 9 | 9 | 4 | 0 | 10 | 1 | 0 | 0 | 0 | 0 | - | 3 | .298 | .365 | .553 |
| 2013 NwBrit | AA | 107 | 386 | 119 | 23 | 1 | 14 | (- | -) | 186 | 59 | 68 | 78 | 64 | 1 | 71 | 3 | 0 | 0 | 0 | 2 | .00 | 8 | .308 | .411 | .482 |
| 2013 Roch | AAA | 19 | 70 | 22 | 9 | 0 | 1 | (- | -) | 34 | 6 | 6 | 11 | 2 | 0 | 12 | 1 | 0 | 2 | 0 | 0 | - | 6 | .314 | .333 | .486 |
| 2013 Min | AL | 21 | 76 | 26 | 5 | 0 | 4 | (3 | 1) | 43 | 10 | 12 | 15 | 6 | 0 | 22 | 1 | 0 | 0 | 0 | 0 | - | 3 | .342 | .398 | .566 |

## Trevor Plouffe

**Bats:** R **Throws:** R **Pos:** 3B-120;DH-9;PH-3;1B-2 PLOOF **Ht:** 6'2" **Wt:** 205 **Born:** 6/15/1986 **Age:** 28

| BATTING | | | | | | | | | | | | | | | | | | | | BASERUNNING | | | | AVERAGES | | |
|---|---|---|---|---|---|---|---|---|---|---|---|---|---|---|---|---|---|---|---|---|---|---|---|---|---|---|
| Year Team | Lg | G | AB | H | 2B | 3B | HR | (Hm | Rd) | TB | R | RBI | RC | TBB | IBB | SO | HBP | SH | SF | SB | CS | SB% | GDP | Avg | OBP | Slg |
| 2013 Roch* | AAA | 4 | 15 | 5 | 0 | 0 | 1 | (- | -) | 8 | 3 | 3 | 3 | 2 | 0 | 3 | 0 | 0 | 0 | 0 | 0 | - | 0 | .333 | .412 | .533 |
| 2010 Min | AL | 22 | 41 | 6 | 1 | 0 | 2 | (1 | 1) | 13 | 7 | 6 | 2 | 0 | 0 | 14 | 0 | 2 | 1 | 0 | 0 | - | 0 | .146 | .143 | .317 |
| 2011 Min | AL | 81 | 286 | 68 | 18 | 1 | 8 | (3 | 5) | 112 | 47 | 31 | 31 | 25 | 0 | 71 | 4 | 2 | 3 | 3 | 3 | .50 | 6 | .238 | .305 | .392 |
| 2012 Min | AL | 119 | 422 | 99 | 19 | 1 | 24 | (15 | 9) | 192 | 56 | 55 | 48 | 37 | 0 | 92 | 4 | 0 | 2 | 1 | 3 | .25 | 9 | .235 | .301 | .455 |
| 2013 Min | AL | 129 | 477 | 121 | 22 | 1 | 14 | (8 | 6) | 187 | 44 | 52 | 49 | 34 | 1 | 112 | 6 | 1 | 4 | 2 | 1 | .67 | 11 | .254 | .309 | .392 |
| 4 ML YEARS | | 351 | 1226 | 294 | 60 | 3 | 48 | (27 | 21) | 504 | 154 | 144 | 130 | 96 | 1 | 289 | 14 | 5 | 10 | 6 | 7 | .46 | 26 | .240 | .300 | .411 |

## Placido Polanco

**Bats:** R **Throws:** R **Pos:** 3B-109;PH-10;PR-1 PLAH-si-doh puh-LAHN-ko **Ht:** 5'9" **Wt:** 190 **Born:** 10/10/1975 **Age:** 38

| BATTING | | | | | | | | | | | | | | | | | | | | BASERUNNING | | | | AVERAGES | | |
|---|---|---|---|---|---|---|---|---|---|---|---|---|---|---|---|---|---|---|---|---|---|---|---|---|---|---|
| Year Team | Lg | G | AB | H | 2B | 3B | HR | (Hm | Rd) | TB | R | RBI | RC | TBB | IBB | SO | HBP | SH | SF | SB | CS | SB% | GDP | Avg | OBP | Slg |
| 1998 StL | NL | 45 | 114 | 29 | 3 | 2 | 1 | (1 | 0) | 39 | 10 | 11 | 12 | 5 | 0 | 9 | 1 | 2 | 0 | 2 | 0 | 1.00 | 1 | .254 | .292 | .342 |
| 1999 StL | NL | 88 | 220 | 61 | 9 | 3 | 1 | (0 | 1) | 79 | 24 | 19 | 23 | 15 | 1 | 24 | 0 | 3 | 2 | 1 | 3 | .25 | 7 | .277 | .321 | .359 |
| 2000 StL | NL | 118 | 323 | 102 | 12 | 3 | 5 | (2 | 3) | 135 | 50 | 39 | 44 | 16 | 0 | 26 | 1 | 7 | 3 | 4 | 4 | .50 | 8 | .316 | .347 | .418 |
| 2001 StL | NL | 144 | 564 | 173 | 26 | 4 | 3 | (1 | 2) | 216 | 87 | 38 | 70 | 25 | 0 | 43 | 6 | 14 | 1 | 12 | 3 | .80 | 22 | .307 | .342 | .383 |
| 2002 2 Tms | NL | 147 | 548 | 158 | 32 | 2 | 9 | (8 | 1) | 221 | 75 | 49 | 64 | 26 | 1 | 41 | 8 | 13 | 0 | 5 | 3 | .63 | 15 | .288 | .330 | .403 |
| 2003 Phi | NL | 122 | 492 | 142 | 30 | 3 | 14 | (7 | 7) | 220 | 87 | 63 | 74 | 42 | 1 | 38 | 8 | 8 | 4 | 14 | 2 | .88 | 16 | .289 | .352 | .447 |
| 2004 Phi | NL | 126 | 503 | 150 | 21 | 0 | 17 | (10 | 7) | 222 | 74 | 55 | 71 | 27 | 0 | 39 | 12 | 7 | 6 | 7 | 4 | .64 | 13 | .298 | .345 | .441 |
| 2005 2 Tms | | 129 | 501 | 166 | 27 | 2 | 9 | (6 | 3) | 224 | 84 | 56 | 86 | 33 | 0 | 25 | 11 | 2 | 4 | 4 | 3 | .57 | 12 | .331 | .383 | .447 |
| 2006 Det | AL | 110 | 461 | 136 | 18 | 1 | 4 | (2 | 2) | 168 | 58 | 52 | 65 | 17 | 0 | 27 | 7 | 8 | 2 | 1 | 2 | .33 | 18 | .295 | .329 | .364 |
| 2007 Det | AL | 142 | 587 | 200 | 36 | 3 | 9 | (7 | 2) | 269 | 105 | 67 | 100 | 37 | 3 | 30 | 11 | 2 | 4 | 7 | 3 | .70 | 9 | .341 | .388 | .458 |
| 2008 Det | AL | 141 | 580 | 178 | 34 | 3 | 8 | (2 | 6) | 242 | 90 | 58 | 81 | 35 | 2 | 43 | 6 | 4 | 4 | 7 | 1 | .88 | 14 | .307 | .350 | .417 |
| 2009 Det | AL | 153 | 618 | 176 | 31 | 4 | 10 | (5 | 5) | 245 | 82 | 72 | 84 | 36 | 2 | 46 | 9 | 7 | 5 | 7 | 2 | .78 | 15 | .285 | .331 | .396 |
| 2010 Phi | NL | 132 | 554 | 165 | 27 | 2 | 6 | (4 | 2) | 214 | 76 | 52 | 68 | 32 | 1 | 47 | 7 | 1 | 8 | 5 | 0 | 1.00 | 14 | .298 | .339 | .386 |
| 2011 Phi | NL | 122 | 469 | 130 | 14 | 0 | 5 | (4 | 1) | 159 | 46 | 50 | 56 | 42 | 0 | 44 | 3 | 1 | 8 | 3 | 0 | 1.00 | 15 | .277 | .335 | .339 |
| 2012 Phi | NL | 90 | 303 | 78 | 15 | 0 | 2 | (2 | 0) | 99 | 28 | 19 | 27 | 18 | 1 | 25 | 2 | 4 | 1 | 0 | 0 | - | 7 | .257 | .302 | .327 |
| 2013 Mia | NL | 118 | 377 | 98 | 13 | 0 | 1 | (1 | 0) | 114 | 33 | 23 | 33 | 23 | 1 | 31 | 9 | 3 | 4 | 2 | 0 | 1.00 | 15 | .260 | .315 | .302 |
| 02 StL | NL | 94 | 342 | 97 | 19 | 1 | 5 | (5 | 0) | 133 | 47 | 27 | 38 | 12 | 1 | 27 | 4 | 9 | 0 | 3 | 1 | .75 | 12 | .284 | .316 | .389 |
| 02 Phi | NL | 53 | 206 | 61 | 13 | 1 | 4 | (3 | 1) | 88 | 28 | 22 | 26 | 14 | 0 | 14 | 4 | 4 | 0 | 2 | 2 | .50 | 3 | .296 | .353 | .427 |
| 05 Phi | NL | 43 | 158 | 50 | 7 | 0 | 3 | (2 | 1) | 66 | 26 | 20 | 26 | 12 | 0 | 9 | 3 | 0 | 0 | 0 | 0 | - | 3 | .316 | .376 | .418 |
| 05 Det | AL | 86 | 343 | 116 | 20 | 2 | 6 | (4 | 2) | 158 | 58 | 36 | 60 | 21 | 0 | 16 | 8 | 2 | 4 | 4 | 3 | .57 | 9 | .338 | .386 | .461 |
| Postseason | | 38 | 129 | 32 | 4 | 0 | 0 | (0 | 0) | 36 | 11 | 13 | 13 | 11 | 2 | 9 | 2 | 3 | 2 | 3 | 1 | .75 | 6 | .248 | .313 | .279 |
| 16 ML YEARS | | 1927 | 7214 | 2142 | 348 | 32 | 104 | (62 | 42) | 2866 | 1009 | 723 | 958 | 429 | 13 | 538 | 101 | 86 | 56 | 81 | 30 | .73 | 201 | .297 | .343 | .397 |

## A.J. Pollock

**Bats:** R **Throws:** R **Pos:** CF-110;PH-24;LF-7;RF-2;PR-2 **Ht:** 6'1" **Wt:** 195 **Born:** 12/5/1987 **Age:** 26

| BATTING | | | | | | | | | | | | | | | | | | | | BASERUNNING | | | | AVERAGES | | |
|---|---|---|---|---|---|---|---|---|---|---|---|---|---|---|---|---|---|---|---|---|---|---|---|---|---|---|
| Year Team | Lg | G | AB | H | 2B | 3B | HR | (Hm | Rd) | TB | R | RBI | RC | TBB | IBB | SO | HBP | SH | SF | SB | CS | SB% | GDP | Avg | OBP | Slg |
| 2009 Sbend | A | 63 | 255 | 69 | 12 | 3 | 3 | (- | -) | 96 | 36 | 22 | 32 | 16 | 0 | 36 | 3 | 1 | 2 | 10 | 4 | .71 | 3 | .271 | .319 | .376 |
| 2011 Mobile | AA | 133 | 550 | 169 | 41 | 5 | 8 | (- | -) | 244 | 103 | 73 | 94 | 44 | 2 | 86 | 4 | 1 | 9 | 36 | 7 | .84 | 11 | .307 | .357 | .444 |
| 2012 Reno | AAA | 106 | 428 | 136 | 25 | 3 | 3 | (- | -) | 176 | 65 | 52 | 68 | 32 | 0 | 52 | 5 | 2 | 4 | 21 | 8 | .72 | 5 | .318 | .369 | .411 |
| 2012 Ari | NL | 31 | 81 | 20 | 4 | 1 | 2 | (2 | 0) | 32 | 8 | 8 | 9 | 9 | 1 | 11 | 0 | 1 | 2 | 1 | 2 | .33 | 2 | .247 | .315 | .395 |
| 2013 Ari | NL | 137 | 443 | 119 | 28 | 5 | 8 | (3 | 5) | 181 | 64 | 38 | 58 | 33 | 1 | 82 | 2 | 3 | 1 | 12 | 3 | .80 | 5 | .269 | .322 | .409 |
| 2 ML YEARS | | 168 | 524 | 139 | 32 | 6 | 10 | (5 | 5) | 213 | 72 | 46 | 67 | 42 | 2 | 93 | 2 | 4 | 3 | 13 | 5 | .72 | 7 | .265 | .320 | .406 |

## Drew Pomeranz

**Pitches:** L **Bats:** R **Pos:** SP-4; RP-4 POMM-er-anze **Ht:** 6'5" **Wt:** 240 **Born:** 11/22/1988 **Age:** 25

| HOW MUCH HE PITCHED | | | | | | | | WHAT HE GAVE UP | | | | | | | | | | | | THE RESULTS | | | | | | | |
|---|---|---|---|---|---|---|---|---|---|---|---|---|---|---|---|---|---|---|---|---|---|---|---|---|---|---|---|
| Year Team | Lg | G | GS | CG | GF | IP | BFP | H | R | ER | HR | SH | SF | HB | TBB | IBB | SO | WP | Bk | W | L | Pct | Sh | Sv-Op | Hld | ERC | ERA |
| 2013 ColSpr* | AAA | 15 | 15 | 0 | 0 | 85.2 | 366 | 83 | 40 | 40 | 6 | 5 | 1 | 3 | 33 | 0 | 96 | 3 | 0 | 8 | 1 | .889 | 0 | 0-- | - | 3.80 | 4.20 |
| 2013 Tulsa* | AA | 1 | 1 | 0 | 0 | 5.1 | 27 | 10 | 7 | 7 | 2 | 1 | 0 | 0 | 1 | 0 | 5 | 0 | 0 | 0 | 1 | .000 | 0 | 0-- | - | 10.86 | 11.81 |
| 2011 Col | NL | 4 | 4 | 0 | 0 | 18.1 | 77 | 19 | 11 | 11 | 0 | 1 | 0 | 1 | 5 | 0 | 13 | 1 | 0 | 2 | 1 | .667 | 0 | 0-0 | 0 | 3.36 | 5.40 |
| 2012 Col | NL | 22 | 22 | 0 | 0 | 96.2 | 434 | 97 | 57 | 53 | 14 | 8 | 4 | 4 | 46 | 2 | 83 | 8 | 1 | 2 | 9 | .182 | 0 | 0-0 | 0 | 4.78 | 4.93 |
| 2013 Col | NL | 8 | 4 | 0 | 0 | 21.2 | 105 | 25 | 15 | 15 | 4 | 1 | 1 | 1 | 19 | 1 | 19 | 0 | 0 | 0 | 4 | .000 | 0 | 0-0 | 0 | 8.04 | 6.23 |
| 3 ML YEARS | | 34 | 30 | 0 | 0 | 136.2 | 616 | 141 | 83 | 79 | 18 | 10 | 5 | 6 | 70 | 3 | 115 | 9 | 1 | 4 | 14 | .222 | 0 | 0-0 | 0 | 5.06 | 5.20 |

## Rick Porcello

**Pitches:** R **Bats:** R **Pos:** SP-29; RP-3 pore-SELL-oh **Ht:** 6'5" **Wt:** 200 **Born:** 12/27/1988 **Age:** 25

| HOW MUCH HE PITCHED | | | | | | | | WHAT HE GAVE UP | | | | | | | | | | | | THE RESULTS | | | | | | | |
|---|---|---|---|---|---|---|---|---|---|---|---|---|---|---|---|---|---|---|---|---|---|---|---|---|---|---|---|
| Year Team | Lg | G | GS | CG | GF | IP | BFP | H | R | ER | HR | SH | SF | HB | TBB | IBB | SO | WP | Bk | W | L | Pct | Sh | Sv-Op | Hld | ERC | ERA |
| 2009 Det | AL | 31 | 31 | 0 | 0 | 170.2 | 720 | 176 | 81 | 75 | 23 | 4 | 2 | 3 | 52 | 0 | 89 | 6 | 1 | 14 | 9 | .609 | 0 | 0-0 | 0 | 4.24 | 3.96 |
| 2010 Det | AL | 27 | 27 | 0 | 0 | 162.2 | 700 | 188 | 96 | 89 | 18 | 1 | 2 | 7 | 38 | 2 | 84 | 11 | 3 | 10 | 12 | .455 | 0 | 0-0 | 0 | 4.56 | 4.92 |
| 2011 Det | AL | 31 | 31 | 0 | 0 | 182.0 | 784 | 210 | 103 | 96 | 18 | 5 | 5 | 8 | 46 | 1 | 104 | 12 | 0 | 14 | 9 | .609 | 0 | 0-0 | 0 | 4.57 | 4.75 |
| 2012 Det | AL | 31 | 31 | 0 | 0 | 176.1 | 783 | **226** | 101 | 90 | 16 | 2 | 3 | 6 | 44 | 3 | 107 | 6 | 0 | 10 | 12 | .455 | 0 | 0-0 | 0 | 5.16 | 4.59 |
| 2013 Det | AL | 32 | 29 | 1 | 1 | 177.0 | 736 | 185 | 87 | 85 | 18 | 4 | 3 | 3 | 42 | 4 | 142 | 6 | 1 | 13 | 8 | .619 | 0 | 0-0 | 0 | 3.79 | 4.32 |
| Postseason | | 6 | 2 | 0 | 2 | 16.1 | 68 | 15 | 9 | 8 | 0 | 0 | 1 | 2 | 2 | 2 | 13 | 0 | 0 | 0 | 1 | .000 | 0 | 0-0 | 0 | 2.19 | 4.41 |
| 5 ML YEARS | | 152 | 149 | 1 | 1 | 868.2 | 3723 | 985 | 468 | 435 | 93 | 16 | 15 | 27 | 222 | 10 | 526 | 41 | 5 | 61 | 50 | .550 | 0 | 0-0 | 0 | 4.46 | 4.51 |

# Buster Posey

**Bats:** R **Throws:** R **Pos:** C-121;1B-21;DH-5;PH-4 **Ht:** 6'1" **Wt:** 220 **Born:** 3/27/1987 **Age:** 27

| | | | BATTING | | | | | | | | | | | | | | | | | | BASERUNNING | | | | AVERAGES | | |
|---|---|---|---|---|---|---|---|---|---|---|---|---|---|---|---|---|---|---|---|---|---|---|---|---|---|---|---|
| Year | Team | Lg | G | AB | H | 2B | 3B | HR | (Hm | Rd) | TB | R | RBI | RC | TBB | IBB | SO | HBP | SH | SF | SB | CS | SB% | GDP | Avg | OBP | Slg |
| 2009 | SF | NL | 7 | 17 | 2 | 0 | 0 | 0 | (0 | 0) | 2 | 1 | 0 | 0 | 0 | 0 | 4 | 0 | 0 | 0 | 0 | 0 | - | 0 | .118 | .118 | .118 |
| 2010 | SF | NL | 108 | 406 | 124 | 23 | 2 | 18 | (6 | 12) | 205 | 58 | 67 | 70 | 30 | 5 | 55 | 4 | 0 | 3 | 0 | 2 | .00 | 12 | .305 | .357 | .505 |
| 2011 | SF | NL | 45 | 162 | 46 | 5 | 0 | 4 | (1 | 3) | 63 | 17 | 21 | 26 | 18 | 3 | 30 | 4 | 0 | 1 | 3 | 0 | 1.00 | 4 | .284 | .368 | .389 |
| 2012 | SF | NL | 148 | 530 | 178 | 39 | 1 | 24 | (7 | 17) | 291 | 78 | 103 | 111 | 69 | 7 | 96 | 2 | 0 | **9** | 1 | 1 | .50 | 19 | .336 | .408 | .549 |
| 2013 | SF | NL | 148 | 520 | 153 | 34 | 1 | 15 | (8 | 7) | 234 | 61 | 72 | 77 | 60 | 8 | 70 | 8 | 0 | 7 | 2 | 1 | .67 | 15 | .294 | .371 | .450 |
| Postseason | | | 31 | 119 | 29 | 3 | 0 | 4 | (1 | 3) | 44 | 11 | 14 | 11 | 14 | 2 | 33 | 0 | 0 | 0 | 1 | 0 | 1.00 | 1 | .244 | .323 | .370 |
| 5 ML YEARS | | | 456 | 1635 | 503 | 101 | 4 | 61 | (22 | 39) | 795 | 215 | 263 | 284 | 177 | 23 | 255 | 18 | 0 | 20 | 6 | 4 | .60 | 50 | .308 | .377 | .486 |

# Martin Prado

mar-TEEN PRAH-doe

**Bats:** R **Throws:** R **Pos:** 3B-113;2B-32;LF-30;PH-4;SS-1 **Ht:** 6'1" **Wt:** 190 **Born:** 10/27/1983 **Age:** 30

| | | | BATTING | | | | | | | | | | | | | | | | | | BASERUNNING | | | | AVERAGES | | |
|---|---|---|---|---|---|---|---|---|---|---|---|---|---|---|---|---|---|---|---|---|---|---|---|---|---|---|---|
| Year | Team | Lg | G | AB | H | 2B | 3B | HR | (Hm | Rd) | TB | R | RBI | RC | TBB | IBB | SO | HBP | SH | SF | SB | CS | SB% | GDP | Avg | OBP | Slg |
| 2006 | Atl | NL | 24 | 42 | 11 | 1 | 1 | 1 | (1 | 0) | 17 | 3 | 9 | 9 | 5 | 0 | 7 | 0 | 2 | 0 | 0 | 0 | - | 2 | .262 | .340 | .405 |
| 2007 | Atl | NL | 28 | 59 | 17 | 3 | 0 | 0 | (0 | 0) | 20 | 5 | 2 | 6 | 3 | 0 | 6 | 0 | 0 | 0 | 0 | 0 | - | 0 | .288 | .323 | .339 |
| 2008 | Atl | NL | 78 | 228 | 73 | 18 | 4 | 2 | (1 | 1) | 105 | 36 | 33 | 39 | 21 | 0 | 29 | 1 | 2 | 2 | 3 | 1 | .75 | 3 | .320 | .377 | .461 |
| 2009 | Atl | NL | 128 | 450 | 138 | 38 | 0 | 11 | (4 | 7) | 209 | 64 | 49 | 57 | 36 | 1 | 59 | 2 | 11 | 4 | 1 | 3 | .25 | 17 | .307 | .358 | .464 |
| 2010 | Atl | NL | 140 | 599 | 184 | 40 | 3 | 15 | (4 | 11) | 275 | 100 | 66 | 86 | 40 | 2 | 86 | 3 | 3 | 6 | 5 | 3 | .63 | 13 | .307 | .350 | .459 |
| 2011 | Atl | NL | 129 | 551 | 143 | 26 | 2 | 13 | (9 | 4) | 212 | 66 | 57 | 57 | 34 | 1 | 52 | 1 | 1 | 3 | 4 | 8 | .33 | 16 | .260 | .302 | .385 |
| 2012 | Atl | NL | 156 | 617 | 186 | 42 | 6 | 10 | (6 | 4) | 270 | 81 | 70 | 96 | 58 | 2 | 69 | 2 | 4 | **9** | 17 | 4 | .81 | 19 | .301 | .359 | .438 |
| 2013 | Ari | NL | 155 | 609 | 172 | 36 | 2 | 14 | (7 | 7) | 254 | 70 | 82 | 72 | 47 | 2 | 53 | 2 | 0 | 6 | 3 | 5 | .38 | 29 | .282 | .333 | .417 |
| Postseason | | | 1 | 5 | 1 | 0 | 0 | 0 | (0 | 0) | 1 | 0 | 0 | 0 | 0 | 0 | 1 | 0 | 0 | 0 | 0 | 0 | - | 0 | .200 | .200 | .200 |
| 8 ML YEARS | | | 838 | 3155 | 924 | 204 | 18 | 66 | (32 | 34) | 1362 | 425 | 368 | 422 | 244 | 8 | 361 | 11 | 23 | 30 | 33 | 24 | .58 | 99 | .293 | .343 | .432 |

# Alex Presley

**Bats:** L **Throws:** L **Pos:** CF-28;LF-12;RF-12;PH-9;PR-4 **Ht:** 5'10" **Wt:** 190 **Born:** 7/25/1985 **Age:** 28

| | | | BATTING | | | | | | | | | | | | | | | | | | BASERUNNING | | | | AVERAGES | | |
|---|---|---|---|---|---|---|---|---|---|---|---|---|---|---|---|---|---|---|---|---|---|---|---|---|---|---|---|
| Year | Team | Lg | G | AB | H | 2B | 3B | HR | (Hm | Rd) | TB | R | RBI | RC | TBB | IBB | SO | HBP | SH | SF | SB | CS | SB% | GDP | Avg | OBP | Slg |
| 2013 | Indy* | AAA | 89 | 342 | 102 | 17 | 6 | 5 | (- | -) | 146 | 57 | 27 | 59 | 40 | 2 | 56 | 4 | 3 | 2 | 17 | 6 | .74 | 1 | .298 | .376 | .427 |
| 2010 | Pit | NL | 19 | 23 | 6 | 1 | 0 | 0 | (0 | 0) | 7 | 2 | 0 | 1 | 1 | 0 | 8 | 0 | 1 | 0 | 1 | 1 | .50 | 0 | .261 | .292 | .304 |
| 2011 | Pit | NL | 52 | 215 | 64 | 12 | 6 | 4 | (1 | 3) | 100 | 27 | 20 | 35 | 13 | 1 | 40 | 1 | 1 | 1 | 9 | 3 | .75 | 1 | .298 | .339 | .465 |
| 2012 | Pit | NL | 104 | 346 | 82 | 14 | 7 | 10 | (2 | 8) | 140 | 46 | 25 | 31 | 18 | 0 | 72 | 2 | 4 | 0 | 9 | 7 | .56 | 5 | .237 | .279 | .405 |
| 2013 | 2 Tms | | 57 | 185 | 51 | 5 | 2 | 3 | (2 | 1) | 69 | 17 | 15 | 17 | 9 | 0 | 39 | 1 | 0 | 0 | 1 | 4 | .20 | 3 | .276 | .313 | .373 |
| 13 | Pit | NL | 29 | 72 | 19 | 1 | 1 | 2 | (2 | 0) | 28 | 8 | 4 | 5 | 1 | 0 | 18 | 0 | 0 | 0 | 0 | 1 | .00 | 1 | .264 | .274 | .389 |
| 13 | Min | AL | 28 | 113 | 32 | 4 | 1 | 1 | (0 | 1) | 41 | 9 | 11 | 12 | 8 | 0 | 21 | 1 | 0 | 0 | 1 | 3 | .25 | 2 | .283 | .336 | .363 |
| 4 ML YEARS | | | 232 | 769 | 203 | 32 | 15 | 17 | (5 | 12) | 316 | 92 | 60 | 84 | 41 | 1 | 159 | 4 | 6 | 1 | 20 | 15 | .57 | 9 | .264 | .304 | .411 |

# Ryan Pressly

**Pitches:** R **Bats:** R **Pos:** RP-49 **Ht:** 6'3" **Wt:** 205 **Born:** 12/15/1988 **Age:** 25

| | | | HOW MUCH HE PITCHED | | | | | | WHAT HE GAVE UP | | | | | | | | | | | | THE RESULTS | | | | | | | |
|---|---|---|---|---|---|---|---|---|---|---|---|---|---|---|---|---|---|---|---|---|---|---|---|---|---|---|---|---|
| Year | Team | Lg | G | GS | CG | GF | IP | BFP | H | R | ER | HR | SH | SF | HB | TBB | IBB | SO | WP | Bk | W | L | Pct | Sh | Sv-Op | Hld | ERC | ERA |
| 2009 | Lowell | A- | 13 | 11 | 0 | 0 | 59.2 | 252 | 48 | 22 | 21 | 1 | 4 | 3 | 2 | 25 | 0 | 64 | 7 | 0 | 6 | 4 | .600 | 0 | 0- - | - | 2.64 | 3.17 |
| 2010 | Grnvlle | A | 26 | 24 | 0 | 2 | 113.2 | 481 | 110 | 55 | 47 | 9 | 3 | 1 | 5 | 43 | 0 | 96 | 5 | 0 | 5 | 7 | .417 | 0 | 0- - | - | 3.91 | 3.72 |
| 2011 | Salem | A+ | 26 | 26 | 0 | 0 | 130.0 | 573 | 125 | 84 | 65 | 9 | 3 | 5 | 13 | 53 | 0 | 72 | 11 | 0 | 6 | 11 | .353 | 0 | 0- - | - | 4.02 | 4.50 |
| 2012 | Salem | A+ | 20 | 12 | 0 | 4 | 76.0 | 334 | 86 | 58 | 53 | 9 | 3 | 1 | 4 | 26 | 0 | 61 | 10 | 0 | 5 | 3 | .625 | 0 | 0- - | - | 4.99 | 6.28 |
| 2012 | Portlnd | AA | 14 | 0 | 0 | 7 | 27.2 | 113 | 23 | 9 | 9 | 2 | 3 | 1 | 0 | 10 | 2 | 21 | 2 | 0 | 2 | 2 | .500 | 0 | 0- - | - | 2.77 | 2.93 |
| 2013 | Min | AL | 49 | 0 | 0 | 18 | 76.2 | 315 | 71 | 37 | 33 | 5 | 2 | 3 | 0 | 27 | 1 | 49 | 7 | 0 | 3 | 3 | .500 | 0 | 0-0 | 1 | 3.31 | 3.87 |

# David Price

**Pitches:** L **Bats:** L **Pos:** SP-27 **Ht:** 6'6" **Wt:** 220 **Born:** 8/26/1985 **Age:** 28

| | | | HOW MUCH HE PITCHED | | | | | | WHAT HE GAVE UP | | | | | | | | | | | | THE RESULTS | | | | | | | |
|---|---|---|---|---|---|---|---|---|---|---|---|---|---|---|---|---|---|---|---|---|---|---|---|---|---|---|---|---|
| Year | Team | Lg | G | GS | CG | GF | IP | BFP | H | R | ER | HR | SH | SF | HB | TBB | IBB | SO | WP | Bk | W | L | Pct | Sh | Sv-Op | Hld | ERC | ERA |
| 2013 | Charltt* | A+ | 2 | 2 | 0 | 0 | 7.1 | 30 | 4 | 2 | 1 | 0 | 0 | 0 | 0 | 3 | 0 | 12 | 1 | 0 | 1 | 0 | 1.000 | 0 | 0- - | - | 1.32 | 1.23 |
| 2008 | TB | AL | 5 | 1 | 0 | 0 | 14.0 | 57 | 9 | 4 | 3 | 1 | 0 | 1 | 1 | 4 | 0 | 12 | 0 | 0 | 0 | 0 | - | 0 | 0-0 | 1 | 1.86 | 1.93 |
| 2009 | TB | AL | 23 | 23 | 0 | 0 | 128.1 | 557 | 119 | 72 | 63 | 17 | 3 | 2 | 4 | 54 | 0 | 102 | 2 | 0 | 10 | 7 | .588 | 0 | 0-0 | 0 | 4.05 | 4.42 |
| 2010 | TB | AL | 32 | 31 | 2 | 0 | 208.2 | 861 | 170 | 71 | 63 | 15 | 4 | 3 | 5 | 79 | 1 | 188 | 5 | 3 | 19 | 6 | .760 | 1 | 0-0 | 0 | 2.91 | 2.72 |
| 2011 | TB | AL | 34 | **34** | 0 | 0 | 224.1 | 918 | 192 | 93 | 87 | 22 | 4 | 7 | 9 | 63 | 5 | 218 | 2 | 0 | 12 | 13 | .480 | 0 | 0-0 | 0 | 2.97 | 3.49 |
| 2012 | TB | AL | 31 | 31 | 2 | 0 | 211.0 | 836 | 173 | 63 | 60 | 16 | 2 | 3 | 5 | 59 | 2 | 205 | 8 | 1 | **20** | 5 | **.800** | 1 | 0-0 | 0 | 2.67 | **2.56** |
| 2013 | TB | AL | 27 | 27 | **4** | 0 | 186.2 | 740 | 178 | 78 | 69 | 16 | 1 | 2 | 3 | 27 | 0 | 151 | 6 | 0 | 10 | 8 | .556 | 0 | 0-0 | 0 | 2.89 | 3.33 |
| Postseason | | | 8 | 3 | 0 | 5 | 25.0 | 106 | 26 | 13 | 11 | 4 | 0 | 0 | 0 | 5 | 0 | 25 | 1 | 0 | 1 | 3 | .250 | 0 | 1-1 | 0 | 3.82 | 3.96 |
| 6 ML YEARS | | | 152 | 147 | 8 | 0 | 973.0 | 3969 | 841 | 381 | 345 | 87 | 14 | 18 | 27 | 286 | 8 | 876 | 23 | 4 | 71 | 39 | .645 | 2 | 0-0 | 1 | 3.00 | 3.19 |

# Jason Pridie

PRY-dee

**Bats:** L **Throws:** R **Pos:** LF-2;CF-2 **Ht:** 6'1" **Wt:** 205 **Born:** 10/9/1983 **Age:** 30

| | | | BATTING | | | | | | | | | | | | | | | | | | BASERUNNING | | | | AVERAGES | | |
|---|---|---|---|---|---|---|---|---|---|---|---|---|---|---|---|---|---|---|---|---|---|---|---|---|---|---|---|
| Year | Team | Lg | G | AB | H | 2B | 3B | HR | (Hm | Rd) | TB | R | RBI | RC | TBB | IBB | SO | HBP | SH | SF | SB | CS | SB% | GDP | Avg | OBP | Slg |
| 2013 | Norfolk* | AAA | 119 | 479 | 129 | 24 | 5 | 15 | (- | -) | 208 | 69 | 57 | 72 | 43 | 0 | 120 | 4 | 2 | 3 | 8 | 2 | .80 | 5 | .269 | .333 | .434 |
| 2008 | Min | AL | 10 | 4 | 0 | 0 | 0 | 0 | (0 | 0) | 0 | 3 | 0 | 0 | 1 | 0 | 1 | 0 | 1 | 0 | 0 | 0 | - | 0 | .000 | .200 | .000 |
| 2009 | Min | AL | 1 | 0 | 0 | 0 | 0 | 0 | (0 | 0) | 0 | 0 | 0 | 0 | 0 | 0 | 0 | 0 | 0 | 0 | 0 | 0 | - | 0 | - | - | - |

| | | | BATTING | | | | | | | | | | | | | | | | | | BASERUNNING | | | | AVERAGES | | |
|---|---|---|---|---|---|---|---|---|---|---|---|---|---|---|---|---|---|---|---|---|---|---|---|---|---|---|---|
| Year | Team | Lg | G | AB | H | 2B | 3B | HR | (Hm | Rd) | TB | R | RBI | RC | TBB | IBB | SO | HBP | SH | SF | SB | CS | SB% | GDP | Avg | OBP | Slg |
| 2011 | NYM | NL | 101 | 208 | 48 | 11 | 3 | 4 | (3 | 1) | 77 | 28 | 20 | 22 | 24 | 2 | 64 | 0 | 3 | 1 | 7 | 1 | .88 | 2 | .231 | .309 | .370 |
| 2012 | Phi | NL | 9 | 10 | 3 | 1 | 0 | 1 | (1 | 0) | 7 | 1 | 3 | 2 | 0 | 0 | 0 | 0 | 0 | 0 | 0 | 0 | - | 0 | .300 | .300 | .700 |
| 2013 | Bal | AL | 4 | 10 | 2 | 0 | 0 | 0 | (0 | 0) | 2 | 0 | 1 | 1 | 0 | 0 | 2 | 0 | 0 | 0 | 0 | 0 | - | 0 | .200 | .200 | .200 |
| 5 ML YEARS | | | 125 | 232 | 53 | 12 | 3 | 5 | (4 | 1) | 86 | 32 | 24 | 25 | 25 | 2 | 67 | 0 | 4 | 1 | 7 | 1 | .88 | 2 | .228 | .302 | .371 |

# Josh Prince

**Bats:** R **Throws:** R **Pos:** PR-4;LF-2;3B-1;RF-1;DH-1;PH-1 **Ht:** 6'0" **Wt:** 180 **Born:** 1/26/1988 **Age:** 26

| | | | BATTING | | | | | | | | | | | | | | | | | | BASERUNNING | | | | AVERAGES | | |
|---|---|---|---|---|---|---|---|---|---|---|---|---|---|---|---|---|---|---|---|---|---|---|---|---|---|---|---|
| Year | Team | Lg | G | AB | H | 2B | 3B | HR | (Hm | Rd) | TB | R | RBI | RC | TBB | IBB | SO | HBP | SH | SF | SB | CS | SB% | GDP | Avg | OBP | Slg |
| 2009 | Helena | R+ | 36 | 141 | 42 | 5 | 1 | 0 | (- | -) | 49 | 32 | 8 | 27 | 33 | 0 | 25 | 0 | 0 | 2 | 26 | 7 | .79 | 1 | .298 | .426 | .348 |
| 2009 | Wisc | A | 31 | 122 | 27 | 5 | 0 | 1 | (- | -) | 35 | 18 | 10 | 12 | 15 | 0 | 21 | 1 | 0 | 2 | 12 | 5 | .71 | 0 | .221 | .307 | .287 |
| 2010 | BrvdCt | A+ | 106 | 408 | 95 | 13 | 2 | 1 | (- | -) | 115 | 62 | 19 | 38 | 32 | 0 | 80 | 0 | 7 | 2 | 44 | 11 | .80 | 5 | .233 | .287 | .282 |
| 2011 | BrvdCt | A+ | 75 | 249 | 70 | 11 | 0 | 5 | (- | -) | 96 | 41 | 24 | 35 | 17 | 0 | 37 | 3 | 7 | 2 | 24 | 8 | .75 | 4 | .281 | .332 | .386 |
| 2012 | Hntsvl | AA | 137 | 505 | 127 | 28 | 3 | 7 | (- | -) | 182 | 74 | 55 | 71 | 74 | 0 | 107 | 3 | 6 | 8 | 41 | 18 | .69 | 9 | .251 | .346 | .360 |
| 2013 | Nashv | AAA | 115 | 418 | 99 | 18 | 2 | 11 | (- | -) | 154 | 68 | 53 | 59 | 60 | 0 | 105 | 5 | 5 | 2 | 25 | 8 | .76 | 4 | .237 | .338 | .368 |
| 2013 | Mil | NL | 8 | 8 | 1 | 1 | 0 | 0 | (0 | 0) | 2 | 3 | 0 | 0 | 1 | 0 | 1 | 0 | 0 | 0 | 0 | 0 | - | 1 | .125 | .222 | .250 |

# Jurickson Profar

JURR-ick-sun PRO-farr

**Bats:** B **Throws:** R **Pos:** 2B-32;DH-19;SS-18;3B-10;PH-9;LF-4 **Ht:** 6'0" **Wt:** 165 **Born:** 2/20/1993 **Age:** 21

| | | | BATTING | | | | | | | | | | | | | | | | | | BASERUNNING | | | | AVERAGES | | |
|---|---|---|---|---|---|---|---|---|---|---|---|---|---|---|---|---|---|---|---|---|---|---|---|---|---|---|---|
| Year | Team | Lg | G | AB | H | 2B | 3B | HR | (Hm | Rd) | TB | R | RBI | RC | TBB | IBB | SO | HBP | SH | SF | SB | CS | SB% | GDP | Avg | OBP | Slg |
| 2010 | Spkane | A- | 63 | 252 | 63 | 19 | 0 | 4 | (- | -) | 94 | 42 | 23 | 33 | 28 | 0 | 46 | 0 | 6 | 2 | 8 | 3 | .73 | 8 | .250 | .323 | .373 |
| 2011 | Hkry | A | 115 | 430 | 123 | 37 | 8 | 12 | (- | -) | 212 | 86 | 65 | 88 | 65 | 2 | 63 | 11 | 6 | 4 | 23 | 9 | .72 | 7 | .286 | .390 | .493 |
| 2012 | Frisco | AA | 126 | 480 | 135 | 26 | 7 | 14 | (- | -) | 217 | 76 | 62 | 86 | 66 | 5 | 79 | 5 | 2 | 9 | 16 | 4 | .80 | 11 | .281 | .368 | .452 |
| 2013 | RdRck | AAA | 37 | 144 | 40 | 7 | 2 | 4 | (- | -) | 63 | 27 | 19 | 25 | 21 | 0 | 24 | 0 | 1 | 0 | 6 | 1 | .86 | 3 | .278 | .370 | .438 |
| 2012 | Tex | AL | 9 | 17 | 3 | 2 | 0 | 1 | (0 | 1) | 8 | 2 | 2 | 1 | 0 | 0 | 4 | 0 | 0 | 0 | 0 | 0 | - | 1 | .176 | .176 | .471 |
| 2013 | Tex | AL | 85 | 286 | 67 | 11 | 0 | 6 | (3 | 3) | 96 | 30 | 26 | 30 | 26 | 0 | 63 | 5 | 6 | 1 | 2 | 4 | .33 | 1 | .234 | .308 | .336 |
| Postseason | | | 1 | 1 | 1 | 0 | 0 | 0 | (0 | 0) | 1 | 0 | 0 | 0 | 0 | 0 | 0 | 0 | 0 | 0 | 0 | 0 | - | 0 | 1.000 | 1.000 | 1.000 |
| 2 ML YEARS | | | 94 | 303 | 70 | 13 | 0 | 7 | (3 | 4) | 104 | 32 | 28 | 31 | 26 | 0 | 67 | 5 | 6 | 1 | 2 | 4 | .33 | 2 | .231 | .301 | .343 |

# Stephen Pryor

**Pitches:** R **Bats:** R **Pos:** RP-7 **Ht:** 6'4" **Wt:** 250 **Born:** 7/23/1989 **Age:** 24

| | | | HOW MUCH HE PITCHED | | | | | | WHAT HE GAVE UP | | | | | | | | | | | | THE RESULTS | | | | | | | |
|---|---|---|---|---|---|---|---|---|---|---|---|---|---|---|---|---|---|---|---|---|---|---|---|---|---|---|---|---|
| Year | Team | Lg | G | GS | CG | GF | IP | BFP | H | R | ER | HR | SH | SF | HB | TBB | IBB | SO | WP | Bk | W | L | Pct | Sh | Sv-Op | Hld | ERC | ERA |
| 2010 | Everett | A- | 11 | 0 | 0 | 7 | 18.1 | 68 | 7 | 1 | 1 | 0 | 2 | 0 | 0 | 7 | 0 | 26 | 1 | 0 | 0 | 0 | - | 0 | 4-- | - | 0.89 | 0.49 |
| 2010 | Clinton | A | 12 | 0 | 0 | 4 | 17.0 | 76 | 17 | 12 | 7 | 0 | 1 | 0 | 1 | 6 | 0 | 29 | 3 | 1 | 0 | 2 | .000 | 0 | 1-- | - | 3.27 | 3.71 |
| 2011 | Hi Dsrt | A+ | 22 | 0 | 0 | 9 | 27.0 | 134 | 28 | 24 | 23 | 2 | 0 | 0 | 2 | 26 | 0 | 34 | 5 | 0 | 1 | 0 | 1.000 | 0 | 4-- | - | 6.66 | 7.67 |
| 2011 | Jacksn | AA | 17 | 0 | 0 | 13 | 22.2 | 84 | 9 | 4 | 3 | 0 | 1 | 2 | 1 | 7 | 0 | 27 | 1 | 0 | 2 | 1 | .667 | 0 | 6-- | - | 0.88 | 1.19 |
| 2012 | Jacksn | AA | 11 | 0 | 0 | 10 | 16.0 | 61 | 7 | 3 | 2 | 0 | 0 | 0 | 0 | 5 | 0 | 24 | 0 | 0 | 1 | 0 | 1.000 | 0 | 7-- | - | 0.88 | 1.13 |
| 2012 | Tacom | AAA | 16 | 0 | 0 | 12 | 20.0 | 80 | 11 | 0 | 0 | 0 | 0 | 0 | 0 | 11 | 0 | 20 | 1 | 0 | 0 | 0 | - | 0 | 3-- | - | 1.72 | 0.00 |
| 2012 | Hi Dsrt | A+ | 2 | 1 | 0 | 0 | 2.2 | 10 | 0 | 2 | 2 | 0 | 0 | 0 | 0 | 3 | 0 | 3 | 0 | 0 | 0 | 0 | - | 0 | 0-- | - | 1.28 | 6.75 |
| 2013 | Everett | A- | 1 | 1 | 0 | 0 | 0.2 | 5 | 3 | 3 | 2 | 1 | 0 | 0 | 0 | 0 | 0 | 1 | 0 | 1 | 0 | 0 | - | 0 | 0-- | - | 46.37 | 27.00 |
| 2013 | Tacom | AAA | 4 | 0 | 0 | 1 | 3.0 | 17 | 5 | 5 | 5 | 0 | 0 | 0 | 0 | 2 | 0 | 1 | 1 | 0 | 0 | 0 | - | 0 | 0-- | - | 7.72 | 15.00 |
| 2012 | Sea | AL | 26 | 0 | 0 | 8 | 23.0 | 104 | 22 | 13 | 10 | 5 | 2 | 2 | 0 | 13 | 2 | 27 | 3 | 0 | 3 | 1 | .750 | 0 | 0-0 | 5 | 5.10 | 3.91 |
| 2013 | Sea | AL | 7 | 0 | 0 | 2 | 7.1 | 26 | 3 | 0 | 0 | 0 | 0 | 0 | 0 | 1 | 0 | 7 | 0 | 0 | 0 | 0 | - | 0 | 0-1 | 3 | 0.55 | 0.00 |
| 2 ML YEARS | | | 33 | 0 | 0 | 10 | 30.1 | 130 | 25 | 13 | 10 | 5 | 2 | 2 | 0 | 14 | 2 | 34 | 3 | 0 | 3 | 1 | .750 | 0 | 0-1 | 8 | 3.61 | 2.97 |

# Yasiel Puig

**Bats:** R **Throws:** R **Pos:** RF-93;CF-10;PH-5;LF-2 yah-SEE-el PWEEG **Ht:** 6'3" **Wt:** 245 **Born:** 12/7/1990 **Age:** 23

| | | | BATTING | | | | | | | | | | | | | | | | | | BASERUNNING | | | | AVERAGES | | |
|---|---|---|---|---|---|---|---|---|---|---|---|---|---|---|---|---|---|---|---|---|---|---|---|---|---|---|---|
| Year | Team | Lg | G | AB | H | 2B | 3B | HR | (Hm | Rd) | TB | R | RBI | RC | TBB | IBB | SO | HBP | SH | SF | SB | CS | SB% | GDP | Avg | OBP | Slg |
| 2012 | Ddgrs | R | 9 | 30 | 12 | 0 | 3 | 4 | (- | -) | 30 | 10 | 11 | 12 | 6 | 1 | 7 | 0 | 0 | 0 | 1 | 1 | .50 | 0 | .400 | .500 | 1.000 |
| 2012 | RCuca | A+ | 14 | 52 | 17 | 2 | 0 | 1 | (- | -) | 22 | 10 | 4 | 9 | 6 | 0 | 8 | 1 | 0 | 0 | 7 | 4 | .64 | 0 | .327 | .407 | .423 |
| 2013 | Chatt | AA | 40 | 147 | 46 | 12 | 3 | 8 | (- | -) | 88 | 26 | 37 | 33 | 15 | 3 | 29 | 3 | 0 | 2 | 13 | 5 | .72 | 0 | .313 | .383 | .599 |
| 2013 | LAD | NL | 104 | 382 | 122 | 21 | 2 | 19 | (9 | 10) | 204 | 66 | 42 | 62 | 36 | 6 | 97 | 11 | 0 | 3 | 11 | 8 | .58 | 6 | .319 | .391 | .534 |

# Albert Pujols

**Bats:** R **Throws:** R **Pos:** DH-65;1B-34 POO-holes **Ht:** 6'3" **Wt:** 230 **Born:** 1/16/1980 **Age:** 34

| | | | BATTING | | | | | | | | | | | | | | | | | | BASERUNNING | | | | AVERAGES | | |
|---|---|---|---|---|---|---|---|---|---|---|---|---|---|---|---|---|---|---|---|---|---|---|---|---|---|---|---|
| Year | Team | Lg | G | AB | H | 2B | 3B | HR | (Hm | Rd) | TB | R | RBI | RC | TBB | IBB | SO | HBP | SH | SF | SB | CS | SB% | GDP | Avg | OBP | Slg |
| 2001 | StL | NL | 161 | 590 | 194 | 47 | 4 | 37 | (18 | 19) | 360 | 112 | 130 | 132 | 69 | 6 | 93 | 9 | 1 | 7 | 1 | 3 | .25 | 21 | .329 | .403 | .610 |
| 2002 | StL | NL | 157 | 590 | 185 | 40 | 2 | 34 | (14 | 20) | 331 | 118 | 127 | 121 | 72 | 13 | 69 | 9 | 0 | 4 | 2 | 4 | .33 | 20 | .314 | .394 | .561 |
| 2003 | StL | NL | 157 | 591 | **212** | **51** | 1 | 43 | (21 | **22)** | **394** | **137** | 124 | **160** | 79 | 12 | 65 | 10 | 0 | 5 | 5 | 1 | .83 | 13 | **.359** | .439 | .667 |
| 2004 | StL | NL | 154 | 592 | 196 | 51 | 2 | 46 | (18 | **28)** | **389** | **133** | 123 | 143 | 84 | 12 | 52 | 7 | 0 | 9 | 5 | 5 | .50 | 21 | .331 | .415 | .657 |
| 2005 | StL | NL | 161 | 591 | 195 | 38 | 2 | 41 | (23 | 18) | 360 | **129** | 117 | **139** | 97 | **27** | 65 | 9 | 0 | 3 | 16 | 2 | .89 | 19 | .330 | .430 | .609 |
| 2006 | StL | NL | 143 | 535 | 177 | 33 | 1 | 49 | (24 | 25) | 359 | 119 | 137 | **146** | 92 | 28 | 50 | 4 | 0 | 3 | 7 | 2 | .78 | 20 | .331 | **.431** | **.671** |
| 2007 | StL | NL | 158 | 565 | 185 | 38 | 1 | 32 | (12 | 20) | 321 | 99 | 103 | 118 | 99 | 22 | 58 | 7 | 0 | 8 | 2 | 6 | .25 | **27** | .327 | .429 | .568 |
| 2008 | StL | NL | 148 | 524 | 187 | 44 | 0 | 37 | (19 | 18) | **342** | 100 | 116 | **130** | 104 | **34** | 54 | 5 | 0 | 8 | 7 | 3 | .70 | 16 | .357 | .462 | **.653** |
| 2009 | StL | NL | 160 | 568 | 186 | 45 | 1 | **47** | (22 | 25) | **374** | **124** | 135 | **145** | 115 | **44** | 64 | 9 | 0 | 8 | 16 | 4 | .80 | 23 | .327 | **.443** | **.658** |
| 2010 | StL | NL | 159 | 587 | 183 | 39 | 1 | **42** | (17 | **25)** | 350 | **115** | **118** | 131 | 103 | **38** | 76 | 4 | 0 | 6 | 14 | 4 | .78 | 23 | .312 | .414 | .596 |
| 2011 | StL | NL | 147 | 579 | 173 | 29 | 0 | 37 | (16 | 21) | 313 | 105 | 99 | 100 | 61 | 15 | 58 | 4 | 0 | 7 | 9 | 1 | .90 | **29** | .299 | .366 | .541 |

| Year | Team | Lg | G | AB | H | 2B | 3B | HR | (Hm | Rd) | TB | R | RBI | RC | TBB | IBB | SO | HBP | SH | SF | SB | CS | SB% | GDP | Avg | OBP | Slg |
|---|---|---|---|---|---|---|---|---|---|---|---|---|---|---|---|---|---|---|---|---|---|---|---|---|---|---|---|
| | | | BATTING | | | | | | | | | | | | | | | | | | BASERUNNING | | | | AVERAGES | | |
| 2012 | LAA | AL | 154 | 607 | 173 | 50 | 0 | 30 | (14 | 16) | 313 | 85 | 105 | 100 | 52 | 16 | 76 | 5 | 0 | 6 | 8 | 1 | .89 | 19 | .285 | .343 | .516 |
| 2013 | LAA | AL | 99 | 391 | 101 | 19 | 0 | 17 | (8 | 9) | 171 | 49 | 64 | 54 | 40 | 8 | 55 | 5 | 0 | 7 | 1 | 1 | .50 | 18 | .258 | .330 | .437 |
| Postseason | | | 74 | 267 | 88 | 18 | 1 | 18 | (7 | 11) | 162 | 54 | 52 | 67 | 48 | 20 | 39 | 5 | 0 | 1 | 1 | 2 | .33 | 6 | .330 | .439 | .607 |
| 13 ML YEARS | | | 1958 | 7310 | 2347 | 524 | 15 | 492 | (226 | 266) | 4377 | 1425 | 1498 | 1619 | 1067 | 275 | 835 | 87 | 1 | 81 | 93 | 37 | .72 | 269 | .321 | .410 | .599 |

## Nick Punto

**Bats:** B **Throws:** R **Pos:** SS-49;3B-35;2B-33;PH-20;PR-3 POON-toh **Ht:** 5'9" **Wt:** 195 **Born:** 11/8/1977 **Age:** 36

| Year | Team | Lg | G | AB | H | 2B | 3B | HR | (Hm | Rd) | TB | R | RBI | RC | TBB | IBB | SO | HBP | SH | SF | SB | CS | SB% | GDP | Avg | OBP | Slg |
|---|---|---|---|---|---|---|---|---|---|---|---|---|---|---|---|---|---|---|---|---|---|---|---|---|---|---|---|
| | | | BATTING | | | | | | | | | | | | | | | | | | BASERUNNING | | | | AVERAGES | | |
| 2001 | Phi | NL | 4 | 5 | 2 | 0 | 0 | 0 | (0 | 0) | 2 | 0 | 0 | 1 | 0 | 0 | 0 | 0 | 0 | 0 | 0 | 0 | - | 0 | .400 | .400 | .400 |
| 2002 | Phi | NL | 9 | 6 | 1 | 0 | 0 | 0 | (0 | 0) | 1 | 0 | 0 | 0 | 0 | 0 | 3 | 0 | 1 | 0 | 0 | 0 | - | 0 | .167 | .167 | .167 |
| 2003 | Phi | NL | 64 | 92 | 20 | 2 | 0 | 1 | (0 | 1) | 25 | 14 | 4 | 7 | 7 | 1 | 22 | 0 | 0 | 0 | 2 | 1 | .67 | 0 | .217 | .273 | .272 |
| 2004 | Min | AL | 38 | 91 | 23 | 0 | 0 | 2 | (2 | 0) | 29 | 17 | 12 | 15 | 12 | 0 | 19 | 0 | 0 | 0 | 6 | 0 | 1.00 | 2 | .253 | .340 | .319 |
| 2005 | Min | AL | 112 | 394 | 94 | 18 | 4 | 4 | (3 | 1) | 132 | 45 | 26 | 35 | 36 | 0 | 86 | 0 | 7 | 2 | 13 | 8 | .62 | 9 | .239 | .301 | .335 |
| 2006 | Min | AL | 135 | 459 | 133 | 21 | 7 | 1 | (0 | 1) | 171 | 73 | 45 | 59 | 47 | 0 | 68 | 1 | 10 | 7 | 17 | 5 | .77 | 8 | .290 | .352 | .373 |
| 2007 | Min | AL | 150 | 472 | 99 | 18 | 4 | 1 | (0 | 1) | 128 | 53 | 25 | 37 | 55 | 1 | 90 | 0 | 6 | 3 | 16 | 6 | .73 | 7 | .210 | .291 | .271 |
| 2008 | Min | AL | 99 | 338 | 96 | 19 | 4 | 2 | (1 | 1) | 129 | 43 | 28 | 42 | 32 | 1 | 57 | 0 | 5 | 2 | 15 | 6 | .71 | 10 | .284 | .344 | .382 |
| 2009 | Min | AL | 125 | 359 | 82 | 15 | 1 | 1 | (0 | 1) | 102 | 56 | 38 | 46 | 61 | 1 | 70 | 1 | 13 | 6 | 16 | 3 | .84 | 7 | .228 | .337 | .284 |
| 2010 | Min | AL | 88 | 252 | 60 | 11 | 1 | 1 | (0 | 1) | 76 | 24 | 20 | 25 | 28 | 2 | 50 | 1 | 4 | 3 | 6 | 2 | .75 | 3 | .238 | .313 | .302 |
| 2011 | StL | NL | 63 | 133 | 37 | 8 | 4 | 1 | (0 | 1) | 56 | 21 | 20 | 25 | 25 | 3 | 21 | 0 | 6 | 2 | 1 | 1 | .50 | 3 | .278 | .388 | .421 |
| 2012 | 2 Tms | | 87 | 160 | 35 | 7 | 0 | 1 | (0 | 1) | 45 | 20 | 10 | 15 | 25 | 0 | 42 | 0 | 4 | 2 | 6 | 0 | 1.00 | 5 | .219 | .321 | .281 |
| 2013 | LAD | NL | 116 | 294 | 75 | 15 | 0 | 2 | (2 | 0) | 96 | 34 | 21 | 30 | 33 | 0 | 67 | 0 | 6 | 2 | 3 | 3 | .50 | 4 | .255 | .328 | .327 |
| 12 | Bos | AL | 65 | 125 | 25 | 6 | 0 | 1 | (0 | 1) | 34 | 14 | 10 | 10 | 19 | 0 | 33 | 0 | 2 | 2 | 5 | 0 | 1.00 | 5 | .200 | .301 | .272 |
| 12 | LAD | NL | 22 | 35 | 10 | 1 | 0 | 0 | (0 | 0) | 11 | 6 | 0 | 5 | 6 | 0 | 9 | 0 | 2 | 0 | 1 | 0 | 1.00 | 0 | .286 | .390 | .314 |
| Postseason | | | 21 | 56 | 12 | 1 | 0 | 0 | (0 | 0) | 13 | 0 | 4 | 4 | 10 | 2 | 19 | 0 | 2 | 1 | 0 | 0 | - | 0 | .214 | .328 | .232 |
| 13 ML YEARS | | | 1090 | 3055 | 757 | 134 | 25 | 17 | (8 | 9) | 992 | 400 | 249 | 337 | 361 | 9 | 595 | 3 | 62 | 29 | 101 | 35 | .74 | 58 | .248 | .325 | .325 |

## David Purcey

**Pitches:** L **Bats:** L **Pos:** RP-24 **Ht:** 6'5" **Wt:** 235 **Born:** 4/22/1982 **Age:** 32

| Year | Team | Lg | G | GS | CG | GF | IP | BFP | H | R | ER | HR | SH | SF | HB | TBB | IBB | SO | WP | Bk | W | L | Pct | Sh | Sv-Op | Hld | ERC | ERA |
|---|---|---|---|---|---|---|---|---|---|---|---|---|---|---|---|---|---|---|---|---|---|---|---|---|---|---|---|---|
| | | | HOW MUCH HE PITCHED | | | | | | WHAT HE GAVE UP | | | | | | | | | | | | THE RESULTS | | | | | | | |
| 2013 | Charltt* | AAA | 26 | 0 | 0 | 12 | 38.2 | 156 | 30 | 14 | 13 | 2 | 2 | 2 | 2 | 12 | 0 | 43 | 5 | 0 | 0 | 2 | .000 | 0 | 3-- | - | 2.48 | 3.03 |
| 2008 | Tor | AL | 12 | 12 | 1 | 0 | 65.0 | 289 | 67 | 41 | 40 | 9 | 2 | 3 | 4 | 29 | 0 | 58 | 3 | 0 | 3 | 6 | .333 | 0 | 0-0 | 0 | 4.96 | 5.54 |
| 2009 | Tor | AL | 9 | 9 | 0 | 0 | 48.0 | 223 | 54 | 35 | 33 | 6 | 3 | 1 | 1 | 30 | 1 | 39 | 3 | 0 | 1 | 3 | .250 | 0 | 0-0 | 0 | 6.00 | 6.19 |
| 2010 | Tor | AL | 33 | 0 | 0 | 18 | 34.0 | 143 | 26 | 16 | 14 | 3 | 2 | 2 | 0 | 15 | 1 | 32 | 3 | 0 | 1 | 1 | .500 | 0 | 1-1 | 3 | 2.80 | 3.71 |
| 2011 | 3 Tms | AL | 33 | 0 | 0 | 9 | 33.2 | 157 | 33 | 21 | 21 | 2 | 2 | 0 | 0 | 27 | 2 | 22 | 0 | 0 | 1 | 2 | .333 | 0 | 0-0 | 3 | 5.14 | 5.61 |
| 2013 | CWS | AL | 24 | 0 | 0 | 7 | 25.1 | 113 | 19 | 7 | 6 | 2 | 1 | 2 | 2 | 17 | 4 | 23 | 5 | 0 | 1 | 1 | .500 | 0 | 0-0 | 0 | 3.56 | 2.13 |
| 11 | Tor | AL | 5 | 0 | 0 | 0 | 2.1 | 14 | 3 | 3 | 3 | 0 | 0 | 0 | 0 | 4 | 0 | 3 | 0 | 0 | 0 | 0 | - | 0 | 0-0 | 0 | 10.22 | 11.57 |
| 11 | Oak | AL | 9 | 0 | 0 | 3 | 12.2 | 50 | 9 | 3 | 3 | 1 | 0 | 0 | 0 | 3 | 0 | 7 | 0 | 0 | 0 | 0 | - | 0 | 0-0 | 1 | 1.86 | 2.13 |
| 11 | Det | AL | 19 | 0 | 0 | 6 | 18.2 | 93 | 21 | 15 | 15 | 1 | 2 | 0 | 0 | 20 | 2 | 12 | 0 | 0 | 1 | 2 | .333 | 0 | 0-0 | 2 | 7.09 | 7.23 |
| 5 ML YEARS | | | 111 | 21 | 1 | 34 | 206.0 | 925 | 199 | 120 | 114 | 22 | 10 | 8 | 7 | 118 | 8 | 174 | 14 | 0 | 7 | 13 | .350 | 0 | 1-1 | 6 | 4.67 | 4.98 |

## Luke Putkonen

**Pitches:** R **Bats:** R **Pos:** RP-30 putt-COE-nen **Ht:** 6'6" **Wt:** 215 **Born:** 5/10/1986 **Age:** 28

| Year | Team | Lg | G | GS | CG | GF | IP | BFP | H | R | ER | HR | SH | SF | HB | TBB | IBB | SO | WP | Bk | W | L | Pct | Sh | Sv-Op | Hld | ERC | ERA |
|---|---|---|---|---|---|---|---|---|---|---|---|---|---|---|---|---|---|---|---|---|---|---|---|---|---|---|---|---|
| | | | HOW MUCH HE PITCHED | | | | | | WHAT HE GAVE UP | | | | | | | | | | | | THE RESULTS | | | | | | | |
| 2009 | WMich | A | 28 | 28 | 1 | 0 | 149.1 | 631 | 148 | 63 | 52 | 3 | 1 | 2 | 9 | 47 | 0 | 115 | 9 | 0 | 7 | 8 | .467 | 1 | 0-- | - | 3.41 | 3.13 |
| 2010 | Lkland | A+ | 27 | 26 | 1 | 0 | 152.2 | 617 | 144 | 55 | 54 | 8 | 3 | 3 | 6 | 44 | 1 | 87 | 6 | 1 | 9 | 7 | .563 | 0 | 0-- | - | 3.29 | 3.18 |
| 2011 | Erie | AA | 11 | 11 | 0 | 0 | 52.1 | 247 | 68 | 50 | 44 | 8 | 4 | 2 | 2 | 22 | 0 | 23 | 2 | 0 | 1 | 7 | .125 | 0 | 0-- | - | 6.42 | 7.57 |
| 2011 | Lkland | A+ | 18 | 8 | 1 | 6 | 65.0 | 285 | 77 | 46 | 40 | 10 | 3 | 2 | 3 | 18 | 1 | 52 | 2 | 1 | 2 | 6 | .250 | 0 | 0-- | - | 5.23 | 5.54 |
| 2012 | Toledo | AAA | 24 | 2 | 0 | 6 | 56.2 | 249 | 68 | 37 | 31 | 3 | 0 | 3 | 2 | 19 | 0 | 46 | 2 | 0 | 3 | 3 | .500 | 0 | 0-- | - | 4.84 | 4.92 |
| 2013 | Toledo | AAA | 20 | 1 | 0 | 5 | 37.2 | 148 | 25 | 10 | 8 | 0 | 0 | 0 | 0 | 13 | 0 | 38 | 2 | 0 | 2 | 0 | 1.000 | 0 | 1-- | - | 1.62 | 1.91 |
| 2012 | Det | AL | 12 | 0 | 0 | 6 | 16.0 | 72 | 19 | 7 | 7 | 0 | 1 | 0 | 0 | 8 | 1 | 10 | 2 | 0 | 0 | 2 | .000 | 0 | 1-2 | 0 | 4.74 | 3.94 |
| 2013 | Det | AL | 30 | 0 | 0 | 12 | 29.2 | 127 | 30 | 11 | 10 | 4 | 2 | 1 | 0 | 9 | 0 | 28 | 5 | 0 | 1 | 3 | .250 | 0 | 0-0 | 1 | 3.94 | 3.03 |
| 2 ML YEARS | | | 42 | 0 | 0 | 18 | 45.2 | 199 | 49 | 18 | 17 | 4 | 3 | 1 | 0 | 17 | 1 | 38 | 7 | 0 | 1 | 5 | .167 | 0 | 1-2 | 1 | 4.24 | 3.35 |

## Zach Putnam

**Pitches:** R **Bats:** R **Pos:** RP-5 **Ht:** 6'2" **Wt:** 225 **Born:** 7/3/1987 **Age:** 26

| Year | Team | Lg | G | GS | CG | GF | IP | BFP | H | R | ER | HR | SH | SF | HB | TBB | IBB | SO | WP | Bk | W | L | Pct | Sh | Sv-Op | Hld | ERC | ERA |
|---|---|---|---|---|---|---|---|---|---|---|---|---|---|---|---|---|---|---|---|---|---|---|---|---|---|---|---|---|
| | | | HOW MUCH HE PITCHED | | | | | | WHAT HE GAVE UP | | | | | | | | | | | | THE RESULTS | | | | | | | |
| 2013 | Iowa* | AAA | 17 | 0 | 0 | 8 | 19.1 | 83 | 20 | 7 | 7 | 0 | 1 | 0 | 0 | 6 | 0 | 22 | 0 | 0 | 1 | 1 | .500 | 0 | 4-- | - | 3.19 | 3.26 |
| 2011 | Cle | AL | 8 | 0 | 0 | 3 | 7.1 | 34 | 10 | 5 | 5 | 1 | 0 | 0 | 2 | 0 | 0 | 9 | 1 | 0 | 1 | 1 | .500 | 0 | 0-1 | 0 | 5.82 | 6.14 |
| 2012 | Col | NL | 2 | 0 | 0 | 0 | 2.0 | 9 | 3 | 0 | 0 | 0 | 1 | 0 | 0 | 1 | 0 | 0 | 0 | 0 | 0 | 0 | - | 0 | 0-0 | 0 | 7.26 | 0.00 |
| 2013 | ChC | NL | 5 | 0 | 0 | 1 | 3.1 | 19 | 9 | 7 | 7 | 1 | 0 | 1 | 0 | 0 | 0 | 4 | 0 | 0 | 0 | 0 | - | 0 | 0-0 | 0 | 15.42 | 18.90 |
| 3 ML YEARS | | | 15 | 0 | 0 | 4 | 12.2 | 62 | 22 | 12 | 12 | 2 | 1 | 1 | 2 | 1 | 0 | 13 | 1 | 0 | 1 | 1 | .500 | 0 | 0-1 | 0 | 8.36 | 8.53 |

## J.J. Putz

**Pitches:** R **Bats:** R **Pos:** RP-40 PUTS **Ht:** 6'5" **Wt:** 250 **Born:** 2/22/1977 **Age:** 37

| Year | Team | Lg | G | GS | CG | GF | IP | BFP | H | R | ER | HR | SH | SF | HB | TBB | IBB | SO | WP | Bk | W | L | Pct | Sh | Sv-Op | Hld | ERC | ERA |
|---|---|---|---|---|---|---|---|---|---|---|---|---|---|---|---|---|---|---|---|---|---|---|---|---|---|---|---|---|
| | | | HOW MUCH HE PITCHED | | | | | | WHAT HE GAVE UP | | | | | | | | | | | | THE RESULTS | | | | | | | |
| 2013 | Reno* | AAA | 4 | 4 | 0 | 0 | 4.0 | 16 | 2 | 1 | 1 | 0 | 0 | 0 | 0 | 3 | 0 | 4 | 0 | 0 | 0 | 0 | - | 0 | 0-- | - | 2.19 | 2.25 |
| 2003 | Sea | AL | 3 | 0 | 0 | 0 | 3.2 | 18 | 4 | 2 | 2 | 0 | 0 | 0 | 0 | 3 | 0 | 3 | 0 | 0 | 0 | 0 | - | 0 | 0-0 | 0 | 5.31 | 4.91 |
| 2004 | Sea | AL | 54 | 0 | 0 | 30 | 63.0 | 275 | 66 | 35 | 33 | 10 | 3 | 2 | 5 | 24 | 4 | 47 | 1 | 0 | 0 | 3 | .000 | 0 | 9-13 | 3 | 4.97 | 4.71 |
| 2005 | Sea | AL | 64 | 0 | 0 | 20 | 60.0 | 259 | 58 | 27 | 24 | 8 | 3 | 3 | 2 | 23 | 2 | 45 | 2 | 0 | 6 | 5 | .545 | 0 | 1-4 | 21 | 4.11 | 3.60 |
| 2006 | Sea | AL | 72 | 0 | 0 | 57 | 78.1 | 303 | 59 | 20 | 20 | 4 | 1 | 2 | 2 | 13 | 1 | 104 | 1 | 0 | 4 | 1 | .800 | 0 | 36-43 | 5 | 1.78 | 2.30 |

| | | | HOW MUCH HE PITCHED | | | | | | WHAT HE GAVE UP | | | | | | | | | | | | THE RESULTS | | | | | | | |
|---|---|---|---|---|---|---|---|---|---|---|---|---|---|---|---|---|---|---|---|---|---|---|---|---|---|---|---|
| Year | Team | Lg | G | GS | CG | GF | IP | BFP | H | R | ER | HR | SH | SF | HB | TBB | IBB | SO | WP | Bk | W | L | Pct | Sh | Sv-Op | Hld | ERC | ERA |
| 2007 | Sea | AL | 68 | 0 | 0 | 65 | 71.2 | 260 | 37 | 11 | 11 | 6 | 2 | 1 | 2 | 13 | 0 | 82 | 3 | 0 | 6 | 1 | .857 | 0 | 40-42 | 0 | 1.21 | 1.38 |
| 2008 | Sea | AL | 47 | 0 | 0 | 35 | 46.1 | 211 | 46 | 20 | 20 | 4 | 0 | 1 | 2 | 28 | 2 | 56 | 2 | 0 | 6 | 5 | .545 | 0 | 15-23 | 0 | 4.82 | 3.88 |
| 2009 | NYM | NL | 29 | 0 | 0 | 6 | 29.1 | 135 | 29 | 18 | 17 | 1 | 1 | 2 | 0 | 19 | 4 | 19 | 1 | 0 | 1 | 4 | .200 | 0 | 2-4 | 10 | 4.16 | 5.22 |
| 2010 | CWS | AL | 60 | 0 | 0 | 16 | 54.0 | 219 | 41 | 18 | 17 | 4 | 1 | 1 | 1 | 15 | 2 | 65 | 4 | 0 | 7 | 5 | .583 | 0 | 3-7 | 14 | 2.19 | 2.83 |
| 2011 | Ari | NL | 60 | 0 | 0 | 52 | 58.0 | 229 | 41 | 15 | 14 | 4 | 2 | 3 | 2 | 12 | 0 | 61 | 2 | 0 | 2 | 2 | .500 | 0 | 45-49 | 0 | 1.80 | 2.17 |
| 2012 | Ari | NL | 57 | 0 | 0 | 52 | 54.1 | 218 | 45 | 18 | 17 | 4 | 2 | 1 | 2 | 11 | 1 | 65 | 3 | 0 | 1 | 5 | .167 | 0 | 32-37 | 0 | 2.38 | 2.82 |
| 2013 | Ari | NL | 40 | 0 | 0 | 16 | 34.1 | 140 | 26 | 9 | 9 | 4 | 0 | 0 | 0 | 17 | 1 | 38 | 3 | 0 | 3 | 1 | .750 | 0 | 6-11 | 6 | 3.29 | 2.36 |
| Postseason | | | 3 | 0 | 0 | 3 | 2.1 | 11 | 3 | 1 | 1 | 0 | 0 | 0 | 0 | 1 | 0 | 0 | 0 | 0 | 0 | 1 | .000 | 0 | 0-0 | 0 | 4.93 | 3.86 |
| 11 ML YEARS | | | 554 | 0 | 0 | 349 | 553.0 | 2267 | 452 | 193 | 184 | 49 | 15 | 16 | 18 | 178 | 17 | 585 | 22 | 0 | 36 | 32 | .529 | 0 | 189-233 | 59 | 2.81 | 2.99 |

# Chad Qualls

**Pitches:** R **Bats:** R **Pos:** RP-66 **Ht:** 6'4" **Wt:** 240 **Born:** 8/17/1978 **Age:** 35

| | | | HOW MUCH HE PITCHED | | | | | | WHAT HE GAVE UP | | | | | | | | | | | | THE RESULTS | | | | | | | |
|---|---|---|---|---|---|---|---|---|---|---|---|---|---|---|---|---|---|---|---|---|---|---|---|---|---|---|---|
| Year | Team | Lg | G | GS | CG | GF | IP | BFP | H | R | ER | HR | SH | SF | HB | TBB | IBB | SO | WP | Bk | W | L | Pct | Sh | Sv-Op | Hld | ERC | ERA |
| 2004 | Hou | NL | 25 | 0 | 0 | 4 | 33.0 | 141 | 34 | 13 | 13 | 3 | 0 | 1 | 4 | 8 | 1 | 24 | 0 | 0 | 4 | 0 | 1.000 | 0 | 1-2 | 9 | 4.02 | 3.55 |
| 2005 | Hou | NL | 77 | 0 | 0 | 19 | 79.2 | 329 | 73 | 33 | 29 | 7 | 4 | 3 | 6 | 23 | 2 | 60 | 1 | 0 | 6 | 4 | .600 | 0 | 0-0 | 22 | 3.42 | 3.28 |
| 2006 | Hou | NL | 81 | 0 | 0 | 13 | 88.2 | 356 | 76 | 38 | 37 | 10 | 4 | 4 | 6 | 28 | 6 | 56 | 0 | 0 | 7 | 3 | .700 | 0 | 0-6 | 23 | 3.36 | 3.76 |
| 2007 | Hou | NL | 79 | 0 | 0 | 16 | 82.2 | 345 | 84 | 29 | 28 | 10 | 6 | 2 | 3 | 25 | 5 | 78 | 2 | 0 | 6 | 5 | .545 | 0 | 5-10 | 21 | 4.07 | 3.05 |
| 2008 | Ari | NL | 77 | 0 | 0 | 21 | 73.2 | 300 | 61 | 29 | 23 | 4 | 4 | 3 | 3 | 18 | 2 | 71 | 6 | 0 | 4 | 8 | .333 | 0 | 9-17 | 22 | 2.40 | 2.81 |
| 2009 | Ari | NL | 51 | 0 | 0 | 44 | 52.0 | 217 | 53 | 23 | 21 | 5 | 1 | 0 | 2 | 7 | 2 | 45 | 2 | 0 | 2 | 2 | .500 | 0 | 24-29 | 0 | 3.17 | 3.63 |
| 2010 | 2 Tms | | 70 | 0 | 0 | 29 | 59.0 | 281 | 85 | 56 | 48 | 7 | 4 | 4 | 2 | 21 | 4 | 49 | 4 | 0 | 3 | 4 | .429 | 0 | 12-19 | 11 | 6.63 | 7.32 |
| 2011 | SD | NL | 77 | 0 | 0 | 20 | 74.1 | 306 | 73 | 30 | 29 | 7 | 7 | 1 | 0 | 20 | 5 | 43 | 4 | 0 | 6 | 8 | .429 | 0 | 0-5 | 22 | 3.38 | 3.51 |
| 2012 | 3 Tms | | 60 | 0 | 0 | 15 | 52.1 | 231 | 63 | 34 | 31 | 7 | 2 | 2 | 0 | 14 | 4 | 27 | 3 | 0 | 2 | 1 | .667 | 0 | 0-5 | 14 | 4.78 | 5.33 |
| 2013 | Mia | NL | 66 | 0 | 0 | 12 | 62.0 | 252 | 57 | 18 | 18 | 4 | 4 | 0 | 2 | 19 | 7 | 49 | 1 | 0 | 5 | 2 | .714 | 0 | 0-2 | 15 | 3.09 | 2.61 |
| 10 | Ari | NL | 43 | 0 | 0 | 28 | 38.0 | 190 | 61 | 41 | 35 | 5 | 4 | 2 | 1 | 15 | 4 | 34 | 3 | 0 | 1 | 4 | .200 | 0 | 12-16 | 3 | 7.80 | 8.29 |
| 10 | TB | AL | 27 | 0 | 0 | 1 | 21.0 | 91 | 24 | 15 | 13 | 2 | 0 | 2 | 1 | 6 | 0 | 15 | 1 | 0 | 2 | 0 | 1.000 | 0 | 0-3 | 8 | 4.64 | 5.57 |
| 12 | Phi | NL | 35 | 0 | 0 | 6 | 31.1 | 140 | 39 | 18 | 16 | 7 | 1 | 0 | 0 | 9 | 3 | 19 | 2 | 0 | 1 | 1 | .500 | 0 | 0-5 | 12 | 5.74 | 4.60 |
| 12 | NYY | AL | 8 | 0 | 0 | 4 | 7.1 | 33 | 10 | 5 | 5 | 0 | 0 | 1 | 0 | 3 | 1 | 2 | 1 | 0 | 1 | 0 | 1.000 | 0 | 0-0 | 0 | 5.38 | 6.14 |
| 12 | Pit | NL | 17 | 0 | 0 | 5 | 13.2 | 58 | 14 | 11 | 10 | 0 | 1 | 1 | 0 | 2 | 0 | 6 | 0 | 0 | 0 | 0 | - | 0 | 0-0 | 2 | 2.48 | 6.59 |
| Postseason | | | 17 | 0 | 0 | 0 | 22.2 | 94 | 24 | 13 | 13 | 3 | 1 | 0 | 0 | 7 | 3 | 17 | 0 | 0 | 1 | 1 | .500 | 0 | 0-2 | 2 | 4.20 | 5.16 |
| 10 ML YEARS | | | 663 | 0 | 0 | 193 | 657.1 | 2758 | 659 | 303 | 277 | 64 | 36 | 20 | 28 | 183 | 38 | 502 | 23 | 0 | 45 | 37 | .549 | 0 | 51-95 | 159 | 3.71 | 3.79 |

# Carlos Quentin

**Bats:** R **Throws:** R **Pos:** LF-69;PH-7;DH-6 **Ht:** 6'2" **Wt:** 240 **Born:** 8/28/1982 **Age:** 31

| | | | BATTING | | | | | | | | | | | | | | | | | BASERUNNING | | | | AVERAGES | | |
|---|---|---|---|---|---|---|---|---|---|---|---|---|---|---|---|---|---|---|---|---|---|---|---|---|---|---|
| Year | Team | Lg | G | AB | H | 2B | 3B | HR | (Hm | Rd) | TB | R | RBI | RC | TBB | IBB | SO | HBP | SH | SF | SB | CS | SB% | GDP | Avg | OBP | Slg |
| 2006 | Ari | NL | 57 | 166 | 42 | 13 | 3 | 9 | (3 | 6) | 88 | 23 | 32 | 29 | 15 | 2 | 34 | 8 | 1 | 1 | 1 | 0 | 1.00 | 6 | .253 | .342 | .530 |
| 2007 | Ari | NL | 81 | 229 | 49 | 16 | 0 | 5 | (5 | 0) | 80 | 29 | 31 | 27 | 18 | 1 | 54 | 11 | 1 | 4 | 2 | 2 | .50 | 5 | .214 | .298 | .349 |
| 2008 | CWS | AL | 130 | 480 | 138 | 26 | 1 | 36 | **(21** | 15) | 274 | 96 | 100 | 104 | 66 | 0 | 80 | 20 | 0 | 3 | 7 | 3 | .70 | 16 | .288 | .394 | .571 |
| 2009 | CWS | AL | 99 | 351 | 83 | 14 | 0 | 21 | (12 | 9) | 160 | 47 | 56 | 47 | 31 | 2 | 52 | 15 | 0 | 2 | 3 | 0 | 1.00 | 11 | .236 | .323 | .456 |
| 2010 | CWS | AL | 131 | 453 | 110 | 25 | 2 | 26 | (19 | 7) | 217 | 73 | 87 | 78 | 50 | 3 | 83 | 20 | 0 | 4 | 2 | 2 | .50 | 16 | .243 | .342 | .479 |
| 2011 | CWS | AL | 118 | 421 | 107 | 31 | 0 | 24 | (7 | 17) | 210 | 53 | 77 | 72 | 34 | 0 | 84 | **23** | 0 | 5 | 1 | 1 | .50 | 7 | .254 | .340 | .499 |
| 2012 | SD | NL | 86 | 284 | 74 | 21 | 0 | 16 | (7 | 9) | 143 | 44 | 46 | 45 | 36 | 2 | 41 | **17** | 0 | 3 | 0 | 1 | .00 | 6 | .261 | .374 | .504 |
| 2013 | SD | NL | 82 | 276 | 76 | 21 | 0 | 13 | (4 | 9) | 136 | 42 | 44 | 47 | 31 | 0 | 55 | 9 | 0 | 4 | 0 | 0 | - | 7 | .275 | .363 | .493 |
| 8 ML YEARS | | | 784 | 2660 | 679 | 167 | 6 | 150 | (78 | 72) | 1308 | 407 | 473 | 449 | 281 | 10 | 483 | 123 | 2 | 26 | 16 | 9 | .64 | 74 | .255 | .350 | .492 |

# Jose Quintana

**Pitches:** L **Bats:** R **Pos:** SP-33 KIN-tahn-ah **Ht:** 6'1" **Wt:** 215 **Born:** 1/24/1989 **Age:** 25

| | | | HOW MUCH HE PITCHED | | | | | | WHAT HE GAVE UP | | | | | | | | | | | | THE RESULTS | | | | | | | |
|---|---|---|---|---|---|---|---|---|---|---|---|---|---|---|---|---|---|---|---|---|---|---|---|---|---|---|---|
| Year | Team | Lg | G | GS | CG | GF | IP | BFP | H | R | ER | HR | SH | SF | HB | TBB | IBB | SO | WP | Bk | W | L | Pct | Sh | Sv-Op | Hld | ERC | ERA |
| 2010 | Yanks | R | 15 | 0 | 0 | 10 | 23.1 | 97 | 14 | 11 | 6 | 0 | 3 | 0 | 3 | 8 | 0 | 32 | 1 | 0 | 3 | 1 | .750 | 0 | 1-- | - | 1.63 | 2.31 |
| 2010 | CtnSC | A | 5 | 3 | 0 | 0 | 15.1 | 68 | 11 | 10 | 8 | 1 | 0 | 0 | 1 | 10 | 0 | 12 | 0 | 0 | 0 | 1 | .000 | 0 | 0-- | - | 3.41 | 4.70 |
| 2011 | Tampa | A+ | 30 | 12 | 0 | 3 | 102.0 | 402 | 86 | 35 | 33 | 5 | 5 | 4 | 1 | 28 | 0 | 88 | 7 | 0 | 10 | 2 | .833 | 0 | 1-- | - | 2.58 | 2.91 |
| 2012 | Brham | AA | 9 | 9 | 0 | 0 | 48.2 | 196 | 43 | 17 | 15 | 1 | 2 | 1 | 0 | 14 | 0 | 41 | 2 | 0 | 1 | 3 | .250 | 0 | 0-- | - | 2.58 | 2.77 |
| 2012 | CWS | AL | 25 | 22 | 0 | 2 | 136.1 | 568 | 142 | 62 | 57 | 14 | 5 | 1 | 3 | 42 | 4 | 81 | 10 | 2 | 6 | 6 | .500 | 0 | 0-0 | 0 | 4.13 | 3.76 |
| 2013 | CWS | AL | 33 | 33 | 0 | 0 | 200.0 | 832 | 188 | 83 | 78 | 23 | 3 | 6 | 5 | 56 | 2 | 164 | 2 | 1 | 9 | 7 | .563 | 0 | 0-0 | 0 | 3.47 | 3.51 |
| 2 ML YEARS | | | 58 | 55 | 0 | 2 | 336.1 | 1400 | 330 | 145 | 135 | 37 | 8 | 7 | 8 | 98 | 6 | 245 | 12 | 3 | 15 | 13 | .536 | 0 | 0-0 | 0 | 3.73 | 3.61 |

# Omar Quintanilla

**Bats:** L **Throws:** R **Pos:** SS-92;PH-2;3B-1;PR-1 keen-tah-NEE-yah **Ht:** 5'9" **Wt:** 185 **Born:** 10/24/1981 **Age:** 32

| | | | BATTING | | | | | | | | | | | | | | | | | BASERUNNING | | | | AVERAGES | | |
|---|---|---|---|---|---|---|---|---|---|---|---|---|---|---|---|---|---|---|---|---|---|---|---|---|---|---|
| Year | Team | Lg | G | AB | H | 2B | 3B | HR | (Hm | Rd) | TB | R | RBI | RC | TBB | IBB | SO | HBP | SH | SF | SB | CS | SB% | GDP | Avg | OBP | Slg |
| 2013 | LsVgs* | AAA | 48 | 126 | 42 | 9 | 2 | 2 | (- | -) | 61 | 26 | 18 | 26 | 20 | 1 | 25 | 0 | 0 | 2 | 1 | 1 | .50 | 3 | .333 | .419 | .484 |
| 2005 | Col | NL | 39 | 128 | 28 | 1 | 1 | 0 | (0 | 0) | 31 | 16 | 7 | 9 | 9 | 0 | 15 | 0 | 6 | 0 | 2 | 1 | .67 | 3 | .219 | .270 | .242 |
| 2006 | Col | NL | 11 | 34 | 6 | 1 | 1 | 0 | (0 | 0) | 9 | 3 | 3 | 2 | 3 | 1 | 9 | 0 | 1 | 0 | 1 | 1 | .50 | 1 | .176 | .243 | .265 |
| 2007 | Col | NL | 27 | 70 | 16 | 4 | 0 | 0 | (0 | 0) | 20 | 6 | 5 | 6 | 5 | 0 | 15 | 0 | 0 | 0 | 0 | 0 | - | 3 | .229 | .280 | .286 |
| 2008 | Col | NL | 81 | 210 | 50 | 17 | 0 | 2 | (1 | 1) | 73 | 28 | 15 | 18 | 15 | 3 | 46 | 0 | 8 | 1 | 0 | 0 | - | 3 | .238 | .288 | .348 |
| 2009 | Col | NL | 58 | 58 | 10 | 2 | 0 | 0 | (0 | 0) | 12 | 7 | 2 | 4 | 8 | 0 | 27 | 0 | 3 | 0 | 0 | 0 | - | 0 | .172 | .273 | .207 |
| 2011 | Tex | AL | 11 | 22 | 1 | 0 | 1 | 0 | (0 | 0) | 3 | 3 | 2 | 0 | 0 | 0 | 9 | 0 | 1 | 0 | 0 | 0 | - | 0 | .045 | .045 | .136 |
| 2012 | 2 Tms | | 65 | 169 | 41 | 8 | 0 | 4 | (3 | 1) | 61 | 25 | 16 | 14 | 16 | 1 | 42 | 2 | 1 | 2 | 0 | 1 | .00 | 3 | .243 | .312 | .361 |
| 2013 | NYM | NL | 95 | 315 | 70 | 9 | 2 | 2 | (1 | 1) | 89 | 28 | 21 | 27 | 38 | 7 | 70 | 1 | 3 | 2 | 2 | 0 | 1.00 | 10 | .222 | .306 | .283 |
| 12 | NYM | NL | 29 | 70 | 18 | 5 | 0 | 1 | (0 | 1) | 26 | 13 | 4 | 6 | 8 | 1 | 17 | 2 | 0 | 0 | 0 | 0 | - | 2 | .257 | .350 | .371 |
| 12 | Bal | AL | 36 | 99 | 23 | 3 | 0 | 3 | (3 | 0) | 35 | 12 | 12 | 8 | 8 | 0 | 25 | 0 | 1 | 2 | 0 | 1 | .00 | 1 | .232 | .284 | .354 |
| 8 ML YEARS | | | 387 | 1006 | 222 | 42 | 5 | 8 | (5 | 3) | 298 | 116 | 71 | 80 | 94 | 12 | 233 | 3 | 23 | 5 | 5 | 3 | .63 | 23 | .221 | .288 | .296 |

## Humberto Quintero

**Bats:** R **Throws:** R **Pos:** C-42;PH-4 oom-BARE-toe keen-TARE-oh **Ht:** 5'9" **Wt:** 215 **Born:** 8/2/1979 **Age:** 34

| BATTING | | | | | | | | | | | | | | | | | | | | BASERUNNING | | | | AVERAGES | | |
|---|---|---|---|---|---|---|---|---|---|---|---|---|---|---|---|---|---|---|---|---|---|---|---|---|---|---|
| Year Team | Lg | G | AB | H | 2B | 3B | HR | (Hm | Rd) | TB | R | RBI | RC | TBB | IBB | SO | HBP | SH | SF | SB | CS | SB% | GDP | Avg | OBP | Slg |
| 2013 LV* | AAA | 8 | 24 | 7 | 1 | 0 | 2 | (- | -) | 14 | 7 | 4 | 6 | 4 | 0 | 5 | 2 | 1 | 1 | 0 | 0 | - | 0 | .292 | .419 | .583 |
| 2003 SD | NL | 12 | 23 | 5 | 0 | 0 | 0 | (0 | 0) | 5 | 1 | 2 | 2 | 1 | 1 | 6 | 0 | 0 | 0 | 0 | 0 | - | 0 | .217 | .250 | .217 |
| 2004 SD | NL | 23 | 72 | 18 | 3 | 0 | 2 | (1 | 1) | 27 | 7 | 10 | 6 | 5 | 0 | 16 | 0 | 0 | 1 | 0 | 2 | .00 | 5 | .250 | .295 | .375 |
| 2005 Hou | NL | 18 | 54 | 10 | 1 | 0 | 1 | (1 | 0) | 14 | 6 | 8 | 2 | 1 | 1 | 10 | 0 | 2 | 0 | 0 | 0 | - | 3 | .185 | .200 | .259 |
| 2006 Hou | NL | 11 | 21 | 7 | 2 | 0 | 0 | (0 | 0) | 9 | 2 | 2 | 1 | 1 | 0 | 3 | 0 | 0 | 0 | 0 | 0 | - | 2 | .333 | .364 | .429 |
| 2007 Hou | NL | 29 | 53 | 12 | 2 | 0 | 0 | (0 | 0) | 14 | 2 | 1 | 3 | 2 | 1 | 13 | 2 | 0 | 0 | 0 | 0 | - | 2 | .226 | .281 | .264 |
| 2008 Hou | NL | 59 | 168 | 38 | 6 | 0 | 2 | (1 | 1) | 50 | 16 | 12 | 10 | 6 | 0 | 34 | 4 | 5 | 0 | 0 | 0 | - | 5 | .226 | .270 | .298 |
| 2009 Hou | NL | 60 | 157 | 37 | 8 | 1 | 4 | (3 | 1) | 59 | 11 | 14 | 13 | 7 | 1 | 41 | 4 | 0 | 0 | 0 | 0 | - | 8 | .236 | .286 | .376 |
| 2010 Hou | NL | 88 | 265 | 62 | 10 | 0 | 4 | (2 | 2) | 84 | 13 | 20 | 20 | 8 | 2 | 59 | 2 | 1 | 0 | 0 | 0 | - | 5 | .234 | .262 | .317 |
| 2011 Hou | NL | 79 | 262 | 63 | 12 | 1 | 2 | (2 | 0) | 83 | 22 | 25 | 14 | 6 | 2 | 53 | 1 | 1 | 2 | 1 | 0 | 1.00 | 10 | .240 | .258 | .317 |
| 2012 KC | AL | 43 | 138 | 32 | 12 | 0 | 1 | (1 | 0) | 47 | 7 | 19 | 10 | 4 | 0 | 28 | 1 | 0 | 1 | 0 | 1 | .00 | 1 | .232 | .257 | .341 |
| 2013 2 Tms | | 46 | 131 | 31 | 5 | 0 | 4 | (2 | 2) | 48 | 8 | 13 | 10 | 6 | 1 | 30 | 1 | 2 | 0 | 0 | 0 | - | 6 | .237 | .275 | .366 |
| 13 Phi | NL | 24 | 64 | 16 | 4 | 0 | 2 | (1 | 1) | 26 | 3 | 9 | 7 | 3 | 1 | 15 | 1 | 0 | 0 | 0 | 0 | - | 3 | .250 | .294 | .406 |
| 13 Sea | AL | 22 | 67 | 15 | 1 | 0 | 2 | (1 | 1) | 22 | 5 | 4 | 3 | 3 | 0 | 15 | 0 | 2 | 0 | 0 | 0 | - | 3 | .224 | .257 | .328 |
| 11 ML YEARS | | 468 | 1344 | 315 | 61 | 2 | 20 | (13 | 7) | 440 | 95 | 126 | 91 | 47 | 9 | 293 | 15 | 11 | 4 | 1 | 3 | .25 | 47 | .234 | .267 | .327 |

## Guillermo Quiroz

**Bats:** R **Throws:** R **Pos:** C-35;PH-10 key-ROSE **Ht:** 6'1" **Wt:** 210 **Born:** 11/29/1981 **Age:** 32

| BATTING | | | | | | | | | | | | | | | | | | | | BASERUNNING | | | | AVERAGES | | |
|---|---|---|---|---|---|---|---|---|---|---|---|---|---|---|---|---|---|---|---|---|---|---|---|---|---|---|
| Year Team | Lg | G | AB | H | 2B | 3B | HR | (Hm | Rd) | TB | R | RBI | RC | TBB | IBB | SO | HBP | SH | SF | SB | CS | SB% | GDP | Avg | OBP | Slg |
| 2013 Fresno* | AAA | 14 | 34 | 10 | 2 | 0 | 0 | (- | -) | 12 | 2 | 8 | 5 | 6 | 0 | 7 | 1 | 0 | 1 | 0 | 0 | - | 1 | .294 | .405 | .353 |
| 2004 Tor | AL | 17 | 52 | 11 | 2 | 0 | 0 | (0 | 0) | 13 | 2 | 6 | 4 | 2 | 0 | 8 | 2 | 0 | 1 | 1 | 0 | 1.00 | 1 | .212 | .263 | .250 |
| 2005 Tor | AL | 12 | 36 | 7 | 2 | 0 | 0 | (0 | 0) | 9 | 3 | 4 | 3 | 2 | 0 | 13 | 1 | 0 | 0 | 0 | 0 | - | 0 | .194 | .256 | .250 |
| 2006 Sea | AL | 1 | 2 | 0 | 0 | 0 | 0 | (0 | 0) | 0 | 0 | 0 | 0 | 0 | 0 | 2 | 0 | 0 | 0 | 0 | 0 | - | 0 | .000 | .000 | .000 |
| 2007 Tex | AL | 9 | 10 | 4 | 1 | 0 | 0 | (0 | 0) | 5 | 1 | 2 | 3 | 1 | 0 | 2 | 0 | 0 | 0 | 0 | 0 | - | 0 | .400 | .455 | .500 |
| 2008 Bal | AL | 56 | 134 | 25 | 5 | 0 | 2 | (1 | 1) | 36 | 12 | 14 | 10 | 12 | 0 | 34 | 1 | 1 | 0 | 0 | 0 | - | 3 | .187 | .259 | .269 |
| 2009 Sea | AL | 4 | 14 | 4 | 0 | 0 | 0 | (0 | 0) | 4 | 0 | 2 | 1 | 0 | 0 | 3 | 0 | 1 | 0 | 0 | 0 | - | 0 | .286 | .286 | .286 |
| 2010 Sea | AL | 2 | 7 | 2 | 1 | 0 | 0 | (0 | 0) | 3 | 1 | 0 | 0 | 0 | 0 | 1 | 0 | 0 | 0 | 0 | 0 | - | 0 | .286 | .286 | .429 |
| 2012 Bos | AL | 2 | 2 | 0 | 0 | 0 | 0 | (0 | 0) | 0 | 0 | 0 | 0 | 0 | 0 | 1 | 0 | 0 | 0 | 0 | 0 | - | 0 | .000 | .000 | .000 |
| 2013 SF | NL | 43 | 86 | 16 | 7 | 0 | 1 | (1 | 0) | 26 | 5 | 6 | 3 | 5 | 1 | 21 | 1 | 2 | 1 | 0 | 0 | - | 4 | .186 | .237 | .302 |
| 9 ML YEARS | | 146 | 343 | 69 | 18 | 0 | 3 | (2 | 1) | 96 | 24 | 34 | 24 | 22 | 1 | 85 | 5 | 4 | 2 | 1 | 0 | 1.00 | 8 | .201 | .258 | .280 |

## Ryan Raburn

RAY-burn

**Bats:** R **Throws:** R **Pos:** RF-54;DH-17;LF-13;PH-11;2B-2;PR-2 **Ht:** 6'0" **Wt:** 185 **Born:** 4/17/1981 **Age:** 33

| BATTING | | | | | | | | | | | | | | | | | | | | BASERUNNING | | | | AVERAGES | | |
|---|---|---|---|---|---|---|---|---|---|---|---|---|---|---|---|---|---|---|---|---|---|---|---|---|---|---|
| Year Team | Lg | G | AB | H | 2B | 3B | HR | (Hm | Rd) | TB | R | RBI | RC | TBB | IBB | SO | HBP | SH | SF | SB | CS | SB% | GDP | Avg | OBP | Slg |
| 2004 Det | AL | 12 | 29 | 4 | 1 | 0 | 0 | (0 | 0) | 5 | 4 | 1 | 1 | 2 | 0 | 15 | 0 | 0 | 0 | 1 | 0 | 1.00 | 0 | .138 | .194 | .172 |
| 2007 Det | AL | 49 | 138 | 42 | 12 | 2 | 4 | (2 | 2) | 70 | 28 | 27 | 21 | 8 | 1 | 33 | 0 | 1 | 1 | 3 | 0 | 1.00 | 7 | .304 | .340 | .507 |
| 2008 Det | AL | 92 | 182 | 43 | 10 | 1 | 4 | (2 | 2) | 67 | 26 | 20 | 20 | 16 | 1 | 49 | 0 | 1 | 0 | 3 | 1 | .75 | 2 | .236 | .298 | .368 |
| 2009 Det | AL | 113 | 261 | 76 | 11 | 2 | 16 | (9 | 7) | 139 | 44 | 45 | 42 | 26 | 2 | 60 | 2 | 1 | 1 | 5 | 4 | .56 | 6 | .291 | .359 | .533 |
| 2010 Det | AL | 113 | 371 | 104 | 25 | 1 | 15 | (5 | 10) | 176 | 54 | 62 | 54 | 27 | 0 | 92 | 8 | 1 | 3 | 2 | 2 | .50 | 8 | .280 | .340 | .474 |
| 2011 Det | AL | 121 | 387 | 99 | 22 | 2 | 14 | (7 | 7) | 167 | 53 | 49 | 48 | 21 | 2 | 114 | 3 | 4 | 3 | 1 | 1 | .50 | 4 | .256 | .297 | .432 |
| 2012 Det | AL | 66 | 205 | 35 | 14 | 0 | 1 | (0 | 1) | 52 | 14 | 12 | 8 | 13 | 0 | 53 | 2 | 1 | 1 | 1 | 1 | .50 | 7 | .171 | .226 | .254 |
| 2013 Cle | AL | 87 | 243 | 66 | 18 | 0 | 16 | (8 | 8) | 132 | 40 | 55 | 47 | 29 | 0 | 67 | 4 | 0 | 1 | 0 | 0 | - | 4 | .272 | .357 | .543 |
| Postseason | | 9 | 28 | 8 | 1 | 0 | 2 | (1 | 1) | 15 | 4 | 5 | 4 | 4 | 0 | 7 | 0 | 0 | 0 | 0 | 0 | - | 3 | .286 | .375 | .536 |
| 8 ML YEARS | | 653 | 1816 | 469 | 113 | 8 | 70 | (33 | 37) | 808 | 263 | 271 | 241 | 142 | 6 | 483 | 19 | 9 | 10 | 16 | 9 | .64 | 38 | .258 | .317 | .445 |

## Brooks Raley

**Pitches:** L **Bats:** L **Pos:** RP-9 RAIL-ee **Ht:** 6'3" **Wt:** 200 **Born:** 6/29/1988 **Age:** 26

| HOW MUCH HE PITCHED | | | | | | | WHAT HE GAVE UP | | | | | | | | | | | | THE RESULTS | | | | | | | |
|---|---|---|---|---|---|---|---|---|---|---|---|---|---|---|---|---|---|---|---|---|---|---|---|---|---|---|
| Year Team | Lg | G | GS | CG | GF | IP | BFP | H | R | ER | HR | SH | SF | HB | TBB | IBB | SO | WP | Bk | W | L | Pct | Sh | Sv-Op | Hld | ERC | ERA |
| 2009 Cubs | R | 3 | 3 | 0 | 0 | 4.1 | 18 | 2 | 4 | 2 | 1 | 0 | 0 | 0 | 2 | 0 | 3 | 1 | 0 | 0 | 1 | .000 | 0 | 0- - | - | 2.12 | 4.15 |
| 2009 Boise | A- | 2 | 0 | 0 | 0 | 6.1 | 21 | 3 | 1 | 1 | 1 | 0 | 0 | 0 | 1 | 0 | 2 | 0 | 0 | 0 | 0 | - | 0 | 0- - | - | 1.29 | 1.42 |
| 2010 Dytona | A+ | 27 | 27 | 0 | 0 | 136.1 | 584 | 151 | 62 | 53 | 9 | 3 | 2 | 4 | 43 | 0 | 97 | 5 | 2 | 8 | 6 | .571 | 0 | 0- - | - | 4.30 | 3.50 |
| 2011 Tenn | AA | 26 | 25 | 0 | 0 | 136.1 | 619 | 170 | 86 | 64 | 16 | 14 | 4 | 3 | 45 | 0 | 80 | 7 | 0 | 8 | 10 | .444 | 0 | 0- - | - | 5.39 | 4.22 |
| 2012 Tenn | AA | 8 | 8 | 0 | 0 | 48.2 | 199 | 47 | 19 | 19 | 2 | 2 | 0 | 4 | 12 | 0 | 29 | 1 | 0 | 2 | 2 | .500 | 0 | 0- - | - | 3.32 | 3.51 |
| 2012 Iowa | AAA | 14 | 14 | 1 | 0 | 82.0 | 356 | 87 | 39 | 33 | 7 | 1 | 4 | 3 | 28 | 0 | 69 | 2 | 0 | 4 | 8 | .333 | 1 | 0- - | - | 4.23 | 3.62 |
| 2013 Iowa | AAA | 27 | 25 | 0 | 1 | 141.1 | 610 | 142 | 73 | 70 | 13 | 8 | 2 | 6 | 45 | 0 | 95 | 6 | 0 | 8 | 10 | .444 | 0 | 1- - | - | 3.85 | 4.46 |
| 2012 ChC | NL | 5 | 5 | 0 | 0 | 24.1 | 116 | 33 | 23 | 22 | 7 | 1 | 0 | 0 | 11 | 0 | 16 | 0 | 0 | 1 | 2 | .333 | 0 | 0-0 | 0 | 7.87 | 8.14 |
| 2013 ChC | NL | 9 | 0 | 0 | 1 | 14.0 | 61 | 11 | 9 | 8 | 2 | 1 | 1 | 2 | 8 | 0 | 14 | 0 | 0 | 0 | 0 | - | 0 | 0-0 | 0 | 4.48 | 5.14 |
| 2 ML YEARS | | 14 | 5 | 0 | 1 | 38.1 | 177 | 44 | 32 | 30 | 9 | 2 | 1 | 2 | 19 | 0 | 30 | 0 | 0 | 1 | 2 | .333 | 0 | 0-0 | 0 | 6.59 | 7.04 |

## Alexei Ramirez

**Bats:** R **Throws:** R **Pos:** SS-158 ah-lexx-AY **Ht:** 6'2" **Wt:** 180 **Born:** 9/22/1981 **Age:** 32

| BATTING | | | | | | | | | | | | | | | | | | | | BASERUNNING | | | | AVERAGES | | |
|---|---|---|---|---|---|---|---|---|---|---|---|---|---|---|---|---|---|---|---|---|---|---|---|---|---|---|
| Year Team | Lg | G | AB | H | 2B | 3B | HR | (Hm | Rd) | TB | R | RBI | RC | TBB | IBB | SO | HBP | SH | SF | SB | CS | SB% | GDP | Avg | OBP | Slg |
| 2008 CWS | AL | 136 | 480 | 139 | 22 | 2 | 21 | (13 | 8) | 228 | 65 | 77 | 78 | 18 | 3 | 61 | 3 | 4 | 4 | 13 | 9 | .59 | 14 | .290 | .317 | .475 |
| 2009 CWS | AL | 148 | 542 | 150 | 14 | 1 | 15 | (9 | 6) | 211 | 71 | 68 | 74 | 49 | 3 | 66 | 1 | 6 | 8 | 14 | 5 | .74 | 15 | .277 | .333 | .389 |
| 2010 CWS | AL | 156 | 585 | 165 | 29 | 2 | 18 | (11 | 7) | 252 | 83 | 70 | 72 | 27 | 2 | 82 | 2 | 7 | 5 | 13 | 8 | .62 | 12 | .282 | .313 | .431 |
| 2011 CWS | AL | 158 | 614 | 165 | 31 | 2 | 15 | (7 | 8) | 245 | 81 | 70 | 74 | 51 | 1 | 84 | 6 | 8 | 5 | 7 | 5 | .58 | 19 | .269 | .328 | .399 |

| | | | BATTING | | | | | | | | | | | | | | | | | | BASERUNNING | | | | AVERAGES | | |
|---|---|---|---|---|---|---|---|---|---|---|---|---|---|---|---|---|---|---|---|---|---|---|---|---|---|---|---|
| Year | Team | Lg | G | AB | H | 2B | 3B | HR | (Hm | Rd) | TB | R | RBI | RC | TBB | IBB | SO | HBP | SH | SF | SB | CS | SB% | GDP | Avg | OBP | Slg |
| 2012 | CWS | AL | 158 | 593 | 157 | 24 | 4 | 9 | (6 | 3) | 216 | 59 | 73 | 70 | 16 | 2 | 77 | 4 | 4 | 4 | 20 | 7 | .74 | 15 | .265 | .287 | .364 |
| 2013 | CWS | AL | 158 | 637 | 181 | 39 | 2 | 6 | (5 | 1) | 242 | 68 | 48 | 67 | 26 | 2 | 68 | 3 | 4 | 4 | 30 | 9 | .77 | 17 | .284 | .313 | .380 |
| Postseason | | | 4 | 12 | 3 | 0 | 0 | 0 | (0 | 0) | 3 | 1 | 2 | 1 | 1 | 0 | 1 | 0 | 0 | 2 | 0 | 0 | - | 0 | .250 | .267 | .250 |
| 6 ML YEARS | | | 914 | 3451 | 957 | 159 | 13 | 84 | (51 | 33) | 1394 | 427 | 406 | 435 | 187 | 13 | 438 | 19 | 33 | 30 | 97 | 43 | .69 | 92 | .277 | .315 | .404 |

# Aramis Ramirez

**Bats:** R **Throws:** R **Pos:** 3B-80;PH-7;DH-5 ah-RAH-miss **Ht:** 6'1" **Wt:** 210 **Born:** 6/25/1978 **Age:** 36

| | | | BATTING | | | | | | | | | | | | | | | | | | BASERUNNING | | | | AVERAGES | | |
|---|---|---|---|---|---|---|---|---|---|---|---|---|---|---|---|---|---|---|---|---|---|---|---|---|---|---|---|
| Year | Team | Lg | G | AB | H | 2B | 3B | HR | (Hm | Rd) | TB | R | RBI | RC | TBB | IBB | SO | HBP | SH | SF | SB | CS | SB% | GDP | Avg | OBP | Slg |
| 1998 | Pit | NL | 72 | 251 | 59 | 9 | 1 | 6 | (3 | 3) | 88 | 23 | 24 | 26 | 18 | 0 | 72 | 4 | 1 | 1 | 0 | 1 | .00 | 3 | .235 | .296 | .351 |
| 1999 | Pit | NL | 18 | 56 | 10 | 2 | 1 | 0 | (0 | 0) | 14 | 2 | 7 | 4 | 6 | 0 | 9 | 0 | 1 | 1 | 0 | 0 | - | 0 | .179 | .254 | .250 |
| 2000 | Pit | NL | 73 | 254 | 65 | 15 | 2 | 6 | (4 | 2) | 102 | 19 | 35 | 28 | 10 | 0 | 36 | 5 | 1 | 4 | 0 | 0 | - | 9 | .256 | .293 | .402 |
| 2001 | Pit | NL | 158 | 603 | 181 | 40 | 0 | 34 | (16 | 18) | 323 | 83 | 112 | 108 | 40 | 4 | 100 | 8 | 0 | 4 | 5 | 4 | .56 | 9 | .300 | .350 | .536 |
| 2002 | Pit | NL | 142 | 522 | 122 | 26 | 0 | 18 | (7 | 11) | 202 | 51 | 71 | 49 | 29 | 3 | 95 | 8 | 0 | **11** | 2 | 0 | 1.00 | 17 | .234 | .279 | .387 |
| 2003 | 2 Tms | NL | 159 | 607 | 165 | 32 | 2 | 27 | (10 | 17) | 282 | 75 | 106 | 88 | 42 | 3 | 99 | 10 | 0 | **11** | 2 | 2 | .50 | 21 | .272 | .324 | .465 |
| 2004 | ChC | NL | 145 | 547 | 174 | 32 | 1 | 36 | (22 | 14) | 316 | 99 | 103 | 100 | 49 | 6 | 62 | 3 | 0 | 7 | 0 | 2 | .00 | 25 | .318 | .373 | .578 |
| 2005 | ChC | NL | 123 | 463 | 140 | 30 | 0 | 31 | (11 | 20) | 263 | 72 | 92 | 79 | 35 | 4 | 60 | 6 | 0 | 2 | 0 | 1 | .00 | 15 | .302 | .358 | .568 |
| 2006 | ChC | NL | 157 | 594 | 173 | 38 | 4 | 38 | (14 | 24) | 333 | 93 | 119 | 109 | 50 | 4 | 63 | 9 | 0 | 7 | 2 | 1 | .67 | 15 | .291 | .352 | .561 |
| 2007 | ChC | NL | 132 | 506 | 157 | 35 | 4 | 26 | (17 | 9) | 278 | 72 | 101 | 95 | 43 | 8 | 66 | 4 | 0 | 5 | 0 | 0 | - | 13 | .310 | .366 | .549 |
| 2008 | ChC | NL | 149 | 554 | 160 | 44 | 1 | 27 | (17 | 10) | 287 | 97 | 111 | 108 | 74 | 7 | 94 | 11 | 0 | 6 | 2 | 2 | .50 | 13 | .289 | .380 | .518 |
| 2009 | ChC | NL | 82 | 306 | 97 | 14 | 1 | 15 | (7 | 8) | 158 | 46 | 65 | 66 | 28 | 3 | 43 | 8 | 0 | 0 | 2 | 1 | .67 | 8 | .317 | .389 | .516 |
| 2010 | ChC | NL | 124 | 465 | 112 | 21 | 1 | 25 | (14 | 11) | 210 | 61 | 83 | 64 | 34 | 3 | 90 | 3 | 0 | 5 | 0 | 0 | - | 10 | .241 | .294 | .452 |
| 2011 | ChC | NL | 149 | 565 | 173 | 35 | 1 | 26 | (14 | 12) | 288 | 80 | 93 | 96 | 43 | 5 | 69 | 10 | 0 | 8 | 1 | 1 | .50 | 12 | .306 | .361 | .510 |
| 2012 | Mil | NL | 149 | 570 | 171 | **50** | 3 | 27 | (15 | 12) | 308 | 92 | 105 | 97 | 44 | 3 | 82 | 12 | 0 | 4 | 9 | 2 | .82 | 14 | .300 | .360 | .540 |
| 2013 | Mil | NL | 92 | 304 | 86 | 18 | 0 | 12 | (5 | 7) | 140 | 43 | 49 | 44 | 36 | 0 | 55 | 8 | 0 | 3 | 0 | 1 | .00 | 8 | .283 | .370 | .461 |
| 03 | Pit | NL | 96 | 375 | 105 | 25 | 1 | 12 | (6 | 6) | 168 | 44 | 67 | 49 | 25 | 3 | 68 | 7 | 0 | 8 | 1 | 1 | .50 | 17 | .280 | .330 | .448 |
| 03 | ChC | NL | 63 | 232 | 60 | 7 | 1 | 15 | (4 | 11) | 114 | 31 | 39 | 39 | 17 | 0 | 31 | 3 | 0 | 3 | 1 | 1 | .50 | 4 | .259 | .314 | .491 |
| Postseason | | | 18 | 67 | 13 | 2 | 1 | 4 | (1 | 3) | 29 | 7 | 10 | 8 | 9 | 0 | 15 | 1 | 0 | 0 | 0 | 0 | - | 5 | .194 | .299 | .433 |
| 16 ML YEARS | | | 1924 | 7167 | 2045 | 441 | 22 | 354 | (176 | 178) | 3592 | 1008 | 1276 | 1161 | 581 | 53 | 1095 | 109 | 3 | 79 | 25 | 18 | .58 | 192 | .285 | .345 | .501 |

# Erasmo Ramirez

**Pitches:** R **Bats:** R **Pos:** SP-13; RP-1 ehh-RAZ-mo **Ht:** 5'11" **Wt:** 200 **Born:** 5/2/1990 **Age:** 24

| | | | HOW MUCH HE PITCHED | | | | | | WHAT HE GAVE UP | | | | | | | | | | | | THE RESULTS | | | | | | | |
|---|---|---|---|---|---|---|---|---|---|---|---|---|---|---|---|---|---|---|---|---|---|---|---|---|---|---|---|---|
| Year | Team | Lg | G | GS | CG | GF | IP | BFP | H | R | ER | HR | SH | SF | HB | TBB | IBB | SO | WP | Bk | W | L | Pct | Sh | Sv-Op | Hld | ERC | ERA |
| 2010 | Clinton | A | 26 | 23 | 1 | 1 | 151.2 | 611 | 142 | 63 | 50 | 13 | 3 | 1 | 13 | 21 | 0 | 117 | 2 | 0 | 10 | 4 | .714 | 0 | 1- - | - | 3.02 | 2.97 |
| 2011 | Jacksn | AA | 19 | 19 | 0 | 0 | 110.1 | 481 | 127 | 74 | 58 | 10 | 6 | 3 | 8 | 19 | 0 | 81 | 5 | 0 | 7 | 6 | .538 | 0 | 0- - | - | 4.18 | 4.73 |
| 2011 | Tacom | AAA | 7 | 7 | 0 | 0 | 42.1 | 184 | 51 | 27 | 24 | 4 | 0 | 1 | 2 | 13 | 0 | 35 | 0 | 0 | 3 | 2 | .600 | 0 | 0- - | - | 5.17 | 5.10 |
| 2012 | Tacom | AAA | 15 | 15 | 0 | 0 | 77.1 | 339 | 81 | 45 | 32 | 5 | 3 | 4 | 4 | 18 | 0 | 58 | 8 | 0 | 6 | 3 | .667 | 0 | 0- - | - | 3.51 | 3.72 |
| 2013 | Jacksn | AA | 1 | 1 | 0 | 0 | 5.0 | 21 | 3 | 2 | 1 | 0 | 0 | 0 | 0 | 2 | 0 | 3 | 0 | 0 | 0 | 0 | - | 0 | 0- - | - | 1.44 | 1.80 |
| 2013 | Tacom | AAA | 7 | 7 | 0 | 0 | 43.2 | 185 | 43 | 17 | 15 | 4 | 2 | 0 | 1 | 14 | 0 | 42 | 0 | 0 | 3 | 3 | .500 | 0 | 0- - | - | 3.72 | 3.09 |
| 2013 | Everett | A- | 1 | 1 | 0 | 0 | 5.1 | 22 | 6 | 2 | 1 | 0 | 0 | 0 | 0 | 1 | 0 | 10 | 1 | 0 | 0 | 0 | - | 0 | 0- - | - | 3.34 | 1.69 |
| 2012 | Sea | AL | 16 | 8 | 0 | 2 | 59.0 | 238 | 47 | 26 | 22 | 6 | 1 | 5 | 3 | 12 | 1 | 48 | 0 | 0 | 1 | 3 | .250 | 0 | 0-0 | 0 | 2.42 | 3.36 |
| 2013 | Sea | AL | 14 | 13 | 0 | 0 | 72.1 | 321 | 79 | 44 | 40 | 12 | 0 | 3 | 3 | 26 | 0 | 57 | 0 | 0 | 5 | 3 | .625 | 0 | 0-0 | 0 | 5.04 | 4.98 |
| 2 ML YEARS | | | 30 | 21 | 0 | 2 | 131.1 | 559 | 126 | 70 | 62 | 18 | 1 | 8 | 6 | 38 | 1 | 105 | 0 | 0 | 6 | 6 | .500 | 0 | 0-0 | 0 | 3.79 | 4.25 |

# Hanley Ramirez

**Bats:** R **Throws:** R **Pos:** SS-76;PH-9;DH-2 **Ht:** 6'2" **Wt:** 225 **Born:** 12/23/1983 **Age:** 30

| | | | BATTING | | | | | | | | | | | | | | | | | | BASERUNNING | | | | AVERAGES | | |
|---|---|---|---|---|---|---|---|---|---|---|---|---|---|---|---|---|---|---|---|---|---|---|---|---|---|---|---|
| Year | Team | Lg | G | AB | H | 2B | 3B | HR | (Hm | Rd) | TB | R | RBI | RC | TBB | IBB | SO | HBP | SH | SF | SB | CS | SB% | GDP | Avg | OBP | Slg |
| 2013 | RCuca* | A+ | 5 | 15 | 5 | 2 | 0 | 0 | (- | -) | 7 | 1 | 6 | 2 | 1 | 0 | 3 | 0 | 0 | 1 | 0 | 0 | - | 0 | .333 | .353 | .467 |
| 2005 | Bos | AL | 2 | 2 | 0 | 0 | 0 | 0 | (0 | 0) | 0 | 0 | 0 | 0 | 0 | 0 | 2 | 0 | 0 | 0 | 0 | 0 | - | 0 | .000 | .000 | .000 |
| 2006 | Fla | NL | 158 | 633 | 185 | 46 | 11 | 17 | (9 | 8) | 304 | 119 | 59 | 101 | 56 | 0 | 128 | 4 | 5 | 2 | 51 | 15 | .77 | 7 | .292 | .353 | .480 |
| 2007 | Fla | NL | 154 | 639 | 212 | 48 | 6 | 29 | (15 | 14) | 359 | 125 | 81 | 115 | 52 | 3 | 95 | 7 | 4 | 4 | 51 | 14 | .78 | 10 | .332 | .386 | .562 |
| 2008 | Fla | NL | 153 | 589 | 177 | 34 | 4 | 33 | (17 | 16) | 318 | **125** | 67 | 116 | 92 | 9 | 122 | 8 | 0 | 4 | 35 | 12 | .74 | 5 | .301 | .400 | .540 |
| 2009 | Fla | NL | 151 | 576 | 197 | 42 | 1 | 24 | (17 | 7) | 313 | 101 | 106 | 122 | 61 | 14 | 101 | 9 | 1 | 5 | 27 | 8 | .77 | 9 | **.342** | .410 | .543 |
| 2010 | Fla | NL | 142 | 543 | 163 | 28 | 2 | 21 | (12 | 9) | 258 | 92 | 76 | 90 | 64 | 12 | 93 | 7 | 0 | 5 | 32 | 10 | .76 | 14 | .300 | .378 | .475 |
| 2011 | Fla | NL | 92 | 338 | 82 | 16 | 0 | 10 | (5 | 5) | 128 | 55 | 45 | 46 | 44 | 3 | 66 | 2 | 1 | 0 | 20 | 10 | .67 | 6 | .243 | .333 | .379 |
| 2012 | 2 Tms | NL | 157 | 604 | 155 | 29 | 4 | 24 | (11 | 13) | 264 | 79 | 92 | 81 | 54 | 4 | 132 | 6 | 0 | 3 | 21 | 7 | .75 | 17 | .257 | .322 | .437 |
| 2013 | LAD | NL | 86 | 304 | 105 | 25 | 2 | 20 | (8 | 12) | 194 | 62 | 57 | 69 | 27 | 3 | 52 | 3 | 0 | 2 | 10 | 2 | .83 | 5 | .345 | .402 | .638 |
| 12 | Mia | NL | 93 | 353 | 87 | 18 | 2 | 14 | (7 | 7) | 151 | 49 | 48 | 42 | 37 | 1 | 72 | 3 | 0 | 2 | 14 | 4 | .78 | 11 | .246 | .322 | .428 |
| 12 | LAD | NL | 64 | 251 | 68 | 11 | 2 | 10 | (4 | 6) | 113 | 30 | 44 | 39 | 17 | 3 | 60 | 3 | 0 | 1 | 7 | 3 | .70 | 6 | .271 | .324 | .450 |
| 9 ML YEARS | | | 1095 | 4228 | 1276 | 268 | 30 | 178 | (94 | 84) | 2138 | 758 | 583 | 740 | 450 | 48 | 791 | 46 | 11 | 25 | 247 | 78 | .76 | 73 | .302 | .373 | .506 |

# J.C. Ramirez

**Pitches:** R **Bats:** R **Pos:** RP-18 **Ht:** 6'4" **Wt:** 250 **Born:** 8/16/1988 **Age:** 25

| | | | HOW MUCH HE PITCHED | | | | | | WHAT HE GAVE UP | | | | | | | | | | | | THE RESULTS | | | | | | | |
|---|---|---|---|---|---|---|---|---|---|---|---|---|---|---|---|---|---|---|---|---|---|---|---|---|---|---|---|---|
| Year | Team | Lg | G | GS | CG | GF | IP | BFP | H | R | ER | HR | SH | SF | HB | TBB | IBB | SO | WP | Bk | W | L | Pct | Sh | Sv-Op | Hld | ERC | ERA |
| 2009 | Hi Dsrt | A+ | 28 | 27 | 1 | 1 | 142.1 | 633 | 153 | 93 | 81 | 18 | 3 | 3 | 17 | 53 | 0 | 111 | 14 | 2 | 8 | 10 | .444 | 0 | 0- - | - | 5.10 | 5.12 |
| 2010 | Clrwtr | A+ | 11 | 11 | 0 | 0 | 64.1 | 273 | 63 | 34 | 29 | 2 | 3 | 2 | 8 | 17 | 0 | 55 | 5 | 0 | 4 | 3 | .571 | 0 | 0- - | - | 3.46 | 4.06 |
| 2010 | Rdng | AA | 13 | 13 | 1 | 0 | 77.2 | 340 | 88 | 51 | 46 | 11 | 5 | 3 | 2 | 24 | 1 | 60 | 0 | 0 | 3 | 4 | .429 | 0 | 0- - | - | 4.85 | 5.33 |
| 2011 | Rdng | AA | 26 | 26 | 3 | 0 | 144.0 | 627 | 144 | 84 | 72 | 15 | 4 | 5 | 4 | 55 | 0 | 89 | 5 | 4 | 11 | 13 | .458 | 1 | 0- - | - | 4.10 | 4.50 |
| 2012 | Rdng | AA | 16 | 0 | 0 | 8 | 27.1 | 115 | 20 | 14 | 11 | 3 | 0 | 0 | 1 | 14 | 0 | 18 | 1 | 0 | 0 | 2 | .000 | 0 | 3- - | - | 3.25 | 3.62 |
| 2012 | LV | AAA | 29 | 0 | 0 | 11 | 40.0 | 164 | 36 | 19 | 19 | 3 | 0 | 1 | 2 | 17 | 1 | 34 | 5 | 0 | 3 | 2 | .600 | 0 | 1- - | - | 3.79 | 4.28 |
| 2013 | Rdng | AA | 4 | 0 | 0 | 1 | 7.0 | 26 | 2 | 0 | 0 | 0 | 0 | 0 | 0 | 2 | 0 | 8 | 1 | 0 | 1 | 0 | 1.000 | 0 | 0- - | - | 0.50 | 0.00 |
| 2013 | LV | AAA | 30 | 0 | 0 | 9 | 42.0 | 191 | 42 | 24 | 22 | 2 | 1 | 1 | 0 | 23 | 1 | 36 | 4 | 0 | 4 | 2 | .667 | 0 | 3- - | - | 4.12 | 4.71 |
| 2013 | Phi | NL | 18 | 0 | 0 | 2 | 24.0 | 116 | 30 | 22 | 20 | 6 | 1 | 4 | 0 | 15 | 1 | 16 | 0 | 0 | 0 | 1 | .000 | 0 | 0-0 | 3 | 7.59 | 7.50 |

## Jose Ramirez

**Bats:** B **Throws:** R **Pos:** PR-7;2B-5;PH-3;3B-2;SS-2;DH-2 **Ht:** 5'9" **Wt:** 165 **Born:** 9/17/1992 **Age:** 21

| BATTING | | | | | | | | | | | | | | | | | | | | | BASERUNNING | | | | AVERAGES | | |
|---|---|---|---|---|---|---|---|---|---|---|---|---|---|---|---|---|---|---|---|---|---|---|---|---|---|---|---|
| Year | Team | Lg | G | AB | H | 2B | 3B | HR | (Hm | Rd) | TB | R | RBI | RC | TBB | IBB | SO | HBP | SH | SF | SB | CS | SB% | GDP | Avg | OBP | Slg |
| 2011 | Indns | R | 48 | 194 | 63 | 13 | 4 | 1 | (- | -) | 87 | 30 | 20 | 30 | 7 | 0 | 17 | 2 | 3 | 2 | 12 | 6 | .67 | 3 | .325 | .351 | .448 |
| 2012 | MhVlly | A- | 3 | 11 | 4 | 2 | 0 | 0 | (- | -) | 6 | 2 | 0 | 2 | 1 | 0 | 0 | 0 | 1 | 0 | 2 | 1 | .67 | 0 | .364 | .417 | .545 |
| 2012 | Lk Cty | A | 67 | 277 | 98 | 13 | 4 | 3 | (- | -) | 128 | 54 | 27 | 53 | 24 | 1 | 26 | 1 | 8 | 3 | 15 | 6 | .71 | 4 | .354 | .403 | .462 |
| 2013 | Akron | AA | 113 | 482 | 131 | 16 | 6 | 3 | (- | -) | 168 | 78 | 38 | 59 | 39 | 1 | 41 | 1 | 7 | 4 | 38 | 16 | .70 | 3 | .272 | .325 | .349 |
| 2013 | Cle | AL | 15 | 12 | 4 | 0 | 1 | 0 | (0 | 0) | 6 | 5 | 0 | 2 | 2 | 0 | 2 | 0 | 0 | 0 | 0 | 1 | .00 | 0 | .333 | .429 | .500 |

## Ramon Ramirez

**Pitches:** R **Bats:** R **Pos:** RP-6 **Ht:** 5'11" **Wt:** 200 **Born:** 8/31/1981 **Age:** 32

| HOW MUCH HE PITCHED | | | | | | | | | WHAT HE GAVE UP | | | | | | | | | | | | THE RESULTS | | | | | | | |
|---|---|---|---|---|---|---|---|---|---|---|---|---|---|---|---|---|---|---|---|---|---|---|---|---|---|---|---|---|
| Year | Team | Lg | G | GS | CG | GF | IP | BFP | H | R | ER | HR | SH | SF | HB | TBB | IBB | SO | WP | Bk | W | L | Pct | Sh | Sv-Op | Hld | ERC | ERA |
| 2013 | Fresno* | AAA | 20 | 0 | 0 | 5 | 26.0 | 109 | 18 | 11 | 10 | 2 | 0 | 1 | 0 | 13 | 0 | 31 | 3 | 1 | 2 | 1 | .667 | 0 | 0-- | - | 2.62 | 3.46 |
| 2013 | Charltt* | A+ | 1 | 0 | 0 | 0 | 3.0 | 12 | 2 | 1 | 1 | 1 | 0 | 0 | 0 | 1 | 0 | 4 | 0 | 0 | 1 | 0 | 1.000 | 0 | 0-- | - | 3.37 | 3.00 |
| 2013 | Drham* | AAA | 6 | 0 | 0 | 3 | 6.1 | 25 | 5 | 2 | 2 | 0 | 0 | 0 | 0 | 1 | 0 | 7 | 0 | 0 | 0 | 0 | - | 0 | 0-- | - | 1.57 | 2.84 |
| 2006 | Col | NL | 61 | 0 | 0 | 14 | 67.2 | 285 | 58 | 28 | 26 | 5 | 2 | 3 | 1 | 27 | 3 | 61 | 2 | 0 | 4 | 3 | .571 | 0 | 0-2 | 10 | 3.09 | 3.46 |
| 2007 | Col | NL | 22 | 0 | 0 | 5 | 17.1 | 78 | 21 | 16 | 16 | 2 | 2 | 2 | 1 | 6 | 2 | 15 | 2 | 0 | 2 | 2 | .500 | 0 | 0-0 | 3 | 5.24 | 8.31 |
| 2008 | KC | AL | 71 | 0 | 0 | 15 | 71.2 | 295 | 57 | 23 | 21 | 2 | 4 | 3 | 0 | 31 | 6 | 70 | 6 | 1 | 3 | 2 | .600 | 0 | 1-5 | 21 | 2.53 | 2.64 |
| 2009 | Bos | AL | 70 | 0 | 0 | 16 | 69.2 | 301 | 61 | 26 | 22 | 7 | 3 | 0 | 4 | 32 | 4 | 52 | 2 | 2 | 7 | 4 | .636 | 0 | 0-4 | 12 | 3.73 | 2.84 |
| 2010 | 2 Tms | | 69 | 0 | 0 | 23 | 69.1 | 284 | 52 | 24 | 23 | 7 | 2 | 4 | 0 | 27 | 3 | 46 | 5 | 2 | 1 | 3 | .250 | 0 | 3-3 | 6 | 2.64 | 2.99 |
| 2011 | SF | NL | 66 | 0 | 0 | 22 | 68.2 | 282 | 54 | 24 | 20 | 3 | 2 | 1 | 3 | 26 | 5 | 66 | 6 | 1 | 3 | 3 | .500 | 0 | 4-5 | 11 | 2.57 | 2.62 |
| 2012 | NYM | NL | 58 | 0 | 0 | 18 | 63.2 | 277 | 58 | 33 | 30 | 4 | 3 | 3 | 0 | 35 | 4 | 52 | 4 | 0 | 3 | 4 | .429 | 0 | 1-3 | 1 | 3.80 | 4.24 |
| 2013 | SF | NL | 6 | 0 | 0 | 1 | 5.2 | 29 | 9 | 8 | 7 | 2 | 1 | 2 | 0 | 5 | 0 | 0 | 1 | 0 | 0 | 0 | - | 0 | 0-0 | 1 | 13.04 | 11.12 |
| 10 | Bos | AL | 44 | 0 | 0 | 17 | 42.1 | 178 | 39 | 21 | 21 | 6 | 2 | 4 | 0 | 16 | 2 | 31 | 4 | 1 | 0 | 3 | .000 | 0 | 2-2 | 2 | 3.78 | 4.46 |
| 10 | SF | NL | 25 | 0 | 0 | 6 | 27.0 | 106 | 13 | 3 | 2 | 1 | 0 | 0 | 0 | 11 | 1 | 15 | 1 | 1 | 1 | 0 | 1.000 | 0 | 1-1 | 4 | 1.28 | 0.67 |
| Postseason | | | 6 | 0 | 0 | 2 | 4.0 | 24 | 6 | 8 | 8 | 2 | 1 | 0 | 1 | 3 | 1 | 2 | 0 | 0 | 0 | 1 | .000 | 0 | 0-0 | 0 | 11.88 | 18.00 |
| 8 ML YEARS | | | 423 | 0 | 0 | 114 | 433.2 | 1831 | 370 | 182 | 165 | 32 | 19 | 18 | 9 | 189 | 27 | 362 | 28 | 6 | 23 | 21 | .523 | 0 | 9-22 | 65 | 3.22 | 3.42 |

## Wilkin Ramirez

**Bats:** R **Throws:** R **Pos:** PH-12;CF-9;RF-9;LF-8;PR-1 **Ht:** 6'2" **Wt:** 230 **Born:** 10/25/1985 **Age:** 28

| BATTING | | | | | | | | | | | | | | | | | | | | | BASERUNNING | | | | AVERAGES | | |
|---|---|---|---|---|---|---|---|---|---|---|---|---|---|---|---|---|---|---|---|---|---|---|---|---|---|---|---|
| Year | Team | Lg | G | AB | H | 2B | 3B | HR | (Hm | Rd) | TB | R | RBI | RC | TBB | IBB | SO | HBP | SH | SF | SB | CS | SB% | GDP | Avg | OBP | Slg |
| 2013 | FtMyrs* | A+ | 3 | 9 | 1 | 0 | 0 | 0 | (- | -) | 1 | 3 | 0 | 0 | 2 | 0 | 2 | 0 | 0 | 0 | 0 | 0 | - | 0 | .111 | .273 | .111 |
| 2013 | Twins* | R | 4 | 11 | 3 | 1 | 0 | 1 | (- | -) | 7 | 2 | 1 | 2 | 1 | 0 | 2 | 0 | 0 | 0 | 0 | 0 | - | 0 | .273 | .333 | .636 |
| 2013 | NwBrit* | AA | 7 | 29 | 5 | 1 | 0 | 0 | (- | -) | 6 | 3 | 0 | 1 | 2 | 0 | 6 | 0 | 0 | 0 | 1 | 0 | 1.00 | 0 | .172 | .226 | .207 |
| 2009 | Det | AL | 15 | 11 | 4 | 0 | 1 | 1 | (1 | 0) | 9 | 6 | 3 | 3 | 1 | 0 | 3 | 0 | 0 | 1 | 0 | 0 | - | 1 | .364 | .385 | .818 |
| 2011 | Atl | NL | 20 | 26 | 6 | 2 | 0 | 0 | (0 | 0) | 8 | 5 | 2 | 1 | 4 | 0 | 11 | 0 | 0 | 0 | 0 | 2 | .00 | 0 | .231 | .333 | .308 |
| 2013 | Min | AL | 35 | 81 | 22 | 6 | 1 | 0 | (0 | 0) | 30 | 5 | 6 | 7 | 3 | 0 | 23 | 1 | 0 | 1 | 0 | 0 | - | 1 | .272 | .302 | .370 |
| 3 ML YEARS | | | 70 | 118 | 32 | 8 | 2 | 1 | (1 | 0) | 47 | 16 | 11 | 11 | 8 | 0 | 37 | 1 | 0 | 2 | 0 | 2 | .00 | 2 | .271 | .318 | .398 |

## A.J. Ramos

**Pitches:** R **Bats:** R **Pos:** RP-68 **Ht:** 5'10" **Wt:** 210 **Born:** 9/20/1986 **Age:** 27

| HOW MUCH HE PITCHED | | | | | | | | | WHAT HE GAVE UP | | | | | | | | | | | | THE RESULTS | | | | | | | |
|---|---|---|---|---|---|---|---|---|---|---|---|---|---|---|---|---|---|---|---|---|---|---|---|---|---|---|---|---|
| Year | Team | Lg | G | GS | CG | GF | IP | BFP | H | R | ER | HR | SH | SF | HB | TBB | IBB | SO | WP | Bk | W | L | Pct | Sh | Sv-Op | Hld | ERC | ERA |
| 2009 | Jmstwn | A- | 25 | 0 | 0 | 21 | 33.2 | 140 | 22 | 9 | 8 | 0 | 1 | 1 | 3 | 14 | 0 | 50 | 6 | 1 | 2 | 2 | .500 | 0 | 9-- | - | 1.98 | 2.14 |
| 2010 | Grnsbr | A | 49 | 0 | 0 | 45 | 58.1 | 245 | 40 | 26 | 24 | 3 | 1 | 5 | 5 | 32 | 3 | 78 | 7 | 1 | 3 | 7 | .300 | 0 | 28-- | - | 2.89 | 3.70 |
| 2011 | Jupiter | A+ | 49 | 0 | 0 | 48 | 50.2 | 212 | 37 | 12 | 10 | 2 | 1 | 2 | 5 | 19 | 1 | 71 | 4 | 0 | 1 | 4 | .200 | 0 | 25-- | - | 2.46 | 1.78 |
| 2012 | Jaxnvl | AA | 55 | 0 | 0 | 46 | 68.2 | 261 | 36 | 14 | 11 | 3 | 1 | 0 | 0 | 21 | 0 | 89 | 2 | 1 | 3 | 3 | .500 | 0 | 21-- | - | 1.27 | 1.44 |
| 2012 | Mia | NL | 11 | 0 | 0 | 4 | 9.1 | 40 | 8 | 4 | 4 | 2 | 0 | 0 | 1 | 4 | 0 | 13 | 0 | 0 | 0 | 0 | - | 0 | 0-1 | 1 | 4.65 | 3.86 |
| 2013 | Mia | NL | 68 | 0 | 0 | 18 | 80.0 | 338 | 58 | 32 | 28 | 4 | 1 | 3 | 2 | 43 | 3 | 86 | 1 | 0 | 3 | 4 | .429 | 0 | 0-4 | 11 | 2.80 | 3.15 |
| 2 ML YEARS | | | 79 | 0 | 0 | 22 | 89.1 | 378 | 66 | 36 | 32 | 6 | 1 | 3 | 3 | 47 | 3 | 99 | 1 | 0 | 3 | 4 | .429 | 0 | 0-5 | 12 | 2.99 | 3.22 |

## Cesar Ramos

**Pitches:** L **Bats:** L **Pos:** RP-48 **Ht:** 6'2" **Wt:** 205 **Born:** 6/22/1984 **Age:** 30

| HOW MUCH HE PITCHED | | | | | | | | | WHAT HE GAVE UP | | | | | | | | | | | | THE RESULTS | | | | | | | |
|---|---|---|---|---|---|---|---|---|---|---|---|---|---|---|---|---|---|---|---|---|---|---|---|---|---|---|---|---|
| Year | Team | Lg | G | GS | CG | GF | IP | BFP | H | R | ER | HR | SH | SF | HB | TBB | IBB | SO | WP | Bk | W | L | Pct | Sh | Sv-Op | Hld | ERC | ERA |
| 2009 | SD | NL | 5 | 2 | 0 | 0 | 14.2 | 62 | 19 | 5 | 5 | 0 | 0 | 0 | 0 | 4 | 0 | 10 | 0 | 0 | 0 | 1 | .000 | 0 | 0-0 | 0 | 4.78 | 3.07 |
| 2010 | SD | NL | 14 | 0 | 0 | 4 | 8.1 | 47 | 18 | 11 | 11 | 1 | 0 | 0 | 0 | 4 | 0 | 9 | 1 | 1 | 0 | 1 | .000 | 0 | 0-0 | 2 | 11.97 | 11.88 |
| 2011 | TB | AL | 59 | 0 | 0 | 9 | 43.2 | 192 | 36 | 22 | 19 | 4 | 1 | 2 | 3 | 25 | 8 | 31 | 1 | 0 | 0 | 1 | .000 | 0 | 0-2 | 3 | 3.64 | 3.92 |
| 2012 | TB | AL | 17 | 1 | 0 | 9 | 30.0 | 120 | 19 | 7 | 7 | 2 | 0 | 0 | 2 | 10 | 0 | 29 | 0 | 0 | 1 | 0 | 1.000 | 0 | 0-0 | 0 | 1.98 | 2.10 |
| 2013 | TB | AL | 48 | 0 | 0 | 25 | 67.1 | 288 | 66 | 31 | 31 | 6 | 2 | 4 | 2 | 22 | 6 | 53 | 3 | 0 | 2 | 2 | .500 | 0 | 1-1 | 1 | 3.55 | 4.14 |
| 5 ML YEARS | | | 143 | 3 | 0 | 47 | 164.0 | 709 | 158 | 76 | 73 | 13 | 3 | 6 | 7 | 65 | 14 | 132 | 5 | 1 | 3 | 5 | .375 | 0 | 1-3 | 6 | 3.73 | 4.01 |

## Wilson Ramos

**Bats:** R **Throws:** R **Pos:** C-77;PH-1 **Ht:** 6'0" **Wt:** 220 **Born:** 8/10/1987 **Age:** 26

| BATTING | | | | | | | | | | | | | | | | | | | | | BASERUNNING | | | | AVERAGES | | |
|---|---|---|---|---|---|---|---|---|---|---|---|---|---|---|---|---|---|---|---|---|---|---|---|---|---|---|---|
| Year | Team | Lg | G | AB | H | 2B | 3B | HR | (Hm | Rd) | TB | R | RBI | RC | TBB | IBB | SO | HBP | SH | SF | SB | CS | SB% | GDP | Avg | OBP | Slg |
| 2013 | Hrsbrg* | AA | 2 | 4 | 2 | 1 | 0 | 0 | (- | -) | 3 | 1 | 0 | 1 | 1 | 0 | 0 | 0 | 0 | 0 | 0 | 0 | - | 0 | .500 | .600 | .750 |
| 2013 | Nats* | R | 2 | 3 | 0 | 0 | 0 | 0 | (- | -) | 0 | 0 | 0 | 0 | 1 | 0 | 0 | 1 | 0 | 0 | 0 | 0 | - | 0 | .000 | .400 | .000 |
| 2013 | Ptomc* | A+ | 3 | 10 | 0 | 0 | 0 | 0 | (- | -) | 0 | 0 | 0 | 0 | 1 | 0 | 1 | 1 | 0 | 0 | 0 | 0 | - | 0 | .000 | .167 | .000 |
| 2010 | 2 Tms | | 22 | 79 | 22 | 7 | 0 | 1 | (1 | 0) | 32 | 5 | 5 | 10 | 2 | 0 | 12 | 1 | 0 | 0 | 0 | 0 | - | 2 | .278 | .305 | .405 |
| 2011 | Was | NL | 113 | 389 | 104 | 22 | 1 | 15 | (8 | 7) | 173 | 48 | 52 | 43 | 38 | 8 | 76 | 2 | 4 | 2 | 0 | 2 | .00 | 19 | .267 | .334 | .445 |
| 2012 | Was | NL | 25 | 83 | 22 | 2 | 0 | 3 | (1 | 2) | 33 | 11 | 10 | 12 | 12 | 2 | 19 | 0 | 0 | 1 | 0 | 0 | - | 1 | .265 | .354 | .398 |

| BATTING | | | | | | | | | | | | | | | | | | | | | | BASERUNNING | | | | AVERAGES | | |
|---|---|---|---|---|---|---|---|---|---|---|---|---|---|---|---|---|---|---|---|---|---|---|---|---|---|---|---|---|
| Year | Team | Lg | G | AB | H | 2B | 3B | HR | (Hm | Rd) | TB | R | RBI | RC | TBB | IBB | SO | HBP | SH | SF | SB | CS | SB% | GDP | Avg | OBP | Slg |
| 2013 | Was | NL | 78 | 287 | 78 | 9 | 0 | 16 | (6 | 10) | 135 | 29 | 59 | 40 | 15 | 1 | 42 | 0 | 0 | 1 | 0 | 1 | .00 | 12 | .272 | .307 | .470 |
| 10 | Min | AL | 7 | 27 | 8 | 3 | 0 | 0 | (0 | 0) | 11 | 2 | 1 | 3 | 0 | 0 | 3 | 1 | 0 | 0 | 0 | 0 | - | 1 | .296 | .321 | .407 |
| 10 | Was | NL | 15 | 52 | 14 | 4 | 0 | 1 | (1 | 0) | 21 | 3 | 4 | 7 | 2 | 0 | 9 | 0 | 0 | 0 | 0 | 0 | - | 1 | .269 | .296 | .404 |
| 4 ML YEARS | | | 238 | 838 | 226 | 40 | 1 | 35 | (16 | 19) | 373 | 93 | 126 | 105 | 67 | 11 | 149 | 3 | 4 | 4 | 0 | 3 | .00 | 34 | .270 | .325 | .445 |

# Cody Ransom

**Bats:** R **Throws:** R **Pos:** 3B-46;PH-13;1B-4;SS-1 **Ht:** 6'2" **Wt:** 200 **Born:** 2/17/1976 **Age:** 38

| BATTING | | | | | | | | | | | | | | | | | | | | | | BASERUNNING | | | | AVERAGES | | |
|---|---|---|---|---|---|---|---|---|---|---|---|---|---|---|---|---|---|---|---|---|---|---|---|---|---|---|---|---|
| Year | Team | Lg | G | AB | H | 2B | 3B | HR | (Hm | Rd) | TB | R | RBI | RC | TBB | IBB | SO | HBP | SH | SF | SB | CS | SB% | GDP | Avg | OBP | Slg |
| 2001 | SF | NL | 9 | 7 | 0 | 0 | 0 | 0 | (0 | 0) | 0 | 1 | 0 | 0 | 0 | 0 | 5 | 0 | 0 | 0 | 0 | 0 | - | 0 | .000 | .000 | .000 |
| 2002 | SF | NL | 7 | 3 | 2 | 0 | 0 | 0 | (0 | 0) | 2 | 2 | 1 | 1 | 1 | 1 | 1 | 0 | 0 | 0 | 0 | 0 | - | 0 | .667 | .750 | .667 |
| 2003 | SF | NL | 20 | 27 | 6 | 1 | 0 | 1 | (1 | 0) | 10 | 7 | 1 | 1 | 1 | 0 | 11 | 0 | 0 | 0 | 0 | 0 | - | 0 | .222 | .250 | .370 |
| 2004 | SF | NL | 78 | 68 | 17 | 6 | 0 | 1 | (0 | 1) | 26 | 13 | 11 | 9 | 6 | 0 | 20 | 1 | 3 | 0 | 2 | 2 | .50 | 2 | .250 | .320 | .382 |
| 2007 | Hou | NL | 19 | 35 | 8 | 2 | 0 | 1 | (1 | 0) | 13 | 9 | 3 | 6 | 9 | 1 | 9 | 2 | 0 | 0 | 0 | 0 | - | 1 | .229 | .413 | .371 |
| 2008 | NYY | AL | 33 | 43 | 13 | 3 | 0 | 4 | (1 | 3) | 28 | 9 | 8 | 10 | 6 | 0 | 12 | 1 | 1 | 0 | 0 | 0 | - | 0 | .302 | .400 | .651 |
| 2009 | NYY | AL | 31 | 79 | 15 | 9 | 1 | 0 | (0 | 0) | 26 | 11 | 10 | 5 | 7 | 0 | 25 | 0 | 0 | 0 | 2 | 0 | 1.00 | 3 | .190 | .256 | .329 |
| 2010 | Phi | NL | 22 | 42 | 8 | 0 | 0 | 2 | (2 | 0) | 14 | 6 | 5 | 5 | 3 | 0 | 11 | 0 | 1 | 0 | 1 | 0 | 1.00 | 0 | .190 | .244 | .333 |
| 2011 | Ari | NL | 12 | 33 | 5 | 2 | 0 | 1 | (1 | 0) | 10 | 3 | 4 | 2 | 3 | 0 | 9 | 1 | 0 | 0 | 1 | 0 | 1.00 | 3 | .152 | .243 | .303 |
| 2012 | 2 Tms | NL | 90 | 246 | 54 | 14 | 0 | 11 | (6 | 5) | 101 | 29 | 42 | 31 | 30 | 0 | 109 | 3 | 3 | 0 | 0 | 1 | .00 | 6 | .220 | .312 | .411 |
| 2013 | 2 Tms | NL | 62 | 169 | 32 | 10 | 1 | 9 | (6 | 3) | 71 | 21 | 20 | 18 | 22 | 0 | 62 | 1 | 1 | 0 | 0 | 0 | - | 4 | .189 | .286 | .420 |
| 12 | Ari | NL | 26 | 78 | 21 | 7 | 0 | 5 | (3 | 2) | 43 | 11 | 16 | 12 | 7 | 0 | 30 | 3 | 0 | 0 | 0 | 0 | - | 1 | .269 | .352 | .551 |
| 12 | Mil | NL | 64 | 168 | 33 | 7 | 0 | 6 | (3 | 3) | 58 | 18 | 26 | 19 | 23 | 0 | 79 | 0 | 3 | 0 | 0 | 1 | .00 | 5 | .196 | .293 | .345 |
| 13 | SD | NL | 5 | 11 | 0 | 0 | 0 | 0 | (0 | 0) | 0 | 0 | 0 | 0 | 0 | 0 | 5 | 0 | 0 | 0 | 0 | 0 | - | 0 | .000 | .000 | .000 |
| 13 | ChC | NL | 57 | 158 | 32 | 10 | 1 | 9 | (6 | 3) | 71 | 21 | 20 | 18 | 22 | 0 | 57 | 1 | 1 | 0 | 0 | 0 | - | 4 | .203 | .304 | .449 |
| 11 ML YEARS | | | 383 | 752 | 160 | 47 | 2 | 30 | (18 | 12) | 301 | 111 | 105 | 88 | 88 | 2 | 274 | 9 | 9 | 0 | 6 | 3 | .67 | 19 | .213 | .303 | .400 |

# Clay Rapada

**Pitches:** L **Bats:** R **Pos:** RP-4 ruh-PAH-duh **Ht:** 6'5" **Wt:** 195 **Born:** 3/9/1981 **Age:** 33

| HOW MUCH HE PITCHED | | | | | | | | | WHAT HE GAVE UP | | | | | | | | | | | | THE RESULTS | | | | | | | |
|---|---|---|---|---|---|---|---|---|---|---|---|---|---|---|---|---|---|---|---|---|---|---|---|---|---|---|---|---|
| Year | Team | Lg | G | GS | CG | GF | IP | BFP | H | R | ER | HR | SH | SF | HB | TBB | IBB | SO | WP | Bk | W | L | Pct | Sh | Sv-Op | Hld | ERC | ERA |
| 2013 | S-WB* | AAA | 10 | 0 | 0 | 2 | 9.2 | 44 | 13 | 5 | 5 | 1 | 1 | 2 | 0 | 4 | 0 | 4 | 0 | 0 | 1 | 0 | 1.000 | 0 | 1-- | - | 6.35 | 4.66 |
| 2013 | Clmbs* | AAA | 27 | 0 | 0 | 7 | 24.0 | 95 | 18 | 5 | 3 | 1 | 4 | 0 | 0 | 9 | 0 | 20 | 0 | 0 | 0 | 0 | - | 0 | 1-- | - | 2.38 | 1.13 |
| 2007 | 2 Tms | | 5 | 0 | 0 | 2 | 2.2 | 13 | 3 | 3 | 3 | 2 | 0 | 0 | 0 | 2 | 0 | 4 | 2 | 0 | 0 | 0 | - | 0 | 0-0 | 0 | 11.59 | 10.13 |
| 2008 | Det | AL | 25 | 0 | 0 | 3 | 21.1 | 94 | 19 | 11 | 10 | 0 | 1 | 0 | 1 | 14 | 1 | 15 | 1 | 0 | 3 | 0 | 1.000 | 0 | 0-0 | 2 | 3.87 | 4.22 |
| 2009 | Det | AL | 3 | 0 | 0 | 1 | 3.1 | 16 | 4 | 2 | 2 | 1 | 0 | 0 | 0 | 2 | 1 | 2 | 0 | 0 | 0 | 0 | - | 0 | 0-0 | 0 | 7.00 | 5.40 |
| 2010 | Tex | AL | 13 | 0 | 0 | 2 | 9.0 | 39 | 6 | 4 | 4 | 2 | 0 | 0 | 0 | 7 | 1 | 5 | 0 | 0 | 0 | 0 | - | 0 | 0-1 | 3 | 4.42 | 4.00 |
| 2011 | Bal | AL | 32 | 0 | 0 | 4 | 16.1 | 69 | 14 | 11 | 11 | 3 | 0 | 1 | 0 | 7 | 0 | 18 | 0 | 0 | 2 | 0 | 1.000 | 0 | 0-0 | 5 | 3.95 | 6.06 |
| 2012 | NYY | AL | 70 | 0 | 0 | 7 | 38.1 | 155 | 29 | 14 | 12 | 2 | 1 | 1 | 1 | 17 | 1 | 38 | 1 | 2 | 3 | 0 | 1.000 | 0 | 0-0 | 6 | 2.77 | 2.82 |
| 2013 | Cle | AL | 4 | 0 | 0 | 2 | 2.0 | 9 | 1 | 0 | 0 | 0 | 0 | 0 | 0 | 2 | 0 | 0 | 0 | 0 | 0 | 0 | - | 0 | 0-0 | 0 | 2.80 | 0.00 |
| 07 | ChC | NL | 1 | 0 | 0 | 0 | 0.1 | 1 | 0 | 0 | 0 | 0 | 0 | 0 | 0 | 0 | 0 | 0 | 0 | 0 | 0 | 0 | - | 0 | 0-0 | 0 | 0.00 | 0.00 |
| 07 | Det | AL | 4 | 0 | 0 | 2 | 2.1 | 12 | 3 | 3 | 3 | 2 | 0 | 0 | 0 | 2 | 0 | 4 | 2 | 0 | 0 | 0 | - | 0 | 0-0 | 0 | 14.48 | 11.57 |
| Postseason | | | 8 | 0 | 0 | 0 | 2.0 | 10 | 1 | 0 | 0 | 0 | 0 | 0 | 0 | 3 | 1 | 2 | 0 | 0 | 0 | 0 | - | 0 | 0-1 | 0 | 3.47 | 0.00 |
| 7 ML YEARS | | | 152 | 0 | 0 | 21 | 93.0 | 395 | 76 | 45 | 42 | 10 | 2 | 2 | 2 | 51 | 4 | 82 | 4 | 2 | 8 | 0 | 1.000 | 0 | 0-1 | 16 | 3.76 | 4.06 |

# Colby Rasmus

**Bats:** L **Throws:** L **Pos:** CF-114;PH-4 **Ht:** 6'2" **Wt:** 190 **Born:** 8/11/1986 **Age:** 27

| BATTING | | | | | | | | | | | | | | | | | | | | | | BASERUNNING | | | | AVERAGES | | |
|---|---|---|---|---|---|---|---|---|---|---|---|---|---|---|---|---|---|---|---|---|---|---|---|---|---|---|---|---|
| Year | Team | Lg | G | AB | H | 2B | 3B | HR | (Hm | Rd) | TB | R | RBI | RC | TBB | IBB | SO | HBP | SH | SF | SB | CS | SB% | GDP | Avg | OBP | Slg |
| 2009 | StL | NL | 147 | 474 | 119 | 22 | 2 | 16 | (7 | 9) | 193 | 72 | 52 | 60 | 36 | 3 | 95 | 3 | 5 | 2 | 3 | 1 | .75 | 5 | .251 | .307 | .407 |
| 2010 | StL | NL | 144 | 464 | 128 | 28 | 3 | 23 | (11 | 12) | 231 | 85 | 66 | 76 | 63 | 9 | 148 | 1 | 2 | 4 | 12 | 8 | .60 | 5 | .276 | .361 | .498 |
| 2011 | 2 Tms | | 129 | 471 | 106 | 24 | 6 | 14 | (4 | 10) | 184 | 75 | 53 | 50 | 50 | 2 | 116 | 0 | 2 | 3 | 5 | 2 | .71 | 10 | .225 | .298 | .391 |
| 2012 | Tor | AL | 151 | 565 | 126 | 21 | 5 | 23 | (8 | 15) | 226 | 75 | 75 | 74 | 47 | 5 | 149 | 7 | 2 | 4 | 4 | 3 | .57 | 7 | .223 | .289 | .400 |
| 2013 | Tor | AL | 118 | 417 | 115 | 26 | 1 | 22 | (14 | 8) | 209 | 57 | 66 | 76 | 37 | 0 | 135 | 3 | 0 | 1 | 0 | 1 | .00 | 4 | .276 | .338 | .501 |
| 11 | StL | NL | 94 | 338 | 83 | 14 | 6 | 11 | (4 | 7) | 142 | 61 | 40 | 43 | 45 | 2 | 77 | 0 | 1 | 2 | 5 | 2 | .71 | 8 | .246 | .332 | .420 |
| 11 | Tor | AL | 35 | 133 | 23 | 10 | 0 | 3 | (0 | 3) | 42 | 14 | 13 | 7 | 5 | 0 | 39 | 0 | 1 | 1 | 0 | 0 | - | 2 | .173 | .201 | .316 |
| Postseason | | | 3 | 9 | 4 | 3 | 0 | 0 | (0 | 0) | 7 | 1 | 1 | 1 | 2 | 0 | 1 | 0 | 0 | 0 | 0 | 0 | - | 1 | .444 | .545 | .778 |
| 5 ML YEARS | | | 689 | 2391 | 594 | 121 | 17 | 98 | (44 | 54) | 1043 | 364 | 312 | 336 | 233 | 19 | 643 | 14 | 11 | 14 | 24 | 15 | .62 | 31 | .248 | .317 | .436 |

# Cory Rasmus

**Pitches:** R **Bats:** R **Pos:** RP-19 **Ht:** 6'0" **Wt:** 200 **Born:** 11/6/1987 **Age:** 26

| HOW MUCH HE PITCHED | | | | | | | | | WHAT HE GAVE UP | | | | | | | | | | | | THE RESULTS | | | | | | | |
|---|---|---|---|---|---|---|---|---|---|---|---|---|---|---|---|---|---|---|---|---|---|---|---|---|---|---|---|---|
| Year | Team | Lg | G | GS | CG | GF | IP | BFP | H | R | ER | HR | SH | SF | HB | TBB | IBB | SO | WP | Bk | W | L | Pct | Sh | Sv-Op | Hld | ERC | ERA |
| 2009 | Danvle | R | 13 | 6 | 1 | 2 | 51.2 | 215 | 34 | 21 | 20 | 1 | 3 | 0 | 5 | 26 | 2 | 57 | 3 | 0 | 4 | 2 | .667 | 1 | 1-- | - | 2.42 | 3.48 |
| 2010 | Rome | A | 20 | 12 | 0 | 3 | 83.0 | 353 | 77 | 39 | 29 | 6 | 2 | 2 | 2 | 29 | 0 | 72 | 6 | 0 | 6 | 6 | .500 | 0 | 1-- | - | 3.36 | 3.14 |
| 2010 | MrtlBh | A+ | 8 | 8 | 0 | 0 | 41.1 | 183 | 38 | 19 | 15 | 3 | 3 | 2 | 6 | 18 | 0 | 30 | 1 | 0 | 0 | 3 | .000 | 0 | 0-- | - | 4.10 | 3.27 |
| 2011 | Lynbrg | A+ | 7 | 7 | 0 | 0 | 26.2 | 123 | 28 | 28 | 21 | 5 | 1 | 0 | 4 | 12 | 0 | 40 | 5 | 0 | 1 | 5 | .167 | 0 | 0-- | - | 5.77 | 7.09 |
| 2011 | Braves | R | 1 | 0 | 0 | 0 | 0.2 | 5 | 2 | 2 | 2 | 0 | 0 | 0 | 0 | 1 | 0 | 2 | 0 | 0 | 0 | 0 | - | 0 | 0-- | - | 22.07 | 27.00 |
| 2012 | Missi | AA | 50 | 0 | 0 | 27 | 58.2 | 247 | 45 | 24 | 24 | 3 | 3 | 5 | 2 | 32 | 2 | 62 | 3 | 0 | 3 | 5 | .375 | 0 | 7-- | - | 3.15 | 3.68 |
| 2013 | Gwnntt | AAA | 37 | 0 | 0 | 30 | 36.2 | 148 | 20 | 8 | 7 | 2 | 0 | 0 | 1 | 22 | 0 | 48 | 1 | 0 | 3 | 1 | .750 | 0 | 14-- | - | 2.30 | 1.72 |
| 2013 | Salt Lk | AAA | 9 | 0 | 0 | 6 | 9.2 | 40 | 6 | 3 | 3 | 0 | 0 | 0 | 0 | 5 | 0 | 8 | 1 | 1 | 1 | 1 | .500 | 0 | 3-- | - | 1.87 | 2.79 |
| 2013 | 2 Tms | | 19 | 0 | 0 | 6 | 21.2 | 103 | 24 | 15 | 13 | 6 | 0 | 1 | 0 | 13 | 2 | 20 | 0 | 1 | 1 | 1 | .500 | 0 | 0-1 | 2 | 6.55 | 5.40 |
| 13 | Atl | NL | 3 | 0 | 0 | 2 | 6.2 | 31 | 8 | 6 | 6 | 4 | 0 | 0 | 0 | 3 | 0 | 6 | 0 | 0 | 0 | 0 | - | 0 | 0-0 | 0 | 9.21 | 8.10 |
| 13 | LAA | AL | 16 | 0 | 0 | 4 | 15.0 | 72 | 16 | 9 | 7 | 2 | 0 | 1 | 0 | 10 | 2 | 14 | 0 | 1 | 1 | 1 | .500 | 0 | 0-1 | 2 | 5.34 | 4.20 |

## Jon Rauch

**Pitches:** R **Bats:** R **Pos:** RP-15 RAUSH **Ht:** 6'11" **Wt:** 290 **Born:** 9/27/1978 **Age:** 35

| | | | HOW MUCH HE PITCHED | | | | | | WHAT HE GAVE UP | | | | | | | | | | | | THE RESULTS | | | | | | | |
|---|---|---|---|---|---|---|---|---|---|---|---|---|---|---|---|---|---|---|---|---|---|---|---|---|---|---|---|---|
| Year | Team | Lg | G | GS | CG | GF | IP | BFP | H | R | ER | HR | SH | SF | HB | TBB | IBB | SO | WP | Bk | W | L | Pct | Sh | Sv-Op | Hld | ERC | ERA |
| 2013 | Norfolk* | AAA | 10 | 0 | 0 | 5 | 9.1 | 40 | 9 | 3 | 3 | 2 | 1 | 0 | 0 | 4 | 1 | 10 | 2 | 0 | 1 | 0 | 1.000 | 0 | 0-- | - | 4.65 | 2.89 |
| 2002 | CWS | AL | 8 | 6 | 0 | 1 | 28.2 | 130 | 28 | 26 | 21 | 7 | 0 | 1 | 2 | 14 | 2 | 19 | 1 | 1 | 2 | 1 | .667 | 0 | 0-0 | 0 | 5.41 | 6.59 |
| 2004 | 2 Tms | | 11 | 4 | 0 | 1 | 32.0 | 131 | 30 | 10 | 10 | 1 | 2 | 1 | 0 | 11 | 2 | 22 | 2 | 0 | 4 | 1 | .800 | 0 | 0-0 | 0 | 3.05 | 2.81 |
| 2005 | Was | NL | 15 | 1 | 0 | 4 | 30.0 | 124 | 24 | 12 | 12 | 3 | 1 | 1 | 1 | 11 | 2 | 23 | 2 | 0 | 2 | 4 | .333 | 0 | 0-0 | 0 | 2.90 | 3.60 |
| 2006 | Was | NL | 85 | 0 | 0 | 19 | 91.1 | 383 | 78 | 37 | 34 | 13 | 1 | 6 | 2 | 36 | 6 | 86 | 4 | 1 | 4 | 5 | .444 | 0 | 2-5 | 18 | 3.52 | 3.35 |
| 2007 | Was | NL | **88** | 0 | 0 | 26 | 87.1 | 354 | 75 | 37 | 35 | 7 | 2 | 5 | 0 | 21 | 4 | 71 | 2 | 0 | 8 | 4 | .667 | 0 | 4-10 | 33 | 2.53 | 3.61 |
| 2008 | 2 Tms | NL | 74 | 0 | 0 | 51 | 71.2 | 295 | 69 | 36 | 33 | 11 | 6 | 3 | 0 | 16 | 2 | 66 | 1 | 0 | 4 | 8 | .333 | 0 | 18-24 | 6 | 3.48 | 4.14 |
| 2009 | 2 Tms | | 75 | 0 | 0 | 15 | 70.0 | 299 | 70 | 30 | 28 | 6 | 3 | 4 | 2 | 23 | 1 | 49 | 6 | 0 | 7 | 3 | .700 | 0 | 2-5 | 17 | 3.78 | 3.60 |
| 2010 | Min | AL | 59 | 0 | 0 | 41 | 57.2 | 245 | 61 | 20 | 20 | 3 | 1 | 1 | 1 | 14 | 0 | 46 | 1 | 0 | 3 | 1 | .750 | 0 | 21-25 | 2 | 3.50 | 3.12 |
| 2011 | Tor | AL | 53 | 0 | 0 | 28 | 52.0 | 225 | 56 | 28 | 28 | 11 | 2 | 0 | 1 | 14 | 1 | 36 | 2 | 0 | 5 | 4 | .556 | 0 | 11-16 | 4 | 4.75 | 4.85 |
| 2012 | NYM | NL | 73 | 0 | 0 | 22 | 57.2 | 233 | 45 | 28 | 23 | 7 | 1 | 4 | 1 | 12 | 2 | 42 | 1 | 0 | 3 | 7 | .300 | 0 | 4-8 | 16 | 2.30 | 3.59 |
| 2013 | Mia | NL | 15 | 0 | 0 | 6 | 16.2 | 80 | 23 | 14 | 14 | 1 | 2 | 0 | 1 | 7 | 3 | 15 | 1 | 0 | 1 | 2 | .333 | 0 | 0-0 | 1 | 5.91 | 7.56 |
| 04 | CWS | AL | 2 | 2 | 0 | 0 | 8.2 | 43 | 16 | 6 | 6 | 0 | 1 | 1 | 0 | 4 | 0 | 4 | 1 | 0 | 1 | 1 | .500 | 0 | 0-0 | 0 | 9.15 | 6.23 |
| 04 | Mon | NL | 9 | 2 | 0 | 1 | 23.1 | 88 | 14 | 4 | 4 | 1 | 1 | 0 | 0 | 7 | 2 | 18 | 1 | 0 | 3 | 0 | 1.000 | 0 | 0-0 | 0 | 1.44 | 1.54 |
| 08 | Was | NL | 48 | 0 | 0 | 41 | 48.1 | 192 | 42 | 18 | 16 | 5 | 3 | 1 | 0 | 7 | 1 | 44 | 0 | 0 | 4 | 2 | .667 | 0 | 17-22 | 0 | 2.41 | 2.98 |
| 08 | Ari | NL | 26 | 0 | 0 | 10 | 23.1 | 103 | 27 | 18 | 17 | 6 | 3 | 2 | 0 | 9 | 1 | 22 | 1 | 0 | 0 | 6 | .000 | 0 | 1-2 | 6 | 6.09 | 6.56 |
| 09 | Ari | NL | 58 | 0 | 0 | 13 | 54.1 | 235 | 57 | 27 | 25 | 5 | 1 | 2 | 1 | 17 | 0 | 35 | 6 | 0 | 2 | 2 | .500 | 0 | 2-3 | 12 | 3.98 | 4.14 |
| 09 | Min | AL | 17 | 0 | 0 | 2 | 15.2 | 64 | 13 | 3 | 3 | 1 | 2 | 2 | 1 | 6 | 1 | 14 | 0 | 0 | 5 | 1 | .833 | 0 | 0-2 | 5 | 3.09 | 1.72 |
| Postseason | | | 5 | 0 | 0 | 1 | 3.0 | 12 | 1 | 1 | 1 | 0 | 0 | 0 | 0 | 2 | 0 | 1 | 0 | 0 | 0 | 0 | - | 0 | 0-0 | 0 | 1.26 | 3.00 |
| 11 ML YEARS | | | 556 | 11 | 0 | 214 | 595.0 | 2499 | 559 | 278 | 258 | 70 | 21 | 26 | 11 | 179 | 25 | 475 | 23 | 2 | 43 | 40 | .518 | 0 | 62-93 | 97 | 3.46 | 3.90 |

## Anthony Recker

**Bats:** R **Throws:** R **Pos:** C-38;PH-11;DH-1;PR-1 **Ht:** 6'2" **Wt:** 240 **Born:** 8/29/1983 **Age:** 30

| | | | BATTING | | | | | | | | | | | | | | | | | | BASERUNNING | | | | AVERAGES | | |
|---|---|---|---|---|---|---|---|---|---|---|---|---|---|---|---|---|---|---|---|---|---|---|---|---|---|---|---|
| Year | Team | Lg | G | AB | H | 2B | 3B | HR | (Hm | Rd) | TB | R | RBI | RC | TBB | IBB | SO | HBP | SH | SF | SB | CS | SB% | GDP | Avg | OBP | Slg |
| 2013 | LsVgs* | AAA | 5 | 10 | 4 | 0 | 1 | 1 | (- | -) | 9 | 3 | 4 | 3 | 2 | 0 | 2 | 0 | 0 | 0 | 0 | 0 | - | 0 | .400 | .500 | .900 |
| 2011 | Oak | AL | 5 | 17 | 3 | 1 | 0 | 0 | (0 | 0) | 4 | 3 | 0 | 0 | 4 | 0 | 7 | 0 | 0 | 0 | 0 | 0 | - | 0 | .176 | .333 | .235 |
| 2012 | 2 Tms | | 22 | 49 | 7 | 2 | 0 | 1 | (0 | 1) | 12 | 4 | 4 | 0 | 6 | 0 | 15 | 2 | 1 | 0 | 0 | 0 | - | 1 | .143 | .263 | .245 |
| 2013 | NYM | NL | 50 | 135 | 29 | 7 | 0 | 6 | (4 | 2) | 54 | 17 | 19 | 13 | 13 | 1 | 49 | 0 | 1 | 2 | 0 | 1 | .00 | 1 | .215 | .280 | .400 |
| 12 | Oak | AL | 13 | 31 | 4 | 1 | 0 | 0 | (0 | 0) | 5 | 3 | 0 | 0 | 4 | 0 | 13 | 1 | 1 | 0 | 0 | 0 | - | 0 | .129 | .250 | .161 |
| 12 | ChC | NL | 9 | 18 | 3 | 1 | 0 | 1 | (0 | 1) | 7 | 1 | 4 | 0 | 2 | 0 | 2 | 1 | 0 | 0 | 0 | 0 | - | 1 | .167 | .286 | .389 |
| 3 ML YEARS | | | 77 | 201 | 39 | 10 | 0 | 7 | (4 | 3) | 70 | 24 | 23 | 13 | 23 | 1 | 71 | 2 | 2 | 2 | 0 | 1 | .00 | 2 | .194 | .281 | .348 |

## Josh Reddick

**Bats:** L **Throws:** R **Pos:** RF-113;PH-2;DH-1 **Ht:** 6'2" **Wt:** 180 **Born:** 2/19/1987 **Age:** 27

| | | | BATTING | | | | | | | | | | | | | | | | | | BASERUNNING | | | | AVERAGES | | |
|---|---|---|---|---|---|---|---|---|---|---|---|---|---|---|---|---|---|---|---|---|---|---|---|---|---|---|---|
| Year | Team | Lg | G | AB | H | 2B | 3B | HR | (Hm | Rd) | TB | R | RBI | RC | TBB | IBB | SO | HBP | SH | SF | SB | CS | SB% | GDP | Avg | OBP | Slg |
| 2013 | Stcktn* | A+ | 1 | 3 | 1 | 0 | 0 | 0 | (- | -) | 1 | 0 | 0 | 0 | 0 | 0 | 0 | 0 | 0 | 0 | 0 | 0 | - | 0 | .333 | .333 | .333 |
| 2013 | Scrmto* | AAA | 3 | 11 | 2 | 0 | 0 | 0 | (- | -) | 2 | 5 | 0 | 1 | 3 | 0 | 1 | 0 | 0 | 0 | 2 | 0 | 1.00 | 1 | .182 | .357 | .182 |
| 2009 | Bos | AL | 27 | 59 | 10 | 4 | 0 | 2 | (0 | 2) | 20 | 5 | 4 | 4 | 2 | 0 | 17 | 1 | 0 | 0 | 0 | 0 | - | 0 | .169 | .210 | .339 |
| 2010 | Bos | AL | 29 | 62 | 12 | 3 | 1 | 1 | (1 | 0) | 20 | 5 | 5 | 1 | 1 | 0 | 15 | 0 | 0 | 0 | 1 | 0 | 1.00 | 1 | .194 | .206 | .323 |
| 2011 | Bos | AL | 87 | 254 | 71 | 18 | 3 | 7 | (2 | 5) | 116 | 41 | 28 | 33 | 19 | 1 | 50 | 1 | 0 | 4 | 1 | 2 | .33 | 1 | .280 | .327 | .457 |
| 2012 | Oak | AL | 156 | 611 | 148 | 29 | 5 | 32 | (18 | 14) | 283 | 85 | 85 | 73 | 55 | 8 | 151 | 2 | 1 | 4 | 11 | 1 | .92 | 15 | .242 | .305 | .463 |
| 2013 | Oak | AL | 114 | 385 | 87 | 19 | 2 | 12 | (2 | 10) | 146 | 54 | 56 | 53 | 46 | 1 | 86 | 2 | 1 | 7 | 9 | 2 | .82 | 4 | .226 | .307 | .379 |
| Postseason | | | 5 | 17 | 2 | 0 | 0 | 1 | (0 | 1) | 5 | 2 | 1 | 0 | 1 | 0 | 10 | 0 | 0 | 0 | 0 | 0 | - | 1 | .118 | .167 | .294 |
| 5 ML YEARS | | | 413 | 1371 | 328 | 73 | 11 | 54 | (23 | 31) | 585 | 190 | 178 | 164 | 123 | 10 | 319 | 6 | 2 | 15 | 22 | 5 | .81 | 21 | .239 | .302 | .427 |

## Todd Redmond

**Pitches:** R **Bats:** R **Pos:** SP-14; RP-3 **Ht:** 6'3" **Wt:** 235 **Born:** 5/17/1985 **Age:** 29

| | | | HOW MUCH HE PITCHED | | | | | | WHAT HE GAVE UP | | | | | | | | | | | | THE RESULTS | | | | | | | |
|---|---|---|---|---|---|---|---|---|---|---|---|---|---|---|---|---|---|---|---|---|---|---|---|---|---|---|---|---|
| Year | Team | Lg | G | GS | CG | GF | IP | BFP | H | R | ER | HR | SH | SF | HB | TBB | IBB | SO | WP | Bk | W | L | Pct | Sh | Sv-Op | Hld | ERC | ERA |
| 2009 | Gwnntt | AAA | 27 | 24 | 0 | 0 | 145.0 | 635 | 152 | 85 | 71 | 21 | 6 | 9 | 7 | 47 | 1 | 106 | 1 | 0 | 9 | 6 | .600 | 0 | 0-- | - | 4.49 | 4.41 |
| 2010 | Gwnntt | AAA | 28 | 28 | 1 | 0 | 162.2 | 679 | 156 | 86 | 77 | 21 | 3 | 6 | 1 | 44 | 0 | 142 | 1 | 0 | 9 | 10 | .474 | 1 | 0-- | - | 3.55 | 4.26 |
| 2011 | Gwnntt | AAA | 28 | 27 | 2 | 1 | 169.2 | 693 | 152 | 58 | 55 | 18 | 3 | 4 | 8 | 47 | 0 | 142 | 1 | 1 | 10 | 8 | .556 | 1 | 0-- | - | 3.31 | 2.92 |
| 2012 | Gwnntt | AAA | 18 | 18 | 1 | 0 | 105.2 | 446 | 107 | 50 | 42 | 11 | 4 | 2 | 2 | 28 | 5 | 96 | 1 | 0 | 6 | 6 | .500 | 1 | 0-- | - | 3.64 | 3.58 |
| 2012 | Lsvlle | AAA | 8 | 7 | 0 | 0 | 43.0 | 178 | 43 | 21 | 18 | 7 | 1 | 0 | 1 | 11 | 0 | 40 | 0 | 0 | 2 | 5 | .286 | 0 | 0-- | - | 4.09 | 3.77 |
| 2013 | Buffalo | AAA | 6 | 5 | 0 | 0 | 26.2 | 109 | 29 | 15 | 15 | 2 | 1 | 1 | 0 | 5 | 0 | 29 | 0 | 0 | 3 | 1 | .750 | 0 | 0-- | - | 3.66 | 5.06 |
| 2012 | Cin | NL | 1 | 1 | 0 | 0 | 3.1 | 22 | 7 | 4 | 4 | 1 | 0 | 0 | 0 | 5 | 0 | 2 | 0 | 0 | 0 | 1 | .000 | 0 | 0-0 | 0 | 18.68 | 10.80 |
| 2013 | Tor | AL | 17 | 14 | 0 | 2 | 77.0 | 324 | 70 | 38 | 37 | 13 | 1 | 1 | 6 | 23 | 2 | 76 | 1 | 0 | 4 | 3 | .571 | 0 | 0-0 | 0 | 3.91 | 4.32 |
| 2 ML YEARS | | | 18 | 15 | 0 | 2 | 80.1 | 346 | 77 | 42 | 41 | 14 | 1 | 1 | 6 | 28 | 2 | 78 | 1 | 0 | 4 | 4 | .500 | 0 | 0-0 | 0 | 4.40 | 4.59 |

## Addison Reed

**Pitches:** R **Bats:** L **Pos:** RP-68 **Ht:** 6'4" **Wt:** 220 **Born:** 12/27/1988 **Age:** 25

| | | | HOW MUCH HE PITCHED | | | | | | WHAT HE GAVE UP | | | | | | | | | | | | THE RESULTS | | | | | | | |
|---|---|---|---|---|---|---|---|---|---|---|---|---|---|---|---|---|---|---|---|---|---|---|---|---|---|---|---|---|
| Year | Team | Lg | G | GS | CG | GF | IP | BFP | H | R | ER | HR | SH | SF | HB | TBB | IBB | SO | WP | Bk | W | L | Pct | Sh | Sv-Op | Hld | ERC | ERA |
| 2011 | CWS | AL | 6 | 0 | 0 | 2 | 7.1 | 33 | 10 | 3 | 3 | 1 | 0 | 0 | 0 | 1 | 0 | 12 | 0 | 0 | 0 | 0 | - | 0 | 0-0 | 0 | 5.24 | 3.68 |
| 2012 | CWS | AL | 62 | 0 | 0 | 44 | 55.0 | 238 | 57 | 30 | 29 | 6 | 0 | 4 | 2 | 18 | 3 | 54 | 0 | 1 | 3 | 2 | .600 | 0 | 29-33 | 4 | 4.09 | 4.75 |
| 2013 | CWS | AL | 68 | 0 | 0 | 59 | 71.1 | 295 | 56 | 31 | 30 | 6 | 3 | 6 | 2 | 23 | 2 | 72 | 2 | 0 | 5 | 4 | .556 | 0 | 40-48 | 0 | 2.56 | 3.79 |
| 3 ML YEARS | | | 136 | 0 | 0 | 105 | 133.2 | 566 | 123 | 64 | 62 | 13 | 3 | 10 | 4 | 42 | 5 | 138 | 2 | 1 | 8 | 6 | .571 | 0 | 69-81 | 4 | 3.30 | 4.17 |

# Evan Reed

**Pitches:** R **Bats:** R **Pos:** RP-16 **Ht:** 6'4" **Wt:** 255 **Born:** 12/31/1985 **Age:** 28

| HOW MUCH HE PITCHED | | | | | | | | | WHAT HE GAVE UP | | | | | | | | | | | | THE RESULTS | | | | | | | |
|---|---|---|---|---|---|---|---|---|---|---|---|---|---|---|---|---|---|---|---|---|---|---|---|---|---|---|---|---|
| Year | Team | Lg | G | GS | CG | GF | IP | BFP | H | R | ER | HR | SH | SF | HB | TBB | IBB | SO | WP | Bk | W | L | Pct | Sh | Sv-Op | Hld | ERC | ERA |
| 2009 | Bkrsfld | A+ | 46 | 0 | 0 | 41 | 48.2 | 213 | 44 | 17 | 16 | 1 | 3 | 1 | 1 | 28 | 3 | 65 | 5 | 0 | 2 | 2 | .500 | 0 | 25- - | - | 3.63 | 2.96 |
| 2010 | Frisco | AA | 30 | 0 | 0 | 15 | 39.0 | 160 | 35 | 7 | 7 | 0 | 0 | 0 | 0 | 13 | 0 | 34 | 3 | 0 | 1 | 1 | .500 | 0 | 5- - | - | 2.65 | 1.62 |
| 2010 | OKCity | AAA | 1 | 0 | 0 | 0 | 2.0 | 7 | 1 | 1 | 1 | 1 | 0 | 0 | 0 | 0 | 0 | 2 | 0 | 0 | 1 | 0 | 1.000 | 0 | 0- - | - | 1.73 | 4.50 |
| 2010 | Jaxnvl | AA | 1 | 0 | 0 | 0 | 1.2 | 6 | 1 | 0 | 0 | 0 | 0 | 0 | 0 | 1 | 0 | 1 | 0 | 0 | 0 | 0 | - | 0 | 0- - | - | 2.46 | 0.00 |
| 2011 | Mrlns | R | 8 | 3 | 0 | 0 | 8.2 | 38 | 15 | 4 | 3 | 0 | 0 | 0 | 0 | 0 | 0 | 11 | 1 | 0 | 0 | 0 | - | 0 | 0- - | - | 6.31 | 3.12 |
| 2011 | Jupiter | A+ | 11 | 0 | 0 | 1 | 15.2 | 63 | 9 | 7 | 7 | 0 | 0 | 1 | 1 | 10 | 1 | 13 | 2 | 0 | 0 | 1 | .000 | 0 | 0- - | - | 2.29 | 4.02 |
| 2012 | Jaxnvl | AA | 27 | 0 | 0 | 23 | 34.2 | 137 | 24 | 10 | 9 | 1 | 1 | 2 | 0 | 11 | 0 | 43 | 1 | 0 | 3 | 1 | .750 | 0 | 12- - | - | 1.79 | 2.34 |
| 2012 | NewOr | AAA | 23 | 0 | 0 | 7 | 32.2 | 156 | 43 | 27 | 26 | 2 | 0 | 2 | 0 | 16 | 2 | 27 | 3 | 0 | 2 | 3 | .400 | 0 | 1- - | - | 5.77 | 7.16 |
| 2013 | Toledo | AAA | 32 | 0 | 0 | 11 | 49.2 | 195 | 38 | 17 | 14 | 1 | 2 | 1 | 0 | 20 | 0 | 49 | 4 | 1 | 1 | 4 | .200 | 0 | 1- - | - | 2.46 | 2.54 |
| 2013 | Det | AL | 16 | 0 | 0 | 10 | 23.1 | 105 | 28 | 16 | 11 | 2 | 1 | 2 | 1 | 8 | 0 | 17 | 1 | 1 | 0 | 1 | .000 | 0 | 0-0 | 0 | 5.04 | 4.24 |

# Ryan Reid

**Pitches:** R **Bats:** L **Pos:** RP-7 **Ht:** 5'11" **Wt:** 210 **Born:** 4/24/1985 **Age:** 29

| HOW MUCH HE PITCHED | | | | | | | | | WHAT HE GAVE UP | | | | | | | | | | | | THE RESULTS | | | | | | | |
|---|---|---|---|---|---|---|---|---|---|---|---|---|---|---|---|---|---|---|---|---|---|---|---|---|---|---|---|---|
| Year | Team | Lg | G | GS | CG | GF | IP | BFP | H | R | ER | HR | SH | SF | HB | TBB | IBB | SO | WP | Bk | W | L | Pct | Sh | Sv-Op | Hld | ERC | ERA |
| 2009 | Mont | AA | 42 | 0 | 0 | 19 | 58.1 | 258 | 65 | 32 | 27 | 3 | 1 | 4 | 2 | 28 | 1 | 50 | 5 | 0 | 0 | 1 | .000 | 0 | 1- - | - | 4.90 | 4.17 |
| 2010 | Mont | AA | 43 | 0 | 0 | 20 | 72.1 | 325 | 71 | 39 | 33 | 2 | 3 | 4 | 6 | 39 | 3 | 61 | 13 | 0 | 3 | 3 | .500 | 0 | 2- - | - | 4.22 | 4.11 |
| 2011 | Mont | AA | 9 | 0 | 0 | 2 | 16.0 | 77 | 27 | 12 | 12 | 4 | 0 | 0 | 3 | 4 | 1 | 12 | 2 | 0 | 2 | 0 | 1.000 | 0 | 1- - | - | 10.19 | 6.75 |
| 2011 | Drham | AAA | 26 | 5 | 0 | 4 | 55.1 | 237 | 58 | 31 | 28 | 5 | 1 | 2 | 2 | 18 | 0 | 51 | 2 | 0 | 1 | 1 | .500 | 0 | 0- - | - | 4.16 | 4.55 |
| 2012 | Drham | AAA | 46 | 3 | 0 | 14 | 79.1 | 336 | 75 | 36 | 31 | 8 | 2 | 0 | 3 | 28 | 2 | 79 | 4 | 0 | 6 | 3 | .667 | 0 | 1- - | - | 3.72 | 3.52 |
| 2013 | Indy | AAA | 36 | 0 | 0 | 9 | 59.1 | 245 | 49 | 22 | 18 | 4 | 1 | 1 | 1 | 22 | 0 | 56 | 4 | 1 | 7 | 2 | .778 | 0 | 2- - | - | 2.89 | 2.73 |
| 2013 | Pit | NL | 7 | 0 | 0 | 3 | 11.0 | 47 | 9 | 2 | 2 | 1 | 2 | 1 | 2 | 3 | 1 | 7 | 0 | 0 | 0 | 0 | - | 0 | 1-2 | 0 | 3.03 | 1.64 |

# Nolan Reimold

**Bats:** R **Throws:** R **Pos:** DH-28;LF-11;PH-2 RYE-mold **Ht:** 6'4" **Wt:** 205 **Born:** 10/12/1983 **Age:** 30

| BATTING | | | | | | | | | | | | | | | | | | | | | BASERUNNING | | | | AVERAGES | | |
|---|---|---|---|---|---|---|---|---|---|---|---|---|---|---|---|---|---|---|---|---|---|---|---|---|---|---|---|
| Year | Team | Lg | G | AB | H | 2B | 3B | HR | (Hm | Rd) | TB | R | RBI | RC | TBB | IBB | SO | HBP | SH | SF | SB | CS | SB% | GDP | Avg | OBP | Slg |
| 2013 | Bowie* | AA | 12 | 46 | 9 | 0 | 1 | 1 | (- | -) | 14 | 3 | 5 | 3 | 4 | 0 | 13 | 0 | 0 | 1 | 0 | 0 | - | 2 | .196 | .255 | .304 |
| 2009 | Bal | AL | 104 | 358 | 100 | 18 | 2 | 15 | (8 | 7) | 167 | 49 | 45 | 57 | 47 | 1 | 77 | 3 | 0 | 3 | 8 | 2 | .80 | 8 | .279 | .365 | .466 |
| 2010 | Bal | AL | 39 | 116 | 24 | 5 | 0 | 3 | (0 | 3) | 38 | 9 | 14 | 6 | 12 | 0 | 26 | 1 | 0 | 2 | 0 | 0 | - | 6 | .207 | .282 | .328 |
| 2011 | Bal | AL | 87 | 267 | 66 | 10 | 3 | 13 | (8 | 5) | 121 | 40 | 45 | 48 | 28 | 1 | 57 | 6 | 0 | 4 | 7 | 2 | .78 | 4 | .247 | .328 | .453 |
| 2012 | Bal | AL | 16 | 67 | 21 | 6 | 0 | 5 | (0 | 5) | 42 | 10 | 10 | 15 | 2 | 0 | 14 | 0 | 0 | 0 | 1 | 0 | 1.00 | 3 | .313 | .333 | .627 |
| 2013 | Bal | AL | 40 | 128 | 25 | 3 | 0 | 5 | (3 | 2) | 43 | 17 | 12 | 7 | 10 | 2 | 41 | 0 | 0 | 2 | 0 | 1 | .00 | 4 | .195 | .250 | .336 |
| 5 ML YEARS | | | 286 | 936 | 236 | 42 | 5 | 41 | (19 | 22) | 411 | 125 | 126 | 133 | 99 | 4 | 215 | 10 | 0 | 11 | 16 | 5 | .76 | 25 | .252 | .327 | .439 |

# Anthony Rendon

**Bats:** R **Throws:** R **Pos:** 2B-82;3B-15;SS-4;PH-2 ren-DOAN **Ht:** 6'0" **Wt:** 195 **Born:** 6/6/1990 **Age:** 24

| BATTING | | | | | | | | | | | | | | | | | | | | | BASERUNNING | | | | AVERAGES | | |
|---|---|---|---|---|---|---|---|---|---|---|---|---|---|---|---|---|---|---|---|---|---|---|---|---|---|---|---|
| Year | Team | Lg | G | AB | H | 2B | 3B | HR | (Hm | Rd) | TB | R | RBI | RC | TBB | IBB | SO | HBP | SH | SF | SB | CS | SB% | GDP | Avg | OBP | Slg |
| 2012 | Ptomc | A+ | 9 | 27 | 9 | 2 | 3 | 0 | (- | -) | 17 | 5 | 0 | 7 | 5 | 0 | 4 | 0 | 0 | 0 | 0 | 0 | - | 0 | .333 | .438 | .630 |
| 2012 | Nats | R | 5 | 11 | 4 | 1 | 0 | 2 | (- | -) | 11 | 2 | 6 | 4 | 3 | 0 | 3 | 0 | 0 | 0 | 0 | 0 | - | 0 | .364 | .500 | 1.000 |
| 2012 | Auburn | A- | 8 | 27 | 7 | 2 | 0 | 1 | (- | -) | 12 | 7 | 3 | 4 | 4 | 0 | 6 | 1 | 0 | 0 | 0 | 0 | - | 0 | .259 | .375 | .444 |
| 2012 | Hrsbrg | AA | 21 | 68 | 11 | 3 | 1 | 3 | (- | -) | 25 | 14 | 3 | 8 | 11 | 0 | 16 | 3 | 0 | 0 | 0 | 0 | - | 3 | .162 | .305 | .368 |
| 2013 | Hrsbrg | AA | 33 | 116 | 37 | 11 | 2 | 6 | (- | -) | 70 | 17 | 24 | 33 | 30 | 0 | 25 | 3 | 0 | 3 | 1 | 0 | 1.00 | 1 | .319 | .461 | .603 |
| 2013 | Syrcse | AAA | 3 | 11 | 2 | 1 | 0 | 0 | (- | -) | 3 | 2 | 0 | 1 | 2 | 0 | 3 | 1 | 0 | 0 | 0 | 0 | - | 0 | .182 | .357 | .273 |
| 2013 | Was | NL | 98 | 351 | 93 | 23 | 1 | 7 | (3 | 4) | 139 | 40 | 35 | 43 | 31 | 3 | 69 | 5 | 2 | 5 | 1 | 1 | .50 | 7 | .265 | .329 | .396 |

# Chris Resop

**Pitches:** R **Bats:** R **Pos:** RP-18 REE-sawp **Ht:** 6'3" **Wt:** 225 **Born:** 11/4/1982 **Age:** 31

| HOW MUCH HE PITCHED | | | | | | | | | WHAT HE GAVE UP | | | | | | | | | | | | THE RESULTS | | | | | | | |
|---|---|---|---|---|---|---|---|---|---|---|---|---|---|---|---|---|---|---|---|---|---|---|---|---|---|---|---|---|
| Year | Team | Lg | G | GS | CG | GF | IP | BFP | H | R | ER | HR | SH | SF | HB | TBB | IBB | SO | WP | Bk | W | L | Pct | Sh | Sv-Op | Hld | ERC | ERA |
| 2013 | Scrmto* | AAA | 26 | 1 | 0 | 9 | 35.2 | 165 | 48 | 27 | 27 | 5 | 0 | 1 | 2 | 13 | 0 | 29 | 2 | 0 | 1 | 2 | .333 | 0 | 0- - | - | 6.59 | 6.81 |
| 2005 | Fla | NL | 15 | 0 | 0 | 6 | 17.0 | 80 | 22 | 16 | 16 | 1 | 0 | 2 | 1 | 9 | 0 | 15 | 3 | 0 | 2 | 0 | 1.000 | 0 | 0-0 | 0 | 6.35 | 8.47 |
| 2006 | Fla | NL | 22 | 0 | 0 | 10 | 21.1 | 101 | 26 | 9 | 8 | 1 | 0 | 0 | 1 | 16 | 5 | 10 | 0 | 0 | 1 | 2 | .333 | 0 | 0-1 | 2 | 6.30 | 3.38 |
| 2007 | LAA | AL | 4 | 0 | 0 | 3 | 4.1 | 17 | 4 | 2 | 2 | 1 | 2 | 1 | 0 | 1 | 0 | 2 | 0 | 0 | 0 | 0 | - | 0 | 0-0 | 0 | 4.00 | 4.15 |
| 2008 | Atl | NL | 16 | 0 | 0 | 9 | 18.1 | 82 | 16 | 12 | 12 | 2 | 2 | 1 | 2 | 10 | 2 | 13 | 0 | 0 | 0 | 1 | .000 | 0 | 0-0 | 2 | 4.19 | 5.89 |
| 2010 | 2 Tms | NL | 23 | 0 | 0 | 5 | 21.0 | 91 | 15 | 9 | 9 | 1 | 1 | 2 | 0 | 13 | 0 | 26 | 0 | 1 | 0 | 0 | - | 0 | 0-0 | 5 | 2.93 | 3.86 |
| 2011 | Pit | NL | 76 | 0 | 0 | 12 | 69.2 | 309 | 73 | 34 | 34 | 8 | 0 | 5 | 3 | 30 | **9** | 79 | 4 | 1 | 5 | 4 | .556 | 0 | 1-6 | 15 | 4.52 | 4.39 |
| 2012 | Pit | NL | 61 | 0 | 0 | 13 | 73.2 | 330 | 81 | 35 | 32 | 6 | 5 | 6 | 2 | 24 | 6 | 46 | 2 | 0 | 1 | 4 | .200 | 0 | 1-2 | 8 | 4.05 | 3.91 |
| 2013 | Oak | AL | 18 | 0 | 0 | 5 | 18.0 | 87 | 22 | 13 | 12 | 3 | 0 | 0 | 2 | 10 | 1 | 13 | 2 | 0 | 1 | 1 | .500 | 0 | 0-0 | 0 | 6.88 | 6.00 |
| 10 | Atl | NL | 1 | 0 | 0 | 0 | 2.0 | 14 | 5 | 5 | 5 | 0 | 0 | 0 | 0 | 3 | 0 | 2 | 0 | 0 | 0 | 0 | - | 0 | 0-0 | 0 | 18.12 | 22.50 |
| 10 | Pit | NL | 22 | 0 | 0 | 5 | 19.0 | 77 | 10 | 4 | 4 | 1 | 1 | 2 | 0 | 10 | 0 | 24 | 0 | 1 | 0 | 0 | - | 0 | 0-0 | 5 | 1.80 | 1.89 |
| 8 ML YEARS | | | 235 | 0 | 0 | 63 | 243.1 | 1097 | 259 | 130 | 125 | 23 | 10 | 17 | 11 | 113 | 23 | 204 | 11 | 2 | 10 | 12 | .455 | 0 | 2-9 | 32 | 4.63 | 4.62 |

# Ben Revere

**Bats:** L **Throws:** R **Pos:** CF-87;PR-3 **Ht:** 5'9" **Wt:** 170 **Born:** 5/3/1988 **Age:** 26

| BATTING | | | | | | | | | | | | | | | | | | | | | BASERUNNING | | | | AVERAGES | | |
|---|---|---|---|---|---|---|---|---|---|---|---|---|---|---|---|---|---|---|---|---|---|---|---|---|---|---|---|
| Year | Team | Lg | G | AB | H | 2B | 3B | HR | (Hm | Rd) | TB | R | RBI | RC | TBB | IBB | SO | HBP | SH | SF | SB | CS | SB% | GDP | Avg | OBP | Slg |
| 2010 | Min | AL | 13 | 28 | 5 | 0 | 0 | 0 | (0 | 0) | 5 | 1 | 2 | 0 | 2 | 0 | 5 | 0 | 0 | 0 | 0 | 1 | .00 | 1 | .179 | .233 | .179 |

| | | | BATTING | | | | | | | | | | | | | | | | | | BASERUNNING | | | | AVERAGES | | |
|---|---|---|---|---|---|---|---|---|---|---|---|---|---|---|---|---|---|---|---|---|---|---|---|---|---|---|---|
| Year | Team | Lg | G | AB | H | 2B | 3B | HR | (Hm | Rd) | TB | R | RBI | RC | TBB | IBB | SO | HBP | SH | SF | SB | CS | SB% | GDP | Avg | OBP | Slg |
| 2011 | Min | AL | 117 | 450 | 120 | 9 | 5 | 0 | (0 | 0) | 139 | 56 | 30 | 51 | 26 | 1 | 41 | 2 | 3 | 0 | 34 | 9 | .79 | 7 | .267 | .310 | .309 |
| 2012 | Min | AL | 124 | 511 | 150 | 13 | 6 | 0 | (0 | 0) | 175 | 70 | 32 | 62 | 29 | 0 | 54 | 3 | 6 | 4 | 40 | 9 | .82 | 8 | .294 | .333 | .342 |
| 2013 | Phi | NL | 88 | 315 | 96 | 9 | 3 | 0 | (0 | 0) | 111 | 37 | 17 | 39 | 16 | 1 | 36 | 0 | 5 | 0 | 22 | 8 | .73 | 10 | .305 | .338 | .352 |
| 4 ML YEARS | | | 342 | 1304 | 371 | 31 | 14 | 0 | (0 | 0) | 430 | 164 | 81 | 152 | 73 | 2 | 136 | 5 | 14 | 4 | 96 | 27 | .78 | 26 | .285 | .324 | .330 |

# Jose Reyes

**Bats:** B **Throws:** R **Pos:** SS-92;PH-1 **Ht:** 6'1" **Wt:** 195 **Born:** 6/11/1983 **Age:** 31

| | | | BATTING | | | | | | | | | | | | | | | | | | BASERUNNING | | | | AVERAGES | | |
|---|---|---|---|---|---|---|---|---|---|---|---|---|---|---|---|---|---|---|---|---|---|---|---|---|---|---|---|
| Year | Team | Lg | G | AB | H | 2B | 3B | HR | (Hm | Rd) | TB | R | RBI | RC | TBB | IBB | SO | HBP | SH | SF | SB | CS | SB% | GDP | Avg | OBP | Slg |
| 2013 | Dnedin* | A+ | 3 | 12 | 5 | 0 | 0 | 0 | (- | -) | 5 | 3 | 1 | 2 | 0 | 0 | 2 | 0 | 0 | 0 | 1 | 0 | 1.00 | 0 | .417 | .417 | .417 |
| 2013 | Buffalo* | AAA | 4 | 17 | 7 | 1 | 0 | 0 | (- | -) | 8 | 3 | 1 | 3 | 0 | 0 | 0 | 0 | 0 | 0 | 1 | 0 | 1.00 | 0 | .412 | .412 | .471 |
| 2003 | NYM | NL | 69 | 274 | 84 | 12 | 4 | 5 | (1 | 4) | 119 | 47 | 32 | 46 | 13 | 0 | 36 | 0 | 2 | 3 | 13 | 3 | .81 | 1 | .307 | .334 | .434 |
| 2004 | NYM | NL | 53 | 220 | 56 | 16 | 2 | 2 | (1 | 1) | 82 | 33 | 14 | 25 | 5 | 0 | 31 | 0 | 4 | 0 | 19 | 2 | .90 | 1 | .255 | .271 | .373 |
| 2005 | NYM | NL | 161 | **696** | 190 | 24 | **17** | 7 | (2 | 5) | 269 | 99 | 58 | 84 | 27 | 0 | 78 | 2 | 4 | 4 | **60** | 15 | .80 | 7 | .273 | .300 | .386 |
| 2006 | NYM | NL | 153 | 647 | 194 | 30 | **17** | 19 | (9 | 10) | 315 | 122 | 81 | 121 | 53 | 6 | 81 | 1 | 2 | 0 | **64** | 17 | .79 | 6 | .300 | .354 | .487 |
| 2007 | NYM | NL | 160 | 681 | 191 | 36 | 12 | 12 | (7 | 5) | 287 | 119 | 57 | 99 | 77 | 13 | 78 | 1 | 5 | 1 | **78** | **21** | .79 | 6 | .280 | .354 | .421 |
| 2008 | NYM | NL | 159 | **688** | **204** | 37 | **19** | 16 | (9 | 7) | 327 | 113 | 68 | 117 | 66 | 8 | 82 | 1 | 5 | 3 | 56 | **15** | .79 | 9 | .297 | .358 | .475 |
| 2009 | NYM | NL | 36 | 147 | 41 | 7 | 2 | 2 | (1 | 1) | 58 | 18 | 15 | 20 | 18 | 1 | 19 | 0 | 0 | 1 | 11 | 2 | .85 | 2 | .279 | .355 | .395 |
| 2010 | NYM | NL | 133 | 563 | 159 | 29 | 10 | 11 | (8 | 3) | 241 | 83 | 54 | 76 | 31 | 4 | 63 | 2 | 4 | 3 | 30 | 10 | .75 | 8 | .282 | .321 | .428 |
| 2011 | NYM | NL | 126 | 537 | 181 | 31 | **16** | 7 | (4 | 3) | 265 | 101 | 44 | 90 | 43 | 9 | 41 | 0 | 2 | 4 | 39 | 7 | .85 | 5 | **.337** | .384 | .493 |
| 2012 | Mia | NL | 160 | 642 | 184 | 37 | 12 | 11 | (4 | 7) | 278 | 86 | 57 | 92 | 63 | 9 | 56 | 0 | 5 | 6 | 40 | 11 | .78 | 10 | .287 | .347 | .433 |
| 2013 | Tor | AL | 93 | 382 | 113 | 20 | 0 | 10 | (7 | 3) | 163 | 58 | 37 | 61 | 34 | 2 | 47 | 1 | 0 | 2 | 15 | 6 | .71 | 6 | .296 | .353 | .427 |
| Postseason | | | 10 | 44 | 11 | 1 | 1 | 1 | (1 | 0) | 17 | 7 | 5 | 6 | 3 | 1 | 5 | 0 | 0 | 0 | 3 | 1 | .75 | 0 | .250 | .298 | .386 |
| 11 ML YEARS | | | 1303 | 5477 | 1597 | 279 | 111 | 102 | (53 | 49) | 2404 | 879 | 517 | 831 | 430 | 52 | 612 | 8 | 33 | 27 | 425 | 109 | .80 | 61 | .292 | .342 | .439 |

# Greg Reynolds

**Pitches:** R **Bats:** R **Pos:** SP-5; RP-1 **Ht:** 6'7" **Wt:** 225 **Born:** 7/3/1985 **Age:** 28

| | | | HOW MUCH HE PITCHED | | | | | | WHAT HE GAVE UP | | | | | | | | | | | | THE RESULTS | | | | | | | |
|---|---|---|---|---|---|---|---|---|---|---|---|---|---|---|---|---|---|---|---|---|---|---|---|---|---|---|---|---|
| Year | Team | Lg | G | GS | CG | GF | IP | BFP | H | R | ER | HR | SH | SF | HB | TBB | IBB | SO | WP | Bk | W | L | Pct | Sh | Sv-Op | Hld | ERC | ERA |
| 2013 | Lsvlle* | AAA | 23 | 21 | 3 | 0 | 156.1 | 618 | 139 | 45 | 42 | 6 | 1 | 3 | 1 | 26 | 0 | 97 | 2 | 0 | 12 | 3 | .800 | 1 | 0- - | - | 2.30 | 2.42 |
| 2008 | Col | NL | 14 | 13 | 0 | 0 | 62.0 | 294 | 83 | 58 | 56 | 14 | 4 | 2 | 4 | 26 | 3 | 22 | 2 | 0 | 2 | 8 | .200 | 0 | 0-0 | 0 | 7.36 | 8.13 |
| 2011 | Col | NL | 13 | 3 | 0 | 3 | 32.0 | 144 | 40 | 22 | 22 | 6 | 0 | 1 | 1 | 10 | 2 | 18 | 1 | 0 | 3 | 0 | 1.000 | 0 | 0-0 | 0 | 5.85 | 6.19 |
| 2013 | Cin | NL | 6 | 5 | 0 | 0 | 29.1 | 133 | 38 | 19 | 18 | 5 | 3 | 2 | 4 | 6 | 1 | 13 | 0 | 0 | 1 | 3 | .250 | 0 | 0-0 | 0 | 6.05 | 5.52 |
| 3 ML YEARS | | | 33 | 21 | 0 | 3 | 123.1 | 571 | 161 | 99 | 96 | 25 | 7 | 5 | 9 | 42 | 6 | 53 | 3 | 0 | 6 | 11 | .353 | 0 | 0-0 | 0 | 6.65 | 7.01 |

# Mark Reynolds

**Bats:** R **Throws:** R **Pos:** 1B-65;3B-54;DH-19;PH-8;2B-2;PR-2 **Ht:** 6'2" **Wt:** 220 **Born:** 8/3/1983 **Age:** 30

| | | | BATTING | | | | | | | | | | | | | | | | | | BASERUNNING | | | | AVERAGES | | |
|---|---|---|---|---|---|---|---|---|---|---|---|---|---|---|---|---|---|---|---|---|---|---|---|---|---|---|---|
| Year | Team | Lg | G | AB | H | 2B | 3B | HR | (Hm | Rd) | TB | R | RBI | RC | TBB | IBB | SO | HBP | SH | SF | SB | CS | SB% | GDP | Avg | OBP | Slg |
| 2007 | Ari | NL | 111 | 366 | 102 | 20 | 4 | 17 | (7 | 10) | 181 | 62 | 62 | 62 | 37 | 4 | 129 | 5 | 1 | 5 | 0 | 1 | .00 | 5 | .279 | .349 | .495 |
| 2008 | Ari | NL | 152 | 539 | 129 | 28 | 3 | 28 | (13 | 15) | 247 | 87 | 97 | 82 | 64 | 0 | **204** | 3 | 1 | 6 | 11 | 2 | .85 | 10 | .239 | .320 | .458 |
| 2009 | Ari | NL | 155 | 578 | 150 | 30 | 1 | 44 | (19 | 25) | 314 | 98 | 102 | 94 | 76 | 3 | **223** | 5 | 0 | 3 | 24 | 9 | .73 | 8 | .260 | .349 | .543 |
| 2010 | Ari | NL | 145 | 499 | 99 | 17 | 2 | 32 | (21 | 11) | 216 | 79 | 85 | 77 | 83 | 7 | **211** | 9 | 0 | 5 | 7 | 4 | .64 | 8 | .198 | .320 | .433 |
| 2011 | Bal | AL | 155 | 534 | 118 | 27 | 1 | 37 | (17 | 20) | 258 | 84 | 86 | 77 | 75 | 2 | **196** | 7 | 0 | 4 | 6 | 4 | .60 | 11 | .221 | .323 | .483 |
| 2012 | Bal | AL | 135 | 457 | 101 | 26 | 0 | 23 | (11 | 12) | 196 | 65 | 69 | 68 | 73 | 2 | 159 | 6 | 0 | 2 | 1 | 3 | .25 | 19 | .221 | .335 | .429 |
| 2013 | 2 Tms | AL | 135 | 445 | 98 | 14 | 0 | 21 | (9 | 12) | 175 | 55 | 67 | 55 | 51 | 1 | 154 | 5 | 0 | 3 | 3 | 1 | .75 | 9 | .220 | .306 | .393 |
| 13 | Cle | AL | 99 | 335 | 72 | 8 | 0 | 15 | (8 | 7) | 125 | 40 | 48 | 39 | 43 | 1 | 123 | 3 | 0 | 3 | 3 | 0 | 1.00 | 7 | .215 | .307 | .373 |
| 13 | NYY | AL | 36 | 110 | 26 | 6 | 0 | 6 | (1 | 5) | 50 | 15 | 19 | 16 | 8 | 0 | 31 | 2 | 0 | 0 | 0 | 1 | .00 | 2 | .236 | .300 | .455 |
| Postseason | | | 13 | 48 | 7 | 0 | 0 | 2 | (1 | 1) | 13 | 3 | 3 | 2 | 3 | 0 | 19 | 3 | 0 | 0 | 1 | 0 | 1.00 | 1 | .146 | .241 | .271 |
| 7 ML YEARS | | | 988 | 3418 | 797 | 162 | 11 | 202 | (97 | 105) | 1587 | 530 | 568 | 515 | 459 | 19 | 1276 | 40 | 2 | 28 | 52 | 24 | .68 | 70 | .233 | .329 | .464 |

# Matt Reynolds

**Pitches:** L **Bats:** L **Pos:** RP-30 **Ht:** 6'5" **Wt:** 240 **Born:** 10/2/1984 **Age:** 29

| | | | HOW MUCH HE PITCHED | | | | | | WHAT HE GAVE UP | | | | | | | | | | | | THE RESULTS | | | | | | | |
|---|---|---|---|---|---|---|---|---|---|---|---|---|---|---|---|---|---|---|---|---|---|---|---|---|---|---|---|---|
| Year | Team | Lg | G | GS | CG | GF | IP | BFP | H | R | ER | HR | SH | SF | HB | TBB | IBB | SO | WP | Bk | W | L | Pct | Sh | Sv-Op | Hld | ERC | ERA |
| 2010 | Col | NL | 21 | 0 | 0 | 2 | 18.0 | 70 | 10 | 4 | 4 | 2 | 1 | 1 | 2 | 5 | 0 | 17 | 1 | 0 | 1 | 0 | 1.000 | 0 | 0-0 | 2 | 1.87 | 2.00 |
| 2011 | Col | NL | 73 | 0 | 0 | 9 | 50.2 | 211 | 48 | 24 | 23 | 10 | 1 | 4 | 0 | 18 | 5 | 50 | 5 | 2 | 1 | 2 | .333 | 0 | 0-2 | 18 | 4.18 | 4.09 |
| 2012 | Col | NL | 71 | 0 | 0 | 16 | 57.1 | 249 | 65 | 31 | 28 | 11 | 6 | 3 | 0 | 17 | 4 | 51 | 5 | 1 | 3 | 1 | .750 | 0 | 0-0 | 2 | 4.96 | 4.40 |
| 2013 | Ari | NL | 30 | 0 | 0 | 9 | 27.1 | 111 | 25 | 7 | 6 | 2 | 0 | 1 | 1 | 5 | 1 | 23 | 0 | 0 | 0 | 2 | .000 | 0 | 2-3 | 5 | 2.71 | 1.98 |
| 4 ML YEARS | | | 195 | 0 | 0 | 36 | 153.1 | 641 | 148 | 66 | 61 | 25 | 8 | 9 | 3 | 45 | 10 | 141 | 11 | 3 | 5 | 5 | .500 | 0 | 2-5 | 27 | 3.88 | 3.58 |

# Scott Rice

**Pitches:** L **Bats:** L **Pos:** RP-73 **Ht:** 6'6" **Wt:** 225 **Born:** 9/21/1981 **Age:** 32

| | | | HOW MUCH HE PITCHED | | | | | | WHAT HE GAVE UP | | | | | | | | | | | | THE RESULTS | | | | | | | |
|---|---|---|---|---|---|---|---|---|---|---|---|---|---|---|---|---|---|---|---|---|---|---|---|---|---|---|---|---|
| Year | Team | Lg | G | GS | CG | GF | IP | BFP | H | R | ER | HR | SH | SF | HB | TBB | IBB | SO | WP | Bk | W | L | Pct | Sh | Sv-Op | Hld | ERC | ERA |
| 2009 | SnAnt | AA | 25 | 0 | 0 | 6 | 29.1 | 144 | 33 | 26 | 24 | 1 | 1 | 2 | 3 | 22 | 2 | 21 | 2 | 0 | 1 | 4 | .200 | 0 | 0- - | - | 5.89 | 7.36 |
| 2010 | Tulsa | AA | 35 | 0 | 0 | 12 | 46.2 | 182 | 23 | 8 | 5 | 0 | 3 | 0 | 2 | 18 | 1 | 33 | 7 | 1 | 2 | 0 | 1.000 | 0 | 4- - | - | 1.24 | 0.96 |
| 2010 | ColSpr | AAA | 23 | 0 | 0 | 5 | 22.2 | 108 | 27 | 17 | 17 | 0 | 1 | 1 | 2 | 15 | 0 | 15 | 2 | 0 | 0 | 1 | .000 | 0 | 3- - | - | 5.86 | 6.75 |
| 2011 | Chatt | AA | 34 | 0 | 0 | 7 | 50.2 | 208 | 42 | 17 | 11 | 3 | 1 | 1 | 1 | 17 | 0 | 42 | 3 | 2 | 4 | 4 | .500 | 0 | 1- - | - | 2.74 | 1.95 |
| 2012 | Albq | AAA | 54 | 0 | 0 | 27 | 59.1 | 260 | 58 | 33 | 29 | 3 | 5 | 2 | 4 | 22 | 1 | 47 | 9 | 0 | 2 | 3 | .400 | 0 | 9- - | - | 3.66 | 4.40 |
| 2013 | NYM | NL | 73 | 0 | 0 | 7 | 51.0 | 213 | 42 | 22 | 21 | 1 | 3 | 2 | 2 | 27 | 4 | 41 | 3 | 1 | 4 | 5 | .444 | 0 | 0-2 | 17 | 3.17 | 3.71 |

# Clayton Richard

**Pitches:** L **Bats:** L **Pos:** SP-11; RP-1 **Ht:** 6'5" **Wt:** 245 **Born:** 9/12/1983 **Age:** 30

| HOW MUCH HE PITCHED | | | | | | | | | WHAT HE GAVE UP | | | | | | | | | | | | THE RESULTS | | | | | | | |
|---|---|---|---|---|---|---|---|---|---|---|---|---|---|---|---|---|---|---|---|---|---|---|---|---|---|---|---|---|
| Year | Team | Lg | G | GS | CG | GF | IP | BFP | H | R | ER | HR | SH | SF | HB | TBB | IBB | SO | WP | Bk | W | L | Pct | Sh | Sv-Op | Hld | ERC | ERA |
| 2013 | Tucsn* | AAA | 2 | 2 | 0 | 0 | 12.0 | 46 | 10 | 3 | 3 | 0 | 0 | 1 | 1 | 0 | 0 | 12 | 1 | 0 | 0 | 1 | .000 | 0 | 0-- | - | 1.58 | 2.25 |
| 2008 | CWS | AL | 13 | 8 | 0 | 3 | 47.2 | 215 | 61 | 37 | 32 | 5 | 0 | 1 | 0 | 13 | 2 | 29 | 1 | 1 | 2 | 5 | .286 | 0 | 0-0 | 0 | 5.06 | 6.04 |
| 2009 | 2 Tms | | 38 | 26 | 1 | 3 | 153.0 | 663 | 154 | 81 | 75 | 17 | 8 | 5 | 3 | 71 | 0 | 114 | 7 | 3 | 9 | 5 | .643 | 0 | 0-0 | 0 | 4.60 | 4.41 |
| 2010 | SD | NL | 33 | 33 | 1 | 0 | 201.2 | 861 | 206 | 89 | 84 | 16 | 6 | 2 | 4 | 78 | 6 | 153 | 4 | 2 | 14 | 9 | .609 | 1 | 0-0 | 0 | 4.09 | 3.75 |
| 2011 | SD | NL | 18 | 18 | 0 | 0 | 99.2 | 427 | 104 | 52 | 43 | 8 | 4 | 1 | 2 | 38 | 2 | 53 | 3 | 1 | 5 | 9 | .357 | 0 | 0-0 | 0 | 4.22 | 3.88 |
| 2012 | SD | NL | 33 | **33** | 1 | 0 | 218.2 | 910 | **228** | 110 | 97 | **31** | 3 | 6 | 6 | 42 | 4 | 107 | 4 | 2 | 14 | 14 | .500 | 1 | 0-0 | 0 | 3.87 | 3.99 |
| 2013 | SD | NL | 12 | 11 | 0 | 1 | 52.2 | 239 | 65 | 44 | 41 | 13 | 6 | 1 | 0 | 21 | 1 | 24 | 0 | 0 | 2 | 5 | .286 | 0 | 0-0 | 0 | 6.55 | 7.01 |
| 09 | CWS | AL | 26 | 14 | 1 | 3 | 89.0 | 387 | 94 | 50 | 46 | 10 | 3 | 4 | 3 | 37 | 0 | 66 | 5 | 2 | 4 | 3 | .571 | 0 | 0-0 | 0 | 4.76 | 4.65 |
| 09 | SD | NL | 12 | 12 | 0 | 0 | 64.0 | 276 | 60 | 31 | 29 | 7 | 5 | 1 | 0 | 34 | 0 | 48 | 2 | 1 | 5 | 2 | .714 | 0 | 0-0 | 0 | 4.38 | 4.08 |
| Postseason | | | 2 | 0 | 0 | 0 | 6.1 | 25 | 5 | 1 | 1 | 0 | 0 | 0 | 0 | 3 | 0 | 6 | 0 | 0 | 0 | 0 | - | 0 | 0-0 | 0 | 2.74 | 1.42 |
| 6 ML YEARS | | | 147 | 129 | 3 | 7 | 773.1 | 3315 | 818 | 413 | 372 | 90 | 27 | 16 | 15 | 263 | 15 | 480 | 19 | 9 | 46 | 47 | .495 | 2 | 0-0 | 0 | 4.37 | 4.33 |

# Garrett Richards

**Pitches:** R **Bats:** R **Pos:** RP-30; SP-17 **Ht:** 6'3" **Wt:** 215 **Born:** 5/27/1988 **Age:** 26

| HOW MUCH HE PITCHED | | | | | | | | | WHAT HE GAVE UP | | | | | | | | | | | | THE RESULTS | | | | | | | |
|---|---|---|---|---|---|---|---|---|---|---|---|---|---|---|---|---|---|---|---|---|---|---|---|---|---|---|---|---|
| Year | Team | Lg | G | GS | CG | GF | IP | BFP | H | R | ER | HR | SH | SF | HB | TBB | IBB | SO | WP | Bk | W | L | Pct | Sh | Sv-Op | Hld | ERC | ERA |
| 2011 | LAA | AL | 7 | 3 | 0 | 2 | 14.0 | 62 | 16 | 11 | 9 | 4 | 0 | 0 | 0 | 7 | 0 | 9 | 2 | 0 | 0 | 2 | .000 | 0 | 0-0 | 0 | 6.97 | 5.79 |
| 2012 | LAA | AL | 30 | 9 | 0 | 4 | 71.0 | 318 | 77 | 46 | 37 | 7 | 2 | 4 | 3 | 34 | 1 | 47 | 2 | 0 | 4 | 3 | .571 | 0 | 1-3 | 5 | 5.04 | 4.69 |
| 2013 | LAA | AL | 47 | 17 | 1 | 6 | 145.0 | 620 | 151 | 73 | 67 | 12 | **9** | 3 | 1 | 44 | 4 | 101 | 11 | 0 | 7 | 8 | .467 | 0 | 1-2 | 5 | 3.78 | 4.16 |
| 3 ML YEARS | | | 84 | 29 | 1 | 12 | 230.0 | 1000 | 244 | 130 | 113 | 23 | 11 | 7 | 4 | 85 | 5 | 157 | 15 | 0 | 11 | 13 | .458 | 0 | 2-5 | 10 | 4.34 | 4.42 |

# Andre Rienzo

**Pitches:** R **Bats:** R **Pos:** SP-10 ree-ENN-zo **Ht:** 6'3" **Wt:** 190 **Born:** 6/5/1988 **Age:** 26

| HOW MUCH HE PITCHED | | | | | | | | | WHAT HE GAVE UP | | | | | | | | | | | | THE RESULTS | | | | | | | |
|---|---|---|---|---|---|---|---|---|---|---|---|---|---|---|---|---|---|---|---|---|---|---|---|---|---|---|---|---|
| Year | Team | Lg | G | GS | CG | GF | IP | BFP | H | R | ER | HR | SH | SF | HB | TBB | IBB | SO | WP | Bk | W | L | Pct | Sh | Sv-Op | Hld | ERC | ERA |
| 2009 | Bristol | R | 13 | 9 | 0 | 2 | 54.1 | 226 | 55 | 28 | 25 | 4 | 2 | 1 | 0 | 13 | 0 | 49 | 5 | 0 | 2 | 6 | .250 | 0 | 0-- | - | 3.35 | 4.14 |
| 2010 | Knapol | A | 20 | 18 | 2 | 0 | 101.0 | 432 | 95 | 45 | 41 | 5 | 3 | 2 | 2 | 32 | 0 | 125 | 6 | 4 | 8 | 4 | .667 | 2 | 0-- | - | 3.10 | 3.65 |
| 2011 | WinSa | A+ | 25 | 22 | 1 | 0 | 116.0 | 512 | 108 | 50 | 44 | 4 | 2 | 4 | 3 | 66 | 0 | 118 | 16 | 0 | 6 | 5 | .545 | 1 | 0-- | - | 3.97 | 3.41 |
| 2012 | WinSa | A+ | 4 | 4 | 0 | 0 | 25.0 | 96 | 17 | 3 | 3 | 0 | 0 | 1 | 0 | 7 | 0 | 31 | 3 | 1 | 3 | 0 | 1.000 | 0 | 0-- | - | 1.55 | 1.08 |
| 2012 | Brham | AA | 13 | 13 | 1 | 0 | 71.2 | 307 | 56 | 31 | 26 | 2 | 3 | 2 | 1 | 33 | 0 | 72 | 3 | 0 | 4 | 3 | .571 | 0 | 0-- | - | 2.62 | 3.27 |
| 2012 | Charltt | AAA | 1 | 1 | 0 | 0 | 6.2 | 26 | 5 | 1 | 0 | 0 | 1 | 1 | 0 | 2 | 0 | 10 | 1 | 0 | 0 | 0 | - | 0 | 0-- | - | 1.88 | 0.00 |
| 2013 | Charltt | AAA | 20 | 20 | 3 | 0 | 113.0 | 488 | 105 | 62 | 51 | 7 | 2 | 4 | 4 | 46 | 0 | 113 | 4 | 1 | 8 | 6 | .571 | 1 | 0-- | - | 3.55 | 4.06 |
| 2013 | CWS | AL | 10 | 10 | 0 | 0 | 56.0 | 250 | 55 | 34 | 30 | 11 | 2 | 1 | 2 | 28 | 0 | 38 | 4 | 0 | 2 | 3 | .400 | 0 | 0-0 | 0 | 5.18 | 4.82 |

# Alex Rios

**Bats:** R **Throws:** R **Pos:** RF-155;CF-1;PH-1 **Ht:** 6'5" **Wt:** 210 **Born:** 2/18/1981 **Age:** 33

| BATTING | | | | | | | | | | | | | | | | | | | | BASERUNNING | | | | AVERAGES | | |
|---|---|---|---|---|---|---|---|---|---|---|---|---|---|---|---|---|---|---|---|---|---|---|---|---|---|---|
| Year | Team | Lg | G | AB | H | 2B | 3B | HR | (Hm | Rd) | TB | R | RBI | RC | TBB | IBB | SO | HBP | SH | SF | SB | CS | SB% | GDP | Avg | OBP | Slg |
| 2004 | Tor | AL | 111 | 426 | 122 | 24 | 7 | 1 | (0 | 1) | 163 | 55 | 28 | 49 | 31 | 0 | 84 | 2 | 1 | 0 | 15 | 3 | .83 | 14 | .286 | .338 | .383 |
| 2005 | Tor | AL | 146 | 481 | 126 | 23 | 6 | 10 | (5 | 5) | 191 | 71 | 59 | 56 | 28 | 1 | 101 | 5 | 0 | 5 | 14 | 9 | .61 | 14 | .262 | .306 | .397 |
| 2006 | Tor | AL | 128 | 450 | 136 | 33 | 6 | 17 | (12 | 5) | 232 | 68 | 82 | 83 | 35 | 1 | 89 | 3 | 0 | 10 | 15 | 6 | .71 | 10 | .302 | .349 | .516 |
| 2007 | Tor | AL | 161 | 643 | 191 | 43 | 7 | 24 | (13 | 11) | 320 | 114 | 85 | 105 | 55 | 3 | 103 | 6 | 0 | 7 | 17 | 4 | .81 | 9 | .297 | .354 | .498 |
| 2008 | Tor | AL | 155 | 635 | 185 | 47 | 8 | 15 | (9 | 6) | 293 | 91 | 79 | 92 | 44 | 2 | 112 | 2 | 0 | 5 | 32 | 8 | .80 | 20 | .291 | .337 | .461 |
| 2009 | 2 Tms | AL | 149 | 582 | 144 | 31 | 2 | 17 | (15 | 2) | 230 | 63 | 71 | 64 | 37 | 1 | 107 | 6 | 1 | 7 | 24 | 5 | .83 | 21 | .247 | .296 | .395 |
| 2010 | CWS | AL | 147 | 567 | 161 | 29 | 3 | 21 | (10 | 11) | 259 | 89 | 88 | 84 | 38 | 4 | 93 | 7 | 0 | 5 | 34 | 14 | .71 | 21 | .284 | .334 | .457 |
| 2011 | CWS | AL | 145 | 537 | 122 | 22 | 2 | 13 | (7 | 6) | 187 | 64 | 44 | 35 | 27 | 4 | 68 | 2 | 0 | 4 | 11 | 6 | .65 | 20 | .227 | .265 | .348 |
| 2012 | CWS | AL | 157 | 605 | 184 | 37 | 8 | 25 | (16 | 9) | 312 | 93 | 91 | 103 | 26 | 3 | 92 | 4 | 0 | 5 | 23 | 6 | .79 | 18 | .304 | .334 | .516 |
| 2013 | 2 Tms | AL | 156 | 616 | 171 | 33 | 4 | 18 | (7 | 11) | 266 | 83 | 81 | 78 | 41 | 2 | 108 | 2 | 0 | 2 | 42 | 7 | .86 | 17 | .278 | .324 | .432 |
| 09 | Tor | AL | 108 | 436 | 115 | 25 | 2 | 14 | (12 | 2) | 186 | 52 | 62 | 60 | 31 | 1 | 78 | 6 | 0 | 6 | 19 | 3 | .86 | 14 | .264 | .317 | .427 |
| 09 | CWS | AL | 41 | 146 | 29 | 6 | 0 | 3 | (3 | 0) | 44 | 11 | 9 | 4 | 6 | 0 | 29 | 0 | 1 | 1 | 5 | 2 | .71 | 7 | .199 | .229 | .301 |
| 13 | CWS | AL | 109 | 430 | 119 | 22 | 2 | 12 | (6 | 6) | 181 | 57 | 55 | 51 | 32 | 2 | 78 | 1 | 0 | 1 | 26 | 6 | .81 | 12 | .277 | .328 | .421 |
| 13 | Tex | AL | 47 | 186 | 52 | 11 | 2 | 6 | (1 | 5) | 85 | 26 | 26 | 27 | 9 | 0 | 30 | 1 | 0 | 1 | 16 | 1 | .94 | 5 | .280 | .315 | .457 |
| 10 ML YEARS | | | 1455 | 5542 | 1542 | 322 | 53 | 161 | (94 | 67) | 2453 | 791 | 708 | 749 | 362 | 21 | 957 | 39 | 2 | 50 | 227 | 68 | .77 | 164 | .278 | .324 | .443 |

# Mariano Rivera

**Pitches:** R **Bats:** R **Pos:** RP-64 **Ht:** 6'2" **Wt:** 195 **Born:** 11/29/1969 **Age:** 44

| HOW MUCH HE PITCHED | | | | | | | | | WHAT HE GAVE UP | | | | | | | | | | | | THE RESULTS | | | | | | | |
|---|---|---|---|---|---|---|---|---|---|---|---|---|---|---|---|---|---|---|---|---|---|---|---|---|---|---|---|---|
| Year | Team | Lg | G | GS | CG | GF | IP | BFP | H | R | ER | HR | SH | SF | HB | TBB | IBB | SO | WP | Bk | W | L | Pct | Sh | Sv-Op | Hld | ERC | ERA |
| 1995 | NYY | AL | 19 | 10 | 0 | 2 | 67.0 | 301 | 71 | 43 | 41 | 11 | 0 | 2 | 2 | 30 | 0 | 51 | 0 | 1 | 5 | 3 | .625 | 0 | 0-1 | 0 | 5.14 | 5.51 |
| 1996 | NYY | AL | 61 | 0 | 0 | 14 | 107.2 | 425 | 73 | 25 | 25 | 1 | 2 | 1 | 2 | 34 | 3 | 130 | 1 | 0 | 8 | 3 | .727 | 0 | 5-8 | **26** | 1.65 | 2.09 |
| 1997 | NYY | AL | 66 | 0 | 0 | 56 | 71.2 | 301 | 65 | 17 | 15 | 5 | 3 | 4 | 0 | 20 | 6 | 68 | 2 | 0 | 6 | 4 | .600 | 0 | 43-**52** | 0 | 2.73 | 1.88 |
| 1998 | NYY | AL | 54 | 0 | 0 | 49 | 61.1 | 246 | 48 | 13 | 13 | 3 | 2 | 3 | 1 | 17 | 1 | 36 | 0 | 0 | 3 | 0 | 1.000 | 0 | 36-41 | 0 | 2.21 | 1.91 |
| 1999 | NYY | AL | 66 | 0 | 0 | 63 | 69.0 | 268 | 43 | 15 | 14 | 2 | 0 | 2 | 3 | 18 | 3 | 52 | 2 | 1 | 4 | 3 | .571 | 0 | **45**-49 | 0 | 1.47 | 1.83 |
| 2000 | NYY | AL | 66 | 0 | 0 | 61 | 75.2 | 311 | 58 | 26 | 24 | 4 | 5 | 2 | 0 | 25 | 3 | 58 | 2 | 0 | 7 | 4 | .636 | 0 | 36-41 | 0 | 2.20 | 2.85 |
| 2001 | NYY | AL | 71 | 0 | 0 | 66 | 80.2 | 310 | 61 | 24 | 21 | 5 | 4 | 1 | 1 | 12 | 2 | 83 | 1 | 0 | 4 | 6 | .400 | 0 | **50-57** | 0 | 1.74 | 2.34 |
| 2002 | NYY | AL | 45 | 0 | 0 | 36 | 46.0 | 187 | 35 | 16 | 14 | 3 | 2 | 0 | 2 | 11 | 2 | 41 | 1 | 1 | 1 | 4 | .200 | 0 | 28-32 | 2 | 2.08 | 2.74 |
| 2003 | NYY | AL | 64 | 0 | 0 | 57 | 70.2 | 277 | 61 | 15 | 13 | 3 | 1 | 2 | 4 | 10 | 1 | 63 | 0 | 0 | 5 | 2 | .714 | 0 | 40-46 | 0 | 2.29 | 1.66 |
| 2004 | NYY | AL | 74 | 0 | 0 | 69 | 78.2 | 316 | 65 | 17 | 17 | 3 | 2 | 0 | 5 | 20 | 3 | 66 | 0 | 0 | 4 | 2 | .667 | 0 | **53-57** | 0 | 2.45 | 1.94 |
| 2005 | NYY | AL | 71 | 0 | 0 | 67 | 78.1 | 306 | 50 | 18 | 12 | 2 | 0 | 1 | 4 | 18 | 0 | 80 | 0 | 0 | 7 | 4 | .636 | 0 | 43-47 | 0 | 1.48 | 1.38 |
| 2006 | NYY | AL | 63 | 0 | 0 | 59 | 75.0 | 293 | 61 | 16 | 15 | 3 | 1 | 2 | 5 | 11 | 4 | 55 | 0 | 0 | 5 | 5 | .500 | 0 | 34-37 | 0 | 2.03 | 1.80 |
| 2007 | NYY | AL | 67 | 0 | 0 | 59 | 71.1 | 295 | 68 | 25 | 25 | 4 | 1 | 1 | 6 | 12 | 2 | 74 | 1 | 0 | 3 | 4 | .429 | 0 | 30-34 | 0 | 2.92 | 3.15 |
| 2008 | NYY | AL | 64 | 0 | 0 | 60 | 70.2 | 259 | 41 | 11 | 11 | 4 | 1 | 1 | 2 | 6 | 0 | 77 | 1 | 0 | 6 | 5 | .545 | 0 | 39-40 | 0 | 1.09 | 1.40 |
| 2009 | NYY | AL | 66 | 0 | 0 | 55 | 66.1 | 257 | 48 | 14 | 13 | 7 | 0 | 0 | 1 | 12 | 1 | 72 | 1 | 0 | 3 | 3 | .500 | 0 | 44-46 | 0 | 1.93 | 1.76 |
| 2010 | NYY | AL | 61 | 0 | 0 | 55 | 60.0 | 230 | 39 | 14 | 12 | 2 | 0 | 1 | 5 | 11 | 3 | 45 | 0 | 0 | 3 | 3 | .500 | 0 | 33-38 | 0 | 1.50 | 1.80 |

| Year | Team | Lg | G | GS | CG | GF | IP | BFP | H | R | ER | HR | SH | SF | HB | TBB | IBB | SO | WP | Bk | W | L | Pct | Sh | Sv-Op | Hld | ERC | ERA |
|---|---|---|---|---|---|---|---|---|---|---|---|---|---|---|---|---|---|---|---|---|---|---|---|---|---|---|---|---|
| | | | HOW MUCH HE PITCHED | | | | | | WHAT HE GAVE UP | | | | | | | | | | | | THE RESULTS | | | | | | | |
| 2011 | NYY | AL | 64 | 0 | 0 | 54 | 61.1 | 233 | 47 | 13 | 13 | 3 | 2 | 2 | 2 | 8 | 2 | 60 | 1 | 0 | 1 | 2 | .333 | 0 | 44-**49** | 0 | 1.75 | 1.91 |
| 2012 | NYY | AL | 9 | 0 | 0 | 9 | 8.1 | 32 | 6 | 2 | 2 | 0 | 0 | 0 | 0 | 2 | 2 | 8 | 0 | 0 | 1 | 1 | .500 | 0 | 5-6 | 0 | 1.36 | 2.16 |
| 2013 | NYY | AL | 64 | 0 | 0 | 60 | 64.0 | 256 | 58 | 16 | 15 | 6 | 0 | 0 | 1 | 9 | 3 | 54 | 0 | 0 | 6 | 2 | .750 | 0 | 44-51 | 0 | 2.55 | 2.11 |
| Postseason | | | 96 | 0 | 0 | 78 | 141.0 | 527 | 86 | 13 | 11 | 2 | 7 | 3 | 3 | 21 | 4 | 110 | 3 | 0 | 8 | 1 | .889 | 0 | 42-47 | 4 | 1.12 | 0.70 |
| 19 ML YEARS | | | 1115 | 10 | 0 | 951 | 1283.2 | 5103 | 998 | 340 | 315 | 71 | 26 | 25 | 46 | 286 | 41 | 1173 | 13 | 3 | 82 | 60 | .577 | 0 | 652-732 | 28 | 2.09 | 2.21 |

## Rene Rivera

**Bats:** R **Throws:** R **Pos:** C-21;PH-2 ruh-NAY **Ht:** 5'10" **Wt:** 230 **Born:** 7/31/1983 **Age:** 30

| Year | Team | Lg | G | AB | H | 2B | 3B | HR | (Hm | Rd) | TB | R | RBI | RC | TBB | IBB | SO | HBP | SH | SF | SB | CS | SB% | GDP | Avg | OBP | Slg |
|---|---|---|---|---|---|---|---|---|---|---|---|---|---|---|---|---|---|---|---|---|---|---|---|---|---|---|---|
| | | | BATTING | | | | | | | | | | | | | | | | | | BASERUNNING | | | | AVERAGES | | |
| 2013 | Tucsn* | AAA | 74 | 251 | 86 | 18 | 0 | 5 | (- | -) | 119 | 36 | 38 | 45 | 17 | 0 | 42 | 2 | 1 | 5 | 0 | 2 | .00 | 9 | .343 | .382 | .474 |
| 2004 | Sea | AL | 2 | 3 | 0 | 0 | 0 | 0 | (0 | 0) | 0 | 0 | 0 | 0 | 0 | 0 | 1 | 0 | 0 | 0 | 0 | 0 | - | 0 | .000 | .000 | .000 |
| 2005 | Sea | AL | 16 | 48 | 19 | 3 | 0 | 1 | (0 | 1) | 25 | 3 | 6 | 8 | 1 | 0 | 11 | 0 | 1 | 0 | 0 | 0 | - | 0 | .396 | .408 | .521 |
| 2006 | Sea | AL | 35 | 99 | 15 | 4 | 0 | 2 | (1 | 1) | 25 | 8 | 4 | 4 | 3 | 0 | 29 | 1 | 3 | 0 | 1 | 0 | 1.00 | 2 | .152 | .184 | .253 |
| 2011 | Min | AL | 45 | 104 | 15 | 3 | 0 | 1 | (0 | 1) | 21 | 9 | 5 | 3 | 8 | 0 | 32 | 1 | 0 | 1 | 0 | 0 | - | 2 | .144 | .211 | .202 |
| 2013 | SD | NL | 23 | 67 | 17 | 3 | 1 | 0 | (0 | 0) | 22 | 4 | 7 | 6 | 2 | 1 | 16 | 0 | 0 | 2 | 0 | 0 | - | 1 | .254 | .268 | .328 |
| 5 ML YEARS | | | 121 | 321 | 66 | 13 | 1 | 4 | (1 | 3) | 93 | 24 | 22 | 21 | 14 | 1 | 89 | 2 | 4 | 3 | 1 | 0 | 1.00 | 5 | .206 | .241 | .290 |

## Anthony Rizzo

**Bats:** L **Throws:** L **Pos:** 1B-159;PH-2 **Ht:** 6'3" **Wt:** 240 **Born:** 8/8/1989 **Age:** 24

| Year | Team | Lg | G | AB | H | 2B | 3B | HR | (Hm | Rd) | TB | R | RBI | RC | TBB | IBB | SO | HBP | SH | SF | SB | CS | SB% | GDP | Avg | OBP | Slg |
|---|---|---|---|---|---|---|---|---|---|---|---|---|---|---|---|---|---|---|---|---|---|---|---|---|---|---|---|
| | | | BATTING | | | | | | | | | | | | | | | | | | BASERUNNING | | | | AVERAGES | | |
| 2011 | SD | NL | 49 | 128 | 18 | 8 | 1 | 1 | (1 | 0) | 31 | 9 | 9 | 7 | 21 | 1 | 46 | 4 | 0 | 0 | 2 | 1 | .67 | 2 | .141 | .281 | .242 |
| 2012 | ChC | NL | 87 | 337 | 96 | 15 | 0 | 15 | (7 | 8) | 156 | 44 | 48 | 57 | 27 | 1 | 62 | 3 | 0 | 1 | 3 | 2 | .60 | 7 | .285 | .342 | .463 |
| 2013 | ChC | NL | 160 | 606 | 141 | 40 | 2 | 23 | (13 | 10) | 254 | 71 | 80 | 74 | 76 | 7 | 127 | 6 | 0 | 2 | 6 | 5 | .55 | 12 | .233 | .323 | .419 |
| 3 ML YEARS | | | 296 | 1071 | 255 | 63 | 3 | 39 | (21 | 18) | 441 | 124 | 137 | 138 | 124 | 9 | 235 | 13 | 0 | 3 | 11 | 8 | .58 | 21 | .238 | .324 | .412 |

## Tanner Roark

**Pitches:** R **Bats:** R **Pos:** RP-9; SP-5 ROW-ark **Ht:** 6'2" **Wt:** 220 **Born:** 10/5/1986 **Age:** 27

| Year | Team | Lg | G | GS | CG | GF | IP | BFP | H | R | ER | HR | SH | SF | HB | TBB | IBB | SO | WP | Bk | W | L | Pct | Sh | Sv-Op | Hld | ERC | ERA |
|---|---|---|---|---|---|---|---|---|---|---|---|---|---|---|---|---|---|---|---|---|---|---|---|---|---|---|---|---|
| | | | HOW MUCH HE PITCHED | | | | | | WHAT HE GAVE UP | | | | | | | | | | | | THE RESULTS | | | | | | | |
| 2009 | Bkrsfld | A+ | 29 | 9 | 0 | 7 | 86.2 | 354 | 68 | 27 | 26 | 5 | 1 | 5 | 7 | 27 | 0 | 91 | 5 | 0 | 10 | 0 | 1.000 | 0 | 0-- | - | 2.65 | 2.70 |
| 2009 | Frisco | AA | 5 | 4 | 0 | 0 | 17.2 | 75 | 17 | 9 | 9 | 1 | 0 | 2 | 1 | 7 | 0 | 9 | 2 | 0 | 1 | 1 | .500 | 0 | 0-- | - | 3.84 | 4.58 |
| 2010 | Frisco | AA | 22 | 17 | 0 | 0 | 105.0 | 448 | 113 | 57 | 49 | 8 | 2 | 2 | 2 | 33 | 0 | 75 | 4 | 0 | 10 | 5 | .667 | 0 | 0-- | - | 4.12 | 4.20 |
| 2010 | Hrsbrg | AA | 6 | 6 | 0 | 0 | 36.0 | 148 | 35 | 13 | 10 | 5 | 0 | 1 | 0 | 9 | 0 | 33 | 0 | 1 | 1 | 1 | .500 | 0 | 0-- | - | 3.63 | 2.50 |
| 2011 | Hrsbrg | AA | 21 | 21 | 0 | 0 | 117.0 | 502 | 125 | 64 | 61 | 10 | 5 | 3 | 4 | 39 | 3 | 92 | 6 | 0 | 9 | 9 | .500 | 0 | 0-- | - | 4.24 | 4.69 |
| 2012 | Syrcse | AAA | 28 | 26 | 1 | 0 | 147.2 | 645 | 161 | 89 | 72 | 14 | 8 | 7 | 11 | 47 | 3 | 130 | 5 | 0 | 6 | 17 | .261 | 0 | 0-- | - | 4.51 | 4.39 |
| 2013 | Syrcse | AAA | 33 | 11 | 0 | 9 | 105.2 | 419 | 85 | 43 | 37 | 6 | 2 | 2 | 3 | 20 | 0 | 84 | 2 | 0 | 9 | 3 | .750 | 0 | 2-- | - | 2.13 | 3.15 |
| 2013 | Was | NL | 14 | 5 | 0 | 1 | 53.2 | 204 | 38 | 11 | 9 | 1 | 3 | 2 | 0 | 11 | 0 | 40 | 0 | 0 | 7 | 1 | .875 | 0 | 0-0 | 1 | 1.54 | 1.51 |

## Brian Roberts

**Bats:** B **Throws:** R **Pos:** 2B-60;DH-15;PH-3 **Ht:** 5'9" **Wt:** 175 **Born:** 10/9/1977 **Age:** 36

| Year | Team | Lg | G | AB | H | 2B | 3B | HR | (Hm | Rd) | TB | R | RBI | RC | TBB | IBB | SO | HBP | SH | SF | SB | CS | SB% | GDP | Avg | OBP | Slg |
|---|---|---|---|---|---|---|---|---|---|---|---|---|---|---|---|---|---|---|---|---|---|---|---|---|---|---|---|
| | | | BATTING | | | | | | | | | | | | | | | | | | BASERUNNING | | | | AVERAGES | | |
| 2013 | Norfolk* | AAA | 4 | 13 | 3 | 1 | 0 | 0 | (- | -) | 4 | 2 | 1 | 1 | 2 | 0 | 3 | 0 | 0 | 0 | 0 | 0 | - | 0 | .231 | .333 | .308 |
| 2001 | Bal | AL | 75 | 273 | 69 | 12 | 3 | 2 | (0 | 2) | 93 | 42 | 17 | 27 | 13 | 0 | 36 | 0 | 3 | 3 | 12 | 3 | .80 | 3 | .253 | .284 | .341 |
| 2002 | Bal | AL | 38 | 128 | 29 | 6 | 0 | 1 | (1 | 0) | 38 | 18 | 11 | 12 | 15 | 0 | 21 | 1 | 3 | 2 | 9 | 2 | .82 | 3 | .227 | .308 | .297 |
| 2003 | Bal | AL | 112 | 460 | 124 | 22 | 4 | 5 | (3 | 2) | 169 | 65 | 41 | 62 | 46 | 1 | 58 | 1 | 4 | 1 | 23 | 6 | .79 | 9 | .270 | .337 | .367 |
| 2004 | Bal | AL | 159 | 641 | 175 | **50** | 2 | 4 | (0 | 4) | 241 | 107 | 53 | 91 | 71 | 1 | 95 | 1 | 15 | 6 | 29 | 12 | .71 | 3 | .273 | .344 | .376 |
| 2005 | Bal | AL | 143 | 561 | 176 | 45 | 7 | 18 | (9 | 9) | 289 | 92 | 73 | 106 | 67 | 5 | 83 | 3 | 5 | 4 | 27 | 10 | .73 | 6 | .314 | .387 | .515 |
| 2006 | Bal | AL | 138 | 563 | 161 | 34 | 3 | 10 | (6 | 4) | 231 | 85 | 55 | 74 | 55 | 4 | 66 | 0 | 6 | 5 | 36 | 7 | .84 | 16 | .286 | .347 | .410 |
| 2007 | Bal | AL | 156 | 621 | 180 | 42 | 5 | 12 | (6 | 6) | 268 | 103 | 57 | 105 | 89 | 6 | 99 | 0 | 2 | 4 | **50** | 7 | .88 | 8 | .290 | .377 | .432 |
| 2008 | Bal | AL | 155 | 611 | 181 | 51 | 8 | 9 | (6 | 3) | 275 | 107 | 57 | 101 | 82 | 3 | 104 | 2 | 3 | 6 | 40 | 10 | .80 | 8 | .296 | .378 | .450 |
| 2009 | Bal | AL | 159 | 632 | 179 | **56** | 1 | 16 | (4 | 12) | 285 | 110 | 79 | 106 | 74 | 3 | 112 | 2 | 1 | 8 | 30 | 7 | .81 | 7 | .283 | .356 | .451 |
| 2010 | Bal | AL | 59 | 230 | 64 | 14 | 0 | 4 | (2 | 2) | 90 | 28 | 15 | 31 | 26 | 1 | 40 | 2 | 1 | 2 | 12 | 2 | .86 | 2 | .278 | .354 | .391 |
| 2011 | Bal | AL | 39 | 163 | 36 | 7 | 1 | 3 | (1 | 2) | 54 | 18 | 19 | 18 | 12 | 0 | 21 | 0 | 2 | 1 | 6 | 1 | .86 | 4 | .221 | .273 | .331 |
| 2012 | Bal | AL | 17 | 66 | 12 | 0 | 0 | 0 | (0 | 0) | 12 | 2 | 5 | 3 | 5 | 0 | 12 | 0 | 1 | 2 | 1 | 1 | .50 | 0 | .182 | .233 | .182 |
| 2013 | Bal | AL | 77 | 265 | 66 | 12 | 1 | 8 | (6 | 2) | 104 | 33 | 39 | 36 | 26 | 1 | 44 | 0 | 1 | 4 | 3 | 1 | .75 | 4 | .249 | .312 | .392 |
| 13 ML YEARS | | | 1327 | 5214 | 1452 | 351 | 35 | 92 | (44 | 48) | 2149 | 810 | 521 | 772 | 581 | 25 | 791 | 12 | 47 | 48 | 278 | 69 | .80 | 73 | .278 | .349 | .412 |

## Ryan Roberts

**Bats:** R **Throws:** R **Pos:** 2B-48;PH-16;3B-9;1B-3;DH-1;PR-1 **Ht:** 5'11" **Wt:** 185 **Born:** 9/19/1980 **Age:** 33

| Year | Team | Lg | G | AB | H | 2B | 3B | HR | (Hm | Rd) | TB | R | RBI | RC | TBB | IBB | SO | HBP | SH | SF | SB | CS | SB% | GDP | Avg | OBP | Slg |
|---|---|---|---|---|---|---|---|---|---|---|---|---|---|---|---|---|---|---|---|---|---|---|---|---|---|---|---|
| | | | BATTING | | | | | | | | | | | | | | | | | | BASERUNNING | | | | AVERAGES | | |
| 2013 | Drham* | AAA | 37 | 124 | 26 | 5 | 0 | 1 | (- | -) | 34 | 12 | 13 | 13 | 21 | 0 | 30 | 0 | 1 | 2 | 3 | 1 | .75 | 3 | .210 | .320 | .274 |
| 2006 | Tor | AL | 9 | 13 | 1 | 0 | 0 | 1 | (0 | 1) | 4 | 1 | 1 | 0 | 1 | 0 | 4 | 0 | 0 | 0 | 0 | 0 | - | 1 | .077 | .143 | .308 |
| 2007 | Tor | AL | 8 | 13 | 1 | 0 | 0 | 0 | (0 | 0) | 1 | 2 | 0 | 0 | 2 | 0 | 7 | 1 | 0 | 0 | 0 | 0 | - | 0 | .077 | .250 | .077 |
| 2008 | Tex | AL | 1 | 1 | 0 | 0 | 0 | 0 | (0 | 0) | 0 | 0 | 0 | 0 | 0 | 0 | 1 | 0 | 0 | 0 | 0 | 0 | - | 0 | .000 | .000 | .000 |
| 2009 | Ari | NL | 110 | 305 | 85 | 17 | 2 | 7 | (3 | 4) | 127 | 41 | 25 | 41 | 40 | 1 | 55 | 3 | 2 | 1 | 7 | 3 | .70 | 2 | .279 | .367 | .416 |
| 2010 | Ari | NL | 36 | 66 | 13 | 4 | 0 | 2 | (1 | 1) | 23 | 8 | 9 | 7 | 3 | 1 | 17 | 0 | 1 | 1 | 0 | 0 | - | 0 | .197 | .229 | .348 |
| 2011 | Ari | NL | 143 | 482 | 120 | 25 | 2 | 19 | (9 | 10) | 206 | 86 | 65 | 75 | 66 | 2 | 98 | 2 | 3 | 2 | 18 | 9 | .67 | 6 | .249 | .341 | .427 |
| 2012 | 2 Tms | | 143 | 439 | 103 | 19 | 0 | 12 | (5 | 7) | 158 | 51 | 52 | 46 | 40 | 1 | 92 | 1 | 3 | 6 | 10 | 6 | .63 | 13 | .235 | .296 | .360 |
| 2013 | TB | AL | 60 | 162 | 40 | 6 | 0 | 5 | (3 | 2) | 61 | 15 | 17 | 17 | 11 | 0 | 39 | 0 | 0 | 0 | 0 | 2 | .00 | 3 | .247 | .295 | .377 |

| Year | Team | Lg | G | AB | H | 2B | 3B | HR | (Hm | Rd) | TB | R | RBI | RC | TBB | IBB | SO | HBP | SH | SF | SB | CS | SB% | GDP | Avg | OBP | Slg |
|---|---|---|---|---|---|---|---|---|---|---|---|---|---|---|---|---|---|---|---|---|---|---|---|---|---|---|---|
| BATTING | | | | | | | | | | | | | | | | | | | | | BASERUNNING | | | | AVERAGES | | |
| 12 | Ari | NL | 83 | 252 | 63 | 9 | 0 | 6 | (4 | 2) | 90 | 28 | 34 | 25 | 22 | 1 | 45 | 0 | 2 | 4 | 6 | 3 | .67 | 10 | .250 | .306 | .357 |
| 12 | TB | AL | 60 | 187 | 40 | 10 | 0 | 6 | (1 | 5) | 68 | 23 | 18 | 21 | 18 | 0 | 47 | 1 | 1 | 2 | 4 | 3 | .57 | 3 | .214 | .284 | .364 |
| Postseason | | | 5 | 20 | 7 | 1 | 0 | 2 | (1 | 1) | 14 | 2 | 6 | 2 | 0 | 0 | 4 | 0 | 0 | 0 | 0 | 1 | .00 | 0 | .350 | .350 | .700 |
| 8 ML YEARS | | | 510 | 1481 | 363 | 71 | 4 | 46 | (21 | 25) | 580 | 204 | 169 | 186 | 163 | 5 | 313 | 7 | 9 | 10 | 35 | 20 | .64 | 25 | .245 | .321 | .392 |

## David Robertson

**Pitches:** R **Bats:** R **Pos:** RP-70 **Ht:** 5'11" **Wt:** 195 **Born:** 4/9/1985 **Age:** 29

| Year | Team | Lg | G | GS | CG | GF | IP | BFP | H | R | ER | HR | SH | SF | HB | TBB | IBB | SO | WP | Bk | W | L | Pct | Sh | Sv-Op | Hld | ERC | ERA |
|---|---|---|---|---|---|---|---|---|---|---|---|---|---|---|---|---|---|---|---|---|---|---|---|---|---|---|---|---|
| HOW MUCH HE PITCHED | | | | | | | | | WHAT HE GAVE UP | | | | | | | | | | | | THE RESULTS | | | | | | | |
| 2008 | NYY | AL | 25 | 0 | 0 | 8 | 30.1 | 131 | 29 | 18 | 18 | 3 | 0 | 3 | 0 | 15 | 2 | 36 | 6 | 0 | 4 | 0 | 1.000 | 0 | 0-0 | 0 | 4.12 | 5.34 |
| 2009 | NYY | AL | 45 | 0 | 0 | 20 | 43.2 | 191 | 36 | 19 | 16 | 4 | 0 | 0 | 1 | 23 | 1 | 63 | 6 | 0 | 2 | 1 | .667 | 0 | 1-1 | 5 | 3.51 | 3.30 |
| 2010 | NYY | AL | 64 | 0 | 0 | 10 | 61.1 | 273 | 59 | 26 | 26 | 5 | 5 | 3 | 3 | 33 | 6 | 71 | 7 | 2 | 4 | 5 | .444 | 0 | 1-3 | 14 | 4.29 | 3.82 |
| 2011 | NYY | AL | 70 | 0 | 0 | 8 | 66.2 | 272 | 40 | 9 | 8 | 1 | 1 | 0 | 1 | 35 | 6 | 100 | 6 | 1 | 4 | 0 | 1.000 | 0 | 1-4 | **34** | 1.85 | 1.08 |
| 2012 | NYY | AL | 65 | 0 | 0 | 17 | 60.2 | 248 | 52 | 19 | 18 | 5 | 0 | 1 | 1 | 19 | 0 | 81 | 1 | 1 | 2 | 7 | .222 | 0 | 2-5 | 30 | 2.95 | 2.67 |
| 2013 | NYY | AL | 70 | 0 | 0 | 9 | 66.1 | 262 | 51 | 15 | 15 | 5 | 3 | 0 | 2 | 18 | 1 | 77 | 1 | 0 | 5 | 1 | .833 | 0 | 3-5 | 33 | 2.37 | 2.04 |
| Postseason | | | 19 | 0 | 0 | 7 | 17.0 | 73 | 15 | 7 | 7 | 2 | 1 | 0 | 1 | 5 | 3 | 17 | 1 | 0 | 3 | 0 | 1.000 | 0 | 0-0 | 2 | 2.99 | 3.71 |
| 6 ML YEARS | | | 339 | 0 | 0 | 72 | 329.0 | 1377 | 267 | 106 | 101 | 23 | 9 | 7 | 8 | 143 | 16 | 428 | 27 | 4 | 21 | 14 | .600 | 0 | 8-18 | 116 | 3.01 | 2.76 |

## Tyler Robertson

**Pitches:** L **Bats:** L **Pos:** RP-2 **Ht:** 6'5" **Wt:** 255 **Born:** 12/23/1987 **Age:** 26

| Year | Team | Lg | G | GS | CG | GF | IP | BFP | H | R | ER | HR | SH | SF | HB | TBB | IBB | SO | WP | Bk | W | L | Pct | Sh | Sv-Op | Hld | ERC | ERA |
|---|---|---|---|---|---|---|---|---|---|---|---|---|---|---|---|---|---|---|---|---|---|---|---|---|---|---|---|---|
| HOW MUCH HE PITCHED | | | | | | | | | WHAT HE GAVE UP | | | | | | | | | | | | THE RESULTS | | | | | | | |
| 2009 | FtMyrs | A+ | 26 | 26 | 0 | 0 | 143.1 | 606 | 139 | 64 | 53 | 7 | 8 | 4 | 7 | 51 | 0 | 103 | 7 | 0 | 8 | 8 | .500 | 0 | 0-- | - | 3.62 | 3.33 |
| 2010 | NwBrit | AA | 27 | 27 | 0 | 0 | 144.2 | 658 | 181 | 100 | 87 | 17 | 1 | 6 | 7 | 57 | 1 | 91 | 13 | 1 | 4 | 13 | .235 | 0 | 0-- | - | 5.90 | 5.41 |
| 2010 | Roch | AAA | 1 | 1 | 0 | 0 | 5.0 | 25 | 6 | 3 | 3 | 0 | 0 | 0 | 1 | 2 | 0 | 6 | 0 | 0 | 0 | 1 | .000 | 0 | 0-- | - | 4.87 | 5.40 |
| 2011 | NwBrit | AA | 55 | 0 | 0 | 43 | 89.2 | 384 | 87 | 42 | 36 | 6 | 5 | 2 | 3 | 29 | 1 | 88 | 13 | 1 | 10 | 3 | .769 | 0 | 16-- | - | 3.46 | 3.61 |
| 2012 | Roch | AAA | 33 | 0 | 0 | 13 | 28.2 | 129 | 26 | 18 | 12 | 2 | 2 | 1 | 0 | 13 | 2 | 33 | 1 | 0 | 2 | 2 | .500 | 0 | 2-- | - | 3.24 | 3.77 |
| 2013 | Roch | AAA | 21 | 0 | 0 | 5 | 20.2 | 95 | 22 | 7 | 7 | 0 | 3 | 0 | 0 | 16 | 4 | 20 | 1 | 0 | 2 | 0 | 1.000 | 0 | 1-- | - | 4.89 | 3.05 |
| 2013 | Syrcse | AAA | 26 | 1 | 0 | 5 | 26.2 | 119 | 33 | 12 | 9 | 2 | 2 | 0 | 0 | 8 | 0 | 24 | 2 | 0 | 2 | 2 | .500 | 0 | 1-- | - | 4.82 | 3.04 |
| 2012 | Min | AL | 40 | 0 | 0 | 2 | 25.0 | 111 | 21 | 16 | 15 | 4 | 1 | 1 | 1 | 14 | 3 | 26 | 1 | 0 | 2 | 2 | .500 | 0 | 0-1 | 5 | 4.10 | 5.40 |
| 2013 | Min | AL | 2 | 0 | 0 | 1 | 1.0 | 4 | 1 | 1 | 1 | 1 | 0 | 0 | 0 | 0 | 0 | 2 | 0 | 0 | 0 | 0 | - | 0 | 0-0 | 1 | 7.45 | 9.00 |
| 2 ML YEARS | | | 42 | 0 | 0 | 3 | 26.0 | 115 | 22 | 17 | 16 | 5 | 1 | 1 | 1 | 14 | 3 | 28 | 1 | 0 | 2 | 2 | .500 | 0 | 0-1 | 6 | 4.29 | 5.54 |

## Chris Robinson

**Bats:** R **Throws:** R **Pos:** PH-7;C-2 **Ht:** 6'0" **Wt:** 220 **Born:** 5/12/1984 **Age:** 30

| Year | Team | Lg | G | AB | H | 2B | 3B | HR | (Hm | Rd) | TB | R | RBI | RC | TBB | IBB | SO | HBP | SH | SF | SB | CS | SB% | GDP | Avg | OBP | Slg |
|---|---|---|---|---|---|---|---|---|---|---|---|---|---|---|---|---|---|---|---|---|---|---|---|---|---|---|---|
| BATTING | | | | | | | | | | | | | | | | | | | | | BASERUNNING | | | | AVERAGES | | |
| 2009 | Iowa | AAA | 91 | 310 | 101 | 22 | 3 | 2 | (- | -) | 135 | 37 | 48 | 48 | 13 | 2 | 44 | 0 | 1 | 7 | 9 | 3 | .75 | 11 | .326 | .345 | .435 |
| 2010 | Iowa | AAA | 67 | 230 | 57 | 10 | 1 | 2 | (- | -) | 75 | 15 | 26 | 24 | 17 | 0 | 34 | 1 | 6 | 2 | 1 | 0 | 1.00 | 12 | .248 | .300 | .326 |
| 2011 | Iowa | AAA | 66 | 225 | 71 | 15 | 0 | 1 | (- | -) | 89 | 26 | 29 | 31 | 6 | 0 | 33 | 5 | 2 | 2 | 1 | 1 | .50 | 11 | .316 | .345 | .396 |
| 2012 | Norfolk | AAA | 52 | 177 | 41 | 10 | 2 | 0 | (- | -) | 55 | 18 | 18 | 17 | 15 | 0 | 27 | 3 | 0 | 3 | 0 | 2 | .00 | 8 | .232 | .298 | .311 |
| 2013 | Norfolk | AAA | 29 | 108 | 26 | 4 | 0 | 0 | (- | -) | 30 | 9 | 5 | 7 | 4 | 0 | 24 | 0 | 1 | 0 | 0 | 0 | - | 3 | .241 | .268 | .278 |
| 2013 | Tucsn | AAA | 39 | 133 | 42 | 5 | 0 | 0 | (- | -) | 47 | 20 | 17 | 16 | 3 | 0 | 18 | 2 | 3 | 1 | 2 | 2 | .50 | 5 | .316 | .338 | .353 |
| 2013 | SD | NL | 8 | 12 | 2 | 0 | 0 | 1 | (1 | 0) | 5 | 1 | 3 | 2 | 0 | 0 | 3 | 0 | 0 | 0 | 0 | 0 | - | 0 | .167 | .167 | .417 |

## Derrick Robinson

**Bats:** B **Throws:** L **Pos:** LF-60;PH-37;CF-15;PR-6;RF-2 **Ht:** 5'11" **Wt:** 190 **Born:** 9/28/1987 **Age:** 26

| Year | Team | Lg | G | AB | H | 2B | 3B | HR | (Hm | Rd) | TB | R | RBI | RC | TBB | IBB | SO | HBP | SH | SF | SB | CS | SB% | GDP | Avg | OBP | Slg |
|---|---|---|---|---|---|---|---|---|---|---|---|---|---|---|---|---|---|---|---|---|---|---|---|---|---|---|---|
| BATTING | | | | | | | | | | | | | | | | | | | | | BASERUNNING | | | | AVERAGES | | |
| 2009 | Wilmg | A+ | 128 | 522 | 125 | 19 | 5 | 5 | (- | -) | 169 | 72 | 47 | 55 | 35 | 1 | 90 | 3 | 9 | 2 | 69 | 23 | .75 | 5 | .239 | .290 | .324 |
| 2010 | NWArk | AA | 127 | 511 | 146 | 26 | 8 | 2 | (- | -) | 194 | 74 | 48 | 74 | 45 | 1 | 86 | 4 | 5 | 5 | 50 | 17 | .75 | 6 | .286 | .345 | .380 |
| 2011 | NWArk | AA | 107 | 419 | 105 | 6 | 2 | 1 | (- | -) | 118 | 56 | 25 | 47 | 46 | 3 | 87 | 0 | 15 | 3 | 56 | 15 | .79 | 5 | .251 | .323 | .282 |
| 2012 | Omha | AAA | 116 | 422 | 113 | 12 | 3 | 2 | (- | -) | 137 | 73 | 28 | 54 | 50 | 2 | 84 | 2 | 8 | 6 | 23 | 9 | .72 | 8 | .268 | .344 | .325 |
| 2013 | Lsvlle | AAA | 15 | 59 | 13 | 3 | 0 | 0 | (- | -) | 16 | 5 | 3 | 4 | 3 | 0 | 20 | 0 | 1 | 0 | 3 | 0 | 1.00 | 0 | .220 | .258 | .271 |
| 2013 | Cin | NL | 102 | 192 | 49 | 7 | 3 | 0 | (0 | 0) | 62 | 21 | 8 | 20 | 18 | 0 | 44 | 1 | 5 | 0 | 4 | 5 | .44 | 0 | .255 | .322 | .323 |

## Shane Robinson

**Bats:** R **Throws:** R **Pos:** RF-34;CF-27;LF-26;PH-23;PR-11 **Ht:** 5'9" **Wt:** 165 **Born:** 10/30/1984 **Age:** 29

| Year | Team | Lg | G | AB | H | 2B | 3B | HR | (Hm | Rd) | TB | R | RBI | RC | TBB | IBB | SO | HBP | SH | SF | SB | CS | SB% | GDP | Avg | OBP | Slg |
|---|---|---|---|---|---|---|---|---|---|---|---|---|---|---|---|---|---|---|---|---|---|---|---|---|---|---|---|
| BATTING | | | | | | | | | | | | | | | | | | | | | BASERUNNING | | | | AVERAGES | | |
| 2013 | Sprgfld* | AA | 3 | 10 | 2 | 0 | 0 | 0 | (- | -) | 2 | 0 | 0 | 0 | 2 | 0 | 1 | 0 | 0 | 0 | 0 | 0 | - | 0 | .200 | .333 | .200 |
| 2009 | StL | NL | 11 | 25 | 6 | 1 | 0 | 0 | (0 | 0) | 7 | 1 | 1 | 1 | 0 | 0 | 2 | 0 | 0 | 1 | 1 | 0 | 1.00 | 1 | .240 | .231 | .280 |
| 2011 | StL | NL | 9 | 7 | 0 | 0 | 0 | 0 | (0 | 0) | 0 | 0 | 0 | 0 | 1 | 0 | 2 | 0 | 0 | 0 | 0 | 0 | - | 1 | .000 | .125 | .000 |
| 2012 | StL | NL | 102 | 166 | 42 | 8 | 0 | 3 | (1 | 2) | 59 | 20 | 16 | 15 | 14 | 2 | 32 | 0 | 0 | 1 | 1 | 0 | 1.00 | 5 | .253 | .309 | .355 |
| 2013 | StL | NL | 99 | 144 | 36 | 2 | 1 | 2 | (1 | 1) | 46 | 22 | 16 | 18 | 23 | 0 | 17 | 0 | 0 | 4 | 5 | 1 | .83 | 2 | .250 | .345 | .319 |
| Postseason | | | 10 | 8 | 0 | 0 | 0 | 0 | (0 | 0) | 0 | 1 | 1 | 0 | 1 | 0 | 2 | 0 | 0 | 0 | 0 | 0 | - | 0 | .000 | .111 | .000 |
| 4 ML YEARS | | | 221 | 342 | 84 | 11 | 1 | 5 | (2 | 3) | 112 | 43 | 33 | 34 | 38 | 2 | 53 | 0 | 0 | 6 | 7 | 1 | .88 | 9 | .246 | .316 | .327 |

# Mauricio Robles

**Pitches:** L **Bats:** L **Pos:** RP-3 more-EE-see-oh ROW-bless **Ht:** 5'10" **Wt:** 215 **Born:** 3/5/1989 **Age:** 25

| | | | HOW MUCH HE PITCHED | | | | | | WHAT HE GAVE UP | | | | | | | | | | | | THE RESULTS | | | | | | | |
|---|---|---|---|---|---|---|---|---|---|---|---|---|---|---|---|---|---|---|---|---|---|---|---|---|---|---|---|---|
| Year | Team | Lg | G | GS | CG | GF | IP | BFP | H | R | ER | HR | SH | SF | HB | TBB | IBB | SO | WP | Bk | W | L | Pct | Sh | Sv-Op | Hld | ERC | ERA |
| 2009 | WMich | A | 11 | 11 | 0 | 0 | 56.1 | 235 | 45 | 29 | 29 | 6 | 2 | 1 | 1 | 27 | 0 | 71 | 2 | 1 | 4 | 4 | .500 | 0 | 0-- | - | 3.44 | 4.63 |
| 2009 | Lkland | A+ | 7 | 7 | 0 | 0 | 35.0 | 151 | 34 | 16 | 14 | 3 | 1 | 0 | 3 | 14 | 0 | 40 | 1 | 0 | 4 | 2 | .667 | 0 | 0-- | - | 4.20 | 3.60 |
| 2009 | Hi Dsrt | A+ | 7 | 6 | 0 | 0 | 32.1 | 134 | 23 | 14 | 10 | 1 | 1 | 0 | 0 | 19 | 0 | 34 | 1 | 0 | 3 | 2 | .600 | 0 | 0-- | - | 2.82 | 2.78 |
| 2010 | WTenn | AA | 22 | 22 | 0 | 0 | 114.0 | 489 | 102 | 58 | 52 | 10 | 2 | 3 | 6 | 51 | 3 | 120 | 6 | 2 | 6 | 6 | .500 | 0 | 0-- | - | 3.77 | 4.11 |
| 2010 | Tacom | AAA | 5 | 5 | 0 | 0 | 28.0 | 122 | 19 | 12 | 11 | 2 | 1 | 0 | 0 | 20 | 0 | 34 | 0 | 0 | 3 | 1 | .750 | 0 | 0-- | - | 3.27 | 3.54 |
| 2011 | Hi Dsrt | A+ | 4 | 4 | 0 | 0 | 12.1 | 64 | 19 | 18 | 17 | 2 | 1 | 0 | 1 | 11 | 0 | 9 | 2 | 0 | 0 | 2 | .000 | 0 | 0-- | - | 11.04 | 12.41 |
| 2011 | Jacksn | AA | 2 | 2 | 0 | 0 | 8.2 | 41 | 7 | 4 | 4 | 1 | 0 | 0 | 1 | 8 | 0 | 6 | 1 | 0 | 0 | 1 | .000 | 0 | 0-- | - | 5.64 | 4.15 |
| 2011 | Tacom | AAA | 4 | 4 | 0 | 0 | 11.1 | 52 | 7 | 11 | 11 | 3 | 0 | 0 | 1 | 14 | 0 | 8 | 1 | 1 | 1 | 2 | .333 | 0 | 0-- | - | 7.35 | 8.74 |
| 2012 | Tacom | AAA | 6 | 5 | 0 | 0 | 21.0 | 105 | 22 | 23 | 23 | 3 | 0 | 1 | 2 | 22 | 0 | 19 | 1 | 1 | 0 | 3 | .000 | 0 | 0-- | - | 7.95 | 9.86 |
| 2012 | Jacksn | AA | 37 | 1 | 0 | 10 | 50.2 | 227 | 36 | 24 | 23 | 2 | 2 | 0 | 3 | 41 | 2 | 50 | 5 | 0 | 2 | 2 | .500 | 0 | 0-- | - | 3.74 | 4.09 |
| 2013 | Rdng | AA | 17 | 0 | 0 | 7 | 26.0 | 107 | 19 | 8 | 8 | 1 | 0 | 1 | 0 | 13 | 0 | 37 | 2 | 1 | 3 | 1 | .750 | 0 | 2-- | - | 2.64 | 2.77 |
| 2013 | LV | AAA | 34 | 0 | 0 | 19 | 38.0 | 156 | 16 | 7 | 6 | 0 | 5 | 1 | 1 | 31 | 2 | 26 | 6 | 0 | 2 | 2 | .500 | 0 | 7-- | - | 1.97 | 1.42 |
| 2013 | Phi | NL | 3 | 0 | 0 | 0 | 4.2 | 25 | 7 | 3 | 1 | 0 | 0 | 0 | 0 | 3 | 0 | 6 | 2 | 1 | 0 | 0 | - | 0 | 0-0 | 0 | 6.77 | 1.93 |

# Fernando Rodney

**Pitches:** R **Bats:** R **Pos:** RP-68 **Ht:** 5'11" **Wt:** 220 **Born:** 3/18/1977 **Age:** 37

| | | | HOW MUCH HE PITCHED | | | | | | WHAT HE GAVE UP | | | | | | | | | | | | THE RESULTS | | | | | | | |
|---|---|---|---|---|---|---|---|---|---|---|---|---|---|---|---|---|---|---|---|---|---|---|---|---|---|---|---|---|
| Year | Team | Lg | G | GS | CG | GF | IP | BFP | H | R | ER | HR | SH | SF | HB | TBB | IBB | SO | WP | Bk | W | L | Pct | Sh | Sv-Op | Hld | ERC | ERA |
| 2002 | Det | AL | 20 | 0 | 0 | 10 | 18.0 | 89 | 25 | 15 | 12 | 2 | 2 | 1 | 0 | 10 | 2 | 10 | 0 | 1 | 1 | 3 | .250 | 0 | 0-4 | 0 | 6.77 | 6.00 |
| 2003 | Det | AL | 27 | 0 | 0 | 11 | 29.2 | 143 | 35 | 20 | 20 | 2 | 3 | 3 | 1 | 17 | 1 | 33 | 0 | 0 | 1 | 3 | .250 | 0 | 3-6 | 3 | 5.46 | 6.07 |
| 2005 | Det | AL | 39 | 0 | 0 | 26 | 44.0 | 185 | 39 | 14 | 14 | 5 | 2 | 0 | 2 | 17 | 3 | 42 | 2 | 0 | 2 | 3 | .400 | 0 | 9-15 | 3 | 3.59 | 2.86 |
| 2006 | Det | AL | 63 | 0 | 0 | 30 | 71.2 | 304 | 51 | 36 | 28 | 6 | 2 | 0 | 8 | 34 | 4 | 65 | 3 | 0 | 7 | 4 | .636 | 0 | 7-11 | 18 | 3.01 | 3.52 |
| 2007 | Det | AL | 48 | 0 | 0 | 12 | 50.2 | 223 | 46 | 27 | 24 | 5 | 4 | 2 | 3 | 21 | 0 | 54 | 4 | 0 | 2 | 6 | .250 | 0 | 1-3 | 12 | 3.74 | 4.26 |
| 2008 | Det | AL | 38 | 0 | 0 | 25 | 40.1 | 188 | 34 | 22 | 22 | 3 | 1 | 2 | 3 | 30 | 5 | 49 | 3 | 0 | 0 | 6 | .000 | 0 | 13-19 | 5 | 4.29 | 4.91 |
| 2009 | Det | AL | 73 | 0 | 0 | 65 | 75.2 | 330 | 70 | 38 | 37 | 8 | 4 | 2 | 2 | 41 | 4 | 61 | 5 | 0 | 2 | 5 | .286 | 0 | 37-38 | 0 | 4.31 | 4.40 |
| 2010 | LAA | AL | 72 | 0 | 0 | 30 | 68.0 | 308 | 70 | 33 | 32 | 4 | 1 | 0 | 5 | 35 | 1 | 53 | 4 | 0 | 4 | 3 | .571 | 0 | 14-21 | 21 | 4.63 | 4.24 |
| 2011 | LAA | AL | 39 | 0 | 0 | 15 | 32.0 | 150 | 26 | 18 | 16 | 1 | 3 | 0 | 3 | 28 | 0 | 26 | 2 | 0 | 3 | 5 | .375 | 0 | 3-7 | 10 | 4.66 | 4.50 |
| 2012 | TB | AL | 76 | 0 | 0 | 65 | 74.2 | 282 | 43 | 9 | 5 | 2 | 4 | 2 | 3 | 15 | 1 | 76 | 4 | 0 | 2 | 2 | .500 | 0 | 48-50 | 0 | 1.22 | 0.60 |
| 2013 | TB | AL | 68 | 0 | 0 | 55 | 66.2 | 290 | 53 | 27 | 25 | 3 | 1 | 1 | 1 | 36 | 3 | 82 | 4 | 1 | 5 | 4 | .556 | 0 | 37-45 | 0 | 3.02 | 3.38 |
| Postseason | | | 7 | 0 | 0 | 0 | 7.2 | 33 | 6 | 4 | 2 | 0 | 2 | 0 | 0 | 5 | 1 | 9 | 0 | 0 | 0 | 0 | - | 0 | 0-1 | 2 | 2.94 | 2.35 |
| 11 ML YEARS | | | 563 | 0 | 0 | 344 | 571.1 | 2492 | 492 | 259 | 235 | 41 | 27 | 13 | 31 | 284 | 24 | 551 | 31 | 2 | 29 | 44 | .397 | 0 | 172-219 | 72 | 3.59 | 3.70 |

# Alex Rodriguez

**Bats:** R **Throws:** R **Pos:** 3B-27;DH-16;PH-1 **Ht:** 6'3" **Wt:** 225 **Born:** 7/27/1975 **Age:** 38

| | | | BATTING | | | | | | | | | | | | | | | | | | | BASERUNNING | | | | AVERAGES | | |
|---|---|---|---|---|---|---|---|---|---|---|---|---|---|---|---|---|---|---|---|---|---|---|---|---|---|---|---|---|
| Year | Team | Lg | G | AB | H | 2B | 3B | HR | (Hm | Rd) | TB | R | RBI | RC | TBB | IBB | SO | HBP | SH | SF | SB | CS | SB% | GDP | Avg | OBP | Slg |
| 2013 | Tampa* | A+ | 6 | 17 | 3 | 1 | 0 | 0 | (- | -) | 4 | 2 | 3 | 1 | 1 | 0 | 5 | 2 | 0 | 0 | 0 | 0 | - | 1 | .176 | .300 | .235 |
| 2013 | CtnSC* | A | 2 | 4 | 0 | 0 | 0 | 0 | (- | -) | 0 | 0 | 0 | 0 | 0 | 0 | 1 | 0 | 0 | 0 | 0 | 0 | - | 1 | .000 | .000 | .000 |
| 2013 | Trntn* | AA | 4 | 9 | 3 | 0 | 0 | 2 | (- | -) | 9 | 3 | 5 | 4 | 5 | 0 | 2 | 0 | 0 | 1 | 0 | 0 | - | 0 | .333 | .533 | 1.000 |
| 2013 | S-WB* | AAA | 3 | 12 | 3 | 0 | 0 | 1 | (- | -) | 6 | 1 | 2 | 1 | 0 | 0 | 5 | 0 | 0 | 0 | 0 | 0 | - | 0 | .250 | .250 | .500 |
| 1994 | Sea | AL | 17 | 54 | 11 | 0 | 0 | 0 | (0 | 0) | 11 | 4 | 2 | 3 | 3 | 0 | 20 | 0 | 1 | 1 | 3 | 0 | 1.00 | 0 | .204 | .241 | .204 |
| 1995 | Sea | AL | 48 | 142 | 33 | 6 | 2 | 5 | (1 | 4) | 58 | 15 | 19 | 15 | 6 | 0 | 42 | 0 | 1 | 0 | 4 | 2 | .67 | 0 | .232 | .264 | .408 |
| 1996 | Sea | AL | 146 | 601 | 215 | **54** | 1 | 36 | (18 | 18) | **379** | **141** | 123 | 144 | 59 | 1 | 104 | 4 | 6 | 7 | 15 | 4 | .79 | 15 | **.358** | .414 | .631 |
| 1997 | Sea | AL | 141 | 587 | 176 | 40 | 3 | 23 | (16 | 7) | 291 | 100 | 84 | 100 | 41 | 1 | 99 | 5 | 4 | 1 | 29 | 6 | .83 | 14 | .300 | .350 | .496 |
| 1998 | Sea | AL | 161 | **686** | **213** | 35 | 5 | 42 | (18 | 24) | 384 | 123 | 124 | 135 | 45 | 0 | 121 | 10 | 3 | 4 | 46 | 13 | .78 | 12 | .310 | .360 | .560 |
| 1999 | Sea | AL | 129 | 502 | 143 | 25 | 0 | 42 | (20 | 22) | 294 | 110 | 111 | 102 | 56 | 2 | 109 | 5 | 1 | 8 | 21 | 7 | .75 | 12 | .285 | .357 | .586 |
| 2000 | Sea | AL | 148 | 554 | 175 | 34 | 2 | 41 | (13 | **28)** | 336 | 134 | 132 | 138 | 100 | 5 | 121 | 7 | 0 | 11 | 15 | 4 | .79 | 10 | .316 | .420 | .606 |
| 2001 | Tex | AL | **162** | 632 | 201 | 34 | 1 | **52** | (26 | **26)** | **393** | **133** | 135 | 148 | 75 | 6 | 131 | 16 | 0 | 9 | 18 | 3 | .86 | 17 | .318 | .399 | .622 |
| 2002 | Tex | AL | **162** | 624 | 187 | 27 | 2 | **57** | **(34** | **23)** | **389** | 125 | **142** | **152** | 87 | 12 | 122 | 10 | 0 | 4 | 9 | 4 | .69 | 14 | .300 | .392 | .623 |
| 2003 | Tex | AL | 161 | 607 | 181 | 30 | 6 | **47** | (26 | 21) | 364 | **124** | 118 | 131 | 87 | 10 | 126 | 15 | 0 | 6 | 17 | 3 | .85 | 16 | .298 | .396 | **.600** |
| 2004 | NYY | AL | 155 | 601 | 172 | 24 | 2 | 36 | (17 | 19) | 308 | 112 | 106 | 112 | 80 | 6 | 131 | 10 | 0 | 7 | 28 | 4 | .88 | 18 | .286 | .375 | .512 |
| 2005 | NYY | AL | **162** | 605 | 194 | 29 | 1 | **48** | (26 | 22) | 369 | **124** | 130 | 137 | 91 | 8 | 139 | 16 | 0 | 3 | 21 | 6 | .78 | 8 | .321 | .421 | **.610** |
| 2006 | NYY | AL | 154 | 572 | 166 | 26 | 1 | 35 | (20 | 15) | 299 | 113 | 121 | 112 | 90 | 8 | 139 | 8 | 0 | 4 | 15 | 4 | .79 | 22 | .290 | .392 | .523 |
| 2007 | NYY | AL | 158 | 583 | 183 | 31 | 0 | **54** | **(26** | **28)** | **376** | **143** | **156** | **159** | 95 | 11 | 120 | 21 | 0 | 9 | 24 | 4 | .86 | 15 | .314 | .422 | **.645** |
| 2008 | NYY | AL | 138 | 510 | 154 | 33 | 0 | 35 | **(21** | 14) | 292 | 104 | 103 | 97 | 65 | 9 | 117 | 14 | 0 | 5 | 18 | 3 | .86 | 16 | .302 | .392 | **.573** |
| 2009 | NYY | AL | 124 | 444 | 127 | 17 | 1 | 30 | (18 | 12) | 236 | 78 | 100 | 89 | 80 | 7 | 97 | 8 | 0 | 3 | 14 | 2 | .88 | 13 | .286 | .402 | .532 |
| 2010 | NYY | AL | 137 | 522 | 141 | 29 | 2 | 30 | (15 | 15) | 264 | 74 | 125 | 93 | 59 | 1 | 98 | 3 | 0 | 11 | 4 | 3 | .57 | 7 | .270 | .341 | .506 |
| 2011 | NYY | AL | 99 | 373 | 103 | 21 | 0 | 16 | (9 | 7) | 172 | 67 | 62 | 61 | 47 | 1 | 80 | 5 | 0 | 3 | 4 | 1 | .80 | 13 | .276 | .362 | .461 |
| 2012 | NYY | AL | 122 | 463 | 126 | 17 | 1 | 18 | (8 | 10) | 199 | 74 | 57 | 66 | 51 | 3 | 116 | 10 | 0 | 5 | 13 | 1 | .93 | 13 | .272 | .353 | .430 |
| 2013 | NYY | AL | 44 | 156 | 38 | 7 | 0 | 7 | (2 | 5) | 66 | 21 | 19 | 19 | 23 | 1 | 43 | 2 | 0 | 0 | 4 | 2 | .67 | 5 | .244 | .348 | .423 |
| Postseason | | | 75 | 274 | 72 | 16 | 0 | 13 | (5 | 8) | 127 | 43 | 41 | 43 | 39 | 4 | 75 | 9 | 1 | 3 | 8 | 3 | .73 | 6 | .263 | .369 | .464 |
| 20 ML YEARS | | | 2568 | 9818 | 2939 | 519 | 30 | 654 | (334 | 320) | 5480 | 1919 | 1969 | 2013 | 1240 | 92 | 2075 | 169 | 16 | 101 | 322 | 76 | .81 | 240 | .299 | .384 | .558 |

# Francisco Rodriguez

**Pitches:** R **Bats:** R **Pos:** RP-48 **Ht:** 6'0" **Wt:** 195 **Born:** 1/7/1982 **Age:** 32

| | | | HOW MUCH HE PITCHED | | | | | | WHAT HE GAVE UP | | | | | | | | | | | | THE RESULTS | | | | | | | |
|---|---|---|---|---|---|---|---|---|---|---|---|---|---|---|---|---|---|---|---|---|---|---|---|---|---|---|---|---|
| Year | Team | Lg | G | GS | CG | GF | IP | BFP | H | R | ER | HR | SH | SF | HB | TBB | IBB | SO | WP | Bk | W | L | Pct | Sh | Sv-Op | Hld | ERC | ERA |
| 2013 | BrvdCt* | A+ | 2 | 0 | 0 | 0 | 2.0 | 7 | 0 | 0 | 0 | 0 | 0 | 0 | 0 | 1 | 0 | 4 | 0 | 0 | 0 | 0 | - | 0 | 0-- | - | 0.27 | 0.00 |
| 2013 | Nashv* | AAA | 2 | 0 | 0 | 0 | 2.0 | 9 | 1 | 0 | 0 | 0 | 0 | 0 | 0 | 2 | 0 | 3 | 0 | 0 | 0 | 0 | - | 0 | 0-- | - | 2.80 | 0.00 |
| 2002 | LAA | AL | 5 | 0 | 0 | 4 | 5.2 | 21 | 3 | 0 | 0 | 0 | 0 | 0 | 1 | 2 | 1 | 13 | 0 | 0 | 0 | 0 | - | 0 | 0-0 | 0 | 1.52 | 0.00 |
| 2003 | LAA | AL | 59 | 0 | 0 | 23 | 86.0 | 334 | 50 | 30 | 29 | 12 | 2 | 4 | 2 | 35 | 5 | 95 | 7 | 0 | 8 | 3 | .727 | 0 | 2-6 | 7 | 2.25 | 3.03 |
| 2004 | LAA | AL | 69 | 0 | 0 | 29 | 84.0 | 335 | 51 | 21 | 17 | 2 | 2 | 1 | 1 | 33 | 1 | 123 | 5 | 0 | 4 | 1 | .800 | 0 | 12-19 | 27 | 1.64 | 1.82 |
| 2005 | LAA | AL | 66 | 0 | 0 | 58 | 67.1 | 279 | 45 | 20 | 20 | 7 | 1 | 1 | 0 | 32 | 3 | 91 | 8 | 0 | 2 | 5 | .286 | 0 | **45-50** | 0 | 2.52 | 2.67 |
| 2006 | LAA | AL | 69 | 0 | 0 | 58 | 73.0 | 296 | 52 | 16 | 14 | 6 | 3 | 0 | 1 | 28 | 5 | 98 | 10 | 0 | 2 | 3 | .400 | 0 | **47-51** | 0 | 2.35 | 1.73 |
| 2007 | LAA | AL | 64 | 0 | 0 | 56 | 67.1 | 285 | 50 | 22 | 21 | 3 | 1 | 4 | 1 | 34 | 0 | 90 | 7 | 1 | 5 | 2 | .714 | 0 | 40-46 | 0 | 2.74 | 2.81 |
| 2008 | LAA | AL | **76** | 0 | 0 | 69 | 68.1 | 288 | 54 | 21 | 17 | 4 | 1 | 1 | 2 | 34 | 4 | 77 | 6 | 0 | 2 | 3 | .400 | 0 | **62-69** | 0 | 3.06 | 2.24 |

| | | | HOW MUCH HE PITCHED | | | | | | WHAT HE GAVE UP | | | | | | | | | | THE RESULTS | | | | | | | |
|---|---|---|---|---|---|---|---|---|---|---|---|---|---|---|---|---|---|---|---|---|---|---|---|---|---|---|
| Year | Team | Lg | G | GS | CG | GF | IP | BFP | H | R | ER | HR | SH | SF | HB | TBB | IBB | SO | WP | Bk | W | L | Pct | Sh | Sv-Op | Hld | ERC | ERA |
| 2009 | NYM | NL | 70 | 0 | 0 | 66 | 68.0 | 295 | 51 | 34 | 28 | 7 | 4 | 1 | 1 | 38 | 6 | 73 | 1 | 0 | 3 | 6 | .333 | 0 | 35-42 | 0 | 3.18 | 3.71 |
| 2010 | NYM | NL | 53 | 0 | 0 | 46 | 57.1 | 236 | 45 | 14 | 14 | 3 | 1 | 1 | 2 | 21 | 4 | 67 | 3 | 1 | 4 | 2 | .667 | 0 | 25-30 | 0 | 2.53 | 2.20 |
| 2011 | 2 Tms | NL | 73 | 0 | 0 | 36 | 71.2 | 307 | 67 | 22 | 21 | 4 | 2 | 1 | 2 | 26 | 4 | 79 | 4 | 0 | 6 | 2 | .750 | 0 | 23-29 | 17 | 3.25 | 2.64 |
| 2012 | Mil | NL | 78 | 0 | 0 | 13 | 72.0 | 305 | 65 | 37 | 35 | 8 | 1 | 3 | 0 | 31 | 1 | 72 | 6 | 0 | 2 | 7 | .222 | 0 | 3-10 | 32 | 3.73 | 4.38 |
| 2013 | 2 Tms | | 48 | 0 | 0 | 23 | 46.2 | 193 | 42 | 14 | 14 | 7 | 3 | 0 | 1 | 14 | 4 | 54 | 2 | 0 | 3 | 2 | .600 | 0 | 10-10 | 5 | 3.44 | 2.70 |
| 11 | NYM | NL | 42 | 0 | 0 | 34 | 42.2 | 187 | 44 | 15 | 15 | 3 | 2 | 1 | 2 | 16 | 4 | 46 | 2 | 0 | 2 | 2 | .500 | 0 | 23-26 | 0 | 3.94 | 3.16 |
| 11 | Mil | NL | 31 | 0 | 0 | 2 | 29.0 | 120 | 23 | 7 | 6 | 1 | 0 | 0 | 0 | 10 | 0 | 33 | 2 | 0 | 4 | 0 | 1.000 | 0 | 0-3 | 17 | 2.32 | 1.86 |
| 13 | Mil | NL | 25 | 0 | 0 | 18 | 24.2 | 97 | 17 | 3 | 3 | 2 | 2 | 0 | 0 | 9 | 3 | 26 | 0 | 0 | 1 | 1 | .500 | 0 | 10-10 | 1 | 2.10 | 1.09 |
| 13 | Bal | AL | 23 | 0 | 0 | 5 | 22.0 | 96 | 25 | 11 | 11 | 5 | 1 | 0 | 1 | 5 | 1 | 28 | 2 | 0 | 2 | 1 | .667 | 0 | 0-0 | 4 | 5.11 | 4.50 |
| Postseason | | | 26 | 0 | 0 | 8 | 36.2 | 158 | 32 | 15 | 12 | 5 | 1 | 3 | 1 | 18 | 2 | 49 | 5 | 0 | 5 | 4 | .556 | 0 | 3-5 | 6 | 3.99 | 2.95 |
| 12 ML YEARS | | | 730 | 0 | 0 | 481 | 767.1 | 3174 | 575 | 251 | 230 | 63 | 21 | 17 | 14 | 328 | 38 | 932 | 59 | 2 | 41 | 36 | .532 | 0 | 304-362 | 88 | 2.71 | 2.70 |

# Henry Rodriguez

**Bats:** B **Throws:** R **Pos:** PH-6;2B-3;PR-1 **Ht:** 5'8" **Wt:** 200 **Born:** 2/9/1990 **Age:** 24

| | | | BATTING | | | | | | | | | | | | | | | | | | BASERUNNING | | | | AVERAGES | | |
|---|---|---|---|---|---|---|---|---|---|---|---|---|---|---|---|---|---|---|---|---|---|---|---|---|---|---|---|
| Year | Team | Lg | G | AB | H | 2B | 3B | HR | (Hm | Rd) | TB | R | RBI | RC | TBB | IBB | SO | HBP | SH | SF | SB | CS | SB% | GDP | Avg | OBP | Slg |
| 2009 | Reds | R | 42 | 152 | 49 | 10 | 1 | 1 | (- | -) | 64 | 24 | 19 | 24 | 7 | 0 | 18 | 1 | 0 | 1 | 9 | 0 | 1.00 | 6 | .322 | .354 | .421 |
| 2010 | Dayton | A | 124 | 514 | 158 | 37 | 3 | 14 | (- | -) | 243 | 76 | 78 | 84 | 22 | 3 | 70 | 4 | 1 | 6 | 33 | 13 | .72 | 13 | .307 | .337 | .473 |
| 2010 | Lynbrg | A+ | 6 | 24 | 6 | 0 | 0 | 0 | (- | -) | 6 | 2 | 4 | 1 | 0 | 0 | 4 | 0 | 0 | 0 | 0 | 0 | - | 1 | .250 | .250 | .250 |
| 2011 | Bkrsfld | A+ | 58 | 238 | 81 | 17 | 0 | 8 | (- | -) | 122 | 37 | 44 | 44 | 14 | 0 | 35 | 1 | 0 | 1 | 12 | 7 | .63 | 4 | .340 | .378 | .513 |
| 2011 | Carlina | AA | 69 | 278 | 84 | 19 | 1 | 5 | (- | -) | 120 | 39 | 37 | 48 | 25 | 1 | 43 | 4 | 4 | 1 | 18 | 3 | .86 | 4 | .302 | .367 | .432 |
| 2012 | Pnscla | AA | 33 | 132 | 46 | 6 | 0 | 2 | (- | -) | 58 | 19 | 15 | 23 | 9 | 2 | 18 | 0 | 1 | 2 | 3 | 0 | 1.00 | 5 | .348 | .385 | .439 |
| 2012 | Reds | R | 5 | 17 | 4 | 1 | 0 | 0 | (- | -) | 5 | 1 | 1 | 1 | 1 | 0 | 2 | 0 | 0 | 0 | 0 | 0 | - | 0 | .235 | .278 | .294 |
| 2012 | Lsvlle | AAA | 51 | 213 | 52 | 10 | 0 | 3 | (- | -) | 71 | 23 | 20 | 18 | 6 | 0 | 35 | 0 | 1 | 1 | 5 | 4 | .56 | 4 | .244 | .264 | .333 |
| 2013 | Lsvlle | AAA | 126 | 478 | 131 | 17 | 0 | 4 | (- | -) | 160 | 45 | 41 | 53 | 28 | 0 | 69 | 5 | 0 | 3 | 6 | 5 | .55 | 20 | .274 | .319 | .335 |
| 2012 | Cin | NL | 12 | 14 | 3 | 1 | 0 | 0 | (0 | 0) | 4 | 0 | 2 | 1 | 2 | 0 | 2 | 0 | 0 | 0 | 0 | 0 | - | 1 | .214 | .313 | .286 |
| 2013 | Cin | NL | 9 | 9 | 1 | 0 | 0 | 0 | (0 | 0) | 1 | 0 | 0 | 0 | 1 | 0 | 4 | 0 | 0 | 0 | 0 | 0 | - | 0 | .111 | .200 | .111 |
| 2 ML YEARS | | | 21 | 23 | 4 | 1 | 0 | 0 | (0 | 0) | 5 | 0 | 2 | 1 | 3 | 0 | 6 | 0 | 0 | 0 | 0 | 0 | - | 1 | .174 | .269 | .217 |

# Henry Rodriguez

**Pitches:** R **Bats:** R **Pos:** RP-22 **Ht:** 6'1" **Wt:** 225 **Born:** 2/25/1987 **Age:** 27

| | | | HOW MUCH HE PITCHED | | | | | | WHAT HE GAVE UP | | | | | | | | | | THE RESULTS | | | | | | | |
|---|---|---|---|---|---|---|---|---|---|---|---|---|---|---|---|---|---|---|---|---|---|---|---|---|---|---|
| Year | Team | Lg | G | GS | CG | GF | IP | BFP | H | R | ER | HR | SH | SF | HB | TBB | IBB | SO | WP | Bk | W | L | Pct | Sh | Sv-Op | Hld | ERC | ERA |
| 2013 | Iowa* | AAA | 3 | 0 | 0 | 2 | 3.1 | 15 | 5 | 2 | 2 | 0 | 2 | 0 | 0 | 1 | 0 | 0 | 1 | 0 | 0 | 1 | .000 | 0 | 0- - | - | 6.08 | 5.40 |
| 2009 | Oak | AL | 3 | 0 | 0 | 1 | 4.0 | 20 | 4 | 2 | 1 | 0 | 0 | 0 | 1 | 2 | 0 | 4 | 3 | 0 | 0 | 0 | - | 0 | 0-0 | 0 | 4.28 | 2.25 |
| 2010 | Oak | AL | 29 | 0 | 0 | 8 | 27.2 | 121 | 25 | 16 | 14 | 2 | 2 | 1 | 1 | 13 | 0 | 33 | 7 | 0 | 1 | 0 | 1.000 | 0 | 0-1 | 3 | 3.70 | 4.55 |
| 2011 | Was | NL | 59 | 0 | 0 | 21 | 65.2 | 295 | 54 | 30 | 26 | 1 | 1 | 1 | 2 | 45 | 1 | 70 | **14** | 1 | 3 | 3 | .500 | 0 | 2-5 | 10 | 3.59 | 3.56 |
| 2012 | Was | NL | 35 | 0 | 0 | 20 | 29.1 | 131 | 19 | 20 | 19 | 4 | 2 | 1 | 1 | 22 | 0 | 31 | 10 | 1 | 1 | 3 | .250 | 0 | 9-12 | 2 | 3.76 | 5.83 |
| 2013 | 2 Tms | NL | 22 | 0 | 0 | 10 | 22.0 | 109 | 20 | 12 | 10 | 2 | 0 | 1 | 2 | 20 | 1 | 12 | 2 | 1 | 0 | 1 | .000 | 0 | 0-0 | 1 | 5.59 | 4.09 |
| 13 | Was | NL | 17 | 0 | 0 | 8 | 18.0 | 86 | 14 | 8 | 8 | 1 | 0 | 0 | 1 | 16 | 0 | 11 | 2 | 1 | 0 | 1 | .000 | 0 | 0-0 | 1 | 4.41 | 4.00 |
| 13 | ChC | NL | 5 | 0 | 0 | 2 | 4.0 | 23 | 6 | 4 | 2 | 1 | 0 | 1 | 1 | 4 | 1 | 1 | 0 | 0 | 0 | 0 | - | 0 | 0-0 | 0 | 11.69 | 4.50 |
| 5 ML YEARS | | | 148 | 0 | 0 | 60 | 148.2 | 676 | 122 | 80 | 70 | 9 | 5 | 4 | 7 | 102 | 2 | 150 | 36 | 3 | 5 | 7 | .417 | 0 | 11-18 | 16 | 3.95 | 4.24 |

# Paco Rodriguez

**Pitches:** L **Bats:** L **Pos:** RP-76 **Ht:** 6'3" **Wt:** 220 **Born:** 4/16/1991 **Age:** 23

| | | | HOW MUCH HE PITCHED | | | | | | WHAT HE GAVE UP | | | | | | | | | | THE RESULTS | | | | | | | |
|---|---|---|---|---|---|---|---|---|---|---|---|---|---|---|---|---|---|---|---|---|---|---|---|---|---|---|
| Year | Team | Lg | G | GS | CG | GF | IP | BFP | H | R | ER | HR | SH | SF | HB | TBB | IBB | SO | WP | Bk | W | L | Pct | Sh | Sv-Op | Hld | ERC | ERA |
| 2012 | Gt Lks | A | 6 | 0 | 0 | 4 | 6.0 | 22 | 4 | 0 | 0 | 0 | 0 | 0 | 0 | 0 | 0 | 10 | 0 | 0 | 0 | 0 | - | 0 | 2- - | - | 0.91 | 0.00 |
| 2012 | Chatt | AA | 16 | 0 | 0 | 5 | 13.2 | 55 | 7 | 2 | 2 | 0 | 1 | 0 | 1 | 6 | 1 | 22 | 0 | 0 | 1 | 0 | 1.000 | 0 | 3- - | - | 1.41 | 1.32 |
| 2012 | LAD | NL | 11 | 0 | 0 | 2 | 6.2 | 26 | 3 | 1 | 1 | 0 | 0 | 0 | 0 | 4 | 1 | 6 | 0 | 0 | 0 | 1 | .000 | 0 | 0-0 | 0 | 1.37 | 1.35 |
| 2013 | LAD | NL | 76 | 0 | 0 | 11 | 54.1 | 208 | 30 | 15 | 14 | 5 | 3 | 1 | 2 | 19 | 4 | 63 | 3 | 0 | 3 | 4 | .429 | 0 | 2-5 | 20 | 1.68 | 2.32 |
| 2 ML YEARS | | | 87 | 0 | 0 | 13 | 61.0 | 234 | 33 | 16 | 15 | 5 | 3 | 1 | 2 | 23 | 5 | 69 | 3 | 0 | 3 | 5 | .375 | 0 | 2-5 | 20 | 1.65 | 2.21 |

# Sean Rodriguez

**Bats:** R **Throws:** R **Pos:** LF-47;PH-31;1B-23;RF-8;SS-7;2B-5;PR-5;DH-4 **Ht:** 6'0" **Wt:** 200 **Born:** 4/26/1985 **Age:** 29

| | | | BATTING | | | | | | | | | | | | | | | | | | BASERUNNING | | | | AVERAGES | | |
|---|---|---|---|---|---|---|---|---|---|---|---|---|---|---|---|---|---|---|---|---|---|---|---|---|---|---|---|
| Year | Team | Lg | G | AB | H | 2B | 3B | HR | (Hm | Rd) | TB | R | RBI | RC | TBB | IBB | SO | HBP | SH | SF | SB | CS | SB% | GDP | Avg | OBP | Slg |
| 2008 | LAA | AL | 59 | 167 | 34 | 8 | 1 | 3 | (2 | 1) | 53 | 18 | 10 | 12 | 14 | 0 | 55 | 3 | 2 | 1 | 3 | 1 | .75 | 3 | .204 | .276 | .317 |
| 2009 | LAA | AL | 12 | 25 | 5 | 0 | 0 | 2 | (0 | 2) | 11 | 4 | 4 | 2 | 3 | 0 | 7 | 0 | 0 | 1 | 0 | 0 | - | 2 | .200 | .276 | .440 |
| 2010 | TB | AL | 118 | 343 | 86 | 19 | 2 | 9 | (5 | 4) | 136 | 53 | 40 | 38 | 21 | 1 | 97 | 8 | 5 | 1 | 13 | 3 | .81 | 10 | .251 | .308 | .397 |
| 2011 | TB | AL | 131 | 373 | 83 | 20 | 3 | 8 | (4 | 4) | 133 | 45 | 36 | 41 | 38 | 2 | 87 | 18 | 5 | 2 | 11 | 7 | .61 | 8 | .223 | .323 | .357 |
| 2012 | TB | AL | 112 | 301 | 64 | 14 | 1 | 6 | (3 | 3) | 98 | 36 | 32 | 32 | 27 | 1 | 75 | 3 | 8 | 3 | 5 | 0 | 1.00 | 7 | .213 | .281 | .326 |
| 2013 | TB | AL | 96 | 195 | 48 | 10 | 1 | 5 | (3 | 2) | 75 | 21 | 23 | 21 | 17 | 0 | 59 | 5 | 3 | 2 | 1 | 3 | .25 | 3 | .246 | .320 | .385 |
| Postseason | | | 8 | 22 | 4 | 1 | 0 | 0 | (0 | 0) | 5 | 5 | 1 | 1 | 2 | 0 | 5 | 0 | 0 | 0 | 0 | 0 | - | 0 | .182 | .250 | .227 |
| 6 ML YEARS | | | 528 | 1404 | 320 | 71 | 8 | 33 | (17 | 16) | 506 | 177 | 145 | 146 | 120 | 4 | 380 | 37 | 23 | 10 | 33 | 14 | .70 | 33 | .228 | .304 | .360 |

# Wandy Rodriguez

**Pitches:** L **Bats:** B **Pos:** SP-12 WAHN-dee **Ht:** 5'10" **Wt:** 195 **Born:** 1/18/1979 **Age:** 35

| | | | HOW MUCH HE PITCHED | | | | | | WHAT HE GAVE UP | | | | | | | | | | THE RESULTS | | | | | | | |
|---|---|---|---|---|---|---|---|---|---|---|---|---|---|---|---|---|---|---|---|---|---|---|---|---|---|---|
| Year | Team | Lg | G | GS | CG | GF | IP | BFP | H | R | ER | HR | SH | SF | HB | TBB | IBB | SO | WP | Bk | W | L | Pct | Sh | Sv-Op | Hld | ERC | ERA |
| 2013 | Indy* | AAA | 1 | 1 | 0 | 0 | 4.0 | 18 | 4 | 1 | 1 | 0 | 0 | 0 | 0 | 1 | 0 | 5 | 0 | 0 | 0 | 0 | - | 0 | 0- - | - | 2.58 | 2.25 |
| 2005 | Hou | NL | 25 | 22 | 0 | 0 | 128.2 | 560 | 135 | 82 | 79 | 19 | 3 | 3 | 8 | 53 | 2 | 80 | 3 | 3 | 10 | 10 | .500 | 0 | 0-0 | 0 | 5.08 | 5.53 |
| 2006 | Hou | NL | 30 | 24 | 0 | 1 | 135.2 | 611 | 154 | 96 | 85 | 17 | 7 | 4 | 6 | 63 | 7 | 98 | 6 | 0 | 9 | 10 | .474 | 0 | 0-0 | 0 | 5.45 | 5.64 |
| 2007 | Hou | NL | 31 | 31 | 1 | 0 | 182.2 | 782 | 179 | 102 | 93 | 22 | 6 | 4 | 5 | 62 | 2 | 158 | 3 | 0 | 9 | 13 | .409 | 1 | 0-0 | 0 | 3.94 | 4.58 |
| 2008 | Hou | NL | 25 | 25 | 0 | 0 | 137.1 | 587 | 136 | 65 | 54 | 14 | 2 | 5 | 5 | 44 | 3 | 131 | 2 | 3 | 9 | 7 | .563 | 0 | 0-0 | 0 | 3.82 | 3.54 |

| | | | HOW MUCH HE PITCHED | | | | | | WHAT HE GAVE UP | | | | | | | | | | | | THE RESULTS | | | | | | | |
|---|---|---|---|---|---|---|---|---|---|---|---|---|---|---|---|---|---|---|---|---|---|---|---|---|---|---|---|---|
| Year | Team | Lg | G | GS | CG | GF | IP | BFP | H | R | ER | HR | SH | SF | HB | TBB | IBB | SO | WP | Bk | W | L | Pct | Sh | Sv-Op | Hld | ERC | ERA |
| 2009 | Hou | NL | 33 | 33 | 1 | 0 | 205.2 | 849 | 192 | 77 | 69 | 21 | 8 | 4 | 5 | 63 | 5 | 193 | 2 | 1 | 14 | 12 | .538 | 1 | 0-0 | 0 | 3.47 | 3.02 |
| 2010 | Hou | NL | 32 | 32 | 0 | 0 | 195.0 | 822 | 183 | 95 | 78 | 16 | 6 | 5 | 9 | 68 | 3 | 178 | 8 | 0 | 11 | 12 | .478 | 0 | 0-0 | 0 | 3.60 | 3.60 |
| 2011 | Hou | NL | 30 | 30 | 0 | 0 | 191.0 | 808 | 182 | 81 | 74 | 25 | 7 | 3 | 5 | 69 | 7 | 166 | 5 | 0 | 11 | 11 | .500 | 0 | 0-0 | 0 | 3.95 | 3.49 |
| 2012 | 2 Tms | NL | 34 | **33** | 0 | 1 | 205.2 | 875 | 205 | 99 | 86 | 21 | 6 | 5 | 3 | 56 | 4 | 139 | 5 | 0 | 12 | 13 | .480 | 0 | 0-0 | 0 | 3.55 | 3.76 |
| 2013 | Pit | NL | 12 | 12 | 0 | 0 | 62.2 | 260 | 58 | 26 | 25 | 10 | 1 | 1 | 4 | 12 | 1 | 46 | 1 | 1 | 6 | 4 | .600 | 0 | 0-0 | 0 | 3.43 | 3.59 |
| 12 | Hou | NL | 21 | 21 | 0 | 0 | 130.2 | 558 | 134 | 66 | 55 | 13 | 5 | 3 | 2 | 32 | 2 | 89 | 5 | 0 | 7 | 9 | .438 | 0 | 0-0 | 0 | 3.57 | 3.79 |
| 12 | Pit | NL | 13 | 12 | 0 | 1 | 75.0 | 317 | 71 | 33 | 31 | 8 | 1 | 2 | 1 | 24 | 2 | 50 | 0 | 0 | 5 | 4 | .556 | 0 | 0-0 | 0 | 3.50 | 3.72 |
| Postseason | | | 3 | 0 | 0 | 1 | 4.2 | 22 | 5 | 2 | 2 | 2 | 1 | 0 | 0 | 5 | 1 | 4 | 0 | 0 | 0 | 1 | .000 | 0 | 0-0 | 0 | 10.58 | 3.86 |
| 9 ML YEARS | | | 252 | 242 | 2 | 2 | 1444.1 | 6154 | 1424 | 723 | 643 | 165 | 46 | 34 | 50 | 490 | 34 | 1189 | 35 | 8 | 91 | 92 | .497 | 2 | 0-0 | 0 | 3.97 | 4.01 |

## Chaz Roe

**Pitches:** R **Bats:** R **Pos:** RP-21 ROW **Ht:** 6'5" **Wt:** 190 **Born:** 10/9/1986 **Age:** 27

| | | | HOW MUCH HE PITCHED | | | | | | WHAT HE GAVE UP | | | | | | | | | | | | THE RESULTS | | | | | | | |
|---|---|---|---|---|---|---|---|---|---|---|---|---|---|---|---|---|---|---|---|---|---|---|---|---|---|---|---|---|
| Year | Team | Lg | G | GS | CG | GF | IP | BFP | H | R | ER | HR | SH | SF | HB | TBB | IBB | SO | WP | Bk | W | L | Pct | Sh | Sv-Op | Hld | ERC | ERA |
| 2009 | Tulsa | AA | 20 | 20 | 1 | 0 | 117.0 | 491 | 105 | 47 | 41 | 7 | 5 | 1 | 6 | 43 | 0 | 77 | 5 | 1 | 7 | 3 | .700 | 0 | 0-- | - | 3.34 | 3.15 |
| 2010 | ColSpr | AAA | 27 | 27 | 2 | 0 | 158.0 | 725 | 210 | 115 | 105 | 18 | 8 | 10 | 7 | 53 | 2 | 115 | 9 | 0 | 9 | 13 | .409 | 0 | 0-- | - | 6.04 | 5.98 |
| 2011 | Tacom | AAA | 33 | 10 | 0 | 9 | 99.2 | 467 | 133 | 85 | 73 | 16 | 2 | 6 | 4 | 38 | 0 | 83 | 11 | 1 | 0 | 7 | .000 | 0 | 2-- | - | 6.59 | 6.59 |
| 2013 | Mobile | AA | 3 | 0 | 0 | 3 | 2.1 | 10 | 2 | 1 | 0 | 0 | 0 | 0 | 0 | 0 | 0 | 3 | 0 | 0 | 0 | 1 | .000 | 0 | 1-- | - | 1.29 | 0.00 |
| 2013 | Reno | AAA | 22 | 0 | 0 | 21 | 22.0 | 87 | 15 | 3 | 3 | 0 | 0 | 1 | 3 | 4 | 0 | 20 | 5 | 0 | 0 | 0 | - | 0 | 7-- | - | 1.60 | 1.23 |
| 2013 | Ari | NL | 21 | 0 | 0 | 4 | 22.1 | 95 | 18 | 10 | 10 | 3 | 2 | 1 | 0 | 13 | 3 | 24 | 1 | 0 | 1 | 0 | 1.000 | 0 | 0-2 | 1 | 3.78 | 4.03 |

## Josh Roenicke

**Pitches:** R **Bats:** R **Pos:** RP-63 RENN-ick-kee **Ht:** 6'3" **Wt:** 200 **Born:** 8/4/1982 **Age:** 31

| | | | HOW MUCH HE PITCHED | | | | | | WHAT HE GAVE UP | | | | | | | | | | | | THE RESULTS | | | | | | | |
|---|---|---|---|---|---|---|---|---|---|---|---|---|---|---|---|---|---|---|---|---|---|---|---|---|---|---|---|---|
| Year | Team | Lg | G | GS | CG | GF | IP | BFP | H | R | ER | HR | SH | SF | HB | TBB | IBB | SO | WP | Bk | W | L | Pct | Sh | Sv-Op | Hld | ERC | ERA |
| 2008 | Cin | NL | 5 | 0 | 0 | 0 | 3.0 | 18 | 6 | 3 | 3 | 0 | 0 | 0 | 1 | 2 | 0 | 6 | 0 | 0 | 0 | 0 | - | 0 | 0-0 | 0 | 12.01 | 9.00 |
| 2009 | 2 Tms | | 24 | 0 | 0 | 5 | 31.0 | 138 | 32 | 19 | 18 | 2 | 0 | 1 | 1 | 16 | 1 | 33 | 2 | 0 | 0 | 0 | - | 0 | 0-0 | 1 | 4.55 | 5.23 |
| 2010 | Tor | AL | 16 | 0 | 0 | 3 | 19.0 | 91 | 18 | 15 | 12 | 1 | 0 | 0 | 2 | 13 | 0 | 18 | 1 | 0 | 1 | 0 | 1.000 | 0 | 0-0 | 2 | 4.76 | 5.68 |
| 2011 | Col | NL | 19 | 0 | 0 | 6 | 16.2 | 68 | 14 | 7 | 7 | 1 | 0 | 0 | 1 | 7 | 1 | 12 | 1 | 0 | 0 | 0 | - | 0 | 0-0 | 4 | 3.28 | 3.78 |
| 2012 | Col | NL | 63 | 0 | 0 | 14 | 88.2 | 383 | 85 | 40 | 32 | 9 | 6 | 4 | 2 | 43 | 3 | 54 | 8 | 0 | 4 | 2 | .667 | 0 | 1-3 | 8 | 4.28 | 3.25 |
| 2013 | Min | AL | 63 | 0 | 0 | 12 | 62.0 | 282 | 63 | 31 | 30 | 6 | 1 | 4 | 1 | 36 | 5 | 45 | 7 | 0 | 3 | 1 | .750 | 0 | 1-3 | 12 | 4.74 | 4.35 |
| 09 | Cin | NL | 11 | 0 | 0 | 2 | 13.1 | 54 | 13 | 4 | 4 | 0 | 0 | 0 | 0 | 4 | 0 | 14 | 1 | 0 | 0 | 0 | - | 0 | 0-0 | 0 | 3.00 | 2.70 |
| 09 | Tor | AL | 13 | 0 | 0 | 3 | 17.2 | 84 | 19 | 15 | 14 | 2 | 0 | 1 | 1 | 12 | 1 | 19 | 1 | 0 | 0 | 0 | - | 0 | 0-0 | 1 | 5.81 | 7.13 |
| 6 ML YEARS | | | 190 | 0 | 0 | 40 | 220.1 | 980 | 218 | 115 | 102 | 19 | 7 | 9 | 8 | 117 | 10 | 168 | 19 | 0 | 8 | 3 | .727 | 0 | 2-6 | 27 | 4.51 | 4.17 |

## Esmil Rogers

**Pitches:** R **Bats:** R **Pos:** RP-24; SP-20 ESS-mill **Ht:** 6'1" **Wt:** 190 **Born:** 8/14/1985 **Age:** 28

| | | | HOW MUCH HE PITCHED | | | | | | WHAT HE GAVE UP | | | | | | | | | | | | THE RESULTS | | | | | | | |
|---|---|---|---|---|---|---|---|---|---|---|---|---|---|---|---|---|---|---|---|---|---|---|---|---|---|---|---|---|
| Year | Team | Lg | G | GS | CG | GF | IP | BFP | H | R | ER | HR | SH | SF | HB | TBB | IBB | SO | WP | Bk | W | L | Pct | Sh | Sv-Op | Hld | ERC | ERA |
| 2009 | Col | NL | 1 | 1 | 0 | 0 | 4.0 | 16 | 3 | 2 | 2 | 0 | 0 | 1 | 0 | 2 | 0 | 3 | 0 | 0 | 0 | 0 | - | 0 | 0-0 | 0 | 2.58 | 4.50 |
| 2010 | Col | NL | 28 | 8 | 0 | 5 | 72.0 | 333 | 94 | 59 | 49 | 5 | 3 | 3 | 5 | 26 | 2 | 66 | 5 | 2 | 2 | 3 | .400 | 0 | 0-1 | 1 | 5.70 | 6.13 |
| 2011 | Col | NL | 18 | 13 | 0 | 1 | 83.0 | 404 | 110 | 65 | 65 | 14 | 4 | 3 | 6 | 47 | 5 | 63 | 5 | 1 | 6 | 6 | .500 | 0 | 0-0 | 0 | 7.49 | 7.05 |
| 2012 | 2 Tms | | 67 | 0 | 0 | 19 | 78.2 | 348 | 83 | 42 | 41 | 7 | 2 | 2 | 5 | 30 | 4 | 83 | 10 | 0 | 3 | 3 | .500 | 0 | 0-2 | 8 | 4.37 | 4.69 |
| 2013 | Tor | AL | 44 | 20 | 0 | 5 | 137.2 | 598 | 152 | 76 | 73 | 21 | 0 | 4 | 6 | 44 | 2 | 96 | 7 | **2** | 5 | 9 | .357 | 0 | 0-1 | 4 | 4.92 | 4.77 |
| 12 | Col | NL | 23 | 0 | 0 | 6 | 25.2 | 131 | 36 | 23 | 23 | 2 | 0 | 0 | 2 | 18 | 2 | 29 | 5 | 0 | 0 | 2 | .000 | 0 | 0-2 | 2 | 7.71 | 8.06 |
| 12 | Cle | AL | 44 | 0 | 0 | 13 | 53.0 | 217 | 47 | 19 | 18 | 5 | 2 | 2 | 3 | 12 | 2 | 54 | 5 | 0 | 3 | 1 | .750 | 0 | 0-0 | 6 | 2.93 | 3.06 |
| 5 ML YEARS | | | 158 | 42 | 0 | 30 | 375.1 | 1699 | 442 | 244 | 230 | 47 | 9 | 13 | 22 | 149 | 13 | 311 | 27 | 5 | 16 | 21 | .432 | 0 | 0-4 | 13 | 5.47 | 5.52 |

## Jimmy Rollins

**Bats:** B **Throws:** R **Pos:** SS-153;PH-9 **Ht:** 5'8" **Wt:** 180 **Born:** 11/27/1978 **Age:** 35

| | | | BATTING | | | | | | | | | | | | | | | | | | BASERUNNING | | | | AVERAGES | | |
|---|---|---|---|---|---|---|---|---|---|---|---|---|---|---|---|---|---|---|---|---|---|---|---|---|---|---|---|
| Year | Team | Lg | G | AB | H | 2B | 3B | HR | (Hm | Rd) | TB | R | RBI | RC | TBB | IBB | SO | HBP | SH | SF | SB | CS | SB% | GDP | Avg | OBP | Slg |
| 2000 | Phi | NL | 14 | 53 | 17 | 1 | 1 | 0 | (0 | 0) | 20 | 5 | 5 | 8 | 2 | 0 | 7 | 0 | 0 | 0 | 3 | 0 | 1.00 | 0 | .321 | .345 | .377 |
| 2001 | Phi | NL | 158 | **656** | 180 | 29 | **12** | 14 | (8 | 6) | 275 | 97 | 54 | 96 | 48 | 2 | 108 | 2 | 9 | 5 | **46** | 8 | .85 | 5 | .274 | .323 | .419 |
| 2002 | Phi | NL | 154 | **637** | 156 | 33 | **10** | 11 | (3 | 8) | 242 | 82 | 60 | 72 | 54 | 3 | 103 | 4 | 6 | 4 | 31 | 13 | .70 | 14 | .245 | .306 | .380 |
| 2003 | Phi | NL | 156 | 628 | 165 | 42 | 6 | 8 | (5 | 3) | 243 | 85 | 62 | 76 | 54 | 4 | 113 | 0 | 5 | 2 | 20 | 12 | .63 | 9 | .263 | .320 | .387 |
| 2004 | Phi | NL | 154 | 657 | 190 | 43 | **12** | 14 | (8 | 6) | 299 | 119 | 73 | 108 | 57 | 3 | 73 | 3 | 6 | 2 | 30 | 9 | .77 | 4 | .289 | .348 | .455 |
| 2005 | Phi | NL | 158 | 677 | 196 | 38 | 11 | 12 | (5 | 7) | 292 | 115 | 54 | 100 | 47 | 8 | 71 | 4 | 2 | 2 | 41 | 6 | .87 | 9 | .290 | .338 | .431 |
| 2006 | Phi | NL | 158 | 689 | 191 | 45 | 9 | 25 | (15 | 10) | 329 | 127 | 83 | 114 | 57 | 2 | 80 | 5 | 0 | 7 | 36 | 4 | .90 | 12 | .277 | .334 | .478 |
| 2007 | Phi | NL | **162** | **716** | 212 | 38 | **20** | 30 | (18 | 12) | 380 | **139** | 94 | 124 | 49 | 5 | 85 | 7 | 0 | 6 | 41 | 6 | .87 | 11 | .296 | .344 | .531 |
| 2008 | Phi | NL | 137 | 556 | 154 | 38 | 9 | 11 | (5 | 6) | 243 | 76 | 59 | 95 | 58 | 7 | 55 | 5 | 3 | 3 | 47 | 3 | .94 | 11 | .277 | .349 | .437 |
| 2009 | Phi | NL | 155 | **672** | 168 | 43 | 5 | 21 | (10 | 11) | 284 | 100 | 77 | 88 | 44 | 1 | 70 | 2 | 2 | 5 | 31 | 8 | .79 | 7 | .250 | .296 | .423 |
| 2010 | Phi | NL | 88 | 350 | 85 | 16 | 3 | 8 | (4 | 4) | 131 | 48 | 41 | 54 | 40 | 2 | 32 | 1 | 0 | 3 | 17 | 1 | .94 | 4 | .243 | .320 | .374 |
| 2011 | Phi | NL | 142 | 567 | 152 | 22 | 2 | 16 | (7 | 9) | 226 | 87 | 63 | 82 | 58 | 5 | 59 | 3 | 0 | 3 | 30 | 8 | .79 | 9 | .268 | .338 | .399 |
| 2012 | Phi | NL | 156 | 632 | 158 | 33 | 5 | 23 | (11 | 12) | 270 | 102 | 68 | 88 | 62 | 2 | 96 | 0 | 2 | 3 | 30 | 5 | .86 | 9 | .250 | .316 | .427 |
| 2013 | Phi | NL | 160 | 600 | 151 | 36 | 2 | 6 | (4 | 2) | 209 | 65 | 39 | 70 | 59 | 6 | 93 | 1 | 3 | 3 | 22 | 6 | .79 | 12 | .252 | .318 | .348 |
| Postseason | | | 46 | 188 | 47 | 12 | 1 | 3 | (1 | 2) | 70 | 27 | 15 | 16 | 16 | 0 | 34 | 2 | 1 | 1 | 11 | 4 | .73 | 5 | .250 | .314 | .372 |
| 14 ML YEARS | | | 1952 | 8090 | 2175 | 457 | 107 | 199 | (103 | 96) | 3443 | 1247 | 832 | 1175 | 689 | 50 | 1045 | 37 | 38 | 48 | 425 | 89 | .83 | 116 | .269 | .327 | .426 |

# Enny Romero

**Pitches:** L **Bats:** L **Pos:** SP-1 ENN-nee **Ht:** 6'3" **Wt:** 165 **Born:** 1/24/1991 **Age:** 23

| HOW MUCH HE PITCHED | | | | | | | | WHAT HE GAVE UP | | | | | | | | | | | | THE RESULTS | | | | | | | |
|---|---|---|---|---|---|---|---|---|---|---|---|---|---|---|---|---|---|---|---|---|---|---|---|---|---|---|---|
| Year | Team | Lg | G | GS | CG | GF | IP | BFP | H | R | ER | HR | SH | SF | HB | TBB | IBB | SO | WP | Bk | W | L | Pct | Sh | Sv-Op | Hld | ERC | ERA |
| 2009 | Rays | R | 11 | 4 | 0 | 1 | 39.1 | 175 | 38 | 25 | 21 | 2 | 1 | 1 | 3 | 21 | 0 | 33 | 6 | 1 | 2 | 4 | .333 | 0 | 0- - | - | 4.37 | 4.81 |
| 2010 | Princtn | R | 13 | 13 | 0 | 0 | 69.1 | 270 | 51 | 15 | 15 | 2 | 0 | 0 | 6 | 14 | 0 | 72 | 4 | 3 | 4 | 1 | .800 | 0 | 0- - | - | 1.93 | 1.95 |
| 2010 | HudVal | A- | 1 | 1 | 0 | 0 | 5.0 | 20 | 1 | 1 | 1 | 0 | 0 | 0 | 1 | 5 | 0 | 4 | 0 | 0 | 1 | 0 | 1.000 | 0 | 0- - | - | 2.26 | 1.80 |
| 2011 | BG | A | 26 | 26 | 0 | 0 | 114.0 | 503 | 104 | 67 | 54 | 9 | 3 | 3 | 4 | 68 | 0 | 140 | 14 | 3 | 5 | 5 | .500 | 0 | 0- - | - | 4.37 | 4.26 |
| 2012 | Charltt | A+ | 25 | 23 | 1 | 0 | 126.0 | 539 | 89 | 67 | 55 | 5 | 3 | 10 | 7 | 76 | 0 | 107 | 12 | 0 | 5 | 7 | .417 | 1 | 0- - | - | 3.04 | 3.93 |
| 2013 | Mont | AA | 27 | 27 | 0 | 0 | 140.1 | 594 | 110 | 51 | 43 | 9 | 5 | 3 | 2 | 73 | 1 | 110 | 4 | 3 | 11 | 7 | .611 | 0 | 0- - | - | 3.16 | 2.76 |
| 2013 | Drham | AAA | 1 | 1 | 0 | 0 | 8.0 | 28 | 4 | 0 | 0 | 0 | 0 | 0 | 0 | 2 | 0 | 2 | 1 | 0 | 0 | 0 | - | 0 | 0- - | - | 1.01 | 0.00 |
| 2013 | TB | AL | 1 | 1 | 0 | 0 | 4.2 | 18 | 1 | 0 | 0 | 0 | 0 | 0 | 0 | 4 | 0 | 0 | 0 | 0 | 0 | 0 | - | 0 | 0-0 | 0 | 1.35 | 0.00 |

# Ricky Romero

**Pitches:** L **Bats:** R **Pos:** SP-2; RP-2 **Ht:** 6'0" **Wt:** 225 **Born:** 11/6/1984 **Age:** 29

| HOW MUCH HE PITCHED | | | | | | | | WHAT HE GAVE UP | | | | | | | | | | | | THE RESULTS | | | | | | | |
|---|---|---|---|---|---|---|---|---|---|---|---|---|---|---|---|---|---|---|---|---|---|---|---|---|---|---|---|
| Year | Team | Lg | G | GS | CG | GF | IP | BFP | H | R | ER | HR | SH | SF | HB | TBB | IBB | SO | WP | Bk | W | L | Pct | Sh | Sv-Op | Hld | ERC | ERA |
| 2013 | Dnedin* | A+ | 1 | 1 | 0 | 0 | 7.0 | 25 | 6 | 1 | 1 | 0 | 0 | 0 | 0 | 0 | 0 | 4 | 0 | 0 | 0 | 0 | - | 0 | 0- - | - | 1.55 | 1.29 |
| 2013 | Buffalo* | AAA | 22 | 22 | 1 | 0 | 113.2 | 526 | 136 | 81 | 73 | 11 | 4 | 6 | 4 | 63 | 0 | 81 | 10 | 1 | 5 | 8 | .385 | 0 | 0- - | - | 6.05 | 5.78 |
| 2009 | Tor | AL | 29 | 29 | 0 | 0 | 178.0 | 771 | 192 | 88 | 85 | 18 | 3 | 3 | 10 | 79 | 0 | 141 | 6 | 1 | 13 | 9 | .591 | 0 | 0-0 | 0 | 5.12 | 4.30 |
| 2010 | Tor | AL | 32 | 32 | 3 | 0 | 210.0 | 882 | 189 | 98 | 87 | 15 | **9** | 3 | 8 | 82 | 3 | 174 | **18** | 1 | 14 | 9 | .609 | 1 | 0-0 | 0 | 3.46 | 3.73 |
| 2011 | Tor | AL | 32 | 32 | 4 | 0 | 225.0 | 917 | 176 | 85 | 73 | 26 | 6 | 1 | 14 | 80 | 2 | 178 | 9 | 1 | 15 | 11 | .577 | 2 | 0-0 | 0 | 3.11 | 2.92 |
| 2012 | Tor | AL | 32 | 32 | 1 | 0 | 181.0 | 829 | 198 | 122 | 116 | 21 | **7** | 4 | 10 | **105** | 1 | 124 | 8 | 0 | 9 | 14 | .391 | 0 | 0-0 | 0 | 5.75 | 5.77 |
| 2013 | Tor | AL | 4 | 2 | 0 | 1 | 7.1 | 40 | 11 | 9 | 9 | 2 | 0 | 0 | 1 | 8 | 0 | 5 | 1 | 0 | 0 | 2 | .000 | 0 | 0-0 | 0 | 13.07 | 11.05 |
| 5 ML YEARS | | | 129 | 127 | 8 | 1 | 801.1 | 3439 | 766 | 402 | 370 | 82 | 25 | 11 | 43 | 354 | 6 | 622 | 42 | 3 | 51 | 45 | .531 | 3 | 0-0 | 0 | 4.28 | 4.16 |

# Andrew Romine

**Bats:** B **Throws:** R **Pos:** 3B-24;SS-17;PR-6;2B-4;PH-1 ROW-mine **Ht:** 6'1" **Wt:** 190 **Born:** 12/24/1985 **Age:** 28

| BATTING | | | | | | | | | | | | | | | | | | | | | BASERUNNING | | | | AVERAGES | | |
|---|---|---|---|---|---|---|---|---|---|---|---|---|---|---|---|---|---|---|---|---|---|---|---|---|---|---|---|
| Year | Team | Lg | G | AB | H | 2B | 3B | HR | (Hm | Rd) | TB | R | RBI | RC | TBB | IBB | SO | HBP | SH | SF | SB | CS | SB% | GDP | Avg | OBP | Slg |
| 2013 | Salt Lk* | AAA | 89 | 363 | 104 | 16 | 5 | 4 | (- | -) | 142 | 61 | 39 | 56 | 43 | 3 | 68 | 4 | 4 | 2 | 15 | 6 | .71 | 6 | .287 | .367 | .391 |
| 2010 | LAA | AL | 5 | 11 | 1 | 0 | 0 | 0 | (0 | 0) | 1 | 0 | 0 | 0 | 0 | 0 | 4 | 0 | 1 | 0 | 0 | 0 | - | 0 | .091 | .091 | .091 |
| 2011 | LAA | AL | 10 | 16 | 2 | 0 | 0 | 0 | (0 | 0) | 2 | 2 | 0 | 0 | 1 | 0 | 6 | 0 | 1 | 0 | 1 | 0 | 1.00 | 0 | .125 | .176 | .125 |
| 2012 | LAA | AL | 12 | 17 | 7 | 0 | 0 | 0 | (0 | 0) | 7 | 2 | 1 | 5 | 3 | 0 | 3 | 0 | 1 | 0 | 1 | 0 | 1.00 | 0 | .412 | .500 | .412 |
| 2013 | LAA | AL | 47 | 108 | 28 | 3 | 0 | 0 | (0 | 0) | 31 | 9 | 10 | 12 | 7 | 0 | 24 | 1 | 6 | 1 | 1 | 0 | 1.00 | 2 | .259 | .308 | .287 |
| 4 ML YEARS | | | 74 | 152 | 38 | 3 | 0 | 0 | (0 | 0) | 41 | 13 | 11 | 17 | 11 | 0 | 37 | 1 | 9 | 1 | 3 | 0 | 1.00 | 2 | .250 | .303 | .270 |

# Austin Romine

**Bats:** R **Throws:** R **Pos:** C-59;PH-3 ROW-mine **Ht:** 6'0" **Wt:** 215 **Born:** 11/22/1988 **Age:** 25

| BATTING | | | | | | | | | | | | | | | | | | | | | BASERUNNING | | | | AVERAGES | | |
|---|---|---|---|---|---|---|---|---|---|---|---|---|---|---|---|---|---|---|---|---|---|---|---|---|---|---|---|
| Year | Team | Lg | G | AB | H | 2B | 3B | HR | (Hm | Rd) | TB | R | RBI | RC | TBB | IBB | SO | HBP | SH | SF | SB | CS | SB% | GDP | Avg | OBP | Slg |
| 2009 | Tampa | A+ | 118 | 442 | 122 | 28 | 3 | 13 | (- | -) | 195 | 61 | 72 | 65 | 29 | 2 | 78 | 4 | 0 | 6 | 11 | 5 | .69 | 13 | .276 | .322 | .441 |
| 2010 | Trntn | AA | 115 | 455 | 122 | 31 | 0 | 10 | (- | -) | 183 | 61 | 69 | 62 | 37 | 1 | 94 | 2 | 0 | 3 | 2 | 0 | 1.00 | 13 | .268 | .324 | .402 |
| 2011 | Trntn | AA | 85 | 336 | 96 | 13 | 0 | 6 | (- | -) | 127 | 43 | 47 | 47 | 32 | 1 | 60 | 3 | 0 | 2 | 2 | 2 | .50 | 5 | .286 | .351 | .378 |
| 2011 | S-WB | AAA | 4 | 15 | 2 | 0 | 0 | 0 | (- | -) | 2 | 1 | 1 | 0 | 0 | 0 | 3 | 0 | 0 | 0 | 0 | 0 | - | 2 | .133 | .133 | .133 |
| 2012 | Yanks | R | 9 | 24 | 5 | 3 | 0 | 0 | (- | -) | 8 | 3 | 5 | 3 | 5 | 0 | 3 | 1 | 0 | 0 | 0 | 0 | - | 1 | .208 | .367 | .333 |
| 2012 | Tampa | A+ | 5 | 18 | 7 | 0 | 0 | 1 | (- | -) | 10 | 2 | 1 | 3 | 1 | 0 | 3 | 0 | 0 | 0 | 0 | 0 | - | 2 | .389 | .421 | .556 |
| 2012 | S-WB | AAA | 17 | 61 | 13 | 2 | 0 | 3 | (- | -) | 24 | 6 | 9 | 7 | 8 | 0 | 10 | 0 | 0 | 2 | 0 | 0 | - | 2 | .213 | .296 | .393 |
| 2013 | S-WB | AAA | 14 | 42 | 14 | 0 | 0 | 1 | (- | -) | 17 | 5 | 4 | 6 | 4 | 0 | 12 | 0 | 0 | 0 | 0 | 0 | - | 0 | .333 | .391 | .405 |
| 2011 | NYY | AL | 9 | 19 | 3 | 0 | 0 | 0 | (0 | 0) | 3 | 2 | 0 | 0 | 1 | 0 | 5 | 0 | 0 | 0 | 0 | 0 | - | 0 | .158 | .200 | .158 |
| 2013 | NYY | AL | 60 | 135 | 28 | 9 | 0 | 1 | (0 | 1) | 40 | 15 | 10 | 8 | 8 | 0 | 37 | 1 | 3 | 1 | 1 | 0 | 1.00 | 7 | .207 | .255 | .296 |
| 2 ML YEARS | | | 69 | 154 | 31 | 9 | 0 | 1 | (0 | 1) | 43 | 17 | 10 | 8 | 9 | 0 | 42 | 1 | 3 | 1 | 1 | 0 | 1.00 | 7 | .201 | .248 | .279 |

# Sergio Romo

**Pitches:** R **Bats:** R **Pos:** RP-65 **Ht:** 5'10" **Wt:** 185 **Born:** 3/4/1983 **Age:** 31

| HOW MUCH HE PITCHED | | | | | | | | WHAT HE GAVE UP | | | | | | | | | | | | THE RESULTS | | | | | | | |
|---|---|---|---|---|---|---|---|---|---|---|---|---|---|---|---|---|---|---|---|---|---|---|---|---|---|---|---|
| Year | Team | Lg | G | GS | CG | GF | IP | BFP | H | R | ER | HR | SH | SF | HB | TBB | IBB | SO | WP | Bk | W | L | Pct | Sh | Sv-Op | Hld | ERC | ERA |
| 2008 | SF | NL | 29 | 0 | 0 | 8 | 34.0 | 130 | 16 | 13 | 8 | 3 | 2 | 1 | 3 | 8 | 1 | 33 | 0 | 0 | 3 | 1 | .750 | 0 | 0-0 | 5 | 1.27 | 2.12 |
| 2009 | SF | NL | 45 | 0 | 0 | 9 | 34.0 | 143 | 30 | 15 | 15 | 1 | 2 | 0 | 1 | 11 | 0 | 41 | 2 | 0 | 5 | 2 | .714 | 0 | 2-2 | 10 | 2.76 | 3.97 |
| 2010 | SF | NL | 68 | 0 | 0 | 13 | 62.0 | 247 | 46 | 16 | 15 | 6 | 2 | 2 | 4 | 14 | 2 | 70 | 0 | 0 | 5 | 3 | .625 | 0 | 0-4 | 21 | 2.26 | 2.18 |
| 2011 | SF | NL | 65 | 0 | 0 | 16 | 48.0 | 175 | 29 | 8 | 8 | 2 | 2 | 0 | 0 | 5 | 1 | 70 | 0 | 0 | 3 | 1 | .750 | 0 | 1-2 | 23 | 1.08 | 1.50 |
| 2012 | SF | NL | 69 | 0 | 0 | 27 | 55.1 | 215 | 37 | 11 | 11 | 5 | 2 | 0 | 3 | 10 | 1 | 63 | 2 | 0 | 4 | 2 | .667 | 0 | 14-15 | 23 | 1.72 | 1.79 |
| 2013 | SF | NL | 65 | 0 | 0 | 52 | 60.1 | 250 | 53 | 20 | 17 | 5 | 1 | 1 | 1 | 12 | 3 | 58 | 1 | 0 | 5 | 8 | .385 | 0 | 38-43 | 0 | 2.47 | 2.54 |
| Postseason | | | 16 | 0 | 0 | 11 | 14.1 | 54 | 10 | 4 | 4 | 1 | 0 | 0 | 0 | 2 | 0 | 13 | 1 | 0 | 2 | 0 | 1.000 | 0 | 4-6 | 0 | 1.54 | 2.51 |
| 6 ML YEARS | | | 341 | 0 | 0 | 125 | 293.2 | 1160 | 211 | 83 | 74 | 22 | 11 | 4 | 12 | 60 | 8 | 335 | 5 | 0 | 25 | 17 | .595 | 0 | 55-66 | 82 | 1.87 | 2.27 |

# Bruce Rondon

**Pitches:** R **Bats:** R **Pos:** RP-30 ron-DOAN **Ht:** 6'3" **Wt:** 275 **Born:** 12/9/1990 **Age:** 23

| HOW MUCH HE PITCHED | | | | | | | | WHAT HE GAVE UP | | | | | | | | | | | | THE RESULTS | | | | | | | |
|---|---|---|---|---|---|---|---|---|---|---|---|---|---|---|---|---|---|---|---|---|---|---|---|---|---|---|---|
| Year | Team | Lg | G | GS | CG | GF | IP | BFP | H | R | ER | HR | SH | SF | HB | TBB | IBB | SO | WP | Bk | W | L | Pct | Sh | Sv-Op | Hld | ERC | ERA |
| 2009 | Tigers | R | 3 | 3 | 0 | 0 | 11.1 | 53 | 12 | 6 | 6 | 0 | 0 | 0 | 0 | 8 | 0 | 15 | 0 | 0 | 0 | 1 | .000 | 0 | 0- - | - | 4.80 | 4.76 |
| 2010 | Tigers | R | 24 | 0 | 0 | 22 | 25.2 | 105 | 11 | 2 | 2 | 1 | 3 | 0 | 5 | 14 | 0 | 26 | 1 | 1 | 0 | 0 | - | 0 | 15- - | - | 1.98 | 0.70 |
| 2010 | Lkland | A+ | 4 | 0 | 0 | 2 | 6.2 | 23 | 2 | 1 | 1 | 1 | 0 | 0 | 0 | 2 | 0 | 7 | 0 | 0 | 0 | 0 | - | 0 | 2- - | - | 1.02 | 1.35 |
| 2011 | WMich | A | 41 | 0 | 0 | 33 | 40.0 | 179 | 22 | 11 | 9 | 0 | 4 | 2 | 5 | 34 | 1 | 61 | 11 | 1 | 2 | 2 | .500 | 0 | 19- - | - | 2.96 | 2.03 |
| 2012 | Lkland | A+ | 22 | 0 | 0 | 21 | 23.1 | 92 | 12 | 5 | 5 | 1 | 1 | 1 | 1 | 10 | 1 | 34 | 1 | 0 | 1 | 0 | 1.000 | 0 | 15- - | - | 1.55 | 1.93 |

| | | | HOW MUCH HE PITCHED | | | | | | WHAT HE GAVE UP | | | | | | | | | | | | THE RESULTS | | | | | | | |
|---|---|---|---|---|---|---|---|---|---|---|---|---|---|---|---|---|---|---|---|---|---|---|---|---|---|---|---|---|
| Year | Team | Lg | G | GS | CG | GF | IP | BFP | H | R | ER | HR | SH | SF | HB | TBB | IBB | SO | WP | Bk | W | L | Pct | Sh | Sv-Op | Hld | ERC | ERA |
| 2012 | Erie | AA | 21 | 0 | 0 | 19 | 21.2 | 90 | 15 | 4 | 2 | 1 | 0 | 0 | 4 | 9 | 0 | 23 | 2 | 1 | 0 | 1 | .000 | 0 | 12- - | - | 2.86 | 0.83 |
| 2012 | Toledo | AAA | 9 | 0 | 0 | 8 | 8.0 | 37 | 5 | 3 | 2 | 1 | 0 | 0 | 0 | 7 | 1 | 9 | 0 | 0 | 1 | 0 | 1.000 | 0 | 2- - | - | 3.60 | 2.25 |
| 2013 | Toledo | AAA | 30 | 0 | 0 | 26 | 29.2 | 118 | 14 | 6 | 5 | 1 | 1 | 1 | 2 | 13 | 0 | 40 | 2 | 0 | 1 | 1 | .500 | 0 | 14- - | - | 1.48 | 1.52 |
| 2013 | Det | AL | 30 | 0 | 0 | 12 | 28.2 | 122 | 28 | 11 | 11 | 2 | 1 | 2 | 0 | 11 | 0 | 30 | 7 | 1 | 1 | 2 | .333 | 0 | 1-3 | 5 | 3.69 | 3.45 |

## Hector Rondon

**Pitches:** R **Bats:** R **Pos:** RP-45 ron-DOAN **Ht:** 6'3" **Wt:** 180 **Born:** 2/26/1988 **Age:** 26

| | | | HOW MUCH HE PITCHED | | | | | | WHAT HE GAVE UP | | | | | | | | | | | | THE RESULTS | | | | | | | |
|---|---|---|---|---|---|---|---|---|---|---|---|---|---|---|---|---|---|---|---|---|---|---|---|---|---|---|---|---|
| Year | Team | Lg | G | GS | CG | GF | IP | BFP | H | R | ER | HR | SH | SF | HB | TBB | IBB | SO | WP | Bk | W | L | Pct | Sh | Sv-Op | Hld | ERC | ERA |
| 2009 | Akron | AA | 15 | 13 | 1 | 0 | 72.0 | 287 | 60 | 23 | 22 | 3 | 2 | 2 | 3 | 16 | 0 | 73 | 3 | 0 | 7 | 5 | .583 | 0 | 0- - | - | 2.36 | 2.75 |
| 2009 | Clmbs | AAA | 12 | 12 | 0 | 0 | 74.1 | 314 | 83 | 38 | 33 | 8 | 1 | 1 | 4 | 13 | 0 | 64 | 0 | 0 | 4 | 5 | .444 | 0 | 0- - | - | 4.14 | 4.00 |
| 2010 | Clmbs | AAA | 7 | 7 | 0 | 0 | 31.2 | 152 | 48 | 32 | 30 | 12 | 0 | 0 | 2 | 10 | 0 | 33 | 0 | 0 | 1 | 3 | .250 | 0 | 0- - | - | 9.50 | 8.53 |
| 2011 | MhVlly | A- | 2 | 2 | 0 | 0 | 3.0 | 12 | 3 | 1 | 1 | 0 | 0 | 0 | 0 | 0 | 0 | 2 | 0 | 0 | 0 | 0 | - | 0 | 0- - | - | 1.95 | 3.00 |
| 2012 | Indns | R | 2 | 2 | 0 | 0 | 3.0 | 10 | 0 | 0 | 0 | 0 | 0 | 0 | 0 | 1 | 0 | 6 | 0 | 0 | 0 | 0 | - | 0 | 0- - | - | 0.13 | 0.00 |
| 2012 | Akron | AA | 2 | 0 | 0 | 0 | 4.0 | 16 | 4 | 1 | 1 | 0 | 1 | 0 | 0 | 1 | 0 | 3 | 1 | 0 | 0 | 0 | - | 0 | 0- - | - | 2.98 | 2.25 |
| 2013 | ChC | NL | 45 | 0 | 0 | 14 | 54.2 | 242 | 52 | 29 | 29 | 6 | 4 | 3 | 3 | 25 | 5 | 44 | 4 | 0 | 2 | 1 | .667 | 0 | 0-1 | 2 | 4.10 | 4.77 |

## Adam Rosales

**Bats:** R **Throws:** R **Pos:** SS-39;PH-17;2B-15;PR-6;1B-4;3B-4;DH-3;LF-1 **Ht:** 6'1" **Wt:** 195 **Born:** 5/20/1983 **Age:** 31

| | | | BATTING | | | | | | | | | | | | | | | | | | BASERUNNING | | | | AVERAGES | | |
|---|---|---|---|---|---|---|---|---|---|---|---|---|---|---|---|---|---|---|---|---|---|---|---|---|---|---|---|
| Year | Team | Lg | G | AB | H | 2B | 3B | HR | (Hm | Rd) | TB | R | RBI | RC | TBB | IBB | SO | HBP | SH | SF | SB | CS | SB% | GDP | Avg | OBP | Slg |
| 2013 | Stcktn* | A+ | 3 | 12 | 6 | 2 | 0 | 1 | (- | -) | 11 | 3 | 1 | 4 | 0 | 0 | 1 | 0 | 0 | 0 | 0 | 0 | - | 0 | .500 | .500 | .917 |
| 2013 | Scrmto* | AAA | 9 | 38 | 8 | 2 | 0 | 0 | (- | -) | 10 | 4 | 6 | 2 | 3 | 0 | 7 | 0 | 0 | 1 | 1 | 1 | .50 | 1 | .211 | .262 | .263 |
| 2008 | Cin | NL | 18 | 29 | 6 | 1 | 0 | 0 | (0 | 0) | 7 | 0 | 2 | 2 | 1 | 0 | 4 | 0 | 0 | 0 | 1 | 0 | 1.00 | 0 | .207 | .233 | .241 |
| 2009 | Cin | NL | 87 | 230 | 49 | 10 | 1 | 4 | (2 | 2) | 73 | 23 | 19 | 22 | 26 | 0 | 46 | 5 | 2 | 3 | 1 | 2 | .33 | 2 | .213 | .303 | .317 |
| 2010 | Oak | AL | 80 | 255 | 69 | 8 | 2 | 7 | (1 | 6) | 102 | 31 | 31 | 31 | 19 | 0 | 65 | 1 | 2 | 2 | 2 | 2 | .50 | 1 | .271 | .321 | .400 |
| 2011 | Oak | AL | 24 | 61 | 6 | 0 | 0 | 2 | (0 | 2) | 12 | 5 | 8 | 0 | 4 | 0 | 13 | 1 | 0 | 2 | 0 | 0 | - | 4 | .098 | .162 | .197 |
| 2012 | Oak | AL | 42 | 99 | 22 | 5 | 0 | 2 | (1 | 1) | 33 | 12 | 8 | 6 | 11 | 1 | 24 | 0 | 0 | 1 | 0 | 0 | - | 4 | .222 | .297 | .333 |
| 2013 | 2 Tms | AL | 68 | 147 | 28 | 5 | 0 | 5 | (2 | 3) | 48 | 15 | 12 | 6 | 10 | 1 | 34 | 4 | 4 | 1 | 0 | 0 | - | 4 | .190 | .259 | .327 |
| 13 | Oak | AL | 51 | 136 | 26 | 5 | 0 | 4 | (2 | 2) | 43 | 11 | 8 | 5 | 10 | 1 | 31 | 4 | 4 | 0 | 0 | 0 | - | 4 | .191 | .267 | .316 |
| 13 | Tex | AL | 17 | 11 | 2 | 0 | 0 | 1 | (0 | 1) | 5 | 4 | 4 | 1 | 0 | 0 | 3 | 0 | 0 | 1 | 0 | 0 | - | 0 | .182 | .167 | .455 |
| 6 ML YEARS | | | 319 | 821 | 180 | 29 | 3 | 20 | (6 | 14) | 275 | 86 | 80 | 67 | 71 | 2 | 186 | 11 | 8 | 9 | 4 | 4 | .50 | 15 | .219 | .287 | .335 |

## Sandy Rosario

**Pitches:** R **Bats:** R **Pos:** RP-43 roh-SORRY-oh **Ht:** 6'1" **Wt:** 210 **Born:** 8/22/1985 **Age:** 28

| | | | HOW MUCH HE PITCHED | | | | | | WHAT HE GAVE UP | | | | | | | | | | | | THE RESULTS | | | | | | | |
|---|---|---|---|---|---|---|---|---|---|---|---|---|---|---|---|---|---|---|---|---|---|---|---|---|---|---|---|---|
| Year | Team | Lg | G | GS | CG | GF | IP | BFP | H | R | ER | HR | SH | SF | HB | TBB | IBB | SO | WP | Bk | W | L | Pct | Sh | Sv-Op | Hld | ERC | ERA |
| 2013 | Fresno* | AAA | 21 | 0 | 0 | 8 | 32.1 | 133 | 30 | 11 | 10 | 1 | 0 | 0 | 0 | 10 | 0 | 35 | 0 | 0 | 1 | 1 | .500 | 0 | 4- - | - | 2.92 | 2.78 |
| 2010 | Fla | NL | 2 | 0 | 0 | 0 | 1.0 | 12 | 9 | 6 | 6 | 2 | 0 | 0 | 0 | 1 | 0 | 0 | 0 | 0 | 0 | 0 | - | 0 | 0-0 | 0 | 115.7 | 54.00 |
| 2011 | Fla | NL | 4 | 0 | 0 | 1 | 3.2 | 18 | 5 | 1 | 1 | 0 | 0 | 0 | 0 | 2 | 0 | 2 | 0 | 0 | 0 | 0 | - | 0 | 0-0 | 0 | 5.84 | 2.45 |
| 2012 | Mia | NL | 4 | 0 | 0 | 1 | 3.0 | 17 | 8 | 6 | 6 | 0 | 0 | 0 | 0 | 0 | 0 | 2 | 0 | 0 | 0 | 0 | - | 0 | 0-0 | 0 | 12.05 | 18.00 |
| 2013 | SF | NL | 43 | 0 | 0 | 14 | 41.2 | 180 | 38 | 15 | 14 | 1 | 3 | 2 | 0 | 20 | 5 | 24 | 2 | 0 | 3 | 2 | .600 | 0 | 0-0 | 6 | 3.15 | 3.02 |
| 4 ML YEARS | | | 53 | 0 | 0 | 16 | 49.1 | 227 | 60 | 28 | 27 | 3 | 3 | 2 | 0 | 23 | 5 | 28 | 2 | 0 | 3 | 2 | .600 | 0 | 0-0 | 6 | 5.07 | 4.93 |

## Wilin Rosario

**Bats:** R **Throws:** R **Pos:** C-106;PH-9;1B-4;DH-4 wih-LEAN roh-SORRY-oh **Ht:** 5'11" **Wt:** 220 **Born:** 2/23/1989 **Age:** 25

| | | | BATTING | | | | | | | | | | | | | | | | | | BASERUNNING | | | | AVERAGES | | |
|---|---|---|---|---|---|---|---|---|---|---|---|---|---|---|---|---|---|---|---|---|---|---|---|---|---|---|---|
| Year | Team | Lg | G | AB | H | 2B | 3B | HR | (Hm | Rd) | TB | R | RBI | RC | TBB | IBB | SO | HBP | SH | SF | SB | CS | SB% | GDP | Avg | OBP | Slg |
| 2011 | Col | NL | 16 | 54 | 11 | 3 | 1 | 3 | (1 | 2) | 25 | 6 | 8 | 4 | 2 | 0 | 20 | 0 | 0 | 1 | 0 | 0 | - | 1 | .204 | .228 | .463 |
| 2012 | Col | NL | 117 | 396 | 107 | 19 | 0 | 28 | (18 | 10) | 210 | 67 | 71 | 56 | 25 | 2 | 99 | 1 | 0 | 4 | 4 | 5 | .44 | 10 | .270 | .312 | .530 |
| 2013 | Col | NL | 121 | 449 | 131 | 22 | 1 | 21 | (10 | 11) | 218 | 63 | 79 | 62 | 15 | 0 | 109 | 1 | 0 | 1 | 4 | 1 | .80 | 7 | .292 | .315 | .486 |
| 3 ML YEARS | | | 254 | 899 | 249 | 44 | 2 | 52 | (29 | 23) | 453 | 136 | 158 | 122 | 42 | 2 | 228 | 2 | 0 | 6 | 8 | 6 | .57 | 18 | .277 | .309 | .504 |

## B.J. Rosenberg

**Pitches:** R **Bats:** R **Pos:** RP-22 **Ht:** 6'3" **Wt:** 220 **Born:** 9/17/1985 **Age:** 28

| | | | HOW MUCH HE PITCHED | | | | | | WHAT HE GAVE UP | | | | | | | | | | | | THE RESULTS | | | | | | | |
|---|---|---|---|---|---|---|---|---|---|---|---|---|---|---|---|---|---|---|---|---|---|---|---|---|---|---|---|---|
| Year | Team | Lg | G | GS | CG | GF | IP | BFP | H | R | ER | HR | SH | SF | HB | TBB | IBB | SO | WP | Bk | W | L | Pct | Sh | Sv-Op | Hld | ERC | ERA |
| 2009 | Lakwd | A | 37 | 0 | 0 | 31 | 50.1 | 198 | 37 | 7 | 5 | 0 | 0 | 1 | 2 | 10 | 1 | 65 | 5 | 0 | 7 | 2 | .778 | 0 | 19- - | - | 1.58 | 0.89 |
| 2009 | Rdng | AA | 10 | 0 | 0 | 6 | 10.2 | 43 | 10 | 3 | 3 | 0 | 0 | 0 | 1 | 4 | 0 | 8 | 0 | 0 | 0 | 1 | .000 | 0 | 3- - | - | 3.55 | 2.53 |
| 2010 | Rdng | AA | 11 | 0 | 0 | 3 | 13.2 | 60 | 15 | 14 | 14 | 6 | 0 | 0 | 1 | 5 | 0 | 15 | 0 | 0 | 1 | 0 | 1.000 | 0 | 0- - | - | 7.45 | 9.22 |
| 2010 | Clrwtr | A+ | 8 | 0 | 0 | 4 | 13.0 | 51 | 9 | 2 | 2 | 2 | 0 | 0 | 0 | 4 | 0 | 17 | 1 | 0 | 1 | 0 | 1.000 | 0 | 1- - | - | 2.47 | 1.38 |
| 2010 | Phillies | R | 1 | 0 | 0 | 0 | 1.0 | 4 | 1 | 0 | 0 | 0 | 0 | 0 | 0 | 0 | 0 | 1 | 0 | 0 | 0 | 0 | - | 0 | 0- - | - | 1.95 | 0.00 |
| 2011 | Rdng | AA | 39 | 14 | 0 | 9 | 109.1 | 474 | 114 | 56 | 52 | 11 | 8 | 3 | 8 | 38 | 1 | 103 | 1 | 0 | 5 | 7 | .417 | 0 | 2- - | - | 4.43 | 4.28 |
| 2012 | Rdng | AA | 5 | 0 | 0 | 4 | 8.0 | 32 | 5 | 1 | 1 | 1 | 0 | 0 | 0 | 2 | 0 | 10 | 2 | 0 | 1 | 0 | 1.000 | 0 | 3- - | - | 1.69 | 1.13 |
| 2012 | LV | AAA | 20 | 6 | 0 | 4 | 54.0 | 221 | 49 | 14 | 12 | 4 | 1 | 0 | 3 | 16 | 0 | 63 | 2 | 0 | 4 | 2 | .667 | 0 | 0- - | - | 3.29 | 2.00 |
| 2013 | LV | AAA | 28 | 10 | 0 | 8 | 75.2 | 340 | 80 | 41 | 38 | 5 | 3 | 1 | 6 | 34 | 2 | 59 | 2 | 0 | 3 | 6 | .333 | 0 | 2- - | - | 4.60 | 4.52 |
| 2012 | Phi | NL | 22 | 1 | 0 | 3 | 25.0 | 106 | 18 | 17 | 17 | 4 | 2 | 0 | 2 | 14 | 0 | 24 | 0 | 0 | 1 | 2 | .333 | 0 | 0-0 | 2 | 3.92 | 6.12 |
| 2013 | Phi | NL | 22 | 0 | 0 | 5 | 19.2 | 86 | 20 | 10 | 10 | 0 | 1 | 0 | 0 | 9 | 1 | 19 | 2 | 0 | 2 | 0 | 1.000 | 0 | 1-1 | 2 | 3.58 | 4.58 |
| 2 ML YEARS | | | 44 | 1 | 0 | 8 | 44.2 | 192 | 38 | 27 | 27 | 4 | 3 | 0 | 2 | 23 | 1 | 43 | 2 | 0 | 3 | 2 | .600 | 0 | 1-1 | 4 | 3.78 | 5.44 |

# Trevor Rosenthal

**Pitches:** R **Bats:** R **Pos:** RP-74 **Ht:** 6'2" **Wt:** 220 **Born:** 5/29/1990 **Age:** 24

| HOW MUCH HE PITCHED | | | | | | | | | WHAT HE GAVE UP | | | | | | | | | | | | THE RESULTS | | | | | | | |
|---|---|---|---|---|---|---|---|---|---|---|---|---|---|---|---|---|---|---|---|---|---|---|---|---|---|---|---|---|
| Year | Team | Lg | G | GS | CG | GF | IP | BFP | H | R | ER | HR | SH | SF | HB | TBB | IBB | SO | WP | Bk | W | L | Pct | Sh | Sv-Op | Hld | ERC | ERA |
| 2009 | Cards | R | 14 | 0 | 0 | 2 | 24.0 | 111 | 25 | 17 | 13 | 0 | 1 | 1 | 4 | 10 | 0 | 26 | 3 | 1 | 4 | 1 | .800 | 0 | 0-- | - | 4.15 | 4.88 |
| 2010 | JhsCty | R | 10 | 6 | 0 | 1 | 32.0 | 125 | 23 | 10 | 8 | 1 | 0 | 0 | 2 | 7 | 0 | 30 | 0 | 1 | 3 | 0 | 1.000 | 0 | 1-- | - | 1.83 | 2.25 |
| 2011 | QuadC | A | 22 | 22 | 1 | 0 | 120.1 | 509 | 111 | 62 | 55 | 7 | 4 | 3 | 13 | 39 | 0 | 133 | 7 | 0 | 7 | 7 | .500 | 0 | 0-- | - | 3.52 | 4.11 |
| 2012 | Sprgfld | AA | 17 | 17 | 0 | 0 | 94.0 | 379 | 67 | 33 | 29 | 6 | 5 | 3 | 2 | 37 | 0 | 83 | 5 | 1 | 8 | 6 | .571 | 0 | 0-- | - | 2.42 | 2.78 |
| 2012 | Memp | AAA | 3 | 3 | 0 | 0 | 15.0 | 61 | 11 | 7 | 7 | 1 | 1 | 0 | 2 | 5 | 0 | 21 | 1 | 0 | 0 | 0 | - | 0 | 0-- | - | 2.74 | 4.20 |
| 2012 | StL | NL | 19 | 0 | 0 | 7 | 22.2 | 89 | 14 | 7 | 7 | 2 | 1 | 0 | 1 | 7 | 0 | 25 | 1 | 0 | 0 | 2 | .000 | 0 | 0-0 | 3 | 1.89 | 2.78 |
| 2013 | StL | NL | 74 | 0 | 0 | 15 | 75.1 | 311 | 63 | 25 | 22 | 4 | 3 | 0 | 6 | 20 | 0 | 108 | 3 | 0 | 2 | 4 | .333 | 0 | 3-8 | 29 | 2.68 | 2.63 |
| Postseason | | | 7 | 0 | 0 | 1 | 8.2 | 30 | 2 | 0 | 0 | 0 | 0 | 0 | 0 | 2 | 0 | 15 | 0 | 0 | 0 | 0 | - | 0 | 0-0 | 2 | 0.35 | 0.00 |
| 2 ML YEARS | | | 93 | 0 | 0 | 22 | 98.0 | 400 | 77 | 32 | 29 | 6 | 4 | 0 | 7 | 27 | 0 | 133 | 4 | 0 | 2 | 6 | .250 | 0 | 3-8 | 32 | 2.49 | 2.66 |

# Cody Ross

**Bats:** R **Throws:** L **Pos:** LF-46;RF-44;PH-13 **Ht:** 5'10" **Wt:** 195 **Born:** 12/23/1980 **Age:** 33

| BATTING | | | | | | | | | | | | | | | | | | | | | BASERUNNING | | | | AVERAGES | | |
|---|---|---|---|---|---|---|---|---|---|---|---|---|---|---|---|---|---|---|---|---|---|---|---|---|---|---|---|
| Year | Team | Lg | G | AB | H | 2B | 3B | HR | (Hm | Rd) | TB | R | RBI | RC | TBB | IBB | SO | HBP | SH | SF | SB | CS | SB% | GDP | Avg | OBP | Slg |
| 2013 | Visalia* | A+ | 6 | 16 | 2 | 0 | 0 | 0 | (- | -) | 2 | 2 | 2 | 0 | 1 | 0 | 4 | 1 | 0 | 1 | 0 | 0 | - | 0 | .125 | .211 | .125 |
| 2013 | Reno* | AAA | 1 | 3 | 2 | 1 | 0 | 0 | (- | -) | 3 | 1 | 2 | 1 | 1 | 0 | 0 | 0 | 0 | 0 | 0 | 0 | - | 0 | .667 | .750 | 1.000 |
| 2003 | Det | AL | 6 | 19 | 4 | 1 | 0 | 1 | (1 | 0) | 8 | 1 | 5 | 4 | 1 | 0 | 3 | 1 | 1 | 0 | 0 | 0 | - | 0 | .211 | .286 | .421 |
| 2005 | LAD | NL | 14 | 25 | 4 | 1 | 0 | 0 | (0 | 0) | 5 | 1 | 1 | 0 | 1 | 0 | 10 | 0 | 0 | 0 | 0 | 0 | - | 1 | .160 | .192 | .200 |
| 2006 | 3 Tms | NL | 101 | 269 | 61 | 12 | 2 | 13 | (6 | 7) | 116 | 34 | 46 | 36 | 22 | 0 | 65 | 4 | 1 | 2 | 1 | 1 | .50 | 8 | .227 | .293 | .431 |
| 2007 | Fla | NL | 66 | 173 | 58 | 19 | 0 | 12 | (8 | 4) | 113 | 35 | 39 | 42 | 20 | 3 | 38 | 3 | 0 | 1 | 2 | 0 | 1.00 | 2 | .335 | .411 | .653 |
| 2008 | Fla | NL | 145 | 461 | 120 | 29 | 5 | 22 | (7 | 15) | 225 | 59 | 73 | 68 | 33 | 2 | 116 | 7 | 0 | 5 | 6 | 1 | .86 | 5 | .260 | .316 | .488 |
| 2009 | Fla | NL | 151 | 559 | 151 | 37 | 1 | 24 | (13 | 11) | 262 | 73 | 90 | 75 | 34 | 1 | 122 | 9 | 0 | 2 | 5 | 2 | .71 | 18 | .270 | .321 | .469 |
| 2010 | 2 Tms | NL | 153 | 525 | 141 | 28 | 3 | 14 | (5 | 9) | 217 | 71 | 65 | 68 | 37 | 4 | 121 | 5 | 0 | 2 | 9 | 2 | .82 | 9 | .269 | .322 | .413 |
| 2011 | SF | NL | 121 | 405 | 97 | 25 | 0 | 14 | (6 | 8) | 164 | 54 | 52 | 53 | 49 | 4 | 96 | 4 | 0 | 3 | 5 | 2 | .71 | 10 | .240 | .325 | .405 |
| 2012 | Bos | AL | 130 | 476 | 127 | 34 | 1 | 22 | (13 | 9) | 229 | 70 | 81 | 76 | 42 | 3 | 129 | 3 | 1 | 6 | 2 | 3 | .40 | 11 | .267 | .326 | .481 |
| 2013 | Ari | NL | 94 | 317 | 88 | 17 | 1 | 8 | (4 | 4) | 131 | 33 | 38 | 37 | 25 | 1 | 50 | 3 | 1 | 5 | 3 | 2 | .60 | 10 | .278 | .331 | .413 |
| 06 | LAD | NL | 8 | 14 | 7 | 1 | 1 | 2 | (0 | 2) | 16 | 4 | 9 | 6 | 0 | 0 | 2 | 0 | 0 | 0 | 1 | 0 | 1.00 | 0 | .500 | .500 | 1.143 |
| 06 | Cin | NL | 2 | 5 | 1 | 0 | 0 | 0 | (0 | 0) | 1 | 0 | 0 | 1 | 0 | 0 | 2 | 0 | 0 | 0 | 0 | 0 | - | 0 | .200 | .200 | .200 |
| 06 | Fla | NL | 91 | 250 | 53 | 11 | 1 | 11 | (6 | 5) | 99 | 30 | 37 | 29 | 22 | 0 | 61 | 4 | 1 | 2 | 0 | 1 | .00 | 8 | .212 | .284 | .396 |
| 10 | Fla | NL | 120 | 452 | 120 | 24 | 3 | 11 | (5 | 6) | 183 | 60 | 58 | 58 | 30 | 4 | 100 | 4 | 0 | 1 | 9 | 1 | .90 | 7 | .265 | .316 | .405 |
| 10 | SF | NL | 33 | 73 | 21 | 4 | 0 | 3 | (0 | 3) | 34 | 11 | 7 | 10 | 7 | 0 | 21 | 1 | 0 | 1 | 0 | 1 | .00 | 2 | .288 | .354 | .466 |
| Postseason | | | 15 | 51 | 15 | 5 | 0 | 5 | (0 | 5) | 35 | 11 | 10 | 12 | 7 | 0 | 11 | 1 | 0 | 0 | 0 | 0 | - | 1 | .294 | .390 | .686 |
| 10 ML YEARS | | | 981 | 3229 | 851 | 203 | 13 | 130 | (63 | 67) | 1470 | 431 | 490 | 459 | 264 | 18 | 750 | 39 | 4 | 26 | 33 | 13 | .72 | 74 | .264 | .324 | .455 |

# David Ross

**Bats:** R **Throws:** R **Pos:** C-36;PH-1 **Ht:** 6'2" **Wt:** 230 **Born:** 3/19/1977 **Age:** 37

| BATTING | | | | | | | | | | | | | | | | | | | | | BASERUNNING | | | | AVERAGES | | |
|---|---|---|---|---|---|---|---|---|---|---|---|---|---|---|---|---|---|---|---|---|---|---|---|---|---|---|---|
| Year | Team | Lg | G | AB | H | 2B | 3B | HR | (Hm | Rd) | TB | R | RBI | RC | TBB | IBB | SO | HBP | SH | SF | SB | CS | SB% | GDP | Avg | OBP | Slg |
| 2013 | Portlnd* | AA | 3 | 6 | 2 | 2 | 0 | 0 | (- | -) | 4 | 3 | 2 | 1 | 1 | 0 | 2 | 0 | 0 | 0 | 0 | 0 | - | 0 | .333 | .429 | .667 |
| 2013 | Pwtckt* | AAA | 4 | 13 | 0 | 0 | 0 | 0 | (- | -) | 0 | 0 | 0 | 0 | 1 | 0 | 5 | 0 | 0 | 0 | 0 | 0 | - | 0 | .000 | .071 | .000 |
| 2002 | LAD | NL | 8 | 10 | 2 | 1 | 0 | 1 | (0 | 1) | 6 | 2 | 2 | 2 | 2 | 0 | 4 | 1 | 0 | 0 | 0 | 0 | - | 0 | .200 | .385 | .600 |
| 2003 | LAD | NL | 40 | 124 | 32 | 7 | 0 | 10 | (5 | 5) | 69 | 19 | 18 | 18 | 13 | 0 | 42 | 2 | 0 | 1 | 0 | 0 | - | 4 | .258 | .336 | .556 |
| 2004 | LAD | NL | 70 | 165 | 28 | 3 | 1 | 5 | (2 | 3) | 48 | 13 | 15 | 11 | 15 | 1 | 62 | 5 | 0 | 5 | 0 | 0 | - | 3 | .170 | .253 | .291 |
| 2005 | 2 Tms | NL | 51 | 125 | 30 | 8 | 1 | 3 | (2 | 1) | 49 | 11 | 15 | 13 | 6 | 0 | 28 | 2 | 2 | 3 | 0 | 0 | - | 3 | .240 | .279 | .392 |
| 2006 | Cin | NL | 90 | 247 | 63 | 15 | 1 | 21 | (13 | 8) | 143 | 37 | 52 | 43 | 37 | 7 | 75 | 3 | 4 | 5 | 0 | 0 | - | 4 | .255 | .353 | .579 |
| 2007 | Cin | NL | 112 | 311 | 63 | 10 | 0 | 17 | (12 | 5) | 124 | 32 | 39 | 27 | 30 | 4 | 92 | 0 | 5 | 2 | 0 | 0 | - | 9 | .203 | .271 | .399 |
| 2008 | 2 Tms | | 60 | 142 | 32 | 9 | 0 | 3 | (1 | 2) | 50 | 18 | 13 | 19 | 32 | 4 | 39 | 1 | 6 | 1 | 0 | 1 | .00 | 3 | .225 | .369 | .352 |
| 2009 | Atl | NL | 54 | 128 | 35 | 9 | 0 | 7 | (2 | 5) | 65 | 18 | 20 | 20 | 21 | 0 | 39 | 1 | 1 | 0 | 0 | 0 | - | 1 | .273 | .380 | .508 |
| 2010 | Atl | NL | 59 | 121 | 35 | 13 | 2 | 2 | (2 | 0) | 58 | 15 | 28 | 22 | 20 | 0 | 28 | 1 | 2 | 1 | 0 | 1 | .00 | 5 | .289 | .392 | .479 |
| 2011 | Atl | NL | 52 | 152 | 40 | 7 | 0 | 6 | (2 | 4) | 65 | 14 | 23 | 22 | 16 | 0 | 51 | 0 | 2 | 0 | 0 | 1 | .00 | 4 | .263 | .333 | .428 |
| 2012 | Atl | NL | 62 | 176 | 45 | 7 | 0 | 9 | (4 | 5) | 79 | 18 | 23 | 21 | 18 | 0 | 60 | 0 | 0 | 2 | 1 | 0 | 1.00 | 5 | .256 | .321 | .449 |
| 2013 | Bos | AL | 36 | 102 | 22 | 5 | 0 | 4 | (3 | 1) | 39 | 11 | 10 | 7 | 11 | 0 | 42 | 1 | 2 | 0 | 1 | 0 | 1.00 | 3 | .216 | .298 | .382 |
| 05 | Pit | NL | 40 | 108 | 24 | 8 | 0 | 3 | (2 | 1) | 41 | 9 | 15 | 9 | 6 | 0 | 24 | 1 | 1 | 3 | 0 | 0 | - | 3 | .222 | .263 | .380 |
| 05 | SD | NL | 11 | 17 | 6 | 0 | 1 | 0 | (0 | 0) | 8 | 2 | 0 | 4 | 0 | 0 | 4 | 1 | 1 | 0 | 0 | 0 | - | 0 | .353 | .389 | .471 |
| 08 | Cin | NL | 52 | 134 | 31 | 9 | 0 | 3 | (1 | 2) | 49 | 17 | 13 | 19 | 32 | 4 | 36 | 1 | 5 | 1 | 0 | 1 | .00 | 3 | .231 | .381 | .366 |
| 08 | Bos | AL | 8 | 8 | 1 | 0 | 0 | 0 | (0 | 0) | 1 | 1 | 0 | 0 | 0 | 0 | 3 | 0 | 1 | 0 | 0 | 0 | - | 0 | .125 | .125 | .125 |
| Postseason | | | 6 | 7 | 3 | 0 | 0 | 1 | (1 | 0) | 6 | 1 | 2 | 1 | 1 | 0 | 0 | 0 | 0 | 0 | 0 | 0 | - | 0 | .429 | .500 | .857 |
| 12 ML YEARS | | | 694 | 1803 | 427 | 94 | 5 | 88 | (48 | 40) | 795 | 208 | 258 | 225 | 221 | 16 | 562 | 17 | 24 | 20 | 2 | 3 | .40 | 44 | .237 | .323 | .441 |

# Robbie Ross

**Pitches:** L **Bats:** L **Pos:** RP-65 **Ht:** 5'11" **Wt:** 215 **Born:** 6/24/1989 **Age:** 25

| HOW MUCH HE PITCHED | | | | | | | | | WHAT HE GAVE UP | | | | | | | | | | | | THE RESULTS | | | | | | | |
|---|---|---|---|---|---|---|---|---|---|---|---|---|---|---|---|---|---|---|---|---|---|---|---|---|---|---|---|---|
| Year | Team | Lg | G | GS | CG | GF | IP | BFP | H | R | ER | HR | SH | SF | HB | TBB | IBB | SO | WP | Bk | W | L | Pct | Sh | Sv-Op | Hld | ERC | ERA |
| 2009 | Spkane | A- | 15 | 15 | 0 | 0 | 74.1 | 315 | 68 | 28 | 22 | 5 | 4 | 1 | 10 | 17 | 0 | 76 | 6 | 2 | 4 | 4 | .500 | 0 | 0-- | - | 3.21 | 2.66 |
| 2010 | Hkry | A | 16 | 16 | 0 | 0 | 94.0 | 401 | 89 | 38 | 27 | 2 | 5 | 1 | 11 | 20 | 0 | 62 | 2 | 1 | 8 | 7 | .533 | 0 | 0-- | - | 2.93 | 2.59 |
| 2010 | Bkrsfld | A+ | 11 | 11 | 0 | 0 | 52.0 | 242 | 67 | 38 | 31 | 4 | 1 | 0 | 4 | 17 | 0 | 49 | 4 | 1 | 4 | 4 | .500 | 0 | 0-- | - | 5.51 | 5.37 |
| 2011 | MrtlBh | A+ | 21 | 20 | 1 | 0 | 123.1 | 491 | 102 | 37 | 31 | 1 | 6 | 2 | 6 | 28 | 0 | 98 | 5 | 0 | 9 | 4 | .692 | 0 | 0-- | - | 2.18 | 2.26 |
| 2011 | Frisco | AA | 6 | 6 | 0 | 0 | 38.0 | 149 | 33 | 13 | 11 | 5 | 0 | 1 | 0 | 5 | 0 | 36 | 1 | 0 | 1 | 1 | .500 | 0 | 0-- | - | 2.57 | 2.61 |
| 2012 | Tex | AL | 58 | 0 | 0 | 9 | 65.0 | 265 | 55 | 21 | 16 | 3 | 1 | 2 | 2 | 23 | 3 | 47 | 1 | 1 | 6 | 0 | 1.000 | 0 | 0-0 | 9 | 2.83 | 2.22 |
| 2013 | Tex | AL | 65 | 0 | 0 | 16 | 62.1 | 267 | 63 | 21 | 21 | 4 | 0 | 0 | 5 | 19 | 2 | 58 | 2 | 0 | 4 | 2 | .667 | 0 | 0-1 | 15 | 3.79 | 3.03 |
| 2 ML YEARS | | | 123 | 0 | 0 | 25 | 127.1 | 532 | 118 | 42 | 37 | 7 | 1 | 2 | 7 | 42 | 5 | 105 | 3 | 1 | 10 | 2 | .833 | 0 | 0-1 | 24 | 3.29 | 2.62 |

## Tyson Ross

**Pitches:** R **Bats:** R **Pos:** RP-19; SP-16 **Ht:** 6'6" **Wt:** 230 **Born:** 4/22/1987 **Age:** 27

| HOW MUCH HE PITCHED | | | | | | | | WHAT HE GAVE UP | | | | | | | | | | | | THE RESULTS | | | | | | | |
|---|---|---|---|---|---|---|---|---|---|---|---|---|---|---|---|---|---|---|---|---|---|---|---|---|---|---|---|
| Year Team | Lg | G | GS | CG | GF | IP | BFP | H | R | ER | HR | SH | SF | HB | TBB | IBB | SO | WP | Bk | W | L | Pct | Sh | Sv-Op | Hld | ERC | ERA |
| 2013 Tucsn* | AAA | 4 | 2 | 0 | 0 | 11.2 | 50 | 12 | 6 | 6 | 0 | 0 | 0 | 0 | 6 | 0 | 9 | 1 | 0 | 1 | 1 | .500 | 0 | 0- - | - | 4.10 | 4.63 |
| 2010 Oak | AL | 26 | 2 | 0 | 9 | 39.1 | 169 | 39 | 24 | 24 | 4 | 1 | 4 | 0 | 20 | 0 | 32 | 5 | 0 | 1 | 4 | .200 | 0 | 1-2 | 2 | 4.60 | 5.49 |
| 2011 Oak | AL | 9 | 6 | 0 | 1 | 36.0 | 145 | 33 | 12 | 11 | 1 | 1 | 0 | 0 | 13 | 1 | 24 | 2 | 0 | 3 | 3 | .500 | 0 | 0-0 | 0 | 3.09 | 2.75 |
| 2012 Oak | AL | 18 | 13 | 0 | 3 | 73.1 | 342 | 96 | 56 | 53 | 7 | 3 | 3 | 5 | 37 | 3 | 46 | 2 | 1 | 2 | 11 | .154 | 0 | 0-0 | 0 | 6.68 | 6.50 |
| 2013 SD | NL | 35 | 16 | 0 | 8 | 125.0 | 504 | 100 | 51 | 44 | 8 | 3 | 5 | 7 | 44 | 4 | 119 | 7 | 0 | 3 | 8 | .273 | 0 | 0-0 | 0 | 2.84 | 3.17 |
| 4 ML YEARS | | 88 | 37 | 0 | 21 | 273.2 | 1160 | 268 | 143 | 132 | 20 | 8 | 12 | 12 | 114 | 8 | 221 | 16 | 1 | 9 | 26 | .257 | 0 | 1-2 | 2 | 4.07 | 4.34 |

## Zac Rosscup

**Pitches:** L **Bats:** R **Pos:** RP-10 **Ht:** 6'2" **Wt:** 205 **Born:** 6/9/1988 **Age:** 26

| HOW MUCH HE PITCHED | | | | | | | | WHAT HE GAVE UP | | | | | | | | | | | | THE RESULTS | | | | | | | |
|---|---|---|---|---|---|---|---|---|---|---|---|---|---|---|---|---|---|---|---|---|---|---|---|---|---|---|---|
| Year Team | Lg | G | GS | CG | GF | IP | BFP | H | R | ER | HR | SH | SF | HB | TBB | IBB | SO | WP | Bk | W | L | Pct | Sh | Sv-Op | Hld | ERC | ERA |
| 2009 Princtn | R | 10 | 9 | 0 | 1 | 40.1 | 168 | 41 | 20 | 12 | 0 | 2 | 3 | 1 | 6 | 0 | 27 | 4 | 0 | 3 | 4 | .429 | 0 | 0- - | - | 2.61 | 2.68 |
| 2010 Rays | R | 3 | 1 | 0 | 0 | 8.2 | 36 | 5 | 3 | 1 | 0 | 1 | 0 | 1 | 2 | 1 | 6 | 0 | 0 | 0 | 0 | - | 0 | 0- - | - | 1.16 | 1.04 |
| 2010 HudVal | A- | 9 | 7 | 0 | 1 | 35.2 | 142 | 27 | 16 | 12 | 0 | 1 | 2 | 0 | 7 | 0 | 35 | 2 | 0 | 3 | 1 | .750 | 0 | 1- - | - | 1.54 | 3.03 |
| 2011 Dytona | A+ | 11 | 9 | 0 | 0 | 49.2 | 211 | 43 | 17 | 14 | 4 | 2 | 1 | 2 | 19 | 0 | 50 | 0 | 0 | 4 | 2 | .667 | 0 | 0- - | - | 3.26 | 2.54 |
| 2012 Cubs | R | 1 | 0 | 0 | 0 | 1.2 | 5 | 0 | 0 | 0 | 0 | 0 | 0 | 0 | 0 | 0 | 4 | 0 | 0 | 0 | 0 | - | 0 | 0- - | - | 0.00 | 0.00 |
| 2012 Peoria | A | 3 | 0 | 0 | 0 | 7.1 | 24 | 3 | 0 | 0 | 0 | 0 | 0 | 0 | 0 | 0 | 12 | 0 | 0 | 2 | 0 | 1.000 | 0 | 0- - | - | 0.39 | 0.00 |
| 2012 Tenn | AA | 11 | 1 | 0 | 0 | 22.1 | 99 | 14 | 12 | 12 | 1 | 0 | 1 | 1 | 19 | 0 | 29 | 3 | 0 | 0 | 1 | .000 | 0 | 0- - | - | 3.49 | 4.84 |
| 2013 Tenn | AA | 37 | 0 | 0 | 11 | 43.1 | 177 | 31 | 12 | 12 | 2 | 0 | 0 | 0 | 19 | 0 | 66 | 3 | 0 | 2 | 1 | .667 | 0 | 3- - | - | 2.38 | 2.49 |
| 2013 Iowa | AAA | 9 | 0 | 0 | 2 | 7.2 | 36 | 5 | 5 | 0 | 0 | 1 | 1 | 0 | 6 | 0 | 17 | 0 | 0 | 0 | 1 | .000 | 0 | 0- - | - | 2.65 | 0.00 |
| 2013 ChC | NL | 10 | 0 | 0 | 3 | 6.2 | 30 | 3 | 1 | 1 | 1 | 0 | 0 | 0 | 7 | 1 | 7 | 0 | 0 | 0 | 0 | - | 0 | 0-0 | 0 | 3.56 | 1.35 |

## Michael Roth

**Pitches:** L **Bats:** L **Pos:** RP-14; SP-1 **Ht:** 6'1" **Wt:** 210 **Born:** 2/15/1990 **Age:** 24

| HOW MUCH HE PITCHED | | | | | | | | WHAT HE GAVE UP | | | | | | | | | | | | THE RESULTS | | | | | | | |
|---|---|---|---|---|---|---|---|---|---|---|---|---|---|---|---|---|---|---|---|---|---|---|---|---|---|---|---|
| Year Team | Lg | G | GS | CG | GF | IP | BFP | H | R | ER | HR | SH | SF | HB | TBB | IBB | SO | WP | Bk | W | L | Pct | Sh | Sv-Op | Hld | ERC | ERA |
| 2012 Orem | R+ | 11 | 9 | 0 | 0 | 22.0 | 99 | 23 | 13 | 12 | 2 | 0 | 1 | 3 | 11 | 0 | 21 | 2 | 0 | 0 | 2 | .000 | 0 | 0- - | - | 5.31 | 4.91 |
| 2013 Ark | AA | 17 | 15 | 0 | 0 | 79.1 | 342 | 77 | 42 | 37 | 8 | 3 | 0 | 9 | 36 | 1 | 51 | 6 | 1 | 6 | 3 | .667 | 0 | 0- - | - | 4.71 | 4.20 |
| 2013 LAA | AL | 15 | 1 | 0 | 5 | 20.0 | 89 | 24 | 16 | 16 | 0 | 1 | 0 | 1 | 6 | 0 | 17 | 2 | 0 | 1 | 1 | .500 | 0 | 0-0 | 0 | 4.26 | 7.20 |

## Darin Ruf

**Bats:** R **Throws:** R **Pos:** 1B-36;RF-29;LF-20;PH-1 ROUGH **Ht:** 6'3" **Wt:** 220 **Born:** 7/28/1986 **Age:** 27

| BATTING | | | | | | | | | | | | | | | | | | | | BASERUNNING | | | | AVERAGES | | |
|---|---|---|---|---|---|---|---|---|---|---|---|---|---|---|---|---|---|---|---|---|---|---|---|---|---|---|
| Year Team | Lg | G | AB | H | 2B | 3B | HR | (Hm | Rd) | TB | R | RBI | RC | TBB | IBB | SO | HBP | SH | SF | SB | CS | SB% | GDP | Avg | OBP | Slg |
| 2009 Phillies | R | 20 | 43 | 14 | 3 | 0 | 0 | (- | -) | 17 | 5 | 6 | 7 | 3 | 0 | 8 | 3 | 0 | 1 | 0 | 0 | - | 2 | .326 | .400 | .395 |
| 2009 Wmspt | A- | 37 | 133 | 40 | 17 | 0 | 3 | (- | -) | 66 | 17 | 24 | 25 | 14 | 1 | 22 | 3 | 0 | 1 | 0 | 1 | .00 | 2 | .301 | .377 | .496 |
| 2010 Lakwd | A | 32 | 115 | 38 | 7 | 3 | 4 | (- | -) | 63 | 25 | 17 | 28 | 21 | 0 | 23 | 3 | 1 | 1 | 3 | 2 | .60 | 1 | .330 | .443 | .548 |
| 2010 Clrwtr | A+ | 97 | 368 | 102 | 34 | 2 | 5 | (- | -) | 155 | 45 | 50 | 53 | 26 | 0 | 87 | 8 | 0 | 4 | 2 | 2 | .50 | 10 | .277 | .335 | .421 |
| 2011 Clrwtr | A+ | 133 | 484 | 149 | 43 | 1 | 17 | (- | -) | 245 | 72 | 82 | 96 | 56 | 1 | 95 | 10 | 0 | 4 | 0 | 1 | .00 | 15 | .308 | .388 | .506 |
| 2012 Rdng | AA | 139 | 489 | 155 | 32 | 1 | 38 | (- | -) | 303 | 93 | 104 | 122 | 65 | 2 | 102 | 18 | 0 | 11 | 2 | 0 | 1.00 | 17 | .317 | .408 | .620 |
| 2013 LV | AAA | 83 | 305 | 81 | 22 | 0 | 7 | (- | -) | 124 | 44 | 46 | 45 | 36 | 1 | 88 | 3 | 0 | 6 | 1 | 2 | .33 | 6 | .266 | .343 | .407 |
| 2012 Phi | NL | 12 | 33 | 11 | 2 | 1 | 3 | (1 | 2) | 24 | 4 | 10 | 5 | 2 | 1 | 12 | 0 | 0 | 2 | 0 | 0 | - | 1 | .333 | .351 | .727 |
| 2013 Phi | NL | 73 | 251 | 62 | 11 | 0 | 14 | (11 | 3) | 115 | 36 | 30 | 33 | 33 | 1 | 91 | 7 | 0 | 2 | 0 | 0 | - | 4 | .247 | .348 | .458 |
| 2 ML YEARS | | 85 | 284 | 73 | 13 | 1 | 17 | (12 | 5) | 139 | 40 | 40 | 38 | 35 | 2 | 103 | 7 | 0 | 4 | 0 | 0 | - | 5 | .257 | .348 | .489 |

## Chance Ruffin

**Pitches:** R **Bats:** R **Pos:** RP-9 **Ht:** 6'0" **Wt:** 195 **Born:** 9/8/1988 **Age:** 25

| HOW MUCH HE PITCHED | | | | | | | | WHAT HE GAVE UP | | | | | | | | | | | | THE RESULTS | | | | | | | |
|---|---|---|---|---|---|---|---|---|---|---|---|---|---|---|---|---|---|---|---|---|---|---|---|---|---|---|---|
| Year Team | Lg | G | GS | CG | GF | IP | BFP | H | R | ER | HR | SH | SF | HB | TBB | IBB | SO | WP | Bk | W | L | Pct | Sh | Sv-Op | Hld | ERC | ERA |
| 2011 Erie | AA | 31 | 0 | 0 | 28 | 34.0 | 139 | 23 | 9 | 8 | 2 | 1 | 0 | 1 | 16 | 2 | 43 | 2 | 0 | 3 | 3 | .500 | 0 | 10- - | - | 2.41 | 2.12 |
| 2011 Toledo | AAA | 13 | 0 | 0 | 9 | 14.2 | 65 | 14 | 4 | 3 | 1 | 1 | 0 | 0 | 6 | 0 | 17 | 1 | 0 | 0 | 0 | - | 0 | 9- - | - | 3.49 | 1.84 |
| 2012 Tacom | AAA | 50 | 0 | 0 | 24 | 70.2 | 323 | 75 | 55 | 47 | 8 | 2 | 3 | 3 | 35 | 0 | 54 | 7 | 0 | 0 | 5 | .000 | 0 | 1- - | - | 4.99 | 5.99 |
| 2013 Jacksn | AA | 16 | 16 | 1 | 0 | 83.0 | 357 | 82 | 40 | 36 | 11 | 4 | 3 | 7 | 23 | 0 | 57 | 2 | 1 | 4 | 4 | .500 | 0 | 0- - | - | 4.04 | 3.90 |
| 2013 Tacom | AAA | 15 | 2 | 0 | 5 | 29.2 | 123 | 28 | 13 | 13 | 3 | 0 | 1 | 3 | 6 | 0 | 25 | 2 | 0 | 1 | 2 | .333 | 0 | 0- - | - | 3.42 | 3.94 |
| 2011 2 Tms | AL | 15 | 0 | 0 | 2 | 17.2 | 78 | 18 | 8 | 8 | 4 | 0 | 0 | 0 | 9 | 0 | 18 | 1 | 0 | 1 | 0 | 1.000 | 0 | 0-0 | 1 | 5.60 | 4.08 |
| 2013 Sea | AL | 9 | 0 | 0 | 1 | 9.2 | 49 | 14 | 10 | 9 | 3 | 0 | 0 | 2 | 5 | 1 | 15 | 1 | 0 | 0 | 2 | .000 | 0 | 0-1 | 0 | 9.94 | 8.38 |
| 11 Det | AL | 2 | 0 | 0 | 0 | 3.2 | 16 | 5 | 2 | 2 | 2 | 0 | 0 | 0 | 0 | 0 | 3 | 0 | 0 | 0 | 0 | - | 0 | 0-0 | 0 | 7.47 | 4.91 |
| 11 Sea | AL | 13 | 0 | 0 | 2 | 14.0 | 62 | 13 | 6 | 6 | 2 | 0 | 0 | 0 | 9 | 0 | 15 | 1 | 0 | 1 | 0 | 1.000 | 0 | 0-0 | 1 | 5.02 | 3.86 |
| 2 ML YEARS | | 24 | 0 | 0 | 3 | 27.1 | 127 | 32 | 18 | 17 | 7 | 0 | 0 | 2 | 14 | 1 | 33 | 2 | 0 | 1 | 2 | .333 | 0 | 0-1 | 1 | 7.06 | 5.60 |

## Justin Ruggiano

**Bats:** R **Throws:** R **Pos:** CF-84;LF-23;PH-20;RF-5;DH-1 rouge-ee-AH-no **Ht:** 6'1" **Wt:** 210 **Born:** 4/12/1982 **Age:** 32

| BATTING | | | | | | | | | | | | | | | | | | | | BASERUNNING | | | | AVERAGES | | |
|---|---|---|---|---|---|---|---|---|---|---|---|---|---|---|---|---|---|---|---|---|---|---|---|---|---|---|
| Year Team | Lg | G | AB | H | 2B | 3B | HR | (Hm | Rd) | TB | R | RBI | RC | TBB | IBB | SO | HBP | SH | SF | SB | CS | SB% | GDP | Avg | OBP | Slg |
| 2007 TB | AL | 7 | 14 | 3 | 0 | 0 | 0 | (0 | 0) | 3 | 2 | 3 | 1 | 1 | 0 | 5 | 0 | 0 | 0 | 0 | 0 | - | 0 | .214 | .267 | .214 |
| 2008 TB | AL | 45 | 76 | 15 | 4 | 0 | 2 | (2 | 0) | 25 | 9 | 7 | 4 | 4 | 0 | 27 | 1 | 0 | 0 | 2 | 0 | 1.00 | 2 | .197 | .247 | .329 |
| 2011 TB | AL | 46 | 105 | 26 | 4 | 0 | 4 | (3 | 1) | 42 | 11 | 13 | 16 | 4 | 0 | 26 | 0 | 1 | 1 | 1 | 1 | .50 | 2 | .248 | .273 | .400 |
| 2012 Mia | NL | 91 | 288 | 90 | 23 | 1 | 13 | (4 | 9) | 154 | 38 | 36 | 46 | 29 | 0 | 84 | 0 | 1 | 1 | 14 | 8 | .64 | 6 | .313 | .374 | .535 |
| 2013 Mia | NL | 128 | 424 | 94 | 18 | 1 | 18 | (3 | 15) | 168 | 49 | 50 | 42 | 41 | 1 | 114 | 5 | 1 | 0 | 15 | 8 | .65 | 9 | .222 | .298 | .396 |
| 5 ML YEARS | | 317 | 907 | 228 | 49 | 2 | 37 | (12 | 25) | 392 | 109 | 109 | 109 | 79 | 1 | 256 | 6 | 3 | 2 | 32 | 17 | .65 | 19 | .251 | .315 | .432 |

# Carlos Ruiz

**Bats:** R **Throws:** R **Pos:** C-86;PH-7 **Ht:** 5'10" **Wt:** 205 **Born:** 1/22/1979 **Age:** 35

| BATTING | | | | | | | | | | | | | | | | | | | | | BASERUNNING | | | | AVERAGES | | |
|---|---|---|---|---|---|---|---|---|---|---|---|---|---|---|---|---|---|---|---|---|---|---|---|---|---|---|---|
| Year | Team | Lg | G | AB | H | 2B | 3B | HR | (Hm | Rd) | TB | R | RBI | RC | TBB | IBB | SO | HBP | SH | SF | SB | CS | SB% | GDP | Avg | OBP | Slg |
| 2013 | Clrwtr* | A+ | 2 | 8 | 1 | 0 | 0 | 1 | (- | -) | 4 | 1 | 3 | 1 | 2 | 0 | 0 | 0 | 0 | 0 | 0 | 0 | - | 0 | .125 | .300 | .500 |
| 2013 | Rdng* | AA | 2 | 6 | 1 | 1 | 0 | 0 | (- | -) | 2 | 0 | 0 | 0 | 1 | 0 | 0 | 0 | 0 | 0 | 0 | 0 | - | 0 | .167 | .286 | .333 |
| 2013 | LV* | AAA | 2 | 5 | 1 | 0 | 0 | 0 | (- | -) | 1 | 1 | 0 | 0 | 0 | 0 | 0 | 0 | 0 | 0 | 0 | 0 | - | 0 | .200 | .200 | .200 |
| 2006 | Phi | NL | 27 | 69 | 18 | 1 | 1 | 3 | (2 | 1) | 30 | 5 | 10 | 10 | 5 | 2 | 8 | 1 | 2 | 1 | 0 | 0 | - | 3 | .261 | .316 | .435 |
| 2007 | Phi | NL | 115 | 374 | 97 | 29 | 2 | 6 | (4 | 2) | 148 | 42 | 54 | 49 | 42 | 10 | 49 | 5 | 5 | 3 | 6 | 1 | .86 | 17 | .259 | .340 | .396 |
| 2008 | Phi | NL | 117 | 320 | 70 | 14 | 0 | 4 | (2 | 2) | 96 | 47 | 31 | 28 | 44 | 6 | 38 | 4 | 4 | 1 | 1 | 2 | .33 | 14 | .219 | .320 | .300 |
| 2009 | Phi | NL | 107 | 322 | 82 | 26 | 1 | 9 | (5 | 4) | 137 | 32 | 43 | 49 | 47 | 8 | 39 | 4 | 4 | 2 | 3 | 2 | .60 | 8 | .255 | .355 | .425 |
| 2010 | Phi | NL | 121 | 371 | 112 | 28 | 1 | 8 | (3 | 5) | 166 | 43 | 53 | 62 | 55 | 13 | 54 | 6 | 0 | 1 | 0 | 1 | .00 | 8 | .302 | .400 | .447 |
| 2011 | Phi | NL | 132 | 410 | 116 | 23 | 0 | 6 | (1 | 5) | 157 | 49 | 40 | 59 | 48 | 10 | 48 | 10 | 3 | 1 | 1 | 0 | 1.00 | 7 | .283 | .371 | .383 |
| 2012 | Phi | NL | 114 | 372 | 121 | 32 | 0 | 16 | (8 | 8) | 201 | 56 | 68 | 75 | 29 | 6 | 50 | 16 | 0 | 4 | 4 | 0 | 1.00 | 6 | .325 | .394 | .540 |
| 2013 | Phi | NL | 92 | 310 | 83 | 16 | 0 | 5 | (4 | 1) | 114 | 30 | 37 | 34 | 18 | 3 | 39 | 7 | 4 | 2 | 1 | 0 | 1.00 | 11 | .268 | .320 | .368 |
| Postseason | | | 46 | 142 | 36 | 8 | 1 | 4 | (3 | 1) | 58 | 19 | 15 | 24 | 24 | 3 | 16 | 5 | 1 | 0 | 3 | 0 | 1.00 | 2 | .254 | .380 | .408 |
| 8 ML YEARS | | | 825 | 2548 | 699 | 169 | 5 | 57 | (29 | 28) | 1049 | 304 | 336 | 366 | 288 | 58 | 325 | 53 | 22 | 15 | 16 | 6 | .73 | 74 | .274 | .358 | .412 |

# Cameron Rupp

**Bats:** R **Throws:** R **Pos:** C-3;PH-1 **Ht:** 6'1" **Wt:** 240 **Born:** 9/28/1988 **Age:** 25

| BATTING | | | | | | | | | | | | | | | | | | | | | BASERUNNING | | | | AVERAGES | | |
|---|---|---|---|---|---|---|---|---|---|---|---|---|---|---|---|---|---|---|---|---|---|---|---|---|---|---|---|
| Year | Team | Lg | G | AB | H | 2B | 3B | HR | (Hm | Rd) | TB | R | RBI | RC | TBB | IBB | SO | HBP | SH | SF | SB | CS | SB% | GDP | Avg | OBP | Slg |
| 2010 | Wmspt | A- | 55 | 193 | 42 | 16 | 0 | 5 | (- | -) | 73 | 20 | 28 | 25 | 25 | 0 | 51 | 4 | 0 | 1 | 0 | 0 | - | 2 | .218 | .318 | .378 |
| 2011 | Lakwd | A | 99 | 324 | 88 | 19 | 1 | 4 | (- | -) | 121 | 33 | 44 | 45 | 31 | 0 | 96 | 8 | 1 | 4 | 0 | 0 | - | 5 | .272 | .346 | .373 |
| 2012 | Clrwtr | A+ | 104 | 344 | 92 | 22 | 1 | 10 | (- | -) | 146 | 32 | 49 | 53 | 40 | 0 | 77 | 2 | 2 | 2 | 0 | 0 | - | 9 | .267 | .345 | .424 |
| 2013 | Rdng | AA | 41 | 143 | 35 | 6 | 0 | 8 | (- | -) | 65 | 18 | 21 | 22 | 14 | 1 | 36 | 4 | 0 | 0 | 0 | 0 | - | 7 | .245 | .329 | .455 |
| 2013 | LV | AAA | 53 | 182 | 49 | 10 | 0 | 6 | (- | -) | 77 | 18 | 24 | 24 | 10 | 0 | 55 | 1 | 0 | 1 | 1 | 1 | .50 | 5 | .269 | .309 | .423 |
| 2013 | Phi | NL | 4 | 13 | 4 | 1 | 0 | 0 | (0 | 0) | 5 | 1 | 2 | 2 | 1 | 0 | 4 | 0 | 0 | 0 | 0 | 0 | - | 0 | .308 | .357 | .385 |

# Chris Rusin

**Pitches:** L **Bats:** L **Pos:** SP-13 RUSS-inn **Ht:** 6'2" **Wt:** 195 **Born:** 10/22/1986 **Age:** 27

| HOW MUCH HE PITCHED | | | | | | | | | WHAT HE GAVE UP | | | | | | | | | | | | THE RESULTS | | | | | | | |
|---|---|---|---|---|---|---|---|---|---|---|---|---|---|---|---|---|---|---|---|---|---|---|---|---|---|---|---|---|
| Year | Team | Lg | G | GS | CG | GF | IP | BFP | H | R | ER | HR | SH | SF | HB | TBB | IBB | SO | WP | Bk | W | L | Pct | Sh | Sv-Op | Hld | ERC | ERA |
| 2009 | Cubs | R | 2 | 1 | 0 | 0 | 5.0 | 18 | 1 | 0 | 0 | 0 | 0 | 0 | 0 | 3 | 0 | 2 | 0 | 0 | 0 | 0 | - | 0 | 0- - | - | 0.84 | 0.00 |
| 2009 | Boise | A- | 8 | 8 | 0 | 0 | 31.0 | 136 | 33 | 14 | 12 | 1 | 0 | 1 | 4 | 9 | 0 | 27 | 3 | 0 | 0 | 4 | .000 | 0 | 0- - | - | 4.01 | 3.48 |
| 2010 | Dytona | A+ | 20 | 17 | 0 | 1 | 91.0 | 366 | 79 | 43 | 34 | 6 | 2 | 0 | 7 | 15 | 0 | 84 | 1 | 0 | 4 | 3 | .571 | 0 | 0- - | - | 2.58 | 3.36 |
| 2010 | Tenn | AA | 4 | 4 | 0 | 0 | 19.0 | 81 | 21 | 8 | 4 | 0 | 2 | 0 | 1 | 4 | 0 | 15 | 0 | 0 | 2 | 1 | .667 | 0 | 0- - | - | 3.43 | 1.89 |
| 2011 | Tenn | AA | 15 | 15 | 0 | 0 | 76.0 | 324 | 80 | 39 | 33 | 5 | 4 | 1 | 5 | 16 | 0 | 49 | 2 | 0 | 3 | 2 | .600 | 0 | 0- - | - | 3.62 | 3.91 |
| 2011 | Iowa | AAA | 11 | 9 | 0 | 1 | 62.2 | 259 | 70 | 29 | 28 | 8 | 5 | 0 | 1 | 14 | 0 | 46 | 0 | 1 | 5 | 2 | .714 | 0 | 0- - | - | 4.44 | 4.02 |
| 2012 | Iowa | AAA | 25 | 25 | 0 | 0 | 140.1 | 615 | 146 | 81 | 71 | 17 | 4 | 4 | 8 | 53 | 2 | 94 | 7 | 1 | 8 | 9 | .471 | 0 | 0- - | - | 4.57 | 4.55 |
| 2012 | Tenn | AA | 1 | 1 | 0 | 0 | 3.0 | 9 | 0 | 0 | 0 | 0 | 0 | 0 | 0 | 0 | 0 | 1 | 0 | 0 | 0 | 0 | - | 0 | 0- - | - | 0.00 | 0.00 |
| 2013 | Iowa | AAA | 19 | 18 | 1 | 1 | 121.0 | 493 | 113 | 49 | 45 | 8 | 3 | 4 | 3 | 27 | 0 | 69 | 9 | 0 | 8 | 7 | .533 | 1 | 0- - | - | 2.95 | 3.35 |
| 2012 | ChC | NL | 7 | 7 | 0 | 0 | 29.2 | 135 | 38 | 22 | 21 | 4 | 0 | 0 | 3 | 11 | 0 | 21 | 0 | 0 | 2 | 3 | .400 | 0 | 0-0 | 0 | 6.46 | 6.37 |
| 2013 | ChC | NL | 13 | 13 | 0 | 0 | 66.1 | 282 | 66 | 30 | 29 | 8 | 1 | 1 | 3 | 24 | 3 | 36 | 1 | 0 | 2 | 6 | .250 | 0 | 0-0 | 0 | 4.21 | 3.93 |
| 2 ML YEARS | | | 20 | 20 | 0 | 0 | 96.0 | 417 | 104 | 52 | 50 | 12 | 1 | 1 | 6 | 35 | 3 | 57 | 1 | 0 | 4 | 9 | .308 | 0 | 0-0 | 0 | 4.88 | 4.69 |

# James Russell

**Pitches:** L **Bats:** L **Pos:** RP-74 **Ht:** 6'4" **Wt:** 200 **Born:** 1/8/1986 **Age:** 28

| HOW MUCH HE PITCHED | | | | | | | | | WHAT HE GAVE UP | | | | | | | | | | | | THE RESULTS | | | | | | | |
|---|---|---|---|---|---|---|---|---|---|---|---|---|---|---|---|---|---|---|---|---|---|---|---|---|---|---|---|---|
| Year | Team | Lg | G | GS | CG | GF | IP | BFP | H | R | ER | HR | SH | SF | HB | TBB | IBB | SO | WP | Bk | W | L | Pct | Sh | Sv-Op | Hld | ERC | ERA |
| 2010 | ChC | NL | 57 | 0 | 0 | 11 | 49.0 | 219 | 55 | 37 | 27 | 11 | 3 | 4 | 4 | 11 | 0 | 42 | 2 | 0 | 1 | 1 | .500 | 0 | 0-2 | 6 | 5.12 | 4.96 |
| 2011 | ChC | NL | 64 | 5 | 0 | 10 | 67.2 | 292 | 76 | 37 | 31 | 12 | 4 | 6 | 2 | 14 | 4 | 43 | 1 | 0 | 1 | 6 | .143 | 0 | 0-2 | 6 | 4.51 | 4.12 |
| 2012 | ChC | NL | 77 | 0 | 0 | 19 | 69.1 | 292 | 67 | 28 | 25 | 5 | 2 | 3 | 1 | 23 | 7 | 55 | 1 | 1 | 7 | 1 | .875 | 0 | 2-5 | 13 | 3.35 | 3.25 |
| 2013 | ChC | NL | 74 | 0 | 0 | 7 | 52.2 | 214 | 46 | 21 | 21 | 7 | 1 | 1 | 1 | 18 | 6 | 37 | 1 | 0 | 1 | 6 | .143 | 0 | 0-8 | 19 | 3.37 | 3.59 |
| 4 ML YEARS | | | 272 | 5 | 0 | 47 | 238.2 | 1017 | 244 | 123 | 104 | 35 | 10 | 14 | 8 | 66 | 17 | 177 | 5 | 1 | 10 | 14 | .417 | 0 | 2-17 | 44 | 4.04 | 3.92 |

# Josh Rutledge

**Bats:** R **Throws:** R **Pos:** 2B-58;SS-14;PH-13;PR-3 **Ht:** 6'1" **Wt:** 190 **Born:** 4/21/1989 **Age:** 25

| BATTING | | | | | | | | | | | | | | | | | | | | | BASERUNNING | | | | AVERAGES | | |
|---|---|---|---|---|---|---|---|---|---|---|---|---|---|---|---|---|---|---|---|---|---|---|---|---|---|---|---|
| Year | Team | Lg | G | AB | H | 2B | 3B | HR | (Hm | Rd) | TB | R | RBI | RC | TBB | IBB | SO | HBP | SH | SF | SB | CS | SB% | GDP | Avg | OBP | Slg |
| 2010 | TriCity | A- | 11 | 39 | 5 | 0 | 0 | 0 | (- | -) | 5 | 6 | 4 | 0 | 4 | 0 | 10 | 1 | 1 | 0 | 1 | 0 | 1.00 | 1 | .128 | .227 | .128 |
| 2011 | Mdest | A+ | 113 | 460 | 160 | 33 | 9 | 9 | (- | -) | 238 | 91 | 71 | 99 | 41 | 1 | 91 | 12 | 8 | 2 | 16 | 3 | .84 | 5 | .348 | .414 | .517 |
| 2012 | Tulsa | AA | 87 | 356 | 109 | 27 | 3 | 13 | (- | -) | 181 | 57 | 35 | 62 | 14 | 1 | 69 | 5 | 0 | 4 | 14 | 4 | .78 | 6 | .306 | .338 | .508 |
| 2013 | ColSpr | AAA | 38 | 143 | 53 | 17 | 1 | 4 | (- | -) | 84 | 24 | 24 | 34 | 12 | 0 | 21 | 7 | 0 | 0 | 1 | 2 | .33 | 1 | .371 | .444 | .587 |
| 2012 | Col | NL | 73 | 277 | 76 | 20 | 5 | 8 | (5 | 3) | 130 | 37 | 37 | 37 | 9 | 0 | 54 | 4 | 0 | 1 | 7 | 0 | 1.00 | 8 | .274 | .306 | .469 |
| 2013 | Col | NL | 88 | 285 | 67 | 6 | 1 | 7 | (5 | 2) | 96 | 45 | 19 | 28 | 22 | 1 | 62 | 2 | 4 | 1 | 12 | 0 | 1.00 | 2 | .235 | .294 | .337 |
| 2 ML YEARS | | | 161 | 562 | 143 | 26 | 6 | 15 | (10 | 5) | 226 | 82 | 56 | 65 | 31 | 1 | 116 | 6 | 4 | 2 | 19 | 0 | 1.00 | 10 | .254 | .300 | .402 |

# Brendan Ryan

**Bats:** R **Throws:** R **Pos:** SS-101;PR-3;DH-2;PH-2 **Ht:** 6'2" **Wt:** 195 **Born:** 3/26/1982 **Age:** 32

| BATTING | | | | | | | | | | | | | | | | | | | | | BASERUNNING | | | | AVERAGES | | |
|---|---|---|---|---|---|---|---|---|---|---|---|---|---|---|---|---|---|---|---|---|---|---|---|---|---|---|---|
| Year | Team | Lg | G | AB | H | 2B | 3B | HR | (Hm | Rd) | TB | R | RBI | RC | TBB | IBB | SO | HBP | SH | SF | SB | CS | SB% | GDP | Avg | OBP | Slg |
| 2007 | StL | NL | 67 | 180 | 52 | 9 | 0 | 4 | (2 | 2) | 73 | 30 | 12 | 21 | 15 | 0 | 19 | 1 | 3 | 0 | 7 | 0 | 1.00 | 3 | .289 | .347 | .406 |
| 2008 | StL | NL | 80 | 197 | 48 | 9 | 0 | 0 | (0 | 0) | 57 | 30 | 10 | 12 | 16 | 0 | 31 | 2 | 3 | 0 | 7 | 2 | .78 | 4 | .244 | .307 | .289 |
| 2009 | StL | NL | 129 | 390 | 114 | 19 | 7 | 3 | (1 | 2) | 156 | 55 | 37 | 48 | 24 | 3 | 56 | 6 | 6 | 3 | 14 | 7 | .67 | 9 | .292 | .340 | .400 |
| 2010 | StL | NL | 139 | 439 | 98 | 19 | 3 | 2 | (0 | 2) | 129 | 50 | 36 | 37 | 33 | 5 | 60 | 2 | 9 | 3 | 11 | 4 | .73 | 6 | .223 | .279 | .294 |

| Year | Team | Lg | G | AB | H | 2B | 3B | HR | (Hm | Rd) | TB | R | RBI | RC | TBB | IBB | SO | HBP | SH | SF | SB | CS | SB% | GDP | Avg | OBP | Slg |
|---|---|---|---|---|---|---|---|---|---|---|---|---|---|---|---|---|---|---|---|---|---|---|---|---|---|---|---|
| 2011 | Sea | AL | 123 | 436 | 108 | 19 | 3 | 3 | (0 | 3) | 142 | 51 | 39 | 46 | 34 | 0 | 87 | 10 | 9 | 5 | 13 | 3 | .81 | 7 | .248 | .313 | .326 |
| 2012 | Sea | AL | 141 | 407 | 79 | 19 | 3 | 3 | (2 | 1) | 113 | 42 | 31 | 35 | 44 | 0 | 98 | 5 | 8 | 6 | 11 | 5 | .69 | 4 | .194 | .277 | .278 |
| 2013 | 2 Tms | AL | 104 | 319 | 63 | 12 | 0 | 4 | (1 | 3) | 87 | 30 | 22 | 17 | 23 | 1 | 73 | 2 | 4 | 1 | 4 | 2 | .67 | 11 | .197 | .255 | .273 |
| 13 | Sea | AL | 87 | 260 | 50 | 10 | 0 | 3 | (1 | 2) | 69 | 23 | 21 | 14 | 21 | 1 | 60 | 1 | 4 | 1 | 4 | 2 | .67 | 11 | .192 | .254 | .265 |
| 13 | NYY | AL | 17 | 59 | 13 | 2 | 0 | 1 | (0 | 1) | 18 | 7 | 1 | 3 | 2 | 0 | 13 | 1 | 0 | 0 | 0 | 0 | - | 0 | .220 | .258 | .305 |
| Postseason | | | 3 | 12 | 1 | 1 | 0 | 0 | (0 | 0) | 2 | 0 | 0 | 0 | 0 | 0 | 2 | 0 | 0 | 0 | 0 | 0 | - | 0 | .083 | .083 | .167 |
| 7 ML YEARS | | | 783 | 2368 | 562 | 106 | 16 | 19 | (6 | 13) | 757 | 288 | 187 | 216 | 189 | 9 | 424 | 28 | 42 | 18 | 67 | 23 | .74 | 44 | .237 | .299 | .320 |

## Hyun-Jin Ryu

**Pitches:** L **Bats:** R **Pos:** SP-30 he-YUN-jin ree-YOO **Ht:** 6'2" **Wt:** 255 **Born:** 3/25/1987 **Age:** 27

| Year | Team | Lg | G | GS | CG | GF | IP | BFP | H | R | ER | HR | SH | SF | HB | TBB | IBB | SO | WP | Bk | W | L | Pct | Sh | Sv-Op | Hld | ERC | ERA |
|---|---|---|---|---|---|---|---|---|---|---|---|---|---|---|---|---|---|---|---|---|---|---|---|---|---|---|---|---|
| 2013 | LAD | NL | 30 | 30 | 2 | 0 | 192.0 | 783 | 182 | 67 | 64 | 15 | 7 | 3 | 1 | 49 | 4 | 154 | 5 | 0 | 14 | 8 | .636 | 1 | 0-0 | 0 | 3.13 | 3.00 |

## Marc Rzepczynski

**Pitches:** L **Bats:** L **Pos:** RP-38 zepp-CHINN-ski **Ht:** 6'1" **Wt:** 215 **Born:** 8/29/1985 **Age:** 28

| Year | Team | Lg | G | GS | CG | GF | IP | BFP | H | R | ER | HR | SH | SF | HB | TBB | IBB | SO | WP | Bk | W | L | Pct | Sh | Sv-Op | Hld | ERC | ERA |
|---|---|---|---|---|---|---|---|---|---|---|---|---|---|---|---|---|---|---|---|---|---|---|---|---|---|---|---|---|
| 2013 | Memp* | AAA | 32 | 0 | 0 | 10 | 44.0 | 196 | 44 | 23 | 15 | 1 | 7 | 3 | 1 | 18 | 2 | 31 | 2 | 0 | 1 | 2 | .333 | 0 | 0-- | - | 3.46 | 3.07 |
| 2009 | Tor | AL | 11 | 11 | 0 | 0 | 61.1 | 261 | 51 | 27 | 25 | 7 | 2 | 1 | 1 | 30 | 0 | 60 | 4 | 1 | 2 | 4 | .333 | 0 | 0-0 | 0 | 3.65 | 3.67 |
| 2010 | Tor | AL | 14 | 12 | 0 | 0 | 63.2 | 287 | 72 | 37 | 35 | 8 | 1 | 2 | 5 | 30 | 1 | 57 | 4 | 1 | 4 | 4 | .500 | 0 | 0-0 | 2 | 5.71 | 4.95 |
| 2011 | 2 Tms | | 71 | 0 | 0 | 7 | 62.0 | 256 | 50 | 27 | 23 | 3 | 2 | 0 | 4 | 26 | 1 | 61 | 6 | 0 | 2 | 6 | .250 | 0 | 0-4 | 18 | 3.04 | 3.34 |
| 2012 | StL | NL | 70 | 0 | 0 | 14 | 46.2 | 196 | 46 | 22 | 22 | 7 | 0 | 0 | 0 | 17 | 2 | 33 | 3 | 0 | 1 | 3 | .250 | 0 | 0-5 | 18 | 4.21 | 4.24 |
| 2013 | 2 Tms | | 38 | 0 | 0 | 10 | 30.2 | 129 | 27 | 13 | 11 | 2 | 1 | 1 | 4 | 10 | 3 | 29 | 0 | 0 | 0 | 0 | - | 0 | 0-0 | 6 | 3.28 | 3.23 |
| 11 | Tor | AL | 43 | 0 | 0 | 6 | 39.1 | 158 | 28 | 16 | 13 | 2 | 1 | 0 | 3 | 15 | 0 | 33 | 5 | 0 | 2 | 3 | .400 | 0 | 0-3 | 10 | 2.52 | 2.97 |
| 11 | StL | NL | 28 | 0 | 0 | 1 | 22.2 | 98 | 22 | 11 | 10 | 1 | 1 | 0 | 1 | 11 | 1 | 28 | 1 | 0 | 0 | 3 | .000 | 0 | 0-1 | 8 | 4.01 | 3.97 |
| 13 | StL | NL | 11 | 0 | 0 | 4 | 10.1 | 50 | 16 | 9 | 9 | 1 | 0 | 1 | 1 | 4 | 1 | 9 | 0 | 0 | 0 | 0 | - | 0 | 0-0 | 0 | 7.69 | 7.84 |
| 13 | Cle | AL | 27 | 0 | 0 | 6 | 20.1 | 79 | 11 | 4 | 2 | 1 | 1 | 0 | 3 | 6 | 2 | 20 | 0 | 0 | 0 | 0 | - | 0 | 0-0 | 6 | 1.57 | 0.89 |
| Postseason | | | 17 | 0 | 0 | 1 | 10.1 | 43 | 10 | 5 | 5 | 0 | 0 | 0 | 1 | 2 | 0 | 12 | 1 | 0 | 1 | 0 | 1.000 | 0 | 0-1 | 7 | 2.82 | 4.35 |
| 5 ML YEARS | | | 204 | 23 | 0 | 31 | 264.1 | 1129 | 246 | 126 | 116 | 27 | 6 | 4 | 14 | 113 | 7 | 240 | 17 | 2 | 9 | 17 | .346 | 0 | 0-9 | 44 | 4.03 | 3.95 |

## CC Sabathia

**Pitches:** L **Bats:** L **Pos:** SP-32 **Ht:** 6'7" **Wt:** 290 **Born:** 7/21/1980 **Age:** 33

| Year | Team | Lg | G | GS | CG | GF | IP | BFP | H | R | ER | HR | SH | SF | HB | TBB | IBB | SO | WP | Bk | W | L | Pct | Sh | Sv-Op | Hld | ERC | ERA |
|---|---|---|---|---|---|---|---|---|---|---|---|---|---|---|---|---|---|---|---|---|---|---|---|---|---|---|---|---|
| 2001 | Cle | AL | 33 | 33 | 0 | 0 | 180.1 | 763 | 149 | 93 | 88 | 19 | 3 | 5 | 7 | 95 | 1 | 171 | 7 | 3 | 17 | 5 | .773 | 0 | 0-0 | 0 | 3.86 | 4.39 |
| 2002 | Cle | AL | 33 | 33 | 2 | 0 | 210.0 | 891 | 198 | 109 | 102 | 17 | 5 | 10 | 1 | 88 | 2 | 149 | 6 | **3** | 13 | 11 | .542 | 0 | 0-0 | 0 | 3.74 | 4.37 |
| 2003 | Cle | AL | 30 | 30 | 2 | 0 | 197.2 | 832 | 190 | 85 | 79 | 19 | 10 | 4 | 6 | 66 | 3 | 141 | 4 | 2 | 13 | 9 | .591 | 1 | 0-0 | 0 | 3.70 | 3.60 |
| 2004 | Cle | AL | 30 | 30 | 1 | 0 | 188.0 | 787 | 176 | 90 | 86 | 20 | 3 | 6 | 7 | 72 | 3 | 139 | 1 | 1 | 11 | 10 | .524 | 1 | 0-0 | 0 | 3.91 | 4.12 |
| 2005 | Cle | AL | 31 | 31 | 1 | 0 | 196.2 | 823 | 185 | 92 | 88 | 19 | 6 | 3 | 7 | 62 | 1 | 161 | 7 | 0 | 15 | 10 | .600 | 0 | 0-0 | 0 | 3.55 | 4.03 |
| 2006 | Cle | AL | 28 | 28 | **6** | 0 | 192.2 | 802 | 182 | 83 | 69 | 17 | 8 | 5 | 7 | 44 | 3 | 172 | 3 | 0 | 12 | 11 | .522 | **2** | 0-0 | 0 | 3.13 | 3.22 |
| 2007 | Cle | AL | 34 | **34** | 4 | 0 | **241.0** | **975** | 238 | 94 | 86 | 20 | 6 | 6 | 8 | 37 | 1 | 209 | 1 | 0 | 19 | 7 | .731 | 1 | 0-0 | 0 | 3.12 | 3.21 |
| 2008 | 2 Tms | | 35 | 35 | 10 | 0 | 253.0 | 1023 | 223 | 85 | 76 | 19 | 9 | 6 | 7 | 59 | 1 | 251 | 2 | 2 | 17 | 10 | .630 | 5 | 0-0 | 0 | 2.78 | 2.70 |
| 2009 | NYY | AL | 34 | 34 | 2 | 0 | 230.0 | 938 | 197 | 96 | 86 | 18 | 4 | 9 | 9 | 67 | 7 | 197 | 5 | 0 | **19** | 8 | .704 | 1 | 0-0 | 0 | 2.89 | 3.37 |
| 2010 | NYY | AL | 34 | **34** | 2 | 0 | 237.2 | 970 | 209 | 92 | 84 | 20 | 5 | 8 | 7 | 74 | 6 | 197 | 8 | 1 | **21** | 7 | .750 | 0 | 0-0 | 0 | 3.11 | 3.18 |
| 2011 | NYY | AL | 33 | 33 | 3 | 0 | 237.1 | **985** | 230 | 87 | 79 | 17 | 8 | 7 | 7 | 61 | 4 | 230 | 2 | 1 | 19 | 8 | .704 | 1 | 0-0 | 0 | 3.27 | 3.00 |
| 2012 | NYY | AL | 28 | 28 | 2 | 0 | 200.0 | 833 | 184 | 89 | 75 | 22 | 4 | 3 | 8 | 44 | 2 | 197 | 4 | 1 | 15 | 6 | .714 | 0 | 0-0 | 0 | 3.10 | 3.38 |
| 2013 | NYY | AL | 32 | 32 | 2 | 0 | 211.0 | 908 | 224 | **122** | **112** | 28 | 8 | 8 | 4 | 65 | 5 | 175 | 7 | 1 | 14 | 13 | .519 | 0 | 0-0 | 0 | 4.32 | 4.78 |
| 08 | Cle | AL | 18 | 18 | 3 | 0 | 122.1 | 507 | 117 | 54 | 52 | 13 | 3 | 3 | 3 | 34 | 1 | 123 | 1 | 2 | 6 | 8 | .429 | 2 | 0-0 | 0 | 3.52 | 3.83 |
| 08 | Mil | NL | 17 | 17 | 7 | 0 | 130.2 | 516 | 106 | 31 | 24 | 6 | 6 | 3 | 4 | 25 | 0 | 128 | 1 | 0 | 11 | 2 | .846 | 3 | 0-0 | 0 | 2.13 | 1.65 |
| Postseason | | | 19 | 18 | 1 | 0 | 107.1 | 478 | 116 | 57 | 54 | 14 | 5 | 0 | 5 | 51 | 8 | 101 | 4 | 1 | 9 | 5 | .643 | 0 | 0-0 | 0 | 5.19 | 4.53 |
| 13 ML YEARS | | | 415 | 415 | 37 | 0 | 2775.1 | 11530 | 2585 | 1217 | 1110 | 255 | 79 | 80 | 85 | 834 | 39 | 2389 | 57 | 15 | 205 | 115 | .641 | 12 | 0-0 | 0 | 3.39 | 3.60 |

## Fernando Salas

**Pitches:** R **Bats:** R **Pos:** RP-27 SAH-lahss **Ht:** 6'2" **Wt:** 210 **Born:** 5/30/1985 **Age:** 29

| Year | Team | Lg | G | GS | CG | GF | IP | BFP | H | R | ER | HR | SH | SF | HB | TBB | IBB | SO | WP | Bk | W | L | Pct | Sh | Sv-Op | Hld | ERC | ERA |
|---|---|---|---|---|---|---|---|---|---|---|---|---|---|---|---|---|---|---|---|---|---|---|---|---|---|---|---|---|
| 2013 | Memp* | AAA | 22 | 0 | 0 | 19 | 23.2 | 91 | 15 | 8 | 5 | 1 | 2 | 0 | 1 | 5 | 0 | 21 | 0 | 0 | 1 | 2 | .333 | 0 | 12-- | - | 1.48 | 1.90 |
| 2010 | StL | NL | 27 | 0 | 0 | 11 | 30.2 | 133 | 28 | 13 | 12 | 4 | 1 | 1 | 0 | 15 | 2 | 29 | 2 | 0 | 0 | 0 | - | 0 | 0-1 | 1 | 4.03 | 3.52 |
| 2011 | StL | NL | 68 | 0 | 0 | 46 | 75.0 | 295 | 50 | 20 | 19 | 7 | 3 | 0 | 2 | 21 | 3 | 75 | 2 | 0 | 5 | 6 | .455 | 0 | 24-30 | 6 | 1.94 | 2.28 |
| 2012 | StL | NL | 65 | 0 | 0 | 23 | 58.2 | 256 | 56 | 28 | 28 | 5 | 5 | 0 | 1 | 27 | 5 | 60 | 4 | 0 | 1 | 4 | .200 | 0 | 0-3 | 7 | 3.85 | 4.30 |
| 2013 | StL | NL | 27 | 0 | 0 | 14 | 28.0 | 118 | 27 | 15 | 14 | 3 | 1 | 4 | 1 | 6 | 1 | 22 | 2 | 0 | 0 | 3 | .000 | 0 | 0-2 | 2 | 3.22 | 4.50 |
| Postseason | | | 16 | 0 | 0 | 2 | 19.0 | 78 | 15 | 9 | 7 | 1 | 0 | 0 | 0 | 4 | 1 | 17 | 1 | 1 | 0 | 0 | - | 0 | 0-0 | 4 | 1.85 | 3.32 |
| 4 ML YEARS | | | 187 | 0 | 0 | 94 | 192.1 | 802 | 161 | 76 | 73 | 19 | 10 | 5 | 4 | 69 | 11 | 186 | 10 | 0 | 6 | 13 | .316 | 0 | 24-36 | 16 | 3.00 | 3.42 |

## Danny Salazar

**Pitches:** R **Bats:** L **Pos:** SP-10 **Ht:** 6'0" **Wt:** 190 **Born:** 1/11/1990 **Age:** 24

| Year | Team | Lg | G | GS | CG | GF | IP | BFP | H | R | ER | HR | SH | SF | HB | TBB | IBB | SO | WP | Bk | W | L | Pct | Sh | Sv-Op | Hld | ERC | ERA |
|---|---|---|---|---|---|---|---|---|---|---|---|---|---|---|---|---|---|---|---|---|---|---|---|---|---|---|---|---|
| 2009 | Lk Cty | A | 21 | 20 | 0 | 1 | 107.1 | 474 | 114 | 60 | 53 | 10 | 2 | 4 | 7 | 40 | 0 | 65 | 11 | 2 | 5 | 7 | .417 | 0 | 0-- | - | 4.51 | 4.44 |
| 2010 | Lk Cty | A | 7 | 7 | 0 | 0 | 32.1 | 140 | 34 | 16 | 16 | 7 | 1 | 0 | 1 | 13 | 0 | 23 | 3 | 0 | 1 | 1 | .500 | 0 | 0-- | - | 5.44 | 4.45 |
| 2011 | Indns | R | 5 | 5 | 0 | 0 | 6.2 | 30 | 6 | 3 | 2 | 1 | 0 | 1 | 1 | 2 | 0 | 11 | 1 | 0 | 0 | 0 | - | 0 | 0-- | - | 3.82 | 2.70 |
| 2011 | Lk Cty | A | 3 | 3 | 0 | 0 | 8.0 | 35 | 8 | 4 | 3 | 0 | 0 | 0 | 2 | 2 | 0 | 7 | 2 | 0 | 0 | 2 | .000 | 0 | 0-- | - | 3.75 | 3.38 |
| 2012 | Carlina | A+ | 16 | 16 | 0 | 0 | 53.2 | 215 | 46 | 17 | 16 | 3 | 1 | 1 | 0 | 19 | 0 | 53 | 4 | 1 | 1 | 2 | .333 | 0 | 0-- | - | 2.96 | 2.68 |

| Year | Team | Lg | G | GS | CG | GF | IP | BFP | H | R | ER | HR | SH | SF | HB | TBB | IBB | SO | WP | Bk | W | L | Pct | Sh | Sv-Op | Hld | ERC | ERA |
|---|---|---|---|---|---|---|---|---|---|---|---|---|---|---|---|---|---|---|---|---|---|---|---|---|---|---|---|---|
| HOW MUCH HE PITCHED | | | | | | | | | WHAT HE GAVE UP | | | | | | | | | | | | THE RESULTS | | | | | | | |
| 2012 | Akron | AA | 6 | 6 | 0 | 0 | 34.0 | 132 | 25 | 8 | 7 | 1 | 1 | 0 | 0 | 8 | 0 | 23 | 1 | 0 | 4 | 0 | 1.000 | 0 | 0-- | - | 1.75 | 1.85 |
| 2013 | Akron | AA | 7 | 7 | 0 | 0 | 33.2 | 133 | 27 | 10 | 10 | 1 | 0 | 0 | 0 | 10 | 0 | 51 | 0 | 1 | 2 | 3 | .400 | 0 | 0-- | - | 2.28 | 2.67 |
| 2013 | Clmbs | AAA | 14 | 13 | 0 | 1 | 59.1 | 230 | 44 | 21 | 18 | 4 | 0 | 1 | 2 | 14 | 0 | 78 | 0 | 0 | 4 | 2 | .667 | 0 | 1-- | - | 2.13 | 2.73 |
| 2013 | Cle | AL | 10 | 10 | 0 | 0 | 52.0 | 211 | 44 | 18 | 18 | 7 | 1 | 0 | 0 | 15 | 0 | 65 | 3 | 0 | 2 | 3 | .400 | 0 | 0-0 | 0 | 3.05 | 3.12 |

# Chris Sale

**Pitches:** L **Bats:** L **Pos:** SP-30 SAIL **Ht:** 6'6" **Wt:** 180 **Born:** 3/30/1989 **Age:** 25

| Year | Team | Lg | G | GS | CG | GF | IP | BFP | H | R | ER | HR | SH | SF | HB | TBB | IBB | SO | WP | Bk | W | L | Pct | Sh | Sv-Op | Hld | ERC | ERA |
|---|---|---|---|---|---|---|---|---|---|---|---|---|---|---|---|---|---|---|---|---|---|---|---|---|---|---|---|---|
| HOW MUCH HE PITCHED | | | | | | | | | WHAT HE GAVE UP | | | | | | | | | | | | THE RESULTS | | | | | | | |
| 2010 | CWS | AL | 21 | 0 | 0 | 8 | 23.1 | 92 | 15 | 5 | 5 | 2 | 1 | 0 | 0 | 10 | 0 | 32 | 1 | 0 | 2 | 1 | .667 | 0 | 4-4 | 2 | 2.30 | 1.93 |
| 2011 | CWS | AL | 58 | 0 | 0 | 17 | 71.0 | 288 | 52 | 22 | 22 | 6 | 3 | 0 | 2 | 27 | 3 | 79 | 2 | 0 | 2 | 2 | .500 | 0 | 8-10 | 16 | 2.55 | 2.79 |
| 2012 | CWS | AL | 30 | 29 | 1 | 0 | 192.0 | 772 | 167 | 66 | 65 | 19 | 1 | 3 | 6 | 51 | 5 | 192 | 6 | 0 | 17 | 8 | .680 | 0 | 0-1 | 0 | 3.00 | 3.05 |
| 2013 | CWS | AL | 30 | 30 | **4** | 0 | 214.1 | 866 | 184 | 81 | 73 | 23 | 2 | 4 | 14 | 46 | 2 | 226 | 8 | 1 | 11 | 14 | .440 | 1 | 0-0 | 0 | 2.92 | 3.07 |
| 4 ML YEARS | | | 139 | 59 | 5 | 25 | 500.2 | 2018 | 418 | 174 | 165 | 50 | 7 | 7 | 22 | 134 | 10 | 529 | 17 | 1 | 32 | 25 | .561 | 1 | 12-15 | 18 | 2.87 | 2.97 |

# Jarrod Saltalamacchia

**Bats:** B **Throws:** R **Pos:** C-119;PH-4;DH-1 salt-ah-luh-MOCK-ee-ah **Ht:** 6'4" **Wt:** 235 **Born:** 5/2/1985 **Age:** 29

| Year | Team | Lg | G | AB | H | 2B | 3B | HR | (Hm | Rd) | TB | R | RBI | RC | TBB | IBB | SO | HBP | SH | SF | SB | CS | SB% | GDP | Avg | OBP | Slg |
|---|---|---|---|---|---|---|---|---|---|---|---|---|---|---|---|---|---|---|---|---|---|---|---|---|---|---|---|
| BATTING | | | | | | | | | | | | | | | | | | | | | BASERUNNING | | | | AVERAGES | | |
| 2007 | 2 Tms | | 93 | 308 | 82 | 13 | 1 | 11 | (6 | 5) | 130 | 39 | 33 | 32 | 19 | 1 | 75 | 1 | 0 | 1 | 0 | 0 | - | 8 | .266 | .310 | .422 |
| 2008 | Tex | AL | 61 | 198 | 50 | 13 | 0 | 3 | (2 | 1) | 72 | 27 | 26 | 29 | 31 | 1 | 74 | 0 | 0 | 1 | 0 | 2 | .00 | 1 | .253 | .352 | .364 |
| 2009 | Tex | AL | 84 | 283 | 66 | 12 | 0 | 9 | (6 | 3) | 105 | 34 | 34 | 30 | 22 | 1 | 97 | 1 | 3 | 1 | 0 | 2 | .00 | 3 | .233 | .290 | .371 |
| 2010 | 2 Tms | AL | 12 | 24 | 4 | 3 | 0 | 0 | (0 | 0) | 7 | 2 | 2 | 3 | 6 | 0 | 5 | 0 | 0 | 0 | 0 | 0 | - | 0 | .167 | .333 | .292 |
| 2011 | Bos | AL | 103 | 358 | 84 | 23 | 3 | 16 | (6 | 10) | 161 | 52 | 56 | 43 | 24 | 1 | 119 | 3 | 0 | 1 | 1 | 0 | 1.00 | 7 | .235 | .288 | .450 |
| 2012 | Bos | AL | 121 | 405 | 90 | 17 | 1 | 25 | (12 | 13) | 184 | 55 | 59 | 49 | 38 | 0 | 139 | 1 | 0 | 4 | 0 | 1 | .00 | 5 | .222 | .288 | .454 |
| 2013 | Bos | AL | 121 | 425 | 116 | 40 | 0 | 14 | (9 | 5) | 198 | 68 | 65 | 60 | 43 | 3 | 139 | 0 | 0 | 2 | 4 | 1 | .80 | 7 | .273 | .338 | .466 |
| 07 | Atl | NL | 47 | 141 | 40 | 6 | 0 | 4 | (4 | 0) | 58 | 11 | 12 | 13 | 10 | 1 | 28 | 1 | 0 | 1 | 0 | 0 | - | 4 | .284 | .333 | .411 |
| 07 | Tex | AL | 46 | 167 | 42 | 7 | 1 | 7 | (2 | 5) | 72 | 28 | 21 | 19 | 9 | 0 | 47 | 0 | 0 | 0 | 0 | 0 | - | 4 | .251 | .290 | .431 |
| 10 | Tex | AL | 2 | 5 | 1 | 0 | 0 | 0 | (0 | 0) | 1 | 0 | 1 | 1 | 0 | 0 | 1 | 0 | 0 | 0 | 0 | 0 | - | 0 | .200 | .200 | .200 |
| 10 | Bos | AL | 10 | 19 | 3 | 3 | 0 | 0 | (0 | 0) | 6 | 2 | 1 | 2 | 6 | 0 | 4 | 0 | 0 | 0 | 0 | 0 | - | 0 | .158 | .360 | .316 |
| 7 ML YEARS | | | 595 | 2001 | 492 | 121 | 5 | 78 | (41 | 37) | 857 | 277 | 275 | 246 | 183 | 7 | 648 | 6 | 3 | 10 | 5 | 6 | .45 | 31 | .246 | .310 | .428 |

# Jeff Samardzija

**Pitches:** R **Bats:** R **Pos:** SP-33 suh-MAHR-jah **Ht:** 6'5" **Wt:** 225 **Born:** 1/23/1985 **Age:** 29

| Year | Team | Lg | G | GS | CG | GF | IP | BFP | H | R | ER | HR | SH | SF | HB | TBB | IBB | SO | WP | Bk | W | L | Pct | Sh | Sv-Op | Hld | ERC | ERA |
|---|---|---|---|---|---|---|---|---|---|---|---|---|---|---|---|---|---|---|---|---|---|---|---|---|---|---|---|---|
| HOW MUCH HE PITCHED | | | | | | | | | WHAT HE GAVE UP | | | | | | | | | | | | THE RESULTS | | | | | | | |
| 2008 | ChC | NL | 26 | 0 | 0 | 6 | 27.2 | 124 | 24 | 12 | 7 | 0 | 1 | 1 | 1 | 15 | 2 | 25 | 2 | 0 | 1 | 0 | 1.000 | 0 | 1-4 | 3 | 3.08 | 2.28 |
| 2009 | ChC | NL | 20 | 2 | 0 | 7 | 34.2 | 161 | 46 | 29 | 29 | 7 | 4 | 1 | 1 | 15 | 1 | 21 | 2 | 0 | 1 | 3 | .250 | 0 | 0-0 | 0 | 7.13 | 7.53 |
| 2010 | ChC | NL | 7 | 3 | 0 | 0 | 19.1 | 100 | 21 | 22 | 18 | 4 | 0 | 0 | 2 | 20 | 1 | 9 | 1 | 0 | 2 | 2 | .500 | 0 | 0-0 | 0 | 8.45 | 8.38 |
| 2011 | ChC | NL | 75 | 0 | 0 | 18 | 88.0 | 380 | 64 | 35 | 29 | 5 | 3 | 2 | 5 | 50 | 3 | 87 | 8 | 0 | 8 | 4 | .667 | 0 | 0-2 | 13 | 3.05 | 2.97 |
| 2012 | ChC | NL | 28 | 28 | 1 | 0 | 174.2 | 723 | 157 | 79 | 74 | 20 | 5 | 4 | 4 | 56 | 2 | 180 | 10 | 0 | 9 | 13 | .409 | 0 | 0-0 | 0 | 3.41 | 3.81 |
| 2013 | ChC | NL | 33 | 33 | 2 | 0 | 213.2 | 914 | 210 | 109 | 103 | 25 | 4 | 2 | 8 | 78 | 3 | 214 | 11 | 0 | 8 | 13 | .381 | 1 | 0-0 | 0 | 4.11 | 4.34 |
| Postseason | | | 1 | 0 | 0 | 0 | 1.0 | 4 | 2 | 1 | 1 | 0 | 0 | 0 | 0 | 0 | 0 | 0 | 0 | 0 | 0 | 0 | - | 0 | 0-0 | 0 | 9.49 | 9.00 |
| 6 ML YEARS | | | 189 | 66 | 3 | 31 | 558.0 | 2402 | 522 | 286 | 260 | 61 | 17 | 10 | 21 | 234 | 12 | 536 | 34 | 0 | 29 | 35 | .453 | 1 | 1-6 | 16 | 3.97 | 4.19 |

# Alex Sanabia

**Pitches:** R **Bats:** R **Pos:** SP-10 suh-NAH-bee-ah **Ht:** 6'2" **Wt:** 210 **Born:** 9/8/1988 **Age:** 25

| Year | Team | Lg | G | GS | CG | GF | IP | BFP | H | R | ER | HR | SH | SF | HB | TBB | IBB | SO | WP | Bk | W | L | Pct | Sh | Sv-Op | Hld | ERC | ERA |
|---|---|---|---|---|---|---|---|---|---|---|---|---|---|---|---|---|---|---|---|---|---|---|---|---|---|---|---|---|
| HOW MUCH HE PITCHED | | | | | | | | | WHAT HE GAVE UP | | | | | | | | | | | | THE RESULTS | | | | | | | |
| 2010 | Fla | NL | 15 | 12 | 0 | 0 | 72.1 | 307 | 74 | 32 | 30 | 6 | 3 | 1 | 3 | 16 | 2 | 47 | 0 | 0 | 5 | 3 | .625 | 0 | 0-0 | 0 | 3.47 | 3.73 |
| 2011 | Fla | NL | 3 | 2 | 0 | 0 | 11.0 | 48 | 13 | 4 | 4 | 2 | 0 | 0 | 0 | 3 | 0 | 8 | 2 | 0 | 0 | 0 | - | 0 | 0-0 | 0 | 5.19 | 3.27 |
| 2013 | Mia | NL | 10 | 10 | 0 | 0 | 55.1 | 251 | 69 | 33 | 30 | 10 | 2 | 2 | 4 | 25 | 3 | 31 | 1 | 0 | 3 | 7 | .300 | 0 | 0-0 | 0 | 6.81 | 4.88 |
| 3 ML YEARS | | | 28 | 24 | 0 | 0 | 138.2 | 606 | 156 | 69 | 64 | 18 | 5 | 3 | 7 | 44 | 5 | 86 | 3 | 0 | 8 | 10 | .444 | 0 | 0-0 | 0 | 4.85 | 4.15 |

# Angel Sanchez

**Bats:** R **Throws:** R **Pos:** 2B-1 ahn-HELL **Ht:** 6'1" **Wt:** 205 **Born:** 9/20/1983 **Age:** 30

| Year | Team | Lg | G | AB | H | 2B | 3B | HR | (Hm | Rd) | TB | R | RBI | RC | TBB | IBB | SO | HBP | SH | SF | SB | CS | SB% | GDP | Avg | OBP | Slg |
|---|---|---|---|---|---|---|---|---|---|---|---|---|---|---|---|---|---|---|---|---|---|---|---|---|---|---|---|
| BATTING | | | | | | | | | | | | | | | | | | | | | BASERUNNING | | | | AVERAGES | | |
| 2013 | Charltt* | AAA | 43 | 148 | 28 | 5 | 0 | 1 | (- | -) | 36 | 19 | 16 | 9 | 12 | 0 | 25 | 3 | 0 | 0 | 0 | 1 | .00 | 5 | .189 | .264 | .243 |
| 2006 | KC | AL | 8 | 27 | 6 | 0 | 0 | 0 | (0 | 0) | 6 | 2 | 1 | 0 | 0 | 0 | 4 | 0 | 0 | 1 | 0 | 0 | - | 0 | .222 | .214 | .222 |
| 2010 | 2 Tms | | 66 | 253 | 70 | 9 | 4 | 0 | (0 | 0) | 87 | 30 | 25 | 29 | 11 | 0 | 45 | 2 | 6 | 0 | 0 | 1 | .00 | 8 | .277 | .312 | .344 |
| 2011 | Hou | NL | 110 | 288 | 69 | 10 | 0 | 1 | (1 | 0) | 82 | 35 | 28 | 27 | 27 | 1 | 44 | 1 | 10 | 2 | 3 | 0 | 1.00 | 3 | .240 | .305 | .285 |
| 2013 | CWS | AL | 1 | 2 | 0 | 0 | 0 | 0 | (0 | 0) | 0 | 0 | 0 | 0 | 0 | 0 | 0 | 0 | 0 | 0 | 0 | 0 | - | 0 | .000 | .000 | .000 |
| 10 | Bos | AL | 1 | 3 | 0 | 0 | 0 | 0 | (0 | 0) | 0 | 0 | 0 | 0 | 0 | 0 | 0 | 0 | 0 | 0 | 0 | 0 | - | 0 | .000 | .000 | .000 |
| 10 | Hou | NL | 65 | 250 | 70 | 9 | 4 | 0 | (0 | 0) | 87 | 30 | 25 | 29 | 11 | 0 | 45 | 2 | 6 | 0 | 0 | 1 | .00 | 8 | .280 | .316 | .348 |
| 4 ML YEARS | | | 185 | 570 | 145 | 19 | 4 | 1 | (1 | 0) | 175 | 67 | 54 | 56 | 38 | 1 | 93 | 3 | 16 | 3 | 3 | 1 | .75 | 11 | .254 | .303 | .307 |

# Anibal Sanchez

**Pitches:** R **Bats:** R **Pos:** SP-29 ah-NEE-bahl **Ht:** 6'0" **Wt:** 205 **Born:** 2/27/1984 **Age:** 30

| | | | HOW MUCH HE PITCHED | | | | | | WHAT HE GAVE UP | | | | | | | | | | | | THE RESULTS | | | | | | | |
|---|---|---|---|---|---|---|---|---|---|---|---|---|---|---|---|---|---|---|---|---|---|---|---|---|---|---|---|---|
| Year | Team | Lg | G | GS | CG | GF | IP | BFP | H | R | ER | HR | SH | SF | HB | TBB | IBB | SO | WP | Bk | W | L | Pct | Sh | Sv-Op | Hld | ERC | ERA |
| 2013 | Lkland* | A+ | 1 | 0 | 0 | 0 | 1.2 | 6 | 2 | 0 | 0 | 0 | 0 | 0 | 0 | 0 | 0 | 0 | 0 | 0 | 0 | 0 | - | 0 | 0-- | - | 3.46 | 0.00 |
| 2006 | Fla | NL | 18 | 17 | 2 | 0 | 114.1 | 469 | 90 | 39 | 36 | 9 | 3 | 1 | 4 | 46 | 1 | 72 | 4 | 1 | 10 | 3 | .769 | 1 | 0-0 | 0 | 2.96 | 2.83 |
| 2007 | Fla | NL | 6 | 6 | 0 | 0 | 30.0 | 151 | 43 | 17 | 16 | 3 | 2 | 2 | 2 | 19 | 1 | 14 | 3 | 0 | 2 | 1 | .667 | 0 | 0-0 | 0 | 7.90 | 4.80 |
| 2008 | Fla | NL | 10 | 10 | 0 | 0 | 51.2 | 241 | 54 | 35 | 32 | 7 | 4 | 2 | 6 | 27 | 2 | 50 | 1 | 0 | 2 | 5 | .286 | 0 | 0-0 | 0 | 5.40 | 5.57 |
| 2009 | Fla | NL | 16 | 16 | 0 | 0 | 86.0 | 383 | 84 | 39 | 37 | 10 | 2 | 2 | 1 | 46 | 5 | 71 | 0 | 1 | 4 | 8 | .333 | 0 | 0-0 | 0 | 4.51 | 3.87 |
| 2010 | Fla | NL | 32 | 32 | 1 | 0 | 195.0 | 841 | 192 | 89 | 77 | 10 | 13 | 3 | 7 | 70 | 5 | 157 | 7 | 0 | 13 | 12 | .520 | 1 | 0-0 | 0 | 3.56 | 3.55 |
| 2011 | Fla | NL | 32 | 32 | 3 | 0 | 196.1 | 830 | 187 | 85 | 80 | 20 | 12 | 1 | 5 | 64 | 8 | 202 | 4 | **5** | 8 | 9 | .471 | 2 | 0-0 | 0 | 3.57 | 3.67 |
| 2012 | 2 Tms | | 31 | 31 | 1 | 0 | 195.2 | 820 | 200 | 95 | 84 | 20 | 5 | 7 | 5 | 48 | 3 | 167 | 7 | 1 | 9 | 13 | .409 | 1 | 0-0 | 0 | 3.70 | 3.86 |
| 2013 | Det | AL | 29 | 29 | 1 | 0 | 182.0 | 746 | 156 | 56 | 52 | 9 | 4 | 4 | 2 | 54 | 1 | 202 | 7 | 0 | 14 | 8 | .636 | 1 | 0-0 | 0 | 2.63 | **2.57** |
| 12 | Mia | NL | 19 | 19 | 0 | 0 | 121.0 | 504 | 119 | 59 | 53 | 12 | 4 | 5 | 2 | 33 | 2 | 110 | 4 | 1 | 5 | 7 | .417 | 0 | 0-0 | 0 | 3.55 | 3.94 |
| 12 | Det | AL | 12 | 12 | 1 | 0 | 74.2 | 316 | 81 | 36 | 31 | 8 | 1 | 2 | 3 | 15 | 1 | 57 | 3 | 0 | 4 | 6 | .400 | 1 | 0-0 | 0 | 3.95 | 3.74 |
| Postseason | | | 3 | 3 | 0 | 0 | 20.1 | 79 | 14 | 4 | 4 | 1 | 0 | 0 | 0 | 6 | 1 | 18 | 1 | 0 | 1 | 2 | .333 | 0 | 0-0 | 0 | 1.78 | 1.77 |
| 8 ML YEARS | | | 174 | 173 | 8 | 0 | 1051.0 | 4481 | 1006 | 455 | 414 | 88 | 45 | 22 | 32 | 374 | 26 | 935 | 33 | 8 | 62 | 59 | .512 | 6 | 0-0 | 0 | 3.63 | 3.55 |

# Eduardo Sanchez

**Pitches:** R **Bats:** R **Pos:** RP-4 **Ht:** 5'11" **Wt:** 175 **Born:** 2/16/1989 **Age:** 25

| | | | HOW MUCH HE PITCHED | | | | | | WHAT HE GAVE UP | | | | | | | | | | | | THE RESULTS | | | | | | | |
|---|---|---|---|---|---|---|---|---|---|---|---|---|---|---|---|---|---|---|---|---|---|---|---|---|---|---|---|---|
| Year | Team | Lg | G | GS | CG | GF | IP | BFP | H | R | ER | HR | SH | SF | HB | TBB | IBB | SO | WP | Bk | W | L | Pct | Sh | Sv-Op | Hld | ERC | ERA |
| 2013 | Memp* | AAA | 9 | 0 | 0 | 3 | 9.2 | 44 | 10 | 4 | 4 | 2 | 0 | 1 | 2 | 4 | 0 | 7 | 4 | 0 | 0 | 0 | - | 0 | 1-- | - | 6.01 | 3.72 |
| 2013 | Iowa* | AAA | 24 | 0 | 0 | 13 | 30.1 | 131 | 21 | 12 | 11 | 1 | 1 | 0 | 3 | 19 | 3 | 28 | 2 | 0 | 1 | 1 | .500 | 0 | 2-- | - | 3.00 | 3.26 |
| 2011 | StL | NL | 26 | 0 | 0 | 11 | 30.0 | 118 | 14 | 6 | 6 | 1 | 0 | 2 | 3 | 16 | 0 | 35 | 5 | 0 | 3 | 1 | .750 | 0 | 5-7 | 7 | 1.85 | 1.80 |
| 2012 | StL | NL | 17 | 0 | 0 | 4 | 15.0 | 70 | 11 | 11 | 11 | 2 | 1 | 1 | 1 | 13 | 4 | 13 | 4 | 0 | 0 | 1 | .000 | 0 | 0-0 | 4 | 4.32 | 6.60 |
| 2013 | ChC | NL | 4 | 0 | 0 | 1 | 6.1 | 29 | 5 | 4 | 4 | 1 | 2 | 1 | 0 | 5 | 0 | 5 | 1 | 1 | 0 | 1 | .000 | 0 | 0-0 | 0 | 4.75 | 5.68 |
| 3 ML YEARS | | | 47 | 0 | 0 | 16 | 51.1 | 217 | 30 | 21 | 21 | 4 | 3 | 4 | 4 | 34 | 4 | 53 | 10 | 1 | 3 | 3 | .500 | 0 | 5-7 | 11 | 2.86 | 3.68 |

# Gaby Sanchez

**Bats:** R **Throws:** R **Pos:** 1B-113;PH-42;3B-1 GABB-ee **Ht:** 6'1" **Wt:** 235 **Born:** 9/2/1983 **Age:** 30

| | | | BATTING | | | | | | | | | | | | | | | | | | | BASERUNNING | | | | AVERAGES | | |
|---|---|---|---|---|---|---|---|---|---|---|---|---|---|---|---|---|---|---|---|---|---|---|---|---|---|---|---|---|
| Year | Team | Lg | G | AB | H | 2B | 3B | HR | (Hm | Rd) | TB | R | RBI | RC | TBB | IBB | SO | HBP | SH | SF | SB | CS | SB% | GDP | Avg | OBP | Slg |
| 2008 | Fla | NL | 5 | 8 | 3 | 2 | 0 | 0 | (0 | 0) | 5 | 0 | 1 | 2 | 0 | 0 | 2 | 0 | 0 | 0 | 0 | 0 | - | 0 | .375 | .375 | .625 |
| 2009 | Fla | NL | 21 | 21 | 5 | 0 | 0 | 2 | (2 | 0) | 11 | 2 | 3 | 3 | 2 | 0 | 3 | 0 | 0 | 0 | 0 | 0 | - | 1 | .238 | .304 | .524 |
| 2010 | Fla | NL | 151 | 572 | 156 | 37 | 3 | 19 | (7 | 12) | 256 | 72 | 85 | 88 | 57 | 2 | 101 | 5 | 3 | 6 | 5 | 0 | 1.00 | 14 | .273 | .341 | .448 |
| 2011 | Fla | NL | 159 | 572 | 152 | 35 | 0 | 19 | (11 | 8) | 244 | 72 | 78 | 77 | 74 | 4 | 97 | 6 | 2 | 7 | 3 | 1 | .75 | 18 | .266 | .352 | .427 |
| 2012 | 2 Tms | NL | 105 | 299 | 65 | 16 | 0 | 7 | (1 | 6) | 102 | 30 | 30 | 21 | 25 | 2 | 56 | 1 | 0 | 1 | 1 | 0 | 1.00 | 13 | .217 | .279 | .341 |
| 2013 | Pit | NL | 136 | 264 | 67 | 18 | 0 | 7 | (1 | 6) | 106 | 29 | 36 | 38 | 44 | 1 | 51 | 4 | 0 | 7 | 1 | 0 | 1.00 | 3 | .254 | .361 | .402 |
| 12 | Mia | NL | 55 | 183 | 37 | 10 | 0 | 3 | (1 | 2) | 56 | 12 | 17 | 10 | 12 | 1 | 36 | 0 | 0 | 1 | 1 | 0 | 1.00 | 7 | .202 | .250 | .306 |
| 12 | Pit | NL | 50 | 116 | 28 | 6 | 0 | 4 | (0 | 4) | 46 | 18 | 13 | 11 | 13 | 1 | 20 | 1 | 0 | 0 | 0 | 0 | - | 6 | .241 | .323 | .397 |
| 6 ML YEARS | | | 577 | 1736 | 448 | 108 | 3 | 54 | (22 | 32) | 724 | 205 | 233 | 229 | 202 | 9 | 310 | 16 | 5 | 21 | 10 | 1 | .91 | 49 | .258 | .337 | .417 |

# Hector Sanchez

**Bats:** B **Throws:** R **Pos:** C-33;PH-32;DH-1 **Ht:** 6'0" **Wt:** 235 **Born:** 11/17/1989 **Age:** 24

| | | | BATTING | | | | | | | | | | | | | | | | | | | BASERUNNING | | | | AVERAGES | | |
|---|---|---|---|---|---|---|---|---|---|---|---|---|---|---|---|---|---|---|---|---|---|---|---|---|---|---|---|---|
| Year | Team | Lg | G | AB | H | 2B | 3B | HR | (Hm | Rd) | TB | R | RBI | RC | TBB | IBB | SO | HBP | SH | SF | SB | CS | SB% | GDP | Avg | OBP | Slg |
| 2013 | Fresno* | AAA | 32 | 85 | 23 | 4 | 0 | 3 | (- | -) | 36 | 10 | 11 | 14 | 12 | 1 | 15 | 1 | 0 | 1 | 0 | 0 | - | 3 | .271 | .364 | .424 |
| 2013 | Giants* | R | 1 | 3 | 1 | 1 | 0 | 0 | (- | -) | 2 | 0 | 2 | 0 | 0 | 0 | 1 | 0 | 0 | 0 | 0 | 0 | - | 0 | .333 | .333 | .667 |
| 2013 | SnJos* | A+ | 4 | 12 | 3 | 1 | 0 | 0 | (- | -) | 4 | 1 | 3 | 1 | 1 | 0 | 4 | 0 | 0 | 1 | 0 | 0 | - | 0 | .250 | .286 | .333 |
| 2011 | SF | NL | 13 | 31 | 8 | 2 | 0 | 0 | (0 | 0) | 10 | 0 | 1 | 2 | 3 | 0 | 6 | 0 | 0 | 0 | 0 | 0 | - | 1 | .258 | .324 | .323 |
| 2012 | SF | NL | 74 | 218 | 61 | 15 | 0 | 3 | (1 | 2) | 85 | 22 | 34 | 22 | 5 | 0 | 52 | 1 | 0 | 3 | 0 | 0 | - | 8 | .280 | .295 | .390 |
| 2013 | SF | NL | 63 | 129 | 32 | 4 | 0 | 3 | (0 | 3) | 45 | 8 | 19 | 14 | 7 | 0 | 29 | 3 | 0 | 1 | 0 | 0 | - | 1 | .248 | .300 | .349 |
| Postseason | | | 4 | 11 | 1 | 0 | 0 | 0 | (0 | 0) | 1 | 1 | 0 | 1 | 2 | 0 | 7 | 0 | 0 | 0 | 0 | 0 | - | 0 | .091 | .231 | .091 |
| 3 ML YEARS | | | 150 | 378 | 101 | 21 | 0 | 6 | (1 | 5) | 140 | 30 | 54 | 38 | 15 | 0 | 87 | 4 | 0 | 4 | 0 | 0 | - | 10 | .267 | .299 | .370 |

# Jonathan Sanchez

**Pitches:** L **Bats:** L **Pos:** SP-4; RP-1 **Ht:** 6'0" **Wt:** 195 **Born:** 11/19/1982 **Age:** 31

| | | | HOW MUCH HE PITCHED | | | | | | WHAT HE GAVE UP | | | | | | | | | | | | THE RESULTS | | | | | | | |
|---|---|---|---|---|---|---|---|---|---|---|---|---|---|---|---|---|---|---|---|---|---|---|---|---|---|---|---|---|
| Year | Team | Lg | G | GS | CG | GF | IP | BFP | H | R | ER | HR | SH | SF | HB | TBB | IBB | SO | WP | Bk | W | L | Pct | Sh | Sv-Op | Hld | ERC | ERA |
| 2013 | Albq* | AAA | 14 | 14 | 1 | 0 | 66.2 | 307 | 72 | 40 | 38 | 12 | 4 | 2 | 3 | 42 | 0 | 79 | 3 | 0 | 7 | 3 | .700 | 0 | 0-- | - | 6.38 | 5.13 |
| 2006 | SF | NL | 27 | 4 | 0 | 4 | 40.0 | 185 | 39 | 26 | 22 | 2 | 0 | 2 | 4 | 23 | 0 | 33 | 2 | 0 | 3 | 1 | .750 | 0 | 0-0 | 5 | 4.54 | 4.95 |
| 2007 | SF | NL | 33 | 4 | 0 | 8 | 52.0 | 238 | 57 | 34 | 34 | 8 | 2 | 2 | 5 | 28 | 1 | 62 | 4 | 0 | 1 | 5 | .167 | 0 | 0-0 | 2 | 6.06 | 5.88 |
| 2008 | SF | NL | 29 | 29 | 0 | 0 | 158.0 | 695 | 154 | 90 | 88 | 14 | 9 | 5 | 7 | 75 | 1 | 157 | 7 | 0 | 9 | 12 | .429 | 0 | 0-0 | 0 | 4.31 | 5.01 |
| 2009 | SF | NL | 32 | 29 | 1 | 2 | 163.1 | 710 | 135 | 82 | 77 | 19 | 3 | 1 | 6 | 88 | 5 | 177 | 11 | 0 | 8 | 12 | .400 | 1 | 0-0 | 1 | 3.83 | 4.24 |
| 2010 | SF | NL | 34 | 33 | 0 | 0 | 193.1 | 812 | 142 | 74 | 66 | 21 | 7 | 4 | 9 | **96** | 4 | 205 | 15 | 1 | 13 | 9 | .591 | 0 | 0-0 | 1 | 3.21 | 3.07 |
| 2011 | SF | NL | 19 | 19 | 0 | 0 | 101.1 | 444 | 80 | 54 | 48 | 9 | 4 | 4 | 6 | 66 | 2 | 102 | 5 | 0 | 4 | 7 | .364 | 0 | 0-0 | 0 | 4.02 | 4.26 |
| 2012 | 2 Tms | | 15 | 15 | 0 | 0 | 64.2 | 327 | 82 | 60 | 58 | 11 | 2 | 6 | 5 | 53 | 2 | 45 | 6 | 1 | 1 | 9 | .100 | 0 | 0-0 | 0 | 8.37 | 8.07 |
| 2013 | Pit | NL | 5 | 4 | 0 | 0 | 13.2 | 75 | 25 | 18 | 18 | 7 | 2 | 0 | 2 | 8 | 0 | 15 | 0 | 0 | 0 | 3 | .000 | 0 | 0-0 | 0 | 15.00 | 11.85 |
| 12 | KC | AL | 12 | 12 | 0 | 0 | 53.1 | 270 | 65 | 47 | 46 | 8 | 2 | 4 | 5 | 44 | 1 | 36 | 4 | 1 | 1 | 6 | .143 | 0 | 0-0 | 0 | 7.92 | 7.76 |
| 12 | Col | NL | 3 | 3 | 0 | 0 | 11.1 | 57 | 17 | 13 | 12 | 3 | 0 | 2 | 0 | 9 | 1 | 9 | 2 | 0 | 0 | 3 | .000 | 0 | 0-0 | 0 | 10.60 | 9.53 |
| Postseason | | | 4 | 4 | 0 | 0 | 20.0 | 86 | 16 | 10 | 9 | 2 | 0 | 2 | 1 | 9 | 0 | 22 | 1 | 0 | 0 | 2 | .000 | 0 | 0-0 | 0 | 3.30 | 4.05 |
| 8 ML YEARS | | | 194 | 137 | 1 | 14 | 786.1 | 3486 | 714 | 438 | 411 | 91 | 29 | 24 | 44 | 437 | 15 | 796 | 50 | 2 | 39 | 58 | .402 | 1 | 0-0 | 9 | 4.47 | 4.70 |

## Tony Sanchez

**Bats:** R **Throws:** R **Pos:** C-16;PH-5;DH-2 **Ht:** 5'11" **Wt:** 230 **Born:** 5/20/1988 **Age:** 26

| BATTING | | | | | | | | | | | | | | | | | | | | | | BASERUNNING | | | | AVERAGES | | |
|---|---|---|---|---|---|---|---|---|---|---|---|---|---|---|---|---|---|---|---|---|---|---|---|---|---|---|---|---|
| Year | Team | Lg | G | AB | H | 2B | 3B | HR | (Hm | Rd) | TB | R | RBI | RC | TBB | IBB | SO | HBP | SH | SF | SB | CS | SB% | GDP | Avg | OBP | Slg |
| 2009 | StCol | A- | 4 | 13 | 4 | 1 | 0 | 0 | (- | -) | 5 | 2 | 1 | 1 | 1 | 0 | 2 | 0 | 0 | 0 | 0 | 0 | - | 0 | .308 | .357 | .385 |
| 2009 | WV | A | 41 | 155 | 49 | 15 | 1 | 7 | (- | -) | 87 | 29 | 46 | 37 | 21 | 2 | 34 | 8 | 0 | 4 | 1 | 0 | 1.00 | 0 | .316 | .415 | .561 |
| 2009 | Lynbrg | A+ | 3 | 10 | 2 | 2 | 0 | 0 | (- | -) | 4 | 2 | 1 | 1 | 1 | 0 | 4 | 2 | 0 | 0 | 0 | 0 | - | 0 | .200 | .385 | .400 |
| 2010 | Bradtn | A+ | 59 | 207 | 65 | 17 | 0 | 4 | (- | -) | 94 | 31 | 35 | 42 | 28 | 1 | 41 | 11 | 0 | 4 | 2 | 1 | .67 | 4 | .314 | .416 | .454 |
| 2011 | Altna | AA | 118 | 402 | 97 | 14 | 1 | 5 | (- | -) | 128 | 46 | 44 | 48 | 47 | 2 | 76 | 14 | 4 | 2 | 5 | 5 | .50 | 13 | .241 | .340 | .318 |
| 2012 | Altna | AA | 40 | 141 | 39 | 14 | 1 | 0 | (- | -) | 55 | 22 | 17 | 21 | 18 | 0 | 33 | 3 | 0 | 0 | 1 | 1 | .50 | 3 | .277 | .370 | .390 |
| 2012 | Indy | AAA | 63 | 206 | 48 | 12 | 0 | 8 | (- | -) | 84 | 21 | 26 | 28 | 23 | 0 | 46 | 3 | 2 | 2 | 0 | 0 | - | 3 | .233 | .316 | .408 |
| 2013 | Indy | AAA | 76 | 260 | 75 | 26 | 0 | 10 | (- | -) | 131 | 35 | 42 | 49 | 28 | 2 | 60 | 6 | 0 | 2 | 0 | 0 | - | 10 | .288 | .368 | .504 |
| 2013 | Altna | AA | 4 | 17 | 3 | 1 | 0 | 0 | (- | -) | 4 | 2 | 0 | 0 | 0 | 0 | 3 | 0 | 0 | 0 | 0 | 0 | - | 0 | .176 | .176 | .235 |
| 2013 | Pit | NL | 22 | 60 | 14 | 4 | 0 | 2 | (1 | 1) | 24 | 9 | 5 | 4 | 3 | 0 | 14 | 2 | 0 | 1 | 0 | 0 | - | 2 | .233 | .288 | .400 |

## Pablo Sandoval

**Bats:** B **Throws:** R **Pos:** 3B-137;PH-3;DH-1 **Ht:** 5'11" **Wt:** 240 **Born:** 8/11/1986 **Age:** 27

| BATTING | | | | | | | | | | | | | | | | | | | | | | BASERUNNING | | | | AVERAGES | | |
|---|---|---|---|---|---|---|---|---|---|---|---|---|---|---|---|---|---|---|---|---|---|---|---|---|---|---|---|---|
| Year | Team | Lg | G | AB | H | 2B | 3B | HR | (Hm | Rd) | TB | R | RBI | RC | TBB | IBB | SO | HBP | SH | SF | SB | CS | SB% | GDP | Avg | OBP | Slg |
| 2013 | SnJos* | A+ | 2 | 6 | 4 | 0 | 0 | 2 | (- | -) | 10 | 2 | 2 | 4 | 0 | 0 | 0 | 0 | 0 | 0 | 0 | 0 | - | 0 | .667 | .667 | 1.667 |
| 2008 | SF | NL | 41 | 145 | 50 | 10 | 1 | 3 | (1 | 2) | 71 | 24 | 24 | 24 | 4 | 1 | 14 | 1 | 0 | 4 | 0 | 0 | - | 6 | .345 | .357 | .490 |
| 2009 | SF | NL | 153 | 572 | 189 | 44 | 5 | 25 | (13 | 12) | 318 | 79 | 90 | 113 | 52 | 13 | 83 | 4 | 0 | 5 | 5 | 5 | .50 | 10 | .330 | .387 | .556 |
| 2010 | SF | NL | 152 | 563 | 151 | 34 | 3 | 13 | (9 | 4) | 230 | 61 | 63 | 55 | 47 | 12 | 81 | 1 | 0 | 5 | 3 | 2 | .60 | **26** | .268 | .323 | .409 |
| 2011 | SF | NL | 117 | 426 | 134 | 26 | 3 | 23 | (7 | 16) | 235 | 55 | 70 | 72 | 32 | 9 | 63 | 0 | 1 | 7 | 2 | 4 | .33 | 12 | .315 | .357 | .552 |
| 2012 | SF | NL | 108 | 396 | 112 | 25 | 2 | 12 | (7 | 5) | 177 | 59 | 63 | 60 | 38 | 4 | 59 | 1 | 0 | 7 | 1 | 1 | .50 | 13 | .283 | .342 | .447 |
| 2013 | SF | NL | 141 | 525 | 146 | 27 | 2 | 14 | (6 | 8) | 219 | 52 | 79 | 78 | 47 | 5 | 79 | 6 | 0 | 6 | 0 | 0 | - | 19 | .278 | .341 | .417 |
| Postseason | | | 22 | 83 | 27 | 6 | 0 | 6 | (3 | 3) | 51 | 9 | 15 | 16 | 5 | 2 | 11 | 0 | 0 | 1 | 0 | 0 | - | 5 | .325 | .360 | .614 |
| 6 ML YEARS | | | 712 | 2627 | 782 | 166 | 16 | 90 | (43 | 47) | 1250 | 330 | 389 | 402 | 220 | 44 | 379 | 13 | 1 | 34 | 11 | 12 | .48 | 86 | .298 | .351 | .476 |

## Carlos Santana

**Bats:** B **Throws:** R **Pos:** C-84;DH-47;1B-29;PH-2 **Ht:** 5'11" **Wt:** 210 **Born:** 4/8/1986 **Age:** 28

| BATTING | | | | | | | | | | | | | | | | | | | | | | BASERUNNING | | | | AVERAGES | | |
|---|---|---|---|---|---|---|---|---|---|---|---|---|---|---|---|---|---|---|---|---|---|---|---|---|---|---|---|---|
| Year | Team | Lg | G | AB | H | 2B | 3B | HR | (Hm | Rd) | TB | R | RBI | RC | TBB | IBB | SO | HBP | SH | SF | SB | CS | SB% | GDP | Avg | OBP | Slg |
| 2010 | Cle | AL | 46 | 150 | 39 | 13 | 0 | 6 | (2 | 4) | 70 | 23 | 22 | 25 | 37 | 2 | 29 | 1 | 0 | 4 | 3 | 0 | 1.00 | 3 | .260 | .401 | .467 |
| 2011 | Cle | AL | 155 | 552 | 132 | 35 | 2 | 27 | (14 | 13) | 252 | 84 | 79 | 81 | 97 | 7 | 133 | 2 | 0 | 7 | 5 | 3 | .63 | 15 | .239 | .351 | .457 |
| 2012 | Cle | AL | 143 | 507 | 128 | 27 | 2 | 18 | (7 | 11) | 213 | 72 | 76 | 77 | 91 | 4 | 101 | 3 | 0 | 8 | 3 | 5 | .38 | 21 | .252 | .365 | .420 |
| 2013 | Cle | AL | 154 | 541 | 145 | 39 | 1 | 20 | (12 | 8) | 246 | 75 | 74 | 93 | 93 | 6 | 110 | 4 | 0 | 4 | 3 | 1 | .75 | 7 | .268 | .377 | .455 |
| 4 ML YEARS | | | 498 | 1750 | 444 | 114 | 5 | 71 | (35 | 36) | 781 | 254 | 251 | 276 | 318 | 19 | 373 | 10 | 0 | 23 | 14 | 9 | .61 | 46 | .254 | .367 | .446 |

## Ervin Santana

**Pitches:** R **Bats:** R **Pos:** SP-32 **Ht:** 6'2" **Wt:** 185 **Born:** 12/12/1982 **Age:** 31

| HOW MUCH HE PITCHED | | | | | | | | | WHAT HE GAVE UP | | | | | | | | | | | | THE RESULTS | | | | | | | |
|---|---|---|---|---|---|---|---|---|---|---|---|---|---|---|---|---|---|---|---|---|---|---|---|---|---|---|---|
| Year | Team | Lg | G | GS | CG | GF | IP | BFP | H | R | ER | HR | SH | SF | HB | TBB | IBB | SO | WP | Bk | W | L | Pct | Sh | Sv-Op | Hld | ERC | ERA |
| 2005 | LAA | AL | 23 | 23 | 1 | 0 | 133.2 | 583 | 139 | 73 | 69 | 17 | 1 | 4 | 8 | 47 | 2 | 99 | 4 | 0 | 12 | 8 | .600 | 1 | 0-0 | 0 | 4.51 | 4.65 |
| 2006 | LAA | AL | 33 | 33 | 0 | 0 | 204.0 | 846 | 181 | 106 | 97 | 21 | 4 | 10 | 11 | 70 | 2 | 141 | 10 | 2 | 16 | 8 | .667 | 0 | 0-0 | 0 | 3.51 | 4.28 |
| 2007 | LAA | AL | 28 | 26 | 0 | 1 | 150.0 | 675 | 174 | 103 | 96 | 26 | 3 | 2 | 8 | 58 | 3 | 126 | 7 | 0 | 7 | 14 | .333 | 0 | 0-0 | 0 | 5.69 | 5.76 |
| 2008 | LAA | AL | 32 | 32 | 2 | 0 | 219.0 | 897 | 198 | 89 | 85 | 23 | 3 | 5 | 8 | 47 | 2 | 214 | 5 | 1 | 16 | 7 | .696 | 1 | 0-0 | 0 | 3.00 | 3.49 |
| 2009 | LAA | AL | 24 | 23 | 2 | 0 | 139.2 | 614 | 159 | 83 | 78 | 24 | 2 | 1 | 10 | 47 | 4 | 107 | 4 | 0 | 8 | 8 | .500 | 2 | 0-0 | 1 | 5.47 | 5.03 |
| 2010 | LAA | AL | 33 | 33 | 4 | 0 | 222.2 | 954 | 221 | 104 | 97 | 27 | 8 | 8 | 12 | 73 | 2 | 169 | 11 | 1 | 17 | 10 | .630 | 1 | 0-0 | 0 | 4.10 | 3.92 |
| 2011 | LAA | AL | 33 | 33 | 4 | 0 | 228.2 | 949 | 207 | 95 | 86 | 26 | 4 | 7 | 8 | 72 | 4 | 178 | 10 | 1 | 11 | 12 | .478 | 1 | 0-0 | 0 | 3.45 | 3.38 |
| 2012 | LAA | AL | 30 | 30 | 1 | 0 | 178.0 | 764 | 165 | 109 | 102 | **39** | 2 | 2 | 9 | 61 | 2 | 133 | 4 | 0 | 9 | 13 | .409 | 1 | 0-0 | 0 | 4.38 | 5.16 |
| 2013 | KC | AL | 32 | 32 | 0 | 0 | 211.0 | 859 | 190 | 85 | 76 | 26 | 2 | 3 | 6 | 51 | 3 | 161 | 6 | 0 | 9 | 10 | .474 | 0 | 0-0 | 0 | 3.19 | 3.24 |
| Postseason | | | 8 | 2 | 0 | 3 | 22.2 | 101 | 21 | 17 | 14 | 4 | 1 | 1 | 3 | 9 | 1 | 14 | 0 | 0 | 2 | 2 | .500 | 0 | 0-0 | 0 | 4.55 | 5.56 |
| 9 ML YEARS | | | 268 | 265 | 14 | 1 | 1686.2 | 7141 | 1634 | 847 | 786 | 229 | 29 | 42 | 80 | 526 | 24 | 1328 | 61 | 5 | 105 | 90 | .538 | 7 | 0-0 | 1 | 3.98 | 4.19 |

## Johan Santana

**Pitches:** L **Bats:** L **Pos:** P **Ht:** 6'0" **Wt:** 210 **Born:** 3/13/1979 **Age:** 35

| HOW MUCH HE PITCHED | | | | | | | | | WHAT HE GAVE UP | | | | | | | | | | | | THE RESULTS | | | | | | | |
|---|---|---|---|---|---|---|---|---|---|---|---|---|---|---|---|---|---|---|---|---|---|---|---|---|---|---|---|
| Year | Team | Lg | G | GS | CG | GF | IP | BFP | H | R | ER | HR | SH | SF | HB | TBB | IBB | SO | WP | Bk | W | L | Pct | Sh | Sv-Op | Hld | ERC | ERA |
| 2000 | Min | AL | 30 | 5 | 0 | 9 | 86.0 | 398 | 102 | 64 | 62 | 11 | 1 | 3 | 2 | 54 | 0 | 64 | 5 | 2 | 2 | 3 | .400 | 0 | 0-0 | 0 | 6.59 | 6.49 |
| 2001 | Min | AL | 15 | 4 | 0 | 5 | 43.2 | 195 | 50 | 25 | 23 | 6 | 2 | 3 | 3 | 16 | 0 | 28 | 3 | 0 | 1 | 0 | 1.000 | 0 | 0-0 | 0 | 5.36 | 4.74 |
| 2002 | Min | AL | 27 | 14 | 0 | 2 | 108.1 | 452 | 84 | 41 | 36 | 7 | 3 | 3 | 1 | 49 | 0 | 137 | **15** | 2 | 8 | 6 | .571 | 0 | 1-1 | 3 | 2.86 | 2.99 |
| 2003 | Min | AL | 45 | 18 | 0 | 7 | 158.1 | 644 | 127 | 56 | 54 | 17 | 2 | 4 | 3 | 47 | 1 | 169 | 6 | 2 | 12 | 3 | **.800** | 0 | 0-0 | 5 | 2.73 | 3.07 |
| 2004 | Min | AL | 34 | 34 | 1 | 0 | 228.0 | 881 | 156 | 70 | 66 | 24 | 3 | 3 | 9 | 54 | 0 | **265** | 7 | 0 | 20 | 6 | .769 | 1 | 0-0 | 0 | **2.07** | **2.61** |
| 2005 | Min | AL | 33 | 33 | 3 | 0 | 231.2 | 910 | 180 | 77 | 74 | 22 | 6 | 2 | 1 | 45 | 1 | **238** | 8 | 0 | 16 | 7 | .696 | 2 | 0-0 | 0 | **2.14** | 2.87 |
| 2006 | Min | AL | 34 | **34** | 1 | 0 | **233.2** | 923 | 186 | 79 | 72 | 24 | 6 | 4 | 4 | 47 | 0 | **245** | 4 | 1 | **19** | 6 | .760 | 0 | 0-0 | 0 | **2.36** | **2.77** |
| 2007 | Min | AL | 33 | 33 | 1 | 0 | 219.0 | 878 | 183 | 88 | 81 | **33** | 4 | 4 | 4 | 52 | 0 | 235 | 7 | 1 | 15 | 13 | .536 | 1 | 0-0 | 0 | 2.98 | 3.33 |
| 2008 | NYM | NL | 34 | **34** | 3 | 0 | **234.1** | **964** | 206 | 74 | 66 | 23 | 9 | 1 | 4 | 63 | 5 | 206 | 9 | 2 | 16 | 7 | .696 | 2 | 0-0 | 0 | 2.93 | **2.53** |
| 2009 | NYM | NL | 25 | 25 | 0 | 0 | 166.2 | 701 | 156 | 67 | 58 | 20 | 8 | 3 | 3 | 46 | 3 | 146 | 1 | 0 | 13 | 9 | .591 | 0 | 0-0 | 0 | 3.37 | 3.13 |
| 2010 | NYM | NL | 29 | 29 | 4 | 0 | 199.0 | 817 | 179 | 67 | 66 | 16 | 10 | 5 | 2 | 55 | 2 | 144 | 2 | 2 | 11 | 9 | .550 | 2 | 0-0 | 0 | 2.96 | 2.98 |
| 2012 | NYM | NL | 21 | 21 | 2 | 0 | 117.0 | 499 | 117 | 65 | 63 | 17 | 4 | 3 | 0 | 39 | 1 | 111 | 1 | 0 | 6 | 9 | .400 | 2 | 0-0 | 0 | 4.09 | 4.85 |
| Postseason | | | 11 | 5 | 0 | 0 | 34.0 | 143 | 35 | 15 | 15 | 2 | 0 | 0 | 1 | 10 | 1 | 32 | 2 | 0 | 1 | 3 | .250 | 0 | 0-0 | 1 | 3.66 | 3.97 |
| 12 ML YEARS | | | 360 | 284 | 15 | 23 | 2025.2 | 8262 | 1726 | 773 | 721 | 220 | 58 | 38 | 36 | 567 | 13 | 1988 | 68 | 12 | 139 | 78 | .641 | 10 | 1-1 | 8 | 2.94 | 3.20 |

# Hector Santiago

**Pitches:** L **Bats:** R **Pos:** SP-23; RP-11 **Ht:** 6'0" **Wt:** 210 **Born:** 12/16/1987 **Age:** 26

| HOW MUCH HE PITCHED | | | | | | | | | WHAT HE GAVE UP | | | | | | | | | | | | THE RESULTS | | | | | | | |
|---|---|---|---|---|---|---|---|---|---|---|---|---|---|---|---|---|---|---|---|---|---|---|---|---|---|---|---|---|
| Year | Team | Lg | G | GS | CG | GF | IP | BFP | H | R | ER | HR | SH | SF | HB | TBB | IBB | SO | WP | Bk | W | L | Pct | Sh | Sv-Op | Hld | ERC | ERA |
| 2011 | CWS | AL | 2 | 0 | 0 | 1 | 5.1 | 18 | 1 | 0 | 0 | 0 | 0 | 0 | 0 | 1 | 1 | 2 | 1 | 0 | 0 | 0 | - | 0 | 0-0 | 0 | 0.16 | 0.00 |
| 2012 | CWS | AL | 42 | 4 | 0 | 19 | 70.1 | 306 | 54 | 26 | 26 | 10 | 2 | 1 | 7 | 40 | 1 | 79 | 5 | 2 | 4 | 1 | .800 | 0 | 4-6 | 4 | 4.11 | 3.33 |
| 2013 | CWS | AL | 34 | 23 | 0 | 4 | 149.0 | 656 | 137 | 69 | 59 | 17 | 3 | 3 | 15 | 72 | 2 | 137 | 2 | 0 | 4 | 9 | .308 | 0 | 0-0 | 0 | 4.43 | 3.56 |
| 3 ML YEARS | | | 78 | 27 | 0 | 24 | 224.2 | 980 | 192 | 95 | 85 | 27 | 5 | 4 | 22 | 113 | 4 | 218 | 8 | 2 | 8 | 10 | .444 | 0 | 4-6 | 4 | 4.17 | 3.41 |

# Ramon Santiago

**Bats:** B **Throws:** R **Pos:** 2B-33;3B-27;SS-27;PH-4;PR-1 **Ht:** 5'11" **Wt:** 175 **Born:** 8/31/1979 **Age:** 34

| BATTING | | | | | | | | | | | | | | | | | | | | | BASERUNNING | | | | AVERAGES | | |
|---|---|---|---|---|---|---|---|---|---|---|---|---|---|---|---|---|---|---|---|---|---|---|---|---|---|---|---|
| Year | Team | Lg | G | AB | H | 2B | 3B | HR | (Hm | Rd) | TB | R | RBI | RC | TBB | IBB | SO | HBP | SH | SF | SB | CS | SB% | GDP | Avg | OBP | Slg |
| 2002 | Det | AL | 65 | 222 | 54 | 5 | 5 | 4 | (3 | 1) | 81 | 33 | 20 | 23 | 13 | 0 | 48 | 8 | 4 | 2 | 8 | 5 | .62 | 2 | .243 | .306 | .365 |
| 2003 | Det | AL | 141 | 444 | 100 | 18 | 1 | 2 | (1 | 1) | 126 | 41 | 29 | 38 | 33 | 0 | 66 | 10 | **18** | 2 | 10 | 4 | .71 | 9 | .225 | .292 | .284 |
| 2004 | Sea | AL | 19 | 39 | 7 | 1 | 0 | 0 | (0 | 0) | 8 | 8 | 2 | 1 | 3 | 0 | 3 | 1 | 2 | 0 | 0 | 0 | - | 1 | .179 | .256 | .205 |
| 2005 | Sea | AL | 8 | 8 | 1 | 0 | 0 | 0 | (0 | 0) | 1 | 2 | 0 | 1 | 1 | 0 | 2 | 3 | 1 | 0 | 0 | 0 | - | 0 | .125 | .417 | .125 |
| 2006 | Det | AL | 43 | 80 | 18 | 1 | 1 | 0 | (0 | 0) | 21 | 9 | 3 | 3 | 1 | 0 | 14 | 1 | 4 | 0 | 2 | 0 | 1.00 | 1 | .225 | .244 | .263 |
| 2007 | Det | AL | 32 | 67 | 19 | 5 | 1 | 0 | (0 | 0) | 26 | 10 | 7 | 11 | 1 | 0 | 10 | 3 | 3 | 0 | 3 | 0 | 1.00 | 0 | .284 | .324 | .388 |
| 2008 | Det | AL | 58 | 124 | 35 | 6 | 2 | 4 | (4 | 0) | 57 | 30 | 18 | 26 | 22 | 0 | 17 | 5 | 5 | 0 | 1 | 0 | 1.00 | 1 | .282 | .411 | .460 |
| 2009 | Det | AL | 93 | 262 | 70 | 6 | 2 | 7 | (4 | 3) | 101 | 29 | 35 | 33 | 17 | 1 | 57 | 4 | 10 | 3 | 1 | 2 | .33 | 3 | .267 | .318 | .385 |
| 2010 | Det | AL | 112 | 320 | 84 | 9 | 1 | 3 | (3 | 0) | 104 | 38 | 22 | 37 | 30 | 0 | 56 | 7 | 8 | 2 | 2 | 2 | .50 | 6 | .263 | .337 | .325 |
| 2011 | Det | AL | 101 | 258 | 67 | 11 | 3 | 5 | (3 | 2) | 99 | 29 | 30 | 25 | 17 | 0 | 38 | 4 | 11 | 4 | 0 | 0 | - | 5 | .260 | .311 | .384 |
| 2012 | Det | AL | 93 | 228 | 47 | 7 | 1 | 2 | (1 | 1) | 62 | 19 | 17 | 17 | 20 | 1 | 39 | 5 | 5 | 1 | 1 | 0 | 1.00 | 7 | .206 | .283 | .272 |
| 2013 | Det | AL | 80 | 205 | 46 | 8 | 1 | 1 | (1 | 0) | 59 | 27 | 14 | 14 | 21 | 0 | 32 | 1 | 6 | 1 | 0 | 1 | .00 | 3 | .224 | .298 | .288 |
| Postseason | | | 17 | 51 | 12 | 2 | 0 | 0 | (0 | 0) | 14 | 1 | 2 | 3 | 1 | 0 | 9 | 0 | 3 | 0 | 0 | 0 | - | 3 | .235 | .250 | .275 |
| 12 ML YEARS | | | 845 | 2257 | 548 | 77 | 18 | 28 | (20 | 8) | 745 | 275 | 197 | 229 | 179 | 2 | 382 | 52 | 77 | 15 | 28 | 14 | .67 | 38 | .243 | .311 | .330 |

# Omir Santos

**Bats:** R **Throws:** R **Pos:** C-1 OH-meer **Ht:** 6'0" **Wt:** 215 **Born:** 4/29/1981 **Age:** 33

| BATTING | | | | | | | | | | | | | | | | | | | | | BASERUNNING | | | | AVERAGES | | |
|---|---|---|---|---|---|---|---|---|---|---|---|---|---|---|---|---|---|---|---|---|---|---|---|---|---|---|---|
| Year | Team | Lg | G | AB | H | 2B | 3B | HR | (Hm | Rd) | TB | R | RBI | RC | TBB | IBB | SO | HBP | SH | SF | SB | CS | SB% | GDP | Avg | OBP | Slg |
| 2013 | Clmbs* | AAA | 62 | 206 | 51 | 9 | 2 | 3 | (- | -) | 73 | 14 | 23 | 21 | 10 | 0 | 47 | 2 | 1 | 3 | 0 | 0 | - | 4 | .248 | .285 | .354 |
| 2008 | Bal | AL | 11 | 10 | 1 | 0 | 0 | 0 | (0 | 0) | 1 | 0 | 0 | 0 | 0 | 0 | 2 | 0 | 0 | 0 | 0 | 0 | - | 0 | .100 | .100 | .100 |
| 2009 | NYM | NL | 96 | 281 | 73 | 14 | 1 | 7 | (2 | 5) | 110 | 28 | 40 | 29 | 15 | 1 | 44 | 2 | 2 | 6 | 0 | 0 | - | 9 | .260 | .296 | .391 |
| 2011 | Det | AL | 11 | 22 | 5 | 0 | 0 | 0 | (0 | 0) | 5 | 1 | 0 | 0 | 0 | 0 | 4 | 0 | 0 | 0 | 0 | 0 | - | 0 | .227 | .227 | .227 |
| 2012 | Det | AL | 3 | 8 | 1 | 0 | 0 | 0 | (0 | 0) | 1 | 0 | 1 | 0 | 0 | 0 | 1 | 0 | 1 | 1 | 0 | 0 | - | 2 | .125 | .111 | .125 |
| 2013 | Cle | AL | 1 | 1 | 0 | 0 | 0 | 0 | (0 | 0) | 0 | 0 | 0 | 0 | 0 | 0 | 0 | 0 | 0 | 0 | 0 | 0 | - | 0 | .000 | .000 | .000 |
| Postseason | | | 1 | 0 | 0 | 0 | 0 | 0 | (0 | 0) | 0 | 0 | 0 | 0 | 0 | 0 | 0 | 0 | 0 | 0 | 0 | 0 | - | 0 | - | - | - |
| 5 ML YEARS | | | 122 | 322 | 80 | 14 | 1 | 7 | (2 | 5) | 117 | 29 | 41 | 29 | 15 | 1 | 51 | 2 | 3 | 7 | 0 | 0 | - | 11 | .248 | .280 | .363 |

# Sergio Santos

**Pitches:** R **Bats:** R **Pos:** RP-29 **Ht:** 6'3" **Wt:** 240 **Born:** 7/4/1983 **Age:** 30

| HOW MUCH HE PITCHED | | | | | | | | | WHAT HE GAVE UP | | | | | | | | | | | | THE RESULTS | | | | | | | |
|---|---|---|---|---|---|---|---|---|---|---|---|---|---|---|---|---|---|---|---|---|---|---|---|---|---|---|---|---|
| Year | Team | Lg | G | GS | CG | GF | IP | BFP | H | R | ER | HR | SH | SF | HB | TBB | IBB | SO | WP | Bk | W | L | Pct | Sh | Sv-Op | Hld | ERC | ERA |
| 2013 | B Jays* | R | 1 | 1 | 0 | 0 | 1.0 | 5 | 1 | 0 | 0 | 0 | 0 | 0 | 0 | 0 | 0 | 2 | 0 | 0 | 0 | 0 | - | 0 | 0-- | - | 1.51 | 0.00 |
| 2013 | Dnedin* | A+ | 5 | 4 | 0 | 0 | 4.2 | 20 | 4 | 3 | 3 | 0 | 0 | 2 | 0 | 2 | 0 | 2 | 0 | 1 | 0 | 0 | - | 0 | 0-- | - | 2.67 | 5.79 |
| 2013 | Buffalo* | AAA | 6 | 0 | 0 | 0 | 6.0 | 29 | 8 | 7 | 5 | 0 | 0 | 1 | 0 | 2 | 0 | 5 | 1 | 0 | 0 | 0 | - | 0 | 0-- | - | 4.64 | 7.50 |
| 2010 | CWS | AL | 56 | 0 | 0 | 13 | 51.2 | 235 | 53 | 18 | 17 | 2 | 2 | 1 | 3 | 26 | 3 | 56 | 8 | 0 | 2 | 2 | .500 | 0 | 1-3 | 14 | 4.22 | 2.96 |
| 2011 | CWS | AL | 63 | 0 | 0 | 50 | 63.1 | 260 | 41 | 25 | 25 | 6 | 1 | 1 | 3 | 29 | 5 | 92 | 5 | 0 | 4 | 5 | .444 | 0 | 30-36 | 2 | 2.46 | 3.55 |
| 2012 | Tor | AL | 6 | 0 | 0 | 4 | 5.0 | 24 | 6 | 5 | 5 | 1 | 0 | 1 | 0 | 4 | 0 | 4 | 1 | 0 | 0 | 1 | .000 | 0 | 2-4 | 0 | 7.98 | 9.00 |
| 2013 | Tor | AL | 29 | 0 | 0 | 6 | 25.2 | 90 | 11 | 5 | 5 | 1 | 0 | 2 | 0 | 4 | 2 | 28 | 1 | 0 | 1 | 1 | .500 | 0 | 1-3 | 8 | 0.69 | 1.75 |
| 4 ML YEARS | | | 154 | 0 | 0 | 73 | 145.2 | 609 | 111 | 53 | 52 | 10 | 3 | 5 | 6 | 63 | 10 | 180 | 15 | 0 | 7 | 9 | .438 | 0 | 34-46 | 24 | 2.75 | 3.21 |

# Dave Sappelt

**Bats:** R **Throws:** R **Pos:** PH-14;CF-13;RF-7;LF-2 sap-PELT **Ht:** 5'9" **Wt:** 195 **Born:** 1/2/1987 **Age:** 27

| BATTING | | | | | | | | | | | | | | | | | | | | | BASERUNNING | | | | AVERAGES | | |
|---|---|---|---|---|---|---|---|---|---|---|---|---|---|---|---|---|---|---|---|---|---|---|---|---|---|---|---|
| Year | Team | Lg | G | AB | H | 2B | 3B | HR | (Hm | Rd) | TB | R | RBI | RC | TBB | IBB | SO | HBP | SH | SF | SB | CS | SB% | GDP | Avg | OBP | Slg |
| 2013 | Iowa* | AAA | 90 | 321 | 81 | 15 | 3 | 5 | (- | -) | 117 | 39 | 45 | 36 | 27 | 1 | 38 | 0 | 1 | 6 | 4 | 7 | .36 | 1 | .252 | .305 | .364 |
| 2011 | Cin | NL | 38 | 107 | 26 | 8 | 0 | 0 | (0 | 0) | 34 | 14 | 5 | 9 | 7 | 0 | 17 | 0 | 4 | 0 | 1 | 1 | .50 | 1 | .243 | .289 | .318 |
| 2012 | ChC | NL | 26 | 69 | 19 | 6 | 0 | 2 | (0 | 2) | 31 | 8 | 8 | 11 | 7 | 1 | 9 | 1 | 1 | 0 | 0 | 0 | - | 1 | .275 | .351 | .449 |
| 2013 | ChC | NL | 31 | 75 | 18 | 3 | 0 | 0 | (0 | 0) | 21 | 6 | 4 | 7 | 3 | 0 | 14 | 0 | 0 | 0 | 3 | 1 | .75 | 1 | .240 | .269 | .280 |
| 3 ML YEARS | | | 95 | 251 | 63 | 17 | 0 | 2 | (0 | 2) | 86 | 28 | 17 | 27 | 17 | 1 | 40 | 1 | 5 | 0 | 4 | 2 | .67 | 3 | .251 | .301 | .343 |

# Josh Satin

**Bats:** R **Throws:** R **Pos:** 1B-33;PH-29;3B-17;DH-2 SAT-inn **Ht:** 6'2" **Wt:** 200 **Born:** 12/23/1984 **Age:** 29

| BATTING | | | | | | | | | | | | | | | | | | | | | BASERUNNING | | | | AVERAGES | | |
|---|---|---|---|---|---|---|---|---|---|---|---|---|---|---|---|---|---|---|---|---|---|---|---|---|---|---|---|
| Year | Team | Lg | G | AB | H | 2B | 3B | HR | (Hm | Rd) | TB | R | RBI | RC | TBB | IBB | SO | HBP | SH | SF | SB | CS | SB% | GDP | Avg | OBP | Slg |
| 2013 | LsVgs* | AAA | 60 | 220 | 67 | 14 | 0 | 9 | (- | -) | 108 | 46 | 32 | 46 | 43 | 0 | 45 | 1 | 0 | 0 | 0 | 2 | .00 | 6 | .305 | .420 | .491 |
| 2011 | NYM | NL | 15 | 25 | 5 | 1 | 0 | 0 | (0 | 0) | 6 | 3 | 2 | 1 | 1 | 0 | 11 | 0 | 0 | 0 | 0 | 0 | - | 1 | .200 | .259 | .240 |
| 2012 | NYM | NL | 1 | 1 | 0 | 0 | 0 | 0 | (0 | 0) | 0 | 0 | 0 | 0 | 0 | 0 | 1 | 0 | 0 | 0 | 0 | 0 | - | 0 | .000 | .000 | .000 |
| 2013 | NYM | NL | 75 | 190 | 53 | 15 | 0 | 3 | (3 | 0) | 77 | 23 | 17 | 27 | 30 | 2 | 56 | 0 | 0 | 1 | 1 | 1 | .50 | 4 | .279 | .376 | .405 |
| 3 ML YEARS | | | 91 | 216 | 58 | 16 | 0 | 3 | (3 | 0) | 83 | 26 | 19 | 28 | 31 | 2 | 68 | 1 | 0 | 1 | 1 | 1 | .50 | 5 | .269 | .361 | .384 |

## Joe Saunders

**Pitches:** L **Bats:** L **Pos:** SP-32 **Ht:** 6'3" **Wt:** 215 **Born:** 6/16/1981 **Age:** 33

| HOW MUCH HE PITCHED | | | | | | | | WHAT HE GAVE UP | | | | | | | | | | | THE RESULTS | | | | | | | |
|---|---|---|---|---|---|---|---|---|---|---|---|---|---|---|---|---|---|---|---|---|---|---|---|---|---|---|
| Year Team | Lg | G | GS | CG | GF | IP | BFP | H | R | ER | HR | SH | SF | HB | TBB | IBB | SO | WP | Bk | W | L | Pct | Sh | Sv-Op | Hld | ERC | ERA |
| 2005 LAA | AL | 2 | 2 | 0 | 0 | 9.1 | 41 | 10 | 8 | 8 | 3 | 0 | 0 | 0 | 4 | 0 | 4 | 1 | 0 | 0 | 0 | - | 0 | 0-0 | 0 | 6.27 | 7.71 |
| 2006 LAA | AL | 13 | 13 | 0 | 0 | 70.2 | 302 | 71 | 42 | 37 | 6 | 1 | 2 | 1 | 29 | 1 | 51 | 2 | 1 | 7 | 3 | .700 | 0 | 0-0 | 0 | 4.13 | 4.71 |
| 2007 LAA | AL | 18 | 18 | 0 | 0 | 107.1 | 473 | 129 | 56 | 53 | 11 | 0 | 5 | 1 | 34 | 1 | 69 | 3 | 0 | 8 | 5 | .615 | 0 | 0-0 | 0 | 4.96 | 4.44 |
| 2008 LAA | AL | 31 | 31 | 1 | 0 | 198.0 | 807 | 187 | 82 | 75 | 21 | 5 | 2 | 6 | 53 | 2 | 103 | 3 | 0 | 17 | 7 | .708 | 0 | 0-0 | 0 | 3.49 | 3.41 |
| 2009 LAA | AL | 31 | 31 | 1 | 0 | 186.0 | 805 | 202 | 102 | 95 | 29 | 6 | 4 | 6 | 64 | 2 | 101 | 5 | 1 | 16 | 7 | .696 | 1 | 0-0 | 0 | 4.91 | 4.60 |
| 2010 2 Tms | | 33 | 33 | 3 | 0 | 203.1 | 880 | 232 | 120 | 101 | 25 | 6 | 8 | 5 | 64 | 1 | 114 | 6 | 0 | 9 | 17 | .346 | 1 | 0-0 | 0 | 4.86 | 4.47 |
| 2011 Ari | NL | 33 | 33 | 1 | 0 | 212.0 | 874 | 210 | 94 | 87 | 29 | 9 | 5 | 3 | 67 | 4 | 108 | 3 | 0 | 12 | 13 | .480 | 0 | 0-0 | 0 | 4.10 | 3.69 |
| 2012 2 Tms | | 28 | 28 | 1 | 0 | 174.2 | 745 | 195 | 88 | 79 | 21 | 7 | 3 | 2 | 39 | 2 | 112 | 3 | 0 | 9 | 13 | .409 | 1 | 0-0 | 0 | 4.19 | 4.07 |
| 2013 Sea | AL | 32 | 32 | 2 | 0 | 183.0 | 820 | 232 | 117 | 107 | 25 | 6 | 3 | 4 | 61 | 5 | 107 | 5 | 0 | 11 | 16 | .407 | 0 | 0-0 | 0 | 5.74 | 5.26 |
| 10 LAA | AL | 20 | 20 | 2 | 0 | 120.2 | 522 | 135 | 70 | 62 | 14 | 5 | 5 | 1 | 45 | 1 | 64 | 3 | 0 | 6 | 10 | .375 | 1 | 0-0 | 0 | 4.88 | 4.62 |
| 10 Ari | NL | 13 | 13 | 1 | 0 | 82.2 | 358 | 97 | 50 | 39 | 11 | 1 | 3 | 4 | 19 | 0 | 50 | 3 | 0 | 3 | 7 | .300 | 0 | 0-0 | 0 | 4.84 | 4.25 |
| 12 Ari | NL | 21 | 21 | 1 | 0 | 130.0 | 561 | 146 | 68 | 61 | 17 | 5 | 2 | 2 | 31 | 1 | 89 | 2 | 0 | 6 | 10 | .375 | 1 | 0-0 | 0 | 4.36 | 4.22 |
| 12 Bal | AL | 7 | 7 | 0 | 0 | 44.2 | 184 | 49 | 20 | 18 | 4 | 2 | 1 | 0 | 8 | 1 | 23 | 1 | 0 | 3 | 3 | .500 | 0 | 0-0 | 0 | 3.71 | 3.63 |
| Postseason | | 6 | 6 | 0 | 0 | 29.1 | 130 | 32 | 14 | 14 | 1 | 2 | 0 | 1 | 17 | 0 | 17 | 0 | 0 | 1 | 1 | .500 | 0 | 0-0 | 0 | 5.14 | 4.30 |
| 9 ML YEARS | | 221 | 221 | 9 | 0 | 1344.1 | 5747 | 1468 | 709 | 642 | 170 | 40 | 32 | 28 | 415 | 18 | 769 | 31 | 2 | 89 | 81 | .524 | 3 | 0-0 | 0 | 4.54 | 4.30 |

## Michael Saunders

**Bats:** L **Throws:** R **Pos:** CF-78;RF-34;LF-24;PR-7;PH-4;DH-2 **Ht:** 6'4" **Wt:** 225 **Born:** 11/19/1986 **Age:** 27

| BATTING | | | | | | | | | | | | | | | | | | | | BASERUNNING | | | | AVERAGES | | |
|---|---|---|---|---|---|---|---|---|---|---|---|---|---|---|---|---|---|---|---|---|---|---|---|---|---|---|
| Year Team | Lg | G | AB | H | 2B | 3B | HR | (Hm | Rd) | TB | R | RBI | RC | TBB | IBB | SO | HBP | SH | SF | SB | CS | SB% | GDP | Avg | OBP | Slg |
| 2013 Tacom* | AAA | 3 | 11 | 2 | 1 | 1 | 0 | (- | -) | 5 | 2 | 2 | 2 | 3 | 0 | 1 | 1 | 0 | 1 | 0 | 0 | - | 0 | .182 | .375 | .455 |
| 2009 Sea | AL | 46 | 122 | 27 | 1 | 3 | 0 | (0 | 0) | 34 | 13 | 4 | 8 | 6 | 0 | 40 | 0 | 1 | 0 | 4 | 1 | .80 | 1 | .221 | .258 | .279 |
| 2010 Sea | AL | 100 | 289 | 61 | 11 | 2 | 10 | (5 | 5) | 106 | 29 | 33 | 31 | 35 | 0 | 84 | 0 | 2 | 1 | 6 | 3 | .67 | 1 | .211 | .295 | .367 |
| 2011 Sea | AL | 58 | 161 | 24 | 5 | 0 | 2 | (1 | 1) | 35 | 16 | 8 | 2 | 12 | 1 | 56 | 0 | 5 | 1 | 6 | 2 | .75 | 1 | .149 | .207 | .217 |
| 2012 Sea | AL | 139 | 507 | 125 | 31 | 3 | 19 | (8 | 11) | 219 | 71 | 57 | 67 | 43 | 0 | 132 | 1 | 1 | 1 | 21 | 4 | .84 | 6 | .247 | .306 | .432 |
| 2013 Sea | AL | 132 | 406 | 96 | 23 | 3 | 12 | (5 | 7) | 161 | 59 | 46 | 49 | 54 | 4 | 118 | 1 | 1 | 6 | 13 | 5 | .72 | 6 | .236 | .323 | .397 |
| 5 ML YEARS | | 475 | 1485 | 333 | 71 | 11 | 43 | (19 | 24) | 555 | 188 | 148 | 157 | 150 | 5 | 430 | 2 | 10 | 9 | 50 | 15 | .77 | 15 | .224 | .295 | .374 |

## Joe Savery

**Pitches:** L **Bats:** L **Pos:** RP-18 SAVE-uh-ree **Ht:** 6'3" **Wt:** 235 **Born:** 11/4/1985 **Age:** 28

| HOW MUCH HE PITCHED | | | | | | | | WHAT HE GAVE UP | | | | | | | | | | | THE RESULTS | | | | | | | |
|---|---|---|---|---|---|---|---|---|---|---|---|---|---|---|---|---|---|---|---|---|---|---|---|---|---|---|
| Year Team | Lg | G | GS | CG | GF | IP | BFP | H | R | ER | HR | SH | SF | HB | TBB | IBB | SO | WP | Bk | W | L | Pct | Sh | Sv-Op | Hld | ERC | ERA |
| 2013 LV* | AAA | 20 | 0 | 0 | 8 | 23.2 | 97 | 18 | 11 | 10 | 2 | 1 | 1 | 0 | 9 | 1 | 29 | 0 | 0 | 3 | 1 | .750 | 0 | 2-- | - | 2.56 | 3.80 |
| 2013 Phillies* | R | 1 | 1 | 0 | 0 | 1.0 | 3 | 0 | 0 | 0 | 0 | 0 | 0 | 0 | 0 | 0 | 1 | 0 | 0 | 0 | 0 | - | 0 | 0-- | - | 0.00 | 0.00 |
| 2013 Clrwtr* | A+ | 1 | 0 | 0 | 0 | 1.0 | 3 | 0 | 0 | 0 | 0 | 0 | 0 | 0 | 0 | 0 | 1 | 0 | 0 | 0 | 0 | - | 0 | 0-- | - | 0.00 | 0.00 |
| 2011 Phi | NL | 4 | 0 | 0 | 1 | 2.2 | 9 | 1 | 0 | 0 | 0 | 1 | 0 | 0 | 0 | 0 | 2 | 0 | 0 | 0 | 0 | - | 0 | 0-0 | 1 | 0.31 | 0.00 |
| 2012 Phi | NL | 19 | 0 | 0 | 8 | 25.0 | 108 | 26 | 17 | 15 | 4 | 2 | 2 | 1 | 8 | 1 | 16 | 0 | 1 | 1 | 2 | .333 | 0 | 0-0 | 1 | 4.49 | 5.40 |
| 2013 Phi | NL | 18 | 0 | 0 | 8 | 20.0 | 86 | 15 | 11 | 7 | 1 | 1 | 1 | 0 | 11 | 0 | 14 | 0 | 0 | 2 | 0 | 1.000 | 0 | 0-0 | 1 | 2.89 | 3.15 |
| 3 ML YEARS | | 41 | 0 | 0 | 17 | 47.2 | 203 | 42 | 28 | 22 | 5 | 4 | 3 | 1 | 19 | 1 | 32 | 0 | 1 | 3 | 2 | .600 | 0 | 0-0 | 3 | 3.46 | 4.15 |

## Rob Scahill

**Pitches:** R **Bats:** L **Pos:** RP-23 SKAY-hill **Ht:** 6'2" **Wt:** 220 **Born:** 2/15/1987 **Age:** 27

| HOW MUCH HE PITCHED | | | | | | | | WHAT HE GAVE UP | | | | | | | | | | | THE RESULTS | | | | | | | |
|---|---|---|---|---|---|---|---|---|---|---|---|---|---|---|---|---|---|---|---|---|---|---|---|---|---|---|
| Year Team | Lg | G | GS | CG | GF | IP | BFP | H | R | ER | HR | SH | SF | HB | TBB | IBB | SO | WP | Bk | W | L | Pct | Sh | Sv-Op | Hld | ERC | ERA |
| 2009 TriCity | A- | 15 | 15 | 0 | 0 | 63.0 | 267 | 58 | 30 | 22 | 2 | 1 | 1 | 8 | 20 | 0 | 58 | 7 | 0 | 1 | 4 | .200 | 0 | 0-- | - | 3.37 | 3.14 |
| 2010 Mdest | A+ | 27 | 27 | 1 | 0 | 156.0 | 689 | 173 | 91 | 82 | 9 | 1 | 9 | 10 | 59 | 0 | 140 | 13 | 0 | 10 | 7 | .588 | 0 | 0-- | - | 4.58 | 4.73 |
| 2011 Tulsa | AA | 27 | 26 | 1 | 1 | 160.2 | 693 | 164 | 81 | 70 | 12 | 7 | 5 | 5 | 60 | 0 | 104 | 16 | 0 | 12 | 11 | .522 | 0 | 0-- | - | 4.05 | 3.92 |
| 2012 ColSpr | AAA | 29 | 29 | 1 | 0 | 152.0 | 693 | 168 | 109 | 96 | 11 | 10 | 3 | 7 | 74 | 0 | 159 | 8 | 0 | 9 | 11 | .450 | 0 | 0-- | - | 4.97 | 5.68 |
| 2013 ColSpr | AAA | 23 | 0 | 0 | 6 | 46.0 | 197 | 53 | 25 | 23 | 6 | 3 | 2 | 1 | 11 | 1 | 45 | 7 | 0 | 5 | 1 | .833 | 0 | 1-- | - | 4.61 | 4.50 |
| 2012 Col | NL | 6 | 0 | 0 | 3 | 8.2 | 33 | 7 | 1 | 1 | 0 | 0 | 0 | 0 | 3 | 0 | 4 | 0 | 0 | 0 | 0 | - | 0 | 0-0 | 0 | 2.43 | 1.04 |
| 2013 Col | NL | 23 | 0 | 0 | 6 | 33.1 | 149 | 40 | 19 | 19 | 5 | 3 | 0 | 4 | 9 | 1 | 20 | 1 | 0 | 1 | 0 | 1.000 | 0 | 0-0 | 1 | 5.55 | 5.13 |
| 2 ML YEARS | | 29 | 0 | 0 | 9 | 42.0 | 182 | 47 | 20 | 20 | 5 | 3 | 0 | 4 | 12 | 1 | 24 | 1 | 0 | 1 | 0 | 1.000 | 0 | 0-0 | 1 | 4.86 | 4.29 |

## Jordan Schafer

**Bats:** L **Throws:** L **Pos:** CF-30;RF-29;PH-28;LF-15;PR-7 **Ht:** 6'1" **Wt:** 190 **Born:** 9/4/1986 **Age:** 27

| BATTING | | | | | | | | | | | | | | | | | | | | BASERUNNING | | | | AVERAGES | | |
|---|---|---|---|---|---|---|---|---|---|---|---|---|---|---|---|---|---|---|---|---|---|---|---|---|---|---|
| Year Team | Lg | G | AB | H | 2B | 3B | HR | (Hm | Rd) | TB | R | RBI | RC | TBB | IBB | SO | HBP | SH | SF | SB | CS | SB% | GDP | Avg | OBP | Slg |
| 2013 Gwnntt* | AAA | 8 | 32 | 2 | 2 | 0 | 0 | (- | -) | 4 | 0 | 2 | 0 | 1 | 0 | 4 | 0 | 0 | 0 | 0 | 0 | - | 0 | .063 | .091 | .125 |
| 2009 Atl | NL | 50 | 167 | 34 | 8 | 0 | 2 | (0 | 2) | 48 | 18 | 8 | 11 | 27 | 3 | 63 | 0 | 0 | 1 | 2 | 1 | .67 | 2 | .204 | .313 | .287 |
| 2011 2 Tms | NL | 82 | 302 | 73 | 10 | 3 | 2 | (0 | 2) | 95 | 46 | 13 | 34 | 28 | 0 | 70 | 2 | 4 | 1 | 22 | 4 | .85 | 4 | .242 | .309 | .315 |
| 2012 Hou | NL | 106 | 313 | 66 | 10 | 2 | 4 | (4 | 0) | 92 | 40 | 23 | 32 | 36 | 3 | 106 | 3 | 6 | 1 | 27 | 9 | .75 | 3 | .211 | .297 | .294 |
| 2013 Atl | NL | 94 | 231 | 57 | 8 | 3 | 3 | (0 | 3) | 80 | 32 | 21 | 31 | 29 | 2 | 73 | 0 | 5 | 0 | 22 | 6 | .79 | 1 | .247 | .331 | .346 |
| 11 Atl | NL | 52 | 196 | 47 | 6 | 3 | 1 | (0 | 1) | 62 | 32 | 7 | 22 | 18 | 0 | 42 | 1 | 4 | 0 | 15 | 4 | .79 | 3 | .240 | .307 | .316 |
| 11 Hou | NL | 30 | 106 | 26 | 4 | 0 | 1 | (0 | 1) | 33 | 14 | 6 | 12 | 10 | 0 | 28 | 1 | 0 | 1 | 7 | 0 | 1.00 | 1 | .245 | .314 | .311 |
| 4 ML YEARS | | 332 | 1013 | 230 | 36 | 8 | 11 | (4 | 7) | 315 | 136 | 65 | 108 | 120 | 8 | 312 | 5 | 15 | 3 | 73 | 20 | .78 | 10 | .227 | .311 | .311 |

# Logan Schafer

**Bats:** L **Throws:** L **Pos:** LF-56;PH-49;CF-28;RF-13;PR-1 **Ht:** 6'1" **Wt:** 180 **Born:** 9/8/1986 **Age:** 27

| BATTING | | | | | | | | | | | | | | | | | | | | BASERUNNING | | | | AVERAGES | | |
|---|---|---|---|---|---|---|---|---|---|---|---|---|---|---|---|---|---|---|---|---|---|---|---|---|---|---|
| Year Team | Lg | G | AB | H | 2B | 3B | HR | (Hm | Rd) | TB | R | RBI | RC | TBB | IBB | SO | HBP | SH | SF | SB | CS | SB% | GDP | Avg | OBP | Slg |
| 2011 Mil | NL | 8 | 3 | 1 | 0 | 0 | 0 | (0 | 0) | 1 | 1 | 0 | 0 | 1 | 0 | 1 | 0 | 1 | 0 | 0 | 0 | - | 0 | .333 | .500 | .333 |
| 2012 Mil | NL | 16 | 23 | 7 | 1 | 2 | 0 | (0 | 0) | 12 | 3 | 5 | 4 | 1 | 0 | 3 | 0 | 0 | 1 | 0 | 1 | .00 | 0 | .304 | .320 | .522 |
| 2013 Mil | NL | 134 | 298 | 63 | 15 | 3 | 4 | (2 | 2) | 96 | 29 | 33 | 31 | 25 | 1 | 60 | 3 | 11 | 0 | 7 | 1 | .88 | 5 | .211 | .279 | .322 |
| 3 ML YEARS | | 158 | 324 | 71 | 16 | 5 | 4 | (2 | 2) | 109 | 33 | 38 | 35 | 27 | 1 | 64 | 3 | 12 | 1 | 7 | 2 | .78 | 5 | .219 | .285 | .336 |

# Tanner Scheppers

**Pitches:** R **Bats:** R **Pos:** RP-76 **Ht:** 6'4" **Wt:** 200 **Born:** 1/17/1987 **Age:** 27

| HOW MUCH HE PITCHED | | | | | | | | WHAT HE GAVE UP | | | | | | | | | | | | THE RESULTS | | | | | | | |
|---|---|---|---|---|---|---|---|---|---|---|---|---|---|---|---|---|---|---|---|---|---|---|---|---|---|---|---|
| Year Team | Lg | G | GS | CG | GF | IP | BFP | H | R | ER | HR | SH | SF | HB | TBB | IBB | SO | WP | Bk | W | L | Pct | Sh | Sv-Op | Hld | ERC | ERA |
| 2010 Frisco | AA | 6 | 0 | 0 | 5 | 11.0 | 38 | 3 | 1 | 1 | 1 | 0 | 0 | 0 | 0 | 0 | 19 | 1 | 0 | 0 | 0 | - | 0 | 2-- | - | 0.28 | 0.82 |
| 2010 OKCity | AAA | 30 | 7 | 0 | 11 | 69.0 | 320 | 82 | 45 | 42 | 5 | 2 | 4 | 8 | 30 | 0 | 71 | 7 | 0 | 1 | 3 | .250 | 0 | 4-- | - | 5.56 | 5.48 |
| 2011 RdRck | AAA | 11 | 1 | 0 | 6 | 20.2 | 94 | 23 | 10 | 10 | 0 | 1 | 1 | 2 | 12 | 0 | 20 | 2 | 0 | 2 | 0 | 1.000 | 0 | 2-- | - | 5.19 | 4.35 |
| 2011 Frisco | AA | 17 | 0 | 0 | 8 | 23.0 | 97 | 18 | 10 | 8 | 1 | 1 | 1 | 1 | 9 | 1 | 24 | 2 | 1 | 2 | 1 | .667 | 0 | 0-- | - | 2.56 | 3.13 |
| 2012 RdRck | AAA | 27 | 0 | 0 | 26 | 31.0 | 127 | 30 | 12 | 12 | 2 | 2 | 1 | 3 | 4 | 0 | 31 | 2 | 0 | 1 | 2 | .333 | 0 | 11-- | - | 3.02 | 3.48 |
| 2012 Tex | AL | 39 | 0 | 0 | 13 | 32.1 | 152 | 47 | 18 | 16 | 6 | 3 | 1 | 2 | 9 | 3 | 30 | 4 | 0 | 1 | 1 | .500 | 0 | 1-1 | 4 | 7.05 | 4.45 |
| 2013 Tex | AL | 76 | 0 | 0 | 11 | 76.2 | 302 | 58 | 21 | 16 | 6 | 0 | 0 | 7 | 24 | 4 | 59 | 4 | 0 | 6 | 2 | .750 | 0 | 1-3 | 27 | 2.71 | 1.88 |
| 2 ML YEARS | | 115 | 0 | 0 | 24 | 109.0 | 454 | 105 | 39 | 32 | 12 | 3 | 1 | 9 | 33 | 7 | 89 | 8 | 0 | 7 | 3 | .700 | 0 | 2-4 | 31 | 3.88 | 2.64 |

# Max Scherzer

**Pitches:** R **Bats:** R **Pos:** SP-32 SHERR-zer **Ht:** 6'3" **Wt:** 220 **Born:** 7/27/1984 **Age:** 29

| HOW MUCH HE PITCHED | | | | | | | | WHAT HE GAVE UP | | | | | | | | | | | | THE RESULTS | | | | | | | |
|---|---|---|---|---|---|---|---|---|---|---|---|---|---|---|---|---|---|---|---|---|---|---|---|---|---|---|---|
| Year Team | Lg | G | GS | CG | GF | IP | BFP | H | R | ER | HR | SH | SF | HB | TBB | IBB | SO | WP | Bk | W | L | Pct | Sh | Sv-Op | Hld | ERC | ERA |
| 2008 Ari | NL | 16 | 7 | 0 | 2 | 56.0 | 237 | 48 | 24 | 19 | 5 | 4 | 2 | 5 | 21 | 1 | 66 | 2 | 0 | 0 | 4 | .000 | 0 | 0-0 | 0 | 3.45 | 3.05 |
| 2009 Ari | NL | 30 | 30 | 0 | 0 | 170.1 | 741 | 166 | 94 | 78 | 20 | 5 | 6 | 10 | 63 | 1 | 174 | 5 | 1 | 9 | 11 | .450 | 0 | 0-0 | 0 | 4.12 | 4.12 |
| 2010 Det | AL | 31 | 31 | 0 | 0 | 195.2 | 800 | 174 | 84 | 76 | 20 | 5 | 5 | 7 | 70 | 1 | 184 | 8 | 0 | 12 | 11 | .522 | 0 | 0-0 | 0 | 3.56 | 3.50 |
| 2011 Det | AL | 33 | 33 | 0 | 0 | 195.0 | 833 | 207 | 101 | 96 | 29 | 3 | 7 | 7 | 56 | 1 | 174 | 12 | 0 | 15 | 9 | .625 | 0 | 0-0 | 0 | 4.48 | 4.43 |
| 2012 Det | AL | 32 | 32 | 0 | 0 | 187.2 | 787 | 179 | 82 | 78 | 23 | 5 | 1 | 5 | 60 | 2 | 231 | 2 | 1 | 16 | 7 | .696 | 0 | 0-0 | 0 | 3.77 | 3.74 |
| 2013 Det | AL | 32 | 32 | 0 | 0 | 214.1 | 836 | 152 | 73 | 69 | 18 | 2 | 8 | 4 | 56 | 0 | 240 | 6 | 1 | **21** | 3 | **.875** | 0 | 0-0 | 0 | **2.07** | 2.90 |
| Postseason | | 7 | 6 | 0 | 0 | 33.0 | 140 | 27 | 15 | 14 | 2 | 0 | 0 | 1 | 13 | 0 | 40 | 1 | 0 | 2 | 1 | .667 | 0 | 0-0 | 1 | 2.87 | 3.82 |
| 6 ML YEARS | | 174 | 165 | 0 | 2 | 1019.0 | 4234 | 926 | 458 | 416 | 115 | 24 | 29 | 38 | 326 | 6 | 1069 | 35 | 3 | 73 | 45 | .619 | 0 | 0-0 | 0 | 3.52 | 3.67 |

# Nate Schierholtz

**Bats:** L **Throws:** R **Pos:** RF-126;PH-18 SHEER-holtz **Ht:** 6'2" **Wt:** 215 **Born:** 2/15/1984 **Age:** 30

| BATTING | | | | | | | | | | | | | | | | | | | | BASERUNNING | | | | AVERAGES | | |
|---|---|---|---|---|---|---|---|---|---|---|---|---|---|---|---|---|---|---|---|---|---|---|---|---|---|---|
| Year Team | Lg | G | AB | H | 2B | 3B | HR | (Hm | Rd) | TB | R | RBI | RC | TBB | IBB | SO | HBP | SH | SF | SB | CS | SB% | GDP | Avg | OBP | Slg |
| 2007 SF | NL | 39 | 112 | 34 | 5 | 3 | 0 | (0 | 0) | 45 | 9 | 10 | 14 | 2 | 0 | 19 | 1 | 0 | 2 | 3 | 1 | .75 | 0 | .304 | .316 | .402 |
| 2008 SF | NL | 19 | 75 | 24 | 8 | 1 | 1 | (1 | 0) | 37 | 12 | 5 | 12 | 3 | 0 | 8 | 3 | 0 | 0 | 0 | 1 | .00 | 1 | .320 | .370 | .493 |
| 2009 SF | NL | 116 | 285 | 76 | 19 | 2 | 5 | (1 | 4) | 114 | 33 | 29 | 35 | 16 | 3 | 58 | 1 | 0 | 6 | 3 | 1 | .75 | 5 | .267 | .302 | .400 |
| 2010 SF | NL | 137 | 227 | 55 | 13 | 3 | 3 | (0 | 3) | 83 | 34 | 17 | 26 | 20 | 5 | 38 | 3 | 1 | 1 | 4 | 5 | .44 | 3 | .242 | .311 | .366 |
| 2011 SF | NL | 115 | 335 | 93 | 22 | 1 | 9 | (4 | 5) | 144 | 42 | 41 | 46 | 21 | 3 | 61 | 4 | 0 | 2 | 7 | 4 | .64 | 5 | .278 | .326 | .430 |
| 2012 2 Tms | NL | 114 | 241 | 62 | 8 | 5 | 6 | (0 | 6) | 98 | 20 | 21 | 31 | 23 | 2 | 46 | 1 | 1 | 3 | 3 | 2 | .60 | 1 | .257 | .321 | .407 |
| 2013 ChC | NL | 137 | 462 | 116 | 32 | 3 | 21 | (11 | 10) | 217 | 56 | 68 | 65 | 29 | 3 | 94 | 6 | 1 | 5 | 6 | 3 | .67 | 6 | .251 | .301 | .470 |
| 12 SF | NL | 77 | 175 | 44 | 4 | 5 | 5 | (0 | 5) | 73 | 15 | 16 | 23 | 18 | 2 | 36 | 1 | 0 | 2 | 3 | 2 | .60 | 1 | .251 | .321 | .417 |
| 12 Phi | NL | 37 | 66 | 18 | 4 | 0 | 1 | (0 | 1) | 25 | 5 | 5 | 8 | 5 | 0 | 10 | 0 | 1 | 1 | 0 | 0 | - | 0 | .273 | .319 | .379 |
| Postseason | | 11 | 12 | 2 | 0 | 0 | 0 | (0 | 0) | 2 | 2 | 1 | 1 | 1 | 0 | 5 | 0 | 0 | 0 | 0 | 0 | - | 0 | .167 | .231 | .167 |
| 7 ML YEARS | | 677 | 1737 | 460 | 107 | 18 | 45 | (17 | 28) | 738 | 206 | 191 | 229 | 114 | 16 | 324 | 19 | 3 | 19 | 26 | 17 | .60 | 21 | .265 | .314 | .425 |

# Jonathan Schoop

**Bats:** R **Throws:** R **Pos:** 2B-4;PH-1 SCOPE **Ht:** 6'2" **Wt:** 210 **Born:** 10/16/1991 **Age:** 22

| BATTING | | | | | | | | | | | | | | | | | | | | BASERUNNING | | | | AVERAGES | | |
|---|---|---|---|---|---|---|---|---|---|---|---|---|---|---|---|---|---|---|---|---|---|---|---|---|---|---|
| Year Team | Lg | G | AB | H | 2B | 3B | HR | (Hm | Rd) | TB | R | RBI | RC | TBB | IBB | SO | HBP | SH | SF | SB | CS | SB% | GDP | Avg | OBP | Slg |
| 2010 Orioles | R | 17 | 60 | 15 | 4 | 0 | 3 | (- | -) | 28 | 11 | 16 | 9 | 7 | 1 | 7 | 1 | 0 | 2 | 0 | 0 | - | 0 | .250 | .329 | .467 |
| 2010 Bluefld | R | 39 | 133 | 42 | 11 | 1 | 2 | (- | -) | 61 | 16 | 16 | 22 | 12 | 0 | 14 | 0 | 3 | 0 | 1 | 1 | .50 | 6 | .316 | .372 | .459 |
| 2010 Frdrck | A+ | 6 | 21 | 5 | 3 | 0 | 0 | (- | -) | 8 | 5 | 3 | 2 | 1 | 0 | 4 | 0 | 0 | 0 | 0 | 0 | - | 2 | .238 | .273 | .381 |
| 2011 Dlmrva | A | 51 | 212 | 67 | 12 | 3 | 8 | (- | -) | 109 | 45 | 34 | 41 | 20 | 0 | 32 | 2 | 1 | 3 | 6 | 4 | .60 | 13 | .316 | .376 | .514 |
| 2011 Frdrck | A+ | 77 | 299 | 81 | 12 | 2 | 5 | (- | -) | 112 | 37 | 37 | 38 | 22 | 1 | 44 | 4 | 4 | 0 | 6 | 3 | .67 | 4 | .271 | .329 | .375 |
| 2012 Bowie | AA | 124 | 485 | 119 | 24 | 1 | 14 | (- | -) | 187 | 68 | 56 | 65 | 50 | 1 | 103 | 9 | 6 | 5 | 5 | 3 | .63 | 12 | .245 | .324 | .386 |
| 2013 Norfolk | AAA | 70 | 270 | 69 | 11 | 0 | 9 | (- | -) | 107 | 30 | 34 | 32 | 13 | 1 | 55 | 5 | 0 | 1 | 1 | 2 | .33 | 7 | .256 | .301 | .396 |
| 2013 Orioles | R | 8 | 25 | 9 | 2 | 0 | 3 | (- | -) | 20 | 9 | 9 | 8 | 6 | 0 | 6 | 0 | 0 | 1 | 0 | 0 | - | 2 | .360 | .469 | .800 |
| 2013 Abrdn | A- | 3 | 14 | 8 | 1 | 0 | 2 | (- | -) | 15 | 3 | 9 | 6 | 1 | 0 | 1 | 0 | 0 | 0 | 0 | 1 | .00 | 0 | .571 | .600 | 1.071 |
| 2013 Bal | AL | 5 | 14 | 4 | 0 | 0 | 1 | (1 | 0) | 7 | 5 | 1 | 1 | 1 | 0 | 2 | 0 | 0 | 0 | 0 | 0 | - | 2 | .286 | .333 | .500 |

# Skip Schumaker

SHOO-mock-er

**Bats:** L **Throws:** R **Pos:** 2B-44;LF-35;CF-29;PH-21;RF-18;PR-2;DH-1 **Ht:** 5'10" **Wt:** 195 **Born:** 2/3/1980 **Age:** 34

| BATTING | | | | | | | | | | | | | | | | | | | | BASERUNNING | | | | AVERAGES | | |
|---|---|---|---|---|---|---|---|---|---|---|---|---|---|---|---|---|---|---|---|---|---|---|---|---|---|---|
| Year Team | Lg | G | AB | H | 2B | 3B | HR | (Hm | Rd) | TB | R | RBI | RC | TBB | IBB | SO | HBP | SH | SF | SB | CS | SB% | GDP | Avg | OBP | Slg |
| 2005 StL | NL | 27 | 24 | 6 | 1 | 0 | 0 | (0 | 0) | 7 | 9 | 1 | 2 | 2 | 0 | 2 | 0 | 0 | 0 | 1 | 0 | 1.00 | 0 | .250 | .308 | .292 |
| 2006 StL | NL | 28 | 54 | 10 | 1 | 0 | 1 | (0 | 1) | 14 | 3 | 2 | 2 | 5 | 1 | 6 | 0 | 1 | 0 | 2 | 1 | .67 | 1 | .185 | .254 | .259 |
| 2007 StL | NL | 88 | 177 | 59 | 12 | 2 | 2 | (1 | 1) | 81 | 19 | 19 | 30 | 8 | 0 | 20 | 0 | 1 | 2 | 1 | 1 | .50 | 5 | .333 | .358 | .458 |
| 2008 StL | NL | 153 | 540 | 163 | 22 | 5 | 8 | (4 | 4) | 219 | 87 | 46 | 74 | 47 | 2 | 60 | 2 | 4 | 1 | 8 | 2 | .80 | 19 | .302 | .359 | .406 |
| 2009 StL | NL | 153 | 532 | 161 | 34 | 1 | 4 | (2 | 2) | 209 | 85 | 35 | 74 | 52 | 2 | 69 | 0 | 1 | 1 | 2 | 2 | .50 | 4 | .303 | .364 | .393 |

| BATTING | | | | | | | | | | | | | | | | | | | | | | BASERUNNING | | | | AVERAGES | | |
|---|---|---|---|---|---|---|---|---|---|---|---|---|---|---|---|---|---|---|---|---|---|---|---|---|---|---|---|---|
| Year Team | Lg | G | AB | H | 2B | 3B | HR | (Hm | Rd) | TB | R | RBI | RC | TBB | IBB | SO | HBP | SH | SF | SB | CS | SB% | GDP | Avg | OBP | Slg |
| 2010 StL | NL | 137 | 476 | 126 | 18 | 1 | 5 | (1 | 4) | 161 | 66 | 42 | 61 | 43 | 2 | 64 | 4 | 2 | 4 | 5 | 3 | .63 | 7 | .265 | .328 | .338 |
| 2011 StL | NL | 117 | 367 | 104 | 19 | 0 | 2 | (1 | 1) | 129 | 34 | 38 | 43 | 27 | 3 | 50 | 2 | 1 | 3 | 0 | 2 | .00 | 10 | .283 | .333 | .351 |
| 2012 StL | NL | 107 | 272 | 75 | 14 | 4 | 1 | (1 | 0) | 100 | 37 | 28 | 34 | 27 | 2 | 50 | 0 | 3 | 2 | 1 | 1 | .50 | 6 | .276 | .339 | .368 |
| 2013 LAD | NL | 125 | 319 | 84 | 16 | 0 | 2 | (1 | 1) | 106 | 31 | 30 | 34 | 28 | 0 | 54 | 5 | 3 | 0 | 2 | 2 | .50 | 11 | .263 | .332 | .332 |
| Postseason | | 22 | 36 | 10 | 3 | 0 | 0 | (0 | 0) | 13 | 3 | 6 | 5 | 1 | 0 | 6 | 1 | 0 | 0 | 0 | 0 | - | 1 | .278 | .316 | .361 |
| 9 ML YEARS | | 935 | 2761 | 788 | 137 | 13 | 25 | (11 | 14) | 1026 | 371 | 241 | 354 | 239 | 12 | 375 | 13 | 16 | 13 | 22 | 14 | .61 | 63 | .285 | .344 | .372 |

# Luke Scott

**Bats:** L **Throws:** R **Pos:** DH-63;PH-25;LF-6;1B-5 **Ht:** 6'0" **Wt:** 220 **Born:** 6/25/1978 **Age:** 36

| BATTING | | | | | | | | | | | | | | | | | | | | | | BASERUNNING | | | | AVERAGES | | |
|---|---|---|---|---|---|---|---|---|---|---|---|---|---|---|---|---|---|---|---|---|---|---|---|---|---|---|
| Year Team | Lg | G | AB | H | 2B | 3B | HR | (Hm | Rd) | TB | R | RBI | RC | TBB | IBB | SO | HBP | SH | SF | SB | CS | SB% | GDP | Avg | OBP | Slg |
| 2013 Charltt* | A+ | 5 | 18 | 4 | 1 | 0 | 0 | (- | -) | 5 | 2 | 2 | 1 | 0 | 0 | 5 | 1 | 0 | 0 | 0 | 0 | - | 1 | .222 | .263 | .278 |
| 2013 Drham* | AAA | 3 | 12 | 4 | 0 | 0 | 0 | (- | -) | 4 | 2 | 0 | 1 | 2 | 1 | 1 | 0 | 0 | 0 | 0 | 0 | - | 0 | .333 | .429 | .333 |
| 2005 Hou | NL | 34 | 80 | 15 | 4 | 2 | 0 | (0 | 0) | 23 | 6 | 4 | 6 | 9 | 1 | 23 | 0 | 0 | 0 | 1 | 1 | .50 | 0 | .188 | .270 | .288 |
| 2006 Hou | NL | 65 | 214 | 72 | 19 | 6 | 10 | (8 | 2) | 133 | 31 | 37 | 48 | 30 | 4 | 43 | 4 | 0 | 1 | 2 | 1 | .67 | 2 | .336 | .426 | .621 |
| 2007 Hou | NL | 132 | 369 | 94 | 28 | 5 | 18 | (8 | 10) | 186 | 49 | 64 | 55 | 53 | 4 | 95 | 2 | 0 | 1 | 3 | 1 | .75 | 8 | .255 | .351 | .504 |
| 2008 Bal | AL | 148 | 475 | 122 | 29 | 2 | 23 | (11 | 12) | 224 | 67 | 65 | 68 | 53 | 10 | 102 | 5 | 0 | 3 | 2 | 2 | .50 | 7 | .257 | .336 | .472 |
| 2009 Bal | AL | 128 | 449 | 116 | 26 | 1 | 25 | (18 | 7) | 219 | 61 | 77 | 69 | 55 | 5 | 104 | 1 | 0 | 1 | 0 | 0 | - | 4 | .258 | .340 | .488 |
| 2010 Bal | AL | 131 | 447 | 127 | 29 | 1 | 27 | (19 | 8) | 239 | 70 | 72 | 71 | 59 | 4 | 98 | 4 | 0 | 7 | 2 | 0 | 1.00 | 9 | .284 | .368 | .535 |
| 2011 Bal | AL | 64 | 209 | 46 | 11 | 0 | 9 | (5 | 4) | 84 | 24 | 22 | 24 | 24 | 1 | 54 | 1 | 0 | 2 | 1 | 1 | .50 | 2 | .220 | .301 | .402 |
| 2012 TB | AL | 96 | 314 | 72 | 22 | 1 | 14 | (6 | 8) | 138 | 35 | 55 | 40 | 21 | 3 | 80 | 5 | 0 | 4 | 5 | 0 | 1.00 | 9 | .229 | .285 | .439 |
| 2013 TB | AL | 91 | 253 | 61 | 13 | 2 | 9 | (6 | 3) | 105 | 27 | 40 | 37 | 30 | 1 | 63 | 4 | 0 | 4 | 1 | 1 | .50 | 5 | .241 | .326 | .415 |
| Postseason | | 2 | 2 | 0 | 0 | 0 | 0 | (0 | 0) | 0 | 1 | 0 | 0 | 1 | 0 | 1 | 0 | 0 | 0 | 0 | 0 | - | 0 | .000 | .333 | .000 |
| 9 ML YEARS | | 889 | 2810 | 725 | 181 | 20 | 135 | (81 | 54) | 1351 | 370 | 436 | 418 | 334 | 33 | 662 | 26 | 0 | 23 | 17 | 7 | .71 | 46 | .258 | .340 | .481 |

# Evan Scribner

**Pitches:** R **Bats:** R **Pos:** RP-18 SKRIBB-nurr **Ht:** 6'3" **Wt:** 190 **Born:** 7/19/1985 **Age:** 28

| HOW MUCH HE PITCHED | | | | | | | | WHAT HE GAVE UP | | | | | | | | | | | | THE RESULTS | | | | | | | |
|---|---|---|---|---|---|---|---|---|---|---|---|---|---|---|---|---|---|---|---|---|---|---|---|---|---|---|---|
| Year Team | Lg | G | GS | CG | GF | IP | BFP | H | R | ER | HR | SH | SF | HB | TBB | IBB | SO | WP | Bk | W | L | Pct | Sh | Sv-Op | Hld | ERC | ERA |
| 2013 Scrmto* | AAA | 31 | 0 | 0 | 10 | 44.2 | 177 | 32 | 12 | 11 | 2 | 0 | 1 | 0 | 9 | 0 | 58 | 1 | 0 | 3 | 1 | .750 | 0 | 1-- | - | 1.60 | 2.22 |
| 2011 SD | NL | 10 | 0 | 0 | 5 | 14.0 | 64 | 18 | 11 | 11 | 1 | 0 | 0 | 0 | 4 | 0 | 10 | 0 | 0 | 0 | 0 | - | 0 | 0-0 | 0 | 4.92 | 7.07 |
| 2012 Oak | AL | 30 | 0 | 0 | 13 | 35.1 | 148 | 30 | 11 | 10 | 2 | 0 | 0 | 0 | 12 | 0 | 30 | 1 | 0 | 2 | 0 | 1.000 | 0 | 1-1 | 1 | 2.70 | 2.55 |
| 2013 Oak | AL | 18 | 0 | 0 | 12 | 26.2 | 114 | 26 | 13 | 13 | 3 | 0 | 0 | 0 | 7 | 0 | 19 | 2 | 0 | 0 | 0 | - | 0 | 0-0 | 0 | 3.38 | 4.39 |
| Postseason | | 1 | 0 | 0 | 1 | 2.0 | 6 | 0 | 0 | 0 | 0 | 0 | 0 | 0 | 0 | 0 | 3 | 0 | 0 | 0 | 0 | - | 0 | 0-0 | 0 | 0.00 | 0.00 |
| 3 ML YEARS | | 58 | 0 | 0 | 30 | 76.0 | 326 | 74 | 35 | 34 | 6 | 0 | 0 | 0 | 23 | 0 | 59 | 3 | 0 | 2 | 0 | 1.000 | 0 | 1-1 | 1 | 3.32 | 4.03 |

# Marco Scutaro

**Bats:** R **Throws:** R **Pos:** 2B-121;DH-3;PH-3 SKOO-tah-row **Ht:** 5'10" **Wt:** 185 **Born:** 10/30/1975 **Age:** 38

| BATTING | | | | | | | | | | | | | | | | | | | | | | BASERUNNING | | | | AVERAGES | | |
|---|---|---|---|---|---|---|---|---|---|---|---|---|---|---|---|---|---|---|---|---|---|---|---|---|---|---|
| Year Team | Lg | G | AB | H | 2B | 3B | HR | (Hm | Rd) | TB | R | RBI | RC | TBB | IBB | SO | HBP | SH | SF | SB | CS | SB% | GDP | Avg | OBP | Slg |
| 2002 NYM | NL | 27 | 36 | 8 | 0 | 1 | 1 | (1 | 0) | 13 | 2 | 6 | 2 | 0 | 0 | 11 | 0 | 1 | 1 | 0 | 1 | .00 | 1 | .222 | .216 | .361 |
| 2003 NYM | NL | 48 | 75 | 16 | 4 | 0 | 2 | (0 | 2) | 26 | 10 | 6 | 10 | 13 | 2 | 14 | 1 | 1 | 1 | 2 | 0 | 1.00 | 1 | .213 | .333 | .347 |
| 2004 Oak | AL | 137 | 455 | 124 | 32 | 1 | 7 | (6 | 1) | 179 | 50 | 43 | 48 | 16 | 1 | 58 | 0 | 5 | 1 | 0 | 0 | - | 9 | .273 | .297 | .393 |
| 2005 Oak | AL | 118 | 381 | 94 | 22 | 3 | 9 | (5 | 4) | 149 | 48 | 37 | 45 | 36 | 1 | 48 | 0 | 4 | 2 | 5 | 2 | .71 | 6 | .247 | .310 | .391 |
| 2006 Oak | AL | 117 | 365 | 97 | 21 | 6 | 5 | (1 | 4) | 145 | 52 | 41 | 47 | 50 | 0 | 66 | 0 | 3 | 5 | 5 | 1 | .83 | 16 | .266 | .350 | .397 |
| 2007 Oak | AL | 104 | 338 | 88 | 13 | 0 | 7 | (2 | 5) | 122 | 49 | 41 | 42 | 35 | 1 | 40 | 2 | 2 | 2 | 2 | 1 | .67 | 13 | .260 | .332 | .361 |
| 2008 Tor | AL | 145 | 517 | 138 | 23 | 1 | 7 | (5 | 2) | 184 | 76 | 60 | 72 | 57 | 0 | 65 | 5 | 6 | 7 | 7 | 2 | .78 | 8 | .267 | .341 | .356 |
| 2009 Tor | AL | 144 | 574 | 162 | 35 | 1 | 12 | (7 | 5) | 235 | 100 | 60 | 97 | 90 | 0 | 75 | 4 | 5 | 7 | 14 | 5 | .74 | 12 | .282 | .379 | .409 |
| 2010 Bos | AL | 150 | 632 | 174 | 38 | 0 | 11 | (6 | 5) | 245 | 92 | 56 | 81 | 53 | 1 | 71 | 3 | 4 | 3 | 5 | 4 | .56 | 13 | .275 | .333 | .388 |
| 2011 Bos | AL | 113 | 395 | 118 | 26 | 1 | 7 | (3 | 4) | 167 | 59 | 54 | 56 | 38 | 1 | 36 | 1 | 7 | 4 | 4 | 2 | .67 | 12 | .299 | .358 | .423 |
| 2012 2 Tms | NL | 156 | 620 | 190 | 32 | 4 | 7 | (4 | 3) | 251 | 87 | 74 | 86 | 40 | 0 | 49 | 4 | 10 | **9** | 9 | 4 | .69 | 12 | .306 | .348 | .405 |
| 2013 SF | NL | 127 | 488 | 145 | 23 | 3 | 2 | (1 | 1) | 180 | 57 | 31 | 61 | 45 | 0 | 34 | 2 | 9 | 3 | 2 | 0 | 1.00 | 13 | .297 | .357 | .369 |
| 12 Col | NL | 95 | 377 | 102 | 16 | 3 | 4 | (3 | 1) | 136 | 47 | 30 | 40 | 27 | 0 | 35 | 4 | 4 | 3 | 7 | 3 | .70 | 5 | .271 | .324 | .361 |
| 12 SF | NL | 61 | 243 | 88 | 16 | 1 | 3 | (1 | 2) | 115 | 40 | 44 | 46 | 13 | 0 | 14 | 0 | 6 | 6 | 2 | 1 | .67 | 7 | .362 | .385 | .473 |
| Postseason | | 23 | 91 | 26 | 8 | 0 | 0 | (0 | 0) | 34 | 12 | 14 | 17 | 5 | 0 | 7 | 0 | 1 | 0 | 0 | 0 | - | 1 | .286 | .323 | .374 |
| 12 ML YEARS | | 1386 | 4876 | 1354 | 269 | 21 | 77 | (41 | 36) | 1896 | 682 | 509 | 647 | 473 | 7 | 567 | 22 | 57 | 45 | 55 | 22 | .71 | 116 | .278 | .341 | .389 |

# Kyle Seager

**Bats:** L **Throws:** R **Pos:** 3B-160;PH-2 SEE-gurr **Ht:** 6'0" **Wt:** 215 **Born:** 11/3/1987 **Age:** 26

| BATTING | | | | | | | | | | | | | | | | | | | | | | BASERUNNING | | | | AVERAGES | | |
|---|---|---|---|---|---|---|---|---|---|---|---|---|---|---|---|---|---|---|---|---|---|---|---|---|---|---|
| Year Team | Lg | G | AB | H | 2B | 3B | HR | (Hm | Rd) | TB | R | RBI | RC | TBB | IBB | SO | HBP | SH | SF | SB | CS | SB% | GDP | Avg | OBP | Slg |
| 2011 Sea | AL | 53 | 182 | 47 | 13 | 0 | 3 | (0 | 3) | 69 | 22 | 13 | 16 | 13 | 0 | 36 | 2 | 2 | 2 | 3 | 1 | .75 | 4 | .258 | .312 | .379 |
| 2012 Sea | AL | 155 | 594 | 154 | 35 | 1 | 20 | (5 | 15) | 251 | 62 | 86 | 88 | 46 | 1 | 110 | 5 | 2 | 4 | 13 | 5 | .72 | 9 | .259 | .316 | .423 |
| 2013 Sea | AL | 160 | 615 | 160 | 32 | 2 | 22 | (8 | 14) | 262 | 79 | 69 | 90 | 68 | 1 | 122 | 7 | 0 | 5 | 9 | 3 | .75 | 8 | .260 | .338 | .426 |
| 3 ML YEARS | | 368 | 1391 | 361 | 80 | 3 | 45 | (13 | 32) | 582 | 163 | 168 | 194 | 127 | 2 | 268 | 14 | 4 | 11 | 25 | 9 | .74 | 21 | .260 | .325 | .418 |

# Jean Segura

**Bats:** R **Throws:** R **Pos:** SS-144;PH-3 GENE seg-ER-uh **Ht:** 5'10" **Wt:** 200 **Born:** 3/17/1990 **Age:** 24

| BATTING | | | | | | | | | | | | | | | | | | | | | | BASERUNNING | | | | AVERAGES | | |
|---|---|---|---|---|---|---|---|---|---|---|---|---|---|---|---|---|---|---|---|---|---|---|---|---|---|---|
| Year Team | Lg | G | AB | H | 2B | 3B | HR | (Hm | Rd) | TB | R | RBI | RC | TBB | IBB | SO | HBP | SH | SF | SB | CS | SB% | GDP | Avg | OBP | Slg |
| 2009 Salt Lk | AAA | 7 | 19 | 8 | 2 | 0 | 0 | (- | -) | 10 | 2 | 2 | 3 | 0 | 0 | 4 | 0 | 0 | 0 | 0 | 0 | - | 0 | .421 | .421 | .526 |
| 2009 Orem | R+ | 36 | 162 | 56 | 10 | 4 | 3 | (- | -) | 83 | 33 | 21 | 33 | 11 | 1 | 11 | 2 | 1 | 1 | 11 | 3 | .79 | 1 | .346 | .392 | .512 |
| 2010 CRpds | A | 130 | 515 | 161 | 24 | 12 | 10 | (- | -) | 239 | 89 | 79 | 95 | 45 | 3 | 72 | 2 | 11 | 8 | 50 | 10 | .83 | 5 | .313 | .365 | .464 |
| 2011 InldEm | A+ | 44 | 185 | 52 | 9 | 4 | 3 | (- | -) | 78 | 26 | 21 | 28 | 15 | 3 | 26 | 1 | 0 | 1 | 18 | 6 | .75 | 4 | .281 | .337 | .422 |
| 2011 Angels | R | 8 | 30 | 11 | 4 | 0 | 1 | (- | -) | 18 | 5 | 5 | 6 | 0 | 0 | 3 | 0 | 0 | 0 | 0 | 0 | - | 0 | .367 | .367 | .600 |

| | | | | | | | | BATTING | | | | | | | | | | | | | | BASERUNNING | | | | AVERAGES | | |
|---|---|---|---|---|---|---|---|---|---|---|---|---|---|---|---|---|---|---|---|---|---|---|---|---|---|---|---|---|
| Year | Team | Lg | G | AB | H | 2B | 3B | HR | (Hm | Rd) | TB | R | RBI | RC | TBB | IBB | SO | HBP | SH | SF | SB | CS | SB% | GDP | Avg | OBP | Slg |
| 2012 | Ark | AA | 94 | 374 | 110 | 10 | 5 | 7 | (- | -) | 151 | 50 | 40 | 55 | 23 | 3 | 57 | 8 | 6 | 3 | 33 | 13 | .72 | 6 | .294 | .346 | .404 |
| 2012 | Hntsvl | AA | 8 | 30 | 13 | 3 | 0 | 0 | (- | -) | 16 | 7 | 4 | 8 | 4 | 0 | 4 | 1 | 1 | 1 | 4 | 0 | 1.00 | 0 | .433 | .500 | .533 |
| 2012 | 2 Tms | | 45 | 151 | 39 | 4 | 3 | 0 | (0 | 0) | 49 | 19 | 14 | 16 | 13 | 3 | 23 | 0 | 1 | 1 | 7 | 1 | .88 | 1 | .258 | .315 | .325 |
| 2013 | Mil | NL | 146 | 588 | 173 | 20 | 10 | 12 | (7 | 5) | 249 | 74 | 49 | 72 | 25 | 1 | 84 | 6 | 2 | 2 | 44 | 13 | .77 | 17 | .294 | .329 | .423 |
| 12 | LAA | AL | 1 | 3 | 0 | 0 | 0 | 0 | (0 | 0) | 0 | 0 | 0 | 0 | 0 | 0 | 2 | 0 | 0 | 0 | 0 | 0 | - | 0 | .000 | .000 | .000 |
| 12 | Mil | NL | 44 | 148 | 39 | 4 | 3 | 0 | (0 | 0) | 49 | 19 | 14 | 16 | 13 | 3 | 21 | 0 | 1 | 1 | 7 | 1 | .88 | 1 | .264 | .321 | .331 |
| 2 ML YEARS | | | 191 | 739 | 212 | 24 | 13 | 12 | (7 | 5) | 298 | 93 | 63 | 88 | 38 | 4 | 107 | 6 | 3 | 3 | 51 | 14 | .78 | 18 | .287 | .326 | .403 |

# Justin Sellers

**Bats:** R **Throws:** R **Pos:** SS-22;PH-4;3B-1;PR-1 **Ht:** 5'10" **Wt:** 160 **Born:** 2/1/1986 **Age:** 28

| | | | | | | | | BATTING | | | | | | | | | | | | | | BASERUNNING | | | | AVERAGES | | |
|---|---|---|---|---|---|---|---|---|---|---|---|---|---|---|---|---|---|---|---|---|---|---|---|---|---|---|---|---|
| Year | Team | Lg | G | AB | H | 2B | 3B | HR | (Hm | Rd) | TB | R | RBI | RC | TBB | IBB | SO | HBP | SH | SF | SB | CS | SB% | GDP | Avg | OBP | Slg |
| 2013 | Albq* | AAA | 89 | 326 | 88 | 26 | 4 | 6 | (- | -) | 140 | 39 | 65 | 49 | 25 | 3 | 54 | 5 | 4 | 6 | 4 | 0 | 1.00 | 4 | .270 | .326 | .429 |
| 2011 | LAD | NL | 36 | 123 | 25 | 9 | 0 | 1 | (1 | 0) | 37 | 20 | 13 | 15 | 12 | 0 | 21 | 2 | 1 | 1 | 1 | 0 | 1.00 | 1 | .203 | .283 | .301 |
| 2012 | LAD | NL | 19 | 44 | 9 | 3 | 1 | 1 | (1 | 0) | 17 | 6 | 2 | 2 | 5 | 1 | 14 | 0 | 1 | 0 | 0 | 0 | - | 0 | .205 | .286 | .386 |
| 2013 | LAD | NL | 27 | 69 | 13 | 1 | 0 | 1 | (1 | 0) | 17 | 6 | 2 | 4 | 5 | 0 | 20 | 2 | 1 | 0 | 0 | 0 | - | 3 | .188 | .263 | .246 |
| 3 ML YEARS | | | 82 | 236 | 47 | 13 | 1 | 3 | (3 | 0) | 71 | 32 | 17 | 21 | 22 | 1 | 55 | 4 | 3 | 1 | 1 | 0 | 1.00 | 4 | .199 | .278 | .301 |

# Marcus Semien

**Bats:** R **Throws:** R **Pos:** 3B-17;2B-3;SS-3 SIM-ee-inn **Ht:** 6'1" **Wt:** 190 **Born:** 9/17/1990 **Age:** 23

| | | | | | | | | BATTING | | | | | | | | | | | | | | BASERUNNING | | | | AVERAGES | | |
|---|---|---|---|---|---|---|---|---|---|---|---|---|---|---|---|---|---|---|---|---|---|---|---|---|---|---|---|---|
| Year | Team | Lg | G | AB | H | 2B | 3B | HR | (Hm | Rd) | TB | R | RBI | RC | TBB | IBB | SO | HBP | SH | SF | SB | CS | SB% | GDP | Avg | OBP | Slg |
| 2011 | Knapol | A | 60 | 229 | 58 | 15 | 2 | 3 | (- | -) | 86 | 35 | 26 | 28 | 22 | 0 | 53 | 2 | 6 | 3 | 3 | 4 | .43 | 4 | .253 | .320 | .376 |
| 2012 | WinSa | A+ | 107 | 418 | 114 | 31 | 5 | 14 | (- | -) | 197 | 80 | 59 | 74 | 55 | 1 | 97 | 5 | 6 | 3 | 11 | 5 | .69 | 7 | .273 | .362 | .471 |
| 2013 | Brham | AA | 105 | 393 | 114 | 22 | 5 | 15 | (- | -) | 191 | 90 | 49 | 87 | 84 | 3 | 66 | 4 | 2 | 0 | 20 | 5 | .80 | 7 | .290 | .420 | .486 |
| 2013 | Charltt | AAA | 32 | 125 | 33 | 11 | 1 | 4 | (- | -) | 58 | 20 | 17 | 21 | 14 | 0 | 24 | 1 | 0 | 2 | 4 | 0 | 1.00 | 6 | .264 | .338 | .464 |
| 2013 | CWS | AL | 21 | 69 | 18 | 4 | 0 | 2 | (2 | 0) | 28 | 7 | 7 | 7 | 1 | 0 | 22 | 0 | 0 | 1 | 2 | 2 | .50 | 1 | .261 | .268 | .406 |

# Bryan Shaw

**Pitches:** R **Bats:** B **Pos:** RP-70 **Ht:** 6'1" **Wt:** 210 **Born:** 11/8/1987 **Age:** 26

| | | | HOW MUCH HE PITCHED | | | | | | WHAT HE GAVE UP | | | | | | | | | | | THE RESULTS | | | | | | | |
|---|---|---|---|---|---|---|---|---|---|---|---|---|---|---|---|---|---|---|---|---|---|---|---|---|---|---|---|
| Year | Team | Lg | G | GS | CG | GF | IP | BFP | H | R | ER | HR | SH | SF | HB | TBB | IBB | SO | WP | Bk | W | L | Pct | Sh | Sv-Op | Hld | ERC | ERA |
| 2011 | Ari | NL | 33 | 0 | 0 | 8 | 28.1 | 122 | 30 | 9 | 8 | 2 | 0 | 0 | 4 | 8 | 1 | 24 | 1 | 0 | 1 | 0 | 1.000 | 0 | 0-0 | 9 | 4.31 | 2.54 |
| 2012 | Ari | NL | 64 | 0 | 0 | 19 | 59.1 | 252 | 60 | 29 | 23 | 4 | 4 | 2 | 2 | 24 | 3 | 41 | 4 | 1 | 1 | 6 | .143 | 0 | 2-4 | 10 | 4.08 | 3.49 |
| 2013 | Cle | AL | 70 | 0 | 0 | 11 | 75.0 | 316 | 60 | 31 | 27 | 4 | 4 | 2 | 4 | 28 | 2 | 73 | 5 | 0 | 7 | 3 | .700 | 0 | 1-5 | 12 | 2.71 | 3.24 |
| Postseason | | | 4 | 0 | 0 | 1 | 4.0 | 13 | 0 | 0 | 0 | 0 | 0 | 1 | 0 | 1 | 0 | 3 | 0 | 0 | 0 | 0 | - | 0 | 0-0 | 1 | 0.07 | 0.00 |
| 3 ML YEARS | | | 167 | 0 | 0 | 38 | 162.2 | 690 | 150 | 69 | 58 | 10 | 8 | 4 | 10 | 60 | 6 | 138 | 10 | 1 | 9 | 9 | .500 | 0 | 3-9 | 31 | 3.46 | 3.21 |

# James Shields

**Pitches:** R **Bats:** R **Pos:** SP-34 **Ht:** 6'4" **Wt:** 215 **Born:** 12/20/1981 **Age:** 32

| | | | HOW MUCH HE PITCHED | | | | | | WHAT HE GAVE UP | | | | | | | | | | | THE RESULTS | | | | | | | |
|---|---|---|---|---|---|---|---|---|---|---|---|---|---|---|---|---|---|---|---|---|---|---|---|---|---|---|---|
| Year | Team | Lg | G | GS | CG | GF | IP | BFP | H | R | ER | HR | SH | SF | HB | TBB | IBB | SO | WP | Bk | W | L | Pct | Sh | Sv-Op | Hld | ERC | ERA |
| 2006 | TB | AL | 21 | 21 | 1 | 0 | 124.2 | 540 | 141 | 69 | 67 | 18 | 4 | 3 | 5 | 38 | 5 | 104 | 9 | 0 | 6 | 8 | .429 | 0 | 0-0 | 0 | 4.92 | 4.84 |
| 2007 | TB | AL | 31 | 31 | 1 | 0 | 215.0 | 874 | 202 | 98 | 92 | 28 | 4 | 5 | 10 | 36 | 0 | 184 | 9 | 0 | 12 | 8 | .600 | 0 | 0-0 | 0 | 3.24 | 3.85 |
| 2008 | TB | AL | 33 | 33 | 3 | 0 | 215.0 | 877 | 208 | 94 | 85 | 24 | 6 | 0 | 12 | 40 | 0 | 160 | 6 | 0 | 14 | 8 | .636 | **2** | 0-0 | 0 | 3.41 | 3.56 |
| 2009 | TB | AL | 33 | 33 | 0 | 0 | 219.2 | 930 | 239 | 113 | 101 | 29 | 6 | 3 | 1 | 52 | 1 | 167 | 3 | 1 | 11 | 12 | .478 | 0 | 0-0 | 0 | 4.16 | 4.14 |
| 2010 | TB | AL | 34 | 33 | 0 | 0 | 203.1 | 899 | **246** | **128** | **117** | **34** | 5 | 2 | 5 | 51 | 2 | 187 | 13 | 2 | 13 | 15 | .464 | 0 | 0-0 | 0 | 5.21 | 5.18 |
| 2011 | TB | AL | 33 | 33 | **11** | 0 | 249.1 | 975 | 195 | 83 | 78 | 26 | 5 | 3 | 5 | 65 | 1 | 225 | 4 | 0 | 16 | 12 | .571 | **4** | 0-0 | 0 | 2.58 | 2.82 |
| 2012 | TB | AL | 33 | 33 | 3 | 0 | 227.2 | 944 | 208 | 103 | 89 | 25 | 3 | 2 | 11 | 58 | 2 | 223 | 7 | 1 | 15 | 10 | .600 | 2 | 0-0 | 0 | 3.28 | 3.52 |
| 2013 | KC | AL | 34 | **34** | 2 | 0 | **228.2** | **946** | 215 | 82 | 80 | 20 | 6 | 7 | 8 | 68 | 0 | 196 | 11 | **2** | 13 | 9 | .591 | 0 | 0-0 | 0 | 3.45 | 3.15 |
| Postseason | | | 6 | 6 | 0 | 0 | 34.1 | 152 | 40 | 20 | 19 | 4 | 1 | 1 | 5 | 8 | 0 | 25 | 3 | 0 | 2 | 4 | .333 | 0 | 0-0 | 0 | 5.08 | 4.98 |
| 8 ML YEARS | | | 252 | 251 | 21 | 0 | 1683.1 | 6985 | 1654 | 770 | 709 | 204 | 39 | 25 | 57 | 408 | 11 | 1446 | 62 | 6 | 100 | 82 | .549 | 8 | 0-0 | 0 | 3.66 | 3.79 |

# Matt Shoemaker

**Pitches:** R **Bats:** R **Pos:** SP-1 SHOO-may-kerr **Ht:** 6'2" **Wt:** 225 **Born:** 9/27/1986 **Age:** 27

| | | | HOW MUCH HE PITCHED | | | | | | WHAT HE GAVE UP | | | | | | | | | | | THE RESULTS | | | | | | | |
|---|---|---|---|---|---|---|---|---|---|---|---|---|---|---|---|---|---|---|---|---|---|---|---|---|---|---|---|
| Year | Team | Lg | G | GS | CG | GF | IP | BFP | H | R | ER | HR | SH | SF | HB | TBB | IBB | SO | WP | Bk | W | L | Pct | Sh | Sv-Op | Hld | ERC | ERA |
| 2009 | CRpds | A | 20 | 5 | 0 | 0 | 63.2 | 269 | 53 | 29 | 24 | 5 | 1 | 4 | 8 | 23 | 0 | 54 | 5 | 0 | 4 | 1 | .800 | 0 | 0- - | - | 3.36 | 3.39 |
| 2009 | RCuca | A+ | 3 | 3 | 0 | 0 | 17.1 | 67 | 14 | 7 | 6 | 2 | 0 | 0 | 0 | 1 | 0 | 13 | 0 | 0 | 1 | 0 | 1.000 | 0 | 0- - | - | 1.89 | 3.12 |
| 2010 | RCuca | A+ | 20 | 20 | 2 | 0 | 122.1 | 531 | 138 | 75 | 67 | 14 | 0 | 0 | 4 | 39 | 1 | 119 | 10 | 1 | 7 | 8 | .467 | 0 | 0- - | - | 4.75 | 4.93 |
| 2010 | Salt Lk | AAA | 3 | 2 | 0 | 0 | 15.1 | 69 | 20 | 10 | 10 | 0 | 0 | 0 | 0 | 8 | 0 | 9 | 0 | 0 | 2 | 1 | .667 | 0 | 0- - | - | 5.83 | 5.87 |
| 2011 | Salt Lk | AAA | 4 | 4 | 0 | 0 | 21.0 | 100 | 28 | 19 | 19 | 3 | 0 | 1 | 1 | 12 | 0 | 12 | 2 | 0 | 0 | 2 | .000 | 0 | 0- - | - | 7.50 | 8.14 |
| 2011 | Ark | AA | 23 | 23 | 5 | 0 | 156.1 | 629 | 132 | 47 | 43 | 17 | 5 | 1 | 8 | 35 | 0 | 129 | 6 | 3 | 12 | 5 | .706 | 2 | 0- - | - | 2.85 | 2.48 |
| 2012 | Salt Lk | AAA | 29 | 29 | 1 | 0 | 176.2 | 782 | 230 | 123 | 113 | 25 | 3 | 9 | 5 | 45 | 0 | 124 | 4 | 1 | 11 | 10 | .524 | 0 | 0- - | - | 5.75 | 5.76 |
| 2013 | Salt Lk | AAA | 29 | 29 | 0 | 0 | 184.1 | 782 | 212 | 99 | 95 | 27 | 1 | 11 | 8 | 29 | 0 | 160 | 5 | 0 | 11 | 13 | .458 | 0 | 0- - | - | 4.47 | 4.64 |
| 2013 | LAA | AL | 1 | 1 | 0 | 0 | 5.0 | 19 | 2 | 0 | 0 | 0 | 0 | 0 | 0 | 2 | 0 | 5 | 1 | 0 | 0 | 0 | - | 0 | 0-0 | 0 | 0.95 | 0.00 |

## Kelly Shoppach

**Bats:** R **Throws:** R **Pos:** C-36;PH-1 SHOP-ick **Ht:** 6'0" **Wt:** 220 **Born:** 4/29/1980 **Age:** 34

| BATTING | | | | | | | | | | | | | | | | | | | | | BASERUNNING | | | | AVERAGES | | |
|---|---|---|---|---|---|---|---|---|---|---|---|---|---|---|---|---|---|---|---|---|---|---|---|---|---|---|---|
| Year Team | Lg | G | AB | H | 2B | 3B | HR | (Hm | Rd) | TB | R | RBI | RC | TBB | IBB | SO | HBP | SH | SF | SB | CS | SB% | GDP | Avg | OBP | Slg |
| 2013 Syrcse* | AAA | 10 | 32 | 7 | 0 | 0 | 0 | (- | -) | 7 | 3 | 2 | 3 | 5 | 0 | 8 | 2 | 1 | 0 | 0 | 0 | - | 0 | .219 | .359 | .219 |
| 2013 Indy* | AAA | 7 | 26 | 5 | 1 | 0 | 0 | (- | -) | 6 | 0 | 2 | 1 | 1 | 0 | 9 | 0 | 0 | 0 | 0 | 0 | - | 1 | .192 | .222 | .231 |
| 2013 Clmbs* | AAA | 1 | 3 | 1 | 0 | 0 | 0 | (- | -) | 1 | 0 | 0 | 0 | 0 | 0 | 1 | 0 | 0 | 0 | 0 | 0 | - | 0 | .333 | .333 | .333 |
| 2005 Bos | AL | 9 | 15 | 0 | 0 | 0 | 0 | (0 | 0) | 0 | 1 | 0 | 0 | 0 | 0 | 7 | 1 | 0 | 0 | 0 | 0 | - | 0 | .000 | .063 | .000 |
| 2006 Cle | AL | 41 | 110 | 27 | 6 | 0 | 3 | (2 | 1) | 42 | 7 | 16 | 13 | 8 | 0 | 45 | 0 | 2 | 0 | 0 | 0 | - | 2 | .245 | .297 | .382 |
| 2007 Cle | AL | 59 | 161 | 42 | 13 | 0 | 7 | (4 | 3) | 76 | 26 | 30 | 24 | 11 | 0 | 56 | 1 | 3 | 1 | 0 | 0 | - | 2 | .261 | .310 | .472 |
| 2008 Cle | AL | 112 | 352 | 92 | 27 | 0 | 21 | (9 | 12) | 182 | 67 | 55 | 58 | 36 | 3 | 133 | 11 | 3 | 1 | 0 | 0 | - | 7 | .261 | .348 | .517 |
| 2009 Cle | AL | 89 | 271 | 58 | 14 | 0 | 12 | (5 | 7) | 108 | 33 | 40 | 32 | 33 | 0 | 98 | **18** | 2 | 3 | 0 | 0 | - | 8 | .214 | .335 | .399 |
| 2010 TB | AL | 63 | 158 | 31 | 8 | 0 | 5 | (4 | 1) | 54 | 17 | 17 | 18 | 20 | 0 | 71 | 6 | 2 | 1 | 0 | 0 | - | 2 | .196 | .308 | .342 |
| 2011 TB | AL | 87 | 221 | 39 | 3 | 0 | 11 | (4 | 7) | 75 | 23 | 22 | 15 | 19 | 0 | 79 | 9 | 3 | 1 | 0 | 0 | - | 5 | .176 | .268 | .339 |
| 2012 2 Tms | | 76 | 219 | 51 | 14 | 2 | 8 | (3 | 5) | 93 | 23 | 27 | 31 | 16 | 3 | 89 | 8 | 2 | 0 | 1 | 0 | 1.00 | 2 | .233 | .309 | .425 |
| 2013 2 Tms | AL | 36 | 109 | 21 | 7 | 0 | 3 | (3 | 0) | 37 | 11 | 9 | 8 | 12 | 1 | 46 | 3 | 2 | 1 | 0 | 0 | - | 0 | .193 | .288 | .339 |
| 12 Bos | AL | 48 | 140 | 35 | 12 | 2 | 5 | (3 | 2) | 66 | 16 | 17 | 22 | 11 | 1 | 62 | 5 | 2 | 0 | 1 | 0 | 1.00 | 2 | .250 | .327 | .471 |
| 12 NYM | NL | 28 | 79 | 16 | 2 | 0 | 3 | (0 | 3) | 27 | 7 | 10 | 9 | 5 | 2 | 27 | 3 | 0 | 0 | 0 | 0 | - | 0 | .203 | .276 | .342 |
| 13 Sea | AL | 35 | 107 | 21 | 7 | 0 | 3 | (3 | 0) | 37 | 11 | 9 | 8 | 12 | 1 | 45 | 3 | 2 | 1 | 0 | 0 | - | 0 | .196 | .293 | .346 |
| 13 Cle | AL | 1 | 2 | 0 | 0 | 0 | 0 | (0 | 0) | 0 | 0 | 0 | 0 | 0 | 0 | 1 | 0 | 0 | 0 | 0 | 0 | - | 0 | .000 | .000 | .000 |
| Postseason | | 9 | 25 | 7 | 2 | 0 | 2 | (0 | 2) | 15 | 4 | 6 | 6 | 2 | 0 | 9 | 2 | 0 | 0 | 0 | 0 | - | 1 | .280 | .379 | .600 |
| 9 ML YEARS | | 572 | 1616 | 361 | 92 | 2 | 70 | (34 | 36) | 667 | 208 | 216 | 199 | 155 | 7 | 624 | 57 | 19 | 8 | 1 | 0 | 1.00 | 28 | .223 | .312 | .413 |

## J.B. Shuck

**Bats:** L **Throws:** L **Pos:** LF-97;DH-16;PH-13;RF-9;PR-2 **Ht:** 5'11" **Wt:** 195 **Born:** 6/18/1987 **Age:** 27

| BATTING | | | | | | | | | | | | | | | | | | | | | BASERUNNING | | | | AVERAGES | | |
|---|---|---|---|---|---|---|---|---|---|---|---|---|---|---|---|---|---|---|---|---|---|---|---|---|---|---|---|
| Year Team | Lg | G | AB | H | 2B | 3B | HR | (Hm | Rd) | TB | R | RBI | RC | TBB | IBB | SO | HBP | SH | SF | SB | CS | SB% | GDP | Avg | OBP | Slg |
| 2009 Lancst | A+ | 133 | 556 | 175 | 30 | 11 | 1 | (- | -) | 230 | 98 | 36 | 94 | 64 | 5 | 55 | 4 | 4 | 0 | 18 | 9 | .67 | 10 | .315 | .389 | .414 |
| 2010 CpChr | AA | 101 | 389 | 116 | 14 | 2 | 2 | (- | -) | 140 | 52 | 28 | 54 | 46 | 1 | 56 | 0 | 0 | 0 | 9 | 9 | .50 | 3 | .298 | .372 | .360 |
| 2010 RdRck | AAA | 36 | 139 | 38 | 2 | 2 | 0 | (- | -) | 44 | 15 | 7 | 17 | 16 | 1 | 15 | 0 | 1 | 0 | 7 | 3 | .70 | 4 | .273 | .348 | .317 |
| 2011 OKCity | AAA | 108 | 354 | 105 | 11 | 7 | 0 | (- | -) | 130 | 60 | 30 | 58 | 56 | 1 | 30 | 4 | 4 | 1 | 20 | 11 | .65 | 6 | .297 | .398 | .367 |
| 2012 OKCity | AAA | 115 | 315 | 94 | 11 | 3 | 0 | (- | -) | 111 | 49 | 33 | 45 | 39 | 1 | 20 | 0 | 2 | 2 | 12 | 8 | .60 | 3 | .298 | .374 | .352 |
| 2011 Hou | NL | 37 | 81 | 22 | 2 | 1 | 0 | (0 | 0) | 26 | 9 | 3 | 9 | 11 | 1 | 7 | 0 | 0 | 0 | 2 | 0 | 1.00 | 3 | .272 | .359 | .321 |
| 2013 LAA | AL | 129 | 437 | 128 | 20 | 3 | 2 | (1 | 1) | 160 | 60 | 39 | 54 | 27 | 0 | 54 | 1 | 6 | 7 | 8 | 4 | .67 | 10 | .293 | .331 | .366 |
| 2 ML YEARS | | 166 | 518 | 150 | 22 | 4 | 2 | (1 | 1) | 186 | 69 | 42 | 63 | 38 | 1 | 61 | 1 | 6 | 7 | 10 | 4 | .71 | 13 | .290 | .335 | .359 |

## Kevin Siegrist

**Pitches:** L **Bats:** L **Pos:** RP-45 SEE-grist **Ht:** 6'5" **Wt:** 215 **Born:** 7/20/1989 **Age:** 24

| HOW MUCH HE PITCHED | | | | | | | | WHAT HE GAVE UP | | | | | | | | | | | | THE RESULTS | | | | | | | |
|---|---|---|---|---|---|---|---|---|---|---|---|---|---|---|---|---|---|---|---|---|---|---|---|---|---|---|---|
| Year Team | Lg | G | GS | CG | GF | IP | BFP | H | R | ER | HR | SH | SF | HB | TBB | IBB | SO | WP | Bk | W | L | Pct | Sh | Sv-Op | Hld | ERC | ERA |
| 2009 Batvia | A- | 10 | 4 | 0 | 2 | 28.0 | 128 | 30 | 14 | 12 | 4 | 2 | 0 | 5 | 11 | 0 | 23 | 2 | 0 | 1 | 0 | 1.000 | 0 | 2-- | - | 5.47 | 3.86 |
| 2010 Batvia | A- | 7 | 4 | 0 | 0 | 21.0 | 105 | 24 | 17 | 17 | 1 | 1 | 0 | 3 | 16 | 0 | 14 | 2 | 0 | 0 | 1 | .000 | 0 | 0-- | - | 6.44 | 7.29 |
| 2010 JhsCty | R | 7 | 5 | 0 | 0 | 32.2 | 128 | 28 | 12 | 7 | 3 | 0 | 0 | 4 | 6 | 0 | 31 | 1 | 0 | 4 | 3 | .571 | 0 | 0-- | - | 3.06 | 1.93 |
| 2011 QuadC | A | 9 | 8 | 0 | 1 | 54.2 | 213 | 38 | 12 | 7 | 1 | 1 | 0 | 0 | 15 | 0 | 34 | 4 | 0 | 8 | 1 | .889 | 0 | 0-- | - | 1.64 | 1.15 |
| 2011 PlmBh | A+ | 11 | 11 | 0 | 0 | 52.2 | 228 | 44 | 23 | 20 | 3 | 3 | 3 | 2 | 30 | 0 | 45 | 4 | 0 | 0 | 3 | .000 | 0 | 0-- | - | 3.68 | 3.42 |
| 2012 PlmBh | A+ | 10 | 10 | 0 | 0 | 55.1 | 222 | 33 | 18 | 14 | 3 | 0 | 3 | 6 | 22 | 0 | 41 | 1 | 1 | 6 | 0 | 1.000 | 0 | 0-- | - | 2.12 | 2.28 |
| 2012 Sprgfld | AA | 8 | 5 | 0 | 0 | 32.1 | 135 | 26 | 14 | 13 | 4 | 2 | 0 | 5 | 9 | 0 | 27 | 2 | 0 | 1 | 2 | .333 | 0 | 0-- | - | 3.29 | 3.62 |
| 2013 Sprgfld | AA | 13 | 0 | 0 | 3 | 20.0 | 74 | 8 | 5 | 5 | 2 | 0 | 0 | 1 | 7 | 0 | 35 | 1 | 0 | 1 | 1 | .500 | 0 | 1-- | - | 1.34 | 2.25 |
| 2013 Memp | AAA | 5 | 0 | 0 | 1 | 7.2 | 30 | 3 | 2 | 1 | 0 | 0 | 0 | 0 | 3 | 0 | 9 | 1 | 0 | 1 | 0 | 1.000 | 0 | 0-- | - | 0.89 | 1.17 |
| 2013 StL | NL | 45 | 0 | 0 | 15 | 39.2 | 152 | 17 | 2 | 2 | 1 | 0 | 0 | 1 | 18 | 1 | 50 | 0 | 0 | 3 | 1 | .750 | 0 | 0-0 | 11 | 1.27 | 0.45 |

## Moises Sierra

**Bats:** R **Throws:** R **Pos:** RF-29;DH-4;LF-2;PH-2 **Ht:** 6'0" **Wt:** 230 **Born:** 9/24/1988 **Age:** 25

| BATTING | | | | | | | | | | | | | | | | | | | | | BASERUNNING | | | | AVERAGES | | |
|---|---|---|---|---|---|---|---|---|---|---|---|---|---|---|---|---|---|---|---|---|---|---|---|---|---|---|---|
| Year Team | Lg | G | AB | H | 2B | 3B | HR | (Hm | Rd) | TB | R | RBI | RC | TBB | IBB | SO | HBP | SH | SF | SB | CS | SB% | GDP | Avg | OBP | Slg |
| 2009 Dnedin | A+ | 110 | 405 | 116 | 24 | 2 | 5 | (- | -) | 159 | 56 | 56 | 62 | 34 | 3 | 66 | 15 | 1 | 4 | 10 | 2 | .83 | 11 | .286 | .360 | .393 |
| 2009 NHam | AA | 8 | 34 | 12 | 1 | 0 | 1 | (- | -) | 16 | 1 | 6 | 5 | 1 | 0 | 8 | 0 | 0 | 1 | 0 | 1 | .00 | 2 | .353 | .361 | .471 |
| 2010 B Jays | R | 10 | 34 | 9 | 2 | 0 | 1 | (- | -) | 14 | 4 | 3 | 5 | 4 | 0 | 8 | 0 | 0 | 0 | 0 | 0 | - | 2 | .265 | .342 | .412 |
| 2010 Dnedin | A+ | 10 | 37 | 6 | 1 | 0 | 1 | (- | -) | 10 | 4 | 5 | 1 | 1 | 0 | 11 | 0 | 0 | 2 | 0 | 1 | .00 | 0 | .162 | .175 | .270 |
| 2011 NHam | AA | 133 | 495 | 137 | 19 | 3 | 18 | (- | -) | 216 | 81 | 67 | 74 | 39 | 2 | 93 | 12 | 1 | 4 | 16 | 14 | .53 | 12 | .277 | .342 | .436 |
| 2012 LsVgs | AAA | 100 | 377 | 109 | 16 | 1 | 17 | (- | -) | 178 | 62 | 63 | 64 | 39 | 2 | 86 | 4 | 0 | 2 | 7 | 6 | .54 | 12 | .289 | .360 | .472 |
| 2013 Buffalo | AAA | 100 | 379 | 99 | 18 | 5 | 11 | (- | -) | 160 | 57 | 51 | 51 | 16 | 0 | 106 | 12 | 1 | 4 | 12 | 4 | .75 | 8 | .261 | .309 | .422 |
| 2013 B Jays | R | 3 | 6 | 2 | 1 | 0 | 0 | (- | -) | 3 | 2 | 3 | 2 | 1 | 0 | 1 | 2 | 0 | 1 | 1 | 0 | 1.00 | 0 | .333 | .500 | .500 |
| 2012 Tor | AL | 49 | 147 | 33 | 4 | 0 | 6 | (3 | 3) | 55 | 14 | 15 | 10 | 8 | 0 | 44 | 2 | 0 | 0 | 1 | 0 | 1.00 | 3 | .224 | .274 | .374 |
| 2013 Tor | AL | 35 | 107 | 31 | 13 | 1 | 1 | (0 | 1) | 49 | 11 | 13 | 22 | 14 | 1 | 29 | 0 | 0 | 1 | 1 | 0 | 1.00 | 0 | .290 | .369 | .458 |
| 2 ML YEARS | | 84 | 254 | 64 | 17 | 1 | 7 | (3 | 4) | 104 | 25 | 28 | 32 | 22 | 1 | 73 | 2 | 0 | 1 | 2 | 0 | 1.00 | 3 | .252 | .315 | .409 |

## Andrelton Simmons

**Bats:** R **Throws:** R **Pos:** SS-156;PR-2;PH-1 ANN-drel-ton **Ht:** 6'2" **Wt:** 170 **Born:** 9/4/1989 **Age:** 24

| BATTING | | | | | | | | | | | | | | | | | | | | | BASERUNNING | | | | AVERAGES | | |
|---|---|---|---|---|---|---|---|---|---|---|---|---|---|---|---|---|---|---|---|---|---|---|---|---|---|---|---|
| Year Team | Lg | G | AB | H | 2B | 3B | HR | (Hm | Rd) | TB | R | RBI | RC | TBB | IBB | SO | HBP | SH | SF | SB | CS | SB% | GDP | Avg | OBP | Slg |
| 2010 Danvle | R | 62 | 239 | 66 | 11 | 1 | 2 | (- | -) | 85 | 36 | 26 | 33 | 16 | 0 | 14 | 9 | 1 | 4 | 18 | 4 | .82 | 3 | .276 | .340 | .356 |
| 2011 Lynbrg | A+ | 131 | 517 | 161 | 35 | 6 | 1 | (- | -) | 211 | 69 | 52 | 76 | 29 | 2 | 43 | 6 | 12 | 6 | 26 | 18 | .59 | 12 | .311 | .351 | .408 |
| 2012 Missi | AA | 44 | 174 | 51 | 9 | 2 | 3 | (- | -) | 73 | 29 | 21 | 30 | 20 | 1 | 20 | 3 | 4 | 2 | 10 | 2 | .83 | 4 | .293 | .372 | .420 |
| 2012 Atl | NL | 49 | 166 | 48 | 8 | 2 | 3 | (3 | 0) | 69 | 17 | 19 | 23 | 12 | 1 | 21 | 1 | 0 | 3 | 1 | 0 | 1.00 | 5 | .289 | .335 | .416 |
| 2013 Atl | NL | 157 | 606 | 150 | 27 | 6 | 17 | (5 | 12) | 240 | 76 | 59 | 60 | 40 | 1 | 55 | 3 | 5 | 4 | 6 | 5 | .55 | 16 | .248 | .296 | .396 |
| Postseason | | 1 | 4 | 1 | 0 | 0 | 0 | (0 | 0) | 1 | 0 | 0 | 0 | 0 | 0 | 0 | 0 | 0 | 0 | 0 | 0 | - | 0 | .250 | .250 | .250 |
| 2 ML YEARS | | 206 | 772 | 198 | 35 | 8 | 20 | (8 | 12) | 309 | 93 | 78 | 83 | 52 | 2 | 76 | 4 | 5 | 7 | 7 | 5 | .58 | 21 | .256 | .304 | .400 |

# Alfredo Simon

**Pitches:** R **Bats:** R **Pos:** RP-63 — si-MOHN — **Ht:** 6'6" **Wt:** 265 **Born:** 5/8/1981 **Age:** 33

| HOW MUCH HE PITCHED | | | | | | | | WHAT HE GAVE UP | | | | | | | | | | | | THE RESULTS | | | | | | | |
|---|---|---|---|---|---|---|---|---|---|---|---|---|---|---|---|---|---|---|---|---|---|---|---|---|---|---|---|
| Year Team | Lg | G | GS | CG | GF | IP | BFP | H | R | ER | HR | SH | SF | HB | TBB | IBB | SO | WP | Bk | W | L | Pct | Sh | Sv-Op | Hld | ERC | ERA |
| 2008 Bal | AL | 4 | 1 | 0 | 0 | 13.0 | 59 | 16 | 10 | 9 | 4 | 0 | 1 | 2 | 2 | 0 | 8 | 2 | 0 | 0 | 0 | - | 0 | 0-0 | 0 | 6.45 | 6.23 |
| 2009 Bal | AL | 2 | 2 | 0 | 0 | 6.1 | 28 | 8 | 7 | 7 | 5 | 0 | 0 | 0 | 2 | 0 | 3 | 0 | 0 | 0 | 1 | .000 | 0 | 0-0 | 0 | 10.74 | 9.95 |
| 2010 Bal | AL | 49 | 0 | 0 | 35 | 49.1 | 222 | 54 | 30 | 27 | 10 | 1 | 2 | 2 | 22 | 2 | 37 | 1 | 0 | 4 | 2 | .667 | 0 | 17-21 | 0 | 5.66 | 4.93 |
| 2011 Bal | AL | 23 | 16 | 0 | 1 | 115.2 | 499 | 128 | 69 | 63 | 15 | 1 | 4 | 4 | 40 | 6 | 83 | 2 | **2** | 4 | 9 | .308 | 0 | 0-0 | 0 | 4.83 | 4.90 |
| 2012 Cin | NL | 36 | 0 | 0 | 13 | 61.0 | 269 | 65 | 22 | 18 | 2 | 2 | 3 | 6 | 22 | 1 | 52 | 9 | 0 | 3 | 2 | .600 | 0 | 1-1 | 1 | 4.16 | 2.66 |
| 2013 Cin | NL | 63 | 0 | 0 | 20 | 87.2 | 359 | 68 | 31 | 28 | 8 | 5 | 2 | 8 | 26 | 2 | 63 | 4 | 0 | 6 | 4 | .600 | 0 | 1-3 | 6 | 2.75 | 2.87 |
| Postseason | | 1 | 0 | 0 | 1 | 1.0 | 5 | 1 | 0 | 0 | 0 | 0 | 0 | 0 | 1 | 0 | 1 | 0 | 0 | 0 | 0 | - | 0 | 0-0 | 0 | 5.48 | 0.00 |
| 6 ML YEARS | | 177 | 19 | 0 | 69 | 333.0 | 1436 | 339 | 169 | 152 | 44 | 9 | 12 | 22 | 114 | 11 | 246 | 18 | 2 | 17 | 18 | .486 | 0 | 19-25 | 7 | 4.41 | 4.11 |

# Tony Sipp

**Pitches:** L **Bats:** L **Pos:** RP-56 — **Ht:** 6'0" **Wt:** 190 **Born:** 7/12/1983 **Age:** 30

| HOW MUCH HE PITCHED | | | | | | | | WHAT HE GAVE UP | | | | | | | | | | | | THE RESULTS | | | | | | | |
|---|---|---|---|---|---|---|---|---|---|---|---|---|---|---|---|---|---|---|---|---|---|---|---|---|---|---|---|
| Year Team | Lg | G | GS | CG | GF | IP | BFP | H | R | ER | HR | SH | SF | HB | TBB | IBB | SO | WP | Bk | W | L | Pct | Sh | Sv-Op | Hld | ERC | ERA |
| 2013 Reno* | AAA | 9 | 0 | 0 | 1 | 10.0 | 40 | 3 | 1 | 0 | 0 | 1 | 0 | 0 | 5 | 0 | 12 | 1 | 0 | 1 | 0 | 1.000 | 0 | 1-- | - | 0.83 | 0.00 |
| 2009 Cle | AL | 46 | 0 | 0 | 8 | 40.0 | 168 | 27 | 16 | 13 | 5 | 3 | 1 | 0 | 25 | 2 | 48 | 3 | 0 | 2 | 0 | 1.000 | 0 | 0-0 | 9 | 3.29 | 2.93 |
| 2010 Cle | AL | 70 | 0 | 0 | 16 | 63.0 | 266 | 48 | 30 | 29 | 12 | 3 | 2 | 2 | 39 | 3 | 69 | 4 | 0 | 2 | 2 | .500 | 0 | 1-3 | 15 | 4.42 | 4.14 |
| 2011 Cle | AL | 69 | 0 | 0 | 17 | 62.1 | 251 | 45 | 22 | 21 | 10 | 1 | 2 | 0 | 24 | 3 | 57 | 2 | 1 | 6 | 3 | .667 | 0 | 0-1 | 24 | 2.87 | 3.03 |
| 2012 Cle | AL | 63 | 0 | 0 | 7 | 55.0 | 233 | 47 | 29 | 27 | 9 | 2 | 1 | 1 | 23 | 1 | 51 | 3 | 0 | 1 | 2 | .333 | 0 | 1-2 | 12 | 3.80 | 4.42 |
| 2013 Ari | NL | 56 | 0 | 0 | 11 | 37.2 | 175 | 35 | 22 | 20 | 6 | 3 | 1 | 3 | 22 | 2 | 42 | 3 | 1 | 3 | 2 | .600 | 0 | 0-2 | 3 | 4.90 | 4.78 |
| 5 ML YEARS | | 304 | 0 | 0 | 59 | 258.0 | 1093 | 202 | 119 | 110 | 42 | 12 | 7 | 6 | 133 | 11 | 267 | 15 | 2 | 14 | 9 | .609 | 0 | 2-8 | 63 | 3.79 | 3.84 |

# Scott Sizemore

**Bats:** R **Throws:** R **Pos:** 2B-2 — **Ht:** 6'0" **Wt:** 185 **Born:** 1/4/1985 **Age:** 29

| BATTING | | | | | | | | | | | | | | | | | | | | BASERUNNING | | | | AVERAGES | | |
|---|---|---|---|---|---|---|---|---|---|---|---|---|---|---|---|---|---|---|---|---|---|---|---|---|---|---|
| Year Team | Lg | G | AB | H | 2B | 3B | HR | (Hm | Rd) | TB | R | RBI | RC | TBB | IBB | SO | HBP | SH | SF | SB | CS | SB% | GDP | Avg | OBP | Slg |
| 2010 Det | AL | 48 | 143 | 32 | 7 | 0 | 3 | (1 | 2) | 48 | 19 | 14 | 13 | 15 | 0 | 40 | 0 | 4 | 1 | 0 | 0 | - | 4 | .224 | .296 | .336 |
| 2011 2 Tms | AL | 110 | 368 | 90 | 22 | 1 | 11 | (4 | 7) | 147 | 50 | 56 | 60 | 53 | 0 | 112 | 2 | 5 | 1 | 5 | 3 | .63 | 8 | .245 | .342 | .399 |
| 2013 Oak | AL | 2 | 6 | 1 | 1 | 0 | 0 | (0 | 0) | 2 | 0 | 0 | 0 | 0 | 0 | 2 | 0 | 0 | 0 | 0 | 0 | - | 0 | .167 | .167 | .333 |
| 11 Det | AL | 17 | 63 | 14 | 1 | 0 | 0 | (0 | 0) | 15 | 8 | 4 | 8 | 10 | 0 | 19 | 0 | 1 | 0 | 1 | 1 | .50 | 0 | .222 | .329 | .238 |
| 11 Oak | AL | 93 | 305 | 76 | 21 | 1 | 11 | (4 | 7) | 132 | 42 | 52 | 52 | 43 | 0 | 93 | 2 | 4 | 1 | 4 | 2 | .67 | 8 | .249 | .345 | .433 |
| 3 ML YEARS | | 160 | 517 | 123 | 30 | 1 | 14 | (5 | 9) | 197 | 69 | 70 | 73 | 68 | 0 | 154 | 2 | 9 | 2 | 5 | 3 | .63 | 12 | .238 | .328 | .381 |

# Tyler Skaggs

**Pitches:** L **Bats:** L **Pos:** SP-7 — **Ht:** 6'5" **Wt:** 215 **Born:** 7/13/1991 **Age:** 22

| HOW MUCH HE PITCHED | | | | | | | | WHAT HE GAVE UP | | | | | | | | | | | | THE RESULTS | | | | | | | |
|---|---|---|---|---|---|---|---|---|---|---|---|---|---|---|---|---|---|---|---|---|---|---|---|---|---|---|---|
| Year Team | Lg | G | GS | CG | GF | IP | BFP | H | R | ER | HR | SH | SF | HB | TBB | IBB | SO | WP | Bk | W | L | Pct | Sh | Sv-Op | Hld | ERC | ERA |
| 2009 Angels | R | 3 | 2 | 0 | 0 | 6.0 | 24 | 4 | 0 | 0 | 0 | 0 | 0 | 1 | 1 | 0 | 7 | 0 | 1 | 0 | 0 | - | 0 | 0-- | - | 1.57 | 0.00 |
| 2009 Orem | R+ | 2 | 0 | 0 | 0 | 4.0 | 19 | 5 | 4 | 2 | 0 | 0 | 0 | 0 | 1 | 0 | 6 | 0 | 0 | 0 | 0 | - | 0 | 0-- | - | 3.81 | 4.50 |
| 2010 CRpds | A | 19 | 14 | 0 | 3 | 82.1 | 341 | 78 | 35 | 33 | 6 | 7 | 0 | 4 | 21 | 1 | 82 | 1 | 1 | 8 | 4 | .667 | 0 | 0-- | - | 3.24 | 3.61 |
| 2010 Sbend | A | 4 | 4 | 0 | 0 | 16.0 | 62 | 13 | 3 | 3 | 1 | 0 | 0 | 0 | 4 | 0 | 20 | 1 | 0 | 1 | 1 | .500 | 0 | 0-- | - | 2.40 | 1.69 |
| 2011 Visalia | A+ | 17 | 17 | 0 | 0 | 100.2 | 413 | 81 | 39 | 36 | 6 | 1 | 3 | 5 | 34 | 0 | 125 | 4 | 1 | 5 | 5 | .500 | 0 | 0-- | - | 2.74 | 3.22 |
| 2011 Mobile | AA | 10 | 10 | 0 | 0 | 57.2 | 228 | 45 | 20 | 16 | 4 | 2 | 1 | 2 | 15 | 0 | 73 | 2 | 0 | 4 | 1 | .800 | 0 | 0-- | - | 2.39 | 2.50 |
| 2012 Mobile | AA | 13 | 13 | 0 | 0 | 69.2 | 290 | 63 | 27 | 22 | 8 | 5 | 2 | 1 | 21 | 1 | 71 | 8 | 1 | 5 | 4 | .556 | 0 | 0-- | - | 3.29 | 2.84 |
| 2012 Reno | AAA | 9 | 9 | 0 | 0 | 52.2 | 213 | 49 | 22 | 17 | 4 | 1 | 1 | 1 | 16 | 0 | 45 | 2 | 2 | 4 | 2 | .667 | 0 | 0-- | - | 3.36 | 2.91 |
| 2013 Reno | AAA | 19 | 17 | 0 | 0 | 104.0 | 466 | 114 | 62 | 53 | 5 | 5 | 2 | 6 | 39 | 0 | 107 | 3 | 2 | 6 | 10 | .375 | 0 | 0-- | - | 4.30 | 4.59 |
| 2013 Visalia | A+ | 1 | 1 | 0 | 0 | 5.2 | 30 | 5 | 4 | 3 | 0 | 0 | 0 | 1 | 8 | 0 | 8 | 0 | 0 | 0 | 0 | - | 0 | 0-- | - | 7.31 | 4.76 |
| 2012 Ari | NL | 6 | 6 | 0 | 0 | 29.1 | 133 | 30 | 20 | 19 | 6 | 1 | 0 | 2 | 13 | 0 | 21 | 1 | 0 | 1 | 3 | .250 | 0 | 0-0 | 0 | 5.31 | 5.83 |
| 2013 Ari | NL | 7 | 7 | 0 | 0 | 38.2 | 170 | 38 | 23 | 22 | 7 | 0 | 2 | 2 | 15 | 2 | 36 | 2 | 0 | 2 | 3 | .400 | 0 | 0-0 | 0 | 4.56 | 5.12 |
| 2 ML YEARS | | 13 | 13 | 0 | 0 | 68.0 | 303 | 68 | 43 | 41 | 13 | 1 | 2 | 4 | 28 | 2 | 57 | 3 | 0 | 3 | 6 | .333 | 0 | 0-0 | 0 | 4.88 | 5.43 |

# Kyle Skipworth

**Bats:** L **Throws:** R **Pos:** PH-4;C-1 — **Ht:** 6'4" **Wt:** 225 **Born:** 3/1/1990 **Age:** 24

| BATTING | | | | | | | | | | | | | | | | | | | | BASERUNNING | | | | AVERAGES | | |
|---|---|---|---|---|---|---|---|---|---|---|---|---|---|---|---|---|---|---|---|---|---|---|---|---|---|---|
| Year Team | Lg | G | AB | H | 2B | 3B | HR | (Hm | Rd) | TB | R | RBI | RC | TBB | IBB | SO | HBP | SH | SF | SB | CS | SB% | GDP | Avg | OBP | Slg |
| 2009 Grnsbr | A | 70 | 264 | 55 | 14 | 1 | 7 | (- | -) | 92 | 28 | 37 | 23 | 18 | 1 | 91 | 2 | 1 | 1 | 1 | 2 | .33 | 4 | .208 | .263 | .348 |
| 2010 Grnsbr | A | 107 | 397 | 99 | 17 | 1 | 17 | (- | -) | 169 | 55 | 59 | 53 | 32 | 3 | 132 | 5 | 0 | 2 | 1 | 2 | .33 | 11 | .249 | .312 | .426 |
| 2010 Jaxnvl | AA | 2 | 7 | 0 | 0 | 0 | 0 | (- | -) | 0 | 1 | 0 | 0 | 1 | 0 | 3 | 0 | 0 | 0 | 0 | 0 | - | 0 | .000 | .125 | .000 |
| 2011 Jaxnvl | AA | 106 | 396 | 82 | 12 | 2 | 11 | (- | -) | 131 | 35 | 49 | 34 | 34 | 5 | 143 | 2 | 1 | 1 | 0 | 4 | .00 | 10 | .207 | .273 | .331 |
| 2012 Jaxnvl | AA | 116 | 420 | 90 | 16 | 2 | 21 | (- | -) | 173 | 59 | 63 | 51 | 36 | 2 | 143 | 6 | 0 | 5 | 1 | 1 | .50 | 8 | .214 | .283 | .412 |
| 2013 NewOr | AAA | 73 | 239 | 45 | 13 | 2 | 11 | (- | -) | 95 | 22 | 30 | 23 | 12 | 0 | 82 | 5 | 0 | 1 | 0 | 0 | - | 1 | .188 | .241 | .397 |
| 2013 Mia | NL | 4 | 3 | 0 | 0 | 0 | 0 | (0 | 0) | 0 | 0 | 0 | 0 | 1 | 0 | 1 | 0 | 0 | 0 | 0 | 0 | - | 1 | .000 | .250 | .000 |

# Kevin Slowey

**Pitches:** R **Bats:** R **Pos:** SP-14; RP-6 — **Ht:** 6'2" **Wt:** 200 **Born:** 5/4/1984 **Age:** 30

| HOW MUCH HE PITCHED | | | | | | | | WHAT HE GAVE UP | | | | | | | | | | | | THE RESULTS | | | | | | | |
|---|---|---|---|---|---|---|---|---|---|---|---|---|---|---|---|---|---|---|---|---|---|---|---|---|---|---|---|
| Year Team | Lg | G | GS | CG | GF | IP | BFP | H | R | ER | HR | SH | SF | HB | TBB | IBB | SO | WP | Bk | W | L | Pct | Sh | Sv-Op | Hld | ERC | ERA |
| 2007 Min | AL | 13 | 11 | 0 | 0 | 66.2 | 297 | 82 | 39 | 35 | 16 | 0 | 1 | 0 | 11 | 0 | 47 | 3 | 0 | 4 | 1 | .800 | 0 | 0-0 | 0 | 5.22 | 4.73 |
| 2008 Min | AL | 27 | 27 | 3 | 0 | 160.1 | 653 | 161 | 74 | 71 | 22 | 1 | 5 | 4 | 24 | 1 | 123 | 1 | 0 | 12 | 11 | .522 | **2** | 0-0 | 0 | 3.48 | 3.99 |
| 2009 Min | AL | 16 | 16 | 0 | 0 | 90.2 | 394 | 113 | 50 | 49 | 15 | 3 | 5 | 5 | 15 | 1 | 75 | 3 | 0 | 10 | 3 | .769 | 0 | 0-0 | 0 | 5.25 | 4.86 |

| Year | Team | Lg | G | GS | CG | GF | IP | BFP | H | R | ER | HR | SH | SF | HB | TBB | IBB | SO | WP | Bk | W | L | Pct | Sh | Sv-Op | Hld | ERC | ERA |
|---|---|---|---|---|---|---|---|---|---|---|---|---|---|---|---|---|---|---|---|---|---|---|---|---|---|---|---|---|
| | | | HOW MUCH HE PITCHED | | | | | | WHAT HE GAVE UP | | | | | | | | | | | | THE RESULTS | | | | | | | |
| 2010 | Min | AL | 30 | 28 | 0 | 0 | 155.2 | 662 | 172 | 80 | 77 | 21 | 2 | **11** | 4 | 29 | 0 | 116 | 3 | 0 | 13 | 6 | .684 | 0 | 0-0 | 0 | 4.13 | 4.45 |
| 2011 | Min | AL | 14 | 8 | 0 | 1 | 59.1 | 258 | 78 | 44 | 44 | 10 | 3 | 4 | 3 | 5 | 0 | 34 | 0 | 0 | 0 | 8 | .000 | 0 | 0-0 | 0 | 5.31 | 6.67 |
| 2013 | Mia | NL | 20 | 14 | 0 | 2 | 92.0 | 395 | 106 | 44 | 42 | 12 | 3 | 6 | 4 | 18 | 0 | 76 | 1 | 0 | 3 | 6 | .333 | 0 | 0-0 | 0 | 4.51 | 4.11 |
| 6 ML YEARS | | | 120 | 104 | 3 | 3 | 624.2 | 2659 | 712 | 331 | 318 | 96 | 12 | 32 | 20 | 102 | 2 | 471 | 11 | 0 | 42 | 35 | .545 | 2 | 0-0 | 0 | 4.40 | 4.58 |

## Burch Smith

**Pitches:** R **Bats:** R **Pos:** SP-7; RP-3 — **Ht:** 6'4" **Wt:** 215 **Born:** 4/12/1990 **Age:** 24

| Year | Team | Lg | G | GS | CG | GF | IP | BFP | H | R | ER | HR | SH | SF | HB | TBB | IBB | SO | WP | Bk | W | L | Pct | Sh | Sv-Op | Hld | ERC | ERA |
|---|---|---|---|---|---|---|---|---|---|---|---|---|---|---|---|---|---|---|---|---|---|---|---|---|---|---|---|---|
| | | | HOW MUCH HE PITCHED | | | | | | WHAT HE GAVE UP | | | | | | | | | | | | THE RESULTS | | | | | | | |
| 2011 | Padres | R | 2 | 0 | 0 | 1 | 2.0 | 11 | 3 | 2 | 1 | 0 | 0 | 0 | 0 | 1 | 0 | 4 | 1 | 0 | 0 | 0 | - | 0 | 1-- | - | 5.84 | 4.50 |
| 2012 | Lk Els | A+ | 26 | 26 | 0 | 0 | 128.2 | 534 | 127 | 62 | 55 | 11 | 2 | 2 | 7 | 27 | 1 | 137 | 4 | 0 | 9 | 6 | .600 | 0 | 0-- | - | 3.39 | 3.85 |
| 2013 | SnAnt | AA | 6 | 6 | 0 | 0 | 31.1 | 118 | 17 | 8 | 4 | 1 | 0 | 0 | 2 | 6 | 0 | 37 | 1 | 0 | 1 | 2 | .333 | 0 | 0-- | - | 1.18 | 1.15 |
| 2013 | Tucsn | AAA | 12 | 12 | 0 | 0 | 61.0 | 247 | 56 | 24 | 23 | 4 | 0 | 1 | 1 | 17 | 0 | 65 | 3 | 0 | 5 | 1 | .833 | 0 | 0-- | - | 3.08 | 3.39 |
| 2013 | SD | NL | 10 | 7 | 0 | 3 | 36.1 | 167 | 39 | 26 | 26 | 9 | 1 | 0 | 0 | 21 | 1 | 46 | 0 | 0 | 1 | 3 | .250 | 0 | 0-0 | 0 | 6.27 | 6.44 |

## Joe Smith

**Pitches:** R **Bats:** R **Pos:** RP-70 — **Ht:** 6'2" **Wt:** 205 **Born:** 3/22/1984 **Age:** 30

| Year | Team | Lg | G | GS | CG | GF | IP | BFP | H | R | ER | HR | SH | SF | HB | TBB | IBB | SO | WP | Bk | W | L | Pct | Sh | Sv-Op | Hld | ERC | ERA |
|---|---|---|---|---|---|---|---|---|---|---|---|---|---|---|---|---|---|---|---|---|---|---|---|---|---|---|---|---|
| | | | HOW MUCH HE PITCHED | | | | | | WHAT HE GAVE UP | | | | | | | | | | | | THE RESULTS | | | | | | | |
| 2007 | NYM | NL | 54 | 0 | 0 | 14 | 44.1 | 205 | 48 | 18 | 17 | 3 | 2 | 0 | 7 | 21 | 4 | 45 | 2 | 0 | 3 | 2 | .600 | 0 | 0-0 | 10 | 5.04 | 3.45 |
| 2008 | NYM | NL | 82 | 0 | 0 | 12 | 63.1 | 271 | 51 | 28 | 25 | 4 | 4 | 0 | 4 | 31 | 4 | 52 | 1 | 0 | 6 | 3 | .667 | 0 | 0-3 | 18 | 3.23 | 3.55 |
| 2009 | Cle | AL | 37 | 0 | 0 | 5 | 34.0 | 142 | 30 | 16 | 13 | 4 | 1 | 1 | 0 | 13 | 0 | 30 | 2 | 0 | 0 | 0 | - | 0 | 0-1 | 10 | 3.49 | 3.44 |
| 2010 | Cle | AL | 53 | 0 | 0 | 7 | 40.0 | 170 | 30 | 18 | 17 | 4 | 1 | 0 | 1 | 24 | 2 | 32 | 0 | 1 | 2 | 2 | .500 | 0 | 0-1 | 17 | 3.53 | 3.83 |
| 2011 | Cle | AL | 71 | 0 | 0 | 13 | 67.0 | 267 | 52 | 16 | 15 | 1 | 2 | 2 | 2 | 21 | 1 | 45 | 2 | 0 | 3 | 3 | .500 | 0 | 0-3 | 16 | 2.19 | 2.01 |
| 2012 | Cle | AL | 72 | 0 | 0 | 12 | 67.0 | 278 | 53 | 27 | 22 | 4 | 1 | 1 | 2 | 25 | 4 | 53 | 1 | 1 | 7 | 4 | .636 | 0 | 0-3 | 21 | 2.60 | 2.96 |
| 2013 | Cle | AL | 70 | 0 | 0 | 20 | 63.0 | 259 | 54 | 17 | 16 | 5 | 3 | 0 | 3 | 23 | 2 | 54 | 3 | 0 | 6 | 2 | .750 | 0 | 3-8 | 25 | 3.23 | 2.29 |
| 7 ML YEARS | | | 439 | 0 | 0 | 83 | 378.2 | 1592 | 318 | 140 | 125 | 25 | 14 | 4 | 19 | 158 | 17 | 311 | 11 | 2 | 27 | 16 | .628 | 0 | 3-19 | 117 | 3.18 | 2.97 |

## Seth Smith

**Bats:** L **Throws:** L **Pos:** DH-53;LF-50;PH-15;RF-9;PR-1 — **Ht:** 6'3" **Wt:** 210 **Born:** 9/30/1982 **Age:** 31

| Year | Team | Lg | G | AB | H | 2B | 3B | HR | (Hm | Rd) | TB | R | RBI | RC | TBB | IBB | SO | HBP | SH | SF | SB | CS | SB% | GDP | Avg | OBP | Slg |
|---|---|---|---|---|---|---|---|---|---|---|---|---|---|---|---|---|---|---|---|---|---|---|---|---|---|---|---|
| | | | BATTING | | | | | | | | | | | | | | | | | | BASERUNNING | | | | AVERAGES | | |
| 2007 | Col | NL | 7 | 8 | 5 | 0 | 1 | 0 | (0 | 0) | 7 | 4 | 0 | 3 | 0 | 0 | 1 | 0 | 0 | 0 | 0 | 0 | - | 0 | .625 | .625 | .875 |
| 2008 | Col | NL | 67 | 108 | 28 | 7 | 0 | 4 | (2 | 2) | 47 | 13 | 15 | 18 | 15 | 0 | 23 | 0 | 0 | 0 | 1 | 0 | 1.00 | 0 | .259 | .350 | .435 |
| 2009 | Col | NL | 133 | 335 | 98 | 20 | 4 | 15 | (8 | 7) | 171 | 61 | 55 | 63 | 46 | 3 | 67 | 2 | 1 | 3 | 4 | 1 | .80 | 5 | .293 | .378 | .510 |
| 2010 | Col | NL | 133 | 358 | 88 | 19 | 5 | 17 | (12 | 5) | 168 | 55 | 52 | 51 | 35 | 1 | 67 | 2 | 0 | 3 | 2 | 1 | .67 | 5 | .246 | .314 | .469 |
| 2011 | Col | NL | 147 | 476 | 135 | 32 | 9 | 15 | (9 | 6) | 230 | 67 | 59 | 73 | 46 | 7 | 93 | 4 | 0 | 7 | 10 | 2 | .83 | 9 | .284 | .347 | .483 |
| 2012 | Oak | AL | 125 | 383 | 92 | 23 | 2 | 14 | (6 | 8) | 161 | 55 | 52 | 52 | 50 | 7 | 98 | 5 | 0 | 3 | 2 | 2 | .50 | 4 | .240 | .333 | .420 |
| 2013 | Oak | AL | 117 | 368 | 93 | 27 | 0 | 8 | (3 | 5) | 144 | 49 | 40 | 46 | 39 | 4 | 94 | 3 | 0 | 0 | 0 | 0 | - | 10 | .253 | .329 | .391 |
| Postseason | | | 14 | 26 | 6 | 2 | 0 | 1 | (1 | 0) | 11 | 5 | 5 | 5 | 4 | 1 | 8 | 1 | 0 | 0 | 0 | 0 | - | 0 | .231 | .355 | .423 |
| 7 ML YEARS | | | 729 | 2036 | 539 | 128 | 21 | 73 | (40 | 33) | 928 | 304 | 273 | 306 | 231 | 22 | 443 | 16 | 1 | 16 | 19 | 6 | .76 | 33 | .265 | .342 | .456 |

## Will Smith

**Pitches:** L **Bats:** R **Pos:** RP-18; SP-1 — **Ht:** 6'5" **Wt:** 250 **Born:** 7/10/1989 **Age:** 24

| Year | Team | Lg | G | GS | CG | GF | IP | BFP | H | R | ER | HR | SH | SF | HB | TBB | IBB | SO | WP | Bk | W | L | Pct | Sh | Sv-Op | Hld | ERC | ERA |
|---|---|---|---|---|---|---|---|---|---|---|---|---|---|---|---|---|---|---|---|---|---|---|---|---|---|---|---|---|
| | | | HOW MUCH HE PITCHED | | | | | | WHAT HE GAVE UP | | | | | | | | | | | | THE RESULTS | | | | | | | |
| 2009 | CRpds | A | 20 | 19 | 0 | 0 | 115.0 | 473 | 109 | 61 | 48 | 11 | 2 | 7 | 2 | 24 | 0 | 95 | 3 | 0 | 10 | 5 | .667 | 0 | 0-- | - | 3.08 | 3.76 |
| 2010 | RCuca | A+ | 6 | 6 | 0 | 0 | 37.1 | 156 | 36 | 23 | 19 | 4 | 3 | 1 | 0 | 13 | 0 | 31 | 1 | 0 | 2 | 2 | .500 | 0 | 0-- | - | 3.78 | 4.58 |
| 2010 | Salt Lk | AAA | 9 | 9 | 0 | 0 | 53.0 | 239 | 65 | 39 | 33 | 6 | 4 | 2 | 0 | 20 | 3 | 40 | 0 | 1 | 2 | 4 | .333 | 0 | 0-- | - | 5.28 | 5.60 |
| 2010 | Ark | AA | 4 | 4 | 0 | 0 | 18.2 | 96 | 33 | 16 | 15 | 3 | 3 | 0 | 1 | 9 | 0 | 8 | 2 | 0 | 1 | 2 | .333 | 0 | 0-- | - | 10.19 | 7.23 |
| 2010 | Wilmg | A+ | 8 | 8 | 0 | 0 | 54.2 | 213 | 48 | 20 | 17 | 6 | 1 | 1 | 1 | 4 | 0 | 51 | 1 | 0 | 4 | 1 | .800 | 0 | 0-- | - | 2.35 | 2.80 |
| 2011 | NWArk | AA | 27 | 27 | 2 | 0 | 161.1 | 678 | 171 | 78 | 69 | 13 | 6 | 7 | 6 | 45 | 2 | 108 | 4 | 0 | 13 | 9 | .591 | 1 | 0-- | - | 4.01 | 3.85 |
| 2012 | Omha | AAA | 15 | 15 | 0 | 0 | 89.2 | 388 | 104 | 44 | 36 | 8 | 3 | 2 | 2 | 22 | 0 | 74 | 1 | 0 | 4 | 4 | .500 | 0 | 0-- | - | 4.38 | 3.61 |
| 2013 | Omha | AAA | 28 | 10 | 0 | 9 | 89.0 | 362 | 81 | 32 | 30 | 7 | 1 | 1 | 3 | 24 | 0 | 100 | 4 | 0 | 6 | 4 | .600 | 0 | 4-- | - | 3.14 | 3.03 |
| 2012 | KC | AL | 16 | 16 | 0 | 0 | 89.2 | 396 | 111 | 54 | 53 | 12 | 2 | 5 | 1 | 33 | 1 | 59 | 4 | 0 | 6 | 9 | .400 | 0 | 0-0 | 0 | 5.75 | 5.32 |
| 2013 | KC | AL | 19 | 1 | 0 | 4 | 33.1 | 131 | 24 | 16 | 12 | 6 | 0 | 4 | 1 | 7 | 0 | 43 | 0 | 0 | 2 | 1 | .667 | 0 | 0-3 | 6 | 2.47 | 3.24 |
| 2 ML YEARS | | | 35 | 17 | 0 | 4 | 123.0 | 527 | 135 | 70 | 65 | 18 | 2 | 9 | 2 | 40 | 1 | 102 | 4 | 0 | 8 | 10 | .444 | 0 | 0-3 | 6 | 4.79 | 4.76 |

## Justin Smoak

**Bats:** B **Throws:** L **Pos:** 1B-125;DH-3;PH-3 — SMOKE — **Ht:** 6'4" **Wt:** 220 **Born:** 12/5/1986 **Age:** 27

| Year | Team | Lg | G | AB | H | 2B | 3B | HR | (Hm | Rd) | TB | R | RBI | RC | TBB | IBB | SO | HBP | SH | SF | SB | CS | SB% | GDP | Avg | OBP | Slg |
|---|---|---|---|---|---|---|---|---|---|---|---|---|---|---|---|---|---|---|---|---|---|---|---|---|---|---|---|
| | | | BATTING | | | | | | | | | | | | | | | | | | BASERUNNING | | | | AVERAGES | | |
| 2013 | Tacom* | AAA | 5 | 21 | 5 | 2 | 0 | 0 | (- | -) | 7 | 2 | 1 | 1 | 0 | 0 | 5 | 1 | 0 | 0 | 0 | 0 | - | 0 | .238 | .273 | .333 |
| 2010 | 2 Tms | AL | 100 | 348 | 76 | 14 | 0 | 13 | (4 | 9) | 129 | 40 | 48 | 42 | 46 | 4 | 91 | 0 | 0 | 3 | 1 | 0 | 1.00 | 9 | .218 | .307 | .371 |
| 2011 | Sea | AL | 123 | 427 | 100 | 24 | 0 | 15 | (10 | 5) | 169 | 38 | 55 | 55 | 55 | 4 | 105 | 3 | 0 | 4 | 0 | 0 | - | 10 | .234 | .323 | .396 |
| 2012 | Sea | AL | 132 | 483 | 105 | 14 | 0 | 19 | (4 | 15) | 176 | 49 | 51 | 50 | 49 | 2 | 111 | 1 | 0 | 2 | 1 | 0 | 1.00 | 12 | .217 | .290 | .364 |
| 2013 | Sea | AL | 131 | 454 | 108 | 19 | 0 | 20 | (9 | 11) | 187 | 53 | 50 | 60 | 64 | 1 | 119 | 2 | 0 | 1 | 0 | 0 | - | 11 | .238 | .334 | .412 |
| 10 | Tex | AL | 70 | 235 | 49 | 10 | 0 | 8 | (4 | 4) | 83 | 29 | 34 | 30 | 38 | 4 | 57 | 0 | 0 | 2 | 1 | 0 | 1.00 | 6 | .209 | .316 | .353 |
| 10 | Sea | AL | 30 | 113 | 27 | 4 | 0 | 5 | (0 | 5) | 46 | 11 | 14 | 12 | 8 | 0 | 34 | 0 | 0 | 1 | 0 | 0 | - | 3 | .239 | .287 | .407 |
| 4 ML YEARS | | | 486 | 1712 | 389 | 71 | 0 | 67 | (27 | 40) | 661 | 180 | 204 | 207 | 214 | 11 | 426 | 6 | 0 | 10 | 2 | 0 | 1.00 | 42 | .227 | .314 | .386 |

## Drew Smyly

**Pitches:** L **Bats:** L **Pos:** RP-63 SMILE-ee **Ht:** 6'3" **Wt:** 190 **Born:** 6/13/1989 **Age:** 25

| HOW MUCH HE PITCHED | | | | | | | | WHAT HE GAVE UP | | | | | | | | | | | | THE RESULTS | | | | | | | |
|---|---|---|---|---|---|---|---|---|---|---|---|---|---|---|---|---|---|---|---|---|---|---|---|---|---|---|---|
| Year Team | Lg | G | GS | CG | GF | IP | BFP | H | R | ER | HR | SH | SF | HB | TBB | IBB | SO | WP | Bk | W | L | Pct | Sh | Sv-Op | Hld | ERC | ERA |
| 2011 Lkland | A+ | 14 | 14 | 0 | 0 | 80.1 | 323 | 71 | 32 | 23 | 1 | 4 | 1 | 3 | 21 | 0 | 77 | 5 | 0 | 7 | 3 | .700 | 0 | 0- - | - | 2.58 | 2.58 |
| 2011 Erie | AA | 8 | 7 | 0 | 0 | 45.2 | 178 | 31 | 10 | 6 | 1 | 2 | 1 | 1 | 15 | 0 | 53 | 2 | 0 | 4 | 3 | .571 | 0 | 0- - | - | 1.84 | 1.18 |
| 2012 Toledo | AAA | 7 | 7 | 0 | 0 | 17.2 | 83 | 22 | 13 | 12 | 3 | 3 | 0 | 1 | 8 | 0 | 25 | 2 | 1 | 0 | 2 | .000 | 0 | 0- - | - | 6.47 | 6.11 |
| 2012 Det | AL | 23 | 18 | 0 | 0 | 99.1 | 416 | 93 | 49 | 44 | 12 | 2 | 3 | 2 | 33 | 1 | 94 | 3 | 0 | 4 | 3 | .571 | 0 | 0-0 | 1 | 3.68 | 3.99 |
| 2013 Det | AL | 63 | 0 | 0 | 9 | 76.0 | 303 | 62 | 20 | 20 | 4 | 0 | 1 | 1 | 17 | 1 | 81 | 5 | 0 | 6 | 0 | 1.000 | 0 | 2-6 | 21 | 2.21 | 2.37 |
| Postseason | | 4 | 0 | 0 | 1 | 4.0 | 16 | 2 | 1 | 1 | 0 | 0 | 0 | 0 | 3 | 1 | 4 | 0 | 0 | 1 | 0 | 1.000 | 0 | 0-0 | 0 | 1.80 | 2.25 |
| 2 ML YEARS | | 86 | 18 | 0 | 9 | 175.1 | 719 | 155 | 69 | 64 | 16 | 2 | 4 | 3 | 50 | 2 | 175 | 8 | 0 | 10 | 3 | .769 | 0 | 2-6 | 22 | 3.02 | 3.29 |

## Travis Snider

**Bats:** L **Throws:** L **Pos:** RF-79;PH-46;LF-5 **Ht:** 6'0" **Wt:** 235 **Born:** 2/2/1988 **Age:** 26

| BATTING | | | | | | | | | | | | | | | | | | | | BASERUNNING | | | | AVERAGES | | |
|---|---|---|---|---|---|---|---|---|---|---|---|---|---|---|---|---|---|---|---|---|---|---|---|---|---|---|
| Year Team | Lg | G | AB | H | 2B | 3B | HR | (Hm | Rd) | TB | R | RBI | RC | TBB | IBB | SO | HBP | SH | SF | SB | CS | SB% | GDP | Avg | OBP | Slg |
| 2013 Altna* | AA | 2 | 6 | 2 | 0 | 0 | 0 | (- | -) | 2 | 1 | 0 | 0 | 0 | 0 | 0 | 0 | 0 | 0 | 0 | 0 | - | 0 | .333 | .333 | .333 |
| 2013 Indy* | AAA | 8 | 32 | 11 | 1 | 0 | 0 | (- | -) | 12 | 4 | 5 | 5 | 5 | 0 | 8 | 0 | 0 | 1 | 1 | 1 | .50 | 0 | .344 | .421 | .375 |
| 2008 Tor | AL | 24 | 73 | 22 | 6 | 0 | 2 | (1 | 1) | 34 | 9 | 13 | 13 | 5 | 0 | 23 | 0 | 0 | 2 | 0 | 0 | - | 0 | .301 | .338 | .466 |
| 2009 Tor | AL | 77 | 241 | 58 | 14 | 1 | 9 | (5 | 4) | 101 | 34 | 29 | 30 | 29 | 1 | 78 | 3 | 2 | 1 | 1 | 1 | .50 | 5 | .241 | .328 | .419 |
| 2010 Tor | AL | 82 | 298 | 76 | 20 | 0 | 14 | (9 | 5) | 138 | 36 | 32 | 40 | 21 | 2 | 79 | 0 | 0 | 0 | 6 | 3 | .67 | 3 | .255 | .304 | .463 |
| 2011 Tor | AL | 49 | 187 | 42 | 14 | 0 | 3 | (2 | 1) | 65 | 23 | 30 | 21 | 11 | 1 | 56 | 1 | 1 | 2 | 9 | 3 | .75 | 5 | .225 | .269 | .348 |
| 2012 2 Tms | | 60 | 164 | 41 | 7 | 1 | 4 | (3 | 1) | 62 | 23 | 17 | 21 | 17 | 0 | 48 | 1 | 0 | 3 | 2 | 0 | 1.00 | 2 | .250 | .319 | .378 |
| 2013 Pit | NL | 111 | 261 | 56 | 12 | 2 | 5 | (4 | 1) | 87 | 28 | 25 | 23 | 24 | 3 | 75 | 0 | 0 | 0 | 2 | 3 | .40 | 1 | .215 | .281 | .333 |
| 12 Tor | AL | 10 | 36 | 9 | 2 | 0 | 3 | (2 | 1) | 20 | 6 | 8 | 7 | 3 | 0 | 14 | 0 | 0 | 1 | 0 | 0 | - | 0 | .250 | .300 | .556 |
| 12 Pit | NL | 50 | 128 | 32 | 5 | 1 | 1 | (1 | 0) | 42 | 17 | 9 | 14 | 14 | 0 | 34 | 1 | 0 | 2 | 2 | 0 | 1.00 | 2 | .250 | .324 | .328 |
| 6 ML YEARS | | 403 | 1224 | 295 | 73 | 4 | 37 | (24 | 13) | 487 | 153 | 146 | 148 | 107 | 7 | 359 | 5 | 3 | 8 | 20 | 10 | .67 | 16 | .241 | .303 | .398 |

## Brandon Snyder

**Bats:** R **Throws:** R **Pos:** 3B-17;1B-6;PH-6;PR-5;DH-3;LF-1 **Ht:** 6'2" **Wt:** 225 **Born:** 11/23/1986 **Age:** 27

| BATTING | | | | | | | | | | | | | | | | | | | | BASERUNNING | | | | AVERAGES | | |
|---|---|---|---|---|---|---|---|---|---|---|---|---|---|---|---|---|---|---|---|---|---|---|---|---|---|---|
| Year Team | Lg | G | AB | H | 2B | 3B | HR | (Hm | Rd) | TB | R | RBI | RC | TBB | IBB | SO | HBP | SH | SF | SB | CS | SB% | GDP | Avg | OBP | Slg |
| 2013 Pwtckt* | AAA | 68 | 249 | 65 | 16 | 1 | 10 | (- | -) | 113 | 37 | 37 | 38 | 20 | 2 | 69 | 7 | 0 | 1 | 3 | 1 | .75 | 7 | .261 | .332 | .454 |
| 2010 Bal | AL | 10 | 20 | 6 | 2 | 0 | 0 | (0 | 0) | 8 | 1 | 3 | 3 | 0 | 0 | 3 | 0 | 0 | 0 | 0 | 1 | .00 | 0 | .300 | .300 | .400 |
| 2011 Bal | AL | 6 | 13 | 3 | 1 | 0 | 0 | (0 | 0) | 4 | 2 | 1 | 1 | 3 | 0 | 4 | 1 | 0 | 0 | 0 | 0 | - | 0 | .231 | .412 | .308 |
| 2012 Tex | AL | 40 | 65 | 18 | 2 | 0 | 3 | (1 | 2) | 29 | 11 | 9 | 7 | 3 | 0 | 26 | 0 | 1 | 0 | 0 | 0 | - | 1 | .277 | .309 | .446 |
| 2013 Bos | AL | 27 | 50 | 9 | 3 | 0 | 2 | (2 | 0) | 18 | 5 | 7 | 1 | 0 | 0 | 16 | 2 | 0 | 0 | 0 | 0 | - | 0 | .180 | .212 | .360 |
| 4 ML YEARS | | 83 | 148 | 36 | 8 | 0 | 5 | (3 | 2) | 59 | 19 | 20 | 12 | 6 | 0 | 49 | 3 | 1 | 0 | 0 | 1 | .00 | 1 | .243 | .287 | .399 |

## Chris Snyder

**Bats:** R **Throws:** R **Pos:** C-8;PH-1 **Ht:** 6'4" **Wt:** 235 **Born:** 2/12/1981 **Age:** 33

| BATTING | | | | | | | | | | | | | | | | | | | | BASERUNNING | | | | AVERAGES | | |
|---|---|---|---|---|---|---|---|---|---|---|---|---|---|---|---|---|---|---|---|---|---|---|---|---|---|---|
| Year Team | Lg | G | AB | H | 2B | 3B | HR | (Hm | Rd) | TB | R | RBI | RC | TBB | IBB | SO | HBP | SH | SF | SB | CS | SB% | GDP | Avg | OBP | Slg |
| 2013 Salt Lk* | AAA | 21 | 79 | 27 | 6 | 0 | 7 | (- | -) | 54 | 14 | 21 | 19 | 6 | 0 | 22 | 0 | 1 | 0 | 0 | 1 | .00 | 1 | .342 | .388 | .684 |
| 2013 Norfolk* | AAA | 52 | 180 | 44 | 8 | 0 | 6 | (- | -) | 70 | 16 | 24 | 22 | 17 | 0 | 46 | 0 | 0 | 2 | 0 | 0 | - | 6 | .244 | .307 | .389 |
| 2004 Ari | NL | 29 | 96 | 23 | 6 | 0 | 5 | (1 | 4) | 44 | 10 | 15 | 11 | 13 | 1 | 25 | 0 | 0 | 1 | 0 | 0 | - | 0 | .240 | .327 | .458 |
| 2005 Ari | NL | 115 | 326 | 66 | 14 | 0 | 6 | (2 | 4) | 98 | 24 | 28 | 25 | 40 | 5 | 87 | 4 | 3 | 0 | 0 | 1 | .00 | 6 | .202 | .297 | .301 |
| 2006 Ari | NL | 61 | 184 | 51 | 9 | 0 | 6 | (4 | 2) | 78 | 19 | 32 | 27 | 22 | 4 | 39 | 1 | 1 | 5 | 0 | 0 | - | 5 | .277 | .349 | .424 |
| 2007 Ari | NL | 110 | 326 | 82 | 20 | 0 | 13 | (4 | 9) | 141 | 37 | 47 | 48 | 40 | 3 | 67 | 7 | 3 | 4 | 0 | 1 | .00 | 9 | .252 | .342 | .433 |
| 2008 Ari | NL | 115 | 334 | 79 | 22 | 1 | 16 | (6 | 10) | 151 | 47 | 64 | 53 | 56 | 5 | 101 | 4 | 5 | 5 | 0 | 0 | - | 7 | .237 | .348 | .452 |
| 2009 Ari | NL | 61 | 165 | 33 | 7 | 0 | 6 | (3 | 3) | 58 | 20 | 22 | 17 | 32 | 4 | 47 | 2 | 1 | 2 | 0 | 0 | - | 5 | .200 | .333 | .352 |
| 2010 2 Tms | NL | 105 | 319 | 66 | 9 | 0 | 15 | (6 | 9) | 120 | 34 | 48 | 38 | 52 | 10 | 94 | 2 | 1 | 2 | 0 | 0 | - | 11 | .207 | .320 | .376 |
| 2011 Pit | NL | 34 | 96 | 26 | 3 | 0 | 3 | (0 | 3) | 38 | 13 | 17 | 17 | 17 | 0 | 23 | 1 | 2 | 3 | 0 | 1 | .00 | 2 | .271 | .376 | .396 |
| 2012 Hou | NL | 76 | 221 | 39 | 8 | 0 | 7 | (3 | 4) | 68 | 23 | 24 | 21 | 33 | 4 | 70 | 4 | 0 | 0 | 0 | 0 | - | 5 | .176 | .295 | .308 |
| 2013 Bal | AL | 9 | 20 | 2 | 0 | 0 | 0 | (0 | 0) | 2 | 0 | 1 | 1 | 4 | 0 | 7 | 0 | 0 | 0 | 0 | 0 | - | 0 | .100 | .250 | .100 |
| 10 Ari | NL | 65 | 195 | 45 | 8 | 0 | 10 | (5 | 5) | 83 | 22 | 32 | 30 | 36 | 6 | 61 | 1 | 1 | 1 | 0 | 0 | - | 5 | .231 | .352 | .426 |
| 10 Pit | NL | 40 | 124 | 21 | 1 | 0 | 5 | (1 | 4) | 37 | 12 | 16 | 8 | 16 | 4 | 33 | 1 | 0 | 1 | 0 | 0 | - | 6 | .169 | .268 | .298 |
| Postseason | | 6 | 19 | 5 | 2 | 0 | 1 | (0 | 1) | 10 | 3 | 3 | 2 | 2 | 0 | 6 | 0 | 0 | 0 | 0 | 0 | - | 3 | .263 | .333 | .526 |
| 10 ML YEARS | | 715 | 2087 | 467 | 98 | 1 | 77 | (29 | 48) | 798 | 227 | 298 | 258 | 309 | 36 | 560 | 25 | 16 | 22 | 0 | 3 | .00 | 50 | .224 | .328 | .382 |

## Eric Sogard

**Bats:** L **Throws:** R **Pos:** 2B-113;SS-15;PH-8;PR-2 SO-guard **Ht:** 5'10" **Wt:** 190 **Born:** 5/22/1986 **Age:** 28

| BATTING | | | | | | | | | | | | | | | | | | | | BASERUNNING | | | | AVERAGES | | |
|---|---|---|---|---|---|---|---|---|---|---|---|---|---|---|---|---|---|---|---|---|---|---|---|---|---|---|
| Year Team | Lg | G | AB | H | 2B | 3B | HR | (Hm | Rd) | TB | R | RBI | RC | TBB | IBB | SO | HBP | SH | SF | SB | CS | SB% | GDP | Avg | OBP | Slg |
| 2010 Oak | AL | 4 | 7 | 3 | 0 | 0 | 0 | (0 | 0) | 3 | 0 | 0 | 1 | 2 | 0 | 1 | 0 | 0 | 0 | 0 | 1 | .00 | 0 | .429 | .556 | .429 |
| 2011 Oak | AL | 27 | 70 | 14 | 3 | 0 | 2 | (0 | 2) | 23 | 7 | 4 | 3 | 4 | 0 | 13 | 0 | 0 | 0 | 0 | 0 | - | 2 | .200 | .243 | .329 |
| 2012 Oak | AL | 37 | 102 | 17 | 3 | 1 | 2 | (0 | 2) | 28 | 8 | 7 | 7 | 5 | 0 | 17 | 0 | 1 | 0 | 2 | 0 | 1.00 | 1 | .167 | .206 | .275 |
| 2013 Oak | AL | 130 | 368 | 98 | 24 | 3 | 2 | (0 | 2) | 134 | 45 | 35 | 43 | 27 | 2 | 51 | 5 | 6 | 4 | 10 | 5 | .67 | 4 | .266 | .322 | .364 |
| 4 ML YEARS | | 198 | 547 | 132 | 30 | 4 | 6 | (0 | 6) | 188 | 60 | 46 | 54 | 38 | 2 | 82 | 5 | 7 | 4 | 12 | 6 | .67 | 7 | .241 | .295 | .344 |

# Donovan Solano

**Bats:** R **Throws:** R **Pos:** 2B-93;PH-7;3B-2 sol-ON-oh **Ht:** 5'9" **Wt:** 195 **Born:** 12/17/1987 **Age:** 26

| BATTING | | | | | | | | | | | | | | | | | | | | | | BASERUNNING | | | | AVERAGES | | |
|---|---|---|---|---|---|---|---|---|---|---|---|---|---|---|---|---|---|---|---|---|---|---|---|---|---|---|---|---|
| Year | Team | Lg | G | AB | H | 2B | 3B | HR | (Hm | Rd) | TB | R | RBI | RC | TBB | IBB | SO | HBP | SH | SF | SB | CS | SB% | GDP | Avg | OBP | Slg |
| 2009 | Sprgfld | AA | 64 | 251 | 52 | 7 | 1 | 1 | (- | -) | 64 | 27 | 16 | 17 | 21 | 0 | 39 | 1 | 3 | 0 | 1 | 0 | 1.00 | 8 | .207 | .271 | .255 |
| 2009 | Memp | AAA | 52 | 164 | 52 | 7 | 0 | 0 | (- | -) | 59 | 22 | 14 | 23 | 10 | 0 | 27 | 2 | 2 | 0 | 3 | 0 | 1.00 | 0 | .317 | .364 | .360 |
| 2010 | Memp | AAA | 102 | 330 | 84 | 12 | 1 | 4 | (- | -) | 110 | 41 | 27 | 31 | 11 | 1 | 35 | 2 | 1 | 0 | 2 | 1 | .67 | 9 | .255 | .283 | .333 |
| 2011 | Memp | AAA | 81 | 229 | 65 | 21 | 1 | 1 | (- | -) | 91 | 22 | 23 | 33 | 19 | 0 | 35 | 1 | 5 | 4 | 2 | 0 | 1.00 | 6 | .284 | .336 | .397 |
| 2011 | Sprgfld | AA | 27 | 101 | 23 | 7 | 0 | 2 | (- | -) | 36 | 5 | 10 | 8 | 3 | 0 | 16 | 0 | 0 | 0 | 0 | 0 | - | 3 | .228 | .250 | .356 |
| 2012 | NewOr | AAA | 36 | 141 | 37 | 7 | 1 | 0 | (- | -) | 46 | 14 | 14 | 17 | 10 | 0 | 27 | 4 | 4 | 1 | 4 | 0 | 1.00 | 3 | .262 | .327 | .326 |
| 2013 | Jupiter | A+ | 4 | 14 | 6 | 1 | 0 | 0 | (- | -) | 7 | 0 | 1 | 2 | 0 | 0 | 2 | 0 | 0 | 0 | 0 | 0 | - | 0 | .429 | .429 | .500 |
| 2013 | NewOr | AAA | 17 | 66 | 25 | 3 | 1 | 2 | (- | -) | 36 | 8 | 9 | 14 | 4 | 0 | 11 | 1 | 0 | 2 | 0 | 0 | - | 3 | .379 | .411 | .545 |
| 2012 | Mia | NL | 93 | 285 | 84 | 11 | 3 | 2 | (0 | 2) | 107 | 29 | 28 | 35 | 21 | 1 | 58 | 2 | 3 | 5 | 7 | 0 | 1.00 | 5 | .295 | .342 | .375 |
| 2013 | Mia | NL | 102 | 361 | 90 | 13 | 1 | 3 | (0 | 3) | 114 | 33 | 34 | 38 | 23 | 3 | 57 | 7 | 2 | 2 | 3 | 1 | .75 | 11 | .249 | .305 | .316 |
| 2 ML YEARS | | | 195 | 646 | 174 | 24 | 4 | 5 | (0 | 5) | 221 | 62 | 62 | 73 | 44 | 4 | 115 | 9 | 5 | 7 | 10 | 1 | .91 | 16 | .269 | .322 | .342 |

# Jhonatan Solano

**Bats:** R **Throws:** R **Pos:** C-19;PH-5 JOHN-uh-tun sol-ON-oh **Ht:** 5'9" **Wt:** 205 **Born:** 8/12/1985 **Age:** 28

| BATTING | | | | | | | | | | | | | | | | | | | | | | BASERUNNING | | | | AVERAGES | | |
|---|---|---|---|---|---|---|---|---|---|---|---|---|---|---|---|---|---|---|---|---|---|---|---|---|---|---|---|---|
| Year | Team | Lg | G | AB | H | 2B | 3B | HR | (Hm | Rd) | TB | R | RBI | RC | TBB | IBB | SO | HBP | SH | SF | SB | CS | SB% | GDP | Avg | OBP | Slg |
| 2009 | Hrsbrg | AA | 26 | 93 | 26 | 6 | 0 | 1 | (- | -) | 35 | 7 | 11 | 10 | 2 | 0 | 16 | 0 | 0 | 0 | 0 | 0 | - | 5 | .280 | .295 | .376 |
| 2009 | Syrcse | AAA | 63 | 183 | 37 | 11 | 0 | 1 | (- | -) | 51 | 17 | 17 | 12 | 9 | 0 | 24 | 1 | 2 | 4 | 2 | 1 | .67 | 10 | .202 | .239 | .279 |
| 2010 | Hrsbrg | AA | 90 | 317 | 80 | 15 | 0 | 6 | (- | -) | 113 | 28 | 42 | 35 | 21 | 1 | 29 | 3 | 1 | 3 | 1 | 1 | .50 | 9 | .252 | .302 | .356 |
| 2011 | Syrcse | AAA | 78 | 255 | 70 | 14 | 0 | 5 | (- | -) | 99 | 27 | 33 | 33 | 19 | 1 | 36 | 1 | 2 | 2 | 1 | 1 | .50 | 11 | .275 | .325 | .388 |
| 2012 | Syrcse | AAA | 13 | 52 | 13 | 2 | 0 | 0 | (- | -) | 15 | 8 | 2 | 4 | 3 | 0 | 6 | 1 | 0 | 1 | 0 | 0 | - | 1 | .250 | .298 | .288 |
| 2012 | Nats | R | 2 | 3 | 1 | 1 | 0 | 0 | (- | -) | 2 | 1 | 1 | 0 | 0 | 0 | 0 | 0 | 0 | 1 | 0 | 0 | - | 0 | .333 | .250 | .667 |
| 2012 | Hrsbrg | AA | 11 | 41 | 8 | 1 | 0 | 1 | (- | -) | 12 | 4 | 7 | 2 | 0 | 0 | 12 | 1 | 0 | 1 | 0 | 0 | - | 1 | .195 | .209 | .293 |
| 2013 | Syrcse | AAA | 40 | 140 | 30 | 7 | 1 | 0 | (- | -) | 39 | 9 | 10 | 9 | 5 | 1 | 17 | 1 | 1 | 1 | 0 | 0 | - | 3 | .214 | .245 | .279 |
| 2012 | Was | NL | 12 | 35 | 11 | 3 | 0 | 2 | (1 | 1) | 20 | 6 | 6 | 6 | 2 | 1 | 5 | 0 | 0 | 0 | 1 | 0 | 1.00 | 0 | .314 | .351 | .571 |
| 2013 | Was | NL | 24 | 48 | 7 | 2 | 0 | 0 | (0 | 0) | 9 | 2 | 2 | 0 | 2 | 0 | 7 | 0 | 0 | 0 | 0 | 1 | .00 | 4 | .146 | .180 | .188 |
| 2 ML YEARS | | | 36 | 83 | 18 | 5 | 0 | 2 | (1 | 1) | 29 | 8 | 8 | 6 | 4 | 1 | 12 | 0 | 0 | 0 | 1 | 1 | .50 | 4 | .217 | .253 | .349 |

# Joakim Soria

**Pitches:** R **Bats:** R **Pos:** RP-26 wah-KEEM SORE-ee-uh **Ht:** 6'3" **Wt:** 200 **Born:** 5/18/1984 **Age:** 30

| HOW MUCH HE PITCHED | | | | | | | | | WHAT HE GAVE UP | | | | | | | | | | | | | THE RESULTS | | | | | | | | |
|---|---|---|---|---|---|---|---|---|---|---|---|---|---|---|---|---|---|---|---|---|---|---|---|---|---|---|---|---|---|---|
| Year | Team | Lg | G | GS | CG | GF | IP | BFP | H | R | ER | HR | SH | SF | HB | TBB | IBB | SO | WP | Bk | W | L | Pct | Sh | Sv-Op | Hld | ERC | ERA |
| 2013 | Frisco* | AA | 4 | 0 | 0 | 0 | 4.0 | 12 | 0 | 0 | 0 | 0 | 0 | 0 | 0 | 0 | 0 | 4 | 0 | 0 | 0 | 0 | - | 0 | 0- - | - | 0.00 | 0.00 |
| 2013 | Rngrs* | R | 1 | 1 | 0 | 0 | 1.0 | 3 | 0 | 0 | 0 | 0 | 0 | 0 | 0 | 0 | 0 | 1 | 0 | 0 | 0 | 0 | - | 0 | 0- - | - | 0.00 | 0.00 |
| 2013 | RdRck* | AAA | 2 | 0 | 0 | 0 | 2.0 | 7 | 1 | 0 | 0 | 0 | 0 | 0 | 0 | 0 | 0 | 3 | 0 | 0 | 0 | 0 | - | 0 | 0- - | - | 0.54 | 0.00 |
| 2007 | KC | AL | 62 | 0 | 0 | 38 | 69.0 | 270 | 46 | 20 | 19 | 3 | 1 | 3 | 1 | 19 | 3 | 75 | 2 | 0 | 2 | 3 | .400 | 0 | 17-21 | 9 | 1.63 | 2.48 |
| 2008 | KC | AL | 63 | 0 | 0 | 57 | 67.1 | 260 | 39 | 13 | 12 | 5 | 2 | 2 | 6 | 19 | 1 | 66 | 1 | 1 | 2 | 3 | .400 | 0 | 42-45 | 0 | 1.72 | 1.60 |
| 2009 | KC | AL | 47 | 0 | 0 | 41 | 53.0 | 222 | 44 | 14 | 13 | 5 | 1 | 2 | 2 | 16 | 1 | 69 | 3 | 0 | 3 | 2 | .600 | 0 | 30-33 | 0 | 2.80 | 2.21 |
| 2010 | KC | AL | 66 | 0 | 0 | 56 | 65.2 | 270 | 53 | 13 | 13 | 4 | 3 | 4 | 2 | 16 | 1 | 71 | 3 | 1 | 1 | 2 | .333 | 0 | 43-46 | 0 | 2.27 | 1.78 |
| 2011 | KC | AL | 60 | 0 | 0 | 47 | 60.1 | 256 | 60 | 29 | 27 | 7 | 3 | 2 | 2 | 17 | 0 | 60 | 1 | 0 | 5 | 5 | .500 | 0 | 28-35 | 0 | 3.80 | 4.03 |
| 2013 | Tex | AL | 26 | 0 | 0 | 9 | 23.2 | 101 | 18 | 10 | 10 | 2 | 1 | 0 | 1 | 14 | 2 | 28 | 2 | 0 | 1 | 0 | 1.000 | 0 | 0-0 | 6 | 3.45 | 3.80 |
| 6 ML YEARS | | | 324 | 0 | 0 | 248 | 339.0 | 1379 | 260 | 99 | 94 | 26 | 11 | 13 | 14 | 101 | 8 | 369 | 12 | 2 | 14 | 15 | .483 | 0 | 160-180 | 15 | 2.43 | 2.50 |

# Alfonso Soriano

**Bats:** R **Throws:** R **Pos:** LF-134;DH-13;PH-4 **Ht:** 6'1" **Wt:** 195 **Born:** 1/7/1976 **Age:** 38

| BATTING | | | | | | | | | | | | | | | | | | | | | | BASERUNNING | | | | AVERAGES | | |
|---|---|---|---|---|---|---|---|---|---|---|---|---|---|---|---|---|---|---|---|---|---|---|---|---|---|---|---|---|
| Year | Team | Lg | G | AB | H | 2B | 3B | HR | (Hm | Rd) | TB | R | RBI | RC | TBB | IBB | SO | HBP | SH | SF | SB | CS | SB% | GDP | Avg | OBP | Slg |
| 1999 | NYY | AL | 9 | 8 | 1 | 0 | 0 | 1 | (1 | 0) | 4 | 2 | 1 | 0 | 0 | 0 | 3 | 0 | 0 | 0 | 0 | 1 | .00 | 0 | .125 | .125 | .500 |
| 2000 | NYY | AL | 22 | 50 | 9 | 3 | 0 | 2 | (0 | 2) | 18 | 5 | 3 | 4 | 1 | 0 | 15 | 0 | 2 | 0 | 2 | 0 | 1.00 | 0 | .180 | .196 | .360 |
| 2001 | NYY | AL | 158 | 574 | 154 | 34 | 3 | 18 | (8 | 10) | 248 | 77 | 73 | 77 | 29 | 0 | 125 | 3 | 3 | 5 | 43 | 14 | .75 | 7 | .268 | .304 | .432 |
| 2002 | NYY | AL | 156 | **696** | **209** | 51 | 2 | 39 | (17 | 22) | 381 | **128** | 102 | 121 | 23 | 1 | 157 | 14 | 1 | 7 | **41** | 13 | .76 | 8 | .300 | .332 | .547 |
| 2003 | NYY | AL | 156 | **682** | 198 | 36 | 5 | 38 | (15 | 23) | 358 | 114 | 91 | 110 | 38 | 7 | 130 | 12 | 0 | 2 | 35 | 8 | .81 | 8 | .290 | .338 | .525 |
| 2004 | Tex | AL | 145 | 608 | 170 | 32 | 4 | 28 | (12 | 16) | 294 | 77 | 91 | 90 | 33 | 4 | 121 | 10 | 0 | 7 | 18 | 5 | .78 | 7 | .280 | .324 | .484 |
| 2005 | Tex | AL | 156 | 637 | 171 | 43 | 2 | 36 | (25 | 11) | 326 | 102 | 104 | 93 | 33 | 3 | 125 | 7 | 0 | 5 | 30 | 2 | **.94** | 6 | .268 | .309 | .512 |
| 2006 | Was | NL | 159 | 647 | 179 | 41 | 2 | 46 | (24 | 22) | 362 | 119 | 95 | 114 | 67 | 16 | 160 | 9 | 2 | 3 | 41 | 17 | .71 | 3 | .277 | .351 | .560 |
| 2007 | ChC | NL | 135 | 579 | 173 | 42 | 5 | 33 | (13 | 20) | 324 | 97 | 70 | 91 | 31 | 4 | 130 | 4 | 0 | 3 | 19 | 6 | .76 | 9 | .299 | .337 | .560 |
| 2008 | ChC | NL | 109 | 453 | 127 | 27 | 0 | 29 | (17 | 12) | 241 | 76 | 75 | 77 | 43 | 11 | 103 | 3 | 0 | 4 | 19 | 3 | .86 | 9 | .280 | .344 | .532 |
| 2009 | ChC | NL | 117 | 477 | 115 | 25 | 1 | 20 | (7 | 13) | 202 | 64 | 55 | 61 | 40 | 6 | 118 | 3 | 0 | 2 | 9 | 2 | .82 | 7 | .241 | .303 | .423 |
| 2010 | ChC | NL | 147 | 496 | 128 | 40 | 3 | 24 | (11 | 13) | 246 | 67 | 79 | 75 | 45 | 3 | 123 | 3 | 1 | 3 | 5 | 1 | .83 | 12 | .258 | .322 | .496 |
| 2011 | ChC | NL | 137 | 475 | 116 | 27 | 1 | 26 | (12 | 14) | 223 | 50 | 88 | 59 | 27 | 4 | 113 | 4 | 0 | 2 | 2 | 1 | .67 | 15 | .244 | .289 | .469 |
| 2012 | ChC | NL | 151 | 561 | 147 | 33 | 2 | 32 | (15 | 17) | 280 | 68 | 108 | 89 | 44 | 5 | 153 | 7 | 0 | 3 | 6 | 2 | .75 | 18 | .262 | .322 | .499 |
| 2013 | 2 Tms | | 151 | 581 | 148 | 32 | 1 | 34 | (22 | 12) | 284 | 84 | 101 | 90 | 36 | 3 | 156 | 5 | 0 | 4 | 18 | 9 | .67 | 11 | .255 | .302 | .489 |
| 13 | ChC | NL | 93 | 362 | 92 | 24 | 1 | 17 | (11 | 6) | 169 | 47 | 51 | 45 | 15 | 2 | 89 | 3 | 0 | 3 | 10 | 5 | .67 | 9 | .254 | .287 | .467 |
| 13 | NYY | AL | 58 | 219 | 56 | 8 | 0 | 17 | (11 | 6) | 115 | 37 | 50 | 45 | 21 | 1 | 67 | 2 | 0 | 1 | 8 | 4 | .67 | 2 | .256 | .325 | .525 |
| Postseason | | | 44 | 174 | 37 | 3 | 0 | 4 | (3 | 1) | 52 | 14 | 18 | 14 | 9 | 0 | 53 | 3 | 0 | 0 | 10 | 3 | .77 | 3 | .213 | .263 | .299 |
| 15 ML YEARS | | | 1908 | 7524 | 2045 | 466 | 31 | 406 | (199 | 207) | 3791 | 1130 | 1136 | 1151 | 490 | 67 | 1732 | 84 | 9 | 50 | 288 | 84 | .77 | 120 | .272 | .321 | .504 |

## Rafael Soriano

**Pitches:** R **Bats:** R **Pos:** RP-68 **Ht:** 6'1" **Wt:** 210 **Born:** 12/19/1979 **Age:** 34

| HOW MUCH HE PITCHED | | | | | | | | | WHAT HE GAVE UP | | | | | | | | | | | | THE RESULTS | | | | | | | |
|---|---|---|---|---|---|---|---|---|---|---|---|---|---|---|---|---|---|---|---|---|---|---|---|---|---|---|---|---|
| Year | Team | Lg | G | GS | CG | GF | IP | BFP | H | R | ER | HR | SH | SF | HB | TBB | IBB | SO | WP | Bk | W | L | Pct | Sh | Sv-Op | Hld | ERC | ERA |
| 2002 | Sea | AL | 10 | 8 | 0 | 1 | 47.1 | 202 | 45 | 25 | 24 | 8 | 1 | 0 | 0 | 16 | 1 | 32 | 2 | 0 | 0 | 3 | .000 | 0 | 1-1 | 0 | 3.93 | 4.56 |
| 2003 | Sea | AL | 40 | 0 | 0 | 12 | 53.0 | 201 | 30 | 9 | 9 | 2 | 0 | 1 | 3 | 12 | 1 | 68 | 0 | 0 | 3 | 0 | 1.000 | 0 | 1-2 | 5 | 1.32 | 1.53 |
| 2004 | Sea | AL | 6 | 0 | 0 | 0 | 3.1 | 23 | 9 | 6 | 5 | 0 | 0 | 0 | 0 | 3 | 0 | 3 | 0 | 0 | 0 | 3 | .000 | 0 | 0-1 | 0 | 15.97 | 13.50 |
| 2005 | Sea | AL | 7 | 0 | 0 | 4 | 7.1 | 30 | 6 | 2 | 2 | 0 | 0 | 1 | 1 | 1 | 0 | 9 | 0 | 0 | 0 | 0 | - | 0 | 0-0 | 1 | 2.00 | 2.45 |
| 2006 | Sea | AL | 53 | 0 | 0 | 14 | 60.0 | 241 | 44 | 15 | 15 | 6 | 1 | 1 | 2 | 21 | 0 | 65 | 2 | 0 | 1 | 2 | .333 | 0 | 2-6 | 18 | 2.64 | 2.25 |
| 2007 | Atl | NL | 71 | 0 | 0 | 28 | 72.0 | 276 | 47 | 26 | 24 | 12 | 0 | 0 | 2 | 15 | 2 | 70 | 0 | 0 | 3 | 3 | .500 | 0 | 9-12 | 19 | 2.05 | 3.00 |
| 2008 | Atl | NL | 14 | 0 | 0 | 5 | 14.0 | 57 | 7 | 5 | 4 | 1 | 0 | 0 | 1 | 9 | 2 | 16 | 1 | 0 | 0 | 1 | .000 | 0 | 3-4 | 0 | 2.27 | 2.57 |
| 2009 | Atl | NL | 77 | 0 | 0 | 52 | 75.2 | 307 | 53 | 25 | 25 | 6 | 4 | 2 | 1 | 27 | 4 | 102 | 0 | 0 | 1 | 6 | .143 | 0 | 27-31 | 6 | 2.18 | 2.97 |
| 2010 | TB | AL | 64 | 0 | 0 | 56 | 62.1 | 237 | 36 | 14 | 12 | 4 | 0 | 1 | 1 | 14 | 2 | 57 | 0 | 0 | 3 | 2 | .600 | 0 | **45-48** | 0 | 1.33 | 1.73 |
| 2011 | NYY | AL | 42 | 0 | 0 | 8 | 39.1 | 164 | 33 | 18 | 18 | 4 | 1 | 0 | 1 | 18 | 2 | 36 | 0 | 0 | 2 | 3 | .400 | 0 | 2-5 | 23 | 3.51 | 4.12 |
| 2012 | NYY | AL | 69 | 0 | 0 | 54 | 67.2 | 279 | 55 | 17 | 17 | 6 | 0 | 1 | 1 | 24 | 4 | 69 | 3 | 0 | 2 | 1 | .667 | 0 | 42-46 | 4 | 2.79 | 2.26 |
| 2013 | Was | NL | 68 | 0 | 0 | 58 | 66.2 | 277 | 65 | 24 | 23 | 7 | 1 | 0 | 0 | 17 | 2 | 51 | 3 | 0 | 3 | 3 | .500 | 0 | 43-49 | 0 | 3.36 | 3.11 |
| Postseason | | | 9 | 0 | 0 | 3 | 12.0 | 40 | 7 | 4 | 4 | 3 | 1 | 0 | 0 | 0 | 0 | 7 | 0 | 0 | 0 | 1 | .000 | 0 | 1-1 | 1 | 1.49 | 3.00 |
| 12 ML YEARS | | | 521 | 8 | 0 | 292 | 568.2 | 2294 | 430 | 186 | 178 | 56 | 8 | 7 | 13 | 177 | 20 | 578 | 11 | 0 | 18 | 27 | .400 | 0 | 175-205 | 76 | 2.49 | 2.82 |

## Geovany Soto

**Bats:** R **Throws:** R **Pos:** C-53;3B-1 **Ht:** 6'1" **Wt:** 235 **Born:** 1/20/1983 **Age:** 31

| BATTING | | | | | | | | | | | | | | | | | | | | | BASERUNNING | | | | AVERAGES | | |
|---|---|---|---|---|---|---|---|---|---|---|---|---|---|---|---|---|---|---|---|---|---|---|---|---|---|---|---|
| Year | Team | Lg | G | AB | H | 2B | 3B | HR | (Hm | Rd) | TB | R | RBI | RC | TBB | IBB | SO | HBP | SH | SF | SB | CS | SB% | GDP | Avg | OBP | Slg |
| 2005 | ChC | NL | 1 | 1 | 0 | 0 | 0 | 0 | (0 | 0) | 0 | 0 | 0 | 0 | 0 | 0 | 0 | 0 | 0 | 0 | 0 | 0 | - | 0 | .000 | .000 | .000 |
| 2006 | ChC | NL | 11 | 25 | 5 | 1 | 0 | 0 | (0 | 0) | 6 | 1 | 2 | 0 | 0 | 0 | 5 | 1 | 0 | 0 | 0 | 0 | - | 0 | .200 | .231 | .240 |
| 2007 | ChC | NL | 18 | 54 | 21 | 6 | 0 | 3 | (2 | 1) | 36 | 12 | 8 | 13 | 5 | 0 | 14 | 0 | 0 | 1 | 0 | 0 | - | 1 | .389 | .433 | .667 |
| 2008 | ChC | NL | 141 | 494 | 141 | 35 | 2 | 23 | (11 | 12) | 249 | 66 | 86 | 81 | 62 | 6 | 121 | 2 | 0 | 5 | 0 | 1 | .00 | 11 | .285 | .364 | .504 |
| 2009 | ChC | NL | 102 | 331 | 72 | 19 | 1 | 11 | (6 | 5) | 126 | 27 | 47 | 34 | 50 | 3 | 77 | 3 | 0 | 5 | 1 | 0 | 1.00 | 19 | .218 | .321 | .381 |
| 2010 | ChC | NL | 105 | 322 | 90 | 19 | 0 | 17 | (12 | 5) | 160 | 47 | 53 | 59 | 62 | 4 | 83 | 0 | 0 | 3 | 0 | 1 | .00 | 5 | .280 | .393 | .497 |
| 2011 | ChC | NL | 125 | 421 | 96 | 26 | 0 | 17 | (7 | 10) | 173 | 46 | 54 | 43 | 45 | 3 | 124 | 6 | 0 | 2 | 0 | 0 | - | 12 | .228 | .310 | .411 |
| 2012 | 2 Tms | | 99 | 324 | 64 | 12 | 1 | 11 | (3 | 8) | 111 | 45 | 39 | 30 | 30 | 1 | 76 | 3 | 2 | 2 | 1 | 0 | 1.00 | 12 | .198 | .270 | .343 |
| 2013 | Tex | AL | 54 | 163 | 40 | 9 | 0 | 9 | (7 | 2) | 76 | 20 | 22 | 23 | 20 | 0 | 60 | 0 | 1 | 0 | 1 | 2 | .33 | 2 | .245 | .328 | .466 |
| 12 | ChC | NL | 52 | 176 | 35 | 6 | 1 | 6 | (2 | 4) | 61 | 26 | 14 | 15 | 19 | 1 | 35 | 2 | 0 | 0 | 0 | 0 | - | 6 | .199 | .284 | .347 |
| 12 | Tex | AL | 47 | 148 | 29 | 6 | 0 | 5 | (1 | 4) | 50 | 19 | 25 | 15 | 11 | 0 | 41 | 1 | 2 | 2 | 1 | 0 | 1.00 | 6 | .196 | .253 | .338 |
| Postseason | | | 6 | 19 | 3 | 1 | 0 | 1 | (0 | 1) | 7 | 1 | 2 | 1 | 3 | 0 | 5 | 0 | 0 | 0 | 0 | 0 | - | 0 | .158 | .273 | .368 |
| 9 ML YEARS | | | 656 | 2135 | 529 | 127 | 4 | 91 | (48 | 43) | 937 | 264 | 311 | 283 | 274 | 17 | 560 | 15 | 3 | 18 | 3 | 4 | .43 | 62 | .248 | .335 | .439 |

## Neftali Soto

**Bats:** R **Throws:** R **Pos:** PH-8;1B-5 neff-TAH-lee **Ht:** 6'1" **Wt:** 215 **Born:** 2/28/1989 **Age:** 25

| BATTING | | | | | | | | | | | | | | | | | | | | | BASERUNNING | | | | AVERAGES | | |
|---|---|---|---|---|---|---|---|---|---|---|---|---|---|---|---|---|---|---|---|---|---|---|---|---|---|---|---|
| Year | Team | Lg | G | AB | H | 2B | 3B | HR | (Hm | Rd) | TB | R | RBI | RC | TBB | IBB | SO | HBP | SH | SF | SB | CS | SB% | GDP | Avg | OBP | Slg |
| 2009 | Srsota | A+ | 131 | 505 | 125 | 21 | 2 | 11 | (- | -) | 183 | 53 | 57 | 52 | 23 | 0 | 95 | 3 | 2 | 4 | 1 | 3 | .25 | 23 | .248 | .282 | .362 |
| 2010 | Lynbrg | A+ | 134 | 522 | 140 | 33 | 2 | 21 | (- | -) | 240 | 73 | 73 | 78 | 32 | 3 | 105 | 8 | 0 | 3 | 0 | 0 | - | 10 | .268 | .319 | .460 |
| 2011 | Carlina | AA | 102 | 379 | 103 | 19 | 3 | 30 | (- | -) | 218 | 70 | 76 | 71 | 25 | 0 | 96 | 8 | 0 | 2 | 0 | 1 | .00 | 8 | .272 | .329 | .575 |
| 2011 | Lsvlle | AAA | 4 | 17 | 7 | 0 | 0 | 1 | (- | -) | 10 | 1 | 4 | 4 | 1 | 0 | 2 | 0 | 0 | 0 | 0 | 0 | - | 0 | .412 | .444 | .588 |
| 2012 | Lsvlle | AAA | 122 | 465 | 114 | 30 | 0 | 14 | (- | -) | 186 | 55 | 59 | 60 | 41 | 3 | 116 | 5 | 0 | 1 | 2 | 1 | .67 | 18 | .245 | .313 | .400 |
| 2013 | Lsvlle | AAA | 118 | 461 | 125 | 21 | 0 | 15 | (- | -) | 191 | 54 | 61 | 61 | 26 | 1 | 103 | 4 | 0 | 4 | 3 | 1 | .75 | 20 | .271 | .313 | .414 |
| 2013 | Cin | NL | 13 | 12 | 0 | 0 | 0 | 0 | (0 | 0) | 0 | 0 | 0 | 0 | 0 | 0 | 6 | 1 | 0 | 0 | 0 | 0 | - | 1 | .000 | .077 | .000 |

## Denard Span

**Bats:** L **Throws:** L **Pos:** CF-153;PH-4 **Ht:** 6'0" **Wt:** 210 **Born:** 2/27/1984 **Age:** 30

| BATTING | | | | | | | | | | | | | | | | | | | | | BASERUNNING | | | | AVERAGES | | |
|---|---|---|---|---|---|---|---|---|---|---|---|---|---|---|---|---|---|---|---|---|---|---|---|---|---|---|---|
| Year | Team | Lg | G | AB | H | 2B | 3B | HR | (Hm | Rd) | TB | R | RBI | RC | TBB | IBB | SO | HBP | SH | SF | SB | CS | SB% | GDP | Avg | OBP | Slg |
| 2008 | Min | AL | 93 | 347 | 102 | 16 | 7 | 6 | (2 | 4) | 150 | 70 | 47 | 68 | 50 | 3 | 60 | 4 | 8 | 2 | 18 | 7 | .72 | 3 | .294 | .387 | .432 |
| 2009 | Min | AL | 145 | 578 | 180 | 16 | **10** | 8 | (5 | 3) | 240 | 97 | 68 | 100 | 70 | 3 | 89 | 10 | 12 | 6 | 23 | 10 | .70 | 7 | .311 | .392 | .415 |
| 2010 | Min | AL | 153 | 629 | 166 | 24 | 10 | 3 | (0 | 3) | 219 | 85 | 58 | 85 | 60 | 0 | 74 | 4 | 10 | 2 | 26 | 4 | .87 | 12 | .264 | .331 | .348 |
| 2011 | Min | AL | 70 | 284 | 75 | 11 | 5 | 2 | (1 | 1) | 102 | 37 | 16 | 32 | 27 | 0 | 36 | 0 | 0 | 0 | 6 | 1 | .86 | 3 | .264 | .328 | .359 |
| 2012 | Min | AL | 128 | 516 | 146 | 38 | 4 | 4 | (2 | 2) | 204 | 71 | 41 | 69 | 47 | 0 | 62 | 0 | 4 | 1 | 17 | 6 | .74 | 10 | .283 | .342 | .395 |
| 2013 | Was | NL | 153 | 610 | 170 | 28 | **11** | 4 | (2 | 2) | 232 | 75 | 47 | 74 | 42 | 0 | 77 | 2 | 7 | 1 | 20 | 6 | .77 | 11 | .279 | .327 | .380 |
| Postseason | | | 6 | 28 | 10 | 1 | 0 | 0 | (0 | 0) | 11 | 1 | 1 | 2 | 0 | 0 | 2 | 0 | 0 | 0 | 1 | 0 | 1.00 | 1 | .357 | .357 | .393 |
| 6 ML YEARS | | | 742 | 2964 | 839 | 133 | 47 | 27 | (12 | 15) | 1147 | 435 | 277 | 428 | 296 | 6 | 398 | 20 | 41 | 12 | 110 | 34 | .76 | 46 | .283 | .351 | .387 |

## Zeke Spruill

**Pitches:** R **Bats:** R **Pos:** RP-4; SP-2 ZEEK SPROO-ill **Ht:** 6'5" **Wt:** 190 **Born:** 9/11/1989 **Age:** 24

| HOW MUCH HE PITCHED | | | | | | | | | WHAT HE GAVE UP | | | | | | | | | | | | THE RESULTS | | | | | | | |
|---|---|---|---|---|---|---|---|---|---|---|---|---|---|---|---|---|---|---|---|---|---|---|---|---|---|---|---|---|
| Year | Team | Lg | G | GS | CG | GF | IP | BFP | H | R | ER | HR | SH | SF | HB | TBB | IBB | SO | WP | Bk | W | L | Pct | Sh | Sv-Op | Hld | ERC | ERA |
| 2009 | Rome | A | 20 | 19 | 0 | 1 | 116.0 | 496 | 120 | 54 | 39 | 9 | 3 | 2 | 7 | 24 | 1 | 95 | 2 | 1 | 8 | 6 | .571 | 0 | 1-- | - | 3.52 | 3.03 |
| 2009 | Braves | R | 4 | 4 | 0 | 0 | 19.2 | 91 | 24 | 15 | 10 | 2 | 0 | 0 | 3 | 5 | 0 | 23 | 3 | 1 | 1 | 0 | 1.000 | 0 | 0-- | - | 5.26 | 4.58 |
| 2010 | MrtlBh | A+ | 14 | 13 | 1 | 0 | 65.0 | 295 | 83 | 44 | 40 | 4 | 3 | 7 | 4 | 13 | 2 | 41 | 1 | 0 | 3 | 5 | .375 | 0 | 0-- | - | 4.64 | 5.54 |
| 2010 | Braves | R | 2 | 2 | 0 | 0 | 3.0 | 14 | 4 | 1 | 1 | 0 | 0 | 1 | 0 | 1 | 0 | 1 | 0 | 0 | 0 | 0 | - | 0 | 0-- | - | 4.83 | 3.00 |
| 2011 | Lynbrg | A+ | 20 | 20 | 5 | 0 | 129.2 | 520 | 108 | 56 | 46 | 7 | 7 | 7 | 8 | 23 | 0 | 92 | 5 | 1 | 7 | 9 | .438 | 1 | 0-- | - | 2.32 | 3.19 |
| 2011 | Missi | AA | 7 | 7 | 1 | 0 | 45.0 | 195 | 45 | 18 | 16 | 3 | 1 | 3 | 5 | 17 | 0 | 16 | 1 | 0 | 3 | 2 | .600 | 0 | 0-- | - | 4.24 | 3.20 |
| 2012 | Missi | AA | 27 | 27 | 1 | 0 | 161.2 | 674 | 158 | 81 | 66 | 8 | 6 | 9 | 6 | 46 | 2 | 106 | 5 | 1 | 9 | 11 | .450 | 0 | 0-- | - | 3.33 | 3.67 |
| 2013 | Mobile | AA | 5 | 5 | 0 | 0 | 31.2 | 122 | 24 | 7 | 5 | 0 | 2 | 1 | 0 | 12 | 1 | 20 | 1 | 0 | 0 | 3 | .000 | 0 | 0-- | - | 2.20 | 1.42 |
| 2013 | Reno | AAA | 16 | 16 | 1 | 0 | 92.0 | 402 | 98 | 48 | 43 | 8 | 9 | 3 | 3 | 33 | 0 | 48 | 0 | 2 | 6 | 5 | .545 | 1 | 0-- | - | 4.30 | 4.21 |
| 2013 | Ari | NL | 6 | 2 | 0 | 1 | 11.1 | 55 | 17 | 11 | 7 | 3 | 1 | 0 | 1 | 5 | 0 | 9 | 0 | 0 | 0 | 2 | .000 | 0 | 0-0 | 0 | 9.30 | 5.56 |

## Craig Stammen

**Pitches:** R **Bats:** R **Pos:** RP-55 STAMM-enn **Ht:** 6'3" **Wt:** 215 **Born:** 3/9/1984 **Age:** 30

| HOW MUCH HE PITCHED | | | | | | | | WHAT HE GAVE UP | | | | | | | | | | | | THE RESULTS | | | | | | | |
|---|---|---|---|---|---|---|---|---|---|---|---|---|---|---|---|---|---|---|---|---|---|---|---|---|---|---|---|
| Year Team | Lg | G | GS | CG | GF | IP | BFP | H | R | ER | HR | SH | SF | HB | TBB | IBB | SO | WP | Bk | W | L | Pct | Sh | Sv-Op | Hld | ERC | ERA |
| 2009 Was | NL | 19 | 19 | 1 | 0 | 105.2 | 448 | 112 | 67 | 60 | 14 | 4 | 3 | 3 | 24 | 1 | 48 | 7 | 0 | 4 | 7 | .364 | 0 | 0-0 | 0 | 4.03 | 5.11 |
| 2010 Was | NL | 35 | 19 | 0 | 3 | 128.0 | 562 | 151 | 78 | 73 | 13 | 5 | 6 | 1 | 41 | 4 | 85 | 3 | 0 | 4 | 4 | .500 | 0 | 0-0 | 1 | 4.79 | 5.13 |
| 2011 Was | NL | 7 | 0 | 0 | 2 | 10.1 | 38 | 3 | 1 | 1 | 0 | 0 | 0 | 0 | 4 | 0 | 12 | 1 | 0 | 1 | 1 | .500 | 0 | 0-0 | 1 | 0.67 | 0.87 |
| 2012 Was | NL | 59 | 0 | 0 | 15 | 88.1 | 370 | 70 | 27 | 23 | 7 | 5 | 1 | 2 | 36 | 4 | 87 | 3 | 0 | 6 | 1 | .857 | 0 | 1-2 | 10 | 2.84 | 2.34 |
| 2013 Was | NL | 55 | 0 | 0 | 14 | 81.2 | 339 | 78 | 30 | 25 | 4 | 8 | 4 | 2 | 27 | 3 | 79 | 2 | 1 | 7 | 6 | .538 | 0 | 0-1 | 7 | 3.32 | 2.76 |
| Postseason | | 4 | 0 | 0 | 0 | 3.0 | 21 | 5 | 3 | 3 | 1 | 1 | 1 | 3 | 2 | 0 | 3 | 0 | 0 | 0 | 0 | - | 0 | 0-0 | 1 | 14.91 | 9.00 |
| 5 ML YEARS | | 175 | 38 | 1 | 34 | 414.0 | 1757 | 414 | 203 | 182 | 38 | 22 | 14 | 8 | 132 | 12 | 311 | 16 | 1 | 22 | 19 | .537 | 0 | 1-3 | 19 | 3.74 | 3.96 |

## Daniel Stange

**Pitches:** R **Bats:** R **Pos:** RP-3 STANG **Ht:** 6'2" **Wt:** 210 **Born:** 12/22/1985 **Age:** 28

| HOW MUCH HE PITCHED | | | | | | | | WHAT HE GAVE UP | | | | | | | | | | | | THE RESULTS | | | | | | | |
|---|---|---|---|---|---|---|---|---|---|---|---|---|---|---|---|---|---|---|---|---|---|---|---|---|---|---|---|
| Year Team | Lg | G | GS | CG | GF | IP | BFP | H | R | ER | HR | SH | SF | HB | TBB | IBB | SO | WP | Bk | W | L | Pct | Sh | Sv-Op | Hld | ERC | ERA |
| 2009 Mobile | AA | 39 | 0 | 0 | 21 | 51.2 | 235 | 66 | 35 | 29 | 4 | 5 | 4 | 1 | 15 | 1 | 44 | 3 | 1 | 0 | 4 | .000 | 0 | 10- - | - | 5.03 | 5.05 |
| 2010 Reno | AAA | 19 | 0 | 0 | 14 | 23.1 | 106 | 29 | 17 | 16 | 3 | 1 | 1 | 0 | 10 | 2 | 16 | 4 | 0 | 4 | 3 | .571 | 0 | 2- - | - | 5.71 | 6.17 |
| 2010 Mobile | AA | 30 | 0 | 0 | 23 | 32.0 | 116 | 14 | 6 | 6 | 1 | 1 | 2 | 2 | 11 | 0 | 18 | 3 | 2 | 4 | 1 | .800 | 0 | 13- - | - | 1.25 | 1.69 |
| 2011 Reno | AAA | 25 | 1 | 0 | 6 | 36.2 | 173 | 41 | 27 | 25 | 6 | 1 | 0 | 1 | 27 | 0 | 29 | 5 | 0 | 3 | 1 | .750 | 0 | 1- - | - | 6.89 | 6.14 |
| 2012 Reno | AAA | 3 | 0 | 0 | 1 | 2.2 | 19 | 8 | 8 | 7 | 0 | 0 | 0 | 1 | 5 | 0 | 2 | 0 | 0 | 0 | 0 | - | 0 | 0- - | - | 30.02 | 23.63 |
| 2012 SnAnt | AA | 46 | 0 | 0 | 20 | 53.2 | 228 | 50 | 23 | 20 | 3 | 3 | 0 | 6 | 12 | 1 | 64 | 3 | 1 | 3 | 6 | .333 | 0 | 6- - | - | 3.08 | 3.35 |
| 2012 Tucsn | AAA | 2 | 0 | 0 | 0 | 1.1 | 9 | 1 | 1 | 0 | 0 | 0 | 0 | 0 | 3 | 0 | 1 | 0 | 0 | 0 | 0 | - | 0 | 0- - | - | 7.83 | 0.00 |
| 2013 Tucsn | AAA | 26 | 0 | 0 | 4 | 39.0 | 171 | 34 | 21 | 18 | 5 | 0 | 0 | 1 | 24 | 0 | 43 | 2 | 0 | 1 | 0 | 1.000 | 0 | 0- - | - | 4.55 | 4.15 |
| 2013 Salt Lk | AAA | 26 | 0 | 0 | 21 | 26.2 | 122 | 31 | 16 | 15 | 1 | 0 | 0 | 2 | 13 | 1 | 30 | 1 | 0 | 4 | 1 | .800 | 0 | 5- - | - | 5.15 | 5.06 |
| 2010 Ari | NL | 4 | 0 | 0 | 1 | 4.0 | 22 | 4 | 6 | 6 | 1 | 0 | 0 | 0 | 6 | 0 | 2 | 1 | 0 | 0 | 0 | - | 0 | 0-0 | 0 | 9.94 | 13.50 |
| 2013 LAA | AL | 3 | 0 | 0 | 3 | 1.2 | 9 | 2 | 3 | 3 | 1 | 0 | 0 | 0 | 2 | 0 | 1 | 0 | 0 | 0 | 1 | .000 | 0 | 0-0 | 0 | 13.35 | 16.20 |
| 2 ML YEARS | | 7 | 0 | 0 | 4 | 5.2 | 31 | 6 | 9 | 9 | 2 | 0 | 0 | 0 | 8 | 0 | 3 | 0 | 0 | 0 | 1 | .000 | 0 | 0-0 | 0 | 10.96 | 14.29 |

## Giancarlo Stanton

**Bats:** R **Throws:** R **Pos:** RF-116 john-CAHR-loh **Ht:** 6'6" **Wt:** 240 **Born:** 11/8/1989 **Age:** 24

| BATTING | | | | | | | | | | | | | | | | | | | | BASERUNNING | | | | AVERAGES | | |
|---|---|---|---|---|---|---|---|---|---|---|---|---|---|---|---|---|---|---|---|---|---|---|---|---|---|---|
| Year Team | Lg | G | AB | H | 2B | 3B | HR | (Hm | Rd) | TB | R | RBI | RC | TBB | IBB | SO | HBP | SH | SF | SB | CS | SB% | GDP | Avg | OBP | Slg |
| 2013 Jupiter* | A+ | 5 | 15 | 0 | 0 | 0 | 0 | (- | -) | 0 | 0 | 0 | 0 | 2 | 0 | 5 | 0 | 0 | 0 | 1 | 0 | 1.00 | 0 | .000 | .118 | .000 |
| 2010 Fla | NL | 100 | 359 | 93 | 21 | 1 | 22 | (7 | 15) | 182 | 45 | 59 | 56 | 34 | 6 | 123 | 2 | 0 | 1 | 5 | 2 | .71 | 7 | .259 | .326 | .507 |
| 2011 Fla | NL | 150 | 516 | 135 | 30 | 5 | 34 | (16 | 18) | 277 | 79 | 87 | 81 | 70 | 6 | 166 | 9 | 0 | 6 | 5 | 5 | .50 | 11 | .262 | .356 | .537 |
| 2012 Mia | NL | 123 | 449 | 130 | 30 | 1 | 37 | (16 | **21)** | 273 | 75 | 86 | 79 | 46 | 9 | 143 | 5 | 0 | 1 | 6 | 2 | .75 | 5 | .290 | .361 | **.608** |
| 2013 Mia | NL | 116 | 425 | 106 | 26 | 0 | 24 | (15 | 9) | 204 | 62 | 62 | 66 | 74 | 5 | 140 | 4 | 0 | 1 | 1 | 0 | 1.00 | 10 | .249 | .365 | .480 |
| 4 ML YEARS | | 489 | 1749 | 464 | 107 | 7 | 117 | (54 | 63) | 936 | 261 | 294 | 282 | 224 | 26 | 572 | 20 | 0 | 9 | 17 | 9 | .65 | 33 | .265 | .354 | .535 |

## Max Stassi

**Bats:** R **Throws:** R **Pos:** DH-2;C-1 STASS-ee **Ht:** 5'10" **Wt:** 205 **Born:** 3/15/1991 **Age:** 23

| BATTING | | | | | | | | | | | | | | | | | | | | BASERUNNING | | | | AVERAGES | | |
|---|---|---|---|---|---|---|---|---|---|---|---|---|---|---|---|---|---|---|---|---|---|---|---|---|---|---|
| Year Team | Lg | G | AB | H | 2B | 3B | HR | (Hm | Rd) | TB | R | RBI | RC | TBB | IBB | SO | HBP | SH | SF | SB | CS | SB% | GDP | Avg | OBP | Slg |
| 2009 As | R | 1 | 1 | 0 | 0 | 0 | 0 | (- | -) | 0 | 0 | 0 | 0 | 1 | 0 | 1 | 0 | 0 | 0 | 0 | 0 | - | 0 | .000 | .500 | .000 |
| 2009 Vancvr | A- | 13 | 49 | 14 | 4 | 0 | 0 | (- | -) | 18 | 3 | 8 | 6 | 2 | 0 | 11 | 2 | 0 | 0 | 0 | 0 | - | 3 | .286 | .340 | .367 |
| 2010 Kane | A | 110 | 411 | 94 | 21 | 1 | 13 | (- | -) | 156 | 54 | 51 | 50 | 45 | 1 | 141 | 5 | 1 | 3 | 3 | 3 | .50 | 12 | .229 | .310 | .380 |
| 2011 Stcktn | A+ | 31 | 121 | 28 | 6 | 0 | 2 | (- | -) | 40 | 22 | 19 | 14 | 16 | 0 | 22 | 2 | 0 | 0 | 1 | 1 | .50 | 4 | .231 | .331 | .331 |
| 2012 Stcktn | A+ | 84 | 314 | 84 | 18 | 0 | 15 | (- | -) | 147 | 48 | 45 | 51 | 27 | 0 | 83 | 8 | 0 | 11 | 3 | 1 | .75 | 5 | .268 | .331 | .468 |
| 2013 CpChr | AA | 76 | 289 | 80 | 20 | 1 | 17 | (- | -) | 153 | 40 | 60 | 52 | 19 | 1 | 68 | 8 | 2 | 5 | 1 | 1 | .50 | 11 | .277 | .333 | .529 |
| 2013 Hou | AL | 3 | 7 | 2 | 0 | 0 | 0 | (0 | 0) | 2 | 0 | 1 | 0 | 0 | 0 | 2 | 1 | 0 | 0 | 0 | 0 | - | 1 | .286 | .375 | .286 |

## Tim Stauffer

**Pitches:** R **Bats:** R **Pos:** RP-43 STOFF-er **Ht:** 6'1" **Wt:** 215 **Born:** 6/2/1982 **Age:** 32

| HOW MUCH HE PITCHED | | | | | | | | WHAT HE GAVE UP | | | | | | | | | | | | THE RESULTS | | | | | | | |
|---|---|---|---|---|---|---|---|---|---|---|---|---|---|---|---|---|---|---|---|---|---|---|---|---|---|---|---|
| Year Team | Lg | G | GS | CG | GF | IP | BFP | H | R | ER | HR | SH | SF | HB | TBB | IBB | SO | WP | Bk | W | L | Pct | Sh | Sv-Op | Hld | ERC | ERA |
| 2013 Tucsn* | AAA | 8 | 8 | 0 | 0 | 42.2 | 185 | 50 | 16 | 15 | 1 | 2 | 0 | 1 | 15 | 0 | 38 | 2 | 0 | 2 | 2 | .500 | 0 | 0- - | - | 4.50 | 3.16 |
| 2005 SD | NL | 15 | 14 | 0 | 0 | 81.0 | 355 | 92 | 50 | 48 | 10 | 2 | 0 | 2 | 29 | 0 | 49 | 0 | 0 | 3 | 6 | .333 | 0 | 0-0 | 0 | 5.00 | 5.33 |
| 2006 SD | NL | 1 | 1 | 0 | 0 | 6.0 | 21 | 3 | 2 | 1 | 0 | 0 | 0 | 0 | 1 | 0 | 2 | 0 | 0 | 1 | 0 | 1.000 | 0 | 0-0 | 0 | 0.84 | 1.50 |
| 2007 SD | NL | 2 | 2 | 0 | 0 | 7.2 | 45 | 15 | 18 | 18 | 5 | 0 | 0 | 1 | 6 | 0 | 6 | 0 | 0 | 0 | 1 | .000 | 0 | 0-0 | 0 | 18.32 | 21.13 |
| 2009 SD | NL | 14 | 14 | 0 | 0 | 73.0 | 316 | 71 | 31 | 29 | 8 | 2 | 1 | 5 | 34 | 1 | 53 | 1 | 0 | 4 | 7 | .364 | 0 | 0-0 | 0 | 4.60 | 3.58 |
| 2010 SD | NL | 32 | 7 | 0 | 12 | 82.2 | 326 | 65 | 18 | 17 | 3 | 3 | 0 | 2 | 24 | 5 | 61 | 0 | 0 | 6 | 5 | .545 | 0 | 0-0 | 0 | 2.23 | 1.85 |
| 2011 SD | NL | 31 | 31 | 0 | 0 | 185.2 | 777 | 180 | 81 | 77 | 20 | 14 | 3 | 8 | 53 | 5 | 128 | 4 | 1 | 9 | 12 | .429 | 0 | 0-0 | 0 | 3.67 | 3.73 |
| 2012 SD | NL | 1 | 1 | 0 | 0 | 5.0 | 24 | 7 | 4 | 3 | 1 | 0 | 0 | 0 | 3 | 0 | 5 | 0 | 0 | 0 | 0 | - | 0 | 0-0 | 0 | 8.40 | 5.40 |
| 2013 SD | NL | 43 | 0 | 0 | 8 | 69.2 | 284 | 59 | 29 | 29 | 7 | 3 | 2 | 4 | 20 | 1 | 64 | 0 | 0 | 3 | 1 | .750 | 0 | 0-1 | 7 | 3.06 | 3.75 |
| 8 ML YEARS | | 139 | 70 | 0 | 20 | 510.2 | 2148 | 492 | 233 | 222 | 54 | 24 | 6 | 22 | 170 | 12 | 368 | 5 | 1 | 26 | 32 | .448 | 0 | 0-1 | 7 | 3.83 | 3.91 |

## Chris Stewart

**Bats:** R **Throws:** R **Pos:** C-108;1B-2;PH-2 **Ht:** 6'4" **Wt:** 210 **Born:** 2/19/1982 **Age:** 32

| BATTING | | | | | | | | | | | | | | | | | | | | BASERUNNING | | | | AVERAGES | | |
|---|---|---|---|---|---|---|---|---|---|---|---|---|---|---|---|---|---|---|---|---|---|---|---|---|---|---|
| Year Team | Lg | G | AB | H | 2B | 3B | HR | (Hm | Rd) | TB | R | RBI | RC | TBB | IBB | SO | HBP | SH | SF | SB | CS | SB% | GDP | Avg | OBP | Slg |
| 2006 CWS | AL | 6 | 8 | 0 | 0 | 0 | 0 | (0 | 0) | 0 | 0 | 0 | 0 | 0 | 0 | 2 | 0 | 0 | 0 | 0 | 0 | - | 0 | .000 | .000 | .000 |
| 2007 Tex | AL | 17 | 37 | 9 | 2 | 0 | 0 | (0 | 0) | 11 | 4 | 3 | 3 | 3 | 0 | 6 | 0 | 3 | 0 | 0 | 0 | - | 2 | .243 | .300 | .297 |
| 2008 NYY | AL | 1 | 3 | 0 | 0 | 0 | 0 | (0 | 0) | 0 | 0 | 0 | 0 | 0 | 0 | 1 | 0 | 0 | 0 | 0 | 0 | - | 0 | .000 | .000 | .000 |
| 2010 SD | NL | 2 | 0 | 0 | 0 | 0 | 0 | (0 | 0) | 0 | 0 | 0 | 0 | 0 | 0 | 0 | 0 | 0 | 0 | 0 | 0 | - | 0 | - | - | - |
| 2011 SF | NL | 67 | 162 | 33 | 8 | 0 | 3 | (1 | 2) | 50 | 20 | 10 | 10 | 16 | 4 | 18 | 2 | 3 | 0 | 0 | 0 | - | 2 | .204 | .283 | .309 |

| Year Team | Lg | BATTING G | AB | H | 2B | 3B | HR | (Hm | Rd) | TB | R | RBI | RC | TBB | IBB | SO | HBP | SH | SF | BASERUNNING SB | CS | SB% | GDP | AVERAGES Avg | OBP | Slg |
|---|---|---|---|---|---|---|---|---|---|---|---|---|---|---|---|---|---|---|---|---|---|---|---|---|---|---|
| 2012 NYY | AL | 55 | 141 | 34 | 8 | 0 | 1 | (1 | 0) | 45 | 15 | 13 | 10 | 10 | 0 | 21 | 1 | 3 | 2 | 2 | 0 | 1.00 | 1 | .241 | .292 | .319 |
| 2013 NYY | AL | 109 | 294 | 62 | 6 | 0 | 4 | (3 | 1) | 80 | 28 | 25 | 24 | 30 | 0 | 49 | 6 | 6 | 4 | 4 | 0 | 1.00 | 8 | .211 | .293 | .272 |
| Postseason | | 1 | 0 | 0 | 0 | 0 | 0 | (0 | 0) | 0 | 0 | 0 | 0 | 0 | 0 | 0 | 0 | 0 | 0 | 0 | 0 | - | 0 | - | - | - |
| 7 ML YEARS | | 257 | 645 | 138 | 24 | 0 | 8 | (5 | 3) | 186 | 67 | 51 | 47 | 59 | 4 | 97 | 9 | 15 | 6 | 6 | 0 | 1.00 | 13 | .214 | .287 | .288 |

# Josh Stinson

**Pitches:** R **Bats:** R **Pos:** RP-10; SP-1 **Ht:** 6'4" **Wt:** 210 **Born:** 3/14/1988 **Age:** 26

| Year Team | Lg | HOW MUCH HE PITCHED G | GS | CG | GF | IP | BFP | WHAT HE GAVE UP H | R | ER | HR | SH | SF | HB | TBB | IBB | SO | WP | Bk | THE RESULTS W | L | Pct | Sh | Sv-Op | Hld | ERC | ERA |
|---|---|---|---|---|---|---|---|---|---|---|---|---|---|---|---|---|---|---|---|---|---|---|---|---|---|---|---|
| 2013 Norfolk* | AAA | 23 | 23 | 0 | 0 | 131.0 | 555 | 126 | 60 | 55 | 11 | 5 | 2 | 4 | 54 | 0 | 87 | 5 | 0 | 7 | 6 | .538 | 0 | 0-- | - | 4.00 | 3.78 |
| 2013 Frdrck* | A+ | 1 | 0 | 0 | 0 | 2.0 | 10 | 4 | 1 | 1 | 0 | 0 | 0 | 0 | 0 | 0 | 1 | 0 | 0 | 0 | 0 | - | 0 | 0-- | - | 7.48 | 4.50 |
| 2011 NYM | NL | 14 | 0 | 0 | 3 | 13.0 | 57 | 14 | 10 | 10 | 1 | 1 | 0 | 0 | 7 | 0 | 8 | 0 | 0 | 0 | 2 | .000 | 0 | 1-2 | 4 | 5.05 | 6.92 |
| 2012 Mil | NL | 6 | 1 | 0 | 2 | 9.1 | 38 | 7 | 1 | 1 | 1 | 0 | 0 | 0 | 5 | 0 | 3 | 0 | 0 | 0 | 0 | - | 0 | 0-0 | 0 | 3.42 | 0.96 |
| 2013 Bal | AL | 11 | 1 | 0 | 2 | 17.0 | 63 | 10 | 7 | 6 | 4 | 0 | 0 | 1 | 3 | 0 | 12 | 0 | 0 | 0 | 0 | - | 0 | 0-1 | 2 | 2.17 | 3.18 |
| 3 ML YEARS | | 31 | 2 | 0 | 7 | 39.1 | 158 | 31 | 18 | 17 | 6 | 1 | 0 | 1 | 15 | 0 | 23 | 0 | 0 | 0 | 2 | .000 | 0 | 1-3 | 6 | 3.40 | 3.89 |

# Drew Storen

**Pitches:** R **Bats:** B **Pos:** RP-68 STORE-inn **Ht:** 6'1" **Wt:** 225 **Born:** 8/11/1987 **Age:** 26

| Year Team | Lg | HOW MUCH HE PITCHED G | GS | CG | GF | IP | BFP | WHAT HE GAVE UP H | R | ER | HR | SH | SF | HB | TBB | IBB | SO | WP | Bk | THE RESULTS W | L | Pct | Sh | Sv-Op | Hld | ERC | ERA |
|---|---|---|---|---|---|---|---|---|---|---|---|---|---|---|---|---|---|---|---|---|---|---|---|---|---|---|---|
| 2013 Syrcse* | AAA | 6 | 1 | 0 | 0 | 6.1 | 27 | 7 | 5 | 4 | 1 | 1 | 0 | 0 | 0 | 0 | 11 | 0 | 0 | 0 | 0 | - | 0 | 0-- | - | 3.22 | 5.68 |
| 2010 Was | NL | 54 | 0 | 0 | 22 | 55.1 | 232 | 48 | 24 | 22 | 3 | 6 | 2 | 3 | 22 | 3 | 52 | 3 | 0 | 4 | 4 | .500 | 0 | 5-7 | 10 | 3.19 | 3.58 |
| 2011 Was | NL | 73 | 0 | 0 | 52 | 75.1 | 303 | 57 | 24 | 23 | 8 | 1 | 1 | 2 | 20 | 4 | 74 | 2 | 0 | 6 | 3 | .667 | 0 | 43-48 | 3 | 2.35 | 2.75 |
| 2012 Was | NL | 37 | 0 | 0 | 17 | 30.1 | 116 | 22 | 8 | 8 | 0 | 0 | 2 | 1 | 8 | 0 | 24 | 1 | 0 | 3 | 1 | .750 | 0 | 4-5 | 10 | 1.79 | 2.37 |
| 2013 Was | NL | 68 | 0 | 0 | 20 | 61.2 | 267 | 65 | 34 | 31 | 7 | 3 | 1 | 1 | 19 | 2 | 58 | 2 | 0 | 4 | 2 | .667 | 0 | 3-8 | 24 | 4.08 | 4.52 |
| Postseason | | 4 | 0 | 0 | 4 | 4.0 | 18 | 3 | 4 | 4 | 0 | 0 | 0 | 0 | 3 | 0 | 6 | 0 | 0 | 1 | 1 | .500 | 0 | 1-2 | 0 | 3.21 | 9.00 |
| 4 ML YEARS | | 232 | 0 | 0 | 111 | 222.2 | 918 | 192 | 90 | 84 | 18 | 10 | 6 | 7 | 69 | 9 | 208 | 8 | 0 | 17 | 10 | .630 | 0 | 55-68 | 47 | 2.93 | 3.40 |

# Mickey Storey

**Pitches:** R **Bats:** R **Pos:** RP-3 STORY **Ht:** 6'1" **Wt:** 185 **Born:** 3/16/1986 **Age:** 28

| Year Team | Lg | HOW MUCH HE PITCHED G | GS | CG | GF | IP | BFP | WHAT HE GAVE UP H | R | ER | HR | SH | SF | HB | TBB | IBB | SO | WP | Bk | THE RESULTS W | L | Pct | Sh | Sv-Op | Hld | ERC | ERA |
|---|---|---|---|---|---|---|---|---|---|---|---|---|---|---|---|---|---|---|---|---|---|---|---|---|---|---|---|
| 2009 Kane | A | 13 | 0 | 0 | 10 | 17.1 | 60 | 5 | 1 | 1 | 0 | 0 | 0 | 2 | 1 | 0 | 23 | 0 | 0 | 0 | 0 | - | 0 | 9-- | - | 0.38 | 0.52 |
| 2009 Stcktn | A+ | 22 | 0 | 0 | 19 | 23.2 | 97 | 19 | 10 | 6 | 2 | 1 | 0 | 1 | 6 | 0 | 35 | 1 | 0 | 1 | 1 | .500 | 0 | 9-- | - | 2.50 | 2.28 |
| 2009 Scrmto | AAA | 2 | 0 | 0 | 1 | 3.0 | 9 | 0 | 0 | 0 | 0 | 0 | 0 | 0 | 0 | 0 | 4 | 0 | 0 | 0 | 0 | - | 0 | 0-- | - | 0.00 | 0.00 |
| 2009 Mdlnd | AA | 4 | 0 | 0 | 0 | 7.2 | 27 | 3 | 0 | 0 | 0 | 0 | 0 | 1 | 1 | 0 | 9 | 0 | 0 | 1 | 0 | 1.000 | 0 | 0-- | - | 0.73 | 0.00 |
| 2010 Mdlnd | AA | 43 | 1 | 0 | 23 | 71.0 | 294 | 58 | 31 | 26 | 5 | 2 | 6 | 3 | 22 | 2 | 63 | 5 | 1 | 5 | 4 | .556 | 0 | 8-- | - | 2.66 | 3.30 |
| 2010 Scrmto | AAA | 11 | 0 | 0 | 6 | 13.0 | 60 | 15 | 10 | 8 | 3 | 0 | 1 | 0 | 5 | 0 | 14 | 1 | 1 | 1 | 1 | .500 | 0 | 1-- | - | 5.64 | 5.54 |
| 2011 Mdlnd | AA | 27 | 0 | 0 | 12 | 38.0 | 165 | 41 | 17 | 17 | 3 | 1 | 2 | 3 | 13 | 2 | 31 | 3 | 1 | 3 | 3 | .500 | 0 | 4-- | - | 4.43 | 4.03 |
| 2011 OKCity | AAA | 23 | 0 | 0 | 7 | 29.1 | 130 | 35 | 13 | 13 | 3 | 0 | 0 | 0 | 12 | 0 | 28 | 1 | 0 | 1 | 0 | 1.000 | 0 | 2-- | - | 5.33 | 3.99 |
| 2012 OKCity | AAA | 38 | 2 | 0 | 9 | 65.0 | 273 | 62 | 24 | 22 | 8 | 4 | 2 | 3 | 14 | 1 | 72 | 3 | 1 | 7 | 4 | .636 | 0 | 2-- | - | 3.36 | 3.05 |
| 2013 Buffalo | AAA | 36 | 0 | 0 | 13 | 59.2 | 236 | 43 | 21 | 17 | 5 | 1 | 0 | 2 | 16 | 0 | 70 | 1 | 0 | 0 | 2 | .000 | 0 | 2-- | - | 2.18 | 2.56 |
| 2012 Hou | NL | 26 | 0 | 0 | 3 | 30.1 | 127 | 27 | 14 | 13 | 2 | 2 | 0 | 1 | 10 | 0 | 34 | 0 | 0 | 0 | 1 | .000 | 0 | 0-0 | 3 | 3.10 | 3.86 |
| 2013 Tor | AL | 3 | 0 | 0 | 3 | 4.0 | 19 | 6 | 3 | 3 | 0 | 0 | 1 | 0 | 1 | 0 | 6 | 0 | 0 | 0 | 0 | - | 0 | 0-0 | 0 | 5.46 | 6.75 |
| 2 ML YEARS | | 29 | 0 | 0 | 6 | 34.1 | 146 | 33 | 17 | 16 | 2 | 2 | 1 | 1 | 11 | 0 | 40 | 0 | 0 | 0 | 1 | .000 | 0 | 0-0 | 3 | 3.36 | 4.19 |

# Dan Straily

**Pitches:** R **Bats:** R **Pos:** SP-27 STRAY-lee **Ht:** 6'2" **Wt:** 215 **Born:** 12/1/1988 **Age:** 25

| Year Team | Lg | HOW MUCH HE PITCHED G | GS | CG | GF | IP | BFP | WHAT HE GAVE UP H | R | ER | HR | SH | SF | HB | TBB | IBB | SO | WP | Bk | THE RESULTS W | L | Pct | Sh | Sv-Op | Hld | ERC | ERA |
|---|---|---|---|---|---|---|---|---|---|---|---|---|---|---|---|---|---|---|---|---|---|---|---|---|---|---|---|
| 2009 Vancvr | A- | 16 | 11 | 0 | 1 | 59.0 | 256 | 66 | 27 | 27 | 5 | 1 | 1 | 5 | 18 | 0 | 66 | 2 | 0 | 5 | 3 | .625 | 0 | 0-- | - | 4.68 | 4.12 |
| 2010 Kane | A | 28 | 28 | 0 | 0 | 148.0 | 623 | 138 | 75 | 71 | 13 | 5 | 6 | 7 | 61 | 3 | 149 | 10 | 1 | 10 | 7 | .588 | 0 | 0-- | - | 3.91 | 4.32 |
| 2011 Stcktn | A+ | 28 | 26 | 0 | 0 | 160.2 | 683 | 160 | 78 | 69 | 10 | 6 | 8 | 14 | 40 | 0 | 154 | 5 | 0 | 11 | 9 | .550 | 0 | 0-- | - | 3.54 | 3.87 |
| 2012 Mdlnd | AA | 14 | 14 | 0 | 0 | 85.1 | 347 | 69 | 36 | 32 | 6 | 3 | 4 | 5 | 23 | 1 | 108 | 6 | 0 | 3 | 4 | .429 | 0 | 0-- | - | 2.59 | 3.38 |
| 2012 Scrmto | AAA | 11 | 11 | 0 | 0 | 66.2 | 255 | 40 | 15 | 15 | 3 | 2 | 0 | 1 | 19 | 0 | 82 | 3 | 0 | 6 | 3 | .667 | 0 | 0-- | - | 1.51 | 2.03 |
| 2013 Scrmto | AAA | 5 | 5 | 0 | 0 | 31.2 | 130 | 24 | 11 | 4 | 1 | 2 | 0 | 0 | 9 | 1 | 33 | 2 | 0 | 3 | 1 | .750 | 0 | 0-- | - | 1.87 | 1.14 |
| 2012 Oak | AL | 7 | 7 | 0 | 0 | 39.1 | 172 | 36 | 19 | 17 | 11 | 1 | 1 | 2 | 16 | 1 | 32 | 0 | 0 | 2 | 1 | .667 | 0 | 0-0 | 0 | 4.94 | 3.89 |
| 2013 Oak | AL | 27 | 27 | 0 | 0 | 152.1 | 640 | 132 | 74 | 67 | 16 | 4 | 5 | 7 | 57 | 0 | 124 | 7 | 0 | 10 | 8 | .556 | 0 | 0-0 | 0 | 3.46 | 3.96 |
| 2 ML YEARS | | 34 | 34 | 0 | 0 | 191.2 | 812 | 168 | 93 | 84 | 27 | 5 | 6 | 9 | 73 | 1 | 156 | 7 | 0 | 12 | 9 | .571 | 0 | 0-0 | 0 | 3.76 | 3.94 |

# Stephen Strasburg

**Pitches:** R **Bats:** R **Pos:** SP-30 STRAHS-berg **Ht:** 6'4" **Wt:** 200 **Born:** 7/20/1988 **Age:** 25

| Year Team | Lg | HOW MUCH HE PITCHED G | GS | CG | GF | IP | BFP | WHAT HE GAVE UP H | R | ER | HR | SH | SF | HB | TBB | IBB | SO | WP | Bk | THE RESULTS W | L | Pct | Sh | Sv-Op | Hld | ERC | ERA |
|---|---|---|---|---|---|---|---|---|---|---|---|---|---|---|---|---|---|---|---|---|---|---|---|---|---|---|---|
| 2010 Was | NL | 12 | 12 | 0 | 0 | 68.0 | 274 | 56 | 25 | 22 | 5 | 2 | 2 | 0 | 17 | 0 | 92 | 2 | 0 | 5 | 3 | .625 | 0 | 0-0 | 0 | 2.41 | 2.91 |
| 2011 Was | NL | 5 | 5 | 0 | 0 | 24.0 | 88 | 15 | 5 | 4 | 0 | 1 | 1 | 0 | 2 | 0 | 24 | 0 | 0 | 1 | 1 | .500 | 0 | 0-0 | 0 | 0.97 | 1.50 |
| 2012 Was | NL | 28 | 28 | 0 | 0 | 159.1 | 653 | 136 | 62 | 56 | 15 | 6 | 4 | 4 | 48 | 1 | 197 | 5 | 0 | 15 | 6 | .714 | 0 | 0-0 | 0 | 2.97 | 3.16 |
| 2013 Was | NL | 30 | 30 | 1 | 0 | 183.0 | 731 | 136 | 71 | 61 | 16 | 5 | 1 | 12 | 56 | 1 | 191 | 7 | **3** | 8 | 9 | .471 | 1 | 0-0 | 0 | 2.58 | 3.00 |
| 4 ML YEARS | | 75 | 75 | 1 | 0 | 434.1 | 1746 | 343 | 163 | 143 | 36 | 14 | 8 | 16 | 123 | 2 | 504 | 14 | 3 | 29 | 19 | .604 | 1 | 0-0 | 0 | 2.57 | 2.96 |

## Huston Street

**Pitches:** R **Bats:** R **Pos:** RP-58 **Ht:** 6'0" **Wt:** 195 **Born:** 8/2/1983 **Age:** 30

| HOW MUCH HE PITCHED | | | | | | | | WHAT HE GAVE UP | | | | | | | | | | | | THE RESULTS | | | | | | | |
|---|---|---|---|---|---|---|---|---|---|---|---|---|---|---|---|---|---|---|---|---|---|---|---|---|---|---|---|
| Year Team | Lg | G | GS | CG | GF | IP | BFP | H | R | ER | HR | SH | SF | HB | TBB | IBB | SO | WP | Bk | W | L | Pct | Sh | Sv-Op | Hld | ERC | ERA |
| 2013 Lk Els* | A+ | 1 | 1 | 0 | 0 | 1.0 | 3 | 0 | 0 | 0 | 0 | 0 | 0 | 0 | 0 | 0 | 0 | 0 | 0 | 0 | 0 | - | 0 | 0- - | - | 0.00 | 0.00 |
| 2005 Oak | AL | 67 | 0 | 0 | 47 | 78.1 | 306 | 53 | 17 | 15 | 3 | 3 | 2 | 2 | 26 | 4 | 72 | 1 | 0 | 5 | 1 | .833 | 0 | 23-27 | 0 | 1.87 | 1.72 |
| 2006 Oak | AL | 69 | 0 | 0 | 55 | 70.2 | 290 | 64 | 28 | 26 | 4 | 3 | 3 | 2 | 13 | 3 | 67 | 4 | 0 | 4 | 4 | .500 | 0 | 37-48 | 1 | 2.49 | 3.31 |
| 2007 Oak | AL | 48 | 0 | 0 | 35 | 50.0 | 199 | 35 | 20 | 16 | 5 | 2 | 1 | 0 | 12 | 3 | 63 | 0 | 0 | 5 | 2 | .714 | 0 | 16-21 | 5 | 1.84 | 2.88 |
| 2008 Oak | AL | 63 | 0 | 0 | 37 | 70.0 | 287 | 58 | 29 | 29 | 6 | 3 | 3 | 1 | 27 | 6 | 69 | 2 | 0 | 7 | 5 | .583 | 0 | 18-25 | 6 | 2.98 | 3.73 |
| 2009 Col | NL | 64 | 0 | 0 | 52 | 61.2 | 240 | 43 | 22 | 21 | 7 | 3 | 2 | 0 | 13 | 4 | 70 | 0 | 0 | 4 | 1 | .800 | 0 | 35-37 | 2 | 1.83 | 3.06 |
| 2010 Col | NL | 44 | 0 | 0 | 39 | 47.1 | 187 | 39 | 21 | 19 | 5 | 0 | 1 | 2 | 11 | 4 | 45 | 2 | 1 | 4 | 4 | .500 | 0 | 20-25 | 0 | 2.66 | 3.61 |
| 2011 Col | NL | 62 | 0 | 0 | 47 | 58.1 | 239 | 62 | 28 | 25 | 10 | 3 | 1 | 1 | 9 | 1 | 55 | 0 | 0 | 1 | 4 | .200 | 0 | 29-33 | 4 | 4.03 | 3.86 |
| 2012 SD | NL | 40 | 0 | 0 | 36 | 39.0 | 144 | 17 | 8 | 8 | 2 | 1 | 1 | 0 | 11 | 1 | 47 | 1 | 0 | 2 | 1 | .667 | 0 | 23-24 | 0 | 0.99 | 1.85 |
| 2013 SD | NL | 58 | 0 | 0 | 52 | 56.2 | 222 | 44 | 17 | 17 | 12 | 0 | 1 | 0 | 14 | 1 | 46 | 4 | 0 | 2 | 5 | .286 | 0 | 33-35 | 0 | 3.00 | 2.70 |
| Postseason | | 8 | 0 | 0 | 7 | 9.0 | 43 | 14 | 9 | 9 | 2 | 1 | 1 | 0 | 4 | 0 | 5 | 0 | 0 | 0 | 3 | .000 | 0 | 3-4 | 0 | 8.97 | 9.00 |
| 9 ML YEARS | | 515 | 0 | 0 | 400 | 532.0 | 2114 | 415 | 190 | 176 | 54 | 18 | 15 | 8 | 136 | 27 | 534 | 14 | 1 | 34 | 27 | .557 | 0 | 234-275 | 18 | 2.40 | 2.98 |

## Pedro Strop

**Pitches:** R **Bats:** R **Pos:** RP-66 STROPE **Ht:** 6'0" **Wt:** 215 **Born:** 6/13/1985 **Age:** 29

| HOW MUCH HE PITCHED | | | | | | | | WHAT HE GAVE UP | | | | | | | | | | | | THE RESULTS | | | | | | | |
|---|---|---|---|---|---|---|---|---|---|---|---|---|---|---|---|---|---|---|---|---|---|---|---|---|---|---|---|
| Year Team | Lg | G | GS | CG | GF | IP | BFP | H | R | ER | HR | SH | SF | HB | TBB | IBB | SO | WP | Bk | W | L | Pct | Sh | Sv-Op | Hld | ERC | ERA |
| 2009 Tex | AL | 7 | 0 | 0 | 3 | 7.0 | 30 | 6 | 6 | 6 | 0 | 0 | 0 | 0 | 4 | 0 | 9 | 0 | 0 | 0 | 0 | - | 0 | 0-0 | 0 | 3.27 | 7.71 |
| 2010 Tex | AL | 15 | 0 | 0 | 5 | 10.2 | 60 | 17 | 12 | 12 | 2 | 1 | 0 | 1 | 11 | 0 | 11 | 5 | 1 | 0 | 0 | - | 0 | 0-0 | 1 | 11.92 | 10.13 |
| 2011 2 Tms | AL | 23 | 0 | 0 | 6 | 22.0 | 90 | 15 | 5 | 5 | 0 | 2 | 1 | 1 | 10 | 0 | 21 | 2 | **2** | 2 | 1 | .667 | 0 | 0-2 | 4 | 2.15 | 2.05 |
| 2012 Bal | AL | 70 | 0 | 0 | 17 | 66.1 | 283 | 52 | 18 | 18 | 2 | 1 | 1 | 4 | 37 | 2 | 58 | 5 | 0 | 5 | 2 | .714 | 0 | 3-10 | 24 | 3.22 | 2.44 |
| 2013 2 Tms | | 66 | 0 | 0 | 22 | 57.1 | 254 | 45 | 30 | 29 | 5 | 7 | 0 | 6 | 26 | 2 | 66 | 8 | 1 | 2 | 5 | .286 | 0 | 1-4 | 17 | 3.21 | 4.55 |
| 11 Tex | AL | 11 | 0 | 0 | 4 | 9.2 | 44 | 7 | 4 | 4 | 0 | 1 | 1 | 1 | 7 | 0 | 9 | 2 | 2 | 0 | 1 | .000 | 0 | 0-1 | 0 | 3.34 | 3.72 |
| 11 Bal | AL | 12 | 0 | 0 | 2 | 12.1 | 46 | 8 | 1 | 1 | 0 | 1 | 0 | 0 | 3 | 0 | 12 | 0 | 0 | 2 | 0 | 1.000 | 0 | 0-1 | 4 | 1.39 | 0.73 |
| 13 Bal | AL | 29 | 0 | 0 | 15 | 22.1 | 111 | 23 | 19 | 18 | 4 | 4 | 0 | 2 | 15 | 2 | 24 | 5 | 1 | 0 | 3 | .000 | 0 | 0-3 | 3 | 5.81 | 7.25 |
| 13 ChC | NL | 37 | 0 | 0 | 7 | 35.0 | 143 | 22 | 11 | 11 | 1 | 3 | 0 | 4 | 11 | 0 | 42 | 3 | 0 | 2 | 2 | .500 | 0 | 1-1 | 14 | 1.80 | 2.83 |
| Postseason | | 2 | 0 | 0 | 0 | 2.1 | 9 | 1 | 0 | 0 | 0 | 0 | 0 | 0 | 1 | 0 | 2 | 0 | 0 | 1 | 0 | 1.000 | 0 | 0-0 | 0 | 1.08 | 0.00 |
| 5 ML YEARS | | 181 | 0 | 0 | 53 | 163.1 | 717 | 135 | 71 | 70 | 9 | 11 | 2 | 12 | 88 | 4 | 165 | 20 | 4 | 9 | 8 | .529 | 0 | 4-16 | 46 | 3.53 | 3.86 |

## Drew Stubbs

**Bats:** R **Throws:** R **Pos:** RF-105;CF-43;PR-11;DH-1 **Ht:** 6'4" **Wt:** 205 **Born:** 10/4/1984 **Age:** 29

| BATTING | | | | | | | | | | | | | | | | | | | | BASERUNNING | | | | AVERAGES | | |
|---|---|---|---|---|---|---|---|---|---|---|---|---|---|---|---|---|---|---|---|---|---|---|---|---|---|---|
| Year Team | Lg | G | AB | H | 2B | 3B | HR | (Hm | Rd) | TB | R | RBI | RC | TBB | IBB | SO | HBP | SH | SF | SB | CS | SB% | GDP | Avg | OBP | Slg |
| 2009 Cin | NL | 42 | 180 | 48 | 5 | 1 | 8 | (7 | 1) | 79 | 27 | 17 | 22 | 15 | 0 | 49 | 0 | 1 | 0 | 10 | 4 | .71 | 1 | .267 | .323 | .439 |
| 2010 Cin | NL | 150 | 514 | 131 | 19 | 6 | 22 | (13 | 9) | 228 | 91 | 77 | 74 | 55 | 2 | 168 | 5 | 3 | 6 | 30 | 6 | .83 | 6 | .255 | .329 | .444 |
| 2011 Cin | NL | 158 | 604 | 147 | 22 | 3 | 15 | (9 | 6) | 220 | 92 | 44 | 66 | 63 | 1 | **205** | 7 | 6 | 1 | 40 | 10 | .80 | 2 | .243 | .321 | .364 |
| 2012 Cin | NL | 136 | 493 | 105 | 13 | 2 | 14 | (6 | 8) | 164 | 75 | 40 | 45 | 42 | 0 | 166 | 2 | 6 | 1 | 30 | 7 | .81 | 2 | .213 | .277 | .333 |
| 2013 Cle | AL | 146 | 430 | 100 | 21 | 2 | 10 | (4 | 6) | 155 | 59 | 45 | 50 | 44 | 1 | 141 | 2 | 2 | 3 | 17 | 2 | .89 | 3 | .233 | .305 | .360 |
| Postseason | | 8 | 28 | 5 | 1 | 1 | 0 | (0 | 0) | 8 | 4 | 1 | 1 | 2 | 0 | 7 | 0 | 0 | 0 | 0 | 0 | - | 0 | .179 | .233 | .286 |
| 5 ML YEARS | | 632 | 2221 | 531 | 80 | 14 | 69 | (39 | 30) | 846 | 344 | 223 | 257 | 219 | 4 | 729 | 16 | 18 | 11 | 127 | 29 | .81 | 14 | .239 | .310 | .381 |

## Eric Stults

**Pitches:** L **Bats:** L **Pos:** SP-33 **Ht:** 6'0" **Wt:** 230 **Born:** 12/9/1979 **Age:** 34

| HOW MUCH HE PITCHED | | | | | | | | WHAT HE GAVE UP | | | | | | | | | | | | THE RESULTS | | | | | | | |
|---|---|---|---|---|---|---|---|---|---|---|---|---|---|---|---|---|---|---|---|---|---|---|---|---|---|---|---|
| Year Team | Lg | G | GS | CG | GF | IP | BFP | H | R | ER | HR | SH | SF | HB | TBB | IBB | SO | WP | Bk | W | L | Pct | Sh | Sv-Op | Hld | ERC | ERA |
| 2006 LAD | NL | 6 | 2 | 0 | 2 | 17.2 | 73 | 17 | 12 | 11 | 4 | 2 | 0 | 0 | 7 | 0 | 5 | 0 | 0 | 1 | 0 | 1.000 | 0 | 0-0 | 0 | 4.91 | 5.60 |
| 2007 LAD | NL | 12 | 5 | 0 | 0 | 38.2 | 179 | 50 | 26 | 25 | 5 | 1 | 1 | 1 | 17 | 2 | 30 | 2 | 0 | 1 | 4 | .200 | 0 | 0-0 | 1 | 6.25 | 5.82 |
| 2008 LAD | NL | 7 | 7 | 1 | 0 | 38.2 | 167 | 38 | 18 | 15 | 6 | 2 | 0 | 1 | 13 | 2 | 30 | 0 | 0 | 2 | 3 | .400 | 1 | 0-0 | 0 | 4.07 | 3.49 |
| 2009 LAD | NL | 10 | 10 | 1 | 0 | 50.0 | 223 | 51 | 27 | 27 | 3 | 3 | 0 | 4 | 26 | 2 | 33 | 2 | 0 | 4 | 3 | .571 | 1 | 0-0 | 0 | 4.67 | 4.86 |
| 2011 Col | NL | 6 | 0 | 0 | 2 | 12.0 | 53 | 11 | 8 | 8 | 4 | 0 | 0 | 1 | 4 | 1 | 7 | 0 | 0 | 0 | 0 | - | 0 | 0-0 | 0 | 4.94 | 6.00 |
| 2012 2 Tms | | 20 | 15 | 0 | 2 | 99.0 | 413 | 92 | 38 | 32 | 7 | 9 | 5 | 2 | 27 | 0 | 55 | 1 | 1 | 8 | 3 | .727 | 0 | 0-0 | 0 | 3.06 | 2.91 |
| 2013 SD | NL | 33 | 33 | 2 | 0 | 203.2 | 857 | 219 | 97 | 89 | 18 | 10 | 6 | 2 | 40 | 2 | 131 | 2 | 1 | 11 | 13 | .458 | 0 | 0-0 | 0 | 3.63 | 3.93 |
| 12 CWS | AL | 2 | 1 | 0 | 1 | 6.2 | 30 | 6 | 2 | 2 | 0 | 0 | 0 | 1 | 4 | 0 | 4 | 0 | 0 | 0 | 0 | - | 0 | 0-0 | 0 | 4.14 | 2.70 |
| 12 SD | NL | 18 | 14 | 0 | 1 | 92.1 | 383 | 86 | 36 | 30 | 7 | 9 | 5 | 1 | 23 | 0 | 51 | 1 | 1 | 8 | 3 | .727 | 0 | 0-0 | 0 | 2.98 | 2.92 |
| 7 ML YEARS | | 94 | 72 | 4 | 6 | 459.2 | 1965 | 478 | 226 | 207 | 47 | 27 | 12 | 11 | 134 | 9 | 291 | 7 | 2 | 27 | 26 | .509 | 2 | 0-0 | 1 | 3.94 | 4.05 |

## Michael Stutes

**Pitches:** R **Bats:** R **Pos:** RP-16 STOOTS **Ht:** 6'1" **Wt:** 185 **Born:** 9/4/1986 **Age:** 27

| HOW MUCH HE PITCHED | | | | | | | | WHAT HE GAVE UP | | | | | | | | | | | | THE RESULTS | | | | | | | |
|---|---|---|---|---|---|---|---|---|---|---|---|---|---|---|---|---|---|---|---|---|---|---|---|---|---|---|---|
| Year Team | Lg | G | GS | CG | GF | IP | BFP | H | R | ER | HR | SH | SF | HB | TBB | IBB | SO | WP | Bk | W | L | Pct | Sh | Sv-Op | Hld | ERC | ERA |
| 2013 LV* | AAA | 20 | 0 | 0 | 10 | 27.0 | 117 | 21 | 11 | 10 | 1 | 3 | 0 | 2 | 11 | 1 | 25 | 6 | 3 | 1 | 2 | .333 | 0 | 2- - | - | 2.60 | 3.33 |
| 2011 Phi | NL | 57 | 0 | 0 | 11 | 62.0 | 259 | 49 | 25 | 25 | 7 | 2 | 2 | 2 | 28 | 2 | 58 | 0 | 0 | 6 | 2 | .750 | 0 | 0-0 | 13 | 3.31 | 3.63 |
| 2012 Phi | NL | 6 | 0 | 0 | 4 | 5.2 | 29 | 7 | 6 | 4 | 0 | 0 | 0 | 0 | 4 | 0 | 5 | 1 | 0 | 0 | 0 | - | 0 | 0-0 | 1 | 5.50 | 6.35 |
| 2013 Phi | NL | 16 | 0 | 0 | 4 | 17.2 | 75 | 14 | 11 | 9 | 1 | 0 | 0 | 1 | 8 | 1 | 9 | 1 | 0 | 3 | 1 | .750 | 0 | 0-0 | 3 | 2.96 | 4.58 |
| Postseason | | 1 | 0 | 0 | 0 | 0.1 | 5 | 3 | 3 | 3 | 0 | 0 | 0 | 0 | 1 | 0 | 0 | 0 | 0 | 0 | 0 | - | 0 | 0-0 | 0 | 83.91 | 81.00 |
| 3 ML YEARS | | 79 | 0 | 0 | 19 | 85.1 | 363 | 70 | 42 | 38 | 8 | 2 | 2 | 3 | 40 | 3 | 72 | 2 | 0 | 9 | 3 | .750 | 0 | 0-0 | 17 | 3.38 | 4.01 |

# Jesus Sucre

**Bats:** R **Throws:** R **Pos:** C-8 SUE-cray **Ht:** 6'0" **Wt:** 225 **Born:** 4/30/1988 **Age:** 26

| | | | BATTING | | | | | | | | | | | | | | | | | | BASERUNNING | | | | AVERAGES | | |
|---|---|---|---|---|---|---|---|---|---|---|---|---|---|---|---|---|---|---|---|---|---|---|---|---|---|---|---|
| Year | Team | Lg | G | AB | H | 2B | 3B | HR | (Hm | Rd) | TB | R | RBI | RC | TBB | IBB | SO | HBP | SH | SF | SB | CS | SB% | GDP | Avg | OBP | Slg |
| 2009 | Rome | A | 45 | 169 | 55 | 15 | 0 | 1 | (- | -) | 73 | 14 | 18 | 24 | 6 | 0 | 17 | 1 | 0 | 0 | 1 | 4 | .20 | 8 | .325 | .352 | .432 |
| 2009 | MrtlBh | A+ | 53 | 197 | 51 | 8 | 1 | 5 | (- | -) | 76 | 17 | 20 | 22 | 8 | 0 | 33 | 0 | 0 | 1 | 3 | 1 | .75 | 11 | .259 | .286 | .386 |
| 2010 | MrtlBh | A+ | 48 | 191 | 42 | 9 | 0 | 5 | (- | -) | 66 | 14 | 22 | 16 | 7 | 0 | 26 | 1 | 1 | 0 | 1 | 0 | 1.00 | 8 | .220 | .251 | .346 |
| 2010 | Missi | AA | 38 | 145 | 43 | 11 | 1 | 2 | (- | -) | 62 | 20 | 12 | 17 | 1 | 1 | 17 | 0 | 1 | 0 | 0 | 2 | .00 | 5 | .297 | .301 | .428 |
| 2011 | Missi | AA | 40 | 137 | 30 | 5 | 0 | 0 | (- | -) | 35 | 13 | 10 | 8 | 6 | 0 | 12 | 1 | 1 | 1 | 0 | 1 | .00 | 7 | .219 | .255 | .255 |
| 2011 | Jacksn | AA | 32 | 84 | 18 | 3 | 0 | 1 | (- | -) | 24 | 4 | 9 | 5 | 5 | 0 | 7 | 0 | 2 | 0 | 0 | 1 | .00 | 5 | .214 | .258 | .286 |
| 2012 | Jacksn | AA | 90 | 321 | 87 | 11 | 0 | 1 | (- | -) | 101 | 27 | 30 | 34 | 20 | 2 | 39 | 3 | 4 | 1 | 1 | 1 | .50 | 9 | .271 | .319 | .315 |
| 2013 | Tacom | AAA | 23 | 87 | 26 | 3 | 0 | 0 | (- | -) | 29 | 10 | 8 | 10 | 7 | 0 | 10 | 0 | 1 | 0 | 1 | 1 | .50 | 2 | .299 | .351 | .333 |
| 2013 | Ms | R | 6 | 19 | 6 | 1 | 0 | 0 | (- | -) | 7 | 1 | 3 | 2 | 1 | 0 | 2 | 0 | 0 | 0 | 0 | 0 | - | 0 | .316 | .350 | .368 |
| 2013 | Sea | AL | 8 | 26 | 5 | 0 | 0 | 0 | (0 | 0) | 5 | 1 | 3 | 1 | 2 | 0 | 1 | 0 | 0 | 1 | 0 | 0 | - | 2 | .192 | .241 | .192 |

# Eric Surkamp

**Pitches:** L **Bats:** L **Pos:** SP-1 SIR-camp **Ht:** 6'5" **Wt:** 215 **Born:** 7/16/1987 **Age:** 26

| | | | HOW MUCH HE PITCHED | | | | | | WHAT HE GAVE UP | | | | | | | | | | | | THE RESULTS | | | | | | | |
|---|---|---|---|---|---|---|---|---|---|---|---|---|---|---|---|---|---|---|---|---|---|---|---|---|---|---|---|---|
| Year | Team | Lg | G | GS | CG | GF | IP | BFP | H | R | ER | HR | SH | SF | HB | TBB | IBB | SO | WP | Bk | W | L | Pct | Sh | Sv-Op | Hld | ERC | ERA |
| 2009 | Augsta | A | 23 | 23 | 2 | 0 | 131.0 | 551 | 129 | 57 | 48 | 6 | 2 | 4 | 4 | 39 | 0 | 169 | 9 | 0 | 11 | 5 | .688 | 0 | 0- - | - | 3.36 | 3.30 |
| 2010 | SnJos | A+ | 17 | 17 | 1 | 0 | 101.1 | 398 | 79 | 39 | 35 | 5 | 4 | 2 | 6 | 22 | 0 | 108 | 5 | 0 | 4 | 2 | .667 | 1 | 0- - | - | 2.21 | 3.11 |
| 2011 | Rchmd | AA | 23 | 22 | 1 | 0 | 142.1 | 572 | 110 | 37 | 32 | 5 | 6 | 0 | 5 | 44 | 0 | 165 | 5 | 1 | 10 | 4 | .714 | 0 | 0- - | - | 2.30 | 2.02 |
| 2011 | SnJos | A+ | 1 | 1 | 0 | 0 | 6.0 | 22 | 4 | 0 | 0 | 0 | 0 | 0 | 0 | 1 | 0 | 5 | 0 | 0 | 1 | 0 | 1.000 | 0 | 0- - | - | 1.29 | 0.00 |
| 2013 | SnJos | A+ | 5 | 5 | 0 | 0 | 15.1 | 55 | 8 | 6 | 5 | 2 | 0 | 1 | 0 | 3 | 0 | 17 | 0 | 0 | 0 | 0 | - | 0 | 0- - | - | 1.36 | 2.93 |
| 2013 | Fresno | AAA | 11 | 11 | 0 | 0 | 71.1 | 282 | 56 | 23 | 22 | 4 | 4 | 2 | 2 | 20 | 0 | 54 | 1 | 0 | 7 | 1 | .875 | 0 | 0- - | - | 2.39 | 2.78 |
| 2011 | SF | NL | 6 | 6 | 0 | 0 | 26.2 | 126 | 32 | 18 | 17 | 1 | 2 | 2 | 2 | 17 | 1 | 13 | 0 | 0 | 2 | 2 | .500 | 0 | 0-0 | 0 | 6.03 | 5.74 |
| 2013 | SF | NL | 1 | 1 | 0 | 0 | 2.2 | 18 | 9 | 7 | 7 | 2 | 0 | 0 | 2 | 0 | 0 | 0 | 0 | 0 | 0 | 1 | .000 | 0 | 0-0 | 0 | 32.56 | 23.63 |
| 2 ML YEARS | | | 7 | 7 | 0 | 0 | 29.1 | 144 | 41 | 25 | 24 | 3 | 2 | 2 | 4 | 17 | 1 | 13 | 0 | 0 | 2 | 3 | .400 | 0 | 0-0 | 0 | 7.94 | 7.36 |

# Steve Susdorf

**Bats:** L **Throws:** L **Pos:** LF-2;PH-1 SUSS-dorff **Ht:** 6'1" **Wt:** 195 **Born:** 3/28/1986 **Age:** 28

| | | | BATTING | | | | | | | | | | | | | | | | | | BASERUNNING | | | | AVERAGES | | |
|---|---|---|---|---|---|---|---|---|---|---|---|---|---|---|---|---|---|---|---|---|---|---|---|---|---|---|---|
| Year | Team | Lg | G | AB | H | 2B | 3B | HR | (Hm | Rd) | TB | R | RBI | RC | TBB | IBB | SO | HBP | SH | SF | SB | CS | SB% | GDP | Avg | OBP | Slg |
| 2009 | Lakwd | A | 21 | 78 | 26 | 5 | 1 | 2 | (- | -) | 39 | 9 | 15 | 16 | 7 | 0 | 15 | 2 | 0 | 0 | 2 | 0 | 1.00 | 1 | .333 | .402 | .500 |
| 2009 | Clrwtr | A+ | 40 | 151 | 56 | 12 | 0 | 3 | (- | -) | 77 | 20 | 22 | 32 | 11 | 1 | 23 | 2 | 0 | 0 | 3 | 0 | 1.00 | 5 | .371 | .421 | .510 |
| 2009 | Rdng | AA | 24 | 77 | 17 | 4 | 0 | 2 | (- | -) | 27 | 12 | 7 | 8 | 7 | 1 | 26 | 4 | 0 | 0 | 0 | 1 | .00 | 1 | .221 | .318 | .351 |
| 2010 | Clrwtr | A+ | 128 | 489 | 136 | 28 | 2 | 11 | (- | -) | 201 | 60 | 77 | 71 | 46 | 1 | 109 | 4 | 0 | 4 | 6 | 4 | .60 | 10 | .278 | .343 | .411 |
| 2011 | Rdng | AA | 78 | 242 | 82 | 20 | 0 | 6 | (- | -) | 120 | 51 | 35 | 49 | 25 | 1 | 48 | 3 | 1 | 1 | 7 | 1 | .88 | 5 | .339 | .406 | .496 |
| 2012 | Rdng | AA | 33 | 111 | 33 | 9 | 1 | 1 | (- | -) | 47 | 11 | 15 | 16 | 9 | 0 | 15 | 1 | 1 | 1 | 2 | 2 | .50 | 2 | .297 | .352 | .423 |
| 2012 | LV | AAA | 84 | 266 | 75 | 18 | 0 | 1 | (- | -) | 96 | 38 | 26 | 36 | 27 | 3 | 42 | 3 | 0 | 4 | 4 | 4 | .50 | 3 | .282 | .350 | .361 |
| 2013 | LV | AAA | 102 | 310 | 97 | 20 | 1 | 2 | (- | -) | 125 | 43 | 36 | 52 | 37 | 0 | 52 | 6 | 0 | 6 | 11 | 7 | .61 | 2 | .313 | .390 | .403 |
| 2013 | Phi | NL | 3 | 7 | 1 | 1 | 0 | 0 | (0 | 0) | 2 | 1 | 0 | 0 | 0 | 0 | 1 | 0 | 0 | 0 | 0 | 0 | - | 1 | .143 | .143 | .286 |

# Ichiro Suzuki

EE-chee-row soo-ZOO-kee

**Bats:** L **Throws:** R **Pos:** RF-128;CF-13;PH-13;LF-9;DH-3;PR-1 **Ht:** 5'11" **Wt:** 170 **Born:** 10/22/1973 **Age:** 40

| | | | BATTING | | | | | | | | | | | | | | | | | | BASERUNNING | | | | AVERAGES | | |
|---|---|---|---|---|---|---|---|---|---|---|---|---|---|---|---|---|---|---|---|---|---|---|---|---|---|---|---|
| Year | Team | Lg | G | AB | H | 2B | 3B | HR | (Hm | Rd) | TB | R | RBI | RC | TBB | IBB | SO | HBP | SH | SF | SB | CS | SB% | GDP | Avg | OBP | Slg |
| 2001 | Sea | AL | 157 | **692** | **242** | 34 | 8 | 8 | (5 | 3) | 316 | 127 | 69 | 124 | 30 | 10 | 53 | 8 | 4 | 4 | **56** | 14 | .80 | 3 | **.350** | .381 | .457 |
| 2002 | Sea | AL | 157 | 647 | 208 | 27 | 8 | 8 | (4 | 4) | 275 | 111 | 51 | 110 | 68 | **27** | 62 | 5 | 3 | 5 | 31 | **15** | .67 | 8 | .321 | .388 | .425 |
| 2003 | Sea | AL | 159 | 679 | 212 | 29 | 8 | 13 | (8 | 5) | 296 | 111 | 62 | 107 | 36 | 7 | 69 | 6 | 3 | 1 | 34 | 8 | .81 | 3 | .312 | .352 | .436 |
| 2004 | Sea | AL | 161 | **704** | **262** | 24 | 5 | 8 | (4 | 4) | 320 | 101 | 60 | 125 | 49 | **19** | 63 | 4 | 2 | 3 | 36 | 11 | .77 | 6 | **.372** | .414 | .455 |
| 2005 | Sea | AL | **162** | **679** | 206 | 21 | 12 | 15 | (8 | 7) | 296 | 111 | 68 | 109 | 48 | 23 | 66 | 4 | 2 | 6 | 33 | 8 | .80 | 5 | .303 | .350 | .436 |
| 2006 | Sea | AL | 161 | **695** | **224** | 20 | 9 | 9 | (6 | 3) | 289 | 110 | 49 | 107 | 49 | 16 | 71 | 5 | 1 | 2 | 45 | 2 | **.96** | 2 | .322 | .370 | .416 |
| 2007 | Sea | AL | 161 | **678** | **238** | 22 | 7 | 6 | (3 | 3) | 292 | 111 | 68 | 128 | 49 | 13 | 77 | 3 | 4 | 2 | 37 | 8 | .82 | 7 | .351 | .396 | .431 |
| 2008 | Sea | AL | 162 | **686** | **213** | 20 | 7 | 6 | (3 | 3) | 265 | 103 | 42 | 100 | 51 | 12 | 65 | 5 | 3 | 4 | 43 | 4 | .91 | 8 | .310 | .361 | .386 |
| 2009 | Sea | AL | 146 | 639 | **225** | 31 | 4 | 11 | (6 | 5) | 297 | 88 | 46 | 111 | 32 | **15** | 71 | 4 | 2 | 1 | 26 | 9 | .74 | 1 | .352 | .386 | .465 |
| 2010 | Sea | AL | **162** | **680** | **214** | 30 | 3 | 6 | (1 | 5) | 268 | 74 | 43 | 96 | 45 | 13 | 86 | 3 | 3 | 1 | 42 | 9 | .82 | 3 | .315 | .359 | .394 |
| 2011 | Sea | AL | **161** | **677** | 184 | 22 | 3 | 5 | (4 | 1) | 227 | 80 | 47 | 80 | 39 | 13 | 69 | 0 | 1 | 4 | 40 | 7 | .85 | 11 | .272 | .310 | .335 |
| 2012 | 2 Tms | AL | **162** | 629 | 178 | 28 | 6 | 9 | (6 | 3) | 245 | 77 | 55 | 63 | 22 | 5 | 61 | 2 | 5 | 5 | 29 | 7 | .81 | 12 | .283 | .307 | .390 |
| 2013 | NYY | AL | 150 | 520 | 136 | 15 | 3 | 7 | (5 | 2) | 178 | 57 | 35 | 56 | 26 | 4 | 63 | 1 | 6 | 2 | 20 | 4 | .83 | 6 | .262 | .297 | .342 |
| 12 | Sea | AL | 95 | 402 | 105 | 15 | 5 | 4 | (1 | 3) | 142 | 49 | 28 | 33 | 17 | 4 | 40 | 0 | 0 | 4 | 15 | 2 | .88 | 10 | .261 | .288 | .353 |
| 12 | NYY | AL | 67 | 227 | 73 | 13 | 1 | 5 | (5 | 0) | 103 | 28 | 27 | 30 | 5 | 1 | 21 | 2 | 5 | 1 | 14 | 5 | .74 | 2 | .322 | .340 | .454 |
| Postseason | | | 19 | 78 | 27 | 4 | 0 | 1 | (1 | 0) | 34 | 10 | 8 | 11 | 7 | 2 | 9 | 0 | 1 | 0 | 4 | 3 | .57 | 0 | .346 | .400 | .436 |
| 13 ML YEARS | | | 2061 | 8605 | 2742 | 323 | 83 | 111 | (63 | 48) | 3564 | 1261 | 695 | 1316 | 544 | 177 | 876 | 50 | 39 | 40 | 472 | 106 | .82 | 75 | .319 | .361 | .414 |

# Kurt Suzuki

**Bats:** R **Throws:** R **Pos:** C-93;PR-3;PH-1 **Ht:** 5'11" **Wt:** 205 **Born:** 10/4/1983 **Age:** 30

| | | | BATTING | | | | | | | | | | | | | | | | | | BASERUNNING | | | | AVERAGES | | |
|---|---|---|---|---|---|---|---|---|---|---|---|---|---|---|---|---|---|---|---|---|---|---|---|---|---|---|---|
| Year | Team | Lg | G | AB | H | 2B | 3B | HR | (Hm | Rd) | TB | R | RBI | RC | TBB | IBB | SO | HBP | SH | SF | SB | CS | SB% | GDP | Avg | OBP | Slg |
| 2007 | Oak | AL | 68 | 213 | 53 | 13 | 0 | 7 | (4 | 3) | 87 | 27 | 39 | 33 | 24 | 0 | 39 | 3 | 3 | 5 | 0 | 0 | - | 4 | .249 | .327 | .408 |
| 2008 | Oak | AL | 148 | 530 | 148 | 25 | 1 | 7 | (5 | 2) | 196 | 54 | 42 | 66 | 44 | 2 | 69 | 11 | 2 | 1 | 2 | 3 | .40 | 20 | .279 | .346 | .370 |
| 2009 | Oak | AL | 147 | 570 | 156 | 37 | 1 | 15 | (8 | 7) | 240 | 74 | 88 | 77 | 28 | 0 | 59 | 8 | 1 | 7 | 8 | 2 | .80 | 14 | .274 | .313 | .421 |
| 2010 | Oak | AL | 131 | 495 | 120 | 18 | 2 | 13 | (8 | 5) | 181 | 55 | 71 | 54 | 33 | 3 | 49 | 12 | 0 | 4 | 3 | 2 | .60 | 22 | .242 | .303 | .366 |
| 2011 | Oak | AL | 134 | 460 | 109 | 26 | 0 | 14 | (8 | 6) | 177 | 54 | 44 | 42 | 38 | 1 | 64 | 7 | 3 | 7 | 2 | 2 | .50 | 14 | .237 | .301 | .385 |
| 2012 | 2 Tms | | 118 | 408 | 96 | 20 | 0 | 6 | (3 | 3) | 134 | 36 | 43 | 39 | 20 | 3 | 73 | 5 | 4 | 5 | 2 | 0 | 1.00 | 5 | .235 | .276 | .328 |
| 2013 | 2 Tms | | 94 | 285 | 66 | 13 | 1 | 5 | (2 | 3) | 96 | 25 | 32 | 34 | 22 | 6 | 35 | 3 | 2 | 4 | 2 | 0 | 1.00 | 2 | .232 | .290 | .337 |

| BATTING | | | | | | | | | | | | | | | | | | | | | | BASERUNNING | | | | AVERAGES | | |
|---|---|---|---|---|---|---|---|---|---|---|---|---|---|---|---|---|---|---|---|---|---|---|---|---|---|---|---|---|
| Year Team | Lg | G | AB | H | 2B | 3B | HR | (Hm | Rd) | TB | R | RBI | RC | TBB | IBB | SO | HBP | SH | SF | SB | CS | SB% | GDP | Avg | OBP | Slg | | |
| 12 Oak | AL | 75 | 262 | 57 | 15 | 0 | 1 | (1 | 0) | 75 | 19 | 18 | 16 | 9 | 0 | 53 | 3 | 2 | 2 | 1 | 0 | 1.00 | 3 | .218 | .250 | .286 | | |
| 12 Was | NL | 43 | 146 | 39 | 5 | 0 | 5 | (2 | 3) | 59 | 17 | 25 | 23 | 11 | 3 | 20 | 2 | 2 | 3 | 1 | 0 | 1.00 | 2 | .267 | .321 | .404 | | |
| 13 Was | NL | 79 | 252 | 56 | 11 | 1 | 3 | (0 | 3) | 78 | 19 | 25 | 26 | 20 | 6 | 32 | 3 | 2 | 4 | 2 | 0 | 1.00 | 2 | .222 | .283 | .310 | | |
| 13 Oak | AL | 15 | 33 | 10 | 2 | 0 | 2 | (2 | 0) | 18 | 6 | 7 | 8 | 2 | 0 | 3 | 0 | 0 | 0 | 0 | 0 | - | 0 | .303 | .343 | .545 | | |
| Postseason | | 5 | 17 | 4 | 0 | 0 | 0 | (0 | 0) | 4 | 0 | 2 | 2 | 2 | 0 | 4 | 0 | 0 | 0 | 0 | 0 | - | 0 | .235 | .316 | .235 | | |
| 7 ML YEARS | | 840 | 2961 | 748 | 152 | 5 | 67 | (38 | 29) | 1111 | 325 | 359 | 345 | 209 | 15 | 388 | 49 | 15 | 33 | 19 | 9 | .68 | 81 | .253 | .309 | .375 | | |

## Anthony Swarzak

**Pitches:** R **Bats:** R **Pos:** RP-48 SWORE-zack **Ht:** 6'4" **Wt:** 210 **Born:** 9/10/1985 **Age:** 28

| HOW MUCH HE PITCHED | | | | | | | | WHAT HE GAVE UP | | | | | | | | | | | | THE RESULTS | | | | | | | |
|---|---|---|---|---|---|---|---|---|---|---|---|---|---|---|---|---|---|---|---|---|---|---|---|---|---|---|---|
| Year | Team | Lg | G | GS | CG | GF | IP | BFP | H | R | ER | HR | SH | SF | HB | TBB | IBB | SO | WP | Bk | W | L | Pct | Sh | Sv-Op | Hld | ERC | ERA |
| 2009 | Min | AL | 12 | 12 | 0 | 0 | 59.0 | 268 | 76 | 43 | 41 | 12 | 1 | 1 | 2 | 20 | 0 | 34 | 0 | 0 | 3 | 7 | .300 | 0 | 0-0 | 0 | 6.50 | 6.25 |
| 2011 | Min | AL | 27 | 11 | 0 | 2 | 102.0 | 441 | 111 | 53 | 49 | 9 | 2 | 3 | 6 | 26 | 1 | 55 | 3 | 1 | 4 | 7 | .364 | 0 | 0-0 | 0 | 4.11 | 4.32 |
| 2012 | Min | AL | 44 | 5 | 0 | 9 | 96.2 | 413 | 106 | 57 | 54 | 15 | 3 | 6 | 0 | 31 | **8** | 62 | 3 | 0 | 3 | 6 | .333 | 0 | 0-1 | 1 | 4.63 | 5.03 |
| 2013 | Min | AL | 48 | 0 | 0 | 8 | 96.0 | 387 | 89 | 33 | 31 | 7 | 2 | 5 | 1 | 22 | 1 | 69 | 1 | 0 | 3 | 2 | .600 | 0 | 0-2 | 3 | 2.94 | 2.91 |
| 4 ML YEARS | | | 131 | 28 | 0 | 19 | 353.2 | 1509 | 382 | 186 | 175 | 43 | 8 | 15 | 9 | 99 | 10 | 220 | 7 | 1 | 13 | 22 | .371 | 0 | 0-3 | 4 | 4.29 | 4.45 |

## Ryan Sweeney

**Bats:** L **Throws:** L **Pos:** CF-45;PH-17;LF-10;RF-4 **Ht:** 6'4" **Wt:** 225 **Born:** 2/20/1985 **Age:** 29

| BATTING | | | | | | | | | | | | | | | | | | | | | BASERUNNING | | | | AVERAGES | | |
|---|---|---|---|---|---|---|---|---|---|---|---|---|---|---|---|---|---|---|---|---|---|---|---|---|---|---|---|
| Year Team | Lg | G | AB | H | 2B | 3B | HR | (Hm | Rd) | TB | R | RBI | RC | TBB | IBB | SO | HBP | SH | SF | SB | CS | SB% | GDP | Avg | OBP | Slg | |
| 2013 Iowa* | AAA | 23 | 83 | 28 | 2 | 2 | 6 | (- | -) | 52 | 12 | 16 | 19 | 8 | 0 | 15 | 0 | 0 | 0 | 1 | 0 | 1.00 | 3 | .337 | .396 | .627 | |
| 2013 Cubs* | R | 4 | 14 | 4 | 2 | 0 | 0 | (- | -) | 6 | 4 | 2 | 2 | 3 | 0 | 1 | 0 | 0 | 0 | 0 | 0 | - | 1 | .286 | .412 | .429 | |
| 2013 Kane* | A | 1 | 4 | 1 | 0 | 0 | 0 | (- | -) | 1 | 0 | 0 | 0 | 0 | 0 | 0 | 0 | 0 | 0 | 0 | 0 | - | 1 | .250 | .250 | .250 | |
| 2006 CWS | AL | 18 | 35 | 8 | 0 | 0 | 0 | (0 | 0) | 8 | 1 | 5 | 1 | 0 | 0 | 7 | 0 | 0 | 0 | 0 | 0 | - | 1 | .229 | .229 | .229 | |
| 2007 CWS | AL | 15 | 45 | 9 | 3 | 0 | 1 | (1 | 0) | 15 | 5 | 5 | 2 | 4 | 0 | 5 | 0 | 0 | 0 | 0 | 1 | .00 | 2 | .200 | .265 | .333 | |
| 2008 Oak | AL | 115 | 384 | 110 | 18 | 2 | 5 | (1 | 4) | 147 | 53 | 45 | 56 | 38 | 3 | 67 | 3 | 2 | 6 | 9 | 1 | .90 | 9 | .286 | .350 | .383 | |
| 2009 Oak | AL | 134 | 484 | 142 | 31 | 3 | 6 | (2 | 4) | 197 | 68 | 53 | 63 | 40 | 1 | 67 | 3 | 2 | 5 | 6 | 5 | .55 | 14 | .293 | .348 | .407 | |
| 2010 Oak | AL | 82 | 303 | 89 | 20 | 2 | 1 | (1 | 0) | 116 | 41 | 36 | 38 | 24 | 2 | 41 | 0 | 1 | 3 | 1 | 1 | .50 | 14 | .294 | .342 | .383 | |
| 2011 Oak | AL | 108 | 264 | 70 | 11 | 3 | 1 | (1 | 0) | 90 | 34 | 25 | 35 | 33 | 3 | 48 | 0 | 1 | 1 | 1 | 1 | .50 | 7 | .265 | .346 | .341 | |
| 2012 Bos | AL | 63 | 204 | 53 | 19 | 2 | 0 | (0 | 0) | 76 | 22 | 16 | 20 | 12 | 0 | 43 | 1 | 1 | 1 | 0 | 0 | - | 1 | .260 | .303 | .373 | |
| 2013 ChC | NL | 70 | 192 | 51 | 13 | 2 | 6 | (3 | 3) | 86 | 19 | 19 | 23 | 17 | 0 | 31 | 0 | 2 | 1 | 1 | 0 | 1.00 | 3 | .266 | .324 | .448 | |
| 8 ML YEARS | | 605 | 1911 | 532 | 115 | 14 | 20 | (9 | 11) | 735 | 243 | 204 | 238 | 168 | 9 | 309 | 7 | 9 | 17 | 18 | 9 | .67 | 51 | .278 | .336 | .385 | |

## Nick Swisher

**Bats:** B **Throws:** L **Pos:** 1B-112;RF-27;DH-17;PH-1 **Ht:** 6'0" **Wt:** 200 **Born:** 11/25/1980 **Age:** 33

| BATTING | | | | | | | | | | | | | | | | | | | | | BASERUNNING | | | | AVERAGES | | |
|---|---|---|---|---|---|---|---|---|---|---|---|---|---|---|---|---|---|---|---|---|---|---|---|---|---|---|---|
| Year Team | Lg | G | AB | H | 2B | 3B | HR | (Hm | Rd) | TB | R | RBI | RC | TBB | IBB | SO | HBP | SH | SF | SB | CS | SB% | GDP | Avg | OBP | Slg | |
| 2004 Oak | AL | 20 | 60 | 15 | 4 | 0 | 2 | (1 | 1) | 25 | 11 | 8 | 8 | 8 | 0 | 11 | 2 | 0 | 1 | 0 | 0 | - | 2 | .250 | .352 | .417 | |
| 2005 Oak | AL | 131 | 462 | 109 | 32 | 1 | 21 | (11 | 10) | 206 | 66 | 74 | 62 | 55 | 3 | 110 | 4 | 0 | 1 | 0 | 1 | .00 | 9 | .236 | .322 | .446 | |
| 2006 Oak | AL | 157 | 556 | 141 | 24 | 2 | 35 | (17 | 18) | 274 | 106 | 95 | 95 | 97 | 7 | 152 | 11 | 2 | 6 | 1 | 2 | .33 | 13 | .254 | .372 | .493 | |
| 2007 Oak | AL | 150 | 539 | 141 | 36 | 1 | 22 | (8 | 14) | 245 | 84 | 78 | 89 | 100 | 12 | 131 | 10 | 1 | 9 | 3 | 2 | .60 | 13 | .262 | .381 | .455 | |
| 2008 CWS | AL | 153 | 497 | 109 | 21 | 1 | 24 | (19 | 5) | 204 | 86 | 69 | 69 | 82 | 6 | 135 | 4 | 1 | 4 | 3 | 3 | .50 | 14 | .219 | .332 | .410 | |
| 2009 NYY | AL | 150 | 498 | 124 | 35 | 1 | 29 | (8 | **21**) | 248 | 84 | 82 | 84 | 97 | 2 | 126 | 3 | 3 | 6 | 0 | 0 | - | 13 | .249 | .371 | .498 | |
| 2010 NYY | AL | 150 | 566 | 163 | 33 | 3 | 29 | (15 | 14) | 289 | 91 | 89 | 100 | 58 | 0 | 139 | 6 | 3 | 2 | 1 | 2 | .33 | 13 | .288 | .359 | .511 | |
| 2011 NYY | AL | 150 | 526 | 137 | 30 | 0 | 23 | (12 | 11) | 236 | 81 | 85 | 90 | 95 | 6 | 125 | 5 | 1 | 8 | 2 | 2 | .50 | 18 | .260 | .374 | .449 | |
| 2012 NYY | AL | 148 | 537 | 146 | 36 | 0 | 24 | (11 | 13) | 254 | 75 | 93 | 98 | 77 | 2 | 141 | 4 | 1 | 5 | 2 | 3 | .40 | 9 | .272 | .364 | .473 | |
| 2013 Cle | AL | 145 | 549 | 135 | 27 | 2 | 22 | (11 | 11) | 232 | 74 | 63 | 75 | 77 | 3 | 138 | 4 | 0 | 4 | 1 | 0 | 1.00 | 11 | .246 | .341 | .423 | |
| Postseason | | 46 | 154 | 26 | 9 | 0 | 4 | (3 | 1) | 47 | 16 | 8 | 10 | 24 | 0 | 46 | 1 | 1 | 1 | 0 | 0 | - | 4 | .169 | .283 | .305 | |
| 10 ML YEARS | | 1354 | 4790 | 1220 | 278 | 11 | 231 | (113 | 118) | 2213 | 758 | 736 | 770 | 746 | 41 | 1208 | 53 | 12 | 46 | 13 | 15 | .46 | 115 | .255 | .358 | .462 | |

## Jose Tabata

**Bats:** R **Throws:** R **Pos:** RF-50;LF-40;PH-29 TAH-bah-tah **Ht:** 5'11" **Wt:** 210 **Born:** 8/12/1988 **Age:** 25

| BATTING | | | | | | | | | | | | | | | | | | | | | BASERUNNING | | | | AVERAGES | | |
|---|---|---|---|---|---|---|---|---|---|---|---|---|---|---|---|---|---|---|---|---|---|---|---|---|---|---|---|
| Year Team | Lg | G | AB | H | 2B | 3B | HR | (Hm | Rd) | TB | R | RBI | RC | TBB | IBB | SO | HBP | SH | SF | SB | CS | SB% | GDP | Avg | OBP | Slg | |
| 2013 Indy* | AAA | 9 | 28 | 5 | 1 | 0 | 0 | (- | -) | 6 | 1 | 0 | 1 | 3 | 0 | 7 | 1 | 0 | 0 | 1 | 0 | 1.00 | 2 | .179 | .281 | .214 | |
| 2010 Pit | NL | 102 | 405 | 121 | 21 | 4 | 4 | (3 | 1) | 162 | 61 | 35 | 59 | 28 | 0 | 57 | 2 | 5 | 1 | 19 | 7 | .73 | 7 | .299 | .346 | .400 | |
| 2011 Pit | NL | 91 | 334 | 89 | 18 | 1 | 4 | (3 | 1) | 121 | 53 | 21 | 41 | 40 | 1 | 61 | 4 | 1 | 3 | 16 | 7 | .70 | 8 | .266 | .349 | .362 | |
| 2012 Pit | NL | 103 | 333 | 81 | 20 | 3 | 3 | (1 | 2) | 116 | 43 | 16 | 31 | 29 | 0 | 58 | 6 | 6 | 0 | 8 | 12 | .40 | 7 | .243 | .315 | .348 | |
| 2013 Pit | NL | 106 | 308 | 87 | 17 | 5 | 6 | (4 | 2) | 132 | 35 | 33 | 45 | 23 | 0 | 45 | 5 | 5 | 0 | 3 | 1 | .75 | 6 | .282 | .342 | .429 | |
| 4 ML YEARS | | 402 | 1380 | 378 | 76 | 13 | 17 | (11 | 6) | 531 | 192 | 105 | 176 | 120 | 1 | 221 | 17 | 17 | 4 | 46 | 27 | .63 | 28 | .274 | .339 | .385 | |

## Hisanori Takahashi

**Pitches:** L **Bats:** L **Pos:** RP-3 EES-ah-nore-ee tah-ka-HA-shee **Ht:** 5'10" **Wt:** 180 **Born:** 4/2/1975 **Age:** 39

| HOW MUCH HE PITCHED | | | | | | | | WHAT HE GAVE UP | | | | | | | | | | | | THE RESULTS | | | | | | | |
|---|---|---|---|---|---|---|---|---|---|---|---|---|---|---|---|---|---|---|---|---|---|---|---|---|---|---|---|
| Year | Team | Lg | G | GS | CG | GF | IP | BFP | H | R | ER | HR | SH | SF | HB | TBB | IBB | SO | WP | Bk | W | L | Pct | Sh | Sv-Op | Hld | ERC | ERA |
| 2013 | Iowa* | AAA | 20 | 0 | 0 | 3 | 27.1 | 103 | 14 | 7 | 6 | 3 | 1 | 1 | 0 | 9 | 0 | 25 | 2 | 0 | 1 | 0 | 1.000 | 0 | 0- - | - | 1.54 | 1.98 |
| 2013 | ColSpr* | AAA | 18 | 0 | 0 | 4 | 25.2 | 127 | 39 | 26 | 19 | 2 | 1 | 0 | 0 | 13 | 2 | 36 | 3 | 0 | 1 | 1 | .500 | 0 | 0- - | - | 7.28 | 6.66 |
| 2010 | NYM | NL | 53 | 12 | 0 | 21 | 122.0 | 516 | 116 | 51 | 49 | 13 | 10 | 3 | 0 | 43 | 7 | 114 | 1 | 1 | 10 | 6 | .625 | 0 | 8-8 | 3 | 3.57 | 3.61 |
| 2011 | LAA | AL | 61 | 0 | 0 | 18 | 68.0 | 281 | 58 | 30 | 26 | 7 | 3 | 3 | 0 | 25 | 8 | 52 | 1 | 0 | 4 | 3 | .571 | 0 | 2-5 | 7 | 3.01 | 3.44 |
| 2012 | 2 Tms | | 51 | 0 | 0 | 11 | 50.1 | 212 | 49 | 32 | 31 | 8 | 2 | 1 | 0 | 14 | 1 | 52 | 0 | 0 | 0 | 3 | .000 | 0 | 0-1 | 3 | 3.77 | 5.54 |
| 2013 | ChC | NL | 3 | 0 | 0 | 2 | 3.0 | 14 | 3 | 2 | 2 | 1 | 0 | 1 | 0 | 2 | 0 | 3 | 0 | 0 | 0 | 0 | - | 0 | 0-0 | 0 | 6.85 | 6.00 |
| 12 | LAA | AL | 42 | 0 | 0 | 9 | 42.0 | 173 | 39 | 24 | 23 | 6 | 1 | 1 | 0 | 10 | 1 | 41 | 0 | 0 | 0 | 3 | .000 | 0 | 0-1 | 3 | 3.28 | 4.93 |
| 12 | Pit | NL | 9 | 0 | 0 | 2 | 8.1 | 39 | 10 | 8 | 8 | 2 | 1 | 0 | 0 | 4 | 0 | 11 | 0 | 0 | 0 | 0 | - | 0 | 0-0 | 0 | 6.53 | 8.64 |
| 4 ML YEARS | | | 168 | 12 | 0 | 52 | 243.1 | 1023 | 226 | 115 | 108 | 29 | 15 | 8 | 0 | 84 | 16 | 221 | 2 | 1 | 14 | 12 | .538 | 0 | 10-14 | 13 | 3.49 | 3.99 |

## Kensuke Tanaka

**Bats:** L **Throws:** R **Pos:** LF-9;PH-5;PR-1 — kin-SOO-kay teh-NAH-kah — **Ht:** 5'9" **Wt:** 170 **Born:** 5/20/1981 **Age:** 33

| BATTING | | | | | | | | | | | | | | | | | | | | | | BASERUNNING | | | | AVERAGES | | |
|---|---|---|---|---|---|---|---|---|---|---|---|---|---|---|---|---|---|---|---|---|---|---|---|---|---|---|---|---|
| Year | Team | Lg | G | AB | H | 2B | 3B | HR | (Hm | Rd) | TB | R | RBI | RC | TBB | IBB | SO | HBP | SH | SF | SB | CS | SB% | GDP | Avg | OBP | Slg |
| 2009 | Hokado | Jap | 144 | 575 | 163 | 34 | 4 | 3 | (- | -) | 214 | 93 | 49 | 90 | 79 | 4 | 105 | 5 | 17 | 4 | 31 | 11 | .74 | 0 | .283 | .373 | .372 |
| 2010 | Hokado | Jap | 143 | 576 | 193 | 24 | 4 | 5 | (- | -) | 240 | 88 | 54 | 107 | 72 | 4 | 66 | 2 | 7 | 5 | 34 | 10 | .77 | 6 | .335 | .408 | .417 |
| 2011 | Hokado | Jap | 49 | 200 | 58 | 6 | 1 | 1 | (- | -) | 69 | 25 | 10 | 25 | 17 | 0 | 21 | 0 | 2 | 1 | 8 | 3 | .73 | 1 | .290 | .344 | .345 |
| 2012 | Hokado | Jap | 114 | 457 | 137 | 14 | 3 | 3 | (- | -) | 166 | 49 | 32 | 61 | 35 | 2 | 36 | 2 | 8 | 3 | 13 | 9 | .59 | 2 | .300 | .350 | .363 |
| 2013 | Fresno | AAA | 107 | 343 | 113 | 14 | 3 | 1 | (- | -) | 136 | 54 | 31 | 60 | 42 | 2 | 36 | 3 | 5 | 7 | 22 | 10 | .69 | 6 | .329 | .400 | .397 |
| 2013 | SF | NL | 15 | 30 | 8 | 0 | 0 | 0 | (0 | 0) | 8 | 4 | 2 | 4 | 4 | 0 | 3 | 0 | 0 | 0 | 2 | 0 | 1.00 | 0 | .267 | .353 | .267 |

## Masahiro Tanaka

**Pitches:** R **Bats:** R **Pos:** P — mah-sah-HEE-roh tah-NAH-kah — **Ht:** 6'2" **Wt:** 205 **Born:** 11/1/1988 **Age:** 25

| HOW MUCH HE PITCHED | | | | | | | | | WHAT HE GAVE UP | | | | | | | | | | | | | THE RESULTS | | | | | | | |
|---|---|---|---|---|---|---|---|---|---|---|---|---|---|---|---|---|---|---|---|---|---|---|---|---|---|---|---|---|---|
| Year | Team | Lg | G | GS | CG | GF | IP | BFP | H | R | ER | HR | SH | SF | HB | TBB | IBB | SO | WP | Bk | W | L | Pct | Sh | Sv-Op | Hld | ERC | ERA |
| 2009 | Tohoku | Jap | 25 | 24 | 6 | 1 | 189.2 | 771 | 170 | 51 | 49 | 13 | - | - | 7 | 43 | 0 | 171 | 3 | 0 | 15 | 6 | .714 | 3 | 1-- | - | 2.82 | 2.33 |
| 2010 | Tohoku | Jap | 20 | 20 | 8 | 0 | 155.0 | 643 | 159 | 47 | 43 | 9 | - | - | 5 | 32 | 1 | 119 | 1 | 0 | 11 | 6 | .647 | 1 | 0-- | - | 3.33 | 2.50 |
| 2011 | Tohoku | Jap | 27 | 27 | 14 | 0 | 226.1 | 866 | 171 | 35 | 32 | 8 | - | - | 5 | 27 | 0 | 241 | 7 | 0 | 19 | 5 | .792 | 6 | 0-- | - | 1.60 | 1.27 |
| 2012 | Tohoku | Jap | 22 | 22 | 8 | 0 | 173.0 | 696 | 160 | 45 | 36 | 4 | - | - | 2 | 19 | 0 | 169 | 4 | 0 | 10 | 4 | .714 | 3 | 0-- | - | 2.15 | 1.87 |
| 2013 | Tohoku | Jap | 26 | 25 | 8 | 1 | 199.0 | 770 | 157 | 31 | 27 | 6 | - | - | 3 | 30 | 0 | 173 | 9 | 0 | 22 | 0 | 1.000 | 2 | 1-- | - | 1.77 | 1.22 |

## Michael Taylor

**Bats:** R **Throws:** R **Pos:** RF-6;LF-5;PH-1 — **Ht:** 6'5" **Wt:** 255 **Born:** 12/19/1985 **Age:** 28

| BATTING | | | | | | | | | | | | | | | | | | | | | | BASERUNNING | | | | AVERAGES | | |
|---|---|---|---|---|---|---|---|---|---|---|---|---|---|---|---|---|---|---|---|---|---|---|---|---|---|---|---|---|
| Year | Team | Lg | G | AB | H | 2B | 3B | HR | (Hm | Rd) | TB | R | RBI | RC | TBB | IBB | SO | HBP | SH | SF | SB | CS | SB% | GDP | Avg | OBP | Slg |
| 2013 | Scrmto* | AAA | 112 | 420 | 118 | 25 | 1 | 18 | (- | -) | 199 | 54 | 85 | 74 | 50 | 0 | 88 | 5 | 0 | 6 | 5 | 2 | .71 | 9 | .281 | .360 | .474 |
| 2011 | Oak | AL | 11 | 30 | 6 | 0 | 0 | 1 | (1 | 0) | 9 | 4 | 1 | 4 | 5 | 0 | 11 | 0 | 0 | 0 | 0 | 0 | - | 0 | .200 | .314 | .300 |
| 2012 | Oak | AL | 6 | 21 | 3 | 1 | 0 | 0 | (0 | 0) | 4 | 2 | 0 | 0 | 0 | 0 | 10 | 0 | 0 | 0 | 0 | 0 | - | 1 | .143 | .143 | .190 |
| 2013 | Oak | AL | 9 | 23 | 1 | 0 | 0 | 0 | (0 | 0) | 1 | 0 | 0 | 0 | 2 | 0 | 5 | 0 | 0 | 0 | 0 | 0 | - | 1 | .043 | .120 | .043 |
| 3 ML YEARS | | | 26 | 74 | 10 | 1 | 0 | 1 | (1 | 0) | 14 | 6 | 1 | 4 | 7 | 0 | 26 | 0 | 0 | 0 | 0 | 0 | - | 2 | .135 | .210 | .189 |

## Junichi Tazawa

**Pitches:** R **Bats:** R **Pos:** RP-71 — joo-NEE-chee tuh-ZAH-wah — **Ht:** 5'11" **Wt:** 200 **Born:** 6/6/1986 **Age:** 28

| HOW MUCH HE PITCHED | | | | | | | | | WHAT HE GAVE UP | | | | | | | | | | | | | THE RESULTS | | | | | | | |
|---|---|---|---|---|---|---|---|---|---|---|---|---|---|---|---|---|---|---|---|---|---|---|---|---|---|---|---|---|---|
| Year | Team | Lg | G | GS | CG | GF | IP | BFP | H | R | ER | HR | SH | SF | HB | TBB | IBB | SO | WP | Bk | W | L | Pct | Sh | Sv-Op | Hld | ERC | ERA |
| 2009 | Bos | AL | 6 | 4 | 0 | 1 | 25.1 | 130 | 43 | 23 | 21 | 4 | 0 | 3 | 3 | 9 | 0 | 13 | 0 | 0 | 2 | 3 | .400 | 0 | 0-0 | 0 | 9.14 | 7.46 |
| 2011 | Bos | AL | 3 | 0 | 0 | 2 | 3.0 | 13 | 3 | 2 | 2 | 1 | 0 | 0 | 0 | 1 | 0 | 4 | 0 | 0 | 0 | 0 | - | 0 | 0-0 | 0 | 5.31 | 6.00 |
| 2012 | Bos | AL | 37 | 0 | 0 | 13 | 44.0 | 172 | 37 | 7 | 7 | 1 | 1 | 1 | 2 | 5 | 0 | 45 | 0 | 0 | 1 | 1 | .500 | 0 | 1-1 | 5 | 1.94 | 1.43 |
| 2013 | Bos | AL | 71 | 0 | 0 | 10 | 68.1 | 284 | 70 | 25 | 24 | 9 | 2 | 5 | 1 | 12 | 1 | 72 | 3 | 1 | 5 | 4 | .556 | 0 | 0-8 | 25 | 3.55 | 3.16 |
| 4 ML YEARS | | | 117 | 4 | 0 | 26 | 140.2 | 599 | 153 | 57 | 54 | 15 | 3 | 9 | 6 | 27 | 1 | 134 | 3 | 1 | 8 | 8 | .500 | 0 | 1-9 | 30 | 3.92 | 3.45 |

## Everett Teaford

**Pitches:** L **Bats:** L **Pos:** RP-1 — **Ht:** 6'0" **Wt:** 165 **Born:** 5/15/1984 **Age:** 30

| HOW MUCH HE PITCHED | | | | | | | | | WHAT HE GAVE UP | | | | | | | | | | | | | THE RESULTS | | | | | | | |
|---|---|---|---|---|---|---|---|---|---|---|---|---|---|---|---|---|---|---|---|---|---|---|---|---|---|---|---|---|---|
| Year | Team | Lg | G | GS | CG | GF | IP | BFP | H | R | ER | HR | SH | SF | HB | TBB | IBB | SO | WP | Bk | W | L | Pct | Sh | Sv-Op | Hld | ERC | ERA |
| 2013 | Omha* | AAA | 31 | 14 | 0 | 4 | 95.1 | 416 | 92 | 39 | 37 | 7 | 2 | 2 | 5 | 39 | 2 | 99 | 5 | 0 | 4 | 6 | .400 | 0 | 0-- | - | 3.87 | 3.49 |
| 2011 | KC | AL | 26 | 3 | 0 | 7 | 44.0 | 175 | 36 | 17 | 16 | 8 | 1 | 3 | 1 | 14 | 0 | 28 | 2 | 0 | 2 | 1 | .667 | 0 | 1-1 | 1 | 3.50 | 3.27 |
| 2012 | KC | AL | 18 | 5 | 0 | 3 | 61.1 | 263 | 68 | 34 | 34 | 11 | 0 | 1 | 2 | 21 | 0 | 35 | 2 | 1 | 1 | 4 | .200 | 0 | 0-0 | 0 | 5.31 | 4.99 |
| 2013 | KC | AL | 1 | 0 | 0 | 0 | 0.2 | 3 | 1 | 0 | 0 | 0 | 0 | 0 | 0 | 0 | 0 | 0 | 0 | 0 | 0 | 0 | - | 0 | 0-0 | 0 | 4.47 | 0.00 |
| 3 ML YEARS | | | 45 | 8 | 0 | 10 | 106.0 | 441 | 105 | 51 | 50 | 19 | 1 | 4 | 3 | 35 | 0 | 63 | 4 | 1 | 3 | 5 | .375 | 0 | 1-1 | 1 | 4.53 | 4.25 |

## Taylor Teagarden

**Bats:** R **Throws:** R **Pos:** C-23;PH-1 — **Ht:** 6'0" **Wt:** 215 **Born:** 12/21/1983 **Age:** 30

| BATTING | | | | | | | | | | | | | | | | | | | | | | BASERUNNING | | | | AVERAGES | | |
|---|---|---|---|---|---|---|---|---|---|---|---|---|---|---|---|---|---|---|---|---|---|---|---|---|---|---|---|---|
| Year | Team | Lg | G | AB | H | 2B | 3B | HR | (Hm | Rd) | TB | R | RBI | RC | TBB | IBB | SO | HBP | SH | SF | SB | CS | SB% | GDP | Avg | OBP | Slg |
| 2013 | Norfolk* | AAA | 3 | 13 | 1 | 0 | 0 | 0 | (- | -) | 1 | 0 | 0 | 0 | 0 | 0 | 2 | 0 | 0 | 0 | 0 | 0 | - | 1 | .077 | .077 | .077 |
| 2008 | Tex | AL | 16 | 47 | 15 | 5 | 0 | 6 | (3 | 3) | 38 | 10 | 17 | 15 | 5 | 0 | 19 | 1 | 0 | 0 | 0 | 0 | - | 0 | .319 | .396 | .809 |
| 2009 | Tex | AL | 60 | 198 | 43 | 13 | 0 | 6 | (2 | 4) | 74 | 26 | 24 | 16 | 14 | 0 | 76 | 1 | 3 | 2 | 0 | 0 | - | 6 | .217 | .270 | .374 |
| 2010 | Tex | AL | 28 | 71 | 11 | 1 | 0 | 4 | (1 | 3) | 24 | 10 | 6 | 5 | 8 | 0 | 34 | 2 | 4 | 0 | 0 | 0 | - | 0 | .155 | .259 | .338 |
| 2011 | Tex | AL | 14 | 34 | 8 | 2 | 0 | 0 | (0 | 0) | 10 | 3 | 2 | 2 | 2 | 0 | 13 | 0 | 0 | 0 | 0 | 0 | - | 0 | .235 | .278 | .294 |
| 2012 | Bal | AL | 22 | 57 | 9 | 3 | 0 | 2 | (2 | 0) | 18 | 4 | 9 | 6 | 5 | 0 | 23 | 0 | 2 | 0 | 0 | 0 | - | 1 | .158 | .226 | .316 |
| 2013 | Bal | AL | 23 | 60 | 10 | 2 | 0 | 2 | (0 | 2) | 18 | 3 | 5 | 2 | 1 | 0 | 18 | 0 | 1 | 0 | 0 | 1 | .00 | 0 | .167 | .180 | .300 |
| 6 ML YEARS | | | 163 | 467 | 96 | 26 | 0 | 20 | (8 | 12) | 182 | 56 | 63 | 46 | 35 | 0 | 183 | 4 | 10 | 2 | 0 | 1 | .00 | 7 | .206 | .266 | .390 |

## Julio Teheran

**Pitches:** R **Bats:** R **Pos:** SP-30 — tay-RONN — **Ht:** 6'2" **Wt:** 175 **Born:** 1/27/1991 **Age:** 23

| HOW MUCH HE PITCHED | | | | | | | | | WHAT HE GAVE UP | | | | | | | | | | | | | THE RESULTS | | | | | | | |
|---|---|---|---|---|---|---|---|---|---|---|---|---|---|---|---|---|---|---|---|---|---|---|---|---|---|---|---|---|---|
| Year | Team | Lg | G | GS | CG | GF | IP | BFP | H | R | ER | HR | SH | SF | HB | TBB | IBB | SO | WP | Bk | W | L | Pct | Sh | Sv-Op | Hld | ERC | ERA |
| 2011 | Atl | NL | 5 | 3 | 0 | 0 | 19.2 | 87 | 21 | 11 | 11 | 4 | 2 | 1 | 0 | 8 | 0 | 10 | 1 | 0 | 1 | 1 | .500 | 0 | 0-0 | 0 | 5.19 | 5.03 |
| 2012 | Atl | NL | 2 | 1 | 0 | 0 | 6.1 | 24 | 5 | 4 | 4 | 0 | 0 | 0 | 0 | 1 | 0 | 5 | 0 | 0 | 0 | 0 | - | 0 | 0-0 | 0 | 1.64 | 5.68 |
| 2013 | Atl | NL | 30 | 30 | 0 | 0 | 185.2 | 774 | 173 | 69 | 66 | 22 | 8 | 5 | 13 | 45 | 4 | 170 | 2 | 0 | 14 | 8 | .636 | 0 | 0-0 | 0 | 3.45 | 3.20 |
| 3 ML YEARS | | | 37 | 34 | 0 | 0 | 211.2 | 885 | 199 | 84 | 81 | 26 | 10 | 6 | 13 | 54 | 4 | 185 | 3 | 0 | 15 | 9 | .625 | 0 | 0-0 | 0 | 3.54 | 3.44 |

# Mark Teixeira

**Bats:** B **Throws:** R **Pos:** 1B-14;DH-1 tuh-SHARE-uh **Ht:** 6'3" **Wt:** 215 **Born:** 4/11/1980 **Age:** 34

| BATTING | | | | | | | | | | | | | | | | | | | | | | BASERUNNING | | | | AVERAGES | | |
|---|---|---|---|---|---|---|---|---|---|---|---|---|---|---|---|---|---|---|---|---|---|---|---|---|---|---|---|---|
| Year | Team | Lg | G | AB | H | 2B | 3B | HR | (Hm | Rd) | TB | R | RBI | RC | TBB | IBB | SO | HBP | SH | SF | SB | CS | SB% | GDP | Avg | OBP | Slg |
| 2013 | Trntn* | AA | 2 | 5 | 1 | 0 | 0 | 0 | (- | -) | 1 | 0 | 0 | 0 | 1 | 0 | 1 | 0 | 0 | 0 | 0 | 0 | - | 1 | .200 | .333 | .200 |
| 2003 | Tex | AL | 146 | 529 | 137 | 29 | 5 | 26 | (19 | 7) | 254 | 66 | 84 | 78 | 44 | 5 | 120 | 14 | 0 | 2 | 1 | 2 | .33 | 14 | .259 | .331 | .480 |
| 2004 | Tex | AL | 145 | 545 | 153 | 34 | 2 | 38 | (18 | 20) | 305 | 101 | 112 | 120 | 68 | 12 | 117 | 10 | 0 | 2 | 4 | 1 | .80 | 6 | .281 | .370 | .560 |
| 2005 | Tex | AL | **162** | 644 | 194 | 41 | 3 | 43 | **(30** | 13) | **370** | 112 | 144 | **148** | 72 | 5 | 124 | 11 | 0 | 3 | 4 | 0 | 1.00 | 18 | .301 | .379 | .575 |
| 2006 | Tex | AL | **162** | 628 | 177 | 45 | 1 | 33 | (12 | 21) | 323 | 99 | 110 | 114 | 89 | 12 | 128 | 4 | 0 | 6 | 2 | 0 | 1.00 | 17 | .282 | .371 | .514 |
| 2007 | 2 Tms | | 132 | 494 | 151 | 33 | 2 | 30 | (14 | 16) | 278 | 86 | 105 | 116 | 72 | 13 | 112 | 7 | 0 | 2 | 0 | 0 | - | 7 | .306 | .400 | .563 |
| 2008 | 2 Tms | | 157 | 574 | 177 | 41 | 0 | 33 | (19 | 14) | 317 | 102 | 121 | 119 | 97 | 13 | 93 | 7 | 0 | 7 | 2 | 0 | 1.00 | 17 | .308 | .410 | .552 |
| 2009 | NYY | AL | 156 | 609 | 178 | 43 | 3 | **39** | **(24** | 15) | **344** | 103 | **122** | 112 | 81 | 9 | 114 | 12 | 0 | 5 | 2 | 0 | 1.00 | 13 | .292 | .383 | .565 |
| 2010 | NYY | AL | 158 | 601 | 154 | 36 | 0 | 33 | (19 | 14) | 289 | **113** | 108 | 110 | 93 | 6 | 122 | 13 | 0 | 5 | 0 | 1 | .00 | 15 | .256 | .365 | .481 |
| 2011 | NYY | AL | 156 | 589 | 146 | 26 | 1 | 39 | (22 | 17) | 291 | 90 | 111 | 106 | 76 | 3 | 110 | 11 | 0 | 8 | 4 | 1 | .80 | 12 | .248 | .341 | .494 |
| 2012 | NYY | AL | 123 | 451 | 113 | 27 | 1 | 24 | (12 | 12) | 214 | 66 | 84 | 69 | 54 | 1 | 83 | 7 | 0 | **12** | 2 | 1 | .67 | 11 | .251 | .332 | .475 |
| 2013 | NYY | AL | 15 | 53 | 8 | 1 | 0 | 3 | (2 | 1) | 18 | 5 | 12 | 6 | 8 | 2 | 19 | 1 | 0 | 1 | 0 | 0 | - | 1 | .151 | .270 | .340 |
| 07 | Tex | AL | 78 | 286 | 85 | 24 | 1 | 13 | (5 | 8) | 150 | 48 | 49 | 58 | 45 | 10 | 66 | 3 | 0 | 1 | 0 | 0 | - | 5 | .297 | .397 | .524 |
| 07 | Atl | NL | 54 | 208 | 66 | 9 | 1 | 17 | (9 | 8) | 128 | 38 | 56 | 58 | 27 | 3 | 46 | 4 | 0 | 1 | 0 | 0 | - | 2 | .317 | .404 | .615 |
| 08 | Atl | NL | 103 | 381 | 108 | 27 | 0 | 20 | (11 | 9) | 195 | 63 | 78 | 69 | 65 | 9 | 70 | 3 | 0 | 2 | 0 | 0 | - | 13 | .283 | .390 | .512 |
| 08 | LAA | AL | 54 | 193 | 69 | 14 | 0 | 13 | (8 | 5) | 122 | 39 | 43 | 50 | 32 | 4 | 23 | 4 | 0 | 5 | 2 | 0 | 1.00 | 4 | .358 | .449 | .632 |
| Postseason | | | 40 | 153 | 34 | 6 | 0 | 3 | (2 | 1) | 49 | 21 | 14 | 15 | 24 | 2 | 34 | 4 | 0 | 2 | 1 | 0 | 1.00 | 3 | .222 | .339 | .320 |
| 11 ML YEARS | | | 1512 | 5717 | 1588 | 356 | 18 | 341 | (191 | 150) | 3003 | 943 | 1113 | 1098 | 754 | 81 | 1142 | 97 | 0 | 53 | 21 | 6 | .78 | 131 | .278 | .368 | .525 |

# Miguel Tejada

**Bats:** R **Throws:** R **Pos:** 2B-26;3B-22;PH-12;1B-1 **Ht:** 5'9" **Wt:** 220 **Born:** 5/25/1974 **Age:** 40

| BATTING | | | | | | | | | | | | | | | | | | | | | | BASERUNNING | | | | AVERAGES | | |
|---|---|---|---|---|---|---|---|---|---|---|---|---|---|---|---|---|---|---|---|---|---|---|---|---|---|---|---|---|
| Year | Team | Lg | G | AB | H | 2B | 3B | HR | (Hm | Rd) | TB | R | RBI | RC | TBB | IBB | SO | HBP | SH | SF | SB | CS | SB% | GDP | Avg | OBP | Slg |
| 1997 | Oak | AL | 26 | 99 | 20 | 3 | 2 | 2 | (1 | 1) | 33 | 10 | 10 | 7 | 2 | 0 | 22 | 3 | 0 | 0 | 2 | 0 | 1.00 | 3 | .202 | .240 | .333 |
| 1998 | Oak | AL | 105 | 365 | 85 | 20 | 1 | 11 | (5 | 6) | 140 | 53 | 45 | 40 | 28 | 0 | 86 | 7 | 4 | 3 | 5 | 6 | .45 | 8 | .233 | .298 | .384 |
| 1999 | Oak | AL | 159 | 593 | 149 | 33 | 4 | 21 | (12 | 9) | 253 | 93 | 84 | 82 | 57 | 3 | 94 | 10 | 9 | 5 | 8 | 7 | .53 | 11 | .251 | .325 | .427 |
| 2000 | Oak | AL | 160 | 607 | 167 | 32 | 1 | 30 | (16 | 14) | 291 | 105 | 115 | 99 | 66 | 6 | 102 | 4 | 2 | 2 | 6 | 0 | 1.00 | 15 | .275 | .349 | .479 |
| 2001 | Oak | AL | **162** | 622 | 166 | 31 | 3 | 31 | (17 | 14) | 296 | 107 | 113 | 94 | 43 | 5 | 89 | 13 | 1 | 4 | 11 | 5 | .69 | 14 | .267 | .326 | .476 |
| 2002 | Oak | AL | **162** | 662 | 204 | 30 | 0 | 34 | (17 | 17) | 336 | 108 | 131 | 123 | 38 | 3 | 84 | 11 | 0 | 4 | 7 | 2 | .78 | 21 | .308 | .354 | .508 |
| 2003 | Oak | AL | 162 | 636 | 177 | 42 | 0 | 27 | (15 | 12) | 300 | 98 | 106 | 103 | 53 | 7 | 65 | 6 | 0 | 8 | 10 | 0 | 1.00 | 12 | .278 | .336 | .472 |
| 2004 | Bal | AL | **162** | 653 | 203 | 40 | 2 | 34 | (17 | 17) | 349 | 107 | **150** | 124 | 48 | 6 | 73 | 10 | 0 | **14** | 4 | 1 | .80 | **24** | .311 | .360 | .534 |
| 2005 | Bal | AL | **162** | 654 | 199 | **50** | 5 | 26 | (16 | 10) | 337 | 89 | 98 | 102 | 40 | 9 | 83 | 7 | 0 | 3 | 5 | 1 | .83 | **26** | .304 | .349 | .515 |
| 2006 | Bal | AL | **162** | 648 | 214 | 37 | 0 | 24 | (17 | 7) | 323 | 99 | 100 | 99 | 46 | 10 | 79 | 9 | 0 | 6 | 6 | 2 | .75 | **28** | .330 | .379 | .498 |
| 2007 | Bal | AL | 133 | 514 | 152 | 19 | 1 | 18 | (12 | 6) | 227 | 72 | 81 | 76 | 41 | 9 | 55 | 10 | 0 | 3 | 2 | 1 | .67 | 22 | .296 | .357 | .442 |
| 2008 | Hou | NL | 158 | 632 | 179 | 38 | 3 | 13 | (8 | 5) | 262 | 92 | 66 | 61 | 24 | 4 | 72 | 6 | 1 | 3 | 7 | 7 | .50 | **32** | .283 | .314 | .415 |
| 2009 | Hou | NL | 158 | 635 | 199 | **46** | 1 | 14 | (10 | 4) | 289 | 83 | 86 | 84 | 19 | 2 | 48 | 11 | 0 | 8 | 5 | 2 | .71 | **29** | .313 | .340 | .455 |
| 2010 | 2 Tms | | 156 | 636 | 171 | 26 | 0 | 15 | (7 | 8) | 242 | 71 | 71 | 73 | 30 | 3 | 67 | 11 | 1 | 3 | 2 | 0 | 1.00 | 16 | .269 | .312 | .381 |
| 2011 | SF | NL | 91 | 322 | 77 | 16 | 0 | 4 | (1 | 3) | 105 | 28 | 26 | 24 | 12 | 5 | 35 | 3 | 2 | 4 | 4 | 4 | .50 | 10 | .239 | .270 | .326 |
| 2013 | KC | AL | 53 | 156 | 45 | 5 | 0 | 3 | (2 | 1) | 59 | 15 | 20 | 18 | 6 | 1 | 25 | 1 | 3 | 1 | 1 | 0 | 1.00 | 6 | .288 | .317 | .378 |
| 10 | Bal | AL | 97 | 401 | 108 | 16 | 0 | 7 | (5 | 2) | 145 | 40 | 39 | 38 | 15 | 3 | 39 | 9 | 0 | 3 | 0 | 0 | - | 13 | .269 | .308 | .362 |
| 10 | SD | NL | 59 | 235 | 63 | 10 | 0 | 8 | (2 | 6) | 97 | 31 | 32 | 35 | 15 | 0 | 28 | 2 | 1 | 0 | 2 | 0 | 1.00 | 3 | .268 | .317 | .413 |
| Postseason | | | 20 | 85 | 18 | 7 | 0 | 1 | (0 | 1) | 28 | 9 | 8 | 6 | 3 | 0 | 16 | 1 | 0 | 2 | 1 | 0 | 1.00 | 2 | .212 | .242 | .329 |
| 16 ML YEARS | | | 2171 | 8434 | 2407 | 468 | 23 | 307 | (173 | 134) | 3842 | 1230 | 1302 | 1209 | 553 | 73 | 1079 | 122 | 23 | 71 | 85 | 38 | .69 | 277 | .285 | .336 | .456 |

# Ruben Tejada

**Bats:** R **Throws:** R **Pos:** SS-55;PH-2 **Ht:** 5'11" **Wt:** 185 **Born:** 10/27/1989 **Age:** 24

| BATTING | | | | | | | | | | | | | | | | | | | | | | BASERUNNING | | | | AVERAGES | | |
|---|---|---|---|---|---|---|---|---|---|---|---|---|---|---|---|---|---|---|---|---|---|---|---|---|---|---|---|---|
| Year | Team | Lg | G | AB | H | 2B | 3B | HR | (Hm | Rd) | TB | R | RBI | RC | TBB | IBB | SO | HBP | SH | SF | SB | CS | SB% | GDP | Avg | OBP | Slg |
| 2013 | LsVgs* | AAA | 60 | 240 | 69 | 14 | 1 | 2 | (- | -) | 91 | 38 | 24 | 32 | 14 | 0 | 30 | 6 | 5 | 4 | 1 | 1 | .50 | 3 | .288 | .337 | .379 |
| 2013 | Mets* | R | 3 | 9 | 3 | 1 | 0 | 0 | (- | -) | 4 | 1 | 2 | 1 | 0 | 0 | 5 | 1 | 0 | 0 | 0 | 0 | - | 0 | .333 | .400 | .444 |
| 2010 | NYM | NL | 78 | 216 | 46 | 12 | 0 | 1 | (0 | 1) | 61 | 28 | 15 | 16 | 22 | 3 | 38 | 8 | 6 | 3 | 2 | 2 | .50 | 2 | .213 | .305 | .282 |
| 2011 | NYM | NL | 96 | 328 | 93 | 15 | 1 | 0 | (0 | 0) | 110 | 31 | 36 | 41 | 35 | 3 | 50 | 6 | 4 | 3 | 5 | 1 | .83 | 6 | .284 | .360 | .335 |
| 2012 | NYM | NL | 114 | 464 | 134 | 26 | 0 | 1 | (0 | 1) | 163 | 53 | 25 | 49 | 27 | 0 | 73 | 5 | 3 | 2 | 4 | 4 | .50 | 9 | .289 | .333 | .351 |
| 2013 | NYM | NL | 57 | 208 | 42 | 12 | 0 | 0 | (0 | 0) | 54 | 20 | 10 | 15 | 15 | 0 | 24 | 1 | 3 | 0 | 2 | 1 | .67 | 3 | .202 | .259 | .260 |
| 4 ML YEARS | | | 345 | 1216 | 315 | 65 | 1 | 2 | (0 | 2) | 388 | 132 | 86 | 121 | 99 | 6 | 185 | 20 | 16 | 8 | 13 | 8 | .62 | 20 | .259 | .323 | .319 |

# Blake Tekotte

**Bats:** L **Throws:** R **Pos:** CF-16;PR-6;PH-2;LF-1 tee-COAT-ee **Ht:** 5'11" **Wt:** 180 **Born:** 5/24/1987 **Age:** 27

| BATTING | | | | | | | | | | | | | | | | | | | | | | BASERUNNING | | | | AVERAGES | | |
|---|---|---|---|---|---|---|---|---|---|---|---|---|---|---|---|---|---|---|---|---|---|---|---|---|---|---|---|---|
| Year | Team | Lg | G | AB | H | 2B | 3B | HR | (Hm | Rd) | TB | R | RBI | RC | TBB | IBB | SO | HBP | SH | SF | SB | CS | SB% | GDP | Avg | OBP | Slg |
| 2013 | Charltt* | AAA | 76 | 296 | 70 | 27 | 3 | 4 | (- | -) | 115 | 32 | 33 | 39 | 31 | 2 | 74 | 6 | 3 | 2 | 12 | 5 | .71 | 4 | .236 | .319 | .389 |
| 2011 | SD | NL | 19 | 34 | 6 | 1 | 1 | 0 | (0 | 0) | 9 | 1 | 1 | 1 | 4 | 0 | 21 | 0 | 2 | 0 | 2 | 1 | .67 | 0 | .176 | .263 | .265 |
| 2012 | SD | NL | 11 | 15 | 2 | 0 | 0 | 0 | (0 | 0) | 2 | 0 | 0 | 0 | 0 | 0 | 4 | 0 | 0 | 0 | 1 | 0 | 1.00 | 0 | .133 | .133 | .133 |
| 2013 | CWS | AL | 20 | 31 | 7 | 1 | 0 | 1 | (1 | 0) | 11 | 4 | 2 | 1 | 3 | 0 | 9 | 1 | 0 | 1 | 1 | 3 | .25 | 0 | .226 | .306 | .355 |
| 3 ML YEARS | | | 50 | 80 | 15 | 2 | 1 | 1 | (1 | 0) | 22 | 5 | 3 | 2 | 7 | 0 | 34 | 1 | 2 | 1 | 4 | 4 | .50 | 0 | .188 | .258 | .275 |

# Nick Tepesch

**Pitches:** R **Bats:** R **Pos:** SP-17; RP-2 TEP-ish **Ht:** 6'4" **Wt:** 225 **Born:** 10/12/1988 **Age:** 25

| HOW MUCH HE PITCHED | | | | | | | | WHAT HE GAVE UP | | | | | | | | | | | | THE RESULTS | | | | | | | |
|---|---|---|---|---|---|---|---|---|---|---|---|---|---|---|---|---|---|---|---|---|---|---|---|---|---|---|---|
| Year | Team | Lg | G | GS | CG | GF | IP | BFP | H | R | ER | HR | SH | SF | HB | TBB | IBB | SO | WP | Bk | W | L | Pct | Sh | Sv-Op | Hld | ERC | ERA |
| 2011 | Hkry | A | 29 | 23 | 2 | 1 | 138.1 | 583 | 147 | 70 | 62 | 14 | 6 | 4 | 13 | 33 | 0 | 118 | 1 | 0 | 7 | 5 | .583 | 0 | 0-- | - | 4.27 | 4.03 |
| 2012 | MrtlBh | A+ | 12 | 12 | 1 | 0 | 71.2 | 299 | 68 | 27 | 23 | 3 | 3 | 2 | 7 | 18 | 0 | 59 | 3 | 0 | 5 | 3 | .625 | 1 | 0-- | - | 3.24 | 2.89 |

| Year | Team | Lg | G | GS | CG | GF | IP | BFP | H | R | ER | HR | SH | SF | HB | TBB | IBB | SO | WP | Bk | W | L | Pct | Sh | Sv-Op | Hld | ERC | ERA |
|---|---|---|---|---|---|---|---|---|---|---|---|---|---|---|---|---|---|---|---|---|---|---|---|---|---|---|---|---|
| | | | **HOW MUCH HE PITCHED** | | | | | | **WHAT HE GAVE UP** | | | | | | | | | | | | **THE RESULTS** | | | | | | | |
| 2012 | Frisco | AA | 16 | 14 | 0 | 0 | 90.1 | 382 | 97 | 47 | 43 | 10 | 3 | 3 | 3 | 26 | 0 | 68 | 3 | 2 | 6 | 3 | .667 | 0 | 0- - | - | 4.34 | 4.28 |
| 2013 | RdRck | AAA | 1 | 1 | 0 | 0 | 5.0 | 20 | 5 | 1 | 0 | 0 | 0 | 0 | 0 | 0 | 0 | 5 | 0 | 0 | 1 | 0 | 1.000 | 0 | 0- - | - | 1.95 | 0.00 |
| 2013 | Frisco | AA | 2 | 2 | 0 | 0 | 6.0 | 27 | 7 | 1 | 1 | 0 | 0 | 0 | 0 | 2 | 0 | 3 | 0 | 0 | 0 | 0 | - | 0 | 0- - | - | 3.91 | 1.50 |
| 2013 | Tex | AL | 19 | 17 | 0 | 1 | 93.0 | 407 | 100 | 53 | 50 | 12 | 1 | 4 | 7 | 27 | 3 | 76 | 0 | 0 | 4 | 6 | .400 | 0 | 0-0 | 0 | 4.49 | 4.84 |

# Joey Terdoslavich

**Bats:** B **Throws:** R **Pos:** PH-36;LF-13;1B-6;RF-4;PR-1 ter-DOSS-low-vitch **Ht:** 6'0" **Wt:** 200 **Born:** 9/9/1988 **Age:** 25

| Year | Team | Lg | G | AB | H | 2B | 3B | HR | (Hm | Rd) | TB | R | RBI | RC | TBB | IBB | SO | HBP | SH | SF | SB | CS | SB% | GDP | Avg | OBP | Slg |
|---|---|---|---|---|---|---|---|---|---|---|---|---|---|---|---|---|---|---|---|---|---|---|---|---|---|---|---|
| | | | **BATTING** | | | | | | | | | | | | | | | | | | **BASERUNNING** | | | | **AVERAGES** | | |
| 2010 | Danvle | R | 49 | 189 | 56 | 10 | 2 | 2 | (- | -) | 76 | 27 | 24 | 27 | 15 | 0 | 27 | 1 | 0 | 0 | 3 | 3 | .50 | 2 | .296 | .351 | .402 |
| 2010 | Rome | A | 21 | 79 | 25 | 9 | 0 | 0 | (- | -) | 34 | 7 | 10 | 12 | 5 | 0 | 18 | 1 | 0 | 0 | 0 | 0 | - | 4 | .316 | .365 | .430 |
| 2011 | Lynbrg | A+ | 131 | 483 | 138 | 52 | 2 | 20 | (- | -) | 254 | 72 | 82 | 88 | 41 | 4 | 107 | 4 | 0 | 8 | 2 | 0 | 1.00 | 7 | .286 | .341 | .526 |
| 2012 | Gwnntt | AAA | 53 | 194 | 35 | 4 | 0 | 4 | (- | -) | 51 | 19 | 20 | 13 | 19 | 0 | 50 | 0 | 1 | 1 | 3 | 0 | 1.00 | 3 | .180 | .252 | .263 |
| 2012 | Missi | AA | 78 | 298 | 94 | 24 | 5 | 5 | (- | -) | 143 | 43 | 51 | 55 | 27 | 0 | 62 | 3 | 0 | 5 | 4 | 0 | 1.00 | 8 | .315 | .372 | .480 |
| 2013 | Gwnntt | AAA | 85 | 321 | 102 | 24 | 1 | 18 | (- | -) | 182 | 48 | 58 | 62 | 23 | 1 | 65 | 1 | 0 | 6 | 3 | 6 | .33 | 7 | .318 | .359 | .567 |
| 2013 | Atl | NL | 55 | 79 | 17 | 4 | 0 | 0 | (0 | 0) | 21 | 11 | 4 | 6 | 12 | 1 | 24 | 0 | 0 | 1 | 1 | 0 | 1.00 | 2 | .215 | .315 | .266 |

# Joe Thatcher

**Pitches:** L **Bats:** L **Pos:** RP-72 **Ht:** 6'2" **Wt:** 230 **Born:** 10/4/1981 **Age:** 32

| Year | Team | Lg | G | GS | CG | GF | IP | BFP | H | R | ER | HR | SH | SF | HB | TBB | IBB | SO | WP | Bk | W | L | Pct | Sh | Sv-Op | Hld | ERC | ERA |
|---|---|---|---|---|---|---|---|---|---|---|---|---|---|---|---|---|---|---|---|---|---|---|---|---|---|---|---|---|
| | | | **HOW MUCH HE PITCHED** | | | | | | **WHAT HE GAVE UP** | | | | | | | | | | | | **THE RESULTS** | | | | | | | |
| 2007 | SD | NL | 22 | 0 | 0 | 5 | 21.0 | 85 | 13 | 6 | 3 | 1 | 0 | 0 | 1 | 6 | 2 | 16 | 0 | 0 | 2 | 2 | .500 | 0 | 0-0 | 2 | 1.49 | 1.29 |
| 2008 | SD | NL | 25 | 0 | 0 | 7 | 25.2 | 128 | 42 | 25 | 24 | 4 | 2 | 3 | 0 | 13 | 2 | 17 | 0 | 0 | 0 | 4 | .000 | 0 | 0-3 | 5 | 8.91 | 8.42 |
| 2009 | SD | NL | 52 | 0 | 0 | 7 | 45.0 | 188 | 37 | 14 | 14 | 2 | 1 | 2 | 4 | 18 | 7 | 55 | 2 | 1 | 1 | 0 | 1.000 | 0 | 0-1 | 9 | 2.87 | 2.80 |
| 2010 | SD | NL | 65 | 0 | 0 | 12 | 35.0 | 137 | 23 | 5 | 5 | 1 | 3 | 2 | 1 | 7 | 2 | 45 | 0 | 0 | 1 | 0 | 1.000 | 0 | 0-0 | 11 | 1.37 | 1.29 |
| 2011 | SD | NL | 18 | 0 | 0 | 5 | 10.0 | 44 | 8 | 5 | 5 | 1 | 0 | 0 | 0 | 7 | 1 | 9 | 0 | 0 | 0 | 0 | - | 0 | 0-0 | 2 | 3.96 | 4.50 |
| 2012 | SD | NL | 55 | 0 | 0 | 13 | 31.2 | 141 | 30 | 13 | 12 | 2 | 2 | 2 | 3 | 14 | 3 | 39 | 0 | 1 | 1 | 4 | .200 | 0 | 1-1 | 14 | 3.82 | 3.41 |
| 2013 | 2 Tms | NL | 72 | 0 | 0 | 16 | 39.1 | 164 | 40 | 14 | 14 | 4 | 1 | 2 | 1 | 10 | 0 | 36 | 3 | 0 | 3 | 2 | .600 | 0 | 0-4 | 15 | 3.75 | 3.20 |
| 13 | SD | NL | 50 | 0 | 0 | 13 | 30.0 | 121 | 28 | 7 | 7 | 3 | 0 | 1 | 1 | 4 | 0 | 29 | 2 | 0 | 3 | 1 | .750 | 0 | 0-2 | 11 | 2.83 | 2.10 |
| 13 | Ari | NL | 22 | 0 | 0 | 3 | 9.1 | 43 | 12 | 7 | 7 | 1 | 1 | 1 | 0 | 6 | 0 | 7 | 1 | 0 | 0 | 1 | .000 | 0 | 0-2 | 4 | 7.19 | 6.75 |
| 7 ML YEARS | | | 309 | 0 | 0 | 65 | 207.2 | 887 | 193 | 82 | 77 | 15 | 9 | 11 | 10 | 75 | 17 | 217 | 5 | 2 | 8 | 12 | .400 | 0 | 1-9 | 58 | 3.38 | 3.34 |

# Dale Thayer

**Pitches:** R **Bats:** R **Pos:** RP-69 **Ht:** 6'0" **Wt:** 215 **Born:** 12/17/1980 **Age:** 33

| Year | Team | Lg | G | GS | CG | GF | IP | BFP | H | R | ER | HR | SH | SF | HB | TBB | IBB | SO | WP | Bk | W | L | Pct | Sh | Sv-Op | Hld | ERC | ERA |
|---|---|---|---|---|---|---|---|---|---|---|---|---|---|---|---|---|---|---|---|---|---|---|---|---|---|---|---|---|
| | | | **HOW MUCH HE PITCHED** | | | | | | **WHAT HE GAVE UP** | | | | | | | | | | | | **THE RESULTS** | | | | | | | |
| 2009 | TB | AL | 11 | 0 | 0 | 3 | 13.2 | 59 | 18 | 9 | 7 | 3 | 0 | 0 | 0 | 1 | 0 | 8 | 1 | 0 | 0 | 0 | - | 0 | 1-1 | 0 | 5.38 | 4.61 |
| 2010 | TB | AL | 1 | 0 | 0 | 0 | 2.0 | 13 | 7 | 6 | 6 | 1 | 0 | 0 | 0 | 0 | 0 | 2 | 0 | 0 | 0 | 0 | - | 0 | 0-0 | 0 | 24.30 | 27.00 |
| 2011 | NYM | NL | 11 | 0 | 0 | 7 | 10.1 | 42 | 12 | 4 | 4 | 0 | 1 | 2 | 0 | 0 | 0 | 5 | 0 | 0 | 0 | 3 | .000 | 0 | 0-0 | 0 | 2.78 | 3.48 |
| 2012 | SD | NL | 64 | 0 | 0 | 21 | 57.2 | 235 | 53 | 24 | 22 | 4 | 4 | 4 | 1 | 12 | 4 | 47 | 2 | 0 | 2 | 2 | .500 | 0 | 7-10 | 22 | 2.68 | 3.43 |
| 2013 | SD | NL | 69 | 0 | 0 | 13 | 65.0 | 270 | 59 | 25 | 24 | 8 | 3 | 1 | 2 | 22 | 2 | 64 | 2 | 0 | 3 | 5 | .375 | 0 | 1-4 | 18 | 3.60 | 3.32 |
| 5 ML YEARS | | | 156 | 0 | 0 | 44 | 148.2 | 619 | 149 | 68 | 63 | 16 | 8 | 7 | 3 | 35 | 6 | 126 | 5 | 0 | 5 | 10 | .333 | 0 | 9-15 | 40 | 3.53 | 3.81 |

# Caleb Thielbar

**Pitches:** L **Bats:** R **Pos:** RP-49 THEEL-bar **Ht:** 6'0" **Wt:** 195 **Born:** 1/31/1987 **Age:** 27

| Year | Team | Lg | G | GS | CG | GF | IP | BFP | H | R | ER | HR | SH | SF | HB | TBB | IBB | SO | WP | Bk | W | L | Pct | Sh | Sv-Op | Hld | ERC | ERA |
|---|---|---|---|---|---|---|---|---|---|---|---|---|---|---|---|---|---|---|---|---|---|---|---|---|---|---|---|---|
| | | | **HOW MUCH HE PITCHED** | | | | | | **WHAT HE GAVE UP** | | | | | | | | | | | | **THE RESULTS** | | | | | | | |
| 2009 | Brewrs | R | 14 | 2 | 0 | 2 | 45.1 | 187 | 44 | 16 | 8 | 1 | 0 | 1 | 0 | 7 | 0 | 46 | 3 | 0 | 6 | 1 | .857 | 0 | 0- - | - | 2.45 | 1.59 |
| 2009 | Helena | R+ | 2 | 0 | 0 | 0 | 1.2 | 5 | 0 | 0 | 0 | 0 | 0 | 0 | 0 | 1 | 0 | 2 | 0 | 0 | 0 | 0 | - | 0 | 0- - | - | 0.45 | 0.00 |
| 2010 | Wisc | A | 30 | 0 | 0 | 9 | 53.0 | 241 | 65 | 41 | 33 | 6 | 5 | 1 | 0 | 14 | 3 | 43 | 0 | 0 | 0 | 2 | .000 | 0 | 3- - | - | 4.64 | 5.60 |
| 2010 | Helena | R+ | 9 | 0 | 0 | 4 | 14.2 | 56 | 16 | 7 | 6 | 2 | 0 | 0 | 0 | 0 | 0 | 9 | 1 | 0 | 0 | 0 | - | 0 | 0- - | - | 3.43 | 3.68 |
| 2011 | FtMyrs | A+ | 3 | 1 | 0 | 1 | 7.1 | 29 | 1 | 0 | 0 | 0 | 0 | 0 | 0 | 5 | 0 | 5 | 1 | 0 | 1 | 0 | 1.000 | 0 | 0- - | - | 0.75 | 0.00 |
| 2012 | FtMyrs | A+ | 7 | 0 | 0 | 6 | 12.1 | 45 | 4 | 1 | 0 | 0 | 1 | 0 | 2 | 2 | 0 | 16 | 0 | 0 | 1 | 1 | .500 | 0 | 1- - | - | 0.65 | 0.00 |
| 2012 | NwBrit | AA | 16 | 0 | 0 | 11 | 25.0 | 95 | 18 | 5 | 5 | 1 | 1 | 0 | 0 | 3 | 1 | 26 | 0 | 0 | 2 | 0 | 1.000 | 0 | 4- - | - | 1.41 | 1.80 |
| 2012 | Roch | AAA | 25 | 1 | 0 | 5 | 40.1 | 178 | 42 | 19 | 16 | 5 | 1 | 2 | 1 | 16 | 2 | 32 | 3 | 0 | 3 | 1 | .750 | 0 | 1- - | - | 4.43 | 3.57 |
| 2013 | Roch | AAA | 17 | 0 | 0 | 4 | 26.1 | 114 | 27 | 13 | 11 | 1 | 0 | 1 | 1 | 8 | 0 | 34 | 2 | 0 | 1 | 1 | .500 | 0 | 1- - | - | 3.50 | 3.76 |
| 2013 | Min | AL | 49 | 0 | 0 | 16 | 46.0 | 171 | 24 | 11 | 9 | 4 | 0 | 1 | 0 | 14 | 4 | 39 | 1 | 0 | 3 | 2 | .600 | 0 | 0-0 | 1 | 1.38 | 1.76 |

# Josh Thole

**Bats:** L **Throws:** R **Pos:** C-39;PH-5;1B-2;DH-1 TOE-lee **Ht:** 6'0" **Wt:** 215 **Born:** 10/28/1986 **Age:** 27

| Year | Team | Lg | G | AB | H | 2B | 3B | HR | (Hm | Rd) | TB | R | RBI | RC | TBB | IBB | SO | HBP | SH | SF | SB | CS | SB% | GDP | Avg | OBP | Slg |
|---|---|---|---|---|---|---|---|---|---|---|---|---|---|---|---|---|---|---|---|---|---|---|---|---|---|---|---|
| | | | **BATTING** | | | | | | | | | | | | | | | | | | **BASERUNNING** | | | | **AVERAGES** | | |
| 2013 | Buffalo* | AAA | 41 | 149 | 48 | 5 | 1 | 7 | (- | -) | 76 | 18 | 31 | 29 | 14 | 1 | 25 | 2 | 0 | 2 | 0 | 1 | .00 | 6 | .322 | .383 | .510 |
| 2009 | NYM | NL | 17 | 53 | 17 | 2 | 1 | 0 | (0 | 0) | 21 | 2 | 9 | 9 | 4 | 0 | 5 | 0 | 0 | 2 | 1 | 0 | 1.00 | 1 | .321 | .356 | .396 |
| 2010 | NYM | NL | 73 | 202 | 56 | 7 | 1 | 3 | (2 | 1) | 74 | 17 | 17 | 28 | 24 | 1 | 25 | 1 | 0 | 0 | 1 | 0 | 1.00 | 8 | .277 | .357 | .366 |
| 2011 | NYM | NL | 114 | 340 | 91 | 17 | 0 | 3 | (1 | 2) | 117 | 22 | 40 | 39 | 38 | 6 | 47 | 4 | 1 | 3 | 0 | 2 | .00 | 8 | .268 | .345 | .344 |
| 2012 | NYM | NL | 104 | 321 | 75 | 15 | 0 | 1 | (0 | 1) | 93 | 24 | 21 | 24 | 27 | 6 | 50 | 1 | 4 | 1 | 0 | 0 | - | 12 | .234 | .294 | .290 |
| 2013 | Tor | AL | 45 | 120 | 21 | 3 | 1 | 1 | (0 | 1) | 29 | 11 | 8 | 7 | 12 | 0 | 25 | 1 | 2 | 0 | 0 | 0 | - | 3 | .175 | .256 | .242 |
| 5 ML YEARS | | | 353 | 1036 | 260 | 44 | 3 | 8 | (3 | 5) | 334 | 76 | 95 | 107 | 105 | 13 | 152 | 7 | 7 | 6 | 2 | 2 | .50 | 32 | .251 | .322 | .322 |

## Clete Thomas

**Bats:** L **Throws:** R **Pos:** CF-50;LF-26;RF-10;PR-5;PH-3;DH-2 **Ht:** 5'11" **Wt:** 195 **Born:** 11/14/1983 **Age:** 30

| BATTING | | | | | | | | | | | | | | | | | | | | | BASERUNNING | | | | AVERAGES | | |
|---|---|---|---|---|---|---|---|---|---|---|---|---|---|---|---|---|---|---|---|---|---|---|---|---|---|---|---|
| Year Team | Lg | G | AB | H | 2B | 3B | HR | (Hm | Rd) | TB | R | RBI | RC | TBB | IBB | SO | HBP | SH | SF | | SB | CS | SB% | GDP | Avg | OBP | Slg |
| 2013 Roch* | AAA | 36 | 125 | 37 | 8 | 0 | 9 | (- | -) | 72 | 17 | 25 | 27 | 18 | 0 | 35 | 0 | 0 | 0 | | 6 | 3 | .67 | 2 | .296 | .385 | .576 |
| 2008 Det | AL | 40 | 116 | 33 | 9 | 1 | 1 | (1 | 0) | 47 | 7 | 9 | 17 | 14 | 1 | 26 | 1 | 2 | 0 | | 2 | 0 | 1.00 | 1 | .284 | .366 | .405 |
| 2009 Det | AL | 102 | 275 | 66 | 13 | 3 | 7 | (4 | 3) | 106 | 46 | 39 | 36 | 33 | 0 | 77 | 1 | 1 | 0 | | 3 | 0 | 1.00 | 3 | .240 | .324 | .385 |
| 2012 2 Tms | AL | 15 | 28 | 4 | 1 | 0 | 1 | (1 | 0) | 8 | 3 | 4 | 4 | 0 | 0 | 16 | 1 | 0 | 0 | | 0 | 0 | - | 0 | .143 | .172 | .286 |
| 2013 Min | AL | 92 | 290 | 62 | 15 | 0 | 4 | (3 | 1) | 89 | 39 | 13 | 17 | 30 | 1 | 92 | 1 | 1 | 0 | | 1 | 3 | .25 | 4 | .214 | .290 | .307 |
| 12 Det | AL | 3 | 0 | 0 | 0 | 0 | 0 | (0 | 0) | 0 | 1 | 0 | 0 | 0 | 0 | 0 | 0 | 0 | 0 | | 0 | 0 | - | 0 | - | - | - |
| 12 Min | AL | 12 | 28 | 4 | 1 | 0 | 1 | (1 | 0) | 8 | 2 | 4 | 4 | 0 | 0 | 16 | 1 | 0 | 0 | | 0 | 0 | - | 0 | .143 | .172 | .286 |
| 4 ML YEARS | | 249 | 709 | 165 | 38 | 4 | 13 | (9 | 4) | 250 | 95 | 65 | 74 | 77 | 2 | 211 | 4 | 4 | 0 | | 6 | 3 | .67 | 8 | .233 | .311 | .353 |

## Tyler Thornburg

**Pitches:** R **Bats:** R **Pos:** RP-11; SP-7 **Ht:** 5'11" **Wt:** 190 **Born:** 9/29/1988 **Age:** 25

| HOW MUCH HE PITCHED | | | | | | | | WHAT HE GAVE UP | | | | | | | | | | | | THE RESULTS | | | | | | | |
|---|---|---|---|---|---|---|---|---|---|---|---|---|---|---|---|---|---|---|---|---|---|---|---|---|---|---|---|
| Year Team | Lg | G | GS | CG | GF | IP | BFP | H | R | ER | HR | SH | SF | HB | TBB | IBB | SO | WP | Bk | W | L | Pct | Sh | Sv-Op | Hld | ERC | ERA |
| 2010 Helena | R+ | 9 | 6 | 0 | 1 | 23.1 | 97 | 15 | 6 | 5 | 2 | 0 | 0 | 2 | 11 | 0 | 38 | 3 | 2 | 1 | 0 | 1.000 | 0 | 1- | - | 2.66 | 1.93 |
| 2011 Wisc | A | 12 | 12 | 2 | 0 | 68.2 | 274 | 49 | 14 | 12 | 3 | 3 | 1 | 4 | 25 | 0 | 76 | 5 | 3 | 7 | 0 | 1.000 | 1 | 0- - | - | 2.36 | 1.57 |
| 2011 BrvdCt | A+ | 12 | 12 | 0 | 0 | 68.0 | 282 | 45 | 30 | 27 | 5 | 3 | 0 | 4 | 33 | 0 | 84 | 4 | 0 | 3 | 6 | .333 | 0 | 0- - | - | 2.64 | 3.57 |
| 2012 Hntsvl | AA | 13 | 13 | 0 | 0 | 75.0 | 307 | 57 | 36 | 25 | 6 | 5 | 7 | 2 | 24 | 0 | 71 | 2 | 0 | 8 | 1 | .889 | 0 | 0- - | - | 2.45 | 3.00 |
| 2012 Nashv | AAA | 8 | 8 | 0 | 0 | 37.2 | 162 | 38 | 16 | 15 | 1 | 3 | 0 | 2 | 13 | 0 | 42 | 0 | 0 | 2 | 3 | .400 | 0 | 0- - | - | 3.61 | 3.58 |
| 2013 Nashv | AAA | 15 | 15 | 1 | 0 | 74.2 | 339 | 90 | 54 | 48 | 11 | 2 | 1 | 4 | 29 | 0 | 87 | 6 | 0 | 0 | 9 | .000 | 0 | 0- - | - | 5.82 | 5.79 |
| 2012 Mil | NL | 8 | 3 | 0 | 3 | 22.0 | 95 | 24 | 11 | 11 | 8 | 1 | 0 | 1 | 7 | 0 | 20 | 1 | 0 | 0 | 0 | - | 0 | 0-0 | 0 | 6.44 | 4.50 |
| 2013 Mil | NL | 18 | 7 | 0 | 4 | 66.2 | 270 | 53 | 17 | 15 | 1 | 4 | 1 | 3 | 26 | 2 | 48 | 2 | 1 | 3 | 1 | .750 | 0 | 0-0 | 0 | 2.59 | 2.03 |
| 2 ML YEARS | | 26 | 10 | 0 | 7 | 88.2 | 365 | 77 | 28 | 26 | 9 | 5 | 1 | 4 | 33 | 2 | 68 | 3 | 1 | 3 | 1 | .750 | 0 | 0-0 | 0 | 3.49 | 2.64 |

## Matt Thornton

**Pitches:** L **Bats:** L **Pos:** RP-60 **Ht:** 6'6" **Wt:** 235 **Born:** 9/15/1976 **Age:** 37

| HOW MUCH HE PITCHED | | | | | | | | WHAT HE GAVE UP | | | | | | | | | | | | THE RESULTS | | | | | | | |
|---|---|---|---|---|---|---|---|---|---|---|---|---|---|---|---|---|---|---|---|---|---|---|---|---|---|---|---|
| Year Team | Lg | G | GS | CG | GF | IP | BFP | H | R | ER | HR | SH | SF | HB | TBB | IBB | SO | WP | Bk | W | L | Pct | Sh | Sv-Op | Hld | ERC | ERA |
| 2004 Sea | AL | 19 | 1 | 0 | 8 | 32.2 | 148 | 30 | 15 | 15 | 2 | 2 | 1 | 0 | 25 | 1 | 30 | 2 | 0 | 1 | 2 | .333 | 0 | 0-0 | 0 | 4.75 | 4.13 |
| 2005 Sea | AL | 55 | 0 | 0 | 15 | 57.0 | 262 | 54 | 33 | 33 | 13 | 1 | 1 | 0 | 42 | 2 | 57 | 7 | 0 | 0 | 4 | .000 | 0 | 0-1 | 5 | 6.06 | 5.21 |
| 2006 CWS | AL | 63 | 0 | 0 | 20 | 54.0 | 227 | 46 | 20 | 20 | 5 | 1 | 3 | 1 | 21 | 4 | 49 | 1 | 0 | 5 | 3 | .625 | 0 | 2-5 | 18 | 3.12 | 3.33 |
| 2007 CWS | AL | 68 | 0 | 0 | 13 | 56.1 | 249 | 59 | 31 | 30 | 4 | 0 | 2 | 2 | 26 | 6 | 55 | 3 | 0 | 4 | 4 | .500 | 0 | 2-7 | 17 | 4.35 | 4.79 |
| 2008 CWS | AL | 74 | 0 | 0 | 12 | 67.1 | 268 | 48 | 20 | 20 | 5 | 1 | 1 | 2 | 19 | 2 | 77 | 3 | 0 | 5 | 3 | .625 | 0 | 1-6 | 20 | 2.07 | 2.67 |
| 2009 CWS | AL | 70 | 0 | 0 | 17 | 72.1 | 291 | 58 | 22 | 22 | 5 | 2 | 1 | 1 | 20 | 2 | 87 | 4 | 0 | 6 | 3 | .667 | 0 | 4-9 | 24 | 2.40 | 2.74 |
| 2010 CWS | AL | 61 | 0 | 0 | 13 | 60.2 | 239 | 41 | 18 | 18 | 3 | 0 | 2 | 2 | 20 | 5 | 81 | 1 | 0 | 5 | 4 | .556 | 0 | 8-10 | 21 | 1.89 | 2.67 |
| 2011 CWS | AL | 62 | 0 | 0 | 20 | 59.2 | 262 | 60 | 34 | 22 | 3 | 3 | 3 | 0 | 21 | 5 | 63 | 2 | 0 | 2 | 5 | .286 | 0 | 3-7 | 20 | 3.32 | 3.32 |
| 2012 CWS | AL | 74 | 0 | 0 | 18 | 65.0 | 266 | 63 | 27 | 25 | 4 | 1 | 0 | 3 | 17 | 4 | 53 | 2 | 0 | 4 | 10 | .286 | 0 | 3-7 | 26 | 3.29 | 3.46 |
| 2013 2 Tms | AL | 60 | 0 | 0 | 6 | 43.1 | 187 | 47 | 20 | 18 | 4 | 4 | 1 | 2 | 15 | 1 | 30 | 2 | 0 | 0 | 4 | .000 | 0 | 0-1 | 19 | 4.50 | 3.74 |
| 13 CWS | AL | 40 | 0 | 0 | 3 | 28.0 | 116 | 25 | 14 | 12 | 4 | 2 | 0 | 2 | 10 | 1 | 21 | 1 | 0 | 0 | 3 | .000 | 0 | 0-1 | 18 | 3.94 | 3.86 |
| 13 Bos | AL | 20 | 0 | 0 | 3 | 15.1 | 71 | 22 | 6 | 6 | 0 | 2 | 1 | 0 | 5 | 0 | 9 | 1 | 0 | 0 | 1 | .000 | 0 | 0-0 | 1 | 5.55 | 3.52 |
| Postseason | | 3 | 0 | 0 | 1 | 3.1 | 14 | 2 | 0 | 0 | 0 | 0 | 0 | 0 | 2 | 1 | 2 | 0 | 0 | 0 | 0 | - | 0 | 0-0 | 1 | 1.62 | 0.00 |
| 10 ML YEARS | | 606 | 1 | 0 | 142 | 568.1 | 2399 | 506 | 240 | 223 | 48 | 15 | 15 | 13 | 226 | 32 | 582 | 27 | 0 | 32 | 42 | .432 | 0 | 23-53 | 170 | 3.37 | 3.53 |

## Chris Tillman

**Pitches:** R **Bats:** R **Pos:** SP-33 **Ht:** 6'5" **Wt:** 210 **Born:** 4/15/1988 **Age:** 26

| HOW MUCH HE PITCHED | | | | | | | | WHAT HE GAVE UP | | | | | | | | | | | | THE RESULTS | | | | | | | |
|---|---|---|---|---|---|---|---|---|---|---|---|---|---|---|---|---|---|---|---|---|---|---|---|---|---|---|---|
| Year Team | Lg | G | GS | CG | GF | IP | BFP | H | R | ER | HR | SH | SF | HB | TBB | IBB | SO | WP | Bk | W | L | Pct | Sh | Sv-Op | Hld | ERC | ERA |
| 2009 Bal | AL | 12 | 12 | 0 | 0 | 65.0 | 285 | 77 | 40 | 39 | 15 | 0 | 0 | 2 | 24 | 1 | 39 | 4 | 0 | 2 | 5 | .286 | 0 | 0-0 | 0 | 6.28 | 5.40 |
| 2010 Bal | AL | 11 | 11 | 0 | 0 | 53.2 | 236 | 51 | 37 | 35 | 9 | 1 | 3 | 1 | 31 | 1 | 31 | 2 | 0 | 2 | 5 | .286 | 0 | 0-0 | 0 | 5.12 | 5.87 |
| 2011 Bal | AL | 13 | 13 | 0 | 0 | 62.0 | 287 | 77 | 41 | 38 | 5 | 1 | 1 | 4 | 25 | 0 | 46 | 1 | 1 | 3 | 5 | .375 | 0 | 0-0 | 0 | 5.58 | 5.52 |
| 2012 Bal | AL | 15 | 15 | 0 | 0 | 86.0 | 347 | 66 | 38 | 28 | 12 | 1 | 2 | 1 | 24 | 0 | 66 | 5 | 0 | 9 | 3 | .750 | 0 | 0-0 | 0 | 2.65 | 2.93 |
| 2013 Bal | AL | 33 | 33 | 1 | 0 | 206.1 | 845 | 184 | 87 | 85 | 33 | 4 | 6 | 3 | 68 | 2 | 179 | 6 | 1 | 16 | 7 | .696 | 0 | 0-0 | 0 | 3.72 | 3.71 |
| 5 ML YEARS | | 84 | 84 | 1 | 0 | 473.0 | 2000 | 455 | 243 | 225 | 74 | 7 | 12 | 11 | 172 | 4 | 361 | 18 | 2 | 32 | 25 | .561 | 0 | 0-0 | 0 | 4.23 | 4.28 |

## Shawn Tolleson

**Pitches:** R **Bats:** R **Pos:** RP-1 TAHL-eh-son **Ht:** 6'2" **Wt:** 210 **Born:** 1/19/1988 **Age:** 26

| HOW MUCH HE PITCHED | | | | | | | | WHAT HE GAVE UP | | | | | | | | | | | | THE RESULTS | | | | | | | |
|---|---|---|---|---|---|---|---|---|---|---|---|---|---|---|---|---|---|---|---|---|---|---|---|---|---|---|---|
| Year Team | Lg | G | GS | CG | GF | IP | BFP | H | R | ER | HR | SH | SF | HB | TBB | IBB | SO | WP | Bk | W | L | Pct | Sh | Sv-Op | Hld | ERC | ERA |
| 2010 Ogden | R+ | 26 | 0 | 0 | 25 | 28.2 | 104 | 17 | 2 | 2 | 1 | 1 | 1 | 0 | 5 | 0 | 39 | 2 | 0 | 1 | 1 | .500 | 0 | 17- - | - | 1.21 | 0.63 |
| 2011 Gt Lks | A | 14 | 0 | 0 | 13 | 15.0 | 56 | 8 | 1 | 0 | 0 | 0 | 0 | 0 | 4 | 0 | 33 | 2 | 0 | 1 | 0 | 1.000 | 0 | 10- - | - | 1.08 | 0.00 |
| 2011 RCuca | A+ | 5 | 0 | 0 | 5 | 9.2 | 36 | 2 | 3 | 1 | 1 | 0 | 0 | 0 | 3 | 0 | 17 | 0 | 0 | 2 | 0 | 1.000 | 0 | 3- - | - | 0.62 | 0.93 |
| 2011 Chatt | AA | 38 | 0 | 0 | 22 | 44.1 | 181 | 42 | 14 | 8 | 2 | 1 | 0 | 2 | 11 | 1 | 55 | 2 | 0 | 4 | 2 | .667 | 0 | 12- - | - | 3.05 | 1.62 |
| 2012 Chatt | AA | 11 | 0 | 0 | 9 | 13.0 | 49 | 8 | 2 | 2 | 2 | 0 | 0 | 0 | 4 | 0 | 19 | 0 | 0 | 0 | 0 | - | 0 | 5- - | - | 2.16 | 1.38 |
| 2012 Albq | AAA | 8 | 0 | 0 | 2 | 9.1 | 37 | 8 | 5 | 5 | 1 | 0 | 0 | 0 | 1 | 0 | 15 | 3 | 0 | 0 | 1 | .000 | 0 | 0- - | - | 2.24 | 4.82 |
| 2013 Albq | AAA | 3 | 0 | 0 | 2 | 5.2 | 19 | 2 | 0 | 0 | 0 | 1 | 0 | 0 | 2 | 0 | 6 | 0 | 0 | 0 | 0 | - | 0 | 2- - | - | 0.84 | 0.00 |
| 2013 Ddgrs | R | 1 | 0 | 0 | 0 | 1.0 | 4 | 0 | 0 | 0 | 0 | 0 | 0 | 0 | 1 | 0 | 0 | 0 | 0 | 0 | 0 | - | 0 | 0- - | - | 0.95 | 0.00 |
| 2013 RCuca | A+ | 1 | 0 | 0 | 0 | 1.0 | 4 | 1 | 1 | 1 | 1 | 0 | 0 | 0 | 0 | 0 | 1 | 0 | 0 | 1 | 0 | 1.000 | 0 | 0- - | - | 7.45 | 9.00 |
| 2012 LAD | NL | 40 | 0 | 0 | 12 | 37.2 | 160 | 30 | 19 | 18 | 4 | 2 | 1 | 1 | 20 | 1 | 39 | 0 | 0 | 3 | 1 | .750 | 0 | 0-0 | 2 | 3.59 | 4.30 |
| 2013 LAD | NL | 1 | 0 | 0 | 0 | 0.0 | 2 | 0 | 0 | 0 | 0 | 0 | 0 | 0 | 2 | 0 | 0 | 0 | 0 | 0 | 0 | - | 0 | 0-0 | 0 | - | - |
| 2 ML YEARS | | 41 | 0 | 0 | 12 | 37.2 | 162 | 30 | 19 | 18 | 4 | 2 | 1 | 1 | 22 | 1 | 39 | 0 | 0 | 3 | 1 | .750 | 0 | 0-0 | 2 | 3.79 | 4.30 |

# Josh Tomlin

**Pitches:** R **Bats:** R **Pos:** RP-1 **Ht:** 6'1" **Wt:** 190 **Born:** 10/19/1984 **Age:** 29

| HOW MUCH HE PITCHED | | | | | | | | | WHAT HE GAVE UP | | | | | | | | | | | | THE RESULTS | | | | | | | |
|---|---|---|---|---|---|---|---|---|---|---|---|---|---|---|---|---|---|---|---|---|---|---|---|---|---|---|---|---|
| Year | Team | Lg | G | GS | CG | GF | IP | BFP | H | R | ER | HR | SH | SF | HB | TBB | IBB | SO | WP | Bk | W | L | Pct | Sh | Sv-Op | Hld | ERC | ERA |
| 2013 | Indns* | R | 2 | 2 | 0 | 0 | 2.0 | 7 | 1 | 0 | 0 | 0 | 0 | 0 | 0 | 0 | 0 | 2 | 0 | 0 | 0 | 0 | - | 0 | 0-- | - | 0.54 | 0.00 |
| 2013 | Lk Cty* | A | 3 | 1 | 0 | 0 | 4.1 | 15 | 1 | 0 | 0 | 0 | 0 | 0 | 0 | 0 | 0 | 4 | 0 | 0 | 0 | 0 | - | 0 | 0-- | - | 0.12 | 0.00 |
| 2013 | Akron* | AA | 2 | 2 | 0 | 0 | 6.0 | 22 | 3 | 1 | 1 | 0 | 0 | 0 | 1 | 0 | 0 | 4 | 0 | 0 | 0 | 0 | - | 0 | 0-- | - | 0.80 | 1.50 |
| 2013 | Clmbs* | AAA | 3 | 3 | 0 | 0 | 15.0 | 56 | 12 | 4 | 4 | 0 | 0 | 0 | 2 | 0 | 0 | 11 | 0 | 0 | 2 | 0 | 1.000 | 0 | 0-- | - | 1.63 | 2.40 |
| 2010 | Cle | AL | 12 | 12 | 1 | 0 | 73.0 | 301 | 72 | 38 | 37 | 10 | 3 | 3 | 3 | 19 | 3 | 43 | 1 | 0 | 6 | 4 | .600 | 0 | 0-0 | 0 | 3.89 | 4.56 |
| 2011 | Cle | AL | 26 | 26 | 0 | 0 | 165.1 | 662 | 157 | 80 | 78 | 24 | 1 | 3 | 3 | 21 | 2 | 89 | 3 | 0 | 12 | 7 | .632 | 0 | 0-0 | 0 | 3.11 | 4.25 |
| 2012 | Cle | AL | 21 | 16 | 0 | 0 | 103.1 | 452 | 126 | 74 | 73 | 18 | 2 | 3 | 3 | 25 | 3 | 56 | 4 | 0 | 5 | 8 | .385 | 0 | 0-0 | 0 | 5.34 | 6.36 |
| 2013 | Cle | AL | 1 | 0 | 0 | 0 | 2.0 | 9 | 2 | 0 | 0 | 0 | 0 | 0 | 0 | 0 | 0 | 0 | 0 | 0 | 0 | 0 | - | 0 | 0-0 | 0 | 1.68 | 0.00 |
| 4 ML YEARS | | | 60 | 54 | 1 | 0 | 343.2 | 1424 | 357 | 192 | 188 | 52 | 6 | 9 | 9 | 65 | 8 | 188 | 8 | 0 | 23 | 19 | .548 | 0 | 0-0 | 0 | 3.90 | 4.92 |

# Michael Tonkin

**Pitches:** R **Bats:** R **Pos:** RP-9 TAHN-kin **Ht:** 6'7" **Wt:** 220 **Born:** 11/19/1989 **Age:** 24

| HOW MUCH HE PITCHED | | | | | | | | | WHAT HE GAVE UP | | | | | | | | | | | | THE RESULTS | | | | | | | |
|---|---|---|---|---|---|---|---|---|---|---|---|---|---|---|---|---|---|---|---|---|---|---|---|---|---|---|---|---|
| Year | Team | Lg | G | GS | CG | GF | IP | BFP | H | R | ER | HR | SH | SF | HB | TBB | IBB | SO | WP | Bk | W | L | Pct | Sh | Sv-Op | Hld | ERC | ERA |
| 2009 | Twins | R | 11 | 9 | 0 | 0 | 54.2 | 231 | 55 | 30 | 22 | 2 | 1 | 4 | 4 | 9 | 0 | 60 | 5 | 0 | 3 | 4 | .429 | 0 | 0-- | - | 3.01 | 3.62 |
| 2010 | Beloit | A | 13 | 12 | 0 | 0 | 65.0 | 292 | 76 | 43 | 31 | 7 | 1 | 0 | 8 | 18 | 0 | 40 | 7 | 0 | 3 | 6 | .333 | 0 | 0-- | - | 5.08 | 4.29 |
| 2010 | Elizab | R | 10 | 0 | 0 | 3 | 25.0 | 101 | 18 | 6 | 3 | 1 | 1 | 0 | 4 | 4 | 1 | 26 | 1 | 0 | 1 | 0 | 1.000 | 0 | 1-- | - | 1.89 | 1.08 |
| 2011 | Beloit | A | 48 | 3 | 0 | 17 | 76.2 | 338 | 82 | 41 | 33 | 3 | 3 | 0 | 8 | 24 | 1 | 69 | 6 | 0 | 4 | 3 | .571 | 0 | 2-- | - | 4.04 | 3.87 |
| 2012 | Beloit | A | 22 | 0 | 0 | 7 | 39.0 | 154 | 29 | 8 | 6 | 1 | 1 | 2 | 1 | 9 | 1 | 53 | 5 | 0 | 3 | 0 | 1.000 | 0 | 6-- | - | 1.77 | 1.38 |
| 2012 | FtMyrs | A+ | 22 | 0 | 0 | 18 | 30.1 | 127 | 24 | 12 | 10 | 2 | 1 | 0 | 2 | 11 | 0 | 44 | 1 | 0 | 1 | 1 | .500 | 0 | 6-- | - | 2.81 | 2.97 |
| 2013 | NwBrit | AA | 22 | 0 | 0 | 20 | 24.1 | 108 | 21 | 10 | 6 | 0 | 0 | 0 | 3 | 8 | 0 | 30 | 2 | 0 | 1 | 2 | .333 | 0 | 7-- | - | 2.69 | 2.22 |
| 2013 | Roch | AAA | 30 | 0 | 0 | 21 | 32.2 | 139 | 33 | 18 | 16 | 3 | 0 | 1 | 1 | 8 | 1 | 36 | 0 | 0 | 1 | 2 | .333 | 0 | 14-- | - | 3.49 | 4.41 |
| 2013 | Min | AL | 9 | 0 | 0 | 6 | 11.1 | 47 | 9 | 6 | 1 | 0 | 0 | 0 | 0 | 3 | 0 | 10 | 1 | 0 | 0 | 0 | - | 0 | 0-0 | 0 | 1.82 | 0.79 |

# Takashi Toritani

**Bats:** L **Throws:** R **Pos:** IF tah-KAH-shee toor-ih-TAHN-ee **Ht:** 5'11" **Wt:** 170 **Born:** 6/26/1981 **Age:** 33

| BATTING | | | | | | | | | | | | | | | | | | | | | BASERUNNING | | | | AVERAGES | | |
|---|---|---|---|---|---|---|---|---|---|---|---|---|---|---|---|---|---|---|---|---|---|---|---|---|---|---|---|
| Year | Team | Lg | G | AB | H | 2B | 3B | HR | (Hm | Rd) | TB | R | RBI | RC | TBB | IBB | SO | HBP | SH | SF | SB | CS | SB% | GDP | Avg | OBP | Slg |
| 2009 | Hnshn | Jap | 144 | 538 | 155 | 31 | 2 | 20 | (- | -) | 250 | 84 | 75 | 94 | 65 | 0 | 83 | 5 | 5 | 4 | 7 | 7 | .50 | 13 | .288 | .368 | .465 |
| 2010 | Hnshn | Jap | 144 | 575 | 173 | 31 | 6 | 19 | (- | -) | 273 | 98 | 104 | 106 | 66 | 1 | 93 | 3 | 2 | 5 | 13 | 3 | .81 | 14 | .301 | .373 | .475 |
| 2011 | Hnshn | Jap | 144 | 500 | 150 | 28 | 7 | 5 | (- | -) | 207 | 71 | 51 | 91 | 78 | 0 | 72 | 4 | 3 | 5 | 16 | 3 | .84 | 10 | .300 | .395 | .414 |
| 2012 | Hnshn | Jap | 144 | 515 | 135 | 22 | 6 | 8 | (- | -) | 193 | 62 | 59 | 83 | 94 | 2 | 91 | 2 | 5 | 8 | 15 | 4 | .79 | 12 | .262 | .373 | .375 |
| 2013 | Hnshn | Jap | 138 | 508 | 143 | 30 | 4 | 8 | (- | -) | 205 | 66 | 61 | 92 | 99 | 1 | 63 | 4 | 1 | 2 | 15 | 7 | .68 | 12 | .281 | .401 | .404 |

# Yorvit Torrealba

**Bats:** R **Throws:** R **Pos:** C-50;PH-11;1B-3 your-VEET tore-ree-AL-bah **Ht:** 5'11" **Wt:** 200 **Born:** 7/19/1978 **Age:** 35

| BATTING | | | | | | | | | | | | | | | | | | | | | BASERUNNING | | | | AVERAGES | | |
|---|---|---|---|---|---|---|---|---|---|---|---|---|---|---|---|---|---|---|---|---|---|---|---|---|---|---|---|
| Year | Team | Lg | G | AB | H | 2B | 3B | HR | (Hm | Rd) | TB | R | RBI | RC | TBB | IBB | SO | HBP | SH | SF | SB | CS | SB% | GDP | Avg | OBP | Slg |
| 2001 | SF | NL | 3 | 4 | 2 | 0 | 1 | 0 | (0 | 0) | 4 | 0 | 2 | 2 | 0 | 0 | 0 | 0 | 0 | 0 | 0 | 0 | - | 0 | .500 | .500 | 1.000 |
| 2002 | SF | NL | 53 | 136 | 38 | 10 | 0 | 2 | (0 | 2) | 54 | 17 | 14 | 16 | 14 | 2 | 20 | 2 | 3 | 0 | 0 | 0 | - | 11 | .279 | .355 | .397 |
| 2003 | SF | NL | 66 | 200 | 52 | 10 | 2 | 4 | (3 | 1) | 78 | 22 | 29 | 25 | 14 | 1 | 39 | 2 | 3 | 2 | 1 | 0 | 1.00 | 3 | .260 | .312 | .390 |
| 2004 | SF | NL | 64 | 172 | 39 | 7 | 3 | 6 | (3 | 3) | 70 | 19 | 23 | 18 | 17 | 3 | 31 | 2 | 4 | 1 | 2 | 0 | 1.00 | 7 | .227 | .302 | .407 |
| 2005 | 2 Tms | | 76 | 201 | 47 | 12 | 0 | 3 | (2 | 1) | 68 | 32 | 15 | 14 | 16 | 1 | 50 | 2 | 5 | 0 | 1 | 0 | 1.00 | 8 | .234 | .297 | .338 |
| 2006 | Col | NL | 65 | 223 | 55 | 16 | 3 | 7 | (3 | 4) | 98 | 23 | 43 | 30 | 11 | 1 | 49 | 4 | 2 | 1 | 4 | 3 | .57 | 7 | .247 | .293 | .439 |
| 2007 | Col | NL | 113 | 396 | 101 | 22 | 1 | 8 | (6 | 2) | 149 | 47 | 47 | 34 | 34 | 1 | 73 | 6 | 6 | 1 | 2 | 1 | .67 | 19 | .255 | .323 | .376 |
| 2008 | Col | NL | 70 | 236 | 58 | 17 | 0 | 6 | (5 | 1) | 93 | 19 | 31 | 23 | 12 | 0 | 44 | 5 | 5 | 3 | 0 | 4 | .00 | 10 | .246 | .293 | .394 |
| 2009 | Col | NL | 64 | 213 | 62 | 11 | 1 | 2 | (1 | 1) | 81 | 27 | 31 | 37 | 21 | 5 | 42 | 1 | 3 | 4 | 1 | 1 | .50 | 4 | .291 | .351 | .380 |
| 2010 | SD | NL | 95 | 325 | 88 | 14 | 0 | 7 | (4 | 3) | 123 | 31 | 37 | 41 | 33 | 2 | 67 | 3 | 1 | 1 | 7 | 5 | .58 | 12 | .271 | .343 | .378 |
| 2011 | Tex | AL | 113 | 396 | 108 | 27 | 1 | 7 | (7 | 0) | 158 | 40 | 37 | 41 | 20 | 0 | 65 | 0 | 1 | 2 | 0 | 2 | .00 | 11 | .273 | .306 | .399 |
| 2012 | 3 Tms | | 64 | 194 | 44 | 8 | 0 | 4 | (2 | 2) | 64 | 19 | 14 | 17 | 17 | 0 | 40 | 2 | 3 | 2 | 1 | 1 | .50 | 2 | .227 | .293 | .330 |
| 2013 | Col | NL | 61 | 179 | 43 | 8 | 0 | 0 | (0 | 0) | 51 | 10 | 16 | 14 | 13 | 2 | 24 | 1 | 3 | 0 | 0 | 0 | - | 6 | .240 | .295 | .285 |
| 05 | SF | NL | 34 | 93 | 21 | 8 | 0 | 1 | (1 | 0) | 32 | 18 | 7 | 7 | 9 | 1 | 25 | 1 | 2 | 0 | 1 | 0 | 1.00 | 3 | .226 | .301 | .344 |
| 05 | Sea | AL | 42 | 108 | 26 | 4 | 0 | 2 | (1 | 1) | 36 | 14 | 8 | 7 | 7 | 0 | 25 | 1 | 3 | 0 | 0 | 0 | - | 5 | .241 | .293 | .333 |
| 12 | Tex | AL | 49 | 161 | 38 | 8 | 0 | 3 | (2 | 1) | 55 | 16 | 12 | 15 | 14 | 0 | 31 | 2 | 3 | 2 | 1 | 1 | .50 | 2 | .236 | .302 | .342 |
| 12 | Tor | AL | 10 | 28 | 6 | 0 | 0 | 1 | (0 | 1) | 9 | 3 | 2 | 2 | 2 | 0 | 7 | 0 | 0 | 0 | 0 | 0 | - | 0 | .214 | .267 | .321 |
| 12 | Mil | NL | 5 | 5 | 0 | 0 | 0 | 0 | (0 | 0) | 0 | 0 | 0 | 0 | 1 | 0 | 2 | 0 | 0 | 0 | 0 | 0 | - | 0 | .000 | .167 | .000 |
| Postseason | | | 24 | 73 | 21 | 5 | 0 | 2 | (1 | 1) | 32 | 7 | 13 | 12 | 5 | 1 | 16 | 0 | 3 | 1 | 0 | 0 | - | 2 | .288 | .329 | .438 |
| 13 ML YEARS | | | 907 | 2875 | 737 | 162 | 12 | 56 | (36 | 20) | 1091 | 306 | 339 | 312 | 222 | 18 | 544 | 30 | 39 | 17 | 19 | 17 | .53 | 100 | .256 | .315 | .379 |

# Alex Torres

**Pitches:** L **Bats:** L **Pos:** RP-39 **Ht:** 5'10" **Wt:** 175 **Born:** 12/8/1987 **Age:** 26

| HOW MUCH HE PITCHED | | | | | | | | | WHAT HE GAVE UP | | | | | | | | | | | | THE RESULTS | | | | | | | |
|---|---|---|---|---|---|---|---|---|---|---|---|---|---|---|---|---|---|---|---|---|---|---|---|---|---|---|---|---|
| Year | Team | Lg | G | GS | CG | GF | IP | BFP | H | R | ER | HR | SH | SF | HB | TBB | IBB | SO | WP | Bk | W | L | Pct | Sh | Sv-Op | Hld | ERC | ERA |
| 2009 | RCuca | A+ | 21 | 19 | 0 | 1 | 121.1 | 506 | 93 | 43 | 37 | 4 | 6 | 2 | 6 | 63 | 0 | 124 | 9 | 1 | 10 | 3 | .769 | 0 | 0-- | - | 3.06 | 2.74 |
| 2009 | Ark | AA | 5 | 5 | 0 | 0 | 26.0 | 113 | 23 | 10 | 8 | 0 | 0 | 1 | 1 | 17 | 0 | 25 | 1 | 0 | 3 | 1 | .750 | 0 | 0-- | - | 3.93 | 2.77 |
| 2009 | Mont | AA | 2 | 2 | 0 | 0 | 8.2 | 38 | 7 | 6 | 3 | 1 | 1 | 0 | 0 | 5 | 0 | 7 | 1 | 0 | 0 | 2 | .000 | 0 | 0-- | - | 3.72 | 3.12 |
| 2010 | Mont | AA | 27 | 27 | 0 | 0 | 142.2 | 612 | 136 | 63 | 55 | 9 | 5 | 1 | 4 | 70 | 2 | 150 | 12 | 1 | 11 | 6 | .647 | 0 | 0-- | - | 4.08 | 3.47 |
| 2011 | Drham | AAA | 27 | 27 | 1 | 0 | 146.1 | 636 | 134 | 61 | 50 | 7 | 4 | 5 | 6 | 83 | 0 | 156 | 10 | 3 | 9 | 7 | .563 | 0 | 0-- | - | 4.11 | 3.08 |
| 2012 | Drham | AAA | 26 | 14 | 0 | 2 | 69.0 | 337 | 70 | 58 | 56 | 6 | 1 | 2 | 3 | 63 | 1 | 91 | 5 | 1 | 3 | 7 | .300 | 0 | 0-- | - | 6.24 | 7.30 |
| 2012 | Rays | R | 4 | 4 | 0 | 0 | 11.1 | 44 | 7 | 4 | 4 | 0 | 0 | 0 | 0 | 4 | 0 | 17 | 0 | 0 | 0 | 1 | .000 | 0 | 0-- | - | 1.50 | 3.18 |
| 2013 | Drham | AAA | 9 | 9 | 0 | 0 | 46.0 | 197 | 34 | 23 | 18 | 2 | 2 | 2 | 2 | 21 | 1 | 61 | 2 | 0 | 2 | 2 | .500 | 0 | 0-- | - | 2.56 | 3.52 |
| 2011 | TB | AL | 4 | 0 | 0 | 2 | 8.0 | 39 | 8 | 4 | 3 | 0 | 0 | 0 | 1 | 7 | 2 | 9 | 0 | 0 | 1 | 1 | .500 | 0 | 0-0 | 0 | 5.11 | 3.38 |
| 2013 | TB | AL | 39 | 0 | 0 | 5 | 58.0 | 226 | 32 | 12 | 11 | 1 | 1 | 1 | 3 | 20 | 1 | 62 | 1 | 0 | 4 | 2 | .667 | 0 | 0-1 | 5 | 1.43 | 1.71 |
| 2 ML YEARS | | | 43 | 0 | 0 | 7 | 66.0 | 265 | 40 | 16 | 14 | 1 | 1 | 1 | 4 | 27 | 3 | 71 | 1 | 0 | 5 | 3 | .625 | 0 | 0-1 | 5 | 1.73 | 1.91 |

# Andres Torres

**Bats:** B **Throws:** R **Pos:** LF-56;CF-30;PH-21;PR-4;RF-2 **Ht:** 5'10" **Wt:** 195 **Born:** 1/26/1978 **Age:** 36

| BATTING | | | | | | | | | | | | | | | | | | | | | | BASERUNNING | | | | AVERAGES | | |
|---|---|---|---|---|---|---|---|---|---|---|---|---|---|---|---|---|---|---|---|---|---|---|---|---|---|---|---|---|
| Year | Team | Lg | G | AB | H | 2B | 3B | HR | (Hm | Rd) | TB | R | RBI | RC | TBB | IBB | SO | HBP | SH | SF | | SB | CS | SB% | GDP | Avg | OBP | Slg |
| 2002 | Det | AL | 19 | 70 | 14 | 1 | 1 | 0 | (0 | 0) | 17 | 7 | 3 | 2 | 6 | 0 | 16 | 1 | 0 | 2 | | 2 | 2 | .50 | 2 | .200 | .266 | .243 |
| 2003 | Det | AL | 59 | 168 | 37 | 4 | 3 | 1 | (1 | 0) | 50 | 23 | 9 | 9 | 10 | 0 | 35 | 0 | 6 | 1 | | 5 | 5 | .50 | 5 | .220 | .263 | .298 |
| 2004 | Det | AL | 3 | 0 | 0 | 0 | 0 | 0 | (0 | 0) | 0 | 1 | 0 | 0 | 0 | 0 | 0 | 0 | 0 | 0 | | 1 | 0 | 1.00 | 0 | - | - | - |
| 2005 | Tex | AL | 8 | 19 | 3 | 1 | 0 | 0 | (0 | 0) | 4 | 2 | 1 | 1 | 1 | 0 | 6 | 0 | 0 | 1 | | 1 | 0 | 1.00 | 0 | .158 | .190 | .211 |
| 2009 | SF | NL | 75 | 152 | 41 | 6 | 8 | 6 | (4 | 2) | 81 | 30 | 23 | 31 | 16 | 0 | 45 | 1 | 1 | 0 | | 6 | 1 | .86 | 0 | .270 | .343 | .533 |
| 2010 | SF | NL | 139 | 507 | 136 | 43 | 8 | 16 | (7 | 9) | 243 | 84 | 63 | 87 | 56 | 2 | 128 | 2 | 5 | 0 | | 26 | 7 | .79 | 10 | .268 | .343 | .479 |
| 2011 | SF | NL | 112 | 348 | 77 | 24 | 1 | 4 | (1 | 3) | 115 | 50 | 19 | 38 | 42 | 0 | 95 | 4 | 4 | 0 | | 19 | 6 | .76 | 3 | .221 | .312 | .330 |
| 2012 | NYM | NL | 132 | 374 | 86 | 17 | 7 | 3 | (1 | 2) | 126 | 47 | 35 | 45 | 52 | 2 | 90 | 3 | 1 | 2 | | 13 | 5 | .72 | 9 | .230 | .327 | .337 |
| 2013 | SF | NL | 103 | 272 | 68 | 17 | 1 | 2 | (2 | 0) | 93 | 33 | 21 | 23 | 22 | 1 | 61 | 0 | 2 | 4 | | 4 | 3 | .57 | 7 | .250 | .302 | .342 |
| Postseason | | | 15 | 58 | 16 | 4 | 0 | 1 | (0 | 1) | 23 | 6 | 3 | 6 | 3 | 0 | 18 | 1 | 1 | 0 | | 2 | 3 | .40 | 0 | .276 | .323 | .397 |
| 9 ML YEARS | | | 650 | 1910 | 462 | 113 | 29 | 32 | (16 | 16) | 729 | 277 | 174 | 236 | 205 | 5 | 476 | 11 | 19 | 10 | | 77 | 29 | .73 | 36 | .242 | .317 | .382 |

# Carlos Torres

**Pitches:** R **Bats:** R **Pos:** RP-24; SP-9 **Ht:** 6'1" **Wt:** 185 **Born:** 10/22/1982 **Age:** 31

| HOW MUCH HE PITCHED | | | | | | | | | WHAT HE GAVE UP | | | | | | | | | | | THE RESULTS | | | | | | | |
|---|---|---|---|---|---|---|---|---|---|---|---|---|---|---|---|---|---|---|---|---|---|---|---|---|---|---|---|
| Year | Team | Lg | G | GS | CG | GF | IP | BFP | H | R | ER | HR | SH | SF | HB | TBB | IBB | SO | WP | Bk | W | L | Pct | Sh | Sv-Op | Hld | ERC | ERA |
| 2013 | LsVgs* | AAA | 12 | 12 | 2 | 0 | 71.2 | 303 | 71 | 36 | 31 | 7 | 0 | 1 | 2 | 19 | 0 | 67 | 7 | 0 | 6 | 3 | .667 | 1 | 0-- | - | 3.56 | 3.89 |
| 2009 | CWS | AL | 8 | 5 | 0 | 2 | 28.1 | 130 | 30 | 20 | 19 | 5 | 3 | 3 | 2 | 17 | 2 | 22 | 0 | 0 | 1 | 2 | .333 | 0 | 0-0 | 0 | 6.05 | 6.04 |
| 2010 | CWS | AL | 5 | 1 | 0 | 1 | 13.2 | 71 | 23 | 13 | 13 | 2 | 0 | 1 | 0 | 9 | 1 | 13 | 0 | 0 | 0 | 1 | .000 | 0 | 0-0 | 0 | 9.84 | 8.56 |
| 2012 | Col | NL | 31 | 0 | 0 | 9 | 53.0 | 231 | 49 | 31 | 31 | 2 | 6 | 4 | 4 | 26 | 1 | 42 | 6 | 0 | 5 | 3 | .625 | 0 | 0-0 | 1 | 3.85 | 5.26 |
| 2013 | NYM | NL | 33 | 9 | 0 | 6 | 86.1 | 352 | 79 | 34 | 33 | 15 | 4 | 1 | 4 | 17 | 1 | 75 | 4 | 1 | 4 | 6 | .400 | 0 | 0-0 | 3 | 3.47 | 3.44 |
| 4 ML YEARS | | | 77 | 15 | 0 | 18 | 181.1 | 784 | 181 | 98 | 96 | 24 | 13 | 9 | 10 | 69 | 5 | 152 | 10 | 1 | 10 | 12 | .455 | 0 | 0-0 | 4 | 4.41 | 4.76 |

# Wilfredo Tovar

**Bats:** R **Throws:** R **Pos:** SS-7;PH-1 will-FRAY-doe TOE-varr **Ht:** 5'10" **Wt:** 160 **Born:** 8/11/1991 **Age:** 22

| BATTING | | | | | | | | | | | | | | | | | | | | | | BASERUNNING | | | | AVERAGES | | |
|---|---|---|---|---|---|---|---|---|---|---|---|---|---|---|---|---|---|---|---|---|---|---|---|---|---|---|---|---|
| Year | Team | Lg | G | AB | H | 2B | 3B | HR | (Hm | Rd) | TB | R | RBI | RC | TBB | IBB | SO | HBP | SH | SF | | SB | CS | SB% | GDP | Avg | OBP | Slg |
| 2009 | Mets | R | 38 | 148 | 36 | 5 | 3 | 0 | (- | -) | 47 | 21 | 14 | 14 | 8 | 0 | 19 | 3 | 1 | 1 | | 16 | 8 | .67 | 5 | .243 | .294 | .318 |
| 2010 | StLuci | A+ | 30 | 118 | 29 | 5 | 1 | 0 | (- | -) | 36 | 14 | 6 | 9 | 3 | 1 | 22 | 2 | 1 | 0 | | 4 | 3 | .57 | 2 | .246 | .276 | .305 |
| 2010 | Savann | A | 44 | 160 | 45 | 10 | 0 | 0 | (- | -) | 55 | 12 | 17 | 17 | 8 | 0 | 12 | 3 | 2 | 0 | | 4 | 5 | .44 | 1 | .281 | .327 | .344 |
| 2010 | Bklyn | A- | 18 | 68 | 18 | 2 | 1 | 0 | (- | -) | 22 | 11 | 6 | 7 | 2 | 0 | 9 | 3 | 3 | 1 | | 4 | 3 | .57 | 0 | .265 | .311 | .324 |
| 2011 | Savann | A | 131 | 491 | 123 | 21 | 3 | 2 | (- | -) | 156 | 70 | 41 | 54 | 44 | 1 | 53 | 8 | 3 | 7 | | 15 | 9 | .63 | 11 | .251 | .318 | .318 |
| 2012 | StLuci | A+ | 65 | 218 | 62 | 17 | 1 | 1 | (- | -) | 84 | 31 | 23 | 34 | 29 | 0 | 17 | 4 | 4 | 1 | | 12 | 7 | .63 | 8 | .284 | .377 | .385 |
| 2012 | Bnghtn | AA | 57 | 193 | 49 | 11 | 2 | 0 | (- | -) | 64 | 20 | 27 | 21 | 11 | 0 | 22 | 6 | 3 | 4 | | 2 | 1 | .67 | 6 | .254 | .308 | .332 |
| 2013 | Bnghtn | AA | 133 | 441 | 116 | 14 | 4 | 4 | (- | -) | 150 | 70 | 36 | 51 | 33 | 0 | 49 | 7 | 3 | 2 | | 12 | 7 | .63 | 11 | .263 | .323 | .340 |
| 2013 | NYM | NL | 7 | 15 | 3 | 0 | 0 | 0 | (0 | 0) | 3 | 1 | 2 | 2 | 1 | 1 | 3 | 1 | 2 | 0 | | 1 | 0 | 1.00 | 2 | .200 | .294 | .200 |

# Chad Tracy

**Bats:** L **Throws:** R **Pos:** PH-71;3B-14;1B-10;DH-3 **Ht:** 6'1" **Wt:** 205 **Born:** 5/22/1980 **Age:** 34

| BATTING | | | | | | | | | | | | | | | | | | | | | | BASERUNNING | | | | AVERAGES | | |
|---|---|---|---|---|---|---|---|---|---|---|---|---|---|---|---|---|---|---|---|---|---|---|---|---|---|---|---|---|
| Year | Team | Lg | G | AB | H | 2B | 3B | HR | (Hm | Rd) | TB | R | RBI | RC | TBB | IBB | SO | HBP | SH | SF | | SB | CS | SB% | GDP | Avg | OBP | Slg |
| 2004 | Ari | NL | 143 | 481 | 137 | 29 | 3 | 8 | (6 | 2) | 196 | 45 | 53 | 63 | 45 | 3 | 60 | 0 | 1 | 5 | | 2 | 3 | .40 | 11 | .285 | .343 | .407 |
| 2005 | Ari | NL | 145 | 503 | 155 | 34 | 4 | 27 | (9 | 18) | 278 | 73 | 72 | 82 | 35 | 4 | 78 | 8 | 1 | 6 | | 3 | 1 | .75 | 10 | .308 | .359 | .553 |
| 2006 | Ari | NL | 154 | 597 | 168 | 41 | 0 | 20 | (14 | 6) | 269 | 91 | 80 | 85 | 54 | 5 | 129 | 5 | 1 | 5 | | 5 | 1 | .83 | 11 | .281 | .343 | .451 |
| 2007 | Ari | NL | 76 | 227 | 60 | 18 | 2 | 7 | (3 | 4) | 103 | 30 | 35 | 33 | 29 | 4 | 43 | 1 | 0 | 3 | | 0 | 0 | - | 8 | .264 | .346 | .454 |
| 2008 | Ari | NL | 88 | 273 | 73 | 16 | 0 | 8 | (3 | 5) | 113 | 25 | 39 | 32 | 16 | 2 | 49 | 1 | 0 | 2 | | 0 | 0 | - | 5 | .267 | .308 | .414 |
| 2009 | Ari | NL | 98 | 257 | 61 | 15 | 0 | 8 | (7 | 1) | 100 | 29 | 39 | 28 | 26 | 7 | 38 | 1 | 0 | 4 | | 1 | 0 | 1.00 | 3 | .237 | .306 | .389 |
| 2010 | 2 Tms | NL | 69 | 146 | 36 | 8 | 0 | 1 | (0 | 1) | 47 | 11 | 15 | 14 | 11 | 0 | 36 | 2 | 0 | 1 | | 0 | 0 | - | 2 | .247 | .306 | .322 |
| 2012 | Was | NL | 73 | 93 | 25 | 7 | 0 | 3 | (3 | 0) | 41 | 7 | 14 | 14 | 10 | 3 | 15 | 1 | 0 | 1 | | 0 | 0 | - | 1 | .269 | .343 | .441 |
| 2013 | Was | NL | 92 | 129 | 26 | 4 | 0 | 4 | (0 | 4) | 42 | 6 | 11 | 4 | 7 | 0 | 25 | 0 | 0 | 0 | | 0 | 2 | .00 | 2 | .202 | .243 | .326 |
| 10 | ChC | NL | 28 | 44 | 11 | 2 | 0 | 0 | (0 | 0) | 13 | 6 | 5 | 6 | 5 | 0 | 15 | 0 | 0 | 0 | | 0 | 0 | - | 0 | .250 | .327 | .295 |
| 10 | Fla | NL | 41 | 102 | 25 | 6 | 0 | 1 | (0 | 1) | 34 | 5 | 10 | 8 | 6 | 0 | 21 | 2 | 0 | 1 | | 0 | 0 | - | 2 | .245 | .297 | .333 |
| Postseason | | | 5 | 4 | 0 | 0 | 0 | 0 | (0 | 0) | 0 | 0 | 0 | 0 | 0 | 0 | 1 | 0 | 0 | 0 | | 0 | 0 | - | 0 | .000 | .000 | .000 |
| 9 ML YEARS | | | 938 | 2706 | 741 | 172 | 9 | 86 | (45 | 41) | 1189 | 317 | 358 | 355 | 233 | 28 | 473 | 19 | 3 | 27 | | 11 | 7 | .61 | 53 | .274 | .333 | .439 |

# Carlos Triunfel

**Bats:** R **Throws:** R **Pos:** SS-10;2B-4;PH-2;3B-1;DH-1;PR-1 TRUE-en-fell **Ht:** 5'11" **Wt:** 205 **Born:** 2/27/1990 **Age:** 24

| BATTING | | | | | | | | | | | | | | | | | | | | | | BASERUNNING | | | | AVERAGES | | |
|---|---|---|---|---|---|---|---|---|---|---|---|---|---|---|---|---|---|---|---|---|---|---|---|---|---|---|---|---|
| Year | Team | Lg | G | AB | H | 2B | 3B | HR | (Hm | Rd) | TB | R | RBI | RC | TBB | IBB | SO | HBP | SH | SF | | SB | CS | SB% | GDP | Avg | OBP | Slg |
| 2009 | WTenn | AA | 7 | 26 | 6 | 1 | 0 | 0 | (- | -) | 7 | 2 | 4 | 2 | 1 | 0 | 2 | 1 | 0 | 0 | | 0 | 0 | - | 0 | .231 | .286 | .269 |
| 2009 | Ms | R | 4 | 16 | 4 | 1 | 0 | 0 | (- | -) | 5 | 0 | 4 | 1 | 0 | 0 | 2 | 0 | 0 | 0 | | 1 | 0 | 1.00 | 1 | .250 | .250 | .313 |
| 2010 | WTenn | AA | 129 | 470 | 121 | 12 | 1 | 7 | (- | -) | 156 | 51 | 42 | 43 | 13 | 1 | 54 | 7 | 5 | 3 | | 2 | 8 | .20 | 18 | .257 | .286 | .332 |
| 2011 | Jacksn | AA | 105 | 395 | 111 | 22 | 2 | 6 | (- | -) | 155 | 45 | 35 | 53 | 25 | 2 | 71 | 10 | 3 | 0 | | 5 | 7 | .42 | 2 | .281 | .340 | .392 |
| 2011 | Tacom | AAA | 27 | 111 | 31 | 6 | 1 | 0 | (- | -) | 39 | 7 | 10 | 12 | 2 | 0 | 17 | 2 | 1 | 1 | | 1 | 0 | 1.00 | 3 | .279 | .302 | .351 |
| 2012 | Tacom | AAA | 131 | 496 | 129 | 31 | 2 | 10 | (- | -) | 194 | 74 | 63 | 62 | 23 | 0 | 89 | 13 | 7 | 4 | | 3 | 2 | .60 | 12 | .260 | .308 | .391 |
| 2013 | Tacom | AAA | 100 | 383 | 108 | 22 | 3 | 5 | (- | -) | 151 | 55 | 31 | 50 | 17 | 0 | 76 | 10 | 2 | 1 | | 6 | 4 | .60 | 9 | .282 | .328 | .394 |
| 2012 | Sea | AL | 10 | 22 | 5 | 2 | 0 | 0 | (0 | 0) | 7 | 2 | 3 | 3 | 1 | 0 | 4 | 0 | 1 | 0 | | 0 | 0 | - | 0 | .227 | .261 | .318 |
| 2013 | Sea | AL | 17 | 44 | 6 | 1 | 0 | 0 | (0 | 0) | 7 | 1 | 2 | 0 | 0 | 0 | 11 | 1 | 1 | 1 | | 0 | 0 | - | 1 | .136 | .152 | .159 |
| 2 ML YEARS | | | 27 | 66 | 11 | 3 | 0 | 0 | (0 | 0) | 14 | 3 | 5 | 3 | 1 | 0 | 15 | 1 | 2 | 1 | | 0 | 0 | - | 1 | .167 | .188 | .212 |

# Ramon Troncoso

**Pitches:** R **Bats:** R **Pos:** RP-29 tronn-KOE-soe **Ht:** 6'2" **Wt:** 215 **Born:** 2/16/1983 **Age:** 31

| HOW MUCH HE PITCHED | | | | | | | | | WHAT HE GAVE UP | | | | | | | | | | | | THE RESULTS | | | | | | | |
|---|---|---|---|---|---|---|---|---|---|---|---|---|---|---|---|---|---|---|---|---|---|---|---|---|---|---|---|---|
| Year | Team | Lg | G | GS | CG | GF | IP | BFP | H | R | ER | HR | SH | SF | HB | TBB | IBB | SO | WP | Bk | W | L | Pct | Sh | Sv-Op | Hld | ERC | ERA |
| 2013 | Charltt* | AAA | 21 | 0 | 0 | 18 | 24.2 | 102 | 18 | 9 | 6 | 2 | 1 | 0 | 1 | 7 | 0 | 17 | 1 | 0 | 1 | 1 | .500 | 0 | 8- - | - | 2.18 | 2.19 |
| 2008 | LAD | NL | 32 | 0 | 0 | 12 | 38.0 | 160 | 37 | 19 | 18 | 2 | 4 | 3 | 3 | 12 | 1 | 38 | 2 | 0 | 1 | 1 | .500 | 0 | 0-0 | 2 | 3.60 | 4.26 |
| 2009 | LAD | NL | 73 | 0 | 0 | 20 | 82.2 | 357 | 83 | 30 | 25 | 3 | 7 | 3 | 3 | 34 | 9 | 55 | 4 | 0 | 5 | 4 | .556 | 0 | 6-7 | 14 | 3.67 | 2.72 |
| 2010 | LAD | NL | 52 | 0 | 0 | 13 | 54.0 | 234 | 55 | 28 | 26 | 7 | 1 | 2 | 3 | 18 | 5 | 34 | 2 | 0 | 2 | 3 | .400 | 0 | 0-1 | 8 | 4.18 | 4.33 |
| 2011 | LAD | NL | 18 | 0 | 0 | 13 | 22.2 | 103 | 38 | 18 | 17 | 5 | 1 | 0 | 0 | 4 | 1 | 14 | 2 | 0 | 0 | 0 | - | 0 | 0-0 | 0 | 8.56 | 6.75 |
| 2013 | CWS | AL | 29 | 0 | 0 | 15 | 30.0 | 137 | 30 | 22 | 15 | 4 | 2 | 1 | 1 | 16 | 1 | 18 | 1 | 0 | 1 | 4 | .200 | 0 | 0-0 | 1 | 4.82 | 4.50 |
| Postseason | | | 3 | 0 | 0 | 0 | 3.0 | 12 | 0 | 0 | 0 | 0 | 1 | 0 | 1 | 3 | 0 | 3 | 0 | 0 | 0 | 0 | - | 0 | 0-0 | 0 | 1.68 | 0.00 |
| 5 ML YEARS | | | 204 | 0 | 0 | 73 | 227.1 | 991 | 243 | 117 | 101 | 21 | 15 | 9 | 10 | 84 | 17 | 159 | 11 | 0 | 9 | 12 | .429 | 0 | 6-8 | 25 | 4.37 | 4.00 |

# Mike Trout

**Bats:** R **Throws:** R **Pos:** CF-111;LF-47;DH-9 **Ht:** 6'2" **Wt:** 230 **Born:** 8/7/1991 **Age:** 22

| BATTING | | | | | | | | | | | | | | | | | | | | BASERUNNING | | | | AVERAGES | | |
|---|---|---|---|---|---|---|---|---|---|---|---|---|---|---|---|---|---|---|---|---|---|---|---|---|---|---|
| Year | Team | Lg | G | AB | H | 2B | 3B | HR | (Hm | Rd) | TB | R | RBI | RC | TBB | IBB | SO | HBP | SH | SF | SB | CS | SB% | GDP | Avg | OBP | Slg |
| 2011 | LAA | AL | 40 | 123 | 27 | 6 | 0 | 5 | (1 | 4) | 48 | 20 | 16 | 14 | 9 | 0 | 30 | 2 | 0 | 1 | 4 | 0 | 1.00 | 2 | .220 | .281 | .390 |
| 2012 | LAA | AL | 139 | 559 | 182 | 27 | 8 | 30 | (16 | 14) | 315 | **129** | 83 | **127** | 67 | 4 | 139 | 6 | 0 | 7 | **49** | 5 | .91 | 7 | .326 | .399 | .564 |
| 2013 | LAA | AL | 157 | 589 | 190 | 39 | 9 | 27 | (13 | 14) | 328 | **109** | 97 | 141 | **110** | 10 | 136 | 9 | 0 | 8 | 33 | 7 | .83 | 8 | .323 | .432 | .557 |
| 3 ML YEARS | | | 336 | 1271 | 399 | 72 | 17 | 62 | (30 | 32) | 691 | 258 | 196 | 282 | 186 | 14 | 305 | 17 | 0 | 16 | 86 | 12 | .88 | 17 | .314 | .404 | .544 |

2014 157 602 173 39 9 36 338 115 111 83 184 16 287 377 561

# Mark Trumbo

**Bats:** R **Throws:** R **Pos:** 1B-123;RF-19;DH-17;LF-8;3B-1 **Ht:** 6'4" **Wt:** 235 **Born:** 1/16/1986 **Age:** 28

| BATTING | | | | | | | | | | | | | | | | | | | | BASERUNNING | | | | AVERAGES | | |
|---|---|---|---|---|---|---|---|---|---|---|---|---|---|---|---|---|---|---|---|---|---|---|---|---|---|---|
| Year | Team | Lg | G | AB | H | 2B | 3B | HR | (Hm | Rd) | TB | R | RBI | RC | TBB | IBB | SO | HBP | SH | SF | SB | CS | SB% | GDP | Avg | OBP | Slg |
| 2010 | LAA | AL | 8 | 15 | 1 | 0 | 0 | 0 | (0 | 0) | 1 | 2 | 2 | 0 | 1 | 0 | 8 | 0 | 0 | 0 | 0 | 0 | - | 0 | .067 | .125 | .067 |
| 2011 | LAA | AL | 149 | 539 | 137 | 31 | 1 | 29 | (14 | 15) | 257 | 65 | 87 | 69 | 25 | 6 | 120 | 5 | 0 | 4 | 9 | 4 | .69 | 17 | .254 | .291 | .477 |
| 2012 | LAA | AL | 144 | 544 | 146 | 19 | 3 | 32 | (12 | 20) | 267 | 66 | 95 | 80 | 36 | 3 | 153 | 4 | 0 | 2 | 4 | 5 | .44 | 12 | .268 | .317 | .491 |
| 2013 | LAA | AL | 159 | 620 | 145 | 30 | 2 | 34 | (19 | 15) | 281 | 85 | 100 | 74 | 54 | 6 | 184 | 0 | 0 | 4 | 5 | 2 | .71 | 18 | .234 | .294 | .453 |
| 4 ML YEARS | | | 460 | 1718 | 429 | 80 | 6 | 95 | (45 | 50) | 806 | 218 | 284 | 223 | 116 | 15 | 465 | 9 | 0 | 10 | 18 | 11 | .62 | 47 | .250 | .299 | .469 |

# Matt Tuiasosopo

too-ee-ah-suh-SOH-poe

**Bats:** R **Throws:** R **Pos:** LF-63;PH-20;1B-13;PR-5;3B-1;DH-1 **Ht:** 6'2" **Wt:** 225 **Born:** 5/10/1986 **Age:** 28

| BATTING | | | | | | | | | | | | | | | | | | | | BASERUNNING | | | | AVERAGES | | |
|---|---|---|---|---|---|---|---|---|---|---|---|---|---|---|---|---|---|---|---|---|---|---|---|---|---|---|
| Year | Team | Lg | G | AB | H | 2B | 3B | HR | (Hm | Rd) | TB | R | RBI | RC | TBB | IBB | SO | HBP | SH | SF | SB | CS | SB% | GDP | Avg | OBP | Slg |
| 2013 | Toledo* | AAA | 2 | 5 | 2 | 1 | 0 | 0 | (- | -) | 3 | 3 | 0 | 2 | 2 | 0 | 2 | 1 | 0 | 0 | 0 | 0 | - | 0 | .400 | .625 | .600 |
| 2008 | Sea | AL | 14 | 44 | 7 | 2 | 1 | 0 | (0 | 0) | 11 | 1 | 2 | 1 | 2 | 0 | 16 | 1 | 0 | 0 | 0 | 0 | - | 0 | .159 | .213 | .250 |
| 2009 | Sea | AL | 7 | 22 | 5 | 1 | 0 | 1 | (0 | 1) | 9 | 2 | 2 | 2 | 2 | 0 | 5 | 0 | 0 | 1 | 0 | 0 | - | 0 | .227 | .280 | .409 |
| 2010 | Sea | AL | 50 | 127 | 22 | 5 | 0 | 4 | (0 | 4) | 39 | 12 | 11 | 8 | 9 | 0 | 49 | 1 | 1 | 0 | 0 | 0 | - | 3 | .173 | .234 | .307 |
| 2013 | Det | AL | 81 | 164 | 40 | 7 | 0 | 7 | (5 | 2) | 68 | 26 | 30 | 26 | 25 | 0 | 57 | 2 | 0 | 0 | 0 | 0 | - | 3 | .244 | .351 | .415 |
| 4 ML YEARS | | | 152 | 357 | 74 | 15 | 1 | 12 | (5 | 7) | 127 | 41 | 45 | 37 | 38 | 0 | 127 | 4 | 1 | 1 | 0 | 0 | - | 6 | .207 | .290 | .356 |

# Troy Tulowitzki

**Bats:** R **Throws:** R **Pos:** SS-121;PH-7 too-luh-WIT-skee **Ht:** 6'3" **Wt:** 215 **Born:** 10/10/1984 **Age:** 29

| BATTING | | | | | | | | | | | | | | | | | | | | BASERUNNING | | | | AVERAGES | | |
|---|---|---|---|---|---|---|---|---|---|---|---|---|---|---|---|---|---|---|---|---|---|---|---|---|---|---|
| Year | Team | Lg | G | AB | H | 2B | 3B | HR | (Hm | Rd) | TB | R | RBI | RC | TBB | IBB | SO | HBP | SH | SF | SB | CS | SB% | GDP | Avg | OBP | Slg |
| 2013 | ColSpr* | AAA | 2 | 5 | 4 | 0 | 0 | 0 | (- | -) | 4 | 2 | 0 | 2 | 1 | 0 | 0 | 0 | 0 | 0 | 0 | 0 | - | 0 | .800 | .833 | .800 |
| 2006 | Col | NL | 25 | 96 | 23 | 2 | 0 | 1 | (0 | 1) | 28 | 15 | 6 | 10 | 10 | 3 | 25 | 1 | 1 | 0 | 3 | 0 | 1.00 | 1 | .240 | .318 | .292 |
| 2007 | Col | NL | 155 | 609 | 177 | 33 | 5 | 24 | (15 | 9) | 292 | 104 | 99 | 95 | 57 | 3 | 130 | 9 | 5 | 2 | 7 | 6 | .54 | 14 | .291 | .359 | .479 |
| 2008 | Col | NL | 101 | 377 | 99 | 24 | 2 | 8 | (4 | 4) | 151 | 48 | 46 | 42 | 38 | 5 | 56 | 2 | 2 | 2 | 1 | 6 | .14 | 16 | .263 | .332 | .401 |
| 2009 | Col | NL | 151 | 543 | 161 | 25 | 9 | 32 | (17 | 15) | 300 | 101 | 92 | 96 | 73 | 4 | 112 | 3 | 0 | 9 | 20 | 11 | .65 | 20 | .297 | .377 | .552 |
| 2010 | Col | NL | 122 | 470 | 148 | 32 | 3 | 27 | (15 | 12) | 267 | 89 | 95 | 88 | 48 | 4 | 78 | 5 | 1 | 5 | 11 | 2 | .85 | 17 | .315 | .381 | .568 |
| 2011 | Col | NL | 143 | 537 | 162 | 36 | 2 | 30 | (17 | 13) | 292 | 81 | 105 | 101 | 59 | 12 | 79 | 4 | 1 | 5 | 9 | 3 | .75 | 16 | .302 | .372 | .544 |
| 2012 | Col | NL | 47 | 181 | 52 | 8 | 2 | 8 | (3 | 5) | 88 | 33 | 27 | 27 | 19 | 1 | 19 | 2 | 0 | 1 | 2 | 2 | .50 | 7 | .287 | .360 | .486 |
| 2013 | Col | NL | 126 | 446 | 139 | 27 | 0 | 25 | (14 | 11) | 241 | 72 | 82 | 80 | 57 | 5 | 85 | 4 | 0 | 5 | 1 | 0 | 1.00 | 9 | .312 | .391 | .540 |
| Postseason | | | 15 | 57 | 12 | 5 | 0 | 1 | (0 | 1) | 20 | 3 | 6 | 3 | 4 | 0 | 17 | 1 | 0 | 1 | 0 | 1 | .00 | 3 | .211 | .270 | .351 |
| 8 ML YEARS | | | 870 | 3259 | 961 | 187 | 23 | 155 | (85 | 70) | 1659 | 543 | 552 | 539 | 361 | 37 | 584 | 30 | 10 | 29 | 54 | 30 | .64 | 100 | .295 | .367 | .509 |

# Jacob Turner

**Pitches:** R **Bats:** R **Pos:** SP-20 **Ht:** 6'5" **Wt:** 215 **Born:** 5/21/1991 **Age:** 23

| HOW MUCH HE PITCHED | | | | | | | | | WHAT HE GAVE UP | | | | | | | | | | | | THE RESULTS | | | | | | | |
|---|---|---|---|---|---|---|---|---|---|---|---|---|---|---|---|---|---|---|---|---|---|---|---|---|---|---|---|---|
| Year | Team | Lg | G | GS | CG | GF | IP | BFP | H | R | ER | HR | SH | SF | HB | TBB | IBB | SO | WP | Bk | W | L | Pct | Sh | Sv-Op | Hld | ERC | ERA |
| 2013 | NewOr* | AAA | 10 | 10 | 0 | 0 | 56.1 | 242 | 59 | 35 | 28 | 7 | 3 | 2 | 3 | 14 | 1 | 35 | 4 | 1 | 3 | 4 | .429 | 0 | 0- - | - | 4.05 | 4.47 |
| 2011 | Det | AL | 3 | 3 | 0 | 0 | 12.2 | 60 | 17 | 13 | 12 | 3 | 0 | 1 | 1 | 4 | 0 | 8 | 0 | 0 | 0 | 1 | .000 | 0 | 0-0 | 0 | 7.03 | 8.53 |
| 2012 | 2 Tms | | 10 | 10 | 0 | 0 | 55.0 | 231 | 50 | 32 | 27 | 9 | 1 | 2 | 0 | 16 | 3 | 36 | 5 | 0 | 2 | 5 | .286 | 0 | 0-0 | 0 | 3.42 | 4.42 |
| 2013 | Mia | NL | 20 | 20 | 1 | 0 | 118.0 | 514 | 116 | 55 | 49 | 11 | 8 | 5 | 4 | 54 | 5 | 77 | 11 | 0 | 3 | 8 | .273 | 0 | 0-0 | 0 | 4.25 | 3.74 |
| 12 | Det | AL | 3 | 3 | 0 | 0 | 12.1 | 61 | 17 | 11 | 11 | 4 | 0 | 1 | 0 | 7 | 1 | 7 | 1 | 0 | 1 | 1 | .500 | 0 | 0-0 | 0 | 8.66 | 8.03 |
| 12 | Mia | NL | 7 | 7 | 0 | 0 | 42.2 | 170 | 33 | 21 | 16 | 5 | 1 | 1 | 0 | 9 | 2 | 29 | 4 | 0 | 1 | 4 | .200 | 0 | 0-0 | 0 | 2.20 | 3.38 |
| 3 ML YEARS | | | 33 | 33 | 1 | 0 | 185.2 | 805 | 183 | 100 | 88 | 23 | 9 | 8 | 5 | 74 | 8 | 121 | 16 | 0 | 5 | 14 | .263 | 0 | 0-0 | 0 | 4.18 | 4.27 |

# Justin Turner

**Bats:** R **Throws:** R **Pos:** PH-35;3B-23;SS-18;1B-15;2B-12;LF-1;DH-1;PR-1 **Ht:** 6'0" **Wt:** 210 **Born:** 11/23/1984 **Age:** 29

| BATTING | | | | | | | | | | | | | | | | | | | | BASERUNNING | | | | AVERAGES | | |
|---|---|---|---|---|---|---|---|---|---|---|---|---|---|---|---|---|---|---|---|---|---|---|---|---|---|---|
| Year Team | Lg | G | AB | H | 2B | 3B | HR | (Hm | Rd) | TB | R | RBI | RC | TBB | IBB | SO | HBP | SH | SF | SB | CS | SB% | GDP | Avg | OBP | Slg |
| 2013 Mets* | R | 1 | 4 | 0 | 0 | 0 | 0 | (- | -) | 0 | 0 | 0 | 0 | 1 | 0 | 2 | 0 | 0 | 0 | 0 | 0 | - | 0 | .000 | .200 | .000 |
| 2013 StLuci* | A+ | 1 | 1 | 0 | 0 | 0 | 0 | (- | -) | 0 | 0 | 0 | 0 | 0 | 0 | 0 | 0 | 0 | 0 | 0 | 0 | - | 0 | .000 | .000 | .000 |
| 2013 Bnghtn* | AA | 4 | 15 | 6 | 2 | 0 | 0 | (- | -) | 8 | 5 | 1 | 3 | 1 | 0 | 2 | 1 | 0 | 0 | 0 | 0 | - | 3 | .400 | .471 | .533 |
| 2013 Bklyn* | A- | 3 | 10 | 3 | 1 | 0 | 0 | (- | -) | 4 | 2 | 0 | 1 | 2 | 0 | 3 | 0 | 0 | 0 | 0 | 0 | - | 0 | .300 | .417 | .400 |
| 2009 Bal | AL | 12 | 18 | 3 | 0 | 0 | 0 | (0 | 0) | 3 | 2 | 3 | 1 | 4 | 0 | 3 | 0 | 0 | 0 | 0 | 0 | - | 1 | .167 | .318 | .167 |
| 2010 2 Tms | | 9 | 17 | 1 | 1 | 0 | 0 | (0 | 0) | 2 | 1 | 0 | 0 | 1 | 0 | 3 | 0 | 0 | 0 | 0 | 0 | - | 0 | .059 | .111 | .118 |
| 2011 NYM | NL | 117 | 435 | 113 | 30 | 0 | 4 | (3 | 1) | 155 | 49 | 51 | 59 | 39 | 2 | 59 | 10 | 2 | 1 | 7 | 2 | .78 | 9 | .260 | .334 | .356 |
| 2012 NYM | NL | 94 | 171 | 46 | 13 | 1 | 2 | (2 | 0) | 67 | 20 | 19 | 19 | 9 | 0 | 24 | 4 | 0 | 1 | 1 | 1 | .50 | 9 | .269 | .319 | .392 |
| 2013 NYM | NL | 86 | 200 | 56 | 13 | 1 | 2 | (0 | 2) | 77 | 12 | 16 | 17 | 11 | 1 | 34 | 1 | 1 | 1 | 0 | 1 | .00 | 6 | .280 | .319 | .385 |
| 10 Bal | AL | 5 | 9 | 0 | 0 | 0 | 0 | (0 | 0) | 0 | 0 | 0 | 0 | 0 | 0 | 3 | 0 | 0 | 0 | 0 | 0 | - | 0 | .000 | .000 | .000 |
| 10 NYM | NL | 4 | 8 | 1 | 1 | 0 | 0 | (0 | 0) | 2 | 1 | 0 | 0 | 1 | 0 | 0 | 0 | 0 | 0 | 0 | 0 | - | 0 | .125 | .222 | .250 |
| 5 ML YEARS | | 318 | 841 | 219 | 57 | 2 | 8 | (5 | 3) | 304 | 84 | 89 | 96 | 64 | 3 | 123 | 15 | 3 | 3 | 8 | 4 | .67 | 25 | .260 | .323 | .361 |

# Koji Uehara

**Pitches:** R **Bats:** R **Pos:** RP-73 KOH-jee ooh-ih-HAR-uh **Ht:** 6'2" **Wt:** 195 **Born:** 4/3/1975 **Age:** 39

| HOW MUCH HE PITCHED | | | | | | | | WHAT HE GAVE UP | | | | | | | | | | | | THE RESULTS | | | | | | | |
|---|---|---|---|---|---|---|---|---|---|---|---|---|---|---|---|---|---|---|---|---|---|---|---|---|---|---|---|
| Year Team | Lg | G | GS | CG | GF | IP | BFP | H | R | ER | HR | SH | SF | HB | TBB | IBB | SO | WP | Bk | W | L | Pct | Sh | Sv-Op | Hld | ERC | ERA |
| 2009 Bal | AL | 12 | 12 | 0 | 0 | 66.2 | 279 | 71 | 33 | 30 | 7 | 1 | 3 | 0 | 12 | 1 | 48 | 0 | 0 | 2 | 4 | .333 | 0 | 0-0 | 0 | 3.56 | 4.05 |
| 2010 Bal | AL | 43 | 0 | 0 | 22 | 44.0 | 174 | 37 | 15 | 14 | 5 | 1 | 0 | 0 | 5 | 0 | 55 | 1 | 0 | 1 | 2 | .333 | 0 | 13-15 | 6 | 2.22 | 2.86 |
| 2011 2 Tms | AL | 65 | 0 | 0 | 22 | 65.0 | 243 | 38 | 17 | 17 | 11 | 1 | 1 | 0 | 9 | 1 | 85 | 0 | 0 | 2 | 3 | .400 | 0 | 0-1 | 22 | 1.48 | 2.35 |
| 2012 Tex | AL | 37 | 0 | 0 | 13 | 36.0 | 130 | 20 | 7 | 7 | 4 | 1 | 1 | 0 | 3 | 0 | 43 | 1 | 0 | 0 | 0 | - | 0 | 1-1 | 7 | 1.12 | 1.75 |
| 2013 Bos | AL | 73 | 0 | 0 | 40 | 74.1 | 265 | 33 | 10 | 9 | 5 | 1 | 1 | 1 | 9 | 2 | 101 | 1 | 0 | 4 | 1 | .800 | 0 | 21-24 | 13 | 0.79 | 1.09 |
| 11 Bal | AL | 43 | 0 | 0 | 19 | 47.0 | 174 | 25 | 9 | 9 | 6 | 1 | 1 | 0 | 8 | 1 | 62 | 0 | 0 | 1 | 1 | .500 | 0 | 0-1 | 13 | 1.27 | 1.72 |
| 11 Tex | AL | 22 | 0 | 0 | 3 | 18.0 | 69 | 13 | 8 | 8 | 5 | 0 | 0 | 0 | 1 | 0 | 23 | 0 | 0 | 1 | 2 | .333 | 0 | 0-0 | 9 | 2.21 | 4.00 |
| Postseason | | 4 | 0 | 0 | 0 | 2.1 | 14 | 5 | 5 | 5 | 3 | 0 | 0 | 0 | 2 | 0 | 4 | 0 | 0 | 0 | 0 | - | 0 | 0-0 | 0 | 26.51 | 19.29 |
| 5 ML YEARS | | 230 | 12 | 0 | 97 | 286.0 | 1091 | 199 | 82 | 77 | 32 | 5 | 6 | 1 | 38 | 4 | 332 | 3 | 0 | 9 | 10 | .474 | 0 | 35-41 | 48 | 1.65 | 2.42 |

# Dan Uggla

**Bats:** R **Throws:** R **Pos:** 2B-133;PH-2;DH-1 UGG-luh **Ht:** 5'11" **Wt:** 205 **Born:** 3/11/1980 **Age:** 34

| BATTING | | | | | | | | | | | | | | | | | | | | BASERUNNING | | | | AVERAGES | | |
|---|---|---|---|---|---|---|---|---|---|---|---|---|---|---|---|---|---|---|---|---|---|---|---|---|---|---|
| Year Team | Lg | G | AB | H | 2B | 3B | HR | (Hm | Rd) | TB | R | RBI | RC | TBB | IBB | SO | HBP | SH | SF | SB | CS | SB% | GDP | Avg | OBP | Slg |
| 2013 Gwnntt* | AAA | 2 | 7 | 2 | 0 | 0 | 1 | (- | -) | 5 | 1 | 1 | 1 | 0 | 0 | 4 | 0 | 0 | 0 | 0 | 0 | - | 1 | .286 | .286 | .714 |
| 2006 Fla | NL | 154 | 611 | 172 | 26 | 7 | 27 | (10 | 17) | 293 | 105 | 90 | 97 | 48 | 1 | 123 | 9 | 7 | 8 | 6 | 6 | .50 | 5 | .282 | .339 | .480 |
| 2007 Fla | NL | 159 | 632 | 155 | 49 | 3 | 31 | (18 | 13) | 303 | 113 | 88 | 81 | 68 | 0 | 167 | 13 | 4 | 11 | 2 | 1 | .67 | 10 | .245 | .326 | .479 |
| 2008 Fla | NL | 146 | 531 | 138 | 37 | 1 | 32 | (15 | 17) | 273 | 97 | 92 | 93 | 77 | 6 | 171 | 8 | 0 | 3 | 5 | 5 | .50 | 10 | .260 | .360 | .514 |
| 2009 Fla | NL | 158 | 564 | 137 | 27 | 1 | 31 | (21 | 10) | 259 | 84 | 90 | 81 | 92 | 4 | 150 | 7 | 1 | 4 | 2 | 1 | .67 | 10 | .243 | .354 | .459 |
| 2010 Fla | NL | 159 | 589 | 169 | 31 | 0 | 33 | (14 | 19) | 299 | 100 | 105 | 101 | 78 | 2 | 149 | 2 | 0 | 5 | 4 | 1 | .80 | 10 | .287 | .369 | .508 |
| 2011 Atl | NL | 161 | 600 | 140 | 22 | 1 | 36 | (18 | 18) | 272 | 88 | 82 | 78 | 62 | 2 | 156 | 7 | 0 | 3 | 1 | 3 | .25 | 9 | .233 | .311 | .453 |
| 2012 Atl | NL | 154 | 523 | 115 | 29 | 0 | 19 | (7 | 12) | 201 | 86 | 78 | 83 | **94** | 5 | 168 | 10 | 0 | 3 | 4 | 3 | .57 | 8 | .220 | .348 | .384 |
| 2013 Atl | NL | 136 | 448 | 80 | 10 | 3 | 22 | (8 | 14) | 162 | 60 | 55 | 48 | 77 | 2 | 171 | 9 | 0 | 3 | 2 | 0 | 1.00 | 7 | .179 | .309 | .362 |
| Postseason | | 1 | 4 | 0 | 0 | 0 | 0 | (0 | 0) | 0 | 1 | 0 | 0 | 1 | 0 | 0 | 0 | 0 | 0 | 0 | 0 | - | 0 | .000 | .200 | .000 |
| 8 ML YEARS | | 1227 | 4498 | 1106 | 231 | 16 | 231 | (111 | 120) | 2062 | 733 | 680 | 662 | 596 | 22 | 1255 | 65 | 12 | 40 | 26 | 20 | .57 | 69 | .246 | .340 | .458 |

# B.J. Upton

**Bats:** R **Throws:** R **Pos:** CF-118;PH-6;PR-6 **Ht:** 6'3" **Wt:** 185 **Born:** 8/21/1984 **Age:** 29

| BATTING | | | | | | | | | | | | | | | | | | | | BASERUNNING | | | | AVERAGES | | |
|---|---|---|---|---|---|---|---|---|---|---|---|---|---|---|---|---|---|---|---|---|---|---|---|---|---|---|
| Year Team | Lg | G | AB | H | 2B | 3B | HR | (Hm | Rd) | TB | R | RBI | RC | TBB | IBB | SO | HBP | SH | SF | SB | CS | SB% | GDP | Avg | OBP | Slg |
| 2013 Gwnntt* | AAA | 3 | 12 | 4 | 3 | 0 | 0 | (- | -) | 7 | 3 | 2 | 2 | 0 | 0 | 4 | 0 | 0 | 0 | 0 | 0 | - | 0 | .333 | .333 | .583 |
| 2004 TB | AL | 45 | 159 | 41 | 8 | 2 | 4 | (2 | 2) | 65 | 19 | 12 | 22 | 15 | 0 | 46 | 1 | 1 | 1 | 4 | 1 | .80 | 1 | .258 | .324 | .409 |
| 2006 TB | AL | 50 | 175 | 43 | 5 | 0 | 1 | (1 | 0) | 51 | 20 | 10 | 17 | 13 | 0 | 40 | 1 | 0 | 0 | 11 | 3 | .79 | 1 | .246 | .302 | .291 |
| 2007 TB | AL | 129 | 474 | 142 | 25 | 1 | 24 | (13 | 11) | 241 | 86 | 82 | 93 | 65 | 4 | 154 | 4 | 1 | 4 | 22 | 8 | .73 | 14 | .300 | .386 | .508 |
| 2008 TB | AL | 145 | 531 | 145 | 37 | 2 | 9 | (4 | 5) | 213 | 85 | 67 | 87 | 97 | 4 | 134 | 2 | 3 | 7 | 44 | **16** | .73 | 13 | .273 | .383 | .401 |
| 2009 TB | AL | 144 | 560 | 135 | 33 | 4 | 11 | (7 | 4) | 209 | 79 | 55 | 68 | 57 | 0 | 152 | 3 | 3 | 3 | 42 | 14 | .75 | 7 | .241 | .313 | .373 |
| 2010 TB | AL | 154 | 536 | 127 | 38 | 4 | 18 | (7 | 11) | 227 | 89 | 62 | 74 | 67 | 1 | 164 | 2 | 1 | 4 | 42 | 9 | .82 | 13 | .237 | .322 | .424 |
| 2011 TB | AL | 153 | 560 | 136 | 27 | 4 | 23 | (9 | 14) | 240 | 82 | 81 | 79 | 71 | 4 | 161 | 4 | 2 | 3 | 36 | 12 | .75 | 16 | .243 | .331 | .429 |
| 2012 TB | AL | 146 | 573 | 141 | 29 | 3 | 28 | (17 | 11) | 260 | 79 | 78 | 71 | 45 | 0 | 169 | 1 | 4 | 8 | 31 | 6 | .84 | 13 | .246 | .298 | .454 |
| 2013 Atl | NL | 126 | 391 | 72 | 14 | 0 | 9 | (7 | 2) | 113 | 30 | 26 | 21 | 44 | 2 | 151 | 3 | 1 | 6 | 12 | 5 | .71 | 7 | .184 | .268 | .289 |
| Postseason | | 25 | 101 | 27 | 6 | 1 | 7 | (2 | 5) | 56 | 19 | 18 | 17 | 9 | 1 | 29 | 0 | 0 | 1 | 9 | 2 | .82 | 4 | .267 | .324 | .554 |
| 9 ML YEARS | | 1092 | 3959 | 982 | 216 | 20 | 127 | (67 | 60) | 1619 | 569 | 473 | 532 | 474 | 15 | 1171 | 21 | 16 | 36 | 244 | 74 | .77 | 85 | .248 | .329 | .409 |

# Justin Upton

**Bats:** R **Throws:** R **Pos:** LF-108;RF-54;PH-3;DH-2 **Ht:** 6'2" **Wt:** 205 **Born:** 8/25/1987 **Age:** 26

| BATTING | | | | | | | | | | | | | | | | | | | | BASERUNNING | | | | AVERAGES | | |
|---|---|---|---|---|---|---|---|---|---|---|---|---|---|---|---|---|---|---|---|---|---|---|---|---|---|---|
| Year Team | Lg | G | AB | H | 2B | 3B | HR | (Hm | Rd) | TB | R | RBI | RC | TBB | IBB | SO | HBP | SH | SF | SB | CS | SB% | GDP | Avg | OBP | Slg |
| 2007 Ari | NL | 43 | 140 | 31 | 8 | 3 | 2 | (2 | 0) | 51 | 17 | 11 | 13 | 11 | 4 | 37 | 1 | 0 | 0 | 2 | 0 | 1.00 | 3 | .221 | .283 | .364 |
| 2008 Ari | NL | 108 | 356 | 89 | 19 | 6 | 15 | (12 | 3) | 165 | 52 | 42 | 47 | 54 | 6 | 121 | 4 | 0 | 3 | 1 | 4 | .20 | 3 | .250 | .353 | .463 |
| 2009 Ari | NL | 138 | 526 | 158 | 30 | 7 | 26 | (14 | 12) | 280 | 84 | 86 | 94 | 55 | 3 | 137 | 2 | 1 | 4 | 20 | 5 | .80 | 10 | .300 | .366 | .532 |
| 2010 Ari | NL | 133 | 495 | 135 | 27 | 3 | 17 | (8 | 9) | 219 | 73 | 69 | 73 | 64 | 5 | 152 | 4 | 1 | 7 | 18 | 8 | .69 | 20 | .273 | .356 | .442 |
| 2011 Ari | NL | 159 | 592 | 171 | 39 | 5 | 31 | (20 | 11) | 313 | 105 | 88 | 103 | 59 | 9 | 126 | **19** | 0 | 4 | 21 | 9 | .70 | 8 | .289 | .369 | .529 |
| 2012 Ari | NL | 150 | 554 | 155 | 24 | 4 | 17 | (11 | 6) | 238 | 107 | 67 | 82 | 63 | 5 | 121 | 5 | 0 | 6 | 18 | 8 | .69 | 7 | .280 | .355 | .430 |
| 2013 Atl | NL | 149 | 558 | 147 | 27 | 2 | 27 | (13 | 14) | 259 | 94 | 70 | 84 | 75 | 4 | 161 | 5 | 1 | 4 | 8 | 1 | .89 | 12 | .263 | .354 | .464 |
| Postseason | | 11 | 34 | 9 | 1 | 1 | 2 | (0 | 2) | 18 | 5 | 4 | 6 | 6 | 0 | 9 | 2 | 0 | 0 | 1 | 0 | 1.00 | 0 | .265 | .405 | .529 |
| 7 ML YEARS | | 880 | 3221 | 886 | 174 | 30 | 135 | (80 | 55) | 1525 | 532 | 433 | 496 | 381 | 36 | 855 | 40 | 3 | 28 | 88 | 35 | .72 | 63 | .275 | .356 | .473 |

# Juan Uribe

**Bats:** R **Throws:** R **Pos:** 3B-123;PH-15;1B-4;PR-1 yer-EE-bay **Ht:** 6'0" **Wt:** 235 **Born:** 3/22/1979 **Age:** 35

| BATTING | | | | | | | | | | | | | | | | | | | | | | BASERUNNING | | | | AVERAGES | | |
|---|---|---|---|---|---|---|---|---|---|---|---|---|---|---|---|---|---|---|---|---|---|---|---|---|---|---|---|---|
| Year | Team | Lg | G | AB | H | 2B | 3B | HR | (Hm | Rd) | TB | R | RBI | RC | TBB | IBB | SO | HBP | SH | SF | | SB | CS | SB% | GDP | Avg | OBP | Slg |
| 2001 | Col | NL | 72 | 273 | 82 | 15 | 11 | 8 | (3 | 5) | 143 | 32 | 53 | 44 | 8 | 1 | 55 | 2 | 0 | 0 | | 3 | 0 | 1.00 | 6 | .300 | .325 | .524 |
| 2002 | Col | NL | 155 | 566 | 136 | 25 | 7 | 6 | (4 | 2) | 193 | 69 | 49 | 53 | 34 | 1 | 120 | 5 | 7 | 6 | | 9 | 2 | .82 | 17 | .240 | .286 | .341 |
| 2003 | Col | NL | 87 | 316 | 80 | 19 | 3 | 10 | (6 | 4) | 135 | 45 | 33 | 45 | 17 | 0 | 60 | 3 | 6 | 1 | | 7 | 2 | .78 | 3 | .253 | .297 | .427 |
| 2004 | CWS | AL | 134 | 502 | 142 | 31 | 6 | 23 | (16 | 7) | 254 | 82 | 74 | 81 | 32 | 1 | 96 | 3 | 11 | 5 | | 9 | 11 | .45 | 10 | .283 | .327 | .506 |
| 2005 | CWS | AL | 146 | 481 | 121 | 23 | 3 | 16 | (10 | 6) | 198 | 58 | 71 | 59 | 34 | 0 | 77 | 4 | 11 | 10 | | 4 | 6 | .40 | 7 | .252 | .301 | .412 |
| 2006 | CWS | AL | 132 | 463 | 109 | 28 | 2 | 21 | (13 | 8) | 204 | 53 | 71 | 52 | 13 | 1 | 82 | 3 | 9 | 7 | | 1 | 1 | .50 | 10 | .235 | .257 | .441 |
| 2007 | CWS | AL | 150 | 513 | 120 | 18 | 2 | 20 | (15 | 5) | 202 | 55 | 68 | 52 | 34 | 2 | 112 | 4 | 7 | 5 | | 1 | 9 | .10 | 6 | .234 | .284 | .394 |
| 2008 | CWS | AL | 110 | 324 | 80 | 22 | 1 | 7 | (5 | 2) | 125 | 38 | 40 | 43 | 22 | 0 | 64 | 1 | 5 | 1 | | 1 | 3 | .25 | 5 | .247 | .296 | .386 |
| 2009 | SF | NL | 122 | 398 | 115 | 26 | 4 | 16 | (9 | 7) | 197 | 50 | 55 | 55 | 25 | 2 | 82 | 1 | 3 | 5 | | 3 | 1 | .75 | 7 | .289 | .329 | .495 |
| 2010 | SF | NL | 148 | 521 | 129 | 24 | 2 | 24 | (13 | 11) | 229 | 64 | 85 | 68 | 45 | 6 | 92 | 4 | 0 | 5 | | 1 | 2 | .33 | 20 | .248 | .310 | .440 |
| 2011 | LAD | NL | 77 | 270 | 55 | 12 | 0 | 4 | (3 | 1) | 79 | 21 | 28 | 13 | 17 | 2 | 60 | 6 | 0 | 2 | | 2 | 0 | 1.00 | 12 | .204 | .264 | .293 |
| 2012 | LAD | NL | 66 | 162 | 31 | 9 | 0 | 2 | (1 | 1) | 46 | 15 | 17 | 13 | 13 | 0 | 37 | 2 | 1 | 1 | | 0 | 1 | .00 | 6 | .191 | .258 | .284 |
| 2013 | LAD | NL | 132 | 388 | 108 | 22 | 2 | 12 | (6 | 6) | 170 | 47 | 50 | 51 | 30 | 3 | 81 | 2 | 3 | 3 | | 5 | 0 | 1.00 | 12 | .278 | .331 | .438 |
| Postseason | | | 30 | 101 | 21 | 5 | 0 | 3 | (2 | 1) | 35 | 11 | 16 | 11 | 7 | 0 | 27 | 1 | 2 | 1 | | 2 | 0 | 1.00 | 2 | .208 | .264 | .347 |
| 13 ML YEARS | | | 1531 | 5177 | 1308 | 274 | 43 | 169 | (104 | 65) | 2175 | 629 | 694 | 629 | 324 | 19 | 1018 | 40 | 63 | 51 | | 46 | 38 | .55 | 121 | .253 | .299 | .420 |

# Henry Urrutia

**Bats:** L **Throws:** R **Pos:** DH-13;PH-12;LF-2 oo-ROOT-ee-ah **Ht:** 6'5" **Wt:** 200 **Born:** 2/13/1987 **Age:** 27

| BATTING | | | | | | | | | | | | | | | | | | | | | | BASERUNNING | | | | AVERAGES | | |
|---|---|---|---|---|---|---|---|---|---|---|---|---|---|---|---|---|---|---|---|---|---|---|---|---|---|---|---|---|
| Year | Team | Lg | G | AB | H | 2B | 3B | HR | (Hm | Rd) | TB | R | RBI | RC | TBB | IBB | SO | HBP | SH | SF | | SB | CS | SB% | GDP | Avg | OBP | Slg |
| 2013 | Bowie | AA | 52 | 200 | 73 | 16 | 0 | 7 | (- | -) | 110 | 33 | 37 | 45 | 24 | 2 | 36 | 0 | 0 | 0 | | 1 | 1 | .50 | 4 | .365 | .433 | .550 |
| 2013 | Norfolk | AAA | 29 | 114 | 36 | 5 | 1 | 2 | (- | -) | 49 | 16 | 13 | 17 | 8 | 0 | 15 | 0 | 0 | 1 | | 0 | 0 | - | 2 | .316 | .358 | .430 |
| 2013 | Bal | AL | 24 | 58 | 16 | 0 | 1 | 0 | (0 | 0) | 18 | 5 | 2 | 4 | 0 | 0 | 11 | 0 | 0 | 0 | | 0 | 0 | - | 2 | .276 | .276 | .310 |

# Chase Utley

**Bats:** L **Throws:** R **Pos:** 2B-125;PH-7;DH-1 UTT-lee **Ht:** 6'1" **Wt:** 200 **Born:** 12/17/1978 **Age:** 35

| BATTING | | | | | | | | | | | | | | | | | | | | | | BASERUNNING | | | | AVERAGES | | |
|---|---|---|---|---|---|---|---|---|---|---|---|---|---|---|---|---|---|---|---|---|---|---|---|---|---|---|---|---|
| Year | Team | Lg | G | AB | H | 2B | 3B | HR | (Hm | Rd) | TB | R | RBI | RC | TBB | IBB | SO | HBP | SH | SF | | SB | CS | SB% | GDP | Avg | OBP | Slg |
| 2013 | Rdng* | AA | 2 | 9 | 0 | 0 | 0 | 0 | (- | -) | 0 | 0 | 0 | 0 | 0 | 0 | 1 | 0 | 0 | 0 | | 0 | 0 | - | 0 | .000 | .000 | .000 |
| 2003 | Phi | NL | 43 | 134 | 32 | 10 | 1 | 2 | (1 | 1) | 50 | 13 | 21 | 19 | 11 | 0 | 22 | 6 | 0 | 1 | | 2 | 0 | 1.00 | 3 | .239 | .322 | .373 |
| 2004 | Phi | NL | 94 | 267 | 71 | 11 | 2 | 13 | (8 | 5) | 125 | 36 | 57 | 37 | 15 | 1 | 40 | 2 | 1 | 2 | | 4 | 1 | .80 | 6 | .266 | .308 | .468 |
| 2005 | Phi | NL | 147 | 543 | 158 | 39 | 6 | 28 | (12 | 16) | 293 | 93 | 105 | 102 | 69 | 5 | 109 | 9 | 0 | 7 | | 16 | 3 | .84 | 10 | .291 | .376 | .540 |
| 2006 | Phi | NL | 160 | 658 | 203 | 40 | 4 | 32 | (16 | 16) | 347 | **131** | 102 | 122 | 63 | 1 | 132 | 14 | 0 | 4 | | 15 | 4 | .79 | 9 | .309 | .379 | .527 |
| 2007 | Phi | NL | 132 | 530 | 176 | 48 | 5 | 22 | (14 | 8) | 300 | 104 | 103 | 111 | 50 | 1 | 89 | **25** | 1 | 7 | | 9 | 1 | .90 | 7 | .332 | .410 | .566 |
| 2008 | Phi | NL | 159 | 607 | 177 | 41 | 4 | 33 | (20 | 13) | 325 | 113 | 104 | 113 | 64 | 14 | 104 | **27** | 1 | 8 | | 14 | 2 | .88 | 9 | .292 | .380 | .535 |
| 2009 | Phi | NL | 156 | 571 | 161 | 28 | 4 | 31 | (16 | 15) | 290 | 112 | 93 | 115 | 88 | 3 | 110 | **24** | 0 | 4 | | 23 | 0 | **1.00** | 5 | .282 | .397 | .508 |
| 2010 | Phi | NL | 115 | 425 | 117 | 20 | 2 | 16 | (10 | 6) | 189 | 75 | 65 | 83 | 63 | 3 | 63 | 18 | 0 | 5 | | 13 | 2 | .87 | 4 | .275 | .387 | .445 |
| 2011 | Phi | NL | 103 | 398 | 103 | 21 | 6 | 11 | (8 | 3) | 169 | 54 | 44 | 57 | 39 | 4 | 47 | 14 | 1 | 2 | | 14 | 0 | 1.00 | 3 | .259 | .344 | .425 |
| 2012 | Phi | NL | 83 | 301 | 77 | 15 | 2 | 11 | (8 | 3) | 129 | 48 | 45 | 49 | 43 | 7 | 43 | 12 | 0 | 6 | | 11 | 1 | .92 | 4 | .256 | .365 | .429 |
| 2013 | Phi | NL | 131 | 476 | 135 | 25 | 6 | 18 | (8 | 10) | 226 | 73 | 69 | 78 | 45 | 4 | 79 | 5 | 0 | 5 | | 8 | 3 | .73 | 12 | .284 | .348 | .475 |
| Postseason | | | 46 | 164 | 43 | 7 | 1 | 10 | (5 | 5) | 82 | 38 | 25 | 34 | 34 | 3 | 38 | 5 | 0 | 1 | | 10 | 2 | .83 | 3 | .262 | .402 | .500 |
| 11 ML YEARS | | | 1323 | 4910 | 1410 | 298 | 42 | 217 | (121 | 96) | 2443 | 852 | 808 | 886 | 550 | 43 | 838 | 156 | 4 | 51 | | 129 | 17 | .88 | 72 | .287 | .373 | .498 |

# Chris Valaika

**Bats:** R **Throws:** R **Pos:** 2B-6;SS-6;3B-5;PH-4;1B-3;PR-1 vuh-LAKE-uh **Ht:** 5'11" **Wt:** 210 **Born:** 8/14/1985 **Age:** 28

| BATTING | | | | | | | | | | | | | | | | | | | | | | BASERUNNING | | | | AVERAGES | | |
|---|---|---|---|---|---|---|---|---|---|---|---|---|---|---|---|---|---|---|---|---|---|---|---|---|---|---|---|---|
| Year | Team | Lg | G | AB | H | 2B | 3B | HR | (Hm | Rd) | TB | R | RBI | RC | TBB | IBB | SO | HBP | SH | SF | | SB | CS | SB% | GDP | Avg | OBP | Slg |
| 2013 | Jupiter* | A+ | 11 | 40 | 8 | 1 | 0 | 1 | (- | -) | 12 | 3 | 4 | 2 | 2 | 0 | 6 | 1 | 0 | 0 | | 0 | 1 | .00 | 2 | .200 | .256 | .300 |
| 2013 | NewOr* | AAA | 37 | 130 | 32 | 6 | 0 | 3 | (- | -) | 47 | 17 | 11 | 15 | 10 | 0 | 25 | 2 | 0 | 1 | | 1 | 1 | .50 | 2 | .246 | .308 | .362 |
| 2010 | Cin | NL | 19 | 38 | 10 | 1 | 0 | 1 | (1 | 0) | 14 | 3 | 2 | 2 | 1 | 0 | 9 | 0 | 1 | 0 | | 0 | 0 | - | 2 | .263 | .282 | .368 |
| 2011 | Cin | NL | 14 | 25 | 7 | 1 | 1 | 0 | (0 | 0) | 10 | 3 | 0 | 3 | 2 | 0 | 3 | 0 | 0 | 0 | | 0 | 0 | - | 0 | .280 | .333 | .400 |
| 2013 | Mia | NL | 22 | 64 | 14 | 5 | 0 | 1 | (0 | 1) | 22 | 4 | 9 | 5 | 3 | 0 | 16 | 1 | 1 | 1 | | 0 | 0 | - | 2 | .219 | .261 | .344 |
| 3 ML YEARS | | | 55 | 127 | 31 | 7 | 1 | 2 | (1 | 1) | 46 | 10 | 11 | 10 | 6 | 0 | 28 | 1 | 2 | 1 | | 0 | 0 | - | 4 | .244 | .281 | .362 |

# Luis Valbuena

**Bats:** L **Throws:** R **Pos:** 3B-94;PH-13;2B-6;LF-1;DH-1 val-BWAY-nah **Ht:** 5'10" **Wt:** 170 **Born:** 11/30/1985 **Age:** 28

| BATTING | | | | | | | | | | | | | | | | | | | | | | BASERUNNING | | | | AVERAGES | | |
|---|---|---|---|---|---|---|---|---|---|---|---|---|---|---|---|---|---|---|---|---|---|---|---|---|---|---|---|---|
| Year | Team | Lg | G | AB | H | 2B | 3B | HR | (Hm | Rd) | TB | R | RBI | RC | TBB | IBB | SO | HBP | SH | SF | | SB | CS | SB% | GDP | Avg | OBP | Slg |
| 2013 | Cubs* | R | 2 | 7 | 5 | 2 | 0 | 0 | (- | -) | 7 | 2 | 3 | 3 | 1 | 0 | 1 | 0 | 0 | 0 | | 1 | 0 | 1.00 | 0 | .714 | .750 | 1.000 |
| 2013 | Kane* | A | 1 | 3 | 1 | 0 | 0 | 0 | (- | -) | 1 | 0 | 0 | 0 | 1 | 0 | 0 | 0 | 0 | 0 | | 0 | 0 | - | 1 | .333 | .500 | .333 |
| 2008 | Sea | AL | 18 | 49 | 12 | 5 | 0 | 0 | (0 | 0) | 17 | 6 | 1 | 5 | 4 | 0 | 11 | 1 | 0 | 0 | | 0 | 0 | - | 0 | .245 | .315 | .347 |
| 2009 | Cle | AL | 103 | 368 | 92 | 25 | 3 | 10 | (2 | 8) | 153 | 52 | 31 | 35 | 26 | 0 | 83 | 0 | 2 | 2 | | 2 | 3 | .40 | 8 | .250 | .298 | .416 |
| 2010 | Cle | AL | 91 | 275 | 53 | 12 | 0 | 2 | (1 | 1) | 71 | 22 | 24 | 21 | 28 | 1 | 61 | 3 | 2 | 2 | | 1 | 2 | .33 | 5 | .193 | .273 | .258 |
| 2011 | Cle | AL | 17 | 43 | 9 | 0 | 0 | 1 | (0 | 1) | 12 | 4 | 1 | 2 | 1 | 0 | 9 | 0 | 0 | 0 | | 1 | 0 | 1.00 | 0 | .209 | .227 | .279 |
| 2012 | ChC | NL | 90 | 265 | 58 | 20 | 0 | 4 | (2 | 2) | 90 | 26 | 28 | 27 | 36 | 1 | 55 | 0 | 0 | 2 | | 0 | 2 | .00 | 6 | .219 | .310 | .340 |
| 2013 | ChC | NL | 108 | 331 | 72 | 15 | 1 | 12 | (4 | 8) | 125 | 34 | 37 | 43 | 53 | 4 | 63 | 4 | 1 | 2 | | 1 | 4 | .20 | 4 | .218 | .331 | .378 |
| 6 ML YEARS | | | 427 | 1331 | 296 | 77 | 4 | 29 | (9 | 20) | 468 | 144 | 122 | 133 | 148 | 6 | 282 | 8 | 5 | 8 | | 5 | 11 | .31 | 23 | .222 | .302 | .352 |

## Raul Valdes

**Pitches:** L **Bats:** L **Pos:** RP-16; SP-1 **Ht:** 5'11" **Wt:** 190 **Born:** 11/27/1977 **Age:** 36

| | | | HOW MUCH HE PITCHED | | | | | | WHAT HE GAVE UP | | | | | | | | | | | | THE RESULTS | | | | | | | |
|---|---|---|---|---|---|---|---|---|---|---|---|---|---|---|---|---|---|---|---|---|---|---|---|---|---|---|---|---|
| Year | Team | Lg | G | GS | CG | GF | IP | BFP | H | R | ER | HR | SH | SF | HB | TBB | IBB | SO | WP | Bk | W | L | Pct | Sh | Sv-Op | Hld | ERC | ERA |
| 2013 | LV* | AAA | 14 | 14 | 0 | 0 | 78.2 | 323 | 67 | 26 | 25 | 5 | 2 | 3 | 2 | 22 | 1 | 66 | 3 | 0 | 4 | 5 | .444 | 0 | 0- - | - | 2.66 | 2.86 |
| 2010 | NYM | NL | 38 | 1 | 0 | 8 | 58.2 | 262 | 59 | 33 | 32 | 7 | 2 | 2 | 4 | 27 | 1 | 56 | 2 | 0 | 3 | 3 | .500 | 0 | 1-3 | 1 | 4.70 | 4.91 |
| 2011 | 2 Tms | | 13 | 0 | 0 | 3 | 12.0 | 55 | 14 | 4 | 4 | 1 | 0 | 0 | 1 | 6 | 2 | 15 | 0 | 0 | 0 | 1 | .000 | 0 | 0-0 | 0 | 5.42 | 3.00 |
| 2012 | Phi | NL | 27 | 1 | 0 | 7 | 31.0 | 113 | 18 | 10 | 10 | 3 | 1 | 0 | 0 | 5 | 1 | 35 | 0 | 0 | 3 | 2 | .600 | 0 | 0-1 | 2 | 1.32 | 2.90 |
| 2013 | Phi | NL | 17 | 1 | 0 | 7 | 35.0 | 152 | 42 | 29 | 29 | 7 | 1 | 1 | 2 | 8 | 0 | 37 | 1 | 0 | 1 | 1 | .500 | 0 | 0-0 | 0 | 5.56 | 7.46 |
| 11 | StL | NL | 7 | 0 | 0 | 3 | 5.1 | 27 | 6 | 2 | 2 | 0 | 0 | 0 | 1 | 4 | 2 | 7 | 0 | 0 | 0 | 1 | .000 | 0 | 0-0 | 0 | 5.20 | 3.38 |
| 11 | NYY | AL | 6 | 0 | 0 | 0 | 6.2 | 28 | 8 | 2 | 2 | 1 | 0 | 0 | 0 | 2 | 0 | 8 | 0 | 0 | 0 | 0 | - | 0 | 0-0 | 0 | 5.47 | 2.70 |
| 4 ML YEARS | | | 95 | 3 | 0 | 25 | 136.2 | 582 | 133 | 76 | 75 | 18 | 4 | 3 | 7 | 46 | 4 | 143 | 3 | 0 | 7 | 7 | .500 | 0 | 1-4 | 3 | 4.07 | 4.94 |

## Jordany Valdespin

jor-DAN-ee VAL-dah-spin

**Bats:** L **Throws:** R **Pos:** PH-35;CF-16;2B-12;RF-8;LF-5;SS-1 **Ht:** 6'0" **Wt:** 190 **Born:** 12/23/1987 **Age:** 26

| | | | BATTING | | | | | | | | | | | | | | | | | | BASERUNNING | | | | AVERAGES | | |
|---|---|---|---|---|---|---|---|---|---|---|---|---|---|---|---|---|---|---|---|---|---|---|---|---|---|---|---|
| Year | Team | Lg | G | AB | H | 2B | 3B | HR | (Hm | Rd) | TB | R | RBI | RC | TBB | IBB | SO | HBP | SH | SF | SB | CS | SB% | GDP | Avg | OBP | Slg |
| 2009 | Savann | A | 39 | 152 | 49 | 9 | 3 | 3 | (- | -) | 73 | 30 | 18 | 27 | 11 | 0 | 32 | 0 | 0 | 1 | 7 | 2 | .78 | 1 | .322 | .366 | .480 |
| 2009 | Mets | R | 6 | 23 | 4 | 0 | 0 | 0 | (- | -) | 4 | 0 | 0 | 0 | 1 | 0 | 3 | 0 | 0 | 0 | 1 | 0 | 1.00 | 0 | .174 | .208 | .174 |
| 2009 | Bklyn | A- | 18 | 68 | 19 | 3 | 1 | 1 | (- | -) | 27 | 10 | 5 | 9 | 5 | 0 | 16 | 1 | 2 | 0 | 4 | 3 | .57 | 3 | .279 | .338 | .397 |
| 2010 | StLuci | A+ | 65 | 270 | 78 | 16 | 3 | 6 | (- | -) | 118 | 40 | 33 | 37 | 8 | 0 | 45 | 6 | 3 | 1 | 13 | 10 | .57 | 1 | .289 | .323 | .437 |
| 2010 | Bnghtn | AA | 28 | 112 | 26 | 8 | 0 | 0 | (- | -) | 34 | 8 | 8 | 7 | 2 | 0 | 23 | 0 | 2 | 1 | 4 | 2 | .67 | 4 | .232 | .243 | .304 |
| 2011 | Bnghtn | AA | 107 | 404 | 120 | 23 | 3 | 15 | (- | -) | 194 | 62 | 51 | 67 | 21 | 2 | 68 | 7 | 7 | 2 | 33 | 14 | .70 | 5 | .297 | .341 | .480 |
| 2011 | Buffalo | AAA | 27 | 107 | 30 | 8 | 0 | 2 | (- | -) | 44 | 7 | 9 | 12 | 4 | 0 | 25 | 0 | 1 | 1 | 4 | 4 | .50 | 1 | .280 | .304 | .411 |
| 2012 | Buffalo | AAA | 39 | 151 | 43 | 2 | 1 | 5 | (- | -) | 62 | 22 | 23 | 20 | 10 | 0 | 22 | 1 | 0 | 1 | 10 | 8 | .56 | 3 | .285 | .331 | .411 |
| 2013 | LsVgs | AAA | 16 | 58 | 27 | 4 | 2 | 3 | (- | -) | 44 | 14 | 24 | 19 | 8 | 0 | 7 | 1 | 0 | 0 | 2 | 3 | .40 | 0 | .466 | .537 | .759 |
| 2012 | NYM | NL | 94 | 191 | 46 | 9 | 1 | 8 | (5 | 3) | 81 | 28 | 26 | 20 | 10 | 0 | 44 | 2 | 3 | 0 | 10 | 3 | .77 | 2 | .241 | .286 | .424 |
| 2013 | NYM | NL | 66 | 133 | 25 | 3 | 1 | 4 | (2 | 2) | 42 | 16 | 16 | 10 | 8 | 0 | 28 | 3 | 0 | 0 | 4 | 3 | .57 | 1 | .188 | .250 | .316 |
| 2 ML YEARS | | | 160 | 324 | 71 | 12 | 2 | 12 | (7 | 5) | 123 | 44 | 42 | 30 | 18 | 0 | 72 | 5 | 3 | 0 | 14 | 6 | .70 | 3 | .219 | .271 | .380 |

## Danny Valencia

vuh-LENN-see-yah

**Bats:** R **Throws:** R **Pos:** DH-41;PH-9;3B-6;PR-1 **Ht:** 6'2" **Wt:** 220 **Born:** 9/19/1984 **Age:** 29

| | | | BATTING | | | | | | | | | | | | | | | | | | BASERUNNING | | | | AVERAGES | | |
|---|---|---|---|---|---|---|---|---|---|---|---|---|---|---|---|---|---|---|---|---|---|---|---|---|---|---|---|
| Year | Team | Lg | G | AB | H | 2B | 3B | HR | (Hm | Rd) | TB | R | RBI | RC | TBB | IBB | SO | HBP | SH | SF | SB | CS | SB% | GDP | Avg | OBP | Slg |
| 2013 | Norfolk* | AAA | 65 | 262 | 75 | 20 | 1 | 14 | (- | -) | 139 | 40 | 51 | 45 | 17 | 2 | 48 | 0 | 0 | 3 | 1 | 1 | .50 | 8 | .286 | .326 | .531 |
| 2010 | Min | AL | 85 | 299 | 93 | 18 | 1 | 7 | (4 | 3) | 134 | 30 | 40 | 50 | 20 | 0 | 46 | 0 | 0 | 3 | 2 | 0 | 1.00 | 11 | .311 | .351 | .448 |
| 2011 | Min | AL | 154 | 564 | 139 | 28 | 2 | 15 | (9 | 6) | 216 | 63 | 72 | 57 | 40 | 2 | 102 | 0 | 0 | 4 | 2 | 6 | .25 | 15 | .246 | .294 | .383 |
| 2012 | 2 Tms | AL | 44 | 154 | 29 | 6 | 1 | 3 | (3 | 0) | 46 | 14 | 21 | 7 | 3 | 0 | 38 | 0 | 0 | 4 | 0 | 1 | .00 | 6 | .188 | .199 | .299 |
| 2013 | Bal | AL | 52 | 161 | 49 | 14 | 1 | 8 | (4 | 4) | 89 | 20 | 23 | 25 | 8 | 0 | 33 | 0 | 0 | 1 | 0 | 2 | .00 | 5 | .304 | .335 | .553 |
| 12 | Min | AL | 34 | 126 | 25 | 6 | 1 | 2 | (2 | 0) | 39 | 13 | 17 | 7 | 3 | 0 | 32 | 0 | 0 | 3 | 0 | 1 | .00 | 5 | .198 | .212 | .310 |
| 12 | Bos | AL | 10 | 28 | 4 | 0 | 0 | 1 | (1 | 0) | 7 | 1 | 4 | 0 | 0 | 0 | 6 | 0 | 0 | 1 | 0 | 0 | - | 1 | .143 | .138 | .250 |
| Postseason | | | 3 | 9 | 2 | 1 | 0 | 0 | (0 | 0) | 3 | 1 | 2 | 1 | 1 | 0 | 3 | 0 | 0 | 1 | 0 | 0 | - | 0 | .222 | .273 | .333 |
| 4 ML YEARS | | | 335 | 1178 | 310 | 66 | 5 | 33 | (20 | 13) | 485 | 127 | 156 | 139 | 71 | 2 | 219 | 0 | 0 | 12 | 4 | 9 | .31 | 37 | .263 | .302 | .412 |

## Jose Valverde

val-VARE-day

**Pitches:** R **Bats:** R **Pos:** RP-20 **Ht:** 6'4" **Wt:** 255 **Born:** 3/24/1978 **Age:** 36

| | | | HOW MUCH HE PITCHED | | | | | | WHAT HE GAVE UP | | | | | | | | | | | | THE RESULTS | | | | | | | |
|---|---|---|---|---|---|---|---|---|---|---|---|---|---|---|---|---|---|---|---|---|---|---|---|---|---|---|---|---|
| Year | Team | Lg | G | GS | CG | GF | IP | BFP | H | R | ER | HR | SH | SF | HB | TBB | IBB | SO | WP | Bk | W | L | Pct | Sh | Sv-Op | Hld | ERC | ERA |
| 2013 | Lkland* | A+ | 3 | 0 | 0 | 0 | 3.0 | 10 | 1 | 0 | 0 | 0 | 0 | 0 | 0 | 2 | 0 | 4 | 0 | 0 | 0 | 0 | - | 0 | 0- - | - | 1.51 | 0.00 |
| 2013 | Toledo* | AAA | 11 | 0 | 0 | 11 | 11.0 | 50 | 14 | 5 | 5 | 1 | 0 | 1 | 1 | 6 | 0 | 10 | 0 | 0 | 0 | 0 | - | 0 | 7- - | - | 7.00 | 4.09 |
| 2003 | Ari | NL | 54 | 0 | 0 | 33 | 50.1 | 204 | 24 | 16 | 12 | 4 | 0 | 1 | 2 | 26 | 2 | 71 | 2 | 0 | 2 | 1 | .667 | 0 | 10-11 | 8 | 1.77 | 2.15 |
| 2004 | Ari | NL | 29 | 0 | 0 | 20 | 29.2 | 131 | 23 | 17 | 14 | 7 | 3 | 2 | 1 | 17 | 4 | 38 | 4 | 0 | 1 | 2 | .333 | 0 | 8-10 | 5 | 4.25 | 4.25 |
| 2005 | Ari | NL | 61 | 0 | 0 | 34 | 66.1 | 268 | 51 | 19 | 18 | 5 | 3 | 1 | 2 | 20 | 1 | 75 | 3 | 0 | 3 | 4 | .429 | 0 | 15-17 | 7 | 2.43 | 2.44 |
| 2006 | Ari | NL | 44 | 0 | 0 | 35 | 49.1 | 223 | 50 | 32 | 32 | 6 | 1 | 3 | 2 | 22 | 3 | 69 | 2 | 0 | 2 | 3 | .400 | 0 | 18-22 | 1 | 4.42 | 5.84 |
| 2007 | Ari | NL | 65 | 0 | 0 | 59 | 64.1 | 265 | 46 | 21 | 19 | 7 | 0 | 1 | 3 | 26 | 1 | 78 | 1 | 0 | 1 | 4 | .200 | 0 | **47-54** | 0 | 2.77 | 2.66 |
| 2008 | Hou | NL | 74 | 0 | 0 | 71 | 72.0 | 303 | 62 | 28 | 27 | 10 | 0 | 2 | 2 | 23 | 6 | 83 | 3 | 2 | 6 | 3 | .667 | 0 | **44-51** | 0 | 3.18 | 3.38 |
| 2009 | Hou | NL | 52 | 0 | 0 | 45 | 54.0 | 219 | 40 | 15 | 14 | 5 | 1 | 2 | 2 | 21 | 1 | 56 | 1 | 0 | 4 | 2 | .667 | 0 | 25-29 | 1 | 2.76 | 2.33 |
| 2010 | Det | AL | 60 | 0 | 0 | 55 | 63.0 | 259 | 41 | 24 | 21 | 5 | 0 | 1 | 3 | 32 | 1 | 63 | 3 | 0 | 2 | 4 | .333 | 0 | 26-29 | 0 | 2.67 | 3.00 |
| 2011 | Det | AL | **75** | 0 | 0 | 70 | 72.1 | 301 | 52 | 21 | 18 | 5 | 2 | 0 | 3 | 34 | 4 | 69 | 3 | 1 | 2 | 4 | .333 | 0 | **49-49** | 0 | 2.71 | 2.24 |
| 2012 | Det | AL | 71 | 0 | 0 | 67 | 69.0 | 294 | 59 | 34 | 29 | 3 | 2 | 3 | 4 | 27 | 5 | 48 | 1 | 0 | 3 | 4 | .429 | 0 | 35-40 | 0 | 2.95 | 3.78 |
| 2013 | Det | AL | 20 | 0 | 0 | 18 | 19.1 | 84 | 18 | 12 | 12 | 6 | 0 | 0 | 2 | 6 | 0 | 19 | 0 | 0 | 0 | 1 | .000 | 0 | 9-12 | 0 | 5.09 | 5.59 |
| Postseason | | | 14 | 0 | 0 | 9 | 14.2 | 76 | 20 | 16 | 16 | 4 | 0 | 1 | 1 | 11 | 2 | 20 | 0 | 0 | 0 | 3 | .000 | 0 | 5-6 | 0 | 9.18 | 9.82 |
| 11 ML YEARS | | | 605 | 0 | 0 | 507 | 609.2 | 2551 | 466 | 239 | 216 | 63 | 12 | 16 | 26 | 254 | 28 | 669 | 23 | 3 | 26 | 32 | .448 | 0 | 286-324 | 22 | 2.96 | 3.19 |

## Scott Van Slyke

**Bats:** R **Throws:** R **Pos:** LF-30;RF-13;PH-11;1B-4;PR-2 **Ht:** 6'5" **Wt:** 250 **Born:** 7/24/1986 **Age:** 27

| | | | BATTING | | | | | | | | | | | | | | | | | | BASERUNNING | | | | AVERAGES | | |
|---|---|---|---|---|---|---|---|---|---|---|---|---|---|---|---|---|---|---|---|---|---|---|---|---|---|---|---|
| Year | Team | Lg | G | AB | H | 2B | 3B | HR | (Hm | Rd) | TB | R | RBI | RC | TBB | IBB | SO | HBP | SH | SF | SB | CS | SB% | GDP | Avg | OBP | Slg |
| 2009 | InldEm | A+ | 132 | 496 | 146 | 42 | 4 | 23 | (- | -) | 265 | 75 | 100 | 98 | 61 | 0 | 128 | 3 | 0 | 3 | 10 | 7 | .59 | 10 | .294 | .373 | .534 |
| 2009 | Albq | AAA | 3 | 6 | 1 | 0 | 0 | 0 | (- | -) | 1 | 1 | 0 | 0 | 2 | 0 | 1 | 0 | 0 | 0 | 0 | 0 | - | 0 | .167 | .375 | .167 |
| 2010 | Chatt | AA | 65 | 217 | 51 | 7 | 3 | 4 | (- | -) | 76 | 28 | 29 | 24 | 18 | 1 | 37 | 3 | 1 | 2 | 4 | 2 | .67 | 5 | .235 | .300 | .350 |
| 2010 | InldEm | A+ | 48 | 189 | 58 | 12 | 2 | 9 | (- | -) | 101 | 34 | 35 | 37 | 17 | 1 | 39 | 2 | 0 | 1 | 3 | 1 | .75 | 7 | .307 | .368 | .534 |
| 2010 | Albq | AAA | 12 | 38 | 11 | 4 | 0 | 1 | (- | -) | 18 | 5 | 5 | 5 | 0 | 0 | 7 | 0 | 0 | 0 | 0 | 0 | - | 0 | .289 | .289 | .474 |
| 2011 | Chatt | AA | 130 | 457 | 158 | 45 | 4 | 20 | (- | -) | 271 | 81 | 92 | 111 | 65 | 7 | 100 | 2 | 0 | 5 | 6 | 5 | .55 | 5 | .346 | .425 | .593 |
| 2012 | Albq | AAA | 95 | 358 | 117 | 34 | 1 | 18 | (- | -) | 207 | 68 | 67 | 82 | 46 | 1 | 64 | 3 | 0 | 4 | 5 | 3 | .63 | 9 | .327 | .404 | .578 |
| 2013 | Albq | AAA | 61 | 204 | 71 | 17 | 2 | 12 | (- | -) | 128 | 55 | 48 | 61 | 50 | 1 | 61 | 5 | 0 | 4 | 8 | 2 | .80 | 6 | .348 | .479 | .627 |

| | | | BATTING | | | | | | | | | | | | | | | | | | BASERUNNING | | | | AVERAGES | | |
|---|---|---|---|---|---|---|---|---|---|---|---|---|---|---|---|---|---|---|---|---|---|---|---|---|---|---|---|
| Year | Team | Lg | G | AB | H | 2B | 3B | HR | (Hm | Rd) | TB | R | RBI | RC | TBB | IBB | SO | HBP | SH | SF | SB | CS | SB% | GDP | Avg | OBP | Slg |
| 2013 | RCuca | A+ | 2 | 7 | 3 | 0 | 0 | 0 | (- | -) | 3 | 2 | 0 | 1 | 2 | 0 | 1 | 0 | 0 | 0 | 0 | 0 | - | 0 | .429 | .556 | .429 |
| 2012 | LAD | NL | 27 | 54 | 9 | 2 | 0 | 2 | (1 | 1) | 17 | 4 | 7 | 4 | 2 | 0 | 14 | 0 | 1 | 0 | 1 | 0 | 1.00 | 2 | .167 | .196 | .315 |
| 2013 | LAD | NL | 53 | 129 | 31 | 8 | 0 | 7 | (4 | 3) | 60 | 13 | 19 | 15 | 20 | 0 | 37 | 1 | 0 | 2 | 1 | 1 | .50 | 7 | .240 | .342 | .465 |
| 2 ML YEARS | | | 80 | 183 | 40 | 10 | 0 | 9 | (5 | 4) | 77 | 17 | 26 | 19 | 22 | 0 | 51 | 1 | 1 | 2 | 2 | 1 | .67 | 9 | .219 | .303 | .421 |

## Jason Vargas

**Pitches:** L **Bats:** L **Pos:** SP-24 **Ht:** 6'0" **Wt:** 215 **Born:** 2/2/1983 **Age:** 31

| | | | HOW MUCH HE PITCHED | | | | | | WHAT HE GAVE UP | | | | | | | | | | | | THE RESULTS | | | | | | | |
|---|---|---|---|---|---|---|---|---|---|---|---|---|---|---|---|---|---|---|---|---|---|---|---|---|---|---|---|---|
| Year | Team | Lg | G | GS | CG | GF | IP | BFP | H | R | ER | HR | SH | SF | HB | TBB | IBB | SO | WP | Bk | W | L | Pct | Sh | Sv-Op | Hld | ERC | ERA |
| 2013 | Salt Lk* | AAA | 1 | 1 | 0 | 0 | 4.2 | 20 | 4 | 4 | 4 | 3 | 0 | 0 | 0 | 3 | 0 | 2 | 1 | 0 | 0 | 0 | - | 0 | 0-- | - | 8.54 | 7.71 |
| 2005 | Fla | NL | 17 | 13 | 1 | 0 | 73.2 | 325 | 71 | 34 | 33 | 4 | 4 | 1 | 4 | 31 | 4 | 59 | 0 | 0 | 5 | 5 | .500 | 0 | 0-0 | 0 | 3.68 | 4.03 |
| 2006 | Fla | NL | 12 | 5 | 0 | 3 | 43.0 | 213 | 50 | 39 | 35 | 9 | 4 | 4 | 4 | 30 | 3 | 25 | 2 | 0 | 1 | 2 | .333 | 0 | 0-0 | 0 | 7.30 | 7.33 |
| 2007 | NYM | NL | 2 | 2 | 0 | 0 | 10.1 | 51 | 17 | 14 | 14 | 4 | 0 | 0 | 0 | 2 | 1 | 4 | 1 | 0 | 0 | 1 | .000 | 0 | 0-0 | 0 | 8.95 | 12.19 |
| 2009 | Sea | AL | 23 | 14 | 0 | 4 | 91.2 | 385 | 98 | 53 | 50 | 16 | 3 | 6 | 3 | 24 | 1 | 54 | 1 | 1 | 3 | 6 | .333 | 0 | 0-0 | 0 | 4.64 | 4.91 |
| 2010 | Sea | AL | 31 | 31 | 0 | 0 | 192.2 | 811 | 187 | 86 | 81 | 18 | 4 | 7 | 1 | 54 | 3 | 116 | 1 | 4 | 9 | 12 | .429 | 0 | 0-0 | 0 | 3.37 | 3.78 |
| 2011 | Sea | AL | 32 | 32 | 4 | 0 | 201.0 | 857 | 205 | 105 | 95 | 22 | 3 | 4 | 4 | 59 | 4 | 131 | 3 | 1 | 10 | 13 | .435 | 3 | 0-0 | 0 | 3.86 | 4.25 |
| 2012 | Sea | AL | 33 | 33 | 2 | 0 | 217.1 | 887 | 201 | 94 | 93 | 35 | 3 | 6 | 3 | 55 | 1 | 141 | 5 | 0 | 14 | 11 | .560 | 0 | 0-0 | 0 | 3.57 | 3.85 |
| 2013 | LAA | AL | 24 | 24 | 3 | 0 | 150.0 | 644 | 162 | 68 | 67 | 17 | 3 | 3 | 5 | 46 | 2 | 109 | 0 | 1 | 9 | 8 | .529 | 2 | 0-0 | 0 | 4.40 | 4.02 |
| 8 ML YEARS | | | 174 | 154 | 10 | 7 | 979.2 | 4173 | 991 | 493 | 468 | 125 | 24 | 31 | 24 | 301 | 19 | 639 | 13 | 7 | 51 | 58 | .468 | 5 | 0-0 | 0 | 4.03 | 4.30 |

## Anthony Varvaro

**Pitches:** R **Bats:** R **Pos:** RP-62 var-VAR-oh **Ht:** 6'0" **Wt:** 195 **Born:** 10/31/1984 **Age:** 29

| | | | HOW MUCH HE PITCHED | | | | | | WHAT HE GAVE UP | | | | | | | | | | | | THE RESULTS | | | | | | | |
|---|---|---|---|---|---|---|---|---|---|---|---|---|---|---|---|---|---|---|---|---|---|---|---|---|---|---|---|---|
| Year | Team | Lg | G | GS | CG | GF | IP | BFP | H | R | ER | HR | SH | SF | HB | TBB | IBB | SO | WP | Bk | W | L | Pct | Sh | Sv-Op | Hld | ERC | ERA |
| 2010 | Sea | AL | 4 | 0 | 0 | 2 | 4.0 | 24 | 6 | 5 | 5 | 2 | 0 | 0 | 0 | 6 | 0 | 5 | 1 | 0 | 0 | 1 | .000 | 0 | 0-0 | 0 | 16.26 | 11.25 |
| 2011 | Atl | NL | 18 | 0 | 0 | 9 | 24.0 | 96 | 15 | 7 | 7 | 3 | 2 | 1 | 0 | 11 | 4 | 23 | 1 | 0 | 0 | 2 | .000 | 0 | 0-1 | 1 | 2.28 | 2.63 |
| 2012 | Atl | NL | 12 | 0 | 0 | 5 | 16.2 | 76 | 16 | 11 | 10 | 2 | 1 | 0 | 2 | 9 | 1 | 21 | 3 | 0 | 1 | 1 | .500 | 0 | 0-0 | 0 | 4.88 | 5.40 |
| 2013 | Atl | NL | 62 | 0 | 0 | 30 | 73.1 | 306 | 68 | 25 | 23 | 3 | 2 | 0 | 1 | 25 | 3 | 43 | 7 | 0 | 3 | 1 | .750 | 0 | 1-3 | 6 | 3.07 | 2.82 |
| 4 ML YEARS | | | 96 | 0 | 0 | 46 | 118.0 | 502 | 105 | 48 | 45 | 10 | 5 | 1 | 3 | 51 | 8 | 92 | 12 | 0 | 4 | 5 | .444 | 0 | 1-4 | 7 | 3.49 | 3.43 |

## Donnie Veal

**Pitches:** L **Bats:** L **Pos:** RP-50 VEEL **Ht:** 6'4" **Wt:** 235 **Born:** 9/18/1984 **Age:** 29

| | | | HOW MUCH HE PITCHED | | | | | | WHAT HE GAVE UP | | | | | | | | | | | | THE RESULTS | | | | | | | |
|---|---|---|---|---|---|---|---|---|---|---|---|---|---|---|---|---|---|---|---|---|---|---|---|---|---|---|---|---|
| Year | Team | Lg | G | GS | CG | GF | IP | BFP | H | R | ER | HR | SH | SF | HB | TBB | IBB | SO | WP | Bk | W | L | Pct | Sh | Sv-Op | Hld | ERC | ERA |
| 2013 | Charltt* | AAA | 17 | 0 | 0 | 12 | 26.2 | 112 | 23 | 8 | 8 | 1 | 4 | 0 | 2 | 14 | 0 | 30 | 1 | 0 | 2 | 2 | .500 | 0 | 2-- | - | 3.80 | 2.70 |
| 2009 | Pit | NL | 19 | 0 | 0 | 10 | 16.1 | 87 | 18 | 13 | 13 | 2 | 0 | 1 | 2 | 20 | 0 | 16 | 2 | 0 | 1 | 0 | 1.000 | 0 | 0-0 | 1 | 8.89 | 7.16 |
| 2012 | CWS | AL | 24 | 0 | 0 | 5 | 13.0 | 49 | 5 | 2 | 2 | 0 | 0 | 0 | 0 | 4 | 0 | 19 | 0 | 0 | 0 | 0 | - | 0 | 1-1 | 4 | 0.75 | 1.38 |
| 2013 | CWS | AL | 50 | 0 | 0 | 5 | 29.1 | 126 | 26 | 16 | 15 | 3 | 0 | 0 | 0 | 16 | 1 | 29 | 4 | 0 | 2 | 3 | .400 | 0 | 0-1 | 13 | 4.02 | 4.60 |
| 3 ML YEARS | | | 93 | 0 | 0 | 20 | 58.2 | 262 | 49 | 31 | 30 | 5 | 0 | 1 | 2 | 40 | 1 | 64 | 6 | 0 | 3 | 3 | .500 | 0 | 1-2 | 18 | 4.23 | 4.60 |

## Gil Velazquez

**Bats:** R **Throws:** R **Pos:** 3B-1 veh-LAZZ-kezz **Ht:** 6'2" **Wt:** 185 **Born:** 10/17/1979 **Age:** 34

| | | | BATTING | | | | | | | | | | | | | | | | | | BASERUNNING | | | | AVERAGES | | |
|---|---|---|---|---|---|---|---|---|---|---|---|---|---|---|---|---|---|---|---|---|---|---|---|---|---|---|---|
| Year | Team | Lg | G | AB | H | 2B | 3B | HR | (Hm | Rd) | TB | R | RBI | RC | TBB | IBB | SO | HBP | SH | SF | SB | CS | SB% | GDP | Avg | OBP | Slg |
| 2013 | S-WB* | AAA | 27 | 75 | 13 | 0 | 0 | 0 | (- | -) | 13 | 4 | 2 | 2 | 8 | 0 | 11 | 0 | 2 | 0 | 0 | 1 | .00 | 4 | .173 | .253 | .173 |
| 2013 | NewOr* | AAA | 74 | 256 | 71 | 8 | 0 | 0 | (- | -) | 79 | 30 | 24 | 34 | 43 | 1 | 53 | 0 | 4 | 4 | 3 | 5 | .38 | 4 | .277 | .376 | .309 |
| 2008 | Bos | AL | 3 | 8 | 1 | 0 | 0 | 0 | (0 | 0) | 1 | 0 | 1 | 1 | 0 | 0 | 0 | 0 | 0 | 0 | 0 | 0 | - | 0 | .125 | .125 | .125 |
| 2009 | Bos | AL | 6 | 2 | 0 | 0 | 0 | 0 | (0 | 0) | 0 | 0 | 0 | 0 | 0 | 0 | 0 | 1 | 0 | 0 | 0 | 0 | - | 0 | .000 | .333 | .000 |
| 2011 | LAA | AL | 4 | 6 | 3 | 0 | 0 | 0 | (0 | 0) | 3 | 0 | 1 | 1 | 0 | 0 | 0 | 0 | 0 | 1 | 0 | 0 | - | 0 | .500 | .429 | .500 |
| 2012 | Mia | NL | 19 | 56 | 13 | 1 | 0 | 0 | (0 | 0) | 14 | 2 | 2 | 3 | 1 | 0 | 11 | 0 | 0 | 0 | 0 | 0 | - | 0 | .232 | .246 | .250 |
| 2013 | Mia | NL | 1 | 1 | 0 | 0 | 0 | 0 | (0 | 0) | 0 | 0 | 0 | 0 | 0 | 0 | 0 | 0 | 0 | 0 | 0 | 0 | - | 0 | .000 | .000 | .000 |
| 5 ML YEARS | | | 33 | 73 | 17 | 1 | 0 | 0 | (0 | 0) | 18 | 2 | 4 | 5 | 1 | 0 | 11 | 1 | 0 | 1 | 0 | 0 | - | 0 | .233 | .250 | .247 |

## Will Venable

**Bats:** L **Throws:** L **Pos:** RF-97;CF-80;PH-10;PR-6 VENN-uh-bull **Ht:** 6'2" **Wt:** 210 **Born:** 10/29/1982 **Age:** 31

| | | | BATTING | | | | | | | | | | | | | | | | | | BASERUNNING | | | | AVERAGES | | |
|---|---|---|---|---|---|---|---|---|---|---|---|---|---|---|---|---|---|---|---|---|---|---|---|---|---|---|---|
| Year | Team | Lg | G | AB | H | 2B | 3B | HR | (Hm | Rd) | TB | R | RBI | RC | TBB | IBB | SO | HBP | SH | SF | SB | CS | SB% | GDP | Avg | OBP | Slg |
| 2008 | SD | NL | 28 | 110 | 29 | 4 | 2 | 2 | (0 | 2) | 43 | 16 | 10 | 15 | 13 | 1 | 21 | 0 | 0 | 1 | 1 | 1 | .50 | 1 | .264 | .339 | .391 |
| 2009 | SD | NL | 95 | 293 | 75 | 14 | 2 | 12 | (5 | 7) | 129 | 38 | 38 | 34 | 25 | 2 | 89 | 4 | 2 | 0 | 6 | 1 | .86 | 6 | .256 | .323 | .440 |
| 2010 | SD | NL | 131 | 392 | 96 | 11 | 7 | 13 | (6 | 7) | 160 | 60 | 51 | 57 | 45 | 8 | 128 | 3 | 0 | 5 | 29 | 7 | .81 | 3 | .245 | .324 | .408 |
| 2011 | SD | NL | 121 | 370 | 91 | 14 | 7 | 9 | (6 | 3) | 146 | 49 | 44 | 52 | 31 | 4 | 92 | 5 | 1 | 4 | 26 | 3 | .90 | 2 | .246 | .310 | .395 |
| 2012 | SD | NL | 148 | 417 | 110 | 26 | 8 | 9 | (2 | 7) | 179 | 62 | 45 | 66 | 41 | 2 | 94 | 5 | 5 | 2 | 24 | 6 | .80 | 2 | .264 | .335 | .429 |
| 2013 | SD | NL | 151 | 481 | 129 | 22 | 8 | 22 | (15 | 7) | 233 | 64 | 53 | 56 | 29 | 4 | 118 | 2 | 2 | 1 | 22 | 6 | .79 | 6 | .268 | .312 | .484 |
| 6 ML YEARS | | | 674 | 2063 | 530 | 91 | 34 | 67 | (34 | 33) | 890 | 289 | 241 | 280 | 184 | 21 | 542 | 19 | 10 | 13 | 108 | 24 | .82 | 20 | .257 | .322 | .431 |

## Jonny Venters

**Pitches:** L **Bats:** L **Pos:** P **Ht:** 6'3" **Wt:** 195 **Born:** 3/20/1985 **Age:** 29

| | | | HOW MUCH HE PITCHED | | | | | | WHAT HE GAVE UP | | | | | | | | | | | | THE RESULTS | | | | | | | |
|---|---|---|---|---|---|---|---|---|---|---|---|---|---|---|---|---|---|---|---|---|---|---|---|---|---|---|---|---|
| Year | Team | Lg | G | GS | CG | GF | IP | BFP | H | R | ER | HR | SH | SF | HB | TBB | IBB | SO | WP | Bk | W | L | Pct | Sh | Sv-Op | Hld | ERC | ERA |
| 2010 | Atl | NL | 79 | 0 | 0 | 17 | 83.0 | 350 | 61 | 30 | 18 | 1 | 2 | 1 | 8 | 39 | 2 | 93 | 4 | 0 | 4 | 4 | .500 | 0 | 1-5 | 24 | 2.64 | 1.95 |

| | | | HOW MUCH HE PITCHED | | | | | | WHAT HE GAVE UP | | | | | | | | | | | | THE RESULTS | | | | | | | |
|---|---|---|---|---|---|---|---|---|---|---|---|---|---|---|---|---|---|---|---|---|---|---|---|---|---|---|---|---|
| Year | Team | Lg | G | GS | CG | GF | IP | BFP | H | R | ER | HR | SH | SF | HB | TBB | IBB | SO | WP | Bk | W | L | Pct | Sh | Sv-Op | Hld | ERC | ERA |
| 2011 | Atl | NL | **85** | 0 | 0 | 10 | 88.0 | 357 | 53 | 19 | 18 | 2 | 7 | 1 | 5 | 43 | 7 | 96 | 4 | 0 | 6 | 2 | .750 | 0 | 5-9 | 35 | 1.96 | 1.84 |
| 2012 | Atl | NL | 66 | 0 | 0 | 12 | 58.2 | 262 | 61 | 23 | 21 | 6 | 3 | 0 | 5 | 28 | 3 | 69 | 9 | 0 | 5 | 4 | .556 | 0 | 0-3 | 20 | 4.92 | 3.22 |
| Postseason | | | 5 | 0 | 0 | 0 | 6.0 | 22 | 8 | 0 | 0 | 0 | 0 | 0 | 0 | 0 | 0 | 8 | 0 | 0 | 0 | 0 | - | 0 | 0-0 | 0 | 4.31 | 0.00 |
| 3 ML YEARS | | | 230 | 0 | 0 | 39 | 229.2 | 969 | 175 | 72 | 57 | 9 | 12 | 2 | 18 | 110 | 12 | 258 | 17 | 0 | 15 | 10 | .600 | 0 | 6-17 | 79 | 2.90 | 2.23 |

## Yordano Ventura

**Pitches:** R **Bats:** R **Pos:** SP-3 your-DON-oh ven-TOUR-uh **Ht:** 5'11" **Wt:** 180 **Born:** 6/3/1991 **Age:** 23

| | | | HOW MUCH HE PITCHED | | | | | | WHAT HE GAVE UP | | | | | | | | | | | | THE RESULTS | | | | | | | |
|---|---|---|---|---|---|---|---|---|---|---|---|---|---|---|---|---|---|---|---|---|---|---|---|---|---|---|---|---|
| Year | Team | Lg | G | GS | CG | GF | IP | BFP | H | R | ER | HR | SH | SF | HB | TBB | IBB | SO | WP | Bk | W | L | Pct | Sh | Sv-Op | Hld | ERC | ERA |
| 2010 | Royals | R | 14 | 6 | 0 | 0 | 52.2 | 228 | 49 | 28 | 19 | 3 | 0 | 0 | 3 | 17 | 0 | 58 | 3 | 0 | 4 | 2 | .667 | 0 | 0- | - | 3.23 | 3.25 |
| 2011 | Kane | A | 19 | 19 | 0 | 0 | 84.1 | 351 | 82 | 43 | 40 | 8 | 1 | 3 | 5 | 24 | 0 | 88 | 13 | 1 | 4 | 6 | .400 | 0 | 0- | - | 3.74 | 4.27 |
| 2012 | Wilmg | A+ | 16 | 16 | 0 | 0 | 76.1 | 326 | 66 | 32 | 28 | 7 | 3 | 2 | 5 | 28 | 0 | 98 | 3 | 1 | 3 | 5 | .375 | 0 | 0- | - | 3.35 | 3.30 |
| 2012 | NWArk | AA | 6 | 6 | 0 | 0 | 29.1 | 123 | 23 | 16 | 15 | 1 | 0 | 2 | 4 | 13 | 0 | 25 | 3 | 0 | 1 | 2 | .333 | 0 | 0- | - | 3.20 | 4.60 |
| 2012 | Royals | R | 1 | 1 | 0 | 0 | 3.2 | 15 | 3 | 1 | 1 | 0 | 0 | 0 | 0 | 1 | 0 | 7 | 1 | 0 | 0 | 0 | - | 0 | 0- | - | 2.00 | 2.45 |
| 2013 | NWArk | AA | 11 | 11 | 0 | 0 | 57.2 | 230 | 39 | 17 | 15 | 3 | 0 | 0 | 4 | 20 | 0 | 74 | 2 | 2 | 3 | 2 | .600 | 0 | 0- | - | 2.19 | 2.34 |
| 2013 | Omha | AAA | 15 | 14 | 0 | 0 | 77.0 | 334 | 80 | 35 | 32 | 4 | 1 | 2 | 3 | 33 | 1 | 81 | 5 | 1 | 5 | 4 | .556 | 0 | 0- | - | 4.26 | 3.74 |
| 2013 | KC | AL | 3 | 3 | 0 | 0 | 15.1 | 64 | 13 | 6 | 6 | 3 | 0 | 0 | 0 | 6 | 0 | 11 | 1 | 0 | 0 | 1 | .000 | 0 | 0-0 | 0 | 3.83 | 3.52 |

## Jose Veras

**Pitches:** R **Bats:** R **Pos:** RP-67 **Ht:** 6'6" **Wt:** 240 **Born:** 10/20/1980 **Age:** 33

| | | | HOW MUCH HE PITCHED | | | | | | WHAT HE GAVE UP | | | | | | | | | | | | THE RESULTS | | | | | | | |
|---|---|---|---|---|---|---|---|---|---|---|---|---|---|---|---|---|---|---|---|---|---|---|---|---|---|---|---|---|
| Year | Team | Lg | G | GS | CG | GF | IP | BFP | H | R | ER | HR | SH | SF | HB | TBB | IBB | SO | WP | Bk | W | L | Pct | Sh | Sv-Op | Hld | ERC | ERA |
| 2006 | NYY | AL | 12 | 0 | 0 | 4 | 11.0 | 43 | 8 | 5 | 5 | 2 | 0 | 0 | 0 | 5 | 0 | 6 | 1 | 1 | 0 | 0 | - | 0 | 1-1 | 1 | 3.55 | 4.09 |
| 2007 | NYY | AL | 9 | 0 | 0 | 3 | 9.1 | 41 | 6 | 6 | 6 | 0 | 0 | 0 | 0 | 7 | 1 | 7 | 1 | 0 | 0 | 0 | - | 0 | 2-2 | 1 | 2.52 | 5.79 |
| 2008 | NYY | AL | 60 | 0 | 0 | 15 | 57.2 | 253 | 52 | 23 | 23 | 7 | 2 | 1 | 3 | 29 | 6 | 63 | 4 | 0 | 5 | 3 | .625 | 0 | 0-2 | 10 | 4.09 | 3.59 |
| 2009 | 2 Tms | AL | 47 | 0 | 0 | 19 | 50.1 | 225 | 42 | 33 | 29 | 8 | 4 | 0 | 6 | 28 | 0 | 40 | 0 | 1 | 4 | 3 | .571 | 0 | 0-0 | 6 | 4.60 | 5.19 |
| 2010 | Fla | NL | 48 | 0 | 0 | 11 | 48.0 | 201 | 32 | 20 | 20 | 5 | 1 | 0 | 1 | 29 | 0 | 54 | 2 | 0 | 3 | 3 | .500 | 0 | 0-2 | 19 | 3.19 | 3.75 |
| 2011 | Pit | NL | 79 | 0 | 0 | 19 | 71.0 | 305 | 54 | 32 | 30 | 6 | 2 | 3 | 4 | 34 | 3 | 79 | 5 | 1 | 2 | 4 | .333 | 0 | 1-8 | 27 | 3.06 | 3.80 |
| 2012 | Mil | NL | 72 | 0 | 0 | 17 | 67.0 | 300 | 61 | 29 | 27 | 5 | 1 | 2 | 2 | 40 | 1 | 79 | 1 | 0 | 5 | 4 | .556 | 0 | 1-2 | 10 | 4.20 | 3.63 |
| 2013 | 2 Tms | AL | 67 | 0 | 0 | 45 | 62.2 | 254 | 45 | 23 | 21 | 6 | 2 | 0 | 4 | 22 | 1 | 60 | 2 | 0 | 0 | 5 | .000 | 0 | 21-25 | 9 | 2.61 | 3.02 |
| 09 | NYY | AL | 25 | 0 | 0 | 10 | 25.2 | 118 | 23 | 17 | 17 | 5 | 2 | 0 | 4 | 14 | 0 | 18 | 0 | 0 | 3 | 1 | .750 | 0 | 0-0 | 3 | 5.29 | 5.96 |
| 09 | Cle | AL | 22 | 0 | 0 | 9 | 24.2 | 107 | 19 | 16 | 12 | 3 | 2 | 0 | 2 | 14 | 0 | 22 | 0 | 1 | 1 | 2 | .333 | 0 | 0-0 | 3 | 3.92 | 4.38 |
| 13 | Hou | AL | 42 | 0 | 0 | 38 | 43.0 | 169 | 29 | 15 | 14 | 4 | 1 | 0 | 3 | 14 | 0 | 44 | 2 | 0 | 0 | 4 | .000 | 0 | 19-22 | 0 | 2.38 | 2.93 |
| 13 | Det | AL | 25 | 0 | 0 | 7 | 19.2 | 85 | 16 | 8 | 7 | 2 | 1 | 0 | 1 | 8 | 1 | 16 | 0 | 0 | 0 | 1 | .000 | 0 | 2-3 | 9 | 3.11 | 3.20 |
| Postseason | | | 2 | 0 | 0 | 0 | 0.2 | 4 | 1 | 0 | 0 | 0 | 0 | 0 | 0 | 1 | 1 | 1 | 0 | 0 | 0 | 0 | - | 0 | 0-0 | 0 | 6.98 | 0.00 |
| 8 ML YEARS | | | 394 | 0 | 0 | 133 | 377.0 | 1622 | 300 | 171 | 161 | 39 | 12 | 6 | 20 | 194 | 12 | 388 | 16 | 3 | 19 | 22 | .463 | 0 | 26-42 | 83 | 3.55 | 3.84 |

## Justin Verlander

**Pitches:** R **Bats:** R **Pos:** SP-34 **Ht:** 6'5" **Wt:** 225 **Born:** 2/20/1983 **Age:** 31

| | | | HOW MUCH HE PITCHED | | | | | | WHAT HE GAVE UP | | | | | | | | | | | | THE RESULTS | | | | | | | |
|---|---|---|---|---|---|---|---|---|---|---|---|---|---|---|---|---|---|---|---|---|---|---|---|---|---|---|---|---|
| Year | Team | Lg | G | GS | CG | GF | IP | BFP | H | R | ER | HR | SH | SF | HB | TBB | IBB | SO | WP | Bk | W | L | Pct | Sh | Sv-Op | Hld | ERC | ERA |
| 2005 | Det | AL | 2 | 2 | 0 | 0 | 11.1 | 54 | 15 | 9 | 9 | 1 | 0 | 0 | 1 | 5 | 0 | 7 | 1 | 0 | 0 | 2 | .000 | 0 | 0-0 | 0 | 6.41 | 7.15 |
| 2006 | Det | AL | 30 | 30 | 1 | 0 | 186.0 | 776 | 187 | 78 | 75 | 21 | 2 | 4 | 6 | 60 | 1 | 124 | 5 | 1 | 17 | 9 | .654 | 1 | 0-0 | 0 | 4.12 | 3.63 |
| 2007 | Det | AL | 32 | 32 | 1 | 0 | 201.2 | 866 | 181 | 88 | 82 | 20 | 3 | 1 | **19** | 67 | 3 | 183 | **17** | 2 | 18 | 6 | **.750** | 1 | 0-0 | 0 | 3.53 | 3.66 |
| 2008 | Det | AL | 33 | 33 | 1 | 0 | 201.0 | 880 | 195 | 119 | 108 | 18 | 4 | 6 | 14 | 87 | 8 | 163 | 6 | **3** | 11 | **17** | .393 | 0 | 0-0 | 0 | 4.17 | 4.84 |
| 2009 | Det | AL | 35 | **35** | 3 | 0 | **240.0** | **982** | 219 | 99 | 92 | 20 | 6 | 4 | 6 | 63 | 5 | **269** | 8 | **4** | **19** | 9 | .679 | 1 | 0-0 | 0 | 3.06 | 3.45 |
| 2010 | Det | AL | 33 | 33 | 4 | 0 | 224.1 | 925 | 190 | 89 | 84 | 14 | 6 | 8 | 6 | 71 | 0 | 219 | 11 | 2 | 18 | 9 | .667 | 0 | 0-0 | 0 | 2.79 | 3.37 |
| 2011 | Det | AL | 34 | **34** | 4 | 0 | **251.0** | 969 | 174 | 73 | 67 | 24 | 2 | 3 | 3 | 57 | 0 | **250** | 7 | **2** | **24** | 5 | **.828** | 2 | 0-0 | 0 | **1.92** | **2.40** |
| 2012 | Det | AL | 33 | 33 | **6** | 0 | **238.1** | **956** | 192 | 81 | 70 | 19 | 4 | 3 | 5 | 60 | 2 | **239** | 2 | 1 | 17 | 8 | .680 | 1 | 0-0 | 0 | **2.45** | 2.64 |
| 2013 | Det | AL | 34 | **34** | 0 | 0 | 218.1 | 925 | 212 | 94 | 84 | 19 | 2 | 6 | 4 | 75 | 1 | 217 | 3 | 1 | 13 | 12 | .520 | 0 | 0-0 | 0 | 3.68 | 3.46 |
| Postseason | | | 12 | 12 | 1 | 0 | 70.1 | 297 | 61 | 36 | 33 | 11 | 1 | 1 | 1 | 26 | 0 | 77 | 5 | 1 | 6 | 4 | .600 | 1 | 0-0 | 0 | 3.62 | 4.22 |
| 9 ML YEARS | | | 266 | 266 | 20 | 0 | 1772.0 | 7333 | 1565 | 730 | 671 | 156 | 29 | 35 | 64 | 545 | 20 | 1671 | 60 | 16 | 137 | 77 | .640 | 6 | 0-0 | 0 | 3.14 | 3.41 |

## Dayan Viciedo

**Bats:** R **Throws:** R **Pos:** LF-109;DH-13;PH-2 DYE-yahn vee-see-AY-doe **Ht:** 5'11" **Wt:** 230 **Born:** 3/10/1989 **Age:** 25

| | | | BATTING | | | | | | | | | | | | | | | | | | BASERUNNING | | | | AVERAGES | | |
|---|---|---|---|---|---|---|---|---|---|---|---|---|---|---|---|---|---|---|---|---|---|---|---|---|---|---|---|
| Year | Team | Lg | G | AB | H | 2B | 3B | HR | (Hm | Rd) | TB | R | RBI | RC | TBB | IBB | SO | HBP | SH | SF | SB | CS | SB% | GDP | Avg | OBP | Slg |
| 2013 | Charltt* | AAA | 4 | 15 | 3 | 0 | 0 | 0 | (- | -) | 3 | 2 | 0 | 0 | 1 | 0 | 3 | 1 | 0 | 0 | 0 | 0 | - | 0 | .200 | .294 | .200 |
| 2010 | CWS | AL | 38 | 104 | 32 | 7 | 0 | 5 | (4 | 1) | 54 | 17 | 13 | 15 | 2 | 0 | 25 | 0 | 0 | 0 | 1 | 0 | 1.00 | 5 | .308 | .321 | .519 |
| 2011 | CWS | AL | 29 | 102 | 26 | 3 | 0 | 1 | (0 | 1) | 32 | 11 | 6 | 12 | 9 | 0 | 23 | 2 | 0 | 0 | 1 | 0 | 1.00 | 4 | .255 | .327 | .314 |
| 2012 | CWS | AL | 147 | 505 | 129 | 18 | 1 | 25 | (13 | 12) | 224 | 64 | 78 | 65 | 28 | 0 | 120 | 6 | 0 | 4 | 0 | 2 | .00 | 19 | .255 | .300 | .444 |
| 2013 | CWS | AL | 124 | 441 | 117 | 23 | 3 | 14 | (5 | 9) | 188 | 43 | 56 | 56 | 24 | 0 | 98 | 3 | 0 | 5 | 0 | 0 | - | 11 | .265 | .304 | .426 |
| 4 ML YEARS | | | 338 | 1152 | 304 | 51 | 4 | 45 | (22 | 23) | 498 | 135 | 153 | 148 | 63 | 0 | 266 | 11 | 0 | 9 | 2 | 2 | .50 | 39 | .264 | .306 | .432 |

## Shane Victorino

**Bats:** B **Throws:** R **Pos:** RF-110;CF-15;PR-3;PH-1 **Ht:** 5'9" **Wt:** 190 **Born:** 11/30/1980 **Age:** 33

| | | | BATTING | | | | | | | | | | | | | | | | | | BASERUNNING | | | | AVERAGES | | |
|---|---|---|---|---|---|---|---|---|---|---|---|---|---|---|---|---|---|---|---|---|---|---|---|---|---|---|---|
| Year | Team | Lg | G | AB | H | 2B | 3B | HR | (Hm | Rd) | TB | R | RBI | RC | TBB | IBB | SO | HBP | SH | SF | SB | CS | SB% | GDP | Avg | OBP | Slg |
| 2013 | Pwtckt* | AAA | 1 | 4 | 2 | 0 | 0 | 1 | (- | -) | 5 | 1 | 1 | 1 | 0 | 0 | 1 | 0 | 0 | 0 | 0 | 0 | - | 0 | .500 | .500 | 1.250 |
| 2003 | SD | NL | 36 | 73 | 11 | 2 | 0 | 0 | (0 | 0) | 13 | 8 | 4 | 1 | 7 | 0 | 17 | 1 | 1 | 1 | 7 | 2 | .78 | 5 | .151 | .232 | .178 |
| 2005 | Phi | NL | 21 | 17 | 5 | 0 | 0 | 2 | (1 | 1) | 11 | 5 | 8 | 4 | 0 | 0 | 3 | 0 | 0 | 2 | 0 | 0 | - | 0 | .294 | .263 | .647 |
| 2006 | Phi | NL | 153 | 415 | 119 | 19 | 8 | 6 | (3 | 3) | 172 | 70 | 46 | 58 | 24 | 0 | 54 | 14 | 8 | 1 | 4 | 3 | .57 | 5 | .287 | .346 | .414 |
| 2007 | Phi | NL | 131 | 456 | 128 | 23 | 3 | 12 | (6 | 6) | 193 | 78 | 46 | 65 | 37 | 1 | 62 | 10 | 5 | 2 | 37 | 4 | .90 | 10 | .281 | .347 | .423 |
| 2008 | Phi | NL | 146 | 570 | 167 | 30 | 8 | 14 | (6 | 8) | 255 | 102 | 58 | 86 | 45 | 2 | 69 | 7 | 5 | 0 | 36 | 11 | .77 | 8 | .293 | .352 | .447 |
| 2009 | Phi | NL | 156 | 620 | 181 | 39 | **13** | 10 | (4 | 6) | 276 | 102 | 62 | 99 | 60 | 1 | 71 | 6 | 4 | 4 | 25 | 8 | .76 | 5 | .292 | .358 | .445 |

| Year | Team | Lg | G | AB | H | 2B | 3B | HR | (Hm | Rd) | TB | R | RBI | RC | TBB | IBB | SO | HBP | SH | SF | SB | CS | SB% | GDP | Avg | OBP | Slg |
|---|---|---|---|---|---|---|---|---|---|---|---|---|---|---|---|---|---|---|---|---|---|---|---|---|---|---|---|
| | | | BATTING | | | | | | | | | | | | | | | | | | BASERUNNING | | | | AVERAGES | | |
| 2010 | Phi | NL | 147 | 587 | 152 | 26 | 10 | 18 | (13 | 5) | 252 | 84 | 69 | 89 | 53 | 5 | 79 | 7 | 0 | 1 | 34 | 6 | .85 | 7 | .259 | .327 | .429 |
| 2011 | Phi | NL | 132 | 519 | 145 | 27 | **16** | 17 | (6 | 11) | 255 | 95 | 61 | 86 | 55 | 1 | 63 | 6 | 6 | 0 | 19 | 3 | .86 | 4 | .279 | .355 | .491 |
| 2012 | 2 Tms | NL | 154 | 595 | 152 | 29 | 7 | 11 | (4 | 7) | 228 | 72 | 55 | 76 | 53 | 1 | 80 | 6 | 9 | 3 | 39 | 6 | .87 | 5 | .255 | .321 | .383 |
| 2013 | Bos | AL | 122 | 477 | 140 | 26 | 2 | 15 | (7 | 8) | 215 | 82 | 61 | 77 | 25 | 0 | 75 | **18** | 10 | 2 | 21 | 3 | .88 | 5 | .294 | .351 | .451 |
| 12 | Phi | NL | 101 | 387 | 101 | 17 | 5 | 9 | (3 | 6) | 155 | 46 | 40 | 50 | 35 | 1 | 49 | 2 | 5 | 2 | 24 | 4 | .86 | 4 | .261 | .324 | .401 |
| 12 | LAD | NL | 53 | 208 | 51 | 12 | 2 | 2 | (1 | 1) | 73 | 26 | 15 | 26 | 18 | 0 | 31 | 4 | 4 | 1 | 15 | 2 | .88 | 1 | .245 | .316 | .351 |
| Postseason | | | 46 | 175 | 47 | 9 | 2 | 6 | (3 | 3) | 78 | 25 | 30 | 29 | 15 | 4 | 15 | 4 | 3 | 1 | 8 | 1 | .89 | 3 | .269 | .338 | .446 |
| 10 ML YEARS | | | 1198 | 4329 | 1200 | 221 | 67 | 105 | (50 | 55) | 1870 | 698 | 470 | 641 | 359 | 11 | 573 | 75 | 48 | 16 | 222 | 46 | .83 | 54 | .277 | .342 | .432 |

# Carlos Villanueva

**Pitches:** R **Bats:** R **Pos:** RP-32; SP-15 vee-ah-nue-AY-vah **Ht:** 6'2" **Wt:** 215 **Born:** 11/28/1983 **Age:** 30

| Year | Team | Lg | G | GS | CG | GF | IP | BFP | H | R | ER | HR | SH | SF | HB | TBB | IBB | SO | WP | Bk | W | L | Pct | Sh | Sv-Op | Hld | ERC | ERA |
|---|---|---|---|---|---|---|---|---|---|---|---|---|---|---|---|---|---|---|---|---|---|---|---|---|---|---|---|---|
| | | | HOW MUCH HE PITCHED | | | | | | WHAT HE GAVE UP | | | | | | | | | | | | THE RESULTS | | | | | | | |
| 2006 | Mil | NL | 10 | 6 | 0 | 2 | 53.2 | 215 | 43 | 22 | 22 | 8 | 1 | 0 | 4 | 11 | 1 | 39 | 0 | 0 | 2 | 2 | .500 | 0 | 0-0 | 0 | 2.85 | 3.69 |
| 2007 | Mil | NL | 59 | 6 | 0 | 8 | 114.1 | 489 | 101 | 52 | 50 | 16 | 4 | 1 | 3 | 53 | 3 | 99 | 3 | 0 | 8 | 5 | .615 | 0 | 1-3 | 16 | 4.03 | 3.94 |
| 2008 | Mil | NL | 47 | 9 | 0 | 9 | 108.1 | 464 | 112 | 53 | 49 | 18 | 9 | 1 | 3 | 30 | 1 | 93 | 4 | 0 | 4 | 7 | .364 | 0 | 1-1 | 11 | 4.29 | 4.07 |
| 2009 | Mil | NL | 64 | 6 | 0 | 23 | 96.0 | 422 | 102 | 58 | 57 | 13 | 4 | 0 | 2 | 35 | 8 | 83 | 4 | 0 | 4 | 10 | .286 | 0 | 3-8 | 9 | 4.44 | 5.34 |
| 2010 | Mil | NL | 50 | 0 | 0 | 5 | 52.2 | 231 | 48 | 27 | 27 | 7 | 0 | 3 | 4 | 22 | 1 | 67 | 5 | 0 | 2 | 0 | 1.000 | 0 | 1-4 | 14 | 4.08 | 4.61 |
| 2011 | Tor | AL | 33 | 13 | 0 | 3 | 107.0 | 454 | 103 | 49 | 48 | 11 | 1 | 6 | 4 | 32 | 3 | 68 | 4 | 0 | 6 | 4 | .600 | 0 | 0-1 | 0 | 3.57 | 4.04 |
| 2012 | Tor | AL | 38 | 16 | 0 | 9 | 125.1 | 521 | 113 | 59 | 58 | 23 | 2 | 4 | 3 | 46 | 4 | 122 | 6 | 1 | 7 | 7 | .500 | 0 | 0-0 | 2 | 4.08 | 4.16 |
| 2013 | ChC | NL | 47 | 15 | 0 | 5 | 128.2 | 524 | 117 | 58 | 58 | 14 | 7 | 3 | 3 | 40 | 4 | 103 | 0 | 0 | 7 | 8 | .467 | 0 | 0-1 | 2 | 3.43 | 4.06 |
| Postseason | | | 2 | 0 | 0 | 0 | 3.2 | 11 | 0 | 0 | 0 | 0 | 0 | 0 | 0 | 0 | 0 | 3 | 0 | 0 | 0 | 0 | - | 0 | 0-0 | 1 | 0.00 | 0.00 |
| 8 ML YEARS | | | 348 | 71 | 0 | 64 | 786.0 | 3320 | 739 | 378 | 369 | 110 | 28 | 18 | 26 | 269 | 25 | 674 | 26 | 1 | 40 | 43 | .482 | 0 | 6-18 | 54 | 3.88 | 4.23 |

# Jonathan Villar

**Bats:** B **Throws:** R **Pos:** SS-58;PR-1 vee-YARR **Ht:** 6'1" **Wt:** 195 **Born:** 5/2/1991 **Age:** 23

| Year | Team | Lg | G | AB | H | 2B | 3B | HR | (Hm | Rd) | TB | R | RBI | RC | TBB | IBB | SO | HBP | SH | SF | SB | CS | SB% | GDP | Avg | OBP | Slg |
|---|---|---|---|---|---|---|---|---|---|---|---|---|---|---|---|---|---|---|---|---|---|---|---|---|---|---|---|
| | | | BATTING | | | | | | | | | | | | | | | | | | BASERUNNING | | | | AVERAGES | | |
| 2009 | Phillies | R | 31 | 94 | 26 | 7 | 1 | 0 | (- | -) | 35 | 14 | 14 | 15 | 13 | 0 | 24 | 1 | 1 | 2 | 11 | 2 | .85 | 1 | .277 | .364 | .372 |
| 2009 | Wmspt | A- | 11 | 39 | 9 | 1 | 1 | 0 | (- | -) | 12 | 6 | 5 | 4 | 4 | 1 | 14 | 0 | 1 | 0 | 6 | 0 | 1.00 | 1 | .231 | .302 | .308 |
| 2010 | Lakwd | A | 100 | 371 | 101 | 18 | 4 | 2 | (- | -) | 133 | 61 | 36 | 49 | 26 | 1 | 103 | 8 | 13 | 2 | 38 | 13 | .75 | 5 | .272 | .332 | .358 |
| 2010 | Lancst | A+ | 32 | 129 | 29 | 6 | 2 | 3 | (- | -) | 48 | 18 | 19 | 15 | 12 | 0 | 50 | 1 | 0 | 1 | 7 | 2 | .78 | 2 | .225 | .294 | .372 |
| 2011 | Lancst | A+ | 47 | 174 | 45 | 7 | 4 | 4 | (- | -) | 72 | 26 | 26 | 29 | 25 | 0 | 56 | 2 | 3 | 3 | 20 | 6 | .77 | 0 | .259 | .353 | .414 |
| 2011 | CpChr | AA | 83 | 324 | 75 | 16 | 2 | 10 | (- | -) | 125 | 52 | 26 | 40 | 29 | 0 | 100 | 4 | 8 | 2 | 14 | 6 | .70 | 2 | .231 | .301 | .386 |
| 2012 | CpChr | AA | 86 | 326 | 85 | 7 | 2 | 11 | (- | -) | 129 | 54 | 50 | 50 | 35 | 1 | 87 | 4 | 8 | 4 | 39 | 8 | .83 | 2 | .261 | .336 | .396 |
| 2013 | OKCity | AAA | 91 | 339 | 94 | 16 | 8 | 8 | (- | -) | 150 | 47 | 41 | 56 | 32 | 0 | 93 | 2 | 11 | 2 | 31 | 7 | .82 | 7 | .277 | .341 | .442 |
| 2013 | Hou | AL | 58 | 210 | 51 | 9 | 2 | 1 | (0 | 1) | 67 | 26 | 8 | 22 | 24 | 1 | 71 | 0 | 7 | 0 | 18 | 8 | .69 | 5 | .243 | .321 | .319 |

# Brayan Villarreal

**Pitches:** R **Bats:** R **Pos:** RP-8 BRIAN VEE-yuh-ray-al **Ht:** 6'0" **Wt:** 170 **Born:** 5/10/1987 **Age:** 27

| Year | Team | Lg | G | GS | CG | GF | IP | BFP | H | R | ER | HR | SH | SF | HB | TBB | IBB | SO | WP | Bk | W | L | Pct | Sh | Sv-Op | Hld | ERC | ERA |
|---|---|---|---|---|---|---|---|---|---|---|---|---|---|---|---|---|---|---|---|---|---|---|---|---|---|---|---|---|
| | | | HOW MUCH HE PITCHED | | | | | | WHAT HE GAVE UP | | | | | | | | | | | | THE RESULTS | | | | | | | |
| 2013 | Toledo* | AAA | 28 | 0 | 0 | 9 | 34.1 | 152 | 26 | 13 | 12 | 0 | 2 | 0 | 3 | 26 | 1 | 41 | 3 | 1 | 2 | 2 | .500 | 0 | 1-- | - | 3.68 | 3.15 |
| 2013 | Lowell* | A- | 2 | 0 | 0 | 0 | 2.2 | 9 | 1 | 0 | 0 | 0 | 0 | 0 | 0 | 0 | 0 | 3 | 1 | 0 | 0 | 0 | - | 0 | 0-- | - | 0.31 | 0.00 |
| 2013 | Pwtckt* | AAA | 5 | 0 | 0 | 2 | 5.1 | 21 | 3 | 1 | 1 | 0 | 1 | 0 | 0 | 4 | 0 | 6 | 0 | 0 | 0 | 1 | .000 | 0 | 1-- | - | 2.58 | 1.69 |
| 2011 | Det | AL | 16 | 0 | 0 | 4 | 16.0 | 76 | 21 | 12 | 12 | 3 | 1 | 0 | 0 | 10 | 2 | 14 | 1 | 0 | 1 | 1 | .500 | 0 | 0-0 | 1 | 7.53 | 6.75 |
| 2012 | Det | AL | 50 | 0 | 0 | 15 | 54.2 | 226 | 38 | 20 | 16 | 3 | 1 | 6 | 1 | 28 | 3 | 66 | 9 | 2 | 3 | 5 | .375 | 0 | 0-0 | 9 | 2.58 | 2.63 |
| 2013 | 2 Tms | AL | 8 | 0 | 0 | 4 | 4.1 | 29 | 8 | 10 | 10 | 1 | 1 | 1 | 0 | 9 | 0 | 6 | 1 | 0 | 0 | 2 | .000 | 0 | 0-0 | 1 | 19.43 | 20.77 |
| 13 | Det | AL | 7 | 0 | 0 | 3 | 4.1 | 28 | 8 | 10 | 10 | 1 | 1 | 1 | 0 | 8 | 0 | 6 | 1 | 0 | 0 | 2 | .000 | 0 | 0-0 | 1 | 18.26 | 20.77 |
| 13 | Bos | AL | 1 | 0 | 0 | 1 | 0.0 | 1 | 0 | 0 | 0 | 0 | 0 | 0 | 0 | 1 | 0 | 0 | 0 | 0 | 0 | 0 | - | 0 | 0-0 | 0 | - | - |
| 3 ML YEARS | | | 74 | 0 | 0 | 23 | 75.0 | 331 | 67 | 42 | 38 | 7 | 3 | 7 | 1 | 47 | 5 | 86 | 11 | 2 | 4 | 8 | .333 | 0 | 0-0 | 11 | 4.28 | 4.56 |

# Pedro Villarreal

**Pitches:** R **Bats:** R **Pos:** SP-1; RP-1 VEE-uh-ree-al **Ht:** 6'1" **Wt:** 230 **Born:** 12/9/1987 **Age:** 26

| Year | Team | Lg | G | GS | CG | GF | IP | BFP | H | R | ER | HR | SH | SF | HB | TBB | IBB | SO | WP | Bk | W | L | Pct | Sh | Sv-Op | Hld | ERC | ERA |
|---|---|---|---|---|---|---|---|---|---|---|---|---|---|---|---|---|---|---|---|---|---|---|---|---|---|---|---|---|
| | | | HOW MUCH HE PITCHED | | | | | | WHAT HE GAVE UP | | | | | | | | | | | | THE RESULTS | | | | | | | |
| 2009 | Reds | R | 5 | 5 | 0 | 0 | 18.1 | 71 | 15 | 6 | 3 | 1 | 0 | 1 | 2 | 6 | 0 | 9 | 0 | 0 | 1 | 2 | .333 | 0 | 0-- | - | 3.21 | 1.47 |
| 2009 | Srsota | A+ | 9 | 3 | 0 | 2 | 31.1 | 145 | 30 | 20 | 19 | 2 | 1 | 2 | 5 | 18 | 0 | 12 | 1 | 0 | 0 | 3 | .000 | 0 | 0-- | - | 4.82 | 5.46 |
| 2010 | Dayton | A | 26 | 14 | 0 | 7 | 96.0 | 414 | 89 | 52 | 41 | 7 | 3 | 2 | 9 | 29 | 0 | 77 | 10 | 0 | 4 | 7 | .364 | 0 | 2-- | - | 3.40 | 3.84 |
| 2010 | Lynbrg | A+ | 6 | 5 | 0 | 0 | 19.2 | 91 | 26 | 17 | 15 | 3 | 1 | 0 | 1 | 8 | 0 | 16 | 0 | 0 | 0 | 3 | .000 | 0 | 0-- | - | 6.73 | 6.86 |
| 2011 | Bkrsfld | A+ | 10 | 10 | 0 | 0 | 58.0 | 242 | 68 | 31 | 28 | 9 | 0 | 1 | 2 | 8 | 0 | 41 | 2 | 1 | 4 | 3 | .571 | 0 | 0-- | - | 4.62 | 4.34 |
| 2011 | Carlina | AA | 17 | 17 | 1 | 0 | 91.2 | 391 | 92 | 52 | 45 | 11 | 2 | 5 | 7 | 20 | 0 | 68 | 4 | 2 | 7 | 4 | .636 | 0 | 0-- | - | 3.77 | 4.42 |
| 2012 | Pnscla | AA | 6 | 6 | 0 | 0 | 35.1 | 138 | 31 | 16 | 14 | 2 | 1 | 1 | 1 | 6 | 0 | 26 | 2 | 0 | 1 | 2 | .333 | 0 | 0-- | - | 2.49 | 3.57 |
| 2012 | Lsvlle | AAA | 20 | 20 | 0 | 0 | 113.1 | 499 | 129 | 70 | 58 | 9 | 6 | 5 | 3 | 32 | 0 | 81 | 3 | 1 | 3 | 12 | .200 | 0 | 0-- | - | 4.29 | 4.61 |
| 2013 | Lsvlle | AAA | 33 | 18 | 0 | 10 | 109.2 | 465 | 115 | 56 | 54 | 17 | 4 | 3 | 5 | 28 | 1 | 84 | 1 | 2 | 4 | 9 | .308 | 0 | 2-- | - | 4.35 | 4.43 |
| 2012 | Cin | NL | 1 | 0 | 0 | 1 | 1.0 | 3 | 0 | 0 | 0 | 0 | 0 | 0 | 0 | 0 | 0 | 1 | 0 | 0 | 0 | 0 | - | 0 | 0-0 | 0 | 0.00 | 0.00 |
| 2013 | Cin | NL | 2 | 1 | 0 | 0 | 5.2 | 32 | 13 | 8 | 8 | 4 | 0 | 0 | 0 | 3 | 0 | 4 | 0 | 0 | 0 | 1 | .000 | 0 | 0-0 | 0 | 20.07 | 12.71 |
| 2 ML YEARS | | | 3 | 1 | 0 | 1 | 6.2 | 35 | 13 | 8 | 8 | 4 | 0 | 0 | 0 | 3 | 0 | 5 | 0 | 0 | 0 | 1 | .000 | 0 | 0-0 | 0 | 15.47 | 10.80 |

# Nick Vincent

**Pitches:** R **Bats:** R **Pos:** RP-45 **Ht:** 6'0" **Wt:** 185 **Born:** 7/12/1986 **Age:** 27

| HOW MUCH HE PITCHED | | | | | | | | | WHAT HE GAVE UP | | | | | | | | | | | | THE RESULTS | | | | | | | |
|---|---|---|---|---|---|---|---|---|---|---|---|---|---|---|---|---|---|---|---|---|---|---|---|---|---|---|---|---|
| Year | Team | Lg | G | GS | CG | GF | IP | BFP | H | R | ER | HR | SH | SF | HB | TBB | IBB | SO | WP | Bk | W | L | Pct | Sh | Sv-Op | Hld | ERC | ERA |
| 2009 | Lk Els | A+ | 59 | 0 | 0 | 24 | 64.1 | 270 | 66 | 27 | 22 | 3 | 3 | 0 | 1 | 18 | 1 | 74 | 0 | 0 | 4 | 2 | .667 | 0 | 2-- | - | 3.45 | 3.08 |
| 2010 | Lk Els | A+ | 48 | 1 | 0 | 5 | 81.2 | 333 | 60 | 24 | 17 | 7 | 4 | 2 | 5 | 23 | 0 | 76 | 1 | 1 | 4 | 0 | 1.000 | 0 | 0-- | - | 2.35 | 1.87 |
| 2011 | SnAnt | AA | 66 | 0 | 0 | 16 | 79.1 | 310 | 54 | 20 | 20 | 6 | 7 | 4 | 3 | 20 | 2 | 89 | 1 | 0 | 8 | 2 | .800 | 0 | 3-- | - | 1.88 | 2.27 |
| 2012 | Tucsn | AAA | 23 | 0 | 0 | 7 | 21.2 | 102 | 27 | 14 | 14 | 2 | 2 | 1 | 2 | 11 | 0 | 19 | 1 | 0 | 1 | 1 | .500 | 0 | 2-- | - | 6.33 | 5.82 |
| 2012 | SnAnt | AA | 9 | 0 | 0 | 0 | 9.2 | 34 | 4 | 2 | 2 | 0 | 0 | 0 | 1 | 0 | 0 | 15 | 0 | 0 | 1 | 0 | 1.000 | 0 | 0-- | - | 0.52 | 1.86 |
| 2013 | Tucsn | AAA | 24 | 0 | 0 | 6 | 25.1 | 115 | 26 | 11 | 10 | 4 | 1 | 0 | 1 | 12 | 0 | 24 | 1 | 0 | 4 | 3 | .571 | 0 | 0-- | - | 4.99 | 3.55 |
| 2012 | SD | NL | 27 | 0 | 0 | 3 | 26.1 | 105 | 19 | 5 | 5 | 2 | 1 | 0 | 1 | 7 | 0 | 28 | 1 | 0 | 2 | 0 | 1.000 | 0 | 0-1 | 5 | 2.13 | 1.71 |
| 2013 | SD | NL | 45 | 0 | 0 | 7 | 46.1 | 180 | 33 | 11 | 11 | 1 | 4 | 0 | 2 | 11 | 3 | 49 | 0 | 0 | 6 | 3 | .667 | 0 | 1-1 | 10 | 1.67 | 2.14 |
| 2 ML YEARS | | | 72 | 0 | 0 | 10 | 72.2 | 285 | 52 | 16 | 16 | 3 | 5 | 0 | 3 | 18 | 3 | 77 | 1 | 0 | 8 | 3 | .727 | 0 | 1-2 | 15 | 1.83 | 1.98 |

# Ryan Vogelsong

**Pitches:** R **Bats:** R **Pos:** SP-19 VOH-gull-song **Ht:** 6'4" **Wt:** 215 **Born:** 7/22/1977 **Age:** 36

| HOW MUCH HE PITCHED | | | | | | | | | WHAT HE GAVE UP | | | | | | | | | | | | THE RESULTS | | | | | | | |
|---|---|---|---|---|---|---|---|---|---|---|---|---|---|---|---|---|---|---|---|---|---|---|---|---|---|---|---|---|
| Year | Team | Lg | G | GS | CG | GF | IP | BFP | H | R | ER | HR | SH | SF | HB | TBB | IBB | SO | WP | Bk | W | L | Pct | Sh | Sv-Op | Hld | ERC | ERA |
| 2013 | Giants* | R | 1 | 1 | 0 | 0 | 2.0 | 7 | 2 | 0 | 0 | 0 | 0 | 0 | 0 | 0 | 0 | 2 | 0 | 0 | 0 | 0 | - | 0 | 0-- | - | 2.31 | 0.00 |
| 2013 | SnJos* | A+ | 1 | 1 | 0 | 0 | 2.2 | 11 | 1 | 2 | 2 | 1 | 0 | 0 | 1 | 1 | 0 | 3 | 0 | 0 | 0 | 1 | .000 | 0 | 0-- | - | 3.75 | 6.75 |
| 2013 | Rchmd* | AA | 2 | 2 | 0 | 0 | 11.0 | 42 | 10 | 1 | 1 | 1 | 1 | 0 | 0 | 2 | 0 | 8 | 0 | 0 | 2 | 0 | 1.000 | 0 | 0-- | - | 2.88 | 0.82 |
| 2000 | SF | NL | 4 | 0 | 0 | 3 | 6.0 | 24 | 4 | 0 | 0 | 0 | 0 | 0 | 0 | 2 | 0 | 6 | 0 | 0 | 0 | 0 | - | 0 | 0-0 | 0 | 1.57 | 0.00 |
| 2001 | 2 Tms | NL | 15 | 2 | 0 | 8 | 34.2 | 164 | 39 | 31 | 26 | 6 | 0 | 1 | 2 | 20 | 1 | 24 | 2 | 0 | 0 | 5 | .000 | 0 | 0-0 | 1 | 6.20 | 6.75 |
| 2003 | Pit | NL | 6 | 5 | 0 | 0 | 22.0 | 108 | 30 | 19 | 16 | 1 | 3 | 1 | 2 | 9 | 3 | 15 | 1 | 0 | 2 | 2 | .500 | 0 | 0-0 | 0 | 5.72 | 6.55 |
| 2004 | Pit | NL | 31 | 26 | 0 | 4 | 133.0 | 610 | 148 | 97 | 96 | 22 | 8 | 6 | 10 | 67 | 7 | 92 | 3 | 0 | 6 | 13 | .316 | 0 | 0-0 | 0 | 5.89 | 6.50 |
| 2005 | Pit | NL | 44 | 0 | 0 | 19 | 81.1 | 369 | 82 | 43 | 40 | 5 | 1 | 4 | 8 | 40 | 1 | 52 | 7 | 0 | 2 | 2 | .500 | 0 | 0-1 | 1 | 4.51 | 4.43 |
| 2006 | Pit | NL | 20 | 0 | 0 | 7 | 38.0 | 178 | 44 | 27 | 27 | 2 | 5 | 4 | 7 | 16 | 2 | 27 | 4 | 1 | 0 | 0 | - | 0 | 0-0 | 0 | 5.31 | 6.39 |
| 2011 | SF | NL | 30 | 28 | 1 | 1 | 179.2 | 752 | 164 | 62 | 54 | 15 | 10 | 3 | 5 | 61 | 6 | 139 | 1 | 1 | 13 | 7 | .650 | 1 | 0-0 | 0 | 3.32 | 2.71 |
| 2012 | SF | NL | 31 | 31 | 0 | 0 | 189.2 | 788 | 171 | 76 | 71 | 17 | 7 | 4 | 8 | 62 | 7 | 158 | 3 | 0 | 14 | 9 | .609 | 0 | 0-0 | 0 | 3.33 | 3.37 |
| 2013 | SF | NL | 19 | 19 | 0 | 0 | 103.2 | 467 | 124 | 73 | 66 | 15 | 4 | 4 | 6 | 38 | 2 | 67 | 3 | 0 | 4 | 6 | .400 | 0 | 0-0 | 0 | 5.64 | 5.73 |
| 01 | SF | NL | 13 | 0 | 0 | 8 | 28.2 | 130 | 29 | 21 | 18 | 5 | 0 | 1 | 2 | 14 | 0 | 17 | 2 | 0 | 0 | 3 | .000 | 0 | 0-0 | 1 | 5.26 | 5.65 |
| 01 | Pit | NL | 2 | 2 | 0 | 0 | 6.0 | 34 | 10 | 10 | 8 | 1 | 0 | 0 | 0 | 6 | 1 | 7 | 0 | 0 | 0 | 2 | .000 | 0 | 0-0 | 0 | 11.03 | 12.00 |
| Postseason | | | 4 | 4 | 0 | 0 | 24.2 | 99 | 16 | 3 | 3 | 0 | 0 | 0 | 1 | 10 | 0 | 21 | 0 | 0 | 3 | 0 | 1.000 | 0 | 0-0 | 0 | 1.83 | 1.09 |
| 9 ML YEARS | | | 200 | 111 | 1 | 42 | 788.0 | 3460 | 806 | 428 | 396 | 83 | 38 | 27 | 48 | 315 | 29 | 580 | 24 | 2 | 41 | 44 | .482 | 1 | 0-1 | 2 | 4.42 | 4.52 |

# Stephen Vogt

**Bats:** L **Throws:** R **Pos:** C-44;PH-5;DH-1 VOTE **Ht:** 6'0" **Wt:** 215 **Born:** 11/1/1984 **Age:** 29

| BATTING | | | | | | | | | | | | | | | | | | | | | | BASERUNNING | | | | AVERAGES | | |
|---|---|---|---|---|---|---|---|---|---|---|---|---|---|---|---|---|---|---|---|---|---|---|---|---|---|---|---|---|
| Year | Team | Lg | G | AB | H | 2B | 3B | HR | (Hm | Rd) | TB | R | RBI | RC | TBB | IBB | SO | HBP | SH | SF | SB | CS | SB% | GDP | Avg | OBP | Slg |
| 2009 | Charltt | A+ | 10 | 35 | 6 | 2 | 0 | 0 | (- | -) | 8 | 0 | 3 | 1 | 2 | 0 | 4 | 0 | 0 | 0 | 0 | 1 | .00 | 2 | .171 | .216 | .229 |
| 2010 | Charltt | A+ | 106 | 368 | 127 | 31 | 3 | 8 | (- | -) | 188 | 56 | 47 | 75 | 31 | 4 | 46 | 6 | 3 | 6 | 3 | 1 | .75 | 5 | .345 | .399 | .511 |
| 2011 | Mont | AA | 97 | 386 | 116 | 21 | 6 | 13 | (- | -) | 188 | 52 | 85 | 66 | 30 | 3 | 51 | 1 | 0 | 10 | 4 | 2 | .67 | 9 | .301 | .344 | .487 |
| 2011 | Drham | AAA | 31 | 124 | 36 | 14 | 1 | 4 | (- | -) | 64 | 15 | 20 | 19 | 4 | 0 | 29 | 0 | 0 | 3 | 0 | 0 | - | 4 | .290 | .305 | .516 |
| 2012 | Drham | AAA | 94 | 349 | 95 | 18 | 4 | 9 | (- | -) | 148 | 48 | 43 | 54 | 42 | 2 | 61 | 1 | 2 | 2 | 1 | 0 | 1.00 | 3 | .272 | .350 | .424 |
| 2013 | Scrmto | AAA | 75 | 296 | 96 | 21 | 3 | 13 | (- | -) | 162 | 55 | 58 | 63 | 38 | 0 | 45 | 0 | 1 | 3 | 0 | 1 | .00 | 7 | .324 | .398 | .547 |
| 2012 | TB | AL | 18 | 25 | 0 | 0 | 0 | 0 | (0 | 0) | 0 | 0 | 0 | 0 | 2 | 0 | 2 | 0 | 0 | 0 | 0 | 0 | - | 0 | .000 | .074 | .000 |
| 2013 | Oak | AL | 47 | 135 | 34 | 6 | 1 | 4 | (3 | 1) | 54 | 18 | 16 | 15 | 9 | 1 | 28 | 0 | 2 | 2 | 0 | 1 | .00 | 2 | .252 | .295 | .400 |
| 2 ML YEARS | | | 65 | 160 | 34 | 6 | 1 | 4 | (3 | 1) | 54 | 18 | 16 | 15 | 11 | 1 | 30 | 0 | 2 | 2 | 0 | 1 | .00 | 2 | .213 | .260 | .338 |

# Edinson Volquez

**Pitches:** R **Bats:** R **Pos:** SP-32; RP-1 VOLE-kezz **Ht:** 6'0" **Wt:** 225 **Born:** 7/3/1983 **Age:** 30

| HOW MUCH HE PITCHED | | | | | | | | | WHAT HE GAVE UP | | | | | | | | | | | | THE RESULTS | | | | | | | |
|---|---|---|---|---|---|---|---|---|---|---|---|---|---|---|---|---|---|---|---|---|---|---|---|---|---|---|---|---|
| Year | Team | Lg | G | GS | CG | GF | IP | BFP | H | R | ER | HR | SH | SF | HB | TBB | IBB | SO | WP | Bk | W | L | Pct | Sh | Sv-Op | Hld | ERC | ERA |
| 2005 | Tex | AL | 6 | 3 | 0 | 0 | 12.2 | 75 | 25 | 22 | 20 | 3 | 0 | 1 | 2 | 10 | 0 | 11 | 0 | 0 | 0 | 4 | .000 | 0 | 0-0 | 0 | 14.15 | 14.21 |
| 2006 | Tex | AL | 8 | 8 | 0 | 0 | 33.1 | 164 | 52 | 28 | 27 | 7 | 0 | 1 | 1 | 17 | 0 | 15 | 0 | 0 | 1 | 6 | .143 | 0 | 0-0 | 0 | 9.27 | 7.29 |
| 2007 | Tex | AL | 6 | 6 | 0 | 0 | 34.0 | 149 | 34 | 18 | 17 | 4 | 0 | 2 | 2 | 15 | 0 | 29 | 0 | 0 | 2 | 1 | .667 | 0 | 0-0 | 0 | 4.63 | 4.50 |
| 2008 | Cin | NL | 33 | 32 | 0 | 1 | 196.0 | 838 | 167 | 82 | 70 | 14 | 6 | 5 | **14** | 93 | 5 | 206 | 10 | 1 | 17 | 6 | .739 | 0 | 0-0 | 0 | 3.61 | 3.21 |
| 2009 | Cin | NL | 9 | 9 | 0 | 0 | 49.2 | 218 | 34 | 25 | 24 | 6 | 2 | 1 | 5 | 32 | 0 | 47 | 2 | 1 | 4 | 2 | .667 | 0 | 0-0 | 0 | 3.77 | 4.35 |
| 2010 | Cin | NL | 12 | 12 | 0 | 0 | 62.2 | 275 | 59 | 30 | 30 | 6 | 3 | 1 | 3 | 35 | 0 | 67 | 5 | 0 | 4 | 3 | .571 | 0 | 0-0 | 0 | 4.60 | 4.31 |
| 2011 | Cin | NL | 20 | 20 | 0 | 0 | 108.2 | 489 | 106 | 72 | 69 | 19 | 5 | 6 | 4 | 65 | 3 | 104 | 5 | 2 | 5 | 7 | .417 | 0 | 0-0 | 0 | 5.42 | 5.71 |
| 2012 | SD | NL | 32 | 32 | 1 | 0 | 182.2 | 802 | 160 | 88 | 84 | 14 | 5 | 4 | 9 | **105** | 6 | 174 | 9 | 1 | 11 | 11 | .500 | 1 | 0-0 | 0 | 4.04 | 4.14 |
| 2013 | 2 Tms | NL | 33 | 32 | 0 | 0 | 170.1 | 777 | 193 | **114** | **108** | 19 | 9 | 4 | 3 | 77 | 2 | 142 | 16 | 0 | 9 | 12 | .429 | 0 | 0-0 | 0 | 5.11 | 5.71 |
| 13 | SD | NL | 27 | 27 | 0 | 0 | 142.1 | 659 | 168 | 100 | 95 | 14 | 7 | 3 | 3 | 69 | 2 | 116 | 11 | 0 | 9 | 10 | .474 | 0 | 0-0 | 0 | 5.45 | 6.01 |
| 13 | LAD | NL | 6 | 5 | 0 | 0 | 28.0 | 118 | 25 | 14 | 13 | 5 | 2 | 1 | 0 | 8 | 0 | 26 | 5 | 0 | 0 | 2 | .000 | 0 | 0-0 | 0 | 3.45 | 4.18 |
| Postseason | | | 1 | 1 | 0 | 0 | 1.2 | 11 | 4 | 4 | 4 | 0 | 0 | 1 | 0 | 2 | 0 | 0 | 0 | 0 | 0 | 1 | .000 | 0 | 0-0 | 0 | 15.90 | 21.60 |
| 9 ML YEARS | | | 159 | 154 | 1 | 1 | 850.0 | 3787 | 830 | 479 | 449 | 92 | 30 | 25 | 43 | 449 | 16 | 795 | 47 | 5 | 53 | 52 | .505 | 1 | 0-0 | 0 | 4.68 | 4.75 |

# Chris Volstad

**Pitches:** R **Bats:** R **Pos:** RP-6 VOHL-stadd **Ht:** 6'8" **Wt:** 230 **Born:** 9/23/1986 **Age:** 27

| HOW MUCH HE PITCHED | | | | | | | | | WHAT HE GAVE UP | | | | | | | | | | | | THE RESULTS | | | | | | | |
|---|---|---|---|---|---|---|---|---|---|---|---|---|---|---|---|---|---|---|---|---|---|---|---|---|---|---|---|---|
| Year | Team | Lg | G | GS | CG | GF | IP | BFP | H | R | ER | HR | SH | SF | HB | TBB | IBB | SO | WP | Bk | W | L | Pct | Sh | Sv-Op | Hld | ERC | ERA |
| 2013 | ColSpr* | AAA | 23 | 22 | 2 | 0 | 127.2 | 561 | 156 | 68 | 65 | 12 | 8 | 1 | 2 | 44 | 1 | 57 | 5 | 0 | 7 | 6 | .538 | 0 | 0-- | - | 5.25 | 4.58 |
| 2008 | Fla | NL | 15 | 14 | 0 | 0 | 84.1 | 365 | 76 | 30 | 27 | 3 | 6 | 1 | 5 | 36 | 4 | 52 | 0 | 0 | 6 | 4 | .600 | 0 | 0-0 | 0 | 3.30 | 2.88 |
| 2009 | Fla | NL | 29 | 29 | 1 | 0 | 159.0 | 682 | 169 | 100 | 92 | 29 | 8 | 3 | 3 | 59 | 3 | 107 | 8 | 0 | 9 | 13 | .409 | 1 | 0-0 | 0 | 5.05 | 5.21 |
| 2010 | Fla | NL | 30 | 30 | 2 | 0 | 175.0 | 758 | 187 | 94 | 89 | 17 | 8 | 7 | 8 | 60 | 5 | 102 | 8 | 1 | 12 | 9 | .571 | 1 | 0-0 | 0 | 4.38 | 4.58 |

| Year Team | Lg | G | GS | CG | GF | IP | BFP | H | R | ER | HR | SH | SF | HB | TBB | IBB | SO | WP | Bk | W | L | Pct | Sh | Sv-Op | Hld | ERC | ERA |
|---|---|---|---|---|---|---|---|---|---|---|---|---|---|---|---|---|---|---|---|---|---|---|---|---|---|---|---|
| HOW MUCH HE PITCHED | | | | | | | | WHAT HE GAVE UP | | | | | | | | | | | | THE RESULTS | | | | | | | |
| 2011 Fla | NL | 29 | 29 | 0 | 0 | 165.2 | 719 | 187 | 96 | 90 | 23 | 12 | **10** | 1 | 49 | 6 | 117 | 2 | 1 | 5 | 13 | .278 | 0 | 0-0 | 0 | 4.63 | 4.89 |
| 2012 ChC | NL | 21 | 21 | 0 | 0 | 111.1 | 507 | 137 | 81 | 78 | 16 | 5 | 8 | 3 | 43 | 4 | 61 | 2 | 1 | 3 | 12 | .200 | 0 | 0-0 | 0 | 5.73 | 6.31 |
| 2013 Col | NL | 6 | 0 | 0 | 1 | 8.1 | 47 | 19 | 10 | 10 | 1 | 0 | 0 | 2 | 1 | 0 | 3 | 0 | 0 | 0 | 0 | - | 0 | 0-0 | 1 | 12.25 | 10.80 |
| 6 ML YEARS | | 130 | 123 | 3 | 1 | 703.2 | 3078 | 775 | 411 | 386 | 89 | 39 | 29 | 22 | 248 | 22 | 442 | 20 | 3 | 35 | 51 | .407 | 2 | 0-0 | 1 | 4.75 | 4.94 |

## Joey Votto

**Bats:** L **Throws:** R **Pos:** 1B-161;PH-1 — VAH-toe — **Ht:** 6'2" **Wt:** 220 **Born:** 9/10/1983 **Age:** 30

| Year Team | Lg | G | AB | H | 2B | 3B | HR | (Hm | Rd) | TB | R | RBI | RC | TBB | IBB | SO | HBP | SH | SF | SB | CS | SB% | GDP | Avg | OBP | Slg |
|---|---|---|---|---|---|---|---|---|---|---|---|---|---|---|---|---|---|---|---|---|---|---|---|---|---|---|
| BATTING | | | | | | | | | | | | | | | | | | | | BASERUNNING | | | | AVERAGES | | |
| 2007 Cin | NL | 24 | 84 | 27 | 7 | 0 | 4 | (4 | 0) | 46 | 11 | 17 | 17 | 5 | 1 | 15 | 0 | 0 | 0 | 1 | 0 | 1.00 | 0 | .321 | .360 | .548 |
| 2008 Cin | NL | 151 | 526 | 156 | 32 | 3 | 24 | (14 | 10) | 266 | 69 | 84 | 91 | 59 | 9 | 102 | 2 | 0 | 2 | 7 | 5 | .58 | 7 | .297 | .368 | .506 |
| 2009 Cin | NL | 131 | 469 | 151 | 38 | 1 | 25 | (14 | 11) | 266 | 82 | 84 | 99 | 70 | 10 | 106 | 4 | 0 | 1 | 4 | 1 | .80 | 8 | .322 | .414 | .567 |
| 2010 Cin | NL | 150 | 547 | 177 | 36 | 2 | 37 | (18 | 19) | 328 | 106 | 113 | **132** | 91 | 8 | 125 | 7 | 0 | 3 | 16 | 5 | .76 | 11 | .324 | **.424** | **.600** |
| 2011 Cin | NL | 161 | 599 | 185 | **40** | 3 | 29 | (13 | 16) | 318 | 101 | 103 | **131** | **110** | 15 | 129 | 4 | 0 | 6 | 8 | 6 | .57 | 20 | .309 | **.416** | .531 |
| 2012 Cin | NL | 111 | 374 | 126 | 44 | 0 | 14 | (10 | 4) | 212 | 59 | 56 | 97 | **94** | **18** | 85 | 5 | 0 | 2 | 5 | 3 | .63 | 8 | .337 | **.474** | .567 |
| 2013 Cin | NL | **162** | 581 | 177 | 30 | 3 | 24 | (11 | 13) | 285 | 101 | 73 | 121 | **135** | **19** | 138 | 4 | 0 | 6 | 6 | 3 | .67 | 15 | .305 | **.435** | .491 |
| Postseason | | 8 | 28 | 8 | 0 | 0 | 0 | (0 | 0) | 8 | 3 | 1 | 3 | 4 | 0 | 7 | 0 | 0 | 1 | 0 | 0 | - | 1 | .286 | .364 | .286 |
| 7 ML YEARS | | 890 | 3180 | 999 | 227 | 12 | 157 | (84 | 73) | 1721 | 529 | 530 | 688 | 564 | 80 | 700 | 26 | 0 | 20 | 47 | 23 | .67 | 69 | .314 | .419 | .541 |

## Michael Wacha

**Pitches:** R **Bats:** R **Pos:** SP-9; RP-6 — WOCK-uh — **Ht:** 6'6" **Wt:** 210 **Born:** 7/1/1991 **Age:** 22

| Year Team | Lg | G | GS | CG | GF | IP | BFP | H | R | ER | HR | SH | SF | HB | TBB | IBB | SO | WP | Bk | W | L | Pct | Sh | Sv-Op | Hld | ERC | ERA |
|---|---|---|---|---|---|---|---|---|---|---|---|---|---|---|---|---|---|---|---|---|---|---|---|---|---|---|---|
| HOW MUCH HE PITCHED | | | | | | | | WHAT HE GAVE UP | | | | | | | | | | | | THE RESULTS | | | | | | | |
| 2012 Cards | R | 3 | 2 | 0 | 0 | 5.0 | 19 | 4 | 1 | 1 | 1 | 1 | 0 | 0 | 0 | 0 | 7 | 0 | 0 | 0 | 0 | - | 0 | 0-- | - | 2.06 | 1.80 |
| 2012 PlmBh | A+ | 4 | 0 | 0 | 2 | 8.0 | 26 | 1 | 0 | 0 | 0 | 0 | 0 | 0 | 1 | 0 | 16 | 1 | 0 | 0 | 0 | - | 0 | 0-- | - | 0.11 | 0.00 |
| 2012 Sprgfld | AA | 4 | 0 | 0 | 0 | 8.0 | 30 | 3 | 1 | 1 | 0 | 0 | 0 | 0 | 3 | 0 | 17 | 1 | 0 | 0 | 0 | - | 0 | 0-- | - | 0.85 | 1.13 |
| 2013 Memp | AAA | 15 | 15 | 0 | 0 | 85.0 | 333 | 65 | 26 | 25 | 9 | 3 | 2 | 0 | 19 | 0 | 73 | 5 | 0 | 5 | 3 | .625 | 0 | 0-- | - | 2.25 | 2.65 |
| 2013 StL | NL | 15 | 9 | 0 | 2 | 64.2 | 260 | 52 | 20 | 20 | 5 | 1 | 3 | 0 | 19 | 0 | 65 | 3 | 0 | 4 | 1 | .800 | 0 | 0-1 | 0 | 2.52 | 2.78 |

## Neil Wagner

**Pitches:** R **Bats:** R **Pos:** RP-36 — **Ht:** 6'0" **Wt:** 215 **Born:** 1/1/1984 **Age:** 30

| Year Team | Lg | G | GS | CG | GF | IP | BFP | H | R | ER | HR | SH | SF | HB | TBB | IBB | SO | WP | Bk | W | L | Pct | Sh | Sv-Op | Hld | ERC | ERA |
|---|---|---|---|---|---|---|---|---|---|---|---|---|---|---|---|---|---|---|---|---|---|---|---|---|---|---|---|
| HOW MUCH HE PITCHED | | | | | | | | WHAT HE GAVE UP | | | | | | | | | | | | THE RESULTS | | | | | | | |
| 2009 Akron | AA | 46 | 0 | 0 | 24 | 61.0 | 262 | 48 | 24 | 20 | 3 | 3 | 2 | 1 | 32 | 2 | 69 | 6 | 0 | 1 | 3 | .250 | 0 | 2-- | - | 3.01 | 2.95 |
| 2010 Akron | AA | 13 | 0 | 0 | 9 | 14.1 | 70 | 17 | 12 | 10 | 0 | 2 | 0 | 1 | 7 | 0 | 15 | 0 | 0 | 1 | 1 | .500 | 0 | 4-- | - | 4.70 | 6.28 |
| 2010 Mdlnd | AA | 33 | 0 | 0 | 8 | 48.2 | 223 | 55 | 25 | 20 | 1 | 1 | 0 | 0 | 27 | 4 | 45 | 3 | 0 | 6 | 2 | .750 | 0 | 1-- | - | 4.66 | 3.70 |
| 2011 Mdlnd | AA | 28 | 0 | 0 | 14 | 37.1 | 155 | 31 | 18 | 14 | 0 | 3 | 0 | 1 | 13 | 2 | 53 | 2 | 0 | 1 | 3 | .250 | 0 | 4-- | - | 2.33 | 3.38 |
| 2011 Scrmto | AAA | 22 | 0 | 0 | 9 | 29.0 | 122 | 27 | 10 | 10 | 2 | 0 | 0 | 0 | 10 | 0 | 34 | 0 | 0 | 2 | 1 | .667 | 0 | 2-- | - | 3.27 | 3.10 |
| 2012 Scrmto | AAA | 15 | 0 | 0 | 6 | 19.2 | 85 | 20 | 13 | 12 | 1 | 0 | 1 | 2 | 6 | 1 | 24 | 4 | 0 | 1 | 1 | .500 | 0 | 1-- | - | 3.77 | 5.49 |
| 2012 Tucsn | AAA | 31 | 0 | 0 | 6 | 43.0 | 200 | 57 | 30 | 29 | 2 | 0 | 4 | 0 | 17 | 1 | 32 | 5 | 1 | 3 | 1 | .750 | 0 | 0-- | - | 5.44 | 6.07 |
| 2013 Buffalo | AAA | 23 | 0 | 0 | 22 | 23.2 | 90 | 13 | 2 | 2 | 0 | 1 | 0 | 2 | 9 | 0 | 38 | 1 | 0 | 1 | 0 | 1.000 | 0 | 16-- | - | 1.57 | 0.76 |
| 2011 Oak | AL | 6 | 0 | 0 | 5 | 5.0 | 24 | 6 | 7 | 4 | 1 | 0 | 0 | 1 | 3 | 0 | 4 | 0 | 0 | 0 | 0 | - | 0 | 0-0 | 0 | 7.98 | 7.20 |
| 2013 Tor | AL | 36 | 0 | 0 | 8 | 38.0 | 161 | 39 | 17 | 16 | 5 | 2 | 1 | 1 | 13 | 1 | 33 | 3 | 1 | 2 | 4 | .333 | 0 | 0-1 | 10 | 4.36 | 3.79 |
| 2 ML YEARS | | 42 | 0 | 0 | 13 | 43.0 | 185 | 45 | 24 | 20 | 6 | 2 | 1 | 2 | 16 | 1 | 37 | 3 | 1 | 2 | 4 | .333 | 0 | 0-1 | 10 | 4.75 | 4.19 |

## Adam Wainwright

**Pitches:** R **Bats:** R **Pos:** SP-34 — **Ht:** 6'7" **Wt:** 235 **Born:** 8/30/1981 **Age:** 32

| Year Team | Lg | G | GS | CG | GF | IP | BFP | H | R | ER | HR | SH | SF | HB | TBB | IBB | SO | WP | Bk | W | L | Pct | Sh | Sv-Op | Hld | ERC | ERA |
|---|---|---|---|---|---|---|---|---|---|---|---|---|---|---|---|---|---|---|---|---|---|---|---|---|---|---|---|
| HOW MUCH HE PITCHED | | | | | | | | WHAT HE GAVE UP | | | | | | | | | | | | THE RESULTS | | | | | | | |
| 2005 StL | NL | 2 | 0 | 0 | 1 | 2.0 | 9 | 2 | 3 | 3 | 1 | 0 | 0 | 0 | 1 | 0 | 0 | 0 | 0 | 0 | 0 | - | 0 | 0-0 | 0 | 7.30 | 13.50 |
| 2006 StL | NL | 61 | 0 | 0 | 10 | 75.0 | 309 | 64 | 26 | 26 | 6 | 4 | 1 | 4 | 22 | 2 | 72 | 3 | 0 | 2 | 1 | .667 | 0 | 3-5 | 17 | 2.92 | 3.12 |
| 2007 StL | NL | 32 | 32 | 1 | 0 | 202.0 | 882 | 212 | 93 | 83 | 13 | 9 | 5 | 9 | 70 | 4 | 136 | 6 | 0 | 14 | 12 | .538 | 0 | 0-0 | 0 | 4.01 | 3.70 |
| 2008 StL | NL | 20 | 20 | 1 | 0 | 132.0 | 544 | 122 | 51 | 47 | 12 | 6 | 4 | 3 | 34 | 1 | 91 | 3 | 0 | 11 | 3 | .786 | 0 | 0-0 | 0 | 3.14 | 3.20 |
| 2009 StL | NL | 34 | **34** | 1 | 0 | **233.0** | **970** | 216 | 75 | 68 | 17 | 10 | 5 | 3 | 66 | 1 | 212 | 7 | 0 | **19** | 8 | .704 | 0 | 0-0 | 0 | 3.08 | 2.63 |
| 2010 StL | NL | 33 | 33 | 5 | 0 | 230.1 | 910 | 186 | 68 | 62 | 15 | 13 | 6 | 4 | 56 | 2 | 213 | 2 | 0 | 20 | 11 | .645 | 2 | 0-0 | 0 | **2.36** | 2.42 |
| 2012 StL | NL | 32 | 32 | 3 | 0 | 198.2 | 831 | 196 | 96 | 87 | 15 | 9 | 6 | 6 | 52 | 3 | 184 | 5 | 2 | 14 | 13 | .519 | 2 | 0-0 | 0 | 3.41 | 3.94 |
| 2013 StL | NL | 34 | **34** | **5** | 0 | **241.2** | **956** | **223** | 83 | 79 | 15 | **13** | 2 | 6 | 35 | 2 | 219 | 5 | 0 | **19** | 9 | .679 | **2** | 0-0 | 0 | 2.60 | 2.94 |
| Postseason | | 13 | 4 | 0 | 9 | 32.2 | 132 | 27 | 9 | 9 | 5 | 0 | 0 | 1 | 6 | 0 | 42 | 2 | 0 | 2 | 0 | 1.000 | 0 | 4-5 | 0 | 2.73 | 2.48 |
| 8 ML YEARS | | 248 | 185 | 16 | 11 | 1314.2 | 5411 | 1221 | 495 | 455 | 94 | 64 | 29 | 35 | 336 | 15 | 1127 | 31 | 2 | 99 | 57 | .635 | 6 | 3-5 | 17 | 3.05 | 3.11 |

## Jordan Walden

**Pitches:** R **Bats:** R **Pos:** RP-50 — **Ht:** 6'5" **Wt:** 235 **Born:** 11/16/1987 **Age:** 26

| Year Team | Lg | G | GS | CG | GF | IP | BFP | H | R | ER | HR | SH | SF | HB | TBB | IBB | SO | WP | Bk | W | L | Pct | Sh | Sv-Op | Hld | ERC | ERA |
|---|---|---|---|---|---|---|---|---|---|---|---|---|---|---|---|---|---|---|---|---|---|---|---|---|---|---|---|
| HOW MUCH HE PITCHED | | | | | | | | WHAT HE GAVE UP | | | | | | | | | | | | THE RESULTS | | | | | | | |
| 2013 Gwnntt* | AAA | 1 | 0 | 0 | 0 | 1.0 | 3 | 0 | 0 | 0 | 0 | 0 | 0 | 0 | 0 | 0 | 1 | 0 | 0 | 0 | 0 | - | 0 | 0-- | - | 0.00 | 0.00 |
| 2010 LAA | AL | 16 | 0 | 0 | 5 | 15.1 | 65 | 13 | 4 | 4 | 1 | 0 | 0 | 0 | 7 | 0 | 23 | 1 | 1 | 0 | 1 | .000 | 0 | 1-1 | 6 | 3.21 | 2.35 |
| 2011 LAA | AL | 62 | 0 | 0 | 42 | 60.1 | 253 | 49 | 22 | 20 | 3 | 4 | 2 | 1 | 26 | 3 | 67 | 6 | 0 | 5 | 5 | .500 | 0 | 32-42 | 2 | 2.82 | 2.98 |
| 2012 LAA | AL | 45 | 0 | 0 | 20 | 39.0 | 172 | 35 | 15 | 15 | 3 | 0 | 1 | 0 | 18 | 1 | 48 | 7 | 0 | 3 | 2 | .600 | 0 | 1-2 | 8 | 3.42 | 3.46 |
| 2013 Atl | NL | 50 | 0 | 0 | 9 | 47.0 | 193 | 39 | 19 | 18 | 4 | 1 | 0 | 1 | 14 | 4 | 54 | 6 | 0 | 4 | 3 | .571 | 0 | 1-3 | 14 | 2.63 | 3.45 |
| 4 ML YEARS | | 173 | 0 | 0 | 76 | 161.2 | 683 | 136 | 60 | 57 | 11 | 5 | 3 | 2 | 65 | 8 | 192 | 20 | 1 | 12 | 11 | .522 | 0 | 35-48 | 30 | 2.94 | 3.17 |

# Neil Walker

**Bats:** B **Throws:** R **Pos:** 2B-132;PH-7 **Ht:** 6'3" **Wt:** 210 **Born:** 9/10/1985 **Age:** 28

| BATTING | | | | | | | | | | | | | | | | | | | | BASERUNNING | | | | AVERAGES | | |
|---|---|---|---|---|---|---|---|---|---|---|---|---|---|---|---|---|---|---|---|---|---|---|---|---|---|---|
| Year Team | Lg | G | AB | H | 2B | 3B | HR | (Hm | Rd) | TB | R | RBI | RC | TBB | IBB | SO | HBP | SH | SF | SB | CS | SB% | GDP | Avg | OBP | Slg |
| 2013 Altna* | AA | 4 | 12 | 5 | 1 | 0 | 0 | (- | -) | 6 | 0 | 1 | 2 | 1 | 0 | 2 | 0 | 0 | 0 | 0 | 0 | - | 0 | .417 | .462 | .500 |
| 2013 Indy* | AAA | 3 | 9 | 2 | 1 | 0 | 0 | (- | -) | 3 | 0 | 0 | 1 | 2 | 0 | 1 | 0 | 0 | 0 | 0 | 0 | - | 0 | .222 | .364 | .333 |
| 2009 Pit | NL | 17 | 36 | 7 | 1 | 0 | 0 | (0 | 0) | 8 | 5 | 0 | 2 | 4 | 0 | 11 | 0 | 0 | 0 | 1 | 0 | 1.00 | 1 | .194 | .275 | .222 |
| 2010 Pit | NL | 110 | 426 | 126 | 29 | 3 | 12 | (5 | 7) | 197 | 57 | 66 | 66 | 34 | 1 | 83 | 3 | 2 | 4 | 2 | 3 | .40 | 4 | .296 | .349 | .462 |
| 2011 Pit | NL | 159 | 596 | 163 | 36 | 4 | 12 | (4 | 8) | 243 | 76 | 83 | 77 | 54 | 5 | 112 | 4 | 0 | 8 | 9 | 6 | .60 | 15 | .273 | .334 | .408 |
| 2012 Pit | NL | 129 | 472 | 132 | 27 | 0 | 14 | (7 | 7) | 201 | 62 | 69 | 72 | 47 | 1 | 104 | 2 | 1 | 8 | 7 | 5 | .58 | 11 | .280 | .342 | .426 |
| 2013 Pit | NL | 133 | 478 | 120 | 24 | 4 | 16 | (8 | 8) | 200 | 62 | 53 | 62 | 50 | 4 | 85 | 15 | 5 | 3 | 1 | 2 | .33 | 14 | .251 | .339 | .418 |
| 5 ML YEARS | | 548 | 2008 | 548 | 117 | 11 | 54 | (24 | 30) | 849 | 262 | 271 | 279 | 189 | 11 | 395 | 24 | 8 | 23 | 20 | 16 | .56 | 45 | .273 | .339 | .423 |

# Taijuan Walker

**Pitches:** R **Bats:** R **Pos:** SP-3 TIE-wahn **Ht:** 6'4" **Wt:** 210 **Born:** 8/13/1992 **Age:** 21

| HOW MUCH HE PITCHED | | | | | | | | WHAT HE GAVE UP | | | | | | | | | | | | THE RESULTS | | | | | | | |
|---|---|---|---|---|---|---|---|---|---|---|---|---|---|---|---|---|---|---|---|---|---|---|---|---|---|---|---|
| Year Team | Lg | G | GS | CG | GF | IP | BFP | H | R | ER | HR | SH | SF | HB | TBB | IBB | SO | WP | Bk | W | L | Pct | Sh | Sv-Op | Hld | ERC | ERA |
| 2010 Ms | R | 4 | 0 | 0 | 0 | 7.0 | 27 | 2 | 3 | 1 | 0 | 0 | 0 | 1 | 3 | 0 | 9 | 3 | 0 | 1 | 1 | .500 | 0 | 0-- | - | 0.96 | 1.29 |
| 2011 Clinton | A | 18 | 18 | 1 | 0 | 96.2 | 384 | 69 | 33 | 31 | 4 | 0 | 1 | 3 | 39 | 0 | 113 | 6 | 2 | 6 | 5 | .545 | 0 | 0-- | - | 2.41 | 2.89 |
| 2012 Jacksn | AA | 25 | 25 | 0 | 0 | 126.2 | 550 | 124 | 70 | 66 | 12 | 4 | 3 | 12 | 50 | 0 | 118 | 5 | 0 | 7 | 10 | .412 | 0 | 0-- | - | 4.31 | 4.69 |
| 2013 Jacksn | AA | 14 | 14 | 0 | 0 | 84.0 | 339 | 58 | 31 | 23 | 6 | 3 | 2 | 6 | 30 | 1 | 96 | 4 | 0 | 4 | 7 | .364 | 0 | 0-- | - | 2.38 | 2.46 |
| 2013 Tacom | AAA | 11 | 11 | 0 | 0 | 57.1 | 246 | 54 | 25 | 23 | 5 | 0 | 0 | 2 | 27 | 0 | 64 | 2 | 0 | 5 | 3 | .625 | 0 | 0-- | - | 4.14 | 3.61 |
| 2013 Sea | AL | 3 | 3 | 0 | 0 | 15.0 | 60 | 11 | 7 | 6 | 0 | 0 | 2 | 0 | 4 | 0 | 12 | 0 | 0 | 1 | 0 | 1.000 | 0 | 0-0 | 0 | 1.63 | 3.60 |

# Josh Wall

**Pitches:** R **Bats:** R **Pos:** RP-6 **Ht:** 6'6" **Wt:** 215 **Born:** 1/21/1987 **Age:** 27

| HOW MUCH HE PITCHED | | | | | | | | WHAT HE GAVE UP | | | | | | | | | | | | THE RESULTS | | | | | | | |
|---|---|---|---|---|---|---|---|---|---|---|---|---|---|---|---|---|---|---|---|---|---|---|---|---|---|---|---|
| Year Team | Lg | G | GS | CG | GF | IP | BFP | H | R | ER | HR | SH | SF | HB | TBB | IBB | SO | WP | Bk | W | L | Pct | Sh | Sv-Op | Hld | ERC | ERA |
| 2009 InldEm | A+ | 23 | 22 | 0 | 0 | 111.1 | 506 | 135 | 85 | 74 | 9 | 5 | 4 | 11 | 51 | 1 | 77 | 10 | 1 | 5 | 8 | .385 | 0 | 0-- | - | 5.95 | 5.98 |
| 2010 Gt Lks | A | 26 | 26 | 1 | 0 | 153.0 | 670 | 144 | 80 | 72 | 11 | 1 | 6 | 14 | 68 | 0 | 151 | 20 | 0 | 9 | 7 | .563 | 1 | 0-- | - | 4.08 | 4.24 |
| 2011 Chatt | AA | 51 | 0 | 0 | 22 | 68.2 | 299 | 71 | 34 | 30 | 6 | 3 | 0 | 3 | 27 | 1 | 57 | 4 | 0 | 4 | 5 | .444 | 0 | 1-- | - | 4.32 | 3.93 |
| 2012 Albq | AAA | 55 | 0 | 0 | 48 | 53.2 | 231 | 50 | 30 | 27 | 7 | 1 | 1 | 2 | 20 | 0 | 52 | 4 | 0 | 2 | 1 | .667 | 0 | 28-- | - | 3.90 | 4.53 |
| 2013 Albq | AAA | 25 | 0 | 0 | 11 | 27.1 | 121 | 27 | 19 | 17 | 3 | 2 | 3 | 0 | 16 | 1 | 25 | 6 | 0 | 1 | 2 | .333 | 0 | 3-- | - | 4.81 | 5.60 |
| 2013 NewOr | AAA | 20 | 0 | 0 | 10 | 22.0 | 98 | 23 | 9 | 8 | 0 | 1 | 1 | 1 | 8 | 0 | 21 | 4 | 0 | 1 | 1 | .500 | 0 | 1-- | - | 3.54 | 3.27 |
| 2012 LAD | NL | 7 | 0 | 0 | 6 | 5.2 | 21 | 3 | 3 | 3 | 1 | 0 | 0 | 1 | 1 | 0 | 4 | 2 | 0 | 1 | 0 | 1.000 | 0 | 0-0 | 0 | 2.05 | 4.76 |
| 2013 LAD | NL | 6 | 0 | 0 | 4 | 7.0 | 44 | 17 | 14 | 14 | 2 | 2 | 1 | 0 | 6 | 3 | 7 | 0 | 0 | 0 | 1 | .000 | 0 | 0-0 | 0 | 16.61 | 18.00 |
| 2 ML YEARS | | 13 | 0 | 0 | 10 | 12.2 | 65 | 20 | 17 | 17 | 3 | 2 | 1 | 1 | 7 | 3 | 11 | 2 | 0 | 1 | 1 | .500 | 0 | 0-0 | 0 | 9.38 | 12.08 |

# Brett Wallace

**Bats:** L **Throws:** R **Pos:** 1B-61;3B-9;PH-8;DH-7 **Ht:** 6'2" **Wt:** 235 **Born:** 8/26/1986 **Age:** 27

| BATTING | | | | | | | | | | | | | | | | | | | | BASERUNNING | | | | AVERAGES | | |
|---|---|---|---|---|---|---|---|---|---|---|---|---|---|---|---|---|---|---|---|---|---|---|---|---|---|---|
| Year Team | Lg | G | AB | H | 2B | 3B | HR | (Hm | Rd) | TB | R | RBI | RC | TBB | IBB | SO | HBP | SH | SF | SB | CS | SB% | GDP | Avg | OBP | Slg |
| 2013 OKCity* | AAA | 60 | 233 | 76 | 16 | 2 | 11 | (- | -) | 129 | 36 | 37 | 50 | 24 | 1 | 69 | 4 | 0 | 0 | 1 | 0 | 1.00 | 2 | .326 | .398 | .554 |
| 2010 Hou | NL | 51 | 144 | 32 | 6 | 1 | 2 | (1 | 1) | 46 | 14 | 13 | 10 | 8 | 3 | 50 | 7 | 0 | 0 | 0 | 0 | - | 3 | .222 | .296 | .319 |
| 2011 Hou | NL | 115 | 336 | 87 | 22 | 0 | 5 | (2 | 3) | 124 | 37 | 29 | 31 | 36 | 4 | 91 | 3 | 1 | 2 | 1 | 1 | .50 | 12 | .259 | .334 | .369 |
| 2012 Hou | NL | 66 | 229 | 58 | 10 | 1 | 9 | (1 | 8) | 97 | 24 | 24 | 27 | 18 | 1 | 73 | 6 | 0 | 1 | 0 | 0 | - | 2 | .253 | .323 | .424 |
| 2013 Hou | AL | 79 | 262 | 58 | 14 | 1 | 13 | (7 | 6) | 113 | 35 | 36 | 34 | 18 | 0 | 104 | 5 | 0 | 0 | 1 | 1 | .50 | 5 | .221 | .284 | .431 |
| 4 ML YEARS | | 311 | 971 | 235 | 52 | 3 | 29 | (11 | 18) | 380 | 110 | 102 | 102 | 80 | 8 | 318 | 21 | 1 | 3 | 2 | 2 | .50 | 22 | .242 | .313 | .391 |

# P.J. Walters

**Pitches:** R **Bats:** R **Pos:** SP-8 **Ht:** 6'4" **Wt:** 215 **Born:** 3/12/1985 **Age:** 29

| HOW MUCH HE PITCHED | | | | | | | | WHAT HE GAVE UP | | | | | | | | | | | | THE RESULTS | | | | | | | |
|---|---|---|---|---|---|---|---|---|---|---|---|---|---|---|---|---|---|---|---|---|---|---|---|---|---|---|---|
| Year Team | Lg | G | GS | CG | GF | IP | BFP | H | R | ER | HR | SH | SF | HB | TBB | IBB | SO | WP | Bk | W | L | Pct | Sh | Sv-Op | Hld | ERC | ERA |
| 2013 Roch* | AAA | 19 | 19 | 1 | 0 | 103.1 | 457 | 110 | 54 | 48 | 5 | 4 | 4 | 8 | 46 | 0 | 82 | 6 | 0 | 7 | 5 | .583 | 1 | 0-- | - | 4.61 | 4.18 |
| 2009 StL | NL | 8 | 1 | 0 | 4 | 16.0 | 80 | 21 | 19 | 17 | 6 | 1 | 1 | 0 | 9 | 1 | 14 | 0 | 0 | 0 | 0 | - | 0 | 0-0 | 0 | 8.42 | 9.56 |
| 2010 StL | NL | 7 | 3 | 0 | 3 | 30.0 | 129 | 32 | 20 | 20 | 5 | 1 | 2 | 0 | 10 | 0 | 22 | 0 | 0 | 2 | 0 | 1.000 | 0 | 0-0 | 0 | 4.67 | 6.00 |
| 2011 2 Tms | | 5 | 0 | 0 | 2 | 5.0 | 21 | 3 | 4 | 4 | 1 | 0 | 0 | 0 | 3 | 0 | 4 | 0 | 0 | 0 | 0 | - | 0 | 0-0 | 0 | 3.28 | 7.20 |
| 2012 Min | AL | 12 | 12 | 1 | 0 | 61.2 | 271 | 71 | 41 | 39 | 12 | 1 | 1 | 3 | 22 | 1 | 42 | 1 | 0 | 2 | 5 | .286 | 0 | 0-0 | 0 | 5.75 | 5.69 |
| 2013 Min | AL | 8 | 8 | 0 | 0 | 39.1 | 183 | 51 | 30 | 26 | 5 | 0 | 0 | 1 | 18 | 0 | 22 | 0 | 0 | 2 | 5 | .286 | 0 | 0-0 | 0 | 6.43 | 5.95 |
| 11 StL | NL | 4 | 0 | 0 | 2 | 4.0 | 18 | 3 | 4 | 4 | 1 | 0 | 0 | 0 | 2 | 0 | 3 | 0 | 0 | 0 | 0 | - | 0 | 0-0 | 0 | 3.76 | 9.00 |
| 11 Tor | AL | 1 | 0 | 0 | 0 | 1.0 | 3 | 0 | 0 | 0 | 0 | 0 | 0 | 0 | 1 | 0 | 1 | 0 | 0 | 0 | 0 | - | 0 | 0-0 | 0 | 1.26 | 0.00 |
| 5 ML YEARS | | 40 | 24 | 1 | 9 | 152.0 | 684 | 178 | 114 | 106 | 29 | 3 | 4 | 4 | 62 | 2 | 104 | 1 | 0 | 6 | 10 | .375 | 0 | 0-0 | 0 | 5.89 | 6.28 |

# Zach Walters

**Bats:** B **Throws:** R **Pos:** PH-4;3B-2;SS-2;PR-2 **Ht:** 6'2" **Wt:** 220 **Born:** 9/5/1989 **Age:** 24

| BATTING | | | | | | | | | | | | | | | | | | | | BASERUNNING | | | | AVERAGES | | |
|---|---|---|---|---|---|---|---|---|---|---|---|---|---|---|---|---|---|---|---|---|---|---|---|---|---|---|
| Year Team | Lg | G | AB | H | 2B | 3B | HR | (Hm | Rd) | TB | R | RBI | RC | TBB | IBB | SO | HBP | SH | SF | SB | CS | SB% | GDP | Avg | OBP | Slg |
| 2010 Yakima | A- | 69 | 275 | 83 | 18 | 4 | 4 | (- | -) | 121 | 44 | 43 | 42 | 16 | 1 | 59 | 1 | 1 | 4 | 14 | 4 | .78 | 3 | .302 | .338 | .440 |
| 2011 Sbend | A | 97 | 361 | 109 | 27 | 6 | 9 | (- | -) | 175 | 69 | 56 | 66 | 42 | 1 | 96 | 3 | 3 | 3 | 12 | 10 | .55 | 4 | .302 | .377 | .485 |
| 2011 Ptomc | A+ | 30 | 116 | 34 | 7 | 1 | 0 | (- | -) | 43 | 15 | 11 | 15 | 8 | 0 | 33 | 0 | 1 | 1 | 7 | 1 | .88 | 0 | .293 | .336 | .371 |
| 2012 Ptomc | A+ | 54 | 193 | 52 | 8 | 1 | 5 | (- | -) | 77 | 24 | 24 | 24 | 10 | 1 | 43 | 1 | 0 | 3 | 6 | 3 | .67 | 2 | .269 | .304 | .399 |
| 2012 Hrsbrg | AA | 43 | 164 | 48 | 11 | 4 | 6 | (- | -) | 85 | 23 | 19 | 27 | 8 | 1 | 38 | 0 | 0 | 0 | 1 | 0 | 1.00 | 5 | .293 | .326 | .518 |
| 2012 Syrcse | AAA | 29 | 98 | 21 | 4 | 0 | 1 | (- | -) | 28 | 9 | 6 | 7 | 6 | 0 | 28 | 0 | 1 | 0 | 0 | 0 | - | 2 | .214 | .260 | .286 |
| 2013 Syrcse | AAA | 134 | 487 | 123 | 32 | 5 | 29 | (- | -) | 252 | 69 | 77 | 73 | 20 | 2 | 134 | 5 | 3 | 6 | 4 | 3 | .57 | 7 | .253 | .286 | .517 |
| 2013 Was | NL | 8 | 8 | 3 | 0 | 1 | 0 | (0 | 0) | 5 | 2 | 1 | 2 | 1 | 0 | 0 | 0 | 0 | 0 | 0 | 0 | - | 1 | .375 | .444 | .625 |

## Chien-Ming Wang

**Pitches:** R **Bats:** R **Pos:** SP-6 CHENN-MING WONG **Ht:** 6'4" **Wt:** 225 **Born:** 3/31/1980 **Age:** 34

| HOW MUCH HE PITCHED | | | | | | | | | WHAT HE GAVE UP | | | | | | | | | | | | THE RESULTS | | | | | | | |
|---|---|---|---|---|---|---|---|---|---|---|---|---|---|---|---|---|---|---|---|---|---|---|---|---|---|---|---|---|
| Year | Team | Lg | G | GS | CG | GF | IP | BFP | H | R | ER | HR | SH | SF | HB | TBB | IBB | SO | WP | Bk | W | L | Pct | Sh | Sv-Op | Hld | ERC | ERA |
| 2013 | S-WB* | AAA | 9 | 9 | 1 | 0 | 58.0 | 238 | 57 | 17 | 15 | 2 | 3 | 1 | 1 | 10 | 0 | 25 | 4 | 1 | 4 | 4 | .500 | 0 | 0-- | - | 2.75 | 2.33 |
| 2013 | Buffalo* | AAA | 9 | 8 | 1 | 0 | 51.2 | 210 | 46 | 22 | 20 | 3 | 2 | 1 | 1 | 12 | 0 | 30 | 1 | 0 | 4 | 3 | .571 | 0 | 0-- | - | 2.67 | 3.48 |
| 2005 | NYY | AL | 18 | 17 | 0 | 0 | 116.1 | 486 | 113 | 58 | 52 | 9 | 3 | 4 | 6 | 32 | 3 | 47 | 3 | 0 | 8 | 5 | .615 | 0 | 0-0 | 0 | 3.47 | 4.02 |
| 2006 | NYY | AL | 34 | 33 | 2 | 1 | 218.0 | 900 | 233 | 92 | 88 | 12 | 3 | 2 | 2 | 52 | 4 | 76 | 6 | 1 | **19** | 6 | .760 | 1 | 1-1 | 0 | 3.62 | 3.63 |
| 2007 | NYY | AL | 30 | 30 | 1 | 0 | 199.1 | 823 | 199 | 84 | 82 | 9 | 2 | 3 | 8 | 59 | 1 | 104 | 9 | 1 | 19 | 7 | .731 | 0 | 0-0 | 0 | 3.54 | 3.70 |
| 2008 | NYY | AL | 15 | 15 | 1 | 0 | 95.0 | 402 | 90 | 44 | 43 | 4 | 0 | 3 | 3 | 35 | 1 | 54 | 0 | 0 | 8 | 2 | .800 | 0 | 0-0 | 0 | 3.39 | 4.07 |
| 2009 | NYY | AL | 12 | 9 | 0 | 2 | 42.0 | 206 | 66 | 46 | 45 | 7 | 3 | 1 | 2 | 19 | 1 | 29 | 3 | 0 | 1 | 6 | .143 | 0 | 0-0 | 0 | 8.67 | 9.64 |
| 2011 | Was | NL | 11 | 11 | 0 | 0 | 62.1 | 264 | 67 | 35 | 28 | 8 | 2 | 2 | 1 | 13 | 0 | 25 | 2 | 0 | 4 | 3 | .571 | 0 | 0-0 | 0 | 3.97 | 4.04 |
| 2012 | Was | NL | 10 | 5 | 0 | 0 | 32.1 | 158 | 50 | 24 | 24 | 5 | 4 | 3 | 3 | 15 | 0 | 15 | 5 | 0 | 2 | 3 | .400 | 0 | 0-0 | 0 | 8.80 | 6.68 |
| 2013 | Tor | AL | 6 | 6 | 0 | 0 | 27.0 | 123 | 40 | 24 | 23 | 5 | 0 | 0 | 0 | 9 | 0 | 14 | 2 | 0 | 1 | 2 | .333 | 0 | 0-0 | 0 | 7.66 | 7.67 |
| Postseason | | | 4 | 4 | 0 | 0 | 19.0 | 90 | 28 | 19 | 16 | 5 | 2 | 0 | 3 | 5 | 0 | 7 | 0 | 0 | 1 | 3 | .250 | 0 | 0-0 | 0 | 8.53 | 7.58 |
| 8 ML YEARS | | | 136 | 126 | 4 | 3 | 792.1 | 3362 | 858 | 407 | 385 | 59 | 17 | 18 | 25 | 234 | 10 | 364 | 30 | 2 | 62 | 34 | .646 | 1 | 1-1 | 0 | 4.13 | 4.37 |

## Adam Warren

**Pitches:** R **Bats:** R **Pos:** RP-32; SP-2 **Ht:** 6'1" **Wt:** 200 **Born:** 8/25/1987 **Age:** 26

| HOW MUCH HE PITCHED | | | | | | | | | WHAT HE GAVE UP | | | | | | | | | | | | THE RESULTS | | | | | | | |
|---|---|---|---|---|---|---|---|---|---|---|---|---|---|---|---|---|---|---|---|---|---|---|---|---|---|---|---|---|
| Year | Team | Lg | G | GS | CG | GF | IP | BFP | H | R | ER | HR | SH | SF | HB | TBB | IBB | SO | WP | Bk | W | L | Pct | Sh | Sv-Op | Hld | ERC | ERA |
| 2009 | StlsInd | A- | 12 | 12 | 0 | 0 | 56.2 | 220 | 49 | 12 | 9 | 1 | 1 | 1 | 0 | 10 | 0 | 50 | 3 | 0 | 4 | 2 | .667 | 0 | 0-- | - | 2.11 | 1.43 |
| 2010 | Tampa | A+ | 15 | 15 | 1 | 0 | 81.0 | 333 | 72 | 23 | 20 | 2 | 3 | 1 | 6 | 17 | 0 | 67 | 0 | 0 | 7 | 5 | .583 | 1 | 0-- | - | 2.55 | 2.22 |
| 2010 | Trntn | AA | 10 | 10 | 0 | 0 | 54.1 | 232 | 49 | 26 | 19 | 2 | 0 | 2 | 3 | 16 | 0 | 59 | 4 | 0 | 4 | 2 | .667 | 0 | 0-- | - | 2.85 | 3.15 |
| 2011 | S-WB | AAA | 27 | 27 | 1 | 0 | 152.1 | 650 | 145 | 68 | 61 | 13 | 4 | 3 | 8 | 53 | 0 | 111 | 4 | 0 | 6 | 8 | .429 | 0 | 0-- | - | 3.71 | 3.60 |
| 2012 | S-WB | AAA | 26 | 26 | 2 | 0 | 152.2 | 657 | 167 | 64 | 63 | 11 | 0 | 3 | 4 | 46 | 1 | 107 | 9 | 0 | 7 | 8 | .467 | 1 | 0-- | - | 4.13 | 3.71 |
| 2012 | NYY | AL | 1 | 1 | 0 | 0 | 2.1 | 17 | 8 | 6 | 6 | 2 | 0 | 0 | 0 | 2 | 0 | 1 | 0 | 0 | 0 | 0 | - | 0 | 0-0 | 0 | 33.34 | 23.14 |
| 2013 | NYY | AL | 34 | 2 | 0 | 17 | 77.0 | 331 | 80 | 29 | 29 | 10 | 0 | 0 | 2 | 30 | 2 | 64 | 3 | 0 | 3 | 2 | .600 | 0 | 1-1 | 1 | 4.60 | 3.39 |
| 2 ML YEARS | | | 35 | 3 | 0 | 17 | 79.1 | 348 | 88 | 35 | 35 | 12 | 0 | 0 | 2 | 32 | 2 | 65 | 3 | 0 | 3 | 2 | .600 | 0 | 1-1 | 1 | 5.23 | 3.97 |

## Logan Watkins

**Bats:** L **Throws:** R **Pos:** PH-16;2B-9;PR-2 **Ht:** 5'11" **Wt:** 175 **Born:** 8/29/1989 **Age:** 24

| BATTING | | | | | | | | | | | | | | | | | | | | | BASERUNNING | | | | AVERAGES | | |
|---|---|---|---|---|---|---|---|---|---|---|---|---|---|---|---|---|---|---|---|---|---|---|---|---|---|---|---|
| Year | Team | Lg | G | AB | H | 2B | 3B | HR | (Hm | Rd) | TB | R | RBI | RC | TBB | IBB | SO | HBP | SH | SF | SB | CS | SB% | GDP | Avg | OBP | Slg |
| 2009 | Boise | A- | 72 | 279 | 91 | 14 | 2 | 0 | (- | -) | 109 | 48 | 29 | 45 | 27 | 1 | 31 | 3 | 7 | 2 | 14 | 7 | .67 | 1 | .326 | .389 | .391 |
| 2010 | Peoria | A | 118 | 440 | 115 | 15 | 8 | 1 | (- | -) | 149 | 69 | 30 | 58 | 58 | 0 | 97 | 3 | 18 | 1 | 19 | 10 | .66 | 5 | .261 | .351 | .339 |
| 2011 | Dytona | A+ | 125 | 441 | 124 | 15 | 12 | 5 | (- | -) | 178 | 70 | 45 | 68 | 44 | 0 | 97 | 7 | 5 | 5 | 21 | 5 | .81 | 0 | .281 | .352 | .404 |
| 2012 | Tenn | AA | 133 | 488 | 137 | 20 | 11 | 9 | (- | -) | 206 | 93 | 52 | 88 | 76 | 0 | 97 | 7 | 14 | 3 | 28 | 7 | .80 | 7 | .281 | .383 | .422 |
| 2013 | Iowa | AAA | 107 | 412 | 100 | 18 | 7 | 8 | (- | -) | 156 | 51 | 26 | 54 | 52 | 1 | 98 | 4 | 3 | 1 | 10 | 9 | .53 | 3 | .243 | .333 | .379 |
| 2013 | ChC | NL | 27 | 38 | 8 | 1 | 0 | 0 | (0 | 0) | 9 | 2 | 0 | 3 | 3 | 0 | 14 | 0 | 1 | 0 | 0 | 0 | - | 0 | .211 | .268 | .237 |

## Tony Watson

**Pitches:** L **Bats:** L **Pos:** RP-67 **Ht:** 6'4" **Wt:** 225 **Born:** 5/30/1985 **Age:** 29

| HOW MUCH HE PITCHED | | | | | | | | | WHAT HE GAVE UP | | | | | | | | | | | | THE RESULTS | | | | | | | |
|---|---|---|---|---|---|---|---|---|---|---|---|---|---|---|---|---|---|---|---|---|---|---|---|---|---|---|---|---|
| Year | Team | Lg | G | GS | CG | GF | IP | BFP | H | R | ER | HR | SH | SF | HB | TBB | IBB | SO | WP | Bk | W | L | Pct | Sh | Sv-Op | Hld | ERC | ERA |
| 2011 | Pit | NL | 43 | 0 | 0 | 6 | 41.0 | 174 | 34 | 18 | 18 | 6 | 2 | 1 | 1 | 20 | 4 | 37 | 0 | 0 | 2 | 2 | .500 | 0 | 0-1 | 10 | 3.75 | 3.95 |
| 2012 | Pit | NL | 68 | 0 | 0 | 10 | 53.1 | 215 | 37 | 21 | 20 | 5 | 2 | 2 | 1 | 23 | 1 | 53 | 1 | 0 | 5 | 2 | .714 | 0 | 0-2 | 16 | 2.62 | 3.38 |
| 2013 | Pit | NL | 67 | 0 | 0 | 14 | 71.2 | 280 | 51 | 19 | 19 | 5 | 3 | 1 | 6 | 12 | 1 | 54 | 2 | 0 | 3 | 1 | .750 | 0 | 2-4 | 22 | 1.88 | 2.39 |
| 3 ML YEARS | | | 178 | 0 | 0 | 30 | 166.0 | 669 | 122 | 58 | 57 | 16 | 7 | 4 | 8 | 55 | 6 | 144 | 3 | 0 | 10 | 5 | .667 | 0 | 2-7 | 48 | 2.55 | 3.09 |

## Jered Weaver

**Pitches:** R **Bats:** R **Pos:** SP-24 **Ht:** 6'7" **Wt:** 210 **Born:** 10/4/1982 **Age:** 31

| HOW MUCH HE PITCHED | | | | | | | | | WHAT HE GAVE UP | | | | | | | | | | | | THE RESULTS | | | | | | | |
|---|---|---|---|---|---|---|---|---|---|---|---|---|---|---|---|---|---|---|---|---|---|---|---|---|---|---|---|---|
| Year | Team | Lg | G | GS | CG | GF | IP | BFP | H | R | ER | HR | SH | SF | HB | TBB | IBB | SO | WP | Bk | W | L | Pct | Sh | Sv-Op | Hld | ERC | ERA |
| 2006 | LAA | AL | 19 | 19 | 0 | 0 | 123.0 | 490 | 94 | 36 | 35 | 15 | 2 | 2 | 3 | 33 | 1 | 105 | 2 | 0 | 11 | 2 | .846 | 0 | 0-0 | 0 | 2.57 | 2.56 |
| 2007 | LAA | AL | 28 | 28 | 0 | 0 | 161.0 | 695 | 178 | 77 | 70 | 17 | 5 | 5 | 2 | 45 | 3 | 115 | 4 | 0 | 13 | 7 | .650 | 0 | 0-0 | 0 | 4.24 | 3.91 |
| 2008 | LAA | AL | 30 | 30 | 0 | 0 | 176.2 | 745 | 173 | 88 | 85 | 20 | 1 | 4 | 6 | 54 | 4 | 152 | 3 | 0 | 11 | 10 | .524 | 0 | 0-0 | 0 | 3.80 | 4.33 |
| 2009 | LAA | AL | 33 | 33 | 4 | 0 | 211.0 | 882 | 196 | 91 | 88 | 26 | 6 | 8 | 4 | 66 | 3 | 174 | 3 | 0 | 16 | 8 | .667 | 2 | 0-0 | 0 | 3.56 | 3.75 |
| 2010 | LAA | AL | 34 | **34** | 0 | 0 | 224.1 | 905 | 187 | 83 | 75 | 23 | 2 | 5 | 0 | 54 | 0 | **233** | 7 | 1 | 13 | 12 | .520 | 0 | 0-0 | 0 | 2.59 | 3.01 |
| 2011 | LAA | AL | 33 | 33 | 4 | 0 | 235.2 | 926 | 182 | 65 | 63 | 20 | 5 | 5 | 3 | 56 | 0 | 198 | 8 | 0 | 18 | 8 | .692 | 2 | 0-0 | 0 | 2.27 | 2.41 |
| 2012 | LAA | AL | 30 | 30 | 3 | 0 | 188.2 | 739 | 147 | 63 | 59 | 20 | 0 | 4 | 4 | 45 | 0 | 142 | 2 | 0 | **20** | 5 | **.800** | 2 | 0-0 | 0 | 2.48 | 2.81 |
| 2013 | LAA | AL | 24 | 24 | 0 | 0 | 154.1 | 634 | 139 | 58 | 56 | 17 | 1 | 3 | 7 | 37 | 0 | 117 | 2 | 0 | 11 | 8 | .579 | 0 | 0-0 | 0 | 3.17 | 3.27 |
| Postseason | | | 6 | 3 | 0 | 2 | 20.2 | 83 | 12 | 6 | 6 | 5 | 0 | 0 | 0 | 10 | 0 | 22 | 0 | 0 | 2 | 1 | .667 | 0 | 0-0 | 1 | 3.04 | 2.61 |
| 8 ML YEARS | | | 231 | 231 | 11 | 0 | 1474.2 | 6016 | 1296 | 561 | 531 | 158 | 22 | 36 | 29 | 390 | 11 | 1236 | 31 | 1 | 113 | 60 | .653 | 6 | 0-0 | 0 | 3.03 | 3.24 |

## Daniel Webb

**Pitches:** R **Bats:** R **Pos:** RP-9 **Ht:** 6'3" **Wt:** 210 **Born:** 8/18/1989 **Age:** 24

| HOW MUCH HE PITCHED | | | | | | | | | WHAT HE GAVE UP | | | | | | | | | | | | THE RESULTS | | | | | | | |
|---|---|---|---|---|---|---|---|---|---|---|---|---|---|---|---|---|---|---|---|---|---|---|---|---|---|---|---|---|
| Year | Team | Lg | G | GS | CG | GF | IP | BFP | H | R | ER | HR | SH | SF | HB | TBB | IBB | SO | WP | Bk | W | L | Pct | Sh | Sv-Op | Hld | ERC | ERA |
| 2010 | Auburn | A- | 13 | 13 | 0 | 0 | 56.2 | 270 | 69 | 43 | 33 | 4 | 4 | 0 | 9 | 26 | 0 | 39 | 2 | 1 | 0 | 6 | .000 | 0 | 0-- | - | 5.95 | 5.24 |
| 2010 | Lnsng | A | 2 | 2 | 0 | 0 | 11.2 | 50 | 8 | 7 | 3 | 0 | 1 | 1 | 1 | 6 | 0 | 4 | 2 | 0 | 1 | 1 | .500 | 0 | 0-- | - | 2.42 | 2.31 |
| 2011 | Lnsng | A | 18 | 12 | 0 | 3 | 66.0 | 299 | 80 | 53 | 41 | 7 | 2 | 3 | 6 | 24 | 0 | 51 | 3 | 1 | 4 | 5 | .444 | 0 | 2-- | - | 5.62 | 5.59 |
| 2011 | B Jays | R | 1 | 0 | 0 | 1 | 1.1 | 6 | 2 | 0 | 0 | 0 | 0 | 0 | 0 | 0 | 0 | 0 | 1 | 0 | 0 | 0 | - | 0 | 0-- | - | 4.47 | 0.00 |
| 2012 | Knapol | A | 31 | 4 | 0 | 12 | 62.0 | 287 | 73 | 51 | 40 | 2 | 5 | 3 | 3 | 27 | 0 | 50 | 7 | 0 | 1 | 8 | .111 | 0 | 3-- | - | 4.82 | 5.81 |

| | | | HOW MUCH HE PITCHED | | | | | | WHAT HE GAVE UP | | | | | | | | | | | | THE RESULTS | | | | | | | |
|---|---|---|---|---|---|---|---|---|---|---|---|---|---|---|---|---|---|---|---|---|---|---|---|---|---|---|---|---|
| Year | Team | Lg | G | GS | CG | GF | IP | BFP | H | R | ER | HR | SH | SF | HB | TBB | IBB | SO | WP | Bk | W | L | Pct | Sh | Sv-Op | Hld | ERC | ERA |
| 2013 | WinSa | A+ | 8 | 0 | 0 | 4 | 15.0 | 60 | 10 | 2 | 0 | 0 | 0 | 0 | 0 | 5 | 0 | 19 | 1 | 1 | 1 | 0 | 1.000 | 0 | 2-- | - | 1.57 | 0.00 |
| 2013 | Brham | AA | 13 | 0 | 0 | 10 | 20.1 | 78 | 11 | 4 | 4 | 0 | 1 | 0 | 1 | 5 | 0 | 21 | 1 | 0 | 0 | 0 | - | 0 | 4-- | - | 1.13 | 1.77 |
| 2013 | Charltt | AAA | 21 | 0 | 0 | 14 | 27.1 | 125 | 24 | 15 | 9 | 1 | 2 | 0 | 0 | 17 | 0 | 38 | 5 | 0 | 1 | 1 | .500 | 0 | 4-- | - | 3.63 | 2.96 |
| 2013 | CWS | AL | 9 | 0 | 0 | 4 | 11.1 | 46 | 9 | 4 | 4 | 0 | 0 | 1 | 0 | 4 | 0 | 10 | 1 | 0 | 0 | 0 | - | 0 | 0-0 | 1 | 2.20 | 3.18 |

# Ryan Webb

**Pitches:** R **Bats:** R **Pos:** RP-66 **Ht:** 6'6" **Wt:** 245 **Born:** 2/5/1986 **Age:** 28

| | | | HOW MUCH HE PITCHED | | | | | | WHAT HE GAVE UP | | | | | | | | | | | | THE RESULTS | | | | | | | |
|---|---|---|---|---|---|---|---|---|---|---|---|---|---|---|---|---|---|---|---|---|---|---|---|---|---|---|---|---|
| Year | Team | Lg | G | GS | CG | GF | IP | BFP | H | R | ER | HR | SH | SF | HB | TBB | IBB | SO | WP | Bk | W | L | Pct | Sh | Sv-Op | Hld | ERC | ERA |
| 2009 | SD | NL | 28 | 0 | 0 | 9 | 25.2 | 117 | 27 | 14 | 11 | 3 | 2 | 1 | 1 | 11 | 1 | 19 | 4 | 0 | 2 | 1 | .667 | 0 | 0-0 | 6 | 4.54 | 3.86 |
| 2010 | SD | NL | 54 | 0 | 0 | 15 | 59.0 | 253 | 64 | 21 | 19 | 1 | 1 | 1 | 1 | 19 | 5 | 44 | 2 | 1 | 3 | 1 | .750 | 0 | 0-2 | 9 | 3.61 | 2.90 |
| 2011 | Fla | NL | 53 | 0 | 0 | 10 | 50.2 | 214 | 48 | 20 | 18 | 2 | 3 | 1 | 2 | 20 | 5 | 31 | 1 | 1 | 2 | 4 | .333 | 0 | 0-4 | 8 | 3.39 | 3.20 |
| 2012 | Mia | NL | 65 | 0 | 0 | 21 | 60.1 | 270 | 72 | 30 | 27 | 2 | 0 | 2 | 4 | 20 | 8 | 44 | 0 | 0 | 4 | 3 | .571 | 0 | 0-0 | 10 | 4.44 | 4.03 |
| 2013 | Mia | NL | 66 | 0 | 0 | 19 | 80.1 | 332 | 70 | 30 | 26 | 5 | 11 | 5 | 2 | 27 | 5 | 54 | 4 | 0 | 2 | 6 | .250 | 0 | 0-3 | 4 | 2.91 | 2.91 |
| 5 ML YEARS | | | 266 | 0 | 0 | 74 | 276.0 | 1186 | 281 | 115 | 101 | 13 | 17 | 10 | 10 | 97 | 24 | 192 | 11 | 2 | 13 | 15 | .464 | 0 | 0-9 | 37 | 3.62 | 3.29 |

# Thad Weber

**Pitches:** R **Bats:** R **Pos:** RP-8 **Ht:** 6'2" **Wt:** 205 **Born:** 9/28/1984 **Age:** 29

| | | | HOW MUCH HE PITCHED | | | | | | WHAT HE GAVE UP | | | | | | | | | | | | THE RESULTS | | | | | | | |
|---|---|---|---|---|---|---|---|---|---|---|---|---|---|---|---|---|---|---|---|---|---|---|---|---|---|---|---|---|
| Year | Team | Lg | G | GS | CG | GF | IP | BFP | H | R | ER | HR | SH | SF | HB | TBB | IBB | SO | WP | Bk | W | L | Pct | Sh | Sv-Op | Hld | ERC | ERA |
| 2009 | Lkland | A+ | 12 | 12 | 1 | 0 | 67.2 | 262 | 54 | 19 | 16 | 6 | 0 | 1 | 1 | 11 | 0 | 40 | 5 | 0 | 4 | 4 | .500 | 0 | 0-- | - | 2.18 | 2.13 |
| 2009 | Erie | AA | 13 | 13 | 1 | 0 | 75.1 | 311 | 78 | 38 | 34 | 7 | 1 | 2 | 4 | 18 | 1 | 44 | 2 | 0 | 7 | 3 | .700 | 1 | 0-- | - | 3.90 | 4.06 |
| 2010 | Erie | AA | 25 | 25 | 2 | 0 | 167.2 | 707 | 176 | 87 | 76 | 17 | 7 | 7 | 8 | 41 | 1 | 113 | 7 | 1 | 9 | 12 | .429 | 0 | 0-- | - | 3.97 | 4.08 |
| 2010 | Toledo | AAA | 3 | 3 | 0 | 0 | 22.0 | 78 | 14 | 4 | 4 | 2 | 0 | 0 | 0 | 3 | 0 | 17 | 2 | 0 | 2 | 1 | .667 | 0 | 0-- | - | 1.48 | 1.64 |
| 2011 | Toledo | AAA | 27 | 27 | 1 | 0 | 151.1 | 667 | 176 | 98 | 95 | 28 | 4 | 3 | 5 | 49 | 1 | 111 | 4 | 1 | 5 | 11 | .313 | 0 | 0-- | - | 5.48 | 5.65 |
| 2012 | Toledo | AAA | 22 | 21 | 1 | 0 | 128.2 | 536 | 123 | 62 | 60 | 16 | 2 | 6 | 6 | 31 | 0 | 97 | 5 | 1 | 7 | 11 | .389 | 0 | 0-- | - | 3.56 | 4.20 |
| 2012 | Tucsn | AAA | 3 | 3 | 0 | 0 | 18.1 | 78 | 22 | 9 | 9 | 1 | 3 | 0 | 1 | 3 | 0 | 14 | 0 | 0 | 1 | 0 | 1.000 | 0 | 0-- | - | 4.23 | 4.42 |
| 2013 | Tucsn | AAA | 6 | 6 | 0 | 0 | 34.1 | 143 | 38 | 16 | 15 | 0 | 0 | 1 | 1 | 4 | 0 | 26 | 3 | 0 | 4 | 1 | .800 | 0 | 0-- | - | 3.01 | 3.93 |
| 2013 | Buffalo | AAA | 18 | 15 | 1 | 0 | 100.0 | 400 | 91 | 35 | 29 | 5 | 3 | 2 | 0 | 21 | 0 | 88 | 12 | 1 | 8 | 5 | .615 | 0 | 0-- | - | 2.61 | 2.61 |
| 2012 | Det | AL | 2 | 0 | 0 | 1 | 4.0 | 24 | 10 | 4 | 4 | 0 | 0 | 0 | 0 | 2 | 0 | 1 | 0 | 0 | 0 | 1 | .000 | 0 | 0-0 | 0 | 13.27 | 9.00 |
| 2013 | 2 Tms | | 8 | 0 | 0 | 5 | 15.0 | 61 | 12 | 5 | 4 | 2 | 0 | 2 | 0 | 8 | 0 | 10 | 0 | 0 | 0 | 1 | .000 | 0 | 0-0 | 0 | 3.92 | 2.40 |
| 13 | SD | NL | 3 | 0 | 0 | 1 | 9.0 | 35 | 5 | 2 | 2 | 1 | 0 | 1 | 0 | 5 | 0 | 6 | 0 | 0 | 0 | 0 | - | 0 | 0-0 | 0 | 2.53 | 2.00 |
| 13 | Tor | AL | 5 | 0 | 0 | 4 | 6.0 | 26 | 7 | 3 | 2 | 1 | 0 | 1 | 0 | 3 | 0 | 4 | 0 | 0 | 0 | 1 | .000 | 0 | 0-0 | 0 | 6.33 | 3.00 |
| 2 ML YEARS | | | 10 | 0 | 0 | 6 | 19.0 | 85 | 22 | 9 | 8 | 2 | 0 | 2 | 0 | 10 | 0 | 11 | 0 | 0 | 0 | 2 | .000 | 0 | 0-0 | 0 | 5.69 | 3.79 |

# Allen Webster

**Pitches:** R **Bats:** R **Pos:** SP-7; RP-1 **Ht:** 6'2" **Wt:** 190 **Born:** 2/10/1990 **Age:** 24

| | | | HOW MUCH HE PITCHED | | | | | | WHAT HE GAVE UP | | | | | | | | | | | | THE RESULTS | | | | | | | |
|---|---|---|---|---|---|---|---|---|---|---|---|---|---|---|---|---|---|---|---|---|---|---|---|---|---|---|---|---|
| Year | Team | Lg | G | GS | CG | GF | IP | BFP | H | R | ER | HR | SH | SF | HB | TBB | IBB | SO | WP | Bk | W | L | Pct | Sh | Sv-Op | Hld | ERC | ERA |
| 2009 | Ddgrs | R | 12 | 8 | 0 | 0 | 47.2 | 203 | 35 | 19 | 11 | 0 | 3 | 2 | 5 | 14 | 0 | 56 | 4 | 0 | 2 | 1 | .667 | 0 | 0-- | - | 1.94 | 2.08 |
| 2009 | Ogden | R+ | 4 | 3 | 0 | 0 | 21.0 | 87 | 23 | 8 | 7 | 1 | 0 | 0 | 0 | 4 | 0 | 21 | 1 | 0 | 2 | 0 | 1.000 | 0 | 0-- | - | 3.48 | 3.00 |
| 2010 | Gt Lks | A | 26 | 23 | 0 | 1 | 131.1 | 568 | 119 | 55 | 42 | 6 | 4 | 4 | 10 | 53 | 1 | 114 | 5 | 1 | 12 | 9 | .571 | 0 | 0-- | - | 3.44 | 2.88 |
| 2011 | RCuca | A+ | 9 | 9 | 0 | 0 | 54.0 | 228 | 46 | 18 | 14 | 2 | 0 | 1 | 4 | 21 | 0 | 62 | 1 | 1 | 5 | 2 | .714 | 0 | 0-- | - | 3.09 | 2.33 |
| 2011 | Chatt | AA | 18 | 17 | 1 | 0 | 91.0 | 407 | 101 | 53 | 51 | 7 | 9 | 1 | 8 | 36 | 2 | 73 | 5 | 0 | 6 | 3 | .667 | 1 | 0-- | - | 4.85 | 5.04 |
| 2012 | Chatt | AA | 27 | 22 | 0 | 2 | 121.2 | 546 | 120 | 63 | 48 | 1 | 9 | 1 | 17 | 57 | 2 | 117 | 10 | 1 | 6 | 8 | .429 | 0 | 0-- | - | 4.09 | 3.55 |
| 2012 | Portlnd | AA | 2 | 2 | 0 | 0 | 9.0 | 46 | 13 | 8 | 8 | 1 | 0 | 0 | 2 | 4 | 0 | 12 | 1 | 0 | 0 | 1 | .000 | 0 | 0-- | - | 7.83 | 8.00 |
| 2013 | Pwtckt | AAA | 21 | 21 | 0 | 0 | 105.0 | 436 | 71 | 45 | 42 | 9 | 1 | 2 | 16 | 43 | 0 | 116 | 9 | 1 | 8 | 4 | .667 | 0 | 0-- | - | 2.87 | 3.60 |
| 2013 | Bos | AL | 8 | 7 | 0 | 1 | 30.1 | 145 | 37 | 30 | 29 | 7 | 0 | 5 | 2 | 18 | 0 | 23 | 1 | 0 | 1 | 2 | .333 | 0 | 0-0 | 0 | 7.56 | 8.60 |

# Jemile Weeks

**Bats:** B **Throws:** R **Pos:** 2B-4;PR-3;CF-2;DH-2;PH-1 jah-MYLE **Ht:** 5'9" **Wt:** 160 **Born:** 1/26/1987 **Age:** 27

| | | | BATTING | | | | | | | | | | | | | | | | | | BASERUNNING | | | | AVERAGES | | |
|---|---|---|---|---|---|---|---|---|---|---|---|---|---|---|---|---|---|---|---|---|---|---|---|---|---|---|---|
| Year | Team | Lg | G | AB | H | 2B | 3B | HR | (Hm | Rd) | TB | R | RBI | RC | TBB | IBB | SO | HBP | SH | SF | SB | CS | SB% | GDP | Avg | OBP | Slg |
| 2013 | Scrmto* | AAA | 130 | 520 | 141 | 19 | 10 | 4 | (- | -) | 192 | 96 | 40 | 83 | 80 | 1 | 99 | 8 | 5 | 1 | 17 | 2 | .89 | 14 | .271 | .376 | .369 |
| 2011 | Oak | AL | 97 | 406 | 123 | 26 | 8 | 2 | (1 | 1) | 171 | 50 | 36 | 64 | 21 | 1 | 62 | 4 | 2 | 4 | 22 | 11 | .67 | 3 | .303 | .340 | .421 |
| 2012 | Oak | AL | 118 | 444 | 98 | 15 | 8 | 2 | (1 | 1) | 135 | 54 | 20 | 42 | 50 | 0 | 70 | 5 | 9 | 3 | 16 | 5 | .76 | 5 | .221 | .305 | .304 |
| 2013 | Oak | AL | 8 | 9 | 1 | 0 | 0 | 0 | (0 | 0) | 1 | 3 | 0 | 0 | 0 | 0 | 5 | 0 | 0 | 0 | 0 | 0 | - | 0 | .111 | .111 | .111 |
| 3 ML YEARS | | | 223 | 859 | 222 | 41 | 16 | 4 | (2 | 2) | 307 | 107 | 56 | 106 | 71 | 1 | 137 | 9 | 11 | 7 | 38 | 16 | .70 | 8 | .258 | .319 | .357 |

# Rickie Weeks

**Bats:** R **Throws:** R **Pos:** 2B-95;PH-10 **Ht:** 5'10" **Wt:** 215 **Born:** 9/13/1982 **Age:** 31

| | | | BATTING | | | | | | | | | | | | | | | | | | BASERUNNING | | | | AVERAGES | | |
|---|---|---|---|---|---|---|---|---|---|---|---|---|---|---|---|---|---|---|---|---|---|---|---|---|---|---|---|
| Year | Team | Lg | G | AB | H | 2B | 3B | HR | (Hm | Rd) | TB | R | RBI | RC | TBB | IBB | SO | HBP | SH | SF | SB | CS | SB% | GDP | Avg | OBP | Slg |
| 2003 | Mil | NL | 7 | 12 | 2 | 1 | 0 | 0 | (0 | 0) | 3 | 1 | 0 | 0 | 1 | 0 | 6 | 1 | 0 | 0 | 0 | 0 | - | 0 | .167 | .286 | .250 |
| 2005 | Mil | NL | 96 | 360 | 86 | 13 | 2 | 13 | (8 | 5) | 142 | 56 | 42 | 49 | 40 | 2 | 96 | 11 | 2 | 1 | 15 | 2 | .88 | 11 | .239 | .333 | .394 |
| 2006 | Mil | NL | 95 | 359 | 100 | 15 | 3 | 8 | (6 | 2) | 145 | 73 | 34 | 53 | 30 | 1 | 92 | **19** | 2 | 3 | 19 | 5 | .79 | 6 | .279 | .363 | .404 |
| 2007 | Mil | NL | 118 | 409 | 96 | 21 | 6 | 16 | (5 | 11) | 177 | 87 | 36 | 65 | 78 | 5 | 116 | 14 | 3 | 2 | 25 | 2 | .93 | 3 | .235 | .374 | .433 |
| 2008 | Mil | NL | 129 | 475 | 111 | 22 | 7 | 14 | (3 | 11) | 189 | 89 | 46 | 67 | 66 | 0 | 115 | 14 | 1 | 4 | 19 | 5 | .79 | 5 | .234 | .342 | .398 |
| 2009 | Mil | NL | 37 | 147 | 40 | 5 | 2 | 9 | (7 | 2) | 76 | 28 | 24 | 27 | 12 | 0 | 39 | 3 | 0 | 0 | 2 | 2 | .50 | 1 | .272 | .340 | .517 |
| 2010 | Mil | NL | 160 | **651** | 175 | 32 | 4 | 29 | (16 | 13) | 302 | 112 | 83 | 110 | 76 | 0 | 184 | **25** | 0 | 2 | 11 | 4 | .73 | 5 | .269 | .366 | .464 |
| 2011 | Mil | NL | 118 | 453 | 122 | 26 | 2 | 20 | (10 | 10) | 212 | 77 | 49 | 68 | 50 | 3 | 107 | 8 | 1 | 3 | 9 | 2 | .82 | 6 | .269 | .350 | .468 |
| 2012 | Mil | NL | 157 | 588 | 135 | 29 | 4 | 21 | (10 | 11) | 235 | 85 | 63 | 77 | 74 | 2 | 169 | 13 | 0 | 2 | 16 | 3 | .84 | 9 | .230 | .328 | .400 |
| 2013 | Mil | NL | 104 | 350 | 73 | 20 | 1 | 10 | (6 | 4) | 125 | 40 | 24 | 28 | 40 | 0 | 105 | 9 | 0 | 0 | 7 | 3 | .70 | 13 | .209 | .306 | .357 |
| Postseason | | | 14 | 45 | 6 | 1 | 1 | 2 | (2 | 0) | 15 | 5 | 4 | 2 | 2 | 0 | 8 | 2 | 0 | 0 | 0 | 0 | - | 3 | .133 | .204 | .333 |
| 10 ML YEARS | | | 1021 | 3804 | 940 | 184 | 31 | 140 | (71 | 69) | 1606 | 648 | 401 | 544 | 467 | 13 | 1029 | 117 | 9 | 17 | 123 | 28 | .81 | 59 | .247 | .346 | .422 |

# Duke Welker

**Pitches:** R **Bats:** L **Pos:** RP-2 **Ht:** 6'7" **Wt:** 240 **Born:** 2/10/1986 **Age:** 28

| HOW MUCH HE PITCHED | | | | | | | | | WHAT HE GAVE UP | | | | | | | | | | | | THE RESULTS | | | | | | | |
|---|---|---|---|---|---|---|---|---|---|---|---|---|---|---|---|---|---|---|---|---|---|---|---|---|---|---|---|---|
| Year | Team | Lg | G | GS | CG | GF | IP | BFP | H | R | ER | HR | SH | SF | HB | TBB | IBB | SO | WP | Bk | W | L | Pct | Sh | Sv-Op | Hld | ERC | ERA |
| 2009 | WV | A | 31 | 15 | 0 | 7 | 101.0 | 470 | 96 | 80 | 65 | 7 | 6 | 4 | 13 | 67 | 0 | 69 | 22 | 1 | 0 | 11 | .000 | 0 | 2-- | - | 5.08 | 5.79 |
| 2010 | WV | A | 20 | 0 | 0 | 13 | 22.1 | 107 | 16 | 14 | 9 | 0 | 0 | 1 | 1 | 24 | 0 | 25 | 3 | 0 | 1 | 1 | .500 | 0 | 5-- | - | 4.36 | 3.63 |
| 2010 | Bradtn | A+ | 20 | 0 | 0 | 5 | 24.1 | 113 | 16 | 12 | 10 | 2 | 1 | 0 | 1 | 23 | 0 | 20 | 3 | 0 | 0 | 1 | .000 | 0 | 0-- | - | 4.18 | 3.70 |
| 2011 | Bradtn | A+ | 36 | 0 | 0 | 22 | 52.0 | 208 | 33 | 18 | 13 | 2 | 3 | 1 | 2 | 25 | 0 | 41 | 6 | 1 | 3 | 5 | .375 | 0 | 6-- | - | 2.28 | 2.25 |
| 2011 | Altna | AA | 8 | 0 | 0 | 2 | 10.0 | 45 | 11 | 7 | 6 | 0 | 0 | 0 | 1 | 1 | 0 | 9 | 1 | 0 | 1 | 0 | 1.000 | 0 | 0-- | - | 2.93 | 5.40 |
| 2012 | Altna | AA | 15 | 0 | 0 | 12 | 23.1 | 97 | 18 | 7 | 6 | 0 | 2 | 2 | 0 | 7 | 0 | 19 | 1 | 1 | 2 | 1 | .667 | 0 | 5-- | - | 1.83 | 2.31 |
| 2012 | Indy | AAA | 26 | 0 | 0 | 4 | 31.2 | 131 | 24 | 8 | 8 | 1 | 0 | 0 | 1 | 18 | 0 | 30 | 3 | 0 | 0 | 1 | .000 | 0 | 0-- | - | 3.16 | 2.27 |
| 2013 | Indy | AAA | 48 | 0 | 0 | 30 | 63.0 | 266 | 53 | 28 | 25 | 3 | 2 | 2 | 2 | 31 | 1 | 65 | 4 | 1 | 3 | 4 | .429 | 0 | 9-- | - | 3.34 | 3.57 |
| 2013 | Pit | NL | 2 | 0 | 0 | 1 | 1.1 | 4 | 0 | 0 | 0 | 0 | 0 | 0 | 0 | 0 | 0 | 1 | 0 | 0 | 0 | 0 | - | 0 | 0-0 | 0 | 0.00 | 0.00 |

# Casper Wells

**Bats:** R **Throws:** R **Pos:** PH-17;LF-16;RF-11;PR-9;CF-5;DH-4 **Ht:** 6'2" **Wt:** 220 **Born:** 11/23/1984 **Age:** 29

| BATTING | | | | | | | | | | | | | | | | | | | | | BASERUNNING | | | | AVERAGES | | |
|---|---|---|---|---|---|---|---|---|---|---|---|---|---|---|---|---|---|---|---|---|---|---|---|---|---|---|---|
| Year | Team | Lg | G | AB | H | 2B | 3B | HR | (Hm | Rd) | TB | R | RBI | RC | TBB | IBB | SO | HBP | SH | SF | SB | CS | SB% | GDP | Avg | OBP | Slg |
| 2010 | Det | AL | 36 | 93 | 30 | 6 | 1 | 4 | (1 | 3) | 50 | 14 | 17 | 16 | 6 | 0 | 19 | 0 | 0 | 0 | 0 | 1 | .00 | 2 | .323 | .364 | .538 |
| 2011 | 2 Tms | AL | 95 | 215 | 51 | 11 | 0 | 11 | (7 | 4) | 95 | 30 | 27 | 30 | 18 | 2 | 71 | 7 | 1 | 0 | 3 | 2 | .60 | 3 | .237 | .317 | .442 |
| 2012 | Sea | AL | 93 | 285 | 65 | 12 | 3 | 10 | (4 | 6) | 113 | 42 | 36 | 39 | 26 | 0 | 80 | 4 | 1 | 0 | 3 | 0 | 1.00 | 3 | .228 | .302 | .396 |
| 2013 | 3 Tms | | 53 | 95 | 12 | 2 | 0 | 0 | (0 | 0) | 14 | 6 | 1 | 1 | 7 | 0 | 31 | 0 | 0 | 0 | 0 | 1 | .00 | 1 | .126 | .186 | .147 |
| 11 | Det | AL | 64 | 113 | 29 | 10 | 0 | 4 | (1 | 3) | 51 | 16 | 12 | 15 | 9 | 0 | 29 | 2 | 1 | 0 | 1 | 0 | 1.00 | 2 | .257 | .323 | .451 |
| 11 | Sea | AL | 31 | 102 | 22 | 1 | 0 | 7 | (6 | 1) | 44 | 14 | 15 | 15 | 9 | 2 | 42 | 5 | 0 | 0 | 2 | 2 | .50 | 1 | .216 | .310 | .431 |
| 13 | Oak | AL | 3 | 5 | 0 | 0 | 0 | 0 | (0 | 0) | 0 | 0 | 0 | 0 | 0 | 0 | 1 | 0 | 0 | 0 | 0 | 0 | - | 0 | .000 | .000 | .000 |
| 13 | CWS | AL | 38 | 66 | 11 | 1 | 0 | 0 | (0 | 0) | 12 | 4 | 1 | 1 | 5 | 0 | 22 | 0 | 0 | 0 | 0 | 1 | .00 | 1 | .167 | .225 | .182 |
| 13 | Phi | NL | 12 | 24 | 1 | 1 | 0 | 0 | (0 | 0) | 2 | 2 | 0 | 0 | 2 | 0 | 8 | 0 | 0 | 0 | 0 | 0 | - | 0 | .042 | .115 | .083 |
| 4 ML YEARS | | | 277 | 688 | 158 | 31 | 4 | 25 | (12 | 13) | 272 | 92 | 81 | 86 | 57 | 2 | 201 | 11 | 2 | 0 | 6 | 4 | .60 | 9 | .230 | .299 | .395 |

# Vernon Wells

**Bats:** R **Throws:** R **Pos:** LF-73;RF-23;PH-23;DH-22;1B-1;2B-1;3B-1 **Ht:** 6'1" **Wt:** 230 **Born:** 12/8/1978 **Age:** 35

| BATTING | | | | | | | | | | | | | | | | | | | | | BASERUNNING | | | | AVERAGES | | |
|---|---|---|---|---|---|---|---|---|---|---|---|---|---|---|---|---|---|---|---|---|---|---|---|---|---|---|---|
| Year | Team | Lg | G | AB | H | 2B | 3B | HR | (Hm | Rd) | TB | R | RBI | RC | TBB | IBB | SO | HBP | SH | SF | SB | CS | SB% | GDP | Avg | OBP | Slg |
| 1999 | Tor | AL | 24 | 88 | 23 | 5 | 0 | 1 | (1 | 0) | 31 | 8 | 8 | 7 | 4 | 0 | 18 | 0 | 0 | 0 | 1 | 1 | .50 | 6 | .261 | .293 | .352 |
| 2000 | Tor | AL | 3 | 2 | 0 | 0 | 0 | 0 | (0 | 0) | 0 | 0 | 0 | 0 | 0 | 0 | 0 | 0 | 0 | 0 | 0 | 0 | - | 0 | .000 | .000 | .000 |
| 2001 | Tor | AL | 30 | 96 | 30 | 8 | 0 | 1 | (1 | 0) | 41 | 14 | 6 | 16 | 5 | 0 | 15 | 1 | 0 | 1 | 5 | 0 | 1.00 | 0 | .313 | .350 | .427 |
| 2002 | Tor | AL | 159 | 608 | 167 | 34 | 4 | 23 | (10 | 13) | 278 | 87 | 100 | 88 | 27 | 0 | 85 | 3 | 2 | 8 | 9 | 4 | .69 | 15 | .275 | .305 | .457 |
| 2003 | Tor | AL | 161 | 678 | **215** | **49** | 5 | 33 | (13 | 20) | **373** | 118 | 117 | 124 | 42 | 2 | 80 | 7 | 0 | 8 | 4 | 1 | .80 | 21 | .317 | .359 | .550 |
| 2004 | Tor | AL | 134 | 536 | 146 | 34 | 2 | 23 | (14 | 9) | 253 | 82 | 67 | 72 | 51 | 2 | 83 | 2 | 0 | 1 | 9 | 2 | .82 | 17 | .272 | .337 | .472 |
| 2005 | Tor | AL | 156 | 620 | 167 | 30 | 3 | 28 | (14 | 14) | 287 | 78 | 97 | 96 | 47 | 3 | 86 | 3 | 0 | 8 | 8 | 3 | .73 | 13 | .269 | .320 | .463 |
| 2006 | Tor | AL | 154 | 611 | 185 | 40 | 5 | 32 | (24 | 8) | 331 | 91 | 106 | 107 | 54 | 0 | 90 | 3 | 0 | 9 | 17 | 4 | .81 | 13 | .303 | .357 | .542 |
| 2007 | Tor | AL | 149 | 584 | 143 | 36 | 4 | 16 | (8 | 8) | 235 | 85 | 80 | 74 | 49 | 4 | 89 | 3 | 0 | 6 | 10 | 4 | .71 | 9 | .245 | .304 | .402 |
| 2008 | Tor | AL | 108 | 427 | 128 | 22 | 1 | 20 | (11 | 9) | 212 | 63 | 78 | 68 | 29 | 5 | 46 | 3 | 0 | 7 | 4 | 2 | .67 | 16 | .300 | .343 | .496 |
| 2009 | Tor | AL | 158 | 630 | 164 | 37 | 3 | 15 | (8 | 7) | 252 | 84 | 66 | 65 | 48 | 2 | 86 | 1 | 0 | 5 | 17 | 4 | .81 | 18 | .260 | .311 | .400 |
| 2010 | Tor | AL | 157 | 590 | 161 | 44 | 3 | 31 | (20 | 11) | 304 | 79 | 88 | 92 | 50 | 5 | 84 | 3 | 0 | 3 | 6 | 4 | .60 | 18 | .273 | .331 | .515 |
| 2011 | LAA | AL | 131 | 505 | 110 | 15 | 4 | 25 | (8 | 17) | 208 | 60 | 66 | 52 | 20 | 0 | 86 | 1 | 0 | 3 | 9 | 4 | .69 | 8 | .218 | .248 | .412 |
| 2012 | LAA | AL | 77 | 243 | 56 | 9 | 0 | 11 | (5 | 6) | 98 | 36 | 29 | 17 | 16 | 0 | 35 | 1 | 0 | 2 | 3 | 1 | .75 | 5 | .230 | .279 | .403 |
| 2013 | NYY | AL | 130 | 424 | 99 | 16 | 0 | 11 | (5 | 6) | 148 | 45 | 50 | 39 | 30 | 1 | 73 | 0 | 0 | 4 | 7 | 3 | .70 | 9 | .233 | .282 | .349 |
| 15 ML YEARS | | | 1731 | 6642 | 1794 | 379 | 34 | 270 | (142 | 128) | 3051 | 930 | 958 | 917 | 472 | 24 | 956 | 31 | 2 | 65 | 109 | 37 | .75 | 168 | .270 | .319 | .459 |

# Jayson Werth

**Bats:** R **Throws:** R **Pos:** RF-126;DH-2;PH-1 **Ht:** 6'5" **Wt:** 225 **Born:** 5/20/1979 **Age:** 35

| BATTING | | | | | | | | | | | | | | | | | | | | | BASERUNNING | | | | AVERAGES | | |
|---|---|---|---|---|---|---|---|---|---|---|---|---|---|---|---|---|---|---|---|---|---|---|---|---|---|---|---|
| Year | Team | Lg | G | AB | H | 2B | 3B | HR | (Hm | Rd) | TB | R | RBI | RC | TBB | IBB | SO | HBP | SH | SF | SB | CS | SB% | GDP | Avg | OBP | Slg |
| 2013 | Ptomc* | A+ | 6 | 18 | 10 | 1 | 0 | 2 | (- | -) | 17 | 6 | 8 | 7 | 2 | 0 | 0 | 0 | 0 | 0 | 0 | 0 | - | 0 | .556 | .600 | .944 |
| 2002 | Tor | AL | 15 | 46 | 12 | 2 | 1 | 0 | (0 | 0) | 16 | 4 | 6 | 5 | 6 | 0 | 11 | 0 | 0 | 1 | 1 | 0 | 1.00 | 4 | .261 | .340 | .348 |
| 2003 | Tor | AL | 26 | 48 | 10 | 4 | 0 | 2 | (0 | 2) | 20 | 7 | 10 | 6 | 3 | 0 | 22 | 0 | 0 | 0 | 1 | 0 | 1.00 | 0 | .208 | .255 | .417 |
| 2004 | LAD | NL | 89 | 290 | 76 | 11 | 3 | 16 | (11 | 5) | 141 | 56 | 47 | 47 | 30 | 0 | 85 | 4 | 1 | 1 | 4 | 1 | .80 | 1 | .262 | .338 | .486 |
| 2005 | LAD | NL | 102 | 337 | 79 | 22 | 2 | 7 | (1 | 6) | 126 | 46 | 43 | 44 | 48 | 2 | 114 | 6 | 1 | 3 | 11 | 2 | .85 | 10 | .234 | .338 | .374 |
| 2007 | Phi | NL | 94 | 255 | 76 | 11 | 3 | 8 | (1 | 7) | 117 | 43 | 49 | 57 | 44 | 1 | 73 | 2 | 2 | 1 | 7 | 1 | .88 | 0 | .298 | .404 | .459 |
| 2008 | Phi | NL | 134 | 418 | 114 | 16 | 3 | 24 | (11 | 13) | 208 | 73 | 67 | 74 | 57 | 1 | 119 | 4 | 0 | 3 | 20 | 1 | **.95** | 2 | .273 | .363 | .498 |
| 2009 | Phi | NL | 159 | 571 | 153 | 26 | 1 | 36 | (21 | 15) | 289 | 98 | 99 | 107 | 91 | 8 | 156 | 8 | 0 | 6 | 20 | 3 | .87 | 11 | .268 | .373 | .506 |
| 2010 | Phi | NL | 156 | 554 | 164 | **46** | 2 | 27 | (18 | 9) | 295 | 106 | 85 | 91 | 82 | 6 | 147 | 7 | 0 | 9 | 13 | 3 | .81 | 11 | .296 | .388 | .532 |
| 2011 | Was | NL | 150 | 561 | 130 | 26 | 1 | 20 | (10 | 10) | 218 | 69 | 58 | 74 | 74 | 5 | 160 | 10 | 0 | 4 | 19 | 3 | .86 | 10 | .232 | .330 | .389 |
| 2012 | Was | NL | 81 | 300 | 90 | 21 | 3 | 5 | (4 | 1) | 132 | 42 | 31 | 48 | 42 | 2 | 57 | 1 | 0 | 1 | 8 | 2 | .80 | 3 | .300 | .387 | .440 |
| 2013 | Was | NL | 129 | 462 | 147 | 24 | 0 | 25 | (13 | 12) | 246 | 84 | 82 | 94 | 60 | 3 | 101 | 5 | 0 | 5 | 10 | 1 | .91 | 9 | .318 | .398 | .532 |
| Postseason | | | 49 | 174 | 46 | 10 | 2 | 14 | (10 | 4) | 102 | 33 | 27 | 30 | 30 | 4 | 58 | 1 | 0 | 1 | 5 | 0 | 1.00 | 3 | .264 | .374 | .586 |
| 11 ML YEARS | | | 1135 | 3842 | 1051 | 209 | 19 | 170 | (90 | 80) | 1808 | 628 | 577 | 647 | 537 | 28 | 1045 | 47 | 4 | 34 | 114 | 17 | .87 | 61 | .274 | .367 | .471 |

# Jake Westbrook

**Pitches:** R **Bats:** R **Pos:** SP-19; RP-2 **Ht:** 6'3" **Wt:** 210 **Born:** 9/29/1977 **Age:** 36

| HOW MUCH HE PITCHED | | | | | | | | | WHAT HE GAVE UP | | | | | | | | | | | | THE RESULTS | | | | | | | |
|---|---|---|---|---|---|---|---|---|---|---|---|---|---|---|---|---|---|---|---|---|---|---|---|---|---|---|---|---|
| Year | Team | Lg | G | GS | CG | GF | IP | BFP | H | R | ER | HR | SH | SF | HB | TBB | IBB | SO | WP | Bk | W | L | Pct | Sh | Sv-Op | Hld | ERC | ERA |
| 2013 | Sprgfld* | AA | 1 | 1 | 0 | 0 | 3.2 | 16 | 6 | 1 | 1 | 0 | 0 | 0 | 0 | 0 | 0 | 5 | 1 | 0 | 0 | 0 | - | 0 | 0-- | - | 5.61 | 2.45 |
| 2013 | Peoria* | A | 1 | 1 | 0 | 0 | 7.0 | 24 | 4 | 1 | 1 | 0 | 0 | 0 | 0 | 0 | 0 | 5 | 0 | 0 | 1 | 0 | 1.000 | 0 | 0-- | - | 0.72 | 1.29 |
| 2000 | NYY | AL | 3 | 2 | 0 | 1 | 6.2 | 38 | 15 | 10 | 10 | 1 | 0 | 2 | 0 | 4 | 1 | 1 | 0 | 0 | 0 | 2 | .000 | 0 | 0-0 | 0 | 13.53 | 13.50 |
| 2001 | Cle | AL | 23 | 6 | 0 | 3 | 64.2 | 290 | 79 | 43 | 42 | 6 | 1 | 5 | 4 | 22 | 4 | 48 | 4 | 0 | 4 | 4 | .500 | 0 | 0-0 | 5 | 5.25 | 5.85 |
| 2002 | Cle | AL | 11 | 4 | 0 | 1 | 41.2 | 185 | 50 | 30 | 27 | 6 | 2 | 1 | 1 | 12 | 1 | 20 | 1 | 0 | 1 | 3 | .250 | 0 | 0-2 | 1 | 5.12 | 5.83 |

| Year | Team | Lg | G | GS | CG | GF | IP | BFP | H | R | ER | HR | SH | SF | HB | TBB | IBB | SO | WP | Bk | W | L | Pct | Sh | Sv-Op | Hld | ERC | ERA |
|---|---|---|---|---|---|---|---|---|---|---|---|---|---|---|---|---|---|---|---|---|---|---|---|---|---|---|---|---|
| | | | HOW MUCH HE PITCHED | | | | | | WHAT HE GAVE UP | | | | | | | | | | | | THE RESULTS | | | | | | | |
| 2003 | Cle | AL | 34 | 22 | 1 | 4 | 133.0 | 580 | 142 | 70 | 64 | 9 | 4 | 3 | 12 | 56 | 1 | 58 | 3 | 0 | 7 | 10 | .412 | 0 | 0-0 | 1 | 4.78 | 4.33 |
| 2004 | Cle | AL | 33 | 30 | **5** | 2 | 215.2 | 895 | 208 | 95 | 81 | 19 | 6 | 6 | 5 | 61 | 3 | 116 | 4 | 1 | 14 | 9 | .609 | 1 | 0-0 | 0 | 3.45 | 3.38 |
| 2005 | Cle | AL | 34 | 34 | 2 | 0 | 210.2 | 895 | 218 | 121 | 105 | 19 | 5 | 4 | 7 | 56 | 3 | 119 | 3 | 0 | 15 | 15 | .500 | 0 | 0-0 | 0 | 3.78 | 4.49 |
| 2006 | Cle | AL | 32 | 32 | 3 | 0 | 211.1 | 904 | **247** | 106 | 98 | 15 | 5 | 4 | 4 | 55 | 4 | 109 | 5 | 0 | 15 | 10 | .600 | **2** | 0-0 | 0 | 4.39 | 4.17 |
| 2007 | Cle | AL | 25 | 25 | 0 | 0 | 152.0 | 648 | 159 | 78 | 73 | 13 | 6 | 4 | 6 | 55 | 5 | 93 | 3 | 0 | 6 | 9 | .400 | 0 | 0-0 | 0 | 4.28 | 4.32 |
| 2008 | Cle | AL | 5 | 5 | 1 | 0 | 34.2 | 139 | 33 | 13 | 12 | 5 | 0 | 2 | 1 | 7 | 0 | 19 | 1 | 0 | 1 | 2 | .333 | 0 | 0-0 | 0 | 3.54 | 3.12 |
| 2010 | 2 Tms | | 33 | 33 | 1 | 0 | 202.2 | 860 | 203 | 99 | 95 | 20 | 5 | 3 | 8 | 68 | 4 | 128 | 8 | 0 | 10 | 11 | .476 | 0 | 0-0 | 0 | 3.99 | 4.22 |
| 2011 | StL | NL | 33 | 33 | 0 | 0 | 183.1 | 809 | 208 | 103 | 95 | 16 | 11 | 5 | 2 | 73 | 8 | 104 | 3 | 0 | 12 | 9 | .571 | 0 | 0-0 | 0 | 4.75 | 4.66 |
| 2012 | StL | NL | 28 | 28 | 1 | 0 | 174.2 | 751 | 191 | 85 | 77 | 12 | 8 | 5 | 8 | 52 | 0 | 106 | 5 | 0 | 13 | 11 | .542 | 0 | 0-0 | 0 | 4.20 | 3.97 |
| 2013 | StL | NL | 21 | 19 | 1 | 0 | 116.2 | 523 | 132 | 69 | 60 | 7 | 8 | 4 | 10 | 50 | 3 | 44 | 1 | 0 | 7 | 8 | .467 | 1 | 0-0 | 0 | 5.00 | 4.63 |
| 10 | Cle | AL | 21 | 21 | 1 | 0 | 127.2 | 543 | 133 | 68 | 66 | 15 | 3 | 3 | 6 | 44 | 4 | 73 | 6 | 0 | 6 | 7 | .462 | 0 | 0-0 | 0 | 4.45 | 4.65 |
| 10 | StL | NL | 12 | 12 | 0 | 0 | 75.0 | 317 | 70 | 31 | 29 | 5 | 2 | 0 | 2 | 24 | 0 | 55 | 2 | 0 | 4 | 4 | .500 | 0 | 0-0 | 0 | 3.25 | 3.48 |
| Postseason | | | 5 | 3 | 0 | 2 | 19.2 | 82 | 27 | 11 | 11 | 2 | 0 | 1 | 0 | 5 | 1 | 8 | 0 | 0 | 2 | 2 | .500 | 0 | 0-0 | 0 | 6.10 | 5.03 |
| 13 ML YEARS | | | 315 | 273 | 15 | 11 | 1747.2 | 7517 | 1885 | 922 | 839 | 148 | 61 | 48 | 68 | 571 | 37 | 965 | 41 | 1 | 105 | 103 | .505 | 4 | 0-2 | 7 | 4.29 | 4.32 |

## Ryan Wheeler

**Bats:** L **Throws:** R **Pos:** PH-20;1B-7;3B-1;LF-1 **Ht:** 6'3" **Wt:** 235 **Born:** 7/10/1988 **Age:** 25

| Year | Team | Lg | G | AB | H | 2B | 3B | HR | (Hm | Rd) | TB | R | RBI | RC | TBB | IBB | SO | HBP | SH | SF | SB | CS | SB% | GDP | Avg | OBP | Slg |
|---|---|---|---|---|---|---|---|---|---|---|---|---|---|---|---|---|---|---|---|---|---|---|---|---|---|---|---|
| | | | BATTING | | | | | | | | | | | | | | | | | | BASERUNNING | | | | AVERAGES | | |
| 2009 | Yakima | A- | 64 | 234 | 85 | 20 | 3 | 5 | (- | -) | 126 | 44 | 36 | 58 | 37 | 3 | 28 | 7 | 0 | 2 | 7 | 4 | .64 | 4 | .363 | .461 | .538 |
| 2009 | Sbend | A | 8 | 29 | 10 | 1 | 1 | 1 | (- | -) | 16 | 4 | 5 | 7 | 5 | 0 | 4 | 2 | 0 | 0 | 0 | 1 | .00 | 1 | .345 | .472 | .552 |
| 2010 | Visalia | A+ | 113 | 465 | 132 | 25 | 2 | 9 | (- | -) | 188 | 62 | 57 | 66 | 35 | 2 | 98 | 5 | 0 | 1 | 3 | 1 | .75 | 15 | .284 | .340 | .404 |
| 2010 | Mobile | AA | 19 | 67 | 17 | 3 | 0 | 3 | (- | -) | 29 | 8 | 10 | 9 | 5 | 0 | 16 | 1 | 0 | 0 | 0 | 0 | - | 1 | .254 | .315 | .433 |
| 2011 | Mobile | AA | 131 | 480 | 141 | 30 | 2 | 16 | (- | -) | 223 | 69 | 89 | 80 | 45 | 7 | 102 | 4 | 0 | 2 | 3 | 3 | .50 | 14 | .294 | .358 | .465 |
| 2012 | Reno | AAA | 93 | 362 | 127 | 27 | 4 | 15 | (- | -) | 207 | 56 | 90 | 78 | 26 | 2 | 67 | 2 | 0 | 9 | 3 | 1 | .75 | 9 | .351 | .388 | .572 |
| 2013 | ColSpr | AAA | 116 | 438 | 134 | 29 | 2 | 12 | (- | -) | 203 | 74 | 89 | 73 | 31 | 1 | 91 | 3 | 1 | 7 | 4 | 1 | .80 | 9 | .306 | .351 | .463 |
| 2012 | Ari | NL | 50 | 109 | 26 | 6 | 1 | 1 | (0 | 1) | 37 | 11 | 10 | 7 | 9 | 0 | 22 | 0 | 0 | 1 | 1 | 0 | 1.00 | 4 | .239 | .294 | .339 |
| 2013 | Col | NL | 28 | 41 | 9 | 2 | 0 | 0 | (0 | 0) | 11 | 1 | 7 | 4 | 1 | 0 | 10 | 0 | 0 | 0 | 0 | 0 | - | 1 | .220 | .238 | .268 |
| 2 ML YEARS | | | 78 | 150 | 35 | 8 | 1 | 1 | (0 | 1) | 48 | 12 | 17 | 11 | 10 | 0 | 32 | 0 | 0 | 1 | 1 | 0 | 1.00 | 5 | .233 | .280 | .320 |

## Zack Wheeler

**Pitches:** R **Bats:** L **Pos:** SP-17 **Ht:** 6'4" **Wt:** 185 **Born:** 5/30/1990 **Age:** 24

| Year | Team | Lg | G | GS | CG | GF | IP | BFP | H | R | ER | HR | SH | SF | HB | TBB | IBB | SO | WP | Bk | W | L | Pct | Sh | Sv-Op | Hld | ERC | ERA |
|---|---|---|---|---|---|---|---|---|---|---|---|---|---|---|---|---|---|---|---|---|---|---|---|---|---|---|---|---|
| | | | HOW MUCH HE PITCHED | | | | | | WHAT HE GAVE UP | | | | | | | | | | | | THE RESULTS | | | | | | | |
| 2010 | Augsta | A | 21 | 13 | 0 | 2 | 58.2 | 262 | 47 | 27 | 26 | 0 | 1 | 0 | 7 | 38 | 0 | 70 | 13 | 2 | 3 | 3 | .500 | 0 | 0- - | - | 3.63 | 3.99 |
| 2011 | SnJos | A+ | 16 | 16 | 0 | 0 | 88.0 | 385 | 74 | 44 | 39 | 7 | 2 | 2 | 4 | 47 | 1 | 98 | 6 | 0 | 7 | 5 | .583 | 0 | 0- - | - | 3.68 | 3.99 |
| 2011 | StLuci | A+ | 6 | 6 | 0 | 0 | 27.0 | 110 | 26 | 6 | 6 | 0 | 0 | 0 | 2 | 5 | 0 | 31 | 3 | 0 | 2 | 2 | .500 | 0 | 0- - | - | 2.74 | 2.00 |
| 2012 | Bnghtn | AA | 19 | 19 | 1 | 0 | 116.0 | 474 | 92 | 46 | 42 | 2 | 2 | 8 | 11 | 43 | 0 | 117 | 6 | 1 | 10 | 6 | .625 | 1 | 0- - | - | 2.74 | 3.26 |
| 2012 | Buffalo | AAA | 6 | 6 | 1 | 0 | 33.0 | 134 | 23 | 13 | 12 | 2 | 3 | 2 | 1 | 16 | 0 | 31 | 2 | 0 | 2 | 2 | .500 | 1 | 0- - | - | 2.70 | 3.27 |
| 2013 | LsVgs | AAA | 13 | 13 | 0 | 0 | 68.2 | 291 | 61 | 35 | 30 | 9 | 1 | 2 | 2 | 27 | 0 | 73 | 1 | 0 | 4 | 2 | .667 | 0 | 0- - | - | 3.75 | 3.93 |
| 2013 | NYM | NL | 17 | 17 | 0 | 0 | 100.0 | 431 | 90 | 42 | 38 | 10 | 3 | 7 | 4 | 46 | 2 | 84 | 6 | 0 | 7 | 5 | .583 | 0 | 0-0 | 0 | 3.88 | 3.42 |

## Matt Wieters

**Bats:** B **Throws:** R **Pos:** C-140;PH-9;DH-5 WEE-ters **Ht:** 6'5" **Wt:** 240 **Born:** 5/21/1986 **Age:** 28

| Year | Team | Lg | G | AB | H | 2B | 3B | HR | (Hm | Rd) | TB | R | RBI | RC | TBB | IBB | SO | HBP | SH | SF | SB | CS | SB% | GDP | Avg | OBP | Slg |
|---|---|---|---|---|---|---|---|---|---|---|---|---|---|---|---|---|---|---|---|---|---|---|---|---|---|---|---|
| | | | BATTING | | | | | | | | | | | | | | | | | | BASERUNNING | | | | AVERAGES | | |
| 2009 | Bal | AL | 96 | 354 | 102 | 15 | 1 | 9 | (5 | 4) | 146 | 35 | 43 | 43 | 28 | 2 | 86 | 1 | 0 | 2 | 0 | 0 | - | 11 | .288 | .340 | .412 |
| 2010 | Bal | AL | 130 | 446 | 111 | 22 | 1 | 11 | (3 | 8) | 168 | 37 | 55 | 47 | 47 | 7 | 94 | 2 | 0 | 7 | 0 | 1 | .00 | 13 | .249 | .319 | .377 |
| 2011 | Bal | AL | 139 | 500 | 131 | 28 | 0 | 22 | (13 | 9) | 225 | 72 | 68 | 76 | 48 | 3 | 84 | 2 | 0 | 1 | 1 | 0 | 1.00 | 16 | .262 | .328 | .450 |
| 2012 | Bal | AL | 144 | 526 | 131 | 27 | 1 | 23 | (11 | 12) | 229 | 67 | 83 | 73 | 60 | 4 | 112 | 4 | 0 | 3 | 3 | 0 | 1.00 | 17 | .249 | .329 | .435 |
| 2013 | Bal | AL | 148 | 523 | 123 | 29 | 0 | 22 | (13 | 9) | 218 | 59 | 79 | 65 | 43 | 5 | 104 | 0 | 1 | **12** | 2 | 0 | 1.00 | 7 | .235 | .287 | .417 |
| Postseason | | | 6 | 24 | 3 | 1 | 0 | 0 | (0 | 0) | 4 | 2 | 0 | 0 | 2 | 0 | 4 | 0 | 0 | 0 | 0 | 0 | - | 0 | .125 | .192 | .167 |
| 5 ML YEARS | | | 657 | 2349 | 598 | 121 | 3 | 87 | (45 | 42) | 986 | 270 | 328 | 304 | 226 | 21 | 480 | 9 | 1 | 25 | 6 | 1 | .86 | 64 | .255 | .319 | .420 |

## Ty Wigginton

**Bats:** R **Throws:** R **Pos:** PH-35;1B-7;LF-6;3B-5 **Ht:** 6'0" **Wt:** 225 **Born:** 10/11/1977 **Age:** 36

| Year | Team | Lg | G | AB | H | 2B | 3B | HR | (Hm | Rd) | TB | R | RBI | RC | TBB | IBB | SO | HBP | SH | SF | SB | CS | SB% | GDP | Avg | OBP | Slg |
|---|---|---|---|---|---|---|---|---|---|---|---|---|---|---|---|---|---|---|---|---|---|---|---|---|---|---|---|
| | | | BATTING | | | | | | | | | | | | | | | | | | BASERUNNING | | | | AVERAGES | | |
| 2002 | NYM | NL | 46 | 116 | 35 | 8 | 0 | 6 | (4 | 2) | 61 | 18 | 18 | 15 | 8 | 0 | 19 | 2 | 0 | 1 | 2 | 1 | .67 | 4 | .302 | .354 | .526 |
| 2003 | NYM | NL | 156 | 573 | 146 | 36 | 6 | 11 | (4 | 7) | 227 | 73 | 71 | 76 | 46 | 2 | 124 | 9 | 1 | 4 | 12 | 2 | .86 | 15 | .255 | .318 | .396 |
| 2004 | 2 Tms | NL | 144 | 494 | 129 | 30 | 2 | 17 | (6 | 11) | 214 | 63 | 66 | 59 | 45 | 6 | 82 | 2 | 1 | 3 | 7 | 1 | .88 | 15 | .261 | .324 | .433 |
| 2005 | Pit | NL | 57 | 155 | 40 | 9 | 1 | 7 | (1 | 6) | 72 | 20 | 25 | 22 | 14 | 0 | 30 | 1 | 1 | 0 | 0 | 1 | .00 | 3 | .258 | .324 | .465 |
| 2006 | TB | AL | 122 | 444 | 122 | 25 | 1 | 24 | (18 | 6) | 221 | 55 | 79 | 69 | 32 | 3 | 97 | 6 | 1 | 3 | 4 | 3 | .57 | 11 | .275 | .330 | .498 |
| 2007 | 2 Tms | | 148 | 547 | 152 | 33 | 0 | 22 | (15 | 7) | 251 | 71 | 67 | 64 | 41 | 0 | 113 | 8 | 0 | 8 | 3 | 4 | .43 | 16 | .278 | .333 | .459 |
| 2008 | Hou | NL | 111 | 386 | 110 | 22 | 1 | 23 | (15 | 8) | 203 | 50 | 58 | 57 | 32 | 1 | 69 | 8 | 0 | 3 | 4 | 6 | .40 | 9 | .285 | .350 | .526 |
| 2009 | Bal | AL | 122 | 410 | 112 | 19 | 0 | 11 | (9 | 2) | 164 | 44 | 41 | 41 | 23 | 1 | 57 | 2 | 0 | 1 | 1 | 2 | .33 | 16 | .273 | .314 | .400 |
| 2010 | Bal | AL | 154 | 581 | 144 | 29 | 1 | 22 | (12 | 10) | 241 | 63 | 76 | 62 | 50 | 3 | 116 | 8 | 1 | 9 | 0 | 1 | .00 | 23 | .248 | .312 | .415 |
| 2011 | Col | NL | 130 | 401 | 97 | 21 | 2 | 15 | (7 | 8) | 167 | 52 | 47 | 38 | 38 | 4 | 84 | 5 | 1 | 1 | 8 | 1 | .89 | 10 | .242 | .315 | .416 |
| 2012 | Phi | NL | 125 | 315 | 74 | 11 | 0 | 11 | (5 | 6) | 118 | 40 | 43 | 32 | 37 | 2 | 81 | 2 | 0 | 6 | 1 | 0 | 1.00 | 5 | .235 | .314 | .375 |
| 2013 | StL | NL | 47 | 57 | 9 | 2 | 0 | 0 | (0 | 0) | 11 | 9 | 3 | 4 | 5 | 1 | 19 | 1 | 0 | 0 | 0 | 1 | .00 | 1 | .158 | .238 | .193 |
| 04 | NYM | NL | 86 | 312 | 89 | 23 | 2 | 12 | (5 | 7) | 152 | 46 | 42 | 38 | 23 | 4 | 48 | 1 | 1 | 2 | 6 | 1 | .86 | 11 | .285 | .334 | .487 |
| 04 | Pit | NL | 58 | 182 | 40 | 7 | 0 | 5 | (1 | 4) | 62 | 17 | 24 | 21 | 22 | 2 | 34 | 1 | 0 | 1 | 1 | 0 | 1.00 | 4 | .220 | .306 | .341 |
| 07 | TB | AL | 98 | 378 | 104 | 21 | 0 | 16 | (9 | 7) | 173 | 47 | 49 | 42 | 28 | 0 | 73 | 5 | 0 | 6 | 1 | 4 | .20 | 8 | .275 | .329 | .458 |
| 07 | Hou | NL | 50 | 169 | 48 | 12 | 0 | 6 | (6 | 0) | 78 | 24 | 18 | 22 | 13 | 0 | 40 | 3 | 0 | 2 | 2 | 0 | 1.00 | 8 | .284 | .342 | .462 |
| 12 ML YEARS | | | 1362 | 4479 | 1170 | 245 | 14 | 169 | (96 | 73) | 1950 | 558 | 594 | 539 | 371 | 23 | 891 | 54 | 6 | 39 | 42 | 23 | .65 | 128 | .261 | .323 | .435 |

# Tom Wilhelmsen

**Pitches:** R **Bats:** R **Pos:** RP-59 will-HELM-senn **Ht:** 6'6" **Wt:** 220 **Born:** 12/16/1983 **Age:** 30

| | | | HOW MUCH HE PITCHED | | | | | | WHAT HE GAVE UP | | | | | | | | | | | | THE RESULTS | | | | | | | |
|---|---|---|---|---|---|---|---|---|---|---|---|---|---|---|---|---|---|---|---|---|---|---|---|---|---|---|---|---|
| Year | Team | Lg | G | GS | CG | GF | IP | BFP | H | R | ER | HR | SH | SF | HB | TBB | IBB | SO | WP | Bk | W | L | Pct | Sh | Sv-Op | Hld | ERC | ERA |
| 2013 | Tacom* | AAA | 8 | 2 | 0 | 0 | 12.0 | 58 | 19 | 14 | 14 | 3 | 1 | 0 | 2 | 5 | 0 | 15 | 5 | 0 | 0 | 1 | .000 | 0 | 0- - | - | 10.36 | 10.50 |
| 2011 | Sea | AL | 25 | 0 | 0 | 10 | 32.2 | 136 | 25 | 13 | 12 | 2 | 0 | 2 | 2 | 13 | 0 | 30 | 6 | 1 | 2 | 0 | 1.000 | 0 | 0-0 | 3 | 2.78 | 3.31 |
| 2012 | Sea | AL | 73 | 0 | 0 | 48 | 79.1 | 326 | 59 | 24 | 22 | 5 | 1 | 2 | 2 | 29 | 3 | 87 | 3 | 0 | 4 | 3 | .571 | 0 | 29-34 | 7 | 2.38 | 2.50 |
| 2013 | Sea | AL | 59 | 0 | 0 | 40 | 59.0 | 251 | 45 | 28 | 27 | 2 | 3 | 3 | 1 | 33 | 5 | 45 | 6 | 0 | 0 | 3 | .000 | 0 | 24-29 | 2 | 2.87 | 4.12 |
| 3 ML YEARS | | | 157 | 0 | 0 | 98 | 171.0 | 713 | 129 | 65 | 61 | 9 | 4 | 7 | 5 | 75 | 8 | 162 | 15 | 1 | 6 | 6 | .500 | 0 | 53-63 | 12 | 2.62 | 3.21 |

# Jerome Williams

**Pitches:** R **Bats:** R **Pos:** SP-25; RP-12 **Ht:** 6'3" **Wt:** 240 **Born:** 12/4/1981 **Age:** 32

| | | | HOW MUCH HE PITCHED | | | | | | WHAT HE GAVE UP | | | | | | | | | | | | THE RESULTS | | | | | | | |
|---|---|---|---|---|---|---|---|---|---|---|---|---|---|---|---|---|---|---|---|---|---|---|---|---|---|---|---|---|
| Year | Team | Lg | G | GS | CG | GF | IP | BFP | H | R | ER | HR | SH | SF | HB | TBB | IBB | SO | WP | Bk | W | L | Pct | Sh | Sv-Op | Hld | ERC | ERA |
| 2003 | SF | NL | 21 | 21 | 2 | 0 | 131.0 | 545 | 116 | 54 | 48 | 10 | 6 | 3 | 7 | 49 | 3 | 88 | 2 | 1 | 7 | 5 | .583 | 1 | 0-0 | 0 | 3.42 | 3.30 |
| 2004 | SF | NL | 22 | 22 | 0 | 0 | 129.1 | 559 | 123 | 69 | 61 | 14 | 4 | 9 | 17 | 44 | 1 | 80 | 2 | 1 | 10 | 7 | .588 | 0 | 0-0 | 0 | 4.14 | 4.24 |
| 2005 | 2 Tms | NL | 22 | 20 | 0 | 0 | 122.2 | 532 | 119 | 62 | 58 | 14 | 11 | 8 | 10 | 49 | 1 | 70 | 2 | 0 | 6 | 10 | .375 | 0 | 0-0 | 1 | 4.34 | 4.26 |
| 2006 | ChC | NL | 5 | 2 | 0 | 1 | 12.1 | 61 | 15 | 12 | 10 | 2 | 0 | 3 | 1 | 11 | 1 | 5 | 0 | 0 | 0 | 2 | .000 | 0 | 0-0 | 0 | 8.42 | 7.30 |
| 2007 | Was | NL | 6 | 6 | 0 | 0 | 30.0 | 140 | 34 | 26 | 24 | 6 | 1 | 1 | 0 | 18 | 0 | 15 | 2 | 1 | 0 | 5 | .000 | 0 | 0-0 | 0 | 6.43 | 7.20 |
| 2011 | LAA | AL | 10 | 6 | 0 | 1 | 44.0 | 184 | 45 | 20 | 18 | 6 | 0 | 1 | 1 | 15 | 0 | 28 | 0 | 0 | 4 | 0 | 1.000 | 0 | 0-0 | 0 | 4.45 | 3.68 |
| 2012 | LAA | AL | 32 | 15 | 1 | 7 | 137.2 | 572 | 139 | 73 | 70 | 17 | 0 | 4 | 5 | 35 | 1 | 98 | 1 | 0 | 6 | 8 | .429 | 1 | 1-1 | 0 | 3.91 | 4.58 |
| 2013 | LAA | AL | 37 | 25 | 0 | 8 | 169.1 | 728 | 181 | 93 | 86 | 23 | 1 | 3 | 4 | 55 | 2 | 107 | 5 | 0 | 9 | 10 | .474 | 0 | 0-0 | 0 | 4.53 | 4.57 |
| 05 | SF | NL | 4 | 3 | 0 | 0 | 16.2 | 73 | 21 | 12 | 12 | 2 | 1 | 0 | 1 | 4 | 1 | 11 | 0 | 0 | 0 | 2 | .000 | 0 | 0-0 | 0 | 5.32 | 6.48 |
| 05 | ChC | NL | 18 | 17 | 0 | 0 | 106.0 | 459 | 98 | 50 | 46 | 12 | 10 | 8 | 9 | 45 | 0 | 59 | 2 | 0 | 6 | 8 | .429 | 0 | 0-0 | 1 | 4.19 | 3.91 |
| Postseason | | | 1 | 1 | 0 | 0 | 2.0 | 13 | 5 | 3 | 3 | 0 | 1 | 0 | 0 | 1 | 0 | 1 | 0 | 0 | 0 | 0 | - | 0 | 0-0 | 0 | 12.20 | 13.50 |
| 8 ML YEARS | | | 155 | 117 | 3 | 17 | 776.1 | 3321 | 772 | 409 | 375 | 92 | 23 | 32 | 45 | 276 | 9 | 491 | 14 | 3 | 42 | 47 | .472 | 2 | 1-1 | 1 | 4.25 | 4.35 |

# Josh Willingham

**Bats:** R **Throws:** R **Pos:** LF-72;DH-35;PH-5 **Ht:** 6'2" **Wt:** 230 **Born:** 2/17/1979 **Age:** 35

| | | | BATTING | | | | | | | | | | | | | | | | | | BASERUNNING | | | | AVERAGES | | |
|---|---|---|---|---|---|---|---|---|---|---|---|---|---|---|---|---|---|---|---|---|---|---|---|---|---|---|---|
| Year | Team | Lg | G | AB | H | 2B | 3B | HR | (Hm | Rd) | TB | R | RBI | RC | TBB | IBB | SO | HBP | SH | SF | SB | CS | SB% | GDP | Avg | OBP | Slg |
| 2013 | Roch* | AAA | 3 | 9 | 1 | 0 | 0 | 1 | (- | -) | 4 | 1 | 1 | 1 | 2 | 0 | 2 | 0 | 0 | 0 | 0 | 0 | - | 0 | .111 | .273 | .444 |
| 2004 | Fla | NL | 12 | 25 | 5 | 0 | 0 | 1 | (0 | 1) | 8 | 2 | 1 | 1 | 4 | 0 | 8 | 0 | 0 | 0 | 0 | 0 | - | 1 | .200 | .310 | .320 |
| 2005 | Fla | NL | 16 | 23 | 7 | 1 | 0 | 0 | (0 | 0) | 8 | 3 | 4 | 3 | 2 | 0 | 5 | 2 | 1 | 0 | 0 | 0 | - | 1 | .304 | .407 | .348 |
| 2006 | Fla | NL | 142 | 502 | 139 | 28 | 2 | 26 | (11 | 15) | 249 | 62 | 74 | 74 | 54 | 2 | 109 | 11 | 0 | 6 | 2 | 0 | 1.00 | 13 | .277 | .356 | .496 |
| 2007 | Fla | NL | 144 | 521 | 138 | 32 | 4 | 21 | (10 | 11) | 241 | 75 | 89 | 94 | 66 | 1 | 122 | 16 | 0 | 1 | 8 | 1 | .89 | 11 | .265 | .364 | .463 |
| 2008 | Fla | NL | 102 | 351 | 89 | 21 | 5 | 15 | (6 | 9) | 165 | 54 | 51 | 56 | 48 | 2 | 82 | 14 | 1 | 2 | 3 | 2 | .60 | 7 | .254 | .364 | .470 |
| 2009 | Was | NL | 133 | 427 | 111 | 29 | 0 | 24 | (7 | 17) | 212 | 70 | 61 | 61 | 61 | 2 | 104 | 12 | 0 | 2 | 4 | 3 | .57 | 11 | .260 | .367 | .496 |
| 2010 | Was | NL | 114 | 370 | 99 | 19 | 2 | 16 | (11 | 5) | 170 | 54 | 56 | 65 | 67 | 3 | 85 | 9 | 0 | 4 | 8 | 0 | 1.00 | 8 | .268 | .389 | .459 |
| 2011 | Oak | AL | 136 | 488 | 120 | 26 | 0 | 29 | (15 | 14) | 233 | 69 | 98 | 86 | 56 | 3 | 150 | 11 | 0 | 8 | 4 | 1 | .80 | 6 | .246 | .332 | .477 |
| 2012 | Min | AL | 145 | 519 | 135 | 30 | 1 | 35 | (21 | 14) | 272 | 85 | 110 | 99 | 76 | 4 | 141 | 14 | 0 | 6 | 3 | 2 | .60 | 15 | .260 | .366 | .524 |
| 2013 | Min | AL | 111 | 389 | 81 | 20 | 0 | 14 | (7 | 7) | 143 | 42 | 48 | 51 | 66 | 2 | 128 | 14 | 0 | 2 | 1 | 0 | 1.00 | 8 | .208 | .342 | .368 |
| 10 ML YEARS | | | 1055 | 3615 | 924 | 206 | 14 | 181 | (88 | 93) | 1701 | 516 | 592 | 590 | 500 | 19 | 934 | 103 | 2 | 31 | 33 | 9 | .79 | 81 | .256 | .359 | .471 |

# Alex Wilson

**Pitches:** R **Bats:** R **Pos:** RP-26 **Ht:** 6'0" **Wt:** 215 **Born:** 11/3/1986 **Age:** 27

| | | | HOW MUCH HE PITCHED | | | | | | WHAT HE GAVE UP | | | | | | | | | | | | THE RESULTS | | | | | | | |
|---|---|---|---|---|---|---|---|---|---|---|---|---|---|---|---|---|---|---|---|---|---|---|---|---|---|---|---|---|
| Year | Team | Lg | G | GS | CG | GF | IP | BFP | H | R | ER | HR | SH | SF | HB | TBB | IBB | SO | WP | Bk | W | L | Pct | Sh | Sv-Op | Hld | ERC | ERA |
| 2009 | Lowell | A- | 13 | 13 | 0 | 0 | 36.0 | 126 | 10 | 3 | 2 | 0 | 1 | 0 | 0 | 7 | 0 | 33 | 0 | 0 | 0 | 1 | .000 | 0 | 0- - | - | 0.38 | 0.50 |
| 2010 | Salem | A+ | 11 | 11 | 0 | 0 | 55.2 | 224 | 43 | 24 | 21 | 4 | 1 | 2 | 2 | 15 | 0 | 50 | 1 | 0 | 2 | 1 | .667 | 0 | 0- - | - | 2.36 | 3.40 |
| 2010 | Portlnd | AA | 16 | 16 | 0 | 0 | 78.1 | 354 | 95 | 59 | 58 | 15 | 1 | 2 | 2 | 34 | 0 | 56 | 3 | 0 | 4 | 5 | .444 | 0 | 0- - | - | 6.37 | 6.66 |
| 2011 | Portlnd | AA | 21 | 21 | 0 | 0 | 112.0 | 458 | 103 | 42 | 38 | 8 | 0 | 1 | 1 | 37 | 0 | 99 | 6 | 1 | 9 | 4 | .692 | 0 | 0- - | - | 3.30 | 3.05 |
| 2011 | Pwtckt | AAA | 4 | 4 | 0 | 0 | 21.0 | 89 | 19 | 8 | 8 | 2 | 0 | 1 | 0 | 7 | 0 | 24 | 1 | 0 | 1 | 0 | 1.000 | 0 | 0- - | - | 3.20 | 3.43 |
| 2012 | Pwtckt | AAA | 40 | 3 | 0 | 10 | 72.2 | 321 | 76 | 40 | 30 | 3 | 0 | 7 | 0 | 33 | 1 | 78 | 4 | 3 | 5 | 3 | .625 | 0 | 1- - | - | 4.07 | 3.72 |
| 2013 | Pwtckt | AAA | 14 | 0 | 0 | 2 | 17.0 | 71 | 17 | 7 | 7 | 2 | 0 | 1 | 0 | 5 | 2 | 16 | 2 | 0 | 3 | 1 | .750 | 0 | 0- - | - | 3.63 | 3.71 |
| 2013 | Bos | AL | 26 | 0 | 0 | 9 | 27.2 | 127 | 34 | 16 | 15 | 0 | 0 | 1 | 1 | 14 | 1 | 22 | 1 | 0 | 1 | 1 | .500 | 0 | 0-0 | 1 | 5.19 | 4.88 |

# Brian Wilson

**Pitches:** R **Bats:** R **Pos:** RP-18 **Ht:** 6'2" **Wt:** 205 **Born:** 3/16/1982 **Age:** 32

| | | | HOW MUCH HE PITCHED | | | | | | WHAT HE GAVE UP | | | | | | | | | | | | THE RESULTS | | | | | | | |
|---|---|---|---|---|---|---|---|---|---|---|---|---|---|---|---|---|---|---|---|---|---|---|---|---|---|---|---|---|
| Year | Team | Lg | G | GS | CG | GF | IP | BFP | H | R | ER | HR | SH | SF | HB | TBB | IBB | SO | WP | Bk | W | L | Pct | Sh | Sv-Op | Hld | ERC | ERA |
| 2013 | RCuca* | A+ | 1 | 1 | 0 | 0 | 1.0 | 3 | 0 | 0 | 0 | 0 | 0 | 0 | 0 | 0 | 0 | 1 | 0 | 0 | 0 | 0 | - | 0 | 0- - | - | 0.00 | 0.00 |
| 2013 | Albq* | AAA | 3 | 0 | 0 | 0 | 3.1 | 11 | 1 | 0 | 0 | 0 | 0 | 0 | 0 | 0 | 0 | 2 | 0 | 0 | 0 | 0 | - | 0 | 0- - | - | 0.21 | 0.00 |
| 2006 | SF | NL | 31 | 0 | 0 | 9 | 30.0 | 141 | 32 | 19 | 18 | 1 | 1 | 4 | 1 | 21 | 2 | 23 | 0 | 0 | 2 | 3 | .400 | 0 | 1-2 | 4 | 5.11 | 5.40 |
| 2007 | SF | NL | 24 | 0 | 0 | 9 | 23.2 | 93 | 16 | 6 | 6 | 1 | 0 | 0 | 1 | 7 | 0 | 18 | 0 | 0 | 1 | 2 | .333 | 0 | 6-7 | 9 | 1.87 | 2.28 |
| 2008 | SF | NL | 63 | 0 | 0 | 54 | 62.1 | 274 | 62 | 32 | 32 | 7 | 2 | 5 | 3 | 28 | 4 | 67 | 2 | 0 | 3 | 2 | .600 | 0 | 41-47 | 0 | 4.41 | 4.62 |
| 2009 | SF | NL | 68 | 0 | 0 | 60 | 72.1 | 303 | 60 | 27 | 22 | 3 | 4 | 2 | 1 | 27 | 4 | 83 | 4 | 0 | 5 | 6 | .455 | 0 | 38-45 | 1 | 2.61 | 2.74 |
| 2010 | SF | NL | 70 | 0 | 0 | 59 | 74.2 | 311 | 62 | 16 | 15 | 3 | 1 | 0 | 1 | 26 | 5 | 93 | 0 | 0 | 3 | 3 | .500 | 0 | **48-53** | 0 | 2.51 | 1.81 |
| 2011 | SF | NL | 57 | 0 | 0 | 45 | 55.0 | 243 | 50 | 20 | 19 | 2 | 1 | 1 | 2 | 31 | 0 | 54 | 2 | 0 | 6 | 4 | .600 | 0 | 36-41 | 0 | 3.87 | 3.11 |
| 2012 | SF | NL | 2 | 0 | 0 | 2 | 2.0 | 12 | 4 | 2 | 2 | 0 | 0 | 0 | 0 | 2 | 0 | 2 | 1 | 0 | 0 | 0 | - | 0 | 1-1 | 0 | 12.01 | 9.00 |
| 2013 | LAD | NL | 18 | 0 | 0 | 8 | 13.2 | 49 | 8 | 1 | 1 | 0 | 0 | 0 | 0 | 4 | 0 | 13 | 0 | 0 | 2 | 1 | .667 | 0 | 0-0 | 3 | 1.35 | 0.66 |
| Postseason | | | 10 | 0 | 0 | 9 | 11.2 | 44 | 5 | 1 | 0 | 0 | 1 | 1 | 1 | 4 | 0 | 16 | 0 | 0 | 1 | 0 | 1.000 | 0 | 6-7 | 0 | 1.10 | 0.00 |
| 8 ML YEARS | | | 333 | 0 | 0 | 246 | 333.2 | 1426 | 294 | 123 | 115 | 17 | 9 | 12 | 9 | 146 | 15 | 353 | 9 | 0 | 22 | 21 | .512 | 0 | 171-196 | 17 | 3.25 | 3.10 |

# C.J. Wilson

**Pitches:** L **Bats:** L **Pos:** SP-33 — **Ht:** 6'1" **Wt:** 210 **Born:** 11/18/1980 **Age:** 33

| | | | HOW MUCH HE PITCHED | | | | | | WHAT HE GAVE UP | | | | | | | | | | | | THE RESULTS | | | | | | | |
|---|---|---|---|---|---|---|---|---|---|---|---|---|---|---|---|---|---|---|---|---|---|---|---|---|---|---|---|---|
| Year | Team | Lg | G | GS | CG | GF | IP | BFP | H | R | ER | HR | SH | SF | HB | TBB | IBB | SO | WP | Bk | W | L | Pct | Sh | Sv-Op | Hld | ERC | ERA |
| 2005 | Tex | AL | 24 | 6 | 0 | 5 | 48.0 | 220 | 63 | 39 | 37 | 5 | 1 | 2 | 2 | 18 | 1 | 30 | 4 | 1 | 1 | 7 | .125 | 0 | 1-1 | 4 | 6.03 | 6.94 |
| 2006 | Tex | AL | 44 | 0 | 0 | 12 | 44.1 | 191 | 39 | 23 | 20 | 7 | 1 | 0 | 5 | 18 | 1 | 43 | 0 | 0 | 2 | 4 | .333 | 0 | 1-2 | 7 | 4.25 | 4.06 |
| 2007 | Tex | AL | 66 | 0 | 0 | 22 | 68.1 | 285 | 50 | 25 | 23 | 4 | 2 | 4 | 6 | 33 | 1 | 63 | 5 | 0 | 2 | 1 | .667 | 0 | 12-14 | 15 | 3.01 | 3.03 |
| 2008 | Tex | AL | 50 | 0 | 0 | 41 | 46.1 | 214 | 49 | 35 | 31 | 8 | 1 | 1 | 2 | 27 | 2 | 41 | 3 | 0 | 2 | 2 | .500 | 0 | 24-28 | 1 | 5.77 | 6.02 |
| 2009 | Tex | AL | 74 | 0 | 0 | 30 | 73.2 | 323 | 66 | 29 | 23 | 3 | 3 | 0 | 6 | 32 | 3 | 84 | 3 | 0 | 5 | 6 | .455 | 0 | 14-18 | 19 | 3.40 | 2.81 |
| 2010 | Tex | AL | 33 | 33 | 3 | 0 | 204.0 | 850 | 161 | 83 | 76 | 10 | 1 | 3 | 10 | **93** | 0 | 170 | 7 | 1 | 15 | 8 | .652 | 0 | 0-0 | 0 | 3.03 | 3.35 |
| 2011 | Tex | AL | 34 | **34** | 3 | 0 | 223.1 | 915 | 191 | 89 | 73 | 16 | 3 | 5 | 10 | 74 | 0 | 206 | 6 | 0 | 16 | 7 | .696 | 1 | 0-0 | 0 | 3.07 | 2.94 |
| 2012 | LAA | AL | 34 | **34** | 0 | 0 | 202.1 | 865 | 181 | 102 | 86 | 19 | 4 | 6 | 6 | 91 | 2 | 173 | 4 | 1 | 13 | 10 | .565 | 0 | 0-0 | 0 | 3.75 | 3.83 |
| 2013 | LAA | AL | 33 | 33 | 0 | 0 | 212.1 | 913 | 200 | 93 | 80 | 15 | 4 | 2 | 8 | 85 | 3 | 188 | 14 | **2** | 17 | 7 | .708 | 0 | 0-0 | 0 | 3.66 | 3.39 |
| Postseason | | | 10 | 9 | 0 | 0 | 52.1 | 231 | 46 | 32 | 28 | 10 | 3 | 1 | 4 | 29 | 6 | 43 | 3 | 0 | 1 | 5 | .167 | 0 | 0-0 | 0 | 4.79 | 4.82 |
| 9 ML YEARS | | | 392 | 140 | 6 | 110 | 1122.2 | 4776 | 1000 | 518 | 449 | 87 | 20 | 23 | 55 | 471 | 13 | 998 | 46 | 5 | 73 | 52 | .584 | 1 | 52-63 | 46 | 3.58 | 3.60 |

# Josh Wilson

**Bats:** R **Throws:** R **Pos:** 2B-17;PH-8;3B-4;PR-3;SS-2 — **Ht:** 6'0" **Wt:** 175 **Born:** 3/26/1981 **Age:** 33

| | | | BATTING | | | | | | | | | | | | | | | | | BASERUNNING | | | | AVERAGES | | |
|---|---|---|---|---|---|---|---|---|---|---|---|---|---|---|---|---|---|---|---|---|---|---|---|---|---|---|
| Year | Team | Lg | G | AB | H | 2B | 3B | HR | (Hm | Rd) | TB | R | RBI | RC | TBB | IBB | SO | HBP | SH | SF | SB | CS | SB% | GDP | Avg | OBP | Slg |
| 2013 | Reno* | AAA | 59 | 192 | 42 | 8 | 0 | 4 | (- | -) | 62 | 17 | 20 | 15 | 13 | 1 | 44 | 0 | 1 | 0 | 1 | 3 | .25 | 2 | .219 | .268 | .323 |
| 2005 | Fla | NL | 11 | 10 | 1 | 1 | 0 | 0 | (0 | 0) | 2 | 2 | 0 | 0 | 0 | 0 | 4 | 1 | 0 | 0 | 0 | 0 | - | 0 | .100 | .182 | .200 |
| 2007 | 2 Tms | | 105 | 282 | 67 | 15 | 3 | 2 | (0 | 2) | 94 | 28 | 24 | 24 | 17 | 0 | 57 | 5 | 3 | 3 | 6 | 2 | .75 | 5 | .238 | .290 | .333 |
| 2009 | 3 Tms | | 72 | 192 | 42 | 11 | 1 | 3 | (1 | 2) | 64 | 19 | 13 | 14 | 12 | 1 | 44 | 4 | 3 | 0 | 1 | 2 | .33 | 4 | .219 | .279 | .333 |
| 2010 | Sea | AL | 108 | 361 | 82 | 14 | 2 | 2 | (1 | 1) | 106 | 22 | 25 | 31 | 14 | 0 | 74 | 12 | 0 | 1 | 5 | 0 | 1.00 | 6 | .227 | .278 | .294 |
| 2011 | 2 Tms | NL | 60 | 85 | 19 | 5 | 0 | 2 | (0 | 2) | 30 | 13 | 5 | 7 | 4 | 0 | 22 | 0 | 3 | 0 | 1 | 0 | 1.00 | 0 | .224 | .258 | .353 |
| 2013 | Ari | NL | 30 | 60 | 12 | 1 | 1 | 1 | (1 | 0) | 18 | 9 | 4 | 2 | 5 | 0 | 17 | 0 | 0 | 0 | 0 | 0 | - | 6 | .200 | .262 | .300 |
| 07 | Was | NL | 15 | 19 | 1 | 0 | 0 | 0 | (0 | 0) | 1 | 3 | 0 | 0 | 5 | 0 | 6 | 1 | 0 | 0 | 0 | 0 | - | 0 | .053 | .280 | .053 |
| 07 | TB | AL | 90 | 263 | 66 | 15 | 3 | 2 | (0 | 2) | 93 | 25 | 24 | 24 | 12 | 0 | 51 | 4 | 3 | 3 | 6 | 2 | .75 | 5 | .251 | .291 | .354 |
| 09 | Ari | NL | 11 | 26 | 6 | 1 | 0 | 0 | (0 | 0) | 7 | 1 | 2 | 4 | 3 | 0 | 3 | 1 | 0 | 0 | 0 | 0 | - | 2 | .231 | .333 | .269 |
| 09 | SD | NL | 16 | 38 | 4 | 2 | 0 | 0 | (0 | 0) | 6 | 2 | 1 | 1 | 3 | 1 | 9 | 1 | 1 | 0 | 0 | 0 | - | 0 | .105 | .190 | .158 |
| 09 | Sea | AL | 45 | 128 | 32 | 8 | 1 | 3 | (1 | 2) | 51 | 16 | 10 | 9 | 6 | 0 | 32 | 2 | 2 | 0 | 1 | 2 | .33 | 2 | .250 | .294 | .398 |
| 11 | Ari | NL | 6 | 10 | 2 | 1 | 0 | 0 | (0 | 0) | 3 | 3 | 1 | 1 | 0 | 0 | 1 | 0 | 0 | 0 | 0 | 0 | - | 0 | .200 | .200 | .300 |
| 11 | Mil | NL | 54 | 75 | 17 | 4 | 0 | 2 | (0 | 2) | 27 | 10 | 4 | 6 | 4 | 0 | 21 | 0 | 3 | 0 | 1 | 0 | 1.00 | 0 | .227 | .266 | .360 |
| 6 ML YEARS | | | 386 | 990 | 223 | 47 | 7 | 10 | (3 | 7) | 314 | 93 | 71 | 78 | 52 | 1 | 218 | 22 | 9 | 4 | 13 | 4 | .76 | 21 | .225 | .278 | .317 |

# Justin Wilson

**Pitches:** L **Bats:** L **Pos:** RP-58 — **Ht:** 6'2" **Wt:** 195 **Born:** 8/18/1987 **Age:** 26

| | | | HOW MUCH HE PITCHED | | | | | | WHAT HE GAVE UP | | | | | | | | | | | | THE RESULTS | | | | | | | |
|---|---|---|---|---|---|---|---|---|---|---|---|---|---|---|---|---|---|---|---|---|---|---|---|---|---|---|---|---|
| Year | Team | Lg | G | GS | CG | GF | IP | BFP | H | R | ER | HR | SH | SF | HB | TBB | IBB | SO | WP | Bk | W | L | Pct | Sh | Sv-Op | Hld | ERC | ERA |
| 2009 | Lynbrg | A+ | 26 | 26 | 0 | 0 | 116.0 | 514 | 118 | 64 | 58 | 14 | 1 | 0 | 7 | 55 | 0 | 94 | 6 | 0 | 6 | 8 | .429 | 0 | 0-- | - | 4.89 | 4.50 |
| 2010 | Altna | AA | 27 | 26 | 0 | 0 | 142.2 | 600 | 109 | 59 | 49 | 4 | 8 | 7 | 7 | 71 | 0 | 134 | 6 | 1 | 11 | 8 | .579 | 0 | 0-- | - | 2.88 | 3.09 |
| 2011 | Indy | AAA | 30 | 21 | 0 | 5 | 124.1 | 557 | 121 | 68 | 57 | 12 | 7 | 3 | 4 | 67 | 1 | 94 | 4 | 0 | 10 | 8 | .556 | 0 | 3-- | - | 4.52 | 4.13 |
| 2012 | Indy | AAA | 29 | 25 | 1 | 0 | 135.2 | 564 | 91 | 60 | 57 | 12 | 4 | 6 | 7 | 66 | 1 | 138 | 6 | 0 | 9 | 6 | .600 | 1 | 0-- | - | 2.74 | 3.78 |
| 2012 | Pit | NL | 8 | 0 | 0 | 3 | 4.2 | 26 | 10 | 1 | 1 | 0 | 1 | 0 | 0 | 3 | 0 | 7 | 1 | 0 | 0 | 0 | - | 0 | 0-0 | 0 | 11.83 | 1.93 |
| 2013 | Pit | NL | 58 | 0 | 0 | 8 | 73.2 | 295 | 50 | 17 | 17 | 4 | 3 | 1 | 3 | 28 | 1 | 59 | 5 | 0 | 6 | 1 | .857 | 0 | 0-3 | 14 | 2.20 | 2.08 |
| 2 ML YEARS | | | 66 | 0 | 0 | 11 | 78.1 | 321 | 60 | 18 | 18 | 4 | 4 | 1 | 3 | 31 | 1 | 66 | 6 | 0 | 6 | 1 | .857 | 0 | 0-3 | 14 | 2.65 | 2.07 |

# DeWayne Wise

**Bats:** L **Throws:** L **Pos:** CF-22;PR-6;LF-4;PH-4;RF-1;DH-1 — **Ht:** 6'0" **Wt:** 200 **Born:** 2/24/1978 **Age:** 36

| | | | BATTING | | | | | | | | | | | | | | | | | BASERUNNING | | | | AVERAGES | | |
|---|---|---|---|---|---|---|---|---|---|---|---|---|---|---|---|---|---|---|---|---|---|---|---|---|---|---|
| Year | Team | Lg | G | AB | H | 2B | 3B | HR | (Hm | Rd) | TB | R | RBI | RC | TBB | IBB | SO | HBP | SH | SF | SB | CS | SB% | GDP | Avg | OBP | Slg |
| 2013 | Charltt* | AAA | 16 | 53 | 9 | 3 | 1 | 0 | (- | -) | 14 | 4 | 2 | 2 | 3 | 0 | 17 | 1 | 0 | 0 | 1 | 1 | .50 | 2 | .170 | .228 | .264 |
| 2000 | Tor | AL | 28 | 22 | 3 | 0 | 0 | 0 | (0 | 0) | 3 | 3 | 0 | 0 | 1 | 0 | 5 | 1 | 0 | 0 | 1 | 0 | 1.00 | 0 | .136 | .208 | .136 |
| 2002 | Tor | AL | 42 | 112 | 20 | 4 | 1 | 3 | (2 | 1) | 35 | 14 | 13 | 8 | 4 | 0 | 15 | 0 | 0 | 0 | 5 | 0 | 1.00 | 0 | .179 | .207 | .313 |
| 2004 | Atl | NL | 77 | 162 | 37 | 9 | 4 | 6 | (3 | 3) | 72 | 24 | 17 | 20 | 9 | 1 | 28 | 1 | 2 | 1 | 6 | 1 | .86 | 1 | .228 | .272 | .444 |
| 2006 | Cin | NL | 31 | 38 | 7 | 2 | 0 | 0 | (0 | 0) | 9 | 3 | 1 | 0 | 0 | 0 | 6 | 0 | 2 | 0 | 0 | 0 | - | 2 | .184 | .184 | .237 |
| 2007 | Cin | NL | 5 | 5 | 1 | 0 | 1 | 0 | (0 | 0) | 3 | 1 | 1 | 1 | 1 | 1 | 1 | 0 | 0 | 0 | 0 | 0 | - | 0 | .200 | .333 | .600 |
| 2008 | CWS | AL | 57 | 129 | 32 | 4 | 2 | 6 | (2 | 4) | 58 | 20 | 18 | 14 | 8 | 0 | 32 | 1 | 3 | 2 | 9 | 0 | 1.00 | 5 | .248 | .293 | .450 |
| 2009 | CWS | AL | 84 | 142 | 32 | 8 | 3 | 2 | (2 | 0) | 52 | 17 | 11 | 10 | 3 | 0 | 27 | 4 | 4 | 0 | 4 | 5 | .44 | 1 | .225 | .262 | .366 |
| 2010 | Tor | AL | 52 | 112 | 28 | 3 | 2 | 3 | (1 | 2) | 44 | 20 | 14 | 17 | 4 | 0 | 29 | 1 | 1 | 0 | 4 | 0 | 1.00 | 1 | .250 | .282 | .393 |
| 2011 | 2 Tms | | 69 | 99 | 20 | 2 | 1 | 2 | (0 | 2) | 30 | 10 | 7 | 5 | 3 | 0 | 36 | 1 | 0 | 1 | 6 | 2 | .75 | 0 | .202 | .231 | .303 |
| 2012 | 2 Tms | AL | 101 | 224 | 58 | 10 | 2 | 8 | (5 | 3) | 96 | 31 | 30 | 29 | 11 | 0 | 52 | 1 | 0 | 3 | 19 | 4 | .83 | 2 | .259 | .293 | .429 |
| 2013 | CWS | AL | 30 | 64 | 15 | 3 | 0 | 1 | (0 | 1) | 21 | 6 | 3 | 4 | 2 | 0 | 14 | 0 | 0 | 0 | 1 | 1 | .50 | 1 | .234 | .258 | .328 |
| 11 | Fla | NL | 49 | 67 | 16 | 2 | 0 | 0 | (0 | 0) | 18 | 6 | 5 | 5 | 3 | 0 | 21 | 1 | 0 | 1 | 4 | 2 | .67 | 0 | .239 | .278 | .269 |
| 11 | Tor | AL | 20 | 32 | 4 | 0 | 1 | 2 | (0 | 2) | 12 | 4 | 2 | 0 | 0 | 0 | 15 | 0 | 0 | 0 | 2 | 0 | 1.00 | 0 | .125 | .125 | .375 |
| 12 | NYY | AL | 56 | 61 | 16 | 3 | 1 | 3 | (2 | 1) | 30 | 11 | 8 | 10 | 2 | 0 | 12 | 0 | 0 | 0 | 7 | 0 | 1.00 | 1 | .262 | .286 | .492 |
| 12 | CWS | AL | 45 | 163 | 42 | 7 | 1 | 5 | (3 | 2) | 66 | 20 | 22 | 19 | 9 | 0 | 40 | 1 | 0 | 3 | 12 | 4 | .75 | 1 | .258 | .295 | .405 |
| Postseason | | | 8 | 12 | 3 | 2 | 0 | 1 | (0 | 1) | 8 | 3 | 5 | 3 | 1 | 0 | 4 | 0 | 0 | 0 | 1 | 0 | 1.00 | 0 | .250 | .308 | .667 |
| 11 ML YEARS | | | 576 | 1109 | 253 | 45 | 16 | 31 | (15 | 16) | 423 | 149 | 115 | 108 | 46 | 2 | 245 | 10 | 12 | 7 | 55 | 13 | .81 | 13 | .228 | .264 | .381 |

# Chris Withrow

**Pitches:** R **Bats:** R **Pos:** RP-26 **Ht:** 6'4" **Wt:** 215 **Born:** 4/1/1989 **Age:** 25

| HOW MUCH HE PITCHED | | | | | | | | WHAT HE GAVE UP | | | | | | | | | | | | THE RESULTS | | | | | | | |
|---|---|---|---|---|---|---|---|---|---|---|---|---|---|---|---|---|---|---|---|---|---|---|---|---|---|---|---|
| Year | Team | Lg | G | GS | CG | GF | IP | BFP | H | R | ER | HR | SH | SF | HB | TBB | IBB | SO | WP | Bk | W | L | Pct | Sh | Sv-Op | Hld | ERC | ERA |
| 2009 | InldEm | A+ | 19 | 16 | 0 | 1 | 86.1 | 373 | 80 | 50 | 45 | 3 | 5 | 1 | 5 | 45 | 0 | 105 | 4 | 0 | 6 | 6 | .500 | 0 | 0- - | - | 3.97 | 4.69 |
| 2009 | Chatt | AA | 6 | 6 | 0 | 0 | 27.1 | 114 | 24 | 14 | 12 | 2 | 1 | 0 | 1 | 12 | 0 | 26 | 2 | 1 | 2 | 2 | .500 | 0 | 0- - | - | 3.60 | 3.95 |
| 2010 | Chatt | AA | 27 | 27 | 1 | 0 | 129.2 | 604 | 146 | 92 | 86 | 13 | 4 | 8 | 11 | 69 | 1 | 120 | 6 | 0 | 4 | 9 | .308 | 1 | 0- - | - | 5.65 | 5.97 |
| 2011 | Chatt | AA | 25 | 25 | 1 | 0 | 128.2 | 553 | 111 | 68 | 60 | 8 | 4 | 4 | 5 | 75 | 1 | 130 | 10 | 1 | 6 | 6 | .500 | 0 | 0- - | - | 3.98 | 4.20 |
| 2012 | Chatt | AA | 22 | 7 | 0 | 4 | 60.0 | 265 | 52 | 34 | 31 | 3 | 4 | 0 | 2 | 36 | 1 | 64 | 3 | 0 | 3 | 3 | .500 | 0 | 2- - | - | 3.83 | 4.65 |
| 2013 | Albq | AAA | 25 | 0 | 0 | 11 | 26.1 | 115 | 25 | 10 | 5 | 0 | 1 | 0 | 0 | 13 | 0 | 33 | 2 | 0 | 4 | 0 | 1.000 | 0 | 0- - | - | 3.42 | 1.71 |
| 2013 | LAD | NL | 26 | 0 | 0 | 4 | 34.2 | 134 | 20 | 10 | 10 | 5 | 0 | 0 | 0 | 13 | 0 | 43 | 2 | 0 | 3 | 0 | 1.000 | 0 | 1-2 | 4 | 2.11 | 2.60 |

# Ross Wolf

**Pitches:** R **Bats:** R **Pos:** RP-19; SP-3 **Ht:** 6'0" **Wt:** 180 **Born:** 10/18/1982 **Age:** 31

| HOW MUCH HE PITCHED | | | | | | | | WHAT HE GAVE UP | | | | | | | | | | | | THE RESULTS | | | | | | | |
|---|---|---|---|---|---|---|---|---|---|---|---|---|---|---|---|---|---|---|---|---|---|---|---|---|---|---|---|
| Year | Team | Lg | G | GS | CG | GF | IP | BFP | H | R | ER | HR | SH | SF | HB | TBB | IBB | SO | WP | Bk | W | L | Pct | Sh | Sv-Op | Hld | ERC | ERA |
| 2013 | Frisco* | AA | 1 | 0 | 0 | 1 | 1.2 | 8 | 3 | 1 | 1 | 0 | 1 | 0 | 0 | 0 | 0 | 1 | 0 | 0 | 0 | 1 | .000 | 0 | 0- - | - | 6.23 | 5.40 |
| 2013 | RdRck* | AAA | 7 | 6 | 0 | 0 | 35.2 | 140 | 27 | 8 | 7 | 1 | 1 | 2 | 1 | 10 | 0 | 26 | 1 | 0 | 1 | 1 | .500 | 0 | 0- - | - | 2.09 | 1.77 |
| 2007 | Fla | NL | 14 | 0 | 0 | 2 | 12.1 | 66 | 24 | 16 | 16 | 4 | 1 | 0 | 1 | 3 | 0 | 6 | 1 | 0 | 0 | 1 | .000 | 0 | 0-0 | 0 | 11.46 | 11.68 |
| 2010 | Oak | AL | 11 | 0 | 0 | 7 | 12.2 | 56 | 12 | 6 | 6 | 1 | 1 | 0 | 1 | 6 | 1 | 9 | 0 | 0 | 0 | 0 | - | 0 | 0-0 | 0 | 4.07 | 4.26 |
| 2013 | Tex | AL | 22 | 3 | 0 | 10 | 47.2 | 207 | 58 | 24 | 22 | 5 | 0 | 2 | 1 | 15 | 1 | 21 | 2 | 0 | 1 | 3 | .250 | 0 | 0-0 | 1 | 5.20 | 4.15 |
| 3 ML YEARS | | | 47 | 3 | 0 | 19 | 72.2 | 329 | 94 | 46 | 44 | 10 | 2 | 2 | 3 | 24 | 2 | 36 | 3 | 0 | 1 | 4 | .200 | 0 | 0-0 | 1 | 5.97 | 5.45 |

# Kolten Wong

**Bats:** L **Throws:** R **Pos:** 2B-18;PH-17;PR-1 COLT-enn **Ht:** 5'9" **Wt:** 185 **Born:** 10/10/1990 **Age:** 23

| BATTING | | | | | | | | | | | | | | | | | | | | BASERUNNING | | | | AVERAGES | | |
|---|---|---|---|---|---|---|---|---|---|---|---|---|---|---|---|---|---|---|---|---|---|---|---|---|---|---|
| Year | Team | Lg | G | AB | H | 2B | 3B | HR | (Hm | Rd) | TB | R | RBI | RC | TBB | IBB | SO | HBP | SH | SF | SB | CS | SB% | GDP | Avg | OBP | Slg |
| 2011 | QuadC | A | 47 | 194 | 65 | 15 | 2 | 5 | (- | -) | 99 | 39 | 25 | 40 | 21 | 1 | 24 | 3 | 0 | 4 | 9 | 5 | .64 | 4 | .335 | .401 | .510 |
| 2012 | Sprgfld | AA | 126 | 523 | 150 | 23 | 6 | 9 | (- | -) | 212 | 79 | 52 | 77 | 44 | 2 | 74 | 7 | 2 | 3 | 21 | 11 | .66 | 6 | .287 | .348 | .405 |
| 2013 | Memp | AAA | 107 | 412 | 125 | 21 | 8 | 10 | (- | -) | 192 | 68 | 45 | 76 | 41 | 3 | 60 | 4 | 2 | 4 | 20 | 1 | .95 | 9 | .303 | .369 | .466 |
| 2013 | StL | NL | 32 | 59 | 9 | 1 | 0 | 0 | (0 | 0) | 10 | 6 | 0 | 0 | 3 | 0 | 12 | 0 | 0 | 0 | 3 | 0 | 1.00 | 2 | .153 | .194 | .169 |

# Alex Wood

**Pitches:** L **Bats:** R **Pos:** RP-20; SP-11 **Ht:** 6'4" **Wt:** 215 **Born:** 1/12/1991 **Age:** 23

| HOW MUCH HE PITCHED | | | | | | | | WHAT HE GAVE UP | | | | | | | | | | | | THE RESULTS | | | | | | | |
|---|---|---|---|---|---|---|---|---|---|---|---|---|---|---|---|---|---|---|---|---|---|---|---|---|---|---|---|
| Year | Team | Lg | G | GS | CG | GF | IP | BFP | H | R | ER | HR | SH | SF | HB | TBB | IBB | SO | WP | Bk | W | L | Pct | Sh | Sv-Op | Hld | ERC | ERA |
| 2012 | Rome | A | 13 | 13 | 0 | 0 | 52.2 | 206 | 39 | 18 | 13 | 1 | 1 | 0 | 2 | 14 | 0 | 52 | 1 | 0 | 4 | 3 | .571 | 0 | 0- - | - | 1.95 | 2.22 |
| 2013 | Missi | AA | 10 | 10 | 0 | 0 | 57.0 | 227 | 41 | 10 | 8 | 1 | 0 | 1 | 1 | 15 | 0 | 57 | 1 | 0 | 4 | 2 | .667 | 0 | 0- - | - | 1.71 | 1.26 |
| 2013 | Gwnntt | AAA | 1 | 1 | 0 | 0 | 5.0 | 20 | 3 | 1 | 1 | 0 | 0 | 1 | 2 | 2 | 0 | 5 | 3 | 0 | 1 | 0 | 1.000 | 0 | 0- - | - | 2.96 | 1.80 |
| 2013 | Atl | NL | 31 | 11 | 0 | 9 | 77.2 | 327 | 76 | 29 | 27 | 3 | 6 | 4 | 1 | 27 | 1 | 77 | 4 | 2 | 3 | 3 | .500 | 0 | 0-0 | 1 | 3.40 | 3.13 |

# Blake Wood

**Pitches:** R **Bats:** R **Pos:** RP-2 **Ht:** 6'5" **Wt:** 240 **Born:** 8/8/1985 **Age:** 28

| HOW MUCH HE PITCHED | | | | | | | | WHAT HE GAVE UP | | | | | | | | | | | | THE RESULTS | | | | | | | |
|---|---|---|---|---|---|---|---|---|---|---|---|---|---|---|---|---|---|---|---|---|---|---|---|---|---|---|---|
| Year | Team | Lg | G | GS | CG | GF | IP | BFP | H | R | ER | HR | SH | SF | HB | TBB | IBB | SO | WP | Bk | W | L | Pct | Sh | Sv-Op | Hld | ERC | ERA |
| 2013 | Akron* | AA | 7 | 3 | 0 | 0 | 6.0 | 32 | 8 | 7 | 3 | 0 | 0 | 0 | 0 | 5 | 0 | 6 | 0 | 1 | 0 | 0 | - | 0 | 0- - | - | 6.59 | 4.50 |
| 2013 | Lk Cty* | A | 3 | 3 | 0 | 0 | 2.2 | 12 | 1 | 0 | 0 | 0 | 0 | 0 | 0 | 3 | 0 | 3 | 0 | 0 | 0 | 0 | - | 0 | 0- - | - | 2.59 | 0.00 |
| 2013 | MhVlly* | A- | 1 | 0 | 0 | 0 | 1.0 | 4 | 2 | 0 | 0 | 0 | 0 | 0 | 0 | 0 | 0 | 0 | 0 | 0 | 0 | 0 | - | 0 | 0- - | - | 9.49 | 0.00 |
| 2013 | Clmbs* | AAA | 18 | 0 | 0 | 6 | 16.2 | 71 | 11 | 4 | 4 | 0 | 0 | 1 | 1 | 10 | 0 | 23 | 1 | 0 | 2 | 0 | 1.000 | 0 | 0- - | - | 2.53 | 2.16 |
| 2010 | KC | AL | 51 | 0 | 0 | 13 | 49.2 | 220 | 54 | 29 | 28 | 6 | 2 | 6 | 1 | 22 | 5 | 31 | 3 | 0 | 1 | 3 | .250 | 0 | 0-4 | 15 | 4.83 | 5.07 |
| 2011 | KC | AL | 55 | 0 | 0 | 20 | 69.2 | 303 | 66 | 30 | 29 | 5 | 5 | 3 | 3 | 32 | 7 | 62 | 2 | 0 | 5 | 3 | .625 | 0 | 1-3 | 5 | 3.82 | 3.75 |
| 2013 | Cle | AL | 2 | 0 | 0 | 1 | 1.1 | 8 | 1 | 0 | 0 | 0 | 0 | 0 | 0 | 3 | 0 | 1 | 0 | 0 | 0 | 0 | - | 0 | 0-0 | 0 | 8.88 | 0.00 |
| 3 ML YEARS | | | 108 | 0 | 0 | 34 | 120.2 | 531 | 121 | 59 | 57 | 11 | 7 | 9 | 4 | 57 | 12 | 94 | 5 | 0 | 6 | 6 | .500 | 0 | 1-7 | 20 | 4.28 | 4.25 |

# Travis Wood

**Pitches:** L **Bats:** R **Pos:** SP-32 **Ht:** 5'11" **Wt:** 175 **Born:** 2/6/1987 **Age:** 27

| HOW MUCH HE PITCHED | | | | | | | | WHAT HE GAVE UP | | | | | | | | | | | | THE RESULTS | | | | | | | |
|---|---|---|---|---|---|---|---|---|---|---|---|---|---|---|---|---|---|---|---|---|---|---|---|---|---|---|---|
| Year | Team | Lg | G | GS | CG | GF | IP | BFP | H | R | ER | HR | SH | SF | HB | TBB | IBB | SO | WP | Bk | W | L | Pct | Sh | Sv-Op | Hld | ERC | ERA |
| 2010 | Cin | NL | 17 | 17 | 0 | 0 | 102.2 | 419 | 85 | 45 | 40 | 9 | 3 | 3 | 4 | 26 | 1 | 86 | 0 | 1 | 5 | 4 | .556 | 0 | 0-0 | 0 | 2.64 | 3.51 |
| 2011 | Cin | NL | 22 | 18 | 0 | 2 | 106.0 | 463 | 118 | 57 | 57 | 10 | 9 | 7 | 4 | 40 | 5 | 76 | 2 | 0 | 6 | 6 | .500 | 0 | 0-0 | 0 | 4.73 | 4.84 |
| 2012 | ChC | NL | 26 | 26 | 0 | 0 | 156.0 | 649 | 133 | 80 | 74 | 25 | 9 | 4 | 8 | 54 | 3 | 119 | 2 | 1 | 6 | 13 | .316 | 0 | 0-0 | 0 | 3.65 | 4.27 |
| 2013 | ChC | NL | 32 | 32 | 0 | 0 | 200.0 | 821 | 163 | 73 | 69 | 18 | 7 | 4 | 8 | 66 | 2 | 144 | 6 | 0 | 9 | 12 | .429 | 0 | 0-0 | 0 | 2.90 | 3.11 |
| Postseason | | | 1 | 0 | 0 | 0 | 3.1 | 12 | 1 | 0 | 0 | 0 | 0 | 0 | 0 | 1 | 1 | 3 | 0 | 0 | 0 | 0 | - | 0 | 0-0 | 0 | 0.38 | 0.00 |
| 4 ML YEARS | | | 97 | 93 | 0 | 2 | 564.2 | 2352 | 499 | 255 | 240 | 62 | 28 | 18 | 24 | 186 | 11 | 425 | 10 | 2 | 26 | 35 | .426 | 0 | 0-0 | 0 | 3.38 | 3.83 |

# Rob Wooten

**Pitches:** R **Bats:** R **Pos:** RP-27 WOOT-enn **Ht:** 6'1" **Wt:** 210 **Born:** 7/21/1985 **Age:** 28

| HOW MUCH HE PITCHED | | | | | | | | WHAT HE GAVE UP | | | | | | | | | | | | THE RESULTS | | | | | | | |
|---|---|---|---|---|---|---|---|---|---|---|---|---|---|---|---|---|---|---|---|---|---|---|---|---|---|---|---|
| Year | Team | Lg | G | GS | CG | GF | IP | BFP | H | R | ER | HR | SH | SF | HB | TBB | IBB | SO | WP | Bk | W | L | Pct | Sh | Sv-Op | Hld | ERC | ERA |
| 2009 | BrvdCt | A+ | 26 | 0 | 0 | 25 | 30.0 | 129 | 21 | 7 | 4 | 0 | 2 | 0 | 4 | 13 | 0 | 44 | 2 | 1 | 1 | 1 | .500 | 0 | 18- - | - | 2.35 | 1.20 |
| 2009 | Hntsvl | AA | 27 | 0 | 0 | 23 | 27.1 | 117 | 26 | 15 | 13 | 3 | 1 | 0 | 1 | 9 | 1 | 34 | 1 | 1 | 0 | 1 | .000 | 0 | 11- - | - | 3.64 | 4.28 |
| 2011 | BrvdCt | A+ | 12 | 0 | 0 | 6 | 21.1 | 83 | 15 | 6 | 6 | 0 | 0 | 1 | 0 | 3 | 0 | 18 | 0 | 0 | 2 | 0 | 1.000 | 0 | 1- - | - | 1.26 | 2.53 |
| 2011 | Hntsvl | AA | 36 | 0 | 0 | 27 | 42.2 | 188 | 41 | 20 | 16 | 3 | 5 | 0 | 5 | 15 | 2 | 41 | 3 | 1 | 3 | 3 | .500 | 0 | 7- - | - | 3.77 | 3.38 |

| Year Team | Lg | G | GS | CG | GF | IP | BFP | H | R | ER | HR | SH | SF | HB | TBB | IBB | SO | WP | Bk | W | L | Pct | Sh | Sv-Op | Hld | ERC | ERA |
|---|---|---|---|---|---|---|---|---|---|---|---|---|---|---|---|---|---|---|---|---|---|---|---|---|---|---|---|
| HOW MUCH HE PITCHED | | | | | | | | WHAT HE GAVE UP | | | | | | | | | | | | THE RESULTS | | | | | | | |
| 2012 Hntsvl | AA | 17 | 0 | 0 | 14 | 20.2 | 88 | 18 | 4 | 4 | 1 | 1 | 0 | 1 | 7 | 1 | 21 | 2 | 0 | 3 | 0 | 1.000 | 0 | 8- - | - | 2.85 | 1.74 |
| 2012 Nashv | AAA | 40 | 0 | 0 | 23 | 52.2 | 221 | 49 | 23 | 23 | 4 | 3 | 2 | 2 | 16 | 2 | 49 | 1 | 1 | 0 | 2 | .000 | 0 | 7- - | - | 3.25 | 3.93 |
| 2013 Nashv | AAA | 40 | 0 | 0 | 36 | 52.0 | 208 | 40 | 17 | 17 | 4 | 3 | 0 | 2 | 12 | 1 | 45 | 5 | 0 | 0 | 1 | .000 | 0 | 20- - | - | 2.21 | 2.94 |
| 2013 Mil | NL | 27 | 0 | 0 | 6 | 27.2 | 115 | 27 | 12 | 12 | 1 | 1 | 0 | 1 | 8 | 2 | 18 | 0 | 0 | 3 | 1 | .750 | 0 | 0-1 | 8 | 3.16 | 3.90 |

## Brandon Workman

**Pitches:** R **Bats:** R **Pos:** RP-17; SP-3 **Ht:** 6'4" **Wt:** 195 **Born:** 8/13/1988 **Age:** 25

| HOW MUCH HE PITCHED | | | | | | | | WHAT HE GAVE UP | | | | | | | | | | | | THE RESULTS | | | | | | | |
|---|---|---|---|---|---|---|---|---|---|---|---|---|---|---|---|---|---|---|---|---|---|---|---|---|---|---|---|
| Year Team | Lg | G | GS | CG | GF | IP | BFP | H | R | ER | HR | SH | SF | HB | TBB | IBB | SO | WP | Bk | W | L | Pct | Sh | Sv-Op | Hld | ERC | ERA |
| 2011 Grnvlle | A | 26 | 26 | 0 | 0 | 131.0 | 540 | 128 | 67 | 54 | 10 | 5 | 4 | 5 | 33 | 0 | 115 | 6 | 1 | 6 | 7 | .462 | 0 | 0- - | - | 3.42 | 3.71 |
| 2012 Salem | A+ | 20 | 20 | 0 | 0 | 113.2 | 454 | 104 | 47 | 43 | 10 | 4 | 3 | 1 | 20 | 0 | 107 | 6 | 1 | 7 | 7 | .500 | 0 | 0- - | - | 2.76 | 3.40 |
| 2012 Portlnd | AA | 5 | 5 | 0 | 0 | 25.0 | 101 | 23 | 12 | 11 | 2 | 1 | 2 | 0 | 5 | 0 | 23 | 0 | 0 | 3 | 1 | .750 | 0 | 0- - | - | 2.77 | 3.96 |
| 2013 Portlnd | AA | 11 | 10 | 0 | 0 | 65.2 | 259 | 51 | 29 | 25 | 6 | 2 | 2 | 1 | 17 | 0 | 74 | 3 | 0 | 5 | 1 | .833 | 0 | 0- - | - | 2.42 | 3.43 |
| 2013 Pwtckt | AAA | 6 | 6 | 0 | 0 | 35.1 | 152 | 39 | 13 | 11 | 6 | 2 | 0 | 2 | 13 | 0 | 34 | 1 | 0 | 3 | 1 | .750 | 0 | 0- - | - | 5.47 | 2.80 |
| 2013 Bos | AL | 20 | 3 | 0 | 5 | 41.2 | 180 | 44 | 23 | 23 | 5 | 2 | 1 | 0 | 15 | 1 | 47 | 1 | 0 | 6 | 3 | .667 | 0 | 0-1 | 1 | 4.34 | 4.97 |

## Vance Worley

**Pitches:** R **Bats:** R **Pos:** SP-10 **Ht:** 6'2" **Wt:** 230 **Born:** 9/25/1987 **Age:** 26

| HOW MUCH HE PITCHED | | | | | | | | WHAT HE GAVE UP | | | | | | | | | | | | THE RESULTS | | | | | | | |
|---|---|---|---|---|---|---|---|---|---|---|---|---|---|---|---|---|---|---|---|---|---|---|---|---|---|---|---|
| Year Team | Lg | G | GS | CG | GF | IP | BFP | H | R | ER | HR | SH | SF | HB | TBB | IBB | SO | WP | Bk | W | L | Pct | Sh | Sv-Op | Hld | ERC | ERA |
| 2013 Roch* | AAA | 9 | 9 | 3 | 0 | 58.0 | 251 | 65 | 31 | 25 | 3 | 1 | 1 | 1 | 17 | 1 | 34 | 1 | 0 | 6 | 3 | .667 | 1 | 0- - | - | 4.03 | 3.88 |
| 2010 Phi | NL | 5 | 2 | 0 | 2 | 13.0 | 51 | 8 | 2 | 2 | 1 | 2 | 0 | 0 | 4 | 0 | 12 | 1 | 0 | 1 | 1 | .500 | 0 | 0-0 | 0 | 1.66 | 1.38 |
| 2011 Phi | NL | 25 | 21 | 1 | 0 | 131.2 | 553 | 116 | 47 | 44 | 10 | 9 | 5 | 3 | 46 | 2 | 119 | 2 | 1 | 11 | 3 | .786 | 0 | 0-0 | 2 | 3.12 | 3.01 |
| 2012 Phi | NL | 23 | 23 | 0 | 0 | 133.0 | 590 | 154 | 69 | 62 | 12 | 11 | 3 | 6 | 47 | 4 | 107 | 1 | 0 | 6 | 9 | .400 | 0 | 0-0 | 0 | 4.87 | 4.20 |
| 2013 Min | AL | 10 | 10 | 0 | 0 | 48.2 | 234 | 82 | 43 | 39 | 9 | 0 | 1 | 3 | 15 | 1 | 25 | 1 | 0 | 1 | 5 | .167 | 0 | 0-0 | 0 | 9.17 | 7.21 |
| Postseason | | 2 | 0 | 0 | 0 | 1.1 | 8 | 3 | 1 | 1 | 0 | 0 | 0 | 0 | 1 | 0 | 0 | 0 | 0 | 0 | 0 | - | 0 | 0-0 | 1 | 12.64 | 6.75 |
| 4 ML YEARS | | 63 | 56 | 1 | 2 | 326.1 | 1428 | 360 | 161 | 147 | 32 | 22 | 9 | 12 | 112 | 7 | 263 | 5 | 1 | 19 | 18 | .514 | 0 | 0-0 | 2 | 4.54 | 4.05 |

## Danny Worth

**Bats:** R **Throws:** R **Pos:** 3B-2;DH-1;PR-1 **Ht:** 6'1" **Wt:** 185 **Born:** 9/30/1985 **Age:** 28

| BATTING | | | | | | | | | | | | | | | | | | | | BASERUNNING | | | | AVERAGES | | |
|---|---|---|---|---|---|---|---|---|---|---|---|---|---|---|---|---|---|---|---|---|---|---|---|---|---|---|
| Year Team | Lg | G | AB | H | 2B | 3B | HR | (Hm | Rd) | TB | R | RBI | RC | TBB | IBB | SO | HBP | SH | SF | SB | CS | SB% | GDP | Avg | OBP | Slg |
| 2013 Toledo* | AAA | 82 | 305 | 68 | 19 | 2 | 1 | (- | -) | 94 | 33 | 22 | 30 | 35 | 0 | 91 | 1 | 4 | 0 | 9 | 5 | .64 | 5 | .223 | .305 | .308 |
| 2013 Lkland* | A+ | 4 | 17 | 3 | 1 | 0 | 0 | (- | -) | 4 | 2 | 3 | 0 | 0 | 0 | 3 | 0 | 0 | 0 | 0 | 0 | - | 1 | .176 | .176 | .235 |
| 2010 Det | AL | 39 | 106 | 27 | 5 | 0 | 2 | (2 | 0) | 38 | 10 | 8 | 11 | 6 | 0 | 13 | 0 | 3 | 0 | 1 | 2 | .33 | 0 | .255 | .295 | .358 |
| 2011 Det | AL | 30 | 37 | 10 | 2 | 0 | 0 | (0 | 0) | 12 | 6 | 3 | 3 | 2 | 0 | 9 | 0 | 0 | 0 | 0 | 0 | - | 0 | .270 | .308 | .324 |
| 2012 Det | AL | 43 | 74 | 16 | 3 | 0 | 0 | (0 | 0) | 19 | 9 | 3 | 7 | 13 | 0 | 23 | 0 | 2 | 1 | 0 | 0 | - | 1 | .216 | .330 | .257 |
| 2013 Det | AL | 3 | 2 | 0 | 0 | 0 | 0 | (0 | 0) | 0 | 0 | 0 | 0 | 0 | 0 | 1 | 0 | 0 | 0 | 0 | 0 | - | 1 | .000 | .000 | .000 |
| Postseason | | 4 | 1 | 0 | 0 | 0 | 0 | (0 | 0) | 0 | 0 | 0 | 0 | 0 | 0 | 1 | 0 | 0 | 0 | 0 | 0 | - | 0 | .000 | .000 | .000 |
| 4 ML YEARS | | 115 | 219 | 53 | 10 | 0 | 2 | (2 | 0) | 69 | 25 | 14 | 21 | 21 | 0 | 46 | 0 | 5 | 1 | 1 | 2 | .33 | 2 | .242 | .307 | .315 |

## David Wright

**Bats:** R **Throws:** R **Pos:** 3B-111;PH-1 **Ht:** 6'0" **Wt:** 210 **Born:** 12/20/1982 **Age:** 31

| BATTING | | | | | | | | | | | | | | | | | | | | BASERUNNING | | | | AVERAGES | | |
|---|---|---|---|---|---|---|---|---|---|---|---|---|---|---|---|---|---|---|---|---|---|---|---|---|---|---|
| Year Team | Lg | G | AB | H | 2B | 3B | HR | (Hm | Rd) | TB | R | RBI | RC | TBB | IBB | SO | HBP | SH | SF | SB | CS | SB% | GDP | Avg | OBP | Slg |
| 2004 NYM | NL | 69 | 263 | 77 | 17 | 1 | 14 | (8 | 6) | 138 | 41 | 40 | 42 | 14 | 0 | 40 | 3 | 0 | 3 | 6 | 0 | 1.00 | 7 | .293 | .332 | .525 |
| 2005 NYM | NL | 160 | 575 | 176 | 42 | 1 | 27 | (12 | 15) | 301 | 99 | 102 | 105 | 72 | 2 | 113 | 7 | 0 | 3 | 17 | 7 | .71 | 16 | .306 | .388 | .523 |
| 2006 NYM | NL | 154 | 582 | 181 | 40 | 5 | 26 | (13 | 13) | 309 | 96 | 116 | 119 | 66 | 13 | 113 | 5 | 0 | 8 | 20 | 5 | .80 | 15 | .311 | .381 | .531 |
| 2007 NYM | NL | 160 | 604 | 196 | 42 | 1 | 30 | (16 | 14) | 330 | 113 | 107 | 127 | 94 | 6 | 115 | 6 | 0 | 7 | 34 | 5 | .87 | 14 | .325 | .416 | .546 |
| 2008 NYM | NL | 160 | 626 | 189 | 42 | 2 | 33 | (21 | 12) | 334 | 115 | 124 | 116 | 94 | 5 | 118 | 4 | 0 | **11** | 15 | 5 | .75 | 15 | .302 | .390 | .534 |
| 2009 NYM | NL | 144 | 535 | 164 | 39 | 3 | 10 | (5 | 5) | 239 | 88 | 72 | 86 | 74 | 8 | 140 | 3 | 0 | 6 | 27 | 9 | .75 | 16 | .307 | .390 | .447 |
| 2010 NYM | NL | 157 | 587 | 166 | 36 | 3 | 29 | (12 | 17) | 295 | 87 | 103 | 97 | 69 | 9 | 161 | 2 | 0 | **12** | 19 | 11 | .63 | 12 | .283 | .354 | .503 |
| 2011 NYM | NL | 102 | 389 | 99 | 23 | 1 | 14 | (5 | 9) | 166 | 60 | 61 | 58 | 52 | 4 | 97 | 3 | 0 | 3 | 13 | 2 | .87 | 5 | .254 | .345 | .427 |
| 2012 NYM | NL | 156 | 581 | 178 | 41 | 2 | 21 | (12 | 9) | 286 | 91 | 93 | 105 | 81 | 16 | 112 | 3 | 0 | 5 | 15 | 10 | .60 | 15 | .306 | .391 | .492 |
| 2013 NYM | NL | 112 | 430 | 132 | 23 | 6 | 18 | (6 | 12) | 221 | 63 | 58 | 78 | 55 | 5 | 79 | 5 | 0 | 2 | 17 | 3 | .85 | 11 | .307 | .390 | .514 |
| Postseason | | 10 | 37 | 8 | 3 | 0 | 1 | (0 | 1) | 14 | 3 | 6 | 5 | 5 | 1 | 8 | 0 | 0 | 0 | 0 | 0 | - | 0 | .216 | .310 | .378 |
| 10 ML YEARS | | 1374 | 5172 | 1558 | 345 | 25 | 222 | (110 | 112) | 2619 | 853 | 876 | 933 | 671 | 68 | 1088 | 41 | 0 | 60 | 183 | 57 | .76 | 126 | .301 | .382 | .506 |

## Jamey Wright

**Pitches:** R **Bats:** R **Pos:** RP-65; SP-1 **Ht:** 6'6" **Wt:** 235 **Born:** 12/24/1974 **Age:** 39

| HOW MUCH HE PITCHED | | | | | | | | WHAT HE GAVE UP | | | | | | | | | | | | THE RESULTS | | | | | | | |
|---|---|---|---|---|---|---|---|---|---|---|---|---|---|---|---|---|---|---|---|---|---|---|---|---|---|---|---|
| Year Team | Lg | G | GS | CG | GF | IP | BFP | H | R | ER | HR | SH | SF | HB | TBB | IBB | SO | WP | Bk | W | L | Pct | Sh | Sv-Op | Hld | ERC | ERA |
| 1996 Col | NL | 16 | 15 | 0 | 0 | 91.1 | 406 | 105 | 60 | 50 | 8 | 4 | 2 | 7 | 41 | 1 | 45 | 1 | 2 | 4 | 4 | .500 | 0 | 0-0 | 1 | 5.50 | 4.93 |
| 1997 Col | NL | 26 | 26 | 1 | 0 | 149.2 | 698 | 198 | 113 | 104 | 19 | 8 | 3 | 11 | 71 | 3 | 59 | 6 | 2 | 8 | 12 | .400 | 0 | 0-0 | 0 | 6.96 | 6.25 |
| 1998 Col | NL | 34 | 34 | 1 | 0 | 206.1 | 919 | 235 | 143 | 130 | 24 | 8 | 6 | 11 | 95 | 3 | 86 | 6 | 3 | 9 | 14 | .391 | 0 | 0-0 | 0 | 5.57 | 5.67 |
| 1999 Col | NL | 16 | 16 | 0 | 0 | 94.1 | 423 | 110 | 52 | 51 | 10 | 3 | 4 | 4 | 54 | 3 | 49 | 3 | 0 | 4 | 3 | .571 | 0 | 0-0 | 0 | 6.19 | 4.87 |
| 2000 Mil | NL | 26 | 25 | 0 | 1 | 164.2 | 718 | 157 | 81 | 75 | 12 | 4 | 6 | **18** | 88 | 5 | 96 | 9 | 2 | 7 | 9 | .438 | 0 | 0-0 | 0 | 4.67 | 4.10 |
| 2001 Mil | NL | 33 | 33 | 1 | 0 | 194.2 | 868 | 201 | 115 | 106 | 26 | 7 | 5 | **20** | 98 | 10 | 129 | 6 | 1 | 11 | 12 | .478 | 1 | 0-0 | 0 | 5.36 | 4.90 |
| 2002 2 Tms | NL | 23 | 22 | 1 | 0 | 129.1 | 585 | 130 | 80 | 76 | 17 | 9 | 6 | 11 | 75 | 9 | 77 | 9 | 0 | 7 | 13 | .350 | 1 | 0-0 | 0 | 5.35 | 5.29 |
| 2003 KC | AL | 4 | 4 | 2 | 0 | 25.1 | 106 | 23 | 14 | 12 | 1 | 0 | 0 | 1 | 11 | 0 | 19 | 0 | 0 | 1 | 2 | .333 | 1 | 0-0 | 0 | 3.53 | 4.26 |
| 2004 Col | NL | 14 | 14 | 0 | 0 | 78.2 | 361 | 82 | 39 | 36 | 8 | 1 | 1 | 6 | 45 | 3 | 41 | 3 | 0 | 2 | 3 | .400 | 0 | 0-0 | 0 | 5.26 | 4.12 |
| 2005 Col | NL | 34 | 27 | 0 | 1 | 171.1 | 782 | 201 | 119 | 104 | 22 | 4 | 3 | 15 | 81 | 4 | 101 | 2 | 2 | 8 | 16 | .333 | 0 | 0-0 | 1 | 6.02 | 5.46 |
| 2006 SF | NL | 34 | 21 | 0 | 2 | 156.0 | 676 | 167 | 95 | 90 | 16 | 5 | 4 | 10 | 64 | 4 | 79 | 6 | 0 | 6 | 10 | .375 | 0 | 0-0 | 0 | 4.89 | 5.19 |
| 2007 Tex | AL | 20 | 9 | 0 | 3 | 77.0 | 330 | 72 | 35 | 31 | 6 | 3 | 2 | 5 | 41 | 2 | 39 | 4 | 0 | 4 | 5 | .444 | 0 | 0-0 | 1 | 4.44 | 3.62 |
| 2008 Tex | AL | 75 | 0 | 0 | 17 | 84.1 | 379 | 93 | 57 | 48 | 5 | 3 | 4 | 8 | 35 | 3 | 60 | 5 | 0 | 8 | 7 | .533 | 0 | 0-6 | 17 | 4.74 | 5.12 |

| HOW MUCH HE PITCHED | | | | | | | | | WHAT HE GAVE UP | | | | | | | | | | | | THE RESULTS | | | | | | | |
|---|---|---|---|---|---|---|---|---|---|---|---|---|---|---|---|---|---|---|---|---|---|---|---|---|---|---|---|
| Year | Team | Lg | G | GS | CG | GF | IP | BFP | H | R | ER | HR | SH | SF | HB | TBB | IBB | SO | WP | Bk | W | L | Pct | Sh | Sv-Op | Hld | ERC | ERA |
| 2009 | KC | AL | 65 | 0 | 0 | 14 | 79.0 | 350 | 73 | 51 | 38 | 8 | 4 | 0 | 7 | 44 | 5 | 60 | 7 | 0 | 3 | 5 | .375 | 0 | 0-3 | 12 | 4.56 | 4.33 |
| 2010 | 2 Tms | AL | 46 | 0 | 0 | 17 | 58.1 | 249 | 55 | 33 | 27 | 3 | 3 | 3 | 3 | 25 | 1 | 28 | 4 | 1 | 1 | 3 | .250 | 0 | 0-1 | 9 | 3.75 | 4.17 |
| 2011 | Sea | AL | 60 | 0 | 0 | 19 | 68.1 | 286 | 61 | 26 | 24 | 6 | 2 | 1 | 5 | 30 | 3 | 48 | 4 | 0 | 2 | 3 | .400 | 0 | 1-5 | 16 | 3.89 | 3.16 |
| 2012 | LAD | NL | 66 | 0 | 0 | 22 | 67.2 | 306 | 72 | 35 | 28 | 2 | 3 | 2 | 4 | 30 | 7 | 54 | 2 | 0 | 5 | 3 | .625 | 0 | 0-0 | 6 | 4.07 | 3.72 |
| 2013 | TB | AL | 66 | 1 | 0 | 15 | 70.0 | 288 | 61 | 25 | 24 | 4 | 3 | 3 | 5 | 23 | 3 | 65 | 5 | 0 | 2 | 2 | .500 | 0 | 0-1 | 6 | 3.09 | 3.09 |
| 02 | Mil | NL | 19 | 19 | 1 | 0 | 114.1 | 515 | 115 | 72 | 68 | 15 | 9 | 6 | 11 | 63 | 8 | 69 | 8 | 0 | 5 | 13 | .278 | 1 | 0-0 | 0 | 5.28 | 5.35 |
| 02 | StL | NL | 4 | 3 | 0 | 0 | 15.0 | 70 | 15 | 8 | 8 | 2 | 0 | 0 | 0 | 12 | 1 | 8 | 1 | 0 | 2 | 0 | 1.000 | 0 | 0-0 | 0 | 5.87 | 4.80 |
| 10 | Cle | AL | 18 | 0 | 0 | 9 | 21.1 | 98 | 25 | 18 | 13 | 1 | 1 | 1 | 2 | 9 | 0 | 9 | 1 | 0 | 1 | 2 | .333 | 0 | 0-0 | 1 | 5.10 | 5.48 |
| 10 | Sea | AL | 28 | 0 | 0 | 8 | 37.0 | 151 | 30 | 15 | 14 | 2 | 2 | 2 | 1 | 16 | 1 | 19 | 3 | 1 | 0 | 1 | .000 | 0 | 0-1 | 8 | 3.03 | 3.41 |
| 18 ML YEARS | | | 658 | 247 | 6 | 111 | 1966.1 | 8730 | 2096 | 1173 | 1054 | 197 | 74 | 55 | 151 | 951 | 69 | 1135 | 82 | 13 | 92 | 126 | .422 | 3 | 1-16 | 69 | 5.14 | 4.82 |

## Steven Wright

**Pitches:** R **Bats:** R **Pos:** RP-3; SP-1 **Ht:** 6'1" **Wt:** 220 **Born:** 8/30/1984 **Age:** 29

| HOW MUCH HE PITCHED | | | | | | | | | WHAT HE GAVE UP | | | | | | | | | | | | THE RESULTS | | | | | | | |
|---|---|---|---|---|---|---|---|---|---|---|---|---|---|---|---|---|---|---|---|---|---|---|---|---|---|---|---|---|
| Year | Team | Lg | G | GS | CG | GF | IP | BFP | H | R | ER | HR | SH | SF | HB | TBB | IBB | SO | WP | Bk | W | L | Pct | Sh | Sv-Op | Hld | ERC | ERA |
| 2009 | Akron | AA | 36 | 5 | 0 | 9 | 81.1 | 331 | 72 | 24 | 21 | 1 | 2 | 1 | 2 | 20 | 0 | 64 | 0 | 0 | 10 | 0 | 1.000 | 0 | 2-- | - | 2.43 | 2.32 |
| 2009 | Clmbs | AAA | 2 | 1 | 0 | 0 | 5.2 | 24 | 5 | 3 | 3 | 0 | 0 | 0 | 1 | 0 | 0 | 4 | 0 | 0 | 0 | 0 | - | 0 | 0-- | - | 1.88 | 4.76 |
| 2010 | Clmbs | AAA | 9 | 0 | 0 | 4 | 10.2 | 49 | 13 | 9 | 9 | 2 | 0 | 0 | 0 | 5 | 0 | 10 | 0 | 0 | 0 | 1 | .000 | 0 | 0-- | - | 6.32 | 7.59 |
| 2010 | Akron | AA | 39 | 2 | 0 | 18 | 64.2 | 282 | 73 | 33 | 31 | 4 | 2 | 1 | 3 | 21 | 1 | 48 | 2 | 1 | 2 | 2 | .500 | 0 | 5-- | - | 4.43 | 4.31 |
| 2011 | Lk Cty | A | 9 | 9 | 0 | 0 | 46.0 | 205 | 48 | 30 | 16 | 3 | 0 | 2 | 3 | 24 | 0 | 33 | 5 | 0 | 1 | 2 | .333 | 0 | 0-- | - | 4.88 | 3.13 |
| 2011 | Clmbs | AAA | 1 | 0 | 0 | 0 | 2.2 | 12 | 5 | 2 | 2 | 0 | 0 | 0 | 0 | 0 | 0 | 2 | 1 | 0 | 0 | 0 | - | 0 | 0-- | - | 7.29 | 6.75 |
| 2011 | Akron | AA | 8 | 7 | 0 | 0 | 46.2 | 212 | 47 | 32 | 31 | 8 | 1 | 2 | 5 | 28 | 0 | 35 | 14 | 0 | 2 | 4 | .333 | 0 | 0-- | - | 6.03 | 5.98 |
| 2011 | Knstn | A+ | 7 | 4 | 0 | 3 | 38.1 | 172 | 47 | 28 | 19 | 7 | 0 | 1 | 1 | 16 | 0 | 27 | 7 | 0 | 1 | 2 | .333 | 0 | 0-- | - | 6.35 | 4.46 |
| 2012 | Akron | AA | 20 | 20 | 1 | 0 | 115.2 | 488 | 86 | 44 | 34 | 8 | 3 | 2 | 5 | 62 | 0 | 101 | 11 | 0 | 9 | 6 | .600 | 1 | 0-- | - | 3.18 | 2.65 |
| 2012 | Portlnd | AA | 1 | 1 | 0 | 0 | 6.0 | 24 | 5 | 1 | 1 | 0 | 0 | 0 | 1 | 2 | 0 | 2 | 0 | 0 | 1 | 0 | 1.000 | 0 | 0-- | - | 3.07 | 1.50 |
| 2012 | Pwtckt | AAA | 4 | 4 | 0 | 0 | 20.0 | 88 | 19 | 10 | 7 | 1 | 1 | 0 | 2 | 5 | 0 | 16 | 1 | 0 | 0 | 1 | .000 | 0 | 0-- | - | 3.11 | 3.15 |
| 2013 | Pwtckt | AAA | 24 | 24 | 3 | 0 | 135.1 | 586 | 130 | 64 | 52 | 10 | 0 | 6 | 4 | 65 | 0 | 99 | 15 | 0 | 8 | 7 | .533 | 3 | 0-- | - | 4.14 | 3.46 |
| 2013 | Bos | AL | 4 | 1 | 0 | 2 | 13.1 | 59 | 12 | 8 | 8 | 0 | 0 | 0 | 1 | 9 | 0 | 10 | 2 | 0 | 2 | 0 | 1.000 | 0 | 0-0 | 0 | 4.22 | 5.40 |

## Wesley Wright

**Pitches:** L **Bats:** R **Pos:** RP-71 **Ht:** 5'11" **Wt:** 185 **Born:** 1/28/1985 **Age:** 29

| HOW MUCH HE PITCHED | | | | | | | | | WHAT HE GAVE UP | | | | | | | | | | | | THE RESULTS | | | | | | | |
|---|---|---|---|---|---|---|---|---|---|---|---|---|---|---|---|---|---|---|---|---|---|---|---|---|---|---|---|---|
| Year | Team | Lg | G | GS | CG | GF | IP | BFP | H | R | ER | HR | SH | SF | HB | TBB | IBB | SO | WP | Bk | W | L | Pct | Sh | Sv-Op | Hld | ERC | ERA |
| 2008 | Hou | NL | 71 | 0 | 0 | 15 | 55.2 | 250 | 45 | 34 | 31 | 8 | 1 | 1 | 4 | 34 | 4 | 57 | 2 | 1 | 4 | 3 | .571 | 0 | 1-1 | 13 | 4.21 | 5.01 |
| 2009 | Hou | NL | 49 | 0 | 0 | 5 | 44.2 | 204 | 53 | 27 | 27 | 9 | 0 | 2 | 0 | 25 | 3 | 47 | 2 | 0 | 3 | 4 | .429 | 0 | 0-2 | 6 | 6.64 | 5.44 |
| 2010 | Hou | NL | 14 | 4 | 0 | 3 | 33.0 | 148 | 37 | 27 | 21 | 6 | 2 | 1 | 3 | 13 | 0 | 29 | 0 | 0 | 1 | 2 | .333 | 0 | 0-0 | 0 | 5.78 | 5.73 |
| 2011 | Hou | NL | 21 | 0 | 0 | 5 | 12.0 | 44 | 6 | 2 | 2 | 1 | 0 | 0 | 0 | 5 | 0 | 11 | 1 | 0 | 0 | 0 | - | 0 | 0-1 | 3 | 1.68 | 1.50 |
| 2012 | Hou | NL | 77 | 0 | 0 | 13 | 52.1 | 223 | 45 | 20 | 19 | 4 | 1 | 0 | 6 | 17 | 0 | 54 | 1 | 0 | 2 | 2 | .500 | 0 | 1-2 | 19 | 3.26 | 3.27 |
| 2013 | 2 Tms | AL | 71 | 0 | 0 | 17 | 53.2 | 232 | 54 | 24 | 22 | 7 | 1 | 2 | 3 | 19 | 2 | 55 | 2 | 0 | 0 | 4 | .000 | 0 | 0-4 | 9 | 4.31 | 3.69 |
| 13 | Hou | AL | 55 | 0 | 0 | 13 | 41.1 | 184 | 45 | 20 | 18 | 5 | 1 | 2 | 3 | 16 | 2 | 40 | 2 | 0 | 0 | 4 | .000 | 0 | 0-4 | 8 | 4.89 | 3.92 |
| 13 | TB | AL | 16 | 0 | 0 | 4 | 12.1 | 48 | 9 | 4 | 4 | 2 | 0 | 0 | 0 | 3 | 0 | 15 | 0 | 0 | 0 | 0 | - | 0 | 0-0 | 1 | 2.47 | 2.92 |
| 6 ML YEARS | | | 303 | 4 | 0 | 58 | 251.1 | 1101 | 240 | 134 | 122 | 35 | 5 | 6 | 16 | 113 | 9 | 253 | 8 | 1 | 10 | 15 | .400 | 0 | 2-10 | 50 | 4.49 | 4.37 |

## Yao-Hsun Yang

**Pitches:** L **Bats:** L **Pos:** P YOW-shun YAYNG **Ht:** 5'10" **Wt:** 191 **Born:** 1/22/1983 **Age:** 31

| HOW MUCH HE PITCHED | | | | | | | | | WHAT HE GAVE UP | | | | | | | | | | | | THE RESULTS | | | | | | | |
|---|---|---|---|---|---|---|---|---|---|---|---|---|---|---|---|---|---|---|---|---|---|---|---|---|---|---|---|---|
| Year | Team | Lg | G | GS | CG | GF | IP | BFP | H | R | ER | HR | SH | SF | HB | TBB | IBB | SO | WP | Bk | W | L | Pct | Sh | Sv-Op | Hld | ERC | ERA |
| 2009 | Fkuoka | Jap | 4 | 0 | 0 | - | 9.2 | 48 | 12 | 10 | 7 | 0 | - | - | 2 | 6 | 0 | 10 | 0 | 0 | 0 | 0 | - | 0 | 0-- | - | 6.38 | 6.52 |
| 2010 | Fkuoka | Jap | 14 | 4 | 0 | 4 | 32.2 | 149 | 33 | 18 | 8 | 2 | - | - | 3 | 18 | 0 | 28 | 1 | 0 | 2 | 0 | 1.000 | 0 | 0-- | - | 4.78 | 2.20 |
| 2012 | Fkuoka | Jap | 9 | 7 | 1 | 0 | 42.2 | 168 | 24 | 10 | 7 | 1 | - | - | 4 | 18 | 0 | 45 | 1 | 0 | 2 | 3 | .400 | 1 | 0-- | - | 1.84 | 1.48 |

## Christian Yelich

**Bats:** L **Throws:** R **Pos:** LF-59;CF-5;PH-1 YELL-itch **Ht:** 6'4" **Wt:** 195 **Born:** 12/5/1991 **Age:** 22

| BATTING | | | | | | | | | | | | | | | | | | | | | BASERUNNING | | | | AVERAGES | | |
|---|---|---|---|---|---|---|---|---|---|---|---|---|---|---|---|---|---|---|---|---|---|---|---|---|---|---|---|
| Year | Team | Lg | G | AB | H | 2B | 3B | HR | (Hm | Rd) | TB | R | RBI | RC | TBB | IBB | SO | HBP | SH | SF | SB | CS | SB% | GDP | Avg | OBP | Slg |
| 2010 | Mrlns | R | 6 | 24 | 9 | 1 | 1 | 0 | (- | -) | 12 | 3 | 3 | 5 | 2 | 0 | 7 | 0 | 0 | 0 | 1 | 0 | 1.00 | 3 | .375 | .423 | .500 |
| 2010 | Grnsbr | A | 6 | 23 | 8 | 2 | 0 | 0 | (- | -) | 10 | 2 | 2 | 3 | 1 | 0 | 6 | 0 | 0 | 0 | 0 | 0 | - | 1 | .348 | .375 | .435 |
| 2011 | Grnsbr | A | 122 | 461 | 144 | 32 | 1 | 15 | (- | -) | 223 | 73 | 77 | 92 | 55 | 1 | 102 | 3 | 0 | 2 | 32 | 5 | .86 | 10 | .312 | .388 | .484 |
| 2012 | Jupiter | A+ | 106 | 397 | 131 | 29 | 5 | 12 | (- | -) | 206 | 76 | 48 | 83 | 49 | 2 | 85 | 0 | 1 | 0 | 20 | 6 | .77 | 10 | .330 | .404 | .519 |
| 2012 | Mrlns | R | 1 | 4 | 1 | 0 | 0 | 0 | (- | -) | 1 | 0 | 0 | 0 | 0 | 0 | 0 | 0 | 0 | 0 | 0 | 0 | - | 0 | .250 | .250 | .250 |
| 2013 | Jupiter | A+ | 7 | 26 | 6 | 0 | 0 | 2 | (- | -) | 12 | 3 | 4 | 4 | 4 | 0 | 8 | 0 | 0 | 0 | 0 | 0 | - | 1 | .231 | .333 | .462 |
| 2013 | Jaxnvl | AA | 49 | 193 | 54 | 13 | 6 | 7 | (- | -) | 100 | 33 | 29 | 36 | 26 | 1 | 52 | 1 | 0 | 2 | 5 | 5 | .50 | 2 | .280 | .365 | .518 |
| 2013 | Mrlns | R | 5 | 17 | 5 | 0 | 1 | 0 | (- | -) | 7 | 2 | 0 | 2 | 1 | 0 | 5 | 0 | 0 | 0 | 0 | 0 | - | 0 | .294 | .333 | .412 |
| 2013 | Mia | NL | 62 | 240 | 69 | 12 | 1 | 4 | (0 | 4) | 95 | 34 | 16 | 35 | 31 | 1 | 66 | 1 | 0 | 1 | 10 | 0 | 1.00 | 4 | .288 | .370 | .396 |

## Kevin Youkilis

**Bats:** R **Throws:** R **Pos:** 3B-22;1B-6;DH-2 YOU-kih-liss **Ht:** 6'1" **Wt:** 220 **Born:** 3/15/1979 **Age:** 35

| BATTING | | | | | | | | | | | | | | | | | | | | | BASERUNNING | | | | AVERAGES | | |
|---|---|---|---|---|---|---|---|---|---|---|---|---|---|---|---|---|---|---|---|---|---|---|---|---|---|---|---|
| Year | Team | Lg | G | AB | H | 2B | 3B | HR | (Hm | Rd) | TB | R | RBI | RC | TBB | IBB | SO | HBP | SH | SF | SB | CS | SB% | GDP | Avg | OBP | Slg |
| 2013 | Trntn* | AA | 2 | 5 | 1 | 0 | 0 | 0 | (- | -) | 1 | 1 | 1 | 0 | 1 | 0 | 0 | 0 | 0 | 0 | 0 | 0 | - | 0 | .200 | .333 | .200 |
| 2004 | Bos | AL | 72 | 208 | 54 | 11 | 0 | 7 | (2 | 5) | 86 | 38 | 35 | 36 | 33 | 0 | 45 | 4 | 0 | 3 | 0 | 1 | .00 | 1 | .260 | .367 | .413 |
| 2005 | Bos | AL | 44 | 79 | 22 | 7 | 0 | 1 | (0 | 1) | 32 | 11 | 9 | 13 | 14 | 0 | 19 | 2 | 0 | 0 | 0 | 1 | .00 | 0 | .278 | .400 | .405 |
| 2006 | Bos | AL | 147 | 569 | 159 | 42 | 2 | 13 | (6 | 7) | 244 | 100 | 72 | 104 | 91 | 0 | 120 | 9 | 0 | **11** | 5 | 2 | .71 | 12 | .279 | .381 | .429 |
| 2007 | Bos | AL | 145 | 528 | 152 | 35 | 2 | 16 | (8 | 8) | 239 | 85 | 83 | 101 | 77 | 0 | 105 | 15 | 0 | 5 | 4 | 2 | .67 | 9 | .288 | .390 | .453 |
| 2008 | Bos | AL | 145 | 538 | 168 | 43 | 4 | 29 | (17 | 12) | 306 | 91 | 115 | 120 | 62 | 7 | 108 | 12 | 0 | 9 | 3 | 5 | .38 | 11 | .312 | .390 | .569 |

| Year Team | Lg | G | AB | H | 2B | 3B | HR | (Hm | Rd) | TB | R | RBI | RC | TBB | IBB | SO | HBP | SH | SF | SB | CS | SB% | GDP | Avg | OBP | Slg |
|---|---|---|---|---|---|---|---|---|---|---|---|---|---|---|---|---|---|---|---|---|---|---|---|---|---|---|
| BATTING | | | | | | | | | | | | | | | | | | | | BASERUNNING | | | | AVERAGES | | |
| 2009 Bos | AL | 136 | 491 | 150 | 36 | 1 | 27 | (14 | 13) | 269 | 99 | 94 | 114 | 77 | 6 | 125 | 16 | 0 | 4 | 7 | 2 | .78 | 9 | .305 | .413 | .548 |
| 2010 Bos | AL | 102 | 362 | 111 | 26 | 5 | 19 | (8 | 11) | 204 | 77 | 62 | 77 | 58 | 3 | 67 | 10 | 0 | 5 | 4 | 1 | .80 | 4 | .307 | .411 | .564 |
| 2011 Bos | AL | 120 | 431 | 111 | 32 | 2 | 17 | (8 | 9) | 198 | 68 | 80 | 81 | 68 | 3 | 100 | 14 | 0 | 4 | 3 | 0 | 1.00 | 14 | .258 | .373 | .459 |
| 2012 2 Tms | AL | 122 | 438 | 103 | 15 | 2 | 19 | (12 | 7) | 179 | 72 | 60 | 63 | 51 | 2 | 108 | **17** | 0 | 3 | 0 | 0 | - | 10 | .235 | .336 | .409 |
| 2013 NYY | AL | 28 | 105 | 23 | 7 | 0 | 2 | (0 | 2) | 36 | 12 | 8 | 11 | 8 | 1 | 31 | 5 | 0 | 0 | 0 | 0 | - | 4 | .219 | .305 | .343 |
| 12 Bos | AL | 42 | 146 | 34 | 7 | 1 | 4 | (2 | 2) | 55 | 25 | 14 | 17 | 14 | 0 | 39 | 4 | 0 | 1 | 0 | 0 | - | 4 | .233 | .315 | .377 |
| 12 CWS | AL | 80 | 292 | 69 | 8 | 1 | 15 | (10 | 5) | 124 | 47 | 46 | 46 | 37 | 2 | 69 | 13 | 0 | 2 | 0 | 0 | - | 6 | .236 | .346 | .425 |
| Postseason | | 29 | 111 | 34 | 9 | 1 | 6 | (2 | 4) | 63 | 22 | 17 | 20 | 13 | 0 | 18 | 0 | 0 | 1 | 0 | 0 | - | 4 | .306 | .376 | .568 |
| 10 ML YEARS | | 1061 | 3749 | 1053 | 254 | 18 | 150 | (75 | 75) | 1793 | 653 | 618 | 720 | 539 | 22 | 828 | 104 | 0 | 44 | 26 | 14 | .65 | 74 | .281 | .382 | .478 |

# Chris Young

**Bats:** R **Throws:** R **Pos:** CF-54;RF-26;LF-24;PH-19;DH-5;PR-1 **Ht:** 6'2" **Wt:** 190 **Born:** 9/5/1983 **Age:** 30

| Year Team | Lg | G | AB | H | 2B | 3B | HR | (Hm | Rd) | TB | R | RBI | RC | TBB | IBB | SO | HBP | SH | SF | SB | CS | SB% | GDP | Avg | OBP | Slg |
|---|---|---|---|---|---|---|---|---|---|---|---|---|---|---|---|---|---|---|---|---|---|---|---|---|---|---|
| BATTING | | | | | | | | | | | | | | | | | | | | BASERUNNING | | | | AVERAGES | | |
| 2013 Scrmto* | AAA | 1 | 1 | 1 | 0 | 0 | 0 | (- | -) | 1 | 1 | 0 | 1 | 2 | 0 | 0 | 0 | 0 | 0 | 1 | 0 | 1.00 | 0 | 1.000 | 1.000 | 1.000 |
| 2006 Ari | NL | 30 | 70 | 17 | 4 | 0 | 2 | (1 | 1) | 27 | 10 | 10 | 11 | 6 | 0 | 12 | 1 | 0 | 1 | 2 | 1 | .67 | 0 | .243 | .308 | .386 |
| 2007 Ari | NL | 148 | 569 | 135 | 29 | 3 | 32 | (14 | 18) | 266 | 85 | 68 | 68 | 43 | 1 | 141 | 6 | 1 | 5 | 27 | 6 | .82 | 5 | .237 | .295 | .467 |
| 2008 Ari | NL | 160 | 625 | 155 | 42 | 7 | 22 | (9 | 13) | 277 | 85 | 85 | 84 | 62 | 2 | 165 | 1 | 6 | 5 | 14 | 5 | .74 | 10 | .248 | .315 | .443 |
| 2009 Ari | NL | 134 | 433 | 92 | 28 | 4 | 15 | (7 | 8) | 173 | 54 | 42 | 47 | 59 | 2 | 133 | 4 | 3 | 2 | 11 | 4 | .73 | 3 | .212 | .311 | .400 |
| 2010 Ari | NL | 156 | 584 | 150 | 33 | 0 | 27 | (20 | 7) | 264 | 94 | 91 | 86 | 74 | 0 | 145 | 2 | 1 | 3 | 28 | 7 | .80 | 10 | .257 | .341 | .452 |
| 2011 Ari | NL | 156 | 567 | 134 | 38 | 3 | 20 | (14 | 6) | 238 | 89 | 71 | 84 | 80 | 4 | 139 | 4 | 1 | 7 | 22 | 9 | .71 | 3 | .236 | .331 | .420 |
| 2012 Ari | NL | 101 | 325 | 75 | 24 | 0 | 14 | (5 | 9) | 141 | 36 | 41 | 46 | 36 | 0 | 79 | 2 | 0 | 0 | 8 | 3 | .73 | 4 | .231 | .311 | .434 |
| 2013 Oak | AL | 107 | 335 | 67 | 18 | 3 | 12 | (4 | 8) | 127 | 46 | 40 | 32 | 36 | 3 | 93 | 2 | 0 | 2 | 10 | 3 | .77 | 7 | .200 | .280 | .379 |
| Postseason | | 12 | 43 | 14 | 2 | 0 | 5 | (3 | 2) | 31 | 9 | 9 | 12 | 9 | 0 | 18 | 1 | 0 | 0 | 3 | 2 | .60 | 0 | .326 | .453 | .721 |
| 8 ML YEARS | | 992 | 3508 | 825 | 216 | 20 | 144 | (74 | 70) | 1513 | 499 | 448 | 458 | 396 | 12 | 907 | 22 | 12 | 25 | 122 | 38 | .76 | 42 | .235 | .315 | .431 |

# Delmon Young

**Bats:** R **Throws:** R **Pos:** RF-65;DH-28;PH-16 **Ht:** 6'3" **Wt:** 240 **Born:** 9/14/1985 **Age:** 28

| Year Team | Lg | G | AB | H | 2B | 3B | HR | (Hm | Rd) | TB | R | RBI | RC | TBB | IBB | SO | HBP | SH | SF | SB | CS | SB% | GDP | Avg | OBP | Slg |
|---|---|---|---|---|---|---|---|---|---|---|---|---|---|---|---|---|---|---|---|---|---|---|---|---|---|---|
| BATTING | | | | | | | | | | | | | | | | | | | | BASERUNNING | | | | AVERAGES | | |
| 2013 Clrwtr* | A+ | 3 | 13 | 6 | 1 | 0 | 0 | (- | -) | 7 | 1 | 1 | 2 | 0 | 0 | 3 | 0 | 0 | 1 | 0 | 0 | - | 0 | .462 | .429 | .538 |
| 2013 LV* | AAA | 4 | 17 | 5 | 1 | 0 | 0 | (- | -) | 6 | 2 | 1 | 1 | 0 | 0 | 4 | 0 | 0 | 0 | 0 | 0 | - | 1 | .294 | .294 | .353 |
| 2013 Mont* | AA | 7 | 30 | 7 | 0 | 0 | 1 | (- | -) | 10 | 4 | 3 | 2 | 1 | 0 | 7 | 0 | 0 | 0 | 0 | 0 | - | 1 | .233 | .258 | .333 |
| 2006 TB | AL | 30 | 126 | 40 | 9 | 1 | 3 | (1 | 2) | 60 | 16 | 10 | 15 | 1 | 0 | 24 | 3 | 0 | 1 | 2 | 2 | .50 | 0 | .317 | .336 | .476 |
| 2007 TB | AL | **162** | 645 | 186 | 38 | 0 | 13 | (9 | 4) | 263 | 65 | 93 | 90 | 26 | 2 | 127 | 3 | 0 | 7 | 10 | 3 | .77 | **23** | .288 | .316 | .408 |
| 2008 Min | AL | 152 | 575 | 167 | 28 | 4 | 10 | (7 | 3) | 233 | 80 | 69 | 74 | 35 | 7 | 105 | 7 | 1 | 5 | 14 | 5 | .74 | 19 | .290 | .336 | .405 |
| 2009 Min | AL | 108 | 395 | 112 | 16 | 2 | 12 | (7 | 5) | 168 | 50 | 60 | 46 | 12 | 1 | 92 | 4 | 0 | 5 | 2 | 5 | .29 | 17 | .284 | .308 | .425 |
| 2010 Min | AL | 153 | 570 | 170 | 46 | 1 | 21 | (6 | 15) | 281 | 77 | 112 | 94 | 28 | 5 | 81 | 6 | 0 | 9 | 5 | 4 | .56 | 16 | .298 | .333 | .493 |
| 2011 2 Tms | AL | 124 | 473 | 127 | 21 | 1 | 12 | (8 | 4) | 186 | 54 | 64 | 57 | 23 | 2 | 85 | 2 | 0 | 5 | 1 | 0 | 1.00 | 19 | .268 | .302 | .393 |
| 2012 Det | AL | 151 | 574 | 153 | 27 | 1 | 18 | (9 | 9) | 236 | 54 | 74 | 62 | 20 | 1 | 112 | 7 | 0 | 7 | 0 | 2 | .00 | 20 | .267 | .296 | .411 |
| 2013 2 Tms | | 103 | 334 | 87 | 16 | 0 | 11 | (3 | 8) | 136 | 30 | 38 | 36 | 20 | 0 | 78 | 4 | 0 | 3 | 0 | 0 | - | 8 | .260 | .307 | .407 |
| 11 Min | AL | 84 | 305 | 81 | 16 | 0 | 4 | (1 | 3) | 109 | 26 | 32 | 32 | 18 | 2 | 55 | 0 | 0 | 2 | 1 | 0 | 1.00 | 12 | .266 | .305 | .357 |
| 11 Det | AL | 40 | 168 | 46 | 5 | 1 | 8 | (7 | 1) | 77 | 28 | 32 | 25 | 5 | 0 | 30 | 2 | 0 | 3 | 0 | 0 | - | 7 | .274 | .298 | .458 |
| 13 Phi | NL | 80 | 272 | 71 | 13 | 0 | 8 | (3 | 5) | 108 | 22 | 31 | 30 | 14 | 0 | 69 | 3 | 0 | 2 | 0 | 0 | - | 7 | .261 | .302 | .397 |
| 13 TB | AL | 23 | 62 | 16 | 3 | 0 | 3 | (0 | 3) | 28 | 8 | 7 | 6 | 6 | 0 | 9 | 1 | 0 | 1 | 0 | 0 | - | 1 | .258 | .329 | .452 |
| Postseason | | 28 | 106 | 28 | 3 | 1 | 8 | (5 | 3) | 57 | 13 | 15 | 11 | 7 | 1 | 24 | 2 | 0 | 0 | 1 | 1 | .50 | 2 | .264 | .322 | .538 |
| 8 ML YEARS | | 983 | 3692 | 1042 | 201 | 10 | 100 | (50 | 50) | 1563 | 426 | 520 | 474 | 165 | 18 | 704 | 36 | 1 | 42 | 34 | 21 | .62 | 122 | .282 | .316 | .423 |

# Eric Young

**Bats:** B **Throws:** R **Pos:** LF-95;RF-20;PH-19;CF-18;2B-4;PR-3;DH-1 **Ht:** 5'10" **Wt:** 180 **Born:** 5/25/1985 **Age:** 29

| Year Team | Lg | G | AB | H | 2B | 3B | HR | (Hm | Rd) | TB | R | RBI | RC | TBB | IBB | SO | HBP | SH | SF | SB | CS | SB% | GDP | Avg | OBP | Slg |
|---|---|---|---|---|---|---|---|---|---|---|---|---|---|---|---|---|---|---|---|---|---|---|---|---|---|---|
| BATTING | | | | | | | | | | | | | | | | | | | | BASERUNNING | | | | AVERAGES | | |
| 2009 Col | NL | 30 | 57 | 14 | 1 | 0 | 1 | (1 | 0) | 18 | 7 | 1 | 2 | 4 | 0 | 12 | 0 | 0 | 0 | 4 | 4 | .50 | 1 | .246 | .295 | .316 |
| 2010 Col | NL | 51 | 172 | 42 | 5 | 1 | 0 | (0 | 0) | 49 | 26 | 8 | 16 | 17 | 0 | 32 | 0 | 0 | 0 | 17 | 6 | .74 | 2 | .244 | .312 | .285 |
| 2011 Col | NL | 77 | 198 | 49 | 4 | 3 | 0 | (0 | 0) | 59 | 34 | 10 | 27 | 26 | 0 | 38 | 3 | 1 | 1 | 27 | 4 | .87 | 1 | .247 | .342 | .298 |
| 2012 Col | NL | 98 | 174 | 55 | 7 | 2 | 4 | (2 | 2) | 78 | 36 | 15 | 29 | 13 | 0 | 31 | 4 | 5 | 0 | 14 | 2 | .88 | 1 | .316 | .377 | .448 |
| 2013 2 Tms | NL | 148 | 539 | 134 | 27 | 7 | 2 | (1 | 1) | 181 | 70 | 32 | 58 | 46 | 1 | 100 | 2 | 10 | 1 | **46** | 11 | .81 | 6 | .249 | .310 | .336 |
| 13 Col | NL | 57 | 165 | 40 | 9 | 3 | 1 | (0 | 1) | 58 | 22 | 6 | 14 | 11 | 0 | 33 | 0 | 4 | 0 | 8 | 4 | .67 | 1 | .242 | .290 | .352 |
| 13 NYM | NL | 91 | 374 | 94 | 18 | 4 | 1 | (1 | 0) | 123 | 48 | 26 | 44 | 35 | 1 | 67 | 2 | 6 | 1 | 38 | 7 | .84 | 5 | .251 | .318 | .329 |
| Postseason | | 2 | 1 | 0 | 0 | 0 | 0 | (0 | 0) | 0 | 0 | 0 | 0 | 0 | 0 | 0 | 0 | 0 | 0 | 0 | 0 | - | 0 | .000 | .000 | .000 |
| 5 ML YEARS | | 404 | 1140 | 294 | 44 | 13 | 7 | (4 | 3) | 385 | 173 | 66 | 132 | 106 | 1 | 213 | 9 | 16 | 2 | 108 | 27 | .80 | 11 | .258 | .325 | .338 |

# Michael Young

**Bats:** R **Throws:** R **Pos:** 3B-107;1B-34;PH-14;2B-2;SS-1 **Ht:** 6'1" **Wt:** 200 **Born:** 10/19/1976 **Age:** 37

| Year Team | Lg | G | AB | H | 2B | 3B | HR | (Hm | Rd) | TB | R | RBI | RC | TBB | IBB | SO | HBP | SH | SF | SB | CS | SB% | GDP | Avg | OBP | Slg |
|---|---|---|---|---|---|---|---|---|---|---|---|---|---|---|---|---|---|---|---|---|---|---|---|---|---|---|
| BATTING | | | | | | | | | | | | | | | | | | | | BASERUNNING | | | | AVERAGES | | |
| 2000 Tex | AL | 2 | 2 | 0 | 0 | 0 | 0 | (0 | 0) | 0 | 0 | 0 | 0 | 0 | 0 | 1 | 0 | 0 | 0 | 0 | 0 | - | 0 | .000 | .000 | .000 |
| 2001 Tex | AL | 106 | 386 | 96 | 18 | 4 | 11 | (7 | 4) | 155 | 57 | 49 | 45 | 26 | 0 | 91 | 3 | 9 | 5 | 3 | 1 | .75 | 9 | .249 | .298 | .402 |
| 2002 Tex | AL | 156 | 573 | 150 | 26 | 8 | 9 | (3 | 6) | 219 | 77 | 62 | 64 | 41 | 1 | 112 | 0 | 13 | 6 | 6 | 7 | .46 | 14 | .262 | .308 | .382 |
| 2003 Tex | AL | 160 | 666 | 204 | 33 | 9 | 14 | (9 | 5) | 297 | 106 | 72 | 106 | 36 | 1 | 103 | 1 | 3 | 7 | 13 | 2 | .87 | 14 | .306 | .339 | .446 |
| 2004 Tex | AL | 160 | 690 | 216 | 33 | 9 | 22 | (9 | 13) | 333 | 114 | 99 | 124 | 44 | 1 | 89 | 1 | 0 | 4 | 12 | 3 | .80 | 11 | .313 | .353 | .483 |
| 2005 Tex | AL | 159 | 668 | **221** | 40 | 5 | 24 | (12 | 12) | 343 | 114 | 91 | 131 | 58 | 0 | 91 | 3 | 0 | 3 | 5 | 2 | .71 | 20 | **.331** | .385 | .513 |
| 2006 Tex | AL | **162** | 691 | 217 | 52 | 3 | 14 | (8 | 6) | 317 | 93 | 103 | 120 | 48 | 0 | 96 | 1 | 0 | 8 | 7 | 3 | .70 | 27 | .314 | .356 | .459 |
| 2007 Tex | AL | 156 | 639 | 201 | 37 | 1 | 9 | (8 | 1) | 267 | 80 | 94 | 107 | 47 | 5 | 107 | 5 | 0 | 1 | 13 | 3 | .81 | 21 | .315 | .366 | .418 |
| 2008 Tex | AL | 155 | 645 | 183 | 36 | 2 | 12 | (8 | 4) | 259 | 102 | 82 | 86 | 55 | 0 | 109 | 2 | 0 | 6 | 10 | 0 | 1.00 | 19 | .284 | .339 | .402 |
| 2009 Tex | AL | 135 | 541 | 174 | 36 | 2 | 22 | (10 | 12) | 280 | 76 | 68 | 87 | 47 | 2 | 90 | 1 | 0 | 4 | 8 | 3 | .73 | 16 | .322 | .374 | .518 |
| 2010 Tex | AL | 157 | 656 | 186 | 36 | 3 | 21 | (16 | 5) | 291 | 99 | 91 | 85 | 50 | 4 | 115 | 1 | 0 | 11 | 4 | 2 | .67 | 21 | .284 | .330 | .444 |

| | | | BATTING | | | | | | | | | | | | | | | | | | BASERUNNING | | | | AVERAGES | | |
|---|---|---|---|---|---|---|---|---|---|---|---|---|---|---|---|---|---|---|---|---|---|---|---|---|---|---|---|
| Year | Team | Lg | G | AB | H | 2B | 3B | HR | (Hm | Rd) | TB | R | RBI | RC | TBB | IBB | SO | HBP | SH | SF | SB | CS | SB% | GDP | Avg | OBP | Slg |
| 2011 | Tex | AL | 159 | 631 | **213** | 41 | 6 | 11 | (10 | 1) | 299 | 88 | 106 | 118 | 47 | 7 | 78 | 2 | 0 | 9 | 6 | 2 | .75 | 17 | .338 | .380 | .474 |
| 2012 | Tex | AL | 156 | 611 | 169 | 27 | 3 | 8 | (1 | 7) | 226 | 79 | 67 | 67 | 33 | 3 | 70 | 1 | 0 | 6 | 2 | 2 | .50 | 26 | .277 | .312 | .370 |
| 2013 | 2 Tms | NL | 147 | 519 | 145 | 26 | 5 | 8 | (5 | 3) | 205 | 52 | 46 | 62 | 43 | 4 | 83 | 1 | 0 | 2 | 1 | 0 | 1.00 | 22 | .279 | .335 | .395 |
| 13 | Phi | NL | 126 | 468 | 129 | 24 | 4 | 8 | (5 | 3) | 185 | 49 | 42 | 57 | 42 | 4 | 78 | 1 | 0 | 1 | 1 | 0 | 1.00 | 19 | .276 | .336 | .395 |
| 13 | LAD | NL | 21 | 51 | 16 | 2 | 1 | 0 | (0 | 0) | 20 | 3 | 4 | 5 | 1 | 0 | 5 | 0 | 0 | 1 | 0 | 0 | - | 3 | .314 | .321 | .392 |
| Postseason | | | 34 | 141 | 35 | 10 | 0 | 3 | (2 | 1) | 54 | 11 | 19 | 12 | 5 | 0 | 30 | 0 | 0 | 1 | 0 | 0 | - | 5 | .248 | .272 | .383 |
| 14 ML YEARS | | | 1970 | 7918 | 2375 | 441 | 60 | 185 | (106 | 79) | 3491 | 1137 | 1030 | 1202 | 575 | 28 | 1235 | 22 | 25 | 72 | 90 | 30 | .75 | 237 | .300 | .346 | .441 |

# Mike Zagurski

**Pitches:** L **Bats:** L **Pos:** RP-7

zah-GURR-skee

**Ht:** 6'0" **Wt:** 240 **Born:** 1/27/1983 **Age:** 31

| | | | HOW MUCH HE PITCHED | | | | | | WHAT HE GAVE UP | | | | | | | | | | | | THE RESULTS | | | | | | | |
|---|---|---|---|---|---|---|---|---|---|---|---|---|---|---|---|---|---|---|---|---|---|---|---|---|---|---|---|---|
| Year | Team | Lg | G | GS | CG | GF | IP | BFP | H | R | ER | HR | SH | SF | HB | TBB | IBB | SO | WP | Bk | W | L | Pct | Sh | Sv-Op | Hld | ERC | ERA |
| 2013 | Indy* | AAA | 19 | 0 | 0 | 6 | 21.0 | 91 | 15 | 5 | 5 | 2 | 0 | 1 | 1 | 9 | 0 | 37 | 0 | 0 | 1 | 0 | 1.000 | 0 | 1-- | - | 2.65 | 2.14 |
| 2013 | S-WB* | AAA | 20 | 0 | 0 | 9 | 26.1 | 108 | 22 | 11 | 9 | 2 | 0 | 2 | 1 | 12 | 0 | 38 | 1 | 0 | 5 | 3 | .625 | 0 | 1-- | - | 3.51 | 3.08 |
| 2013 | Scrmto* | AAA | 6 | 0 | 0 | 2 | 6.0 | 30 | 7 | 6 | 4 | 0 | 0 | 0 | 2 | 3 | 1 | 8 | 2 | 0 | 0 | 0 | - | 0 | 0-- | - | 5.48 | 6.00 |
| 2007 | Phi | NL | 25 | 0 | 0 | 4 | 21.1 | 101 | 25 | 14 | 14 | 3 | 1 | 1 | 1 | 11 | 2 | 21 | 2 | 0 | 1 | 0 | 1.000 | 0 | 0-2 | 5 | 5.75 | 5.91 |
| 2010 | Phi | NL | 8 | 0 | 0 | 3 | 7.0 | 34 | 8 | 8 | 8 | 1 | 1 | 1 | 2 | 5 | 0 | 11 | 1 | 0 | 0 | 0 | - | 0 | 0-0 | 0 | 8.12 | 10.29 |
| 2011 | Phi | NL | 4 | 0 | 0 | 1 | 3.1 | 17 | 4 | 2 | 2 | 1 | 0 | 0 | 0 | 3 | 0 | 4 | 0 | 0 | 0 | 0 | - | 0 | 0-0 | 0 | 8.99 | 5.40 |
| 2012 | Ari | NL | 45 | 0 | 0 | 13 | 37.1 | 163 | 37 | 24 | 23 | 5 | 2 | 5 | 1 | 19 | 0 | 34 | 5 | 0 | 0 | 0 | - | 0 | 0-1 | 4 | 4.90 | 5.54 |
| 2013 | 2 Tms | | 7 | 0 | 0 | 2 | 6.1 | 40 | 11 | 12 | 12 | 1 | 1 | 1 | 2 | 8 | 0 | 5 | 3 | 0 | 0 | 0 | - | 0 | 0-0 | 0 | 14.61 | 17.05 |
| 13 | Pit | NL | 6 | 0 | 0 | 2 | 6.0 | 37 | 10 | 10 | 10 | 1 | 1 | 1 | 1 | 8 | 0 | 5 | 3 | 0 | 0 | 0 | - | 0 | 0-0 | 0 | 13.81 | 15.00 |
| 13 | NYY | AL | 1 | 0 | 0 | 0 | 0.1 | 3 | 1 | 2 | 2 | 0 | 0 | 0 | 1 | 0 | 0 | 0 | 0 | 0 | 0 | 0 | - | 0 | 0-0 | 0 | 29.63 | 54.00 |
| 5 ML YEARS | | | 89 | 0 | 0 | 23 | 75.1 | 355 | 85 | 60 | 59 | 11 | 5 | 8 | 6 | 46 | 2 | 75 | 11 | 0 | 1 | 0 | 1.000 | 0 | 0-3 | 9 | 6.35 | 7.05 |

# Josh Zeid

**Pitches:** R **Bats:** R **Pos:** RP-25

ZIDE

**Ht:** 6'4" **Wt:** 220 **Born:** 3/24/1987 **Age:** 27

| | | | HOW MUCH HE PITCHED | | | | | | WHAT HE GAVE UP | | | | | | | | | | | | THE RESULTS | | | | | | | |
|---|---|---|---|---|---|---|---|---|---|---|---|---|---|---|---|---|---|---|---|---|---|---|---|---|---|---|---|---|
| Year | Team | Lg | G | GS | CG | GF | IP | BFP | H | R | ER | HR | SH | SF | HB | TBB | IBB | SO | WP | Bk | W | L | Pct | Sh | Sv-Op | Hld | ERC | ERA |
| 2009 | Wmspt | A- | 15 | 15 | 0 | 0 | 79.2 | 323 | 64 | 27 | 26 | 1 | 2 | 2 | 4 | 20 | 0 | 72 | 7 | 0 | 8 | 5 | .615 | 0 | 0-- | - | 2.13 | 2.94 |
| 2010 | Lakwd | A | 43 | 12 | 0 | 15 | 107.1 | 440 | 95 | 41 | 35 | 7 | 7 | 2 | 4 | 27 | 2 | 111 | 7 | 1 | 8 | 4 | .667 | 0 | 8-- | - | 2.79 | 2.93 |
| 2011 | Rdng | AA | 21 | 11 | 0 | 6 | 63.2 | 275 | 63 | 43 | 40 | 9 | 3 | 4 | 3 | 27 | 0 | 56 | 6 | 0 | 2 | 3 | .400 | 0 | 2-- | - | 4.66 | 5.65 |
| 2011 | CpChr | AA | 14 | 1 | 0 | 5 | 16.0 | 78 | 23 | 21 | 18 | 5 | 2 | 0 | 1 | 6 | 1 | 15 | 2 | 0 | 0 | 1 | .000 | 0 | 0-- | - | 8.37 | 10.13 |
| 2012 | CpChr | AA | 47 | 0 | 0 | 20 | 56.1 | 247 | 57 | 35 | 35 | 6 | 0 | 6 | 4 | 20 | 3 | 66 | 9 | 1 | 2 | 0 | 1.000 | 0 | 1-- | - | 4.16 | 5.59 |
| 2013 | OKCity | AAA | 43 | 0 | 0 | 24 | 43.2 | 189 | 36 | 17 | 17 | 3 | 1 | 5 | 0 | 27 | 1 | 53 | 6 | 0 | 4 | 1 | .800 | 0 | 13-- | - | 3.71 | 3.50 |
| 2013 | Hou | AL | 25 | 0 | 0 | 6 | 27.2 | 118 | 26 | 12 | 12 | 3 | 1 | 0 | 1 | 12 | 1 | 24 | 2 | 0 | 0 | 1 | .000 | 0 | 1-2 | 6 | 4.07 | 3.90 |

# Brad Ziegler

**Pitches:** R **Bats:** R **Pos:** RP-78

ZIGG-lerr

**Ht:** 6'4" **Wt:** 210 **Born:** 10/10/1979 **Age:** 34

| | | | HOW MUCH HE PITCHED | | | | | | WHAT HE GAVE UP | | | | | | | | | | | | THE RESULTS | | | | | | | |
|---|---|---|---|---|---|---|---|---|---|---|---|---|---|---|---|---|---|---|---|---|---|---|---|---|---|---|---|---|
| Year | Team | Lg | G | GS | CG | GF | IP | BFP | H | R | ER | HR | SH | SF | HB | TBB | IBB | SO | WP | Bk | W | L | Pct | Sh | Sv-Op | Hld | ERC | ERA |
| 2008 | Oak | AL | 47 | 0 | 0 | 21 | 59.2 | 229 | 47 | 8 | 7 | 2 | 4 | 3 | 1 | 22 | 3 | 30 | 0 | 0 | 3 | 0 | 1.000 | 0 | 11-13 | 9 | 2.60 | 1.06 |
| 2009 | Oak | AL | 69 | 0 | 0 | 23 | 73.1 | 313 | 82 | 27 | 25 | 2 | 1 | 3 | 1 | 28 | 4 | 54 | 0 | 0 | 2 | 4 | .333 | 0 | 7-10 | 14 | 4.25 | 3.07 |
| 2010 | Oak | AL | 64 | 0 | 0 | 12 | 60.2 | 257 | 54 | 24 | 22 | 4 | 1 | 1 | 3 | 28 | **9** | 41 | 0 | 1 | 3 | 7 | .300 | 0 | 0-4 | 18 | 3.48 | 3.26 |
| 2011 | 2 Tms | | 66 | 0 | 0 | 16 | 58.1 | 239 | 53 | 21 | 14 | 0 | 1 | 2 | 1 | 19 | 3 | 44 | 1 | 0 | 3 | 2 | .600 | 0 | 1-2 | 10 | 2.68 | 2.16 |
| 2012 | Ari | NL | 77 | 0 | 0 | 15 | 68.2 | 263 | 54 | 21 | 19 | 2 | 2 | 2 | 1 | 21 | 2 | 42 | 1 | 0 | 6 | 1 | .857 | 0 | 0-2 | 17 | 2.33 | 2.49 |
| 2013 | Ari | NL | **78** | 0 | 0 | 33 | 73.0 | 297 | 61 | 20 | 18 | 3 | 2 | 2 | 3 | 22 | 6 | 44 | 0 | 0 | 8 | 1 | .889 | 0 | 13-15 | 11 | 2.51 | 2.22 |
| 11 | Oak | AL | 43 | 0 | 0 | 12 | 37.2 | 160 | 38 | 14 | 10 | 0 | 1 | 1 | 1 | 13 | 3 | 29 | 1 | 0 | 3 | 2 | .600 | 0 | 1-2 | 6 | 3.21 | 2.39 |
| 11 | Ari | NL | 23 | 0 | 0 | 4 | 20.2 | 79 | 15 | 7 | 4 | 0 | 0 | 1 | 0 | 6 | 0 | 15 | 0 | 0 | 0 | 0 | - | 0 | 0-0 | 4 | 1.77 | 1.74 |
| Postseason | | | 2 | 0 | 0 | 0 | 0.1 | 7 | 4 | 4 | 4 | 0 | 0 | 0 | 0 | 2 | 1 | 0 | 0 | 1 | 0 | 0 | - | 0 | 0-0 | 0 | 115.8 | 108.0 |
| 6 ML YEARS | | | 401 | 0 | 0 | 120 | 393.2 | 1598 | 351 | 121 | 105 | 13 | 11 | 13 | 10 | 140 | 27 | 255 | 2 | 1 | 25 | 15 | .625 | 0 | 32-46 | 79 | 2.97 | 2.40 |

# Ryan Zimmerman

**Bats:** R **Throws:** R **Pos:** 3B-141;DH-4;PH-2

**Ht:** 6'3" **Wt:** 230 **Born:** 9/28/1984 **Age:** 29

| | | | BATTING | | | | | | | | | | | | | | | | | | BASERUNNING | | | | AVERAGES | | |
|---|---|---|---|---|---|---|---|---|---|---|---|---|---|---|---|---|---|---|---|---|---|---|---|---|---|---|---|
| Year | Team | Lg | G | AB | H | 2B | 3B | HR | (Hm | Rd) | TB | R | RBI | RC | TBB | IBB | SO | HBP | SH | SF | SB | CS | SB% | GDP | Avg | OBP | Slg |
| 2013 | Ptomc* | A+ | 1 | 3 | 0 | 0 | 0 | 0 | (- | -) | 0 | 0 | 0 | 0 | 0 | 0 | 0 | 0 | 0 | 0 | 0 | 0 | - | 0 | .000 | .000 | .000 |
| 2005 | Was | NL | 20 | 58 | 23 | 10 | 0 | 0 | (0 | 0) | 33 | 6 | 6 | 9 | 3 | 0 | 12 | 0 | 0 | 1 | 0 | 0 | - | 1 | .397 | .419 | .569 |
| 2006 | Was | NL | 157 | 614 | 176 | 47 | 3 | 20 | (10 | 10) | 289 | 84 | 110 | 101 | 61 | 7 | 120 | 2 | 1 | 4 | 11 | 8 | .58 | 15 | .287 | .351 | .471 |
| 2007 | Was | NL | **162** | 653 | 174 | 43 | 5 | 24 | (11 | 13) | 299 | 99 | 91 | 83 | 61 | 3 | 125 | 3 | 0 | 5 | 4 | 1 | .80 | 26 | .266 | .330 | .458 |
| 2008 | Was | NL | 106 | 428 | 121 | 24 | 1 | 14 | (7 | 7) | 189 | 51 | 51 | 48 | 31 | 1 | 71 | 3 | 0 | 4 | 1 | 1 | .50 | 12 | .283 | .333 | .442 |
| 2009 | Was | NL | 157 | 610 | 178 | 37 | 3 | 33 | (17 | 16) | 320 | 110 | 106 | 96 | 72 | 9 | 119 | 2 | 0 | 9 | 2 | 0 | 1.00 | 22 | .292 | .364 | .525 |
| 2010 | Was | NL | 142 | 525 | 161 | 32 | 0 | 25 | (9 | 16) | 268 | 85 | 85 | 97 | 69 | 6 | 98 | 4 | 0 | 5 | 4 | 1 | .80 | 16 | .307 | .388 | .510 |
| 2011 | Was | NL | 101 | 395 | 114 | 21 | 2 | 12 | (7 | 5) | 175 | 52 | 49 | 58 | 41 | 4 | 73 | 1 | 0 | 3 | 3 | 1 | .75 | 14 | .289 | .355 | .443 |
| 2012 | Was | NL | 145 | 578 | 163 | 36 | 1 | 25 | (16 | 9) | 276 | 93 | 95 | 84 | 57 | 8 | 116 | 2 | 0 | 4 | 5 | 2 | .71 | **20** | .282 | .346 | .478 |
| 2013 | Was | NL | 147 | 568 | 156 | 26 | 2 | 26 | (7 | 19) | 264 | 84 | 79 | 83 | 60 | 2 | 133 | 2 | 0 | 3 | 6 | 0 | 1.00 | 16 | .275 | .344 | .465 |
| Postseason | | | 5 | 21 | 8 | 1 | 0 | 2 | (1 | 1) | 15 | 3 | 4 | 5 | 0 | 0 | 6 | 0 | 0 | 1 | 0 | 0 | - | 0 | .381 | .364 | .714 |
| 9 ML YEARS | | | 1137 | 4429 | 1266 | 276 | 17 | 179 | (84 | 95) | 2113 | 664 | 672 | 659 | 455 | 40 | 867 | 19 | 1 | 38 | 36 | 14 | .72 | 142 | .286 | .352 | .477 |

# Jordan Zimmermann

**Pitches:** R **Bats:** R **Pos:** SP-32 **Ht:** 6'2" **Wt:** 220 **Born:** 5/23/1986 **Age:** 28

| HOW MUCH HE PITCHED | | | | | | | | | WHAT HE GAVE UP | | | | | | | | | | | | THE RESULTS | | | | | | | |
|---|---|---|---|---|---|---|---|---|---|---|---|---|---|---|---|---|---|---|---|---|---|---|---|---|---|---|---|---|
| Year | Team | Lg | G | GS | CG | GF | IP | BFP | H | R | ER | HR | SH | SF | HB | TBB | IBB | SO | WP | Bk | W | L | Pct | Sh | Sv-Op | Hld | ERC | ERA |
| 2009 | Was | NL | 16 | 16 | 0 | 0 | 91.1 | 391 | 95 | 51 | 47 | 10 | 5 | 3 | 4 | 29 | 0 | 92 | 0 | 0 | 3 | 5 | .375 | 0 | 0-0 | 0 | 4.25 | 4.63 |
| 2010 | Was | NL | 7 | 7 | 0 | 0 | 31.0 | 135 | 31 | 20 | 17 | 8 | 1 | 1 | 2 | 10 | 1 | 27 | 0 | 0 | 1 | 2 | .333 | 0 | 0-0 | 0 | 5.02 | 4.94 |
| 2011 | Was | NL | 26 | 26 | 1 | 0 | 161.1 | 662 | 154 | 62 | 57 | 12 | 8 | 2 | 7 | 31 | 2 | 124 | 3 | 1 | 8 | 11 | .421 | 0 | 0-0 | 0 | 3.02 | 3.18 |
| 2012 | Was | NL | 32 | 32 | 0 | 0 | 195.2 | 805 | 186 | 69 | 64 | 18 | 8 | 4 | 8 | 43 | 2 | 153 | 3 | 0 | 12 | 8 | .600 | 0 | 0-0 | 0 | 3.22 | 2.94 |
| 2013 | Was | NL | 32 | 32 | 4 | 0 | 213.1 | 865 | 192 | 81 | 77 | 19 | 9 | 4 | 7 | 40 | 0 | 161 | 3 | 0 | **19** | 9 | .679 | **2** | 0-0 | 0 | 2.79 | 3.25 |
| Postseason | | | 2 | 1 | 0 | 0 | 4.0 | 18 | 7 | 5 | 5 | 1 | 0 | 0 | 0 | 0 | 0 | 5 | 0 | 0 | 0 | 1 | .000 | 0 | 0-0 | 0 | 8.42 | 11.25 |
| 5 ML YEARS | | | 113 | 113 | 5 | 0 | 692.2 | 2858 | 658 | 283 | 262 | 67 | 31 | 14 | 28 | 153 | 5 | 557 | 9 | 1 | 43 | 35 | .551 | 2 | 0-0 | 0 | 3.24 | 3.40 |

# Barry Zito

**Pitches:** L **Bats:** L **Pos:** SP-25; RP-5 **Ht:** 6'2" **Wt:** 205 **Born:** 5/13/1978 **Age:** 36

| HOW MUCH HE PITCHED | | | | | | | | | WHAT HE GAVE UP | | | | | | | | | | | | THE RESULTS | | | | | | | |
|---|---|---|---|---|---|---|---|---|---|---|---|---|---|---|---|---|---|---|---|---|---|---|---|---|---|---|---|---|
| Year | Team | Lg | G | GS | CG | GF | IP | BFP | H | R | ER | HR | SH | SF | HB | TBB | IBB | SO | WP | Bk | W | L | Pct | Sh | Sv-Op | Hld | ERC | ERA |
| 2000 | Oak | AL | 14 | 14 | 1 | 0 | 92.2 | 376 | 64 | 30 | 28 | 6 | 1 | 0 | 2 | 45 | 2 | 78 | 2 | 0 | 7 | 4 | .636 | 1 | 0-0 | 0 | 2.63 | 2.72 |
| 2001 | Oak | AL | 35 | **35** | 3 | 0 | 214.1 | 902 | 184 | 92 | 83 | 18 | 5 | 4 | 13 | 80 | 0 | 205 | 6 | 1 | 17 | 8 | .680 | 2 | 0-0 | 0 | 3.33 | 3.49 |
| 2002 | Oak | AL | 35 | **35** | 1 | 0 | 229.1 | 939 | 182 | 79 | 70 | 24 | 9 | 7 | 9 | 78 | 2 | 182 | 2 | 1 | **23** | 5 | .821 | 0 | 0-0 | 0 | 2.92 | 2.75 |
| 2003 | Oak | AL | 35 | 35 | 4 | 0 | 231.2 | 957 | 186 | 98 | 85 | 19 | 7 | 7 | 6 | 88 | 3 | 146 | 4 | 0 | 14 | 12 | .538 | 1 | 0-0 | 0 | 2.91 | 3.30 |
| 2004 | Oak | AL | 34 | 34 | 0 | 0 | 213.0 | 926 | 216 | 116 | 106 | 28 | 7 | 9 | 9 | 81 | 2 | 163 | 4 | 1 | 11 | 11 | .500 | 0 | 0-0 | 0 | 4.45 | 4.48 |
| 2005 | Oak | AL | 35 | **35** | 0 | 0 | 228.1 | 953 | 185 | 106 | 98 | 26 | 8 | 7 | 13 | 89 | 0 | 171 | 4 | 0 | 14 | 13 | .519 | 0 | 0-0 | 0 | 3.32 | 3.86 |
| 2006 | Oak | AL | 34 | **34** | 0 | 0 | 221.0 | **945** | 211 | 99 | 94 | 27 | 7 | 6 | 13 | 99 | 5 | 151 | 4 | 2 | 16 | 10 | .615 | 0 | 0-0 | 0 | 4.47 | 3.83 |
| 2007 | SF | NL | 34 | 33 | 0 | 0 | 196.2 | 850 | 182 | 105 | 99 | 24 | 12 | 4 | 4 | 83 | 4 | 131 | 5 | 0 | 11 | 13 | .458 | 0 | 0-0 | 0 | 3.91 | 4.53 |
| 2008 | SF | NL | 32 | 32 | 0 | 0 | 180.0 | 818 | 186 | 115 | 103 | 16 | 8 | **14** | 4 | 102 | 10 | 120 | 3 | 0 | 10 | **17** | .370 | 0 | 0-0 | 0 | 4.81 | 5.15 |
| 2009 | SF | NL | 33 | 33 | 1 | 0 | 192.0 | 818 | 179 | 89 | 86 | 21 | 11 | 1 | 8 | 81 | 8 | 154 | 2 | 2 | 10 | 13 | .435 | 0 | 0-0 | 0 | 4.00 | 4.03 |
| 2010 | SF | NL | 34 | 33 | 1 | 1 | 199.1 | 848 | 184 | 97 | 92 | 20 | 13 | 7 | 7 | 84 | 7 | 150 | 7 | 0 | 9 | 14 | .391 | 0 | 0-0 | 0 | 3.85 | 4.15 |
| 2011 | SF | NL | 13 | 9 | 0 | 3 | 53.2 | 225 | 51 | 35 | 35 | 10 | 0 | 2 | 0 | 24 | 1 | 32 | 1 | 0 | 3 | 4 | .429 | 0 | 0-0 | 0 | 4.71 | 5.87 |
| 2012 | SF | NL | 32 | 32 | 1 | 0 | 184.1 | 799 | 186 | 91 | 85 | 20 | 12 | 4 | 5 | 70 | 6 | 114 | 1 | 0 | 15 | 8 | .652 | 1 | 0-0 | 0 | 4.15 | 4.15 |
| 2013 | SF | NL | 30 | 25 | 0 | 4 | 133.1 | 608 | 173 | 94 | 85 | 19 | 5 | 1 | 4 | 54 | 2 | 86 | 5 | 1 | 5 | 11 | .313 | 0 | 0-0 | 0 | 6.39 | 5.74 |
| Postseason | | | 10 | 10 | 0 | 0 | 60.1 | 252 | 50 | 19 | 19 | 7 | 1 | 0 | 3 | 23 | 1 | 46 | 1 | 0 | 6 | 3 | .667 | 0 | 0-0 | 0 | 3.35 | 2.83 |
| 14 ML YEARS | | | 430 | 419 | 12 | 8 | 2569.2 | 10964 | 2369 | 1246 | 1149 | 278 | 105 | 73 | 97 | 1058 | 52 | 1883 | 50 | 8 | 165 | 143 | .536 | 5 | 0-0 | 0 | 3.88 | 4.02 |

# Ben Zobrist

ZOH-brist

**Bats:** B **Throws:** R **Pos:** 2B-125;RF-39;SS-21;LF-4;DH-2;CF-1;PH-1 **Ht:** 6'3" **Wt:** 210 **Born:** 5/26/1981 **Age:** 33

| BATTING | | | | | | | | | | | | | | | | | | | | | BASERUNNING | | | | AVERAGES | | |
|---|---|---|---|---|---|---|---|---|---|---|---|---|---|---|---|---|---|---|---|---|---|---|---|---|---|---|---|
| Year | Team | Lg | G | AB | H | 2B | 3B | HR | (Hm | Rd) | TB | R | RBI | RC | TBB | IBB | SO | HBP | SH | SF | SB | CS | SB% | GDP | Avg | OBP | Slg |
| 2006 | TB | AL | 52 | 183 | 41 | 6 | 2 | 2 | (2 | 0) | 57 | 10 | 18 | 13 | 10 | 1 | 26 | 0 | 2 | 3 | 2 | 3 | .40 | 2 | .224 | .260 | .311 |
| 2007 | TB | AL | 31 | 97 | 15 | 2 | 0 | 1 | (0 | 1) | 20 | 8 | 9 | 0 | 3 | 0 | 21 | 1 | 2 | 2 | 2 | 0 | 1.00 | 1 | .155 | .184 | .206 |
| 2008 | TB | AL | 62 | 198 | 50 | 10 | 2 | 12 | (4 | 8) | 100 | 32 | 30 | 31 | 25 | 1 | 37 | 2 | 0 | 2 | 3 | 0 | 1.00 | 4 | .253 | .339 | .505 |
| 2009 | TB | AL | 152 | 501 | 149 | 28 | 7 | 27 | (18 | 9) | 272 | 91 | 91 | 109 | 91 | 4 | 104 | 2 | 1 | 4 | 17 | 6 | .74 | 7 | .297 | .405 | .543 |
| 2010 | TB | AL | 151 | 541 | 129 | 28 | 2 | 10 | (3 | 7) | 191 | 77 | 75 | 84 | 92 | 1 | 107 | 3 | 7 | **12** | 24 | 3 | .89 | 10 | .238 | .346 | .353 |
| 2011 | TB | AL | 156 | 588 | 158 | 46 | 6 | 20 | (9 | 11) | 276 | 99 | 91 | 100 | 77 | 1 | 128 | 2 | 2 | 5 | 19 | 6 | .76 | 9 | .269 | .353 | .469 |
| 2012 | TB | AL | 157 | 560 | 151 | 39 | 7 | 20 | (8 | 12) | 264 | 88 | 74 | 102 | 97 | 7 | 103 | 3 | 2 | 6 | 14 | 9 | .61 | 13 | .270 | .377 | .471 |
| 2013 | TB | AL | 157 | 612 | 168 | 36 | 3 | 12 | (7 | 5) | 246 | 77 | 71 | 85 | 72 | 4 | 91 | 7 | 1 | 6 | 11 | 3 | .79 | 18 | .275 | .354 | .402 |
| Postseason | | | 16 | 48 | 11 | 2 | 0 | 1 | (1 | 0) | 16 | 4 | 2 | 2 | 4 | 0 | 10 | 1 | 0 | 0 | 0 | 0 | - | 0 | .229 | .302 | .333 |
| 8 ML YEARS | | | 918 | 3280 | 861 | 195 | 29 | 104 | (51 | 53) | 1426 | 482 | 459 | 524 | 467 | 19 | 617 | 20 | 17 | 40 | 92 | 30 | .75 | 64 | .263 | .354 | .435 |

# Mike Zunino

**Bats:** R **Throws:** R **Pos:** C-50;PH-3 zoo-NEE-no **Ht:** 6'2" **Wt:** 220 **Born:** 3/25/1991 **Age:** 23

| BATTING | | | | | | | | | | | | | | | | | | | | | BASERUNNING | | | | AVERAGES | | |
|---|---|---|---|---|---|---|---|---|---|---|---|---|---|---|---|---|---|---|---|---|---|---|---|---|---|---|---|
| Year | Team | Lg | G | AB | H | 2B | 3B | HR | (Hm | Rd) | TB | R | RBI | RC | TBB | IBB | SO | HBP | SH | SF | SB | CS | SB% | GDP | Avg | OBP | Slg |
| 2012 | Everett | A- | 29 | 110 | 41 | 10 | 0 | 10 | (- | -) | 81 | 29 | 35 | 35 | 18 | 1 | 26 | 4 | 0 | 1 | 1 | 0 | 1.00 | 2 | .373 | .474 | .736 |
| 2012 | Jacksn | AA | 15 | 51 | 17 | 4 | 0 | 3 | (- | -) | 30 | 6 | 8 | 11 | 5 | 1 | 7 | 0 | 0 | 1 | 0 | 0 | - | 0 | .333 | .386 | .588 |
| 2013 | Tacom | AAA | 52 | 203 | 46 | 12 | 3 | 11 | (- | -) | 97 | 38 | 43 | 30 | 17 | 1 | 66 | 5 | 0 | 4 | 0 | 0 | - | 3 | .227 | .297 | .478 |
| 2013 | Sea | AL | 52 | 173 | 37 | 5 | 0 | 5 | (3 | 2) | 57 | 22 | 14 | 13 | 16 | 0 | 49 | 3 | 0 | 1 | 1 | 0 | 1.00 | 5 | .214 | .290 | .329 |

# 2013 Fielding Statistics

In this section, Plus/Minus (PM) and Defensive Runs Saved (Runs Saved for short) numbers are supplied for each player, as well as traditional stats such as putouts, assists, and errors. We split fielders between "Regulars" and "All Others". The thresholds that we use to distinguish the two are 750 innings played at a given position or 600 innings as a catcher. For lineup regulars, we list players by position in order of best-to-worst Runs Saved.

For each position, we evaluate at least three separate aspects of defensive play at the position and report the corresponding component of Runs Saved individually in the following pages. For catchers, we have grouped Bunt Runs Saved and Good Fielding Play/Defensive Misplay Runs Saved together into the "Other" category. A more detailed explanation of Runs Saved can be found in the Baseball Glossary at the end of the book.

Fielding data for pitchers can be found in the "Pitchers Hitting, Fielding, and Holding Runners" section.

## First Basemen - Regulars

| [illegible] | Tm | G | GS | Inn | PO | A | E | DP | Pct. | PM | Runs Saved +/- | Runs Saved GFP/ DME | Runs Saved Bunts/ GDP | Runs Saved Total |
|---|---|---|---|---|---|---|---|---|---|---|---|---|---|---|
| [illegible]y | ChC | 159 | 158 | 1415.0 | 1287 | 149 | 5 | 114 | .997 | +22 | 16 | 3 | -3 | 16 |
| [illegible]aul | Ari | 159 | 158 | 1446.0 | 1494 | 99 | 5 | 118 | .997 | +15 | 11 | 2 | 0 | 13 |
| [illegible]an | LAD | 151 | 148 | 1291.0 | 1294 | 84 | 11 | 133 | .992 | +15 | 11 | 1 | -1 | 11 |
| [illegible]poli,Mike | Bos | 131 | 123 | 1097.1 | 977 | 87 | 6 | 96 | .994 | +12 | 9 | 0 | 1 | 10 |
| Alonso,Yonder | SD | 92 | 86 | 771.0 | 761 | 58 | 3 | 72 | .996 | +10 | 8 | -1 | 0 | 7 |
| Freeman,Freddie | Atl | 147 | 145 | 1290.2 | 1228 | 107 | 10 | 114 | .993 | +7 | 6 | 2 | -1 | 7 |
| Votto,Joey | Cin | 161 | 161 | 1430.2 | 1245 | 154 | 14 | 115 | .990 | +9 | 7 | 1 | -2 | 6 |
| Swisher,Nick | Cle | 112 | 101 | 910.1 | 812 | 88 | 8 | 70 | .991 | +6 | 5 | 1 | 0 | 6 |
| Overbay,Lyle | NYY | 130 | 114 | 1031.0 | 933 | 67 | 4 | 93 | .996 | +3 | 3 | 2 | 0 | 5 |
| Morneau,Justin | TOT | 137 | 133 | 1189.1 | 1222 | 100 | 4 | 133 | .997 | +3 | 2 | 2 | 1 | 5 |
| Belt,Brandon | SF | 143 | 132 | 1174.1 | 1066 | 88 | 8 | 100 | .993 | +9 | 7 | -4 | 1 | 4 |
| Loney,James | TB | 154 | 143 | 1277.2 | 1203 | 98 | 7 | 115 | .995 | -1 | -1 | 3 | 2 | 4 |
| Hosmer,Eric | KC | 158 | 153 | 1372.1 | 1205 | 122 | 8 | 118 | .994 | +4 | 3 | -1 | 1 | 3 |
| Trumbo,Mark | LAA | 123 | 114 | 1030.2 | 915 | 79 | 8 | 87 | .992 | +4 | 3 | -2 | 1 | 2 |
| Davis,Ike | NYM | 96 | 87 | 781.0 | 805 | 38 | 9 | 62 | .989 | +1 | 1 | -1 | 1 | 1 |
| Moreland,Mitch | Tex | 146 | 129 | 1176.0 | 1045 | 96 | 5 | 108 | .996 | +1 | 1 | -1 | 1 | 1 |
| LaRoche,Adam | Was | 149 | 143 | 1272.0 | 1164 | 76 | 11 | 117 | .991 | -3 | -2 | 2 | 1 | 1 |
| Helton,Todd | Col | 110 | 104 | 910.1 | 941 | 92 | 2 | 96 | .998 | -7 | -5 | 4 | 1 | 0 |
| Craig,Allen | StL | 95 | 90 | 775.2 | 780 | 57 | 1 | 85 | .999 | -3 | -2 | 0 | 1 | -1 |
| Davis,Chris | Bal | 155 | 155 | 1377.2 | 1339 | 75 | 6 | 153 | .996 | -8 | -6 | 0 | -1 | -7 |
| Smoak,Justin | Sea | 125 | 121 | 1084.1 | 1036 | 60 | 5 | 101 | .995 | -7 | -6 | -1 | -1 | -8 |
| Moss,Brandon | Oak | 111 | 88 | 801.2 | 663 | 47 | 7 | 52 | .990 | -16 | -12 | 0 | 0 | -12 |
| Fielder,Prince | Det | 151 | 151 | 1323.2 | 1152 | 96 | 6 | 119 | .995 | -18 | -13 | 1 | -1 | -13 |

## Second Basemen - Regulars

| Player | Tm | G | GS | Inn | PO | A | E | DP | Pct. | Range | PM | Runs Saved +/- | Runs Saved GFP/ DME | Runs Saved GDP | Runs Saved Total |
|---|---|---|---|---|---|---|---|---|---|---|---|---|---|---|---|
| Pedroia,Dustin | Bos | 160 | 159 | 1398.0 | 254 | 429 | 5 | 102 | .993 | 4.40 | +17 | 13 | 2 | 0 | 15 |
| Ellis,Mark | LAD | 119 | 106 | 950.0 | 225 | 302 | 6 | 78 | .989 | 4.99 | +14 | 10 | 2 | 0 | 12 |
| Barney,Darwin | ChC | 141 | 139 | 1237.1 | 236 | 363 | 4 | 72 | .993 | 4.36 | +15 | 11 | 0 | 0 | 11 |
| Kinsler,Ian | Tex | 124 | 124 | 1095.1 | 211 | 371 | 13 | 89 | .978 | 4.78 | +10 | 8 | 1 | 2 | 11 |
| LeMahieu,DJ | Col | 90 | 86 | 750.0 | 168 | 271 | 3 | 57 | .993 | 5.27 | +9 | 7 | 2 | 1 | 10 |
| Dozier,Brian | Min | 146 | 141 | 1255.1 | 267 | 461 | 6 | 110 | .992 | 5.22 | +14 | 11 | 0 | -2 | 9 |
| Walker,Neil | Pit | 132 | 125 | 1144.0 | 256 | 397 | 7 | 88 | .989 | 5.14 | +10 | 8 | 3 | -2 | 9 |
| Zobrist,Ben | TB | 125 | 117 | 1017.1 | 218 | 332 | 4 | 73 | .993 | 4.87 | +8 | 6 | 2 | -1 | 7 |
| Cano,Robinson | NYY | 153 | 153 | 1350.1 | 247 | 404 | 6 | 88 | .991 | 4.34 | +8 | 6 | 2 | -2 | 6 |
| Sogard,Eric | Oak | 113 | 98 | 865.0 | 207 | 258 | 7 | 68 | .985 | 4.84 | +4 | 3 | 3 | -1 | 5 |
| Solano,Donovan | Mia | 93 | 92 | 806.1 | 172 | 284 | 8 | 69 | .983 | 5.09 | +4 | 3 | 1 | 0 | 4 |
| Phillips,Brandon | Cin | 151 | 151 | 1347.0 | 278 | 428 | 9 | 84 | .987 | 4.72 | +6 | 5 | -1 | -3 | 1 |
| Franklin,Nick | Sea | 96 | 90 | 828.1 | 139 | 326 | 12 | 64 | .975 | 5.05 | +2 | 1 | 1 | -2 | 0 |
| Carpenter,Matt | StL | 132 | 128 | 1108.0 | 211 | 370 | 9 | 97 | .985 | 4.72 | 0 | 0 | -2 | 2 | 0 |
| Gyorko,Jedd | SD | 117 | 114 | 1008.0 | 196 | 302 | 4 | 54 | .992 | 4.45 | +2 | 1 | 0 | -2 | -1 |
| Kipnis,Jason | Cle | 147 | 146 | 1292.1 | 242 | 395 | 12 | 91 | .982 | 4.44 | +1 | 1 | -1 | -1 | -1 |
| Kendrick,Howie | LAA | 118 | 118 | 1043.1 | 222 | 321 | 10 | 68 | .982 | 4.68 | 0 | 0 | -2 | -1 | -3 |
| Beckham,Gordon | CWS | 103 | 100 | 884.1 | 212 | 255 | 12 | 69 | .975 | 4.75 | -2 | -2 | -2 | 1 | -3 |
| Altuve,Jose | Hou | 145 | 145 | 1261.2 | 273 | 393 | 9 | 114 | .987 | 4.75 | -9 | -7 | 1 | 3 | -3 |
| Utley,Chase | Phi | 125 | 123 | 1071.0 | 247 | 317 | 17 | 65 | .971 | 4.74 | -3 | -3 | 0 | -1 | -4 |
| Infante,Omar | Det | 118 | 116 | 1025.1 | 157 | 342 | 10 | 73 | .980 | 4.38 | -4 | -3 | -3 | 1 | -5 |
| Scutaro,Marco | SF | 121 | 121 | 1033.2 | 221 | 299 | 13 | 69 | .976 | 4.53 | -9 | -7 | 1 | -1 | -7 |
| Murphy,Daniel | NYM | 150 | 148 | 1334.1 | 263 | 391 | 16 | 86 | .976 | 4.41 | -13 | -10 | -3 | 0 | -13 |
| Weeks,Rickie | Mil | 95 | 92 | 815.2 | 143 | 254 | 10 | 56 | .975 | 4.38 | -18 | -14 | 0 | -1 | -15 |
| Uggla,Dan | Atl | 133 | 130 | 1161.2 | 247 | 334 | 14 | 81 | .976 | 4.50 | -20 | -15 | -6 | 2 | -19 |

## Third Basemen - Regulars

| Player | Tm | G | GS | Inn | PO | A | E | DP | Pct. | Range | PM | Runs Saved +/- | Runs Saved GFP/ DME | Runs Saved Bunts/ GDP | Runs Saved Total |
|---|---|---|---|---|---|---|---|---|---|---|---|---|---|---|---|
| Machado,Manny | Bal | 156 | 156 | 1390.0 | 116 | 355 | 13 | 42 | .973 | 3.05 | +47 | 36 | -2 | 1 | 35 |
| Arenado,Nolan | Col | 130 | 128 | 1110.0 | 91 | 309 | 11 | 27 | .973 | 3.24 | +36 | 27 | 1 | 2 | 30 |
| Uribe,Juan | LAD | 123 | 101 | 900.1 | 62 | 230 | 5 | 22 | .983 | 2.92 | +24 | 18 | -2 | -1 | 15 |
| Longoria,Evan | TB | 147 | 145 | 1289.0 | 96 | 279 | 11 | 27 | .972 | 2.62 | +14 | 10 | 1 | 1 | 12 |
| Donaldson,Josh | Oak | 155 | 155 | 1373.0 | 143 | 255 | 16 | 22 | .961 | 2.61 | +13 | 10 | 1 | 0 | 11 |
| Dominguez,Matt | Hou | 149 | 149 | 1312.1 | 92 | 323 | 16 | 28 | .963 | 2.85 | +7 | 6 | 2 | 0 | 8 |
| Valbuena,Luis | ChC | 94 | 85 | 760.2 | 56 | 150 | 7 | 13 | .967 | 2.44 | +5 | 4 | 0 | 2 | 6 |
| Wright,David | NYM | 111 | 111 | 1003.1 | 86 | 235 | 9 | 18 | .973 | 2.88 | +9 | 7 | -3 | 1 | 5 |
| Headley,Chase | SD | 140 | 138 | 1235.0 | 83 | 252 | 11 | 18 | .968 | 2.44 | +8 | 6 | 1 | -2 | 5 |
| Frazier,Todd | Cin | 147 | 140 | 1256.2 | 86 | 241 | 10 | 27 | .970 | 2.34 | +6 | 5 | 1 | -1 | 5 |

| Player | Tm | G | GS | Inn | PO | A | E | DP | Pct. | Range | PM | Runs Saved +/- | GFP/ DME | Bunts/ GDP | Total |
|---|---|---|---|---|---|---|---|---|---|---|---|---|---|---|---|
| Lawrie,Brett | Tor | 103 | 101 | 888.2 | 68 | 189 | 10 | 19 | .963 | 2.60 | +5 | 3 | 2 | -1 | 4 |
| Alvarez,Pedro | Pit | 150 | 148 | 1328.1 | 72 | 359 | 27 | 27 | .941 | 2.92 | +8 | 6 | -1 | -2 | 3 |
| Polanco,Placido | Mia | 109 | 92 | 849.2 | 52 | 153 | 2 | 13 | .990 | 2.17 | +4 | 3 | 0 | 0 | 3 |
| Prado,Martin | Ari | 113 | 96 | 881.1 | 60 | 202 | 6 | 21 | .978 | 2.68 | +2 | 1 | 1 | -2 | 0 |
| Plouffe,Trevor | Min | 120 | 118 | 1035.2 | 91 | 194 | 13 | 25 | .956 | 2.48 | +1 | 1 | -2 | 1 | 0 |
| Zimmerman,Ryan | Was | 141 | 141 | 1245.2 | 98 | 260 | 21 | 28 | .945 | 2.59 | -10 | -8 | 4 | 3 | -1 |
| Moustakas,Mike | KC | 134 | 126 | 1129.2 | 114 | 210 | 16 | 19 | .953 | 2.58 | -4 | -3 | -1 | 1 | -3 |
| Gillaspie,Conor | CWS | 113 | 107 | 940.0 | 64 | 200 | 16 | 16 | .943 | 2.53 | -9 | -7 | 3 | 0 | -4 |
| Sandoval,Pablo | SF | 137 | 137 | 1152.0 | 77 | 206 | 18 | 14 | .940 | 2.21 | -4 | -3 | 0 | -2 | -5 |
| Beltre,Adrian | Tex | 146 | 146 | 1289.2 | 93 | 232 | 14 | 25 | .959 | 2.27 | -10 | -7 | 1 | 1 | -5 |
| Callaspo,Alberto | TOT | 93 | 87 | 769.0 | 66 | 152 | 13 | 8 | .944 | 2.55 | -7 | -5 | 0 | -1 | -6 |
| Johnson,Chris | Atl | 125 | 123 | 1020.0 | 62 | 210 | 14 | 14 | .951 | 2.40 | -8 | -6 | 0 | 0 | -6 |
| Middlebrooks,Will | Bos | 92 | 90 | 797.2 | 52 | 156 | 10 | 12 | .954 | 2.35 | -7 | -5 | -2 | -1 | -8 |
| Seager,Kyle | Sea | 160 | 158 | 1425.0 | 94 | 308 | 15 | 38 | .964 | 2.54 | -13 | -10 | 0 | 2 | -8 |
| Freese,David | StL | 132 | 129 | 1050.2 | 55 | 190 | 11 | 21 | .957 | 2.10 | -22 | -17 | 1 | 2 | -14 |
| Cabrera,Miguel | Det | 145 | 145 | 1234.2 | 87 | 184 | 12 | 24 | .958 | 1.98 | -25 | -19 | -1 | 2 | -18 |
| Young,Michael | TOT | 107 | 104 | 890.2 | 58 | 175 | 10 | 13 | .959 | 2.35 | -21 | -17 | -2 | -1 | -20 |

## Shortstops - Regulars

| Player | Tm | G | GS | Inn | PO | A | E | DP | Pct. | Range | PM | Runs Saved +/- | GFP/ DME | GDP | Total |
|---|---|---|---|---|---|---|---|---|---|---|---|---|---|---|---|
| Simmons,Andrelton | Atl | 156 | 150 | 1352.1 | 240 | 499 | 14 | 94 | .981 | 4.92 | +49 | 37 | 2 | 2 | 41 |
| Barmes,Clint | Pit | 106 | 91 | 804.1 | 107 | 282 | 13 | 53 | .968 | 4.35 | +17 | 13 | -1 | 0 | 12 |
| Florimon,Pedro | Min | 133 | 127 | 1099.2 | 245 | 401 | 18 | 101 | .973 | 5.29 | +15 | 12 | 0 | 0 | 12 |
| Andrus,Elvis | Tex | 146 | 145 | 1288.2 | 212 | 362 | 14 | 97 | .976 | 4.01 | +11 | 8 | 1 | 2 | 11 |
| Kozma,Pete | StL | 139 | 113 | 1051.0 | 155 | 397 | 9 | 98 | .984 | 4.73 | +10 | 8 | -2 | 2 | 8 |
| Hardy,J.J. | Bal | 159 | 159 | 1417.0 | 230 | 403 | 12 | 108 | .981 | 4.02 | +4 | 3 | 2 | 3 | 8 |
| Tulowitzki,Troy | Col | 121 | 119 | 1029.1 | 183 | 379 | 8 | 84 | .986 | 4.91 | +9 | 7 | -1 | 0 | 6 |
| Ryan,Brendan | TOT | 101 | 96 | 854.0 | 111 | 301 | 12 | 64 | .972 | 4.34 | +7 | 5 | 2 | -1 | 6 |
| Cozart,Zack | Cin | 150 | 147 | 1308.0 | 222 | 386 | 14 | 83 | .977 | 4.18 | +6 | 5 | 1 | -2 | 4 |
| Escobar,Yunel | TB | 153 | 149 | 1320.0 | 208 | 395 | 7 | 88 | .989 | 4.11 | +7 | 5 | -1 | 0 | 4 |
| Escobar,Alcides | KC | 158 | 156 | 1388.1 | 221 | 395 | 13 | 89 | .979 | 3.99 | +5 | 4 | -1 | 1 | 4 |
| Segura,Jean | Mil | 144 | 143 | 1251.0 | 199 | 459 | 15 | 96 | .978 | 4.73 | +4 | 3 | -1 | 1 | 3 |
| Crawford,Brandon | SF | 147 | 139 | 1226.0 | 185 | 388 | 15 | 75 | .974 | 4.21 | +5 | 4 | -1 | -1 | 2 |
| Ramirez,Alexei | CWS | 158 | 157 | 1400.2 | 236 | 433 | 22 | 100 | .968 | 4.30 | 0 | 0 | -1 | 2 | 1 |
| Peralta,Jhonny | Det | 106 | 103 | 935.2 | 140 | 294 | 4 | 54 | .991 | 4.17 | 0 | 0 | 0 | 0 | 0 |
| Gregorius,Didi | Ari | 100 | 97 | 894.2 | 152 | 279 | 13 | 51 | .971 | 4.34 | +4 | 2 | -2 | -1 | -1 |
| Drew,Stephen | Bos | 124 | 122 | 1093.1 | 176 | 332 | 8 | 82 | .984 | 4.18 | -3 | -2 | 1 | -1 | -2 |
| Desmond,Ian | Was | 158 | 158 | 1400.0 | 234 | 446 | 20 | 96 | .971 | 4.37 | -2 | -2 | -2 | 1 | -3 |
| Hechavarria,Adeiny | Mia | 148 | 145 | 1297.1 | 197 | 401 | 15 | 89 | .976 | 4.15 | -4 | -2 | -1 | 0 | -3 |
| Cabrera,Everth | SD | 95 | 95 | 847.2 | 143 | 298 | 6 | 59 | .987 | 4.68 | -4 | -4 | 1 | 0 | -3 |
| Reyes,Jose | Tor | 92 | 92 | 793.0 | 95 | 240 | 9 | 51 | .974 | 3.80 | -9 | -7 | 1 | 2 | -4 |
| Aybar,Erick | LAA | 138 | 138 | 1203.0 | 218 | 328 | 15 | 78 | .973 | 4.08 | -7 | -5 | 0 | -2 | -7 |
| Castro,Starlin | ChC | 159 | 159 | 1418.0 | 238 | 416 | 22 | 77 | .967 | 4.15 | -6 | -5 | -3 | 0 | -8 |
| Quintanilla,Omar | NYM | 92 | 89 | 814.0 | 107 | 248 | 8 | 45 | .978 | 3.93 | -8 | -6 | 0 | -2 | -8 |
| Rollins,Jimmy | Phi | 153 | 151 | 1318.1 | 190 | 424 | 11 | 89 | .982 | 4.19 | -23 | -18 | 2 | 1 | -15 |
| Cabrera,Asdrubal | Cle | 129 | 127 | 1099.2 | 180 | 314 | 9 | 70 | .982 | 4.04 | -21 | -16 | 0 | 0 | -16 |
| Lowrie,Jed | Oak | 119 | 115 | 1023.1 | 139 | 266 | 16 | 56 | .962 | 3.56 | -22 | -17 | 2 | -3 | -18 |

## Left Fielders - Regulars

| Player | Tm | G | GS | Inn | PO | A | E | DP | Pct. | Range | PM | Runs Saved +/- | GFP/ DME | Throws | Total |
|---|---|---|---|---|---|---|---|---|---|---|---|---|---|---|---|
| Marte,Starling | Pit | 124 | 113 | 1038.1 | 176 | 5 | 6 | 0 | .968 | 1.57 | +34 | 19 | 2 | -1 | 20 |
| Gordon,Alex | KC | 155 | 155 | 1364.1 | 323 | 17 | 1 | 2 | .997 | 2.24 | +8 | 5 | 5 | 6 | 16 |
| Gonzalez,Carlos | Col | 106 | 99 | 857.0 | 172 | 11 | 3 | 0 | .984 | 1.92 | +5 | 3 | 3 | 4 | 10 |
| Murphy,David | Tex | 128 | 106 | 980.1 | 191 | 10 | 2 | 1 | .990 | 1.85 | +9 | 5 | 1 | 2 | 8 |
| Dirks,Andy | Det | 116 | 95 | 868.2 | 211 | 7 | 2 | 0 | .991 | 2.26 | +8 | 5 | 0 | 1 | 6 |
| Cespedes,Yoenis | Oak | 94 | 91 | 801.1 | 187 | 9 | 4 | 1 | .980 | 2.20 | +8 | 4 | -3 | 3 | 4 |
| Harper,Bryce | Was | 97 | 89 | 800.1 | 150 | 11 | 5 | 1 | .970 | 1.81 | -2 | -1 | 1 | 4 | 4 |
| Young,Eric | TOT | 95 | 88 | 790.1 | 180 | 7 | 2 | 0 | .989 | 2.13 | +6 | 4 | -1 | -1 | 2 |
| Brantley,Michael | Cle | 151 | 144 | 1293.1 | 257 | 11 | 0 | 1 | 1.000 | 1.86 | -10 | -6 | 4 | 4 | 2 |
| Crawford,Carl | LAD | 107 | 96 | 835.2 | 165 | 3 | 4 | 0 | .977 | 1.81 | +11 | 6 | -2 | -3 | 1 |
| Soriano,Alfonso | TOT | 134 | 134 | 1163.1 | 266 | 12 | 6 | 2 | .979 | 2.15 | 0 | 0 | 1 | 0 | 1 |
| McLouth,Nate | Bal | 136 | 124 | 1138.2 | 250 | 4 | 1 | 0 | .996 | 2.01 | +3 | 2 | -1 | -1 | 0 |
| Shuck,J.B. | LAA | 97 | 87 | 765.2 | 151 | 7 | 2 | 0 | .988 | 1.86 | -5 | -3 | 2 | 1 | 0 |
| Viciedo,Dayan | CWS | 109 | 109 | 892.2 | 147 | 12 | 5 | 0 | .970 | 1.60 | -20 | -11 | 2 | 4 | -5 |
| Brown,Domonic | Phi | 132 | 129 | 1123.2 | 185 | 9 | 5 | 0 | .975 | 1.55 | -22 | -13 | 2 | 4 | -7 |
| Upton,Justin | Atl | 108 | 91 | 839.2 | 174 | 0 | 4 | 0 | .978 | 1.87 | -3 | -2 | -3 | -3 | -8 |

| | | | | | | | | | | | | Runs Saved | | | |
|---|---|---|---|---|---|---|---|---|---|---|---|---|---|---|---|
| Player | Tm | G | GS | Inn | PO | A | E | DP | Pct. | Range | PM | +/- | GFP/ DME | Throws | Total |
| Holliday,Matt | StL | 136 | 136 | 1150.1 | 212 | 2 | 1 | 1 | .995 | 1.67 | -7 | -4 | -2 | -7 | -13 |
| Ibanez,Raul | Sea | 99 | 97 | 824.1 | 164 | 6 | 4 | 1 | .977 | 1.86 | -22 | -12 | -2 | -5 | -19 |

## Center Fielders - Regulars

| | | | | | | | | | | | | Runs Saved | | | |
|---|---|---|---|---|---|---|---|---|---|---|---|---|---|---|---|
| Player | Tm | G | GS | Inn | PO | A | E | DP | Pct. | Range | PM | +/- | GFP/ DME | Throws | Total |
| Gomez,Carlos | Mil | 145 | 142 | 1242.0 | 391 | 11 | 5 | 2 | .988 | 2.91 | +44 | 25 | 7 | 6 | 38 |
| Lagares,Juan | NYM | 108 | 88 | 819.2 | 257 | 14 | 5 | 0 | .982 | 2.98 | +19 | 11 | 4 | 11 | 26 |
| Cain,Lorenzo | KC | 92 | 88 | 761.1 | 247 | 7 | 1 | 0 | .996 | 3.00 | +18 | 10 | 3 | 4 | 17 |
| Pollock,A.J. | Ari | 110 | 98 | 915.2 | 238 | 8 | 2 | 1 | .992 | 2.42 | +26 | 14 | 0 | 1 | 15 |
| Martin,Leonys | Tex | 127 | 109 | 974.1 | 287 | 11 | 5 | 1 | .983 | 2.75 | +16 | 9 | -1 | 6 | 14 |
| Ellsbury,Jacoby | Bos | 134 | 134 | 1188.1 | 347 | 3 | 3 | 2 | .992 | 2.65 | +22 | 12 | 1 | 0 | 13 |
| Rasmus,Colby | Tor | 114 | 111 | 1002.2 | 308 | 1 | 4 | 1 | .987 | 2.77 | +12 | 7 | 2 | 2 | 11 |
| McCutchen,Andrew | Pit | 155 | 154 | 1378.0 | 321 | 11 | 6 | 3 | .982 | 2.17 | +10 | 5 | -1 | 3 | 7 |
| Barnes,Brandon | Hou | 116 | 102 | 913.0 | 298 | 8 | 3 | 4 | .990 | 3.02 | +5 | 3 | 0 | 4 | 7 |
| Crisp,Coco | Oak | 110 | 107 | 919.0 | 307 | 2 | 0 | 1 | 1.000 | 3.03 | +17 | 10 | 0 | -4 | 6 |
| Gardner,Brett | NYY | 138 | 130 | 1166.1 | 327 | 5 | 3 | 1 | .991 | 2.56 | +7 | 4 | 3 | -1 | 6 |
| Span,Denard | Was | 153 | 145 | 1300.2 | 379 | 5 | 0 | 1 | 1.000 | 2.66 | +8 | 5 | 2 | -4 | 3 |
| Bourn,Michael | Cle | 128 | 124 | 1098.1 | 272 | 6 | 3 | 2 | .989 | 2.28 | +5 | 3 | 0 | 0 | 3 |
| Jackson,Austin | Det | 129 | 127 | 1145.2 | 300 | 5 | 2 | 1 | .993 | 2.40 | +4 | 2 | -1 | 2 | 3 |
| Upton,B.J. | Atl | 118 | 111 | 975.1 | 230 | 3 | 4 | 3 | .983 | 2.15 | +3 | 2 | 0 | 0 | 2 |
| Jones,Adam | Bal | 156 | 156 | 1394.0 | 352 | 11 | 2 | 0 | .995 | 2.34 | -16 | -9 | 0 | 7 | -2 |
| Fowler,Dexter | Col | 110 | 106 | 921.1 | 231 | 3 | 3 | 2 | .987 | 2.29 | +1 | 1 | 0 | -4 | -3 |
| Jennings,Desmond | TB | 136 | 132 | 1188.2 | 320 | 2 | 3 | 2 | .991 | 2.44 | -4 | -2 | -2 | -2 | -6 |
| Trout,Mike | LAA | 111 | 108 | 952.2 | 275 | 0 | 1 | 0 | .996 | 2.60 | -6 | -3 | -3 | -3 | -9 |
| Jay,Jon | StL | 152 | 141 | 1285.2 | 335 | 4 | 1 | 3 | .997 | 2.37 | -8 | -4 | -1 | -5 | -10 |
| Choo,Shin-Soo | Cin | 150 | 150 | 1333.0 | 349 | 8 | 4 | 0 | .989 | 2.41 | -29 | -16 | -2 | 1 | -17 |
| De Aza,Alejandro | CWS | 107 | 105 | 888.2 | 271 | 3 | 5 | 2 | .982 | 2.77 | -16 | -9 | -5 | -4 | -18 |

## Right Fielders - Regulars

| | | | | | | | | | | | | Runs Saved | | | |
|---|---|---|---|---|---|---|---|---|---|---|---|---|---|---|---|
| Player | Tm | G | GS | Inn | PO | A | E | DP | Pct. | Range | PM | +/- | GFP/ DME | Throws | Total |
| Parra,Gerardo | Ari | 123 | 114 | 1042.1 | 256 | 15 | 3 | 1 | .989 | 2.34 | +39 | 23 | 3 | 10 | 36 |
| Victorino,Shane | Bos | 110 | 106 | 913.1 | 264 | 9 | 3 | 3 | .989 | 2.69 | +33 | 19 | 1 | 4 | 24 |
| Bruce,Jay | Cin | 160 | 160 | 1438.2 | 330 | 13 | 3 | 3 | .991 | 2.15 | +18 | 11 | 3 | 4 | 18 |
| Aoki,Norichika | Mil | 149 | 145 | 1288.1 | 289 | 9 | 3 | 0 | .990 | 2.08 | +16 | 9 | -1 | 5 | 13 |
| Reddick,Josh | Oak | 113 | 108 | 966.1 | 244 | 9 | 5 | 3 | .981 | 2.36 | +12 | 7 | 3 | 3 | 13 |
| Byrd,Marlon | TOT | 138 | 129 | 1168.1 | 237 | 10 | 5 | 3 | .980 | 1.90 | +11 | 7 | 2 | 3 | 12 |
| Puig,Yasiel | LAD | 93 | 89 | 773.1 | 148 | 8 | 4 | 1 | .975 | 1.82 | +13 | 8 | 1 | 1 | 10 |
| Suzuki,Ichiro | NYY | 128 | 109 | 993.1 | 217 | 5 | 3 | 0 | .987 | 2.01 | +6 | 3 | 3 | 1 | 7 |
| Bautista,Jose | Tor | 109 | 109 | 966.0 | 192 | 8 | 5 | 4 | .976 | 1.86 | -7 | -4 | -1 | 9 | 4 |
| Werth,Jayson | Was | 126 | 126 | 1072.0 | 235 | 7 | 2 | 1 | .992 | 2.03 | +4 | 2 | 1 | -2 | 1 |
| Schierholtz,Nate | ChC | 126 | 117 | 1041.0 | 242 | 5 | 3 | 1 | .988 | 2.14 | +3 | 2 | 1 | -3 | 0 |
| Cruz,Nelson | Tex | 102 | 102 | 906.1 | 195 | 1 | 3 | 0 | .985 | 1.95 | -1 | -1 | 0 | -2 | -3 |
| Rios,Alex | TOT | 155 | 155 | 1365.2 | 327 | 9 | 3 | 1 | .991 | 2.21 | -15 | -9 | 2 | 2 | -5 |
| Beltran,Carlos | StL | 137 | 135 | 1138.1 | 242 | 4 | 5 | 1 | .980 | 1.94 | -4 | -2 | -1 | -3 | -6 |
| Stubbs,Drew | Cle | 105 | 86 | 785.0 | 163 | 4 | 6 | 0 | .965 | 1.91 | -8 | -5 | -1 | 0 | -6 |
| Pence,Hunter | SF | 162 | 162 | 1431.1 | 374 | 2 | 7 | 1 | .982 | 2.36 | +1 | 1 | -2 | -6 | -7 |
| Stanton,Giancarlo | Mia | 116 | 116 | 1031.1 | 233 | 7 | 8 | 0 | .968 | 2.09 | -1 | 0 | -5 | -2 | -7 |
| Markakis,Nick | Bal | 155 | 154 | 1381.0 | 312 | 7 | 0 | 1 | 1.000 | 2.08 | -21 | -12 | 5 | 0 | -7 |
| Hunter,Torii | Det | 143 | 138 | 1236.1 | 223 | 9 | 3 | 3 | .987 | 1.69 | -15 | -9 | -1 | 0 | -10 |
| Cuddyer,Michael | Col | 118 | 113 | 992.0 | 191 | 6 | 2 | 1 | .990 | 1.79 | -20 | -12 | -1 | -3 | -16 |

## Catchers - Regulars

| | | | | | | | | | | | | | | | | Runs Saved | | | |
|---|---|---|---|---|---|---|---|---|---|---|---|---|---|---|---|---|---|---|---|
| Player | Tm | G | GS | Inn | PO | A | E | DP | PB | Pct. | SBA | CS | PCS | CS% | CERA | GFP/ DME | SB | Other | Total |
| Castillo,Welington | ChC | 111 | 107 | 956.0 | 730 | 85 | 10 | 3 | 8 | .988 | 88 | 21 | 7 | .24 | 4.02 | 10 | 4 | 5 | 19 |
| Martin,Russell | Pit | 120 | 117 | 1051.1 | 885 | 103 | 2 | 6 | 4 | .998 | 82 | 29 | 7 | .35 | 3.13 | 4 | 9 | 3 | 16 |
| Molina,Yadier | StL | 132 | 128 | 1115.1 | 976 | 63 | 4 | 11 | 3 | .996 | 45 | 19 | 1 | .42 | 3.16 | 3 | 2 | 7 | 12 |
| Perez,Salvador | KC | 137 | 126 | 1115.1 | 930 | 71 | 7 | 4 | 3 | .993 | 69 | 23 | 2 | .33 | 3.36 | 3 | 4 | 4 | 11 |
| Gomes,Yan | Cle | 85 | 79 | 710.0 | 663 | 65 | 3 | 1 | 4 | .996 | 47 | 18 | 2 | .38 | 3.56 | 0 | 7 | 4 | 11 |
| Mathis,Jeff | Mia | 73 | 70 | 615.0 | 520 | 30 | 1 | 2 | 5 | .998 | 43 | 13 | 2 | .30 | 3.15 | -1 | 2 | 4 | 5 |
| Ramos,Wilson | Was | 77 | 77 | 667.2 | 593 | 35 | 8 | 1 | 5 | .987 | 45 | 11 | 3 | .24 | 3.26 | -1 | 2 | 4 | 5 |
| Mauer,Joe | Min | 75 | 73 | 658.2 | 495 | 30 | 2 | 7 | 3 | .996 | 38 | 15 | 2 | .39 | 4.04 | -2 | 3 | 4 | 5 |
| Posey,Buster | SF | 121 | 119 | 1031.0 | 907 | 53 | 7 | 5 | 3 | .993 | 80 | 17 | 10 | .21 | 3.84 | -2 | -1 | 7 | 4 |
| Ruiz,Carlos | Phi | 86 | 83 | 745.0 | 657 | 44 | 3 | 9 | 4 | .996 | 75 | 12 | 9 | .16 | 4.14 | 3 | -2 | 2 | 3 |

| Player | Tm | G | GS | Inn | PO | A | E | DP | PB | Pct. | SBA | CS | PCS | CS% | CERA | Runs Saved GFP/ DME | SB | Other | Total |
|---|---|---|---|---|---|---|---|---|---|---|---|---|---|---|---|---|---|---|---|
| Arencibia,J.P. | Tor | 131 | 115 | 1058.2 | 891 | 49 | 11 | 6 | 13 | .988 | 74 | 12 | 9 | .16 | 4.10 | 1 | -4 | 5 | 2 |
| Castro,Jason | Hou | 98 | 95 | 827.1 | 630 | 44 | 5 | 6 | 10 | .993 | 75 | 17 | 2 | .23 | 4.84 | 4 | 0 | -2 | 2 |
| Flowers,Tyler | CWS | 84 | 77 | 687.2 | 640 | 42 | 4 | 4 | 8 | .994 | 65 | 13 | 3 | .20 | 3.86 | -2 | 0 | 4 | 2 |
| Stewart,Chris | NYY | 108 | 97 | 844.1 | 741 | 55 | 2 | 6 | 12 | .997 | 54 | 17 | 0 | .31 | 4.05 | 4 | 2 | -5 | 1 |
| Ellis,A.J. | LAD | 113 | 109 | 972.1 | 855 | 73 | 3 | 8 | 6 | .997 | 59 | 24 | 4 | .41 | 3.05 | -4 | 4 | 0 | 0 |
| Mesoraco,Devin | Cin | 97 | 84 | 782.0 | 668 | 55 | 5 | 2 | 4 | .993 | 58 | 13 | 5 | .22 | 3.40 | 1 | -2 | 0 | -1 |
| Lucroy,Jonathan | Mil | 126 | 122 | 1074.0 | 857 | 56 | 8 | 5 | 7 | .991 | 101 | 21 | 1 | .21 | 4.06 | 6 | -2 | -6 | -2 |
| Rosario,Wilin | Col | 106 | 103 | 910.1 | 646 | 63 | 9 | 2 | 9 | .987 | 69 | 16 | 3 | .23 | 4.31 | -2 | -2 | 2 | -2 |
| Suzuki,Kurt | TOT | 93 | 82 | 748.0 | 621 | 35 | 6 | 5 | 3 | .991 | 61 | 4 | 4 | .07 | 3.89 | 6 | -6 | -2 | -2 |
| McCann,Brian | Atl | 92 | 91 | 806.1 | 729 | 34 | 4 | 1 | 3 | .995 | 60 | 13 | 2 | .22 | 2.98 | -2 | -1 | 1 | -2 |
| Molina,Jose | TB | 96 | 87 | 749.1 | 674 | 34 | 4 | 5 | 8 | .994 | 73 | 17 | 6 | .23 | 3.74 | -4 | 2 | 0 | -2 |
| Pierzynski,A.J. | Tex | 119 | 111 | 1005.0 | 892 | 65 | 2 | 8 | 6 | .998 | 66 | 17 | 7 | .26 | 3.60 | -2 | 0 | -1 | -3 |
| Hundley,Nick | SD | 112 | 102 | 928.0 | 729 | 63 | 10 | 12 | 4 | .988 | 106 | 25 | 3 | .24 | 4.26 | 3 | 1 | -7 | -3 |
| Avila,Alex | Det | 98 | 96 | 836.2 | 815 | 29 | 6 | 4 | 9 | .993 | 84 | 11 | 4 | .13 | 3.38 | 0 | -7 | 3 | -4 |
| Lobaton,Jose | TB | 96 | 76 | 713.2 | 643 | 40 | 3 | 6 | 2 | .996 | 72 | 9 | 1 | .13 | 3.73 | 0 | -3 | -1 | -4 |
| Montero,Miguel | Ari | 112 | 111 | 1006.2 | 823 | 70 | 5 | 5 | 9 | .994 | 40 | 9 | 6 | .23 | 4.02 | -2 | 1 | -4 | -5 |
| Saltalamacchia,J | Bos | 119 | 111 | 1004.0 | 908 | 46 | 6 | 4 | 7 | .994 | 110 | 21 | 3 | .19 | 3.86 | 2 | -4 | -4 | -6 |
| Norris,Derek | Oak | 91 | 71 | 663.0 | 562 | 30 | 3 | 4 | 6 | .995 | 42 | 7 | 5 | .17 | 3.65 | -3 | -1 | -2 | -6 |
| Iannetta,Chris | LAA | 113 | 102 | 921.2 | 725 | 51 | 5 | 6 | 6 | .994 | 99 | 15 | 5 | .15 | 4.55 | 1 | -4 | -4 | -7 |
| Buck,John | TOT | 104 | 101 | 922.2 | 746 | 41 | 4 | 1 | 6 | .995 | 48 | 9 | 7 | .19 | 4.00 | -3 | -1 | -6 | -10 |
| Santana,Carlos | Cle | 84 | 81 | 712.2 | 694 | 33 | 4 | 2 | 5 | .995 | 61 | 10 | 1 | .16 | 4.05 | -7 | -2 | -3 | -12 |
| Wieters,Matt | Bal | 140 | 134 | 1201.0 | 1021 | 58 | 3 | 6 | 5 | .997 | 66 | 22 | 2 | .33 | 4.30 | -3 | 2 | -12 | -13 |

# All Other Fielders

| Player | Tm | Pos | G | GS | Inn | PO | A | E | DP | Pct. | Rng | +/- | RS |
|---|---|---|---|---|---|---|---|---|---|---|---|---|---|
| Abreu, T | SF | 2B | 30 | 22 | 220 | 45 | 57 | 2 | 15 | .981 | 4.17 | -6 | -3 |
| | SF | 3B | 3 | 1 | 13 | 0 | 2 | 0 | 0 | 1.000 | 1.35 | -1 | 0 |
| | SF | SS | 3 | 2 | 18 | 2 | 7 | 1 | 0 | .900 | 4.50 | -1 | -2 |
| Ackley, D | Sea | 1B | 6 | 0 | 14 | 11 | 1 | 0 | 0 | 1.000 | - | 0 | 0 |
| | Sea | 2B | 53 | 49 | 441 | 81 | 150 | 0 | 30 | 1.000 | 4.72 | +4 | 3 |
| | Sea | LF | 11 | 8 | 81 | 20 | 1 | 0 | 1 | 1.000 | 2.32 | +1 | 0 |
| | Sea | CF | 50 | 46 | 414 | 114 | 0 | 1 | 0 | .991 | 2.48 | -9 | -8 |
| Adams, D | NYY | 1B | 4 | 3 | 27 | 26 | 4 | 0 | 2 | 1.000 | - | +1 | 1 |
| | NYY | 2B | 9 | 6 | 60 | 16 | 19 | 0 | 4 | 1.000 | 5.25 | 0 | 1 |
| | NYY | 3B | 31 | 29 | 253 | 14 | 53 | 1 | 6 | .985 | 2.38 | +3 | 1 |
| Adams, M | StL | 1B | 74 | 63 | 598 | 598 | 50 | 2 | 70 | .997 | - | 0 | -2 |
| Adduci, J | Tex | 1B | 4 | 1 | 12 | 12 | 0 | 1 | 3 | .923 | - | 0 | -1 |
| | Tex | LF | 8 | 6 | 50 | 10 | 0 | 0 | 0 | 1.000 | 1.80 | +1 | 1 |
| Adrianza, E | SF | SS | 6 | 4 | 45 | 4 | 12 | 1 | 4 | .941 | 3.20 | +2 | 1 |
| Almonte, A | Sea | LF | 2 | 1 | 10 | 1 | 0 | 0 | 0 | 1.000 | .90 | 0 | 0 |
| | Sea | CF | 15 | 12 | 112 | 19 | 1 | 2 | 0 | .909 | 1.61 | -2 | -1 |
| | Sea | RF | 7 | 5 | 46 | 13 | 0 | 2 | 0 | .867 | 2.54 | +1 | -1 |
| Almonte, Z | NYY | LF | 25 | 24 | 207 | 49 | 0 | 0 | 0 | 1.000 | 2.13 | +4 | 1 |
| | NYY | RF | 3 | 3 | 32 | 7 | 0 | 0 | 0 | 1.000 | 1.97 | +1 | 0 |
| Alonso, Y | SD | 2B | 1 | 0 | 1 | 0 | 0 | 0 | 0 | - | .00 | -1 | -1 |
| | SD | 3B | 1 | 0 | 0 | 0 | 0 | 0 | 0 | - | - | 0 | 0 |
| | SD | LF | 1 | 0 | 0 | 0 | 0 | 0 | 0 | - | - | -1 | 0 |
| Amarista, A | SD | 2B | 23 | 16 | 153 | 40 | 48 | 1 | 10 | .989 | 5.19 | +1 | 1 |
| | SD | 3B | 9 | 2 | 27 | 3 | 5 | 0 | 1 | 1.000 | 2.63 | 0 | 0 |
| | SD | SS | 13 | 8 | 84 | 11 | 26 | 1 | 5 | .974 | 3.98 | -3 | -2 |
| | SD | LF | 11 | 5 | 48 | 11 | 0 | 0 | 0 | 1.000 | 2.05 | +3 | 1 |
| | SD | CF | 87 | 53 | 507 | 149 | 5 | 3 | 1 | .981 | 2.73 | -8 | -5 |
| Andino, R | Sea | 2B | 8 | 8 | 67 | 15 | 27 | 0 | 9 | 1.000 | 5.64 | -2 | -1 |
| | Sea | 3B | 4 | 3 | 26 | 1 | 5 | 0 | 0 | 1.000 | 2.08 | 0 | 0 |
| | Sea | SS | 18 | 11 | 109 | 12 | 29 | 2 | 8 | .953 | 3.38 | 0 | 0 |
| Ankiel, R | TOT | CF | 17 | 17 | 142 | 35 | 1 | 0 | 0 | 1.000 | 2.28 | -7 | -3 |
| | TOT | RF | 26 | 16 | 166 | 42 | 3 | 2 | 0 | .957 | 2.44 | -6 | -2 |
| Aoki, N | Mil | CF | 2 | 1 | 9 | 1 | 0 | 0 | 0 | 1.000 | 1.00 | -1 | 0 |
| Arcia, O | Min | LF | 56 | 54 | 476 | 113 | 3 | 1 | 2 | .991 | 2.19 | -16 | -9 |
| | Min | RF | 29 | 28 | 236 | 54 | 2 | 1 | 0 | .982 | 2.13 | -11 | -6 |
| Arias, J | SF | 1B | 6 | 4 | 40 | 41 | 1 | 0 | 4 | 1.000 | - | 0 | 0 |
| | SF | 2B | 13 | 8 | 78 | 28 | 21 | 1 | 9 | .980 | 5.65 | +1 | 0 |
| | SF | 3B | 55 | 18 | 218 | 15 | 55 | 3 | 4 | .959 | 2.89 | +7 | 5 |
| | SF | SS | 24 | 17 | 156 | 21 | 42 | 1 | 12 | .984 | 3.63 | -4 | -2 |
| Asche, C | Phi | 3B | 44 | 44 | 384 | 29 | 87 | 5 | 3 | .959 | 2.72 | -11 | -7 |
| Aviles, M | Cle | 2B | 12 | 11 | 94 | 13 | 31 | 1 | 5 | .978 | 4.21 | 0 | 0 |
| | Cle | 3B | 56 | 37 | 376 | 29 | 63 | 3 | 6 | .968 | 2.20 | -5 | -5 |
| | Cle | SS | 46 | 35 | 340 | 55 | 106 | 4 | 26 | .976 | 4.27 | 0 | 0 |
| | Cle | LF | 4 | 4 | 33 | 12 | 0 | 0 | 0 | 1.000 | 3.27 | +2 | 1 |
| | Cle | RF | 1 | 0 | 2 | 1 | 0 | 0 | 0 | 1.000 | 4.50 | 0 | 0 |
| Baker, J | Tex | 1B | 21 | 15 | 114 | 109 | 3 | 0 | 7 | 1.000 | - | +1 | 0 |
| | Tex | 2B | 1 | 1 | 9 | 1 | 1 | 0 | 1 | 1.000 | 2.00 | -1 | -1 |
| | Tex | 3B | 10 | 5 | 59 | 5 | 14 | 1 | 1 | .950 | 2.91 | -3 | -2 |
| | Tex | LF | 21 | 15 | 101 | 18 | 0 | 0 | 0 | 1.000 | 1.60 | -2 | -1 |
| | Tex | RF | 1 | 1 | 8 | 2 | 0 | 0 | 0 | 1.000 | 2.25 | -1 | 0 |
| Barnes, B | Hou | LF | 8 | 2 | 35 | 8 | 0 | 0 | 0 | 1.000 | 2.08 | +1 | 1 |
| | Hou | RF | 13 | 11 | 87 | 22 | 1 | 0 | 0 | 1.000 | 2.38 | -2 | -1 |
| Barton, D | Oak | 1B | 36 | 30 | 268 | 232 | 23 | 1 | 25 | .996 | - | 0 | -1 |
| Bautista, J | Tor | 1B | 1 | 0 | 2 | 2 | 0 | 0 | 0 | 1.000 | - | 0 | 0 |
| | Tor | 3B | 3 | 2 | 21 | 1 | 1 | 0 | 0 | 1.000 | .84 | 0 | 0 |
| Baxter, M | NYM | LF | 17 | 4 | 62 | 28 | 0 | 0 | 0 | 1.000 | 4.09 | +3 | 2 |
| | NYM | RF | 30 | 24 | 207 | 56 | 1 | 1 | 0 | .983 | 2.48 | +3 | 2 |
| Bay, J | Sea | LF | 38 | 31 | 299 | 57 | 1 | 0 | 0 | 1.000 | 1.75 | +2 | 0 |
| | Sea | CF | 1 | 0 | 1 | 0 | 0 | 0 | 0 | - | .00 | 0 | 0 |
| | Sea | RF | 25 | 19 | 181 | 46 | 1 | 0 | 0 | 1.000 | 2.33 | -2 | -1 |
| Beckham, G | CWS | SS | 2 | 0 | 6 | 2 | 0 | 0 | 0 | 1.000 | 3.00 | 0 | 0 |
| Beckham, T | TB | 2B | 3 | 1 | 13 | 0 | 5 | 0 | 0 | 1.000 | 3.46 | 0 | 0 |
| | TB | SS | 1 | 0 | 1 | 0 | 0 | 0 | 0 | - | .00 | 0 | 0 |
| Beltre, E | Tex | LF | 5 | 4 | 34 | 6 | 0 | 0 | 0 | 1.000 | 1.59 | +2 | 2 |
| | Tex | CF | 5 | 5 | 44 | 16 | 0 | 0 | 0 | 1.000 | 3.27 | -2 | -1 |
| | Tex | RF | 6 | 1 | 17 | 4 | 0 | 0 | 0 | 1.000 | 2.12 | 0 | 0 |
| Berkman, L | Tex | 1B | 4 | 4 | 42 | 38 | 6 | 1 | 3 | .978 | - | +1 | 1 |
| Bernadina, R | TOT | LF | 29 | 14 | 146 | 29 | 0 | 0 | 0 | 1.000 | 1.79 | +2 | -1 |
| | TOT | CF | 18 | 14 | 139 | 43 | 2 | 0 | 0 | 1.000 | 2.91 | -4 | 1 |
| | TOT | RF | 40 | 19 | 223 | 44 | 4 | 0 | 1 | 1.000 | 1.94 | +2 | 4 |
| Bernier, D | Min | 2B | 4 | 1 | 17 | 1 | 2 | 0 | 0 | 1.000 | 1.59 | +1 | 1 |
| | Min | 3B | 7 | 1 | 16 | 0 | 2 | 0 | 0 | 1.000 | 1.13 | 0 | 0 |
| | Min | SS | 20 | 12 | 117 | 17 | 46 | 0 | 9 | 1.000 | 4.85 | +4 | 3 |
| Berry, Q | Bos | LF | 4 | 0 | 6 | 1 | 0 | 0 | 0 | 1.000 | 1.50 | 0 | 0 |
| | Bos | CF | 3 | 0 | 4 | 2 | 0 | 0 | 0 | 1.000 | 4.91 | +1 | 1 |
| | Bos | RF | 4 | 1 | 12 | 1 | 0 | 0 | 0 | 1.000 | .75 | -1 | 0 |
| Betancourt, Y | Mil | 1B | 68 | 46 | 409 | 389 | 25 | 3 | 38 | .993 | - | -3 | -2 |
| | Mil | 2B | 5 | 3 | 28 | 5 | 7 | 0 | 0 | 1.000 | 3.86 | 0 | 0 |
| | Mil | 3B | 59 | 43 | 417 | 29 | 84 | 8 | 3 | .934 | 2.44 | +2 | -1 |
| | Mil | SS | 3 | 0 | 5 | 3 | 1 | 0 | 0 | 1.000 | 7.20 | 0 | 0 |
| | Mil | LF | 2 | 0 | 4 | 0 | 0 | 0 | 0 | - | .00 | 0 | 0 |
| Betemit, W | Bal | 1B | 1 | 0 | 1 | 1 | 0 | 0 | 0 | 1.000 | - | 0 | 0 |
| Bianchi, J | Mil | 2B | 19 | 11 | 111 | 25 | 40 | 2 | 10 | .970 | 5.25 | 0 | 1 |
| | Mil | 3B | 42 | 26 | 263 | 27 | 84 | 4 | 9 | .965 | 3.79 | +16 | 11 |
| | Mil | SS | 20 | 17 | 164 | 35 | 55 | 4 | 16 | .957 | 4.95 | +6 | 4 |
| | Mil | LF | 3 | 0 | 5 | 0 | 1 | 0 | 0 | 1.000 | 1.69 | -1 | 0 |
| Blackmon, C | Col | LF | 17 | 8 | 84 | 13 | 0 | 0 | 0 | 1.000 | 1.40 | +1 | 0 |
| | Col | CF | 25 | 22 | 197 | 46 | 0 | 3 | 0 | .939 | 2.11 | -7 | -5 |
| | Col | RF | 34 | 26 | 243 | 53 | 0 | 1 | 0 | .981 | 1.96 | +6 | 1 |
| Blanco, G | SF | LF | 72 | 50 | 471 | 90 | 4 | 0 | 1 | 1.000 | 1.80 | +8 | 5 |
| | SF | CF | 76 | 63 | 550 | 142 | 2 | 0 | 0 | 1.000 | 2.36 | +11 | 5 |
| | SF | RF | 1 | 0 | 2 | 0 | 0 | 0 | 0 | - | .00 | 0 | 0 |
| Blanks, K | SD | 1B | 34 | 21 | 209 | 199 | 14 | 2 | 19 | .991 | - | +4 | 3 |
| | SD | LF | 35 | 16 | 161 | 29 | 1 | 0 | 1 | 1.000 | 1.68 | -1 | 0 |
| | SD | RF | 37 | 33 | 261 | 65 | 1 | 2 | 1 | .971 | 2.28 | -2 | -1 |
| Bloomquist, W | Ari | 2B | 15 | 15 | 136 | 32 | 37 | 0 | 10 | 1.000 | 4.57 | +1 | 0 |
| | Ari | SS | 9 | 8 | 74 | 12 | 29 | 1 | 7 | .976 | 4.99 | -2 | -2 |
| | Ari | LF | 7 | 6 | 55 | 9 | 0 | 0 | 0 | 1.000 | 1.46 | +2 | 1 |
| Boesch, B | NYY | RF | 15 | 12 | 103 | 28 | 1 | 1 | 1 | .967 | 2.53 | -3 | -2 |
| Bogaerts, X | Bos | 3B | 9 | 6 | 57 | 9 | 9 | 0 | 1 | 1.000 | 2.83 | -4 | -3 |
| | Bos | SS | 8 | 6 | 53 | 6 | 20 | 0 | 1 | 1.000 | 4.44 | +2 | 2 |
| Bogusevic, B | ChC | LF | 29 | 27 | 248 | 56 | 3 | 0 | 0 | 1.000 | 2.14 | -6 | -3 |
| | ChC | CF | 10 | 10 | 76 | 28 | 0 | 0 | 0 | 1.000 | 3.33 | -4 | -2 |
| | ChC | RF | 1 | 0 | 4 | 2 | 0 | 0 | 0 | 1.000 | 4.15 | +3 | 1 |
| Bonifacio, E | TOT | 2B | 90 | 78 | 711 | 141 | 230 | 10 | 58 | .974 | 4.70 | +10 | 10 |
| | TOT | 3B | 6 | 5 | 44 | 3 | 8 | 0 | 2 | 1.000 | 2.25 | 0 | 0 |
| | TOT | SS | 1 | 0 | 4 | 1 | 1 | 0 | 0 | 1.000 | 4.50 | 0 | 0 |
| | TOT | LF | 20 | 11 | 114 | 30 | 0 | 0 | 0 | 1.000 | 2.37 | -2 | -1 |
| | TOT | CF | 15 | 13 | 118 | 32 | 0 | 0 | 0 | 1.000 | 2.44 | -3 | -2 |
| | TOT | RF | 5 | 3 | 26 | 6 | 0 | 0 | 0 | 1.000 | 2.05 | 0 | 0 |
| Borbon, J | TOT | LF | 9 | 3 | 33 | 4 | 1 | 0 | 0 | 1.000 | 1.38 | 0 | 1 |
| | TOT | CF | 12 | 10 | 103 | 29 | 0 | 1 | 0 | .967 | 2.53 | +1 | 0 |
| | TOT | RF | 8 | 0 | 15 | 4 | 0 | 1 | 0 | .800 | 2.35 | -2 | -1 |
| Bourgeois, J | TB | LF | 6 | 3 | 26 | 6 | 0 | 0 | 0 | 1.000 | 2.08 | -2 | -1 |
| | TB | RF | 1 | 1 | 8 | 2 | 0 | 0 | 0 | 1.000 | 2.25 | -2 | -1 |
| Bourjos, P | LAA | CF | 53 | 45 | 415 | 117 | 2 | 1 | 0 | .992 | 2.58 | 0 | -1 |
| Bradley, J | Bos | LF | 14 | 10 | 94 | 15 | 1 | 1 | 0 | .941 | 1.53 | -1 | -1 |
| | Bos | CF | 19 | 16 | 146 | 42 | 0 | 0 | 0 | 1.000 | 2.59 | -2 | -2 |
| | Bos | RF | 2 | 0 | 2 | 0 | 0 | 0 | 0 | - | .00 | 0 | 0 |
| Brantley, M | Cle | CF | 1 | 0 | 4 | 0 | 0 | 0 | 0 | - | .00 | 0 | 0 |
| Braun, R | Mil | LF | 59 | 59 | 503 | 116 | 5 | 2 | 1 | .984 | 2.17 | +2 | 4 |
| Brignac, R | TOT | 2B | 3 | 3 | 26 | 6 | 8 | 0 | 1 | 1.000 | 4.85 | -1 | -1 |
| | TOT | 3B | 8 | 4 | 43 | 4 | 10 | 2 | 1 | .875 | 2.95 | -2 | -2 |
| | TOT | SS | 20 | 14 | 128 | 21 | 30 | 1 | 7 | .981 | 3.58 | -2 | -2 |
| | TOT | LF | 1 | 0 | 2 | 1 | 0 | 0 | 0 | 1.000 | 4.50 | +1 | 0 |
| Brown, A | NYM | 1B | 1 | 0 | 2 | 1 | 0 | 0 | 0 | 1.000 | - | 0 | 0 |
| | NYM | LF | 14 | 10 | 93 | 13 | 1 | 0 | 0 | 1.000 | 1.35 | -3 | 0 |
| | NYM | RF | 25 | 17 | 155 | 39 | 3 | 2 | 0 | .955 | 2.44 | -2 | 0 |
| Brown, C | Was | LF | 5 | 1 | 16 | 2 | 0 | 0 | 0 | 1.000 | 1.13 | 0 | 0 |
| | Was | CF | 1 | 1 | 8 | 3 | 0 | 0 | 0 | 1.000 | 3.38 | 0 | 0 |
| | Was | RF | 3 | 0 | 6 | 2 | 0 | 0 | 0 | 1.000 | 3.00 | +1 | 1 |
| Brown, D | Phi | RF | 2 | 2 | 15 | 5 | 0 | 0 | 0 | 1.000 | 3.00 | +1 | 1 |
| Buss, N | LAD | LF | 3 | 1 | 16 | 4 | 0 | 0 | 0 | 1.000 | 2.25 | +1 | 0 |
| | LAD | CF | 1 | 1 | 6 | 1 | 0 | 0 | 0 | 1.000 | 1.42 | 0 | 0 |
| | LAD | RF | 3 | 2 | 20 | 2 | 0 | 0 | 0 | 1.000 | .92 | +1 | 0 |
| Butera, D | TOT | 1B | 2 | 1 | 11 | 15 | 0 | 0 | 1 | 1.000 | - | 0 | 0 |
| Butler, B | KC | 1B | 7 | 7 | 53 | 56 | 0 | 0 | 4 | 1.000 | - | 0 | 0 |
| Butler, J | Tex | LF | 3 | 3 | 19 | 2 | 0 | 0 | 0 | 1.000 | .95 | +1 | 0 |
| | Tex | RF | 2 | 0 | 2 | 1 | 0 | 0 | 0 | 1.000 | 4.50 | +1 | 0 |
| Byrd, M | TOT | LF | 2 | 2 | 15 | 2 | 0 | 0 | 0 | 1.000 | 1.20 | -1 | 0 |
| | TOT | CF | 2 | 2 | 17 | 1 | 0 | 0 | 0 | 1.000 | .54 | +1 | 0 |
| Cabrera, M | Tor | LF | 77 | 76 | 621 | 126 | 3 | 1 | 0 | .992 | 1.87 | -12 | -5 |
| Cain, L | KC | RF | 32 | 18 | 187 | 49 | 0 | 2 | 0 | .961 | 2.36 | +13 | 7 |
| Calhoun, K | LAA | 1B | 6 | 4 | 37 | 44 | 4 | 2 | 3 | .960 | - | -1 | -1 |

# All Other Fielders

| Player | Tm | Pos | G | GS | Inn | PO | A | E | DP | Pct. | Rng | +/- | RS |
|---|---|---|---|---|---|---|---|---|---|---|---|---|---|
| | LAA | RF | 54 | 45 | 421 | 108 | 4 | 6 | 3 | .949 | 2.40 | -2 | -5 |
| Callaspo, A | TOT | 2B | 33 | 29 | 248 | 39 | 56 | 3 | 9 | .969 | 3.45 | -9 | -8 |
| Campana, T | Ari | LF | 2 | 0 | 3 | 1 | 0 | 0 | 0 | 1.000 | 2.70 | 0 | 0 |
| | Ari | CF | 8 | 7 | 75 | 13 | 1 | 1 | 0 | .933 | 1.68 | 0 | -1 |
| Cano, R | NYY | SS | 1 | 0 | 1 | 0 | 0 | 0 | 0 | - | .00 | 0 | 0 |
| Carp, M | Bos | 1B | 29 | 23 | 202 | 188 | 12 | 2 | 19 | .990 | - | -2 | -1 |
| | Bos | LF | 41 | 31 | 249 | 41 | 0 | 0 | 0 | 1.000 | 1.48 | -4 | -3 |
| | Bos | RF | 2 | 2 | 11 | 2 | 0 | 0 | 0 | 1.000 | 1.64 | 0 | 0 |
| Carpenter, M | StL | 1B | 2 | 1 | 12 | 10 | 0 | 0 | 0 | 1.000 | - | -1 | -1 |
| | StL | 3B | 42 | 24 | 253 | 11 | 58 | 3 | 9 | .958 | 2.45 | -1 | 1 |
| | StL | RF | 2 | 1 | 7 | 1 | 1 | 0 | 0 | 1.000 | 2.57 | -1 | 0 |
| Carrera, E | TOT | LF | 1 | 0 | 5 | 1 | 0 | 0 | 0 | 1.000 | 1.80 | 0 | 0 |
| | TOT | CF | 1 | 1 | 9 | 6 | 0 | 0 | 0 | 1.000 | 6.00 | +1 | 0 |
| | TOT | RF | 6 | 2 | 24 | 4 | 0 | 0 | 0 | 1.000 | 1.50 | -3 | -2 |
| Carroll, J | TOT | 2B | 18 | 16 | 147 | 25 | 33 | 0 | 10 | 1.000 | 3.56 | -1 | 0 |
| | TOT | 3B | 47 | 38 | 349 | 30 | 70 | 2 | 13 | .980 | 2.58 | -4 | -3 |
| | TOT | SS | 3 | 2 | 17 | 2 | 9 | 0 | 2 | 1.000 | 5.82 | +1 | 1 |
| Carson, M | Cle | LF | 4 | 0 | 12 | 2 | 0 | 0 | 0 | 1.000 | 1.50 | +1 | 0 |
| | Cle | RF | 14 | 1 | 38 | 8 | 0 | 0 | 0 | 1.000 | 1.89 | 0 | 0 |
| Carter, C | Hou | 1B | 61 | 54 | 492 | 472 | 17 | 2 | 45 | .996 | - | -7 | -5 |
| | Hou | LF | 49 | 41 | 336 | 55 | 0 | 2 | 0 | .965 | 1.47 | -4 | -3 |
| | Hou | RF | 2 | 2 | 17 | 6 | 0 | 1 | 0 | .857 | 3.18 | -2 | -1 |
| Casilla, A | Bal | 2B | 51 | 31 | 300 | 70 | 99 | 0 | 22 | 1.000 | 5.08 | +4 | 4 |
| | Bal | SS | 2 | 0 | 3 | 0 | 1 | 0 | 0 | 1.000 | 3.00 | 0 | 0 |
| Castellanos, A | LAD | LF | 2 | 2 | 14 | 1 | 0 | 0 | 0 | 1.000 | .64 | -1 | -1 |
| | LAD | RF | 6 | 2 | 24 | 1 | 0 | 0 | 0 | 1.000 | .37 | -1 | -1 |
| Castellanos, N | Det | LF | 9 | 4 | 39 | 5 | 0 | 0 | 0 | 1.000 | 1.16 | -1 | -1 |
| Cedeno, R | TOT | 1B | 1 | 0 | 1 | 0 | 1 | 0 | 0 | 1.000 | - | 0 | 0 |
| | TOT | 3B | 1 | 0 | 1 | 0 | 0 | 0 | 0 | - | .00 | -1 | -1 |
| | TOT | SS | 76 | 71 | 628 | 111 | 197 | 13 | 44 | .960 | 4.42 | -7 | -5 |
| Cervelli, F | NYY | 2B | 1 | 0 | 1 | 0 | 0 | 0 | 0 | - | .00 | 0 | 0 |
| Cespedes, Y | Oak | CF | 18 | 16 | 133 | 37 | 1 | 0 | 0 | 1.000 | 2.57 | -6 | -4 |
| Chambers, A | StL | LF | 11 | 0 | 25 | 3 | 0 | 1 | 0 | .750 | 1.08 | -1 | -1 |
| | StL | RF | 6 | 1 | 18 | 4 | 0 | 0 | 0 | 1.000 | 2.00 | -2 | -1 |
| Chavez, E | Sea | LF | 16 | 4 | 44 | 9 | 1 | 0 | 0 | 1.000 | 2.05 | -1 | 0 |
| | Sea | CF | 24 | 20 | 179 | 54 | 0 | 0 | 0 | 1.000 | 2.71 | -8 | -7 |
| | Sea | RF | 50 | 35 | 349 | 86 | 3 | 4 | 2 | .957 | 2.29 | -1 | 1 |
| Chavez, E | Ari | 1B | 6 | 2 | 23 | 20 | 2 | 0 | 3 | 1.000 | - | 0 | 0 |
| | Ari | 3B | 52 | 46 | 429 | 30 | 104 | 1 | 6 | .993 | 2.81 | -9 | -10 |
| Chirinos, R | Tex | 1B | 4 | 4 | 30 | 23 | 4 | 1 | 2 | .964 | - | 0 | 0 |
| | Tex | 3B | 3 | 0 | 5 | 0 | 1 | 0 | 0 | 1.000 | 1.80 | 0 | 0 |
| Chisenhall, L | Cle | 3B | 88 | 83 | 697 | 55 | 134 | 9 | 18 | .955 | 2.44 | -4 | 1 |
| Choice, M | Oak | LF | 2 | 1 | 12 | 3 | 0 | 0 | 0 | 1.000 | 2.25 | 0 | 0 |
| | Oak | CF | 2 | 0 | 7 | 1 | 0 | 0 | 0 | 1.000 | 1.29 | 0 | 0 |
| | Oak | RF | 4 | 2 | 22 | 6 | 0 | 0 | 0 | 1.000 | 2.45 | +1 | 0 |
| Choo, S | Cin | LF | 3 | 3 | 28 | 4 | 1 | 0 | 0 | 1.000 | 1.61 | 0 | 0 |
| Ciriaco, P | TOT | 1B | 1 | 0 | 3 | 3 | 1 | 0 | 1 | 1.000 | - | 0 | 0 |
| | TOT | 2B | 5 | 1 | 15 | 7 | 7 | 0 | 1 | 1.000 | 8.40 | +1 | 0 |
| | TOT | 3B | 10 | 5 | 56 | 3 | 11 | 4 | 0 | .778 | 2.25 | -1 | 0 |
| | TOT | SS | 29 | 25 | 238 | 42 | 58 | 6 | 19 | .943 | 3.79 | -14 | -9 |
| Clevenger, S | TOT | 3B | 2 | 1 | 8 | 1 | 2 | 0 | 0 | 1.000 | 3.38 | 0 | 1 |
| Coghlan, C | Mia | 2B | 1 | 0 | 1 | 0 | 1 | 0 | 0 | 1.000 | 13.50 | 0 | 0 |
| | Mia | 3B | 8 | 8 | 67 | 4 | 16 | 3 | 3 | .870 | 2.67 | -1 | -1 |
| | Mia | LF | 18 | 17 | 146 | 43 | 1 | 0 | 0 | 1.000 | 2.71 | -3 | -2 |
| | Mia | CF | 17 | 17 | 150 | 48 | 3 | 0 | 0 | 1.000 | 3.06 | -8 | -3 |
| | Mia | RF | 4 | 3 | 30 | 8 | 0 | 0 | 0 | 1.000 | 2.40 | +1 | 0 |
| Colabello, C | Min | 1B | 26 | 23 | 206 | 206 | 16 | 2 | 19 | .991 | - | +3 | 1 |
| | Min | RF | 11 | 9 | 78 | 14 | 1 | 1 | 0 | .938 | 1.73 | -1 | 0 |
| Colvin, T | Col | 1B | 1 | 0 | 3 | 4 | 0 | 0 | 0 | 1.000 | - | 0 | 0 |
| | Col | LF | 4 | 2 | 21 | 5 | 0 | 0 | 0 | 1.000 | 2.14 | 0 | 0 |
| | Col | CF | 16 | 14 | 121 | 36 | 0 | 0 | 0 | 1.000 | 2.68 | -1 | -3 |
| | Col | RF | 4 | 2 | 21 | 2 | 0 | 0 | 0 | 1.000 | .86 | +1 | 0 |
| Constanza, J | Atl | LF | 9 | 3 | 38 | 9 | 0 | 0 | 0 | 1.000 | 2.13 | +4 | 2 |
| | Atl | CF | 2 | 2 | 14 | 2 | 0 | 0 | 0 | 1.000 | 1.29 | 0 | 0 |
| Corporan, C | Hou | 1B | 1 | 0 | 1 | 0 | 0 | 0 | 0 | - | - | 0 | 0 |
| Cousins, S | LAA | LF | 3 | 0 | 5 | 0 | 0 | 0 | 0 | - | .00 | 0 | 0 |
| | LAA | RF | 1 | 0 | 1 | 0 | 0 | 0 | 0 | - | .00 | 0 | 0 |
| Cowgill, C | TOT | LF | 32 | 10 | 124 | 17 | 0 | 1 | 0 | .944 | 1.23 | +2 | 0 |
| | TOT | CF | 24 | 13 | 136 | 36 | 0 | 0 | 0 | 1.000 | 2.38 | +2 | 1 |
| | TOT | RF | 17 | 13 | 106 | 30 | 3 | 0 | 0 | 1.000 | 2.80 | +2 | 2 |
| Craig, A | StL | LF | 25 | 20 | 181 | 35 | 1 | 0 | 1 | 1.000 | 1.79 | -2 | -2 |
| | StL | RF | 22 | 21 | 180 | 32 | 0 | 0 | 0 | 1.000 | 1.60 | 0 | -1 |

| Player | Tm | Pos | G | GS | Inn | PO | A | E | DP | Pct. | Rng | +/- | RS |
|---|---|---|---|---|---|---|---|---|---|---|---|---|---|
| Crowe, T | Hou | LF | 24 | 14 | 150 | 27 | 2 | 0 | 1 | 1.000 | 1.74 | -2 | -3 |
| | Hou | CF | 14 | 10 | 99 | 40 | 0 | 1 | 0 | .976 | 3.65 | +3 | 1 |
| | Hou | RF | 25 | 16 | 141 | 36 | 1 | 2 | 0 | .949 | 2.36 | +5 | 2 |
| Cruz, L | TOT | 1B | 1 | 0 | 4 | 5 | 0 | 0 | 1 | 1.000 | - | 0 | 0 |
| | TOT | 3B | 41 | 30 | 276 | 30 | 78 | 3 | 6 | .973 | 3.52 | +6 | 6 |
| | TOT | SS | 20 | 15 | 140 | 21 | 59 | 3 | 10 | .964 | 5.14 | +4 | 5 |
| | TOT | LF | 1 | 0 | 0 | 0 | 0 | 0 | 0 | - | - | 0 | 0 |
| Cruz, T | StL | 3B | 3 | 0 | 5 | 0 | 1 | 0 | 0 | 1.000 | 1.80 | 0 | 0 |
| Cuddyer, M | Col | 1B | 15 | 13 | 109 | 112 | 6 | 0 | 15 | 1.000 | - | 0 | 0 |
| Culberson, C | Col | 2B | 4 | 1 | 8 | 3 | 3 | 1 | 1 | .857 | 6.75 | -1 | -1 |
| | Col | LF | 27 | 20 | 177 | 39 | 2 | 1 | 1 | .976 | 2.08 | -3 | -3 |
| Cunningham, T | Atl | LF | 5 | 0 | 12 | 0 | 0 | 0 | 0 | - | .00 | 0 | 0 |
| | Atl | RF | 2 | 0 | 4 | 0 | 0 | 0 | 0 | - | .00 | 0 | 0 |
| Curtis, J | StL | LF | 1 | 0 | 2 | 0 | 0 | 0 | 0 | - | .00 | 0 | 0 |
| Danks, J | CWS | LF | 2 | 2 | 19 | 1 | 0 | 0 | 0 | 1.000 | .47 | 0 | 0 |
| | CWS | CF | 47 | 21 | 233 | 62 | 0 | 1 | 0 | .984 | 2.40 | -2 | -2 |
| | CWS | RF | 20 | 17 | 156 | 37 | 1 | 0 | 1 | 1.000 | 2.20 | +2 | 1 |
| Davidson, M | Ari | 3B | 20 | 18 | 155 | 10 | 28 | 1 | 3 | .974 | 2.20 | +1 | -1 |
| Davis, K | Mil | LF | 34 | 30 | 265 | 47 | 1 | 1 | 0 | .980 | 1.63 | +1 | -2 |
| Davis, R | Tor | LF | 57 | 38 | 381 | 89 | 2 | 2 | 1 | .978 | 2.15 | +5 | 2 |
| | Tor | CF | 16 | 14 | 114 | 34 | 1 | 0 | 0 | 1.000 | 2.76 | +6 | 5 |
| | Tor | RF | 35 | 23 | 227 | 50 | 1 | 0 | 0 | 1.000 | 2.02 | -4 | -1 |
| De Aza, A | CWS | LF | 79 | 41 | 427 | 97 | 2 | 3 | 0 | .971 | 2.09 | +4 | -2 |
| Decker, J | SD | LF | 8 | 7 | 62 | 15 | 2 | 0 | 0 | 1.000 | 2.45 | -1 | -1 |
| DeJesus, D | TOT | LF | 30 | 21 | 205 | 37 | 1 | 0 | 0 | 1.000 | 1.67 | -1 | 0 |
| | TOT | CF | 81 | 69 | 617 | 186 | 1 | 1 | 0 | .995 | 2.73 | -4 | -6 |
| | TOT | RF | 6 | 3 | 31 | 7 | 0 | 0 | 0 | 1.000 | 2.03 | +2 | 1 |
| den Dekker, M | NYM | LF | 1 | 0 | 1 | 0 | 0 | 0 | 0 | - | .00 | 0 | 0 |
| | NYM | CF | 16 | 12 | 112 | 28 | 0 | 0 | 0 | 1.000 | 2.24 | +2 | 0 |
| | NYM | RF | 7 | 2 | 24 | 6 | 0 | 0 | 0 | 1.000 | 2.25 | +1 | 1 |
| Denorfia, C | SD | LF | 58 | 18 | 215 | 42 | 3 | 1 | 1 | .978 | 1.88 | +7 | 6 |
| | SD | CF | 41 | 36 | 279 | 78 | 2 | 2 | 0 | .976 | 2.58 | +5 | 5 |
| | SD | RF | 97 | 51 | 530 | 127 | 8 | 2 | 2 | .985 | 2.29 | +10 | 9 |
| DeRosa, M | Tor | 1B | 17 | 10 | 96 | 82 | 9 | 0 | 7 | 1.000 | - | +1 | 1 |
| | Tor | 2B | 29 | 15 | 153 | 28 | 47 | 0 | 8 | 1.000 | 4.42 | 0 | -2 |
| | Tor | 3B | 25 | 16 | 154 | 13 | 30 | 4 | 2 | .915 | 2.51 | -8 | -6 |
| | Tor | LF | 1 | 0 | 1 | 0 | 0 | 0 | 0 | - | .00 | 0 | 0 |
| Descalso, D | StL | 2B | 39 | 24 | 238 | 55 | 92 | 4 | 22 | .974 | 5.57 | -4 | -3 |
| | StL | 3B | 38 | 6 | 119 | 6 | 29 | 3 | 4 | .921 | 2.65 | +3 | 4 |
| | StL | SS | 55 | 48 | 402 | 51 | 135 | 7 | 28 | .964 | 4.17 | -8 | -7 |
| DeWitt, B | Atl | 3B | 1 | 0 | 1 | 0 | 0 | 0 | 0 | - | .00 | 0 | 0 |
| Diaz, J | Bos | 2B | 1 | 0 | 1 | 0 | 0 | 0 | 0 | - | .00 | 0 | 0 |
| | Bos | 3B | 3 | 1 | 12 | 2 | 3 | 0 | 0 | 1.000 | 3.75 | +1 | 0 |
| Diaz, M | Mia | LF | 4 | 3 | 27 | 4 | 2 | 0 | 1 | 1.000 | 2.00 | -1 | 1 |
| Dickerson, C | Bal | LF | 17 | 2 | 46 | 12 | 0 | 0 | 0 | 1.000 | 2.35 | +2 | 1 |
| | Bal | CF | 5 | 4 | 37 | 17 | 0 | 0 | 0 | 1.000 | 4.14 | +4 | 2 |
| | Bal | RF | 6 | 5 | 48 | 12 | 1 | 0 | 0 | 1.000 | 2.44 | 0 | 0 |
| Dickerson, C | Col | LF | 36 | 28 | 238 | 52 | 0 | 0 | 0 | 1.000 | 1.96 | 0 | -1 |
| | Col | CF | 15 | 12 | 116 | 38 | 0 | 0 | 0 | 1.000 | 2.95 | +4 | 1 |
| | Col | RF | 4 | 1 | 12 | 4 | 0 | 0 | 0 | 1.000 | 3.00 | +1 | 0 |
| Dietrich, D | Mia | 2B | 57 | 56 | 502 | 98 | 158 | 2 | 31 | .992 | 4.59 | -8 | -6 |
| Dirks, A | Det | CF | 4 | 1 | 13 | 5 | 0 | 0 | 0 | 1.000 | 3.46 | +1 | 1 |
| | Det | RF | 15 | 7 | 69 | 16 | 0 | 0 | 0 | 1.000 | 2.10 | +1 | 1 |
| Dobbs, G | Mia | 1B | 51 | 47 | 423 | 363 | 50 | 1 | 33 | .998 | - | +6 | 7 |
| | Mia | RF | 1 | 0 | 5 | 1 | 0 | 0 | 0 | 1.000 | 1.80 | 0 | 0 |
| Donaldson, J | Oak | 1B | 1 | 0 | 1 | 0 | 0 | 0 | 0 | - | - | 0 | 0 |
| | Oak | SS | 1 | 0 | 1 | 0 | 1 | 0 | 0 | 1.000 | 9.00 | 0 | 0 |
| Doumit, R | Min | LF | 1 | 0 | 3 | 0 | 0 | 0 | 0 | - | .00 | -2 | -1 |
| | Min | RF | 32 | 29 | 264 | 55 | 5 | 1 | 2 | .984 | 2.05 | -14 | -6 |
| Duda, L | NYM | 1B | 34 | 31 | 280 | 237 | 18 | 0 | 19 | 1.000 | - | -2 | -1 |
| | NYM | LF | 58 | 58 | 494 | 90 | 1 | 2 | 1 | .978 | 1.66 | -16 | -11 |
| Duncan, S | TB | 1B | 4 | 1 | 13 | 14 | 1 | 0 | 2 | 1.000 | - | 0 | 0 |
| Dunn, A | CWS | 1B | 71 | 70 | 627 | 548 | 31 | 8 | 54 | .986 | - | -12 | -12 |
| | CWS | LF | 3 | 2 | 17 | 2 | 0 | 0 | 0 | 1.000 | 1.06 | -1 | -1 |
| Dyson, J | KC | CF | 73 | 61 | 572 | 176 | 3 | 5 | 2 | .973 | 2.82 | +12 | 6 |
| Eaton, A | Ari | LF | 35 | 25 | 266 | 44 | 2 | 2 | 1 | .958 | 1.56 | +3 | 1 |
| | Ari | CF | 30 | 28 | 232 | 44 | 4 | 2 | 0 | .960 | 1.86 | -3 | -5 |
| | Ari | RF | 4 | 3 | 28 | 15 | 0 | 0 | 0 | 1.000 | 4.76 | +4 | 2 |
| Ellis, M | LAD | 3B | 1 | 0 | 0 | 0 | 0 | 0 | 0 | - | .00 | 0 | 0 |
| Elmore, J | Hou | 1B | 1 | 0 | 1 | 0 | 0 | 0 | 0 | - | - | 0 | 0 |
| | Hou | 2B | 12 | 10 | 97 | 20 | 36 | 1 | 5 | .982 | 5.21 | -2 | -2 |
| | Hou | 3B | 1 | 0 | 1 | 0 | 0 | 0 | 0 | - | .00 | 0 | 0 |

# All Other Fielders

| Player | Tm | Pos | G | GS | Inn | PO | A | E | DP | Pct. | Rng | +/- | RS |
|---|---|---|---|---|---|---|---|---|---|---|---|---|---|
| | Hou | SS | 20 | 18 | 160 | 33 | 55 | 7 | 12 | .926 | 4.95 | -4 | -2 |
| | Hou | LF | 9 | 2 | 33 | 4 | 0 | 0 | 0 | 1.000 | 1.10 | 0 | 0 |
| | Hou | CF | 2 | 0 | 3 | 1 | 0 | 0 | 0 | 1.000 | 3.00 | 0 | 0 |
| | Hou | RF | 1 | 0 | 2 | 0 | 0 | 0 | 0 | - | .00 | 0 | 0 |
| Encarnacion, E | Tor | 1B | 79 | 78 | 699 | 689 | 44 | 6 | 66 | .992 | - | -9 | -8 |
| | Tor | 3B | 10 | 9 | 88 | 12 | 26 | 2 | 2 | .950 | 3.90 | +1 | 1 |
| Escobar, E | Min | 2B | 7 | 5 | 40 | 8 | 17 | 0 | 4 | 1.000 | 5.58 | -1 | 0 |
| | Min | 3B | 23 | 14 | 135 | 4 | 18 | 2 | 3 | .917 | 1.46 | -6 | -5 |
| | Min | SS | 38 | 21 | 217 | 31 | 69 | 5 | 9 | .952 | 4.15 | +4 | 3 |
| | Min | LF | 1 | 0 | 4 | 0 | 0 | 0 | 0 | - | .00 | 0 | 0 |
| Espinosa, D | Was | 2B | 43 | 43 | 372 | 96 | 119 | 2 | 32 | .991 | 5.21 | +2 | 3 |
| | Was | SS | 1 | 1 | 8 | 1 | 0 | 0 | 0 | 1.000 | 1.13 | -1 | 0 |
| Ethier, A | LAD | LF | 8 | 7 | 52 | 10 | 1 | 0 | 0 | 1.000 | 1.90 | 0 | 0 |
| | LAD | CF | 74 | 70 | 645 | 132 | 5 | 2 | 2 | .986 | 1.91 | -7 | -3 |
| | LAD | RF | 54 | 50 | 444 | 105 | 2 | 0 | 2 | 1.000 | 2.17 | +4 | 4 |
| Falu, I | KC | 3B | 1 | 1 | 9 | 1 | 0 | 0 | 0 | 1.000 | 1.00 | 0 | 0 |
| Federowicz, T | LAD | 1B | 2 | 0 | 3 | 0 | 0 | 0 | 0 | - | - | 0 | 0 |
| Field, T | LAA | 2B | 9 | 3 | 30 | 8 | 1 | 0 | 1 | 1.000 | 2.67 | -2 | -2 |
| | LAA | 3B | 3 | 1 | 14 | 1 | 2 | 0 | 0 | 1.000 | 1.88 | -1 | -1 |
| | LAA | SS | 5 | 1 | 20 | 3 | 2 | 0 | 0 | 1.000 | 2.25 | 0 | 0 |
| Flaherty, R | Bal | 1B | 4 | 1 | 20 | 26 | 0 | 0 | 1 | 1.000 | - | 0 | -1 |
| | Bal | 2B | 65 | 59 | 515 | 105 | 176 | 2 | 52 | .993 | 4.91 | 0 | 3 |
| | Bal | 3B | 7 | 3 | 34 | 5 | 7 | 0 | 1 | 1.000 | 3.18 | +1 | 0 |
| | Bal | SS | 9 | 3 | 33 | 4 | 8 | 0 | 3 | 1.000 | 3.27 | +1 | 1 |
| Flores, W | NYM | 2B | 2 | 1 | 11 | 3 | 2 | 0 | 1 | 1.000 | 4.09 | -2 | -1 |
| | NYM | 3B | 26 | 25 | 208 | 13 | 55 | 2 | 4 | .971 | 2.94 | -1 | -2 |
| Forsythe, L | SD | 2B | 34 | 31 | 282 | 59 | 99 | 2 | 21 | .988 | 5.04 | +4 | 2 |
| | SD | 3B | 11 | 8 | 67 | 5 | 14 | 1 | 0 | .950 | 2.54 | 0 | -1 |
| | SD | SS | 11 | 9 | 79 | 15 | 34 | 2 | 4 | .961 | 5.58 | -2 | -1 |
| | SD | LF | 11 | 7 | 64 | 9 | 0 | 0 | 0 | 1.000 | 1.26 | -4 | -2 |
| | SD | RF | 3 | 2 | 13 | 2 | 0 | 0 | 0 | 1.000 | 1.38 | 0 | 0 |
| Francisco, B | NYY | LF | 3 | 0 | 6 | 3 | 0 | 0 | 0 | 1.000 | 4.50 | 0 | 0 |
| | NYY | RF | 5 | 4 | 27 | 5 | 0 | 0 | 0 | 1.000 | 1.69 | +2 | 1 |
| Francisco, J | TOT | 1B | 67 | 62 | 532 | 538 | 25 | 10 | 57 | .983 | - | -2 | -3 |
| | TOT | 3B | 34 | 33 | 256 | 19 | 65 | 7 | 8 | .923 | 2.96 | -3 | -4 |
| Francoeur, J | TOT | LF | 16 | 14 | 116 | 23 | 2 | 1 | 0 | .962 | 1.95 | -3 | 0 |
| | TOT | CF | 2 | 1 | 9 | 0 | 0 | 0 | 0 | - | .00 | 0 | 0 |
| | TOT | RF | 55 | 49 | 440 | 96 | 3 | 1 | 0 | .990 | 2.02 | -8 | -1 |
| Frandsen, K | Phi | 1B | 40 | 35 | 286 | 256 | 16 | 1 | 18 | .996 | - | +3 | 4 |
| | Phi | 2B | 20 | 13 | 128 | 38 | 43 | 2 | 13 | .976 | 5.70 | +1 | 1 |
| | Phi | 3B | 4 | 4 | 33 | 2 | 4 | 1 | 0 | .857 | 1.64 | -1 | 0 |
| Franklin, N | Sea | SS | 3 | 2 | 21 | 4 | 10 | 0 | 3 | 1.000 | 6.10 | +2 | 3 |
| Frazier, T | Cin | LF | 2 | 1 | 6 | 0 | 0 | 0 | 0 | - | .00 | 0 | 0 |
| Freiman, N | Oak | 1B | 59 | 42 | 358 | 292 | 17 | 1 | 23 | .997 | - | -3 | -3 |
| Fuentes, R | SD | LF | 2 | 0 | 6 | 4 | 0 | 0 | 0 | 1.000 | 6.00 | 0 | 0 |
| | SD | CF | 15 | 7 | 70 | 19 | 0 | 1 | 0 | .950 | 2.45 | 0 | 0 |
| Fuld, S | TB | LF | 55 | 17 | 205 | 42 | 2 | 0 | 1 | 1.000 | 1.93 | +1 | 1 |
| | TB | CF | 29 | 20 | 186 | 52 | 0 | 1 | 0 | .981 | 2.51 | +1 | -1 |
| | TB | RF | 28 | 11 | 121 | 32 | 0 | 0 | 0 | 1.000 | 2.37 | +1 | 1 |
| Galvis, F | Phi | 2B | 23 | 19 | 167 | 40 | 56 | 2 | 13 | .980 | 5.16 | -4 | -2 |
| | Phi | 3B | 16 | 14 | 133 | 7 | 33 | 1 | 2 | .976 | 2.70 | -1 | -1 |
| | Phi | SS | 11 | 6 | 67 | 11 | 26 | 0 | 7 | 1.000 | 4.97 | -2 | -2 |
| | Phi | LF | 10 | 10 | 80 | 20 | 0 | 0 | 0 | 1.000 | 2.26 | +3 | 2 |
| Garcia, A | TOT | LF | 3 | 2 | 21 | 6 | 0 | 0 | 0 | 1.000 | 2.57 | 0 | 0 |
| | TOT | CF | 31 | 22 | 202 | 49 | 0 | 1 | 0 | .980 | 2.19 | -3 | -3 |
| | TOT | RF | 41 | 36 | 329 | 73 | 1 | 2 | 0 | .974 | 2.03 | -1 | 0 |
| Garcia, L | TOT | 2B | 21 | 15 | 142 | 30 | 56 | 2 | 14 | .977 | 5.45 | -1 | 1 |
| | TOT | 3B | 6 | 2 | 22 | 0 | 2 | 0 | 0 | 1.000 | .82 | 0 | 0 |
| | TOT | SS | 7 | 4 | 42 | 4 | 13 | 0 | 1 | 1.000 | 3.64 | 0 | 1 |
| | TOT | CF | 6 | 4 | 38 | 9 | 0 | 0 | 0 | 1.000 | 2.13 | +2 | 1 |
| Gattis, E | Atl | 1B | 4 | 4 | 33 | 34 | 0 | 1 | 2 | .971 | - | 0 | 0 |
| | Atl | LF | 48 | 47 | 342 | 63 | 3 | 4 | 1 | .943 | 1.74 | -14 | -10 |
| Gennett, S | Mil | 2B | 59 | 56 | 488 | 113 | 146 | 5 | 39 | .981 | 4.78 | +2 | 2 |
| Gentry, C | Tex | LF | 34 | 20 | 203 | 38 | 3 | 1 | 0 | .976 | 1.82 | +3 | 4 |
| | Tex | CF | 71 | 49 | 445 | 145 | 4 | 1 | 1 | .993 | 3.02 | +14 | 8 |
| Getz, C | KC | 2B | 68 | 62 | 541 | 106 | 181 | 4 | 39 | .986 | 4.77 | +5 | 5 |
| Giavotella, J | KC | 2B | 13 | 12 | 97 | 20 | 37 | 0 | 9 | 1.000 | 5.29 | 0 | -1 |
| Gillaspie, C | CWS | 1B | 12 | 2 | 42 | 45 | 6 | 1 | 3 | .981 | - | -1 | -1 |
| Gillespie, C | TOT | LF | 6 | 5 | 47 | 6 | 0 | 0 | 0 | 1.000 | 1.15 | -2 | -2 |
| | TOT | CF | 1 | 0 | 1 | 1 | 0 | 0 | 0 | 1.000 | 9.00 | 0 | 0 |
| | TOT | RF | 13 | 9 | 84 | 19 | 2 | 0 | 1 | 1.000 | 2.24 | +3 | 4 |
| Gimenez, C | TB | 1B | 1 | 0 | 3 | 3 | 0 | 0 | 0 | 1.000 | - | +1 | 0 |
| | TB | 3B | 1 | 0 | 2 | 0 | 1 | 0 | 0 | 1.000 | 4.50 | 0 | 0 |
| Gindl, C | Mil | LF | 30 | 30 | 256 | 45 | 3 | 2 | 0 | .960 | 1.69 | -3 | 0 |
| | Mil | RF | 5 | 4 | 36 | 4 | 0 | 0 | 0 | 1.000 | 1.00 | -1 | -1 |
| Goins, R | Tor | 2B | 32 | 29 | 262 | 53 | 94 | 1 | 27 | .993 | 5.04 | +11 | 12 |
| | Tor | SS | 2 | 1 | 10 | 1 | 3 | 0 | 0 | 1.000 | 3.60 | 0 | 0 |
| Gomes, J | Bos | LF | 98 | 65 | 634 | 114 | 5 | 1 | 2 | .992 | 1.69 | -11 | 0 |
| | Bos | RF | 4 | 2 | 22 | 5 | 0 | 0 | 0 | 1.000 | 2.05 | -1 | 0 |
| Gomes, Y | Cle | 1B | 1 | 0 | 3 | 6 | 0 | 0 | 0 | 1.000 | - | 0 | 0 |
| Gonzalez, A | TOT | 2B | 10 | 6 | 58 | 14 | 21 | 0 | 5 | 1.000 | 5.40 | +3 | 1 |
| | TOT | 3B | 7 | 6 | 51 | 3 | 5 | 1 | 1 | .889 | 1.41 | -2 | -2 |
| | TOT | SS | 5 | 5 | 43 | 13 | 14 | 0 | 2 | 1.000 | 5.70 | +4 | 3 |
| | TOT | LF | 1 | 0 | 4 | 0 | 0 | 0 | 0 | - | .00 | 0 | 0 |
| | TOT | RF | 1 | 0 | 2 | 0 | 0 | 0 | 0 | - | .00 | 0 | 0 |
| Gonzalez, A | Mil | 1B | 22 | 16 | 146 | 145 | 9 | 1 | 13 | .994 | - | -1 | -1 |
| | Mil | 3B | 11 | 9 | 72 | 5 | 14 | 3 | 1 | .864 | 2.38 | 0 | 0 |
| | Mil | SS | 3 | 2 | 23 | 2 | 12 | 1 | 0 | .933 | 5.48 | +1 | 1 |
| Gonzalez, M | Hou | 2B | 10 | 6 | 70 | 17 | 38 | 0 | 6 | 1.000 | 7.11 | +1 | 1 |
| | Hou | 3B | 4 | 1 | 17 | 3 | 1 | 0 | 0 | 1.000 | 2.16 | -1 | -1 |
| | Hou | SS | 53 | 50 | 450 | 75 | 143 | 10 | 38 | .956 | 4.36 | 0 | 2 |
| Gordon, D | LAD | 2B | 3 | 0 | 4 | 0 | 4 | 0 | 1 | 1.000 | 9.82 | +1 | 1 |
| | LAD | SS | 27 | 23 | 207 | 29 | 73 | 7 | 11 | .936 | 4.44 | -4 | -4 |
| Gose, A | Tor | LF | 15 | 7 | 75 | 13 | 1 | 0 | 0 | 1.000 | 1.68 | -2 | 1 |
| | Tor | CF | 34 | 30 | 269 | 68 | 3 | 4 | 0 | .947 | 2.37 | -4 | -1 |
| | Tor | RF | 2 | 0 | 3 | 0 | 0 | 0 | 0 | - | .00 | 0 | 0 |
| Gosselin, P | Atl | 2B | 3 | 1 | 15 | 2 | 5 | 0 | 1 | 1.000 | 4.20 | +1 | 1 |
| Grandal, Y | SD | 1B | 1 | 0 | 5 | 4 | 0 | 0 | 1 | 1.000 | - | 0 | 0 |
| Granderson, C | NYY | LF | 13 | 11 | 101 | 21 | 1 | 0 | 0 | 1.000 | 1.97 | 0 | 0 |
| | NYY | CF | 25 | 22 | 197 | 62 | 0 | 0 | 0 | 1.000 | 2.83 | +6 | 2 |
| | NYY | RF | 14 | 9 | 85 | 24 | 0 | 0 | 0 | 1.000 | 2.54 | +4 | 1 |
| Green, G | TOT | 2B | 45 | 40 | 362 | 75 | 92 | 4 | 17 | .977 | 4.16 | -7 | -7 |
| Green, N | Mia | 1B | 6 | 5 | 46 | 47 | 3 | 0 | 4 | 1.000 | - | -1 | 0 |
| | Mia | 2B | 2 | 1 | 9 | 5 | 1 | 0 | 1 | 1.000 | 6.00 | 0 | 0 |
| | Mia | 3B | 2 | 2 | 17 | 1 | 2 | 0 | 0 | 1.000 | 1.59 | 0 | 0 |
| | Mia | SS | 8 | 8 | 80 | 15 | 23 | 0 | 6 | 1.000 | 4.29 | 0 | 0 |
| Greene, T | CWS | 2B | 19 | 14 | 128 | 24 | 33 | 2 | 11 | .966 | 4.01 | -5 | -4 |
| Grossman, R | Hou | LF | 45 | 37 | 340 | 65 | 1 | 2 | 0 | .971 | 1.75 | -2 | 0 |
| | Hou | CF | 29 | 25 | 210 | 54 | 1 | 1 | 0 | .982 | 2.35 | -4 | -4 |
| | Hou | RF | 2 | 0 | 5 | 3 | 0 | 0 | 0 | 1.000 | 5.40 | 0 | 0 |
| Gutierrez, F | Sea | CF | 17 | 15 | 132 | 41 | 0 | 0 | 0 | 1.000 | 2.80 | -7 | -4 |
| | Sea | RF | 21 | 19 | 174 | 37 | 0 | 1 | 0 | .974 | 1.92 | +1 | -2 |
| Guzman, J | SD | 1B | 38 | 33 | 280 | 280 | 15 | 3 | 24 | .990 | - | +2 | 3 |
| | SD | 2B | 1 | 0 | 2 | 1 | 0 | 0 | 0 | 1.000 | 4.50 | 0 | 0 |
| | SD | 3B | 3 | 2 | 11 | 3 | 2 | 2 | 0 | .714 | 3.97 | -2 | -1 |
| | SD | LF | 35 | 25 | 224 | 45 | 0 | 1 | 0 | .978 | 1.81 | -4 | -4 |
| | SD | RF | 5 | 3 | 22 | 5 | 0 | 0 | 0 | 1.000 | 2.01 | +1 | 1 |
| Gyorko, J | SD | 3B | 13 | 9 | 92 | 1 | 27 | 2 | 0 | .933 | 2.74 | -3 | -3 |
| Hairston, J | LAD | 1B | 13 | 7 | 65 | 57 | 4 | 0 | 2 | 1.000 | - | +1 | 1 |
| | LAD | 2B | 1 | 0 | 1 | 0 | 0 | 0 | 0 | - | .00 | 0 | 0 |
| | LAD | 3B | 28 | 19 | 160 | 12 | 35 | 6 | 5 | .887 | 2.64 | -1 | -1 |
| | LAD | LF | 23 | 15 | 137 | 28 | 1 | 0 | 0 | 1.000 | 1.91 | +1 | 0 |
| | LAD | RF | 4 | 2 | 21 | 5 | 0 | 0 | 0 | 1.000 | 2.11 | 0 | 0 |
| Hairston, S | TOT | LF | 16 | 9 | 80 | 16 | 0 | 0 | 0 | 1.000 | 1.81 | +4 | 1 |
| | TOT | RF | 31 | 26 | 205 | 28 | 2 | 1 | 0 | .968 | 1.32 | -7 | -6 |
| Halton, S | Mil | 1B | 25 | 19 | 167 | 168 | 8 | 0 | 18 | 1.000 | - | +4 | 2 |
| | Mil | 3B | 1 | 0 | 1 | 0 | 0 | 0 | 0 | - | .00 | 0 | 0 |
| | Mil | LF | 3 | 3 | 23 | 4 | 1 | 0 | 0 | 1.000 | 1.96 | -1 | 0 |
| | Mil | RF | 3 | 2 | 20 | 2 | 0 | 0 | 0 | 1.000 | .90 | -1 | 0 |
| Hamilton, B | Cin | CF | 7 | 3 | 45 | 16 | 0 | 0 | 0 | 1.000 | 3.20 | +2 | 1 |
| Hamilton, J | LAA | LF | 19 | 19 | 161 | 52 | 0 | 0 | 0 | 1.000 | 2.90 | +5 | 2 |
| | LAA | CF | 6 | 6 | 53 | 13 | 1 | 0 | 0 | 1.000 | 2.38 | +1 | 1 |
| | LAA | RF | 83 | 80 | 717 | 171 | 3 | 8 | 0 | .956 | 2.18 | -10 | -8 |
| Hannahan, J | Cin | 1B | 10 | 1 | 29 | 30 | 0 | 0 | 6 | 1.000 | - | +1 | 1 |
| | Cin | 2B | 1 | 1 | 9 | 0 | 6 | 0 | 1 | 1.000 | 6.00 | +2 | 1 |
| | Cin | 3B | 37 | 22 | 215 | 15 | 44 | 4 | 5 | .937 | 2.47 | -2 | -2 |
| Harper, B | Was | CF | 9 | 8 | 61 | 16 | 1 | 0 | 0 | 1.000 | 2.51 | -2 | -2 |
| | Was | RF | 16 | 16 | 132 | 36 | 1 | 1 | 0 | .974 | 2.52 | +5 | 3 |
| Harris, B | LAA | 1B | 6 | 4 | 36 | 20 | 2 | 0 | 2 | 1.000 | - | -1 | -2 |
| | LAA | 2B | 6 | 2 | 25 | 2 | 8 | 0 | 2 | 1.000 | 3.60 | +1 | 1 |
| | LAA | 3B | 7 | 4 | 48 | 3 | 11 | 1 | 1 | .933 | 2.64 | +1 | 0 |
| | LAA | SS | 21 | 17 | 145 | 22 | 40 | 2 | 9 | .969 | 3.85 | -8 | -5 |
| | LAA | LF | 1 | 0 | 3 | 1 | 0 | 0 | 0 | 1.000 | 3.00 | -1 | 0 |
| Harrison, J | Pit | 2B | 11 | 7 | 53 | 18 | 24 | 0 | 5 | 1.000 | 7.13 | +2 | 2 |

# All Other Fielders

| Player | Tm | Pos | G | GS | Inn | PO | A | E | DP | Pct. | Rng | +/- | RS |
|---|---|---|---|---|---|---|---|---|---|---|---|---|---|
| | Pit | 3B | 7 | 3 | 31 | 1 | 11 | 1 | 0 | .923 | 3.48 | 0 | 0 |
| | Pit | SS | 4 | 0 | 5 | 1 | 1 | 0 | 0 | 1.000 | 3.38 | +1 | 0 |
| | Pit | LF | 1 | 0 | 1 | 1 | 0 | 0 | 0 | 1.000 | 9.00 | 0 | 0 |
| | Pit | RF | 14 | 5 | 59 | 6 | 2 | 0 | 1 | 1.000 | 1.22 | -3 | -1 |
| Hawpe, B | LAA | 1B | 7 | 4 | 34 | 31 | 3 | 0 | 3 | 1.000 | - | 0 | 0 |
| | LAA | LF | 1 | 1 | 8 | 2 | 0 | 1 | 0 | .667 | 2.25 | -2 | -1 |
| | LAA | RF | 5 | 2 | 28 | 4 | 0 | 0 | 0 | 1.000 | 1.29 | 0 | 0 |
| Heisey, C | Cin | LF | 69 | 42 | 423 | 90 | 1 | 0 | 1 | 1.000 | 1.94 | +11 | 5 |
| | Cin | CF | 1 | 1 | 9 | 3 | 0 | 0 | 0 | 1.000 | 3.00 | 0 | 0 |
| | Cin | RF | 6 | 1 | 23 | 8 | 0 | 0 | 0 | 1.000 | 3.13 | +3 | 2 |
| Hernandez, C | Phi | 2B | 10 | 7 | 67 | 12 | 19 | 2 | 4 | .939 | 4.16 | -2 | -1 |
| | Phi | CF | 22 | 22 | 190 | 45 | 0 | 4 | 0 | .918 | 2.13 | -4 | -3 |
| Hernandez, R | LAD | 1B | 2 | 0 | 3 | 3 | 0 | 0 | 0 | 1.000 | - | 0 | 0 |
| Herrera, E | LAD | LF | 2 | 2 | 17 | 0 | 0 | 1 | 0 | .000 | .00 | 0 | 0 |
| Herrera, J | Col | 2B | 22 | 16 | 152 | 34 | 56 | 3 | 11 | .968 | 5.32 | +5 | 4 |
| | Col | 3B | 5 | 1 | 18 | 1 | 1 | 0 | 0 | 1.000 | 1.02 | -3 | -2 |
| | Col | SS | 42 | 28 | 274 | 50 | 94 | 2 | 27 | .986 | 4.72 | -2 | 0 |
| | Col | LF | 2 | 0 | 7 | 0 | 0 | 0 | 0 | - | .00 | 0 | 0 |
| Herrmann, C | Min | LF | 3 | 1 | 15 | 6 | 0 | 0 | 0 | 1.000 | 3.60 | +1 | 1 |
| | Min | RF | 21 | 14 | 135 | 23 | 3 | 0 | 2 | 1.000 | 1.73 | -6 | -4 |
| Heyward, J | Atl | CF | 20 | 20 | 164 | 38 | 1 | 0 | 0 | 1.000 | 2.14 | +3 | 1 |
| | Atl | RF | 86 | 76 | 698 | 173 | 3 | 0 | 0 | 1.000 | 2.27 | +32 | 15 |
| Hicks, A | Min | CF | 81 | 78 | 701 | 215 | 9 | 0 | 2 | 1.000 | 2.87 | -8 | 2 |
| Hill, A | Ari | 2B | 84 | 82 | 741 | 150 | 232 | 2 | 48 | .995 | 4.64 | -10 | -9 |
| Hinske, E | Ari | 1B | 6 | 2 | 26 | 32 | 2 | 0 | 5 | 1.000 | - | +1 | 1 |
| Hoes, L | TOT | LF | 3 | 1 | 14 | 4 | 0 | 0 | 0 | 1.000 | 2.63 | +1 | 1 |
| | TOT | CF | 2 | 1 | 12 | 4 | 0 | 0 | 0 | 1.000 | 3.00 | 0 | 0 |
| | TOT | RF | 44 | 40 | 362 | 81 | 0 | 4 | 0 | .953 | 2.02 | -2 | -6 |
| Holt, B | Bos | 2B | 5 | 0 | 8 | 2 | 2 | 0 | 0 | 1.000 | 4.50 | 0 | 0 |
| | Bos | 3B | 20 | 17 | 152 | 14 | 25 | 2 | 4 | .951 | 2.31 | -4 | -5 |
| Hosmer, E | KC | RF | 1 | 1 | 6 | 0 | 0 | 0 | 0 | - | .00 | 0 | 0 |
| Howard, R | Phi | 1B | 76 | 74 | 650 | 618 | 42 | 1 | 55 | .998 | - | 0 | -1 |
| Ibanez, R | Sea | RF | 1 | 1 | 8 | 1 | 0 | 0 | 0 | 1.000 | 1.13 | -1 | 0 |
| Iglesias, J | TOT | 2B | 3 | 1 | 12 | 2 | 2 | 0 | 0 | 1.000 | 3.00 | 0 | 0 |
| | TOT | 3B | 37 | 36 | 309 | 20 | 65 | 3 | 6 | .966 | 2.48 | -1 | -1 |
| | TOT | SS | 71 | 67 | 572 | 93 | 173 | 3 | 47 | .989 | 4.19 | -4 | 0 |
| Inge, B | Pit | 1B | 4 | 0 | 5 | 6 | 1 | 0 | 1 | 1.000 | - | 0 | 0 |
| | Pit | 2B | 13 | 9 | 81 | 18 | 26 | 0 | 6 | 1.000 | 4.89 | +2 | 2 |
| | Pit | 3B | 10 | 8 | 78 | 4 | 25 | 0 | 2 | 1.000 | 3.33 | +2 | 2 |
| | Pit | SS | 1 | 0 | 1 | 0 | 1 | 0 | 1 | 1.000 | 9.00 | -1 | -1 |
| | Pit | RF | 6 | 5 | 33 | 6 | 1 | 0 | 0 | 1.000 | 1.91 | -1 | 0 |
| Ishikawa, T | TOT | 1B | 5 | 4 | 34 | 26 | 1 | 0 | 1 | 1.000 | - | -1 | -1 |
| Izturis, C | Cin | 2B | 21 | 10 | 108 | 23 | 37 | 0 | 9 | 1.000 | 5.02 | +4 | 3 |
| | Cin | 3B | 1 | 0 | 2 | 0 | 1 | 1 | 0 | .500 | 4.50 | -1 | 0 |
| | Cin | SS | 29 | 15 | 166 | 23 | 45 | 1 | 10 | .986 | 3.69 | +4 | 4 |
| Izturis, M | Tor | 2B | 59 | 47 | 413 | 73 | 123 | 5 | 28 | .975 | 4.27 | -6 | -6 |
| | Tor | 3B | 36 | 33 | 291 | 18 | 42 | 2 | 3 | .968 | 1.85 | -1 | -1 |
| | Tor | SS | 28 | 18 | 174 | 22 | 51 | 3 | 8 | .961 | 3.77 | -3 | -2 |
| Jackson, R | StL | 2B | 2 | 0 | 3 | 1 | 2 | 0 | 0 | 1.000 | 9.00 | 0 | 0 |
| | StL | 3B | 3 | 0 | 5 | 0 | 0 | 0 | 0 | - | .00 | 0 | 0 |
| | StL | SS | 1 | 1 | 7 | 0 | 1 | 0 | 0 | 1.000 | 1.29 | -1 | -1 |
| Janish, P | Atl | 2B | 9 | 5 | 54 | 11 | 11 | 0 | 2 | 1.000 | 3.67 | 0 | 0 |
| | Atl | 3B | 36 | 2 | 69 | 3 | 17 | 0 | 2 | 1.000 | 2.60 | +1 | 1 |
| | Atl | SS | 6 | 3 | 24 | 2 | 8 | 0 | 1 | 1.000 | 3.75 | -1 | -1 |
| Jaso, J | Oak | 1B | 1 | 0 | 1 | 1 | 0 | 0 | 0 | 1.000 | - | 0 | 0 |
| Jeter, D | NYY | SS | 13 | 13 | 110 | 23 | 27 | 2 | 6 | .962 | 4.10 | -7 | -5 |
| Jimenez, L | LAA | 1B | 2 | 1 | 8 | 2 | 0 | 0 | 0 | 1.000 | - | 0 | 0 |
| | LAA | 3B | 29 | 28 | 247 | 34 | 71 | 4 | 13 | .963 | 3.83 | +6 | 4 |
| | LAA | SS | 1 | 0 | 3 | 1 | 0 | 0 | 0 | 1.000 | 3.00 | 0 | 0 |
| Johnson, C | Atl | 1B | 12 | 10 | 100 | 103 | 9 | 0 | 12 | 1.000 | - | +1 | 0 |
| Johnson, D | Bal | 1B | 1 | 0 | 1 | 1 | 0 | 0 | 1 | 1.000 | - | 0 | 0 |
| Johnson, E | TOT | 2B | 74 | 52 | 483 | 92 | 151 | 5 | 27 | .980 | 4.52 | +11 | 10 |
| | TOT | 3B | 8 | 6 | 65 | 5 | 18 | 1 | 1 | .958 | 3.17 | +2 | 1 |
| | TOT | SS | 10 | 5 | 48 | 9 | 15 | 0 | 4 | 1.000 | 4.50 | +2 | 2 |
| | TOT | LF | 8 | 3 | 37 | 8 | 0 | 0 | 0 | 1.000 | 1.95 | -2 | -1 |
| | TOT | RF | 3 | 1 | 13 | 1 | 0 | 0 | 0 | 1.000 | .71 | 0 | 0 |
| Johnson, K | TB | 1B | 3 | 2 | 18 | 21 | 0 | 0 | 2 | 1.000 | - | -1 | 0 |
| | TB | 2B | 22 | 14 | 135 | 21 | 37 | 0 | 8 | 1.000 | 3.86 | +3 | 2 |
| | TB | 3B | 16 | 12 | 118 | 13 | 31 | 1 | 3 | .978 | 3.36 | 0 | 1 |
| | TB | LF | 53 | 50 | 408 | 77 | 6 | 3 | 1 | .965 | 1.83 | -6 | -1 |
| Johnson, R | Atl | LF | 10 | 3 | 37 | 8 | 0 | 0 | 0 | 1.000 | 1.93 | +2 | 1 |
| | Atl | CF | 12 | 6 | 80 | 21 | 0 | 0 | 0 | 1.000 | 2.36 | -2 | -2 |

| Player | Tm | Pos | G | GS | Inn | PO | A | E | DP | Pct. | Rng | +/- | RS |
|---|---|---|---|---|---|---|---|---|---|---|---|---|---|
| | Atl | RF | 15 | 10 | 93 | 24 | 0 | 0 | 0 | 1.000 | 2.33 | +1 | 1 |
| Jones, G | Pit | 1B | 83 | 80 | 618 | 671 | 52 | 6 | 73 | .992 | - | -5 | -1 |
| | Pit | RF | 32 | 25 | 196 | 37 | 1 | 1 | 0 | .974 | 1.74 | +1 | -3 |
| Joseph, C | NYY | 1B | 1 | 1 | 8 | 7 | 2 | 0 | 1 | 1.000 | - | 0 | 0 |
| | NYY | 2B | 1 | 1 | 9 | 1 | 4 | 0 | 0 | 1.000 | 5.00 | 0 | 0 |
| Joyce, M | TB | LF | 58 | 41 | 365 | 80 | 0 | 0 | 0 | 1.000 | 1.97 | +9 | 2 |
| | TB | RF | 58 | 51 | 439 | 88 | 2 | 1 | 1 | .989 | 1.85 | -9 | -7 |
| Kawasaki, M | Tor | 2B | 18 | 16 | 126 | 26 | 45 | 1 | 6 | .986 | 5.07 | +1 | 1 |
| | Tor | SS | 60 | 51 | 471 | 79 | 136 | 5 | 39 | .977 | 4.11 | +2 | 2 |
| Kearns, A | Mia | LF | 1 | 1 | 9 | 4 | 0 | 0 | 0 | 1.000 | 4.00 | 0 | 0 |
| | Mia | RF | 3 | 3 | 28 | 9 | 0 | 0 | 0 | 1.000 | 2.89 | +1 | 0 |
| Kelly, D | Det | 1B | 4 | 0 | 11 | 17 | 0 | 0 | 2 | 1.000 | - | 0 | 0 |
| | Det | 2B | 3 | 0 | 4 | 1 | 0 | 0 | 0 | 1.000 | 2.45 | -1 | -1 |
| | Det | 3B | 22 | 7 | 98 | 8 | 17 | 0 | 2 | 1.000 | 2.30 | +1 | 1 |
| | Det | LF | 38 | 11 | 150 | 22 | 0 | 0 | 0 | 1.000 | 1.32 | -4 | -1 |
| | Det | CF | 25 | 19 | 162 | 34 | 0 | 0 | 0 | 1.000 | 1.89 | -2 | -2 |
| | Det | RF | 22 | 15 | 132 | 30 | 0 | 2 | 0 | .938 | 2.04 | -3 | -3 |
| Kemp, M | LAD | CF | 70 | 68 | 576 | 133 | 2 | 5 | 0 | .964 | 2.11 | -16 | -6 |
| Kendrick, H | LAA | LF | 1 | 0 | 1 | 1 | 0 | 0 | 0 | 1.000 | 9.00 | 0 | 0 |
| Keppinger, J | CWS | 1B | 20 | 14 | 126 | 120 | 14 | 1 | 16 | .993 | - | 0 | 0 |
| | CWS | 2B | 45 | 41 | 371 | 74 | 107 | 1 | 24 | .995 | 4.39 | -7 | -7 |
| | CWS | 3B | 41 | 35 | 325 | 25 | 67 | 3 | 8 | .968 | 2.55 | -7 | -3 |
| Kiermaier, K | TB | CF | 1 | 0 | 1 | 0 | 0 | 0 | 0 | - | .00 | 0 | 0 |
| Kieschnick, R | SF | LF | 25 | 21 | 190 | 38 | 1 | 0 | 0 | 1.000 | 1.85 | -4 | 0 |
| Kobernus, J | Was | LF | 6 | 5 | 31 | 7 | 0 | 0 | 0 | 1.000 | 2.03 | -1 | -1 |
| | Was | CF | 3 | 3 | 23 | 6 | 0 | 0 | 0 | 1.000 | 2.35 | -1 | -1 |
| | Was | RF | 2 | 0 | 3 | 0 | 0 | 0 | 0 | - | .00 | 0 | 0 |
| Konerko, P | CWS | 1B | 76 | 76 | 653 | 600 | 48 | 4 | 70 | .994 | - | -4 | -3 |
| Kotchman, C | Mia | 1B | 6 | 5 | 47 | 39 | 2 | 1 | 4 | .976 | - | 0 | -1 |
| Kotsay, M | SD | 1B | 5 | 3 | 26 | 26 | 2 | 0 | 2 | 1.000 | - | 0 | 0 |
| | SD | LF | 19 | 15 | 118 | 13 | 1 | 0 | 0 | 1.000 | 1.07 | -6 | -3 |
| | SD | RF | 6 | 5 | 35 | 4 | 0 | 0 | 0 | 1.000 | 1.03 | -5 | -4 |
| Kozma, P | StL | LF | 1 | 0 | 4 | 2 | 0 | 0 | 0 | 1.000 | 4.50 | -2 | -1 |
| Krauss, M | Hou | 1B | 2 | 0 | 4 | 2 | 0 | 0 | 1 | 1.000 | - | 0 | 0 |
| | Hou | LF | 18 | 14 | 115 | 22 | 3 | 1 | 2 | .962 | 1.95 | -2 | 1 |
| | Hou | RF | 9 | 8 | 63 | 16 | 0 | 1 | 0 | .941 | 2.29 | -2 | -2 |
| Kubel, J | TOT | LF | 56 | 53 | 450 | 70 | 6 | 1 | 0 | .987 | 1.52 | -5 | 1 |
| | TOT | RF | 8 | 6 | 64 | 14 | 1 | 2 | 0 | .882 | 2.10 | -1 | 0 |
| Lagares, J | NYM | RF | 14 | 9 | 84 | 24 | 1 | 0 | 0 | 1.000 | 2.67 | +2 | 2 |
| Laird, B | Hou | 1B | 13 | 8 | 76 | 71 | 2 | 0 | 8 | 1.000 | - | -2 | -1 |
| | Hou | 3B | 4 | 3 | 27 | 1 | 8 | 1 | 1 | .900 | 3.00 | 0 | 0 |
| Lake, J | ChC | LF | 32 | 29 | 260 | 53 | 1 | 0 | 0 | 1.000 | 1.87 | 0 | -1 |
| | ChC | CF | 27 | 27 | 238 | 66 | 1 | 3 | 1 | .957 | 2.53 | -3 | -3 |
| Lalli, B | Mil | 1B | 5 | 3 | 33 | 45 | 0 | 2 | 1 | .957 | - | -1 | -1 |
| Lambo, A | Pit | LF | 2 | 0 | 6 | 3 | 0 | 0 | 0 | 1.000 | 4.50 | 0 | 0 |
| | Pit | RF | 6 | 6 | 42 | 3 | 0 | 0 | 0 | 1.000 | .64 | -3 | -2 |
| Langerhans, R | Tor | 1B | 4 | 3 | 27 | 28 | 0 | 0 | 4 | 1.000 | - | 0 | 0 |
| LaRoche, A | Tor | 3B | 1 | 1 | 9 | 1 | 3 | 0 | 1 | 1.000 | 4.00 | +1 | 1 |
| Lawrie, B | Tor | 2B | 6 | 6 | 50 | 12 | 9 | 2 | 2 | .913 | 3.78 | 0 | -1 |
| LeMahieu, D | Col | 1B | 1 | 0 | 1 | 2 | 0 | 0 | 0 | 1.000 | - | 0 | 0 |
| | Col | 3B | 14 | 9 | 101 | 6 | 24 | 0 | 2 | 1.000 | 2.68 | +1 | 1 |
| | Col | SS | 1 | 0 | 1 | 0 | 0 | 0 | 0 | - | .00 | 0 | 0 |
| Liddi, A | Sea | 1B | 6 | 4 | 41 | 34 | 0 | 0 | 4 | 1.000 | - | -1 | -1 |
| Lillibridge, B | TOT | 1B | 1 | 1 | 8 | 7 | 0 | 0 | 1 | 1.000 | - | -1 | -1 |
| | TOT | 2B | 5 | 5 | 39 | 11 | 12 | 1 | 3 | .958 | 5.31 | -1 | -1 |
| | TOT | 3B | 12 | 11 | 89 | 10 | 16 | 1 | 0 | .963 | 2.64 | +1 | 1 |
| | TOT | RF | 1 | 0 | 4 | 1 | 0 | 0 | 0 | 1.000 | 2.25 | 0 | 0 |
| Lind, A | Tor | 1B | 76 | 71 | 620 | 579 | 51 | 7 | 56 | .989 | - | -11 | -7 |
| Lombardozzi, S | Was | 2B | 48 | 38 | 360 | 92 | 129 | 3 | 28 | .987 | 5.53 | +2 | 2 |
| | Was | 3B | 4 | 2 | 21 | 1 | 4 | 0 | 0 | 1.000 | 2.14 | +1 | 1 |
| | Was | LF | 23 | 20 | 170 | 32 | 1 | 0 | 0 | 1.000 | 1.75 | -3 | -4 |
| Lough, D | KC | LF | 15 | 7 | 83 | 27 | 2 | 0 | 1 | 1.000 | 3.14 | +9 | 5 |
| | KC | CF | 7 | 5 | 47 | 13 | 0 | 1 | 0 | .929 | 2.47 | 0 | 0 |
| | KC | RF | 74 | 68 | 578 | 124 | 6 | 1 | 0 | .992 | 2.03 | +11 | 10 |
| Lowrie, J | Oak | 2B | 24 | 23 | 199 | 33 | 36 | 2 | 10 | .972 | 3.12 | -4 | -3 |
| Lucas, E | Mia | 1B | 25 | 19 | 179 | 180 | 14 | 0 | 17 | 1.000 | - | +2 | 1 |
| | Mia | 2B | 20 | 8 | 96 | 17 | 30 | 0 | 5 | 1.000 | 4.39 | +3 | 2 |
| | Mia | 3B | 61 | 56 | 483 | 37 | 111 | 6 | 14 | .961 | 2.76 | +3 | 4 |
| | Mia | SS | 6 | 3 | 30 | 7 | 18 | 1 | 4 | .962 | 7.50 | 0 | 1 |
| | Mia | LF | 1 | 0 | 10 | 5 | 0 | 0 | 0 | 1.000 | 4.35 | +3 | 2 |
| Lucroy, J | Mil | 1B | 14 | 9 | 82 | 66 | 4 | 2 | 5 | .972 | - | +2 | 1 |
| Ludwick, R | Cin | LF | 32 | 32 | 250 | 39 | 0 | 0 | 0 | 1.000 | 1.40 | -2 | -3 |

# All Other Fielders

| Player | Tm | Pos | G | GS | Inn | PO | A | E | DP | Pct. | Rng | +/- | RS |
|---|---|---|---|---|---|---|---|---|---|---|---|---|---|
| Lutz, D | Cin | LF | 17 | 6 | 76 | 22 | 0 | 0 | 0 | 1.000 | 2.62 | +2 | 1 |
| | Cin | RF | 1 | 1 | 9 | 5 | 0 | 0 | 0 | 1.000 | 5.00 | +1 | 0 |
| Lutz, Z | NYM | 1B | 1 | 0 | 2 | 1 | 0 | 0 | 0 | 1.000 | - | 0 | 0 |
| | NYM | 3B | 3 | 3 | 27 | 0 | 5 | 0 | 1 | 1.000 | 1.67 | +1 | 1 |
| Mahoney, J | Mia | 1B | 7 | 7 | 58 | 44 | 3 | 1 | 6 | .979 | - | +1 | 0 |
| Maldonado, M | Mil | 1B | 10 | 7 | 73 | 62 | 3 | 3 | 4 | .956 | - | 0 | 0 |
| Marisnick, J | Mia | CF | 32 | 30 | 261 | 75 | 5 | 0 | 2 | 1.000 | 2.76 | +5 | 6 |
| Marrero, C | Was | 1B | 3 | 2 | 17 | 12 | 2 | 0 | 1 | 1.000 | - | 0 | 0 |
| Marte, A | Ari | LF | 9 | 9 | 75 | 10 | 0 | 0 | 0 | 1.000 | 1.20 | -2 | -2 |
| | Ari | RF | 1 | 0 | 3 | 1 | 0 | 0 | 0 | 1.000 | 3.00 | 0 | 0 |
| Marte, S | Pit | CF | 13 | 6 | 70 | 17 | 1 | 1 | 0 | .947 | 2.33 | +4 | 2 |
| Martin, L | Tex | LF | 6 | 5 | 42 | 9 | 1 | 0 | 0 | 1.000 | 2.14 | -1 | -1 |
| | Tex | RF | 21 | 11 | 111 | 21 | 2 | 0 | 0 | 1.000 | 1.86 | 0 | 0 |
| Martin, R | Pit | 3B | 3 | 2 | 20 | 3 | 3 | 0 | 0 | 1.000 | 2.70 | 0 | 0 |
| | Pit | RF | 1 | 1 | 6 | 1 | 0 | 0 | 0 | 1.000 | 1.59 | 0 | 0 |
| Martinez, F | Hou | LF | 8 | 6 | 49 | 10 | 0 | 0 | 0 | 1.000 | 1.84 | -4 | -2 |
| | Hou | RF | 2 | 2 | 16 | 2 | 0 | 0 | 0 | 1.000 | 1.13 | -3 | -2 |
| Martinez, J | Hou | LF | 50 | 46 | 378 | 65 | 3 | 1 | 1 | .986 | 1.62 | -7 | -5 |
| | Hou | RF | 25 | 21 | 186 | 33 | 1 | 1 | 0 | .971 | 1.65 | -5 | -6 |
| Martinez, M | Phi | 3B | 2 | 0 | 6 | 1 | 1 | 0 | 0 | 1.000 | 3.00 | 0 | 0 |
| | Phi | SS | 3 | 2 | 19 | 5 | 3 | 0 | 1 | 1.000 | 3.79 | 0 | 0 |
| | Phi | LF | 2 | 0 | 4 | 0 | 0 | 0 | 0 | - | .00 | 0 | 0 |
| | Phi | CF | 13 | 5 | 52 | 18 | 1 | 0 | 1 | 1.000 | 3.29 | -3 | -1 |
| | Phi | RF | 1 | 0 | 1 | 0 | 0 | 0 | 0 | - | .00 | 0 | 0 |
| Martinez, V | Det | 1B | 11 | 11 | 97 | 85 | 14 | 0 | 3 | 1.000 | - | +2 | 2 |
| Mastroianni, D | Min | 2B | 1 | 0 | 1 | 0 | 0 | 0 | 0 | - | .00 | 0 | 0 |
| | Min | LF | 19 | 7 | 82 | 17 | 1 | 0 | 0 | 1.000 | 1.97 | 0 | 1 |
| | Min | CF | 3 | 3 | 21 | 7 | 0 | 0 | 0 | 1.000 | 3.00 | -4 | -2 |
| | Min | RF | 9 | 7 | 62 | 16 | 0 | 0 | 0 | 1.000 | 2.34 | -2 | -2 |
| Mauer, J | Min | 1B | 8 | 8 | 70 | 78 | 3 | 1 | 9 | .988 | - | +1 | 1 |
| Maxwell, J | TOT | CF | 27 | 26 | 219 | 80 | 2 | 2 | 1 | .976 | 3.37 | -7 | -5 |
| | TOT | RF | 47 | 39 | 348 | 73 | 4 | 3 | 1 | .963 | 1.99 | +2 | 0 |
| Mayberry, J | Phi | 1B | 7 | 5 | 44 | 36 | 3 | 1 | 7 | .975 | - | 0 | 0 |
| | Phi | LF | 9 | 3 | 39 | 13 | 0 | 0 | 0 | 1.000 | 3.00 | +1 | 0 |
| | Phi | CF | 46 | 41 | 344 | 101 | 0 | 0 | 0 | 1.000 | 2.64 | -13 | -10 |
| | Phi | RF | 79 | 40 | 428 | 89 | 3 | 1 | 0 | .989 | 1.93 | -3 | -4 |
| Maybin, C | SD | CF | 14 | 14 | 120 | 33 | 0 | 0 | 0 | 1.000 | 2.47 | -6 | -5 |
| McDonald, D | ChC | LF | 7 | 5 | 45 | 18 | 0 | 0 | 0 | 1.000 | 3.57 | +4 | 1 |
| | ChC | RF | 8 | 6 | 55 | 15 | 0 | 0 | 0 | 1.000 | 2.45 | +1 | 0 |
| McDonald, J | TOT | 2B | 11 | 3 | 42 | 14 | 12 | 0 | 2 | 1.000 | 5.57 | -1 | -1 |
| | TOT | 3B | 16 | 2 | 52 | 4 | 13 | 1 | 5 | .944 | 2.94 | 0 | 0 |
| | TOT | SS | 19 | 11 | 98 | 14 | 32 | 3 | 9 | .939 | 4.22 | -1 | 1 |
| | TOT | LF | 1 | 0 | 1 | 1 | 0 | 0 | 0 | 1.000 | 13.50 | 0 | 0 |
| McGuiness, C | Tex | 1B | 10 | 9 | 82 | 77 | 6 | 0 | 5 | 1.000 | - | 0 | 0 |
| McLouth, N | Bal | CF | 3 | 1 | 12 | 4 | 0 | 0 | 0 | 1.000 | 3.00 | 0 | 0 |
| Medica, T | SD | 1B | 19 | 19 | 164 | 153 | 13 | 0 | 6 | 1.000 | - | +1 | 1 |
| Mercer, J | Pit | 1B | 1 | 0 | 1 | 1 | 0 | 0 | 0 | 1.000 | - | 0 | 0 |
| | Pit | 2B | 26 | 20 | 179 | 31 | 72 | 3 | 13 | .972 | 5.19 | -1 | 0 |
| | Pit | 3B | 1 | 1 | 9 | 0 | 3 | 0 | 0 | 1.000 | 3.00 | 0 | 0 |
| | Pit | SS | 78 | 63 | 594 | 89 | 214 | 12 | 49 | .962 | 4.59 | 0 | -2 |
| Mesa, M | NYY | LF | 3 | 2 | 18 | 7 | 0 | 0 | 0 | 1.000 | 3.50 | 0 | 0 |
| | NYY | CF | 1 | 1 | 8 | 3 | 0 | 0 | 0 | 1.000 | 3.38 | 0 | 0 |
| | NYY | RF | 1 | 0 | 2 | 1 | 0 | 0 | 0 | 1.000 | 4.50 | 0 | 0 |
| Middlebrooks, W | Bos | 1B | 1 | 1 | 9 | 10 | 1 | 0 | 0 | 1.000 | - | 0 | 0 |
| | Bos | 2B | 2 | 0 | 4 | 1 | 3 | 0 | 1 | 1.000 | 9.00 | +1 | 1 |
| Miller, B | Sea | 2B | 13 | 11 | 96 | 22 | 25 | 1 | 5 | .979 | 4.41 | -1 | -1 |
| | Sea | 3B | 3 | 0 | 8 | 0 | 1 | 0 | 0 | 1.000 | 1.13 | 0 | 0 |
| | Sea | SS | 68 | 62 | 561 | 87 | 155 | 7 | 30 | .972 | 3.88 | +4 | -2 |
| Molina, Y | StL | 1B | 5 | 2 | 18 | 17 | 1 | 0 | 1 | 1.000 | - | 0 | 0 |
| Montz, L | Oak | 1B | 1 | 0 | 1 | 0 | 0 | 0 | 0 | - | - | 0 | 0 |
| Moore, T | Was | 1B | 14 | 11 | 96 | 97 | 4 | 0 | 12 | 1.000 | - | -1 | -1 |
| | Was | LF | 29 | 24 | 201 | 31 | 0 | 1 | 0 | .969 | 1.39 | 0 | -2 |
| | Was | RF | 6 | 6 | 47 | 3 | 0 | 0 | 0 | 1.000 | .57 | -1 | -1 |
| Morales, K | Sea | 1B | 31 | 31 | 274 | 293 | 13 | 1 | 26 | .997 | - | -4 | -2 |
| Morel, B | CWS | 1B | 3 | 0 | 7 | 5 | 0 | 0 | 0 | 1.000 | - | +1 | 0 |
| | CWS | 3B | 9 | 7 | 65 | 4 | 16 | 1 | 2 | .952 | 2.76 | -1 | -1 |
| Moreland, M | Tex | RF | 1 | 0 | 0 | 0 | 0 | 0 | 0 | - | .00 | 0 | 0 |
| Morrison, L | Mia | 1B | 79 | 78 | 692 | 678 | 68 | 3 | 65 | .996 | - | -3 | -4 |
| Morse, M | TOT | 1B | 7 | 6 | 51 | 59 | 3 | 0 | 9 | 1.000 | - | +2 | 0 |
| | TOT | LF | 19 | 16 | 124 | 30 | 0 | 0 | 0 | 1.000 | 2.17 | -1 | -1 |
| | TOT | RF | 55 | 55 | 456 | 91 | 1 | 1 | 0 | .989 | 1.82 | -19 | -15 |
| Moss, B | Oak | 3B | 2 | 0 | 4 | 0 | 0 | 0 | 0 | - | .00 | 0 | 0 |

| Player | Tm | Pos | G | GS | Inn | PO | A | E | DP | Pct. | Rng | +/- | RS |
|---|---|---|---|---|---|---|---|---|---|---|---|---|---|
| | Oak | LF | 8 | 5 | 54 | 10 | 0 | 0 | 0 | 1.000 | 1.67 | +1 | 1 |
| | Oak | CF | 2 | 0 | 7 | 2 | 0 | 0 | 0 | 1.000 | 2.57 | +1 | 1 |
| | Oak | RF | 27 | 20 | 177 | 44 | 1 | 1 | 0 | .978 | 2.29 | -4 | -4 |
| Murphy, D | NYM | 1B | 7 | 7 | 62 | 70 | 5 | 2 | 3 | .974 | - | -2 | -2 |
| Murphy, D | Tex | RF | 1 | 1 | 8 | 4 | 0 | 0 | 0 | 1.000 | 4.50 | -1 | -1 |
| Murphy, D | ChC | 2B | 2 | 2 | 17 | 2 | 3 | 0 | 0 | 1.000 | 2.65 | -3 | -2 |
| | ChC | 3B | 40 | 34 | 307 | 27 | 60 | 4 | 10 | .956 | 2.55 | -1 | -1 |
| | ChC | SS | 3 | 2 | 22 | 2 | 2 | 0 | 1 | 1.000 | 1.64 | +1 | 1 |
| Myers, W | TB | CF | 8 | 6 | 51 | 22 | 1 | 0 | 1 | 1.000 | 4.06 | +3 | 1 |
| | TB | RF | 72 | 68 | 605 | 118 | 1 | 0 | 0 | 1.000 | 1.77 | -4 | -4 |
| Nava, D | Bos | 1B | 19 | 8 | 87 | 63 | 6 | 1 | 5 | .986 | - | -2 | -2 |
| | Bos | LF | 63 | 56 | 469 | 90 | 2 | 1 | 0 | .989 | 1.76 | -1 | -1 |
| | Bos | CF | 1 | 1 | 8 | 3 | 0 | 1 | 0 | .750 | 3.38 | -3 | -2 |
| | Bos | RF | 69 | 51 | 494 | 88 | 3 | 1 | 0 | .989 | 1.66 | -3 | -1 |
| Navarro, E | LAA | 1B | 2 | 1 | 10 | 7 | 2 | 0 | 2 | 1.000 | - | 0 | 0 |
| Navarro, Y | Bal | 2B | 8 | 8 | 62 | 17 | 18 | 2 | 4 | .946 | 5.08 | +2 | 1 |
| Neal, T | TOT | LF | 2 | 2 | 14 | 3 | 0 | 0 | 0 | 1.000 | 1.93 | 0 | 0 |
| | TOT | RF | 2 | 2 | 16 | 6 | 0 | 0 | 0 | 1.000 | 3.38 | -2 | -1 |
| Nelson, C | TOT | 2B | 2 | 0 | 3 | 0 | 2 | 0 | 0 | 1.000 | 6.00 | 0 | 0 |
| | TOT | 3B | 57 | 55 | 481 | 25 | 89 | 6 | 3 | .950 | 2.13 | -4 | -3 |
| Nieuwenhuis, K | NYM | LF | 9 | 3 | 35 | 4 | 0 | 0 | 0 | 1.000 | 1.03 | +1 | 1 |
| | NYM | CF | 25 | 18 | 152 | 40 | 1 | 0 | 0 | 1.000 | 2.43 | -3 | -1 |
| | NYM | RF | 2 | 1 | 12 | 2 | 1 | 0 | 0 | 1.000 | 2.25 | -2 | 0 |
| Nix, J | NYY | 2B | 4 | 0 | 9 | 3 | 6 | 0 | 3 | 1.000 | 9.35 | 0 | 0 |
| | NYY | 3B | 41 | 33 | 285 | 24 | 66 | 3 | 8 | .968 | 2.84 | +3 | 1 |
| | NYY | SS | 48 | 41 | 380 | 58 | 133 | 4 | 26 | .979 | 4.52 | +3 | 1 |
| Nix, L | Phi | 1B | 8 | 1 | 20 | 24 | 0 | 0 | 2 | 1.000 | - | 0 | 0 |
| | Phi | LF | 2 | 2 | 16 | 3 | 0 | 0 | 0 | 1.000 | 1.69 | 0 | 0 |
| | Phi | CF | 1 | 0 | 1 | 0 | 0 | 0 | 0 | - | .00 | 0 | 0 |
| | Phi | RF | 25 | 19 | 162 | 44 | 0 | 1 | 0 | .978 | 2.44 | +2 | 2 |
| Noonan, N | SF | 2B | 22 | 11 | 116 | 22 | 30 | 1 | 11 | .981 | 4.05 | -1 | -1 |
| | SF | 3B | 15 | 6 | 64 | 7 | 16 | 0 | 2 | 1.000 | 3.23 | +4 | 3 |
| | SF | SS | 1 | 0 | 2 | 0 | 0 | 0 | 0 | - | .00 | -1 | -1 |
| Norris, D | Oak | 1B | 1 | 0 | 4 | 4 | 0 | 0 | 0 | 1.000 | - | 0 | 0 |
| Nunez, E | NYY | 2B | 2 | 1 | 9 | 6 | 3 | 0 | 2 | 1.000 | 9.00 | -1 | -1 |
| | NYY | 3B | 14 | 14 | 120 | 5 | 23 | 2 | 1 | .933 | 2.10 | +2 | 2 |
| | NYY | SS | 75 | 69 | 608 | 88 | 156 | 12 | 34 | .953 | 3.61 | -33 | -28 |
| Olivo, M | Mia | 1B | 1 | 0 | 3 | 4 | 0 | 0 | 0 | 1.000 | - | 0 | 0 |
| Orr, P | Phi | 3B | 2 | 1 | 11 | 0 | 2 | 1 | 0 | .667 | 1.59 | 0 | 0 |
| | Phi | LF | 2 | 2 | 12 | 4 | 0 | 0 | 0 | 1.000 | 3.00 | -1 | 0 |
| Ortiz, D | Bos | 1B | 6 | 6 | 39 | 36 | 1 | 0 | 4 | 1.000 | - | -2 | -1 |
| Overbay, L | NYY | RF | 4 | 4 | 26 | 5 | 0 | 0 | 0 | 1.000 | 1.73 | -2 | -2 |
| Owings, C | Ari | 2B | 3 | 3 | 30 | 2 | 10 | 0 | 0 | 1.000 | 3.60 | +2 | 2 |
| | Ari | SS | 13 | 10 | 93 | 18 | 31 | 1 | 4 | .980 | 4.74 | -1 | -2 |
| Ozuna, M | Mia | CF | 33 | 33 | 301 | 77 | 3 | 0 | 2 | 1.000 | 2.39 | -4 | -2 |
| | Mia | RF | 36 | 36 | 328 | 80 | 5 | 2 | 2 | .977 | 2.33 | +8 | 4 |
| Pacheco, J | Col | 1B | 43 | 39 | 352 | 385 | 28 | 5 | 28 | .988 | - | -1 | -2 |
| | Col | LF | 1 | 0 | 1 | 0 | 0 | 0 | 0 | - | .00 | 0 | 0 |
| Pagan, A | SF | CF | 71 | 66 | 580 | 149 | 5 | 4 | 1 | .975 | 2.39 | -13 | -9 |
| Paredes, J | Hou | 2B | 3 | 1 | 12 | 0 | 5 | 0 | 0 | 1.000 | 3.75 | 0 | 0 |
| | Hou | 3B | 1 | 1 | 9 | 0 | 3 | 0 | 0 | 1.000 | 3.00 | +1 | 1 |
| | Hou | RF | 39 | 32 | 286 | 61 | 0 | 1 | 0 | .984 | 1.92 | -2 | -4 |
| Parmelee, C | Min | 1B | 23 | 20 | 177 | 152 | 12 | 0 | 15 | 1.000 | - | +1 | 2 |
| | Min | CF | 1 | 0 | 1 | 0 | 0 | 0 | 0 | - | .00 | 0 | 0 |
| | Min | RF | 68 | 59 | 525 | 105 | 6 | 2 | 0 | .982 | 1.90 | -4 | 4 |
| Parra, G | Ari | LF | 6 | 4 | 41 | 7 | 0 | 0 | 0 | 1.000 | 1.54 | +2 | 1 |
| | Ari | CF | 33 | 29 | 272 | 80 | 2 | 2 | 0 | .976 | 2.71 | +4 | 4 |
| Parrino, A | Oak | 2B | 5 | 4 | 37 | 12 | 8 | 1 | 2 | .952 | 4.86 | -2 | -2 |
| | Oak | 3B | 2 | 1 | 13 | 1 | 2 | 0 | 0 | 1.000 | 2.08 | 0 | 0 |
| | Oak | SS | 7 | 2 | 28 | 1 | 12 | 0 | 1 | 1.000 | 4.18 | 0 | -3 |
| Pastornicky, T | Atl | 2B | 6 | 4 | 30 | 4 | 5 | 0 | 2 | 1.000 | 2.70 | 0 | 0 |
| | Atl | SS | 1 | 1 | 8 | 2 | 5 | 0 | 1 | 1.000 | 7.88 | -1 | 0 |
| | Atl | CF | 1 | 0 | 2 | 0 | 0 | 0 | 0 | - | .00 | 0 | 0 |
| Paul, X | Cin | LF | 59 | 49 | 385 | 69 | 3 | 2 | 0 | .973 | 1.68 | -15 | -12 |
| Pearce, S | Bal | 1B | 3 | 3 | 26 | 23 | 0 | 0 | 2 | 1.000 | - | 0 | -1 |
| | Bal | LF | 15 | 15 | 107 | 21 | 0 | 0 | 0 | 1.000 | 1.76 | +1 | 1 |
| | Bal | RF | 3 | 1 | 10 | 2 | 0 | 0 | 0 | 1.000 | 1.80 | 0 | 0 |
| Peguero, C | Sea | RF | 2 | 2 | 18 | 3 | 0 | 0 | 0 | 1.000 | 1.50 | -2 | -1 |
| Peguero, F | SF | LF | 13 | 6 | 62 | 15 | 0 | 0 | 0 | 1.000 | 2.18 | +2 | 2 |
| | SF | RF | 2 | 0 | 4 | 0 | 0 | 0 | 0 | - | .00 | 0 | 0 |
| Pena, B | Det | 1B | 1 | 0 | 1 | 1 | 0 | 0 | 0 | 1.000 | - | 0 | 0 |
| Pena, C | TOT | 1B | 46 | 43 | 383 | 399 | 30 | 0 | 47 | 1.000 | - | -8 | -5 |

# All Other Fielders

| Player | Tm | Pos | G | GS | Inn | PO | A | E | DP | Pct. | Rng | +/- | RS |
|---|---|---|---|---|---|---|---|---|---|---|---|---|---|
| Pena, R | Atl | 2B | 10 | 6 | 59 | 12 | 17 | 0 | 4 | 1.000 | 4.40 | -3 | -2 |
| | Atl | 3B | 32 | 5 | 99 | 7 | 25 | 0 | 4 | 1.000 | 2.92 | +2 | 3 |
| | Atl | SS | 7 | 7 | 56 | 5 | 24 | 0 | 3 | 1.000 | 4.66 | +1 | 1 |
| Pennington, C | Ari | 2B | 29 | 20 | 199 | 33 | 64 | 2 | 14 | .980 | 4.38 | +3 | 3 |
| | Ari | 3B | 2 | 2 | 20 | 0 | 6 | 1 | 0 | .857 | 2.70 | +1 | 0 |
| | Ari | SS | 51 | 47 | 429 | 58 | 152 | 5 | 30 | .977 | 4.40 | +12 | 9 |
| Peralta, J | Det | LF | 3 | 3 | 19 | 2 | 0 | 0 | 0 | 1.000 | .96 | -1 | 0 |
| Perez, E | Was | LF | 3 | 0 | 4 | 3 | 0 | 0 | 0 | 1.000 | 6.75 | +1 | 1 |
| | Was | CF | 4 | 2 | 19 | 7 | 0 | 0 | 0 | 1.000 | 3.32 | 0 | 0 |
| | Was | RF | 1 | 0 | 1 | 1 | 0 | 0 | 0 | 1.000 | 9.00 | +2 | 1 |
| Perez, H | Det | 2B | 25 | 16 | 164 | 30 | 48 | 2 | 9 | .975 | 4.27 | 0 | 1 |
| | Det | 3B | 2 | 0 | 1 | 0 | 1 | 0 | 0 | 1.000 | 6.75 | 0 | 0 |
| | Det | SS | 2 | 0 | 3 | 0 | 0 | 0 | 0 | - | .00 | 0 | 0 |
| Perez, J | SF | LF | 11 | 9 | 75 | 17 | 2 | 0 | 0 | 1.000 | 2.28 | +1 | 4 |
| | SF | CF | 20 | 15 | 142 | 50 | 6 | 1 | 1 | .982 | 3.55 | +4 | 6 |
| | SF | RF | 1 | 0 | 1 | 0 | 0 | 0 | 0 | - | .00 | 0 | 0 |
| Perez, S | KC | 1B | 1 | 1 | 9 | 2 | 0 | 1 | 0 | .667 | - | 0 | 0 |
| Peterson, B | StL | 1B | 4 | 2 | 17 | 17 | 2 | 0 | 1 | 1.000 | - | 0 | 0 |
| | StL | LF | 5 | 1 | 17 | 2 | 0 | 0 | 0 | 1.000 | 1.06 | -1 | 0 |
| Peterson, S | Oak | 1B | 2 | 2 | 18 | 8 | 2 | 0 | 1 | 1.000 | - | -1 | 1 |
| Phegley, J | CWS | 2B | 1 | 0 | 1 | 0 | 0 | 0 | 0 | - | .00 | 0 | 0 |
| Phelps, C | Cle | 2B | 3 | 2 | 22 | 3 | 2 | 1 | 0 | .833 | 2.05 | -1 | -1 |
| Pie, F | Pit | LF | 13 | 1 | 31 | 4 | 0 | 0 | 0 | 1.000 | 1.16 | 0 | 0 |
| | Pit | CF | 5 | 2 | 23 | 6 | 0 | 0 | 0 | 1.000 | 2.35 | -2 | -1 |
| | Pit | RF | 1 | 0 | 3 | 0 | 0 | 0 | 0 | - | .00 | 0 | 0 |
| Pierre, J | Mia | LF | 64 | 63 | 564 | 146 | 0 | 0 | 0 | 1.000 | 2.33 | +17 | 4 |
| Pill, B | SF | 1B | 13 | 10 | 95 | 73 | 6 | 0 | 6 | 1.000 | - | 0 | 0 |
| | SF | LF | 8 | 6 | 39 | 8 | 0 | 0 | 0 | 1.000 | 1.85 | +1 | 0 |
| Pillar, K | Tor | LF | 33 | 28 | 243 | 56 | 1 | 0 | 0 | 1.000 | 2.11 | -1 | 2 |
| | Tor | RF | 1 | 1 | 8 | 1 | 0 | 0 | 0 | 1.000 | 1.13 | +1 | 1 |
| Plouffe, T | Min | 1B | 2 | 0 | 2 | 2 | 0 | 0 | 0 | 1.000 | - | 0 | 0 |
| Pollock, A | Ari | LF | 7 | 3 | 38 | 3 | 0 | 0 | 0 | 1.000 | .71 | +1 | 0 |
| | Ari | RF | 2 | 1 | 12 | 5 | 0 | 0 | 0 | 1.000 | 3.75 | +1 | 0 |
| Posey, B | SF | 1B | 21 | 16 | 139 | 137 | 6 | 2 | 11 | .986 | - | -1 | 0 |
| Prado, M | Ari | 2B | 32 | 27 | 257 | 53 | 66 | 3 | 12 | .975 | 4.17 | +2 | 4 |
| | Ari | SS | 1 | 0 | 1 | 0 | 0 | 0 | 0 | - | .00 | 0 | 0 |
| | Ari | LF | 30 | 26 | 233 | 35 | 1 | 1 | 0 | .973 | 1.39 | +2 | 0 |
| Presley, A | TOT | LF | 12 | 8 | 72 | 17 | 0 | 1 | 0 | .944 | 2.13 | +7 | 3 |
| | TOT | CF | 28 | 27 | 241 | 80 | 2 | 0 | 1 | 1.000 | 3.06 | -12 | -8 |
| | TOT | RF | 12 | 6 | 65 | 13 | 0 | 0 | 0 | 1.000 | 1.79 | +1 | 0 |
| Pridie, J | Bal | LF | 2 | 2 | 17 | 1 | 1 | 2 | 0 | .500 | 1.06 | -3 | -2 |
| | Bal | CF | 2 | 1 | 10 | 1 | 0 | 0 | 0 | 1.000 | .90 | -2 | -1 |
| Prince, J | Mil | 3B | 1 | 0 | 2 | 0 | 0 | 0 | 0 | - | .00 | 0 | 0 |
| | Mil | LF | 2 | 1 | 12 | 2 | 0 | 0 | 0 | 1.000 | 1.50 | 0 | 0 |
| | Mil | RF | 1 | 0 | 1 | 0 | 0 | 0 | 0 | - | .00 | 0 | 0 |
| Profar, J | Tex | 2B | 32 | 29 | 269 | 54 | 75 | 4 | 16 | .970 | 4.32 | -3 | -4 |
| | Tex | 3B | 10 | 10 | 88 | 8 | 16 | 2 | 1 | .923 | 2.45 | +2 | 0 |
| | Tex | SS | 18 | 16 | 148 | 22 | 43 | 2 | 9 | .970 | 3.96 | +2 | 3 |
| | Tex | LF | 4 | 4 | 34 | 8 | 0 | 0 | 0 | 1.000 | 2.12 | -3 | -2 |
| Puig, Y | LAD | LF | 2 | 1 | 10 | 3 | 0 | 0 | 0 | 1.000 | 2.70 | 0 | 0 |
| | LAD | CF | 10 | 6 | 55 | 11 | 0 | 1 | 0 | .917 | 1.79 | 0 | 0 |
| Pujols, A | LAA | 1B | 34 | 34 | 302 | 265 | 29 | 3 | 24 | .990 | - | 0 | 1 |
| Punto, N | LAD | 2B | 33 | 21 | 187 | 41 | 47 | 1 | 15 | .989 | 4.24 | -1 | -1 |
| | LAD | 3B | 35 | 17 | 165 | 15 | 40 | 4 | 3 | .932 | 3.00 | +6 | 5 |
| | LAD | SS | 49 | 33 | 309 | 47 | 109 | 3 | 30 | .981 | 4.54 | +5 | 6 |
| Quentin, C | SD | LF | 69 | 69 | 556 | 105 | 1 | 1 | 0 | .991 | 1.72 | +4 | -5 |
| Quintanilla, O | NYM | 3B | 1 | 0 | 2 | 0 | 0 | 0 | 0 | - | .00 | 0 | 0 |
| Raburn, R | Cle | 2B | 2 | 2 | 17 | 7 | 3 | 0 | 1 | 1.000 | 5.29 | 0 | 0 |
| | Cle | LF | 13 | 12 | 85 | 17 | 0 | 0 | 0 | 1.000 | 1.80 | +3 | 1 |
| | Cle | RF | 54 | 46 | 392 | 75 | 3 | 2 | 2 | .975 | 1.79 | -5 | -3 |
| Ramirez, A | Mil | 3B | 80 | 80 | 657 | 45 | 103 | 7 | 7 | .955 | 2.03 | -12 | -12 |
| Ramirez, H | LAD | SS | 76 | 75 | 651 | 105 | 210 | 13 | 43 | .960 | 4.35 | +8 | 3 |
| Ramirez, J | Cle | 2B | 5 | 1 | 16 | 2 | 7 | 0 | 0 | 1.000 | 5.06 | +1 | 1 |
| | Cle | 3B | 2 | 1 | 10 | 0 | 3 | 1 | 0 | .750 | 2.70 | +1 | 0 |
| | Cle | SS | 2 | 0 | 2 | 0 | 0 | 0 | 0 | - | .00 | 0 | 0 |
| Ramirez, W | Min | LF | 8 | 6 | 52 | 8 | 0 | 0 | 0 | 1.000 | 1.39 | 0 | 0 |
| | Min | CF | 9 | 6 | 50 | 19 | 0 | 0 | 0 | 1.000 | 3.42 | +2 | 1 |
| | Min | RF | 9 | 8 | 70 | 22 | 1 | 0 | 0 | 1.000 | 2.96 | -3 | -1 |
| Ransom, C | TOT | 1B | 4 | 4 | 33 | 31 | 0 | 0 | 5 | 1.000 | - | 0 | 0 |
| | TOT | 3B | 46 | 41 | 363 | 22 | 88 | 7 | 8 | .940 | 2.73 | +4 | 1 |
| | TOT | SS | 1 | 1 | 8 | 1 | 3 | 0 | 0 | 1.000 | 4.50 | +1 | 1 |
| Reimold, N | Bal | LF | 11 | 11 | 90 | 24 | 2 | 0 | 1 | 1.000 | 2.60 | -5 | -4 |

| Player | Tm | Pos | G | GS | Inn | PO | A | E | DP | Pct. | Rng | +/- | RS |
|---|---|---|---|---|---|---|---|---|---|---|---|---|---|
| Rendon, A | Was | 2B | 82 | 81 | 714 | 147 | 213 | 9 | 50 | .976 | 4.54 | -7 | -5 |
| | Was | 3B | 15 | 10 | 98 | 7 | 26 | 5 | 4 | .868 | 3.03 | -7 | -5 |
| | Was | SS | 4 | 2 | 28 | 9 | 2 | 2 | 1 | .846 | 3.58 | -1 | -1 |
| Revere, B | Phi | CF | 87 | 79 | 708 | 220 | 6 | 2 | 3 | .991 | 2.87 | -9 | -5 |
| Reynolds, M | TOT | 1B | 65 | 58 | 500 | 505 | 17 | 4 | 44 | .992 | - | -6 | -5 |
| | TOT | 2B | 2 | 1 | 9 | 4 | 3 | 0 | 1 | 1.000 | 7.00 | 0 | 0 |
| | TOT | 3B | 54 | 46 | 410 | 25 | 68 | 7 | 15 | .930 | 2.04 | -5 | -6 |
| Rios, A | TOT | CF | 1 | 0 | 0 | 0 | 0 | 0 | 0 | - | .00 | 0 | 0 |
| Roberts, B | Bal | 2B | 60 | 60 | 540 | 110 | 190 | 1 | 43 | .997 | 5.00 | -2 | 0 |
| Roberts, R | TB | 1B | 3 | 0 | 4 | 2 | 1 | 0 | 0 | 1.000 | - | 0 | 0 |
| | TB | 2B | 48 | 30 | 286 | 46 | 84 | 4 | 17 | .970 | 4.09 | -2 | -1 |
| | TB | 3B | 9 | 6 | 55 | 3 | 14 | 0 | 3 | 1.000 | 2.78 | -1 | -1 |
| Robinson, D | Cin | LF | 60 | 29 | 306 | 82 | 0 | 0 | 0 | 1.000 | 2.41 | +12 | 5 |
| | Cin | CF | 15 | 8 | 87 | 18 | 0 | 0 | 0 | 1.000 | 1.87 | +2 | 1 |
| | Cin | RF | 2 | 0 | 3 | 1 | 0 | 0 | 0 | 1.000 | 3.00 | +1 | 0 |
| Robinson, S | StL | LF | 26 | 5 | 70 | 15 | 0 | 0 | 0 | 1.000 | 1.94 | +2 | 1 |
| | StL | CF | 27 | 21 | 174 | 52 | 0 | 2 | 0 | .963 | 2.69 | +12 | 5 |
| | StL | RF | 34 | 4 | 117 | 41 | 0 | 1 | 0 | .976 | 3.16 | +5 | 2 |
| Rodriguez, A | NYY | 3B | 27 | 27 | 233 | 22 | 52 | 1 | 9 | .987 | 2.86 | -3 | -3 |
| Rodriguez, H | Cin | 2B | 3 | 0 | 10 | 3 | 3 | 0 | 2 | 1.000 | 5.40 | -1 | 0 |
| Rodriguez, S | TB | 1B | 23 | 17 | 136 | 124 | 3 | 0 | 11 | 1.000 | - | -1 | 0 |
| | TB | 2B | 5 | 1 | 12 | 1 | 5 | 0 | 1 | 1.000 | 4.50 | +1 | 0 |
| | TB | SS | 7 | 3 | 28 | 3 | 8 | 1 | 1 | .917 | 3.54 | 0 | 0 |
| | TB | LF | 47 | 30 | 248 | 48 | 1 | 0 | 0 | 1.000 | 1.78 | +1 | 2 |
| | TB | RF | 8 | 5 | 39 | 8 | 0 | 0 | 0 | 1.000 | 1.85 | 0 | 0 |
| Romine, A | LAA | 2B | 4 | 4 | 32 | 5 | 15 | 0 | 4 | 1.000 | 5.57 | +1 | 1 |
| | LAA | 3B | 24 | 20 | 189 | 16 | 34 | 3 | 4 | .943 | 2.39 | 0 | 0 |
| | LAA | SS | 17 | 6 | 87 | 18 | 29 | 1 | 8 | .979 | 4.88 | 0 | 0 |
| Rosales, A | TOT | 1B | 4 | 1 | 8 | 4 | 1 | 0 | 1 | 1.000 | - | 0 | 0 |
| | TOT | 2B | 15 | 0 | 40 | 8 | 17 | 0 | 1 | 1.000 | 5.58 | -1 | -1 |
| | TOT | 3B | 4 | 1 | 12 | 1 | 2 | 0 | 0 | 1.000 | 2.25 | 0 | 0 |
| | TOT | SS | 39 | 33 | 293 | 46 | 101 | 7 | 14 | .955 | 4.52 | +1 | 1 |
| | TOT | LF | 1 | 0 | 2 | 2 | 0 | 0 | 0 | 1.000 | 9.00 | 0 | 0 |
| Rosario, W | Col | 1B | 4 | 3 | 22 | 21 | 2 | 2 | 3 | .920 | - | 0 | 0 |
| Ross, C | Ari | LF | 46 | 38 | 351 | 68 | 1 | 0 | 0 | 1.000 | 1.77 | +7 | 5 |
| | Ari | RF | 44 | 40 | 361 | 96 | 4 | 0 | 1 | 1.000 | 2.49 | +24 | 15 |
| Ruf, D | Phi | 1B | 36 | 28 | 251 | 248 | 21 | 2 | 29 | .993 | - | -1 | -2 |
| | Phi | LF | 20 | 15 | 145 | 27 | 0 | 0 | 0 | 1.000 | 1.68 | -4 | -2 |
| | Phi | RF | 29 | 27 | 223 | 47 | 4 | 0 | 0 | 1.000 | 2.06 | -12 | -7 |
| Ruggiano, J | Mia | LF | 23 | 22 | 198 | 37 | 1 | 1 | 0 | .974 | 1.73 | +2 | -1 |
| | Mia | CF | 84 | 77 | 709 | 197 | 2 | 3 | 0 | .985 | 2.53 | -5 | -5 |
| | Mia | RF | 5 | 4 | 38 | 8 | 0 | 0 | 0 | 1.000 | 1.89 | 0 | 0 |
| Rutledge, J | Col | 2B | 58 | 56 | 498 | 98 | 171 | 5 | 40 | .982 | 4.86 | -11 | -9 |
| | Col | SS | 14 | 13 | 115 | 23 | 37 | 1 | 8 | .984 | 4.68 | 0 | 0 |
| Sanchez, A | CWS | 2B | 1 | 0 | 3 | 0 | 1 | 0 | 0 | 1.000 | 2.70 | 0 | 0 |
| Sanchez, G | Pit | 1B | 113 | 60 | 652 | 696 | 58 | 3 | 55 | .996 | - | -1 | -3 |
| | Pit | 3B | 1 | 0 | 4 | 0 | 0 | 0 | 0 | - | .00 | 0 | 0 |
| Santana, C | Cle | 1B | 29 | 24 | 215 | 185 | 9 | 1 | 29 | .995 | - | -1 | 0 |
| Santiago, R | Det | 2B | 33 | 30 | 269 | 55 | 90 | 0 | 19 | 1.000 | 4.85 | 0 | -2 |
| | Det | 3B | 27 | 7 | 91 | 5 | 19 | 0 | 1 | 1.000 | 2.38 | +4 | 3 |
| | Det | SS | 27 | 19 | 193 | 20 | 49 | 2 | 7 | .972 | 3.22 | +6 | 6 |
| Sappelt, D | ChC | LF | 2 | 0 | 4 | 2 | 0 | 0 | 0 | 1.000 | 4.50 | -1 | 0 |
| | ChC | CF | 13 | 10 | 85 | 17 | 0 | 0 | 0 | 1.000 | 1.80 | 0 | 0 |
| | ChC | RF | 7 | 5 | 45 | 11 | 0 | 1 | 0 | .917 | 2.20 | 0 | 0 |
| Satin, J | NYM | 1B | 33 | 28 | 262 | 257 | 16 | 2 | 27 | .993 | - | +4 | 3 |
| | NYM | 3B | 17 | 12 | 109 | 10 | 21 | 3 | 0 | .912 | 2.56 | -1 | -1 |
| Saunders, M | Sea | LF | 24 | 12 | 124 | 22 | 2 | 0 | 0 | 1.000 | 1.74 | 0 | 1 |
| | Sea | CF | 78 | 69 | 628 | 173 | 4 | 1 | 2 | .994 | 2.54 | -23 | -14 |
| | Sea | RF | 34 | 28 | 247 | 60 | 1 | 0 | 0 | 1.000 | 2.23 | +5 | 2 |
| Schafer, J | Atl | LF | 15 | 8 | 75 | 12 | 0 | 0 | 0 | 1.000 | 1.45 | +1 | 0 |
| | Atl | CF | 30 | 23 | 215 | 60 | 2 | 0 | 0 | 1.000 | 2.60 | +3 | 1 |
| | Atl | RF | 29 | 20 | 204 | 54 | 3 | 1 | 1 | .983 | 2.51 | 0 | 2 |
| Schafer, L | Mil | LF | 56 | 39 | 374 | 96 | 3 | 0 | 1 | 1.000 | 2.38 | +13 | 8 |
| | Mil | CF | 28 | 19 | 192 | 56 | 1 | 0 | 1 | 1.000 | 2.68 | +6 | 3 |
| | Mil | RF | 13 | 11 | 97 | 22 | 0 | 0 | 0 | 1.000 | 2.03 | +2 | 1 |
| Schoop, J | Bal | 2B | 4 | 4 | 36 | 8 | 12 | 1 | 4 | .952 | 5.00 | -2 | -1 |
| Schumaker, S | LAD | 2B | 44 | 34 | 298 | 85 | 79 | 5 | 25 | .970 | 4.95 | -16 | -14 |
| | LAD | LF | 35 | 14 | 157 | 24 | 0 | 0 | 0 | 1.000 | 1.37 | +2 | 3 |
| | LAD | CF | 29 | 17 | 167 | 39 | 1 | 2 | 1 | .952 | 2.16 | -4 | -3 |
| | LAD | RF | 18 | 8 | 88 | 17 | 0 | 0 | 0 | 1.000 | 1.75 | -5 | -4 |
| Scott, L | TB | 1B | 5 | 0 | 12 | 12 | 0 | 0 | 0 | 1.000 | - | 0 | 0 |
| | TB | LF | 6 | 2 | 21 | 5 | 0 | 1 | 0 | .833 | 2.14 | -2 | -1 |

# All Other Fielders

| Player | Tm | Pos | G | GS | Inn | PO | A | E | DP | Pct. | Rng | +/- | RS |
|---|---|---|---|---|---|---|---|---|---|---|---|---|---|
| Sellers, J | LAD | 3B | 1 | 0 | 1 | 0 | 0 | 0 | 0 | - | .00 | 0 | 0 |
| | LAD | SS | 22 | 20 | 177 | 22 | 48 | 3 | 11 | .959 | 3.55 | -1 | 0 |
| Semien, M | CWS | 2B | 3 | 1 | 13 | 1 | 7 | 0 | 0 | 1.000 | 5.54 | 0 | 0 |
| | CWS | 3B | 17 | 13 | 122 | 5 | 30 | 3 | 2 | .921 | 2.59 | +3 | 2 |
| | CWS | SS | 3 | 3 | 27 | 7 | 13 | 0 | 0 | 1.000 | 6.59 | +4 | 3 |
| Shuck, J | LAA | RF | 9 | 5 | 42 | 7 | 0 | 0 | 0 | 1.000 | 1.50 | -1 | -1 |
| Sierra, M | Tor | LF | 2 | 2 | 17 | 6 | 0 | 0 | 0 | 1.000 | 3.18 | +1 | 0 |
| | Tor | RF | 29 | 26 | 222 | 51 | 0 | 2 | 0 | .962 | 2.07 | +2 | -1 |
| Sizemore, S | Oak | 2B | 2 | 2 | 12 | 4 | 2 | 0 | 2 | 1.000 | 4.50 | -3 | -2 |
| Smith, S | Oak | LF | 50 | 43 | 382 | 101 | 1 | 0 | 0 | 1.000 | 2.40 | +2 | 0 |
| | Oak | RF | 9 | 8 | 65 | 13 | 0 | 0 | 0 | 1.000 | 1.80 | 0 | -1 |
| Snider, T | Pit | LF | 5 | 4 | 33 | 5 | 0 | 0 | 0 | 1.000 | 1.36 | 0 | -1 |
| | Pit | RF | 79 | 49 | 494 | 112 | 5 | 1 | 0 | .992 | 2.13 | 0 | 1 |
| Snyder, B | Bos | 1B | 6 | 1 | 17 | 15 | 1 | 0 | 3 | 1.000 | - | 0 | 0 |
| | Bos | 3B | 17 | 10 | 100 | 8 | 24 | 1 | 4 | .970 | 2.87 | +1 | -1 |
| | Bos | LF | 1 | 0 | 2 | 0 | 0 | 0 | 0 | - | .00 | 0 | 0 |
| Sogard, E | Oak | SS | 15 | 12 | 113 | 27 | 29 | 2 | 2 | .966 | 4.47 | +1 | -1 |
| Solano, D | Mia | 3B | 2 | 0 | 3 | 0 | 0 | 0 | 0 | - | .00 | 0 | 0 |
| Soto, G | Tex | 3B | 1 | 0 | 1 | 0 | 0 | 0 | 0 | - | .00 | 0 | 0 |
| Soto, N | Cin | 1B | 5 | 0 | 14 | 14 | 0 | 0 | 2 | 1.000 | - | +1 | 0 |
| Stewart, C | NYY | 1B | 2 | 0 | 4 | 4 | 0 | 0 | 2 | 1.000 | - | 0 | 0 |
| Stubbs, D | Cle | CF | 43 | 38 | 339 | 95 | 2 | 0 | 1 | 1.000 | 2.58 | -3 | -3 |
| Susdorf, S | Phi | LF | 2 | 1 | 12 | 3 | 0 | 1 | 0 | .750 | 2.25 | 0 | 0 |
| Suzuki, I | NYY | LF | 9 | 8 | 64 | 15 | 0 | 0 | 0 | 1.000 | 2.11 | 0 | 1 |
| | NYY | CF | 13 | 9 | 76 | 22 | 0 | 0 | 0 | 1.000 | 2.61 | +1 | 1 |
| Sweeney, R | ChC | LF | 10 | 5 | 48 | 15 | 1 | 0 | 0 | 1.000 | 3.00 | -3 | -2 |
| | ChC | CF | 45 | 41 | 365 | 121 | 0 | 1 | 0 | .992 | 2.98 | -8 | -2 |
| | ChC | RF | 4 | 1 | 15 | 4 | 0 | 0 | 0 | 1.000 | 2.35 | 0 | 0 |
| Swisher, N | Cle | RF | 27 | 26 | 199 | 41 | 2 | 1 | 1 | .977 | 1.94 | -1 | 1 |
| Tabata, J | Pit | LF | 40 | 34 | 275 | 51 | 0 | 0 | 0 | 1.000 | 1.67 | +6 | 4 |
| | Pit | RF | 50 | 39 | 341 | 55 | 0 | 0 | 0 | 1.000 | 1.45 | -8 | -5 |
| Tanaka, K | SF | LF | 9 | 7 | 55 | 6 | 0 | 0 | 0 | 1.000 | .98 | -1 | 2 |
| Taylor, M | Oak | LF | 5 | 3 | 25 | 8 | 0 | 0 | 0 | 1.000 | 2.88 | -1 | -1 |
| | Oak | RF | 6 | 3 | 28 | 4 | 0 | 0 | 0 | 1.000 | 1.29 | -3 | -2 |
| Teixeira, M | NYY | 1B | 14 | 14 | 121 | 100 | 8 | 0 | 9 | 1.000 | - | 0 | 0 |
| Tejada, M | KC | 1B | 1 | 1 | 9 | 10 | 0 | 0 | 0 | 1.000 | - | 0 | 0 |
| | KC | 2B | 26 | 22 | 184 | 28 | 50 | 0 | 10 | 1.000 | 3.81 | 0 | 0 |
| | KC | 3B | 22 | 18 | 150 | 5 | 27 | 2 | 1 | .941 | 1.92 | 0 | 1 |
| Tejada, R | NYM | SS | 55 | 55 | 499 | 72 | 177 | 8 | 37 | .969 | 4.49 | -9 | -6 |
| Tekotte, B | CWS | LF | 1 | 1 | 7 | 0 | 0 | 0 | 0 | - | .00 | -2 | -1 |
| | CWS | CF | 16 | 8 | 85 | 21 | 0 | 0 | 0 | 1.000 | 2.21 | +2 | 1 |
| Terdoslavich, J | Atl | 1B | 6 | 3 | 27 | 32 | 1 | 0 | 3 | 1.000 | - | +1 | 1 |
| | Atl | LF | 13 | 7 | 70 | 15 | 0 | 0 | 0 | 1.000 | 1.92 | -1 | 0 |
| | Atl | RF | 4 | 4 | 31 | 6 | 1 | 0 | 0 | 1.000 | 2.03 | -1 | -1 |
| Thole, J | Tor | 1B | 2 | 0 | 8 | 9 | 0 | 1 | 0 | .900 | - | -1 | -1 |
| Thomas, C | Min | LF | 26 | 23 | 211 | 62 | 2 | 0 | 1 | 1.000 | 2.73 | +2 | 5 |
| | Min | CF | 50 | 48 | 436 | 132 | 3 | 3 | 0 | .978 | 2.79 | 0 | 0 |
| | Min | RF | 10 | 8 | 81 | 18 | 1 | 0 | 0 | 1.000 | 2.12 | -4 | -2 |
| Torrealba, Y | Col | 1B | 3 | 0 | 4 | 4 | 0 | 0 | 0 | 1.000 | - | 0 | 0 |
| Torres, A | SF | LF | 56 | 47 | 417 | 94 | 1 | 5 | 0 | .950 | 2.05 | +9 | 0 |
| | SF | CF | 30 | 17 | 166 | 57 | 0 | 0 | 0 | 1.000 | 3.08 | -1 | -1 |
| | SF | RF | 2 | 0 | 8 | 1 | 0 | 0 | 0 | 1.000 | 1.13 | 0 | 0 |
| Tovar, W | NYM | SS | 7 | 5 | 46 | 5 | 15 | 0 | 4 | 1.000 | 3.88 | +2 | 1 |
| Tracy, C | Was | 1B | 10 | 6 | 61 | 55 | 4 | 1 | 5 | .983 | - | +1 | 0 |
| | Was | 3B | 14 | 9 | 78 | 5 | 13 | 1 | 3 | .947 | 2.08 | 0 | -1 |
| Triunfel, C | Sea | 2B | 4 | 4 | 33 | 5 | 6 | 0 | 2 | 1.000 | 3.00 | -2 | -1 |
| | Sea | 3B | 1 | 1 | 6 | 1 | 0 | 0 | 0 | 1.000 | 1.50 | 0 | 0 |
| | Sea | SS | 10 | 8 | 72 | 11 | 23 | 2 | 6 | .944 | 4.25 | -3 | -2 |
| Trout, M | LAA | LF | 47 | 40 | 356 | 84 | 0 | 1 | 0 | .988 | 2.12 | +3 | 0 |
| Trumbo, M | LAA | 3B | 1 | 0 | 2 | 0 | 0 | 0 | 0 | - | .00 | 0 | 0 |
| | LAA | LF | 8 | 7 | 58 | 19 | 0 | 1 | 0 | .950 | 2.93 | +3 | 0 |
| | LAA | RF | 19 | 17 | 143 | 31 | 1 | 0 | 0 | 1.000 | 2.01 | 0 | -1 |
| Tuiasosopo, M | Det | 1B | 13 | 0 | 30 | 27 | 1 | 0 | 3 | 1.000 | - | +2 | 1 |
| | Det | 3B | 1 | 0 | 2 | 0 | 1 | 0 | 0 | 1.000 | 4.50 | 0 | 0 |
| | Det | LF | 63 | 47 | 366 | 97 | 0 | 1 | 0 | .990 | 2.39 | +8 | -3 |
| Turner, J | NYM | 1B | 15 | 9 | 88 | 87 | 6 | 1 | 9 | .989 | - | +1 | 1 |
| | NYM | 2B | 12 | 4 | 46 | 5 | 7 | 0 | 1 | 1.000 | 2.35 | -3 | -2 |
| | NYM | 3B | 23 | 11 | 127 | 9 | 21 | 1 | 1 | .968 | 2.12 | -1 | 0 |
| | NYM | SS | 18 | 13 | 115 | 19 | 32 | 0 | 8 | 1.000 | 3.98 | +2 | 1 |
| | NYM | LF | 1 | 0 | 1 | 0 | 0 | 0 | 0 | - | .00 | 0 | 0 |
| Upton, J | Atl | RF | 54 | 52 | 419 | 89 | 2 | 0 | 0 | 1.000 | 1.95 | +5 | 2 |
| Uribe, J | LAD | 1B | 4 | 1 | 16 | 18 | 1 | 1 | 1 | .950 | - | -1 | 0 |

| Player | Tm | Pos | G | GS | Inn | PO | A | E | DP | Pct. | Rng | +/- | RS |
|---|---|---|---|---|---|---|---|---|---|---|---|---|---|
| Urrutia, H | Bal | LF | 2 | 0 | 3 | 0 | 0 | 0 | 0 | - | .00 | 0 | 0 |
| Valaika, C | Mia | 1B | 3 | 1 | 12 | 8 | 2 | 1 | 2 | .909 | - | -2 | 0 |
| | Mia | 2B | 6 | 5 | 45 | 8 | 11 | 0 | 3 | 1.000 | 3.77 | 0 | 0 |
| | Mia | 3B | 5 | 4 | 37 | 0 | 3 | 1 | 0 | .750 | .72 | -3 | -2 |
| | Mia | SS | 6 | 6 | 53 | 5 | 13 | 1 | 3 | .947 | 3.06 | -3 | -3 |
| Valbuena, L | ChC | 2B | 6 | 5 | 40 | 13 | 13 | 0 | 4 | 1.000 | 5.85 | 0 | 0 |
| | ChC | LF | 1 | 0 | 2 | 0 | 0 | 0 | 0 | - | .00 | 0 | 0 |
| Valdespin, J | NYM | 2B | 12 | 8 | 73 | 14 | 24 | 1 | 4 | .974 | 4.71 | 0 | 0 |
| | NYM | SS | 1 | 0 | 2 | 0 | 0 | 0 | 0 | - | .00 | 0 | 0 |
| | NYM | LF | 5 | 1 | 17 | 2 | 0 | 1 | 0 | .667 | 1.08 | 0 | -1 |
| | NYM | CF | 16 | 10 | 91 | 25 | 1 | 0 | 0 | 1.000 | 2.58 | -4 | -2 |
| | NYM | RF | 8 | 6 | 47 | 7 | 0 | 0 | 0 | 1.000 | 1.34 | -1 | -3 |
| Valencia, D | Bal | 3B | 6 | 3 | 29 | 2 | 2 | 0 | 1 | 1.000 | 1.24 | 0 | 0 |
| Van Slyke, S | LAD | 1B | 4 | 2 | 23 | 24 | 0 | 0 | 4 | 1.000 | - | +2 | 1 |
| | LAD | LF | 30 | 24 | 211 | 40 | 0 | 2 | 0 | .952 | 1.70 | +7 | 3 |
| | LAD | RF | 13 | 9 | 80 | 19 | 1 | 0 | 0 | 1.000 | 2.24 | +2 | -1 |
| Velazquez, G | Mia | 3B | 1 | 0 | 3 | 0 | 0 | 0 | 0 | - | .00 | 0 | 0 |
| Venable, W | SD | CF | 80 | 52 | 478 | 132 | 0 | 1 | 0 | .992 | 2.48 | +10 | 4 |
| | SD | RF | 97 | 68 | 594 | 139 | 3 | 2 | 1 | .986 | 2.15 | -4 | -4 |
| Victorino, S | Bos | CF | 15 | 11 | 108 | 32 | 1 | 0 | 0 | 1.000 | 2.75 | -1 | -1 |
| Villar, J | Hou | SS | 58 | 57 | 499 | 95 | 141 | 16 | 38 | .937 | 4.26 | -2 | -5 |
| Wallace, B | Hou | 1B | 61 | 57 | 488 | 452 | 40 | 4 | 53 | .992 | - | -5 | -4 |
| | Hou | 3B | 9 | 8 | 74 | 4 | 12 | 0 | 3 | 1.000 | 1.95 | -3 | -2 |
| Walters, Z | Was | 3B | 2 | 0 | 3 | 0 | 1 | 0 | 0 | 1.000 | 3.00 | 0 | 0 |
| | Was | SS | 2 | 1 | 10 | 0 | 6 | 0 | 1 | 1.000 | 5.40 | 0 | 0 |
| Watkins, L | ChC | 2B | 9 | 5 | 56 | 2 | 11 | 1 | 1 | .929 | 2.08 | +2 | 0 |
| Weeks, J | Oak | 2B | 4 | 1 | 16 | 5 | 6 | 0 | 1 | 1.000 | 6.19 | -1 | -1 |
| | Oak | CF | 2 | 0 | 5 | 2 | 0 | 0 | 0 | 1.000 | 3.60 | 0 | 0 |
| Wells, C | TOT | LF | 16 | 8 | 97 | 21 | 1 | 1 | 1 | .957 | 2.04 | +1 | 5 |
| | TOT | CF | 5 | 5 | 35 | 9 | 1 | 0 | 1 | 1.000 | 2.57 | -1 | 0 |
| | TOT | RF | 11 | 5 | 66 | 16 | 0 | 0 | 0 | 1.000 | 2.18 | +2 | 0 |
| Wells, V | NYY | 1B | 1 | 1 | 8 | 6 | 0 | 0 | 0 | 1.000 | - | 0 | 0 |
| | NYY | 2B | 1 | 0 | 0 | 0 | 0 | 0 | 0 | - | .00 | 0 | 0 |
| | NYY | 3B | 1 | 0 | 1 | 0 | 1 | 0 | 0 | 1.000 | 9.00 | 0 | 0 |
| | NYY | LF | 73 | 68 | 623 | 137 | 6 | 0 | 1 | 1.000 | 2.07 | +3 | 5 |
| | NYY | RF | 23 | 19 | 157 | 40 | 2 | 0 | 0 | 1.000 | 2.41 | -8 | -5 |
| Wheeler, R | Col | 1B | 7 | 3 | 34 | 39 | 0 | 0 | 4 | 1.000 | - | -1 | -1 |
| | Col | 3B | 1 | 1 | 8 | 0 | 1 | 1 | 1 | .500 | 1.13 | -3 | -2 |
| | Col | LF | 1 | 1 | 8 | 1 | 0 | 0 | 0 | 1.000 | 1.13 | -1 | -1 |
| Wigginton, T | StL | 1B | 7 | 4 | 40 | 36 | 3 | 0 | 6 | 1.000 | - | -1 | -1 |
| | StL | 3B | 5 | 3 | 27 | 0 | 9 | 1 | 0 | .900 | 3.00 | -1 | -1 |
| | StL | LF | 6 | 0 | 11 | 1 | 0 | 0 | 0 | 1.000 | .82 | 0 | 0 |
| Willingham, J | Min | LF | 72 | 71 | 608 | 125 | 5 | 1 | 1 | .992 | 1.93 | -14 | -8 |
| Wilson, J | Ari | 2B | 17 | 15 | 132 | 22 | 43 | 1 | 11 | .985 | 4.43 | +4 | 4 |
| | Ari | 3B | 4 | 0 | 9 | 0 | 2 | 0 | 0 | 1.000 | 2.00 | +1 | 1 |
| | Ari | SS | 2 | 0 | 3 | 0 | 2 | 1 | 0 | .667 | 6.00 | 0 | 0 |
| Wise, D | CWS | LF | 4 | 0 | 7 | 4 | 0 | 1 | 0 | .800 | 5.40 | -1 | 0 |
| | CWS | CF | 22 | 15 | 141 | 47 | 0 | 0 | 0 | 1.000 | 2.99 | +2 | 0 |
| | CWS | RF | 1 | 0 | 1 | 0 | 0 | 0 | 0 | - | .00 | 0 | 0 |
| Wong, K | StL | 2B | 18 | 10 | 111 | 22 | 43 | 0 | 8 | 1.000 | 5.27 | 0 | 0 |
| Worth, D | Det | 3B | 2 | 0 | 6 | 0 | 3 | 1 | 0 | .750 | 4.50 | -1 | -1 |
| Yelich, C | Mia | LF | 59 | 56 | 505 | 103 | 0 | 0 | 0 | 1.000 | 1.83 | +6 | -2 |
| | Mia | CF | 5 | 5 | 39 | 11 | 0 | 0 | 0 | 1.000 | 2.54 | +1 | 1 |
| Youkilis, K | NYY | 1B | 6 | 6 | 46 | 45 | 1 | 0 | 1 | 1.000 | - | 0 | 0 |
| | NYY | 3B | 22 | 20 | 185 | 12 | 25 | 3 | 1 | .925 | 1.80 | -2 | -2 |
| Young, C | Oak | LF | 24 | 18 | 164 | 44 | 0 | 0 | 0 | 1.000 | 2.41 | 0 | -1 |
| | Oak | CF | 54 | 39 | 381 | 130 | 2 | 0 | 0 | 1.000 | 3.12 | -4 | -5 |
| | Oak | RF | 26 | 21 | 194 | 66 | 0 | 2 | 0 | .971 | 3.06 | +4 | 0 |
| Young, D | TOT | RF | 65 | 64 | 503 | 115 | 4 | 5 | 2 | .960 | 2.13 | -19 | -10 |
| Young, E | TOT | 2B | 4 | 1 | 15 | 2 | 4 | 0 | 1 | 1.000 | 3.68 | 0 | 0 |
| | TOT | CF | 18 | 13 | 125 | 33 | 0 | 1 | 0 | .971 | 2.38 | -3 | -3 |
| | TOT | RF | 20 | 20 | 168 | 26 | 0 | 1 | 0 | .963 | 1.39 | -6 | -6 |
| Young, M | TOT | 1B | 34 | 22 | 220 | 204 | 10 | 0 | 21 | 1.000 | - | -5 | -3 |
| | TOT | 2B | 2 | 1 | 11 | 0 | 4 | 0 | 0 | 1.000 | 3.38 | 0 | 0 |
| | TOT | SS | 1 | 1 | 7 | 0 | 2 | 0 | 0 | 1.000 | 2.57 | -1 | -1 |
| Zobrist, B | TB | SS | 21 | 11 | 115 | 11 | 37 | 1 | 5 | .980 | 3.76 | +4 | 3 |
| | TB | LF | 4 | 2 | 15 | 4 | 2 | 0 | 0 | 1.000 | 3.52 | -3 | 2 |
| | TB | CF | 1 | 0 | 1 | 0 | 0 | 0 | 0 | - | .00 | 0 | 0 |
| | TB | RF | 39 | 24 | 228 | 45 | 2 | 0 | 1 | 1.000 | 1.86 | -6 | -4 |

# All Other Catchers

| | | | | | | | | | | | | | | | | Runs Saved | | | |
|---|---|---|---|---|---|---|---|---|---|---|---|---|---|---|---|---|---|---|---|
| Player | Tm | G | GS | Inn | PO | A | E | DP | PB | Pct. | SBA | CS | PCS | CS% | CERA | GFP/ DME | SB | Other | Total |
| Anderson,Bryan | CWS | 10 | 6 | 54.1 | 49 | 2 | 1 | 0 | 0 | .981 | 3 | 0 | 0 | .00 | 3.15 | 0 | 0 | -1 | -1 |
| Baker,John | SD | 14 | 12 | 106.0 | 81 | 9 | 0 | 2 | 0 | 1.000 | 13 | 5 | 0 | .38 | 3.74 | 0 | 2 | 0 | 2 |
| Bantz,Brandon | Sea | 1 | 1 | 8.0 | 5 | 0 | 0 | 0 | 0 | 1.000 | 2 | 0 | 0 | .00 | 3.38 | 0 | 0 | 0 | 0 |
| Blanco,Henry | TOT | 47 | 42 | 368.0 | 331 | 17 | 3 | 4 | 10 | .991 | 18 | 5 | 1 | .28 | 5.14 | -1 | 0 | -4 | -5 |
| Boscan,J.C. | ChC | 4 | 2 | 22.0 | 19 | 2 | 0 | 0 | 0 | 1.000 | 4 | 1 | 0 | .25 | 2.45 | 0 | 0 | 0 | 0 |
| Brantly,Rob | Mia | 65 | 61 | 556.0 | 440 | 42 | 5 | 5 | 9 | .990 | 49 | 13 | 1 | .27 | 4.37 | -1 | 0 | -2 | -3 |
| Butera,Drew | TOT | 4 | 1 | 15.0 | 6 | 0 | 0 | 0 | 0 | 1.000 | 0 | 0 | 0 | - | 3.60 | 0 | 0 | 0 | 0 |
| Centeno,Juan | NYM | 4 | 3 | 26.0 | 28 | 2 | 0 | 0 | 0 | 1.000 | 5 | 1 | 0 | .20 | 2.42 | 1 | 0 | 0 | 1 |
| Cervelli,Francisco | NYY | 17 | 16 | 138.0 | 121 | 6 | 4 | 1 | 0 | .969 | 3 | 1 | 1 | .33 | 3.13 | 0 | 0 | 1 | 1 |
| Chirinos,Robinson | Tex | 3 | 3 | 27.0 | 22 | 0 | 0 | 0 | 0 | 1.000 | 0 | 0 | 0 | - | 3.67 | 0 | 0 | 0 | 0 |
| Clark,Cody | Hou | 16 | 10 | 102.0 | 87 | 11 | 1 | 2 | 2 | .990 | 13 | 7 | 0 | .54 | 4.85 | 1 | 2 | 0 | 3 |
| Clevenger,Steve | TOT | 4 | 4 | 35.0 | 30 | 1 | 1 | 0 | 1 | .969 | 2 | 0 | 0 | .00 | 4.63 | 0 | 0 | 0 | 0 |
| Conger,Hank | LAA | 71 | 60 | 535.0 | 480 | 30 | 7 | 5 | 1 | .986 | 60 | 13 | 2 | .22 | 3.68 | -1 | -1 | 2 | 0 |
| Corporan,Carlos | Hou | 57 | 51 | 449.2 | 356 | 17 | 6 | 3 | 2 | .984 | 41 | 10 | 0 | .24 | 4.78 | 2 | -1 | 0 | 1 |
| Cruz,Tony | StL | 44 | 28 | 267.0 | 234 | 14 | 1 | 1 | 2 | .996 | 18 | 6 | 0 | .33 | 4.11 | 1 | -1 | -1 | -1 |
| d'Arnaud,Travis | NYM | 30 | 30 | 258.1 | 214 | 10 | 0 | 0 | 3 | 1.000 | 24 | 5 | 0 | .21 | 4.11 | -1 | 0 | -1 | -2 |
| Doumit,Ryan | Min | 43 | 43 | 373.2 | 229 | 20 | 2 | 2 | 3 | .992 | 32 | 4 | 3 | .13 | 4.77 | 1 | -2 | -1 | -2 |
| Elmore,Jake | Hou | 1 | 0 | 4.0 | 1 | 0 | 0 | 0 | 0 | 1.000 | 0 | 0 | 0 | - | 6.75 | 0 | 0 | 0 | 0 |
| Federowicz,Tim | LAD | 45 | 42 | 374.0 | 323 | 40 | 5 | 0 | 2 | .986 | 33 | 9 | 1 | .27 | 3.59 | 3 | 0 | 1 | 4 |
| Fryer,Eric | Min | 5 | 4 | 40.0 | 28 | 2 | 0 | 0 | 0 | 1.000 | 5 | 2 | 0 | .40 | 5.63 | 0 | 1 | 0 | 1 |
| Gattis,Evan | Atl | 42 | 38 | 349.2 | 279 | 26 | 2 | 0 | 2 | .993 | 24 | 8 | 0 | .33 | 2.99 | -1 | 1 | 3 | 3 |
| Gimenez,Chris | TB | 1 | 0 | 1.0 | 1 | 0 | 0 | 0 | 0 | 1.000 | 0 | 0 | 0 | - | 9.00 | 0 | 0 | 0 | 0 |
| Gimenez,Hector | CWS | 23 | 19 | 179.0 | 146 | 12 | 2 | 3 | 5 | .988 | 20 | 5 | 1 | .25 | 4.37 | 1 | 1 | 0 | 2 |
| Gonzalez,Miguel | CWS | 4 | 1 | 18.0 | 12 | 1 | 0 | 0 | 0 | 1.000 | 2 | 0 | 0 | .00 | 3.50 | 0 | 0 | 0 | 0 |
| Gosewisch,Tuffy | Ari | 13 | 11 | 107.2 | 87 | 2 | 1 | 1 | 0 | .989 | 6 | 2 | 0 | .33 | 2.93 | 1 | 0 | 0 | 1 |
| Grandal,Yasmani | SD | 26 | 26 | 231.0 | 195 | 11 | 2 | 1 | 1 | .990 | 12 | 1 | 0 | .08 | 3.78 | 0 | -1 | 0 | -1 |
| Hanigan,Ryan | Cin | 72 | 66 | 589.2 | 538 | 33 | 1 | 1 | 3 | .998 | 30 | 12 | 3 | .40 | 3.40 | -4 | 2 | 1 | -1 |
| Hayes,Brett | KC | 5 | 4 | 44.0 | 45 | 1 | 0 | 0 | 0 | 1.000 | 3 | 0 | 1 | .00 | 2.05 | 0 | -1 | 0 | -1 |
| Hernandez,Ramon | LAD | 11 | 11 | 98.0 | 89 | 8 | 1 | 0 | 2 | .990 | 6 | 2 | 0 | .33 | 3.67 | -1 | 1 | 0 | 0 |
| Herrmann,Chris | Min | 27 | 23 | 209.2 | 136 | 13 | 2 | 0 | 0 | .987 | 20 | 7 | 0 | .35 | 4.94 | 0 | 1 | -1 | 0 |
| Hester,John | LAA | 1 | 0 | 1.0 | 1 | 0 | 0 | 0 | 0 | 1.000 | 0 | 0 | 0 | - | 0.00 | 0 | 0 | 0 | 0 |
| Hill,Koyie | Mia | 18 | 16 | 145.2 | 107 | 6 | 1 | 0 | 1 | .991 | 12 | 1 | 1 | .08 | 3.27 | 0 | 0 | 0 | 0 |
| Holaday,Bryan | Det | 14 | 8 | 84.0 | 73 | 3 | 2 | 0 | 0 | .974 | 13 | 1 | 0 | .08 | 5.14 | 0 | -1 | 0 | -1 |
| Jaso,John | Oak | 48 | 42 | 364.1 | 269 | 12 | 3 | 1 | 0 | .989 | 30 | 2 | 2 | .07 | 3.66 | -4 | -2 | 0 | -6 |
| Johnson,Rob | StL | 15 | 6 | 75.1 | 52 | 3 | 0 | 0 | 1 | 1.000 | 1 | 0 | 0 | .00 | 5.02 | -1 | 0 | 0 | -1 |
| Kottaras,George | KC | 39 | 29 | 262.0 | 212 | 14 | 4 | 0 | 3 | .983 | 31 | 6 | 3 | .19 | 3.98 | 1 | -1 | -1 | -1 |
| Kratz,Erik | Phi | 60 | 54 | 478.1 | 414 | 26 | 1 | 5 | 1 | .998 | 39 | 6 | 3 | .15 | 4.61 | -1 | -2 | -1 | -4 |
| Laird,Gerald | Atl | 40 | 33 | 294.1 | 241 | 16 | 0 | 6 | 1 | 1.000 | 23 | 7 | 2 | .30 | 3.94 | -2 | 1 | -1 | -2 |
| Lalli,Blake | Mil | 1 | 0 | 2.0 | 2 | 0 | 0 | 0 | 0 | 1.000 | 0 | 0 | 0 | - | 4.50 | 0 | 0 | 0 | 0 |
| Lavarnway,Ryan | Bos | 22 | 18 | 164.0 | 131 | 8 | 1 | 4 | 6 | .993 | 30 | 5 | 1 | .17 | 4.55 | 0 | -1 | 0 | -1 |
| Leon,Sandy | Was | 1 | 0 | 1.0 | 2 | 0 | 0 | 0 | 0 | 1.000 | 0 | 0 | 0 | - | 0.00 | 0 | 0 | 0 | 0 |
| Lerud,Steven | Phi | 5 | 1 | 15.0 | 7 | 0 | 0 | 0 | 0 | 1.000 | 2 | 0 | 0 | .00 | 4.20 | -1 | 0 | 0 | -1 |
| Maldonado,Martin | Mil | 47 | 40 | 366.2 | 281 | 35 | 1 | 3 | 3 | .997 | 27 | 8 | 0 | .30 | 3.17 | 2 | 1 | 3 | 6 |
| Marson,Lou | Cle | 3 | 2 | 11.2 | 11 | 1 | 0 | 1 | 0 | 1.000 | 4 | 0 | 0 | .00 | 3.09 | 1 | 0 | -1 | 0 |
| Martinez,Victor | Det | 3 | 3 | 22.0 | 18 | 4 | 0 | 0 | 0 | 1.000 | 1 | 0 | 0 | .00 | 3.27 | 0 | 0 | 0 | 0 |
| McKenry,Michael | Pit | 31 | 27 | 253.1 | 210 | 16 | 2 | 0 | 1 | .991 | 38 | 3 | 3 | .08 | 3.23 | 0 | -5 | 1 | -4 |
| Miller,Corky | Cin | 16 | 12 | 102.0 | 103 | 6 | 1 | 1 | 1 | .991 | 8 | 1 | 1 | .13 | 3.18 | 2 | 0 | 0 | 2 |
| Monell,Johnny | SF | 1 | 0 | 3.0 | 4 | 0 | 0 | 0 | 0 | 1.000 | 0 | 0 | 0 | - | 0.00 | 0 | 0 | 0 | 0 |
| Montero,Jesus | Sea | 26 | 25 | 225.1 | 207 | 11 | 1 | 0 | 3 | .995 | 24 | 1 | 0 | .04 | 3.39 | 0 | -3 | 0 | -3 |
| Moore,Adam | KC | 5 | 3 | 27.0 | 22 | 3 | 1 | 0 | 0 | .962 | 4 | 1 | 0 | .25 | 4.00 | 0 | 0 | 0 | 0 |
| Murphy,J.R. | NYY | 15 | 6 | 70.2 | 65 | 7 | 0 | 0 | 0 | 1.000 | 6 | 3 | 0 | .50 | 2.55 | -1 | 1 | 0 | 0 |
| Navarro,Dioner | ChC | 55 | 53 | 470.0 | 425 | 36 | 5 | 7 | 5 | .989 | 48 | 11 | 2 | .23 | 4.02 | -1 | 1 | 1 | 1 |
| Nickeas,Mike | Tor | 1 | 0 | 1.0 | 0 | 0 | 0 | 0 | 0 | - | 0 | 0 | 0 | - | 0.00 | 0 | 0 | 0 | 0 |
| Nieves,Wil | Ari | 47 | 40 | 380.2 | 323 | 14 | 2 | 0 | 1 | .994 | 15 | 2 | 3 | .13 | 3.92 | -5 | -2 | 1 | -6 |
| Olivo,Miguel | Mia | 21 | 15 | 141.1 | 114 | 12 | 3 | 1 | 1 | .977 | 17 | 4 | 2 | .24 | 4.01 | 0 | -1 | 1 | 0 |
| Pacheco,Jordan | Col | 15 | 11 | 103.2 | 84 | 8 | 2 | 2 | 2 | .979 | 5 | 1 | 0 | .20 | 4.34 | 1 | -1 | -1 | -1 |
| Pagnozzi,Matt | Hou | 7 | 6 | 54.0 | 37 | 2 | 1 | 0 | 0 | .975 | 4 | 1 | 0 | .25 | 3.50 | 0 | 0 | 0 | 0 |
| Pena,Brayan | Det | 64 | 55 | 520.0 | 528 | 27 | 3 | 4 | 5 | .995 | 51 | 9 | 4 | .18 | 3.76 | 1 | -3 | -1 | -3 |
| Perez,Audry | StL | 1 | 0 | 2.0 | 1 | 0 | 0 | 0 | 0 | 1.000 | 0 | 0 | 0 | - | 0.00 | 0 | 0 | 0 | 0 |
| Phegley,Josh | CWS | 64 | 59 | 516.0 | 415 | 29 | 5 | 4 | 8 | .989 | 40 | 10 | 3 | .25 | 4.10 | 1 | 2 | -1 | 2 |
| Pinto,Josmil | Min | 20 | 18 | 159.1 | 112 | 4 | 2 | 1 | 0 | .983 | 8 | 2 | 3 | .25 | 5.54 | -2 | 0 | -1 | -3 |
| Quintero,Humberto | TOT | 42 | 40 | 347.0 | 280 | 27 | 5 | 4 | 2 | .984 | 33 | 12 | 0 | .36 | 4.56 | 1 | 3 | -1 | 3 |
| Quiroz,Guillermo | SF | 35 | 19 | 193.0 | 144 | 13 | 0 | 0 | 0 | 1.000 | 17 | 6 | 2 | .35 | 4.71 | -1 | 1 | -1 | -1 |
| Recker,Anthony | NYM | 38 | 34 | 323.1 | 289 | 17 | 3 | 2 | 2 | .990 | 33 | 6 | 1 | .18 | 3.28 | 1 | -2 | 2 | 1 |
| Rivera,Rene | SD | 21 | 21 | 180.0 | 185 | 13 | 0 | 1 | 2 | 1.000 | 16 | 9 | 0 | .56 | 3.00 | 0 | 4 | 1 | 5 |
| Robinson,Chris | SD | 2 | 1 | 10.0 | 8 | 0 | 0 | 0 | 0 | 1.000 | 0 | 0 | 0 | - | 2.70 | 0 | 0 | 0 | 0 |
| Romine,Austin | NYY | 59 | 43 | 394.1 | 315 | 24 | 3 | 1 | 4 | .991 | 37 | 7 | 1 | .19 | 4.22 | 0 | -1 | -2 | -3 |
| Ross,David | Bos | 36 | 33 | 286.0 | 288 | 13 | 1 | 2 | 2 | .997 | 29 | 10 | 3 | .34 | 3.12 | 0 | 2 | 1 | 3 |
| Rupp,Cameron | Phi | 3 | 3 | 27.0 | 25 | 1 | 0 | 0 | 0 | 1.000 | 2 | 0 | 0 | .00 | 4.33 | 1 | 0 | 0 | 1 |
| Sanchez,Hector | SF | 33 | 24 | 220.1 | 210 | 15 | 1 | 0 | 5 | .996 | 26 | 5 | 1 | .19 | 4.17 | 0 | 0 | 0 | 0 |
| Sanchez,Tony | Pit | 16 | 12 | 112.1 | 98 | 7 | 0 | 0 | 2 | 1.000 | 5 | 0 | 1 | .00 | 3.20 | 0 | -1 | 0 | -1 |
| Santos,Omir | Cle | 1 | 0 | 3.0 | 2 | 0 | 0 | 0 | 0 | 1.000 | 0 | 0 | 0 | - | 15.00 | 0 | 0 | 0 | 0 |
| Shoppach,Kelly | TOT | 36 | 32 | 295.0 | 265 | 14 | 2 | 0 | 3 | .993 | 25 | 8 | 2 | .32 | 4.42 | -4 | 1 | 0 | -3 |
| Skipworth,Kyle | Mia | 1 | 0 | 2.0 | 2 | 0 | 0 | 0 | 0 | 1.000 | 0 | 0 | 0 | - | 4.50 | 0 | 0 | 0 | 0 |
| Snyder,Chris | Bal | 8 | 6 | 55.0 | 39 | 5 | 0 | 2 | 1 | 1.000 | 7 | 3 | 0 | .43 | 2.62 | 0 | 1 | 1 | 2 |
| Solano,Jhonatan | Was | 19 | 12 | 118.0 | 96 | 6 | 1 | 0 | 0 | .990 | 8 | 0 | 0 | .00 | 3.43 | 2 | -1 | 0 | 1 |
| Soto,Geovany | Tex | 53 | 49 | 431.1 | 395 | 27 | 2 | 3 | 1 | .995 | 34 | 10 | 0 | .29 | 3.67 | 0 | 1 | 1 | 2 |
| Stassi,Max | Hou | 1 | 0 | 3.0 | 1 | 1 | 0 | 0 | 0 | 1.000 | 0 | 0 | 0 | - | 9.00 | 0 | 0 | 0 | 0 |
| Sucre,Jesus | Sea | 8 | 8 | 71.0 | 60 | 6 | 0 | 1 | 0 | 1.000 | 2 | 0 | 0 | .00 | 4.06 | 0 | 0 | 0 | 0 |

| Player | Tm | G | GS | Inn | PO | A | E | DP | PB | Pct. | SBA | CS | PCS | CS% | CERA | Runs Saved GFP/ DME | SB | Other | Total |
|---|---|---|---|---|---|---|---|---|---|---|---|---|---|---|---|---|---|---|---|
| Teagarden,Taylor | Bal | 23 | 18 | 162.0 | 108 | 9 | 1 | 0 | 1 | .992 | 17 | 4 | 1 | .24 | 3.89 | 0 | 0 | 0 | 0 |
| Thole,Josh | Tor | 39 | 34 | 288.1 | 253 | 13 | 2 | 2 | 9 | .993 | 26 | 4 | 4 | .15 | 4.40 | -1 | 0 | -1 | -2 |
| Torrealba,Yorvit | Col | 50 | 48 | 422.0 | 336 | 20 | 3 | 4 | 2 | .992 | 41 | 9 | 4 | .22 | 4.73 | 2 | 0 | -1 | 1 |
| Vogt,Stephen | Oak | 44 | 40 | 335.2 | 299 | 14 | 1 | 2 | 6 | .997 | 28 | 8 | 1 | .29 | 3.30 | 0 | 1 | 0 | 1 |
| Zunino,Mike | Sea | 50 | 48 | 429.2 | 363 | 22 | 2 | 1 | 2 | .995 | 32 | 4 | 2 | .13 | 4.13 | -3 | -3 | 1 | -5 |

# Baserunning

The best baserunner of 2013 was also the best baserunner of 2012: Mike Trout. He went first-to-third successfully in 61 percent of his 44 opportunities (the league averaged just 28 percent), second-to-home in 75 percent of 20 opportunities (league average of 59 percent), and first-to-home in 36 percent of 14 opportunities (league at 43 percent). Additionally, he was thrown out just once and doubled off three times, a relatively small number of outs on the basepaths considering he was on base a league-leading 312 times. To top it off, Trout had another efficient year as a stolen base threat (33 for 40).

Baserunning is usually a fairly consistent ability. Rajai Davis, Jacoby Ellsbury, and Alex Rios are very good, year after year. Hunter Pence doesn't get enough credit for being a good baserunner. Paul Konerko, Victor Martinez, and David Ortiz are consistently bad. A small handful of players can't make up their minds. Martin Prado, it seems, is a good baserunner in even-numbered years and a bad baserunner in odd years. In 2013, he was the league's worst. He was worse than the league average advancing first-to-third, second-to-home, and first-to-home, and he was thrown out seven times on the basepaths. He was just 3-for-8 on stolen base attempts, and worst of all, he grounded into more double plays (29) than both Billy Butler and Miguel Cabrera.

Trout was tops going first-to-third (27 for 44), while Victor Martinez was the worst (3 for 43), though teammate Miguel Cabrera wasn't much better (6 for 50). That's essentially a 23-base difference between Trout and Cabrera for those of you tracking the AL MVP debate. Elvis Andrus was an amazing 19 for 20 going second-to-home, while Adrian Gonzalez was just 2 for 17. Jason Heyward was 8 for 8 going first-to-home on a double, the only aspect of baserunning in which he excelled. The aforementioned Butler, on the other hand, scored just thrice in 17 such chances. Despite Billy Boy, the Royals were the best baserunning team in baseball thanks largely to a league-leading 153 stolen bases against just 32 times caught (83 percent).

There's only so much a runner can do above and beyond his natural ability. Paul Konerko can try as hard as he can, but he's never going to be Mike Trout's equal on the basepaths. However, there are baserunning instincts that can help a player exceed his raw speed, and the lack of such instincts can be equally harmful. The easiest way for a fast runner to become a bad baserunner is to get overly aggressive. For example, Yasiel Puig gave the entire league a two months head start but he still led the league with 11 outs on the basepaths. Howie Kendrick was nearly as reckless on the bases, running into 10 outs of his own, as did Allen Craig. Considering the offensive firepower of their respective lineups, all three would benefit from being more conservative on the basepaths.

# 2013 Baserunning

| | 1st to 3rd | | 2nd to Home | | 1st to Home | | | | | | | | | | |
|---|---|---|---|---|---|---|---|---|---|---|---|---|---|---|---|
| Player | Moved | Chances | Moved | Chances | Moved | Chances | Bases Taken | Out Adv | Doubled Off | BR Outs | GDP | GDP Opps | BR Gain | SB Gain | Net Gain |
| Ackley,Dustin | 5 | 20 | 6 | 9 | 5 | 7 | 13 | 0 | 1 | 1 | 6 | 80 | +12 | -4 | +8 |
| Adams,Matt | 1 | 17 | 8 | 16 | 4 | 8 | 6 | 0 | 0 | 0 | 9 | 70 | -2 | -2 | -4 |
| Alonso,Yonder | 4 | 16 | 6 | 11 | 1 | 6 | 16 | 2 | 2 | 4 | 9 | 66 | -3 | +6 | +3 |
| Altuve,Jose | 9 | 26 | 6 | 9 | 5 | 11 | 17 | 7 | 1 | 8 | 24 | 105 | -22 | +9 | -13 |
| Alvarez,Pedro | 4 | 20 | 7 | 13 | 4 | 8 | 8 | 1 | 1 | 2 | 16 | 109 | -7 | +2 | -5 |
| Amarista,Alexi | 7 | 19 | 8 | 13 | 1 | 1 | 16 | 0 | 1 | 1 | 7 | 64 | +13 | 0 | +13 |
| Andrus,Elvis | 22 | 49 | 19 | 20 | 2 | 4 | 36 | 3 | 4 | 8 | 19 | 129 | +18 | +26 | +44 |
| Aoki,Norichika | 13 | 51 | 8 | 19 | 1 | 9 | 18 | 1 | 2 | 3 | 9 | 72 | -5 | -4 | -9 |
| Arcia,Oswaldo | 2 | 18 | 4 | 9 | 2 | 3 | 11 | 3 | 0 | 3 | 4 | 64 | -1 | -3 | -4 |
| Arenado,Nolan | 5 | 29 | 7 | 15 | 2 | 4 | 14 | 1 | 1 | 2 | 16 | 90 | -6 | +2 | -4 |
| Arencibia,J.P. | 4 | 15 | 5 | 7 | 1 | 5 | 8 | 1 | 2 | 3 | 8 | 93 | -2 | -4 | -6 |
| Arias,Joaquin | 6 | 15 | 5 | 6 | 2 | 4 | 6 | 0 | 0 | 0 | 4 | 46 | +9 | +1 | +10 |
| Asche,Cody | 2 | 6 | 4 | 6 | 0 | 0 | 6 | 1 | 0 | 1 | 1 | 41 | +6 | +1 | +7 |
| Avila,Alex | 3 | 27 | 6 | 11 | 1 | 4 | 12 | 1 | 1 | 2 | 10 | 84 | -3 | 0 | -3 |
| Aviles,Mike | 5 | 15 | 10 | 15 | 4 | 9 | 14 | 2 | 5 | 7 | 11 | 83 | -10 | -2 | -12 |
| Aybar,Erick | 6 | 15 | 17 | 24 | 1 | 3 | 17 | 3 | 2 | 5 | 14 | 108 | 0 | -2 | -2 |
| Baker,Jeff | 0 | 7 | 2 | 5 | 0 | 2 | 4 | 1 | 0 | 1 | 5 | 33 | -5 | +1 | -4 |
| Barmes,Clint | 2 | 8 | 3 | 7 | 1 | 3 | 5 | 0 | 2 | 2 | 5 | 52 | -4 | 0 | -4 |
| Barnes,Brandon | 10 | 27 | 4 | 12 | 1 | 4 | 21 | 2 | 1 | 3 | 5 | 72 | +11 | -11 | 0 |
| Barney,Darwin | 6 | 21 | 11 | 15 | 4 | 5 | 9 | 1 | 0 | 1 | 22 | 110 | -3 | 0 | -3 |
| Bautista,Jose | 12 | 26 | 10 | 12 | 6 | 10 | 8 | 2 | 3 | 5 | 13 | 102 | -3 | +3 | 0 |
| Baxter,Mike | 3 | 10 | 1 | 2 | 1 | 2 | 3 | 2 | 0 | 2 | 1 | 21 | -3 | +1 | -2 |
| Bay,Jason | 4 | 11 | 3 | 9 | 0 | 1 | 7 | 0 | 0 | 0 | 6 | 46 | +3 | +1 | +4 |
| Beckham,Gordon | 5 | 17 | 14 | 20 | 0 | 4 | 15 | 4 | 0 | 4 | 10 | 73 | -1 | +3 | +2 |
| Belt,Brandon | 7 | 35 | 16 | 23 | 1 | 4 | 13 | 4 | 1 | 5 | 4 | 124 | +2 | +1 | +3 |
| Beltran,Carlos | 7 | 32 | 14 | 20 | 3 | 7 | 10 | 2 | 2 | 4 | 12 | 123 | -4 | 0 | -4 |
| Beltre,Adrian | 18 | 45 | 11 | 19 | 2 | 9 | 22 | 2 | 0 | 2 | 17 | 116 | +10 | +1 | +11 |
| Berkman,Lance | 4 | 20 | 1 | 5 | 3 | 3 | 11 | 3 | 0 | 3 | 7 | 62 | -2 | 0 | -2 |
| Bernadina,Roger | 8 | 15 | 4 | 5 | 0 | 2 | 6 | 2 | 0 | 2 | 4 | 37 | +3 | +4 | +7 |
| Betancourt,Yuniesky | 1 | 7 | 0 | 9 | 1 | 2 | 6 | 1 | 1 | 2 | 9 | 67 | -10 | 0 | -10 |
| Bianchi,Jeff | 4 | 11 | 3 | 7 | 1 | 1 | 5 | 1 | 0 | 1 | 4 | 32 | 0 | -4 | -4 |
| Blackmon,Charlie | 4 | 12 | 9 | 12 | 3 | 4 | 9 | 1 | 0 | 1 | 1 | 32 | +10 | +7 | +17 |
| Blanco,Gregor | 11 | 28 | 11 | 15 | 6 | 7 | 14 | 4 | 4 | 8 | 10 | 87 | -6 | -4 | -10 |
| Blanks,Kyle | 6 | 17 | 5 | 7 | 1 | 5 | 7 | 0 | 0 | 0 | 2 | 51 | +9 | -1 | +8 |
| Bloomquist,Willie | 2 | 7 | 2 | 2 | 2 | 3 | 5 | 1 | 0 | 1 | 3 | 23 | +2 | -4 | -2 |
| Bogusevic,Brian | 0 | 5 | 1 | 1 | 2 | 2 | 5 | 1 | 1 | 2 | 4 | 28 | -3 | +2 | -1 |
| Bonifacio,Emilio | 7 | 17 | 12 | 17 | 4 | 4 | 10 | 0 | 1 | 1 | 4 | 72 | +14 | +12 | +26 |
| Bourjos,Peter | 4 | 10 | 6 | 8 | 0 | 0 | 8 | 1 | 0 | 1 | 8 | 39 | +2 | +6 | +8 |
| Bourn,Michael | 12 | 27 | 16 | 23 | 3 | 6 | 26 | 2 | 2 | 4 | 2 | 75 | +23 | -1 | +22 |
| Brantley,Michael | 10 | 24 | 7 | 12 | 4 | 10 | 13 | 1 | 0 | 1 | 11 | 123 | +11 | +9 | +20 |
| Brantly,Rob | 1 | 14 | 4 | 5 | 2 | 4 | 5 | 1 | 2 | 3 | 8 | 43 | -10 | 0 | -10 |
| Braun,Ryan | 4 | 15 | 4 | 6 | 4 | 7 | 6 | 0 | 0 | 0 | 8 | 72 | +5 | -6 | -1 |
| Brown,Domonic | 4 | 25 | 4 | 9 | 3 | 4 | 17 | 3 | 1 | 4 | 5 | 102 | +5 | +2 | +7 |
| Bruce,Jay | 9 | 29 | 13 | 23 | 2 | 7 | 18 | 1 | 1 | 2 | 9 | 139 | +13 | +1 | +14 |
| Buck,John | 5 | 15 | 9 | 10 | 1 | 3 | 3 | 0 | 1 | 1 | 13 | 86 | -3 | 0 | -3 |
| Butler,Billy | 4 | 39 | 9 | 18 | 3 | 17 | 13 | 1 | 1 | 2 | 28 | 142 | -24 | 0 | -24 |
| Byrd,Marlon | 6 | 29 | 13 | 20 | 5 | 8 | 9 | 4 | 0 | 4 | 11 | 108 | -6 | -6 | -12 |
| Cabrera,Asdrubal | 5 | 22 | 14 | 22 | 2 | 10 | 20 | 4 | 2 | 7 | 10 | 109 | -5 | +3 | -2 |
| Cabrera,Everth | 7 | 22 | 10 | 17 | 2 | 3 | 16 | 1 | 1 | 2 | 1 | 48 | +12 | +13 | +25 |
| Cabrera,Melky | 7 | 20 | 5 | 8 | 0 | 3 | 13 | 3 | 0 | 3 | 7 | 59 | +1 | -2 | -1 |
| Cabrera,Miguel | 6 | 50 | 10 | 19 | 7 | 12 | 25 | 3 | 0 | 3 | 19 | 143 | 0 | +3 | +3 |
| Cain,Lorenzo | 9 | 23 | 10 | 15 | 2 | 6 | 15 | 1 | 1 | 2 | 10 | 92 | +9 | +2 | +11 |
| Calhoun,Kole | 7 | 13 | 6 | 9 | 1 | 1 | 4 | 1 | 0 | 1 | 6 | 46 | +3 | -2 | +1 |
| Callaspo,Alberto | 8 | 32 | 7 | 22 | 1 | 4 | 11 | 5 | 0 | 5 | 12 | 104 | -16 | -4 | -20 |
| Cano,Robinson | 7 | 29 | 14 | 26 | 2 | 6 | 19 | 6 | 2 | 8 | 18 | 137 | -16 | +5 | -11 |
| Carp,Mike | 3 | 9 | 3 | 9 | 3 | 6 | 6 | 0 | 0 | 0 | 3 | 50 | +5 | +1 | +6 |
| Carpenter,Matt | 22 | 58 | 25 | 35 | 4 | 8 | 30 | 3 | 3 | 6 | 4 | 74 | +21 | -3 | +18 |
| Carroll,Jamey | 5 | 12 | 3 | 6 | 1 | 7 | 5 | 2 | 0 | 2 | 3 | 26 | -4 | 0 | -4 |
| Carter,Chris | 5 | 19 | 5 | 12 | 1 | 7 | 11 | 4 | 0 | 4 | 8 | 111 | -5 | +2 | -3 |
| Casilla,Alexi | 1 | 8 | 3 | 8 | 4 | 4 | 8 | 1 | 1 | 2 | 1 | 23 | +2 | +5 | +7 |
| Castillo,Welington | 8 | 21 | 6 | 9 | 3 | 5 | 9 | 3 | 0 | 3 | 13 | 65 | -5 | +2 | -3 |
| Castro,Jason | 11 | 24 | 2 | 7 | 3 | 5 | 10 | 0 | 1 | 1 | 4 | 82 | +12 | 0 | +12 |
| Castro,Starlin | 7 | 27 | 10 | 14 | 4 | 6 | 19 | 4 | 2 | 6 | 21 | 113 | -10 | -3 | -13 |

# 2013 Baserunning

| | 1st to 3rd | | 2nd to Home | | 1st to Home | | | | | | | | | | |
|---|---|---|---|---|---|---|---|---|---|---|---|---|---|---|---|
| Player | Moved | Chances | Moved | Chances | Moved | Chances | Bases Taken | Out Adv | Doubled Off | BR Outs | GDP | GDP Opps | BR Gain | SB Gain | Net Gain |
| Cedeno,Ronny | 3 | 12 | 8 | 10 | 0 | 2 | 12 | 0 | 0 | 0 | 6 | 52 | +11 | -3 | +8 |
| Cespedes,Yoenis | 9 | 27 | 9 | 14 | 4 | 7 | 14 | 1 | 1 | 2 | 8 | 121 | +13 | -7 | +6 |
| Chavez,Endy | 2 | 14 | 3 | 4 | 0 | 2 | 5 | 1 | 0 | 1 | 9 | 47 | -6 | -5 | -11 |
| Chavez,Eric | 5 | 12 | 3 | 4 | 2 | 5 | 5 | 3 | 0 | 3 | 7 | 66 | -3 | +1 | -2 |
| Chisenhall,Lonnie | 4 | 14 | 4 | 7 | 1 | 2 | 8 | 2 | 0 | 2 | 8 | 54 | -2 | +1 | -1 |
| Choo,Shin-Soo | 11 | 36 | 17 | 30 | 2 | 10 | 29 | 1 | 2 | 3 | 3 | 75 | +17 | -2 | +15 |
| Ciriaco,Pedro | 1 | 5 | 0 | 2 | 0 | 1 | 4 | 1 | 0 | 1 | 2 | 31 | -1 | +7 | +6 |
| Coghlan,Chris | 4 | 10 | 0 | 5 | 1 | 1 | 6 | 2 | 0 | 2 | 2 | 34 | -1 | +2 | +1 |
| Colabello,Chris | 1 | 5 | 0 | 0 | 1 | 2 | 5 | 0 | 0 | 0 | 5 | 40 | +3 | -2 | +1 |
| Conger,Hank | 5 | 14 | 1 | 6 | 0 | 0 | 4 | 1 | 2 | 4 | 6 | 45 | -12 | -2 | -14 |
| Corporan,Carlos | 1 | 7 | 0 | 1 | 0 | 6 | 4 | 2 | 0 | 2 | 3 | 41 | -6 | 0 | -6 |
| Cozart,Zack | 11 | 27 | 9 | 14 | 5 | 10 | 16 | 3 | 2 | 5 | 18 | 114 | -4 | 0 | -4 |
| Craig,Allen | 14 | 54 | 12 | 18 | 5 | 14 | 10 | 8 | 1 | 10 | 12 | 109 | -25 | +2 | -23 |
| Crawford,Brandon | 4 | 24 | 10 | 15 | 0 | 2 | 19 | 2 | 0 | 2 | 10 | 101 | +8 | -3 | +5 |
| Crawford,Carl | 11 | 31 | 13 | 18 | 5 | 8 | 13 | 2 | 0 | 2 | 4 | 58 | +12 | +7 | +19 |
| Crisp,Coco | 10 | 31 | 16 | 22 | 6 | 9 | 14 | 1 | 1 | 3 | 7 | 79 | +9 | +11 | +20 |
| Crowe,Trevor | 3 | 10 | 2 | 3 | 2 | 3 | 7 | 3 | 0 | 3 | 3 | 36 | -1 | +4 | +3 |
| Cruz,Nelson | 3 | 16 | 1 | 2 | 1 | 5 | 9 | 4 | 1 | 5 | 14 | 82 | -17 | +3 | -14 |
| Cuddyer,Michael | 15 | 38 | 11 | 16 | 8 | 11 | 23 | 5 | 3 | 8 | 13 | 99 | +2 | +4 | +6 |
| Danks,Jordan | 3 | 11 | 1 | 4 | 0 | 1 | 5 | 1 | 0 | 1 | 5 | 35 | -2 | +3 | +1 |
| Davis,Chris | 9 | 30 | 10 | 15 | 6 | 9 | 14 | 0 | 1 | 3 | 4 | 127 | +15 | +2 | +17 |
| Davis,Ike | 2 | 20 | 7 | 12 | 4 | 6 | 6 | 2 | 0 | 2 | 9 | 62 | -7 | +4 | -3 |
| Davis,Khris | 0 | 7 | 6 | 6 | 0 | 3 | 2 | 0 | 0 | 0 | 4 | 30 | -1 | +3 | +2 |
| Davis,Rajai | 2 | 13 | 5 | 7 | 2 | 3 | 17 | 0 | 0 | 0 | 8 | 77 | +15 | +33 | +48 |
| De Aza,Alejandro | 11 | 36 | 12 | 17 | 5 | 7 | 18 | 2 | 6 | 8 | 8 | 89 | -4 | +4 | 0 |
| DeJesus,David | 7 | 16 | 7 | 15 | 8 | 11 | 14 | 1 | 0 | 1 | 6 | 55 | +12 | -1 | +11 |
| Denorfia,Chris | 11 | 32 | 10 | 13 | 4 | 7 | 13 | 0 | 2 | 2 | 14 | 77 | +3 | +11 | +14 |
| DeRosa,Mark | 1 | 11 | 3 | 10 | 2 | 2 | 5 | 1 | 0 | 1 | 8 | 49 | -6 | 0 | -6 |
| Descalso,Daniel | 6 | 16 | 10 | 16 | 3 | 3 | 9 | 1 | 0 | 1 | 7 | 59 | +7 | 0 | +7 |
| Desmond,Ian | 12 | 32 | 15 | 21 | 4 | 5 | 21 | 3 | 3 | 6 | 16 | 116 | +3 | +9 | +12 |
| Dickerson,Corey | 8 | 16 | 4 | 5 | 2 | 4 | 7 | 1 | 0 | 1 | 1 | 36 | +10 | -2 | +8 |
| Dietrich,Derek | 3 | 14 | 5 | 9 | 5 | 7 | 5 | 2 | 1 | 3 | 1 | 47 | 0 | +1 | +1 |
| Dirks,Andy | 3 | 28 | 6 | 17 | 4 | 7 | 10 | 1 | 1 | 2 | 6 | 110 | -1 | +5 | +4 |
| Dobbs,Greg | 4 | 15 | 3 | 8 | 2 | 4 | 6 | 2 | 0 | 2 | 5 | 54 | -3 | -1 | -4 |
| Dominguez,Matt | 4 | 16 | 7 | 16 | 1 | 5 | 13 | 4 | 2 | 6 | 17 | 94 | -19 | -2 | -21 |
| Donaldson,Josh | 14 | 36 | 8 | 15 | 5 | 14 | 18 | 5 | 1 | 6 | 15 | 132 | -4 | +1 | -3 |
| Doumit,Ryan | 4 | 20 | 10 | 20 | 2 | 3 | 18 | 8 | 0 | 8 | 13 | 110 | -13 | +1 | -12 |
| Dozier,Brian | 12 | 23 | 12 | 17 | 5 | 7 | 16 | 1 | 3 | 4 | 14 | 103 | +7 | 0 | +7 |
| Drew,Stephen | 10 | 30 | 14 | 22 | 1 | 6 | 11 | 5 | 1 | 6 | 9 | 93 | -8 | +6 | -2 |
| Duda,Lucas | 4 | 14 | 5 | 7 | 2 | 6 | 6 | 0 | 0 | 0 | 1 | 61 | +10 | -6 | +4 |
| Dunn,Adam | 3 | 27 | 7 | 17 | 1 | 7 | 17 | 0 | 0 | 0 | 2 | 84 | +11 | -1 | +10 |
| Dyson,Jarrod | 5 | 14 | 9 | 11 | 2 | 2 | 8 | 0 | 0 | 0 | 4 | 31 | +10 | +22 | +32 |
| Eaton,Adam | 7 | 17 | 7 | 9 | 5 | 7 | 7 | 2 | 0 | 2 | 4 | 37 | +5 | +1 | +6 |
| Ellis,A.J. | 7 | 21 | 11 | 18 | 1 | 5 | 13 | 1 | 0 | 1 | 11 | 95 | +7 | -4 | +3 |
| Ellis,Mark | 9 | 34 | 8 | 14 | 2 | 6 | 17 | 1 | 0 | 1 | 5 | 87 | +14 | +2 | +16 |
| Ellsbury,Jacoby | 11 | 35 | 17 | 31 | 3 | 8 | 23 | 3 | 1 | 4 | 12 | 88 | +3 | +44 | +47 |
| Elmore,Jake | 3 | 9 | 2 | 5 | 0 | 0 | 9 | 0 | 0 | 0 | 1 | 22 | +9 | -11 | -2 |
| Encarnacion,Edwin | 9 | 29 | 15 | 20 | 1 | 7 | 20 | 3 | 1 | 4 | 20 | 118 | -1 | +5 | +4 |
| Escobar,Alcides | 14 | 29 | 13 | 18 | 4 | 7 | 22 | 1 | 3 | 4 | 12 | 101 | +14 | +22 | +36 |
| Escobar,Eduardo | 4 | 10 | 2 | 3 | 1 | 2 | 8 | 0 | 1 | 1 | 0 | 28 | +8 | -4 | +4 |
| Escobar,Yunel | 4 | 26 | 14 | 19 | 4 | 7 | 12 | 3 | 3 | 6 | 19 | 115 | -16 | -4 | -20 |
| Ethier,Andre | 6 | 35 | 11 | 22 | 3 | 6 | 12 | 1 | 1 | 2 | 9 | 120 | +1 | -2 | -1 |
| Fielder,Prince | 11 | 46 | 6 | 15 | 5 | 15 | 25 | 3 | 0 | 3 | 20 | 147 | +1 | -1 | 0 |
| Flaherty,Ryan | 5 | 13 | 4 | 6 | 1 | 2 | 2 | 1 | 1 | 2 | 2 | 56 | 0 | +2 | +2 |
| Florimon,Pedro | 6 | 12 | 12 | 15 | 3 | 4 | 12 | 0 | 1 | 1 | 7 | 79 | +15 | +3 | +18 |
| Flowers,Tyler | 5 | 12 | 2 | 6 | 0 | 2 | 10 | 0 | 2 | 2 | 9 | 50 | -2 | -2 | -4 |
| Forsythe,Logan | 4 | 15 | 4 | 4 | 0 | 1 | 4 | 2 | 1 | 3 | 5 | 42 | -6 | +4 | -2 |
| Fowler,Dexter | 21 | 31 | 10 | 21 | 2 | 3 | 16 | 5 | 2 | 7 | 5 | 51 | +2 | +1 | +3 |
| Francisco,Juan | 1 | 14 | 5 | 8 | 2 | 4 | 3 | 3 | 0 | 3 | 3 | 58 | -7 | -4 | -11 |
| Francoeur,Jeff | 1 | 9 | 5 | 8 | 0 | 4 | 2 | 0 | 0 | 0 | 7 | 52 | -4 | +3 | -1 |
| Frandsen,Kevin | 4 | 13 | 3 | 9 | 2 | 3 | 2 | 1 | 1 | 2 | 10 | 58 | -11 | +1 | -10 |
| Franklin,Nick | 5 | 10 | 3 | 9 | 0 | 4 | 12 | 3 | 0 | 3 | 2 | 68 | +4 | +4 | +8 |
| Frazier,Todd | 5 | 28 | 8 | 14 | 2 | 2 | 19 | 2 | 1 | 3 | 14 | 110 | +2 | -4 | -2 |
| Freeman,Freddie | 8 | 35 | 13 | 20 | 3 | 11 | 23 | 1 | 1 | 2 | 11 | 124 | +12 | +1 | +13 |

# 2013 Baserunning

| | 1st to 3rd | | 2nd to Home | | 1st to Home | | | | | | | | | | |
|---|---|---|---|---|---|---|---|---|---|---|---|---|---|---|---|
| Player | Moved | Chances | Moved | Chances | Moved | Chances | Bases Taken | Out Adv | Doubled Off | BR Outs | GDP | GDP Opps | BR Gain | SB Gain | Net Gain |
| Freese,David | 11 | 35 | 8 | 14 | 2 | 12 | 10 | 3 | 1 | 4 | 26 | 115 | -21 | -3 | -24 |
| Freiman,Nate | 1 | 10 | 2 | 3 | 0 | 1 | 3 | 2 | 0 | 2 | 8 | 47 | -9 | 0 | -9 |
| Fuld,Sam | 4 | 14 | 7 | 7 | 4 | 7 | 7 | 0 | 0 | 0 | 6 | 36 | +7 | +4 | +11 |
| Galvis,Freddy | 4 | 8 | 1 | 2 | 0 | 0 | 1 | 2 | 0 | 2 | 5 | 36 | -6 | +1 | -5 |
| Garcia,Avisail | 6 | 14 | 6 | 10 | 1 | 3 | 5 | 0 | 1 | 1 | 8 | 59 | +1 | -3 | -2 |
| Gardner,Brett | 8 | 23 | 10 | 17 | 3 | 7 | 19 | 2 | 3 | 5 | 8 | 89 | +3 | +8 | +11 |
| Gattis,Evan | 2 | 10 | 3 | 4 | 0 | 2 | 11 | 2 | 0 | 2 | 10 | 87 | +1 | 0 | +1 |
| Gennett,Scooter | 6 | 14 | 6 | 9 | 2 | 2 | 8 | 1 | 0 | 1 | 0 | 40 | +12 | 0 | +12 |
| Gentry,Craig | 4 | 15 | 5 | 8 | 5 | 5 | 5 | 1 | 2 | 3 | 5 | 58 | -2 | +18 | +16 |
| Getz,Chris | 8 | 15 | 4 | 10 | 0 | 1 | 8 | 2 | 1 | 3 | 9 | 40 | -6 | +10 | +4 |
| Giambi,Jason | 0 | 3 | 2 | 5 | 0 | 3 | 4 | 1 | 0 | 1 | 8 | 38 | -7 | -2 | -9 |
| Gillaspie,Conor | 11 | 39 | 7 | 8 | 2 | 5 | 14 | 1 | 1 | 2 | 7 | 83 | +10 | -2 | +8 |
| Gindl,Caleb | 2 | 7 | 4 | 5 | 0 | 2 | 1 | 0 | 0 | 0 | 0 | 25 | +3 | 0 | +3 |
| Goldschmidt,Paul | 9 | 41 | 17 | 23 | 3 | 6 | 24 | 0 | 0 | 0 | 25 | 164 | +13 | +1 | +14 |
| Gomes,Jonny | 5 | 16 | 11 | 13 | 1 | 7 | 8 | 1 | 1 | 2 | 6 | 83 | +4 | +1 | +5 |
| Gomes,Yan | 4 | 18 | 4 | 7 | 3 | 7 | 7 | 0 | 0 | 0 | 12 | 73 | 0 | +2 | +2 |
| Gomez,Carlos | 4 | 19 | 9 | 14 | 5 | 7 | 16 | 4 | 1 | 5 | 11 | 118 | 0 | +26 | +26 |
| Gonzalez,Adrian | 5 | 26 | 2 | 17 | 7 | 19 | 19 | 5 | 1 | 6 | 12 | 147 | -11 | +1 | -10 |
| Gonzalez,Carlos | 9 | 21 | 9 | 15 | 5 | 9 | 9 | 1 | 0 | 1 | 7 | 82 | +9 | +15 | +24 |
| Gonzalez,Marwin | 3 | 12 | 4 | 8 | 0 | 1 | 7 | 1 | 1 | 2 | 5 | 38 | -3 | +2 | -1 |
| Gordon,Alex | 8 | 32 | 19 | 26 | 5 | 10 | 25 | 2 | 2 | 4 | 4 | 95 | +18 | +5 | +23 |
| Gose,Anthony | 1 | 5 | 2 | 4 | 1 | 2 | 2 | 0 | 0 | 0 | 5 | 24 | -2 | -2 | -4 |
| Granderson,Curtis | 2 | 10 | 8 | 14 | 2 | 3 | 6 | 0 | 0 | 0 | 1 | 45 | +8 | +4 | +12 |
| Green,Grant | 0 | 2 | 2 | 3 | 2 | 3 | 8 | 0 | 1 | 1 | 3 | 32 | +5 | 0 | +5 |
| Gregorius,Didi | 8 | 24 | 9 | 11 | 4 | 6 | 14 | 1 | 0 | 1 | 4 | 70 | +17 | -4 | +13 |
| Grossman,Robbie | 5 | 17 | 4 | 7 | 0 | 1 | 14 | 0 | 0 | 0 | 2 | 36 | +14 | -8 | +6 |
| Guzman,Jesus | 2 | 11 | 4 | 8 | 6 | 8 | 5 | 2 | 0 | 3 | 4 | 61 | -2 | +3 | +1 |
| Gyorko,Jedd | 5 | 21 | 8 | 13 | 3 | 5 | 12 | 1 | 0 | 1 | 14 | 100 | +3 | -1 | +2 |
| Hafner,Travis | 3 | 10 | 4 | 7 | 0 | 2 | 4 | 1 | 0 | 1 | 5 | 63 | 0 | +2 | +2 |
| Hairston,Jerry | 2 | 10 | 8 | 10 | 0 | 2 | 1 | 1 | 1 | 2 | 7 | 43 | -8 | 0 | -8 |
| Hamilton,Billy | 0 | 0 | 5 | 5 | 0 | 0 | 4 | 0 | 1 | 1 | 0 | 1 | +3 | +11 | +14 |
| Hamilton,Josh | 4 | 29 | 11 | 14 | 8 | 11 | 16 | 1 | 2 | 4 | 16 | 136 | +1 | +4 | +5 |
| Hanigan,Ryan | 1 | 5 | 2 | 4 | 2 | 3 | 5 | 0 | 1 | 1 | 7 | 47 | -2 | -2 | -4 |
| Hannahan,Jack | 1 | 8 | 0 | 2 | 1 | 7 | 7 | 1 | 1 | 2 | 6 | 35 | -7 | 0 | -7 |
| Hardy,J.J. | 5 | 29 | 8 | 16 | 0 | 6 | 12 | 1 | 2 | 3 | 14 | 107 | -10 | 0 | -10 |
| Harper,Bryce | 11 | 24 | 9 | 10 | 5 | 9 | 15 | 5 | 2 | 7 | 4 | 101 | +6 | +3 | +9 |
| Headley,Chase | 9 | 33 | 9 | 18 | 2 | 9 | 13 | 3 | 2 | 6 | 9 | 106 | -10 | 0 | -10 |
| Hechavarria,Adeiny | 5 | 24 | 6 | 8 | 5 | 7 | 8 | 3 | 0 | 3 | 19 | 103 | -11 | -9 | -20 |
| Heisey,Chris | 2 | 6 | 4 | 5 | 3 | 4 | 5 | 0 | 0 | 0 | 4 | 43 | +7 | +3 | +10 |
| Helton,Todd | 3 | 23 | 5 | 14 | 1 | 6 | 4 | 2 | 3 | 5 | 4 | 85 | -17 | 0 | -17 |
| Herrera,Jonathan | 6 | 10 | 4 | 6 | 1 | 2 | 4 | 0 | 2 | 2 | 6 | 37 | -2 | -1 | -3 |
| Herrmann,Chris | 1 | 4 | 5 | 5 | 1 | 2 | 4 | 1 | 1 | 2 | 3 | 28 | -1 | -2 | -3 |
| Heyward,Jason | 7 | 22 | 11 | 20 | 8 | 8 | 13 | 4 | 0 | 4 | 7 | 73 | +3 | -6 | -3 |
| Hicks,Aaron | 2 | 9 | 8 | 12 | 2 | 3 | 13 | 1 | 0 | 1 | 0 | 60 | +16 | +3 | +19 |
| Hill,Aaron | 7 | 24 | 4 | 9 | 3 | 7 | 8 | 0 | 0 | 0 | 6 | 68 | +6 | -7 | -1 |
| Hoes,L.J. | 1 | 7 | 5 | 8 | 5 | 5 | 5 | 1 | 0 | 1 | 4 | 27 | +2 | +5 | +7 |
| Holliday,Matt | 13 | 39 | 24 | 33 | 7 | 13 | 15 | 4 | 0 | 4 | 31 | 143 | -9 | +4 | -5 |
| Hosmer,Eric | 11 | 41 | 21 | 29 | 6 | 9 | 11 | 3 | 1 | 6 | 15 | 130 | -7 | +3 | -4 |
| Howard,Ryan | 0 | 12 | 4 | 8 | 1 | 4 | 7 | 2 | 1 | 3 | 6 | 61 | -8 | 0 | -8 |
| Hundley,Nick | 1 | 20 | 9 | 16 | 0 | 0 | 10 | 2 | 1 | 3 | 7 | 68 | -6 | +1 | -5 |
| Hunter,Torii | 9 | 29 | 19 | 25 | 4 | 8 | 18 | 6 | 2 | 8 | 11 | 136 | -1 | -1 | -2 |
| Iannetta,Chris | 4 | 31 | 3 | 9 | 1 | 6 | 13 | 2 | 0 | 2 | 8 | 61 | -6 | -2 | -8 |
| Ibanez,Raul | 3 | 10 | 6 | 10 | 2 | 2 | 6 | 4 | 1 | 5 | 8 | 79 | -10 | 0 | -10 |
| Iglesias,Jose | 7 | 21 | 9 | 11 | 1 | 5 | 12 | 5 | 0 | 5 | 7 | 64 | -4 | +1 | -3 |
| Infante,Omar | 11 | 24 | 10 | 19 | 2 | 5 | 12 | 3 | 2 | 5 | 11 | 98 | -4 | +1 | -3 |
| Izturis,Maicer | 0 | 16 | 7 | 8 | 3 | 4 | 5 | 0 | 2 | 2 | 11 | 62 | -9 | -9 | -18 |
| Jackson,Austin | 14 | 53 | 18 | 22 | 5 | 6 | 23 | 2 | 2 | 4 | 12 | 100 | +12 | 0 | +12 |
| Jaso,John | 8 | 17 | 8 | 11 | 2 | 3 | 12 | 2 | 0 | 2 | 5 | 39 | +9 | 0 | +9 |
| Jay,Jon | 14 | 40 | 17 | 22 | 9 | 14 | 21 | 3 | 0 | 3 | 13 | 115 | +17 | 0 | +17 |
| Jennings,Desmond | 9 | 19 | 13 | 21 | 7 | 12 | 22 | 3 | 0 | 3 | 6 | 77 | +17 | +4 | +21 |
| Johnson,Chris | 5 | 20 | 8 | 14 | 1 | 6 | 8 | 2 | 1 | 3 | 20 | 102 | -16 | 0 | -16 |
| Johnson,Elliot | 3 | 7 | 1 | 4 | 0 | 1 | 16 | 3 | 1 | 4 | 4 | 42 | +2 | +18 | +20 |
| Johnson,Kelly | 2 | 16 | 4 | 6 | 2 | 3 | 8 | 1 | 0 | 1 | 4 | 73 | +5 | -1 | +4 |
| Jones,Adam | 9 | 30 | 8 | 14 | 8 | 13 | 22 | 2 | 2 | 4 | 15 | 146 | +9 | +8 | +17 |

# 2013 Baserunning

| | 1st to 3rd | | 2nd to Home | | 1st to Home | | | | | | | | | | |
|---|---|---|---|---|---|---|---|---|---|---|---|---|---|---|---|
| Player | Moved | Chances | Moved | Chances | Moved | Chances | Bases Taken | Out Adv | Doubled Off | BR Outs | GDP | GDP Opps | BR Gain | SB Gain | Net Gain |
| Jones,Garrett | 2 | 18 | 6 | 10 | 2 | 4 | 6 | 1 | 0 | 1 | 10 | 84 | -3 | +2 | -1 |
| Joyce,Matt | 13 | 28 | 11 | 13 | 2 | 7 | 15 | 2 | 0 | 2 | 8 | 96 | +16 | +1 | +17 |
| Kawasaki,Munenori | 7 | 20 | 4 | 4 | 1 | 3 | 7 | 0 | 1 | 1 | 5 | 53 | +5 | +5 | +10 |
| Kelly,Don | 3 | 17 | 5 | 7 | 1 | 4 | 6 | 0 | 1 | 1 | 4 | 59 | +2 | +2 | +4 |
| Kemp,Matt | 3 | 14 | 10 | 11 | 1 | 3 | 11 | 3 | 0 | 3 | 11 | 69 | -1 | +9 | +8 |
| Kendrick,Howie | 13 | 25 | 9 | 16 | 3 | 9 | 14 | 7 | 2 | 10 | 16 | 96 | -21 | 0 | -21 |
| Keppinger,Jeff | 5 | 25 | 12 | 23 | 1 | 7 | 11 | 5 | 1 | 6 | 14 | 95 | -19 | -2 | -21 |
| Kinsler,Ian | 16 | 34 | 25 | 32 | 0 | 1 | 20 | 5 | 0 | 5 | 5 | 87 | +17 | -7 | +10 |
| Kipnis,Jason | 8 | 38 | 13 | 20 | 4 | 9 | 18 | 1 | 5 | 6 | 10 | 130 | -2 | +16 | +14 |
| Konerko,Paul | 3 | 29 | 2 | 11 | 0 | 10 | 11 | 3 | 0 | 3 | 12 | 85 | -18 | 0 | -18 |
| Kozma,Pete | 5 | 15 | 9 | 13 | 0 | 3 | 6 | 1 | 1 | 2 | 6 | 79 | +1 | +1 | +2 |
| Kratz,Erik | 0 | 4 | 1 | 2 | 1 | 2 | 4 | 0 | 0 | 0 | 11 | 37 | -5 | 0 | -5 |
| Kubel,Jason | 3 | 15 | 5 | 5 | 1 | 3 | 7 | 0 | 0 | 0 | 6 | 62 | +7 | -2 | +5 |
| Lagares,Juan | 6 | 13 | 8 | 12 | 2 | 4 | 6 | 2 | 2 | 4 | 6 | 75 | -3 | 0 | -3 |
| Laird,Gerald | 1 | 10 | 2 | 6 | 0 | 2 | 7 | 0 | 0 | 0 | 4 | 27 | +1 | -1 | 0 |
| Lake,Junior | 9 | 14 | 3 | 3 | 0 | 1 | 11 | 2 | 1 | 3 | 2 | 47 | +9 | -4 | +5 |
| LaRoche,Adam | 6 | 33 | 8 | 11 | 2 | 8 | 15 | 0 | 2 | 2 | 13 | 118 | +2 | +2 | +4 |
| Lawrie,Brett | 8 | 18 | 3 | 6 | 6 | 8 | 10 | 0 | 1 | 1 | 8 | 72 | +9 | -1 | +8 |
| LeMahieu,DJ | 6 | 18 | 13 | 18 | 0 | 1 | 13 | 2 | 1 | 3 | 13 | 82 | 0 | +4 | +4 |
| Lind,Adam | 5 | 18 | 11 | 16 | 4 | 14 | 4 | 4 | 1 | 5 | 20 | 96 | -25 | +1 | -24 |
| Lobaton,Jose | 3 | 20 | 4 | 13 | 3 | 6 | 11 | 1 | 1 | 2 | 5 | 58 | -2 | -2 | -4 |
| Lombardozzi,Steve | 5 | 10 | 3 | 7 | 1 | 2 | 6 | 1 | 2 | 3 | 6 | 56 | -4 | -2 | -6 |
| Loney,James | 6 | 25 | 11 | 16 | 1 | 9 | 23 | 2 | 0 | 2 | 16 | 107 | +6 | +1 | +7 |
| Longoria,Evan | 4 | 37 | 10 | 22 | 4 | 11 | 12 | 2 | 1 | 3 | 16 | 128 | -14 | +1 | -13 |
| Lough,David | 8 | 15 | 8 | 11 | 2 | 5 | 12 | 0 | 1 | 1 | 3 | 53 | +15 | +1 | +16 |
| Lowrie,Jed | 6 | 32 | 8 | 17 | 3 | 9 | 19 | 2 | 0 | 2 | 17 | 151 | +2 | +1 | +3 |
| Lucas,Ed | 8 | 18 | 12 | 15 | 4 | 4 | 6 | 0 | 1 | 1 | 6 | 70 | +10 | -1 | +9 |
| Lucroy,Jonathan | 4 | 31 | 7 | 23 | 2 | 7 | 14 | 6 | 3 | 9 | 16 | 106 | -34 | +7 | -27 |
| Machado,Manny | 8 | 32 | 14 | 29 | 5 | 11 | 25 | 4 | 1 | 5 | 15 | 136 | +1 | -8 | -7 |
| Maldonado,Martin | 1 | 4 | 2 | 3 | 0 | 2 | 1 | 0 | 0 | 0 | 2 | 29 | 0 | 0 | 0 |
| Markakis,Nick | 12 | 47 | 9 | 13 | 7 | 18 | 17 | 2 | 0 | 2 | 17 | 125 | +2 | -3 | -1 |
| Marte,Starling | 8 | 23 | 11 | 18 | 8 | 11 | 19 | 0 | 1 | 1 | 6 | 70 | +19 | +11 | +30 |
| Martin,Leonys | 6 | 20 | 20 | 26 | 3 | 5 | 16 | 2 | 1 | 4 | 6 | 91 | +10 | +18 | +28 |
| Martin,Russell | 3 | 25 | 12 | 15 | 4 | 9 | 5 | 2 | 1 | 3 | 13 | 107 | -10 | -1 | -11 |
| Martinez,J.D. | 1 | 6 | 2 | 7 | 2 | 5 | 9 | 1 | 0 | 1 | 8 | 72 | +1 | +2 | +3 |
| Martinez,Victor | 3 | 43 | 13 | 26 | 1 | 8 | 18 | 3 | 0 | 3 | 23 | 130 | -19 | -4 | -23 |
| Mathis,Jeff | 3 | 8 | 1 | 3 | 0 | 2 | 1 | 3 | 0 | 3 | 5 | 49 | -10 | 0 | -10 |
| Mauer,Joe | 12 | 31 | 10 | 18 | 3 | 11 | 16 | 0 | 0 | 0 | 7 | 87 | +15 | -2 | +13 |
| Maxwell,Justin | 6 | 14 | 3 | 8 | 0 | 2 | 5 | 1 | 1 | 2 | 4 | 33 | -4 | +2 | -2 |
| Mayberry,John | 4 | 17 | 14 | 17 | 3 | 4 | 11 | 0 | 0 | 0 | 6 | 78 | +15 | -1 | +14 |
| McCann,Brian | 1 | 21 | 0 | 4 | 0 | 6 | 9 | 1 | 1 | 2 | 9 | 89 | -9 | -2 | -11 |
| McCutchen,Andrew | 16 | 33 | 20 | 24 | 8 | 9 | 16 | 2 | 2 | 4 | 13 | 133 | +17 | +7 | +24 |
| McLouth,Nate | 8 | 27 | 10 | 19 | 4 | 8 | 13 | 1 | 2 | 3 | 7 | 90 | +3 | +16 | +19 |
| Mercer,Jordy | 7 | 19 | 5 | 11 | 2 | 4 | 8 | 3 | 3 | 6 | 7 | 56 | -13 | -1 | -14 |
| Mesoraco,Devin | 3 | 16 | 3 | 6 | 2 | 3 | 5 | 2 | 1 | 3 | 9 | 53 | -11 | -4 | -15 |
| Middlebrooks,Will | 1 | 12 | 4 | 5 | 4 | 7 | 8 | 1 | 1 | 2 | 13 | 71 | -6 | +1 | -5 |
| Miller,Brad | 4 | 12 | 10 | 13 | 1 | 1 | 13 | 0 | 1 | 1 | 2 | 46 | +14 | -1 | +13 |
| Molina,Jose | 2 | 12 | 4 | 8 | 0 | 2 | 11 | 0 | 0 | 0 | 11 | 58 | +2 | 0 | +2 |
| Molina,Yadier | 10 | 28 | 9 | 23 | 2 | 9 | 13 | 2 | 0 | 2 | 14 | 117 | -3 | -1 | -4 |
| Montero,Miguel | 3 | 26 | 6 | 12 | 1 | 7 | 11 | 0 | 4 | 4 | 18 | 92 | -19 | 0 | -19 |
| Moore,Tyler | 1 | 5 | 1 | 2 | 2 | 4 | 1 | 2 | 0 | 2 | 1 | 36 | -3 | 0 | -3 |
| Morales,Kendrys | 14 | 34 | 4 | 8 | 0 | 6 | 12 | 6 | 0 | 6 | 21 | 126 | -16 | 0 | -16 |
| Moreland,Mitch | 5 | 25 | 5 | 10 | 1 | 5 | 9 | 3 | 1 | 4 | 11 | 80 | -12 | 0 | -12 |
| Morneau,Justin | 5 | 30 | 10 | 17 | 2 | 11 | 14 | 3 | 1 | 4 | 13 | 147 | -5 | 0 | -5 |
| Morrison,Logan | 3 | 17 | 8 | 11 | 1 | 1 | 7 | 1 | 2 | 3 | 10 | 62 | -7 | 0 | -7 |
| Morse,Michael | 2 | 15 | 4 | 11 | 1 | 8 | 3 | 1 | 0 | 1 | 12 | 60 | -14 | 0 | -14 |
| Moss,Brandon | 2 | 20 | 12 | 16 | 3 | 11 | 15 | 4 | 0 | 4 | 4 | 109 | +5 | 0 | +5 |
| Moustakas,Mike | 5 | 23 | 6 | 13 | 3 | 7 | 17 | 2 | 3 | 5 | 13 | 108 | -5 | -6 | -11 |
| Murphy,Daniel | 16 | 32 | 17 | 21 | 5 | 9 | 22 | 4 | 1 | 5 | 13 | 120 | +15 | +17 | +32 |
| Murphy,David | 5 | 25 | 9 | 15 | 4 | 8 | 7 | 3 | 0 | 3 | 11 | 86 | -8 | -7 | -15 |
| Myers,Wil | 6 | 22 | 10 | 15 | 5 | 8 | 14 | 4 | 1 | 5 | 10 | 83 | -2 | +1 | -1 |
| Napoli,Mike | 6 | 29 | 14 | 20 | 2 | 5 | 15 | 3 | 1 | 4 | 15 | 135 | -1 | -1 | -2 |
| Nava,Daniel | 5 | 37 | 16 | 24 | 7 | 14 | 29 | 4 | 0 | 4 | 10 | 111 | +12 | -4 | +8 |
| Navarro,Dioner | 0 | 15 | 0 | 6 | 1 | 2 | 7 | 2 | 0 | 2 | 4 | 42 | -8 | -2 | -10 |

# 2013 Baserunning

| | 1st to 3rd | | 2nd to Home | | 1st to Home | | | | | | | | | | |
|---|---|---|---|---|---|---|---|---|---|---|---|---|---|---|---|
| Player | Moved | Chances | Moved | Chances | Moved | Chances | Bases Taken | Out Adv | Doubled Off | BR Outs | GDP | GDP Opps | BR Gain | SB Gain | Net Gain |
| Nelson,Chris | 2 | 11 | 0 | 3 | 0 | 1 | 9 | 1 | 1 | 2 | 8 | 36 | -6 | 0 | -6 |
| Nieves,Wil | 3 | 14 | 1 | 4 | 1 | 2 | 3 | 1 | 1 | 2 | 7 | 39 | -9 | 0 | -9 |
| Nix,Jayson | 6 | 17 | 2 | 5 | 1 | 3 | 11 | 1 | 1 | 2 | 4 | 46 | +4 | +11 | +15 |
| Norris,Derek | 6 | 14 | 9 | 12 | 1 | 3 | 6 | 0 | 1 | 1 | 5 | 59 | +6 | +5 | +11 |
| Nunez,Eduardo | 3 | 18 | 7 | 7 | 0 | 0 | 14 | 1 | 0 | 1 | 3 | 61 | +13 | +4 | +17 |
| Ortiz,David | 2 | 22 | 10 | 22 | 0 | 9 | 13 | 4 | 0 | 4 | 21 | 138 | -20 | +4 | -16 |
| Overbay,Lyle | 1 | 21 | 8 | 14 | 0 | 3 | 7 | 0 | 1 | 2 | 16 | 97 | -14 | +2 | -12 |
| Ozuna,Marcell | 4 | 17 | 5 | 8 | 2 | 2 | 8 | 1 | 0 | 1 | 6 | 64 | +5 | +3 | +8 |
| Pacheco,Jordan | 1 | 9 | 1 | 7 | 4 | 7 | 2 | 1 | 0 | 1 | 4 | 45 | -5 | 0 | -5 |
| Pagan,Angel | 4 | 16 | 8 | 13 | 2 | 3 | 8 | 1 | 2 | 3 | 1 | 36 | 0 | +1 | +1 |
| Parmelee,Chris | 2 | 17 | 1 | 3 | 0 | 2 | 5 | 1 | 0 | 1 | 6 | 60 | -4 | -1 | -5 |
| Parra,Gerardo | 6 | 27 | 13 | 17 | 2 | 5 | 19 | 0 | 1 | 1 | 12 | 113 | +13 | -10 | +3 |
| Paul,Xavier | 1 | 7 | 3 | 8 | 0 | 2 | 8 | 1 | 0 | 1 | 6 | 47 | -1 | -2 | -3 |
| Pearce,Steve | 2 | 9 | 2 | 4 | 3 | 4 | 4 | 0 | 0 | 0 | 0 | 27 | +6 | +1 | +7 |
| Pedroia,Dustin | 16 | 42 | 11 | 20 | 7 | 20 | 20 | 4 | 3 | 8 | 24 | 168 | -14 | +7 | -7 |
| Pena,Brayan | 1 | 16 | 5 | 10 | 0 | 4 | 2 | 3 | 1 | 4 | 7 | 55 | -19 | -4 | -23 |
| Pena,Carlos | 5 | 17 | 3 | 6 | 2 | 5 | 17 | 3 | 0 | 3 | 5 | 50 | +6 | -5 | +1 |
| Pence,Hunter | 10 | 40 | 10 | 21 | 7 | 8 | 25 | 1 | 0 | 1 | 17 | 137 | +15 | +16 | +31 |
| Pennington,Cliff | 3 | 14 | 7 | 9 | 2 | 5 | 10 | 2 | 2 | 4 | 7 | 65 | -3 | +2 | -1 |
| Peralta,Jhonny | 10 | 33 | 7 | 18 | 2 | 4 | 15 | 1 | 2 | 3 | 9 | 91 | +1 | -3 | -2 |
| Perez,Salvador | 5 | 30 | 10 | 15 | 3 | 6 | 9 | 2 | 0 | 2 | 13 | 103 | -4 | 0 | -4 |
| Phillips,Brandon | 9 | 33 | 11 | 18 | 10 | 14 | 27 | 4 | 2 | 6 | 19 | 161 | +7 | -1 | +6 |
| Pierre,Juan | 8 | 14 | 7 | 9 | 1 | 2 | 6 | 0 | 1 | 1 | 4 | 33 | +6 | +11 | +17 |
| Pierzynski,A.J. | 3 | 23 | 5 | 13 | 1 | 5 | 10 | 3 | 1 | 5 | 14 | 100 | -18 | -1 | -19 |
| Plouffe,Trevor | 6 | 17 | 4 | 13 | 0 | 3 | 20 | 3 | 0 | 3 | 11 | 102 | +4 | 0 | +4 |
| Polanco,Placido | 8 | 25 | 3 | 10 | 3 | 4 | 8 | 1 | 3 | 4 | 15 | 72 | -15 | +2 | -13 |
| Pollock,A.J. | 7 | 26 | 9 | 17 | 4 | 7 | 17 | 2 | 1 | 3 | 5 | 62 | +6 | +6 | +12 |
| Posey,Buster | 7 | 31 | 5 | 21 | 6 | 13 | 11 | 3 | 0 | 3 | 15 | 121 | -13 | 0 | -13 |
| Prado,Martin | 7 | 34 | 13 | 22 | 4 | 11 | 17 | 4 | 3 | 7 | 29 | 140 | -26 | -7 | -33 |
| Presley,Alex | 4 | 14 | 3 | 4 | 3 | 4 | 6 | 1 | 0 | 1 | 3 | 30 | +4 | -7 | -3 |
| Profar,Jurickson | 3 | 18 | 6 | 11 | 0 | 4 | 9 | 1 | 0 | 1 | 1 | 53 | +4 | -6 | -2 |
| Puig,Yasiel | 12 | 26 | 7 | 10 | 4 | 4 | 8 | 7 | 3 | 11 | 6 | 66 | -19 | -5 | -24 |
| Pujols,Albert | 1 | 13 | 6 | 11 | 0 | 10 | 10 | 3 | 1 | 4 | 18 | 107 | -19 | -1 | -20 |
| Punto,Nick | 6 | 16 | 4 | 7 | 5 | 6 | 9 | 0 | 0 | 0 | 4 | 63 | +13 | -3 | +10 |
| Quentin,Carlos | 8 | 19 | 8 | 16 | 1 | 5 | 6 | 0 | 0 | 0 | 7 | 60 | +3 | 0 | +3 |
| Quintanilla,Omar | 1 | 11 | 6 | 9 | 2 | 4 | 9 | 1 | 0 | 1 | 10 | 63 | -1 | +2 | +1 |
| Raburn,Ryan | 2 | 10 | 4 | 11 | 0 | 1 | 8 | 1 | 0 | 1 | 4 | 49 | +1 | 0 | +1 |
| Ramirez,Alexei | 5 | 26 | 20 | 25 | 8 | 12 | 21 | 2 | 2 | 4 | 17 | 136 | +8 | +12 | +20 |
| Ramirez,Aramis | 5 | 21 | 1 | 10 | 1 | 6 | 3 | 3 | 0 | 3 | 8 | 70 | -16 | -2 | -18 |
| Ramirez,Hanley | 5 | 21 | 11 | 17 | 0 | 3 | 15 | 6 | 2 | 8 | 5 | 64 | -11 | +6 | -5 |
| Ramos,Wilson | 3 | 12 | 2 | 5 | 1 | 4 | 5 | 3 | 0 | 3 | 12 | 50 | -14 | -2 | -16 |
| Ransom,Cody | 1 | 2 | 2 | 2 | 2 | 2 | 6 | 1 | 0 | 1 | 4 | 27 | +3 | 0 | +3 |
| Rasmus,Colby | 12 | 23 | 6 | 9 | 3 | 5 | 8 | 0 | 4 | 4 | 4 | 80 | +5 | -2 | +3 |
| Reddick,Josh | 5 | 13 | 6 | 12 | 5 | 6 | 14 | 0 | 0 | 0 | 4 | 77 | +18 | +5 | +23 |
| Rendon,Anthony | 4 | 17 | 6 | 11 | 4 | 6 | 11 | 2 | 0 | 2 | 7 | 67 | +3 | -1 | +2 |
| Revere,Ben | 11 | 22 | 5 | 8 | 2 | 5 | 8 | 1 | 4 | 5 | 10 | 53 | -9 | +6 | -3 |
| Reyes,Jose | 7 | 22 | 12 | 14 | 3 | 5 | 15 | 5 | 1 | 6 | 6 | 59 | 0 | +3 | +3 |
| Reynolds,Mark | 10 | 26 | 5 | 9 | 0 | 6 | 9 | 2 | 0 | 2 | 9 | 92 | +1 | +1 | +2 |
| Rios,Alex | 7 | 23 | 16 | 21 | 1 | 5 | 31 | 4 | 1 | 5 | 17 | 115 | +10 | +28 | +38 |
| Rizzo,Anthony | 7 | 28 | 7 | 11 | 5 | 11 | 17 | 5 | 2 | 7 | 12 | 138 | -5 | -4 | -9 |
| Roberts,Brian | 2 | 13 | 4 | 6 | 2 | 3 | 7 | 1 | 1 | 2 | 4 | 53 | 0 | +1 | +1 |
| Roberts,Ryan | 3 | 10 | 1 | 4 | 0 | 1 | 6 | 0 | 0 | 0 | 3 | 29 | +4 | -4 | 0 |
| Robinson,Derrick | 5 | 13 | 2 | 4 | 1 | 2 | 6 | 2 | 1 | 3 | 0 | 36 | 0 | -6 | -6 |
| Robinson,Shane | 5 | 11 | 5 | 10 | 1 | 1 | 7 | 0 | 2 | 2 | 2 | 23 | +2 | +3 | +5 |
| Rodriguez,Alex | 1 | 6 | 1 | 5 | 1 | 6 | 1 | 1 | 1 | 2 | 5 | 27 | -12 | 0 | -12 |
| Rodriguez,Sean | 6 | 13 | 4 | 6 | 2 | 4 | 10 | 0 | 0 | 0 | 3 | 41 | +13 | -5 | +8 |
| Rollins,Jimmy | 14 | 26 | 10 | 20 | 2 | 4 | 23 | 4 | 1 | 5 | 12 | 101 | +8 | +10 | +18 |
| Rosales,Adam | 3 | 7 | 0 | 1 | 3 | 4 | 8 | 0 | 0 | 0 | 4 | 31 | +8 | 0 | +8 |
| Rosario,Wilin | 4 | 16 | 8 | 12 | 4 | 6 | 12 | 1 | 3 | 4 | 7 | 92 | +2 | +2 | +4 |
| Ross,Cody | 1 | 16 | 7 | 9 | 1 | 5 | 9 | 2 | 1 | 3 | 10 | 72 | -8 | -1 | -9 |
| Ruf,Darin | 1 | 8 | 5 | 7 | 1 | 6 | 11 | 3 | 1 | 4 | 4 | 48 | -4 | 0 | -4 |
| Ruggiano,Justin | 8 | 24 | 7 | 12 | 2 | 3 | 8 | 2 | 0 | 2 | 9 | 83 | +1 | -1 | 0 |
| Ruiz,Carlos | 7 | 15 | 7 | 8 | 1 | 4 | 9 | 1 | 1 | 3 | 11 | 64 | -2 | +1 | -1 |
| Rutledge,Josh | 10 | 21 | 9 | 11 | 0 | 4 | 13 | 1 | 1 | 2 | 2 | 53 | +13 | +12 | +25 |

# 2013 Baserunning

| | 1st to 3rd | | 2nd to Home | | 1st to Home | | | | | | | | | | |
|---|---|---|---|---|---|---|---|---|---|---|---|---|---|---|---|
| Player | Moved | Chances | Moved | Chances | Moved | Chances | Bases Taken | Out Adv | Doubled Off | BR Outs | GDP | GDP Opps | BR Gain | SB Gain | Net Gain |
| Ryan,Brendan | 4 | 12 | 3 | 8 | 3 | 4 | 10 | 0 | 1 | 1 | 11 | 63 | +1 | 0 | +1 |
| Saltalamacchia,Jarrod | 6 | 24 | 9 | 16 | 4 | 12 | 15 | 1 | 1 | 2 | 7 | 91 | +6 | +2 | +8 |
| Sanchez,Gaby | 4 | 25 | 1 | 2 | 2 | 7 | 7 | 1 | 0 | 1 | 3 | 70 | +2 | +1 | +3 |
| Sandoval,Pablo | 8 | 33 | 2 | 7 | 1 | 6 | 18 | 3 | 1 | 4 | 19 | 126 | -8 | 0 | -8 |
| Santana,Carlos | 12 | 36 | 9 | 17 | 0 | 6 | 20 | 5 | 0 | 5 | 7 | 115 | +4 | +1 | +5 |
| Santiago,Ramon | 5 | 20 | 4 | 10 | 0 | 0 | 5 | 0 | 0 | 0 | 3 | 43 | +3 | -2 | +1 |
| Satin,Josh | 2 | 11 | 8 | 12 | 0 | 3 | 5 | 2 | 2 | 4 | 4 | 42 | -10 | -1 | -11 |
| Saunders,Michael | 7 | 22 | 4 | 9 | 5 | 8 | 16 | 0 | 1 | 1 | 6 | 87 | +14 | +3 | +17 |
| Schafer,Jordan | 1 | 14 | 9 | 13 | 0 | 0 | 12 | 2 | 0 | 2 | 1 | 34 | +5 | +10 | +15 |
| Schafer,Logan | 6 | 14 | 5 | 8 | 1 | 3 | 10 | 2 | 0 | 2 | 5 | 56 | +5 | +5 | +10 |
| Schierholtz,Nate | 3 | 20 | 7 | 11 | 3 | 4 | 7 | 2 | 0 | 2 | 6 | 99 | +2 | 0 | +2 |
| Schumaker,Skip | 2 | 15 | 9 | 15 | 1 | 3 | 16 | 2 | 0 | 2 | 11 | 74 | +2 | -2 | 0 |
| Scott,Luke | 1 | 14 | 7 | 10 | 0 | 0 | 7 | 0 | 1 | 1 | 5 | 59 | +2 | -1 | +1 |
| Scutaro,Marco | 21 | 49 | 8 | 15 | 5 | 12 | 16 | 3 | 1 | 4 | 13 | 99 | +4 | +2 | +6 |
| Seager,Kyle | 14 | 32 | 14 | 20 | 3 | 8 | 25 | 5 | 0 | 6 | 8 | 137 | +16 | +3 | +19 |
| Segura,Jean | 13 | 32 | 12 | 17 | 5 | 7 | 22 | 6 | 3 | 9 | 17 | 143 | -3 | +18 | +15 |
| Shuck,J.B. | 15 | 27 | 14 | 19 | 4 | 4 | 13 | 4 | 1 | 5 | 10 | 79 | +6 | 0 | +6 |
| Simmons,Andrelton | 8 | 26 | 14 | 16 | 3 | 10 | 18 | 3 | 1 | 4 | 16 | 111 | +2 | -4 | -2 |
| Smith,Seth | 5 | 24 | 11 | 15 | 5 | 9 | 11 | 2 | 1 | 3 | 10 | 75 | -1 | 0 | -1 |
| Smoak,Justin | 5 | 32 | 4 | 10 | 1 | 6 | 5 | 3 | 0 | 3 | 11 | 98 | -15 | 0 | -15 |
| Snider,Travis | 3 | 14 | 3 | 8 | 1 | 2 | 9 | 1 | 0 | 1 | 1 | 40 | +5 | -4 | +1 |
| Sogard,Eric | 6 | 19 | 7 | 11 | 1 | 5 | 14 | 5 | 2 | 7 | 4 | 79 | -5 | 0 | -5 |
| Solano,Donovan | 2 | 28 | 9 | 14 | 2 | 4 | 7 | 2 | 1 | 3 | 11 | 74 | -12 | +1 | -11 |
| Soriano,Alfonso | 7 | 26 | 11 | 15 | 1 | 5 | 19 | 3 | 2 | 5 | 11 | 109 | +2 | 0 | +2 |
| Soto,Geovany | 1 | 7 | 3 | 9 | 2 | 5 | 3 | 1 | 0 | 1 | 2 | 22 | -4 | -3 | -7 |
| Span,Denard | 10 | 34 | 13 | 19 | 1 | 4 | 33 | 2 | 2 | 4 | 11 | 64 | +14 | +8 | +22 |
| Stanton,Giancarlo | 5 | 22 | 8 | 13 | 1 | 4 | 15 | 2 | 0 | 2 | 10 | 123 | +7 | +1 | +8 |
| Stewart,Chris | 2 | 17 | 3 | 10 | 1 | 3 | 6 | 2 | 0 | 2 | 8 | 66 | -9 | +4 | -5 |
| Stubbs,Drew | 13 | 30 | 13 | 19 | 2 | 2 | 14 | 1 | 3 | 4 | 3 | 78 | +12 | +13 | +25 |
| Suzuki,Ichiro | 9 | 34 | 10 | 20 | 4 | 7 | 19 | 0 | 1 | 2 | 6 | 100 | +13 | +12 | +25 |
| Suzuki,Kurt | 2 | 8 | 5 | 10 | 2 | 3 | 8 | 2 | 0 | 2 | 2 | 50 | +3 | +2 | +5 |
| Sweeney,Ryan | 2 | 9 | 2 | 6 | 0 | 2 | 2 | 3 | 1 | 4 | 3 | 33 | -14 | +1 | -13 |
| Swisher,Nick | 14 | 39 | 7 | 16 | 4 | 11 | 17 | 3 | 0 | 3 | 11 | 121 | +6 | +1 | +7 |
| Tabata,Jose | 8 | 21 | 7 | 10 | 1 | 5 | 9 | 3 | 1 | 4 | 6 | 46 | -4 | +1 | -3 |
| Tejada,Miguel | 4 | 11 | 4 | 5 | 1 | 2 | 2 | 0 | 1 | 1 | 6 | 35 | -2 | +1 | -1 |
| Tejada,Ruben | 4 | 10 | 2 | 5 | 2 | 2 | 8 | 1 | 0 | 1 | 3 | 35 | +6 | 0 | +6 |
| Thomas,Clete | 4 | 16 | 4 | 8 | 1 | 3 | 7 | 0 | 0 | 0 | 4 | 52 | +5 | -5 | 0 |
| Torrealba,Yorvit | 1 | 11 | 4 | 6 | 0 | 0 | 6 | 1 | 0 | 1 | 6 | 37 | -2 | 0 | -2 |
| Torres,Andres | 4 | 15 | 6 | 8 | 2 | 4 | 7 | 1 | 0 | 1 | 7 | 49 | +2 | -2 | 0 |
| Trout,Mike | 27 | 44 | 15 | 20 | 5 | 14 | 26 | 1 | 3 | 4 | 8 | 127 | +30 | +19 | +49 |
| Trumbo,Mark | 7 | 36 | 13 | 19 | 0 | 6 | 16 | 1 | 1 | 2 | 18 | 125 | -2 | +1 | -1 |
| Tuiasosopo,Matt | 4 | 14 | 2 | 5 | 2 | 4 | 4 | 2 | 0 | 2 | 3 | 39 | -3 | 0 | -3 |
| Tulowitzki,Troy | 9 | 36 | 8 | 13 | 4 | 10 | 15 | 3 | 1 | 4 | 9 | 93 | -1 | +1 | 0 |
| Turner,Justin | 5 | 12 | 3 | 3 | 0 | 1 | 7 | 2 | 0 | 2 | 6 | 40 | 0 | -2 | -2 |
| Uggla,Dan | 9 | 30 | 8 | 13 | 1 | 5 | 14 | 6 | 1 | 7 | 7 | 92 | -8 | +2 | -6 |
| Upton,B.J.` | 2 | 14 | 7 | 11 | 0 | 2 | 8 | 0 | 3 | 3 | 7 | 67 | -6 | +2 | -4 |
| Upton,Justin | 15 | 45 | 15 | 17 | 9 | 13 | 12 | 3 | 3 | 6 | 12 | 123 | +2 | +6 | +8 |
| Uribe,Juan | 2 | 18 | 6 | 11 | 4 | 5 | 12 | 0 | 1 | 2 | 12 | 103 | +1 | +5 | +6 |
| Utley,Chase | 10 | 31 | 12 | 18 | 4 | 6 | 19 | 2 | 1 | 3 | 12 | 100 | +9 | +2 | +11 |
| Valbuena,Luis | 5 | 18 | 9 | 11 | 2 | 2 | 6 | 1 | 1 | 2 | 4 | 60 | +4 | -7 | -3 |
| Valencia,Danny | 2 | 8 | 1 | 5 | 2 | 3 | 3 | 0 | 0 | 0 | 5 | 30 | -1 | -4 | -5 |
| Van Slyke,Scott | 1 | 2 | 0 | 3 | 0 | 2 | 2 | 1 | 0 | 1 | 7 | 34 | -8 | -1 | -9 |
| Venable,Will | 4 | 20 | 12 | 16 | 1 | 2 | 22 | 1 | 0 | 1 | 6 | 75 | +19 | +10 | +29 |
| Viciedo,Dayan | 7 | 17 | 7 | 14 | 0 | 3 | 13 | 1 | 0 | 1 | 11 | 84 | +5 | 0 | +5 |
| Victorino,Shane | 10 | 37 | 17 | 25 | 2 | 8 | 17 | 1 | 2 | 4 | 5 | 101 | +8 | +15 | +23 |
| Villar,Jonathan | 6 | 10 | 5 | 8 | 2 | 2 | 4 | 3 | 0 | 3 | 5 | 31 | -4 | +2 | -2 |
| Votto,Joey | 16 | 56 | 15 | 27 | 10 | 18 | 28 | 6 | 2 | 8 | 15 | 149 | +1 | 0 | +1 |
| Walker,Neil | 4 | 17 | 10 | 18 | 3 | 7 | 17 | 3 | 0 | 3 | 14 | 94 | -1 | -3 | -4 |
| Wallace,Brett | 3 | 10 | 3 | 8 | 1 | 2 | 3 | 0 | 1 | 1 | 5 | 57 | -2 | -1 | -3 |
| Weeks,Rickie | 4 | 20 | 3 | 4 | 1 | 3 | 6 | 1 | 2 | 3 | 13 | 67 | -13 | +1 | -12 |
| Wells,Vernon | 3 | 16 | 8 | 11 | 2 | 6 | 13 | 1 | 1 | 2 | 9 | 83 | +4 | +1 | +5 |
| Werth,Jayson | 8 | 31 | 10 | 18 | 4 | 7 | 7 | 4 | 0 | 4 | 9 | 103 | -7 | +8 | +1 |
| Wieters,Matt | 3 | 22 | 11 | 20 | 0 | 5 | 10 | 2 | 0 | 2 | 7 | 106 | -1 | +2 | +1 |
| Willingham,Josh | 7 | 35 | 8 | 14 | 4 | 9 | 9 | 3 | 1 | 4 | 8 | 109 | -5 | +1 | -4 |

# 2013 Baserunning

| | 1st to 3rd | | 2nd to Home | | 1st to Home | | | | | | | | | | |
|---|---|---|---|---|---|---|---|---|---|---|---|---|---|---|---|
| Player | Moved | Chances | Moved | Chances | Moved | Chances | Bases Taken | Out Adv | Doubled Off | BR Outs | GDP | GDP Opps | BR Gain | SB Gain | Net Gain |
| Wright,David | 10 | 28 | 5 | 7 | 2 | 4 | 11 | 2 | 1 | 3 | 11 | 103 | +2 | +11 | +13 |
| Yelich,Christian | 6 | 10 | 6 | 9 | 2 | 4 | 6 | 1 | 2 | 3 | 4 | 42 | -1 | +10 | +9 |
| Young,Chris | 2 | 10 | 6 | 8 | 4 | 6 | 10 | 2 | 0 | 2 | 7 | 83 | +6 | +4 | +10 |
| Young,Delmon | 4 | 15 | 5 | 7 | 1 | 4 | 4 | 3 | 0 | 3 | 8 | 59 | -9 | 0 | -9 |
| Young,Eric | 9 | 26 | 16 | 20 | 4 | 7 | 14 | 1 | 2 | 3 | 6 | 65 | +9 | +24 | +33 |
| Young,Michael | 9 | 33 | 8 | 14 | 1 | 5 | 17 | 6 | 1 | 7 | 22 | 109 | -20 | +1 | -19 |
| Zimmerman,Ryan | 11 | 30 | 10 | 18 | 5 | 10 | 23 | 4 | 1 | 5 | 16 | 121 | +4 | +6 | +10 |
| Zobrist,Ben | 13 | 35 | 12 | 26 | 5 | 11 | 28 | 0 | 0 | 0 | 18 | 138 | +20 | +5 | +25 |
| Zunino,Mike | 6 | 15 | 2 | 4 | 4 | 6 | 7 | 0 | 0 | 0 | 5 | 44 | +8 | +1 | +9 |

# Career Baserunning

Players with 1000 Career Games
(Data goes back to 2002)

| | 1st to 3rd | | 2nd to Home | | 1st to Home | | | | | | | | | | |
|---|---|---|---|---|---|---|---|---|---|---|---|---|---|---|---|
| Player | Moved | Chances | Moved | Chances | Moved | Chances | Bases Taken | Out Adv | Doubled Off | BR Outs | GDP | GDP Opps | BR Gain | SB Gain | Net Gain |
| Barmes,Clint | 54 | 150 | 63 | 92 | 26 | 40 | 91 | 7 | 9 | 16 | 52 | 627 | +66 | -14 | +52 |
| Bautista,Jose | 71 | 213 | 77 | 117 | 37 | 67 | 96 | 20 | 17 | 37 | 94 | 810 | -22 | +4 | -18 |
| Bay,Jason | 85 | 290 | 90 | 178 | 43 | 103 | 136 | 14 | 9 | 23 | 84 | 1063 | +49 | +61 | +110 |
| Beltran,Carlos | 133 | 375 | 144 | 223 | 56 | 104 | 202 | 16 | 14 | 31 | 114 | 1369 | +148 | +156 | +304 |
| Beltre,Adrian | 111 | 347 | 121 | 205 | 41 | 99 | 182 | 35 | 3 | 38 | 186 | 1494 | +9 | +24 | +33 |
| Berkman,Lance | 93 | 432 | 112 | 212 | 49 | 106 | 170 | 41 | 9 | 50 | 131 | 1325 | -53 | -4 | -57 |
| Betancourt,Yuniesky | 71 | 208 | 74 | 141 | 18 | 33 | 101 | 25 | 17 | 43 | 110 | 807 | -68 | -30 | -98 |
| Bourn,Michael | 65 | 202 | 100 | 149 | 40 | 52 | 138 | 13 | 9 | 22 | 21 | 477 | +113 | +147 | +260 |
| Buck,John | 31 | 150 | 61 | 115 | 13 | 31 | 69 | 11 | 7 | 19 | 85 | 681 | -39 | -18 | -57 |
| Butler,Billy | 29 | 220 | 49 | 125 | 14 | 81 | 104 | 23 | 4 | 27 | 147 | 802 | -145 | -1 | -146 |
| Byrd,Marlon | 64 | 251 | 106 | 164 | 43 | 82 | 138 | 20 | 6 | 27 | 98 | 907 | +34 | -5 | +29 |
| Cabrera,Melky | 71 | 222 | 75 | 122 | 33 | 65 | 130 | 22 | 7 | 30 | 85 | 786 | +28 | +22 | +50 |
| Cabrera,Miguel | 106 | 462 | 140 | 254 | 42 | 117 | 189 | 30 | 11 | 42 | 213 | 1458 | -84 | 0 | -84 |
| Cano,Robinson | 80 | 280 | 136 | 209 | 33 | 70 | 148 | 30 | 19 | 49 | 171 | 1248 | -56 | -18 | -74 |
| Carroll,Jamey | 87 | 275 | 118 | 175 | 37 | 82 | 135 | 16 | 9 | 26 | 61 | 656 | +61 | +2 | +63 |
| Chavez,Endy | 34 | 123 | 69 | 103 | 21 | 40 | 75 | 12 | 4 | 16 | 56 | 517 | +18 | +25 | +43 |
| Chavez,Eric | 69 | 221 | 77 | 117 | 33 | 67 | 86 | 13 | 7 | 21 | 106 | 999 | +17 | +14 | +31 |
| Crawford,Carl | 68 | 267 | 157 | 222 | 56 | 104 | 241 | 34 | 19 | 56 | 68 | 1182 | +119 | +247 | +366 |
| Crisp,Coco | 84 | 247 | 129 | 187 | 51 | 85 | 171 | 17 | 9 | 27 | 79 | 853 | +115 | +140 | +255 |
| Cuddyer,Michael | 125 | 299 | 105 | 170 | 46 | 82 | 151 | 43 | 12 | 57 | 164 | 1097 | -46 | +25 | -21 |
| DeJesus,David | 132 | 333 | 108 | 173 | 42 | 76 | 171 | 25 | 13 | 38 | 91 | 799 | +70 | -51 | +19 |
| DeRosa,Mark | 51 | 219 | 80 | 128 | 25 | 60 | 107 | 20 | 11 | 31 | 93 | 755 | -30 | -13 | -43 |
| Dunn,Adam | 66 | 369 | 104 | 204 | 38 | 113 | 160 | 20 | 6 | 27 | 91 | 1452 | +35 | +14 | +49 |
| Ellis,Mark | 92 | 298 | 122 | 210 | 50 | 91 | 164 | 18 | 6 | 25 | 89 | 1024 | +92 | +22 | +114 |
| Encarnacion,Edwin | 61 | 204 | 67 | 108 | 27 | 67 | 94 | 19 | 7 | 26 | 92 | 821 | -10 | +27 | +17 |
| Ethier,Andre | 55 | 283 | 111 | 157 | 32 | 66 | 98 | 16 | 8 | 25 | 87 | 954 | +6 | -21 | -15 |
| Fielder,Prince | 41 | 338 | 57 | 143 | 29 | 95 | 135 | 25 | 9 | 34 | 121 | 1061 | -104 | -4 | -108 |
| Francoeur,Jeff | 78 | 223 | 85 | 138 | 29 | 78 | 119 | 27 | 14 | 43 | 112 | 980 | -31 | -18 | -49 |
| Furcal,Rafael | 136 | 359 | 156 | 241 | 36 | 73 | 204 | 21 | 15 | 36 | 76 | 756 | +113 | +104 | +217 |
| Giambi,Jason | 54 | 263 | 59 | 105 | 14 | 76 | 84 | 25 | 6 | 32 | 80 | 1054 | -51 | -1 | -52 |
| Gonzalez,Adrian | 48 | 295 | 70 | 178 | 40 | 109 | 130 | 29 | 12 | 42 | 145 | 1172 | -128 | +1 | -127 |
| Gonzalez,Alex | 47 | 149 | 73 | 121 | 22 | 43 | 82 | 25 | 4 | 29 | 101 | 889 | -25 | -10 | -35 |
| Granderson,Curtis | 74 | 244 | 98 | 168 | 47 | 78 | 137 | 10 | 15 | 25 | 39 | 878 | +106 | +54 | +160 |
| Hafner,Travis | 57 | 270 | 73 | 129 | 35 | 85 | 99 | 28 | 7 | 36 | 86 | 950 | -47 | -3 | -50 |
| Hairston,Jerry | 66 | 194 | 74 | 125 | 24 | 50 | 98 | 18 | 11 | 29 | 60 | 629 | +7 | +5 | +12 |
| Hardy,J.J. | 63 | 209 | 64 | 111 | 20 | 62 | 100 | 14 | 9 | 24 | 112 | 844 | -24 | -8 | -32 |
| Helton,Todd | 91 | 421 | 141 | 224 | 52 | 153 | 180 | 42 | 12 | 54 | 130 | 1319 | -52 | -7 | -59 |
| Hernandez,Ramon | 45 | 223 | 59 | 136 | 16 | 67 | 75 | 34 | 7 | 43 | 122 | 885 | -161 | -2 | -163 |
| Hill,Aaron | 67 | 239 | 82 | 131 | 28 | 58 | 124 | 15 | 7 | 22 | 101 | 950 | +37 | +3 | +40 |
| Hinske,Eric | 61 | 232 | 93 | 135 | 25 | 52 | 106 | 13 | 11 | 24 | 91 | 920 | +28 | +19 | +47 |
| Holliday,Matt | 124 | 364 | 160 | 233 | 51 | 91 | 168 | 31 | 14 | 45 | 168 | 1285 | +16 | +31 | +47 |
| Howard,Ryan | 32 | 244 | 68 | 148 | 29 | 96 | 99 | 26 | 9 | 35 | 88 | 1016 | -82 | +4 | -78 |
| Hunter,Torii | 148 | 322 | 141 | 217 | 46 | 90 | 203 | 52 | 17 | 70 | 195 | 1383 | -20 | +16 | -4 |
| Ibanez,Raul | 91 | 357 | 124 | 230 | 55 | 94 | 160 | 27 | 12 | 40 | 149 | 1380 | -11 | -8 | -19 |
| Infante,Omar | 74 | 207 | 84 | 143 | 26 | 54 | 99 | 18 | 16 | 35 | 74 | 821 | -2 | +13 | +11 |
| Inge,Brandon | 57 | 243 | 72 | 136 | 25 | 49 | 116 | 12 | 15 | 29 | 100 | 1009 | -9 | -28 | -37 |
| Izturis,Cesar | 60 | 234 | 99 | 139 | 20 | 50 | 80 | 22 | 8 | 30 | 88 | 735 | -37 | -2 | -39 |
| Jeter,Derek | 144 | 466 | 151 | 240 | 56 | 128 | 231 | 28 | 11 | 40 | 193 | 1317 | +27 | +103 | +130 |
| Johnson,Kelly | 52 | 200 | 60 | 116 | 31 | 55 | 121 | 12 | 7 | 19 | 53 | 713 | +57 | +13 | +70 |
| Johnson,Reed | 57 | 211 | 83 | 127 | 36 | 68 | 118 | 20 | 5 | 26 | 73 | 592 | +18 | -15 | +3 |
| Kearns,Austin | 53 | 203 | 74 | 117 | 36 | 70 | 102 | 12 | 9 | 22 | 115 | 881 | -5 | -9 | -14 |
| Kinsler,Ian | 103 | 229 | 123 | 175 | 35 | 68 | 168 | 14 | 14 | 28 | 94 | 786 | +108 | +88 | +196 |
| Konerko,Paul | 61 | 411 | 80 | 192 | 15 | 102 | 131 | 26 | 10 | 36 | 206 | 1340 | -201 | 0 | -201 |
| Kotsay,Mark | 78 | 250 | 78 | 138 | 22 | 59 | 126 | 32 | 6 | 38 | 95 | 931 | -13 | -32 | -45 |
| LaRoche,Adam | 47 | 250 | 68 | 135 | 20 | 66 | 111 | 21 | 9 | 30 | 105 | 1030 | -47 | -12 | -59 |
| Loney,James | 57 | 203 | 65 | 105 | 25 | 53 | 107 | 16 | 8 | 25 | 114 | 780 | -18 | -2 | -20 |
| Markakis,Nick | 81 | 319 | 115 | 173 | 36 | 85 | 130 | 20 | 4 | 25 | 121 | 987 | +9 | +11 | +20 |
| Martin,Russell | 58 | 224 | 91 | 144 | 29 | 52 | 107 | 21 | 12 | 33 | 119 | 801 | -45 | +17 | -28 |
| Martinez,Victor | 53 | 320 | 83 | 171 | 22 | 97 | 144 | 27 | 6 | 33 | 176 | 1182 | -115 | -6 | -121 |
| Mauer,Joe | 97 | 302 | 116 | 171 | 40 | 95 | 168 | 12 | 8 | 22 | 137 | 1032 | +64 | +11 | +75 |
| McCann,Brian | 38 | 208 | 31 | 102 | 11 | 73 | 65 | 25 | 8 | 34 | 116 | 943 | -148 | +7 | -141 |

# Career Baserunning

Players with 1000 Career Games
(Data goes back to 2002)

| | 1st to 3rd | | 2nd to Home | | 1st to Home | | | | | | | | | | |
|---|---|---|---|---|---|---|---|---|---|---|---|---|---|---|---|
| Player | Moved | Chances | Moved | Chances | Moved | Chances | Bases Taken | Out Adv | Doubled Off | BR Outs | GDP | GDP Opps | BR Gain | SB Gain | Net Gain |
| McDonald,John | 33 | 113 | 47 | 75 | 9 | 25 | 60 | 18 | 3 | 21 | 45 | 435 | -15 | -1 | -16 |
| Molina,Yadier | 48 | 237 | 50 | 128 | 17 | 52 | 90 | 23 | 7 | 31 | 159 | 897 | -144 | -12 | -156 |
| Morneau,Justin | 45 | 245 | 80 | 148 | 21 | 78 | 130 | 32 | 5 | 37 | 125 | 1158 | -58 | -9 | -67 |
| Olivo,Miguel | 45 | 142 | 52 | 88 | 16 | 28 | 94 | 24 | 7 | 32 | 76 | 785 | -5 | -15 | -20 |
| Ortiz,David | 56 | 361 | 84 | 210 | 25 | 116 | 156 | 40 | 14 | 55 | 150 | 1586 | -144 | -4 | -148 |
| Overbay,Lyle | 58 | 282 | 68 | 141 | 30 | 84 | 117 | 19 | 9 | 29 | 141 | 1021 | -79 | +3 | -76 |
| Pedroia,Dustin | 60 | 222 | 94 | 145 | 37 | 100 | 129 | 26 | 11 | 39 | 97 | 841 | -27 | +57 | +30 |
| Pena,Carlos | 104 | 306 | 67 | 129 | 31 | 88 | 160 | 27 | 9 | 36 | 69 | 1097 | +70 | -16 | +54 |
| Pence,Hunter | 67 | 230 | 84 | 126 | 44 | 59 | 128 | 15 | 9 | 24 | 107 | 854 | +42 | +5 | +47 |
| Peralta,Jhonny | 52 | 275 | 91 | 176 | 27 | 83 | 136 | 31 | 10 | 41 | 151 | 1144 | -97 | -29 | -126 |
| Phillips,Brandon | 103 | 249 | 105 | 155 | 39 | 61 | 183 | 36 | 12 | 50 | 159 | 1067 | +14 | +35 | +49 |
| Pierre,Juan | 168 | 424 | 178 | 264 | 49 | 85 | 245 | 28 | 23 | 52 | 84 | 978 | +142 | +201 | +343 |
| Pierzynski,A.J. | 56 | 295 | 81 | 180 | 18 | 65 | 141 | 43 | 5 | 50 | 188 | 1266 | -159 | -14 | -173 |
| Polanco,Placido | 114 | 403 | 149 | 234 | 48 | 112 | 194 | 23 | 12 | 37 | 163 | 1211 | +17 | +22 | +39 |
| Pujols,Albert | 150 | 431 | 173 | 236 | 53 | 126 | 215 | 55 | 14 | 71 | 248 | 1812 | -45 | +24 | -21 |
| Punto,Nick | 73 | 220 | 79 | 127 | 25 | 46 | 121 | 11 | 10 | 21 | 58 | 670 | +69 | +31 | +100 |
| Ramirez,Aramis | 65 | 316 | 83 | 191 | 28 | 107 | 132 | 36 | 10 | 46 | 171 | 1341 | -146 | -6 | -152 |
| Ramirez,Hanley | 76 | 221 | 116 | 178 | 37 | 63 | 141 | 37 | 11 | 48 | 73 | 809 | +13 | +91 | +104 |
| Reyes,Jose | 100 | 281 | 146 | 212 | 37 | 57 | 216 | 43 | 16 | 59 | 61 | 769 | +75 | +207 | +282 |
| Rios,Alex | 73 | 243 | 134 | 196 | 36 | 70 | 160 | 18 | 14 | 32 | 164 | 1222 | +23 | +91 | +114 |
| Roberts,Brian | 90 | 295 | 127 | 205 | 34 | 81 | 167 | 24 | 19 | 43 | 70 | 841 | +33 | +134 | +167 |
| Rodriguez,Alex | 114 | 352 | 147 | 223 | 47 | 117 | 182 | 33 | 15 | 48 | 160 | 1521 | +21 | +97 | +118 |
| Rollins,Jimmy | 140 | 406 | 188 | 274 | 47 | 93 | 261 | 32 | 9 | 41 | 111 | 1084 | +153 | +214 | +367 |
| Scutaro,Marco | 97 | 315 | 106 | 173 | 45 | 109 | 162 | 23 | 12 | 35 | 116 | 968 | +18 | +11 | +29 |
| Soriano,Alfonso | 108 | 278 | 139 | 213 | 28 | 67 | 181 | 26 | 16 | 42 | 113 | 1240 | +76 | +105 | +181 |
| Suzuki,Ichiro | 147 | 547 | 198 | 317 | 61 | 126 | 289 | 29 | 15 | 45 | 72 | 1249 | +164 | +232 | +396 |
| Swisher,Nick | 101 | 309 | 80 | 147 | 38 | 87 | 139 | 23 | 16 | 39 | 115 | 1161 | +5 | -17 | -12 |
| Teixeira,Mark | 73 | 325 | 115 | 188 | 41 | 105 | 157 | 36 | 8 | 44 | 131 | 1476 | -8 | +9 | +1 |
| Tejada,Miguel | 122 | 380 | 113 | 202 | 54 | 114 | 195 | 41 | 6 | 49 | 226 | 1433 | -53 | +13 | -40 |
| Uggla,Dan | 90 | 274 | 92 | 135 | 53 | 94 | 129 | 30 | 9 | 39 | 69 | 916 | +48 | -14 | +34 |
| Upton,B.J. | 80 | 195 | 88 | 134 | 24 | 48 | 146 | 22 | 10 | 33 | 85 | 832 | +61 | +96 | +157 |
| Uribe,Juan | 75 | 220 | 83 | 131 | 18 | 48 | 121 | 12 | 12 | 26 | 115 | 1017 | +24 | -33 | -9 |
| Utley,Chase | 129 | 274 | 123 | 166 | 51 | 82 | 159 | 20 | 11 | 31 | 72 | 1133 | +171 | +95 | +266 |
| Victorino,Shane | 92 | 248 | 103 | 150 | 40 | 72 | 156 | 8 | 14 | 25 | 54 | 794 | +126 | +130 | +256 |
| Weeks,Rickie | 76 | 224 | 108 | 147 | 33 | 63 | 135 | 29 | 22 | 51 | 59 | 653 | +4 | +67 | +71 |
| Wells,Vernon | 108 | 293 | 125 | 182 | 54 | 94 | 171 | 29 | 11 | 41 | 162 | 1404 | +52 | +31 | +83 |
| Werth,Jayson | 71 | 241 | 81 | 125 | 28 | 59 | 107 | 16 | 4 | 21 | 61 | 803 | +53 | +80 | +133 |
| Wigginton,Ty | 41 | 221 | 77 | 140 | 26 | 60 | 91 | 29 | 10 | 39 | 128 | 954 | -108 | -4 | -112 |
| Willingham,Josh | 77 | 248 | 62 | 115 | 27 | 70 | 76 | 16 | 11 | 27 | 81 | 902 | -18 | +15 | -3 |
| Wright,David | 99 | 307 | 110 | 164 | 50 | 109 | 161 | 28 | 14 | 45 | 126 | 1236 | +21 | +69 | +90 |
| Youkilis,Kevin | 73 | 262 | 87 | 149 | 41 | 96 | 140 | 22 | 10 | 32 | 74 | 931 | +37 | -2 | +35 |
| Young,Michael | 103 | 438 | 162 | 259 | 72 | 135 | 199 | 23 | 12 | 35 | 228 | 1458 | -30 | +29 | -1 |
| Zimmerman,Ryan | 73 | 235 | 97 | 148 | 42 | 85 | 130 | 17 | 6 | 23 | 142 | 1063 | +23 | +8 | +31 |

## 2002-2013 MLB Averages

| 1st to 3rd | 2nd to Home | 1st to Home |
|---|---|---|
| 28% | 59% | 44% |

# 2013 Team Baserunning

| | 1st to 3rd | | 2nd to Home | | 1st to Home | | | | | | | | | | |
|---|---|---|---|---|---|---|---|---|---|---|---|---|---|---|---|
| Team | Moved | Chances | Moved | Chances | Moved | Chances | Bases Taken | Out Adv | Doubled Off | BR Outs | GDP | GDP Opps | BR Gain | SB Gain | Net Gain |
| Kansas City Royals | 93 | 316 | 130 | 203 | 34 | 82 | 165 | 17 | 16 | 35 | 131 | 1092 | +20 | +89 | +109 |
| San Diego Padres | 78 | 299 | 106 | 180 | 25 | 60 | 169 | 19 | 11 | 32 | 100 | 1035 | +40 | +50 | +90 |
| Boston Red Sox | 92 | 340 | 143 | 234 | 37 | 112 | 185 | 34 | 11 | 47 | 137 | 1282 | -9 | +85 | +76 |
| Cleveland Indians | 95 | 301 | 109 | 184 | 29 | 84 | 177 | 25 | 17 | 43 | 106 | 1133 | +27 | +45 | +72 |
| New York Mets | 83 | 261 | 115 | 165 | 32 | 64 | 121 | 23 | 10 | 33 | 106 | 1081 | +26 | +44 | +70 |
| Oakland Athletics | 84 | 288 | 113 | 189 | 47 | 96 | 170 | 30 | 7 | 38 | 108 | 1189 | +47 | +18 | +65 |
| Colorado Rockies | 112 | 329 | 114 | 193 | 39 | 77 | 162 | 27 | 19 | 46 | 110 | 1070 | +15 | +48 | +63 |
| Tampa Bay Rays | 81 | 303 | 118 | 199 | 40 | 91 | 196 | 19 | 7 | 26 | 139 | 1156 | +60 | -3 | +57 |
| Texas Rangers | 98 | 322 | 120 | 189 | 27 | 68 | 178 | 36 | 11 | 50 | 125 | 1082 | -7 | +57 | +50 |
| New York Yankees | 65 | 275 | 94 | 172 | 20 | 64 | 162 | 21 | 14 | 37 | 121 | 1096 | -17 | +53 | +36 |
| Baltimore Orioles | 74 | 295 | 93 | 169 | 45 | 92 | 145 | 18 | 13 | 33 | 104 | 1105 | +13 | +21 | +34 |
| Minnesota Twins | 75 | 271 | 99 | 171 | 33 | 77 | 169 | 26 | 8 | 34 | 104 | 1145 | +44 | -14 | +30 |
| Washington Nationals | 82 | 270 | 87 | 143 | 33 | 71 | 157 | 29 | 15 | 44 | 115 | 1053 | -3 | +32 | +29 |
| San Francisco Giants | 91 | 335 | 96 | 184 | 33 | 71 | 169 | 22 | 12 | 34 | 131 | 1183 | +9 | +15 | +24 |
| Cincinnati Reds | 81 | 287 | 99 | 172 | 41 | 88 | 195 | 26 | 16 | 42 | 129 | 1175 | +27 | -3 | +24 |
| Chicago White Sox | 72 | 297 | 109 | 186 | 20 | 70 | 179 | 24 | 15 | 39 | 124 | 1070 | -6 | +21 | +15 |
| Toronto Blue Jays | 84 | 274 | 109 | 154 | 39 | 81 | 138 | 26 | 17 | 43 | 133 | 1093 | -16 | +30 | +14 |
| Seattle Mariners | 78 | 263 | 71 | 135 | 29 | 71 | 146 | 25 | 5 | 31 | 122 | 1139 | +11 | +3 | +14 |
| Los Angeles Angels | 110 | 318 | 114 | 184 | 30 | 80 | 178 | 30 | 16 | 49 | 150 | 1190 | -10 | +14 | +4 |
| Pittsburgh Pirates | 70 | 264 | 98 | 160 | 44 | 87 | 134 | 22 | 12 | 34 | 120 | 1061 | -6 | +10 | +4 |
| Atlanta Braves | 70 | 288 | 104 | 163 | 28 | 72 | 164 | 29 | 14 | 43 | 120 | 1111 | -11 | +2 | -9 |
| Los Angeles Dodgers | 76 | 305 | 113 | 196 | 36 | 84 | 160 | 35 | 11 | 48 | 130 | 1219 | -35 | +22 | -13 |
| Chicago Cubs | 67 | 236 | 80 | 130 | 38 | 63 | 130 | 27 | 11 | 38 | 120 | 1045 | -13 | -1 | -14 |
| St Louis Cardinals | 115 | 372 | 153 | 238 | 40 | 97 | 151 | 28 | 10 | 39 | 155 | 1160 | -17 | +1 | -16 |
| Houston Astros | 81 | 245 | 64 | 136 | 25 | 66 | 167 | 33 | 9 | 42 | 110 | 1005 | -4 | -12 | -16 |
| Milwaukee Brewers | 71 | 282 | 80 | 158 | 27 | 65 | 128 | 29 | 13 | 42 | 116 | 1052 | -61 | +42 | -19 |
| Arizona D-Backs | 77 | 327 | 107 | 165 | 36 | 82 | 170 | 19 | 14 | 33 | 160 | 1209 | -5 | -20 | -25 |
| Philadelphia Phillies | 84 | 277 | 91 | 151 | 26 | 58 | 154 | 34 | 14 | 49 | 132 | 1051 | -40 | +15 | -25 |
| Miami Marlins | 75 | 282 | 90 | 153 | 35 | 60 | 109 | 25 | 14 | 39 | 130 | 1092 | -52 | +20 | -32 |
| Detroit Tigers | 89 | 419 | 115 | 213 | 37 | 88 | 186 | 29 | 12 | 41 | 147 | 1320 | -27 | -5 | -32 |
| MLB Totals | 2503 | 8941 | 3134 | 5269 | 1005 | 2321 | 4814 | 787 | 374 | 1182 | 3735 | 33694 | | | |

# Relief Pitching

This section documents the bullpen performance of each major league team and all of their most used relievers. For each team we have included only pitchers with at least 10 relief appearances in 2013. We show each relief pitcher's role on his team along with his performance in twenty-some bullpen specific performance categories. A modern bullpen consists of a Closer (CL), a Set-up Man or two set-up men (SU), some left-handers whose job is to get out left handed hitters (LT), a Long Man (LM), and some auditioning relievers who pitch as they are needed, categorized as Utility Relievers (UR).

The data contained in this section includes:

**Usage:** Games in Relief (Rel G), the number of times the pitcher entered the game before the seventh inning (Early Entry), pitching on consecutive days (Cons Days), long outings (LO), and Leverage Index (Lev Ind). We use the Leverage Index calculated by Tom Tango and published on Fangraphs.com. An average Leverage Index is 1.0. If a pitcher pitches frequently in late innings with the game on the line, his leverage index will be high. If he generally pitches in the 6th inning of 7-2 ballgames, his leverage index will be very low.

**Inherited Runners:** The total (#), the number that scored (Scrd), and the percentage that scored (Pct).

**Saves:** The conversions and opportunities for three different classifications of Saves: "Easy", "Regular", and "Tough". The definitions of each of these save types can be found in the Baseball Glossary at the end of the book.

**Relief Results:** Clean Outings (Clean), Blown Save Wins (BS Wins), Saves and Save Opportunities (Sv-Opp), Holds, Save/Hold Percentage (Sv/Hld Pct), Opponent OPS (Opp OPS), and reliever ERA (Rel ERA). The definitions of several of these categories can be found in the Baseball Glossary at the end of the book.

## Arizona Diamondbacks

| | | | Usage | | | | | Inherited Runners | | | Saves | | | Relief Results | | | | | | |
|---|---|---|---|---|---|---|---|---|---|---|---|---|---|---|---|---|---|---|---|---|
| Pitcher | Pos | T | Rel G | Early Entry | Cons Days | Long | Lev Ind | # | Scrd | Pct | Easy | Reg | Tough | Clean | BS Win | Sv-Opp | Holds | Sv/Hld Pct | Opp OPS | Rel ERA |
| Bell, Heath | CL | R | 69 | 1 | 18 | 5 | 1.6 | 30 | 9 | 0.30 | 9 - 12 | 6 - 10 | 0 - 0 | 46 | 0 | 15 - 22 | 8 | 0.77 | .802 | 4.11 |
| Ziegler, Brad | SU | R | 78 | 7 | 21 | 3 | 1.8 | 41 | 9 | 0.22 | 5 - 6 | 8 - 9 | 0 - 0 | 60 | 1 | 13 - 15 | 11 | 0.92 | .594 | 2.22 |
| Hernandez, David | SU | R | 62 | 0 | 16 | 8 | 1.7 | 4 | 0 | 0.00 | 0 - 2 | 2 - 6 | 0 - 0 | 44 | 1 | 2 - 8 | 15 | 0.74 | .702 | 4.48 |
| Putz, J.J. | SU | R | 40 | 2 | 5 | 1 | 1.7 | 10 | 3 | 0.30 | 4 - 6 | 2 - 4 | 0 - 1 | 32 | 0 | 6 - 11 | 6 | 0.71 | .665 | 2.36 |
| Sipp, Tony | LT | L | 56 | 9 | 16 | 2 | 0.7 | 34 | 10 | 0.29 | 0 - 0 | 0 - 0 | 0 - 2 | 38 | 0 | 0 - 2 | 3 | 0.60 | .780 | 4.78 |
| Reynolds, Matt | LT | L | 30 | 7 | 7 | 1 | 0.9 | 9 | 3 | 0.33 | 1 - 1 | 1 - 1 | 0 - 1 | 22 | 0 | 2 - 3 | 5 | 0.88 | .645 | 1.98 |
| Thatcher, Joe | LT | L | 22 | 3 | 7 | 1 | 1.3 | 19 | 3 | 0.16 | 0 - 0 | 0 - 1 | 0 - 1 | 16 | 0 | 0 - 2 | 4 | 0.67 | .886 | 6.75 |
| De la Rosa, Eury | LT | L | 19 | 3 | 5 | 2 | 0.6 | 8 | 1 | 0.13 | 0 - 0 | 0 - 0 | 0 - 0 | 11 | 0 | 0 - 0 | 2 | 1.00 | .849 | 7.36 |
| Collmenter, Josh | LM | R | 49 | 20 | 5 | 28 | 1.3 | 22 | 2 | 0.09 | 0 - 0 | 0 - 0 | 0 - 1 | 27 | 0 | 0 - 1 | 5 | 0.83 | .649 | 3.13 |
| Harris, Will | UR | R | 61 | 13 | 16 | 2 | 0.8 | 34 | 10 | 0.29 | 0 - 0 | 0 - 0 | 0 - 1 | 44 | 0 | 0 - 1 | 4 | 0.80 | .661 | 2.91 |
| Roe, Chaz | UR | R | 21 | 7 | 5 | 2 | 1.0 | 9 | 3 | 0.33 | 0 - 0 | 0 - 1 | 0 - 1 | 14 | 1 | 0 - 2 | 1 | 0.33 | .726 | 4.03 |

## Atlanta Braves

| | | | Usage | | | | | Inherited Runners | | | Saves | | | Relief Results | | | | | | |
|---|---|---|---|---|---|---|---|---|---|---|---|---|---|---|---|---|---|---|---|---|
| Pitcher | Pos | T | Rel G | Early Entry | Cons Days | Long | Lev Ind | # | Scrd | Pct | Easy | Reg | Tough | Clean | BS Win | Sv-Opp | Holds | Sv/Hld Pct | Opp OPS | Rel ERA |
| Kimbrel, Craig | CL | R | 68 | 0 | 21 | 5 | 2.0 | 3 | 1 | 0.33 | 36 - 38 | 14 - 16 | 0 - 0 | 61 | 0 | 50 - 54 | 0 | 0.93 | .487 | 1.21 |
| Avilan, Luis | SU | L | 75 | 4 | 22 | 5 | 1.3 | 32 | 7 | 0.22 | 0 - 0 | 0 - 2 | 0 - 0 | 60 | 0 | 0 - 2 | 27 | 0.93 | .478 | 1.52 |
| Walden, Jordan | SU | R | 50 | 2 | 13 | 2 | 1.4 | 13 | 2 | 0.15 | 0 - 0 | 1 - 3 | 0 - 0 | 35 | 0 | 1 - 3 | 14 | 0.88 | .620 | 3.45 |
| Ayala, Luis | SU | R | 37 | 9 | 6 | 2 | 0.9 | 21 | 3 | 0.14 | 0 - 0 | 0 - 0 | 0 - 2 | 26 | 0 | 0 - 2 | 10 | 0.83 | .709 | 2.90 |
| Downs, Scott | SU | L | 25 | 5 | 7 | 0 | 1.3 | 18 | 5 | 0.28 | 0 - 0 | 0 - 0 | 0 - 1 | 17 | 0 | 0 - 1 | 8 | 0.89 | .790 | 3.86 |
| OFlaherty, Eric | SU | L | 19 | 0 | 6 | 0 | 1.5 | 6 | 2 | 0.33 | 0 - 0 | 0 - 1 | 0 - 0 | 12 | 0 | 0 - 1 | 12 | 0.92 | .555 | 2.50 |
| Wood, Alex | LT | L | 20 | 3 | 4 | 5 | 0.9 | 12 | 4 | 0.33 | 0 - 0 | 0 - 0 | 0 - 0 | 13 | 0 | 0 - 0 | 1 | 1.00 | .563 | 2.08 |
| Varvaro, Anthony | UR | R | 62 | 7 | 15 | 14 | 0.5 | 19 | 4 | 0.21 | 0 - 0 | 1 - 3 | 0 - 0 | 45 | 1 | 1 - 3 | 6 | 0.78 | .644 | 2.82 |
| Carpenter, David | UR | R | 56 | 9 | 18 | 14 | 0.9 | 34 | 11 | 0.32 | 0 - 0 | 0 - 0 | 0 - 0 | 41 | 0 | 0 - 0 | 12 | 1.00 | .558 | 1.78 |
| Gearrin, Cory | UR | R | 37 | 7 | 13 | 3 | 0.7 | 28 | 7 | 0.25 | 1 - 1 | 0 - 1 | 0 - 1 | 29 | 0 | 1 - 3 | 1 | 0.50 | .754 | 3.77 |

## Baltimore Orioles

| | | | Usage | | | | | Inherited Runners | | | Saves | | | Relief Results | | | | | | |
|---|---|---|---|---|---|---|---|---|---|---|---|---|---|---|---|---|---|---|---|---|
| Pitcher | Pos | T | Rel G | Early Entry | Cons Days | Long | Lev Ind | # | Scrd | Pct | Easy | Reg | Tough | Clean | BS Win | Sv-Opp | Holds | Sv/Hld Pct | Opp OPS | Rel ERA |
| Johnson, Jim | CL | R | 74 | 0 | 21 | 3 | 2.2 | 11 | 4 | 0.36 | 37 - 39 | 13 - 20 | 0 - 0 | 55 | 1 | 50 - 59 | 0 | 0.85 | .699 | 2.94 |
| ODay, Darren | SU | R | 68 | 1 | 14 | 8 | 1.4 | 31 | 10 | 0.32 | 0 - 0 | 2 - 4 | 0 - 2 | 50 | 0 | 2 - 6 | 20 | 0.85 | .617 | 2.18 |
| Hunter, Tommy | SU | R | 68 | 8 | 10 | 13 | 1.3 | 28 | 4 | 0.14 | 1 - 2 | 2 - 3 | 1 - 1 | 47 | 0 | 4 - 6 | 21 | 0.93 | .617 | 2.81 |
| Matusz, Brian | SU | L | 65 | 7 | 15 | 1 | 1.0 | 37 | 5 | 0.14 | 0 - 0 | 0 - 3 | 0 - 1 | 47 | 0 | 0 - 4 | 18 | 0.82 | .616 | 3.53 |
| Patton, Troy | LT | L | 56 | 17 | 7 | 7 | 0.8 | 31 | 12 | 0.39 | 0 - 0 | 0 - 0 | 0 - 1 | 35 | 0 | 0 - 1 | 8 | 0.89 | .757 | 3.70 |
| McFarland, T.J. | LM | L | 37 | 24 | 3 | 22 | 0.8 | 27 | 15 | 0.56 | 0 - 0 | 0 - 0 | 0 - 0 | 19 | 0 | 0 - 0 | 0 | | .722 | 4.00 |
| Strop, Pedro | UR | R | 29 | 1 | 5 | 0 | 1.0 | 17 | 10 | 0.59 | 0 - 0 | 0 - 2 | 0 - 1 | 17 | 0 | 0 - 3 | 3 | 0.50 | .861 | 7.25 |
| Rodriguez, Francisco | UR | R | 23 | 4 | 4 | 1 | 0.9 | 6 | 1 | 0.17 | 0 - 0 | 0 - 0 | 0 - 0 | 14 | 0 | 0 - 0 | 4 | 1.00 | .899 | 4.50 |
| Gausman, Kevin | UR | R | 15 | 6 | 2 | 7 | 1.0 | 6 | 0 | 0.00 | 0 - 0 | 0 - 2 | 0 - 0 | 10 | 0 | 0 - 2 | 2 | 0.50 | .556 | 3.52 |
| Stinson, Josh | UR | R | 10 | 4 | 2 | 2 | 1.0 | 6 | 1 | 0.17 | 0 - 0 | 0 - 0 | 0 - 1 | 8 | 0 | 0 - 1 | 2 | 0.67 | .335 | 0.79 |

## Boston Red Sox

| | | | Usage | | | | | Inherited Runners | | | Saves | | | Relief Results | | | | | | |
|---|---|---|---|---|---|---|---|---|---|---|---|---|---|---|---|---|---|---|---|---|
| Pitcher | Pos | T | Rel G | Early Entry | Cons Days | Long | Lev Ind | # | Scrd | Pct | Easy | Reg | Tough | Clean | BS Win | Sv-Opp | Holds | Sv/Hld Pct | Opp OPS | Rel ERA |
| Uehara, Koji | CL | R | 73 | 3 | 15 | 4 | 1.3 | 23 | 7 | 0.30 | 11 - 11 | 9 - 12 | 1 - 1 | 62 | 1 | 21 - 24 | 13 | 0.92 | .400 | 1.09 |
| Tazawa, Junichi | SU | R | 71 | 6 | 11 | 2 | 1.3 | 34 | 11 | 0.32 | 0 - 0 | 0 - 7 | 0 - 1 | 44 | 1 | 0 - 8 | 25 | 0.76 | .741 | 3.16 |
| Bailey, Andrew | SU | R | 30 | 1 | 5 | 2 | 1.9 | 5 | 0 | 0.00 | 6 - 7 | 2 - 6 | 0 - 0 | 21 | 2 | 8 - 13 | 8 | 0.76 | .761 | 3.77 |
| Breslow, Craig | LT | L | 61 | 10 | 14 | 6 | 1.2 | 39 | 12 | 0.31 | 0 - 0 | 0 - 0 | 0 - 1 | 46 | 0 | 0 - 1 | 13 | 0.93 | .635 | 1.81 |
| Miller, Andrew | LT | L | 37 | 4 | 7 | 3 | 1.2 | 27 | 6 | 0.22 | 0 - 0 | 0 - 0 | 0 - 1 | 26 | 0 | 0 - 1 | 6 | 0.86 | .624 | 2.64 |
| Thornton, Matt | LT | L | 20 | 4 | 4 | 0 | 1.1 | 14 | 8 | 0.57 | 0 - 0 | 0 - 0 | 0 - 0 | 12 | 0 | 0 - 0 | 1 | 1.00 | .756 | 3.52 |
| Morales, Franklin | LT | L | 19 | 4 | 1 | 4 | 1.2 | 10 | 3 | 0.30 | 0 - 0 | 0 - 0 | 0 - 1 | 13 | 0 | 0 - 1 | 4 | 0.80 | .738 | 4.87 |
| Britton, Drake | LT | L | 18 | 3 | 1 | 4 | 1.0 | 11 | 6 | 0.55 | 0 - 0 | 0 - 0 | 0 - 2 | 11 | 0 | 0 - 2 | 1 | 0.33 | .720 | 3.86 |
| Mortensen, Clayton | LM | R | 24 | 7 | 3 | 9 | 0.8 | 12 | 4 | 0.33 | 0 - 0 | 0 - 0 | 0 - 0 | 13 | 0 | 0 - 0 | 0 | | .739 | 5.34 |
| Wilson, Alex | UR | R | 26 | 3 | 6 | 8 | 0.6 | 19 | 11 | 0.58 | 0 - 0 | 0 - 0 | 0 - 0 | 13 | 0 | 0 - 0 | 1 | 1.00 | .818 | 4.88 |
| Workman, Brandon | UR | R | 17 | 4 | 2 | 6 | 1.1 | 13 | 2 | 0.15 | 0 - 0 | 0 - 1 | 0 - 0 | 8 | 0 | 0 - 1 | 1 | 0.50 | .884 | 6.94 |
| de la Rosa, Rubby | UR | R | 11 | 3 | 1 | 3 | 0.4 | 6 | 0 | 0.00 | 0 - 0 | 0 - 0 | 0 - 0 | 6 | 0 | 0 - 0 | 0 | | .877 | 5.56 |
| Beato, Pedro | UR | R | 10 | 2 | 1 | 2 | 0.5 | 2 | 1 | 0.50 | 0 - 0 | 0 - 0 | 0 - 0 | 5 | 0 | 0 - 0 | 0 | | .698 | 3.60 |

## Chicago Cubs

| | | | Usage | | | | | Inherited Runners | | | Saves | | | Relief Results | | | | | | |
|---|---|---|---|---|---|---|---|---|---|---|---|---|---|---|---|---|---|---|---|---|
| Pitcher | Pos | T | Rel G | Early Entry | Cons Days | Long | Lev Ind | # | Scrd | Pct | Easy | Reg | Tough | Clean | BS Win | Sv-Opp | Holds | Sv/Hld Pct | Opp OPS | Rel ERA |
| Gregg, Kevin | CL | R | 62 | 0 | 17 | 9 | 2.0 | 9 | 2 | 0.22 | 19 - 20 | 13 - 17 | 1 - 1 | 43 | 0 | 33 - 38 | 0 | 0.87 | .695 | 3.48 |
| Russell, James | SU | L | 74 | 4 | 25 | 1 | 1.4 | 51 | 15 | 0.29 | 0 - 1 | 0 - 3 | 0 - 4 | 55 | 0 | 0 - 8 | 19 | 0.70 | .746 | 3.59 |
| Strop, Pedro | SU | R | 37 | 2 | 9 | 3 | 1.5 | 9 | 0 | 0.00 | 1 - 1 | 0 - 0 | 0 - 0 | 32 | 0 | 1 - 1 | 14 | 1.00 | .520 | 2.83 |
| Marmol, Carlos | SU | R | 31 | 2 | 7 | 3 | 1.6 | 2 | 1 | 0.50 | 1 - 2 | 1 - 2 | 0 - 1 | 21 | 1 | 2 - 5 | 5 | 0.70 | .876 | 5.86 |
| Guerrier, Matt | SU | R | 15 | 1 | 6 | 0 | 1.5 | 12 | 1 | 0.08 | 0 - 0 | 0 - 1 | 0 - 1 | 11 | 0 | 0 - 2 | 5 | 0.71 | .640 | 2.13 |
| Rosscup, Zac | LT | L | 10 | 3 | 2 | 0 | 0.7 | 7 | 1 | 0.14 | 0 - 0 | 0 - 0 | 0 - 0 | 9 | 0 | 0 - 0 | 0 | | .638 | 1.35 |
| Rondon, Hector | LM | R | 45 | 13 | 3 | 14 | 0.8 | 12 | 6 | 0.50 | 0 - 0 | 0 - 0 | 0 - 1 | 27 | 0 | 0 - 1 | 2 | 0.67 | .737 | 4.77 |
| Parker, Blake | UR | R | 49 | 7 | 16 | 10 | 0.8 | 21 | 6 | 0.29 | 1 - 1 | 0 - 0 | 0 - 0 | 33 | 0 | 1 - 1 | 7 | 1.00 | .626 | 2.72 |
| Bowden, Michael | UR | R | 34 | 11 | 8 | 7 | 0.9 | 21 | 8 | 0.38 | 0 - 0 | 0 - 0 | 0 - 2 | 18 | 0 | 0 - 2 | 0 | 0.00 | .713 | 4.30 |
| Villanueva, Carlos | UR | R | 32 | 9 | 6 | 8 | 1.0 | 15 | 3 | 0.20 | 0 - 0 | 0 - 1 | 0 - 0 | 22 | 0 | 0 - 1 | 2 | 0.67 | .656 | 3.03 |
| Camp, Shawn | UR | R | 26 | 2 | 7 | 4 | 1.2 | 17 | 7 | 0.41 | 0 - 0 | 0 - 1 | 0 - 2 | 15 | 0 | 0 - 3 | 4 | 0.57 | 1.065 | 7.04 |
| Fujikawa, Kyuji | UR | R | 12 | 0 | 1 | 2 | 1.5 | 2 | 0 | 0.00 | 1 - 2 | 0 - 0 | 1 - 1 | 9 | 1 | 2 - 3 | 1 | 0.75 | .691 | 5.25 |
| Grimm, Justin | UR | R | 10 | 1 | 1 | 0 | 1.2 | 3 | 0 | 0.00 | 0 - 0 | 0 - 0 | 0 - 0 | 8 | 0 | 0 - 0 | 3 | 1.00 | .402 | 2.00 |

## Chicago White Sox

| | | | Usage | | | | | Inherited Runners | | | Saves | | | Relief Results | | | | | | |
|---|---|---|---|---|---|---|---|---|---|---|---|---|---|---|---|---|---|---|---|---|
| Pitcher | Pos | T | Rel G | Early Entry | Cons Days | Long | Lev Ind | # | Scrd | Pct | Easy | Reg | Tough | Clean | BS Win | Sv-Opp | Holds | Sv/Hld Pct | Opp OPS | Rel ERA |
| Reed, Addison | CL | R | 68 | 0 | 23 | 8 | 2.1 | 2 | 0 | 0.00 | 28 - 31 | 12 - 17 | 0 - 0 | 49 | 1 | 40 - 48 | 0 | 0.83 | .603 | 3.79 |
| Lindstrom, Matt | SU | R | 76 | 12 | 23 | 5 | 1.3 | 50 | 19 | 0.38 | 0 - 0 | 0 - 2 | 0 - 2 | 52 | 0 | 0 - 4 | 20 | 0.83 | .683 | 3.12 |
| Thornton, Matt | SU | L | 40 | 2 | 11 | 2 | 1.6 | 28 | 5 | 0.18 | 0 - 0 | 0 - 1 | 0 - 0 | 28 | 0 | 0 - 1 | 18 | 0.95 | .727 | 3.86 |
| Crain, Jesse | SU | R | 38 | 0 | 14 | 7 | 2.0 | 20 | 7 | 0.35 | 0 - 1 | 0 - 0 | 0 - 0 | 31 | 0 | 0 - 1 | 19 | 0.95 | .562 | 0.74 |
| Veal, Donnie | LT | L | 50 | 4 | 18 | 1 | 1.3 | 48 | 11 | 0.23 | 0 - 0 | 0 - 0 | 0 - 1 | 36 | 0 | 0 - 1 | 13 | 0.93 | .688 | 4.60 |
| Purcey, David | LT | L | 24 | 6 | 5 | 6 | 0.7 | 12 | 5 | 0.42 | 0 - 0 | 0 - 0 | 0 - 0 | 16 | 0 | 0 - 0 | 0 | | .691 | 2.13 |
| Jones, Nate | UR | R | 70 | 13 | 20 | 16 | 1.4 | 51 | 15 | 0.29 | 0 - 1 | 0 - 2 | 0 - 1 | 45 | 0 | 0 - 4 | 16 | 0.80 | .659 | 4.15 |
| Troncoso, Ramon | UR | R | 29 | 7 | 9 | 7 | 0.8 | 20 | 4 | 0.20 | 0 - 0 | 0 - 0 | 0 - 0 | 16 | 0 | 0 - 0 | 1 | 1.00 | .750 | 4.50 |
| Petricka, Jake | UR | R | 16 | 8 | 3 | 5 | 0.9 | 14 | 7 | 0.50 | 0 - 0 | 0 - 1 | 0 - 0 | 7 | 0 | 0 - 1 | 0 | 0.00 | .688 | 3.26 |
| Omogrosso, Brian | UR | R | 12 | 2 | 3 | 5 | 0.8 | 4 | 1 | 0.25 | 0 - 0 | 0 - 0 | 0 - 0 | 5 | 0 | 0 - 0 | 0 | | 1.060 | 9.37 |
| Santiago, Hector | UR | L | 11 | 5 | 3 | 4 | 1.1 | 7 | 0 | 0.00 | 0 - 0 | 0 - 0 | 0 - 0 | 6 | 0 | 0 - 0 | 0 | | .755 | 3.93 |
| Axelrod, Dylan | UR | R | 10 | 4 | 1 | 7 | 0.9 | 3 | 3 | 1.00 | 0 - 0 | 0 - 0 | 0 - 0 | 2 | 0 | 0 - 0 | 0 | | .946 | 5.32 |

## Cincinnati Reds

| | | | Usage | | | | | Inherited Runners | | | Saves | | | Relief Results | | | | | | |
|---|---|---|---|---|---|---|---|---|---|---|---|---|---|---|---|---|---|---|---|---|
| Pitcher | Pos | T | Rel G | Early Entry | Cons Days | Long | Lev Ind | # | Scrd | Pct | Easy | Reg | Tough | Clean | BS Win | Sv-Opp | Holds | Sv/Hld Pct | Opp OPS | Rel ERA |
| Chapman, Aroldis | CL | L | 68 | 0 | 20 | 5 | 1.7 | 8 | 3 | 0.38 | 25 - 25 | 13 - 17 | 0 - 1 | 53 | 1 | 38 - 43 | 0 | 0.88 | .544 | 2.54 |
| LeCure, Sam | SU | R | 63 | 5 | 8 | 7 | 1.4 | 27 | 3 | 0.11 | 0 - 0 | 1 - 3 | 0 - 0 | 51 | 0 | 1 - 3 | 17 | 0.90 | .624 | 2.66 |
| Broxton, Jonathan | SU | R | 34 | 0 | 9 | 2 | 1.5 | 5 | 2 | 0.40 | 0 - 2 | 0 - 1 | 0 - 0 | 23 | 0 | 0 - 3 | 12 | 0.80 | .712 | 4.11 |
| Marshall, Sean | SU | L | 16 | 1 | 4 | 0 | 1.3 | 13 | 2 | 0.15 | 0 - 0 | 0 - 0 | 0 - 0 | 13 | 0 | 0 - 0 | 7 | 1.00 | .307 | 1.74 |
| Parra, Manny | LT | L | 57 | 5 | 10 | 4 | 0.9 | 30 | 5 | 0.17 | 0 - 0 | 0 - 1 | 0 - 0 | 42 | 0 | 0 - 1 | 16 | 0.94 | .684 | 3.33 |
| Duke, Zach | LT | L | 14 | 3 | 5 | 2 | 1.1 | 11 | 1 | 0.09 | 0 - 0 | 0 - 0 | 0 - 0 | 12 | 0 | 0 - 0 | 1 | 1.00 | .552 | 0.84 |
| Partch, Curtis | LM | R | 14 | 7 | 0 | 8 | 0.7 | 6 | 5 | 0.83 | 0 - 0 | 0 - 0 | 0 - 0 | 7 | 0 | 0 - 0 | 0 | | .937 | 6.17 |
| Hoover, J.J. | UR | R | 69 | 7 | 13 | 13 | 1.4 | 36 | 15 | 0.42 | 2 - 2 | 0 - 1 | 1 - 2 | 53 | 0 | 3 - 5 | 13 | 0.89 | .627 | 2.86 |
| Simon, Alfredo | UR | R | 63 | 19 | 13 | 20 | 0.9 | 25 | 4 | 0.16 | 0 - 0 | 1 - 2 | 0 - 1 | 39 | 0 | 1 - 3 | 6 | 0.78 | .625 | 2.87 |
| Ondrusek, Logan | UR | R | 52 | 16 | 7 | 11 | 0.7 | 18 | 4 | 0.22 | 0 - 1 | 0 - 0 | 0 - 0 | 38 | 0 | 0 - 1 | 5 | 0.83 | .730 | 4.09 |

## Cleveland Indians

| | | | Usage | | | | | Inherited Runners | | | Saves | | | Relief Results | | | | | | |
|---|---|---|---|---|---|---|---|---|---|---|---|---|---|---|---|---|---|---|---|---|
| Pitcher | Pos | T | Rel G | Early Entry | Cons Days | Long | Lev Ind | # | Scrd | Pct | Easy | Reg | Tough | Clean | BS Win | Sv-Opp | Holds | Sv/Hld Pct | Opp OPS | Rel ERA |
| Perez, Chris | CL | R | 54 | 0 | 20 | 4 | 2.0 | 0 | 0 | 0.00 | 16 - 18 | 9 - 12 | 0 - 0 | 40 | 2 | 25 - 30 | 1 | 0.84 | .847 | 4.33 |
| Smith, Joe | SU | R | 70 | 0 | 17 | 4 | 1.5 | 23 | 5 | 0.22 | 0 - 2 | 3 - 5 | 0 - 1 | 55 | 1 | 3 - 8 | 25 | 0.85 | .643 | 2.29 |
| Pestano, Vinnie | SU | R | 37 | 1 | 7 | 5 | 1.0 | 2 | 2 | 1.00 | 3 - 4 | 3 - 5 | 0 - 0 | 25 | 0 | 6 - 9 | 6 | 0.80 | .838 | 4.08 |
| Hill, Rich | LT | L | 63 | 17 | 18 | 6 | 0.9 | 63 | 12 | 0.19 | 0 - 0 | 0 - 1 | 0 - 1 | 40 | 0 | 0 - 2 | 13 | 0.87 | .719 | 6.28 |
| Rzepczynski, Marc | LT | L | 27 | 6 | 9 | 1 | 0.6 | 20 | 3 | 0.15 | 0 - 0 | 0 - 0 | 0 - 0 | 22 | 0 | 0 - 0 | 6 | 1.00 | .517 | 0.89 |
| Hagadone, Nick | LM | L | 36 | 19 | 7 | 4 | 0.7 | 34 | 6 | 0.18 | 0 - 0 | 0 - 0 | 0 - 1 | 20 | 0 | 0 - 1 | 2 | 0.67 | .710 | 5.46 |
| Allen, Cody | UR | R | 77 | 16 | 20 | 11 | 1.1 | 52 | 19 | 0.37 | 1 - 1 | 1 - 2 | 0 - 1 | 55 | 0 | 2 - 4 | 11 | 0.87 | .679 | 2.43 |
| Shaw, Bryan | UR | R | 70 | 24 | 11 | 7 | 1.0 | 44 | 11 | 0.25 | 0 - 0 | 1 - 2 | 0 - 3 | 48 | 0 | 1 - 5 | 12 | 0.76 | .586 | 3.24 |
| Albers, Matt | UR | R | 56 | 17 | 11 | 8 | 0.5 | 44 | 18 | 0.41 | 0 - 0 | 0 - 0 | 0 - 0 | 28 | 0 | 0 - 0 | 1 | 1.00 | .621 | 3.14 |

## Colorado Rockies

| | | | Usage | | | | | Inherited Runners | | | Saves | | | Relief Results | | | | | | |
|---|---|---|---|---|---|---|---|---|---|---|---|---|---|---|---|---|---|---|---|---|
| Pitcher | Pos | T | Rel G | Early Entry | Cons Days | Long | Lev Ind | # | Scrd | Pct | Easy | Reg | Tough | Clean | BS Win | Sv-Opp | Holds | Sv/Hld Pct | Opp OPS | Rel ERA |
| Brothers, Rex | CL | L | 72 | 0 | 19 | 6 | 1.7 | 17 | 7 | 0.41 | 8 - 8 | 10 - 11 | 1 - 2 | 54 | 0 | 19 - 21 | 12 | 0.94 | .618 | 1.74 |
| Betancourt, Rafael | CL | R | 32 | 0 | 7 | 1 | 1.9 | 2 | 0 | 0.00 | 14 - 14 | 2 - 5 | 0 - 0 | 21 | 0 | 16 - 19 | 0 | 0.84 | .669 | 4.08 |
| Belisle, Matt | SU | R | 72 | 1 | 20 | 8 | 1.4 | 15 | 4 | 0.27 | 0 - 0 | 0 - 4 | 0 - 1 | 50 | 1 | 0 - 5 | 24 | 0.83 | .707 | 4.32 |
| Outman, Josh | LT | L | 61 | 16 | 14 | 8 | 0.8 | 34 | 6 | 0.18 | 0 - 0 | 0 - 0 | 0 - 1 | 42 | 0 | 0 - 1 | 13 | 0.93 | .700 | 4.33 |
| Ottavino, Adam | LM | R | 51 | 29 | 3 | 25 | 0.9 | 30 | 12 | 0.40 | 0 - 0 | 0 - 0 | 0 - 0 | 26 | 0 | 0 - 0 | 8 | 1.00 | .672 | 2.64 |
| Escalona, Edgmer | LM | R | 37 | 14 | 3 | 15 | 0.8 | 13 | 2 | 0.15 | 0 - 1 | 0 - 0 | 0 - 0 | 20 | 0 | 0 - 1 | 7 | 0.88 | .835 | 5.67 |
| Corpas, Manny | LM | R | 31 | 12 | 4 | 11 | 0.7 | 12 | 3 | 0.25 | 0 - 0 | 0 - 0 | 0 - 0 | 17 | 0 | 0 - 0 | 3 | 1.00 | .730 | 4.54 |
| Scahill, Rob | LM | R | 23 | 11 | 2 | 9 | 0.6 | 12 | 1 | 0.08 | 0 - 0 | 0 - 0 | 0 - 0 | 15 | 0 | 0 - 0 | 1 | 1.00 | .867 | 5.13 |
| Lopez, Wilton | UR | R | 75 | 9 | 22 | 10 | 0.9 | 43 | 14 | 0.33 | 0 - 2 | 0 - 3 | 0 - 0 | 50 | 1 | 0 - 5 | 8 | 0.62 | .754 | 4.06 |
| Francis, Jeff | UR | L | 11 | 5 | 0 | 5 | 0.8 | 3 | 2 | 0.67 | 0 - 0 | 0 - 0 | 0 - 0 | 4 | 0 | 0 - 0 | 0 | | .862 | 6.75 |

## Detroit Tigers

| | | | Usage | | | | | Inherited Runners | | | Saves | | | Relief Results | | | | | | |
|---|---|---|---|---|---|---|---|---|---|---|---|---|---|---|---|---|---|---|---|---|
| Pitcher | Pos | T | Rel G | Early Entry | Cons Days | Long | Lev Ind | # | Scrd | Pct | Easy | Reg | Tough | Clean | BS Win | Sv-Opp | Holds | Sv/Hld Pct | Opp OPS | Rel ERA |
| Benoit, Joaquin | CL | R | 66 | 0 | 15 | 5 | 1.7 | 21 | 3 | 0.14 | 12 - 12 | 10 - 11 | 2 - 3 | 53 | 0 | 24 - 26 | 9 | 0.94 | .575 | 2.01 |
| Veras, Jose | SU | R | 25 | 0 | 5 | 1 | 1.4 | 8 | 0 | 0.00 | 1 - 1 | 1 - 2 | 0 - 0 | 19 | 0 | 2 - 3 | 9 | 0.92 | .644 | 3.20 |
| Smyly, Drew | LT | L | 63 | 9 | 13 | 18 | 0.9 | 26 | 3 | 0.12 | 0 - 0 | 2 - 5 | 0 - 1 | 47 | 1 | 2 - 6 | 21 | 0.85 | .601 | 2.37 |
| Coke, Phil | LT | L | 49 | 3 | 8 | 3 | 1.2 | 27 | 9 | 0.33 | 1 - 1 | 0 - 0 | 0 - 2 | 30 | 0 | 1 - 3 | 4 | 0.71 | .809 | 5.40 |
| Downs, Darin | LT | L | 29 | 11 | 5 | 8 | 0.9 | 25 | 9 | 0.36 | 0 - 0 | 0 - 0 | 0 - 0 | 15 | 0 | 0 - 0 | 4 | 1.00 | .768 | 4.84 |
| Alburquerque, Al | UR | R | 53 | 8 | 10 | 5 | 1.0 | 40 | 14 | 0.35 | 0 - 0 | 0 - 0 | 0 - 0 | 35 | 0 | 0 - 0 | 10 | 1.00 | .674 | 4.59 |
| Putkonen, Luke | UR | R | 30 | 6 | 4 | 4 | 0.8 | 12 | 4 | 0.33 | 0 - 0 | 0 - 0 | 0 - 0 | 20 | 0 | 0 - 0 | 1 | 1.00 | .677 | 3.03 |
| Rondon, Bruce | UR | R | 30 | 1 | 6 | 0 | 1.2 | 8 | 3 | 0.38 | 1 - 1 | 0 - 1 | 0 - 1 | 19 | 0 | 1 - 3 | 5 | 0.75 | .720 | 3.45 |
| Valverde, Jose | UR | R | 20 | 0 | 6 | 2 | 2.0 | 3 | 1 | 0.33 | 4 - 5 | 5 - 7 | 0 - 0 | 15 | 0 | 9 - 12 | 0 | 0.75 | .796 | 5.59 |
| Reed, Evan | UR | R | 16 | 3 | 1 | 7 | 0.3 | 9 | 3 | 0.33 | 0 - 0 | 0 - 0 | 0 - 0 | 7 | 0 | 0 - 0 | 0 | | .775 | 4.24 |
| Bonderman, Jeremy | UR | R | 11 | 4 | 2 | 6 | 0.6 | 8 | 0 | 0.00 | 0 - 0 | 0 - 0 | 0 - 0 | 4 | 0 | 0 - 0 | 0 | | .873 | 6.48 |
| Ortega, Jose | UR | R | 11 | 2 | 2 | 4 | 1.3 | 4 | 0 | 0.00 | 0 - 1 | 0 - 0 | 0 - 0 | 9 | 0 | 0 - 1 | 2 | 0.67 | .697 | 3.86 |

## Houston Astros

| | | | Usage | | | | | Inherited Runners | | | Saves | | | Relief Results | | | | | | |
|---|---|---|---|---|---|---|---|---|---|---|---|---|---|---|---|---|---|---|---|---|
| Pitcher | Pos | T | Rel G | Early Entry | Cons Days | Long | Lev Ind | # | Scrd | Pct | Easy | Reg | Tough | Clean | BS Win | Sv-Opp | Holds | Sv/Hld Pct | Opp OPS | Rel ERA |
| Veras, Jose | CL | R | 42 | 0 | 9 | 3 | 1.7 | 4 | 0 | 0.00 | 7 - 8 | 11 - 13 | 1 - 1 | 33 | 0 | 19 - 22 | 0 | 0.86 | .585 | 2.93 |
| Ambriz, Hector | SU | R | 43 | 2 | 9 | 6 | 1.1 | 27 | 11 | 0.41 | 1 - 1 | 1 - 2 | 0 - 2 | 24 | 0 | 2 - 5 | 13 | 0.83 | .913 | 5.70 |
| Blackley, Travis | SU | L | 42 | 11 | 8 | 3 | 1.1 | 37 | 7 | 0.19 | 0 - 0 | 0 - 0 | 0 - 1 | 26 | 0 | 0 - 1 | 13 | 0.93 | .830 | 4.89 |
| Zeid, Josh | SU | R | 25 | 3 | 7 | 4 | 1.2 | 17 | 2 | 0.12 | 0 - 0 | 1 - 1 | 0 - 1 | 15 | 0 | 1 - 2 | 6 | 0.88 | .708 | 3.90 |
| Chapman, Kevin | LT | L | 25 | 2 | 10 | 3 | 1.6 | 19 | 3 | 0.16 | 0 - 1 | 0 - 0 | 1 - 3 | 19 | 0 | 1 - 4 | 4 | 0.63 | .585 | 1.77 |
| Wright, Wesley | LM | L | 55 | 11 | 14 | 2 | 0.8 | 36 | 15 | 0.42 | 0 - 0 | 0 - 2 | 0 - 2 | 31 | 0 | 0 - 4 | 8 | 0.67 | .794 | 3.92 |
| Clemens, Paul | LM | R | 30 | 13 | 4 | 11 | 0.8 | 20 | 3 | 0.15 | 0 - 0 | 0 - 1 | 0 - 1 | 15 | 0 | 0 - 2 | 7 | 0.78 | .885 | 6.36 |
| Cisnero, Jose | LM | R | 28 | 4 | 2 | 14 | 1.0 | 16 | 10 | 0.63 | 0 - 0 | 0 - 1 | 0 - 1 | 15 | 0 | 0 - 2 | 5 | 0.71 | .826 | 4.12 |
| Harrell, Lucas | LM | R | 14 | 9 | 2 | 12 | 0.9 | 9 | 2 | 0.22 | 0 - 0 | 0 - 1 | 0 - 0 | 4 | 0 | 0 - 1 | 0 | 0.00 | .826 | 5.49 |
| Fields, Josh | UR | R | 41 | 4 | 8 | 5 | 1.4 | 17 | 2 | 0.12 | 2 - 2 | 1 - 2 | 2 - 2 | 27 | 0 | 5 - 6 | 6 | 0.92 | .783 | 4.97 |
| Cruz, Rhiner | UR | R | 20 | 3 | 5 | 3 | 0.5 | 7 | 4 | 0.57 | 0 - 0 | 0 - 0 | 0 - 0 | 11 | 0 | 0 - 0 | 1 | 1.00 | .843 | 3.38 |
| Lo, Chia-Jen | UR | R | 19 | 1 | 4 | 4 | 2.0 | 6 | 2 | 0.33 | 1 - 1 | 0 - 2 | 1 - 2 | 13 | 0 | 2 - 5 | 1 | 0.50 | .615 | 4.19 |
| De Leon, Jorge | UR | R | 11 | 1 | 0 | 3 | 0.9 | 7 | 2 | 0.29 | 0 - 0 | 0 - 0 | 0 - 0 | 5 | 0 | 0 - 0 | 1 | 1.00 | .863 | 5.40 |
| Humber, Philip | UR | R | 10 | 7 | 0 | 6 | 0.8 | 14 | 4 | 0.29 | 0 - 0 | 0 - 2 | 0 - 0 | 2 | 0 | 0 - 2 | 0 | 0.00 | .906 | 6.43 |

## Kansas City Royals

| | | | Usage | | | | | Inherited Runners | | | Saves | | | Relief Results | | | | | | |
|---|---|---|---|---|---|---|---|---|---|---|---|---|---|---|---|---|---|---|---|---|
| Pitcher | Pos | T | Rel G | Early Entry | Cons Days | Long | Lev Ind | # | Scrd | Pct | Easy | Reg | Tough | Clean | BS Win | Sv-Opp | Holds | Sv/Hld Pct | Opp OPS | Rel ERA |
| Holland, Greg | CL | R | 68 | 0 | 20 | 5 | 2.1 | 6 | 1 | 0.17 | 26 - 27 | 21 - 23 | 0 - 0 | 59 | 0 | 47 - 50 | 1 | 0.94 | .479 | 1.21 |
| Collins, Tim | SU | L | 66 | 8 | 17 | 5 | 1.3 | 39 | 8 | 0.21 | 0 - 1 | 0 - 2 | 0 - 2 | 46 | 0 | 0 - 5 | 21 | 0.81 | .677 | 3.54 |
| Herrera, Kelvin | SU | R | 59 | 3 | 13 | 6 | 1.3 | 18 | 6 | 0.33 | 1 - 2 | 0 - 0 | 1 - 2 | 39 | 0 | 2 - 4 | 20 | 0.92 | .701 | 3.86 |
| Crow, Aaron | SU | R | 57 | 1 | 8 | 0 | 1.8 | 44 | 15 | 0.34 | 1 - 3 | 0 - 0 | 0 - 1 | 37 | 1 | 1 - 4 | 19 | 0.87 | .776 | 3.38 |
| Smith, Will | LT | L | 18 | 6 | 1 | 6 | 0.9 | 22 | 6 | 0.27 | 0 - 0 | 0 - 0 | 0 - 3 | 9 | 1 | 0 - 3 | 6 | 0.67 | .558 | 2.45 |
| Chen, Bruce | LM | L | 19 | 9 | 1 | 10 | 0.8 | 13 | 10 | 0.77 | 0 - 0 | 0 - 0 | 0 - 2 | 11 | 0 | 0 - 2 | 2 | 0.50 | .751 | 2.41 |
| Hochevar, Luke | UR | R | 58 | 6 | 4 | 11 | 0.7 | 28 | 6 | 0.21 | 0 - 1 | 2 - 3 | 0 - 1 | 43 | 0 | 2 - 5 | 9 | 0.79 | .533 | 1.92 |
| Coleman, Louis | UR | R | 27 | 6 | 4 | 2 | 0.5 | 20 | 6 | 0.30 | 0 - 0 | 0 - 0 | 0 - 0 | 22 | 0 | 0 - 0 | 4 | 1.00 | .493 | 0.61 |
| Gutierrez, J.C. | UR | R | 25 | 6 | 2 | 4 | 0.4 | 11 | 0 | 0.00 | 0 - 0 | 0 - 0 | 0 - 0 | 19 | 0 | 0 - 0 | 2 | 1.00 | .692 | 3.38 |

## Los Angeles Angels

| | | | Usage | | | | | Inherited Runners | | | Saves | | | Relief Results | | | | | | |
|---|---|---|---|---|---|---|---|---|---|---|---|---|---|---|---|---|---|---|---|---|
| Pitcher | Pos | T | Rel G | Early Entry | Cons Days | Long | Lev Ind | # | Scrd | Pct | Easy | Reg | Tough | Clean | BS Win | Sv-Opp | Holds | Sv/Hld Pct | Opp OPS | Rel ERA |
| Frieri, Ernesto | CL | R | 67 | 0 | 20 | 17 | 2.0 | 23 | 3 | 0.13 | 19 - 20 | 13 - 15 | 5 - 6 | 50 | 0 | 37 - 41 | 2 | 0.91 | .684 | 3.80 |
| de la Rosa, Dane | SU | R | 75 | 9 | 25 | 8 | 1.1 | 41 | 18 | 0.44 | 1 - 1 | 1 - 3 | 0 - 1 | 51 | 0 | 2 - 5 | 20 | 0.88 | .571 | 2.86 |
| Downs, Scott | SU | L | 43 | 3 | 10 | 1 | 1.5 | 31 | 9 | 0.29 | 0 - 0 | 0 - 1 | 0 - 2 | 32 | 0 | 0 - 3 | 18 | 0.86 | .643 | 1.84 |
| Burnett, Sean | SU | L | 13 | 1 | 2 | 0 | 1.2 | 11 | 3 | 0.27 | 0 - 0 | 0 - 0 | 0 - 0 | 10 | 0 | 0 - 0 | 5 | 1.00 | .695 | 0.93 |
| Boshers, Buddy | LT | L | 25 | 10 | 11 | 0 | 1.0 | 20 | 6 | 0.30 | 0 - 0 | 0 - 0 | 0 - 0 | 15 | 0 | 0 - 0 | 6 | 1.00 | .646 | 4.70 |
| Roth, Michael | LT | L | 14 | 4 | 1 | 5 | 0.5 | 8 | 1 | 0.13 | 0 - 0 | 0 - 0 | 0 - 0 | 8 | 0 | 0 - 0 | 0 | | .661 | 5.94 |
| Maronde, Nick | LT | L | 10 | 4 | 2 | 0 | 0.9 | 10 | 4 | 0.40 | 0 - 0 | 0 - 0 | 0 - 0 | 4 | 0 | 0 - 0 | 2 | 1.00 | .829 | 6.75 |
| Kohn, Michael | UR | R | 63 | 20 | 19 | 8 | 1.0 | 44 | 11 | 0.25 | 0 - 0 | 0 - 0 | 0 - 2 | 40 | 0 | 0 - 2 | 8 | 0.80 | .711 | 3.74 |
| Jepsen, Kevin | UR | R | 45 | 5 | 14 | 0 | 1.3 | 16 | 5 | 0.31 | 0 - 0 | 0 - 1 | 0 - 1 | 29 | 0 | 0 - 2 | 8 | 0.80 | .769 | 4.50 |
| Richards, Garrett | UR | R | 30 | 9 | 4 | 11 | 0.9 | 16 | 8 | 0.50 | 0 - 0 | 1 - 2 | 0 - 0 | 16 | 0 | 1 - 2 | 5 | 0.86 | .712 | 4.10 |
| Gutierrez, J.C. | UR | R | 28 | 8 | 9 | 2 | 1.2 | 13 | 5 | 0.38 | 0 - 0 | 0 - 1 | 0 - 0 | 16 | 0 | 0 - 1 | 2 | 0.67 | .703 | 5.19 |
| Coello, Robert | UR | R | 16 | 3 | 4 | 3 | 0.9 | 12 | 1 | 0.08 | 0 - 0 | 0 - 0 | 1 - 1 | 12 | 0 | 1 - 1 | 0 | 1.00 | .602 | 3.71 |
| Rasmus, Cory | UR | R | 16 | 4 | 5 | 2 | 0.7 | 5 | 4 | 0.80 | 0 - 0 | 0 - 0 | 0 - 1 | 9 | 0 | 0 - 1 | 2 | 0.67 | .804 | 4.20 |
| Williams, Jerome | UR | R | 12 | 3 | 1 | 8 | 1.0 | 3 | 0 | 0.00 | 0 - 0 | 0 - 0 | 0 - 0 | 6 | 0 | 0 - 0 | 0 | | .552 | 2.35 |
| Lowe, Mark | UR | R | 11 | 5 | 1 | 3 | 1.1 | 8 | 7 | 0.88 | 0 - 0 | 0 - 0 | 0 - 0 | 5 | 0 | 0 - 0 | 1 | 1.00 | .849 | 9.26 |

## Los Angeles Dodgers

| | | | Usage | | | | | Inherited Runners | | | Saves | | | Relief Results | | | | | | |
|---|---|---|---|---|---|---|---|---|---|---|---|---|---|---|---|---|---|---|---|---|
| Pitcher | Pos | T | Rel G | Early Entry | Cons Days | Long | Lev Ind | # | Scrd | Pct | Easy | Reg | Tough | Clean | BS Win | Sv-Opp | Holds | Sv/Hld Pct | Opp OPS | Rel ERA |
| Jansen, Kenley | CL | R | 75 | 0 | 27 | 5 | 1.6 | 14 | 2 | 0.14 | 15 - 15 | 11 - 14 | 2 - 3 | 62 | 1 | 28 - 32 | 16 | 0.92 | .509 | 1.88 |
| Belisario, Ronald | SU | R | 77 | 7 | 24 | 5 | 1.3 | 43 | 13 | 0.30 | 1 - 2 | 0 - 3 | 0 - 0 | 48 | 0 | 1 - 5 | 21 | 0.85 | .725 | 3.97 |
| Rodriguez, Paco | SU | L | 76 | 9 | 20 | 2 | 1.4 | 69 | 14 | 0.20 | 0 - 0 | 0 - 1 | 2 - 4 | 57 | 0 | 2 - 5 | 20 | 0.88 | .511 | 2.32 |
| Howell, J.P. | LT | L | 67 | 25 | 13 | 5 | 0.8 | 45 | 8 | 0.18 | 0 - 0 | 0 - 0 | 0 - 0 | 54 | 0 | 0 - 0 | 11 | 1.00 | .531 | 2.18 |
| Guerrier, Matt | LM | R | 34 | 12 | 8 | 4 | 0.6 | 18 | 5 | 0.28 | 0 - 0 | 0 - 0 | 0 - 1 | 20 | 0 | 0 - 1 | 3 | 0.75 | .776 | 4.80 |
| League, Brandon | UR | R | 58 | 8 | 10 | 6 | 1.2 | 12 | 6 | 0.50 | 11 - 13 | 3 - 5 | 0 - 1 | 34 | 1 | 14 - 19 | 2 | 0.76 | .818 | 5.30 |
| Withrow, Chris | UR | R | 26 | 9 | 2 | 8 | 1.2 | 10 | 0 | 0.00 | 1 - 1 | 0 - 1 | 0 - 0 | 18 | 0 | 1 - 2 | 4 | 0.83 | .536 | 2.60 |
| Marmol, Carlos | UR | R | 21 | 3 | 2 | 6 | 0.4 | 8 | 1 | 0.13 | 0 - 0 | 0 - 0 | 0 - 0 | 17 | 0 | 0 - 0 | 1 | 1.00 | .608 | 2.53 |
| Wilson, Brian | UR | R | 18 | 1 | 5 | 0 | 1.1 | 11 | 1 | 0.09 | 0 - 0 | 0 - 0 | 0 - 0 | 16 | 0 | 0 - 0 | 3 | 1.00 | .467 | 0.66 |
| Moylan, Peter | UR | R | 14 | 4 | 3 | 3 | 0.6 | 11 | 4 | 0.36 | 0 - 0 | 0 - 0 | 0 - 0 | 8 | 0 | 0 - 0 | 1 | 1.00 | .984 | 6.46 |

## Miami Marlins

| | | | Usage | | | | | Inherited Runners | | | Saves | | | Relief Results | | | | | | |
|---|---|---|---|---|---|---|---|---|---|---|---|---|---|---|---|---|---|---|---|---|
| Pitcher | Pos | T | Rel G | Early Entry | Cons Days | Long | Lev Ind | # | Scrd | Pct | Easy | Reg | Tough | Clean | BS Win | Sv-Opp | Holds | Sv/Hld Pct | Opp OPS | Rel ERA |
| Cishek, Steve | CL | R | 69 | 0 | 20 | 6 | 1.7 | 10 | 3 | 0.30 | 18 - 18 | 16 - 18 | 0 - 0 | 54 | 0 | 34 - 36 | 1 | 0.95 | .568 | 2.33 |
| Dunn, Mike | SU | L | 75 | 1 | 18 | 7 | 1.4 | 30 | 10 | 0.33 | 0 - 0 | 0 - 3 | 2 - 2 | 56 | 0 | 2 - 5 | 18 | 0.87 | .604 | 2.66 |
| Jennings, Dan | LT | L | 47 | 13 | 11 | 6 | 0.8 | 24 | 7 | 0.29 | 0 - 0 | 0 - 1 | 0 - 1 | 31 | 0 | 0 - 2 | 1 | 0.33 | .714 | 3.76 |
| Ramos, A.J. | UR | R | 68 | 7 | 9 | 16 | 1.0 | 15 | 7 | 0.47 | 0 - 0 | 0 - 1 | 0 - 3 | 48 | 0 | 0 - 4 | 11 | 0.73 | .603 | 3.15 |
| Webb, Ryan | UR | R | 66 | 24 | 12 | 16 | 1.1 | 48 | 14 | 0.29 | 0 - 0 | 0 - 1 | 0 - 2 | 38 | 0 | 0 - 3 | 4 | 0.57 | .695 | 2.91 |
| Qualls, Chad | UR | R | 66 | 1 | 11 | 2 | 1.5 | 23 | 3 | 0.13 | 0 - 1 | 0 - 1 | 0 - 0 | 51 | 0 | 0 - 2 | 15 | 0.88 | .658 | 2.61 |
| Rauch, Jon | UR | R | 15 | 3 | 2 | 4 | 1.0 | 7 | 3 | 0.43 | 0 - 0 | 0 - 0 | 0 - 0 | 8 | 0 | 0 - 0 | 1 | 1.00 | .840 | 7.56 |
| Caminero, Arquimedes | UR | R | 13 | 5 | 2 | 2 | 0.6 | 6 | 0 | 0.00 | 0 - 0 | 0 - 1 | 0 - 0 | 10 | 0 | 0 - 1 | 1 | 0.50 | .603 | 2.77 |

## Milwaukee Brewers

| | | | Usage | | | | | Inherited Runners | | | Saves | | | Relief Results | | | | | | |
|---|---|---|---|---|---|---|---|---|---|---|---|---|---|---|---|---|---|---|---|---|
| Pitcher | Pos | T | Rel G | Early Entry | Cons Days | Long | Lev Ind | # | Scrd | Pct | Easy | Reg | Tough | Clean | BS Win | Sv-Opp | Holds | Sv/Hld Pct | Opp OPS | Rel ERA |
| Henderson, Jim | CL | R | 61 | 0 | 10 | 6 | 1.5 | 10 | 1 | 0.10 | 21 - 21 | 6 - 10 | 1 - 1 | 46 | 0 | 28 - 32 | 5 | 0.89 | .625 | 2.70 |
| Rodriguez, Francisco | CL | R | 25 | 0 | 5 | 1 | 1.8 | 1 | 0 | 0.00 | 7 - 7 | 2 - 2 | 1 - 1 | 22 | 0 | 10 - 10 | 1 | 1.00 | .564 | 1.09 |
| Kintzler, Brandon | SU | R | 71 | 10 | 14 | 8 | 1.2 | 21 | 5 | 0.24 | 0 - 0 | 0 - 2 | 0 - 2 | 55 | 0 | 0 - 4 | 26 | 0.87 | .567 | 2.69 |
| Axford, John | SU | R | 62 | 8 | 18 | 5 | 1.3 | 19 | 8 | 0.42 | 0 - 1 | 0 - 4 | 0 - 1 | 43 | 0 | 0 - 6 | 19 | 0.76 | .816 | 4.45 |
| Wooten, Rob | SU | R | 27 | 4 | 8 | 4 | 1.1 | 14 | 7 | 0.50 | 0 - 0 | 0 - 1 | 0 - 0 | 20 | 0 | 0 - 1 | 8 | 0.89 | .659 | 3.90 |
| Gonzalez, Michael | LT | L | 75 | 8 | 19 | 2 | 0.9 | 38 | 18 | 0.47 | 0 - 0 | 0 - 0 | 0 - 3 | 47 | 0 | 0 - 3 | 11 | 0.79 | .853 | 4.68 |
| Gorzelanny, Tom | LT | L | 33 | 8 | 5 | 6 | 0.7 | 12 | 1 | 0.08 | 0 - 0 | 0 - 1 | 0 - 0 | 25 | 0 | 0 - 1 | 6 | 0.86 | .574 | 2.70 |
| Figaro, Alfredo | LM | R | 28 | 13 | 1 | 14 | 0.6 | 17 | 6 | 0.35 | 1 - 1 | 0 - 0 | 0 - 0 | 13 | 0 | 1 - 1 | 0 | 1.00 | .710 | 2.94 |
| Badenhop, Burke | UR | R | 63 | 18 | 13 | 11 | 0.7 | 41 | 14 | 0.34 | 0 - 0 | 0 - 1 | 1 - 3 | 40 | 1 | 1 - 4 | 5 | 0.67 | .694 | 3.47 |
| Hand, Donovan | UR | R | 24 | 8 | 3 | 7 | 0.9 | 17 | 3 | 0.18 | 0 - 0 | 0 - 1 | 0 - 0 | 14 | 1 | 0 - 1 | 2 | 0.67 | .685 | 3.13 |
| Thornburg, Tyler | UR | R | 11 | 6 | 1 | 5 | 0.9 | 6 | 1 | 0.17 | 0 - 0 | 0 - 0 | 0 - 0 | 8 | 0 | 0 - 0 | 0 | | .600 | 3.04 |

## Minnesota Twins

| | | | Usage | | | | | Inherited Runners | | | Saves | | | Relief Results | | | | | | |
|---|---|---|---|---|---|---|---|---|---|---|---|---|---|---|---|---|---|---|---|---|
| Pitcher | Pos | T | Rel G | Early Entry | Cons Days | Long | Lev Ind | # | Scrd | Pct | Easy | Reg | Tough | Clean | BS Win | Sv-Opp | Holds | Sv/Hld Pct | Opp OPS | Rel ERA |
| Perkins, Glen | CL | L | 61 | 0 | 16 | 5 | 1.7 | 4 | 3 | 0.75 | 19 - 20 | 16 - 19 | 1 - 1 | 48 | 1 | 36 - 40 | 0 | 0.90 | .562 | 2.30 |
| Burton, Jared | SU | R | 71 | 2 | 14 | 4 | 1.5 | 11 | 2 | 0.18 | 2 - 2 | 0 - 4 | 0 - 1 | 53 | 1 | 2 - 7 | 27 | 0.85 | .688 | 3.82 |
| Duensing, Brian | LT | L | 73 | 16 | 14 | 6 | 1.1 | 57 | 18 | 0.32 | 0 - 0 | 1 - 3 | 0 - 1 | 46 | 1 | 1 - 4 | 15 | 0.84 | .750 | 3.98 |
| Thielbar, Caleb | LT | L | 49 | 6 | 9 | 2 | 0.7 | 33 | 12 | 0.36 | 0 - 0 | 0 - 0 | 0 - 0 | 36 | 0 | 0 - 0 | 1 | 1.00 | .530 | 1.76 |
| Pressly, Ryan | LM | R | 49 | 21 | 1 | 19 | 0.5 | 28 | 10 | 0.36 | 0 - 0 | 0 - 0 | 0 - 0 | 25 | 0 | 0 - 0 | 1 | 1.00 | .677 | 3.87 |
| Swarzak, Anthony | LM | R | 48 | 32 | 1 | 27 | 0.7 | 29 | 12 | 0.41 | 0 - 0 | 0 - 1 | 0 - 1 | 24 | 0 | 0 - 2 | 3 | 0.60 | .649 | 2.91 |
| Fien, Casey | UR | R | 73 | 5 | 16 | 3 | 1.1 | 44 | 6 | 0.14 | 0 - 0 | 0 - 1 | 0 - 1 | 54 | 0 | 0 - 2 | 17 | 0.89 | .627 | 3.92 |
| Roenicke, Josh | UR | R | 63 | 17 | 7 | 8 | 0.9 | 41 | 15 | 0.37 | 1 - 2 | 0 - 1 | 0 - 0 | 36 | 0 | 1 - 3 | 12 | 0.87 | .773 | 4.35 |

## New York Mets

| | | | Usage | | | | | Inherited Runners | | | Saves | | | Relief Results | | | | | | |
|---|---|---|---|---|---|---|---|---|---|---|---|---|---|---|---|---|---|---|---|---|
| Pitcher | Pos | T | Rel G | Early Entry | Cons Days | Long | Lev Ind | # | Scrd | Pct | Easy | Reg | Tough | Clean | BS Win | Sv-Opp | Holds | Sv/Hld Pct | Opp OPS | Rel ERA |
| Parnell, Bobby | CL | R | 49 | 0 | 14 | 5 | 2.1 | 13 | 4 | 0.31 | 11 - 11 | 9 - 12 | 2 - 3 | 37 | 0 | 22 - 26 | 0 | 0.85 | .555 | 2.16 |
| Hawkins, LaTroy | SU | R | 72 | 9 | 16 | 9 | 1.2 | 23 | 9 | 0.39 | 6 - 7 | 7 - 9 | 0 - 0 | 49 | 0 | 13 - 16 | 12 | 0.89 | .656 | 2.93 |
| Rice, Scott | LT | L | 73 | 4 | 30 | 3 | 1.3 | 47 | 7 | 0.15 | 0 - 1 | 0 - 1 | 0 - 0 | 53 | 0 | 0 - 2 | 17 | 0.89 | .634 | 3.71 |
| Edgin, Josh | LT | L | 34 | 3 | 11 | 4 | 0.9 | 22 | 4 | 0.18 | 0 - 0 | 1 - 1 | 0 - 1 | 24 | 0 | 1 - 2 | 3 | 0.80 | .686 | 3.77 |
| Feliciano, Pedro | LT | L | 25 | 3 | 9 | 0 | 1.4 | 22 | 1 | 0.05 | 0 - 0 | 0 - 0 | 0 - 0 | 20 | 0 | 0 - 0 | 5 | 1.00 | .812 | 3.97 |
| Torres, Carlos | LM | R | 24 | 7 | 4 | 11 | 0.9 | 15 | 3 | 0.20 | 0 - 0 | 0 - 0 | 0 - 0 | 18 | 0 | 0 - 0 | 3 | 1.00 | .548 | 1.47 |
| Carson, Robert | LM | L | 14 | 9 | 2 | 6 | 0.4 | 11 | 4 | 0.36 | 0 - 0 | 0 - 0 | 0 - 0 | 4 | 0 | 0 - 0 | 1 | 1.00 | .974 | 8.24 |
| Atchison, Scott | UR | R | 51 | 8 | 10 | 6 | 0.9 | 30 | 12 | 0.40 | 0 - 0 | 0 - 0 | 0 - 0 | 29 | 0 | 0 - 0 | 10 | 1.00 | .647 | 4.37 |
| Aardsma, David | UR | R | 43 | 10 | 11 | 5 | 1.0 | 19 | 0 | 0.00 | 0 - 0 | 0 - 2 | 0 - 0 | 31 | 0 | 0 - 2 | 4 | 0.67 | .800 | 4.31 |
| Lyon, Brandon | UR | R | 37 | 4 | 6 | 5 | 1.3 | 18 | 8 | 0.44 | 0 - 0 | 0 - 1 | 0 - 2 | 22 | 0 | 0 - 3 | 7 | 0.70 | .860 | 4.98 |
| Burke, Greg | UR | R | 32 | 6 | 8 | 6 | 0.8 | 15 | 6 | 0.40 | 0 - 0 | 0 - 0 | 0 - 0 | 16 | 0 | 0 - 0 | 1 | 1.00 | .857 | 5.68 |
| Germen, Gonzalez | UR | R | 29 | 7 | 6 | 6 | 0.8 | 10 | 2 | 0.20 | 0 - 0 | 1 - 1 | 0 - 2 | 19 | 0 | 1 - 3 | 1 | 0.50 | .676 | 3.93 |
| Black, Vic | UR | R | 15 | 2 | 6 | 1 | 1.6 | 6 | 1 | 0.17 | 1 - 1 | 0 - 0 | 0 - 1 | 10 | 0 | 1 - 2 | 4 | 0.83 | .617 | 3.46 |

## New York Yankees

| | | | Usage | | | | | Inherited Runners | | | Saves | | | Relief Results | | | | | | |
|---|---|---|---|---|---|---|---|---|---|---|---|---|---|---|---|---|---|---|---|---|
| Pitcher | Pos | T | Rel G | Early Entry | Cons Days | Long | Lev Ind | # | Scrd | Pct | Easy | Reg | Tough | Clean | BS Win | Sv-Opp | Holds | Sv/Hld Pct | Opp OPS | Rel ERA |
| Rivera, Mariano | CL | R | 64 | 0 | 17 | 4 | 1.9 | 15 | 5 | 0.33 | 28 - 30 | 14 - 19 | 2 - 2 | 51 | 2 | 44 - 51 | 0 | 0.86 | .615 | 2.11 |
| Robertson, David | SU | R | 70 | 0 | 19 | 3 | 1.7 | 12 | 6 | 0.50 | 1 - 3 | 2 - 2 | 0 - 0 | 59 | 0 | 3 - 5 | 33 | 0.95 | .584 | 2.04 |
| Logan, Boone | LT | L | 61 | 12 | 13 | 0 | 1.1 | 55 | 17 | 0.31 | 0 - 0 | 0 - 1 | 0 - 1 | 45 | 0 | 0 - 2 | 11 | 0.85 | .709 | 3.23 |
| Warren, Adam | LM | R | 32 | 13 | 1 | 20 | 0.6 | 12 | 5 | 0.42 | 0 - 0 | 1 - 1 | 0 - 0 | 17 | 0 | 1 - 1 | 1 | 1.00 | .786 | 3.52 |
| Kelley, Shawn | UR | R | 57 | 11 | 8 | 13 | 0.9 | 40 | 4 | 0.10 | 0 - 0 | 0 - 1 | 0 - 0 | 37 | 0 | 0 - 1 | 11 | 0.92 | .729 | 4.39 |
| Chamberlain, Joba | UR | R | 45 | 3 | 10 | 7 | 0.7 | 20 | 9 | 0.45 | 0 - 0 | 1 - 1 | 0 - 0 | 27 | 0 | 1 - 1 | 5 | 1.00 | .825 | 4.93 |
| Claiborne, Preston | UR | R | 44 | 15 | 9 | 9 | 0.6 | 32 | 6 | 0.19 | 0 - 0 | 0 - 0 | 0 - 0 | 31 | 0 | 0 - 0 | 4 | 1.00 | .734 | 4.11 |
| Phelps, David | UR | R | 10 | 6 | 0 | 7 | 1.0 | 9 | 6 | 0.67 | 0 - 0 | 0 - 0 | 0 - 1 | 3 | 0 | 0 - 1 | 1 | 0.50 | .753 | 5.14 |

## Oakland Athletics

| | | | Usage | | | | | Inherited Runners | | | Saves | | | Relief Results | | | | | | |
|---|---|---|---|---|---|---|---|---|---|---|---|---|---|---|---|---|---|---|---|---|
| Pitcher | Pos | T | Rel G | Early Entry | Cons Days | Long | Lev Ind | # | Scrd | Pct | Easy | Reg | Tough | Clean | BS Win | Sv-Opp | Holds | Sv/Hld Pct | Opp OPS | Rel ERA |
| Balfour, Grant | CL | R | 65 | 0 | 20 | 5 | 1.8 | 6 | 5 | 0.83 | 20 - 23 | 18 - 18 | 0 - 0 | 50 | 0 | 38 - 41 | 0 | 0.93 | .610 | 2.59 |
| Cook, Ryan | SU | R | 71 | 3 | 13 | 11 | 1.6 | 30 | 15 | 0.50 | 0 - 0 | 1 - 2 | 1 - 7 | 51 | 2 | 2 - 9 | 23 | 0.78 | .616 | 2.54 |
| Doolittle, Sean | SU | L | 70 | 0 | 14 | 1 | 1.4 | 32 | 2 | 0.06 | 0 - 2 | 0 - 2 | 2 - 3 | 55 | 2 | 2 - 7 | 26 | 0.85 | .573 | 3.13 |
| Blevins, Jerry | LT | L | 67 | 25 | 14 | 3 | 0.9 | 45 | 16 | 0.36 | 0 - 0 | 0 - 1 | 0 - 3 | 43 | 0 | 0 - 4 | 4 | 0.50 | .651 | 3.15 |
| Anderson, Brett | LT | L | 11 | 3 | 1 | 5 | 0.9 | 5 | 1 | 0.20 | 0 - 0 | 3 - 3 | 0 - 0 | 4 | 0 | 3 - 3 | 1 | 1.00 | .732 | 4.71 |
| Chavez, Jesse | LM | R | 35 | 14 | 4 | 16 | 0.8 | 26 | 8 | 0.31 | 0 - 0 | 1 - 1 | 0 - 1 | 17 | 0 | 1 - 2 | 1 | 0.67 | .620 | 3.92 |
| Neshek, Pat | UR | R | 45 | 8 | 5 | 7 | 0.3 | 25 | 7 | 0.28 | 0 - 0 | 0 - 0 | 0 - 0 | 30 | 0 | 0 - 0 | 1 | 1.00 | .738 | 3.35 |
| Otero, Dan | UR | R | 33 | 11 | 9 | 6 | 0.8 | 19 | 7 | 0.37 | 0 - 0 | 0 - 0 | 0 - 1 | 23 | 0 | 0 - 1 | 8 | 0.89 | .613 | 1.38 |
| Scribner, Evan | UR | R | 18 | 4 | 2 | 8 | 0.2 | 9 | 3 | 0.33 | 0 - 0 | 0 - 0 | 0 - 0 | 10 | 0 | 0 - 0 | 0 | | .747 | 4.39 |
| Resop, Chris | UR | R | 18 | 7 | 2 | 5 | 0.5 | 13 | 3 | 0.23 | 0 - 0 | 0 - 0 | 0 - 0 | 9 | 0 | 0 - 0 | 0 | | .871 | 6.00 |

## Philadelphia Phillies

| | | | Usage | | | | | Inherited Runners | | | Saves | | | Relief Results | | | | | | |
|---|---|---|---|---|---|---|---|---|---|---|---|---|---|---|---|---|---|---|---|---|
| Pitcher | Pos | T | Rel G | Early Entry | Cons Days | Long | Lev Ind | # | Scrd | Pct | Easy | Reg | Tough | Clean | BS Win | Sv-Opp | Holds | Sv/Hld Pct | Opp OPS | Rel ERA |
| Papelbon, Jonathan | CL | R | 61 | 0 | 16 | 5 | 1.8 | 4 | 3 | 0.75 | 16 - 18 | 13 - 18 | 0 - 0 | 46 | 3 | 29 - 36 | 0 | 0.81 | .631 | 2.92 |
| Bastardo, Antonio | SU | L | 48 | 2 | 10 | 1 | 1.3 | 13 | 2 | 0.15 | 2 - 2 | 0 - 1 | 0 - 2 | 35 | 0 | 2 - 5 | 14 | 0.84 | .637 | 2.32 |
| Adams, Mike | SU | R | 28 | 0 | 7 | 1 | 1.4 | 5 | 2 | 0.40 | 0 - 0 | 0 - 1 | 0 - 0 | 17 | 0 | 0 - 1 | 8 | 0.89 | .759 | 3.96 |
| Diekman, Jake | LT | L | 45 | 5 | 14 | 2 | 1.2 | 19 | 3 | 0.16 | 0 - 0 | 0 - 1 | 0 - 0 | 34 | 0 | 0 - 1 | 11 | 0.92 | .598 | 2.58 |
| Horst, Jeremy | LT | L | 28 | 10 | 6 | 6 | 0.7 | 29 | 9 | 0.31 | 0 - 0 | 0 - 0 | 0 - 1 | 14 | 0 | 0 - 1 | 2 | 0.67 | .905 | 6.23 |
| Jimenez, Cesar | LT | L | 19 | 5 | 4 | 3 | 0.6 | 15 | 4 | 0.27 | 0 - 0 | 0 - 0 | 0 - 0 | 13 | 0 | 0 - 0 | 0 | | .688 | 3.71 |
| Savery, Joe | LT | L | 18 | 6 | 0 | 3 | 0.4 | 2 | 1 | 0.50 | 0 - 0 | 0 - 0 | 0 - 0 | 13 | 0 | 0 - 0 | 1 | 1.00 | .607 | 3.15 |
| Garcia, Luis | LM | R | 24 | 10 | 3 | 7 | 1.0 | 18 | 7 | 0.39 | 0 - 0 | 0 - 0 | 0 - 0 | 14 | 0 | 0 - 0 | 1 | 1.00 | .764 | 3.73 |
| Valdes, Raul | LM | L | 16 | 9 | 1 | 9 | 0.2 | 6 | 2 | 0.33 | 0 - 0 | 0 - 0 | 0 - 0 | 6 | 0 | 0 - 0 | 0 | | .800 | 5.74 |
| De Fratus, Justin | UR | R | 58 | 11 | 14 | 4 | 1.1 | 48 | 16 | 0.33 | 0 - 0 | 0 - 1 | 0 - 0 | 35 | 0 | 0 - 1 | 9 | 0.90 | .738 | 3.86 |
| Rosenberg, B.J. | UR | R | 22 | 0 | 7 | 2 | 1.0 | 4 | 1 | 0.25 | 0 - 0 | 1 - 1 | 0 - 0 | 16 | 0 | 1 - 1 | 2 | 1.00 | .683 | 4.58 |
| Aumont, Phillippe | UR | R | 22 | 2 | 4 | 3 | 0.9 | 3 | 3 | 1.00 | 0 - 0 | 0 - 0 | 0 - 0 | 15 | 0 | 0 - 0 | 1 | 1.00 | .818 | 4.19 |
| Ramirez, J.C. | UR | R | 18 | 7 | 0 | 7 | 0.7 | 7 | 2 | 0.29 | 0 - 0 | 0 - 0 | 0 - 0 | 6 | 0 | 0 - 0 | 3 | 1.00 | .975 | 7.50 |
| Stutes, Michael | UR | R | 16 | 7 | 4 | 3 | 0.9 | 4 | 1 | 0.25 | 0 - 0 | 0 - 0 | 0 - 0 | 12 | 0 | 0 - 0 | 3 | 1.00 | .640 | 4.58 |
| Durbin, Chad | UR | R | 16 | 7 | 2 | 4 | 0.5 | 17 | 9 | 0.53 | 0 - 0 | 0 - 0 | 0 - 0 | 4 | 0 | 0 - 0 | 0 | | 1.063 | 9.00 |
| Miner, Zach | UR | R | 13 | 9 | 1 | 8 | 0.7 | 9 | 7 | 0.78 | 0 - 0 | 0 - 1 | 0 - 0 | 6 | 0 | 0 - 1 | 0 | 0.00 | .787 | 3.72 |

# Pittsburgh Pirates

| | | | Usage | | | | | Inherited Runners | | | Saves | | | Relief Results | | | | | | |
|---|---|---|---|---|---|---|---|---|---|---|---|---|---|---|---|---|---|---|---|---|
| Pitcher | Pos | T | Rel G | Early Entry | Cons Days | Long | Lev Ind | # | Scrd | Pct | Easy | Reg | Tough | Clean | BS Win | Sv-Opp | Holds | Sv/Hld Pct | Opp OPS | Rel ERA |
| Grilli, Jason | CL | R | 54 | 0 | 13 | 2 | 1.4 | 2 | 0 | 0.00 | 24 - 24 | 9 - 11 | 0 - 0 | 44 | 0 | 33 - 35 | 2 | 0.95 | .595 | 2.70 |
| Melancon, Mark | SU | R | 72 | 0 | 22 | 1 | 1.9 | 0 | 0 | 0.00 | 10 - 11 | 6 - 10 | 0 - 0 | 61 | 1 | 16 - 21 | 26 | 0.89 | .511 | 1.39 |
| Watson, Tony | SU | L | 67 | 6 | 12 | 8 | 1.2 | 27 | 6 | 0.22 | 0 - 1 | 2 - 2 | 0 - 1 | 47 | 1 | 2 - 4 | 22 | 0.92 | .544 | 2.39 |
| Wilson, Justin | LM | L | 58 | 24 | 5 | 17 | 1.2 | 31 | 11 | 0.35 | 0 - 0 | 0 - 1 | 0 - 2 | 42 | 1 | 0 - 3 | 14 | 0.82 | .543 | 2.08 |
| Mazzaro, Vin | LM | R | 57 | 23 | 7 | 15 | 1.0 | 32 | 4 | 0.13 | 0 - 0 | 0 - 1 | 1 - 2 | 44 | 0 | 1 - 3 | 6 | 0.78 | .628 | 2.81 |
| Gomez, Jeanmar | LM | R | 26 | 14 | 1 | 12 | 0.9 | 11 | 3 | 0.27 | 0 - 0 | 0 - 0 | 0 - 0 | 17 | 0 | 0 - 0 | 3 | 1.00 | .628 | 3.77 |
| Morris, Bryan | UR | R | 55 | 7 | 10 | 10 | 1.0 | 36 | 8 | 0.22 | 0 - 0 | 0 - 0 | 0 - 0 | 37 | 0 | 0 - 0 | 7 | 1.00 | .705 | 3.46 |
| Hughes, Jared | UR | R | 29 | 10 | 5 | 4 | 0.6 | 17 | 3 | 0.18 | 0 - 0 | 0 - 0 | 0 - 0 | 16 | 0 | 0 - 0 | 3 | 1.00 | .786 | 4.78 |

# San Diego Padres

| | | | Usage | | | | | Inherited Runners | | | Saves | | | Relief Results | | | | | | |
|---|---|---|---|---|---|---|---|---|---|---|---|---|---|---|---|---|---|---|---|---|
| Pitcher | Pos | T | Rel G | Early Entry | Cons Days | Long | Lev Ind | # | Scrd | Pct | Easy | Reg | Tough | Clean | BS Win | Sv-Opp | Holds | Sv/Hld Pct | Opp OPS | Rel ERA |
| Street, Huston | CL | R | 58 | 0 | 15 | 2 | 1.3 | 4 | 2 | 0.50 | 22 - 22 | 11 - 13 | 0 - 0 | 45 | 0 | 33 - 35 | 0 | 0.94 | .691 | 2.70 |
| Gregerson, Luke | SU | R | 73 | 0 | 21 | 1 | 1.7 | 19 | 5 | 0.26 | 3 - 5 | 1 - 3 | 0 - 1 | 55 | 1 | 4 - 9 | 25 | 0.85 | .572 | 2.71 |
| Thayer, Dale | SU | R | 69 | 9 | 15 | 4 | 1.1 | 33 | 7 | 0.21 | 1 - 2 | 0 - 2 | 0 - 0 | 49 | 0 | 1 - 4 | 18 | 0.86 | .691 | 3.32 |
| Thatcher, Joe | LT | L | 50 | 4 | 15 | 1 | 1.1 | 36 | 4 | 0.11 | 0 - 0 | 0 - 0 | 0 - 2 | 40 | 0 | 0 - 2 | 11 | 0.85 | .629 | 2.10 |
| Hynes, Colt | LT | L | 22 | 5 | 4 | 4 | 0.3 | 15 | 6 | 0.40 | 0 - 0 | 0 - 0 | 0 - 0 | 12 | 0 | 0 - 0 | 1 | 1.00 | .971 | 9.00 |
| Layne, Tom | LT | L | 14 | 6 | 2 | 1 | 1.0 | 13 | 1 | 0.08 | 0 - 0 | 0 - 0 | 0 - 0 | 10 | 0 | 0 - 0 | 0 | | .899 | 2.08 |
| Stauffer, Tim | LM | R | 43 | 18 | 7 | 17 | 0.8 | 14 | 4 | 0.29 | 0 - 0 | 0 - 0 | 0 - 1 | 24 | 1 | 0 - 1 | 7 | 0.88 | .644 | 3.75 |
| Bass, Anthony | LM | R | 24 | 9 | 0 | 14 | 0.3 | 21 | 14 | 0.67 | 0 - 0 | 0 - 0 | 0 - 0 | 9 | 0 | 0 - 0 | 0 | | .829 | 5.36 |
| Ross, Tyson | LM | R | 19 | 10 | 2 | 7 | 1.0 | 19 | 4 | 0.21 | 0 - 0 | 0 - 0 | 0 - 0 | 11 | 0 | 0 - 0 | 0 | | .706 | 3.48 |
| Boxberger, Brad | LM | R | 18 | 6 | 2 | 7 | 0.7 | 13 | 2 | 0.15 | 0 - 0 | 1 - 1 | 0 - 0 | 11 | 0 | 1 - 1 | 0 | 1.00 | .760 | 2.86 |
| Vincent, Nick | UR | R | 45 | 2 | 10 | 3 | 1.1 | 21 | 4 | 0.19 | 0 - 0 | 0 - 0 | 1 - 1 | 36 | 0 | 1 - 1 | 10 | 1.00 | .525 | 2.14 |
| Brach, Brad | UR | R | 33 | 10 | 8 | 5 | 0.6 | 22 | 8 | 0.36 | 0 - 0 | 0 - 0 | 0 - 0 | 23 | 0 | 0 - 0 | 2 | 1.00 | .819 | 3.19 |

# San Francisco Giants

| | | | Usage | | | | | Inherited Runners | | | Saves | | | Relief Results | | | | | | |
|---|---|---|---|---|---|---|---|---|---|---|---|---|---|---|---|---|---|---|---|---|
| Pitcher | Pos | T | Rel G | Early Entry | Cons Days | Long | Lev Ind | # | Scrd | Pct | Easy | Reg | Tough | Clean | BS Win | Sv-Opp | Holds | Sv/Hld Pct | Opp OPS | Rel ERA |
| Romo, Sergio | CL | R | 65 | 0 | 19 | 1 | 2.3 | 15 | 4 | 0.27 | 22 - 23 | 15 - 19 | 1 - 1 | 50 | 0 | 38 - 43 | 0 | 0.88 | .614 | 2.54 |
| Casilla, Santiago | SU | R | 57 | 3 | 20 | 4 | 1.8 | 32 | 5 | 0.16 | 0 - 1 | 1 - 1 | 1 - 1 | 44 | 0 | 2 - 3 | 22 | 0.96 | .627 | 2.16 |
| Affeldt, Jeremy | SU | L | 39 | 2 | 12 | 2 | 1.7 | 15 | 8 | 0.53 | 0 - 0 | 0 - 2 | 0 - 2 | 28 | 0 | 0 - 4 | 11 | 0.73 | .646 | 3.74 |
| Lopez, Javier | LT | L | 69 | 7 | 22 | 2 | 1.4 | 57 | 6 | 0.11 | 0 - 0 | 0 - 0 | 1 - 1 | 57 | 0 | 1 - 1 | 15 | 1.00 | .573 | 1.83 |
| Mijares, Jose | LT | L | 60 | 26 | 17 | 8 | 0.8 | 45 | 19 | 0.42 | 0 - 0 | 0 - 0 | 0 - 0 | 36 | 0 | 0 - 0 | 6 | 1.00 | .844 | 4.22 |
| Gaudin, Chad | LM | R | 18 | 7 | 1 | 10 | 0.8 | 6 | 1 | 0.17 | 0 - 0 | 0 - 0 | 0 - 0 | 13 | 0 | 0 - 0 | 2 | 1.00 | .586 | 2.05 |
| Moscoso, Guillermo | LM | R | 11 | 10 | 1 | 7 | 0.9 | 1 | 1 | 1.00 | 0 - 0 | 0 - 0 | 0 - 0 | 5 | 0 | 0 - 0 | 0 | | .668 | 3.86 |
| Kontos, George | UR | R | 52 | 18 | 13 | 12 | 0.6 | 44 | 15 | 0.34 | 0 - 0 | 0 - 0 | 0 - 1 | 29 | 0 | 0 - 1 | 5 | 0.83 | .788 | 4.39 |
| Machi, Jean | UR | R | 51 | 10 | 15 | 7 | 1.0 | 35 | 12 | 0.34 | 0 - 0 | 0 - 0 | 0 - 2 | 37 | 0 | 0 - 2 | 11 | 0.85 | .586 | 2.38 |
| Rosario, Sandy | UR | R | 43 | 2 | 11 | 7 | 1.1 | 14 | 3 | 0.21 | 0 - 0 | 0 - 0 | 0 - 0 | 28 | 0 | 0 - 0 | 6 | 1.00 | .644 | 3.02 |
| Dunning, Jake | UR | R | 29 | 9 | 9 | 1 | 0.7 | 25 | 11 | 0.44 | 0 - 0 | 0 - 0 | 0 - 0 | 21 | 0 | 0 - 0 | 2 | 1.00 | .664 | 2.84 |

## Seattle Mariners

| | | | Usage | | | | | Inherited Runners | | | Saves | | | Relief Results | | | | | | |
|---|---|---|---|---|---|---|---|---|---|---|---|---|---|---|---|---|---|---|---|---|
| Pitcher | Pos | T | Rel G | Early Entry | Cons Days | Long | Lev Ind | # | Scrd | Pct | Easy | Reg | Tough | Clean | BS Win | Sv-Opp | Holds | Sv/Hld Pct | Opp OPS | Rel ERA |
| Wilhelmsen, Tom | CL | R | 59 | 4 | 11 | 5 | 1.6 | 10 | 4 | 0.40 | 15 - 16 | 9 - 13 | 0 - 0 | 40 | 0 | 24 - 29 | 2 | 0.84 | .603 | 4.12 |
| Farquhar, Danny | CL | R | 46 | 7 | 8 | 15 | 1.3 | 15 | 6 | 0.40 | 10 - 10 | 5 - 8 | 1 - 2 | 31 | 0 | 16 - 20 | 2 | 0.82 | .586 | 4.20 |
| Furbush, Charlie | SU | L | 71 | 14 | 16 | 10 | 1.3 | 57 | 18 | 0.32 | 0 - 0 | 0 - 4 | 0 - 2 | 45 | 0 | 0 - 6 | 20 | 0.77 | .603 | 3.74 |
| Medina, Yoervis | SU | R | 63 | 6 | 11 | 9 | 1.7 | 53 | 16 | 0.30 | 0 - 0 | 1 - 3 | 0 - 1 | 38 | 1 | 1 - 4 | 19 | 0.87 | .629 | 2.91 |
| Perez, Oliver | LT | L | 61 | 5 | 13 | 8 | 1.1 | 39 | 14 | 0.36 | 1 - 1 | 1 - 1 | 0 - 1 | 44 | 0 | 2 - 3 | 8 | 0.91 | .731 | 3.74 |
| Luetge, Lucas | LT | L | 35 | 5 | 8 | 5 | 0.8 | 23 | 9 | 0.39 | 0 - 0 | 0 - 0 | 0 - 0 | 22 | 0 | 0 - 0 | 1 | 1.00 | .784 | 4.86 |
| LaFromboise, Bobby | LT | L | 10 | 3 | 0 | 2 | 0.6 | 10 | 4 | 0.40 | 0 - 0 | 0 - 0 | 0 - 0 | 4 | 0 | 0 - 0 | 1 | 1.00 | .681 | 5.91 |
| Capps, Carter | UR | R | 53 | 13 | 10 | 17 | 1.0 | 29 | 5 | 0.17 | 0 - 0 | 0 - 1 | 0 - 1 | 30 | 1 | 0 - 2 | 9 | 0.82 | .878 | 5.49 |
| Noesi, Hector | UR | R | 11 | 7 | 0 | 8 | 0.6 | 8 | 7 | 0.88 | 0 - 0 | 0 - 0 | 0 - 0 | 1 | 0 | 0 - 0 | 0 | | .998 | 7.83 |
| Beavan, Blake | UR | R | 10 | 8 | 1 | 8 | 0.5 | 9 | 3 | 0.33 | 0 - 0 | 0 - 0 | 0 - 0 | 1 | 0 | 0 - 0 | 0 | | .720 | 5.28 |

## St Louis Cardinals

| | | | Usage | | | | | Inherited Runners | | | Saves | | | Relief Results | | | | | | |
|---|---|---|---|---|---|---|---|---|---|---|---|---|---|---|---|---|---|---|---|---|
| Pitcher | Pos | T | Rel G | Early Entry | Cons Days | Long | Lev Ind | # | Scrd | Pct | Easy | Reg | Tough | Clean | BS Win | Sv-Opp | Holds | Sv/Hld Pct | Opp OPS | Rel ERA |
| Mujica, Edward | CL | R | 65 | 1 | 19 | 1 | 1.8 | 25 | 4 | 0.16 | 22 - 22 | 13 - 16 | 2 - 3 | 48 | 1 | 37 - 41 | 5 | 0.91 | .674 | 2.78 |
| Rosenthal, Trevor | SU | R | 74 | 0 | 19 | 8 | 1.5 | 21 | 5 | 0.24 | 1 - 2 | 2 - 6 | 0 - 0 | 55 | 0 | 3 - 8 | 29 | 0.86 | .608 | 2.63 |
| Choate, Randy | LT | L | 64 | 12 | 19 | 0 | 1.0 | 59 | 9 | 0.15 | 0 - 0 | 0 - 0 | 0 - 1 | 53 | 0 | 0 - 1 | 15 | 0.94 | .537 | 2.29 |
| Siegrist, Kevin | LT | L | 45 | 7 | 9 | 3 | 0.9 | 19 | 4 | 0.21 | 0 - 0 | 0 - 0 | 0 - 0 | 39 | 0 | 0 - 0 | 11 | 1.00 | .432 | 0.45 |
| Freeman, Sam | LT | L | 13 | 4 | 3 | 1 | 0.6 | 5 | 1 | 0.20 | 0 - 0 | 0 - 0 | 0 - 0 | 10 | 0 | 0 - 0 | 1 | 1.00 | .515 | 2.19 |
| Rzepczynski, Marc | LT | L | 11 | 2 | 3 | 2 | 0.5 | 7 | 6 | 0.86 | 0 - 0 | 0 - 0 | 0 - 0 | 5 | 0 | 0 - 0 | 0 | | .920 | 7.84 |
| Maness, Seth | UR | R | 66 | 24 | 21 | 7 | 1.2 | 58 | 7 | 0.12 | 1 - 2 | 0 - 0 | 0 - 1 | 48 | 1 | 1 - 3 | 15 | 0.89 | .725 | 2.32 |
| Salas, Fernando | UR | R | 27 | 4 | 5 | 5 | 0.8 | 24 | 8 | 0.33 | 0 - 0 | 0 - 0 | 0 - 2 | 11 | 0 | 0 - 2 | 2 | 0.50 | .715 | 4.50 |
| Kelly, Joe | UR | R | 22 | 10 | 1 | 6 | 0.9 | 16 | 2 | 0.13 | 0 - 1 | 0 - 0 | 0 - 0 | 14 | 0 | 0 - 1 | 2 | 0.67 | .777 | 3.65 |
| Martinez, Carlos | UR | R | 20 | 5 | 0 | 3 | 0.9 | 7 | 3 | 0.43 | 0 - 0 | 1 - 1 | 0 - 0 | 13 | 0 | 1 - 1 | 3 | 1.00 | .656 | 4.56 |
| Boggs, Mitchell | UR | R | 18 | 0 | 7 | 3 | 1.3 | 2 | 1 | 0.50 | 2 - 2 | 0 - 3 | 0 - 0 | 9 | 0 | 2 - 5 | 0 | 0.40 | 1.007 | 11.05 |
| Butler, Keith | UR | R | 16 | 1 | 3 | 5 | 0.2 | 3 | 0 | 0.00 | 0 - 0 | 0 - 0 | 0 - 0 | 13 | 0 | 0 - 0 | 0 | | .572 | 4.05 |
| Axford, John | UR | R | 13 | 0 | 3 | 0 | 0.7 | 5 | 3 | 0.60 | 0 - 0 | 0 - 0 | 0 - 1 | 9 | 1 | 0 - 1 | 0 | 0.00 | .682 | 1.74 |
| Blazek, Michael | UR | R | 11 | 1 | 1 | 2 | 0.5 | 7 | 1 | 0.14 | 0 - 0 | 0 - 0 | 0 - 0 | 7 | 0 | 0 - 0 | 0 | | .818 | 6.97 |

## Tampa Bay Rays

| | | | Usage | | | | | Inherited Runners | | | Saves | | | Relief Results | | | | | | |
|---|---|---|---|---|---|---|---|---|---|---|---|---|---|---|---|---|---|---|---|---|
| Pitcher | Pos | T | Rel G | Early Entry | Cons Days | Long | Lev Ind | # | Scrd | Pct | Easy | Reg | Tough | Clean | BS Win | Sv-Opp | Holds | Sv/Hld Pct | Opp OPS | Rel ERA |
| Rodney, Fernando | CL | R | 68 | 0 | 22 | 7 | 2.2 | 18 | 6 | 0.33 | 27 - 30 | 9 - 12 | 1 - 3 | 51 | 1 | 37 - 45 | 0 | 0.82 | .634 | 3.38 |
| Peralta, Joel | SU | R | 80 | 0 | 25 | 1 | 1.6 | 30 | 4 | 0.13 | 0 - 2 | 1 - 2 | 0 - 0 | 58 | 0 | 1 - 4 | 41 | 0.93 | .586 | 3.41 |
| McGee, Jake | SU | L | 71 | 10 | 17 | 8 | 1.4 | 39 | 18 | 0.46 | 0 - 1 | 1 - 2 | 0 - 2 | 49 | 0 | 1 - 5 | 27 | 0.88 | .659 | 4.02 |
| Ramos, Cesar | LT | L | 48 | 10 | 8 | 17 | 0.4 | 23 | 7 | 0.30 | 0 - 0 | 1 - 1 | 0 - 0 | 26 | 0 | 1 - 1 | 1 | 1.00 | .687 | 4.14 |
| Torres, Alex | LM | L | 39 | 25 | 3 | 16 | 0.9 | 27 | 7 | 0.26 | 0 - 0 | 0 - 0 | 0 - 1 | 27 | 0 | 0 - 1 | 5 | 0.83 | .468 | 1.71 |
| Wright, Wesley | LM | L | 16 | 10 | 2 | 1 | 0.4 | 6 | 1 | 0.17 | 0 - 0 | 0 - 0 | 0 - 0 | 12 | 0 | 0 - 0 | 1 | 1.00 | .672 | 2.92 |
| Wright, Jamey | UR | R | 65 | 21 | 16 | 7 | 0.7 | 24 | 9 | 0.38 | 0 - 0 | 0 - 0 | 0 - 1 | 46 | 0 | 0 - 1 | 6 | 0.86 | .622 | 3.03 |
| Farnsworth, Kyle | UR | R | 39 | 6 | 3 | 0 | 0.9 | 17 | 6 | 0.35 | 0 - 0 | 0 - 1 | 0 - 0 | 25 | 0 | 0 - 1 | 2 | 0.67 | .828 | 5.76 |
| Gomes, Brandon | UR | R | 26 | 9 | 8 | 2 | 0.8 | 18 | 3 | 0.17 | 0 - 0 | 0 - 0 | 0 - 0 | 17 | 0 | 0 - 0 | 0 | | .784 | 6.52 |
| Lueke, Josh | UR | R | 19 | 7 | 5 | 5 | 0.9 | 22 | 9 | 0.41 | 0 - 0 | 0 - 0 | 0 - 0 | 8 | 0 | 0 - 0 | 2 | 1.00 | .861 | 5.06 |

# Texas Rangers

| | | | Usage | | | | | Inherited Runners | | | Saves | | | Relief Results | | | | | | |
|---|---|---|---|---|---|---|---|---|---|---|---|---|---|---|---|---|---|---|---|---|
| Pitcher | Pos | T | Rel G | Early Entry | Cons Days | Long | Lev Ind | # | Scrd | Pct | Easy | Reg | Tough | Clean | BS Win | Sv-Opp | Holds | Sv/Hld Pct | Opp OPS | Rel ERA |
| Nathan, Joe | CL | R | 67 | 0 | 27 | 3 | 2.0 | 10 | 6 | 0.60 | 27 - 27 | 16 - 19 | 0 - 0 | 57 | 0 | 43 - 46 | 0 | 0.93 | .464 | 1.39 |
| Scheppers, Tanner | SU | R | 76 | 0 | 24 | 7 | 1.4 | 18 | 3 | 0.17 | 0 - 1 | 1 - 2 | 0 - 0 | 59 | 0 | 1 - 3 | 27 | 0.93 | .605 | 1.88 |
| Ross, Robbie | LT | L | 65 | 14 | 10 | 9 | 1.3 | 42 | 10 | 0.24 | 0 - 0 | 0 - 0 | 0 - 1 | 49 | 0 | 0 - 1 | 15 | 0.94 | .684 | 3.03 |
| Cotts, Neal | LT | L | 58 | 12 | 15 | 7 | 1.3 | 30 | 5 | 0.17 | 0 - 0 | 0 - 2 | 1 - 2 | 49 | 1 | 1 - 4 | 11 | 0.80 | .499 | 1.11 |
| Kirkman, Michael | LT | L | 25 | 4 | 6 | 7 | 0.6 | 13 | 6 | 0.46 | 0 - 0 | 1 - 1 | 0 - 1 | 10 | 0 | 1 - 2 | 0 | 0.50 | .979 | 8.18 |
| Ortiz, Joe | LM | L | 32 | 16 | 2 | 10 | 0.5 | 20 | 7 | 0.35 | 0 - 0 | 0 - 0 | 0 - 0 | 14 | 0 | 0 - 0 | 2 | 1.00 | .747 | 4.23 |
| Frasor, Jason | UR | R | 61 | 14 | 10 | 2 | 1.0 | 38 | 9 | 0.24 | 0 - 0 | 0 - 0 | 0 - 1 | 43 | 0 | 0 - 1 | 10 | 0.91 | .598 | 2.57 |
| Soria, Joakim | UR | R | 26 | 3 | 5 | 3 | 0.9 | 11 | 4 | 0.36 | 0 - 0 | 0 - 0 | 0 - 0 | 18 | 0 | 0 - 0 | 6 | 1.00 | .624 | 3.80 |
| Wolf, Ross | UR | R | 19 | 7 | 2 | 6 | 0.9 | 14 | 5 | 0.36 | 0 - 0 | 0 - 0 | 0 - 0 | 7 | 0 | 0 - 0 | 1 | 1.00 | .751 | 3.12 |
| Burns, Cory | UR | R | 10 | 4 | 3 | 4 | 0.3 | 8 | 2 | 0.25 | 0 - 0 | 0 - 0 | 0 - 0 | 7 | 0 | 0 - 0 | 0 | | .762 | 3.18 |

# Toronto Blue Jays

| | | | Usage | | | | | Inherited Runners | | | Saves | | | Relief Results | | | | | | |
|---|---|---|---|---|---|---|---|---|---|---|---|---|---|---|---|---|---|---|---|---|
| Pitcher | Pos | T | Rel G | Early Entry | Cons Days | Long | Lev Ind | # | Scrd | Pct | Easy | Reg | Tough | Clean | BS Win | Sv-Opp | Holds | Sv/Hld Pct | Opp OPS | Rel ERA |
| Janssen, Casey | CL | R | 56 | 0 | 7 | 3 | 1.9 | 10 | 2 | 0.20 | 24 - 25 | 10 - 11 | 0 - 0 | 44 | 0 | 34 - 36 | 1 | 0.95 | .558 | 2.56 |
| Santos, Sergio | SU | R | 29 | 3 | 5 | 0 | 1.2 | 22 | 1 | 0.05 | 0 - 0 | 1 - 2 | 0 - 1 | 24 | 0 | 1 - 3 | 8 | 0.82 | .393 | 1.75 |
| Loup, Aaron | LT | L | 64 | 24 | 9 | 10 | 1.1 | 40 | 14 | 0.35 | 1 - 1 | 1 - 2 | 0 - 0 | 38 | 0 | 2 - 3 | 8 | 0.91 | .670 | 2.47 |
| Cecil, Brett | LT | L | 60 | 11 | 8 | 5 | 1.1 | 34 | 7 | 0.21 | 1 - 2 | 0 - 1 | 0 - 0 | 44 | 0 | 1 - 3 | 11 | 0.86 | .594 | 2.82 |
| Oliver, Darren | LT | L | 50 | 0 | 6 | 3 | 1.1 | 17 | 4 | 0.24 | 0 - 1 | 0 - 2 | 0 - 0 | 32 | 2 | 0 - 3 | 8 | 0.73 | .745 | 3.86 |
| Lincoln, Brad | LM | R | 22 | 10 | 5 | 11 | 0.9 | 20 | 5 | 0.25 | 0 - 0 | 0 - 0 | 0 - 0 | 11 | 0 | 0 - 0 | 0 | | .757 | 3.98 |
| Perez, Juan | LM | L | 19 | 8 | 3 | 12 | 0.7 | 10 | 0 | 0.00 | 0 - 0 | 0 - 1 | 0 - 0 | 12 | 0 | 0 - 1 | 0 | 0.00 | .611 | 3.69 |
| Delabar, Steve | UR | R | 55 | 5 | 8 | 12 | 1.3 | 28 | 11 | 0.39 | 0 - 0 | 0 - 3 | 1 - 3 | 38 | 2 | 1 - 6 | 6 | 0.58 | .680 | 3.22 |
| Wagner, Neil | UR | R | 36 | 13 | 6 | 7 | 0.9 | 24 | 6 | 0.25 | 0 - 0 | 0 - 0 | 0 - 1 | 25 | 0 | 0 - 1 | 10 | 0.91 | .750 | 3.79 |
| McGowan, Dustin | UR | R | 25 | 4 | 2 | 4 | 0.9 | 9 | 3 | 0.33 | 0 - 1 | 0 - 0 | 0 - 0 | 16 | 0 | 0 - 1 | 6 | 0.86 | .609 | 2.45 |
| Rogers, Esmil | UR | R | 24 | 6 | 6 | 7 | 0.9 | 9 | 4 | 0.44 | 0 - 0 | 0 - 1 | 0 - 0 | 15 | 0 | 0 - 1 | 4 | 0.80 | .763 | 4.35 |
| Jeffress, Jeremy | UR | R | 10 | 3 | 1 | 4 | 0.6 | 7 | 3 | 0.43 | 0 - 0 | 0 - 0 | 0 - 0 | 7 | 0 | 0 - 0 | 0 | | .592 | 0.87 |

# Washington Nationals

| | | | Usage | | | | | Inherited Runners | | | Saves | | | Relief Results | | | | | | |
|---|---|---|---|---|---|---|---|---|---|---|---|---|---|---|---|---|---|---|---|---|
| Pitcher | Pos | T | Rel G | Early Entry | Cons Days | Long | Lev Ind | # | Scrd | Pct | Easy | Reg | Tough | Clean | BS Win | Sv-Opp | Holds | Sv/Hld Pct | Opp OPS | Rel ERA |
| Soriano, Rafael | CL | R | 68 | 0 | 28 | 2 | 1.7 | 2 | 2 | 1.00 | 28 - 32 | 15 - 17 | 0 - 0 | 53 | 1 | 43 - 49 | 0 | 0.88 | .668 | 3.11 |
| Clippard, Tyler | SU | R | 72 | 0 | 20 | 7 | 1.4 | 9 | 2 | 0.22 | 0 - 0 | 0 - 3 | 0 - 0 | 57 | 0 | 0 - 3 | 33 | 0.92 | .517 | 2.41 |
| Storen, Drew | SU | R | 68 | 0 | 18 | 3 | 1.3 | 17 | 6 | 0.35 | 1 - 2 | 2 - 4 | 0 - 2 | 48 | 1 | 3 - 8 | 24 | 0.84 | .729 | 4.52 |
| Abad, Fernando | LT | L | 39 | 8 | 7 | 5 | 0.6 | 15 | 6 | 0.40 | 0 - 0 | 0 - 0 | 0 - 1 | 26 | 0 | 0 - 1 | 2 | 0.67 | .687 | 3.35 |
| Krol, Ian | LT | L | 32 | 1 | 4 | 2 | 0.9 | 10 | 7 | 0.70 | 0 - 0 | 0 - 0 | 0 - 1 | 17 | 1 | 0 - 1 | 2 | 0.67 | .785 | 3.95 |
| Cedeno, Xavier | LT | L | 11 | 1 | 2 | 0 | 0.4 | 6 | 1 | 0.17 | 0 - 0 | 0 - 0 | 0 - 0 | 9 | 0 | 0 - 0 | 2 | 1.00 | .488 | 1.50 |
| Duke, Zach | LT | L | 11 | 7 | 1 | 5 | 0.4 | 4 | 1 | 0.25 | 0 - 0 | 0 - 0 | 0 - 0 | 5 | 0 | 0 - 0 | 0 | | .924 | 8.31 |
| Stammen, Craig | LM | R | 55 | 24 | 9 | 21 | 1.0 | 24 | 8 | 0.33 | 0 - 0 | 0 - 1 | 0 - 0 | 33 | 1 | 0 - 1 | 7 | 0.88 | .682 | 2.76 |
| Mattheus, Ryan | UR | R | 37 | 6 | 6 | 6 | 0.7 | 13 | 4 | 0.31 | 0 - 0 | 0 - 3 | 0 - 0 | 19 | 0 | 0 - 3 | 6 | 0.67 | .829 | 6.37 |
| Rodriguez, Henry | UR | R | 17 | 1 | 3 | 3 | 0.4 | 2 | 2 | 1.00 | 0 - 0 | 0 - 0 | 0 - 0 | 11 | 0 | 0 - 0 | 1 | 1.00 | .636 | 4.00 |
| Davis, Erik | UR | R | 10 | 4 | 1 | 1 | 0.4 | 5 | 0 | 0.00 | 0 - 0 | 0 - 0 | 0 - 0 | 9 | 0 | 0 - 0 | 0 | | .714 | 3.12 |

# Pitchers Hitting, Fielding, & Holding Runners, and Hitters Pitching

Pitchers are notoriously weak hitters, so it's pretty exciting when a pitcher makes solid contact at the plate. Zack Greinke took this to the extreme in 2013. Over 58 at bats, Greinke hit .328, which would have trailed only Michael Cuddyer in the National League had Greinke qualified for the batting title. In addition, Greinke drove in four runs, though he failed to hit a home run. Greinke's teammate Clayton Kershaw led all pitchers with 10 RBI, and Travis Wood of the Cubs led all pitchers with three home runs. Theirs and all other pitchers' hitting statistics are included in the following tables.

This section also includes 2013 fielding statistics for pitchers and data on how well they held runners last season. A pitcher's Runs Saved (RS) is the sum of Plus/Minus Runs Saved to evaluate range, Stolen Base Runs Saved, which measures the ability to control the running game, and Good Fielding Play/Defensive Misplay Runs Saved, which account for the good defensive plays made by the player as well as the mistakes made on the field that are not counted by normal errors. Patrick Corbin of the Diamondbacks led all pitchers with eight Runs Saved.

The final piece of this section is Hitters Pitching. In 2013, no hitter "dominated" on the mound quite like Chris Davis did in 2012. However, a handful of pitching hitters recorded a strikeout, including Rob Johnson, John McDonald, David Murphy, Ryan Raburn, Skip Schumaker, and Casper Wells. Raburn even made it through a full inning without allowing a baserunner. Career statistics are listed for all active position players who have pitched, as well as any 2013 pitching statistics that they may have accrued.

# Pitchers Hitting, Fielding and Holding Runners

| | | 2013 Hitting | | | | | | Career Hitting | | | | | | | | | | 2013 Fielding and Holding Runners | | | | | | | | | | | |
|---|---|---|---|---|---|---|---|---|---|---|---|---|---|---|---|---|---|---|---|---|---|---|---|---|---|---|---|---|---|
| Pitcher | T | Avg | AB | H | HR | RBI | SH | Avg | AB | H | 2B | 3B | HR | RBI | BB | SO | SH | Inn | PO | A | E | DP | Pct | SBA | CS | PCS | PPO | CS% | RS |
| Aardsma,David, NYM | R | - | 0 | 0 | 0 | 0 | 0 | .000 | 3 | 0 | 0 | 0 | 0 | 0 | 0 | 1 | 1 | 39.2 | 1 | 5 | 0 | 0 | 1.000 | 6 | 0 | 0 | 0 | .00 | 0 |
| Abad,Fernando, Was | L | - | 0 | 0 | 0 | 0 | 0 | .125 | 8 | 1 | 0 | 0 | 0 | 0 | 0 | 4 | 0 | 37.2 | 1 | 4 | 0 | 0 | 1.000 | 2 | 0 | 0 | 0 | .00 | -2 |
| Aceves,Alfredo, Bos | R | - | 0 | 0 | 0 | 0 | 0 | .000 | 2 | 0 | 0 | 0 | 0 | 0 | 0 | 1 | 0 | 37.0 | 2 | 7 | 2 | 0 | .818 | 2 | 0 | 0 | 0 | .00 | 0 |
| Adams,Mike, Phi | R | - | 0 | 0 | 0 | 0 | 0 | .000 | 2 | 0 | 0 | 0 | 0 | 0 | 0 | 0 | 0 | 25.0 | 5 | 3 | 1 | 0 | .889 | 5 | 2 | 0 | 0 | .40 | 0 |
| Affeldt,Jeremy, SF | L | - | 0 | 0 | 0 | 0 | 0 | .200 | 15 | 3 | 0 | 0 | 0 | 2 | 2 | 4 | 0 | 33.2 | 1 | 9 | 0 | 0 | 1.000 | 2 | 1 | 1 | 0 | .50 | 1 |
| Albers,Andrew, Min | L | - | 0 | 0 | 0 | 0 | 0 | - | 0 | 0 | 0 | 0 | 0 | 0 | 0 | 0 | 0 | 60.0 | 4 | 9 | 0 | 1 | 1.000 | 2 | 0 | 0 | 0 | .00 | 1 |
| Albers,Matt, Cle | R | - | 0 | 0 | 0 | 0 | 0 | .059 | 34 | 2 | 0 | 0 | 0 | 0 | 0 | 21 | 3 | 63.0 | 4 | 11 | 1 | 1 | .938 | 5 | 3 | 0 | 0 | .60 | 1 |
| Alburquerque,Al, Det | R | - | 0 | 0 | 0 | 0 | 0 | - | 0 | 0 | 0 | 0 | 0 | 0 | 0 | 0 | 0 | 49.0 | 4 | 2 | 1 | 0 | .857 | 3 | 0 | 0 | 0 | .00 | -3 |
| Allen,Cody, Cle | R | - | 0 | 0 | 0 | 0 | 0 | - | 0 | 0 | 0 | 0 | 0 | 0 | 0 | 0 | 0 | 70.1 | 0 | 5 | 3 | 0 | .625 | 6 | 0 | 0 | 0 | .00 | -2 |
| Alvarez,Henderson, Mia | R | .300 | 30 | 9 | 1 | 6 | 4 | .290 | 31 | 9 | 3 | 0 | 1 | 6 | 0 | 13 | 4 | 102.2 | 14 | 19 | 1 | 1 | .971 | 2 | 0 | 0 | 0 | .00 | 2 |
| Alvarez,Jose, Det | L | .000 | 1 | 0 | 0 | 0 | 0 | .000 | 1 | 0 | 0 | 0 | 0 | 0 | 1 | 0 | 0 | 38.2 | 0 | 3 | 0 | 0 | 1.000 | 3 | 0 | 0 | 0 | .00 | 0 |
| Ambriz,Hector, Hou | R | - | 0 | 0 | 0 | 0 | 0 | - | 0 | 0 | 0 | 0 | 0 | 0 | 0 | 0 | 0 | 36.1 | 1 | 9 | 0 | 1 | 1.000 | 4 | 0 | 0 | 0 | .00 | 0 |
| Ames,Steven, Mia | R | - | 0 | 0 | 0 | 0 | 0 | - | 0 | 0 | 0 | 0 | 0 | 0 | 0 | 0 | 0 | 4.0 | 1 | 0 | 0 | 0 | 1.000 | 1 | 0 | 0 | 0 | .00 | 0 |
| Anderson,Brett, Oak | L | - | 0 | 0 | 0 | 0 | 0 | .000 | 4 | 0 | 0 | 0 | 0 | 0 | 0 | 2 | 0 | 44.2 | 0 | 4 | 0 | 0 | 1.000 | 2 | 0 | 0 | 0 | .00 | -3 |
| Archer,Chris, TB | R | .000 | 1 | 0 | 0 | 0 | 0 | .000 | 4 | 0 | 0 | 0 | 0 | 0 | 0 | 2 | 0 | 128.2 | 6 | 13 | 2 | 1 | .905 | 18 | 2 | 0 | 0 | .11 | -1 |
| Arrieta,Jake, Bal-ChC | R | .133 | 15 | 2 | 0 | 2 | 4 | .120 | 25 | 3 | 0 | 0 | 0 | 3 | 2 | 14 | 5 | 75.1 | 12 | 15 | 1 | 0 | .964 | 9 | 2 | 0 | 0 | .22 | 3 |
| Arroyo,Bronson, Cin | R | .068 | 59 | 4 | 0 | 0 | 16 | .123 | 576 | 71 | 16 | 0 | 6 | 29 | 14 | 254 | 78 | 202.0 | 15 | 29 | 1 | 1 | .978 | 7 | 4 | 0 | 1 | .57 | 2 |
| Asencio,Jairo, Bal | R | - | 0 | 0 | 0 | 0 | 0 | - | 0 | 0 | 0 | 0 | 0 | 0 | 0 | 0 | 0 | 2.1 | 0 | 1 | 0 | 0 | 1.000 | 0 | 0 | 0 | 0 | - | -1 |
| Atchison,Scott, NYM | R | - | 0 | 0 | 0 | 0 | 0 | .000 | 2 | 0 | 0 | 0 | 0 | 0 | 0 | 1 | 0 | 45.1 | 5 | 13 | 1 | 0 | .947 | 6 | 0 | 0 | 0 | .00 | 0 |
| Aumont,Phillippe, Phi | R | - | 0 | 0 | 0 | 0 | 0 | - | 0 | 0 | 0 | 0 | 0 | 0 | 0 | 0 | 0 | 19.1 | 1 | 3 | 0 | 0 | 1.000 | 2 | 1 | 0 | 0 | .50 | 1 |
| Avilan,Luis, Atl | L | - | 0 | 0 | 0 | 0 | 1 | .333 | 3 | 1 | 0 | 0 | 0 | 0 | 0 | 0 | 1 | 65.0 | 11 | 16 | 0 | 0 | 1.000 | 3 | 2 | 1 | 0 | .67 | 4 |
| Axelrod,Dylan, CWS | R | .500 | 2 | 1 | 0 | 0 | 0 | .500 | 2 | 1 | 0 | 0 | 0 | 0 | 0 | 1 | 0 | 128.1 | 13 | 12 | 1 | 1 | .962 | 17 | 5 | 0 | 0 | .29 | -3 |
| Axford,John, Mil-StL | R | - | 0 | 0 | 0 | 0 | 0 | .000 | 1 | 0 | 0 | 0 | 0 | 0 | 0 | 1 | 0 | 65.0 | 1 | 3 | 0 | 0 | 1.000 | 5 | 2 | 0 | 0 | .40 | 0 |
| Ayala,Luis, Bal-Atl | R | - | 0 | 0 | 0 | 0 | 0 | .286 | 14 | 4 | 1 | 0 | 0 | 0 | 0 | 3 | 3 | 33.0 | 0 | 10 | 0 | 1 | 1.000 | 5 | 1 | 0 | 0 | .20 | 2 |
| Badenhop,Burke, Mil | R | .000 | 1 | 0 | 0 | 0 | 0 | .094 | 32 | 3 | 1 | 0 | 0 | 2 | 1 | 19 | 5 | 62.1 | 1 | 15 | 2 | 2 | .889 | 7 | 4 | 0 | 0 | .57 | 3 |
| Bailey,Andrew, Bos | R | - | 0 | 0 | 0 | 0 | 0 | - | 0 | 0 | 0 | 0 | 0 | 0 | 0 | 0 | 0 | 28.2 | 1 | 0 | 0 | 1 | 1.000 | 3 | 1 | 0 | 0 | .33 | 0 |
| Bailey,Homer, Cin | R | .155 | 58 | 9 | 0 | 1 | 11 | .162 | 259 | 42 | 6 | 0 | 0 | 14 | 7 | 100 | 33 | 209.0 | 20 | 26 | 1 | 2 | .979 | 17 | 3 | 1 | 0 | .18 | 1 |
| Baker,Scott, ChC | R | .000 | 3 | 0 | 0 | 0 | 1 | .107 | 28 | 3 | 1 | 0 | 0 | 0 | 0 | 11 | 5 | 15.0 | 2 | 1 | 0 | 0 | 1.000 | 1 | 1 | 0 | 0 | 1.00 | -1 |
| Balfour,Grant, Oak | R | - | 0 | 0 | 0 | 0 | 0 | .000 | 2 | 0 | 0 | 0 | 0 | 0 | 0 | 2 | 0 | 62.2 | 1 | 5 | 1 | 1 | .857 | 1 | 1 | 0 | 0 | 1.00 | 1 |
| Bard,Daniel, Bos | R | - | 0 | 0 | 0 | 0 | 0 | .000 | 2 | 0 | 0 | 0 | 0 | 0 | 0 | 1 | 0 | 1.0 | 0 | 1 | 0 | 0 | 1.000 | 0 | 0 | 0 | 0 | - | 1 |
| Barnes,Scott, Cle | L | - | 0 | 0 | 0 | 0 | 0 | - | 0 | 0 | 0 | 0 | 0 | 0 | 0 | 0 | 0 | 8.2 | 1 | 3 | 0 | 0 | 1.000 | 0 | 0 | 0 | 0 | - | 1 |
| Bass,Anthony, SD | R | .000 | 2 | 0 | 0 | 1 | 0 | .105 | 38 | 4 | 0 | 1 | 0 | 6 | 0 | 17 | 1 | 42.0 | 5 | 5 | 0 | 0 | 1.000 | 4 | 2 | 0 | 0 | .50 | -1 |
| Bastardo,Antonio, Phi | L | - | 0 | 0 | 0 | 0 | 0 | .000 | 6 | 0 | 0 | 0 | 0 | 0 | 0 | 3 | 1 | 42.2 | 1 | 1 | 0 | 0 | 1.000 | 5 | 2 | 1 | 0 | .40 | -2 |
| Bauer,Trevor, Cle | R | .000 | 1 | 0 | 0 | 0 | 0 | .000 | 5 | 0 | 0 | 0 | 0 | 0 | 0 | 2 | 1 | 17.0 | 2 | 2 | 0 | 0 | 1.000 | 5 | 1 | 0 | 0 | .20 | 1 |
| Beachy,Brandon, Atl | R | .125 | 8 | 1 | 0 | 0 | 3 | .120 | 83 | 10 | 1 | 0 | 0 | 5 | 5 | 46 | 11 | 30.0 | 2 | 8 | 0 | 1 | 1.000 | 5 | 0 | 0 | 0 | .00 | 0 |
| Beato,Pedro, Bos | R | - | 0 | 0 | 0 | 0 | 0 | - | 0 | 0 | 0 | 0 | 0 | 0 | 0 | 0 | 0 | 10.0 | 0 | 1 | 0 | 0 | 1.000 | 2 | 1 | 0 | 0 | .50 | 0 |
| Beavan,Blake, Sea | R | - | 0 | 0 | 0 | 0 | 0 | .000 | 2 | 0 | 0 | 0 | 0 | 0 | 0 | 1 | 1 | 39.2 | 0 | 4 | 0 | 0 | 1.000 | 5 | 1 | 0 | 0 | .20 | 0 |
| Beckett,Josh, LAD | R | .125 | 8 | 1 | 0 | 0 | 3 | .136 | 250 | 34 | 9 | 0 | 3 | 16 | 11 | 96 | 30 | 43.1 | 2 | 7 | 1 | 0 | .900 | 5 | 2 | 0 | 0 | .40 | 0 |
| Bedard,Erik, Hou | L | .000 | 3 | 0 | 0 | 0 | 1 | .150 | 60 | 9 | 1 | 0 | 0 | 1 | 2 | 22 | 8 | 151.0 | 3 | 9 | 3 | 0 | .800 | 6 | 1 | 0 | 0 | .17 | -2 |
| Belfiore,Mike, Bal | L | - | 0 | 0 | 0 | 0 | 0 | - | 0 | 0 | 0 | 0 | 0 | 0 | 0 | 0 | 0 | 1.1 | 0 | 0 | 0 | 0 | - | 0 | 0 | 0 | 0 | - | 0 |
| Belisario,Ronald, LAD | R | .000 | 1 | 0 | 0 | 0 | 0 | .000 | 5 | 0 | 0 | 0 | 0 | 0 | 0 | 3 | 0 | 68.0 | 6 | 15 | 2 | 1 | .913 | 6 | 2 | 0 | 0 | .33 | -2 |
| Belisle,Matt, Col | R | .000 | 1 | 0 | 0 | 0 | 0 | .083 | 84 | 7 | 3 | 0 | 0 | 3 | 3 | 47 | 18 | 73.0 | 8 | 13 | 0 | 2 | 1.000 | 3 | 0 | 0 | 0 | .00 | 2 |
| Beliveau,Jeff, TB | L | - | 0 | 0 | 0 | 0 | 0 | - | 0 | 0 | 0 | 0 | 0 | 0 | 0 | 0 | 0 | 0.2 | 0 | 0 | 0 | 0 | - | 0 | 0 | 0 | 0 | - | 0 |
| Bell,Heath, Ari | R | - | 0 | 0 | 0 | 0 | 0 | .000 | 6 | 0 | 0 | 0 | 0 | 0 | 0 | 2 | 1 | 65.2 | 8 | 7 | 1 | 1 | .938 | 2 | 1 | 0 | 0 | .50 | 1 |
| Below,Duane, Mia | L | - | 0 | 0 | 0 | 0 | 0 | .000 | 1 | 0 | 0 | 0 | 0 | 0 | 0 | 0 | 0 | 2.2 | 0 | 1 | 0 | 0 | 1.000 | 1 | 1 | 1 | 0 | 1.00 | 0 |
| Benoit,Joaquin, Det | R | - | 0 | 0 | 0 | 0 | 0 | .000 | 9 | 0 | 0 | 0 | 0 | 0 | 0 | 4 | 0 | 67.0 | 6 | 8 | 0 | 0 | 1.000 | 10 | 0 | 0 | 1 | .00 | 0 |
| Betances,Dellin, NYY | R | - | 0 | 0 | 0 | 0 | 0 | - | 0 | 0 | 0 | 0 | 0 | 0 | 0 | 0 | 0 | 5.0 | 0 | 0 | 0 | 0 | - | 0 | 0 | 0 | 0 | - | 0 |
| Betancourt,Rafael, Col | R | - | 0 | 0 | 0 | 0 | 0 | .000 | 1 | 0 | 0 | 0 | 0 | 0 | 0 | 1 | 0 | 28.2 | 0 | 6 | 0 | 0 | 1.000 | 4 | 1 | 0 | 0 | .25 | 1 |
| Bettis,Chad, Col | R | .000 | 11 | 0 | 0 | 0 | 3 | .000 | 11 | 0 | 0 | 0 | 0 | 0 | 0 | 4 | 3 | 44.2 | 3 | 9 | 0 | 0 | 1.000 | 2 | 2 | 0 | 0 | 1.00 | 1 |
| Billingsley,Chad, LAD | R | .000 | 3 | 0 | 0 | 0 | 2 | .140 | 342 | 48 | 8 | 0 | 2 | 20 | 19 | 165 | 35 | 12.0 | 0 | 2 | 0 | 0 | 1.000 | 0 | 0 | 0 | 0 | - | 0 |
| Black,Vic, Pit-NYM | R | - | 0 | 0 | 0 | 0 | 0 | - | 0 | 0 | 0 | 0 | 0 | 0 | 0 | 0 | 0 | 17.0 | 1 | 2 | 1 | 1 | .750 | 1 | 0 | 0 | 0 | .00 | 0 |
| Blackley,Travis, Hou-Tex | L | - | 0 | 0 | 0 | 0 | 0 | .200 | 5 | 1 | 0 | 0 | 0 | 0 | 0 | 3 | 0 | 50.1 | 3 | 12 | 0 | 0 | 1.000 | 4 | 3 | 3 | 0 | .75 | 3 |
| Blanton,Joe, LAA | R | .167 | 6 | 1 | 0 | 0 | 0 | .108 | 212 | 23 | 0 | 0 | 0 | 6 | 8 | 91 | 31 | 132.2 | 12 | 10 | 2 | 2 | .917 | 17 | 0 | 0 | 0 | .00 | -3 |
| Blazek,Michael, StL-Mil | R | - | 0 | 0 | 0 | 0 | 0 | - | 0 | 0 | 0 | 0 | 0 | 0 | 0 | 0 | 0 | 17.1 | 1 | 0 | 0 | 0 | 1.000 | 1 | 0 | 0 | 0 | .00 | 0 |
| Blevins,Jerry, Oak | L | .000 | 1 | 0 | 0 | 0 | 0 | .000 | 1 | 0 | 0 | 0 | 0 | 0 | 0 | 1 | 0 | 60.0 | 0 | 4 | 2 | 0 | .667 | 4 | 2 | 1 | 0 | .50 | -1 |
| Boggs,Mitchell, StL-Col | R | - | 0 | 0 | 0 | 0 | 0 | .037 | 27 | 1 | 1 | 0 | 0 | 0 | 0 | 14 | 3 | 23.1 | 3 | 4 | 0 | 0 | 1.000 | 1 | 0 | 0 | 0 | .00 | 0 |
| Bonderman,Jeremy, Sea-Det | R | .000 | 2 | 0 | 0 | 0 | 0 | .033 | 30 | 1 | 0 | 0 | 0 | 0 | 0 | 18 | 1 | 55.0 | 4 | 4 | 1 | 1 | .889 | 2 | 2 | 0 | 0 | 1.00 | 0 |
| Bootcheck,Chris, NYY | R | - | 0 | 0 | 0 | 0 | 0 | .000 | 2 | 0 | 0 | 0 | 0 | 0 | 0 | 2 | 0 | 1.0 | 0 | 0 | 0 | 0 | - | 0 | 0 | 0 | 0 | - | 0 |
| Boshers,Buddy, LAA | L | - | 0 | 0 | 0 | 0 | 0 | - | 0 | 0 | 0 | 0 | 0 | 0 | 0 | 0 | 0 | 15.1 | 1 | 4 | 0 | 0 | 1.000 | 3 | 3 | 2 | 0 | 1.00 | 1 |
| Bowden,Michael, ChC | R | - | 0 | 0 | 0 | 0 | 0 | .000 | 2 | 0 | 0 | 0 | 0 | 0 | 0 | 2 | 0 | 37.2 | 5 | 8 | 0 | 1 | 1.000 | 2 | 2 | 0 | 0 | 1.00 | 3 |
| Boxberger,Brad, SD | R | .000 | 1 | 0 | 0 | 0 | 0 | .000 | 2 | 0 | 0 | 0 | 0 | 0 | 0 | 1 | 1 | 22.0 | 3 | 3 | 0 | 1 | 1.000 | 3 | 2 | 0 | 1 | .67 | 1 |
| Brach,Brad, SD | R | - | 0 | 0 | 0 | 0 | 0 | - | 0 | 0 | 0 | 0 | 0 | 0 | 0 | 0 | 0 | 31.0 | 2 | 5 | 0 | 1 | 1.000 | 7 | 1 | 0 | 0 | .14 | 0 |
| Brasier,Ryan, LAA | R | - | 0 | 0 | 0 | 0 | 0 | - | 0 | 0 | 0 | 0 | 0 | 0 | 0 | 0 | 0 | 9.0 | 0 | 1 | 0 | 0 | 1.000 | 2 | 1 | 1 | 0 | .50 | 0 |
| Breslow,Craig, Bos | L | - | 0 | 0 | 0 | 0 | 0 | .000 | 4 | 0 | 0 | 0 | 0 | 0 | 0 | 2 | 0 | 59.2 | 5 | 9 | 0 | 2 | 1.000 | 4 | 3 | 2 | 0 | .75 | 2 |
| Brewer,Charles, Ari | R | - | 0 | 0 | 0 | 0 | 0 | - | 0 | 0 | 0 | 0 | 0 | 0 | 0 | 0 | 0 | 6.0 | 0 | 2 | 0 | 0 | 1.000 | 1 | 0 | 0 | 0 | .00 | 0 |
| Britton,Drake, Bos | L | - | 0 | 0 | 0 | 0 | 0 | - | 0 | 0 | 0 | 0 | 0 | 0 | 0 | 0 | 0 | 21.0 | 0 | 3 | 0 | 1 | 1.000 | 5 | 2 | 0 | 0 | .40 | 0 |
| Britton,Zach, Bal | L | - | 0 | 0 | 0 | 0 | 0 | .625 | 8 | 5 | 1 | 0 | 1 | 2 | 0 | 1 | 0 | 40.0 | 1 | 4 | 0 | 0 | 1.000 | 3 | 1 | 1 | 0 | .33 | -2 |
| Brothers,Rex, Col | L | .000 | 1 | 0 | 0 | 0 | 0 | .000 | 4 | 0 | 0 | 0 | 0 | 0 | 0 | 4 | 1 | 67.1 | 2 | 7 | 2 | 1 | .818 | 6 | 3 | 1 | 0 | .50 | -2 |
| Broxton,Jonathan, Cin | R | - | 0 | 0 | 0 | 0 | 0 | .000 | 5 | 0 | 0 | 0 | 0 | 0 | 2 | 2 | 1 | 30.2 | 4 | 3 | 0 | 0 | 1.000 | 6 | 1 | 0 | 0 | .17 | -1 |

# Pitchers Hitting, Fielding and Holding Runners

| | | 2013 Hitting | | | | | | Career Hitting | | | | | | | | | | 2013 Fielding and Holding Runners | | | | | | | | | | | |
|---|---|---|---|---|---|---|---|---|---|---|---|---|---|---|---|---|---|---|---|---|---|---|---|---|---|---|---|
| Pitcher | T | Avg | AB | H | HR | RBI | SH | Avg | AB | H | 2B | 3B | HR | RBI | BB | SO | SH | Inn | PO | A | E | DP | Pct | SBA | CS | PCS | PPO | CS% | RS |
| Buchholz,Clay, Bos | R | - | 0 | 0 | 0 | 0 | 0 | .333 | 3 | 1 | 0 | 0 | 0 | 0 | 0 | 1 | 1 | 108.1 | 17 | 13 | 2 | 1 | .938 | 12 | 6 | 0 | 0 | .50 | 0 |
| Buckner,Billy, LAA | R | - | 0 | 0 | 0 | 0 | 0 | .231 | 26 | 6 | 2 | 0 | 0 | 6 | 1 | 8 | 2 | 17.1 | 0 | 1 | 0 | 0 | 1.000 | 2 | 1 | 0 | 0 | .50 | 0 |
| Buehrle,Mark, Tor | L | .000 | 4 | 0 | 0 | 0 | 0 | .068 | 118 | 8 | 2 | 0 | 1 | 3 | 1 | 55 | 12 | 203.2 | 12 | 35 | 2 | 1 | .959 | 9 | 5 | 4 | 2 | .56 | 4 |
| Bueno,Francisley, KC | L | - | 0 | 0 | 0 | 0 | 0 | - | 0 | 0 | 0 | 0 | 0 | 0 | 0 | 0 | 0 | 8.1 | 2 | 2 | 0 | 0 | 1.000 | 0 | 0 | 0 | 0 | - | 1 |
| Bumgarner,Madison, SF | L | .107 | 56 | 6 | 0 | 4 | 7 | .138 | 224 | 31 | 6 | 0 | 2 | 16 | 13 | 85 | 27 | 201.1 | 7 | 33 | 3 | 1 | .930 | 15 | 7 | 6 | 0 | .47 | 5 |
| Burgos,Hiram, Mil | R | .125 | 8 | 1 | 0 | 0 | 2 | .125 | 8 | 1 | 0 | 0 | 0 | 0 | 0 | 6 | 2 | 29.1 | 2 | 4 | 0 | 0 | 1.000 | 2 | 0 | 0 | 0 | .00 | -1 |
| Burke,Greg, NYM | R | .000 | 2 | 0 | 0 | 0 | 0 | .000 | 2 | 0 | 0 | 0 | 0 | 0 | 0 | 1 | 0 | 31.2 | 1 | 2 | 0 | 0 | 1.000 | 5 | 0 | 0 | 0 | .00 | -3 |
| Burnett,A.J., Pit | R | .068 | 59 | 4 | 0 | 2 | 6 | .110 | 391 | 43 | 6 | 3 | 3 | 13 | 17 | 198 | 48 | 191.0 | 12 | 19 | 2 | 0 | .939 | 24 | 2 | 0 | 1 | .08 | -4 |
| Burnett,Alex, Bal-ChC | R | - | 0 | 0 | 0 | 0 | 0 | - | 0 | 0 | 0 | 0 | 0 | 0 | 0 | 0 | 0 | 2.1 | 1 | 0 | 0 | 0 | 1.000 | 0 | 0 | 0 | 0 | - | 0 |
| Burnett,Sean, LAA | L | - | 0 | 0 | 0 | 0 | 0 | .069 | 29 | 2 | 1 | 0 | 0 | 0 | 4 | 9 | 2 | 9.2 | 1 | 0 | 0 | 0 | 1.000 | 0 | 0 | 0 | 0 | - | 0 |
| Burns,Cory, Tex | R | - | 0 | 0 | 0 | 0 | 0 | .000 | 1 | 0 | 0 | 0 | 0 | 0 | 0 | 1 | 0 | 11.1 | 0 | 0 | 1 | 0 | .000 | 1 | 1 | 0 | 0 | 1.00 | -2 |
| Burton,Jared, Min | R | - | 0 | 0 | 0 | 0 | 0 | .000 | 2 | 0 | 0 | 0 | 0 | 0 | 0 | 2 | 0 | 66.0 | 6 | 10 | 1 | 0 | .941 | 17 | 3 | 0 | 0 | .18 | -1 |
| Bush,Dave, Tor | R | - | 0 | 0 | 0 | 0 | 0 | .129 | 263 | 34 | 7 | 0 | 0 | 13 | 9 | 96 | 27 | 3.0 | 0 | 0 | 0 | 0 | - | 0 | 0 | 0 | 0 | - | 0 |
| Butler,Keith, StL | R | - | 0 | 0 | 0 | 0 | 0 | - | 0 | 0 | 0 | 0 | 0 | 0 | 0 | 0 | 0 | 20.0 | 2 | 1 | 0 | 0 | 1.000 | 2 | 0 | 0 | 0 | .00 | 0 |
| Byrdak,Tim, NYM | L | - | 0 | 0 | 0 | 0 | 0 | .154 | 13 | 2 | 1 | 0 | 0 | 0 | 0 | 4 | 0 | 4.2 | 0 | 0 | 0 | 0 | - | 1 | 0 | 0 | 0 | .00 | 0 |
| Cabral,Cesar, NYY | L | - | 0 | 0 | 0 | 0 | 0 | - | 0 | 0 | 0 | 0 | 0 | 0 | 0 | 0 | 0 | 3.2 | 0 | 0 | 0 | 0 | - | 0 | 0 | 0 | 0 | - | 0 |
| Cabrera,Alberto, ChC | R | - | 0 | 0 | 0 | 0 | 0 | - | 0 | 0 | 0 | 0 | 0 | 0 | 0 | 0 | 0 | 6.0 | 1 | 2 | 0 | 0 | 1.000 | 2 | 0 | 0 | 0 | .00 | 1 |
| Cahill,Trevor, Ari | R | .082 | 49 | 4 | 0 | 5 | 4 | .103 | 126 | 13 | 1 | 1 | 0 | 9 | 1 | 47 | 11 | 146.2 | 4 | 36 | 0 | 3 | 1.000 | 17 | 1 | 1 | 1 | .06 | 3 |
| Cain,Matt, SF | R | .096 | 52 | 5 | 0 | 2 | 10 | .124 | 509 | 63 | 10 | 1 | 6 | 26 | 19 | 249 | 67 | 184.1 | 12 | 25 | 1 | 2 | .974 | 21 | 4 | 1 | 0 | .19 | 1 |
| Caminero,Arquimedes, Mia | R | - | 0 | 0 | 0 | 0 | 0 | - | 0 | 0 | 0 | 0 | 0 | 0 | 0 | 0 | 0 | 13.0 | 0 | 0 | 0 | 0 | - | 2 | 0 | 0 | 0 | .00 | -1 |
| Camp,Shawn, ChC | R | - | 0 | 0 | 0 | 0 | 0 | 1.000 | 1 | 1 | 0 | 0 | 0 | 0 | 0 | 0 | 1 | 23.0 | 4 | 3 | 2 | 0 | .778 | 3 | 2 | 1 | 0 | .67 | -1 |
| Capps,Carter, Sea | R | - | 0 | 0 | 0 | 0 | 0 | - | 0 | 0 | 0 | 0 | 0 | 0 | 0 | 0 | 0 | 59.0 | 2 | 6 | 0 | 0 | 1.000 | 12 | 1 | 1 | 1 | .08 | -2 |
| Capuano,Chris, LAD | L | .042 | 24 | 1 | 0 | 0 | 4 | .124 | 370 | 46 | 10 | 0 | 1 | 20 | 9 | 176 | 38 | 105.2 | 5 | 14 | 0 | 1 | 1.000 | 3 | 1 | 0 | 0 | .33 | -1 |
| Carpenter,David, Atl | R | .000 | 3 | 0 | 0 | 0 | 1 | .200 | 5 | 1 | 0 | 0 | 0 | 0 | 0 | 1 | 1 | 65.2 | 1 | 3 | 0 | 0 | 1.000 | 9 | 4 | 0 | 0 | .44 | -1 |
| Carpenter,David, LAA | R | - | 0 | 0 | 0 | 0 | 0 | - | 0 | 0 | 0 | 0 | 0 | 0 | 0 | 0 | 0 | 0.1 | 0 | 0 | 0 | 0 | - | 0 | 0 | 0 | 0 | - | 0 |
| Carrasco,Carlos, Cle | R | - | 0 | 0 | 0 | 0 | 0 | .000 | 5 | 0 | 0 | 0 | 0 | 0 | 0 | 3 | 2 | 46.2 | 3 | 7 | 2 | 0 | .833 | 3 | 0 | 0 | 1 | .00 | -1 |
| Carson,Robert, NYM | L | - | 0 | 0 | 0 | 0 | 0 | - | 0 | 0 | 0 | 0 | 0 | 0 | 1 | 0 | 0 | 19.2 | 1 | 3 | 0 | 0 | 1.000 | 0 | 0 | 0 | 2 | - | 0 |
| Cashner,Andrew, SD | R | .245 | 53 | 13 | 1 | 3 | 6 | .222 | 63 | 14 | 1 | 0 | 1 | 3 | 2 | 30 | 8 | 175.0 | 10 | 37 | 1 | 4 | .979 | 21 | 5 | 0 | 1 | .24 | 5 |
| Casilla,Santiago, SF | R | - | 0 | 0 | 0 | 0 | 0 | .333 | 3 | 1 | 0 | 0 | 0 | 1 | 1 | 1 | 0 | 50.0 | 1 | 8 | 0 | 2 | 1.000 | 3 | 1 | 0 | 0 | .33 | 1 |
| Castro,Simon, CWS | R | - | 0 | 0 | 0 | 0 | 0 | - | 0 | 0 | 0 | 0 | 0 | 0 | 0 | 0 | 0 | 6.2 | 0 | 0 | 0 | 0 | - | 1 | 1 | 0 | 0 | 1.00 | 0 |
| Cecil,Brett, Tor | L | - | 0 | 0 | 0 | 0 | 0 | .000 | 6 | 0 | 0 | 0 | 0 | 0 | 0 | 6 | 0 | 60.2 | 0 | 3 | 0 | 0 | 1.000 | 8 | 2 | 1 | 0 | .25 | -2 |
| Cedeno,Xavier, Hou-Was | L | - | 0 | 0 | 0 | 0 | 0 | .000 | 1 | 0 | 0 | 0 | 0 | 0 | 0 | 1 | 0 | 12.1 | 3 | 2 | 0 | 0 | 1.000 | 0 | 0 | 0 | 0 | - | 0 |
| Chacin,Jhoulys, Col | R | .190 | 63 | 12 | 1 | 7 | 2 | .170 | 188 | 32 | 4 | 0 | 1 | 15 | 6 | 39 | 12 | 197.1 | 15 | 22 | 1 | 2 | .974 | 9 | 3 | 1 | 0 | .33 | 2 |
| Chamberlain,Joba, NYY | R | - | 0 | 0 | 0 | 0 | 0 | .000 | 5 | 0 | 0 | 0 | 0 | 0 | 1 | 1 | 2 | 42.0 | 3 | 4 | 0 | 0 | 1.000 | 10 | 1 | 0 | 0 | .10 | 0 |
| Chapman,Aroldis, Cin | L | .000 | 1 | 0 | 0 | 0 | 0 | .000 | 1 | 0 | 0 | 0 | 0 | 0 | 0 | 1 | 0 | 63.2 | 1 | 3 | 1 | 0 | .800 | 2 | 1 | 1 | 0 | .50 | -1 |
| Chapman,Kevin, Hou | L | - | 0 | 0 | 0 | 0 | 0 | - | 0 | 0 | 0 | 0 | 0 | 0 | 0 | 0 | 0 | 20.1 | 0 | 2 | 0 | 0 | 1.000 | 1 | 0 | 0 | 0 | .00 | 0 |
| Chatwood,Tyler, Col | R | .300 | 40 | 12 | 0 | 7 | 3 | .305 | 59 | 18 | 2 | 0 | 0 | 8 | 3 | 11 | 11 | 111.1 | 13 | 22 | 3 | 1 | .921 | 11 | 2 | 0 | 0 | .18 | -2 |
| Chavez,Jesse, Oak | R | .000 | 1 | 0 | 0 | 0 | 0 | .000 | 5 | 0 | 0 | 0 | 0 | 0 | 0 | 5 | 1 | 57.1 | 7 | 7 | 0 | 0 | 1.000 | 1 | 0 | 0 | 0 | .00 | -1 |
| Chen,Bruce, KC | L | .500 | 2 | 1 | 0 | 0 | 0 | .152 | 125 | 19 | 1 | 0 | 0 | 3 | 3 | 58 | 19 | 121.0 | 5 | 15 | 0 | 0 | 1.000 | 11 | 6 | 5 | 0 | .55 | 5 |
| Chen,Wei-Yin, Bal | L | .000 | 2 | 0 | 0 | 0 | 0 | .000 | 5 | 0 | 0 | 0 | 0 | 0 | 0 | 2 | 1 | 137.0 | 4 | 16 | 0 | 3 | 1.000 | 7 | 3 | 1 | 0 | .43 | 4 |
| Choate,Randy, StL | L | - | 0 | 0 | 0 | 0 | 0 | .000 | 5 | 0 | 0 | 0 | 0 | 0 | 0 | 3 | 0 | 35.1 | 4 | 5 | 0 | 0 | 1.000 | 1 | 0 | 0 | 0 | .00 | -1 |
| Christiani,Nick, Cin | R | - | 0 | 0 | 0 | 0 | 0 | - | 0 | 0 | 0 | 0 | 0 | 0 | 0 | 0 | 0 | 4.0 | 0 | 0 | 0 | 0 | - | 0 | 0 | 0 | 0 | - | 0 |
| Cingrani,Tony, Cin | L | .250 | 28 | 7 | 0 | 1 | 7 | .241 | 29 | 7 | 1 | 0 | 0 | 1 | 0 | 10 | 7 | 104.2 | 9 | 13 | 0 | 1 | 1.000 | 11 | 6 | 6 | 0 | .55 | 3 |
| Cishek,Steve, Mia | R | - | 0 | 0 | 0 | 0 | 0 | .000 | 1 | 0 | 0 | 0 | 0 | 0 | 0 | 0 | 0 | 69.2 | 9 | 6 | 1 | 0 | .938 | 3 | 2 | 0 | 0 | .67 | 1 |
| Cisnero,Jose, Hou | R | .000 | 1 | 0 | 0 | 0 | 0 | .000 | 1 | 0 | 0 | 0 | 0 | 0 | 0 | 1 | 0 | 43.2 | 4 | 3 | 0 | 0 | 1.000 | 6 | 1 | 0 | 1 | .17 | -1 |
| Claiborne,Preston, NYY | R | - | 0 | 0 | 0 | 0 | 0 | - | 0 | 0 | 0 | 0 | 0 | 0 | 0 | 0 | 0 | 50.1 | 6 | 7 | 0 | 2 | 1.000 | 6 | 2 | 0 | 0 | .33 | 0 |
| Clark,Zach, Bal | R | - | 0 | 0 | 0 | 0 | 0 | - | 0 | 0 | 0 | 0 | 0 | 0 | 0 | 0 | 0 | 1.2 | 0 | 0 | 0 | 0 | - | 0 | 0 | 0 | 0 | - | 0 |
| Clemens,Paul, Hou | R | - | 0 | 0 | 0 | 0 | 0 | - | 0 | 0 | 0 | 0 | 0 | 0 | 0 | 0 | 0 | 73.1 | 1 | 4 | 1 | 0 | .833 | 9 | 2 | 0 | 0 | .22 | 0 |
| Cleto,Maikel, StL | R | .000 | 1 | 0 | 0 | 0 | 0 | .000 | 3 | 0 | 0 | 0 | 0 | 0 | 0 | 3 | 0 | 2.1 | 0 | 0 | 0 | 0 | - | 0 | 0 | 0 | 0 | - | 0 |
| Clippard,Tyler, Was | R | - | 0 | 0 | 0 | 0 | 0 | .214 | 14 | 3 | 1 | 0 | 0 | 0 | 0 | 6 | 3 | 71.0 | 3 | 5 | 0 | 2 | 1.000 | 2 | 0 | 0 | 0 | .00 | 0 |
| Cloyd,Tyler, Phi | R | .111 | 18 | 2 | 0 | 1 | 2 | .103 | 29 | 3 | 1 | 0 | 0 | 1 | 5 | 7 | 2 | 60.1 | 5 | 10 | 0 | 0 | 1.000 | 4 | 0 | 0 | 0 | .00 | 0 |
| Cobb,Alex, TB | R | .000 | 3 | 0 | 0 | 0 | 0 | .000 | 3 | 0 | 0 | 0 | 0 | 0 | 0 | 0 | 0 | 143.1 | 7 | 20 | 1 | 1 | .964 | 16 | 4 | 2 | 0 | .25 | 1 |
| Coello,Robert, LAA | R | - | 0 | 0 | 0 | 0 | 0 | - | 0 | 0 | 0 | 0 | 0 | 0 | 0 | 0 | 0 | 17.0 | 1 | 0 | 0 | 0 | 1.000 | 1 | 0 | 0 | 0 | .00 | 0 |
| Coke,Phil, Det | L | - | 0 | 0 | 0 | 0 | 0 | .000 | 3 | 0 | 0 | 0 | 0 | 0 | 0 | 3 | 0 | 38.1 | 0 | 6 | 1 | 0 | .857 | 1 | 1 | 1 | 0 | 1.00 | -2 |
| Cole,Gerrit, Pit | R | .206 | 34 | 7 | 0 | 5 | 1 | .206 | 34 | 7 | 0 | 0 | 0 | 5 | 1 | 14 | 1 | 117.1 | 7 | 13 | 1 | 2 | .952 | 14 | 5 | 0 | 0 | .36 | 0 |
| Coleman,Louis, KC | R | - | 0 | 0 | 0 | 0 | 0 | .000 | 1 | 0 | 0 | 0 | 0 | 0 | 0 | 1 | 0 | 29.2 | 1 | 2 | 0 | 2 | 1.000 | 2 | 0 | 0 | 0 | .00 | 1 |
| Collins,Tim, KC | L | - | 0 | 0 | 0 | 0 | 0 | .000 | 1 | 0 | 0 | 0 | 0 | 0 | 0 | 0 | 0 | 53.1 | 2 | 5 | 0 | 0 | 1.000 | 2 | 0 | 0 | 0 | .00 | -1 |
| Collmenter,Josh, Ari | R | .091 | 11 | 1 | 0 | 0 | 0 | .119 | 67 | 8 | 0 | 0 | 0 | 3 | 3 | 26 | 10 | 92.0 | 4 | 11 | 0 | 0 | 1.000 | 7 | 3 | 0 | 0 | .43 | 0 |
| Colome,Alex, TB | R | .000 | 2 | 0 | 0 | 0 | 0 | .000 | 2 | 0 | 0 | 0 | 0 | 0 | 0 | 1 | 0 | 16.0 | 1 | 0 | 1 | 0 | .500 | 0 | 0 | 0 | 0 | - | 0 |
| Colon,Bartolo, Oak | R | .000 | 6 | 0 | 0 | 0 | 0 | .104 | 96 | 10 | 0 | 0 | 0 | 5 | 0 | 56 | 6 | 190.1 | 6 | 22 | 1 | 1 | .966 | 9 | 2 | 1 | 1 | .22 | -2 |
| Contreras,Jose, Pit | R | - | 0 | 0 | 0 | 0 | 0 | .000 | 29 | 0 | 0 | 0 | 0 | 0 | 3 | 18 | 1 | 5.0 | 1 | 2 | 0 | 0 | 1.000 | 0 | 0 | 0 | 0 | - | 1 |
| Cook,Ryan, Oak | R | - | 0 | 0 | 0 | 0 | 0 | - | 0 | 0 | 0 | 0 | 0 | 0 | 0 | 0 | 0 | 67.1 | 4 | 8 | 0 | 1 | 1.000 | 17 | 1 | 0 | 0 | .06 | -2 |
| Corbin,Patrick, Ari | L | .123 | 65 | 8 | 0 | 3 | 5 | .119 | 101 | 12 | 4 | 1 | 0 | 7 | 3 | 40 | 11 | 208.1 | 10 | 40 | 2 | 2 | .962 | 8 | 6 | 4 | 0 | .75 | 8 |
| Corpas,Manny, Col | R | .000 | 3 | 0 | 0 | 0 | 1 | .000 | 10 | 0 | 0 | 0 | 0 | 0 | 2 | 7 | 1 | 41.2 | 4 | 7 | 1 | 1 | .917 | 1 | 1 | 0 | 0 | 1.00 | 1 |
| Correia,Kevin, Min | R | .000 | 7 | 0 | 0 | 0 | 3 | .113 | 283 | 32 | 5 | 0 | 0 | 12 | 11 | 121 | 44 | 185.1 | 18 | 16 | 2 | 1 | .944 | 11 | 5 | 1 | 0 | .45 | -4 |
| Cosart,Jarred, Hou | R | - | 0 | 0 | 0 | 0 | 0 | - | 0 | 0 | 0 | 0 | 0 | 0 | 0 | 0 | 0 | 60.0 | 6 | 8 | 0 | 1 | 1.000 | 8 | 3 | 0 | 0 | .38 | 2 |
| Cotts,Neal, Tex | L | - | 0 | 0 | 0 | 0 | 0 | .500 | 2 | 1 | 1 | 0 | 0 | 0 | 0 | 1 | 0 | 57.0 | 5 | 5 | 0 | 0 | 1.000 | 4 | 1 | 0 | 0 | .25 | 0 |
| Crain,Jesse, CWS | R | - | 0 | 0 | 0 | 0 | 0 | .000 | 1 | 0 | 0 | 0 | 0 | 0 | 0 | 1 | 0 | 36.2 | 1 | 2 | 1 | 0 | .750 | 4 | 1 | 0 | 1 | .25 | -2 |
| Crow,Aaron, KC | R | - | 0 | 0 | 0 | 0 | 0 | - | 0 | 0 | 0 | 0 | 0 | 0 | 0 | 0 | 0 | 48.0 | 3 | 4 | 0 | 1 | 1.000 | 10 | 2 | 0 | 0 | .20 | -1 |
| Cruz,Rhiner, Hou | R | - | 0 | 0 | 0 | 0 | 0 | .000 | 1 | 0 | 0 | 0 | 0 | 0 | 0 | 1 | 0 | 21.1 | 0 | 1 | 0 | 0 | 1.000 | 1 | 1 | 0 | 0 | 1.00 | 0 |

# Pitchers Hitting, Fielding and Holding Runners

| | | 2013 Hitting | | | | | | Career Hitting | | | | | | | | | | 2013 Fielding and Holding Runners | | | | | | | | | | | |
|---|---|---|---|---|---|---|---|---|---|---|---|---|---|---|---|---|---|---|---|---|---|---|---|---|---|---|---|---|---|
| Pitcher | T | Avg | AB | H | HR | RBI | SH | Avg | AB | H | 2B | 3B | HR | RBI | BB | SO | SH | Inn | PO | A | E | DP | Pct | SBA | CS | PCS | PPO | CS% | RS |
| Cueto,Johnny, Cin | R | .150 | 20 | 3 | 0 | 1 | 2 | .093 | 279 | 26 | 1 | 0 | 0 | 7 | 8 | 94 | 52 | 60.2 | 7 | 8 | 1 | 0 | .938 | 4 | 2 | 0 | 0 | .50 | 2 |
| Cumpton,Brandon, Pit | R | .000 | 9 | 0 | 0 | 0 | 2 | .000 | 9 | 0 | 0 | 0 | 0 | 0 | 1 | 4 | 2 | 30.2 | 2 | 1 | 0 | 0 | 1.000 | 3 | 2 | 0 | 0 | .67 | -1 |
| Daley,Matt, NYY | R | - | 0 | 0 | 0 | 0 | 0 | - | 0 | 0 | 0 | 0 | 0 | 0 | 0 | 0 | 0 | 6.0 | 0 | 1 | 0 | 0 | 1.000 | 0 | 0 | 0 | 0 | - | 0 |
| Danks,John, CWS | L | .000 | 2 | 0 | 0 | 0 | 2 | .048 | 21 | 1 | 0 | 0 | 0 | 0 | 1 | 7 | 3 | 138.1 | 8 | 13 | 0 | 1 | 1.000 | 5 | 3 | 0 | 1 | .60 | 1 |
| Darvish,Yu, Tex | R | .000 | 3 | 0 | 0 | 0 | 0 | .167 | 6 | 1 | 0 | 0 | 0 | 0 | 0 | 3 | 0 | 209.2 | 9 | 14 | 0 | 1 | 1.000 | 25 | 7 | 0 | 0 | .28 | 0 |
| Davis,Erik, Was | R | - | 0 | 0 | 0 | 0 | 0 | - | 0 | 0 | 0 | 0 | 0 | 0 | 0 | 0 | 0 | 8.2 | 0 | 3 | 0 | 0 | 1.000 | 1 | 0 | 0 | 0 | .00 | 1 |
| Davis,Wade, KC | R | .000 | 3 | 0 | 0 | 0 | 1 | .250 | 8 | 2 | 0 | 0 | 0 | 0 | 0 | 4 | 3 | 135.1 | 12 | 13 | 1 | 2 | .962 | 8 | 3 | 0 | 1 | .38 | -1 |
| De Fratus,Justin, Phi | R | - | 0 | 0 | 0 | 0 | 0 | - | 0 | 0 | 0 | 0 | 0 | 0 | 0 | 0 | 0 | 46.2 | 1 | 6 | 1 | 1 | .875 | 4 | 1 | 1 | 0 | .25 | -1 |
| de la Rosa,Dane, LAA | R | - | 0 | 0 | 0 | 0 | 0 | - | 0 | 0 | 0 | 0 | 0 | 0 | 0 | 0 | 0 | 72.1 | 6 | 12 | 1 | 2 | .947 | 8 | 3 | 0 | 1 | .38 | 2 |
| De la Rosa,Eury, Ari | L | .000 | 1 | 0 | 0 | 0 | 0 | .000 | 1 | 0 | 0 | 0 | 0 | 0 | 0 | 0 | 0 | 14.2 | 0 | 2 | 1 | 0 | .667 | 0 | 0 | 0 | 0 | - | 0 |
| de la Rosa,Jorge, Col | L | .038 | 52 | 2 | 0 | 0 | 5 | .125 | 232 | 29 | 4 | 0 | 0 | 17 | 3 | 102 | 20 | 167.2 | 7 | 30 | 1 | 2 | .974 | 23 | 10 | 5 | 0 | .43 | 5 |
| de la Rosa,Rubby, Bos | R | - | 0 | 0 | 0 | 0 | 0 | .214 | 14 | 3 | 0 | 0 | 0 | 0 | 1 | 1 | 1 | 11.1 | 1 | 1 | 1 | 0 | .667 | 2 | 0 | 0 | 0 | .00 | 0 |
| De La Torre,Jose, Bos | R | - | 0 | 0 | 0 | 0 | 0 | - | 0 | 0 | 0 | 0 | 0 | 0 | 0 | 0 | 0 | 11.1 | 1 | 0 | 0 | 0 | 1.000 | 3 | 1 | 0 | 0 | .33 | 0 |
| De Leon,Jorge, Hou | R | - | 0 | 0 | 0 | 0 | 0 | - | 0 | 0 | 0 | 0 | 0 | 0 | 0 | 0 | 0 | 10.0 | 1 | 1 | 0 | 0 | 1.000 | 1 | 0 | 0 | 0 | .00 | -1 |
| Deduno,Samuel, Min | R | .000 | 1 | 0 | 0 | 0 | 1 | .000 | 1 | 0 | 0 | 0 | 0 | 0 | 0 | 1 | 1 | 108.0 | 13 | 21 | 1 | 1 | .971 | 7 | 2 | 0 | 0 | .29 | -2 |
| Delabar,Steve, Tor | R | - | 0 | 0 | 0 | 0 | 0 | - | 0 | 0 | 0 | 0 | 0 | 0 | 0 | 0 | 0 | 58.2 | 1 | 6 | 0 | 0 | 1.000 | 7 | 2 | 0 | 0 | .29 | 1 |
| Delgado,Randall, Ari | R | .219 | 32 | 7 | 0 | 1 | 4 | .194 | 67 | 13 | 0 | 0 | 0 | 2 | 1 | 28 | 8 | 116.1 | 6 | 10 | 1 | 1 | .941 | 2 | 1 | 0 | 0 | .50 | 1 |
| Dempster,Ryan, Bos | R | - | 0 | 0 | 0 | 0 | 0 | .099 | 588 | 58 | 9 | 2 | 0 | 17 | 13 | 221 | 85 | 171.1 | 12 | 19 | 3 | 2 | .912 | 17 | 1 | 0 | 0 | .06 | -3 |
| Detwiler,Ross, Was | L | .091 | 22 | 2 | 0 | 0 | 2 | .063 | 112 | 7 | 0 | 0 | 0 | 3 | 2 | 57 | 8 | 71.1 | 4 | 7 | 0 | 1 | 1.000 | 2 | 0 | 0 | 0 | .00 | -1 |
| DeVries,Cole, Min | R | - | 0 | 0 | 0 | 0 | 0 | - | 0 | 0 | 0 | 0 | 0 | 0 | 0 | 0 | 0 | 15.0 | 1 | 2 | 0 | 0 | 1.000 | 0 | 0 | 0 | 0 | - | 0 |
| Diamond,Scott, Min | L | .143 | 7 | 1 | 0 | 0 | 0 | .143 | 14 | 2 | 0 | 0 | 0 | 0 | 0 | 7 | 1 | 131.0 | 7 | 16 | 2 | 0 | .920 | 8 | 4 | 0 | 0 | .50 | 0 |
| Dickey,R.A., Tor | R | .333 | 6 | 2 | 0 | 1 | 0 | .187 | 193 | 36 | 3 | 0 | 0 | 11 | 4 | 33 | 26 | 224.2 | 11 | 40 | 2 | 1 | .962 | 11 | 3 | 0 | 2 | .27 | 7 |
| Diekman,Jake, Phi | L | - | 0 | 0 | 0 | 0 | 0 | - | 0 | 0 | 0 | 0 | 0 | 0 | 0 | 0 | 0 | 38.1 | 0 | 5 | 2 | 0 | .714 | 2 | 0 | 0 | 0 | .00 | -2 |
| Dolis,Rafael, ChC | R | - | 0 | 0 | 0 | 0 | 0 | - | 0 | 0 | 0 | 0 | 0 | 0 | 0 | 0 | 0 | 5.0 | 0 | 0 | 0 | 0 | - | 0 | 0 | 0 | 0 | - | 0 |
| Dominguez,Jose, LAD | R | .000 | 1 | 0 | 0 | 0 | 0 | .000 | 1 | 0 | 0 | 0 | 0 | 0 | 0 | 1 | 0 | 8.1 | 0 | 2 | 0 | 0 | 1.000 | 0 | 0 | 0 | 0 | - | 0 |
| Doolittle,Sean, Oak | L | - | 0 | 0 | 0 | 0 | 0 | - | 0 | 0 | 0 | 0 | 0 | 0 | 0 | 0 | 0 | 69.0 | 1 | 6 | 0 | 0 | 1.000 | 9 | 3 | 2 | 0 | .33 | -1 |
| Dotel,Octavio, Det | R | - | 0 | 0 | 0 | 0 | 0 | .065 | 77 | 5 | 0 | 0 | 0 | 1 | 5 | 44 | 9 | 4.2 | 0 | 1 | 0 | 0 | 1.000 | 2 | 0 | 0 | 0 | .00 | 0 |
| Doubront,Felix, Bos | L | .000 | 3 | 0 | 0 | 0 | 1 | .000 | 4 | 0 | 0 | 0 | 0 | 0 | 0 | 1 | 2 | 162.1 | 5 | 18 | 1 | 1 | .958 | 20 | 5 | 4 | 0 | .25 | 0 |
| Downs,Darin, Det | L | - | 0 | 0 | 0 | 0 | 0 | - | 0 | 0 | 0 | 0 | 0 | 0 | 0 | 0 | 0 | 35.1 | 1 | 2 | 0 | 0 | 1.000 | 1 | 1 | 1 | 0 | 1.00 | 1 |
| Downs,Scott, LAA-Atl | L | - | 0 | 0 | 0 | 0 | 0 | .067 | 45 | 3 | 0 | 0 | 0 | 1 | 3 | 17 | 10 | 43.1 | 7 | 6 | 1 | 3 | .929 | 1 | 0 | 0 | 0 | .00 | 0 |
| Drabek,Kyle, Tor | R | - | 0 | 0 | 0 | 0 | 0 | .000 | 2 | 0 | 0 | 0 | 0 | 0 | 0 | 1 | 0 | 2.1 | 0 | 1 | 0 | 0 | 1.000 | 1 | 0 | 0 | 0 | .00 | 0 |
| Duensing,Brian, Min | L | - | 0 | 0 | 0 | 0 | 0 | .000 | 6 | 0 | 0 | 0 | 0 | 0 | 0 | 4 | 0 | 61.0 | 7 | 12 | 0 | 1 | 1.000 | 5 | 3 | 2 | 0 | .60 | 1 |
| Duffy,Danny, KC | L | - | 0 | 0 | 0 | 0 | 0 | .000 | 3 | 0 | 0 | 0 | 0 | 0 | 0 | 2 | 0 | 24.1 | 1 | 2 | 0 | 1 | 1.000 | 3 | 1 | 0 | 0 | .33 | 1 |
| Duke,Zach, Was-Cin | L | 1.000 | 2 | 2 | 0 | 0 | 0 | .180 | 316 | 57 | 7 | 0 | 2 | 23 | 12 | 116 | 42 | 31.1 | 1 | 5 | 0 | 0 | 1.000 | 2 | 0 | 0 | 0 | .00 | 0 |
| Dunn,Mike, Mia | L | - | 0 | 0 | 0 | 0 | 0 | .000 | 4 | 0 | 0 | 0 | 0 | 0 | 0 | 1 | 0 | 67.2 | 2 | 4 | 2 | 0 | .750 | 2 | 1 | 0 | 0 | .50 | 0 |
| Dunning,Jake, SF | R | - | 0 | 0 | 0 | 0 | 0 | - | 0 | 0 | 0 | 0 | 0 | 0 | 0 | 0 | 0 | 25.1 | 1 | 5 | 1 | 0 | .857 | 2 | 1 | 0 | 0 | .50 | 1 |
| Durbin,Chad, Phi | R | - | 0 | 0 | 0 | 0 | 0 | .083 | 24 | 2 | 0 | 0 | 0 | 1 | 0 | 8 | 1 | 16.0 | 0 | 1 | 0 | 0 | 1.000 | 0 | 0 | 0 | 0 | - | -1 |
| Dwyer,Chris, KC | L | - | 0 | 0 | 0 | 0 | 0 | - | 0 | 0 | 0 | 0 | 0 | 0 | 0 | 0 | 0 | 3.0 | 0 | 3 | 0 | 1 | 1.000 | 1 | 0 | 0 | 0 | .00 | 1 |
| Dyson,Sam, Mia | R | .000 | 1 | 0 | 0 | 0 | 0 | .000 | 1 | 0 | 0 | 0 | 0 | 0 | 0 | 0 | 0 | 11.0 | 1 | 0 | 0 | 0 | 1.000 | 2 | 0 | 0 | 0 | .00 | -1 |
| Edgin,Josh, NYM | L | - | 0 | 0 | 0 | 0 | 0 | - | 0 | 0 | 0 | 0 | 0 | 0 | 0 | 0 | 0 | 28.2 | 0 | 0 | 0 | 0 | - | 0 | 0 | 0 | 0 | - | -1 |
| Enright,Barry, LAA | R | - | 0 | 0 | 0 | 0 | 0 | .222 | 45 | 10 | 1 | 0 | 1 | 8 | 2 | 11 | 4 | 8.1 | 1 | 1 | 0 | 0 | 1.000 | 0 | 0 | 0 | 0 | - | 0 |
| Eovaldi,Nathan, Mia | R | .065 | 31 | 2 | 0 | 1 | 3 | .081 | 74 | 6 | 0 | 0 | 0 | 1 | 3 | 46 | 6 | 106.1 | 8 | 20 | 2 | 1 | .933 | 1 | 0 | 0 | 1 | .00 | 1 |
| Eppley,Cody, NYY | R | - | 0 | 0 | 0 | 0 | 0 | - | 0 | 0 | 0 | 0 | 0 | 0 | 0 | 0 | 0 | 1.2 | 0 | 0 | 0 | 0 | - | 1 | 0 | 0 | 0 | .00 | 0 |
| Erlin,Robbie, SD | L | .063 | 16 | 1 | 0 | 1 | 2 | .063 | 16 | 1 | 0 | 0 | 0 | 1 | 1 | 5 | 2 | 54.2 | 1 | 5 | 0 | 0 | 1.000 | 8 | 2 | 1 | 0 | .25 | 1 |
| Escalona,Edgmer, Col | R | .000 | 6 | 0 | 0 | 0 | 1 | .000 | 9 | 0 | 0 | 0 | 0 | 0 | 0 | 6 | 2 | 46.0 | 2 | 5 | 1 | 0 | .875 | 2 | 0 | 0 | 0 | .00 | 0 |
| Estrada,Marco, Mil | R | .206 | 34 | 7 | 0 | 2 | 5 | .161 | 87 | 14 | 4 | 0 | 0 | 5 | 4 | 42 | 15 | 128.0 | 5 | 9 | 1 | 1 | .933 | 10 | 1 | 0 | 0 | .10 | -3 |
| Familia,Jeurys, NYM | R | - | 0 | 0 | 0 | 0 | 0 | .000 | 1 | 0 | 0 | 0 | 0 | 0 | 0 | 1 | 0 | 10.2 | 1 | 0 | 0 | 1 | 1.000 | 2 | 0 | 0 | 0 | .00 | 0 |
| Farnsworth,Kyle, TB-Pit | R | - | 0 | 0 | 0 | 0 | 0 | .074 | 54 | 4 | 1 | 0 | 0 | 3 | 2 | 18 | 8 | 38.1 | 4 | 6 | 0 | 0 | 1.000 | 7 | 0 | 0 | 1 | .00 | -1 |
| Farquhar,Danny, Sea | R | - | 0 | 0 | 0 | 0 | 0 | - | 0 | 0 | 0 | 0 | 0 | 0 | 0 | 0 | 0 | 55.2 | 4 | 8 | 0 | 2 | 1.000 | 4 | 1 | 0 | 0 | .25 | 0 |
| Feldman,Scott, ChC-Bal | R | .162 | 37 | 6 | 1 | 8 | 1 | .164 | 55 | 9 | 3 | 0 | 1 | 9 | 0 | 20 | 5 | 181.2 | 11 | 29 | 3 | 2 | .930 | 33 | 3 | 0 | 0 | .09 | -1 |
| Feliciano,Pedro, NYM | L | - | 0 | 0 | 0 | 0 | 0 | .000 | 6 | 0 | 0 | 0 | 0 | 0 | 2 | 2 | 1 | 11.1 | 1 | 3 | 0 | 0 | 1.000 | 0 | 0 | 0 | 0 | - | -1 |
| Feliz,Neftali, Tex | R | - | 0 | 0 | 0 | 0 | 0 | .000 | 2 | 0 | 0 | 0 | 0 | 0 | 0 | 1 | 0 | 4.2 | 0 | 0 | 0 | 0 | - | 1 | 1 | 0 | 0 | 1.00 | 0 |
| Fernandez,Jose, Mia | R | .220 | 50 | 11 | 1 | 5 | 7 | .220 | 50 | 11 | 1 | 1 | 1 | 5 | 0 | 20 | 7 | 172.2 | 22 | 15 | 1 | 0 | .974 | 10 | 4 | 1 | 1 | .40 | 3 |
| Fields,Josh, Hou | R | - | 0 | 0 | 0 | 0 | 0 | - | 0 | 0 | 0 | 0 | 0 | 0 | 0 | 0 | 0 | 38.0 | 3 | 1 | 0 | 0 | 1.000 | 4 | 2 | 0 | 0 | .50 | 0 |
| Fien,Casey, Min | R | - | 0 | 0 | 0 | 0 | 0 | - | 0 | 0 | 0 | 0 | 0 | 0 | 0 | 0 | 0 | 62.0 | 3 | 7 | 0 | 0 | 1.000 | 6 | 1 | 0 | 0 | .17 | 0 |
| Fiers,Mike, Mil | R | .000 | 4 | 0 | 0 | 0 | 1 | .083 | 36 | 3 | 0 | 0 | 0 | 2 | 0 | 21 | 7 | 22.1 | 2 | 5 | 0 | 0 | 1.000 | 3 | 0 | 0 | 0 | .00 | 1 |
| Fife,Stephen, LAD | R | .059 | 17 | 1 | 0 | 0 | 0 | .125 | 24 | 3 | 1 | 0 | 0 | 0 | 1 | 14 | 1 | 58.1 | 1 | 4 | 0 | 0 | 1.000 | 8 | 6 | 0 | 0 | .75 | -3 |
| Figaro,Alfredo, Mil | R | .250 | 12 | 3 | 0 | 2 | 0 | .214 | 14 | 3 | 0 | 0 | 0 | 2 | 0 | 7 | 0 | 74.0 | 5 | 7 | 1 | 1 | .923 | 5 | 1 | 0 | 0 | .20 | -1 |
| Figueroa,Pedro, Oak | L | - | 0 | 0 | 0 | 0 | 0 | - | 0 | 0 | 0 | 0 | 0 | 0 | 0 | 0 | 0 | 3.0 | 0 | 0 | 0 | 0 | - | 0 | 0 | 0 | 0 | - | 0 |
| Fister,Doug, Det | R | .400 | 5 | 2 | 0 | 1 | 2 | .267 | 15 | 4 | 1 | 0 | 0 | 2 | 0 | 5 | 3 | 208.2 | 23 | 29 | 0 | 5 | 1.000 | 13 | 5 | 0 | 1 | .38 | 1 |
| Floyd,Gavin, CWS | R | .000 | 2 | 0 | 0 | 0 | 0 | .054 | 56 | 3 | 0 | 0 | 0 | 0 | 2 | 31 | 4 | 24.1 | 2 | 6 | 0 | 1 | 1.000 | 2 | 0 | 0 | 0 | .00 | 1 |
| Flynn,Brian, Mia | L | .400 | 5 | 2 | 0 | 0 | 1 | .400 | 5 | 2 | 0 | 0 | 0 | 0 | 0 | 2 | 1 | 18.0 | 0 | 1 | 0 | 0 | 1.000 | 1 | 1 | 0 | 0 | 1.00 | 0 |
| Font,Wilmer, Tex | R | - | 0 | 0 | 0 | 0 | 0 | - | 0 | 0 | 0 | 0 | 0 | 0 | 0 | 0 | 0 | 1.1 | 0 | 0 | 0 | 0 | - | 0 | 0 | 0 | 0 | - | 0 |
| Francis,Jeff, Col | L | .071 | 14 | 1 | 0 | 1 | 2 | .116 | 301 | 35 | 7 | 0 | 0 | 16 | 25 | 100 | 53 | 70.1 | 6 | 12 | 0 | 1 | 1.000 | 4 | 0 | 0 | 0 | .00 | 0 |
| Francisco,Frank, NYM | R | - | 0 | 0 | 0 | 0 | 0 | - | 0 | 0 | 0 | 0 | 0 | 0 | 0 | 0 | 0 | 6.1 | 0 | 1 | 0 | 0 | 1.000 | 2 | 0 | 0 | 0 | .00 | 0 |
| Frasor,Jason, Tex | R | - | 0 | 0 | 0 | 0 | 0 | - | 0 | 0 | 0 | 0 | 0 | 0 | 0 | 0 | 0 | 49.0 | 3 | 5 | 1 | 0 | .889 | 8 | 1 | 0 | 0 | .13 | -3 |
| Freeman,Justin, Cin | R | - | 0 | 0 | 0 | 0 | 0 | - | 0 | 0 | 0 | 0 | 0 | 0 | 0 | 0 | 0 | 1.0 | 0 | 0 | 0 | 0 | - | 0 | 0 | 0 | 0 | - | 0 |
| Freeman,Sam, StL | L | - | 0 | 0 | 0 | 0 | 0 | - | 0 | 0 | 0 | 0 | 0 | 0 | 0 | 0 | 0 | 12.1 | 0 | 3 | 1 | 0 | .750 | 0 | 0 | 0 | 0 | - | -1 |
| Frieri,Ernesto, LAA | R | - | 0 | 0 | 0 | 0 | 0 | .000 | 1 | 0 | 0 | 0 | 0 | 0 | 0 | 1 | 0 | 68.2 | 2 | 6 | 0 | 1 | 1.000 | 6 | 1 | 0 | 0 | .17 | 0 |
| Fujikawa,Kyuji, ChC | R | - | 0 | 0 | 0 | 0 | 0 | - | 0 | 0 | 0 | 0 | 0 | 0 | 0 | 0 | 0 | 12.0 | 1 | 1 | 0 | 0 | 1.000 | 0 | 0 | 0 | 0 | - | 1 |

# Pitchers Hitting, Fielding and Holding Runners

| | | 2013 Hitting | | | | | | Career Hitting | | | | | | | | | | 2013 Fielding and Holding Runners | | | | | | | | | | | |
|---|---|---|---|---|---|---|---|---|---|---|---|---|---|---|---|---|---|---|---|---|---|---|---|---|---|---|---|---|---|
| Pitcher | T | Avg | AB | H | HR | RBI | SH | Avg | AB | H | 2B | 3B | HR | RBI | BB | SO | SH | Inn | PO | A | E | DP | Pct | SBA | CS | PCS | PPO | CS% | RS |
| Furbush,Charlie, Sea | L | - | 0 | 0 | 0 | 0 | 0 | - | 0 | 0 | 0 | 0 | 0 | 0 | 0 | 0 | 0 | 65.0 | 2 | 9 | 0 | 1 | 1.000 | 7 | 1 | 1 | 0 | .14 | -1 |
| Gallardo,Yovani, Mil | R | .211 | 57 | 12 | 2 | 4 | 7 | .207 | 362 | 75 | 19 | 0 | 12 | 41 | 11 | 129 | 30 | 180.2 | 14 | 22 | 1 | 1 | .973 | 15 | 0 | 0 | 1 | .00 | -1 |
| Garcia,Freddy, Bal-Atl | R | .000 | 8 | 0 | 0 | 0 | 2 | .156 | 77 | 12 | 2 | 0 | 0 | 4 | 2 | 26 | 19 | 80.1 | 9 | 11 | 1 | 1 | .952 | 10 | 1 | 0 | 0 | .10 | -1 |
| Garcia,Jaime, StL | L | .000 | 21 | 0 | 0 | 0 | 0 | .146 | 178 | 26 | 2 | 1 | 2 | 11 | 7 | 57 | 13 | 55.1 | 0 | 11 | 0 | 0 | 1.000 | 2 | 1 | 1 | 0 | .50 | 0 |
| Garcia,Luis, Phi | R | .000 | 2 | 0 | 0 | 0 | 0 | .000 | 2 | 0 | 0 | 0 | 0 | 0 | 0 | 1 | 0 | 31.1 | 0 | 10 | 0 | 0 | 1.000 | 4 | 2 | 1 | 1 | .50 | 1 |
| Garcia,Onelki, LAD | L | - | 0 | 0 | 0 | 0 | 0 | - | 0 | 0 | 0 | 0 | 0 | 0 | 0 | 0 | 0 | 1.1 | 0 | 1 | 0 | 0 | 1.000 | 1 | 0 | 0 | 0 | .00 | 0 |
| Garland,Jon, Col | R | .158 | 19 | 3 | 0 | 0 | 2 | .137 | 175 | 24 | 2 | 0 | 1 | 7 | 10 | 65 | 22 | 68.0 | 6 | 21 | 0 | 0 | 1.000 | 4 | 2 | 0 | 1 | .50 | 3 |
| Garza,Matt, ChC-Tex | R | .222 | 18 | 4 | 0 | 2 | 1 | .098 | 123 | 12 | 2 | 0 | 0 | 3 | 2 | 83 | 13 | 155.1 | 13 | 11 | 2 | 0 | .923 | 8 | 3 | 0 | 0 | .38 | -4 |
| Gast,John, StL | L | .000 | 5 | 0 | 0 | 0 | 0 | .000 | 5 | 0 | 0 | 0 | 0 | 0 | 1 | 3 | 0 | 12.1 | 1 | 0 | 0 | 0 | 1.000 | 1 | 1 | 0 | 0 | 1.00 | -1 |
| Gaudin,Chad, SF | R | .040 | 25 | 1 | 0 | 1 | 2 | .031 | 65 | 2 | 0 | 0 | 0 | 1 | 4 | 34 | 5 | 97.0 | 3 | 7 | 1 | 1 | .909 | 7 | 5 | 0 | 0 | .71 | -2 |
| Gausman,Kevin, Bal | R | .000 | 1 | 0 | 0 | 0 | 0 | .000 | 1 | 0 | 0 | 0 | 0 | 0 | 0 | 1 | 0 | 47.2 | 4 | 8 | 0 | 1 | 1.000 | 0 | 0 | 0 | 0 | - | 0 |
| Gearrin,Cory, Atl | R | - | 0 | 0 | 0 | 0 | 0 | - | 0 | 0 | 0 | 0 | 0 | 0 | 0 | 0 | 0 | 31.0 | 0 | 5 | 0 | 1 | 1.000 | 4 | 2 | 0 | 0 | .50 | 0 |
| Gee,Dillon, NYM | R | .133 | 60 | 8 | 0 | 4 | 8 | .131 | 145 | 19 | 3 | 1 | 0 | 10 | 7 | 67 | 21 | 199.0 | 12 | 37 | 1 | 1 | .980 | 17 | 5 | 1 | 2 | .29 | 3 |
| Germano,Justin, Tor | R | - | 0 | 0 | 0 | 0 | 0 | .149 | 67 | 10 | 2 | 0 | 0 | 3 | 4 | 31 | 17 | 2.0 | 0 | 0 | 0 | 0 | - | 0 | 0 | 0 | 0 | - | 0 |
| Germen,Gonzalez, NYM | R | .000 | 1 | 0 | 0 | 0 | 0 | .000 | 1 | 0 | 0 | 0 | 0 | 0 | 0 | 1 | 0 | 34.1 | 5 | 1 | 0 | 0 | 1.000 | 2 | 0 | 0 | 0 | .00 | 0 |
| Gibson,Kyle, Min | R | - | 0 | 0 | 0 | 0 | 0 | - | 0 | 0 | 0 | 0 | 0 | 0 | 0 | 0 | 0 | 51.0 | 1 | 4 | 0 | 1 | 1.000 | 6 | 2 | 0 | 0 | .33 | -2 |
| Gomes,Brandon, TB | R | - | 0 | 0 | 0 | 0 | 0 | .000 | 1 | 0 | 0 | 0 | 0 | 1 | 1 | 1 | 0 | 19.1 | 0 | 4 | 0 | 0 | 1.000 | 3 | 0 | 0 | 0 | .00 | 0 |
| Gomez,Jeanmar, Pit | R | .077 | 13 | 1 | 0 | 0 | 0 | .118 | 17 | 2 | 0 | 0 | 0 | 0 | 0 | 10 | 0 | 80.2 | 7 | 13 | 0 | 0 | 1.000 | 9 | 2 | 0 | 0 | .22 | 1 |
| Gonzalez,Edgar, Tor-Hou | R | - | 0 | 0 | 0 | 0 | 0 | .167 | 72 | 12 | 1 | 0 | 0 | 3 | 2 | 18 | 8 | 18.0 | 3 | 2 | 1 | 1 | .833 | 0 | 0 | 0 | 0 | - | 1 |
| Gonzalez,Gio, Was | L | .089 | 56 | 5 | 1 | 1 | 8 | .087 | 127 | 11 | 2 | 0 | 2 | 5 | 2 | 45 | 19 | 195.2 | 6 | 16 | 1 | 1 | .957 | 16 | 5 | 3 | 0 | .31 | -2 |
| Gonzalez,Michael, Mil | L | - | 0 | 0 | 0 | 0 | 0 | .333 | 3 | 1 | 1 | 0 | 0 | 2 | 0 | 0 | 0 | 50.0 | 0 | 5 | 0 | 0 | 1.000 | 8 | 2 | 1 | 0 | .25 | -2 |
| Gonzalez,Miguel, Bal | R | .000 | 3 | 0 | 0 | 0 | 1 | .000 | 3 | 0 | 0 | 0 | 0 | 0 | 0 | 1 | 1 | 171.1 | 6 | 24 | 1 | 1 | .968 | 5 | 3 | 0 | 0 | .60 | 2 |
| Gorzelanny,Tom, Mil | L | .059 | 17 | 1 | 0 | 0 | 1 | .093 | 216 | 20 | 0 | 0 | 0 | 13 | 9 | 101 | 24 | 85.1 | 6 | 11 | 1 | 2 | .944 | 6 | 1 | 0 | 0 | .17 | 2 |
| Gray,Sonny, Oak | R | - | 0 | 0 | 0 | 0 | 0 | - | 0 | 0 | 0 | 0 | 0 | 0 | 0 | 0 | 0 | 64.0 | 9 | 10 | 1 | 0 | .950 | 2 | 1 | 0 | 1 | .50 | 2 |
| Gregerson,Luke, SD | R | - | 0 | 0 | 0 | 0 | 0 | .000 | 2 | 0 | 0 | 0 | 0 | 0 | 0 | 1 | 1 | 66.1 | 2 | 14 | 1 | 1 | .941 | 10 | 0 | 0 | 0 | .00 | 0 |
| Gregg,Kevin, ChC | R | - | 0 | 0 | 0 | 0 | 0 | .000 | 6 | 0 | 0 | 0 | 0 | 0 | 0 | 5 | 0 | 62.0 | 4 | 6 | 2 | 0 | .833 | 6 | 2 | 0 | 0 | .33 | -1 |
| Greinke,Zack, LAD | R | .328 | 58 | 19 | 0 | 4 | 6 | .226 | 164 | 37 | 8 | 0 | 3 | 8 | 10 | 33 | 19 | 177.2 | 16 | 31 | 0 | 4 | 1.000 | 7 | 4 | 0 | 2 | .57 | 7 |
| Griffin,A.J., Oak | R | .000 | 4 | 0 | 0 | 0 | 0 | .000 | 4 | 0 | 0 | 0 | 0 | 0 | 1 | 3 | 0 | 200.0 | 8 | 15 | 0 | 0 | 1.000 | 7 | 2 | 1 | 0 | .29 | 0 |
| Grilli,Jason, Pit | R | - | 0 | 0 | 0 | 0 | 0 | .200 | 15 | 3 | 0 | 0 | 1 | 3 | 0 | 3 | 3 | 50.0 | 3 | 2 | 0 | 0 | 1.000 | 1 | 0 | 0 | 0 | .00 | 0 |
| Grimm,Justin, Tex-ChC | R | .000 | 1 | 0 | 0 | 0 | 0 | .000 | 1 | 0 | 0 | 0 | 0 | 0 | 0 | 0 | 0 | 98.0 | 12 | 11 | 2 | 1 | .920 | 8 | 4 | 1 | 1 | .50 | 0 |
| Guerra,Javy, LAD | R | - | 0 | 0 | 0 | 0 | 0 | - | 0 | 0 | 0 | 0 | 0 | 0 | 1 | 0 | 0 | 10.2 | 1 | 2 | 1 | 0 | .750 | 0 | 0 | 0 | 0 | - | 0 |
| Guerrier,Matt, LAD-ChC | R | .000 | 1 | 0 | 0 | 0 | 0 | .000 | 3 | 0 | 0 | 0 | 0 | 1 | 1 | 2 | 0 | 42.2 | 4 | 6 | 0 | 0 | 1.000 | 6 | 3 | 0 | 1 | .50 | -1 |
| Guilmet,Preston, Cle | R | - | 0 | 0 | 0 | 0 | 0 | - | 0 | 0 | 0 | 0 | 0 | 0 | 0 | 0 | 0 | 5.1 | 1 | 1 | 0 | 0 | 1.000 | 0 | 0 | 0 | 0 | - | -1 |
| Guthrie,Jeremy, KC | R | .250 | 4 | 1 | 0 | 0 | 0 | .098 | 51 | 5 | 2 | 0 | 0 | 1 | 1 | 26 | 4 | 211.2 | 17 | 22 | 0 | 2 | 1.000 | 12 | 3 | 0 | 1 | .25 | -1 |
| Gutierrez,Juan, KC-LAA | R | - | 0 | 0 | 0 | 0 | 0 | .000 | 6 | 0 | 0 | 0 | 0 | 0 | 0 | 4 | 1 | 55.1 | 3 | 3 | 2 | 0 | .750 | 11 | 2 | 0 | 0 | .18 | -7 |
| Hagadone,Nick, Cle | L | - | 0 | 0 | 0 | 0 | 0 | - | 0 | 0 | 0 | 0 | 0 | 0 | 0 | 0 | 0 | 31.1 | 0 | 4 | 0 | 0 | 1.000 | 1 | 1 | 1 | 0 | 1.00 | 0 |
| Hale,David, Atl | R | .000 | 4 | 0 | 0 | 0 | 0 | .000 | 4 | 0 | 0 | 0 | 0 | 0 | 0 | 3 | 0 | 11.0 | 1 | 1 | 0 | 0 | 1.000 | 1 | 0 | 0 | 0 | .00 | 0 |
| Halladay,Roy, Phi | R | .000 | 18 | 0 | 0 | 1 | 1 | .124 | 275 | 34 | 2 | 0 | 0 | 12 | 4 | 137 | 26 | 62.0 | 4 | 7 | 1 | 0 | .917 | 13 | 1 | 0 | 0 | .08 | -2 |
| Hamels,Cole, Phi | L | .179 | 56 | 10 | 0 | 5 | 13 | .170 | 506 | 86 | 12 | 2 | 1 | 28 | 17 | 212 | 51 | 220.0 | 9 | 29 | 1 | 0 | .974 | 35 | 10 | 5 | 0 | .29 | -2 |
| Hammel,Jason, Bal | R | .000 | 3 | 0 | 0 | 0 | 1 | .120 | 166 | 20 | 4 | 0 | 1 | 7 | 4 | 74 | 26 | 139.1 | 4 | 7 | 0 | 0 | 1.000 | 11 | 3 | 0 | 0 | .27 | -3 |
| Hand,Brad, Mia | L | .000 | 4 | 0 | 0 | 0 | 0 | .091 | 22 | 2 | 0 | 0 | 0 | 1 | 0 | 9 | 3 | 20.2 | 1 | 2 | 0 | 0 | 1.000 | 1 | 0 | 0 | 0 | .00 | 0 |
| Hand,Donovan, Mil | R | .091 | 11 | 1 | 0 | 0 | 2 | .091 | 11 | 1 | 0 | 0 | 0 | 0 | 0 | 3 | 2 | 68.1 | 3 | 15 | 1 | 0 | .947 | 14 | 4 | 0 | 1 | .29 | 2 |
| Hanrahan,Joel, Bos | R | - | 0 | 0 | 0 | 0 | 0 | .235 | 17 | 4 | 2 | 1 | 0 | 3 | 0 | 5 | 4 | 7.1 | 1 | 1 | 0 | 0 | 1.000 | 1 | 0 | 0 | 0 | .00 | 0 |
| Hanson,Tommy, LAA | R | - | 0 | 0 | 0 | 0 | 0 | .059 | 187 | 11 | 0 | 0 | 0 | 5 | 5 | 92 | 32 | 73.0 | 7 | 7 | 1 | 0 | .933 | 25 | 4 | 0 | 0 | .16 | -4 |
| Happ,J.A., Tor | L | - | 0 | 0 | 0 | 0 | 0 | .092 | 152 | 14 | 2 | 0 | 1 | 6 | 8 | 62 | 24 | 92.2 | 2 | 9 | 0 | 0 | 1.000 | 9 | 0 | 0 | 0 | .00 | -1 |
| Harang,Aaron, Sea-NYM | R | .182 | 11 | 2 | 0 | 0 | 0 | .093 | 561 | 52 | 7 | 0 | 1 | 20 | 3 | 247 | 51 | 143.1 | 10 | 14 | 1 | 1 | .960 | 10 | 2 | 1 | 0 | .20 | -1 |
| Haren,Dan, Was | R | .170 | 47 | 8 | 0 | 2 | 6 | .215 | 311 | 67 | 24 | 0 | 2 | 29 | 9 | 85 | 28 | 169.2 | 9 | 14 | 0 | 0 | 1.000 | 12 | 1 | 0 | 0 | .08 | -2 |
| Harrell,Lucas, Hou | R | .250 | 4 | 1 | 0 | 0 | 0 | .152 | 66 | 10 | 0 | 0 | 0 | 1 | 3 | 37 | 3 | 153.2 | 6 | 22 | 1 | 5 | .966 | 18 | 4 | 0 | 0 | .22 | -2 |
| Harris,Will, Ari | R | - | 0 | 0 | 0 | 0 | 0 | - | 0 | 0 | 0 | 0 | 0 | 0 | 0 | 0 | 0 | 52.2 | 2 | 9 | 0 | 1 | 1.000 | 4 | 0 | 0 | 0 | .00 | 0 |
| Harrison,Matt, Tex | L | - | 0 | 0 | 0 | 0 | 0 | .000 | 16 | 0 | 0 | 0 | 0 | 0 | 1 | 11 | 2 | 10.2 | 1 | 1 | 0 | 0 | 1.000 | 0 | 0 | 0 | 0 | - | -1 |
| Harvey,Matt, NYM | R | .086 | 58 | 5 | 0 | 2 | 5 | .145 | 76 | 11 | 4 | 0 | 0 | 5 | 1 | 34 | 8 | 178.1 | 9 | 19 | 0 | 1 | 1.000 | 4 | 2 | 1 | 1 | .50 | 0 |
| Hatcher,Chris, Mia | R | - | 0 | 0 | 0 | 0 | 0 | .000 | 7 | 0 | 0 | 0 | 0 | 0 | 2 | 6 | 0 | 8.2 | 0 | 2 | 0 | 0 | 1.000 | 0 | 0 | 0 | 0 | - | 0 |
| Hawkins,LaTroy, NYM | R | - | 0 | 0 | 0 | 0 | 0 | .000 | 6 | 0 | 0 | 0 | 0 | 0 | 0 | 5 | 1 | 70.2 | 3 | 16 | 2 | 1 | .905 | 8 | 3 | 0 | 0 | .38 | 2 |
| Heath,Deunte, CWS | R | - | 0 | 0 | 0 | 0 | 0 | - | 0 | 0 | 0 | 0 | 0 | 0 | 0 | 0 | 0 | 7.2 | 0 | 0 | 0 | 0 | - | 0 | 0 | 0 | 0 | - | -1 |
| Hefner,Jeremy, NYM | R | .000 | 32 | 0 | 0 | 1 | 5 | .038 | 52 | 2 | 0 | 0 | 1 | 2 | 1 | 32 | 11 | 130.2 | 5 | 19 | 0 | 1 | 1.000 | 6 | 2 | 0 | 0 | .33 | 3 |
| Hellickson,Jeremy, TB | R | .333 | 3 | 1 | 0 | 0 | 0 | .167 | 6 | 1 | 0 | 0 | 0 | 0 | 0 | 3 | 1 | 174.0 | 9 | 14 | 0 | 1 | 1.000 | 10 | 4 | 0 | 1 | .40 | 1 |
| Hellweg,John, Mil | R | .000 | 10 | 0 | 0 | 0 | 1 | .000 | 10 | 0 | 0 | 0 | 0 | 0 | 0 | 4 | 1 | 30.2 | 1 | 1 | 0 | 0 | 1.000 | 3 | 1 | 0 | 0 | .33 | -1 |
| Hembree,Heath, SF | R | - | 0 | 0 | 0 | 0 | 0 | - | 0 | 0 | 0 | 0 | 0 | 0 | 0 | 0 | 0 | 7.2 | 0 | 0 | 0 | 0 | - | 1 | 0 | 0 | 0 | .00 | 0 |
| Henderson,Jim, Mil | R | - | 0 | 0 | 0 | 0 | 0 | - | 0 | 0 | 0 | 0 | 0 | 0 | 0 | 0 | 0 | 60.0 | 2 | 8 | 0 | 1 | 1.000 | 10 | 2 | 0 | 0 | .20 | 1 |
| Hendriks,Liam, Min | R | - | 0 | 0 | 0 | 0 | 0 | .000 | 2 | 0 | 0 | 0 | 0 | 0 | 0 | 1 | 0 | 47.1 | 5 | 4 | 0 | 0 | 1.000 | 9 | 2 | 0 | 0 | .22 | -1 |
| Henn,Sean, NYM | L | - | 0 | 0 | 0 | 0 | 0 | .000 | 1 | 0 | 0 | 0 | 0 | 0 | 0 | 1 | 0 | 2.2 | 0 | 0 | 0 | 0 | - | 0 | 0 | 0 | 0 | - | 0 |
| Hernandez,David, Ari | R | - | 0 | 0 | 0 | 0 | 0 | .250 | 4 | 1 | 0 | 0 | 0 | 0 | 0 | 1 | 0 | 62.1 | 2 | 2 | 0 | 0 | 1.000 | 2 | 0 | 0 | 0 | .00 | 0 |
| Hernandez,Felix, Sea | R | .000 | 5 | 0 | 0 | 0 | 0 | .125 | 32 | 4 | 1 | 0 | 1 | 7 | 2 | 16 | 4 | 204.1 | 7 | 15 | 2 | 2 | .917 | 22 | 5 | 0 | 0 | .23 | -3 |
| Hernandez,Pedro, Min | L | - | 0 | 0 | 0 | 0 | 0 | - | 0 | 0 | 0 | 0 | 0 | 0 | 0 | 0 | 0 | 56.2 | 1 | 11 | 0 | 0 | 1.000 | 4 | 3 | 2 | 0 | .75 | 0 |
| Hernandez,Roberto, TB | R | .000 | 4 | 0 | 0 | 0 | 0 | .000 | 18 | 0 | 0 | 0 | 0 | 0 | 0 | 11 | 2 | 151.0 | 8 | 15 | 0 | 2 | 1.000 | 23 | 5 | 0 | 1 | .22 | -1 |
| Herrera,Kelvin, KC | R | - | 0 | 0 | 0 | 0 | 0 | - | 0 | 0 | 0 | 0 | 0 | 0 | 0 | 0 | 0 | 58.1 | 4 | 4 | 1 | 0 | .889 | 10 | 2 | 0 | 0 | .20 | -1 |
| Hill,Rich, Cle | L | - | 0 | 0 | 0 | 0 | 0 | .123 | 114 | 14 | 3 | 0 | 0 | 6 | 2 | 51 | 6 | 38.2 | 3 | 4 | 1 | 0 | .875 | 9 | 2 | 1 | 0 | .22 | -2 |
| Hochevar,Luke, KC | R | - | 0 | 0 | 0 | 0 | 0 | .063 | 16 | 1 | 0 | 0 | 0 | 0 | 0 | 10 | 1 | 70.1 | 4 | 3 | 1 | 0 | .875 | 7 | 3 | 0 | 0 | .43 | 1 |
| Holland,Derek, Tex | L | .000 | 5 | 0 | 0 | 0 | 1 | .000 | 12 | 0 | 0 | 0 | 0 | 0 | 2 | 6 | 2 | 213.0 | 3 | 17 | 2 | 0 | .909 | 12 | 4 | 4 | 0 | .33 | 0 |
| Holland,Greg, KC | R | - | 0 | 0 | 0 | 0 | 0 | - | 0 | 0 | 0 | 0 | 0 | 0 | 0 | 0 | 0 | 67.0 | 5 | 6 | 0 | 1 | 1.000 | 3 | 0 | 0 | 0 | .00 | 0 |

# Pitchers Hitting, Fielding and Holding Runners

| | | 2013 Hitting | | | | | | Career Hitting | | | | | | | | | | 2013 Fielding and Holding Runners | | | | | | | | | | | |
|---|---|---|---|---|---|---|---|---|---|---|---|---|---|---|---|---|---|---|---|---|---|---|---|---|---|---|---|---|---|
| Pitcher | T | Avg | AB | H | HR | RBI | SH | Avg | AB | H | 2B | 3B | HR | RBI | BB | SO | SH | Inn | PO | A | E | DP | Pct | SBA | CS | PCS | PPO | CS% | RS |
| Holmberg,David, Ari | L | .000 | 1 | 0 | 0 | 0 | 0 | .000 | 1 | 0 | 0 | 0 | 0 | 0 | 0 | 1 | 0 | 3.2 | 1 | 0 | 0 | 0 | 1.000 | 0 | 0 | 0 | 0 | - | 0 |
| Hoover,J.J., Cin | R | - | 0 | 0 | 0 | 0 | 0 | - | 0 | 0 | 0 | 0 | 0 | 0 | 0 | 0 | 0 | 66.0 | 7 | 4 | 1 | 1 | .917 | 2 | 1 | 0 | 0 | .50 | -1 |
| Horst,Jeremy, Phi | L | - | 0 | 0 | 0 | 0 | 0 | 1.000 | 1 | 1 | 0 | 0 | 0 | 1 | 0 | 0 | 0 | 26.0 | 0 | 4 | 0 | 2 | 1.000 | 2 | 0 | 0 | 0 | .00 | -1 |
| Howell,J.P., LAD | L | .000 | 1 | 0 | 0 | 0 | 0 | .182 | 11 | 2 | 0 | 0 | 0 | 1 | 0 | 5 | 0 | 62.0 | 6 | 10 | 0 | 1 | 1.000 | 5 | 2 | 0 | 0 | .40 | 1 |
| Hudson,Tim, Atl | R | .158 | 38 | 6 | 1 | 3 | 6 | .170 | 522 | 89 | 17 | 1 | 3 | 40 | 23 | 159 | 58 | 131.1 | 5 | 16 | 1 | 0 | .955 | 8 | 1 | 0 | 0 | .13 | -3 |
| Huff,David, Cle-NYY | L | - | 0 | 0 | 0 | 0 | 0 | .000 | 4 | 0 | 0 | 0 | 0 | 0 | 0 | 2 | 2 | 37.2 | 2 | 3 | 0 | 0 | 1.000 | 3 | 1 | 0 | 0 | .33 | 0 |
| Hughes,Jared, Pit | R | .000 | 2 | 0 | 0 | 0 | 0 | .000 | 3 | 0 | 0 | 0 | 0 | 0 | 0 | 3 | 0 | 32.0 | 1 | 7 | 2 | 0 | .800 | 6 | 2 | 1 | 0 | .33 | 0 |
| Hughes,Phil, NYY | R | .000 | 3 | 0 | 0 | 0 | 1 | .000 | 6 | 0 | 0 | 0 | 0 | 0 | 0 | 2 | 2 | 145.2 | 3 | 10 | 0 | 0 | 1.000 | 11 | 3 | 0 | 0 | .27 | -2 |
| Humber,Philip, Hou | R | - | 0 | 0 | 0 | 0 | 0 | .091 | 11 | 1 | 0 | 0 | 0 | 1 | 0 | 4 | 2 | 54.2 | 7 | 4 | 0 | 0 | 1.000 | 6 | 0 | 0 | 0 | .00 | -1 |
| Hunter,Tommy, Bal | R | - | 0 | 0 | 0 | 0 | 0 | .000 | 3 | 0 | 0 | 0 | 0 | 0 | 0 | 2 | 0 | 86.1 | 3 | 10 | 1 | 0 | .929 | 7 | 4 | 0 | 0 | .57 | 0 |
| Hynes,Colt, SD | L | - | 0 | 0 | 0 | 0 | 0 | - | 0 | 0 | 0 | 0 | 0 | 0 | 0 | 0 | 0 | 17.0 | 1 | 4 | 0 | 0 | 1.000 | 1 | 0 | 0 | 0 | .00 | 1 |
| Irwin,Phil, Pit | R | .000 | 1 | 0 | 0 | 0 | 0 | .000 | 1 | 0 | 0 | 0 | 0 | 0 | 0 | 1 | 0 | 4.2 | 0 | 2 | 0 | 0 | 1.000 | 3 | 0 | 0 | 0 | .00 | 0 |
| Iwakuma,Hisashi, Sea | R | .000 | 3 | 0 | 0 | 0 | 0 | .000 | 3 | 0 | 0 | 0 | 0 | 0 | 0 | 2 | 0 | 219.2 | 13 | 26 | 1 | 2 | .975 | 7 | 2 | 0 | 0 | .29 | 5 |
| Jackson,Edwin, ChC | R | .077 | 52 | 4 | 1 | 4 | 5 | .169 | 207 | 35 | 1 | 0 | 2 | 11 | 11 | 79 | 18 | 175.1 | 16 | 24 | 4 | 1 | .909 | 20 | 2 | 0 | 2 | .10 | -3 |
| Jansen,Kenley, LAD | R | .000 | 1 | 0 | 0 | 0 | 0 | .500 | 2 | 1 | 0 | 0 | 0 | 0 | 1 | 0 | 0 | 76.2 | 3 | 1 | 0 | 0 | 1.000 | 9 | 2 | 0 | 0 | .22 | -2 |
| Janssen,Casey, Tor | R | - | 0 | 0 | 0 | 0 | 0 | .000 | 3 | 0 | 0 | 0 | 0 | 0 | 0 | 2 | 1 | 52.2 | 4 | 8 | 0 | 0 | 1.000 | 2 | 2 | 0 | 0 | 1.00 | 3 |
| Jeffress,Jeremy, Tor | R | - | 0 | 0 | 0 | 0 | 0 | - | 0 | 0 | 0 | 0 | 0 | 0 | 0 | 0 | 0 | 10.1 | 0 | 2 | 0 | 0 | 1.000 | 3 | 0 | 0 | 0 | .00 | -1 |
| Jenkins,Chad, Tor | R | .000 | 2 | 0 | 0 | 0 | 0 | .000 | 2 | 0 | 0 | 0 | 0 | 0 | 0 | 2 | 0 | 33.1 | 2 | 8 | 1 | 2 | .909 | 1 | 0 | 0 | 0 | .00 | 1 |
| Jennings,Dan, Mia | L | - | 0 | 0 | 0 | 0 | 0 | .000 | 1 | 0 | 0 | 0 | 0 | 0 | 0 | 0 | 0 | 40.2 | 3 | 6 | 0 | 0 | 1.000 | 7 | 1 | 0 | 0 | .14 | 1 |
| Jepsen,Kevin, LAA | R | - | 0 | 0 | 0 | 0 | 0 | - | 0 | 0 | 0 | 0 | 0 | 0 | 0 | 0 | 0 | 36.0 | 0 | 2 | 0 | 0 | 1.000 | 5 | 0 | 0 | 0 | .00 | -2 |
| Jimenez,Cesar, Phi | L | - | 0 | 0 | 0 | 0 | 0 | - | 0 | 0 | 0 | 0 | 0 | 0 | 0 | 0 | 0 | 17.0 | 1 | 1 | 0 | 0 | 1.000 | 2 | 0 | 0 | 0 | .00 | 0 |
| Jimenez,Ubaldo, Cle | R | .000 | 3 | 0 | 0 | 0 | 1 | .114 | 273 | 31 | 0 | 0 | 0 | 9 | 17 | 94 | 33 | 182.2 | 5 | 14 | 2 | 1 | .905 | 22 | 6 | 0 | 0 | .27 | -4 |
| Johnson,Erik, CWS | R | - | 0 | 0 | 0 | 0 | 0 | - | 0 | 0 | 0 | 0 | 0 | 0 | 0 | 0 | 0 | 27.2 | 2 | 2 | 1 | 0 | .800 | 1 | 0 | 0 | 0 | .00 | 1 |
| Johnson,Jim, Bal | R | - | 0 | 0 | 0 | 0 | 0 | - | 0 | 0 | 0 | 0 | 0 | 0 | 0 | 0 | 0 | 70.1 | 3 | 17 | 2 | 2 | .909 | 2 | 1 | 0 | 0 | .50 | -1 |
| Johnson,Josh, Tor | R | .000 | 1 | 0 | 0 | 0 | 0 | .125 | 272 | 34 | 5 | 0 | 3 | 25 | 14 | 146 | 32 | 81.1 | 12 | 4 | 2 | 1 | .889 | 12 | 1 | 0 | 0 | .08 | -5 |
| Johnson,Kris, Pit | L | .000 | 2 | 0 | 0 | 0 | 1 | .000 | 2 | 0 | 0 | 0 | 0 | 0 | 0 | 1 | 1 | 10.1 | 1 | 0 | 0 | 0 | 1.000 | 1 | 1 | 0 | 0 | 1.00 | 0 |
| Johnson,Steve, Bal | R | - | 0 | 0 | 0 | 0 | 0 | - | 0 | 0 | 0 | 0 | 0 | 0 | 0 | 0 | 0 | 15.2 | 0 | 1 | 0 | 0 | 1.000 | 0 | 0 | 0 | 0 | - | 0 |
| Jones,Nate, CWS | R | - | 0 | 0 | 0 | 0 | 0 | - | 0 | 0 | 0 | 0 | 0 | 0 | 0 | 0 | 0 | 78.0 | 2 | 8 | 0 | 0 | 1.000 | 10 | 3 | 1 | 0 | .30 | -1 |
| Jordan,Taylor, Was | R | .143 | 14 | 2 | 0 | 0 | 4 | .143 | 14 | 2 | 0 | 0 | 0 | 0 | 0 | 3 | 4 | 51.2 | 2 | 3 | 0 | 0 | 1.000 | 3 | 0 | 0 | 0 | .00 | -3 |
| Joseph,Donnie, KC | L | - | 0 | 0 | 0 | 0 | 0 | - | 0 | 0 | 0 | 0 | 0 | 0 | 0 | 0 | 0 | 5.2 | 0 | 2 | 0 | 0 | 1.000 | 0 | 0 | 0 | 0 | - | 0 |
| Jurrjens,Jair, Bal | R | - | 0 | 0 | 0 | 0 | 0 | .113 | 222 | 25 | 3 | 1 | 0 | 7 | 18 | 75 | 28 | 7.1 | 0 | 0 | 0 | 0 | - | 0 | 0 | 0 | 0 | - | 0 |
| Karns,Nate, Was | R | .000 | 3 | 0 | 0 | 0 | 2 | .000 | 3 | 0 | 0 | 0 | 0 | 0 | 0 | 1 | 2 | 12.0 | 3 | 0 | 0 | 0 | 1.000 | 2 | 0 | 0 | 0 | .00 | 0 |
| Kazmir,Scott, Cle | L | .250 | 4 | 1 | 0 | 0 | 0 | .111 | 18 | 2 | 0 | 0 | 0 | 1 | 0 | 7 | 1 | 158.0 | 10 | 12 | 3 | 0 | .880 | 8 | 2 | 0 | 0 | .25 | 1 |
| Kelley,Shawn, NYY | R | - | 0 | 0 | 0 | 0 | 0 | - | 0 | 0 | 0 | 0 | 0 | 0 | 0 | 0 | 0 | 53.1 | 6 | 3 | 0 | 1 | 1.000 | 4 | 3 | 0 | 0 | .75 | 1 |
| Kelly,Joe, StL | R | .152 | 33 | 5 | 0 | 2 | 5 | .152 | 66 | 10 | 3 | 0 | 0 | 4 | 0 | 21 | 7 | 124.0 | 13 | 16 | 3 | 2 | .906 | 3 | 1 | 0 | 0 | .33 | -1 |
| Kendrick,Kyle, Phi | R | .125 | 56 | 7 | 0 | 2 | 8 | .133 | 264 | 35 | 6 | 1 | 0 | 6 | 14 | 110 | 37 | 182.0 | 13 | 43 | 2 | 5 | .966 | 12 | 2 | 0 | 0 | .17 | 4 |
| Kennedy,Ian, Ari-SD | R | .132 | 53 | 7 | 0 | 1 | 6 | .137 | 219 | 30 | 7 | 1 | 0 | 13 | 27 | 105 | 30 | 181.1 | 7 | 20 | 0 | 1 | 1.000 | 6 | 4 | 0 | 0 | .67 | 0 |
| Kensing,Logan, Col | R | - | 0 | 0 | 0 | 0 | 0 | .000 | 8 | 0 | 0 | 0 | 0 | 0 | 0 | 2 | 1 | 0.2 | 0 | 0 | 0 | 0 | - | 1 | 1 | 0 | 0 | 1.00 | 0 |
| Kershaw,Clayton, LAD | L | .182 | 77 | 14 | 1 | 10 | 9 | .154 | 338 | 52 | 4 | 0 | 1 | 19 | 14 | 102 | 69 | 236.0 | 7 | 27 | 1 | 2 | .971 | 9 | 4 | 3 | 4 | .44 | 4 |
| Keuchel,Dallas, Hou | L | .000 | 2 | 0 | 0 | 0 | 0 | .091 | 22 | 2 | 0 | 0 | 0 | 1 | 1 | 12 | 5 | 153.2 | 7 | 24 | 0 | 3 | 1.000 | 11 | 4 | 0 | 0 | .36 | 3 |
| Kickham,Mike, SF | L | .167 | 6 | 1 | 0 | 0 | 0 | .167 | 6 | 1 | 1 | 0 | 0 | 0 | 0 | 1 | 0 | 28.1 | 2 | 5 | 1 | 0 | .875 | 2 | 0 | 0 | 0 | .00 | -1 |
| Kimbrel,Craig, Atl | R | - | 0 | 0 | 0 | 0 | 0 | - | 0 | 0 | 0 | 0 | 0 | 0 | 0 | 0 | 0 | 67.0 | 3 | 4 | 0 | 0 | 1.000 | 5 | 2 | 0 | 0 | .40 | -1 |
| Kintzler,Brandon, Mil | R | - | 0 | 0 | 0 | 0 | 0 | .000 | 1 | 0 | 0 | 0 | 0 | 0 | 0 | 1 | 0 | 77.0 | 5 | 10 | 0 | 2 | 1.000 | 3 | 0 | 0 | 0 | .00 | 2 |
| Kirkman,Michael, Tex | L | - | 0 | 0 | 0 | 0 | 0 | - | 0 | 0 | 0 | 0 | 0 | 0 | 0 | 0 | 0 | 22.0 | 0 | 0 | 0 | 0 | - | 2 | 0 | 0 | 0 | .00 | -1 |
| Kluber,Corey, Cle | R | .000 | 2 | 0 | 0 | 0 | 0 | .000 | 2 | 0 | 0 | 0 | 0 | 0 | 1 | 1 | 0 | 147.1 | 12 | 18 | 1 | 1 | .968 | 9 | 3 | 0 | 0 | .33 | 1 |
| Koehler,Tom, Mia | R | .077 | 39 | 3 | 0 | 0 | 2 | .075 | 40 | 3 | 0 | 0 | 0 | 0 | 0 | 18 | 2 | 143.0 | 16 | 15 | 1 | 3 | .969 | 10 | 5 | 0 | 2 | .50 | -1 |
| Kohn,Michael, LAA | R | - | 0 | 0 | 0 | 0 | 0 | - | 0 | 0 | 0 | 0 | 0 | 0 | 0 | 0 | 0 | 53.0 | 2 | 4 | 0 | 0 | 1.000 | 2 | 2 | 0 | 0 | 1.00 | 0 |
| Kontos,George, SF | R | .000 | 1 | 0 | 0 | 0 | 1 | .000 | 2 | 0 | 0 | 0 | 0 | 0 | 0 | 1 | 1 | 55.1 | 4 | 7 | 0 | 0 | 1.000 | 1 | 0 | 0 | 0 | .00 | 0 |
| Krol,Ian, Was | L | - | 0 | 0 | 0 | 0 | 0 | - | 0 | 0 | 0 | 0 | 0 | 0 | 0 | 0 | 0 | 27.1 | 2 | 3 | 0 | 0 | 1.000 | 2 | 0 | 0 | 0 | .00 | 1 |
| Kuroda,Hiroki, NYY | R | .000 | 6 | 0 | 0 | 0 | 0 | .102 | 206 | 21 | 1 | 0 | 0 | 3 | 13 | 72 | 32 | 201.1 | 12 | 25 | 0 | 3 | 1.000 | 12 | 6 | 0 | 2 | .50 | 6 |
| Lackey,John, Bos | R | .000 | 5 | 0 | 0 | 0 | 1 | .093 | 43 | 4 | 2 | 0 | 0 | 2 | 0 | 14 | 3 | 189.1 | 18 | 29 | 2 | 0 | .959 | 43 | 7 | 0 | 0 | .16 | -5 |
| Laffey,Aaron, NYM-Tor | L | .000 | 3 | 0 | 0 | 0 | 0 | .143 | 7 | 1 | 0 | 0 | 0 | 0 | 0 | 1 | 0 | 12.2 | 0 | 2 | 0 | 0 | 1.000 | 3 | 1 | 0 | 0 | .33 | 0 |
| LaFromboise,Bobby, Sea | L | - | 0 | 0 | 0 | 0 | 0 | - | 0 | 0 | 0 | 0 | 0 | 0 | 0 | 0 | 0 | 10.2 | 0 | 2 | 0 | 0 | 1.000 | 0 | 0 | 0 | 0 | - | 0 |
| Langwell,Matt, Cle-Ari | R | .000 | 1 | 0 | 0 | 0 | 0 | .000 | 1 | 0 | 0 | 0 | 0 | 0 | 0 | 0 | 0 | 14.0 | 0 | 2 | 0 | 0 | 1.000 | 1 | 0 | 0 | 0 | .00 | 0 |
| Lannan,John, Phi | L | .190 | 21 | 4 | 0 | 1 | 2 | .105 | 247 | 26 | 5 | 0 | 1 | 11 | 16 | 111 | 21 | 74.1 | 0 | 9 | 1 | 0 | .900 | 7 | 2 | 1 | 1 | .29 | -1 |
| Latos,Mat, Cin | R | .127 | 71 | 9 | 0 | 4 | 6 | .121 | 265 | 32 | 6 | 0 | 3 | 12 | 5 | 126 | 32 | 210.2 | 26 | 20 | 1 | 2 | .979 | 19 | 5 | 0 | 0 | .26 | -2 |
| Layne,Tom, SD | L | - | 0 | 0 | 0 | 0 | 0 | - | 0 | 0 | 0 | 0 | 0 | 0 | 0 | 0 | 0 | 8.2 | 0 | 1 | 0 | 0 | 1.000 | 1 | 0 | 0 | 0 | .00 | 0 |
| League,Brandon, LAD | R | - | 0 | 0 | 0 | 0 | 0 | - | 0 | 0 | 0 | 0 | 0 | 0 | 1 | 0 | 0 | 54.1 | 4 | 8 | 2 | 0 | .857 | 4 | 2 | 0 | 0 | .50 | -3 |
| Leake,Mike, Cin | R | .190 | 63 | 12 | 0 | 2 | 4 | .251 | 227 | 57 | 8 | 1 | 2 | 10 | 9 | 77 | 27 | 192.1 | 26 | 28 | 1 | 2 | .982 | 13 | 4 | 0 | 0 | .31 | 6 |
| LeBlanc,Wade, Mia-Hou | L | .167 | 12 | 2 | 0 | 0 | 1 | .252 | 111 | 28 | 1 | 0 | 0 | 2 | 3 | 25 | 15 | 55.0 | 4 | 5 | 1 | 1 | .900 | 6 | 3 | 1 | 0 | .50 | -2 |
| LeCure,Sam, Cin | R | - | 0 | 0 | 0 | 0 | 0 | .095 | 21 | 2 | 2 | 0 | 0 | 0 | 1 | 8 | 2 | 61.0 | 2 | 3 | 0 | 1 | 1.000 | 1 | 1 | 0 | 0 | 1.00 | 0 |
| Lee,C.C., Cle | R | - | 0 | 0 | 0 | 0 | 0 | - | 0 | 0 | 0 | 0 | 0 | 0 | 0 | 0 | 0 | 4.1 | 0 | 0 | 0 | 0 | - | 0 | 0 | 0 | 0 | - | 0 |
| Lee,Cliff, Phi | L | .183 | 60 | 11 | 0 | 6 | 10 | .169 | 267 | 45 | 7 | 1 | 2 | 18 | 5 | 101 | 23 | 222.2 | 7 | 28 | 1 | 1 | .972 | 5 | 2 | 1 | 0 | .40 | 2 |
| Leesman,Charlie, CWS | L | - | 0 | 0 | 0 | 0 | 0 | - | 0 | 0 | 0 | 0 | 0 | 0 | 0 | 0 | 0 | 15.1 | 1 | 2 | 0 | 0 | 1.000 | 2 | 0 | 0 | 0 | .00 | 0 |
| Leroux,Chris, Pit | R | .000 | 1 | 0 | 0 | 0 | 0 | .000 | 2 | 0 | 0 | 0 | 0 | 0 | 0 | 0 | 0 | 4.0 | 0 | 0 | 0 | 0 | - | 1 | 0 | 0 | 0 | .00 | 0 |
| Lester,Jon, Bos | L | .000 | 6 | 0 | 0 | 0 | 1 | .000 | 31 | 0 | 0 | 0 | 0 | 1 | 1 | 19 | 5 | 213.1 | 12 | 18 | 2 | 1 | .938 | 16 | 4 | 1 | 0 | .25 | -3 |
| Lilly,Ted, LAD | L | .000 | 5 | 0 | 0 | 0 | 0 | .101 | 347 | 35 | 6 | 1 | 0 | 17 | 8 | 149 | 37 | 23.0 | 0 | 3 | 1 | 0 | .750 | 2 | 0 | 0 | 0 | .00 | 1 |
| Lim,Chang-Yong, ChC | R | - | 0 | 0 | 0 | 0 | 0 | - | 0 | 0 | 0 | 0 | 0 | 0 | 0 | 0 | 0 | 5.0 | 0 | 0 | 0 | 0 | - | 1 | 0 | 0 | 0 | .00 | 0 |
| Lincecum,Tim, SF | R | .105 | 57 | 6 | 0 | 1 | 7 | .115 | 409 | 47 | 3 | 2 | 0 | 18 | 28 | 208 | 63 | 197.2 | 11 | 17 | 4 | 0 | .875 | 23 | 2 | 0 | 0 | .09 | -8 |
| Lincoln,Brad, Tor | R | .000 | 1 | 0 | 0 | 0 | 0 | .237 | 38 | 9 | 1 | 0 | 0 | 4 | 1 | 14 | 4 | 31.2 | 5 | 6 | 0 | 1 | 1.000 | 5 | 1 | 1 | 0 | .20 | 0 |

# Pitchers Hitting, Fielding and Holding Runners

| | | 2013 Hitting | | | | | | Career Hitting | | | | | | | | | | 2013 Fielding and Holding Runners | | | | | | | | | | | |
|---|---|---|---|---|---|---|---|---|---|---|---|---|---|---|---|---|---|---|---|---|---|---|---|---|---|---|---|---|---|
| Pitcher | T | Avg | AB | H | HR | RBI | SH | Avg | AB | H | 2B | 3B | HR | RBI | BB | SO | SH | Inn | PO | A | E | DP | Pct | SBA | CS | PCS | PPO | CS% | RS |
| Lindblom,Josh, Tex | R | - | 0 | 0 | 0 | 0 | 0 | .000 | 1 | 0 | 0 | 0 | 0 | 0 | 0 | 1 | 0 | 31.1 | 1 | 5 | 0 | 0 | 1.000 | 2 | 0 | 0 | 0 | .00 | 0 |
| Lindstrom,Matt, CWS | R | - | 0 | 0 | 0 | 0 | 0 | .000 | 1 | 0 | 0 | 0 | 0 | 0 | 0 | 1 | 0 | 60.2 | 2 | 8 | 0 | 1 | 1.000 | 10 | 0 | 0 | 0 | .00 | -1 |
| Liriano,Francisco, Pit | L | .064 | 47 | 3 | 0 | 1 | 5 | .078 | 64 | 5 | 0 | 0 | 0 | 3 | 6 | 27 | 7 | 161.0 | 7 | 30 | 1 | 5 | .974 | 11 | 4 | 2 | 0 | .36 | 4 |
| Lo,Chia-Jen, Hou | R | - | 0 | 0 | 0 | 0 | 0 | - | 0 | 0 | 0 | 0 | 0 | 0 | 0 | 0 | 0 | 19.1 | 1 | 2 | 0 | 0 | 1.000 | 1 | 1 | 0 | 0 | 1.00 | -1 |
| Locke,Jeff, Pit | L | .106 | 47 | 5 | 0 | 0 | 5 | .095 | 63 | 6 | 0 | 0 | 0 | 0 | 2 | 30 | 5 | 166.1 | 15 | 30 | 1 | 0 | .978 | 15 | 7 | 5 | 1 | .47 | 2 |
| Loe,Kameron, Sea-ChC-Atl | R | .000 | 1 | 0 | 0 | 0 | 0 | .167 | 6 | 1 | 0 | 0 | 0 | 0 | 1 | 3 | 1 | 26.2 | 1 | 3 | 0 | 0 | 1.000 | 3 | 0 | 0 | 0 | .00 | 0 |
| Logan,Boone, NYY | L | - | 0 | 0 | 0 | 0 | 0 | - | 0 | 0 | 0 | 0 | 0 | 0 | 0 | 0 | 1 | 39.0 | 1 | 3 | 0 | 0 | 1.000 | 5 | 1 | 0 | 0 | .20 | -2 |
| Lohse,Kyle, Mil | R | .145 | 55 | 8 | 0 | 3 | 12 | .152 | 409 | 62 | 8 | 0 | 0 | 25 | 7 | 130 | 63 | 198.2 | 7 | 16 | 0 | 0 | 1.000 | 9 | 1 | 0 | 0 | .11 | 1 |
| Lopez,Javier, SF | L | - | 0 | 0 | 0 | 0 | 0 | .091 | 11 | 1 | 0 | 0 | 0 | 1 | 0 | 5 | 1 | 39.1 | 5 | 9 | 0 | 1 | 1.000 | 3 | 1 | 0 | 0 | .33 | 1 |
| Lopez,Wilton, Col | R | .000 | 1 | 0 | 0 | 0 | 0 | .000 | 6 | 0 | 0 | 0 | 0 | 0 | 0 | 3 | 0 | 75.1 | 9 | 7 | 1 | 0 | .941 | 4 | 2 | 0 | 0 | .50 | -1 |
| Loup,Aaron, Tor | L | - | 0 | 0 | 0 | 0 | 0 | .000 | 1 | 0 | 0 | 0 | 0 | 0 | 0 | 0 | 0 | 69.1 | 5 | 23 | 3 | 2 | .903 | 10 | 7 | 5 | 0 | .70 | 2 |
| Lowe,Derek, Tex | R | - | 0 | 0 | 0 | 0 | 0 | .149 | 436 | 65 | 13 | 0 | 1 | 25 | 29 | 129 | 67 | 13.0 | 0 | 2 | 0 | 0 | 1.000 | 0 | 0 | 0 | 0 | - | 0 |
| Lowe,Mark, LAA | R | - | 0 | 0 | 0 | 0 | 0 | .000 | 1 | 0 | 0 | 0 | 0 | 0 | 0 | 1 | 0 | 11.2 | 0 | 4 | 0 | 0 | 1.000 | 5 | 0 | 0 | 0 | .00 | -1 |
| Lueke,Josh, TB | R | - | 0 | 0 | 0 | 0 | 0 | - | 0 | 0 | 0 | 0 | 0 | 0 | 0 | 0 | 0 | 21.1 | 1 | 3 | 0 | 0 | 1.000 | 2 | 1 | 0 | 0 | .50 | -1 |
| Luetge,Lucas, Sea | L | - | 0 | 0 | 0 | 0 | 0 | - | 0 | 0 | 0 | 0 | 0 | 0 | 0 | 0 | 0 | 37.0 | 2 | 3 | 0 | 1 | 1.000 | 3 | 0 | 0 | 0 | .00 | -1 |
| Lyles,Jordan, Hou | R | .000 | 6 | 0 | 0 | 0 | 1 | .130 | 69 | 9 | 1 | 0 | 1 | 4 | 3 | 32 | 10 | 141.2 | 12 | 18 | 1 | 1 | .968 | 8 | 3 | 0 | 0 | .38 | 2 |
| Lynn,Lance, StL | R | .074 | 54 | 4 | 0 | 2 | 11 | .065 | 108 | 7 | 0 | 0 | 0 | 3 | 7 | 67 | 21 | 201.2 | 14 | 26 | 1 | 5 | .976 | 14 | 7 | 0 | 1 | .50 | -3 |
| Lyon,Brandon, NYM | R | - | 0 | 0 | 0 | 0 | 0 | 1.000 | 1 | 1 | 1 | 0 | 0 | 1 | 1 | 0 | 0 | 34.1 | 1 | 5 | 1 | 0 | .857 | 2 | 1 | 0 | 0 | .50 | -1 |
| Lyons,Tyler, StL | L | .167 | 12 | 2 | 0 | 0 | 1 | .167 | 12 | 2 | 0 | 0 | 0 | 0 | 0 | 4 | 1 | 53.0 | 2 | 12 | 0 | 0 | 1.000 | 2 | 0 | 0 | 0 | .00 | 2 |
| Machi,Jean, SF | R | .000 | 1 | 0 | 0 | 0 | 0 | .000 | 1 | 0 | 0 | 0 | 0 | 0 | 0 | 1 | 0 | 53.0 | 3 | 11 | 1 | 0 | .933 | 4 | 0 | 0 | 1 | .00 | 2 |
| Magill,Matt, LAD | R | .000 | 7 | 0 | 0 | 0 | 1 | .000 | 7 | 0 | 0 | 0 | 0 | 0 | 0 | 5 | 1 | 27.2 | 0 | 3 | 0 | 0 | 1.000 | 5 | 3 | 0 | 0 | .60 | -2 |
| Maholm,Paul, Atl | L | .135 | 52 | 7 | 0 | 2 | 4 | .111 | 469 | 52 | 4 | 0 | 2 | 18 | 22 | 246 | 30 | 153.0 | 7 | 18 | 1 | 2 | .962 | 12 | 2 | 1 | 0 | .17 | 0 |
| Maine,John, Mia | R | - | 0 | 0 | 0 | 0 | 1 | .096 | 166 | 16 | 1 | 0 | 1 | 8 | 11 | 84 | 29 | 7.1 | 1 | 1 | 0 | 0 | 1.000 | 0 | 0 | 0 | 0 | - | 0 |
| Maness,Seth, StL | R | .200 | 5 | 1 | 0 | 0 | 0 | .200 | 5 | 1 | 0 | 0 | 0 | 0 | 0 | 3 | 0 | 62.0 | 7 | 9 | 0 | 0 | 1.000 | 2 | 0 | 0 | 0 | .00 | -1 |
| Manship,Jeff, Col | R | .000 | 7 | 0 | 0 | 0 | 0 | .000 | 8 | 0 | 0 | 0 | 0 | 0 | 0 | 3 | 0 | 30.2 | 5 | 2 | 0 | 0 | 1.000 | 2 | 0 | 0 | 0 | .00 | -1 |
| Marcum,Shaun, NYM | R | .136 | 22 | 3 | 0 | 0 | 4 | .132 | 129 | 17 | 5 | 0 | 1 | 8 | 9 | 44 | 20 | 78.1 | 4 | 13 | 0 | 0 | 1.000 | 7 | 5 | 1 | 0 | .71 | 2 |
| Marmol,Carlos, ChC-LAD | R | .000 | 1 | 0 | 0 | 0 | 0 | .194 | 31 | 6 | 1 | 0 | 1 | 1 | 0 | 11 | 3 | 49.0 | 6 | 11 | 1 | 1 | .944 | 14 | 4 | 1 | 0 | .29 | 2 |
| Maronde,Nick, LAA | L | - | 0 | 0 | 0 | 0 | 0 | - | 0 | 0 | 0 | 0 | 0 | 0 | 0 | 0 | 0 | 5.1 | 0 | 1 | 0 | 0 | 1.000 | 1 | 0 | 0 | 0 | .00 | 0 |
| Marquis,Jason, SD | R | .119 | 42 | 5 | 0 | 2 | 1 | .196 | 647 | 127 | 34 | 2 | 5 | 56 | 13 | 163 | 41 | 117.2 | 8 | 20 | 0 | 2 | 1.000 | 10 | 4 | 0 | 0 | .40 | 2 |
| Marshall,Brett, NYY | R | - | 0 | 0 | 0 | 0 | 0 | - | 0 | 0 | 0 | 0 | 0 | 0 | 0 | 0 | 0 | 12.0 | 1 | 1 | 0 | 1 | 1.000 | 0 | 0 | 0 | 0 | - | 0 |
| Marshall,Sean, Cin | L | - | 0 | 0 | 0 | 0 | 0 | .158 | 101 | 16 | 1 | 0 | 1 | 5 | 2 | 48 | 8 | 10.1 | 0 | 3 | 0 | 0 | 1.000 | 0 | 0 | 0 | 0 | - | 1 |
| Marte,Victor, StL | R | - | 0 | 0 | 0 | 0 | 0 | - | 0 | 0 | 0 | 0 | 0 | 0 | 0 | 0 | 0 | 3.0 | 0 | 0 | 1 | 0 | .000 | 0 | 0 | 0 | 0 | - | -1 |
| Martin,Ethan, Phi | R | .000 | 9 | 0 | 0 | 0 | 1 | .000 | 9 | 0 | 0 | 0 | 0 | 0 | 0 | 6 | 1 | 40.0 | 0 | 6 | 0 | 0 | 1.000 | 5 | 0 | 0 | 0 | .00 | 0 |
| Martinez,Carlos, StL | R | .000 | 2 | 0 | 0 | 0 | 0 | .000 | 2 | 0 | 0 | 0 | 0 | 0 | 0 | 1 | 0 | 28.1 | 4 | 3 | 0 | 1 | 1.000 | 2 | 1 | 0 | 0 | .50 | -2 |
| Martinez,Cristhian, Atl | R | - | 0 | 0 | 0 | 0 | 0 | .133 | 15 | 2 | 1 | 0 | 0 | 2 | 0 | 5 | 2 | 2.1 | 0 | 1 | 0 | 0 | 1.000 | 0 | 0 | 0 | 0 | - | 0 |
| Martinez,David, Hou | R | - | 0 | 0 | 0 | 0 | 0 | - | 0 | 0 | 0 | 0 | 0 | 0 | 0 | 0 | 0 | 11.1 | 0 | 4 | 0 | 0 | 1.000 | 1 | 0 | 0 | 0 | .00 | 0 |
| Martinez,Joe, Cle | R | - | 0 | 0 | 0 | 0 | 0 | .182 | 11 | 2 | 1 | 0 | 0 | 0 | 0 | 2 | 1 | 5.0 | 0 | 0 | 0 | 0 | - | 0 | 0 | 0 | 0 | - | 0 |
| Martis,Shairon, Min | R | - | 0 | 0 | 0 | 0 | 0 | .161 | 31 | 5 | 1 | 0 | 0 | 2 | 1 | 8 | 3 | 9.2 | 2 | 0 | 0 | 0 | 1.000 | 0 | 0 | 0 | 0 | - | 0 |
| Masterson,Justin, Cle | R | .500 | 2 | 1 | 0 | 0 | 0 | .158 | 19 | 3 | 0 | 0 | 0 | 0 | 0 | 8 | 1 | 193.0 | 21 | 27 | 1 | 3 | .980 | 12 | 3 | 0 | 1 | .25 | 1 |
| Matsuzaka,Daisuke, NYM | R | .250 | 12 | 3 | 0 | 1 | 1 | .192 | 26 | 5 | 0 | 0 | 0 | 2 | 0 | 10 | 2 | 38.2 | 1 | 4 | 0 | 0 | 1.000 | 6 | 1 | 0 | 0 | .17 | -1 |
| Mattheus,Ryan, Was | R | - | 0 | 0 | 0 | 0 | 0 | .000 | 1 | 0 | 0 | 0 | 0 | 0 | 0 | 1 | 0 | 35.1 | 3 | 3 | 0 | 1 | 1.000 | 3 | 0 | 0 | 0 | .00 | -3 |
| Matusz,Brian, Bal | L | - | 0 | 0 | 0 | 0 | 0 | .125 | 8 | 1 | 0 | 0 | 0 | 0 | 0 | 2 | 0 | 51.0 | 0 | 6 | 0 | 1 | 1.000 | 2 | 1 | 0 | 0 | .50 | 0 |
| Maurer,Brandon, Sea | R | - | 0 | 0 | 0 | 0 | 0 | - | 0 | 0 | 0 | 0 | 0 | 0 | 0 | 0 | 0 | 90.0 | 6 | 10 | 0 | 0 | 1.000 | 11 | 5 | 0 | 0 | .45 | 1 |
| Maya,Yunesky, Was | R | - | 0 | 0 | 0 | 0 | 0 | .067 | 15 | 1 | 0 | 0 | 0 | 0 | 0 | 9 | 3 | 0.1 | 0 | 0 | 0 | 0 | - | 0 | 0 | 0 | 0 | - | 0 |
| Mazzaro,Vin, Pit | R | .167 | 6 | 1 | 0 | 0 | 0 | .188 | 16 | 3 | 0 | 0 | 0 | 1 | 0 | 10 | 5 | 73.2 | 9 | 8 | 0 | 1 | 1.000 | 2 | 2 | 0 | 0 | 1.00 | 1 |
| McAllister,Zach, Cle | R | .000 | 4 | 0 | 0 | 0 | 0 | .000 | 4 | 0 | 0 | 0 | 0 | 0 | 0 | 2 | 0 | 134.1 | 8 | 6 | 2 | 0 | .875 | 9 | 2 | 0 | 0 | .22 | -3 |
| McCarthy,Brandon, Ari | R | .027 | 37 | 1 | 0 | 0 | 2 | .022 | 46 | 1 | 0 | 0 | 0 | 0 | 3 | 19 | 3 | 135.0 | 8 | 16 | 0 | 0 | 1.000 | 2 | 0 | 0 | 0 | .00 | -2 |
| McClellan,Kyle, Tex | R | - | 0 | 0 | 0 | 0 | 0 | .130 | 46 | 6 | 1 | 0 | 0 | 4 | 1 | 18 | 6 | 9.1 | 1 | 0 | 0 | 0 | 1.000 | 2 | 0 | 0 | 0 | .00 | 0 |
| McDonald,James, Pit | R | .273 | 11 | 3 | 0 | 0 | 0 | .110 | 145 | 16 | 2 | 0 | 0 | 4 | 13 | 75 | 13 | 29.2 | 2 | 1 | 1 | 0 | .750 | 4 | 2 | 1 | 0 | .50 | 0 |
| McFarland,T.J., Bal | L | - | 0 | 0 | 0 | 0 | 0 | - | 0 | 0 | 0 | 0 | 0 | 0 | 0 | 0 | 0 | 74.2 | 3 | 12 | 0 | 0 | 1.000 | 7 | 1 | 0 | 0 | .14 | -2 |
| McGee,Jake, TB | L | - | 0 | 0 | 0 | 0 | 0 | - | 0 | 0 | 0 | 0 | 0 | 0 | 0 | 0 | 0 | 62.2 | 1 | 5 | 0 | 0 | 1.000 | 3 | 0 | 0 | 0 | .00 | -1 |
| McGowan,Dustin, Tor | R | - | 0 | 0 | 0 | 0 | 0 | .200 | 10 | 2 | 0 | 0 | 0 | 0 | 0 | 4 | 1 | 25.2 | 2 | 6 | 2 | 0 | .800 | 3 | 1 | 0 | 0 | .33 | 1 |
| McHugh,Collin, NYM-Col | R | .167 | 6 | 1 | 0 | 0 | 0 | .100 | 10 | 1 | 0 | 0 | 0 | 0 | 0 | 4 | 0 | 26.0 | 3 | 6 | 0 | 0 | 1.000 | 6 | 0 | 0 | 0 | .00 | -1 |
| Medina,Yoervis, Sea | R | - | 0 | 0 | 0 | 0 | 0 | - | 0 | 0 | 0 | 0 | 0 | 0 | 0 | 0 | 0 | 68.0 | 2 | 7 | 0 | 0 | 1.000 | 8 | 3 | 0 | 0 | .38 | 0 |
| Medlen,Kris, Atl | R | .164 | 55 | 9 | 1 | 4 | 7 | .141 | 128 | 18 | 4 | 0 | 1 | 8 | 11 | 59 | 11 | 197.0 | 9 | 30 | 2 | 2 | .951 | 14 | 5 | 0 | 3 | .36 | 1 |
| Mejia,Jenrry, NYM | R | .000 | 11 | 0 | 0 | 0 | 0 | .059 | 17 | 1 | 0 | 0 | 0 | 1 | 0 | 9 | 2 | 27.1 | 2 | 1 | 0 | 0 | 1.000 | 1 | 0 | 0 | 0 | .00 | -1 |
| Melancon,Mark, Pit | R | - | 0 | 0 | 0 | 0 | 0 | - | 0 | 0 | 0 | 0 | 0 | 0 | 1 | 0 | 0 | 71.0 | 7 | 11 | 0 | 2 | 1.000 | 3 | 0 | 0 | 0 | .00 | 2 |
| Mendoza,Luis, KC | R | .400 | 5 | 2 | 0 | 1 | 0 | .250 | 8 | 2 | 0 | 0 | 0 | 1 | 0 | 5 | 1 | 94.0 | 10 | 8 | 0 | 2 | 1.000 | 6 | 0 | 0 | 1 | .00 | 0 |
| Mijares,Jose, SF | L | - | 0 | 0 | 0 | 0 | 0 | .000 | 1 | 0 | 0 | 0 | 0 | 0 | 0 | 1 | 0 | 49.0 | 0 | 4 | 2 | 0 | .667 | 5 | 1 | 0 | 0 | .20 | 0 |
| Mikolas,Miles, SD | R | - | 0 | 0 | 0 | 0 | 0 | .000 | 3 | 0 | 0 | 0 | 0 | 0 | 0 | 1 | 0 | 1.2 | 0 | 0 | 0 | 0 | - | 0 | 0 | 0 | 0 | - | 0 |
| Miley,Wade, Ari | L | .133 | 60 | 8 | 1 | 8 | 8 | .145 | 138 | 20 | 5 | 0 | 1 | 11 | 5 | 38 | 17 | 202.2 | 14 | 24 | 0 | 0 | 1.000 | 10 | 5 | 3 | 2 | .50 | -1 |
| Miller,Andrew, Bos | L | - | 0 | 0 | 0 | 0 | 0 | .056 | 72 | 4 | 0 | 0 | 0 | 3 | 0 | 36 | 4 | 30.2 | 2 | 2 | 1 | 0 | .800 | 3 | 1 | 0 | 0 | .33 | -2 |
| Miller,Jim, NYY | R | - | 0 | 0 | 0 | 0 | 0 | - | 0 | 0 | 0 | 0 | 0 | 0 | 0 | 0 | 0 | 1.1 | 0 | 0 | 0 | 0 | - | 0 | 0 | 0 | 0 | - | 0 |
| Miller,Shelby, StL | R | .075 | 53 | 4 | 1 | 2 | 8 | .107 | 56 | 6 | 2 | 0 | 1 | 2 | 1 | 29 | 8 | 173.1 | 10 | 13 | 1 | 0 | .958 | 13 | 4 | 0 | 0 | .31 | -3 |
| Milone,Tommy, Oak | L | .250 | 8 | 2 | 0 | 1 | 0 | .211 | 19 | 4 | 0 | 0 | 1 | 6 | 0 | 3 | 4 | 156.1 | 6 | 11 | 1 | 0 | .944 | 12 | 3 | 2 | 0 | .25 | -1 |
| Miner,Zach, Phi | R | .333 | 6 | 2 | 0 | 0 | 0 | .231 | 13 | 3 | 1 | 0 | 0 | 0 | 0 | 7 | 0 | 28.2 | 1 | 5 | 0 | 1 | 1.000 | 6 | 2 | 0 | 0 | .33 | 0 |
| Minor,Mike, Atl | L | .164 | 61 | 10 | 1 | 6 | 7 | .111 | 153 | 17 | 4 | 0 | 1 | 6 | 8 | 73 | 13 | 204.2 | 5 | 20 | 0 | 1 | 1.000 | 12 | 8 | 1 | 0 | .67 | 3 |
| Moore,Matt, TB | L | .000 | 2 | 0 | 0 | 0 | 0 | .000 | 6 | 0 | 0 | 0 | 0 | 1 | 0 | 2 | 1 | 150.1 | 9 | 17 | 0 | 1 | 1.000 | 7 | 0 | 0 | 0 | .00 | 2 |
| Morales,Franklin, Bos | L | .000 | 2 | 0 | 0 | 0 | 0 | .250 | 32 | 8 | 0 | 0 | 0 | 2 | 1 | 12 | 2 | 25.1 | 1 | 4 | 0 | 0 | 1.000 | 2 | 1 | 0 | 3 | .50 | 0 |
| Morris,Bryan, Pit | R | .200 | 5 | 1 | 0 | 0 | 0 | .200 | 5 | 1 | 0 | 0 | 0 | 0 | 0 | 2 | 0 | 65.0 | 3 | 12 | 0 | 2 | 1.000 | 3 | 2 | 0 | 0 | .67 | 1 |

# Pitchers Hitting, Fielding and Holding Runners

| | | 2013 Hitting | | | | | | Career Hitting | | | | | | | | | | 2013 Fielding and Holding Runners | | | | | | | | | | | |
|---|---|---|---|---|---|---|---|---|---|---|---|---|---|---|---|---|---|---|---|---|---|---|---|---|---|---|---|---|---|
| Pitcher | T | Avg | AB | H | HR | RBI | SH | Avg | AB | H | 2B | 3B | HR | RBI | BB | SO | SH | Inn | PO | A | E | DP | Pct | SBA | CS | PCS | PPO | CS% | RS |
| Morrow,Brandon, Tor | R | - | 0 | 0 | 0 | 0 | 0 | .000 | 12 | 0 | 0 | 0 | 0 | 0 | 0 | 4 | 0 | 54.1 | 2 | 3 | 0 | 1 | 1.000 | 3 | 1 | 1 | 0 | .33 | -1 |
| Mortensen,Clayton, Bos | R | .000 | 1 | 0 | 0 | 0 | 0 | .000 | 16 | 0 | 0 | 0 | 0 | 1 | 1 | 11 | 0 | 30.1 | 3 | 4 | 1 | 0 | .875 | 3 | 0 | 0 | 0 | .00 | -2 |
| Morton,Charlie, Pit | R | .139 | 36 | 5 | 0 | 1 | 2 | .087 | 173 | 15 | 4 | 0 | 0 | 4 | 1 | 90 | 22 | 116.0 | 4 | 13 | 0 | 0 | 1.000 | 17 | 6 | 0 | 0 | .35 | -1 |
| Moscoso,Guillermo, SF | R | .000 | 2 | 0 | 0 | 0 | 1 | .133 | 15 | 2 | 1 | 0 | 0 | 1 | 0 | 8 | 3 | 30.0 | 0 | 2 | 1 | 1 | .667 | 3 | 2 | 0 | 1 | .67 | 1 |
| Moylan,Peter, LAD | R | - | 0 | 0 | 0 | 0 | 0 | .000 | 7 | 0 | 0 | 0 | 0 | 0 | 1 | 6 | 0 | 15.1 | 0 | 0 | 0 | 0 | - | 3 | 3 | 0 | 0 | 1.00 | 1 |
| Mujica,Edward, StL | R | .000 | 2 | 0 | 0 | 0 | 0 | .182 | 11 | 2 | 0 | 0 | 0 | 0 | 0 | 4 | 2 | 64.2 | 6 | 9 | 0 | 0 | 1.000 | 4 | 2 | 0 | 0 | .50 | 1 |
| Myers,Brett, Cle | R | - | 0 | 0 | 0 | 0 | 0 | .134 | 471 | 63 | 11 | 0 | 0 | 12 | 25 | 161 | 60 | 21.1 | 1 | 4 | 0 | 0 | 1.000 | 3 | 1 | 0 | 0 | .33 | 1 |
| Narveson,Chris, Mil | L | - | 0 | 0 | 0 | 0 | 0 | .227 | 110 | 25 | 3 | 0 | 0 | 12 | 5 | 42 | 15 | 2.0 | 0 | 0 | 0 | 0 | - | 0 | 0 | 0 | 0 | - | 0 |
| Nathan,Joe, Tex | R | - | 0 | 0 | 0 | 0 | 0 | .159 | 63 | 10 | 3 | 0 | 2 | 4 | 3 | 17 | 10 | 64.2 | 5 | 7 | 0 | 0 | 1.000 | 5 | 1 | 0 | 0 | .20 | 1 |
| Nelson,Jimmy, Mil | R | .000 | 2 | 0 | 0 | 0 | 0 | .000 | 2 | 0 | 0 | 0 | 0 | 0 | 0 | 2 | 0 | 10.0 | 0 | 1 | 0 | 0 | 1.000 | 2 | 0 | 0 | 0 | .00 | 0 |
| Neshek,Pat, Oak | R | - | 0 | 0 | 0 | 0 | 0 | - | 0 | 0 | 0 | 0 | 0 | 0 | 0 | 0 | 0 | 40.1 | 0 | 5 | 0 | 0 | 1.000 | 3 | 1 | 0 | 0 | .33 | 0 |
| Nicasio,Juan, Col | R | .139 | 36 | 5 | 0 | 3 | 10 | .132 | 76 | 10 | 2 | 0 | 0 | 4 | 6 | 49 | 12 | 157.2 | 9 | 15 | 0 | 1 | 1.000 | 11 | 3 | 0 | 0 | .27 | -1 |
| Niese,Jon, NYM | L | .205 | 39 | 8 | 0 | 4 | 2 | .167 | 210 | 35 | 4 | 1 | 0 | 10 | 22 | 103 | 22 | 143.0 | 5 | 26 | 2 | 1 | .939 | 3 | 1 | 1 | 0 | .33 | -1 |
| Noesi,Hector, Sea | R | - | 0 | 0 | 0 | 0 | 0 | .500 | 4 | 2 | 0 | 0 | 0 | 0 | 0 | 2 | 0 | 27.1 | 0 | 3 | 1 | 0 | .750 | 2 | 1 | 0 | 0 | .50 | 0 |
| Nolasco,Ricky, Mia-LAD | R | .120 | 50 | 6 | 0 | 1 | 8 | .138 | 369 | 51 | 12 | 0 | 1 | 26 | 21 | 171 | 62 | 199.1 | 14 | 27 | 2 | 0 | .953 | 15 | 6 | 1 | 1 | .40 | 0 |
| Nolin,Sean, Tor | L | - | 0 | 0 | 0 | 0 | 0 | - | 0 | 0 | 0 | 0 | 0 | 0 | 0 | 0 | 0 | 1.1 | 0 | 0 | 0 | 0 | - | 0 | 0 | 0 | 0 | - | 0 |
| Norris,Bud, Hou-Bal | R | .429 | 7 | 3 | 0 | 0 | 0 | .147 | 170 | 25 | 5 | 0 | 0 | 10 | 4 | 57 | 30 | 176.2 | 9 | 21 | 1 | 2 | .968 | 21 | 5 | 0 | 2 | .24 | 2 |
| Nova,Ivan, NYY | R | .000 | 3 | 0 | 0 | 0 | 0 | .071 | 14 | 1 | 0 | 0 | 0 | 0 | 0 | 13 | 3 | 139.1 | 8 | 18 | 0 | 1 | 1.000 | 12 | 5 | 0 | 0 | .42 | 2 |
| Nuno,Vidal, NYY | L | - | 0 | 0 | 0 | 0 | 0 | - | 0 | 0 | 0 | 0 | 0 | 0 | 0 | 0 | 0 | 20.0 | 0 | 2 | 0 | 0 | 1.000 | 0 | 0 | 0 | 0 | - | 0 |
| Oberholtzer,Brett, Hou | L | - | 0 | 0 | 0 | 0 | 0 | - | 0 | 0 | 0 | 0 | 0 | 0 | 0 | 0 | 0 | 71.2 | 4 | 6 | 0 | 0 | 1.000 | 5 | 4 | 0 | 0 | .80 | 2 |
| O'Day,Darren, Bal | R | .000 | 1 | 0 | 0 | 0 | 0 | .000 | 1 | 0 | 0 | 0 | 0 | 0 | 0 | 1 | 0 | 62.0 | 4 | 3 | 1 | 2 | .875 | 10 | 4 | 0 | 0 | .40 | 0 |
| Odorizzi,Jake, TB | R | - | 0 | 0 | 0 | 0 | 0 | - | 0 | 0 | 0 | 0 | 0 | 0 | 0 | 0 | 0 | 29.2 | 3 | 4 | 0 | 0 | 1.000 | 0 | 0 | 0 | 0 | - | 1 |
| O'Flaherty,Eric, Atl | L | - | 0 | 0 | 0 | 0 | 0 | .000 | 2 | 0 | 0 | 0 | 0 | 0 | 0 | 2 | 0 | 18.0 | 0 | 5 | 0 | 0 | 1.000 | 2 | 1 | 0 | 0 | .50 | 0 |
| Ogando,Alexi, Tex | R | .000 | 1 | 0 | 0 | 0 | 0 | .500 | 6 | 3 | 0 | 0 | 0 | 0 | 0 | 3 | 0 | 104.1 | 9 | 12 | 0 | 1 | 1.000 | 5 | 2 | 0 | 1 | .40 | 2 |
| Ohlendorf,Ross, Was | R | .000 | 15 | 0 | 0 | 1 | 3 | .073 | 137 | 10 | 0 | 0 | 1 | 5 | 4 | 67 | 11 | 60.1 | 4 | 4 | 4 | 0 | .667 | 1 | 0 | 0 | 0 | .00 | -1 |
| Okajima,Hideki, Oak | L | - | 0 | 0 | 0 | 0 | 0 | .000 | 1 | 0 | 0 | 0 | 0 | 0 | 0 | 0 | 0 | 4.0 | 0 | 2 | 0 | 0 | 1.000 | 0 | 0 | 0 | 0 | - | 0 |
| Oliver,Darren, Tor | L | - | 0 | 0 | 0 | 0 | 0 | .221 | 217 | 48 | 11 | 0 | 1 | 20 | 8 | 74 | 15 | 49.0 | 0 | 11 | 0 | 0 | 1.000 | 6 | 2 | 1 | 0 | .33 | 1 |
| Olmos,Edgar, Mia | L | - | 0 | 0 | 0 | 0 | 0 | - | 0 | 0 | 0 | 0 | 0 | 0 | 0 | 0 | 0 | 5.0 | 0 | 1 | 1 | 0 | .500 | 0 | 0 | 0 | 0 | - | -1 |
| Omogrosso,Brian, CWS | R | - | 0 | 0 | 0 | 0 | 0 | - | 0 | 0 | 0 | 0 | 0 | 0 | 0 | 0 | 0 | 16.1 | 2 | 1 | 0 | 0 | 1.000 | 3 | 1 | 0 | 0 | .33 | -1 |
| Ondrusek,Logan, Cin | R | - | 0 | 0 | 0 | 0 | 0 | .000 | 4 | 0 | 0 | 0 | 0 | 0 | 0 | 4 | 0 | 55.0 | 4 | 8 | 0 | 1 | 1.000 | 2 | 1 | 0 | 0 | .50 | -1 |
| Ortega,Jose, Det | R | - | 0 | 0 | 0 | 0 | 0 | - | 0 | 0 | 0 | 0 | 0 | 0 | 0 | 0 | 0 | 11.2 | 1 | 2 | 1 | 0 | .750 | 1 | 0 | 0 | 0 | .00 | 0 |
| Ortiz,Joe, Tex | L | - | 0 | 0 | 0 | 0 | 0 | - | 0 | 0 | 0 | 0 | 0 | 0 | 0 | 0 | 0 | 44.2 | 3 | 5 | 0 | 0 | 1.000 | 0 | 0 | 0 | 0 | - | 1 |
| Ortiz,Ramon, Tor | R | .000 | 1 | 0 | 0 | 0 | 0 | .076 | 144 | 11 | 2 | 0 | 1 | 4 | 5 | 62 | 15 | 25.1 | 3 | 2 | 1 | 1 | .833 | 0 | 0 | 0 | 0 | - | 1 |
| O'Sullivan,Sean, SD | R | .167 | 6 | 1 | 0 | 0 | 0 | .200 | 10 | 2 | 1 | 0 | 0 | 0 | 0 | 5 | 0 | 25.0 | 0 | 4 | 0 | 0 | 1.000 | 5 | 2 | 0 | 0 | .40 | 0 |
| Oswalt,Roy, Col | R | .333 | 6 | 2 | 0 | 0 | 1 | .154 | 657 | 101 | 7 | 0 | 1 | 36 | 27 | 181 | 106 | 32.1 | 5 | 3 | 0 | 1 | 1.000 | 3 | 1 | 0 | 1 | .33 | -2 |
| Otero,Dan, Oak | R | - | 0 | 0 | 0 | 0 | 0 | .000 | 1 | 0 | 0 | 0 | 0 | 0 | 0 | 1 | 0 | 39.0 | 1 | 7 | 0 | 2 | 1.000 | 1 | 0 | 0 | 0 | .00 | -1 |
| Ottavino,Adam, Col | R | .111 | 9 | 1 | 0 | 0 | 0 | .083 | 24 | 2 | 0 | 0 | 0 | 0 | 1 | 17 | 3 | 78.1 | 8 | 8 | 1 | 1 | .941 | 13 | 2 | 0 | 0 | .15 | -3 |
| Outman,Josh, Col | L | .000 | 5 | 0 | 0 | 0 | 0 | .042 | 24 | 1 | 0 | 0 | 0 | 1 | 1 | 12 | 0 | 54.0 | 3 | 8 | 0 | 2 | 1.000 | 6 | 0 | 0 | 0 | .00 | -3 |
| Papelbon,Jonathan, Phi | R | - | 0 | 0 | 0 | 0 | 0 | - | 0 | 0 | 0 | 0 | 0 | 0 | 0 | 0 | 0 | 61.2 | 2 | 5 | 0 | 0 | 1.000 | 7 | 1 | 1 | 0 | .14 | 0 |
| Parker,Blake, ChC | R | - | 0 | 0 | 0 | 0 | 0 | - | 0 | 0 | 0 | 0 | 0 | 0 | 0 | 0 | 0 | 46.1 | 4 | 2 | 0 | 0 | 1.000 | 3 | 0 | 0 | 0 | .00 | -1 |
| Parker,Jarrod, Oak | R | - | 0 | 0 | 0 | 0 | 0 | .125 | 8 | 1 | 1 | 0 | 0 | 0 | 0 | 5 | 1 | 197.0 | 14 | 21 | 4 | 0 | .897 | 17 | 6 | 2 | 0 | .35 | 0 |
| Parnell,Bobby, NYM | R | - | 0 | 0 | 0 | 0 | 0 | .111 | 9 | 1 | 0 | 0 | 0 | 0 | 0 | 3 | 5 | 50.0 | 2 | 8 | 0 | 1 | 1.000 | 4 | 0 | 0 | 0 | .00 | 0 |
| Parra,Manny, Cin | L | .500 | 2 | 1 | 0 | 0 | 0 | .188 | 144 | 27 | 11 | 1 | 0 | 13 | 6 | 58 | 10 | 46.0 | 4 | 6 | 0 | 0 | 1.000 | 7 | 1 | 1 | 0 | .14 | -1 |
| Partch,Curtis, Cin | R | .000 | 1 | 0 | 0 | 0 | 0 | .000 | 1 | 0 | 0 | 0 | 0 | 0 | 0 | 0 | 0 | 23.1 | 2 | 4 | 0 | 0 | 1.000 | 5 | 0 | 0 | 0 | .00 | -1 |
| Paterson,Joe, Ari | L | - | 0 | 0 | 0 | 0 | 0 | - | 0 | 0 | 0 | 0 | 0 | 0 | 0 | 0 | 0 | 2.1 | 0 | 0 | 0 | 0 | - | 0 | 0 | 0 | 0 | - | 0 |
| Patton,Troy, Bal | L | .000 | 1 | 0 | 0 | 0 | 0 | .250 | 4 | 1 | 0 | 0 | 0 | 0 | 0 | 1 | 0 | 56.0 | 3 | 10 | 0 | 2 | 1.000 | 0 | 0 | 0 | 0 | - | 2 |
| Paxton,James, Sea | L | .000 | 1 | 0 | 0 | 0 | 0 | .000 | 1 | 0 | 0 | 0 | 0 | 0 | 1 | 1 | 0 | 24.0 | 0 | 3 | 0 | 0 | 1.000 | 0 | 0 | 0 | 0 | - | 0 |
| Peacock,Brad, Hou | R | - | 0 | 0 | 0 | 0 | 1 | .000 | 4 | 0 | 0 | 0 | 0 | 0 | 0 | 2 | 1 | 83.1 | 4 | 10 | 1 | 0 | .933 | 13 | 1 | 0 | 0 | .08 | -2 |
| Peavy,Jake, CWS-Bos | R | .067 | 15 | 1 | 0 | 0 | 0 | .173 | 433 | 75 | 15 | 1 | 2 | 27 | 19 | 122 | 45 | 144.2 | 10 | 10 | 0 | 0 | 1.000 | 15 | 6 | 0 | 1 | .40 | -1 |
| Pelfrey,Mike, Min | R | .000 | 1 | 0 | 0 | 0 | 0 | .098 | 265 | 26 | 5 | 0 | 0 | 13 | 13 | 71 | 24 | 152.2 | 11 | 14 | 2 | 3 | .926 | 13 | 3 | 1 | 0 | .23 | 0 |
| Peralta,Joel, TB | R | - | 0 | 0 | 0 | 0 | 0 | .250 | 4 | 1 | 1 | 0 | 0 | 2 | 0 | 2 | 0 | 71.1 | 3 | 4 | 0 | 0 | 1.000 | 3 | 1 | 0 | 0 | .33 | 0 |
| Peralta,Wily, Mil | R | .140 | 50 | 7 | 0 | 0 | 9 | .131 | 61 | 8 | 1 | 0 | 0 | 0 | 1 | 25 | 9 | 183.1 | 10 | 19 | 1 | 2 | .967 | 13 | 5 | 0 | 1 | .38 | -1 |
| Perez,Chris, Cle | R | - | 0 | 0 | 0 | 0 | 0 | .000 | 1 | 0 | 0 | 0 | 0 | 0 | 0 | 1 | 0 | 54.0 | 2 | 6 | 0 | 0 | 1.000 | 4 | 1 | 0 | 1 | .25 | 0 |
| Perez,Juan, Tor | L | - | 0 | 0 | 0 | 0 | 0 | .000 | 1 | 0 | 0 | 0 | 0 | 0 | 0 | 1 | 0 | 31.2 | 3 | 5 | 0 | 0 | 1.000 | 5 | 0 | 0 | 0 | .00 | 0 |
| Perez,Luis, Tor | L | - | 0 | 0 | 0 | 0 | 0 | - | 0 | 0 | 0 | 0 | 0 | 0 | 0 | 0 | 0 | 5.0 | 0 | 1 | 0 | 0 | 1.000 | 0 | 0 | 0 | 0 | - | 0 |
| Perez,Martin, Tex | L | .000 | 5 | 0 | 0 | 0 | 0 | .000 | 5 | 0 | 0 | 0 | 0 | 0 | 0 | 4 | 0 | 124.1 | 4 | 22 | 1 | 1 | .963 | 3 | 1 | 1 | 1 | .33 | 2 |
| Perez,Oliver, Sea | L | - | 0 | 0 | 0 | 0 | 0 | .158 | 341 | 54 | 1 | 0 | 0 | 15 | 14 | 116 | 39 | 53.0 | 1 | 4 | 1 | 0 | .833 | 2 | 1 | 1 | 0 | .50 | 1 |
| Perkins,Glen, Min | L | - | 0 | 0 | 0 | 0 | 0 | .000 | 4 | 0 | 0 | 0 | 0 | 0 | 0 | 4 | 3 | 62.2 | 2 | 5 | 0 | 0 | 1.000 | 0 | 0 | 0 | 0 | - | 0 |
| Pestano,Vinnie, Cle | R | - | 0 | 0 | 0 | 0 | 0 | - | 0 | 0 | 0 | 0 | 0 | 0 | 0 | 0 | 0 | 35.1 | 2 | 5 | 0 | 0 | 1.000 | 0 | 0 | 0 | 0 | - | 1 |
| Petit,Yusmeiro, SF | R | .063 | 16 | 1 | 0 | 2 | 0 | .051 | 78 | 4 | 0 | 0 | 0 | 3 | 2 | 31 | 4 | 48.0 | 1 | 5 | 0 | 1 | 1.000 | 3 | 1 | 0 | 0 | .33 | 0 |
| Petricka,Jake, CWS | R | - | 0 | 0 | 0 | 0 | 0 | - | 0 | 0 | 0 | 0 | 0 | 0 | 0 | 0 | 0 | 19.1 | 0 | 4 | 0 | 0 | 1.000 | 2 | 1 | 0 | 0 | .50 | 1 |
| Pettibone,Jonathan, Phi | R | .103 | 29 | 3 | 0 | 0 | 0 | .103 | 29 | 3 | 1 | 0 | 0 | 0 | 3 | 14 | 0 | 100.1 | 9 | 14 | 1 | 0 | .958 | 16 | 4 | 0 | 0 | .25 | -1 |
| Pettitte,Andy, NYY | L | .000 | 2 | 0 | 0 | 0 | 0 | .138 | 196 | 27 | 6 | 0 | 1 | 13 | 6 | 66 | 34 | 185.1 | 7 | 30 | 3 | 4 | .925 | 10 | 1 | 0 | 1 | .10 | 3 |
| Phelps,David, NYY | R | .000 | 2 | 0 | 0 | 0 | 0 | .000 | 2 | 0 | 0 | 0 | 0 | 0 | 0 | 2 | 0 | 86.2 | 13 | 9 | 1 | 2 | .957 | 6 | 3 | 0 | 3 | .50 | 2 |
| Phillips,Zach, Mia | L | - | 0 | 0 | 0 | 0 | 0 | - | 0 | 0 | 0 | 0 | 0 | 0 | 0 | 0 | 0 | 1.2 | 0 | 0 | 0 | 0 | - | 0 | 0 | 0 | 0 | - | -1 |
| Pimentel,Stolmy, Pit | R | .000 | 1 | 0 | 0 | 0 | 0 | .000 | 1 | 0 | 0 | 0 | 0 | 0 | 0 | 0 | 0 | 9.1 | 0 | 0 | 0 | 0 | - | 1 | 0 | 0 | 0 | .00 | 0 |
| Pomeranz,Drew, Col | L | .000 | 3 | 0 | 0 | 0 | 1 | .206 | 34 | 7 | 2 | 0 | 1 | 1 | 1 | 19 | 7 | 21.2 | 0 | 2 | 0 | 0 | 1.000 | 3 | 0 | 0 | 0 | .00 | 1 |
| Porcello,Rick, Det | R | .333 | 3 | 1 | 0 | 0 | 0 | .235 | 17 | 4 | 0 | 0 | 0 | 2 | 0 | 6 | 2 | 177.0 | 15 | 21 | 1 | 2 | .973 | 17 | 5 | 1 | 1 | .29 | -4 |
| Pressly,Ryan, Min | R | - | 0 | 0 | 0 | 0 | 0 | - | 0 | 0 | 0 | 0 | 0 | 0 | 0 | 0 | 0 | 76.2 | 8 | 13 | 1 | 2 | .955 | 2 | 1 | 0 | 0 | .50 | 1 |
| Price,David, TB | L | .000 | 6 | 0 | 0 | 0 | 0 | .083 | 24 | 2 | 0 | 0 | 0 | 0 | 2 | 11 | 0 | 186.2 | 7 | 25 | 0 | 0 | 1.000 | 21 | 10 | 4 | 1 | .48 | 4 |

# Pitchers Hitting, Fielding and Holding Runners

| | | 2013 Hitting | | | | | | Career Hitting | | | | | | | | | | 2013 Fielding and Holding Runners | | | | | | | | | | | |
|---|---|---|---|---|---|---|---|---|---|---|---|---|---|---|---|---|---|---|---|---|---|---|---|---|---|---|---|---|---|
| Pitcher | T | Avg | AB | H | HR | RBI | SH | Avg | AB | H | 2B | 3B | HR | RBI | BB | SO | SH | Inn | PO | A | E | DP | Pct | SBA | CS | PCS | PPO | CS% | RS |
| Pryor,Stephen, Sea | R | - | 0 | 0 | 0 | 0 | 0 | - | 0 | 0 | 0 | 0 | 0 | 0 | 0 | 0 | 0 | 7.1 | 1 | 0 | 0 | 0 | 1.000 | 0 | 0 | 0 | 0 | - | 0 |
| Purcey,David, CWS | L | - | 0 | 0 | 0 | 0 | 0 | .000 | 1 | 0 | 0 | 0 | 0 | 0 | 0 | 1 | 0 | 25.1 | 1 | 3 | 0 | 0 | 1.000 | 1 | 0 | 0 | 0 | .00 | 0 |
| Putkonen,Luke, Det | R | - | 0 | 0 | 0 | 0 | 0 | - | 0 | 0 | 0 | 0 | 0 | 0 | 0 | 0 | 0 | 29.2 | 2 | 1 | 0 | 0 | 1.000 | 2 | 0 | 0 | 0 | .00 | -1 |
| Putnam,Zach, ChC | R | - | 0 | 0 | 0 | 0 | 0 | - | 0 | 0 | 0 | 0 | 0 | 0 | 0 | 0 | 0 | 3.1 | 0 | 0 | 0 | 0 | - | 0 | 0 | 0 | 0 | - | 0 |
| Putz,J.J., Ari | R | - | 0 | 0 | 0 | 0 | 0 | - | 0 | 0 | 0 | 0 | 0 | 0 | 0 | 0 | 0 | 34.1 | 0 | 5 | 0 | 0 | 1.000 | 4 | 2 | 0 | 0 | .50 | 1 |
| Qualls,Chad, Mia | R | - | 0 | 0 | 0 | 0 | 0 | .000 | 6 | 0 | 0 | 0 | 0 | 0 | 0 | 5 | 0 | 62.0 | 4 | 18 | 0 | 3 | 1.000 | 6 | 1 | 0 | 0 | .17 | 1 |
| Quintana,Jose, CWS | L | .000 | 2 | 0 | 0 | 0 | 0 | .000 | 5 | 0 | 0 | 0 | 0 | 0 | 1 | 4 | 1 | 200.0 | 4 | 23 | 2 | 1 | .931 | 12 | 5 | 5 | 0 | .42 | 3 |
| Raley,Brooks, ChC | L | .000 | 3 | 0 | 0 | 0 | 1 | .154 | 13 | 2 | 0 | 0 | 0 | 0 | 0 | 2 | 1 | 14.0 | 2 | 1 | 1 | 0 | .750 | 0 | 0 | 0 | 0 | - | 0 |
| Ramirez,Erasmo, Sea | R | .000 | 1 | 0 | 0 | 0 | 0 | .000 | 4 | 0 | 0 | 0 | 0 | 0 | 0 | 1 | 0 | 72.1 | 2 | 7 | 0 | 0 | 1.000 | 3 | 0 | 0 | 0 | .00 | 1 |
| Ramirez,J.C., Phi | R | .000 | 1 | 0 | 0 | 0 | 0 | .000 | 1 | 0 | 0 | 0 | 0 | 0 | 0 | 0 | 0 | 24.0 | 1 | 3 | 1 | 0 | .800 | 1 | 1 | 0 | 0 | 1.00 | -1 |
| Ramirez,Ramon, SF | R | - | 0 | 0 | 0 | 0 | 0 | .333 | 6 | 2 | 0 | 0 | 0 | 0 | 0 | 3 | 1 | 5.2 | 0 | 1 | 0 | 1 | 1.000 | 1 | 0 | 0 | 0 | .00 | 0 |
| Ramos,A.J., Mia | R | - | 0 | 0 | 0 | 0 | 0 | - | 0 | 0 | 0 | 0 | 0 | 0 | 0 | 0 | 0 | 80.0 | 5 | 9 | 2 | 0 | .875 | 10 | 3 | 1 | 0 | .30 | -2 |
| Ramos,Cesar, TB | L | - | 0 | 0 | 0 | 0 | 0 | .000 | 5 | 0 | 0 | 0 | 0 | 0 | 0 | 3 | 0 | 67.1 | 7 | 8 | 0 | 0 | 1.000 | 6 | 0 | 0 | 0 | .00 | 0 |
| Rapada,Clay, Cle | L | - | 0 | 0 | 0 | 0 | 0 | - | 0 | 0 | 0 | 0 | 0 | 0 | 0 | 0 | 0 | 2.0 | 1 | 0 | 0 | 0 | 1.000 | 0 | 0 | 0 | 0 | - | 0 |
| Rasmus,Cory, Atl-LAA | R | - | 0 | 0 | 0 | 0 | 0 | - | 0 | 0 | 0 | 0 | 0 | 0 | 0 | 0 | 0 | 21.2 | 0 | 1 | 0 | 0 | 1.000 | 1 | 0 | 0 | 0 | .00 | 0 |
| Rauch,Jon, Mia | R | - | 0 | 0 | 0 | 0 | 1 | .095 | 21 | 2 | 0 | 0 | 1 | 3 | 0 | 15 | 3 | 16.2 | 1 | 4 | 0 | 0 | 1.000 | 2 | 0 | 0 | 0 | .00 | 0 |
| Redmond,Todd, Tor | R | .000 | 3 | 0 | 0 | 0 | 0 | .000 | 4 | 0 | 0 | 0 | 0 | 0 | 1 | 2 | 0 | 77.0 | 2 | 7 | 1 | 1 | .900 | 8 | 0 | 0 | 0 | .00 | -1 |
| Reed,Addison, CWS | R | - | 0 | 0 | 0 | 0 | 0 | - | 0 | 0 | 0 | 0 | 0 | 0 | 0 | 0 | 0 | 71.1 | 6 | 5 | 0 | 0 | 1.000 | 12 | 0 | 0 | 0 | .00 | -3 |
| Reed,Evan, Det | R | - | 0 | 0 | 0 | 0 | 0 | - | 0 | 0 | 0 | 0 | 0 | 0 | 0 | 0 | 0 | 23.1 | 2 | 6 | 3 | 0 | .727 | 7 | 2 | 2 | 0 | .29 | 0 |
| Reid,Ryan, Pit | R | .000 | 1 | 0 | 0 | 0 | 0 | .000 | 1 | 0 | 0 | 0 | 0 | 0 | 0 | 0 | 0 | 11.0 | 1 | 1 | 0 | 0 | 1.000 | 0 | 0 | 0 | 0 | - | 0 |
| Resop,Chris, Oak | R | - | 0 | 0 | 0 | 0 | 0 | .000 | 4 | 0 | 0 | 0 | 0 | 0 | 1 | 3 | 1 | 18.0 | 1 | 1 | 0 | 0 | 1.000 | 6 | 0 | 0 | 0 | .00 | -2 |
| Reynolds,Greg, Cin | R | .143 | 7 | 1 | 0 | 0 | 2 | .167 | 30 | 5 | 3 | 0 | 0 | 0 | 1 | 13 | 7 | 29.1 | 5 | 4 | 0 | 2 | 1.000 | 2 | 1 | 0 | 0 | .50 | 0 |
| Reynolds,Matt, Ari | L | - | 0 | 0 | 0 | 0 | 0 | .000 | 5 | 0 | 0 | 0 | 0 | 0 | 1 | 3 | 1 | 27.1 | 0 | 3 | 0 | 0 | 1.000 | 0 | 0 | 0 | 0 | - | 0 |
| Rice,Scott, NYM | L | - | 0 | 0 | 0 | 0 | 0 | - | 0 | 0 | 0 | 0 | 0 | 0 | 0 | 0 | 0 | 51.0 | 4 | 16 | 0 | 0 | 1.000 | 7 | 4 | 4 | 0 | .57 | 2 |
| Richard,Clayton, SD | L | .214 | 14 | 3 | 0 | 1 | 1 | .118 | 195 | 23 | 6 | 0 | 1 | 17 | 3 | 88 | 23 | 52.2 | 4 | 12 | 1 | 1 | .941 | 3 | 1 | 0 | 1 | .33 | 0 |
| Richards,Garrett, LAA | R | - | 0 | 0 | 0 | 0 | 0 | .000 | 2 | 0 | 0 | 0 | 0 | 0 | 0 | 1 | 0 | 145.0 | 16 | 21 | 2 | 1 | .949 | 15 | 5 | 0 | 0 | .33 | 0 |
| Rienzo,Andre, CWS | R | - | 0 | 0 | 0 | 0 | 0 | - | 0 | 0 | 0 | 0 | 0 | 0 | 0 | 0 | 0 | 56.0 | 8 | 10 | 1 | 1 | .947 | 1 | 0 | 0 | 1 | .00 | 0 |
| Rivera,Mariano, NYY | R | - | 0 | 0 | 0 | 0 | 0 | .000 | 3 | 0 | 0 | 0 | 0 | 1 | 1 | 1 | 0 | 64.0 | 5 | 12 | 0 | 0 | 1.000 | 3 | 0 | 0 | 1 | .00 | 2 |
| Roark,Tanner, Was | R | .286 | 14 | 4 | 0 | 1 | 1 | .286 | 14 | 4 | 1 | 0 | 0 | 1 | 0 | 5 | 1 | 53.2 | 6 | 7 | 1 | 2 | .929 | 1 | 0 | 0 | 0 | .00 | -1 |
| Robertson,David, NYY | R | - | 0 | 0 | 0 | 0 | 0 | - | 0 | 0 | 0 | 0 | 0 | 0 | 0 | 0 | 0 | 66.1 | 4 | 4 | 0 | 0 | 1.000 | 8 | 1 | 0 | 0 | .13 | -1 |
| Robertson,Tyler, Min | L | - | 0 | 0 | 0 | 0 | 0 | - | 0 | 0 | 0 | 0 | 0 | 0 | 0 | 0 | 0 | 1.0 | 0 | 0 | 0 | 0 | - | 0 | 0 | 0 | 0 | - | 0 |
| Robles,Mauricio, Phi | L | - | 0 | 0 | 0 | 0 | 0 | - | 0 | 0 | 0 | 0 | 0 | 0 | 0 | 0 | 0 | 4.2 | 0 | 0 | 0 | 0 | - | 1 | 0 | 0 | 0 | .00 | 0 |
| Rodney,Fernando, TB | R | - | 0 | 0 | 0 | 0 | 0 | .000 | 1 | 0 | 0 | 0 | 0 | 0 | 0 | 0 | 0 | 66.2 | 4 | 7 | 2 | 1 | .846 | 11 | 2 | 0 | 0 | .18 | -1 |
| Rodriguez,Francisco, Mil-Bal | R | - | 0 | 0 | 0 | 0 | 0 | .500 | 2 | 1 | 0 | 0 | 0 | 0 | 0 | 1 | 0 | 46.2 | 2 | 4 | 0 | 0 | 1.000 | 4 | 1 | 0 | 1 | .25 | 0 |
| Rodriguez,Henry, Was-ChC | R | - | 0 | 0 | 0 | 0 | 0 | .000 | 2 | 0 | 0 | 0 | 0 | 0 | 0 | 2 | 0 | 22.0 | 0 | 1 | 0 | 0 | 1.000 | 9 | 0 | 0 | 0 | .00 | -2 |
| Rodriguez,Paco, LAD | L | .000 | 1 | 0 | 0 | 0 | 0 | .000 | 1 | 0 | 0 | 0 | 0 | 0 | 0 | 1 | 0 | 54.1 | 4 | 7 | 0 | 1 | 1.000 | 10 | 2 | 0 | 0 | .20 | 0 |
| Rodriguez,Wandy, Pit | L | .091 | 22 | 2 | 0 | 1 | 2 | .130 | 437 | 57 | 10 | 0 | 0 | 21 | 10 | 128 | 53 | 62.2 | 2 | 8 | 0 | 0 | 1.000 | 2 | 0 | 0 | 0 | .00 | 0 |
| Roe,Chaz, Ari | R | .000 | 1 | 0 | 0 | 0 | 0 | .000 | 1 | 0 | 0 | 0 | 0 | 0 | 0 | 1 | 0 | 22.1 | 2 | 1 | 0 | 0 | 1.000 | 1 | 0 | 0 | 0 | .00 | -1 |
| Roenicke,Josh, Min | R | .000 | 1 | 0 | 0 | 0 | 0 | .077 | 13 | 1 | 0 | 0 | 0 | 0 | 0 | 6 | 0 | 62.0 | 4 | 10 | 0 | 0 | 1.000 | 5 | 2 | 0 | 0 | .40 | 1 |
| Rogers,Esmil, Tor | R | .000 | 3 | 0 | 0 | 0 | 3 | .212 | 52 | 11 | 3 | 0 | 0 | 1 | 0 | 21 | 10 | 137.2 | 11 | 16 | 0 | 2 | 1.000 | 4 | 1 | 0 | 0 | .25 | 1 |
| Romero,Enny, TB | L | - | 0 | 0 | 0 | 0 | 0 | - | 0 | 0 | 0 | 0 | 0 | 0 | 0 | 0 | 0 | 4.2 | 0 | 1 | 0 | 1 | 1.000 | 1 | 1 | 0 | 0 | 1.00 | 0 |
| Romero,Ricky, Tor | L | - | 0 | 0 | 0 | 0 | 0 | .095 | 21 | 2 | 0 | 0 | 0 | 2 | 0 | 11 | 0 | 7.1 | 0 | 2 | 0 | 0 | 1.000 | 0 | 0 | 0 | 0 | - | 0 |
| Romo,Sergio, SF | R | - | 0 | 0 | 0 | 0 | 0 | .000 | 4 | 0 | 0 | 0 | 0 | 0 | 0 | 3 | 0 | 60.1 | 2 | 6 | 0 | 0 | 1.000 | 4 | 1 | 1 | 0 | .25 | -2 |
| Rondon,Bruce, Det | R | - | 0 | 0 | 0 | 0 | 0 | - | 0 | 0 | 0 | 0 | 0 | 0 | 0 | 0 | 0 | 28.2 | 1 | 1 | 1 | 0 | .667 | 4 | 0 | 0 | 0 | .00 | -3 |
| Rondon,Hector, ChC | R | - | 0 | 0 | 0 | 0 | 0 | - | 0 | 0 | 0 | 0 | 0 | 0 | 0 | 0 | 0 | 54.2 | 9 | 8 | 0 | 1 | 1.000 | 5 | 1 | 0 | 0 | .20 | 1 |
| Rosario,Sandy, SF | R | .000 | 1 | 0 | 0 | 0 | 0 | .000 | 1 | 0 | 0 | 0 | 0 | 0 | 0 | 1 | 0 | 41.2 | 1 | 11 | 0 | 0 | 1.000 | 2 | 1 | 0 | 0 | .50 | 1 |
| Rosenberg,B.J., Phi | R | - | 0 | 0 | 0 | 0 | 0 | .333 | 3 | 1 | 0 | 0 | 0 | 1 | 0 | 1 | 1 | 19.2 | 0 | 3 | 0 | 1 | 1.000 | 2 | 0 | 0 | 0 | .00 | 0 |
| Rosenthal,Trevor, StL | R | .000 | 1 | 0 | 0 | 0 | 0 | .000 | 1 | 0 | 0 | 0 | 0 | 0 | 0 | 1 | 0 | 75.1 | 6 | 3 | 1 | 0 | .900 | 2 | 2 | 0 | 0 | 1.00 | -2 |
| Ross,Robbie, Tex | L | - | 0 | 0 | 0 | 0 | 0 | .000 | 2 | 0 | 0 | 0 | 0 | 0 | 0 | 1 | 0 | 62.1 | 5 | 10 | 0 | 0 | 1.000 | 1 | 0 | 0 | 0 | .00 | 3 |
| Ross,Tyson, SD | R | .182 | 33 | 6 | 0 | 0 | 3 | .167 | 36 | 6 | 0 | 0 | 0 | 0 | 0 | 20 | 3 | 125.0 | 12 | 17 | 2 | 2 | .935 | 18 | 7 | 1 | 0 | .39 | 1 |
| Rosscup,Zac, ChC | L | - | 0 | 0 | 0 | 0 | 0 | - | 0 | 0 | 0 | 0 | 0 | 0 | 0 | 0 | 0 | 6.2 | 0 | 0 | 0 | 0 | - | 3 | 0 | 0 | 0 | .00 | -1 |
| Roth,Michael, LAA | L | - | 0 | 0 | 0 | 0 | 0 | - | 0 | 0 | 0 | 0 | 0 | 0 | 0 | 0 | 0 | 20.0 | 2 | 4 | 0 | 0 | 1.000 | 2 | 1 | 0 | 0 | .50 | 1 |
| Ruffin,Chance, Sea | R | - | 0 | 0 | 0 | 0 | 0 | - | 0 | 0 | 0 | 0 | 0 | 0 | 0 | 0 | 0 | 9.2 | 0 | 0 | 0 | 0 | - | 0 | 0 | 0 | 0 | - | 0 |
| Rusin,Chris, ChC | L | .105 | 19 | 2 | 0 | 2 | 2 | .129 | 31 | 4 | 0 | 1 | 0 | 2 | 0 | 8 | 2 | 66.1 | 3 | 11 | 0 | 0 | 1.000 | 4 | 2 | 2 | 0 | .50 | 2 |
| Russell,James, ChC | L | - | 0 | 0 | 0 | 0 | 0 | .077 | 13 | 1 | 0 | 0 | 0 | 0 | 0 | 5 | 0 | 52.2 | 4 | 8 | 0 | 1 | 1.000 | 11 | 5 | 3 | 0 | .45 | 1 |
| Ryu,Hyun-Jin, LAD | L | .207 | 58 | 12 | 0 | 5 | 6 | .207 | 58 | 12 | 3 | 1 | 0 | 5 | 2 | 23 | 6 | 192.0 | 8 | 29 | 0 | 3 | 1.000 | 3 | 2 | 1 | 0 | .67 | 2 |
| Rzepczynski,Marc, StL-Cle | L | .000 | 1 | 0 | 0 | 0 | 0 | .000 | 1 | 0 | 0 | 0 | 0 | 0 | 0 | 1 | 0 | 30.2 | 1 | 2 | 0 | 0 | 1.000 | 3 | 1 | 0 | 0 | .33 | 0 |
| Sabathia,CC, NYY | L | .000 | 4 | 0 | 0 | 1 | 0 | .229 | 109 | 25 | 3 | 0 | 3 | 15 | 1 | 30 | 3 | 211.0 | 1 | 30 | 2 | 2 | .939 | 10 | 4 | 2 | 0 | .40 | 1 |
| Salas,Fernando, StL | R | .000 | 2 | 0 | 0 | 0 | 0 | .000 | 4 | 0 | 0 | 0 | 0 | 0 | 0 | 2 | 0 | 28.0 | 1 | 3 | 0 | 0 | 1.000 | 1 | 0 | 0 | 0 | .00 | 0 |
| Salazar,Danny, Cle | R | .000 | 2 | 0 | 0 | 0 | 0 | .000 | 2 | 0 | 0 | 0 | 0 | 0 | 0 | 2 | 0 | 52.0 | 3 | 2 | 0 | 1 | 1.000 | 3 | 0 | 0 | 0 | .00 | -1 |
| Sale,Chris, CWS | L | - | 0 | 0 | 0 | 0 | 0 | .000 | 2 | 0 | 0 | 0 | 0 | 0 | 0 | 2 | 1 | 214.1 | 5 | 19 | 1 | 1 | .960 | 21 | 2 | 0 | 1 | .10 | -3 |
| Samardzija,Jeff, ChC | R | .113 | 62 | 7 | 1 | 2 | 10 | .111 | 126 | 14 | 2 | 0 | 2 | 7 | 6 | 54 | 19 | 213.2 | 23 | 16 | 3 | 2 | .929 | 22 | 7 | 0 | 0 | .32 | -6 |
| Sanabia,Alex, Mia | R | .063 | 16 | 1 | 0 | 0 | 1 | .049 | 41 | 2 | 0 | 0 | 0 | 0 | 1 | 21 | 5 | 55.1 | 1 | 9 | 0 | 0 | 1.000 | 3 | 0 | 0 | 1 | .00 | 2 |
| Sanchez,Anibal, Det | R | .000 | 4 | 0 | 0 | 0 | 2 | .089 | 236 | 21 | 0 | 1 | 0 | 6 | 16 | 109 | 31 | 182.0 | 17 | 19 | 1 | 0 | .973 | 26 | 1 | 0 | 2 | .04 | -6 |
| Sanchez,Eduardo, ChC | R | - | 0 | 0 | 0 | 0 | 0 | .000 | 2 | 0 | 0 | 0 | 0 | 0 | 0 | 1 | 0 | 6.1 | 0 | 1 | 0 | 0 | 1.000 | 1 | 0 | 0 | 0 | .00 | 0 |
| Sanchez,Jonathan, Pit | L | .000 | 5 | 0 | 0 | 0 | 0 | .115 | 200 | 23 | 6 | 1 | 0 | 9 | 8 | 103 | 22 | 13.2 | 0 | 2 | 1 | 0 | .667 | 3 | 2 | 0 | 0 | .67 | 0 |
| Santana,Ervin, KC | R | .250 | 4 | 1 | 0 | 0 | 0 | .160 | 25 | 4 | 1 | 0 | 0 | 2 | 0 | 15 | 1 | 211.0 | 22 | 19 | 1 | 2 | .976 | 21 | 8 | 0 | 0 | .38 | 0 |
| Santiago,Hector, CWS | L | .000 | 4 | 0 | 0 | 0 | 2 | .000 | 4 | 0 | 0 | 0 | 0 | 0 | 0 | 1 | 2 | 149.0 | 8 | 17 | 1 | 0 | .962 | 15 | 6 | 1 | 0 | .40 | 6 |
| Santos,Sergio, Tor | R | .000 | 1 | 0 | 0 | 0 | 0 | .000 | 1 | 0 | 0 | 0 | 0 | 0 | 0 | 0 | 0 | 25.2 | 1 | 3 | 0 | 1 | 1.000 | 5 | 0 | 0 | 0 | .00 | 0 |
| Saunders,Joe, Sea | L | .000 | 5 | 0 | 0 | 0 | 1 | .133 | 128 | 17 | 1 | 0 | 0 | 6 | 6 | 34 | 15 | 183.0 | 8 | 35 | 1 | 3 | .977 | 21 | 5 | 1 | 1 | .24 | 1 |

# Pitchers Hitting, Fielding and Holding Runners

| | | 2013 Hitting | | | | | | Career Hitting | | | | | | | | | | 2013 Fielding and Holding Runners | | | | | | | | | | | |
|---|---|---|---|---|---|---|---|---|---|---|---|---|---|---|---|---|---|---|---|---|---|---|---|---|---|---|---|---|---|
| Pitcher | T | Avg | AB | H | HR | RBI | SH | Avg | AB | H | 2B | 3B | HR | RBI | BB | SO | SH | Inn | PO | A | E | DP | Pct | SBA | CS | PCS | PPO | CS% | RS |
| Savery,Joe, Phi | L | - | 0 | 0 | 0 | 0 | 1 | .000 | 2 | 0 | 0 | 0 | 0 | 0 | 0 | 1 | 1 | 20.0 | 1 | 2 | 1 | 0 | .750 | 4 | 1 | 0 | 0 | .25 | 0 |
| Scahill,Rob, Col | R | .000 | 1 | 0 | 0 | 0 | 0 | .000 | 2 | 0 | 0 | 0 | 0 | 0 | 1 | 0 | 1 | 33.1 | 7 | 4 | 0 | 1 | 1.000 | 3 | 0 | 0 | 0 | .00 | 0 |
| Scheppers,Tanner, Tex | R | - | 0 | 0 | 0 | 0 | 0 | - | 0 | 0 | 0 | 0 | 0 | 0 | 0 | 0 | 0 | 76.2 | 7 | 8 | 2 | 1 | .882 | 8 | 6 | 0 | 0 | .75 | 1 |
| Scherzer,Max, Det | R | .333 | 3 | 1 | 0 | 1 | 0 | .169 | 77 | 13 | 3 | 0 | 0 | 4 | 4 | 22 | 8 | 214.1 | 17 | 21 | 3 | 0 | .927 | 22 | 8 | 2 | 1 | .36 | 1 |
| Scribner,Evan, Oak | R | - | 0 | 0 | 0 | 0 | 0 | - | 0 | 0 | 0 | 0 | 0 | 0 | 0 | 0 | 0 | 26.2 | 1 | 0 | 0 | 0 | 1.000 | 6 | 0 | 0 | 0 | .00 | -2 |
| Shaw,Bryan, Cle | R | - | 0 | 0 | 0 | 0 | 0 | - | 0 | 0 | 0 | 0 | 0 | 0 | 0 | 0 | 0 | 75.0 | 4 | 5 | 2 | 0 | .818 | 6 | 2 | 0 | 0 | .33 | -2 |
| Shields,James, KC | R | .333 | 3 | 1 | 0 | 0 | 0 | .200 | 40 | 8 | 0 | 0 | 0 | 3 | 2 | 12 | 1 | 228.2 | 11 | 21 | 3 | 2 | .914 | 10 | 5 | 0 | 3 | .50 | 0 |
| Shoemaker,Matt, LAA | R | - | 0 | 0 | 0 | 0 | 0 | - | 0 | 0 | 0 | 0 | 0 | 0 | 0 | 0 | 0 | 5.0 | 0 | 1 | 0 | 0 | 1.000 | 1 | 0 | 0 | 0 | .00 | 1 |
| Siegrist,Kevin, StL | L | .000 | 1 | 0 | 0 | 0 | 0 | .000 | 1 | 0 | 0 | 0 | 0 | 0 | 0 | 1 | 0 | 39.2 | 1 | 4 | 0 | 1 | 1.000 | 1 | 1 | 0 | 0 | 1.00 | 1 |
| Simon,Alfredo, Cin | R | .143 | 7 | 1 | 0 | 0 | 0 | .091 | 11 | 1 | 0 | 0 | 0 | 0 | 0 | 6 | 0 | 87.2 | 5 | 13 | 0 | 0 | 1.000 | 7 | 4 | 0 | 1 | .57 | 2 |
| Sipp,Tony, Ari | L | - | 0 | 0 | 0 | 0 | 0 | - | 0 | 0 | 0 | 0 | 0 | 0 | 0 | 0 | 0 | 37.2 | 4 | 2 | 1 | 0 | .857 | 2 | 0 | 0 | 0 | .00 | -1 |
| Skaggs,Tyler, Ari | L | .200 | 10 | 2 | 0 | 1 | 3 | .118 | 17 | 2 | 0 | 0 | 0 | 1 | 0 | 9 | 5 | 38.2 | 1 | 5 | 0 | 0 | 1.000 | 3 | 1 | 0 | 0 | .33 | 0 |
| Slowey,Kevin, Mia | R | .048 | 21 | 1 | 0 | 0 | 5 | .088 | 34 | 3 | 1 | 0 | 0 | 2 | 2 | 15 | 7 | 92.0 | 7 | 15 | 0 | 1 | 1.000 | 6 | 4 | 0 | 0 | .67 | 1 |
| Smith,Burch, SD | R | .111 | 9 | 1 | 0 | 0 | 0 | .111 | 9 | 1 | 0 | 0 | 0 | 0 | 1 | 2 | 0 | 36.1 | 2 | 3 | 1 | 0 | .833 | 4 | 1 | 0 | 1 | .25 | 0 |
| Smith,Joe, Cle | R | - | 0 | 0 | 0 | 0 | 0 | .000 | 2 | 0 | 0 | 0 | 0 | 0 | 0 | 2 | 0 | 63.0 | 2 | 14 | 1 | 1 | .941 | 3 | 2 | 1 | 1 | .67 | 0 |
| Smith,Will, KC | L | - | 0 | 0 | 0 | 0 | 0 | - | 0 | 0 | 0 | 0 | 0 | 0 | 0 | 0 | 0 | 33.1 | 2 | 4 | 1 | 1 | .857 | 2 | 1 | 1 | 0 | .50 | -1 |
| Smyly,Drew, Det | L | - | 0 | 0 | 0 | 0 | 0 | .000 | 1 | 0 | 0 | 0 | 0 | 0 | 0 | 0 | 0 | 76.0 | 6 | 6 | 0 | 0 | 1.000 | 10 | 2 | 1 | 0 | .20 | -1 |
| Soria,Joakim, Tex | R | - | 0 | 0 | 0 | 0 | 0 | - | 0 | 0 | 0 | 0 | 0 | 0 | 0 | 0 | 0 | 23.2 | 1 | 1 | 0 | 0 | 1.000 | 5 | 0 | 0 | 0 | .00 | -2 |
| Soriano,Rafael, Was | R | - | 0 | 0 | 0 | 0 | 0 | .000 | 4 | 0 | 0 | 0 | 0 | 0 | 0 | 1 | 0 | 66.2 | 3 | 6 | 0 | 0 | 1.000 | 3 | 0 | 0 | 0 | .00 | 0 |
| Spruill,Zeke, Ari | R | .000 | 1 | 0 | 0 | 0 | 0 | .000 | 1 | 0 | 0 | 0 | 0 | 0 | 0 | 1 | 0 | 11.1 | 0 | 2 | 0 | 0 | 1.000 | 0 | 0 | 0 | 0 | - | 0 |
| Stammen,Craig, Was | R | .000 | 5 | 0 | 0 | 0 | 0 | .195 | 82 | 16 | 6 | 0 | 0 | 10 | 4 | 31 | 9 | 81.2 | 0 | 8 | 0 | 0 | 1.000 | 12 | 3 | 0 | 0 | .25 | -4 |
| Stange,Daniel, LAA | R | - | 0 | 0 | 0 | 0 | 0 | - | 0 | 0 | 0 | 0 | 0 | 0 | 0 | 0 | 0 | 1.2 | 0 | 0 | 0 | 0 | - | 0 | 0 | 0 | 0 | - | 0 |
| Stauffer,Tim, SD | R | .000 | 8 | 0 | 0 | 0 | 0 | .150 | 133 | 20 | 3 | 0 | 0 | 12 | 4 | 61 | 16 | 69.2 | 6 | 10 | 0 | 0 | 1.000 | 3 | 3 | 0 | 0 | 1.00 | 0 |
| Stinson,Josh, Bal | R | - | 0 | 0 | 0 | 0 | 0 | .000 | 1 | 0 | 0 | 0 | 0 | 0 | 1 | 1 | 0 | 17.0 | 3 | 1 | 0 | 0 | 1.000 | 0 | 0 | 0 | 0 | - | 0 |
| Storen,Drew, Was | R | - | 0 | 0 | 0 | 0 | 0 | .500 | 2 | 1 | 0 | 0 | 0 | 0 | 0 | 1 | 0 | 61.2 | 4 | 8 | 1 | 2 | .923 | 5 | 1 | 0 | 0 | .20 | 0 |
| Storey,Mickey, Tor | R | - | 0 | 0 | 0 | 0 | 0 | - | 0 | 0 | 0 | 0 | 0 | 0 | 0 | 0 | 0 | 4.0 | 0 | 0 | 0 | 0 | - | 0 | 0 | 0 | 0 | - | 0 |
| Straily,Dan, Oak | R | .000 | 2 | 0 | 0 | 0 | 0 | .000 | 2 | 0 | 0 | 0 | 0 | 0 | 1 | 2 | 0 | 152.1 | 8 | 8 | 0 | 0 | 1.000 | 17 | 5 | 1 | 0 | .29 | -1 |
| Strasburg,Stephen, Was | R | .143 | 49 | 7 | 0 | 2 | 10 | .172 | 122 | 21 | 6 | 0 | 1 | 10 | 5 | 46 | 16 | 183.0 | 9 | 19 | 0 | 0 | 1.000 | 18 | 5 | 0 | 0 | .28 | -3 |
| Street,Huston, SD | R | - | 0 | 0 | 0 | 0 | 0 | .000 | 2 | 0 | 0 | 0 | 0 | 0 | 0 | 1 | 0 | 56.2 | 3 | 9 | 0 | 0 | 1.000 | 4 | 2 | 0 | 0 | .50 | 2 |
| Strop,Pedro, Bal-ChC | R | - | 0 | 0 | 0 | 0 | 0 | - | 0 | 0 | 0 | 0 | 0 | 0 | 0 | 0 | 0 | 57.1 | 1 | 6 | 0 | 0 | 1.000 | 1 | 0 | 0 | 0 | .00 | -2 |
| Stults,Eric, SD | L | .164 | 61 | 10 | 1 | 4 | 7 | .203 | 138 | 28 | 6 | 0 | 1 | 11 | 5 | 51 | 16 | 203.2 | 5 | 32 | 2 | 5 | .949 | 8 | 2 | 0 | 0 | .25 | 3 |
| Stutes,Michael, Phi | R | .000 | 1 | 0 | 0 | 0 | 0 | .000 | 1 | 0 | 0 | 0 | 0 | 0 | 0 | 0 | 0 | 17.2 | 3 | 3 | 0 | 0 | 1.000 | 4 | 0 | 0 | 0 | .00 | -1 |
| Surkamp,Eric, SF | L | .000 | 1 | 0 | 0 | 0 | 0 | .111 | 9 | 1 | 0 | 0 | 0 | 1 | 1 | 5 | 0 | 2.2 | 0 | 0 | 0 | 0 | - | 1 | 0 | 0 | 0 | .00 | 0 |
| Swarzak,Anthony, Min | R | .000 | 1 | 0 | 0 | 0 | 0 | .000 | 5 | 0 | 0 | 0 | 0 | 0 | 0 | 4 | 0 | 96.0 | 6 | 9 | 1 | 1 | .938 | 7 | 4 | 1 | 0 | .57 | 1 |
| Takahashi,Hisanori, ChC | L | - | 0 | 0 | 0 | 0 | 0 | .063 | 16 | 1 | 0 | 0 | 0 | 0 | 0 | 3 | 4 | 3.0 | 0 | 1 | 0 | 0 | 1.000 | 0 | 0 | 0 | 0 | - | 0 |
| Tazawa,Junichi, Bos | R | - | 0 | 0 | 0 | 0 | 0 | - | 0 | 0 | 0 | 0 | 0 | 0 | 0 | 0 | 0 | 68.1 | 2 | 6 | 0 | 1 | 1.000 | 5 | 2 | 0 | 0 | .40 | 0 |
| Teaford,Everett, KC | L | - | 0 | 0 | 0 | 0 | 0 | - | 0 | 0 | 0 | 0 | 0 | 0 | 0 | 0 | 0 | 0.2 | 0 | 0 | 0 | 0 | - | 0 | 0 | 0 | 0 | - | 0 |
| Teheran,Julio, Atl | R | .224 | 58 | 13 | 0 | 2 | 5 | .206 | 63 | 13 | 3 | 0 | 0 | 2 | 3 | 17 | 6 | 185.2 | 12 | 25 | 0 | 0 | 1.000 | 8 | 1 | 0 | 8 | .13 | 6 |
| Tepesch,Nick, Tex | R | .000 | 3 | 0 | 0 | 0 | 0 | .000 | 3 | 0 | 0 | 0 | 0 | 0 | 0 | 1 | 0 | 93.0 | 10 | 6 | 0 | 0 | 1.000 | 5 | 0 | 0 | 1 | .00 | -1 |
| Thatcher,Joe, SD-Ari | L | - | 0 | 0 | 0 | 0 | 0 | .000 | 1 | 0 | 0 | 0 | 0 | 0 | 0 | 1 | 0 | 39.1 | 0 | 4 | 0 | 0 | 1.000 | 2 | 0 | 0 | 0 | .00 | 2 |
| Thayer,Dale, SD | R | .000 | 1 | 0 | 0 | 0 | 0 | .000 | 2 | 0 | 0 | 0 | 0 | 0 | 0 | 0 | 0 | 65.0 | 2 | 6 | 1 | 2 | .889 | 8 | 1 | 1 | 0 | .13 | -2 |
| Thielbar,Caleb, Min | L | - | 0 | 0 | 0 | 0 | 0 | - | 0 | 0 | 0 | 0 | 0 | 0 | 0 | 0 | 0 | 46.0 | 3 | 3 | 0 | 0 | 1.000 | 3 | 1 | 1 | 0 | .33 | 0 |
| Thornburg,Tyler, Mil | R | .000 | 16 | 0 | 0 | 0 | 2 | .048 | 21 | 1 | 1 | 0 | 0 | 0 | 0 | 10 | 2 | 66.2 | 3 | 8 | 0 | 1 | 1.000 | 9 | 4 | 0 | 0 | .44 | 0 |
| Thornton,Matt, CWS-Bos | L | - | 0 | 0 | 0 | 0 | 0 | .000 | 1 | 0 | 0 | 0 | 0 | 0 | 0 | 1 | 0 | 43.1 | 3 | 6 | 2 | 0 | .818 | 6 | 1 | 0 | 0 | .17 | 1 |
| Tillman,Chris, Bal | R | .000 | 5 | 0 | 0 | 0 | 2 | .000 | 6 | 0 | 0 | 0 | 0 | 0 | 0 | 1 | 2 | 206.1 | 8 | 18 | 0 | 1 | 1.000 | 9 | 8 | 1 | 0 | .89 | 2 |
| Tolleson,Shawn, LAD | R | - | 0 | 0 | 0 | 0 | 0 | - | 0 | 0 | 0 | 0 | 0 | 0 | 0 | 0 | 0 | 0.0 | 0 | 0 | 0 | 0 | - | 0 | 0 | 0 | 0 | - | 0 |
| Tomlin,Josh, Cle | R | - | 0 | 0 | 0 | 0 | 0 | .571 | 7 | 4 | 0 | 0 | 0 | 1 | 0 | 3 | 0 | 2.0 | 0 | 0 | 0 | 0 | - | 0 | 0 | 0 | 0 | - | 0 |
| Tonkin,Michael, Min | R | - | 0 | 0 | 0 | 0 | 0 | - | 0 | 0 | 0 | 0 | 0 | 0 | 0 | 0 | 0 | 11.1 | 0 | 2 | 0 | 1 | 1.000 | 2 | 0 | 0 | 0 | .00 | -1 |
| Torres,Alex, TB | L | - | 0 | 0 | 0 | 0 | 0 | - | 0 | 0 | 0 | 0 | 0 | 0 | 0 | 0 | 0 | 58.0 | 2 | 9 | 1 | 0 | .917 | 2 | 0 | 0 | 0 | .00 | 1 |
| Torres,Carlos, NYM | R | .063 | 16 | 1 | 0 | 1 | 1 | .107 | 28 | 3 | 0 | 0 | 0 | 2 | 2 | 15 | 4 | 86.1 | 5 | 9 | 0 | 0 | 1.000 | 5 | 1 | 0 | 0 | .20 | 1 |
| Troncoso,Ramon, CWS | R | - | 0 | 0 | 0 | 0 | 0 | .000 | 8 | 0 | 0 | 0 | 0 | 1 | 1 | 7 | 1 | 30.0 | 3 | 6 | 2 | 0 | .818 | 6 | 2 | 0 | 0 | .33 | 0 |
| Turner,Jacob, Mia | R | .086 | 35 | 3 | 0 | 0 | 3 | .061 | 49 | 3 | 0 | 1 | 0 | 0 | 0 | 24 | 5 | 118.0 | 14 | 21 | 5 | 1 | .875 | 23 | 5 | 2 | 2 | .22 | -3 |
| Uehara,Koji, Bos | R | - | 0 | 0 | 0 | 0 | 0 | .000 | 2 | 0 | 0 | 0 | 0 | 0 | 1 | 1 | 0 | 74.1 | 2 | 7 | 0 | 0 | 1.000 | 2 | 1 | 0 | 0 | .50 | 0 |
| Valdes,Raul, Phi | L | .333 | 3 | 1 | 0 | 0 | 1 | .385 | 13 | 5 | 2 | 0 | 0 | 1 | 0 | 3 | 5 | 35.0 | 1 | 7 | 0 | 1 | 1.000 | 1 | 1 | 1 | 0 | 1.00 | 2 |
| Valverde,Jose, Det | R | - | 0 | 0 | 0 | 0 | 0 | .500 | 2 | 1 | 1 | 0 | 0 | 0 | 0 | 1 | 0 | 19.1 | 0 | 1 | 0 | 0 | 1.000 | 4 | 0 | 0 | 0 | .00 | -1 |
| Vargas,Jason, LAA | L | - | 0 | 0 | 0 | 0 | 0 | .262 | 61 | 16 | 3 | 0 | 0 | 4 | 3 | 16 | 2 | 150.0 | 7 | 19 | 1 | 2 | .963 | 16 | 4 | 3 | 1 | .25 | -2 |
| Varvaro,Anthony, Atl | R | .000 | 1 | 0 | 0 | 0 | 0 | .000 | 1 | 0 | 0 | 0 | 0 | 0 | 0 | 1 | 0 | 73.1 | 13 | 9 | 1 | 2 | .957 | 5 | 0 | 0 | 0 | .00 | 3 |
| Veal,Donnie, CWS | L | - | 0 | 0 | 0 | 0 | 0 | - | 0 | 0 | 0 | 0 | 0 | 0 | 0 | 0 | 1 | 29.1 | 1 | 2 | 1 | 0 | .750 | 2 | 0 | 0 | 0 | .00 | -1 |
| Ventura,Yordano, KC | R | - | 0 | 0 | 0 | 0 | 0 | - | 0 | 0 | 0 | 0 | 0 | 0 | 0 | 0 | 0 | 15.1 | 1 | 2 | 1 | 2 | .750 | 0 | 0 | 0 | 0 | - | 1 |
| Veras,Jose, Hou-Det | R | - | 0 | 0 | 0 | 0 | 0 | - | 0 | 0 | 0 | 0 | 0 | 0 | 1 | 0 | 0 | 62.2 | 6 | 7 | 0 | 0 | 1.000 | 7 | 0 | 0 | 1 | .00 | -1 |
| Verlander,Justin, Det | R | .000 | 2 | 0 | 0 | 0 | 0 | .000 | 26 | 0 | 0 | 0 | 0 | 0 | 0 | 15 | 9 | 218.1 | 19 | 17 | 2 | 5 | .947 | 25 | 4 | 0 | 3 | .16 | -1 |
| Villanueva,Carlos, ChC | R | .156 | 32 | 5 | 0 | 1 | 2 | .112 | 98 | 11 | 0 | 0 | 0 | 4 | 3 | 46 | 12 | 128.2 | 9 | 9 | 0 | 2 | 1.000 | 16 | 6 | 1 | 0 | .38 | 0 |
| Villarreal,Brayan, Det-Bos | R | - | 0 | 0 | 0 | 0 | 0 | - | 0 | 0 | 0 | 0 | 0 | 0 | 0 | 0 | 0 | 4.1 | 0 | 2 | 0 | 1 | 1.000 | 2 | 0 | 0 | 0 | .00 | 0 |
| Villarreal,Pedro, Cin | R | .000 | 1 | 0 | 0 | 0 | 0 | .000 | 1 | 0 | 0 | 0 | 0 | 0 | 0 | 0 | 0 | 5.2 | 0 | 0 | 0 | 0 | - | 0 | 0 | 0 | 0 | - | 0 |
| Vincent,Nick, SD | R | - | 0 | 0 | 0 | 0 | 0 | .000 | 1 | 0 | 0 | 0 | 0 | 0 | 0 | 1 | 0 | 46.1 | 4 | 7 | 0 | 0 | 1.000 | 3 | 2 | 0 | 1 | .67 | 2 |
| Vogelsong,Ryan, SF | R | .069 | 29 | 2 | 0 | 2 | 4 | .154 | 195 | 30 | 6 | 0 | 0 | 7 | 12 | 87 | 29 | 103.2 | 8 | 9 | 0 | 0 | 1.000 | 9 | 4 | 0 | 0 | .44 | -1 |
| Volquez,Edinson, SD-LAD | R | .119 | 42 | 5 | 1 | 4 | 9 | .096 | 218 | 21 | 2 | 0 | 1 | 6 | 4 | 111 | 35 | 170.1 | 11 | 21 | 0 | 0 | 1.000 | 26 | 2 | 0 | 0 | .08 | -7 |
| Volstad,Chris, Col | R | - | 0 | 0 | 0 | 0 | 0 | .139 | 201 | 28 | 6 | 0 | 0 | 7 | 2 | 94 | 28 | 8.1 | 0 | 0 | 0 | 0 | - | 1 | 0 | 0 | 0 | .00 | 0 |
| Wacha,Michael, StL | R | .143 | 21 | 3 | 0 | 3 | 1 | .143 | 21 | 3 | 0 | 0 | 0 | 3 | 0 | 10 | 1 | 64.2 | 3 | 6 | 1 | 0 | .900 | 1 | 0 | 0 | 0 | .00 | 0 |
| Wagner,Neil, Tor | R | - | 0 | 0 | 0 | 0 | 0 | - | 0 | 0 | 0 | 0 | 0 | 0 | 0 | 0 | 0 | 38.0 | 0 | 7 | 0 | 2 | 1.000 | 1 | 1 | 0 | 0 | 1.00 | 0 |

# Pitchers Hitting, Fielding and Holding Runners

| | | 2013 Hitting | | | | | | Career Hitting | | | | | | | | | | 2013 Fielding and Holding Runners | | | | | | | | | | | |
|---|---|---|---|---|---|---|---|---|---|---|---|---|---|---|---|---|---|---|---|---|---|---|---|---|---|---|---|---|---|
| Pitcher | T | Avg | AB | H | HR | RBI | SH | Avg | AB | H | 2B | 3B | HR | RBI | BB | SO | SH | Inn | PO | A | E | DP | Pct | SBA | CS | PCS | PPO | CS% | RS |
| Wainwright,Adam, StL | R | .211 | 71 | 15 | 0 | 6 | 9 | .205 | 438 | 90 | 22 | 1 | 6 | 33 | 16 | 142 | 34 | 241.2 | 25 | 36 | 0 | 6 | 1.000 | 6 | 3 | 0 | 0 | .50 | 4 |
| Walden,Jordan, Atl | R | - | 0 | 0 | 0 | 0 | 0 | - | 0 | 0 | 0 | 0 | 0 | 0 | 0 | 0 | 0 | 47.0 | 0 | 4 | 2 | 0 | .667 | 8 | 0 | 0 | 1 | .00 | -1 |
| Walker,Taijuan, Sea | R | - | 0 | 0 | 0 | 0 | 0 | - | 0 | 0 | 0 | 0 | 0 | 0 | 0 | 0 | 0 | 15.0 | 0 | 1 | 0 | 0 | 1.000 | 1 | 1 | 0 | 0 | 1.00 | -1 |
| Wall,Josh, LAD | R | - | 0 | 0 | 0 | 0 | 0 | - | 0 | 0 | 0 | 0 | 0 | 0 | 0 | 0 | 0 | 7.0 | 0 | 0 | 0 | 0 | - | 1 | 0 | 0 | 0 | .00 | -1 |
| Walters,P.J., Min | R | - | 0 | 0 | 0 | 0 | 0 | .000 | 10 | 0 | 0 | 0 | 0 | 0 | 1 | 6 | 3 | 39.1 | 3 | 4 | 0 | 0 | 1.000 | 1 | 0 | 0 | 0 | .00 | -1 |
| Wang,Chien-Ming, Tor | R | - | 0 | 0 | 0 | 0 | 0 | .051 | 39 | 2 | 1 | 0 | 0 | 1 | 2 | 21 | 1 | 27.0 | 3 | 8 | 0 | 2 | 1.000 | 2 | 0 | 0 | 1 | .00 | 1 |
| Warren,Adam, NYY | R | - | 0 | 0 | 0 | 0 | 0 | - | 0 | 0 | 0 | 0 | 0 | 0 | 0 | 0 | 0 | 77.0 | 4 | 12 | 0 | 1 | 1.000 | 2 | 0 | 0 | 1 | .00 | 1 |
| Watson,Tony, Pit | L | .000 | 1 | 0 | 0 | 0 | 2 | .000 | 3 | 0 | 0 | 0 | 0 | 0 | 0 | 3 | 2 | 71.2 | 2 | 12 | 0 | 0 | 1.000 | 4 | 1 | 1 | 0 | .25 | 1 |
| Weaver,Jered, LAA | R | .000 | 4 | 0 | 0 | 0 | 0 | .125 | 32 | 4 | 0 | 0 | 0 | 1 | 2 | 13 | 0 | 154.1 | 6 | 5 | 1 | 1 | .917 | 14 | 1 | 0 | 0 | .07 | -3 |
| Webb,Daniel, CWS | R | - | 0 | 0 | 0 | 0 | 0 | - | 0 | 0 | 0 | 0 | 0 | 0 | 0 | 0 | 0 | 11.1 | 0 | 0 | 0 | 0 | - | 0 | 0 | 0 | 0 | - | 0 |
| Webb,Ryan, Mia | R | .333 | 3 | 1 | 0 | 0 | 0 | .200 | 5 | 1 | 0 | 0 | 0 | 0 | 0 | 4 | 0 | 80.1 | 3 | 19 | 0 | 1 | 1.000 | 16 | 2 | 0 | 0 | .13 | -2 |
| Weber,Thad, SD-Tor | R | .000 | 3 | 0 | 0 | 0 | 0 | .000 | 3 | 0 | 0 | 0 | 0 | 0 | 0 | 0 | 0 | 15.0 | 2 | 3 | 1 | 0 | .833 | 3 | 1 | 0 | 0 | .33 | 0 |
| Webster,Allen, Bos | R | - | 0 | 0 | 0 | 0 | 0 | - | 0 | 0 | 0 | 0 | 0 | 0 | 0 | 0 | 0 | 30.1 | 3 | 2 | 0 | 0 | 1.000 | 5 | 2 | 0 | 0 | .40 | -1 |
| Welker,Duke, Pit | R | - | 0 | 0 | 0 | 0 | 0 | - | 0 | 0 | 0 | 0 | 0 | 0 | 0 | 0 | 0 | 1.1 | 0 | 1 | 0 | 0 | 1.000 | 0 | 0 | 0 | 0 | - | 0 |
| Westbrook,Jake, StL | R | .176 | 34 | 6 | 0 | 4 | 4 | .130 | 169 | 22 | 7 | 0 | 1 | 14 | 13 | 79 | 23 | 116.2 | 11 | 24 | 0 | 2 | 1.000 | 7 | 3 | 0 | 1 | .43 | 4 |
| Wheeler,Zack, NYM | R | .133 | 30 | 4 | 0 | 2 | 3 | .133 | 30 | 4 | 1 | 0 | 0 | 2 | 1 | 13 | 3 | 100.0 | 1 | 5 | 0 | 1 | 1.000 | 12 | 2 | 0 | 0 | .17 | -4 |
| Wilhelmsen,Tom, Sea | R | - | 0 | 0 | 0 | 0 | 0 | - | 0 | 0 | 0 | 0 | 0 | 0 | 0 | 0 | 0 | 59.0 | 3 | 6 | 1 | 0 | .900 | 5 | 0 | 0 | 0 | .00 | -2 |
| Williams,Jerome, LAA | R | .000 | 2 | 0 | 0 | 0 | 0 | .115 | 122 | 14 | 3 | 0 | 0 | 1 | 1 | 55 | 19 | 169.1 | 15 | 16 | 1 | 0 | .969 | 16 | 7 | 0 | 1 | .44 | 1 |
| Wilson,Alex, Bos | R | - | 0 | 0 | 0 | 0 | 0 | - | 0 | 0 | 0 | 0 | 0 | 0 | 0 | 0 | 0 | 27.2 | 1 | 6 | 0 | 1 | 1.000 | 2 | 1 | 0 | 0 | .50 | 2 |
| Wilson,Brian, LAD | R | - | 0 | 0 | 0 | 0 | 0 | .000 | 9 | 0 | 0 | 0 | 0 | 0 | 0 | 2 | 1 | 13.2 | 1 | 3 | 0 | 1 | 1.000 | 1 | 0 | 0 | 0 | .00 | -1 |
| Wilson,C.J., LAA | L | .125 | 8 | 1 | 0 | 0 | 2 | .095 | 21 | 2 | 0 | 1 | 0 | 0 | 2 | 7 | 4 | 212.1 | 9 | 24 | 1 | 1 | .971 | 17 | 2 | 1 | 0 | .12 | 0 |
| Wilson,Justin, Pit | L | .000 | 5 | 0 | 0 | 0 | 1 | .000 | 5 | 0 | 0 | 0 | 0 | 0 | 0 | 5 | 1 | 73.2 | 5 | 10 | 0 | 0 | 1.000 | 10 | 3 | 1 | 0 | .30 | 0 |
| Withrow,Chris, LAD | R | .000 | 1 | 0 | 0 | 0 | 1 | .000 | 1 | 0 | 0 | 0 | 0 | 0 | 0 | 1 | 1 | 34.2 | 0 | 1 | 0 | 0 | 1.000 | 4 | 1 | 0 | 0 | .25 | 0 |
| Wolf,Ross, Tex | R | - | 0 | 0 | 0 | 0 | 0 | .000 | 1 | 0 | 0 | 0 | 0 | 0 | 0 | 1 | 0 | 47.2 | 7 | 5 | 1 | 3 | .923 | 3 | 2 | 0 | 0 | .67 | -1 |
| Wood,Alex, Atl | L | .000 | 21 | 0 | 0 | 0 | 1 | .000 | 21 | 0 | 0 | 0 | 0 | 0 | 0 | 15 | 1 | 77.2 | 0 | 13 | 0 | 0 | 1.000 | 6 | 3 | 1 | 2 | .50 | 3 |
| Wood,Blake, Cle | R | - | 0 | 0 | 0 | 0 | 0 | .000 | 1 | 0 | 0 | 0 | 0 | 0 | 0 | 1 | 0 | 1.1 | 0 | 0 | 0 | 0 | - | 2 | 0 | 0 | 0 | .00 | 0 |
| Wood,Travis, ChC | L | .222 | 63 | 14 | 3 | 8 | 1 | .180 | 183 | 33 | 6 | 1 | 6 | 18 | 3 | 70 | 13 | 200.0 | 20 | 14 | 1 | 0 | .971 | 7 | 3 | 1 | 0 | .43 | 1 |
| Wooten,Rob, Mil | R | .000 | 1 | 0 | 0 | 0 | 0 | .000 | 1 | 0 | 0 | 0 | 0 | 0 | 0 | 1 | 0 | 27.2 | 0 | 2 | 0 | 0 | 1.000 | 2 | 1 | 0 | 0 | .50 | 0 |
| Workman,Brandon, Bos | R | - | 0 | 0 | 0 | 0 | 0 | - | 0 | 0 | 0 | 0 | 0 | 0 | 0 | 0 | 0 | 41.2 | 0 | 1 | 0 | 0 | 1.000 | 12 | 2 | 0 | 1 | .17 | -2 |
| Worley,Vance, Min | R | .000 | 1 | 0 | 0 | 0 | 0 | .151 | 86 | 13 | 2 | 0 | 0 | 7 | 1 | 30 | 9 | 48.2 | 2 | 11 | 1 | 1 | .929 | 3 | 2 | 0 | 0 | .67 | 1 |
| Wright,Jamey, TB | R | - | 0 | 0 | 0 | 0 | 0 | .146 | 438 | 64 | 15 | 1 | 1 | 17 | 12 | 176 | 51 | 70.0 | 8 | 13 | 0 | 2 | 1.000 | 19 | 3 | 1 | 2 | .16 | -1 |
| Wright,Steven, Bos | R | - | 0 | 0 | 0 | 0 | 0 | - | 0 | 0 | 0 | 0 | 0 | 0 | 0 | 0 | 0 | 13.1 | 0 | 1 | 0 | 0 | 1.000 | 1 | 0 | 0 | 0 | .00 | 1 |
| Wright,Wesley, Hou-TB | L | .000 | 1 | 0 | 0 | 0 | 0 | .063 | 16 | 1 | 0 | 0 | 0 | 0 | 0 | 8 | 1 | 53.2 | 2 | 10 | 0 | 0 | 1.000 | 6 | 1 | 0 | 0 | .17 | 0 |
| Zagurski,Mike, Pit-NYY | L | - | 0 | 0 | 0 | 0 | 0 | - | 0 | 0 | 0 | 0 | 0 | 0 | 0 | 0 | 0 | 6.1 | 0 | 1 | 0 | 0 | 1.000 | 1 | 0 | 0 | 0 | .00 | 0 |
| Zeid,Josh, Hou | R | - | 0 | 0 | 0 | 0 | 0 | - | 0 | 0 | 0 | 0 | 0 | 0 | 0 | 0 | 0 | 27.2 | 2 | 5 | 1 | 0 | .875 | 6 | 2 | 0 | 0 | .33 | 0 |
| Ziegler,Brad, Ari | R | .000 | 2 | 0 | 0 | 0 | 0 | .167 | 6 | 1 | 0 | 0 | 0 | 0 | 0 | 2 | 0 | 73.0 | 3 | 21 | 2 | 0 | .923 | 3 | 1 | 1 | 0 | .33 | 3 |
| Zimmermann,Jordan, Was | R | .123 | 65 | 8 | 0 | 2 | 6 | .168 | 202 | 34 | 4 | 0 | 1 | 11 | 8 | 58 | 28 | 213.1 | 12 | 28 | 2 | 1 | .952 | 19 | 5 | 2 | 0 | .26 | 3 |
| Zito,Barry, SF | L | .147 | 34 | 5 | 0 | 2 | 9 | .102 | 344 | 35 | 0 | 0 | 0 | 11 | 18 | 99 | 56 | 133.1 | 3 | 20 | 0 | 0 | 1.000 | 24 | 9 | 4 | 0 | .38 | 1 |

# Hitters Pitching

| | 2013 Pitching | | | | | | | | | | | Career Pitching | | | | | | | | | | |
|---|---|---|---|---|---|---|---|---|---|---|---|---|---|---|---|---|---|---|---|---|---|---|
| Player | G | W | L | Sv | IP | H | R | ER | BB | SO | ERA | G | W | L | Sv | IP | H | R | ER | BB | SO | ERA |
| Ankiel,Rick, Hou-NYM | - | - | - | - | - | - | - | - | - | - | - | 51 | 13 | 10 | 1 | 242.0 | 198 | 119 | 105 | 130 | 269 | 3.90 |
| Bogusevic,Brian, ChC | - | - | - | - | - | - | - | - | - | - | - | 1 | 0 | 0 | 0 | 1.0 | 3 | 2 | 2 | 0 | 0 | 18.00 |
| Butera,Drew, Min-LAD | - | - | - | - | - | - | - | - | - | - | - | 1 | 0 | 0 | 0 | 1.0 | 0 | 0 | 0 | 1 | 1 | 0.00 |
| Carroll,Jamey, Min-KC | 1 | - | - | - | 1.0 | - | - | - | - | - | 0.00 | 1 | 0 | 0 | 0 | 1.0 | 0 | 0 | 0 | 0 | 0 | 0.00 |
| Cuddyer,Michael, Col | - | - | - | - | - | - | - | - | - | - | - | 1 | 0 | 0 | 0 | 1.0 | 2 | 0 | 0 | 1 | 0 | 0.00 |
| Davis,Chris, Bal | - | - | - | - | - | - | - | - | - | - | - | 1 | 1 | 0 | 0 | 2.0 | 2 | 0 | 0 | 1 | 2 | 0.00 |
| Elmore,Jake, Hou | 1 | - | - | - | 1.0 | - | - | - | - | - | 0.00 | 1 | 0 | 0 | 0 | 1.0 | 0 | 0 | 0 | 0 | 0 | 0.00 |
| Fuld,Sam, TB | 1 | - | - | - | 0.1 | - | - | - | - | - | 0.00 | 1 | 0 | 0 | 0 | 0.1 | 0 | 0 | 0 | 0 | 0 | 0.00 |
| Gentry,Craig, Tex | - | - | - | - | - | - | - | - | - | - | - | 1 | 0 | 0 | 0 | 1.0 | 3 | 2 | 2 | 1 | 0 | 18.00 |
| Gonzalez,Alberto, ChC-NYY | 1 | - | - | - | 0.1 | - | - | - | - | - | 0.00 | 1 | 0 | 0 | 0 | 0.1 | 0 | 0 | 0 | 0 | 0 | 0.00 |
| Green,Nick, Mia | - | - | - | - | - | - | - | - | - | - | - | 1 | 0 | 0 | 0 | 2.0 | 0 | 0 | 0 | 3 | 0 | 0.00 |
| Harrison,Josh, Pit | 1 | - | - | - | 0.1 | - | - | - | - | - | 0.00 | 1 | 0 | 0 | 0 | 0.1 | 0 | 0 | 0 | 0 | 0 | 0.00 |
| Janish,Paul, Atl | - | - | - | - | - | - | - | - | - | - | - | 2 | 0 | 0 | 0 | 2.0 | 9 | 11 | 11 | 2 | 3 | 49.50 |
| Johnson,Rob, StL | 1 | - | - | - | 0.1 | - | - | - | - | 1 | 0.00 | 2 | 0 | 0 | 0 | 1.1 | 0 | 0 | 0 | 0 | 2 | 0.00 |
| Kelly,Don, Det | - | - | - | - | - | - | - | - | - | - | - | 1 | 0 | 0 | 0 | 0.1 | 0 | 0 | 0 | 0 | 0 | 0.00 |
| Mathis,Jeff, Mia | - | - | - | - | - | - | - | - | - | - | - | 2 | 0 | 0 | 0 | 2.0 | 4 | 2 | 2 | 1 | 0 | 9.00 |
| McDonald,Darnell, ChC | - | - | - | - | - | - | - | - | - | - | - | 2 | 0 | 1 | 0 | 2.0 | 3 | 5 | 5 | 4 | 0 | 22.50 |
| McDonald,John, Pit-Cle-Phi-Bos | 1 | - | - | - | 0.1 | 2 | - | - | - | 1 | 0.00 | 1 | 0 | 0 | 0 | 0.1 | 2 | 0 | 0 | 0 | 1 | 0.00 |
| Murphy,David, Tex | 1 | - | - | - | 1.0 | 1 | - | - | - | 1 | 0.00 | 1 | 0 | 0 | 0 | 1.0 | 1 | 0 | 0 | 0 | 1 | 0.00 |
| Raburn,Ryan, Cle | 1 | - | - | - | 1.0 | - | - | - | - | 1 | 0.00 | 1 | 0 | 0 | 0 | 1.0 | 0 | 0 | 0 | 0 | 1 | 0.00 |
| Recker,Anthony, NYM | 1 | - | - | - | 1.0 | 1 | 2 | 2 | 1 | - | 18.00 | 1 | 0 | 0 | 0 | 1.0 | 1 | 2 | 2 | 1 | 0 | 18.00 |
| Ross,Cody, Ari | - | - | - | - | - | - | - | - | - | - | - | 1 | 0 | 0 | 0 | 1.0 | 1 | 0 | 0 | 0 | 0 | 0.00 |
| Schumaker,Skip, LAD | 2 | - | - | - | 2.0 | 3 | - | - | 3 | 1 | 0.00 | 3 | 0 | 0 | 0 | 3.0 | 4 | 2 | 2 | 4 | 3 | 6.00 |
| Swisher,Nick, Cle | - | - | - | - | - | - | - | - | - | - | - | 1 | 0 | 0 | 0 | 1.0 | 1 | 0 | 0 | 1 | 1 | 0.00 |
| Wells,Casper, Oak-CWS-Phi | 2 | - | 1 | - | 1.2 | 3 | 5 | 5 | 4 | 1 | 27.00 | 2 | 0 | 1 | 0 | 1.2 | 3 | 5 | 5 | 4 | 1 | 27.00 |
| Wilson,Josh, Ari | - | - | - | - | - | - | - | - | - | - | - | 3 | 0 | 1 | 0 | 3.0 | 4 | 3 | 3 | 3 | 0 | 9.00 |
| Wise,DeWayne, CWS | - | - | - | - | - | - | - | - | - | - | - | 2 | 0 | 0 | 0 | 1.2 | 1 | 0 | 0 | 1 | 0 | 0.00 |

# Hitter Analysis

**Bill James**

What follows here is a new feature, the "Hitter Analysis". It's a straightforward section, merely intended to put on record some basic information about each major league hitter with 100 or more plate appearances. It's simple information, which was not recorded when Ty Cobb was playing merely because the level of granularity involved exceeds what was practical before the computer age. The categories of these records are:

PA-Plate Appearances

Pit-Pitches Seen

T-Pitches Taken

Sw-Pitches Swung at, or, for you Dizzy Dean fans, Swang at

St-Pitches Taken for a Strike

B-Pitches Taken for a Ball

S/M-Swing and a Miss

F-Foul Balls Hit

InP - Pitches Hit In Play

P/PA-Pitches Per Plate Appearance

GB-Ground Balls Hit

LD-Line Drives

FB-Fly Balls

We have summarized some of this data to characterize hitters as:

a) Aggressive, Patient, Very Aggressive, Very Patient, or Neutral

b) Ground Ball Hitters, Fly Ball Hitters (Air), or Medium

There are some things you can learn by studying this data, and I guess we'll start with names. The major league hitters who saw the most pitches in 2013 were 1. Joey Votto, 2. Mike Trout, 3. Shin Soo Choo Choo, 4. Matt (If I were a) Carpenter, and 5. Dustin Pedroia. The hitters who saw the most pitches per plate appearance were 1. Mike Napoli, 2. Marc Krauss, 3. Josh Satin, 4. George Kottaras, and 5. A. J. Ellis. The hitters who saw the fewest pitches per plate appearance were 1. Cesar Izturis, 2. Joaquin Arias, 3. Steve Lombardozzi, 4. Tony Abreu, and 5. A. J. Pierzynski.

Trout, Votto, Carpenter and Choo, who were among the five players who saw the most pitchers, were also among the five who took the most pitches without offering at them; they were joined on that list by Paul Goldschmidt. Pitches taken as a percentage of pitches seen: 1. Kottaras, 2. Satin, 3. John Jaso, 4. Geovany Soto, and 5. Trout.

Those who Swung at the most pitches were 1. Adam Jones, 2. Jay Bruce, 3. Chris Davis, 4. Torii Hunter, and 5. Josh Hamilton. Pitches swung at as a percentage of pitches seen: 1. Pierzynski, 2. Charlie Culberson, 3. Humberto Quintero, 4. Jimmy Paredes, 5. Adam Jones.

Pitches taken for a strike: 1. Matt Carpenter, 2. Brian Dozier, 3. Martin Prado, 4. Trout, 5. Pedroia. As a percentage of pitches seen: 1. Kottaras, 2. Marco Scutaro, 3. Jamey Carroll, 4. Jose Iglesias, 5. Prado. Scutaro is really interesting; he takes an exceptional number of pitches for a strike (25.2%—the highest of any major league regular) but makes contact when he does swing with fantastic consistency. He swung and missed only 40 times in 2013, or 1.9% of his pitches seen. Every other major league player swung and missed at least 75% more often than Scutaro, per plate appearance.

Pitches taken for a ball: 1. Shin Soo, 2. Goldschmidt, 3. Carlos Santana, 4. Carpenter, 5. Jason Kipnis. As a percentage of pitches seen: 1. Chris Iannetta, 2. Yasmani Grandal, 3. Trout, 4. Choo, 5. Giancarlo Stanton.

Swings and misses: 1. Chris Davis (417), 2. Pedro Alvarez, 3. Jay Bruce, 4. Josh Hamilton, 5. Chris Carter. As a percentage of pitches seen: 1. Rick Ankiel (21.7%), 2. Kelly Shoppach, 3. Jimmy Paredes, 4. Tyler Flowers, 5. Casper Wells. The fewest swings and misses, as a percentage of pitches seen: 1. Scutaro (1.9%), 2. Nonchika Aoki, 3. Prado, 4. Ben Revere, 5. Jeff Keppinger.

Most foul balls hit: 1. Freddie Freeman (561), 2. Panda Bear, 3. Pedroia, 4. Justin Morneau, 5. Adam Jones. Freeman is interesting, too; he led the majors in foul balls hit, and also had extraordinary judgment as to what he should swing at. Freeman took 925 pitches for balls, whereas he took only 185 pitches for called strikes—easily the highest ratio of called balls to strikes in the major leagues. The combination of these two suggests. .. .I haven't seen Freddie Freeman play a whole lot, so I'm reconstructing from the data. The combination suggests that he has an exceptional ability to spoil a borderline pitch by fouling it off, and great confidence in his ability to do this.

Anyway, foul balls as a percentage of pitches seen: 1. Pablo Sandoval, 2. Pierzynski, 3. Jake Marisnick, 4. Corey Dickerson, 5. Humberto Quintero. Fewest foul balls as a percentage of pitches seen: 1. Kottaras, 2. Omar Infante, 3. Adam Rosales, 4. Lance Berkman, 5. Jonny Gomes.

Most balls put into play: Alexei Ramirez, 2. Pedroia, 3. Daniel Murphy, 4. Norichika Aoki, 5. Nick Markakis. As a percentage of pitches seen: 1. Cesar Izutris (27.6%), 2. Lombardozzi, 3. Joaquin Arias, 4. Omar Infante, 5. Alexei Ramirez. Fewest balls put in play as a percentage of pitches seen: 1. Kottaras (10.3%), 2. Napoli, 3. Chris Carter, 4. Dan Uggla, 5. Ankiel. Highest ratios of balls in play to foul balls: 1. Infante (2.15 to 1), 2. Ben Revere, 3. Prado, 4. Keppinger, 5. Cesar Izturis. Highest ratios of foul balls to balls in play: 1. Rick Ankiel (1.60 to 1), 2. Jason Giambi, 3. Juan Francisco, 3. Layce Nix, 4. Brett Wallace.

Norichika Aoki hit 328 ground balls in 2013, the only major league player to hit 300; he was followed on that list by Elvis Andrus, Jean Segura, Pedroia and Denard Span. Per pitches seen, the major league leader in ground balls was Wil Nieves, followed by Cesar Izturis, Ben Revere, Wilson Ramos and Aoki. The fewest ground balls, per pitch seen: 1. Rick Ankiel, 2. Chris Carter, 3. Geovany Soto, 4. Kottaras, 5. Lucas Duda.

At this point we can definitely conclude that if Cesar Izturis is on a list, George Kottaras will be on the other end of the list. The polar opposite of Cesar Izturis is George Kottaras. More on that in a moment, but a few more lists first. The major league leader in the number of line drives hit was Matt Carpenter (145), followed by James Loney, Robinson Cano, Nick Markakis and Alexei Ramirez. Per pitches seen the leader was Loney (64 per 1000 pitches), followed by four guys who don't play very much (more on that later, too.) Well...Infante was on that list; I guess he's a regular. Fewest line drives, per 1000 pitches seen:

1. Dan Uggla, 2. David Ross, 3. Kelly Shoppach, 4. Collin Cowgill (I must have more Cowgill), and 5. Chris Colabello.

Kyle Seager hit 223 fly balls and pop outs in 2013, the most of any major league player; he was followed by Adrian Beltre, Jed Lowrie, Andrelton Simmons and Daniel Murphy. Per pitches seen, the #1 fly ball maniac was Chad Tracy (118 fly balls per 1000 pitches), followed by Scott Hairston, Luis Cruz, Omar Infante and Yuniesky Betancourt. Infante makes both the list of hitters hitting the most fly balls (per pitch seen) and the most line drives, and he does this because a) he is a very good hitter, and b) he almost never fouls the pitch off. He's kind of the opposite of Freddie Freeman, among the good hitters; he's the guy who doesn't foul anything off. Fewest fly balls per 1000 pitches seen: 1. Jonathan Villar, 2-5, a bunch of guys who are a great deal like Jonathan Villar. Young players who are still trying to figure out the game.

I hope you got something out of that; I know I went on too long with the lists, but it's interesting to me. But I should have cut it off to get to some general conclusions we can draw from studying this data.

First, fly ball hitters are patient hitters, and impatient hitters hit the ball on the ground. We sort of intuitively knew this anyway, of course; we know that a guy like Joey Votto, Babe Ruth or Ted Williams is sorting through pitches, trying to find something he can hit into the air. But the data clearly shows that these two biases go together. Aggressive hitters are ground ball hitters.

When we sort the hitters into five groups one way and three groups the other way, we have 15 possible "groups" or "codes" to describe each hitter. There were 453 major league hitters in 2013 who had 100 or more plate appearances. Those 453 hitters can be sorted into 15 groups in this way:

| | Very Patient | Patient | Neutral | Aggressive | Very Aggressive |
|---|---|---|---|---|---|
| Air | 51 | 42 | 39 | 28 | 22 |
| Medium | 21 | 19 | 20 | 16 | 15 |
| Ground | 19 | 30 | 32 | 46 | 53 |

That's about as crystal clear as data can get, isn't it? The more patient a hitter is, the more likely he is to hit the ball in the air. There were 51 major league hitters who were Very Patient and had a strong tendency to hit the ball in the air, whereas there were only 19 major league hitters who were Very Patient, but hit the ball on the ground. On the other end of the aggressiveness spectrum, the ratio was 53-22 going the other way.

So that's worth knowing, and that relates to the Kottaras/Izturis thing I was talking about a minute ago; Kottaras is an extreme type of a patient/fly ball hitter, while Izturis the Elder is an extreme type of an aggressive ground ball hitter.

There's a second general point here, which has to do with Line Drive hitters. When I was young and naïve and didn't have access to good data, I would have sorted hitters into three groups: Fly Ball Hitters, Ground Ball Hitters, and Line Drive Hitters. The fallacy in doing that, though, is this: Hitting Line Drives is a dramatically better outcome than hitting fly balls or ground balls. When you hit a ground ball or a fly ball, your batting average is going to be around .250. When you hit a line drive, it's going to be around .750.

Because this is true, everybody is trying to hit line drives. Fly ball hitter or ground ball hitter, the line drive is the preferred outcome for all of them. Thus, getting the line drive is, in a certain sense, an accident. It is the "intended accident", the outcome that the hitter is trying to make happen, but it happens so rarely that it is, to an extent, a fluke outcome. No major league hitter hits more than 6 line drives per 100 pitches seen. No hitter can hit a line drive whenever he wants to hit one. It's just. . .every hitter is trying to do that, and once in a while the bat collides with the ball dead center, and the result is a line drive.

James Loney led the majors in Line Drives per pitches seen in 2013, and that's because he is good hitter, but it also means that he was hitting in good luck. Second on the list was Willie Bloomquist, third was DJ LeMahieu. Not saying those guys aren't good hitters, but they were hitting in good luck. Line drives are, to a certain extent, luck.

That's why I am reluctant to describe anyone as a "line drive hitter". Everybody is a line drive hitter.

In the chart I showed you before, of the 15 types of hitters, there are good hitters and weak hitters in every group. Some groups are better than others. Probably the very aggressive/ground ball hitters are the weakest group of hitters, but Robinson Cano is a very aggressive/ground ball hitter, and he's pretty good. OK, it's kind of a phony example, because Cano is right on the cutoff lines both ways, but still. . . that's where we put him.

But because the line drive is the best outcome, the best hitters do tend to be in the "medium" categories. If a hitter is very prone to hit ground balls, generally speaking, he is somebody that the pitcher is very happy to see coming to the plate. If he is very prone to hit fly balls, not so much, because some of the fly balls will turn out to be Big Flies.

But if the hitter is TOO prone either to hit ground balls or to hit fly balls, that will reduce the number of Line Drives. The best hitters are the "medium" group. We put only 20% of the hitters in the "medium" group, with 40% in the "Ground" group and 40% in the "Air" group. But the "medium" 20% group includes more than its share of the best hitters.

# Hitter Analysis

| Hitter | PA | Pit | T | Sw | St | B | S/M | F | In P | P/PA | Group | GB | LD | FB | Hits |
|---|---|---|---|---|---|---|---|---|---|---|---|---|---|---|---|
| Tony Abreu# | 147 | 470 | 211 | 259 | 73 | 138 | 53 | 99 | 107 | 3.20 | Very Aggressive | 49 | 27 | 30 | Ground |
| Dustin Ackley* | 427 | 1738 | 1069 | 669 | 393 | 676 | 94 | 258 | 317 | 4.07 | Very Patient | 159 | 68 | 84 | Ground |
| David Adams | 152 | 602 | 344 | 258 | 131 | 213 | 56 | 104 | 98 | 3.96 | Patient | 54 | 16 | 27 | Ground |
| Matt Adams* | 319 | 1343 | 754 | 589 | 233 | 521 | 143 | 230 | 216 | 4.21 | Very Patient | 96 | 42 | 78 | Medium |
| Zoilo Almonte# | 113 | 388 | 197 | 191 | 67 | 130 | 34 | 69 | 88 | 3.43 | Very Aggressive | 47 | 20 | 21 | Ground |
| Yonder Alonso* | 375 | 1334 | 708 | 626 | 183 | 525 | 102 | 230 | 294 | 3.56 | Very Aggressive | 135 | 60 | 97 | Ground |
| Jose Altuve | 672 | 2207 | 1138 | 1069 | 407 | 731 | 147 | 369 | 553 | 3.28 | Very Aggressive | 268 | 123 | 154 | Ground |
| Pedro Alvarez* | 614 | 2415 | 1231 | 1184 | 326 | 905 | 412 | 396 | 376 | 3.93 | Patient | 162 | 77 | 137 | Medium |
| Alexi Amarista* | 396 | 1514 | 765 | 749 | 247 | 518 | 118 | 316 | 315 | 3.82 | Neutral | 130 | 70 | 105 | Medium |
| Elvis Andrus | 698 | 2780 | 1666 | 1114 | 595 | 1071 | 158 | 411 | 545 | 3.98 | Patient | 291 | 110 | 116 | Ground |
| Rick Ankiel* | 136 | 539 | 245 | 294 | 64 | 181 | 117 | 109 | 68 | 3.96 | Patient | 18 | 14 | 35 | Air |
| Norichika Aoki* | 674 | 2439 | 1389 | 1050 | 453 | 936 | 82 | 400 | 568 | 3.62 | Very Aggressive | 328 | 96 | 119 | Ground |
| Oswaldo Arcia* | 378 | 1543 | 762 | 781 | 229 | 533 | 250 | 297 | 234 | 4.08 | Very Patient | 99 | 40 | 95 | Air |
| Nolan Arenado | 514 | 1726 | 767 | 959 | 238 | 529 | 179 | 362 | 418 | 3.36 | Very Aggressive | 177 | 99 | 140 | Medium |
| J.P. Arencibia | 497 | 1912 | 901 | 1011 | 274 | 627 | 295 | 388 | 328 | 3.85 | Neutral | 120 | 64 | 144 | Air |
| Joaquin Arias | 236 | 749 | 328 | 421 | 120 | 208 | 69 | 154 | 198 | 3.17 | Very Aggressive | 100 | 40 | 54 | Ground |
| Cody Asche* | 179 | 635 | 332 | 303 | 98 | 234 | 74 | 109 | 120 | 3.55 | Very Aggressive | 52 | 25 | 42 | Medium |
| Alex Avila* | 379 | 1550 | 907 | 643 | 272 | 635 | 188 | 233 | 222 | 4.09 | Very Patient | 92 | 61 | 65 | Ground |
| Mike Aviles | 394 | 1375 | 694 | 681 | 265 | 429 | 88 | 258 | 335 | 3.49 | Very Aggressive | 142 | 65 | 121 | Medium |
| Erick Aybar# | 589 | 2045 | 1033 | 1012 | 375 | 658 | 126 | 382 | 504 | 3.47 | Very Aggressive | 237 | 109 | 131 | Ground |
| Jeff Baker | 175 | 715 | 407 | 308 | 134 | 273 | 79 | 122 | 107 | 4.09 | Very Patient | 52 | 19 | 36 | Ground |
| Clint Barmes | 330 | 1168 | 571 | 597 | 220 | 351 | 118 | 235 | 244 | 3.54 | Very Aggressive | 89 | 52 | 93 | Air |
| Brandon Barnes | 445 | 1699 | 829 | 870 | 278 | 551 | 250 | 331 | 289 | 3.82 | Neutral | 133 | 55 | 88 | Ground |
| Darwin Barney | 555 | 2128 | 1154 | 974 | 446 | 708 | 98 | 427 | 447 | 3.83 | Neutral | 201 | 84 | 157 | Medium |
| Daric Barton* | 120 | 453 | 275 | 178 | 97 | 178 | 26 | 64 | 88 | 3.78 | Aggressive | 36 | 19 | 32 | Air |
| Jose Bautista | 528 | 2236 | 1377 | 859 | 469 | 908 | 138 | 349 | 372 | 4.23 | Very Patient | 153 | 60 | 159 | Air |
| Mike Baxter* | 155 | 647 | 370 | 277 | 114 | 256 | 39 | 133 | 105 | 4.17 | Very Patient | 33 | 25 | 46 | Air |
| Jason Bay | 236 | 959 | 571 | 388 | 200 | 371 | 106 | 136 | 146 | 4.06 | Very Patient | 60 | 26 | 58 | Air |
| Gordon Beckham | 408 | 1555 | 785 | 770 | 231 | 554 | 115 | 335 | 320 | 3.81 | Neutral | 113 | 74 | 132 | Air |
| Brandon Belt* | 571 | 2271 | 1118 | 1153 | 252 | 866 | 244 | 521 | 388 | 3.98 | Patient | 133 | 94 | 160 | Air |
| Carlos Beltran# | 600 | 2181 | 1168 | 1013 | 359 | 809 | 190 | 352 | 471 | 3.64 | Very Aggressive | 165 | 112 | 192 | Air |
| Adrian Beltre | 690 | 2534 | 1314 | 1220 | 411 | 903 | 183 | 482 | 555 | 3.67 | Aggressive | 212 | 121 | 222 | Air |
| Lance Berkman# | 294 | 1159 | 708 | 451 | 220 | 488 | 105 | 142 | 204 | 3.94 | Patient | 90 | 30 | 80 | Air |
| Roger Bernadina* | 250 | 976 | 561 | 415 | 185 | 376 | 105 | 146 | 164 | 3.90 | Neutral | 78 | 26 | 50 | Ground |
| Yuniesky Betancourt | 409 | 1387 | 634 | 753 | 191 | 443 | 143 | 287 | 323 | 3.39 | Very Aggressive | 139 | 52 | 132 | Air |
| Jeff Bianchi | 252 | 889 | 400 | 489 | 133 | 267 | 99 | 196 | 194 | 3.53 | Very Aggressive | 89 | 38 | 62 | Ground |
| Charlie Blackmon* | 258 | 936 | 450 | 486 | 158 | 292 | 84 | 203 | 199 | 3.63 | Very Aggressive | 81 | 53 | 61 | Medium |
| Gregor Blanco* | 511 | 1943 | 1079 | 864 | 340 | 739 | 135 | 366 | 363 | 3.80 | Neutral | 155 | 97 | 98 | Ground |
| Henry Blanco | 150 | 584 | 314 | 270 | 105 | 209 | 75 | 96 | 99 | 3.89 | Neutral | 33 | 21 | 44 | Air |
| Kyle Blanks | 308 | 1220 | 593 | 627 | 151 | 442 | 183 | 247 | 197 | 3.96 | Patient | 90 | 44 | 63 | Ground |
| Willie Bloomquist | 150 | 515 | 262 | 253 | 81 | 181 | 38 | 86 | 129 | 3.43 | Very Aggressive | 63 | 32 | 33 | Ground |
| Brian Bogusevic* | 155 | 595 | 286 | 309 | 92 | 194 | 86 | 114 | 109 | 3.84 | Neutral | 55 | 25 | 28 | Ground |
| Emilio Bonifacio# | 461 | 1747 | 871 | 876 | 279 | 592 | 174 | 376 | 326 | 3.79 | Neutral | 161 | 60 | 80 | Ground |
| Julio Borbon* | 118 | 442 | 241 | 201 | 84 | 157 | 47 | 70 | 84 | 3.75 | Aggressive | 38 | 14 | 20 | Ground |
| Peter Bourjos | 196 | 726 | 394 | 332 | 147 | 247 | 75 | 120 | 137 | 3.70 | Aggressive | 74 | 18 | 34 | Ground |
| Michael Bourn* | 575 | 2233 | 1266 | 967 | 462 | 804 | 226 | 340 | 401 | 3.88 | Neutral | 216 | 75 | 91 | Ground |
| Jackie Bradley Jr.* | 107 | 436 | 246 | 190 | 91 | 155 | 52 | 74 | 64 | 4.07 | Very Patient | 40 | 10 | 14 | Ground |
| Michael Brantley* | 611 | 2243 | 1308 | 935 | 452 | 856 | 87 | 348 | 500 | 3.67 | Aggressive | 232 | 115 | 147 | Ground |
| Rob Brantly* | 243 | 854 | 455 | 399 | 145 | 310 | 94 | 132 | 173 | 3.51 | Very Aggressive | 83 | 33 | 55 | Ground |
| Ryan Braun | 253 | 973 | 537 | 436 | 159 | 378 | 93 | 173 | 170 | 3.85 | Neutral | 88 | 27 | 55 | Ground |
| Andrew Brown | 165 | 641 | 311 | 330 | 90 | 221 | 112 | 110 | 108 | 3.88 | Neutral | 49 | 16 | 41 | Medium |
| Domonic Brown* | 540 | 2080 | 1064 | 1016 | 265 | 799 | 215 | 398 | 403 | 3.85 | Neutral | 171 | 92 | 140 | Medium |
| Jay Bruce* | 697 | 2762 | 1422 | 1340 | 363 | 1059 | 404 | 489 | 446 | 3.96 | Patient | 163 | 106 | 175 | Air |
| John Buck | 431 | 1682 | 844 | 838 | 217 | 627 | 238 | 310 | 290 | 3.90 | Neutral | 126 | 55 | 108 | Medium |
| Billy Butler | 668 | 2609 | 1500 | 1109 | 475 | 1025 | 189 | 436 | 484 | 3.91 | Neutral | 257 | 99 | 128 | Ground |
| Marlon Byrd | 579 | 2115 | 961 | 1154 | 291 | 670 | 326 | 432 | 396 | 3.65 | Aggressive | 155 | 94 | 146 | Air |
| Asdrubal Cabrera# | 562 | 2162 | 1105 | 1057 | 337 | 768 | 215 | 437 | 405 | 3.85 | Neutral | 144 | 91 | 161 | Air |
| Everth Cabrera# | 435 | 1749 | 1019 | 730 | 355 | 664 | 101 | 306 | 323 | 4.02 | Patient | 182 | 62 | 57 | Ground |
| Melky Cabrera# | 372 | 1391 | 734 | 657 | 251 | 483 | 83 | 272 | 302 | 3.74 | Aggressive | 139 | 66 | 94 | Ground |
| Miguel Cabrera | 652 | 2425 | 1219 | 1206 | 259 | 960 | 238 | 505 | 463 | 3.72 | Aggressive | 179 | 111 | 173 | Air |
| Lorenzo Cain | 442 | 1760 | 988 | 772 | 375 | 613 | 149 | 308 | 315 | 3.98 | Patient | 155 | 69 | 91 | Ground |
| Kole Calhoun* | 222 | 867 | 481 | 386 | 155 | 326 | 75 | 152 | 159 | 3.91 | Neutral | 65 | 36 | 57 | Air |
| Alberto Callaspo# | 516 | 1975 | 1173 | 802 | 382 | 791 | 78 | 309 | 415 | 3.83 | Neutral | 164 | 101 | 146 | Air |
| Robinson Cano* | 681 | 2476 | 1280 | 1196 | 352 | 928 | 166 | 505 | 525 | 3.64 | Very Aggressive | 232 | 136 | 156 | Ground |
| Mike Carp* | 243 | 964 | 561 | 403 | 185 | 376 | 92 | 159 | 152 | 3.97 | Patient | 63 | 37 | 52 | Medium |
| Matt Carpenter* | 717 | 2954 | 1854 | 1100 | 717 | 1137 | 128 | 434 | 538 | 4.12 | Very Patient | 206 | 145 | 181 | Air |
| Jamey Carroll | 249 | 999 | 596 | 403 | 251 | 345 | 40 | 171 | 192 | 4.01 | Patient | 107 | 47 | 36 | Ground |
| Chris Carter | 585 | 2464 | 1356 | 1108 | 412 | 944 | 395 | 414 | 299 | 4.21 | Very Patient | 92 | 67 | 140 | Air |
| Alexi Casilla# | 125 | 412 | 210 | 202 | 77 | 133 | 33 | 73 | 96 | 3.30 | Very Aggressive | 51 | 15 | 24 | Ground |
| Welington Castillo | 428 | 1638 | 927 | 711 | 312 | 615 | 157 | 268 | 286 | 3.83 | Neutral | 125 | 62 | 98 | Medium |
| Jason Castro* | 491 | 2023 | 1109 | 914 | 331 | 778 | 261 | 344 | 309 | 4.12 | Very Patient | 122 | 78 | 109 | Air |
| Starlin Castro | 705 | 2716 | 1433 | 1283 | 498 | 935 | 248 | 496 | 539 | 3.85 | Neutral | 273 | 107 | 158 | Ground |

# Hitter Analysis

| Hitter | PA | Pit | T | Sw | St | B | S/M | F | In P | P/PA | Group | GB | LD | FB | Hits |
|---|---|---|---|---|---|---|---|---|---|---|---|---|---|---|---|
| Ronny Cedeno | 288 | 1068 | 532 | 536 | 204 | 328 | 111 | 227 | 198 | 3.71 | Aggressive | 98 | 42 | 50 | Ground |
| Yoenis Cespedes | 574 | 2169 | 1071 | 1098 | 309 | 762 | 296 | 407 | 395 | 3.78 | Aggressive | 149 | 66 | 180 | Air |
| Endy Chavez* | 279 | 994 | 521 | 473 | 204 | 317 | 74 | 160 | 239 | 3.56 | Very Aggressive | 123 | 50 | 59 | Ground |
| Eric Chavez* | 254 | 998 | 518 | 480 | 168 | 350 | 80 | 211 | 188 | 3.93 | Patient | 78 | 42 | 68 | Air |
| Lonnie Chisenhall* | 308 | 1168 | 553 | 615 | 175 | 378 | 108 | 273 | 234 | 3.79 | Neutral | 89 | 46 | 98 | Air |
| Shin-Soo Choo* | 712 | 3010 | 1820 | 1190 | 537 | 1283 | 248 | 501 | 441 | 4.23 | Very Patient | 215 | 92 | 128 | Ground |
| Pedro Ciriaco | 137 | 474 | 229 | 245 | 68 | 161 | 57 | 84 | 104 | 3.46 | Very Aggressive | 45 | 20 | 34 | Medium |
| Chris Coghlan* | 214 | 793 | 459 | 334 | 153 | 306 | 77 | 104 | 153 | 3.71 | Aggressive | 76 | 32 | 45 | Ground |
| Chris Colabello | 181 | 731 | 393 | 338 | 107 | 286 | 121 | 115 | 102 | 4.04 | Patient | 65 | 14 | 23 | Ground |
| Hank Conger# | 255 | 1023 | 548 | 475 | 169 | 379 | 123 | 179 | 173 | 4.01 | Patient | 66 | 33 | 69 | Air |
| Carlos Corporan# | 210 | 807 | 389 | 418 | 117 | 272 | 114 | 171 | 133 | 3.84 | Neutral | 58 | 26 | 48 | Medium |
| Collin Cowgill | 162 | 630 | 357 | 273 | 133 | 224 | 72 | 88 | 113 | 3.89 | Neutral | 55 | 12 | 40 | Ground |
| Zack Cozart | 618 | 2272 | 1196 | 1076 | 434 | 762 | 188 | 400 | 488 | 3.68 | Aggressive | 237 | 85 | 149 | Ground |
| Allen Craig | 563 | 2134 | 1168 | 966 | 393 | 775 | 177 | 376 | 413 | 3.79 | Neutral | 186 | 111 | 116 | Ground |
| Brandon Crawford* | 550 | 2070 | 1101 | 969 | 376 | 725 | 208 | 354 | 407 | 3.76 | Aggressive | 198 | 76 | 128 | Ground |
| Carl Crawford* | 469 | 1699 | 873 | 826 | 262 | 611 | 130 | 324 | 371 | 3.62 | Very Aggressive | 173 | 85 | 111 | Ground |
| Coco Crisp# | 584 | 2355 | 1391 | 964 | 468 | 923 | 123 | 383 | 458 | 4.03 | Patient | 183 | 88 | 178 | Air |
| Trevor Crowe# | 181 | 674 | 353 | 321 | 123 | 230 | 69 | 126 | 126 | 3.72 | Aggressive | 61 | 24 | 37 | Ground |
| Luis Cruz | 187 | 634 | 304 | 330 | 97 | 207 | 59 | 127 | 144 | 3.39 | Very Aggressive | 51 | 25 | 65 | Air |
| Nelson Cruz | 456 | 1797 | 961 | 836 | 297 | 664 | 233 | 295 | 308 | 3.94 | Patient | 129 | 52 | 127 | Air |
| Tony Cruz | 129 | 459 | 225 | 234 | 77 | 148 | 47 | 89 | 98 | 3.56 | Very Aggressive | 53 | 18 | 27 | Ground |
| Michael Cuddyer | 540 | 2112 | 1136 | 976 | 371 | 765 | 210 | 374 | 392 | 3.91 | Patient | 195 | 79 | 118 | Ground |
| Charlie Culberson | 104 | 356 | 146 | 210 | 44 | 102 | 61 | 72 | 77 | 3.42 | Very Aggressive | 42 | 17 | 18 | Ground |
| Jordan Danks* | 179 | 685 | 357 | 328 | 86 | 271 | 112 | 113 | 103 | 3.83 | Neutral | 40 | 28 | 34 | Medium |
| Travis dArnaud' | 112 | 453 | 258 | 195 | 80 | 178 | 43 | 73 | 79 | 4.04 | Patient | 37 | 14 | 28 | Medium |
| Chris Davis* | 673 | 2679 | 1355 | 1324 | 303 | 1052 | 417 | 515 | 392 | 3.98 | Patient | 127 | 86 | 179 | Air |
| Ike Davis* | 377 | 1565 | 913 | 652 | 253 | 660 | 171 | 263 | 218 | 4.15 | Very Patient | 98 | 43 | 76 | Medium |
| Khris Davis | 153 | 620 | 311 | 309 | 82 | 229 | 84 | 122 | 103 | 4.05 | Patient | 44 | 21 | 38 | Medium |
| Rajai Davis | 360 | 1298 | 625 | 673 | 213 | 412 | 128 | 278 | 267 | 3.61 | Very Aggressive | 104 | 60 | 100 | Air |
| Alejandro De Aza* | 675 | 2749 | 1541 | 1208 | 527 | 1014 | 243 | 493 | 472 | 4.07 | Very Patient | 185 | 112 | 157 | Medium |
| David DeJesus* | 439 | 1773 | 1067 | 706 | 399 | 668 | 108 | 283 | 315 | 4.04 | Patient | 130 | 60 | 122 | Air |
| Chris Denorfia | 520 | 2034 | 1192 | 842 | 432 | 760 | 169 | 280 | 393 | 3.91 | Patient | 217 | 81 | 93 | Ground |
| Mark DeRosa | 236 | 952 | 507 | 445 | 135 | 372 | 127 | 160 | 158 | 4.03 | Patient | 72 | 32 | 54 | Medium |
| Daniel Descalso* | 358 | 1271 | 666 | 605 | 215 | 451 | 111 | 217 | 277 | 3.55 | Very Aggressive | 130 | 49 | 94 | Ground |
| Ian Desmond | 655 | 2422 | 1202 | 1220 | 366 | 836 | 309 | 449 | 462 | 3.70 | Aggressive | 197 | 102 | 155 | Medium |
| Chris Dickerson* | 109 | 424 | 217 | 207 | 74 | 143 | 70 | 68 | 69 | 3.89 | Neutral | 24 | 17 | 26 | Air |
| Corey Dickerson* | 213 | 868 | 417 | 451 | 142 | 275 | 87 | 208 | 156 | 4.08 | Very Patient | 62 | 40 | 52 | Medium |
| Derek Dietrich* | 233 | 865 | 430 | 435 | 143 | 287 | 100 | 176 | 159 | 3.71 | Aggressive | 64 | 39 | 56 | Air |
| Andy Dirks* | 484 | 1770 | 906 | 864 | 256 | 650 | 185 | 323 | 356 | 3.66 | Aggressive | 147 | 86 | 114 | Medium |
| Greg Dobbs* | 267 | 1005 | 493 | 512 | 138 | 355 | 85 | 227 | 200 | 3.76 | Aggressive | 87 | 46 | 67 | Medium |
| Matt Dominguez | 589 | 2184 | 1177 | 1007 | 428 | 749 | 170 | 381 | 456 | 3.71 | Aggressive | 191 | 85 | 178 | Air |
| Josh Donaldson | 668 | 2697 | 1506 | 1191 | 447 | 1059 | 252 | 463 | 476 | 4.04 | Patient | 208 | 98 | 169 | Medium |
| Ryan Doumit# | 538 | 2118 | 1158 | 960 | 349 | 809 | 232 | 338 | 390 | 3.94 | Patient | 185 | 76 | 129 | Ground |
| Brian Dozier | 623 | 2595 | 1548 | 1047 | 607 | 941 | 169 | 432 | 445 | 4.17 | Very Patient | 166 | 91 | 181 | Air |
| Stephen Drew* | 501 | 2052 | 1224 | 828 | 428 | 796 | 191 | 315 | 322 | 4.10 | Very Patient | 107 | 81 | 134 | Air |
| Lucas Duda* | 384 | 1614 | 1007 | 607 | 321 | 686 | 179 | 210 | 218 | 4.20 | Very Patient | 69 | 43 | 105 | Air |
| Adam Dunn* | 607 | 2606 | 1557 | 1049 | 457 | 1100 | 326 | 384 | 339 | 4.29 | Very Patient | 130 | 66 | 143 | Air |
| Jarrod Dyson* | 239 | 933 | 540 | 393 | 213 | 327 | 60 | 161 | 172 | 3.90 | Neutral | 88 | 26 | 37 | Ground |
| Adam Eaton* | 277 | 1091 | 630 | 461 | 235 | 395 | 56 | 195 | 210 | 3.94 | Patient | 113 | 37 | 49 | Ground |
| A.J. Ellis | 448 | 1958 | 1224 | 734 | 458 | 766 | 111 | 301 | 322 | 4.37 | Very Patient | 140 | 59 | 117 | Medium |
| Mark Ellis | 480 | 1983 | 1123 | 860 | 439 | 684 | 120 | 370 | 370 | 4.13 | Very Patient | 153 | 88 | 119 | Medium |
| Jacoby Ellsbury* | 636 | 2454 | 1340 | 1114 | 442 | 898 | 135 | 487 | 488 | 3.86 | Neutral | 247 | 102 | 137 | Ground |
| Jake Elmore | 136 | 526 | 328 | 198 | 128 | 200 | 28 | 67 | 103 | 3.87 | Neutral | 40 | 26 | 31 | Medium |
| Edwin Encarnacion | 621 | 2461 | 1454 | 1007 | 439 | 1015 | 159 | 375 | 473 | 3.96 | Patient | 166 | 102 | 205 | Air |
| Alcides Escobar | 642 | 2245 | 1082 | 1163 | 412 | 670 | 178 | 449 | 536 | 3.50 | Very Aggressive | 238 | 119 | 160 | Ground |
| Eduardo Escobar# | 179 | 709 | 350 | 359 | 112 | 238 | 67 | 158 | 134 | 3.96 | Patient | 54 | 27 | 48 | Air |
| Yunel Escobar | 578 | 2129 | 1183 | 946 | 334 | 849 | 159 | 342 | 445 | 3.68 | Aggressive | 233 | 85 | 118 | Ground |
| Danny Espinosa# | 167 | 563 | 251 | 312 | 74 | 177 | 97 | 102 | 113 | 3.37 | Very Aggressive | 56 | 11 | 42 | Ground |
| Andre Ethier* | 553 | 2162 | 1170 | 992 | 318 | 852 | 203 | 399 | 390 | 3.91 | Neutral | 152 | 95 | 143 | Air |
| Tim Federowicz | 173 | 635 | 338 | 297 | 116 | 222 | 95 | 95 | 107 | 3.67 | Aggressive | 47 | 23 | 35 | Medium |
| Prince Fielder* | 712 | 2618 | 1445 | 1173 | 404 | 1041 | 261 | 401 | 511 | 3.68 | Aggressive | 209 | 117 | 185 | Air |
| Ryan Flaherty* | 271 | 1040 | 550 | 490 | 150 | 400 | 128 | 177 | 185 | 3.84 | Neutral | 89 | 29 | 65 | Ground |
| Wilmer Flores | 101 | 395 | 194 | 201 | 71 | 123 | 42 | 86 | 73 | 3.91 | Neutral | 37 | 16 | 20 | Ground |
| Pedro Florimon# | 446 | 1801 | 1003 | 798 | 338 | 665 | 192 | 310 | 296 | 4.04 | Patient | 129 | 64 | 83 | Ground |
| Tyler Flowers | 275 | 1018 | 490 | 528 | 157 | 333 | 183 | 182 | 163 | 3.70 | Aggressive | 68 | 28 | 67 | Air |
| Logan Forsythe | 243 | 956 | 550 | 406 | 195 | 355 | 85 | 153 | 168 | 3.93 | Patient | 70 | 47 | 48 | Ground |
| Dexter Fowler# | 492 | 1953 | 1048 | 905 | 241 | 807 | 223 | 366 | 316 | 3.97 | Patient | 130 | 72 | 106 | Medium |
| Juan Francisco* | 385 | 1511 | 759 | 752 | 212 | 547 | 233 | 307 | 212 | 3.92 | Patient | 96 | 37 | 78 | Medium |
| Jeff Francoeur | 256 | 958 | 413 | 545 | 114 | 299 | 143 | 218 | 184 | 3.74 | Aggressive | 86 | 32 | 66 | Medium |
| Kevin Frandsen | 278 | 960 | 459 | 501 | 154 | 305 | 70 | 205 | 226 | 3.45 | Very Aggressive | 126 | 41 | 55 | Ground |
| Nick Franklin# | 412 | 1690 | 974 | 716 | 334 | 640 | 190 | 269 | 257 | 4.10 | Very Patient | 88 | 62 | 105 | Air |
| Todd Frazier | 600 | 2297 | 1167 | 1130 | 330 | 837 | 278 | 441 | 411 | 3.83 | Neutral | 172 | 74 | 162 | Air |
| Freddie Freeman* | 629 | 2398 | 1107 | 1291 | 185 | 922 | 295 | 561 | 435 | 3.81 | Neutral | 166 | 116 | 153 | Air |
| David Freese | 521 | 2023 | 1099 | 924 | 327 | 772 | 207 | 358 | 359 | 3.88 | Neutral | 198 | 75 | 86 | Ground |
| Nate Freiman | 208 | 772 | 426 | 346 | 134 | 292 | 68 | 117 | 161 | 3.71 | Aggressive | 61 | 38 | 62 | Air |

# Hitter Analysis

| Hitter | PA | Pit | T | Sw | St | B | S/M | F | In P | P/PA | Group | GB | LD | FB | Hits |
|---|---|---|---|---|---|---|---|---|---|---|---|---|---|---|---|
| Sam Fuld* | 200 | 770 | 460 | 310 | 189 | 271 | 36 | 120 | 154 | 3.85 | Neutral | 76 | 34 | 37 | Ground |
| Freddy Galvis# | 222 | 844 | 411 | 433 | 146 | 265 | 79 | 191 | 163 | 3.80 | Neutral | 56 | 29 | 71 | Air |
| Avisail Garcia | 256 | 919 | 389 | 530 | 99 | 290 | 149 | 194 | 187 | 3.59 | Very Aggressive | 105 | 34 | 48 | Ground |
| Leury Garcia# | 111 | 400 | 205 | 195 | 79 | 126 | 58 | 67 | 70 | 3.60 | Very Aggressive | 31 | 17 | 20 | Ground |
| Brett Gardner* | 609 | 2577 | 1518 | 1059 | 559 | 959 | 151 | 486 | 422 | 4.23 | Very Patient | 165 | 93 | 141 | Medium |
| Evan Gattis | 382 | 1313 | 594 | 719 | 165 | 429 | 166 | 277 | 276 | 3.44 | Very Aggressive | 113 | 40 | 123 | Air |
| Scooter Gennett* | 230 | 763 | 338 | 425 | 109 | 229 | 73 | 175 | 177 | 3.32 | Very Aggressive | 64 | 40 | 60 | Air |
| Craig Gentry | 287 | 1168 | 701 | 467 | 234 | 467 | 70 | 193 | 204 | 4.07 | Very Patient | 97 | 38 | 60 | Ground |
| Chris Getz* | 237 | 897 | 521 | 376 | 207 | 314 | 39 | 144 | 193 | 3.78 | Neutral | 80 | 38 | 58 | Ground |
| Jason Giambi* | 216 | 913 | 494 | 419 | 142 | 352 | 91 | 195 | 133 | 4.23 | Very Patient | 45 | 21 | 67 | Air |
| Conor Gillaspie* | 452 | 1641 | 904 | 737 | 272 | 632 | 125 | 277 | 335 | 3.63 | Very Aggressive | 125 | 68 | 141 | Air |
| Caleb Gindl* | 155 | 606 | 323 | 283 | 77 | 246 | 59 | 114 | 110 | 3.91 | Neutral | 42 | 23 | 43 | Air |
| Ryan Goins* | 121 | 465 | 261 | 204 | 111 | 150 | 46 | 67 | 91 | 3.84 | Neutral | 50 | 17 | 22 | Ground |
| Paul Goldschmidt | 710 | 2930 | 1739 | 1191 | 546 | 1193 | 257 | 471 | 462 | 4.13 | Very Patient | 204 | 98 | 160 | Medium |
| Jonny Gomes | 366 | 1416 | 869 | 547 | 337 | 532 | 139 | 180 | 228 | 3.87 | Neutral | 68 | 45 | 115 | Air |
| Yan Gomes | 322 | 1232 | 632 | 600 | 219 | 413 | 125 | 245 | 230 | 3.83 | Neutral | 100 | 41 | 89 | Air |
| Carlos Gomez | 590 | 2173 | 972 | 1201 | 233 | 739 | 318 | 486 | 397 | 3.68 | Aggressive | 154 | 81 | 146 | Air |
| Adrian Gonzalez* | 641 | 2361 | 1168 | 1193 | 306 | 862 | 234 | 464 | 495 | 3.68 | Aggressive | 189 | 113 | 193 | Air |
| Alex Gonzalez | 118 | 396 | 192 | 204 | 78 | 114 | 48 | 68 | 88 | 3.36 | Very Aggressive | 37 | 24 | 26 | Ground |
| Carlos Gonzalez* | 436 | 1686 | 870 | 816 | 239 | 631 | 230 | 310 | 276 | 3.87 | Neutral | 102 | 58 | 109 | Air |
| Marwin Gonzalez# | 222 | 804 | 406 | 398 | 157 | 249 | 67 | 155 | 176 | 3.62 | Very Aggressive | 89 | 25 | 50 | Ground |
| Alex Gordon* | 700 | 2805 | 1545 | 1260 | 490 | 1055 | 272 | 490 | 498 | 4.01 | Patient | 201 | 101 | 196 | Air |
| Dee Gordon* | 106 | 389 | 214 | 175 | 81 | 133 | 25 | 76 | 74 | 3.67 | Aggressive | 31 | 13 | 19 | Ground |
| Anthony Gose* | 153 | 614 | 295 | 319 | 103 | 192 | 65 | 143 | 111 | 4.01 | Patient | 55 | 23 | 27 | Ground |
| Yasmani Grandal# | 108 | 401 | 231 | 170 | 56 | 175 | 33 | 66 | 71 | 3.71 | Aggressive | 34 | 17 | 20 | Ground |
| Curtis Granderson* | 245 | 978 | 539 | 439 | 178 | 361 | 141 | 150 | 148 | 3.99 | Patient | 48 | 32 | 62 | Air |
| Grant Green | 153 | 577 | 293 | 284 | 101 | 192 | 79 | 107 | 98 | 3.77 | Aggressive | 40 | 20 | 34 | Medium |
| Didi Gregorius* | 404 | 1648 | 833 | 815 | 216 | 617 | 171 | 348 | 295 | 4.08 | Very Patient | 108 | 61 | 122 | Air |
| Robbie Grossman# | 288 | 1073 | 636 | 437 | 237 | 399 | 98 | 146 | 193 | 3.73 | Aggressive | 88 | 43 | 55 | Ground |
| Franklin Gutierrez | 151 | 625 | 324 | 301 | 113 | 211 | 86 | 112 | 103 | 4.14 | Very Patient | 45 | 13 | 44 | Air |
| Jesus Guzman | 318 | 1289 | 719 | 570 | 238 | 481 | 154 | 206 | 210 | 4.05 | Patient | 88 | 45 | 76 | Medium |
| Jedd Gyorko | 525 | 2040 | 1033 | 1007 | 317 | 716 | 271 | 371 | 365 | 3.89 | Neutral | 137 | 82 | 145 | Air |
| Travis Hafner* | 299 | 1230 | 710 | 520 | 215 | 495 | 133 | 204 | 183 | 4.11 | Very Patient | 68 | 34 | 80 | Air |
| Jerry Hairston | 226 | 834 | 446 | 388 | 153 | 293 | 46 | 154 | 188 | 3.69 | Aggressive | 79 | 30 | 75 | Air |
| Scott Hairston | 174 | 681 | 376 | 305 | 133 | 243 | 71 | 115 | 119 | 3.91 | Patient | 31 | 17 | 70 | Air |
| Sean Halton | 111 | 427 | 215 | 212 | 69 | 146 | 59 | 81 | 72 | 3.85 | Neutral | 30 | 14 | 27 | Air |
| Josh Hamilton* | 636 | 2380 | 1072 | 1308 | 219 | 853 | 396 | 485 | 427 | 3.74 | Aggressive | 166 | 95 | 166 | Air |
| Ryan Hanigan | 260 | 984 | 584 | 400 | 202 | 382 | 38 | 164 | 198 | 3.78 | Neutral | 96 | 42 | 57 | Ground |
| Jack Hannahan* | 162 | 674 | 382 | 292 | 114 | 268 | 70 | 119 | 102 | 4.16 | Very Patient | 54 | 19 | 29 | Ground |
| J.J. Hardy | 644 | 2405 | 1406 | 999 | 556 | 850 | 128 | 338 | 533 | 3.73 | Aggressive | 239 | 88 | 202 | Medium |
| Bryce Harper* | 497 | 1960 | 1012 | 948 | 224 | 788 | 224 | 387 | 337 | 3.94 | Patient | 155 | 66 | 111 | Ground |
| Brendan Harris | 117 | 446 | 263 | 183 | 105 | 158 | 37 | 65 | 81 | 3.81 | Neutral | 39 | 18 | 20 | Ground |
| Chase Headley# | 600 | 2374 | 1292 | 1082 | 339 | 953 | 287 | 415 | 380 | 3.96 | Patient | 175 | 86 | 119 | Ground |
| Adeiny Hechavarria | 578 | 2124 | 1059 | 1065 | 348 | 711 | 165 | 448 | 452 | 3.67 | Aggressive | 229 | 90 | 123 | Ground |
| Chris Heisey | 244 | 843 | 387 | 456 | 126 | 261 | 111 | 166 | 179 | 3.45 | Very Aggressive | 68 | 27 | 75 | Air |
| Todd Helton* | 442 | 1840 | 964 | 876 | 290 | 674 | 166 | 395 | 315 | 4.16 | Very Patient | 106 | 79 | 130 | Air |
| Cesar Hernandez# | 131 | 495 | 264 | 231 | 88 | 176 | 46 | 90 | 95 | 3.78 | Aggressive | 48 | 23 | 21 | Ground |
| Jonathan Herrera# | 215 | 757 | 429 | 328 | 158 | 271 | 40 | 111 | 177 | 3.52 | Very Aggressive | 64 | 43 | 57 | Air |
| Chris Herrmann* | 178 | 715 | 391 | 324 | 115 | 276 | 115 | 98 | 111 | 4.02 | Patient | 46 | 21 | 41 | Air |
| Jason Heyward* | 440 | 1791 | 1003 | 788 | 280 | 723 | 167 | 310 | 310 | 4.07 | Very Patient | 135 | 66 | 108 | Medium |
| Aaron Hicks# | 313 | 1271 | 754 | 517 | 270 | 484 | 115 | 199 | 203 | 4.06 | Patient | 87 | 32 | 74 | Medium |
| Aaron Hill | 362 | 1378 | 780 | 598 | 264 | 516 | 94 | 224 | 280 | 3.81 | Neutral | 108 | 61 | 111 | Air |
| L.J. Hoes | 184 | 706 | 399 | 307 | 141 | 258 | 63 | 108 | 136 | 3.84 | Neutral | 84 | 27 | 25 | Ground |
| Matt Holliday | 602 | 2236 | 1129 | 1107 | 276 | 853 | 219 | 450 | 438 | 3.71 | Aggressive | 200 | 91 | 147 | Medium |
| Eric Hosmer* | 680 | 2566 | 1360 | 1206 | 419 | 941 | 231 | 447 | 528 | 3.77 | Aggressive | 277 | 118 | 131 | Ground |
| Ryan Howard* | 317 | 1262 | 644 | 618 | 155 | 489 | 218 | 203 | 197 | 3.98 | Patient | 76 | 47 | 74 | Air |
| Nick Hundley | 408 | 1529 | 723 | 806 | 205 | 518 | 201 | 326 | 279 | 3.75 | Aggressive | 117 | 55 | 103 | Air |
| Torii Hunter | 652 | 2363 | 1052 | 1311 | 301 | 751 | 283 | 522 | 506 | 3.62 | Very Aggressive | 246 | 99 | 152 | Ground |
| Chris Iannetta | 399 | 1663 | 959 | 704 | 225 | 734 | 203 | 272 | 229 | 4.17 | Very Patient | 85 | 44 | 99 | Air |
| Raul Ibanez* | 496 | 2047 | 1140 | 907 | 380 | 760 | 243 | 338 | 326 | 4.13 | Very Patient | 116 | 70 | 140 | Air |
| Jose Iglesias | 382 | 1422 | 792 | 630 | 354 | 438 | 89 | 245 | 296 | 3.72 | Aggressive | 157 | 50 | 71 | Ground |
| Omar Infante | 476 | 1572 | 854 | 718 | 319 | 535 | 114 | 192 | 412 | 3.30 | Very Aggressive | 156 | 96 | 154 | Air |
| Brandon Inge | 110 | 439 | 248 | 191 | 105 | 143 | 52 | 64 | 75 | 3.99 | Patient | 24 | 16 | 33 | Air |
| Cesar Izturis# | 142 | 434 | 216 | 218 | 58 | 158 | 30 | 68 | 120 | 3.06 | Very Aggressive | 60 | 25 | 31 | Ground |
| Maicer Izturis# | 399 | 1408 | 796 | 612 | 283 | 513 | 70 | 209 | 333 | 3.53 | Very Aggressive | 171 | 74 | 84 | Ground |
| Austin Jackson | 614 | 2390 | 1337 | 1053 | 480 | 857 | 208 | 416 | 429 | 3.89 | Neutral | 177 | 117 | 130 | Medium |
| John Jaso* | 249 | 1061 | 679 | 382 | 237 | 442 | 76 | 142 | 164 | 4.26 | Very Patient | 65 | 41 | 56 | Air |
| Jon Jay* | 628 | 2358 | 1306 | 1052 | 403 | 903 | 184 | 409 | 459 | 3.75 | Aggressive | 223 | 118 | 101 | Ground |
| Desmond Jennings | 602 | 2428 | 1421 | 1007 | 483 | 938 | 224 | 363 | 420 | 4.03 | Patient | 192 | 70 | 147 | Medium |
| Luis Jimenez | 110 | 398 | 195 | 203 | 75 | 120 | 48 | 78 | 77 | 3.62 | Very Aggressive | 36 | 13 | 28 | Medium |
| Chris Johnson | 547 | 2049 | 963 | 1086 | 283 | 680 | 268 | 418 | 400 | 3.75 | Aggressive | 182 | 108 | 110 | Ground |
| Elliot Johnson# | 275 | 991 | 506 | 485 | 177 | 329 | 120 | 173 | 192 | 3.60 | Very Aggressive | 84 | 37 | 61 | Ground |
| Kelly Johnson* | 407 | 1684 | 928 | 756 | 286 | 642 | 172 | 314 | 270 | 4.14 | Very Patient | 104 | 41 | 124 | Air |
| Reed Johnson | 136 | 489 | 236 | 253 | 81 | 155 | 65 | 96 | 92 | 3.60 | Very Aggressive | 50 | 13 | 26 | Ground |
| Adam Jones | 689 | 2450 | 1035 | 1415 | 265 | 770 | 373 | 522 | 520 | 3.56 | Very Aggressive | 250 | 102 | 166 | Ground |

# Hitter Analysis

| Hitter | PA | Pit | T | Sw | St | B | S/M | F | In P | P/PA | Group | GB | LD | FB | Hits |
|---|---|---|---|---|---|---|---|---|---|---|---|---|---|---|---|
| Garrett Jones* | 440 | 1751 | 877 | 874 | 252 | 625 | 217 | 351 | 306 | 3.98 | Patient | 123 | 73 | 110 | Air |
| Matt Joyce* | 481 | 2003 | 1153 | 850 | 336 | 817 | 189 | 328 | 333 | 4.16 | Very Patient | 121 | 67 | 142 | Air |
| Munenori Kawasaki* | 289 | 1207 | 726 | 481 | 257 | 469 | 55 | 214 | 212 | 4.18 | Very Patient | 112 | 42 | 39 | Ground |
| Don Kelly* | 251 | 1007 | 582 | 425 | 183 | 399 | 48 | 183 | 194 | 4.01 | Patient | 74 | 29 | 88 | Air |
| Matt Kemp | 290 | 1094 | 572 | 522 | 163 | 409 | 170 | 162 | 190 | 3.77 | Aggressive | 76 | 48 | 66 | Air |
| Howie Kendrick | 513 | 1925 | 901 | 1024 | 292 | 609 | 207 | 422 | 395 | 3.75 | Aggressive | 200 | 107 | 83 | Ground |
| Jeff Keppinger | 451 | 1604 | 938 | 666 | 359 | 579 | 57 | 219 | 389 | 3.56 | Very Aggressive | 172 | 94 | 119 | Ground |
| Ian Kinsler | 614 | 2384 | 1415 | 969 | 509 | 906 | 99 | 374 | 496 | 3.88 | Neutral | 182 | 117 | 194 | Air |
| Jason Kipnis* | 658 | 2763 | 1694 | 1069 | 573 | 1121 | 202 | 431 | 436 | 4.20 | Very Patient | 183 | 105 | 137 | Medium |
| Paul Konerko | 520 | 1948 | 1088 | 860 | 359 | 729 | 165 | 298 | 397 | 3.75 | Aggressive | 144 | 97 | 156 | Air |
| Mark Kotsay* | 171 | 619 | 326 | 293 | 103 | 223 | 53 | 107 | 133 | 3.62 | Very Aggressive | 60 | 28 | 44 | Ground |
| George Kottaras* | 126 | 563 | 394 | 169 | 142 | 252 | 48 | 63 | 58 | 4.47 | Very Patient | 24 | 12 | 21 | Air |
| Pete Kozma | 448 | 1620 | 875 | 745 | 292 | 583 | 127 | 295 | 323 | 3.62 | Very Aggressive | 131 | 72 | 113 | Medium |
| Erik Kratz | 218 | 879 | 431 | 448 | 133 | 298 | 109 | 185 | 154 | 4.03 | Patient | 68 | 22 | 64 | Air |
| Marc Krauss* | 146 | 665 | 379 | 286 | 121 | 258 | 70 | 126 | 90 | 4.55 | Very Patient | 38 | 22 | 30 | Medium |
| Jason Kubel* | 290 | 1252 | 682 | 570 | 201 | 481 | 177 | 224 | 169 | 4.32 | Very Patient | 55 | 45 | 69 | Air |
| Juan Lagares | 421 | 1656 | 859 | 797 | 328 | 531 | 150 | 344 | 303 | 3.93 | Patient | 140 | 45 | 102 | Ground |
| Gerald Laird | 141 | 522 | 300 | 222 | 98 | 202 | 42 | 79 | 101 | 3.70 | Aggressive | 45 | 21 | 31 | Ground |
| Junior Lake | 254 | 984 | 492 | 492 | 147 | 345 | 167 | 156 | 169 | 3.87 | Neutral | 66 | 44 | 48 | Medium |
| Adam LaRoche* | 590 | 2400 | 1409 | 991 | 415 | 994 | 225 | 382 | 384 | 4.07 | Very Patient | 141 | 83 | 159 | Air |
| Brett Lawrie | 442 | 1621 | 863 | 758 | 280 | 583 | 139 | 282 | 337 | 3.67 | Aggressive | 162 | 58 | 114 | Ground |
| DJ LeMahieu | 434 | 1505 | 734 | 771 | 266 | 468 | 108 | 316 | 347 | 3.47 | Very Aggressive | 185 | 92 | 61 | Ground |
| Adam Lind* | 521 | 2131 | 1264 | 867 | 452 | 812 | 181 | 320 | 366 | 4.09 | Very Patient | 168 | 78 | 120 | Ground |
| Jose Lobaton# | 311 | 1174 | 615 | 559 | 176 | 439 | 132 | 211 | 216 | 3.77 | Aggressive | 94 | 50 | 69 | Medium |
| Steve Lombardozzi# | 307 | 976 | 456 | 520 | 151 | 305 | 67 | 189 | 264 | 3.18 | Very Aggressive | 125 | 50 | 77 | Ground |
| James Loney* | 598 | 2221 | 1197 | 1024 | 407 | 790 | 120 | 427 | 477 | 3.71 | Aggressive | 201 | 142 | 133 | Ground |
| Evan Longoria | 693 | 2779 | 1645 | 1134 | 536 | 1109 | 277 | 399 | 458 | 4.01 | Patient | 169 | 85 | 204 | Air |
| David Lough* | 335 | 1194 | 601 | 593 | 219 | 382 | 106 | 217 | 270 | 3.56 | Very Aggressive | 108 | 58 | 91 | Medium |
| Jed Lowrie# | 662 | 2449 | 1281 | 1168 | 352 | 929 | 173 | 476 | 519 | 3.70 | Aggressive | 171 | 120 | 221 | Air |
| Ed Lucas | 384 | 1505 | 752 | 753 | 252 | 500 | 150 | 325 | 278 | 3.92 | Patient | 127 | 67 | 78 | Ground |
| Jonathan Lucroy | 580 | 2331 | 1333 | 998 | 510 | 823 | 128 | 410 | 460 | 4.02 | Patient | 180 | 105 | 175 | Air |
| Ryan Ludwick | 140 | 464 | 209 | 255 | 56 | 153 | 69 | 85 | 101 | 3.31 | Very Aggressive | 36 | 24 | 41 | Air |
| Manny Machado | 710 | 2505 | 1295 | 1210 | 414 | 881 | 229 | 415 | 566 | 3.53 | Very Aggressive | 258 | 113 | 177 | Ground |
| Martin Maldonado | 202 | 796 | 406 | 390 | 134 | 272 | 92 | 165 | 133 | 3.94 | Patient | 53 | 17 | 55 | Air |
| Jake Marisnick | 118 | 472 | 221 | 251 | 74 | 147 | 51 | 116 | 84 | 4.00 | Patient | 35 | 21 | 27 | Medium |
| Nick Markakis* | 700 | 2664 | 1525 | 1139 | 557 | 968 | 128 | 445 | 566 | 3.81 | Neutral | 264 | 128 | 174 | Ground |
| Starling Marte | 566 | 2168 | 1061 | 1107 | 379 | 682 | 284 | 444 | 379 | 3.83 | Neutral | 181 | 77 | 98 | Ground |
| Leonys Martin* | 508 | 1848 | 926 | 922 | 327 | 599 | 208 | 346 | 368 | 3.64 | Aggressive | 172 | 71 | 95 | Ground |
| Russell Martin | 506 | 2027 | 1232 | 795 | 388 | 844 | 186 | 277 | 332 | 4.01 | Patient | 168 | 55 | 108 | Ground |
| J.D. Martinez | 310 | 1173 | 564 | 609 | 187 | 377 | 157 | 234 | 217 | 3.78 | Neutral | 96 | 47 | 74 | Medium |
| Victor Martinez# | 668 | 2601 | 1454 | 1147 | 480 | 974 | 116 | 480 | 551 | 3.89 | Neutral | 233 | 123 | 195 | Medium |
| Jeff Mathis | 256 | 985 | 516 | 469 | 170 | 346 | 137 | 174 | 158 | 3.85 | Neutral | 66 | 31 | 58 | Air |
| Joe Mauer* | 508 | 2158 | 1352 | 806 | 505 | 847 | 136 | 312 | 358 | 4.25 | Very Patient | 168 | 99 | 91 | Ground |
| Justin Maxwell | 262 | 1017 | 540 | 477 | 151 | 389 | 161 | 159 | 157 | 3.88 | Neutral | 75 | 31 | 50 | Ground |
| John Mayberry | 384 | 1506 | 835 | 671 | 291 | 544 | 166 | 241 | 264 | 3.92 | Patient | 113 | 54 | 97 | Medium |
| Brian McCann* | 402 | 1631 | 954 | 677 | 300 | 654 | 106 | 279 | 292 | 4.06 | Patient | 103 | 65 | 123 | Air |
| Andrew McCutchen | 674 | 2562 | 1393 | 1169 | 369 | 1024 | 236 | 447 | 486 | 3.80 | Neutral | 198 | 119 | 169 | Medium |
| Michael McKenry | 122 | 494 | 245 | 249 | 85 | 160 | 50 | 108 | 91 | 4.05 | Patient | 34 | 19 | 38 | Air |
| Nate McLouth* | 593 | 2269 | 1346 | 923 | 481 | 865 | 120 | 353 | 450 | 3.83 | Neutral | 171 | 110 | 162 | Air |
| Jordy Mercer | 365 | 1399 | 778 | 621 | 315 | 463 | 102 | 242 | 277 | 3.83 | Neutral | 125 | 61 | 81 | Ground |
| Devin Mesoraco | 352 | 1300 | 641 | 659 | 177 | 464 | 133 | 259 | 267 | 3.69 | Aggressive | 120 | 56 | 90 | Medium |
| Will Middlebrooks | 374 | 1537 | 831 | 706 | 301 | 530 | 182 | 270 | 254 | 4.11 | Very Patient | 103 | 51 | 99 | Air |
| Brad Miller* | 335 | 1189 | 597 | 592 | 196 | 401 | 105 | 229 | 258 | 3.55 | Very Aggressive | 115 | 54 | 81 | Ground |
| Jose Molina | 313 | 1157 | 564 | 593 | 178 | 386 | 135 | 232 | 226 | 3.70 | Aggressive | 120 | 43 | 57 | Ground |
| Yadier Molina | 541 | 1884 | 883 | 1001 | 235 | 648 | 131 | 417 | 453 | 3.48 | Very Aggressive | 190 | 110 | 153 | Medium |
| Jesus Montero | 110 | 373 | 194 | 179 | 66 | 128 | 48 | 50 | 81 | 3.39 | Very Aggressive | 34 | 16 | 31 | Air |
| Miguel Montero* | 475 | 1929 | 997 | 932 | 236 | 761 | 248 | 375 | 309 | 4.06 | Patient | 146 | 66 | 97 | Ground |
| Tyler Moore | 178 | 687 | 318 | 369 | 105 | 213 | 116 | 142 | 111 | 3.86 | Neutral | 44 | 20 | 46 | Air |
| Kendrys Morales# | 657 | 2464 | 1287 | 1177 | 373 | 914 | 280 | 408 | 489 | 3.75 | Aggressive | 238 | 92 | 159 | Ground |
| Mitch Moreland* | 518 | 2139 | 1197 | 942 | 383 | 814 | 238 | 351 | 353 | 4.13 | Very Patient | 152 | 61 | 139 | Air |
| Justin Morneau* | 635 | 2421 | 1182 | 1239 | 338 | 844 | 248 | 523 | 468 | 3.81 | Neutral | 191 | 99 | 178 | Air |
| Logan Morrison* | 333 | 1258 | 705 | 553 | 207 | 498 | 102 | 214 | 237 | 3.78 | Aggressive | 113 | 48 | 76 | Ground |
| Michael Morse | 337 | 1287 | 603 | 684 | 164 | 439 | 193 | 265 | 226 | 3.82 | Neutral | 101 | 44 | 81 | Medium |
| Brandon Moss* | 505 | 2017 | 1017 | 1000 | 261 | 756 | 304 | 387 | 309 | 3.99 | Patient | 93 | 56 | 160 | Air |
| Mike Moustakas* | 514 | 1962 | 1001 | 961 | 281 | 720 | 178 | 389 | 394 | 3.82 | Neutral | 144 | 74 | 175 | Air |
| Daniel Murphy* | 697 | 2531 | 1353 | 1178 | 444 | 909 | 146 | 464 | 568 | 3.63 | Very Aggressive | 241 | 121 | 206 | Medium |
| David Murphy* | 476 | 1856 | 1044 | 812 | 342 | 702 | 116 | 317 | 378 | 3.90 | Neutral | 163 | 73 | 142 | Air |
| Donnie Murphy | 163 | 640 | 313 | 327 | 101 | 212 | 89 | 137 | 101 | 3.93 | Patient | 35 | 19 | 45 | Air |
| Wil Myers | 373 | 1476 | 813 | 663 | 255 | 558 | 170 | 245 | 248 | 3.96 | Patient | 114 | 50 | 84 | Medium |
| Mike Napoli | 578 | 2652 | 1555 | 1097 | 505 | 1050 | 358 | 427 | 312 | 4.59 | Very Patient | 115 | 76 | 121 | Air |
| Daniel Nava# | 536 | 2204 | 1336 | 868 | 492 | 844 | 137 | 354 | 377 | 4.11 | Very Patient | 127 | 97 | 147 | Air |
| Dioner Navarro# | 266 | 961 | 525 | 436 | 158 | 367 | 90 | 141 | 205 | 3.61 | Very Aggressive | 84 | 52 | 69 | Medium |
| Chris Nelson | 227 | 908 | 504 | 404 | 179 | 325 | 96 | 161 | 147 | 4.00 | Patient | 74 | 29 | 44 | Ground |
| Kirk Nieuwenhuis* | 108 | 447 | 260 | 187 | 87 | 173 | 54 | 69 | 64 | 4.14 | Very Patient | 29 | 12 | 22 | Medium |
| Wil Nieves | 206 | 698 | 299 | 399 | 87 | 212 | 96 | 137 | 166 | 3.39 | Very Aggressive | 102 | 29 | 35 | Ground |

# Hitter Analysis

| Hitter | PA | Pit | T | Sw | St | B | S/M | F | In P | P/PA | Group | GB | LD | FB | Hits |
|---|---|---|---|---|---|---|---|---|---|---|---|---|---|---|---|
| Jayson Nix | 303 | 1140 | 601 | 539 | 196 | 405 | 113 | 232 | 194 | 3.76 | Aggressive | 74 | 49 | 67 | Air |
| Laynce Nix* | 136 | 543 | 265 | 278 | 92 | 173 | 75 | 119 | 84 | 3.99 | Patient | 39 | 19 | 26 | Ground |
| Nick Noonan* | 111 | 415 | 200 | 215 | 53 | 147 | 58 | 76 | 81 | 3.74 | Aggressive | 28 | 24 | 27 | Air |
| Derek Norris | 308 | 1313 | 777 | 536 | 241 | 536 | 112 | 228 | 196 | 4.26 | Very Patient | 69 | 41 | 84 | Air |
| Eduardo Nunez | 336 | 1211 | 634 | 577 | 224 | 410 | 89 | 226 | 262 | 3.60 | Very Aggressive | 106 | 54 | 96 | Air |
| David Ortiz* | 600 | 2311 | 1299 | 1012 | 318 | 981 | 208 | 369 | 435 | 3.85 | Neutral | 168 | 98 | 168 | Air |
| Lyle Overbay* | 486 | 1850 | 962 | 888 | 265 | 697 | 222 | 327 | 339 | 3.81 | Neutral | 148 | 74 | 117 | Medium |
| Marcell Ozuna | 291 | 1104 | 556 | 548 | 180 | 376 | 137 | 192 | 219 | 3.79 | Neutral | 101 | 46 | 71 | Ground |
| Jordan Pacheco | 262 | 957 | 512 | 445 | 192 | 320 | 60 | 174 | 211 | 3.65 | Aggressive | 102 | 53 | 54 | Ground |
| Angel Pagan# | 305 | 1171 | 680 | 491 | 249 | 431 | 47 | 198 | 246 | 3.84 | Neutral | 105 | 57 | 83 | Medium |
| Jimmy Paredes# | 135 | 495 | 205 | 290 | 59 | 146 | 90 | 116 | 84 | 3.67 | Aggressive | 50 | 16 | 17 | Ground |
| Chris Parmelee* | 333 | 1425 | 789 | 636 | 254 | 535 | 134 | 286 | 216 | 4.28 | Very Patient | 84 | 46 | 85 | Air |
| Gerardo Parra* | 663 | 2307 | 1166 | 1141 | 410 | 756 | 205 | 424 | 512 | 3.48 | Very Aggressive | 272 | 98 | 122 | Ground |
| Xavier Paul* | 239 | 954 | 515 | 439 | 137 | 378 | 125 | 158 | 156 | 3.99 | Patient | 77 | 35 | 44 | Ground |
| Steve Pearce | 138 | 562 | 314 | 248 | 98 | 216 | 58 | 96 | 94 | 4.07 | Very Patient | 37 | 16 | 41 | Air |
| Dustin Pedroia | 724 | 2934 | 1684 | 1250 | 598 | 1086 | 141 | 536 | 573 | 4.05 | Patient | 289 | 124 | 160 | Ground |
| Brayan Pena# | 243 | 911 | 484 | 427 | 165 | 319 | 56 | 162 | 209 | 3.75 | Aggressive | 107 | 41 | 58 | Ground |
| Carlos Pena* | 328 | 1308 | 705 | 603 | 178 | 527 | 205 | 209 | 189 | 3.99 | Patient | 91 | 40 | 52 | Ground |
| Ramiro Pena# | 107 | 380 | 182 | 198 | 60 | 122 | 41 | 76 | 81 | 3.55 | Very Aggressive | 37 | 19 | 21 | Ground |
| Hunter Pence | 687 | 2590 | 1408 | 1182 | 441 | 967 | 279 | 386 | 517 | 3.77 | Aggressive | 243 | 89 | 185 | Medium |
| Cliff Pennington# | 299 | 1152 | 622 | 530 | 197 | 425 | 93 | 219 | 218 | 3.85 | Neutral | 90 | 48 | 77 | Medium |
| Jhonny Peralta | 448 | 1742 | 914 | 828 | 272 | 642 | 200 | 314 | 314 | 3.89 | Neutral | 122 | 79 | 112 | Air |
| Salvador Perez | 526 | 1771 | 905 | 866 | 314 | 591 | 112 | 316 | 438 | 3.37 | Very Aggressive | 204 | 90 | 144 | Ground |
| Josh Phegley | 213 | 723 | 333 | 390 | 124 | 209 | 91 | 132 | 167 | 3.39 | Very Aggressive | 65 | 32 | 68 | Air |
| Brandon Phillips | 666 | 2422 | 1137 | 1285 | 303 | 834 | 271 | 493 | 521 | 3.64 | Very Aggressive | 239 | 99 | 178 | Medium |
| Juan Pierre* | 330 | 1137 | 606 | 531 | 235 | 371 | 49 | 195 | 287 | 3.45 | Very Aggressive | 132 | 65 | 64 | Ground |
| A.J. Pierzynski* | 529 | 1728 | 688 | 1040 | 181 | 507 | 179 | 428 | 433 | 3.27 | Very Aggressive | 184 | 97 | 152 | Medium |
| Kevin Pillar | 110 | 437 | 218 | 219 | 83 | 135 | 54 | 90 | 75 | 3.97 | Patient | 26 | 12 | 34 | Air |
| Trevor Plouffe | 522 | 1926 | 1095 | 831 | 423 | 672 | 161 | 300 | 370 | 3.69 | Aggressive | 142 | 91 | 135 | Air |
| Placido Polanco | 416 | 1506 | 817 | 689 | 290 | 527 | 56 | 280 | 353 | 3.62 | Very Aggressive | 169 | 87 | 94 | Ground |
| A.J. Pollock | 482 | 1853 | 1063 | 790 | 398 | 665 | 145 | 280 | 365 | 3.84 | Neutral | 170 | 65 | 121 | Ground |
| Buster Posey | 595 | 2405 | 1453 | 952 | 480 | 973 | 129 | 366 | 457 | 4.04 | Patient | 216 | 91 | 150 | Ground |
| Martin Prado | 664 | 2459 | 1497 | 962 | 607 | 890 | 85 | 315 | 562 | 3.70 | Aggressive | 268 | 123 | 170 | Ground |
| Alex Presley* | 195 | 778 | 433 | 345 | 170 | 263 | 57 | 142 | 146 | 3.99 | Patient | 74 | 33 | 35 | Ground |
| Jurickson Profar# | 324 | 1358 | 793 | 565 | 267 | 526 | 81 | 254 | 230 | 4.19 | Very Patient | 92 | 52 | 78 | Medium |
| Yasiel Puig | 432 | 1547 | 730 | 817 | 145 | 585 | 272 | 257 | 288 | 3.58 | Very Aggressive | 142 | 54 | 87 | Ground |
| Albert Pujols | 443 | 1677 | 907 | 770 | 267 | 640 | 135 | 292 | 343 | 3.79 | Neutral | 131 | 68 | 144 | Air |
| Nick Punto# | 335 | 1440 | 831 | 609 | 314 | 517 | 69 | 305 | 235 | 4.30 | Very Patient | 88 | 66 | 67 | Medium |
| Carlos Quentin | 320 | 1158 | 544 | 614 | 106 | 438 | 155 | 234 | 225 | 3.62 | Very Aggressive | 80 | 44 | 101 | Air |
| Omar Quintanilla* | 359 | 1477 | 824 | 653 | 255 | 569 | 121 | 282 | 250 | 4.11 | Very Patient | 131 | 48 | 65 | Ground |
| Humberto Quintero | 140 | 482 | 199 | 283 | 56 | 143 | 66 | 114 | 103 | 3.44 | Very Aggressive | 48 | 23 | 29 | Ground |
| Ryan Raburn | 277 | 1122 | 628 | 494 | 194 | 434 | 133 | 184 | 177 | 4.05 | Patient | 79 | 31 | 67 | Medium |
| Alexei Ramirez | 674 | 2216 | 1005 | 1211 | 331 | 674 | 151 | 483 | 577 | 3.29 | Very Aggressive | 277 | 126 | 166 | Ground |
| Aramis Ramirez | 351 | 1289 | 663 | 626 | 167 | 496 | 126 | 248 | 252 | 3.67 | Aggressive | 104 | 49 | 99 | Air |
| Hanley Ramirez | 336 | 1194 | 576 | 618 | 161 | 415 | 124 | 240 | 254 | 3.55 | Very Aggressive | 103 | 56 | 95 | Air |
| Wilson Ramos | 303 | 1038 | 481 | 557 | 122 | 359 | 107 | 204 | 246 | 3.43 | Very Aggressive | 140 | 48 | 58 | Ground |
| Cody Ransom | 193 | 807 | 436 | 371 | 112 | 324 | 116 | 147 | 108 | 4.18 | Very Patient | 45 | 19 | 43 | Air |
| Colby Rasmus* | 458 | 1903 | 1051 | 852 | 332 | 719 | 235 | 334 | 283 | 4.16 | Very Patient | 93 | 62 | 127 | Air |
| Anthony Recker | 151 | 618 | 365 | 253 | 134 | 231 | 71 | 93 | 89 | 4.09 | Very Patient | 33 | 18 | 37 | Air |
| Josh Reddick* | 441 | 1794 | 997 | 797 | 311 | 686 | 159 | 331 | 307 | 4.07 | Very Patient | 108 | 61 | 135 | Air |
| Nolan Reimold | 140 | 603 | 340 | 263 | 105 | 235 | 87 | 87 | 89 | 4.31 | Very Patient | 43 | 12 | 34 | Medium |
| Anthony Rendon | 394 | 1599 | 967 | 632 | 348 | 619 | 82 | 261 | 289 | 4.06 | Patient | 116 | 73 | 97 | Medium |
| Ben Revere* | 336 | 1155 | 679 | 476 | 268 | 411 | 41 | 151 | 284 | 3.44 | Very Aggressive | 156 | 61 | 46 | Ground |
| Jose Reyes# | 419 | 1548 | 874 | 674 | 295 | 579 | 93 | 244 | 337 | 3.69 | Aggressive | 153 | 71 | 111 | Ground |
| Mark Reynolds | 504 | 2126 | 1120 | 1006 | 315 | 805 | 338 | 374 | 294 | 4.22 | Very Patient | 115 | 53 | 124 | Air |
| Alex Rios | 662 | 2497 | 1422 | 1075 | 510 | 912 | 167 | 397 | 510 | 3.77 | Aggressive | 223 | 109 | 178 | Medium |
| Anthony Rizzo* | 690 | 2615 | 1450 | 1165 | 456 | 994 | 237 | 447 | 481 | 3.79 | Neutral | 204 | 94 | 182 | Air |
| Brian Roberts# | 296 | 1235 | 714 | 521 | 260 | 454 | 57 | 238 | 226 | 4.17 | Very Patient | 81 | 54 | 88 | Air |
| Ryan Roberts | 173 | 675 | 379 | 296 | 135 | 244 | 64 | 109 | 123 | 3.90 | Neutral | 53 | 20 | 49 | Air |
| Derrick Robinson# | 216 | 753 | 363 | 390 | 115 | 248 | 74 | 163 | 153 | 3.49 | Very Aggressive | 61 | 33 | 37 | Ground |
| Shane Robinson | 171 | 639 | 385 | 254 | 117 | 268 | 29 | 94 | 131 | 3.74 | Aggressive | 59 | 33 | 39 | Ground |
| Alex Rodriguez | 181 | 744 | 431 | 313 | 132 | 299 | 92 | 108 | 113 | 4.11 | Very Patient | 45 | 23 | 45 | Air |
| Sean Rodriguez | 222 | 891 | 507 | 384 | 163 | 344 | 102 | 141 | 141 | 4.01 | Patient | 50 | 32 | 56 | Air |
| Jimmy Rollins# | 666 | 2523 | 1451 | 1072 | 483 | 968 | 159 | 400 | 513 | 3.79 | Neutral | 193 | 120 | 196 | Air |
| Andrew Romine# | 123 | 463 | 229 | 234 | 72 | 157 | 49 | 94 | 91 | 3.76 | Aggressive | 48 | 21 | 15 | Ground |
| Austin Romine | 148 | 522 | 254 | 268 | 88 | 166 | 57 | 109 | 102 | 3.53 | Very Aggressive | 54 | 23 | 22 | Ground |
| Adam Rosales | 166 | 564 | 317 | 247 | 127 | 190 | 60 | 69 | 118 | 3.40 | Very Aggressive | 54 | 17 | 42 | Medium |
| Wilin Rosario | 466 | 1630 | 754 | 876 | 218 | 536 | 240 | 295 | 341 | 3.50 | Very Aggressive | 140 | 78 | 123 | Air |
| Cody Ross | 351 | 1323 | 713 | 610 | 220 | 493 | 102 | 235 | 273 | 3.77 | Aggressive | 117 | 58 | 96 | Medium |
| David Ross | 116 | 490 | 261 | 229 | 81 | 180 | 82 | 85 | 62 | 4.22 | Very Patient | 23 | 9 | 27 | Air |
| Darin Ruf | 293 | 1223 | 716 | 507 | 249 | 467 | 151 | 194 | 162 | 4.17 | Very Patient | 66 | 30 | 66 | Air |
| Justin Ruggiano | 472 | 1877 | 968 | 909 | 251 | 717 | 262 | 335 | 311 | 3.98 | Patient | 138 | 51 | 119 | Medium |
| Carlos Ruiz | 341 | 1270 | 697 | 573 | 224 | 473 | 68 | 228 | 277 | 3.72 | Aggressive | 127 | 53 | 91 | Ground |
| Josh Rutledge | 314 | 1165 | 638 | 527 | 218 | 420 | 106 | 193 | 228 | 3.71 | Aggressive | 109 | 41 | 72 | Ground |
| Brendan Ryan | 349 | 1270 | 650 | 620 | 234 | 416 | 146 | 223 | 251 | 3.64 | Aggressive | 95 | 48 | 98 | Air |

# Hitter Analysis

| Hitter | PA | Pit | T | Sw | St | B | S/M | F | In P | P/PA | Group | GB | LD | FB | Hits |
|---|---|---|---|---|---|---|---|---|---|---|---|---|---|---|---|
| Jarrod Saltalamacchia# | 470 | 1892 | 1007 | 885 | 301 | 706 | 271 | 326 | 288 | 4.03 | Patient | 94 | 82 | 111 | Air |
| Gaby Sanchez | 320 | 1293 | 777 | 516 | 248 | 529 | 83 | 212 | 220 | 4.04 | Patient | 80 | 50 | 90 | Air |
| Hector Sanchez# | 140 | 525 | 242 | 283 | 72 | 170 | 71 | 111 | 101 | 3.75 | Aggressive | 43 | 27 | 31 | Medium |
| Pablo Sandoval# | 584 | 2164 | 970 | 1194 | 204 | 766 | 202 | 540 | 452 | 3.71 | Aggressive | 187 | 96 | 168 | Air |
| Carlos Santana# | 642 | 2760 | 1686 | 1074 | 528 | 1158 | 193 | 446 | 435 | 4.30 | Very Patient | 183 | 94 | 154 | Medium |
| Ramon Santiago# | 234 | 878 | 505 | 373 | 167 | 338 | 36 | 157 | 180 | 3.75 | Aggressive | 81 | 40 | 44 | Ground |
| Josh Satin | 221 | 992 | 653 | 339 | 241 | 412 | 66 | 138 | 135 | 4.49 | Very Patient | 63 | 24 | 48 | Medium |
| Michael Saunders* | 468 | 1884 | 1057 | 827 | 307 | 750 | 215 | 317 | 295 | 4.03 | Patient | 117 | 63 | 106 | Air |
| Jordan Schafer* | 265 | 1113 | 617 | 496 | 185 | 432 | 143 | 190 | 163 | 4.20 | Very Patient | 70 | 31 | 44 | Ground |
| Logan Schafer* | 337 | 1272 | 657 | 615 | 225 | 432 | 112 | 254 | 249 | 3.77 | Aggressive | 106 | 46 | 77 | Ground |
| Nate Schierholtz* | 503 | 1971 | 987 | 984 | 283 | 704 | 204 | 406 | 374 | 3.92 | Patient | 147 | 75 | 148 | Air |
| Skip Schumaker* | 356 | 1375 | 760 | 615 | 272 | 488 | 101 | 245 | 268 | 3.86 | Neutral | 144 | 72 | 49 | Ground |
| Luke Scott* | 291 | 1145 | 646 | 499 | 202 | 444 | 125 | 180 | 194 | 3.93 | Patient | 73 | 37 | 80 | Air |
| Marco Scutaro | 547 | 2142 | 1318 | 824 | 539 | 779 | 40 | 318 | 466 | 3.92 | Patient | 221 | 96 | 135 | Ground |
| Kyle Seager* | 695 | 2823 | 1638 | 1185 | 531 | 1107 | 210 | 477 | 498 | 4.06 | Patient | 170 | 103 | 223 | Air |
| Jean Segura | 623 | 2266 | 1177 | 1089 | 437 | 740 | 167 | 414 | 508 | 3.64 | Aggressive | 290 | 89 | 115 | Ground |
| Kelly Shoppach | 127 | 489 | 254 | 235 | 76 | 178 | 90 | 79 | 66 | 3.85 | Neutral | 22 | 9 | 33 | Air |
| J.B. Shuck* | 478 | 1717 | 988 | 729 | 397 | 591 | 92 | 241 | 396 | 3.59 | Very Aggressive | 207 | 76 | 96 | Ground |
| Moises Sierra | 122 | 477 | 229 | 248 | 61 | 168 | 59 | 110 | 79 | 3.91 | Neutral | 38 | 16 | 25 | Ground |
| Andrelton Simmons | 658 | 2307 | 1239 | 1068 | 437 | 802 | 135 | 373 | 560 | 3.51 | Very Aggressive | 232 | 101 | 214 | Air |
| Seth Smith* | 410 | 1741 | 980 | 761 | 317 | 663 | 189 | 298 | 274 | 4.25 | Very Patient | 124 | 54 | 95 | Medium |
| Justin Smoak# | 521 | 2101 | 1169 | 932 | 331 | 838 | 208 | 388 | 336 | 4.03 | Patient | 117 | 66 | 153 | Air |
| Travis Snider* | 285 | 1172 | 644 | 528 | 215 | 429 | 135 | 207 | 186 | 4.11 | Very Patient | 95 | 28 | 61 | Ground |
| Eric Sogard* | 410 | 1486 | 857 | 629 | 326 | 531 | 63 | 239 | 327 | 3.62 | Very Aggressive | 111 | 78 | 125 | Air |
| Donovan Solano | 395 | 1462 | 747 | 715 | 247 | 500 | 116 | 291 | 308 | 3.70 | Aggressive | 150 | 71 | 82 | Ground |
| Alfonso Soriano | 626 | 2347 | 1102 | 1245 | 326 | 776 | 360 | 456 | 429 | 3.75 | Aggressive | 163 | 86 | 180 | Air |
| Geovany Soto | 184 | 782 | 493 | 289 | 182 | 311 | 67 | 118 | 104 | 4.25 | Very Patient | 33 | 23 | 47 | Air |
| Denard Span* | 662 | 2435 | 1373 | 1062 | 498 | 875 | 95 | 426 | 541 | 3.68 | Aggressive | 283 | 120 | 119 | Ground |
| Giancarlo Stanton | 504 | 2087 | 1228 | 859 | 340 | 888 | 283 | 290 | 286 | 4.14 | Very Patient | 124 | 52 | 110 | Air |
| Chris Stewart | 340 | 1287 | 784 | 503 | 276 | 508 | 77 | 171 | 255 | 3.79 | Neutral | 101 | 45 | 96 | Air |
| Drew Stubbs | 481 | 1874 | 1085 | 789 | 397 | 688 | 229 | 266 | 294 | 3.90 | Neutral | 133 | 56 | 97 | Ground |
| Ichiro Suzuki* | 555 | 2055 | 1016 | 1039 | 345 | 671 | 147 | 427 | 465 | 3.70 | Aggressive | 235 | 94 | 120 | Ground |
| Kurt Suzuki | 316 | 1224 | 712 | 512 | 271 | 441 | 56 | 200 | 256 | 3.87 | Neutral | 94 | 57 | 102 | Air |
| Ryan Sweeney* | 212 | 870 | 528 | 342 | 196 | 332 | 44 | 134 | 164 | 4.10 | Very Patient | 77 | 34 | 51 | Ground |
| Nick Swisher# | 634 | 2522 | 1482 | 1040 | 451 | 1031 | 255 | 370 | 415 | 3.98 | Patient | 158 | 96 | 161 | Air |
| Jose Tabata | 341 | 1269 | 691 | 578 | 218 | 473 | 100 | 210 | 268 | 3.72 | Aggressive | 153 | 48 | 59 | Ground |
| Miguel Tejada | 167 | 585 | 280 | 305 | 103 | 177 | 47 | 123 | 135 | 3.50 | Very Aggressive | 65 | 27 | 39 | Ground |
| Ruben Tejada | 227 | 857 | 477 | 380 | 179 | 298 | 46 | 147 | 187 | 3.78 | Aggressive | 85 | 35 | 62 | Ground |
| Josh Thole* | 135 | 553 | 312 | 241 | 99 | 213 | 32 | 112 | 97 | 4.10 | Very Patient | 41 | 18 | 35 | Medium |
| Clete Thomas* | 322 | 1326 | 736 | 590 | 258 | 478 | 158 | 233 | 199 | 4.12 | Very Patient | 86 | 42 | 67 | Medium |
| Yorvit Torrealba | 196 | 703 | 356 | 347 | 112 | 244 | 62 | 127 | 158 | 3.59 | Very Aggressive | 76 | 32 | 46 | Ground |
| Andres Torres# | 300 | 1111 | 558 | 553 | 175 | 383 | 121 | 215 | 217 | 3.70 | Aggressive | 90 | 41 | 82 | Air |
| Chad Tracy* | 136 | 486 | 253 | 233 | 81 | 172 | 47 | 82 | 104 | 3.57 | Very Aggressive | 32 | 16 | 56 | Air |
| Mike Trout | 716 | 3015 | 1899 | 1116 | 604 | 1295 | 208 | 447 | 461 | 4.21 | Very Patient | 191 | 106 | 164 | Medium |
| Mark Trumbo | 678 | 2521 | 1268 | 1253 | 402 | 866 | 383 | 430 | 440 | 3.72 | Aggressive | 202 | 75 | 163 | Medium |
| Matt Tuiasosopo | 191 | 836 | 501 | 335 | 161 | 340 | 99 | 129 | 107 | 4.38 | Very Patient | 62 | 20 | 25 | Ground |
| Troy Tulowitzki | 512 | 1967 | 1183 | 784 | 399 | 784 | 135 | 283 | 366 | 3.84 | Neutral | 152 | 76 | 138 | Air |
| Justin Turner | 214 | 885 | 458 | 427 | 158 | 300 | 58 | 201 | 168 | 4.14 | Very Patient | 77 | 37 | 53 | Ground |
| Dan Uggla | 537 | 2224 | 1289 | 935 | 357 | 932 | 319 | 336 | 280 | 4.14 | Very Patient | 111 | 37 | 132 | Air |
| B.J. Upton | 446 | 1722 | 923 | 799 | 266 | 657 | 264 | 287 | 247 | 3.86 | Neutral | 110 | 46 | 88 | Medium |
| Justin Upton | 643 | 2628 | 1481 | 1147 | 439 | 1042 | 334 | 411 | 402 | 4.09 | Very Patient | 163 | 86 | 151 | Air |
| Juan Uribe | 426 | 1540 | 739 | 801 | 183 | 556 | 187 | 301 | 313 | 3.62 | Very Aggressive | 132 | 62 | 114 | Medium |
| Chase Utley* | 531 | 2033 | 1186 | 847 | 433 | 753 | 146 | 299 | 402 | 3.83 | Neutral | 152 | 78 | 170 | Air |
| Luis Valbuena* | 391 | 1646 | 985 | 661 | 312 | 673 | 110 | 280 | 271 | 4.21 | Very Patient | 107 | 42 | 121 | Air |
| Jordany Valdespin* | 144 | 576 | 327 | 249 | 130 | 197 | 43 | 101 | 105 | 4.00 | Patient | 47 | 13 | 37 | Medium |
| Danny Valencia | 170 | 706 | 413 | 293 | 152 | 261 | 63 | 101 | 129 | 4.15 | Very Patient | 49 | 28 | 52 | Air |
| Scott Van Slyke | 152 | 633 | 377 | 256 | 118 | 259 | 64 | 98 | 94 | 4.16 | Very Patient | 34 | 16 | 44 | Air |
| Will Venable* | 515 | 1997 | 966 | 1031 | 283 | 683 | 246 | 419 | 366 | 3.88 | Neutral | 166 | 75 | 111 | Ground |
| Dayan Viciedo | 473 | 1810 | 826 | 984 | 218 | 608 | 236 | 400 | 348 | 3.83 | Neutral | 165 | 65 | 118 | Ground |
| Shane Victorino# | 532 | 2039 | 1159 | 880 | 465 | 694 | 134 | 332 | 414 | 3.83 | Neutral | 169 | 89 | 139 | Medium |
| Jonathan Villar# | 241 | 949 | 556 | 393 | 191 | 365 | 123 | 124 | 146 | 3.94 | Patient | 84 | 26 | 18 | Ground |
| Stephen Vogt* | 148 | 599 | 314 | 285 | 109 | 205 | 45 | 129 | 111 | 4.05 | Patient | 32 | 26 | 49 | Air |
| Joey Votto* | 726 | 3033 | 1852 | 1181 | 493 | 1359 | 233 | 499 | 449 | 4.18 | Very Patient | 196 | 122 | 131 | Ground |
| Neil Walker# | 551 | 2042 | 1116 | 926 | 329 | 787 | 182 | 343 | 401 | 3.71 | Aggressive | 151 | 90 | 151 | Air |
| Brett Wallace* | 285 | 1140 | 568 | 572 | 167 | 401 | 192 | 222 | 158 | 4.00 | Patient | 64 | 35 | 59 | Air |
| Rickie Weeks | 399 | 1625 | 963 | 662 | 314 | 649 | 180 | 237 | 245 | 4.07 | Very Patient | 121 | 44 | 80 | Ground |
| Casper Wells | 102 | 369 | 188 | 181 | 60 | 128 | 65 | 52 | 64 | 3.62 | Very Aggressive | 37 | 9 | 18 | Ground |
| Vernon Wells | 458 | 1570 | 774 | 796 | 226 | 548 | 151 | 290 | 355 | 3.43 | Very Aggressive | 148 | 64 | 143 | Air |
| Jayson Werth | 532 | 2258 | 1348 | 910 | 479 | 869 | 174 | 370 | 366 | 4.24 | Very Patient | 132 | 95 | 139 | Air |
| Matt Wieters# | 579 | 2283 | 1181 | 1102 | 345 | 836 | 214 | 456 | 432 | 3.94 | Patient | 166 | 76 | 189 | Air |
| Josh Willingham | 471 | 1988 | 1232 | 756 | 401 | 831 | 213 | 280 | 263 | 4.22 | Very Patient | 96 | 48 | 119 | Air |
| David Wright | 492 | 1867 | 1030 | 837 | 279 | 751 | 148 | 336 | 353 | 3.79 | Neutral | 134 | 81 | 138 | Air |
| Christian Yelich* | 273 | 1172 | 682 | 490 | 202 | 480 | 121 | 194 | 175 | 4.29 | Very Patient | 110 | 40 | 24 | Ground |
| Kevin Youkilis | 118 | 479 | 285 | 194 | 109 | 176 | 39 | 81 | 74 | 4.06 | Patient | 29 | 15 | 30 | Air |
| Chris Young | 375 | 1563 | 887 | 676 | 297 | 590 | 160 | 272 | 244 | 4.17 | Very Patient | 69 | 52 | 120 | Air |

# Hitter Analysis

| Hitter | PA | Pit | T | Sw | St | B | S/M | F | In P | P/PA | Group | GB | LD | FB | Hits |
|---|---|---|---|---|---|---|---|---|---|---|---|---|---|---|---|
| Delmon Young | 361 | 1328 | 570 | 758 | 145 | 425 | 217 | 282 | 259 | 3.68 | Aggressive | 110 | 57 | 92 | Medium |
| Eric Young# | 598 | 2239 | 1184 | 1055 | 388 | 796 | 221 | 384 | 450 | 3.74 | Aggressive | 231 | 88 | 105 | Ground |
| Michael Young | 565 | 2111 | 1167 | 944 | 375 | 792 | 165 | 341 | 438 | 3.74 | Aggressive | 234 | 100 | 104 | Ground |
| Ryan Zimmerman | 633 | 2540 | 1491 | 1049 | 548 | 943 | 232 | 379 | 438 | 4.01 | Patient | 196 | 94 | 148 | Medium |
| Ben Zobrist# | 698 | 2550 | 1532 | 1018 | 512 | 1020 | 142 | 348 | 528 | 3.65 | Aggressive | 224 | 103 | 196 | Air |
| Mike Zunino | 193 | 767 | 398 | 369 | 115 | 283 | 110 | 134 | 125 | 3.97 | Patient | 53 | 23 | 48 | Air |

For some players Swings and Misses, Fouls, and Balls in Play do not add up to overall Swings. This is because of the rare occasions when a swing results in a Catcher Interference.

# Pitcher Analysis

**Bill James**

The custom of counting a ball in play as a strike is something of a nuisance as we try to make use of this data, the Pitcher Analysis data. The pitcher analysis. . .perhaps it should be called pitch analysis. . .records how many strikes each pitcher threw, how many balls, how many swinging strikes, how many ground balls, etc. It counts balls in play as strikes, which could tend to cause pitchers who get hit hard to show up in the data as throwing lots of strikes. To be honest, I don't know how else you would do it.

The value of data depends upon what questions it answers, so let's ask a few questions of this data, and see what we get.

***1) Can you throw too many strikes?***

Not really, as much as we can tell from the data. The "strike" percentages of major league pitchers in 2013 ranged from 54% (Jeurys Famila) to 74% (Koji Uehara), but really, almost everybody is in the 60s. Of the 556 pitchers in this chart,

8 threw 70% strikes,

54 threw less than 60% strikes, and

The other 494 threw 60 to 69% strikes.

The real data, then, is in the 60 to 69% range. Suppose that we divide these pitchers into ten groups, according to the percentage of strikes thrown. Group 1, led by Koji Uehara, threw 68% strikes or more than 68%. Group 2 threw 67%, Group 3 66%, Group 4 65%, etc.; Group 10 threw less than 60% strikes. There are about 55 pitchers in each group, with the largest group being Group 5 (87 pitchers) and the smallest group Group 2 (28 pitchers).

As you would expect, the strikeout to walk ratio improves steadily with more strikes:

| Group | 1 | 2 | 3 | 4 | 5 | 6 | 7 | 8 | 9 | 10 |
|---|---|---|---|---|---|---|---|---|---|---|
| Strike Pct | 68%> | 67% | 66% | 65% | 64% | 63% | 62% | 61% | 60% | <60% |
| SO/BB | 4.8 | 4.1 | 3.2 | 3 | 2.8 | 2.5 | 2.1 | 1.9 | 1.6 | 1.3 |

We can say, then, that if a pitcher throws 61-62% strikes, he will have a strikeout/walk ratio of 2-1, whereas if he throws 65% strikes, he will have a strikeout/walk ratio of 3-1, and 67%, 4-1. One would expect there to be some predictable relationship there, and there is.

OK, but as the strikeout/walk ratio increases, the ERA improves with almost equal regularity:

| Group | 1 | 2 | 3 | 4 | 5 | 6 | 7 | 8 | 9 | 10 |
|---|---|---|---|---|---|---|---|---|---|---|
| Strike Pct | 68%> | 67% | 66% | 65% | 64% | 63% | 62% | 61% | 60% | <60% |
| ERA | 4.8 | 4.1 | 3.2 | 3 | 2.8 | 2.5 | 2.1 | 1.9 | 1.6 | 1.3 |
| Winning Pct | 3.03 | 3.28 | 3.47 | 3.78 | 3.62 | 3.81 | 4.20 | 4.57 | 4.42 | 4.61 |

The winning percentage improves. Group 1, the strike throwers, had a .574 winning percentage, highest of any group, while Group 10 had a .395 winning percentage, lowest of any group. Group 1 relievers got saves in 79% of their Save Opportunities; Group 10, in 55%.

Perhaps more surprisingly, even the Home Run rates improved as the pitchers threw more strikes. Group 1 allowed 0.84 Home Runs per 9 innings, the lowest home run rate of any group. Group 10 allowed 1.04 Home Runs per 9 innings, the worst home run rate of any group. There is no evidence in this study that you can throw too many strikes. This is the full data from the study:

| Group | 1 | 2 | 3 | 4 | 5 | 6 | 7 | 8 | 9 | 10 |
|---|---|---|---|---|---|---|---|---|---|---|
| Strike Pct | 68%> | 67% | 66% | 65% | 64% | 63% | 62% | 61% | 60% | <60% |
| ERA | 3.03 | 3.28 | 3.47 | 3.78 | 3.62 | 3.81 | 4.20 | 4.57 | 4.42 | 4.61 |
| Winning Pct | .574 | .514 | .548 | .494 | .536 | .512 | .479 | .435 | .478 | .395 |
| Save Pct | 79% | 69% | 79% | 66% | 65% | 65% | 74% | 44% | 11% | 55% |
| SO/BB | 4.8 | 4.1 | 3.2 | 3.0 | 2.8 | 2.5 | 2.1 | 1.9 | 1.6 | 1.3 |
| HR Rate | .84 | .91 | .96 | 1.00 | .93 | .95 | .99 | .98 | .93 | 1.04 |

***2) Which is more of a key to success: Throwing Strikes, or Having a Swing and Miss Pitch?***

Koji Uehara, who led the majors in the percentage of strikes thrown in 2013, also had the highest swing-and-miss percentage of any major league pitcher, 27%. The "central range" for swing-and-miss percentages is 12 to 20%. Of the 556 pitchers in this data, 58 have swing-and-miss percentages over 20%, and 54 have swing-and-miss percentages under 12%. The other 444 are in the 12-to-20 class.

Suppose that we sort those the same way that we did before, with Group 1 being Swing-and-Miss Percentages over 20 and Group 10 being Swing-and-Miss Percentages under 12.

This second sort immediately reveals some interesting anomalies. Scott Rice of the Mets and Jose de la Torre of the Red Sox had very high swing-and-miss percentages, but nonetheless did not throw strikes. Brandon McCarthy, on the other hand, had a very low swing-and-miss percentage (9%), but nonetheless did throw strikes (69%). Bartolo Colon has a low swing-and-miss percentage (10%), but nonetheless pounds the strike zone.

Throwing strikes and having a swing-and-miss pitch are of comparable importance to a major league pitcher. Neither one is substantially more important than the other.

However, to answer the question rather than ducking it, Throwing Strikes is more important to the success of a major league pitcher than Having a Swing-and-Miss Pitch. This is the data from the Swing-and-Miss Study, parallel to the Strike Percentage Data:

| Group | 1 | 2 | 3 | 4 | 5 | 6 | 7 | 8 | 9 | 10 |
|---|---|---|---|---|---|---|---|---|---|---|
| S/M Pct | 21%> | 19-20% | 18% | 17% | 16 | 15 | 14 | 13 | 12 | 12 |
| ERA | 3.12 | 3.37 | 3.15 | 3.72 | 3.66 | 3.98 | 4.09 | 4.17 | 4.20 | 4.41 |
| Winning Pct | .516 | .534 | .529 | .540 | .542 | .486 | .472 | .488 | .483 | .453 |
| Save Pct | 78% | 48% | 77% | 51% | 63% | 41% | 76% | 75% | 65% | 10% |
| SO/BB | 3.2 | 2.7 | 2.9 | 2.9 | 2.6 | 2.5 | 2.4 | 2.3 | 2.1 | 2.0 |
| HR Rate | .85 | .84 | .78 | .94 | .95 | .92 | 1.06 | 1.09 | 1.00 | 1.02 |

When we slice the pitchers into groups by the percentage of strikes thrown, the ERA improves from 4.61 from the worst group to 3.03 for the best group. When we divide them by the swing-and-miss percentages, the improvement is from 4.41 to 3.12, which is comparable but less. This is true across the board: the improvements in all areas of performance are larger and more consistent with improving strike percentages than with improving swing-and-miss rates. The one exception is the Home Run Rates. Home Run rates probably improve more with more swings and misses than they do with more strikes.

We might generalize that "young" pitchers have high swing-and-miss percentages but low strike percentages, whereas "old" pitchers have low swing-and-miss percentages but high strike percentages. In this way, we could assign each pitcher an "age" based not on his calendar age, but on his pitching patterns. If we do that, the ten "oldest" pitchers in the majors in 2013 were 1. Brandon McCarthy, 2. Bartolo Colon, 3. Tanner Roark, 4. Ian Krol, 5. Brandon Crumpton, 6. Kevin Slowey, 7. David Price, 8. Bronson Arroyo, 9. Andrew Albers, and 10. Scott Baker. The ten "youngest" pitchers in the majors were 1. Jose De La Torre, 2. Scott Rice, 3. Luis Garcia, 4. Matt Harrison, 5. Marc Rzepczynski, 6. Buddy Boshers, 7. Donnie Veal, 8. J. J. Putz, 9. Matt Magill, and 10. Keith Butler.

### *3. How important is Ground Ball Rate to Success as a pitcher?*

It isn't. At all.

Look, whether Ground Ball Rates correlate with success in pitching depends entirely on whether or not you remove the strikeouts from the process before you figure Ground Ball Rates. But let's start with "not".

The highest Ground Ball rate in the majors in 2013 was for Sam Dyson of Miami, who faced 54 batters and got 29 Ground Balls. Dyson, however, only pitched 11 innings; the highest ground ball rate for a real pitcher was 53%, for Seth Maness of the Cardinals. The lowest ground ball rate in the majors was 8%, for Guillermo Moscoso, and the lowest ground ball rate for a pitcher pitching 50 or more innings was 13%, for Ernesto Frieri of the Angels. Most of the data is in the range of 22 to 39%, ground balls divided by batters faced.

We'll say that a Ground Ball rate of 40% or higher represents Group 1, 37-39% is Group 2, 35-36% is Group 3, 33-34% is Group 4, 31-32%, is Group 5, 29-30% is Group 6, 27-28% is Group 7, 24-26% is Group 8, 21-23% is Group 9, and 20% or less is Group 10.

One can see, in this data, that as pitchers throw more ground balls, they do not become more effective. The two most effective groups of pitchers are Groups 9 and Groups 10, the two groups which throw the fewest ground balls. They have the best ERAs, the best Save Percentages and the best strikeout/walk ratios in the study. :

| Group | 1 | 2 | 3 | 4 | 5 | 6 | 7 | 8 | 9 | 10 |
|---|---|---|---|---|---|---|---|---|---|---|
| GB Pct | 40%> | 37-39% | 35-36% | 33-34% | 31-32% | 29-30% | 27-28% | 24-26% | 21-23% | <20% |
| ERA | 3.83 | 4.06 | 3.65 | 3.87 | 3.90 | 3.90 | 4.03 | 3.88 | 3.48 | 3.46 |
| Winning Pct | .518 | .450 | .521 | .510 | .503 | .511 | .505 | .476 | .535 | .503 |
| Save Pct | 64% | 13% | 70% | 67% | 55% | 70% | 59% | 68% | 75% | 79% |
| SO/BB | 2.1 | 2.0 | 2.5 | 2.6 | 2.7 | 2.5 | 2.7 | 2.3 | 3.0 | 2.8 |
| HR Rate | .69 | .90 | .87 | .95 | .98 | .98 | 1.15 | 1.00 | 1.02 | 1.10 |

Ground Ball pitchers allow fewer home runs, but their mediocre strikeout/walk ratios more than offset this benefit. I have had this argument, with those I work with and with others in the sabermetric community, for many years. I have never liked Ground Ball pitchers; basically, I don't want to have anything to do with Ground Ball pitchers.

But it does depend on how you look at the data. Those who like Ground Ball pitchers will defend their position by arguing that I should have excluded strikeouts from the data before I figured the Ground Ball rates. "You should either exclude strikeouts, or you should figure Ground Ball rates by focusing *only* on the outs," they will say. "If you do either of those things, then the Ground Ball pitchers look better. You have made the Ground Ball pitchers look worse by including Ground Ball singles as Ground Ball outs."

Well, that's true as far as it goes. If you remove the strikeouts and walks from the data before figuring Ground Ball Rates, then the Ground Ball pitchers do have a small advantage over the Fly Ball pitchers. For convenience, this time we'll just divide the pitchers into 10 equal groups; the "1" group is the pitchers getting the most ground balls:

| Group | 1 | 2 | 3 | 4 | 5 | 6 | 7 | 8 | 9 | 10 |
|---|---|---|---|---|---|---|---|---|---|---|
| ERA | 3.44 | 3.77 | 3.79 | 3.71 | 3.85 | 3.83 | 4.18 | 4.13 | 3.96 | 3.77 |
| Winning Pct | .548 | .489 | .512 | .516 | .504 | .503 | .494 | .490 | .474 | .493 |
| Save Pct | 61% | 68% | 47% | 77% | 52% | 71% | 70% | 67% | 77% | 70% |
| SO/BB | 2.3 | 2.2 | 2.5 | 2.7 | 2.7 | 2.6 | 2.5 | 2.4 | 2.7 | 2.6 |
| HR Rate | .63 | .77 | .88 | .90 | .95 | 1.00 | 1.07 | 1.16 | 1.14 | 1.15 |

Even interpreted in this way, the advantage of Ground Ball pitchers is small compared to the advantage of throwing strikes or the advantage of a swing and miss pitch. But the real question is, what is the right way to interpret the data?

To me, excluding strikeouts from the data before determining who is and who is not a ground ball pitcher is like excluding home runs from the data. The problem with ground ball pitchers is that they give up too much hard contact. What you really need to avoid is line drives. When a pitcher gets more ground balls, that generally doesn't mean fewer line drives, it generally means fewer strikeouts.

Well. ..enough arguing; let's look at some fun stuff in the data.

***James Shields*** was behind the hitter 1-0 after one pitch 401 times in 2013, more than any other major league pitcher.

***Ryan Pressly*** was behind the hitter 1-0 54% of the time, the worst percentage for a pitcher with a reasonable number of innings.

***Edward Mujica*** was behind the hitter 1-0 only 27% of the time, the best percentage in the major leagues.

***Adam Wainwright*** was ahead of the hitter 0-1 504 times, the most of any major league pitcher. ***Cliff Lee*** was right behind him, with 498, and that was in 20 fewer innings.

***Doug Fister*** got the most ground balls of any major league pitcher, 352.

***Jeremy Guthrie*** gave up the most line drives, 160.

***A. J. Griffin*** gave up the most fly balls, 288.

***C. J. Wilson*** had by far the most full counts, 155.

***Verlander*** and ***Scherzer*** had the most two-strike counts on hitters, 525 for Verlander, 504 for Scherzer. ***Yu Darvish***, with 277 strikeouts, had "only" 498 two-strike counts.

***C. J. Wilson*** (206) and ***Lucas Harrell*** (200) were the only major league pitchers to have 200 three-ball counts.

What we are trying to do, with this data, is nurture an understanding of pitching on a more molecular level. Let us take a memorable season from the past. . .let's say Steve Carlton in 1972, or Nolan Ryan in 1973. How many pitches did he throw? How many of them were strikes? How many swings and misses did he probably get?

Steve Carlton in 1972 had a strikeout/walk ratio of 3.6 to 1, so it is likely, based on what we now know, that he threw about 66-67% strikes. Nolan Ryan in '73 had a strikeout/walk ratio of 2.4 to 1, so it seems likely that he threw about 62-63% strikes.

Except that we don't really know enough, yet, to make these estimates with confidence. Ryan had 383 strikeouts, 162 walks—but other pitchers in 200+

innings have had 128 strikeouts and 54 walks, the same ratio but very different numbers. Were their strike percentages the same as Ryan's, or different?

We have not had access to this type of data long enough yet to have a deep understanding of it. It will take years or decades of studying this data to really understand the ball-and-strike economics of the game on the same level that we understand the hits-and-outs economics. Printing this kind of data, and writing a little bit about it, is intended to start people thinking about these kind of questions, so that a better understanding will eventually emerge.

The "highest" level of outcomes is wins and losses, and next is runs and innings. Below that are the "category"outcomes of batters faced, strikeouts, walks, home runs allowed, hit batsmen, etc. Modern analysis has shown that, while the higher-level outcomes are more important, the lower-level outcomes are better predictors of future outcomes—including the future higher-level outcomes.

But below the third-level data (batters faced, strikeouts, walks, etc.) there is another level of data—pitches, strikes, balls, line drives, etc. It is likely that the fourth-level outcomes are better predictors than the third-level outcomes, for the same reason that the third-level outcomes are better predictors than the first-and second-level outcomes. So it is likely that, over time, analysis will slide toward the fourth-level outcomes. I'm just trying to push the process along a little bit.

# Pitcher Analysis

## Pitchers with 50+ Batters Faced in 2013

| | | | | | | | | | | Counts | | | | |
|---|---|---|---|---|---|---|---|---|---|---|---|---|---|---|
| Pitcher | BF | Pitches | K | BB | GB | LD | FB | Str% | S/Str | 1-0 | 0-1 | Full | 2 Strike | 3 Ball |
| David Aardsma | 178 | 728 | 36 | 19 | 38 | 30 | 48 | 61% | 20% | 77 | 85 | 23 | 96 | 40 |
| Fernando Abad | 166 | 654 | 32 | 10 | 48 | 26 | 48 | 67% | 15% | 59 | 87 | 24 | 98 | 27 |
| Alfredo Aceves | 169 | 625 | 24 | 22 | 56 | 25 | 40 | 61% | 12% | 72 | 75 | 23 | 76 | 41 |
| Mike Adams | 107 | 412 | 23 | 11 | 39 | 11 | 21 | 64% | 15% | 47 | 50 | 14 | 55 | 20 |
| Jeremy Affeldt | 146 | 523 | 21 | 17 | 54 | 25 | 20 | 59% | 14% | 66 | 62 | 14 | 54 | 32 |
| Andrew Albers | 249 | 917 | 25 | 7 | 91 | 41 | 77 | 67% | 10% | 79 | 138 | 25 | 116 | 37 |
| Matt Albers | 262 | 943 | 35 | 23 | 127 | 38 | 34 | 62% | 13% | 100 | 120 | 29 | 109 | 49 |
| Al Alburquerque | 220 | 879 | 70 | 34 | 46 | 29 | 39 | 62% | 26% | 93 | 110 | 27 | 127 | 54 |
| Cody Allen | 301 | 1204 | 88 | 26 | 54 | 44 | 81 | 62% | 20% | 134 | 135 | 42 | 165 | 61 |
| Henderson Alvarez | 418 | 1451 | 57 | 27 | 170 | 70 | 78 | 65% | 11% | 164 | 194 | 40 | 180 | 63 |
| Jose Alvarez | 172 | 696 | 31 | 16 | 48 | 27 | 44 | 60% | 18% | 77 | 75 | 29 | 81 | 47 |
| Hector Ambriz | 171 | 649 | 27 | 14 | 59 | 25 | 43 | 62% | 14% | 80 | 76 | 23 | 85 | 31 |
| Brett Anderson | 200 | 768 | 46 | 21 | 83 | 21 | 28 | 62% | 15% | 85 | 90 | 27 | 98 | 43 |
| Chris Archer | 525 | 2103 | 101 | 38 | 176 | 72 | 128 | 63% | 15% | 219 | 260 | 64 | 272 | 100 |
| Jake Arrieta | 324 | 1265 | 60 | 41 | 86 | 54 | 73 | 62% | 12% | 131 | 155 | 43 | 163 | 73 |
| Bronson Arroyo | 823 | 2873 | 124 | 34 | 287 | 131 | 228 | 67% | 10% | 283 | 419 | 80 | 374 | 110 |
| Scott Atchison | 194 | 740 | 28 | 12 | 73 | 30 | 47 | 63% | 12% | 79 | 97 | 28 | 98 | 36 |
| Phillippe Aumont | 95 | 371 | 19 | 13 | 29 | 17 | 13 | 60% | 16% | 36 | 44 | 11 | 45 | 26 |
| Luis Avilan | 256 | 1001 | 38 | 22 | 109 | 35 | 45 | 60% | 14% | 118 | 113 | 39 | 121 | 60 |
| Dylan Axelrod | 586 | 2269 | 73 | 43 | 186 | 97 | 179 | 61% | 13% | 244 | 269 | 100 | 280 | 126 |
| John Axford | 289 | 1170 | 65 | 26 | 86 | 46 | 58 | 61% | 17% | 132 | 131 | 44 | 144 | 69 |
| Luis Ayala | 143 | 555 | 22 | 13 | 63 | 23 | 21 | 63% | 13% | 55 | 77 | 19 | 73 | 29 |
| Burke Badenhop | 254 | 922 | 42 | 12 | 97 | 42 | 51 | 63% | 10% | 90 | 124 | 30 | 116 | 40 |
| Andrew Bailey | 116 | 488 | 39 | 12 | 14 | 15 | 34 | 64% | 19% | 51 | 55 | 18 | 74 | 24 |
| Homer Bailey | 849 | 3292 | 199 | 54 | 263 | 111 | 196 | 67% | 17% | 302 | 448 | 99 | 456 | 136 |
| Scott Baker | 57 | 200 | 6 | 4 | 13 | 6 | 27 | 70% | 13% | 20 | 27 | 6 | 28 | 7 |
| Grant Balfour | 262 | 1145 | 72 | 27 | 61 | 37 | 63 | 62% | 18% | 117 | 123 | 52 | 164 | 75 |
| Anthony Bass | 193 | 710 | 31 | 20 | 63 | 38 | 39 | 61% | 20% | 91 | 81 | 20 | 80 | 38 |
| Antonio Bastardo | 179 | 702 | 47 | 21 | 33 | 19 | 53 | 64% | 22% | 58 | 99 | 28 | 104 | 38 |
| Trevor Bauer | 81 | 350 | 11 | 16 | 18 | 10 | 23 | 56% | 12% | 35 | 42 | 20 | 45 | 28 |
| Brandon Beachy | 120 | 448 | 23 | 4 | 37 | 15 | 37 | 67% | 14% | 45 | 63 | 13 | 63 | 14 |
| Blake Beavan | 174 | 647 | 27 | 8 | 52 | 28 | 57 | 68% | 13% | 53 | 105 | 22 | 86 | 28 |
| Josh Beckett | 195 | 739 | 41 | 15 | 52 | 32 | 49 | 63% | 18% | 73 | 103 | 15 | 95 | 28 |
| Erik Bedard | 663 | 2679 | 138 | 75 | 157 | 77 | 197 | 62% | 14% | 266 | 331 | 117 | 370 | 162 |
| Ronald Belisario | 300 | 1088 | 49 | 28 | 132 | 45 | 38 | 64% | 15% | 116 | 142 | 28 | 141 | 49 |
| Matt Belisle | 301 | 1126 | 62 | 15 | 107 | 58 | 55 | 69% | 16% | 100 | 170 | 30 | 165 | 40 |
| Heath Bell | 287 | 1126 | 72 | 16 | 83 | 45 | 65 | 64% | 16% | 115 | 140 | 48 | 145 | 58 |
| Joaquin Benoit | 265 | 1068 | 73 | 22 | 69 | 32 | 62 | 64% | 23% | 99 | 146 | 39 | 152 | 50 |
| Rafael Betancourt | 123 | 481 | 27 | 11 | 28 | 13 | 40 | 66% | 14% | 42 | 71 | 7 | 65 | 16 |
| Chad Bettis | 208 | 778 | 30 | 20 | 71 | 32 | 49 | 63% | 13% | 81 | 97 | 23 | 94 | 39 |
| Vic Black | 76 | 285 | 15 | 6 | 16 | 12 | 25 | 64% | 15% | 30 | 40 | 8 | 39 | 11 |
| Travis Blackley | 211 | 829 | 40 | 22 | 63 | 30 | 51 | 61% | 19% | 89 | 99 | 33 | 106 | 47 |
| Joe Blanton | 611 | 2221 | 108 | 34 | 203 | 103 | 152 | 65% | 15% | 221 | 317 | 60 | 273 | 90 |
| Michael Blazek | 84 | 334 | 14 | 13 | 24 | 6 | 25 | 61% | 18% | 36 | 40 | 9 | 43 | 19 |
| Jerry Blevins | 245 | 972 | 52 | 17 | 52 | 31 | 83 | 62% | 16% | 101 | 108 | 33 | 131 | 53 |
| Mitchell Boggs | 120 | 453 | 16 | 20 | 43 | 17 | 19 | 59% | 14% | 39 | 64 | 13 | 51 | 29 |
| Jeremy Bonderman | 246 | 904 | 32 | 27 | 75 | 40 | 68 | 59% | 13% | 115 | 100 | 26 | 94 | 53 |
| Buddy Boshers | 63 | 252 | 13 | 8 | 18 | 10 | 13 | 54% | 19% | 36 | 23 | 10 | 28 | 19 |
| Michael Bowden | 158 | 606 | 23 | 15 | 34 | 28 | 49 | 64% | 18% | 55 | 82 | 19 | 78 | 30 |
| Brad Boxberger | 94 | 394 | 24 | 13 | 22 | 9 | 21 | 60% | 22% | 36 | 50 | 12 | 52 | 22 |
| Brad Brach | 141 | 617 | 31 | 19 | 34 | 21 | 35 | 60% | 16% | 65 | 66 | 37 | 83 | 45 |
| Craig Breslow | 237 | 867 | 33 | 18 | 81 | 38 | 62 | 63% | 14% | 99 | 98 | 27 | 105 | 46 |
| Drake Britton | 84 | 312 | 17 | 7 | 28 | 15 | 17 | 61% | 17% | 41 | 33 | 14 | 40 | 19 |
| Zach Britton | 182 | 663 | 18 | 17 | 83 | 28 | 32 | 60% | 11% | 84 | 79 | 20 | 72 | 37 |
| Rex Brothers | 281 | 1119 | 76 | 36 | 81 | 31 | 54 | 62% | 21% | 120 | 135 | 41 | 152 | 63 |
| Jonathan Broxton | 133 | 509 | 25 | 12 | 42 | 15 | 34 | 60% | 21% | 60 | 56 | 17 | 63 | 29 |
| Clay Buchholz | 416 | 1629 | 96 | 36 | 132 | 57 | 88 | 64% | 15% | 169 | 195 | 78 | 234 | 96 |
| Billy Buckner | 73 | 289 | 7 | 7 | 20 | 12 | 25 | 61% | 8% | 35 | 33 | 11 | 32 | 16 |
| Mark Buehrle | 876 | 3299 | 139 | 51 | 302 | 137 | 227 | 63% | 12% | 361 | 419 | 110 | 405 | 156 |
| Madison Bumgarner | 803 | 3204 | 199 | 62 | 242 | 93 | 182 | 64% | 18% | 317 | 408 | 119 | 445 | 154 |
| Hiram Burgos | 139 | 534 | 18 | 11 | 42 | 15 | 48 | 63% | 12% | 44 | 82 | 23 | 73 | 32 |
| Greg Burke | 156 | 612 | 28 | 15 | 57 | 24 | 29 | 61% | 17% | 61 | 77 | 28 | 79 | 38 |
| A.J. Burnett | 801 | 3021 | 209 | 67 | 282 | 96 | 121 | 65% | 17% | 301 | 398 | 92 | 435 | 149 |
| Cory Burns | 54 | 210 | 5 | 7 | 14 | 5 | 22 | 60% | 19% | 27 | 23 | 6 | 24 | 11 |
| Jared Burton | 281 | 1062 | 61 | 22 | 78 | 37 | 73 | 65% | 21% | 100 | 149 | 23 | 142 | 44 |
| Keith Butler | 85 | 334 | 16 | 11 | 14 | 11 | 32 | 59% | 20% | 41 | 33 | 14 | 43 | 24 |
| Trevor Cahill | 636 | 2373 | 102 | 65 | 250 | 88 | 107 | 59% | 14% | 258 | 294 | 93 | 276 | 143 |
| Matt Cain | 760 | 2922 | 158 | 55 | 200 | 119 | 212 | 64% | 14% | 282 | 384 | 103 | 380 | 140 |

# Pitcher Analysis

## Pitchers with 50+ Batters Faced in 2013

| | | | | | | | | | | Counts | | | | |
|---|---|---|---|---|---|---|---|---|---|---|---|---|---|---|
| Pitcher | BF | Pitches | K | BB | GB | LD | FB | Str% | S/Str | 1-0 | 0-1 | Full | 2 Strike | 3 Ball |
| Arquimedes Caminero | 52 | 205 | 12 | 3 | 9 | 6 | 21 | 63% | 16% | 24 | 21 | 7 | 25 | 11 |
| Shawn Camp | 108 | 391 | 13 | 9 | 41 | 12 | 31 | 65% | 11% | 47 | 48 | 13 | 48 | 20 |
| Carter Capps | 270 | 1057 | 66 | 23 | 71 | 42 | 64 | 63% | 21% | 108 | 141 | 30 | 135 | 52 |
| Chris Capuano | 457 | 1699 | 81 | 24 | 159 | 70 | 114 | 63% | 16% | 178 | 226 | 48 | 212 | 78 |
| David Carpenter | 256 | 1061 | 74 | 20 | 60 | 36 | 61 | 66% | 20% | 87 | 145 | 34 | 166 | 48 |
| Carlos Carrasco | 218 | 787 | 30 | 18 | 84 | 37 | 46 | 66% | 14% | 72 | 119 | 23 | 94 | 38 |
| Robert Carson | 88 | 326 | 8 | 7 | 25 | 12 | 34 | 62% | 12% | 33 | 48 | 10 | 34 | 16 |
| Andrew Cashner | 707 | 2687 | 128 | 47 | 273 | 98 | 149 | 64% | 14% | 284 | 353 | 86 | 346 | 130 |
| Santiago Casilla | 208 | 807 | 38 | 25 | 74 | 24 | 40 | 61% | 16% | 95 | 88 | 29 | 106 | 44 |
| Brett Cecil | 250 | 919 | 70 | 23 | 77 | 30 | 43 | 63% | 19% | 103 | 120 | 30 | 118 | 51 |
| Xavier Cedeno | 60 | 221 | 9 | 8 | 24 | 6 | 10 | 62% | 15% | 23 | 30 | 6 | 25 | 13 |
| Jhoulys Chacin | 816 | 2962 | 126 | 61 | 288 | 151 | 177 | 64% | 12% | 319 | 408 | 91 | 363 | 150 |
| Joba Chamberlain | 198 | 769 | 38 | 26 | 54 | 32 | 44 | 62% | 16% | 57 | 108 | 34 | 105 | 46 |
| Aroldis Chapman | 258 | 1099 | 112 | 29 | 38 | 27 | 48 | 65% | 26% | 105 | 138 | 38 | 179 | 52 |
| Kevin Chapman | 87 | 322 | 15 | 13 | 21 | 12 | 21 | 58% | 12% | 38 | 38 | 9 | 38 | 19 |
| Tyler Chatwood | 476 | 1782 | 66 | 41 | 210 | 74 | 75 | 61% | 12% | 212 | 212 | 55 | 197 | 100 |
| Jesse Chavez | 248 | 948 | 55 | 20 | 70 | 28 | 63 | 66% | 15% | 95 | 121 | 28 | 137 | 39 |
| Bruce Chen | 498 | 1962 | 78 | 36 | 104 | 77 | 195 | 66% | 11% | 169 | 280 | 62 | 259 | 81 |
| Wei-Yin Chen | 572 | 2192 | 104 | 39 | 144 | 103 | 172 | 66% | 13% | 236 | 277 | 61 | 274 | 96 |
| Randy Choate | 141 | 487 | 28 | 11 | 65 | 11 | 19 | 64% | 19% | 55 | 70 | 12 | 66 | 23 |
| Tony Cingrani | 420 | 1816 | 120 | 43 | 85 | 52 | 111 | 62% | 17% | 179 | 207 | 71 | 247 | 102 |
| Steve Cishek | 281 | 1107 | 74 | 22 | 94 | 31 | 52 | 63% | 16% | 104 | 148 | 27 | 147 | 50 |
| Jose Cisnero | 198 | 791 | 41 | 22 | 50 | 33 | 50 | 60% | 20% | 100 | 87 | 30 | 95 | 52 |
| Preston Claiborne | 214 | 839 | 42 | 14 | 69 | 28 | 57 | 63% | 18% | 85 | 114 | 27 | 113 | 41 |
| Paul Clemens | 323 | 1168 | 49 | 26 | 87 | 40 | 119 | 62% | 13% | 135 | 141 | 43 | 144 | 67 |
| Tyler Clippard | 275 | 1166 | 73 | 24 | 48 | 28 | 96 | 66% | 23% | 111 | 136 | 43 | 168 | 59 |
| Tyler Cloyd | 282 | 1066 | 41 | 25 | 82 | 47 | 79 | 62% | 11% | 110 | 135 | 37 | 132 | 56 |
| Alex Cobb | 578 | 2221 | 134 | 45 | 218 | 85 | 88 | 65% | 15% | 238 | 289 | 66 | 312 | 99 |
| Robert Coello | 73 | 305 | 23 | 8 | 8 | 13 | 19 | 62% | 19% | 32 | 36 | 12 | 44 | 17 |
| Phil Coke | 177 | 629 | 30 | 21 | 55 | 25 | 41 | 62% | 19% | 73 | 86 | 12 | 78 | 33 |
| Gerrit Cole | 469 | 1727 | 100 | 28 | 162 | 82 | 86 | 65% | 15% | 172 | 242 | 58 | 231 | 82 |
| Louis Coleman | 110 | 420 | 32 | 6 | 29 | 17 | 24 | 66% | 27% | 37 | 58 | 13 | 65 | 18 |
| Tim Collins | 233 | 963 | 52 | 28 | 57 | 31 | 63 | 60% | 16% | 112 | 105 | 33 | 129 | 54 |
| Josh Collmenter | 384 | 1555 | 85 | 33 | 81 | 51 | 116 | 64% | 18% | 156 | 193 | 58 | 210 | 82 |
| Alex Colome | 71 | 265 | 12 | 9 | 21 | 11 | 17 | 61% | 19% | 28 | 32 | 11 | 32 | 16 |
| Bartolo Colon | 769 | 2777 | 117 | 29 | 255 | 126 | 233 | 69% | 10% | 271 | 417 | 62 | 381 | 98 |
| Ryan Cook | 294 | 1146 | 67 | 25 | 91 | 37 | 67 | 64% | 18% | 124 | 144 | 34 | 151 | 60 |
| Patrick Corbin | 860 | 3082 | 178 | 54 | 282 | 134 | 188 | 66% | 17% | 256 | 467 | 96 | 395 | 134 |
| Manny Corpas | 178 | 643 | 30 | 16 | 57 | 30 | 40 | 60% | 16% | 77 | 73 | 28 | 75 | 46 |
| Kevin Correia | 792 | 2921 | 101 | 45 | 279 | 149 | 206 | 63% | 10% | 334 | 355 | 94 | 335 | 137 |
| Jarred Cosart | 246 | 1024 | 33 | 35 | 96 | 37 | 43 | 57% | 10% | 117 | 112 | 39 | 121 | 68 |
| Neal Cotts | 223 | 929 | 65 | 18 | 60 | 30 | 46 | 68% | 19% | 81 | 123 | 34 | 148 | 39 |
| Jesse Crain | 152 | 669 | 46 | 11 | 32 | 22 | 38 | 64% | 18% | 59 | 78 | 30 | 102 | 36 |
| Aaron Crow | 210 | 807 | 44 | 22 | 68 | 27 | 43 | 61% | 18% | 88 | 95 | 26 | 100 | 52 |
| Rhiner Cruz | 98 | 381 | 10 | 11 | 24 | 16 | 34 | 62% | 16% | 45 | 41 | 14 | 46 | 21 |
| Johnny Cueto | 242 | 958 | 51 | 18 | 86 | 42 | 41 | 64% | 18% | 94 | 130 | 36 | 128 | 43 |
| Brandon Cumpton | 124 | 449 | 22 | 5 | 51 | 16 | 27 | 68% | 10% | 47 | 61 | 8 | 56 | 17 |
| John Danks | 583 | 2202 | 89 | 27 | 189 | 101 | 167 | 66% | 14% | 223 | 293 | 70 | 278 | 98 |
| Yu Darvish | 841 | 3451 | 277 | 80 | 194 | 99 | 180 | 62% | 21% | 360 | 420 | 107 | 498 | 171 |
| Wade Davis | 618 | 2470 | 114 | 58 | 177 | 120 | 140 | 62% | 13% | 256 | 304 | 100 | 317 | 140 |
| Justin De Fratus | 208 | 835 | 42 | 25 | 58 | 35 | 40 | 62% | 19% | 91 | 105 | 28 | 114 | 47 |
| Dane de la Rosa | 291 | 1196 | 65 | 28 | 99 | 39 | 55 | 63% | 19% | 133 | 140 | 42 | 174 | 65 |
| Eury De la Rosa | 62 | 254 | 16 | 5 | 15 | 4 | 21 | 62% | 18% | 24 | 32 | 10 | 36 | 10 |
| Jorge de la Rosa | 714 | 2774 | 112 | 62 | 245 | 130 | 143 | 62% | 16% | 285 | 339 | 109 | 334 | 156 |
| Rubby de la Rosa | 53 | 189 | 6 | 2 | 20 | 6 | 16 | 67% | 16% | 18 | 26 | 5 | 26 | 10 |
| Jose De La Torre | 53 | 229 | 15 | 10 | 13 | 4 | 10 | 57% | 25% | 24 | 24 | 12 | 33 | 19 |
| Jorge De Leon | 50 | 181 | 6 | 7 | 13 | 7 | 15 | 56% | 16% | 23 | 19 | 5 | 20 | 10 |
| Samuel Deduno | 461 | 1743 | 67 | 41 | 203 | 69 | 68 | 61% | 13% | 224 | 205 | 58 | 209 | 93 |
| Steve Delabar | 253 | 1002 | 82 | 29 | 40 | 31 | 65 | 64% | 24% | 96 | 136 | 38 | 148 | 58 |
| Randall Delgado | 473 | 1811 | 79 | 23 | 153 | 71 | 139 | 65% | 14% | 187 | 239 | 57 | 236 | 86 |
| Ryan Dempster | 754 | 2997 | 157 | 79 | 205 | 109 | 189 | 62% | 16% | 301 | 382 | 113 | 384 | 172 |
| Ross Detwiler | 316 | 1115 | 39 | 14 | 113 | 57 | 78 | 64% | 11% | 139 | 140 | 31 | 123 | 45 |
| Cole DeVries | 76 | 301 | 12 | 9 | 13 | 9 | 33 | 60% | 13% | 36 | 31 | 10 | 37 | 19 |
| Scott Diamond | 576 | 2206 | 52 | 36 | 227 | 103 | 154 | 62% | 10% | 242 | 276 | 78 | 259 | 122 |
| R.A. Dickey | 943 | 3505 | 177 | 71 | 275 | 131 | 276 | 65% | 15% | 371 | 467 | 114 | 461 | 173 |
| Jake Diekman | 164 | 637 | 41 | 16 | 51 | 29 | 20 | 64% | 22% | 68 | 80 | 16 | 87 | 28 |
| Sean Doolittle | 266 | 1019 | 60 | 13 | 61 | 37 | 87 | 72% | 17% | 93 | 146 | 21 | 151 | 28 |
| Felix Doubront | 705 | 2845 | 139 | 71 | 220 | 96 | 166 | 61% | 13% | 328 | 310 | 115 | 370 | 159 |
| Darin Downs | 151 | 576 | 37 | 11 | 45 | 17 | 38 | 63% | 21% | 53 | 78 | 22 | 80 | 36 |

# Pitcher Analysis

Pitchers with 50+ Batters Faced in 2013

| | | | | | | | | | | Counts | | | | |
|---|---|---|---|---|---|---|---|---|---|---|---|---|---|---|
| Pitcher | BF | Pitches | K | BB | GB | LD | FB | Str% | S/Str | 1-0 | 0-1 | Full | 2 Strike | 3 Ball |
| Scott Downs | 189 | 712 | 37 | 19 | 81 | 29 | 16 | 60% | 17% | 78 | 84 | 27 | 77 | 43 |
| Brian Duensing | 268 | 996 | 56 | 22 | 75 | 49 | 59 | 63% | 17% | 102 | 126 | 30 | 129 | 47 |
| Danny Duffy | 104 | 470 | 22 | 14 | 21 | 18 | 27 | 60% | 18% | 48 | 53 | 22 | 66 | 30 |
| Zach Duke | 142 | 516 | 18 | 10 | 56 | 23 | 32 | 60% | 17% | 62 | 58 | 23 | 53 | 36 |
| Mike Dunn | 282 | 1193 | 72 | 28 | 70 | 31 | 76 | 66% | 19% | 112 | 149 | 47 | 176 | 59 |
| Jake Dunning | 104 | 387 | 16 | 11 | 40 | 20 | 14 | 61% | 17% | 50 | 44 | 10 | 51 | 19 |
| Chad Durbin | 81 | 329 | 16 | 9 | 25 | 10 | 20 | 62% | 17% | 33 | 35 | 17 | 45 | 21 |
| Sam Dyson | 54 | 173 | 5 | 5 | 29 | 2 | 11 | 60% | 11% | 27 | 13 | 3 | 15 | 9 |
| Josh Edgin | 122 | 486 | 20 | 12 | 37 | 14 | 35 | 60% | 13% | 53 | 60 | 21 | 58 | 34 |
| Nathan Eovaldi | 451 | 1696 | 78 | 40 | 141 | 71 | 110 | 64% | 13% | 186 | 223 | 52 | 211 | 83 |
| Robbie Erlin | 227 | 902 | 40 | 15 | 63 | 43 | 63 | 65% | 11% | 87 | 117 | 35 | 120 | 47 |
| Edgmer Escalona | 205 | 803 | 34 | 14 | 61 | 29 | 63 | 65% | 13% | 81 | 102 | 27 | 106 | 43 |
| Marco Estrada | 512 | 1995 | 118 | 29 | 135 | 65 | 159 | 65% | 17% | 205 | 254 | 75 | 278 | 94 |
| Jeurys Familia | 52 | 196 | 8 | 9 | 17 | 5 | 11 | 54% | 13% | 25 | 23 | 5 | 22 | 14 |
| Kyle Farnsworth | 162 | 576 | 28 | 10 | 55 | 30 | 36 | 65% | 15% | 54 | 81 | 18 | 74 | 24 |
| Danny Farquhar | 228 | 934 | 79 | 22 | 53 | 32 | 41 | 62% | 22% | 104 | 115 | 29 | 127 | 51 |
| Scott Feldman | 758 | 2993 | 132 | 56 | 271 | 103 | 172 | 61% | 12% | 330 | 354 | 109 | 373 | 154 |
| Pedro Feliciano | 51 | 179 | 9 | 6 | 13 | 6 | 12 | 61% | 15% | 15 | 30 | 5 | 22 | 10 |
| Jose Fernandez | 681 | 2609 | 187 | 58 | 190 | 91 | 140 | 66% | 16% | 260 | 341 | 73 | 371 | 115 |
| Josh Fields | 160 | 638 | 40 | 18 | 37 | 11 | 51 | 61% | 17% | 78 | 64 | 31 | 83 | 44 |
| Casey Fien | 244 | 962 | 73 | 12 | 57 | 31 | 65 | 68% | 22% | 81 | 134 | 29 | 145 | 40 |
| Mike Fiers | 103 | 402 | 15 | 6 | 28 | 21 | 31 | 64% | 14% | 41 | 52 | 12 | 49 | 21 |
| Stephen Fife | 258 | 954 | 45 | 20 | 94 | 40 | 47 | 63% | 11% | 109 | 119 | 29 | 122 | 45 |
| Alfredo Figaro | 316 | 1187 | 54 | 15 | 116 | 46 | 76 | 66% | 12% | 129 | 156 | 27 | 155 | 42 |
| Doug Fister | 881 | 3351 | 159 | 44 | 352 | 138 | 158 | 64% | 13% | 359 | 440 | 106 | 440 | 151 |
| Gavin Floyd | 110 | 420 | 25 | 12 | 35 | 15 | 20 | 63% | 18% | 36 | 64 | 11 | 55 | 18 |
| Brian Flynn | 88 | 340 | 15 | 13 | 22 | 19 | 17 | 59% | 17% | 38 | 40 | 16 | 45 | 21 |
| Jeff Francis | 324 | 1245 | 63 | 24 | 108 | 46 | 77 | 63% | 15% | 126 | 166 | 45 | 154 | 61 |
| Jason Frasor | 200 | 867 | 48 | 20 | 58 | 25 | 47 | 63% | 15% | 76 | 104 | 31 | 130 | 43 |
| Sam Freeman | 50 | 204 | 8 | 5 | 14 | 7 | 15 | 67% | 17% | 23 | 22 | 8 | 34 | 9 |
| Ernesto Frieri | 292 | 1262 | 98 | 30 | 37 | 27 | 93 | 68% | 25% | 106 | 160 | 47 | 198 | 62 |
| Kyuji Fujikawa | 50 | 207 | 14 | 2 | 16 | 6 | 10 | 62% | 20% | 21 | 24 | 9 | 28 | 10 |
| Charlie Furbush | 280 | 1128 | 80 | 29 | 65 | 35 | 62 | 64% | 20% | 115 | 138 | 47 | 168 | 60 |
| Yovani Gallardo | 773 | 3048 | 144 | 66 | 269 | 127 | 151 | 60% | 12% | 345 | 349 | 121 | 389 | 171 |
| Freddy Garcia | 331 | 1161 | 46 | 17 | 112 | 62 | 84 | 66% | 13% | 112 | 171 | 30 | 142 | 46 |
| Jaime Garcia | 234 | 826 | 43 | 15 | 109 | 25 | 39 | 67% | 18% | 76 | 126 | 24 | 110 | 35 |
| Luis Garcia | 138 | 550 | 23 | 23 | 50 | 15 | 24 | 56% | 21% | 73 | 53 | 25 | 59 | 39 |
| Jon Garland | 303 | 1090 | 32 | 23 | 115 | 53 | 66 | 62% | 10% | 110 | 145 | 43 | 126 | 64 |
| Matt Garza | 652 | 2425 | 136 | 42 | 175 | 105 | 173 | 65% | 16% | 238 | 337 | 87 | 315 | 118 |
| John Gast | 52 | 184 | 8 | 5 | 21 | 6 | 12 | 62% | 11% | 27 | 23 | 4 | 24 | 7 |
| Chad Gaudin | 406 | 1550 | 88 | 40 | 104 | 63 | 104 | 62% | 16% | 166 | 193 | 50 | 198 | 86 |
| Kevin Gausman | 201 | 796 | 49 | 13 | 55 | 33 | 43 | 64% | 16% | 78 | 98 | 33 | 108 | 47 |
| Cory Gearrin | 133 | 493 | 23 | 16 | 44 | 22 | 21 | 59% | 17% | 59 | 61 | 20 | 56 | 34 |
| Dillon Gee | 841 | 2985 | 142 | 47 | 268 | 123 | 238 | 66% | 15% | 317 | 401 | 78 | 371 | 123 |
| Gonzalez Germen | 149 | 592 | 33 | 16 | 37 | 21 | 41 | 62% | 25% | 63 | 69 | 24 | 81 | 36 |
| Kyle Gibson | 238 | 900 | 29 | 20 | 92 | 39 | 52 | 59% | 14% | 114 | 104 | 43 | 105 | 56 |
| Brandon Gomes | 83 | 344 | 29 | 7 | 10 | 6 | 29 | 67% | 27% | 25 | 48 | 9 | 56 | 14 |
| Jeanmar Gomez | 333 | 1233 | 53 | 28 | 134 | 45 | 63 | 62% | 15% | 122 | 166 | 44 | 156 | 61 |
| Edgar Gonzalez | 87 | 313 | 11 | 8 | 19 | 20 | 28 | 64% | 13% | 41 | 34 | 11 | 39 | 16 |
| Gio Gonzalez | 819 | 3315 | 192 | 76 | 232 | 120 | 176 | 63% | 16% | 323 | 397 | 130 | 449 | 189 |
| Michael Gonzalez | 235 | 944 | 60 | 25 | 46 | 35 | 59 | 61% | 19% | 88 | 123 | 40 | 128 | 58 |
| Miguel Gonzalez | 712 | 2713 | 120 | 53 | 204 | 110 | 211 | 64% | 13% | 296 | 335 | 79 | 345 | 126 |
| Tom Gorzelanny | 356 | 1351 | 83 | 31 | 104 | 46 | 86 | 64% | 17% | 119 | 193 | 37 | 177 | 67 |
| Sonny Gray | 261 | 995 | 67 | 20 | 92 | 34 | 48 | 63% | 16% | 105 | 132 | 39 | 143 | 52 |
| Luke Gregerson | 268 | 955 | 64 | 18 | 80 | 35 | 61 | 67% | 22% | 104 | 126 | 29 | 134 | 42 |
| Kevin Gregg | 269 | 1134 | 56 | 32 | 64 | 41 | 70 | 59% | 12% | 109 | 132 | 55 | 146 | 75 |
| Zack Greinke | 717 | 2814 | 148 | 46 | 226 | 118 | 152 | 63% | 17% | 300 | 342 | 111 | 368 | 143 |
| A.J. Griffin | 823 | 3212 | 171 | 54 | 187 | 107 | 288 | 64% | 14% | 333 | 411 | 100 | 431 | 150 |
| Jason Grilli | 202 | 837 | 74 | 13 | 37 | 28 | 47 | 68% | 22% | 78 | 107 | 23 | 135 | 33 |
| Justin Grimm | 442 | 1642 | 76 | 34 | 140 | 70 | 116 | 62% | 13% | 186 | 206 | 47 | 198 | 86 |
| Javy Guerra | 55 | 233 | 12 | 6 | 14 | 12 | 10 | 63% | 21% | 27 | 23 | 7 | 29 | 11 |
| Matt Guerrier | 181 | 670 | 30 | 17 | 56 | 27 | 48 | 61% | 18% | 86 | 79 | 24 | 81 | 36 |
| Jeremy Guthrie | 905 | 3370 | 111 | 59 | 307 | 160 | 248 | 63% | 9% | 343 | 464 | 111 | 384 | 160 |
| Juan Gutierrez | 236 | 880 | 45 | 20 | 72 | 35 | 62 | 63% | 16% | 92 | 116 | 34 | 118 | 46 |
| Nick Hagadone | 133 | 534 | 30 | 21 | 30 | 14 | 35 | 62% | 17% | 52 | 67 | 20 | 73 | 31 |
| Roy Halladay | 282 | 1112 | 51 | 36 | 72 | 38 | 67 | 59% | 16% | 130 | 125 | 47 | 133 | 73 |
| Cole Hamels | 905 | 3423 | 202 | 50 | 268 | 129 | 230 | 68% | 19% | 331 | 459 | 109 | 502 | 146 |
| Jason Hammel | 611 | 2302 | 96 | 48 | 182 | 100 | 172 | 63% | 12% | 265 | 271 | 70 | 288 | 116 |
| Brad Hand | 82 | 300 | 15 | 8 | 25 | 12 | 22 | 60% | 16% | 39 | 36 | 8 | 36 | 17 |

# Pitcher Analysis

## Pitchers with 50+ Batters Faced in 2013

| | | | | | | | | | | Counts | | | | |
|---|---|---|---|---|---|---|---|---|---|---|---|---|---|---|
| Pitcher | BF | Pitches | K | BB | GB | LD | FB | Str% | S/Str | 1-0 | 0-1 | Full | 2 Strike | 3 Ball |
| Donovan Hand | 286 | 1032 | 37 | 21 | 103 | 44 | 73 | 65% | 11% | 101 | 148 | 33 | 126 | 49 |
| Tommy Hanson | 327 | 1261 | 56 | 30 | 77 | 53 | 105 | 62% | 12% | 120 | 175 | 46 | 160 | 67 |
| J.A. Happ | 415 | 1723 | 77 | 45 | 104 | 51 | 130 | 63% | 14% | 167 | 205 | 63 | 237 | 96 |
| Aaron Harang | 626 | 2445 | 113 | 40 | 166 | 91 | 204 | 64% | 13% | 259 | 300 | 86 | 326 | 120 |
| Dan Haren | 717 | 2778 | 151 | 31 | 184 | 112 | 215 | 65% | 15% | 250 | 385 | 89 | 372 | 116 |
| Lucas Harrell | 707 | 2860 | 89 | 88 | 263 | 108 | 140 | 57% | 9% | 320 | 312 | 124 | 327 | 200 |
| Will Harris | 217 | 882 | 53 | 15 | 69 | 34 | 43 | 63% | 18% | 91 | 110 | 34 | 120 | 49 |
| Matt Harrison | 51 | 196 | 12 | 7 | 14 | 7 | 10 | 59% | 24% | 22 | 24 | 3 | 25 | 10 |
| Matt Harvey | 690 | 2697 | 191 | 31 | 217 | 90 | 148 | 67% | 20% | 245 | 384 | 83 | 384 | 112 |
| LaTroy Hawkins | 288 | 1030 | 55 | 10 | 105 | 52 | 60 | 69% | 13% | 95 | 155 | 24 | 138 | 34 |
| Jeremy Hefner | 556 | 2140 | 99 | 37 | 182 | 77 | 149 | 64% | 13% | 198 | 295 | 52 | 268 | 93 |
| Jeremy Hellickson | 737 | 2887 | 135 | 50 | 216 | 109 | 220 | 64% | 16% | 294 | 373 | 90 | 375 | 134 |
| John Hellweg | 162 | 614 | 9 | 26 | 64 | 29 | 23 | 56% | 7% | 81 | 62 | 21 | 64 | 43 |
| Jim Henderson | 247 | 1063 | 75 | 24 | 40 | 41 | 64 | 62% | 23% | 131 | 97 | 34 | 155 | 53 |
| Liam Hendriks | 224 | 891 | 34 | 14 | 63 | 37 | 72 | 63% | 14% | 91 | 109 | 32 | 99 | 49 |
| David Hernandez | 263 | 1054 | 66 | 24 | 52 | 35 | 78 | 64% | 20% | 97 | 138 | 37 | 152 | 53 |
| Felix Hernandez | 823 | 3175 | 216 | 46 | 283 | 118 | 150 | 64% | 18% | 317 | 417 | 126 | 422 | 169 |
| Pedro Hernandez | 263 | 1021 | 29 | 23 | 83 | 45 | 80 | 60% | 10% | 118 | 123 | 32 | 110 | 62 |
| Roberto Hernandez | 643 | 2394 | 113 | 38 | 251 | 106 | 115 | 65% | 13% | 249 | 328 | 73 | 306 | 111 |
| Kelvin Herrera | 245 | 1010 | 74 | 21 | 70 | 27 | 50 | 65% | 23% | 107 | 122 | 29 | 143 | 50 |
| Rich Hill | 182 | 787 | 51 | 29 | 41 | 20 | 37 | 59% | 16% | 96 | 79 | 31 | 108 | 52 |
| Luke Hochevar | 262 | 1044 | 82 | 17 | 56 | 31 | 73 | 66% | 21% | 81 | 150 | 41 | 151 | 52 |
| Derek Holland | 894 | 3281 | 189 | 64 | 256 | 143 | 228 | 65% | 16% | 326 | 465 | 112 | 419 | 162 |
| Greg Holland | 255 | 1063 | 103 | 18 | 52 | 36 | 44 | 65% | 27% | 106 | 135 | 36 | 173 | 49 |
| J.J. Hoover | 269 | 1141 | 67 | 26 | 52 | 36 | 81 | 62% | 17% | 105 | 138 | 50 | 161 | 67 |
| Jeremy Horst | 123 | 474 | 21 | 12 | 31 | 13 | 42 | 63% | 12% | 51 | 55 | 16 | 60 | 26 |
| J.P. Howell | 246 | 961 | 54 | 23 | 95 | 25 | 46 | 59% | 18% | 105 | 106 | 50 | 119 | 72 |
| Tim Hudson | 534 | 2006 | 95 | 36 | 220 | 69 | 105 | 65% | 15% | 189 | 281 | 58 | 265 | 97 |
| David Huff | 151 | 562 | 31 | 9 | 44 | 26 | 39 | 66% | 17% | 45 | 88 | 15 | 79 | 23 |
| Jared Hughes | 148 | 524 | 23 | 16 | 58 | 21 | 24 | 61% | 19% | 63 | 64 | 14 | 61 | 27 |
| Phil Hughes | 642 | 2550 | 121 | 42 | 144 | 106 | 217 | 67% | 14% | 185 | 403 | 74 | 343 | 98 |
| Philip Humber | 259 | 914 | 36 | 20 | 86 | 42 | 69 | 64% | 15% | 109 | 122 | 21 | 114 | 43 |
| Tommy Hunter | 336 | 1274 | 68 | 14 | 98 | 52 | 101 | 69% | 16% | 122 | 173 | 34 | 171 | 48 |
| Colt Hynes | 84 | 311 | 13 | 9 | 28 | 11 | 22 | 65% | 14% | 34 | 39 | 10 | 42 | 16 |
| Hisashi Iwakuma | 866 | 3102 | 185 | 42 | 305 | 110 | 211 | 68% | 16% | 317 | 438 | 69 | 426 | 100 |
| Edwin Jackson | 777 | 2932 | 135 | 59 | 291 | 115 | 161 | 61% | 15% | 345 | 339 | 113 | 337 | 169 |
| Kenley Jansen | 292 | 1245 | 111 | 18 | 59 | 38 | 61 | 68% | 23% | 106 | 167 | 32 | 193 | 46 |
| Casey Janssen | 210 | 817 | 50 | 13 | 68 | 32 | 42 | 64% | 13% | 75 | 113 | 25 | 117 | 37 |
| Chad Jenkins | 132 | 471 | 15 | 6 | 49 | 22 | 36 | 65% | 11% | 56 | 62 | 15 | 56 | 21 |
| Dan Jennings | 171 | 677 | 38 | 16 | 57 | 23 | 37 | 60% | 18% | 80 | 77 | 26 | 88 | 40 |
| Kevin Jepsen | 164 | 674 | 36 | 14 | 44 | 22 | 43 | 61% | 15% | 76 | 69 | 31 | 89 | 41 |
| Cesar Jimenez | 76 | 302 | 11 | 10 | 20 | 8 | 24 | 59% | 16% | 30 | 38 | 14 | 33 | 20 |
| Ubaldo Jimenez | 777 | 3163 | 194 | 80 | 215 | 97 | 178 | 62% | 15% | 327 | 386 | 123 | 427 | 182 |
| Erik Johnson | 128 | 503 | 18 | 11 | 45 | 18 | 34 | 61% | 13% | 61 | 53 | 18 | 63 | 30 |
| Jim Johnson | 291 | 1114 | 56 | 18 | 119 | 42 | 44 | 63% | 14% | 113 | 141 | 46 | 139 | 64 |
| Josh Johnson | 384 | 1470 | 83 | 30 | 119 | 64 | 81 | 61% | 17% | 148 | 193 | 58 | 185 | 82 |
| Steve Johnson | 73 | 306 | 20 | 13 | 10 | 11 | 18 | 59% | 17% | 30 | 36 | 11 | 41 | 20 |
| Nate Jones | 315 | 1247 | 89 | 26 | 99 | 42 | 55 | 64% | 22% | 125 | 166 | 41 | 178 | 60 |
| Taylor Jordan | 220 | 773 | 29 | 11 | 100 | 34 | 40 | 66% | 17% | 95 | 93 | 19 | 100 | 33 |
| Nate Karns | 61 | 247 | 11 | 6 | 15 | 13 | 14 | 61% | 16% | 22 | 35 | 9 | 31 | 13 |
| Scott Kazmir | 672 | 2742 | 162 | 47 | 186 | 105 | 164 | 66% | 16% | 264 | 348 | 86 | 401 | 123 |
| Shawn Kelley | 227 | 982 | 71 | 23 | 44 | 28 | 61 | 62% | 19% | 80 | 135 | 45 | 145 | 59 |
| Joe Kelly | 532 | 1967 | 79 | 44 | 203 | 82 | 112 | 61% | 12% | 236 | 227 | 76 | 226 | 114 |
| Kyle Kendrick | 800 | 2874 | 110 | 47 | 302 | 120 | 189 | 65% | 11% | 294 | 386 | 98 | 346 | 138 |
| Ian Kennedy | 794 | 3089 | 163 | 73 | 202 | 123 | 204 | 63% | 16% | 296 | 399 | 119 | 415 | 177 |
| Clayton Kershaw | 908 | 3428 | 232 | 52 | 278 | 137 | 189 | 67% | 18% | 318 | 471 | 103 | 495 | 141 |
| Dallas Keuchel | 682 | 2506 | 123 | 52 | 277 | 104 | 115 | 63% | 15% | 253 | 348 | 72 | 309 | 116 |
| Mike Kickham | 144 | 559 | 29 | 10 | 46 | 31 | 26 | 61% | 17% | 60 | 65 | 24 | 67 | 34 |
| Craig Kimbrel | 258 | 1039 | 98 | 20 | 64 | 32 | 39 | 64% | 22% | 113 | 123 | 39 | 164 | 52 |
| Brandon Kintzler | 305 | 1100 | 58 | 16 | 128 | 54 | 41 | 65% | 14% | 122 | 144 | 27 | 131 | 43 |
| Michael Kirkman | 115 | 440 | 25 | 15 | 28 | 21 | 26 | 61% | 16% | 44 | 59 | 14 | 55 | 27 |
| Corey Kluber | 608 | 2290 | 136 | 33 | 193 | 110 | 121 | 65% | 17% | 245 | 299 | 73 | 310 | 111 |
| Tom Koehler | 601 | 2256 | 92 | 54 | 210 | 97 | 134 | 62% | 13% | 245 | 282 | 72 | 281 | 113 |
| Michael Kohn | 231 | 975 | 52 | 28 | 34 | 33 | 80 | 63% | 20% | 99 | 114 | 29 | 135 | 52 |
| George Kontos | 238 | 873 | 47 | 18 | 64 | 42 | 62 | 65% | 17% | 83 | 118 | 30 | 113 | 46 |
| Ian Krol | 117 | 475 | 22 | 8 | 33 | 17 | 35 | 68% | 10% | 50 | 60 | 16 | 76 | 19 |
| Hiroki Kuroda | 824 | 3202 | 150 | 43 | 290 | 137 | 195 | 63% | 16% | 320 | 424 | 97 | 402 | 142 |
| John Lackey | 778 | 2873 | 161 | 40 | 262 | 102 | 196 | 67% | 16% | 279 | 403 | 96 | 375 | 127 |
| Aaron Laffey | 64 | 257 | 9 | 10 | 17 | 11 | 12 | 58% | 11% | 30 | 28 | 9 | 28 | 16 |

# Pitcher Analysis

## Pitchers with 50+ Batters Faced in 2013

| | | | | | | | | | | Counts | | | | |
|---|---|---|---|---|---|---|---|---|---|---|---|---|---|---|
| Pitcher | BF | Pitches | K | BB | GB | LD | FB | Str% | S/Str | 1-0 | 0-1 | Full | 2 Strike | 3 Ball |
| Matt Langwell | 62 | 248 | 12 | 7 | 14 | 12 | 16 | 62% | 14% | 23 | 35 | 9 | 31 | 11 |
| John Lannan | 332 | 1231 | 38 | 27 | 132 | 44 | 76 | 61% | 12% | 150 | 136 | 45 | 140 | 66 |
| Mat Latos | 881 | 3239 | 187 | 58 | 274 | 129 | 204 | 66% | 17% | 317 | 452 | 89 | 436 | 127 |
| Brandon League | 249 | 923 | 28 | 15 | 119 | 38 | 42 | 62% | 16% | 111 | 103 | 31 | 110 | 52 |
| Mike Leake | 801 | 2911 | 122 | 48 | 297 | 131 | 182 | 63% | 11% | 330 | 366 | 92 | 341 | 140 |
| Wade LeBlanc | 259 | 971 | 33 | 20 | 77 | 43 | 77 | 62% | 15% | 92 | 128 | 36 | 117 | 50 |
| Sam LeCure | 251 | 1005 | 66 | 24 | 68 | 36 | 54 | 61% | 17% | 95 | 132 | 36 | 138 | 58 |
| Cliff Lee | 876 | 3253 | 222 | 32 | 269 | 136 | 202 | 71% | 14% | 276 | 498 | 71 | 499 | 93 |
| Charlie Leesman | 77 | 335 | 13 | 16 | 27 | 11 | 9 | 55% | 15% | 43 | 31 | 16 | 40 | 24 |
| Jon Lester | 903 | 3559 | 177 | 67 | 291 | 127 | 229 | 64% | 14% | 354 | 444 | 134 | 466 | 185 |
| Ted Lilly | 109 | 407 | 18 | 10 | 28 | 17 | 34 | 65% | 14% | 45 | 56 | 12 | 56 | 18 |
| Tim Lincecum | 841 | 3281 | 193 | 76 | 249 | 127 | 174 | 62% | 19% | 368 | 395 | 117 | 431 | 192 |
| Brad Lincoln | 148 | 575 | 25 | 22 | 35 | 11 | 48 | 59% | 14% | 65 | 67 | 20 | 72 | 34 |
| Josh Lindblom | 137 | 555 | 21 | 11 | 38 | 27 | 40 | 61% | 14% | 61 | 66 | 24 | 70 | 36 |
| Matt Lindstrom | 260 | 943 | 46 | 23 | 104 | 32 | 51 | 64% | 16% | 90 | 135 | 23 | 128 | 38 |
| Francisco Liriano | 666 | 2496 | 163 | 63 | 217 | 104 | 109 | 62% | 22% | 278 | 310 | 77 | 324 | 131 |
| Chia-Jen Lo | 84 | 344 | 16 | 13 | 20 | 12 | 21 | 62% | 12% | 40 | 34 | 14 | 47 | 21 |
| Jeff Locke | 711 | 2715 | 125 | 84 | 256 | 101 | 124 | 59% | 15% | 296 | 332 | 92 | 326 | 173 |
| Kameron Loe | 127 | 454 | 15 | 10 | 51 | 18 | 32 | 64% | 12% | 56 | 56 | 11 | 50 | 20 |
| Boone Logan | 159 | 668 | 50 | 13 | 43 | 13 | 35 | 63% | 21% | 65 | 85 | 31 | 92 | 45 |
| Kyle Lohse | 806 | 3013 | 125 | 36 | 251 | 133 | 240 | 66% | 12% | 276 | 447 | 77 | 384 | 119 |
| Javier Lopez | 161 | 621 | 37 | 12 | 64 | 17 | 24 | 63% | 20% | 68 | 70 | 16 | 76 | 28 |
| Wilton Lopez | 321 | 1129 | 48 | 18 | 124 | 62 | 64 | 67% | 15% | 109 | 162 | 31 | 144 | 41 |
| Aaron Loup | 282 | 1037 | 53 | 13 | 124 | 36 | 47 | 65% | 14% | 113 | 143 | 27 | 131 | 42 |
| Derek Lowe | 57 | 199 | 8 | 3 | 24 | 7 | 12 | 63% | 11% | 23 | 22 | 5 | 22 | 11 |
| Mark Lowe | 56 | 247 | 7 | 11 | 13 | 6 | 16 | 54% | 14% | 33 | 18 | 14 | 29 | 20 |
| Josh Lueke | 99 | 406 | 25 | 12 | 19 | 9 | 32 | 61% | 15% | 46 | 48 | 20 | 57 | 26 |
| Lucas Luetge | 165 | 554 | 27 | 16 | 58 | 29 | 30 | 60% | 17% | 63 | 74 | 11 | 58 | 29 |
| Jordan Lyles | 642 | 2445 | 93 | 49 | 234 | 103 | 146 | 61% | 12% | 283 | 283 | 93 | 275 | 140 |
| Lance Lynn | 856 | 3351 | 198 | 76 | 237 | 124 | 189 | 64% | 16% | 311 | 454 | 131 | 466 | 184 |
| Brandon Lyon | 153 | 570 | 23 | 13 | 43 | 27 | 41 | 61% | 15% | 71 | 60 | 29 | 74 | 36 |
| Tyler Lyons | 223 | 787 | 43 | 16 | 74 | 30 | 52 | 66% | 14% | 92 | 101 | 22 | 101 | 32 |
| Jean Machi | 211 | 754 | 51 | 12 | 80 | 29 | 38 | 64% | 18% | 84 | 100 | 23 | 97 | 38 |
| Matt Magill | 137 | 549 | 26 | 28 | 34 | 10 | 35 | 57% | 19% | 65 | 59 | 26 | 73 | 42 |
| Paul Maholm | 670 | 2498 | 105 | 47 | 254 | 118 | 123 | 64% | 11% | 241 | 345 | 84 | 304 | 125 |
| Seth Maness | 249 | 886 | 35 | 13 | 132 | 37 | 24 | 66% | 11% | 81 | 133 | 24 | 109 | 35 |
| Jeff Manship | 139 | 519 | 18 | 12 | 49 | 28 | 31 | 61% | 14% | 54 | 66 | 17 | 59 | 29 |
| Shaun Marcum | 334 | 1235 | 60 | 21 | 84 | 57 | 100 | 66% | 15% | 119 | 175 | 40 | 176 | 51 |
| Carlos Marmol | 225 | 926 | 59 | 40 | 44 | 30 | 43 | 59% | 19% | 108 | 100 | 44 | 130 | 67 |
| Jason Marquis | 518 | 1912 | 72 | 68 | 191 | 75 | 99 | 57% | 14% | 238 | 208 | 69 | 198 | 130 |
| Brett Marshall | 54 | 207 | 7 | 7 | 20 | 5 | 14 | 58% | 17% | 24 | 21 | 6 | 18 | 15 |
| Ethan Martin | 190 | 772 | 47 | 26 | 35 | 26 | 53 | 59% | 18% | 91 | 79 | 26 | 88 | 47 |
| Carlos Martinez | 124 | 475 | 24 | 9 | 45 | 16 | 25 | 65% | 15% | 48 | 58 | 14 | 68 | 20 |
| David Martinez | 52 | 167 | 6 | 3 | 16 | 6 | 17 | 60% | 15% | 26 | 18 | 4 | 16 | 10 |
| Justin Masterson | 803 | 3018 | 195 | 76 | 290 | 89 | 121 | 63% | 15% | 328 | 381 | 89 | 392 | 147 |
| Daisuke Matsuzaka | 166 | 663 | 33 | 16 | 30 | 24 | 52 | 65% | 12% | 65 | 86 | 20 | 92 | 28 |
| Ryan Mattheus | 166 | 622 | 22 | 15 | 75 | 28 | 25 | 61% | 11% | 67 | 74 | 27 | 73 | 40 |
| Brian Matusz | 208 | 856 | 50 | 16 | 53 | 28 | 54 | 63% | 20% | 84 | 109 | 32 | 118 | 46 |
| Brandon Maurer | 402 | 1541 | 70 | 27 | 130 | 56 | 109 | 61% | 16% | 166 | 191 | 54 | 193 | 83 |
| Vin Mazzaro | 304 | 1186 | 46 | 21 | 120 | 44 | 66 | 63% | 13% | 115 | 143 | 48 | 150 | 73 |
| Zach McAllister | 579 | 2292 | 101 | 49 | 155 | 90 | 173 | 63% | 12% | 227 | 299 | 82 | 293 | 124 |
| Brandon McCarthy | 577 | 2009 | 76 | 21 | 224 | 115 | 126 | 69% | 9% | 186 | 310 | 45 | 260 | 63 |
| James McDonald | 138 | 513 | 25 | 20 | 38 | 15 | 37 | 58% | 13% | 67 | 54 | 16 | 59 | 31 |
| T.J. McFarland | 331 | 1229 | 58 | 28 | 137 | 42 | 58 | 62% | 15% | 137 | 146 | 41 | 145 | 70 |
| Jake McGee | 260 | 1150 | 75 | 22 | 68 | 30 | 62 | 67% | 18% | 95 | 148 | 44 | 166 | 59 |
| Dustin McGowan | 114 | 454 | 26 | 12 | 34 | 10 | 29 | 59% | 20% | 39 | 61 | 21 | 58 | 30 |
| Collin McHugh | 125 | 435 | 11 | 5 | 41 | 29 | 33 | 67% | 13% | 57 | 51 | 13 | 54 | 16 |
| Yoervis Medina | 291 | 1128 | 71 | 40 | 93 | 33 | 47 | 58% | 18% | 140 | 122 | 36 | 134 | 76 |
| Kris Medlen | 820 | 3049 | 157 | 47 | 267 | 142 | 181 | 66% | 17% | 291 | 424 | 79 | 412 | 122 |
| Jenrry Mejia | 112 | 437 | 27 | 4 | 47 | 18 | 16 | 67% | 19% | 45 | 56 | 7 | 63 | 14 |
| Mark Melancon | 279 | 988 | 70 | 8 | 120 | 48 | 31 | 70% | 18% | 98 | 143 | 23 | 140 | 32 |
| Luis Mendoza | 419 | 1576 | 54 | 43 | 158 | 64 | 94 | 60% | 12% | 174 | 188 | 53 | 179 | 91 |
| Jose Mijares | 236 | 868 | 54 | 20 | 53 | 41 | 59 | 63% | 16% | 109 | 98 | 30 | 122 | 43 |
| Wade Miley | 847 | 3239 | 147 | 66 | 321 | 128 | 168 | 63% | 13% | 345 | 423 | 106 | 403 | 169 |
| Andrew Miller | 135 | 555 | 48 | 17 | 37 | 14 | 15 | 64% | 21% | 56 | 67 | 15 | 86 | 27 |
| Shelby Miller | 722 | 2968 | 169 | 57 | 184 | 97 | 198 | 66% | 15% | 272 | 382 | 109 | 443 | 146 |
| Tommy Milone | 667 | 2598 | 126 | 39 | 174 | 99 | 221 | 64% | 14% | 222 | 369 | 93 | 355 | 117 |
| Zach Miner | 133 | 558 | 20 | 17 | 45 | 19 | 28 | 56% | 15% | 51 | 65 | 35 | 60 | 49 |
| Mike Minor | 820 | 3126 | 181 | 46 | 204 | 129 | 250 | 66% | 15% | 296 | 440 | 92 | 420 | 125 |

# Pitcher Analysis

## Pitchers with 50+ Batters Faced in 2013

| | | | | | | | | | | Counts | | | | |
|---|---|---|---|---|---|---|---|---|---|---|---|---|---|---|
| Pitcher | BF | Pitches | K | BB | GB | LD | FB | Str% | S/Str | 1-0 | 0-1 | Full | 2 Strike | 3 Ball |
| Matt Moore | 642 | 2621 | 143 | 76 | 162 | 75 | 174 | 60% | 17% | 314 | 284 | 100 | 348 | 156 |
| Franklin Morales | 112 | 447 | 21 | 15 | 28 | 17 | 27 | 60% | 17% | 48 | 56 | 16 | 61 | 26 |
| Bryan Morris | 270 | 962 | 37 | 28 | 115 | 35 | 50 | 62% | 20% | 113 | 125 | 25 | 121 | 48 |
| Brandon Morrow | 242 | 910 | 42 | 18 | 67 | 37 | 77 | 63% | 14% | 115 | 102 | 23 | 111 | 46 |
| Clayton Mortensen | 141 | 560 | 21 | 16 | 45 | 21 | 33 | 60% | 14% | 58 | 67 | 26 | 73 | 34 |
| Charlie Morton | 493 | 1715 | 85 | 36 | 219 | 64 | 65 | 63% | 14% | 198 | 222 | 46 | 204 | 81 |
| Guillermo Moscoso | 128 | 522 | 31 | 21 | 10 | 13 | 50 | 59% | 18% | 63 | 54 | 18 | 71 | 32 |
| Peter Moylan | 70 | 247 | 6 | 7 | 16 | 16 | 25 | 59% | 12% | 27 | 35 | 8 | 27 | 15 |
| Edward Mujica | 255 | 901 | 46 | 5 | 90 | 32 | 77 | 73% | 18% | 70 | 147 | 16 | 132 | 20 |
| Brett Myers | 97 | 319 | 12 | 5 | 30 | 14 | 34 | 61% | 13% | 47 | 33 | 9 | 36 | 15 |
| Joe Nathan | 250 | 1021 | 73 | 22 | 48 | 35 | 67 | 64% | 18% | 94 | 131 | 37 | 145 | 48 |
| Pat Neshek | 177 | 669 | 29 | 15 | 44 | 25 | 63 | 66% | 16% | 81 | 84 | 10 | 91 | 24 |
| Juan Nicasio | 703 | 2867 | 119 | 64 | 228 | 108 | 170 | 62% | 13% | 299 | 332 | 114 | 359 | 170 |
| Jon Niese | 621 | 2343 | 105 | 48 | 233 | 97 | 122 | 64% | 12% | 240 | 311 | 66 | 295 | 109 |
| Hector Noesi | 134 | 495 | 21 | 12 | 36 | 27 | 36 | 62% | 15% | 56 | 62 | 13 | 64 | 23 |
| Ricky Nolasco | 834 | 3183 | 165 | 46 | 258 | 146 | 196 | 64% | 17% | 335 | 416 | 105 | 426 | 153 |
| Bud Norris | 773 | 3017 | 147 | 67 | 219 | 117 | 209 | 64% | 15% | 302 | 377 | 117 | 409 | 159 |
| Ivan Nova | 586 | 2093 | 116 | 44 | 219 | 83 | 107 | 63% | 15% | 268 | 261 | 57 | 253 | 99 |
| Vidal Nuno | 82 | 314 | 9 | 6 | 23 | 12 | 31 | 64% | 7% | 28 | 45 | 7 | 35 | 12 |
| Brett Oberholtzer | 293 | 1101 | 45 | 13 | 83 | 51 | 99 | 67% | 13% | 101 | 168 | 32 | 146 | 42 |
| Darren O'Day | 247 | 977 | 59 | 15 | 60 | 36 | 67 | 67% | 18% | 90 | 125 | 34 | 145 | 45 |
| Jake Odorizzi | 122 | 534 | 22 | 8 | 29 | 23 | 38 | 63% | 13% | 52 | 59 | 26 | 74 | 30 |
| Eric O'Flaherty | 70 | 244 | 11 | 5 | 30 | 7 | 15 | 62% | 14% | 29 | 34 | 8 | 26 | 12 |
| Alexi Ogando | 428 | 1710 | 72 | 41 | 124 | 55 | 126 | 63% | 13% | 193 | 198 | 63 | 218 | 94 |
| Ross Ohlendorf | 247 | 974 | 45 | 14 | 70 | 36 | 73 | 65% | 15% | 89 | 129 | 33 | 126 | 44 |
| Darren Oliver | 204 | 714 | 40 | 15 | 66 | 27 | 46 | 64% | 12% | 74 | 103 | 25 | 93 | 35 |
| Brian Omogrosso | 84 | 332 | 16 | 9 | 25 | 12 | 21 | 61% | 17% | 42 | 37 | 8 | 47 | 16 |
| Logan Ondrusek | 233 | 879 | 53 | 16 | 71 | 29 | 56 | 64% | 19% | 95 | 111 | 28 | 116 | 42 |
| Jose Ortega | 52 | 202 | 10 | 6 | 16 | 6 | 12 | 57% | 13% | 25 | 24 | 7 | 25 | 13 |
| Joe Ortiz | 187 | 688 | 27 | 10 | 58 | 46 | 43 | 64% | 17% | 79 | 86 | 19 | 79 | 32 |
| Ramon Ortiz | 117 | 438 | 8 | 11 | 38 | 18 | 40 | 60% | 13% | 52 | 51 | 12 | 47 | 26 |
| Sean O'Sullivan | 118 | 435 | 12 | 14 | 41 | 17 | 32 | 60% | 11% | 56 | 49 | 11 | 46 | 24 |
| Roy Oswalt | 151 | 595 | 34 | 9 | 41 | 28 | 36 | 66% | 14% | 52 | 87 | 21 | 90 | 28 |
| Dan Otero | 159 | 580 | 27 | 6 | 70 | 25 | 30 | 66% | 9% | 59 | 85 | 13 | 69 | 20 |
| Adam Ottavino | 335 | 1284 | 78 | 31 | 98 | 47 | 70 | 63% | 20% | 130 | 167 | 49 | 173 | 69 |
| Josh Outman | 238 | 910 | 53 | 23 | 79 | 32 | 43 | 62% | 22% | 92 | 119 | 32 | 125 | 52 |
| Jonathan Papelbon | 254 | 962 | 57 | 11 | 73 | 32 | 78 | 67% | 17% | 92 | 136 | 24 | 128 | 38 |
| Blake Parker | 195 | 810 | 55 | 15 | 35 | 27 | 60 | 64% | 18% | 76 | 101 | 36 | 119 | 47 |
| Jarrod Parker | 818 | 2994 | 134 | 63 | 249 | 117 | 239 | 63% | 16% | 324 | 389 | 97 | 362 | 152 |
| Bobby Parnell | 198 | 806 | 44 | 12 | 72 | 31 | 36 | 66% | 15% | 70 | 110 | 23 | 111 | 33 |
| Manny Parra | 188 | 761 | 56 | 15 | 49 | 25 | 38 | 65% | 22% | 58 | 109 | 24 | 105 | 37 |
| Curtis Partch | 106 | 417 | 16 | 17 | 27 | 10 | 29 | 59% | 17% | 44 | 52 | 18 | 51 | 28 |
| Troy Patton | 235 | 843 | 42 | 16 | 77 | 30 | 63 | 66% | 17% | 78 | 133 | 26 | 113 | 38 |
| James Paxton | 94 | 384 | 21 | 7 | 39 | 11 | 16 | 64% | 16% | 43 | 48 | 8 | 52 | 14 |
| Brad Peacock | 365 | 1488 | 77 | 37 | 91 | 46 | 110 | 61% | 13% | 159 | 175 | 53 | 189 | 84 |
| Jake Peavy | 590 | 2367 | 121 | 36 | 139 | 88 | 198 | 66% | 13% | 200 | 319 | 89 | 337 | 110 |
| Mike Pelfrey | 680 | 2727 | 101 | 53 | 222 | 107 | 185 | 61% | 10% | 306 | 310 | 109 | 330 | 149 |
| Joel Peralta | 291 | 1173 | 74 | 34 | 48 | 35 | 97 | 65% | 17% | 121 | 153 | 38 | 168 | 58 |
| Wily Peralta | 802 | 2987 | 129 | 73 | 293 | 122 | 159 | 61% | 15% | 334 | 376 | 116 | 358 | 174 |
| Chris Perez | 243 | 895 | 54 | 21 | 67 | 36 | 55 | 64% | 13% | 94 | 120 | 31 | 125 | 45 |
| Juan Perez | 131 | 563 | 33 | 15 | 49 | 12 | 21 | 61% | 17% | 56 | 68 | 22 | 78 | 32 |
| Martin Perez | 529 | 1858 | 84 | 37 | 193 | 83 | 125 | 63% | 16% | 203 | 248 | 54 | 219 | 100 |
| Oliver Perez | 229 | 973 | 74 | 26 | 38 | 25 | 61 | 64% | 20% | 89 | 124 | 38 | 147 | 59 |
| Glen Perkins | 240 | 944 | 77 | 15 | 51 | 37 | 53 | 69% | 21% | 73 | 141 | 28 | 141 | 40 |
| Vinnie Pestano | 159 | 664 | 37 | 21 | 35 | 21 | 44 | 62% | 19% | 69 | 74 | 26 | 87 | 41 |
| Yusmeiro Petit | 196 | 731 | 47 | 11 | 41 | 35 | 60 | 70% | 19% | 61 | 118 | 19 | 109 | 24 |
| Jake Petricka | 85 | 326 | 10 | 10 | 39 | 13 | 10 | 60% | 15% | 42 | 38 | 8 | 38 | 16 |
| Jonathan Pettibone | 437 | 1674 | 66 | 38 | 155 | 65 | 94 | 62% | 10% | 169 | 210 | 62 | 198 | 98 |
| Andy Pettitte | 784 | 2896 | 128 | 48 | 273 | 134 | 186 | 66% | 13% | 299 | 402 | 79 | 365 | 123 |
| David Phelps | 376 | 1500 | 79 | 35 | 107 | 55 | 90 | 61% | 11% | 152 | 193 | 57 | 193 | 85 |
| Drew Pomeranz | 105 | 417 | 19 | 19 | 33 | 11 | 21 | 60% | 14% | 48 | 51 | 12 | 51 | 27 |
| Rick Porcello | 736 | 2836 | 142 | 42 | 299 | 114 | 128 | 64% | 14% | 292 | 375 | 93 | 371 | 132 |
| Ryan Pressly | 315 | 1194 | 49 | 27 | 103 | 50 | 82 | 61% | 13% | 171 | 120 | 29 | 142 | 58 |
| David Price | 740 | 2707 | 151 | 27 | 249 | 120 | 185 | 69% | 12% | 240 | 412 | 72 | 375 | 96 |
| David Purcey | 113 | 472 | 23 | 17 | 28 | 11 | 31 | 57% | 18% | 55 | 47 | 21 | 55 | 32 |
| Luke Putkonen | 127 | 479 | 28 | 9 | 49 | 9 | 30 | 63% | 14% | 50 | 60 | 16 | 68 | 22 |
| J.J. Putz | 140 | 535 | 38 | 17 | 43 | 15 | 27 | 59% | 21% | 61 | 62 | 17 | 66 | 30 |
| Chad Qualls | 252 | 838 | 49 | 19 | 112 | 30 | 35 | 66% | 17% | 86 | 128 | 11 | 102 | 32 |
| Jose Quintana | 832 | 3335 | 164 | 56 | 256 | 121 | 225 | 63% | 15% | 286 | 456 | 120 | 414 | 169 |

# Pitcher Analysis

Pitchers with 50+ Batters Faced in 2013

| | | | | | | | | | | Counts | | | | |
|---|---|---|---|---|---|---|---|---|---|---|---|---|---|---|
| Pitcher | BF | Pitches | K | BB | GB | LD | FB | Str% | S/Str | 1-0 | 0-1 | Full | 2 Strike | 3 Ball |
| Brooks Raley | 61 | 237 | 14 | 8 | 17 | 10 | 9 | 60% | 16% | 35 | 20 | 5 | 29 | 10 |
| Erasmo Ramirez | 321 | 1277 | 57 | 26 | 99 | 50 | 84 | 63% | 15% | 131 | 159 | 46 | 164 | 68 |
| J.C. Ramirez | 116 | 417 | 16 | 15 | 32 | 18 | 33 | 61% | 17% | 54 | 50 | 12 | 50 | 23 |
| A.J. Ramos | 338 | 1370 | 86 | 43 | 79 | 38 | 87 | 62% | 20% | 132 | 173 | 56 | 192 | 88 |
| Cesar Ramos | 288 | 1026 | 53 | 22 | 85 | 50 | 73 | 64% | 15% | 100 | 146 | 26 | 130 | 42 |
| Cory Rasmus | 103 | 408 | 20 | 13 | 21 | 13 | 35 | 60% | 22% | 49 | 42 | 9 | 50 | 22 |
| Jon Rauch | 80 | 308 | 15 | 7 | 25 | 12 | 18 | 66% | 14% | 31 | 41 | 6 | 44 | 12 |
| Todd Redmond | 324 | 1290 | 76 | 23 | 66 | 42 | 110 | 64% | 17% | 128 | 157 | 46 | 184 | 65 |
| Addison Reed | 295 | 1173 | 72 | 23 | 64 | 42 | 88 | 66% | 18% | 104 | 171 | 30 | 171 | 47 |
| Evan Reed | 105 | 387 | 17 | 8 | 41 | 17 | 20 | 62% | 15% | 44 | 45 | 9 | 51 | 17 |
| Chris Resop | 87 | 353 | 13 | 10 | 26 | 16 | 20 | 59% | 13% | 39 | 42 | 17 | 47 | 23 |
| Greg Reynolds | 133 | 472 | 13 | 6 | 45 | 18 | 42 | 64% | 9% | 50 | 64 | 10 | 50 | 19 |
| Matt Reynolds | 111 | 418 | 23 | 5 | 31 | 23 | 26 | 66% | 15% | 45 | 59 | 8 | 62 | 12 |
| Scott Rice | 213 | 785 | 41 | 27 | 82 | 29 | 25 | 58% | 25% | 98 | 92 | 20 | 89 | 48 |
| Clayton Richard | 239 | 854 | 24 | 21 | 97 | 39 | 51 | 62% | 10% | 112 | 94 | 24 | 97 | 41 |
| Garrett Richards | 620 | 2351 | 101 | 44 | 267 | 88 | 106 | 62% | 15% | 288 | 280 | 75 | 281 | 122 |
| Andre Rienzo | 250 | 941 | 38 | 28 | 86 | 34 | 60 | 58% | 13% | 129 | 102 | 37 | 115 | 58 |
| Mariano Rivera | 256 | 941 | 54 | 9 | 88 | 44 | 59 | 70% | 14% | 79 | 154 | 20 | 130 | 28 |
| Tanner Roark | 204 | 756 | 40 | 11 | 74 | 36 | 38 | 68% | 10% | 60 | 121 | 16 | 105 | 26 |
| David Robertson | 262 | 1054 | 77 | 18 | 82 | 32 | 47 | 64% | 15% | 108 | 130 | 34 | 157 | 48 |
| Fernando Rodney | 290 | 1212 | 82 | 36 | 86 | 42 | 42 | 62% | 21% | 128 | 150 | 48 | 171 | 74 |
| Francisco Rodriguez | 193 | 754 | 54 | 14 | 43 | 29 | 46 | 66% | 17% | 77 | 101 | 21 | 112 | 30 |
| Henry Rodriguez | 109 | 450 | 12 | 20 | 32 | 20 | 22 | 54% | 12% | 62 | 42 | 17 | 49 | 36 |
| Paco Rodriguez | 208 | 840 | 63 | 19 | 55 | 22 | 41 | 64% | 25% | 91 | 100 | 36 | 124 | 47 |
| Wandy Rodriguez | 260 | 1026 | 46 | 12 | 83 | 37 | 76 | 64% | 10% | 99 | 137 | 25 | 131 | 41 |
| Chaz Roe | 95 | 348 | 24 | 13 | 32 | 7 | 17 | 64% | 16% | 43 | 46 | 12 | 49 | 20 |
| Josh Roenicke | 282 | 1117 | 45 | 36 | 81 | 29 | 87 | 60% | 14% | 141 | 117 | 43 | 130 | 72 |
| Esmil Rogers | 598 | 2258 | 96 | 44 | 212 | 104 | 133 | 62% | 12% | 261 | 281 | 73 | 279 | 111 |
| Sergio Romo | 250 | 973 | 58 | 12 | 72 | 42 | 63 | 67% | 20% | 77 | 157 | 31 | 142 | 41 |
| Bruce Rondon | 122 | 442 | 30 | 11 | 37 | 19 | 23 | 63% | 24% | 65 | 45 | 12 | 55 | 20 |
| Hector Rondon | 242 | 935 | 44 | 25 | 72 | 36 | 58 | 61% | 17% | 110 | 107 | 34 | 119 | 54 |
| Sandy Rosario | 180 | 675 | 24 | 20 | 59 | 35 | 38 | 61% | 13% | 84 | 75 | 20 | 74 | 36 |
| B.J. Rosenberg | 86 | 350 | 19 | 9 | 21 | 10 | 26 | 61% | 18% | 42 | 34 | 13 | 44 | 19 |
| Trevor Rosenthal | 311 | 1287 | 108 | 20 | 76 | 33 | 62 | 68% | 23% | 114 | 165 | 41 | 199 | 56 |
| Robbie Ross | 267 | 1003 | 58 | 19 | 83 | 52 | 48 | 68% | 16% | 86 | 149 | 28 | 134 | 41 |
| Tyson Ross | 504 | 1981 | 119 | 44 | 179 | 50 | 97 | 62% | 19% | 233 | 219 | 64 | 267 | 108 |
| Michael Roth | 89 | 370 | 17 | 6 | 26 | 19 | 18 | 61% | 12% | 44 | 37 | 13 | 48 | 22 |
| Chris Rusin | 282 | 1021 | 36 | 24 | 103 | 49 | 62 | 61% | 13% | 118 | 132 | 31 | 115 | 52 |
| James Russell | 214 | 850 | 37 | 18 | 52 | 25 | 79 | 65% | 15% | 81 | 118 | 25 | 124 | 38 |
| Hyun-Jin Ryu | 783 | 3070 | 154 | 49 | 287 | 107 | 173 | 64% | 13% | 321 | 383 | 113 | 424 | 150 |
| Marc Rzepczynski | 129 | 474 | 29 | 10 | 47 | 14 | 23 | 59% | 23% | 66 | 52 | 21 | 57 | 32 |
| CC Sabathia | 908 | 3336 | 175 | 65 | 291 | 145 | 215 | 65% | 15% | 320 | 482 | 98 | 440 | 159 |
| Fernando Salas | 118 | 446 | 22 | 6 | 28 | 13 | 46 | 68% | 15% | 36 | 66 | 14 | 65 | 18 |
| Danny Salazar | 211 | 821 | 65 | 15 | 44 | 33 | 51 | 68% | 22% | 69 | 121 | 20 | 120 | 29 |
| Chris Sale | 866 | 3248 | 226 | 46 | 268 | 123 | 184 | 67% | 17% | 316 | 462 | 82 | 465 | 122 |
| Jeff Samardzija | 914 | 3462 | 214 | 78 | 288 | 122 | 188 | 63% | 18% | 369 | 436 | 118 | 446 | 182 |
| Alex Sanabia | 251 | 908 | 31 | 25 | 73 | 42 | 73 | 62% | 17% | 95 | 120 | 32 | 109 | 47 |
| Anibal Sanchez | 746 | 2974 | 202 | 54 | 215 | 104 | 155 | 64% | 20% | 287 | 390 | 118 | 417 | 159 |
| Jonathan Sanchez | 75 | 320 | 15 | 8 | 19 | 10 | 19 | 60% | 13% | 29 | 41 | 13 | 43 | 22 |
| Ervin Santana | 859 | 3199 | 161 | 51 | 294 | 133 | 209 | 65% | 16% | 295 | 460 | 108 | 414 | 148 |
| Hector Santiago | 656 | 2697 | 137 | 72 | 154 | 85 | 184 | 62% | 15% | 279 | 325 | 92 | 347 | 146 |
| Sergio Santos | 90 | 310 | 28 | 4 | 29 | 5 | 24 | 69% | 27% | 31 | 42 | 4 | 47 | 9 |
| Joe Saunders | 820 | 3110 | 107 | 61 | 325 | 138 | 172 | 59% | 11% | 324 | 404 | 119 | 341 | 179 |
| Joe Savery | 86 | 349 | 14 | 11 | 33 | 10 | 17 | 60% | 13% | 38 | 36 | 13 | 36 | 23 |
| Rob Scahill | 149 | 504 | 20 | 9 | 52 | 26 | 33 | 65% | 13% | 60 | 64 | 14 | 61 | 23 |
| Tanner Scheppers | 302 | 1084 | 59 | 24 | 106 | 39 | 65 | 64% | 16% | 120 | 147 | 25 | 140 | 43 |
| Max Scherzer | 836 | 3388 | 240 | 56 | 193 | 101 | 237 | 66% | 19% | 298 | 461 | 114 | 505 | 151 |
| Evan Scribner | 114 | 481 | 19 | 7 | 31 | 16 | 41 | 65% | 11% | 50 | 54 | 15 | 66 | 20 |
| Bryan Shaw | 316 | 1235 | 73 | 28 | 85 | 49 | 66 | 64% | 18% | 137 | 156 | 51 | 166 | 69 |
| James Shields | 946 | 3657 | 196 | 68 | 276 | 154 | 233 | 63% | 16% | 401 | 445 | 137 | 474 | 194 |
| Kevin Siegrist | 152 | 678 | 50 | 18 | 32 | 20 | 30 | 61% | 16% | 60 | 82 | 30 | 99 | 41 |
| Alfredo Simon | 359 | 1318 | 63 | 26 | 116 | 47 | 93 | 64% | 16% | 149 | 169 | 38 | 170 | 60 |
| Tony Sipp | 175 | 718 | 42 | 22 | 27 | 17 | 60 | 61% | 20% | 69 | 88 | 28 | 102 | 43 |
| Tyler Skaggs | 170 | 659 | 36 | 15 | 52 | 23 | 41 | 64% | 15% | 65 | 90 | 14 | 88 | 31 |
| Kevin Slowey | 395 | 1467 | 76 | 18 | 83 | 78 | 128 | 68% | 11% | 119 | 225 | 40 | 212 | 63 |
| Burch Smith | 167 | 641 | 46 | 21 | 27 | 23 | 49 | 64% | 21% | 66 | 79 | 21 | 84 | 36 |
| Joe Smith | 259 | 995 | 54 | 23 | 85 | 36 | 52 | 64% | 14% | 105 | 130 | 36 | 137 | 53 |
| Will Smith | 131 | 489 | 43 | 7 | 34 | 13 | 32 | 65% | 24% | 49 | 69 | 13 | 69 | 19 |
| Drew Smyly | 303 | 1284 | 81 | 17 | 85 | 35 | 76 | 65% | 17% | 124 | 153 | 45 | 179 | 62 |

# Pitcher Analysis

## Pitchers with 50+ Batters Faced in 2013

| | | | | | | | | | | Counts | | | | |
|---|---|---|---|---|---|---|---|---|---|---|---|---|---|---|
| Pitcher | BF | Pitches | K | BB | GB | LD | FB | Str% | S/Str | 1-0 | 0-1 | Full | 2 Strike | 3 Ball |
| Joakim Soria | 101 | 442 | 28 | 14 | 29 | 10 | 17 | 60% | 17% | 44 | 50 | 20 | 59 | 30 |
| Rafael Soriano | 277 | 1137 | 51 | 17 | 69 | 51 | 86 | 66% | 14% | 125 | 129 | 40 | 164 | 56 |
| Zeke Spruill | 55 | 197 | 9 | 5 | 15 | 8 | 15 | 63% | 15% | 17 | 31 | 5 | 23 | 10 |
| Craig Stammen | 339 | 1280 | 79 | 27 | 132 | 35 | 54 | 63% | 21% | 131 | 164 | 46 | 165 | 73 |
| Tim Stauffer | 284 | 1127 | 64 | 20 | 95 | 44 | 49 | 64% | 15% | 111 | 137 | 37 | 148 | 52 |
| Josh Stinson | 63 | 230 | 12 | 3 | 22 | 8 | 17 | 66% | 22% | 24 | 31 | 6 | 31 | 11 |
| Drew Storen | 267 | 955 | 58 | 19 | 74 | 36 | 71 | 65% | 15% | 109 | 119 | 29 | 122 | 43 |
| Dan Straily | 640 | 2465 | 124 | 57 | 162 | 89 | 194 | 64% | 18% | 259 | 318 | 78 | 336 | 124 |
| Stephen Strasburg | 731 | 2851 | 191 | 56 | 239 | 81 | 144 | 63% | 17% | 295 | 347 | 95 | 394 | 138 |
| Huston Street | 222 | 855 | 46 | 14 | 48 | 35 | 76 | 66% | 18% | 81 | 120 | 27 | 116 | 37 |
| Pedro Strop | 254 | 981 | 66 | 26 | 70 | 37 | 37 | 61% | 21% | 115 | 111 | 35 | 123 | 57 |
| Eric Stults | 857 | 3234 | 131 | 40 | 270 | 137 | 261 | 65% | 12% | 329 | 442 | 107 | 415 | 147 |
| Michael Stutes | 75 | 293 | 9 | 8 | 22 | 9 | 24 | 60% | 19% | 40 | 27 | 10 | 39 | 15 |
| Anthony Swarzak | 387 | 1499 | 69 | 22 | 132 | 56 | 104 | 65% | 13% | 153 | 201 | 41 | 197 | 64 |
| Junichi Tazawa | 284 | 1064 | 72 | 12 | 66 | 53 | 76 | 68% | 19% | 107 | 133 | 31 | 152 | 43 |
| Julio Teheran | 774 | 2885 | 170 | 45 | 201 | 113 | 218 | 67% | 17% | 267 | 417 | 82 | 386 | 121 |
| Nick Tepesch | 407 | 1537 | 76 | 27 | 139 | 66 | 89 | 64% | 14% | 155 | 207 | 51 | 202 | 73 |
| Joe Thatcher | 164 | 676 | 36 | 10 | 41 | 29 | 43 | 66% | 16% | 62 | 86 | 25 | 99 | 32 |
| Dale Thayer | 270 | 1138 | 64 | 22 | 73 | 39 | 65 | 64% | 15% | 110 | 143 | 41 | 158 | 55 |
| Caleb Thielbar | 171 | 659 | 39 | 14 | 31 | 22 | 63 | 62% | 19% | 77 | 74 | 19 | 80 | 33 |
| Tyler Thornburg | 270 | 1069 | 48 | 26 | 68 | 46 | 74 | 61% | 12% | 109 | 133 | 31 | 134 | 56 |
| Matt Thornton | 187 | 706 | 30 | 15 | 69 | 26 | 41 | 64% | 13% | 63 | 94 | 20 | 96 | 34 |
| Chris Tillman | 845 | 3477 | 179 | 68 | 225 | 126 | 232 | 64% | 13% | 361 | 406 | 120 | 477 | 172 |
| Alex Torres | 226 | 893 | 62 | 20 | 56 | 26 | 51 | 63% | 21% | 98 | 98 | 36 | 122 | 50 |
| Carlos Torres | 352 | 1324 | 75 | 17 | 109 | 49 | 92 | 67% | 16% | 117 | 200 | 42 | 178 | 59 |
| Ramon Troncoso | 137 | 533 | 18 | 16 | 50 | 18 | 30 | 59% | 15% | 56 | 68 | 21 | 66 | 34 |
| Jacob Turner | 514 | 1855 | 77 | 54 | 169 | 72 | 129 | 60% | 15% | 234 | 219 | 47 | 209 | 101 |
| Koji Uehara | 265 | 1049 | 101 | 9 | 61 | 17 | 73 | 74% | 27% | 78 | 170 | 22 | 178 | 25 |
| Raul Valdes | 152 | 588 | 37 | 8 | 32 | 21 | 50 | 66% | 17% | 57 | 83 | 19 | 80 | 23 |
| Jose Valverde | 84 | 341 | 19 | 6 | 23 | 9 | 25 | 65% | 13% | 37 | 39 | 15 | 47 | 19 |
| Jason Vargas | 644 | 2386 | 109 | 46 | 192 | 102 | 184 | 63% | 14% | 249 | 316 | 85 | 297 | 121 |
| Anthony Varvaro | 306 | 1106 | 43 | 25 | 111 | 57 | 67 | 64% | 13% | 115 | 159 | 35 | 130 | 55 |
| Donnie Veal | 126 | 501 | 29 | 16 | 41 | 13 | 24 | 56% | 19% | 65 | 52 | 19 | 56 | 35 |
| Yordano Ventura | 64 | 243 | 11 | 6 | 23 | 7 | 17 | 62% | 13% | 30 | 28 | 7 | 29 | 14 |
| Jose Veras | 254 | 1007 | 60 | 22 | 69 | 24 | 72 | 62% | 16% | 100 | 131 | 43 | 137 | 58 |
| Justin Verlander | 925 | 3692 | 217 | 75 | 240 | 142 | 243 | 66% | 17% | 325 | 495 | 120 | 524 | 170 |
| Carlos Villanueva | 524 | 1985 | 103 | 40 | 148 | 79 | 143 | 63% | 17% | 221 | 236 | 66 | 239 | 101 |
| Nick Vincent | 180 | 705 | 49 | 11 | 48 | 26 | 38 | 65% | 18% | 79 | 84 | 24 | 96 | 31 |
| Ryan Vogelsong | 467 | 1748 | 67 | 38 | 143 | 95 | 112 | 62% | 9% | 185 | 230 | 56 | 217 | 90 |
| Edinson Volquez | 777 | 3013 | 142 | 77 | 257 | 123 | 160 | 61% | 15% | 334 | 362 | 107 | 377 | 173 |
| Michael Wacha | 260 | 1034 | 65 | 19 | 77 | 29 | 68 | 65% | 18% | 109 | 132 | 31 | 142 | 42 |
| Neil Wagner | 161 | 649 | 33 | 13 | 49 | 31 | 31 | 64% | 17% | 60 | 84 | 24 | 87 | 35 |
| Adam Wainwright | 956 | 3533 | 219 | 35 | 332 | 158 | 186 | 67% | 15% | 337 | 504 | 113 | 486 | 141 |
| Jordan Walden | 193 | 780 | 54 | 14 | 38 | 22 | 62 | 64% | 24% | 74 | 104 | 30 | 108 | 40 |
| Taijuan Walker | 60 | 233 | 12 | 4 | 16 | 9 | 17 | 62% | 17% | 26 | 29 | 6 | 26 | 10 |
| P.J. Walters | 183 | 677 | 22 | 18 | 56 | 32 | 53 | 61% | 10% | 81 | 79 | 24 | 76 | 37 |
| Chien-Ming Wang | 123 | 409 | 14 | 9 | 58 | 21 | 21 | 62% | 11% | 45 | 63 | 9 | 44 | 17 |
| Adam Warren | 331 | 1298 | 64 | 30 | 106 | 52 | 76 | 61% | 19% | 144 | 154 | 49 | 173 | 75 |
| Tony Watson | 280 | 1072 | 54 | 12 | 88 | 38 | 75 | 67% | 18% | 104 | 150 | 29 | 149 | 36 |
| Jered Weaver | 634 | 2396 | 117 | 37 | 143 | 104 | 217 | 64% | 16% | 256 | 307 | 80 | 309 | 109 |
| Ryan Webb | 332 | 1208 | 54 | 27 | 134 | 45 | 59 | 62% | 15% | 139 | 152 | 37 | 141 | 68 |
| Thad Weber | 61 | 238 | 10 | 8 | 23 | 9 | 11 | 59% | 15% | 28 | 29 | 7 | 28 | 14 |
| Allen Webster | 145 | 535 | 23 | 18 | 44 | 21 | 37 | 60% | 21% | 55 | 69 | 18 | 64 | 36 |
| Jake Westbrook | 523 | 1862 | 44 | 50 | 229 | 83 | 95 | 61% | 9% | 213 | 233 | 72 | 207 | 109 |
| Zack Wheeler | 431 | 1728 | 84 | 46 | 127 | 69 | 98 | 61% | 15% | 207 | 180 | 69 | 221 | 95 |
| Tom Wilhelmsen | 251 | 982 | 45 | 33 | 73 | 38 | 57 | 61% | 18% | 112 | 116 | 39 | 130 | 59 |
| Jerome Williams | 728 | 2637 | 107 | 55 | 260 | 117 | 175 | 63% | 15% | 308 | 331 | 74 | 305 | 121 |
| Alex Wilson | 127 | 479 | 22 | 14 | 28 | 27 | 35 | 61% | 15% | 56 | 59 | 12 | 63 | 22 |
| C.J. Wilson | 913 | 3651 | 188 | 85 | 276 | 138 | 208 | 62% | 14% | 368 | 469 | 155 | 472 | 206 |
| Justin Wilson | 295 | 1191 | 59 | 28 | 106 | 34 | 60 | 65% | 15% | 119 | 152 | 39 | 170 | 54 |
| Chris Withrow | 134 | 604 | 43 | 13 | 28 | 16 | 34 | 64% | 19% | 60 | 70 | 22 | 85 | 30 |
| Ross Wolf | 207 | 688 | 21 | 15 | 80 | 45 | 44 | 65% | 10% | 84 | 94 | 10 | 82 | 23 |
| Alex Wood | 327 | 1310 | 77 | 27 | 106 | 51 | 59 | 63% | 16% | 124 | 168 | 52 | 175 | 73 |
| Travis Wood | 821 | 3090 | 144 | 66 | 195 | 131 | 261 | 65% | 13% | 319 | 404 | 96 | 397 | 141 |
| Rob Wooten | 115 | 410 | 18 | 8 | 38 | 18 | 31 | 67% | 15% | 38 | 63 | 11 | 52 | 17 |
| Brandon Workman | 180 | 772 | 47 | 15 | 45 | 31 | 40 | 62% | 16% | 67 | 101 | 31 | 98 | 47 |
| Vance Worley | 234 | 918 | 25 | 15 | 89 | 42 | 58 | 63% | 7% | 96 | 122 | 31 | 116 | 51 |
| Jamey Wright | 288 | 1115 | 65 | 23 | 97 | 38 | 56 | 61% | 16% | 118 | 143 | 32 | 148 | 53 |
| Steven Wright | 59 | 244 | 10 | 9 | 15 | 10 | 14 | 60% | 16% | 32 | 23 | 13 | 33 | 17 |

# Pitcher Analysis
Pitchers with 50+ Batters Faced in 2013

| | | | | | | | | | | Counts | | | | |
|---|---|---|---|---|---|---|---|---|---|---|---|---|---|---|
| Pitcher | BF | Pitches | K | BB | GB | LD | FB | Str% | S/Str | 1-0 | 0-1 | Full | 2 Strike | 3 Ball |
| Wesley Wright | 232 | 910 | 55 | 19 | 77 | 33 | 43 | 64% | 12% | 104 | 104 | 25 | 123 | 41 |
| Josh Zeid | 118 | 466 | 24 | 12 | 38 | 19 | 22 | 62% | 20% | 50 | 53 | 20 | 70 | 28 |
| Brad Ziegler | 297 | 982 | 44 | 22 | 157 | 42 | 24 | 65% | 16% | 109 | 139 | 24 | 116 | 42 |
| Jordan Zimmermann | 865 | 3083 | 161 | 40 | 304 | 135 | 200 | 68% | 13% | 284 | 465 | 78 | 413 | 108 |
| Barry Zito | 608 | 2355 | 86 | 54 | 165 | 118 | 171 | 62% | 12% | 264 | 279 | 81 | 292 | 123 |

# Notes on the Pitchers' Repertoires

**Bill James**

1) Using modern radar guns, 72% of major league pitchers have an average fastball velocity over 90 miles an hour.

I suppose that most of you know this, but modern radar guns are about 3 to 5 MPH "faster" than the first generation of radar guns, which was used in the late 1970s. The reason they are faster is that they pick up the ball much quicker out of the pitcher's hand. Since the ball decelerates as it travels to home plate, if you read the speed earlier you get a bigger number. It is very likely that Goose Gossage and Nolan Ryan would read consistently over 100 with the modern radar guns.

2) The major league leaders in terms of having a good fastball and not using it are Al Alburquerque and Nate Jones. Alburquerque's fastball averaged 94.3 miles per hour, putting it in the top 10% of major league fastballs in terms of velocity, but he threw the fastball only 35% of the time. Jones' fastball averaged a stunning 97.7, but he threw it only 53% of the time.

3) The opposite of Alburquerque and Jones—that is, the pitchers who don't have much of a fastball, but who throw it a lot anyway—are Javy Lopez and Scott Downs. Lopez' fastball averaged 86.1 MPH, but he throws it 80% of the time and had a 1.83 ERA. Downs' fastball averaged 88.0, but he threw it 83% of the time, and he also was very effective.

4) Only two real major league pitchers in 2013 threw their fastball 90% of the time or more: Kenley Jansen and Jake McGee. Several other pitchers did so who just threw a couple of innings or less.

5) If you treat the cutter as a separate pitch. . .about 7% of major league pitchers throw their fastball 80% of the time or more, and about 21% throw it 70% or more. 51% throw the fastball 60% or more, and 80% throw the fastball 50% or more.

6) These numbers, however, are very different if you treat the cutter as a fastball. If you do that, then 3% of pitchers throw the fastball 90% or more, 13% are 80% or more, 33% are 70% or more, and 68% of pitchers throw the fastball 60% or more. Including the cutter, 91% of major league pitchers throw the fastball 50% or more.

7) By our data, the two major league pitchers who throw a splitter the highest percentage of the time, Edward Mujica and Koji Uehara, are also the two pitchers who throw the highest percentage of strikes in the major leagues. This, however, is potentially misleading, since their splitters are quite a bit different from what might be called a traditional splitter. It's a splitter, but. . .not really. They're not using it in the same way that many pitchers are using the pitch.

8) 39% of major league pitchers throw a curve ball 10% of the time or more.

9) 61% of major league pitchers throw a slider 10% of the time or more. If you add up the curve ball percentage (39%) and the slider (61%) it totals up to 100%, which is a coincidence but not totally. 86% of major league pitchers throw one or the other at least 10% of the time.

10) 39% of major league pitchers throw a changeup at least 10% of the time.

11) Only 7% of major league pitchers throw a splitter 10% of the time or more.

12) There were two "real" knuckleball pitchers in the majors last year, Dickey and Steven Wright, and two pitchers who threw the screwball occasionally, Hector Santiago and Trevor Bauer. Thus, one could argue that the screwball is now more uncommon than the knuckleball. But a lot of pitchers now throw a circle change which is not that far from the pitch that used to be called a screwball. It is as much a change of the vocabulary as it is of the pitches.

13) The most common description of a pitcher's repertoire used to be "sinker/slider", as in "he's your basic sinker/slider pitcher." Our data doesn't really identify anyone as a sinker/slider pitcher because the sinker is coded as a two-seam fastball.

14) I cobbled together a formula to identify pitchers who had similar repertoires. Most similar to Clayton Kershaw, if you ignore the left/right thing, is Mat Latos. But you can't really ignore the left/right difference, so most similar to Kershaw is David Purcey. Kershaw: 92.6 MPH fastball, 61% fastballs, 24% sliders, 13% curves, 2% changes. Purcey: 92.6 MPH fastball, 66% fastballs, 25% sliders, 2% curves, 7% changes. Purcey was effective with the White Sox last year, but he's a long way from being Clayton Kershaw.

15) Most-similar repertoire to Max Scherzer is Justin Verlander, and most-similar to Verlander is Scherzer.

16) Most-similar repertoire to Felix Hernandez is Erasmo Ramirez. Actually Hector Santiago, but that, again, ignores the left/right difference.

17) Did you know there are now six major league players named "Hector"?

18) Most-similar repertoire to Zack Greinke is Clay Buchholz.

19) Most-similar repertoire to Jon Lester is David Price.

20) Most-similar repertoire to Craig Kimbrel is Jeremy Jeffress. That's very intriguing, because Jeffress did have an 0.87 ERA in 10 innings for Toronto, but still. . .it's 10 innings. Next on that list is Cody Allen of the Indians.

21) Most-similar to Jason Marquis is Greg Burke.

22) You can measure how "varied" a pitcher's repertoire is by squaring the number of times a pitcher throws each pitch, and then dividing the square of all his pitches by the sum of the squares of the individual pitches. The higher the result, the more varied the pitcher's repertoire.

In other words, suppose that a pitcher throws 100 pitches, all fastballs. His "repertoire variance score" would be 1.00, since 100 squared divided by 100 squared is 1.00.

But suppose that he throws 25 fastballs, 25 curves, 25 sliders, 25 changes. That would be a score of 4.00, since 100 squared (10,000) divided by 625+625+625+625 is 4.00.

I remember that I did this study one other time, several years ago, and the most-varied repertoire in the majors at that time was Shaun Marcum. I repeated the study now, and the most-varied repertoire in the majors in 2013 was: Shaun Marcum. The top 10: Shaun Marcum (4.13), Roy Halladay (3.92), Mike Leake (3.64), Yu Darvish (3.56), Alfredo Aceves (3.54), Freddy Garcia (3.53), Jamey Wright (3.48), Jon Garland (3.46), James Shields (3.41), and Daisuke Matsuzaka (3.40). That's very much an "old pitcher's trait", so I could have combined that with the "pitcher age score" that I introduced in the Pitcher Analysis Section, and made a better "pitcher age score". But I have no way to sync up the two data bases.

| | Fastball Velocity | Pitch Repertoire | | | | | | |
|---|---|---|---|---|---|---|---|---|
| Player | | Fastball | Cutter | Curve | Slider | Change | Splitter | Other |
| Aardsma,David | 91.2 | 64% | - | - | 27% | - | 10% | |
| Abad,Fernando | 93.1 | 63% | - | 23% | - | 14% | - | |
| Aceves,Alfredo | 91.6 | 44% | 16% | 20% | - | 14% | 6% | |
| Adams,Mike | 89.8 | 41% | 41% | 8% | - | 10% | - | |
| Affeldt,Jeremy | 91.1 | 70% | - | 19% | - | - | 10% | |
| Albers,Andrew | 86.2 | 67% | - | 6% | 18% | 8% | - | |
| Albers,Matt | 93.4 | 77% | - | 12% | 7% | 3% | - | |
| Alburquerque,Al | 94.3 | 35% | - | - | 65% | - | - | |
| Allen,Cody | 95.4 | 72% | - | 28% | - | - | - | |
| Alvarez,Henderson | 93.2 | 70% | - | 3% | 15% | 12% | - | |
| Alvarez,Jose | 89.4 | 50% | - | 4% | 17% | 29% | - | |
| Ambriz,Hector | 92.9 | 62% | - | 9% | 29% | - | - | |
| Ames,Steven | 88.6 | 50% | - | - | 32% | 18% | - | |
| Anderson,Brett | 91.7 | 55% | - | 8% | 33% | 4% | - | |
| Archer,Chris | 95.0 | 60% | - | - | 33% | 7% | - | |
| Arrieta,Jake | 93.9 | 65% | 6% | 16% | 9% | 4% | - | |
| Arroyo,Bronson | 87.2 | 44% | <1% | 13% | 27% | 16% | - | |
| Asencio,Jairo | 91.9 | 26% | - | - | 20% | 54% | - | |
| Atchison,Scott | 91.2 | 42% | 44% | 12% | - | 3% | - | |
| Aumont,Phillippe | 94.0 | 64% | - | 33% | - | - | 2% | |
| Avilan,Luis | 93.1 | 81% | - | 14% | - | 5% | - | |
| Axelrod,Dylan | 88.1 | 43% | - | 15% | 27% | 16% | - | |
| Axford,John | 95.4 | 66% | - | 21% | 13% | - | - | |
| Ayala,Luis | 89.7 | 56% | 12% | 3% | 20% | 10% | - | |
| Badenhop,Burke | 89.1 | 68% | - | - | 27% | 5% | - | |
| Bailey,Andrew | 94.0 | 63% | 30% | 7% | - | <1% | - | |
| Bailey,Homer | 94.1 | 60% | - | 12% | 15% | - | 13% | |
| Baker,Scott | 88.4 | 78% | - | 3% | 15% | 5% | - | |
| Balfour,Grant | 93.4 | 65% | - | 8% | 27% | <1% | - | |
| Bard,Daniel | 93.7 | 93% | - | - | 7% | - | - | |
| Barnes,Scott | 90.6 | 57% | - | - | 35% | 8% | - | |
| Bass,Anthony | 92.3 | 55% | - | <1% | 36% | 10% | - | |
| Bastardo,Antonio | 91.7 | 59% | - | - | 38% | 3% | - | |
| Bauer,Trevor | 92.8 | 46% | - | 9% | 17% | 7% | - | Screwball 22% |
| Beachy,Brandon | 90.2 | 59% | - | 11% | 8% | 22% | - | |
| Beato,Pedro | 93.1 | 66% | 16% | 4% | - | 14% | - | |
| Beavan,Blake | 89.7 | 52% | - | 4% | 40% | 3% | - | |
| Beckett,Josh | 92.0 | 45% | 18% | 19% | - | 18% | - | |
| Bedard,Erik | 89.3 | 50% | 17% | 19% | - | 13% | - | |
| Belfiore,Mike | 88.1 | 71% | - | - | 26% | 3% | - | |
| Belisario,Ronald | 94.4 | 78% | - | - | 17% | - | 5% | |
| Belisle,Matt | 90.6 | 64% | - | 8% | 27% | 2% | - | |
| Beliveau,Jeff | 89.3 | 82% | 18% | - | - | - | - | |
| Bell,Heath | 93.2 | 67% | - | 32% | - | <1% | - | |
| Below,Duane | 90.2 | 52% | 28% | 9% | - | 12% | - | |
| Benoit,Joaquin | 94.1 | 61% | - | - | 11% | 28% | - | |
| Betances,Dellin | 95.8 | 61% | - | 38% | - | 2% | - | |
| Betancourt,Rafael | 89.9 | 70% | - | 23% | - | 7% | - | |
| Bettis,Chad | 93.2 | 68% | 13% | 12% | - | 7% | - | |
| Billingsley,Chad | 91.1 | 64% | 13% | 16% | - | 7% | - | |
| Black,Vic | 95.5 | 75% | - | 25% | - | - | - | |
| Blackley,Travis | 90.3 | 48% | - | 12% | 26% | 15% | - | |
| Blanton,Joe | 89.4 | 48% | 9% | 11% | 6% | 27% | - | |
| Blazek,Michael | 94.8 | 65% | - | 18% | 14% | 3% | - | |
| Blevins,Jerry | 90.1 | 44% | 30% | 15% | - | 11% | - | |
| Boggs,Mitchell | 94.2 | 66% | - | - | 22% | 12% | - | |

| | Fastball Velocity | Pitch Repertoire | | | | | | |
|---|---|---|---|---|---|---|---|---|
| Player | | Fastball | Cutter | Curve | Slider | Change | Splitter | Other |
| Bonderman,Jeremy | 91.0 | 61% | - | - | 31% | 8% | - | |
| Bootcheck,Chris | 89.4 | 47% | 33% | - | 17% | 3% | - | |
| Boshers,Buddy | 92.6 | 54% | - | 43% | - | 3% | - | |
| Bowden,Michael | 90.7 | 64% | 4% | - | 19% | - | 13% | |
| Boxberger,Brad | 91.6 | 55% | - | 3% | 10% | 32% | - | |
| Brach,Brad | 92.0 | 69% | - | - | 17% | 14% | - | |
| Brasier,Ryan | 94.5 | 71% | - | - | 25% | 4% | - | |
| Breslow,Craig | 89.9 | 63% | 25% | 3% | - | 9% | - | |
| Brewer,Charles | 90.6 | 75% | - | 16% | - | 8% | - | |
| Britton,Drake | 92.7 | 63% | - | - | 33% | 4% | - | |
| Britton,Zach | 91.6 | 68% | - | - | 19% | 13% | - | |
| Brothers,Rex | 93.4 | 66% | - | - | 29% | 5% | - | |
| Broxton,Jonathan | 93.8 | 60% | 29% | 1% | 9% | - | - | |
| Buchholz,Clay | 91.9 | 49% | 24% | 14% | - | 11% | 3% | |
| Buckner,Billy | 86.8 | 57% | - | 19% | - | 24% | - | |
| Buehrle,Mark | 84.2 | 45% | 27% | 7% | - | 20% | - | |
| Bueno,Francisley | 89.8 | 68% | - | 13% | 8% | 11% | - | |
| Bumgarner,Madison | 91.4 | 38% | - | 13% | 38% | 10% | - | |
| Burgos,Hiram | 87.8 | 50% | 11% | 22% | - | 16% | - | |
| Burke,Greg | 87.7 | 63% | - | - | 33% | 4% | - | |
| Burnett,A.J. | 92.5 | 58% | - | 35% | - | 6% | - | |
| Burnett,Alex | 90.3 | 69% | - | 4% | 20% | 8% | - | |
| Burnett,Sean | 87.7 | 79% | - | - | 18% | 3% | - | |
| Burns,Cory | 90.0 | 49% | - | - | 5% | 43% | - | Knuckleball 4% |
| Burton,Jared | 92.1 | 48% | - | - | 19% | 33% | - | |
| Bush,Dave | 86.8 | 47% | - | 27% | 24% | 2% | - | |
| Butler,Keith | 90.7 | 58% | - | 15% | - | 27% | - | |
| Byrdak,Tim | 85.4 | 54% | - | - | 40% | 6% | - | |
| Cabral,Cesar | 91.8 | 36% | - | - | 44% | 20% | - | |
| Cabrera,Alberto | 92.9 | 64% | - | - | 31% | 5% | - | |
| Cahill,Trevor | 89.3 | 61% | - | 9% | 15% | 15% | - | |
| Cain,Matt | 91.2 | 49% | - | 12% | 28% | 11% | - | |
| Caminero,Arquimedes | 95.4 | 72% | 2% | - | 11% | - | 15% | |
| Camp,Shawn | 86.3 | 50% | - | - | 45% | 5% | - | |
| Capps,Carter | 95.6 | 68% | - | 2% | 26% | 4% | - | |
| Capuano,Chris | 88.9 | 52% | - | 5% | 13% | 30% | - | |
| Carpenter,David | 95.1 | 71% | - | - | 26% | 3% | - | |
| Carpenter,David | 89.0 | 84% | - | - | 11% | 5% | - | |
| Carrasco,Carlos | 94.9 | 63% | - | 9% | 10% | 19% | - | |
| Carroll,Jamey | 76.9 | 100% | - | - | - | - | - | |
| Carson,Robert | 92.9 | 67% | - | - | 32% | 2% | - | |
| Cashner,Andrew | 94.5 | 63% | - | 3% | 14% | 19% | - | |
| Casilla,Santiago | 93.4 | 58% | - | 14% | 26% | 2% | - | |
| Castro,Simon | 89.5 | 58% | - | - | 39% | 3% | - | |
| Cecil,Brett | 92.3 | 41% | 19% | 33% | - | 7% | - | |
| Cedeno,Xavier | 89.3 | 52% | 10% | 9% | 24% | 5% | - | |
| Chacin,Jhoulys | 89.8 | 63% | - | 5% | 24% | 9% | - | |
| Chamberlain,Joba | 94.7 | 56% | - | 9% | 35% | <1% | - | |
| Chapman,Aroldis | 98.3 | 85% | - | - | 15% | - | - | |
| Chapman,Kevin | 92.4 | 59% | - | - | 41% | - | - | |
| Chatwood,Tyler | 93.0 | 72% | - | 12% | 12% | 4% | - | |
| Chavez,Jesse | 92.3 | 31% | 42% | 18% | <1% | 9% | - | |
| Chen,Bruce | 85.4 | 44% | - | 18% | 26% | 12% | - | |
| Chen,Wei-Yin | 91.4 | 68% | - | 8% | 12% | 12% | - | |
| Choate,Randy | 85.8 | 70% | - | - | 30% | <1% | - | |
| Christiani,Nick | 92.6 | 80% | 9% | - | 9% | 2% | - | |
| Cingrani,Tony | 91.9 | 81% | - | 7% | 4% | 7% | - | |

| | Fastball Velocity | Pitch Repertoire | | | | | | |
|---|---|---|---|---|---|---|---|---|
| Player | | Fastball | Cutter | Curve | Slider | Change | Splitter | Other |
| Cishek,Steve | 92.3 | 60% | - | - | 37% | 3% | - | |
| Cisnero,Jose | 92.8 | 70% | - | 10% | 12% | 8% | - | |
| Claiborne,Preston | 93.1 | 55% | - | - | 27% | 18% | - | |
| Clark,Zach | 88.1 | 81% | - | 3% | 11% | 6% | - | |
| Clemens,Paul | 93.0 | 68% | - | 17% | - | 15% | - | |
| Cleto,Maikel | 95.4 | 58% | - | - | 34% | 8% | - | |
| Clippard,Tyler | 92.1 | 60% | 5% | 6% | - | 28% | <1% | |
| Cloyd,Tyler | 86.3 | 47% | 32% | 11% | - | 10% | - | |
| Cobb,Alex | 91.0 | 43% | - | 24% | - | 33% | - | |
| Coello,Robert | 90.8 | 82% | - | 6% | - | - | 12% | |
| Coke,Phil | 93.4 | 58% | - | - | 25% | 17% | - | |
| Cole,Gerrit | 96.1 | 65% | - | 12% | 15% | 8% | - | |
| Coleman,Louis | 90.1 | 54% | - | - | 46% | <1% | - | |
| Collins,Tim | 93.1 | 54% | - | 25% | - | 20% | - | |
| Collmenter,Josh | 87.5 | 71% | - | 3% | - | 26% | - | |
| Colome,Alex | 94.7 | 57% | - | - | 17% | 25% | - | |
| Colon,Bartolo | 89.9 | 85% | - | - | 9% | 5% | - | |
| Contreras,Jose | 91.1 | 49% | - | - | 37% | - | 14% | |
| Cook,Ryan | 94.9 | 68% | - | - | 25% | 7% | - | |
| Corbin,Patrick | 92.1 | 67% | - | - | 23% | 10% | - | |
| Corpas,Manny | 90.0 | 58% | - | - | 42% | - | - | |
| Correia,Kevin | 90.5 | 38% | 35% | 14% | - | 14% | - | |
| Cosart,Jarred | 94.5 | 70% | - | 22% | - | 8% | - | |
| Cotts,Neal | 92.2 | 59% | 31% | - | 9% | <1% | - | |
| Crain,Jesse | 94.5 | 47% | - | 16% | 31% | 6% | - | |
| Crow,Aaron | 94.6 | 58% | - | - | 42% | <1% | - | |
| Cruz,Rhiner | 96.0 | 72% | - | - | 17% | 12% | - | |
| Cueto,Johnny | 92.5 | 46% | 20% | - | 16% | 18% | - | |
| Cumpton,Brandon | 91.7 | 66% | - | - | 24% | 10% | - | |
| Daley,Matt | 87.1 | 64% | - | 34% | - | 2% | - | |
| Danks,John | 89.3 | 46% | 17% | 10% | - | 26% | - | |
| Darvish,Yu | 92.9 | 38% | 16% | 8% | 32% | 2% | 4% | |
| Davis,Erik | 92.9 | 62% | - | 11% | - | 28% | - | |
| Davis,Wade | 92.1 | 55% | 20% | 22% | - | 4% | - | |
| De Fratus,Justin | 93.1 | 61% | - | - | 37% | 2% | - | |
| de la Rosa,Dane | 94.6 | 79% | - | 14% | - | 7% | - | |
| De la Rosa,Eury | 88.5 | 35% | - | 20% | 25% | 20% | - | |
| de la Rosa,Jorge | 91.1 | 51% | - | 7% | 14% | 28% | - | |
| de la Rosa,Rubby | 95.2 | 59% | - | 1% | 17% | 23% | - | |
| De La Torre,Jose | 91.5 | 52% | - | - | 30% | 19% | - | |
| De Leon,Jorge | 94.9 | 63% | - | - | 30% | 7% | - | |
| Deduno,Samuel | 90.3 | 61% | - | 25% | 2% | 12% | - | |
| Delabar,Steve | 94.7 | 70% | - | - | 11% | - | 19% | |
| Delgado,Randall | 91.7 | 66% | - | 8% | <1% | 26% | - | |
| Dempster,Ryan | 89.2 | 49% | 6% | - | 28% | - | 18% | |
| Detwiler,Ross | 92.1 | 88% | - | 8% | - | 4% | - | |
| DeVries,Cole | 89.1 | 67% | - | 8% | 14% | 11% | - | |
| Diamond,Scott | 88.6 | 65% | - | 23% | - | 11% | - | |
| Dickey,R.A. | 81.9 | 12% | - | - | - | 1% | - | Knuckleball 87% |
| Diekman,Jake | 96.0 | 72% | - | - | 21% | 7% | - | |
| Dolis,Rafael | 94.7 | 84% | - | - | 16% | - | - | |
| Dominguez,Jose | 98.5 | 78% | - | - | 19% | 3% | - | |
| Doolittle,Sean | 94.3 | 88% | - | - | 9% | 3% | - | |
| Dotel,Octavio | 89.5 | 79% | - | 8% | 13% | - | - | |
| Doubront,Felix | 90.5 | 63% | 8% | 14% | - | 14% | - | |
| Downs,Darin | 89.7 | 48% | - | 6% | 32% | 14% | - | |
| Downs,Scott | 88.0 | 83% | - | 15% | 2% | - | - | |

| | Fastball Velocity | Pitch Repertoire | | | | | | |
|---|---|---|---|---|---|---|---|---|
| Player | | Fastball | Cutter | Curve | Slider | Change | Splitter | Other |
| Drabek,Kyle | 93.0 | 65% | - | 19% | - | 16% | - | |
| Duensing,Brian | 92.2 | 57% | - | 5% | 30% | 9% | - | |
| Duffy,Danny | 93.7 | 67% | - | 12% | 3% | 18% | - | |
| Duke,Zach | 88.7 | 59% | - | 13% | 15% | 12% | - | |
| Dunn,Mike | 94.4 | 62% | - | 2% | 35% | - | - | |
| Dunning,Jake | 90.2 | 62% | - | - | 28% | 10% | - | |
| Durbin,Chad | 89.0 | 45% | 35% | 13% | - | 8% | - | |
| Dwyer,Chris | 89.3 | 52% | - | 46% | - | 2% | - | |
| Dyson,Sam | 91.7 | 85% | - | 1% | 5% | 8% | - | |
| Edgin,Josh | 92.7 | 68% | - | - | 26% | 6% | - | |
| Elmore,Jake | 81.0 | 73% | - | 9% | - | 18% | - | |
| Enright,Barry | 90.5 | 61% | - | 8% | 20% | 12% | - | |
| Eovaldi,Nathan | 96.2 | 71% | - | 9% | 19% | 2% | - | |
| Eppley,Cody | 85.7 | 84% | - | - | 13% | 3% | - | |
| Erlin,Robbie | 89.6 | 61% | - | 21% | 7% | 12% | - | |
| Escalona,Edgmer | 94.2 | 70% | - | - | 27% | 3% | - | |
| Estrada,Marco | 89.2 | 59% | <1% | 17% | - | 24% | - | |
| Familia,Jeurys | 94.8 | 74% | - | - | 22% | 4% | - | |
| Farnsworth,Kyle | 92.6 | 61% | 13% | - | 24% | 2% | - | |
| Farquhar,Danny | 94.5 | 30% | 50% | 20% | - | <1% | - | |
| Feldman,Scott | 89.9 | 36% | 33% | 26% | - | - | 5% | |
| Feliciano,Pedro | 83.4 | 49% | - | - | 40% | 12% | - | |
| Feliz,Neftali | 93.6 | 51% | - | - | 20% | 29% | - | |
| Fernandez,Jose | 94.9 | 57% | - | 21% | 13% | 9% | - | |
| Fields,Josh | 93.7 | 75% | - | 20% | <1% | 5% | - | |
| Fien,Casey | 91.0 | 50% | 42% | - | 8% | - | - | |
| Fiers,Mike | 88.2 | 53% | 12% | 22% | - | 13% | - | |
| Fife,Stephen | 89.4 | 54% | - | 29% | 3% | 14% | - | |
| Figaro,Alfredo | 95.2 | 66% | - | 9% | 19% | 6% | - | |
| Figueroa,Pedro | 95.5 | 83% | - | - | 12% | 5% | - | |
| Fister,Doug | 88.8 | 51% | - | 20% | 14% | 15% | - | |
| Floyd,Gavin | 91.4 | 55% | 19% | 21% | - | 5% | - | |
| Flynn,Brian | 90.5 | 63% | - | 10% | 19% | 8% | - | |
| Font,Wilmer | 94.6 | 86% | - | - | 4% | 11% | - | |
| Francis,Jeff | 85.8 | 53% | 6% | 22% | - | 19% | - | |
| Francisco,Frank | 92.1 | 63% | - | 4% | 2% | - | 31% | |
| Frasor,Jason | 92.5 | 65% | - | - | 15% | - | 20% | |
| Freeman,Justin | 92.3 | 69% | - | - | 6% | 25% | - | |
| Freeman,Sam | 95.2 | 73% | - | - | 3% | 25% | - | |
| Frieri,Ernesto | 94.4 | 87% | - | - | 11% | 2% | - | |
| Fujikawa,Kyuji | 92.3 | 64% | 12% | 2% | - | - | 22% | |
| Fuld,Sam | 86.8 | 100% | - | - | - | - | - | |
| Furbush,Charlie | 92.0 | 55% | - | 2% | 42% | 1% | - | |
| Gallardo,Yovani | 90.7 | 53% | - | 21% | 24% | 1% | - | |
| Garcia,Freddy | 87.5 | 45% | - | 11% | 15% | 10% | 19% | |
| Garcia,Jaime | 88.7 | 52% | 24% | 9% | - | 15% | - | |
| Garcia,Luis | 94.1 | 65% | - | - | 35% | - | - | |
| Garcia,Onelki | 93.3 | 78% | - | 22% | - | - | - | |
| Garland,Jon | 87.5 | 47% | 12% | 15% | 15% | 9% | 3% | |
| Garza,Matt | 93.1 | 64% | - | 8% | 24% | 4% | - | |
| Gast,John | 87.0 | 64% | - | 8% | - | 28% | - | |
| Gaudin,Chad | 90.8 | 67% | - | - | 24% | 10% | - | |
| Gausman,Kevin | 95.9 | 66% | - | - | 11% | 4% | 20% | |
| Gearrin,Cory | 88.2 | 58% | - | - | 34% | 8% | - | |
| Gee,Dillon | 89.3 | 54% | - | 10% | 18% | 18% | - | |
| Germano,Justin | 87.0 | 60% | - | 17% | 3% | 20% | - | |
| Germen,Gonzalez | 93.0 | 55% | - | - | 16% | 28% | - | |

| | Fastball Velocity | Pitch Repertoire | | | | | | |
|---|---|---|---|---|---|---|---|---|
| Player | | Fastball | Cutter | Curve | Slider | Change | Splitter | Other |
| Gibson,Kyle | 92.1 | 69% | - | 1% | 17% | 13% | - | |
| Gomes,Brandon | 91.5 | 45% | - | - | 35% | - | 20% | |
| Gomez,Jeanmar | 90.8 | 62% | 3% | <1% | 19% | 15% | - | |
| Gonzalez,Alberto | 80.4 | 100% | - | - | - | - | - | |
| Gonzalez,Edgar | 88.1 | 56% | 5% | 8% | 10% | 21% | - | |
| Gonzalez,Gio | 92.6 | 69% | - | 21% | - | 10% | - | |
| Gonzalez,Michael | 90.9 | 55% | - | 2% | 36% | 7% | - | |
| Gonzalez,Miguel | 91.4 | 62% | - | 8% | 10% | - | 20% | |
| Gorzelanny,Tom | 91.1 | 55% | <1% | - | 30% | 14% | - | |
| Gray,Sonny | 93.1 | 65% | - | 26% | 2% | 7% | - | |
| Gregerson,Luke | 88.2 | 34% | - | 2% | 56% | 8% | - | |
| Gregg,Kevin | 90.8 | 66% | 9% | - | 16% | - | 9% | |
| Greinke,Zack | 91.7 | 55% | 17% | 13% | 3% | 12% | - | |
| Griffin,A.J. | 88.9 | 59% | 2% | 16% | 9% | 14% | - | |
| Grilli,Jason | 93.4 | 68% | - | - | 32% | <1% | - | |
| Grimm,Justin | 91.6 | 59% | - | 26% | 4% | 11% | - | |
| Guerra,Javy | 92.8 | 75% | - | 3% | 20% | 2% | - | |
| Guerrier,Matt | 89.7 | 48% | - | 15% | 30% | 7% | - | |
| Guilmet,Preston | 89.6 | 59% | - | - | 34% | - | 7% | |
| Guthrie,Jeremy | 91.8 | 59% | - | 9% | 20% | 11% | - | |
| Gutierrez,Juan | 95.0 | 62% | - | 16% | 19% | 3% | - | |
| Hagadone,Nick | 94.1 | 81% | - | - | 19% | - | - | |
| Hale,David | 91.1 | 72% | - | - | 14% | 14% | - | |
| Halladay,Roy | 88.8 | 29% | 30% | 22% | - | - | 18% | |
| Hamels,Cole | 91.6 | 50% | 18% | 7% | - | 25% | - | |
| Hammel,Jason | 92.7 | 60% | - | 11% | 21% | 8% | - | |
| Hand,Brad | 93.0 | 68% | - | 21% | - | 11% | - | |
| Hand,Donovan | 89.6 | 55% | - | 21% | 22% | 2% | - | |
| Hanrahan,Joel | 96.6 | 78% | - | - | 23% | - | - | |
| Hanson,Tommy | 89.6 | 49% | - | 16% | 32% | 3% | - | |
| Happ,J.A. | 91.1 | 66% | - | 8% | 11% | 16% | - | |
| Harang,Aaron | 89.8 | 59% | 3% | 11% | 19% | 9% | - | |
| Haren,Dan | 88.9 | 40% | 39% | 4% | - | - | 17% | |
| Harrell,Lucas | 91.9 | 72% | 9% | 9% | - | 10% | - | |
| Harris,Will | 91.8 | 71% | - | 29% | - | <1% | - | |
| Harrison,Josh | - | - | - | - | - | 100% | - | |
| Harrison,Matt | 91.2 | 63% | - | 5% | 9% | 23% | - | |
| Harvey,Matt | 95.8 | 57% | - | 13% | 18% | 11% | - | |
| Hatcher,Chris | 94.9 | 62% | <1% | - | 22% | 15% | - | |
| Hawkins,LaTroy | 92.6 | 72% | - | 5% | 19% | 4% | - | |
| Heath,Deunte | 92.1 | 67% | - | 15% | 15% | 2% | - | |
| Hefner,Jeremy | 90.8 | 55% | - | 11% | 22% | 12% | - | |
| Hellickson,Jeremy | 90.5 | 54% | <1% | 15% | - | 31% | - | |
| Hellweg,John | 93.9 | 79% | - | 13% | - | 8% | - | |
| Hembree,Heath | 92.1 | 70% | - | - | 27% | 3% | - | |
| Henderson,Jim | 95.3 | 77% | - | - | 23% | - | - | |
| Hendriks,Liam | 90.6 | 74% | - | 7% | 12% | 8% | - | |
| Henn,Sean | 89.9 | 56% | - | - | 37% | 7% | - | |
| Hernandez,David | 94.8 | 64% | - | 33% | - | 3% | - | |
| Hernandez,Felix | 91.9 | 53% | - | 13% | 10% | 23% | - | |
| Hernandez,Pedro | 88.7 | 57% | 13% | 10% | - | 19% | - | |
| Hernandez,Roberto | 91.5 | 55% | - | - | 15% | 30% | - | |
| Herrera,Kelvin | 98.2 | 68% | - | 7% | <1% | 25% | - | |
| Hill,Rich | 90.9 | 51% | 10% | 39% | - | <1% | - | |
| Hochevar,Luke | 95.5 | 50% | 35% | 14% | <1% | <1% | - | |
| Holland,Derek | 93.6 | 62% | - | 5% | 24% | 8% | - | |
| Holland,Greg | 96.1 | 58% | - | - | 40% | - | 3% | |

| | Fastball Velocity | Pitch Repertoire | | | | | | |
|---|---|---|---|---|---|---|---|---|
| Player | | Fastball | Cutter | Curve | Slider | Change | Splitter | Other |
| Holmberg,David | 88.1 | 59% | - | 6% | 8% | 28% | - | |
| Hoover,J.J. | 92.8 | 75% | - | 21% | 2% | 3% | - | |
| Horst,Jeremy | 89.0 | 64% | - | - | 21% | 15% | - | |
| Howell,J.P. | 87.4 | 59% | - | 34% | - | 7% | - | |
| Hudson,Tim | 89.7 | 56% | - | 10% | 21% | - | 12% | |
| Huff,David | 91.4 | 56% | 13% | 9% | - | 23% | - | |
| Hughes,Jared | 92.0 | 86% | - | - | 13% | 2% | - | |
| Hughes,Phil | 92.4 | 62% | - | 9% | 24% | 5% | <1% | |
| Humber,Philip | 90.1 | 57% | - | 17% | 16% | 9% | - | |
| Hunter,Tommy | 96.2 | 61% | 19% | 16% | - | 4% | - | |
| Hynes,Colt | 89.9 | 53% | - | - | 41% | 6% | - | |
| Irwin,Phil | 89.9 | 51% | - | 42% | - | 8% | - | |
| Iwakuma,Hisashi | 89.5 | 53% | - | 6% | 18% | - | 23% | |
| Jackson,Edwin | 93.1 | 60% | 7% | 3% | 28% | 2% | - | |
| Jansen,Kenley | 92.4 | 94% | - | - | 6% | - | - | |
| Janssen,Casey | 90.1 | 49% | 31% | 13% | 3% | 4% | - | |
| Jeffress,Jeremy | 96.7 | 77% | - | 16% | - | 6% | - | |
| Jenkins,Chad | 90.0 | 71% | - | - | 5% | 24% | - | |
| Jennings,Dan | 92.0 | 61% | - | - | 38% | <1% | - | |
| Jepsen,Kevin | 95.7 | 80% | 11% | 10% | - | - | - | |
| Jimenez,Cesar | 89.2 | 58% | - | - | 26% | 15% | - | |
| Jimenez,Ubaldo | 91.7 | 54% | - | 3% | 25% | 8% | 10% | |
| Johnson,Erik | 92.0 | 58% | - | 13% | 23% | 7% | - | |
| Johnson,Jim | 93.8 | 75% | - | 13% | - | 12% | - | |
| Johnson,Josh | 92.8 | 62% | - | 14% | 21% | 3% | - | |
| Johnson,Kris | 92.1 | 56% | 23% | 2% | - | 19% | - | |
| Johnson,Rob | 88.7 | 75% | 25% | - | - | - | - | |
| Johnson,Steve | 88.6 | 71% | - | 10% | 2% | 18% | - | |
| Jones,Nate | 97.7 | 53% | - | <1% | 42% | 4% | - | |
| Jordan,Taylor | 92.0 | 59% | - | - | 21% | 20% | - | |
| Joseph,Donnie | 91.1 | 49% | - | - | 51% | - | - | |
| Jurrjens,Jair | 88.6 | 54% | - | - | 7% | 39% | - | |
| Karns,Nate | 93.4 | 67% | - | 22% | - | 11% | - | |
| Kazmir,Scott | 92.5 | 64% | 6% | 3% | 13% | 14% | <1% | |
| Kelley,Shawn | 92.2 | 50% | - | - | 50% | <1% | - | |
| Kelly,Joe | 94.9 | 67% | - | 8% | 11% | 14% | - | |
| Kendrick,Kyle | 89.8 | 54% | 21% | 2% | - | 23% | - | |
| Kennedy,Ian | 90.3 | 60% | 7% | 12% | - | 21% | - | |
| Kensing,Logan | 94.4 | 42% | - | - | 50% | 8% | - | |
| Kershaw,Clayton | 92.6 | 61% | - | 13% | 24% | 2% | - | |
| Keuchel,Dallas | 89.5 | 53% | 8% | 7% | 19% | 13% | - | |
| Kickham,Mike | 89.9 | 58% | - | 6% | 28% | 9% | - | |
| Kimbrel,Craig | 96.9 | 71% | - | 29% | - | - | - | |
| Kintzler,Brandon | 92.2 | 77% | - | - | 15% | 8% | - | |
| Kirkman,Michael | 93.4 | 64% | - | 2% | 34% | - | <1% | |
| Kluber,Corey | 93.2 | 53% | 24% | 13% | - | 10% | - | |
| Koehler,Tom | 92.9 | 56% | - | 27% | 11% | 6% | - | |
| Kohn,Michael | 94.6 | 78% | - | - | 14% | 7% | - | |
| Kontos,George | 90.5 | 48% | 6% | - | 44% | 2% | - | |
| Krol,Ian | 93.5 | 73% | <1% | 17% | - | 10% | - | |
| Kuroda,Hiroki | 91.5 | 49% | - | 3% | 26% | - | 21% | |
| Lackey,John | 91.7 | 58% | - | 10% | 30% | 2% | - | |
| Laffey,Aaron | 85.6 | 47% | 35% | 7% | - | 11% | - | |
| LaFromboise,Bobby | 89.9 | 63% | - | - | 29% | 8% | - | |
| Langwell,Matt | 90.4 | 60% | 8% | 10% | 14% | 9% | - | |
| Lannan,John | 87.8 | 59% | - | 9% | 10% | 22% | - | |
| Latos,Mat | 92.6 | 61% | - | 10% | 24% | 4% | - | |

| | Fastball Velocity | Pitch Repertoire | | | | | | |
|---|---|---|---|---|---|---|---|---|
| Player | | Fastball | Cutter | Curve | Slider | Change | Splitter | Other |
| Layne,Tom | 88.7 | 45% | 35% | 20% | - | - | - | |
| League,Brandon | 94.5 | 65% | - | - | 9% | - | 26% | |
| Leake,Mike | 90.2 | 42% | 23% | 15% | 6% | 14% | - | |
| LeBlanc,Wade | 86.1 | 45% | 24% | 8% | - | 23% | - | |
| LeCure,Sam | 89.3 | 55% | - | 27% | 12% | 6% | - | |
| Lee,C.C. | 92.6 | 67% | - | - | 33% | - | - | |
| Lee,Cliff | 90.7 | 55% | 21% | 8% | <1% | 16% | - | |
| Leesman,Charlie | 90.4 | 60% | - | - | 34% | 5% | - | |
| Leroux,Chris | 92.1 | 50% | - | - | 50% | - | - | |
| Lester,Jon | 92.7 | 52% | 23% | 12% | - | 12% | - | |
| Lilly,Ted | 87.2 | 53% | - | 18% | 11% | 17% | - | |
| Lim,Chang-Yong | 89.9 | 85% | - | - | 12% | - | 3% | |
| Lincecum,Tim | 90.2 | 50% | - | 8% | 18% | 24% | - | |
| Lincoln,Brad | 93.3 | 60% | - | 31% | - | - | 9% | |
| Lindblom,Josh | 90.2 | 48% | - | 13% | 29% | 10% | - | |
| Lindstrom,Matt | 95.0 | 58% | - | - | 41% | - | 1% | |
| Liriano,Francisco | 93.0 | 41% | - | - | 36% | 22% | - | |
| Lo,Chia-Jen | 94.1 | 74% | - | 23% | - | - | 4% | |
| Locke,Jeff | 90.4 | 65% | - | 19% | - | 16% | - | |
| Loe,Kameron | 89.1 | 74% | 8% | 13% | - | 4% | <1% | |
| Logan,Boone | 93.6 | 59% | - | - | 41% | - | - | |
| Lohse,Kyle | 89.6 | 47% | - | 10% | 28% | 15% | - | |
| Lopez,Javier | 86.1 | 58% | 25% | - | 11% | 6% | - | |
| Lopez,Wilton | 91.5 | 72% | - | - | 8% | 20% | - | |
| Loup,Aaron | 91.5 | 73% | - | - | 11% | 16% | - | |
| Lowe,Derek | 87.9 | 80% | 8% | - | 12% | <1% | - | |
| Lowe,Mark | 92.9 | 68% | - | - | 30% | 2% | - | |
| Lueke,Josh | 94.9 | 56% | - | - | 23% | - | 21% | |
| Luetge,Lucas | 91.1 | 43% | - | 17% | 31% | 8% | - | |
| Lyles,Jordan | 92.2 | 59% | 2% | 18% | 11% | 9% | - | |
| Lynn,Lance | 92.4 | 73% | - | 10% | 13% | 4% | - | |
| Lyon,Brandon | 87.8 | 48% | 23% | 16% | - | 13% | - | |
| Lyons,Tyler | 89.8 | 61% | - | 5% | 22% | 12% | - | |
| Machi,Jean | 92.8 | 52% | - | - | 12% | - | 37% | |
| Magill,Matt | 90.8 | 57% | - | 6% | 31% | 6% | - | |
| Maholm,Paul | 87.1 | 48% | - | 11% | 24% | 17% | - | |
| Maine,John | 90.5 | 78% | - | - | 19% | 3% | - | |
| Maness,Seth | 90.5 | 71% | - | 4% | 4% | 20% | - | |
| Manship,Jeff | 89.0 | 57% | - | 10% | 23% | 10% | - | |
| Marcum,Shaun | 85.3 | 31% | 24% | 12% | 8% | 26% | - | |
| Marmol,Carlos | 93.7 | 46% | - | - | 54% | - | - | |
| Maronde,Nick | 90.7 | 69% | - | - | 25% | 6% | - | |
| Marquis,Jason | 87.3 | 57% | <1% | - | 27% | 4% | 12% | |
| Marshall,Brett | 88.9 | 62% | 3% | 5% | 15% | 14% | - | |
| Marshall,Sean | 88.9 | 31% | - | 40% | 29% | - | - | |
| Marte,Victor | 94.4 | 52% | - | - | 28% | - | 20% | |
| Martin,Ethan | 93.3 | 65% | - | 10% | 19% | 6% | - | |
| Martinez,Carlos | 96.7 | 78% | - | 16% | - | 6% | - | |
| Martinez,Cristhian | 90.0 | 54% | - | - | 16% | 30% | - | |
| Martinez,David | 91.1 | 67% | - | - | 17% | 8% | 8% | |
| Martinez,Joe | 90.2 | 42% | 12% | 32% | - | 14% | - | |
| Martis,Shairon | 88.4 | 60% | - | 1% | 19% | 20% | - | |
| Masterson,Justin | 91.6 | 73% | - | - | 27% | <1% | - | |
| Matsuzaka,Daisuke | 88.9 | 46% | 16% | 16% | 17% | 2% | 4% | |
| Mattheus,Ryan | 92.7 | 76% | - | - | 13% | - | 11% | |
| Matusz,Brian | 91.5 | 57% | - | 5% | 27% | 10% | - | |
| Maurer,Brandon | 92.8 | 49% | - | 12% | 30% | 8% | - | |

| | Fastball Velocity | Pitch Repertoire | | | | | | |
|---|---|---|---|---|---|---|---|---|
| Player | | Fastball | Cutter | Curve | Slider | Change | Splitter | Other |
| Maya,Yunesky | 91.0 | 64% | - | - | 14% | 21% | - | |
| Mazzaro,Vin | 93.1 | 60% | - | - | 38% | 2% | - | |
| McAllister,Zach | 91.3 | 73% | 4% | 13% | - | 6% | 4% | |
| McCarthy,Brandon | 90.8 | 46% | 35% | 15% | - | 4% | <1% | |
| McClellan,Kyle | 88.8 | 50% | 28% | 16% | - | 6% | - | |
| McDonald,James | 90.5 | 61% | - | 22% | 12% | 5% | - | |
| McDonald,John | 78.3 | 100% | - | - | - | - | - | |
| McFarland,T.J. | 88.4 | 68% | - | 21% | - | 12% | - | |
| McGee,Jake | 96.3 | 93% | 7% | - | - | - | - | |
| McGowan,Dustin | 94.7 | 69% | - | - | 23% | 8% | - | |
| McHugh,Collin | 90.4 | 52% | - | 15% | 23% | 9% | - | |
| Medina,Yoervis | 94.1 | 64% | - | - | 31% | 5% | - | |
| Medlen,Kris | 89.4 | 55% | 4% | 18% | <1% | 23% | - | |
| Mejia,Jenrry | 92.1 | 59% | - | 4% | 24% | 13% | - | |
| Melancon,Mark | 92.9 | 27% | 56% | 17% | - | <1% | - | |
| Mendoza,Luis | 91.5 | 68% | - | 27% | - | 5% | - | |
| Mijares,Jose | 90.2 | 72% | - | - | 22% | 6% | - | |
| Mikolas,Miles | 94.0 | 77% | - | 23% | - | - | - | |
| Miley,Wade | 91.0 | 69% | - | 2% | 16% | 13% | - | |
| Miller,Andrew | 94.9 | 57% | - | - | 43% | - | - | |
| Miller,Jim | 91.9 | 61% | - | 10% | 20% | 10% | - | |
| Miller,Shelby | 93.7 | 71% | 4% | 18% | - | 6% | - | |
| Milone,Tommy | 87.2 | 51% | 10% | 12% | - | 28% | - | |
| Miner,Zach | 92.3 | 53% | - | 5% | 19% | 24% | - | |
| Minor,Mike | 90.4 | 57% | - | 14% | 14% | 15% | - | |
| Moore,Matt | 92.4 | 62% | - | 20% | - | 18% | - | |
| Morales,Franklin | 92.7 | 62% | - | 13% | 11% | 15% | - | |
| Morris,Bryan | 94.1 | 41% | 52% | - | 8% | - | - | |
| Morrow,Brandon | 93.3 | 57% | 3% | 3% | 22% | 14% | - | |
| Mortensen,Clayton | 89.1 | 42% | - | - | 31% | 27% | - | |
| Morton,Charlie | 92.8 | 71% | <1% | 22% | - | 7% | - | |
| Moscoso,Guillermo | 91.3 | 53% | - | 9% | 24% | 13% | - | |
| Moylan,Peter | 90.1 | 60% | - | - | 36% | 4% | - | |
| Mujica,Edward | 91.9 | 40% | - | - | 4% | - | 56% | |
| Murphy,David | 76.6 | 80% | - | - | - | - | - | Knuckleball 20% |
| Myers,Brett | 88.0 | 54% | - | 17% | 12% | 17% | - | |
| Narveson,Chris | 86.2 | 49% | - | 3% | 3% | 46% | - | |
| Nathan,Joe | 92.2 | 55% | - | 10% | 35% | - | - | |
| Nelson,Jimmy | 93.7 | 78% | - | - | 20% | 2% | - | |
| Neshek,Pat | 88.9 | 16% | - | - | 73% | 11% | - | |
| Nicasio,Juan | 91.9 | 74% | - | - | 20% | 6% | - | |
| Niese,Jon | 90.2 | 49% | 25% | 17% | - | 9% | - | |
| Noesi,Hector | 93.7 | 63% | - | 5% | 17% | 14% | - | |
| Nolasco,Ricky | 90.3 | 44% | - | 17% | 27% | - | 12% | |
| Nolin,Sean | 89.2 | 54% | - | 9% | 11% | 26% | - | |
| Norris,Bud | 92.5 | 55% | 4% | 3% | 29% | 10% | - | |
| Nova,Ivan | 93.0 | 61% | - | 35% | 1% | 3% | - | |
| Nuno,Vidal | 88.0 | 48% | - | 14% | 32% | 6% | - | |
| O'Day,Darren | 85.9 | 47% | - | - | 53% | - | - | |
| O'Flaherty,Eric | 90.2 | 83% | - | - | 16% | 1% | - | |
| O'Sullivan,Sean | 90.0 | 53% | 7% | 9% | 17% | 14% | - | |
| Oberholtzer,Brett | 90.4 | 62% | - | 17% | - | 21% | - | |
| Odorizzi,Jake | 90.8 | 60% | - | 8% | 16% | 16% | - | |
| Ogando,Alexi | 93.4 | 54% | - | - | 31% | 15% | - | |
| Ohlendorf,Ross | 92.3 | 66% | - | - | 21% | 13% | - | |
| Okajima,Hideki | 86.3 | 49% | - | 23% | - | - | 28% | |
| Oliver,Darren | 87.7 | 47% | 25% | - | 25% | 3% | - | |

| | Fastball Velocity | Pitch Repertoire | | | | | | |
|---|---|---|---|---|---|---|---|---|
| Player | | Fastball | Cutter | Curve | Slider | Change | Splitter | Other |
| Olmos,Edgar | 95.5 | 82% | - | - | 13% | 6% | - | |
| Omogrosso,Brian | 93.0 | 59% | - | 13% | 20% | 9% | - | |
| Ondrusek,Logan | 93.9 | 49% | 23% | 22% | - | - | 6% | |
| Ortega,Jose | 95.7 | 70% | - | - | 25% | 6% | - | |
| Ortiz,Joe | 90.7 | 48% | - | - | 31% | 21% | - | |
| Ortiz,Ramon | 88.6 | 43% | - | - | 39% | 18% | - | |
| Oswalt,Roy | 90.9 | 59% | - | 18% | 6% | 16% | - | |
| Otero,Dan | 90.0 | 81% | - | 2% | 9% | 8% | - | |
| Ottavino,Adam | 91.4 | 48% | - | - | 48% | 4% | - | |
| Outman,Josh | 92.4 | 53% | - | - | 30% | 17% | - | |
| Papelbon,Jonathan | 92.0 | 70% | - | - | 11% | - | 18% | |
| Parker,Blake | 91.9 | 62% | - | - | 32% | - | 6% | |
| Parker,Jarrod | 91.5 | 64% | - | <1% | 14% | 21% | - | |
| Parnell,Bobby | 95.0 | 71% | - | 27% | - | 2% | - | |
| Parra,Manny | 93.4 | 47% | - | 40% | - | - | 13% | |
| Partch,Curtis | 95.1 | 70% | - | - | 20% | 10% | - | |
| Paterson,Joe | 83.3 | 58% | - | - | 42% | - | - | |
| Patton,Troy | 88.9 | 55% | - | 3% | 33% | 8% | - | |
| Paxton,James | 94.9 | 69% | 4% | 16% | - | 10% | - | |
| Peacock,Brad | 92.6 | 63% | - | 18% | 10% | 9% | - | |
| Peavy,Jake | 90.7 | 52% | 21% | 9% | 7% | 10% | - | |
| Pelfrey,Mike | 92.4 | 73% | - | 8% | 10% | - | 9% | |
| Peralta,Joel | 90.2 | 42% | - | 25% | - | - | 34% | |
| Peralta,Wily | 94.8 | 67% | - | - | 27% | 7% | - | |
| Perez,Chris | 92.7 | 68% | - | - | 32% | - | - | |
| Perez,Juan | 93.3 | 56% | - | - | 42% | 1% | - | |
| Perez,Luis | 92.0 | 66% | - | - | 31% | 4% | - | |
| Perez,Martin | 93.0 | 58% | - | 5% | 13% | 24% | - | |
| Perez,Oliver | 92.2 | 66% | - | - | 34% | - | - | |
| Perkins,Glen | 94.9 | 73% | - | - | 27% | - | - | |
| Pestano,Vinnie | 91.2 | 71% | - | - | 29% | - | - | |
| Petit,Yusmeiro | 88.1 | 52% | - | 20% | 20% | 7% | - | |
| Petricka,Jake | 93.4 | 63% | - | - | 32% | 5% | - | |
| Pettibone,Jonathan | 90.8 | 57% | 19% | - | 5% | 19% | - | |
| Pettitte,Andy | 89.0 | 50% | 30% | 13% | - | 7% | - | |
| Phelps,David | 89.9 | 55% | 19% | 19% | - | 7% | - | |
| Phillips,Zach | 90.3 | 76% | - | - | 17% | 7% | - | |
| Pimentel,Stolmy | 95.4 | 63% | 17% | - | - | 20% | - | |
| Pomeranz,Drew | 91.3 | 67% | - | 30% | - | 3% | - | |
| Porcello,Rick | 91.2 | 62% | - | 17% | 6% | 15% | - | |
| Pressly,Ryan | 93.3 | 61% | - | 19% | 14% | 6% | - | |
| Price,David | 93.5 | 54% | 18% | 11% | - | 17% | - | |
| Pryor,Stephen | 95.8 | 72% | 20% | 9% | - | - | - | |
| Purcey,David | 92.6 | 66% | - | 2% | 25% | 7% | - | |
| Putkonen,Luke | 94.1 | 64% | - | 23% | - | - | 14% | |
| Putnam,Zach | 90.5 | 61% | - | - | 4% | - | 34% | |
| Putz,J.J. | 91.7 | 66% | - | - | 13% | - | 20% | |
| Qualls,Chad | 94.0 | 63% | - | - | 37% | - | - | |
| Quintana,Jose | 91.4 | 56% | 14% | 20% | - | 11% | - | |
| Raburn,Ryan | 85.8 | 92% | - | - | - | 8% | - | |
| Raley,Brooks | 89.1 | 59% | 2% | 8% | 25% | 7% | - | |
| Ramirez,Erasmo | 92.2 | 58% | - | 8% | 18% | 16% | - | |
| Ramirez,J.C. | 94.2 | 65% | - | - | 33% | - | 1% | |
| Ramirez,Ramon | 91.3 | 39% | - | - | 38% | 22% | - | |
| Ramos,A.J. | 93.3 | 58% | - | 6% | 21% | 14% | - | |
| Ramos,Cesar | 91.1 | 62% | - | 11% | 11% | 17% | - | |
| Rapada,Clay | 84.9 | 74% | - | - | 23% | 3% | - | |

| | Fastball Velocity | Pitch Repertoire | | | | | | |
|---|---|---|---|---|---|---|---|---|
| Player | | Fastball | Cutter | Curve | Slider | Change | Splitter | Other |
| Rasmus,Cory | 93.0 | 51% | - | 15% | 17% | 18% | - | |
| Rauch,Jon | 90.4 | 60% | - | 11% | 21% | 7% | - | |
| Recker,Anthony | 84.9 | 100% | - | - | - | - | - | |
| Redmond,Todd | 90.6 | 64% | - | - | 30% | 6% | - | |
| Reed,Addison | 92.8 | 61% | - | - | 33% | 7% | - | |
| Reed,Evan | 95.5 | 64% | - | - | 26% | 10% | - | |
| Reid,Ryan | 91.9 | 70% | - | - | 28% | 2% | - | |
| Resop,Chris | 91.5 | 63% | 11% | 7% | - | 19% | - | |
| Reynolds,Greg | 88.8 | 58% | 24% | 12% | - | 7% | - | |
| Reynolds,Matt | 88.9 | 51% | - | - | 23% | 7% | 19% | |
| Rice,Scott | 89.3 | 57% | - | - | 26% | - | 17% | |
| Richard,Clayton | 90.2 | 64% | 10% | - | 13% | 13% | - | |
| Richards,Garrett | 94.8 | 68% | - | 5% | 26% | 1% | - | |
| Rienzo,Andre | 90.8 | 45% | 29% | 20% | - | 6% | - | |
| Rivera,Mariano | 91.9 | 11% | 89% | - | - | - | - | |
| Roark,Tanner | 92.6 | 63% | - | 10% | 20% | 8% | - | |
| Robertson,David | 91.7 | 73% | - | 27% | - | <1% | - | |
| Robertson,Tyler | 84.8 | 46% | - | - | 38% | 15% | - | |
| Robles,Mauricio | 90.7 | 67% | - | - | 15% | 18% | - | |
| Rodney,Fernando | 96.5 | 64% | - | - | - | 36% | - | |
| Rodriguez,Francisco | 91.4 | 54% | - | 21% | - | 25% | - | |
| Rodriguez,Henry | 97.1 | 73% | - | - | 19% | 8% | - | |
| Rodriguez,Paco | 89.6 | 19% | 35% | - | 39% | 8% | - | |
| Rodriguez,Wandy | 89.4 | 60% | - | 31% | - | 9% | - | |
| Roe,Chaz | 91.4 | 60% | - | - | 40% | - | - | |
| Roenicke,Josh | 91.4 | 61% | 25% | 11% | - | 2% | - | |
| Rogers,Esmil | 93.4 | 59% | 5% | 12% | 22% | 2% | - | |
| Romero,Enny | 93.9 | 79% | - | - | 10% | 11% | - | |
| Romero,Ricky | 89.4 | 59% | 16% | 4% | - | 20% | - | |
| Romo,Sergio | 87.7 | 39% | 5% | - | 49% | 6% | - | |
| Rondon,Bruce | 99.3 | 67% | - | - | 22% | 11% | - | |
| Rondon,Hector | 93.8 | 68% | 14% | - | 17% | <1% | - | |
| Rosario,Sandy | 92.8 | 55% | - | - | 38% | 7% | - | |
| Rosenberg,B.J. | 94.0 | 62% | - | 12% | 21% | 5% | - | |
| Rosenthal,Trevor | 97.3 | 79% | 1% | 5% | - | 15% | - | |
| Ross,Robbie | 92.5 | 79% | - | <1% | 19% | 2% | - | |
| Ross,Tyson | 94.2 | 61% | - | - | 33% | 6% | - | |
| Rosscup,Zac | 92.5 | 75% | - | - | 25% | - | - | |
| Roth,Michael | 88.4 | 60% | 10% | 2% | 14% | 15% | - | |
| Ruffin,Chance | 92.5 | 57% | - | 17% | 18% | 8% | - | |
| Rusin,Chris | 87.8 | 51% | 25% | 6% | 5% | 13% | - | |
| Russell,James | 89.1 | 36% | 11% | 4% | 38% | 12% | - | |
| Ryu,Hyun-Jin | 90.3 | 54% | - | 9% | 14% | 22% | - | |
| Rzepczynski,Marc | 91.9 | 64% | - | - | 30% | 6% | - | |
| Sabathia,CC | 91.1 | 57% | - | 6% | 22% | 15% | - | |
| Salas,Fernando | 90.4 | 59% | - | - | 19% | 22% | - | |
| Salazar,Danny | 96.2 | 68% | - | - | 11% | 21% | - | |
| Sale,Chris | 93.1 | 51% | - | - | 30% | 19% | - | |
| Samardzija,Jeff | 94.5 | 53% | 11% | - | 18% | - | 17% | |
| Sanabia,Alex | 89.6 | 54% | - | - | 20% | 25% | - | |
| Sanchez,Anibal | 93.0 | 47% | - | 7% | 21% | 24% | - | |
| Sanchez,Eduardo | 91.6 | 68% | - | 29% | - | 3% | - | |
| Sanchez,Jonathan | 89.9 | 66% | - | - | 19% | 15% | - | |
| Santana,Ervin | 92.4 | 54% | - | - | 39% | 7% | - | |
| Santiago,Hector | 91.8 | 59% | 6% | - | 9% | 22% | - | Screwball 4% |
| Santos,Sergio | 94.6 | 54% | - | - | 43% | 4% | - | |
| Saunders,Joe | 89.6 | 56% | - | 10% | 13% | 20% | - | |

| | Fastball Velocity | Pitch Repertoire | | | | | | |
|---|---|---|---|---|---|---|---|---|
| Player | | Fastball | Cutter | Curve | Slider | Change | Splitter | Other |
| Savery,Joe | 90.5 | 66% | - | - | 24% | 9% | - | |
| Scahill,Rob | 94.5 | 71% | - | - | 23% | 6% | - | |
| Scheppers,Tanner | 96.3 | 81% | - | <1% | 17% | <1% | - | |
| Scherzer,Max | 93.3 | 56% | - | 8% | 15% | 21% | - | |
| Schumaker,Skip | 88.3 | 69% | - | 12% | - | 18% | - | |
| Scribner,Evan | 88.6 | 64% | - | 29% | 5% | 3% | - | |
| Shaw,Bryan | 90.9 | 3% | 74% | <1% | 21% | 2% | - | |
| Shields,James | 92.2 | 41% | 22% | 12% | - | 25% | - | |
| Shoemaker,Matt | 90.9 | 51% | - | 3% | 17% | 3% | 26% | |
| Siegrist,Kevin | 95.2 | 85% | - | - | 9% | 6% | - | |
| Simon,Alfredo | 94.5 | 53% | 21% | 17% | - | - | 8% | |
| Sipp,Tony | 90.3 | 62% | - | - | 35% | 4% | - | |
| Skaggs,Tyler | 89.2 | 61% | - | 20% | - | 20% | - | |
| Slowey,Kevin | 89.3 | 65% | - | 10% | 16% | 9% | - | |
| Smith,Burch | 91.8 | 67% | - | 15% | - | 19% | - | |
| Smith,Joe | 89.6 | 68% | - | - | 32% | - | - | |
| Smith,Will | 91.0 | 58% | - | 11% | 30% | <1% | - | |
| Smyly,Drew | 90.9 | 56% | 29% | 14% | - | <1% | - | |
| Soria,Joakim | 90.8 | 68% | - | 11% | 19% | 3% | - | |
| Soriano,Rafael | 91.5 | 30% | 54% | - | 16% | - | - | |
| Spruill,Zeke | 91.2 | 68% | - | 8% | 22% | 2% | - | |
| Stammen,Craig | 91.7 | 57% | - | 13% | 30% | <1% | - | |
| Stange,Daniel | 94.2 | 64% | - | - | 30% | 6% | - | |
| Stauffer,Tim | 91.7 | 52% | 26% | 6% | - | 17% | - | |
| Stinson,Josh | 92.5 | 54% | - | 11% | 20% | 14% | - | |
| Storen,Drew | 93.9 | 59% | - | - | 32% | 10% | - | |
| Storey,Mickey | 89.2 | 34% | - | 19% | 45% | 1% | - | |
| Straily,Dan | 90.3 | 59% | - | 2% | 28% | 11% | - | |
| Strasburg,Stephen | 95.3 | 61% | - | 23% | - | 16% | - | |
| Street,Huston | 89.4 | 48% | - | - | 35% | 18% | - | |
| Strop,Pedro | 95.8 | 62% | - | - | 34% | - | 5% | |
| Stults,Eric | 86.7 | 49% | - | 11% | 16% | 23% | - | |
| Stutes,Michael | 91.2 | 53% | - | - | 47% | <1% | - | |
| Surkamp,Eric | 86.8 | 57% | 11% | 18% | - | 14% | - | |
| Swarzak,Anthony | 92.0 | 66% | - | 3% | 28% | 3% | - | |
| Takahashi,Hisanori | 88.1 | 36% | 4% | 4% | 16% | 41% | - | |
| Tazawa,Junichi | 93.5 | 61% | - | 8% | 4% | - | 28% | |
| Teaford,Everett | 92.3 | 46% | 23% | 31% | - | - | - | |
| Teheran,Julio | 91.5 | 64% | - | 11% | 20% | 5% | - | |
| Tepesch,Nick | 91.1 | 50% | 27% | 18% | - | 5% | - | |
| Thatcher,Joe | 85.9 | 70% | - | - | 30% | - | - | |
| Thayer,Dale | 92.9 | 76% | - | - | 23% | <1% | - | |
| Thielbar,Caleb | 89.8 | 69% | - | 8% | 18% | 4% | - | |
| Thornburg,Tyler | 92.0 | 60% | - | 26% | - | 14% | - | |
| Thornton,Matt | 94.2 | 76% | 5% | - | 18% | <1% | - | |
| Tillman,Chris | 91.6 | 62% | 6% | 17% | - | 15% | - | |
| Tolleson,Shawn | 92.1 | 64% | 27% | - | 9% | - | - | |
| Tomlin,Josh | 89.9 | 44% | 33% | 11% | - | 11% | - | |
| Tonkin,Michael | 94.4 | 82% | - | - | 14% | 3% | - | |
| Torres,Alex | 92.5 | 60% | - | - | 5% | 35% | - | |
| Torres,Carlos | 90.7 | 39% | 45% | 13% | - | 3% | - | |
| Troncoso,Ramon | 92.9 | 66% | - | 11% | 23% | - | - | |
| Turner,Jacob | 91.9 | 68% | - | 15% | 12% | 5% | - | |
| Uehara,Koji | 89.2 | 46% | 5% | <1% | - | - | 48% | |
| Valdes,Raul | 86.5 | 62% | - | - | 28% | 10% | - | |
| Valverde,Jose | 92.8 | 85% | - | - | - | - | 15% | |
| Vargas,Jason | 87.7 | 56% | 1% | 15% | - | 28% | - | |

| | Fastball Velocity | Pitch Repertoire | | | | | | |
|---|---|---|---|---|---|---|---|---|
| Player | | Fastball | Cutter | Curve | Slider | Change | Splitter | Other |
| Varvaro,Anthony | 92.9 | 69% | - | 21% | - | 10% | - | |
| Veal,Donnie | 92.5 | 56% | - | 40% | - | 4% | - | |
| Ventura,Yordano | 97.5 | 65% | 10% | 18% | - | 7% | - | |
| Veras,Jose | 93.4 | 54% | - | 32% | - | - | 14% | |
| Verlander,Justin | 93.3 | 56% | - | 14% | 13% | 17% | - | |
| Villanueva,Carlos | 87.7 | 44% | - | 13% | 19% | 24% | - | |
| Villarreal,Brayan | 95.5 | 84% | - | - | 16% | - | - | |
| Villarreal,Pedro | 91.6 | 56% | 22% | - | 21% | <1% | - | |
| Vincent,Nick | 90.0 | 33% | 62% | - | - | 5% | - | |
| Vogelsong,Ryan | 89.0 | 47% | 22% | 19% | - | 12% | - | |
| Volquez,Edinson | 92.5 | 55% | - | 25% | - | 21% | - | |
| Volstad,Chris | 91.5 | 67% | - | 22% | - | 11% | - | |
| Wacha,Michael | 93.5 | 65% | 3% | 5% | - | 27% | - | |
| Wagner,Neil | 95.8 | 70% | - | - | 22% | 8% | - | |
| Wainwright,Adam | 91.1 | 40% | 28% | 27% | - | 4% | - | |
| Walden,Jordan | 95.5 | 67% | - | - | 22% | 11% | - | |
| Walker,Taijuan | 94.7 | 60% | 26% | 10% | - | 5% | - | |
| Wall,Josh | 91.9 | 55% | - | - | 45% | - | - | |
| Walters,P.J. | 89.4 | 50% | 9% | 32% | - | 9% | - | |
| Wang,Chien-Ming | 89.9 | 75% | - | 8% | <1% | 9% | 8% | |
| Warren,Adam | 92.7 | 50% | - | 11% | 20% | 19% | - | |
| Watson,Tony | 93.6 | 64% | - | - | 18% | 18% | - | |
| Weaver,Jered | 86.5 | 57% | - | 16% | 12% | 15% | - | |
| Webb,Daniel | 95.9 | 64% | - | - | 30% | 6% | - | |
| Webb,Ryan | 92.3 | 61% | - | - | 35% | 4% | - | |
| Weber,Thad | 90.1 | 52% | - | 43% | - | 5% | - | |
| Webster,Allen | 94.0 | 62% | - | 3% | 9% | 26% | - | |
| Welker,Duke | 97.0 | 55% | - | - | 45% | - | - | |
| Wells,Casper | 90.3 | 83% | - | - | - | 17% | - | |
| Westbrook,Jake | 89.5 | 66% | 12% | - | 5% | 2% | 15% | |
| Wheeler,Zack | 94.4 | 71% | - | 10% | 16% | 3% | - | |
| Wilhelmsen,Tom | 96.2 | 63% | 2% | 23% | - | 12% | - | |
| Williams,Jerome | 92.4 | 55% | 21% | 13% | - | 12% | - | |
| Wilson,Alex | 92.4 | 70% | - | - | 26% | 4% | - | |
| Wilson,Brian | 93.2 | 25% | 75% | - | <1% | - | - | |
| Wilson,C.J. | 91.2 | 50% | 11% | 15% | 18% | 6% | - | |
| Wilson,Justin | 95.3 | 73% | 14% | 12% | - | <1% | - | |
| Withrow,Chris | 96.1 | 61% | - | 10% | 27% | 2% | - | |
| Wolf,Ross | 90.7 | 66% | - | - | 8% | 26% | - | |
| Wood,Alex | 91.7 | 64% | - | 14% | - | 22% | - | |
| Wood,Blake | 97.2 | 93% | - | - | 5% | 2% | - | |
| Wood,Travis | 88.9 | 46% | 34% | 2% | 10% | 8% | - | |
| Wooten,Rob | 88.7 | 26% | 53% | - | 5% | - | 15% | |
| Workman,Brandon | 92.3 | 62% | 13% | 18% | - | 7% | - | |
| Worley,Vance | 89.5 | 71% | 19% | 5% | - | 3% | 2% | |
| Wright,Jamey | 89.5 | 23% | 41% | 24% | 3% | 9% | - | |
| Wright,Steven | 85.2 | 14% | - | <1% | - | - | - | Knuckleball 86% |
| Wright,Wesley | 90.2 | 59% | - | 9% | 22% | 10% | - | |
| Zagurski,Mike | 92.5 | 66% | - | - | 33% | <1% | - | |
| Zeid,Josh | 94.6 | 61% | - | - | 23% | 16% | - | |
| Ziegler,Brad | 86.1 | 69% | - | - | 13% | 19% | - | |
| Zimmermann,Jordan | 93.9 | 64% | - | 12% | 20% | 5% | - | |
| Zito,Barry | 83.2 | 39% | - | 18% | 33% | 10% | - | |

# Pinch Hitting

This section contains a record of the performance of all active major league baseball players in their pinch hit plate appearances. The seasonal lines of players were included only if they accumulated at least 10 plate appearances or at least 10 total bases as a pinch hitter in the most recent season. Career lines were included for players who have at least 100 career pinch hit plate appearances.

Who was called on the most to hit in a pinch in 2013? Mark Kotsay with 72 pinch hit plate appearances. Unfortunately, Kotsay was not very successful in that role for the Padres, as he only managed a .185 batting average. However, Kotsay's teammate, Jesus Guzman, was able to provide the Padres with more production. Guzman had the fifth most pinch hit plate appearances in baseball with 53, and batted .250 with three doubles and three home runs.

The scariest pinch hitter for an opposing pitcher to see coming to the plate may have been Evan Gattis. Gattis only logged 13 plate appearances as a pinch hitter, but he managed six hits, four of which were home runs and another of which was a double. Unsurprisingly he was also intentionally walked twice. The only other player to be intentionally walked more than once was Greg Dobbs, who was intentionally walked four times, though that was in 57 plate appearances.

# Pinch Hitting

Pinch Hitters with 10+ PAs or 10+ Total Bases in 2013

| | | Pinch Hitting | | | | | | | | | | | | | |
|---|---|---|---|---|---|---|---|---|---|---|---|---|---|---|---|
| Batter | B | AB | H | 2B | 3B | HR | RBI | TBB | IBB | SO | GDP | Avg | OBP | Slg | OPS |
| Tony Abreu | B | 22 | 5 | 1 | 1 | 0 | 2 | 0 | 0 | 6 | 3 | .227 | .261 | .364 | .625 |
| Matt Adams | L | 35 | 11 | 1 | 0 | 3 | 9 | 3 | 0 | 13 | 1 | .314 | .368 | .600 | .968 |
| Alexi Amarista | L | 26 | 5 | 2 | 0 | 0 | 0 | 2 | 0 | 6 | 0 | .192 | .250 | .269 | .519 |
| J.P. Arencibia | R | 13 | 1 | 0 | 0 | 0 | 0 | 2 | 0 | 3 | 0 | .077 | .250 | .077 | .327 |
| Joaquin Arias | R | 21 | 5 | 1 | 0 | 0 | 4 | 0 | 0 | 1 | 1 | .238 | .261 | .286 | .547 |
| Mike Aviles | R | 13 | 4 | 0 | 0 | 0 | 1 | 0 | 0 | 1 | 1 | .308 | .308 | .308 | .615 |
| Jeff Baker | R | 21 | 6 | 2 | 0 | 0 | 1 | 3 | 1 | 10 | 0 | .286 | .375 | .381 | .756 |
| Mike Baxter | L | 28 | 8 | 2 | 0 | 0 | 2 | 3 | 0 | 6 | 0 | .286 | .412 | .357 | .769 |
| Jason Bay | R | 10 | 3 | 0 | 0 | 0 | 0 | 0 | 0 | 3 | 0 | .300 | .300 | .300 | .600 |
| Brandon Belt | L | 11 | 3 | 1 | 0 | 1 | 6 | 1 | 0 | 6 | 0 | .273 | .333 | .636 | .970 |
| Roger Bernadina | L | 28 | 5 | 2 | 0 | 0 | 1 | 2 | 0 | 11 | 0 | .179 | .233 | .250 | .483 |
| Yuniesky Betancourt | R | 27 | 7 | 2 | 0 | 0 | 1 | 2 | 0 | 5 | 1 | .259 | .310 | .333 | .644 |
| Jeff Bianchi | R | 21 | 4 | 0 | 0 | 0 | 2 | 0 | 0 | 9 | 0 | .190 | .227 | .190 | .418 |
| Charlie Blackmon | L | 13 | 4 | 1 | 0 | 1 | 2 | 1 | 0 | 2 | 0 | .308 | .400 | .615 | 1.015 |
| Gregor Blanco | L | 19 | 8 | 2 | 1 | 0 | 5 | 1 | 0 | 3 | 0 | .421 | .450 | .632 | 1.082 |
| Willie Bloomquist | R | 15 | 3 | 0 | 1 | 0 | 4 | 1 | 0 | 0 | 1 | .200 | .278 | .333 | .611 |
| Brian Bogusevic | L | 10 | 2 | 0 | 0 | 1 | 1 | 0 | 0 | 4 | 1 | .200 | .200 | .500 | .700 |
| Julio Borbon | L | 38 | 8 | 1 | 0 | 0 | 1 | 5 | 0 | 9 | 0 | .211 | .302 | .237 | .539 |
| Reid Brignac | L | 16 | 4 | 1 | 0 | 1 | 4 | 0 | 0 | 6 | 1 | .250 | .250 | .500 | .750 |
| Andrew Brown | R | 24 | 6 | 1 | 0 | 2 | 5 | 2 | 0 | 10 | 0 | .250 | .308 | .542 | .849 |
| Jordan Brown | L | 11 | 2 | 1 | 0 | 0 | 3 | 1 | 0 | 1 | 0 | .182 | .231 | .273 | .503 |
| Marlon Byrd | R | 11 | 4 | 1 | 0 | 0 | 0 | 0 | 0 | 5 | 0 | .364 | .364 | .455 | .818 |
| Tony Campana | L | 15 | 4 | 0 | 0 | 0 | 0 | 0 | 0 | 5 | 0 | .267 | .267 | .267 | .533 |
| Mike Carp | L | 19 | 5 | 1 | 0 | 2 | 9 | 5 | 0 | 10 | 0 | .263 | .417 | .632 | 1.048 |
| Adron Chambers | L | 11 | 1 | 0 | 0 | 0 | 0 | 2 | 1 | 4 | 0 | .091 | .231 | .091 | .322 |
| Endy Chavez | L | 14 | 5 | 1 | 0 | 1 | 1 | 0 | 0 | 2 | 2 | .357 | .357 | .643 | 1.000 |
| Eric Chavez | L | 16 | 5 | 1 | 0 | 1 | 6 | 2 | 1 | 0 | 0 | .313 | .350 | .563 | .913 |
| Chris Coghlan | L | 21 | 7 | 1 | 0 | 0 | 0 | 1 | 0 | 8 | 2 | .333 | .364 | .381 | .745 |
| Hank Conger | B | 19 | 4 | 0 | 0 | 1 | 3 | 1 | 0 | 6 | 0 | .211 | .286 | .368 | .654 |
| Carl Crawford | L | 10 | 2 | 0 | 0 | 0 | 1 | 2 | 0 | 2 | 1 | .200 | .308 | .200 | .508 |
| Tony Cruz | R | 15 | 5 | 0 | 1 | 0 | 1 | 1 | 0 | 4 | 0 | .333 | .375 | .467 | .842 |
| Charlie Culberson | R | 20 | 6 | 0 | 0 | 1 | 4 | 0 | 0 | 2 | 1 | .300 | .300 | .450 | .750 |
| Matt Davidson | R | 9 | 1 | 1 | 0 | 0 | 1 | 3 | 0 | 2 | 0 | .111 | .333 | .222 | .556 |
| Ike Davis | L | 8 | 1 | 0 | 0 | 0 | 0 | 2 | 0 | 5 | 1 | .125 | .300 | .125 | .425 |
| Khris Davis | R | 18 | 6 | 2 | 0 | 1 | 2 | 1 | 0 | 7 | 0 | .333 | .429 | .611 | 1.040 |
| David DeJesus | L | 24 | 2 | 1 | 0 | 0 | 2 | 1 | 0 | 5 | 0 | .083 | .120 | .125 | .245 |
| Chris Denorfia | R | 20 | 3 | 1 | 0 | 1 | 4 | 4 | 0 | 2 | 0 | .150 | .292 | .350 | .642 |
| Mark DeRosa | R | 21 | 6 | 1 | 0 | 1 | 8 | 7 | 1 | 7 | 1 | .286 | .448 | .476 | .924 |
| Daniel Descalso | L | 25 | 5 | 1 | 0 | 0 | 3 | 1 | 0 | 5 | 0 | .200 | .231 | .240 | .471 |
| Chris Dickerson | L | 9 | 2 | 1 | 0 | 0 | 0 | 2 | 0 | 3 | 0 | .222 | .364 | .333 | .697 |
| Corey Dickerson | L | 21 | 5 | 1 | 1 | 0 | 1 | 0 | 0 | 7 | 0 | .238 | .238 | .381 | .619 |
| Andy Dirks | L | 16 | 3 | 0 | 0 | 1 | 4 | 3 | 0 | 4 | 0 | .188 | .316 | .375 | .691 |
| Greg Dobbs | L | 48 | 10 | 2 | 0 | 0 | 7 | 6 | 4 | 10 | 0 | .208 | .298 | .250 | .548 |
| Ryan Doumit | B | 12 | 1 | 1 | 0 | 0 | 1 | 4 | 1 | 2 | 0 | .083 | .313 | .167 | .479 |
| Mark Ellis | R | 13 | 4 | 0 | 0 | 0 | 1 | 0 | 0 | 2 | 1 | .308 | .357 | .308 | .665 |
| Tim Federowicz | R | 10 | 2 | 0 | 0 | 0 | 0 | 0 | 0 | 2 | 0 | .200 | .200 | .200 | .400 |
| Ryan Flaherty | L | 10 | 2 | 0 | 0 | 0 | 0 | 0 | 0 | 4 | 1 | .200 | .200 | .200 | .400 |
| Logan Forsythe | R | 11 | 3 | 0 | 0 | 1 | 3 | 1 | 0 | 1 | 0 | .273 | .333 | .545 | .879 |
| Juan Francisco | L | 22 | 4 | 1 | 0 | 0 | 0 | 1 | 0 | 9 | 0 | .182 | .217 | .227 | .445 |
| Jeff Francoeur | R | 11 | 2 | 1 | 0 | 0 | 1 | 0 | 0 | 5 | 0 | .182 | .182 | .273 | .455 |
| Kevin Frandsen | R | 56 | 14 | 3 | 1 | 1 | 10 | 2 | 0 | 8 | 1 | .250 | .311 | .393 | .704 |
| Nate Freiman | R | 21 | 4 | 1 | 0 | 0 | 3 | 0 | 0 | 5 | 1 | .190 | .227 | .238 | .465 |
| Sam Fuld | L | 12 | 3 | 0 | 1 | 0 | 3 | 0 | 0 | 1 | 0 | .250 | .250 | .417 | .667 |
| Freddy Galvis | B | 13 | 1 | 1 | 0 | 0 | 0 | 0 | 0 | 3 | 0 | .077 | .077 | .154 | .231 |
| Avisail Garcia | R | 9 | 2 | 0 | 1 | 0 | 4 | 0 | 0 | 3 | 0 | .222 | .200 | .444 | .644 |
| Evan Gattis | R | 10 | 6 | 1 | 0 | 4 | 11 | 3 | 2 | 1 | 0 | .600 | .692 | 1.900 | 2.592 |
| Scooter Gennett | L | 10 | 1 | 0 | 0 | 1 | 4 | 1 | 0 | 1 | 0 | .100 | .182 | .400 | .582 |
| Craig Gentry | R | 22 | 6 | 1 | 1 | 0 | 2 | 6 | 0 | 3 | 0 | .273 | .429 | .409 | .838 |
| Jason Giambi | L | 14 | 3 | 0 | 0 | 3 | 4 | 2 | 0 | 2 | 1 | .214 | .353 | .857 | 1.210 |
| Conor Gillaspie | L | 12 | 1 | 0 | 0 | 1 | 1 | 1 | 0 | 4 | 0 | .083 | .154 | .333 | .487 |
| Cole Gillespie | R | 10 | 3 | 0 | 0 | 0 | 1 | 1 | 0 | 5 | 0 | .300 | .364 | .300 | .664 |
| Caleb Gindl | L | 17 | 2 | 0 | 0 | 1 | 2 | 4 | 0 | 9 | 0 | .118 | .273 | .294 | .567 |
| Jonny Gomes | R | 21 | 6 | 1 | 0 | 4 | 7 | 7 | 1 | 6 | 0 | .286 | .500 | .905 | 1.405 |
| Jesus Guzman | R | 48 | 12 | 3 | 0 | 3 | 14 | 4 | 0 | 13 | 1 | .250 | .321 | .500 | .821 |
| Travis Hafner | L | 12 | 2 | 1 | 0 | 1 | 1 | 3 | 1 | 3 | 0 | .167 | .333 | .500 | .833 |
| Jerry Hairston | R | 39 | 7 | 2 | 0 | 0 | 4 | 0 | 0 | 9 | 1 | .179 | .179 | .231 | .410 |
| Scott Hairston | R | 42 | 10 | 2 | 0 | 3 | 8 | 2 | 0 | 17 | 0 | .238 | .267 | .500 | .767 |
| Sean Halton | R | 14 | 3 | 1 | 0 | 0 | 1 | 2 | 0 | 6 | 0 | .214 | .313 | .286 | .598 |

# Pinch Hitting

Pinch Hitters with 10+ PAs or 10+ Total Bases in 2013

| | | Pinch Hitting | | | | | | | | | | | | | |
|---|---|---|---|---|---|---|---|---|---|---|---|---|---|---|---|
| Batter | B | AB | H | 2B | 3B | HR | RBI | TBB | IBB | SO | GDP | Avg | OBP | Slg | OPS |
| Jack Hannahan | L | 36 | 9 | 0 | 1 | 1 | 7 | 7 | 0 | 11 | 0 | .250 | .386 | .389 | .775 |
| Josh Harrison | R | 29 | 6 | 1 | 1 | 2 | 6 | 0 | 0 | 3 | 1 | .207 | .233 | .517 | .751 |
| Chris Heisey | R | 18 | 2 | 1 | 0 | 0 | 2 | 1 | 0 | 6 | 0 | .111 | .190 | .167 | .357 |
| Todd Helton | L | 13 | 4 | 1 | 0 | 2 | 5 | 1 | 0 | 3 | 0 | .308 | .357 | .846 | 1.203 |
| Jonathan Herrera | B | 15 | 7 | 1 | 0 | 0 | 0 | 2 | 0 | 1 | 1 | .467 | .529 | .533 | 1.063 |
| Chris Herrmann | L | 10 | 1 | 0 | 0 | 0 | 2 | 2 | 0 | 5 | 0 | .100 | .250 | .100 | .350 |
| Eric Hinske | L | 40 | 9 | 3 | 0 | 1 | 5 | 5 | 0 | 11 | 2 | .225 | .311 | .375 | .686 |
| Brandon Inge | R | 21 | 3 | 0 | 0 | 0 | 1 | 0 | 0 | 8 | 1 | .143 | .143 | .143 | .286 |
| Cesar Izturis | B | 22 | 6 | 2 | 0 | 0 | 2 | 0 | 0 | 4 | 0 | .273 | .261 | .364 | .625 |
| John Jaso | L | 11 | 2 | 0 | 0 | 1 | 3 | 3 | 0 | 3 | 0 | .182 | .357 | .455 | .812 |
| Kelly Johnson | L | 16 | 2 | 1 | 0 | 0 | 1 | 1 | 0 | 5 | 1 | .125 | .176 | .188 | .364 |
| Reed Johnson | R | 37 | 11 | 1 | 0 | 1 | 6 | 2 | 0 | 7 | 3 | .297 | .395 | .405 | .801 |
| Garrett Jones | L | 29 | 4 | 2 | 0 | 0 | 4 | 1 | 0 | 5 | 0 | .138 | .194 | .207 | .400 |
| Matt Joyce | L | 27 | 5 | 2 | 0 | 0 | 0 | 3 | 0 | 6 | 1 | .185 | .267 | .259 | .526 |
| Munenori Kawasaki | L | 11 | 1 | 0 | 0 | 0 | 0 | 1 | 0 | 5 | 0 | .091 | .167 | .091 | .258 |
| Austin Kearns | R | 11 | 3 | 0 | 0 | 0 | 0 | 4 | 0 | 3 | 0 | .273 | .467 | .273 | .739 |
| Don Kelly | L | 15 | 0 | 0 | 0 | 0 | 0 | 1 | 0 | 1 | 0 | .000 | .063 | .000 | .063 |
| Jeff Keppinger | R | 7 | 2 | 1 | 0 | 0 | 2 | 2 | 0 | 1 | 0 | .286 | .444 | .429 | .873 |
| Roger Kieschnick | L | 12 | 2 | 0 | 0 | 0 | 1 | 1 | 0 | 7 | 0 | .167 | .231 | .167 | .397 |
| Mark Kotsay | L | 65 | 12 | 1 | 0 | 1 | 4 | 7 | 0 | 11 | 0 | .185 | .264 | .246 | .510 |
| George Kottaras | L | 8 | 2 | 0 | 0 | 0 | 1 | 4 | 0 | 3 | 0 | .250 | .500 | .250 | .750 |
| Erik Kratz | R | 8 | 2 | 1 | 0 | 0 | 1 | 2 | 0 | 2 | 0 | .250 | .400 | .375 | .775 |
| Marc Krauss | L | 15 | 4 | 1 | 0 | 0 | 0 | 1 | 0 | 6 | 0 | .267 | .313 | .333 | .646 |
| Jason Kubel | L | 28 | 6 | 1 | 0 | 0 | 5 | 1 | 0 | 13 | 1 | .214 | .241 | .250 | .491 |
| Juan Lagares | R | 10 | 2 | 1 | 0 | 0 | 0 | 0 | 0 | 4 | 0 | .200 | .200 | .300 | .500 |
| Gerald Laird | R | 8 | 3 | 1 | 0 | 0 | 2 | 2 | 0 | 1 | 0 | .375 | .500 | .500 | 1.000 |
| Blake Lalli | L | 10 | 3 | 0 | 0 | 0 | 2 | 0 | 0 | 2 | 0 | .300 | .300 | .300 | .600 |
| Andrew Lambo | L | 10 | 2 | 1 | 0 | 1 | 1 | 0 | 0 | 6 | 0 | .200 | .200 | .600 | .800 |
| Adam Lind | L | 19 | 7 | 2 | 0 | 2 | 5 | 3 | 0 | 4 | 3 | .368 | .455 | .789 | 1.244 |
| Steve Lombardozzi | B | 44 | 13 | 2 | 1 | 1 | 1 | 2 | 0 | 6 | 0 | .295 | .326 | .455 | .781 |
| David Lough | L | 8 | 1 | 0 | 0 | 0 | 1 | 2 | 0 | 2 | 0 | .125 | .300 | .125 | .425 |
| Jonathan Lucroy | R | 11 | 2 | 0 | 0 | 0 | 2 | 1 | 1 | 3 | 0 | .182 | .250 | .182 | .432 |
| Donald Lutz | L | 23 | 5 | 0 | 0 | 0 | 3 | 1 | 0 | 8 | 0 | .217 | .250 | .217 | .467 |
| Zach Lutz | R | 7 | 4 | 2 | 0 | 0 | 2 | 3 | 0 | 1 | 0 | .571 | .700 | .857 | 1.557 |
| Martin Maldonado | R | 12 | 1 | 0 | 0 | 0 | 1 | 0 | 0 | 2 | 0 | .083 | .083 | .083 | .167 |
| Alfredo Marte | R | 9 | 1 | 1 | 0 | 0 | 1 | 2 | 0 | 1 | 0 | .111 | .273 | .222 | .495 |
| Leonys Martin | L | 18 | 5 | 0 | 1 | 0 | 2 | 0 | 0 | 3 | 0 | .278 | .278 | .389 | .667 |
| John Mayberry | R | 12 | 3 | 0 | 0 | 0 | 0 | 1 | 0 | 2 | 0 | .250 | .308 | .250 | .558 |
| Darnell McDonald | R | 12 | 4 | 0 | 0 | 0 | 0 | 1 | 0 | 2 | 2 | .333 | .385 | .333 | .718 |
| Michael McKenry | R | 10 | 0 | 0 | 0 | 0 | 0 | 0 | 0 | 1 | 0 | .000 | .000 | .000 | .000 |
| Nate McLouth | L | 9 | 2 | 2 | 0 | 0 | 1 | 1 | 1 | 1 | 0 | .222 | .300 | .444 | .744 |
| Devin Mesoraco | R | 9 | 4 | 0 | 0 | 1 | 4 | 0 | 0 | 2 | 0 | .444 | .400 | .778 | 1.178 |
| Tyler Moore | R | 18 | 1 | 0 | 0 | 0 | 0 | 0 | 0 | 12 | 0 | .056 | .056 | .056 | .111 |
| Brandon Moss | L | 16 | 1 | 1 | 0 | 0 | 0 | 3 | 0 | 6 | 0 | .063 | .211 | .125 | .336 |
| David Murphy | L | 12 | 4 | 2 | 0 | 0 | 1 | 2 | 1 | 3 | 0 | .333 | .429 | .500 | .929 |
| Dioner Navarro | B | 28 | 8 | 2 | 0 | 2 | 5 | 3 | 0 | 9 | 0 | .286 | .344 | .571 | .915 |
| Kirk Nieuwenhuis | L | 15 | 5 | 1 | 0 | 0 | 1 | 1 | 0 | 8 | 0 | .333 | .375 | .400 | .775 |
| Wil Nieves | R | 22 | 6 | 1 | 0 | 0 | 4 | 1 | 0 | 5 | 0 | .273 | .292 | .318 | .610 |
| Laynce Nix | L | 50 | 10 | 3 | 0 | 2 | 5 | 1 | 0 | 22 | 1 | .200 | .216 | .380 | .596 |
| Nick Noonan | L | 31 | 4 | 0 | 0 | 0 | 3 | 1 | 0 | 9 | 0 | .129 | .156 | .129 | .285 |
| Derek Norris | R | 15 | 3 | 0 | 0 | 3 | 5 | 3 | 0 | 0 | 0 | .200 | .333 | .800 | 1.133 |
| Miguel Olivo | R | 8 | 2 | 0 | 0 | 1 | 4 | 3 | 0 | 3 | 1 | .250 | .455 | .625 | 1.080 |
| Pete Orr | L | 11 | 3 | 0 | 0 | 0 | 0 | 0 | 0 | 5 | 0 | .273 | .273 | .273 | .545 |
| Lyle Overbay | L | 13 | 3 | 0 | 0 | 1 | 3 | 2 | 0 | 5 | 0 | .231 | .333 | .462 | .795 |
| Jordan Pacheco | R | 38 | 10 | 4 | 0 | 0 | 5 | 2 | 0 | 7 | 2 | .263 | .300 | .368 | .668 |
| Chris Parmelee | L | 13 | 2 | 0 | 0 | 0 | 1 | 0 | 0 | 5 | 0 | .154 | .143 | .154 | .297 |
| Tyler Pastornicky | R | 10 | 2 | 0 | 0 | 0 | 0 | 0 | 0 | 1 | 0 | .200 | .200 | .200 | .400 |
| Xavier Paul | L | 33 | 9 | 1 | 0 | 3 | 9 | 2 | 0 | 12 | 2 | .273 | .333 | .576 | .909 |
| Brayan Pena | B | 12 | 3 | 1 | 0 | 0 | 1 | 0 | 0 | 1 | 0 | .250 | .231 | .333 | .564 |
| Ramiro Pena | B | 11 | 3 | 0 | 0 | 0 | 0 | 0 | 0 | 4 | 0 | .273 | .273 | .273 | .545 |
| Cliff Pennington | B | 18 | 5 | 2 | 0 | 0 | 1 | 1 | 0 | 3 | 0 | .278 | .316 | .389 | .705 |
| Brock Peterson | R | 16 | 1 | 0 | 0 | 0 | 2 | 2 | 0 | 8 | 0 | .063 | .167 | .063 | .229 |
| Juan Pierre | L | 44 | 12 | 3 | 0 | 0 | 0 | 0 | 0 | 3 | 0 | .273 | .273 | .341 | .614 |
| A.J. Pierzynski | L | 10 | 5 | 1 | 0 | 1 | 3 | 0 | 0 | 2 | 0 | .500 | .545 | .900 | 1.445 |
| Brett Pill | R | 23 | 2 | 0 | 0 | 1 | 2 | 2 | 0 | 4 | 1 | .087 | .192 | .217 | .410 |
| Placido Polanco | R | 10 | 5 | 0 | 0 | 0 | 1 | 0 | 0 | 2 | 0 | .500 | .500 | .500 | 1.000 |
| A.J. Pollock | R | 20 | 3 | 1 | 0 | 0 | 0 | 4 | 0 | 5 | 0 | .150 | .292 | .200 | .492 |
| Nick Punto | B | 17 | 3 | 1 | 0 | 0 | 2 | 3 | 0 | 7 | 0 | .176 | .300 | .235 | .535 |
| Guillermo Quiroz | R | 9 | 5 | 1 | 0 | 1 | 2 | 0 | 0 | 1 | 0 | .556 | .556 | 1.000 | 1.556 |

# Pinch Hitting

Pinch Hitters with 10+ PAs or 10+ Total Bases in 2013

| | | Pinch Hitting | | | | | | | | | | | | | |
|---|---|---|---|---|---|---|---|---|---|---|---|---|---|---|---|
| Batter | B | AB | H | 2B | 3B | HR | RBI | TBB | IBB | SO | GDP | Avg | OBP | Slg | OPS |
| Ryan Raburn | R | 8 | 1 | 0 | 0 | 0 | 2 | 3 | 0 | 4 | 0 | .125 | .364 | .125 | .489 |
| Wilkin Ramirez | R | 12 | 2 | 1 | 0 | 0 | 1 | 0 | 0 | 5 | 0 | .167 | .167 | .250 | .417 |
| Cody Ransom | R | 9 | 2 | 1 | 0 | 1 | 3 | 3 | 0 | 4 | 0 | .222 | .462 | .667 | 1.128 |
| Anthony Recker | R | 9 | 0 | 0 | 0 | 0 | 0 | 2 | 0 | 5 | 0 | .000 | .182 | .000 | .182 |
| Ryan Roberts | R | 15 | 4 | 0 | 0 | 0 | 1 | 1 | 0 | 3 | 0 | .267 | .313 | .267 | .579 |
| Derrick Robinson | B | 31 | 9 | 1 | 0 | 0 | 1 | 5 | 0 | 8 | 0 | .290 | .389 | .323 | .711 |
| Shane Robinson | R | 18 | 5 | 0 | 0 | 0 | 1 | 4 | 0 | 3 | 0 | .278 | .391 | .278 | .669 |
| Sean Rodriguez | R | 24 | 3 | 0 | 0 | 0 | 1 | 2 | 0 | 11 | 0 | .125 | .250 | .125 | .375 |
| Adam Rosales | R | 14 | 0 | 0 | 0 | 0 | 1 | 1 | 0 | 5 | 1 | .000 | .067 | .000 | .067 |
| Cody Ross | R | 10 | 3 | 1 | 0 | 1 | 4 | 2 | 0 | 2 | 0 | .300 | .385 | .700 | 1.085 |
| Justin Ruggiano | R | 20 | 2 | 1 | 0 | 0 | 1 | 0 | 0 | 7 | 0 | .100 | .100 | .150 | .250 |
| Josh Rutledge | R | 12 | 4 | 0 | 0 | 1 | 1 | 1 | 0 | 5 | 0 | .333 | .385 | .583 | .968 |
| Gaby Sanchez | R | 29 | 5 | 3 | 0 | 0 | 6 | 10 | 1 | 9 | 1 | .172 | .381 | .276 | .657 |
| Hector Sanchez | B | 30 | 5 | 1 | 0 | 1 | 5 | 0 | 0 | 9 | 1 | .167 | .219 | .300 | .519 |
| Dave Sappelt | R | 13 | 2 | 1 | 0 | 0 | 0 | 1 | 0 | 2 | 0 | .154 | .214 | .231 | .445 |
| Josh Satin | R | 26 | 6 | 1 | 0 | 1 | 2 | 3 | 0 | 8 | 0 | .231 | .310 | .385 | .695 |
| Jordan Schafer | L | 25 | 7 | 0 | 0 | 1 | 3 | 1 | 0 | 9 | 0 | .280 | .308 | .400 | .708 |
| Logan Schafer | L | 39 | 10 | 0 | 0 | 1 | 5 | 2 | 0 | 8 | 3 | .256 | .293 | .333 | .626 |
| Nate Schierholtz | L | 16 | 6 | 2 | 0 | 1 | 4 | 2 | 1 | 2 | 1 | .375 | .444 | .688 | 1.132 |
| Skip Schumaker | L | 21 | 3 | 2 | 0 | 0 | 0 | 0 | 0 | 3 | 2 | .143 | .143 | .238 | .381 |
| Luke Scott | L | 23 | 6 | 2 | 0 | 0 | 1 | 2 | 0 | 8 | 1 | .261 | .320 | .348 | .668 |
| J.B. Shuck | L | 12 | 3 | 0 | 0 | 0 | 0 | 1 | 0 | 2 | 0 | .250 | .308 | .250 | .558 |
| Seth Smith | L | 11 | 3 | 0 | 0 | 1 | 1 | 3 | 0 | 3 | 0 | .273 | .467 | .545 | 1.012 |
| Travis Snider | L | 44 | 9 | 1 | 0 | 3 | 7 | 2 | 0 | 12 | 0 | .205 | .239 | .432 | .671 |
| Ichiro Suzuki | L | 12 | 5 | 0 | 0 | 0 | 0 | 1 | 1 | 1 | 0 | .417 | .462 | .417 | .878 |
| Ryan Sweeney | L | 14 | 4 | 1 | 0 | 0 | 2 | 3 | 0 | 3 | 1 | .286 | .412 | .357 | .769 |
| Jose Tabata | R | 25 | 6 | 2 | 1 | 0 | 3 | 2 | 0 | 5 | 0 | .240 | .321 | .400 | .721 |
| Miguel Tejada | R | 11 | 3 | 1 | 0 | 0 | 0 | 1 | 0 | 3 | 1 | .273 | .333 | .364 | .697 |
| Joey Terdoslavich | B | 30 | 4 | 1 | 0 | 0 | 2 | 5 | 0 | 10 | 1 | .133 | .250 | .167 | .417 |
| Yorvit Torrealba | R | 10 | 4 | 0 | 0 | 0 | 1 | 0 | 0 | 1 | 0 | .400 | .455 | .400 | .855 |
| Andres Torres | B | 18 | 3 | 1 | 0 | 0 | 2 | 3 | 0 | 3 | 1 | .167 | .286 | .222 | .508 |
| Chad Tracy | L | 64 | 11 | 2 | 0 | 2 | 5 | 4 | 0 | 12 | 1 | .172 | .221 | .297 | .517 |
| Matt Tuiasosopo | R | 14 | 4 | 2 | 0 | 1 | 7 | 4 | 0 | 6 | 0 | .286 | .444 | .643 | 1.087 |
| Justin Turner | R | 33 | 5 | 1 | 0 | 0 | 3 | 1 | 0 | 8 | 2 | .152 | .171 | .182 | .353 |
| Juan Uribe | R | 14 | 4 | 1 | 0 | 1 | 2 | 1 | 0 | 6 | 0 | .286 | .333 | .571 | .905 |
| Henry Urrutia | L | 12 | 3 | 0 | 0 | 0 | 0 | 0 | 0 | 4 | 1 | .250 | .250 | .250 | .500 |
| Luis Valbuena | L | 11 | 2 | 0 | 0 | 0 | 2 | 2 | 0 | 6 | 0 | .182 | .308 | .182 | .490 |
| Jordany Valdespin | L | 29 | 3 | 0 | 0 | 1 | 5 | 5 | 0 | 11 | 0 | .103 | .257 | .207 | .464 |
| Scott Van Slyke | R | 10 | 4 | 1 | 0 | 1 | 4 | 0 | 0 | 3 | 1 | .400 | .400 | .800 | 1.200 |
| Will Venable | L | 9 | 2 | 1 | 1 | 0 | 0 | 1 | 0 | 3 | 0 | .222 | .300 | .556 | .856 |
| Logan Watkins | L | 13 | 0 | 0 | 0 | 0 | 0 | 2 | 0 | 8 | 0 | .000 | .133 | .000 | .133 |
| Rickie Weeks | R | 9 | 1 | 1 | 0 | 0 | 0 | 1 | 0 | 3 | 1 | .111 | .200 | .222 | .422 |
| Casper Wells | R | 16 | 3 | 0 | 0 | 0 | 0 | 1 | 0 | 3 | 0 | .188 | .235 | .188 | .423 |
| Vernon Wells | R | 23 | 6 | 1 | 0 | 0 | 4 | 0 | 0 | 7 | 0 | .261 | .261 | .304 | .565 |
| Ryan Wheeler | L | 19 | 5 | 0 | 0 | 0 | 5 | 1 | 0 | 5 | 1 | .263 | .300 | .263 | .563 |
| Ty Wigginton | R | 32 | 5 | 2 | 0 | 0 | 0 | 2 | 1 | 12 | 0 | .156 | .206 | .219 | .425 |
| Kolten Wong | L | 15 | 1 | 0 | 0 | 0 | 0 | 2 | 0 | 6 | 0 | .067 | .176 | .067 | .243 |
| Chris Young | R | 13 | 3 | 0 | 0 | 0 | 3 | 4 | 0 | 7 | 0 | .231 | .412 | .231 | .643 |
| Delmon Young | R | 14 | 2 | 0 | 0 | 0 | 0 | 2 | 0 | 3 | 1 | .143 | .250 | .143 | .393 |
| Eric Young | B | 19 | 2 | 0 | 0 | 0 | 0 | 0 | 0 | 10 | 0 | .105 | .105 | .105 | .211 |
| Michael Young | R | 11 | 4 | 0 | 0 | 0 | 3 | 1 | 0 | 1 | 0 | .364 | .357 | .364 | .721 |

# Career Pinch Hitting

Active Pinch Hitters with 100+ PAs in their careers

| | | Pinch Hitting | | | | | | | | | | | | | |
|---|---|---|---|---|---|---|---|---|---|---|---|---|---|---|---|
| Batter | B | AB | H | 2B | 3B | HR | RBI | TBB | IBB | SO | GDP | Avg | OBP | Slg | OPS |
| Jeff Baker | R | 184 | 36 | 8 | 1 | 5 | 20 | 18 | 3 | 71 | 6 | .196 | .270 | .332 | .601 |
| Wilson Betemit | B | 154 | 36 | 9 | 0 | 5 | 20 | 26 | 0 | 59 | 3 | .234 | .343 | .390 | .732 |
| Willie Bloomquist | R | 91 | 22 | 1 | 1 | 1 | 10 | 6 | 1 | 15 | 3 | .242 | .290 | .308 | .598 |
| Jamey Carroll | R | 122 | 41 | 4 | 0 | 1 | 14 | 17 | 0 | 24 | 4 | .336 | .414 | .393 | .808 |
| Endy Chavez | L | 133 | 36 | 7 | 3 | 2 | 14 | 7 | 1 | 15 | 5 | .271 | .307 | .414 | .721 |
| Eric Chavez | L | 101 | 22 | 5 | 0 | 2 | 16 | 6 | 2 | 25 | 1 | .218 | .257 | .327 | .584 |
| Chris Denorfia | R | 103 | 27 | 7 | 0 | 3 | 16 | 11 | 0 | 21 | 4 | .262 | .325 | .417 | .742 |
| Mark DeRosa | R | 162 | 45 | 7 | 0 | 3 | 27 | 25 | 1 | 33 | 1 | .278 | .377 | .377 | .754 |
| Blake DeWitt | L | 113 | 25 | 6 | 1 | 3 | 17 | 6 | 0 | 20 | 6 | .221 | .270 | .372 | .642 |
| Matt Diaz | R | 232 | 59 | 8 | 2 | 1 | 24 | 9 | 0 | 56 | 9 | .254 | .289 | .319 | .608 |
| Greg Dobbs | L | 375 | 95 | 21 | 2 | 10 | 75 | 33 | 8 | 79 | 7 | .253 | .311 | .400 | .711 |
| Ryan Doumit | B | 107 | 28 | 5 | 0 | 3 | 21 | 12 | 3 | 29 | 5 | .262 | .344 | .393 | .737 |
| Ben Francisco | R | 120 | 28 | 10 | 1 | 1 | 18 | 15 | 0 | 37 | 3 | .233 | .326 | .358 | .684 |
| Juan Francisco | L | 104 | 19 | 3 | 0 | 3 | 12 | 11 | 0 | 41 | 3 | .183 | .267 | .298 | .565 |
| Kevin Frandsen | R | 102 | 27 | 3 | 1 | 1 | 17 | 5 | 1 | 16 | 2 | .265 | .318 | .343 | .661 |
| Jason Giambi | L | 173 | 41 | 3 | 0 | 11 | 36 | 31 | 5 | 62 | 3 | .237 | .362 | .445 | .807 |
| Jonny Gomes | R | 134 | 22 | 6 | 0 | 7 | 24 | 22 | 2 | 56 | 1 | .164 | .305 | .366 | .671 |
| Jesus Guzman | R | 112 | 30 | 7 | 0 | 6 | 29 | 12 | 1 | 29 | 4 | .268 | .341 | .491 | .832 |
| Jerry Hairston | R | 113 | 20 | 6 | 1 | 0 | 7 | 8 | 2 | 23 | 3 | .177 | .230 | .248 | .477 |
| Scott Hairston | R | 216 | 42 | 7 | 0 | 12 | 28 | 25 | 1 | 81 | 4 | .194 | .280 | .394 | .673 |
| Chris Heisey | R | 94 | 27 | 5 | 1 | 6 | 24 | 9 | 0 | 28 | 1 | .287 | .352 | .553 | .905 |
| Eric Hinske | L | 302 | 66 | 14 | 1 | 9 | 41 | 41 | 1 | 86 | 8 | .219 | .316 | .361 | .677 |
| Raul Ibanez | L | 137 | 27 | 7 | 0 | 5 | 23 | 16 | 2 | 27 | 5 | .197 | .277 | .358 | .635 |
| Travis Ishikawa | L | 119 | 33 | 8 | 1 | 1 | 14 | 9 | 1 | 26 | 1 | .277 | .333 | .387 | .720 |
| Reed Johnson | R | 212 | 61 | 11 | 0 | 5 | 28 | 11 | 1 | 51 | 6 | .288 | .349 | .410 | .759 |
| Austin Kearns | R | 110 | 30 | 3 | 1 | 3 | 18 | 25 | 0 | 39 | 3 | .273 | .424 | .400 | .824 |
| Mark Kotsay | L | 247 | 66 | 11 | 0 | 6 | 34 | 20 | 2 | 43 | 4 | .267 | .322 | .385 | .707 |
| Jason Kubel | L | 100 | 21 | 4 | 0 | 4 | 14 | 14 | 1 | 37 | 4 | .210 | .307 | .370 | .677 |
| Ryan Langerhans | L | 93 | 22 | 4 | 1 | 4 | 8 | 13 | 0 | 35 | 1 | .237 | .330 | .430 | .760 |
| Ryan Ludwick | R | 98 | 27 | 7 | 0 | 5 | 15 | 11 | 2 | 27 | 1 | .276 | .355 | .500 | .855 |
| Nate McLouth | L | 120 | 23 | 6 | 1 | 1 | 11 | 10 | 1 | 30 | 0 | .192 | .263 | .283 | .546 |
| Laynce Nix | L | 210 | 39 | 10 | 0 | 4 | 19 | 19 | 4 | 74 | 5 | .186 | .252 | .290 | .543 |
| Pete Orr | L | 206 | 56 | 6 | 2 | 2 | 15 | 8 | 0 | 52 | 1 | .272 | .296 | .350 | .646 |
| David Ortiz | L | 86 | 16 | 3 | 1 | 5 | 19 | 20 | 1 | 22 | 2 | .186 | .336 | .419 | .755 |
| Lyle Overbay | L | 106 | 22 | 5 | 0 | 3 | 19 | 11 | 2 | 38 | 3 | .208 | .277 | .340 | .617 |
| Xavier Paul | L | 128 | 28 | 7 | 1 | 5 | 13 | 6 | 1 | 42 | 6 | .219 | .259 | .406 | .666 |
| Juan Pierre | L | 150 | 43 | 4 | 2 | 0 | 4 | 12 | 1 | 11 | 0 | .287 | .348 | .340 | .688 |
| A.J. Pierzynski | L | 109 | 27 | 5 | 0 | 4 | 20 | 12 | 5 | 18 | 6 | .248 | .328 | .404 | .732 |
| Placido Polanco | R | 99 | 27 | 3 | 0 | 1 | 17 | 8 | 0 | 11 | 3 | .273 | .324 | .333 | .657 |
| Nick Punto | B | 84 | 17 | 4 | 0 | 0 | 2 | 16 | 0 | 27 | 0 | .202 | .330 | .250 | .580 |
| Ryan Roberts | R | 103 | 27 | 3 | 0 | 0 | 9 | 7 | 0 | 27 | 1 | .262 | .319 | .291 | .610 |
| Nate Schierholtz | L | 147 | 46 | 9 | 1 | 3 | 22 | 12 | 1 | 30 | 2 | .313 | .358 | .449 | .807 |
| Skip Schumaker | L | 157 | 37 | 9 | 0 | 1 | 13 | 8 | 1 | 27 | 4 | .236 | .280 | .312 | .592 |
| Luke Scott | L | 115 | 30 | 12 | 0 | 3 | 15 | 10 | 1 | 32 | 3 | .261 | .320 | .443 | .763 |
| Seth Smith | L | 168 | 53 | 12 | 5 | 6 | 40 | 29 | 2 | 45 | 2 | .315 | .413 | .554 | .967 |
| Chad Tracy | L | 220 | 50 | 14 | 0 | 8 | 40 | 24 | 3 | 49 | 3 | .227 | .306 | .400 | .706 |
| Justin Turner | R | 97 | 22 | 6 | 0 | 0 | 14 | 8 | 0 | 17 | 6 | .227 | .287 | .289 | .576 |
| Ty Wigginton | R | 135 | 29 | 5 | 0 | 3 | 24 | 18 | 4 | 38 | 2 | .215 | .316 | .319 | .635 |
| DeWayne Wise | L | 99 | 29 | 4 | 1 | 3 | 15 | 1 | 0 | 21 | 1 | .293 | .297 | .444 | .741 |
| Eric Young | B | 112 | 25 | 2 | 1 | 1 | 4 | 15 | 0 | 27 | 2 | .223 | .326 | .286 | .611 |

# Manufactured Runs, Productive Outs, & Unproductive Outs

Many managers, coaches, and broadcasters will tell you that teams need to be able to move the runners over and manufacture runs to be successful. Get 'em on, get 'em over, get 'em in. You can't always wait for the long ball to score runs, so they say.

Clearly, some teams do this better than others. The Anaheim/Los Angeles Angels have led the league in manufactured runs five times since 2002 and have finished out of the top four only once in that span. Though it's odd that a team with Mike Trout, Albert Pujols, Josh Hamilton, and Mark Trumbo had to resort to manufacturing runs, only the Texas Rangers manufactured more this year. The Rangers have led the league in manufactured runs three of the past four years, and they've gone to the World Series twice in that span. Erick Aybar, Elvis Andrus, Leonys Martin, and Alberto Callaspo were four of the five most effective run manufacturers in terms of their ratio of Productive to Unproductive Outs. Individuals can't manufacture runs on their own, of course; that's the whole point. They can, however, play a role in manufacturing runs via bunts, stolen bases, and productive outs, among other things.

The Oakland A's of the past two seasons have tried their darnedest to provide a compelling counterexample. Their biggest run manufacturer was Coco Crisp (contributing to only 20 manufactured runs), who by the way hit 22 home runs out of the leadoff spot. The A's also had the fewest Productive Outs and the second-fewest Unproductive Outs. In other words, when they got runners on base, the A's said, "Screw getting them over. I'm going for the three-run homer."

The following pages contain team totals for Manufactured Runs, Productive Outs, and Unproductive Outs as well as the totals allowed by each team. Aside from the above examples, we'll call your attention to the St. Louis Cardinals, who avoided both Productive and Unproductive Outs by hitting an incredible .330 with runners in scoring position. We've also provided the individual leaders in Manufactured Run Contributions, Productive Outs, and Unproductive Outs. Note how traditional sluggers Adrian Gonzalez and Torii Hunter gave themselves up in favor of productive outs more than any other hitters in baseball.

# Players with the most Manufactured Run Contributions, Productive Outs, & Unproductive Outs — 2013

| Manufactured Run Contributions | |
|---|---|
| Andrus, Elvis, Tex | 43 |
| Kinsler, Ian, Tex | 35 |
| Young, Eric, Col-NYM | 31 |
| Choo, Shin-Soo, Cin | 31 |
| Marte, Starling, Pit | 31 |
| Martin, Leonys, Tex | 30 |
| Murphy, Daniel, NYM | 29 |
| Ellsbury, Jacoby, Bos | 28 |
| Gardner, Brett, NYY | 28 |
| Aoki, Norichika, Mil | 27 |
| Bourn, Michael, Cle | 27 |
| McLouth, Nate, Bal | 27 |
| Aybar, Erick, LAA | 27 |
| Jennings, Desmond, TB | 26 |
| Rios, Alex, CWS-Tex | 26 |
| McCutchen, Andrew, Pit | 26 |
| Span, Denard, Was | 26 |
| Trout, Mike, LAA | 25 |
| De Aza, Alejandro, CWS | 25 |
| Bonifacio, Emilio, Tor-KC | 24 |
| Shuck, J.B., LAA | 24 |
| Carpenter, Matt, StL | 24 |
| Gordon, Alex, KC | 24 |
| Fowler, Dexter, Col | 23 |
| Segura, Jean, Mil | 23 |
| Machado, Manny, Bal | 22 |
| Davis, Rajai, Tor | 22 |
| Venable, Will, SD | 22 |
| Revere, Ben, Phi | 22 |
| Jay, Jon, StL | 21 |
| Cabrera, Everth, SD | 21 |
| Pence, Hunter, SF | 21 |
| Jackson, Austin, Det | 21 |
| Goldschmidt, Paul, Ari | 20 |
| Ramirez, Alexei, CWS | 20 |
| Suzuki, Ichiro, NYY | 20 |
| Crawford, Carl, LAD | 20 |
| Crisp, Coco, Oak | 20 |
| Victorino, Shane, Bos | 20 |
| Gomez, Carlos, Mil | 19 |
| Denorfia, Chris, SD | 19 |
| Castro, Starlin, ChC | 19 |
| Crawford, Brandon, SF | 18 |
| Desmond, Ian, Was | 18 |
| Escobar, Alcides, KC | 18 |
| Cuddyer, Michael, Col | 18 |
| Phillips, Brandon, Cin | 18 |
| Hosmer, Eric, KC | 18 |
| Dozier, Brian, Min | 18 |
| Belt, Brandon, SF | 18 |

| Productive Outs | |
|---|---|
| Gonzalez, Adrian, LAD | 45 |
| Hunter, Torii, Det | 44 |
| Cozart, Zack, Cin | 43 |
| Markakis, Nick, Bal | 43 |
| Andrus, Elvis, Tex | 43 |
| Phillips, Brandon, Cin | 39 |
| Votto, Joey, Cin | 38 |
| Prado, Martin, Ari | 37 |
| Kipnis, Jason, Cle | 37 |
| Pedroia, Dustin, Bos | 36 |
| Goldschmidt, Paul, Ari | 35 |
| Rizzo, Anthony, ChC | 35 |
| Aybar, Erick, LAA | 35 |
| Scutaro, Marco, SF | 35 |
| Murphy, Daniel, NYM | 35 |
| Callaspo, Alberto, LAA-Oak | 34 |
| Cano, Robinson, NYY | 34 |
| Aviles, Mike, Cle | 33 |
| Altuve, Jose, Hou | 33 |
| Martin, Leonys, Tex | 33 |
| Zobrist, Ben, TB | 32 |
| Cabrera, Asdrubal, Cle | 32 |
| Hosmer, Eric, KC | 32 |
| Victorino, Shane, Bos | 32 |
| Ellis, Mark, LAD | 31 |
| Escobar, Yunel, TB | 31 |
| Wieters, Matt, Bal | 31 |
| Fielder, Prince, Det | 31 |
| Nava, Daniel, Bos | 31 |
| Escobar, Alcides, KC | 31 |
| McCutchen, Andrew, Pit | 31 |
| Bruce, Jay, Cin | 30 |
| Aoki, Norichika, Mil | 30 |
| Morales, Kendrys, Sea | 29 |
| Seager, Kyle, Sea | 29 |
| Hamilton, Josh, LAA | 29 |
| Crawford, Brandon, SF | 29 |
| Pujols, Albert, LAA | 29 |
| Barney, Darwin, ChC | 29 |
| Suzuki, Ichiro, NYY | 28 |
| Desmond, Ian, Was | 28 |
| Young, Eric, Col-NYM | 28 |
| Lucroy, Jonathan, Mil | 28 |
| Jay, Jon, StL | 28 |
| Machado, Manny, Bal | 28 |
| Trout, Mike, LAA | 27 |
| LeMahieu, DJ, Col | 27 |
| Florimon, Pedro, Min | 27 |
| Parra, Gerardo, Ari | 27 |
| Posey, Buster, SF | 27 |
| Sandoval, Pablo, SF | 27 |
| Ramirez, Alexei, CWS | 27 |
| Swisher, Nick, Cle | 27 |
| Holliday, Matt, StL | 27 |

| Unproductive Outs | |
|---|---|
| Murphy, Daniel, NYM | 97 |
| Pence, Hunter, SF | 95 |
| Pedroia, Dustin, Bos | 93 |
| Lowrie, Jed, Oak | 93 |
| Machado, Manny, Bal | 89 |
| McCutchen, Andrew, Pit | 88 |
| Hamilton, Josh, LAA | 88 |
| Morneau, Justin, Min-Pit | 86 |
| Davis, Chris, Bal | 86 |
| Jones, Adam, Bal | 85 |
| Rios, Alex, CWS-Tex | 85 |
| Longoria, Evan, TB | 84 |
| Segura, Jean, Mil | 84 |
| Carter, Chris, Hou | 84 |
| Belt, Brandon, SF | 83 |
| Willingham, Josh, Min | 83 |
| Napoli, Mike, Bos | 83 |
| Ramirez, Alexei, CWS | 82 |
| Upton, Justin, Atl | 81 |
| Seager, Kyle, Sea | 81 |
| Phillips, Brandon, Cin | 81 |
| Hunter, Torii, Det | 79 |
| Castro, Starlin, ChC | 79 |
| Swisher, Nick, Cle | 78 |
| Hardy, J.J., Bal | 78 |
| Goldschmidt, Paul, Ari | 78 |
| Gyorko, Jedd, SD | 78 |
| Markakis, Nick, Bal | 78 |
| Trumbo, Mark, LAA | 77 |
| Rizzo, Anthony, ChC | 77 |
| Votto, Joey, Cin | 77 |
| Beltran, Carlos, StL | 77 |
| Ortiz, David, Bos | 75 |
| Byrd, Marlon, NYM-Pit | 75 |
| Alvarez, Pedro, Pit | 75 |
| Cozart, Zack, Cin | 75 |
| Stanton, Giancarlo, Mia | 75 |
| Gonzalez, Adrian, LAD | 75 |
| Simmons, Andrelton, Atl | 75 |
| Zobrist, Ben, TB | 74 |
| Cespedes, Yoenis, Oak | 74 |
| LaRoche, Adam, Was | 74 |
| Prado, Martin, Ari | 74 |
| Dunn, Adam, CWS | 74 |
| Soriano, Alfonso, ChC-NYY | 74 |
| Fielder, Prince, Det | 73 |
| Uggla, Dan, Atl | 72 |
| Cano, Robinson, NYY | 72 |
| Bautista, Jose, Tor | 72 |
| Cabrera, Miguel, Det | 71 |
| Arencibia, J.P., Tor | 71 |
| Zimmerman, Ryan, Was | 71 |
| Gomez, Carlos, Mil | 71 |
| Donaldson, Josh, Oak | 71 |
| Bruce, Jay, Cin | 71 |
| Reynolds, Mark, Cle-NYY | 71 |
| Lucroy, Jonathan, Mil | 71 |
| Smoak, Justin, Sea | 71 |
| Butler, Billy, KC | 71 |

## Manufactured Runs, Productive Outs, & Unproductive Outs Produced by Team — 2013

| Team | Manufactured Runs | Productive Outs | Unproductive Outs |
|---|---|---|---|
| Arizona Diamondbacks | 134 | 278 | 702 |
| Atlanta Braves | 131 | 241 | 689 |
| Baltimore Orioles | 128 | 238 | 707 |
| Boston Red Sox | 156 | 259 | 778 |
| Chicago White Sox | 137 | 219 | 715 |
| Chicago Cubs | 115 | 234 | 685 |
| Cincinnati Reds | 164 | 311 | 683 |
| Cleveland Indians | 149 | 270 | 672 |
| Colorado Rockies | 156 | 286 | 669 |
| Detroit Tigers | 145 | 250 | 757 |
| Houston Astros | 139 | 239 | 678 |
| Kansas City Royals | 162 | 237 | 688 |
| Los Angeles Dodgers | 163 | 301 | 726 |
| Los Angeles Angels | 178 | 298 | 668 |
| Miami Marlins | 106 | 237 | 662 |
| Milwaukee Brewers | 158 | 290 | 629 |
| Minnesota Twins | 115 | 238 | 759 |
| New York Yankees | 155 | 244 | 693 |
| New York Mets | 158 | 266 | 721 |
| Oakland Athletics | 124 | 213 | 770 |
| Philadelphia Phillies | 149 | 252 | 641 |
| Pittsburgh Pirates | 148 | 272 | 667 |
| San Diego Padres | 148 | 275 | 655 |
| San Francisco Giants | 148 | 303 | 703 |
| Seattle Mariners | 110 | 216 | 714 |
| St Louis Cardinals | 157 | 266 | 630 |
| Tampa Bay Rays | 138 | 243 | 721 |
| Texas Rangers | 201 | 276 | 678 |
| Toronto Blue Jays | 151 | 247 | 672 |
| Washington Nationals | 141 | 276 | 645 |

# Manufactured Runs, Productive Outs, & Unproductive Outs Allowed by Team — 2013

| Team | Manufactured Runs | Productive Outs | Unproductive Outs |
|---|---|---|---|
| Arizona Diamondbacks | 113 | 292 | 687 |
| Atlanta Braves | 117 | 243 | 685 |
| Baltimore Orioles | 112 | 241 | 672 |
| Boston Red Sox | 146 | 228 | 756 |
| Chicago White Sox | 162 | 226 | 721 |
| Chicago Cubs | 143 | 257 | 659 |
| Cincinnati Reds | 112 | 260 | 629 |
| Cleveland Indians | 141 | 239 | 751 |
| Colorado Rockies | 175 | 320 | 689 |
| Detroit Tigers | 136 | 239 | 688 |
| Houston Astros | 172 | 250 | 734 |
| Kansas City Royals | 124 | 222 | 698 |
| Los Angeles Dodgers | 142 | 262 | 648 |
| Los Angeles Angels | 167 | 271 | 787 |
| Miami Marlins | 160 | 303 | 673 |
| Milwaukee Brewers | 165 | 264 | 662 |
| Minnesota Twins | 154 | 265 | 668 |
| New York Yankees | 132 | 244 | 752 |
| New York Mets | 158 | 281 | 662 |
| Oakland Athletics | 150 | 250 | 680 |
| Philadelphia Phillies | 173 | 298 | 704 |
| Pittsburgh Pirates | 167 | 282 | 643 |
| San Diego Padres | 140 | 280 | 691 |
| San Francisco Giants | 145 | 258 | 698 |
| Seattle Mariners | 158 | 257 | 700 |
| St Louis Cardinals | 134 | 265 | 673 |
| Tampa Bay Rays | 138 | 239 | 693 |
| Texas Rangers | 114 | 229 | 727 |
| Toronto Blue Jays | 160 | 257 | 696 |
| Washington Nationals | 154 | 253 | 651 |

# Managers Record

With the Reds' dismissal of Dusty Baker following their Wild Card loss to the Pirates, the future of one of baseball's most unique and controversial managers is up in the air.

There's no denying that Baker's managerial style is old-school. More than all of his contemporaries, Baker loves to sacrifice bunt (consistently over 100 attempts per season, including the league lead the past two seasons), pitch out (21 pitchouts to lead the league this year), and trust his starting pitchers deep into ballgames (378 long outings since 2002 is far more than any other manager). He gave sabermetricians fits with his frequent bunts and rigidly conventional lineup construction, and he received a lot of blame for ruining the careers of many young pitchers, most notoriously Kerry Wood and Mark Prior. Baker was never a big fan of pinch-runners.

For as much criticism as Baker has received over the years, his record speaks for itself. Currently 16th on the managerial wins list, Baker won National League Manager of the Year three times and finished runner up thrice more and his teams have combined for a .520 winning percentage. He guided teams to the playoffs seven times, including one NL pennant in 2002. More recently, he brought the Reds back to respectability and the playoffs. Perhaps as a product of managing Barry Bonds during his prime, he never abused the intentional walk, and on the rare occasions he opted for the tactic, it very seldom blew up in his face. And, if we've learned anything about pitch counts in the past 25 years it's that we don't really know with much certainty what's best for a pitcher's long-term health.

Whether the old soldier catches on elsewhere in 2014 or fades away MacArthur-style, the beloved skipper and his famous toothpicks will be honorably ingrained in the memories of baseball fans everywhere.

The tools we have to evaluate managers are divided into several categories:

Lineups: Number of Different Lineups Used (LUp), the percentage of players who had the platoon advantage at the start of the game (PL%).

Substitution: Pinch Hitters Used (PH), Pinch Runners Used (PR), Defensive Substitutes Used (DS).

Pitchers Usage: Quick Hooks (Quick), Slow Hooks (Slow), Long Outings by Starting Pitchers (LO), Relievers Used on Consecutive Days (RCD), Long Saves (LS), Relievers Used (Rel).

For Quick Hooks, we calculate a "Damage Score" for each pitcher and each game, which is his pitches thrown, plus 10 times his runs allowed. The bottom 25% of the games in each league are Quick Hooks. If the manager takes his pitcher out after 92 pitches and 1 run allowed (102), that will be a quick hook. The top 25% are Slow Hooks. If a pitcher throws 114 pitches and gives up 4 runs (154), that will be a Slow Hook. If a pitcher throws more than 110 pitches in a start, that's a Long Outing. Yes, this is redundant of Slow Hooks; thanks for noticing.

Tactics: Stolen Base Attempts (SBA), Sacrifice Bunts Attempts (SacA), Runners Moving with the Pitch (RM), Pitchouts ordered (PO).

Intentional Walks: Intentional Walks issued (#), Intentional Walks resulting in a Good Outcome (Good), Intentional Walks resulting Not in a Good Outcome (NG), Intentional Walks Blowing up on the Manager (Bomb). A good result is 1) The next hitter grounds into a double play, or 2) The team in the field gets out of the inning without additional runs scoring. A "Bomb" means that Multiple runs score in the inning after the intentional walk. If the hitter after the IBB grounds into a double play, then we count that intentional walk as a success, even if multiple runs score after the IBB.

Results: Wins (W), Losses (L) and Winning Percentage (Pct.).

## Manny Acta

| | | | | LINEUPS | | SUBSTITUTION | | | PITCHER USAGE | | | | | | TACTICS | | | | INTENTIONAL BB | | | | RESULTS | | |
|---|---|---|---|---|---|---|---|---|---|---|---|---|---|---|---|---|---|---|---|---|---|---|---|---|---|
| Year | Team | Lg | G | LUp | PL% | PH | PR | DS | Quick | Slow | LO | RCD | LS | Rel | SBA | SacA | RM | PO | # | Good | NG | Bomb | W | L | Pct |
| 2007 | Nationals | NL | 162 | 101 | .65 | 295 | 32 | **78** | 53 | 28 | 5 | **183** | 1 | **588** | 92 | 86 | 70 | 28 | 44 | 28 | 16 | 8 | 73 | 89 | .451 |
| 2008 | Nationals | NL | 161 | 133 | .62 | 293 | 31 | 39 | 38 | 46 | 6 | 119 | 4 | 517 | 124 | 95 | 63 | 24 | 44 | 27 | 17 | 8 | 59 | **102** | .366 |
| 2009 | Nationals | NL | 87 | 66 | .62 | 145 | 11 | 20 | 14 | 25 | 1 | 91 | 1 | 282 | 54 | 43 | 62 | 5 | 26 | 13 | 13 | 6 | 26 | 61 | .299 |
| 2010 | Indians | AL | 162 | 142 | .63 | 79 | 20 | 39 | 44 | 49 | 18 | 81 | 6 | 470 | 124 | 41 | 142 | 20 | 36 | 17 | **19** | **10** | 69 | **93** | .426 |
| 2011 | Indians | AL | 162 | 134 | .71 | 76 | 44 | 43 | 47 | **49** | 20 | 107 | 0 | **483** | 131 | 40 | 144 | 29 | 34 | 20 | 14 | **10** | 80 | 82 | .494 |
| 2012 | Indians | AL | 156 | 116 | .76 | 68 | 20 | **72** | 38 | **54** | 14 | 94 | 1 | 464 | 149 | 21 | 135 | 23 | 27 | 12 | 15 | 9 | 65 | 91 | .417 |
| 162-Game Average | | | | 126 | .67 | 174 | 29 | 53 | 43 | 46 | 12 | 123 | 2 | 510 | 123 | 59 | 112 | 23 | 38 | 21 | 17 | 9 | 68 | 94 | .420 |

## Sandy Alomar, Jr.

| | | | | LINEUPS | | SUBSTITUTION | | | PITCHER USAGE | | | | | | TACTICS | | | | INTENTIONAL BB | | | | RESULTS | | |
|---|---|---|---|---|---|---|---|---|---|---|---|---|---|---|---|---|---|---|---|---|---|---|---|---|---|
| Year | Team | Lg | G | LUp | PL% | PH | PR | DS | Quick | Slow | LO | RCD | LS | Rel | SBA | SacA | RM | PO | # | Good | NG | Bomb | W | L | Pct |
| 2012 | Indians | AL | 6 | 6 | .61 | 12 | 2 | 1 | 1 | 1 | 0 | 9 | 0 | 30 | 5 | 3 | 3 | 0 | 0 | 0 | 0 | 0 | 3 | 3 | .500 |
| 162-Game Average | | | | 162 | .61 | 324 | 54 | 27 | 27 | 27 | 0 | 243 | 0 | 810 | 135 | 81 | 81 | 0 | 0 | 0 | 0 | 0 | 81 | 81 | .500 |

## Dusty Baker

| | | | | LINEUPS | | SUBSTITUTION | | | PITCHER USAGE | | | | | | TACTICS | | | | INTENTIONAL BB | | | | RESULTS | | |
|---|---|---|---|---|---|---|---|---|---|---|---|---|---|---|---|---|---|---|---|---|---|---|---|---|---|
| Year | Team | Lg | G | LUp | PL% | PH | PR | DS | Quick | Slow | LO | RCD | LS | Rel | SBA | SacA | RM | PO | # | Good | NG | Bomb | W | L | Pct |
| 1994 | Giants | NL | 115 | 76 | .53 | 177 | 16 | 9 | 29 | 25 | 2 | 86 | 12 | 288 | 154 | 88 | | 78 | 40 | 24 | 16 | 8 | 55 | 60 | .478 |
| 1995 | Giants | NL | 144 | 96 | .41 | 230 | 36 | 13 | 32 | 50 | 8 | 90 | 8 | 381 | 184 | 101 | | 77 | 51 | 32 | 19 | 14 | 67 | 77 | .465 |
| 1996 | Giants | NL | 162 | 129 | .51 | 250 | 17 | 15 | 24 | 58 | 15 | 94 | 8 | 425 | 166 | 103 | | 96 | 60 | 37 | 23 | 15 | 68 | 94 | .420 |
| 1997 | Giants | NL | 162 | 114 | .71 | 212 | 17 | 22 | 46 | 25 | 17 | 132 | 4 | 481 | 170 | 85 | | 93 | 57 | 36 | 21 | 12 | 90 | 72 | .556 |
| 1998 | Giants | NL | 163 | 130 | .62 | 224 | 20 | 12 | 43 | 38 | 8 | 113 | 5 | 433 | 153 | 111 | | 41 | 68 | 42 | 26 | 9 | 89 | 74 | .546 |
| 1999 | Giants | NL | 162 | 120 | .62 | 233 | 16 | 16 | 30 | 51 | 27 | 111 | | 450 | 165 | 113 | | 40 | 41 | 25 | 16 | 10 | 86 | 76 | .531 |
| 2000 | Giants | NL | 162 | 82 | .56 | 233 | 26 | 22 | 38 | 50 | 25 | 91 | 3 | 384 | 118 | 86 | | 37 | 26 | 17 | 9 | 2 | 97 | 65 | .599 |
| 2001 | Giants | NL | 162 | 122 | .48 | 261 | 22 | 19 | 40 | 48 | 10 | 114 | 4 | 439 | 99 | 95 | | 45 | 49 | 33 | 16 | 6 | 90 | 72 | .556 |
| 2002 | Giants | NL | 162 | 118 | .43 | 223 | 32 | 38 | 29 | 56 | **53** | 106 | 8 | 417 | 95 | 89 | 42 | 41 | 44 | 28 | 16 | 10 | 95 | 66 | .590 |
| 2003 | Cubs | NL | 162 | 114 | .49 | 272 | 25 | 43 | 24 | 58 | **65** | 111 | 3 | 420 | 104 | 93 | 31 | 24 | 36 | 23 | 13 | 4 | 88 | 74 | .543 |
| 2004 | Cubs | NL | 162 | 113 | .44 | 254 | 16 | 19 | 37 | 41 | 42 | 129 | 8 | 460 | 94 | 108 | 71 | **62** | 33 | 22 | 11 | 7 | 89 | 73 | .549 |
| 2005 | Cubs | NL | 162 | 121 | .59 | 240 | 21 | 29 | 40 | 46 | 36 | 103 | 2 | 457 | 104 | 88 | 107 | **70** | 48 | 27 | 21 | 7 | 79 | 83 | .488 |
| 2006 | Cubs | NL | 162 | 133 | .56 | 271 | 9 | 26 | 45 | 39 | 22 | **165** | 2 | **542** | 170 | 108 | 139 | 46 | 44 | 28 | 16 | 11 | 66 | **96** | .407 |
| 2008 | Reds | NL | 162 | 119 | .58 | 285 | 28 | 27 | 26 | **63** | 39 | 124 | 2 | 507 | 132 | 100 | 101 | 37 | 40 | 28 | 12 | 4 | 74 | 88 | .457 |
| 2009 | Reds | NL | 162 | 130 | .45 | 252 | 15 | 35 | 30 | **62** | **35** | 115 | 1 | 478 | 136 | 120 | 118 | 23 | 36 | 29 | 7 | 4 | 78 | 84 | .481 |
| 2010 | Reds | NL | 162 | 120 | .46 | 258 | 19 | 49 | 36 | 41 | 22 | 140 | 0 | 502 | 136 | 91 | 157 | 13 | 32 | 22 | 10 | 9 | 91 | 71 | .562 |
| 2011 | Reds | NL | 162 | **142** | .42 | 240 | 29 | 42 | 34 | 51 | 20 | 115 | 0 | 501 | 147 | 102 | 226 | 33 | 47 | 26 | 21 | 5 | 79 | 83 | .488 |
| 2012 | Reds | NL | 162 | 121 | .43 | 201 | 19 | 39 | 33 | 39 | 30 | 78 | 4 | 425 | 114 | **108** | 148 | 19 | 33 | 22 | 11 | 3 | 97 | 65 | .599 |
| 2013 | Reds | NL | 162 | 95 | .54 | 236 | 20 | 27 | 39 | 40 | 14 | 90 | 3 | 461 | 102 | **110** | 157 | **21** | 28 | 23 | 5 | 3 | 90 | 72 | .556 |
| 162-Game Average | | | | 118 | .52 | 245 | 22 | 27 | 35 | 47 | 26 | 113 | 4 | 454 | 137 | 102 | 118 | 48 | 44 | 28 | 16 | 8 | 84 | 78 | .519 |

## Bud Black

| | | | | LINEUPS | | SUBSTITUTION | | | PITCHER USAGE | | | | | | TACTICS | | | | INTENTIONAL BB | | | | RESULTS | | |
|---|---|---|---|---|---|---|---|---|---|---|---|---|---|---|---|---|---|---|---|---|---|---|---|---|---|
| Year | Team | Lg | G | LUp | PL% | PH | PR | DS | Quick | Slow | LO | RCD | LS | Rel | SBA | SacA | RM | PO | # | Good | NG | Bomb | W | L | Pct |
| 2007 | Padres | NL | 163 | 115 | .62 | 279 | 18 | 13 | **63** | 28 | 13 | 122 | 0 | 485 | 79 | 85 | 73 | **56** | 48 | 28 | 20 | 11 | 89 | 74 | .546 |
| 2008 | Padres | NL | 162 | 113 | .63 | 286 | 25 | 20 | 55 | 36 | 17 | 109 | 0 | 491 | 53 | 75 | 78 | 31 | 61 | 30 | 31 | 17 | 63 | 99 | .389 |
| 2009 | Padres | NL | 162 | **137** | .64 | 264 | 8 | 34 | 50 | 37 | 8 | 118 | 5 | 527 | 111 | 99 | 84 | **55** | 58 | 42 | 16 | 6 | 75 | 87 | .463 |
| 2010 | Padres | NL | 162 | 135 | .61 | 285 | 16 | 45 | **55** | 33 | 10 | 132 | 7 | 499 | **174** | 99 | 135 | 31 | 51 | 35 | 16 | 8 | 90 | 72 | .556 |
| 2011 | Padres | NL | 162 | 140 | .58 | 288 | 20 | 43 | 40 | 36 | 10 | 110 | 2 | 490 | **214** | 69 | 184 | **41** | 56 | 31 | 25 | 13 | 71 | 91 | .438 |
| 2012 | Padres | NL | 162 | 132 | .74 | 280 | 26 | 35 | 45 | 49 | 11 | 126 | 5 | 529 | **201** | 89 | 162 | 21 | 48 | 34 | 14 | 7 | 76 | 86 | .469 |
| 2013 | Padres | NL | 162 | **145** | .66 | 271 | 24 | 37 | 35 | 46 | 4 | 102 | 1 | 488 | 152 | 78 | 122 | 12 | 31 | 20 | 11 | **8** | 76 | 86 | .469 |
| 162-Game Average | | | | 131 | .64 | 279 | 20 | 32 | 49 | 38 | 10 | 117 | 3 | 501 | 140 | 85 | 120 | 35 | 50 | 31 | 19 | 10 | 77 | 85 | .475 |

## Bruce Bochy

| | | | | LINEUPS | | SUBSTITUTION | | | PITCHER USAGE | | | | | | TACTICS | | | | INTENTIONAL BB | | | | RESULTS | | |
|---|---|---|---|---|---|---|---|---|---|---|---|---|---|---|---|---|---|---|---|---|---|---|---|---|---|
| Year | Team | Lg | G | LUp | PL% | PH | PR | DS | Quick | Slow | LO | RCD | LS | Rel | SBA | SacA | RM | PO | # | Good | NG | Bomb | W | L | Pct |
| 1995 | Padres | NL | 144 | 96 | .59 | 262 | 30 | 23 | 44 | 41 | 17 | 38 | 3 | 337 | 170 | 68 | | 38 | 37 | 19 | 18 | 11 | 70 | 74 | .486 |
| 1996 | Padres | NL | 162 | 114 | .52 | 289 | 29 | 15 | 51 | 33 | 10 | 67 | 12 | 411 | 164 | 73 | | 65 | 47 | 29 | 18 | 12 | 91 | 71 | .562 |
| 1997 | Padres | NL | 162 | 111 | .60 | 291 | 26 | 9 | 45 | 45 | 3 | 81 | 11 | 426 | 200 | 84 | | 58 | 37 | 20 | 17 | 11 | 76 | 86 | .469 |
| 1998 | Padres | NL | 162 | 110 | .65 | 280 | 62 | 44 | 44 | 45 | 9 | 81 | 12 | 369 | 116 | 84 | | 27 | 45 | 31 | 14 | 10 | 98 | 64 | .605 |
| 1999 | Padres | NL | 162 | 137 | .60 | 298 | 51 | 21 | 44 | 36 | 4 | 68 | 5 | 403 | 241 | 60 | | 29 | 48 | 29 | 19 | 13 | 74 | 88 | .457 |
| 2000 | Padres | NL | 162 | 134 | .52 | 285 | 44 | 14 | 41 | 47 | 14 | 105 | 5 | 443 | 184 | 52 | | 27 | 50 | 21 | 29 | 11 | 76 | 86 | .469 |
| 2001 | Padres | NL | 162 | 116 | .60 | 255 | 54 | 27 | 32 | 47 | 6 | 85 | 10 | 422 | 173 | 43 | | 23 | 54 | 31 | 23 | 13 | 79 | 83 | .488 |
| 2002 | Padres | NL | 162 | 123 | .66 | 259 | 44 | 56 | 39 | 40 | 17 | 106 | 4 | 459 | 115 | 63 | 74 | 14 | 61 | 38 | 23 | 14 | 66 | **96** | .407 |
| 2003 | Padres | NL | 162 | 134 | .58 | 339 | 20 | 29 | 34 | 43 | 16 | 100 | 3 | 473 | 115 | 63 | 41 | 6 | 52 | 33 | 19 | 12 | 64 | **98** | .395 |
| 2004 | Padres | NL | 162 | 96 | .54 | 261 | 28 | 47 | 47 | 32 | 15 | 76 | 3 | 437 | 77 | 75 | 96 | 14 | 39 | 24 | 15 | 10 | 87 | 75 | .537 |
| 2005 | Padres | NL | 162 | 128 | .58 | 285 | 31 | 49 | 46 | 36 | 23 | 87 | 1 | 456 | 143 | 89 | 111 | 16 | 45 | 33 | 12 | 8 | 82 | 80 | .506 |
| 2006 | Padres | NL | 162 | 111 | .60 | 264 | **64** | 48 | 43 | 42 | 24 | 111 | 2 | 475 | 154 | 77 | 110 | 21 | 63 | 43 | 20 | 10 | 88 | 74 | .543 |
| 2007 | Giants | NL | 162 | 128 | .72 | 264 | 50 | 45 | 26 | 50 | **36** | 132 | 2 | 496 | 152 | 86 | 119 | 10 | 41 | 29 | 12 | 3 | 71 | 91 | .438 |

| | | | | LINEUPS | | SUBSTITUTION | | | PITCHER USAGE | | | | | | TACTICS | | | | INTENTIONAL BB | | | | RESULTS | | |
|---|---|---|---|---|---|---|---|---|---|---|---|---|---|---|---|---|---|---|---|---|---|---|---|---|---|
| Year | Team | Lg | G | LUp | PL% | PH | PR | DS | Quick | Slow | LO | RCD | LS | Rel | SBA | SacA | RM | PO | # | Good | NG | Bomb | W | L | Pct |
| 2008 | Giants | NL | 162 | 134 | .68 | 276 | 32 | 39 | 24 | 59 | **42** | 97 | 6 | 478 | 154 | 77 | **155** | 5 | 59 | 40 | 19 | 8 | 72 | 90 | .444 |
| 2009 | Giants | NL | 162 | 134 | .65 | 231 | 21 | 52 | 42 | 40 | 32 | 84 | **8** | 457 | 106 | 93 | 118 | 5 | 49 | 32 | 17 | 10 | 88 | 74 | .543 |
| 2010 | Giants | NL | 162 | 126 | .55 | 224 | 45 | **70** | 29 | 37 | 40 | 118 | **12** | 477 | 87 | 102 | 144 | 12 | 58 | 41 | 17 | 8 | 92 | 70 | .568 |
| 2011 | Giants | NL | 162 | 138 | .62 | 245 | **49** | 42 | 38 | 38 | 44 | 108 | 3 | 480 | 136 | 79 | 175 | 11 | 46 | 36 | 10 | 6 | 86 | 76 | .531 |
| 2012 | Giants | NL | 162 | 112 | .75 | 220 | 32 | 55 | 22 | 50 | **31** | 136 | **9** | 526 | 157 | 87 | **176** | 15 | 42 | 30 | 12 | 5 | 94 | 68 | .580 |
| 2013 | Giants | NL | 162 | 109 | .70 | 263 | 19 | 45 | 33 | **52** | 23 | **143** | **4** | 524 | 93 | 78 | 164 | 7 | **64** | **46** | 18 | 6 | 76 | 86 | .469 |
| 162-Game Average | | | | 121 | .62 | 270 | 39 | 39 | 38 | 43 | 21 | 97 | 6 | 453 | 145 | 76 | 124 | 21 | 50 | 32 | 18 | 10 | 81 | 81 | .500 |

## Daren Brown

| | | | | LINEUPS | | SUBSTITUTION | | | PITCHER USAGE | | | | | | TACTICS | | | | INTENTIONAL BB | | | | RESULTS | | |
|---|---|---|---|---|---|---|---|---|---|---|---|---|---|---|---|---|---|---|---|---|---|---|---|---|---|
| Year | Team | Lg | G | LUp | PL% | PH | PR | DS | Quick | Slow | LO | RCD | LS | Rel | SBA | SacA | RM | PO | # | Good | NG | Bomb | W | L | Pct |
| 2010 | Mariners | AL | 50 | 39 | .60 | 9 | 12 | 2 | 15 | 8 | 6 | 14 | 2 | 104 | 52 | 19 | 71 | 9 | 8 | 5 | 3 | 2 | 19 | 31 | .380 |
| 162-Game Average | | | | 126 | .60 | 29 | 39 | 6 | 49 | 26 | 19 | 45 | 6 | 337 | 168 | 62 | 230 | 29 | 26 | 16 | 10 | 6 | 62 | 100 | .383 |

## Terry Collins

| | | | | LINEUPS | | SUBSTITUTION | | | PITCHER USAGE | | | | | | TACTICS | | | | INTENTIONAL BB | | | | RESULTS | | |
|---|---|---|---|---|---|---|---|---|---|---|---|---|---|---|---|---|---|---|---|---|---|---|---|---|---|
| Year | Team | Lg | G | LUp | PL% | PH | PR | DS | Quick | Slow | LO | RCD | LS | Rel | SBA | SacA | RM | PO | # | Good | NG | Bomb | W | L | Pct |
| 1994 | Astros | NL | 115 | 74 | .54 | 185 | 20 | 13 | 6 | 6 | 0 | 37 | 4 | 268 | 168 | 90 | | 37 | 28 | 17 | 11 | 5 | 66 | 49 | .574 |
| 1995 | Astros | NL | 144 | 106 | .49 | 302 | 38 | 11 | 15 | 7 | 8 | 100 | 8 | 394 | 236 | 97 | | 44 | 39 | 27 | 12 | 8 | 76 | 68 | .528 |
| 1996 | Astros | NL | 162 | 111 | .41 | 257 | 30 | 38 | 13 | 12 | 9 | 70 | 10 | 371 | 243 | 94 | | 35 | 42 | 30 | 12 | 6 | 82 | 80 | .506 |
| 1997 | Angels | AL | 162 | 117 | .70 | 86 | 34 | 22 | 10 | 16 | 15 | 67 | 8 | 400 | 198 | 55 | | 60 | 25 | 13 | 12 | 4 | 84 | 78 | .519 |
| 1998 | Angels | AL | 162 | 119 | .57 | 100 | 64 | 33 | 15 | 11 | 28 | 86 | 11 | 415 | 138 | 69 | | 38 | 16 | 6 | 10 | 4 | 85 | 77 | .525 |
| 1999 | Angels | AL | 133 | 113 | .56 | 93 | 26 | 16 | 10 | 16 | 10 | 68 | 2 | 315 | 93 | 39 | | 7 | 10 | 1 | 9 | 3 | 51 | 82 | .383 |
| 2011 | Mets | NL | 162 | 121 | .68 | **312** | 18 | 28 | 32 | 44 | 23 | 126 | 5 | 514 | 165 | 88 | 151 | 9 | 48 | 35 | 13 | 9 | 77 | 85 | .475 |
| 2012 | Mets | NL | 162 | **141** | .69 | **329** | 16 | 38 | 39 | 36 | 19 | 113 | 0 | 505 | 117 | 75 | 149 | 8 | 29 | 18 | 11 | 3 | 74 | 88 | .457 |
| 2013 | Mets | NL | 162 | 132 | .61 | 266 | 12 | 33 | 33 | 42 | 15 | 131 | **4** | **535** | 149 | 67 | 128 | 3 | 38 | 30 | 8 | 3 | 74 | 88 | .457 |
| 162-Game Average | | | | 123 | .59 | 229 | 31 | 28 | 21 | 23 | 15 | 95 | 6 | 441 | 179 | 80 | 143 | 29 | 33 | 21 | 12 | 5 | 79 | 83 | .488 |

## Don Cooper

| | | | | LINEUPS | | SUBSTITUTION | | | PITCHER USAGE | | | | | | TACTICS | | | | INTENTIONAL BB | | | | RESULTS | | |
|---|---|---|---|---|---|---|---|---|---|---|---|---|---|---|---|---|---|---|---|---|---|---|---|---|---|
| Year | Team | Lg | G | LUp | PL% | PH | PR | DS | Quick | Slow | LO | RCD | LS | Rel | SBA | SacA | RM | PO | # | Good | NG | Bomb | W | L | Pct |
| 2011 | White Sox | AL | 2 | 2 | .39 | 0 | 1 | 0 | 1 | 0 | 0 | 2 | 1 | 6 | 1 | 1 | 1 | 0 | 1 | 0 | 1 | 1 | 1 | 1 | .500 |
| 162-Game Average | | | | 162 | .39 | 0 | 81 | 0 | 81 | 0 | 0 | 162 | 81 | 486 | 81 | 81 | 81 | 0 | 81 | 0 | 81 | 81 | 81 | 81 | .500 |

## Bobby Cox

| | | | | LINEUPS | | SUBSTITUTION | | | PITCHER USAGE | | | | | | TACTICS | | | | INTENTIONAL BB | | | | RESULTS | | |
|---|---|---|---|---|---|---|---|---|---|---|---|---|---|---|---|---|---|---|---|---|---|---|---|---|---|
| Year | Team | Lg | G | LUp | PL% | PH | PR | DS | Quick | Slow | LO | RCD | LS | Rel | SBA | SacA | RM | PO | # | Good | NG | Bomb | W | L | Pct |
| 1994 | Braves | NL | 114 | 64 | .60 | 163 | 30 | 25 | 22 | 31 | 5 | 60 | 5 | 244 | 79 | 83 | | 44 | 52 | 33 | 19 | 9 | 68 | 46 | .596 |
| 1995 | Braves | NL | 144 | 59 | .56 | 224 | 48 | 40 | 41 | 34 | 13 | 80 | 6 | 339 | 116 | 77 | | 41 | 46 | 31 | 15 | 4 | 90 | 54 | .625 |
| 1996 | Braves | NL | 162 | 89 | .62 | 254 | 32 | 27 | 48 | 43 | 19 | 110 | 9 | 408 | 126 | 90 | | 34 | 64 | 38 | 26 | 14 | 96 | 66 | .593 |
| 1997 | Braves | NL | 162 | 87 | .64 | 276 | 58 | 29 | 40 | 37 | 23 | 90 | 4 | 374 | 166 | 112 | | 13 | 56 | 42 | 14 | 10 | 101 | 61 | .623 |
| 1998 | Braves | NL | 162 | 80 | .64 | 245 | 28 | 25 | 44 | 33 | 14 | 70 | 1 | 354 | 141 | 97 | | 40 | 37 | 22 | 15 | 8 | 106 | 56 | .654 |
| 1999 | Braves | NL | 162 | 76 | .58 | 272 | 51 | 34 | 44 | 39 | 13 | 99 | 6 | 394 | 214 | 89 | | 54 | 55 | 35 | 20 | 11 | 103 | 59 | .636 |
| 2000 | Braves | NL | 162 | 103 | .59 | 252 | 72 | 11 | 52 | 41 | 6 | 81 | 13 | 376 | 204 | 109 | | 59 | 52 | 35 | 17 | 5 | 95 | 67 | .586 |
| 2001 | Braves | NL | 162 | 113 | .57 | 278 | 50 | 23 | 49 | 40 | 4 | 93 | 8 | 412 | 131 | 84 | | 90 | 77 | 49 | 28 | 13 | 88 | 74 | .543 |
| 2002 | Braves | NL | 161 | 105 | .48 | 282 | 33 | 44 | 60 | 30 | 20 | 113 | 9 | 469 | 115 | 89 | 47 | 51 | 63 | 41 | 22 | 12 | **101** | 59 | .631 |
| 2003 | Braves | NL | 162 | 69 | .52 | 262 | 49 | 45 | 40 | 45 | 23 | 113 | 10 | 489 | 90 | 85 | 23 | 49 | 69 | **51** | 18 | 11 | **101** | 61 | .623 |
| 2004 | Braves | NL | 162 | 105 | .70 | 243 | **57** | 28 | **50** | 34 | 25 | 128 | **16** | 483 | 118 | 105 | 87 | 25 | 50 | 30 | 20 | 14 | 96 | 66 | .593 |
| 2005 | Braves | NL | 162 | 110 | .69 | 247 | **54** | 35 | 46 | 27 | 20 | 125 | 7 | 484 | 124 | 104 | 93 | 11 | 52 | 34 | 18 | 11 | 90 | 72 | .556 |
| 2006 | Braves | NL | 162 | 85 | .58 | 299 | 24 | 35 | 44 | 38 | 24 | 144 | 3 | 522 | 87 | 99 | 58 | 24 | 69 | 48 | 21 | 12 | 79 | 83 | .488 |
| 2007 | Braves | NL | 162 | 86 | .68 | 290 | 33 | 21 | 60 | 24 | 10 | 143 | 1 | 528 | 94 | 77 | 68 | 28 | **89** | **58** | **31** | **16** | 84 | 78 | .519 |
| 2008 | Braves | NL | 162 | 117 | .67 | **294** | 31 | 17 | 59 | 34 | 6 | **134** | 6 | **545** | 85 | 90 | 77 | 23 | **80** | 45 | **35** | **20** | 72 | 90 | .444 |
| 2009 | Braves | NL | 162 | 112 | .62 | 252 | **37** | 32 | 48 | 34 | 19 | **142** | 1 | 488 | 84 | **125** | 47 | 21 | 59 | 35 | 24 | 14 | 86 | 76 | .531 |
| 2010 | Braves | NL | 162 | 109 | .65 | 263 | **51** | 50 | 49 | 31 | 9 | 140 | 1 | 490 | 92 | 89 | 121 | **48** | 64 | 36 | **28** | **14** | 91 | 71 | .562 |
| 162-Game Average | | | | 95 | .61 | 265 | 45 | 31 | 48 | 36 | 15 | 112 | 6 | 446 | 125 | 97 | 69 | 40 | 62 | 40 | 22 | 12 | 93 | 69 | .574 |

# Tony DeFrancesco

| | | | | LINEUPS | | SUBSTITUTION | | | PITCHER USAGE | | | | | | TACTICS | | | | INTENTIONAL BB | | | | RESULTS | | |
|---|---|---|---|---|---|---|---|---|---|---|---|---|---|---|---|---|---|---|---|---|---|---|---|---|---|
| Year | Team | Lg | G | LUp | PL% | PH | PR | DS | Quick | Slow | LO | RCD | LS | Rel | SBA | SacA | RM | PO | # | Good | NG | Bomb | W | L | Pct |
| 2012 | Astros | NL | 41 | 41 | .64 | 82 | 10 | 12 | 21 | 7 | 2 | 24 | 5 | 150 | 34 | 16 | 45 | 14 | 15 | 9 | 6 | 4 | 16 | 25 | .390 |
| 162-Game Average | | | | 162 | .64 | 324 | 40 | 47 | 83 | 28 | 8 | 95 | 20 | 593 | 134 | 63 | 178 | 55 | 59 | 36 | 24 | 16 | 63 | 99 | .389 |

# John Farrell

| | | | | LINEUPS | | SUBSTITUTION | | | PITCHER USAGE | | | | | | TACTICS | | | | INTENTIONAL BB | | | | RESULTS | | |
|---|---|---|---|---|---|---|---|---|---|---|---|---|---|---|---|---|---|---|---|---|---|---|---|---|---|
| Year | Team | Lg | G | LUp | PL% | PH | PR | DS | Quick | Slow | LO | RCD | LS | Rel | SBA | SacA | RM | PO | # | Good | NG | Bomb | W | L | Pct |
| 2011 | Blue Jays | AL | 162 | 131 | .43 | 64 | **48** | 22 | 40 | 41 | 26 | 62 | 3 | 474 | 183 | 40 | 181 | 22 | 28 | 17 | 11 | 5 | 81 | 81 | .500 |
| 2012 | Blue Jays | AL | 162 | 131 | .50 | 94 | 30 | 16 | 49 | 44 | 7 | 84 | 3 | 495 | 164 | 46 | 211 | 15 | 20 | 11 | 9 | 7 | 73 | 89 | .451 |
| 2013 | Red Sox | AL | 162 | 126 | .68 | 93 | 41 | 20 | 28 | 46 | 34 | 71 | 4 | 450 | 142 | 32 | 147 | 5 | 10 | 5 | 5 | 3 | **97** | 65 | .599 |
| 162-Game Average | | | | 129 | .54 | 84 | 40 | 19 | 39 | 44 | 22 | 72 | 3 | 473 | 163 | 39 | 180 | 14 | 19 | 11 | 8 | 5 | 84 | 78 | .519 |

# Terry Francona

| | | | | LINEUPS | | SUBSTITUTION | | | PITCHER USAGE | | | | | | TACTICS | | | | INTENTIONAL BB | | | | RESULTS | | |
|---|---|---|---|---|---|---|---|---|---|---|---|---|---|---|---|---|---|---|---|---|---|---|---|---|---|
| Year | Team | Lg | G | LUp | PL% | PH | PR | DS | Quick | Slow | LO | RCD | LS | Rel | SBA | SacA | RM | PO | # | Good | NG | Bomb | W | L | Pct |
| 1997 | Phillies | NL | 162 | 98 | .66 | 288 | 19 | 28 | 28 | 54 | 22 | 102 | 9 | 409 | 148 | 91 | | 30 | 42 | 23 | 19 | 9 | 68 | 94 | .420 |
| 1998 | Phillies | NL | 162 | 84 | .53 | 256 | 20 | 19 | 34 | 57 | 20 | 88 | 7 | 385 | 142 | 85 | | 16 | 27 | 10 | 17 | 8 | 75 | 87 | .463 |
| 1999 | Phillies | NL | 162 | 85 | .51 | 239 | 13 | 31 | 29 | 41 | 16 | 111 | 7 | 441 | 160 | 81 | | 27 | 24 | 14 | 10 | 6 | 77 | 85 | .475 |
| 2000 | Phillies | NL | 162 | 108 | .53 | 278 | 17 | 14 | 38 | 43 | 25 | 102 | 5 | 414 | 132 | 89 | | 16 | 32 | 22 | 10 | 7 | 65 | 97 | .401 |
| 2004 | Red Sox | AL | 162 | 141 | .65 | 116 | 65 | **58** | 41 | 48 | 32 | 105 | 8 | 437 | 98 | 18 | 91 | 28 | 28 | 22 | 6 | 4 | 98 | 64 | .605 |
| 2005 | Red Sox | AL | 162 | 104 | .67 | 110 | 46 | 37 | 25 | 55 | 30 | 99 | 3 | 442 | 57 | 21 | 79 | 11 | 28 | 18 | 10 | 5 | 95 | 67 | .586 |
| 2006 | Red Sox | AL | 162 | 116 | .59 | 93 | **54** | 49 | 36 | 44 | 13 | 94 | 9 | 454 | 74 | 33 | 98 | 16 | 25 | 11 | 14 | 7 | 86 | 76 | .531 |
| 2007 | Red Sox | AL | 162 | 109 | .60 | 84 | 34 | 23 | 41 | 35 | 32 | 89 | 4 | 451 | 120 | 45 | 90 | 14 | 20 | 14 | 6 | 4 | **96** | 66 | .593 |
| 2008 | Red Sox | AL | 162 | 131 | .59 | 62 | 40 | 40 | 50 | 30 | 20 | 90 | **11** | 466 | 155 | 40 | 87 | 8 | 17 | 10 | 7 | 4 | 95 | 67 | .586 |
| 2009 | Red Sox | AL | 162 | 113 | .58 | 85 | 47 | 28 | 36 | 50 | 30 | 68 | 6 | 463 | 165 | 29 | 68 | 9 | 24 | 15 | 9 | 6 | 95 | 67 | .586 |
| 2010 | Red Sox | AL | 162 | **143** | .62 | 125 | 48 | 34 | 32 | **63** | **49** | 84 | 3 | 443 | 85 | 36 | 125 | 26 | 30 | 17 | 13 | 4 | 89 | 73 | .549 |
| 2011 | Red Sox | AL | 162 | 123 | .67 | 89 | 44 | 11 | **52** | 46 | 27 | 89 | 4 | 444 | 144 | 29 | 163 | 34 | 11 | 6 | 5 | 2 | 90 | 72 | .556 |
| 2013 | Indians | AL | 162 | 121 | .75 | 78 | 45 | 24 | 47 | 34 | 18 | 122 | 2 | **540** | 153 | 41 | 158 | 5 | 26 | 15 | 11 | 6 | 92 | 70 | .568 |
| 162-Game Average | | | | 114 | .61 | 146 | 38 | 30 | 38 | 46 | 26 | 96 | 6 | 445 | 126 | 49 | 107 | 18 | 26 | 15 | 11 | 6 | 86 | 76 | .531 |

# Ron Gardenhire

| | | | | LINEUPS | | SUBSTITUTION | | | PITCHER USAGE | | | | | | TACTICS | | | | INTENTIONAL BB | | | | RESULTS | | |
|---|---|---|---|---|---|---|---|---|---|---|---|---|---|---|---|---|---|---|---|---|---|---|---|---|---|
| Year | Team | Lg | G | LUp | PL% | PH | PR | DS | Quick | Slow | LO | RCD | LS | Rel | SBA | SacA | RM | PO | # | Good | NG | Bomb | W | L | Pct |
| 2002 | Twins | AL | 161 | 111 | .69 | 141 | 36 | 42 | 54 | 25 | 10 | 84 | 1 | 435 | 141 | 48 | 44 | 11 | 24 | 16 | 8 | 4 | 94 | 67 | .584 |
| 2003 | Twins | AL | 162 | 126 | .63 | 144 | 50 | 26 | 49 | 33 | 13 | 85 | 2 | 399 | 138 | 59 | 37 | 14 | 35 | 16 | 19 | 6 | 90 | 72 | .556 |
| 2004 | Twins | AL | 162 | 131 | .59 | 129 | 45 | 29 | **56** | 21 | 20 | 106 | 4 | 435 | 162 | 66 | 121 | 18 | 27 | 15 | 12 | 7 | 92 | 70 | .568 |
| 2005 | Twins | AL | 162 | **135** | .58 | 104 | 45 | 26 | 50 | 21 | 5 | 87 | 1 | 396 | 146 | 59 | 138 | 16 | 38 | **28** | 10 | 3 | 83 | 79 | .512 |
| 2006 | Twins | AL | 162 | 97 | .62 | 93 | 36 | 21 | **60** | 31 | 3 | 82 | 5 | 421 | 143 | 48 | 130 | 11 | 25 | 14 | 11 | 4 | 96 | 66 | .593 |
| 2007 | Twins | AL | 162 | 139 | .63 | 104 | 42 | 25 | 45 | 30 | 8 | 99 | 4 | 438 | 142 | 45 | 148 | 11 | 33 | 14 | 19 | 9 | 79 | 83 | .488 |
| 2008 | Twins | AL | 163 | 103 | .64 | 109 | 26 | 12 | 47 | 29 | 5 | **115** | 3 | 485 | 144 | **73** | 143 | 17 | 38 | 25 | 13 | 8 | 88 | 75 | .540 |
| 2009 | Twins | AL | 163 | 129 | .63 | 83 | 54 | 34 | 43 | 25 | 12 | 115 | 3 | 480 | 117 | **62** | 100 | 21 | 20 | 9 | 11 | 6 | 87 | 76 | .534 |
| 2010 | Twins | AL | 162 | 112 | .62 | 86 | **55** | 30 | **57** | 28 | 5 | 106 | 1 | 465 | 96 | 47 | 140 | 14 | 19 | 12 | 7 | 4 | 94 | 68 | .580 |
| 2011 | Twins | AL | 162 | 150 | .58 | 93 | **48** | 21 | 34 | 44 | 17 | 82 | 1 | 457 | 131 | 44 | 170 | 5 | 37 | 21 | 16 | 9 | 63 | **99** | .389 |
| 2012 | Twins | AL | 162 | 121 | .62 | 64 | 45 | 24 | 42 | 31 | 4 | 82 | 1 | 499 | 172 | 49 | 207 | 10 | 43 | 27 | 16 | 6 | 66 | **96** | .407 |
| 2013 | Twins | AL | 162 | 139 | .66 | 103 | 42 | 28 | 41 | 43 | 6 | 78 | 1 | 511 | 85 | 37 | 137 | 14 | 31 | 13 | 18 | 7 | 66 | 96 | .407 |
| 162-Game Average | | | | 124 | .62 | 104 | 44 | 26 | 48 | 30 | 9 | 93 | 2 | 452 | 135 | 53 | 126 | 13 | 31 | 17 | 13 | 6 | 83 | 79 | .512 |

# Cito Gaston

| | | | | LINEUPS | | SUBSTITUTION | | | PITCHER USAGE | | | | | | TACTICS | | | | INTENTIONAL BB | | | | RESULTS | | |
|---|---|---|---|---|---|---|---|---|---|---|---|---|---|---|---|---|---|---|---|---|---|---|---|---|---|
| Year | Team | Lg | G | LUp | PL% | PH | PR | DS | Quick | Slow | LO | RCD | LS | Rel | SBA | SacA | RM | PO | # | Good | NG | Bomb | W | L | Pct |
| 1994 | Blue Jays | AL | 115 | 59 | .55 | 41 | 16 | 21 | 7 | 14 | 2 | 23 | 5 | 221 | 105 | 44 | | 48 | 23 | 15 | 8 | 6 | 55 | 60 | .478 |
| 1995 | Blue Jays | AL | 144 | 82 | .65 | 85 | 24 | 7 | 15 | 27 | 40 | 29 | 10 | 265 | 91 | 47 | | 57 | 42 | 24 | 18 | 10 | 56 | 88 | .389 |
| 1996 | Blue Jays | AL | 162 | 87 | .70 | 126 | 23 | 11 | 12 | 27 | 23 | 41 | 4 | 303 | 154 | 63 | | 34 | 37 | 23 | 14 | 9 | 74 | 88 | .457 |
| 1997 | Blue Jays | AL | 157 | 90 | .59 | 71 | 19 | 6 | 13 | 22 | 36 | 74 | 6 | 322 | 177 | 50 | | 30 | 29 | 20 | 9 | 2 | 72 | 85 | .459 |
| 2008 | Blue Jays | AL | 88 | 65 | .59 | 36 | 18 | 30 | 18 | 19 | 25 | 40 | 0 | 216 | 37 | 41 | 37 | 11 | 16 | 8 | 8 | 6 | 51 | 37 | .580 |
| 2009 | Blue Jays | AL | 162 | 105 | .49 | 48 | 36 | 18 | 36 | 47 | 25 | 83 | 3 | 445 | 96 | 32 | 64 | 25 | 26 | 15 | 11 | 6 | 75 | 87 | .463 |
| 2010 | Blue Jays | AL | 162 | 103 | .45 | 40 | 40 | 13 | 51 | 33 | 12 | 77 | 4 | 455 | 78 | 22 | 88 | 23 | 35 | 19 | 16 | 6 | 85 | 77 | .525 |
| 162-Game Average | | | | 97 | .57 | 73 | 29 | 17 | 25 | 31 | 27 | 60 | 5 | 364 | 121 | 49 | 74 | 37 | 34 | 20 | 14 | 7 | 77 | 85 | .475 |

## Bob Geren

| | | | | LINEUPS | | SUBSTITUTION | | | PITCHER USAGE | | | | | | TACTICS | | | | INTENTIONAL BB | | | | RESULTS | | |
|---|---|---|---|---|---|---|---|---|---|---|---|---|---|---|---|---|---|---|---|---|---|---|---|---|---|
| Year | Team | Lg | G | LUp | PL% | PH | PR | DS | Quick | Slow | LO | RCD | LS | Rel | SBA | SacA | RM | PO | # | Good | NG | Bomb | W | L | Pct |
| 2007 | Athletics | AL | 162 | 140 | .57 | 64 | 31 | 24 | 39 | 43 | 14 | 112 | 9 | 446 | 72 | 31 | 91 | 22 | **60** | **38** | 22 | 10 | 76 | 86 | .469 |
| 2008 | Athletics | AL | 161 | 133 | .59 | 91 | **57** | 37 | 49 | 32 | 5 | 87 | 8 | 441 | 109 | 44 | 62 | 18 | 45 | 25 | 20 | 10 | 75 | 86 | .466 |
| 2009 | Athletics | AL | 162 | 129 | .59 | 77 | 27 | 40 | **54** | 40 | 5 | 108 | 11 | 488 | 181 | 37 | 71 | 5 | 30 | 15 | 15 | 7 | 75 | 87 | .463 |
| 2010 | Athletics | AL | 162 | 126 | .63 | 108 | 28 | 26 | **57** | 30 | 19 | 81 | **8** | 423 | 194 | 58 | 138 | 11 | 29 | 16 | 13 | 3 | 81 | 81 | .500 |
| 2011 | Athletics | AL | 63 | 47 | .62 | 42 | 9 | 3 | 25 | 11 | 7 | 50 | 2 | 177 | 57 | 18 | 54 | 9 | 15 | 7 | 8 | 4 | 27 | 36 | .429 |
| 162-Game Average | | | | 131 | .60 | 87 | 35 | 30 | 51 | 36 | 11 | 100 | 9 | 451 | 140 | 43 | 95 | 15 | 41 | 23 | 18 | 8 | 76 | 86 | .469 |

## John Gibbons

| | | | | LINEUPS | | SUBSTITUTION | | | PITCHER USAGE | | | | | | TACTICS | | | | INTENTIONAL BB | | | | RESULTS | | |
|---|---|---|---|---|---|---|---|---|---|---|---|---|---|---|---|---|---|---|---|---|---|---|---|---|---|
| Year | Team | Lg | G | LUp | PL% | PH | PR | DS | Quick | Slow | LO | RCD | LS | Rel | SBA | SacA | RM | PO | # | Good | NG | Bomb | W | L | Pct |
| 2004 | Blue Jays | AL | 50 | 36 | .68 | 42 | 3 | 2 | 16 | 8 | 7 | 22 | 1 | 130 | 34 | 2 | 47 | 21 | 11 | 5 | 6 | 3 | 20 | 30 | .400 |
| 2005 | Blue Jays | AL | 162 | 124 | .66 | **148** | 11 | 37 | **55** | 18 | 9 | 77 | 12 | 432 | 107 | 28 | 128 | 45 | 29 | 13 | 16 | 9 | 80 | 82 | .494 |
| 2006 | Blue Jays | AL | 162 | 120 | .53 | 112 | 32 | 40 | 59 | 33 | 17 | 94 | **16** | 482 | 98 | 20 | 127 | 40 | 56 | 32 | **24** | 12 | 87 | 75 | .537 |
| 2007 | Blue Jays | AL | 162 | 131 | .46 | **139** | **48** | 33 | 45 | 37 | 31 | 75 | 9 | 420 | 79 | 35 | 99 | 37 | 34 | 17 | 17 | 6 | 83 | 79 | .512 |
| 2008 | Blue Jays | AL | 74 | 60 | .48 | 53 | 15 | 18 | 12 | 20 | 12 | 43 | 0 | 205 | 70 | 23 | 39 | 10 | 26 | 16 | 10 | 6 | 35 | 39 | .473 |
| 2013 | Blue Jays | AL | 162 | 136 | .63 | 124 | 31 | 24 | **55** | 44 | 14 | 69 | 2 | 487 | 153 | 41 | 160 | 4 | 33 | 17 | 16 | 6 | 74 | 88 | .457 |
| 162-Game Average | | | | 127 | .57 | 130 | 29 | 32 | 51 | 34 | 19 | 80 | 8 | 452 | 114 | 31 | 126 | 33 | 40 | 21 | 19 | 9 | 80 | 82 | .494 |

## Kirk Gibson

| | | | | LINEUPS | | SUBSTITUTION | | | PITCHER USAGE | | | | | | TACTICS | | | | INTENTIONAL BB | | | | RESULTS | | |
|---|---|---|---|---|---|---|---|---|---|---|---|---|---|---|---|---|---|---|---|---|---|---|---|---|---|
| Year | Team | Lg | G | LUp | PL% | PH | PR | DS | Quick | Slow | LO | RCD | LS | Rel | SBA | SacA | RM | PO | # | Good | NG | Bomb | W | L | Pct |
| 2010 | Diamondbacks | NL | 83 | 57 | .64 | 154 | 7 | 11 | 25 | 21 | 8 | 43 | 1 | 247 | 69 | 28 | 62 | 19 | 19 | 13 | 6 | 2 | 34 | 49 | .410 |
| 2011 | Diamondbacks | NL | 162 | 118 | .57 | 253 | 9 | 13 | 33 | 51 | 15 | 116 | 2 | 463 | 188 | 74 | 143 | 12 | 16 | 10 | 6 | 3 | 94 | 68 | .580 |
| 2012 | Diamondbacks | NL | 162 | 140 | .56 | 231 | 11 | 9 | 35 | 50 | 16 | 104 | 4 | 461 | 144 | 77 | 120 | 8 | 18 | 11 | 7 | 1 | 81 | 81 | .500 |
| 2013 | Diamondbacks | NL | 162 | 138 | .59 | 285 | 22 | 15 | 31 | 44 | 9 | 121 | 0 | 527 | 103 | 67 | 108 | 3 | 42 | 31 | 11 | 5 | 81 | 81 | .500 |
| 162-Game Average | | | | 129 | .58 | 263 | 14 | 14 | 35 | 47 | 14 | 109 | 2 | 483 | 143 | 70 | 123 | 12 | 27 | 19 | 9 | 3 | 83 | 79 | .512 |

## Joe Girardi

| | | | | LINEUPS | | SUBSTITUTION | | | PITCHER USAGE | | | | | | TACTICS | | | | INTENTIONAL BB | | | | RESULTS | | |
|---|---|---|---|---|---|---|---|---|---|---|---|---|---|---|---|---|---|---|---|---|---|---|---|---|---|
| Year | Team | Lg | G | LUp | PL% | PH | PR | DS | Quick | Slow | LO | RCD | LS | Rel | SBA | SacA | RM | PO | # | Good | NG | Bomb | W | L | Pct |
| 2006 | Marlins | NL | 162 | 117 | .50 | 250 | 44 | **66** | 46 | 40 | 28 | 76 | 3 | 438 | 168 | 97 | 108 | 42 | 58 | 37 | 21 | 7 | 78 | 84 | .481 |
| 2008 | Yankees | AL | 162 | 114 | .63 | 97 | 37 | 42 | **60** | 37 | 12 | 88 | 10 | 475 | 157 | 38 | **173** | **36** | 37 | 22 | 15 | 8 | 89 | 73 | .549 |
| 2009 | Yankees | AL | 162 | 106 | .73 | 97 | **61** | 42 | 36 | 45 | 27 | 88 | **13** | 461 | 139 | 44 | 83 | 33 | 28 | 14 | 14 | 9 | **103** | 59 | .636 |
| 2010 | Yankees | AL | 162 | 114 | .72 | 117 | 44 | 31 | 43 | 39 | 33 | 76 | 3 | 430 | 133 | 47 | 152 | 20 | 37 | 26 | 11 | 6 | 95 | 67 | .586 |
| 2011 | Yankees | AL | 162 | 94 | .69 | 72 | 41 | 53 | 51 | 36 | 21 | 88 | 2 | 465 | 193 | 50 | 151 | 26 | 43 | 30 | 13 | 4 | **97** | 65 | .599 |
| 2012 | Yankees | AL | 162 | 107 | .70 | 149 | 33 | 48 | 37 | 53 | 21 | 115 | 7 | 485 | 120 | 47 | 145 | 10 | 32 | 17 | 15 | 6 | **95** | 67 | .586 |
| 2013 | Yankees | AL | 162 | 141 | .59 | 119 | 15 | 29 | 42 | 50 | 23 | 82 | 4 | 428 | 146 | 49 | 131 | 4 | 34 | 20 | 14 | 6 | 85 | 77 | .525 |
| 162-Game Average | | | | 113 | .65 | 129 | 39 | 44 | 45 | 43 | 24 | 88 | 6 | 455 | 151 | 53 | 135 | 24 | 38 | 24 | 15 | 7 | 92 | 70 | .568 |

## Fredi Gonzalez

| | | | | LINEUPS | | SUBSTITUTION | | | PITCHER USAGE | | | | | | TACTICS | | | | INTENTIONAL BB | | | | RESULTS | | |
|---|---|---|---|---|---|---|---|---|---|---|---|---|---|---|---|---|---|---|---|---|---|---|---|---|---|
| Year | Team | Lg | G | LUp | PL% | PH | PR | DS | Quick | Slow | LO | RCD | LS | Rel | SBA | SacA | RM | PO | # | Good | NG | Bomb | W | L | Pct |
| 2007 | Marlins | NL | 162 | 96 | .50 | 284 | 29 | 34 | 33 | **56** | 20 | 138 | 5 | 560 | 139 | 91 | 79 | 22 | 60 | 36 | 24 | **16** | 71 | 91 | .438 |
| 2008 | Marlins | NL | 161 | 106 | .51 | 255 | 38 | 49 | 38 | 39 | 8 | 120 | 3 | 511 | 104 | 61 | 75 | 17 | 66 | 42 | 24 | 14 | 84 | 77 | .522 |
| 2009 | Marlins | NL | 162 | 97 | .58 | 281 | 28 | 49 | 48 | 26 | 12 | 116 | 0 | **530** | 110 | 86 | 88 | 20 | 60 | 38 | 22 | 15 | 87 | 75 | .537 |
| 2010 | Marlins | NL | 70 | 31 | .41 | 104 | 12 | 16 | 14 | 13 | 11 | 35 | 1 | 193 | 56 | 33 | 64 | 10 | 18 | 11 | 7 | 5 | 34 | 36 | .486 |
| 2011 | Braves | NL | 162 | 120 | .60 | 260 | 27 | 29 | 53 | 36 | 21 | **144** | 0 | 510 | 121 | 95 | 139 | 19 | **73** | **49** | 24 | 13 | 89 | 73 | .549 |
| 2012 | Braves | NL | 162 | 110 | .61 | 268 | 18 | 27 | 50 | 34 | 9 | 115 | 4 | 460 | 133 | 67 | 116 | 20 | 40 | 28 | 12 | 11 | 94 | 68 | .580 |
| 2013 | Braves | NL | 162 | 115 | .50 | 214 | **40** | 51 | 50 | 42 | 8 | 124 | 2 | 466 | 95 | 79 | 94 | 11 | 35 | 26 | 9 | 4 | 96 | 66 | .593 |
| 162-Game Average | | | | 105 | .54 | 259 | 30 | 40 | 45 | 38 | 14 | 123 | 2 | 503 | 118 | 80 | 102 | 19 | 55 | 36 | 19 | 12 | 86 | 76 | .531 |

## Ozzie Guillen

| | | | | LINEUPS | | SUBSTITUTION | | | PITCHER USAGE | | | | | | TACTICS | | | | INTENTIONAL BB | | | | RESULTS | | |
|---|---|---|---|---|---|---|---|---|---|---|---|---|---|---|---|---|---|---|---|---|---|---|---|---|---|
| Year | Team | Lg | G | LUp | PL% | PH | PR | DS | Quick | Slow | LO | RCD | LS | Rel | SBA | SacA | RM | PO | # | Good | NG | Bomb | W | L | Pct |
| 2004 | White Sox | AL | 162 | 134 | .58 | **132** | 35 | 15 | 28 | **65** | **48** | 86 | 8 | 399 | 129 | **84** | 97 | 17 | 36 | 15 | **21** | 8 | 83 | 79 | .512 |
| 2005 | White Sox | AL | 162 | 112 | .51 | 100 | 32 | 21 | 31 | **56** | **35** | **114** | 5 | 412 | 204 | **68** | 148 | 15 | **42** | 27 | 15 | 6 | **99** | 63 | .611 |
| 2006 | White Sox | AL | 162 | 87 | .60 | **135** | 42 | 38 | 28 | **68** | **35** | 83 | 7 | 398 | 141 | 61 | 85 | 27 | **59** | **39** | 20 | 9 | 90 | 72 | .556 |
| 2007 | White Sox | AL | 162 | 124 | .56 | 100 | 26 | 23 | 26 | 53 | **33** | **131** | 2 | 463 | 123 | 54 | 92 | 13 | 50 | 24 | **26** | **15** | 72 | 90 | .444 |
| 2008 | White Sox | AL | 163 | 100 | .52 | 75 | 49 | 37 | 42 | 48 | 14 | 100 | 3 | 463 | 101 | 44 | 98 | 8 | 42 | 29 | 13 | 6 | 89 | 74 | .546 |
| 2009 | White Sox | AL | 162 | 124 | .52 | 105 | 48 | 19 | 50 | 37 | 16 | 70 | 4 | 415 | 162 | 45 | 114 | 15 | 41 | 23 | **18** | **10** | 79 | 83 | .488 |
| 2010 | White Sox | AL | 162 | 115 | .51 | 85 | 46 | 36 | 41 | 51 | 24 | 61 | **8** | 407 | **234** | 60 | 220 | 25 | **41** | 26 | 15 | **10** | 88 | 74 | .543 |
| 2011 | White Sox | AL | 160 | 111 | .52 | 73 | 47 | 28 | 34 | 45 | 28 | 63 | **8** | 404 | 133 | 65 | 172 | 40 | **49** | **35** | 14 | 7 | 78 | 82 | .488 |
| 2012 | Marlins | NL | 162 | 116 | .60 | 234 | 23 | 29 | 24 | 39 | 27 | 126 | 2 | 483 | 190 | 89 | 137 | **23** | 61 | **38** | 23 | 13 | 69 | 93 | .426 |
| 162-Game Average | | | | 114 | .55 | 116 | 39 | 27 | 34 | 51 | 29 | 93 | 5 | 427 | 158 | 63 | 129 | 20 | 47 | 28 | 18 | 9 | 83 | 79 | .512 |

## Trey Hillman

| | | | | LINEUPS | | SUBSTITUTION | | | PITCHER USAGE | | | | | | TACTICS | | | | INTENTIONAL BB | | | | RESULTS | | |
|---|---|---|---|---|---|---|---|---|---|---|---|---|---|---|---|---|---|---|---|---|---|---|---|---|---|
| Year | Team | Lg | G | LUp | PL% | PH | PR | DS | Quick | Slow | LO | RCD | LS | Rel | SBA | SacA | RM | PO | # | Good | NG | Bomb | W | L | Pct |
| 2008 | Royals | AL | 162 | 134 | .55 | 71 | 44 | 34 | 35 | 48 | 19 | 78 | 2 | 439 | 117 | 50 | 96 | 15 | 15 | 9 | 6 | 3 | 75 | 87 | .463 |
| 2009 | Royals | AL | 162 | 141 | .63 | 90 | 34 | 38 | 41 | **54** | 34 | 72 | 7 | 426 | 117 | 51 | 110 | 27 | 28 | 13 | 15 | **10** | 65 | 97 | .401 |
| 2010 | Royals | AL | 35 | 24 | .57 | 12 | 12 | 1 | 9 | 13 | 4 | 21 | 2 | 109 | 38 | 25 | 41 | 8 | 3 | 2 | 1 | 1 | 12 | 23 | .343 |
| 162-Game Average | | | | 135 | .59 | 78 | 41 | 33 | 38 | 52 | 26 | 77 | 5 | 440 | 123 | 57 | 111 | 23 | 21 | 11 | 10 | 6 | 69 | 93 | .426 |

## A.J. Hinch

| | | | | LINEUPS | | SUBSTITUTION | | | PITCHER USAGE | | | | | | TACTICS | | | | INTENTIONAL BB | | | | RESULTS | | |
|---|---|---|---|---|---|---|---|---|---|---|---|---|---|---|---|---|---|---|---|---|---|---|---|---|---|
| Year | Team | Lg | G | LUp | PL% | PH | PR | DS | Quick | Slow | LO | RCD | LS | Rel | SBA | SacA | RM | PO | # | Good | NG | Bomb | W | L | Pct |
| 2009 | Diamondbacks | NL | 133 | 115 | .63 | 222 | 10 | 13 | 24 | 50 | 24 | 61 | 5 | 392 | 113 | 64 | 41 | 5 | 24 | 12 | 12 | 6 | 58 | 75 | .436 |
| 2010 | Diamondbacks | NL | 79 | 56 | .53 | 120 | 7 | 4 | 12 | 40 | 21 | 39 | 1 | 207 | 58 | 19 | 51 | 7 | 19 | 9 | 10 | 9 | 31 | 48 | .392 |
| 162-Game Average | | | | 131 | .59 | 261 | 13 | 13 | 28 | 69 | 34 | 76 | 5 | 458 | 131 | 63 | 70 | 9 | 33 | 16 | 17 | 11 | 68 | 94 | .420 |

## Clint Hurdle

| | | | | LINEUPS | | SUBSTITUTION | | | PITCHER USAGE | | | | | | TACTICS | | | | INTENTIONAL BB | | | | RESULTS | | |
|---|---|---|---|---|---|---|---|---|---|---|---|---|---|---|---|---|---|---|---|---|---|---|---|---|---|
| Year | Team | Lg | G | LUp | PL% | PH | PR | DS | Quick | Slow | LO | RCD | LS | Rel | SBA | SacA | RM | PO | # | Good | NG | Bomb | W | L | Pct |
| 2002 | Rockies | NL | 140 | 100 | .52 | 274 | 28 | 41 | 33 | 45 | 17 | 104 | 3 | 437 | 139 | 46 | 50 | 13 | 38 | 22 | 16 | 11 | 67 | 73 | .479 |
| 2003 | Rockies | NL | 162 | 108 | .47 | 317 | 17 | 32 | 35 | 40 | 5 | 87 | 4 | 500 | 100 | 82 | 26 | 16 | 51 | 31 | 20 | 13 | 74 | 88 | .457 |
| 2004 | Rockies | NL | 162 | 131 | .57 | 289 | 18 | 35 | 36 | **63** | 20 | 74 | 1 | 473 | 77 | **128** | 67 | 12 | **84** | **54** | **30** | 12 | 68 | 94 | .420 |
| 2005 | Rockies | NL | 162 | 135 | .60 | 273 | 21 | 40 | 42 | **60** | 17 | 89 | 2 | 459 | 97 | 114 | 119 | 22 | 54 | 28 | 26 | **15** | 67 | **95** | .414 |
| 2006 | Rockies | NL | 162 | 111 | .49 | 259 | 17 | 22 | 34 | **52** | 17 | 107 | 2 | 499 | 135 | **156** | 114 | 28 | 81 | 45 | **36** | **23** | 76 | 86 | .469 |
| 2007 | Rockies | NL | 163 | 96 | .51 | 283 | 32 | 29 | 45 | 37 | 13 | 112 | 1 | 529 | 131 | **112** | 109 | 26 | 61 | 30 | **31** | 14 | **90** | 73 | .552 |
| 2008 | Rockies | NL | 162 | 131 | .49 | 253 | 20 | 31 | 40 | 43 | 16 | 85 | 2 | 485 | **178** | **111** | 116 | **43** | 49 | 31 | 18 | 6 | 74 | 88 | .457 |
| 2009 | Rockies | NL | 46 | 42 | .60 | 73 | 8 | 10 | 11 | 14 | 3 | 31 | 0 | 135 | 45 | 26 | 34 | 3 | 11 | 8 | 3 | 1 | 18 | 28 | .391 |
| 2011 | Pirates | NL | 162 | 134 | .60 | 278 | 26 | 63 | **58** | 27 | 1 | 134 | 3 | **549** | 160 | 101 | 173 | 20 | 65 | 39 | **26** | 13 | 72 | 90 | .444 |
| 2012 | Pirates | NL | 162 | 133 | .55 | 270 | 26 | **60** | 50 | 33 | 3 | 74 | 2 | 483 | 125 | 82 | 120 | 17 | 30 | 18 | 12 | 3 | 79 | 83 | .488 |
| 2013 | Pirates | NL | 162 | 127 | .51 | **289** | 24 | **61** | **61** | 25 | 7 | 76 | 3 | 465 | 136 | 83 | **172** | 20 | 26 | 22 | 4 | 2 | 94 | 68 | .580 |
| 162-Game Average | | | | 123 | .53 | 281 | 23 | 42 | 44 | 43 | 12 | 96 | 2 | 494 | 130 | 103 | 108 | 22 | 54 | 32 | 22 | 11 | 77 | 85 | .475 |

## Brandon Hyde

| | | | | LINEUPS | | SUBSTITUTION | | | PITCHER USAGE | | | | | | TACTICS | | | | INTENTIONAL BB | | | | RESULTS | | |
|---|---|---|---|---|---|---|---|---|---|---|---|---|---|---|---|---|---|---|---|---|---|---|---|---|---|
| Year | Team | Lg | G | LUp | PL% | PH | PR | DS | Quick | Slow | LO | RCD | LS | Rel | SBA | SacA | RM | PO | # | Good | NG | Bomb | W | L | Pct |
| 2011 | Marlins | NL | 1 | 1 | .44 | 0 | 0 | 0 | 0 | 0 | 1 | 1 | 0 | 3 | 0 | 0 | 1 | 0 | 1 | 1 | 0 | 0 | 0 | 1 | .000 |

## Davey Johnson

| | | | | LINEUPS | | SUBSTITUTION | | | PITCHER USAGE | | | | | | TACTICS | | | | INTENTIONAL BB | | | | RESULTS | | |
|---|---|---|---|---|---|---|---|---|---|---|---|---|---|---|---|---|---|---|---|---|---|---|---|---|---|
| Year | Team | Lg | G | LUp | PL% | PH | PR | DS | Quick | Slow | LO | RCD | LS | Rel | SBA | SacA | RM | PO | # | Good | NG | Bomb | W | L | Pct |
| 1994 | Reds | NL | 115 | 79 | .54 | 195 | 22 | 12 | 32 | 28 | 2 | 56 | 12 | 261 | 170 | 86 | 0 | 41 | 23 | 15 | 8 | 1 | 66 | 48 | .579 |
| 1995 | Reds | NL | 144 | 105 | .55 | 257 | 18 | 31 | 56 | 18 | 1 | 60 | 16 | 329 | 258 | 88 | 0 | 10 | 32 | 16 | 16 | 10 | 85 | 59 | .590 |
| 1996 | Orioles | AL | 163 | 99 | .68 | 85 | 33 | 38 | 48 | 48 | 13 | 67 | 9 | 378 | 117 | 62 | 0 | 6 | 35 | 13 | 22 | 11 | 88 | 74 | .543 |
| 1997 | Orioles | AL | 162 | 109 | .56 | 104 | 36 | 43 | 65 | 23 | 5 | 84 | 11 | 400 | 89 | 75 | 0 | 10 | 31 | 16 | 15 | 9 | 98 | 64 | .605 |
| 1999 | Dodgers | NL | 162 | 109 | .53 | 236 | 22 | 9 | 36 | 40 | 8 | 67 | 4 | 399 | 235 | 126 | 0 | 19 | 26 | 17 | 9 | 7 | 77 | 85 | .475 |
| 2000 | Dodgers | NL | 162 | 89 | .59 | 252 | 26 | 11 | 20 | 15 | 10 | | 6 | 371 | 137 | 80 | 51 | 11 | 14 | 8 | 6 | 2 | 86 | 76 | .531 |
| 2011 | Nationals | NL | 83 | 59 | .45 | 143 | 20 | 23 | 40 | 13 | 1 | 51 | 1 | 271 | 58 | 51 | 85 | 6 | 19 | 10 | 9 | 6 | 40 | 43 | .482 |
| 2012 | Nationals | NL | 162 | 93 | .60 | 252 | 30 | 42 | 57 | 30 | 10 | 105 | 1 | 482 | 140 | 67 | 158 | 2 | 32 | 21 | 11 | 7 | **98** | 64 | .605 |
| 2013 | Nationals | NL | 162 | 108 | .54 | 233 | 23 | 33 | 46 | 39 | **27** | 99 | 0 | 440 | 116 | 91 | 148 | 1 | 17 | 8 | 9 | 3 | 86 | 76 | .531 |
| 162-Game Average | | | | 99 | .35 | 226 | 29 | 18 | 47 | 36 | 18 | 66 | 15 | 354 | 173 | 88 | 176 | 18 | 33 | 18 | 15 | 8 | 92 | 70 | .568 |

## Tony LaRussa

| | | | | LINEUPS | | SUBSTITUTION | | | PITCHER USAGE | | | | | | TACTICS | | | | INTENTIONAL BB | | | | RESULTS | | |
|---|---|---|---|---|---|---|---|---|---|---|---|---|---|---|---|---|---|---|---|---|---|---|---|---|---|
| Year | Team | Lg | G | LUp | PL% | PH | PR | DS | Quick | Slow | LO | RCD | LS | Rel | SBA | SacA | RM | PO | # | Good | NG | Bomb | W | L | Pct |
| 1994 | Athletics | AL | 114 | 97 | .62 | 89 | 28 | 14 | 43 | 21 | 5 | 60 | 4 | 308 | 130 | 31 | | 32 | 30 | 20 | 10 | 4 | 51 | 63 | .447 |
| 1995 | Athletics | AL | 144 | 120 | .54 | 113 | 38 | 24 | 33 | 38 | 19 | 46 | 7 | 358 | 158 | 42 | | 42 | 26 | 18 | 8 | 4 | 67 | 77 | .465 |
| 1996 | Cardinals | NL | 162 | 120 | .52 | 246 | 25 | 13 | 32 | 48 | 24 | 90 | 8 | 413 | 207 | 117 | | 41 | 43 | 28 | 15 | 7 | 88 | 74 | .543 |
| 1997 | Cardinals | NL | 162 | 146 | .54 | 307 | 17 | 18 | 34 | 42 | 16 | 81 | 2 | 399 | 224 | 77 | | 79 | 34 | 26 | 8 | 2 | 73 | 89 | .451 |
| 1998 | Cardinals | NL | 162 | 146 | .52 | 259 | 7 | 18 | 62 | 31 | 13 | 82 | 14 | 429 | 174 | 85 | | 34 | 38 | 25 | 13 | 8 | 83 | 79 | .512 |
| 1999 | Cardinals | NL | 161 | 138 | .47 | 264 | 32 | 28 | 50 | 41 | 13 | 96 | 14 | 454 | 182 | 103 | | 30 | 38 | 20 | 18 | 11 | 75 | 86 | .466 |
| 2000 | Cardinals | NL | 162 | 137 | .53 | 240 | 35 | 25 | 40 | 31 | 11 | 63 | 18 | 386 | 138 | 107 | | 34 | 28 | 21 | 7 | 6 | 95 | 67 | .586 |
| 2001 | Cardinals | NL | 162 | 117 | .47 | 256 | 26 | 13 | 46 | 36 | 7 | 140 | 7 | 485 | 126 | 102 | | 25 | 36 | 21 | 15 | 4 | 93 | 69 | .574 |
| 2002 | Cardinals | NL | 162 | 117 | .52 | **340** | 27 | 41 | 58 | 33 | 23 | 110 | 6 | 472 | 128 | 106 | 75 | 13 | 39 | 25 | 14 | 8 | 97 | 65 | .599 |
| 2003 | Cardinals | NL | 162 | 126 | .50 | **352** | 28 | 51 | 38 | 49 | 36 | 113 | 9 | 460 | 114 | **108** | **56** | 9 | 36 | 28 | 8 | 2 | 85 | 77 | .525 |
| 2004 | Cardinals | NL | 162 | 119 | .53 | 275 | 25 | **69** | 30 | 48 | 31 | 120 | **16** | 469 | 158 | 88 | **158** | 9 | 24 | 17 | 7 | 4 | **105** | 57 | .648 |
| 2005 | Cardinals | NL | 162 | 138 | .55 | 270 | 25 | 48 | 40 | 38 | 22 | 88 | 4 | 436 | 119 | 92 | **153** | 9 | 27 | 16 | 11 | 7 | **100** | 62 | .617 |
| 2006 | Cardinals | NL | 161 | 131 | .56 | 272 | 11 | 53 | 50 | 34 | 21 | 95 | 6 | 469 | 91 | 86 | 123 | 13 | 35 | 21 | 14 | 3 | 83 | 78 | .516 |
| 2007 | Cardinals | NL | 162 | **150** | .60 | **317** | 19 | 37 | 46 | 44 | 8 | 102 | 5 | 516 | 89 | 85 | 120 | 23 | 25 | 10 | 15 | 11 | 78 | 84 | .481 |
| 2008 | Cardinals | NL | 162 | **153** | .64 | 275 | 26 | 57 | 52 | 40 | 16 | 101 | **11** | 506 | 105 | 87 | 114 | 18 | 21 | 13 | 8 | 1 | 86 | 76 | .531 |

| | | | | LINEUPS | | SUBSTITUTION | | | PITCHER USAGE | | | | | | TACTICS | | | | INTENTIONAL BB | | | | RESULTS | | |
|---|---|---|---|---|---|---|---|---|---|---|---|---|---|---|---|---|---|---|---|---|---|---|---|---|---|
| Year | Team | Lg | G | LUp | PL% | PH | PR | DS | Quick | Slow | LO | RCD | LS | Rel | SBA | SacA | RM | PO | # | Good | NG | Bomb | W | L | Pct |
| 2009 | Cardinals | NL | 162 | 131 | .52 | **289** | 12 | 51 | 55 | 38 | 17 | 102 | **8** | 481 | 106 | 93 | 91 | 17 | 23 | 15 | 8 | 1 | 91 | 71 | .562 |
| 2010 | Cardinals | NL | 162 | **147** | .55 | **292** | 16 | 28 | 52 | 40 | 16 | 80 | 5 | 455 | 120 | 87 | 151 | 22 | 32 | 17 | 15 | 8 | 86 | 76 | .531 |
| 2011 | Cardinals | NL | 162 | 127 | .57 | 262 | 36 | **86** | 47 | 44 | 20 | 94 | **8** | 468 | 96 | 101 | 179 | 17 | 44 | 23 | 21 | **14** | 90 | 72 | .556 |
| 162-Game Average | | | | 134 | .54 | 268 | 25 | 38 | 46 | 40 | 18 | 95 | 9 | 453 | 140 | 91 | 122 | 27 | 33 | 21 | 12 | 6 | 87 | 75 | .537 |

## Jim Leyland

| | | | | LINEUPS | | SUBSTITUTION | | | PITCHER USAGE | | | | | | TACTICS | | | | INTENTIONAL BB | | | | RESULTS | | |
|---|---|---|---|---|---|---|---|---|---|---|---|---|---|---|---|---|---|---|---|---|---|---|---|---|---|
| Year | Team | Lg | G | LUp | PL% | PH | PR | DS | Quick | Slow | LO | RCD | LS | Rel | SBA | SacA | RM | PO | # | Good | NG | Bomb | W | L | Pct |
| 1994 | Pirates | NL | 114 | 94 | .56 | 170 | 16 | 13 | 12 | 9 | 1 | 48 | 4 | 285 | 78 | 48 | | 38 | 52 | 29 | 23 | 15 | 53 | 61 | .465 |
| 1995 | Pirates | NL | 144 | 124 | .56 | 282 | 8 | 4 | 13 | 12 | 11 | 71 | 4 | 391 | 139 | 69 | | 51 | 50 | 30 | 20 | 10 | 58 | 86 | .403 |
| 1996 | Pirates | NL | 162 | 117 | .53 | 299 | 18 | 14 | 27 | 8 | 11 | 60 | 11 | 422 | 175 | 101 | | 46 | 50 | 23 | 27 | 13 | 73 | 89 | .451 |
| 1997 | Marlins | NL | 162 | 105 | .59 | 258 | 36 | 31 | 21 | 12 | 18 | 65 | 2 | 404 | 173 | 91 | | 38 | 41 | 25 | 16 | 9 | 92 | 70 | .568 |
| 1998 | Marlins | NL | 162 | 96 | .59 | 277 | 13 | 15 | 18 | 24 | 31 | 73 | 8 | 420 | 172 | 91 | | 31 | 61 | 36 | 25 | 11 | 54 | 108 | .333 |
| 1999 | Rockies | NL | 162 | 124 | .56 | 294 | 11 | 12 | 11 | 29 | 21 | 72 | 5 | 421 | 113 | 88 | | 11 | 46 | 24 | 22 | 14 | 72 | 90 | .444 |
| 2006 | Tigers | AL | 162 | 120 | .53 | 81 | 34 | 38 | 52 | 32 | 16 | 52 | 3 | 390 | 100 | 57 | 128 | 9 | 35 | 23 | 12 | 9 | 95 | 67 | .586 |
| 2007 | Tigers | AL | 162 | 108 | .53 | 77 | 31 | 49 | 46 | 43 | 14 | 70 | 5 | 443 | 133 | 35 | 123 | 20 | 41 | 24 | 17 | 13 | 88 | 74 | .543 |
| 2008 | Tigers | AL | 162 | 131 | .51 | 66 | 25 | **50** | 29 | 47 | 20 | 72 | 7 | 440 | 94 | 40 | 114 | 10 | **63** | **37** | **26** | 13 | 74 | 88 | .457 |
| 2009 | Tigers | AL | 163 | 126 | .55 | 125 | 52 | **50** | 47 | 47 | **38** | 86 | 3 | 439 | 105 | 60 | 132 | 19 | 42 | 26 | 16 | 6 | 86 | 77 | .528 |
| 2010 | Tigers | AL | 162 | 129 | .58 | 130 | 11 | **47** | 36 | 54 | 45 | 70 | 6 | 416 | 99 | 54 | 174 | **31** | 29 | 14 | 15 | 9 | 81 | 81 | .500 |
| 2011 | Tigers | AL | 162 | 127 | .63 | 86 | 42 | **87** | 43 | 39 | 39 | 84 | 1 | 421 | 69 | 62 | 172 | 7 | 34 | 17 | **17** | **10** | 95 | 67 | .586 |
| 2012 | Tigers | AL | 162 | 121 | .58 | 76 | 33 | 62 | 38 | 41 | **37** | 103 | 0 | 420 | 82 | 46 | 151 | 14 | 35 | 21 | 14 | 7 | 88 | 74 | .543 |
| 2013 | Tigers | AL | 162 | 109 | .61 | 105 | 40 | 34 | 25 | 48 | **50** | 77 | 6 | 428 | 55 | 42 | 180 | 6 | 29 | 16 | 13 | 8 | 93 | 69 | .574 |
| 162-Game Average | | | | 120 | .57 | 171 | 27 | 37 | 31 | 33 | 26 | 74 | 5 | 422 | 117 | 65 | 147 | 24 | 45 | 25 | 19 | 11 | 81 | 81 | .500 |

## Ken Macha

| | | | | LINEUPS | | SUBSTITUTION | | | PITCHER USAGE | | | | | | TACTICS | | | | INTENTIONAL BB | | | | RESULTS | | |
|---|---|---|---|---|---|---|---|---|---|---|---|---|---|---|---|---|---|---|---|---|---|---|---|---|---|
| Year | Team | Lg | G | LUp | PL% | PH | PR | DS | Quick | Slow | LO | RCD | LS | Rel | SBA | SacA | RM | PO | # | Good | NG | Bomb | W | L | Pct |
| 2003 | Athletics | AL | 162 | 111 | .57 | 140 | 29 | 23 | 44 | 38 | 30 | 72 | 12 | 364 | 62 | 31 | 28 | 9 | 42 | 25 | 17 | 10 | 96 | 66 | .593 |
| 2004 | Athletics | AL | 162 | 119 | .60 | 123 | 13 | 14 | 37 | 47 | 39 | 94 | 5 | 414 | 69 | 30 | 63 | 2 | **49** | 31 | 18 | 9 | 91 | 71 | .562 |
| 2005 | Athletics | AL | 162 | 127 | .62 | 83 | 17 | 11 | 43 | 36 | 30 | 79 | **13** | 410 | 53 | 29 | 53 | 13 | **42** | 27 | 15 | 6 | 88 | 74 | .543 |
| 2006 | Athletics | AL | 162 | 121 | .58 | 62 | 33 | 23 | 39 | 47 | 28 | 104 | 8 | 444 | 81 | 29 | 70 | 22 | 47 | 26 | 21 | 11 | 93 | 69 | .574 |
| 2009 | Brewers | NL | 162 | 111 | .48 | 267 | 7 | 32 | 35 | 51 | 19 | 120 | 1 | 512 | 105 | 70 | 90 | 12 | 60 | 35 | **25** | **17** | 80 | 82 | .494 |
| 2010 | Brewers | NL | 162 | 95 | .47 | 226 | 14 | 22 | 42 | **55** | 27 | 102 | 9 | 495 | 107 | 52 | 138 | 5 | 42 | 27 | 15 | 11 | 77 | 85 | .475 |
| 162-Game Average | | | | 114 | .55 | 150 | 19 | 21 | 40 | 46 | 29 | 95 | 8 | 440 | 80 | 40 | 74 | 11 | 47 | 29 | 18 | 11 | 88 | 75 | .540 |

## Joe Maddon

| | | | | LINEUPS | | SUBSTITUTION | | | PITCHER USAGE | | | | | | TACTICS | | | | INTENTIONAL BB | | | | RESULTS | | |
|---|---|---|---|---|---|---|---|---|---|---|---|---|---|---|---|---|---|---|---|---|---|---|---|---|---|
| Year | Team | Lg | G | LUp | PL% | PH | PR | DS | Quick | Slow | LO | RCD | LS | Rel | SBA | SacA | RM | PO | # | Good | NG | Bomb | W | L | Pct |
| 1996 | Angels | AL | 22 | 19 | .64 | 21 | 5 | 0 | 7 | 6 | 6 | 10 | 3 | 48 | 11 | 20 | | 6 | 4 | 3 | 1 | 1 | 8 | 14 | .364 |
| 1998 | Angels | AL | 8 | 4 | .57 | 2 | 4 | 0 | 1 | 5 | 3 | 5 | 3 | 12 | 2 | 7 | | 0 | 1 | 0 | 1 | 0 | 6 | 2 | .750 |
| 1999 | Angels | AL | 29 | 19 | .58 | 29 | 4 | 1 | 6 | 0 | 4 | 20 | 0 | 85 | 23 | 12 | | 7 | 3 | 1 | 2 | 1 | 19 | 10 | .655 |
| 2006 | Devil Rays | AL | 162 | **145** | .54 | 81 | 26 | 51 | 41 | 39 | 16 | 79 | 10 | 444 | 186 | 51 | 132 | 48 | 39 | 19 | 20 | 13 | 61 | **101** | .377 |
| 2007 | Devil Rays | AL | 162 | 122 | .53 | 80 | 19 | 16 | 31 | **56** | 19 | 113 | 1 | 483 | 179 | 40 | 118 | **50** | 31 | 18 | 13 | 4 | 66 | **96** | .407 |
| 2008 | Rays | AL | 162 | 115 | .69 | **133** | 16 | 39 | 48 | 37 | 14 | 112 | 7 | 448 | **192** | 31 | 113 | 26 | 29 | 15 | 14 | 8 | 97 | 65 | .599 |
| 2009 | Rays | AL | 162 | 123 | .66 | **140** | 21 | 18 | 28 | 51 | 23 | **139** | 3 | **510** | **255** | 29 | 99 | 15 | 22 | 10 | 12 | 7 | 84 | 78 | .519 |
| 2010 | Rays | AL | 162 | 129 | .67 | **174** | 31 | 18 | 41 | 34 | 26 | **135** | 2 | **491** | 219 | 45 | 166 | 12 | 34 | **28** | 6 | 3 | **96** | 66 | .593 |
| 2011 | Rays | AL | 162 | 130 | .67 | **137** | 16 | 31 | 34 | 36 | 47 | **112** | 6 | 438 | **217** | 42 | 187 | 4 | 38 | 23 | 15 | 6 | 91 | 71 | .562 |
| 2012 | Rays | AL | 162 | **151** | .62 | **156** | 37 | 52 | 43 | 38 | 33 | **123** | 3 | 472 | **178** | 40 | 181 | 7 | 35 | 25 | 10 | 6 | 90 | 72 | .556 |
| 2013 | Rays | AL | 163 | **147** | .64 | **193** | 27 | **56** | 52 | 38 | 16 | 111 | 6 | 485 | 111 | 26 | 117 | 6 | 38 | 21 | 17 | 11 | 92 | 71 | .564 |
| 162-Game Average | | | | 132 | .63 | 137 | 25 | 34 | 40 | 41 | 25 | 115 | 5 | 468 | 188 | 41 | 139 | 22 | 33 | 19 | 13 | 7 | 85 | 77 | .525 |

## Charlie Manuel

| | | | | LINEUPS | | SUBSTITUTION | | | PITCHER USAGE | | | | | | TACTICS | | | | INTENTIONAL BB | | | | RESULTS | | |
|---|---|---|---|---|---|---|---|---|---|---|---|---|---|---|---|---|---|---|---|---|---|---|---|---|---|
| Year | Team | Lg | G | LUp | PL% | PH | PR | DS | Quick | Slow | LO | RCD | LS | Rel | SBA | SacA | RM | PO | # | Good | NG | Bomb | W | L | Pct |
| 2000 | Indians | AL | 162 | 102 | .64 | 73 | 40 | 26 | 21 | 12 | 20 | 104 | 7 | 462 | 147 | 59 | | 30 | 45 | 28 | 17 | 9 | 90 | 72 | .556 |
| 2001 | Indians | AL | 162 | 114 | .61 | 105 | 30 | 49 | 28 | 17 | 10 | 120 | 3 | 484 | 120 | 67 | | 43 | 44 | 30 | 14 | 11 | 91 | 71 | .562 |
| 2002 | Indians | AL | 86 | 67 | .61 | 57 | 10 | 19 | 14 | 17 | 25 | 47 | 0 | 222 | 57 | 21 | 34 | 3 | 21 | 12 | 9 | 4 | 39 | 47 | .453 |
| 2005 | Phillies | NL | 162 | 80 | .64 | 265 | 36 | 19 | 42 | 28 | 13 | 119 | 6 | 442 | 143 | 86 | 76 | 11 | 51 | 35 | 16 | 9 | 88 | 74 | .543 |
| 2006 | Phillies | NL | 162 | 81 | .65 | 301 | 42 | 49 | 28 | 43 | 22 | 126 | 2 | 500 | 117 | 79 | 74 | 16 | 63 | 35 | 28 | 12 | 85 | 77 | .525 |
| 2007 | Phillies | NL | 162 | 87 | .64 | 264 | **56** | 75 | 40 | 40 | 19 | 128 | 6 | 498 | 157 | 84 | 90 | 30 | 62 | 41 | 21 | **16** | 89 | 73 | .549 |
| 2008 | Phillies | NL | 162 | 77 | .65 | 291 | **62** | 60 | 33 | 42 | 24 | 124 | 1 | 468 | 161 | 88 | 92 | 34 | 64 | **46** | 18 | 11 | 92 | 70 | .568 |
| 2009 | Phillies | NL | 162 | 68 | .67 | 283 | 20 | 16 | 32 | 55 | 32 | 107 | 3 | 459 | 147 | 74 | 65 | 3 | 31 | 19 | 12 | 3 | 93 | 69 | .574 |
| 2010 | Phillies | NL | 162 | 94 | .64 | 276 | 17 | 19 | 37 | 50 | 39 | 114 | 1 | 451 | 129 | 64 | 120 | 3 | 42 | 27 | 15 | 6 | **97** | 65 | .599 |
| 2011 | Phillies | NL | 162 | 105 | .69 | 264 | 26 | 22 | 49 | 39 | **48** | 74 | 1 | 394 | 120 | 80 | 141 | 5 | 41 | 31 | 10 | 5 | **102** | 60 | .630 |
| 2012 | Phillies | NL | 162 | 131 | .68 | 281 | 22 | 48 | 35 | **56** | 30 | 93 | 5 | 440 | 139 | 91 | 125 | 6 | 33 | 21 | 12 | 5 | 81 | 81 | .500 |
| 2013 | Phillies | NL | 120 | 90 | .61 | 196 | 29 | 29 | 20 | 38 | 16 | 73 | 1 | 331 | 88 | 53 | 90 | 1 | 23 | 13 | 10 | 7 | 53 | 67 | .442 |
| 162-Game Average | | | | 97 | .65 | 236 | 35 | 38 | 34 | 39 | 26 | 109 | 3 | 457 | 135 | 75 | 98 | 16 | 46 | 30 | 16 | 9 | 89 | 73 | .549 |

## Jerry Manuel

| | | | | LINEUPS | | SUBSTITUTION | | | PITCHER USAGE | | | | | | TACTICS | | | | INTENTIONAL BB | | | | RESULTS | | |
|---|---|---|---|---|---|---|---|---|---|---|---|---|---|---|---|---|---|---|---|---|---|---|---|---|---|
| Year | Team | Lg | G | LUp | PL% | PH | PR | DS | Quick | Slow | LO | RCD | LS | Rel | SBA | SacA | RM | PO | # | Good | NG | Bomb | W | L | Pct |
| 1998 | White Sox | AL | 162 | 110 | .56 | 65 | 19 | 31 | 43 | 35 | 6 | 72 | 14 | 405 | 173 | 54 | | 26 | 20 | 14 | 6 | 4 | 80 | 82 | .494 |
| 1999 | White Sox | AL | 161 | 109 | .58 | 79 | 35 | 39 | 35 | 42 | 9 | 78 | 8 | 409 | 160 | 69 | | 22 | 31 | 20 | 11 | 7 | 75 | 86 | .466 |
| 2000 | White Sox | AL | 162 | 84 | .53 | 84 | 35 | 20 | 41 | 31 | 8 | 91 | 18 | 466 | 161 | 75 | | 32 | 27 | 16 | 11 | 10 | 95 | 67 | .586 |
| 2001 | White Sox | AL | 162 | 115 | .53 | 104 | 34 | 50 | 45 | 39 | 5 | 93 | 16 | 406 | 182 | 95 | | 41 | 38 | 24 | 14 | 9 | 83 | 79 | .512 |
| 2002 | White Sox | AL | 162 | 104 | .55 | 86 | 10 | 39 | 50 | 44 | 17 | 86 | 10 | 423 | 106 | **73** | 38 | 18 | 31 | 17 | 14 | **11** | 81 | 81 | .500 |
| 2003 | White Sox | AL | 162 | 105 | .55 | 146 | 40 | **71** | 39 | 36 | 27 | 74 | 10 | 361 | 106 | 66 | 39 | 20 | 30 | 18 | 12 | 7 | 86 | 76 | .531 |
| 2008 | Mets | NL | 93 | 58 | .76 | 167 | 7 | 31 | 12 | 30 | 23 | 95 | 2 | 324 | 89 | 54 | 81 | 6 | 37 | 18 | 19 | 6 | 55 | 38 | .591 |
| 2009 | Mets | NL | 162 | 117 | .72 | **289** | 11 | 37 | 34 | 51 | 22 | 137 | 2 | 511 | **166** | 112 | 104 | 3 | 60 | 38 | 22 | 14 | 70 | 92 | .432 |
| 2010 | Mets | NL | 162 | 124 | .67 | 290 | 19 | 25 | 39 | 47 | 32 | **145** | 5 | 491 | **174** | 100 | 169 | 9 | 55 | 42 | 13 | 6 | 79 | 83 | .488 |
| 162-Game Average | | | | 108 | .60 | 153 | 25 | 40 | 39 | 41 | 17 | 102 | 10 | 443 | 154 | 81 | 94 | 21 | 38 | 24 | 14 | 9 | 82 | 80 | .506 |

## Mike Matheny

| | | | | LINEUPS | | SUBSTITUTION | | | PITCHER USAGE | | | | | | TACTICS | | | | INTENTIONAL BB | | | | RESULTS | | |
|---|---|---|---|---|---|---|---|---|---|---|---|---|---|---|---|---|---|---|---|---|---|---|---|---|---|
| Year | Team | Lg | G | LUp | PL% | PH | PR | DS | Quick | Slow | LO | RCD | LS | Rel | SBA | SacA | RM | PO | # | Good | NG | Bomb | W | L | Pct |
| 2012 | Cardinals | NL | 162 | 122 | .62 | 286 | **37** | 33 | 53 | 37 | 8 | 118 | 5 | 506 | 128 | 95 | 144 | 16 | 28 | 13 | 15 | 7 | 88 | 74 | .543 |
| 2013 | Cardinals | NL | 162 | 89 | .56 | 237 | 30 | 41 | 42 | 49 | 25 | 114 | **4** | 483 | 67 | 73 | 125 | 6 | 26 | 20 | 6 | 6 | **97** | 65 | .599 |
| 162-Game Average | | | | 106 | .59 | 262 | 34 | 37 | 48 | 43 | 17 | 116 | 5 | 495 | 98 | 84 | 135 | 11 | 27 | 17 | 11 | 7 | 93 | 70 | .571 |

## Don Mattingly

| | | | | LINEUPS | | SUBSTITUTION | | | PITCHER USAGE | | | | | | TACTICS | | | | INTENTIONAL BB | | | | RESULTS | | |
|---|---|---|---|---|---|---|---|---|---|---|---|---|---|---|---|---|---|---|---|---|---|---|---|---|---|
| Year | Team | Lg | G | LUp | PL% | PH | PR | DS | Quick | Slow | LO | RCD | LS | Rel | SBA | SacA | RM | PO | # | Good | NG | Bomb | W | L | Pct |
| 2011 | Dodgers | NL | 161 | 140 | .57 | 233 | 29 | 44 | 45 | 40 | 30 | 86 | 1 | 461 | 166 | 93 | 181 | 13 | 48 | 27 | 21 | 12 | 82 | 79 | .509 |
| 2012 | Dodgers | NL | 162 | 127 | .59 | 247 | 22 | 43 | 51 | 39 | 20 | 118 | 2 | 506 | 148 | 105 | 153 | 8 | **62** | **38** | 24 | **15** | 86 | 76 | .531 |
| 2013 | Dodgers | NL | 162 | **145** | .55 | 210 | 18 | 47 | 40 | 30 | 18 | 118 | 3 | 504 | 106 | 99 | 131 | 10 | 44 | 28 | 16 | 7 | 92 | 70 | .568 |
| 162-Game Average | | | | 138 | .57 | 230 | 23 | 45 | 45 | 36 | 23 | 108 | 2 | 491 | 140 | 99 | 155 | 10 | 51 | 31 | 20 | 11 | 87 | 75 | .537 |

## Jack McKeon

| | | | | LINEUPS | | SUBSTITUTION | | | PITCHER USAGE | | | | | | TACTICS | | | | INTENTIONAL BB | | | | RESULTS | | |
|---|---|---|---|---|---|---|---|---|---|---|---|---|---|---|---|---|---|---|---|---|---|---|---|---|---|
| Year | Team | Lg | G | LUp | PL% | PH | PR | DS | Quick | Slow | LO | RCD | LS | Rel | SBA | SacA | RM | PO | # | Good | NG | Bomb | W | L | Pct |
| 1997 | Reds | NL | 63 | 50 | .46 | 102 | 18 | 7 | 23 | 11 | 5 | 44 | 3 | 154 | 79 | 42 | | 18 | 16 | 6 | 10 | 7 | 33 | 30 | .524 |
| 1998 | Reds | NL | 162 | 132 | .55 | 288 | 30 | 25 | 49 | 25 | 10 | 107 | 20 | 366 | 137 | 98 | | 7 | 42 | 29 | 13 | 8 | 77 | 85 | .475 |
| 1999 | Reds | NL | 163 | 95 | .50 | 251 | 30 | 38 | 58 | 23 | 9 | 93 | 28 | 381 | 218 | 88 | | 14 | 46 | 30 | 16 | 5 | 96 | 67 | .589 |
| 2000 | Reds | NL | 163 | 117 | .51 | 270 | 31 | 41 | 52 | 27 | 10 | 96 | 24 | 387 | 138 | 82 | | 24 | 53 | 36 | 17 | 10 | 85 | 77 | .525 |
| 2003 | Marlins | NL | 124 | 57 | .43 | 171 | 26 | 21 | 32 | 35 | 33 | 63 | 6 | 280 | 150 | 92 | 41 | 17 | 28 | 16 | 12 | 10 | 75 | 49 | .605 |
| 2004 | Marlins | NL | 162 | 90 | .48 | 224 | 27 | 34 | 42 | 37 | 20 | 95 | 12 | 404 | 139 | 104 | 96 | 19 | 61 | 40 | 21 | 13 | 83 | 79 | .512 |
| 2005 | Marlins | NL | 162 | 82 | .43 | 246 | 24 | 36 | 44 | 35 | 36 | 103 | 7 | 449 | 134 | 106 | 106 | 16 | 57 | 37 | 20 | 10 | 83 | 79 | .512 |
| 2011 | Marlins | NL | 90 | 65 | .53 | 146 | 22 | 16 | 29 | 15 | 13 | 63 | 0 | 278 | 87 | 74 | 67 | 10 | 43 | 25 | 18 | 10 | 40 | 50 | .444 |
| 162-Game Average | | | | 102 | .49 | 253 | 31 | 32 | 49 | 31 | 20 | 99 | 15 | 402 | 161 | 102 | 93 | 19 | 52 | 33 | 19 | 11 | 85 | 77 | .525 |

## John McLaren

| | | | | LINEUPS | | SUBSTITUTION | | | PITCHER USAGE | | | | | | TACTICS | | | | INTENTIONAL BB | | | | RESULTS | | |
|---|---|---|---|---|---|---|---|---|---|---|---|---|---|---|---|---|---|---|---|---|---|---|---|---|---|
| Year | Team | Lg | G | LUp | PL% | PH | PR | DS | Quick | Slow | LO | RCD | LS | Rel | SBA | SacA | RM | PO | # | Good | NG | Bomb | W | L | Pct |
| 2007 | Mariners | AL | 84 | 52 | .48 | 55 | 40 | 18 | 17 | 23 | 19 | 49 | 6 | 247 | 56 | 20 | 76 | 18 | 19 | 10 | 9 | 5 | 43 | 41 | .512 |
| 2008 | Mariners | AL | 72 | 48 | .50 | 31 | 16 | 4 | 17 | 24 | 9 | 45 | 1 | 197 | 65 | 17 | 63 | 11 | 12 | 6 | 6 | 5 | 25 | 47 | .347 |
| 2011 | Nationals | NL | 3 | 3 | .56 | 2 | 0 | 1 | 1 | 0 | 2 | 3 | 0 | 12 | 6 | 2 | 8 | 1 | 2 | 1 | 1 | 0 | 2 | 1 | .667 |
| 162-Game Average | | | | 105 | .49 | 90 | 57 | 23 | 36 | 48 | 31 | 99 | 7 | 465 | 129 | 40 | 150 | 31 | 34 | 17 | 16 | 10 | 71 | 91 | .438 |

## Bob Melvin

| | | | | LINEUPS | | SUBSTITUTION | | | PITCHER USAGE | | | | | | TACTICS | | | | INTENTIONAL BB | | | | RESULTS | | |
|---|---|---|---|---|---|---|---|---|---|---|---|---|---|---|---|---|---|---|---|---|---|---|---|---|---|
| Year | Team | Lg | G | LUp | PL% | PH | PR | DS | Quick | Slow | LO | RCD | LS | Rel | SBA | SacA | RM | PO | # | Good | NG | Bomb | W | L | Pct |
| 2003 | Mariners | AL | 162 | 111 | .62 | 81 | 62 | 33 | 27 | 46 | 43 | 56 | 6 | 366 | 145 | 44 | 37 | 5 | 24 | 14 | 10 | 4 | 93 | 69 | .574 |
| 2004 | Mariners | AL | 162 | **151** | .59 | 109 | **66** | 26 | 26 | 63 | 43 | 82 | 5 | 414 | 152 | 56 | 123 | 24 | 32 | 18 | 14 | 8 | 63 | 99 | .389 |
| 2005 | Diamondbacks | NL | 162 | 120 | .68 | **310** | 26 | 38 | 26 | 56 | 36 | 123 | **11** | 458 | 93 | 93 | 101 | 30 | 43 | 27 | 16 | 9 | 77 | 85 | .475 |
| 2006 | Diamondbacks | NL | 162 | 114 | .72 | 278 | 11 | 35 | 37 | 42 | 15 | 86 | 0 | 461 | 106 | 83 | 61 | 30 | 44 | 28 | 16 | 8 | 76 | 86 | .469 |
| 2007 | Diamondbacks | NL | 162 | 146 | .57 | 243 | 11 | 61 | 35 | 42 | 31 | 96 | 2 | 469 | 133 | 74 | 70 | 25 | 38 | 30 | 8 | 4 | **90** | 72 | .556 |
| 2008 | Diamondbacks | NL | 162 | 134 | .57 | 263 | 27 | 30 | 41 | 39 | 16 | 102 | 0 | 444 | 81 | 87 | 79 | 28 | 41 | 27 | 14 | 9 | 82 | 80 | .506 |
| 2009 | Diamondbacks | NL | 29 | 29 | .62 | 47 | 6 | 8 | 7 | 4 | 3 | 17 | 0 | 91 | 29 | 17 | 13 | 3 | 3 | 1 | 2 | 2 | 12 | 17 | .414 |
| 2011 | Athletics | AL | 99 | 87 | .71 | 33 | 13 | 17 | 24 | 23 | 18 | 59 | 2 | 283 | 103 | 34 | 87 | 23 | 9 | 5 | 4 | 3 | 47 | 52 | .475 |
| 2012 | Athletics | AL | 162 | 132 | .71 | 111 | 17 | 18 | **63** | 29 | 5 | 93 | 2 | 462 | 154 | 41 | 116 | 30 | 34 | 21 | 13 | 6 | 94 | 68 | .580 |
| 2013 | Athletics | AL | 162 | 133 | .77 | 166 | 14 | 35 | 48 | 28 | 7 | 84 | 7 | 447 | 102 | 32 | 74 | 8 | 23 | 18 | 5 | 3 | 96 | 66 | .593 |
| 162-Game Average | | | | 132 | .66 | 187 | 29 | 34 | 38 | 42 | 25 | 91 | 4 | 443 | 125 | 64 | 87 | 23 | 33 | 22 | 12 | 6 | 83 | 79 | .512 |

# Brad Mills

| | | | | LINEUPS | | SUBSTITUTION | | | PITCHER USAGE | | | | | | TACTICS | | | | INTENTIONAL BB | | | | RESULTS | | |
|---|---|---|---|---|---|---|---|---|---|---|---|---|---|---|---|---|---|---|---|---|---|---|---|---|---|
| Year | Team | Lg | G | LUp | PL% | PH | PR | DS | Quick | Slow | LO | RCD | LS | Rel | SBA | SacA | RM | PO | # | Good | NG | Bomb | W | L | Pct |
| 2010 | Astros | NL | 162 | 128 | .50 | 280 | 17 | 51 | 29 | 52 | **41** | 121 | 1 | 507 | 136 | 90 | 122 | 8 | 39 | 30 | 9 | 5 | 76 | 86 | .469 |
| 2011 | Astros | NL | 162 | 121 | .49 | 284 | 31 | 31 | 25 | **65** | 38 | 125 | 2 | 503 | 151 | 95 | 135 | 11 | 59 | 38 | 21 | 9 | 56 | **106** | .346 |
| 2012 | Astros | NL | 121 | 103 | .60 | 181 | 22 | 22 | 20 | 49 | 12 | 102 | 0 | 391 | 117 | 54 | 115 | 10 | 25 | 12 | 13 | 6 | 39 | 82 | .322 |
| 162-Game Average | | | | 128 | .53 | 271 | 25 | 38 | 27 | 60 | 33 | 127 | 1 | 510 | 147 | 87 | 135 | 11 | 45 | 29 | 16 | 7 | 62 | 100 | .383 |

# Lou Piniella

| | | | | LINEUPS | | SUBSTITUTION | | | PITCHER USAGE | | | | | | TACTICS | | | | INTENTIONAL BB | | | | RESULTS | | |
|---|---|---|---|---|---|---|---|---|---|---|---|---|---|---|---|---|---|---|---|---|---|---|---|---|---|
| Year | Team | Lg | G | LUp | PL% | PH | PR | DS | Quick | Slow | LO | RCD | LS | Rel | SBA | SacA | RM | PO | # | Good | NG | Bomb | W | L | Pct |
| 1994 | Mariners | AL | 112 | 98 | .49 | 113 | 24 | 6 | 30 | 35 | 4 | 54 | 9 | 252 | 69 | 54 | | 37 | 39 | 21 | 18 | 9 | 49 | 63 | .438 |
| 1995 | Mariners | AL | 145 | 98 | .56 | 137 | 41 | 22 | 37 | 39 | 30 | 58 | 20 | 324 | 151 | 66 | | 40 | 37 | 18 | 19 | 12 | 79 | 66 | .545 |
| 1996 | Mariners | AL | 161 | 99 | .55 | 190 | 28 | 14 | 56 | 21 | 15 | 91 | 14 | 403 | 129 | 65 | | 40 | 52 | 31 | 21 | 13 | 85 | 76 | .528 |
| 1997 | Mariners | AL | 162 | 84 | .57 | 147 | 35 | 27 | 38 | 47 | 25 | 79 | 11 | 392 | 129 | 61 | | 32 | 36 | 18 | 18 | 10 | 90 | 72 | .556 |
| 1998 | Mariners | AL | 161 | 111 | .53 | 99 | 38 | 43 | 38 | 54 | 32 | 81 | 4 | 368 | 154 | 58 | | 20 | 23 | 8 | 15 | 7 | 76 | 85 | .472 |
| 1999 | Mariners | AL | 162 | 130 | .46 | 122 | 38 | 30 | 31 | 40 | 21 | 51 | 10 | 346 | 175 | 49 | | 31 | 39 | 15 | 24 | 8 | 79 | 83 | .488 |
| 2000 | Mariners | AL | 162 | 130 | .50 | 109 | 43 | 52 | 51 | 37 | 1 | 64 | 11 | 383 | 178 | 73 | | 22 | 37 | 20 | 17 | 8 | 91 | 71 | .562 |
| 2001 | Mariners | AL | 162 | 115 | .64 | 121 | 44 | 64 | 55 | 33 | 5 | 62 | 9 | 392 | 216 | 62 | | 33 | 28 | 19 | 9 | 3 | 116 | 46 | .716 |
| 2002 | Mariners | AL | 162 | **129** | .64 | 95 | **129** | 50 | 49 | 39 | 34 | 52 | 7 | 343 | **195** | 61 | 43 | 25 | 34 | 15 | **19** | **11** | 93 | 69 | .574 |
| 2003 | Devil Rays | AL | 162 | 124 | .60 | **188** | 43 | 26 | 38 | 41 | 29 | 59 | 5 | 372 | 184 | 53 | 52 | 23 | 37 | 21 | 16 | 10 | 63 | 99 | .389 |
| 2004 | Devil Rays | AL | 161 | 137 | .63 | 97 | 25 | 36 | 51 | 34 | 23 | 57 | **15** | 401 | 174 | 45 | 104 | 16 | 35 | 16 | 19 | 9 | 70 | 91 | .435 |
| 2005 | Devil Rays | AL | 162 | **135** | .54 | 127 | 18 | **52** | 38 | 54 | 32 | 67 | 10 | 401 | 200 | 53 | 128 | 16 | 41 | 19 | **22** | 13 | 67 | **95** | .414 |
| 2007 | Cubs | NL | 162 | 125 | .51 | 263 | 52 | 51 | 35 | 38 | 33 | 98 | 3 | 478 | 119 | 60 | 89 | 17 | 46 | 28 | 18 | 4 | 85 | 77 | .525 |
| 2008 | Cubs | NL | 161 | 112 | .47 | 286 | 22 | 31 | 42 | 37 | 27 | 111 | 3 | 478 | 121 | 93 | 98 | 15 | 45 | 28 | 17 | 9 | **97** | 64 | .602 |
| 2009 | Cubs | NL | 161 | 131 | .57 | 277 | 14 | **55** | 47 | 40 | 20 | 127 | 3 | 480 | 90 | 81 | 92 | 23 | 46 | 21 | **25** | 13 | 83 | 78 | .516 |
| 2010 | Cubs | NL | 125 | 101 | .53 | 192 | 10 | 37 | 31 | 41 | 32 | 93 | 6 | 371 | 68 | 65 | 103 | 16 | 33 | 17 | 16 | 9 | 51 | 74 | .408 |
| 162-Game Average | | | | 121 | .55 | 167 | 39 | 39 | 44 | 41 | 24 | 79 | 9 | 403 | 153 | 65 | 91 | 26 | 40 | 21 | 19 | 10 | 83 | 79 | .512 |

# Bo Porter

| | | | | LINEUPS | | SUBSTITUTION | | | PITCHER USAGE | | | | | | TACTICS | | | | INTENTIONAL BB | | | | RESULTS | | |
|---|---|---|---|---|---|---|---|---|---|---|---|---|---|---|---|---|---|---|---|---|---|---|---|---|---|
| Year | Team | Lg | G | LUp | PL% | PH | PR | DS | Quick | Slow | LO | RCD | LS | Rel | SBA | SacA | RM | PO | # | Good | NG | Bomb | W | L | Pct |
| 2013 | Astros | AL | 162 | 138 | .60 | 107 | 40 | 26 | 48 | 43 | 14 | 84 | 6 | 448 | 171 | 51 | 155 | 22 | 32 | 19 | 13 | 8 | 51 | **111** | .315 |
| 162-Game Average | | | | 138 | .60 | 107 | 40 | 26 | 48 | 43 | 14 | 84 | 6 | 448 | 171 | 51 | 155 | 22 | 32 | 19 | 13 | 8 | 51 | 111 | .315 |

# Mike Quade

| | | | | LINEUPS | | SUBSTITUTION | | | PITCHER USAGE | | | | | | TACTICS | | | | INTENTIONAL BB | | | | RESULTS | | |
|---|---|---|---|---|---|---|---|---|---|---|---|---|---|---|---|---|---|---|---|---|---|---|---|---|---|
| Year | Team | Lg | G | LUp | PL% | PH | PR | DS | Quick | Slow | LO | RCD | LS | Rel | SBA | SacA | RM | PO | # | Good | NG | Bomb | W | L | Pct |
| 2010 | Cubs | NL | 37 | 32 | .52 | 44 | 1 | 15 | 10 | 11 | 6 | 20 | 3 | 111 | 18 | 14 | 16 | 4 | 9 | 8 | 1 | 0 | 24 | 13 | .649 |
| 2011 | Cubs | NL | 162 | 125 | .50 | 259 | 30 | 66 | 30 | 56 | 35 | 125 | 4 | 495 | 92 | 78 | 113 | 23 | 45 | 32 | 13 | 9 | 71 | 91 | .438 |
| 162-Game Average | | | | 128 | .50 | 247 | 25 | 66 | 33 | 55 | 33 | 118 | 6 | 493 | 90 | 75 | 105 | 22 | 44 | 33 | 11 | 7 | 77 | 85 | .475 |

# Mike Redmond

| | | | | LINEUPS | | SUBSTITUTION | | | PITCHER USAGE | | | | | | TACTICS | | | | INTENTIONAL BB | | | | RESULTS | | |
|---|---|---|---|---|---|---|---|---|---|---|---|---|---|---|---|---|---|---|---|---|---|---|---|---|---|
| Year | Team | Lg | G | LUp | PL% | PH | PR | DS | Quick | Slow | LO | RCD | LS | Rel | SBA | SacA | RM | PO | # | Good | NG | Bomb | W | L | Pct |
| 2013 | Marlins | NL | 162 | 132 | .52 | 240 | 8 | 9 | 47 | 30 | 4 | 88 | 1 | 471 | 107 | 81 | 124 | 2 | 58 | 42 | 16 | 7 | 62 | **100** | .383 |
| 162-Game Average | | | | 132 | .52 | 240 | 8 | 9 | 47 | 30 | 4 | 88 | 1 | 471 | 107 | 81 | 124 | 2 | 58 | 42 | 16 | 7 | 62 | 100 | .383 |

## Jim Riggleman

| | | | | LINEUPS | | SUBSTITUTION | | | PITCHER USAGE | | | | | | TACTICS | | | | INTENTIONAL BB | | | | RESULTS | | |
|---|---|---|---|---|---|---|---|---|---|---|---|---|---|---|---|---|---|---|---|---|---|---|---|---|---|
| Year | Team | Lg | G | LUp | PL% | PH | PR | DS | Quick | Slow | LO | RCD | LS | Rel | SBA | SacA | RM | PO | # | Good | NG | Bomb | W | L | Pct |
| 1994 | Padres | NL | 117 | 93 | .63 | 184 | 28 | 19 | 11 | 5 | 3 | 53 | 10 | 273 | 116 | 80 | | 52 | 62 | 34 | 28 | 11 | 47 | 70 | .402 |
| 1995 | Cubs | NL | 144 | 92 | .56 | 196 | 9 | 30 | 15 | 8 | 13 | 119 | 12 | 414 | 142 | 90 | | 53 | 68 | 45 | 23 | 12 | 73 | 71 | .507 |
| 1996 | Cubs | NL | 162 | 87 | .54 | 326 | 34 | 21 | 17 | 11 | 7 | 114 | 11 | 439 | 158 | 79 | | 65 | 55 | 33 | 22 | 10 | 76 | 86 | .469 |
| 1997 | Cubs | NL | 162 | 127 | .50 | 280 | 40 | 44 | 13 | 5 | 2 | 113 | 9 | 441 | 176 | 103 | | 74 | 51 | 38 | 13 | 6 | 68 | 94 | .420 |
| 1998 | Cubs | NL | 163 | 104 | .60 | 273 | 26 | 35 | 16 | 14 | 20 | 133 | 6 | 449 | 109 | 89 | | 26 | 48 | 22 | 26 | 15 | 90 | 73 | .552 |
| 1999 | Cubs | NL | 162 | 122 | .61 | 312 | 25 | 30 | 16 | 19 | 8 | 105 | 4 | 441 | 104 | 94 | | 20 | 48 | 21 | 27 | 15 | 67 | 95 | .414 |
| 2008 | Mariners | AL | 90 | 70 | .60 | 75 | 30 | 22 | 21 | 25 | 19 | 50 | 4 | 272 | 57 | 27 | 88 | 10 | 25 | 17 | 8 | 3 | 36 | 54 | .400 |
| 2009 | Nationals | NL | 75 | 60 | .51 | 115 | 15 | 33 | 24 | 16 | 4 | 63 | 6 | 250 | 59 | 44 | 36 | 8 | 33 | 17 | 16 | 8 | 33 | 42 | .440 |
| 2010 | Nationals | NL | 162 | 131 | .58 | 271 | 33 | 67 | 50 | 32 | 9 | 101 | 5 | 494 | 151 | 101 | 158 | 13 | 57 | 37 | 20 | 10 | 69 | 93 | .426 |
| 2011 | Nationals | NL | 75 | 61 | .58 | 105 | 22 | 23 | 24 | 15 | 2 | 54 | 5 | 220 | 80 | 47 | 89 | 3 | 22 | 16 | 6 | 3 | 38 | 37 | .507 |
| 162-Game Average | | | | 117 | .57 | 264 | 32 | 40 | 26 | 19 | 11 | 112 | 9 | 456 | 142 | 93 | 150 | 40 | 58 | 35 | 23 | 11 | 74 | 88 | .457 |

## Edwin Rodriguez

| | | | | LINEUPS | | SUBSTITUTION | | | PITCHER USAGE | | | | | | TACTICS | | | | INTENTIONAL BB | | | | RESULTS | | |
|---|---|---|---|---|---|---|---|---|---|---|---|---|---|---|---|---|---|---|---|---|---|---|---|---|---|
| Year | Team | Lg | G | LUp | PL% | PH | PR | DS | Quick | Slow | LO | RCD | LS | Rel | SBA | SacA | RM | PO | # | Good | NG | Bomb | W | L | Pct |
| 2010 | Marlins | NL | 92 | 60 | .42 | 152 | 12 | 20 | 22 | 23 | 13 | 72 | 1 | 288 | 62 | 37 | 69 | 9 | 24 | 17 | 7 | 3 | 46 | 46 | .500 |
| 2011 | Marlins | NL | 71 | 50 | .51 | 114 | 10 | 10 | 14 | 17 | 14 | 49 | 0 | 227 | 49 | 47 | 62 | 5 | 28 | 19 | 9 | 4 | 32 | 39 | .451 |
| 162-Game Average | | | | 109 | .46 | 264 | 22 | 30 | 36 | 40 | 27 | 120 | 1 | 512 | 110 | 83 | 130 | 14 | 52 | 36 | 16 | 7 | 78 | 84 | .481 |

## Ron Roenicke

| | | | | LINEUPS | | SUBSTITUTION | | | PITCHER USAGE | | | | | | TACTICS | | | | INTENTIONAL BB | | | | RESULTS | | |
|---|---|---|---|---|---|---|---|---|---|---|---|---|---|---|---|---|---|---|---|---|---|---|---|---|---|
| Year | Team | Lg | G | LUp | PL% | PH | PR | DS | Quick | Slow | LO | RCD | LS | Rel | SBA | SacA | RM | PO | # | Good | NG | Bomb | W | L | Pct |
| 2011 | Brewers | NL | 162 | 105 | .45 | 260 | 31 | 36 | 36 | 43 | 31 | 92 | 1 | 434 | 125 | **104** | 141 | 14 | 16 | 9 | 7 | 4 | 96 | 66 | .593 |
| 2012 | Brewers | NL | 162 | 110 | .45 | 322 | 20 | 25 | 36 | 50 | 23 | **149** | 1 | 512 | 197 | 91 | 152 | 8 | 20 | 12 | 8 | 2 | 83 | 79 | .512 |
| 2013 | Brewers | NL | 162 | 125 | .47 | 275 | 15 | 34 | 39 | 47 | 7 | 96 | 2 | 501 | **192** | 86 | 157 | 6 | 29 | 22 | 7 | 6 | 74 | 88 | .457 |
| 162-Game Average | | | | 113 | .46 | 286 | 22 | 32 | 37 | 47 | 20 | 112 | 1 | 482 | 171 | 94 | 150 | 9 | 22 | 14 | 7 | 4 | 84 | 78 | .519 |

## John Russell

| | | | | LINEUPS | | SUBSTITUTION | | | PITCHER USAGE | | | | | | TACTICS | | | | INTENTIONAL BB | | | | RESULTS | | |
|---|---|---|---|---|---|---|---|---|---|---|---|---|---|---|---|---|---|---|---|---|---|---|---|---|---|
| Year | Team | Lg | G | LUp | PL% | PH | PR | DS | Quick | Slow | LO | RCD | LS | Rel | SBA | SacA | RM | PO | # | Good | NG | Bomb | W | L | Pct |
| 2008 | Pirates | NL | 162 | 128 | .51 | 290 | 17 | 13 | 29 | 47 | 15 | 111 | 0 | 497 | 76 | 92 | 54 | 19 | 31 | 21 | 10 | 4 | 67 | 95 | .414 |
| 2009 | Pirates | NL | 161 | 121 | .60 | 251 | 3 | 5 | 44 | 45 | 12 | 89 | 0 | 456 | 122 | 78 | 97 | 15 | 37 | 20 | 17 | 10 | 62 | **99** | .385 |
| 2010 | Pirates | NL | 162 | 119 | .60 | 275 | 13 | 10 | 48 | 44 | 8 | 122 | 0 | **517** | 123 | 81 | 124 | 32 | 40 | 26 | 14 | 4 | 57 | **105** | .352 |
| 162-Game Average | | | | 123 | .57 | 273 | 11 | 9 | 40 | 45 | 12 | 108 | 0 | 491 | 107 | 84 | 92 | 22 | 36 | 22 | 14 | 6 | 62 | 100 | .383 |

## Juan Samuel

| | | | | LINEUPS | | SUBSTITUTION | | | PITCHER USAGE | | | | | | TACTICS | | | | INTENTIONAL BB | | | | RESULTS | | |
|---|---|---|---|---|---|---|---|---|---|---|---|---|---|---|---|---|---|---|---|---|---|---|---|---|---|
| Year | Team | Lg | G | LUp | PL% | PH | PR | DS | Quick | Slow | LO | RCD | LS | Rel | SBA | SacA | RM | PO | # | Good | NG | Bomb | W | L | Pct |
| 2010 | Orioles | AL | 51 | 39 | .63 | 27 | 14 | 3 | 11 | 17 | 6 | 33 | 0 | 157 | 40 | 18 | 39 | 2 | 18 | 12 | 6 | 5 | 17 | 34 | .333 |
| 162-Game Average | | | | 124 | .63 | 86 | 44 | 10 | 35 | 54 | 19 | 105 | 0 | 499 | 127 | 57 | 124 | 6 | 57 | 38 | 19 | 16 | 54 | 108 | .333 |

## Ryne Sandberg

| | | | | LINEUPS | | SUBSTITUTION | | | PITCHER USAGE | | | | | | TACTICS | | | | INTENTIONAL BB | | | | RESULTS | | |
|---|---|---|---|---|---|---|---|---|---|---|---|---|---|---|---|---|---|---|---|---|---|---|---|---|---|
| Year | Team | Lg | G | LUp | PL% | PH | PR | DS | Quick | Slow | LO | RCD | LS | Rel | SBA | SacA | RM | PO | # | Good | NG | Bomb | W | L | Pct |
| 2013 | Phillies | NL | 42 | 34 | .66 | 66 | 4 | 6 | 6 | 12 | 7 | 18 | 0 | 135 | 14 | 15 | 26 | 0 | 10 | 6 | 4 | 4 | 20 | 22 | .476 |
| 162-Game Average | | | | 131 | .66 | 255 | 15 | 23 | 23 | 46 | 27 | 69 | 0 | 521 | 54 | 58 | 100 | 0 | 39 | 23 | 15 | 15 | 77 | 85 | .475 |

## Mike Scioscia

| | | | | LINEUPS | | SUBSTITUTION | | | PITCHER USAGE | | | | | | TACTICS | | | | INTENTIONAL BB | | | | RESULTS | | |
|---|---|---|---|---|---|---|---|---|---|---|---|---|---|---|---|---|---|---|---|---|---|---|---|---|---|
| Year | Team | Lg | G | LUp | PL% | PH | PR | DS | Quick | Slow | LO | RCD | LS | Rel | SBA | SacA | RM | PO | # | Good | NG | Bomb | W | L | Pct |
| 2000 | Angels | AL | 162 | 75 | .62 | 110 | 41 | 4 | 56 | 42 | 6 | 95 | 9 | 441 | 145 | 63 | | 40 | 44 | 28 | 16 | 7 | 82 | 80 | .506 |
| 2001 | Angels | AL | 162 | 130 | .62 | 118 | 30 | 8 | 29 | 41 | 5 | 81 | 9 | 384 | 168 | 66 | | 50 | 47 | 22 | 25 | 12 | 75 | 87 | .463 |
| 2002 | Angels | AL | 162 | 102 | .64 | **162** | 57 | 26 | 36 | 33 | 34 | 88 | 8 | 400 | 168 | 62 | 52 | 30 | 24 | 15 | 9 | 5 | 99 | 63 | .611 |
| 2003 | Angels | AL | 162 | 130 | .64 | 134 | 54 | 40 | 50 | 48 | 11 | 60 | 4 | 375 | **190** | 64 | 79 | 25 | 38 | 26 | 12 | 3 | 77 | 85 | .475 |
| 2004 | Angels | AL | 162 | 126 | .57 | 94 | 32 | 44 | 37 | 40 | 22 | 61 | 11 | 343 | **189** | 70 | **229** | 33 | 27 | 18 | 9 | 3 | 92 | 70 | .568 |
| 2005 | Angels | AL | 162 | 124 | .65 | 92 | 37 | 37 | 47 | 37 | 24 | 88 | 9 | 379 | **218** | 58 | **160** | 43 | 24 | 15 | 9 | 4 | 95 | 67 | .586 |
| 2006 | Angels | AL | 162 | 114 | .63 | 103 | 45 | 38 | 38 | 49 | 21 | 99 | 9 | 380 | **205** | 37 | **166** | 22 | 27 | 18 | 9 | 6 | 89 | 73 | .549 |
| 2007 | Angels | AL | 162 | 127 | .66 | 103 | 26 | 19 | 39 | 40 | 14 | 94 | 4 | 396 | **194** | 41 | **166** | 44 | 22 | 12 | 10 | 5 | 94 | 68 | .580 |
| 2008 | Angels | AL | 162 | 125 | .63 | 74 | 30 | 36 | 37 | 48 | **21** | 87 | 1 | 383 | 177 | 39 | 151 | 31 | 32 | 22 | 10 | 6 | **100** | 62 | .617 |
| 2009 | Angels | AL | 162 | 123 | .69 | 80 | 26 | 37 | 47 | 47 | 33 | 91 | 1 | 434 | 211 | 55 | **137** | **40** | 35 | 22 | 13 | 6 | 97 | 65 | .599 |
| 2010 | Angels | AL | 162 | 133 | .59 | 96 | 31 | 23 | 41 | 52 | 48 | 76 | 0 | 410 | 156 | 58 | **223** | 28 | 33 | 17 | 16 | 8 | 80 | 82 | .494 |
| 2011 | Angels | AL | 162 | 129 | .64 | 88 | 14 | 24 | 31 | 37 | **55** | 57 | 1 | 386 | 187 | **69** | **212** | **46** | 34 | 25 | 9 | 5 | 86 | 76 | .531 |

| | | | | LINEUPS | | SUBSTITUTION | | | PITCHER USAGE | | | | | | TACTICS | | | | INTENTIONAL BB | | | | RESULTS | | |
|---|---|---|---|---|---|---|---|---|---|---|---|---|---|---|---|---|---|---|---|---|---|---|---|---|---|
| Year | Team | Lg | G | LUp | PL% | PH | PR | DS | Quick | Slow | LO | RCD | LS | Rel | SBA | SacA | RM | PO | # | Good | NG | Bomb | W | L | Pct |
| 2012 | Angels | AL | 162 | 121 | .55 | 73 | 33 | 47 | 37 | 47 | 31 | 96 | **8** | 444 | 167 | **61** | **236** | **33** | 20 | 11 | 9 | 7 | 89 | 73 | .549 |
| 2013 | Angels | AL | 162 | 118 | .56 | 88 | 26 | 39 | 31 | 44 | 29 | 130 | **8** | 496 | 116 | 48 | **205** | **41** | 36 | 19 | 17 | 11 | 78 | 84 | .481 |
| 162-Game Average | | | | 120 | .62 | 101 | 34 | 30 | 40 | 43 | 25 | 86 | 6 | 404 | 178 | 57 | 168 | 36 | 32 | 19 | 12 | 6 | 88 | 74 | .543 |

## Buck Showalter

| | | | | LINEUPS | | SUBSTITUTION | | | PITCHER USAGE | | | | | | TACTICS | | | | INTENTIONAL BB | | | | RESULTS | | |
|---|---|---|---|---|---|---|---|---|---|---|---|---|---|---|---|---|---|---|---|---|---|---|---|---|---|
| Year | Team | Lg | G | LUp | PL% | PH | PR | DS | Quick | Slow | LO | RCD | LS | Rel | SBA | SacA | RM | PO | # | Good | NG | Bomb | W | L | Pct |
| 1994 | Yankees | AL | 113 | 79 | .59 | 95 | 31 | 3 | 24 | 30 | 0 | 38 | 7 | 241 | 95 | 34 | | 22 | 24 | 13 | 11 | 4 | 70 | 43 | .619 |
| 1995 | Yankees | AL | 145 | 107 | .68 | 124 | 30 | 20 | 29 | 42 | 37 | 57 | 6 | 302 | 80 | 27 | | 29 | 21 | 14 | 7 | 1 | 79 | 65 | .549 |
| 1998 | Diamondbacks | NL | 162 | 124 | .62 | 252 | 17 | 15 | 34 | 40 | 7 | 43 | 6 | 368 | 111 | 68 | | 13 | 32 | 16 | 16 | 9 | 65 | 97 | .401 |
| 1999 | Diamondbacks | NL | 162 | 97 | .63 | 220 | 20 | 17 | 37 | 48 | 25 | 74 | 3 | 382 | 176 | 75 | | 15 | 48 | 29 | 19 | 8 | 100 | 62 | .617 |
| 2000 | Diamondbacks | NL | 162 | 99 | .60 | 250 | 32 | 11 | 46 | 26 | 18 | 74 | 12 | 390 | 141 | 89 | | 10 | 53 | 28 | 25 | 16 | 85 | 77 | .525 |
| 2003 | Rangers | AL | 162 | 133 | .61 | 88 | 51 | 41 | 35 | 33 | 12 | 93 | 7 | **494** | 90 | 35 | **80** | 12 | 45 | 24 | 21 | **14** | 71 | 91 | .438 |
| 2004 | Rangers | AL | 162 | 120 | .64 | 86 | 15 | 24 | 53 | 30 | 12 | 82 | 10 | 468 | 105 | 30 | 88 | 5 | 29 | 19 | 10 | 3 | 89 | 73 | .549 |
| 2005 | Rangers | AL | 162 | 98 | .59 | 57 | 22 | 11 | 42 | 39 | 17 | 79 | 8 | **454** | 82 | 11 | 103 | 5 | 31 | 10 | 21 | **16** | 79 | 83 | .488 |
| 2006 | Rangers | AL | 162 | 95 | .57 | 39 | 34 | 22 | 41 | 27 | 10 | 85 | 4 | **489** | 77 | 30 | 72 | 8 | 18 | 11 | 7 | 5 | 80 | 82 | .494 |
| 2010 | Orioles | AL | 57 | 42 | .74 | 20 | 11 | 13 | 23 | 9 | 10 | 24 | 1 | 144 | 38 | 13 | 31 | 1 | 10 | 9 | 1 | 1 | 34 | 23 | .596 |
| 2011 | Orioles | AL | 162 | 117 | .53 | 60 | 39 | 27 | 43 | 40 | 14 | 61 | 2 | 478 | 106 | 32 | 133 | 6 | 42 | 31 | 11 | 5 | 69 | 93 | .426 |
| 2012 | Orioles | AL | 162 | 120 | .62 | 78 | 28 | 31 | 37 | 42 | 10 | 88 | 0 | 492 | 87 | 46 | 145 | 6 | 36 | 25 | 11 | 5 | 93 | 69 | .574 |
| 2013 | Orioles | AL | 162 | 100 | .65 | 90 | 23 | 21 | 31 | 39 | 19 | 84 | 4 | 473 | 108 | 37 | 104 | 4 | 32 | 11 | 21 | **13** | 85 | 77 | .525 |
| 162-Game Average | | | | 111 | .62 | 122 | 30 | 21 | 40 | 37 | 16 | 74 | 6 | 433 | 109 | 44 | 103 | 11 | 35 | 20 | 15 | 8 | 84 | 78 | .519 |

## Dale Sveum

| | | | | LINEUPS | | SUBSTITUTION | | | PITCHER USAGE | | | | | | TACTICS | | | | INTENTIONAL BB | | | | RESULTS | | |
|---|---|---|---|---|---|---|---|---|---|---|---|---|---|---|---|---|---|---|---|---|---|---|---|---|---|
| Year | Team | Lg | G | LUp | PL% | PH | PR | DS | Quick | Slow | LO | RCD | LS | Rel | SBA | SacA | RM | PO | # | Good | NG | Bomb | W | L | Pct |
| 2008 | Brewers | NL | 12 | 3 | .48 | 32 | 2 | 1 | 7 | 2 | 1 | 12 | 0 | 46 | 5 | 13 | 6 | 1 | 2 | 1 | 1 | 0 | 7 | 5 | .583 |
| 2012 | Cubs | NL | 162 | 101 | .60 | 277 | 23 | 44 | 46 | 48 | 8 | 117 | 1 | 493 | 139 | 61 | 153 | 13 | 36 | 24 | 12 | 8 | 61 | **101** | .377 |
| 2013 | Cubs | NL | 162 | 107 | .60 | 277 | 12 | 17 | 42 | 47 | 19 | 112 | 1 | 489 | 95 | 58 | 122 | 8 | 43 | 29 | 14 | **8** | 66 | 96 | .407 |
| 162-Game Average | | | | 102 | .60 | 283 | 18 | 30 | 46 | 47 | 14 | 116 | 1 | 496 | 115 | 64 | 135 | 11 | 39 | 26 | 13 | 8 | 65 | 97 | .401 |

## Joe Torre

| | | | | LINEUPS | | SUBSTITUTION | | | PITCHER USAGE | | | | | | TACTICS | | | | INTENTIONAL BB | | | | RESULTS | | |
|---|---|---|---|---|---|---|---|---|---|---|---|---|---|---|---|---|---|---|---|---|---|---|---|---|---|
| Year | Team | Lg | G | LUp | PL% | PH | PR | DS | Quick | Slow | LO | RCD | LS | Rel | SBA | SacA | RM | PO | # | Good | NG | Bomb | W | L | Pct |
| 1994 | Cardinals | NL | 115 | 79 | .68 | 192 | 9 | 0 | 36 | 29 | 6 | 106 | 4 | 330 | 122 | 57 | | 33 | 28 | 18 | 10 | 6 | 53 | 61 | .465 |
| 1995 | Cardinals | NL | 47 | 36 | .51 | 99 | 6 | 4 | 17 | 11 | 1 | 41 | 2 | 146 | 42 | 26 | | 14 | 16 | 10 | 6 | 2 | 20 | 27 | .426 |
| 1996 | Yankees | AL | 162 | 131 | .57 | 92 | 62 | 55 | 59 | 23 | 22 | 97 | 10 | 411 | 142 | 53 | | 19 | 35 | 17 | 18 | 14 | 92 | 70 | .568 |
| 1997 | Yankees | AL | 162 | 118 | .61 | 75 | 70 | 23 | 35 | 41 | 19 | 84 | 14 | 368 | 157 | 54 | | 14 | 41 | 23 | 18 | 10 | 96 | 66 | .593 |
| 1998 | Yankees | AL | 162 | 96 | .62 | 94 | 36 | 28 | 43 | 38 | 27 | 71 | 17 | 334 | 216 | 44 | | 9 | 25 | 17 | 8 | 4 | 114 | 48 | .704 |
| 1999 | Yankees | AL | 162 | 95 | .63 | 114 | 63 | 10 | 29 | 51 | 26 | 80 | 12 | 359 | 161 | 31 | | 12 | 27 | 17 | 10 | 8 | 98 | 64 | .605 |
| 2000 | Yankees | AL | 161 | 112 | .63 | 86 | 49 | 27 | 43 | 53 | 27 | 92 | 16 | 382 | 147 | 22 | | 8 | 23 | 9 | 14 | 7 | 87 | 74 | .540 |
| 2001 | Yankees | AL | 161 | 94 | .56 | 76 | 33 | 14 | 37 | 45 | 10 | 77 | 17 | 362 | 214 | 41 | | 21 | 29 | 20 | 9 | 6 | 95 | 65 | .594 |
| 2002 | Yankees | AL | 161 | 108 | .58 | 89 | 53 | 31 | 39 | 49 | 44 | 86 | **13** | 334 | 138 | 35 | 46 | 18 | 44 | **33** | 11 | 4 | **103** | 58 | .640 |
| 2003 | Yankees | AL | 163 | 104 | .65 | 118 | 48 | 18 | 26 | 51 | **52** | 75 | 10 | 367 | 131 | 39 | 69 | 33 | 36 | 21 | 15 | 8 | **101** | 61 | .623 |
| 2004 | Yankees | AL | 162 | 116 | .65 | 86 | 35 | 46 | 48 | 35 | 29 | **129** | 10 | 436 | 117 | 50 | 126 | **36** | 32 | 16 | 16 | 9 | **101** | 61 | .623 |
| 2005 | Yankees | AL | 162 | 117 | .65 | 94 | **65** | 47 | 44 | 45 | 28 | 92 | 7 | 418 | 111 | 40 | 123 | **50** | 25 | 11 | 14 | 9 | 95 | 67 | .586 |
| 2006 | Yankees | AL | 162 | 120 | .66 | 108 | 50 | **59** | 50 | 30 | 9 | **109** | 7 | **489** | 174 | 48 | 118 | **50** | 41 | 22 | 19 | 4 | **97** | 65 | .599 |
| 2007 | Yankees | AL | 162 | 102 | .68 | 99 | 34 | 22 | **51** | 29 | 10 | 113 | **13** | **522** | 163 | 51 | 152 | 41 | 33 | 17 | 16 | 7 | 94 | 68 | .580 |
| 2008 | Dodgers | NL | 162 | 124 | .53 | 277 | 43 | **66** | **61** | 30 | 17 | 94 | 8 | 461 | 169 | 75 | 133 | 38 | 58 | **46** | 12 | 5 | 84 | 78 | .519 |
| 2009 | Dodgers | NL | 162 | 113 | .59 | 263 | 22 | 22 | **62** | 23 | 18 | 125 | **8** | 526 | 164 | 107 | **163** | 17 | **68** | **45** | 23 | 12 | **95** | 67 | .586 |
| 2010 | Dodgers | NL | 162 | 127 | .55 | 255 | 18 | 47 | 42 | 37 | 30 | 92 | 5 | 475 | 142 | **108** | **192** | 8 | **75** | **53** | 22 | 11 | 80 | 82 | .494 |
| 162-Game Average | | | | 112 | .61 | 139 | 44 | 33 | 45 | 39 | 23 | 98 | 11 | 421 | 157 | 55 | 125 | 26 | 40 | 25 | 15 | 8 | 94 | 68 | .580 |

## Jim Tracy

| | | | | LINEUPS | | SUBSTITUTION | | | PITCHER USAGE | | | | | | TACTICS | | | | INTENTIONAL BB | | | | RESULTS | | |
|---|---|---|---|---|---|---|---|---|---|---|---|---|---|---|---|---|---|---|---|---|---|---|---|---|---|
| Year | Team | Lg | G | LUp | PL% | PH | PR | DS | Quick | Slow | LO | RCD | LS | Rel | SBA | SacA | RM | PO | # | Good | NG | Bomb | W | L | Pct |
| 2001 | Dodgers | NL | 162 | 111 | .50 | 264 | 34 | 20 | 46 | 42 | 8 | 84 | 4 | 409 | 131 | 81 | | 10 | 37 | 19 | 18 | 9 | 86 | 76 | .531 |
| 2002 | Dodgers | NL | 162 | 102 | .52 | 317 | 39 | 37 | 49 | 36 | 21 | 118 | 9 | 423 | 133 | 81 | 46 | 18 | 45 | 31 | 14 | 5 | 92 | 70 | .568 |
| 2003 | Dodgers | NL | 162 | 103 | .64 | 269 | 22 | 64 | 52 | 29 | 22 | **148** | **11** | 438 | 116 | 97 | 32 | 10 | 35 | 23 | 12 | 8 | 85 | 77 | .525 |
| 2004 | Dodgers | NL | 162 | 94 | .70 | **295** | 25 | 19 | 49 | 34 | 16 | 128 | **16** | 459 | 143 | 81 | 93 | 7 | 47 | 32 | 15 | 8 | 93 | 69 | .574 |
| 2005 | Dodgers | NL | 162 | 129 | .64 | 303 | 31 | 37 | 44 | 40 | 20 | 126 | 2 | 459 | 93 | 76 | 97 | 17 | 34 | 21 | 13 | 6 | 71 | 91 | .438 |
| 2006 | Pirates | NL | 162 | 121 | .43 | 264 | 22 | 22 | 37 | 43 | 12 | 156 | 3 | 505 | 91 | 80 | 75 | 12 | 62 | 39 | 23 | 15 | 67 | 95 | .414 |
| 2007 | Pirates | NL | 162 | 124 | .49 | 240 | 12 | 26 | 33 | 40 | 13 | 113 | 0 | 495 | 98 | 80 | 90 | 12 | 55 | 30 | 25 | 11 | 68 | **94** | .420 |
| 2009 | Rockies | NL | 116 | 87 | .63 | 186 | 25 | 28 | 28 | 27 | 27 | 83 | 3 | 349 | 116 | 73 | 82 | 9 | 40 | 28 | 12 | 7 | 74 | 42 | .638 |
| 2010 | Rockies | NL | 162 | 135 | .65 | 257 | 30 | 41 | 38 | 40 | 34 | 128 | 0 | 513 | 141 | 64 | 135 | 11 | 54 | 34 | 20 | 10 | 83 | 79 | .512 |
| 2011 | Rockies | NL | 162 | 134 | .62 | 252 | 21 | 30 | 35 | 47 | 21 | 129 | 1 | 517 | 160 | 94 | **231** | 18 | 47 | 27 | 20 | 11 | 73 | 89 | .451 |
| 2012 | Rockies | NL | 162 | 140 | .55 | 264 | 33 | 33 | **74** | 33 | 6 | 111 | 2 | **575** | 140 | 88 | 165 | 18 | 61 | 36 | **25** | 12 | 64 | 98 | .395 |
| 162-Game Average | | | | 119 | .58 | 272 | 27 | 33 | 45 | 38 | 19 | 124 | 5 | 480 | 127 | 84 | 108 | 13 | 48 | 30 | 18 | 10 | 80 | 82 | .494 |

## Dave Trembley

| | | | | LINEUPS | | SUBSTITUTION | | | PITCHER USAGE | | | | | | TACTICS | | | | INTENTIONAL BB | | | | RESULTS | | |
|---|---|---|---|---|---|---|---|---|---|---|---|---|---|---|---|---|---|---|---|---|---|---|---|---|---|
| Year | Team | Lg | G | LUp | PL% | PH | PR | DS | Quick | Slow | LO | RCD | LS | Rel | SBA | SacA | RM | PO | # | Good | NG | Bomb | W | L | Pct |
| 2007 | Orioles | AL | 93 | 71 | .60 | 63 | 29 | 16 | 21 | 25 | 16 | 47 | 3 | 279 | 124 | 32 | 83 | 32 | 29 | 15 | 14 | 8 | 40 | 53 | .430 |
| 2008 | Orioles | AL | 161 | 119 | .58 | 117 | 36 | 25 | 41 | 44 | 11 | 87 | 4 | **492** | 118 | 38 | 143 | 11 | 44 | 18 | **26** | 12 | 68 | **93** | .422 |
| 2009 | Orioles | AL | 162 | 132 | .68 | 99 | 26 | 21 | 43 | 39 | 11 | 66 | 4 | 484 | 113 | 20 | 86 | 6 | **45** | **28** | 17 | 9 | 64 | **98** | .395 |
| 2010 | Orioles | AL | 54 | 50 | .62 | 24 | 14 | 7 | 6 | 16 | 10 | 33 | 1 | 153 | 32 | 10 | 24 | 2 | 17 | 7 | 10 | 5 | 15 | 39 | .278 |
| 162-Game Average | | | | 128 | .62 | 104 | 36 | 24 | 38 | 43 | 17 | 80 | 4 | 485 | 133 | 34 | 116 | 18 | 47 | 23 | 23 | 12 | 64 | 98 | .395 |

## Bobby Valentine

| | | | | LINEUPS | | SUBSTITUTION | | | PITCHER USAGE | | | | | | TACTICS | | | | INTENTIONAL BB | | | | RESULTS | | |
|---|---|---|---|---|---|---|---|---|---|---|---|---|---|---|---|---|---|---|---|---|---|---|---|---|---|
| Year | Team | Lg | G | LUp | PL% | PH | PR | DS | Quick | Slow | LO | RCD | LS | Rel | SBA | SacA | RM | PO | # | Good | NG | Bomb | W | L | Pct |
| 1996 | Mets | NL | 31 | 28 | .67 | 88 | 7 | 3 | 7 | 4 | 1 | 11 | 1 | 75 | 20 | 27 | | 2 | 14 | 8 | 6 | 2 | 12 | 19 | .387 |
| 1997 | Mets | NL | 162 | 131 | .65 | 313 | 39 | 23 | 52 | 30 | 8 | 70 | 11 | 376 | 171 | 102 | | 27 | 43 | 28 | 15 | 6 | 88 | 74 | .543 |
| 1998 | Mets | NL | 162 | 124 | .64 | 305 | 42 | 34 | 45 | 36 | 23 | 80 | 7 | 399 | 108 | 157 | | 50 | 59 | 42 | 17 | 10 | 88 | 74 | .543 |
| 1999 | Mets | NL | 163 | 76 | .57 | 323 | 43 | 26 | 56 | 24 | 14 | 108 | 8 | 439 | 211 | 109 | | 43 | 53 | 35 | 18 | 9 | 97 | 66 | .595 |
| 2000 | Mets | NL | 162 | 118 | .34 | 299 | 38 | 32 | 37 | 37 | 18 | 90 | 7 | 411 | 112 | 118 | | 0 | 42 | 27 | 15 | 7 | 94 | 68 | .580 |
| 2001 | Mets | NL | 162 | 143 | .43 | 298 | 33 | 34 | 38 | 40 | 7 | 83 | 6 | 397 | 114 | 88 | | 0 | 60 | 30 | 30 | 16 | 82 | 80 | .506 |
| 2002 | Mets | NL | 161 | 122 | .62 | 323 | **48** | 32 | 15 | 42 | 29 | 87 | 2 | 451 | 129 | 98 | **81** | 41 | 75 | 49 | 26 | 13 | 75 | 86 | .466 |
| 2012 | Red Sox | AL | 162 | 143 | .61 | 107 | 30 | 25 | 34 | 52 | 21 | 91 | 6 | 489 | 128 | 44 | 148 | 18 | 33 | 22 | 11 | 5 | 69 | 93 | .426 |
| 162-Game Average | | | | 125 | .61 | 243 | 45 | 14 | 38 | 46 | 31 | 79 | 14 | 369 | 158 | 90 | 115 | 25 | 45 | 27 | 18 | 10 | 82 | 80 | .506 |

## Robin Ventura

| | | | | LINEUPS | | SUBSTITUTION | | | PITCHER USAGE | | | | | | TACTICS | | | | INTENTIONAL BB | | | | RESULTS | | |
|---|---|---|---|---|---|---|---|---|---|---|---|---|---|---|---|---|---|---|---|---|---|---|---|---|---|
| Year | Team | Lg | G | LUp | PL% | PH | PR | DS | Quick | Slow | LO | RCD | LS | Rel | SBA | SacA | RM | PO | # | Good | NG | Bomb | W | L | Pct |
| 2012 | White Sox | AL | 162 | 75 | .48 | 72 | **64** | 23 | 39 | 44 | 34 | 104 | 4 | 466 | 152 | 42 | 174 | 13 | 29 | 17 | 12 | 7 | 85 | 77 | .525 |
| 2013 | White Sox | AL | 162 | 116 | .47 | 76 | 47 | 33 | 24 | **52** | 38 | **133** | 0 | 470 | 147 | 24 | 132 | 15 | 24 | 12 | 12 | 4 | 63 | 99 | .389 |
| 162-Game Average | | | | 96 | .48 | 74 | 56 | 28 | 32 | 48 | 36 | 119 | 2 | 468 | 150 | 33 | 153 | 14 | 27 | 15 | 12 | 6 | 74 | 88 | .457 |

## Don Wakamatsu

| | | | | LINEUPS | | SUBSTITUTION | | | PITCHER USAGE | | | | | | TACTICS | | | | INTENTIONAL BB | | | | RESULTS | | |
|---|---|---|---|---|---|---|---|---|---|---|---|---|---|---|---|---|---|---|---|---|---|---|---|---|---|
| Year | Team | Lg | G | LUp | PL% | PH | PR | DS | Quick | Slow | LO | RCD | LS | Rel | SBA | SacA | RM | PO | # | Good | NG | Bomb | W | L | Pct |
| 2009 | Mariners | AL | 162 | 138 | .51 | 58 | 31 | 19 | 50 | 27 | 18 | 76 | 1 | 410 | 122 | 61 | 91 | 4 | 13 | 3 | 10 | 6 | 85 | 77 | .525 |
| 2010 | Mariners | AL | 112 | 93 | .61 | 49 | 21 | 12 | 37 | 21 | 20 | 39 | 2 | 254 | 129 | 40 | 124 | 17 | 25 | 11 | 14 | 7 | 42 | 70 | .375 |
| 162-Game Average | | | | 137 | .55 | 63 | 31 | 18 | 51 | 28 | 22 | 68 | 2 | 393 | 148 | 60 | 127 | 12 | 22 | 8 | 14 | 8 | 75 | 87 | .463 |

## Ron Washington

| | | | | LINEUPS | | SUBSTITUTION | | | PITCHER USAGE | | | | | | TACTICS | | | | INTENTIONAL BB | | | | RESULTS | | |
|---|---|---|---|---|---|---|---|---|---|---|---|---|---|---|---|---|---|---|---|---|---|---|---|---|---|
| Year | Team | Lg | G | LUp | PL% | PH | PR | DS | Quick | Slow | LO | RCD | LS | Rel | SBA | SacA | RM | PO | # | Good | NG | Bomb | W | L | Pct |
| 2007 | Rangers | AL | 162 | 139 | .60 | 89 | 30 | **53** | 47 | 46 | 4 | 78 | 9 | 467 | 113 | **76** | 67 | 13 | 38 | 19 | 19 | 11 | 75 | 87 | .463 |
| 2008 | Rangers | AL | 162 | 129 | .64 | 118 | 16 | 14 | 31 | **53** | 11 | 85 | 3 | 458 | 106 | 53 | 74 | 20 | 44 | 19 | 25 | **20** | 79 | 83 | .488 |
| 2009 | Rangers | AL | 162 | 123 | .55 | 48 | 11 | 11 | 39 | 47 | 28 | 80 | 9 | 436 | 185 | 44 | 80 | 5 | 14 | 9 | 5 | 3 | 87 | 75 | .537 |
| 2010 | Rangers | AL | 162 | 112 | .52 | 86 | 39 | 31 | 46 | 42 | 35 | 110 | 4 | 481 | 171 | **68** | 160 | 10 | 24 | 15 | 9 | 0 | 90 | 72 | .556 |
| 2011 | Rangers | AL | 162 | 106 | .48 | 66 | 18 | 23 | 43 | 39 | 40 | 76 | 2 | 417 | 188 | 52 | 182 | 3 | 21 | 12 | 9 | 6 | 96 | 66 | .593 |
| 2012 | Rangers | AL | 162 | 79 | .47 | 94 | 25 | 37 | 30 | 48 | 33 | 91 | 0 | 428 | 135 | 46 | 155 | 22 | 15 | 10 | 5 | 5 | 93 | 69 | .574 |
| 2013 | Rangers | AL | 163 | 113 | .60 | 142 | 23 | 19 | 48 | 41 | 28 | 105 | 3 | 475 | **195** | **53** | 169 | 11 | 35 | **24** | 11 | 6 | 91 | 72 | .558 |
| 162-Game Average | | | | 114 | .55 | 92 | 23 | 27 | 41 | 45 | 26 | 89 | 4 | 451 | 156 | 56 | 127 | 12 | 27 | 15 | 12 | 7 | 87 | 75 | .537 |

## Eric Wedge

| | | | | LINEUPS | | SUBSTITUTION | | | PITCHER USAGE | | | | | | TACTICS | | | | INTENTIONAL BB | | | | RESULTS | | |
|---|---|---|---|---|---|---|---|---|---|---|---|---|---|---|---|---|---|---|---|---|---|---|---|---|---|
| Year | Team | Lg | G | LUp | PL% | PH | PR | DS | Quick | Slow | LO | RCD | LS | Rel | SBA | SacA | RM | PO | # | Good | NG | Bomb | W | L | Pct |
| 2003 | Indians | AL | 162 | **145** | .67 | 117 | 43 | 27 | 47 | 34 | 18 | 89 | 5 | 428 | 147 | 67 | 54 | 12 | 37 | 22 | 15 | 8 | 68 | 94 | .420 |
| 2004 | Indians | AL | 162 | 114 | .72 | 91 | 34 | 20 | 44 | 38 | 22 | 121 | 0 | **479** | 149 | 57 | 129 | 28 | 47 | 26 | **21** | **18** | 80 | 82 | .494 |
| 2005 | Indians | AL | 162 | 111 | .66 | 88 | 18 | 16 | 45 | 45 | 15 | 90 | 3 | 409 | 98 | 53 | 79 | 9 | 20 | 11 | 9 | 7 | 93 | 69 | .574 |
| 2006 | Indians | AL | 162 | 111 | .59 | 98 | 13 | 13 | 31 | 52 | 27 | 48 | 1 | 377 | 78 | 40 | 83 | 15 | 35 | 21 | 14 | 11 | 78 | 84 | .481 |
| 2007 | Indians | AL | 162 | 117 | .60 | 116 | 41 | 25 | 34 | 38 | 20 | 79 | 2 | 395 | 113 | 40 | 108 | 16 | 42 | 24 | 18 | 9 | **96** | 66 | .593 |
| 2008 | Indians | AL | 162 | **136** | .54 | 112 | 31 | 18 | 40 | 35 | 17 | 78 | 4 | 399 | 106 | 56 | 98 | 5 | 28 | 6 | 22 | 11 | 81 | 81 | .500 |
| 2009 | Indians | AL | 162 | **148** | .59 | 63 | 28 | 11 | 32 | 41 | 21 | 67 | 3 | 445 | 115 | 52 | 74 | 8 | 31 | 14 | 17 | 9 | 65 | 97 | .401 |
| 2011 | Mariners | AL | 162 | **152** | .68 | 52 | 30 | 22 | 39 | 45 | 30 | 50 | 1 | 351 | 165 | 43 | 161 | 7 | 27 | 20 | 7 | 6 | 67 | 95 | .414 |
| 2012 | Mariners | AL | 162 | 141 | .69 | 87 | 36 | 21 | 44 | 35 | 14 | 89 | 5 | 451 | 139 | 45 | 116 | 8 | 39 | 20 | **19** | 7 | 75 | 87 | .463 |
| 2013 | Mariners | AL | 162 | 143 | .70 | 78 | 36 | 33 | 50 | 36 | 8 | 82 | 2 | 448 | 72 | 43 | 97 | 3 | **48** | 19 | **29** | 12 | 71 | 91 | .438 |
| 162-Game Average | | | | 132 | .65 | 90 | 31 | 21 | 41 | 40 | 19 | 79 | 3 | 418 | 118 | 50 | 100 | 11 | 35 | 18 | 17 | 10 | 77 | 85 | .475 |

## Walt Weiss

| | | | | LINEUPS | | SUBSTITUTION | | | PITCHER USAGE | | | | | | TACTICS | | | | INTENTIONAL BB | | | | RESULTS | | |
|---|---|---|---|---|---|---|---|---|---|---|---|---|---|---|---|---|---|---|---|---|---|---|---|---|---|
| Year | Team | Lg | G | LUp | PL% | PH | PR | DS | Quick | Slow | LO | RCD | LS | Rel | SBA | SacA | RM | PO | # | Good | NG | Bomb | W | L | Pct |
| 2013 | Rockies | NL | 162 | 136 | .56 | 260 | 18 | 32 | 50 | 42 | 0 | 96 | 2 | 503 | 144 | 80 | 149 | 15 | 52 | 28 | **24** | 7 | 74 | 88 | .457 |
| 162-Game Average | | | | 136 | .56 | 260 | 18 | 32 | 50 | 42 | 0 | 96 | 2 | 503 | 144 | 80 | 149 | 15 | 52 | 28 | 24 | 7 | 74 | 88 | .457 |

## Ned Yost

| | | | | LINEUPS | | SUBSTITUTION | | | PITCHER USAGE | | | | | | TACTICS | | | | INTENTIONAL BB | | | | RESULTS | | |
|---|---|---|---|---|---|---|---|---|---|---|---|---|---|---|---|---|---|---|---|---|---|---|---|---|---|
| Year | Team | Lg | G | LUp | PL% | PH | PR | DS | Quick | Slow | LO | RCD | LS | Rel | SBA | SacA | RM | PO | # | Good | NG | Bomb | W | L | Pct |
| 2003 | Brewers | NL | 162 | 97 | .44 | 304 | 22 | 39 | 23 | **59** | 18 | 90 | 6 | 460 | 138 | 85 | 40 | 23 | 43 | 28 | 15 | 9 | 68 | 94 | .420 |
| 2004 | Brewers | NL | 161 | 131 | .60 | 283 | 25 | 20 | 39 | 41 | 27 | 63 | 2 | 423 | **178** | 79 | 108 | 8 | 27 | 16 | 11 | 8 | 67 | 94 | .416 |
| 2005 | Brewers | NL | 162 | 99 | .46 | 259 | 18 | 35 | 26 | 41 | **42** | 71 | 2 | 395 | 113 | 89 | 97 | 50 | 52 | 23 | **29** | 10 | 81 | 81 | .500 |
| 2006 | Brewers | NL | 162 | 106 | .48 | 238 | 12 | 14 | 33 | 44 | 18 | 77 | 4 | 427 | 108 | 80 | 82 | 16 | 34 | 14 | 20 | 12 | 75 | 87 | .463 |
| 2007 | Brewers | NL | 162 | 109 | .60 | 259 | 11 | 41 | 37 | 42 | 18 | 117 | **7** | 492 | 128 | 74 | 94 | 19 | 37 | 28 | 9 | 9 | 83 | 79 | .512 |
| 2008 | Brewers | NL | 150 | 93 | .48 | 217 | 5 | 16 | 37 | 39 | 23 | 69 | 5 | 399 | 141 | 61 | 105 | 31 | 30 | 17 | 13 | 7 | 83 | 67 | .553 |
| 2010 | Royals | AL | 127 | 80 | .57 | 56 | 25 | 6 | 22 | 39 | 20 | 65 | 0 | 332 | 127 | 40 | 128 | 18 | 25 | 16 | 9 | 5 | 55 | 72 | .433 |
| 2011 | Royals | AL | 162 | 87 | .58 | 36 | 28 | 16 | 42 | 42 | 21 | 56 | 7 | 420 | 211 | 65 | 203 | 19 | 42 | 27 | 15 | 5 | 71 | 91 | .438 |
| 2012 | Royals | AL | 162 | 118 | .57 | 60 | 34 | 15 | 48 | 37 | 10 | 108 | 1 | **500** | 170 | 37 | 149 | 25 | **44** | **29** | 15 | **11** | 72 | 90 | .444 |
| 2013 | Royals | AL | 162 | 127 | .60 | 79 | **48** | 39 | 43 | 44 | 21 | 72 | 2 | 427 | 185 | 48 | 168 | 25 | 21 | 12 | 9 | 5 | 86 | 76 | .531 |
| 162-Game Average | | | | 108 | .54 | 185 | 23 | 25 | 36 | 44 | 22 | 81 | 4 | 441 | 154 | 68 | 121 | 24 | 37 | 22 | 15 | 8 | 76 | 86 | .469 |

Categories of this record are Games Managed (G), Number of Different Lineups Used (LUp), the percentage of players who had the platoon advantage at the start of the game (PL%), Pinch Hitters Used (PH), Pinch Runners Used (PR), Defensive Substitutes Used (DS), Quick Hooks (Quick), Slow Hooks (Slow), Long Outings by Starting Pitchers (LO), Relievers Used on Consecutive Days (RCD), Long Saves (LS), Relievers Used (Rel), Stolen Base Attempts (SBA), Sacrifice Bunt Attempts (SacA), Runners Moving with the Pitch (RM), Pitchouts ordered (PO), Intentional Walks issued (#), Intentional Walks resulting in a Good Outcome (Good), Intentional Walks resulting Not in a Good Outcome (NG), Intentional Walks Blowing Up on the Manager (Bomb), Wins (W), Losses (L), and Winning Percentage (Pct).

# 2013 American League Managers

| | | LINEUPS | | SUBSTITUTION | | | PITCHER USAGE | | | | | | TACTICS | | | | INTENTIONAL BB | | | | RESULTS | | |
|---|---|---|---|---|---|---|---|---|---|---|---|---|---|---|---|---|---|---|---|---|---|---|---|
| Manager | G | LUp | PL% | PH | PR | DS | Quick | Slow | LO | RCD | LS | Rel | SBA | SacA | RM | PO | # | Good | NG | Bomb | W | L | Pct |
| John Farrell, Bos | 162 | 126 | .68 | 93 | 41 | 20 | 28 | 46 | 34 | 71 | 4 | 450 | 142 | 32 | 147 | 5 | 10 | 5 | 5 | 3 | **97** | 65 | .599 |
| Terry Francona, Cle | 162 | 121 | .75 | 78 | 45 | 24 | 47 | 34 | 18 | 122 | 2 | **540** | 153 | 41 | 158 | 5 | 26 | 15 | 11 | 6 | 92 | 70 | .568 |
| Ron Gardenhire, Min | 162 | 139 | .66 | 103 | 42 | 28 | 41 | 43 | 6 | 78 | 1 | 511 | 85 | 37 | 137 | 14 | 31 | 13 | 18 | 7 | 66 | 96 | .407 |
| John Gibbons, Tor | 162 | 136 | .63 | 124 | 31 | 24 | **55** | 44 | 14 | 69 | 2 | 487 | 153 | 41 | 160 | 4 | 33 | 17 | 16 | 6 | 74 | 88 | .457 |
| Joe Girardi, NYY | 162 | 141 | .59 | 119 | 15 | 29 | 42 | 50 | 23 | 82 | 4 | 428 | 146 | 49 | 131 | 4 | 34 | 20 | 14 | 6 | 85 | 77 | .525 |
| Jim Leyland, Det | 162 | 109 | .61 | 105 | 40 | 34 | 25 | 48 | **50** | 77 | 6 | 428 | 55 | 42 | 180 | 6 | 29 | 16 | 13 | 8 | 93 | 69 | .574 |
| Joe Maddon, TB | 163 | **147** | .64 | **193** | 27 | **56** | 52 | 38 | 16 | 111 | 6 | 485 | 111 | 26 | 117 | 6 | 38 | 21 | 17 | 11 | 92 | 71 | .564 |
| Bob Melvin, Oak | 162 | 133 | .77 | 166 | 14 | 35 | 48 | 28 | 7 | 84 | 7 | 447 | 102 | 32 | 74 | 8 | 23 | 18 | 5 | 3 | 96 | 66 | .593 |
| Bo Porter, Hou | 162 | 138 | .60 | 107 | 40 | 26 | 48 | 43 | 14 | 84 | 6 | 448 | 171 | 51 | 155 | 22 | 32 | 19 | 13 | 8 | 51 | **111** | .315 |
| Mike Scioscia, LAA | 162 | 118 | .56 | 88 | 26 | 39 | 31 | 44 | 29 | 130 | **8** | 496 | 116 | 48 | **205** | **41** | 36 | 19 | 17 | 11 | 78 | 84 | .481 |
| Buck Showalter, Bal | 162 | 100 | .65 | 90 | 23 | 21 | 31 | 39 | 19 | 84 | 4 | 473 | 108 | 37 | 104 | 4 | 32 | 11 | 21 | **13** | 85 | 77 | .525 |
| Robin Ventura, CWS | 162 | 116 | .47 | 76 | 47 | 33 | 24 | **52** | 38 | **133** | 0 | 470 | 147 | 24 | 132 | 15 | 24 | 12 | 12 | 4 | 63 | 99 | .389 |
| Ron Washington, Tex | 163 | 113 | .60 | 142 | 23 | 19 | 48 | 41 | 28 | 105 | 3 | 475 | **195** | **53** | 169 | 11 | 35 | **24** | 11 | 6 | 91 | 72 | .558 |
| Eric Wedge, Sea | 162 | 143 | .70 | 78 | 36 | 33 | 50 | 36 | 8 | 82 | 2 | 448 | 72 | 43 | 97 | 3 | **48** | 19 | **29** | 12 | 71 | 91 | .438 |
| Ned Yost, KC | 162 | 127 | .60 | 79 | **48** | 39 | 43 | 44 | 21 | 72 | 2 | 427 | 185 | 48 | 168 | 25 | 21 | 12 | 9 | 5 | 86 | 76 | .531 |
| 162-Game Average | | 127 | .63 | 109 | 33 | 31 | 41 | 42 | 22 | 92 | 4 | 467 | 129 | 40 | 142 | 12 | 30 | 16 | 14 | 7 | 81 | 81 | .500 |

# 2013 National League Managers

| | | LINEUPS | | SUBSTITUTION | | | PITCHER USAGE | | | | | | TACTICS | | | | INTENTIONAL BB | | | | RESULTS | | |
|---|---|---|---|---|---|---|---|---|---|---|---|---|---|---|---|---|---|---|---|---|---|---|---|
| Manager | G | LUp | PL% | PH | PR | DS | Quick | Slow | LO | RCD | LS | Rel | SBA | SacA | RM | PO | # | Good | NG | Bomb | W | L | Pct |
| Dusty Baker, Cin | 162 | 95 | .54 | 236 | 20 | 27 | 39 | 40 | 14 | 90 | 3 | 461 | 102 | **110** | 157 | **21** | 28 | 23 | 5 | 3 | 90 | 72 | .556 |
| Bud Black, SD | 162 | **145** | .66 | 271 | 24 | 37 | 35 | 46 | 4 | 102 | 1 | 488 | 152 | 78 | 122 | 12 | 31 | 20 | 11 | **8** | 76 | 86 | .469 |
| Bruce Bochy, SF | 162 | 109 | .70 | 263 | 19 | 45 | 33 | **52** | 23 | **143** | **4** | 524 | 93 | 78 | 164 | 7 | **64** | **46** | 18 | 6 | 76 | 86 | .469 |
| Terry Collins, NYM | 162 | 132 | .61 | 266 | 12 | 33 | 33 | 42 | 15 | 131 | **4** | **535** | 149 | 67 | 128 | 3 | 38 | 30 | 8 | 3 | 74 | 88 | .457 |
| Kirk Gibson, Ari | 162 | 138 | .59 | 285 | 22 | 15 | 31 | 44 | 9 | 121 | 0 | 527 | 103 | 67 | 108 | 3 | 42 | 31 | 11 | 5 | 81 | 81 | .500 |
| Fredi Gonzalez, Atl | 162 | 115 | .50 | 214 | **40** | 51 | 50 | 42 | 8 | 124 | 2 | 466 | 95 | 79 | 94 | 11 | 35 | 26 | 9 | 4 | 96 | 66 | .593 |
| Clint Hurdle, Pit | 162 | 127 | .51 | **289** | 24 | **61** | **61** | 25 | 7 | 76 | 3 | 465 | 136 | 83 | **172** | 20 | 26 | 22 | 4 | 2 | 94 | 68 | .580 |
| Davey Johnson, Was | 162 | 108 | .54 | 233 | 23 | 33 | 46 | 39 | **27** | 99 | 0 | 440 | 116 | 91 | 148 | 1 | 17 | 8 | 9 | 3 | 86 | 76 | .531 |
| Mike Matheny, StL | 162 | 89 | .56 | 237 | 30 | 41 | 42 | 49 | 25 | 114 | **4** | 483 | 67 | 73 | 125 | 6 | 26 | 20 | 6 | 6 | **97** | 65 | .599 |
| Don Mattingly, LAD | 162 | **145** | .55 | 210 | 18 | 47 | 40 | 30 | 18 | 118 | 3 | 504 | 106 | 99 | 131 | 10 | 44 | 28 | 16 | 7 | 92 | 70 | .568 |
| Mike Redmond, Mia | 162 | 132 | .52 | 240 | 8 | 9 | 47 | 30 | 4 | 88 | 1 | 471 | 107 | 81 | 124 | 2 | 58 | 42 | 16 | 7 | 62 | **100** | .383 |
| Ron Roenicke, Mil | 162 | 125 | .47 | 275 | 15 | 34 | 39 | 47 | 7 | 96 | 2 | 501 | **192** | 86 | 157 | 6 | 29 | 22 | 7 | 6 | 74 | 88 | .457 |
| Dale Sveum, ChC | 162 | 107 | .60 | 277 | 12 | 17 | 42 | 47 | 19 | 112 | 1 | 489 | 95 | 58 | 122 | 8 | 43 | 29 | 14 | **8** | 66 | 96 | .407 |
| Walt Weiss, Col | 162 | 136 | .56 | 260 | 18 | 32 | 50 | 42 | 0 | 96 | 2 | 503 | 144 | 80 | 149 | 15 | 52 | 28 | **24** | 7 | 74 | 88 | .457 |
| 162-Game Average | | 122 | .57 | 255 | 22 | 35 | 41 | 42 | 13 | 107 | 2 | 487 | 118 | 80 | 135 | 8 | 38 | 26 | 12 | 6 | 81 | 81 | .500 |

| | | LINEUPS | | SUBSTITUTION | | | PITCHER USAGE | | | | | | TACTICS | | | | INTENTIONAL BB | | | | RESULTS | | |
|---|---|---|---|---|---|---|---|---|---|---|---|---|---|---|---|---|---|---|---|---|---|---|---|
| Manager | G | LUp | PL% | PH | PR | DS | Quick | Slow | LO | RCD | LS | Rel | SBA | SacA | RM | PO | # | Good | NG | Bomb | W | L | Pct |
| Charlie Manuel, Phi | 120 | 90 | .61 | 196 | 29 | 29 | 20 | 38 | 16 | 73 | 1 | 331 | 88 | 53 | 90 | 1 | 23 | 13 | 10 | 7 | 53 | 67 | .442 |
| Ryne Sandberg, Phi | 42 | 34 | .66 | 66 | 4 | 6 | 6 | 12 | 7 | 18 | 0 | 135 | 14 | 15 | 26 | 0 | 10 | 6 | 4 | 4 | 20 | 22 | .476 |

# Ballparks and Park Indices

A Park Index tells you whether a given park is favorable to hitters or pitchers compared to other MLB parks. For example, Coors Field in Colorado had a park index for scoring runs of 127 in 2013, meaning 27 percent more runs were scored there than other parks. Citizens Bank Park in Philadelphia had a home run park index of 148, which made it the homer-friendliest park in baseball last season.

Park indices are calculated in a way that neutralizes the effect of a team's makeup and isolates the effects of the park. The isolation is figured by comparing what both the team and its opponents accomplished at home, and comparing that to what the same team and its opponents accomplished on the road.

To calculate the park index for home runs in a given ballpark, we take the total home runs of both the home team and its opponents at the ballpark and compare it to the total home runs of the home team and its opponents in other games. We then divide each of those totals by the at-bats in the equivalent situations, so that if there are more at-bats in either situation the index is not skewed. The result is then multiplied by 100 to yield the familiar form.

The park indices for doubles, triples, walks, strikeouts and home runs by lefties and righties are determined like home runs above, relative to at-bats. Indices of at-bats, runs, hits, errors and infield fielding errors (E-Infield) are calculated relative to games. The three batting average indices are calculated as is, since these are already relative to at-bats.

A park with an index of exactly 100 is neutral and can be said to have no effect on that particular stat. An index above 100 means the ballpark favors that statistic. For example, if a park has a home run index of 120, it was 20 percent easier to hit home runs in that park than the rest of the parks in the team's league.

In 2013, both Seattle and San Diego moved in parts of their outfield fences. Compared to 2012, Safeco Field in Seattle went from a park factor of 62 for home runs, tied for second-lowest in baseball, to one of 97 last season. Similarly, PETCO Park in San Diego went from a park factor of 62 for home runs in 2012 to one of 94 in 2013.

Finally, the Astros were realigned into the American League in 2013, which is where you find both their 2013 and their historical park data.

# Arizona Diamondbacks - Chase Field

LF: 330 CF: 407 RF:334

| | 2013 Season | | | | | | | 2011-2013 | | | | | | |
|---|---|---|---|---|---|---|---|---|---|---|---|---|---|---|
| | Home Games | | | Away Games | | | | Home Games | | | Away Games | | | |
| | D'Backs | Opp | Total | D'Backs | Opp | Total | Index | D'Backs | Opp | Total | D'Backs | Opp | Total | Index |
| G | 81 | 81 | 162 | 81 | 81 | 162 | | 243 | 243 | 486 | 243 | 243 | 486 | |
| Avg | .259 | .254 | .256 | .258 | .259 | .259 | 99 | .261 | .260 | .261 | .251 | .256 | .254 | 103 |
| AB | 2701 | 2851 | 5552 | 2975 | 2841 | 5816 | 95 | 8033 | 8524 | 16557 | 8526 | 8157 | 16683 | 99 |
| R | 343 | 338 | 681 | 342 | 357 | 699 | 97 | 1134 | 1058 | 2192 | 1016 | 987 | 2003 | 109 |
| H | 699 | 723 | 1422 | 769 | 737 | 1506 | 94 | 2099 | 2217 | 4316 | 2142 | 2089 | 4231 | 102 |
| 2B | 156 | 146 | 302 | 146 | 153 | 299 | 106 | 475 | 468 | 943 | 427 | 423 | 850 | 112 |
| 3B | 20 | 13 | 33 | 11 | 13 | 24 | 144 | 67 | 46 | 113 | 34 | 53 | 87 | 131 |
| HR | 68 | 81 | 149 | 62 | 95 | 157 | 99 | 245 | 251 | 496 | 222 | 239 | 461 | 108 |
| BB | 270 | 227 | 497 | 249 | 258 | 507 | 103 | 799 | 633 | 1432 | 790 | 711 | 1501 | 96 |
| SO | 535 | 596 | 1131 | 607 | 622 | 1229 | 96 | 1758 | 1758 | 3516 | 1899 | 1718 | 3617 | 98 |
| Foul Outs | 58 | 64 | 122 | 62 | 51 | 113 | 113 | 160 | 196 | 356 | 181 | 160 | 341 | 105 |
| E | 41 | 32 | 73 | 34 | 35 | 69 | 106 | 126 | 107 | 233 | 129 | 124 | 253 | 92 |
| E-Infield | 15 | 16 | 31 | 15 | 15 | 30 | 103 | 52 | 48 | 100 | 52 | 52 | 104 | 96 |
| LHB-Avg | .244 | .256 | .250 | .242 | .265 | .252 | 99 | .251 | .258 | .255 | .246 | .259 | .252 | 101 |
| LHB-HR | 27 | 29 | 56 | 21 | 38 | 59 | 97 | 90 | 90 | 180 | 84 | 86 | 170 | 105 |
| RHB-Avg | .271 | .252 | .261 | .271 | .256 | .264 | 99 | .268 | .261 | .265 | .255 | .254 | .255 | 104 |
| RHB-HR | 41 | 52 | 93 | 41 | 57 | 98 | 101 | 155 | 161 | 316 | 138 | 153 | 291 | 111 |

# Atlanta Braves - Turner Field

LF: 335 CF: 401 RF:330

| | 2013 Season | | | | | | | 2011-2013 | | | | | | |
|---|---|---|---|---|---|---|---|---|---|---|---|---|---|---|
| | Home Games | | | Away Games | | | | Home Games | | | Away Games | | | |
| | Braves | Opp | Total | Braves | Opp | Total | Index | Braves | Opp | Total | Braves | Opp | Total | Index |
| G | 81 | 81 | 162 | 81 | 81 | 162 | | 243 | 243 | 486 | 243 | 243 | 486 | |
| Avg | .260 | .233 | .246 | .238 | .255 | .246 | 100 | .255 | .235 | .245 | .238 | .249 | .244 | 101 |
| AB | 2651 | 2756 | 5407 | 2790 | 2687 | 5477 | 99 | 8003 | 8352 | 16355 | 8391 | 8030 | 16421 | 100 |
| R | 364 | 240 | 604 | 324 | 308 | 632 | 96 | 1040 | 834 | 1874 | 989 | 919 | 1908 | 98 |
| H | 690 | 641 | 1331 | 664 | 685 | 1349 | 99 | 2043 | 1966 | 4009 | 1997 | 2002 | 3999 | 100 |
| 2B | 125 | 118 | 243 | 122 | 141 | 263 | 94 | 391 | 366 | 757 | 363 | 372 | 735 | 103 |
| 3B | 13 | 12 | 25 | 8 | 12 | 20 | 127 | 37 | 33 | 70 | 30 | 45 | 75 | 94 |
| HR | 90 | 58 | 148 | 91 | 69 | 160 | 94 | 250 | 180 | 430 | 253 | 217 | 470 | 92 |
| BB | 278 | 184 | 462 | 264 | 225 | 489 | 96 | 856 | 659 | 1515 | 757 | 735 | 1492 | 102 |
| SO | 675 | 669 | 1344 | 709 | 563 | 1272 | 107 | 1941 | 2049 | 3990 | 1992 | 1747 | 3739 | 107 |
| Foul Outs | 64 | 52 | 116 | 64 | 61 | 125 | 94 | 166 | 154 | 320 | 194 | 145 | 339 | 95 |
| E | 41 | 47 | 88 | 44 | 46 | 90 | 98 | 138 | 158 | 296 | 116 | 129 | 245 | 121 |
| E-Infield | 19 | 21 | 40 | 17 | 23 | 40 | 100 | 56 | 72 | 128 | 54 | 63 | 117 | 109 |
| LHB-Avg | .289 | .242 | .264 | .245 | .248 | .246 | 107 | .269 | .244 | .257 | .247 | .246 | .247 | 104 |
| LHB-HR | 42 | 21 | 63 | 27 | 26 | 53 | 114 | 136 | 80 | 216 | 127 | 79 | 206 | 106 |
| RHB-Avg | .244 | .226 | .235 | .234 | .259 | .246 | 95 | .243 | .229 | .236 | .229 | .252 | .241 | 98 |
| RHB-HR | 48 | 37 | 85 | 64 | 43 | 107 | 83 | 114 | 100 | 214 | 126 | 138 | 264 | 81 |

# Baltimore Orioles - Oriole Park at Camden Yards

LF: 337 CF: 406 RF:320

| | 2013 Season | | | | | | | 2011-2013 | | | | | | |
|---|---|---|---|---|---|---|---|---|---|---|---|---|---|---|
| | Home Games | | | Away Games | | | | Home Games | | | Away Games | | | |
| | Orioles | Opp | Total | Orioles | Opp | Total | Index | Orioles | Opp | Total | D'Backs | Opp | Total | Index |
| G | 81 | 81 | 162 | 81 | 81 | 162 | | 243 | 243 | 486 | 243 | 243 | 486 | |
| Avg | .264 | .256 | .260 | .256 | .263 | .259 | 100 | .259 | .264 | .262 | .251 | .262 | .256 | 102 |
| AB | 2729 | 2808 | 5537 | 2891 | 2735 | 5626 | 98 | 8201 | 8643 | 16844 | 8564 | 8240 | 16804 | 100 |
| R | 382 | 365 | 747 | 363 | 344 | 707 | 106 | 1129 | 1165 | 2294 | 1036 | 1109 | 2145 | 107 |
| H | 720 | 720 | 1440 | 740 | 718 | 1458 | 99 | 2123 | 2283 | 4406 | 2146 | 2156 | 4302 | 102 |
| 2B | 138 | 131 | 269 | 160 | 152 | 312 | 88 | 428 | 447 | 875 | 413 | 461 | 874 | 100 |
| 3B | 6 | 8 | 14 | 8 | 14 | 22 | 65 | 17 | 27 | 44 | 26 | 38 | 64 | 69 |
| HR | 115 | 117 | 232 | 97 | 85 | 182 | 130 | 348 | 324 | 672 | 269 | 272 | 541 | 124 |
| BB | 206 | 241 | 447 | 210 | 232 | 442 | 103 | 676 | 762 | 1438 | 672 | 727 | 1399 | 103 |
| SO | 533 | 604 | 1137 | 592 | 565 | 1157 | 100 | 1701 | 1741 | 3442 | 1859 | 1649 | 3508 | 98 |
| Foul Outs | 71 | 61 | 132 | 71 | 75 | 146 | 92 | 200 | 164 | 364 | 213 | 200 | 413 | 88 |
| E | 28 | 50 | 78 | 26 | 45 | 71 | 110 | 120 | 145 | 265 | 150 | 130 | 280 | 95 |
| E-Infield | 9 | 18 | 27 | 12 | 21 | 33 | 82 | 57 | 61 | 118 | 67 | 50 | 117 | 101 |
| LHB-Avg | .259 | .268 | .264 | .245 | .263 | .254 | 104 | .259 | .266 | .262 | .245 | .254 | .249 | 105 |
| LHB-HR | 63 | 65 | 128 | 42 | 43 | 85 | 145 | 147 | 158 | 305 | 101 | 125 | 226 | 134 |
| RHB-Avg | .268 | .245 | .256 | .266 | .262 | .264 | 97 | .259 | .263 | .261 | .255 | .268 | .261 | 100 |
| RHB-HR | 52 | 52 | 104 | 55 | 42 | 97 | 115 | 201 | 166 | 367 | 168 | 147 | 315 | 117 |

# Boston Red Sox - Fenway Park

LF: 310 CF: 420 RF:302

| | 2013 Season | | | | | | | 2011-2013 | | | | | | |
|---|---|---|---|---|---|---|---|---|---|---|---|---|---|---|
| | Home Games | | | Away Games | | | | Home Games | | | Away Games | | | |
| | Red Sox | Opp | Total | Red Sox | Opp | Total | Index | Red Sox | Opp | Total | Red Sox | Opp | Total | Index |
| G | 81 | 81 | 162 | 81 | 81 | 162 | | 243 | 243 | 486 | 243 | 243 | 486 | |
| Avg | .285 | .243 | .264 | .269 | .253 | .261 | 101 | .287 | .259 | .273 | .259 | .245 | .252 | 108 |
| AB | 2737 | 2801 | 5538 | 2914 | 2708 | 5622 | 99 | 8402 | 8553 | 16955 | 8563 | 8006 | 16569 | 102 |
| R | 419 | 320 | 739 | 434 | 336 | 770 | 96 | 1298 | 1153 | 2451 | 1164 | 1046 | 2210 | 111 |
| H | 781 | 682 | 1463 | 785 | 684 | 1469 | 100 | 2409 | 2216 | 4625 | 2216 | 1965 | 4181 | 111 |
| 2B | 205 | 143 | 348 | 158 | 138 | 296 | 119 | 615 | 473 | 1088 | 439 | 386 | 825 | 129 |
| 3B | 18 | 13 | 31 | 11 | 13 | 24 | 131 | 49 | 38 | 87 | 31 | 38 | 69 | 123 |
| HR | 83 | 70 | 153 | 95 | 86 | 181 | 86 | 262 | 244 | 506 | 284 | 258 | 542 | 91 |
| BB | 278 | 250 | 528 | 303 | 274 | 577 | 93 | 783 | 784 | 1567 | 804 | 809 | 1613 | 95 |
| SO | 631 | 670 | 1301 | 677 | 624 | 1301 | 102 | 1763 | 1888 | 3651 | 1850 | 1795 | 3645 | 98 |
| Foul Outs | 41 | 49 | 90 | 61 | 78 | 139 | 66 | 133 | 160 | 293 | 165 | 216 | 381 | 75 |
| E | 46 | 48 | 94 | 34 | 46 | 80 | 118 | 154 | 152 | 306 | 119 | 131 | 250 | 122 |
| E-Infield | 19 | 17 | 36 | 12 | 15 | 27 | 133 | 66 | 62 | 128 | 44 | 53 | 97 | 132 |
| LHB-Avg | .298 | .227 | .264 | .277 | .247 | .263 | 100 | .296 | .251 | .275 | .268 | .243 | .257 | 107 |
| LHB-HR | 41 | 23 | 64 | 49 | 39 | 88 | 71 | 132 | 84 | 216 | 166 | 117 | 283 | 73 |
| RHB-Avg | .272 | .257 | .264 | .262 | .257 | .260 | 102 | .277 | .266 | .271 | .250 | .247 | .248 | 109 |
| RHB-HR | 42 | 47 | 89 | 46 | 47 | 93 | 100 | 130 | 160 | 290 | 118 | 141 | 259 | 111 |

# Chicago Cubs - Wrigley Field

LF: 355 CF: 400 RF:353

| | 2013 Season | | | | | | | 2011-2013 | | | | | | |
|---|---|---|---|---|---|---|---|---|---|---|---|---|---|---|
| | Home Games | | | Away Games | | | | Home Games | | | Away Games | | | |
| | Cubs | Opp | Total | Cubs | Opp | Total | Index | Cubs | Opp | Total | Cubs | Opp | Total | Index |
| G | 81 | 81 | 162 | 81 | 81 | 162 | | 243 | 243 | 486 | 243 | 243 | 486 | |
| Avg | .251 | .251 | .251 | .225 | .237 | .231 | 109 | .251 | .251 | .251 | .239 | .259 | .248 | 101 |
| AB | 2701 | 2817 | 5518 | 2797 | 2631 | 5428 | 102 | 8058 | 8400 | 16458 | 8400 | 7951 | 16351 | 101 |
| R | 335 | 367 | 702 | 267 | 322 | 589 | 119 | 991 | 1086 | 2077 | 878 | 1118 | 1996 | 104 |
| H | 677 | 708 | 1385 | 630 | 624 | 1254 | 110 | 2022 | 2112 | 4134 | 2005 | 2058 | 4063 | 102 |
| 2B | 150 | 166 | 316 | 147 | 135 | 282 | 110 | 423 | 437 | 860 | 424 | 426 | 850 | 101 |
| 3B | 8 | 16 | 24 | 10 | 17 | 27 | 87 | 52 | 49 | 101 | 38 | 60 | 98 | 102 |
| HR | 102 | 73 | 175 | 70 | 87 | 157 | 110 | 240 | 242 | 482 | 217 | 255 | 472 | 101 |
| BB | 220 | 280 | 500 | 219 | 260 | 479 | 103 | 691 | 865 | 1556 | 620 | 828 | 1448 | 107 |
| SO | 604 | 625 | 1229 | 626 | 559 | 1185 | 102 | 1782 | 1889 | 3671 | 1885 | 1647 | 3532 | 103 |
| Foul Outs | 47 | 43 | 90 | 69 | 62 | 131 | 68 | 131 | 124 | 255 | 171 | 159 | 330 | 77 |
| E | 56 | 49 | 105 | 44 | 57 | 101 | 104 | 186 | 166 | 352 | 153 | 158 | 311 | 113 |
| E-Infield | 27 | 18 | 45 | 18 | 27 | 45 | 100 | 82 | 77 | 159 | 64 | 74 | 138 | 115 |
| LHB-Avg | .262 | .249 | .256 | .220 | .217 | .219 | 117 | .247 | .247 | .247 | .228 | .253 | .241 | 103 |
| LHB-HR | 43 | 25 | 68 | 40 | 25 | 65 | 104 | 91 | 81 | 172 | 95 | 89 | 184 | 94 |
| RHB-Avg | .242 | .253 | .248 | .229 | .252 | .240 | 103 | .253 | .254 | .254 | .246 | .263 | .254 | 100 |
| RHB-HR | 59 | 48 | 107 | 30 | 62 | 92 | 114 | 149 | 161 | 310 | 122 | 166 | 288 | 106 |

# Chicago White Sox - U.S. Cellular Field

LF: 330 CF: 400 RF:335

| | 2013 Season | | | | | | | 2011-2013 | | | | | | |
|---|---|---|---|---|---|---|---|---|---|---|---|---|---|---|
| | Home Games | | | Away Games | | | | Home Games | | | Away Games | | | |
| | White Sox | Opp | Total | White Sox | Opp | Total | Index | White Sox | Opp | Total | White Sox | Opp | Total | Index |
| G | 81 | 81 | 162 | 81 | 81 | 162 | | 243 | 243 | 486 | 243 | 243 | 486 | |
| Avg | .249 | .247 | .248 | .249 | .265 | .257 | 97 | .256 | .251 | .254 | .248 | .260 | .254 | 100 |
| AB | 2686 | 2823 | 5509 | 2877 | 2741 | 5618 | 98 | 8086 | 8463 | 16549 | 8497 | 8184 | 16681 | 99 |
| R | 302 | 358 | 660 | 296 | 365 | 661 | 100 | 1033 | 1100 | 2133 | 967 | 1005 | 1972 | 108 |
| H | 669 | 697 | 1366 | 716 | 727 | 1443 | 95 | 2074 | 2128 | 4202 | 2107 | 2124 | 4231 | 99 |
| 2B | 100 | 113 | 213 | 137 | 143 | 280 | 78 | 340 | 370 | 710 | 377 | 403 | 780 | 92 |
| 3B | 5 | 7 | 12 | 14 | 15 | 29 | 42 | 29 | 25 | 54 | 35 | 48 | 83 | 66 |
| HR | 81 | 98 | 179 | 67 | 84 | 151 | 121 | 287 | 286 | 573 | 226 | 229 | 455 | 127 |
| BB | 232 | 262 | 494 | 179 | 247 | 426 | 118 | 742 | 784 | 1526 | 605 | 667 | 1272 | 121 |
| SO | 567 | 655 | 1222 | 640 | 594 | 1234 | 101 | 1643 | 1969 | 3612 | 1756 | 1746 | 3502 | 104 |
| Foul Outs | 59 | 72 | 131 | 62 | 58 | 120 | 111 | 203 | 193 | 396 | 192 | 168 | 360 | 111 |
| E | 65 | 40 | 105 | 56 | 34 | 90 | 117 | 141 | 132 | 273 | 129 | 128 | 257 | 106 |
| E-Infield | 27 | 17 | 44 | 25 | 13 | 38 | 116 | 55 | 52 | 107 | 54 | 50 | 104 | 103 |
| LHB-Avg | .242 | .242 | .242 | .231 | .280 | .257 | 94 | .249 | .253 | .252 | .242 | .269 | .256 | 98 |
| LHB-HR | 39 | 40 | 79 | 34 | 38 | 72 | 119 | 103 | 122 | 225 | 86 | 103 | 189 | 121 |
| RHB-Avg | .253 | .250 | .251 | .258 | .255 | .257 | 98 | .260 | .250 | .255 | .252 | .252 | .252 | 101 |
| RHB-HR | 42 | 58 | 100 | 33 | 46 | 79 | 125 | 184 | 164 | 348 | 140 | 126 | 266 | 131 |

# Cincinnati Reds - Great American Ballpark

LF: 328 CF: 404 RF:325

| | 2013 Season | | | | | | | 2011-2013 | | | | | | |
|---|---|---|---|---|---|---|---|---|---|---|---|---|---|---|
| | Home Games | | | Away Games | | | | Home Games | | | Away Games | | | |
| | Reds | Opp | Total | Reds | Opp | Total | Index | Reds | Opp | Total | Reds | Opp | Total | Index |
| G | 80 | 80 | 160 | 82 | 82 | 164 | | 242 | 242 | 484 | 244 | 244 | 488 | |
| Avg | .249 | .230 | .239 | .250 | .242 | .246 | 97 | .255 | .244 | .250 | .250 | .248 | .249 | 100 |
| AB | 2676 | 2795 | 5471 | 2823 | 2683 | 5506 | 102 | 8034 | 8420 | 16454 | 8554 | 8096 | 16650 | 100 |
| R | 338 | 294 | 632 | 360 | 295 | 655 | 99 | 1078 | 972 | 2050 | 1024 | 925 | 1949 | 106 |
| H | 665 | 644 | 1309 | 705 | 650 | 1355 | 99 | 2050 | 2056 | 4106 | 2135 | 2008 | 4143 | 100 |
| 2B | 136 | 134 | 270 | 138 | 118 | 256 | 106 | 385 | 391 | 776 | 449 | 402 | 851 | 92 |
| 3B | 8 | 12 | 20 | 12 | 13 | 25 | 81 | 36 | 38 | 74 | 33 | 49 | 82 | 91 |
| HR | 82 | 102 | 184 | 73 | 68 | 141 | 131 | 290 | 302 | 592 | 220 | 205 | 425 | 141 |
| BB | 282 | 221 | 503 | 303 | 214 | 517 | 98 | 794 | 684 | 1478 | 807 | 717 | 1524 | 98 |
| SO | 632 | 725 | 1357 | 613 | 571 | 1184 | 115 | 1871 | 1941 | 3812 | 1890 | 1715 | 3605 | 107 |
| Foul Outs | 44 | 50 | 94 | 51 | 53 | 104 | 91 | 155 | 163 | 318 | 162 | 155 | 317 | 102 |
| E | 38 | 55 | 93 | 38 | 50 | 88 | 108 | 121 | 152 | 273 | 135 | 169 | 304 | 91 |
| E-Infield | 16 | 17 | 33 | 13 | 25 | 38 | 89 | 62 | 57 | 119 | 44 | 82 | 126 | 95 |
| LHB-Avg | .268 | .230 | .249 | .270 | .254 | .262 | 95 | .273 | .248 | .258 | .275 | .252 | .262 | 99 |
| LHB-HR | 43 | 49 | 92 | 41 | 31 | 72 | 130 | 110 | 136 | 246 | 98 | 93 | 191 | 131 |
| RHB-Avg | .233 | .231 | .232 | .233 | .233 | .233 | 100 | .247 | .241 | .244 | .238 | .245 | .241 | 101 |
| RHB-HR | 39 | 53 | 92 | 32 | 37 | 69 | 133 | 180 | 166 | 346 | 122 | 112 | 234 | 149 |

# Cleveland Indians - Progressive Field

LF: 325 CF: 405 RF:325

| | 2013 Season | | | | | | | 2011-2013 | | | | | | |
|---|---|---|---|---|---|---|---|---|---|---|---|---|---|---|
| | Home Games | | | Away Games | | | | Home Games | | | Away Games | | | |
| | Indians | Opp | Total | Indians | Opp | Total | Index | Indians | Opp | Total | Indians | Opp | Total | Index |
| G | 81 | 81 | 162 | 81 | 81 | 162 | | 243 | 243 | 486 | 243 | 243 | 486 | |
| Avg | .254 | .245 | .249 | .255 | .253 | .254 | 98 | .252 | .254 | .253 | .252 | .267 | .259 | 97 |
| AB | 2651 | 2799 | 5450 | 2814 | 2668 | 5482 | 99 | 8068 | 8603 | 16671 | 8431 | 8095 | 16526 | 101 |
| R | 358 | 321 | 679 | 387 | 341 | 728 | 93 | 1029 | 1083 | 2112 | 1087 | 1184 | 2271 | 93 |
| H | 673 | 685 | 1358 | 718 | 674 | 1392 | 98 | 2031 | 2181 | 4212 | 2125 | 2163 | 4288 | 98 |
| 2B | 141 | 137 | 278 | 149 | 130 | 279 | 100 | 414 | 465 | 879 | 432 | 442 | 874 | 100 |
| 3B | 7 | 10 | 17 | 16 | 11 | 27 | 63 | 29 | 24 | 53 | 44 | 61 | 105 | 50 |
| HR | 87 | 78 | 165 | 84 | 69 | 153 | 108 | 240 | 232 | 472 | 221 | 242 | 463 | 101 |
| BB | 269 | 265 | 534 | 293 | 289 | 582 | 92 | 792 | 750 | 1542 | 819 | 810 | 1629 | 94 |
| SO | 644 | 724 | 1368 | 639 | 655 | 1294 | 106 | 1799 | 1851 | 3650 | 1840 | 1638 | 3478 | 104 |
| Foul Outs | 44 | 46 | 90 | 49 | 53 | 102 | 89 | 152 | 162 | 314 | 177 | 168 | 345 | 90 |
| E | 50 | 40 | 90 | 48 | 44 | 92 | 98 | 154 | 131 | 285 | 150 | 118 | 268 | 106 |
| E-Infield | 17 | 12 | 29 | 22 | 21 | 43 | 67 | 58 | 49 | 107 | 66 | 51 | 117 | 91 |
| LHB-Avg | .257 | .240 | .249 | .250 | .256 | .253 | 98 | .256 | .263 | .259 | .251 | .274 | .261 | 99 |
| LHB-HR | 51 | 40 | 91 | 39 | 37 | 76 | 117 | 171 | 132 | 303 | 130 | 118 | 248 | 120 |
| RHB-Avg | .249 | .250 | .249 | .261 | .249 | .255 | 98 | .243 | .244 | .244 | .254 | .261 | .258 | 94 |
| RHB-HR | 36 | 38 | 74 | 45 | 32 | 77 | 100 | 69 | 100 | 169 | 91 | 124 | 215 | 79 |

# Colorado Rockies - Coors Field

LF: 347 CF: 415 RF:350

| | 2013 Season | | | | | | | 2011-2013 | | | | | | |
|---|---|---|---|---|---|---|---|---|---|---|---|---|---|---|
| | Home Games | | | Away Games | | | | Home Games | | | Away Games | | | |
| | Rockies | Opp | Total | Rockies | Opp | Total | Index | Rockies | Opp | Total | Rockies | Opp | Total | Index |
| G | 81 | 81 | 162 | 81 | 81 | 162 | | 243 | 243 | 486 | 243 | 243 | 486 | |
| Avg | .293 | .280 | .286 | .246 | .273 | .260 | 110 | .291 | .289 | .290 | .243 | .265 | .254 | 114 |
| AB | 2836 | 2907 | 5743 | 2763 | 2679 | 5442 | 106 | 8419 | 8784 | 17203 | 8301 | 7992 | 16293 | 106 |
| R | 434 | 387 | 821 | 272 | 373 | 645 | 127 | 1359 | 1337 | 2696 | 840 | 1087 | 1927 | 140 |
| H | 830 | 813 | 1643 | 681 | 732 | 1413 | 116 | 2448 | 2539 | 4987 | 2018 | 2114 | 4132 | 121 |
| 2B | 156 | 177 | 333 | 127 | 171 | 298 | 106 | 477 | 514 | 991 | 386 | 447 | 833 | 113 |
| 3B | 30 | 13 | 43 | 6 | 19 | 25 | 163 | 92 | 67 | 159 | 36 | 66 | 102 | 148 |
| HR | 88 | 71 | 159 | 71 | 65 | 136 | 111 | 282 | 290 | 572 | 206 | 220 | 426 | 127 |
| BB | 229 | 241 | 470 | 198 | 276 | 474 | 94 | 792 | 751 | 1543 | 640 | 854 | 1494 | 98 |
| SO | 518 | 535 | 1053 | 686 | 529 | 1215 | 82 | 1616 | 1653 | 3269 | 2002 | 1673 | 3675 | 84 |
| Foul Outs | 46 | 37 | 83 | 38 | 52 | 90 | 87 | 131 | 137 | 268 | 151 | 160 | 311 | 82 |
| E | 46 | 75 | 121 | 44 | 28 | 72 | 168 | 166 | 200 | 366 | 144 | 129 | 273 | 134 |
| E-Infield | 17 | 26 | 43 | 16 | 14 | 30 | 143 | 56 | 74 | 130 | 58 | 60 | 118 | 110 |
| LHB-Avg | .269 | .262 | .265 | .245 | .272 | .259 | 102 | .292 | .280 | .286 | .247 | .264 | .255 | 112 |
| LHB-HR | 39 | 19 | 58 | 28 | 26 | 54 | 104 | 124 | 114 | 238 | 82 | 87 | 169 | 135 |
| RHB-Avg | .306 | .292 | .299 | .247 | .274 | .260 | 115 | .290 | .295 | .293 | .241 | .265 | .252 | 116 |
| RHB-HR | 49 | 52 | 101 | 43 | 39 | 82 | 115 | 158 | 176 | 334 | 124 | 133 | 257 | 122 |

# Detroit Tigers - Comerica Park

LF: 345 CF: 420 RF:330

| | 2013 Season | | | | | | | 2011-2013 | | | | | | |
|---|---|---|---|---|---|---|---|---|---|---|---|---|---|---|
| | Home Games | | | Away Games | | | | Home Games | | | Away Games | | | |
| | Tigers | Opp | Total | Tigers | Opp | Total | Index | Tigers | Opp | Total | Tigers | Opp | Total | Index |
| G | 81 | 81 | 162 | 81 | 81 | 162 | | 243 | 243 | 486 | 243 | 243 | 486 | |
| Avg | .300 | .250 | .275 | .268 | .244 | .256 | 107 | .289 | .255 | .271 | .264 | .252 | .258 | 105 |
| AB | 2760 | 2803 | 5563 | 2975 | 2736 | 5711 | 97 | 8146 | 8429 | 16575 | 8628 | 8084 | 16712 | 99 |
| R | 425 | 331 | 756 | 371 | 293 | 664 | 114 | 1231 | 1018 | 2249 | 1078 | 987 | 2065 | 109 |
| H | 828 | 702 | 1530 | 797 | 667 | 1464 | 105 | 2351 | 2146 | 4497 | 2281 | 2038 | 4319 | 104 |
| 2B | 141 | 148 | 289 | 151 | 111 | 262 | 113 | 420 | 413 | 833 | 448 | 376 | 824 | 102 |
| 3B | 13 | 19 | 32 | 10 | 9 | 19 | 173 | 63 | 59 | 122 | 33 | 35 | 68 | 181 |
| HR | 88 | 65 | 153 | 88 | 63 | 151 | 104 | 274 | 196 | 470 | 234 | 232 | 466 | 102 |
| BB | 278 | 232 | 510 | 253 | 230 | 483 | 108 | 776 | 673 | 1449 | 787 | 719 | 1506 | 97 |
| SO | 468 | 686 | 1154 | 605 | 742 | 1347 | 88 | 1467 | 1895 | 3362 | 1852 | 1966 | 3818 | 89 |
| Foul Outs | 64 | 54 | 118 | 49 | 43 | 92 | 132 | 196 | 177 | 373 | 163 | 167 | 330 | 114 |
| E | 36 | 37 | 73 | 40 | 44 | 84 | 87 | 151 | 125 | 276 | 127 | 135 | 262 | 105 |
| E-Infield | 13 | 14 | 27 | 14 | 22 | 36 | 75 | 62 | 40 | 102 | 41 | 60 | 101 | 101 |
| LHB-Avg | .288 | .258 | .270 | .250 | .243 | .246 | 110 | .285 | .260 | .271 | .260 | .250 | .255 | 106 |
| LHB-HR | 35 | 37 | 72 | 30 | 30 | 60 | 126 | 108 | 100 | 208 | 86 | 110 | 196 | 108 |
| RHB-Avg | .308 | .242 | .279 | .281 | .244 | .265 | 105 | .291 | .249 | .272 | .267 | .254 | .262 | 104 |
| RHB-HR | 53 | 28 | 81 | 58 | 33 | 91 | 89 | 166 | 96 | 262 | 148 | 122 | 270 | 97 |

# Houston Astros - Minute Maid Park

LF: 315 CF: 435 RF:326

| | 2013 Season | | | | | | | 2011-2013 | | | | | | |
|---|---|---|---|---|---|---|---|---|---|---|---|---|---|---|
| | Home Games | | | Away Games | | | | Home Games | | | Away Games | | | |
| | Astros | Opp | Total | Astros | Opp | Total | Index | Astros | Opp | Total | Astros | Opp | Total | Index |
| G | 81 | 81 | 162 | 81 | 81 | 162 | | 243 | 243 | 486 | 243 | 243 | 486 | |
| Avg | .232 | .273 | .253 | .247 | .272 | .259 | 98 | .245 | .264 | .255 | .244 | .275 | .259 | 98 |
| AB | 2699 | 2938 | 5637 | 2758 | 2682 | 5440 | 104 | 8121 | 8657 | 16778 | 8341 | 8045 | 16386 | 102 |
| R | 298 | 457 | 755 | 312 | 391 | 703 | 107 | 934 | 1226 | 2160 | 874 | 1212 | 2086 | 104 |
| H | 627 | 801 | 1428 | 680 | 729 | 1409 | 101 | 1990 | 2284 | 4274 | 2035 | 2216 | 4251 | 101 |
| 2B | 118 | 157 | 275 | 148 | 157 | 305 | 87 | 397 | 456 | 853 | 416 | 428 | 844 | 99 |
| 3B | 11 | 22 | 33 | 5 | 19 | 24 | 133 | 45 | 49 | 94 | 27 | 62 | 89 | 103 |
| HR | 81 | 106 | 187 | 67 | 85 | 152 | 119 | 206 | 291 | 497 | 183 | 261 | 444 | 109 |
| BB | 215 | 332 | 547 | 211 | 284 | 495 | 107 | 693 | 862 | 1555 | 597 | 854 | 1451 | 105 |
| SO | 768 | 604 | 1372 | 767 | 480 | 1247 | 106 | 2024 | 1866 | 3890 | 2040 | 1579 | 3619 | 105 |
| Foul Outs | 45 | 53 | 98 | 52 | 74 | 126 | 75 | 157 | 159 | 316 | 187 | 177 | 364 | 85 |
| E | 55 | 49 | 104 | 70 | 43 | 113 | 92 | 174 | 163 | 337 | 185 | 141 | 326 | 103 |
| E-Infield | 21 | 24 | 45 | 25 | 20 | 45 | 100 | 79 | 63 | 142 | 69 | 63 | 132 | 108 |
| LHB-Avg | .219 | .283 | .255 | .238 | .269 | .254 | 100 | .238 | .269 | .255 | .240 | .274 | .258 | 99 |
| LHB-HR | 39 | 41 | 80 | 25 | 41 | 66 | 118 | 73 | 108 | 181 | 65 | 106 | 171 | 105 |
| RHB-Avg | .240 | .265 | .252 | .252 | .274 | .262 | 96 | .249 | .260 | .254 | .246 | .277 | .260 | 98 |
| RHB-HR | 42 | 65 | 107 | 42 | 44 | 86 | 119 | 133 | 183 | 316 | 118 | 155 | 273 | 112 |

# Kansas City Royals - Kauffman Stadium

LF: 330 CF: 410 RF:330

| | 2013 Season | | | | | | | 2011-2013 | | | | | | |
|---|---|---|---|---|---|---|---|---|---|---|---|---|---|---|
| | Home Games | | | Away Games | | | | Home Games | | | Away Games | | | |
| | Royals | Opp | Total | Royals | Opp | Total | Index | Royals | Opp | Total | Royals | Opp | Total | Index |
| G | 81 | 81 | 162 | 81 | 81 | 162 | | 243 | 243 | 486 | 243 | 243 | 486 | |
| Avg | .260 | .258 | .259 | .260 | .241 | .251 | 103 | .272 | .262 | .267 | .262 | .263 | .262 | 102 |
| AB | 2687 | 2831 | 5518 | 2862 | 2636 | 5498 | 100 | 8232 | 8553 | 16785 | 8625 | 8044 | 16669 | 101 |
| R | 324 | 325 | 649 | 324 | 276 | 600 | 108 | 1036 | 1079 | 2115 | 1018 | 1030 | 2048 | 103 |
| H | 699 | 730 | 1429 | 744 | 636 | 1380 | 104 | 2238 | 2243 | 4481 | 2257 | 2114 | 4371 | 103 |
| 2B | 118 | 135 | 253 | 136 | 103 | 239 | 105 | 424 | 434 | 858 | 450 | 385 | 835 | 102 |
| 3B | 18 | 17 | 35 | 16 | 7 | 23 | 152 | 65 | 63 | 128 | 47 | 46 | 93 | 137 |
| HR | 55 | 70 | 125 | 57 | 85 | 142 | 88 | 170 | 225 | 395 | 202 | 256 | 458 | 86 |
| BB | 215 | 229 | 444 | 207 | 240 | 447 | 99 | 652 | 786 | 1438 | 616 | 782 | 1398 | 102 |
| SO | 463 | 600 | 1063 | 585 | 608 | 1193 | 89 | 1376 | 1724 | 3100 | 1710 | 1741 | 3451 | 89 |
| Foul Outs | 67 | 65 | 132 | 61 | 55 | 116 | 113 | 183 | 201 | 384 | 189 | 190 | 379 | 101 |
| E | 43 | 45 | 88 | 42 | 46 | 88 | 100 | 145 | 149 | 294 | 148 | 152 | 300 | 98 |
| E-Infield | 15 | 26 | 41 | 17 | 13 | 30 | 137 | 49 | 69 | 118 | 57 | 46 | 103 | 115 |
| LHB-Avg | .257 | .272 | .265 | .262 | .254 | .258 | 103 | .271 | .267 | .269 | .260 | .267 | .263 | 102 |
| LHB-HR | 32 | 37 | 69 | 32 | 48 | 80 | 85 | 80 | 94 | 174 | 101 | 109 | 210 | 81 |
| RHB-Avg | .263 | .242 | .253 | .258 | .228 | .243 | 104 | .273 | .258 | .265 | .263 | .259 | .261 | 102 |
| RHB-HR | 23 | 33 | 56 | 25 | 37 | 62 | 91 | 90 | 131 | 221 | 101 | 147 | 248 | 90 |

# Los Angeles Angels - Angel Stadium of Anaheim

LF: 330 CF: 400 RF:330

| | 2013 Season | | | | | | | 2011-2013 | | | | | | |
|---|---|---|---|---|---|---|---|---|---|---|---|---|---|---|
| | Home Games | | | Away Games | | | | Home Games | | | Away Games | | | |
| | Angels | Opp | Total | Angels | Opp | Total | Index | Angels | Opp | Total | Angels | Opp | Total | Index |
| G | 81 | 81 | 162 | 81 | 81 | 162 | | 243 | 243 | 486 | 243 | 243 | 486 | |
| Avg | .271 | .256 | .263 | .258 | .266 | .262 | 100 | .264 | .245 | .254 | .264 | .262 | .263 | 97 |
| AB | 2738 | 2905 | 5643 | 2850 | 2741 | 5591 | 101 | 8060 | 8449 | 16509 | 8577 | 8156 | 16733 | 99 |
| R | 352 | 371 | 723 | 381 | 366 | 747 | 97 | 1005 | 967 | 1972 | 1162 | 1102 | 2264 | 87 |
| H | 741 | 745 | 1486 | 735 | 730 | 1465 | 101 | 2125 | 2068 | 4193 | 2263 | 2134 | 4397 | 95 |
| 2B | 125 | 147 | 272 | 145 | 139 | 284 | 95 | 396 | 391 | 787 | 436 | 432 | 868 | 92 |
| 3B | 19 | 11 | 30 | 20 | 10 | 30 | 99 | 46 | 28 | 74 | 49 | 35 | 84 | 89 |
| HR | 77 | 80 | 157 | 87 | 87 | 174 | 89 | 221 | 228 | 449 | 285 | 267 | 552 | 82 |
| BB | 256 | 269 | 525 | 267 | 264 | 531 | 98 | 668 | 712 | 1380 | 746 | 780 | 1526 | 92 |
| SO | 587 | 633 | 1220 | 634 | 567 | 1201 | 101 | 1601 | 1835 | 3436 | 1819 | 1580 | 3399 | 102 |
| Foul Outs | 52 | 58 | 110 | 48 | 66 | 114 | 96 | 167 | 149 | 316 | 183 | 207 | 390 | 82 |
| E | 59 | 44 | 103 | 53 | 63 | 116 | 89 | 152 | 153 | 305 | 151 | 186 | 337 | 91 |
| E-Infield | 26 | 15 | 41 | 21 | 22 | 43 | 95 | 70 | 46 | 116 | 62 | 75 | 137 | 85 |
| LHB-Avg | .261 | .250 | .255 | .262 | .261 | .261 | 97 | .259 | .238 | .246 | .263 | .260 | .261 | 94 |
| LHB-HR | 23 | 36 | 59 | 22 | 41 | 63 | 94 | 46 | 103 | 149 | 62 | 121 | 183 | 82 |
| RHB-Avg | .276 | .263 | .270 | .255 | .271 | .263 | 103 | .266 | .251 | .260 | .264 | .263 | .264 | 98 |
| RHB-HR | 54 | 44 | 98 | 65 | 46 | 111 | 87 | 175 | 125 | 300 | 223 | 146 | 369 | 83 |

# Los Angeles Dodgers - Dodger Stadium

LF: 330 CF: 395 RF:330

| | 2013 Season | | | | | | | 2011-2013 | | | | | | |
|---|---|---|---|---|---|---|---|---|---|---|---|---|---|---|
| | Home Games | | | Away Games | | | | Home Games | | | Away Games | | | |
| | Dodgers | Opp | Total | Dodgers | Opp | Total | Index | Dodgers | Opp | Total | Dodgers | Opp | Total | Index |
| G | 81 | 81 | 162 | 81 | 81 | 162 | | 243 | 243 | 486 | 242 | 242 | 484 | |
| Avg | .257 | .244 | .250 | .269 | .243 | .256 | 98 | .256 | .236 | .246 | .259 | .245 | .252 | 98 |
| AB | 2632 | 2780 | 5412 | 2859 | 2654 | 5513 | 98 | 7938 | 8215 | 16153 | 8427 | 7936 | 16363 | 98 |
| R | 284 | 288 | 572 | 365 | 294 | 659 | 87 | 889 | 867 | 1756 | 1041 | 924 | 1965 | 89 |
| H | 677 | 677 | 1354 | 770 | 644 | 1414 | 96 | 2029 | 1942 | 3971 | 2182 | 1943 | 4125 | 96 |
| 2B | 131 | 121 | 252 | 150 | 122 | 272 | 94 | 363 | 369 | 732 | 424 | 386 | 810 | 92 |
| 3B | 5 | 6 | 11 | 12 | 12 | 24 | 47 | 28 | 19 | 47 | 40 | 50 | 90 | 53 |
| HR | 65 | 65 | 130 | 73 | 62 | 135 | 98 | 177 | 199 | 376 | 194 | 182 | 376 | 101 |
| BB | 211 | 217 | 428 | 265 | 243 | 508 | 86 | 711 | 734 | 1445 | 744 | 772 | 1516 | 97 |
| SO | 546 | 669 | 1215 | 600 | 623 | 1223 | 101 | 1633 | 1994 | 3627 | 1756 | 1839 | 3595 | 102 |
| Foul Outs | 59 | 37 | 96 | 61 | 50 | 111 | 88 | 160 | 153 | 313 | 171 | 170 | 341 | 93 |
| E | 53 | 40 | 93 | 56 | 54 | 110 | 85 | 149 | 129 | 278 | 143 | 162 | 305 | 91 |
| E-Infield | 23 | 14 | 37 | 25 | 24 | 49 | 76 | 63 | 51 | 114 | 62 | 69 | 131 | 87 |
| LHB-Avg | .258 | .254 | .256 | .271 | .243 | .258 | 99 | .261 | .244 | .253 | .254 | .253 | .254 | 100 |
| LHB-HR | 27 | 20 | 47 | 19 | 25 | 44 | 109 | 61 | 74 | 135 | 53 | 69 | 122 | 112 |
| RHB-Avg | .256 | .237 | .246 | .268 | .242 | .255 | 96 | .251 | .232 | .241 | .262 | .240 | .251 | 96 |
| RHB-HR | 38 | 45 | 83 | 54 | 37 | 91 | 93 | 116 | 125 | 241 | 141 | 113 | 254 | 96 |

# Miami Marlins - Marlins Park

LF: 340 CF: 416 RF:335

| | 2013 Season | | | | | | | 2012-2013 | | | | | | |
|---|---|---|---|---|---|---|---|---|---|---|---|---|---|---|
| | Home Games | | | Away Games | | | | Home Games | | | Away Games | | | |
| | Marlins | Opp | Total | Marlins | Opp | Total | Index | Marlins | Opp | Total | Marlins | Opp | Total | Index |
| G | 81 | 81 | 162 | 81 | 81 | 162 | | 162 | 162 | 324 | 162 | 162 | 324 | |
| Avg | .233 | .251 | .242 | .229 | .251 | .240 | 101 | .241 | .255 | .248 | .234 | .259 | .246 | 101 |
| AB | 2639 | 2816 | 5455 | 2810 | 2667 | 5477 | 100 | 5280 | 5623 | 10903 | 5606 | 5364 | 10970 | 99 |
| R | 276 | 312 | 588 | 237 | 334 | 571 | 103 | 581 | 675 | 1256 | 541 | 695 | 1236 | 102 |
| H | 614 | 707 | 1321 | 643 | 669 | 1312 | 101 | 1272 | 1433 | 2705 | 1312 | 1391 | 2703 | 100 |
| 2B | 106 | 154 | 260 | 113 | 116 | 229 | 114 | 235 | 282 | 517 | 245 | 258 | 503 | 103 |
| 3B | 20 | 25 | 45 | 11 | 23 | 34 | 133 | 43 | 46 | 89 | 27 | 42 | 69 | 130 |
| HR | 36 | 48 | 84 | 59 | 73 | 132 | 64 | 91 | 106 | 197 | 141 | 148 | 289 | 69 |
| BB | 242 | 247 | 489 | 190 | 279 | 469 | 105 | 497 | 488 | 985 | 419 | 533 | 952 | 104 |
| SO | 581 | 597 | 1178 | 651 | 580 | 1231 | 96 | 1175 | 1172 | 2347 | 1285 | 1118 | 2403 | 98 |
| Foul Outs | 57 | 53 | 110 | 59 | 54 | 113 | 98 | 123 | 101 | 224 | 123 | 105 | 228 | 99 |
| E | 43 | 44 | 87 | 45 | 40 | 85 | 102 | 100 | 89 | 189 | 91 | 94 | 185 | 102 |
| E-Infield | 19 | 17 | 36 | 19 | 13 | 32 | 113 | 47 | 33 | 80 | 36 | 37 | 73 | 110 |
| LHB-Avg | .238 | .252 | .246 | .230 | .258 | .246 | 100 | .235 | .259 | .249 | .238 | .261 | .251 | 99 |
| LHB-HR | 8 | 22 | 30 | 17 | 38 | 55 | 53 | 19 | 46 | 65 | 36 | 71 | 107 | 61 |
| RHB-Avg | .230 | .250 | .239 | .228 | .244 | .235 | 102 | .244 | .252 | .248 | .232 | .258 | .243 | 102 |
| RHB-HR | 28 | 26 | 54 | 42 | 35 | 77 | 72 | 72 | 60 | 132 | 105 | 77 | 182 | 73 |

## Milwaukee Brewers - Miller Park

LF: 344 CF: 400 RF:345

| | 2013 Season | | | | | | | 2011-2013 | | | | | | |
|---|---|---|---|---|---|---|---|---|---|---|---|---|---|---|
| | Home Games | | | Away Games | | | | Home Games | | | Away Games | | | |
| | Brewers | Opp | Total | Brewers | Opp | Total | Index | Brewers | Opp | Total | Brewers | Opp | Total | Index |
| G | 81 | 81 | 162 | 81 | 81 | 162 | | 243 | 243 | 486 | 243 | 243 | 486 | |
| Avg | .255 | .269 | .262 | .250 | .241 | .246 | 107 | .266 | .255 | .260 | .250 | .253 | .251 | 104 |
| AB | 2679 | 2835 | 5514 | 2795 | 2649 | 5444 | 101 | 8057 | 8528 | 16585 | 8421 | 8031 | 16452 | 101 |
| R | 327 | 371 | 698 | 313 | 316 | 629 | 111 | 1153 | 1051 | 2204 | 984 | 1007 | 1991 | 111 |
| H | 682 | 763 | 1445 | 699 | 638 | 1337 | 108 | 2142 | 2175 | 4317 | 2103 | 2032 | 4135 | 104 |
| 2B | 116 | 115 | 231 | 122 | 100 | 222 | 103 | 415 | 390 | 805 | 399 | 378 | 777 | 103 |
| 3B | 24 | 7 | 31 | 19 | 10 | 29 | 106 | 67 | 37 | 104 | 46 | 39 | 85 | 121 |
| HR | 82 | 103 | 185 | 75 | 72 | 147 | 124 | 303 | 283 | 586 | 241 | 208 | 449 | 129 |
| BB | 223 | 247 | 470 | 184 | 219 | 403 | 115 | 736 | 723 | 1459 | 618 | 708 | 1326 | 109 |
| SO | 557 | 585 | 1142 | 626 | 540 | 1166 | 97 | 1700 | 2028 | 3728 | 1806 | 1756 | 3562 | 104 |
| Foul Outs | 48 | 66 | 114 | 54 | 62 | 116 | 97 | 158 | 169 | 327 | 162 | 155 | 317 | 102 |
| E | 49 | 48 | 97 | 65 | 56 | 121 | 80 | 149 | 165 | 314 | 175 | 167 | 342 | 92 |
| E-Infield | 23 | 17 | 40 | 27 | 22 | 49 | 82 | 67 | 65 | 132 | 76 | 66 | 142 | 93 |
| LHB-Avg | .245 | .270 | .261 | .274 | .230 | .247 | 106 | .259 | .255 | .257 | .258 | .249 | .253 | 102 |
| LHB-HR | 16 | 55 | 71 | 20 | 45 | 65 | 108 | 59 | 132 | 191 | 56 | 98 | 154 | 121 |
| RHB-Avg | .258 | .269 | .263 | .241 | .250 | .245 | 107 | .268 | .255 | .262 | .246 | .256 | .251 | 105 |
| RHB-HR | 66 | 48 | 114 | 55 | 27 | 82 | 137 | 244 | 151 | 395 | 185 | 110 | 295 | 134 |

## Minnesota Twins - Target Field

LF: 339 CF: 411 RF:328

| | 2013 Season | | | | | | | 2011-2013 | | | | | | |
|---|---|---|---|---|---|---|---|---|---|---|---|---|---|---|
| | Home Games | | | Away Games | | | | Home Games | | | Away Games | | | |
| | Twins | Opp | Total | Twins | Opp | Total | Index | Twins | Opp | Total | Twins | Opp | Total | Index |
| G | 81 | 81 | 162 | 81 | 81 | 162 | | 243 | 243 | 486 | 243 | 243 | 486 | |
| Avg | .248 | .279 | .264 | .236 | .281 | .258 | 102 | .258 | .274 | .266 | .242 | .283 | .262 | 102 |
| AB | 2722 | 2909 | 5631 | 2842 | 2770 | 5612 | 100 | 8140 | 8647 | 16787 | 8473 | 8213 | 16686 | 101 |
| R | 303 | 405 | 708 | 311 | 383 | 694 | 102 | 959 | 1223 | 2182 | 975 | 1201 | 2176 | 100 |
| H | 676 | 812 | 1488 | 670 | 779 | 1449 | 103 | 2103 | 2367 | 4470 | 2048 | 2324 | 4372 | 102 |
| 2B | 141 | 173 | 314 | 144 | 137 | 281 | 111 | 407 | 448 | 855 | 407 | 438 | 845 | 101 |
| 3B | 8 | 15 | 23 | 7 | 15 | 22 | 104 | 38 | 58 | 96 | 32 | 46 | 78 | 122 |
| HR | 68 | 74 | 142 | 83 | 94 | 177 | 80 | 183 | 252 | 435 | 202 | 275 | 477 | 91 |
| BB | 251 | 202 | 453 | 282 | 256 | 538 | 84 | 739 | 668 | 1407 | 739 | 735 | 1474 | 95 |
| SO | 663 | 502 | 1165 | 767 | 483 | 1250 | 93 | 1674 | 1502 | 3176 | 1873 | 1366 | 3239 | 97 |
| Foul Outs | 49 | 67 | 116 | 52 | 59 | 111 | 104 | 156 | 188 | 344 | 163 | 187 | 350 | 98 |
| E | 46 | 43 | 89 | 35 | 56 | 91 | 98 | 155 | 144 | 299 | 152 | 180 | 332 | 90 |
| E-Infield | 21 | 19 | 40 | 10 | 25 | 35 | 114 | 64 | 59 | 123 | 52 | 76 | 128 | 96 |
| LHB-Avg | .253 | .278 | .264 | .241 | .277 | .257 | 103 | .267 | .260 | .264 | .250 | .284 | .265 | 99 |
| LHB-HR | 36 | 38 | 74 | 50 | 45 | 95 | 78 | 73 | 105 | 178 | 111 | 116 | 227 | 79 |
| RHB-Avg | .242 | .280 | .264 | .229 | .285 | .259 | 102 | .248 | .285 | .269 | .232 | .282 | .259 | 104 |
| RHB-HR | 32 | 36 | 68 | 33 | 49 | 82 | 82 | 110 | 147 | 257 | 91 | 159 | 250 | 101 |

## New York Mets - Citi Field

LF: 335 CF: 408 RF:330

| | 2013 Season | | | | | | | 2012-2013 | | | | | | |
|---|---|---|---|---|---|---|---|---|---|---|---|---|---|---|
| | Home Games | | | Away Games | | | | Home Games | | | Away Games | | | |
| | Mets | Opp | Total | Mets | Opp | Total | Index | Mets | Opp | Total | Mets | Opp | Total | Index |
| G | 81 | 81 | 162 | 81 | 81 | 162 | | 162 | 162 | 324 | 162 | 162 | 324 | |
| Avg | .219 | .246 | .233 | .254 | .268 | .261 | 89 | .230 | .243 | .237 | .255 | .265 | .260 | 91 |
| AB | 2707 | 2890 | 5597 | 2852 | 2733 | 5585 | 100 | 5344 | 5652 | 10996 | 5665 | 5420 | 11085 | 99 |
| R | 268 | 337 | 605 | 351 | 347 | 698 | 87 | 555 | 684 | 1239 | 714 | 709 | 1423 | 87 |
| H | 593 | 710 | 1303 | 725 | 732 | 1457 | 89 | 1231 | 1376 | 2607 | 1444 | 1434 | 2878 | 91 |
| 2B | 119 | 125 | 244 | 144 | 147 | 291 | 84 | 236 | 249 | 485 | 313 | 285 | 598 | 82 |
| 3B | 13 | 8 | 21 | 19 | 11 | 30 | 70 | 23 | 20 | 43 | 30 | 35 | 65 | 67 |
| HR | 59 | 90 | 149 | 71 | 62 | 133 | 112 | 126 | 178 | 304 | 143 | 135 | 278 | 110 |
| BB | 264 | 227 | 491 | 248 | 231 | 479 | 102 | 514 | 464 | 978 | 501 | 482 | 983 | 100 |
| SO | 707 | 654 | 1361 | 677 | 555 | 1232 | 110 | 1331 | 1296 | 2627 | 1303 | 1153 | 2456 | 108 |
| Foul Outs | 58 | 67 | 125 | 46 | 65 | 111 | 112 | 98 | 142 | 240 | 104 | 133 | 237 | 102 |
| E | 44 | 44 | 88 | 49 | 51 | 100 | 88 | 81 | 87 | 168 | 113 | 94 | 207 | 81 |
| E-Infield | 20 | 14 | 34 | 18 | 25 | 43 | 79 | 32 | 34 | 66 | 46 | 49 | 95 | 69 |
| LHB-Avg | .213 | .230 | .221 | .252 | .272 | .261 | 85 | .229 | .240 | .235 | .247 | .273 | .259 | 91 |
| LHB-HR | 26 | 32 | 58 | 24 | 31 | 55 | 108 | 59 | 73 | 132 | 67 | 61 | 128 | 105 |
| RHB-Avg | .224 | .257 | .241 | .256 | .265 | .260 | 93 | .231 | .246 | .239 | .262 | .258 | .260 | 92 |
| RHB-HR | 33 | 58 | 91 | 47 | 31 | 78 | 114 | 67 | 105 | 172 | 76 | 74 | 150 | 115 |

## New York Yankees - Yankee Stadium

LF: 318 CF: 408 RF:314

| | 2013 Season | | | | | | | 2011-2013 | | | | | | |
|---|---|---|---|---|---|---|---|---|---|---|---|---|---|---|
| | Home Games | | | Away Games | | | | Home Games | | | Away Games | | | |
| | Yankees | Opp | Total | Yankees | Opp | Total | Index | Yankees | Opp | Total | Yankees | Opp | Total | Index |
| G | 81 | 81 | 162 | 81 | 81 | 162 | | 243 | 243 | 486 | 243 | 243 | 486 | |
| Avg | .252 | .266 | .259 | .234 | .256 | .244 | 106 | .264 | .253 | .258 | .250 | .260 | .255 | 101 |
| AB | 2615 | 2851 | 5466 | 2834 | 2712 | 5546 | 99 | 7996 | 8482 | 16478 | 8495 | 8184 | 16679 | 99 |
| R | 337 | 351 | 688 | 313 | 320 | 633 | 109 | 1214 | 1016 | 2230 | 1107 | 980 | 2087 | 107 |
| H | 659 | 759 | 1418 | 662 | 693 | 1355 | 105 | 2112 | 2146 | 4258 | 2123 | 2130 | 4253 | 100 |
| 2B | 110 | 159 | 269 | 137 | 144 | 281 | 97 | 364 | 456 | 820 | 430 | 442 | 872 | 95 |
| 3B | 9 | 7 | 16 | 15 | 7 | 22 | 74 | 24 | 29 | 53 | 46 | 33 | 79 | 68 |
| HR | 75 | 92 | 167 | 69 | 79 | 148 | 114 | 335 | 273 | 608 | 276 | 240 | 516 | 119 |
| BB | 259 | 210 | 469 | 207 | 227 | 434 | 110 | 868 | 675 | 1543 | 790 | 700 | 1490 | 105 |
| SO | 577 | 650 | 1227 | 637 | 583 | 1220 | 102 | 1699 | 1948 | 3647 | 1829 | 1825 | 3654 | 101 |
| Foul Outs | 59 | 54 | 113 | 66 | 43 | 109 | 105 | 158 | 167 | 325 | 191 | 163 | 354 | 93 |
| E | 41 | 39 | 80 | 28 | 55 | 83 | 96 | 129 | 132 | 261 | 116 | 140 | 256 | 102 |
| E-Infield | 18 | 15 | 33 | 12 | 20 | 32 | 103 | 50 | 56 | 106 | 61 | 59 | 120 | 88 |
| LHB-Avg | .282 | .255 | .269 | .235 | .261 | .247 | 109 | .275 | .248 | .262 | .251 | .257 | .254 | 103 |
| LHB-HR | 43 | 26 | 69 | 38 | 45 | 83 | 84 | 211 | 121 | 332 | 159 | 107 | 266 | 127 |
| RHB-Avg | .219 | .275 | .250 | .232 | .251 | .242 | 103 | .252 | .257 | .255 | .249 | .263 | .256 | 100 |
| RHB-HR | 32 | 66 | 98 | 31 | 34 | 65 | 153 | 124 | 152 | 276 | 117 | 133 | 250 | 111 |

## Oakland Athletics - O.co Coliseum

LF: 330 CF: 400 RF:330

| | 2013 Season | | | | | | | 2011-2013 | | | | | | |
|---|---|---|---|---|---|---|---|---|---|---|---|---|---|---|
| | Home Games | | | Away Games | | | | Home Games | | | Away Games | | | |
| | Athletics | Opp | Total | Athletics | Opp | Total | Index | Athletics | Opp | Total | Athletics | Opp | Total | Index |
| G | 81 | 81 | 162 | 81 | 81 | 162 | | 241 | 241 | 482 | 245 | 245 | 490 | |
| Avg | .248 | .238 | .243 | .260 | .246 | .254 | 96 | .244 | .235 | .240 | .246 | .257 | .252 | 95 |
| AB | 2706 | 2875 | 5581 | 2815 | 2654 | 5469 | 102 | 7970 | 8391 | 16361 | 8530 | 8191 | 16721 | 99 |
| R | 353 | 302 | 655 | 414 | 323 | 737 | 89 | 1025 | 889 | 1914 | 1100 | 1029 | 2129 | 91 |
| H | 670 | 685 | 1355 | 733 | 654 | 1387 | 98 | 1947 | 1974 | 3921 | 2101 | 2105 | 4206 | 95 |
| 2B | 153 | 126 | 279 | 148 | 103 | 251 | 109 | 413 | 361 | 774 | 435 | 377 | 812 | 97 |
| 3B | 15 | 10 | 25 | 10 | 9 | 19 | 129 | 47 | 28 | 75 | 39 | 31 | 70 | 110 |
| HR | 83 | 74 | 157 | 103 | 89 | 192 | 80 | 222 | 198 | 420 | 273 | 248 | 521 | 82 |
| BB | 291 | 219 | 510 | 282 | 209 | 491 | 102 | 850 | 697 | 1547 | 782 | 712 | 1494 | 106 |
| SO | 559 | 613 | 1172 | 619 | 570 | 1189 | 97 | 1698 | 1781 | 3479 | 1961 | 1698 | 3659 | 97 |
| Foul Outs | 108 | 106 | 214 | 65 | 55 | 120 | 175 | 294 | 303 | 597 | 201 | 213 | 414 | 147 |
| E | 47 | 40 | 87 | 50 | 44 | 94 | 93 | 169 | 132 | 301 | 163 | 134 | 297 | 103 |
| E-Infield | 17 | 14 | 31 | 21 | 13 | 34 | 91 | 68 | 45 | 113 | 66 | 55 | 121 | 95 |
| LHB-Avg | .231 | .238 | .234 | .287 | .263 | .276 | 85 | .239 | .242 | .241 | .261 | .260 | .261 | 92 |
| LHB-HR | 33 | 32 | 65 | 61 | 43 | 104 | 62 | 94 | 89 | 183 | 142 | 120 | 262 | 72 |
| RHB-Avg | .265 | .239 | .251 | .231 | .232 | .231 | 108 | .249 | .230 | .239 | .231 | .254 | .243 | 98 |
| RHB-HR | 50 | 42 | 92 | 42 | 46 | 88 | 102 | 128 | 109 | 237 | 131 | 128 | 259 | 93 |

## Philadelphia Phillies - Citizens Bank Park

LF: 329 CF: 401 RF:329

| | 2013 Season | | | | | | | 2011-2013 | | | | | | |
|---|---|---|---|---|---|---|---|---|---|---|---|---|---|---|
| | Home Games | | | Away Games | | | | Home Games | | | Away Games | | | |
| | Phillies | Opp | Total | Phillies | Opp | Total | Index | Phillies | Opp | Total | Phillies | Opp | Total | Index |
| G | 81 | 81 | 162 | 81 | 81 | 162 | | 243 | 243 | 486 | 243 | 243 | 486 | |
| Avg | .250 | .254 | .252 | .247 | .275 | .261 | 97 | .253 | .243 | .248 | .251 | .261 | .256 | 97 |
| AB | 2691 | 2866 | 5557 | 2765 | 2672 | 5437 | 102 | 8111 | 8465 | 16576 | 8468 | 8099 | 16567 | 100 |
| R | 344 | 370 | 714 | 266 | 379 | 645 | 111 | 1035 | 970 | 2005 | 972 | 988 | 1960 | 102 |
| H | 672 | 729 | 1401 | 683 | 736 | 1419 | 99 | 2051 | 2061 | 4112 | 2127 | 2111 | 4238 | 97 |
| 2B | 133 | 155 | 288 | 122 | 153 | 275 | 102 | 398 | 420 | 818 | 386 | 416 | 802 | 102 |
| 3B | 18 | 17 | 35 | 14 | 19 | 33 | 104 | 53 | 33 | 86 | 45 | 55 | 100 | 86 |
| HR | 84 | 92 | 176 | 56 | 60 | 116 | 148 | 243 | 241 | 484 | 208 | 209 | 417 | 116 |
| BB | 237 | 234 | 471 | 180 | 272 | 452 | 102 | 751 | 643 | 1394 | 659 | 676 | 1335 | 104 |
| SO | 637 | 630 | 1267 | 568 | 569 | 1137 | 109 | 1671 | 2038 | 3709 | 1652 | 1845 | 3497 | 106 |
| Foul Outs | 48 | 73 | 121 | 67 | 63 | 130 | 91 | 160 | 209 | 369 | 191 | 184 | 375 | 98 |
| E | 56 | 51 | 107 | 41 | 49 | 90 | 119 | 147 | 148 | 295 | 125 | 149 | 274 | 108 |
| E-Infield | 24 | 22 | 46 | 13 | 21 | 34 | 135 | 73 | 63 | 136 | 49 | 72 | 121 | 112 |
| LHB-Avg | .257 | .269 | .262 | .253 | .256 | .254 | 103 | .251 | .251 | .251 | .250 | .258 | .253 | 99 |
| LHB-HR | 41 | 27 | 68 | 31 | 17 | 48 | 153 | 135 | 88 | 223 | 106 | 65 | 171 | 133 |
| RHB-Avg | .242 | .247 | .245 | .240 | .287 | .267 | 92 | .255 | .239 | .246 | .253 | .262 | .258 | 95 |
| RHB-HR | 43 | 65 | 108 | 25 | 43 | 68 | 144 | 108 | 153 | 261 | 102 | 144 | 246 | 105 |

# Pittsburgh Pirates - PNC Park

LF: 325 CF: 399 RF:320

| | 2013 Season | | | | | | | 2011-2013 | | | | | | |
|---|---|---|---|---|---|---|---|---|---|---|---|---|---|---|
| | Home Games | | | Away Games | | | | Home Games | | | Away Games | | | |
| | Pirates | Opp | Total | Pirates | Opp | Total | Index | Pirates | Opp | Total | Pirates | Opp | Total | Index |
| G | 81 | 81 | 162 | 81 | 81 | 162 | | 243 | 243 | 486 | 243 | 243 | 486 | |
| Avg | .248 | .232 | .240 | .243 | .243 | .243 | 99 | .243 | .245 | .244 | .245 | .260 | .252 | 97 |
| AB | 2686 | 2792 | 5478 | 2800 | 2676 | 5476 | 100 | 7901 | 8365 | 16266 | 8418 | 8154 | 16572 | 98 |
| R | 309 | 267 | 576 | 325 | 310 | 635 | 91 | 893 | 904 | 1797 | 1002 | 1059 | 2061 | 87 |
| H | 666 | 649 | 1315 | 680 | 650 | 1330 | 99 | 1921 | 2052 | 3973 | 2063 | 2117 | 4180 | 95 |
| 2B | 135 | 94 | 229 | 138 | 129 | 267 | 86 | 399 | 357 | 756 | 392 | 391 | 783 | 98 |
| 3B | 14 | 8 | 22 | 21 | 11 | 32 | 69 | 48 | 26 | 74 | 59 | 45 | 104 | 72 |
| HR | 69 | 37 | 106 | 92 | 64 | 156 | 68 | 185 | 161 | 346 | 253 | 245 | 498 | 71 |
| BB | 223 | 238 | 461 | 246 | 277 | 523 | 88 | 649 | 706 | 1355 | 753 | 834 | 1587 | 87 |
| SO | 594 | 651 | 1245 | 736 | 610 | 1346 | 92 | 1772 | 1740 | 3512 | 2220 | 1744 | 3964 | 90 |
| Foul Outs | 42 | 44 | 86 | 56 | 33 | 89 | 97 | 127 | 126 | 253 | 154 | 137 | 291 | 89 |
| E | 52 | 43 | 95 | 54 | 47 | 101 | 94 | 174 | 154 | 328 | 156 | 146 | 302 | 109 |
| E-Infield | 19 | 21 | 40 | 25 | 23 | 48 | 83 | 70 | 81 | 151 | 67 | 66 | 133 | 114 |
| LHB-Avg | .233 | .221 | .227 | .218 | .266 | .242 | 94 | .243 | .241 | .242 | .237 | .270 | .253 | 95 |
| LHB-HR | 36 | 11 | 47 | 39 | 21 | 60 | 79 | 92 | 60 | 152 | 116 | 91 | 207 | 78 |
| RHB-Avg | .256 | .239 | .248 | .257 | .229 | .243 | 102 | .243 | .248 | .246 | .250 | .253 | .251 | 98 |
| RHB-HR | 33 | 26 | 59 | 53 | 43 | 96 | 61 | 93 | 101 | 194 | 137 | 154 | 291 | 66 |

# San Diego Padres - PETCO Park

LF: 336 CF: 396 RF:322

| | 2013 Season | | | | | | | 2010-2012 | | | | | | |
|---|---|---|---|---|---|---|---|---|---|---|---|---|---|---|
| | Home Games | | | Away Games | | | | Home Games | | | Away Games | | | |
| | Padres | Opp | Total | Padres | Opp | Total | Index | Padres | Opp | Total | Padres | Opp | Total | Index |
| G | 81 | 81 | 162 | 81 | 81 | 162 | | 243 | 243 | 486 | 243 | 243 | 486 | |
| Avg | .238 | .237 | .237 | .251 | .275 | .263 | 90 | .236 | .232 | .234 | .251 | .257 | .253 | 92 |
| AB | 2681 | 2824 | 5505 | 2836 | 2687 | 5523 | 100 | 7897 | 8307 | 16204 | 8376 | 8011 | 16387 | 99 |
| R | 291 | 307 | 598 | 327 | 393 | 720 | 83 | 886 | 867 | 1753 | 1023 | 1035 | 2058 | 85 |
| H | 638 | 668 | 1306 | 711 | 739 | 1450 | 90 | 1862 | 1930 | 3792 | 2099 | 2055 | 4154 | 91 |
| 2B | 115 | 110 | 225 | 131 | 160 | 291 | 78 | 346 | 374 | 720 | 409 | 396 | 805 | 90 |
| 3B | 17 | 17 | 34 | 9 | 21 | 30 | 114 | 62 | 51 | 113 | 47 | 39 | 86 | 133 |
| HR | 66 | 80 | 146 | 80 | 76 | 156 | 94 | 152 | 182 | 334 | 192 | 244 | 436 | 77 |
| BB | 242 | 254 | 496 | 225 | 271 | 496 | 100 | 822 | 791 | 1613 | 756 | 786 | 1542 | 106 |
| SO | 642 | 649 | 1291 | 667 | 522 | 1189 | 109 | 1877 | 1935 | 3812 | 1864 | 1704 | 3568 | 108 |
| Foul Outs | 37 | 47 | 84 | 54 | 45 | 99 | 85 | 150 | 169 | 319 | 178 | 162 | 340 | 95 |
| E | 43 | 46 | 89 | 40 | 44 | 84 | 106 | 148 | 147 | 295 | 139 | 169 | 308 | 96 |
| E-Infield | 17 | 17 | 34 | 11 | 15 | 26 | 131 | 52 | 56 | 108 | 55 | 76 | 131 | 82 |
| LHB-Avg | .244 | .246 | .245 | .240 | .254 | .247 | 99 | .237 | .232 | .234 | .262 | .254 | .258 | 91 |
| LHB-HR | 24 | 42 | 66 | 22 | 28 | 50 | 130 | 53 | 48 | 101 | 90 | 89 | 179 | 57 |
| RHB-Avg | .234 | .229 | .232 | .258 | .291 | .273 | 85 | .235 | .233 | .234 | .243 | .258 | .250 | 93 |
| RHB-HR | 42 | 38 | 80 | 58 | 48 | 106 | 77 | 99 | 134 | 233 | 102 | 155 | 257 | 92 |

# San Francisco Giants - AT&T Park

LF: 339 CF: 399 RF:309

| | 2013 Season | | | | | | | 2011-2013 | | | | | | |
|---|---|---|---|---|---|---|---|---|---|---|---|---|---|---|
| | Home Games | | | Away Games | | | | Home Games | | | Away Games | | | |
| | Giants | Opp | Total | Giants | Opp | Total | Index | Giants | Opp | Total | Giants | Opp | Total | Index |
| G | 82 | 82 | 164 | 80 | 80 | 160 | | 244 | 244 | 488 | 242 | 242 | 484 | |
| Avg | .258 | .244 | .251 | .263 | .260 | .261 | 96 | .255 | .234 | .244 | .259 | .254 | .257 | 95 |
| AB | 2746 | 2852 | 5598 | 2806 | 2639 | 5445 | 100 | 8074 | 8353 | 16427 | 8522 | 8051 | 16573 | 98 |
| R | 287 | 335 | 622 | 342 | 356 | 698 | 87 | 831 | 858 | 1689 | 1086 | 1060 | 2146 | 78 |
| H | 708 | 695 | 1403 | 738 | 685 | 1423 | 96 | 2057 | 1956 | 4013 | 2211 | 2045 | 4256 | 94 |
| 2B | 140 | 145 | 285 | 140 | 132 | 272 | 102 | 422 | 415 | 837 | 427 | 430 | 857 | 99 |
| 3B | 20 | 20 | 40 | 15 | 5 | 20 | 195 | 62 | 47 | 109 | 54 | 44 | 98 | 112 |
| HR | 44 | 67 | 111 | 63 | 78 | 141 | 77 | 117 | 159 | 276 | 214 | 224 | 438 | 64 |
| BB | 256 | 268 | 524 | 213 | 253 | 466 | 109 | 717 | 776 | 1493 | 683 | 793 | 1476 | 102 |
| SO | 500 | 667 | 1167 | 578 | 589 | 1167 | 97 | 1560 | 1992 | 3552 | 1737 | 1817 | 3554 | 101 |
| Foul Outs | 56 | 56 | 112 | 54 | 65 | 119 | 92 | 166 | 168 | 334 | 187 | 168 | 355 | 95 |
| E | 54 | 31 | 85 | 53 | 48 | 101 | 82 | 147 | 129 | 276 | 179 | 161 | 340 | 81 |
| E-Infield | 26 | 12 | 38 | 14 | 21 | 35 | 106 | 73 | 48 | 121 | 74 | 60 | 134 | 90 |
| LHB-Avg | .260 | .236 | .249 | .250 | .243 | .247 | 101 | .259 | .220 | .241 | .252 | .249 | .251 | 96 |
| LHB-HR | 17 | 21 | 38 | 32 | 24 | 56 | 65 | 53 | 49 | 102 | 105 | 73 | 178 | 58 |
| RHB-Avg | .256 | .248 | .252 | .276 | .269 | .272 | 93 | .251 | .243 | .246 | .266 | .257 | .262 | 94 |
| RHB-HR | 27 | 46 | 73 | 31 | 54 | 85 | 85 | 64 | 110 | 174 | 109 | 151 | 260 | 67 |

## Seattle Mariners - Safeco Field

LF: 331 CF: 405 RF:326

| | 2013 Season | | | | | | | 2010-2012 | | | | | | |
|---|---|---|---|---|---|---|---|---|---|---|---|---|---|---|
| | Home Games | | | Away Games | | | | Home Games | | | Away Games | | | |
| | Mariners | Opp | Total | Mariners | Opp | Total | Index | Mariners | Opp | Total | Mariners | Opp | Total | Index |
| G | 81 | 81 | 162 | 81 | 81 | 162 | | 246 | 246 | 492 | 240 | 240 | 480 | |
| Avg | .239 | .254 | .247 | .235 | .265 | .250 | 99 | .226 | .236 | .231 | .242 | .267 | .254 | 91 |
| AB | 2744 | 2920 | 5664 | 2814 | 2738 | 5552 | 102 | 7943 | 8409 | 16352 | 8381 | 8036 | 16417 | 97 |
| R | 310 | 376 | 686 | 314 | 378 | 692 | 99 | 761 | 889 | 1650 | 927 | 1135 | 2062 | 78 |
| H | 656 | 742 | 1398 | 662 | 725 | 1387 | 101 | 1792 | 1986 | 3778 | 2030 | 2144 | 4174 | 88 |
| 2B | 130 | 167 | 297 | 119 | 148 | 267 | 109 | 324 | 356 | 680 | 397 | 436 | 833 | 82 |
| 3B | 6 | 11 | 17 | 11 | 16 | 27 | 62 | 27 | 26 | 53 | 38 | 48 | 86 | 62 |
| HR | 88 | 82 | 170 | 100 | 92 | 192 | 87 | 148 | 206 | 354 | 211 | 262 | 473 | 75 |
| BB | 259 | 232 | 491 | 270 | 246 | 516 | 93 | 730 | 651 | 1381 | 630 | 686 | 1316 | 105 |
| SO | 649 | 720 | 1369 | 704 | 577 | 1281 | 105 | 1902 | 1715 | 3617 | 1821 | 1512 | 3333 | 109 |
| Foul Outs | 72 | 57 | 129 | 54 | 48 | 102 | 124 | 234 | 236 | 470 | 208 | 185 | 393 | 120 |
| E | 41 | 47 | 88 | 47 | 36 | 83 | 106 | 124 | 133 | 257 | 166 | 161 | 327 | 77 |
| E-Infield | 13 | 21 | 34 | 26 | 17 | 43 | 79 | 56 | 59 | 115 | 76 | 71 | 147 | 76 |
| LHB-Avg | .254 | .253 | .253 | .256 | .251 | .254 | 100 | .226 | .239 | .232 | .249 | .269 | .258 | 90 |
| LHB-HR | 58 | 37 | 95 | 68 | 41 | 109 | 86 | 93 | 85 | 178 | 122 | 92 | 214 | 85 |
| RHB-Avg | .215 | .255 | .239 | .202 | .276 | .245 | 98 | .225 | .234 | .230 | .233 | .265 | .251 | 92 |
| RHB-HR | 30 | 45 | 75 | 32 | 51 | 83 | 88 | 55 | 121 | 176 | 89 | 170 | 259 | 67 |

## St Louis Cardinals - Busch Stadium

LF: 336 CF: 400 RF:335

| | 2013 Season | | | | | | | 2011-2013 | | | | | | |
|---|---|---|---|---|---|---|---|---|---|---|---|---|---|---|
| | Home Games | | | Away Games | | | | Home Games | | | Away Games | | | |
| | Cardinals | Opp | Total | Cardinals | Opp | Total | Index | Cardinals | Opp | Total | Cardinals | Opp | Total | Index |
| G | 81 | 81 | 162 | 81 | 81 | 162 | | 243 | 243 | 486 | 243 | 243 | 486 | |
| Avg | .274 | .234 | .254 | .264 | .264 | .264 | 96 | .277 | .242 | .259 | .266 | .268 | .267 | 97 |
| AB | 2680 | 2755 | 5435 | 2877 | 2739 | 5616 | 97 | 8119 | 8422 | 16541 | 8592 | 8251 | 16843 | 98 |
| R | 378 | 272 | 650 | 405 | 324 | 729 | 89 | 1132 | 906 | 2038 | 1178 | 1030 | 2208 | 92 |
| H | 735 | 644 | 1379 | 759 | 722 | 1481 | 93 | 2245 | 2035 | 4280 | 2288 | 2212 | 4500 | 95 |
| 2B | 153 | 119 | 272 | 169 | 144 | 313 | 90 | 458 | 383 | 841 | 462 | 447 | 909 | 94 |
| 3B | 9 | 12 | 21 | 11 | 17 | 28 | 77 | 39 | 35 | 74 | 40 | 61 | 101 | 75 |
| HR | 58 | 50 | 108 | 67 | 62 | 129 | 87 | 201 | 177 | 378 | 245 | 205 | 450 | 86 |
| BB | 229 | 212 | 441 | 252 | 239 | 491 | 93 | 751 | 660 | 1411 | 805 | 675 | 1480 | 97 |
| SO | 487 | 656 | 1143 | 623 | 598 | 1221 | 97 | 1494 | 1864 | 3358 | 1786 | 1706 | 3492 | 98 |
| Foul Outs | 57 | 54 | 111 | 51 | 35 | 86 | 133 | 166 | 144 | 310 | 137 | 123 | 260 | 121 |
| E | 34 | 38 | 72 | 41 | 38 | 79 | 91 | 144 | 118 | 262 | 154 | 145 | 299 | 88 |
| E-Infield | 18 | 13 | 31 | 19 | 14 | 33 | 94 | 74 | 46 | 120 | 75 | 59 | 134 | 90 |
| LHB-Avg | .297 | .243 | .268 | .267 | .264 | .265 | 101 | .281 | .251 | .266 | .265 | .263 | .264 | 101 |
| LHB-HR | 29 | 16 | 45 | 28 | 30 | 58 | 81 | 76 | 76 | 152 | 83 | 85 | 168 | 94 |
| RHB-Avg | .259 | .227 | .243 | .262 | .263 | .263 | 92 | .273 | .235 | .254 | .267 | .272 | .269 | 94 |
| RHB-HR | 29 | 34 | 63 | 39 | 32 | 71 | 91 | 125 | 101 | 226 | 162 | 120 | 282 | 80 |

## Tampa Bay Rays - Tropicana Field Surface: FieldTurf

LF: 315 CF: 404 RF:322

| | 2013 Season | | | | | | | 2011-2013 | | | | | | |
|---|---|---|---|---|---|---|---|---|---|---|---|---|---|---|
| | Home Games | | | Away Games | | | | Home Games | | | Away Games | | | |
| | Rays | Opp | Total | Rays | Opp | Total | Index | Rays | Opp | Total | Rays | Opp | Total | Index |
| G | 81 | 81 | 162 | 82 | 82 | 164 | | 243 | 243 | 486 | 244 | 244 | 488 | |
| Avg | .255 | .229 | .242 | .259 | .251 | .255 | 95 | .241 | .224 | .232 | .252 | .244 | .249 | 93 |
| AB | 2695 | 2812 | 5507 | 2843 | 2670 | 5513 | 101 | 7941 | 8335 | 16276 | 8431 | 7955 | 16386 | 100 |
| R | 343 | 302 | 645 | 357 | 344 | 701 | 93 | 982 | 851 | 1833 | 1122 | 986 | 2108 | 87 |
| H | 686 | 644 | 1330 | 735 | 671 | 1406 | 96 | 1910 | 1867 | 3777 | 2128 | 1944 | 4072 | 93 |
| 2B | 133 | 126 | 259 | 163 | 128 | 291 | 89 | 375 | 354 | 729 | 444 | 379 | 823 | 89 |
| 3B | 17 | 16 | 33 | 6 | 14 | 20 | 165 | 48 | 40 | 88 | 42 | 38 | 80 | 111 |
| HR | 81 | 75 | 156 | 84 | 78 | 162 | 96 | 244 | 207 | 451 | 268 | 246 | 514 | 88 |
| BB | 305 | 218 | 523 | 284 | 264 | 548 | 96 | 889 | 682 | 1571 | 842 | 773 | 1615 | 98 |
| SO | 573 | 687 | 1260 | 598 | 623 | 1221 | 103 | 1755 | 2053 | 3808 | 1932 | 1783 | 3715 | 103 |
| Foul Outs | 63 | 63 | 126 | 52 | 62 | 114 | 111 | 214 | 230 | 444 | 156 | 169 | 325 | 138 |
| E | 20 | 29 | 49 | 39 | 45 | 84 | 59 | 114 | 110 | 224 | 132 | 154 | 286 | 79 |
| E-Infield | 7 | 8 | 15 | 10 | 12 | 22 | 69 | 43 | 48 | 91 | 50 | 63 | 113 | 81 |
| LHB-Avg | .253 | .227 | .240 | .261 | .269 | .265 | 90 | .239 | .221 | .230 | .248 | .253 | .250 | 92 |
| LHB-HR | 41 | 46 | 87 | 36 | 35 | 71 | 116 | 110 | 108 | 218 | 114 | 106 | 220 | 93 |
| RHB-Avg | .256 | .231 | .243 | .256 | .237 | .247 | 98 | .242 | .226 | .234 | .256 | .238 | .247 | 95 |
| RHB-HR | 40 | 29 | 69 | 48 | 43 | 91 | 80 | 134 | 99 | 233 | 154 | 140 | 294 | 85 |

## Texas Rangers - Rangers Ballpark in Arlington

LF: 332 CF: 400 RF:325

| | 2013 Season | | | | | | | 2011-2013 | | | | | | |
|---|---|---|---|---|---|---|---|---|---|---|---|---|---|---|
| | Home Games | | | Away Games | | | | Home Games | | | Away Games | | | |
| | Rangers | Opp | Total | Rangers | Opp | Total | Index | Rangers | Opp | Total | Rangers | Opp | Total | Index |
| G | 82 | 82 | 164 | 81 | 81 | 162 | | 244 | 244 | 488 | 243 | 243 | 486 | |
| Avg | .268 | .247 | .258 | .257 | .249 | .253 | 102 | .283 | .254 | .269 | .262 | .240 | .251 | 107 |
| AB | 2713 | 2798 | 5511 | 2872 | 2728 | 5600 | 97 | 8285 | 8495 | 16780 | 8549 | 7993 | 16542 | 101 |
| R | 374 | 308 | 682 | 356 | 328 | 684 | 98 | 1319 | 1080 | 2399 | 1074 | 940 | 2014 | 119 |
| H | 728 | 692 | 1420 | 737 | 678 | 1415 | 99 | 2347 | 2160 | 4507 | 2243 | 1915 | 4158 | 108 |
| 2B | 115 | 131 | 246 | 147 | 130 | 277 | 90 | 447 | 417 | 864 | 428 | 376 | 804 | 106 |
| 3B | 10 | 7 | 17 | 13 | 12 | 25 | 69 | 49 | 38 | 87 | 38 | 36 | 74 | 116 |
| HR | 85 | 74 | 159 | 91 | 83 | 174 | 93 | 319 | 270 | 589 | 267 | 232 | 499 | 116 |
| BB | 251 | 256 | 507 | 211 | 242 | 453 | 114 | 733 | 711 | 1444 | 682 | 694 | 1376 | 103 |
| SO | 496 | 677 | 1173 | 571 | 632 | 1203 | 99 | 1450 | 1934 | 3384 | 1650 | 1840 | 3490 | 96 |
| Foul Outs | 50 | 46 | 96 | 61 | 70 | 131 | 74 | 134 | 168 | 302 | 183 | 214 | 397 | 75 |
| E | 44 | 60 | 104 | 42 | 50 | 92 | 112 | 147 | 204 | 351 | 138 | 149 | 287 | 122 |
| E-Infield | 22 | 26 | 48 | 15 | 20 | 35 | 135 | 71 | 94 | 165 | 59 | 67 | 126 | 130 |
| LHB-Avg | .256 | .256 | .256 | .234 | .250 | .242 | 106 | .275 | .260 | .267 | .253 | .239 | .245 | 109 |
| LHB-HR | 36 | 38 | 74 | 33 | 41 | 74 | 100 | 109 | 131 | 240 | 95 | 99 | 194 | 120 |
| RHB-Avg | .278 | .240 | .259 | .273 | .247 | .261 | 99 | .287 | .250 | .270 | .267 | .240 | .255 | 106 |
| RHB-HR | 49 | 36 | 85 | 58 | 42 | 100 | 87 | 210 | 139 | 349 | 172 | 133 | 305 | 114 |

## Toronto Blue Jays - Rogers Centre Surface: FieldTurf

LF: 328 CF: 400 RF:328

| | 2013 Season | | | | | | | 2011-2013 | | | | | | |
|---|---|---|---|---|---|---|---|---|---|---|---|---|---|---|
| | Home Games | | | Away Games | | | | Home Games | | | Away Games | | | |
| | Blue Jays | Opp | Total | Blue Jays | Opp | Total | Index | Blue Jays | Opp | Total | Blue Jays | Opp | Total | Index |
| G | 81 | 81 | 162 | 81 | 81 | 162 | | 243 | 243 | 486 | 243 | 243 | 486 | |
| Avg | .258 | .256 | .257 | .247 | .262 | .254 | 101 | .254 | .261 | .258 | .244 | .256 | .250 | 103 |
| AB | 2719 | 2900 | 5619 | 2818 | 2708 | 5526 | 102 | 8123 | 8643 | 16766 | 8460 | 8073 | 16533 | 101 |
| R | 380 | 395 | 775 | 332 | 361 | 693 | 112 | 1135 | 1198 | 2333 | 1036 | 1103 | 2139 | 109 |
| H | 701 | 742 | 1443 | 697 | 709 | 1406 | 103 | 2061 | 2258 | 4319 | 2067 | 2065 | 4132 | 105 |
| 2B | 157 | 187 | 344 | 116 | 117 | 233 | 145 | 436 | 547 | 983 | 369 | 398 | 767 | 126 |
| 3B | 14 | 3 | 17 | 10 | 22 | 32 | 52 | 48 | 32 | 80 | 32 | 41 | 73 | 108 |
| HR | 95 | 119 | 214 | 90 | 76 | 166 | 127 | 300 | 316 | 616 | 269 | 262 | 531 | 114 |
| BB | 277 | 251 | 528 | 233 | 249 | 482 | 108 | 788 | 771 | 1559 | 720 | 843 | 1563 | 98 |
| SO | 553 | 672 | 1225 | 570 | 536 | 1106 | 109 | 1737 | 1875 | 3612 | 1821 | 1644 | 3465 | 103 |
| Foul Outs | 88 | 63 | 151 | 76 | 64 | 140 | 106 | 249 | 177 | 426 | 226 | 175 | 401 | 105 |
| E | 59 | 60 | 119 | 52 | 48 | 100 | 119 | 158 | 180 | 338 | 164 | 150 | 314 | 108 |
| E-Infield | 22 | 20 | 42 | 21 | 17 | 38 | 111 | 62 | 70 | 132 | 61 | 63 | 124 | 106 |
| LHB-Avg | .257 | .261 | .259 | .269 | .266 | .267 | 97 | .247 | .265 | .257 | .249 | .258 | .254 | 101 |
| LHB-HR | 39 | 54 | 93 | 28 | 41 | 69 | 133 | 98 | 133 | 231 | 89 | 118 | 207 | 108 |
| RHB-Avg | .259 | .252 | .255 | .229 | .259 | .244 | 105 | .258 | .258 | .258 | .242 | .254 | .247 | 104 |
| RHB-HR | 56 | 65 | 121 | 62 | 35 | 97 | 122 | 202 | 183 | 385 | 180 | 144 | 324 | 119 |

## Washington Nationals - Nationals Park

LF: 336 CF: 403 RF:335

| | 2013 Season | | | | | | | 2011-2013 | | | | | | |
|---|---|---|---|---|---|---|---|---|---|---|---|---|---|---|
| | Home Games | | | Away Games | | | | Home Games | | | Away Games | | | |
| | Nationals | Opp | Total | Nationals | Opp | Total | Index | Nationals | Opp | Total | Nationals | Opp | Total | Index |
| G | 81 | 81 | 162 | 81 | 81 | 162 | | 242 | 242 | 484 | 243 | 243 | 486 | |
| Avg | .271 | .252 | .261 | .232 | .246 | .239 | 109 | .263 | .249 | .256 | .241 | .245 | .243 | 106 |
| AB | 2660 | 2794 | 5454 | 2776 | 2703 | 5479 | 100 | 8063 | 8403 | 16466 | 8429 | 8053 | 16482 | 100 |
| R | 349 | 296 | 645 | 307 | 330 | 637 | 101 | 1027 | 903 | 1930 | 984 | 960 | 1944 | 100 |
| H | 721 | 703 | 1424 | 644 | 664 | 1308 | 109 | 2123 | 2096 | 4219 | 2029 | 1970 | 3999 | 106 |
| 2B | 124 | 143 | 267 | 135 | 119 | 254 | 106 | 392 | 428 | 820 | 425 | 385 | 810 | 101 |
| 3B | 12 | 3 | 15 | 15 | 11 | 26 | 58 | 32 | 32 | 64 | 42 | 37 | 79 | 81 |
| HR | 70 | 65 | 135 | 91 | 77 | 168 | 81 | 254 | 194 | 448 | 255 | 206 | 461 | 97 |
| BB | 224 | 203 | 427 | 240 | 202 | 442 | 97 | 694 | 609 | 1303 | 719 | 770 | 1489 | 88 |
| SO | 540 | 619 | 1159 | 652 | 617 | 1269 | 92 | 1744 | 1785 | 3529 | 2096 | 1825 | 3921 | 90 |
| Foul Outs | 53 | 64 | 117 | 56 | 52 | 108 | 109 | 180 | 168 | 348 | 156 | 166 | 322 | 108 |
| E | 48 | 55 | 103 | 59 | 36 | 95 | 108 | 145 | 157 | 302 | 160 | 145 | 305 | 99 |
| E-Infield | 19 | 21 | 40 | 19 | 16 | 35 | 114 | 59 | 63 | 122 | 63 | 62 | 125 | 98 |
| LHB-Avg | .269 | .246 | .257 | .226 | .269 | .248 | 104 | .257 | .249 | .253 | .233 | .247 | .240 | 105 |
| LHB-HR | 28 | 23 | 51 | 26 | 42 | 68 | 79 | 100 | 72 | 172 | 92 | 97 | 189 | 94 |
| RHB-Avg | .272 | .255 | .264 | .236 | .228 | .232 | 114 | .267 | .250 | .258 | .246 | .243 | .244 | 106 |
| RHB-HR | 42 | 42 | 84 | 65 | 35 | 100 | 82 | 154 | 122 | 276 | 163 | 109 | 272 | 99 |

# 2013 American League Ballpark Index Rankings

| | TOTALS | | | | | | | | | | | | LHB | | RHB | |
|---|---|---|---|---|---|---|---|---|---|---|---|---|---|---|---|---|
| Home Park | Avg | AB | R | H | 2B | 3B | HR | BB | SO | FO | E | E-Inf | Avg | HR | Avg | HR |
| Tigers (Comerica Park) | 107 | 97 | 114 | 105 | 113 | 173 | 104 | 108 | 88 | 132 | 87 | 75 | 110 | 126 | 105 | 89 |
| Blue Jays (Rogers Centre) | 101 | 102 | 112 | 103 | 145 | 52 | 127 | 108 | 109 | 106 | 119 | 111 | 97 | 133 | 105 | 122 |
| Yankees (Yankee Stadium) | 106 | 99 | 109 | 105 | 97 | 74 | 114 | 110 | 102 | 105 | 96 | 103 | 109 | 84 | 103 | 153 |
| Royals (Kauffman Stadium) | 103 | 100 | 108 | 104 | 105 | 152 | 88 | 99 | 89 | 113 | 100 | 137 | 103 | 85 | 104 | 91 |
| Astros (Minute Maid Park) | 98 | 104 | 107 | 101 | 87 | 133 | 119 | 107 | 106 | 75 | 92 | 100 | 100 | 118 | 96 | 119 |
| Orioles (Oriole Park at Camden Yards) | 100 | 98 | 106 | 99 | 88 | 65 | 130 | 103 | 100 | 92 | 110 | 82 | 104 | 145 | 97 | 115 |
| Twins (Target Field) | 102 | 100 | 102 | 103 | 111 | 104 | 80 | 84 | 93 | 104 | 98 | 114 | 103 | 78 | 102 | 82 |
| White Sox (U.S. Cellular Field) | 97 | 98 | 100 | 95 | 78 | 42 | 121 | 118 | 101 | 111 | 117 | 116 | 94 | 119 | 98 | 125 |
| Mariners (Safeco Field) | 99 | 102 | 99 | 101 | 109 | 62 | 87 | 93 | 105 | 124 | 106 | 79 | 100 | 86 | 98 | 88 |
| Rangers (Rangers Ballpark in Arlington) | 102 | 97 | 98 | 99 | 90 | 69 | 93 | 114 | 99 | 74 | 112 | 135 | 106 | 100 | 99 | 87 |
| Angels (Angel Stadium of Anaheim) | 100 | 101 | 97 | 101 | 95 | 99 | 89 | 98 | 101 | 96 | 89 | 95 | 97 | 94 | 103 | 87 |
| Red Sox (Fenway Park) | 101 | 99 | 96 | 100 | 119 | 131 | 86 | 93 | 102 | 66 | 118 | 133 | 100 | 71 | 102 | 100 |
| Indians (Progressive Field) | 98 | 99 | 93 | 98 | 100 | 63 | 108 | 92 | 106 | 89 | 98 | 67 | 98 | 117 | 98 | 100 |
| Rays (Tropicana Field) | 95 | 101 | 93 | 96 | 89 | 165 | 96 | 96 | 103 | 111 | 59 | 69 | 90 | 116 | 98 | 80 |
| Athletics (O.co Coliseum) | 96 | 102 | 89 | 98 | 109 | 129 | 80 | 102 | 97 | 175 | 93 | 91 | 85 | 62 | 108 | 102 |

# 2013 National League Ballpark Index Rankings

| | TOTALS | | | | | | | | | | | | LHB | | RHB | |
|---|---|---|---|---|---|---|---|---|---|---|---|---|---|---|---|---|
| Home Park | Avg | AB | R | H | 2B | 3B | HR | BB | SO | FO | E | E-Inf | Avg | HR | Avg | HR |
| Rockies (Coors Field) | 110 | 106 | 127 | 116 | 106 | 163 | 111 | 94 | 82 | 87 | 168 | 143 | 102 | 104 | 115 | 115 |
| Cubs (Wrigley Field) | 109 | 102 | 119 | 110 | 110 | 87 | 110 | 103 | 102 | 68 | 104 | 100 | 117 | 104 | 103 | 114 |
| Brewers (Miller Park) | 107 | 101 | 111 | 108 | 103 | 106 | 124 | 115 | 97 | 97 | 80 | 82 | 106 | 108 | 107 | 137 |
| Phillies (Citizens Bank Park) | 97 | 102 | 111 | 99 | 102 | 104 | 148 | 102 | 109 | 91 | 119 | 135 | 103 | 153 | 92 | 144 |
| Marlins (Marlins Park) | 101 | 100 | 103 | 101 | 114 | 133 | 64 | 105 | 96 | 98 | 102 | 113 | 100 | 53 | 102 | 72 |
| Nationals (Nationals Park) | 109 | 100 | 101 | 109 | 106 | 58 | 81 | 97 | 92 | 109 | 108 | 114 | 104 | 79 | 114 | 82 |
| Reds (Great American Ballpark) | 97 | 102 | 99 | 99 | 106 | 81 | 131 | 98 | 115 | 91 | 108 | 89 | 95 | 130 | 100 | 133 |
| Diamondbacks (Chase Field) | 99 | 95 | 97 | 94 | 106 | 144 | 99 | 103 | 96 | 113 | 106 | 103 | 99 | 97 | 99 | 101 |
| Braves (Turner Field) | 100 | 99 | 96 | 99 | 94 | 127 | 94 | 96 | 107 | 94 | 98 | 100 | 107 | 114 | 95 | 83 |
| Pirates (PNC Park) | 99 | 100 | 91 | 99 | 86 | 69 | 68 | 88 | 92 | 97 | 94 | 83 | 94 | 79 | 102 | 61 |
| Cardinals (Busch Stadium) | 96 | 97 | 89 | 93 | 90 | 77 | 87 | 93 | 97 | 133 | 91 | 94 | 101 | 81 | 92 | 91 |
| Giants (AT&T Park) | 96 | 100 | 87 | 96 | 102 | 195 | 77 | 109 | 97 | 92 | 82 | 106 | 101 | 65 | 93 | 85 |
| Dodgers (Dodger Stadium) | 98 | 98 | 87 | 96 | 94 | 47 | 98 | 86 | 101 | 88 | 85 | 76 | 99 | 109 | 96 | 93 |
| Mets (Citi Field) | 89 | 100 | 87 | 89 | 84 | 70 | 112 | 102 | 110 | 112 | 88 | 79 | 85 | 108 | 93 | 114 |
| Padres (PETCO Park) | 90 | 100 | 83 | 90 | 78 | 114 | 94 | 100 | 109 | 85 | 106 | 131 | 99 | 130 | 85 | 77 |

| 2013 AL Home Runs | |
|---|---|
| Home Park | Index |
| Orioles | 130 |
| Blue Jays | 127 |
| White Sox | 121 |
| Astros | 119 |
| Yankees | 114 |
| Indians | 108 |
| Tigers | 104 |
| Rays | 96 |
| Rangers | 93 |
| Angels | 89 |
| Royals | 88 |
| Mariners | 87 |
| Red Sox | 86 |
| Athletics | 80 |
| Twins | 80 |

| 2013 AL LHB Home Runs | |
|---|---|
| Home Park | Index |
| Orioles | 145 |
| Blue Jays | 133 |
| Tigers | 126 |
| White Sox | 119 |
| Astros | 118 |
| Indians | 117 |
| Rays | 116 |
| Rangers | 100 |
| Angels | 94 |
| Mariners | 86 |
| Royals | 85 |
| Yankees | 84 |
| Twins | 78 |
| Red Sox | 71 |
| Athletics | 62 |

| 2013 AL RHB Home Runs | |
|---|---|
| Home Park | Index |
| Yankees | 153 |
| White Sox | 125 |
| Blue Jays | 122 |
| Astros | 119 |
| Orioles | 115 |
| Athletics | 102 |
| Indians | 100 |
| Red Sox | 100 |
| Royals | 91 |
| Tigers | 89 |
| Mariners | 88 |
| Rangers | 87 |
| Angels | 87 |
| Twins | 82 |
| Rays | 80 |

| 2013 NL Home Runs | |
|---|---|
| Home Park | Index |
| Phillies | 148 |
| Reds | 131 |
| Brewers | 124 |
| Mets | 112 |
| Rockies | 111 |
| Cubs | 110 |
| Diamondbacks | 99 |
| Dodgers | 98 |
| Padres | 94 |
| Braves | 94 |
| Cardinals | 87 |
| Nationals | 81 |
| Giants | 77 |
| Pirates | 68 |
| Marlins | 64 |

| 2013 NL LHB Home Runs | |
|---|---|
| Home Park | Index |
| Phillies | 153 |
| Reds | 130 |
| Padres | 130 |
| Braves | 114 |
| Dodgers | 109 |
| Brewers | 108 |
| Mets | 108 |
| Cubs | 104 |
| Rockies | 104 |
| Diamondbacks | 97 |
| Cardinals | 81 |
| Pirates | 79 |
| Nationals | 79 |
| Giants | 65 |
| Marlins | 53 |

| 2013 NL RHB Home Runs | |
|---|---|
| Home Park | Index |
| Phillies | 144 |
| Brewers | 137 |
| Reds | 133 |
| Rockies | 115 |
| Mets | 114 |
| Cubs | 114 |
| Diamondbacks | 101 |
| Dodgers | 93 |
| Cardinals | 91 |
| Giants | 85 |
| Braves | 83 |
| Nationals | 82 |
| Padres | 77 |
| Marlins | 72 |
| Pirates | 61 |

| 2013 AL Avg | |
|---|---|
| Home Park | Index |
| Tigers | 107 |
| Yankees | 106 |
| Royals | 103 |
| Twins | 102 |
| Rangers | 102 |
| Red Sox | 101 |
| Blue Jays | 101 |
| Angels | 100 |
| Orioles | 100 |
| Mariners | 99 |
| Indians | 98 |
| Astros | 98 |
| White Sox | 97 |
| Athletics | 96 |
| Rays | 95 |

| 2013 AL LHB Avg | |
|---|---|
| Home Park | Index |
| Tigers | 110 |
| Yankees | 109 |
| Rangers | 106 |
| Orioles | 104 |
| Twins | 103 |
| Royals | 103 |
| Astros | 100 |
| Red Sox | 100 |
| Mariners | 100 |
| Indians | 98 |
| Angels | 97 |
| Blue Jays | 97 |
| White Sox | 94 |
| Rays | 90 |
| Athletics | 85 |

| 2013 AL RHB Avg | |
|---|---|
| Home Park | Index |
| Athletics | 108 |
| Tigers | 105 |
| Blue Jays | 105 |
| Royals | 104 |
| Yankees | 103 |
| Angels | 103 |
| Twins | 102 |
| Red Sox | 102 |
| Rangers | 99 |
| Rays | 98 |
| White Sox | 98 |
| Indians | 98 |
| Mariners | 98 |
| Orioles | 97 |
| Astros | 96 |

| 2013 NL Avg | |
|---|---|
| Home Park | Index |
| Rockies | 110 |
| Nationals | 109 |
| Cubs | 109 |
| Brewers | 107 |
| Marlins | 101 |
| Braves | 100 |
| Diamondbacks | 99 |
| Pirates | 99 |
| Dodgers | 98 |
| Reds | 97 |
| Phillies | 97 |
| Cardinals | 96 |
| Giants | 96 |
| Padres | 90 |
| Mets | 89 |

| 2013 NL LHB Avg | |
|---|---|
| Home Park | Index |
| Cubs | 117 |
| Braves | 107 |
| Brewers | 106 |
| Nationals | 104 |
| Phillies | 103 |
| Rockies | 102 |
| Cardinals | 101 |
| Giants | 101 |
| Marlins | 100 |
| Padres | 99 |
| Dodgers | 99 |
| Diamondbacks | 99 |
| Reds | 95 |
| Pirates | 94 |
| Mets | 85 |

| 2013 NL RHB Avg | |
|---|---|
| Home Park | Index |
| Rockies | 115 |
| Nationals | 114 |
| Brewers | 107 |
| Cubs | 103 |
| Pirates | 102 |
| Marlins | 102 |
| Reds | 100 |
| Diamondbacks | 99 |
| Dodgers | 96 |
| Braves | 95 |
| Mets | 93 |
| Giants | 93 |
| Cardinals | 92 |
| Phillies | 92 |
| Padres | 85 |

| 2013 AL Doubles | |
|---|---|
| Home Park | Index |
| Blue Jays | 145 |
| Red Sox | 119 |
| Tigers | 113 |
| Twins | 111 |
| Mariners | 109 |
| Athletics | 109 |
| Royals | 105 |
| Indians | 100 |
| Yankees | 97 |
| Angels | 95 |
| Rangers | 90 |
| Rays | 89 |
| Orioles | 88 |
| Astros | 87 |
| White Sox | 78 |

| 2013 AL Triples | |
|---|---|
| Home Park | Index |
| Tigers | 173 |
| Rays | 165 |
| Royals | 152 |
| Astros | 133 |
| Red Sox | 131 |
| Athletics | 129 |
| Twins | 104 |
| Angels | 99 |
| Yankees | 74 |
| Rangers | 69 |
| Orioles | 65 |
| Indians | 63 |
| Mariners | 62 |
| Blue Jays | 52 |
| White Sox | 42 |

| 2013 AL Errors | |
|---|---|
| Home Park | Index |
| Blue Jays | 119 |
| Red Sox | 118 |
| White Sox | 117 |
| Rangers | 112 |
| Orioles | 110 |
| Mariners | 106 |
| Royals | 100 |
| Indians | 98 |
| Twins | 98 |
| Yankees | 96 |
| Athletics | 93 |
| Astros | 92 |
| Angels | 89 |
| Tigers | 87 |
| Rays | 59 |

| 2013 NL Doubles | |
|---|---|
| Home Park | Index |
| Marlins | 114 |
| Cubs | 110 |
| Reds | 106 |
| Rockies | 106 |
| Diamondbacks | 106 |
| Nationals | 106 |
| Brewers | 103 |
| Phillies | 102 |
| Giants | 102 |
| Dodgers | 94 |
| Braves | 94 |
| Cardinals | 90 |
| Pirates | 86 |
| Mets | 84 |
| Padres | 78 |

| 2013 NL Triples | |
|---|---|
| Home Park | Index |
| Giants | 195 |
| Rockies | 163 |
| Diamondbacks | 144 |
| Marlins | 133 |
| Braves | 127 |
| Padres | 114 |
| Brewers | 106 |
| Phillies | 104 |
| Cubs | 87 |
| Reds | 81 |
| Cardinals | 77 |
| Mets | 70 |
| Pirates | 69 |
| Nationals | 58 |
| Dodgers | 47 |

| 2013 NL Errors | |
|---|---|
| Home Park | Index |
| Rockies | 168 |
| Phillies | 119 |
| Nationals | 108 |
| Reds | 108 |
| Padres | 106 |
| Diamondbacks | 106 |
| Cubs | 104 |
| Marlins | 102 |
| Braves | 98 |
| Pirates | 94 |
| Cardinals | 91 |
| Mets | 88 |
| Dodgers | 85 |
| Giants | 82 |
| Brewers | 80 |

# 2011-2013 American League Ballpark Index Rankings

| | TOTALS | | | | | | | | | | | | LHB | | RHB | |
|---|---|---|---|---|---|---|---|---|---|---|---|---|---|---|---|---|
| Home Park | Avg | AB | R | H | 2B | 3B | HR | BB | SO | FO | E | E-Inf | Avg | HR | Avg | HR |
| Rangers (Rangers Ballpark in Arlington) | 106 | 101 | 115 | 107 | 106 | 113 | 117 | 103 | 95 | 81 | 119 | 141 | 106 | 122 | 107 | 113 |
| Red Sox (Fenway Park) | 106 | 101 | 110 | 107 | 130 | 105 | 92 | 96 | 98 | 75 | 118 | 116 | 105 | 79 | 108 | 104 |
| White Sox (U.S. Cellular Field) | 100 | 99 | 109 | 99 | 96 | 71 | 130 | 119 | 105 | 114 | 105 | 102 | 99 | 119 | 100 | 138 |
| Orioles (Oriole Park at Camden Yards) | 104 | 101 | 107 | 105 | 98 | 75 | 122 | 99 | 97 | 90 | 90 | 100 | 105 | 129 | 102 | 116 |
| Yankees (Yankee Stadium) | 101 | 99 | 107 | 101 | 94 | 64 | 125 | 104 | 100 | 97 | 100 | 92 | 103 | 133 | 100 | 116 |
| Tigers (Comerica Park) | 103 | 99 | 105 | 102 | 100 | 143 | 99 | 97 | 91 | 119 | 113 | 106 | 102 | 100 | 103 | 98 |
| Blue Jays (Rogers Centre) | 100 | 100 | 105 | 101 | 113 | 108 | 116 | 98 | 103 | 107 | 106 | 104 | 99 | 106 | 102 | 121 |
| Royals (Kauffman Stadium) | 104 | 101 | 104 | 105 | 104 | 151 | 84 | 99 | 91 | 88 | 100 | 119 | 105 | 75 | 103 | 91 |
| Twins (Target Field) | 102 | 100 | 99 | 102 | 104 | 121 | 84 | 98 | 96 | 92 | 91 | 99 | 101 | 75 | 102 | 91 |
| Mariners (Safeco Field)[1] | 99 | 102 | 99 | 101 | 109 | 62 | 87 | 93 | 105 | 124 | 106 | 79 | 100 | 86 | 98 | 88 |
| Astros (Minute Maid Park) | 98 | 101 | 98 | 99 | 95 | 107 | 109 | 102 | 105 | 87 | 104 | 104 | 101 | 105 | 97 | 111 |
| Athletics (O.co Coliseum) | 95 | 99 | 93 | 94 | 95 | 118 | 83 | 103 | 100 | 137 | 102 | 92 | 93 | 74 | 98 | 91 |
| Indians (Progressive Field) | 97 | 101 | 91 | 97 | 102 | 59 | 91 | 95 | 103 | 93 | 108 | 105 | 97 | 108 | 96 | 75 |
| Angels (Angel Stadium of Anaheim) | 97 | 99 | 90 | 96 | 90 | 73 | 90 | 94 | 101 | 85 | 95 | 88 | 95 | 89 | 98 | 90 |
| Rays (Tropicana Field) | 95 | 99 | 88 | 94 | 91 | 124 | 91 | 98 | 104 | 130 | 77 | 76 | 93 | 93 | 96 | 89 |

# 2011-2013 National League Ballpark Index Rankings

| | TOTALS | | | | | | | | | | | | LHB | | RHB | |
|---|---|---|---|---|---|---|---|---|---|---|---|---|---|---|---|---|
| Home Park | Avg | AB | R | H | 2B | 3B | HR | BB | SO | FO | E | E-Inf | Avg | HR | Avg | HR |
| Rockies (Coors Field) | 115 | 105 | 136 | 120 | 117 | 155 | 125 | 97 | 86 | 81 | 122 | 106 | 113 | 133 | 116 | 120 |
| Diamondbacks (Chase Field) | 104 | 100 | 110 | 104 | 113 | 150 | 106 | 96 | 98 | 108 | 93 | 100 | 105 | 105 | 103 | 107 |
| Cubs (Wrigley Field) | 103 | 101 | 109 | 104 | 102 | 104 | 103 | 105 | 100 | 81 | 112 | 118 | 104 | 102 | 102 | 103 |
| Brewers (Miller Park) | 101 | 100 | 103 | 101 | 103 | 105 | 123 | 106 | 105 | 104 | 92 | 90 | 99 | 123 | 101 | 123 |
| Reds (Great American Ballpark) | 101 | 100 | 103 | 100 | 95 | 96 | 130 | 100 | 106 | 106 | 86 | 92 | 99 | 123 | 102 | 136 |
| Phillies (Citizens Bank Park) | 98 | 100 | 102 | 98 | 102 | 87 | 111 | 102 | 104 | 101 | 102 | 103 | 99 | 117 | 98 | 107 |
| Marlins (Marlins Park) | 101 | 99 | 102 | 100 | 103 | 130 | 69 | 104 | 98 | 99 | 102 | 110 | 99 | 61 | 102 | 73 |
| Nationals (Nationals Park) | 103 | 101 | 99 | 103 | 101 | 88 | 97 | 91 | 93 | 110 | 103 | 96 | 103 | 96 | 102 | 98 |
| Braves (Turner Field) | 99 | 99 | 97 | 99 | 97 | 97 | 93 | 101 | 106 | 99 | 113 | 120 | 100 | 103 | 99 | 85 |
| Pirates (PNC Park) | 99 | 99 | 93 | 98 | 100 | 81 | 78 | 91 | 89 | 93 | 110 | 116 | 99 | 87 | 98 | 72 |
| Cardinals (Busch Stadium) | 97 | 98 | 92 | 96 | 95 | 77 | 81 | 101 | 98 | 114 | 97 | 100 | 100 | 90 | 96 | 77 |
| Dodgers (Dodger Stadium) | 97 | 99 | 89 | 96 | 94 | 49 | 98 | 93 | 101 | 100 | 88 | 79 | 99 | 107 | 96 | 94 |
| Mets (Citi Field)[2] | 91 | 99 | 87 | 91 | 82 | 67 | 110 | 100 | 108 | 102 | 81 | 69 | 91 | 105 | 92 | 115 |
| Giants (AT&T Park) | 97 | 98 | 86 | 96 | 100 | 107 | 76 | 99 | 100 | 87 | 92 | 96 | 98 | 67 | 97 | 82 |
| Padres (PETCO Park)[1] | 90 | 100 | 83 | 90 | 78 | 114 | 94 | 100 | 109 | 85 | 106 | 131 | 99 | 130 | 85 | 77 |

| 2011-2013 AL Home Runs | |
|---|---|
| Home Park | Index |
| White Sox | 130 |
| Yankees | 125 |
| Orioles | 122 |
| Rangers | 117 |
| Blue Jays | 116 |
| Astros | 109 |
| Tigers | 99 |
| Red Sox | 92 |
| Indians | 91 |
| Rays | 91 |
| Angels | 90 |
| Mariners[1] | 87 |
| Twins | 84 |
| Royals | 84 |
| Athletics | 83 |

| 2011-2013 AL LHB Home Runs | |
|---|---|
| Home Park | Index |
| Yankees | 133 |
| Orioles | 129 |
| Rangers | 122 |
| White Sox | 119 |
| Indians | 108 |
| Blue Jays | 106 |
| Astros | 105 |
| Tigers | 100 |
| Rays | 93 |
| Angels | 89 |
| Mariners[1] | 86 |
| Red Sox | 79 |
| Royals | 75 |
| Twins | 75 |
| Athletics | 74 |

| 2011-2013 AL RHB Home Runs | |
|---|---|
| Home Park | Index |
| White Sox | 138 |
| Blue Jays | 121 |
| Yankees | 116 |
| Orioles | 116 |
| Rangers | 113 |
| Astros | 111 |
| Red Sox | 104 |
| Tigers | 98 |
| Twins | 91 |
| Royals | 91 |
| Athletics | 91 |
| Angels | 90 |
| Rays | 89 |
| Mariners[1] | 88 |
| Indians | 75 |

| 2011-2013 NL Home Runs | |
|---|---|
| Home Park | Index |
| Reds | 130 |
| Rockies | 125 |
| Brewers | 123 |
| Phillies | 111 |
| Mets[2] | 110 |
| Diamondbacks | 106 |
| Cubs | 103 |
| Dodgers | 98 |
| Nationals | 97 |
| Padres[1] | 94 |
| Braves | 93 |
| Cardinals | 81 |
| Pirates | 78 |
| Giants | 76 |
| Marlins | 69 |

| 2011-2013 NL LHB Home Runs | |
|---|---|
| Home Park | Index |
| Rockies | 133 |
| Padres[1] | 130 |
| Brewers | 123 |
| Reds | 123 |
| Phillies | 117 |
| Dodgers | 107 |
| Diamondbacks | 105 |
| Mets[2] | 105 |
| Braves | 103 |
| Cubs | 102 |
| Nationals | 96 |
| Cardinals | 90 |
| Pirates | 87 |
| Giants | 67 |
| Marlins | 61 |

| 2011-2013 NL RHB Home Runs | |
|---|---|
| Home Park | Index |
| Reds | 136 |
| Brewers | 123 |
| Rockies | 120 |
| Mets[2] | 115 |
| Diamondbacks | 107 |
| Phillies | 107 |
| Cubs | 103 |
| Nationals | 98 |
| Dodgers | 94 |
| Braves | 85 |
| Giants | 82 |
| Cardinals | 77 |
| Padres[1] | 77 |
| Marlins | 73 |
| Pirates | 72 |

1) 2013 Only
2) 2012 - 2013 Only

| 2011-2013 AL Avg | |
|---|---|
| Home Park | Index |
| Rangers | 106 |
| Red Sox | 106 |
| Orioles | 104 |
| Royals | 104 |
| Tigers | 103 |
| Twins | 102 |
| Yankees | 101 |
| Blue Jays | 100 |
| White Sox | 100 |
| Mariners[1] | 99 |
| Astros | 98 |
| Angels | 97 |
| Indians | 97 |
| Athletics | 95 |
| Rays | 95 |

| 2011-2013 AL LHB Avg | |
|---|---|
| Home Park | Index |
| Rangers | 106 |
| Orioles | 105 |
| Royals | 105 |
| Red Sox | 105 |
| Yankees | 103 |
| Tigers | 102 |
| Twins | 101 |
| Astros | 101 |
| Mariners[1] | 100 |
| White Sox | 99 |
| Blue Jays | 99 |
| Indians | 97 |
| Angels | 95 |
| Rays | 93 |
| Athletics | 93 |

| 2011-2013 AL RHB Avg | |
|---|---|
| Home Park | Index |
| Red Sox | 108 |
| Rangers | 107 |
| Tigers | 103 |
| Royals | 103 |
| Twins | 102 |
| Orioles | 102 |
| Blue Jays | 102 |
| White Sox | 100 |
| Yankees | 100 |
| Angels | 98 |
| Mariners[1] | 98 |
| Athletics | 98 |
| Astros | 97 |
| Rays | 96 |
| Indians | 96 |

| 2011-2013 NL Avg | |
|---|---|
| Home Park | Index |
| Rockies | 115 |
| Diamondbacks | 104 |
| Cubs | 103 |
| Nationals | 103 |
| Reds | 101 |
| Marlins | 101 |
| Brewers | 101 |
| Braves | 99 |
| Pirates | 99 |
| Phillies | 98 |
| Dodgers | 97 |
| Cardinals | 97 |
| Giants | 97 |
| Mets[2] | 91 |
| Padres1 | 90 |

| 2011-2013 NL LHB Avg | |
|---|---|
| Home Park | Index |
| Rockies | 113 |
| Diamondbacks | 105 |
| Cubs | 104 |
| Nationals | 103 |
| Cardinals | 100 |
| Braves | 100 |
| Phillies | 99 |
| Brewers | 99 |
| Dodgers | 99 |
| Padres[1] | 99 |
| Marlins | 99 |
| Pirates | 99 |
| Reds | 99 |
| Giants | 98 |
| Mets[2] | 91 |

| 2011-2013 NL RHB Avg | |
|---|---|
| Home Park | Index |
| Rockies | 116 |
| Diamondbacks | 103 |
| Cubs | 102 |
| Nationals | 102 |
| Reds | 102 |
| Marlins | 102 |
| Brewers | 101 |
| Braves | 99 |
| Pirates | 98 |
| Phillies | 98 |
| Giants | 97 |
| Dodgers | 96 |
| Cardinals | 96 |
| Mets[2] | 92 |
| Padres[1] | 85 |

| 2011-2013 AL Doubles | |
|---|---|
| Home Park | Index |
| Red Sox | 130 |
| Blue Jays | 113 |
| Mariners[1] | 109 |
| Rangers | 106 |
| Royals | 104 |
| Twins | 104 |
| Indians | 102 |
| Tigers | 100 |
| Orioles | 98 |
| White Sox | 96 |
| Astros | 95 |
| Athletics | 95 |
| Yankees | 94 |
| Rays | 91 |
| Angels | 90 |

| 2011-2013 AL Triples | |
|---|---|
| Home Park | Index |
| Royals | 151 |
| Tigers | 143 |
| Rays | 124 |
| Twins | 121 |
| Athletics | 118 |
| Rangers | 113 |
| Blue Jays | 108 |
| Astros | 107 |
| Red Sox | 105 |
| Orioles | 75 |
| Angels | 73 |
| White Sox | 71 |
| Yankees | 64 |
| Mariners[1] | 62 |
| Indians | 59 |

| 2011-2013 AL Errors | |
|---|---|
| Home Park | Index |
| Rangers | 119 |
| Red Sox | 118 |
| Tigers | 113 |
| Indians | 108 |
| Blue Jays | 106 |
| Mariners[1] | 106 |
| White Sox | 105 |
| Astros | 104 |
| Athletics | 102 |
| Yankees | 100 |
| Royals | 100 |
| Angels | 95 |
| Twins | 91 |
| Orioles | 90 |
| Rays | 77 |

| 2011-2013 NL Doubles | |
|---|---|
| Home Park | Index |
| Rockies | 117 |
| Diamondbacks | 113 |
| Marlins | 103 |
| Brewers | 103 |
| Cubs | 102 |
| Phillies | 102 |
| Nationals | 101 |
| Pirates | 100 |
| Giants | 100 |
| Braves | 97 |
| Cardinals | 95 |
| Reds | 95 |
| Dodgers | 94 |
| Mets[2] | 82 |
| Padres[1] | 78 |

| 2011-2013 NL Triples | |
|---|---|
| Home Park | Index |
| Rockies | 155 |
| Diamondbacks | 150 |
| Marlins | 130 |
| Padres[1] | 114 |
| Giants | 107 |
| Brewers | 105 |
| Cubs | 104 |
| Braves | 97 |
| Reds | 96 |
| Nationals | 88 |
| Phillies | 87 |
| Pirates | 81 |
| Cardinals | 77 |
| Mets[2] | 67 |
| Dodgers | 49 |

| 2011-2013 NL Errors | |
|---|---|
| Home Park | Index |
| Rockies | 122 |
| Braves | 113 |
| Cubs | 112 |
| Pirates | 110 |
| Padres[1] | 106 |
| Nationals | 103 |
| Marlins | 102 |
| Phillies | 102 |
| Cardinals | 97 |
| Diamondbacks | 93 |
| Giants | 92 |
| Brewers | 92 |
| Dodgers | 88 |
| Reds | 86 |
| Mets[2] | 81 |

1) 2013 Only
2) 2012 - 2013 Only

# 2013 Lefty/Righty Statistics

What follows are the platoon splits for all hitters with at least 20 plate appearances and pitchers with at least 20 batters faced in 2013. You will find the batting average, on-base percentage, and slugging percentage along with a count of at-bats, hits, doubles, triples, home runs, RBI, walks, and strikeouts for hitters against both right and left-handed pitchers. In particular, Mike Trout, Paul Goldschmidt, and Buster Posey were similarly effective against pitchers of either handedness while Carlos Gomez, David Ortiz, and Chris Davis were much better against opposite-handed pitchers.

For pitchers, these stats reflect the results of opposing batters. For example, James Russell of the Cubs was tremendous against same-handed (left-handed) batters this year, holding them to a .183 average. In contrast, Russell allowed a .321 average versus right-handed hitters. Meanwhile Craig Breslow, also a left-handed pitcher but less of a LOOGY(Left-handed One Out Guy) than Russell, actually fared better against opposing right-handed hitters (.208 average) than he did against left-handed hitters (.253 average).

# Batters vs. Left-Handed and Right-Handed Pitchers

| Batter | vs | Avg | AB | H | 2B | 3B | HR | RBI | BB | SO | OBP | Slg |
|---|---|---|---|---|---|---|---|---|---|---|---|---|
| Abreu,Tony | L | .309 | 55 | 17 | 6 | 0 | 2 | 4 | 4 | 9 | .356 | .527 |
| Bats Both | R | .241 | 83 | 20 | 6 | 3 | 0 | 10 | 2 | 24 | .264 | .386 |
| Ackley,Dustin | L | .259 | 112 | 29 | 4 | 1 | 1 | 8 | 11 | 25 | .325 | .339 |
| Bats Left | R | .250 | 272 | 68 | 14 | 1 | 3 | 23 | 26 | 47 | .317 | .342 |
| Adams,David | L | .197 | 61 | 12 | 3 | 0 | 0 | 8 | 3 | 17 | .246 | .246 |
| Bats Right | R | .190 | 79 | 15 | 2 | 1 | 2 | 5 | 6 | 26 | .256 | .316 |
| Adams,Matt | L | .231 | 52 | 12 | 1 | 0 | 3 | 10 | 0 | 19 | .231 | .423 |
| Bats Left | R | .295 | 244 | 72 | 13 | 0 | 14 | 41 | 23 | 61 | .356 | .520 |
| Adduci,Jim | L | .333 | 6 | 2 | 0 | 0 | 0 | 0 | 0 | 2 | .333 | .333 |
| Bats Left | R | .240 | 25 | 6 | 1 | 0 | 0 | 0 | 3 | 7 | .321 | .280 |
| Almonte,Abraham | L | .207 | 29 | 6 | 1 | 0 | 0 | 1 | 1 | 7 | .233 | .241 |
| Bats Both | R | .302 | 43 | 13 | 3 | 0 | 2 | 8 | 5 | 14 | .360 | .512 |
| Almonte,Zoilo | L | .200 | 30 | 6 | 0 | 0 | 0 | 3 | 1 | 4 | .219 | .200 |
| Bats Both | R | .250 | 76 | 19 | 4 | 0 | 1 | 6 | 5 | 15 | .296 | .342 |
| Alonso,Yonder | L | .242 | 91 | 22 | 3 | 0 | 2 | 15 | 6 | 19 | .296 | .341 |
| Bats Left | R | .296 | 243 | 72 | 8 | 0 | 4 | 30 | 26 | 28 | .357 | .379 |
| Altuve,Jose | L | .287 | 181 | 52 | 11 | 1 | 3 | 19 | 9 | 26 | .325 | .409 |
| Bats Right | R | .281 | 445 | 125 | 20 | 1 | 2 | 33 | 23 | 59 | .312 | .344 |
| Alvarez,Pedro | L | .180 | 133 | 24 | 5 | 0 | 3 | 24 | 13 | 56 | .252 | .286 |
| Bats Left | R | .249 | 425 | 106 | 17 | 2 | 33 | 76 | 35 | 130 | .310 | .532 |
| Amarista,Alexi | L | .220 | 41 | 9 | 2 | 0 | 0 | 4 | 3 | 10 | .289 | .268 |
| Bats Left | R | .239 | 327 | 78 | 12 | 4 | 5 | 28 | 19 | 47 | .282 | .346 |
| Andino,Robert | L | .290 | 31 | 9 | 3 | 0 | 0 | 2 | 2 | 9 | .333 | .387 |
| Bats Right | R | .111 | 45 | 5 | 1 | 0 | 0 | 2 | 5 | 18 | .200 | .133 |
| Andrus,Elvis | L | .273 | 176 | 48 | 6 | 0 | 3 | 20 | 19 | 22 | .340 | .358 |
| Bats Right | R | .270 | 444 | 120 | 11 | 4 | 1 | 47 | 33 | 75 | .324 | .320 |
| Ankiel,Rick | L | .100 | 10 | 1 | 1 | 0 | 0 | 0 | 1 | 6 | .182 | .200 |
| Bats Left | R | .195 | 118 | 23 | 6 | 1 | 7 | 18 | 7 | 54 | .240 | .441 |
| Aoki,Norichika | L | .339 | 180 | 61 | 6 | 1 | 1 | 13 | 11 | 11 | .381 | .400 |
| Bats Left | R | .264 | 417 | 110 | 14 | 2 | 7 | 24 | 44 | 29 | .345 | .357 |
| Arcia,Oswaldo | L | .254 | 114 | 29 | 4 | 1 | 3 | 11 | 2 | 36 | .274 | .386 |
| Bats Left | R | .249 | 237 | 59 | 13 | 1 | 11 | 32 | 21 | 81 | .318 | .451 |
| Arenado,Nolan | L | .296 | 135 | 40 | 9 | 3 | 4 | 20 | 10 | 14 | .349 | .496 |
| Bats Right | R | .256 | 351 | 90 | 20 | 1 | 6 | 32 | 13 | 58 | .281 | .370 |
| Arencibia,J.P. | L | .204 | 137 | 28 | 6 | 0 | 5 | 14 | 5 | 44 | .231 | .358 |
| Bats Right | R | .190 | 337 | 64 | 12 | 0 | 16 | 41 | 13 | 104 | .226 | .368 |
| Arias,Joaquin | L | .270 | 122 | 33 | 6 | 0 | 1 | 13 | 1 | 10 | .274 | .344 |
| Bats Right | R | .272 | 103 | 28 | 3 | 2 | 0 | 6 | 3 | 23 | .296 | .340 |
| Asche,Cody | L | .219 | 32 | 7 | 1 | 0 | 1 | 6 | 2 | 10 | .265 | .344 |
| Bats Left | R | .238 | 130 | 31 | 7 | 1 | 4 | 16 | 13 | 33 | .310 | .400 |
| Avila,Alex | L | .139 | 79 | 11 | 4 | 0 | 1 | 7 | 8 | 32 | .227 | .228 |
| Bats Left | R | .255 | 251 | 64 | 10 | 1 | 10 | 40 | 36 | 80 | .345 | .422 |
| Aviles,Mike | L | .232 | 164 | 38 | 8 | 0 | 3 | 18 | 11 | 17 | .269 | .335 |
| Bats Right | R | .269 | 197 | 53 | 7 | 0 | 6 | 28 | 4 | 24 | .293 | .396 |
| Aybar,Erick | L | .288 | 163 | 47 | 16 | 0 | 2 | 15 | 4 | 19 | .300 | .423 |
| Bats Both | R | .264 | 387 | 102 | 17 | 5 | 4 | 39 | 19 | 40 | .302 | .364 |
| Baker,Jeff | L | .314 | 105 | 33 | 7 | 0 | 10 | 18 | 16 | 37 | .407 | .667 |
| Bats Right | R | .204 | 49 | 10 | 1 | 0 | 1 | 3 | 2 | 11 | .250 | .286 |
| Baker,John | L | .167 | 6 | 1 | 0 | 0 | 0 | 0 | 0 | 4 | .167 | .167 |
| Bats Left | R | .147 | 34 | 5 | 0 | 0 | 0 | 2 | 6 | 8 | .275 | .147 |
| Barmes,Clint | L | .185 | 54 | 10 | 4 | 0 | 1 | 5 | 2 | 16 | .214 | .315 |
| Bats Right | R | .216 | 250 | 54 | 11 | 0 | 4 | 18 | 12 | 54 | .257 | .308 |
| Barnes,Brandon | L | .296 | 135 | 40 | 5 | 1 | 4 | 16 | 9 | 41 | .354 | .437 |
| Bats Right | R | .212 | 273 | 58 | 12 | 0 | 4 | 25 | 12 | 86 | .257 | .300 |
| Barney,Darwin | L | .246 | 130 | 32 | 10 | 0 | 4 | 10 | 11 | 18 | .310 | .415 |
| Bats Right | R | .194 | 371 | 72 | 15 | 1 | 3 | 31 | 25 | 46 | .251 | .264 |
| Barton,Daric | L | .269 | 26 | 7 | 1 | 0 | 0 | 4 | 3 | 6 | .345 | .308 |
| Bats Left | R | .269 | 78 | 21 | 1 | 0 | 3 | 12 | 10 | 12 | .352 | .397 |
| Bautista,Jose | L | .250 | 92 | 23 | 6 | 0 | 7 | 20 | 17 | 12 | .366 | .543 |
| Bats Right | R | .261 | 360 | 94 | 18 | 0 | 21 | 53 | 52 | 72 | .356 | .486 |
| Baxter,Mike | L | .333 | 12 | 4 | 0 | 0 | 0 | 1 | 1 | 4 | .385 | .333 |
| Bats Left | R | .175 | 120 | 21 | 6 | 1 | 0 | 3 | 16 | 24 | .296 | .242 |
| Bay,Jason | L | .226 | 106 | 24 | 4 | 0 | 6 | 8 | 11 | 29 | .299 | .434 |
| Bats Right | R | .180 | 100 | 18 | 2 | 0 | 5 | 12 | 15 | 33 | .297 | .350 |
| Beckham,Gordon | L | .195 | 82 | 16 | 4 | 0 | 1 | 7 | 3 | 17 | .230 | .280 |
| Bats Right | R | .287 | 289 | 83 | 18 | 1 | 4 | 17 | 25 | 39 | .347 | .398 |
| Belt,Brandon | L | .261 | 119 | 31 | 10 | 1 | 3 | 12 | 8 | 33 | .318 | .437 |
| Bats Left | R | .297 | 390 | 116 | 29 | 3 | 14 | 55 | 44 | 92 | .372 | .495 |
| Beltran,Carlos | L | .252 | 163 | 41 | 9 | 1 | 7 | 28 | 7 | 26 | .281 | .448 |
| Bats Both | R | .315 | 391 | 123 | 21 | 2 | 17 | 56 | 31 | 64 | .362 | .509 |
| Beltre,Adrian | L | .325 | 154 | 50 | 10 | 0 | 8 | 22 | 19 | 22 | .402 | .545 |
| Bats Right | R | .312 | 477 | 149 | 22 | 0 | 22 | 70 | 31 | 56 | .360 | .497 |
| Beltre,Engel | L | .167 | 6 | 1 | 0 | 0 | 0 | 1 | 0 | 1 | .167 | .167 |
| Bats Left | R | .265 | 34 | 9 | 1 | 0 | 0 | 1 | 0 | 4 | .286 | .294 |
| Berkman,Lance | L | .254 | 71 | 18 | 5 | 0 | 3 | 10 | 8 | 14 | .329 | .451 |
| Bats Both | R | .238 | 185 | 44 | 5 | 1 | 3 | 24 | 30 | 38 | .344 | .324 |

| Batter | vs | Avg | AB | H | 2B | 3B | HR | RBI | BB | SO | OBP | Slg |
|---|---|---|---|---|---|---|---|---|---|---|---|---|
| Bernadina,Roger | L | .129 | 31 | 4 | 0 | 1 | 0 | 1 | 1 | 10 | .229 | .194 |
| Bats Left | R | .189 | 196 | 37 | 10 | 1 | 4 | 10 | 15 | 55 | .254 | .311 |
| Bernier,Doug | L | .278 | 18 | 5 | 2 | 0 | 0 | 4 | 3 | 4 | .381 | .389 |
| Bats Right | R | .200 | 35 | 7 | 1 | 0 | 0 | 1 | 5 | 11 | .317 | .229 |
| Betancourt,Yuniesky | L | .198 | 126 | 25 | 3 | 0 | 3 | 16 | 7 | 29 | .241 | .294 |
| Bats Right | R | .219 | 265 | 58 | 12 | 1 | 10 | 30 | 7 | 42 | .239 | .385 |
| Bianchi,Jeff | L | .258 | 66 | 17 | 1 | 0 | 0 | 10 | 1 | 13 | .279 | .273 |
| Bats Right | R | .229 | 170 | 39 | 7 | 1 | 1 | 15 | 10 | 33 | .269 | .300 |
| Blackmon,Charlie | L | .296 | 71 | 21 | 1 | 0 | 3 | 7 | 1 | 23 | .315 | .437 |
| Bats Left | R | .314 | 175 | 55 | 16 | 2 | 3 | 15 | 6 | 26 | .344 | .480 |
| Blanco,Gregor | L | .246 | 61 | 15 | 0 | 2 | 0 | 7 | 9 | 17 | .338 | .311 |
| Bats Left | R | .269 | 391 | 105 | 17 | 4 | 3 | 34 | 43 | 78 | .341 | .355 |
| Blanco,Henry | L | .149 | 47 | 7 | 2 | 0 | 1 | 3 | 4 | 9 | .216 | .255 |
| Bats Right | R | .138 | 87 | 12 | 3 | 0 | 2 | 11 | 10 | 27 | .235 | .241 |
| Blanks,Kyle | L | .282 | 103 | 29 | 3 | 0 | 5 | 19 | 14 | 26 | .373 | .456 |
| Bats Right | R | .220 | 177 | 39 | 11 | 0 | 3 | 16 | 7 | 59 | .263 | .333 |
| Bloomquist,Willie | L | .333 | 42 | 14 | 2 | 0 | 0 | 3 | 2 | 1 | .364 | .381 |
| Bats Right | R | .309 | 97 | 30 | 3 | 1 | 0 | 11 | 6 | 10 | .358 | .361 |
| Boesch,Brennan | L | .250 | 12 | 3 | 1 | 0 | 0 | 0 | 1 | 1 | .308 | .333 |
| Bats Left | R | .282 | 39 | 11 | 1 | 1 | 3 | 8 | 1 | 8 | .300 | .590 |
| Bogaerts,Xander | L | .467 | 15 | 7 | 1 | 0 | 0 | 2 | 3 | 1 | .556 | .533 |
| Bats Right | R | .138 | 29 | 4 | 1 | 0 | 1 | 3 | 2 | 12 | .188 | .276 |
| Bogusevic,Brian | L | .125 | 16 | 2 | 1 | 0 | 0 | 1 | 0 | 7 | .125 | .188 |
| Bats Left | R | .291 | 127 | 37 | 6 | 1 | 6 | 15 | 10 | 28 | .345 | .496 |
| Bonifacio,Emilio | L | .231 | 121 | 28 | 3 | 1 | 0 | 7 | 10 | 31 | .295 | .273 |
| Bats Both | R | .247 | 299 | 74 | 19 | 2 | 3 | 24 | 20 | 72 | .294 | .355 |
| Borbon,Julio | L | .206 | 34 | 7 | 1 | 0 | 1 | 2 | 3 | 10 | .270 | .324 |
| Bats Left | R | .197 | 71 | 14 | 2 | 1 | 0 | 1 | 9 | 12 | .288 | .254 |
| Bourjos,Peter | L | .256 | 39 | 10 | 1 | 0 | 0 | 0 | 4 | 11 | .326 | .282 |
| Bats Right | R | .279 | 136 | 38 | 2 | 3 | 3 | 12 | 6 | 32 | .336 | .404 |
| Bourn,Michael | L | .277 | 159 | 44 | 4 | 1 | 1 | 12 | 9 | 39 | .322 | .333 |
| Bats Left | R | .257 | 366 | 94 | 17 | 5 | 5 | 38 | 31 | 93 | .313 | .372 |
| Bradley Jr.,Jackie | L | .080 | 25 | 2 | 1 | 0 | 0 | 3 | 3 | 11 | .207 | .120 |
| Bats Left | R | .229 | 70 | 16 | 4 | 0 | 3 | 7 | 7 | 20 | .308 | .414 |
| Brantley,Michael | L | .276 | 174 | 48 | 6 | 1 | 1 | 16 | 11 | 33 | .325 | .339 |
| Bats Left | R | .288 | 382 | 110 | 20 | 2 | 9 | 57 | 29 | 34 | .336 | .421 |
| Brantly,Rob | L | .056 | 36 | 2 | 2 | 0 | 0 | 1 | 3 | 13 | .128 | .111 |
| Bats Left | R | .241 | 187 | 45 | 7 | 0 | 1 | 17 | 12 | 40 | .289 | .294 |
| Braun,Ryan | L | .368 | 76 | 28 | 7 | 2 | 3 | 10 | 7 | 14 | .422 | .632 |
| Bats Right | R | .262 | 149 | 39 | 7 | 0 | 6 | 28 | 20 | 42 | .347 | .430 |
| Brignac,Reid | L | .231 | 13 | 3 | 0 | 0 | 0 | 0 | 2 | 6 | .333 | .231 |
| Bats Left | R | .177 | 79 | 14 | 4 | 0 | 1 | 6 | 2 | 24 | .198 | .266 |
| Brown,Andrew | L | .234 | 77 | 18 | 3 | 0 | 4 | 13 | 5 | 20 | .280 | .429 |
| Bats Right | R | .219 | 73 | 16 | 2 | 0 | 3 | 11 | 8 | 24 | .296 | .370 |
| Brown,Domonic | L | .252 | 147 | 37 | 6 | 1 | 6 | 21 | 9 | 31 | .296 | .429 |
| Bats Left | R | .281 | 349 | 98 | 15 | 3 | 21 | 62 | 30 | 66 | .336 | .521 |
| Bruce,Jay | L | .246 | 203 | 50 | 10 | 0 | 10 | 30 | 12 | 58 | .291 | .443 |
| Bats Left | R | .270 | 423 | 114 | 33 | 1 | 20 | 79 | 51 | 127 | .347 | .494 |
| Buck,John | L | .173 | 98 | 17 | 1 | 0 | 6 | 16 | 10 | 34 | .250 | .367 |
| Bats Right | R | .238 | 294 | 70 | 10 | 0 | 9 | 46 | 19 | 70 | .300 | .364 |
| Butler,Billy | L | .275 | 149 | 41 | 9 | 0 | 5 | 27 | 21 | 28 | .360 | .436 |
| Bats Right | R | .293 | 433 | 127 | 18 | 0 | 10 | 55 | 58 | 74 | .379 | .404 |
| Byrd,Marlon | L | .344 | 163 | 56 | 11 | 2 | 8 | 31 | 9 | 35 | .376 | .583 |
| Bats Right | R | .268 | 369 | 99 | 24 | 3 | 16 | 57 | 22 | 109 | .318 | .480 |
| Cabrera,Asdrubal | L | .232 | 168 | 39 | 11 | 1 | 3 | 21 | 11 | 37 | .276 | .363 |
| Bats Both | R | .247 | 340 | 84 | 24 | 1 | 11 | 43 | 24 | 77 | .309 | .421 |
| Cabrera,Everth | L | .365 | 115 | 42 | 7 | 2 | 2 | 13 | 10 | 16 | .421 | .513 |
| Bats Both | R | .248 | 266 | 66 | 8 | 3 | 2 | 18 | 31 | 53 | .328 | .323 |
| Cabrera,Melky | L | .253 | 99 | 25 | 3 | 0 | 1 | 6 | 4 | 10 | .282 | .313 |
| Bats Both | R | .290 | 245 | 71 | 12 | 2 | 2 | 24 | 19 | 37 | .337 | .380 |
| Cabrera,Miguel | L | .368 | 133 | 49 | 8 | 0 | 13 | 35 | 30 | 20 | .488 | .722 |
| Bats Right | R | .341 | 422 | 144 | 18 | 1 | 31 | 102 | 60 | 74 | .426 | .609 |
| Cain,Lorenzo | L | .238 | 122 | 29 | 6 | 1 | 0 | 13 | 13 | 20 | .314 | .303 |
| Bats Right | R | .256 | 277 | 71 | 15 | 2 | 4 | 33 | 20 | 70 | .308 | .368 |
| Calhoun,Kole | L | .340 | 50 | 17 | 5 | 0 | 1 | 8 | 3 | 14 | .389 | .500 |
| Bats Left | R | .262 | 145 | 38 | 2 | 2 | 7 | 24 | 18 | 27 | .333 | .448 |
| Callaspo,Alberto | L | .268 | 149 | 40 | 9 | 0 | 5 | 19 | 15 | 10 | .333 | .430 |
| Bats Both | R | .253 | 304 | 77 | 11 | 0 | 5 | 39 | 38 | 37 | .333 | .339 |
| Campana,Tony | L | .300 | 10 | 3 | 0 | 0 | 0 | 0 | 0 | 3 | .300 | .300 |
| Bats Left | R | .250 | 36 | 9 | 0 | 1 | 0 | 0 | 8 | 11 | .386 | .306 |
| Cano,Robinson | L | .291 | 234 | 68 | 12 | 0 | 7 | 37 | 22 | 43 | .356 | .432 |
| Bats Left | R | .329 | 371 | 122 | 29 | 0 | 20 | 70 | 43 | 42 | .400 | .569 |
| Carp,Mike | L | .269 | 26 | 7 | 1 | 0 | 1 | 3 | 2 | 11 | .321 | .423 |
| Bats Left | R | .300 | 190 | 57 | 17 | 2 | 8 | 40 | 20 | 56 | .367 | .537 |
| Carpenter,Matt | L | .294 | 197 | 58 | 18 | 2 | 4 | 22 | 16 | 29 | .353 | .467 |
| Bats Left | R | .329 | 429 | 141 | 37 | 5 | 7 | 56 | 56 | 69 | .410 | .487 |

# Batters vs. Left-Handed and Right-Handed Pitchers

| Batter | vs | Avg | AB | H | 2B | 3B | HR | RBI | BB | SO | OBP | Slg |
|---|---|---|---|---|---|---|---|---|---|---|---|---|
| Carroll,Jamey | L | .258 | 66 | 17 | 5 | 0 | 0 | 4 | 6 | 4 | .315 | .333 |
| Bats Right | R | .193 | 161 | 31 | 4 | 0 | 0 | 7 | 11 | 35 | .247 | .217 |
| Carter,Chris | L | .232 | 151 | 35 | 6 | 0 | 9 | 24 | 23 | 65 | .331 | .450 |
| Bats Right | R | .220 | 355 | 78 | 18 | 2 | 20 | 58 | 47 | 147 | .315 | .451 |
| Casilla,Alexi | L | .227 | 66 | 15 | 4 | 0 | 0 | 4 | 4 | 5 | .268 | .288 |
| Bats Both | R | .196 | 46 | 9 | 0 | 1 | 1 | 6 | 5 | 15 | .269 | .304 |
| Castillo,Welington | L | .247 | 89 | 22 | 5 | 0 | 2 | 8 | 9 | 20 | .337 | .371 |
| Bats Right | R | .282 | 291 | 82 | 18 | 0 | 6 | 24 | 25 | 77 | .353 | .405 |
| Castro,Jason | L | .242 | 99 | 24 | 5 | 0 | 4 | 12 | 12 | 33 | .324 | .414 |
| Bats Left | R | .286 | 336 | 96 | 30 | 1 | 14 | 44 | 38 | 97 | .358 | .506 |
| Castro,Starlin | L | .226 | 168 | 38 | 11 | 0 | 3 | 7 | 10 | 32 | .274 | .345 |
| Bats Right | R | .251 | 498 | 125 | 23 | 2 | 7 | 37 | 20 | 97 | .288 | .347 |
| Cedeno,Ronny | L | .308 | 91 | 28 | 5 | 0 | 2 | 10 | 6 | 23 | .347 | .429 |
| Bats Right | R | .208 | 173 | 36 | 3 | 3 | 1 | 11 | 8 | 50 | .255 | .277 |
| Cervelli,Francisco | L | .227 | 22 | 5 | 0 | 0 | 1 | 4 | 2 | 3 | .320 | .364 |
| Bats Right | R | .300 | 30 | 9 | 3 | 0 | 2 | 4 | 6 | 6 | .417 | .600 |
| Cespedes,Yoenis | L | .280 | 161 | 45 | 3 | 1 | 11 | 26 | 20 | 41 | .364 | .516 |
| Bats Right | R | .223 | 368 | 82 | 18 | 3 | 15 | 54 | 17 | 96 | .262 | .410 |
| Chambers,Adron | L | .000 | 5 | 0 | 0 | 0 | 0 | 0 | 0 | 3 | .000 | .000 |
| Bats Left | R | .190 | 21 | 4 | 1 | 0 | 0 | 1 | 3 | 8 | .292 | .238 |
| Chavez,Endy | L | .254 | 67 | 17 | 1 | 0 | 0 | 1 | 1 | 7 | .261 | .269 |
| Bats Left | R | .271 | 199 | 54 | 9 | 0 | 2 | 13 | 8 | 24 | .300 | .347 |
| Chavez,Eric | L | .290 | 31 | 9 | 1 | 1 | 0 | 4 | 1 | 8 | .313 | .387 |
| Bats Left | R | .279 | 197 | 55 | 13 | 1 | 9 | 40 | 18 | 37 | .335 | .492 |
| Chirinos,Robinson | L | .154 | 13 | 2 | 1 | 0 | 0 | 0 | 1 | 2 | .214 | .231 |
| Bats Right | R | .200 | 15 | 3 | 2 | 0 | 0 | 0 | 1 | 4 | .250 | .333 |
| Chisenhall,Lonnie | L | .111 | 36 | 4 | 2 | 0 | 1 | 6 | 1 | 9 | .158 | .250 |
| Bats Left | R | .241 | 253 | 61 | 15 | 0 | 10 | 30 | 15 | 47 | .286 | .419 |
| Choo,Shin-Soo | L | .215 | 181 | 39 | 7 | 1 | 0 | 8 | 24 | 44 | .347 | .265 |
| Bats Left | R | .317 | 388 | 123 | 27 | 1 | 21 | 46 | 88 | 89 | .457 | .554 |
| Ciriaco,Pedro | L | .218 | 55 | 12 | 2 | 1 | 0 | 1 | 5 | 12 | .283 | .291 |
| Bats Right | R | .229 | 70 | 16 | 2 | 1 | 2 | 7 | 4 | 11 | .276 | .371 |
| Clark,Cody | L | .100 | 20 | 2 | 0 | 0 | 0 | 0 | 1 | 5 | .143 | .100 |
| Bats Right | R | .111 | 18 | 2 | 1 | 0 | 0 | 0 | 0 | 10 | .111 | .167 |
| Coghlan,Chris | L | .333 | 27 | 9 | 2 | 1 | 0 | 1 | 1 | 8 | .379 | .481 |
| Bats Left | R | .244 | 168 | 41 | 8 | 2 | 1 | 9 | 16 | 35 | .308 | .333 |
| Colabello,Chris | L | .191 | 47 | 9 | 1 | 0 | 1 | 2 | 7 | 17 | .296 | .277 |
| Bats Right | R | .195 | 113 | 22 | 2 | 0 | 6 | 15 | 13 | 41 | .283 | .372 |
| Colvin,Tyler | L | .150 | 40 | 6 | 0 | 0 | 0 | 3 | 0 | 11 | .150 | .150 |
| Bats Left | R | .171 | 35 | 6 | 0 | 0 | 3 | 7 | 3 | 16 | .237 | .429 |
| Conger,Hank | L | .250 | 28 | 7 | 1 | 0 | 0 | 3 | 4 | 11 | .344 | .286 |
| Bats Both | R | .249 | 205 | 51 | 12 | 1 | 7 | 18 | 13 | 50 | .305 | .420 |
| Constanza,Jose | L | .000 | 8 | 0 | 0 | 0 | 0 | 0 | 0 | 1 | .000 | .000 |
| Bats Left | R | .348 | 23 | 8 | 0 | 0 | 0 | 3 | 0 | 4 | .348 | .348 |
| Corporan,Carlos | L | .265 | 83 | 22 | 5 | 0 | 1 | 9 | 1 | 34 | .299 | .361 |
| Bats Both | R | .194 | 108 | 21 | 0 | 0 | 6 | 11 | 9 | 26 | .279 | .361 |
| Cowgill,Collin | L | .245 | 98 | 24 | 4 | 2 | 2 | 10 | 5 | 26 | .282 | .388 |
| Bats Right | R | .148 | 54 | 8 | 1 | 0 | 2 | 6 | 2 | 16 | .179 | .278 |
| Cozart,Zack | L | .245 | 151 | 37 | 6 | 2 | 5 | 16 | 6 | 28 | .275 | .411 |
| Bats Right | R | .257 | 416 | 107 | 24 | 1 | 7 | 47 | 20 | 74 | .288 | .370 |
| Craig,Allen | L | .278 | 126 | 35 | 6 | 0 | 6 | 20 | 4 | 28 | .311 | .468 |
| Bats Right | R | .327 | 382 | 125 | 23 | 2 | 7 | 77 | 36 | 72 | .392 | .453 |
| Crawford,Brandon | L | .199 | 146 | 29 | 2 | 1 | 3 | 13 | 12 | 38 | .258 | .288 |
| Bats Left | R | .269 | 353 | 95 | 22 | 2 | 6 | 30 | 30 | 58 | .333 | .394 |
| Crawford,Carl | L | .206 | 107 | 22 | 2 | 2 | 1 | 6 | 7 | 18 | .261 | .290 |
| Bats Left | R | .308 | 328 | 101 | 28 | 1 | 5 | 25 | 21 | 48 | .351 | .445 |
| Crisp,Coco | L | .218 | 188 | 41 | 7 | 0 | 6 | 18 | 21 | 31 | .294 | .351 |
| Bats Both | R | .286 | 325 | 93 | 15 | 3 | 16 | 48 | 40 | 34 | .358 | .498 |
| Crowe,Trevor | L | .314 | 35 | 11 | 0 | 0 | 0 | 6 | 7 | 6 | .429 | .314 |
| Bats Both | R | .192 | 130 | 25 | 7 | 1 | 1 | 7 | 9 | 33 | .245 | .285 |
| Cruz,Luis | L | .133 | 45 | 6 | 1 | 0 | 0 | 0 | 3 | 6 | .188 | .156 |
| Bats Right | R | .148 | 128 | 19 | 2 | 0 | 1 | 11 | 3 | 27 | .191 | .188 |
| Cruz,Nelson | L | .279 | 104 | 29 | 4 | 0 | 5 | 17 | 13 | 20 | .359 | .462 |
| Bats Right | R | .262 | 309 | 81 | 14 | 0 | 22 | 59 | 22 | 89 | .316 | .521 |
| Cruz,Tony | L | .088 | 34 | 3 | 0 | 1 | 0 | 2 | 0 | 7 | .088 | .147 |
| Bats Right | R | .247 | 89 | 22 | 6 | 0 | 1 | 11 | 4 | 18 | .295 | .348 |
| Cuddyer,Michael | L | .276 | 123 | 34 | 11 | 1 | 3 | 16 | 16 | 26 | .360 | .455 |
| Bats Right | R | .350 | 366 | 128 | 20 | 2 | 17 | 68 | 30 | 74 | .399 | .555 |
| Culberson,Charlie | L | .283 | 46 | 13 | 2 | 0 | 1 | 5 | 0 | 6 | .277 | .391 |
| Bats Right | R | .302 | 53 | 16 | 3 | 0 | 1 | 7 | 4 | 17 | .351 | .415 |
| Danks,Jordan | L | .182 | 22 | 4 | 2 | 0 | 0 | 4 | 2 | 7 | .250 | .273 |
| Bats Left | R | .239 | 138 | 33 | 5 | 0 | 5 | 8 | 16 | 50 | .323 | .384 |
| d'Arnaud,Travis | L | .083 | 24 | 2 | 0 | 0 | 0 | 0 | 4 | 9 | .214 | .083 |
| Bats Right | R | .240 | 75 | 18 | 3 | 0 | 1 | 5 | 8 | 12 | .310 | .320 |
| Davidson,Matt | L | .231 | 26 | 6 | 2 | 0 | 0 | 3 | 4 | 9 | .333 | .308 |
| Bats Right | R | .240 | 50 | 12 | 4 | 0 | 3 | 9 | 6 | 15 | .333 | .500 |

| Batter | vs | Avg | AB | H | 2B | 3B | HR | RBI | BB | SO | OBP | Slg |
|---|---|---|---|---|---|---|---|---|---|---|---|---|
| Davis,Chris | L | .235 | 217 | 51 | 13 | 0 | 13 | 45 | 14 | 74 | .289 | .475 |
| Bats Left | R | .316 | 367 | 116 | 29 | 1 | 40 | 93 | 58 | 125 | .415 | .728 |
| Davis,Ike | L | .145 | 69 | 10 | 1 | 0 | 1 | 5 | 4 | 22 | .203 | .203 |
| Bats Left | R | .222 | 248 | 55 | 13 | 0 | 8 | 28 | 53 | 79 | .356 | .371 |
| Davis,Khris | L | .244 | 45 | 11 | 2 | 0 | 6 | 10 | 2 | 14 | .320 | .689 |
| Bats Right | R | .297 | 91 | 27 | 8 | 0 | 5 | 17 | 9 | 20 | .369 | .549 |
| Davis,Rajai | L | .319 | 116 | 37 | 10 | 1 | 2 | 9 | 11 | 19 | .383 | .474 |
| Bats Right | R | .228 | 215 | 49 | 6 | 1 | 4 | 15 | 10 | 48 | .273 | .321 |
| De Aza,Alejandro | L | .302 | 139 | 42 | 8 | 1 | 4 | 13 | 11 | 29 | .355 | .460 |
| Bats Left | R | .252 | 468 | 118 | 19 | 3 | 13 | 49 | 39 | 118 | .313 | .389 |
| Decker,Jaff | L | .000 | 2 | 0 | 0 | 0 | 0 | 0 | 0 | 1 | .000 | .000 |
| Bats Left | R | .167 | 24 | 4 | 0 | 0 | 1 | 2 | 3 | 3 | .250 | .292 |
| DeJesus,David | L | .161 | 56 | 9 | 2 | 0 | 1 | 4 | 2 | 14 | .217 | .250 |
| Bats Left | R | .266 | 335 | 89 | 27 | 3 | 7 | 34 | 37 | 65 | .345 | .427 |
| Den Dekker,Matt | L | .000 | 4 | 0 | 0 | 0 | 0 | 0 | 1 | 1 | .200 | .000 |
| Bats Left | R | .222 | 54 | 12 | 1 | 0 | 1 | 6 | 3 | 22 | .276 | .296 |
| Denorfia,Chris | L | .284 | 190 | 54 | 10 | 0 | 9 | 26 | 21 | 30 | .355 | .479 |
| Bats Right | R | .276 | 283 | 78 | 11 | 2 | 1 | 21 | 21 | 54 | .324 | .339 |
| DeRosa,Mark | L | .267 | 131 | 35 | 8 | 0 | 5 | 27 | 21 | 28 | .368 | .443 |
| Bats Right | R | .178 | 73 | 13 | 4 | 1 | 2 | 9 | 7 | 21 | .247 | .342 |
| Descalso,Daniel | L | .183 | 60 | 11 | 3 | 0 | 1 | 8 | 3 | 11 | .246 | .283 |
| Bats Left | R | .250 | 268 | 67 | 22 | 1 | 4 | 35 | 19 | 45 | .300 | .384 |
| Desmond,Ian | L | .281 | 135 | 38 | 9 | 0 | 4 | 16 | 10 | 36 | .329 | .437 |
| Bats Right | R | .280 | 465 | 130 | 29 | 3 | 16 | 64 | 33 | 109 | .331 | .458 |
| Dickerson,Chris | L | .143 | 7 | 1 | 0 | 0 | 0 | 0 | 0 | 4 | .143 | .143 |
| Bats Left | R | .245 | 98 | 24 | 5 | 0 | 4 | 13 | 4 | 32 | .275 | .418 |
| Dickerson,Corey | L | .194 | 36 | 7 | 1 | 0 | 1 | 2 | 4 | 10 | .275 | .306 |
| Bats Left | R | .278 | 158 | 44 | 12 | 5 | 4 | 15 | 12 | 31 | .326 | .494 |
| Dietrich,Derek | L | .259 | 54 | 14 | 1 | 0 | 4 | 7 | 1 | 16 | .286 | .500 |
| Bats Left | R | .199 | 161 | 32 | 9 | 2 | 5 | 16 | 10 | 40 | .271 | .373 |
| Dirks,Andy | L | .234 | 77 | 18 | 1 | 0 | 2 | 4 | 7 | 20 | .306 | .325 |
| Bats Left | R | .260 | 361 | 94 | 15 | 2 | 7 | 33 | 35 | 64 | .327 | .371 |
| Dobbs,Greg | L | .143 | 49 | 7 | 0 | 0 | 0 | 4 | 5 | 11 | .241 | .143 |
| Bats Left | R | .250 | 188 | 47 | 11 | 0 | 2 | 18 | 17 | 29 | .321 | .340 |
| Dominguez,Matt | L | .235 | 153 | 36 | 6 | 0 | 4 | 28 | 8 | 28 | .274 | .353 |
| Bats Right | R | .244 | 390 | 95 | 19 | 0 | 17 | 49 | 22 | 68 | .291 | .423 |
| Donaldson,Josh | L | .335 | 176 | 59 | 19 | 0 | 11 | 36 | 23 | 25 | .412 | .631 |
| Bats Right | R | .285 | 403 | 115 | 18 | 3 | 13 | 57 | 53 | 85 | .371 | .442 |
| Doumit,Ryan | L | .290 | 145 | 42 | 11 | 0 | 2 | 9 | 12 | 24 | .346 | .407 |
| Bats Both | R | .229 | 340 | 78 | 17 | 1 | 12 | 46 | 36 | 75 | .301 | .391 |
| Dozier,Brian | L | .328 | 128 | 42 | 12 | 2 | 5 | 19 | 17 | 20 | .408 | .570 |
| Bats Right | R | .219 | 430 | 94 | 21 | 2 | 13 | 47 | 34 | 100 | .282 | .367 |
| Drew,Stephen | L | .196 | 153 | 30 | 8 | 1 | 4 | 19 | 10 | 55 | .246 | .340 |
| Bats Left | R | .284 | 289 | 82 | 21 | 7 | 9 | 48 | 44 | 69 | .377 | .498 |
| Duda,Lucas | L | .183 | 93 | 17 | 2 | 0 | 3 | 11 | 16 | 37 | .309 | .301 |
| Bats Left | R | .240 | 225 | 54 | 14 | 0 | 12 | 22 | 39 | 65 | .369 | .462 |
| Duncan,Shelley | L | .080 | 25 | 2 | 0 | 0 | 0 | 0 | 6 | 8 | .258 | .080 |
| Bats Right | R | .267 | 30 | 8 | 1 | 0 | 2 | 6 | 3 | 6 | .333 | .500 |
| Dunn,Adam | L | .197 | 122 | 24 | 5 | 0 | 6 | 22 | 16 | 48 | .296 | .385 |
| Bats Left | R | .226 | 403 | 91 | 10 | 0 | 28 | 64 | 60 | 141 | .327 | .459 |
| Dyson,Jarrod | L | .204 | 49 | 10 | 2 | 0 | 0 | 3 | 5 | 10 | .286 | .245 |
| Bats Left | R | .274 | 164 | 45 | 7 | 4 | 2 | 14 | 16 | 35 | .339 | .402 |
| Eaton,Adam | L | .296 | 54 | 16 | 3 | 0 | 0 | 5 | 4 | 10 | .356 | .352 |
| Bats Left | R | .240 | 196 | 47 | 7 | 4 | 3 | 17 | 13 | 34 | .302 | .362 |
| Ellis,A.J. | L | .200 | 85 | 17 | 9 | 0 | 1 | 10 | 17 | 15 | .330 | .341 |
| Bats Right | R | .249 | 305 | 76 | 8 | 1 | 9 | 42 | 28 | 63 | .314 | .370 |
| Ellis,Mark | L | .282 | 131 | 37 | 5 | 0 | 4 | 15 | 8 | 18 | .331 | .412 |
| Bats Right | R | .265 | 302 | 80 | 8 | 2 | 2 | 33 | 18 | 56 | .319 | .325 |
| Ellsbury,Jacoby | L | .246 | 211 | 52 | 7 | 1 | 2 | 12 | 19 | 38 | .323 | .318 |
| Bats Left | R | .328 | 366 | 120 | 24 | 7 | 7 | 41 | 28 | 54 | .374 | .489 |
| Elmore,Jake | L | .286 | 49 | 14 | 0 | 0 | 1 | 1 | 5 | 3 | .352 | .347 |
| Bats Right | R | .211 | 71 | 15 | 4 | 0 | 1 | 5 | 8 | 17 | .288 | .310 |
| Encarnacion,Edwin | L | .270 | 111 | 30 | 7 | 1 | 5 | 21 | 17 | 6 | .372 | .486 |
| Bats Right | R | .272 | 419 | 114 | 22 | 0 | 31 | 83 | 65 | 56 | .370 | .547 |
| Escobar,Alcides | L | .255 | 184 | 47 | 11 | 1 | 1 | 14 | 5 | 23 | .277 | .342 |
| Bats Right | R | .225 | 423 | 95 | 9 | 3 | 3 | 38 | 14 | 61 | .251 | .281 |
| Escobar,Eduardo | L | .233 | 43 | 10 | 3 | 0 | 1 | 3 | 3 | 10 | .283 | .372 |
| Bats Both | R | .238 | 122 | 29 | 2 | 2 | 2 | 7 | 8 | 24 | .282 | .336 |
| Escobar,Yunel | L | .279 | 165 | 46 | 8 | 0 | 4 | 22 | 17 | 15 | .350 | .400 |
| Bats Right | R | .245 | 343 | 84 | 19 | 1 | 5 | 34 | 40 | 58 | .324 | .350 |
| Espinosa,Danny | L | .125 | 32 | 4 | 3 | 0 | 1 | 3 | 1 | 12 | .216 | .313 |
| Bats Both | R | .167 | 126 | 21 | 6 | 0 | 2 | 9 | 3 | 35 | .186 | .262 |
| Ethier,Andre | L | .221 | 145 | 32 | 8 | 0 | 3 | 11 | 9 | 35 | .275 | .338 |
| Bats Left | R | .294 | 337 | 99 | 25 | 2 | 9 | 41 | 52 | 60 | .394 | .460 |
| Federowicz,Tim | L | .213 | 47 | 10 | 1 | 0 | 2 | 4 | 5 | 15 | .288 | .362 |
| Bats Right | R | .239 | 113 | 27 | 7 | 0 | 2 | 12 | 5 | 41 | .269 | .354 |

# Batters vs. Left-Handed and Right-Handed Pitchers

| Batter | vs | Avg | AB | H | 2B | 3B | HR | RBI | BB | SO | OBP | Slg |
|---|---|---|---|---|---|---|---|---|---|---|---|---|
| Field,Tommy | L | .071 | 14 | 1 | 0 | 0 | 0 | 0 | 1 | 4 | .133 | .071 |
| Bats Right | R | .250 | 12 | 3 | 0 | 0 | 0 | 0 | 0 | 3 | .250 | .250 |
| Fielder,Prince | L | .292 | 233 | 68 | 12 | 0 | 9 | 47 | 22 | 45 | .360 | .459 |
| Bats Left | R | .271 | 391 | 106 | 24 | 0 | 16 | 59 | 53 | 72 | .364 | .455 |
| Flaherty,Ryan | L | .217 | 23 | 5 | 1 | 0 | 1 | 3 | 1 | 4 | .250 | .391 |
| Bats Left | R | .224 | 223 | 50 | 10 | 0 | 9 | 24 | 18 | 58 | .297 | .390 |
| Flores,Wilmer | L | .188 | 32 | 6 | 1 | 0 | 0 | 1 | 2 | 11 | .229 | .219 |
| Bats Right | R | .222 | 63 | 14 | 4 | 0 | 1 | 12 | 3 | 12 | .258 | .333 |
| Florimon,Pedro | L | .180 | 100 | 18 | 5 | 0 | 0 | 12 | 6 | 25 | .229 | .230 |
| Bats Both | R | .234 | 303 | 71 | 12 | 0 | 9 | 32 | 27 | 90 | .298 | .363 |
| Flowers,Tyler | L | .151 | 73 | 11 | 2 | 0 | 2 | 5 | 4 | 26 | .195 | .260 |
| Bats Right | R | .213 | 183 | 39 | 9 | 0 | 8 | 19 | 10 | 68 | .268 | .393 |
| Forsythe,Logan | L | .211 | 76 | 16 | 6 | 0 | 2 | 8 | 8 | 13 | .282 | .368 |
| Bats Right | R | .215 | 144 | 31 | 0 | 1 | 4 | 11 | 11 | 41 | .280 | .313 |
| Fowler,Dexter | L | .323 | 124 | 40 | 7 | 1 | 2 | 8 | 18 | 22 | .417 | .444 |
| Bats Both | R | .237 | 291 | 69 | 11 | 2 | 10 | 34 | 47 | 83 | .349 | .392 |
| Francisco,Ben | L | .088 | 34 | 3 | 0 | 0 | 1 | 1 | 5 | 8 | .225 | .176 |
| Bats Right | R | .200 | 10 | 2 | 0 | 0 | 0 | 0 | 0 | 3 | .200 | .200 |
| Francisco,Juan | L | .156 | 32 | 5 | 2 | 0 | 0 | 2 | 2 | 13 | .206 | .219 |
| Bats Left | R | .234 | 316 | 74 | 10 | 1 | 18 | 46 | 30 | 125 | .305 | .443 |
| Francoeur,Jeff | L | .223 | 94 | 21 | 5 | 0 | 0 | 3 | 5 | 22 | .263 | .277 |
| Bats Right | R | .192 | 151 | 29 | 5 | 2 | 3 | 14 | 4 | 39 | .223 | .311 |
| Frandsen,Kevin | L | .311 | 74 | 23 | 2 | 0 | 3 | 11 | 7 | 6 | .409 | .459 |
| Bats Right | R | .202 | 178 | 36 | 8 | 1 | 2 | 15 | 5 | 23 | .243 | .292 |
| Franklin,Nick | L | .210 | 119 | 25 | 6 | 1 | 1 | 11 | 15 | 36 | .296 | .303 |
| Bats Both | R | .232 | 250 | 58 | 14 | 0 | 11 | 34 | 27 | 77 | .307 | .420 |
| Frazier,Todd | L | .236 | 157 | 37 | 8 | 1 | 9 | 26 | 15 | 44 | .311 | .471 |
| Bats Right | R | .233 | 374 | 87 | 21 | 2 | 10 | 47 | 35 | 81 | .316 | .380 |
| Freeman,Freddie | L | .287 | 174 | 50 | 7 | 0 | 4 | 29 | 17 | 38 | .367 | .397 |
| Bats Left | R | .334 | 377 | 126 | 20 | 2 | 19 | 80 | 49 | 83 | .409 | .549 |
| Freese,David | L | .275 | 120 | 33 | 8 | 1 | 4 | 15 | 14 | 24 | .353 | .458 |
| Bats Right | R | .257 | 342 | 88 | 18 | 0 | 5 | 45 | 33 | 82 | .335 | .354 |
| Freiman,Nate | L | .304 | 148 | 45 | 8 | 1 | 4 | 22 | 11 | 24 | .352 | .453 |
| Bats Right | R | .167 | 42 | 7 | 0 | 0 | 0 | 2 | 3 | 7 | .239 | .167 |
| Fuentes,Reymond | L | .167 | 6 | 1 | 0 | 0 | 0 | 1 | 0 | 2 | .167 | .167 |
| Bats Left | R | .148 | 27 | 4 | 0 | 0 | 0 | 0 | 3 | 14 | .233 | .148 |
| Fuld,Sam | L | .273 | 66 | 18 | 0 | 2 | 1 | 11 | 8 | 14 | .355 | .379 |
| Bats Left | R | .155 | 110 | 17 | 0 | 1 | 1 | 6 | 9 | 14 | .217 | .200 |
| Galvis,Freddy | L | .245 | 53 | 13 | 0 | 0 | 3 | 7 | 2 | 7 | .273 | .415 |
| Bats Both | R | .230 | 152 | 35 | 5 | 4 | 3 | 12 | 11 | 38 | .287 | .375 |
| Garcia,Avisail | L | .219 | 73 | 16 | 2 | 2 | 2 | 12 | 3 | 25 | .256 | .384 |
| Bats Right | R | .310 | 171 | 53 | 5 | 1 | 5 | 19 | 6 | 34 | .331 | .439 |
| Garcia,Leury | L | .269 | 26 | 7 | 0 | 0 | 0 | 0 | 1 | 5 | .296 | .269 |
| Bats Both | R | .173 | 75 | 13 | 1 | 1 | 0 | 2 | 6 | 29 | .232 | .213 |
| Gardner,Brett | L | .247 | 178 | 44 | 12 | 7 | 2 | 19 | 18 | 55 | .317 | .427 |
| Bats Left | R | .285 | 361 | 103 | 21 | 3 | 6 | 33 | 34 | 72 | .357 | .410 |
| Gattis,Evan | L | .260 | 96 | 25 | 8 | 0 | 5 | 16 | 7 | 18 | .308 | .500 |
| Bats Right | R | .236 | 258 | 61 | 13 | 0 | 16 | 49 | 14 | 63 | .284 | .473 |
| Gennett,Scooter | L | .154 | 39 | 6 | 0 | 0 | 0 | 0 | 0 | 13 | .175 | .154 |
| Bats Left | R | .362 | 174 | 63 | 11 | 2 | 6 | 21 | 10 | 29 | .395 | .552 |
| Gentry,Craig | L | .280 | 132 | 37 | 6 | 4 | 1 | 14 | 19 | 21 | .392 | .409 |
| Bats Right | R | .281 | 114 | 32 | 6 | 0 | 1 | 8 | 10 | 25 | .349 | .360 |
| Getz,Chris | L | .264 | 53 | 14 | 2 | 0 | 0 | 2 | 3 | 8 | .304 | .302 |
| Bats Left | R | .205 | 156 | 32 | 4 | 1 | 1 | 16 | 17 | 16 | .283 | .263 |
| Giambi,Jason | L | .077 | 13 | 1 | 0 | 0 | 1 | 3 | 2 | 4 | .200 | .308 |
| Bats Left | R | .191 | 173 | 33 | 8 | 0 | 8 | 28 | 21 | 52 | .289 | .376 |
| Giavotella,Johnny | L | .176 | 17 | 3 | 1 | 0 | 0 | 0 | 2 | 2 | .263 | .235 |
| Bats Right | R | .250 | 24 | 6 | 2 | 0 | 0 | 4 | 3 | 2 | .379 | .333 |
| Gillaspie,Conor | L | .159 | 63 | 10 | 1 | 1 | 1 | 5 | 2 | 15 | .197 | .254 |
| Bats Left | R | .261 | 345 | 90 | 13 | 2 | 12 | 35 | 35 | 64 | .324 | .414 |
| Gillespie,Cole | L | .179 | 39 | 7 | 2 | 0 | 0 | 3 | 4 | 9 | .250 | .231 |
| Bats Right | R | .250 | 20 | 5 | 0 | 0 | 0 | 1 | 3 | 4 | .375 | .250 |
| Gimenez,Hector | L | .200 | 10 | 2 | 1 | 0 | 0 | 1 | 0 | 4 | .182 | .300 |
| Bats Both | R | .190 | 58 | 11 | 3 | 0 | 2 | 9 | 7 | 18 | .290 | .345 |
| Gindl,Caleb | L | .333 | 12 | 4 | 0 | 0 | 1 | 3 | 4 | 1 | .500 | .583 |
| Bats Left | R | .233 | 120 | 28 | 7 | 2 | 4 | 11 | 16 | 24 | .321 | .425 |
| Goins,Ryan | L | .233 | 43 | 10 | 1 | 0 | 1 | 3 | 1 | 11 | .250 | .326 |
| Bats Left | R | .263 | 76 | 20 | 4 | 0 | 1 | 5 | 1 | 17 | .273 | .355 |
| Goldschmidt,Paul | L | .309 | 149 | 46 | 11 | 0 | 11 | 30 | 19 | 25 | .382 | .604 |
| Bats Right | R | .300 | 453 | 136 | 25 | 3 | 25 | 95 | 80 | 120 | .406 | .534 |
| Gomes,Jonny | L | .236 | 161 | 38 | 10 | 0 | 8 | 27 | 24 | 46 | .347 | .447 |
| Bats Right | R | .258 | 151 | 39 | 7 | 0 | 5 | 25 | 19 | 43 | .341 | .404 |
| Gomes,Yan | L | .327 | 104 | 34 | 5 | 2 | 5 | 15 | 7 | 23 | .376 | .558 |
| Bats Right | R | .275 | 189 | 52 | 13 | 0 | 6 | 23 | 11 | 44 | .327 | .439 |
| Gomez,Carlos | L | .315 | 127 | 40 | 7 | 4 | 8 | 16 | 9 | 29 | .371 | .622 |
| Bats Right | R | .274 | 409 | 112 | 20 | 6 | 16 | 57 | 28 | 117 | .327 | .469 |

| Batter | vs | Avg | AB | H | 2B | 3B | HR | RBI | BB | SO | OBP | Slg |
|---|---|---|---|---|---|---|---|---|---|---|---|---|
| Gonzalez,Adrian | L | .273 | 183 | 50 | 17 | 0 | 4 | 39 | 12 | 36 | .315 | .432 |
| Bats Left | R | .303 | 400 | 121 | 15 | 0 | 18 | 61 | 35 | 62 | .354 | .475 |
| Gonzalez,Alberto | L | .167 | 18 | 3 | 1 | 0 | 0 | 0 | 1 | 5 | .211 | .222 |
| Bats Right | R | .205 | 39 | 8 | 1 | 0 | 1 | 6 | 1 | 7 | .220 | .308 |
| Gonzalez,Alex | L | .135 | 37 | 5 | 0 | 0 | 0 | 1 | 0 | 16 | .132 | .135 |
| Bats Right | R | .197 | 76 | 15 | 3 | 0 | 1 | 7 | 3 | 10 | .238 | .276 |
| Gonzalez,Carlos | L | .310 | 142 | 44 | 8 | 0 | 8 | 21 | 8 | 43 | .340 | .535 |
| Bats Left | R | .297 | 249 | 74 | 15 | 6 | 18 | 49 | 33 | 75 | .382 | .622 |
| Gonzalez,Marwin | L | .229 | 35 | 8 | 2 | 0 | 0 | 2 | 3 | 7 | .289 | .286 |
| Bats Both | R | .219 | 169 | 37 | 6 | 0 | 4 | 12 | 6 | 30 | .244 | .325 |
| Gordon,Alex | L | .307 | 215 | 66 | 12 | 4 | 8 | 33 | 15 | 48 | .366 | .512 |
| Bats Left | R | .244 | 418 | 102 | 15 | 2 | 12 | 48 | 37 | 93 | .307 | .376 |
| Gordon,Dee | L | .273 | 22 | 6 | 0 | 0 | 0 | 2 | 1 | 6 | .304 | .273 |
| Bats Left | R | .222 | 72 | 16 | 1 | 1 | 1 | 4 | 9 | 15 | .317 | .306 |
| Gose,Anthony | L | .179 | 39 | 7 | 1 | 0 | 0 | 0 | 2 | 14 | .220 | .205 |
| Bats Left | R | .287 | 108 | 31 | 5 | 5 | 2 | 12 | 3 | 23 | .306 | .481 |
| Gosewisch,Tuffy | L | .263 | 19 | 5 | 1 | 0 | 0 | 1 | 0 | 1 | .263 | .316 |
| Bats Right | R | .115 | 26 | 3 | 1 | 0 | 0 | 2 | 0 | 7 | .111 | .154 |
| Grandal,Yasmani | L | .233 | 43 | 10 | 5 | 0 | 1 | 5 | 7 | 10 | .333 | .419 |
| Bats Both | R | .200 | 45 | 9 | 3 | 0 | 0 | 4 | 11 | 8 | .368 | .267 |
| Granderson,Curtis | L | .242 | 62 | 15 | 4 | 1 | 2 | 4 | 10 | 25 | .356 | .435 |
| Bats Left | R | .224 | 152 | 34 | 9 | 1 | 5 | 11 | 17 | 44 | .300 | .395 |
| Green,Grant | L | .106 | 47 | 5 | 2 | 0 | 0 | 11 | 5 | 15 | .185 | .149 |
| Bats Right | R | .323 | 93 | 30 | 6 | 1 | 1 | 6 | 5 | 29 | .364 | .441 |
| Green,Nick | L | .000 | 17 | 0 | 0 | 0 | 0 | 0 | 1 | 10 | .150 | .000 |
| Bats Right | R | .342 | 38 | 13 | 2 | 0 | 1 | 6 | 2 | 4 | .372 | .474 |
| Greene,Tyler | L | .200 | 25 | 5 | 1 | 0 | 0 | 0 | 1 | 8 | .231 | .240 |
| Bats Right | R | .241 | 29 | 7 | 1 | 1 | 1 | 3 | 2 | 11 | .290 | .448 |
| Gregorius,Didi | L | .200 | 110 | 22 | 5 | 0 | 0 | 3 | 7 | 30 | .267 | .245 |
| Bats Left | R | .275 | 247 | 68 | 11 | 3 | 7 | 25 | 30 | 35 | .359 | .429 |
| Grossman,Robbie | L | .329 | 73 | 24 | 5 | 0 | 1 | 3 | 1 | 9 | .347 | .438 |
| Bats Both | R | .245 | 184 | 45 | 9 | 0 | 3 | 18 | 22 | 61 | .327 | .342 |
| Gutierrez,Franklin | L | .218 | 55 | 12 | 2 | 0 | 3 | 7 | 2 | 15 | .246 | .418 |
| Bats Right | R | .267 | 90 | 24 | 5 | 0 | 7 | 17 | 3 | 28 | .290 | .556 |
| Guzman,Jesus | L | .245 | 139 | 34 | 7 | 0 | 4 | 16 | 13 | 32 | .309 | .381 |
| Bats Right | R | .208 | 149 | 31 | 10 | 0 | 5 | 19 | 14 | 47 | .285 | .376 |
| Gyorko,Jedd | L | .264 | 129 | 34 | 9 | 0 | 8 | 15 | 9 | 40 | .309 | .519 |
| Bats Right | R | .244 | 357 | 87 | 17 | 0 | 15 | 48 | 24 | 83 | .298 | .417 |
| Hafner,Travis | L | .173 | 52 | 9 | 1 | 1 | 2 | 11 | 8 | 15 | .317 | .346 |
| Bats Left | R | .210 | 210 | 44 | 7 | 0 | 10 | 26 | 24 | 64 | .297 | .386 |
| Hairston,Jerry | L | .179 | 78 | 14 | 1 | 0 | 0 | 5 | 8 | 7 | .253 | .192 |
| Bats Right | R | .230 | 126 | 29 | 6 | 0 | 2 | 17 | 6 | 15 | .272 | .325 |
| Hairston,Scott | L | .214 | 126 | 27 | 4 | 0 | 10 | 25 | 7 | 31 | .259 | .484 |
| Bats Right | R | .097 | 31 | 3 | 1 | 0 | 0 | 1 | 2 | 13 | .147 | .129 |
| Halton,Sean | L | .212 | 33 | 7 | 1 | 0 | 2 | 7 | 2 | 11 | .250 | .424 |
| Bats Right | R | .250 | 68 | 17 | 3 | 0 | 2 | 10 | 3 | 20 | .311 | .382 |
| Hamilton,Josh | L | .201 | 179 | 36 | 7 | 2 | 6 | 25 | 8 | 60 | .233 | .363 |
| Bats Left | R | .272 | 397 | 108 | 25 | 3 | 15 | 54 | 39 | 98 | .339 | .463 |
| Hanigan,Ryan | L | .222 | 54 | 12 | 4 | 0 | 0 | 4 | 6 | 5 | .311 | .296 |
| Bats Right | R | .190 | 168 | 32 | 4 | 0 | 2 | 17 | 23 | 22 | .305 | .250 |
| Hannahan,Jack | L | .111 | 9 | 1 | 0 | 1 | 0 | 1 | 1 | 6 | .273 | .333 |
| Bats Left | R | .223 | 130 | 29 | 5 | 0 | 1 | 13 | 18 | 32 | .320 | .285 |
| Hardy,J.J. | L | .264 | 178 | 47 | 14 | 0 | 8 | 28 | 11 | 20 | .305 | .478 |
| Bats Right | R | .262 | 423 | 111 | 13 | 0 | 17 | 48 | 27 | 53 | .306 | .414 |
| Harper,Bryce | L | .214 | 131 | 28 | 8 | 0 | 2 | 16 | 21 | 35 | .327 | .321 |
| Bats Left | R | .300 | 293 | 88 | 16 | 3 | 18 | 42 | 40 | 59 | .388 | .560 |
| Harris,Brendan | L | .028 | 36 | 1 | 1 | 0 | 0 | 0 | 4 | 11 | .125 | .056 |
| Bats Right | R | .296 | 71 | 21 | 3 | 0 | 4 | 9 | 2 | 18 | .320 | .507 |
| Harrison,Josh | L | .350 | 40 | 14 | 0 | 2 | 2 | 10 | 1 | 4 | .381 | .600 |
| Bats Right | R | .167 | 48 | 8 | 1 | 0 | 1 | 4 | 1 | 6 | .216 | .250 |
| Hawpe,Brad | L | .333 | 3 | 1 | 0 | 0 | 0 | 0 | 0 | 1 | .333 | .333 |
| Bats Left | R | .167 | 24 | 4 | 0 | 0 | 0 | 2 | 5 | 13 | .310 | .167 |
| Headley,Chase | L | .248 | 149 | 37 | 9 | 2 | 5 | 16 | 15 | 33 | .327 | .436 |
| Bats Both | R | .251 | 371 | 93 | 26 | 0 | 8 | 34 | 52 | 109 | .354 | .385 |
| Hechavarria,Adeiny | L | .234 | 145 | 34 | 3 | 2 | 0 | 10 | 15 | 32 | .306 | .283 |
| Bats Right | R | .224 | 398 | 89 | 11 | 6 | 3 | 32 | 15 | 64 | .251 | .304 |
| Heisey,Chris | L | .259 | 85 | 22 | 9 | 1 | 3 | 11 | 7 | 14 | .316 | .494 |
| Bats Right | R | .223 | 139 | 31 | 2 | 0 | 6 | 12 | 2 | 37 | .255 | .367 |
| Helton,Todd | L | .299 | 77 | 23 | 3 | 0 | 1 | 9 | 9 | 24 | .372 | .377 |
| Bats Left | R | .238 | 320 | 76 | 19 | 1 | 14 | 52 | 31 | 63 | .301 | .434 |
| Hernandez,Cesar | L | .262 | 42 | 11 | 1 | 0 | 0 | 0 | 1 | 10 | .295 | .286 |
| Bats Both | R | .304 | 79 | 24 | 4 | 0 | 0 | 10 | 8 | 16 | .368 | .354 |
| Hernandez,Ramon | L | .231 | 13 | 3 | 1 | 0 | 1 | 3 | 1 | 1 | .267 | .538 |
| Bats Right | R | .200 | 35 | 7 | 1 | 0 | 2 | 3 | 5 | 6 | .300 | .400 |
| Herrera,Jonathan | L | .220 | 50 | 11 | 1 | 0 | 1 | 2 | 3 | 9 | .264 | .300 |
| Bats Both | R | .317 | 145 | 46 | 6 | 2 | 0 | 14 | 11 | 15 | .361 | .386 |

# Batters vs. Left-Handed and Right-Handed Pitchers

| Batter | vs | Avg | AB | H | 2B | 3B | HR | RBI | BB | SO | OBP | Slg |
|---|---|---|---|---|---|---|---|---|---|---|---|---|
| Herrmann,Chris | L | .172 | 29 | 5 | 2 | 0 | 1 | 3 | 1 | 6 | .200 | .345 |
| Bats Left | R | .211 | 128 | 27 | 5 | 0 | 3 | 15 | 17 | 43 | .303 | .320 |
| Heyward,Jason | L | .264 | 110 | 29 | 10 | 1 | 3 | 11 | 10 | 24 | .347 | .455 |
| Bats Left | R | .250 | 272 | 68 | 12 | 0 | 11 | 27 | 38 | 49 | .350 | .415 |
| Hicks,Aaron | L | .203 | 59 | 12 | 2 | 0 | 4 | 11 | 6 | 18 | .273 | .441 |
| Bats Both | R | .189 | 222 | 42 | 9 | 3 | 4 | 16 | 18 | 66 | .255 | .311 |
| Hill,Aaron | L | .321 | 78 | 25 | 11 | 0 | 2 | 12 | 7 | 11 | .372 | .538 |
| Bats Right | R | .281 | 249 | 70 | 10 | 1 | 9 | 29 | 22 | 37 | .351 | .438 |
| Hill,Koyie | L | .350 | 20 | 7 | 1 | 0 | 0 | 0 | 1 | 1 | .381 | .400 |
| Bats Both | R | .053 | 38 | 2 | 1 | 0 | 0 | 0 | 1 | 17 | .077 | .079 |
| Hinske,Eric | L | .250 | 8 | 2 | 2 | 0 | 0 | 1 | 0 | 3 | .250 | .500 |
| Bats Left | R | .159 | 44 | 7 | 1 | 0 | 1 | 5 | 6 | 14 | .260 | .250 |
| Hoes,L.J. | L | .259 | 58 | 15 | 3 | 0 | 1 | 5 | 4 | 18 | .306 | .362 |
| Bats Right | R | .295 | 112 | 33 | 4 | 2 | 0 | 5 | 8 | 17 | .344 | .366 |
| Holaday,Bryan | L | .308 | 13 | 4 | 0 | 0 | 1 | 2 | 1 | 1 | .400 | .538 |
| Bats Right | R | .286 | 14 | 4 | 1 | 0 | 0 | 0 | 1 | 2 | .333 | .357 |
| Holliday,Matt | L | .298 | 121 | 36 | 9 | 0 | 1 | 13 | 20 | 26 | .403 | .397 |
| Bats Right | R | .301 | 399 | 120 | 22 | 1 | 21 | 81 | 49 | 60 | .384 | .519 |
| Holt,Brock | L | .111 | 9 | 1 | 0 | 0 | 0 | 1 | 2 | 0 | .273 | .111 |
| Bats Left | R | .220 | 50 | 11 | 2 | 0 | 0 | 10 | 5 | 4 | .276 | .260 |
| Hosmer,Eric | L | .323 | 217 | 70 | 11 | 0 | 5 | 30 | 11 | 37 | .355 | .442 |
| Bats Left | R | .291 | 406 | 118 | 23 | 3 | 12 | 49 | 40 | 63 | .353 | .451 |
| Howard,Ryan | L | .173 | 81 | 14 | 3 | 0 | 3 | 11 | 3 | 39 | .218 | .321 |
| Bats Left | R | .302 | 205 | 62 | 17 | 2 | 8 | 32 | 20 | 56 | .357 | .522 |
| Hundley,Nick | L | .183 | 93 | 17 | 3 | 0 | 2 | 5 | 12 | 28 | .274 | .280 |
| Bats Right | R | .250 | 280 | 70 | 16 | 0 | 11 | 39 | 14 | 70 | .296 | .425 |
| Hunter,Torii | L | .300 | 170 | 51 | 7 | 1 | 7 | 18 | 15 | 24 | .353 | .476 |
| Bats Right | R | .305 | 436 | 133 | 30 | 4 | 10 | 66 | 11 | 89 | .327 | .461 |
| Iannetta,Chris | L | .266 | 128 | 34 | 9 | 0 | 5 | 19 | 26 | 35 | .382 | .453 |
| Bats Right | R | .198 | 197 | 39 | 6 | 0 | 6 | 20 | 42 | 65 | .343 | .320 |
| Ibanez,Raul | L | .244 | 127 | 31 | 5 | 1 | 8 | 18 | 13 | 43 | .314 | .488 |
| Bats Left | R | .242 | 327 | 79 | 15 | 1 | 21 | 47 | 29 | 85 | .303 | .486 |
| Iglesias,Jose | L | .294 | 126 | 37 | 7 | 2 | 2 | 8 | 8 | 29 | .341 | .429 |
| Bats Right | R | .308 | 224 | 69 | 9 | 0 | 1 | 21 | 7 | 31 | .354 | .362 |
| Infante,Omar | L | .301 | 146 | 44 | 9 | 1 | 6 | 20 | 7 | 13 | .331 | .500 |
| Bats Right | R | .326 | 307 | 100 | 15 | 2 | 4 | 31 | 13 | 31 | .351 | .427 |
| Inge,Brandon | L | .171 | 35 | 6 | 1 | 0 | 1 | 6 | 0 | 12 | .171 | .286 |
| Bats Right | R | .186 | 70 | 13 | 2 | 0 | 0 | 1 | 2 | 20 | .219 | .214 |
| Izturis,Cesar | L | .257 | 35 | 9 | 3 | 0 | 0 | 3 | 1 | 5 | .278 | .343 |
| Bats Both | R | .191 | 94 | 18 | 5 | 0 | 0 | 8 | 8 | 8 | .252 | .245 |
| Izturis,Maicer | L | .259 | 116 | 30 | 4 | 0 | 1 | 9 | 5 | 8 | .287 | .319 |
| Bats Both | R | .225 | 249 | 56 | 8 | 0 | 4 | 23 | 22 | 30 | .288 | .305 |
| Jackson,Austin | L | .213 | 160 | 34 | 10 | 1 | 4 | 10 | 22 | 37 | .319 | .363 |
| Bats Right | R | .296 | 392 | 116 | 20 | 6 | 8 | 39 | 30 | 92 | .345 | .439 |
| Janish,Paul | L | .000 | 10 | 0 | 0 | 0 | 0 | 1 | 2 | 3 | .154 | .000 |
| Bats Right | R | .226 | 31 | 7 | 2 | 0 | 0 | 1 | 1 | 8 | .250 | .290 |
| Jaso,John | L | .192 | 26 | 5 | 0 | 0 | 0 | 1 | 1 | 9 | .250 | .192 |
| Bats Left | R | .282 | 181 | 51 | 12 | 0 | 3 | 20 | 37 | 36 | .405 | .398 |
| Jay,Jon | L | .220 | 118 | 26 | 5 | 0 | 2 | 14 | 13 | 26 | .306 | .314 |
| Bats Left | R | .291 | 430 | 125 | 22 | 2 | 5 | 53 | 39 | 77 | .363 | .386 |
| Jennings,Desmond | L | .299 | 167 | 50 | 11 | 3 | 4 | 17 | 22 | 34 | .384 | .473 |
| Bats Right | R | .231 | 360 | 83 | 20 | 3 | 10 | 37 | 42 | 81 | .311 | .386 |
| Jeter,Derek | L | .350 | 20 | 7 | 0 | 0 | 1 | 5 | 3 | 3 | .440 | .500 |
| Bats Right | R | .116 | 43 | 5 | 1 | 0 | 0 | 2 | 5 | 7 | .208 | .140 |
| Jimenez,Luis | L | .241 | 29 | 7 | 2 | 0 | 0 | 0 | 0 | 8 | .267 | .310 |
| Bats Right | R | .267 | 75 | 20 | 4 | 0 | 0 | 5 | 2 | 20 | .300 | .320 |
| Johnson,Chris | L | .383 | 133 | 51 | 7 | 0 | 4 | 24 | 8 | 30 | .413 | .526 |
| Bats Right | R | .299 | 381 | 114 | 27 | 0 | 8 | 44 | 21 | 86 | .339 | .433 |
| Johnson,Elliot | L | .224 | 58 | 13 | 0 | 2 | 0 | 5 | 5 | 15 | .286 | .293 |
| Bats Both | R | .204 | 196 | 40 | 7 | 1 | 2 | 14 | 11 | 52 | .245 | .281 |
| Johnson,Kelly | L | .291 | 86 | 25 | 3 | 1 | 0 | 8 | 5 | 17 | .337 | .349 |
| Bats Left | R | .218 | 280 | 61 | 9 | 1 | 16 | 44 | 30 | 82 | .295 | .429 |
| Johnson,Reed | L | .291 | 55 | 16 | 3 | 0 | 0 | 3 | 3 | 15 | .328 | .345 |
| Bats Right | R | .206 | 68 | 14 | 4 | 1 | 1 | 8 | 3 | 17 | .299 | .338 |
| Johnson,Rob | L | .000 | 9 | 0 | 0 | 0 | 0 | 0 | 2 | 1 | .182 | .000 |
| Bats Right | R | .231 | 26 | 6 | 1 | 1 | 0 | 2 | 1 | 5 | .259 | .346 |
| Jones,Adam | L | .251 | 199 | 50 | 12 | 0 | 7 | 23 | 17 | 46 | .315 | .417 |
| Bats Right | R | .300 | 454 | 136 | 23 | 1 | 26 | 85 | 8 | 90 | .319 | .526 |
| Jones,Garrett | L | .095 | 21 | 2 | 1 | 0 | 0 | 1 | 1 | 12 | .174 | .143 |
| Bats Left | R | .241 | 382 | 92 | 25 | 2 | 15 | 50 | 30 | 89 | .295 | .435 |
| Joyce,Matt | L | .164 | 55 | 9 | 2 | 0 | 2 | 7 | 2 | 13 | .190 | .309 |
| Bats Left | R | .246 | 358 | 88 | 20 | 0 | 16 | 40 | 57 | 74 | .348 | .436 |
| Kawasaki,Munenori | L | .152 | 46 | 7 | 1 | 0 | 0 | 4 | 6 | 10 | .264 | .174 |
| Bats Left | R | .247 | 194 | 48 | 5 | 5 | 1 | 20 | 26 | 31 | .341 | .340 |
| Kearns,Austin | L | .200 | 15 | 3 | 0 | 0 | 0 | 0 | 2 | 4 | .294 | .200 |
| Bats Right | R | .167 | 12 | 2 | 0 | 0 | 0 | 0 | 2 | 4 | .286 | .167 |

| Batter | vs | Avg | AB | H | 2B | 3B | HR | RBI | BB | SO | OBP | Slg |
|---|---|---|---|---|---|---|---|---|---|---|---|---|
| Kelly,Don | L | .229 | 48 | 11 | 2 | 0 | 0 | 5 | 6 | 12 | .304 | .271 |
| Bats Left | R | .220 | 168 | 37 | 4 | 1 | 6 | 18 | 21 | 16 | .311 | .363 |
| Kemp,Matt | L | .320 | 75 | 24 | 9 | 0 | 1 | 8 | 7 | 19 | .373 | .480 |
| Bats Right | R | .250 | 188 | 47 | 6 | 0 | 5 | 25 | 15 | 57 | .309 | .362 |
| Kendrick,Howie | L | .295 | 122 | 36 | 9 | 1 | 5 | 17 | 11 | 24 | .353 | .508 |
| Bats Right | R | .298 | 356 | 106 | 12 | 3 | 8 | 37 | 12 | 65 | .329 | .416 |
| Keppinger,Jeff | L | .214 | 103 | 22 | 5 | 0 | 2 | 9 | 8 | 5 | .265 | .320 |
| Bats Right | R | .266 | 320 | 85 | 8 | 1 | 2 | 31 | 12 | 36 | .290 | .316 |
| Kieschnick,Roger | L | .083 | 12 | 1 | 0 | 0 | 0 | 0 | 2 | 3 | .214 | .083 |
| Bats Left | R | .222 | 72 | 16 | 0 | 1 | 0 | 5 | 9 | 26 | .309 | .250 |
| Kinsler,Ian | L | .306 | 157 | 48 | 13 | 1 | 2 | 20 | 17 | 15 | .375 | .439 |
| Bats Right | R | .265 | 388 | 103 | 18 | 1 | 11 | 52 | 34 | 44 | .331 | .402 |
| Kipnis,Jason | L | .308 | 198 | 61 | 18 | 2 | 4 | 33 | 17 | 49 | .370 | .480 |
| Bats Left | R | .270 | 366 | 99 | 18 | 2 | 13 | 51 | 59 | 94 | .364 | .437 |
| Kobernus,Jeff | L | .208 | 24 | 5 | 0 | 0 | 1 | 1 | 4 | 4 | .345 | .333 |
| Bats Right | R | .000 | 6 | 0 | 0 | 0 | 0 | 0 | 1 | 2 | .143 | .000 |
| Konerko,Paul | L | .313 | 99 | 31 | 6 | 0 | 5 | 16 | 14 | 11 | .398 | .525 |
| Bats Right | R | .226 | 368 | 83 | 10 | 0 | 7 | 38 | 31 | 63 | .290 | .310 |
| Kotchman,Casey | L | .000 | 5 | 0 | 0 | 0 | 0 | 0 | 0 | 1 | .000 | .000 |
| Bats Left | R | .000 | 15 | 0 | 0 | 0 | 0 | 1 | 1 | 0 | .063 | .000 |
| Kotsay,Mark | L | .118 | 17 | 2 | 0 | 0 | 0 | 2 | 1 | 4 | .167 | .118 |
| Bats Left | R | .203 | 138 | 28 | 2 | 0 | 1 | 10 | 12 | 21 | .263 | .239 |
| Kottaras,George | L | .143 | 14 | 2 | 1 | 0 | 0 | 3 | 4 | 7 | .400 | .214 |
| Bats Left | R | .186 | 86 | 16 | 3 | 0 | 5 | 9 | 20 | 35 | .340 | .395 |
| Kozma,Pete | L | .184 | 125 | 23 | 9 | 0 | 0 | 8 | 17 | 30 | .280 | .256 |
| Bats Right | R | .232 | 285 | 66 | 11 | 0 | 1 | 27 | 17 | 61 | .273 | .281 |
| Kratz,Erik | L | .079 | 38 | 3 | 1 | 0 | 1 | 1 | 7 | 11 | .222 | .184 |
| Bats Right | R | .245 | 159 | 39 | 6 | 0 | 8 | 25 | 11 | 34 | .295 | .434 |
| Krauss,Marc | L | .133 | 15 | 2 | 1 | 0 | 0 | 0 | 0 | 7 | .133 | .200 |
| Bats Left | R | .218 | 119 | 26 | 8 | 0 | 4 | 13 | 10 | 38 | .282 | .387 |
| Kubel,Jason | L | .162 | 37 | 6 | 1 | 0 | 0 | 6 | 3 | 16 | .225 | .189 |
| Bats Left | R | .225 | 222 | 50 | 8 | 1 | 5 | 26 | 26 | 76 | .304 | .338 |
| Lagares,Juan | L | .241 | 137 | 33 | 10 | 0 | 3 | 11 | 7 | 33 | .278 | .380 |
| Bats Right | R | .243 | 255 | 62 | 11 | 5 | 1 | 23 | 13 | 63 | .283 | .337 |
| Laird,Brandon | L | .184 | 38 | 7 | 3 | 0 | 2 | 5 | 3 | 13 | .262 | .421 |
| Bats Right | R | .152 | 33 | 5 | 0 | 0 | 3 | 6 | 0 | 13 | .176 | .424 |
| Laird,Gerald | L | .244 | 45 | 11 | 4 | 0 | 0 | 3 | 5 | 9 | .333 | .333 |
| Bats Right | R | .303 | 76 | 23 | 4 | 0 | 1 | 10 | 9 | 14 | .386 | .395 |
| Lake,Junior | L | .377 | 61 | 23 | 4 | 0 | 2 | 4 | 3 | 12 | .415 | .541 |
| Bats Right | R | .251 | 175 | 44 | 12 | 0 | 4 | 12 | 10 | 56 | .303 | .389 |
| Lalli,Blake | L | .000 | 3 | 0 | 0 | 0 | 0 | 0 | 0 | 2 | .000 | .000 |
| Bats Left | R | .143 | 21 | 3 | 0 | 0 | 0 | 2 | 0 | 5 | .143 | .143 |
| Lambo,Andrew | L | 1.000 | 1 | 1 | 0 | 0 | 0 | 0 | 0 | 0 | 1.000 | 1.000 |
| Bats Left | R | .207 | 29 | 6 | 2 | 0 | 1 | 2 | 3 | 11 | .281 | .379 |
| LaRoche,Adam | L | .198 | 131 | 26 | 6 | 0 | 3 | 12 | 9 | 38 | .254 | .313 |
| Bats Left | R | .250 | 380 | 95 | 13 | 3 | 17 | 50 | 63 | 93 | .357 | .434 |
| Lavarnway,Ryan | L | .267 | 30 | 8 | 5 | 0 | 0 | 2 | 0 | 3 | .290 | .433 |
| Bats Right | R | .319 | 47 | 15 | 2 | 0 | 1 | 12 | 2 | 14 | .353 | .426 |
| Lawrie,Brett | L | .219 | 96 | 21 | 3 | 0 | 3 | 10 | 6 | 17 | .269 | .344 |
| Bats Right | R | .266 | 305 | 81 | 15 | 3 | 8 | 36 | 24 | 51 | .329 | .413 |
| LeMahieu,DJ | L | .276 | 123 | 34 | 5 | 1 | 0 | 4 | 8 | 22 | .318 | .333 |
| Bats Right | R | .281 | 281 | 79 | 16 | 2 | 2 | 24 | 11 | 45 | .308 | .374 |
| Lillibridge,Brent | L | .091 | 22 | 2 | 1 | 0 | 0 | 1 | 0 | 6 | .091 | .136 |
| Bats Right | R | .135 | 37 | 5 | 0 | 0 | 0 | 4 | 1 | 11 | .158 | .135 |
| Lind,Adam | L | .208 | 96 | 20 | 3 | 0 | 3 | 8 | 4 | 31 | .240 | .333 |
| Bats Left | R | .309 | 369 | 114 | 23 | 1 | 20 | 59 | 47 | 72 | .385 | .539 |
| Lobaton,Jose | L | .242 | 95 | 23 | 4 | 2 | 1 | 12 | 8 | 21 | .295 | .358 |
| Bats Both | R | .253 | 182 | 46 | 11 | 0 | 6 | 20 | 22 | 44 | .333 | .412 |
| Lombardozzi,Steve | L | .273 | 77 | 21 | 5 | 0 | 1 | 8 | 1 | 7 | .282 | .377 |
| Bats Both | R | .254 | 213 | 54 | 10 | 1 | 1 | 14 | 7 | 27 | .277 | .324 |
| Loney,James | L | .299 | 154 | 46 | 5 | 0 | 3 | 21 | 10 | 29 | .339 | .390 |
| Bats Left | R | .299 | 395 | 118 | 28 | 0 | 10 | 54 | 34 | 48 | .352 | .446 |
| Longoria,Evan | L | .301 | 173 | 52 | 16 | 0 | 10 | 31 | 25 | 45 | .383 | .566 |
| Bats Right | R | .256 | 441 | 113 | 23 | 3 | 22 | 57 | 45 | 117 | .327 | .472 |
| Lough,David | L | .292 | 65 | 19 | 3 | 0 | 2 | 8 | 2 | 15 | .314 | .431 |
| Bats Left | R | .284 | 250 | 71 | 14 | 4 | 3 | 25 | 8 | 37 | .310 | .408 |
| Lowrie,Jed | L | .305 | 210 | 64 | 18 | 1 | 1 | 20 | 17 | 27 | .358 | .414 |
| Bats Both | R | .282 | 393 | 111 | 27 | 1 | 14 | 55 | 33 | 64 | .337 | .463 |
| Lucas,Ed | L | .330 | 106 | 35 | 10 | 0 | 3 | 9 | 8 | 15 | .374 | .509 |
| Bats Right | R | .224 | 245 | 55 | 4 | 1 | 1 | 19 | 18 | 63 | .283 | .261 |
| Lucroy,Jonathan | L | .312 | 125 | 39 | 6 | 1 | 5 | 20 | 10 | 14 | .363 | .496 |
| Bats Right | R | .270 | 396 | 107 | 19 | 5 | 13 | 62 | 36 | 55 | .333 | .442 |
| Ludwick,Ryan | L | .269 | 26 | 7 | 2 | 0 | 1 | 2 | 2 | 4 | .321 | .462 |
| Bats Right | R | .233 | 103 | 24 | 3 | 0 | 1 | 10 | 8 | 25 | .286 | .291 |
| Lutz,Donald | L | .267 | 15 | 4 | 0 | 0 | 0 | 2 | 0 | 3 | .267 | .267 |
| Bats Left | R | .233 | 43 | 10 | 1 | 0 | 1 | 6 | 1 | 11 | .250 | .326 |

# Batters vs. Left-Handed and Right-Handed Pitchers

| Batter | vs | Avg | AB | H | 2B | 3B | HR | RBI | BB | SO | OBP | Slg |
|---|---|---|---|---|---|---|---|---|---|---|---|---|
| Lutz,Zach | L | .429 | 7 | 3 | 1 | 0 | 0 | 1 | 4 | 1 | .636 | .571 |
| Bats Right | R | .231 | 13 | 3 | 1 | 0 | 0 | 1 | 2 | 5 | .333 | .308 |
| Machado,Manny | L | .292 | 212 | 62 | 18 | 2 | 3 | 21 | 8 | 26 | .323 | .439 |
| Bats Right | R | .279 | 455 | 127 | 33 | 1 | 11 | 50 | 21 | 87 | .310 | .429 |
| Mahoney,Joe | L | .000 | 4 | 0 | 0 | 0 | 0 | 0 | 0 | 0 | .000 | .000 |
| Bats Left | R | .320 | 25 | 8 | 1 | 0 | 1 | 4 | 0 | 4 | .320 | .480 |
| Maldonado,Martin | L | .159 | 44 | 7 | 2 | 1 | 0 | 5 | 2 | 20 | .196 | .250 |
| Bats Right | R | .173 | 139 | 24 | 5 | 0 | 4 | 17 | 11 | 33 | .248 | .295 |
| Marisnick,Jake | L | .188 | 32 | 6 | 1 | 0 | 0 | 1 | 1 | 10 | .212 | .219 |
| Bats Right | R | .182 | 77 | 14 | 1 | 1 | 1 | 4 | 5 | 17 | .238 | .260 |
| Markakis,Nick | L | .274 | 230 | 63 | 9 | 0 | 1 | 21 | 17 | 36 | .325 | .326 |
| Bats Left | R | .270 | 404 | 109 | 15 | 0 | 9 | 38 | 38 | 40 | .330 | .374 |
| Marte,Alfredo | L | .172 | 29 | 5 | 3 | 0 | 0 | 1 | 3 | 8 | .273 | .276 |
| Bats Right | R | .214 | 14 | 3 | 0 | 0 | 0 | 3 | 1 | 4 | .267 | .214 |
| Marte,Starling | L | .402 | 92 | 37 | 4 | 2 | 3 | 6 | 7 | 24 | .466 | .587 |
| Bats Right | R | .254 | 418 | 106 | 22 | 8 | 9 | 29 | 18 | 114 | .315 | .409 |
| Martin,Leonys | L | .226 | 133 | 30 | 6 | 0 | 1 | 13 | 6 | 31 | .280 | .293 |
| Bats Left | R | .275 | 324 | 89 | 15 | 6 | 7 | 36 | 22 | 73 | .326 | .423 |
| Martin,Russell | L | .194 | 93 | 18 | 4 | 0 | 2 | 11 | 15 | 22 | .309 | .301 |
| Bats Right | R | .235 | 345 | 81 | 17 | 0 | 13 | 44 | 43 | 86 | .332 | .397 |
| Martinez,Fernando | L | .000 | 3 | 0 | 0 | 0 | 0 | 0 | 0 | 1 | .000 | .000 |
| Bats Left | R | .200 | 30 | 6 | 0 | 0 | 1 | 3 | 1 | 11 | .250 | .300 |
| Martinez,J.D. | L | .229 | 96 | 22 | 6 | 0 | 2 | 9 | 5 | 31 | .267 | .354 |
| Bats Right | R | .260 | 200 | 52 | 11 | 0 | 5 | 27 | 5 | 51 | .274 | .390 |
| Martinez,Michael | L | .167 | 6 | 1 | 0 | 0 | 0 | 1 | 0 | 1 | .167 | .167 |
| Bats Both | R | .176 | 34 | 6 | 0 | 0 | 0 | 2 | 0 | 11 | .176 | .176 |
| Martinez,Victor | L | .279 | 226 | 63 | 15 | 0 | 5 | 27 | 16 | 27 | .324 | .412 |
| Bats Both | R | .314 | 379 | 119 | 21 | 0 | 9 | 56 | 38 | 35 | .373 | .441 |
| Mastroianni,Darin | L | .227 | 22 | 5 | 1 | 0 | 0 | 3 | 0 | 12 | .227 | .273 |
| Bats Right | R | .163 | 43 | 7 | 1 | 0 | 0 | 2 | 3 | 11 | .229 | .186 |
| Mathis,Jeff | L | .214 | 70 | 15 | 3 | 0 | 3 | 9 | 9 | 23 | .313 | .386 |
| Bats Right | R | .167 | 162 | 27 | 4 | 1 | 2 | 20 | 12 | 53 | .223 | .241 |
| Mauer,Joe | L | .322 | 121 | 39 | 8 | 0 | 4 | 20 | 15 | 28 | .394 | .488 |
| Bats Left | R | .324 | 324 | 105 | 27 | 0 | 7 | 27 | 46 | 61 | .407 | .472 |
| Maxwell,Justin | L | .236 | 89 | 21 | 7 | 2 | 1 | 7 | 11 | 27 | .317 | .393 |
| Bats Right | R | .262 | 145 | 38 | 9 | 1 | 6 | 18 | 12 | 51 | .335 | .462 |
| Mayberry,John | L | .240 | 100 | 24 | 5 | 1 | 5 | 13 | 8 | 17 | .296 | .460 |
| Bats Right | R | .221 | 253 | 56 | 18 | 0 | 6 | 26 | 19 | 73 | .283 | .364 |
| Maybin,Cameron | L | .133 | 15 | 2 | 1 | 0 | 0 | 0 | 2 | 3 | .235 | .200 |
| Bats Right | R | .167 | 36 | 6 | 0 | 0 | 1 | 5 | 2 | 6 | .231 | .250 |
| McCann,Brian | L | .231 | 104 | 24 | 2 | 0 | 3 | 13 | 4 | 22 | .279 | .337 |
| Bats Left | R | .266 | 252 | 67 | 11 | 0 | 17 | 44 | 35 | 44 | .357 | .512 |
| McCutchen,Andrew | L | .388 | 103 | 40 | 11 | 2 | 4 | 20 | 18 | 11 | .479 | .650 |
| Bats Right | R | .302 | 480 | 145 | 27 | 3 | 17 | 64 | 60 | 90 | .387 | .477 |
| McDonald,Darnell | L | .429 | 28 | 12 | 4 | 0 | 1 | 4 | 4 | 1 | .500 | .679 |
| Bats Right | R | .160 | 25 | 4 | 0 | 0 | 0 | 1 | 0 | 7 | .160 | .160 |
| McDonald,John | L | .000 | 21 | 0 | 0 | 0 | 0 | 0 | 4 | 8 | .160 | .000 |
| Bats Right | R | .167 | 48 | 8 | 1 | 0 | 1 | 4 | 2 | 8 | .216 | .250 |
| McGuiness,Chris | L | .111 | 9 | 1 | 0 | 0 | 0 | 0 | 0 | 4 | .111 | .111 |
| Bats Left | R | .200 | 25 | 5 | 1 | 0 | 0 | 1 | 0 | 9 | .200 | .240 |
| McKenry,Michael | L | .207 | 29 | 6 | 1 | 0 | 0 | 4 | 1 | 7 | .233 | .241 |
| Bats Right | R | .221 | 86 | 19 | 5 | 0 | 3 | 10 | 4 | 17 | .272 | .384 |
| McLouth,Nate | L | .209 | 115 | 24 | 5 | 0 | 4 | 11 | 10 | 25 | .283 | .357 |
| Bats Left | R | .272 | 416 | 113 | 26 | 4 | 8 | 25 | 43 | 61 | .342 | .411 |
| Medica,Tommy | L | .154 | 13 | 2 | 0 | 0 | 1 | 1 | 1 | 7 | .214 | .385 |
| Bats Right | R | .321 | 56 | 18 | 2 | 0 | 2 | 9 | 9 | 16 | .415 | .464 |
| Mercer,Jordy | L | .410 | 78 | 32 | 10 | 0 | 4 | 10 | 8 | 8 | .460 | .692 |
| Bats Right | R | .247 | 255 | 63 | 12 | 2 | 4 | 17 | 14 | 54 | .297 | .357 |
| Mesoraco,Devin | L | .321 | 78 | 25 | 7 | 0 | 2 | 11 | 9 | 8 | .386 | .487 |
| Bats Right | R | .212 | 245 | 52 | 6 | 0 | 7 | 31 | 15 | 53 | .254 | .322 |
| Middlebrooks,Will | L | .273 | 110 | 30 | 5 | 0 | 5 | 9 | 7 | 25 | .328 | .455 |
| Bats Right | R | .206 | 238 | 49 | 13 | 0 | 12 | 40 | 13 | 73 | .244 | .412 |
| Miller,Brad | L | .270 | 100 | 27 | 2 | 3 | 0 | 9 | 7 | 15 | .324 | .350 |
| Bats Left | R | .262 | 206 | 54 | 9 | 3 | 8 | 27 | 17 | 37 | .316 | .451 |
| Miller,Corky | L | .267 | 15 | 4 | 1 | 0 | 0 | 3 | 2 | 1 | .353 | .333 |
| Bats Right | R | .250 | 20 | 5 | 4 | 0 | 0 | 5 | 3 | 5 | .375 | .450 |
| Molina,Jose | L | .242 | 95 | 23 | 8 | 0 | 0 | 8 | 7 | 13 | .302 | .326 |
| Bats Right | R | .229 | 188 | 43 | 6 | 0 | 2 | 10 | 15 | 50 | .284 | .293 |
| Molina,Yadier | L | .333 | 108 | 36 | 10 | 0 | 3 | 21 | 7 | 13 | .374 | .509 |
| Bats Right | R | .315 | 397 | 125 | 34 | 0 | 9 | 59 | 23 | 42 | .354 | .469 |
| Montero,Jesus | L | .167 | 30 | 5 | 1 | 1 | 0 | 1 | 4 | 5 | .265 | .267 |
| Bats Right | R | .225 | 71 | 16 | 0 | 0 | 3 | 8 | 4 | 16 | .263 | .352 |
| Montero,Miguel | L | .190 | 105 | 20 | 2 | 0 | 1 | 8 | 9 | 32 | .254 | .238 |
| Bats Left | R | .244 | 308 | 75 | 12 | 0 | 10 | 34 | 42 | 78 | .339 | .380 |
| Montz,Luke | L | .200 | 25 | 5 | 3 | 0 | 1 | 5 | 1 | 7 | .222 | .440 |
| Bats Right | R | .000 | 3 | 0 | 0 | 0 | 0 | 0 | 0 | 1 | .000 | .000 |

| Batter | vs | Avg | AB | H | 2B | 3B | HR | RBI | BB | SO | OBP | Slg |
|---|---|---|---|---|---|---|---|---|---|---|---|---|
| Moore,Tyler | L | .189 | 74 | 14 | 3 | 0 | 1 | 8 | 5 | 25 | .238 | .270 |
| Bats Right | R | .247 | 93 | 23 | 6 | 0 | 3 | 13 | 3 | 33 | .278 | .409 |
| Morales,Kendrys | L | .282 | 209 | 59 | 15 | 0 | 6 | 23 | 21 | 38 | .353 | .440 |
| Bats Both | R | .275 | 393 | 108 | 19 | 0 | 17 | 57 | 28 | 76 | .327 | .453 |
| Morel,Brent | L | .231 | 13 | 3 | 0 | 0 | 0 | 1 | 5 | 3 | .444 | .231 |
| Bats Right | R | .167 | 12 | 2 | 0 | 0 | 0 | 0 | 0 | 4 | .167 | .167 |
| Moreland,Mitch | L | .241 | 141 | 34 | 14 | 0 | 3 | 14 | 11 | 36 | .297 | .404 |
| Bats Left | R | .227 | 321 | 73 | 10 | 1 | 20 | 46 | 34 | 81 | .300 | .452 |
| Morneau,Justin | L | .207 | 169 | 35 | 6 | 0 | 2 | 16 | 7 | 43 | .247 | .278 |
| Bats Left | R | .280 | 403 | 113 | 30 | 0 | 15 | 61 | 43 | 67 | .352 | .467 |
| Morrison,Logan | L | .183 | 71 | 13 | 3 | 0 | 0 | 6 | 7 | 21 | .266 | .225 |
| Bats Left | R | .261 | 222 | 58 | 10 | 4 | 6 | 30 | 31 | 35 | .354 | .423 |
| Morse,Michael | L | .215 | 121 | 26 | 6 | 0 | 5 | 12 | 10 | 30 | .278 | .388 |
| Bats Right | R | .215 | 191 | 41 | 7 | 0 | 8 | 15 | 11 | 57 | .265 | .377 |
| Moss,Brandon | L | .200 | 80 | 16 | 1 | 1 | 4 | 16 | 6 | 38 | .261 | .388 |
| Bats Left | R | .268 | 366 | 98 | 22 | 2 | 26 | 71 | 44 | 102 | .353 | .552 |
| Moustakas,Mike | L | .196 | 107 | 21 | 4 | 0 | 2 | 10 | 9 | 23 | .256 | .290 |
| Bats Left | R | .244 | 365 | 89 | 22 | 0 | 10 | 32 | 23 | 60 | .295 | .386 |
| Murphy,Daniel | L | .273 | 216 | 59 | 8 | 0 | 1 | 19 | 6 | 48 | .292 | .324 |
| Bats Left | R | .292 | 442 | 129 | 30 | 4 | 12 | 59 | 26 | 47 | .331 | .459 |
| Murphy,David | L | .223 | 103 | 23 | 4 | 0 | 1 | 9 | 7 | 13 | .270 | .291 |
| Bats Left | R | .219 | 333 | 73 | 22 | 1 | 12 | 36 | 30 | 46 | .286 | .399 |
| Murphy,Donnie | L | .257 | 35 | 9 | 3 | 0 | 3 | 3 | 4 | 15 | .350 | .600 |
| Bats Right | R | .254 | 114 | 29 | 5 | 0 | 8 | 20 | 4 | 33 | .309 | .509 |
| Murphy,J.R. | L | .250 | 12 | 3 | 1 | 0 | 0 | 0 | 1 | 5 | .308 | .333 |
| Bats Right | R | .071 | 14 | 1 | 0 | 0 | 0 | 1 | 0 | 4 | .071 | .071 |
| Myers,Wil | L | .293 | 99 | 29 | 5 | 0 | 3 | 20 | 17 | 29 | .387 | .434 |
| Bats Right | R | .292 | 236 | 69 | 18 | 0 | 10 | 33 | 16 | 62 | .339 | .496 |
| Napoli,Mike | L | .284 | 155 | 44 | 13 | 0 | 8 | 25 | 23 | 48 | .376 | .523 |
| Bats Right | R | .248 | 343 | 85 | 25 | 2 | 15 | 67 | 50 | 139 | .353 | .464 |
| Nava,Daniel | L | .252 | 119 | 30 | 4 | 0 | 2 | 13 | 12 | 32 | .311 | .336 |
| Bats Both | R | .322 | 339 | 109 | 25 | 0 | 10 | 53 | 39 | 61 | .411 | .484 |
| Navarro,Dioner | L | .361 | 61 | 22 | 1 | 0 | 6 | 10 | 9 | 5 | .451 | .672 |
| Bats Both | R | .279 | 179 | 50 | 6 | 0 | 7 | 24 | 14 | 31 | .333 | .430 |
| Navarro,Yamaico | L | .300 | 10 | 3 | 0 | 0 | 0 | 1 | 1 | 2 | .364 | .300 |
| Bats Right | R | .278 | 18 | 5 | 0 | 1 | 0 | 1 | 1 | 6 | .316 | .389 |
| Nelson,Chris | L | .264 | 53 | 14 | 1 | 0 | 1 | 11 | 5 | 14 | .322 | .340 |
| Bats Right | R | .215 | 158 | 34 | 3 | 4 | 2 | 13 | 8 | 52 | .256 | .323 |
| Nieuwenhuis,Kirk | L | .000 | 8 | 0 | 0 | 0 | 0 | 0 | 1 | 2 | .111 | .000 |
| Bats Left | R | .207 | 87 | 18 | 3 | 1 | 3 | 14 | 11 | 30 | .293 | .368 |
| Nieves,Wil | L | .307 | 75 | 23 | 3 | 0 | 1 | 13 | 4 | 10 | .333 | .387 |
| Bats Right | R | .292 | 120 | 35 | 8 | 0 | 0 | 9 | 4 | 22 | .312 | .358 |
| Nix,Jayson | L | .266 | 94 | 25 | 3 | 0 | 1 | 13 | 14 | 24 | .357 | .330 |
| Bats Right | R | .220 | 173 | 38 | 6 | 1 | 2 | 11 | 10 | 56 | .278 | .301 |
| Nix,Laynce | L | .111 | 9 | 1 | 0 | 0 | 0 | 0 | 0 | 1 | .111 | .111 |
| Bats Left | R | .185 | 119 | 22 | 4 | 0 | 2 | 7 | 8 | 43 | .236 | .269 |
| Noonan,Nick | L | .300 | 10 | 3 | 0 | 0 | 0 | 0 | 1 | 3 | .364 | .300 |
| Bats Left | R | .211 | 95 | 20 | 2 | 0 | 0 | 5 | 5 | 21 | .250 | .232 |
| Norris,Derek | L | .320 | 150 | 48 | 12 | 0 | 9 | 25 | 22 | 33 | .410 | .580 |
| Bats Right | R | .149 | 114 | 17 | 4 | 0 | 0 | 5 | 15 | 38 | .261 | .184 |
| Nunez,Eduardo | L | .225 | 102 | 23 | 5 | 2 | 2 | 5 | 8 | 20 | .279 | .373 |
| Bats Right | R | .277 | 202 | 56 | 12 | 2 | 1 | 23 | 12 | 31 | .321 | .371 |
| Olivo,Miguel | L | .250 | 32 | 8 | 0 | 0 | 4 | 7 | 3 | 6 | .314 | .625 |
| Bats Right | R | .167 | 42 | 7 | 2 | 0 | 0 | 2 | 2 | 17 | .200 | .214 |
| Orr,Pete | L | .333 | 3 | 1 | 0 | 0 | 0 | 0 | 0 | 2 | .333 | .333 |
| Bats Left | R | .176 | 17 | 3 | 0 | 0 | 0 | 0 | 2 | 6 | .263 | .176 |
| Ortiz,David | L | .260 | 196 | 51 | 10 | 0 | 7 | 36 | 16 | 34 | .315 | .418 |
| Bats Left | R | .339 | 322 | 109 | 28 | 2 | 23 | 67 | 60 | 54 | .440 | .652 |
| Overbay,Lyle | L | .190 | 116 | 22 | 8 | 0 | 1 | 14 | 7 | 34 | .232 | .284 |
| Bats Left | R | .258 | 329 | 85 | 16 | 1 | 13 | 45 | 29 | 77 | .317 | .432 |
| Owings,Chris | L | .125 | 16 | 2 | 0 | 0 | 0 | 0 | 0 | 4 | .125 | .125 |
| Bats Right | R | .359 | 39 | 14 | 5 | 0 | 0 | 5 | 6 | 6 | .444 | .487 |
| Ozuna,Marcell | L | .318 | 66 | 21 | 7 | 1 | 1 | 13 | 2 | 14 | .338 | .500 |
| Bats Right | R | .249 | 209 | 52 | 10 | 3 | 2 | 19 | 11 | 43 | .293 | .354 |
| Pacheco,Jordan | L | .205 | 112 | 23 | 8 | 0 | 1 | 12 | 6 | 23 | .252 | .304 |
| Bats Right | R | .267 | 135 | 36 | 7 | 0 | 0 | 10 | 4 | 15 | .296 | .319 |
| Pagan,Angel | L | .305 | 82 | 25 | 6 | 0 | 2 | 6 | 7 | 9 | .356 | .451 |
| Bats Both | R | .273 | 198 | 54 | 10 | 3 | 3 | 24 | 16 | 27 | .326 | .399 |
| Pagnozzi,Matt | L | .400 | 5 | 2 | 0 | 0 | 0 | 0 | 1 | 2 | .500 | .400 |
| Bats Right | R | .063 | 16 | 1 | 0 | 0 | 0 | 0 | 0 | 1 | .063 | .063 |
| Paredes,Jimmy | L | .105 | 38 | 4 | 1 | 0 | 0 | 1 | 1 | 12 | .150 | .132 |
| Bats Both | R | .230 | 87 | 20 | 3 | 0 | 1 | 9 | 5 | 32 | .266 | .299 |
| Parmelee,Chris | L | .172 | 58 | 10 | 0 | 0 | 2 | 5 | 5 | 21 | .250 | .276 |
| Bats Left | R | .242 | 236 | 57 | 13 | 0 | 6 | 19 | 28 | 60 | .323 | .373 |
| Parra,Gerardo | L | .198 | 177 | 35 | 5 | 0 | 0 | 4 | 17 | 33 | .276 | .226 |
| Bats Left | R | .297 | 424 | 126 | 38 | 4 | 10 | 44 | 31 | 67 | .343 | .476 |

# Batters vs. Left-Handed and Right-Handed Pitchers

| Batter | vs | Avg | AB | H | 2B | 3B | HR | RBI | BB | SO | OBP | Slg |
|---|---|---|---|---|---|---|---|---|---|---|---|---|
| Parrino,Andy | L | .167 | 18 | 3 | 1 | 0 | 0 | 0 | 1 | 5 | .211 | .222 |
| Bats Both | R | .063 | 16 | 1 | 1 | 0 | 0 | 1 | 1 | 7 | .118 | .125 |
| Pastornicky,Tyler | L | .500 | 4 | 2 | 0 | 0 | 0 | 0 | 1 | 0 | .600 | .500 |
| Bats Right | R | .269 | 26 | 7 | 1 | 0 | 0 | 0 | 0 | 5 | .269 | .308 |
| Paul,Xavier | L | .158 | 19 | 3 | 0 | 0 | 0 | 0 | 2 | 8 | .238 | .158 |
| Bats Left | R | .253 | 190 | 48 | 12 | 0 | 7 | 32 | 25 | 45 | .349 | .426 |
| Pearce,Steve | L | .267 | 75 | 20 | 6 | 0 | 2 | 8 | 10 | 13 | .375 | .427 |
| Bats Right | R | .250 | 44 | 11 | 1 | 0 | 2 | 5 | 5 | 12 | .340 | .409 |
| Pedroia,Dustin | L | .354 | 192 | 68 | 21 | 1 | 2 | 28 | 27 | 22 | .432 | .505 |
| Bats Right | R | .278 | 449 | 125 | 21 | 1 | 7 | 56 | 46 | 53 | .345 | .376 |
| Peguero,Francisco | L | .214 | 14 | 3 | 0 | 0 | 0 | 0 | 0 | 0 | .214 | .214 |
| Bats Right | R | .200 | 15 | 3 | 1 | 0 | 1 | 1 | 1 | 2 | .250 | .467 |
| Pena,Brayan | L | .264 | 106 | 28 | 7 | 0 | 0 | 6 | 2 | 14 | .278 | .330 |
| Bats Both | R | .325 | 123 | 40 | 4 | 0 | 4 | 16 | 4 | 12 | .346 | .455 |
| Pena,Carlos | L | .231 | 52 | 12 | 2 | 1 | 3 | 7 | 8 | 19 | .355 | .481 |
| Bats Left | R | .202 | 228 | 46 | 11 | 0 | 5 | 18 | 35 | 73 | .313 | .316 |
| Pena,Ramiro | L | .118 | 17 | 2 | 0 | 0 | 0 | 0 | 2 | 5 | .211 | .118 |
| Bats Both | R | .313 | 80 | 25 | 5 | 1 | 3 | 12 | 6 | 13 | .356 | .513 |
| Pence,Hunter | L | .309 | 162 | 50 | 14 | 1 | 11 | 33 | 15 | 26 | .365 | .611 |
| Bats Right | R | .274 | 467 | 128 | 21 | 4 | 16 | 66 | 37 | 89 | .330 | .439 |
| Pennington,Cliff | L | .247 | 97 | 24 | 7 | 0 | 0 | 5 | 9 | 15 | .318 | .320 |
| Bats Both | R | .238 | 172 | 41 | 6 | 1 | 1 | 13 | 17 | 39 | .305 | .302 |
| Peralta,Jhonny | L | .352 | 125 | 44 | 14 | 0 | 4 | 16 | 10 | 38 | .404 | .560 |
| Bats Right | R | .282 | 284 | 80 | 16 | 0 | 7 | 39 | 25 | 60 | .338 | .412 |
| Perez,Hernan | L | .212 | 33 | 7 | 0 | 1 | 0 | 4 | 1 | 8 | .229 | .273 |
| Bats Right | R | .182 | 33 | 6 | 0 | 0 | 0 | 1 | 1 | 7 | .206 | .182 |
| Perez,Juan | L | .208 | 53 | 11 | 3 | 0 | 0 | 4 | 4 | 14 | .259 | .264 |
| Bats Right | R | .333 | 36 | 12 | 2 | 0 | 1 | 4 | 2 | 7 | .368 | .472 |
| Perez,Salvador | L | .317 | 139 | 44 | 11 | 1 | 5 | 21 | 7 | 12 | .349 | .518 |
| Bats Right | R | .283 | 357 | 101 | 14 | 2 | 8 | 58 | 14 | 51 | .313 | .401 |
| Peterson,Brock | L | .056 | 18 | 1 | 0 | 0 | 0 | 1 | 0 | 8 | .056 | .056 |
| Bats Right | R | .125 | 8 | 1 | 0 | 0 | 0 | 1 | 2 | 3 | .300 | .125 |
| Phegley,Josh | L | .261 | 46 | 12 | 4 | 0 | 1 | 3 | 0 | 6 | .255 | .413 |
| Bats Right | R | .190 | 158 | 30 | 3 | 0 | 3 | 19 | 5 | 35 | .213 | .266 |
| Phillips,Brandon | L | .254 | 177 | 45 | 8 | 0 | 7 | 25 | 17 | 25 | .328 | .418 |
| Bats Right | R | .263 | 429 | 113 | 16 | 2 | 11 | 76 | 22 | 73 | .302 | .387 |
| Pie,Felix | L | .000 | 5 | 0 | 0 | 0 | 0 | 0 | 0 | 1 | .000 | .000 |
| Bats Left | R | .167 | 24 | 4 | 1 | 0 | 0 | 2 | 2 | 12 | .231 | .208 |
| Pierre,Juan | L | .175 | 63 | 11 | 1 | 0 | 0 | 2 | 3 | 8 | .235 | .190 |
| Bats Left | R | .265 | 245 | 65 | 10 | 2 | 1 | 6 | 10 | 19 | .297 | .335 |
| Pierzynski,A.J. | L | .279 | 165 | 46 | 9 | 1 | 3 | 27 | 6 | 34 | .318 | .400 |
| Bats Left | R | .269 | 338 | 91 | 15 | 0 | 14 | 43 | 5 | 42 | .286 | .438 |
| Pill,Brett | L | .193 | 57 | 11 | 2 | 0 | 2 | 7 | 3 | 10 | .233 | .333 |
| Bats Right | R | .286 | 28 | 8 | 2 | 0 | 1 | 5 | 2 | 7 | .344 | .464 |
| Pillar,Kevin | L | .235 | 34 | 8 | 2 | 0 | 1 | 2 | 3 | 5 | .297 | .382 |
| Bats Right | R | .191 | 68 | 13 | 2 | 0 | 2 | 11 | 1 | 24 | .225 | .309 |
| Pinto,Josmil | L | .294 | 17 | 5 | 2 | 0 | 0 | 1 | 1 | 4 | .333 | .412 |
| Bats Right | R | .356 | 59 | 21 | 3 | 0 | 4 | 11 | 5 | 18 | .415 | .610 |
| Plouffe,Trevor | L | .300 | 110 | 33 | 9 | 1 | 2 | 13 | 12 | 26 | .371 | .455 |
| Bats Right | R | .240 | 367 | 88 | 13 | 0 | 12 | 39 | 22 | 86 | .290 | .373 |
| Polanco,Placido | L | .317 | 123 | 39 | 8 | 0 | 0 | 9 | 6 | 11 | .348 | .382 |
| Bats Right | R | .232 | 254 | 59 | 5 | 0 | 1 | 14 | 17 | 20 | .299 | .264 |
| Pollock,A.J. | L | .283 | 173 | 49 | 16 | 3 | 4 | 17 | 12 | 28 | .332 | .480 |
| Bats Right | R | .259 | 270 | 70 | 12 | 2 | 4 | 21 | 21 | 54 | .315 | .363 |
| Posey,Buster | L | .320 | 153 | 49 | 13 | 1 | 4 | 22 | 19 | 20 | .394 | .497 |
| Bats Right | R | .283 | 367 | 104 | 21 | 0 | 11 | 50 | 41 | 50 | .362 | .431 |
| Prado,Martin | L | .291 | 148 | 43 | 10 | 1 | 5 | 20 | 21 | 12 | .379 | .473 |
| Bats Right | R | .280 | 461 | 129 | 26 | 1 | 9 | 62 | 26 | 41 | .317 | .399 |
| Presley,Alex | L | .300 | 50 | 15 | 1 | 0 | 0 | 4 | 0 | 10 | .314 | .320 |
| Bats Left | R | .267 | 135 | 36 | 4 | 2 | 3 | 11 | 9 | 29 | .313 | .393 |
| Profar,Jurickson | L | .188 | 96 | 18 | 3 | 0 | 1 | 9 | 12 | 24 | .291 | .250 |
| Bats Both | R | .258 | 190 | 49 | 8 | 0 | 5 | 17 | 14 | 39 | .317 | .379 |
| Puig,Yasiel | L | .340 | 103 | 35 | 5 | 1 | 6 | 10 | 13 | 25 | .419 | .583 |
| Bats Right | R | .312 | 279 | 87 | 16 | 1 | 13 | 32 | 23 | 72 | .381 | .516 |
| Pujols,Albert | L | .213 | 89 | 19 | 7 | 0 | 3 | 10 | 10 | 10 | .297 | .393 |
| Bats Right | R | .272 | 302 | 82 | 12 | 0 | 14 | 54 | 30 | 45 | .339 | .450 |
| Punto,Nick | L | .309 | 97 | 30 | 5 | 0 | 0 | 5 | 8 | 17 | .362 | .361 |
| Bats Both | R | .228 | 197 | 45 | 10 | 0 | 2 | 16 | 25 | 50 | .313 | .310 |
| Quentin,Carlos | L | .284 | 74 | 21 | 6 | 0 | 3 | 11 | 9 | 12 | .376 | .486 |
| Bats Right | R | .272 | 202 | 55 | 15 | 0 | 10 | 33 | 22 | 43 | .357 | .495 |
| Quintanilla,Omar | L | .203 | 79 | 16 | 4 | 0 | 0 | 2 | 5 | 18 | .247 | .253 |
| Bats Left | R | .229 | 236 | 54 | 5 | 2 | 2 | 19 | 33 | 52 | .325 | .292 |
| Quintero,Humberto | L | .286 | 42 | 12 | 2 | 0 | 2 | 8 | 2 | 9 | .318 | .476 |
| Bats Right | R | .213 | 89 | 19 | 3 | 0 | 2 | 5 | 4 | 21 | .255 | .315 |
| Quiroz,Guillermo | L | .121 | 33 | 4 | 3 | 0 | 0 | 1 | 3 | 9 | .189 | .212 |
| Bats Right | R | .226 | 53 | 12 | 4 | 0 | 1 | 5 | 2 | 12 | .268 | .358 |

| Batter | vs | Avg | AB | H | 2B | 3B | HR | RBI | BB | SO | OBP | Slg |
|---|---|---|---|---|---|---|---|---|---|---|---|---|
| Raburn,Ryan | L | .308 | 107 | 33 | 12 | 0 | 7 | 21 | 14 | 26 | .403 | .617 |
| Bats Right | R | .243 | 136 | 33 | 6 | 0 | 9 | 34 | 15 | 41 | .320 | .485 |
| Ramirez,Alexei | L | .285 | 130 | 37 | 7 | 0 | 2 | 12 | 7 | 13 | .317 | .385 |
| Bats Right | R | .284 | 507 | 144 | 32 | 2 | 4 | 36 | 19 | 55 | .313 | .379 |
| Ramirez,Aramis | L | .299 | 77 | 23 | 7 | 0 | 4 | 19 | 5 | 18 | .341 | .545 |
| Bats Right | R | .278 | 227 | 63 | 11 | 0 | 8 | 30 | 31 | 37 | .379 | .432 |
| Ramirez,Hanley | L | .349 | 83 | 29 | 8 | 1 | 7 | 18 | 10 | 16 | .419 | .723 |
| Bats Right | R | .344 | 221 | 76 | 17 | 1 | 13 | 39 | 17 | 36 | .395 | .606 |
| Ramirez,Wilkin | L | .333 | 30 | 10 | 2 | 1 | 0 | 2 | 1 | 6 | .344 | .467 |
| Bats Right | R | .235 | 51 | 12 | 4 | 0 | 0 | 4 | 2 | 17 | .278 | .314 |
| Ramos,Wilson | L | .282 | 71 | 20 | 4 | 0 | 1 | 11 | 4 | 12 | .320 | .380 |
| Bats Right | R | .269 | 216 | 58 | 5 | 0 | 15 | 48 | 11 | 30 | .303 | .500 |
| Ransom,Cody | L | .220 | 100 | 22 | 8 | 0 | 7 | 13 | 12 | 36 | .304 | .510 |
| Bats Right | R | .145 | 69 | 10 | 2 | 1 | 2 | 7 | 10 | 26 | .263 | .290 |
| Rasmus,Colby | L | .256 | 125 | 32 | 3 | 0 | 6 | 19 | 6 | 42 | .288 | .424 |
| Bats Left | R | .284 | 292 | 83 | 23 | 1 | 16 | 47 | 31 | 93 | .359 | .534 |
| Recker,Anthony | L | .208 | 48 | 10 | 2 | 0 | 4 | 7 | 5 | 19 | .283 | .500 |
| Bats Right | R | .218 | 87 | 19 | 5 | 0 | 2 | 12 | 8 | 30 | .278 | .345 |
| Reddick,Josh | L | .200 | 125 | 25 | 3 | 0 | 6 | 16 | 17 | 26 | .299 | .368 |
| Bats Left | R | .238 | 260 | 62 | 16 | 2 | 6 | 40 | 29 | 60 | .311 | .385 |
| Reimold,Nolan | L | .220 | 50 | 11 | 1 | 0 | 2 | 3 | 1 | 17 | .235 | .360 |
| Bats Right | R | .179 | 78 | 14 | 2 | 0 | 3 | 9 | 9 | 24 | .258 | .321 |
| Rendon,Anthony | L | .294 | 102 | 30 | 6 | 0 | 4 | 11 | 12 | 17 | .359 | .471 |
| Bats Right | R | .253 | 249 | 63 | 17 | 1 | 3 | 24 | 19 | 52 | .316 | .365 |
| Revere,Ben | L | .370 | 73 | 27 | 6 | 1 | 0 | 4 | 1 | 8 | .378 | .479 |
| Bats Left | R | .285 | 242 | 69 | 3 | 2 | 0 | 13 | 15 | 28 | .327 | .314 |
| Reyes,Jose | L | .247 | 93 | 23 | 5 | 0 | 3 | 8 | 8 | 12 | .307 | .398 |
| Bats Both | R | .311 | 289 | 90 | 15 | 0 | 7 | 29 | 26 | 35 | .368 | .436 |
| Reynolds,Mark | L | .225 | 160 | 36 | 5 | 0 | 8 | 30 | 21 | 48 | .319 | .406 |
| Bats Right | R | .218 | 285 | 62 | 9 | 0 | 13 | 37 | 30 | 106 | .298 | .386 |
| Rios,Alex | L | .313 | 147 | 46 | 10 | 0 | 7 | 27 | 12 | 23 | .365 | .524 |
| Bats Right | R | .267 | 469 | 125 | 23 | 4 | 11 | 54 | 29 | 85 | .311 | .403 |
| Rivera,Rene | L | .235 | 17 | 4 | 1 | 0 | 0 | 1 | 0 | 5 | .235 | .294 |
| Bats Right | R | .260 | 50 | 13 | 2 | 1 | 0 | 6 | 2 | 11 | .278 | .340 |
| Rizzo,Anthony | L | .189 | 190 | 36 | 8 | 0 | 7 | 23 | 22 | 44 | .282 | .342 |
| Bats Left | R | .252 | 416 | 105 | 32 | 2 | 16 | 57 | 54 | 83 | .342 | .454 |
| Roberts,Brian | L | .284 | 102 | 29 | 4 | 0 | 4 | 15 | 7 | 13 | .327 | .441 |
| Bats Both | R | .227 | 163 | 37 | 8 | 1 | 4 | 24 | 19 | 31 | .303 | .362 |
| Roberts,Ryan | L | .305 | 82 | 25 | 4 | 0 | 4 | 9 | 5 | 15 | .345 | .500 |
| Bats Right | R | .188 | 80 | 15 | 2 | 0 | 1 | 8 | 6 | 24 | .244 | .250 |
| Robinson,Derrick | L | .288 | 80 | 23 | 5 | 1 | 0 | 6 | 10 | 20 | .367 | .375 |
| Bats Both | R | .232 | 112 | 26 | 2 | 2 | 0 | 2 | 8 | 24 | .289 | .286 |
| Robinson,Shane | L | .228 | 79 | 18 | 1 | 0 | 1 | 7 | 12 | 7 | .319 | .278 |
| Bats Right | R | .277 | 65 | 18 | 1 | 1 | 1 | 9 | 11 | 10 | .377 | .369 |
| Rodriguez,Alex | L | .200 | 50 | 10 | 0 | 0 | 0 | 0 | 14 | 10 | .385 | .200 |
| Bats Right | R | .264 | 106 | 28 | 7 | 0 | 7 | 19 | 9 | 33 | .328 | .528 |
| Rodriguez,Sean | L | .252 | 155 | 39 | 9 | 1 | 5 | 18 | 13 | 46 | .326 | .419 |
| Bats Right | R | .225 | 40 | 9 | 1 | 0 | 0 | 5 | 4 | 13 | .295 | .250 |
| Rollins,Jimmy | L | .252 | 163 | 41 | 7 | 0 | 2 | 7 | 16 | 30 | .317 | .331 |
| Bats Both | R | .252 | 437 | 110 | 29 | 2 | 4 | 32 | 43 | 63 | .319 | .355 |
| Romine,Andrew | L | .290 | 31 | 9 | 2 | 0 | 0 | 6 | 1 | 5 | .313 | .355 |
| Bats Both | R | .247 | 77 | 19 | 1 | 0 | 0 | 4 | 6 | 19 | .306 | .260 |
| Romine,Austin | L | .233 | 43 | 10 | 4 | 0 | 0 | 2 | 1 | 11 | .250 | .326 |
| Bats Right | R | .196 | 92 | 18 | 5 | 0 | 1 | 8 | 7 | 26 | .257 | .283 |
| Rosales,Adam | L | .238 | 84 | 20 | 2 | 0 | 4 | 9 | 8 | 14 | .316 | .405 |
| Bats Right | R | .127 | 63 | 8 | 3 | 0 | 1 | 3 | 2 | 20 | .179 | .222 |
| Rosario,Wilin | L | .323 | 130 | 42 | 8 | 0 | 7 | 29 | 7 | 24 | .355 | .546 |
| Bats Right | R | .279 | 319 | 89 | 14 | 1 | 14 | 50 | 8 | 85 | .299 | .461 |
| Ross,Cody | L | .391 | 110 | 43 | 7 | 1 | 4 | 12 | 9 | 11 | .430 | .582 |
| Bats Right | R | .217 | 207 | 45 | 10 | 0 | 4 | 26 | 16 | 39 | .279 | .324 |
| Ross,David | L | .259 | 54 | 14 | 3 | 0 | 3 | 7 | 5 | 19 | .322 | .481 |
| Bats Right | R | .167 | 48 | 8 | 2 | 0 | 1 | 3 | 6 | 23 | .273 | .271 |
| Ruf,Darin | L | .188 | 69 | 13 | 2 | 0 | 3 | 5 | 12 | 28 | .309 | .348 |
| Bats Right | R | .269 | 182 | 49 | 9 | 0 | 11 | 25 | 21 | 63 | .363 | .500 |
| Ruggiano,Justin | L | .248 | 133 | 33 | 10 | 0 | 8 | 24 | 14 | 29 | .329 | .504 |
| Bats Right | R | .210 | 291 | 61 | 8 | 1 | 10 | 26 | 27 | 85 | .283 | .347 |
| Ruiz,Carlos | L | .300 | 80 | 24 | 7 | 0 | 2 | 16 | 8 | 6 | .374 | .463 |
| Bats Right | R | .257 | 230 | 59 | 9 | 0 | 3 | 21 | 10 | 33 | .301 | .335 |
| Rutledge,Josh | L | .196 | 102 | 20 | 1 | 0 | 3 | 6 | 6 | 29 | .239 | .294 |
| Bats Right | R | .257 | 183 | 47 | 5 | 1 | 4 | 13 | 16 | 33 | .323 | .361 |
| Ryan,Brendan | L | .190 | 105 | 20 | 6 | 0 | 0 | 6 | 8 | 24 | .248 | .248 |
| Bats Right | R | .201 | 214 | 43 | 6 | 0 | 4 | 16 | 15 | 49 | .259 | .285 |
| Saltalamacchia,Jarrod | L | .218 | 119 | 26 | 6 | 0 | 2 | 16 | 16 | 36 | .309 | .319 |
| Bats Both | R | .294 | 306 | 90 | 34 | 0 | 12 | 49 | 27 | 103 | .350 | .523 |
| Sanchez,Gaby | L | .333 | 102 | 34 | 9 | 0 | 4 | 14 | 21 | 16 | .448 | .539 |
| Bats Right | R | .204 | 162 | 33 | 9 | 0 | 3 | 22 | 23 | 35 | .304 | .315 |

# Batters vs. Left-Handed and Right-Handed Pitchers

| Batter | vs | Avg | AB | H | 2B | 3B | HR | RBI | BB | SO | OBP | Slg |
|---|---|---|---|---|---|---|---|---|---|---|---|---|
| Sanchez,Hector | L | .341 | 41 | 14 | 3 | 0 | 1 | 9 | 1 | 8 | .372 | .488 |
| Bats Both | R | .205 | 88 | 18 | 1 | 0 | 2 | 10 | 6 | 21 | .268 | .284 |
| Sanchez,Tony | L | .235 | 17 | 4 | 2 | 0 | 1 | 1 | 0 | 3 | .235 | .529 |
| Bats Right | R | .233 | 43 | 10 | 2 | 0 | 1 | 4 | 3 | 11 | .306 | .349 |
| Sandoval,Pablo | L | .270 | 148 | 40 | 8 | 0 | 1 | 15 | 15 | 25 | .341 | .345 |
| Bats Both | R | .281 | 377 | 106 | 19 | 2 | 13 | 64 | 32 | 54 | .341 | .446 |
| Santana,Carlos | L | .299 | 187 | 56 | 15 | 1 | 6 | 27 | 23 | 30 | .377 | .487 |
| Bats Both | R | .251 | 354 | 89 | 24 | 0 | 14 | 47 | 70 | 80 | .377 | .438 |
| Santiago,Ramon | L | .196 | 51 | 10 | 2 | 1 | 0 | 2 | 9 | 12 | .317 | .275 |
| Bats Both | R | .234 | 154 | 36 | 6 | 0 | 1 | 12 | 12 | 20 | .292 | .292 |
| Sappelt,Dave | L | .240 | 50 | 12 | 2 | 0 | 0 | 1 | 1 | 7 | .255 | .280 |
| Bats Right | R | .240 | 25 | 6 | 1 | 0 | 0 | 3 | 2 | 7 | .296 | .280 |
| Satin,Josh | L | .317 | 82 | 26 | 10 | 0 | 1 | 7 | 12 | 22 | .404 | .476 |
| Bats Right | R | .250 | 108 | 27 | 5 | 0 | 2 | 10 | 18 | 34 | .354 | .352 |
| Saunders,Michael | L | .211 | 133 | 28 | 6 | 1 | 4 | 17 | 16 | 41 | .293 | .361 |
| Bats Left | R | .249 | 273 | 68 | 17 | 2 | 8 | 29 | 38 | 77 | .338 | .414 |
| Schafer,Jordan | L | .129 | 31 | 4 | 0 | 0 | 0 | 1 | 1 | 14 | .156 | .129 |
| Bats Left | R | .265 | 200 | 53 | 8 | 3 | 3 | 20 | 28 | 59 | .355 | .380 |
| Schafer,Logan | L | .175 | 57 | 10 | 1 | 1 | 1 | 7 | 3 | 13 | .217 | .281 |
| Bats Left | R | .220 | 241 | 53 | 14 | 2 | 3 | 26 | 22 | 47 | .293 | .332 |
| Schierholtz,Nate | L | .170 | 53 | 9 | 1 | 0 | 1 | 3 | 10 | 15 | .308 | .245 |
| Bats Left | R | .262 | 409 | 107 | 31 | 3 | 20 | 65 | 19 | 79 | .300 | .499 |
| Schumaker,Skip | L | .255 | 55 | 14 | 4 | 0 | 0 | 5 | 3 | 13 | .305 | .327 |
| Bats Left | R | .265 | 264 | 70 | 12 | 0 | 2 | 25 | 25 | 41 | .338 | .333 |
| Scott,Luke | L | .269 | 78 | 21 | 2 | 2 | 2 | 15 | 4 | 25 | .322 | .423 |
| Bats Left | R | .229 | 175 | 40 | 11 | 0 | 7 | 25 | 26 | 38 | .328 | .411 |
| Scutaro,Marco | L | .309 | 139 | 43 | 5 | 2 | 1 | 9 | 11 | 10 | .362 | .396 |
| Bats Right | R | .292 | 349 | 102 | 18 | 1 | 1 | 22 | 34 | 24 | .355 | .358 |
| Seager,Kyle | L | .235 | 238 | 56 | 9 | 1 | 10 | 24 | 15 | 53 | .282 | .408 |
| Bats Left | R | .276 | 377 | 104 | 23 | 1 | 12 | 45 | 53 | 69 | .370 | .438 |
| Segura,Jean | L | .317 | 142 | 45 | 7 | 4 | 4 | 15 | 9 | 20 | .358 | .507 |
| Bats Right | R | .287 | 446 | 128 | 13 | 6 | 8 | 34 | 16 | 64 | .319 | .397 |
| Sellers,Justin | L | .238 | 21 | 5 | 0 | 0 | 0 | 1 | 0 | 6 | .238 | .238 |
| Bats Right | R | .167 | 48 | 8 | 1 | 0 | 1 | 1 | 5 | 14 | .273 | .250 |
| Semien,Marcus | L | .267 | 15 | 4 | 1 | 0 | 1 | 3 | 0 | 3 | .250 | .533 |
| Bats Right | R | .259 | 54 | 14 | 3 | 0 | 1 | 4 | 1 | 19 | .273 | .370 |
| Shoppach,Kelly | L | .167 | 30 | 5 | 2 | 0 | 1 | 2 | 5 | 10 | .306 | .333 |
| Bats Right | R | .203 | 79 | 16 | 5 | 0 | 2 | 7 | 7 | 36 | .281 | .342 |
| Shuck,J.B. | L | .310 | 100 | 31 | 6 | 1 | 0 | 10 | 7 | 11 | .355 | .390 |
| Bats Left | R | .288 | 337 | 97 | 14 | 2 | 2 | 29 | 20 | 43 | .323 | .359 |
| Sierra,Moises | L | .235 | 34 | 8 | 3 | 1 | 1 | 3 | 4 | 8 | .316 | .471 |
| Bats Right | R | .315 | 73 | 23 | 10 | 0 | 0 | 10 | 10 | 21 | .393 | .452 |
| Simmons,Andrelton | L | .216 | 139 | 30 | 5 | 1 | 6 | 15 | 16 | 11 | .297 | .396 |
| Bats Right | R | .257 | 467 | 120 | 22 | 5 | 11 | 44 | 24 | 44 | .295 | .396 |
| Smith,Seth | L | .235 | 81 | 19 | 2 | 0 | 2 | 6 | 6 | 25 | .287 | .333 |
| Bats Left | R | .258 | 287 | 74 | 25 | 0 | 6 | 34 | 33 | 69 | .341 | .408 |
| Smoak,Justin | L | .192 | 146 | 28 | 6 | 0 | 2 | 11 | 17 | 37 | .274 | .274 |
| Bats Both | R | .260 | 308 | 80 | 13 | 0 | 18 | 39 | 47 | 82 | .361 | .477 |
| Snider,Travis | L | .091 | 22 | 2 | 0 | 0 | 0 | 0 | 3 | 13 | .200 | .091 |
| Bats Left | R | .226 | 239 | 54 | 12 | 2 | 5 | 25 | 21 | 62 | .288 | .356 |
| Snyder,Brandon | L | .273 | 33 | 9 | 3 | 0 | 2 | 7 | 0 | 8 | .273 | .545 |
| Bats Right | R | .000 | 17 | 0 | 0 | 0 | 0 | 0 | 0 | 8 | .105 | .000 |
| Snyder,Chris | L | .111 | 9 | 1 | 0 | 0 | 0 | 1 | 2 | 2 | .273 | .111 |
| Bats Right | R | .091 | 11 | 1 | 0 | 0 | 0 | 0 | 2 | 5 | .231 | .091 |
| Sogard,Eric | L | .230 | 61 | 14 | 2 | 0 | 1 | 8 | 5 | 13 | .329 | .311 |
| Bats Left | R | .274 | 307 | 84 | 22 | 3 | 1 | 27 | 22 | 38 | .320 | .375 |
| Solano,Donovan | L | .216 | 102 | 22 | 5 | 0 | 0 | 8 | 9 | 15 | .279 | .265 |
| Bats Right | R | .263 | 259 | 68 | 8 | 1 | 3 | 26 | 14 | 42 | .316 | .336 |
| Solano,Jhonatan | L | .150 | 20 | 3 | 2 | 0 | 0 | 2 | 0 | 1 | .150 | .250 |
| Bats Right | R | .143 | 28 | 4 | 0 | 0 | 0 | 0 | 2 | 6 | .200 | .143 |
| Soriano,Alfonso | L | .293 | 191 | 56 | 11 | 0 | 13 | 34 | 17 | 51 | .349 | .555 |
| Bats Right | R | .236 | 390 | 92 | 21 | 1 | 21 | 67 | 19 | 105 | .278 | .456 |
| Soto,Geovany | L | .200 | 60 | 12 | 2 | 0 | 3 | 7 | 6 | 23 | .273 | .383 |
| Bats Right | R | .272 | 103 | 28 | 7 | 0 | 6 | 15 | 14 | 37 | .359 | .515 |
| Span,Denard | L | .223 | 157 | 35 | 4 | 1 | 0 | 9 | 12 | 21 | .278 | .261 |
| Bats Left | R | .298 | 453 | 135 | 24 | 10 | 4 | 38 | 30 | 56 | .344 | .422 |
| Stanton,Giancarlo | L | .278 | 108 | 30 | 7 | 0 | 9 | 18 | 25 | 28 | .414 | .593 |
| Bats Right | R | .240 | 317 | 76 | 19 | 0 | 15 | 44 | 49 | 112 | .348 | .442 |
| Stewart,Chris | L | .188 | 85 | 16 | 2 | 0 | 0 | 11 | 13 | 14 | .291 | .212 |
| Bats Right | R | .220 | 209 | 46 | 4 | 0 | 4 | 14 | 17 | 35 | .294 | .297 |
| Stubbs,Drew | L | .266 | 143 | 38 | 7 | 0 | 2 | 15 | 22 | 45 | .361 | .357 |
| Bats Right | R | .216 | 287 | 62 | 14 | 2 | 8 | 30 | 22 | 96 | .275 | .362 |
| Sucre,Jesus | L | .250 | 8 | 2 | 0 | 0 | 0 | 1 | 0 | 1 | .250 | .250 |
| Bats Right | R | .167 | 18 | 3 | 0 | 0 | 0 | 2 | 2 | 0 | .238 | .167 |
| Suzuki,Ichiro | L | .321 | 159 | 51 | 3 | 2 | 3 | 15 | 3 | 14 | .331 | .421 |
| Bats Left | R | .235 | 361 | 85 | 12 | 1 | 4 | 20 | 23 | 49 | .282 | .307 |

| Batter | vs | Avg | AB | H | 2B | 3B | HR | RBI | BB | SO | OBP | Slg |
|---|---|---|---|---|---|---|---|---|---|---|---|---|
| Suzuki,Kurt | L | .246 | 61 | 15 | 3 | 0 | 1 | 4 | 4 | 6 | .309 | .344 |
| Bats Right | R | .228 | 224 | 51 | 10 | 1 | 4 | 28 | 18 | 29 | .285 | .335 |
| Sweeney,Ryan | L | .313 | 48 | 15 | 2 | 1 | 1 | 5 | 4 | 7 | .365 | .458 |
| Bats Left | R | .250 | 144 | 36 | 11 | 1 | 5 | 14 | 13 | 24 | .310 | .444 |
| Swisher,Nick | L | .295 | 190 | 56 | 11 | 1 | 10 | 29 | 31 | 29 | .397 | .521 |
| Bats Both | R | .220 | 359 | 79 | 16 | 1 | 12 | 34 | 46 | 109 | .310 | .370 |
| Tabata,Jose | L | .250 | 68 | 17 | 5 | 2 | 2 | 8 | 1 | 11 | .271 | .471 |
| Bats Right | R | .292 | 240 | 70 | 12 | 3 | 4 | 25 | 22 | 34 | .361 | .417 |
| Tanaka,Kensuke | L | .000 | 2 | 0 | 0 | 0 | 0 | 0 | 0 | 1 | .000 | .000 |
| Bats Left | R | .286 | 28 | 8 | 0 | 0 | 0 | 2 | 4 | 2 | .375 | .286 |
| Taylor,Michael | L | .091 | 11 | 1 | 0 | 0 | 0 | 0 | 2 | 5 | .231 | .091 |
| Bats Right | R | .000 | 12 | 0 | 0 | 0 | 0 | 0 | 0 | 0 | .000 | .000 |
| Teagarden,Taylor | L | .261 | 23 | 6 | 0 | 0 | 1 | 2 | 0 | 6 | .261 | .391 |
| Bats Right | R | .108 | 37 | 4 | 2 | 0 | 1 | 3 | 1 | 12 | .132 | .243 |
| Teixeira,Mark | L | .278 | 18 | 5 | 1 | 0 | 1 | 4 | 4 | 6 | .435 | .500 |
| Bats Both | R | .086 | 35 | 3 | 0 | 0 | 2 | 8 | 4 | 13 | .175 | .257 |
| Tejada,Miguel | L | .253 | 83 | 21 | 2 | 0 | 2 | 11 | 2 | 12 | .267 | .349 |
| Bats Right | R | .329 | 73 | 24 | 3 | 0 | 1 | 9 | 4 | 13 | .372 | .411 |
| Tejada,Ruben | L | .274 | 62 | 17 | 6 | 0 | 0 | 3 | 7 | 7 | .348 | .371 |
| Bats Right | R | .171 | 146 | 25 | 6 | 0 | 0 | 7 | 8 | 17 | .219 | .212 |
| Tekotte,Blake | L | .250 | 12 | 3 | 1 | 0 | 0 | 0 | 0 | 3 | .250 | .333 |
| Bats Left | R | .211 | 19 | 4 | 0 | 0 | 1 | 2 | 3 | 6 | .333 | .368 |
| Terdoslavich,Joey | L | .294 | 17 | 5 | 1 | 0 | 0 | 1 | 6 | 2 | .478 | .353 |
| Bats Both | R | .194 | 62 | 12 | 3 | 0 | 0 | 3 | 6 | 22 | .261 | .242 |
| Thole,Josh | L | .182 | 22 | 4 | 1 | 0 | 0 | 0 | 2 | 7 | .250 | .227 |
| Bats Left | R | .173 | 98 | 17 | 2 | 1 | 1 | 8 | 10 | 18 | .257 | .245 |
| Thomas,Clete | L | .175 | 80 | 14 | 3 | 0 | 1 | 2 | 12 | 32 | .283 | .250 |
| Bats Left | R | .229 | 210 | 48 | 12 | 0 | 3 | 11 | 18 | 60 | .293 | .329 |
| Torrealba,Yorvit | L | .293 | 41 | 12 | 1 | 0 | 0 | 2 | 5 | 3 | .370 | .317 |
| Bats Right | R | .225 | 138 | 31 | 7 | 0 | 0 | 14 | 8 | 21 | .272 | .275 |
| Torres,Andres | L | .291 | 141 | 41 | 10 | 1 | 0 | 11 | 12 | 23 | .342 | .376 |
| Bats Both | R | .206 | 131 | 27 | 7 | 0 | 2 | 10 | 10 | 38 | .259 | .305 |
| Tracy,Chad | L | .333 | 9 | 3 | 1 | 0 | 0 | 1 | 0 | 3 | .333 | .444 |
| Bats Left | R | .192 | 120 | 23 | 3 | 0 | 4 | 10 | 7 | 22 | .236 | .317 |
| Triunfel,Carlos | L | .143 | 21 | 3 | 0 | 0 | 0 | 1 | 0 | 7 | .182 | .143 |
| Bats Right | R | .130 | 23 | 3 | 1 | 0 | 0 | 1 | 0 | 4 | .125 | .174 |
| Trout,Mike | L | .309 | 152 | 47 | 13 | 0 | 6 | 26 | 37 | 39 | .440 | .513 |
| Bats Right | R | .327 | 437 | 143 | 26 | 9 | 21 | 71 | 73 | 97 | .428 | .572 |
| Trumbo,Mark | L | .265 | 162 | 43 | 11 | 2 | 13 | 33 | 14 | 39 | .324 | .599 |
| Bats Right | R | .223 | 458 | 102 | 19 | 0 | 21 | 67 | 40 | 145 | .283 | .402 |
| Tuiasosopo,Matt | L | .216 | 116 | 25 | 3 | 0 | 5 | 15 | 21 | 38 | .336 | .371 |
| Bats Right | R | .313 | 48 | 15 | 4 | 0 | 2 | 15 | 4 | 19 | .389 | .521 |
| Tulowitzki,Troy | L | .318 | 110 | 35 | 6 | 0 | 4 | 20 | 20 | 19 | .424 | .482 |
| Bats Right | R | .310 | 336 | 104 | 21 | 0 | 21 | 62 | 37 | 66 | .379 | .560 |
| Turner,Justin | L | .272 | 92 | 25 | 6 | 1 | 0 | 8 | 5 | 14 | .309 | .359 |
| Bats Right | R | .287 | 108 | 31 | 7 | 0 | 2 | 8 | 6 | 20 | .328 | .407 |
| Uggla,Dan | L | .146 | 103 | 15 | 3 | 1 | 4 | 12 | 21 | 48 | .288 | .311 |
| Bats Right | R | .188 | 345 | 65 | 7 | 2 | 18 | 43 | 56 | 123 | .316 | .377 |
| Upton,B.J. | L | .157 | 108 | 17 | 4 | 0 | 1 | 4 | 9 | 36 | .227 | .222 |
| Bats Right | R | .194 | 283 | 55 | 10 | 0 | 8 | 22 | 35 | 115 | .283 | .314 |
| Upton,Justin | L | .268 | 127 | 34 | 8 | 0 | 10 | 22 | 36 | 36 | .427 | .567 |
| Bats Right | R | .262 | 431 | 113 | 19 | 2 | 17 | 48 | 39 | 125 | .328 | .434 |
| Uribe,Juan | L | .242 | 95 | 23 | 4 | 0 | 6 | 13 | 9 | 29 | .308 | .474 |
| Bats Right | R | .290 | 293 | 85 | 18 | 2 | 6 | 37 | 21 | 52 | .339 | .427 |
| Urrutia,Henry | L | .143 | 7 | 1 | 0 | 0 | 0 | 1 | 0 | 0 | .143 | .143 |
| Bats Left | R | .294 | 51 | 15 | 0 | 1 | 0 | 1 | 0 | 11 | .294 | .333 |
| Utley,Chase | L | .245 | 151 | 37 | 8 | 1 | 6 | 19 | 16 | 25 | .324 | .430 |
| Bats Left | R | .302 | 325 | 98 | 17 | 5 | 12 | 50 | 29 | 54 | .360 | .495 |
| Valaika,Chris | L | .280 | 25 | 7 | 3 | 0 | 1 | 2 | 0 | 6 | .308 | .520 |
| Bats Right | R | .179 | 39 | 7 | 2 | 0 | 0 | 7 | 3 | 10 | .233 | .231 |
| Valbuena,Luis | L | .226 | 31 | 7 | 1 | 1 | 0 | 6 | 4 | 10 | .324 | .323 |
| Bats Left | R | .217 | 300 | 65 | 14 | 0 | 12 | 31 | 49 | 53 | .331 | .383 |
| Valdespin,Jordany | L | .105 | 19 | 2 | 0 | 1 | 0 | 1 | 0 | 5 | .150 | .211 |
| Bats Left | R | .202 | 114 | 23 | 3 | 0 | 4 | 15 | 8 | 23 | .266 | .333 |
| Valencia,Danny | L | .371 | 97 | 36 | 14 | 0 | 4 | 13 | 4 | 15 | .392 | .639 |
| Bats Right | R | .203 | 64 | 13 | 0 | 1 | 4 | 10 | 4 | 18 | .250 | .422 |
| Van Slyke,Scott | L | .234 | 64 | 15 | 3 | 0 | 3 | 9 | 11 | 17 | .342 | .422 |
| Bats Right | R | .246 | 65 | 16 | 5 | 0 | 4 | 10 | 9 | 20 | .342 | .508 |
| Venable,Will | L | .276 | 105 | 29 | 6 | 1 | 6 | 15 | 4 | 26 | .309 | .524 |
| Bats Left | R | .266 | 376 | 100 | 16 | 7 | 16 | 38 | 25 | 92 | .313 | .473 |
| Viciedo,Dayan | L | .257 | 109 | 28 | 6 | 1 | 3 | 14 | 6 | 22 | .297 | .413 |
| Bats Right | R | .268 | 332 | 89 | 17 | 2 | 11 | 42 | 18 | 76 | .307 | .431 |
| Victorino,Shane | L | .314 | 169 | 53 | 12 | 0 | 6 | 27 | 9 | 24 | .370 | .491 |
| Bats Both | R | .282 | 308 | 87 | 14 | 2 | 9 | 34 | 16 | 51 | .340 | .429 |
| Villar,Jonathan | L | .250 | 56 | 14 | 2 | 0 | 1 | 1 | 7 | 16 | .333 | .339 |
| Bats Both | R | .240 | 154 | 37 | 7 | 2 | 0 | 7 | 17 | 55 | .316 | .312 |

# Batters vs. Left-Handed and Right-Handed Pitchers

| Batter | vs | Avg | AB | H | 2B | 3B | HR | RBI | BB | SO | OBP | Slg |
|---|---|---|---|---|---|---|---|---|---|---|---|---|
| Vogt,Stephen | L | .222 | 18 | 4 | 1 | 0 | 1 | 1 | 0 | 4 | .222 | .444 |
| Bats Left | R | .256 | 117 | 30 | 5 | 1 | 3 | 15 | 9 | 24 | .305 | .393 |
| Votto,Joey | L | .251 | 199 | 50 | 10 | 1 | 9 | 20 | 37 | 56 | .377 | .447 |
| Bats Left | R | .332 | 382 | 127 | 20 | 2 | 15 | 53 | 98 | 82 | .464 | .513 |
| Walker,Neil | L | .225 | 80 | 18 | 1 | 0 | 0 | 7 | 6 | 15 | .281 | .238 |
| Bats Both | R | .256 | 398 | 102 | 23 | 4 | 16 | 46 | 44 | 70 | .350 | .455 |
| Wallace,Brett | L | .143 | 56 | 8 | 3 | 0 | 1 | 5 | 1 | 29 | .200 | .250 |
| Bats Left | R | .243 | 206 | 50 | 11 | 1 | 12 | 31 | 17 | 75 | .307 | .481 |
| Watkins,Logan | L | .000 | 4 | 0 | 0 | 0 | 0 | 0 | 0 | 2 | .000 | .000 |
| Bats Left | R | .235 | 34 | 8 | 1 | 0 | 0 | 0 | 3 | 12 | .297 | .265 |
| Weeks,Rickie | L | .226 | 106 | 24 | 5 | 1 | 3 | 8 | 15 | 30 | .328 | .377 |
| Bats Right | R | .201 | 244 | 49 | 15 | 0 | 7 | 16 | 25 | 75 | .296 | .348 |
| Wells,Casper | L | .143 | 42 | 6 | 2 | 0 | 0 | 0 | 2 | 10 | .182 | .190 |
| Bats Right | R | .113 | 53 | 6 | 0 | 0 | 0 | 1 | 5 | 21 | .190 | .113 |
| Wells,Vernon | L | .269 | 182 | 49 | 8 | 0 | 4 | 18 | 14 | 32 | .318 | .379 |
| Bats Right | R | .207 | 242 | 50 | 8 | 0 | 7 | 32 | 16 | 41 | .254 | .326 |
| Werth,Jayson | L | .350 | 103 | 36 | 3 | 0 | 9 | 22 | 20 | 22 | .452 | .641 |
| Bats Right | R | .309 | 359 | 111 | 21 | 0 | 16 | 60 | 40 | 79 | .382 | .501 |
| Wheeler,Ryan | L | .000 | 4 | 0 | 0 | 0 | 0 | 0 | 0 | 2 | .000 | .000 |
| Bats Left | R | .243 | 37 | 9 | 2 | 0 | 0 | 7 | 1 | 8 | .263 | .297 |
| Wieters,Matt | L | .282 | 163 | 46 | 10 | 0 | 11 | 27 | 12 | 39 | .326 | .546 |
| Bats Both | R | .214 | 360 | 77 | 19 | 0 | 11 | 52 | 31 | 65 | .270 | .358 |
| Wigginton,Ty | L | .115 | 26 | 3 | 2 | 0 | 0 | 0 | 1 | 11 | .179 | .192 |
| Bats Right | R | .194 | 31 | 6 | 0 | 0 | 0 | 3 | 4 | 8 | .286 | .194 |
| Willingham,Josh | L | .219 | 96 | 21 | 7 | 0 | 2 | 6 | 17 | 30 | .342 | .354 |
| Bats Right | R | .205 | 293 | 60 | 13 | 0 | 12 | 42 | 49 | 98 | .342 | .372 |
| Wilson,Josh | L | .195 | 41 | 8 | 0 | 1 | 0 | 1 | 4 | 9 | .267 | .244 |
| Bats Right | R | .211 | 19 | 4 | 1 | 0 | 1 | 3 | 1 | 8 | .250 | .421 |
| Wise,DeWayne | L | .200 | 10 | 2 | 1 | 0 | 0 | 0 | 0 | 2 | .200 | .300 |
| Bats Left | R | .241 | 54 | 13 | 2 | 0 | 1 | 3 | 2 | 12 | .268 | .333 |
| Wong,Kolten | L | .000 | 7 | 0 | 0 | 0 | 0 | 0 | 0 | 0 | .000 | .000 |
| Bats Left | R | .173 | 52 | 9 | 1 | 0 | 0 | 0 | 3 | 12 | .218 | .192 |
| Wright,David | L | .336 | 119 | 40 | 10 | 2 | 6 | 15 | 29 | 15 | .467 | .605 |
| Bats Right | R | .296 | 311 | 92 | 13 | 4 | 12 | 43 | 26 | 64 | .357 | .479 |
| Yelich,Christian | L | .165 | 91 | 15 | 3 | 0 | 1 | 5 | 9 | 27 | .245 | .231 |
| Bats Left | R | .362 | 149 | 54 | 9 | 1 | 3 | 11 | 22 | 39 | .444 | .497 |
| Youkilis,Kevin | L | .086 | 35 | 3 | 1 | 0 | 0 | 1 | 4 | 12 | .200 | .114 |
| Bats Right | R | .286 | 70 | 20 | 6 | 0 | 2 | 7 | 4 | 19 | .359 | .457 |
| Young,Chris | L | .209 | 148 | 31 | 7 | 1 | 6 | 17 | 24 | 39 | .320 | .392 |
| Bats Right | R | .193 | 187 | 36 | 11 | 2 | 6 | 23 | 12 | 54 | .245 | .369 |
| Young,Delmon | L | .261 | 88 | 23 | 4 | 0 | 1 | 9 | 11 | 18 | .343 | .341 |
| Bats Right | R | .260 | 246 | 64 | 12 | 0 | 10 | 29 | 9 | 60 | .293 | .431 |
| Young,Eric | L | .259 | 170 | 44 | 11 | 0 | 0 | 5 | 14 | 31 | .319 | .324 |
| Bats Both | R | .244 | 369 | 90 | 16 | 7 | 2 | 27 | 32 | 69 | .305 | .341 |
| Young,Michael | L | .254 | 138 | 35 | 8 | 3 | 2 | 12 | 16 | 18 | .331 | .399 |
| Bats Right | R | .289 | 381 | 110 | 18 | 2 | 6 | 34 | 27 | 65 | .336 | .394 |
| Zimmerman,Ryan | L | .259 | 147 | 38 | 9 | 1 | 7 | 21 | 25 | 25 | .374 | .476 |
| Bats Right | R | .280 | 421 | 118 | 17 | 1 | 19 | 58 | 35 | 108 | .333 | .461 |
| Zobrist,Ben | L | .250 | 204 | 51 | 14 | 0 | 1 | 23 | 17 | 30 | .310 | .333 |
| Bats Both | R | .287 | 408 | 117 | 22 | 3 | 11 | 48 | 55 | 61 | .376 | .436 |
| Zunino,Mike | L | .217 | 46 | 10 | 1 | 0 | 2 | 4 | 4 | 12 | .280 | .370 |
| Bats Right | R | .213 | 127 | 27 | 4 | 0 | 3 | 10 | 12 | 37 | .294 | .315 |
| AL | L | .256 | - | - | - | - | - | - | - | - | .321 | .400 |
| | R | .256 | - | - | - | - | - | - | - | - | .320 | .406 |
| NL | L | .248 | - | - | - | - | - | - | - | - | .312 | .385 |
| | R | .252 | - | - | - | - | - | - | - | - | .316 | .390 |
| MLB | L | .252 | - | - | - | - | - | - | - | - | .317 | .393 |
| | R | .254 | - | - | - | - | - | - | - | - | .318 | .398 |

# Pitchers vs. Left-Handed and Right-Handed Batters

| Pitcher | vs | Avg | AB | H | 2B | 3B | HR | RBI | BB | SO | OBP | Slg |
|---|---|---|---|---|---|---|---|---|---|---|---|---|
| Aardsma,David | L | .218 | 55 | 12 | 2 | 0 | 1 | 3 | 8 | 16 | .317 | .309 |
| Throws Right | R | .278 | 97 | 27 | 6 | 0 | 6 | 12 | 11 | 20 | .372 | .526 |
| Abad,Fernando | L | .306 | 62 | 19 | 3 | 0 | 2 | 10 | 3 | 17 | .338 | .452 |
| Throws Left | R | .247 | 93 | 23 | 3 | 0 | 1 | 9 | 7 | 15 | .307 | .312 |
| Aceves,Alfredo | L | .284 | 95 | 27 | 6 | 1 | 5 | 15 | 14 | 16 | .376 | .526 |
| Throws Right | R | .294 | 51 | 15 | 4 | 0 | 3 | 7 | 8 | 8 | .383 | .549 |
| Adams,Mike | L | .257 | 35 | 9 | 0 | 0 | 3 | 5 | 5 | 8 | .350 | .514 |
| Throws Right | R | .233 | 60 | 14 | 3 | 0 | 2 | 6 | 6 | 15 | .313 | .383 |
| Affeldt,Jeremy | L | .196 | 56 | 11 | 2 | 0 | 0 | 7 | 5 | 8 | .292 | .232 |
| Throws Left | R | .250 | 64 | 16 | 2 | 0 | 2 | 10 | 12 | 13 | .377 | .375 |
| Albers,Andrew | L | .290 | 62 | 18 | 3 | 0 | 1 | 5 | 1 | 4 | .302 | .387 |
| Throws Left | R | .264 | 174 | 46 | 10 | 0 | 5 | 20 | 6 | 21 | .293 | .408 |
| Albers,Matt | L | .262 | 103 | 27 | 4 | 1 | 1 | 14 | 11 | 9 | .333 | .350 |
| Throws Right | R | .226 | 133 | 30 | 4 | 0 | 1 | 21 | 12 | 26 | .295 | .278 |
| Alburquerque,Al | L | .228 | 79 | 18 | 2 | 0 | 2 | 15 | 13 | 31 | .333 | .329 |
| Throws Right | R | .202 | 104 | 21 | 5 | 0 | 3 | 14 | 21 | 39 | .346 | .337 |
| Allen,Cody | L | .228 | 123 | 28 | 6 | 1 | 5 | 15 | 9 | 47 | .276 | .415 |
| Throws Right | R | .238 | 143 | 34 | 6 | 2 | 2 | 24 | 17 | 41 | .319 | .350 |
| Alvarez,Henderson | L | .269 | 186 | 50 | 16 | 3 | 2 | 26 | 15 | 22 | .333 | .419 |
| Throws Right | R | .206 | 194 | 40 | 11 | 0 | 0 | 12 | 12 | 35 | .261 | .263 |
| Alvarez,Jose | L | .265 | 49 | 13 | 2 | 1 | 3 | 8 | 4 | 13 | .321 | .531 |
| Throws Left | R | .287 | 101 | 29 | 6 | 2 | 4 | 14 | 12 | 18 | .368 | .505 |
| Ambriz,Hector | L | .373 | 59 | 22 | 4 | 0 | 2 | 15 | 5 | 10 | .409 | .542 |
| Throws Right | R | .295 | 95 | 28 | 4 | 0 | 6 | 19 | 9 | 17 | .362 | .526 |
| Anderson,Brett | L | .283 | 46 | 13 | 2 | 1 | 2 | 9 | 5 | 15 | .353 | .500 |
| Throws Left | R | .288 | 132 | 38 | 7 | 0 | 3 | 18 | 16 | 31 | .365 | .409 |
| Archer,Chris | L | .261 | 280 | 73 | 14 | 3 | 13 | 38 | 25 | 64 | .329 | .471 |
| Throws Right | R | .176 | 193 | 34 | 2 | 0 | 2 | 10 | 13 | 37 | .237 | .218 |
| Arrieta,Jake | L | .187 | 139 | 26 | 10 | 2 | 3 | 16 | 25 | 30 | .311 | .353 |
| Throws Right | R | .246 | 134 | 33 | 5 | 1 | 6 | 20 | 16 | 30 | .342 | .433 |
| Arroyo,Bronson | L | .295 | 397 | 117 | 22 | 1 | 23 | 49 | 20 | 51 | .327 | .529 |
| Throws Right | R | .219 | 374 | 82 | 18 | 2 | 9 | 35 | 14 | 73 | .257 | .350 |
| Atchison,Scott | L | .254 | 63 | 16 | 4 | 0 | 1 | 11 | 8 | 13 | .338 | .365 |
| Throws Right | R | .254 | 114 | 29 | 1 | 0 | 3 | 21 | 4 | 15 | .273 | .342 |
| Aumont,Phillippe | L | .433 | 30 | 13 | 3 | 0 | 0 | 4 | 4 | 7 | .514 | .533 |
| Throws Right | R | .229 | 48 | 11 | 2 | 1 | 0 | 6 | 9 | 12 | .367 | .313 |
| Avilan,Luis | L | .144 | 104 | 15 | 2 | 0 | 0 | 4 | 7 | 20 | .219 | .163 |
| Throws Left | R | .202 | 124 | 25 | 5 | 0 | 1 | 7 | 15 | 18 | .291 | .266 |
| Axelrod,Dylan | L | .302 | 328 | 99 | 15 | 1 | 18 | 40 | 28 | 43 | .358 | .518 |
| Throws Right | R | .345 | 206 | 71 | 14 | 2 | 6 | 39 | 15 | 30 | .394 | .519 |
| Axford,John | L | .289 | 114 | 33 | 4 | 0 | 5 | 12 | 16 | 31 | .382 | .456 |
| Throws Right | R | .282 | 142 | 40 | 6 | 0 | 5 | 21 | 10 | 34 | .331 | .430 |
| Ayala,Luis | L | .295 | 44 | 13 | 1 | 0 | 1 | 3 | 7 | 5 | .392 | .386 |
| Throws Right | R | .294 | 85 | 25 | 5 | 0 | 1 | 7 | 6 | 17 | .341 | .388 |
| Badenhop,Burke | L | .338 | 80 | 27 | 4 | 1 | 3 | 13 | 8 | 6 | .393 | .525 |
| Throws Right | R | .229 | 153 | 35 | 4 | 1 | 3 | 25 | 4 | 36 | .247 | .327 |
| Bailey,Andrew | L | .185 | 54 | 10 | 1 | 0 | 3 | 6 | 8 | 22 | .290 | .370 |
| Throws Right | R | .265 | 49 | 13 | 2 | 0 | 4 | 5 | 4 | 17 | .321 | .551 |
| Bailey,Homer | L | .264 | 382 | 101 | 23 | 2 | 11 | 42 | 31 | 93 | .325 | .421 |
| Throws Right | R | .205 | 391 | 80 | 15 | 1 | 9 | 38 | 23 | 106 | .258 | .317 |
| Baker,Scott | L | .200 | 20 | 4 | 2 | 0 | 1 | 4 | 2 | 2 | .273 | .450 |
| Throws Right | R | .156 | 32 | 5 | 1 | 0 | 2 | 2 | 2 | 4 | .206 | .375 |
| Balfour,Grant | L | .192 | 125 | 24 | 2 | 0 | 3 | 10 | 13 | 41 | .268 | .280 |
| Throws Right | R | .222 | 108 | 24 | 4 | 0 | 4 | 14 | 14 | 31 | .311 | .370 |
| Barnes,Scott | L | .200 | 15 | 3 | 0 | 0 | 3 | 6 | 2 | 4 | .333 | .800 |
| Throws Left | R | .278 | 18 | 5 | 2 | 0 | 0 | 2 | 1 | 6 | .350 | .389 |
| Bass,Anthony | L | .299 | 77 | 23 | 6 | 1 | 2 | 20 | 13 | 11 | .400 | .481 |
| Throws Right | R | .295 | 95 | 28 | 4 | 2 | 2 | 17 | 7 | 20 | .343 | .442 |
| Bastardo,Antonio | L | .194 | 62 | 12 | 2 | 0 | 2 | 4 | 7 | 18 | .275 | .323 |
| Throws Left | R | .233 | 90 | 21 | 6 | 1 | 0 | 6 | 14 | 29 | .340 | .322 |
| Bauer,Trevor | L | .207 | 29 | 6 | 2 | 0 | 2 | 4 | 11 | 3 | .425 | .483 |
| Throws Right | R | .265 | 34 | 9 | 2 | 0 | 1 | 6 | 5 | 8 | .366 | .412 |
| Beachy,Brandon | L | .286 | 49 | 14 | 4 | 0 | 1 | 6 | 2 | 11 | .308 | .429 |
| Throws Right | R | .203 | 64 | 13 | 2 | 1 | 4 | 8 | 2 | 12 | .227 | .453 |
| Beato,Pedro | L | .158 | 19 | 3 | 0 | 0 | 0 | 0 | 2 | 4 | .238 | .158 |
| Throws Right | R | .375 | 24 | 9 | 1 | 0 | 1 | 4 | 0 | 1 | .400 | .542 |
| Beavan,Blake | L | .279 | 68 | 19 | 3 | 0 | 4 | 11 | 8 | 15 | .364 | .500 |
| Throws Right | R | .287 | 94 | 27 | 4 | 0 | 4 | 16 | 0 | 12 | .281 | .457 |
| Beckett,Josh | L | .318 | 85 | 27 | 6 | 0 | 3 | 11 | 11 | 19 | .402 | .494 |
| Throws Right | R | .261 | 88 | 23 | 6 | 0 | 5 | 19 | 4 | 22 | .290 | .500 |
| Bedard,Erik | L | .309 | 136 | 42 | 8 | 2 | 2 | 13 | 17 | 27 | .391 | .441 |
| Throws Left | R | .244 | 438 | 107 | 23 | 3 | 16 | 57 | 58 | 111 | .335 | .420 |
| Belisario,Ronald | L | .305 | 82 | 25 | 6 | 1 | 0 | 9 | 14 | 14 | .408 | .402 |
| Throws Right | R | .260 | 181 | 47 | 9 | 0 | 3 | 21 | 14 | 35 | .325 | .359 |
| Belisle,Matt | L | .283 | 113 | 32 | 11 | 1 | 1 | 12 | 7 | 23 | .325 | .425 |
| Throws Right | R | .259 | 170 | 44 | 7 | 0 | 5 | 25 | 8 | 39 | .291 | .388 |

| Pitcher | vs | Avg | AB | H | 2B | 3B | HR | RBI | BB | SO | OBP | Slg |
|---|---|---|---|---|---|---|---|---|---|---|---|---|
| Bell,Heath | L | .255 | 106 | 27 | 9 | 0 | 3 | 12 | 8 | 25 | .307 | .425 |
| Throws Right | R | .296 | 159 | 47 | 7 | 0 | 9 | 26 | 8 | 47 | .339 | .509 |
| Benoit,Joaquin | L | .194 | 139 | 27 | 7 | 0 | 1 | 4 | 12 | 44 | .258 | .266 |
| Throws Right | R | .202 | 99 | 20 | 4 | 0 | 4 | 13 | 10 | 29 | .282 | .364 |
| Betances,Dellin | L | .571 | 7 | 4 | 1 | 0 | 0 | 1 | 1 | 2 | .625 | .714 |
| Throws Right | R | .294 | 17 | 5 | 0 | 0 | 1 | 5 | 1 | 8 | .333 | .471 |
| Betancourt,Rafael | L | .267 | 45 | 12 | 1 | 0 | 2 | 6 | 9 | 11 | .389 | .422 |
| Throws Right | R | .222 | 63 | 14 | 6 | 0 | 0 | 7 | 2 | 16 | .242 | .317 |
| Bettis,Chad | L | .275 | 91 | 25 | 7 | 0 | 3 | 12 | 13 | 16 | .362 | .451 |
| Throws Right | R | .330 | 91 | 30 | 4 | 2 | 3 | 17 | 7 | 14 | .390 | .516 |
| Billingsley,Chad | L | .261 | 23 | 6 | 1 | 0 | 1 | 3 | 5 | 5 | .393 | .435 |
| Throws Right | R | .316 | 19 | 6 | 1 | 0 | 0 | 1 | 0 | 1 | .316 | .368 |
| Black,Vic | L | .185 | 27 | 5 | 0 | 0 | 1 | 2 | 4 | 7 | .313 | .296 |
| Throws Right | R | .300 | 40 | 12 | 4 | 0 | 0 | 9 | 2 | 8 | .341 | .400 |
| Blackley,Travis | L | .253 | 75 | 19 | 1 | 0 | 4 | 11 | 4 | 16 | .296 | .427 |
| Throws Left | R | .245 | 110 | 27 | 5 | 0 | 8 | 18 | 18 | 24 | .349 | .509 |
| Blanton,Joe | L | .300 | 310 | 93 | 19 | 2 | 13 | 42 | 21 | 64 | .344 | .500 |
| Throws Right | R | .339 | 257 | 87 | 18 | 1 | 16 | 47 | 13 | 44 | .373 | .603 |
| Blazek,Michael | L | .192 | 26 | 5 | 1 | 0 | 2 | 8 | 8 | 7 | .371 | .462 |
| Throws Right | R | .262 | 42 | 11 | 1 | 0 | 1 | 4 | 5 | 7 | .354 | .357 |
| Blevins,Jerry | L | .253 | 95 | 24 | 3 | 0 | 5 | 20 | 5 | 28 | .299 | .442 |
| Throws Left | R | .190 | 121 | 23 | 7 | 1 | 2 | 12 | 12 | 24 | .267 | .314 |
| Boggs,Mitchell | L | .262 | 42 | 11 | 1 | 0 | 1 | 3 | 12 | 5 | .436 | .357 |
| Throws Right | R | .333 | 51 | 17 | 4 | 1 | 4 | 15 | 8 | 11 | .429 | .686 |
| Bonderman,Jeremy | L | .331 | 121 | 40 | 11 | 1 | 4 | 19 | 15 | 11 | .406 | .537 |
| Throws Right | R | .194 | 93 | 18 | 8 | 0 | 3 | 12 | 12 | 21 | .290 | .376 |
| Boshers,Buddy | L | .286 | 35 | 10 | 2 | 0 | 0 | 6 | 1 | 8 | .324 | .343 |
| Throws Left | R | .158 | 19 | 3 | 1 | 0 | 0 | 1 | 7 | 5 | .385 | .211 |
| Bowden,Michael | L | .233 | 60 | 14 | 4 | 0 | 0 | 11 | 10 | 10 | .356 | .300 |
| Throws Right | R | .243 | 74 | 18 | 5 | 1 | 3 | 15 | 5 | 13 | .296 | .459 |
| Boxberger,Brad | L | .182 | 33 | 6 | 0 | 0 | 1 | 4 | 2 | 14 | .222 | .273 |
| Throws Right | R | .302 | 43 | 13 | 3 | 0 | 2 | 5 | 11 | 10 | .436 | .512 |
| Brach,Brad | L | .232 | 56 | 13 | 1 | 0 | 1 | 5 | 10 | 13 | .343 | .304 |
| Throws Right | R | .365 | 63 | 23 | 5 | 0 | 2 | 14 | 9 | 18 | .432 | .540 |
| Brasier,Ryan | L | .333 | 12 | 4 | 0 | 0 | 1 | 3 | 2 | 1 | .400 | .583 |
| Throws Right | R | .167 | 18 | 3 | 0 | 0 | 0 | 0 | 2 | 6 | .250 | .167 |
| Breslow,Craig | L | .253 | 95 | 24 | 11 | 0 | 1 | 12 | 6 | 16 | .304 | .400 |
| Throws Left | R | .208 | 120 | 25 | 5 | 0 | 2 | 9 | 12 | 17 | .281 | .300 |
| Brewer,Charles | L | .429 | 7 | 3 | 2 | 0 | 0 | 1 | 2 | 1 | .556 | .714 |
| Throws Right | R | .278 | 18 | 5 | 0 | 0 | 0 | 1 | 0 | 4 | .278 | .278 |
| Britton,Drake | L | .278 | 36 | 10 | 1 | 1 | 0 | 8 | 5 | 12 | .349 | .361 |
| Throws Left | R | .282 | 39 | 11 | 2 | 0 | 1 | 5 | 2 | 5 | .317 | .410 |
| Britton,Zach | L | .327 | 49 | 16 | 1 | 1 | 1 | 8 | 5 | 7 | .400 | .449 |
| Throws Left | R | .319 | 113 | 36 | 6 | 0 | 3 | 16 | 12 | 11 | .381 | .451 |
| Brothers,Rex | L | .162 | 74 | 12 | 1 | 0 | 0 | 1 | 13 | 27 | .287 | .176 |
| Throws Left | R | .229 | 170 | 39 | 8 | 0 | 5 | 19 | 23 | 49 | .321 | .365 |
| Broxton,Jonathan | L | .269 | 52 | 14 | 2 | 0 | 2 | 6 | 6 | 13 | .356 | .423 |
| Throws Right | R | .210 | 62 | 13 | 3 | 0 | 2 | 9 | 6 | 12 | .301 | .355 |
| Buchholz,Clay | L | .187 | 209 | 39 | 9 | 0 | 3 | 11 | 22 | 55 | .263 | .273 |
| Throws Right | R | .216 | 167 | 36 | 6 | 1 | 1 | 10 | 14 | 41 | .279 | .281 |
| Buckner,Billy | L | .265 | 34 | 9 | 2 | 0 | 2 | 7 | 3 | 5 | .333 | .500 |
| Throws Right | R | .276 | 29 | 8 | 1 | 0 | 3 | 3 | 4 | 2 | .364 | .621 |
| Buehrle,Mark | L | .256 | 203 | 52 | 9 | 1 | 7 | 27 | 11 | 33 | .311 | .414 |
| Throws Left | R | .283 | 604 | 171 | 41 | 0 | 17 | 59 | 40 | 106 | .329 | .435 |
| Bueno,Francisley | L | .143 | 14 | 2 | 1 | 0 | 0 | 0 | 0 | 4 | .143 | .214 |
| Throws Left | R | .143 | 14 | 2 | 0 | 0 | 0 | 0 | 2 | 1 | .250 | .143 |
| Bumgarner,Madison | L | .161 | 161 | 26 | 5 | 0 | 5 | 10 | 6 | 62 | .201 | .286 |
| Throws Left | R | .215 | 559 | 120 | 21 | 2 | 10 | 44 | 56 | 137 | .289 | .313 |
| Burgos,Hiram | L | .339 | 56 | 19 | 5 | 0 | 4 | 13 | 7 | 9 | .422 | .643 |
| Throws Right | R | .284 | 67 | 19 | 4 | 0 | 1 | 10 | 4 | 9 | .324 | .388 |
| Burke,Greg | L | .319 | 47 | 15 | 4 | 1 | 0 | 3 | 7 | 6 | .407 | .447 |
| Throws Right | R | .308 | 91 | 28 | 6 | 1 | 3 | 23 | 8 | 22 | .364 | .495 |
| Burnett,A.J. | L | .263 | 339 | 89 | 19 | 3 | 4 | 35 | 45 | 89 | .363 | .372 |
| Throws Right | R | .203 | 375 | 76 | 16 | 0 | 7 | 34 | 22 | 120 | .246 | .301 |
| Burnett,Sean | L | .286 | 14 | 4 | 0 | 0 | 0 | 0 | 2 | 4 | .375 | .286 |
| Throws Left | R | .250 | 20 | 5 | 0 | 0 | 1 | 4 | 2 | 3 | .318 | .400 |
| Burns,Cory | L | .286 | 21 | 6 | 1 | 0 | 1 | 4 | 6 | 1 | .464 | .476 |
| Throws Right | R | .240 | 25 | 6 | 2 | 0 | 0 | 1 | 1 | 4 | .269 | .320 |
| Burton,Jared | L | .256 | 121 | 31 | 9 | 0 | 2 | 13 | 13 | 30 | .333 | .380 |
| Throws Right | R | .229 | 131 | 30 | 6 | 0 | 4 | 12 | 9 | 31 | .299 | .366 |
| Butler,Keith | L | .212 | 33 | 7 | 1 | 1 | 0 | 6 | 6 | 8 | .333 | .303 |
| Throws Right | R | .154 | 39 | 6 | 4 | 0 | 0 | 2 | 5 | 8 | .261 | .256 |
| Byrdak,Tim | L | .273 | 11 | 3 | 2 | 0 | 0 | 0 | 1 | 2 | .333 | .455 |
| Throws Left | R | .250 | 8 | 2 | 0 | 0 | 2 | 6 | 1 | 1 | .333 | 1.000 |
| Cabrera,Alberto | L | .375 | 8 | 3 | 2 | 0 | 0 | 0 | 0 | 0 | .444 | .625 |
| Throws Right | R | .250 | 16 | 4 | 3 | 0 | 0 | 3 | 5 | 4 | .429 | .438 |

# Pitchers vs. Left-Handed and Right-Handed Batters

| Pitcher | vs | Avg | AB | H | 2B | 3B | HR | RBI | BB | SO | OBP | Slg |
|---|---|---|---|---|---|---|---|---|---|---|---|---|
| Cahill,Trevor | L | .275 | 287 | 79 | 15 | 3 | 7 | 31 | 29 | 51 | .348 | .422 |
| Throws Right | R | .246 | 260 | 64 | 12 | 3 | 6 | 32 | 36 | 51 | .334 | .385 |
| Cain,Matt | L | .215 | 303 | 65 | 17 | 3 | 6 | 23 | 32 | 74 | .294 | .350 |
| Throws Right | R | .239 | 389 | 93 | 15 | 2 | 17 | 54 | 23 | 84 | .285 | .419 |
| Caminero,Arquimedes | L | .300 | 20 | 6 | 0 | 0 | 1 | 1 | 3 | 4 | .391 | .450 |
| Throws Right | R | .143 | 28 | 4 | 0 | 0 | 1 | 3 | 0 | 8 | .172 | .250 |
| Camp,Shawn | L | .385 | 39 | 15 | 1 | 1 | 4 | 10 | 3 | 4 | .419 | .769 |
| Throws Right | R | .345 | 55 | 19 | 4 | 0 | 3 | 11 | 6 | 9 | .397 | .582 |
| Capps,Carter | L | .323 | 96 | 31 | 7 | 0 | 7 | 15 | 15 | 20 | .414 | .615 |
| Throws Right | R | .288 | 146 | 42 | 8 | 0 | 5 | 17 | 8 | 46 | .331 | .445 |
| Capuano,Chris | L | .248 | 113 | 28 | 5 | 0 | 0 | 9 | 4 | 20 | .274 | .292 |
| Throws Left | R | .312 | 311 | 97 | 24 | 2 | 11 | 45 | 20 | 61 | .350 | .508 |
| Carpenter,David | L | .224 | 85 | 19 | 3 | 0 | 2 | 9 | 12 | 26 | .313 | .329 |
| Throws Right | R | .183 | 142 | 26 | 3 | 0 | 3 | 13 | 8 | 48 | .239 | .268 |
| Carrasco,Carlos | L | .351 | 97 | 34 | 11 | 0 | 3 | 19 | 13 | 10 | .423 | .557 |
| Throws Right | R | .309 | 97 | 30 | 4 | 1 | 1 | 12 | 5 | 20 | .343 | .402 |
| Carson,Robert | L | .265 | 34 | 9 | 0 | 0 | 3 | 12 | 2 | 2 | .297 | .529 |
| Throws Left | R | .273 | 44 | 12 | 2 | 0 | 6 | 9 | 5 | 6 | .360 | .727 |
| Cashner,Andrew | L | .251 | 315 | 79 | 15 | 3 | 8 | 32 | 28 | 65 | .309 | .394 |
| Throws Right | R | .217 | 332 | 72 | 17 | 1 | 4 | 23 | 19 | 63 | .268 | .310 |
| Casilla,Santiago | L | .217 | 69 | 15 | 6 | 0 | 1 | 8 | 9 | 24 | .304 | .348 |
| Throws Right | R | .224 | 107 | 24 | 3 | 0 | 1 | 5 | 16 | 14 | .331 | .280 |
| Castro,Simon | L | .222 | 9 | 2 | 0 | 0 | 1 | 1 | 1 | 1 | .300 | .556 |
| Throws Right | R | .214 | 14 | 3 | 0 | 0 | 0 | 1 | 2 | 5 | .353 | .214 |
| Cecil,Brett | L | .191 | 115 | 22 | 1 | 2 | 0 | 10 | 4 | 35 | .223 | .235 |
| Throws Left | R | .212 | 104 | 22 | 7 | 0 | 4 | 12 | 19 | 35 | .341 | .394 |
| Cedeno,Xavier | L | .231 | 26 | 6 | 1 | 0 | 0 | 4 | 2 | 8 | .333 | .269 |
| Throws Left | R | .391 | 23 | 9 | 1 | 1 | 0 | 5 | 6 | 1 | .517 | .522 |
| Chacin,Jhoulys | L | .275 | 356 | 98 | 25 | 4 | 3 | 38 | 31 | 46 | .329 | .393 |
| Throws Right | R | .233 | 386 | 90 | 20 | 2 | 8 | 38 | 30 | 80 | .292 | .358 |
| Chamberlain,Joba | L | .257 | 74 | 19 | 2 | 0 | 2 | 14 | 16 | 13 | .391 | .365 |
| Throws Right | R | .295 | 95 | 28 | 3 | 0 | 6 | 17 | 10 | 25 | .362 | .516 |
| Chapman,Aroldis | L | .137 | 51 | 7 | 0 | 0 | 0 | 3 | 5 | 29 | .241 | .137 |
| Throws Left | R | .172 | 174 | 30 | 2 | 1 | 7 | 16 | 24 | 83 | .276 | .316 |
| Chapman,Kevin | L | .167 | 36 | 6 | 1 | 0 | 0 | 2 | 5 | 10 | .268 | .194 |
| Throws Left | R | .200 | 35 | 7 | 2 | 0 | 1 | 5 | 8 | 5 | .364 | .343 |
| Chatwood,Tyler | L | .273 | 187 | 51 | 8 | 0 | 4 | 21 | 22 | 25 | .349 | .380 |
| Throws Right | R | .282 | 238 | 67 | 13 | 1 | 1 | 17 | 19 | 41 | .340 | .357 |
| Chavez,Jesse | L | .246 | 118 | 29 | 6 | 0 | 0 | 7 | 14 | 29 | .333 | .297 |
| Throws Right | R | .212 | 99 | 21 | 2 | 1 | 3 | 13 | 6 | 26 | .262 | .343 |
| Chen,Bruce | L | .261 | 153 | 40 | 5 | 2 | 6 | 22 | 12 | 23 | .317 | .438 |
| Throws Left | R | .224 | 299 | 67 | 13 | 2 | 7 | 29 | 24 | 55 | .283 | .351 |
| Chen,Wei-Yin | L | .223 | 121 | 27 | 7 | 0 | 5 | 13 | 10 | 27 | .284 | .405 |
| Throws Left | R | .286 | 402 | 115 | 28 | 1 | 12 | 44 | 29 | 77 | .333 | .450 |
| Choate,Randy | L | .176 | 85 | 15 | 4 | 0 | 0 | 8 | 9 | 21 | .268 | .224 |
| Throws Left | R | .275 | 40 | 11 | 2 | 0 | 0 | 2 | 2 | 7 | .310 | .325 |
| Cingrani,Tony | L | .186 | 102 | 19 | 6 | 1 | 1 | 5 | 6 | 32 | .239 | .294 |
| Throws Left | R | .200 | 265 | 53 | 11 | 1 | 13 | 29 | 37 | 88 | .296 | .396 |
| Cishek,Steve | L | .235 | 132 | 31 | 9 | 0 | 2 | 10 | 16 | 41 | .315 | .348 |
| Throws Right | R | .185 | 119 | 22 | 0 | 1 | 1 | 10 | 6 | 33 | .233 | .227 |
| Cisnero,Jose | L | .293 | 82 | 24 | 4 | 1 | 3 | 13 | 14 | 20 | .396 | .476 |
| Throws Right | R | .275 | 91 | 25 | 10 | 0 | 2 | 14 | 8 | 21 | .333 | .451 |
| Claiborne,Preston | L | .323 | 93 | 30 | 5 | 0 | 2 | 12 | 9 | 22 | .382 | .441 |
| Throws Right | R | .204 | 103 | 21 | 3 | 1 | 5 | 12 | 5 | 20 | .255 | .398 |
| Clemens,Paul | L | .275 | 142 | 39 | 9 | 2 | 8 | 22 | 14 | 24 | .335 | .535 |
| Throws Right | R | .291 | 148 | 43 | 9 | 0 | 8 | 18 | 12 | 25 | .346 | .514 |
| Clippard,Tyler | L | .152 | 125 | 19 | 2 | 0 | 4 | 8 | 14 | 29 | .243 | .264 |
| Throws Right | R | .151 | 119 | 18 | 2 | 0 | 5 | 13 | 10 | 44 | .233 | .294 |
| Cloyd,Tyler | L | .308 | 120 | 37 | 12 | 1 | 2 | 14 | 19 | 21 | .404 | .475 |
| Throws Right | R | .346 | 133 | 46 | 14 | 2 | 5 | 24 | 6 | 20 | .374 | .594 |
| Cobb,Alex | L | .235 | 324 | 76 | 15 | 3 | 9 | 26 | 26 | 81 | .294 | .383 |
| Throws Right | R | .217 | 203 | 44 | 6 | 0 | 4 | 16 | 19 | 53 | .287 | .305 |
| Coello,Robert | L | .231 | 26 | 6 | 1 | 0 | 1 | 6 | 7 | 9 | .394 | .385 |
| Throws Right | R | .211 | 38 | 8 | 1 | 0 | 0 | 2 | 1 | 14 | .231 | .237 |
| Coke,Phil | L | .299 | 77 | 23 | 6 | 0 | 1 | 14 | 7 | 20 | .345 | .416 |
| Throws Left | R | .282 | 71 | 20 | 7 | 0 | 2 | 11 | 14 | 10 | .395 | .465 |
| Cole,Gerrit | L | .250 | 192 | 48 | 7 | 0 | 2 | 14 | 12 | 47 | .296 | .318 |
| Throws Right | R | .255 | 239 | 61 | 8 | 0 | 5 | 22 | 16 | 53 | .306 | .351 |
| Coleman,Louis | L | .235 | 34 | 8 | 1 | 1 | 0 | 1 | 2 | 8 | .278 | .324 |
| Throws Right | R | .162 | 68 | 11 | 1 | 0 | 1 | 6 | 4 | 24 | .219 | .221 |
| Collins,Tim | L | .212 | 99 | 21 | 3 | 0 | 3 | 15 | 14 | 25 | .304 | .333 |
| Throws Left | R | .275 | 102 | 28 | 8 | 0 | 0 | 5 | 14 | 27 | .362 | .353 |
| Collmenter,Josh | L | .250 | 132 | 33 | 5 | 0 | 2 | 8 | 13 | 33 | .327 | .333 |
| Throws Right | R | .220 | 209 | 46 | 10 | 0 | 6 | 21 | 20 | 52 | .288 | .354 |
| Colome,Alex | L | .258 | 31 | 8 | 1 | 0 | 0 | 3 | 6 | 8 | .395 | .290 |
| Throws Right | R | .200 | 30 | 6 | 2 | 0 | 2 | 3 | 3 | 4 | .273 | .467 |

| Pitcher | vs | Avg | AB | H | 2B | 3B | HR | RBI | BB | SO | OBP | Slg |
|---|---|---|---|---|---|---|---|---|---|---|---|---|
| Colon,Bartolo | L | .261 | 380 | 99 | 11 | 3 | 11 | 35 | 17 | 57 | .289 | .392 |
| Throws Right | R | .268 | 351 | 94 | 16 | 1 | 3 | 23 | 12 | 60 | .291 | .345 |
| Contreras,Jose | L | .273 | 11 | 3 | 1 | 0 | 1 | 3 | 3 | 3 | .429 | .636 |
| Throws Right | R | .364 | 11 | 4 | 0 | 0 | 0 | 2 | 3 | 2 | .500 | .364 |
| Cook,Ryan | L | .279 | 111 | 31 | 5 | 0 | 1 | 13 | 19 | 28 | .379 | .351 |
| Throws Right | R | .207 | 150 | 31 | 5 | 1 | 1 | 17 | 6 | 39 | .253 | .273 |
| Corbin,Patrick | L | .203 | 172 | 35 | 5 | 1 | 3 | 17 | 13 | 62 | .263 | .297 |
| Throws Left | R | .250 | 616 | 154 | 35 | 4 | 16 | 55 | 41 | 116 | .305 | .398 |
| Corpas,Manny | L | .219 | 64 | 14 | 3 | 0 | 1 | 6 | 6 | 12 | .282 | .313 |
| Throws Right | R | .280 | 93 | 26 | 6 | 0 | 4 | 17 | 10 | 18 | .349 | .473 |
| Correia,Kevin | L | .295 | 359 | 106 | 24 | 1 | 11 | 40 | 28 | 53 | .346 | .460 |
| Throws Right | R | .299 | 375 | 112 | 21 | 1 | 13 | 42 | 17 | 48 | .328 | .464 |
| Cosart,Jarred | L | .173 | 127 | 22 | 4 | 0 | 0 | 2 | 20 | 29 | .284 | .205 |
| Throws Right | R | .293 | 82 | 24 | 4 | 0 | 3 | 9 | 15 | 4 | .398 | .451 |
| Cotts,Neal | L | .204 | 98 | 20 | 4 | 0 | 2 | 8 | 8 | 36 | .259 | .306 |
| Throws Left | R | .157 | 102 | 16 | 3 | 1 | 0 | 2 | 10 | 29 | .230 | .206 |
| Crain,Jesse | L | .275 | 69 | 19 | 2 | 1 | 0 | 6 | 7 | 18 | .342 | .333 |
| Throws Right | R | .174 | 69 | 12 | 3 | 0 | 0 | 3 | 4 | 28 | .230 | .217 |
| Crow,Aaron | L | .264 | 87 | 23 | 9 | 0 | 4 | 18 | 10 | 19 | .340 | .506 |
| Throws Right | R | .277 | 94 | 26 | 1 | 0 | 2 | 14 | 12 | 25 | .361 | .351 |
| Cruz,Rhiner | L | .225 | 40 | 9 | 2 | 0 | 1 | 6 | 7 | 6 | .354 | .350 |
| Throws Right | R | .381 | 42 | 16 | 2 | 1 | 1 | 7 | 4 | 4 | .429 | .548 |
| Cueto,Johnny | L | .204 | 98 | 20 | 2 | 0 | 2 | 5 | 10 | 21 | .275 | .286 |
| Throws Right | R | .213 | 122 | 26 | 5 | 0 | 5 | 13 | 8 | 30 | .267 | .377 |
| Cumpton,Brandon | L | .259 | 54 | 14 | 1 | 0 | 1 | 6 | 4 | 13 | .305 | .333 |
| Throws Right | R | .197 | 61 | 12 | 2 | 0 | 0 | 1 | 1 | 9 | .222 | .230 |
| Daley,Matt | L | .125 | 8 | 1 | 1 | 0 | 0 | 0 | 0 | 3 | .125 | .250 |
| Throws Right | R | .083 | 12 | 1 | 1 | 0 | 0 | 0 | 0 | 5 | .154 | .167 |
| Danks,John | L | .293 | 150 | 44 | 3 | 2 | 8 | 23 | 8 | 23 | .331 | .500 |
| Throws Left | R | .270 | 396 | 107 | 23 | 0 | 20 | 51 | 19 | 66 | .306 | .480 |
| Darvish,Yu | L | .212 | 457 | 97 | 14 | 3 | 16 | 42 | 49 | 151 | .294 | .361 |
| Throws Right | R | .165 | 291 | 48 | 5 | 1 | 10 | 19 | 31 | 126 | .251 | .292 |
| Davis,Erik | L | .286 | 14 | 4 | 2 | 1 | 0 | 1 | 0 | 5 | .286 | .571 |
| Throws Right | R | .273 | 22 | 6 | 1 | 0 | 0 | 2 | 1 | 7 | .304 | .318 |
| Davis,Wade | L | .326 | 288 | 94 | 21 | 1 | 9 | 48 | 40 | 58 | .410 | .500 |
| Throws Right | R | .286 | 262 | 75 | 9 | 0 | 6 | 29 | 18 | 56 | .332 | .389 |
| De Fratus,Justin | L | .170 | 47 | 8 | 4 | 1 | 1 | 12 | 9 | 10 | .322 | .362 |
| Throws Right | R | .291 | 127 | 37 | 3 | 1 | 2 | 20 | 16 | 32 | .381 | .378 |
| De La Rosa,Dane | L | .191 | 131 | 25 | 2 | 0 | 1 | 14 | 10 | 26 | .246 | .229 |
| Throws Right | R | .248 | 125 | 31 | 4 | 0 | 2 | 18 | 18 | 39 | .340 | .328 |
| De La Rosa,Eury | L | .115 | 26 | 3 | 0 | 0 | 1 | 2 | 3 | 6 | .207 | .231 |
| Throws Left | R | .333 | 30 | 10 | 1 | 1 | 4 | 8 | 2 | 10 | .375 | .833 |
| De La Rosa,Jorge | L | .200 | 120 | 24 | 5 | 0 | 0 | 8 | 12 | 30 | .269 | .242 |
| Throws Left | R | .286 | 511 | 146 | 32 | 1 | 11 | 57 | 50 | 82 | .353 | .417 |
| De La Rosa,Rubby | L | .250 | 16 | 4 | 1 | 0 | 0 | 0 | 1 | 3 | .333 | .313 |
| Throws Right | R | .344 | 32 | 11 | 2 | 0 | 2 | 6 | 1 | 3 | .400 | .594 |
| De La Torre,Jose | L | .300 | 20 | 6 | 3 | 0 | 0 | 3 | 5 | 5 | .462 | .450 |
| Throws Right | R | .190 | 21 | 4 | 0 | 0 | 2 | 5 | 5 | 10 | .333 | .476 |
| De Leon,Jorge | L | .318 | 22 | 7 | 3 | 0 | 1 | 7 | 6 | 4 | .464 | .591 |
| Throws Right | R | .263 | 19 | 5 | 1 | 0 | 0 | 2 | 1 | 2 | .318 | .316 |
| Deduno,Samuel | L | .204 | 230 | 47 | 10 | 1 | 3 | 16 | 25 | 47 | .288 | .296 |
| Throws Right | R | .331 | 175 | 58 | 12 | 1 | 4 | 28 | 16 | 20 | .404 | .480 |
| Delabar,Steve | L | .216 | 97 | 21 | 5 | 1 | 3 | 22 | 17 | 40 | .331 | .381 |
| Throws Right | R | .244 | 119 | 29 | 8 | 0 | 1 | 12 | 12 | 42 | .318 | .336 |
| Delgado,Randall | L | .260 | 208 | 54 | 12 | 2 | 9 | 22 | 12 | 38 | .299 | .466 |
| Throws Right | R | .268 | 231 | 62 | 11 | 1 | 15 | 35 | 11 | 41 | .299 | .519 |
| Dempster,Ryan | L | .235 | 358 | 84 | 16 | 2 | 10 | 43 | 49 | 93 | .328 | .374 |
| Throws Right | R | .281 | 306 | 86 | 21 | 0 | 16 | 44 | 30 | 64 | .352 | .507 |
| Detwiler,Ross | L | .312 | 77 | 24 | 2 | 1 | 0 | 9 | 1 | 11 | .341 | .364 |
| Throws Left | R | .316 | 215 | 68 | 22 | 0 | 5 | 24 | 13 | 28 | .361 | .488 |
| DeVries,Cole | L | .292 | 48 | 14 | 2 | 1 | 5 | 16 | 7 | 10 | .375 | .688 |
| Throws Right | R | .444 | 18 | 8 | 3 | 0 | 1 | 2 | 2 | 2 | .500 | .778 |
| Diamond,Scott | L | .310 | 142 | 44 | 7 | 2 | 8 | 27 | 11 | 19 | .355 | .556 |
| Throws Left | R | .304 | 391 | 119 | 27 | 2 | 13 | 51 | 25 | 33 | .345 | .483 |
| Dickey,R.A. | L | .258 | 453 | 117 | 17 | 2 | 23 | 63 | 40 | 87 | .320 | .457 |
| Throws Right | R | .224 | 401 | 90 | 25 | 1 | 12 | 44 | 31 | 90 | .290 | .382 |
| Diekman,Jake | L | .148 | 61 | 9 | 0 | 0 | 0 | 4 | 6 | 23 | .221 | .148 |
| Throws Left | R | .298 | 84 | 25 | 3 | 1 | 1 | 8 | 10 | 18 | .372 | .393 |
| Dolis,Rafael | L | .000 | 8 | 0 | 0 | 0 | 0 | 0 | 1 | 0 | .111 | .000 |
| Throws Right | R | .273 | 11 | 3 | 1 | 1 | 0 | 1 | 1 | 0 | .333 | .545 |
| Dominguez,Jose | L | .333 | 15 | 5 | 1 | 0 | 0 | 3 | 1 | 2 | .375 | .400 |
| Throws Right | R | .300 | 20 | 6 | 0 | 0 | 0 | 2 | 2 | 2 | .391 | .300 |
| Doolittle,Sean | L | .188 | 85 | 16 | 2 | 0 | 2 | 7 | 5 | 20 | .233 | .282 |
| Throws Left | R | .227 | 163 | 37 | 9 | 1 | 2 | 13 | 8 | 40 | .272 | .331 |
| Dotel,Octavio | L | .273 | 11 | 3 | 0 | 0 | 0 | 0 | 1 | 2 | .333 | .273 |
| Throws Right | R | .538 | 13 | 7 | 3 | 1 | 0 | 9 | 3 | 2 | .625 | .923 |

# Pitchers vs. Left-Handed and Right-Handed Batters

| Pitcher | vs | Avg | AB | H | 2B | 3B | HR | RBI | BB | SO | OBP | Slg |
|---|---|---|---|---|---|---|---|---|---|---|---|---|
| Doubront,Felix | L | .247 | 174 | 43 | 9 | 2 | 1 | 16 | 15 | 44 | .309 | .339 |
| Throws Left | R | .267 | 442 | 118 | 24 | 2 | 12 | 60 | 56 | 95 | .348 | .412 |
| Downs,Darin | L | .219 | 64 | 14 | 3 | 0 | 2 | 10 | 3 | 19 | .265 | .359 |
| Throws Left | R | .306 | 72 | 22 | 7 | 1 | 2 | 14 | 8 | 18 | .378 | .514 |
| Downs,Scott | L | .259 | 81 | 21 | 3 | 0 | 0 | 10 | 8 | 23 | .333 | .296 |
| Throws Left | R | .293 | 82 | 24 | 4 | 0 | 1 | 11 | 11 | 14 | .379 | .378 |
| Duensing,Brian | L | .303 | 122 | 37 | 6 | 1 | 3 | 22 | 7 | 36 | .344 | .443 |
| Throws Left | R | .263 | 118 | 31 | 5 | 2 | 1 | 13 | 15 | 20 | .348 | .364 |
| Duffy,Danny | L | .296 | 27 | 8 | 0 | 1 | 0 | 2 | 1 | 4 | .321 | .370 |
| Throws Left | R | .177 | 62 | 11 | 2 | 1 | 0 | 1 | 13 | 18 | .329 | .242 |
| Duke,Zach | L | .327 | 49 | 16 | 3 | 0 | 0 | 11 | 1 | 14 | .340 | .388 |
| Throws Left | R | .295 | 78 | 23 | 6 | 0 | 3 | 8 | 9 | 4 | .367 | .487 |
| Dunn,Mike | L | .192 | 120 | 23 | 4 | 0 | 2 | 9 | 14 | 36 | .274 | .275 |
| Throws Left | R | .231 | 130 | 30 | 7 | 0 | 3 | 17 | 14 | 36 | .301 | .354 |
| Dunning,Jake | L | .171 | 35 | 6 | 1 | 0 | 0 | 1 | 4 | 6 | .256 | .200 |
| Throws Right | R | .259 | 54 | 14 | 3 | 0 | 2 | 13 | 7 | 10 | .369 | .426 |
| Durbin,Chad | L | .357 | 28 | 10 | 3 | 1 | 2 | 9 | 1 | 6 | .379 | .750 |
| Throws Right | R | .357 | 42 | 15 | 3 | 0 | 2 | 13 | 8 | 10 | .442 | .571 |
| Dyson,Sam | L | .368 | 19 | 7 | 1 | 0 | 1 | 8 | 3 | 1 | .435 | .579 |
| Throws Right | R | .333 | 27 | 9 | 2 | 0 | 1 | 4 | 2 | 4 | .400 | .519 |
| Edgin,Josh | L | .250 | 52 | 13 | 4 | 0 | 2 | 5 | 5 | 16 | .328 | .442 |
| Throws Left | R | .236 | 55 | 13 | 2 | 0 | 0 | 5 | 7 | 4 | .333 | .273 |
| Enright,Barry | L | .438 | 16 | 7 | 2 | 0 | 2 | 6 | 6 | 3 | .591 | .938 |
| Throws Right | R | .250 | 20 | 5 | 3 | 0 | 0 | 3 | 1 | 3 | .286 | .400 |
| Eovaldi,Nathan | L | .246 | 171 | 42 | 6 | 2 | 1 | 16 | 25 | 30 | .343 | .322 |
| Throws Right | R | .251 | 231 | 58 | 11 | 2 | 6 | 24 | 15 | 48 | .297 | .394 |
| Erlin,Robbie | L | .318 | 66 | 21 | 5 | 0 | 2 | 5 | 2 | 13 | .338 | .485 |
| Throws Left | R | .225 | 142 | 32 | 4 | 1 | 4 | 17 | 13 | 27 | .288 | .352 |
| Escalona,Edgmer | L | .312 | 77 | 24 | 4 | 0 | 6 | 15 | 6 | 8 | .376 | .597 |
| Throws Right | R | .257 | 109 | 28 | 9 | 2 | 2 | 13 | 8 | 26 | .305 | .431 |
| Estrada,Marco | L | .214 | 220 | 47 | 7 | 0 | 10 | 23 | 15 | 57 | .269 | .382 |
| Throws Right | R | .242 | 256 | 62 | 9 | 3 | 9 | 28 | 14 | 61 | .280 | .406 |
| Familia,Jeurys | L | .313 | 16 | 5 | 0 | 0 | 1 | 2 | 2 | 2 | .389 | .500 |
| Throws Right | R | .280 | 25 | 7 | 2 | 0 | 1 | 5 | 7 | 6 | .438 | .480 |
| Farnsworth,Kyle | L | .259 | 58 | 15 | 3 | 1 | 2 | 7 | 4 | 10 | .306 | .448 |
| Throws Right | R | .301 | 93 | 28 | 5 | 0 | 3 | 13 | 6 | 18 | .350 | .452 |
| Farquhar,Danny | L | .171 | 105 | 18 | 1 | 1 | 1 | 8 | 12 | 44 | .256 | .229 |
| Throws Right | R | .265 | 98 | 26 | 5 | 1 | 1 | 13 | 10 | 35 | .327 | .367 |
| Feldman,Scott | L | .235 | 349 | 82 | 22 | 1 | 8 | 36 | 27 | 67 | .299 | .372 |
| Throws Right | R | .233 | 330 | 77 | 11 | 1 | 11 | 37 | 29 | 65 | .297 | .373 |
| Feliciano,Pedro | L | .176 | 34 | 6 | 2 | 0 | 1 | 4 | 1 | 7 | .216 | .324 |
| Throws Left | R | .625 | 8 | 5 | 3 | 0 | 0 | 1 | 5 | 2 | .769 | 1.000 |
| Feliz,Neftali | L | .200 | 5 | 1 | 0 | 0 | 0 | 0 | 1 | 1 | .429 | .200 |
| Throws Right | R | .308 | 13 | 4 | 0 | 0 | 0 | 1 | 1 | 3 | .357 | .308 |
| Fernandez,Jose | L | .188 | 319 | 60 | 9 | 0 | 5 | 22 | 40 | 93 | .283 | .263 |
| Throws Right | R | .175 | 292 | 51 | 8 | 2 | 5 | 20 | 18 | 94 | .227 | .267 |
| Fields,Josh | L | .246 | 61 | 15 | 6 | 0 | 4 | 10 | 9 | 10 | .343 | .541 |
| Throws Right | R | .200 | 80 | 16 | 4 | 1 | 4 | 8 | 9 | 30 | .281 | .425 |
| Fien,Casey | L | .242 | 91 | 22 | 2 | 0 | 6 | 12 | 6 | 29 | .289 | .462 |
| Throws Right | R | .213 | 136 | 29 | 3 | 0 | 3 | 15 | 6 | 44 | .243 | .301 |
| Fiers,Mike | L | .304 | 56 | 17 | 1 | 2 | 5 | 14 | 4 | 10 | .339 | .661 |
| Throws Right | R | .289 | 38 | 11 | 3 | 0 | 3 | 6 | 2 | 5 | .325 | .605 |
| Fife,Stephen | L | .336 | 128 | 43 | 6 | 0 | 2 | 9 | 12 | 26 | .401 | .430 |
| Throws Right | R | .263 | 99 | 26 | 5 | 0 | 5 | 17 | 8 | 19 | .330 | .465 |
| Figaro,Alfredo | L | .246 | 142 | 35 | 5 | 0 | 10 | 33 | 7 | 27 | .280 | .493 |
| Throws Right | R | .282 | 149 | 42 | 7 | 1 | 5 | 12 | 8 | 27 | .317 | .443 |
| Fister,Doug | L | .263 | 452 | 119 | 16 | 2 | 10 | 47 | 28 | 95 | .313 | .374 |
| Throws Right | R | .304 | 362 | 110 | 17 | 1 | 4 | 35 | 16 | 64 | .349 | .390 |
| Floyd,Gavin | L | .275 | 51 | 14 | 4 | 1 | 3 | 12 | 9 | 13 | .371 | .569 |
| Throws Right | R | .302 | 43 | 13 | 3 | 1 | 1 | 2 | 3 | 12 | .348 | .488 |
| Flynn,Brian | L | .400 | 15 | 6 | 0 | 0 | 2 | 7 | 4 | 3 | .526 | .800 |
| Throws Left | R | .362 | 58 | 21 | 5 | 0 | 2 | 10 | 9 | 12 | .448 | .552 |
| Francis,Jeff | L | .208 | 77 | 16 | 4 | 0 | 0 | 5 | 4 | 19 | .256 | .260 |
| Throws Left | R | .341 | 214 | 73 | 16 | 2 | 12 | 46 | 20 | 44 | .391 | .603 |
| Francisco,Frank | L | .222 | 9 | 2 | 1 | 0 | 0 | 1 | 1 | 0 | .300 | .333 |
| Throws Right | R | .154 | 13 | 2 | 1 | 0 | 0 | 2 | 2 | 6 | .313 | .231 |
| Frasor,Jason | L | .152 | 66 | 10 | 3 | 0 | 0 | 3 | 7 | 21 | .230 | .197 |
| Throws Right | R | .234 | 111 | 26 | 5 | 0 | 4 | 15 | 13 | 27 | .312 | .387 |
| Freeman,Sam | L | .200 | 20 | 4 | 1 | 0 | 0 | 2 | 1 | 3 | .238 | .250 |
| Throws Left | R | .167 | 24 | 4 | 2 | 0 | 0 | 0 | 4 | 5 | .286 | .250 |
| Frieri,Ernesto | L | .155 | 142 | 22 | 4 | 0 | 6 | 15 | 21 | 62 | .262 | .310 |
| Throws Right | R | .292 | 113 | 33 | 5 | 0 | 5 | 15 | 9 | 36 | .357 | .469 |
| Fujikawa,Kyuji | L | .217 | 23 | 5 | 1 | 0 | 1 | 7 | 1 | 8 | .280 | .391 |
| Throws Right | R | .261 | 23 | 6 | 3 | 0 | 0 | 0 | 1 | 6 | .320 | .391 |
| Furbush,Charlie | L | .173 | 110 | 19 | 4 | 0 | 1 | 13 | 12 | 46 | .266 | .236 |
| Throws Left | R | .221 | 131 | 29 | 9 | 0 | 4 | 22 | 17 | 34 | .307 | .382 |

| Pitcher | vs | Avg | AB | H | 2B | 3B | HR | RBI | BB | SO | OBP | Slg |
|---|---|---|---|---|---|---|---|---|---|---|---|---|
| Gallardo,Yovani | L | .249 | 317 | 79 | 16 | 2 | 9 | 40 | 38 | 67 | .331 | .397 |
| Throws Right | R | .272 | 372 | 101 | 14 | 2 | 9 | 43 | 28 | 77 | .320 | .392 |
| Garcia,Freddy | L | .286 | 154 | 44 | 6 | 1 | 10 | 23 | 11 | 17 | .331 | .532 |
| Throws Right | R | .255 | 153 | 39 | 0 | 0 | 8 | 14 | 6 | 29 | .288 | .412 |
| Garcia,Jaime | L | .333 | 54 | 18 | 3 | 1 | 2 | 8 | 3 | 10 | .368 | .537 |
| Throws Left | R | .239 | 163 | 39 | 10 | 0 | 4 | 15 | 12 | 33 | .291 | .374 |
| Garcia,Luis | L | .214 | 42 | 9 | 2 | 1 | 1 | 3 | 9 | 10 | .365 | .381 |
| Throws Right | R | .250 | 72 | 18 | 5 | 0 | 2 | 15 | 14 | 13 | .372 | .403 |
| Garland,Jon | L | .293 | 140 | 41 | 12 | 2 | 5 | 27 | 14 | 17 | .355 | .514 |
| Throws Right | R | .338 | 130 | 44 | 12 | 0 | 4 | 16 | 9 | 15 | .387 | .523 |
| Garza,Matt | L | .271 | 317 | 86 | 15 | 1 | 10 | 33 | 19 | 75 | .314 | .420 |
| Throws Right | R | .231 | 277 | 64 | 14 | 0 | 10 | 31 | 23 | 61 | .297 | .390 |
| Gast,John | L | .385 | 13 | 5 | 1 | 0 | 0 | 2 | 1 | 1 | .429 | .462 |
| Throws Left | R | .176 | 34 | 6 | 1 | 0 | 1 | 3 | 4 | 7 | .263 | .294 |
| Gaudin,Chad | L | .271 | 155 | 42 | 10 | 1 | 1 | 12 | 26 | 27 | .374 | .368 |
| Throws Right | R | .193 | 202 | 39 | 7 | 1 | 5 | 16 | 14 | 61 | .249 | .312 |
| Gausman,Kevin | L | .269 | 93 | 25 | 6 | 0 | 5 | 14 | 7 | 26 | .317 | .495 |
| Throws Right | R | .283 | 92 | 26 | 6 | 0 | 3 | 10 | 6 | 23 | .327 | .446 |
| Gearrin,Cory | L | .238 | 42 | 10 | 3 | 0 | 0 | 7 | 4 | 6 | .319 | .310 |
| Throws Right | R | .286 | 70 | 20 | 3 | 0 | 2 | 12 | 12 | 17 | .412 | .414 |
| Gee,Dillon | L | .288 | 354 | 102 | 19 | 2 | 14 | 39 | 34 | 64 | .350 | .472 |
| Throws Right | R | .252 | 421 | 106 | 25 | 0 | 10 | 40 | 13 | 78 | .283 | .382 |
| Germen,Gonzalez | L | .226 | 53 | 12 | 5 | 1 | 1 | 8 | 6 | 10 | .305 | .415 |
| Throws Right | R | .250 | 80 | 20 | 5 | 0 | 0 | 8 | 10 | 23 | .333 | .313 |
| Gibson,Kyle | L | .341 | 123 | 42 | 5 | 0 | 3 | 18 | 15 | 13 | .420 | .455 |
| Throws Right | R | .307 | 88 | 27 | 6 | 0 | 4 | 18 | 5 | 16 | .358 | .511 |
| Gomes,Brandon | L | .357 | 28 | 10 | 0 | 1 | 3 | 10 | 2 | 10 | .387 | .750 |
| Throws Right | R | .178 | 45 | 8 | 1 | 1 | 1 | 4 | 5 | 19 | .255 | .311 |
| Gomez,Jeanmar | L | .222 | 126 | 28 | 4 | 1 | 2 | 13 | 14 | 17 | .303 | .317 |
| Throws Right | R | .223 | 166 | 37 | 4 | 1 | 4 | 19 | 14 | 36 | .283 | .331 |
| Gonzalez,Edgar | L | .262 | 42 | 11 | 2 | 0 | 3 | 6 | 4 | 8 | .340 | .524 |
| Throws Right | R | .417 | 36 | 15 | 1 | 0 | 3 | 8 | 4 | 3 | .475 | .694 |
| Gonzalez,Gio | L | .204 | 167 | 34 | 8 | 0 | 4 | 17 | 8 | 48 | .244 | .323 |
| Throws Left | R | .239 | 565 | 135 | 36 | 1 | 13 | 53 | 68 | 144 | .321 | .375 |
| Gonzalez,Michael | L | .274 | 106 | 29 | 6 | 0 | 4 | 21 | 8 | 31 | .336 | .443 |
| Throws Left | R | .293 | 99 | 29 | 6 | 0 | 6 | 11 | 17 | 29 | .393 | .535 |
| Gonzalez,Miguel | L | .241 | 320 | 77 | 20 | 2 | 7 | 26 | 31 | 64 | .308 | .381 |
| Throws Right | R | .245 | 327 | 80 | 12 | 1 | 17 | 47 | 22 | 56 | .293 | .443 |
| Gorzelanny,Tom | L | .184 | 98 | 18 | 1 | 0 | 4 | 6 | 12 | 28 | .283 | .316 |
| Throws Left | R | .266 | 222 | 59 | 11 | 1 | 7 | 32 | 19 | 55 | .322 | .419 |
| Gray,Sonny | L | .226 | 137 | 31 | 7 | 0 | 2 | 12 | 15 | 36 | .301 | .321 |
| Throws Right | R | .198 | 101 | 20 | 1 | 0 | 2 | 9 | 5 | 31 | .231 | .267 |
| Gregerson,Luke | L | .216 | 116 | 25 | 6 | 3 | 0 | 14 | 12 | 34 | .305 | .319 |
| Throws Right | R | .192 | 125 | 24 | 3 | 0 | 3 | 12 | 6 | 30 | .233 | .288 |
| Gregg,Kevin | L | .163 | 104 | 17 | 4 | 0 | 1 | 6 | 17 | 31 | .287 | .231 |
| Throws Right | R | .286 | 126 | 36 | 6 | 2 | 5 | 21 | 15 | 25 | .359 | .484 |
| Greinke,Zack | L | .254 | 307 | 78 | 16 | 1 | 10 | 30 | 28 | 65 | .322 | .410 |
| Throws Right | R | .216 | 343 | 74 | 18 | 2 | 3 | 18 | 18 | 83 | .262 | .306 |
| Griffin,A.J. | L | .226 | 412 | 93 | 18 | 0 | 15 | 33 | 36 | 84 | .288 | .379 |
| Throws Right | R | .226 | 345 | 78 | 12 | 0 | 21 | 51 | 18 | 87 | .270 | .443 |
| Grilli,Jason | L | .244 | 86 | 21 | 3 | 0 | 3 | 9 | 9 | 32 | .323 | .384 |
| Throws Right | R | .188 | 101 | 19 | 2 | 2 | 1 | 5 | 4 | 42 | .219 | .277 |
| Grimm,Justin | L | .298 | 215 | 64 | 15 | 1 | 9 | 37 | 18 | 37 | .357 | .502 |
| Throws Right | R | .303 | 185 | 56 | 14 | 0 | 6 | 25 | 16 | 39 | .355 | .476 |
| Guerra,Javy | L | .333 | 21 | 7 | 1 | 0 | 1 | 4 | 2 | 3 | .391 | .524 |
| Throws Right | R | .308 | 26 | 8 | 1 | 0 | 0 | 3 | 4 | 9 | .406 | .346 |
| Guerrier,Matt | L | .200 | 60 | 12 | 3 | 0 | 1 | 4 | 9 | 11 | .304 | .300 |
| Throws Right | R | .313 | 99 | 31 | 4 | 2 | 2 | 14 | 8 | 19 | .364 | .455 |
| Guilmet,Preston | L | .294 | 17 | 5 | 2 | 0 | 0 | 5 | 1 | 1 | .333 | .412 |
| Throws Right | R | .375 | 8 | 3 | 0 | 1 | 0 | 2 | 2 | 0 | .500 | .625 |
| Guthrie,Jeremy | L | .331 | 472 | 156 | 29 | 2 | 20 | 54 | 35 | 58 | .377 | .528 |
| Throws Right | R | .225 | 356 | 80 | 10 | 1 | 10 | 36 | 24 | 53 | .280 | .343 |
| Gutierrez,Juan | L | .280 | 107 | 30 | 3 | 1 | 3 | 17 | 15 | 24 | .368 | .411 |
| Throws Right | R | .250 | 104 | 26 | 2 | 0 | 2 | 8 | 5 | 21 | .282 | .327 |
| Hagadone,Nick | L | .211 | 57 | 12 | 2 | 0 | 2 | 7 | 10 | 18 | .328 | .351 |
| Throws Left | R | .231 | 52 | 12 | 2 | 0 | 2 | 8 | 11 | 12 | .359 | .385 |
| Hale,David | L | .300 | 20 | 6 | 1 | 0 | 0 | 0 | 1 | 6 | .333 | .350 |
| Throws Right | R | .200 | 25 | 5 | 2 | 0 | 0 | 1 | 0 | 8 | .200 | .280 |
| Halladay,Roy | L | .248 | 105 | 26 | 3 | 1 | 6 | 17 | 20 | 18 | .394 | .467 |
| Throws Right | R | .230 | 126 | 29 | 6 | 1 | 6 | 25 | 16 | 33 | .333 | .437 |
| Hamels,Cole | L | .257 | 191 | 49 | 15 | 1 | 4 | 14 | 12 | 50 | .304 | .408 |
| Throws Left | R | .243 | 641 | 156 | 47 | 2 | 17 | 71 | 38 | 152 | .293 | .402 |
| Hammel,Jason | L | .300 | 317 | 95 | 19 | 1 | 15 | 43 | 36 | 54 | .373 | .508 |
| Throws Right | R | .263 | 228 | 60 | 12 | 0 | 7 | 28 | 12 | 42 | .308 | .408 |
| Hand,Brad | L | .192 | 26 | 5 | 0 | 0 | 1 | 3 | 1 | 8 | .222 | .308 |
| Throws Left | R | .167 | 48 | 8 | 3 | 0 | 1 | 3 | 7 | 7 | .273 | .292 |

# Pitchers vs. Left-Handed and Right-Handed Batters

| Pitcher | vs | Avg | AB | H | 2B | 3B | HR | RBI | BB | SO | OBP | Slg |
|---|---|---|---|---|---|---|---|---|---|---|---|---|
| Hand,Donovan | L | .286 | 126 | 36 | 4 | 2 | 7 | 16 | 13 | 21 | .362 | .516 |
| Throws Right | R | .273 | 128 | 35 | 4 | 0 | 3 | 14 | 8 | 16 | .319 | .375 |
| Hanrahan,Joel | L | .235 | 17 | 4 | 0 | 0 | 1 | 2 | 3 | 5 | .350 | .412 |
| Throws Right | R | .462 | 13 | 6 | 1 | 0 | 3 | 5 | 3 | 0 | .563 | 1.231 |
| Hanson,Tommy | L | .294 | 163 | 48 | 11 | 2 | 6 | 22 | 19 | 33 | .370 | .497 |
| Throws Right | R | .276 | 127 | 35 | 3 | 1 | 4 | 17 | 11 | 23 | .336 | .409 |
| Happ,J.A. | L | .304 | 102 | 31 | 4 | 0 | 3 | 14 | 11 | 21 | .371 | .431 |
| Throws Left | R | .229 | 262 | 60 | 17 | 2 | 7 | 30 | 34 | 56 | .319 | .389 |
| Harang,Aaron | L | .259 | 305 | 79 | 19 | 2 | 16 | 46 | 20 | 50 | .308 | .492 |
| Throws Right | R | .276 | 268 | 74 | 11 | 4 | 10 | 40 | 20 | 63 | .330 | .459 |
| Haren,Dan | L | .253 | 304 | 77 | 19 | 0 | 12 | 36 | 14 | 61 | .288 | .434 |
| Throws Right | R | .281 | 363 | 102 | 19 | 1 | 16 | 50 | 17 | 90 | .321 | .471 |
| Harrell,Lucas | L | .255 | 322 | 82 | 19 | 2 | 10 | 56 | 51 | 47 | .357 | .419 |
| Throws Right | R | .329 | 280 | 92 | 10 | 3 | 10 | 44 | 37 | 42 | .412 | .493 |
| Harris,Will | L | .221 | 77 | 17 | 2 | 0 | 0 | 3 | 5 | 22 | .262 | .247 |
| Throws Right | R | .277 | 119 | 33 | 8 | 0 | 3 | 21 | 10 | 31 | .338 | .420 |
| Harrison,Matt | L | .182 | 11 | 2 | 0 | 0 | 0 | 0 | 1 | 7 | .250 | .182 |
| Throws Left | R | .375 | 32 | 12 | 2 | 1 | 2 | 8 | 6 | 5 | .462 | .688 |
| Harvey,Matt | L | .178 | 321 | 57 | 10 | 2 | 2 | 17 | 16 | 105 | .216 | .240 |
| Throws Right | R | .240 | 325 | 78 | 8 | 2 | 5 | 21 | 15 | 86 | .280 | .323 |
| Hatcher,Chris | L | .308 | 13 | 4 | 1 | 2 | 0 | 5 | 3 | 3 | .438 | .692 |
| Throws Right | R | .333 | 27 | 9 | 2 | 0 | 1 | 9 | 1 | 4 | .357 | .519 |
| Hawkins,LaTroy | L | .248 | 109 | 27 | 2 | 1 | 4 | 17 | 5 | 35 | .276 | .394 |
| Throws Right | R | .275 | 160 | 44 | 6 | 0 | 2 | 15 | 5 | 20 | .296 | .350 |
| Heath,Deunte | L | .294 | 17 | 5 | 2 | 0 | 1 | 6 | 8 | 1 | .520 | .588 |
| Throws Right | R | .250 | 12 | 3 | 1 | 0 | 1 | 5 | 4 | 2 | .438 | .583 |
| Hefner,Jeremy | L | .286 | 220 | 63 | 12 | 1 | 11 | 32 | 21 | 38 | .346 | .500 |
| Throws Right | R | .240 | 287 | 69 | 16 | 1 | 9 | 32 | 16 | 61 | .290 | .397 |
| Hellickson,Jeremy | L | .274 | 369 | 101 | 14 | 5 | 15 | 50 | 27 | 74 | .324 | .461 |
| Throws Right | R | .274 | 307 | 84 | 19 | 2 | 9 | 48 | 23 | 61 | .326 | .436 |
| Hellweg,John | L | .381 | 63 | 24 | 5 | 0 | 3 | 15 | 22 | 4 | .540 | .603 |
| Throws Right | R | .267 | 60 | 16 | 0 | 0 | 0 | 12 | 4 | 5 | .375 | .267 |
| Hembree,Heath | L | .125 | 8 | 1 | 1 | 0 | 0 | 0 | 0 | 1 | .125 | .250 |
| Throws Right | R | .158 | 19 | 3 | 0 | 0 | 0 | 0 | 2 | 11 | .238 | .158 |
| Henderson,Jim | L | .238 | 105 | 25 | 4 | 0 | 6 | 12 | 16 | 40 | .339 | .448 |
| Throws Right | R | .165 | 115 | 19 | 3 | 0 | 2 | 7 | 8 | 35 | .232 | .243 |
| Hendriks,Liam | L | .327 | 113 | 37 | 9 | 0 | 5 | 18 | 11 | 13 | .389 | .540 |
| Throws Right | R | .326 | 92 | 30 | 3 | 0 | 5 | 17 | 3 | 21 | .357 | .522 |
| Hernandez,David | L | .234 | 107 | 25 | 4 | 1 | 8 | 17 | 15 | 30 | .333 | .514 |
| Throws Right | R | .198 | 126 | 25 | 8 | 0 | 2 | 11 | 9 | 36 | .268 | .310 |
| Hernandez,Felix | L | .251 | 410 | 103 | 22 | 2 | 8 | 40 | 29 | 113 | .300 | .373 |
| Throws Right | R | .232 | 353 | 82 | 15 | 1 | 7 | 27 | 17 | 103 | .270 | .340 |
| Hernandez,Pedro | L | .290 | 62 | 18 | 3 | 2 | 0 | 8 | 1 | 15 | .302 | .403 |
| Throws Left | R | .354 | 175 | 62 | 13 | 1 | 10 | 34 | 22 | 14 | .420 | .611 |
| Hernandez,Roberto | L | .305 | 315 | 96 | 18 | 2 | 17 | 46 | 28 | 60 | .369 | .537 |
| Throws Right | R | .253 | 269 | 68 | 11 | 0 | 7 | 28 | 10 | 53 | .297 | .372 |
| Herrera,Kelvin | L | .246 | 114 | 28 | 9 | 1 | 4 | 15 | 8 | 42 | .290 | .447 |
| Throws Right | R | .190 | 105 | 20 | 4 | 0 | 5 | 10 | 13 | 32 | .289 | .371 |
| Hill,Rich | L | .238 | 84 | 20 | 1 | 0 | 2 | 15 | 19 | 29 | .375 | .321 |
| Throws Left | R | .281 | 64 | 18 | 2 | 0 | 1 | 11 | 10 | 22 | .390 | .359 |
| Hochevar,Luke | L | .198 | 126 | 25 | 5 | 1 | 4 | 10 | 10 | 38 | .257 | .349 |
| Throws Right | R | .138 | 116 | 16 | 2 | 0 | 4 | 8 | 7 | 44 | .194 | .259 |
| Holland,Derek | L | .265 | 170 | 45 | 8 | 0 | 2 | 6 | 14 | 46 | .324 | .347 |
| Throws Left | R | .258 | 640 | 165 | 41 | 2 | 18 | 73 | 50 | 143 | .310 | .413 |
| Holland,Greg | L | .172 | 128 | 22 | 4 | 1 | 2 | 5 | 13 | 55 | .246 | .266 |
| Throws Right | R | .168 | 107 | 18 | 2 | 1 | 1 | 6 | 5 | 48 | .205 | .234 |
| Holmberg,David | L | .500 | 4 | 2 | 0 | 0 | 0 | 0 | 1 | 0 | .600 | .500 |
| Throws Left | R | .333 | 12 | 4 | 2 | 0 | 0 | 3 | 2 | 0 | .400 | .500 |
| Hoover,J.J. | L | .163 | 92 | 15 | 4 | 0 | 1 | 7 | 7 | 20 | .238 | .239 |
| Throws Right | R | .224 | 143 | 32 | 8 | 2 | 5 | 25 | 19 | 47 | .309 | .413 |
| Horst,Jeremy | L | .286 | 42 | 12 | 1 | 1 | 1 | 6 | 6 | 11 | .392 | .429 |
| Throws Left | R | .359 | 64 | 23 | 3 | 0 | 3 | 12 | 6 | 10 | .414 | .547 |
| Howell,J.P. | L | .164 | 110 | 18 | 2 | 1 | 1 | 12 | 9 | 36 | .225 | .227 |
| Throws Left | R | .222 | 108 | 24 | 5 | 0 | 1 | 5 | 14 | 18 | .312 | .296 |
| Hudson,Tim | L | .236 | 246 | 58 | 12 | 1 | 5 | 26 | 25 | 46 | .308 | .354 |
| Throws Right | R | .254 | 244 | 62 | 10 | 2 | 5 | 28 | 11 | 49 | .289 | .373 |
| Huff,David | L | .271 | 48 | 13 | 3 | 0 | 3 | 6 | 5 | 10 | .333 | .521 |
| Throws Left | R | .220 | 91 | 20 | 5 | 0 | 4 | 15 | 4 | 21 | .260 | .407 |
| Hughes,Jared | L | .392 | 51 | 20 | 3 | 0 | 1 | 11 | 6 | 3 | .458 | .510 |
| Throws Right | R | .224 | 76 | 17 | 4 | 1 | 1 | 5 | 10 | 20 | .322 | .342 |
| Hughes,Phil | L | .298 | 322 | 96 | 27 | 1 | 13 | 45 | 29 | 68 | .354 | .509 |
| Throws Right | R | .286 | 259 | 74 | 11 | 2 | 11 | 37 | 13 | 53 | .322 | .471 |
| Humber,Philip | L | .433 | 127 | 55 | 15 | 6 | 5 | 36 | 13 | 12 | .483 | .764 |
| Throws Right | R | .189 | 106 | 20 | 5 | 0 | 4 | 15 | 7 | 24 | .239 | .349 |
| Hunter,Tommy | L | .294 | 170 | 50 | 6 | 1 | 11 | 23 | 6 | 29 | .322 | .535 |
| Throws Right | R | .141 | 149 | 21 | 2 | 0 | 0 | 7 | 8 | 39 | .190 | .154 |

| Pitcher | vs | Avg | AB | H | 2B | 3B | HR | RBI | BB | SO | OBP | Slg |
|---|---|---|---|---|---|---|---|---|---|---|---|---|
| Hynes,Colt | L | .156 | 32 | 5 | 0 | 1 | 1 | 6 | 6 | 6 | .289 | .313 |
| Throws Left | R | .476 | 42 | 20 | 3 | 1 | 2 | 13 | 3 | 7 | .522 | .738 |
| Irwin,Phil | L | .286 | 7 | 2 | 1 | 0 | 0 | 1 | 2 | 2 | .444 | .429 |
| Throws Right | R | .333 | 12 | 4 | 0 | 0 | 0 | 3 | 2 | 2 | .429 | .333 |
| Iwakuma,Hisashi | L | .216 | 444 | 96 | 21 | 3 | 10 | 33 | 24 | 94 | .254 | .345 |
| Throws Right | R | .225 | 369 | 83 | 19 | 1 | 15 | 29 | 18 | 91 | .263 | .404 |
| Jackson,Edwin | L | .294 | 313 | 92 | 19 | 5 | 6 | 37 | 35 | 70 | .372 | .444 |
| Throws Right | R | .270 | 389 | 105 | 28 | 2 | 10 | 63 | 24 | 65 | .312 | .429 |
| Jansen,Kenley | L | .204 | 113 | 23 | 3 | 1 | 1 | 2 | 8 | 37 | .256 | .274 |
| Throws Right | R | .158 | 158 | 25 | 3 | 0 | 5 | 11 | 10 | 74 | .222 | .272 |
| Janssen,Casey | L | .244 | 119 | 29 | 6 | 0 | 1 | 10 | 8 | 25 | .300 | .319 |
| Throws Right | R | .135 | 74 | 10 | 2 | 1 | 2 | 5 | 5 | 25 | .188 | .270 |
| Jeffress,Jeremy | L | .118 | 17 | 2 | 0 | 0 | 0 | 2 | 1 | 8 | .167 | .118 |
| Throws Right | R | .286 | 21 | 6 | 0 | 0 | 1 | 2 | 4 | 4 | .400 | .429 |
| Jenkins,Chad | L | .235 | 68 | 16 | 7 | 0 | 1 | 3 | 6 | 6 | .297 | .382 |
| Throws Right | R | .268 | 56 | 15 | 8 | 0 | 2 | 9 | 0 | 9 | .281 | .518 |
| Jennings,Dan | L | .282 | 85 | 24 | 5 | 3 | 0 | 12 | 7 | 20 | .333 | .412 |
| Throws Left | R | .221 | 68 | 15 | 3 | 2 | 1 | 5 | 9 | 18 | .308 | .368 |
| Jepsen,Kevin | L | .286 | 70 | 20 | 7 | 0 | 3 | 11 | 7 | 15 | .351 | .514 |
| Throws Right | R | .280 | 75 | 21 | 4 | 0 | 0 | 10 | 7 | 21 | .345 | .333 |
| Jimenez,Cesar | L | .143 | 28 | 4 | 1 | 0 | 0 | 3 | 2 | 6 | .194 | .179 |
| Throws Left | R | .294 | 34 | 10 | 2 | 1 | 1 | 5 | 8 | 5 | .432 | .500 |
| Jimenez,Ubaldo | L | .223 | 368 | 82 | 17 | 1 | 12 | 35 | 34 | 118 | .289 | .372 |
| Throws Right | R | .258 | 314 | 81 | 18 | 1 | 4 | 30 | 46 | 76 | .348 | .360 |
| Johnson,Erik | L | .348 | 69 | 24 | 3 | 1 | 4 | 12 | 8 | 10 | .418 | .594 |
| Throws Right | R | .178 | 45 | 8 | 1 | 0 | 1 | 3 | 3 | 8 | .224 | .267 |
| Johnson,Jim | L | .279 | 140 | 39 | 8 | 0 | 3 | 13 | 11 | 28 | .340 | .400 |
| Throws Right | R | .266 | 124 | 33 | 1 | 0 | 2 | 14 | 7 | 28 | .331 | .323 |
| Johnson,Josh | L | .275 | 204 | 56 | 8 | 1 | 5 | 31 | 18 | 52 | .330 | .397 |
| Throws Right | R | .350 | 140 | 49 | 6 | 1 | 10 | 30 | 12 | 31 | .410 | .621 |
| Johnson,Kris | L | .267 | 15 | 4 | 2 | 0 | 0 | 3 | 0 | 5 | .294 | .400 |
| Throws Left | R | .320 | 25 | 8 | 1 | 0 | 0 | 4 | 4 | 4 | .414 | .360 |
| Johnson,Steve | L | .258 | 31 | 8 | 2 | 0 | 0 | 5 | 10 | 15 | .439 | .323 |
| Throws Right | R | .207 | 29 | 6 | 4 | 0 | 2 | 5 | 3 | 5 | .281 | .552 |
| Jones,Nate | L | .229 | 118 | 27 | 6 | 1 | 4 | 24 | 15 | 38 | .312 | .398 |
| Throws Right | R | .261 | 161 | 42 | 4 | 1 | 1 | 16 | 11 | 51 | .305 | .317 |
| Jordan,Taylor | L | .308 | 91 | 28 | 2 | 1 | 2 | 9 | 5 | 5 | .344 | .418 |
| Throws Right | R | .277 | 112 | 31 | 3 | 0 | 1 | 10 | 6 | 24 | .328 | .330 |
| Joseph,Donnie | L | .000 | 7 | 0 | 0 | 0 | 0 | 0 | 2 | 5 | .222 | .000 |
| Throws Left | R | .308 | 13 | 4 | 1 | 0 | 0 | 0 | 2 | 2 | .400 | .385 |
| Jurrjens,Jair | L | .294 | 17 | 5 | 4 | 0 | 1 | 3 | 1 | 3 | .333 | .706 |
| Throws Right | R | .308 | 13 | 4 | 3 | 0 | 0 | 1 | 0 | 3 | .308 | .538 |
| Karns,Nate | L | .370 | 27 | 10 | 3 | 0 | 3 | 8 | 4 | 4 | .452 | .815 |
| Throws Right | R | .269 | 26 | 7 | 0 | 0 | 2 | 2 | 2 | 7 | .345 | .500 |
| Kazmir,Scott | L | .226 | 168 | 38 | 7 | 0 | 3 | 11 | 6 | 43 | .251 | .321 |
| Throws Left | R | .275 | 451 | 124 | 27 | 3 | 16 | 51 | 41 | 119 | .339 | .455 |
| Kelley,Shawn | L | .244 | 82 | 20 | 4 | 1 | 3 | 11 | 12 | 28 | .333 | .427 |
| Throws Right | R | .225 | 120 | 27 | 8 | 0 | 5 | 16 | 11 | 43 | .290 | .417 |
| Kelly,Joe | L | .245 | 216 | 53 | 15 | 0 | 5 | 12 | 19 | 38 | .306 | .384 |
| Throws Right | R | .270 | 263 | 71 | 5 | 1 | 5 | 25 | 25 | 41 | .342 | .354 |
| Kendrick,Kyle | L | .246 | 334 | 82 | 17 | 5 | 6 | 36 | 25 | 51 | .298 | .380 |
| Throws Right | R | .318 | 393 | 125 | 13 | 2 | 12 | 58 | 22 | 59 | .359 | .453 |
| Kennedy,Ian | L | .265 | 340 | 90 | 21 | 1 | 19 | 61 | 32 | 81 | .328 | .500 |
| Throws Right | R | .253 | 356 | 90 | 23 | 1 | 8 | 39 | 41 | 82 | .345 | .390 |
| Kershaw,Clayton | L | .165 | 158 | 26 | 6 | 1 | 2 | 8 | 11 | 71 | .224 | .253 |
| Throws Left | R | .202 | 682 | 138 | 24 | 2 | 9 | 41 | 41 | 161 | .249 | .283 |
| Keuchel,Dallas | L | .275 | 149 | 41 | 5 | 1 | 5 | 19 | 10 | 45 | .327 | .423 |
| Throws Left | R | .304 | 471 | 143 | 25 | 4 | 15 | 67 | 42 | 78 | .363 | .469 |
| Kickham,Mike | L | .362 | 47 | 17 | 7 | 0 | 1 | 6 | 1 | 9 | .375 | .574 |
| Throws Left | R | .345 | 84 | 29 | 7 | 0 | 7 | 24 | 9 | 20 | .404 | .679 |
| Kimbrel,Craig | L | .211 | 123 | 26 | 6 | 0 | 2 | 7 | 9 | 51 | .265 | .309 |
| Throws Right | R | .116 | 112 | 13 | 1 | 0 | 2 | 3 | 11 | 47 | .214 | .179 |
| Kintzler,Brandon | L | .220 | 118 | 26 | 4 | 0 | 1 | 12 | 6 | 24 | .260 | .280 |
| Throws Right | R | .244 | 164 | 40 | 6 | 0 | 1 | 8 | 10 | 34 | .287 | .299 |
| Kirkman,Michael | L | .341 | 41 | 14 | 5 | 0 | 2 | 10 | 3 | 10 | .386 | .610 |
| Throws Left | R | .379 | 58 | 22 | 6 | 0 | 0 | 7 | 12 | 15 | .479 | .483 |
| Kluber,Corey | L | .277 | 300 | 83 | 17 | 1 | 8 | 39 | 23 | 72 | .331 | .420 |
| Throws Right | R | .265 | 264 | 70 | 16 | 0 | 7 | 19 | 10 | 64 | .299 | .405 |
| Koehler,Tom | L | .235 | 251 | 59 | 16 | 1 | 6 | 27 | 34 | 42 | .328 | .378 |
| Throws Right | R | .283 | 286 | 81 | 12 | 7 | 8 | 37 | 20 | 50 | .338 | .458 |
| Kohn,Michael | L | .163 | 104 | 17 | 4 | 1 | 3 | 11 | 15 | 23 | .281 | .308 |
| Throws Right | R | .266 | 94 | 25 | 9 | 0 | 4 | 18 | 13 | 29 | .358 | .489 |
| Kontos,George | L | .339 | 62 | 21 | 3 | 1 | 4 | 13 | 9 | 11 | .411 | .613 |
| Throws Right | R | .258 | 151 | 39 | 10 | 0 | 3 | 25 | 9 | 36 | .305 | .384 |
| Krol,Ian | L | .220 | 50 | 11 | 2 | 0 | 1 | 5 | 4 | 10 | .273 | .320 |
| Throws Left | R | .304 | 56 | 17 | 5 | 0 | 4 | 11 | 4 | 12 | .350 | .607 |

# Pitchers vs. Left-Handed and Right-Handed Batters

| Pitcher | vs | Avg | AB | H | 2B | 3B | HR | RBI | BB | SO | OBP | Slg |
|---|---|---|---|---|---|---|---|---|---|---|---|---|
| Kuroda,Hiroki | L | .261 | 444 | 116 | 35 | 0 | 14 | 44 | 28 | 82 | .308 | .435 |
| Throws Right | R | .232 | 323 | 75 | 13 | 1 | 6 | 27 | 15 | 68 | .267 | .334 |
| Lackey,John | L | .238 | 404 | 96 | 19 | 3 | 10 | 37 | 25 | 85 | .285 | .374 |
| Throws Right | R | .258 | 322 | 83 | 18 | 0 | 16 | 31 | 15 | 76 | .297 | .463 |
| Laffey,Aaron | L | .333 | 18 | 6 | 1 | 0 | 1 | 4 | 2 | 2 | .435 | .556 |
| Throws Left | R | .400 | 30 | 12 | 3 | 0 | 0 | 6 | 8 | 7 | .513 | .500 |
| LaFromboise,Bobby | L | .286 | 14 | 4 | 1 | 0 | 0 | 4 | 1 | 6 | .333 | .357 |
| Throws Left | R | .286 | 28 | 8 | 1 | 0 | 0 | 3 | 3 | 5 | .355 | .321 |
| Langwell,Matt | L | .211 | 19 | 4 | 0 | 0 | 0 | 0 | 2 | 3 | .286 | .211 |
| Throws Right | R | .257 | 35 | 9 | 2 | 1 | 2 | 9 | 5 | 9 | .366 | .543 |
| Lannan,John | L | .323 | 65 | 21 | 3 | 0 | 2 | 14 | 2 | 9 | .371 | .462 |
| Throws Left | R | .288 | 226 | 65 | 19 | 1 | 4 | 29 | 25 | 29 | .358 | .434 |
| Latos,Mat | L | .247 | 372 | 92 | 21 | 4 | 8 | 34 | 29 | 81 | .309 | .390 |
| Throws Right | R | .246 | 426 | 105 | 16 | 3 | 6 | 37 | 29 | 106 | .302 | .340 |
| Layne,Tom | L | .333 | 21 | 7 | 0 | 0 | 1 | 3 | 4 | 5 | .481 | .476 |
| Throws Left | R | .300 | 10 | 3 | 1 | 0 | 0 | 0 | 1 | 1 | .364 | .400 |
| League,Brandon | L | .312 | 93 | 29 | 7 | 0 | 5 | 20 | 7 | 14 | .356 | .548 |
| Throws Right | R | .301 | 133 | 40 | 5 | 0 | 3 | 19 | 8 | 14 | .352 | .406 |
| Leake,Mike | L | .263 | 373 | 98 | 15 | 3 | 11 | 27 | 24 | 55 | .309 | .408 |
| Throws Right | R | .263 | 361 | 95 | 18 | 2 | 10 | 41 | 24 | 67 | .314 | .407 |
| LeBlanc,Wade | L | .346 | 78 | 27 | 4 | 2 | 4 | 17 | 5 | 7 | .400 | .603 |
| Throws Left | R | .290 | 155 | 45 | 12 | 0 | 3 | 23 | 15 | 26 | .355 | .426 |
| LeCure,Sam | L | .167 | 96 | 16 | 4 | 0 | 0 | 4 | 9 | 33 | .238 | .208 |
| Throws Right | R | .264 | 129 | 34 | 7 | 0 | 4 | 12 | 15 | 33 | .345 | .411 |
| Lee,C.C. | L | .200 | 5 | 1 | 0 | 1 | 0 | 0 | 1 | 1 | .333 | .600 |
| Throws Right | R | .273 | 11 | 3 | 0 | 0 | 0 | 3 | 2 | 3 | .375 | .273 |
| Lee,Cliff | L | .210 | 195 | 41 | 6 | 1 | 1 | 7 | 12 | 42 | .270 | .267 |
| Throws Left | R | .239 | 637 | 152 | 35 | 2 | 21 | 60 | 20 | 180 | .261 | .399 |
| Leesman,Charlie | L | .286 | 28 | 8 | 2 | 0 | 1 | 3 | 5 | 7 | .412 | .464 |
| Throws Left | R | .250 | 32 | 8 | 2 | 0 | 1 | 5 | 11 | 6 | .442 | .406 |
| Leroux,Chris | L | .286 | 7 | 2 | 0 | 0 | 0 | 3 | 2 | 1 | .444 | .286 |
| Throws Right | R | .250 | 8 | 2 | 0 | 0 | 1 | 2 | 4 | 2 | .500 | .625 |
| Lester,Jon | L | .237 | 186 | 44 | 9 | 1 | 6 | 23 | 11 | 51 | .278 | .392 |
| Throws Left | R | .257 | 641 | 165 | 43 | 1 | 13 | 60 | 56 | 126 | .324 | .388 |
| Lilly,Ted | L | .400 | 20 | 8 | 2 | 0 | 0 | 1 | 0 | 3 | .400 | .500 |
| Throws Left | R | .244 | 78 | 19 | 4 | 1 | 4 | 12 | 10 | 15 | .337 | .474 |
| Lim,Chang-Yong | L | .500 | 6 | 3 | 1 | 0 | 0 | 2 | 3 | 0 | .667 | .667 |
| Throws Right | R | .231 | 13 | 3 | 1 | 0 | 0 | 1 | 4 | 5 | .444 | .308 |
| Lincecum,Tim | L | .235 | 362 | 85 | 12 | 3 | 7 | 34 | 45 | 100 | .321 | .343 |
| Throws Right | R | .260 | 381 | 99 | 20 | 2 | 14 | 47 | 31 | 93 | .322 | .433 |
| Lincoln,Brad | L | .224 | 58 | 13 | 2 | 2 | 2 | 9 | 13 | 16 | .375 | .431 |
| Throws Right | R | .242 | 62 | 15 | 1 | 0 | 2 | 6 | 9 | 9 | .356 | .355 |
| Lindblom,Josh | L | .286 | 84 | 24 | 6 | 0 | 3 | 11 | 7 | 11 | .341 | .464 |
| Throws Right | R | .262 | 42 | 11 | 2 | 1 | 1 | 5 | 4 | 10 | .326 | .429 |
| Lindstrom,Matt | L | .317 | 82 | 26 | 5 | 0 | 0 | 8 | 11 | 14 | .400 | .378 |
| Throws Right | R | .255 | 149 | 38 | 4 | 0 | 2 | 23 | 12 | 32 | .307 | .322 |
| Liriano,Francisco | L | .131 | 130 | 17 | 2 | 0 | 0 | 4 | 7 | 37 | .175 | .146 |
| Throws Left | R | .249 | 469 | 117 | 21 | 2 | 9 | 45 | 56 | 126 | .329 | .360 |
| Lo,Chia-Jen | L | .128 | 39 | 5 | 0 | 0 | 1 | 2 | 8 | 7 | .277 | .205 |
| Throws Right | R | .300 | 30 | 9 | 0 | 0 | 1 | 7 | 5 | 9 | .389 | .400 |
| Locke,Jeff | L | .286 | 140 | 40 | 8 | 0 | 1 | 14 | 17 | 19 | .384 | .364 |
| Throws Left | R | .229 | 463 | 106 | 20 | 2 | 10 | 46 | 67 | 106 | .321 | .346 |
| Loe,Kameron | L | .304 | 46 | 14 | 2 | 1 | 3 | 5 | 4 | 4 | .360 | .587 |
| Throws Right | R | .371 | 70 | 26 | 6 | 1 | 8 | 16 | 6 | 11 | .421 | .829 |
| Logan,Boone | L | .221 | 77 | 17 | 3 | 0 | 3 | 13 | 6 | 34 | .274 | .377 |
| Throws Left | R | .254 | 63 | 16 | 1 | 0 | 4 | 14 | 7 | 16 | .319 | .460 |
| Lohse,Kyle | L | .256 | 356 | 91 | 17 | 0 | 14 | 39 | 25 | 65 | .305 | .421 |
| Throws Right | R | .262 | 401 | 105 | 14 | 1 | 12 | 34 | 11 | 60 | .284 | .392 |
| Lopez,Javier | L | .156 | 90 | 14 | 6 | 0 | 0 | 7 | 6 | 29 | .208 | .222 |
| Throws Left | R | .296 | 54 | 16 | 3 | 1 | 1 | 8 | 6 | 8 | .361 | .444 |
| Lopez,Wilton | L | .278 | 133 | 37 | 6 | 2 | 1 | 14 | 8 | 17 | .317 | .376 |
| Throws Right | R | .305 | 167 | 51 | 10 | 0 | 5 | 29 | 10 | 31 | .348 | .455 |
| Loup,Aaron | L | .200 | 100 | 20 | 2 | 0 | 0 | 8 | 6 | 17 | .286 | .220 |
| Throws Left | R | .295 | 156 | 46 | 6 | 2 | 5 | 20 | 7 | 36 | .321 | .455 |
| Lowe,Derek | L | .368 | 19 | 7 | 2 | 0 | 2 | 7 | 1 | 0 | .455 | .789 |
| Throws Right | R | .273 | 33 | 9 | 1 | 0 | 1 | 6 | 2 | 8 | .314 | .394 |
| Lowe,Mark | L | .316 | 19 | 6 | 2 | 1 | 0 | 3 | 7 | 3 | .500 | .526 |
| Throws Right | R | .208 | 24 | 5 | 1 | 0 | 1 | 10 | 4 | 4 | .321 | .375 |
| Lueke,Josh | L | .250 | 36 | 9 | 1 | 2 | 1 | 5 | 9 | 9 | .400 | .472 |
| Throws Right | R | .298 | 47 | 14 | 4 | 0 | 2 | 13 | 3 | 16 | .340 | .511 |
| Luetge,Lucas | L | .259 | 54 | 14 | 1 | 0 | 1 | 11 | 3 | 9 | .300 | .333 |
| Throws Left | R | .318 | 88 | 28 | 10 | 0 | 1 | 15 | 13 | 18 | .408 | .466 |
| Lyles,Jordan | L | .269 | 308 | 83 | 17 | 1 | 7 | 49 | 38 | 40 | .351 | .399 |
| Throws Right | R | .303 | 271 | 82 | 20 | 3 | 10 | 41 | 11 | 53 | .349 | .509 |
| Lynn,Lance | L | .259 | 317 | 82 | 16 | 6 | 6 | 34 | 49 | 71 | .361 | .404 |
| Throws Right | R | .247 | 433 | 107 | 16 | 3 | 8 | 49 | 27 | 127 | .299 | .353 |

| Pitcher | vs | Avg | AB | H | 2B | 3B | HR | RBI | BB | SO | OBP | Slg |
|---|---|---|---|---|---|---|---|---|---|---|---|---|
| Lyon,Brandon | L | .271 | 48 | 13 | 4 | 0 | 0 | 4 | 7 | 8 | .357 | .354 |
| Throws Right | R | .353 | 85 | 30 | 8 | 0 | 3 | 21 | 6 | 15 | .391 | .553 |
| Lyons,Tyler | L | .228 | 57 | 13 | 4 | 0 | 1 | 5 | 3 | 18 | .279 | .351 |
| Throws Left | R | .247 | 146 | 36 | 9 | 4 | 4 | 18 | 13 | 25 | .317 | .445 |
| Machi,Jean | L | .247 | 73 | 18 | 5 | 1 | 0 | 9 | 6 | 16 | .300 | .342 |
| Throws Right | R | .226 | 124 | 28 | 2 | 0 | 2 | 15 | 6 | 35 | .262 | .290 |
| Magill,Matt | L | .279 | 43 | 12 | 2 | 0 | 4 | 12 | 18 | 13 | .500 | .605 |
| Throws Right | R | .242 | 62 | 15 | 1 | 0 | 2 | 11 | 10 | 13 | .338 | .355 |
| Maholm,Paul | L | .226 | 155 | 35 | 8 | 0 | 1 | 15 | 6 | 35 | .262 | .297 |
| Throws Left | R | .299 | 448 | 134 | 28 | 2 | 16 | 56 | 41 | 70 | .367 | .478 |
| Maine,John | L | .364 | 11 | 4 | 0 | 0 | 0 | 2 | 3 | 3 | .500 | .364 |
| Throws Right | R | .478 | 23 | 11 | 1 | 0 | 2 | 7 | 2 | 4 | .520 | .783 |
| Maness,Seth | L | .274 | 73 | 20 | 3 | 0 | 2 | 7 | 6 | 6 | .329 | .397 |
| Throws Right | R | .285 | 158 | 45 | 13 | 0 | 2 | 14 | 7 | 29 | .319 | .405 |
| Manship,Jeff | L | .304 | 56 | 17 | 1 | 1 | 1 | 8 | 6 | 5 | .371 | .411 |
| Throws Right | R | .294 | 68 | 20 | 4 | 1 | 5 | 19 | 6 | 13 | .338 | .603 |
| Marcum,Shaun | L | .302 | 126 | 38 | 9 | 1 | 3 | 20 | 16 | 21 | .378 | .460 |
| Throws Right | R | .272 | 173 | 47 | 8 | 0 | 4 | 23 | 5 | 39 | .303 | .387 |
| Marmol,Carlos | L | .155 | 71 | 11 | 2 | 0 | 2 | 10 | 15 | 28 | .299 | .268 |
| Throws Right | R | .271 | 107 | 29 | 4 | 1 | 5 | 14 | 25 | 31 | .423 | .467 |
| Maronde,Nick | L | .182 | 11 | 2 | 0 | 0 | 1 | 4 | 5 | 3 | .438 | .455 |
| Throws Left | R | .222 | 9 | 2 | 1 | 0 | 0 | 0 | 3 | 2 | .417 | .333 |
| Marquis,Jason | L | .267 | 187 | 50 | 8 | 0 | 11 | 32 | 35 | 28 | .382 | .487 |
| Throws Right | R | .249 | 245 | 61 | 11 | 0 | 7 | 21 | 33 | 44 | .340 | .380 |
| Marshall,Brett | L | .261 | 23 | 6 | 1 | 0 | 2 | 5 | 4 | 5 | .370 | .565 |
| Throws Right | R | .304 | 23 | 7 | 0 | 0 | 1 | 1 | 3 | 2 | .407 | .435 |
| Marshall,Sean | L | .190 | 21 | 4 | 0 | 0 | 0 | 2 | 1 | 6 | .261 | .190 |
| Throws Left | R | .000 | 13 | 0 | 0 | 0 | 0 | 0 | 1 | 4 | .071 | .000 |
| Martin,Ethan | L | .284 | 74 | 21 | 7 | 0 | 2 | 9 | 13 | 26 | .386 | .459 |
| Throws Right | R | .241 | 87 | 21 | 2 | 0 | 7 | 17 | 13 | 21 | .347 | .506 |
| Martinez,Carlos | L | .326 | 46 | 15 | 3 | 0 | 0 | 6 | 4 | 6 | .373 | .391 |
| Throws Right | R | .250 | 64 | 16 | 2 | 0 | 1 | 12 | 5 | 18 | .333 | .328 |
| Martinez,David | L | .417 | 12 | 5 | 1 | 0 | 0 | 3 | 2 | 3 | .438 | .500 |
| Throws Right | R | .367 | 30 | 11 | 2 | 2 | 1 | 6 | 1 | 3 | .375 | .667 |
| Martis,Shairon | L | .211 | 19 | 4 | 1 | 0 | 3 | 4 | 2 | 3 | .286 | .737 |
| Throws Right | R | .125 | 16 | 2 | 1 | 0 | 0 | 3 | 2 | 4 | .222 | .188 |
| Masterson,Justin | L | .248 | 428 | 106 | 15 | 1 | 10 | 51 | 54 | 96 | .340 | .357 |
| Throws Right | R | .182 | 275 | 50 | 7 | 0 | 3 | 18 | 22 | 99 | .267 | .240 |
| Matsuzaka,Daisuke | L | .250 | 76 | 19 | 4 | 0 | 1 | 8 | 10 | 18 | .337 | .342 |
| Throws Right | R | .200 | 65 | 13 | 3 | 0 | 3 | 9 | 6 | 15 | .316 | .385 |
| Mattheus,Ryan | L | .438 | 64 | 28 | 5 | 0 | 0 | 12 | 6 | 7 | .486 | .516 |
| Throws Right | R | .286 | 84 | 24 | 3 | 0 | 1 | 12 | 9 | 15 | .344 | .357 |
| Matusz,Brian | L | .168 | 101 | 17 | 5 | 0 | 2 | 11 | 7 | 33 | .225 | .277 |
| Throws Left | R | .302 | 86 | 26 | 3 | 0 | 1 | 7 | 9 | 17 | .375 | .372 |
| Maurer,Brandon | L | .321 | 209 | 67 | 14 | 2 | 10 | 40 | 17 | 33 | .368 | .550 |
| Throws Right | R | .299 | 157 | 47 | 7 | 1 | 6 | 21 | 10 | 37 | .364 | .471 |
| Mazzaro,Vin | L | .211 | 114 | 24 | 8 | 2 | 0 | 7 | 13 | 22 | .300 | .316 |
| Throws Right | R | .272 | 162 | 44 | 0 | 0 | 3 | 17 | 8 | 24 | .310 | .327 |
| McAllister,Zach | L | .249 | 281 | 70 | 27 | 1 | 4 | 31 | 40 | 55 | .342 | .395 |
| Throws Right | R | .267 | 240 | 64 | 9 | 2 | 9 | 28 | 9 | 46 | .307 | .433 |
| McCarthy,Brandon | L | .283 | 283 | 80 | 10 | 3 | 6 | 31 | 13 | 48 | .313 | .403 |
| Throws Right | R | .310 | 261 | 81 | 19 | 0 | 7 | 36 | 8 | 28 | .343 | .464 |
| McClellan,Kyle | L | .125 | 16 | 2 | 0 | 1 | 1 | 3 | 3 | 2 | .263 | .438 |
| Throws Right | R | .294 | 17 | 5 | 1 | 0 | 1 | 5 | 2 | 1 | .381 | .529 |
| McDonald,James | L | .232 | 56 | 13 | 5 | 0 | 1 | 9 | 8 | 15 | .328 | .375 |
| Throws Right | R | .271 | 59 | 16 | 8 | 0 | 0 | 12 | 12 | 10 | .419 | .407 |
| McFarland,T.J. | L | .287 | 129 | 37 | 7 | 1 | 4 | 20 | 5 | 33 | .311 | .450 |
| Throws Left | R | .269 | 171 | 46 | 7 | 0 | 3 | 23 | 23 | 25 | .356 | .363 |
| McGee,Jake | L | .235 | 81 | 19 | 3 | 0 | 3 | 13 | 7 | 23 | .295 | .383 |
| Throws Left | R | .217 | 152 | 33 | 5 | 1 | 5 | 26 | 15 | 52 | .287 | .362 |
| McGowan,Dustin | L | .188 | 48 | 9 | 4 | 0 | 2 | 5 | 6 | 8 | .278 | .396 |
| Throws Right | R | .192 | 52 | 10 | 3 | 0 | 0 | 7 | 6 | 18 | .300 | .250 |
| McHugh,Collin | L | .438 | 48 | 21 | 5 | 0 | 4 | 11 | 2 | 5 | .460 | .792 |
| Throws Right | R | .353 | 68 | 24 | 5 | 1 | 2 | 18 | 3 | 6 | .370 | .544 |
| Medina,Yoervis | L | .191 | 110 | 21 | 3 | 1 | 3 | 14 | 22 | 28 | .326 | .318 |
| Throws Right | R | .209 | 134 | 28 | 6 | 0 | 2 | 16 | 18 | 43 | .318 | .299 |
| Medlen,Kris | L | .256 | 390 | 100 | 24 | 3 | 10 | 37 | 33 | 77 | .319 | .410 |
| Throws Right | R | .259 | 363 | 94 | 20 | 1 | 8 | 31 | 14 | 80 | .294 | .386 |
| Mejia,Jenrry | L | .261 | 46 | 12 | 3 | 0 | 1 | 2 | 2 | 8 | .292 | .391 |
| Throws Right | R | .276 | 58 | 16 | 0 | 0 | 1 | 6 | 2 | 19 | .281 | .328 |
| Melancon,Mark | L | .148 | 122 | 18 | 2 | 0 | 1 | 1 | 3 | 34 | .168 | .189 |
| Throws Right | R | .286 | 147 | 42 | 4 | 1 | 0 | 12 | 5 | 36 | .312 | .327 |
| Mendoza,Luis | L | .303 | 201 | 61 | 18 | 0 | 7 | 31 | 26 | 23 | .380 | .498 |
| Throws Right | R | .271 | 166 | 45 | 9 | 2 | 3 | 23 | 17 | 31 | .346 | .404 |
| Mijares,Jose | L | .276 | 98 | 27 | 4 | 1 | 1 | 11 | 8 | 35 | .343 | .367 |
| Throws Left | R | .360 | 111 | 40 | 12 | 1 | 2 | 23 | 12 | 19 | .421 | .541 |

# Pitchers vs. Left-Handed and Right-Handed Batters

| Pitcher | vs | Avg | AB | H | 2B | 3B | HR | RBI | BB | SO | OBP | Slg |
|---|---|---|---|---|---|---|---|---|---|---|---|---|
| Miley,Wade | L | .272 | 158 | 43 | 10 | 0 | 3 | 10 | 7 | 27 | .311 | .392 |
| Throws Left | R | .259 | 611 | 158 | 33 | 2 | 18 | 70 | 59 | 120 | .325 | .408 |
| Miller,Andrew | L | .281 | 57 | 16 | 0 | 0 | 2 | 6 | 5 | 24 | .339 | .386 |
| Throws Left | R | .155 | 58 | 9 | 0 | 0 | 1 | 4 | 12 | 24 | .319 | .207 |
| Miller,Shelby | L | .266 | 308 | 82 | 15 | 1 | 11 | 34 | 30 | 74 | .332 | .429 |
| Throws Right | R | .205 | 342 | 70 | 10 | 1 | 9 | 26 | 27 | 95 | .269 | .319 |
| Milone,Tommy | L | .298 | 131 | 39 | 5 | 1 | 4 | 18 | 12 | 21 | .347 | .443 |
| Throws Left | R | .247 | 489 | 121 | 27 | 1 | 21 | 54 | 27 | 105 | .288 | .436 |
| Miner,Zach | L | .281 | 32 | 9 | 0 | 0 | 0 | 5 | 10 | 7 | .442 | .281 |
| Throws Right | R | .304 | 79 | 24 | 5 | 0 | 4 | 15 | 7 | 13 | .375 | .519 |
| Minor,Mike | L | .217 | 180 | 39 | 7 | 0 | 4 | 15 | 10 | 52 | .260 | .322 |
| Throws Left | R | .237 | 582 | 138 | 37 | 2 | 18 | 63 | 36 | 129 | .279 | .400 |
| Moore,Matt | L | .221 | 172 | 38 | 6 | 0 | 4 | 13 | 15 | 42 | .292 | .326 |
| Throws Left | R | .214 | 379 | 81 | 18 | 2 | 10 | 39 | 61 | 101 | .321 | .351 |
| Morales,Franklin | L | .184 | 38 | 7 | 0 | 0 | 0 | 2 | 2 | 13 | .262 | .184 |
| Throws Left | R | .304 | 56 | 17 | 4 | 0 | 2 | 12 | 13 | 8 | .443 | .482 |
| Morris,Bryan | L | .265 | 102 | 27 | 1 | 0 | 4 | 12 | 14 | 17 | .353 | .392 |
| Throws Right | R | .226 | 133 | 30 | 8 | 0 | 4 | 21 | 14 | 20 | .298 | .376 |
| Morrow,Brandon | L | .301 | 123 | 37 | 10 | 1 | 10 | 21 | 15 | 23 | .371 | .642 |
| Throws Right | R | .268 | 97 | 26 | 8 | 0 | 2 | 12 | 3 | 19 | .294 | .412 |
| Mortensen,Clayton | L | .317 | 63 | 20 | 3 | 0 | 1 | 7 | 10 | 10 | .405 | .413 |
| Throws Right | R | .211 | 57 | 12 | 1 | 0 | 2 | 7 | 6 | 11 | .318 | .333 |
| Morton,Charlie | L | .312 | 186 | 58 | 11 | 0 | 3 | 20 | 25 | 39 | .425 | .419 |
| Throws Right | R | .223 | 247 | 55 | 7 | 0 | 3 | 20 | 11 | 46 | .264 | .287 |
| Moscoso,Guillermo | L | .139 | 36 | 5 | 0 | 0 | 1 | 2 | 14 | 11 | .380 | .222 |
| Throws Right | R | .221 | 68 | 15 | 5 | 0 | 4 | 9 | 7 | 20 | .321 | .471 |
| Moylan,Peter | L | .440 | 25 | 11 | 2 | 0 | 0 | 7 | 3 | 1 | .500 | .520 |
| Throws Right | R | .316 | 38 | 12 | 1 | 0 | 3 | 8 | 4 | 5 | .381 | .579 |
| Mujica,Edward | L | .232 | 112 | 26 | 3 | 0 | 6 | 12 | 1 | 19 | .239 | .420 |
| Throws Right | R | .256 | 133 | 34 | 11 | 0 | 3 | 11 | 4 | 27 | .281 | .406 |
| Myers,Brett | L | .300 | 40 | 12 | 3 | 0 | 3 | 5 | 4 | 5 | .364 | .600 |
| Throws Right | R | .333 | 51 | 17 | 2 | 0 | 7 | 14 | 1 | 7 | .346 | .784 |
| Nathan,Joe | L | .171 | 117 | 20 | 5 | 0 | 2 | 12 | 13 | 41 | .250 | .265 |
| Throws Right | R | .152 | 105 | 16 | 1 | 1 | 0 | 3 | 9 | 32 | .226 | .181 |
| Nelson,Jimmy | L | .125 | 16 | 2 | 1 | 0 | 0 | 1 | 4 | 3 | .286 | .188 |
| Throws Right | R | .000 | 15 | 0 | 0 | 0 | 0 | 0 | 1 | 5 | .063 | .000 |
| Neshek,Pat | L | .315 | 54 | 17 | 1 | 0 | 4 | 10 | 5 | 12 | .367 | .556 |
| Throws Right | R | .219 | 105 | 23 | 3 | 3 | 2 | 9 | 10 | 17 | .282 | .362 |
| Nicasio,Juan | L | .228 | 289 | 66 | 17 | 3 | 10 | 34 | 41 | 63 | .325 | .412 |
| Throws Right | R | .302 | 338 | 102 | 33 | 2 | 7 | 44 | 23 | 56 | .353 | .473 |
| Niese,Jon | L | .239 | 138 | 33 | 6 | 2 | 2 | 11 | 11 | 25 | .305 | .355 |
| Throws Left | R | .294 | 425 | 125 | 24 | 1 | 8 | 44 | 37 | 80 | .353 | .412 |
| Noesi,Hector | L | .373 | 59 | 22 | 3 | 0 | 2 | 14 | 4 | 12 | .413 | .525 |
| Throws Right | R | .333 | 60 | 20 | 8 | 0 | 1 | 12 | 8 | 9 | .414 | .517 |
| Nolasco,Ricky | L | .257 | 408 | 105 | 24 | 3 | 10 | 44 | 31 | 86 | .317 | .404 |
| Throws Right | R | .252 | 357 | 90 | 19 | 1 | 7 | 41 | 15 | 79 | .290 | .370 |
| Norris,Bud | L | .315 | 397 | 125 | 23 | 3 | 16 | 61 | 42 | 72 | .381 | .509 |
| Throws Right | R | .241 | 295 | 71 | 17 | 2 | 1 | 20 | 25 | 75 | .307 | .322 |
| Nova,Ivan | L | .264 | 280 | 74 | 11 | 0 | 3 | 18 | 25 | 55 | .341 | .336 |
| Throws Right | R | .251 | 243 | 61 | 9 | 0 | 6 | 22 | 19 | 61 | .318 | .362 |
| Nuno,Vidal | L | .188 | 16 | 3 | 0 | 0 | 1 | 1 | 2 | 2 | .316 | .375 |
| Throws Left | R | .220 | 59 | 13 | 6 | 0 | 1 | 3 | 4 | 7 | .270 | .373 |
| Oberholtzer,Brett | L | .280 | 82 | 23 | 5 | 1 | 2 | 7 | 2 | 11 | .306 | .439 |
| Throws Left | R | .219 | 196 | 43 | 12 | 0 | 5 | 16 | 11 | 34 | .260 | .357 |
| O'Day,Darren | L | .309 | 81 | 25 | 5 | 0 | 5 | 14 | 7 | 18 | .367 | .556 |
| Throws Right | R | .154 | 143 | 22 | 4 | 0 | 2 | 12 | 8 | 41 | .219 | .224 |
| Odorizzi,Jake | L | .293 | 58 | 17 | 5 | 0 | 2 | 7 | 5 | 9 | .364 | .483 |
| Throws Right | R | .208 | 53 | 11 | 4 | 1 | 1 | 3 | 3 | 13 | .250 | .377 |
| O'Flaherty,Eric | L | .143 | 21 | 3 | 0 | 1 | 0 | 1 | 1 | 4 | .182 | .238 |
| Throws Left | R | .209 | 43 | 9 | 0 | 0 | 2 | 6 | 4 | 7 | .271 | .349 |
| Ogando,Alexi | L | .210 | 214 | 45 | 8 | 1 | 6 | 21 | 18 | 34 | .278 | .341 |
| Throws Right | R | .258 | 163 | 42 | 8 | 0 | 5 | 13 | 23 | 38 | .354 | .399 |
| Ohlendorf,Ross | L | .268 | 97 | 26 | 4 | 1 | 4 | 10 | 8 | 18 | .324 | .454 |
| Throws Right | R | .227 | 132 | 30 | 9 | 0 | 4 | 15 | 6 | 27 | .266 | .386 |
| Okajima,Hideki | L | .444 | 9 | 4 | 3 | 0 | 0 | 2 | 0 | 1 | .444 | .778 |
| Throws Left | R | .300 | 10 | 3 | 0 | 0 | 1 | 1 | 2 | 0 | .417 | .600 |
| Oliver,Darren | L | .324 | 74 | 24 | 5 | 1 | 4 | 11 | 2 | 14 | .351 | .581 |
| Throws Left | R | .211 | 109 | 23 | 4 | 1 | 2 | 13 | 13 | 26 | .298 | .321 |
| Olmos,Edgar | L | .222 | 9 | 2 | 0 | 0 | 0 | 0 | 0 | 1 | .222 | .222 |
| Throws Left | R | .455 | 11 | 5 | 0 | 1 | 2 | 8 | 3 | 1 | .571 | 1.182 |
| Omogrosso,Brian | L | .429 | 42 | 18 | 6 | 0 | 2 | 9 | 7 | 9 | .510 | .714 |
| Throws Right | R | .313 | 32 | 10 | 3 | 1 | 0 | 8 | 2 | 7 | .371 | .469 |
| Ondrusek,Logan | L | .258 | 93 | 24 | 6 | 1 | 6 | 19 | 7 | 30 | .317 | .538 |
| Throws Right | R | .244 | 119 | 29 | 5 | 0 | 2 | 9 | 9 | 23 | .297 | .336 |
| Ortega,Jose | L | .227 | 22 | 5 | 0 | 0 | 2 | 5 | 3 | 2 | .320 | .500 |
| Throws Right | R | .227 | 22 | 5 | 0 | 0 | 0 | 0 | 3 | 8 | .346 | .227 |

| Pitcher | vs | Avg | AB | H | 2B | 3B | HR | RBI | BB | SO | OBP | Slg |
|---|---|---|---|---|---|---|---|---|---|---|---|---|
| Ortiz,Joe | L | .257 | 70 | 18 | 2 | 1 | 2 | 8 | 3 | 10 | .284 | .400 |
| Throws Left | R | .277 | 101 | 28 | 9 | 1 | 3 | 17 | 7 | 17 | .315 | .475 |
| Ortiz,Ramon | L | .327 | 55 | 18 | 2 | 0 | 3 | 5 | 8 | 4 | .406 | .527 |
| Throws Right | R | .348 | 46 | 16 | 5 | 0 | 4 | 11 | 3 | 4 | .385 | .717 |
| O'Sullivan,Sean | L | .348 | 46 | 16 | 5 | 1 | 0 | 5 | 9 | 3 | .464 | .500 |
| Throws Right | R | .278 | 54 | 15 | 4 | 0 | 0 | 9 | 5 | 9 | .328 | .352 |
| Oswalt,Roy | L | .375 | 64 | 24 | 5 | 2 | 1 | 12 | 5 | 13 | .414 | .563 |
| Throws Right | R | .342 | 73 | 25 | 4 | 0 | 2 | 15 | 4 | 21 | .375 | .479 |
| Otero,Dan | L | .269 | 78 | 21 | 3 | 0 | 0 | 7 | 4 | 13 | .305 | .308 |
| Throws Right | R | .284 | 74 | 21 | 2 | 0 | 0 | 7 | 2 | 14 | .303 | .311 |
| Ottavino,Adam | L | .328 | 119 | 39 | 5 | 1 | 2 | 12 | 18 | 23 | .416 | .437 |
| Throws Right | R | .197 | 173 | 34 | 5 | 1 | 3 | 22 | 13 | 55 | .255 | .289 |
| Outman,Josh | L | .198 | 111 | 22 | 4 | 0 | 1 | 11 | 11 | 39 | .278 | .261 |
| Throws Left | R | .347 | 98 | 34 | 5 | 0 | 2 | 14 | 12 | 14 | .423 | .459 |
| Papelbon,Jonathan | L | .241 | 116 | 28 | 5 | 0 | 3 | 10 | 7 | 29 | .282 | .362 |
| Throws Right | R | .252 | 123 | 31 | 2 | 0 | 3 | 14 | 4 | 28 | .277 | .341 |
| Parker,Blake | L | .197 | 71 | 14 | 2 | 0 | 1 | 3 | 10 | 29 | .305 | .268 |
| Throws Right | R | .236 | 106 | 25 | 5 | 1 | 3 | 17 | 5 | 26 | .274 | .387 |
| Parker,Jarrod | L | .257 | 424 | 109 | 17 | 1 | 15 | 46 | 34 | 82 | .317 | .408 |
| Throws Right | R | .221 | 312 | 69 | 14 | 0 | 10 | 36 | 29 | 52 | .292 | .362 |
| Parnell,Bobby | L | .211 | 71 | 15 | 4 | 0 | 1 | 5 | 8 | 21 | .296 | .310 |
| Throws Right | R | .211 | 109 | 23 | 8 | 0 | 0 | 10 | 4 | 23 | .235 | .284 |
| Parra,Manny | L | .167 | 84 | 14 | 0 | 0 | 2 | 6 | 8 | 32 | .237 | .238 |
| Throws Left | R | .310 | 84 | 26 | 9 | 0 | 3 | 11 | 7 | 24 | .370 | .524 |
| Partch,Curtis | L | .161 | 31 | 5 | 4 | 0 | 1 | 5 | 9 | 6 | .366 | .387 |
| Throws Right | R | .240 | 50 | 12 | 1 | 0 | 7 | 16 | 8 | 10 | .371 | .680 |
| Patton,Troy | L | .289 | 97 | 28 | 3 | 0 | 5 | 17 | 3 | 19 | .324 | .474 |
| Throws Left | R | .254 | 114 | 29 | 7 | 0 | 3 | 16 | 13 | 23 | .328 | .395 |
| Paxton,James | L | .313 | 16 | 5 | 2 | 0 | 0 | 0 | 1 | 5 | .353 | .438 |
| Throws Left | R | .141 | 71 | 10 | 3 | 0 | 2 | 5 | 6 | 16 | .208 | .268 |
| Peacock,Brad | L | .286 | 182 | 52 | 13 | 3 | 9 | 28 | 27 | 36 | .381 | .538 |
| Throws Right | R | .184 | 141 | 26 | 5 | 0 | 6 | 16 | 10 | 41 | .247 | .348 |
| Peavy,Jake | L | .243 | 288 | 70 | 20 | 2 | 11 | 33 | 20 | 69 | .290 | .441 |
| Throws Right | R | .232 | 259 | 60 | 7 | 2 | 9 | 29 | 16 | 52 | .281 | .378 |
| Pelfrey,Mike | L | .270 | 337 | 91 | 19 | 2 | 10 | 45 | 31 | 60 | .334 | .427 |
| Throws Right | R | .337 | 276 | 93 | 14 | 2 | 3 | 36 | 22 | 41 | .386 | .435 |
| Peralta,Joel | L | .163 | 147 | 24 | 7 | 0 | 4 | 15 | 20 | 44 | .263 | .293 |
| Throws Right | R | .213 | 108 | 23 | 3 | 0 | 3 | 9 | 14 | 30 | .303 | .324 |
| Peralta,Wily | L | .259 | 348 | 90 | 15 | 1 | 12 | 41 | 43 | 66 | .342 | .411 |
| Throws Right | R | .269 | 360 | 97 | 11 | 0 | 7 | 49 | 30 | 63 | .333 | .358 |
| Perez,Chris | L | .291 | 117 | 34 | 9 | 1 | 7 | 17 | 9 | 30 | .352 | .564 |
| Throws Right | R | .229 | 96 | 22 | 6 | 1 | 4 | 8 | 12 | 24 | .327 | .438 |
| Perez,Juan | L | .200 | 45 | 9 | 1 | 1 | 1 | 8 | 4 | 15 | .280 | .333 |
| Throws Left | R | .200 | 70 | 14 | 1 | 0 | 2 | 6 | 11 | 18 | .309 | .300 |
| Perez,Luis | L | .300 | 10 | 3 | 0 | 0 | 0 | 0 | 0 | 4 | .300 | .300 |
| Throws Left | R | .111 | 9 | 1 | 0 | 0 | 0 | 0 | 2 | 2 | .273 | .111 |
| Perez,Martin | L | .282 | 117 | 33 | 3 | 0 | 4 | 8 | 10 | 21 | .349 | .410 |
| Throws Left | R | .262 | 367 | 96 | 18 | 1 | 11 | 41 | 27 | 63 | .312 | .406 |
| Perez,Oliver | L | .238 | 80 | 19 | 1 | 0 | 1 | 7 | 14 | 30 | .358 | .288 |
| Throws Left | R | .256 | 121 | 31 | 8 | 1 | 5 | 21 | 12 | 44 | .323 | .463 |
| Perkins,Glen | L | .236 | 55 | 13 | 2 | 0 | 0 | 4 | 2 | 18 | .271 | .273 |
| Throws Left | R | .183 | 164 | 30 | 7 | 0 | 5 | 15 | 13 | 59 | .251 | .317 |
| Pestano,Vinnie | L | .292 | 72 | 21 | 3 | 0 | 4 | 9 | 9 | 16 | .378 | .500 |
| Throws Right | R | .254 | 63 | 16 | 5 | 0 | 2 | 11 | 12 | 21 | .364 | .429 |
| Petit,Yusmeiro | L | .209 | 67 | 14 | 4 | 0 | 0 | 4 | 8 | 16 | .293 | .269 |
| Throws Right | R | .276 | 116 | 32 | 5 | 0 | 4 | 13 | 3 | 31 | .294 | .422 |
| Petricka,Jake | L | .292 | 24 | 7 | 2 | 0 | 0 | 5 | 4 | 5 | .400 | .375 |
| Throws Right | R | .271 | 48 | 13 | 1 | 0 | 0 | 6 | 6 | 5 | .352 | .292 |
| Pettibone,Jonathan | L | .306 | 196 | 60 | 10 | 1 | 5 | 31 | 21 | 32 | .381 | .444 |
| Throws Right | R | .261 | 188 | 49 | 12 | 2 | 4 | 18 | 17 | 34 | .325 | .410 |
| Pettitte,Andy | L | .195 | 169 | 33 | 6 | 1 | 5 | 19 | 8 | 41 | .235 | .331 |
| Throws Left | R | .299 | 552 | 165 | 37 | 1 | 12 | 58 | 40 | 87 | .346 | .435 |
| Phelps,David | L | .255 | 200 | 51 | 13 | 2 | 6 | 34 | 18 | 52 | .326 | .430 |
| Throws Right | R | .280 | 132 | 37 | 6 | 0 | 2 | 16 | 17 | 27 | .367 | .371 |
| Pimentel,Stolmy | L | .071 | 14 | 1 | 1 | 0 | 0 | 0 | 0 | 3 | .071 | .143 |
| Throws Right | R | .238 | 21 | 5 | 0 | 0 | 0 | 3 | 2 | 6 | .292 | .238 |
| Pomeranz,Drew | L | .130 | 23 | 3 | 1 | 0 | 0 | 3 | 3 | 10 | .231 | .174 |
| Throws Left | R | .367 | 60 | 22 | 5 | 0 | 4 | 11 | 16 | 9 | .500 | .650 |
| Porcello,Rick | L | .301 | 352 | 106 | 17 | 1 | 11 | 32 | 31 | 60 | .359 | .449 |
| Throws Right | R | .238 | 332 | 79 | 12 | 0 | 7 | 44 | 11 | 82 | .264 | .337 |
| Pressly,Ryan | L | .289 | 135 | 39 | 8 | 0 | 2 | 18 | 14 | 26 | .353 | .393 |
| Throws Right | R | .216 | 148 | 32 | 7 | 1 | 3 | 23 | 13 | 23 | .276 | .338 |
| Price,David | L | .189 | 164 | 31 | 4 | 1 | 2 | 16 | 7 | 40 | .227 | .262 |
| Throws Left | R | .271 | 543 | 147 | 36 | 0 | 14 | 53 | 20 | 111 | .298 | .414 |
| Pryor,Stephen | L | .000 | 6 | 0 | 0 | 0 | 0 | 0 | 0 | 2 | .000 | .000 |
| Throws Right | R | .158 | 19 | 3 | 0 | 0 | 0 | 1 | 1 | 5 | .200 | .158 |

# Pitchers vs. Left-Handed and Right-Handed Batters

| Pitcher | vs | Avg | AB | H | 2B | 3B | HR | RBI | BB | SO | OBP | Slg |
|---|---|---|---|---|---|---|---|---|---|---|---|---|
| Purcey,David | L | .205 | 44 | 9 | 4 | 0 | 1 | 6 | 6 | 12 | .315 | .364 |
| Throws Left | R | .213 | 47 | 10 | 1 | 1 | 1 | 4 | 11 | 11 | .362 | .340 |
| Putkonen,Luke | L | .260 | 50 | 13 | 0 | 0 | 0 | 4 | 3 | 18 | .302 | .260 |
| Throws Right | R | .262 | 65 | 17 | 0 | 0 | 4 | 10 | 6 | 10 | .319 | .446 |
| Putz,J.J. | L | .180 | 50 | 9 | 2 | 0 | 2 | 5 | 7 | 14 | .281 | .340 |
| Throws Right | R | .233 | 73 | 17 | 4 | 0 | 2 | 7 | 10 | 24 | .325 | .370 |
| Qualls,Chad | L | .239 | 92 | 22 | 2 | 0 | 1 | 6 | 8 | 19 | .307 | .293 |
| Throws Right | R | .259 | 135 | 35 | 5 | 1 | 3 | 12 | 11 | 30 | .320 | .378 |
| Quintana,Jose | L | .260 | 208 | 54 | 13 | 1 | 5 | 22 | 17 | 47 | .313 | .404 |
| Throws Left | R | .242 | 554 | 134 | 25 | 2 | 18 | 56 | 39 | 117 | .296 | .392 |
| Raley,Brooks | L | .182 | 22 | 4 | 1 | 0 | 0 | 1 | 2 | 8 | .280 | .227 |
| Throws Left | R | .259 | 27 | 7 | 0 | 1 | 2 | 6 | 6 | 6 | .400 | .556 |
| Ramirez,Erasmo | L | .286 | 175 | 50 | 8 | 0 | 6 | 21 | 19 | 31 | .357 | .434 |
| Throws Right | R | .254 | 114 | 29 | 3 | 0 | 6 | 15 | 7 | 26 | .303 | .439 |
| Ramirez,J.C. | L | .378 | 37 | 14 | 1 | 1 | 1 | 7 | 8 | 3 | .478 | .541 |
| Throws Right | R | .271 | 59 | 16 | 3 | 1 | 5 | 15 | 7 | 13 | .333 | .610 |
| Ramirez,Ramon | L | .455 | 11 | 5 | 1 | 0 | 2 | 4 | 1 | 0 | .429 | 1.091 |
| Throws Right | R | .400 | 10 | 4 | 1 | 0 | 0 | 4 | 4 | 0 | .571 | .500 |
| Ramos,A.J. | L | .220 | 132 | 29 | 6 | 2 | 4 | 19 | 26 | 36 | .354 | .386 |
| Throws Right | R | .185 | 157 | 29 | 6 | 0 | 0 | 11 | 17 | 50 | .261 | .223 |
| Ramos,Cesar | L | .272 | 103 | 28 | 2 | 1 | 2 | 12 | 7 | 22 | .325 | .369 |
| Throws Left | R | .245 | 155 | 38 | 6 | 1 | 4 | 22 | 15 | 31 | .308 | .374 |
| Rasmus,Cory | L | .364 | 44 | 16 | 6 | 0 | 3 | 6 | 6 | 5 | .440 | .705 |
| Throws Right | R | .178 | 45 | 8 | 1 | 0 | 3 | 9 | 7 | 15 | .283 | .400 |
| Rauch,Jon | L | .310 | 29 | 9 | 2 | 1 | 1 | 4 | 5 | 2 | .429 | .552 |
| Throws Right | R | .341 | 41 | 14 | 1 | 0 | 0 | 8 | 2 | 13 | .372 | .366 |
| Redmond,Todd | L | .208 | 154 | 32 | 7 | 2 | 8 | 16 | 15 | 33 | .289 | .435 |
| Throws Right | R | .273 | 139 | 38 | 12 | 0 | 5 | 17 | 8 | 43 | .327 | .468 |
| Reed,Addison | L | .210 | 143 | 30 | 4 | 2 | 3 | 17 | 13 | 37 | .280 | .329 |
| Throws Right | R | .220 | 118 | 26 | 3 | 0 | 3 | 11 | 10 | 35 | .275 | .322 |
| Reed,Evan | L | .289 | 38 | 11 | 3 | 0 | 0 | 3 | 7 | 10 | .391 | .368 |
| Throws Right | R | .309 | 55 | 17 | 2 | 0 | 2 | 11 | 1 | 7 | .328 | .455 |
| Reid,Ryan | L | .333 | 15 | 5 | 1 | 1 | 0 | 0 | 3 | 3 | .444 | .533 |
| Throws Right | R | .167 | 24 | 4 | 0 | 0 | 1 | 3 | 0 | 4 | .222 | .292 |
| Resop,Chris | L | .324 | 34 | 11 | 2 | 0 | 2 | 10 | 7 | 6 | .452 | .559 |
| Throws Right | R | .268 | 41 | 11 | 1 | 1 | 1 | 3 | 3 | 7 | .333 | .415 |
| Reynolds,Greg | L | .222 | 54 | 12 | 3 | 0 | 2 | 9 | 4 | 9 | .279 | .389 |
| Throws Right | R | .406 | 64 | 26 | 4 | 1 | 3 | 9 | 2 | 4 | .449 | .641 |
| Reynolds,Matt | L | .262 | 42 | 11 | 4 | 1 | 1 | 4 | 3 | 13 | .326 | .476 |
| Throws Left | R | .226 | 62 | 14 | 1 | 0 | 1 | 5 | 2 | 10 | .246 | .290 |
| Rice,Scott | L | .174 | 121 | 21 | 3 | 0 | 1 | 10 | 10 | 35 | .244 | .223 |
| Throws Left | R | .362 | 58 | 21 | 5 | 0 | 0 | 5 | 17 | 6 | .507 | .448 |
| Richard,Clayton | L | .226 | 53 | 12 | 1 | 0 | 2 | 5 | 4 | 8 | .281 | .358 |
| Throws Left | R | .335 | 158 | 53 | 13 | 2 | 11 | 35 | 17 | 16 | .398 | .652 |
| Richards,Garrett | L | .281 | 324 | 91 | 12 | 0 | 10 | 37 | 30 | 59 | .341 | .410 |
| Throws Right | R | .252 | 238 | 60 | 11 | 1 | 2 | 23 | 14 | 42 | .294 | .332 |
| Rienzo,Andre | L | .248 | 145 | 36 | 6 | 0 | 8 | 22 | 16 | 26 | .325 | .455 |
| Throws Right | R | .264 | 72 | 19 | 4 | 0 | 3 | 6 | 12 | 12 | .376 | .444 |
| Rivera,Mariano | L | .244 | 135 | 33 | 4 | 0 | 1 | 10 | 5 | 28 | .271 | .296 |
| Throws Right | R | .225 | 111 | 25 | 6 | 0 | 5 | 11 | 4 | 26 | .259 | .414 |
| Roark,Tanner | L | .263 | 80 | 21 | 1 | 0 | 1 | 6 | 7 | 12 | .322 | .313 |
| Throws Right | R | .157 | 108 | 17 | 1 | 0 | 0 | 7 | 4 | 28 | .184 | .167 |
| Robertson,David | L | .175 | 126 | 22 | 5 | 0 | 1 | 6 | 12 | 51 | .246 | .238 |
| Throws Right | R | .257 | 113 | 29 | 3 | 0 | 4 | 13 | 6 | 26 | .306 | .389 |
| Robles,Mauricio | L | .375 | 8 | 3 | 1 | 0 | 0 | 1 | 0 | 2 | .375 | .500 |
| Throws Left | R | .286 | 14 | 4 | 0 | 0 | 0 | 4 | 3 | 4 | .412 | .286 |
| Rodney,Fernando | L | .248 | 133 | 33 | 11 | 0 | 1 | 18 | 24 | 46 | .363 | .353 |
| Throws Right | R | .169 | 118 | 20 | 6 | 1 | 2 | 12 | 12 | 36 | .250 | .288 |
| Rodriguez,Francisco | L | .156 | 96 | 15 | 4 | 0 | 3 | 4 | 8 | 37 | .221 | .292 |
| Throws Right | R | .342 | 79 | 27 | 5 | 2 | 4 | 9 | 6 | 17 | .395 | .608 |
| Rodriguez,Henry | L | .250 | 44 | 11 | 0 | 0 | 1 | 7 | 6 | 6 | .353 | .318 |
| Throws Right | R | .214 | 42 | 9 | 2 | 1 | 1 | 6 | 14 | 6 | .414 | .381 |
| Rodriguez,Paco | L | .131 | 99 | 13 | 2 | 0 | 1 | 5 | 9 | 44 | .218 | .182 |
| Throws Left | R | .202 | 84 | 17 | 1 | 0 | 4 | 12 | 10 | 19 | .284 | .357 |
| Rodriguez,Wandy | L | .250 | 60 | 15 | 1 | 0 | 4 | 4 | 3 | 4 | .318 | .467 |
| Throws Left | R | .236 | 182 | 43 | 11 | 1 | 6 | 21 | 9 | 42 | .275 | .407 |
| Roe,Chaz | L | .346 | 26 | 9 | 1 | 1 | 1 | 5 | 3 | 4 | .414 | .577 |
| Throws Right | R | .170 | 53 | 9 | 1 | 0 | 2 | 7 | 10 | 20 | .297 | .302 |
| Roenicke,Josh | L | .295 | 95 | 28 | 8 | 2 | 4 | 16 | 15 | 18 | .389 | .547 |
| Throws Right | R | .241 | 145 | 35 | 7 | 0 | 2 | 21 | 21 | 27 | .333 | .331 |
| Rogers,Esmil | L | .297 | 296 | 88 | 22 | 1 | 10 | 36 | 36 | 45 | .374 | .480 |
| Throws Right | R | .258 | 248 | 64 | 10 | 1 | 11 | 31 | 8 | 51 | .291 | .440 |
| Romero,Ricky | L | .667 | 12 | 8 | 0 | 0 | 2 | 8 | 2 | 0 | .714 | 1.167 |
| Throws Left | R | .158 | 19 | 3 | 0 | 0 | 0 | 1 | 6 | 5 | .385 | .158 |
| Romo,Sergio | L | .279 | 104 | 29 | 5 | 1 | 3 | 7 | 5 | 15 | .312 | .433 |
| Throws Right | R | .183 | 131 | 24 | 7 | 0 | 2 | 15 | 7 | 43 | .229 | .282 |

| Pitcher | vs | Avg | AB | H | 2B | 3B | HR | RBI | BB | SO | OBP | Slg |
|---|---|---|---|---|---|---|---|---|---|---|---|---|
| Rondon,Bruce | L | .295 | 44 | 13 | 3 | 1 | 1 | 3 | 8 | 10 | .396 | .477 |
| Throws Right | R | .234 | 64 | 15 | 4 | 0 | 1 | 8 | 3 | 20 | .265 | .344 |
| Rondon,Hector | L | .192 | 99 | 19 | 4 | 1 | 1 | 10 | 8 | 22 | .264 | .283 |
| Throws Right | R | .306 | 108 | 33 | 7 | 0 | 5 | 22 | 17 | 22 | .398 | .509 |
| Rosario,Sandy | L | .196 | 51 | 10 | 1 | 0 | 1 | 5 | 10 | 8 | .323 | .275 |
| Throws Right | R | .269 | 104 | 28 | 7 | 0 | 0 | 8 | 10 | 16 | .330 | .337 |
| Rosenberg,B.J. | L | .333 | 24 | 8 | 1 | 0 | 0 | 0 | 5 | 6 | .448 | .375 |
| Throws Right | R | .231 | 52 | 12 | 5 | 0 | 0 | 6 | 4 | 13 | .286 | .327 |
| Rosenthal,Trevor | L | .236 | 127 | 30 | 6 | 1 | 0 | 6 | 7 | 44 | .287 | .299 |
| Throws Right | R | .213 | 155 | 33 | 7 | 0 | 4 | 18 | 13 | 64 | .291 | .335 |
| Ross,Robbie | L | .341 | 91 | 31 | 9 | 0 | 3 | 20 | 7 | 24 | .412 | .538 |
| Throws Left | R | .211 | 152 | 32 | 3 | 0 | 1 | 8 | 12 | 34 | .273 | .250 |
| Ross,Tyson | L | .252 | 218 | 55 | 10 | 2 | 4 | 14 | 24 | 47 | .337 | .372 |
| Throws Right | R | .198 | 227 | 45 | 5 | 1 | 4 | 29 | 20 | 72 | .266 | .282 |
| Rosscup,Zac | L | .100 | 10 | 1 | 0 | 0 | 1 | 2 | 3 | 3 | .308 | .400 |
| Throws Left | R | .154 | 13 | 2 | 1 | 0 | 0 | 0 | 4 | 4 | .353 | .231 |
| Roth,Michael | L | .257 | 35 | 9 | 1 | 0 | 0 | 5 | 1 | 8 | .297 | .286 |
| Throws Left | R | .333 | 45 | 15 | 2 | 0 | 0 | 6 | 5 | 9 | .400 | .378 |
| Ruffin,Chance | L | .333 | 21 | 7 | 0 | 0 | 3 | 8 | 1 | 7 | .364 | .762 |
| Throws Right | R | .333 | 21 | 7 | 3 | 0 | 0 | 2 | 4 | 8 | .481 | .476 |
| Rusin,Chris | L | .203 | 59 | 12 | 4 | 0 | 0 | 3 | 3 | 7 | .250 | .271 |
| Throws Left | R | .278 | 194 | 54 | 10 | 1 | 8 | 23 | 21 | 29 | .355 | .464 |
| Russell,James | L | .183 | 115 | 21 | 6 | 2 | 2 | 14 | 6 | 26 | .221 | .322 |
| Throws Left | R | .321 | 78 | 25 | 8 | 0 | 5 | 20 | 12 | 11 | .418 | .615 |
| Ryu,Hyun-Jin | L | .270 | 185 | 50 | 12 | 0 | 5 | 12 | 14 | 37 | .322 | .416 |
| Throws Left | R | .245 | 538 | 132 | 18 | 2 | 10 | 44 | 35 | 117 | .291 | .342 |
| Rzepczynski,Marc | L | .179 | 56 | 10 | 4 | 0 | 0 | 10 | 1 | 16 | .230 | .250 |
| Throws Left | R | .298 | 57 | 17 | 3 | 0 | 2 | 7 | 9 | 13 | .403 | .456 |
| Sabathia,CC | L | .242 | 194 | 47 | 9 | 0 | 5 | 25 | 13 | 64 | .296 | .366 |
| Throws Left | R | .281 | 629 | 177 | 43 | 3 | 23 | 88 | 52 | 111 | .335 | .469 |
| Salas,Fernando | L | .293 | 41 | 12 | 3 | 1 | 1 | 6 | 3 | 11 | .341 | .488 |
| Throws Right | R | .231 | 65 | 15 | 4 | 0 | 2 | 14 | 3 | 11 | .260 | .385 |
| Salazar,Danny | L | .219 | 105 | 23 | 3 | 1 | 1 | 3 | 11 | 36 | .293 | .295 |
| Throws Right | R | .233 | 90 | 21 | 3 | 0 | 6 | 12 | 4 | 29 | .266 | .467 |
| Sale,Chris | L | .135 | 148 | 20 | 3 | 0 | 0 | 7 | 8 | 48 | .205 | .155 |
| Throws Left | R | .252 | 652 | 164 | 25 | 1 | 23 | 68 | 38 | 178 | .300 | .399 |
| Samardzija,Jeff | L | .266 | 387 | 103 | 23 | 4 | 13 | 52 | 40 | 99 | .336 | .447 |
| Throws Right | R | .246 | 435 | 107 | 18 | 2 | 12 | 43 | 38 | 115 | .316 | .379 |
| Sanabia,Alex | L | .369 | 111 | 41 | 11 | 0 | 9 | 20 | 16 | 11 | .459 | .712 |
| Throws Right | R | .262 | 107 | 28 | 8 | 0 | 1 | 6 | 9 | 20 | .319 | .364 |
| Sanchez,Anibal | L | .246 | 370 | 91 | 13 | 6 | 6 | 28 | 34 | 108 | .310 | .362 |
| Throws Right | R | .208 | 312 | 65 | 13 | 2 | 3 | 26 | 20 | 94 | .256 | .292 |
| Sanchez,Eduardo | L | .250 | 8 | 2 | 0 | 0 | 1 | 5 | 1 | 2 | .300 | .625 |
| Throws Right | R | .231 | 13 | 3 | 1 | 0 | 0 | 0 | 4 | 3 | .412 | .308 |
| Sanchez,Jonathan | L | .375 | 16 | 6 | 1 | 0 | 2 | 4 | 1 | 4 | .412 | .813 |
| Throws Left | R | .404 | 47 | 19 | 4 | 2 | 5 | 11 | 7 | 11 | .500 | .894 |
| Santana,Ervin | L | .247 | 445 | 110 | 21 | 2 | 11 | 46 | 30 | 83 | .298 | .378 |
| Throws Right | R | .227 | 352 | 80 | 10 | 0 | 15 | 33 | 21 | 78 | .276 | .384 |
| Santiago,Hector | L | .241 | 170 | 41 | 4 | 1 | 3 | 20 | 24 | 43 | .356 | .329 |
| Throws Left | R | .244 | 393 | 96 | 27 | 1 | 14 | 37 | 48 | 94 | .337 | .425 |
| Santos,Sergio | L | .118 | 34 | 4 | 2 | 0 | 0 | 4 | 1 | 12 | .135 | .176 |
| Throws Right | R | .140 | 50 | 7 | 1 | 1 | 1 | 2 | 3 | 16 | .189 | .260 |
| Saunders,Joe | L | .214 | 159 | 34 | 7 | 0 | 3 | 17 | 8 | 38 | .251 | .314 |
| Throws Left | R | .337 | 587 | 198 | 54 | 5 | 22 | 87 | 53 | 69 | .394 | .559 |
| Savery,Joe | L | .409 | 22 | 9 | 1 | 0 | 1 | 4 | 2 | 1 | .440 | .591 |
| Throws Left | R | .118 | 51 | 6 | 1 | 1 | 0 | 5 | 9 | 13 | .250 | .176 |
| Scahill,Rob | L | .344 | 64 | 22 | 6 | 1 | 1 | 7 | 3 | 7 | .391 | .516 |
| Throws Right | R | .261 | 69 | 18 | 4 | 0 | 4 | 12 | 6 | 13 | .338 | .493 |
| Scheppers,Tanner | L | .218 | 133 | 29 | 2 | 1 | 3 | 7 | 10 | 29 | .283 | .316 |
| Throws Right | R | .210 | 138 | 29 | 4 | 0 | 3 | 13 | 14 | 30 | .306 | .304 |
| Scherzer,Max | L | .222 | 450 | 100 | 28 | 2 | 11 | 42 | 37 | 133 | .278 | .367 |
| Throws Right | R | .165 | 316 | 52 | 8 | 3 | 7 | 25 | 19 | 107 | .219 | .275 |
| Scribner,Evan | L | .220 | 50 | 11 | 4 | 1 | 0 | 7 | 4 | 12 | .278 | .340 |
| Throws Right | R | .263 | 57 | 15 | 4 | 2 | 3 | 9 | 3 | 7 | .300 | .561 |
| Shaw,Bryan | L | .254 | 130 | 33 | 4 | 0 | 3 | 11 | 14 | 24 | .324 | .354 |
| Throws Right | R | .182 | 148 | 27 | 5 | 0 | 1 | 14 | 14 | 49 | .269 | .236 |
| Shields,James | L | .233 | 463 | 108 | 15 | 1 | 8 | 35 | 39 | 108 | .292 | .322 |
| Throws Right | R | .272 | 394 | 107 | 20 | 2 | 12 | 41 | 29 | 88 | .329 | .424 |
| Siegrist,Kevin | L | .118 | 68 | 8 | 0 | 1 | 0 | 5 | 11 | 27 | .241 | .147 |
| Throws Left | R | .138 | 65 | 9 | 2 | 1 | 1 | 1 | 7 | 23 | .233 | .246 |
| Simon,Alfredo | L | .225 | 138 | 31 | 8 | 0 | 6 | 18 | 16 | 26 | .316 | .413 |
| Throws Right | R | .206 | 180 | 37 | 7 | 0 | 2 | 13 | 10 | 37 | .265 | .278 |
| Sipp,Tony | L | .270 | 74 | 20 | 4 | 0 | 4 | 17 | 10 | 16 | .372 | .486 |
| Throws Left | R | .208 | 72 | 15 | 6 | 0 | 2 | 7 | 12 | 26 | .326 | .375 |
| Skaggs,Tyler | L | .242 | 33 | 8 | 1 | 1 | 1 | 4 | 2 | 6 | .286 | .424 |
| Throws Left | R | .254 | 118 | 30 | 7 | 0 | 6 | 18 | 13 | 30 | .333 | .466 |

# Pitchers vs. Left-Handed and Right-Handed Batters

| Pitcher | vs | Avg | AB | H | 2B | 3B | HR | RBI | BB | SO | OBP | Slg |
|---|---|---|---|---|---|---|---|---|---|---|---|---|
| Slowey,Kevin | L | .307 | 179 | 55 | 12 | 1 | 6 | 16 | 11 | 33 | .342 | .486 |
| Throws Right | R | .276 | 185 | 51 | 11 | 4 | 6 | 24 | 7 | 43 | .312 | .476 |
| Smith,Burch | L | .275 | 69 | 19 | 5 | 1 | 5 | 11 | 12 | 16 | .383 | .594 |
| Throws Right | R | .263 | 76 | 20 | 3 | 1 | 4 | 12 | 9 | 30 | .341 | .487 |
| Smith,Joe | L | .227 | 110 | 25 | 4 | 0 | 4 | 13 | 14 | 29 | .325 | .373 |
| Throws Right | R | .242 | 120 | 29 | 3 | 0 | 1 | 7 | 9 | 25 | .300 | .292 |
| Smith,Will | L | .157 | 51 | 8 | 1 | 0 | 3 | 5 | 2 | 27 | .204 | .353 |
| Throws Left | R | .235 | 68 | 16 | 1 | 1 | 3 | 11 | 5 | 16 | .273 | .412 |
| Smyly,Drew | L | .189 | 122 | 23 | 4 | 0 | 1 | 7 | 6 | 34 | .225 | .246 |
| Throws Left | R | .242 | 161 | 39 | 15 | 1 | 3 | 10 | 11 | 47 | .295 | .404 |
| Soria,Joakim | L | .068 | 44 | 3 | 0 | 0 | 1 | 2 | 6 | 14 | .180 | .136 |
| Throws Right | R | .366 | 41 | 15 | 1 | 0 | 1 | 6 | 8 | 14 | .480 | .463 |
| Soriano,Rafael | L | .274 | 106 | 29 | 2 | 2 | 4 | 12 | 11 | 23 | .342 | .443 |
| Throws Right | R | .235 | 153 | 36 | 4 | 0 | 3 | 10 | 6 | 28 | .264 | .320 |
| Spruill,Zeke | L | .417 | 24 | 10 | 1 | 0 | 3 | 6 | 2 | 3 | .481 | .833 |
| Throws Right | R | .292 | 24 | 7 | 1 | 1 | 0 | 2 | 3 | 6 | .370 | .417 |
| Stammen,Craig | L | .282 | 117 | 33 | 7 | 1 | 2 | 13 | 13 | 32 | .346 | .410 |
| Throws Right | R | .249 | 181 | 45 | 8 | 0 | 2 | 24 | 14 | 47 | .308 | .326 |
| Stauffer,Tim | L | .190 | 121 | 23 | 3 | 1 | 2 | 7 | 9 | 34 | .248 | .281 |
| Throws Right | R | .269 | 134 | 36 | 4 | 0 | 5 | 22 | 11 | 30 | .338 | .410 |
| Stinson,Josh | L | .091 | 22 | 2 | 0 | 0 | 0 | 0 | 1 | 3 | .130 | .091 |
| Throws Right | R | .216 | 37 | 8 | 1 | 0 | 4 | 6 | 2 | 9 | .275 | .568 |
| Storen,Drew | L | .267 | 101 | 27 | 5 | 1 | 5 | 14 | 10 | 24 | .330 | .485 |
| Throws Right | R | .268 | 142 | 38 | 4 | 1 | 2 | 17 | 9 | 34 | .316 | .352 |
| Straily,Dan | L | .244 | 295 | 72 | 15 | 0 | 9 | 36 | 36 | 59 | .324 | .386 |
| Throws Right | R | .221 | 272 | 60 | 8 | 0 | 7 | 26 | 21 | 65 | .290 | .327 |
| Strasburg,Stephen | L | .218 | 307 | 67 | 8 | 0 | 8 | 30 | 37 | 79 | .306 | .322 |
| Throws Right | R | .197 | 350 | 69 | 8 | 1 | 8 | 33 | 19 | 112 | .258 | .294 |
| Street,Huston | L | .208 | 101 | 21 | 6 | 0 | 5 | 8 | 9 | 20 | .273 | .416 |
| Throws Right | R | .217 | 106 | 23 | 3 | 0 | 7 | 11 | 5 | 26 | .250 | .443 |
| Strop,Pedro | L | .215 | 93 | 20 | 5 | 1 | 2 | 13 | 10 | 29 | .298 | .355 |
| Throws Right | R | .207 | 121 | 25 | 8 | 0 | 3 | 17 | 16 | 37 | .324 | .347 |
| Stults,Eric | L | .185 | 184 | 34 | 8 | 2 | 5 | 16 | 7 | 35 | .223 | .332 |
| Throws Left | R | .301 | 615 | 185 | 41 | 5 | 13 | 70 | 33 | 96 | .333 | .447 |
| Stutes,Michael | L | .346 | 26 | 9 | 2 | 1 | 0 | 3 | 3 | 1 | .433 | .500 |
| Throws Right | R | .125 | 40 | 5 | 1 | 0 | 1 | 5 | 5 | 8 | .222 | .225 |
| Swarzak,Anthony | L | .268 | 168 | 45 | 5 | 3 | 7 | 25 | 13 | 28 | .314 | .458 |
| Throws Right | R | .233 | 189 | 44 | 5 | 1 | 0 | 14 | 9 | 41 | .270 | .270 |
| Tazawa,Junichi | L | .264 | 121 | 32 | 5 | 4 | 5 | 14 | 6 | 31 | .295 | .496 |
| Throws Right | R | .266 | 143 | 38 | 8 | 0 | 4 | 16 | 6 | 41 | .294 | .406 |
| Teheran,Julio | L | .289 | 346 | 100 | 17 | 4 | 14 | 42 | 25 | 68 | .340 | .483 |
| Throws Right | R | .204 | 357 | 73 | 12 | 2 | 8 | 25 | 20 | 102 | .264 | .317 |
| Tepesch,Nick | L | .297 | 209 | 62 | 11 | 0 | 10 | 30 | 12 | 40 | .348 | .493 |
| Throws Right | R | .239 | 159 | 38 | 10 | 0 | 2 | 19 | 15 | 36 | .307 | .340 |
| Thatcher,Joe | L | .250 | 84 | 21 | 2 | 0 | 1 | 8 | 9 | 23 | .323 | .310 |
| Throws Left | R | .288 | 66 | 19 | 3 | 0 | 3 | 5 | 1 | 13 | .299 | .470 |
| Thayer,Dale | L | .261 | 111 | 29 | 3 | 0 | 5 | 13 | 14 | 28 | .346 | .423 |
| Throws Right | R | .229 | 131 | 30 | 4 | 1 | 3 | 14 | 8 | 36 | .279 | .344 |
| Thielbar,Caleb | L | .143 | 77 | 11 | 4 | 1 | 2 | 11 | 4 | 23 | .183 | .299 |
| Throws Left | R | .165 | 79 | 13 | 4 | 1 | 2 | 8 | 10 | 16 | .258 | .316 |
| Thornburg,Tyler | L | .192 | 125 | 24 | 1 | 0 | 0 | 4 | 14 | 24 | .279 | .200 |
| Throws Right | R | .261 | 111 | 29 | 6 | 0 | 1 | 13 | 12 | 24 | .341 | .342 |
| Thornton,Matt | L | .235 | 81 | 19 | 2 | 0 | 3 | 15 | 3 | 20 | .267 | .370 |
| Throws Left | R | .333 | 84 | 28 | 3 | 0 | 1 | 9 | 12 | 10 | .423 | .405 |
| Tillman,Chris | L | .247 | 441 | 109 | 19 | 3 | 19 | 47 | 40 | 93 | .311 | .433 |
| Throws Right | R | .232 | 323 | 75 | 18 | 0 | 14 | 36 | 28 | 86 | .293 | .418 |
| Tonkin,Michael | L | .160 | 25 | 4 | 2 | 0 | 0 | 3 | 3 | 6 | .250 | .240 |
| Throws Right | R | .263 | 19 | 5 | 1 | 0 | 0 | 5 | 0 | 4 | .263 | .316 |
| Torres,Alex | L | .175 | 80 | 14 | 4 | 0 | 0 | 7 | 5 | 31 | .241 | .225 |
| Throws Left | R | .149 | 121 | 18 | 6 | 0 | 1 | 8 | 15 | 31 | .246 | .223 |
| Torres,Carlos | L | .268 | 127 | 34 | 3 | 0 | 3 | 8 | 9 | 23 | .316 | .362 |
| Throws Right | R | .226 | 199 | 45 | 8 | 0 | 12 | 29 | 8 | 52 | .269 | .447 |
| Troncoso,Ramon | L | .360 | 50 | 18 | 4 | 0 | 3 | 9 | 10 | 8 | .467 | .620 |
| Throws Right | R | .179 | 67 | 12 | 1 | 0 | 1 | 7 | 6 | 10 | .253 | .239 |
| Turner,Jacob | L | .254 | 201 | 51 | 9 | 1 | 4 | 17 | 29 | 29 | .348 | .368 |
| Throws Right | R | .269 | 242 | 65 | 16 | 1 | 7 | 32 | 25 | 48 | .341 | .430 |
| Uehara,Koji | L | .115 | 130 | 15 | 6 | 0 | 1 | 6 | 6 | 56 | .153 | .185 |
| Throws Right | R | .146 | 123 | 18 | 4 | 1 | 4 | 10 | 3 | 45 | .173 | .293 |
| Valdes,Raul | L | .229 | 48 | 11 | 4 | 0 | 1 | 8 | 2 | 16 | .275 | .375 |
| Throws Left | R | .337 | 92 | 31 | 8 | 1 | 6 | 22 | 6 | 21 | .380 | .641 |
| Valverde,Jose | L | .279 | 43 | 12 | 0 | 0 | 4 | 8 | 4 | 10 | .354 | .558 |
| Throws Right | R | .182 | 33 | 6 | 1 | 0 | 2 | 5 | 2 | 9 | .250 | .394 |
| Vargas,Jason | L | .327 | 162 | 53 | 11 | 3 | 0 | 8 | 8 | 23 | .357 | .432 |
| Throws Left | R | .256 | 425 | 109 | 20 | 0 | 17 | 50 | 38 | 86 | .323 | .424 |
| Varvaro,Anthony | L | .207 | 121 | 25 | 4 | 1 | 1 | 6 | 10 | 24 | .267 | .281 |
| Throws Right | R | .274 | 157 | 43 | 10 | 0 | 2 | 16 | 15 | 19 | .341 | .376 |

| Pitcher | vs | Avg | AB | H | 2B | 3B | HR | RBI | BB | SO | OBP | Slg |
|---|---|---|---|---|---|---|---|---|---|---|---|---|
| Veal,Donnie | L | .257 | 70 | 18 | 3 | 0 | 2 | 10 | 8 | 20 | .333 | .386 |
| Throws Left | R | .200 | 40 | 8 | 1 | 0 | 1 | 6 | 8 | 9 | .333 | .300 |
| Ventura,Yordano | L | .211 | 38 | 8 | 0 | 0 | 2 | 5 | 6 | 9 | .318 | .368 |
| Throws Right | R | .250 | 20 | 5 | 1 | 0 | 1 | 1 | 0 | 2 | .250 | .450 |
| Veras,Jose | L | .231 | 117 | 27 | 5 | 0 | 4 | 13 | 10 | 22 | .308 | .376 |
| Throws Right | R | .165 | 109 | 18 | 3 | 1 | 2 | 10 | 12 | 38 | .254 | .266 |
| Verlander,Justin | L | .237 | 493 | 117 | 28 | 2 | 8 | 43 | 50 | 131 | .307 | .351 |
| Throws Right | R | .275 | 345 | 95 | 10 | 2 | 11 | 48 | 25 | 86 | .327 | .412 |
| Villanueva,Carlos | L | .260 | 196 | 51 | 14 | 2 | 3 | 24 | 22 | 41 | .333 | .398 |
| Throws Right | R | .240 | 275 | 66 | 17 | 1 | 11 | 28 | 18 | 62 | .292 | .429 |
| Villarreal,Brayan | L | .714 | 7 | 5 | 3 | 0 | 0 | 5 | 1 | 1 | .750 | 1.143 |
| Throws Right | R | .273 | 11 | 3 | 1 | 0 | 1 | 6 | 8 | 5 | .550 | .636 |
| Villarreal,Pedro | L | .333 | 12 | 4 | 0 | 0 | 2 | 4 | 3 | 1 | .467 | .833 |
| Throws Right | R | .529 | 17 | 9 | 1 | 0 | 2 | 4 | 0 | 3 | .529 | .941 |
| Vincent,Nick | L | .301 | 73 | 22 | 3 | 1 | 1 | 5 | 7 | 19 | .370 | .411 |
| Throws Right | R | .122 | 90 | 11 | 2 | 0 | 0 | 6 | 4 | 30 | .168 | .144 |
| Vogelsong,Ryan | L | .266 | 192 | 51 | 7 | 1 | 7 | 27 | 14 | 38 | .314 | .422 |
| Throws Right | R | .327 | 223 | 73 | 14 | 3 | 8 | 38 | 24 | 29 | .403 | .525 |
| Volquez,Edinson | L | .294 | 350 | 103 | 25 | 5 | 9 | 53 | 39 | 68 | .365 | .471 |
| Throws Right | R | .269 | 334 | 90 | 18 | 2 | 10 | 49 | 38 | 74 | .346 | .425 |
| Volstad,Chris | L | .440 | 25 | 11 | 5 | 0 | 0 | 4 | 0 | 1 | .462 | .640 |
| Throws Right | R | .421 | 19 | 8 | 3 | 0 | 1 | 6 | 1 | 2 | .476 | .737 |
| Wacha,Michael | L | .197 | 117 | 23 | 2 | 0 | 1 | 4 | 9 | 28 | .254 | .239 |
| Throws Right | R | .242 | 120 | 29 | 7 | 1 | 4 | 16 | 10 | 37 | .293 | .417 |
| Wagner,Neil | L | .270 | 63 | 17 | 5 | 0 | 2 | 7 | 5 | 16 | .324 | .444 |
| Throws Right | R | .272 | 81 | 22 | 1 | 0 | 3 | 11 | 8 | 17 | .341 | .395 |
| Wainwright,Adam | L | .242 | 443 | 107 | 26 | 1 | 6 | 33 | 25 | 108 | .286 | .345 |
| Throws Right | R | .254 | 457 | 116 | 22 | 1 | 9 | 41 | 10 | 111 | .274 | .365 |
| Walden,Jordan | L | .190 | 84 | 16 | 1 | 1 | 2 | 6 | 5 | 30 | .244 | .298 |
| Throws Right | R | .247 | 93 | 23 | 4 | 1 | 2 | 8 | 9 | 24 | .314 | .376 |
| Walker,Taijuan | L | .194 | 36 | 7 | 4 | 0 | 0 | 4 | 2 | 10 | .231 | .306 |
| Throws Right | R | .222 | 18 | 4 | 1 | 0 | 0 | 2 | 2 | 2 | .286 | .278 |
| Wall,Josh | L | .333 | 12 | 4 | 1 | 0 | 1 | 6 | 4 | 4 | .500 | .667 |
| Throws Right | R | .565 | 23 | 13 | 4 | 0 | 1 | 9 | 2 | 3 | .577 | .870 |
| Walters,P.J. | L | .288 | 80 | 23 | 6 | 1 | 1 | 13 | 9 | 8 | .360 | .425 |
| Throws Right | R | .333 | 84 | 28 | 5 | 1 | 4 | 12 | 9 | 14 | .404 | .560 |
| Wang,Chien-Ming | L | .429 | 56 | 24 | 6 | 0 | 3 | 13 | 5 | 7 | .475 | .696 |
| Throws Right | R | .276 | 58 | 16 | 2 | 0 | 2 | 10 | 4 | 7 | .323 | .414 |
| Warren,Adam | L | .301 | 156 | 47 | 12 | 1 | 7 | 21 | 16 | 30 | .370 | .526 |
| Throws Right | R | .231 | 143 | 33 | 4 | 0 | 3 | 11 | 14 | 34 | .304 | .322 |
| Watson,Tony | L | .206 | 102 | 21 | 5 | 0 | 0 | 6 | 3 | 21 | .229 | .255 |
| Throws Left | R | .192 | 156 | 30 | 5 | 0 | 5 | 14 | 9 | 33 | .262 | .321 |
| Weaver,Jered | L | .227 | 362 | 82 | 18 | 0 | 10 | 28 | 21 | 76 | .279 | .359 |
| Throws Right | R | .254 | 224 | 57 | 14 | 1 | 7 | 27 | 16 | 41 | .306 | .420 |
| Webb,Daniel | L | .261 | 23 | 6 | 0 | 0 | 0 | 1 | 1 | 5 | .292 | .261 |
| Throws Right | R | .167 | 18 | 3 | 0 | 0 | 0 | 3 | 3 | 5 | .273 | .167 |
| Webb,Ryan | L | .244 | 123 | 30 | 7 | 4 | 1 | 16 | 15 | 25 | .324 | .390 |
| Throws Right | R | .244 | 164 | 40 | 3 | 4 | 4 | 24 | 12 | 29 | .297 | .384 |
| Weber,Thad | L | .333 | 18 | 6 | 2 | 0 | 1 | 3 | 4 | 2 | .435 | .611 |
| Throws Right | R | .182 | 33 | 6 | 1 | 0 | 1 | 3 | 4 | 8 | .263 | .303 |
| Webster,Allen | L | .391 | 64 | 25 | 5 | 0 | 7 | 21 | 11 | 8 | .456 | .797 |
| Throws Right | R | .214 | 56 | 12 | 1 | 0 | 0 | 6 | 7 | 15 | .318 | .232 |
| Westbrook,Jake | L | .337 | 208 | 70 | 13 | 3 | 3 | 38 | 25 | 16 | .413 | .471 |
| Throws Right | R | .255 | 243 | 62 | 7 | 1 | 4 | 26 | 25 | 28 | .338 | .342 |
| Wheeler,Zack | L | .259 | 162 | 42 | 5 | 1 | 5 | 17 | 31 | 38 | .371 | .395 |
| Throws Right | R | .230 | 209 | 48 | 8 | 1 | 5 | 20 | 15 | 46 | .290 | .349 |
| Wilhelmsen,Tom | L | .287 | 101 | 29 | 3 | 1 | 0 | 12 | 21 | 19 | .407 | .337 |
| Throws Right | R | .145 | 110 | 16 | 4 | 0 | 2 | 11 | 12 | 26 | .232 | .236 |
| Williams,Jerome | L | .283 | 364 | 103 | 26 | 2 | 13 | 47 | 35 | 55 | .346 | .473 |
| Throws Right | R | .259 | 301 | 78 | 10 | 2 | 10 | 34 | 20 | 52 | .311 | .405 |
| Wilson,Alex | L | .200 | 60 | 12 | 3 | 1 | 0 | 6 | 7 | 14 | .284 | .283 |
| Throws Right | R | .431 | 51 | 22 | 5 | 2 | 0 | 13 | 7 | 8 | .500 | .608 |
| Wilson,Brian | L | .091 | 11 | 1 | 1 | 0 | 0 | 0 | 2 | 4 | .231 | .182 |
| Throws Right | R | .206 | 34 | 7 | 1 | 0 | 0 | 2 | 2 | 9 | .250 | .235 |
| Wilson,C.J. | L | .169 | 183 | 31 | 6 | 1 | 2 | 15 | 16 | 57 | .239 | .246 |
| Throws Left | R | .268 | 631 | 169 | 35 | 3 | 13 | 65 | 69 | 131 | .346 | .395 |
| Wilson,Justin | L | .200 | 85 | 17 | 0 | 0 | 1 | 6 | 7 | 17 | .266 | .235 |
| Throws Left | R | .189 | 175 | 33 | 7 | 0 | 3 | 20 | 21 | 42 | .283 | .280 |
| Withrow,Chris | L | .217 | 46 | 10 | 0 | 0 | 1 | 5 | 2 | 11 | .250 | .283 |
| Throws Right | R | .133 | 75 | 10 | 0 | 0 | 4 | 4 | 11 | 32 | .244 | .293 |
| Wolf,Ross | L | .356 | 104 | 37 | 4 | 1 | 3 | 13 | 12 | 13 | .420 | .500 |
| Throws Right | R | .247 | 85 | 21 | 4 | 0 | 2 | 11 | 3 | 8 | .273 | .365 |
| Wood,Alex | L | .267 | 86 | 23 | 3 | 0 | 0 | 5 | 7 | 29 | .320 | .302 |
| Throws Left | R | .261 | 203 | 53 | 12 | 0 | 3 | 24 | 20 | 48 | .326 | .365 |
| Wood,Travis | L | .207 | 174 | 36 | 6 | 1 | 3 | 7 | 18 | 45 | .294 | .305 |
| Throws Left | R | .226 | 561 | 127 | 31 | 1 | 15 | 54 | 48 | 99 | .291 | .365 |

# Pitchers vs. Left-Handed and Right-Handed Batters

| Pitcher | vs | Avg | AB | H | 2B | 3B | HR | RBI | BB | SO | OBP | Slg |
|---|---|---|---|---|---|---|---|---|---|---|---|---|
| Wooten,Rob | L | .245 | 49 | 12 | 3 | 0 | 1 | 7 | 3 | 12 | .302 | .367 |
| Throws Right | R | .268 | 56 | 15 | 3 | 0 | 0 | 8 | 5 | 6 | .328 | .321 |
| Workman,Brandon | L | .253 | 91 | 23 | 4 | 0 | 3 | 11 | 9 | 24 | .317 | .396 |
| Throws Right | R | .296 | 71 | 21 | 3 | 1 | 2 | 12 | 6 | 23 | .351 | .451 |
| Worley,Vance | L | .368 | 114 | 42 | 7 | 0 | 6 | 15 | 10 | 18 | .425 | .588 |
| Throws Right | R | .396 | 101 | 40 | 8 | 0 | 3 | 22 | 5 | 7 | .430 | .564 |
| Wright,Jamey | L | .230 | 152 | 35 | 7 | 0 | 4 | 20 | 15 | 44 | .310 | .355 |
| Throws Right | R | .255 | 102 | 26 | 3 | 1 | 0 | 8 | 8 | 21 | .316 | .304 |
| Wright,Steven | L | .297 | 37 | 11 | 2 | 0 | 0 | 7 | 7 | 6 | .409 | .351 |
| Throws Right | R | .083 | 12 | 1 | 0 | 0 | 0 | 0 | 2 | 4 | .267 | .083 |
| Wright,Wesley | L | .269 | 108 | 29 | 5 | 1 | 3 | 14 | 9 | 28 | .336 | .417 |
| Throws Left | R | .253 | 99 | 25 | 9 | 0 | 4 | 15 | 10 | 27 | .321 | .465 |
| Zagurski,Mike | L | .500 | 12 | 6 | 1 | 0 | 0 | 1 | 2 | 1 | .600 | .583 |
| Throws Left | R | .313 | 16 | 5 | 0 | 0 | 1 | 7 | 6 | 4 | .500 | .500 |
| Zeid,Josh | L | .178 | 45 | 8 | 0 | 0 | 1 | 3 | 6 | 11 | .275 | .244 |
| Throws Right | R | .305 | 59 | 18 | 4 | 0 | 2 | 8 | 6 | 13 | .379 | .475 |
| Ziegler,Brad | L | .246 | 118 | 29 | 8 | 0 | 0 | 11 | 14 | 20 | .333 | .314 |
| Throws Right | R | .213 | 150 | 32 | 3 | 0 | 3 | 14 | 8 | 24 | .256 | .293 |
| Zimmermann,Jordan | L | .262 | 427 | 112 | 26 | 1 | 11 | 48 | 21 | 77 | .297 | .405 |
| Throws Right | R | .212 | 378 | 80 | 23 | 1 | 8 | 28 | 19 | 84 | .259 | .341 |
| Zito,Barry | L | .330 | 115 | 38 | 11 | 0 | 4 | 15 | 13 | 22 | .408 | .530 |
| Throws Left | R | .315 | 429 | 135 | 24 | 1 | 15 | 67 | 41 | 64 | .376 | .480 |
| AL | L | .257 | - | - | - | - | - | - | - | - | .324 | .410 |
| | R | .254 | - | - | - | - | - | - | - | - | .316 | .400 |
| NL | L | .250 | - | - | - | - | - | - | - | - | .321 | .387 |
| | R | .252 | - | - | - | - | - | - | - | - | .312 | .389 |
| MLB | L | .254 | - | - | - | - | - | - | - | - | .322 | .399 |
| | R | .253 | - | - | - | - | - | - | - | - | .314 | .394 |

# 2013 Leader Boards

This section contains all the leaderboards you traditionally see, but way more of those that you never see. For example, Mike Trout hit 27 home runs, 17 fewer than Miguel Cabrera hit. However, when he connected, no one averaged more distance per home run than Trout's 407 feet.

Some of the leaderboards derive from the complex pitch data collected by Baseball Info Solutions. For example, R.A. Dickey has finished runner-up in his league in back-to-back seasons in percentage of pitches thrown in the strike zone. In 2012, he trailed Cliff Lee 51.9 percent to 49.3 percent. In 2013, he trailed Bartolo Colon 48.9 percent to 46.7 percent. That's amazing for a knuckleball pitcher.

Bill James provides his own leaderboards including Runs Created, Tough Losses and Power/Speed Numbers. In short, if there's any kind of leaderboard that we thought would be interesting, we put it here.

Some details:

Our home run distance leaderboards are fueled by Hit Tracker data. Please check out www.hittrackeronline.com and thank you ESPN Stats & Information Group.

In the past we measured hitter performance against various pitch types by result only. The problem with that approach was that if a hitter regularly looked silly on non-result-pitch curveballs, but mashed just a few along the way, he could look like a great curveball hitter, even though nothing was further from the truth. Bill James designed a formula to rate hitters not only on the result pitches, but on every pitch the batter faced. The hitters you'll now see in these leaderboards are a much better representation of the guys who mastered each pitch type this past year.

Here are some definitions to help clarify parts of the leaderboards that may not be familiar to all readers:

**BPS** stands for "Batting Average plus Slugging Percentage." BPS makes more sense than OPS for some leaderboards that involve pitches.

**OutZ** is "Pitches Outside the Strike Zone."

**Holds Adjusted Save Percentage** is calculated by dividing holds plus saves by holds plus save opportunities.

# American League Batting Leaders

**Batting Average** (minimum 502 PA)

| | |
|---|---|
| Cabrera,Miguel, Det | .348 |
| Mauer,Joe, Min | .324 |
| Trout,Mike, LAA | .323 |
| Beltre,Adrian, Tex | .315 |
| Cano,Robinson, NYY | .314 |
| Ortiz,David, Bos | .309 |
| Hunter,Torii, Det | .304 |
| Nava,Daniel, Bos | .303 |
| Hosmer,Eric, KC | .302 |
| Pedroia,Dustin, Bos | .301 |

**On Base Percentage** (minimum 502 PA)

| | |
|---|---|
| Cabrera,Miguel, Det | .442 |
| Trout,Mike, LAA | .432 |
| Mauer,Joe, Min | .404 |
| Ortiz,David, Bos | .395 |
| Nava,Daniel, Bos | .385 |
| Donaldson,Josh, Oak | .384 |
| Cano,Robinson, NYY | .383 |
| Santana,Carlos, Cle | .377 |
| Butler,Billy, KC | .374 |
| Pedroia,Dustin, Bos | .372 |

**Slugging Average** (minimum 502 PA)

| | |
|---|---|
| Cabrera,Miguel, Det | .636 |
| Davis,Chris, Bal | .634 |
| Ortiz,David, Bos | .564 |
| Trout,Mike, LAA | .557 |
| Encarnacion,Edwin, Tor | .534 |
| Moss,Brandon, Oak | .522 |
| Cano,Robinson, NYY | .516 |
| Beltre,Adrian, Tex | .509 |
| Donaldson,Josh, Oak | .499 |
| Longoria,Evan, TB | .498 |

**Home Runs**

| | |
|---|---|
| Davis,Chris, Bal | 53 |
| Cabrera,Miguel, Det | 44 |
| Encarnacion,Edwin, Tor | 36 |
| Dunn,Adam, CWS | 34 |
| Trumbo,Mark, LAA | 34 |
| Jones,Adam, Bal | 33 |
| Longoria,Evan, TB | 32 |
| Beltre,Adrian, Tex | 30 |
| Moss,Brandon, Oak | 30 |
| Ortiz,David, Bos | 30 |

**Games**

| | |
|---|---|
| Butler,Billy, KC | 162 |
| Fielder,Prince, Det | 162 |
| Beltre,Adrian, Tex | 161 |
| Cano,Robinson, NYY | 160 |
| Davis,Chris, Bal | 160 |
| Jones,Adam, Bal | 160 |
| Longoria,Evan, TB | 160 |
| Markakis,Nick, Bal | 160 |
| Pedroia,Dustin, Bos | 160 |
| Seager,Kyle, Sea | 160 |

**Plate Appearances**

| | |
|---|---|
| Pedroia,Dustin, Bos | 724 |
| Trout,Mike, LAA | 716 |
| Fielder,Prince, Det | 712 |
| Machado,Manny, Bal | 710 |
| Gordon,Alex, KC | 700 |
| Markakis,Nick, Bal | 700 |
| Andrus,Elvis, Tex | 698 |
| Zobrist,Ben, TB | 698 |
| Seager,Kyle, Sea | 695 |
| Longoria,Evan, TB | 693 |

**At Bats**

| | |
|---|---|
| Machado,Manny, Bal | 667 |
| Jones,Adam, Bal | 653 |
| Pedroia,Dustin, Bos | 641 |
| Ramirez,Alexei, CWS | 637 |
| Markakis,Nick, Bal | 634 |
| Gordon,Alex, KC | 633 |
| Beltre,Adrian, Tex | 631 |
| Altuve,Jose, Hou | 626 |
| Fielder,Prince, Det | 624 |
| Hosmer,Eric, KC | 623 |

**Hits**

| | |
|---|---|
| Beltre,Adrian, Tex | 199 |
| Cabrera,Miguel, Det | 193 |
| Pedroia,Dustin, Bos | 193 |
| Cano,Robinson, NYY | 190 |
| Trout,Mike, LAA | 190 |
| Machado,Manny, Bal | 189 |
| Hosmer,Eric, KC | 188 |
| Jones,Adam, Bal | 186 |
| Hunter,Torii, Det | 184 |
| Martinez,Victor, Det | 182 |

**Singles**

| | |
|---|---|
| Andrus,Elvis, Tex | 143 |
| Pedroia,Dustin, Bos | 140 |
| Altuve,Jose, Hou | 139 |
| Markakis,Nick, Bal | 138 |
| Beltre,Adrian, Tex | 137 |
| Hosmer,Eric, KC | 134 |
| Ramirez,Alexei, CWS | 134 |
| Martinez,Victor, Det | 132 |
| Butler,Billy, KC | 126 |
| Hunter,Torii, Det | 125 |

**Doubles**

| | |
|---|---|
| Machado,Manny, Bal | 51 |
| Lowrie,Jed, Oak | 45 |
| Davis,Chris, Bal | 42 |
| Pedroia,Dustin, Bos | 42 |
| Cano,Robinson, NYY | 41 |
| Saltalamacchia,J, Bos | 40 |
| Longoria,Evan, TB | 39 |
| Ramirez,Alexei, CWS | 39 |
| Santana,Carlos, Cle | 39 |
| Trout,Mike, LAA | 39 |

**Triples**

| | |
|---|---|
| Gardner,Brett, NYY | 10 |
| Trout,Mike, LAA | 9 |
| Drew,Stephen, Bos | 8 |
| Ellsbury,Jacoby, Bos | 8 |
| Jackson,Austin, Det | 7 |
| Bourn,Michael, Cle | 6 |
| Gordon,Alex, KC | 6 |
| Jennings,Desmond, TB | 6 |
| Martin,Leonys, Tex | 6 |
| Miller,Brad, Sea | 6 |

**Total Bases**

| | |
|---|---|
| Davis,Chris, Bal | 370 |
| Cabrera,Miguel, Det | 353 |
| Trout,Mike, LAA | 328 |
| Jones,Adam, Bal | 322 |
| Beltre,Adrian, Tex | 321 |
| Cano,Robinson, NYY | 312 |
| Longoria,Evan, TB | 306 |
| Ortiz,David, Bos | 292 |
| Donaldson,Josh, Oak | 289 |
| Machado,Manny, Bal | 288 |

**Runs Scored**

| | |
|---|---|
| Trout,Mike, LAA | 109 |
| Cabrera,Miguel, Det | 103 |
| Davis,Chris, Bal | 103 |
| Jones,Adam, Bal | 100 |
| Jackson,Austin, Det | 99 |
| Crisp,Coco, Oak | 93 |
| Ellsbury,Jacoby, Bos | 92 |
| Andrus,Elvis, Tex | 91 |
| Longoria,Evan, TB | 91 |
| Pedroia,Dustin, Bos | 91 |

**RBI**

| | |
|---|---|
| Davis,Chris, Bal | 138 |
| Cabrera,Miguel, Det | 137 |
| Jones,Adam, Bal | 108 |
| Cano,Robinson, NYY | 107 |
| Fielder,Prince, Det | 106 |
| Encarnacion,Edwin, Tor | 104 |
| Ortiz,David, Bos | 103 |
| Trumbo,Mark, LAA | 100 |
| Trout,Mike, LAA | 97 |
| Donaldson,Josh, Oak | 93 |

**Walks**

| | |
|---|---|
| Trout,Mike, LAA | 110 |
| Santana,Carlos, Cle | 93 |
| Cabrera,Miguel, Det | 90 |
| Encarnacion,Edwin, Tor | 82 |
| Butler,Billy, KC | 79 |
| Swisher,Nick, Cle | 77 |
| Donaldson,Josh, Oak | 76 |
| Dunn,Adam, CWS | 76 |
| Kipnis,Jason, Cle | 76 |
| Ortiz,David, Bos | 76 |

**Strikeouts**

| | |
|---|---|
| Carter,Chris, Hou | 212 |
| Davis,Chris, Bal | 199 |
| Dunn,Adam, CWS | 189 |
| Napoli,Mike, Bos | 187 |
| Trumbo,Mark, LAA | 184 |
| Longoria,Evan, TB | 162 |
| Hamilton,Josh, LAA | 158 |
| Reynolds,Mark, Cle-NYY | 154 |
| Arencibia,J.P., Tor | 148 |
| De Aza,Alejandro, CWS | 147 |

# American League Batting Leaders

### Intentional Walks

| | |
|---|---|
| Ortiz,David, Bos | 27 |
| Cabrera,Miguel, Det | 19 |
| Cano,Robinson, NYY | 16 |
| Beltre,Adrian, Tex | 12 |
| Davis,Chris, Bal | 12 |
| Butler,Billy, KC | 11 |
| Longoria,Evan, TB | 10 |
| Martinez,Victor, Det | 10 |
| Trout,Mike, LAA | 10 |
| Pujols,Albert, LAA | 8 |

### BA Bases Loaded
(minimum 10 PA)

| | |
|---|---|
| Morneau,Justin, Min | .769 |
| Donaldson,Josh, Oak | .667 |
| Callaspo,Alberto, LAA-Oak | .625 |
| Keppinger,Jeff, CWS | .556 |
| Profar,Jurickson, Tex | .556 |
| Dominguez,Matt, Hou | .545 |
| 6 tied with | .500 |

### Sacrifice Hits

| | |
|---|---|
| Andrus,Elvis, Tex | 16 |
| Martin,Leonys, Tex | 12 |
| Kawasaki,Munenori, Tor | 10 |
| Victorino,Shane, Bos | 10 |
| Escobar,Alcides, KC | 9 |
| Machado,Manny, Bal | 9 |
| Aybar,Erick, LAA | 8 |
| Getz,Chris, KC | 8 |
| Gonzalez,Marwin, Hou | 8 |
| 3 tied with | 7 |

### Sacrifice Flies

| | |
|---|---|
| Wieters,Matt, Bal | 12 |
| Hunter,Torii, Det | 10 |
| Kipnis,Jason, Cle | 10 |
| Hamilton,Josh, LAA | 9 |
| 9 tied with | 8 |

### BA Close & Late
(minimum 50 PA)

| | |
|---|---|
| Beltre,Adrian, Tex | .416 |
| Hosmer,Eric, KC | .389 |
| Andrus,Elvis, Tex | .368 |
| Doumit,Ryan, Min | .356 |
| Morales,Kendrys, Sea | .352 |
| Myers,Wil, TB | .348 |
| Lawrie,Brett, Tor | .338 |
| Loney,James, TB | .337 |
| Bautista,Jose, Tor | .325 |
| Suzuki,Ichiro, NYY | .325 |

### Batting Average w/ RISP
(minimum 100 PA)

| | |
|---|---|
| Cabrera,Miguel, Det | .400 |
| Perez,Salvador, KC | .377 |
| Brantley,Michael, Cle | .375 |
| Cano,Robinson, NYY | .357 |
| Gardner,Brett, NYY | .356 |
| Gomes,Jonny, Bos | .346 |
| Peralta,Jhonny, Det | .344 |
| Davis,Chris, Bal | .343 |
| Butler,Billy, KC | .341 |
| Jones,Adam, Bal | .337 |

### SLG vs. LHP
(minimum 125 PA)

| | |
|---|---|
| Cabrera,Miguel, Det | .722 |
| Donaldson,Josh, Oak | .631 |
| Trumbo,Mark, LAA | .599 |
| Norris,Derek, Oak | .580 |
| Dozier,Brian, Min | .570 |
| Longoria,Evan, TB | .566 |
| Peralta,Jhonny, Det | .560 |
| Wieters,Matt, Bal | .546 |
| Beltre,Adrian, Tex | .545 |
| Rios,Alex, CWS-Tex | .524 |

### SLG vs. RHP
(minimum 377 PA)

| | |
|---|---|
| Davis,Chris, Bal | .728 |
| Ortiz,David, Bos | .652 |
| Cabrera,Miguel, Det | .609 |
| Trout,Mike, LAA | .572 |
| Cano,Robinson, NYY | .569 |
| Moss,Brandon, Oak | .552 |
| Encarnacion,Edwin, Tor | .547 |
| Lind,Adam, Tor | .539 |
| Jones,Adam, Bal | .526 |
| Castro,Jason, Hou | .506 |

### Leadoff Hitters OBP
(minimum 150 PA)

| | |
|---|---|
| Altuve,Jose, Hou | .376 |
| Kinsler,Ian, Tex | .355 |
| Ellsbury,Jacoby, Bos | .355 |
| Markakis,Nick, Bal | .352 |
| Reyes,Jose, Tor | .352 |
| Gardner,Brett, NYY | .344 |
| Cabrera,Melky, Tor | .337 |
| Jackson,Austin, Det | .337 |
| McLouth,Nate, Bal | .334 |
| Crisp,Coco, Oak | .332 |

### Cleanup Hitters SLG
(minimum 150 PA)

| | |
|---|---|
| Moss,Brandon, Oak | .579 |
| Napoli,Mike, Bos | .574 |
| Ortiz,David, Bos | .556 |
| Longoria,Evan, TB | .550 |
| Beltre,Adrian, Tex | .519 |
| Jones,Adam, Bal | .513 |
| Lind,Adam, Tor | .500 |
| Santana,Carlos, Cle | .497 |
| Trumbo,Mark, LAA | .494 |
| Encarnacion,Edwin, Tor | .492 |

### BA vs. LHP
(minimum 125 PA)

| | |
|---|---|
| Cabrera,Miguel, Det | .368 |
| Pedroia,Dustin, Bos | .354 |
| Peralta,Jhonny, Det | .352 |
| Donaldson,Josh, Oak | .335 |
| Dozier,Brian, Min | .328 |
| Beltre,Adrian, Tex | .325 |
| Hosmer,Eric, KC | .323 |
| Mauer,Joe, Min | .322 |
| Suzuki,Ichiro, NYY | .321 |
| Norris,Derek, Oak | .320 |

### BA vs. RHP
(minimum 377 PA)

| | |
|---|---|
| Cabrera,Miguel, Det | .341 |
| Ortiz,David, Bos | .339 |
| Cano,Robinson, NYY | .329 |
| Ellsbury,Jacoby, Bos | .328 |
| Trout,Mike, LAA | .327 |
| Nava,Daniel, Bos | .322 |
| Davis,Chris, Bal | .316 |
| Martinez,Victor, Det | .314 |
| Beltre,Adrian, Tex | .312 |
| Lind,Adam, Tor | .309 |

### Home BA
(minimum 251 PA)

| | |
|---|---|
| Cabrera,Miguel, Det | .366 |
| Hunter,Torii, Det | .333 |
| Kendrick,Howie, LAA | .327 |
| Cano,Robinson, NYY | .325 |
| Beltre,Adrian, Tex | .325 |
| Mauer,Joe, Min | .323 |
| Victorino,Shane, Bos | .322 |
| Trout,Mike, LAA | .319 |
| Butler,Billy, KC | .318 |
| Pedroia,Dustin, Bos | .315 |

### Away BA
(minimum 251 PA)

| | |
|---|---|
| Loney,James, TB | .351 |
| Cabrera,Miguel, Det | .331 |
| Trout,Mike, LAA | .326 |
| Lind,Adam, Tor | .314 |
| Ortiz,David, Bos | .313 |
| Donaldson,Josh, Oak | .309 |
| Beltre,Adrian, Tex | .307 |
| Hosmer,Eric, KC | .305 |
| Cano,Robinson, NYY | .303 |
| Lowrie,Jed, Oak | .303 |

### OBP vs. LHP
(minimum 125 PA)

| | |
|---|---|
| Cabrera,Miguel, Det | .488 |
| Trout,Mike, LAA | .440 |
| Pedroia,Dustin, Bos | .432 |
| Donaldson,Josh, Oak | .412 |
| Norris,Derek, Oak | .410 |
| Dozier,Brian, Min | .408 |
| Peralta,Jhonny, Det | .404 |
| Beltre,Adrian, Tex | .402 |
| Swisher,Nick, Cle | .397 |
| Mauer,Joe, Min | .394 |

### OBP vs. RHP
(minimum 377 PA)

| | |
|---|---|
| Ortiz,David, Bos | .440 |
| Trout,Mike, LAA | .428 |
| Cabrera,Miguel, Det | .426 |
| Davis,Chris, Bal | .415 |
| Nava,Daniel, Bos | .411 |
| Cano,Robinson, NYY | .400 |
| Lind,Adam, Tor | .385 |
| Butler,Billy, KC | .379 |
| Santana,Carlos, Cle | .377 |
| Zobrist,Ben, TB | .376 |

# American League Batting Leaders

**Stolen Bases**

| | |
|---|---|
| Ellsbury,Jacoby, Bos | 52 |
| Davis,Rajai, Tor | 45 |
| Andrus,Elvis, Tex | 42 |
| Rios,Alex, CWS-Tex | 42 |
| Martin,Leonys, Tex | 36 |
| Altuve,Jose, Hou | 35 |
| Dyson,Jarrod, KC | 34 |
| Trout,Mike, LAA | 33 |
| 3 tied with | 30 |

**Caught Stealing**

| | |
|---|---|
| Altuve,Jose, Hou | 13 |
| Bourn,Michael, Cle | 12 |
| Barnes,Brandon, Hou | 11 |
| Kinsler,Ian, Tex | 11 |
| Martin,Leonys, Tex | 9 |
| Ramirez,Alexei, CWS | 9 |
| 6 tied with | 8 |

**Highest SB Success Pct**
(minimum 20 SBA)

| | |
|---|---|
| Escobar,Alcides, KC | 100.0 |
| Ellsbury,Jacoby, Bos | 92.9 |
| Gentry,Craig, Tex | 88.9 |
| Davis,Rajai, Tor | 88.2 |
| Victorino,Shane, Bos | 87.5 |
| Rios,Alex, CWS-Tex | 85.7 |
| Dyson,Jarrod, KC | 85.0 |
| Andrus,Elvis, Tex | 84.0 |
| Suzuki,Ichiro, NYY | 83.3 |
| Trout,Mike, LAA | 82.5 |

**Lowest SB Success Pct**
(minimum 20 SBA)

| | |
|---|---|
| Barnes,Brandon, Hou | 50.0 |
| Kinsler,Ian, Tex | 57.7 |
| Bourn,Michael, Cle | 65.7 |
| Dozier,Brian, Min | 66.7 |
| Villar,Jonathan, Hou | 69.2 |
| Cain,Lorenzo, KC | 70.0 |
| De Aza,Alejandro, CWS | 71.4 |
| Florimon,Pedro, Min | 71.4 |
| Jennings,Desmond, TB | 71.4 |
| Reyes,Jose, Tor | 71.4 |

**Steals of Third**

| | |
|---|---|
| Davis,Rajai, Tor | 13 |
| Andrus,Elvis, Tex | 9 |
| Altuve,Jose, Hou | 7 |
| Brantley,Michael, Cle | 6 |
| Ellsbury,Jacoby, Bos | 6 |
| Escobar,Alcides, KC | 6 |
| Gardner,Brett, NYY | 6 |
| Trout,Mike, LAA | 6 |
| Crisp,Coco, Oak | 5 |
| Victorino,Shane, Bos | 5 |

**Grounded Into DP**

| | |
|---|---|
| Butler,Billy, KC | 28 |
| Altuve,Jose, Hou | 24 |
| Pedroia,Dustin, Bos | 24 |
| Martinez,Victor, Det | 23 |
| Morales,Kendrys, Sea | 21 |
| Ortiz,David, Bos | 21 |
| Encarnacion,Edwin, Tor | 20 |
| Fielder,Prince, Det | 20 |
| Lind,Adam, Tor | 20 |
| 3 tied with | 19 |

**Grounded Into DP Pct**
(minimum 50 GIDP Ops)

| | |
|---|---|
| Hicks,Aaron, Min | 0.00 |
| Profar,Jurickson, Tex | 1.89 |
| Dunn,Adam, CWS | 2.38 |
| Bourn,Michael, Cle | 2.67 |
| Franklin,Nick, Sea | 2.94 |
| Davis,Chris, Bal | 3.15 |
| Flaherty,Ryan, Bal | 3.57 |
| Moss,Brandon, Oak | 3.67 |
| Stubbs,Drew, Cle | 3.85 |
| Gordon,Alex, KC | 4.21 |

**Hit By Pitch**

| | |
|---|---|
| Victorino,Shane, Bos | 18 |
| Nava,Daniel, Bos | 15 |
| Willingham,Josh, Min | 14 |
| Iglesias,Jose, Bos-Det | 11 |
| Davis,Chris, Bal | 10 |
| Fielder,Prince, Det | 9 |
| Gordon,Alex, KC | 9 |
| Pierzynski,A.J., Tex | 9 |
| Trout,Mike, LAA | 9 |
| 7 tied with | 8 |

**Pitches Seen**

| | |
|---|---|
| Trout,Mike, LAA | 3015 |
| Pedroia,Dustin, Bos | 2934 |
| Seager,Kyle, Sea | 2823 |
| Gordon,Alex, KC | 2805 |
| Andrus,Elvis, Tex | 2780 |
| Longoria,Evan, TB | 2779 |
| Kipnis,Jason, Cle | 2763 |
| Santana,Carlos, Cle | 2760 |
| De Aza,Alejandro, CWS | 2749 |
| Donaldson,Josh, Oak | 2697 |

**At Bats Per Home Run**
(minimum 502 PA)

| | |
|---|---|
| Davis,Chris, Bal | 11.0 |
| Cabrera,Miguel, Det | 12.6 |
| Encarnacion,Edwin, Tor | 14.7 |
| Moss,Brandon, Oak | 14.9 |
| Dunn,Adam, CWS | 15.4 |
| Bautista,Jose, Tor | 16.1 |
| Ortiz,David, Bos | 17.3 |
| Carter,Chris, Hou | 17.4 |
| Trumbo,Mark, LAA | 18.2 |
| Longoria,Evan, TB | 19.2 |

**Highest GB/FB Ratio**
(minimum 502 PA)

| | |
|---|---|
| Andrus,Elvis, Tex | 2.51 |
| Kendrick,Howie, LAA | 2.41 |
| Bourn,Michael, Cle | 2.37 |
| Hosmer,Eric, KC | 2.11 |
| Butler,Billy, KC | 2.01 |
| Escobar,Yunel, TB | 1.97 |
| Suzuki,Ichiro, NYY | 1.96 |
| Mauer,Joe, Min | 1.85 |
| Martin,Leonys, Tex | 1.81 |
| Aybar,Erick, LAA | 1.81 |

**Lowest GB/FB Ratio**
(minimum 502 PA)

| | |
|---|---|
| Moss,Brandon, Oak | 0.58 |
| Carter,Chris, Hou | 0.66 |
| Davis,Chris, Bal | 0.71 |
| Seager,Kyle, Sea | 0.76 |
| Smoak,Justin, Sea | 0.76 |
| Lowrie,Jed, Oak | 0.77 |
| Encarnacion,Edwin, Tor | 0.81 |
| Moustakas,Mike, KC | 0.82 |
| Cespedes,Yoenis, Oak | 0.83 |
| Longoria,Evan, TB | 0.83 |

**Pitches Per Plate App**
(minimum 502 PA)

| | |
|---|---|
| Napoli,Mike, Bos | 4.59 |
| Santana,Carlos, Cle | 4.30 |
| Dunn,Adam, CWS | 4.29 |
| Mauer,Joe, Min | 4.25 |
| Bautista,Jose, Tor | 4.24 |
| Gardner,Brett, NYY | 4.23 |
| Reynolds,Mark, Cle-NYY | 4.22 |
| Carter,Chris, Hou | 4.21 |
| Trout,Mike, LAA | 4.21 |
| Kipnis,Jason, Cle | 4.20 |

**Pct Pitches Taken**
(minimum 1500 Pitches)

| | |
|---|---|
| Trout,Mike, LAA | 63.0 |
| Mauer,Joe, Min | 62.7 |
| Willingham,Josh, Min | 62.0 |
| Bautista,Jose, Tor | 61.6 |
| Ackley,Dustin, Sea | 61.5 |
| Kipnis,Jason, Cle | 61.3 |
| Santana,Carlos, Cle | 61.1 |
| Nava,Daniel, Bos | 60.6 |
| Zobrist,Ben, TB | 60.1 |
| Andrus,Elvis, Tex | 59.9 |

**Best BPS on OutZ**
(minimum 502 PA)

| | |
|---|---|
| Cabrera,Miguel, Det | .743 |
| Trout,Mike, LAA | .678 |
| Beltre,Adrian, Tex | .676 |
| Martinez,Victor, Det | .655 |
| Kendrick,Howie, LAA | .640 |
| Perez,Salvador, KC | .624 |
| Lowrie,Jed, Oak | .614 |
| Jones,Adam, Bal | .601 |
| Loney,James, TB | .596 |
| Aybar,Erick, LAA | .585 |

**Worst BPS on OutZ**
(minimum 502 PA)

| | |
|---|---|
| Reynolds,Mark, Cle-NYY | .289 |
| McLouth,Nate, Bal | .297 |
| Dunn,Adam, CWS | .320 |
| Trumbo,Mark, LAA | .320 |
| Plouffe,Trevor, Min | .331 |
| Swisher,Nick, Cle | .345 |
| De Aza,Alejandro, CWS | .358 |
| Moreland,Mitch, Tex | .361 |
| Cabrera,Asdrubal, Cle | .367 |
| Doumit,Ryan, Min | .389 |

# American League Batting Leaders

**Best OPS vs Fastballs**
(minimum 251 PA)

| | |
|---|---|
| Cabrera,Miguel, Det | 1.084 |
| Trout,Mike, LAA | 1.013 |
| Encarnacion,Edwin, Tor | .987 |
| Ortiz,David, Bos | .987 |
| Donaldson,Josh, Oak | .952 |
| Mauer,Joe, Min | .945 |
| Butler,Billy, KC | .895 |
| Victorino,Shane, Bos | .894 |
| Rasmus,Colby, Tor | .892 |
| 3 tied with | .882 |

**Best OPS vs Curveballs**
(minimum 50 PA)

| | |
|---|---|
| Donaldson,Josh, Oak | 1.122 |
| Hunter,Torii, Det | 1.034 |
| Bautista,Jose, Tor | 1.021 |
| Cano,Robinson, NYY | 1.016 |
| Ortiz,David, Bos | 1.011 |
| Lind,Adam, Tor | .979 |
| Brantley,Michael, Cle | .956 |
| Mauer,Joe, Min | .937 |
| Davis,Chris, Bal | .934 |
| Fielder,Prince, Det | .899 |

**Best OPS vs Changeups**
(minimum 50 PA)

| | |
|---|---|
| Davis,Chris, Bal | 1.235 |
| Cabrera,Miguel, Det | 1.152 |
| Ortiz,David, Bos | 1.148 |
| Moss,Brandon, Oak | 1.138 |
| Cano,Robinson, NYY | 1.137 |
| Kinsler,Ian, Tex | 1.079 |
| Trout,Mike, LAA | 1.043 |
| Castro,Jason, Hou | 1.022 |
| Beltre,Adrian, Tex | .940 |
| Santana,Carlos, Cle | .929 |

**Best OPS vs Sliders**
(minimum 32 PA)

| | |
|---|---|
| Carp,Mike, Bos | 1.327 |
| Davis,Chris, Bal | 1.326 |
| Fielder,Prince, Det | 1.167 |
| Pierzynski,A.J., Tex | 1.043 |
| Cano,Robinson, NYY | 1.037 |
| Jaso,John, Oak | 1.021 |
| Raburn,Ryan, Cle | 1.015 |
| McLouth,Nate, Bal | .991 |
| Gardner,Brett, NYY | .982 |
| Nava,Daniel, Bos | .975 |

**OPS**
(minimum 502 PA)

| | |
|---|---|
| Cabrera,Miguel, Det | 1.078 |
| Davis,Chris, Bal | 1.004 |
| Trout,Mike, LAA | .988 |
| Ortiz,David, Bos | .959 |
| Encarnacion,Edwin, Tor | .904 |
| Cano,Robinson, NYY | .899 |
| Donaldson,Josh, Oak | .883 |
| Mauer,Joe, Min | .880 |
| Beltre,Adrian, Tex | .880 |
| Moss,Brandon, Oak | .859 |

**OPS First Half**
(minimum 260 PA)

| | |
|---|---|
| Cabrera,Miguel, Det | 1.132 |
| Davis,Chris, Bal | 1.109 |
| Ortiz,David, Bos | 1.008 |
| Trout,Mike, LAA | .964 |
| Cano,Robinson, NYY | .917 |
| Beltre,Adrian, Tex | .901 |
| Donaldson,Josh, Oak | .900 |
| Kipnis,Jason, Cle | .897 |
| Ibanez,Raul, Sea | .892 |
| Encarnacion,Edwin, Tor | .885 |

**OPS Second Half**
(minimum 201 PA)

| | |
|---|---|
| Trout,Mike, LAA | 1.023 |
| Moss,Brandon, Oak | .989 |
| Cabrera,Miguel, Det | .975 |
| Encarnacion,Edwin, Tor | .939 |
| Napoli,Mike, Bos | .935 |
| Martinez,Victor, Det | .913 |
| Ortiz,David, Bos | .897 |
| Myers,Wil, TB | .874 |
| Cano,Robinson, NYY | .873 |
| Victorino,Shane, Bos | .864 |

**OPS by Catchers**
(minimum 251 PA)

| | |
|---|---|
| Mauer,Joe, Min | .901 |
| Castro,Jason, Hou | .884 |
| Gomes,Yan, Cle | .837 |
| Santana,Carlos, Cle | .821 |
| Saltalamacchia,J, Bos | .813 |
| Perez,Salvador, KC | .741 |
| Norris,Derek, Oak | .734 |
| Iannetta,Chris, LAA | .727 |
| Wieters,Matt, Bal | .726 |
| Lobaton,Jose, TB | .725 |

**OPS by First Basemen**
(minimum 251 PA)

| | |
|---|---|
| Davis,Chris, Bal | .979 |
| Encarnacion,Edwin, Tor | .894 |
| Dunn,Adam, CWS | .888 |
| Lind,Adam, Tor | .871 |
| Fielder,Prince, Det | .841 |
| Moss,Brandon, Oak | .833 |
| Napoli,Mike, Bos | .827 |
| Hosmer,Eric, KC | .794 |
| Loney,James, TB | .767 |
| Smoak,Justin, Sea | .752 |

**OPS by Second Basemen**
(minimum 251 PA)

| | |
|---|---|
| Cano,Robinson, NYY | .919 |
| Kipnis,Jason, Cle | .817 |
| Infante,Omar, Det | .790 |
| Pedroia,Dustin, Bos | .788 |
| Kendrick,Howie, LAA | .785 |
| Kinsler,Ian, Tex | .778 |
| Zobrist,Ben, TB | .778 |
| Dozier,Brian, Min | .726 |
| Sogard,Eric, Oak | .700 |
| Beckham,Gordon, CWS | .696 |

**OPS by Third Basemen**
(minimum 251 PA)

| | |
|---|---|
| Cabrera,Miguel, Det | 1.079 |
| Donaldson,Josh, Oak | .886 |
| Beltre,Adrian, Tex | .884 |
| Longoria,Evan, TB | .848 |
| Seager,Kyle, Sea | .762 |
| Machado,Manny, Bal | .746 |
| Lawrie,Brett, Tor | .728 |
| Plouffe,Trevor, Min | .727 |
| Middlebrooks,Will, Bos | .706 |
| Callaspo,Alberto, LAA-Oak | .705 |

**OPS by Shortstops**
(minimum 251 PA)

| | |
|---|---|
| Peralta,Jhonny, Det | .821 |
| Lowrie,Jed, Oak | .819 |
| Drew,Stephen, Bos | .778 |
| Reyes,Jose, Tor | .777 |
| Miller,Brad, Sea | .765 |
| Hardy,J.J., Bal | .738 |
| Cabrera,Asdrubal, Cle | .702 |
| Escobar,Yunel, TB | .700 |
| Ramirez,Alexei, CWS | .693 |
| Aybar,Erick, LAA | .683 |

**OPS by Left Fielders**
(minimum 251 PA)

| | |
|---|---|
| Willingham,Josh, Min | .773 |
| Viciedo,Dayan, CWS | .767 |
| Cespedes,Yoenis, Oak | .752 |
| Gordon,Alex, KC | .750 |
| Ibanez,Raul, Sea | .748 |
| Gomes,Jonny, Bos | .744 |
| Brantley,Michael, Cle | .728 |
| McLouth,Nate, Bal | .727 |
| Dirks,Andy, Det | .694 |
| Shuck,J.B., LAA | .676 |

**OPS by Center Fielders**
(minimum 251 PA)

| | |
|---|---|
| Trout,Mike, LAA | 1.078 |
| Rasmus,Colby, Tor | .844 |
| Jones,Adam, Bal | .811 |
| Crisp,Coco, Oak | .791 |
| Ellsbury,Jacoby, Bos | .781 |
| Gardner,Brett, NYY | .772 |
| Jackson,Austin, Det | .754 |
| Jennings,Desmond, TB | .743 |
| De Aza,Alejandro, CWS | .730 |
| Martin,Leonys, Tex | .721 |

**OPS by Right Fielders**
(minimum 251 PA)

| | |
|---|---|
| Bautista,Jose, Tor | .867 |
| Cruz,Nelson, Tex | .852 |
| Myers,Wil, TB | .848 |
| Victorino,Shane, Bos | .815 |
| Hunter,Torii, Det | .804 |
| Lough,David, KC | .783 |
| Rios,Alex, CWS-Tex | .755 |
| Reddick,Josh, Oak | .689 |
| Markakis,Nick, Bal | .688 |
| Hamilton,Josh, LAA | .641 |

**OPS by Designated Hitters**
(minimum 125 PA)

| | |
|---|---|
| Ortiz,David, Bos | .964 |
| Valencia,Danny, Bal | .935 |
| Hamilton,Josh, LAA | .918 |
| Encarnacion,Edwin, Tor | .904 |
| Mauer,Joe, Min | .854 |
| Santana,Carlos, Cle | .819 |
| Butler,Billy, KC | .798 |
| Martinez,Victor, Det | .793 |
| Lind,Adam, Tor | .787 |
| Morales,Kendrys, Sea | .780 |

# American League Batting Leaders

### OPS Batting Left vs. LHP
(minimum 125 PA)

| | |
|---|---|
| Mauer,Joe, Min | .882 |
| Gordon,Alex, KC | .877 |
| Kipnis,Jason, Cle | .850 |
| Fielder,Prince, Det | .819 |
| De Aza,Alejandro, CWS | .816 |
| Ibanez,Raul, Sea | .802 |
| Hosmer,Eric, KC | .797 |
| Cano,Robinson, NYY | .788 |
| Davis,Chris, Bal | .763 |
| Suzuki,Ichiro, NYY | .753 |

### OPS Batting Left vs. RHP
(minimum 377 PA)

| | |
|---|---|
| Davis,Chris, Bal | 1.142 |
| Ortiz,David, Bos | 1.092 |
| Cano,Robinson, NYY | .969 |
| Lind,Adam, Tor | .924 |
| Moss,Brandon, Oak | .904 |
| Nava,Daniel, Bos | .894 |
| Castro,Jason, Hou | .864 |
| Ellsbury,Jacoby, Bos | .863 |
| Morneau,Justin, Min | .831 |
| Fielder,Prince, Det | .819 |

### OPS Batting Right vs. LHP
(minimum 125 PA)

| | |
|---|---|
| Cabrera,Miguel, Det | 1.210 |
| Donaldson,Josh, Oak | 1.042 |
| Norris,Derek, Oak | .990 |
| Dozier,Brian, Min | .978 |
| Peralta,Jhonny, Det | .964 |
| Trout,Mike, LAA | .954 |
| Longoria,Evan, TB | .950 |
| Beltre,Adrian, Tex | .948 |
| Pedroia,Dustin, Bos | .937 |
| Trumbo,Mark, LAA | .923 |

### OPS Batting Right vs. RHP
(minimum 377 PA)

| | |
|---|---|
| Cabrera,Miguel, Det | 1.035 |
| Trout,Mike, LAA | 1.000 |
| Encarnacion,Edwin, Tor | .916 |
| Beltre,Adrian, Tex | .857 |
| Jones,Adam, Bal | .846 |
| Bautista,Jose, Tor | .842 |
| Napoli,Mike, Bos | .816 |
| Donaldson,Josh, Oak | .813 |
| Longoria,Evan, TB | .799 |
| Hunter,Torii, Det | .788 |

### OPS vs. LHP
(minimum 125 PA)

| | |
|---|---|
| Cabrera,Miguel, Det | 1.210 |
| Donaldson,Josh, Oak | 1.042 |
| Norris,Derek, Oak | .990 |
| Dozier,Brian, Min | .978 |
| Peralta,Jhonny, Det | .964 |
| Trout,Mike, LAA | .954 |
| Longoria,Evan, TB | .950 |
| Beltre,Adrian, Tex | .948 |
| Pedroia,Dustin, Bos | .937 |
| Trumbo,Mark, LAA | .923 |

### OPS vs. RHP
(minimum 377 PA)

| | |
|---|---|
| Davis,Chris, Bal | 1.142 |
| Ortiz,David, Bos | 1.092 |
| Cabrera,Miguel, Det | 1.035 |
| Trout,Mike, LAA | 1.000 |
| Cano,Robinson, NYY | .969 |
| Lind,Adam, Tor | .924 |
| Encarnacion,Edwin, Tor | .916 |
| Moss,Brandon, Oak | .904 |
| Nava,Daniel, Bos | .894 |
| Castro,Jason, Hou | .864 |

### RC Per 27 Outs vs. LHP
(minimum 125 PA)

| | |
|---|---|
| Cabrera,Miguel, Det | 13.9 |
| Donaldson,Josh, Oak | 9.2 |
| Dozier,Brian, Min | 9.1 |
| Trout,Mike, LAA | 9.0 |
| Norris,Derek, Oak | 8.6 |
| Peralta,Jhonny, Det | 8.3 |
| Pedroia,Dustin, Bos | 8.1 |
| Rios,Alex, CWS-Tex | 7.4 |
| Longoria,Evan, TB | 7.1 |
| Encarnacion,Edwin, Tor | 7.1 |

### RC Per 27 Outs vs. RHP
(minimum 377 PA)

| | |
|---|---|
| Davis,Chris, Bal | 10.8 |
| Ortiz,David, Bos | 9.6 |
| Cabrera,Miguel, Det | 9.2 |
| Trout,Mike, LAA | 8.9 |
| Cano,Robinson, NYY | 8.2 |
| Nava,Daniel, Bos | 7.7 |
| Moss,Brandon, Oak | 6.9 |
| Lind,Adam, Tor | 6.9 |
| Castro,Jason, Hou | 6.9 |
| Ellsbury,Jacoby, Bos | 6.9 |

### Highest RBI %
(minimum 502 PA)

| | |
|---|---|
| Davis,Chris, Bal | 48.34 |
| Cabrera,Miguel, Det | 48.24 |
| Cano,Robinson, NYY | 43.57 |
| Encarnacion,Edwin, Tor | 43.33 |
| Trout,Mike, LAA | 42.75 |
| Moss,Brandon, Oak | 40.88 |
| Donaldson,Josh, Oak | 40.58 |
| Perez,Salvador, KC | 40.29 |
| Bautista,Jose, Tor | 39.42 |
| Ortiz,David, Bos | 39.36 |

### Lowest RBI %
(minimum 502 PA)

| | |
|---|---|
| Moustakas,Mike, KC | 22.12 |
| Suzuki,Ichiro, NYY | 22.21 |
| McLouth,Nate, Bal | 22.93 |
| Escobar,Alcides, KC | 24.98 |
| Markakis,Nick, Bal | 25.02 |
| Plouffe,Trevor, Min | 25.12 |
| Ramirez,Alexei, CWS | 25.14 |
| Altuve,Jose, Hou | 25.81 |
| Doumit,Ryan, Min | 26.04 |
| Smoak,Justin, Sea | 26.61 |

### Highest Strikeout per PA
(minimum 502 PA)

| | |
|---|---|
| Carter,Chris, Hou | .362 |
| Napoli,Mike, Bos | .324 |
| Dunn,Adam, CWS | .311 |
| Reynolds,Mark, Cle-NYY | .306 |
| Davis,Chris, Bal | .296 |
| Moss,Brandon, Oak | .277 |
| Trumbo,Mark, LAA | .271 |
| Hamilton,Josh, LAA | .248 |
| Cespedes,Yoenis, Oak | .239 |
| Longoria,Evan, TB | .234 |

### Lowest Strikeout per PA
(minimum 502 PA)

| | |
|---|---|
| Callaspo,Alberto, LAA-Oak | .091 |
| Martinez,Victor, Det | .093 |
| Kinsler,Ian, Tex | .096 |
| Aybar,Erick, LAA | .100 |
| Encarnacion,Edwin, Tor | .100 |
| Ramirez,Alexei, CWS | .101 |
| Pedroia,Dustin, Bos | .104 |
| Markakis,Nick, Bal | .109 |
| Brantley,Michael, Cle | .110 |
| Crisp,Coco, Oak | .111 |

### Home Runs At Home

| | |
|---|---|
| Davis,Chris, Bal | 28 |
| Dunn,Adam, CWS | 21 |
| Trumbo,Mark, LAA | 19 |
| Cabrera,Miguel, Det | 17 |
| Ibanez,Raul, Sea | 17 |
| Jones,Adam, Bal | 17 |
| Beltre,Adrian, Tex | 15 |
| Longoria,Evan, TB | 15 |
| 3 tied with | 14 |

### Home Runs Away

| | |
|---|---|
| Cabrera,Miguel, Det | 27 |
| Davis,Chris, Bal | 25 |
| Encarnacion,Edwin, Tor | 24 |
| Moss,Brandon, Oak | 20 |
| Carter,Chris, Hou | 19 |
| Ortiz,David, Bos | 18 |
| Longoria,Evan, TB | 17 |
| Cano,Robinson, NYY | 16 |
| Jones,Adam, Bal | 16 |
| 2 tied with | 15 |

### Longest Avg Home Run
(min 10 over the wall)

| | |
|---|---|
| Trout,Mike, LAA | 420 |
| Hosmer,Eric, KC | 418 |
| Trumbo,Mark, LAA | 413 |
| Napoli,Mike, Bos | 412 |
| Reynolds,Mark, Cle-NYY | 412 |
| Dunn,Adam, CWS | 408 |
| Pujols,Albert, LAA | 408 |
| Cruz,Nelson, Tex | 408 |
| Murphy,David, Tex | 408 |
| Kendrick,Howie, LAA | 408 |

### Shortest Avg Home Run
(min 10 over the wall)

| | |
|---|---|
| Crisp,Coco, Oak | 369 |
| Chisenhall,Lonnie, Cle | 375 |
| Callaspo,Alberto, LAA-Oak | 376 |
| Kinsler,Ian, Tex | 376 |
| Zobrist,Ben, TB | 379 |
| Flaherty,Ryan, Bal | 382 |
| Gillaspie,Conor, CWS | 382 |
| Victorino,Shane, Bos | 382 |
| Joyce,Matt, TB | 383 |
| 6 tied with | 384 |

# American League Batting Leaders

### Under Age 26: AB Per HR
(minimum 502 PA)

| | |
|---|---|
| Trout,Mike, LAA | 21.8 |
| Dominguez,Matt, Hou | 25.9 |
| Seager,Kyle, Sea | 28.0 |
| Hosmer,Eric, KC | 36.6 |
| Perez,Salvador, KC | 38.2 |
| Moustakas,Mike, KC | 39.3 |
| Machado,Manny, Bal | 47.6 |
| Martin,Leonys, Tex | 57.1 |
| Altuve,Jose, Hou | 125.2 |
| Andrus,Elvis, Tex | 155.0 |

### Under Age 26: OPS
(minimum 502 PA)

| | |
|---|---|
| Trout,Mike, LAA | .988 |
| Hosmer,Eric, KC | .801 |
| Seager,Kyle, Sea | .764 |
| Perez,Salvador, KC | .757 |
| Machado,Manny, Bal | .746 |
| Martin,Leonys, Tex | .698 |
| Dominguez,Matt, Hou | .690 |
| Altuve,Jose, Hou | .678 |
| Andrus,Elvis, Tex | .659 |
| Moustakas,Mike, KC | .651 |

### Under Age 26: RC/27 Outs
(minimum 502 PA)

| | |
|---|---|
| Trout,Mike, LAA | 9.0 |
| Perez,Salvador, KC | 5.6 |
| Hosmer,Eric, KC | 5.2 |
| Seager,Kyle, Sea | 5.1 |
| Machado,Manny, Bal | 4.6 |
| Martin,Leonys, Tex | 4.2 |
| Andrus,Elvis, Tex | 3.9 |
| Altuve,Jose, Hou | 3.6 |
| Dominguez,Matt, Hou | 3.6 |
| Moustakas,Mike, KC | 2.4 |

### Longest Home Run

| | |
|---|---|
| Trumbo,Mark, LAA, 4/29 | 475 |
| Napoli,Mike, Bos, 5/1 | 472 |
| Trumbo,Mark, LAA, 9/7 | 471 |
| Rasmus,Colby, Tor, 4/6 | 468 |
| Napoli,Mike, Bos, 5/1 | 467 |
| Davis,Chris, Bal, 8/10 | 466 |
| Rasmus,Colby, Tor, 5/21 | 465 |
| Martinez,J.D., Hou, 5/15 | 464 |
| Hunter,Torii, Det, 4/13 | 463 |
| Trout,Mike, LAA, 5/23 | 463 |

### Swing and Miss %
(minimum 1500 Pitches Seen)

| | |
|---|---|
| Carter,Chris, Hou | 36.3 |
| Reynolds,Mark, Cle-NYY | 33.9 |
| Napoli,Mike, Bos | 33.1 |
| Arcia,Oswaldo, Min | 32.4 |
| Davis,Chris, Bal | 32.0 |
| Dunn,Adam, CWS | 31.3 |
| Saltalamacchia,J, Bos | 31.3 |
| Trumbo,Mark, LAA | 30.9 |
| Moss,Brandon, Oak | 30.8 |
| Hamilton,Josh, LAA | 30.7 |

### Highest First Swing %
(minimum 502 PA)

| | |
|---|---|
| Cabrera,Miguel, Det | 39.7 |
| Hamilton,Josh, LAA | 39.5 |
| Jones,Adam, Bal | 37.6 |
| Pierzynski,A.J., Tex | 37.1 |
| Altuve,Jose, Hou | 36.5 |
| Moss,Brandon, Oak | 36.3 |
| Morneau,Justin, Min | 34.9 |
| Davis,Chris, Bal | 34.7 |
| Trumbo,Mark, LAA | 33.8 |
| Ramirez,Alexei, CWS | 33.7 |

### Lowest First Swing %
(minimum 502 PA)

| | |
|---|---|
| Mauer,Joe, Min | 6.8 |
| Dozier,Brian, Min | 8.6 |
| Hardy,J.J., Bal | 8.7 |
| Pedroia,Dustin, Bos | 9.8 |
| Victorino,Shane, Bos | 10.5 |
| Kipnis,Jason, Cle | 11.2 |
| Trout,Mike, LAA | 12.0 |
| Lind,Adam, Tor | 12.3 |
| Kinsler,Ian, Tex | 12.6 |
| Moreland,Mitch, Tex | 13.2 |

### Home RC Per 27 Outs
(minimum 251 PA)

| | |
|---|---|
| Cabrera,Miguel, Det | 10.1 |
| Davis,Chris, Bal | 9.0 |
| Bautista,Jose, Tor | 8.1 |
| Cano,Robinson, NYY | 7.9 |
| Trout,Mike, LAA | 7.8 |
| Kinsler,Ian, Tex | 7.1 |
| Ortiz,David, Bos | 6.9 |
| Pedroia,Dustin, Bos | 6.8 |
| Mauer,Joe, Min | 6.6 |
| Butler,Billy, KC | 6.5 |

### Road RC Per 27 Outs
(minimum 251 PA)

| | |
|---|---|
| Cabrera,Miguel, Det | 10.2 |
| Trout,Mike, LAA | 10.2 |
| Davis,Chris, Bal | 7.9 |
| Donaldson,Josh, Oak | 7.9 |
| Carter,Chris, Hou | 7.5 |
| Ortiz,David, Bos | 7.4 |
| Loney,James, TB | 7.4 |
| Moss,Brandon, Oak | 7.3 |
| Encarnacion,Edwin, Tor | 6.9 |
| Kipnis,Jason, Cle | 6.8 |

### Lead Changing RBI

| | |
|---|---|
| Cabrera,Miguel, Det | 43 |
| Davis,Chris, Bal | 42 |
| Jones,Adam, Bal | 38 |
| Trout,Mike, LAA | 38 |
| Cano,Robinson, NYY | 37 |
| Beltre,Adrian, Tex | 35 |
| Fielder,Prince, Det | 33 |
| Hunter,Torii, Det | 32 |
| Kipnis,Jason, Cle | 32 |
| Morales,Kendrys, Sea | 32 |

# National League Batting Leaders

### Batting Average
(minimum 502 PA)

| | |
|---|---|
| Cuddyer,Michael, Col | .331 |
| Johnson,Chris, Atl | .321 |
| Freeman,Freddie, Atl | .319 |
| Molina,Yadier, StL | .319 |
| Werth,Jayson, Was | .318 |
| Carpenter,Matt, StL | .318 |
| McCutchen,Andrew, Pit | .317 |
| Craig,Allen, StL | .315 |
| Tulowitzki,Troy, Col | .312 |
| Votto,Joey, Cin | .305 |

### On Base Percentage
(minimum 502 PA)

| | |
|---|---|
| Votto,Joey, Cin | .435 |
| Choo,Shin-Soo, Cin | .423 |
| McCutchen,Andrew, Pit | .404 |
| Goldschmidt,Paul, Ari | .401 |
| Werth,Jayson, Was | .398 |
| Freeman,Freddie, Atl | .396 |
| Carpenter,Matt, StL | .392 |
| Tulowitzki,Troy, Col | .391 |
| Cuddyer,Michael, Col | .389 |
| Holliday,Matt, StL | .389 |

### Slugging Average
(minimum 502 PA)

| | |
|---|---|
| Goldschmidt,Paul, Ari | .551 |
| Tulowitzki,Troy, Col | .540 |
| Werth,Jayson, Was | .532 |
| Cuddyer,Michael, Col | .530 |
| Byrd,Marlon, NYM-Pit | .511 |
| McCutchen,Andrew, Pit | .508 |
| Gomez,Carlos, Mil | .506 |
| Freeman,Freddie, Atl | .501 |
| Brown,Domonic, Phi | .494 |
| Beltran,Carlos, StL | .491 |

### Home Runs

| | |
|---|---|
| Alvarez,Pedro, Pit | 36 |
| Goldschmidt,Paul, Ari | 36 |
| Bruce,Jay, Cin | 30 |
| Brown,Domonic, Phi | 27 |
| Pence,Hunter, SF | 27 |
| Upton,Justin, Atl | 27 |
| Gonzalez,Carlos, Col | 26 |
| Zimmerman,Ryan, Was | 26 |
| Tulowitzki,Troy, Col | 25 |
| Werth,Jayson, Was | 25 |

### Games

| | |
|---|---|
| Pence,Hunter, SF | 162 |
| Votto,Joey, Cin | 162 |
| Castro,Starlin, ChC | 161 |
| Murphy,Daniel, NYM | 161 |
| Bruce,Jay, Cin | 160 |
| Goldschmidt,Paul, Ari | 160 |
| Rizzo,Anthony, ChC | 160 |
| Rollins,Jimmy, Phi | 160 |
| Desmond,Ian, Was | 158 |
| 5 tied with | 157 |

### Plate Appearances

| | |
|---|---|
| Votto,Joey, Cin | 726 |
| Carpenter,Matt, StL | 717 |
| Choo,Shin-Soo, Cin | 712 |
| Goldschmidt,Paul, Ari | 710 |
| Castro,Starlin, ChC | 705 |
| Bruce,Jay, Cin | 697 |
| Murphy,Daniel, NYM | 697 |
| Rizzo,Anthony, ChC | 690 |
| Pence,Hunter, SF | 687 |
| 2 tied with | 674 |

### At Bats

| | |
|---|---|
| Castro,Starlin, ChC | 666 |
| Murphy,Daniel, NYM | 658 |
| Pence,Hunter, SF | 629 |
| Bruce,Jay, Cin | 626 |
| Carpenter,Matt, StL | 626 |
| Span,Denard, Was | 610 |
| Prado,Martin, Ari | 609 |
| Phillips,Brandon, Cin | 606 |
| Rizzo,Anthony, ChC | 606 |
| Simmons,Andrelton, Atl | 606 |

### Hits

| | |
|---|---|
| Carpenter,Matt, StL | 199 |
| Murphy,Daniel, NYM | 188 |
| McCutchen,Andrew, Pit | 185 |
| Goldschmidt,Paul, Ari | 182 |
| Pence,Hunter, SF | 178 |
| Votto,Joey, Cin | 177 |
| Freeman,Freddie, Atl | 176 |
| Segura,Jean, Mil | 173 |
| Prado,Martin, Ari | 172 |
| 2 tied with | 171 |

### Singles

| | |
|---|---|
| Aoki,Norichika, Mil | 140 |
| Murphy,Daniel, NYM | 133 |
| Segura,Jean, Mil | 131 |
| Span,Denard, Was | 127 |
| Carpenter,Matt, StL | 126 |
| Freeman,Freddie, Atl | 124 |
| McCutchen,Andrew, Pit | 121 |
| Prado,Martin, Ari | 120 |
| Votto,Joey, Cin | 120 |
| Johnson,Chris, Atl | 119 |

### Doubles

| | |
|---|---|
| Carpenter,Matt, StL | 55 |
| Molina,Yadier, StL | 44 |
| Bruce,Jay, Cin | 43 |
| Parra,Gerardo, Ari | 43 |
| Rizzo,Anthony, ChC | 40 |
| Belt,Brandon, SF | 39 |
| Desmond,Ian, Was | 38 |
| McCutchen,Andrew, Pit | 38 |
| Murphy,Daniel, NYM | 38 |
| 3 tied with | 36 |

### Triples

| | |
|---|---|
| Span,Denard, Was | 11 |
| Gomez,Carlos, Mil | 10 |
| Marte,Starling, Pit | 10 |
| Segura,Jean, Mil | 10 |
| Hechavarria,Adeiny, Mia | 8 |
| Venable,Will, SD | 8 |
| Carpenter,Matt, StL | 7 |
| Young,Eric, Col-NYM | 7 |
| 6 tied with | 6 |

### Total Bases

| | |
|---|---|
| Goldschmidt,Paul, Ari | 332 |
| Pence,Hunter, SF | 304 |
| Carpenter,Matt, StL | 301 |
| Bruce,Jay, Cin | 299 |
| McCutchen,Andrew, Pit | 296 |
| Votto,Joey, Cin | 285 |
| Freeman,Freddie, Atl | 276 |
| Murphy,Daniel, NYM | 273 |
| 3 tied with | 272 |

### Runs Scored

| | |
|---|---|
| Carpenter,Matt, StL | 126 |
| Choo,Shin-Soo, Cin | 107 |
| Goldschmidt,Paul, Ari | 103 |
| Holliday,Matt, StL | 103 |
| Votto,Joey, Cin | 101 |
| McCutchen,Andrew, Pit | 97 |
| Upton,Justin, Atl | 94 |
| Murphy,Daniel, NYM | 92 |
| Pence,Hunter, SF | 91 |
| 2 tied with | 89 |

### RBI

| | |
|---|---|
| Goldschmidt,Paul, Ari | 125 |
| Bruce,Jay, Cin | 109 |
| Freeman,Freddie, Atl | 109 |
| Phillips,Brandon, Cin | 103 |
| Alvarez,Pedro, Pit | 100 |
| Gonzalez,Adrian, LAD | 100 |
| Pence,Hunter, SF | 99 |
| Craig,Allen, StL | 97 |
| Holliday,Matt, StL | 94 |
| Byrd,Marlon, NYM-Pit | 88 |

### Walks

| | |
|---|---|
| Votto,Joey, Cin | 135 |
| Choo,Shin-Soo, Cin | 112 |
| Goldschmidt,Paul, Ari | 99 |
| McCutchen,Andrew, Pit | 78 |
| Uggla,Dan, Atl | 77 |
| Rizzo,Anthony, ChC | 76 |
| Upton,Justin, Atl | 75 |
| Stanton,Giancarlo, Mia | 74 |
| Carpenter,Matt, StL | 72 |
| LaRoche,Adam, Was | 72 |

### Strikeouts

| | |
|---|---|
| Alvarez,Pedro, Pit | 186 |
| Bruce,Jay, Cin | 185 |
| Uggla,Dan, Atl | 171 |
| Upton,Justin, Atl | 161 |
| Upton,B.J., Atl | 151 |
| Gomez,Carlos, Mil | 146 |
| Desmond,Ian, Was | 145 |
| Goldschmidt,Paul, Ari | 145 |
| Byrd,Marlon, NYM-Pit | 144 |
| Headley,Chase, SD | 142 |

# National League Batting Leaders

### Intentional Walks

| | |
|---|---|
| Goldschmidt,Paul, Ari | 19 |
| Votto,Joey, Cin | 19 |
| Bruce,Jay, Cin | 13 |
| McCutchen,Andrew, Pit | 12 |
| Ethier,Andre, LAD | 11 |
| Freeman,Freddie, Atl | 10 |
| LaRoche,Adam, Was | 10 |
| Hanigan,Ryan, Cin | 9 |
| Kozma,Pete, StL | 8 |
| Posey,Buster, SF | 8 |

### BA Bases Loaded
(minimum 10 PA)

| | |
|---|---|
| Carpenter,Matt, StL | .778 |
| Craig,Allen, StL | .700 |
| Freeman,Freddie, Atl | .700 |
| Phillips,Brandon, Cin | .611 |
| Gattis,Evan, Atl | .556 |
| Ross,Cody, Ari | .556 |
| Ramos,Wilson, Was | .545 |
| Tulowitzki,Troy, Col | .545 |
| 3 tied with | .500 |

### Sacrifice Hits

| | |
|---|---|
| Arroyo,Bronson, Cin | 16 |
| Cozart,Zack, Cin | 13 |
| Hamels,Cole, Phi | 13 |
| Lohse,Kyle, Mil | 12 |
| Bailey,Homer, Cin | 11 |
| Lynn,Lance, StL | 11 |
| Schafer,Logan, Mil | 11 |
| 7 tied with | 10 |

### Sacrifice Flies

| | |
|---|---|
| Cozart,Zack, Cin | 10 |
| Gonzalez,Adrian, LAD | 10 |
| Phillips,Brandon, Cin | 9 |
| Lucroy,Jonathan, Mil | 8 |
| Alonso,Yonder, SD | 7 |
| Byrd,Marlon, NYM-Pit | 7 |
| Carpenter,Matt, StL | 7 |
| Posey,Buster, SF | 7 |
| Sanchez,Gaby, Pit | 7 |
| 10 tied with | 6 |

### BA Close & Late
(minimum 50 PA)

| | |
|---|---|
| Arias,Joaquin, SF | .392 |
| Navarro,Dioner, ChC | .346 |
| Zimmerman,Ryan, Was | .345 |
| Nieves,Wil, Ari | .333 |
| Revere,Ben, Phi | .333 |
| Tabata,Jose, Pit | .327 |
| Choo,Shin-Soo, Cin | .326 |
| Denorfia,Chris, SD | .326 |
| Rosario,Wilin, Col | .325 |
| Lucas,Ed, Mia | .319 |

### Batting Average w/ RISP
(minimum 100 PA)

| | |
|---|---|
| Craig,Allen, StL | .454 |
| Freeman,Freddie, Atl | .443 |
| Holliday,Matt, StL | .390 |
| Carpenter,Matt, StL | .388 |
| Beltran,Carlos, StL | .374 |
| Molina,Yadier, StL | .373 |
| Sandoval,Pablo, SF | .354 |
| Goldschmidt,Paul, Ari | .338 |
| Phillips,Brandon, Cin | .338 |
| Johnson,Chris, Atl | .336 |

### SLG vs. LHP
(minimum 125 PA)

| | |
|---|---|
| Gomez,Carlos, Mil | .622 |
| Pence,Hunter, SF | .611 |
| Wright,David, NYM | .605 |
| Goldschmidt,Paul, Ari | .604 |
| Stanton,Giancarlo, Mia | .593 |
| Byrd,Marlon, NYM-Pit | .583 |
| Upton,Justin, Atl | .567 |
| Rosario,Wilin, Col | .546 |
| Sanchez,Gaby, Pit | .539 |
| Gonzalez,Carlos, Col | .535 |

### SLG vs. RHP
(minimum 377 PA)

| | |
|---|---|
| Tulowitzki,Troy, Col | .560 |
| Cuddyer,Michael, Col | .555 |
| Choo,Shin-Soo, Cin | .554 |
| Freeman,Freddie, Atl | .549 |
| Goldschmidt,Paul, Ari | .534 |
| Alvarez,Pedro, Pit | .532 |
| Brown,Domonic, Phi | .521 |
| Holliday,Matt, StL | .519 |
| Votto,Joey, Cin | .513 |
| Beltran,Carlos, StL | .509 |

### Leadoff Hitters OBP
(minimum 150 PA)

| | |
|---|---|
| Choo,Shin-Soo, Cin | .432 |
| Carpenter,Matt, StL | .398 |
| Fowler,Dexter, Col | .378 |
| Aoki,Norichika, Mil | .367 |
| Denorfia,Chris, SD | .363 |
| Crawford,Carl, LAD | .353 |
| DeJesus,David, ChC-Was | .341 |
| Cabrera,Everth, SD | .340 |
| Marte,Starling, Pit | .336 |
| Pagan,Angel, SF | .336 |

### Cleanup Hitters SLG
(minimum 150 PA)

| | |
|---|---|
| Ramirez,Hanley, LAD | .631 |
| Tulowitzki,Troy, Col | .616 |
| Pence,Hunter, SF | .594 |
| Gonzalez,Adrian, LAD | .588 |
| Werth,Jayson, Was | .581 |
| Byrd,Marlon, NYM-Pit | .515 |
| Headley,Chase, SD | .511 |
| Freeman,Freddie, Atl | .498 |
| Cuddyer,Michael, Col | .496 |
| Quentin,Carlos, SD | .489 |

### BA vs. LHP
(minimum 125 PA)

| | |
|---|---|
| Johnson,Chris, Atl | .383 |
| Cabrera,Everth, SD | .365 |
| Byrd,Marlon, NYM-Pit | .344 |
| Aoki,Norichika, Mil | .339 |
| Wright,David, NYM | .336 |
| Sanchez,Gaby, Pit | .333 |
| Rosario,Wilin, Col | .323 |
| Fowler,Dexter, Col | .323 |
| Posey,Buster, SF | .320 |
| Tulowitzki,Troy, Col | .318 |

### BA vs. RHP
(minimum 377 PA)

| | |
|---|---|
| Cuddyer,Michael, Col | .350 |
| Freeman,Freddie, Atl | .334 |
| Votto,Joey, Cin | .332 |
| Carpenter,Matt, StL | .329 |
| Craig,Allen, StL | .327 |
| Choo,Shin-Soo, Cin | .317 |
| Molina,Yadier, StL | .315 |
| Beltran,Carlos, StL | .315 |
| Tulowitzki,Troy, Col | .310 |
| Werth,Jayson, Was | .309 |

### Home BA
(minimum 251 PA)

| | |
|---|---|
| Carpenter,Matt, StL | .360 |
| Cuddyer,Michael, Col | .356 |
| Freeman,Freddie, Atl | .343 |
| Tulowitzki,Troy, Col | .342 |
| McCutchen,Andrew, Pit | .337 |
| Craig,Allen, StL | .336 |
| Johnson,Chris, Atl | .324 |
| Desmond,Ian, Was | .319 |
| Holliday,Matt, StL | .318 |
| Choo,Shin-Soo, Cin | .318 |

### Away BA
(minimum 251 PA)

| | |
|---|---|
| Molina,Yadier, StL | .325 |
| Byrd,Marlon, NYM-Pit | .325 |
| Wright,David, NYM | .319 |
| Votto,Joey, Cin | .319 |
| Johnson,Chris, Atl | .318 |
| Ethier,Andre, LAD | .311 |
| Cuddyer,Michael, Col | .311 |
| Goldschmidt,Paul, Ari | .311 |
| Murphy,Daniel, NYM | .308 |
| Belt,Brandon, SF | .305 |

### OBP vs. LHP
(minimum 125 PA)

| | |
|---|---|
| Wright,David, NYM | .467 |
| Sanchez,Gaby, Pit | .448 |
| Upton,Justin, Atl | .427 |
| Tulowitzki,Troy, Col | .424 |
| Cabrera,Everth, SD | .421 |
| Fowler,Dexter, Col | .417 |
| Stanton,Giancarlo, Mia | .414 |
| Johnson,Chris, Atl | .413 |
| Holliday,Matt, StL | .403 |
| Posey,Buster, SF | .394 |

### OBP vs. RHP
(minimum 377 PA)

| | |
|---|---|
| Votto,Joey, Cin | .464 |
| Choo,Shin-Soo, Cin | .457 |
| Carpenter,Matt, StL | .410 |
| Freeman,Freddie, Atl | .409 |
| Goldschmidt,Paul, Ari | .406 |
| Cuddyer,Michael, Col | .399 |
| Ethier,Andre, LAD | .394 |
| Craig,Allen, StL | .392 |
| McCutchen,Andrew, Pit | .387 |
| Holliday,Matt, StL | .384 |

# National League Batting Leaders

### Stolen Bases

| | |
|---|---|
| Young,Eric, Col-NYM | 46 |
| Segura,Jean, Mil | 44 |
| Marte,Starling, Pit | 41 |
| Gomez,Carlos, Mil | 40 |
| Cabrera,Everth, SD | 37 |
| McCutchen,Andrew, Pit | 27 |
| Murphy,Daniel, NYM | 23 |
| Pierre,Juan, Mia | 23 |
| 5 tied with | 22 |

### Caught Stealing

| | |
|---|---|
| Marte,Starling, Pit | 15 |
| Segura,Jean, Mil | 13 |
| Aoki,Norichika, Mil | 12 |
| Cabrera,Everth, SD | 12 |
| Choo,Shin-Soo, Cin | 11 |
| Young,Eric, Col-NYM | 11 |
| Hechavarria,Adeiny, Mia | 10 |
| McCutchen,Andrew, Pit | 10 |
| Parra,Gerardo, Ari | 10 |
| 2 tied with | 9 |

### Highest SB Success Pct
(minimum 20 SBA)

| | |
|---|---|
| Murphy,Daniel, NYM | 88.5 |
| Pence,Hunter, SF | 88.0 |
| Gonzalez,Carlos, Col | 87.5 |
| Gomez,Carlos, Mil | 85.1 |
| Wright,David, NYM | 85.0 |
| Young,Eric, Col-NYM | 80.7 |
| Pierre,Juan, Mia | 79.3 |
| Rollins,Jimmy, Phi | 78.6 |
| Schafer,Jordan, Atl | 78.6 |
| Venable,Will, SD | 78.6 |

### Lowest SB Success Pct
(minimum 20 SBA)

| | |
|---|---|
| Parra,Gerardo, Ari | 50.0 |
| Hechavarria,Adeiny, Mia | 52.4 |
| Blanco,Gregor, SF | 60.9 |
| Aoki,Norichika, Mil | 62.5 |
| Choo,Shin-Soo, Cin | 64.5 |
| Ruggiano,Justin, Mia | 65.2 |
| Fowler,Dexter, Col | 67.9 |
| Goldschmidt,Paul, Ari | 68.2 |
| LeMahieu,DJ, Col | 72.0 |
| McCutchen,Andrew, Pit | 73.0 |

### Steals of Third

| | |
|---|---|
| Pierre,Juan, Mia | 8 |
| Gomez,Carlos, Mil | 7 |
| Rollins,Jimmy, Phi | 7 |
| Young,Eric, Col-NYM | 7 |
| Aoki,Norichika, Mil | 6 |
| Cabrera,Everth, SD | 6 |
| McCutchen,Andrew, Pit | 6 |
| Murphy,Daniel, NYM | 6 |
| Segura,Jean, Mil | 5 |
| Soriano,Alfonso, ChC | 5 |

### Grounded Into DP

| | |
|---|---|
| Holliday,Matt, StL | 31 |
| Prado,Martin, Ari | 29 |
| Freese,David, StL | 26 |
| Goldschmidt,Paul, Ari | 25 |
| Barney,Darwin, ChC | 22 |
| Young,Michael, Phi-LAD | 22 |
| Castro,Starlin, ChC | 21 |
| Johnson,Chris, Atl | 20 |
| 3 tied with | 19 |

### Grounded Into DP Pct
(minimum 50 GIDP Ops)

| | |
|---|---|
| Duda,Lucas, NYM | 1.64 |
| Belt,Brandon, SF | 3.23 |
| Rutledge,Josh, Col | 3.77 |
| Blanks,Kyle, SD | 3.92 |
| Harper,Bryce, Was | 3.96 |
| Choo,Shin-Soo, Cin | 4.00 |
| Sanchez,Gaby, Pit | 4.29 |
| Helton,Todd, Col | 4.71 |
| Brown,Domonic, Phi | 4.90 |
| Francisco,Juan, Atl-Mil | 5.17 |

### Hit By Pitch

| | |
|---|---|
| Choo,Shin-Soo, Cin | 26 |
| Marte,Starling, Pit | 24 |
| Walker,Neil, Pit | 15 |
| Frazier,Todd, Cin | 14 |
| Jay,Jon, StL | 14 |
| Aoki,Norichika, Mil | 11 |
| Castillo,Welington, ChC | 11 |
| Frandsen,Kevin, Phi | 11 |
| Headley,Chase, SD | 11 |
| Puig,Yasiel, LAD | 11 |

### Pitches Seen

| | |
|---|---|
| Votto,Joey, Cin | 3033 |
| Choo,Shin-Soo, Cin | 3010 |
| Carpenter,Matt, StL | 2954 |
| Goldschmidt,Paul, Ari | 2930 |
| Bruce,Jay, Cin | 2762 |
| Castro,Starlin, ChC | 2716 |
| Upton,Justin, Atl | 2628 |
| Rizzo,Anthony, ChC | 2615 |
| Pence,Hunter, SF | 2590 |
| McCutchen,Andrew, Pit | 2562 |

### At Bats Per Home Run
(minimum 502 PA)

| | |
|---|---|
| Alvarez,Pedro, Pit | 15.5 |
| Goldschmidt,Paul, Ari | 16.7 |
| Stanton,Giancarlo, Mia | 17.7 |
| Tulowitzki,Troy, Col | 17.8 |
| Brown,Domonic, Phi | 18.4 |
| Werth,Jayson, Was | 18.5 |
| Uggla,Dan, Atl | 20.4 |
| Upton,Justin, Atl | 20.7 |
| Bruce,Jay, Cin | 20.9 |
| Gyorko,Jedd, SD | 21.1 |

### Highest GB/FB Ratio
(minimum 502 PA)

| | |
|---|---|
| Aoki,Norichika, Mil | 2.76 |
| Segura,Jean, Mil | 2.52 |
| Span,Denard, Was | 2.38 |
| Denorfia,Chris, SD | 2.33 |
| Freese,David, StL | 2.30 |
| Young,Michael, Phi-LAD | 2.25 |
| Parra,Gerardo, Ari | 2.23 |
| Jay,Jon, StL | 2.21 |
| Young,Eric, Col-NYM | 2.20 |
| Hechavarria,Adeiny, Mia | 1.86 |

### Lowest GB/FB Ratio
(minimum 502 PA)

| | |
|---|---|
| Belt,Brandon, SF | 0.83 |
| Uggla,Dan, Atl | 0.84 |
| Beltran,Carlos, StL | 0.86 |
| LaRoche,Adam, Was | 0.89 |
| Utley,Chase, Phi | 0.89 |
| Bruce,Jay, Cin | 0.93 |
| Gyorko,Jedd, SD | 0.94 |
| Werth,Jayson, Was | 0.95 |
| Gonzalez,Adrian, LAD | 0.98 |
| Rollins,Jimmy, Phi | 0.98 |

### Pitches Per Plate App
(minimum 502 PA)

| | |
|---|---|
| Werth,Jayson, Was | 4.24 |
| Choo,Shin-Soo, Cin | 4.23 |
| Votto,Joey, Cin | 4.18 |
| Uggla,Dan, Atl | 4.14 |
| Stanton,Giancarlo, Mia | 4.14 |
| Goldschmidt,Paul, Ari | 4.13 |
| Carpenter,Matt, StL | 4.12 |
| Upton,Justin, Atl | 4.09 |
| LaRoche,Adam, Was | 4.07 |
| Posey,Buster, SF | 4.04 |

### Pct Pitches Taken
(minimum 1500 Pitches)

| | |
|---|---|
| Carpenter,Matt, StL | 62.8 |
| Ellis,A.J., LAD | 62.5 |
| Duda,Lucas, NYM | 62.4 |
| Scutaro,Marco, SF | 61.5 |
| Votto,Joey, Cin | 61.1 |
| Prado,Martin, Ari | 60.9 |
| Martin,Russell, Pit | 60.8 |
| Rendon,Anthony, Was | 60.5 |
| Choo,Shin-Soo, Cin | 60.5 |
| Posey,Buster, SF | 60.4 |

### Best BPS on OutZ
(minimum 502 PA)

| | |
|---|---|
| Molina,Yadier, StL | .732 |
| Goldschmidt,Paul, Ari | .731 |
| Cuddyer,Michael, Col | .667 |
| Carpenter,Matt, StL | .626 |
| Prado,Martin, Ari | .624 |
| Pence,Hunter, SF | .610 |
| Span,Denard, Was | .603 |
| Freeman,Freddie, Atl | .592 |
| Sandoval,Pablo, SF | .588 |
| Johnson,Chris, Atl | .585 |

### Worst BPS on OutZ
(minimum 502 PA)

| | |
|---|---|
| Uggla,Dan, Atl | .184 |
| Martin,Russell, Pit | .189 |
| Young,Eric, Col-NYM | .270 |
| Stanton,Giancarlo, Mia | .298 |
| Headley,Chase, SD | .313 |
| Rizzo,Anthony, ChC | .349 |
| Votto,Joey, Cin | .350 |
| Castro,Starlin, ChC | .357 |
| Gyorko,Jedd, SD | .369 |
| Crawford,Brandon, SF | .374 |

# National League Batting Leaders

**Best OPS vs Fastballs**
(minimum 251 PA)

| | |
|---|---|
| Choo,Shin-Soo, Cin | 1.066 |
| Goldschmidt,Paul, Ari | 1.043 |
| Votto,Joey, Cin | 1.024 |
| Werth,Jayson, Was | 1.013 |
| McCutchen,Andrew, Pit | .995 |
| Freeman,Freddie, Atl | .971 |
| Wright,David, NYM | .968 |
| Craig,Allen, StL | .955 |
| Tulowitzki,Troy, Col | .939 |
| Alvarez,Pedro, Pit | .910 |

**Best OPS vs Curveballs**
(minimum 50 PA)

| | |
|---|---|
| Gomez,Carlos, Mil | 1.209 |
| Carpenter,Matt, StL | 1.046 |
| Upton,Justin, Atl | .968 |
| Prado,Martin, Ari | .923 |
| LaRoche,Adam, Was | .914 |
| Goldschmidt,Paul, Ari | .910 |
| Sandoval,Pablo, SF | .900 |
| Harper,Bryce, Was | .861 |
| Phillips,Brandon, Cin | .851 |
| Freeman,Freddie, Atl | .822 |

**Best OPS vs Changeups**
(minimum 50 PA)

| | |
|---|---|
| Desmond,Ian, Was | 1.208 |
| Gonzalez,Carlos, Col | 1.192 |
| Pence,Hunter, SF | 1.141 |
| Tulowitzki,Troy, Col | 1.044 |
| Amarista,Alexi, SD | 1.033 |
| Goldschmidt,Paul, Ari | 1.022 |
| Span,Denard, Was | 1.019 |
| Gyorko,Jedd, SD | .985 |
| Simmons,Andrelton, Atl | .983 |
| Posey,Buster, SF | .955 |

**Best OPS vs Sliders**
(minimum 32 PA)

| | |
|---|---|
| Dickerson,Corey, Col | 1.117 |
| Puig,Yasiel, LAD | 1.105 |
| Heisey,Chris, Cin | 1.063 |
| Blanco,Gregor, SF | 1.035 |
| Ramirez,Hanley, LAD | 1.026 |
| Posey,Buster, SF | 1.015 |
| Blackmon,Charlie, Col | .974 |
| Ethier,Andre, LAD | .965 |
| Johnson,Chris, Atl | .952 |
| Young,Michael, Phi-LAD | .939 |

**OPS**
(minimum 502 PA)

| | |
|---|---|
| Goldschmidt,Paul, Ari | .952 |
| Tulowitzki,Troy, Col | .931 |
| Werth,Jayson, Was | .931 |
| Votto,Joey, Cin | .926 |
| Cuddyer,Michael, Col | .919 |
| McCutchen,Andrew, Pit | .911 |
| Freeman,Freddie, Atl | .897 |
| Choo,Shin-Soo, Cin | .885 |
| Holliday,Matt, StL | .879 |
| Carpenter,Matt, StL | .873 |

**OPS First Half**
(minimum 260 PA)

| | |
|---|---|
| Tulowitzki,Troy, Col | 1.008 |
| Gonzalez,Carlos, Col | .980 |
| Cuddyer,Michael, Col | .960 |
| Goldschmidt,Paul, Ari | .952 |
| Votto,Joey, Cin | .939 |
| Posey,Buster, SF | .931 |
| Wright,David, NYM | .903 |
| Choo,Shin-Soo, Cin | .893 |
| Carpenter,Matt, StL | .891 |
| Beltran,Carlos, StL | .879 |

**OPS Second Half**
(minimum 201 PA)

| | |
|---|---|
| Werth,Jayson, Was | 1.032 |
| McCutchen,Andrew, Pit | 1.001 |
| Holliday,Matt, StL | .994 |
| Freeman,Freddie, Atl | .952 |
| Goldschmidt,Paul, Ari | .952 |
| Belt,Brandon, SF | .915 |
| Pence,Hunter, SF | .912 |
| Venable,Will, SD | .906 |
| Votto,Joey, Cin | .905 |
| Byrd,Marlon, NYM-Pit | .879 |

**OPS by Catchers**
(minimum 251 PA)

| | |
|---|---|
| Molina,Yadier, StL | .836 |
| Lucroy,Jonathan, Mil | .823 |
| McCann,Brian, Atl | .797 |
| Posey,Buster, SF | .795 |
| Rosario,Wilin, Col | .780 |
| Ramos,Wilson, Was | .770 |
| Castillo,Welington, ChC | .750 |
| Martin,Russell, Pit | .696 |
| Ruiz,Carlos, Phi | .685 |
| Ellis,A.J., LAD | .682 |

**OPS by First Basemen**
(minimum 251 PA)

| | |
|---|---|
| Goldschmidt,Paul, Ari | .955 |
| Votto,Joey, Cin | .925 |
| Freeman,Freddie, Atl | .897 |
| Belt,Brandon, SF | .838 |
| Adams,Matt, StL | .821 |
| Gonzalez,Adrian, LAD | .794 |
| Jones,Garrett, Pit | .789 |
| Howard,Ryan, Phi | .787 |
| Sanchez,Gaby, Pit | .777 |
| Craig,Allen, StL | .772 |

**OPS by Second Basemen**
(minimum 251 PA)

| | |
|---|---|
| Carpenter,Matt, StL | .879 |
| Utley,Chase, Phi | .816 |
| Hill,Aaron, Ari | .811 |
| Walker,Neil, Pit | .757 |
| Gyorko,Jedd, SD | .745 |
| Murphy,Daniel, NYM | .744 |
| Rendon,Anthony, Was | .743 |
| Scutaro,Marco, SF | .723 |
| Phillips,Brandon, Cin | .706 |
| LeMahieu,DJ, Col | .697 |

**OPS by Third Basemen**
(minimum 251 PA)

| | |
|---|---|
| Wright,David, NYM | .906 |
| Ramirez,Aramis, Mil | .865 |
| Zimmerman,Ryan, Was | .823 |
| Johnson,Chris, Atl | .808 |
| Alvarez,Pedro, Pit | .774 |
| Uribe,Juan, LAD | .767 |
| Sandoval,Pablo, SF | .765 |
| Young,Michael, Phi-LAD | .757 |
| Headley,Chase, SD | .748 |
| Valbuena,Luis, ChC | .717 |

**OPS by Shortstops**
(minimum 251 PA)

| | |
|---|---|
| Ramirez,Hanley, LAD | 1.033 |
| Tulowitzki,Troy, Col | .927 |
| Desmond,Ian, Was | .784 |
| Segura,Jean, Mil | .752 |
| Mercer,Jordy, Pit | .748 |
| Cabrera,Everth, SD | .736 |
| Gregorius,Didi, Ari | .706 |
| Simmons,Andrelton, Atl | .693 |
| Crawford,Brandon, SF | .674 |
| Cozart,Zack, Cin | .665 |

**OPS by Left Fielders**
(minimum 251 PA)

| | |
|---|---|
| Gonzalez,Carlos, Col | .972 |
| Holliday,Matt, StL | .886 |
| Harper,Bryce, Was | .880 |
| Quentin,Carlos, SD | .879 |
| Braun,Ryan, Mil | .877 |
| Upton,Justin, Atl | .853 |
| Brown,Domonic, Phi | .832 |
| Marte,Starling, Pit | .781 |
| Crawford,Carl, LAD | .749 |
| Yelich,Christian, Mia | .739 |

**OPS by Center Fielders**
(minimum 251 PA)

| | |
|---|---|
| McCutchen,Andrew, Pit | .912 |
| Choo,Shin-Soo, Cin | .888 |
| Gomez,Carlos, Mil | .848 |
| Ethier,Andre, LAD | .837 |
| Fowler,Dexter, Col | .780 |
| DeJesus,David, ChC-Was | .765 |
| Pagan,Angel, SF | .752 |
| Ruggiano,Justin, Mia | .737 |
| Kemp,Matt, LAD | .734 |
| Pollock,A.J., Ari | .728 |

**OPS by Right Fielders**
(minimum 251 PA)

| | |
|---|---|
| Puig,Yasiel, LAD | .932 |
| Werth,Jayson, Was | .930 |
| Cuddyer,Michael, Col | .919 |
| Stanton,Giancarlo, Mia | .845 |
| Byrd,Marlon, NYM-Pit | .840 |
| Beltran,Carlos, StL | .835 |
| Pence,Hunter, SF | .822 |
| Venable,Will, SD | .820 |
| Bruce,Jay, Cin | .807 |
| Schierholtz,Nate, ChC | .757 |

**OPS by Pitchers**
(minimum 50 PA)

| | |
|---|---|
| Greinke,Zack, LAD | .779 |
| Wood,Travis, ChC | .639 |
| Gallardo,Yovani, Mil | .571 |
| Fernandez,Jose, Mia | .556 |
| Cashner,Andrew, SD | .553 |
| Ryu,Hyun-Jin, LAD | .526 |
| Teheran,Julio, Atl | .526 |
| Kershaw,Clayton, LAD | .501 |
| Wainwright,Adam, StL | .483 |
| Medlen,Kris, Atl | .471 |

# National League Batting Leaders

**OPS Batting Left vs. LHP**
(minimum 125 PA)

| | |
|---|---|
| Gonzalez,Carlos, Col | .875 |
| Votto,Joey, Cin | .824 |
| Carpenter,Matt, StL | .820 |
| Aoki,Norichika, Mil | .781 |
| Freeman,Freddie, Atl | .764 |
| Belt,Brandon, SF | .755 |
| Utley,Chase, Phi | .754 |
| Gonzalez,Adrian, LAD | .747 |
| Bruce,Jay, Cin | .734 |
| Brown,Domonic, Phi | .724 |

**OPS Batting Left vs. RHP**
(minimum 377 PA)

| | |
|---|---|
| Choo,Shin-Soo, Cin | 1.011 |
| Votto,Joey, Cin | .977 |
| Freeman,Freddie, Atl | .958 |
| Carpenter,Matt, StL | .897 |
| Beltran,Carlos, StL | .871 |
| Belt,Brandon, SF | .867 |
| Brown,Domonic, Phi | .857 |
| Ethier,Andre, LAD | .854 |
| Alvarez,Pedro, Pit | .842 |
| Bruce,Jay, Cin | .841 |

**OPS Batting Right vs. LHP**
(minimum 125 PA)

| | |
|---|---|
| Wright,David, NYM | 1.072 |
| Stanton,Giancarlo, Mia | 1.006 |
| Upton,Justin, Atl | .994 |
| Gomez,Carlos, Mil | .993 |
| Sanchez,Gaby, Pit | .987 |
| Goldschmidt,Paul, Ari | .986 |
| Pence,Hunter, SF | .976 |
| Byrd,Marlon, NYM-Pit | .959 |
| Johnson,Chris, Atl | .939 |
| Cabrera,Everth, SD | .934 |

**OPS Batting Right vs. RHP**
(minimum 377 PA)

| | |
|---|---|
| Cuddyer,Michael, Col | .954 |
| Goldschmidt,Paul, Ari | .941 |
| Tulowitzki,Troy, Col | .938 |
| Holliday,Matt, StL | .903 |
| Werth,Jayson, Was | .884 |
| McCutchen,Andrew, Pit | .864 |
| Craig,Allen, StL | .845 |
| Molina,Yadier, StL | .823 |
| Byrd,Marlon, NYM-Pit | .797 |
| Gomez,Carlos, Mil | .797 |

**OPS vs. LHP**
(minimum 125 PA)

| | |
|---|---|
| Wright,David, NYM | 1.072 |
| Stanton,Giancarlo, Mia | 1.006 |
| Upton,Justin, Atl | .994 |
| Gomez,Carlos, Mil | .993 |
| Sanchez,Gaby, Pit | .987 |
| Goldschmidt,Paul, Ari | .986 |
| Pence,Hunter, SF | .976 |
| Byrd,Marlon, NYM-Pit | .959 |
| Johnson,Chris, Atl | .939 |
| Cabrera,Everth, SD | .934 |

**OPS vs. RHP**
(minimum 377 PA)

| | |
|---|---|
| Choo,Shin-Soo, Cin | 1.011 |
| Votto,Joey, Cin | .977 |
| Freeman,Freddie, Atl | .958 |
| Cuddyer,Michael, Col | .954 |
| Goldschmidt,Paul, Ari | .941 |
| Tulowitzki,Troy, Col | .938 |
| Holliday,Matt, StL | .903 |
| Carpenter,Matt, StL | .897 |
| Werth,Jayson, Was | .884 |
| Beltran,Carlos, StL | .871 |

**RC Per 27 Outs vs. LHP**
(minimum 125 PA)

| | |
|---|---|
| Sanchez,Gaby, Pit | 8.9 |
| Wright,David, NYM | 8.6 |
| Cabrera,Everth, SD | 8.2 |
| Tulowitzki,Troy, Col | 8.1 |
| Johnson,Chris, Atl | 7.8 |
| Upton,Justin, Atl | 7.6 |
| Goldschmidt,Paul, Ari | 6.9 |
| Pence,Hunter, SF | 6.9 |
| Byrd,Marlon, NYM-Pit | 6.7 |
| Freeman,Freddie, Atl | 6.5 |

**RC Per 27 Outs vs. RHP**
(minimum 377 PA)

| | |
|---|---|
| Freeman,Freddie, Atl | 9.5 |
| Choo,Shin-Soo, Cin | 9.3 |
| Votto,Joey, Cin | 9.1 |
| Craig,Allen, StL | 8.0 |
| Goldschmidt,Paul, Ari | 7.9 |
| Carpenter,Matt, StL | 7.8 |
| Cuddyer,Michael, Col | 7.5 |
| Werth,Jayson, Was | 7.0 |
| Holliday,Matt, StL | 6.8 |
| Beltran,Carlos, StL | 6.3 |

**Highest RBI %**
(minimum 502 PA)

| | |
|---|---|
| Freeman,Freddie, Atl | 45.99 |
| Craig,Allen, StL | 45.91 |
| Goldschmidt,Paul, Ari | 45.13 |
| Holliday,Matt, StL | 41.12 |
| Cuddyer,Michael, Col | 40.29 |
| Tulowitzki,Troy, Col | 39.79 |
| Brown,Domonic, Phi | 39.43 |
| Carpenter,Matt, StL | 39.43 |
| Werth,Jayson, Was | 39.39 |
| Molina,Yadier, StL | 38.97 |

**Lowest RBI %**
(minimum 502 PA)

| | |
|---|---|
| Castro,Starlin, ChC | 20.66 |
| Scutaro,Marco, SF | 20.99 |
| Barney,Darwin, ChC | 21.35 |
| Hechavarria,Adeiny, Mia | 22.19 |
| Rollins,Jimmy, Phi | 22.56 |
| Crawford,Brandon, SF | 23.11 |
| Parra,Gerardo, Ari | 25.18 |
| Headley,Chase, SD | 25.54 |
| Aoki,Norichika, Mil | 25.55 |
| Simmons,Andrelton, Atl | 25.87 |

**Highest Strikeout per PA**
(minimum 502 PA)

| | |
|---|---|
| Uggla,Dan, Atl | .318 |
| Alvarez,Pedro, Pit | .303 |
| Stanton,Giancarlo, Mia | .278 |
| Bruce,Jay, Cin | .265 |
| Upton,Justin, Atl | .250 |
| Byrd,Marlon, NYM-Pit | .249 |
| Gomez,Carlos, Mil | .247 |
| Marte,Starling, Pit | .244 |
| Headley,Chase, SD | .237 |
| Gyorko,Jedd, SD | .234 |

**Lowest Strikeout per PA**
(minimum 502 PA)

| | |
|---|---|
| Aoki,Norichika, Mil | .059 |
| Scutaro,Marco, SF | .062 |
| Prado,Martin, Ari | .080 |
| Simmons,Andrelton, Atl | .084 |
| Molina,Yadier, StL | .102 |
| Barney,Darwin, ChC | .115 |
| Span,Denard, Was | .116 |
| Posey,Buster, SF | .118 |
| Lucroy,Jonathan, Mil | .119 |
| 2 tied with | .135 |

**Home Runs At Home**

| | |
|---|---|
| Goldschmidt,Paul, Ari | 17 |
| Alvarez,Pedro, Pit | 16 |
| Bruce,Jay, Cin | 16 |
| Freeman,Freddie, Atl | 16 |
| Gomez,Carlos, Mil | 15 |
| Stanton,Giancarlo, Mia | 15 |
| Venable,Will, SD | 15 |
| Brown,Domonic, Phi | 14 |
| Holliday,Matt, StL | 14 |
| Tulowitzki,Troy, Col | 14 |

**Home Runs Away**

| | |
|---|---|
| Alvarez,Pedro, Pit | 20 |
| Goldschmidt,Paul, Ari | 19 |
| Zimmerman,Ryan, Was | 19 |
| Pence,Hunter, SF | 17 |
| Byrd,Marlon, NYM-Pit | 15 |
| Ruggiano,Justin, Mia | 15 |
| Bruce,Jay, Cin | 14 |
| Gonzalez,Carlos, Col | 14 |
| Uggla,Dan, Atl | 14 |
| Upton,Justin, Atl | 14 |

**Longest Avg Home Run**
(min 10 over the wall)

| | |
|---|---|
| Upton,Justin, Atl | 416 |
| Stanton,Giancarlo, Mia | 414 |
| Byrd,Marlon, NYM-Pit | 412 |
| Pence,Hunter, SF | 410 |
| Werth,Jayson, Was | 410 |
| Gonzalez,Carlos, Col | 409 |
| Holliday,Matt, StL | 409 |
| Gattis,Evan, Atl | 408 |
| Alvarez,Pedro, Pit | 408 |
| Cuddyer,Michael, Col | 408 |

**Shortest Avg Home Run**
(min 10 over the wall)

| | |
|---|---|
| Mayberry,John, Phi | 384 |
| Murphy,Donnie, ChC | 384 |
| Simmons,Andrelton, Atl | 385 |
| Betancourt,Yuniesky, Mil | 386 |
| Brown,Domonic, Phi | 387 |
| Cozart,Zack, Cin | 387 |
| Hill,Aaron, Ari | 387 |
| Valbuena,Luis, ChC | 387 |
| 3 tied with | 389 |

# National League Batting Leaders

**Under Age 26: AB Per HR**
(minimum 502 PA)

| | |
|---|---|
| Stanton,Giancarlo, Mia | 17.7 |
| Gyorko,Jedd, SD | 21.1 |
| Freeman,Freddie, Atl | 24.0 |
| Rizzo,Anthony, ChC | 26.3 |
| Belt,Brandon, SF | 29.9 |
| Simmons,Andrelton, Atl | 35.6 |
| Marte,Starling, Pit | 42.5 |
| Arenado,Nolan, Col | 48.6 |
| Segura,Jean, Mil | 49.0 |
| Castro,Starlin, ChC | 66.6 |

**Under Age 26: OPS**
(minimum 502 PA)

| | |
|---|---|
| Freeman,Freddie, Atl | .897 |
| Stanton,Giancarlo, Mia | .845 |
| Belt,Brandon, SF | .841 |
| Marte,Starling, Pit | .784 |
| Segura,Jean, Mil | .752 |
| Gyorko,Jedd, SD | .745 |
| Rizzo,Anthony, ChC | .742 |
| Arenado,Nolan, Col | .706 |
| Simmons,Andrelton, Atl | .692 |
| Castro,Starlin, ChC | .631 |

**Under Age 26: RC/27 Outs**
(minimum 502 PA)

| | |
|---|---|
| Freeman,Freddie, Atl | 8.6 |
| Belt,Brandon, SF | 5.9 |
| Stanton,Giancarlo, Mia | 5.4 |
| Marte,Starling, Pit | 5.1 |
| Segura,Jean, Mil | 4.3 |
| Rizzo,Anthony, ChC | 4.1 |
| Arenado,Nolan, Col | 3.4 |
| Gyorko,Jedd, SD | 3.4 |
| Simmons,Andrelton, Atl | 3.3 |
| Castro,Starlin, ChC | 2.8 |

**Longest Home Run**

| | |
|---|---|
| Gattis,Evan, Atl, 9/8 | 486 |
| Pence,Hunter, SF, 8/27 | 476 |
| Rizzo,Anthony, ChC, 4/18 | 475 |
| Bruce,Jay, Cin, 6/22 | 472 |
| Frazier,Todd, Cin, 4/24 | 470 |
| Morrison,Logan, Mia, 9/6 | 467 |
| Sandoval,Pablo, SF, 5/21 | 464 |
| Wright,David, NYM, 5/3 | 464 |
| Stanton,Giancarlo, Mia, 9/18 | 463 |
| Upton,Justin, Atl, 5/17 | 461 |

**Swing and Miss %**
(minimum 1500 Pitches Seen)

| | |
|---|---|
| Alvarez,Pedro, Pit | 35.1 |
| Uggla,Dan, Atl | 34.7 |
| Puig,Yasiel, LAD | 33.8 |
| Upton,B.J., Atl | 33.5 |
| Stanton,Giancarlo, Mia | 33.3 |
| Francisco,Juan, Atl-Mil | 31.5 |
| Bruce,Jay, Cin | 30.6 |
| Ruggiano,Justin, Mia | 29.7 |
| Duda,Lucas, NYM | 29.7 |
| Upton,Justin, Atl | 29.6 |

**Highest First Swing %**
(minimum 502 PA)

| | |
|---|---|
| Gomez,Carlos, Mil | 49.5 |
| Freeman,Freddie, Atl | 45.2 |
| Molina,Yadier, StL | 43.9 |
| Sandoval,Pablo, SF | 41.5 |
| Byrd,Marlon, NYM-Pit | 38.6 |
| Desmond,Ian, Was | 37.0 |
| Holliday,Matt, StL | 35.7 |
| Belt,Brandon, SF | 35.5 |
| Frazier,Todd, Cin | 34.9 |
| Brown,Domonic, Phi | 34.0 |

**Lowest First Swing %**
(minimum 502 PA)

| | |
|---|---|
| Prado,Martin, Ari | 9.4 |
| Carpenter,Matt, StL | 10.5 |
| Scutaro,Marco, SF | 10.6 |
| Utley,Chase, Phi | 11.8 |
| Lucroy,Jonathan, Mil | 13.0 |
| Zimmerman,Ryan, Was | 14.9 |
| Barney,Darwin, ChC | 17.8 |
| Posey,Buster, SF | 18.0 |
| Werth,Jayson, Was | 18.1 |
| Stanton,Giancarlo, Mia | 18.7 |

**Home RC Per 27 Outs**
(minimum 251 PA)

| | |
|---|---|
| Freeman,Freddie, Atl | 10.5 |
| Carpenter,Matt, StL | 8.5 |
| Goldschmidt,Paul, Ari | 8.2 |
| Tulowitzki,Troy, Col | 8.1 |
| Choo,Shin-Soo, Cin | 8.0 |
| Holliday,Matt, StL | 8.0 |
| Cuddyer,Michael, Col | 7.8 |
| Craig,Allen, StL | 7.7 |
| McCutchen,Andrew, Pit | 7.7 |
| Werth,Jayson, Was | 7.2 |

**Road RC Per 27 Outs**
(minimum 251 PA)

| | |
|---|---|
| Votto,Joey, Cin | 8.6 |
| Byrd,Marlon, NYM-Pit | 7.5 |
| Goldschmidt,Paul, Ari | 7.2 |
| Belt,Brandon, SF | 7.2 |
| Wright,David, NYM | 7.1 |
| Craig,Allen, StL | 6.9 |
| Molina,Yadier, StL | 6.6 |
| Freeman,Freddie, Atl | 6.6 |
| Sandoval,Pablo, SF | 6.5 |
| Carpenter,Matt, StL | 6.2 |

**Lead Changing RBI**

| | |
|---|---|
| Goldschmidt,Paul, Ari | 42 |
| Phillips,Brandon, Cin | 41 |
| Freeman,Freddie, Atl | 40 |
| Alvarez,Pedro, Pit | 38 |
| McCutchen,Andrew, Pit | 36 |
| Tulowitzki,Troy, Col | 34 |
| Gonzalez,Adrian, LAD | 33 |
| Bruce,Jay, Cin | 31 |
| Holliday,Matt, StL | 30 |
| Prado,Martin, Ari | 30 |

# American League Pitching Leaders

### Earned Run Average
(minimum 162 IP)

| | |
|---|---|
| Sanchez,Anibal, Det | 2.57 |
| Colon,Bartolo, Oak | 2.65 |
| Iwakuma,Hisashi, Sea | 2.66 |
| Darvish,Yu, Tex | 2.83 |
| Scherzer,Max, Det | 2.90 |
| Hernandez,Felix, Sea | 3.04 |
| Sale,Chris, CWS | 3.07 |
| Shields,James, KC | 3.15 |
| Santana,Ervin, KC | 3.24 |
| Jimenez,Ubaldo, Cle | 3.30 |

### Winning Percentage
(minimum 15 Decisions)

| | |
|---|---|
| Scherzer,Max, Det | .875 |
| Moore,Matt, TB | .810 |
| Colon,Bartolo, Oak | .750 |
| Wilson,C.J., LAA | .708 |
| Peavy,Jake, CWS-Bos | .706 |
| Iwakuma,Hisashi, Sea | .700 |
| Tillman,Chris, Bal | .696 |
| Kluber,Corey, Cle | .688 |
| Lester,Jon, Bos | .652 |
| Doubront,Felix, Bos | .647 |

### Opponent Batting Average
(minimum 162 IP)

| | |
|---|---|
| Darvish,Yu, Tex | .194 |
| Scherzer,Max, Det | .198 |
| Iwakuma,Hisashi, Sea | .220 |
| Masterson,Justin, Cle | .222 |
| Griffin,A.J., Oak | .226 |
| Sanchez,Anibal, Det | .229 |
| Sale,Chris, CWS | .230 |
| Santana,Ervin, KC | .238 |
| Jimenez,Ubaldo, Cle | .239 |
| Tillman,Chris, Bal | .241 |

### Baserunners Per 9 IP
(minimum 162 IP)

| | |
|---|---|
| Scherzer,Max, Det | 8.90 |
| Iwakuma,Hisashi, Sea | 9.14 |
| Darvish,Yu, Tex | 10.00 |
| Price,David, TB | 10.03 |
| Sale,Chris, CWS | 10.25 |
| Griffin,A.J., Oak | 10.31 |
| Hernandez,Felix, Sea | 10.31 |
| Sanchez,Anibal, Det | 10.48 |
| Colon,Bartolo, Oak | 10.50 |
| Santana,Ervin, KC | 10.54 |

### Games

| | |
|---|---|
| Peralta,Joel, TB | 80 |
| Allen,Cody, Cle | 77 |
| Lindstrom,Matt, CWS | 76 |
| Scheppers,Tanner, Tex | 76 |
| de la Rosa,Dane, LAA | 75 |
| Johnson,Jim, Bal | 74 |
| Duensing,Brian, Min | 73 |
| Fien,Casey, Min | 73 |
| Uehara,Koji, Bos | 73 |
| 6 tied with | 71 |

### Games Started

| | |
|---|---|
| Dickey,R.A., Tor | 34 |
| Shields,James, KC | 34 |
| Verlander,Justin, Det | 34 |
| 8 tied with | 33 |

### Complete Games

| | |
|---|---|
| Price,David, TB | 4 |
| Sale,Chris, CWS | 4 |
| Colon,Bartolo, Oak | 3 |
| Dickey,R.A., Tor | 3 |
| Guthrie,Jeremy, KC | 3 |
| Masterson,Justin, Cle | 3 |
| Nova,Ivan, NYY | 3 |
| Vargas,Jason, LAA | 3 |
| 9 tied with | 2 |

### Shutouts

| | |
|---|---|
| Colon,Bartolo, Oak | 3 |
| Masterson,Justin, Cle | 3 |
| Archer,Chris, TB | 2 |
| Guthrie,Jeremy, KC | 2 |
| Harang,Aaron, Sea | 2 |
| Holland,Derek, Tex | 2 |
| Nova,Ivan, NYY | 2 |
| Vargas,Jason, LAA | 2 |
| 12 tied with | 1 |

### Wins

| | |
|---|---|
| Scherzer,Max, Det | 21 |
| Colon,Bartolo, Oak | 18 |
| Moore,Matt, TB | 17 |
| Wilson,C.J., LAA | 17 |
| Tillman,Chris, Bal | 16 |
| Guthrie,Jeremy, KC | 15 |
| Lester,Jon, Bos | 15 |
| 7 tied with | 14 |

### Losses

| | |
|---|---|
| Harrell,Lucas, Hou | 17 |
| Saunders,Joe, Sea | 16 |
| Blanton,Joe, LAA | 14 |
| Danks,John, CWS | 14 |
| Hughes,Phil, NYY | 14 |
| Sale,Chris, CWS | 14 |
| 8 tied with | 13 |

### No Decisions

| | |
|---|---|
| Quintana,Jose, CWS | 17 |
| Holland,Derek, Tex | 14 |
| Iwakuma,Hisashi, Sea | 13 |
| Santana,Ervin, KC | 13 |
| Bedard,Erik, Hou | 12 |
| Dempster,Ryan, Bos | 12 |
| Parker,Jarrod, Oak | 12 |
| Santiago,Hector, CWS | 12 |
| Shields,James, KC | 12 |
| 3 tied with | 11 |

### Wild Pitches

| | |
|---|---|
| Moore,Matt, TB | 17 |
| Wilson,C.J., LAA | 14 |
| Hernandez,Felix, Sea | 13 |
| Richards,Garrett, LAA | 11 |
| Shields,James, KC | 11 |
| Iwakuma,Hisashi, Sea | 10 |
| Mendoza,Luis, KC | 10 |
| 8 tied with | 9 |

### Strikeouts

| | |
|---|---|
| Darvish,Yu, Tex | 277 |
| Scherzer,Max, Det | 240 |
| Sale,Chris, CWS | 226 |
| Verlander,Justin, Det | 217 |
| Hernandez,Felix, Sea | 216 |
| Sanchez,Anibal, Det | 202 |
| Shields,James, KC | 196 |
| Masterson,Justin, Cle | 195 |
| Jimenez,Ubaldo, Cle | 194 |
| Holland,Derek, Tex | 189 |

### Walks Allowed

| | |
|---|---|
| Harrell,Lucas, Hou | 88 |
| Wilson,C.J., LAA | 85 |
| Darvish,Yu, Tex | 80 |
| Jimenez,Ubaldo, Cle | 80 |
| Dempster,Ryan, Bos | 79 |
| Masterson,Justin, Cle | 76 |
| Moore,Matt, TB | 76 |
| Bedard,Erik, Hou | 75 |
| Verlander,Justin, Det | 75 |
| Santiago,Hector, CWS | 72 |

### Intentional Walks Allowed

| | |
|---|---|
| Hernandez,Roberto, TB | 8 |
| Coke,Phil, Det | 7 |
| Medina,Yoervis, Sea | 7 |
| Hill,Rich, Cle | 6 |
| Ramos,Cesar, TB | 6 |
| 11 tied with | 5 |

### Hit Batters

| | |
|---|---|
| Masterson,Justin, Cle | 17 |
| Fister,Doug, Det | 16 |
| Santiago,Hector, CWS | 15 |
| Nova,Ivan, NYY | 14 |
| Sale,Chris, CWS | 14 |
| Hernandez,Roberto, TB | 13 |
| Lyles,Jordan, Hou | 11 |
| Dickey,R.A., Tor | 10 |
| Buehrle,Mark, Tor | 9 |
| Deduno,Samuel, Min | 9 |

# American League Pitching Leaders

### Runs Allowed

| | |
|---|---|
| Sabathia,CC, NYY | 122 |
| Saunders,Joe, Sea | 117 |
| Dickey,R.A., Tor | 113 |
| Harrell,Lucas, Hou | 111 |
| Hellickson,Jeremy, TB | 103 |
| Buehrle,Mark, Tor | 100 |
| Guthrie,Jeremy, KC | 99 |
| Lyles,Jordan, Hou | 98 |
| Dempster,Ryan, Bos | 97 |
| 2 tied with | 96 |

### Hits Allowed

| | |
|---|---|
| Guthrie,Jeremy, KC | 236 |
| Saunders,Joe, Sea | 232 |
| Fister,Doug, Det | 229 |
| Sabathia,CC, NYY | 224 |
| Buehrle,Mark, Tor | 223 |
| Correia,Kevin, Min | 218 |
| Shields,James, KC | 215 |
| Verlander,Justin, Det | 212 |
| Holland,Derek, Tex | 210 |
| Lester,Jon, Bos | 209 |

### Doubles Allowed

| | |
|---|---|
| Saunders,Joe, Sea | 61 |
| Lester,Jon, Bos | 52 |
| Sabathia,CC, NYY | 52 |
| Buehrle,Mark, Tor | 50 |
| Holland,Derek, Tex | 49 |
| Kuroda,Hiroki, NYY | 48 |
| Correia,Kevin, Min | 45 |
| Pettitte,Andy, NYY | 43 |
| Dickey,R.A., Tor | 42 |
| Wilson,C.J., LAA | 41 |

### Home Runs Allowed

| | |
|---|---|
| Griffin,A.J., Oak | 36 |
| Dickey,R.A., Tor | 35 |
| Tillman,Chris, Bal | 33 |
| Guthrie,Jeremy, KC | 30 |
| Blanton,Joe, LAA | 29 |
| Danks,John, CWS | 28 |
| Sabathia,CC, NYY | 28 |
| 4 tied with | 26 |

### Run Support Per Nine IP

(minimum 162 IP)

| | |
|---|---|
| Scherzer,Max, Det | 6.80 |
| Dempster,Ryan, Bos | 6.51 |
| Colon,Bartolo, Oak | 6.38 |
| Sanchez,Anibal, Det | 6.13 |
| Hellickson,Jeremy, TB | 5.74 |
| Wilson,C.J., LAA | 5.72 |
| Doubront,Felix, Bos | 5.66 |
| Verlander,Justin, Det | 5.56 |
| Porcello,Rick, Det | 5.54 |
| Griffin,A.J., Oak | 5.44 |

### % Pitches In Strike Zone

(minimum 162 IP)

| | |
|---|---|
| Colon,Bartolo, Oak | 48.9 |
| Dickey,R.A., Tor | 46.7 |
| Guthrie,Jeremy, KC | 45.9 |
| Price,David, TB | 45.8 |
| Iwakuma,Hisashi, Sea | 45.8 |
| Santana,Ervin, KC | 45.3 |
| Sale,Chris, CWS | 45.1 |
| Sabathia,CC, NYY | 45.1 |
| Griffin,A.J., Oak | 45.0 |
| Holland,Derek, Tex | 45.0 |

### Pitches Per Start

(minimum 30 GS)

| | |
|---|---|
| Wilson,C.J., LAA | 110.6 |
| Verlander,Justin, Det | 108.6 |
| Sale,Chris, CWS | 108.3 |
| Lester,Jon, Bos | 107.8 |
| Darvish,Yu, Tex | 107.8 |
| Shields,James, KC | 107.6 |
| Scherzer,Max, Det | 105.9 |
| Tillman,Chris, Bal | 105.4 |
| Fister,Doug, Det | 104.3 |
| Sabathia,CC, NYY | 104.3 |

### Pitches Per Batter

(minimum 162 IP)

| | |
|---|---|
| Iwakuma,Hisashi, Sea | 3.58 |
| Colon,Bartolo, Oak | 3.61 |
| Williams,Jerome, LAA | 3.62 |
| Price,David, TB | 3.66 |
| Parker,Jarrod, Oak | 3.66 |
| Holland,Derek, Tex | 3.67 |
| Sabathia,CC, NYY | 3.67 |
| Correia,Kevin, Min | 3.69 |
| Lackey,John, Bos | 3.69 |
| Pettitte,Andy, NYY | 3.69 |

### Quality Starts

| | |
|---|---|
| Shields,James, KC | 27 |
| Scherzer,Max, Det | 25 |
| Wilson,C.J., LAA | 24 |
| Colon,Bartolo, Oak | 23 |
| Iwakuma,Hisashi, Sea | 23 |
| Parker,Jarrod, Oak | 23 |
| Sale,Chris, CWS | 23 |
| Santana,Ervin, KC | 23 |
| 4 tied with | 22 |

### Batters Faced

| | |
|---|---|
| Shields,James, KC | 946 |
| Dickey,R.A., Tor | 943 |
| Verlander,Justin, Det | 925 |
| Wilson,C.J., LAA | 913 |
| Sabathia,CC, NYY | 908 |
| Guthrie,Jeremy, KC | 905 |
| Lester,Jon, Bos | 903 |
| Holland,Derek, Tex | 894 |
| Fister,Doug, Det | 881 |
| Buehrle,Mark, Tor | 876 |

### Innings Pitched

| | |
|---|---|
| Shields,James, KC | 228.2 |
| Dickey,R.A., Tor | 224.2 |
| Iwakuma,Hisashi, Sea | 219.2 |
| Verlander,Justin, Det | 218.1 |
| Sale,Chris, CWS | 214.1 |
| Scherzer,Max, Det | 214.1 |
| Lester,Jon, Bos | 213.1 |
| Holland,Derek, Tex | 213.0 |
| Wilson,C.J., LAA | 212.1 |
| Guthrie,Jeremy, KC | 211.2 |

### Most Pitches in a Game

| | |
|---|---|
| Darvish,Yu, Tex | 130 |
| Sanchez,Anibal, Det | 130 |
| Darvish,Yu, Tex | 127 |
| Dempster,Ryan, Bos | 127 |
| Price,David, TB | 127 |
| Verlander,Justin, Det | 126 |
| Holland,Derek, Tex | 125 |
| Sanchez,Anibal, Det | 125 |
| Saunders,Joe, Sea | 125 |
| 6 tied with | 124 |

### Stolen Bases Allowed

| | |
|---|---|
| Lackey,John, Bos | 36 |
| Sanchez,Anibal, Det | 25 |
| Hanson,Tommy, LAA | 21 |
| Verlander,Justin, Det | 21 |
| Sale,Chris, CWS | 19 |
| Darvish,Yu, Tex | 18 |
| Hernandez,Roberto, TB | 18 |
| Blanton,Joe, LAA | 17 |
| Hernandez,Felix, Sea | 17 |
| 7 tied with | 16 |

### Caught Stealing Off

| | |
|---|---|
| Price,David, TB | 10 |
| Santana,Ervin, KC | 8 |
| Scherzer,Max, Det | 8 |
| Tillman,Chris, Bal | 8 |
| Darvish,Yu, Tex | 7 |
| Lackey,John, Bos | 7 |
| Loup,Aaron, Tor | 7 |
| Williams,Jerome, LAA | 7 |
| 8 tied with | 6 |

### Stolen Base Pct Allowed

(minimum 162 IP)

| | |
|---|---|
| Tillman,Chris, Bal | 11.1 |
| Gonzalez,Miguel, Bal | 40.0 |
| Buehrle,Mark, Tor | 44.4 |
| Kuroda,Hiroki, NYY | 50.0 |
| Shields,James, KC | 50.0 |
| Price,David, TB | 52.4 |
| Correia,Kevin, Min | 54.5 |
| Williams,Jerome, LAA | 56.3 |
| Quintana,Jose, CWS | 58.3 |
| 2 tied with | 60.0 |

### Pickoffs

| | |
|---|---|
| Buehrle,Mark, Tor | 6 |
| Chen,Bruce, KC | 5 |
| Loup,Aaron, Tor | 5 |
| Price,David, TB | 5 |
| Quintana,Jose, CWS | 5 |
| Doubront,Felix, Bos | 4 |
| Holland,Derek, Tex | 4 |
| Vargas,Jason, LAA | 4 |
| 7 tied with | 3 |

# American League Pitching Leaders

### Strikeouts Per 9 IP
(minimum 162 IP)

| | |
|---|---|
| Darvish,Yu, Tex | 11.89 |
| Scherzer,Max, Det | 10.08 |
| Sanchez,Anibal, Det | 9.99 |
| Jimenez,Ubaldo, Cle | 9.56 |
| Hernandez,Felix, Sea | 9.51 |
| Sale,Chris, CWS | 9.49 |
| Masterson,Justin, Cle | 9.09 |
| Verlander,Justin, Det | 8.95 |
| Dempster,Ryan, Bos | 8.25 |
| Holland,Derek, Tex | 7.99 |

### Opp On-Base Percentage
(minimum 162 IP)

| | |
|---|---|
| Scherzer,Max, Det | .254 |
| Iwakuma,Hisashi, Sea | .258 |
| Darvish,Yu, Tex | .277 |
| Griffin,A.J., Oak | .280 |
| Price,David, TB | .281 |
| Sale,Chris, CWS | .282 |
| Sanchez,Anibal, Det | .286 |
| Hernandez,Felix, Sea | .286 |
| Santana,Ervin, KC | .288 |
| Colon,Bartolo, Oak | .290 |

### Opp Slugging Average
(minimum 162 IP)

| | |
|---|---|
| Masterson,Justin, Cle | .312 |
| Scherzer,Max, Det | .329 |
| Sanchez,Anibal, Det | .330 |
| Darvish,Yu, Tex | .334 |
| Sale,Chris, CWS | .354 |
| Hernandez,Felix, Sea | .358 |
| Wilson,C.J., LAA | .361 |
| Jimenez,Ubaldo, Cle | .367 |
| Shields,James, KC | .369 |
| Colon,Bartolo, Oak | .369 |

### Opponent OPS
(minimum 162 IP)

| | |
|---|---|
| Scherzer,Max, Det | .583 |
| Darvish,Yu, Tex | .611 |
| Sanchez,Anibal, Det | .616 |
| Masterson,Justin, Cle | .624 |
| Iwakuma,Hisashi, Sea | .630 |
| Sale,Chris, CWS | .636 |
| Hernandez,Felix, Sea | .644 |
| Colon,Bartolo, Oak | .659 |
| Price,David, TB | .661 |
| Santana,Ervin, KC | .668 |

### Home Runs Per Nine IP
(minimum 162 IP)

| | |
|---|---|
| Sanchez,Anibal, Det | 0.45 |
| Fister,Doug, Det | 0.60 |
| Masterson,Justin, Cle | 0.61 |
| Wilson,C.J., LAA | 0.64 |
| Hernandez,Felix, Sea | 0.66 |
| Colon,Bartolo, Oak | 0.66 |
| Doubront,Felix, Bos | 0.72 |
| Scherzer,Max, Det | 0.76 |
| Price,David, TB | 0.77 |
| Verlander,Justin, Det | 0.78 |

### Batting Average vs. LHB
(minimum 125 BF)

| | |
|---|---|
| Uehara,Koji, Bos | .115 |
| Sale,Chris, CWS | .135 |
| Frieri,Ernesto, LAA | .155 |
| Peralta,Joel, TB | .163 |
| Wilson,C.J., LAA | .169 |
| Nathan,Joe, Tex | .171 |
| Holland,Greg, KC | .172 |
| Furbush,Charlie, Sea | .173 |
| Cosart,Jarred, Hou | .173 |
| Robertson,David, NYY | .175 |

### Batting Average vs. RHB
(minimum 225 BF)

| | |
|---|---|
| Scherzer,Max, Det | .165 |
| Darvish,Yu, Tex | .165 |
| Masterson,Justin, Cle | .182 |
| Sanchez,Anibal, Det | .208 |
| Moore,Matt, TB | .214 |
| Straily,Dan, Oak | .221 |
| Parker,Jarrod, Oak | .221 |
| Chen,Bruce, KC | .224 |
| Dickey,R.A., Tor | .224 |
| Guthrie,Jeremy, KC | .225 |

### Opp BA w/ RISP
(minimum 125 BF)

| | |
|---|---|
| Darvish,Yu, Tex | .139 |
| Kuroda,Hiroki, NYY | .166 |
| Hernandez,Felix, Sea | .169 |
| Iwakuma,Hisashi, Sea | .184 |
| Santiago,Hector, CWS | .193 |
| Colon,Bartolo, Oak | .195 |
| Moore,Matt, TB | .200 |
| Jimenez,Ubaldo, Cle | .205 |
| Holland,Derek, Tex | .209 |
| Milone,Tommy, Oak | .216 |

### OBP vs. Leadoff Hitter
(minimum 150 BF)

| | |
|---|---|
| Cobb,Alex, TB | .242 |
| Weaver,Jered, LAA | .242 |
| Griffin,A.J., Oak | .251 |
| Santana,Ervin, KC | .257 |
| Sale,Chris, CWS | .267 |
| Scherzer,Max, Det | .271 |
| Porcello,Rick, Det | .272 |
| Darvish,Yu, Tex | .273 |
| Quintana,Jose, CWS | .278 |
| Sanchez,Anibal, Det | .278 |

### Strikeouts / Walks Ratio
(minimum 162 IP)

| | |
|---|---|
| Price,David, TB | 5.59 |
| Sale,Chris, CWS | 4.91 |
| Hernandez,Felix, Sea | 4.70 |
| Iwakuma,Hisashi, Sea | 4.41 |
| Scherzer,Max, Det | 4.29 |
| Colon,Bartolo, Oak | 4.03 |
| Lackey,John, Bos | 4.03 |
| Sanchez,Anibal, Det | 3.74 |
| Fister,Doug, Det | 3.61 |
| Kuroda,Hiroki, NYY | 3.49 |

### Highest GB/FB Ratio
(minimum 162 IP)

| | |
|---|---|
| Masterson,Justin, Cle | 2.40 |
| Porcello,Rick, Det | 2.34 |
| Fister,Doug, Det | 2.23 |
| Saunders,Joe, Sea | 1.89 |
| Hernandez,Felix, Sea | 1.89 |
| Kuroda,Hiroki, NYY | 1.49 |
| Williams,Jerome, LAA | 1.49 |
| Pettitte,Andy, NYY | 1.47 |
| Sale,Chris, CWS | 1.46 |
| Iwakuma,Hisashi, Sea | 1.45 |

### Lowest GB/FB Ratio
(minimum 162 IP)

| | |
|---|---|
| Griffin,A.J., Oak | 0.65 |
| Scherzer,Max, Det | 0.81 |
| Gonzalez,Miguel, Bal | 0.97 |
| Tillman,Chris, Bal | 0.97 |
| Hellickson,Jeremy, TB | 0.98 |
| Verlander,Justin, Det | 0.99 |
| Dickey,R.A., Tor | 1.00 |
| Parker,Jarrod, Oak | 1.04 |
| Norris,Bud, Hou-Bal | 1.05 |
| Darvish,Yu, Tex | 1.08 |

### Sacrifice Flies Allowed

| | |
|---|---|
| Hughes,Phil, NYY | 11 |
| Jimenez,Ubaldo, Cle | 11 |
| Doubront,Felix, Bos | 10 |
| Holland,Derek, Tex | 9 |
| Guthrie,Jeremy, KC | 8 |
| Hammel,Jason, Bal | 8 |
| Sabathia,CC, NYY | 8 |
| Scherzer,Max, Det | 8 |
| 4 tied with | 7 |

### Sacrifice Hits Allowed

| | |
|---|---|
| Richards,Garrett, LAA | 9 |
| Holland,Derek, Tex | 8 |
| Parker,Jarrod, Oak | 8 |
| Sabathia,CC, NYY | 8 |
| 7 tied with | 6 |

### GIDP Induced

| | |
|---|---|
| Fister,Doug, Det | 27 |
| Correia,Kevin, Min | 26 |
| Saunders,Joe, Sea | 26 |
| Hernandez,Felix, Sea | 24 |
| Harrell,Lucas, Hou | 23 |
| Shields,James, KC | 22 |
| Colon,Bartolo, Oak | 21 |
| Holland,Derek, Tex | 21 |
| Keuchel,Dallas, Hou | 21 |
| 3 tied with | 20 |

### GIDP Per Nine IP
(minimum 162 IP)

| | |
|---|---|
| Saunders,Joe, Sea | 1.28 |
| Correia,Kevin, Min | 1.26 |
| Fister,Doug, Det | 1.17 |
| Hernandez,Felix, Sea | 1.06 |
| Porcello,Rick, Det | 1.02 |
| Colon,Bartolo, Oak | 0.99 |
| Price,David, TB | 0.92 |
| Holland,Derek, Tex | 0.89 |
| Doubront,Felix, Bos | 0.89 |
| Shields,James, KC | 0.87 |

# American League Pitching Leaders

**Saves**

| | |
|---|---|
| Johnson,Jim, Bal | 50 |
| Holland,Greg, KC | 47 |
| Rivera,Mariano, NYY | 44 |
| Nathan,Joe, Tex | 43 |
| Reed,Addison, CWS | 40 |
| Balfour,Grant, Oak | 38 |
| Frieri,Ernesto, LAA | 37 |
| Rodney,Fernando, TB | 37 |
| Perkins,Glen, Min | 36 |
| Janssen,Casey, Tor | 34 |

**Blown Saves**

| | |
|---|---|
| Johnson,Jim, Bal | 9 |
| Reed,Addison, CWS | 8 |
| Rodney,Fernando, TB | 8 |
| Tazawa,Junichi, Bos | 8 |
| Cook,Ryan, Oak | 7 |
| Rivera,Mariano, NYY | 7 |
| Furbush,Charlie, Sea | 6 |
| 8 tied with | 5 |

**Save Pct**

(minimum 20 Save Ops)

| | |
|---|---|
| Janssen,Casey, Tor | 94.4 |
| Holland,Greg, KC | 94.0 |
| Nathan,Joe, Tex | 93.5 |
| Balfour,Grant, Oak | 92.7 |
| Benoit,Joaquin, Det | 92.3 |
| Frieri,Ernesto, LAA | 90.2 |
| Perkins,Glen, Min | 90.0 |
| Uehara,Koji, Bos | 87.5 |
| Rivera,Mariano, NYY | 86.3 |
| Johnson,Jim, Bal | 84.7 |

**Save Opportunities**

| | |
|---|---|
| Johnson,Jim, Bal | 59 |
| Rivera,Mariano, NYY | 51 |
| Holland,Greg, KC | 50 |
| Reed,Addison, CWS | 48 |
| Nathan,Joe, Tex | 46 |
| Rodney,Fernando, TB | 45 |
| Balfour,Grant, Oak | 41 |
| Frieri,Ernesto, LAA | 41 |
| Perkins,Glen, Min | 40 |
| Janssen,Casey, Tor | 36 |

**Easy Saves**

| | |
|---|---|
| Johnson,Jim, Bal | 37 |
| Reed,Addison, CWS | 28 |
| Rivera,Mariano, NYY | 28 |
| Nathan,Joe, Tex | 27 |
| Rodney,Fernando, TB | 27 |
| Holland,Greg, KC | 26 |
| Janssen,Casey, Tor | 24 |
| Balfour,Grant, Oak | 20 |
| Frieri,Ernesto, LAA | 19 |
| Perkins,Glen, Min | 19 |

**Regular Saves**

| | |
|---|---|
| Holland,Greg, KC | 21 |
| Balfour,Grant, Oak | 18 |
| Nathan,Joe, Tex | 16 |
| Perkins,Glen, Min | 16 |
| Rivera,Mariano, NYY | 14 |
| Frieri,Ernesto, LAA | 13 |
| Johnson,Jim, Bal | 13 |
| Reed,Addison, CWS | 12 |
| Veras,Jose, Hou-Det | 12 |
| 2 tied with | 10 |

**Tough Saves**

| | |
|---|---|
| Frieri,Ernesto, LAA | 5 |
| Benoit,Joaquin, Det | 2 |
| Doolittle,Sean, Oak | 2 |
| Fields,Josh, Hou | 2 |
| Rivera,Mariano, NYY | 2 |
| 15 tied with | 1 |

**Holds Adjusted Saves %**

(minimum 20 Save Ops + Holds)

| | |
|---|---|
| Crain,Jesse, CWS | 95.0 |
| Thornton,Matt, CWS-Bos | 95.0 |
| Robertson,David, NYY | 94.7 |
| Janssen,Casey, Tor | 94.6 |
| Benoit,Joaquin, Det | 94.3 |
| Holland,Greg, KC | 94.1 |
| Nathan,Joe, Tex | 93.5 |
| Peralta,Joel, TB | 93.3 |
| Scheppers,Tanner, Tex | 93.3 |
| Balfour,Grant, Oak | 92.7 |

**Relief Wins**

| | |
|---|---|
| Cotts,Neal, Tex | 8 |
| Crow,Aaron, KC | 7 |
| Shaw,Bryan, Cle | 7 |
| 10 tied with | 6 |

**Relief Losses**

| | |
|---|---|
| Burton,Jared, Min | 9 |
| Johnson,Jim, Bal | 8 |
| Peralta,Joel, TB | 8 |
| Herrera,Kelvin, KC | 7 |
| Collins,Tim, KC | 6 |
| Furbush,Charlie, Sea | 6 |
| Loup,Aaron, Tor | 6 |
| Medina,Yoervis, Sea | 6 |
| 9 tied with | 5 |

**Relief Games**

| | |
|---|---|
| Peralta,Joel, TB | 80 |
| Allen,Cody, Cle | 77 |
| Lindstrom,Matt, CWS | 76 |
| Scheppers,Tanner, Tex | 76 |
| de la Rosa,Dane, LAA | 75 |
| Johnson,Jim, Bal | 74 |
| Duensing,Brian, Min | 73 |
| Fien,Casey, Min | 73 |
| Uehara,Koji, Bos | 73 |
| 6 tied with | 71 |

**Holds**

| | |
|---|---|
| Peralta,Joel, TB | 41 |
| Robertson,David, NYY | 33 |
| Burton,Jared, Min | 27 |
| McGee,Jake, TB | 27 |
| Scheppers,Tanner, Tex | 27 |
| Doolittle,Sean, Oak | 26 |
| Smith,Joe, Cle | 25 |
| Tazawa,Junichi, Bos | 25 |
| Cook,Ryan, Oak | 23 |
| 3 tied with | 21 |

**Relief Innings**

| | |
|---|---|
| Swarzak,Anthony, Min | 96.0 |
| Hunter,Tommy, Bal | 86.1 |
| Jones,Nate, CWS | 78.0 |
| Pressly,Ryan, Min | 76.2 |
| Scheppers,Tanner, Tex | 76.2 |
| Smyly,Drew, Det | 76.0 |
| Shaw,Bryan, Cle | 75.0 |
| Uehara,Koji, Bos | 74.1 |
| de la Rosa,Dane, LAA | 72.1 |
| McFarland,T.J., Bal | 72.0 |

**Inherited Runners Scrd %**

(minimum 30 IR)

| | |
|---|---|
| Doolittle,Sean, Oak | 6.3 |
| Kelley,Shawn, NYY | 10.0 |
| Peralta,Joel, TB | 13.3 |
| Matusz,Brian, Bal | 13.5 |
| Fien,Casey, Min | 13.6 |
| Cotts,Neal, Tex | 16.7 |
| Hagadone,Nick, Cle | 17.6 |
| Claiborne,Preston, NYY | 18.8 |
| Blackley,Travis, Hou-Tex | 18.9 |
| Hill,Rich, Cle | 19.0 |

**Relief Opp On Base Pct**

(minimum 50 IP)

| | |
|---|---|
| Uehara,Koji, Bos | .163 |
| Hochevar,Luke, KC | .227 |
| Holland,Greg, KC | .228 |
| Nathan,Joe, Tex | .239 |
| Cotts,Neal, Tex | .244 |
| Torres,Alex, TB | .244 |
| Perkins,Glen, Min | .256 |
| Janssen,Casey, Tor | .257 |
| Doolittle,Sean, Oak | .259 |
| Hunter,Tommy, Bal | .260 |

**Relief Opp Slugging Avg**

(minimum 50 IP)

| | |
|---|---|
| Torres,Alex, TB | .224 |
| Nathan,Joe, Tex | .225 |
| Uehara,Koji, Bos | .237 |
| Holland,Greg, KC | .251 |
| Cotts,Neal, Tex | .255 |
| de la Rosa,Dane, LAA | .277 |
| Wilhelmsen,Tom, Sea | .284 |
| Shaw,Bryan, Cle | .291 |
| Farquhar,Danny, Sea | .296 |
| Janssen,Casey, Tor | .301 |

# American League Pitching Leaders

### Relief Opp BA Vs LHB
(minimum 50 AB)

| | |
|---|---|
| Uehara,Koji, Bos | .115 |
| Thielbar,Caleb, Min | .143 |
| Frasor,Jason, Tex | .152 |
| Frieri,Ernesto, LAA | .155 |
| Peralta,Joel, TB | .163 |
| Kohn,Michael, LAA | .163 |
| Matusz,Brian, Bal | .168 |
| Nathan,Joe, Tex | .171 |
| Farquhar,Danny, Sea | .171 |
| Holland,Greg, KC | .172 |

### Relief Opp BA Vs RHB
(minimum 50 AB)

| | |
|---|---|
| Janssen,Casey, Tor | .135 |
| Hochevar,Luke, KC | .138 |
| Santos,Sergio, Tor | .140 |
| Hunter,Tommy, Bal | .141 |
| Wilhelmsen,Tom, Sea | .145 |
| Uehara,Koji, Bos | .146 |
| Torres,Alex, TB | .149 |
| Nathan,Joe, Tex | .152 |
| O'Day,Darren, Bal | .154 |
| Miller,Andrew, Bos | .155 |

### Relief Opp Batting Average
(minimum 50 IP)

| | |
|---|---|
| Uehara,Koji, Bos | .130 |
| Torres,Alex, TB | .159 |
| Nathan,Joe, Tex | .162 |
| Hochevar,Luke, KC | .169 |
| Holland,Greg, KC | .170 |
| Cotts,Neal, Tex | .180 |
| Peralta,Joel, TB | .184 |
| Perkins,Glen, Min | .196 |
| Benoit,Joaquin, Det | .197 |
| Veras,Jose, Hou-Det | .199 |

### Relief Earned Run Average
(minimum 50 IP)

| | |
|---|---|
| Uehara,Koji, Bos | 1.09 |
| Cotts,Neal, Tex | 1.11 |
| Holland,Greg, KC | 1.21 |
| Nathan,Joe, Tex | 1.39 |
| Torres,Alex, TB | 1.71 |
| Breslow,Craig, Bos | 1.81 |
| Scheppers,Tanner, Tex | 1.88 |
| Hochevar,Luke, KC | 1.92 |
| Benoit,Joaquin, Det | 2.02 |
| Robertson,David, NYY | 2.04 |

### Rel OBP 1st Batter Faced
(minimum 40 BF)

| | |
|---|---|
| Janssen,Casey, Tor | .179 |
| Hochevar,Luke, KC | .190 |
| Uehara,Koji, Bos | .192 |
| Jones,Nate, CWS | .200 |
| Rivera,Mariano, NYY | .203 |
| Fien,Casey, Min | .208 |
| Veras,Jose, Hou-Det | .209 |
| Burton,Jared, Min | .211 |
| Doolittle,Sean, Oak | .214 |
| Matusz,Brian, Bal | .215 |

### Rel Opp BA w/ Runners On
(minimum 50 IP)

| | |
|---|---|
| Hochevar,Luke, KC | .119 |
| Uehara,Koji, Bos | .130 |
| Benoit,Joaquin, Det | .142 |
| Cotts,Neal, Tex | .145 |
| Torres,Alex, TB | .146 |
| Frieri,Ernesto, LAA | .164 |
| Medina,Yoervis, Sea | .165 |
| Smyly,Drew, Det | .171 |
| Holland,Greg, KC | .174 |
| Balfour,Grant, Oak | .181 |

### Relief Opp BA w/ RISP
(minimum 50 IP)

| | |
|---|---|
| Cotts,Neal, Tex | .077 |
| Holland,Greg, KC | .111 |
| Benoit,Joaquin, Det | .114 |
| Smyly,Drew, Det | .136 |
| Tazawa,Junichi, Bos | .143 |
| Uehara,Koji, Bos | .146 |
| Wright,Wesley, Hou-TB | .148 |
| Medina,Yoervis, Sea | .151 |
| Torres,Alex, TB | .156 |
| Frieri,Ernesto, LAA | .159 |

### Fastest Avg Fastball-Relief
(minimum 50 IP)

| | |
|---|---|
| Herrera,Kelvin, KC | 98.2 |
| Jones,Nate, CWS | 97.7 |
| Rodney,Fernando, TB | 96.5 |
| Scheppers,Tanner, Tex | 96.3 |
| McGee,Jake, TB | 96.3 |
| Hunter,Tommy, Bal | 96.2 |
| Wilhelmsen,Tom, Sea | 96.2 |
| Holland,Greg, KC | 96.1 |
| Capps,Carter, Sea | 95.6 |
| Hochevar,Luke, KC | 95.5 |

### Fastest Average Fastball
(minimum 162 IP)

| | |
|---|---|
| Holland,Derek, Tex | 93.6 |
| Price,David, TB | 93.5 |
| Scherzer,Max, Det | 93.3 |
| Verlander,Justin, Det | 93.3 |
| Sale,Chris, CWS | 93.1 |
| Sanchez,Anibal, Det | 93.0 |
| Darvish,Yu, Tex | 92.9 |
| Lester,Jon, Bos | 92.7 |
| Norris,Bud, Hou-Bal | 92.5 |
| Santana,Ervin, KC | 92.4 |

### Slowest Average Fastball
(minimum 162 IP)

| | |
|---|---|
| Dickey,R.A., Tor | 81.9 |
| Buehrle,Mark, Tor | 84.2 |
| Fister,Doug, Det | 88.8 |
| Griffin,A.J., Oak | 88.9 |
| Pettitte,Andy, NYY | 89.0 |
| Dempster,Ryan, Bos | 89.2 |
| Iwakuma,Hisashi, Sea | 89.5 |
| Saunders,Joe, Sea | 89.6 |
| Colon,Bartolo, Oak | 89.9 |
| Doubront,Felix, Bos | 90.5 |

### Pitches 100+ Velocity

| | |
|---|---|
| Rondon,Bruce, Det | 144 |
| Herrera,Kelvin, KC | 110 |
| Jones,Nate, CWS | 35 |
| Rodney,Fernando, TB | 21 |
| Ventura,Yordano, KC | 7 |
| Holland,Greg, KC | 5 |
| Salazar,Danny, Cle | 5 |
| Wood,Blake, Cle | 3 |
| Hunter,Tommy, Bal | 2 |
| Verlander,Justin, Det | 2 |

### Pitches 95+ Velocity

| | |
|---|---|
| Richards,Garrett, LAA | 991 |
| McGee,Jake, TB | 974 |
| Scheppers,Tanner, Tex | 812 |
| Archer,Chris, TB | 800 |
| Gutierrez,J.C., KC-LAA | 744 |
| Allen,Cody, Cle | 725 |
| Hunter,Tommy, Bal | 708 |
| Herrera,Kelvin, KC | 678 |
| Rodney,Fernando, TB | 670 |
| Jones,Nate, CWS | 654 |

### Pitches Less Than 80 MPH

| | |
|---|---|
| Dickey,R.A., Tor | 2835 |
| Buehrle,Mark, Tor | 953 |
| Bedard,Erik, Hou | 844 |
| Fister,Doug, Det | 843 |
| Hellickson,Jeremy, TB | 789 |
| Feldman,Scott, Bal | 777 |
| Weaver,Jered, LAA | 749 |
| Sale,Chris, CWS | 690 |
| Griffin,A.J., Oak | 644 |
| Veras,Jose, Hou-Det | 640 |

### Lowest % Fastballs
(minimum 162 IP)

| | |
|---|---|
| Dickey,R.A., Tor | 11.9 |
| Darvish,Yu, Tex | 38.2 |
| Correia,Kevin, Min | 38.5 |
| Shields,James, KC | 40.7 |
| Buehrle,Mark, Tor | 45.5 |
| Sanchez,Anibal, Det | 47.3 |
| Dempster,Ryan, Bos | 49.0 |
| Kuroda,Hiroki, NYY | 49.4 |
| Pettitte,Andy, NYY | 49.8 |
| Wilson,C.J., LAA | 50.4 |

### Highest % Fastballs
(minimum 162 IP)

| | |
|---|---|
| Colon,Bartolo, Oak | 85.5 |
| Masterson,Justin, Cle | 73.3 |
| Parker,Jarrod, Oak | 63.8 |
| Doubront,Felix, Bos | 63.3 |
| Holland,Derek, Tex | 62.5 |
| Gonzalez,Miguel, Bal | 62.3 |
| Tillman,Chris, Bal | 62.2 |
| Porcello,Rick, Det | 61.7 |
| Guthrie,Jeremy, KC | 59.3 |
| Griffin,A.J., Oak | 58.6 |

### Highest % Curveballs
(minimum 162 IP)

| | |
|---|---|
| Fister,Doug, Det | 20.2 |
| Quintana,Jose, CWS | 19.6 |
| Tillman,Chris, Bal | 17.1 |
| Porcello,Rick, Det | 16.5 |
| Griffin,A.J., Oak | 15.9 |
| Hellickson,Jeremy, TB | 15.0 |
| Wilson,C.J., LAA | 14.8 |
| Doubront,Felix, Bos | 14.2 |
| Verlander,Justin, Det | 13.9 |
| Correia,Kevin, Min | 13.5 |

# American League Pitching Leaders

**Highest % Changeups**
(minimum 162 IP)

| | |
|---|---|
| Hellickson,Jeremy, TB | 30.6 |
| Shields,James, KC | 24.9 |
| Sanchez,Anibal, Det | 24.1 |
| Hernandez,Felix, Sea | 23.0 |
| Parker,Jarrod, Oak | 21.5 |
| Scherzer,Max, Det | 20.9 |
| Saunders,Joe, Sea | 20.3 |
| Buehrle,Mark, Tor | 19.9 |
| Sale,Chris, CWS | 19.0 |
| Verlander,Justin, Det | 16.9 |

**Highest % Sliders**
(minimum 162 IP)

| | |
|---|---|
| Santana,Ervin, KC | 38.5 |
| Darvish,Yu, Tex | 31.6 |
| Lackey,John, Bos | 30.0 |
| Sale,Chris, CWS | 29.6 |
| Norris,Bud, Hou-Bal | 28.6 |
| Dempster,Ryan, Bos | 27.6 |
| Masterson,Justin, Cle | 26.6 |
| Kuroda,Hiroki, NYY | 26.4 |
| Jimenez,Ubaldo, Cle | 25.0 |
| Holland,Derek, Tex | 24.4 |

**Balks**

| | |
|---|---|
| Aceves,Alfredo, Bos | 2 |
| Cisnero,Jose, Hou | 2 |
| Deduno,Samuel, Min | 2 |
| Hellickson,Jeremy, TB | 2 |
| Lyles,Jordan, Hou | 2 |
| Peavy,Jake, CWS-Bos | 2 |
| Perez,Martin, Tex | 2 |
| Rogers,Esmil, Tor | 2 |
| Shields,James, KC | 2 |
| Wilson,C.J., LAA | 2 |

**Strikeout/Hit Ratio**
(minimum 50 IP)

| | |
|---|---|
| Uehara,Koji, Bos | 3.06 |
| Holland,Greg, KC | 2.58 |
| Nathan,Joe, Tex | 2.03 |
| Hochevar,Luke, KC | 2.00 |
| Torres,Alex, TB | 1.94 |
| Darvish,Yu, Tex | 1.91 |
| Cotts,Neal, Tex | 1.81 |
| Farquhar,Danny, Sea | 1.80 |
| Perkins,Glen, Min | 1.79 |
| Frieri,Ernesto, LAA | 1.78 |

**Opp OPS vs Fastballs**
(minimum 251 BF)

| | |
|---|---|
| Scheppers,Tanner, Tex | .581 |
| Scherzer,Max, Det | .596 |
| Archer,Chris, TB | .614 |
| Frieri,Ernesto, LAA | .615 |
| Santiago,Hector, CWS | .631 |
| Quintana,Jose, CWS | .649 |
| Iwakuma,Hisashi, Sea | .650 |
| Weaver,Jered, LAA | .651 |
| Price,David, TB | .652 |
| Wilson,C.J., LAA | .652 |

**Opp OPS vs Curveballs**
(minimum 100 BF)

| | |
|---|---|
| Griffin,A.J., Oak | .523 |
| Wilson,C.J., LAA | .530 |
| Weaver,Jered, LAA | .571 |
| Tillman,Chris, Bal | .636 |
| Nova,Ivan, NYY | .638 |
| Cobb,Alex, TB | .665 |
| Moore,Matt, TB | .688 |
| Bedard,Erik, Hou | .696 |
| Deduno,Samuel, Min | .723 |
| Fister,Doug, Det | .724 |

**Opp OPS vs Changeups**
(minimum 100 BF)

| | |
|---|---|
| Hernandez,Felix, Sea | .472 |
| Moore,Matt, TB | .520 |
| Price,David, TB | .544 |
| Vargas,Jason, LAA | .555 |
| Sanchez,Anibal, Det | .573 |
| Griffin,A.J., Oak | .593 |
| Sale,Chris, CWS | .607 |
| Rodney,Fernando, TB | .621 |
| Cobb,Alex, TB | .624 |
| Lester,Jon, Bos | .635 |

**Opp OPS vs Sliders**
(minimum 64 BF)

| | |
|---|---|
| Cook,Ryan, Oak | .276 |
| Scherzer,Max, Det | .394 |
| Medina,Yoervis, Sea | .410 |
| Holland,Greg, KC | .432 |
| Masterson,Justin, Cle | .501 |
| Perez,Chris, Cle | .501 |
| Darvish,Yu, Tex | .511 |
| Perez,Oliver, Sea | .527 |
| Alburquerque,Al, Det | .531 |
| Nathan,Joe, Tex | .532 |

**Earned Runs**

| | |
|---|---|
| Sabathia,CC, NYY | 112 |
| Saunders,Joe, Sea | 107 |
| Dickey,R.A., Tor | 105 |
| Harrell,Lucas, Hou | 100 |
| Hellickson,Jeremy, TB | 100 |
| Guthrie,Jeremy, KC | 95 |
| Buehrle,Mark, Tor | 94 |
| Blanton,Joe, LAA | 89 |
| Lester,Jon, Bos | 89 |
| 3 tied with | 88 |

**Hits Per Nine Innings**
(minimum 162 IP)

| | |
|---|---|
| Darvish,Yu, Tex | 6.22 |
| Scherzer,Max, Det | 6.38 |
| Masterson,Justin, Cle | 7.27 |
| Iwakuma,Hisashi, Sea | 7.33 |
| Griffin,A.J., Oak | 7.70 |
| Sanchez,Anibal, Det | 7.71 |
| Sale,Chris, CWS | 7.73 |
| Jimenez,Ubaldo, Cle | 8.03 |
| Tillman,Chris, Bal | 8.03 |
| Santana,Ervin, KC | 8.10 |

# National League Pitching Leaders

**Earned Run Average** (minimum 162 IP)

| | |
|---|---|
| Kershaw,Clayton, LAD | 1.83 |
| Fernandez,Jose, Mia | 2.19 |
| Harvey,Matt, NYM | 2.27 |
| Greinke,Zack, LAD | 2.63 |
| Bumgarner,Madison, SF | 2.77 |
| Lee,Cliff, Phi | 2.87 |
| Wainwright,Adam, StL | 2.94 |
| Ryu,Hyun-Jin, LAD | 3.00 |
| Strasburg,Stephen, Was | 3.00 |
| Miller,Shelby, StL | 3.06 |

**Winning Percentage** (minimum 15 Decisions)

| | |
|---|---|
| Greinke,Zack, LAD | .789 |
| de la Rosa,Jorge, Col | .727 |
| Wainwright,Adam, StL | .679 |
| Zimmermann,Jordan, Was | .679 |
| Fernandez,Jose, Mia | .667 |
| Kelly,Joe, StL | .667 |
| Latos,Mat, Cin | .667 |
| Leake,Mike, Cin | .667 |
| Liriano,Francisco, Pit | .667 |
| Kershaw,Clayton, LAD | .640 |

**Opponent Batting Average** (minimum 162 IP)

| | |
|---|---|
| Fernandez,Jose, Mia | .182 |
| Kershaw,Clayton, LAD | .195 |
| Bumgarner,Madison, SF | .203 |
| Strasburg,Stephen, Was | .207 |
| Harvey,Matt, NYM | .209 |
| Wood,Travis, ChC | .222 |
| Cain,Matt, SF | .228 |
| Gonzalez,Gio, Was | .231 |
| Burnett,A.J., Pit | .231 |
| Lee,Cliff, Phi | .232 |

**Baserunners Per 9 IP** (minimum 162 IP)

| | |
|---|---|
| Kershaw,Clayton, LAD | 8.35 |
| Harvey,Matt, NYM | 8.58 |
| Fernandez,Jose, Mia | 9.07 |
| Lee,Cliff, Phi | 9.26 |
| Bumgarner,Madison, SF | 9.57 |
| Wainwright,Adam, StL | 9.83 |
| Minor,Mike, Atl | 9.85 |
| Strasburg,Stephen, Was | 10.03 |
| Zimmermann,Jordan, Was | 10.08 |
| Greinke,Zack, LAD | 10.39 |

**Games**

| | |
|---|---|
| Ziegler,Brad, Ari | 78 |
| Belisario,Ronald, LAD | 77 |
| Rodriguez,Paco, LAD | 76 |
| Avilan,Luis, Atl | 75 |
| Axford,John, Mil-StL | 75 |
| Dunn,Mike, Mia | 75 |
| Gonzalez,Michael, Mil | 75 |
| Jansen,Kenley, LAD | 75 |
| Lopez,Wilton, Col | 75 |
| 2 tied with | 74 |

**Games Started**

| | |
|---|---|
| Wainwright,Adam, StL | 34 |
| Hamels,Cole, Phi | 33 |
| Kershaw,Clayton, LAD | 33 |
| Lynn,Lance, StL | 33 |
| Miley,Wade, Ari | 33 |
| Nolasco,Ricky, Mia-LAD | 33 |
| Samardzija,Jeff, ChC | 33 |
| Stults,Eric, SD | 33 |
| 13 tied with | 32 |

**Complete Games**

| | |
|---|---|
| Wainwright,Adam, StL | 5 |
| Zimmermann,Jordan, Was | 4 |
| Corbin,Patrick, Ari | 3 |
| Kershaw,Clayton, LAD | 3 |
| 12 tied with | 2 |

**Shutouts**

| | |
|---|---|
| Kershaw,Clayton, LAD | 2 |
| Wainwright,Adam, StL | 2 |
| Zimmermann,Jordan, Was | 2 |
| 21 tied with | 1 |

**Wins**

| | |
|---|---|
| Wainwright,Adam, StL | 19 |
| Zimmermann,Jordan, Was | 19 |
| de la Rosa,Jorge, Col | 16 |
| Kershaw,Clayton, LAD | 16 |
| Liriano,Francisco, Pit | 16 |
| Greinke,Zack, LAD | 15 |
| Lynn,Lance, StL | 15 |
| Medlen,Kris, Atl | 15 |
| Miller,Shelby, StL | 15 |
| 8 tied with | 14 |

**Losses**

| | |
|---|---|
| Jackson,Edwin, ChC | 18 |
| Peralta,Wily, Mil | 15 |
| Hamels,Cole, Phi | 14 |
| Haren,Dan, Was | 14 |
| Lincecum,Tim, SF | 14 |
| Kendrick,Kyle, Phi | 13 |
| Samardzija,Jeff, ChC | 13 |
| Stults,Eric, SD | 13 |
| 5 tied with | 12 |

**No Decisions**

| | |
|---|---|
| Kennedy,Ian, Ari-SD | 14 |
| Gonzalez,Gio, Was | 13 |
| Locke,Jeff, Pit | 13 |
| Miley,Wade, Ari | 13 |
| Nicasio,Juan, Col | 13 |
| Strasburg,Stephen, Was | 13 |
| Cain,Matt, SF | 12 |
| Harvey,Matt, NYM | 12 |
| Samardzija,Jeff, ChC | 12 |
| 6 tied with | 11 |

**Wild Pitches**

| | |
|---|---|
| Cahill,Trevor, Ari | 17 |
| Volquez,Edinson, SD-LAD | 16 |
| Jackson,Edwin, ChC | 14 |
| Corbin,Patrick, Ari | 13 |
| Miley,Wade, Ari | 13 |
| Burnett,A.J., Pit | 12 |
| Kershaw,Clayton, LAD | 12 |
| Peralta,Wily, Mil | 12 |
| 3 tied with | 11 |

**Strikeouts**

| | |
|---|---|
| Kershaw,Clayton, LAD | 232 |
| Lee,Cliff, Phi | 222 |
| Wainwright,Adam, StL | 219 |
| Samardzija,Jeff, ChC | 214 |
| Burnett,A.J., Pit | 209 |
| Hamels,Cole, Phi | 202 |
| Bailey,Homer, Cin | 199 |
| Bumgarner,Madison, SF | 199 |
| Lynn,Lance, StL | 198 |
| Lincecum,Tim, SF | 193 |

**Walks Allowed**

| | |
|---|---|
| Locke,Jeff, Pit | 84 |
| Samardzija,Jeff, ChC | 78 |
| Volquez,Edinson, SD-LAD | 77 |
| Gonzalez,Gio, Was | 76 |
| Lincecum,Tim, SF | 76 |
| Lynn,Lance, StL | 76 |
| Kennedy,Ian, Ari-SD | 73 |
| Peralta,Wily, Mil | 73 |
| Marquis,Jason, SD | 68 |
| Burnett,A.J., Pit | 67 |

**Intentional Walks Allowed**

| | |
|---|---|
| Belisario,Ronald, LAD | 10 |
| Collmenter,Josh, Ari | 8 |
| Lincecum,Tim, SF | 8 |
| Jackson,Edwin, ChC | 7 |
| Maness,Seth, StL | 7 |
| Nicasio,Juan, Col | 7 |
| Qualls,Chad, Mia | 7 |
| 7 tied with | 6 |

**Hit Batters**

| | |
|---|---|
| Morton,Charlie, Pit | 16 |
| Teheran,Julio, Atl | 13 |
| Kennedy,Ian, Ari-SD | 12 |
| Strasburg,Stephen, Was | 12 |
| Lynn,Lance, StL | 11 |
| 6 tied with | 10 |

# National League Pitching Leaders

### Runs Allowed

| | |
|---|---|
| Volquez,Edinson, SD-LAD | 114 |
| Jackson,Edwin, ChC | 110 |
| Samardzija,Jeff, ChC | 109 |
| Kennedy,Ian, Ari-SD | 108 |
| Peralta,Wily, Mil | 107 |
| Kendrick,Kyle, Phi | 104 |
| Lincecum,Tim, SF | 102 |
| Nicasio,Juan, Col | 97 |
| Stults,Eric, SD | 97 |
| 2 tied with | 94 |

### Hits Allowed

| | |
|---|---|
| Wainwright,Adam, StL | 223 |
| Stults,Eric, SD | 219 |
| Samardzija,Jeff, ChC | 210 |
| Gee,Dillon, NYM | 208 |
| Kendrick,Kyle, Phi | 207 |
| Hamels,Cole, Phi | 205 |
| Miley,Wade, Ari | 201 |
| Arroyo,Bronson, Cin | 199 |
| Jackson,Edwin, ChC | 197 |
| Latos,Mat, Cin | 197 |

### Doubles Allowed

| | |
|---|---|
| Hamels,Cole, Phi | 62 |
| Nicasio,Juan, Col | 50 |
| Stults,Eric, SD | 49 |
| Zimmermann,Jordan, Was | 49 |
| Wainwright,Adam, StL | 48 |
| Jackson,Edwin, ChC | 47 |
| Chacin,Jhoulys, Col | 45 |
| 5 tied with | 44 |

### Home Runs Allowed

| | |
|---|---|
| Arroyo,Bronson, Cin | 32 |
| Haren,Dan, Was | 28 |
| Kennedy,Ian, Ari-SD | 27 |
| Lohse,Kyle, Mil | 26 |
| Samardzija,Jeff, ChC | 25 |
| Delgado,Randall, Ari | 24 |
| Gee,Dillon, NYM | 24 |
| Cain,Matt, SF | 23 |
| 3 tied with | 22 |

### Run Support Per Nine IP

(minimum 162 IP)

| | |
|---|---|
| de la Rosa,Jorge, Col | 5.85 |
| Miller,Shelby, StL | 5.82 |
| Lynn,Lance, StL | 5.67 |
| Chacin,Jhoulys, Col | 5.47 |
| Minor,Mike, Atl | 5.32 |
| Zimmermann,Jordan, Was | 5.15 |
| Wainwright,Adam, StL | 5.10 |
| Arroyo,Bronson, Cin | 5.08 |
| Gonzalez,Gio, Was | 5.01 |
| Gallardo,Yovani, Mil | 4.93 |

### % Pitches In Strike Zone

(minimum 162 IP)

| | |
|---|---|
| Lee,Cliff, Phi | 51.6 |
| Arroyo,Bronson, Cin | 48.1 |
| Zimmermann,Jordan, Was | 47.1 |
| Cashner,Andrew, SD | 46.1 |
| Kershaw,Clayton, LAD | 45.9 |
| Fernandez,Jose, Mia | 45.8 |
| Miller,Shelby, StL | 45.7 |
| Chacin,Jhoulys, Col | 45.5 |
| Teheran,Julio, Atl | 45.2 |
| Harvey,Matt, NYM | 45.2 |

### Pitches Per Start

(minimum 30 GS)

| | |
|---|---|
| Lee,Cliff, Phi | 104.9 |
| Samardzija,Jeff, ChC | 104.9 |
| Wainwright,Adam, StL | 103.9 |
| Kershaw,Clayton, LAD | 103.9 |
| Hamels,Cole, Phi | 103.7 |
| Gonzalez,Gio, Was | 103.6 |
| Bumgarner,Madison, SF | 103.4 |
| Bailey,Homer, Cin | 102.9 |
| Lincecum,Tim, SF | 102.5 |
| Ryu,Hyun-Jin, LAD | 102.3 |

### Pitches Per Batter

(minimum 162 IP)

| | |
|---|---|
| Arroyo,Bronson, Cin | 3.49 |
| Gee,Dillon, NYM | 3.55 |
| Zimmermann,Jordan, Was | 3.56 |
| Corbin,Patrick, Ari | 3.58 |
| Kendrick,Kyle, Phi | 3.59 |
| Chacin,Jhoulys, Col | 3.63 |
| Leake,Mike, Cin | 3.63 |
| Latos,Mat, Cin | 3.68 |
| Wainwright,Adam, StL | 3.70 |
| Lee,Cliff, Phi | 3.71 |

### Quality Starts

| | |
|---|---|
| Kershaw,Clayton, LAD | 27 |
| Wainwright,Adam, StL | 26 |
| Hamels,Cole, Phi | 25 |
| Lee,Cliff, Phi | 24 |
| Wood,Travis, ChC | 24 |
| Corbin,Patrick, Ari | 23 |
| Minor,Mike, Atl | 23 |
| 5 tied with | 22 |

### Batters Faced

| | |
|---|---|
| Wainwright,Adam, StL | 956 |
| Samardzija,Jeff, ChC | 914 |
| Kershaw,Clayton, LAD | 908 |
| Hamels,Cole, Phi | 905 |
| Latos,Mat, Cin | 881 |
| Lee,Cliff, Phi | 876 |
| Zimmermann,Jordan, Was | 865 |
| Corbin,Patrick, Ari | 860 |
| Stults,Eric, SD | 857 |
| Lynn,Lance, StL | 856 |

### Innings Pitched

| | |
|---|---|
| Wainwright,Adam, StL | 241.2 |
| Kershaw,Clayton, LAD | 236.0 |
| Lee,Cliff, Phi | 222.2 |
| Hamels,Cole, Phi | 220.0 |
| Samardzija,Jeff, ChC | 213.2 |
| Zimmermann,Jordan, Was | 213.1 |
| Latos,Mat, Cin | 210.2 |
| Bailey,Homer, Cin | 209.0 |
| Corbin,Patrick, Ari | 208.1 |
| Minor,Mike, Atl | 204.2 |

### Most Pitches in a Game

| | |
|---|---|
| Lincecum,Tim, SF | 148 |
| Kershaw,Clayton, LAD | 132 |
| Wainwright,Adam, StL | 128 |
| Gonzalez,Gio, Was | 127 |
| Bailey,Homer, Cin | 125 |
| Jackson,Edwin, ChC | 124 |
| Lynn,Lance, StL | 124 |
| Stults,Eric, SD | 124 |
| Westbrook,Jake, StL | 124 |
| 2 tied with | 123 |

### Stolen Bases Allowed

| | |
|---|---|
| Hamels,Cole, Phi | 25 |
| Volquez,Edinson, SD-LAD | 24 |
| Burnett,A.J., Pit | 22 |
| Lincecum,Tim, SF | 21 |
| Jackson,Edwin, ChC | 18 |
| Turner,Jacob, Mia | 18 |
| Cain,Matt, SF | 17 |
| Cahill,Trevor, Ari | 16 |
| Cashner,Andrew, SD | 16 |
| Feldman,Scott, ChC | 16 |

### Caught Stealing Off

| | |
|---|---|
| de la Rosa,Jorge, Col | 10 |
| Hamels,Cole, Phi | 10 |
| Zito,Barry, SF | 9 |
| Minor,Mike, Atl | 8 |
| Bumgarner,Madison, SF | 7 |
| Locke,Jeff, Pit | 7 |
| Lynn,Lance, StL | 7 |
| Ross,Tyson, SD | 7 |
| Samardzija,Jeff, ChC | 7 |
| 6 tied with | 6 |

### Stolen Base Pct Allowed

(minimum 162 IP)

| | |
|---|---|
| Corbin,Patrick, Ari | 25.0 |
| Kennedy,Ian, Ari-SD | 33.3 |
| Minor,Mike, Atl | 33.3 |
| Ryu,Hyun-Jin, LAD | 33.3 |
| Arroyo,Bronson, Cin | 42.9 |
| Greinke,Zack, LAD | 42.9 |
| Harvey,Matt, NYM | 50.0 |
| Lynn,Lance, StL | 50.0 |
| Miley,Wade, Ari | 50.0 |
| Wainwright,Adam, StL | 50.0 |

### Pickoffs

| | |
|---|---|
| Teheran,Julio, Atl | 8 |
| Kershaw,Clayton, LAD | 7 |
| Bumgarner,Madison, SF | 6 |
| Cingrani,Tony, Cin | 6 |
| Locke,Jeff, Pit | 6 |
| de la Rosa,Jorge, Col | 5 |
| Hamels,Cole, Phi | 5 |
| Miley,Wade, Ari | 5 |
| 4 tied with | 4 |

# National League Pitching Leaders

**Strikeouts Per 9 IP**
(minimum 162 IP)

| | |
|---|---|
| Burnett,A.J., Pit | 9.85 |
| Fernandez,Jose, Mia | 9.75 |
| Harvey,Matt, NYM | 9.64 |
| Strasburg,Stephen, Was | 9.39 |
| Samardzija,Jeff, ChC | 9.01 |
| Lee,Cliff, Phi | 8.97 |
| Bumgarner,Madison, SF | 8.90 |
| Kershaw,Clayton, LAD | 8.85 |
| Lynn,Lance, StL | 8.84 |
| Gonzalez,Gio, Was | 8.83 |

**Opp On-Base Percentage**
(minimum 162 IP)

| | |
|---|---|
| Kershaw,Clayton, LAD | .244 |
| Harvey,Matt, NYM | .248 |
| Fernandez,Jose, Mia | .257 |
| Lee,Cliff, Phi | .263 |
| Bumgarner,Madison, SF | .270 |
| Minor,Mike, Atl | .275 |
| Zimmermann,Jordan, Was | .279 |
| Wainwright,Adam, StL | .280 |
| Strasburg,Stephen, Was | .281 |
| Cashner,Andrew, SD | .288 |

**Opp Slugging Average**
(minimum 162 IP)

| | |
|---|---|
| Fernandez,Jose, Mia | .265 |
| Kershaw,Clayton, LAD | .277 |
| Harvey,Matt, NYM | .282 |
| Bumgarner,Madison, SF | .307 |
| Strasburg,Stephen, Was | .307 |
| Burnett,A.J., Pit | .335 |
| Locke,Jeff, Pit | .350 |
| Cashner,Andrew, SD | .351 |
| Wood,Travis, ChC | .351 |
| Greinke,Zack, LAD | .355 |

**Opponent OPS**
(minimum 162 IP)

| | |
|---|---|
| Kershaw,Clayton, LAD | .521 |
| Fernandez,Jose, Mia | .522 |
| Harvey,Matt, NYM | .530 |
| Bumgarner,Madison, SF | .577 |
| Strasburg,Stephen, Was | .588 |
| Lee,Cliff, Phi | .631 |
| Wainwright,Adam, StL | .636 |
| Burnett,A.J., Pit | .639 |
| Cashner,Andrew, SD | .639 |
| Wood,Travis, ChC | .643 |

**Home Runs Per Nine IP**
(minimum 162 IP)

| | |
|---|---|
| Harvey,Matt, NYM | 0.35 |
| Kershaw,Clayton, LAD | 0.42 |
| Chacin,Jhoulys, Col | 0.50 |
| Burnett,A.J., Pit | 0.52 |
| Fernandez,Jose, Mia | 0.52 |
| Wainwright,Adam, StL | 0.56 |
| de la Rosa,Jorge, Col | 0.59 |
| Locke,Jeff, Pit | 0.60 |
| Latos,Mat, Cin | 0.60 |
| Cashner,Andrew, SD | 0.62 |

**Batting Average vs. LHB**
(minimum 125 BF)

| | |
|---|---|
| Liriano,Francisco, Pit | .131 |
| Melancon,Mark, Pit | .148 |
| Clippard,Tyler, Was | .152 |
| Bumgarner,Madison, SF | .161 |
| Kershaw,Clayton, LAD | .165 |
| Rice,Scott, NYM | .174 |
| Harvey,Matt, NYM | .178 |
| Stults,Eric, SD | .185 |
| Fernandez,Jose, Mia | .188 |
| Stauffer,Tim, SD | .190 |

**Batting Average vs. RHB**
(minimum 225 BF)

| | |
|---|---|
| Fernandez,Jose, Mia | .175 |
| Strasburg,Stephen, Was | .197 |
| Ross,Tyson, SD | .198 |
| Cingrani,Tony, Cin | .200 |
| Kershaw,Clayton, LAD | .202 |
| Burnett,A.J., Pit | .203 |
| Teheran,Julio, Atl | .204 |
| Bailey,Homer, Cin | .205 |
| Miller,Shelby, StL | .205 |
| Zimmermann,Jordan, Was | .212 |

**Opp BA w/ RISP**
(minimum 125 BF)

| | |
|---|---|
| Kelly,Joe, StL | .161 |
| Kershaw,Clayton, LAD | .180 |
| Greinke,Zack, LAD | .202 |
| Locke,Jeff, Pit | .203 |
| Bumgarner,Madison, SF | .205 |
| Turner,Jacob, Mia | .206 |
| Latos,Mat, Cin | .207 |
| Cashner,Andrew, SD | .212 |
| Cahill,Trevor, Ari | .214 |
| Teheran,Julio, Atl | .217 |

**OBP vs. Leadoff Hitter**
(minimum 150 BF)

| | |
|---|---|
| Harvey,Matt, NYM | .224 |
| Liriano,Francisco, Pit | .241 |
| Fernandez,Jose, Mia | .241 |
| Haren,Dan, Was | .249 |
| Kershaw,Clayton, LAD | .250 |
| Arroyo,Bronson, Cin | .251 |
| Lee,Cliff, Phi | .262 |
| Miley,Wade, Ari | .263 |
| Corbin,Patrick, Ari | .267 |
| Bailey,Homer, Cin | .269 |

**Strikeouts / Walks Ratio**
(minimum 162 IP)

| | |
|---|---|
| Lee,Cliff, Phi | 6.94 |
| Wainwright,Adam, StL | 6.26 |
| Harvey,Matt, NYM | 6.16 |
| Haren,Dan, Was | 4.87 |
| Kershaw,Clayton, LAD | 4.46 |
| Hamels,Cole, Phi | 4.04 |
| Zimmermann,Jordan, Was | 4.03 |
| Minor,Mike, Atl | 3.94 |
| Teheran,Julio, Atl | 3.78 |
| Bailey,Homer, Cin | 3.69 |

**Highest GB/FB Ratio**
(minimum 162 IP)

| | |
|---|---|
| Burnett,A.J., Pit | 2.33 |
| Locke,Jeff, Pit | 2.06 |
| Miley,Wade, Ari | 1.91 |
| Peralta,Wily, Mil | 1.84 |
| Cashner,Andrew, SD | 1.83 |
| Jackson,Edwin, ChC | 1.81 |
| Wainwright,Adam, StL | 1.78 |
| Gallardo,Yovani, Mil | 1.78 |
| de la Rosa,Jorge, Col | 1.71 |
| Strasburg,Stephen, Was | 1.66 |

**Lowest GB/FB Ratio**
(minimum 162 IP)

| | |
|---|---|
| Wood,Travis, ChC | 0.75 |
| Minor,Mike, Atl | 0.82 |
| Haren,Dan, Was | 0.86 |
| Teheran,Julio, Atl | 0.92 |
| Miller,Shelby, StL | 0.93 |
| Cain,Matt, SF | 0.94 |
| Kennedy,Ian, Ari-SD | 0.99 |
| Stults,Eric, SD | 1.03 |
| Lohse,Kyle, Mil | 1.05 |
| Gee,Dillon, NYM | 1.13 |

**Sacrifice Flies Allowed**

| | |
|---|---|
| Locke,Jeff, Pit | 10 |
| Cahill,Trevor, Ari | 9 |
| Lynn,Lance, StL | 8 |
| Arroyo,Bronson, Cin | 7 |
| Chacin,Jhoulys, Col | 7 |
| Gallardo,Yovani, Mil | 7 |
| Kendrick,Kyle, Phi | 7 |
| Wheeler,Zack, NYM | 7 |
| 5 tied with | 6 |

**Sacrifice Hits Allowed**

| | |
|---|---|
| Greinke,Zack, LAD | 13 |
| Wainwright,Adam, StL | 13 |
| Latos,Mat, Cin | 12 |
| de la Rosa,Jorge, Col | 11 |
| Hamels,Cole, Phi | 11 |
| Kendrick,Kyle, Phi | 11 |
| Lynn,Lance, StL | 11 |
| Peralta,Wily, Mil | 11 |
| Webb,Ryan, Mia | 11 |
| 4 tied with | 10 |

**GIDP Induced**

| | |
|---|---|
| Wainwright,Adam, StL | 32 |
| Chacin,Jhoulys, Col | 30 |
| Ryu,Hyun-Jin, LAD | 26 |
| Leake,Mike, Cin | 23 |
| Miley,Wade, Ari | 23 |
| Lee,Cliff, Phi | 21 |
| Strasburg,Stephen, Was | 21 |
| Kershaw,Clayton, LAD | 20 |
| Maholm,Paul, Atl | 20 |
| Westbrook,Jake, StL | 20 |

**GIDP Per Nine IP**
(minimum 162 IP)

| | |
|---|---|
| Chacin,Jhoulys, Col | 1.37 |
| Ryu,Hyun-Jin, LAD | 1.22 |
| Wainwright,Adam, StL | 1.19 |
| Leake,Mike, Cin | 1.08 |
| Strasburg,Stephen, Was | 1.03 |
| Miley,Wade, Ari | 1.02 |
| de la Rosa,Jorge, Col | 1.02 |
| Peralta,Wily, Mil | 0.93 |
| Locke,Jeff, Pit | 0.87 |
| Lee,Cliff, Phi | 0.85 |

# National League Pitching Leaders

### Saves

| | |
|---|---|
| Kimbrel,Craig, Atl | 50 |
| Soriano,Rafael, Was | 43 |
| Chapman,Aroldis, Cin | 38 |
| Romo,Sergio, SF | 38 |
| Mujica,Edward, StL | 37 |
| Cishek,Steve, Mia | 34 |
| Gregg,Kevin, ChC | 33 |
| Grilli,Jason, Pit | 33 |
| Street,Huston, SD | 33 |
| Papelbon,Jonathan, Phi | 29 |

### Blown Saves

| | |
|---|---|
| Russell,James, ChC | 8 |
| Axford,John, Mil-StL | 7 |
| Bell,Heath, Ari | 7 |
| Papelbon,Jonathan, Phi | 7 |
| Hernandez,David, Ari | 6 |
| Soriano,Rafael, Was | 6 |
| 11 tied with | 5 |

### Save Pct

(minimum 20 Save Ops)

| | |
|---|---|
| Cishek,Steve, Mia | 94.4 |
| Grilli,Jason, Pit | 94.3 |
| Street,Huston, SD | 94.3 |
| Kimbrel,Craig, Atl | 92.6 |
| Brothers,Rex, Col | 90.5 |
| Mujica,Edward, StL | 90.2 |
| Chapman,Aroldis, Cin | 88.4 |
| Romo,Sergio, SF | 88.4 |
| Soriano,Rafael, Was | 87.8 |
| 2 tied with | 87.5 |

### Save Opportunities

| | |
|---|---|
| Kimbrel,Craig, Atl | 54 |
| Soriano,Rafael, Was | 49 |
| Chapman,Aroldis, Cin | 43 |
| Romo,Sergio, SF | 43 |
| Mujica,Edward, StL | 41 |
| Gregg,Kevin, ChC | 38 |
| Cishek,Steve, Mia | 36 |
| Papelbon,Jonathan, Phi | 36 |
| Grilli,Jason, Pit | 35 |
| Street,Huston, SD | 35 |

### Easy Saves

| | |
|---|---|
| Kimbrel,Craig, Atl | 36 |
| Soriano,Rafael, Was | 28 |
| Chapman,Aroldis, Cin | 25 |
| Grilli,Jason, Pit | 24 |
| Mujica,Edward, StL | 22 |
| Romo,Sergio, SF | 22 |
| Street,Huston, SD | 22 |
| Henderson,Jim, Mil | 21 |
| Gregg,Kevin, ChC | 19 |
| Cishek,Steve, Mia | 18 |

### Regular Saves

| | |
|---|---|
| Cishek,Steve, Mia | 16 |
| Romo,Sergio, SF | 15 |
| Soriano,Rafael, Was | 15 |
| Kimbrel,Craig, Atl | 14 |
| Chapman,Aroldis, Cin | 13 |
| Gregg,Kevin, ChC | 13 |
| Mujica,Edward, StL | 13 |
| Papelbon,Jonathan, Phi | 13 |
| Jansen,Kenley, LAD | 11 |
| Street,Huston, SD | 11 |

### Tough Saves

| | |
|---|---|
| Dunn,Mike, Mia | 2 |
| Jansen,Kenley, LAD | 2 |
| Mujica,Edward, StL | 2 |
| Parnell,Bobby, NYM | 2 |
| Rodriguez,Paco, LAD | 2 |
| 12 tied with | 1 |

### Holds Adjusted Saves %

(minimum 20 Save Ops + Holds)

| | |
|---|---|
| Casilla,Santiago, SF | 96.0 |
| Cishek,Steve, Mia | 94.6 |
| Grilli,Jason, Pit | 94.6 |
| Street,Huston, SD | 94.3 |
| Brothers,Rex, Col | 93.9 |
| Avilan,Luis, Atl | 93.1 |
| Kimbrel,Craig, Atl | 92.6 |
| Watson,Tony, Pit | 92.3 |
| Ziegler,Brad, Ari | 92.3 |
| 2 tied with | 91.7 |

### Relief Wins

| | |
|---|---|
| Mazzaro,Vin, Pit | 8 |
| Ziegler,Brad, Ari | 8 |
| Axford,John, Mil-StL | 7 |
| Casilla,Santiago, SF | 7 |
| Stammen,Craig, Was | 7 |
| 7 tied with | 6 |

### Relief Losses

| | |
|---|---|
| Gregerson,Luke, SD | 8 |
| Romo,Sergio, SF | 8 |
| Axford,John, Mil-StL | 7 |
| Belisario,Ronald, LAD | 7 |
| Belisle,Matt, Col | 7 |
| Morris,Bryan, Pit | 7 |
| 6 tied with | 6 |

### Relief Games

| | |
|---|---|
| Ziegler,Brad, Ari | 78 |
| Belisario,Ronald, LAD | 77 |
| Rodriguez,Paco, LAD | 76 |
| Avilan,Luis, Atl | 75 |
| Axford,John, Mil-StL | 75 |
| Dunn,Mike, Mia | 75 |
| Gonzalez,Michael, Mil | 75 |
| Jansen,Kenley, LAD | 75 |
| Lopez,Wilton, Col | 75 |
| 2 tied with | 74 |

### Holds

| | |
|---|---|
| Clippard,Tyler, Was | 33 |
| Rosenthal,Trevor, StL | 29 |
| Avilan,Luis, Atl | 27 |
| Kintzler,Brandon, Mil | 26 |
| Melancon,Mark, Pit | 26 |
| Gregerson,Luke, SD | 25 |
| Belisle,Matt, Col | 24 |
| Storen,Drew, Was | 24 |
| Casilla,Santiago, SF | 22 |
| Watson,Tony, Pit | 22 |

### Relief Innings

| | |
|---|---|
| Collmenter,Josh, Ari | 92.0 |
| Simon,Alfredo, Cin | 87.2 |
| Stammen,Craig, Was | 81.2 |
| Webb,Ryan, Mia | 80.1 |
| Ramos,A.J., Mia | 80.0 |
| Ottavino,Adam, Col | 78.1 |
| Kintzler,Brandon, Mil | 77.0 |
| Jansen,Kenley, LAD | 76.2 |
| Lopez,Wilton, Col | 75.1 |
| Rosenthal,Trevor, StL | 75.1 |

### Inherited Runners Scrd %

(minimum 30 IR)

| | |
|---|---|
| Lopez,Javier, SF | 10.5 |
| Maness,Seth, StL | 12.1 |
| Mazzaro,Vin, Pit | 12.5 |
| Thatcher,Joe, SD-Ari | 12.7 |
| Rice,Scott, NYM | 14.9 |
| Choate,Randy, StL | 15.3 |
| Casilla,Santiago, SF | 15.6 |
| Parra,Manny, Cin | 16.7 |
| Outman,Josh, Col | 17.6 |
| Howell,J.P., LAD | 17.8 |

### Relief Opp On Base Pct

(minimum 50 IP)

| | |
|---|---|
| Jansen,Kenley, LAD | .236 |
| Clippard,Tyler, Was | .238 |
| Kimbrel,Craig, Atl | .240 |
| Melancon,Mark, Pit | .247 |
| Rodriguez,Paco, LAD | .249 |
| Watson,Tony, Pit | .249 |
| Avilan,Luis, Atl | .259 |
| Parnell,Bobby, NYM | .260 |
| Street,Huston, SD | .261 |
| Mujica,Edward, StL | .262 |

### Relief Opp Slugging Avg

(minimum 50 IP)

| | |
|---|---|
| Avilan,Luis, Atl | .219 |
| Kimbrel,Craig, Atl | .247 |
| Howell,J.P., LAD | .261 |
| Rodriguez,Paco, LAD | .262 |
| Melancon,Mark, Pit | .264 |
| Wilson,Justin, Pit | .265 |
| Jansen,Kenley, LAD | .273 |
| Chapman,Aroldis, Cin | .276 |
| Clippard,Tyler, Was | .279 |
| Carpenter,David, Atl | .291 |

# National League Pitching Leaders

### Relief Opp BA Vs LHB
(minimum 50 AB)

| | |
|---|---|
| Siegrist,Kevin, StL | .118 |
| Rodriguez,Paco, LAD | .131 |
| Chapman,Aroldis, Cin | .137 |
| Avilan,Luis, Atl | .144 |
| Diekman,Jake, Phi | .148 |
| Melancon,Mark, Pit | .148 |
| Strop,Pedro, ChC | .148 |
| Clippard,Tyler, Was | .152 |
| Marmol,Carlos, ChC-LAD | .155 |
| Lopez,Javier, SF | .156 |

### Relief Opp BA Vs RHB
(minimum 50 AB)

| | |
|---|---|
| Kimbrel,Craig, Atl | .116 |
| Savery,Joe, Phi | .118 |
| Vincent,Nick, SD | .122 |
| Gaudin,Chad, SF | .130 |
| Withrow,Chris, LAD | .133 |
| Siegrist,Kevin, StL | .138 |
| Clippard,Tyler, Was | .151 |
| Jansen,Kenley, LAD | .158 |
| Gorzelanny,Tom, Mil | .164 |
| Henderson,Jim, Mil | .165 |

### Relief Opp Batting Average
(minimum 50 IP)

| | |
|---|---|
| Clippard,Tyler, Was | .152 |
| Rodriguez,Paco, LAD | .164 |
| Chapman,Aroldis, Cin | .164 |
| Kimbrel,Craig, Atl | .166 |
| Avilan,Luis, Atl | .175 |
| Jansen,Kenley, LAD | .177 |
| Wilson,Justin, Pit | .192 |
| Howell,J.P., LAD | .193 |
| Watson,Tony, Pit | .198 |
| Carpenter,David, Atl | .198 |

### Relief Earned Run Average
(minimum 50 IP)

| | |
|---|---|
| Kimbrel,Craig, Atl | 1.21 |
| Melancon,Mark, Pit | 1.39 |
| Avilan,Luis, Atl | 1.52 |
| Brothers,Rex, Col | 1.74 |
| Carpenter,David, Atl | 1.78 |
| Jansen,Kenley, LAD | 1.88 |
| Wilson,Justin, Pit | 2.08 |
| Casilla,Santiago, SF | 2.16 |
| Parnell,Bobby, NYM | 2.16 |
| Howell,J.P., LAD | 2.18 |

### Rel OBP 1st Batter Faced
(minimum 40 BF)

| | |
|---|---|
| Collmenter,Josh, Ari | .146 |
| Melancon,Mark, Pit | .194 |
| Henderson,Jim, Mil | .197 |
| Siegrist,Kevin, StL | .200 |
| Cishek,Steve, Mia | .203 |
| Grilli,Jason, Pit | .204 |
| Gregerson,Luke, SD | .219 |
| Belisle,Matt, Col | .222 |
| Clippard,Tyler, Was | .222 |
| Ziegler,Brad, Ari | .231 |

### Rel Opp BA w/ Runners On
(minimum 50 IP)

| | |
|---|---|
| Jansen,Kenley, LAD | .127 |
| Kimbrel,Craig, Atl | .130 |
| Rodriguez,Paco, LAD | .138 |
| Street,Huston, SD | .149 |
| Carpenter,David, Atl | .158 |
| Chapman,Aroldis, Cin | .165 |
| Henderson,Jim, Mil | .172 |
| Brothers,Rex, Col | .183 |
| Casilla,Santiago, SF | .185 |
| 3 tied with | .192 |

### Relief Opp BA w/ RISP
(minimum 50 IP)

| | |
|---|---|
| Jansen,Kenley, LAD | .069 |
| Kimbrel,Craig, Atl | .083 |
| Watson,Tony, Pit | .123 |
| Chapman,Aroldis, Cin | .132 |
| Rodriguez,Paco, LAD | .146 |
| Simon,Alfredo, Cin | .152 |
| Casilla,Santiago, SF | .155 |
| LeCure,Sam, Cin | .158 |
| Hernandez,David, Ari | .161 |
| Street,Huston, SD | .162 |

### Fastest Avg Fastball-Relief
(minimum 50 IP)

| | |
|---|---|
| Chapman,Aroldis, Cin | 98.3 |
| Rosenthal,Trevor, StL | 97.3 |
| Kimbrel,Craig, Atl | 96.9 |
| Axford,John, Mil-StL | 95.4 |
| Wilson,Justin, Pit | 95.3 |
| Henderson,Jim, Mil | 95.3 |
| Carpenter,David, Atl | 95.1 |
| Parnell,Bobby, NYM | 95.0 |
| Hernandez,David, Ari | 94.8 |
| Simon,Alfredo, Cin | 94.5 |

### Fastest Average Fastball
(minimum 162 IP)

| | |
|---|---|
| Harvey,Matt, NYM | 95.8 |
| Strasburg,Stephen, Was | 95.3 |
| Fernandez,Jose, Mia | 94.9 |
| Peralta,Wily, Mil | 94.8 |
| Cashner,Andrew, SD | 94.5 |
| Samardzija,Jeff, ChC | 94.5 |
| Bailey,Homer, Cin | 94.1 |
| Zimmermann,Jordan, Was | 93.9 |
| Miller,Shelby, StL | 93.7 |
| Jackson,Edwin, ChC | 93.1 |

### Slowest Average Fastball
(minimum 162 IP)

| | |
|---|---|
| Stults,Eric, SD | 86.7 |
| Arroyo,Bronson, Cin | 87.2 |
| Wood,Travis, ChC | 88.9 |
| Haren,Dan, Was | 88.9 |
| Gee,Dillon, NYM | 89.3 |
| Medlen,Kris, Atl | 89.4 |
| Lohse,Kyle, Mil | 89.6 |
| Chacin,Jhoulys, Col | 89.8 |
| Kendrick,Kyle, Phi | 89.8 |
| Lincecum,Tim, SF | 90.2 |

### Pitches 100+ Velocity

| | |
|---|---|
| Chapman,Aroldis, Cin | 282 |
| Rodriguez,Henry, Was-ChC | 86 |
| Rosenthal,Trevor, StL | 41 |
| Dominguez,Jose, LAD | 17 |
| Martinez,Carlos, StL | 15 |
| Cole,Gerrit, Pit | 14 |
| Eovaldi,Nathan, Mia | 7 |
| Harvey,Matt, NYM | 4 |
| Cashner,Andrew, SD | 2 |
| Wilson,Justin, Pit | 2 |

### Pitches 95+ Velocity

| | |
|---|---|
| Strasburg,Stephen, Was | 1260 |
| Harvey,Matt, NYM | 1241 |
| Peralta,Wily, Mil | 1227 |
| Axford,John, Mil-StL | 1212 |
| Eovaldi,Nathan, Mia | 1056 |
| Rosenthal,Trevor, StL | 987 |
| Cole,Gerrit, Pit | 925 |
| Fernandez,Jose, Mia | 911 |
| Chapman,Aroldis, Cin | 902 |
| Cashner,Andrew, SD | 880 |

### Pitches Less Than 80 MPH

| | |
|---|---|
| Arroyo,Bronson, Cin | 1506 |
| Stults,Eric, SD | 1439 |
| Nolasco,Ricky, Mia-LAD | 1378 |
| Wainwright,Adam, StL | 963 |
| Kennedy,Ian, Ari-SD | 908 |
| Volquez,Edinson, SD-LAD | 886 |
| Zito,Barry, SF | 868 |
| Feldman,Scott, ChC | 777 |
| Estrada,Marco, Mil | 772 |
| Ryu,Hyun-Jin, LAD | 697 |

### Lowest % Fastballs
(minimum 162 IP)

| | |
|---|---|
| Bumgarner,Madison, SF | 38.5 |
| Haren,Dan, Was | 40.1 |
| Wainwright,Adam, StL | 40.5 |
| Leake,Mike, Cin | 41.9 |
| Nolasco,Ricky, Mia-LAD | 43.9 |
| Arroyo,Bronson, Cin | 44.1 |
| Wood,Travis, ChC | 45.9 |
| Lohse,Kyle, Mil | 46.8 |
| Cain,Matt, SF | 48.8 |
| Stults,Eric, SD | 49.1 |

### Highest % Fastballs
(minimum 162 IP)

| | |
|---|---|
| Lynn,Lance, StL | 73.2 |
| Miller,Shelby, StL | 71.3 |
| Miley,Wade, Ari | 68.8 |
| Gonzalez,Gio, Was | 68.5 |
| Corbin,Patrick, Ari | 67.3 |
| Peralta,Wily, Mil | 66.7 |
| Locke,Jeff, Pit | 64.7 |
| Teheran,Julio, Atl | 63.8 |
| Zimmermann,Jordan, Was | 63.6 |
| Cashner,Andrew, SD | 63.4 |

### Highest % Curveballs
(minimum 162 IP)

| | |
|---|---|
| Burnett,A.J., Pit | 35.4 |
| Wainwright,Adam, StL | 27.3 |
| Volquez,Edinson, SD-LAD | 24.7 |
| Strasburg,Stephen, Was | 22.9 |
| Fernandez,Jose, Mia | 21.3 |
| Gonzalez,Gio, Was | 21.2 |
| Gallardo,Yovani, Mil | 20.9 |
| Locke,Jeff, Pit | 18.9 |
| Miller,Shelby, StL | 18.4 |
| Medlen,Kris, Atl | 18.2 |

# National League Pitching Leaders

**Highest % Changeups**
(minimum 162 IP)

| | |
|---|---|
| de la Rosa,Jorge, Col | 28.1 |
| Hamels,Cole, Phi | 24.9 |
| Lincecum,Tim, SF | 23.5 |
| Kendrick,Kyle, Phi | 23.1 |
| Stults,Eric, SD | 23.0 |
| Medlen,Kris, Atl | 22.9 |
| Ryu,Hyun-Jin, LAD | 22.3 |
| Kennedy,Ian, Ari-SD | 21.0 |
| Volquez,Edinson, SD-LAD | 20.7 |
| Cashner,Andrew, SD | 19.3 |

**Highest % Sliders**
(minimum 162 IP)

| | |
|---|---|
| Bumgarner,Madison, SF | 38.0 |
| Cain,Matt, SF | 28.2 |
| Jackson,Edwin, ChC | 28.1 |
| Lohse,Kyle, Mil | 27.8 |
| Nolasco,Ricky, Mia-LAD | 27.1 |
| Arroyo,Bronson, Cin | 27.0 |
| Peralta,Wily, Mil | 26.6 |
| Gallardo,Yovani, Mil | 24.5 |
| Latos,Mat, Cin | 24.5 |
| Kershaw,Clayton, LAD | 24.4 |

**Balks**

| | |
|---|---|
| Brothers,Rex, Col | 3 |
| Escalona,Edgmer, Col | 3 |
| Lopez,Wilton, Col | 3 |
| Strasburg,Stephen, Was | 3 |
| 9 tied with | 2 |

**Strikeout/Hit Ratio**
(minimum 50 IP)

| | |
|---|---|
| Chapman,Aroldis, Cin | 3.03 |
| Kimbrel,Craig, Atl | 2.51 |
| Jansen,Kenley, LAD | 2.31 |
| Rodriguez,Paco, LAD | 2.10 |
| Clippard,Tyler, Was | 1.97 |
| Grilli,Jason, Pit | 1.85 |
| Rosenthal,Trevor, StL | 1.71 |
| Henderson,Jim, Mil | 1.70 |
| Fernandez,Jose, Mia | 1.68 |
| Cingrani,Tony, Cin | 1.67 |

**Opp OPS vs Fastballs**
(minimum 251 BF)

| | |
|---|---|
| Jansen,Kenley, LAD | .497 |
| Harvey,Matt, NYM | .498 |
| Kershaw,Clayton, LAD | .517 |
| Fernandez,Jose, Mia | .557 |
| Bumgarner,Madison, SF | .571 |
| Lee,Cliff, Phi | .582 |
| Alvarez,Henderson, Mia | .588 |
| Collmenter,Josh, Ari | .588 |
| Cashner,Andrew, SD | .597 |
| Gaudin,Chad, SF | .610 |

**Opp OPS vs Curveballs**
(minimum 100 BF)

| | |
|---|---|
| Strasburg,Stephen, Was | .448 |
| Koehler,Tom, Mia | .468 |
| Gonzalez,Gio, Was | .490 |
| Burnett,A.J., Pit | .510 |
| Leake,Mike, Cin | .521 |
| Wainwright,Adam, StL | .525 |
| Fernandez,Jose, Mia | .531 |
| Medlen,Kris, Atl | .549 |
| Greinke,Zack, LAD | .591 |
| Nolasco,Ricky, Mia-LAD | .629 |

**Opp OPS vs Changeups**
(minimum 100 BF)

| | |
|---|---|
| Ryu,Hyun-Jin, LAD | .419 |
| Hamels,Cole, Phi | .461 |
| Estrada,Marco, Mil | .530 |
| Lincecum,Tim, SF | .586 |
| Medlen,Kris, Atl | .586 |
| Minor,Mike, Atl | .595 |
| Greinke,Zack, LAD | .605 |
| de la Rosa,Jorge, Col | .619 |
| Liriano,Francisco, Pit | .619 |
| Lohse,Kyle, Mil | .623 |

**Opp OPS vs Sliders**
(minimum 64 BF)

| | |
|---|---|
| Fernandez,Jose, Mia | .267 |
| Romo,Sergio, SF | .387 |
| Outman,Josh, Col | .408 |
| Rodriguez,Paco, LAD | .453 |
| Dunn,Mike, Mia | .455 |
| Ramos,A.J., Mia | .468 |
| Ross,Tyson, SD | .471 |
| Ottavino,Adam, Col | .485 |
| Slowey,Kevin, Mia | .490 |
| Brothers,Rex, Col | .505 |

**Earned Runs**

| | |
|---|---|
| Volquez,Edinson, SD-LAD | 108 |
| Samardzija,Jeff, ChC | 103 |
| Kennedy,Ian, Ari-SD | 99 |
| Jackson,Edwin, ChC | 97 |
| Lincecum,Tim, SF | 96 |
| Kendrick,Kyle, Phi | 95 |
| Nicasio,Juan, Col | 90 |
| Lynn,Lance, StL | 89 |
| Peralta,Wily, Mil | 89 |
| Stults,Eric, SD | 89 |

**Hits Per Nine Innings**
(minimum 162 IP)

| | |
|---|---|
| Fernandez,Jose, Mia | 5.79 |
| Kershaw,Clayton, LAD | 6.25 |
| Bumgarner,Madison, SF | 6.53 |
| Strasburg,Stephen, Was | 6.69 |
| Harvey,Matt, NYM | 6.81 |
| Wood,Travis, ChC | 7.34 |
| Greinke,Zack, LAD | 7.70 |
| Cain,Matt, SF | 7.71 |
| 3 tied with | 7.77 |

# American League Fielding Leaders

**2B Pivot %**
(minimum 98 G)

| | |
|---|---|
| Kinsler,Ian, Tex | 0.740 |
| Altuve,Jose, Hou | 0.701 |
| Pedroia,Dustin, Bos | 0.696 |
| Beckham,Gordon, CWS | 0.696 |
| Zobrist,Ben, TB | 0.667 |
| Dozier,Brian, Min | 0.653 |
| Infante,Omar, Det | 0.645 |
| Kendrick,Howie, LAA | 0.633 |
| Sogard,Eric, Oak | 0.612 |
| Kipnis,Jason, Cle | 0.570 |

**SS Pivot %**
(minimum 98 G)

| | |
|---|---|
| Florimon,Pedro, Min | 0.670 |
| Cabrera,Asdrubal, Cle | 0.652 |
| Hardy,J.J., Bal | 0.651 |
| Ramirez,Alexei, CWS | 0.643 |
| Ryan,Brendan, Sea-NYY | 0.610 |
| Drew,Stephen, Bos | 0.605 |
| Peralta,Jhonny, Det | 0.579 |
| Andrus,Elvis, Tex | 0.563 |
| Escobar,Yunel, TB | 0.562 |
| Escobar,Alcides, KC | 0.551 |

**Highest Pct CS by Catchers**
(minimum 600 INN or 50 SBA)

| | |
|---|---|
| Mauer,Joe, Min | 39.5 |
| Gomes,Yan, Cle | 38.3 |
| Perez,Salvador, KC | 33.3 |
| Wieters,Matt, Bal | 33.3 |
| Stewart,Chris, NYY | 31.5 |
| Pierzynski,A.J., Tex | 25.8 |
| Molina,Jose, TB | 23.3 |
| Castro,Jason, Hou | 22.7 |
| Conger,Hank, LAA | 21.7 |
| Flowers,Tyler, CWS | 20.0 |

**Lowest Pct CS by Catchers**
(minimum 600 INN or 50 SBA)

| | |
|---|---|
| Lobaton,Jose, TB | 12.5 |
| Avila,Alex, Det | 13.1 |
| Iannetta,Chris, LAA | 15.2 |
| Arencibia,J.P., Tor | 16.2 |
| Santana,Carlos, Cle | 16.4 |
| Norris,Derek, Oak | 16.7 |
| Pena,Brayan, Det | 17.6 |
| Saltalamacchia,J, Bos | 19.1 |
| Flowers,Tyler, CWS | 20.0 |
| Conger,Hank, LAA | 21.7 |

**2B Double Play %**
(minimum 98 G)

| | |
|---|---|
| Kinsler,Ian, Tex | 0.630 |
| Altuve,Jose, Hou | 0.609 |
| Pedroia,Dustin, Bos | 0.604 |
| Beckham,Gordon, CWS | 0.578 |
| Kipnis,Jason, Cle | 0.558 |
| Infante,Omar, Det | 0.551 |
| Dozier,Brian, Min | 0.550 |
| Zobrist,Ben, TB | 0.541 |
| Sogard,Eric, Oak | 0.521 |
| Kendrick,Howie, LAA | 0.488 |

**3B Double Play %**
(minimum 98 G)

| | |
|---|---|
| Cabrera,Miguel, Det | 0.512 |
| Seager,Kyle, Sea | 0.484 |
| Machado,Manny, Bal | 0.475 |
| Beltre,Adrian, Tex | 0.444 |
| Plouffe,Trevor, Min | 0.432 |
| Lawrie,Brett, Tor | 0.415 |
| Dominguez,Matt, Hou | 0.411 |
| Longoria,Evan, TB | 0.410 |
| Gillaspie,Conor, CWS | 0.390 |
| Moustakas,Mike, KC | 0.381 |

**SS Double Play %**
(minimum 98 G)

| | |
|---|---|
| Hardy,J.J., Bal | 0.671 |
| Ramirez,Alexei, CWS | 0.635 |
| Ryan,Brendan, Sea-NYY | 0.612 |
| Florimon,Pedro, Min | 0.608 |
| Drew,Stephen, Bos | 0.603 |
| Andrus,Elvis, Tex | 0.597 |
| Cabrera,Asdrubal, Cle | 0.574 |
| Escobar,Alcides, KC | 0.570 |
| Peralta,Jhonny, Det | 0.559 |
| Escobar,Yunel, TB | 0.552 |

**Errors**

| | |
|---|---|
| Ramirez,Alexei, CWS | 22 |
| Florimon,Pedro, Min | 18 |
| Lowrie,Jed, Oak | 18 |
| Gillaspie,Conor, CWS | 17 |
| Callaspo,Alberto, LAA-Oak | 16 |
| Dominguez,Matt, Hou | 16 |
| Donaldson,Josh, Oak | 16 |
| Moustakas,Mike, KC | 16 |
| Villar,Jonathan, Hou | 16 |
| 2 tied with | 15 |

**Fielding Errors**

| | |
|---|---|
| Ramirez,Alexei, CWS | 14 |
| Andrus,Elvis, Tex | 10 |
| Lowrie,Jed, Oak | 10 |
| Seager,Kyle, Sea | 10 |
| Kendrick,Howie, LAA | 9 |
| Moustakas,Mike, KC | 9 |
| Ryan,Brendan, Sea-NYY | 9 |
| 8 tied with | 8 |

**Throwing Errors**

| | |
|---|---|
| Donaldson,Josh, Oak | 10 |
| Florimon,Pedro, Min | 10 |
| Callaspo,Alberto, LAA-Oak | 9 |
| Dominguez,Matt, Hou | 9 |
| Gillaspie,Conor, CWS | 9 |
| Machado,Manny, Bal | 9 |
| 7 tied with | 8 |

**Range Factor for 2B**
(minimum 98 games)

| | |
|---|---|
| Dozier,Brian, Min | 5.22 |
| Zobrist,Ben, TB | 4.87 |
| Sogard,Eric, Oak | 4.84 |
| Kinsler,Ian, Tex | 4.78 |
| Altuve,Jose, Hou | 4.75 |
| Beckham,Gordon, CWS | 4.75 |
| Kendrick,Howie, LAA | 4.68 |
| Kipnis,Jason, Cle | 4.44 |
| Pedroia,Dustin, Bos | 4.40 |
| Infante,Omar, Det | 4.38 |

**Range Factor for 3B**
(minimum 98 games)

| | |
|---|---|
| Machado,Manny, Bal | 3.05 |
| Dominguez,Matt, Hou | 2.85 |
| Longoria,Evan, TB | 2.62 |
| Donaldson,Josh, Oak | 2.61 |
| Lawrie,Brett, Tor | 2.60 |
| Moustakas,Mike, KC | 2.58 |
| Seager,Kyle, Sea | 2.54 |
| Gillaspie,Conor, CWS | 2.53 |
| Plouffe,Trevor, Min | 2.48 |
| Beltre,Adrian, Tex | 2.27 |

**Range Factor for SS**
(minimum 98 games)

| | |
|---|---|
| Florimon,Pedro, Min | 5.29 |
| Ryan,Brendan, Sea-NYY | 4.34 |
| Ramirez,Alexei, CWS | 4.30 |
| Drew,Stephen, Bos | 4.18 |
| Peralta,Jhonny, Det | 4.17 |
| Escobar,Yunel, TB | 4.11 |
| Aybar,Erick, LAA | 4.08 |
| Cabrera,Asdrubal, Cle | 4.04 |
| Hardy,J.J., Bal | 4.02 |
| Andrus,Elvis, Tex | 4.01 |

# National League Fielding Leaders

### 2B Pivot %
(minimum 98 G)

| | |
|---|---|
| Carpenter,Matt, StL | 0.702 |
| Barney,Darwin, ChC | 0.701 |
| Ellis,Mark, LAD | 0.654 |
| Scutaro,Marco, SF | 0.641 |
| Uggla,Dan, Atl | 0.625 |
| Murphy,Daniel, NYM | 0.610 |
| Walker,Neil, Pit | 0.573 |
| Gyorko,Jedd, SD | 0.566 |
| Phillips,Brandon, Cin | 0.554 |
| Utley,Chase, Phi | 0.551 |

### SS Pivot %
(minimum 98 G)

| | |
|---|---|
| Kozma,Pete, StL | 0.714 |
| Desmond,Ian, Was | 0.709 |
| Cozart,Zack, Cin | 0.679 |
| Hechavarria,Adeiny, Mia | 0.663 |
| Rollins,Jimmy, Phi | 0.629 |
| Segura,Jean, Mil | 0.623 |
| Tulowitzki,Troy, Col | 0.608 |
| Barmes,Clint, Pit | 0.568 |
| Crawford,Brandon, SF | 0.552 |
| Castro,Starlin, ChC | 0.545 |

### Highest Pct CS by Catchers
(minimum 600 INN or 50 SBA)

| | |
|---|---|
| Molina,Yadier, StL | 42.2 |
| Ellis,A.J., LAD | 40.7 |
| Martin,Russell, Pit | 35.4 |
| Mathis,Jeff, Mia | 30.2 |
| Ramos,Wilson, Was | 24.4 |
| Castillo,Welington, ChC | 23.9 |
| Hundley,Nick, SD | 23.6 |
| Rosario,Wilin, Col | 23.2 |
| Montero,Miguel, Ari | 22.5 |
| Mesoraco,Devin, Cin | 22.4 |

### Lowest Pct CS by Catchers
(minimum 600 INN or 50 SBA)

| | |
|---|---|
| Suzuki,Kurt, Was | 7.0 |
| Ruiz,Carlos, Phi | 16.0 |
| Buck,John, NYM-Pit | 18.8 |
| Lucroy,Jonathan, Mil | 20.8 |
| Posey,Buster, SF | 21.3 |
| McCann,Brian, Atl | 21.7 |
| Mesoraco,Devin, Cin | 22.4 |
| Montero,Miguel, Ari | 22.5 |
| Rosario,Wilin, Col | 23.2 |
| Hundley,Nick, SD | 23.6 |

### 2B Double Play %
(minimum 98 G)

| | |
|---|---|
| Carpenter,Matt, StL | 0.559 |
| Ellis,Mark, LAD | 0.522 |
| Barney,Darwin, ChC | 0.500 |
| Murphy,Daniel, NYM | 0.497 |
| Scutaro,Marco, SF | 0.459 |
| Uggla,Dan, Atl | 0.451 |
| Gyorko,Jedd, SD | 0.445 |
| Walker,Neil, Pit | 0.437 |
| Phillips,Brandon, Cin | 0.420 |
| Utley,Chase, Phi | 0.381 |

### 3B Double Play %
(minimum 98 G)

| | |
|---|---|
| Frazier,Todd, Cin | 0.446 |
| Prado,Martin, Ari | 0.442 |
| Zimmerman,Ryan, Was | 0.424 |
| Freese,David, StL | 0.417 |
| Polanco,Placido, Mia | 0.417 |
| Arenado,Nolan, Col | 0.379 |
| Headley,Chase, SD | 0.357 |
| Alvarez,Pedro, Pit | 0.352 |
| Uribe,Juan, LAD | 0.350 |
| Wright,David, NYM | 0.340 |

### SS Double Play %
(minimum 98 G)

| | |
|---|---|
| Kozma,Pete, StL | 0.676 |
| Desmond,Ian, Was | 0.644 |
| Hechavarria,Adeiny, Mia | 0.632 |
| Rollins,Jimmy, Phi | 0.610 |
| Tulowitzki,Troy, Col | 0.586 |
| Segura,Jean, Mil | 0.582 |
| Cozart,Zack, Cin | 0.574 |
| Simmons,Andrelton, Atl | 0.555 |
| Gregorius,Didi, Ari | 0.540 |
| Crawford,Brandon, SF | 0.537 |

### Errors

| | |
|---|---|
| Alvarez,Pedro, Pit | 27 |
| Castro,Starlin, ChC | 22 |
| Zimmerman,Ryan, Was | 21 |
| Desmond,Ian, Was | 20 |
| Murphy,Daniel, NYM | 18 |
| Sandoval,Pablo, SF | 18 |
| Francisco,Juan, Atl-Mil | 17 |
| Utley,Chase, Phi | 17 |
| Rendon,Anthony, Was | 16 |
| 4 tied with | 15 |

### Fielding Errors

| | |
|---|---|
| Alvarez,Pedro, Pit | 15 |
| Castro,Starlin, ChC | 14 |
| Utley,Chase, Phi | 12 |
| Murphy,Daniel, NYM | 11 |
| Carpenter,Matt, StL | 10 |
| Crawford,Brandon, SF | 10 |
| Rendon,Anthony, Was | 10 |
| 6 tied with | 9 |

### Throwing Errors

| | |
|---|---|
| Zimmerman,Ryan, Was | 15 |
| Alvarez,Pedro, Pit | 12 |
| Desmond,Ian, Was | 12 |
| Sandoval,Pablo, SF | 11 |
| Cozart,Zack, Cin | 10 |
| Segura,Jean, Mil | 9 |
| 5 tied with | 8 |

### Range Factor for 2B
(minimum 98 games)

| | |
|---|---|
| Walker,Neil, Pit | 5.14 |
| Ellis,Mark, LAD | 4.99 |
| Utley,Chase, Phi | 4.74 |
| Carpenter,Matt, StL | 4.72 |
| Phillips,Brandon, Cin | 4.72 |
| Scutaro,Marco, SF | 4.53 |
| Uggla,Dan, Atl | 4.50 |
| Gyorko,Jedd, SD | 4.45 |
| Murphy,Daniel, NYM | 4.41 |
| Barney,Darwin, ChC | 4.36 |

### Range Factor for 3B
(minimum 98 games)

| | |
|---|---|
| Arenado,Nolan, Col | 3.24 |
| Alvarez,Pedro, Pit | 2.92 |
| Uribe,Juan, LAD | 2.92 |
| Wright,David, NYM | 2.88 |
| Prado,Martin, Ari | 2.68 |
| Zimmerman,Ryan, Was | 2.59 |
| Headley,Chase, SD | 2.44 |
| Johnson,Chris, Atl | 2.40 |
| Young,Michael, Phi-LAD | 2.35 |
| Frazier,Todd, Cin | 2.34 |

### Range Factor for SS
(minimum 98 games)

| | |
|---|---|
| Simmons,Andrelton, Atl | 4.92 |
| Tulowitzki,Troy, Col | 4.91 |
| Kozma,Pete, StL | 4.73 |
| Segura,Jean, Mil | 4.73 |
| Desmond,Ian, Was | 4.37 |
| Barmes,Clint, Pit | 4.35 |
| Gregorius,Didi, Ari | 4.34 |
| Crawford,Brandon, SF | 4.21 |
| Rollins,Jimmy, Phi | 4.19 |
| Cozart,Zack, Cin | 4.18 |

# Active Career Batting Leaders

**Batting Average** (minimum 1000 PA)

| | |
|---|---|
| Mauer,Joe | .323 |
| Pujols,Albert | .321 |
| Cabrera,Miguel | .321 |
| Suzuki,Ichiro | .319 |
| Helton,Todd | .316 |
| Votto,Joey | .314 |
| Trout,Mike | .314 |
| Jeter,Derek | .312 |
| Braun,Ryan | .312 |
| Holliday,Matt | .311 |

**On Base Percentage** (minimum 1000 PA)

| | |
|---|---|
| Votto,Joey | .419 |
| Helton,Todd | .414 |
| Pujols,Albert | .410 |
| Berkman,Lance | .406 |
| Mauer,Joe | .405 |
| Trout,Mike | .404 |
| Giambi,Jason | .400 |
| Cabrera,Miguel | .399 |
| Choo,Shin-Soo | .389 |
| Fielder,Prince | .389 |

**Slugging Average** (minimum 1000 PA)

| | |
|---|---|
| Pujols,Albert | .599 |
| Cabrera,Miguel | .568 |
| Braun,Ryan | .564 |
| Rodriguez,Alex | .558 |
| Ortiz,David | .549 |
| Howard,Ryan | .545 |
| Trout,Mike | .544 |
| Votto,Joey | .541 |
| Helton,Todd | .539 |
| Berkman,Lance | .537 |

**Home Runs**

| | |
|---|---|
| Rodriguez,Alex | 654 |
| Pujols,Albert | 492 |
| Dunn,Adam | 440 |
| Giambi,Jason | 438 |
| Konerko,Paul | 434 |
| Ortiz,David | 431 |
| Soriano,Alfonso | 406 |
| Beltre,Adrian | 376 |
| Helton,Todd | 369 |
| Berkman,Lance | 366 |

**Games**

| | |
|---|---|
| Jeter,Derek | 2602 |
| Rodriguez,Alex | 2568 |
| Beltre,Adrian | 2276 |
| Konerko,Paul | 2268 |
| Helton,Todd | 2247 |
| Giambi,Jason | 2234 |
| Tejada,Miguel | 2171 |
| Hunter,Torii | 2091 |
| Ibanez,Raul | 2071 |
| Beltran,Carlos | 2064 |

**At Bats**

| | |
|---|---|
| Jeter,Derek | 10614 |
| Rodriguez,Alex | 9818 |
| Suzuki,Ichiro | 8605 |
| Beltre,Adrian | 8596 |
| Tejada,Miguel | 8434 |
| Konerko,Paul | 8185 |
| Rollins,Jimmy | 8090 |
| Helton,Todd | 7962 |
| Young,Michael | 7918 |
| Beltran,Carlos | 7868 |

**Hits**

| | |
|---|---|
| Jeter,Derek | 3316 |
| Rodriguez,Alex | 2939 |
| Suzuki,Ichiro | 2742 |
| Helton,Todd | 2519 |
| Beltre,Adrian | 2426 |
| Tejada,Miguel | 2407 |
| Young,Michael | 2375 |
| Pujols,Albert | 2347 |
| Konerko,Paul | 2297 |
| Beltran,Carlos | 2228 |

**Total Bases**

| | |
|---|---|
| Rodriguez,Alex | 5480 |
| Jeter,Derek | 4739 |
| Pujols,Albert | 4377 |
| Helton,Todd | 4292 |
| Beltre,Adrian | 4109 |
| Konerko,Paul | 4017 |
| Beltran,Carlos | 3902 |
| Ortiz,David | 3872 |
| Tejada,Miguel | 3842 |
| Soriano,Alfonso | 3791 |

**Doubles**

| | |
|---|---|
| Helton,Todd | 592 |
| Jeter,Derek | 525 |
| Pujols,Albert | 524 |
| Ortiz,David | 520 |
| Rodriguez,Alex | 519 |
| Beltre,Adrian | 495 |
| Tejada,Miguel | 468 |
| Soriano,Alfonso | 466 |
| Rollins,Jimmy | 457 |
| Beltran,Carlos | 446 |

**Triples**

| | |
|---|---|
| Crawford,Carl | 117 |
| Reyes,Jose | 111 |
| Rollins,Jimmy | 107 |
| Pierre,Juan | 94 |
| Suzuki,Ichiro | 83 |
| Granderson,Curtis | 80 |
| Beltran,Carlos | 77 |
| Furcal,Rafael | 68 |
| Victorino,Shane | 67 |
| Jeter,Derek | 65 |

**Runs Scored**

| | |
|---|---|
| Rodriguez,Alex | 1919 |
| Jeter,Derek | 1876 |
| Pujols,Albert | 1425 |
| Helton,Todd | 1401 |
| Beltran,Carlos | 1346 |
| Suzuki,Ichiro | 1261 |
| Rollins,Jimmy | 1247 |
| Tejada,Miguel | 1230 |
| Giambi,Jason | 1224 |
| Ortiz,David | 1208 |

**RBI**

| | |
|---|---|
| Rodriguez,Alex | 1969 |
| Pujols,Albert | 1498 |
| Giambi,Jason | 1436 |
| Ortiz,David | 1429 |
| Helton,Todd | 1406 |
| Konerko,Paul | 1390 |
| Beltran,Carlos | 1327 |
| Beltre,Adrian | 1307 |
| Tejada,Miguel | 1302 |
| Ramirez,Aramis | 1276 |

**Walks**

| | |
|---|---|
| Giambi,Jason | 1357 |
| Helton,Todd | 1335 |
| Dunn,Adam | 1246 |
| Rodriguez,Alex | 1240 |
| Berkman,Lance | 1201 |
| Ortiz,David | 1087 |
| Pujols,Albert | 1067 |
| Jeter,Derek | 1047 |
| Beltran,Carlos | 934 |
| Konerko,Paul | 911 |

**Intentional Walks**

| | |
|---|---|
| Pujols,Albert | 275 |
| Helton,Todd | 185 |
| Cabrera,Miguel | 180 |
| Suzuki,Ichiro | 177 |
| Berkman,Lance | 160 |
| Ortiz,David | 156 |
| Howard,Ryan | 143 |
| Fielder,Prince | 138 |
| Gonzalez,Adrian | 126 |
| Dunn,Adam | 117 |

**Hit By Pitch**

| | |
|---|---|
| Giambi,Jason | 179 |
| Rodriguez,Alex | 169 |
| Jeter,Derek | 164 |
| Utley,Chase | 156 |
| Johnson,Reed | 125 |
| Quentin,Carlos | 123 |
| Tejada,Miguel | 122 |
| Weeks,Rickie | 117 |
| Pierzynski,A.J. | 114 |
| Ramirez,Aramis | 109 |

**Strikeouts**

| | |
|---|---|
| Dunn,Adam | 2220 |
| Rodriguez,Alex | 2075 |
| Jeter,Derek | 1753 |
| Soriano,Alfonso | 1732 |
| Pena,Carlos | 1566 |
| Giambi,Jason | 1560 |
| Hunter,Torii | 1547 |
| Ortiz,David | 1474 |
| Beltran,Carlos | 1427 |
| Howard,Ryan | 1401 |

# Active Career Batting Leaders

### Sacrifice Hits

| | |
|---|---|
| Pierre,Juan | 167 |
| Oswalt,Roy | 106 |
| Jeter,Derek | 89 |
| Hairston,Jerry | 88 |
| Polanco,Placido | 86 |
| Dempster,Ryan | 85 |
| Andrus,Elvis | 78 |
| Arroyo,Bronson | 78 |
| Carroll,Jamey | 78 |
| 2 tied with | 77 |

### Sacrifice Flies

| | |
|---|---|
| Rodriguez,Alex | 101 |
| Giambi,Jason | 93 |
| Helton,Todd | 93 |
| Beltran,Carlos | 89 |
| Konerko,Paul | 84 |
| Pujols,Albert | 81 |
| Ramirez,Aramis | 79 |
| Beltre,Adrian | 73 |
| Young,Michael | 72 |
| Tejada,Miguel | 71 |

### Stolen Bases

| | |
|---|---|
| Pierre,Juan | 614 |
| Suzuki,Ichiro | 472 |
| Crawford,Carl | 447 |
| Reyes,Jose | 425 |
| Rollins,Jimmy | 425 |
| Jeter,Derek | 348 |
| Rodriguez,Alex | 322 |
| Furcal,Rafael | 314 |
| Beltran,Carlos | 308 |
| Bourn,Michael | 299 |

### Seasons Played

| | |
|---|---|
| Oliver,Darren | 20 |
| Rodriguez,Alex | 20 |
| Giambi,Jason | 19 |
| Hawkins,LaTroy | 19 |
| Jeter,Derek | 19 |
| Rivera,Mariano | 19 |
| Ibanez,Raul | 18 |
| Pettitte,Andy | 18 |
| Wright,Jamey | 18 |
| 6 tied with | 17 |

### At Bats Per Home Run
(minimum 1000 AB)

| | |
|---|---|
| Howard,Ryan | 14.0 |
| Dunn,Adam | 14.7 |
| Pujols,Albert | 14.9 |
| Stanton,Giancarlo | 14.9 |
| Rodriguez,Alex | 15.0 |
| Davis,Chris | 16.2 |
| Ortiz,David | 16.4 |
| Napoli,Mike | 16.4 |
| Giambi,Jason | 16.5 |
| Fielder,Prince | 16.6 |

### Grounded Into DP

| | |
|---|---|
| Tejada,Miguel | 277 |
| Konerko,Paul | 275 |
| Jeter,Derek | 272 |
| Pujols,Albert | 269 |
| Rodriguez,Alex | 240 |
| Young,Michael | 237 |
| Hunter,Torii | 230 |
| Beltre,Adrian | 216 |
| Cabrera,Miguel | 213 |
| Polanco,Placido | 201 |

### Highest SB Success Pct
(minimum 100 SBA)

| | |
|---|---|
| Utley,Chase | 88.4 |
| Werth,Jayson | 87.0 |
| Beltran,Carlos | 86.5 |
| McLouth,Nate | 84.9 |
| Bay,Jason | 84.8 |
| Ellsbury,Jacoby | 84.0 |
| Escobar,Alcides | 82.9 |
| Getz,Chris | 82.9 |
| Victorino,Shane | 82.8 |
| Rollins,Jimmy | 82.7 |

### Lowest SB Success Pct
(minimum 100 SBA)

| | |
|---|---|
| DeJesus,David | 52.5 |
| Kotsay,Mark | 60.5 |
| Berkman,Lance | 64.2 |
| Castro,Starlin | 64.7 |
| Fowler,Dexter | 66.4 |
| Carroll,Jamey | 67.3 |
| Hart,Corey | 67.5 |
| Izturis,Cesar | 67.5 |
| Hunter,Torii | 67.5 |
| Pence,Hunter | 67.9 |

### Strikeouts / Walks Ratio
(minimum 1000 AB)

| | |
|---|---|
| Pujols,Albert | .783 |
| Hanigan,Ryan | .841 |
| Helton,Todd | .880 |
| Mauer,Joe | .916 |
| Pedroia,Dustin | .957 |
| Aoki,Norichika | .969 |
| Jaso,John | .972 |
| Callaspo,Alberto | .996 |
| Pierre,Juan | 1.032 |
| Keppinger,Jeff | 1.075 |

### At Bats Per GIDP
(minimum 1000 AB)

| | |
|---|---|
| Bourn,Michael | 168.6 |
| Stubbs,Drew | 158.6 |
| Suzuki,Ichiro | 114.7 |
| Granderson,Curtis | 113.8 |
| De Aza,Alejandro | 113.6 |
| Belt,Brandon | 110.7 |
| Ackley,Dustin | 110.3 |
| Bonifacio,Emilio | 108.5 |
| Young,Eric | 103.6 |
| Pagan,Angel | 103.6 |

### OPS
(minimum 1000 PA)

| | |
|---|---|
| Pujols,Albert | 1.008 |
| Cabrera,Miguel | .967 |
| Votto,Joey | .960 |
| Helton,Todd | .953 |
| Trout,Mike | .948 |
| Berkman,Lance | .943 |
| Rodriguez,Alex | .942 |
| Braun,Ryan | .938 |
| Ortiz,David | .930 |
| Giambi,Jason | .919 |

### Secondary Average
(minimum 1000 PA)

| | |
|---|---|
| Dunn,Adam | .459 |
| Trout,Mike | .444 |
| Berkman,Lance | .442 |
| Pujols,Albert | .436 |
| Giambi,Jason | .432 |
| Votto,Joey | .419 |
| Ortiz,David | .418 |
| Rodriguez,Alex | .418 |
| Howard,Ryan | .413 |
| Stanton,Giancarlo | .408 |

### Highest Strikeout per PA
(minimum 1000 PA)

| | |
|---|---|
| Shoppach,Kelly | .336 |
| Reynolds,Mark | .323 |
| Alvarez,Pedro | .306 |
| Davis,Chris | .306 |
| Wallace,Brett | .295 |
| Saltalamacchia,J | .294 |
| Stubbs,Drew | .293 |
| Arencibia,J.P. | .287 |
| Stanton,Giancarlo | .286 |
| Dunn,Adam | .284 |

### Lowest Strikeout per PA
(minimum 1000 PA)

| | |
|---|---|
| Pierre,Juan | .058 |
| Keppinger,Jeff | .068 |
| Polanco,Placido | .068 |
| Aoki,Norichika | .075 |
| Callaspo,Alberto | .087 |
| Molina,Yadier | .088 |
| Frandsen,Kevin | .089 |
| Pedroia,Dustin | .089 |
| Izturis,Cesar | .092 |
| Suzuki,Ichiro | .094 |

### Plate Appearances

| | |
|---|---|
| Jeter,Derek | 11968 |
| Rodriguez,Alex | 11344 |
| Helton,Todd | 9453 |
| Beltre,Adrian | 9387 |
| Konerko,Paul | 9281 |
| Suzuki,Ichiro | 9278 |
| Tejada,Miguel | 9205 |
| Beltran,Carlos | 8949 |
| Rollins,Jimmy | 8902 |
| Giambi,Jason | 8838 |

### At Bats Per RBI
(minimum 1000 AB)

| | |
|---|---|
| Howard,Ryan | 4.5 |
| Pujols,Albert | 4.9 |
| Cabrera,Miguel | 4.9 |
| Ortiz,David | 4.9 |
| Rodriguez,Alex | 5.0 |
| Giambi,Jason | 5.0 |
| Teixeira,Mark | 5.1 |
| Craig,Allen | 5.2 |
| Berkman,Lance | 5.3 |
| Hamilton,Josh | 5.4 |

# Active Career Pitching Leaders

| Earned Run Average (minimum 750 IP) | |
|---|---|
| Rivera,Mariano | 2.21 |
| Kershaw,Clayton | 2.60 |
| Rodriguez,Francisco | 2.70 |
| Nathan,Joe | 2.76 |
| Wainwright,Adam | 3.12 |
| Price,David | 3.19 |
| Hernandez,Felix | 3.20 |
| Santana,Johan | 3.20 |
| Weaver,Jered | 3.24 |
| Latos,Mat | 3.35 |

| Winning Percentage (minimum 100 Decisions) | |
|---|---|
| Halladay,Roy | .659 |
| Weaver,Jered | .653 |
| Hudson,Tim | .649 |
| Price,David | .645 |
| Lester,Jon | .641 |
| Sabathia,CC | .641 |
| Santana,Johan | .641 |
| Verlander,Justin | .640 |
| Wainwright,Adam | .635 |
| Kershaw,Clayton | .626 |

| Opponent Batting Average (minimum 750 IP) | |
|---|---|
| Nathan,Joe | .201 |
| Rodriguez,Francisco | .206 |
| Kershaw,Clayton | .211 |
| Rivera,Mariano | .211 |
| Dotel,Octavio | .219 |
| Cain,Matt | .227 |
| Santana,Johan | .228 |
| Lincecum,Tim | .231 |
| Gonzalez,Gio | .232 |
| Benoit,Joaquin | .232 |

| Baserunners Per 9 IP (minimum 750 IP) | |
|---|---|
| Rivera,Mariano | 9.33 |
| Kershaw,Clayton | 9.98 |
| Nathan,Joe | 10.04 |
| Santana,Johan | 10.35 |
| Weaver,Jered | 10.47 |
| Hamels,Cole | 10.48 |
| Price,David | 10.67 |
| Latos,Mat | 10.71 |
| Rodriguez,Francisco | 10.76 |
| Cain,Matt | 10.79 |

| Games | |
|---|---|
| Rivera,Mariano | 1115 |
| Hawkins,LaTroy | 943 |
| Farnsworth,Kyle | 858 |
| Oliver,Darren | 766 |
| Dotel,Octavio | 758 |
| Rodriguez,Francisco | 730 |
| Nathan,Joe | 714 |
| Lowe,Derek | 681 |
| Qualls,Chad | 663 |
| Affeldt,Jeremy | 660 |

| Games Started | |
|---|---|
| Pettitte,Andy | 521 |
| Buehrle,Mark | 429 |
| Hudson,Tim | 426 |
| Zito,Barry | 419 |
| Sabathia,CC | 415 |
| Colon,Bartolo | 405 |
| Halladay,Roy | 390 |
| Lowe,Derek | 377 |
| Burnett,A.J. | 370 |
| Lohse,Kyle | 363 |

| Complete Games | |
|---|---|
| Halladay,Roy | 67 |
| Sabathia,CC | 37 |
| Colon,Bartolo | 35 |
| Carpenter,Chris | 33 |
| Buehrle,Mark | 29 |
| Lee,Cliff | 28 |
| Pettitte,Andy | 26 |
| Hudson,Tim | 25 |
| Burnett,A.J. | 23 |
| Hernandez,Felix | 23 |

| Shutouts | |
|---|---|
| Halladay,Roy | 20 |
| Carpenter,Chris | 15 |
| Hudson,Tim | 13 |
| Colon,Bartolo | 12 |
| Lee,Cliff | 12 |
| Sabathia,CC | 12 |
| Burnett,A.J. | 10 |
| Santana,Johan | 10 |
| Buehrle,Mark | 9 |
| Hernandez,Felix | 9 |

| Wins | |
|---|---|
| Pettitte,Andy | 256 |
| Hudson,Tim | 205 |
| Sabathia,CC | 205 |
| Halladay,Roy | 203 |
| Colon,Bartolo | 189 |
| Buehrle,Mark | 186 |
| Lowe,Derek | 176 |
| Zito,Barry | 165 |
| Oswalt,Roy | 163 |
| Garcia,Freddy | 156 |

| Losses | |
|---|---|
| Lowe,Derek | 157 |
| Pettitte,Andy | 153 |
| Zito,Barry | 143 |
| Buehrle,Mark | 142 |
| Dempster,Ryan | 133 |
| Burnett,A.J. | 132 |
| Colon,Bartolo | 128 |
| Arroyo,Bronson | 127 |
| Wright,Jamey | 126 |
| Garland,Jon | 125 |

| Innings Pitched | |
|---|---|
| Pettitte,Andy | 3316.0 |
| Buehrle,Mark | 2882.2 |
| Hudson,Tim | 2813.2 |
| Sabathia,CC | 2775.1 |
| Halladay,Roy | 2749.1 |
| Lowe,Derek | 2671.1 |
| Colon,Bartolo | 2583.2 |
| Zito,Barry | 2569.2 |
| Dempster,Ryan | 2387.0 |
| Burnett,A.J. | 2353.2 |

| Batters Faced | |
|---|---|
| Pettitte,Andy | 14074 |
| Buehrle,Mark | 12021 |
| Hudson,Tim | 11691 |
| Sabathia,CC | 11530 |
| Lowe,Derek | 11358 |
| Halladay,Roy | 11287 |
| Zito,Barry | 10964 |
| Colon,Bartolo | 10927 |
| Dempster,Ryan | 10412 |
| Burnett,A.J. | 10031 |

| Strikeouts | |
|---|---|
| Pettitte,Andy | 2448 |
| Sabathia,CC | 2389 |
| Burnett,A.J. | 2180 |
| Halladay,Roy | 2117 |
| Dempster,Ryan | 2075 |
| Santana,Johan | 1988 |
| Colon,Bartolo | 1950 |
| Hudson,Tim | 1896 |
| Zito,Barry | 1883 |
| Peavy,Jake | 1869 |

| Walks Allowed | |
|---|---|
| Dempster,Ryan | 1071 |
| Zito,Barry | 1058 |
| Pettitte,Andy | 1031 |
| Burnett,A.J. | 955 |
| Wright,Jamey | 951 |
| Hudson,Tim | 846 |
| Sabathia,CC | 834 |
| Colon,Bartolo | 802 |
| Lowe,Derek | 794 |
| Marquis,Jason | 755 |

| Hit Batters | |
|---|---|
| Wright,Jamey | 151 |
| Burnett,A.J. | 116 |
| Hudson,Tim | 110 |
| Lackey,John | 107 |
| Arroyo,Bronson | 100 |
| Zito,Barry | 97 |
| Oliver,Darren | 96 |
| Dempster,Ryan | 91 |
| Marquis,Jason | 87 |
| 2 tied with | 85 |

| Wild Pitches | |
|---|---|
| Burnett,A.J. | 146 |
| Lackey,John | 101 |
| Hernandez,Felix | 98 |
| Garcia,Freddy | 95 |
| Haren,Dan | 85 |
| Lincecum,Tim | 84 |
| Wright,Jamey | 82 |
| Dempster,Ryan | 80 |
| Hudson,Tim | 78 |
| Jimenez,Ubaldo | 75 |

# Active Career Pitching Leaders

**Saves**

| | |
|---|---|
| Rivera,Mariano | 652 |
| Nathan,Joe | 341 |
| Rodriguez,Francisco | 304 |
| Papelbon,Jonathan | 286 |
| Valverde,Jose | 286 |
| Street,Huston | 234 |
| Putz,J.J. | 189 |
| Gregg,Kevin | 177 |
| Soriano,Rafael | 175 |
| Rodney,Fernando | 172 |

**Save Pct**
(minimum 50 Save Ops)

| | |
|---|---|
| Kimbrel,Craig | 90.3 |
| Nathan,Joe | 90.0 |
| Cishek,Steve | 89.7 |
| Frieri,Ernesto | 89.6 |
| Rivera,Mariano | 89.1 |
| Soria,Joakim | 88.9 |
| Valverde,Jose | 88.3 |
| Holland,Greg | 88.2 |
| Feliz,Neftali | 88.1 |
| Papelbon,Jonathan | 87.7 |

**Home Runs Allowed**

| | |
|---|---|
| Buehrle,Mark | 324 |
| Arroyo,Bronson | 314 |
| Colon,Bartolo | 308 |
| Lilly,Ted | 293 |
| Pettitte,Andy | 288 |
| Garcia,Freddy | 285 |
| Zito,Barry | 278 |
| Dempster,Ryan | 267 |
| Garland,Jon | 263 |
| Lohse,Kyle | 261 |

**Strikeouts Per 9 IP**
(minimum 750 IP)

| | |
|---|---|
| Rodriguez,Francisco | 10.93 |
| Dotel,Octavio | 10.82 |
| Lincecum,Tim | 9.63 |
| Nathan,Joe | 9.56 |
| Scherzer,Max | 9.44 |
| Perez,Oliver | 9.22 |
| Kershaw,Clayton | 9.20 |
| Sanchez,Jonathan | 9.11 |
| Liriano,Francisco | 9.07 |
| Gallardo,Yovani | 8.86 |

**Opp On-Base Percentage**
(minimum 750 IP)

| | |
|---|---|
| Rivera,Mariano | .262 |
| Nathan,Joe | .277 |
| Kershaw,Clayton | .280 |
| Santana,Johan | .284 |
| Weaver,Jered | .286 |
| Hamels,Cole | .288 |
| Rodriguez,Francisco | .291 |
| Price,David | .292 |
| Latos,Mat | .292 |
| Cain,Matt | .294 |

**Opp Slugging Average**
(minimum 750 IP)

| | |
|---|---|
| Rivera,Mariano | .293 |
| Kershaw,Clayton | .311 |
| Rodriguez,Francisco | .325 |
| Nathan,Joe | .328 |
| Lincecum,Tim | .354 |
| Wilson,C.J. | .354 |
| Gonzalez,Gio | .355 |
| Hernandez,Felix | .356 |
| Price,David | .357 |
| Verlander,Justin | .359 |

**Hits Per Nine Innings**
(minimum 750 IP)

| | |
|---|---|
| Nathan,Joe | 6.55 |
| Rodriguez,Francisco | 6.74 |
| Kershaw,Clayton | 6.83 |
| Rivera,Mariano | 7.00 |
| Dotel,Octavio | 7.24 |
| Cain,Matt | 7.51 |
| Santana,Johan | 7.67 |
| Lincecum,Tim | 7.71 |
| Price,David | 7.78 |
| Latos,Mat | 7.81 |

**Home Runs Per Nine IP**
(minimum 750 IP)

| | |
|---|---|
| Rivera,Mariano | 0.50 |
| Kershaw,Clayton | 0.56 |
| Wainwright,Adam | 0.64 |
| Billingsley,Chad | 0.67 |
| Johnson,Josh | 0.67 |
| Wang,Chien-Ming | 0.67 |
| Masterson,Justin | 0.69 |
| Wilson,C.J. | 0.70 |
| Lincecum,Tim | 0.70 |
| Fister,Doug | 0.70 |

**Strikeouts / Walks Ratio**
(minimum 750 IP)

| | |
|---|---|
| Rivera,Mariano | 4.10 |
| Haren,Dan | 4.08 |
| Lee,Cliff | 3.88 |
| Hamels,Cole | 3.83 |
| Halladay,Roy | 3.58 |
| Oswalt,Roy | 3.56 |
| Shields,James | 3.54 |
| Nolasco,Ricky | 3.52 |
| Santana,Johan | 3.51 |
| Greinke,Zack | 3.48 |

**Stolen Base Pct Allowed**
(minimum 750 IP)

| | |
|---|---|
| Cueto,Johnny | 34.8 |
| Carpenter,Chris | 37.9 |
| Buehrle,Mark | 43.3 |
| Fister,Doug | 51.6 |
| Kershaw,Clayton | 52.3 |
| Garland,Jon | 52.4 |
| Greinke,Zack | 52.8 |
| Duke,Zach | 53.4 |
| Santana,Johan | 54.7 |
| Colon,Bartolo | 54.8 |

**GIDP Induced**

| | |
|---|---|
| Pettitte,Andy | 363 |
| Lowe,Derek | 314 |
| Buehrle,Mark | 310 |
| Hudson,Tim | 297 |
| Wright,Jamey | 265 |
| Garland,Jon | 250 |
| Halladay,Roy | 249 |
| Colon,Bartolo | 247 |
| Sabathia,CC | 247 |
| Westbrook,Jake | 239 |

**GIDP Per Nine IP**
(minimum 750 IP)

| | |
|---|---|
| Westbrook,Jake | 1.23 |
| Wang,Chien-Ming | 1.23 |
| Wright,Jamey | 1.21 |
| Romero,Ricky | 1.20 |
| Lannan,John | 1.19 |
| Maholm,Paul | 1.16 |
| Hernandez,Roberto | 1.12 |
| Porcello,Rick | 1.11 |
| Saunders,Joe | 1.11 |
| Lowe,Derek | 1.06 |

**Complete Game %**
(minimum 100 GS)

| | |
|---|---|
| Halladay,Roy | 0.17 |
| Carpenter,Chris | 0.10 |
| Lee,Cliff | 0.09 |
| Sabathia,CC | 0.09 |
| Wainwright,Adam | 0.09 |
| Colon,Bartolo | 0.09 |
| Hernandez,Felix | 0.09 |
| Shields,James | 0.08 |
| Verlander,Justin | 0.08 |
| Dickey,R.A. | 0.07 |

**Quality Start Pct**
(minimum 100 GS)

| | |
|---|---|
| Wainwright,Adam | 68.6 |
| Kershaw,Clayton | 68.1 |
| Weaver,Jered | 68.0 |
| Price,David | 67.3 |
| Hernandez,Felix | 66.9 |
| Cain,Matt | 66.0 |
| Oswalt,Roy | 66.0 |
| Halladay,Roy | 65.9 |
| Bumgarner,Madison | 65.2 |
| Johnson,Josh | 65.0 |

**Walks Per 9 IP**
(minimum 750 IP)

| | |
|---|---|
| Fister,Doug | 1.81 |
| Haren,Dan | 1.87 |
| Halladay,Roy | 1.94 |
| Lee,Cliff | 1.96 |
| Rivera,Mariano | 2.01 |
| Buehrle,Mark | 2.05 |
| Kuroda,Hiroki | 2.07 |
| Oswalt,Roy | 2.08 |
| Nolasco,Ricky | 2.10 |
| Baker,Scott | 2.11 |

**Games Finished**

| | |
|---|---|
| Rivera,Mariano | 951 |
| Nathan,Joe | 531 |
| Valverde,Jose | 507 |
| Rodriguez,Francisco | 481 |
| Papelbon,Jonathan | 452 |
| Street,Huston | 400 |
| Gregg,Kevin | 378 |
| Putz,J.J. | 349 |
| Rodney,Fernando | 344 |
| Hawkins,LaTroy | 309 |

# Home Run Robberies

No other play in baseball takes you on an emotional roller coaster like a robbed home run. Flash back to Milwaukee on July 8, with Joey Votto striding to the plate against Francisco Rodriguez with two outs in the ninth. The Reds trail 4-3, but with the runner on first base, Votto represents the go-ahead run. Votto works a 2-2 count, and K-Rod is one strike from closing out the game.

From the crack of the bat, everyone in the stadium believes the Reds have just taken the lead. The Brewers' faithful in attendance let out a collective scream of agony and defeat. Votto flips his bat and begins his victory march towards first base. K-Rod doesn't even turn around; he knows it's gone, and it's too late to take it back. There's seemingly nothing between the ball and its destiny over the outfield wall.

There's one man who hasn't completely accepted that fate, though he knows his odds are slim. Carlos Gomez, who is already playing deep with the former NL MVP at the plate in a "no doubles" situation, heads back to the centerfield wall he's come to know so well. The drama builds as the ball hangs in the air for what feels like six minutes but is only six seconds. The rest of the stadium starts to realize that Carlos Gomez is out there, and a glimmer of hope remains.

Gomez has to time his jump perfectly with both the falling baseball and the insufficiently padded wall while he can see at most one of the two at any given time. It's not unlike a wide receiver leaping for the overthrown pass from the quarterback while simultaneously bracing for impact with the tackling defender, except in this case the stakes are much higher than a simple incomplete pass. The entire game hangs in the balance.

In that final instant, as the crowd holds its breath, the ball disappears over the wall and momentarily intersects with Gomez's glove. For a brief moment, there's only one man in the ballpark who knows whether it's a home run or just a long out. The entire ballpark waits for some reaction from Gomez, and they don't have to wait long.

Aside from the final out of the World Series, a home run robbery is one of the few moments when emotions spill out unchecked from both sides of the field. In this case, Gomez can't contain his excitement, bounding up and down looking like a child on Christmas morning. K-Rod's jaw drops in disbelief and, seconds later, relief. Votto literally can't believe it. He points at Gomez and starts running into the outfield yelling at the umpires because he is convinced Gomez didn't actually catch the ball. He couldn't have, the ball was going over the wall. It was a home run. When Gomez opens his glove and proudly displays the baseball, Votto's skepticism evolves into frustration and despair. He even turns to the videoboard in centerfield for the replay because seeing it once wasn't proof enough.

The average home run robbery reduces the offense's scoring expectation by 1.6 runs, which is why John Dewan calls it the "grand slam of defense". While there's no single offensive event more valuable than a four-run home run, there's nothing you can do in a single play on defense that is more impactful than turning a home run into an out. (I guess you could say the true "grand slam of defense" would be robbing a grand slam home run, but that feat is so rare it hasn't happened since Julio Borbon robbed Juan Rivera with the bases full on September 20, 2010.)

Amazingly, Carlos Gomez robbed five (count 'em) home runs this season. At 1.6 runs each, that's 8.0 full runs that Gomez saved on just five plays. No one else robbed more than two this year.

### Home Run Robberies in 2013

| Player | HR Robberies |
|---|---|
| Carlos Gomez | 5 |
| Carlos Gonzalez | 2 |
| Starling Marte | 2 |
| Colby Rasmus | 2 |
| Endy Chavez | 2 |
| Aaron Hicks | 2 |

In fact, no one has robbed five in any one season in our ten-year database. Mike Trout (2012) is one of four players with four such robberies in a season, along with Adam Jones (2009), Gary Matthews (2006) and Nook Logan (2005). Gomez is also climbing the "career" leaderboard, trailing only the master himself. Amazingly, Torii Hunter holds the lead despite the fact that we are missing the first six years of his career.

## Career Home Run Robbery Leaders(2004-2013)

| Player | HR Robberies |
|---|---|
| Torii Hunter | 12 |
| Carlos Gomez | 11 |
| Ichiro Suzuki | 9 |
| Jason Bay | 9 |
| Coco Crisp | 7 |
| Franklin Gutierrez | 7 |

When Nick Markakis victimized Adrian Beltre in July, he probably didn't know it but he set a record. Not his own record, but Beltre's. Markakis's catch was the seventh time in the past decade that Beltre lost a home run due to an outfielder's thievery, surpassing Jim Thome for the lead. Thome had the misfortune of spending much of his career in the same division as Torii Hunter, who was responsible for three of Thome's six lost home runs.

## Most Frequent Victims of Home Run Robberies

| Batter | HR Robberies |
|---|---|
| Adrian Beltre | 7 |
| Jim Thome | 6 |
| Jason Bay | 6 |
| Manny Ramirez | 9 |

There were 46 home run robberies in 2013, roughly one every four days. We've listed them for you on the following page, with some helpful context. It's only fair that Gomez, the league's leading robber, was himself victimized by Aaron Hicks. Kensuke Tanaka, who played all of nine games this year, caught exactly six flyballs and one of them was a robbed home run. Adrian Gonzalez, Jay Bruce, and Juan Uribe (of all people) each had two home runs robbed this year. Chris Davis smashed a league-leading 53 balls over the wall this year, and zero of them were caught. Bronson Arroyo allowed an NL-high 32 home runs, but it would have been 33 if it weren't for Derrick Robinson. Erasmo Ramirez, Anibal Sanchez, Juan Nicasio, Phil Hughes, and Tyler Thornburg benefited twice each from robbed home runs. Clayton Kershaw's league-leading ERA would have risen from 1.83 to 1.94 (which still would have led the league) if Skip Schumaker hadn't spared him that three-run homer in mid-June. Josh Reddick had a game-saver against the White Sox with a one run lead in the ninth. How about a David Murphy HR robbery in the bottom of the 11th inning?

# Home Run Robberies

| Date | Matchup | Fielder | Pos | Pitcher | Batter | Inn. | Outs | Men On | Score |
|---|---|---|---|---|---|---|---|---|---|
| 04/03/2013 | Rockies@Brewers | Carlos Gomez | 8 | Wily Peralta | Carlos Gonzalez | 6 | 0 | ___ | 4-2 |
| 04/07/2013 | Pirates@Dodgers | Starling Marte | 7 | Jeff Locke | Juan Uribe | 6 | 1 | ___ | 2-4 |
| 04/09/2013 | Blue Jays@Tigers | Don Kelly | 7 | Anibal Sanchez | J.P. Arencibia | 2 | 0 | ___ | 0-1 |
| 04/20/2013 | Braves@Pirates | Starling Marte | 7 | James McDonald | B.J. Upton | 5 | 1 | ___ | 1-0 |
| 05/01/2013 | Rockies@Dodgers | Dexter Fowler | 8 | Juan Nicasio | Adrian Gonzalez | 3 | 0 | 12_ | 3-2 |
| 05/01/2013 | Phillies@Indians | Laynce Nix | 9 | Cliff Lee | Drew Stubbs | 4 | 1 | ___ | 0-4 |
| 05/04/2013 | Athletics@Yankees | Ichiro Suzuki | 9 | Phil Hughes | John Jaso | 1 | 0 | ___ | 0-0 |
| 05/12/2013 | Phillies@Diamondbacks | Domonic Brown | 7 | Kyle Kendrick | Eric Chavez | 3 | 2 | ___ | 0-2 |
| 05/13/2013 | White Sox@Twins | Aaron Hicks | 8 | Josh Roenicke | Adam Dunn | 6 | 2 | __3 | 3-5 |
| 05/14/2013 | Padres@Orioles | Adam Jones | 8 | Chris Tillman | Carlos Quentin | 6 | 0 | ___ | 1-1 |
| 05/18/2013 | Dodgers@Braves | Matt Kemp | 8 | Chris Capuano | Jason Heyward | 1 | 1 | ___ | 0-0 |
| 05/22/2013 | Dodgers@Brewers | Ryan Braun | 7 | Burke Badenhop | Adrian Gonzalez | 6 | 0 | ___ | 7-0 |
| 05/26/2013 | Rangers@Mariners | David Murphy | 7 | Joe Nathan | Jason Bay | 11 | 2 | ___ | 3-3 |
| 05/27/2013 | Yankees@Mets | Brett Gardner | 8 | Phil Hughes | Daniel Murphy | 6 | 2 | 1__ | 1-0 |
| 05/28/2013 | Twins@Brewers | Aaron Hicks | 8 | Scott Diamond | Carlos Gomez | 2 | 0 | ___ | 2-0 |
| 05/31/2013 | Blue Jays@Padres | Colby Rasmus | 8 | Chad Jenkins | Yonder Alonso | 2 | 1 | ___ | 2-0 |
| 06/02/2013 | Dodgers@Rockies | Carlos Gonzalez | 7 | Jorge de la Rosa | Juan Uribe | 1 | 1 | ___ | 0-0 |
| 06/07/2013 | Athletics@White Sox | Josh Reddick | 9 | Grant Balfour | Conor Gillaspie | 9 | 1 | ___ | 4-3 |
| 06/08/2013 | Phillies@Brewers | Carlos Gomez | 8 | Tom Gorzelanny | John Mayberry | 2 | 0 | ___ | 1-0 |
| 06/08/2013 | Cardinals@Reds | Jay Bruce | 9 | Mat Latos | David Freese | 6 | 1 | ___ | 2-2 |
| 06/09/2013 | Padres@Rockies | Carlos Gonzalez | 7 | Juan Nicasio | Kyle Blanks | 5 | 0 | ___ | 0-4 |
| 06/11/2013 | Angels@Orioles | Peter Bourjos | 8 | Jason Vargas | J.J. Hardy | 1 | 1 | 1__ | 0-0 |
| 06/15/2013 | Dodgers@Pirates | Skip Schumaker | 7 | Clayton Kershaw | Russell Martin | 6 | 0 | 12_ | 3-1 |
| 06/20/2013 | Cubs@Cardinals | Ryan Sweeney | 8 | Scott Feldman | Matt Adams | 6 | 0 | _2_ | 1-3 |
| 06/29/2013 | Angels@Astros | Josh Hamilton | 9 | Joe Blanton | Matt Dominguez | 7 | 1 | ___ | 5-2 |
| 06/30/2013 | Brewers@Pirates | Logan Schafer | 7 | Tyler Thornburg | Gaby Sanchez | 7 | 1 | ___ | 1-0 |
| 07/05/2013 | Mets@Brewers | Carlos Gomez | 8 | Tyler Thornburg | Marlon Byrd | 7 | 0 | ___ | 8-3 |
| 07/08/2013 | Reds@Brewers | Carlos Gomez | 8 | Francisco Rodriguez | Joey Votto | 9 | 2 | 1__ | 3-4 |
| 07/09/2013 | Mets@Giants | Kensuke Tanaka | 7 | Barry Zito | Andrew Brown | 2 | 2 | ___ | 0-0 |
| 07/19/2013 | Orioles@Rangers | Nick Markakis | 9 | Wei-Yin Chen | Adrian Beltre | 4 | 0 | ___ | 2-0 |
| 07/21/2013 | Braves@White Sox | Casper Wells | 7 | Nate Jones | Reed Johnson | 8 | 1 | 1__ | 1-3 |
| 07/22/2013 | Reds@Giants | Derrick Robinson | 8 | Bronson Arroyo | Jeff Francoeur | 9 | 2 | ___ | 11-0 |
| 07/22/2013 | Twins@Angels | Clete Thomas | 7 | Glen Perkins | Chris Iannetta | 8 | 2 | 12_ | 4-3 |
| 07/28/2013 | Twins@Mariners | Endy Chavez | 9 | Erasmo Ramirez | Chris Colabello | 3 | 2 | 12_ | 2-0 |
| 07/29/2013 | Reds@Padres | Will Venable | 9 | Sean OSullivan' | Jay Bruce | 3 | 1 | ___ | 0-0 |
| 07/29/2013 | Rays@Red Sox | Shane Victorino | 9 | Drake Britton | Luke Scott | 7 | 0 | 1__ | 2-1 |
| 08/01/2013 | Royals@Twins | Lorenzo Cain | 8 | James Shields | Trevor Plouffe | 5 | 2 | 1__ | 5-2 |
| 08/02/2013 | Blue Jays@Angels | J.B. Shuck | 7 | Tommy Hanson | Jose Bautista | 4 | 0 | 1__ | 1-0 |
| 08/05/2013 | Tigers@Indians | Austin Jackson | 8 | Anibal Sanchez | Lonnie Chisenhall | 2 | 2 | 1__ | 0-1 |
| 08/06/2013 | Blue Jays@Mariners | Colby Rasmus | 8 | Juan Perez | Kendrys Morales | 6 | 1 | ___ | 6-0 |
| 08/14/2013 | Astros@Athletics | Robbie Grossman | 7 | Lucas Harrell | Chris Young | 10 | 2 | ___ | 1-1 |
| 08/16/2013 | Astros@Angels | Mike Trout | 7 | Jerome Williams | Brandon Barnes | 2 | 1 | ___ | 0-0 |
| 08/24/2013 | Angels@Mariners | Endy Chavez | 9 | Erasmo Ramirez | Hank Conger | 2 | 1 | ___ | 2-0 |
| 08/25/2013 | Diamondbacks@Phillies | Roger Bernadina | 8 | Roy Halladay | Matt Davidson | 3 | 2 | 1__ | 2-4 |
| 09/12/2013 | Yankees@Orioles | Alfonso Soriano | 7 | David Robertson | Manny Machado | 8 | 0 | ___ | 5-2 |
| 09/15/2013 | Reds@Brewers | Carlos Gomez | 8 | Jim Henderson | Jay Bruce | 9 | 2 | 12_ | 5-5 |

# 2013 No-Hitter Summary

We all know the excitement of no-hitters. When we hear one is happening, we immediately want to drop what we're doing to see how it turns out. The tension builds with each subsequent out. Routine groundballs become cause for celebration, and web gem-quality plays blow the roof off the building. Sometimes the fans of the opposing team even start pulling for it to happen.

Because no-hitters are always some of the most thrilling games of the season, this year we decided to add a section to the book that summarizes the most interesting aspects of all the previous season's no-no's. We provide the batting line for every batter that the triumphant pitcher faced, including a breakdown of the pitch types that each batter saw. And because every pitcher that throws a no-hitter usually owes some portion of his success to the defensive play of his teammates behind him, or even just to dumb luck, we also include a rundown of the most interesting plays of the game.

For reference when looking at the table of opposition batting lines, the data included are: Plate Appearances (PA), Pitches Seen (Pit), Strikes Swinging (Ss), Strikes Taken (St), Fouls (F), Balls (B), Balls put In Play (InP), Strikeouts (K), Total Walks (TBB), Hit By Pitches (HBP), Groundballs (GB), Line Drives (LD), Flyballs (FB), and the assortment of pitches in the pitcher's arsenal.

## Homer Bailey

San Francisco Giants at Cincinnati Reds
July 2, 2013

Homer Bailey threw the first no-hitter of this past season on July 2, 2013. He also threw the last no-hitter of the previous season on September 28, 2012. Exactly 38 years prior, Nolan Ryan threw his third career no-hitter on September 28, 1974, which he then followed up with his fourth career no-hitter on June 1, 1975. It took Bailey an extra month between efforts, but he is now the first pitcher to have thrown two no-hitters without someone else throwing one in between since Ryan accomplished the feat with those two aforementioned outings. Bailey is also now one of four active pitchers to have thrown more than one no-hitter. The other three are Mark Buehrle, Roy Halladay, and Justin Verlander.

Bailey faced only one batter over the minimum in this game. The only blemish on his otherwise perfect performance was a walk to Gregor Blanco to lead off the seventh inning.

### The Opposition

| Batter | PA | Pit | Ss | St | F | B | InP | K | TBB | HBP | GB | LD | FB | Fastball | Slider | Curve | Split |
|---|---|---|---|---|---|---|---|---|---|---|---|---|---|---|---|---|---|
| Blanco,Gregor | 4 | 18 | 1 | 2 | 6 | 7 | 2 | 1 | 1 | 0 | 1 | 1 | 0 | 15 | 1 | 0 | 2 |
| Scutaro,Marco | 3 | 9 | 0 | 1 | 2 | 3 | 3 | 0 | 0 | 0 | 1 | 0 | 2 | 8 | 1 | 0 | 0 |
| Posey,Buster | 3 | 15 | 1 | 5 | 1 | 5 | 3 | 0 | 0 | 0 | 2 | 0 | 1 | 14 | 0 | 0 | 1 |
| Sandoval,Pablo | 3 | 15 | 3 | 1 | 5 | 4 | 2 | 1 | 0 | 0 | 1 | 0 | 1 | 12 | 3 | 0 | 0 |
| Pence,Hunter | 3 | 11 | 3 | 1 | 1 | 4 | 2 | 1 | 0 | 0 | 1 | 0 | 1 | 4 | 7 | 0 | 0 |
| Belt,Brandon | 3 | 5 | 1 | 1 | 1 | 0 | 2 | 1 | 0 | 0 | 0 | 0 | 2 | 1 | 4 | 0 | 0 |
| Torres,Andres | 3 | 7 | 1 | 2 | 0 | 2 | 2 | 1 | 0 | 0 | 0 | 0 | 2 | 7 | 0 | 0 | 0 |
| Crawford,Brandon | 3 | 14 | 1 | 2 | 4 | 5 | 2 | 1 | 0 | 0 | 2 | 0 | 0 | 11 | 1 | 1 | 1 |
| Lincecum,Tim | 2 | 9 | 4 | 2 | 0 | 3 | 0 | 2 | 0 | 0 | 0 | 0 | 0 | 7 | 2 | 0 | 0 |
| Abreu,Tony | 1 | 6 | 1 | 0 | 3 | 2 | 0 | 1 | 0 | 0 | 0 | 0 | 0 | 5 | 1 | 0 | 0 |
| Totals | 28 | 109 | 16 | 17 | 23 | 35 | 18 | 9 | 1 | 0 | 8 | 1 | 9 | 84 | 20 | 1 | 4 |

## Notable Plays:

*Top of the 7th Inning, Buster Posey batting, Gregor Blanco on 2B, 1 Out*

On an 0-2 pitch, Buster Posey hit a soft line drive that Joey Votto fielded on one hop to his right. This should have resulted in an easy out at first base, except that Bailey hesitated in getting over to cover the bag. Blanco froze at second base as he waited to see if Votto would catch the ball. Once he saw the ball drop, he decided to try to advance to third base. When Votto saw Blanco take off, and knowing that Bailey had gotten a late break covering first, he made the crucial decision to forgo the play at first and instead throw to third base. Blanco was easily tagged out, resulting in the play being scored as a fielder's choice and the no-hitter remaining intact. However, Bailey's late break gave Posey a good shot at beating him to the base, and the no-hitter very easily could have ended on this play. If Blanco had not tried to advance to third, or if Votto had not alertly reacted to the play as it developed, the no-hitter may have been over then and there.

## Tim Lincecum

San Francisco Giants at San Diego Padres
July 13, 2013

There were two no-hitters thrown during the month of July in 2013, and Tim Lincecum pitched in both of them. In addition to defeating the San Diego Padres with a hitless performance on July 13, 2013, he was also the losing pitcher 11 days earlier when Homer Bailey did the same to the San Francisco Giants.

Lincecum really had to work for this no-hitter. His 148 pitches is the second-most ever thrown in a no-hitter since pitch counts have officially been recorded, one less than Edwin Jackson's 149 pitches on June 25, 2010. In addition to the 61 fastballs, 45 changeups, 21 sliders, and 20 curveballs that he threw, Lincecum's 148 pitches also included one pitchout.

### The Opposition

| Batter | PA | Pit | Ss | St | F | B | InP | K | TBB | HBP | GB | LD | FB | Fastball | Slider | Curve | Changeup |
|---|---|---|---|---|---|---|---|---|---|---|---|---|---|---|---|---|---|
| Cabrera,Everth | 4 | 25 | 1 | 6 | 6 | 11 | 1 | 1 | 2 | 0 | 1 | 0 | 0 | 11 | 1 | 4 | 9 |
| Amarista,Alexi | 4 | 22 | 4 | 4 | 4 | 8 | 2 | 2 | 0 | 0 | 0 | 1 | 1 | 12 | 3 | 0 | 7 |
| Headley,Chase | 4 | 19 | 3 | 3 | 2 | 11 | 0 | 2 | 2 | 0 | 0 | 0 | 0 | 8 | 2 | 3 | 6 |
| Quentin,Carlos | 4 | 16 | 1 | 2 | 5 | 4 | 4 | 0 | 0 | 0 | 1 | 1 | 2 | 3 | 2 | 3 | 7 |
| Alonso,Yonder | 4 | 25 | 6 | 1 | 7 | 9 | 2 | 2 | 0 | 0 | 0 | 0 | 2 | 9 | 6 | 3 | 7 |
| Gyorko,Jedd | 3 | 11 | 4 | 1 | 2 | 3 | 1 | 1 | 0 | 1 | 0 | 0 | 1 | 5 | 1 | 1 | 4 |
| Venable,Will | 2 | 7 | 3 | 1 | 1 | 1 | 1 | 1 | 0 | 0 | 1 | 0 | 0 | 2 | 1 | 2 | 2 |
| Guzman,Jesus | 1 | 3 | 0 | 0 | 0 | 2 | 1 | 0 | 0 | 0 | 1 | 0 | 0 | 1 | 1 | 0 | 1 |
| Rivera,Rene | 3 | 11 | 3 | 2 | 3 | 2 | 1 | 2 | 0 | 0 | 1 | 0 | 0 | 6 | 3 | 0 | 2 |
| Volquez,Edinson | 1 | 3 | 1 | 2 | 0 | 0 | 0 | 1 | 0 | 0 | 0 | 0 | 0 | 1 | 0 | 2 | 0 |
| Forsythe,Logan | 1 | 4 | 1 | 1 | 2 | 0 | 0 | 1 | 0 | 0 | 0 | 0 | 0 | 2 | 1 | 1 | 0 |
| Denorfia,Chris | 1 | 2 | 0 | 0 | 0 | 1 | 1 | 0 | 0 | 0 | 1 | 0 | 0 | 1 | 0 | 1 | 0 |
| Totals | 32 | 148 | 27 | 23 | 32 | 52 | 14 | 13 | 4 | 1 | 6 | 2 | 6 | 61 | 21 | 20 | 45 |

### Notable Plays:

*Bottom of the 6th Inning, Carlos Quentin batting, Everth Cabrera on 3B, Chase Headley on 1B, 2 Outs*

After a strikeout, a walk, a stolen base, another strikeout, a wild pitch, and another walk, Lincecum had runners on first and third with two out. On his 25th pitch of the inning, Quentin hit a screaming line drive directly at shortstop Brandon Crawford, who caught the ball to preserve not only the no-hitter, but the shutout as well.

*Bottom of the 7th Inning, Jesus Guzman batting, No runners on base, 2 Outs*

Guzman hit a chopper down the third base line that forced Pablo Sandoval to go back and to his right to make a backhanded stop and strong throw, getting Guzman by a step at first.

*Bottom of the 8th Inning, Alexi Amarista batting, Everth Cabrera on 1B, 2 Outs*

On the sixth pitch of the at-bat, Amarista hit a hard sinking line drive to right field. Pence came sprinting in and to his left, and made a half-diving, half-sliding catch that kept the no-hitter intact and provided the most dramatic moment of the game.

## Henderson Alvarez

Detroit Tigers at Miami Marlins
September 29, 2013

On the final day of the regular season (not including the American League Wild Card tie-breaker game between the Tampa Bay Rays and Texas Rangers), Henderson Alvarez threw the third no-hitter of the 2013 season. He got it done against the AL Central Division champion Detroit Tigers, a team that was resting several of its regulars in preparation for the play-offs, including the league's batting champ, Miguel Cabrera.

The perfect game ended early when Alvarez hit Prince Fielder, the third batter of the game, with a pitch. However, after that Alvarez allowed only two more base runners and got through the game throwing only 99 pitches.

### The Opposition

| Batter | PA | Pit | Ss | St | F | B | InP | K | TBB | HBP | GB | LD | FB | Fastball | Slider | Curve | Changeup |
|---|---|---|---|---|---|---|---|---|---|---|---|---|---|---|---|---|---|
| Kelly,Don | 4 | 14 | 0 | 2 | 2 | 6 | 4 | 0 | 0 | 0 | 3 | 0 | 1 | 11 | 0 | 1 | 2 |
| Dirks,Andy | 4 | 13 | 0 | 3 | 0 | 7 | 3 | 0 | 1 | 0 | 3 | 0 | 0 | 9 | 1 | 0 | 3 |
| Fielder,Prince | 2 | 2 | 0 | 0 | 0 | 1 | 1 | 0 | 0 | 1 | 1 | 0 | 0 | 1 | 0 | 1 | 0 |
| Tuiasosopo,Matt | 2 | 10 | 3 | 2 | 1 | 4 | 0 | 2 | 0 | 0 | 0 | 0 | 0 | 7 | 3 | 0 | 0 |
| Peralta,Jhonny | 3 | 11 | 1 | 2 | 1 | 4 | 3 | 0 | 0 | 0 | 0 | 0 | 3 | 7 | 4 | 0 | 0 |
| Infante,Omar | 2 | 8 | 0 | 1 | 5 | 0 | 2 | 0 | 0 | 0 | 0 | 1 | 1 | 3 | 3 | 0 | 2 |
| Perez,Hernan | 1 | 4 | 0 | 1 | 1 | 1 | 1 | 0 | 0 | 0 | 0 | 0 | 1 | 1 | 3 | 0 | 0 |
| Pena,Brayan | 3 | 8 | 0 | 0 | 1 | 4 | 3 | 0 | 0 | 0 | 2 | 1 | 0 | 6 | 0 | 1 | 1 |
| Iglesias,Jose | 2 | 5 | 1 | 1 | 1 | 0 | 2 | 0 | 0 | 0 | 1 | 1 | 0 | 4 | 1 | 0 | 0 |
| Castellanos,Nick | 1 | 2 | 0 | 1 | 0 | 0 | 1 | 0 | 0 | 0 | 1 | 0 | 0 | 0 | 2 | 0 | 0 |
| Santiago,Ramon | 3 | 13 | 0 | 5 | 2 | 4 | 2 | 1 | 0 | 0 | 1 | 1 | 0 | 9 | 2 | 0 | 2 |
| Verlander,Justin | 2 | 7 | 1 | 2 | 1 | 2 | 1 | 1 | 0 | 0 | 1 | 0 | 0 | 4 | 3 | 0 | 0 |
| Avila,Alex | 1 | 2 | 0 | 1 | 0 | 0 | 1 | 0 | 0 | 0 | 1 | 0 | 0 | 2 | 0 | 0 | 0 |
| Totals | 30 | 99 | 6 | 21 | 15 | 33 | 24 | 4 | 1 | 1 | 14 | 4 | 6 | 64 | 22 | 3 | 10 |

## Notable Plays:

*Top of the 3rd Inning, Ramon Santiago batting, No runners on base, No Outs*

On a 1-2 pitch, Santiago hit a hard line drive that was headed for left-center field. However, it was hit in the direction of shortstop Adeiny Hechavarria, who made an outstanding leaping catch to record the out.

*Top of the 6th Inning, Justin Verlander batting, No runners on base, No Outs*

Verlander hit an 0-2 pitch deep into the right field corner that Giancarlo Stanton could not quite get to. Fortunately for Alvarez, the ball landed just foul. Two pitches later Alvarez struck Verlander out.

*Top of the 9th Inning, Don Kelly batting, No runners on base, 1 Out*

Kelly hit a hard chopper back up the middle, forcing Alvarez to react quickly to jump, make the play above his head, and throw to first base. It was the second groundball Alvarez fielded in the inning, and the sixth putout or assist that he made in the game.

*Bottom of the 9th Inning, Greg Dobbs batting, Bases Loaded, 2 Outs*

On the first pitch of the at-bat to Dobbs, Tigers pitcher Luke Putkonen threw a wild pitch. Stanton was able to score from third base, winning the game for the Marlins, and securing the no-hitter for Alvarez. Despite not allowing a hit for nine innings, if the Marlins had not scored in that inning, Alvarez would not have been credited with a no-hitter. He would have had to go out to pitch the 10th inning (and possibly beyond) to try to preserve his chance at history.

# Win Shares

Bill James devised Win Shares as a way to relate a player's individual statistics to the number of wins he contributed to his team. As a single number, Win Shares allows us to easily compare the accomplishments of each player to other players and to compare players across positions.

We credit a team with three Win Shares for each win. If a team wins 100 games, the players on the team will be credited with 300 Win Shares—or 300 thirds of a win. If a team wins 70 games, the players on the team will be credited with 210 Win Shares, and so on.

The following pages contain the sum of a player's Win Shares prior to 2003, followed by his individual season totals from 2003 through 2013. Career totals are also included for each player.

The quality of the team does not affect an individual player's Win Shares. A great player on a bad team will rate just as well as a great player on a good team.

Win Shares are also a great tool for evaluating award voting and Hall of Fame credentials. Generally, 30 or more Win Shares indicates an MVP-caliber season; 20 Win Shares indicates a season worthy of the Cy Young Award.

For example, Mike Trout (league-leading 40 Win Shares) topped Miguel Cabrera (37 Win Shares) for the second straight season despite the fact that the postseason-bound Tigers won 15 more games than the Angels. There's one area where Trout can't touch Cabrera, however: longevity. Miguel Cabrera's streak of 10-straight 19+ Win Share seasons is unparalleled among active players.

Over in the National League, Fielding Bible Award winner Paul Goldschmidt (36 Win Shares) edged a competitive field including Matt Carpenter (35), Freddie Freeman (35), and last year's Win Shares leader Andrew McCutchen (34 in 2013). Except for Goldschmidt of the 81-81 Diamondbacks, each of these NL leaders tasted the playoffs.

| | WIN SHARES BY YEAR | | | | | | | | | | | |
|---|---|---|---|---|---|---|---|---|---|---|---|---|
| Player | <04 | 04 | 05 | 06 | 07 | 08 | 09 | 10 | 11 | 12 | 13 | Career |
| Aardsma,David | | 0 | | 4 | 1 | 1 | 16 | 8 | | 0 | 1 | 31 |
| Abad,Fernando | | | | | | | | 2 | 0 | 0 | 2 | 4 |
| Abreu,Tony | | | | | 4 | | 1 | 1 | | 3 | 3 | 12 |
| Aceves,Alfredo | | | | | | 3 | 7 | 2 | 12 | 6 | 1 | 31 |
| Ackley,Dustin | | | | | | | | | 14 | 16 | 11 | 41 |
| Adams,David | | | | | | | | | | | 2 | 2 |
| Adams,Matt | | | | | | | | | | 1 | 12 | 13 |
| Adams,Mike | | 5 | 1 | 0 | | 6 | 5 | 10 | 12 | 6 | 1 | 46 |
| Affeldt,Jeremy | 17 | 4 | 1 | 3 | 5 | 6 | 10 | 3 | 6 | 5 | 1 | 61 |
| Albers,Andrew | | | | | | | | | | | 2 | 2 |
| Albers,Matt | | | | 0 | 0 | 4 | 2 | 5 | 3 | 6 | 5 | 25 |
| Alburquerque,Al | | | | | | | | | 6 | 2 | 3 | 11 |
| Allen,Cody | | | | | | | | | | 1 | 8 | 9 |
| Almonte,Abraham | | | | | | | | | | | 2 | 2 |
| Almonte,Zoilo | | | | | | | | | | | 1 | 1 |
| Alonso,Yonder | | | | | | | | 0 | 4 | 17 | 12 | 33 |
| Altuve,Jose | | | | | | | | | 2 | 17 | 11 | 30 |
| Alvarez,Henderson | | | | | | | | | 4 | 5 | 7 | 16 |
| Alvarez,Pedro | | | | | | | | 14 | 3 | 22 | 18 | 57 |
| Amarista,Alexi | | | | | | | | | 1 | 6 | 10 | 17 |
| Ambriz,Hector | | | | | | | | 0 | | 1 | 0 | 1 |
| Anderson,Brett | | | | | | | 8 | 9 | 4 | 3 | 0 | 24 |
| Anderson,Bryan | | | | | | | | 1 | | 1 | 0 | 2 |
| Andino,Robert | | | 0 | 0 | 0 | 1 | 3 | 0 | 11 | 4 | 1 | 20 |
| Andrus,Elvis | | | | | | | 17 | 20 | 18 | 23 | 15 | 93 |
| Ankiel,Rick | 17 | 0 | | | 8 | 13 | 5 | 4 | 7 | 3 | 3 | 60 |
| Aoki,Norichika | | | | | | | | | | 15 | 17 | 32 |
| Archer,Chris | | | | | | | | | | 0 | 10 | 10 |
| Arcia,Oswaldo | | | | | | | | | | | 6 | 6 |
| Arenado,Nolan | | | | | | | | | | | 9 | 9 |
| Arencibia,J.P. | | | | | | | | 1 | 14 | 12 | 3 | 30 |
| Arias,Joaquin | | | | 1 | | 3 | 0 | 1 | | 9 | 4 | 18 |
| Arrieta,Jake | | | | | | | | 5 | 5 | 0 | 3 | 13 |
| Arroyo,Bronson | 7 | 11 | 11 | 20 | 11 | 10 | 13 | 14 | 3 | 13 | 9 | 122 |
| Asche,Cody | | | | | | | | | | | 4 | 4 |
| Asencio,Jairo | | | | | | | 0 | | 0 | 1 | 0 | 1 |
| Atchison,Scott | | 2 | 0 | | 2 | | | 2 | 2 | 6 | 1 | 15 |
| Aumont,Phillippe | | | | | | | | | | 2 | 1 | 3 |
| Avila,Alex | | | | | | | 3 | 7 | 27 | 15 | 6 | 58 |
| Avilan,Luis | | | | | | | | | | 4 | 10 | 14 |
| Aviles,Mike | | | | | | 17 | 2 | 10 | 5 | 10 | 8 | 52 |
| Axelrod,Dylan | | | | | | | | | 2 | 1 | 0 | 3 |
| Axford,John | | | | | | | 1 | 11 | 15 | 7 | 3 | 37 |
| Ayala,Luis | 11 | 10 | 8 | | 4 | 2 | 2 | | 5 | 8 | 2 | 52 |
| Aybar,Erick | | | | 1 | 2 | 15 | 20 | 9 | 20 | 16 | 14 | 97 |
| Badenhop,Burke | | | | | | 0 | 5 | 4 | 3 | 4 | 3 | 19 |
| Bailey,Andrew | | | | | | | 17 | 11 | 6 | 0 | 3 | 37 |
| Bailey,Homer | | | | | 2 | 0 | 5 | 5 | 5 | 12 | 11 | 40 |
| Baker,Jeff | | | 1 | 3 | 1 | 7 | 7 | 4 | 3 | 3 | 6 | 35 |
| Baker,John | | | | | | 9 | 13 | 1 | 0 | 4 | 1 | 28 |
| Baker,Scott | | | 4 | 0 | 8 | 13 | 12 | 8 | 11 | | 1 | 57 |
| Balfour,Grant | 2 | 3 | | | 0 | 11 | 5 | 6 | 8 | 15 | 10 | 60 |
| Bard,Daniel | | | | | | | 4 | 11 | 7 | 1 | 0 | 23 |
| Barmes,Clint | 1 | 3 | 9 | 6 | 0 | 12 | 13 | 10 | 10 | 10 | 2 | 76 |
| Barnes,Brandon | | | | | | | | | | 1 | 8 | 9 |
| Barnes,Scott | | | | | | | | | | 1 | 0 | 1 |
| Barney,Darwin | | | | | | | | 1 | 14 | 15 | 5 | 35 |
| Barton,Daric | | | | | 3 | 9 | 6 | 21 | 4 | 3 | 5 | 51 |
| Bass,Anthony | | | | | | | | | 5 | 1 | 0 | 6 |
| Bastardo,Antonio | | | | | | | 0 | 1 | 10 | 3 | 6 | 20 |
| Bautista,Jose | | 0 | 0 | 9 | 12 | 8 | 6 | 34 | 36 | 13 | 18 | 136 |
| Baxter,Mike | | | | | | | | 0 | 1 | 7 | 2 | 10 |
| Bay,Jason | 5 | 15 | 30 | 21 | 12 | 24 | 29 | 11 | 10 | 1 | 2 | 160 |
| Beachy,Brandon | | | | | | | | 0 | 7 | 9 | 1 | 17 |
| Beato,Pedro | | | | | | | | | 2 | 1 | 1 | 4 |
| Beavan,Blake | | | | | | | | | 5 | 5 | 0 | 10 |
| Beckett,Josh | 19 | 9 | 12 | 11 | 18 | 11 | 16 | 2 | 16 | 7 | 0 | 121 |
| Beckham,Gordon | | | | | | | 12 | 11 | 14 | 13 | 7 | 57 |
| Bedard,Erik | 0 | 6 | 8 | 13 | 17 | 6 | 8 | | 6 | 0 | 5 | 69 |
| Belisario,Ronald | | | | | | | 7 | 3 | | 9 | 3 | 22 |
| Belisle,Matt | 0 | | 4 | 3 | 5 | 0 | 1 | 11 | 7 | 8 | 5 | 44 |
| Beliveau,Jeff | | | | | | | | | | 1 | 0 | 1 |
| Bell,Heath | | 2 | 0 | 1 | 13 | 6 | 12 | 15 | 11 | 4 | 5 | 69 |

| | WIN SHARES BY YEAR | | | | | | | | | | | |
|---|---|---|---|---|---|---|---|---|---|---|---|---|
| Player | <04 | 04 | 05 | 06 | 07 | 08 | 09 | 10 | 11 | 12 | 13 | Career |
| Below,Duane | | | | | | | | | 1 | 2 | 0 | 3 |
| Belt,Brandon | | | | | | | | | 5 | 17 | 24 | 46 |
| Beltran,Carlos | 100 | 29 | 21 | 34 | 25 | 29 | 14 | 8 | 26 | 18 | 22 | 326 |
| Beltre,Adrian | 82 | 33 | 13 | 17 | 16 | 13 | 10 | 26 | 16 | 25 | 22 | 273 |
| Benoit,Joaquin | 8 | 4 | 6 | 4 | 10 | 2 | | 9 | 8 | 7 | 14 | 72 |
| Berkman,Lance | 97 | 30 | 20 | 31 | 24 | 36 | 22 | 14 | 30 | 2 | 7 | 313 |
| Bernadina,Roger | | | | | | 1 | 0 | 10 | 7 | 10 | 2 | 30 |
| Bernier,Doug | | | | | | 0 | | | | | 2 | 2 |
| Berry,Quintin | | | | | | | | | | 9 | 1 | 10 |
| Betancourt,Rafael | 4 | 5 | 7 | 5 | 16 | 3 | 8 | 8 | 10 | 11 | 4 | 81 |
| Betancourt,Yuniesky | | | 3 | 13 | 19 | 8 | 8 | 12 | 11 | 2 | 3 | 79 |
| Betemit,Wilson | 0 | 1 | 7 | 9 | 8 | 2 | 0 | 12 | 11 | 7 | 0 | 57 |
| Bianchi,Jeff | | | | | | | | | | 1 | 5 | 6 |
| Billingsley,Chad | | | | 6 | 12 | 16 | 9 | 11 | 6 | 8 | 1 | 69 |
| Black,Vic | | | | | | | | | | | 2 | 2 |
| Blackley,Travis | | 0 | | | 0 | | | | | 5 | 2 | 7 |
| Blackmon,Charlie | | | | | | | | | 1 | 1 | 7 | 9 |
| Blanco,Gregor | | | | | | 11 | 0 | 6 | | 12 | 13 | 42 |
| Blanco,Henry | 27 | 5 | 5 | 6 | 0 | 3 | 6 | 3 | 4 | 1 | 1 | 61 |
| Blanks,Kyle | | | | | | | 5 | 2 | 3 | 0 | 10 | 20 |
| Blanton,Joe | | 0 | 13 | 10 | 13 | 7 | 11 | 4 | 1 | 5 | 0 | 64 |
| Blevins,Jerry | | | | | 0 | 3 | 1 | 3 | 2 | 7 | 5 | 21 |
| Bloomquist,Willie | 6 | 2 | 4 | 5 | 2 | 5 | 7 | 3 | 8 | 9 | 5 | 56 |
| Boesch,Brennan | | | | | | | | 11 | 12 | 6 | 2 | 31 |
| Bogaerts,Xander | | | | | | | | | | | 1 | 1 |
| Boggs,Mitchell | | | | | | 0 | 2 | 4 | 3 | 9 | 1 | 19 |
| Bogusevic,Brian | | | | | | | | 0 | 4 | 4 | 4 | 12 |
| Bonderman,Jeremy | 2 | 8 | 9 | 13 | 7 | 4 | 0 | 3 | | | 1 | 47 |
| Bonifacio,Emilio | | | | | 1 | 2 | 7 | 5 | 20 | 6 | 7 | 48 |
| Bootcheck,Chris | 0 | | 1 | 0 | 4 | 0 | 0 | | | | 0 | 5 |
| Borbon,Julio | | | | | | 0 | 5 | 11 | 3 | | 1 | 20 |
| Boshers,Buddy | | | | | | | | | | | 1 | 1 |
| Bourgeois,Jason | | | | | | 0 | 0 | 0 | 6 | 1 | 0 | 7 |
| Bourjos,Peter | | | | | | | | 3 | 16 | 5 | 4 | 28 |
| Bourn,Michael | | | | 0 | 4 | 7 | 23 | 18 | 22 | 28 | 14 | 116 |
| Bowden,Michael | | | | | | 1 | 0 | 0 | 1 | 3 | 1 | 6 |
| Boxberger,Brad | | | | | | | | | | 2 | 1 | 3 |
| Brach,Brad | | | | | | | | | 0 | 3 | 1 | 4 |
| Bradley Jr.,Jackie | | | | | | | | | | | 1 | 1 |
| Brantley,Michael | | | | | | | 3 | 5 | 11 | 18 | 21 | 58 |
| Brantly,Rob | | | | | | | | | | 3 | 2 | 5 |
| Brasier,Ryan | | | | | | | | | | | 1 | 1 |
| Braun,Ryan | | | | | 22 | 23 | 36 | 25 | 37 | 28 | 9 | 180 |
| Breslow,Craig | | | 1 | 1 | | 6 | 6 | 8 | 3 | 6 | 7 | 38 |
| Brignac,Reid | | | | | | 0 | 2 | 10 | 4 | 1 | 2 | 19 |
| Britton,Drake | | | | | | | | | | | 1 | 1 |
| Britton,Zach | | | | | | | | | 6 | 3 | 1 | 10 |
| Brothers,Rex | | | | | | | | | 4 | 7 | 13 | 24 |
| Brown,Andrew | | | | | | | | | 0 | 1 | 4 | 5 |
| Brown,Corey | | | | | | | | | 0 | 0 | 1 | 1 |
| Brown,Domonic | | | | | | | | 0 | 4 | 5 | 19 | 28 |
| Broxton,Jonathan | | | 0 | 9 | 10 | 10 | 16 | 6 | 0 | 11 | 1 | 63 |
| Bruce,Jay | | | | | | 7 | 9 | 16 | 22 | 18 | 21 | 93 |
| Buchholz,Clay | | | | | 3 | 0 | 6 | 18 | 6 | 9 | 12 | 54 |
| Buck,John | | 4 | 10 | 8 | 7 | 8 | 6 | 17 | 14 | 9 | 12 | 95 |
| Buckner,Billy | | | | | 1 | 1 | 1 | 0 | | | 1 | 4 |
| Buehrle,Mark | 52 | 17 | 22 | 9 | 17 | 16 | 16 | 12 | 15 | 12 | 10 | 198 |
| Bueno,Francisley | | | | | | 0 | | | | 2 | 2 | 4 |
| Bumgarner,Madison | | | | | | | 1 | 8 | 12 | 11 | 12 | 44 |
| Burke,Greg | | | | | | | 2 | | | | 0 | 2 |
| Burnett,A.J. | 31 | 7 | 11 | 9 | 11 | 14 | 12 | 4 | 5 | 11 | 9 | 124 |
| Burnett,Alex | | | | | | | | 1 | 1 | 5 | 0 | 7 |
| Burnett,Sean | | 2 | | | | 2 | 5 | 7 | 5 | 7 | 1 | 29 |
| Burns,Cory | | | | | | | | | | 0 | 1 | 1 |
| Burton,Jared | | | | | 5 | 6 | 3 | 1 | 0 | 8 | 5 | 28 |
| Bush,Dave | | 7 | 6 | 12 | 6 | 8 | 0 | 4 | 0 | | 0 | 43 |
| Butera,Drew | | | | | | | | 3 | 3 | 1 | 0 | 7 |
| Butler,Billy | | | | | 7 | 8 | 18 | 20 | 17 | 21 | 16 | 107 |
| Butler,Keith | | | | | | | | | | | 1 | 1 |
| Byrd,Marlon | 16 | 5 | 6 | 2 | 13 | 12 | 20 | 19 | 8 | 1 | 23 | 125 |
| Byrdak,Tim | 0 | | 1 | 0 | 4 | 4 | 5 | 3 | 2 | 2 | 0 | 21 |
| Cabrera,Asdrubal | | | | | 7 | 12 | 18 | 9 | 25 | 19 | 12 | 102 |
| Cabrera,Everth | | | | | | | 14 | 3 | 0 | 11 | 19 | 47 |

| Player | WIN SHARES BY YEAR <04 | 04 | 05 | 06 | 07 | 08 | 09 | 10 | 11 | 12 | 13 | Career |
|---|---|---|---|---|---|---|---|---|---|---|---|---|
| Cabrera,Melky | | | 0 | 13 | 12 | 5 | 14 | 8 | 19 | 25 | 7 | 103 |
| Cabrera,Miguel | 12 | 19 | 27 | 33 | 29 | 20 | 25 | 30 | 38 | 32 | 37 | 302 |
| Cahill,Trevor | | | | | | | 7 | 16 | 9 | 11 | 6 | 49 |
| Cain,Lorenzo | | | | | | | | 6 | 0 | 7 | 12 | 25 |
| Cain,Matt | | | 5 | 11 | 12 | 14 | 20 | 15 | 15 | 16 | 5 | 113 |
| Calhoun,Kole | | | | | | | | | | 0 | 8 | 8 |
| Callaspo,Alberto | | | | 1 | 1 | 6 | 17 | 11 | 17 | 15 | 13 | 81 |
| Caminero,Arquimedes | | | | | | | | | | | 1 | 1 |
| Camp,Shawn | | 4 | 0 | 5 | 0 | 3 | 5 | 7 | 4 | 6 | 0 | 34 |
| Campana,Tony | | | | | | | | | 3 | 4 | 1 | 8 |
| Cano,Robinson | | | 12 | 17 | 21 | 12 | 18 | 34 | 30 | 34 | 35 | 213 |
| Capps,Carter | | | | | | | | | | 1 | 1 | 2 |
| Capuano,Chris | 2 | 4 | 13 | 14 | 5 | | | 3 | 5 | 9 | 2 | 57 |
| Carp,Mike | | | | | | | 2 | 0 | 7 | 2 | 9 | 20 |
| Carpenter,David | | | | | | | | | | 1 | 0 | 1 |
| Carpenter,David | | | | | | | | | 2 | 0 | 8 | 10 |
| Carpenter,Matt | | | | | | | | | 0 | 9 | 35 | 44 |
| Carrasco,Carlos | | | | | | | 0 | 3 | 5 | | 0 | 8 |
| Carrera,Ezequiel | | | | | | | | | 5 | 4 | 0 | 9 |
| Carroll,Jamey | 6 | 6 | 9 | 13 | 5 | 10 | 8 | 14 | 14 | 13 | 3 | 101 |
| Carson,Matt | | | | | | | 1 | 1 | | 0 | 2 | 4 |
| Carter,Chris | | | | | | | | 0 | 0 | 8 | 13 | 21 |
| Cashner,Andrew | | | | | | | | 2 | 1 | 2 | 10 | 15 |
| Casilla,Alexi | | | | 0 | 1 | 9 | 4 | 6 | 7 | 5 | 2 | 34 |
| Casilla,Santiago | | 0 | 0 | 0 | 4 | 3 | 0 | 8 | 8 | 9 | 6 | 38 |
| Castillo,Welington | | | | | | | | 1 | 0 | 4 | 10 | 15 |
| Castro,Jason | | | | | | | | 4 | | 8 | 18 | 30 |
| Castro,Starlin | | | | | | | | 12 | 25 | 23 | 7 | 67 |
| Cecil,Brett | | | | | | | 3 | 10 | 4 | 1 | 6 | 24 |
| Cedeno,Ronny | | | 2 | 5 | 1 | 5 | 7 | 9 | 10 | 4 | 5 | 48 |
| Cedeno,Xavier | | | | | | | | | 0 | 2 | 1 | 3 |
| Cervelli,Francisco | | | | | | 0 | 3 | 7 | 4 | 0 | 3 | 17 |
| Cespedes,Yoenis | | | | | | | | | | 24 | 14 | 38 |
| Chacin,Jhoulys | | | | | | | 0 | 10 | 12 | 4 | 15 | 41 |
| Chamberlain,Joba | | | | | 5 | 11 | 6 | 5 | 3 | 1 | 2 | 33 |
| Chambers,Adron | | | | | | | | | 1 | 1 | 0 | 2 |
| Chapman,Aroldis | | | | | | | | 2 | 4 | 21 | 12 | 39 |
| Chapman,Kevin | | | | | | | | | | | 2 | 2 |
| Chatwood,Tyler | | | | | | | | | 3 | 3 | 11 | 17 |
| Chavez,Endy | 12 | 10 | 1 | 13 | 4 | 3 | 3 | | 6 | 1 | 2 | 55 |
| Chavez,Eric | 100 | 18 | 20 | 16 | 6 | 3 | 0 | 0 | 6 | 8 | 9 | 186 |
| Chavez,Jesse | | | | | | 0 | 4 | 0 | 0 | 0 | 3 | 7 |
| Chen,Bruce | 18 | 4 | 13 | 0 | 0 | | 1 | 9 | 9 | 6 | 10 | 70 |
| Chen,Wei-Yin | | | | | | | | | | 12 | 7 | 19 |
| Chirinos,Robinson | | | | | | | | | 1 | | 0 | 1 |
| Chisenhall,Lonnie | | | | | | | | | 6 | 4 | 7 | 17 |
| Choate,Randy | 5 | 3 | 0 | 1 | 0 | | 5 | 2 | 4 | 4 | 4 | 28 |
| Choice,Michael | | | | | | | | | | | 1 | 1 |
| Choo,Shin-Soo | | | 0 | 4 | 1 | 16 | 23 | 27 | 8 | 25 | 31 | 135 |
| Cingrani,Tony | | | | | | | | | | 1 | 8 | 9 |
| Ciriaco,Pedro | | | | | | | | 1 | 2 | 6 | 3 | 12 |
| Cishek,Steve | | | | | | | | 1 | 6 | 10 | 14 | 31 |
| Cisnero,Jose | | | | | | | | | | | 2 | 2 |
| Claiborne,Preston | | | | | | | | | | | 3 | 3 |
| Clark,Cody | | | | | | | | | | | 1 | 1 |
| Clemens,Paul | | | | | | | | | | | 1 | 1 |
| Clevenger,Steve | | | | | | | | | 0 | 1 | 0 | 1 |
| Clippard,Tyler | | | | | 1 | 1 | 5 | 9 | 13 | 11 | 10 | 50 |
| Cloyd,Tyler | | | | | | | | | | 1 | 0 | 1 |
| Cobb,Alex | | | | | | | | | 3 | 6 | 13 | 22 |
| Coello,Robert | | | | | | | | 0 | | 0 | 1 | 1 |
| Coghlan,Chris | | | | | | | 21 | 8 | 4 | 1 | 5 | 39 |
| Coke,Phil | | | | | | 3 | 5 | 6 | 4 | 3 | 0 | 21 |
| Colabello,Chris | | | | | | | | | | | 1 | 1 |
| Cole,Gerrit | | | | | | | | | | | 8 | 8 |
| Coleman,Louis | | | | | | | | | 5 | 3 | 5 | 13 |
| Collins,Tim | | | | | | | | | 4 | 6 | 4 | 14 |
| Collmenter,Josh | | | | | | | | | 10 | 5 | 7 | 22 |
| Colome,Alex | | | | | | | | | | | 1 | 1 |
| Colon,Bartolo | 102 | 10 | 18 | 1 | 1 | 2 | 3 | | 8 | 9 | 17 | 171 |
| Colvin,Tyler | | | | | | | 0 | 9 | 1 | 13 | 1 | 24 |
| Conger,Hank | | | | | | | | 1 | 4 | 0 | 5 | 10 |

| Player | WIN SHARES BY YEAR <04 | 04 | 05 | 06 | 07 | 08 | 09 | 10 | 11 | 12 | 13 | Career |
|---|---|---|---|---|---|---|---|---|---|---|---|---|
| Constanza,Jose | | | | | | | | | 3 | 2 | 0 | 5 |
| Contreras,Jose | 7 | 6 | 17 | 13 | 5 | 7 | 4 | 6 | 2 | 0 | 0 | 67 |
| Cook,Ryan | | | | | | | | | 0 | 14 | 7 | 21 |
| Corbin,Patrick | | | | | | | | | | 4 | 13 | 17 |
| Corpas,Manny | | | | 3 | 15 | 6 | 1 | 5 | | 1 | 2 | 33 |
| Corporan,Carlos | | | | | | | 0 | | 1 | 2 | 2 | 5 |
| Correia,Kevin | 3 | 0 | 2 | 6 | 8 | 0 | 8 | 1 | 4 | 5 | 9 | 46 |
| Cosart,Jarred | | | | | | | | | | | 5 | 5 |
| Cotts,Neal | 0 | 2 | 9 | 2 | 1 | 2 | 0 | | | | 10 | 26 |
| Cousins,Scott | | | | | | | | 1 | 0 | 0 | 0 | 1 |
| Cowgill,Collin | | | | | | | | | 2 | 4 | 2 | 8 |
| Cozart,Zack | | | | | | | | | 1 | 11 | 12 | 24 |
| Craig,Allen | | | | | | | | 2 | 10 | 20 | 26 | 58 |
| Crain,Jesse | | 4 | 10 | 7 | 0 | 5 | 4 | 6 | 10 | 6 | 6 | 58 |
| Crawford,Brandon | | | | | | | | | 5 | 13 | 11 | 29 |
| Crawford,Carl | 19 | 20 | 22 | 21 | 20 | 11 | 19 | 32 | 8 | 3 | 13 | 188 |
| Crisp,Coco | 11 | 14 | 20 | 9 | 16 | 11 | 4 | 14 | 15 | 18 | 21 | 153 |
| Crow,Aaron | | | | | | | | | 5 | 6 | 5 | 16 |
| Crowe,Trevor | | | | | | | 2 | 7 | 1 | | 1 | 11 |
| Cruz,Luis | | | | | | 1 | 1 | 0 | | 11 | 3 | 16 |
| Cruz,Nelson | | | 0 | 3 | 4 | 7 | 16 | 19 | 16 | 17 | 16 | 98 |
| Cruz,Rhiner | | | | | | | | | | 0 | 1 | 1 |
| Cruz,Tony | | | | | | | | | 2 | 2 | 2 | 6 |
| Cuddyer,Michael | 4 | 10 | 7 | 22 | 16 | 7 | 17 | 15 | 17 | 6 | 19 | 140 |
| Cueto,Johnny | | | | | | 6 | 7 | 12 | 12 | 21 | 5 | 63 |
| Culberson,Charlie | | | | | | | | | | 0 | 2 | 2 |
| Cumpton,Brandon | | | | | | | | | | | 3 | 3 |
| Daley,Matt | | | | | | | 4 | 1 | 0 | | 1 | 6 |
| Danks,John | | | | | 4 | 17 | 16 | 16 | 8 | 1 | 3 | 65 |
| Danks,Jordan | | | | | | | | | | 1 | 1 | 2 |
| d'Arnaud,Travis | | | | | | | | | | | 1 | 1 |
| Darvish,Yu | | | | | | | | | | 14 | 18 | 32 |
| Davidson,Matt | | | | | | | | | | | 3 | 3 |
| Davis,Chris | | | | | | 8 | 7 | 1 | 4 | 19 | 33 | 72 |
| Davis,Erik | | | | | | | | | | | 1 | 1 |
| Davis,Ike | | | | | | | | 16 | 6 | 15 | 7 | 44 |
| Davis,Khris | | | | | | | | | | | 6 | 6 |
| Davis,Rajai | | | | 0 | 5 | 5 | 13 | 14 | 6 | 11 | 6 | 60 |
| Davis,Wade | | | | | | | 2 | 8 | 6 | 7 | 2 | 25 |
| De Aza,Alejandro | | | | | 1 | | 1 | 1 | 9 | 18 | 16 | 46 |
| De Fratus,Justin | | | | | | | | | 0 | 1 | 3 | 4 |
| de la Rosa,Dane | | | | | | | | | 0 | 0 | 7 | 7 |
| de la Rosa,Jorge | | 0 | 2 | 2 | 3 | 5 | 12 | 8 | 4 | 0 | 12 | 48 |
| de la Rosa,Rubby | | | | | | | | | 3 | 0 | 0 | 3 |
| Deduno,Samuel | | | | | | | | 0 | 0 | 4 | 7 | 11 |
| DeJesus,David | 0 | 9 | 16 | 14 | 15 | 22 | 16 | 11 | 8 | 15 | 12 | 138 |
| Delabar,Steve | | | | | | | | | 1 | 4 | 5 | 10 |
| Delgado,Randall | | | | | | | | | 2 | 3 | 4 | 9 |
| Dempster,Ryan | 34 | 2 | 14 | 6 | 8 | 18 | 12 | 12 | 5 | 12 | 5 | 128 |
| den Dekker,Matt | | | | | | | | | | | 1 | 1 |
| Denorfia,Chris | | | 0 | 2 | | 2 | 0 | 10 | 7 | 12 | 17 | 50 |
| DeRosa,Mark | 19 | 2 | 4 | 14 | 16 | 23 | 13 | 1 | 3 | 1 | 5 | 101 |
| Descalso,Daniel | | | | | | | | 1 | 10 | 5 | 11 | 27 |
| Desmond,Ian | | | | | | | 2 | 11 | 16 | 18 | 25 | 72 |
| Detwiler,Ross | | | | | 0 | | 2 | 0 | 4 | 9 | 2 | 17 |
| DeVries,Cole | | | | | | | | | | 4 | 0 | 4 |
| DeWitt,Blake | | | | | | 12 | 0 | 15 | 5 | 0 | 0 | 32 |
| Diamond,Scott | | | | | | | | | 1 | 11 | 1 | 13 |
| Diaz,Matt | 0 | 0 | 2 | 7 | 11 | 1 | 15 | 6 | 2 | 1 | 0 | 45 |
| Dickerson,Chris | | | | | | 5 | 7 | 0 | 1 | 1 | 2 | 16 |
| Dickerson,Corey | | | | | | | | | | | 4 | 4 |
| Dickey,R.A. | 7 | 4 | 0 | 0 | | 3 | 3 | 15 | 11 | 19 | 11 | 73 |
| Diekman,Jake | | | | | | | | | | 1 | 3 | 4 |
| Dietrich,Derek | | | | | | | | | | | 5 | 5 |
| Dirks,Andy | | | | | | | | | 6 | 10 | 9 | 25 |
| Dobbs,Greg | | 1 | 2 | 1 | 7 | 8 | 2 | 1 | 7 | 6 | 3 | 38 |
| Dolis,Rafael | | | | | | | | | 0 | 0 | 1 | 1 |
| Dominguez,Jose | | | | | | | | | | | 1 | 1 |
| Dominguez,Matt | | | | | | | | | 0 | 3 | 11 | 14 |
| Donaldson,Josh | | | | | | | | 0 | | 8 | 32 | 40 |
| Doolittle,Sean | | | | | | | | | | 5 | 8 | 13 |
| Dotel,Octavio | 51 | 14 | 2 | 0 | 3 | 6 | 6 | 6 | 5 | 6 | 0 | 99 |
| Doubront,Felix | | | | | | | | 1 | 0 | 7 | 7 | 15 |

| | WIN SHARES BY YEAR | | | | | | | | | | | |
|---|---|---|---|---|---|---|---|---|---|---|---|---|
| Player | <04 | 04 | 05 | 06 | 07 | 08 | 09 | 10 | 11 | 12 | 13 | Career |
| Doumit,Ryan | | | 6 | 2 | 6 | 20 | 4 | 9 | 9 | 10 | 9 | 75 |
| Downs,Darin | | | | | | | | | | 2 | 1 | 3 |
| Downs,Scott | 3 | 0 | 5 | 6 | 8 | 11 | 6 | 8 | 10 | 5 | 4 | 66 |
| Dozier,Brian | | | | | | | | | | 4 | 19 | 23 |
| Drabek,Kyle | | | | | | | | 0 | 1 | 2 | 0 | 3 |
| Drew,Stephen | | | | 6 | 16 | 21 | 16 | 20 | 10 | 6 | 17 | 112 |
| Duda,Lucas | | | | | | | | 0 | 11 | 13 | 8 | 32 |
| Duensing,Brian | | | | | | | 6 | 13 | 4 | 2 | 5 | 30 |
| Duffy,Danny | | | | | | | | | 1 | 2 | 3 | 6 |
| Duke,Zach | | | 10 | 10 | 2 | 3 | 12 | 1 | 4 | 2 | 2 | 46 |
| Duncan,Shelley | | | | | 3 | 0 | 0 | 6 | 9 | 3 | 0 | 21 |
| Dunn,Adam | 43 | 29 | 25 | 18 | 18 | 21 | 24 | 18 | 1 | 13 | 13 | 223 |
| Dunn,Mike | | | | | | | 0 | 2 | 5 | 0 | 7 | 14 |
| Dunning,Jake | | | | | | | | | | | 1 | 1 |
| Durbin,Chad | 8 | 1 | | 1 | 6 | 8 | 3 | 5 | 1 | 5 | 0 | 38 |
| Dwyer,Chris | | | | | | | | | | | 1 | 1 |
| Dyson,Jarrod | | | | | | | | 2 | 2 | 8 | 7 | 19 |
| Eaton,Adam | | | | | | | | | | 2 | 5 | 7 |
| Edgin,Josh | | | | | | | | | | 1 | 2 | 3 |
| Ellis,A.J. | | | | | | 0 | 0 | 4 | 3 | 20 | 16 | 43 |
| Ellis,Mark | 32 | | 21 | 14 | 20 | 13 | 11 | 19 | 9 | 12 | 16 | 167 |
| Ellsbury,Jacoby | | | | | 6 | 16 | 21 | 1 | 34 | 6 | 22 | 106 |
| Elmore,Jake | | | | | | | | | | 1 | 2 | 3 |
| Encarnacion,Edwin | | | 4 | 14 | 16 | 14 | 6 | 8 | 11 | 31 | 22 | 126 |
| Enright,Barry | | | | | | | | 6 | 0 | 0 | 0 | 6 |
| Eovaldi,Nathan | | | | | | | | | 2 | 3 | 5 | 10 |
| Eppley,Cody | | | | | | | | | 0 | 3 | 0 | 3 |
| Erlin,Robbie | | | | | | | | | | | 2 | 2 |
| Escalona,Edgmer | | | | | | | | 1 | 3 | 0 | 0 | 4 |
| Escobar,Alcides | | | | | | 0 | 4 | 12 | 8 | 14 | 10 | 48 |
| Escobar,Eduardo | | | | | | | | | 0 | 2 | 2 | 4 |
| Escobar,Yunel | | | | | 12 | 13 | 24 | 14 | 20 | 9 | 18 | 110 |
| Espinosa,Danny | | | | | | | | 4 | 22 | 18 | 2 | 46 |
| Estrada,Marco | | | | | | 0 | 0 | 0 | 4 | 8 | 7 | 19 |
| Ethier,Andre | | | | 11 | 13 | 23 | 21 | 22 | 18 | 22 | 16 | 146 |
| Falu,Irving | | | | | | | | | | 3 | 0 | 3 |
| Farnsworth,Kyle | 21 | 3 | 14 | 5 | 3 | 3 | 2 | 5 | 12 | 1 | 2 | 71 |
| Farquhar,Danny | | | | | | | | | 0 | | 7 | 7 |
| Federowicz,Tim | | | | | | | | | 0 | 0 | 3 | 3 |
| Feldman,Scott | | | 1 | 3 | 1 | 4 | 14 | 2 | 2 | 4 | 10 | 41 |
| Feliciano,Pedro | 3 | 1 | | 8 | 6 | 3 | 7 | 4 | | | 0 | 32 |
| Feliz,Neftali | | | | | | | 6 | 15 | 12 | 4 | 1 | 38 |
| Fernandez,Jose | | | | | | | | | | | 16 | 16 |
| Field,Tommy | | | | | | | | | 1 | 0 | 0 | 1 |
| Fielder,Prince | | | 2 | 16 | 27 | 23 | 36 | 23 | 33 | 27 | 18 | 205 |
| Fields,Josh | | | | | | | | | | | 2 | 2 |
| Fien,Casey | | | | | | | 0 | 0 | | 4 | 5 | 9 |
| Fiers,Mike | | | | | | | | | 0 | 8 | 0 | 8 |
| Fife,Stephen | | | | | | | | | | 2 | 2 | 4 |
| Figaro,Alfredo | | | | | | | 0 | 0 | | | 3 | 3 |
| Figueroa,Pedro | | | | | | | | | | 1 | 0 | 1 |
| Fister,Doug | | | | | | | 4 | 7 | 18 | 11 | 14 | 54 |
| Flaherty,Ryan | | | | | | | | | | 2 | 7 | 9 |
| Flores,Wilmer | | | | | | | | | | | 2 | 2 |
| Florimon,Pedro | | | | | | | | | 0 | 1 | 10 | 11 |
| Flowers,Tyler | | | | | | | 0 | 0 | 3 | 3 | 3 | 9 |
| Floyd,Gavin | | 2 | 0 | 0 | 2 | 15 | 13 | 12 | 11 | 10 | 0 | 65 |
| Forsythe,Logan | | | | | | | | | 3 | 8 | 3 | 14 |
| Fowler,Dexter | | | | | | 0 | 15 | 13 | 16 | 15 | 13 | 72 |
| Francis,Jeff | | 2 | 6 | 13 | 14 | 5 | | 4 | 5 | 4 | 0 | 53 |
| Francisco,Ben | | | | | 1 | 9 | 10 | 5 | 6 | 2 | 0 | 33 |
| Francisco,Frank | | 6 | | 0 | 3 | 6 | 9 | 5 | 7 | 2 | 1 | 39 |
| Francisco,Juan | | | | | | | 2 | 0 | 2 | 3 | 7 | 14 |
| Francoeur,Jeff | | | 12 | 15 | 20 | 5 | 9 | 8 | 17 | 6 | 1 | 93 |
| Frandsen,Kevin | | | | 0 | 4 | 0 | 1 | 3 | | 7 | 3 | 18 |
| Franklin,Nick | | | | | | | | | | | 13 | 13 |
| Frasor,Jason | | 9 | 6 | 4 | 3 | 2 | 10 | 5 | 5 | 2 | 5 | 51 |
| Frazier,Todd | | | | | | | | | 3 | 13 | 15 | 31 |
| Freeman,Freddie | | | | | | | | 0 | 19 | 18 | 35 | 72 |
| Freeman,Sam | | | | | | | | | | 0 | 1 | 1 |
| Freese,David | | | | | | | 1 | 8 | 13 | 19 | 9 | 50 |
| Freiman,Nate | | | | | | | | | | | 4 | 4 |
| Frieri,Ernesto | | | | | | | 0 | 4 | 4 | 11 | 8 | 27 |

| | WIN SHARES BY YEAR | | | | | | | | | | | |
|---|---|---|---|---|---|---|---|---|---|---|---|---|
| Player | <04 | 04 | 05 | 06 | 07 | 08 | 09 | 10 | 11 | 12 | 13 | Career |
| Fryer,Eric | | | | | | | | | 0 | 0 | 2 | 2 |
| Fujikawa,Kyuji | | | | | | | | | | | 1 | 1 |
| Fuld,Sam | | | | | 0 | | 4 | 1 | 9 | 3 | 2 | 19 |
| Furbush,Charlie | | | | | | | | | 1 | 5 | 4 | 10 |
| Gallardo,Yovani | | | | | 9 | 2 | 10 | 11 | 13 | 16 | 8 | 69 |
| Galvis,Freddy | | | | | | | | | | 3 | 4 | 7 |
| Garcia,Avisail | | | | | | | | | | 1 | 5 | 6 |
| Garcia,Freddy | 61 | 15 | 17 | 14 | 1 | 1 | 4 | 9 | 10 | 3 | 3 | 138 |
| Garcia,Jaime | | | | | | 1 | | 12 | 7 | 6 | 2 | 28 |
| Garcia,Leury | | | | | | | | | | | 2 | 2 |
| Garcia,Luis | | | | | | | | | | | 2 | 2 |
| Gardner,Brett | | | | | | 3 | 9 | 17 | 16 | 2 | 22 | 69 |
| Garland,Jon | 27 | 11 | 20 | 15 | 13 | 9 | 10 | 12 | 1 | | 1 | 119 |
| Garza,Matt | | | | 1 | 4 | 12 | 12 | 10 | 10 | 5 | 10 | 64 |
| Gattis,Evan | | | | | | | | | | | 11 | 11 |
| Gaudin,Chad | 3 | 1 | 0 | 7 | 9 | 5 | 3 | 2 | 0 | 3 | 5 | 38 |
| Gausman,Kevin | | | | | | | | | | | 1 | 1 |
| Gearrin,Cory | | | | | | | | | 0 | 2 | 2 | 4 |
| Gee,Dillon | | | | | | | | 3 | 5 | 4 | 10 | 22 |
| Gennett,Scooter | | | | | | | | | | | 9 | 9 |
| Gentry,Craig | | | | | | | 0 | 0 | 5 | 9 | 11 | 25 |
| Germano,Justin | | 0 | | 0 | 4 | 0 | | 2 | 0 | 1 | 0 | 7 |
| Germen,Gonzalez | | | | | | | | | | | 1 | 1 |
| Getz,Chris | | | | | | 0 | 10 | 4 | 8 | 4 | 3 | 29 |
| Giambi,Jason | 228 | 8 | 24 | 22 | 6 | 14 | 7 | 6 | 5 | 2 | 3 | 325 |
| Giavotella,Johnny | | | | | | | | | 2 | 1 | 1 | 4 |
| Gillaspie,Conor | | | | | | 0 | | | 1 | 0 | 9 | 10 |
| Gillespie,Cole | | | | | | | | 1 | 1 | | 1 | 3 |
| Gimenez,Chris | | | | | | | 1 | 1 | 1 | 3 | 0 | 6 |
| Gimenez,Hector | | | | 0 | | | | | 0 | 1 | 1 | 2 |
| Gindl,Caleb | | | | | | | | | | | 4 | 4 |
| Goins,Ryan | | | | | | | | | | | 2 | 2 |
| Goldschmidt,Paul | | | | | | | | | 6 | 17 | 36 | 59 |
| Gomes,Brandon | | | | | | | | | 3 | 0 | 0 | 3 |
| Gomes,Jonny | 0 | 0 | 14 | 6 | 8 | 2 | 10 | 18 | 6 | 13 | 12 | 89 |
| Gomes,Yan | | | | | | | | | | 2 | 14 | 16 |
| Gomez,Carlos | | | | | 2 | 13 | 6 | 4 | 7 | 12 | 21 | 65 |
| Gomez,Jeanmar | | | | | | | | 2 | 3 | 0 | 4 | 9 |
| Gonzalez,Adrian | | 1 | 1 | 16 | 25 | 24 | 34 | 35 | 27 | 24 | 24 | 211 |
| Gonzalez,Alberto | | | | | 0 | 3 | 5 | 2 | 4 | 1 | 0 | 15 |
| Gonzalez,Alex | 48 | 15 | 14 | 10 | 10 | | 8 | 19 | 13 | 3 | 0 | 140 |
| Gonzalez,Carlos | | | | | | 6 | 9 | 25 | 20 | 15 | 15 | 90 |
| Gonzalez,Edgar | 1 | 0 | 0 | 3 | 5 | 0 | 1 | | 0 | 1 | 0 | 11 |
| Gonzalez,Gio | | | | | | 0 | 2 | 15 | 15 | 17 | 11 | 60 |
| Gonzalez,Marwin | | | | | | | | | | 2 | 2 | 4 |
| Gonzalez,Michael | 0 | 8 | 6 | 11 | 3 | 3 | 9 | 3 | 2 | 3 | 1 | 49 |
| Gonzalez,Miguel | | | | | | | | | | 10 | 10 | 20 |
| Gordon,Alex | | | | | 12 | 15 | 2 | 3 | 24 | 20 | 21 | 97 |
| Gordon,Dee | | | | | | | | | 6 | 3 | 2 | 11 |
| Gorzelanny,Tom | | | 0 | 3 | 11 | 0 | 2 | 7 | 4 | 6 | 4 | 37 |
| Gose,Anthony | | | | | | | | | | 4 | 2 | 6 |
| Gosewisch,Tuffy | | | | | | | | | | | 1 | 1 |
| Grandal,Yasmani | | | | | | | | | | 11 | 4 | 15 |
| Granderson,Curtis | | 0 | 6 | 20 | 25 | 20 | 20 | 16 | 26 | 21 | 4 | 158 |
| Gray,Sonny | | | | | | | | | | | 5 | 5 |
| Green,Grant | | | | | | | | | | | 4 | 4 |
| Green,Nick | | 8 | 6 | 2 | 0 | | 6 | 0 | | 0 | 1 | 23 |
| Greene,Tyler | | | | | | | 1 | 2 | 3 | 5 | 0 | 11 |
| Gregerson,Luke | | | | | | | 5 | 9 | 4 | 9 | 7 | 34 |
| Gregg,Kevin | 2 | 6 | 2 | 4 | 10 | 11 | 7 | 9 | 4 | 2 | 8 | 65 |
| Gregorius,Didi | | | | | | | | | | 0 | 10 | 10 |
| Greinke,Zack | | 9 | 3 | 1 | 9 | 15 | 26 | 11 | 10 | 16 | 17 | 117 |
| Griffin,A.J. | | | | | | | | | | 7 | 10 | 17 |
| Grilli,Jason | 1 | 0 | 1 | 4 | 4 | 7 | 2 | | 4 | 6 | 9 | 38 |
| Grimm,Justin | | | | | | | | | | 0 | 1 | 1 |
| Grossman,Robbie | | | | | | | | | | | 7 | 7 |
| Guerra,Javy | | | | | | | | | 8 | 5 | 0 | 13 |
| Guerrier,Matt | | 0 | 5 | 5 | 9 | 2 | 11 | 7 | 4 | 1 | 2 | 46 |
| Guthrie,Jeremy | | 1 | 0 | 0 | 12 | 13 | 7 | 15 | 8 | 7 | 12 | 75 |
| Gutierrez,Franklin | | | 0 | 1 | 6 | 5 | 21 | 14 | 4 | 5 | 3 | 59 |
| Gutierrez,J.C. | | | | | 0 | | 7 | 3 | 0 | | 2 | 12 |
| Guzman,Freddy | | 1 | | 0 | 0 | | 0 | | | | 0 | 1 |
| Guzman,Jesus | | | | | | | 0 | | 13 | 10 | 8 | 31 |

| WIN SHARES BY YEAR | | | | | | | | | | | | |
|---|---|---|---|---|---|---|---|---|---|---|---|---|
| Player | <04 | 04 | 05 | 06 | 07 | 08 | 09 | 10 | 11 | 12 | 13 | Career |
| Gyorko,Jedd | | | | | | | | | | | 12 | 12 |
| Hafner,Travis | 8 | 21 | 26 | 24 | 16 | 2 | 8 | 11 | 15 | 3 | 5 | 139 |
| Hagadone,Nick | | | | | | | | | 1 | 0 | 0 | 1 |
| Hairston,Jerry | 38 | 8 | 9 | 1 | 2 | 12 | 8 | 13 | 10 | 8 | 1 | 110 |
| Hairston,Scott | | 3 | 0 | 0 | 7 | 9 | 14 | 5 | 3 | 12 | 2 | 55 |
| Hale,David | | | | | | | | | | | 1 | 1 |
| Halladay,Roy | 65 | 9 | 15 | 20 | 16 | 23 | 21 | 25 | 22 | 6 | 0 | 222 |
| Halton,Sean | | | | | | | | | | | 1 | 1 |
| Hamels,Cole | | | | 8 | 15 | 18 | 10 | 16 | 17 | 18 | 13 | 115 |
| Hamilton,Billy | | | | | | | | | | | 2 | 2 |
| Hamilton,Josh | | | | | 11 | 26 | 11 | 30 | 15 | 26 | 12 | 131 |
| Hammel,Jason | | | | 0 | 2 | 3 | 10 | 8 | 5 | 10 | 4 | 42 |
| Hand,Brad | | | | | | | | | 1 | 0 | 1 | 2 |
| Hand,Donovan | | | | | | | | | | | 3 | 3 |
| Hanigan,Ryan | | | | | 1 | 4 | 8 | 13 | 11 | 18 | 5 | 60 |
| Hannahan,Jack | | | | 0 | 5 | 5 | 4 | | 14 | 8 | 3 | 39 |
| Hanrahan,Joel | | | | | 2 | 7 | 3 | 7 | 15 | 10 | 0 | 44 |
| Hanson,Tommy | | | | | | | 10 | 12 | 8 | 6 | 1 | 37 |
| Happ,J.A. | | | | | 0 | 2 | 15 | 6 | 1 | 5 | 3 | 32 |
| Harang,Aaron | 7 | 5 | 11 | 18 | 17 | 6 | 7 | 1 | 8 | 8 | 1 | 89 |
| Hardy,J.J. | | | 11 | 3 | 19 | 20 | 6 | 10 | 22 | 20 | 16 | 127 |
| Haren,Dan | 1 | 2 | 13 | 14 | 17 | 19 | 20 | 14 | 18 | 6 | 4 | 128 |
| Harper,Bryce | | | | | | | | | | 21 | 19 | 40 |
| Harrell,Lucas | | | | | | | | 1 | 0 | 10 | 1 | 12 |
| Harris,Brendan | | 0 | 1 | 0 | 13 | 11 | 7 | 1 | | | 1 | 34 |
| Harris,Will | | | | | | | | | | 0 | 5 | 5 |
| Harrison,Josh | | | | | | | | | 5 | 4 | 3 | 12 |
| Harrison,Matt | | | | | | 3 | 1 | 3 | 15 | 18 | 0 | 40 |
| Harvey,Matt | | | | | | | | | | 5 | 14 | 19 |
| Hawkins,LaTroy | 50 | 16 | 5 | 4 | 5 | 6 | 10 | 0 | 6 | 2 | 7 | 111 |
| Hawpe,Brad | | 1 | 8 | 15 | 20 | 16 | 19 | 5 | 2 | | 1 | 87 |
| Hayes,Brett | | | | | | | 0 | 2 | 3 | 1 | 1 | 7 |
| Headley,Chase | | | | | 0 | 8 | 16 | 15 | 16 | 32 | 17 | 104 |
| Hechavarria,Adeiny | | | | | | | | | | 3 | 5 | 8 |
| Hefner,Jeremy | | | | | | | | | | 1 | 1 | 2 |
| Heisey,Chris | | | | | | | | 4 | 8 | 8 | 5 | 25 |
| Hellickson,Jeremy | | | | | | | | 3 | 15 | 11 | 4 | 33 |
| Helton,Todd | 155 | 30 | 25 | 21 | 22 | 8 | 23 | 7 | 13 | 5 | 9 | 318 |
| Hembree,Heath | | | | | | | | | | | 1 | 1 |
| Henderson,Jim | | | | | | | | | | 4 | 11 | 15 |
| Hernandez,Cesar | | | | | | | | | | | 3 | 3 |
| Hernandez,David | | | | | | | 3 | 6 | 10 | 9 | 3 | 31 |
| Hernandez,Felix | | | 8 | 8 | 14 | 13 | 26 | 23 | 16 | 15 | 16 | 139 |
| Hernandez,Ramon | 59 | 13 | 10 | 21 | 11 | 11 | 11 | 13 | 10 | 1 | 1 | 161 |
| Hernandez,Roberto | | | | 1 | 22 | 3 | 0 | 12 | 2 | 0 | 3 | 43 |
| Herrera,Elian | | | | | | | | | | 4 | 0 | 4 |
| Herrera,Jonathan | | | | | | 1 | | 6 | 3 | 3 | 5 | 18 |
| Herrera,Kelvin | | | | | | | | | 0 | 10 | 5 | 15 |
| Herrmann,Chris | | | | | | | | | | 0 | 3 | 3 |
| Hester,John | | | | | | | 1 | 2 | | 1 | 0 | 4 |
| Heyward,Jason | | | | | | | | 23 | 11 | 22 | 14 | 70 |
| Hicks,Aaron | | | | | | | | | | | 4 | 4 |
| Hill,Aaron | | | 9 | 14 | 20 | 5 | 25 | 12 | 13 | 25 | 12 | 135 |
| Hill,Koyie | 0 | 1 | 1 | | 1 | 0 | 7 | 3 | 1 | 0 | 1 | 15 |
| Hill,Rich | | | 0 | 5 | 13 | 1 | 0 | 1 | 1 | 3 | 0 | 24 |
| Hinske,Eric | 34 | 6 | 11 | 7 | 3 | 10 | 5 | 8 | 5 | 0 | 0 | 89 |
| Hochevar,Luke | | | | | 1 | 3 | 1 | 4 | 7 | 1 | 10 | 27 |
| Hoes,L.J. | | | | | | | | | | 0 | 4 | 4 |
| Holland,Derek | | | | | | | 2 | 3 | 14 | 8 | 13 | 40 |
| Holland,Greg | | | | | | | | 0 | 9 | 11 | 18 | 38 |
| Holliday,Matt | | 9 | 17 | 19 | 27 | 21 | 25 | 25 | 21 | 21 | 25 | 210 |
| Holt,Brock | | | | | | | | | | 3 | 1 | 4 |
| Hoover,J.J. | | | | | | | | | | 4 | 7 | 11 |
| Horst,Jeremy | | | | | | | | | 1 | 4 | 0 | 5 |
| Hosmer,Eric | | | | | | | | | 13 | 10 | 18 | 41 |
| Howard,Ryan | | 1 | 10 | 29 | 26 | 24 | 26 | 20 | 21 | 7 | 9 | 173 |
| Howell,J.P. | | | 1 | 2 | 0 | 11 | 11 | | 0 | 3 | 6 | 34 |
| Hudson,Tim | 90 | 16 | 14 | 7 | 17 | 10 | 4 | 20 | 14 | 12 | 6 | 210 |
| Huff,David | | | | | | | 3 | 0 | 1 | 2 | 2 | 8 |
| Hughes,Jared | | | | | | | | | 0 | 6 | 1 | 7 |
| Hughes,Phil | | | | | 4 | 0 | 10 | 11 | 1 | 9 | 2 | 37 |
| Humber,Philip | | | | 0 | 0 | 0 | 0 | 2 | 11 | 1 | 0 | 14 |
| Hundley,Nick | | | | | | 3 | 10 | 10 | 12 | 2 | 10 | 47 |

| WIN SHARES BY YEAR | | | | | | | | | | | | |
|---|---|---|---|---|---|---|---|---|---|---|---|---|
| Player | <04 | 04 | 05 | 06 | 07 | 08 | 09 | 10 | 11 | 12 | 13 | Career |
| Hunter,Tommy | | | | | | 0 | 8 | 10 | 3 | 4 | 10 | 35 |
| Hunter,Torii | 68 | 13 | 11 | 17 | 22 | 21 | 20 | 23 | 17 | 24 | 16 | 252 |
| Iannetta,Chris | | | | 1 | 5 | 17 | 10 | 3 | 16 | 8 | 10 | 70 |
| Ibanez,Raul | 42 | 12 | 17 | 25 | 23 | 21 | 17 | 19 | 12 | 9 | 14 | 211 |
| Iglesias,Jose | | | | | | | | | 0 | 1 | 13 | 14 |
| Infante,Omar | 6 | 12 | 7 | 5 | 4 | 9 | 7 | 19 | 18 | 14 | 16 | 117 |
| Inge,Brandon | 11 | 13 | 17 | 17 | 12 | 10 | 13 | 13 | 3 | 10 | 1 | 120 |
| Ishikawa,Travis | | | | 1 | | 4 | 9 | 4 | | 5 | 0 | 23 |
| Iwakuma,Hisashi | | | | | | | | | | 8 | 20 | 28 |
| Izturis,Cesar | 18 | 25 | 6 | 3 | 5 | 9 | 8 | 6 | 1 | 2 | 1 | 84 |
| Izturis,Maicer | | 1 | 6 | 13 | 16 | 11 | 17 | 7 | 13 | 5 | 3 | 92 |
| Jackson,Austin | | | | | | | | 18 | 14 | 22 | 15 | 69 |
| Jackson,Edwin | 2 | 0 | 0 | 1 | 2 | 10 | 17 | 9 | 12 | 9 | 1 | 63 |
| Janish,Paul | | | | | | 1 | 4 | 8 | 3 | 4 | 1 | 21 |
| Jansen,Kenley | | | | | | | | 6 | 6 | 15 | 16 | 43 |
| Janssen,Casey | | | | 4 | 10 | | 0 | 5 | 8 | 11 | 11 | 49 |
| Jaso,John | | | | | | 0 | | 16 | 5 | 21 | 9 | 51 |
| Jay,Jon | | | | | | | | 8 | 13 | 15 | 17 | 53 |
| Jeffress,Jeremy | | | | | | | | 1 | 1 | 0 | 1 | 3 |
| Jenkins,Chad | | | | | | | | | | 1 | 3 | 4 |
| Jennings,Dan | | | | | | | | | | 2 | 2 | 4 |
| Jennings,Desmond | | | | | | | | 0 | 11 | 13 | 20 | 44 |
| Jepsen,Kevin | | | | | | 0 | 4 | 5 | 0 | 4 | 1 | 14 |
| Jeter,Derek | 194 | 26 | 26 | 32 | 24 | 18 | 28 | 19 | 13 | 23 | 0 | 403 |
| Jimenez,Cesar | | | | 0 | | 2 | | | 0 | | 1 | 3 |
| Jimenez,Luis | | | | | | | | | | | 3 | 3 |
| Jimenez,Ubaldo | | | | 0 | 4 | 11 | 19 | 22 | 6 | 3 | 13 | 78 |
| Johnson,Chris | | | | | | | 0 | 15 | 8 | 17 | 20 | 60 |
| Johnson,Dan | | | 9 | 5 | 10 | 1 | | 4 | 0 | 2 | 0 | 31 |
| Johnson,Elliot | | | | | | 0 | | | 2 | 10 | 5 | 17 |
| Johnson,Erik | | | | | | | | | | | 2 | 2 |
| Johnson,Jim | | | | 0 | 0 | 8 | 7 | 3 | 11 | 17 | 11 | 57 |
| Johnson,Josh | | | 1 | 12 | 0 | 6 | 19 | 16 | 7 | 10 | 0 | 71 |
| Johnson,Kelly | | | 9 | | 19 | 19 | 6 | 21 | 16 | 14 | 12 | 116 |
| Johnson,Reed | 11 | 9 | 10 | 16 | 3 | 13 | 3 | 3 | 8 | 8 | 3 | 87 |
| Johnson,Rob | | | | | 0 | 0 | 9 | 3 | 3 | 0 | 0 | 15 |
| Johnson,Steve | | | | | | | | | | 5 | 0 | 5 |
| Jones,Adam | | | | 1 | 0 | 9 | 13 | 15 | 16 | 26 | 23 | 103 |
| Jones,Garrett | | | | | 0 | | 10 | 13 | 12 | 23 | 8 | 66 |
| Jones,Nate | | | | | | | | | | 9 | 4 | 13 |
| Jordan,Taylor | | | | | | | | | | | 2 | 2 |
| Joseph,Donnie | | | | | | | | | | | 1 | 1 |
| Joyce,Matt | | | | | | 6 | 1 | 10 | 19 | 13 | 11 | 60 |
| Jurrjens,Jair | | | | | 2 | 11 | 17 | 4 | 12 | 0 | 0 | 46 |
| Kawasaki,Munenori | | | | | | | | | | 2 | 6 | 8 |
| Kazmir,Scott | | 1 | 10 | 13 | 13 | 12 | 6 | 0 | 0 | | 8 | 63 |
| Kearns,Austin | 28 | 5 | 10 | 17 | 20 | 3 | 2 | 10 | 1 | 5 | 0 | 101 |
| Kelley,Shawn | | | | | | | 3 | 2 | 2 | 2 | 4 | 13 |
| Kelly,Don | | | | | 0 | | 1 | 5 | 5 | 1 | 5 | 17 |
| Kelly,Joe | | | | | | | | | | 5 | 9 | 14 |
| Kemp,Matt | | | | 3 | 10 | 19 | 26 | 15 | 37 | 21 | 6 | 137 |
| Kendrick,Howie | | | | 6 | 9 | 15 | 15 | 19 | 18 | 16 | 13 | 111 |
| Kendrick,Kyle | | | | | 9 | 3 | 2 | 5 | 7 | 8 | 5 | 39 |
| Kennedy,Ian | | | | | 2 | 0 | 0 | 11 | 20 | 11 | 2 | 46 |
| Kensing,Logan | | 0 | 0 | 2 | 2 | 3 | 0 | | | | 0 | 7 |
| Keppinger,Jeff | | 2 | | 1 | 9 | 10 | 5 | 21 | 8 | 14 | 5 | 75 |
| Kershaw,Clayton | | | | | | 5 | 12 | 15 | 23 | 19 | 22 | 96 |
| Keuchel,Dallas | | | | | | | | | | 0 | 3 | 3 |
| Kieschnick,Roger | | | | | | | | | | | 1 | 1 |
| Kimbrel,Craig | | | | | | | | 4 | 17 | 18 | 17 | 56 |
| Kinsler,Ian | | | | 12 | 17 | 24 | 24 | 13 | 22 | 15 | 20 | 147 |
| Kintzler,Brandon | | | | | | | | 0 | 1 | 2 | 8 | 11 |
| Kipnis,Jason | | | | | | | | | 6 | 24 | 27 | 57 |
| Kirkman,Michael | | | | | | | | 2 | 0 | 2 | 0 | 4 |
| Kluber,Corey | | | | | | | | | 0 | 1 | 9 | 10 |
| Koehler,Tom | | | | | | | | | | 0 | 3 | 3 |
| Kohn,Michael | | | | | | | | 3 | 0 | | 3 | 6 |
| Konerko,Paul | 69 | 20 | 24 | 21 | 16 | 10 | 18 | 29 | 24 | 15 | 9 | 255 |
| Kontos,George | | | | | | | | | 0 | 3 | 1 | 4 |
| Kotchman,Casey | | 2 | 4 | 0 | 15 | 14 | 10 | 6 | 17 | 7 | 0 | 75 |
| Kotsay,Mark | 83 | 21 | 19 | 11 | 3 | 9 | 4 | 4 | 7 | 3 | 0 | 164 |
| Kottaras,George | | | | | | 0 | 1 | 4 | 4 | 7 | 2 | 18 |
| Kozma,Pete | | | | | | | | | 1 | 3 | 11 | 15 |

| | WIN SHARES BY YEAR | | | | | | | | | | | |
|---|---|---|---|---|---|---|---|---|---|---|---|---|
| Player | <04 | 04 | 05 | 06 | 07 | 08 | 09 | 10 | 11 | 12 | 13 | Career |
| Kratz,Erik | | | | | | | | 0 | 0 | 7 | 3 | 10 |
| Krauss,Marc | | | | | | | | | | | 1 | 1 |
| Krol,Ian | | | | | | | | | | | 2 | 2 |
| Kubel,Jason | | 3 | | 1 | 12 | 12 | 19 | 12 | 13 | 13 | 5 | 90 |
| Kuroda,Hiroki | | | | | | 10 | 5 | 11 | 12 | 16 | 16 | 70 |
| Lackey,John | 14 | 10 | 16 | 16 | 21 | 13 | 12 | 11 | 1 | | 10 | 124 |
| Laffey,Aaron | | | | | 3 | 4 | 5 | 2 | 3 | 3 | 0 | 20 |
| Lagares,Juan | | | | | | | | | | | 7 | 7 |
| Laird,Brandon | | | | | | | | | 0 | 1 | 1 | 2 |
| Laird,Gerald | 1 | 3 | 1 | 5 | 10 | 9 | 14 | 6 | 3 | 5 | 6 | 63 |
| Lake,Junior | | | | | | | | | | | 5 | 5 |
| Langerhans,Ryan | 0 | | 12 | 8 | 5 | 4 | 2 | 2 | 1 | 0 | 1 | 35 |
| Lannan,John | | | | | 2 | 9 | 9 | 4 | 8 | 2 | 1 | 35 |
| LaRoche,Adam | | 7 | 11 | 16 | 16 | 16 | 17 | 16 | 1 | 22 | 14 | 136 |
| LaRoche,Andy | | | | | 2 | 2 | 12 | 2 | 1 | | 0 | 19 |
| Latos,Mat | | | | | | | 1 | 13 | 8 | 16 | 13 | 51 |
| Lavarnway,Ryan | | | | | | | | | 0 | 0 | 2 | 2 |
| Lawrie,Brett | | | | | | | | | 10 | 14 | 9 | 33 |
| Layne,Tom | | | | | | | | | | 3 | 0 | 3 |
| League,Brandon | | 1 | 0 | 5 | 0 | 4 | 3 | 8 | 11 | 8 | 0 | 40 |
| Leake,Mike | | | | | | | | 7 | 9 | 8 | 12 | 36 |
| LeBlanc,Wade | | | | | | 0 | 2 | 6 | 2 | 4 | 0 | 14 |
| LeCure,Sam | | | | | | | | 2 | 4 | 5 | 6 | 17 |
| Lee,Cliff | 4 | 6 | 13 | 10 | 1 | 24 | 17 | 16 | 22 | 14 | 19 | 146 |
| LeMahieu,DJ | | | | | | | | | 0 | 6 | 8 | 14 |
| Leroux,Chris | | | | | | | 0 | 0 | 2 | 0 | 0 | 2 |
| Lester,Jon | | | | 5 | 4 | 18 | 17 | 17 | 14 | 8 | 12 | 95 |
| Liddi,Alex | | | | | | | | | 2 | 3 | 0 | 5 |
| Lillibridge,Brent | | | | | | 1 | 1 | 2 | 7 | 1 | 0 | 12 |
| Lilly,Ted | 19 | 15 | 4 | 11 | 15 | 12 | 14 | 11 | 8 | 3 | 0 | 112 |
| Lincecum,Tim | | | | | 8 | 25 | 22 | 14 | 16 | 0 | 4 | 89 |
| Lincoln,Brad | | | | | | | | 1 | 1 | 6 | 1 | 9 |
| Lind,Adam | | | | 3 | 7 | 7 | 21 | 9 | 11 | 9 | 15 | 82 |
| Lindblom,Josh | | | | | | | | | 3 | 5 | 0 | 8 |
| Lindstrom,Matt | | | | | 5 | 6 | 2 | 4 | 5 | 4 | 5 | 31 |
| Liriano,Francisco | | | 0 | 16 | | 4 | 2 | 14 | 4 | 4 | 12 | 56 |
| Lo,Chia-Jen | | | | | | | | | | | 1 | 1 |
| Lobaton,Jose | | | | | | | 0 | | 1 | 5 | 9 | 15 |
| Locke,Jeff | | | | | | | | | 0 | 0 | 8 | 8 |
| Loe,Kameron | | 0 | 8 | 2 | 3 | 2 | | 5 | 6 | 4 | 0 | 30 |
| Logan,Boone | | | | 0 | 3 | 1 | 0 | 4 | 3 | 5 | 5 | 21 |
| Lohse,Kyle | 25 | 6 | 10 | 4 | 9 | 12 | 3 | 0 | 9 | 16 | 12 | 106 |
| Lombardozzi,Steve | | | | | | | | | 0 | 12 | 5 | 17 |
| Loney,James | | | | 3 | 16 | 14 | 18 | 18 | 16 | 5 | 19 | 109 |
| Longoria,Evan | | | | | | 19 | 24 | 28 | 25 | 14 | 24 | 134 |
| Lopez,Javier | 6 | 0 | 0 | 2 | 4 | 6 | 0 | 6 | 6 | 4 | 5 | 39 |
| Lopez,Wilton | | | | | | | 0 | 8 | 5 | 9 | 5 | 27 |
| Lough,David | | | | | | | | | | 0 | 8 | 8 |
| Loup,Aaron | | | | | | | | | | 3 | 7 | 10 |
| Lowe,Derek | 91 | 6 | 11 | 15 | 11 | 16 | 7 | 11 | 2 | 4 | 0 | 174 |
| Lowe,Mark | | | | 3 | 0 | 1 | 8 | 1 | 3 | 3 | 0 | 19 |
| Lowrie,Jed | | | | | | 7 | 1 | 8 | 5 | 11 | 23 | 55 |
| Lucas,Ed | | | | | | | | | | | 7 | 7 |
| Lucroy,Jonathan | | | | | | | | 4 | 15 | 15 | 19 | 53 |
| Ludwick,Ryan | 6 | 0 | 0 | | 10 | 24 | 19 | 17 | 12 | 16 | 1 | 105 |
| Luetge,Lucas | | | | | | | | | | 2 | 1 | 3 |
| Lutz,Donald | | | | | | | | | | | 1 | 1 |
| Lutz,Zach | | | | | | | | | | 0 | 1 | 1 |
| Lyles,Jordan | | | | | | | | | 0 | 1 | 2 | 3 |
| Lynn,Lance | | | | | | | | | 2 | 11 | 7 | 20 |
| Lyon,Brandon | 9 | | 0 | 6 | 11 | 6 | 11 | 14 | 0 | 5 | 0 | 62 |
| Machado,Manny | | | | | | | | | | 7 | 20 | 27 |
| Machi,Jean | | | | | | | | | | 0 | 4 | 4 |
| Maholm,Paul | | | 4 | 7 | 5 | 9 | 8 | 4 | 7 | 11 | 3 | 58 |
| Mahoney,Joe | | | | | | | | | | 0 | 1 | 1 |
| Maine,John | | 0 | 0 | 6 | 11 | 7 | 4 | 0 | | | 0 | 28 |
| Maldonado,Martin | | | | | | | | | 0 | 7 | 3 | 10 |
| Maness,Seth | | | | | | | | | | | 6 | 6 |
| Manship,Jeff | | | | | | | 1 | 1 | 0 | 0 | 0 | 2 |
| Marcum,Shaun | | | 1 | 3 | 10 | 12 | | 14 | 13 | 8 | 0 | 61 |
| Marisnick,Jake | | | | | | | | | | | 2 | 2 |
| Markakis,Nick | | | | 12 | 20 | 23 | 16 | 22 | 19 | 16 | 11 | 139 |
| Marmol,Carlos | | | | 1 | 11 | 12 | 10 | 16 | 8 | 6 | 1 | 65 |

| | WIN SHARES BY YEAR | | | | | | | | | | | |
|---|---|---|---|---|---|---|---|---|---|---|---|---|
| Player | <04 | 04 | 05 | 06 | 07 | 08 | 09 | 10 | 11 | 12 | 13 | Career |
| Maronde,Nick | | | | | | | | | | 1 | 0 | 1 |
| Marquis,Jason | 13 | 14 | 12 | 2 | 8 | 8 | 15 | 0 | 6 | 3 | 4 | 85 |
| Marshall,Brett | | | | | | | | | | | 1 | 1 |
| Marshall,Sean | | | | 2 | 6 | 4 | 5 | 10 | 11 | 11 | 2 | 51 |
| Marson,Lou | | | | | | 1 | 1 | 5 | 5 | 4 | 0 | 16 |
| Marte,Alfredo | | | | | | | | | | | 1 | 1 |
| Marte,Starling | | | | | | | | | | 5 | 20 | 25 |
| Marte,Victor | | | | | | | 0 | 0 | | 1 | 0 | 1 |
| Martin,Leonys | | | | | | | | | 0 | 1 | 14 | 15 |
| Martin,Russell | | | | 14 | 22 | 20 | 16 | 9 | 14 | 12 | 16 | 123 |
| Martinez,Carlos | | | | | | | | | | | 1 | 1 |
| Martinez,Cristhian | | | | | | | 1 | 1 | 5 | 4 | 0 | 11 |
| Martinez,Fernando | | | | | | | 0 | 0 | 0 | 2 | 0 | 2 |
| Martinez,J.D. | | | | | | | | | 6 | 7 | 3 | 16 |
| Martinez,Joe | | | | | | | 0 | 0 | | 0 | 1 | 1 |
| Martinez,Michael | | | | | | | | | 4 | 1 | 0 | 5 |
| Martinez,Victor | 4 | 20 | 22 | 18 | 29 | 7 | 21 | 17 | 24 | | 11 | 173 |
| Martis,Shairon | | | | | | 0 | 2 | | | | 0 | 2 |
| Masterson,Justin | | | | | | 7 | 5 | 5 | 15 | 6 | 14 | 52 |
| Mastroianni,Darin | | | | | | | | | 0 | 5 | 0 | 5 |
| Mathis,Jeff | | | 0 | 0 | 2 | 7 | 4 | 3 | 4 | 5 | 4 | 29 |
| Matsuzaka,Daisuke | | | | | 12 | 16 | 2 | 7 | 1 | 0 | 1 | 39 |
| Mattheus,Ryan | | | | | | | | | 3 | 7 | 0 | 10 |
| Matusz,Brian | | | | | | | 3 | 10 | 0 | 4 | 5 | 22 |
| Mauer,Joe | | 6 | 22 | 30 | 21 | 30 | 32 | 27 | 10 | 25 | 23 | 226 |
| Maxwell,Justin | | | | | 1 | | 3 | 2 | | 12 | 5 | 23 |
| Mayberry,John | | | | | | | 1 | 1 | 11 | 9 | 7 | 29 |
| Maybin,Cameron | | | | | 0 | 3 | 2 | 8 | 17 | 13 | 0 | 43 |
| Mazzaro,Vin | | | | | | | 2 | 4 | 0 | 1 | 7 | 14 |
| McAllister,Zach | | | | | | | | | 0 | 4 | 7 | 11 |
| McCann,Brian | | | 6 | 22 | 15 | 18 | 20 | 19 | 23 | 12 | 16 | 151 |
| McCarthy,Brandon | | | 5 | 5 | 3 | 1 | 5 | | 11 | 7 | 3 | 40 |
| McClellan,Kyle | | | | | | 4 | 6 | 8 | 5 | 0 | 0 | 23 |
| McCutchen,Andrew | | | | | | | 18 | 22 | 28 | 40 | 34 | 142 |
| McDonald,Darnell | | 0 | | | 0 | | 1 | 10 | 3 | 1 | 2 | 17 |
| McDonald,James | | | | | | 1 | 3 | 4 | 6 | 6 | 0 | 20 |
| McDonald,John | 8 | 1 | 4 | 3 | 8 | 1 | 3 | 5 | 6 | 4 | 0 | 43 |
| McFarland,T.J. | | | | | | | | | | | 4 | 4 |
| McGee,Jake | | | | | | | | 0 | 2 | 8 | 5 | 15 |
| McGowan,Dustin | | | 0 | 0 | 11 | 5 | | | 0 | | 2 | 18 |
| McKenry,Michael | | | | | | | | 0 | 2 | 8 | 3 | 13 |
| McLouth,Nate | | | 1 | 2 | 10 | 24 | 19 | 4 | 9 | 6 | 14 | 89 |
| Medica,Tommy | | | | | | | | | | | 4 | 4 |
| Medina,Yoervis | | | | | | | | | | | 7 | 7 |
| Medlen,Kris | | | | | | | 3 | 7 | 0 | 18 | 13 | 41 |
| Mejia,Jenrry | | | | | | | | 1 | | 0 | 2 | 3 |
| Melancon,Mark | | | | | | | 1 | 2 | 10 | 0 | 15 | 28 |
| Mendoza,Luis | | | | | 2 | 0 | 0 | 0 | 2 | 8 | 1 | 13 |
| Mercer,Jordy | | | | | | | | | | 2 | 13 | 15 |
| Mesa,Melky | | | | | | | | | | 0 | 1 | 1 |
| Mesoraco,Devin | | | | | | | | | 1 | 3 | 8 | 12 |
| Middlebrooks,Will | | | | | | | | | | 9 | 4 | 13 |
| Mijares,Jose | | | | | | 1 | 8 | 2 | 1 | 6 | 1 | 19 |
| Mikolas,Miles | | | | | | | | | | 2 | 0 | 2 |
| Miley,Wade | | | | | | | | | 2 | 14 | 10 | 26 |
| Miller,Andrew | | | | 0 | 2 | 0 | 2 | 0 | 2 | 4 | 2 | 12 |
| Miller,Brad | | | | | | | | | | | 10 | 10 |
| Miller,Corky | 8 | 0 | 0 | 0 | 1 | 1 | 3 | 3 | | | 2 | 18 |
| Miller,Jim | | | | | | 1 | | | 1 | 4 | 0 | 6 |
| Miller,Shelby | | | | | | | | | | 2 | 10 | 12 |
| Milone,Tommy | | | | | | | | | 2 | 10 | 6 | 18 |
| Miner,Zach | | | | 4 | 5 | 8 | 6 | | | | 1 | 24 |
| Minor,Mike | | | | | | | | 0 | 3 | 7 | 13 | 23 |
| Molina,Jose | 5 | 6 | 7 | 5 | 4 | 9 | 4 | 4 | 7 | 6 | 4 | 61 |
| Molina,Yadier | | 5 | 14 | 9 | 12 | 15 | 20 | 17 | 18 | 29 | 29 | 168 |
| Montero,Jesus | | | | | | | | | 2 | 10 | 2 | 14 |
| Montero,Miguel | | | | 0 | 3 | 4 | 13 | 9 | 29 | 26 | 10 | 94 |
| Montz,Luke | | | | | | 1 | | | | | 0 | 1 |
| Moore,Adam | | | | | | | 1 | 3 | 0 | 0 | 0 | 4 |
| Moore,Matt | | | | | | | | | 1 | 8 | 13 | 22 |
| Moore,Tyler | | | | | | | | | | 6 | 3 | 9 |
| Morales,Franklin | | | | | 4 | 0 | 4 | 0 | 3 | 5 | 1 | 17 |
| Morales,Kendrys | | | | 2 | 2 | 0 | 23 | 8 | | 14 | 17 | 66 |

| | WIN SHARES BY YEAR | | | | | | | | | | | |
|---|---|---|---|---|---|---|---|---|---|---|---|---|
| Player | <04 | 04 | 05 | 06 | 07 | 08 | 09 | 10 | 11 | 12 | 13 | Career |
| Morel,Brent | | | | | | | | 0 | 4 | 1 | 1 | 6 |
| Moreland,Mitch | | | | | | | | 6 | 8 | 9 | 10 | 33 |
| Morneau,Justin | 1 | 9 | 7 | 26 | 18 | 28 | 18 | 17 | 4 | 10 | 14 | 152 |
| Morris,Bryan | | | | | | | | | | 0 | 4 | 4 |
| Morrison,Logan | | | | | | | | 9 | 11 | 4 | 7 | 31 |
| Morrow,Brandon | | | | | 5 | 7 | 4 | 7 | 7 | 10 | 0 | 40 |
| Morse,Michael | | | 5 | 2 | 2 | 0 | 2 | 9 | 25 | 13 | 3 | 61 |
| Mortensen,Clayton | | | | | | | 0 | 0 | 3 | 3 | 0 | 6 |
| Morton,Charlie | | | | | | 0 | 4 | 0 | 8 | 0 | 6 | 18 |
| Moscoso,Guillermo | | | | | | | 1 | 0 | 8 | 2 | 0 | 11 |
| Moss,Brandon | | | | | 1 | 5 | 5 | 0 | 0 | 13 | 20 | 44 |
| Moustakas,Mike | | | | | | | | | 4 | 14 | 5 | 23 |
| Moylan,Peter | | | | 1 | 9 | 1 | 7 | 6 | 1 | 1 | 0 | 26 |
| Mujica,Edward | | | | 1 | 0 | 0 | 4 | 4 | 8 | 7 | 10 | 34 |
| Murphy,Daniel | | | | | | 6 | 10 | | 14 | 20 | 22 | 72 |
| Murphy,David | | | | 0 | 5 | 11 | 11 | 15 | 9 | 20 | 5 | 76 |
| Murphy,Donnie | | 0 | 0 | | 3 | 1 | | 3 | 1 | 2 | 5 | 15 |
| Murphy,J.R. | | | | | | | | | | | 1 | 1 |
| Myers,Brett | 12 | 4 | 14 | 12 | 9 | 7 | 3 | 17 | 6 | 7 | 0 | 91 |
| Myers,Wil | | | | | | | | | | | 14 | 14 |
| Napoli,Mike | | | | 10 | 8 | 12 | 10 | 12 | 23 | 12 | 16 | 103 |
| Narveson,Chris | | | | 0 | | | 2 | 7 | 6 | 0 | 0 | 15 |
| Nathan,Joe | 19 | 19 | 17 | 20 | 16 | 16 | 16 | | 5 | 12 | 17 | 157 |
| Nava,Daniel | | | | | | | | 5 | | 5 | 18 | 28 |
| Navarro,Dioner | | 0 | 4 | 5 | 6 | 17 | 5 | 2 | 3 | 4 | 11 | 57 |
| Navarro,Yamaico | | | | | | | | 0 | 2 | 0 | 1 | 3 |
| Nelson,Chris | | | | | | | | 0 | 2 | 10 | 3 | 15 |
| Nelson,Jimmy | | | | | | | | | | | 1 | 1 |
| Neshek,Pat | | | | 6 | 8 | 1 | | 0 | 1 | 3 | 2 | 21 |
| Nicasio,Juan | | | | | | | | | 4 | 2 | 4 | 10 |
| Nickeas,Mike | | | | | | | | 0 | 1 | 2 | 0 | 3 |
| Niese,Jon | | | | | | 0 | 1 | 6 | 4 | 13 | 6 | 30 |
| Nieuwenhuis,Kirk | | | | | | | | | | 5 | 1 | 6 |
| Nieves,Wil | 1 | | 0 | 0 | 1 | 4 | 4 | 2 | 1 | 2 | 5 | 20 |
| Nix,Jayson | | | | | | 1 | 6 | 6 | 2 | 5 | 7 | 27 |
| Nix,Laynce | 4 | 7 | 4 | 0 | 0 | 0 | 6 | 4 | 7 | 3 | 0 | 35 |
| Noesi,Hector | | | | | | | | | 2 | 0 | 0 | 2 |
| Nolasco,Ricky | | | | 5 | 0 | 14 | 6 | 7 | 5 | 8 | 9 | 54 |
| Noonan,Nick | | | | | | | | | | | 1 | 1 |
| Norris,Bud | | | | | | | 3 | 3 | 7 | 4 | 8 | 25 |
| Norris,Derek | | | | | | | | | | 7 | 11 | 18 |
| Nova,Ivan | | | | | | | | 2 | 11 | 5 | 13 | 31 |
| Nunez,Eduardo | | | | | | | | 2 | 8 | 4 | 6 | 20 |
| Nuno,Vidal | | | | | | | | | | | 2 | 2 |
| Oberholtzer,Brett | | | | | | | | | | | 5 | 5 |
| O'Day,Darren | | | | | | 2 | 9 | 9 | 0 | 10 | 8 | 38 |
| Odorizzi,Jake | | | | | | | | | | 0 | 1 | 1 |
| O'Flaherty,Eric | | | | 0 | 4 | 0 | 4 | 5 | 12 | 8 | 3 | 36 |
| Ogando,Alexi | | | | | | | | 6 | 13 | 7 | 8 | 34 |
| Ohlendorf,Ross | | | | | 1 | 0 | 11 | 4 | 0 | 0 | 4 | 20 |
| Okajima,Hideki | | | | | 11 | 8 | 7 | 2 | 1 | | 0 | 29 |
| Oliver,Darren | 66 | 1 | | 6 | 5 | 9 | 9 | 6 | 7 | 7 | 3 | 119 |
| Olivo,Miguel | 9 | 7 | 7 | 13 | 7 | 7 | 9 | 11 | 10 | 4 | 1 | 85 |
| Omogrosso,Brian | | | | | | | | | | 2 | 0 | 2 |
| Ondrusek,Logan | | | | | | | | 5 | 5 | 5 | 3 | 18 |
| Orr,Pete | | | 3 | 2 | 0 | 1 | 1 | | 2 | 2 | 0 | 11 |
| Ortega,Jose | | | | | | | | | | 0 | 1 | 1 |
| Ortiz,David | 51 | 24 | 30 | 27 | 27 | 15 | 11 | 18 | 18 | 15 | 22 | 258 |
| Ortiz,Joe | | | | | | | | | | | 2 | 2 |
| Ortiz,Ramon | 38 | 7 | 3 | 3 | 3 | | | 0 | 1 | | 0 | 55 |
| O'Sullivan,Sean | | | | | | | 2 | 2 | 0 | | 0 | 4 |
| Oswalt,Roy | 45 | 18 | 21 | 20 | 17 | 16 | 9 | 18 | 7 | 1 | 0 | 172 |
| Otero,Dan | | | | | | | | | | 0 | 5 | 5 |
| Ottavino,Adam | | | | | | | | 0 | | 5 | 7 | 12 |
| Outman,Josh | | | | | | 1 | 4 | | 3 | 0 | 3 | 11 |
| Overbay,Lyle | 6 | 17 | 17 | 17 | 6 | 14 | 12 | 15 | 6 | 2 | 7 | 119 |
| Owings,Chris | | | | | | | | | | | 2 | 2 |
| Ozuna,Marcell | | | | | | | | | | | 8 | 8 |
| Pacheco,Jordan | | | | | | | | | 2 | 9 | 2 | 13 |
| Pagan,Angel | | | | 3 | 5 | 3 | 12 | 23 | 15 | 27 | 11 | 99 |
| Pagnozzi,Matt | | | | | | | 0 | 2 | 0 | | 0 | 2 |
| Papelbon,Jonathan | | | 4 | 19 | 15 | 15 | 15 | 10 | 12 | 14 | 11 | 115 |
| Paredes,Jimmy | | | | | | | | | 5 | 0 | 0 | 5 |

| | WIN SHARES BY YEAR | | | | | | | | | | | |
|---|---|---|---|---|---|---|---|---|---|---|---|---|
| Player | <04 | 04 | 05 | 06 | 07 | 08 | 09 | 10 | 11 | 12 | 13 | Career |
| Parker,Blake | | | | | | | | | | 0 | 4 | 4 |
| Parker,Jarrod | | | | | | | | | 1 | 12 | 9 | 22 |
| Parmelee,Chris | | | | | | | | | 6 | 2 | 3 | 11 |
| Parnell,Bobby | | | | | | 0 | 2 | 2 | 4 | 8 | 9 | 25 |
| Parra,Gerardo | | | | | | | 9 | 6 | 19 | 9 | 15 | 58 |
| Parra,Manny | | | | | 2 | 8 | 0 | 2 | | 1 | 3 | 16 |
| Parrino,Andy | | | | | | | | | 1 | 1 | 0 | 2 |
| Pastornicky,Tyler | | | | | | | | | | 3 | 1 | 4 |
| Paterson,Joe | | | | | | | | | 3 | 0 | 0 | 3 |
| Patton,Troy | | | | | 1 | | | 0 | 3 | 7 | 4 | 15 |
| Paul,Xavier | | | | | | | 0 | 0 | 4 | 2 | 6 | 12 |
| Paxton,James | | | | | | | | | | | 3 | 3 |
| Peacock,Brad | | | | | | | | | 2 | | 2 | 4 |
| Pearce,Steve | | | | | 2 | 2 | 2 | 1 | 0 | 6 | 4 | 17 |
| Peavy,Jake | 10 | 15 | 16 | 12 | 21 | 13 | 6 | 6 | 5 | 17 | 7 | 128 |
| Pedroia,Dustin | | | | 2 | 18 | 26 | 24 | 12 | 27 | 17 | 25 | 151 |
| Peguero,Carlos | | | | | | | | | 2 | 1 | 0 | 3 |
| Pelfrey,Mike | | | | 0 | 1 | 12 | 4 | 12 | 3 | 2 | 3 | 37 |
| Pena,Brayan | | | 0 | 1 | 0 | 0 | 2 | 4 | 5 | 3 | 2 | 17 |
| Pena,Carlos | 23 | 11 | 7 | 0 | 28 | 22 | 17 | 16 | 18 | 10 | 4 | 156 |
| Pena,Ramiro | | | | | | | 4 | 3 | 1 | 0 | 3 | 11 |
| Pence,Hunter | | | | | 18 | 19 | 17 | 21 | 24 | 18 | 25 | 142 |
| Pennington,Cliff | | | | | | 3 | 7 | 19 | 18 | 10 | 5 | 62 |
| Peralta,Jhonny | 5 | 0 | 25 | 15 | 21 | 19 | 10 | 16 | 22 | 12 | 19 | 164 |
| Peralta,Joel | | | 2 | 5 | 6 | 0 | 0 | 5 | 8 | 6 | 7 | 39 |
| Peralta,Wily | | | | | | | | | | 3 | 5 | 8 |
| Perez,Chris | | | | | | 4 | 3 | 13 | 10 | 8 | 5 | 43 |
| Perez,Hernan | | | | | | | | | | 0 | 1 | 1 |
| Perez,Juan | | | | | | | | | | | 3 | 3 |
| Perez,Juan | | | | 0 | 0 | | | | 1 | 0 | 1 | 2 |
| Perez,Luis | | | | | | | | | 2 | 3 | 0 | 5 |
| Perez,Martin | | | | | | | | | | 1 | 8 | 9 |
| Perez,Oliver | 5 | 16 | 2 | 0 | 10 | 8 | 1 | 0 | | 3 | 4 | 49 |
| Perez,Salvador | | | | | | | | | 7 | 10 | 23 | 40 |
| Perkins,Glen | | | | 1 | 2 | 7 | 2 | 0 | 8 | 10 | 13 | 43 |
| Pestano,Vinnie | | | | | | | | 0 | 8 | 8 | 1 | 17 |
| Petit,Yusmeiro | | | | 0 | 3 | 3 | 1 | | | 0 | 2 | 9 |
| Petricka,Jake | | | | | | | | | | | 1 | 1 |
| Pettibone,Jonathan | | | | | | | | | | | 5 | 5 |
| Pettitte,Andy | 124 | 5 | 21 | 12 | 13 | 10 | 11 | 10 | | 6 | 12 | 224 |
| Phegley,Josh | | | | | | | | | | | 2 | 2 |
| Phelps,Cord | | | | | | | | | 0 | 1 | 0 | 1 |
| Phelps,David | | | | | | | | | | 7 | 3 | 10 |
| Phillips,Brandon | 5 | 0 | 0 | 14 | 17 | 19 | 19 | 18 | 22 | 19 | 22 | 155 |
| Phillips,Zach | | | | | | | | | 1 | 0 | 0 | 1 |
| Pie,Felix | | | | | 5 | 2 | 5 | 6 | 1 | | 0 | 19 |
| Pierre,Juan | 55 | 22 | 14 | 15 | 12 | 9 | 12 | 14 | 14 | 12 | 4 | 183 |
| Pierzynski,A.J. | 59 | 12 | 11 | 14 | 8 | 8 | 10 | 12 | 11 | 19 | 17 | 181 |
| Pill,Brett | | | | | | | | | 2 | 1 | 0 | 3 |
| Pillar,Kevin | | | | | | | | | | | 1 | 1 |
| Pimentel,Stolmy | | | | | | | | | | | 1 | 1 |
| Pinto,Josmil | | | | | | | | | | | 4 | 4 |
| Plouffe,Trevor | | | | | | | | 0 | 6 | 8 | 8 | 22 |
| Polanco,Placido | 64 | 17 | 22 | 14 | 24 | 15 | 21 | 16 | 14 | 5 | 5 | 217 |
| Pollock,A.J. | | | | | | | | | | 2 | 14 | 16 |
| Pomeranz,Drew | | | | | | | | | 1 | 4 | 0 | 5 |
| Porcello,Rick | | | | | | | 13 | 5 | 8 | 7 | 9 | 42 |
| Posey,Buster | | | | | | | 0 | 20 | 9 | 38 | 24 | 91 |
| Prado,Martin | | | | 2 | 1 | 9 | 12 | 22 | 12 | 23 | 15 | 96 |
| Presley,Alex | | | | | | | | 0 | 8 | 5 | 3 | 16 |
| Pressly,Ryan | | | | | | | | | | | 4 | 4 |
| Price,David | | | | | | 1 | 6 | 17 | 13 | 19 | 12 | 68 |
| Pridie,Jason | | | | | | 0 | 0 | | 4 | 0 | 0 | 4 |
| Profar,Jurickson | | | | | | | | | | 0 | 5 | 5 |
| Pryor,Stephen | | | | | | | | | | 1 | 1 | 2 |
| Puig,Yasiel | | | | | | | | | | | 17 | 17 |
| Pujols,Albert | 102 | 37 | 34 | 37 | 32 | 34 | 39 | 32 | 26 | 25 | 10 | 408 |
| Punto,Nick | 1 | 4 | 6 | 12 | 5 | 10 | 11 | 5 | 8 | 3 | 8 | 73 |
| Purcey,David | | | | | | 1 | 0 | 2 | 1 | | 2 | 6 |
| Putkonen,Luke | | | | | | | | | | 1 | 2 | 3 |
| Putz,J.J. | 0 | 3 | 5 | 17 | 20 | 5 | 1 | 8 | 13 | 10 | 5 | 87 |
| Qualls,Chad | | 4 | 7 | 9 | 9 | 11 | 8 | 0 | 5 | 1 | 6 | 60 |
| Quentin,Carlos | | | | 5 | 5 | 23 | 8 | 15 | 16 | 11 | 14 | 97 |

| Player | <04 | 04 | 05 | 06 | 07 | 08 | 09 | 10 | 11 | 12 | 13 | Career |
|---|---|---|---|---|---|---|---|---|---|---|---|---|
| | WIN SHARES BY YEAR | | | | | | | | | | | |
| Quintana,Jose | | | | | | | | | | 9 | 13 | 22 |
| Quintanilla,Omar | | | 1 | 0 | 1 | 3 | 1 | | 1 | 3 | 7 | 17 |
| Quintero,Humberto | 0 | 1 | 1 | 0 | 1 | 3 | 4 | 6 | 1 | 3 | 3 | 23 |
| Quiroz,Guillermo | | 0 | 0 | 0 | 1 | 1 | 0 | 0 | | 0 | 1 | 3 |
| Raburn,Ryan | | 0 | | | 4 | 3 | 9 | 11 | 10 | 1 | 13 | 51 |
| Ramirez,Alexei | | | | | | 18 | 15 | 20 | 20 | 14 | 15 | 102 |
| Ramirez,Aramis | 58 | 19 | 18 | 21 | 21 | 25 | 15 | 13 | 25 | 22 | 10 | 247 |
| Ramirez,Erasmo | | | | | | | | | | 2 | 2 | 4 |
| Ramirez,Hanley | | | 0 | 25 | 27 | 32 | 34 | 22 | 10 | 17 | 23 | 190 |
| Ramirez,Jose | | | | | | | | | | | 1 | 1 |
| Ramirez,Ramon | | | | 7 | 0 | 9 | 8 | 7 | 7 | 2 | 0 | 40 |
| Ramirez,Wilkin | | | | | | | 1 | | 0 | | 1 | 2 |
| Ramos,A.J. | | | | | | | | | | 0 | 5 | 5 |
| Ramos,Cesar | | | | | | | 1 | 0 | 1 | 3 | 3 | 8 |
| Ramos,Wilson | | | | | | | | 3 | 13 | 3 | 8 | 27 |
| Ransom,Cody | 0 | 2 | | | 2 | 3 | 1 | 1 | 1 | 6 | 4 | 20 |
| Rapada,Clay | | | | | 0 | 2 | 0 | 1 | 1 | 4 | 0 | 8 |
| Rasmus,Colby | | | | | | | 13 | 17 | 11 | 15 | 20 | 76 |
| Rauch,Jon | 0 | 4 | 2 | 8 | 10 | 9 | 7 | 9 | 4 | 5 | 0 | 58 |
| Recker,Anthony | | | | | | | | | 0 | 0 | 4 | 4 |
| Reddick,Josh | | | | | | | 0 | 1 | 7 | 16 | 13 | 37 |
| Redmond,Todd | | | | | | | | | | 0 | 4 | 4 |
| Reed,Addison | | | | | | | | | 0 | 7 | 12 | 19 |
| Reid,Ryan | | | | | | | | | | | 1 | 1 |
| Reimold,Nolan | | | | | | | 10 | 0 | 11 | 4 | 0 | 25 |
| Rendon,Anthony | | | | | | | | | | | 12 | 12 |
| Resop,Chris | | | 0 | 1 | 0 | 0 | | 2 | 4 | 3 | 0 | 10 |
| Revere,Ben | | | | | | | | 0 | 9 | 11 | 10 | 30 |
| Reyes,Jose | 12 | 4 | 16 | 28 | 24 | 28 | 5 | 19 | 26 | 23 | 15 | 200 |
| Reynolds,Greg | | | | | | 0 | | | 1 | | 0 | 1 |
| Reynolds,Mark | | | | | 14 | 17 | 20 | 16 | 16 | 12 | 11 | 106 |
| Reynolds,Matt | | | | | | | | 2 | 3 | 4 | 3 | 12 |
| Rice,Scott | | | | | | | | | | | 3 | 3 |
| Richard,Clayton | | | | | | 0 | 8 | 10 | 2 | 7 | 0 | 27 |
| Richards,Garrett | | | | | | | | | 0 | 1 | 6 | 7 |
| Rienzo,Andre | | | | | | | | | | | 1 | 1 |
| Rios,Alex | | 7 | 9 | 18 | 22 | 20 | 11 | 18 | 4 | 22 | 15 | 146 |
| Rivera,Mariano | 127 | 18 | 19 | 16 | 12 | 20 | 15 | 14 | 14 | 2 | 16 | 273 |
| Rivera,Rene | | 0 | 2 | 2 | | | | | 2 | | 2 | 8 |
| Rizzo,Anthony | | | | | | | | | 0 | 12 | 14 | 26 |
| Roark,Tanner | | | | | | | | | | | 7 | 7 |
| Roberts,Brian | 19 | 16 | 28 | 13 | 22 | 20 | 20 | 7 | 3 | 1 | 9 | 158 |
| Roberts,Ryan | | | | 0 | 0 | 0 | 8 | 1 | 19 | 9 | 4 | 41 |
| Robertson,David | | | | | | 2 | 3 | 4 | 11 | 7 | 12 | 39 |
| Robertson,Tyler | | | | | | | | | | 1 | 0 | 1 |
| Robinson,Chris | | | | | | | | | | | 1 | 1 |
| Robinson,Derrick | | | | | | | | | | | 4 | 4 |
| Robinson,Shane | | | | | | | 0 | | 0 | 2 | 4 | 6 |
| Rodney,Fernando | 1 | | 6 | 8 | 3 | 4 | 10 | 6 | 1 | 19 | 11 | 69 |
| Rodriguez,Alex | 251 | 29 | 34 | 25 | 37 | 23 | 23 | 21 | 14 | 14 | 4 | 475 |
| Rodriguez,Francisco | 10 | 17 | 14 | 17 | 15 | 16 | 10 | 11 | 10 | 5 | 7 | 132 |
| Rodriguez,Henry | | | | | | | 0 | 1 | 4 | 1 | 1 | 7 |
| Rodriguez,Paco | | | | | | | | | | 1 | 6 | 7 |
| Rodriguez,Sean | | | | | | 3 | 0 | 9 | 10 | 8 | 4 | 34 |
| Rodriguez,Wandy | | | 2 | 2 | 7 | 9 | 16 | 11 | 10 | 9 | 3 | 69 |
| Roe,Chaz | | | | | | | | | | | 1 | 1 |
| Roenicke,Josh | | | | | | 0 | 1 | 0 | 1 | 7 | 3 | 12 |
| Rogers,Esmil | | | | | | | 0 | 0 | 0 | 4 | 4 | 8 |
| Rollins,Jimmy | 56 | 24 | 21 | 25 | 28 | 24 | 19 | 14 | 25 | 21 | 20 | 277 |
| Romero,Enny | | | | | | | | | | | 1 | 1 |
| Romero,Ricky | | | | | | | 10 | 14 | 20 | 2 | 0 | 46 |
| Romine,Andrew | | | | | | | | 0 | 0 | 2 | 3 | 5 |
| Romine,Austin | | | | | | | | | 0 | | 2 | 2 |
| Romo,Sergio | | | | | | 4 | 4 | 8 | 9 | 11 | 9 | 45 |
| Rondon,Bruce | | | | | | | | | | | 2 | 2 |
| Rondon,Hector | | | | | | | | | | | 2 | 2 |
| Rosales,Adam | | | | | | 0 | 3 | 8 | 0 | 1 | 2 | 14 |
| Rosario,Sandy | | | | | | | | 0 | 0 | 0 | 3 | 3 |
| Rosario,Wilin | | | | | | | | | 1 | 9 | 13 | 23 |
| Rosenberg,B.J. | | | | | | | | | | 0 | 1 | 1 |
| Rosenthal,Trevor | | | | | | | | | | 2 | 7 | 9 |
| Ross,Cody | 1 | | 0 | 6 | 10 | 16 | 16 | 14 | 14 | 13 | 8 | 98 |
| Ross,David | 5 | 2 | 3 | 13 | 7 | 5 | 6 | 6 | 7 | 6 | 2 | 62 |

| Player | <04 | 04 | 05 | 06 | 07 | 08 | 09 | 10 | 11 | 12 | 13 | Career |
|---|---|---|---|---|---|---|---|---|---|---|---|---|
| | WIN SHARES BY YEAR | | | | | | | | | | | |
| Ross,Robbie | | | | | | | | | | 8 | 6 | 14 |
| Ross,Tyson | | | | | | | | 0 | 3 | 0 | 5 | 8 |
| Rosscup,Zac | | | | | | | | | | | 1 | 1 |
| Ruf,Darin | | | | | | | | | | 1 | 8 | 9 |
| Ruffin,Chance | | | | | | | | | 1 | | 0 | 1 |
| Ruggiano,Justin | | | | | 0 | 1 | | | 4 | 11 | 8 | 24 |
| Ruiz,Carlos | | | | 2 | 13 | 6 | 13 | 19 | 18 | 24 | 9 | 104 |
| Rupp,Cameron | | | | | | | | | | | 1 | 1 |
| Rusin,Chris | | | | | | | | | | 0 | 3 | 3 |
| Russell,James | | | | | | | | 1 | 2 | 6 | 4 | 13 |
| Rutledge,Josh | | | | | | | | | | 6 | 5 | 11 |
| Ryan,Brendan | | | | | 5 | 2 | 14 | 8 | 13 | 11 | 4 | 57 |
| Ryu,Hyun-Jin | | | | | | | | | | | 13 | 13 |
| Rzepczynski,Marc | | | | | | | 4 | 2 | 5 | 2 | 3 | 16 |
| Sabathia,CC | 38 | 11 | 12 | 15 | 24 | 23 | 18 | 20 | 19 | 14 | 8 | 202 |
| Salas,Fernando | | | | | | | | 1 | 12 | 2 | 0 | 15 |
| Salazar,Danny | | | | | | | | | | | 4 | 4 |
| Sale,Chris | | | | | | | | 5 | 11 | 19 | 15 | 50 |
| Saltalamacchia,J | | | | | 5 | 6 | 6 | 0 | 7 | 8 | 15 | 47 |
| Samardzija,Jeff | | | | | | 3 | 0 | 0 | 7 | 8 | 7 | 25 |
| Sanabia,Alex | | | | | | | | 4 | 1 | | 0 | 5 |
| Sanchez,Angel | | | | 0 | | | | 7 | 5 | | 0 | 12 |
| Sanchez,Anibal | | | | 10 | 1 | 0 | 5 | 11 | 10 | 10 | 17 | 64 |
| Sanchez,Eduardo | | | | | | | | | 5 | 0 | 0 | 5 |
| Sanchez,Gaby | | | | | | 1 | 1 | 17 | 16 | 3 | 10 | 48 |
| Sanchez,Hector | | | | | | | | | 0 | 5 | 4 | 9 |
| Sanchez,Jonathan | | | | 2 | 0 | 6 | 7 | 14 | 2 | 0 | 0 | 31 |
| Sanchez,Tony | | | | | | | | | | | 1 | 1 |
| Sandoval,Pablo | | | | | | 6 | 27 | 9 | 23 | 18 | 22 | 105 |
| Santana,Carlos | | | | | | | | 7 | 22 | 21 | 26 | 76 |
| Santana,Ervin | | | 6 | 12 | 3 | 19 | 6 | 14 | 14 | 2 | 14 | 90 |
| Santiago,Hector | | | | | | | | | 1 | 7 | 8 | 16 |
| Santiago,Ramon | 9 | 0 | 0 | 1 | 2 | 6 | 7 | 9 | 5 | 3 | 3 | 45 |
| Santos,Omir | | | | | | 0 | 7 | | 0 | 0 | 0 | 7 |
| Santos,Sergio | | | | | | | | 5 | 12 | 0 | 4 | 21 |
| Sappelt,Dave | | | | | | | | | 1 | 2 | 1 | 4 |
| Satin,Josh | | | | | | | | | 0 | 0 | 7 | 7 |
| Saunders,Joe | | | 0 | 4 | 7 | 18 | 11 | 6 | 12 | 8 | 3 | 69 |
| Saunders,Michael | | | | | | | 1 | 6 | 2 | 17 | 10 | 36 |
| Savery,Joe | | | | | | | | | 1 | 0 | 1 | 2 |
| Scahill,Rob | | | | | | | | | | 1 | 1 | 2 |
| Schafer,Jordan | | | | | | | 2 | | 8 | 5 | 8 | 23 |
| Schafer,Logan | | | | | | | | | 0 | 1 | 5 | 6 |
| Scheppers,Tanner | | | | | | | | | | 1 | 10 | 11 |
| Scherzer,Max | | | | | | 4 | 9 | 13 | 10 | 14 | 20 | 70 |
| Schierholtz,Nate | | | | | 2 | 3 | 8 | 5 | 13 | 8 | 14 | 53 |
| Schumaker,Skip | | | 0 | 0 | 7 | 16 | 18 | 14 | 11 | 7 | 8 | 81 |
| Scott,Luke | | | 0 | 11 | 11 | 11 | 11 | 14 | 4 | 6 | 8 | 76 |
| Scribner,Evan | | | | | | | | | 0 | 3 | 1 | 4 |
| Scutaro,Marco | 2 | 11 | 11 | 11 | 8 | 15 | 21 | 15 | 11 | 21 | 16 | 142 |
| Seager,Kyle | | | | | | | | | 3 | 24 | 23 | 50 |
| Segura,Jean | | | | | | | | | | 4 | 21 | 25 |
| Sellers,Justin | | | | | | | | | 4 | 0 | 1 | 5 |
| Semien,Marcus | | | | | | | | | | | 2 | 2 |
| Shaw,Bryan | | | | | | | | | 3 | 4 | 7 | 14 |
| Shields,James | | | | 6 | 12 | 15 | 11 | 3 | 20 | 12 | 18 | 97 |
| Shoemaker,Matt | | | | | | | | | | | 1 | 1 |
| Shoppach,Kelly | | | 0 | 3 | 7 | 14 | 7 | 4 | 4 | 7 | 2 | 48 |
| Shuck,J.B. | | | | | | | | | 2 | | 11 | 13 |
| Siegrist,Kevin | | | | | | | | | | | 6 | 6 |
| Sierra,Moises | | | | | | | | | | 1 | 5 | 6 |
| Simmons,Andrelton | | | | | | | | | | 8 | 19 | 27 |
| Simon,Alfredo | | | | | | 0 | 0 | 4 | 3 | 6 | 7 | 20 |
| Sipp,Tony | | | | | | | 3 | 4 | 7 | 2 | 1 | 17 |
| Sizemore,Scott | | | | | | | | 2 | 14 | | 0 | 16 |
| Skaggs,Tyler | | | | | | | | | | 0 | 1 | 1 |
| Slowey,Kevin | | | | | 3 | 10 | 5 | 8 | 0 | | 3 | 29 |
| Smith,Joe | | | | | 3 | 6 | 2 | 3 | 8 | 6 | 9 | 37 |
| Smith,Seth | | | | | 1 | 3 | 14 | 9 | 13 | 11 | 10 | 61 |
| Smith,Will | | | | | | | | | | 2 | 3 | 5 |
| Smoak,Justin | | | | | | | | 7 | 10 | 9 | 12 | 38 |
| Smyly,Drew | | | | | | | | | | 6 | 10 | 16 |
| Snider,Travis | | | | | | 3 | 4 | 8 | 3 | 5 | 5 | 28 |

| Player | <04 | 04 | 05 | 06 | 07 | 08 | 09 | 10 | 11 | 12 | 13 | Career |
|---|---|---|---|---|---|---|---|---|---|---|---|---|
| | WIN SHARES BY YEAR | | | | | | | | | | | |
| Snyder,Brandon | | | | | | | | 1 | 0 | 1 | 0 | 2 |
| Snyder,Chris | | 2 | 4 | 7 | 16 | 15 | 3 | 8 | 5 | 4 | 1 | 65 |
| Sogard,Eric | | | | | | | | 0 | 1 | 1 | 10 | 12 |
| Solano,Donovan | | | | | | | | | | 8 | 9 | 17 |
| Solano,Jhonatan | | | | | | | | | | 2 | 0 | 2 |
| Soria,Joakim | | | | | 13 | 17 | 12 | 15 | 7 | | 2 | 66 |
| Soriano,Alfonso | 71 | 16 | 16 | 26 | 20 | 16 | 10 | 15 | 11 | 19 | 21 | 241 |
| Soriano,Rafael | 8 | 0 | 1 | 7 | 9 | 2 | 12 | 14 | 4 | 13 | 11 | 81 |
| Soto,Geovany | | | 0 | 0 | 3 | 21 | 8 | 15 | 10 | 5 | 8 | 70 |
| Span,Denard | | | | | | 16 | 21 | 20 | 6 | 15 | 19 | 97 |
| Stammen,Craig | | | | | | | 3 | 3 | 2 | 9 | 7 | 24 |
| Stanton,Giancarlo | | | | | | | | 13 | 19 | 19 | 15 | 66 |
| Stauffer,Tim | | | 0 | 1 | 0 | | 3 | 9 | 7 | 0 | 3 | 23 |
| Stewart,Chris | | | | 0 | 1 | 0 | | 0 | 3 | 2 | 8 | 14 |
| Stinson,Josh | | | | | | | | | 0 | 1 | 1 | 2 |
| Storen,Drew | | | | | | | | 5 | 15 | 5 | 3 | 28 |
| Storey,Mickey | | | | | | | | | | 1 | 0 | 1 |
| Straily,Dan | | | | | | | | | | 2 | 7 | 9 |
| Strasburg,Stephen | | | | | | | | 5 | 2 | 14 | 11 | 32 |
| Street,Huston | | | 16 | 14 | 10 | 10 | 15 | 9 | 7 | 9 | 8 | 98 |
| Strop,Pedro | | | | | | | 0 | 0 | 3 | 10 | 5 | 18 |
| Stubbs,Drew | | | | | | | 5 | 18 | 13 | 6 | 10 | 52 |
| Stults,Eric | | | | 1 | 1 | 2 | 2 | | 0 | 7 | 7 | 20 |
| Stutes,Michael | | | | | | | | | 5 | 0 | 1 | 6 |
| Suzuki,Ichiro | 85 | 27 | 22 | 24 | 33 | 19 | 28 | 23 | 15 | 11 | 10 | 297 |
| Suzuki,Kurt | | | | | 7 | 17 | 17 | 10 | 8 | 10 | 6 | 75 |
| Swarzak,Anthony | | | | | | | 0 | | 4 | 2 | 8 | 14 |
| Sweeney,Ryan | | | | 0 | 0 | 12 | 12 | 8 | 7 | 3 | 6 | 48 |
| Swisher,Nick | | 1 | 12 | 20 | 18 | 12 | 18 | 22 | 19 | 24 | 17 | 163 |
| Tabata,Jose | | | | | | | | 14 | 8 | 6 | 12 | 40 |
| Takahashi,Hisanori | | | | | | | | 9 | 5 | 0 | 0 | 14 |
| Tanaka,Kensuke | | | | | | | | | | | 1 | 1 |
| Taylor,Michael | | | | | | | | | 1 | 0 | 0 | 1 |
| Tazawa,Junichi | | | | | | | 0 | | 0 | 6 | 6 | 12 |
| Teaford,Everett | | | | | | | | | 3 | 2 | 0 | 5 |
| Teagarden,Taylor | | | | | | 4 | 3 | 1 | 1 | 2 | 1 | 12 |
| Teheran,Julio | | | | | | | | | 0 | 0 | 12 | 12 |
| Teixeira,Mark | 12 | 24 | 33 | 21 | 25 | 28 | 26 | 24 | 22 | 16 | 1 | 232 |
| Tejada,Miguel | 134 | 28 | 26 | 23 | 14 | 14 | 22 | 18 | 5 | | 4 | 288 |
| Tejada,Ruben | | | | | | | | 3 | 11 | 14 | 4 | 32 |
| Tepesch,Nick | | | | | | | | | | | 3 | 3 |
| Terdoslavich,Joey | | | | | | | | | | | 1 | 1 |
| Thatcher,Joe | | | | | 2 | 0 | 3 | 5 | 0 | 2 | 3 | 15 |
| Thayer,Dale | | | | | | | 0 | 0 | 0 | 6 | 4 | 10 |
| Thielbar,Caleb | | | | | | | | | | | 5 | 5 |
| Thole,Josh | | | | | | | 2 | 8 | 9 | 4 | 1 | 24 |
| Thomas,Clete | | | | | | 3 | 7 | | | 1 | 2 | 13 |
| Thornburg,Tyler | | | | | | | | | | 1 | 6 | 7 |
| Thornton,Matt | | 2 | 1 | 7 | 4 | 10 | 12 | 12 | 5 | 7 | 3 | 63 |
| Tillman,Chris | | | | | | | 2 | 1 | 1 | 8 | 14 | 26 |
| Tolleson,Shawn | | | | | | | | | | 2 | 0 | 2 |
| Tomlin,Josh | | | | | | | | 4 | 9 | 0 | 0 | 13 |
| Tonkin,Michael | | | | | | | | | | | 1 | 1 |
| Torrealba,Yorvit | 12 | 4 | 4 | 6 | 6 | 4 | 9 | 12 | 7 | 3 | 2 | 69 |
| Torres,Alex | | | | | | | | | 1 | | 8 | 9 |
| Torres,Andres | 0 | 0 | 0 | | | | 8 | 23 | 10 | 10 | 4 | 55 |
| Torres,Carlos | | | | | | | 0 | 0 | | 3 | 4 | 7 |
| Tovar,Wilfredo | | | | | | | | | | | 1 | 1 |
| Tracy,Chad | | 11 | 19 | 14 | 6 | 4 | 3 | 2 | | 3 | 0 | 62 |
| Triunfel,Carlos | | | | | | | | | | 1 | 0 | 1 |
| Troncoso,Ramon | | | | | | 2 | 8 | 2 | 0 | | 0 | 12 |
| Trout,Mike | | | | | | | | | 3 | 38 | 40 | 81 |
| Trumbo,Mark | | | | | | | | 0 | 14 | 19 | 14 | 47 |
| Tuiasosopo,Matt | | | | | | 0 | 0 | 1 | | | 6 | 7 |
| Tulowitzki,Troy | | | | 1 | 24 | 9 | 24 | 25 | 25 | 5 | 21 | 134 |
| Turner,Jacob | | | | | | | | | 0 | 2 | 4 | 6 |
| Turner,Justin | | | | | | | 0 | 0 | 15 | 4 | 3 | 22 |
| Uehara,Koji | | | | | | | 4 | 9 | 8 | 5 | 18 | 44 |
| Uggla,Dan | | | | 23 | 16 | 24 | 18 | 24 | 21 | 23 | 10 | 159 |
| Upton,B.J. | | 4 | | 2 | 22 | 23 | 13 | 18 | 20 | 17 | 3 | 122 |
| Upton,Justin | | | | | 1 | 8 | 19 | 14 | 26 | 16 | 21 | 105 |
| Uribe,Juan | 26 | 18 | 17 | 11 | 13 | 11 | 13 | 16 | 2 | 2 | 15 | 144 |
| Utley,Chase | 5 | 8 | 25 | 27 | 28 | 30 | 32 | 25 | 18 | 13 | 22 | 233 |

| Player | <04 | 04 | 05 | 06 | 07 | 08 | 09 | 10 | 11 | 12 | 13 | Career |
|---|---|---|---|---|---|---|---|---|---|---|---|---|
| | WIN SHARES BY YEAR | | | | | | | | | | | |
| Valaika,Chris | | | | | | | | 0 | 1 | | 1 | 2 |
| Valbuena,Luis | | | | | | 1 | 6 | 4 | 0 | 5 | 9 | 25 |
| Valdes,Raul | | | | | | | | 2 | 1 | 3 | 0 | 6 |
| Valdespin,Jordany | | | | | | | | | | 4 | 1 | 5 |
| Valencia,Danny | | | | | | | | 12 | 10 | 1 | 5 | 28 |
| Valverde,Jose | 11 | 3 | 13 | 4 | 14 | 14 | 11 | 10 | 15 | 11 | 1 | 107 |
| Van Slyke,Scott | | | | | | | | | | 1 | 3 | 4 |
| Vargas,Jason | | | 4 | 1 | 0 | | 3 | 10 | 8 | 11 | 7 | 44 |
| Varvaro,Anthony | | | | | | | | 0 | 2 | 0 | 6 | 8 |
| Veal,Donnie | | | | | | | 0 | | | 3 | 2 | 5 |
| Velazquez,Gil | | | | | | 0 | 0 | | 0 | 1 | 0 | 1 |
| Venable,Will | | | | | | 3 | 8 | 15 | 12 | 17 | 14 | 69 |
| Ventura,Yordano | | | | | | | | | | | 1 | 1 |
| Veras,Jose | | | | 1 | 1 | 5 | 2 | 4 | 5 | 6 | 9 | 33 |
| Verlander,Justin | | | 0 | 15 | 16 | 8 | 21 | 17 | 27 | 23 | 14 | 141 |
| Viciedo,Dayan | | | | | | | | 3 | 2 | 12 | 9 | 26 |
| Victorino,Shane | 0 | | 1 | 11 | 11 | 20 | 22 | 23 | 23 | 17 | 19 | 147 |
| Villanueva,Carlos | | | | 4 | 8 | 6 | 2 | 2 | 7 | 6 | 6 | 41 |
| Villar,Jonathan | | | | | | | | | | | 3 | 3 |
| Villarreal,Brayan | | | | | | | | | 0 | 5 | 0 | 5 |
| Vincent,Nick | | | | | | | | | | 3 | 6 | 9 |
| Vogelsong,Ryan | 1 | 0 | 3 | 0 | | | | | 14 | 10 | 0 | 28 |
| Vogt,Stephen | | | | | | | | | | 0 | 4 | 4 |
| Volquez,Edinson | | | 0 | 0 | 2 | 16 | 2 | 3 | 0 | 6 | 0 | 29 |
| Volstad,Chris | | | | | | 7 | 4 | 6 | 2 | 0 | 0 | 19 |
| Votto,Joey | | | | | 3 | 19 | 24 | 33 | 33 | 27 | 30 | 169 |
| Wacha,Michael | | | | | | | | | | | 4 | 4 |
| Wagner,Neil | | | | | | | | | 0 | | 2 | 2 |
| Wainwright,Adam | | | 0 | 9 | 13 | 11 | 21 | 20 | | 9 | 16 | 99 |
| Walden,Jordan | | | | | | | | 2 | 11 | 3 | 4 | 20 |
| Walker,Neil | | | | | | | 0 | 16 | 20 | 21 | 20 | 77 |
| Walker,Taijuan | | | | | | | | | | | 1 | 1 |
| Wallace,Brett | | | | | | | | 1 | 4 | 5 | 6 | 16 |
| Walters,P.J. | | | | | | | 0 | 0 | 0 | 1 | 0 | 1 |
| Walters,Zach | | | | | | | | | | | 1 | 1 |
| Wang,Chien-Ming | | | 7 | 16 | 15 | 7 | 0 | | 2 | 0 | 0 | 47 |
| Warren,Adam | | | | | | | | | | 0 | 6 | 6 |
| Watson,Tony | | | | | | | | | 3 | 5 | 8 | 16 |
| Weaver,Jered | | | | 14 | 12 | 11 | 17 | 19 | 24 | 16 | 10 | 123 |
| Webb,Daniel | | | | | | | | | | | 1 | 1 |
| Webb,Ryan | | | | | | | 1 | 4 | 4 | 4 | 5 | 18 |
| Weber,Thad | | | | | | | | | | 0 | 1 | 1 |
| Weeks,Jemile | | | | | | | | | 15 | 8 | 0 | 23 |
| Weeks,Rickie | 0 | | 9 | 10 | 14 | 16 | 7 | 29 | 18 | 14 | 4 | 121 |
| Wells,Casper | | | | | | | | 4 | 6 | 10 | 0 | 20 |
| Wells,Vernon | 48 | 13 | 20 | 24 | 15 | 15 | 8 | 21 | 10 | 2 | 5 | 181 |
| Werth,Jayson | 2 | 11 | 9 | | 13 | 17 | 26 | 22 | 17 | 13 | 26 | 156 |
| Westbrook,Jake | 9 | 15 | 8 | 13 | 9 | 3 | | 9 | 4 | 8 | 2 | 80 |
| Wheeler,Zack | | | | | | | | | | | 5 | 5 |
| Wieters,Matt | | | | | | | 9 | 12 | 23 | 23 | 19 | 86 |
| Wigginton,Ty | 17 | 10 | 4 | 13 | 11 | 14 | 4 | 8 | 4 | 5 | 0 | 90 |
| Wilhelmsen,Tom | | | | | | | | | 3 | 13 | 8 | 24 |
| Williams,Jerome | 9 | 7 | 6 | 0 | 0 | | | | 3 | 4 | 5 | 34 |
| Willingham,Josh | | 0 | 0 | 14 | 19 | 13 | 11 | 14 | 18 | 22 | 10 | 121 |
| Wilson,Alex | | | | | | | | | | | 1 | 1 |
| Wilson,Brian | | | | 1 | 5 | 9 | 15 | 17 | 9 | 0 | 2 | 58 |
| Wilson,C.J. | | | 0 | 3 | 9 | 2 | 11 | 15 | 20 | 9 | 13 | 82 |
| Wilson,Josh | | | 0 | | 3 | | 3 | 7 | 1 | | 1 | 15 |
| Wilson,Justin | | | | | | | | | | 0 | 8 | 8 |
| Wise,DeWayne | 1 | 3 | | 0 | 0 | 2 | 2 | 4 | 1 | 6 | 1 | 20 |
| Withrow,Chris | | | | | | | | | | | 4 | 4 |
| Wolf,Ross | | | | | 0 | | | 1 | | | 2 | 3 |
| Wong,Kolten | | | | | | | | | | | 1 | 1 |
| Wood,Alex | | | | | | | | | | | 4 | 4 |
| Wood,Blake | | | | | | | | 2 | 4 | | 0 | 6 |
| Wood,Travis | | | | | | | | 6 | 3 | 5 | 15 | 29 |
| Wooten,Rob | | | | | | | | | | | 2 | 2 |
| Workman,Brandon | | | | | | | | | | | 2 | 2 |
| Worley,Vance | | | | | | | | 2 | 11 | 5 | 0 | 18 |
| Worth,Danny | | | | | | | | 3 | 0 | 2 | 0 | 5 |
| Wright,David | | 9 | 26 | 30 | 34 | 27 | 20 | 25 | 14 | 30 | 26 | 241 |
| Wright,Jamey | 43 | 5 | 4 | 4 | 5 | 3 | 4 | 3 | 6 | 3 | 5 | 85 |
| Wright,Steven | | | | | | | | | | | 1 | 1 |

| WIN SHARES BY YEAR | | | | | | | | | | | | |
|---|---|---|---|---|---|---|---|---|---|---|---|---|
| Player | <04 | 04 | 05 | 06 | 07 | 08 | 09 | 10 | 11 | 12 | 13 | Career |
| Wright,Wesley | | | | | | 3 | 1 | 0 | 1 | 4 | 3 | 12 |
| Yelich,Christian | | | | | | | | | | | 8 | 8 |
| Youkilis,Kevin | | 8 | 3 | 22 | 20 | 27 | 28 | 19 | 18 | 11 | 2 | 158 |
| Young,Chris | | | | 2 | 14 | 17 | 8 | 19 | 21 | 9 | 7 | 97 |
| Young,Delmon | | | | 2 | 17 | 13 | 7 | 22 | 10 | 7 | 7 | 85 |
| Young,Eric | | | | | | | 0 | 2 | 4 | 5 | 11 | 22 |
| Young,Michael | 40 | 25 | 29 | 26 | 23 | 20 | 17 | 16 | 23 | 9 | 14 | 242 |
| Zagurski,Mike | | | | | 1 | | | 0 | 0 | 1 | 0 | 2 |
| Zeid,Josh | | | | | | | | | | | 2 | 2 |
| Ziegler,Brad | | | | | | 12 | 7 | 5 | 6 | 8 | 13 | 51 |
| Zimmerman,Ryan | | | 2 | 24 | 20 | 9 | 21 | 23 | 15 | 22 | 23 | 159 |
| Zimmermann,Jordan | | | | | | | 3 | 1 | 11 | 15 | 15 | 45 |
| Zito,Barry | 67 | 12 | 13 | 17 | 8 | 5 | 10 | 7 | 0 | 6 | 0 | 145 |
| Zobrist,Ben | | | | 2 | 1 | 8 | 27 | 21 | 28 | 27 | 26 | 140 |
| Zunino,Mike | | | | | | | | | | | 2 | 2 |

# Instant Replay

Since their introduction in 2008, instant replays have been used more and more frequently in baseball, even with their limited jurisdiction over disputed home run calls in fair vs. foul, fan interference, and wall border situations. Over a six-year period, 34 percent of 386 reviewed calls have been overturned.

Starting in 2014, MLB is greatly expanding instant replays with the introduction of a challenge system similar to that in the NFL. Look for our own tracking of instant replays to expand, as well.

The chart below summarizes the results from day one of instant replay. The next two pages provide the details of every instant replay from 2013.

### Instant Replay Summary

| Season | Instant Replays | Calls Overturned | Percentage |
|---|---|---|---|
| 2008 | 7 | 2 | 29% |
| 2009 | 59 | 22 | 37% |
| 2010 | 69 | 24 | 35% |
| 2011 | 66 | 17 | 26% |
| 2012 | 88 | 33 | 38% |
| 2013 | 95 | 31 | 33% |
| Totals | 384 | 129 | 34% |

# Instant Replay in 2013

| Date | Matchup | Pitcher | Hitter | Inning | Outs | Men On | Score | Initial Ruling | Video Ruling |
|---|---|---|---|---|---|---|---|---|---|
| 03/31/2013 | TEX@HOU | Harrison,Matt | Maxwell,Justin | 4 | 2 | 12_ | 0-0 | 3B | 3B |
| 04/04/2013 | LAA@CIN | Blanton,Joe | Frazier,Todd | 4 | 0 | ___ | 2-2 | 2B | 2B |
| 04/05/2013 | WAS@CIN | Haren,Dan | Choo,Shin-Soo | 4 | 1 | ___ | 5-0 | HR | HR |
| 04/07/2013 | KC@PHI | Hamels,Cole | Butler,Billy | 5 | 1 | 123 | 2-4 | 2B | HR |
| 04/10/2013 | HOU@SEA | Peacock,Brad | Shoppach,Kelly | 5 | 1 | 1__ | 1-5 | 2B | 2B |
| 04/12/2013 | ATL@WAS | Detwiler,Ross | Upton,Justin | 6 | 2 | ___ | 0-4 | 2B | 2B |
| 04/13/2013 | LAN@ARI | Ryu,Hyun-Jin | Goldschmidt,Paul | 4 | 1 | ___ | 0-1 | 2B | 2B |
| 04/14/2013 | CIN@PIT | Latos,Mat | Snider,Travis | 7 | 2 | 1__ | 1-5 | 2B | 2B |
| 04/17/2013 | PHI@CIN | Lannan,John | Cozart,Zack | 1 | 1 | ___ | 0-0 | 2B | 2B |
| 04/17/2013 | TB@BAL | Moore,Matt | Jones,Adam | 3 | 2 | 1__ | 0-2 | 2B | HR |
| 04/21/2013 | CLE@HOU | Ambriz,Hector | Reynolds,Mark | 7 | 2 | ___ | 4-4 | HR | HR |
| 04/24/2013 | LAN@NYN | Harvey,Matt | Kemp,Matt | 6 | 2 | 1__ | 1-1 | 3B | HR |
| 04/26/2013 | TB@CHA | Reed,Addison | Molina,Jose | 9 | 1 | ___ | 3-5 | 2B | 2B |
| 04/28/2013 | CLE@KC | Guthrie,Jeremy | Santana,Carlos | 2 | 1 | ___ | 0-0 | 2B | 2B |
| 04/28/2013 | PIT@STL | Salas,Fernando | Jones,Garrett | 7 | 2 | ___ | 3-0 | 3B | HR |
| 04/29/2013 | LAA@OAK | Williams,Jerome | Young,Chris | 10 | 2 | ___ | 7-7 | 3B | 3B |
| 04/30/2013 | PIT@MIL | Badenhop,Burke | Marte,Starling | 6 | 2 | 1_3 | 5-7 | 2B | HR |
| 04/30/2013 | SD@CHN | Thayer,Dale | DeJesus,David | 7 | 0 | ___ | 4-10 | 2B | HR |
| 05/01/2013 | LAA@OAK | Milone,Tommy | Trumbo,Mark | 6 | 1 | ___ | 3-2 | 2B | HR |
| 05/03/2013 | BAL@LAA | Gonzalez,Miguel | Aybar,Erick | 3 | 2 | ___ | 1-0 | 2B | 2B |
| 05/03/2013 | DET@HOU | Norris,Bud | Martinez,Victor | 4 | 1 | __3 | 1-0 | 1B | 1B |
| 05/03/2013 | OAK@NYA | Sabathia,CC | Donaldson,Josh | 6 | 0 | 1__ | 1-0 | 1B | 1B |
| 05/05/2013 | MIA@PHI | Halladay,Roy | Ozuna,Marcell | 1 | 1 | 123 | 0-0 | 2B | 2B |
| 05/05/2013 | MIA@PHI | Halladay,Roy | Hechavarria,Adeiny | 3 | 1 | 123 | 5-0 | 2B | HR |
| 05/06/2013 | TOR@TB | Buehrle,Mark | Johnson,Kelly | 3 | 0 | 12_ | 0-0 | 1B | 1B |
| 05/06/2013 | CHA@KC | Shields,James | Ramirez,Alexei | 7 | 2 | 1__ | 0-1 | Foul | Foul |
| 05/07/2013 | MIN@BOS | Dempster,Ryan | Doumit,Ryan | 7 | 1 | ___ | 1-0 | HR | HR |
| 05/07/2013 | TOR@TB | Hernandez,Roberto | Bautista,Jose | 1 | 2 | ___ | 0-0 | 2B | 2B |
| 05/08/2013 | LAA@HOU | Blanton,Joe | Dominguez,Matt | 3 | 1 | ___ | 0-0 | 2B | 2B |
| 05/08/2013 | ATL@CIN | Leake,Mike | Gattis,Evan | 4 | 0 | ___ | 0-1 | Foul | Foul |
| 05/08/2013 | OAK@CLE | Perez,Chris | Rosales,Adam | 9 | 2 | ___ | 3-4 | 2B | 2B |
| 05/10/2013 | MIA@LAN | Belisario,Ronald | Coghlan,Chris | 7 | 0 | 1__ | 3-3 | 2B | 2B |
| 05/10/2013 | PIT@NYN | Marcum,Shaun | Jones,Garrett | 5 | 1 | 1_3 | 3-0 | 3B | HR |
| 05/12/2013 | ATL@SF | Medlen,Kris | Scutaro,Marco | 6 | 1 | ___ | 5-0 | GR2B | GR2B |
| 05/12/2013 | TEX@HOU | Gonzalez,Edgar | Beltre,Adrian | 5 | 1 | 12_ | 9-1 | 2B | HR |
| 05/18/2013 | TB@BAL | Jurrjens,Jair | Molina,Jose | 3 | 1 | ___ | 0-4 | 2B | 2B |
| 05/19/2013 | TB@BAL | Tillman,Chris | Joyce,Matt | 6 | 1 | ___ | 2-1 | 2B | HR |
| 05/22/2013 | ARI@COL | Cahill,Trevor | Fowler,Dexter | 6 | 0 | ___ | 4-1 | Foul | Foul |
| 05/22/2013 | STL@SD | Smith,Burch | Holliday,Matt | 1 | 1 | 1__ | 0-0 | 3B | 3B |
| 05/25/2013 | MIN@DET | Fister,Doug | Mauer,Joe | 1 | 1 | ___ | 0-0 | HR | HR |
| 05/27/2013 | MIN@MIL | Gorzelanny,Tom | Mauer,Joe | 7 | 0 | ___ | 4-3 | 2B | HR |
| 05/31/2013 | KC@TEX | Davis,Wade | Pierzynski,A.J. | 6 | 0 | 1__ | 4-2 | 2B | 2B |
| 06/02/2013 | MIL@PHI | De Fratus,Justin | Lucroy,Jonathan | 8 | 2 | 123 | 1-7 | HR | 3B |
| 06/02/2013 | WAS@ATL | Duke,Zach | Freeman,Freddie | 6 | 1 | 123 | 4-3 | 2B | 2B |
| 06/03/2013 | OAK@MIL | Milone,Tommy | Weeks,Rickie | 7 | 2 | ___ | 2-10 | HR | 3B |
| 06/04/2013 | CHA@SEA | Omogrosso,Brian | Franklin,Nick | 3 | 1 | _2_ | 5-2 | HR | 2B |
| 06/04/2013 | COL@CIN | LeCure,Sam | Tulowitzki,Troy | 8 | 2 | 1__ | 3-4 | GR2B | HR |
| 06/05/2013 | CHN@LAA | Garza,Matt | Shuck,J.B. | 2 | 2 | ___ | 2-0 | HR | Foul |
| 06/12/2013 | SF@PIT | Ramirez,Ramon | Walker,Neil | 7 | 0 | ___ | 10-6 | 2B | HR |
| 06/13/2013 | SF@PIT | Mazzaro,Vin | Noonan,Nick | 9 | 0 | ___ | 9-0 | HR | 2B |
| 06/18/2013 | SEA@LAA | Blanton,Joe | Smoak,Justin | 2 | 0 | ___ | 1-0 | HR | HR |
| 06/25/2013 | COL@BOS | Ottavino,Adam | Drew,Stephen | 4 | 2 | ___ | 7-2 | 3B | 3B |
| 06/28/2013 | CLE@CHA | Crain,Jesse | Brantley,Michael | 8 | 2 | 1__ | 5-6 | Foul | Foul |
| 07/01/2013 | ARI@NYN | Putz,J.J. | Byrd,Marlon | 9 | 1 | ___ | 2-3 | 2B | 2B |
| 07/02/2013 | SF@CIN | Lincecum,Tim | Choo,Shin-Soo | 1 | 0 | ___ | 0-0 | HR | 2B |
| 07/05/2013 | ATL@PHI | Maholm,Paul | Quintero,Humberto | 2 | 1 | _2_ | 1-0 | HR | HR |
| 07/05/2013 | COL@ARI | de la Rosa,Jorge | Pollock,A.J. | 3 | 1 | _2_ | 1-0 | 2B | 2B |
| 07/06/2013 | NYN@MIL | Gallardo,Yovani | Buck,John | 5 | 0 | ___ | 0-5 | HR | HR |
| 07/07/2013 | LAN@SF | Gaudin,Chad | Ramirez,Hanley | 4 | 1 | _2_ | 1-1 | Foul | Foul |
| 07/08/2013 | NYN@SF | Harvey,Matt | Pence,Hunter | 7 | 0 | ___ | 2-3 | 3B | 3B |
| 07/10/2013 | TEX@BAL | Lindblom,Josh | Roberts,Brian | 4 | 0 | 12_ | 2-0 | 1B | 1B |
| 07/13/2013 | CIN@ATL | Minor,Mike | Heisey,Chris | 2 | 2 | ___ | 1-0 | 2B | 2B |
| 07/21/2013 | PHI@NYN | Lee,Cliff | Wright,David | 1 | 2 | ___ | 0-0 | HR | HR |
| 07/21/2013 | PHI@NYN | Lee,Cliff | Lagares,Juan | 4 | 2 | 12_ | 2-0 | 2B | HR |
| 07/27/2013 | BOS@BAL | Patton,Troy | Drew,Stephen | 6 | 1 | 1__ | 4-1 | HR | HR |
| 07/28/2013 | HOU@TOR | Cosart,Jarred | Encarnacion,Edwin | 6 | 0 | ___ | 1-1 | 2B | 2B |
| 07/28/2013 | MIN@SEA | Ramirez,Erasmo | Doumit,Ryan | 2 | 0 | ___ | 0-0 | 2B | 2B |
| 07/31/2013 | NYN@MIA | Alvarez,Henderson | Young,Eric | 3 | 2 | ___ | 0-1 | 3B | 3B |
| 07/31/2013 | STL@PIT | Locke,Jeff | Holliday,Matt | 3 | 0 | ___ | 2-1 | 1B | 1B |
| 08/02/2013 | ARI@BOS | Beato,Pedro | Ross,Cody | 7 | 0 | ___ | 6-6 | HR | HR |

| Date | Matchup | Pitcher | Hitter | Inning | Outs | Men On | Score | Initial Ruling | Video Ruling |
|---|---|---|---|---|---|---|---|---|---|
| 08/02/2013 | ATL@PHI | Medlen,Kris | Utley,Chase | 6 | 1 | ___ | 2-6 | HR | HR |
| 08/02/2013 | SEA@BAL | Harang,Aaron | Flaherty,Ryan | 4 | 2 | ___ | 5-3 | 2B | HR |
| 08/04/2013 | ATL@PHI | Wood,Alex | Ruiz,Carlos | 3 | 0 | ___ | 0-2 | HR | 2B |
| 08/04/2013 | ATL@PHI | Lee,Cliff | Upton,B.J. | 4 | 0 | ___ | 2-1 | HR | GR2B |
| 08/09/2013 | PHI@WAS | Lannan,John | Rendon,Anthony | 2 | 0 | _2_ | 0-0 | HR | HR |
| 08/13/2013 | HOU@OAK | Lo,Chia-Jen | Young,Chris | 9 | 2 | 1__ | 4-5 | Foul | Foul |
| 08/14/2013 | SEA@TB | Farquhar,Danny | Zobrist,Ben | 9 | 0 | ___ | 3-4 | 3B | 3B |
| 08/15/2013 | NYN@SD | Wheeler,Zack | Rivera,Rene | 3 | 1 | ___ | 0-0 | 3B | 3B |
| 08/18/2013 | TOR@TB | Redmond,Todd | Longoria,Evan | 1 | 2 | ___ | 0-0 | HR | HR |
| 08/21/2013 | ARI@CIN | Broxton,Jonathan | Parra,Gerardo | 8 | 0 | ___ | 5-8 | 2B | HR |
| 08/23/2013 | MIL@CIN | Simon,Alfredo | Gennett,Scooter | 8 | 2 | ___ | 5-3 | HR | HR |
| 08/23/2013 | TOR@HOU | Redmond,Todd | Altuve,Jose | 1 | 1 | 1__ | 0-1 | 2B | 2B |
| 08/24/2013 | TOR@HOU | Peacock,Brad | Pillar,Kevin | 5 | 1 | 12_ | 0-7 | 2B | HR |
| 09/02/2013 | TEX@OAK | Holland,Derek | Crisp,Coco | 5 | 0 | 1__ | 2-2 | HR | HR |
| 09/04/2013 | DET@BOS | Bonderman,Jeremy | Lavarnway,Ryan | 7 | 0 | _2_ | 13-4 | 2B | HR |
| 09/06/2013 | DET@KC | Mendoza,Luis | Infante,Omar | 5 | 2 | 123 | 10-1 | 2B | 2B |
| 09/07/2013 | TEX@LAA | Holland,Derek | Trumbo,Mark | 3 | 1 | _2_ | 4-2 | Foul | Foul |
| 09/07/2013 | WAS@MIA | Eovaldi,Nathan | Zimmerman,Ryan | 1 | 0 | 1__ | 0-0 | 2B | HR |
| 09/09/2013 | KC@CLE | Santana,Ervin | Santana,Carlos | 7 | 0 | ___ | 3-1 | Foul | HR |
| 09/11/2013 | OAK@MIN | DeVries,Cole | Reddick,Josh | 5 | 1 | 1__ | 15-1 | HR | 2B |
| 09/12/2013 | WAS@NYN | Harang,Aaron | LaRoche,Adam | 2 | 1 | ___ | 1-1 | 2B | HR |
| 09/15/2013 | SF@LAN | Vogelsong,Ryan | Uribe,Juan | 4 | 0 | ___ | 0-1 | 3B | 3B |
| 09/16/2013 | MIN@CHA | DeVries,Cole | Danks,Jordan | 2 | 2 | 1__ | 7-0 | 2B | 2B |
| 09/26/2013 | MIL@NYN | Henderson,Jim | Satin,Josh | 9 | 0 | ___ | 1-4 | 1B | HR |
| 09/27/2013 | BOS@BAL | Feldman,Scott | Saltalamacchia,Jarrod | 3 | 1 | 12_ | 5-0 | HR | 2B |
| 09/27/2013 | NYA@HOU | Oberholtzer,Brett | Soriano,Alfonso | 6 | 1 | ___ | 3-0 | GR2B | GR2B |
| 09/27/2013 | PIT@CIN | Bailey,Homer | Byrd,Marlon | 6 | 0 | ___ | 2-1 | 2B | 2B |

# Hall of Fame Monitor

**Bill James**

Robinson Cano and Jhonny Peralta were both born in 1982. Which one of them is a better candidate for the Hall of Fame?

Yeah, that's what we thought, too.

We are not attempting, in this feature, to say who should be in the Hall of Fame and who should stay home. We are trying to state the obvious, and to keep track of the obvious. We are trying to monitor players' progress on a Hall of Fame path. For the last several years, the youngest person who could be said to be a fully qualified Hall of Famer has been Albert Pujols. Now it is Miguel Cabrera, 30 years old, born April, 1983. Getting to be a fully-qualified Hall of Famer by the age of 30 is a tremendous accomplishment. Heck, getting to be a fully-qualified Hall of Famer by the age of 70 is a tremendous accomplishment; just ask Joe Torre. Anyway, Pujols and Cabrera are the only players younger than 37 who do appear to be fully-qualified Hall of Famers, and there isn't anyone in line behind them. The next player who might reach that level at that age would appear to be. ..well, no; let's not get ahead of ourselves.

By the method we use, 100 points means "fully qualified Hall of Famer." But even at 100 points, we are not saying a player should be a Hall of Famer. Some people may wish to vote against Derek Jeter, for example, because he never used steroids, and they may feel that you shouldn't go in the Hall of Fame if you didn't use steroids. That's fine; we're not arguing. All we're saying is that, based on his career accomplishments and without consideration of disqualifications, he appears to have done enough good work.

Jim Thome got to 95 points. Again, doesn't mean he shouldn't be in the Hall of Fame. I would vote for him, personally. Many, many players are in the Hall of Fame whose credentials are less impressive than Thome's. Our point is that, based on our interpretation of past voting practices as best we are able to understand them, Thome fell slightly short of the line of being an *automatic* or *obvious* Hall of Famer. 100 points means that the player is an automatic or obvious Hall of Famer, unless he used too many steroids or went potty in the swimming pool.

The Gray Area, in which a player might be a Hall of Famer or might not, is 70 to 100 points. If a player hasn't reached 70 points, in general, then he still has work to do to be considered a viable Hall of Fame candidate. But we also give points for post-season play, and, since this book goes to the printer in early October, we haven't been able to include post-season play from 2013.

The formulas which underlie these points are probably the most complex formulas used in this book. You have probably noticed this before: the obvious is very often difficult to explain. The reason that is true is that the obvious is often the accumulation of a large number of small details. A woman pulls her wedding ring out of her purse when she gets home, goes in the other room to take phone calls, puts on perfume to go to the grocery store and works late three days out of five, it is obvious what is going on, but there's no one thing that explains it. Same here; making the Hall of Fame is not a result of a single dramatic accomplishment, but the accumulation of a long list of accomplishments over a long period of time. We're just trying to piece the picture together.

## Leading Hall of Fame Candidates Born in 1992

| Player | Points |
|---|---|
| Bryce Harper | 4 |
| Manny Machado | 3 |

## Leading Hall of Fame Candidates Born in 1991

| Player | Points |
|---|---|
| Mike Trout | 20 |

## Leading Hall of Fame Candidates Born in 1990

| Player | Points |
|---|---|
| Starlin Castro | 15 |

## Leading Hall of Fame Candidates Born in 1989

| Player | Points |
|---|---|
| Freddie Freeman | 12 |

## Leading Hall of Fame Candidates Born in 1988

| Player | Points |
|---|---|
| Clayton Kershaw | 27 |
| Craig Kimbrel | 25 |
| Elvis Andrus | 17 |
| Neftali Feliz | 15 |
| Aroldis Chapman | 15 |

## Leading Hall of Fame Candidates Born in 1987

| Player | Points |
|---|---|
| Buster Posey | 31 |
| Justin Upton | 14 |
| Paul Goldschmidt | 14 |
| Jay Bruce | 11 |
| Alex Avila | 10 |
| Austin Jackson | 10 |

## Leading Hall of Fame Candidates Born in 1986

| Player | Points |
|---|---|
| Felix Hernandez | 27 |
| Andrew McCutchen | 26 |
| Pablo Sandoval | 17 |
| Matt Wieters | 16 |
| Chris Davis | 16 |
| Billy Butler | 15 |
| Carlos Santana | 12 |

## Leading Hall of Fame Candidates Born in 1985

| Player | Points |
|---|---|
| Evan Longoria | 24 |
| David Price | 19 |
| Carlos Gonzalez | 17 |
| Adam Jones | 16 |
| Asdrubal Cabrera | 14 |
| Chris Perez | 12 |
| Matt Carpenter | 12 |
| Gio Gonzalez | 11 |

## Leading Hall of Fame Candidates Born in 1984

| Player | Points |
|---|---|
| Prince Fielder | 47 |
| Troy Tulowitzki | 30 |
| Tim Lincecum | 29 |
| Brian McCann | 28 |
| Matt Kemp | 28 |
| Joakim Soria | 24 |
| Ryan Zimmerman | 23 |
| Melky Cabrera | 19 |
| Matt Cain | 16 |
| Jon Lester | 16 |
| Chase Headley | 15 |
| B.J. Upton | 14 |
| Alex Gordon | 14 |

## Leading Hall of Fame Candidates Born in 1983

| Player | Points |
|---|---|
| Miguel Cabrera | 109 |
| Joe Mauer | 68 |
| Ryan Braun | 54 |
| Justin Verlander | 50 |
| Hanley Ramirez | 45 |
| Dustin Pedroia | 44 |
| Jose Reyes | 41 |
| Joey Votto | 41 |
| Huston Street | 23 |
| Jacoby Ellsbury | 22 |
| Nick Markakis | 22 |
| Hunter Pence | 21 |

| Leading Hall of Fame Candidates Born in 1982 | |
|---|---|
| Player | Points |
| Robinson Cano | 65 |
| David Wright | 56 |
| Francisco Rodriguez | 55 |
| Adrian Gonzalez | 49 |
| Yadier Molina | 45 |
| Ian Kinsler | 28 |
| Brian Wilson | 26 |
| Jhonny Peralta | 24 |
| Shin-Soo Choo | 21 |
| Jered Weaver | 19 |
| Andre Ethier | 19 |
| Aaron Hill | 17 |

| Leading Hall of Fame Candidates Born in 1980 | |
|---|---|
| Player | Points |
| Albert Pujols | 158 |
| Mark Teixeira | 63 |
| Matt Holliday | 56 |
| Jonathan Papelbon | 46 |
| CC Sabathia | 43 |
| Jose Bautista | 27 |
| Dan Uggla | 27 |
| Shane Victorino | 22 |
| Nick Swisher | 19 |
| Josh Beckett | 18 |
| Dan Haren | 15 |
| C.J. Wilson | 14 |

| Leading Hall of Fame Candidates Born in 1978 | |
|---|---|
| Player | Points |
| Jimmy Rollins | 60 |
| Chase Utley | 53 |
| Aramis Ramirez | 49 |
| Victor Martinez | 42 |
| Cliff Lee | 36 |
| Jose Valverde | 34 |
| Vernon Wells | 33 |
| Jason Bay | 31 |
| Barry Zito | 22 |
| Carlos Pena | 21 |
| John Lackey | 15 |
| Kevin Gregg | 14 |

| Leading Hall of Fame Candidates Born in 1981 | |
|---|---|
| Player | Points |
| Josh Hamilton | 35 |
| Curtis Granderson | 32 |
| Carl Crawford | 30 |
| Justin Morneau | 28 |
| Brandon Phillips | 26 |
| Ben Zobrist | 24 |
| Adam Wainwright | 22 |
| Jake Peavy | 19 |
| Alex Rios | 17 |
| Mike Napoli | 15 |
| James Shields | 15 |

| Leading Hall of Fame Candidates Born in 1979 | |
|---|---|
| Player | Points |
| Adrian Beltre | 60 |
| Ryan Howard | 52 |
| Adam Dunn | 49 |
| Johan Santana | 41 |
| Mark Buehrle | 25 |
| Kevin Youkilis | 24 |
| Rafael Soriano | 23 |
| Jayson Werth | 20 |
| Carlos Ruiz | 18 |
| Michael Cuddyer | 17 |
| Coco Crisp | 16 |

| Leading Hall of Fame Candidates Born in 1977 | |
|---|---|
| Player | Points |
| Carlos Beltran | 70 |
| Andruw Jones | 63 |
| Roy Halladay | 55 |
| Juan Pierre | 36 |
| Rafael Furcal | 32 |
| Roy Oswalt | 28 |
| Eric Chavez | 26 |
| J.J. Putz | 26 |
| Travis Hafner | 24 |
| Brian Roberts | 23 |
| Heath Bell | 23 |

| Leading Hall of Fame Candidates Born in 1976 | |
|---|---|
| Player | Points |
| Lance Berkman | 72 |
| Michael Young | 61 |
| Alfonso Soriano | 57 |
| Paul Konerko | 50 |
| Carlos Lee | 50 |
| A.J. Pierzynski | 29 |
| Kyle Farnsworth | 15 |
| Ramon Hernandez | 15 |
| Freddy Garcia | 14 |

## Leading Hall of Fame Candidates Born in 1975

| Player | Points |
|---|---|
| Alex Rodriguez | 177 |
| Vladimir Guerrero | 108 |
| Scott Rolen | 65 |
| David Ortiz | 65 |
| Edgar Renteria | 46 |
| Francisco Cordero | 44 |
| Derrek Lee | 43 |
| Torii Hunter | 38 |
| Tim Hudson | 33 |
| Placido Polanco | 32 |
| Chris Carpenter | 31 |
| Marco Scutaro | 17 |

## Leading Hall of Fame Candidates Born in 1974

| Player | Points |
|---|---|
| Derek Jeter | 147 |
| Bobby Abreu | 79 |
| Miguel Tejada | 74 |
| Joe Nathan | 72 |
| Magglio Ordonez | 62 |

## Leading Hall of Fame Candidates Born in 1973

| Player | Points |
|---|---|
| Ichiro Suzuki | 109 |
| Todd Helton | 98 |
| Johnny Damon | 56 |
| Bartolo Colon | 29 |
| Derek Lowe | 24 |
| Octavio Dotel | 18 |

## Leading Hall of Fame Candidates Born in 1972

| Player | Points |
|---|---|
| Manny Ramirez | 125 |
| Chipper Jones | 108 |
| Andy Pettitte | 54 |
| Jason Isringhausen | 44 |
| Raul Ibanez | 28 |
| LaTroy Hawkins | 20 |

## Leading Hall of Fame Candidates Born in 1971

| Player | Points |
|---|---|
| Ivan Rodriguez | 90 |
| Jason Giambi | 77 |
| Jorge Posada | 57 |

## Leading Hall of Fame Candidates Born in 1970

| Player | Points |
|---|---|
| Jim Thome | 95 |

## Leading Hall of Fame Candidates Born in 1969

| Player | Points |
|---|---|
| Mariano Rivera | 152 |

# 2014 Player Projections

**Bill James**

Surveys show that these are the pages of the book which are most used by our readers, these pitcher and hitter projections. Surveys show that 37% of readers who buy the book use this section of the book more than any other; not really, we don't really do any surveys like that, I just made that up, but then, that's in keeping with this section of the book, in which—uniquely, in what is otherwise a factual record—we just make stuff up. We don't really know what Asdrubal Cabrera is going to hit next year; heck, we don't even know who he will be playing for. He hit 3 homers one year and 25 the next, hit .242 last year but has hit over .300. We don't really know. We are at the mercy of the Gods, or, in his case, Carthaginians.

We do get a lot of feedback about these pages, particularly at the start of the season when people are figuring out their fantasy draft lists. Our best projection last year was for A. J. Pierzynski, who we projected to hit .269 with 25 doubles, one triple and 17 homers, but who actually hit .272 with 24 doubles, one triple and 17 homers:

| Hitter | Label | G | AB | R | H | D | T | HR | RBI | BB | SO | SB | Avg | Slg |
|---|---|---|---|---|---|---|---|---|---|---|---|---|---|---|
| Pierzynski, A.J. | Actual | 134 | 503 | 48 | 137 | 24 | 1 | 17 | 70 | 11 | 76 | 1 | .272 | .425 |
| | Projected | 137 | 509 | 56 | 137 | 25 | 1 | 17 | 61 | 24 | 69 | 0 | .269 | .422 |

We ran projections last year for 406 players, or maybe for 406 players who did play in the majors and a few who did not; I'm not sure. Anyway, our 50th best projection was for Zack the Cozart:

| Hitter | Label | G | AB | R | H | D | T | HR | RBI | BB | SO | SB | Avg | Slg |
|---|---|---|---|---|---|---|---|---|---|---|---|---|---|---|
| Cozart, Zack | Actual | 151 | 567 | 74 | 144 | 30 | 3 | 12 | 63 | 26 | 102 | 0 | .254 | .381 |
| | Projected | 137 | 547 | 79 | 142 | 34 | 3 | 15 | 49 | 37 | 98 | 9 | .260 | .415 |

Our 100th best projection was for Nate McLouth:

| Hitter | Label | G | AB | R | H | D | T | HR | RBI | BB | SO | SB | Avg | Slg |
|---|---|---|---|---|---|---|---|---|---|---|---|---|---|---|
| McLouth, Nate | Actual | 146 | 531 | 76 | 137 | 31 | 4 | 12 | 36 | 53 | 86 | 30 | .258 | .399 |
| | Projected | 126 | 417 | 64 | 99 | 22 | 2 | 14 | 46 | 50 | 84 | 14 | .237 | .400 |

Our 150th best projection was for Jack Hannahan:

| Hitter | Label | G | AB | R | H | D | T | HR | RBI | BB | SO | SB | Avg | Slg |
|---|---|---|---|---|---|---|---|---|---|---|---|---|---|---|
| Hannahan, Jack | Actual | 83 | 139 | 12 | 30 | 5 | 1 | 1 | 14 | 19 | 38 | 0 | .216 | .288 |
| | Projected | 90 | 223 | 23 | 52 | 13 | 0 | 4 | 25 | 27 | 57 | 1 | .233 | .345 |

Our 200th best projection was for Alcides Escobar:

| Hitter | Label | G | AB | R | H | D | T | HR | RBI | BB | SO | SB | Avg | Slg |
|---|---|---|---|---|---|---|---|---|---|---|---|---|---|---|
| Escobar, Alcides | Actual | 158 | 607 | 57 | 142 | 20 | 4 | 4 | 52 | 19 | 84 | 22 | .234 | .300 |
| | Projected | 152 | 595 | 74 | 162 | 26 | 7 | 5 | 53 | 31 | 91 | 30 | .272 | .365 |

The 250th best was for Colby Rasmus:

| Hitter | Label | G | AB | R | H | D | T | HR | RBI | BB | SO | SB | Avg | Slg |
|---|---|---|---|---|---|---|---|---|---|---|---|---|---|---|
| Rasmus, Colby | Actual | 118 | 417 | 57 | 115 | 26 | 1 | 22 | 66 | 37 | 135 | 0 | .276 | .501 |
| | Projected | 149 | 558 | 87 | 132 | 29 | 4 | 23 | 72 | 58 | 145 | 6 | .237 | .427 |

The 300th best, for L.J. Hoes:

| Hitter | Label | G | AB | R | H | D | T | HR | RBI | BB | SO | SB | Avg | Slg |
|---|---|---|---|---|---|---|---|---|---|---|---|---|---|---|
| Hoes, L.J. | Actual | 47 | 170 | 24 | 48 | 7 | 2 | 1 | 10 | 12 | 35 | 7 | .282 | .365 |
| | Projected | 147 | 559 | 77 | 160 | 26 | 4 | 6 | 63 | 67 | 83 | 24 | .286 | .379 |

L. J. Hoes, if you are wondering, is an outfielder, a right fielder, who was in the Baltimore system, and was traded to Houston as a part of the Bud Norris trade. He was in the minors until the trade; Houston put him in the majors. We had projected that he would bat 559 times last year not because we seriously expected him to bat 559 times, but because our policy is that if a young player might play, then we project that he will play. Our theory. . .well, my theory, actually. . .is that we really don't have any way of knowing which rookies will make the team out of spring training next year, and, unless you are a blithering idiot, you know this. Our job is to tell you what kind of player the man is. We try to tell you, as best we are able, how he will play if he plays. Is he a singles hitter who will steal bases and not return them, or is he a power hitter who will strike out 200 times and ask Adam Dunn for his signature after the game?

If we don't print the projection for the young player, then we're cheating you out of what we know; that's the way I see it. If we project that a young player will bat 550 times and he bats 170 times, well, that happens, and you should expect it to happen. But if a rookie bats 550 times and we haven't told you what kind of player he will be, then we haven't done our jobs.

Anyway, our 350th best projection for 2013 was for Jordany Valdespin:

| Hitter | Label | G | AB | R | H | D | T | HR | RBI | BB | SO | SB | Avg | Slg |
|---|---|---|---|---|---|---|---|---|---|---|---|---|---|---|
| Valdespin, Jordany | Actual | 66 | 133 | 16 | 25 | 3 | 1 | 4 | 16 | 8 | 28 | 4 | .188 | .316 |
| | Projected | 85 | 264 | 34 | 71 | 13 | 1 | 9 | 32 | 13 | 46 | 16 | .269 | .428 |

And our 400th best, out of 406, was for Mike Nickeas:

| Hitter | Label | G | AB | R | H | D | T | HR | RBI | BB | SO | SB | Avg | Slg |
|---|---|---|---|---|---|---|---|---|---|---|---|---|---|---|
| Nickeas, Mike | Actual | 1 | 0 | 0 | 0 | 0 | 0 | 0 | 0 | 0 | 0 | 0 | .000 | .000 |
| | Projected | 50 | 102 | 8 | 22 | 5 | 0 | 1 | 9 | 10 | 18 | 0 | .216 | .294 |

Not sure that's exactly true. Our "scoring" system, for ranking the comparisons, deducts a huge penalty in a case like this because we missed his projected batting average by 216 points, although really. . .it's a pretty decent projection. We said he wouldn't hit much and wouldn't play much, and we were right. We had a lot of projections that were worse than that one. Like Derek Jeter:

| Hitter | Label | G | AB | R | H | D | T | HR | RBI | BB | SO | SB | Avg | Slg |
|---|---|---|---|---|---|---|---|---|---|---|---|---|---|---|
| Jeter, Derek | Actual | 17 | 63 | 8 | 12 | 1 | 0 | 1 | 7 | 8 | 10 | 0 | .190 | .254 |
| | Projected | 154 | 642 | 97 | 191 | 28 | 1 | 12 | 64 | 55 | 96 | 11 | .298 | .400 |

And Travis d'Arnaud:

| Hitter | Label | G | AB | R | H | D | T | HR | RBI | BB | SO | SB | Avg | Slg |
|---|---|---|---|---|---|---|---|---|---|---|---|---|---|---|
| d'Arnaud, Travis | Actual | 31 | 99 | 4 | 20 | 3 | 0 | 1 | 5 | 12 | 21 | 0 | .202 | .263 |
| | Projected | 125 | 443 | 66 | 128 | 30 | 1 | 19 | 74 | 28 | 98 | 3 | .289 | .490 |

D'Arnaud, a catcher traded to the Mets as part of the R. A. Dickey deal, hit a foul ball off his left foot, breaking the foot and costing him 100 games or so on the Disabled List. We had no idea that would happen; sorry. But if d'Arnaud is anything like the hitter we think he is, the Blue Jays are going to take a lot of crap over the next ten years for trading away Yan Gomes and d'Arnaud and keeping J. P. Arencibia. Arencibia had a sub-par year:

| Hitter | Label | G | AB | R | H | D | T | HR | RBI | BB | SO | SB | Avg | Slg |
|---|---|---|---|---|---|---|---|---|---|---|---|---|---|---|
| Arencibia, J.P. | Actual | 138 | 474 | 45 | 92 | 18 | 0 | 21 | 55 | 18 | 148 | 0 | .194 | .365 |
| | Projected | 116 | 419 | 51 | 97 | 24 | 1 | 22 | 67 | 25 | 111 | 1 | .232 | .451 |

That's a below-average projection, if you're wondering. We got a lot of stuff right in there, but we missed his batting average by 38 points and his slugging percentage by 86 points, and those are big misses. There were 170 players for whom we had projections in last year's book, and who had 400 or more at bats in 2013. Of those 170, 24 hit more than 20 points higher (.020 higher) than we had projected that they would, and 43 hit more than 20 points lower than we had said that they would. These are the ten hitters who exceeded our batting average projection by the widest margins:

| Hitter | Projected Avg | Actual Avg | Error |
|---|---|---|---|
| Cuddyer, Michael | .264 | .331 | .067 |
| Donaldson, Josh | .246 | .301 | .055 |
| Werth, Jayson | .267 | .318 | .051 |
| Johnson, Chris | .280 | .321 | .041 |
| Rasmus, Colby | .237 | .276 | .039 |
| Peralta, Jhonny | .264 | .303 | .039 |
| Freeman, Freddie | .282 | .319 | .037 |
| Nava, Daniel | .266 | .303 | .037 |
| Infante, Omar | .282 | .318 | .036 |
| Saltalamacchia, Jarrod | .239 | .273 | .034 |

While these are the hitters whose mothers, aunts and cousins had the most difficult summers:

| Hitter | Projected Avg | Actual Avg | Error |
|---|---|---|---|
| Murphy, David | .281 | .220 | .061 |
| Barney, Darwin | .268 | .208 | .060 |
| Castro, Starlin | .304 | .245 | .059 |
| Uggla, Dan | .238 | .179 | .059 |
| Cespedes, Yoenis | .297 | .240 | .057 |
| Ruggiano, Justin | .278 | .222 | .056 |
| Rizzo, Anthony | .283 | .233 | .050 |
| Montero, Miguel | .272 | .230 | .042 |
| Simmons, Andrelton | .289 | .248 | .041 |
| Freese, David | .301 | .262 | .039 |

Arencibia just misses the list of the most over-projected batting averages by one point. The Cubs had three young infielders on the under-achievers list.

On the other hand, there were ten players who came within one point of hitting for the average we had projected for them:

| Hitter | Projected Avg | Actual Avg |
|---|---|---|
| Desmond, Ian | .279 | .280 |
| Encarnacion, Edwin | .271 | .272 |
| Denorfia, Chris | .278 | .279 |
| Drew, Stephen | .252 | .253 |
| Davis, Chris | .286 | .286 |
| Bautista, Jose | .259 | .259 |
| Bruce, Jay | .263 | .262 |
| Rollins, Jimmy | .253 | .252 |
| Dominguez, Matt | .242 | .241 |
| Holliday, Matt | .301 | .300 |

Chris Davis, we got his batting average exactly right, but missed his slugging percentage by 100 points. 102, actually. He was one of seven players in the majors whose slugging percentage we missed by 100 points. Davis and Jason Castro slugged 100 points better than we thought they would. Nick Markakis, Starlin Castro, Josh Hamilton, Giancarlo Stanton and Paul Konerko slugged 100 points less than expected, with Konerko falling 131 points short of our projection. We expected him to hit 30 home runs; he hit 12.

Davis hit 22 homers more than we projected that he would. Stanton hit 19 less. On the other hand, 15 players with 400 or more at bats hit exactly the number of home runs that we thought they would, and 68% of the players with 400 or more at bats were within 5 home runs of the number we had projected. Just for the heck of it, I randomly scrambled the data, so that each player's projection was compared to some other player. When I did that, only five players hit the "correct" number of home runs (as opposed to 15), only 35% were within 5 home runs (as opposed to 68%), there were discrepancies as large as 46 homers, and 21 players missed their projected home runs by 20 or more (as opposed to one).

We are always right, except when we are wrong. We are always on target, except when we're off. We are always on time, except when we are early, or when we are late. We do the best we can. These are our projections for 2014. Some of them will be pretty much right.

# 2014 Hitter Projections

| PLAYER | | | BATTING | | | | | | | | | | | | BASERUNNING | | | AVERAGES | | | |
|---|---|---|---|---|---|---|---|---|---|---|---|---|---|---|---|---|---|---|---|---|---|
| Hitter | Team | Age | G | AB | H | 2B | 3B | HR | R | RBI | RC | RC27 | BB | SO | SB | CS | SB% | Avg | OBP | Slg | OPS |
| Abreu,Tony | SF | 29 | 65 | 159 | 44 | 11 | 1 | 2 | 19 | 18 | 19 | 4.26 | 6 | 30 | 2 | 1 | .67 | .277 | .307 | .396 | .703 |
| Ackley,Dustin | Sea | 26 | 127 | 442 | 115 | 22 | 3 | 7 | 59 | 40 | 55 | 4.35 | 51 | 77 | 5 | 2 | .71 | .260 | .337 | .371 | .708 |
| Adams,Matt | StL | 25 | 156 | 481 | 138 | 29 | 0 | 28 | 72 | 87 | 83 | 6.27 | 33 | 111 | 1 | 1 | .50 | .287 | .333 | .522 | .855 |
| Almonte,Abraham | Sea | 25 | 122 | 401 | 108 | 21 | 3 | 10 | 59 | 44 | 59 | 5.11 | 47 | 86 | 25 | 7 | .78 | .269 | .346 | .411 | .757 |
| Alonso,Yonder | SD | 27 | 150 | 602 | 179 | 37 | 1 | 15 | 65 | 84 | 96 | 5.85 | 65 | 90 | 8 | 4 | .67 | .297 | .367 | .437 | .804 |
| Altuve,Jose | Hou | 24 | 150 | 603 | 177 | 33 | 3 | 7 | 74 | 49 | 79 | 4.68 | 34 | 73 | 34 | 13 | .72 | .294 | .334 | .393 | .727 |
| Alvarez,Pedro | Pit | 27 | 150 | 549 | 138 | 28 | 2 | 34 | 73 | 100 | 88 | 5.55 | 58 | 168 | 2 | 1 | .67 | .251 | .325 | .495 | .821 |
| Amarista,Alexi | SD | 25 | 96 | 210 | 53 | 10 | 2 | 3 | 24 | 23 | 22 | 3.60 | 12 | 29 | 4 | 2 | .67 | .252 | .296 | .362 | .658 |
| Andrus,Elvis | Tex | 25 | 158 | 626 | 174 | 24 | 5 | 4 | 95 | 63 | 77 | 4.31 | 58 | 94 | 38 | 12 | .76 | .278 | .343 | .351 | .694 |
| Aoki,Norichika | Mil | 32 | 152 | 578 | 167 | 27 | 2 | 9 | 82 | 43 | 79 | 4.88 | 53 | 41 | 20 | 10 | .67 | .289 | .361 | .389 | .750 |
| Arcia,Oswaldo | Min | 23 | 148 | 501 | 142 | 28 | 4 | 24 | 73 | 88 | 85 | 6.10 | 46 | 144 | 4 | 3 | .57 | .283 | .347 | .499 | .846 |
| Arenado,Nolan | Col | 23 | 155 | 578 | 162 | 43 | 3 | 14 | 64 | 70 | 81 | 5.05 | 34 | 74 | 2 | 1 | .67 | .280 | .321 | .438 | .759 |
| Arencibia,J.P. | Tor | 28 | 116 | 364 | 80 | 19 | 1 | 18 | 40 | 53 | 40 | 3.66 | 19 | 100 | 0 | 0 | .00 | .220 | .262 | .426 | .688 |
| Arias,Joaquin | SF | 29 | 104 | 240 | 63 | 9 | 2 | 2 | 25 | 22 | 23 | 3.34 | 8 | 31 | 4 | 2 | .67 | .263 | .289 | .342 | .631 |
| Asche,Cody | Phi | 24 | 140 | 514 | 142 | 32 | 4 | 18 | 65 | 81 | 78 | 5.39 | 42 | 118 | 10 | 4 | .71 | .276 | .332 | .459 | .791 |
| Avila,Alex | Det | 27 | 126 | 432 | 109 | 25 | 2 | 15 | 53 | 65 | 64 | 5.14 | 65 | 120 | 1 | 1 | .50 | .252 | .353 | .424 | .776 |
| Aviles,Mike | Cle | 33 | 110 | 316 | 82 | 16 | 1 | 8 | 39 | 36 | 36 | 3.93 | 14 | 42 | 7 | 4 | .64 | .259 | .295 | .392 | .688 |
| Aybar,Erick | LAA | 30 | 139 | 526 | 146 | 29 | 4 | 7 | 68 | 50 | 63 | 4.23 | 26 | 61 | 15 | 7 | .68 | .278 | .317 | .388 | .704 |
| Baez,Javier | ChC | 21 | 137 | 541 | 146 | 25 | 0 | 22 | 78 | 84 | 77 | 4.97 | 43 | 166 | 21 | 8 | .72 | .270 | .324 | .438 | .762 |
| Barmes,Clint | Pit | 35 | 113 | 327 | 74 | 17 | 1 | 7 | 30 | 32 | 30 | 3.07 | 18 | 74 | 1 | 1 | .50 | .226 | .277 | .349 | .626 |
| Barnes,Brandon | Hou | 28 | 127 | 435 | 108 | 25 | 1 | 10 | 54 | 48 | 48 | 3.73 | 29 | 116 | 13 | 8 | .62 | .248 | .300 | .379 | .679 |
| Barney,Darwin | ChC | 28 | 145 | 521 | 131 | 26 | 2 | 6 | 63 | 44 | 54 | 3.58 | 34 | 59 | 6 | 2 | .75 | .251 | .302 | .344 | .646 |
| Barton,Daric | Oak | 28 | 52 | 112 | 28 | 7 | 0 | 2 | 16 | 13 | 15 | 4.64 | 19 | 21 | 1 | 0 | 1.00 | .250 | .368 | .366 | .734 |
| Bautista,Jose | Tor | 33 | 134 | 496 | 127 | 26 | 1 | 33 | 86 | 85 | 93 | 6.50 | 86 | 103 | 6 | 3 | .67 | .256 | .371 | .512 | .883 |
| Beckham,Gordon | CWS | 27 | 131 | 436 | 111 | 27 | 1 | 9 | 55 | 45 | 52 | 4.12 | 35 | 75 | 5 | 3 | .62 | .255 | .320 | .383 | .703 |
| Belt,Brandon | SF | 26 | 151 | 513 | 150 | 36 | 5 | 18 | 74 | 75 | 93 | 6.59 | 64 | 119 | 8 | 4 | .67 | .292 | .375 | .487 | .863 |
| Beltran,Carlos | StL | 37 | 142 | 525 | 145 | 30 | 2 | 23 | 76 | 84 | 86 | 5.85 | 58 | 98 | 5 | 2 | .71 | .276 | .350 | .472 | .823 |
| Beltre,Adrian | Tex | 35 | 157 | 614 | 183 | 37 | 1 | 29 | 86 | 96 | 106 | 6.38 | 41 | 85 | 2 | 1 | .67 | .298 | .348 | .503 | .851 |
| Bernadina,Roger | Phi | 30 | 100 | 209 | 52 | 10 | 1 | 5 | 27 | 19 | 25 | 4.06 | 19 | 48 | 9 | 3 | .75 | .249 | .320 | .378 | .698 |
| Betancourt,Yuniesky | Mil | 32 | 75 | 180 | 43 | 9 | 1 | 5 | 18 | 21 | 18 | 3.42 | 6 | 26 | 0 | 0 | .00 | .239 | .267 | .383 | .651 |
| Bianchi,Jeff | Mil | 27 | 62 | 112 | 29 | 5 | 0 | 1 | 13 | 11 | 11 | 3.36 | 7 | 20 | 3 | 2 | .60 | .259 | .303 | .330 | .633 |
| Blackmon,Charlie | Col | 27 | 85 | 243 | 67 | 15 | 2 | 5 | 35 | 27 | 33 | 4.79 | 16 | 40 | 8 | 3 | .73 | .276 | .326 | .416 | .741 |
| Blanco,Gregor | SF | 30 | 118 | 338 | 85 | 14 | 3 | 3 | 46 | 26 | 39 | 3.92 | 45 | 77 | 13 | 6 | .68 | .251 | .341 | .337 | .678 |
| Blanks,Kyle | SD | 27 | 60 | 135 | 36 | 8 | 1 | 5 | 20 | 22 | 20 | 5.25 | 13 | 36 | 1 | 0 | 1.00 | .267 | .344 | .452 | .796 |
| Bloomquist,Willie | Ari | 36 | 78 | 232 | 65 | 8 | 1 | 1 | 30 | 17 | 25 | 3.82 | 14 | 33 | 5 | 3 | .62 | .280 | .327 | .336 | .663 |
| Bogaerts,Xander | Bos | 21 | 156 | 598 | 169 | 33 | 5 | 19 | 87 | 84 | 96 | 5.75 | 69 | 130 | 10 | 5 | .67 | .283 | .357 | .450 | .807 |
| Bogusevic,Brian | ChC | 30 | 92 | 212 | 56 | 11 | 1 | 5 | 29 | 22 | 29 | 4.74 | 23 | 47 | 9 | 3 | .75 | .264 | .342 | .396 | .738 |
| Bonifacio,Emilio | KC | 29 | 138 | 489 | 127 | 20 | 4 | 3 | 65 | 31 | 55 | 3.84 | 42 | 113 | 33 | 10 | .77 | .260 | .320 | .335 | .655 |
| Borbon,Julio | ChC | 28 | 78 | 154 | 41 | 6 | 1 | 1 | 20 | 12 | 17 | 3.81 | 11 | 23 | 9 | 3 | .75 | .266 | .319 | .338 | .657 |
| Bourjos,Peter | LAA | 27 | 140 | 493 | 127 | 19 | 9 | 11 | 74 | 46 | 61 | 4.26 | 34 | 115 | 18 | 6 | .75 | .258 | .312 | .400 | .712 |
| Bourn,Michael | Cle | 31 | 154 | 620 | 164 | 26 | 6 | 6 | 91 | 48 | 74 | 4.10 | 59 | 153 | 37 | 13 | .74 | .265 | .330 | .355 | .685 |
| Bradley Jr.,Jackie | Bos | 24 | 131 | 512 | 127 | 37 | 3 | 15 | 84 | 55 | 70 | 4.63 | 61 | 122 | 13 | 8 | .62 | .248 | .329 | .420 | .749 |
| Brantley,Michael | Cle | 27 | 150 | 553 | 153 | 28 | 3 | 8 | 72 | 60 | 72 | 4.61 | 49 | 66 | 18 | 6 | .75 | .277 | .338 | .382 | .719 |
| Brantly,Rob | Mia | 24 | 85 | 348 | 87 | 20 | 0 | 4 | 29 | 31 | 35 | 3.49 | 23 | 59 | 0 | 0 | .00 | .250 | .298 | .342 | .640 |
| Braun,Ryan | Mil | 30 | 155 | 598 | 185 | 41 | 3 | 33 | 101 | 108 | 123 | 7.60 | 60 | 127 | 18 | 8 | .69 | .309 | .377 | .554 | .931 |
| Brown,Andrew | NYM | 29 | 75 | 178 | 47 | 10 | 1 | 8 | 26 | 29 | 27 | 5.32 | 17 | 46 | 1 | 1 | .50 | .264 | .328 | .466 | .794 |
| Brown,Domonic | Phi | 26 | 151 | 528 | 145 | 28 | 4 | 25 | 78 | 85 | 87 | 5.83 | 52 | 97 | 11 | 5 | .69 | .275 | .341 | .485 | .826 |
| Bruce,Jay | Cin | 27 | 160 | 607 | 157 | 36 | 3 | 34 | 92 | 102 | 100 | 5.73 | 67 | 170 | 7 | 4 | .64 | .259 | .335 | .496 | .831 |
| Buck,John | Pit | 33 | 65 | 221 | 48 | 10 | 0 | 8 | 21 | 31 | 23 | 3.46 | 20 | 62 | 1 | 0 | 1.00 | .217 | .300 | .371 | .671 |
| Butler,Billy | KC | 28 | 158 | 582 | 173 | 38 | 1 | 19 | 69 | 89 | 100 | 6.36 | 68 | 99 | 1 | 0 | 1.00 | .297 | .375 | .464 | .839 |
| Byrd,Marlon | Pit | 36 | 134 | 420 | 110 | 25 | 2 | 12 | 52 | 53 | 53 | 4.42 | 26 | 103 | 2 | 2 | .50 | .262 | .317 | .417 | .734 |
| Cabrera,Asdrubal | Cle | 28 | 149 | 582 | 154 | 37 | 2 | 16 | 79 | 73 | 78 | 4.68 | 49 | 118 | 12 | 5 | .71 | .265 | .328 | .418 | .746 |
| Cabrera,Everth | SD | 27 | 150 | 560 | 156 | 26 | 6 | 4 | 83 | 45 | 76 | 4.72 | 60 | 108 | 52 | 15 | .78 | .279 | .350 | .368 | .718 |
| Cabrera,Melky | Tor | 29 | 116 | 428 | 126 | 24 | 3 | 8 | 59 | 50 | 62 | 5.27 | 32 | 58 | 7 | 4 | .64 | .294 | .345 | .421 | .765 |
| Cabrera,Miguel | Det | 31 | 158 | 595 | 198 | 40 | 1 | 40 | 107 | 131 | 150 | 9.77 | 87 | 102 | 3 | 2 | .60 | .333 | .421 | .605 | 1.026 |
| Cain,Lorenzo | KC | 28 | 142 | 508 | 138 | 26 | 4 | 9 | 69 | 59 | 66 | 4.55 | 42 | 107 | 19 | 7 | .73 | .272 | .330 | .392 | .721 |
| Calhoun,Kole | LAA | 26 | 84 | 277 | 78 | 15 | 3 | 10 | 42 | 42 | 45 | 5.79 | 27 | 49 | 8 | 3 | .73 | .282 | .348 | .466 | .813 |
| Callaspo,Alberto | Oak | 31 | 146 | 503 | 135 | 26 | 1 | 9 | 60 | 56 | 64 | 4.51 | 53 | 53 | 2 | 1 | .67 | .268 | .339 | .378 | .717 |
| Campana,Tony | Ari | 28 | 75 | 163 | 44 | 5 | 1 | 0 | 24 | 8 | 18 | 3.77 | 12 | 36 | 18 | 5 | .78 | .270 | .320 | .313 | .633 |
| Cano,Robinson | NYY | 31 | 161 | 625 | 191 | 45 | 2 | 27 | 94 | 101 | 115 | 6.84 | 53 | 89 | 5 | 3 | .62 | .306 | .366 | .514 | .880 |
| Carp,Mike | Bos | 28 | 126 | 342 | 88 | 20 | 1 | 13 | 41 | 49 | 49 | 5.00 | 35 | 85 | 2 | 1 | .67 | .257 | .330 | .436 | .765 |
| Carpenter,Matt | StL | 28 | 155 | 612 | 189 | 49 | 5 | 13 | 106 | 82 | 112 | 6.85 | 82 | 95 | 4 | 2 | .67 | .309 | .395 | .469 | .864 |
| Carroll,Jamey | KC | 40 | 86 | 224 | 57 | 8 | 1 | 0 | 30 | 15 | 22 | 3.38 | 23 | 37 | 3 | 2 | .60 | .254 | .332 | .299 | .631 |
| Carter,Chris | Hou | 27 | 145 | 502 | 120 | 28 | 1 | 27 | 73 | 84 | 76 | 5.15 | 68 | 172 | 3 | 2 | .60 | .239 | .332 | .460 | .792 |
| Casilla,Alexi | Bal | 29 | 79 | 184 | 45 | 8 | 1 | 1 | 24 | 15 | 18 | 3.27 | 15 | 30 | 11 | 4 | .73 | .245 | .305 | .315 | .620 |
| Castellanos,Nick | Det | 22 | 134 | 512 | 133 | 31 | 1 | 14 | 64 | 57 | 65 | 4.44 | 39 | 96 | 5 | 2 | .71 | .260 | .312 | .406 | .718 |
| Castillo,Welington | ChC | 27 | 123 | 415 | 109 | 24 | 0 | 13 | 46 | 50 | 55 | 4.66 | 37 | 100 | 1 | 1 | .50 | .263 | .330 | .414 | .745 |
| Castro,Jason | Hou | 27 | 125 | 453 | 119 | 30 | 2 | 15 | 63 | 53 | 68 | 5.28 | 55 | 112 | 2 | 1 | .67 | .263 | .344 | .437 | .781 |
| Castro,Starlin | ChC | 24 | 156 | 648 | 181 | 37 | 7 | 11 | 75 | 63 | 83 | 4.54 | 35 | 108 | 15 | 8 | .65 | .279 | .321 | .409 | .730 |

# 2014 Hitter Projections

| PLAYER | | | BATTING | | | | | | | | | | | | BASERUNNING | | | AVERAGES | | | |
|---|---|---|---|---|---|---|---|---|---|---|---|---|---|---|---|---|---|---|---|---|---|
| Hitter | Team | Age | G | AB | H | 2B | 3B | HR | R | RBI | RC | RC27 | BB | SO | SB | CS | SB% | Avg | OBP | Slg | OPS |
| Cedeno,Ronny | SD | 31 | 63 | 198 | 49 | 10 | 1 | 3 | 21 | 19 | 20 | 3.44 | 12 | 49 | 3 | 2 | .60 | .247 | .297 | .354 | .651 |
| Cervelli,Francisco | NYY | 28 | 73 | 205 | 52 | 9 | 1 | 3 | 26 | 26 | 24 | 4.05 | 22 | 41 | 2 | 1 | .67 | .254 | .329 | .351 | .680 |
| Cespedes,Yoenis | Oak | 28 | 142 | 551 | 147 | 25 | 4 | 29 | 82 | 92 | 85 | 5.39 | 44 | 123 | 10 | 6 | .62 | .267 | .328 | .485 | .812 |
| Chavez,Eric | Ari | 36 | 80 | 250 | 64 | 13 | 1 | 9 | 28 | 36 | 34 | 4.75 | 24 | 54 | 1 | 0 | 1.00 | .256 | .324 | .424 | .748 |
| Chisenhall,Lonnie | Cle | 25 | 132 | 455 | 121 | 28 | 2 | 18 | 65 | 69 | 65 | 5.04 | 32 | 85 | 3 | 1 | .75 | .266 | .316 | .455 | .771 |
| Choice,Michael | Oak | 24 | 140 | 533 | 144 | 27 | 1 | 12 | 76 | 73 | 70 | 4.67 | 51 | 122 | 2 | 1 | .67 | .270 | .334 | .392 | .726 |
| Choo,Shin-Soo | Cin | 31 | 150 | 574 | 161 | 35 | 2 | 19 | 92 | 71 | 97 | 5.98 | 89 | 141 | 18 | 9 | .67 | .280 | .391 | .448 | .839 |
| Ciriaco,Pedro | KC | 28 | 85 | 231 | 61 | 10 | 2 | 2 | 26 | 19 | 23 | 3.44 | 7 | 37 | 11 | 4 | .73 | .264 | .286 | .351 | .636 |
| Clevenger,Steve | Bal | 28 | 62 | 173 | 47 | 12 | 1 | 3 | 20 | 21 | 23 | 4.75 | 16 | 24 | 0 | 0 | .00 | .272 | .333 | .405 | .738 |
| Coghlan,Chris | Mia | 29 | 101 | 305 | 81 | 19 | 2 | 5 | 38 | 28 | 40 | 4.58 | 33 | 49 | 7 | 3 | .70 | .266 | .341 | .390 | .731 |
| Colabello,Chris | Min | 30 | 141 | 509 | 140 | 31 | 0 | 23 | 66 | 85 | 82 | 5.76 | 52 | 131 | 1 | 1 | .50 | .275 | .343 | .472 | .815 |
| Colon,Christian | KC | 25 | 146 | 533 | 136 | 14 | 2 | 11 | 64 | 54 | 58 | 3.73 | 42 | 57 | 17 | 7 | .71 | .255 | .310 | .351 | .660 |
| Conger,Hank | LAA | 26 | 92 | 292 | 74 | 16 | 1 | 9 | 33 | 35 | 38 | 4.53 | 26 | 59 | 1 | 0 | 1.00 | .253 | .319 | .408 | .726 |
| Corporan,Carlos | Hou | 30 | 74 | 209 | 48 | 11 | 0 | 6 | 19 | 24 | 21 | 3.39 | 12 | 54 | 1 | 0 | 1.00 | .230 | .281 | .368 | .650 |
| Cowgill,Collin | LAA | 28 | 70 | 150 | 39 | 8 | 1 | 4 | 20 | 18 | 20 | 4.60 | 13 | 31 | 5 | 2 | .71 | .260 | .319 | .407 | .726 |
| Cozart,Zack | Cin | 28 | 150 | 563 | 146 | 33 | 3 | 14 | 78 | 56 | 69 | 4.29 | 34 | 96 | 5 | 1 | .83 | .259 | .303 | .403 | .706 |
| Craig,Allen | StL | 29 | 136 | 505 | 156 | 33 | 1 | 19 | 75 | 94 | 89 | 6.61 | 40 | 90 | 2 | 1 | .67 | .309 | .364 | .491 | .855 |
| Crawford,Brandon | SF | 27 | 148 | 496 | 124 | 25 | 3 | 8 | 55 | 46 | 56 | 3.89 | 44 | 92 | 3 | 2 | .60 | .250 | .315 | .361 | .676 |
| Crawford,Carl | LAD | 32 | 128 | 443 | 126 | 24 | 4 | 9 | 66 | 49 | 62 | 4.99 | 29 | 75 | 19 | 6 | .76 | .284 | .333 | .418 | .750 |
| Crisp,Coco | Oak | 34 | 140 | 537 | 139 | 26 | 4 | 15 | 84 | 60 | 73 | 4.69 | 55 | 75 | 26 | 7 | .79 | .259 | .328 | .406 | .734 |
| Cruz,Luis | NYY | 30 | 59 | 131 | 32 | 8 | 0 | 2 | 13 | 14 | 12 | 3.12 | 5 | 17 | 1 | 1 | .50 | .244 | .283 | .351 | .634 |
| Cruz,Nelson | Tex | 33 | 142 | 540 | 141 | 31 | 1 | 30 | 73 | 92 | 84 | 5.42 | 48 | 141 | 8 | 4 | .67 | .261 | .325 | .489 | .814 |
| Cruz,Tony | StL | 27 | 58 | 114 | 26 | 7 | 1 | 2 | 11 | 12 | 11 | 3.25 | 6 | 21 | 0 | 0 | .00 | .228 | .273 | .360 | .632 |
| Cuddyer,Michael | Col | 35 | 138 | 523 | 146 | 32 | 3 | 19 | 74 | 79 | 82 | 5.61 | 49 | 109 | 8 | 3 | .73 | .279 | .344 | .461 | .805 |
| Danks,Jordan | CWS | 27 | 90 | 227 | 59 | 12 | 1 | 6 | 31 | 23 | 31 | 4.71 | 27 | 69 | 7 | 3 | .70 | .260 | .339 | .401 | .739 |
| dArnaud,Travis' | NYM | 25 | 116 | 365 | 103 | 27 | 1 | 14 | 50 | 52 | 60 | 5.93 | 37 | 81 | 1 | 1 | .50 | .282 | .348 | .477 | .825 |
| Davidson,Matt | Ari | 23 | 136 | 482 | 120 | 31 | 2 | 19 | 58 | 67 | 67 | 4.80 | 48 | 141 | 2 | 1 | .67 | .249 | .318 | .440 | .758 |
| Davis,Chris | Bal | 28 | 160 | 582 | 161 | 38 | 1 | 41 | 92 | 113 | 110 | 6.76 | 57 | 193 | 3 | 2 | .60 | .277 | .346 | .557 | .903 |
| Davis,Ike | NYM | 27 | 137 | 562 | 138 | 33 | 0 | 29 | 79 | 86 | 89 | 5.43 | 86 | 149 | 4 | 2 | .67 | .246 | .347 | .459 | .806 |
| Davis,Khris | Mil | 26 | 136 | 460 | 126 | 31 | 1 | 26 | 72 | 77 | 82 | 6.29 | 51 | 108 | 10 | 5 | .67 | .274 | .350 | .515 | .865 |
| Davis,Rajai | Tor | 33 | 97 | 254 | 65 | 14 | 2 | 3 | 35 | 22 | 29 | 3.83 | 16 | 53 | 26 | 8 | .76 | .256 | .310 | .362 | .672 |
| De Aza,Alejandro | CWS | 30 | 142 | 547 | 155 | 32 | 4 | 13 | 82 | 57 | 79 | 5.11 | 47 | 113 | 20 | 10 | .67 | .283 | .344 | .428 | .772 |
| DeJesus,David | TB | 34 | 124 | 382 | 98 | 22 | 3 | 7 | 51 | 39 | 47 | 4.26 | 39 | 73 | 4 | 3 | .57 | .257 | .338 | .385 | .723 |
| Denorfia,Chris | SD | 33 | 138 | 412 | 113 | 20 | 2 | 8 | 57 | 41 | 53 | 4.55 | 35 | 72 | 9 | 4 | .69 | .274 | .333 | .391 | .723 |
| Descalso,Daniel | StL | 27 | 138 | 370 | 92 | 23 | 3 | 5 | 47 | 41 | 42 | 3.89 | 32 | 61 | 6 | 3 | .67 | .249 | .314 | .368 | .681 |
| Desmond,Ian | Was | 28 | 153 | 591 | 162 | 36 | 3 | 19 | 75 | 72 | 84 | 5.01 | 41 | 139 | 20 | 7 | .74 | .274 | .324 | .442 | .766 |
| Dickerson,Corey | Col | 25 | 69 | 230 | 68 | 15 | 4 | 8 | 35 | 27 | 38 | 5.95 | 16 | 41 | 4 | 4 | .50 | .296 | .341 | .500 | .841 |
| Dietrich,Derek | Mia | 24 | 123 | 450 | 112 | 25 | 4 | 21 | 73 | 64 | 64 | 4.89 | 39 | 114 | 4 | 2 | .67 | .249 | .316 | .462 | .778 |
| Dirks,Andy | Det | 28 | 111 | 334 | 92 | 17 | 2 | 9 | 49 | 36 | 47 | 5.01 | 28 | 56 | 7 | 2 | .78 | .275 | .335 | .419 | .754 |
| Dobbs,Greg | Mia | 35 | 83 | 168 | 43 | 8 | 0 | 3 | 16 | 20 | 18 | 3.71 | 12 | 32 | 1 | 1 | .50 | .256 | .313 | .357 | .670 |
| Dominguez,Matt | Hou | 24 | 148 | 540 | 131 | 29 | 1 | 18 | 59 | 79 | 63 | 4.00 | 36 | 82 | 0 | 0 | .00 | .243 | .294 | .400 | .694 |
| Donaldson,Josh | Oak | 28 | 155 | 560 | 153 | 34 | 1 | 22 | 81 | 88 | 89 | 5.64 | 64 | 104 | 6 | 3 | .67 | .273 | .351 | .455 | .806 |
| Doumit,Ryan | Min | 33 | 112 | 337 | 87 | 21 | 1 | 11 | 37 | 44 | 45 | 4.68 | 29 | 69 | 1 | 0 | 1.00 | .258 | .324 | .424 | .749 |
| Dozier,Brian | Min | 27 | 145 | 548 | 136 | 32 | 4 | 16 | 71 | 63 | 68 | 4.22 | 46 | 102 | 13 | 7 | .65 | .248 | .310 | .409 | .719 |
| Drew,Stephen | Bos | 31 | 125 | 458 | 113 | 28 | 5 | 12 | 59 | 54 | 60 | 4.48 | 50 | 113 | 5 | 3 | .62 | .247 | .322 | .408 | .730 |
| Duda,Lucas | NYM | 28 | 120 | 449 | 114 | 28 | 1 | 18 | 57 | 61 | 69 | 5.34 | 65 | 115 | 1 | 1 | .50 | .254 | .356 | .441 | .797 |
| Dunn,Adam | CWS | 34 | 153 | 540 | 114 | 23 | 0 | 32 | 70 | 86 | 76 | 4.63 | 93 | 211 | 1 | 1 | .50 | .211 | .331 | .431 | .763 |
| Dyson,Jarrod | KC | 29 | 85 | 195 | 49 | 7 | 2 | 1 | 31 | 12 | 22 | 3.76 | 18 | 36 | 25 | 6 | .81 | .251 | .318 | .323 | .641 |
| Eaton,Adam | Ari | 25 | 131 | 450 | 131 | 26 | 5 | 7 | 78 | 39 | 66 | 5.25 | 40 | 73 | 20 | 8 | .71 | .291 | .354 | .418 | .772 |
| Ellis,A.J. | LAD | 33 | 121 | 413 | 107 | 19 | 1 | 9 | 47 | 53 | 55 | 4.67 | 59 | 78 | 0 | 0 | .00 | .259 | .356 | .375 | .731 |
| Ellis,Mark | LAD | 37 | 128 | 440 | 110 | 20 | 1 | 7 | 50 | 44 | 46 | 3.60 | 32 | 76 | 5 | 2 | .71 | .250 | .311 | .348 | .659 |
| Ellsbury,Jacoby | Bos | 30 | 138 | 580 | 170 | 33 | 4 | 12 | 92 | 59 | 88 | 5.43 | 45 | 88 | 43 | 11 | .80 | .293 | .348 | .426 | .774 |
| Elmore,Jake | Hou | 27 | 86 | 290 | 78 | 15 | 2 | 3 | 41 | 28 | 37 | 4.37 | 34 | 41 | 15 | 8 | .65 | .269 | .346 | .366 | .711 |
| Encarnacion,Edwin | Tor | 31 | 150 | 554 | 152 | 32 | 1 | 34 | 89 | 98 | 104 | 6.68 | 74 | 82 | 7 | 3 | .70 | .274 | .366 | .520 | .886 |
| Escobar,Alcides | KC | 27 | 155 | 594 | 155 | 24 | 5 | 5 | 68 | 52 | 62 | 3.62 | 27 | 87 | 25 | 6 | .81 | .261 | .298 | .343 | .641 |
| Escobar,Eduardo | Min | 25 | 66 | 202 | 51 | 10 | 2 | 3 | 25 | 18 | 22 | 3.74 | 13 | 41 | 4 | 2 | .67 | .252 | .298 | .366 | .664 |
| Escobar,Yunel | TB | 31 | 141 | 516 | 137 | 25 | 1 | 9 | 65 | 53 | 64 | 4.36 | 54 | 72 | 4 | 3 | .57 | .266 | .340 | .370 | .710 |
| Espinosa,Danny | Was | 27 | 93 | 288 | 67 | 15 | 1 | 8 | 36 | 30 | 31 | 3.60 | 21 | 85 | 8 | 3 | .73 | .233 | .303 | .375 | .678 |
| Ethier,Andre | LAD | 32 | 136 | 499 | 139 | 33 | 1 | 16 | 66 | 69 | 78 | 5.60 | 58 | 103 | 3 | 2 | .60 | .279 | .361 | .445 | .805 |
| Federowicz,Tim | LAD | 26 | 56 | 199 | 52 | 13 | 0 | 6 | 24 | 28 | 27 | 4.78 | 18 | 54 | 0 | 0 | .00 | .261 | .323 | .417 | .740 |
| Fielder,Prince | Det | 30 | 158 | 589 | 171 | 35 | 1 | 32 | 87 | 108 | 117 | 7.26 | 90 | 111 | 1 | 1 | .50 | .290 | .396 | .516 | .912 |
| Flaherty,Ryan | Bal | 27 | 92 | 242 | 58 | 11 | 1 | 10 | 29 | 32 | 30 | 4.22 | 19 | 55 | 2 | 1 | .67 | .240 | .303 | .417 | .720 |
| Flores,Wilmer | NYM | 22 | 140 | 502 | 137 | 36 | 2 | 13 | 59 | 71 | 67 | 4.76 | 27 | 80 | 1 | 1 | .50 | .273 | .310 | .430 | .740 |
| Florimon,Pedro | Min | 27 | 142 | 440 | 105 | 21 | 1 | 8 | 49 | 46 | 45 | 3.41 | 38 | 113 | 15 | 8 | .65 | .239 | .301 | .345 | .646 |
| Flowers,Tyler | CWS | 28 | 82 | 226 | 52 | 12 | 0 | 11 | 28 | 28 | 30 | 4.46 | 25 | 78 | 1 | 1 | .50 | .230 | .315 | .429 | .744 |
| Forsythe,Logan | SD | 27 | 103 | 311 | 81 | 15 | 2 | 7 | 46 | 33 | 42 | 4.69 | 38 | 69 | 9 | 3 | .75 | .260 | .347 | .389 | .736 |
| Fowler,Dexter | Col | 28 | 142 | 513 | 139 | 30 | 9 | 11 | 87 | 51 | 81 | 5.48 | 78 | 135 | 19 | 10 | .66 | .271 | .371 | .429 | .800 |
| Francisco,Juan | Mil | 27 | 100 | 252 | 64 | 15 | 1 | 13 | 31 | 41 | 36 | 4.98 | 17 | 80 | 0 | 0 | .00 | .254 | .306 | .476 | .782 |
| Frandsen,Kevin | Phi | 32 | 67 | 124 | 34 | 7 | 0 | 2 | 14 | 12 | 14 | 4.00 | 6 | 11 | 1 | 1 | .50 | .274 | .333 | .379 | .712 |
| Franklin,Nick | Sea | 23 | 142 | 526 | 136 | 31 | 3 | 15 | 65 | 60 | 74 | 4.87 | 61 | 125 | 15 | 5 | .75 | .259 | .336 | .414 | .750 |

# 2014 Hitter Projections

| PLAYER | | | BATTING | | | | | | | | | | | | BASERUNNING | | | AVERAGES | | | |
|---|---|---|---|---|---|---|---|---|---|---|---|---|---|---|---|---|---|---|---|---|---|
| Hitter | Team | Age | G | AB | H | 2B | 3B | HR | R | RBI | RC | RC27 | BB | SO | SB | CS | SB% | Avg | OBP | Slg | OPS |
| Frazier,Todd | Cin | 28 | 148 | 525 | 134 | 34 | 3 | 21 | 68 | 76 | 75 | 4.94 | 48 | 115 | 8 | 4 | .67 | .255 | .326 | .451 | .777 |
| Freeman,Freddie | Atl | 24 | 152 | 564 | 170 | 35 | 2 | 24 | 90 | 104 | 105 | 6.91 | 64 | 117 | 2 | 1 | .67 | .301 | .378 | .498 | .876 |
| Freese,David | StL | 31 | 142 | 492 | 143 | 29 | 1 | 14 | 63 | 76 | 77 | 5.72 | 49 | 105 | 2 | 1 | .67 | .291 | .362 | .439 | .801 |
| Freiman,Nate | Oak | 27 | 61 | 131 | 37 | 7 | 0 | 5 | 15 | 22 | 20 | 5.53 | 11 | 22 | 0 | 0 | .00 | .282 | .343 | .450 | .793 |
| Fuld,Sam | TB | 32 | 92 | 158 | 37 | 6 | 1 | 1 | 22 | 12 | 15 | 3.15 | 18 | 21 | 7 | 3 | .70 | .234 | .316 | .304 | .620 |
| Furcal,Rafael | StL | 36 | 91 | 357 | 94 | 16 | 2 | 6 | 52 | 31 | 43 | 4.17 | 35 | 47 | 10 | 5 | .67 | .263 | .331 | .370 | .701 |
| Galvis,Freddy | Phi | 24 | 69 | 170 | 40 | 8 | 1 | 3 | 17 | 16 | 16 | 3.18 | 9 | 31 | 3 | 1 | .75 | .235 | .274 | .347 | .621 |
| Garcia,Avisail | CWS | 23 | 144 | 535 | 167 | 18 | 5 | 16 | 76 | 70 | 82 | 5.69 | 25 | 111 | 11 | 7 | .61 | .312 | .344 | .454 | .798 |
| Garcia,Leury | CWS | 23 | 121 | 426 | 108 | 13 | 7 | 4 | 54 | 27 | 45 | 3.57 | 25 | 110 | 33 | 10 | .77 | .254 | .295 | .345 | .640 |
| Gardner,Brett | NYY | 30 | 150 | 557 | 149 | 26 | 7 | 7 | 95 | 48 | 75 | 4.65 | 67 | 125 | 33 | 11 | .75 | .268 | .351 | .377 | .728 |
| Gattis,Evan | Atl | 27 | 125 | 468 | 117 | 33 | 2 | 27 | 57 | 87 | 70 | 5.19 | 32 | 93 | 0 | 0 | .00 | .250 | .302 | .502 | .804 |
| Gennett,Scooter | Mil | 24 | 143 | 536 | 152 | 25 | 4 | 7 | 66 | 41 | 66 | 4.40 | 28 | 89 | 12 | 6 | .67 | .284 | .320 | .384 | .705 |
| Gentry,Craig | Tex | 30 | 104 | 237 | 66 | 10 | 2 | 2 | 36 | 22 | 30 | 4.43 | 21 | 40 | 18 | 5 | .78 | .278 | .352 | .363 | .715 |
| Getz,Chris | KC | 30 | 86 | 229 | 59 | 9 | 1 | 1 | 28 | 19 | 24 | 3.57 | 19 | 23 | 13 | 5 | .72 | .258 | .317 | .319 | .636 |
| Giavotella,Johnny | KC | 26 | 56 | 199 | 55 | 12 | 1 | 3 | 26 | 24 | 26 | 4.63 | 19 | 29 | 4 | 2 | .67 | .276 | .342 | .392 | .734 |
| Gillaspie,Conor | CWS | 26 | 84 | 217 | 55 | 9 | 2 | 6 | 25 | 23 | 27 | 4.33 | 20 | 36 | 1 | 0 | 1.00 | .253 | .316 | .396 | .713 |
| Gindl,Caleb | Mil | 25 | 131 | 477 | 127 | 29 | 3 | 14 | 58 | 57 | 68 | 5.01 | 48 | 99 | 5 | 3 | .62 | .266 | .333 | .428 | .761 |
| Goins,Ryan | Tor | 26 | 82 | 260 | 67 | 15 | 1 | 4 | 27 | 26 | 29 | 3.87 | 17 | 51 | 3 | 2 | .60 | .258 | .303 | .369 | .672 |
| Goldschmidt,Paul | Ari | 26 | 160 | 610 | 184 | 42 | 2 | 37 | 113 | 128 | 136 | 8.19 | 98 | 139 | 15 | 6 | .71 | .302 | .401 | .559 | .960 |
| Gomes,Jonny | Bos | 33 | 122 | 342 | 81 | 17 | 1 | 16 | 48 | 53 | 48 | 4.76 | 44 | 110 | 3 | 1 | .75 | .237 | .336 | .433 | .769 |
| Gomes,Yan | Cle | 26 | 120 | 421 | 118 | 31 | 2 | 17 | 55 | 64 | 67 | 5.73 | 30 | 97 | 3 | 1 | .75 | .280 | .336 | .485 | .820 |
| Gomez,Carlos | Mil | 28 | 142 | 528 | 137 | 25 | 6 | 19 | 81 | 62 | 72 | 4.68 | 35 | 137 | 35 | 9 | .80 | .259 | .313 | .438 | .750 |
| Gonzalez,Adrian | LAD | 32 | 160 | 622 | 185 | 39 | 1 | 26 | 86 | 106 | 111 | 6.59 | 67 | 114 | 1 | 1 | .50 | .297 | .368 | .489 | .857 |
| Gonzalez,Carlos | Col | 28 | 138 | 523 | 153 | 32 | 5 | 27 | 91 | 89 | 99 | 6.83 | 51 | 134 | 21 | 7 | .75 | .293 | .358 | .528 | .885 |
| Gonzalez,Marwin | Hou | 25 | 85 | 222 | 54 | 12 | 1 | 3 | 21 | 18 | 21 | 3.19 | 12 | 31 | 5 | 3 | .62 | .243 | .282 | .347 | .629 |
| Gordon,Alex | KC | 30 | 157 | 628 | 174 | 40 | 3 | 20 | 93 | 80 | 97 | 5.49 | 67 | 144 | 11 | 5 | .69 | .277 | .352 | .446 | .798 |
| Gordon,Dee | LAD | 26 | 55 | 186 | 49 | 6 | 2 | 0 | 25 | 11 | 21 | 3.82 | 15 | 33 | 22 | 6 | .79 | .263 | .322 | .317 | .639 |
| Gose,Anthony | Tor | 23 | 138 | 526 | 130 | 23 | 8 | 7 | 79 | 43 | 60 | 3.80 | 46 | 149 | 39 | 15 | .72 | .247 | .309 | .361 | .670 |
| Grandal,Yasmani | SD | 25 | 63 | 221 | 58 | 18 | 0 | 6 | 33 | 34 | 34 | 5.42 | 33 | 43 | 0 | 0 | .00 | .262 | .361 | .425 | .786 |
| Granderson,Curtis | NYY | 33 | 156 | 593 | 144 | 26 | 6 | 31 | 101 | 79 | 90 | 5.14 | 74 | 178 | 15 | 6 | .71 | .243 | .331 | .464 | .795 |
| Green,Grant | LAA | 26 | 140 | 507 | 137 | 30 | 3 | 10 | 62 | 55 | 63 | 4.38 | 30 | 102 | 6 | 4 | .60 | .270 | .312 | .400 | .713 |
| Gregorius,Didi | Ari | 24 | 145 | 497 | 130 | 22 | 6 | 9 | 68 | 45 | 61 | 4.30 | 44 | 78 | 2 | 2 | .50 | .262 | .325 | .384 | .710 |
| Grossman,Robbie | Hou | 24 | 149 | 501 | 133 | 26 | 2 | 8 | 69 | 41 | 65 | 4.42 | 67 | 127 | 20 | 14 | .59 | .265 | .353 | .373 | .727 |
| Gutierrez,Franklin | Sea | 31 | 46 | 105 | 25 | 6 | 0 | 3 | 13 | 11 | 12 | 3.85 | 7 | 28 | 3 | 1 | .75 | .238 | .292 | .381 | .673 |
| Guzman,Jesus | SD | 30 | 93 | 199 | 55 | 13 | 1 | 6 | 25 | 29 | 29 | 5.20 | 17 | 43 | 2 | 1 | .67 | .276 | .336 | .442 | .779 |
| Gyorko,Jedd | SD | 25 | 142 | 533 | 148 | 29 | 0 | 28 | 78 | 85 | 86 | 5.79 | 42 | 116 | 2 | 1 | .67 | .278 | .333 | .490 | .822 |
| Hairston,Jerry | LAD | 38 | 70 | 139 | 34 | 6 | 0 | 2 | 15 | 14 | 14 | 3.43 | 11 | 18 | 1 | 1 | .50 | .245 | .314 | .331 | .645 |
| Hairston,Scott | Was | 34 | 83 | 155 | 36 | 8 | 0 | 8 | 20 | 22 | 19 | 4.12 | 11 | 39 | 2 | 1 | .67 | .232 | .292 | .439 | .730 |
| Hamilton,Billy | Cin | 23 | 145 | 584 | 156 | 21 | 5 | 6 | 97 | 48 | 78 | 4.54 | 57 | 116 | 96 | 19 | .83 | .267 | .332 | .351 | .683 |
| Hamilton,Josh | LAA | 33 | 150 | 572 | 157 | 34 | 3 | 28 | 85 | 99 | 94 | 5.86 | 52 | 152 | 5 | 2 | .71 | .274 | .339 | .491 | .830 |
| Hanigan,Ryan | Cin | 33 | 95 | 262 | 67 | 10 | 0 | 3 | 25 | 26 | 30 | 4.00 | 36 | 29 | 0 | 0 | .00 | .256 | .354 | .328 | .683 |
| Hannahan,Jack | Cin | 34 | 61 | 105 | 24 | 6 | 0 | 2 | 10 | 11 | 11 | 3.53 | 13 | 28 | 0 | 0 | .00 | .229 | .325 | .343 | .668 |
| Hardy,J.J. | Bal | 31 | 157 | 623 | 160 | 30 | 1 | 24 | 78 | 77 | 80 | 4.48 | 43 | 91 | 1 | 1 | .50 | .257 | .306 | .424 | .730 |
| Harper,Bryce | Was | 21 | 152 | 546 | 151 | 31 | 7 | 25 | 99 | 70 | 99 | 6.42 | 74 | 111 | 16 | 6 | .73 | .277 | .366 | .496 | .862 |
| Harris,Brendan | LAA | 33 | 64 | 174 | 40 | 9 | 0 | 3 | 20 | 17 | 17 | 3.30 | 15 | 35 | 0 | 0 | .00 | .230 | .295 | .333 | .628 |
| Hart,Corey | Mil | 32 | 142 | 547 | 148 | 34 | 3 | 26 | 84 | 80 | 86 | 5.53 | 46 | 135 | 8 | 5 | .62 | .271 | .333 | .486 | .819 |
| Headley,Chase | SD | 30 | 150 | 556 | 153 | 36 | 2 | 17 | 74 | 73 | 87 | 5.54 | 71 | 148 | 10 | 5 | .67 | .275 | .363 | .439 | .802 |
| Hechavarria,Adeiny | Mia | 25 | 150 | 563 | 142 | 22 | 5 | 5 | 55 | 54 | 54 | 3.27 | 31 | 98 | 12 | 8 | .60 | .252 | .291 | .336 | .627 |
| Heisey,Chris | Cin | 29 | 95 | 221 | 59 | 11 | 1 | 9 | 31 | 27 | 30 | 4.76 | 13 | 48 | 4 | 2 | .67 | .267 | .322 | .448 | .770 |
| Hernandez,Cesar | Phi | 24 | 69 | 179 | 51 | 8 | 2 | 1 | 23 | 16 | 23 | 4.53 | 14 | 33 | 11 | 4 | .73 | .285 | .340 | .369 | .709 |
| Herrera,Jonathan | Col | 29 | 112 | 322 | 83 | 10 | 2 | 2 | 36 | 23 | 32 | 3.44 | 26 | 41 | 6 | 3 | .67 | .258 | .315 | .320 | .635 |
| Herrmann,Chris | Min | 26 | 55 | 130 | 30 | 6 | 1 | 2 | 17 | 13 | 13 | 3.35 | 14 | 30 | 1 | 1 | .50 | .231 | .306 | .338 | .644 |
| Heyward,Jason | Atl | 24 | 152 | 575 | 155 | 33 | 4 | 24 | 97 | 77 | 95 | 5.81 | 77 | 123 | 10 | 5 | .67 | .270 | .362 | .466 | .828 |
| Hicks,Aaron | Min | 24 | 130 | 472 | 113 | 21 | 6 | 13 | 76 | 50 | 60 | 4.25 | 55 | 124 | 21 | 8 | .72 | .239 | .320 | .392 | .712 |
| Hill,Aaron | Ari | 32 | 139 | 525 | 143 | 31 | 2 | 18 | 72 | 68 | 75 | 5.05 | 41 | 78 | 6 | 4 | .60 | .272 | .331 | .442 | .773 |
| Hoes,L.J. | Hou | 24 | 132 | 448 | 128 | 24 | 3 | 4 | 64 | 45 | 62 | 4.91 | 54 | 71 | 14 | 8 | .64 | .286 | .363 | .379 | .742 |
| Holliday,Matt | StL | 34 | 151 | 570 | 170 | 39 | 1 | 25 | 98 | 99 | 108 | 6.97 | 72 | 110 | 6 | 3 | .67 | .298 | .386 | .502 | .887 |
| Hosmer,Eric | KC | 24 | 156 | 614 | 178 | 33 | 3 | 20 | 86 | 83 | 97 | 5.72 | 56 | 92 | 12 | 5 | .71 | .290 | .350 | .451 | .801 |
| Howard,Ryan | Phi | 34 | 130 | 476 | 119 | 24 | 1 | 26 | 63 | 93 | 74 | 5.39 | 57 | 164 | 1 | 0 | 1.00 | .250 | .335 | .468 | .804 |
| Hundley,Nick | SD | 30 | 90 | 262 | 63 | 14 | 1 | 8 | 28 | 35 | 30 | 3.90 | 21 | 62 | 1 | 1 | .50 | .240 | .304 | .393 | .697 |
| Hunter,Torii | Det | 38 | 152 | 594 | 167 | 31 | 1 | 19 | 81 | 87 | 84 | 5.08 | 43 | 126 | 5 | 3 | .62 | .281 | .336 | .433 | .769 |
| Iannetta,Chris | LAA | 31 | 120 | 391 | 90 | 20 | 1 | 15 | 51 | 55 | 54 | 4.65 | 70 | 113 | 1 | 1 | .50 | .230 | .353 | .402 | .754 |
| Ibanez,Raul | Sea | 42 | 128 | 418 | 99 | 22 | 1 | 17 | 49 | 61 | 52 | 4.23 | 39 | 102 | 1 | 1 | .50 | .237 | .305 | .416 | .721 |
| Iglesias,Jose | Det | 24 | 148 | 533 | 137 | 18 | 2 | 5 | 61 | 42 | 52 | 3.36 | 29 | 82 | 13 | 6 | .68 | .257 | .303 | .326 | .629 |
| Infante,Omar | Det | 32 | 145 | 559 | 163 | 26 | 3 | 10 | 66 | 58 | 74 | 4.82 | 30 | 64 | 7 | 3 | .70 | .292 | .329 | .403 | .731 |
| Izturis,Cesar | Cin | 34 | 59 | 109 | 25 | 4 | 0 | 0 | 9 | 7 | 8 | 2.45 | 6 | 11 | 1 | 1 | .50 | .229 | .276 | .266 | .542 |
| Izturis,Maicer | Tor | 33 | 104 | 308 | 79 | 16 | 1 | 4 | 37 | 32 | 34 | 3.81 | 26 | 37 | 5 | 3 | .62 | .256 | .320 | .354 | .674 |
| Jackson,Austin | Det | 27 | 144 | 566 | 159 | 30 | 8 | 12 | 97 | 58 | 84 | 5.30 | 57 | 141 | 12 | 5 | .71 | .281 | .350 | .426 | .776 |
| Jackson,Ryan | StL | 26 | 126 | 439 | 111 | 23 | 1 | 5 | 46 | 38 | 48 | 3.78 | 39 | 81 | 6 | 2 | .75 | .253 | .314 | .344 | .658 |
| Jaso,John | Oak | 30 | 108 | 337 | 88 | 19 | 1 | 7 | 45 | 43 | 47 | 4.87 | 54 | 55 | 3 | 2 | .60 | .261 | .366 | .386 | .752 |

# 2014 Hitter Projections

| PLAYER | | | BATTING | | | | | | | | | | | | | BASERUNNING | | | AVERAGES | | | |
|---|---|---|---|---|---|---|---|---|---|---|---|---|---|---|---|---|---|---|---|---|---|---|
| Hitter | Team | Age | G | AB | H | 2B | 3B | HR | R | RBI | RC | RC27 | BB | SO | SB | CS | SB% | Avg | OBP | Slg | OPS |
| Jay,Jon | StL | 29 | 151 | 530 | 150 | 29 | 2 | 8 | 74 | 56 | 70 | 4.72 | 45 | 93 | 11 | 6 | .65 | .283 | .349 | .391 | .740 |
| Jennings,Desmond | TB | 27 | 135 | 498 | 130 | 28 | 5 | 13 | 85 | 51 | 72 | 5.01 | 58 | 100 | 25 | 6 | .81 | .261 | .342 | .416 | .757 |
| Jeter,Derek | NYY | 40 | 129 | 529 | 155 | 23 | 1 | 9 | 79 | 53 | 73 | 5.02 | 48 | 80 | 9 | 4 | .69 | .293 | .357 | .391 | .749 |
| Johnson,Chris | Atl | 29 | 152 | 539 | 161 | 34 | 2 | 15 | 58 | 75 | 82 | 5.63 | 30 | 119 | 2 | 1 | .67 | .299 | .339 | .453 | .792 |
| Johnson,Elliot | Atl | 30 | 110 | 348 | 85 | 15 | 2 | 7 | 41 | 35 | 38 | 3.63 | 26 | 87 | 23 | 9 | .72 | .244 | .299 | .359 | .658 |
| Johnson,Kelly | TB | 32 | 108 | 321 | 76 | 16 | 2 | 12 | 43 | 38 | 42 | 4.40 | 37 | 90 | 6 | 3 | .67 | .237 | .321 | .411 | .733 |
| Johnson,Reed | Atl | 37 | 82 | 151 | 40 | 9 | 1 | 2 | 18 | 14 | 17 | 3.95 | 7 | 37 | 1 | 1 | .50 | .265 | .327 | .377 | .705 |
| Jones,Adam | Bal | 28 | 160 | 633 | 178 | 33 | 3 | 29 | 94 | 93 | 96 | 5.43 | 32 | 131 | 13 | 5 | .72 | .281 | .325 | .480 | .805 |
| Jones,Garrett | Pit | 33 | 127 | 351 | 87 | 22 | 1 | 15 | 42 | 52 | 48 | 4.71 | 30 | 85 | 3 | 1 | .75 | .248 | .309 | .444 | .753 |
| Joyce,Matt | TB | 29 | 133 | 406 | 101 | 26 | 1 | 17 | 59 | 59 | 61 | 5.13 | 56 | 95 | 6 | 4 | .60 | .249 | .344 | .443 | .787 |
| Kawasaki,Munenori | Tor | 33 | 68 | 124 | 28 | 2 | 1 | 0 | 14 | 10 | 11 | 2.95 | 17 | 20 | 3 | 1 | .75 | .226 | .333 | .258 | .591 |
| Kelly,Don | Det | 34 | 71 | 156 | 37 | 5 | 1 | 3 | 20 | 15 | 16 | 3.47 | 15 | 21 | 3 | 1 | .75 | .237 | .308 | .340 | .648 |
| Kemp,Matt | LAD | 29 | 142 | 543 | 157 | 30 | 3 | 23 | 87 | 85 | 92 | 6.07 | 50 | 147 | 20 | 8 | .71 | .289 | .352 | .483 | .835 |
| Kendrick,Howie | LAA | 30 | 145 | 559 | 162 | 34 | 3 | 13 | 69 | 68 | 78 | 5.04 | 28 | 109 | 9 | 5 | .64 | .290 | .331 | .431 | .762 |
| Keppinger,Jeff | CWS | 34 | 115 | 420 | 116 | 19 | 1 | 6 | 44 | 40 | 50 | 4.28 | 27 | 37 | 1 | 0 | 1.00 | .276 | .323 | .369 | .692 |
| Kieschnick,Roger | SF | 27 | 77 | 175 | 44 | 9 | 2 | 5 | 22 | 21 | 22 | 4.33 | 15 | 50 | 2 | 1 | .67 | .251 | .311 | .411 | .722 |
| Kinsler,Ian | Tex | 32 | 152 | 615 | 163 | 36 | 2 | 20 | 103 | 76 | 89 | 5.03 | 67 | 78 | 19 | 8 | .70 | .265 | .345 | .428 | .773 |
| Kipnis,Jason | Cle | 27 | 144 | 555 | 153 | 32 | 5 | 17 | 90 | 80 | 90 | 5.72 | 70 | 117 | 26 | 7 | .79 | .276 | .360 | .443 | .803 |
| Konerko,Paul | CWS | 38 | 147 | 539 | 146 | 24 | 0 | 23 | 62 | 80 | 83 | 5.49 | 62 | 92 | 0 | 0 | .00 | .271 | .353 | .443 | .796 |
| Kottaras,George | KC | 31 | 94 | 280 | 63 | 17 | 1 | 12 | 36 | 39 | 40 | 4.77 | 47 | 81 | 1 | 1 | .50 | .225 | .338 | .421 | .760 |
| Kozma,Pete | StL | 26 | 84 | 195 | 43 | 9 | 1 | 2 | 23 | 21 | 17 | 2.89 | 17 | 38 | 2 | 1 | .67 | .221 | .283 | .308 | .591 |
| Kratz,Erik | Phi | 34 | 79 | 230 | 56 | 14 | 0 | 10 | 28 | 34 | 31 | 4.63 | 20 | 47 | 1 | 0 | 1.00 | .243 | .307 | .435 | .742 |
| Krauss,Marc | Hou | 26 | 61 | 153 | 28 | 10 | 1 | 6 | 22 | 22 | 17 | 3.51 | 23 | 39 | 2 | 1 | .67 | .183 | .294 | .379 | .673 |
| Kubel,Jason | Cle | 32 | 132 | 440 | 107 | 24 | 2 | 17 | 52 | 69 | 59 | 4.61 | 47 | 129 | 1 | 0 | 1.00 | .243 | .318 | .423 | .740 |
| Lagares,Juan | NYM | 25 | 142 | 490 | 132 | 27 | 5 | 6 | 54 | 45 | 57 | 4.06 | 27 | 101 | 13 | 7 | .65 | .269 | .309 | .382 | .691 |
| Laird,Gerald | Atl | 34 | 74 | 192 | 47 | 11 | 0 | 2 | 22 | 18 | 19 | 3.38 | 16 | 36 | 1 | 1 | .50 | .245 | .313 | .333 | .646 |
| Lake,Junior | ChC | 24 | 138 | 508 | 140 | 32 | 2 | 13 | 72 | 48 | 68 | 4.65 | 32 | 124 | 27 | 12 | .69 | .276 | .321 | .423 | .744 |
| LaRoche,Adam | Was | 34 | 151 | 508 | 126 | 29 | 1 | 22 | 65 | 75 | 74 | 5.02 | 62 | 136 | 2 | 1 | .67 | .248 | .332 | .439 | .771 |
| Lavarnway,Ryan | Bos | 26 | 112 | 415 | 107 | 25 | 0 | 13 | 54 | 64 | 56 | 4.73 | 44 | 80 | 0 | 0 | .00 | .258 | .330 | .412 | .742 |
| Lawrie,Brett | Tor | 24 | 147 | 519 | 145 | 29 | 6 | 16 | 75 | 63 | 78 | 5.32 | 41 | 89 | 16 | 7 | .70 | .279 | .338 | .451 | .789 |
| LeMahieu,DJ | Col | 25 | 131 | 520 | 152 | 28 | 5 | 4 | 58 | 46 | 66 | 4.54 | 27 | 74 | 22 | 10 | .69 | .292 | .328 | .388 | .717 |
| Lind,Adam | Tor | 30 | 134 | 467 | 129 | 27 | 1 | 21 | 58 | 74 | 74 | 5.68 | 42 | 103 | 1 | 1 | .50 | .276 | .339 | .473 | .812 |
| Lobaton,Jose | TB | 29 | 94 | 262 | 64 | 14 | 1 | 6 | 30 | 31 | 32 | 4.20 | 32 | 60 | 0 | 0 | .00 | .244 | .329 | .374 | .703 |
| Lombardozzi,Steve | Was | 25 | 73 | 198 | 56 | 10 | 2 | 2 | 24 | 17 | 24 | 4.33 | 10 | 23 | 5 | 2 | .71 | .283 | .324 | .384 | .708 |
| Loney,James | TB | 30 | 158 | 536 | 151 | 32 | 1 | 11 | 56 | 73 | 73 | 4.90 | 45 | 73 | 3 | 2 | .60 | .282 | .338 | .407 | .745 |
| Longoria,Evan | TB | 28 | 141 | 535 | 144 | 36 | 2 | 29 | 82 | 94 | 96 | 6.37 | 70 | 132 | 3 | 1 | .75 | .269 | .358 | .507 | .865 |
| Lough,David | KC | 28 | 78 | 218 | 60 | 10 | 3 | 4 | 28 | 23 | 27 | 4.36 | 11 | 30 | 6 | 3 | .67 | .275 | .313 | .404 | .717 |
| Lowrie,Jed | Oak | 30 | 139 | 526 | 143 | 39 | 2 | 15 | 70 | 70 | 78 | 5.28 | 54 | 89 | 1 | 1 | .50 | .272 | .342 | .439 | .781 |
| Lucas,Ed | Mia | 32 | 58 | 139 | 35 | 7 | 0 | 3 | 17 | 14 | 15 | 3.71 | 11 | 29 | 1 | 1 | .50 | .252 | .311 | .367 | .678 |
| Lucroy,Jonathan | Mil | 28 | 135 | 476 | 136 | 24 | 3 | 15 | 58 | 74 | 73 | 5.53 | 43 | 64 | 7 | 3 | .70 | .286 | .349 | .443 | .792 |
| Ludwick,Ryan | Cin | 35 | 115 | 401 | 100 | 22 | 1 | 16 | 47 | 64 | 54 | 4.65 | 37 | 101 | 1 | 1 | .50 | .249 | .319 | .429 | .748 |
| Lutz,Donald | Cin | 25 | 54 | 204 | 50 | 9 | 2 | 7 | 28 | 26 | 25 | 4.17 | 16 | 46 | 4 | 2 | .67 | .245 | .300 | .412 | .712 |
| Machado,Manny | Bal | 21 | 156 | 636 | 177 | 46 | 5 | 16 | 85 | 76 | 89 | 4.99 | 38 | 101 | 8 | 5 | .62 | .278 | .320 | .442 | .762 |
| Maldonado,Martin | Mil | 27 | 68 | 161 | 37 | 8 | 0 | 5 | 15 | 21 | 17 | 3.56 | 12 | 40 | 0 | 0 | .00 | .230 | .291 | .373 | .664 |
| Marisnick,Jake | Mia | 23 | 142 | 536 | 133 | 24 | 5 | 15 | 67 | 62 | 61 | 3.84 | 31 | 125 | 22 | 10 | .69 | .248 | .290 | .396 | .686 |
| Markakis,Nick | Bal | 30 | 160 | 632 | 183 | 38 | 1 | 15 | 86 | 78 | 95 | 5.48 | 64 | 82 | 3 | 2 | .60 | .290 | .359 | .424 | .783 |
| Marte,Starling | Pit | 25 | 149 | 556 | 163 | 31 | 11 | 15 | 90 | 55 | 84 | 5.31 | 29 | 131 | 41 | 18 | .69 | .293 | .343 | .469 | .812 |
| Martin,Leonys | Tex | 26 | 146 | 452 | 125 | 26 | 5 | 9 | 70 | 55 | 61 | 4.66 | 32 | 87 | 34 | 13 | .72 | .277 | .330 | .416 | .746 |
| Martin,Russell | Pit | 31 | 135 | 474 | 111 | 23 | 0 | 16 | 61 | 60 | 59 | 4.17 | 64 | 104 | 9 | 5 | .64 | .234 | .334 | .384 | .718 |
| Martinez,J.D. | Hou | 26 | 78 | 211 | 56 | 12 | 1 | 6 | 21 | 31 | 27 | 4.50 | 15 | 47 | 1 | 1 | .50 | .265 | .317 | .417 | .734 |
| Martinez,Victor | Det | 35 | 150 | 575 | 173 | 36 | 0 | 15 | 70 | 92 | 92 | 5.95 | 55 | 64 | 0 | 0 | .00 | .301 | .364 | .442 | .806 |
| Mathis,Jeff | Mia | 31 | 85 | 256 | 50 | 12 | 0 | 6 | 24 | 30 | 20 | 2.52 | 19 | 83 | 1 | 0 | 1.00 | .195 | .254 | .313 | .566 |
| Mauer,Joe | Min | 31 | 130 | 495 | 157 | 35 | 1 | 11 | 75 | 69 | 92 | 7.06 | 72 | 83 | 2 | 1 | .67 | .317 | .406 | .459 | .865 |
| Maxwell,Justin | KC | 30 | 112 | 392 | 96 | 20 | 2 | 17 | 62 | 52 | 56 | 4.82 | 46 | 125 | 15 | 6 | .71 | .245 | .327 | .436 | .763 |
| Mayberry,John | Phi | 30 | 117 | 297 | 75 | 18 | 1 | 11 | 39 | 38 | 39 | 4.53 | 23 | 67 | 5 | 2 | .71 | .253 | .311 | .431 | .742 |
| Maybin,Cameron | SD | 27 | 142 | 510 | 135 | 23 | 6 | 12 | 81 | 53 | 70 | 4.74 | 51 | 118 | 26 | 9 | .74 | .265 | .334 | .404 | .738 |
| McCann,Brian | Atl | 30 | 125 | 464 | 122 | 25 | 0 | 23 | 54 | 79 | 73 | 5.53 | 52 | 83 | 1 | 1 | .50 | .263 | .342 | .466 | .808 |
| McCutchen,Andrew | Pit | 27 | 159 | 599 | 178 | 36 | 5 | 22 | 99 | 81 | 110 | 6.62 | 80 | 114 | 25 | 11 | .69 | .297 | .385 | .484 | .870 |
| McKenry,Michael | Pit | 29 | 79 | 219 | 53 | 14 | 0 | 7 | 22 | 27 | 27 | 4.23 | 21 | 50 | 0 | 0 | .00 | .242 | .311 | .402 | .713 |
| McLouth,Nate | Bal | 32 | 125 | 453 | 111 | 24 | 2 | 13 | 67 | 44 | 59 | 4.41 | 52 | 83 | 19 | 6 | .76 | .245 | .329 | .393 | .722 |
| Mercer,Jordy | Pit | 27 | 104 | 351 | 96 | 23 | 1 | 8 | 43 | 41 | 47 | 4.74 | 27 | 61 | 5 | 3 | .62 | .274 | .329 | .413 | .742 |
| Mesoraco,Devin | Cin | 26 | 115 | 390 | 98 | 23 | 1 | 14 | 46 | 55 | 52 | 4.63 | 35 | 69 | 0 | 0 | .00 | .251 | .313 | .423 | .736 |
| Middlebrooks,Will | Bos | 25 | 145 | 557 | 148 | 27 | 1 | 32 | 74 | 104 | 84 | 5.31 | 34 | 134 | 6 | 2 | .75 | .266 | .310 | .490 | .800 |
| Miller,Brad | Sea | 24 | 141 | 523 | 153 | 22 | 6 | 17 | 81 | 73 | 86 | 5.95 | 56 | 89 | 11 | 6 | .65 | .293 | .362 | .455 | .817 |
| Molina,Jose | TB | 39 | 95 | 249 | 56 | 12 | 0 | 4 | 23 | 20 | 22 | 2.95 | 18 | 59 | 1 | 1 | .50 | .225 | .283 | .321 | .604 |
| Molina,Yadier | StL | 31 | 140 | 519 | 153 | 32 | 0 | 13 | 57 | 73 | 77 | 5.43 | 40 | 55 | 5 | 3 | .62 | .295 | .350 | .432 | .782 |
| Montero,Jesus | Sea | 24 | 131 | 479 | 130 | 26 | 2 | 18 | 55 | 70 | 70 | 5.21 | 38 | 99 | 0 | 0 | .00 | .271 | .326 | .447 | .773 |
| Montero,Miguel | Ari | 30 | 130 | 452 | 118 | 26 | 1 | 14 | 54 | 65 | 64 | 4.98 | 54 | 113 | 0 | 0 | .00 | .261 | .348 | .416 | .764 |
| Moore,Tyler | Was | 27 | 57 | 161 | 44 | 11 | 1 | 9 | 21 | 31 | 28 | 6.22 | 13 | 42 | 1 | 0 | 1.00 | .273 | .331 | .522 | .853 |
| Morales,Kendrys | Sea | 31 | 148 | 572 | 161 | 34 | 1 | 24 | 69 | 86 | 89 | 5.63 | 42 | 114 | 0 | 0 | .00 | .281 | .335 | .470 | .805 |

# 2014 Hitter Projections

| PLAYER | | | BATTING | | | | | | | | | | | | BASERUNNING | | | AVERAGES | | | |
|---|---|---|---|---|---|---|---|---|---|---|---|---|---|---|---|---|---|---|---|---|---|
| Hitter | Team | Age | G | AB | H | 2B | 3B | HR | R | RBI | RC | RC27 | BB | SO | SB | CS | SB% | Avg | OBP | Slg | OPS |
| Moreland,Mitch | Tex | 28 | 152 | 490 | 128 | 29 | 1 | 22 | 67 | 71 | 73 | 5.23 | 47 | 103 | 1 | 1 | .50 | .261 | .328 | .459 | .788 |
| Morneau,Justin | Pit | 33 | 138 | 525 | 141 | 33 | 1 | 19 | 65 | 85 | 79 | 5.35 | 55 | 101 | 0 | 0 | .00 | .269 | .344 | .444 | .787 |
| Morrison,Logan | Mia | 26 | 120 | 446 | 112 | 26 | 5 | 15 | 56 | 63 | 66 | 5.12 | 61 | 78 | 1 | 1 | .50 | .251 | .345 | .433 | .778 |
| Morse,Michael | Bal | 32 | 146 | 508 | 134 | 28 | 1 | 23 | 62 | 72 | 72 | 5.01 | 33 | 132 | 1 | 0 | 1.00 | .264 | .314 | .459 | .772 |
| Moss,Brandon | Oak | 30 | 146 | 452 | 119 | 28 | 2 | 25 | 67 | 78 | 75 | 5.80 | 47 | 123 | 4 | 3 | .57 | .263 | .337 | .500 | .837 |
| Moustakas,Mike | KC | 25 | 147 | 552 | 142 | 36 | 1 | 20 | 65 | 73 | 73 | 4.61 | 39 | 94 | 3 | 2 | .60 | .257 | .311 | .435 | .746 |
| Murphy,Daniel | NYM | 29 | 155 | 597 | 173 | 41 | 3 | 11 | 76 | 75 | 85 | 5.15 | 37 | 84 | 16 | 5 | .76 | .290 | .332 | .424 | .756 |
| Murphy,David | Tex | 32 | 144 | 442 | 118 | 26 | 1 | 14 | 56 | 56 | 62 | 4.93 | 43 | 70 | 5 | 3 | .62 | .267 | .333 | .425 | .759 |
| Murphy,Donnie | ChC | 31 | 45 | 127 | 31 | 8 | 0 | 6 | 16 | 18 | 17 | 4.56 | 9 | 33 | 2 | 1 | .67 | .244 | .309 | .449 | .758 |
| Myers,Wil | TB | 23 | 154 | 585 | 166 | 35 | 2 | 27 | 90 | 102 | 101 | 6.21 | 62 | 153 | 12 | 4 | .75 | .284 | .353 | .489 | .842 |
| Napoli,Mike | Bos | 32 | 137 | 480 | 118 | 28 | 1 | 26 | 72 | 79 | 77 | 5.52 | 69 | 170 | 2 | 1 | .67 | .246 | .348 | .471 | .819 |
| Nava,Daniel | Bos | 31 | 121 | 418 | 119 | 28 | 1 | 11 | 66 | 59 | 66 | 5.72 | 53 | 79 | 2 | 1 | .67 | .285 | .377 | .435 | .812 |
| Navarro,Dioner | ChC | 30 | 90 | 269 | 70 | 12 | 0 | 8 | 29 | 33 | 34 | 4.44 | 25 | 41 | 1 | 0 | 1.00 | .260 | .328 | .394 | .722 |
| Nelson,Chris | LAA | 28 | 92 | 261 | 70 | 13 | 2 | 6 | 31 | 34 | 33 | 4.45 | 16 | 58 | 4 | 2 | .67 | .268 | .313 | .402 | .715 |
| Nieves,Wil | Ari | 36 | 67 | 175 | 44 | 7 | 0 | 2 | 13 | 17 | 16 | 3.18 | 9 | 28 | 0 | 0 | .00 | .251 | .288 | .326 | .614 |
| Nix,Jayson | NYY | 31 | 74 | 204 | 47 | 10 | 0 | 5 | 25 | 21 | 21 | 3.41 | 17 | 52 | 7 | 3 | .70 | .230 | .299 | .353 | .652 |
| Norris,Derek | Oak | 25 | 98 | 326 | 78 | 18 | 1 | 14 | 54 | 47 | 47 | 4.89 | 46 | 83 | 7 | 2 | .78 | .239 | .337 | .429 | .766 |
| Nunez,Eduardo | NYY | 27 | 102 | 307 | 83 | 16 | 2 | 4 | 39 | 31 | 37 | 4.20 | 19 | 44 | 14 | 5 | .74 | .270 | .315 | .375 | .690 |
| Olt,Mike | ChC | 25 | 135 | 485 | 109 | 25 | 1 | 24 | 65 | 70 | 66 | 4.55 | 66 | 158 | 2 | 1 | .67 | .225 | .318 | .429 | .746 |
| Ortiz,David | Bos | 38 | 146 | 520 | 149 | 35 | 1 | 30 | 84 | 98 | 106 | 7.41 | 81 | 99 | 2 | 1 | .67 | .287 | .384 | .531 | .914 |
| Overbay,Lyle | NYY | 37 | 93 | 222 | 53 | 14 | 0 | 6 | 24 | 27 | 27 | 4.15 | 24 | 56 | 1 | 0 | 1.00 | .239 | .316 | .383 | .699 |
| Owings,Chris | Ari | 22 | 140 | 481 | 136 | 24 | 3 | 8 | 62 | 50 | 59 | 4.36 | 18 | 94 | 18 | 7 | .72 | .283 | .309 | .395 | .704 |
| Ozuna,Marcell | Mia | 23 | 115 | 452 | 127 | 30 | 7 | 11 | 56 | 70 | 65 | 5.15 | 24 | 86 | 9 | 3 | .75 | .281 | .320 | .451 | .771 |
| Pacheco,Jordan | Col | 28 | 125 | 473 | 132 | 29 | 2 | 5 | 48 | 52 | 57 | 4.32 | 24 | 57 | 5 | 2 | .71 | .279 | .317 | .381 | .697 |
| Pagan,Angel | SF | 32 | 150 | 577 | 161 | 32 | 6 | 9 | 84 | 60 | 78 | 4.77 | 48 | 87 | 22 | 9 | .71 | .279 | .334 | .402 | .736 |
| Paredes,Jimmy | Hou | 25 | 55 | 168 | 44 | 9 | 1 | 3 | 21 | 15 | 19 | 3.86 | 9 | 39 | 9 | 4 | .69 | .262 | .303 | .381 | .684 |
| Parker,Kyle | Col | 24 | 143 | 500 | 139 | 25 | 2 | 24 | 70 | 75 | 78 | 5.54 | 39 | 102 | 6 | 5 | .55 | .278 | .330 | .480 | .810 |
| Parmelee,Chris | Min | 26 | 87 | 233 | 60 | 14 | 1 | 7 | 27 | 29 | 33 | 4.93 | 28 | 50 | 1 | 1 | .50 | .258 | .342 | .416 | .759 |
| Parra,Gerardo | Ari | 27 | 159 | 605 | 169 | 37 | 6 | 11 | 81 | 60 | 83 | 4.86 | 51 | 105 | 13 | 8 | .62 | .279 | .338 | .415 | .753 |
| Paul,Xavier | Cin | 29 | 100 | 216 | 60 | 13 | 1 | 6 | 28 | 28 | 32 | 5.27 | 20 | 47 | 5 | 2 | .71 | .278 | .342 | .431 | .772 |
| Pearce,Steve | Bal | 31 | 75 | 184 | 49 | 13 | 0 | 6 | 23 | 27 | 27 | 5.16 | 21 | 36 | 2 | 1 | .67 | .266 | .348 | .435 | .783 |
| Pedroia,Dustin | Bos | 30 | 157 | 625 | 186 | 45 | 2 | 14 | 95 | 77 | 103 | 6.02 | 69 | 70 | 16 | 6 | .73 | .298 | .371 | .443 | .814 |
| Peguero,Francisco | SF | 26 | 120 | 461 | 125 | 19 | 5 | 6 | 48 | 48 | 51 | 3.92 | 14 | 83 | 7 | 2 | .78 | .271 | .293 | .373 | .666 |
| Pena,Brayan | Det | 32 | 87 | 260 | 70 | 14 | 0 | 4 | 23 | 29 | 29 | 3.95 | 13 | 27 | 1 | 1 | .50 | .269 | .307 | .369 | .676 |
| Pena,Carlos | KC | 36 | 99 | 261 | 55 | 12 | 1 | 12 | 36 | 39 | 34 | 4.27 | 46 | 91 | 1 | 1 | .50 | .211 | .344 | .402 | .746 |
| Pence,Hunter | SF | 31 | 157 | 597 | 168 | 33 | 3 | 24 | 84 | 91 | 94 | 5.62 | 51 | 119 | 15 | 6 | .71 | .281 | .341 | .467 | .808 |
| Pennington,Cliff | Ari | 30 | 105 | 352 | 85 | 18 | 2 | 4 | 40 | 29 | 37 | 3.55 | 35 | 71 | 9 | 4 | .69 | .241 | .312 | .338 | .650 |
| Peralta,Jhonny | Det | 32 | 142 | 527 | 139 | 32 | 1 | 14 | 64 | 71 | 70 | 4.67 | 48 | 117 | 2 | 2 | .50 | .264 | .328 | .408 | .736 |
| Perez,Salvador | KC | 24 | 138 | 523 | 156 | 29 | 2 | 15 | 61 | 81 | 77 | 5.46 | 23 | 57 | 0 | 0 | .00 | .298 | .332 | .447 | .779 |
| Phegley,Josh | CWS | 26 | 105 | 351 | 89 | 20 | 1 | 11 | 38 | 46 | 41 | 4.05 | 17 | 60 | 2 | 1 | .67 | .254 | .288 | .410 | .698 |
| Phillips,Brandon | Cin | 33 | 154 | 617 | 167 | 30 | 2 | 19 | 86 | 87 | 81 | 4.63 | 40 | 96 | 9 | 5 | .64 | .271 | .323 | .418 | .741 |
| Pierre,Juan | Mia | 36 | 97 | 263 | 71 | 8 | 1 | 1 | 33 | 15 | 27 | 3.53 | 15 | 20 | 18 | 7 | .72 | .270 | .324 | .319 | .643 |
| Pierzynski,A.J. | Tex | 37 | 128 | 474 | 126 | 23 | 1 | 14 | 48 | 56 | 56 | 4.17 | 18 | 68 | 1 | 1 | .50 | .266 | .303 | .407 | .710 |
| Pinto,Josmil | Min | 25 | 121 | 384 | 107 | 27 | 1 | 13 | 50 | 57 | 60 | 5.63 | 38 | 75 | 0 | 0 | .00 | .279 | .345 | .456 | .801 |
| Plouffe,Trevor | Min | 28 | 125 | 422 | 104 | 23 | 2 | 15 | 52 | 50 | 53 | 4.31 | 33 | 87 | 2 | 2 | .50 | .246 | .306 | .417 | .723 |
| Polanco,Placido | Mia | 38 | 93 | 264 | 72 | 11 | 0 | 2 | 29 | 23 | 28 | 3.77 | 17 | 23 | 1 | 1 | .50 | .273 | .331 | .337 | .668 |
| Pollock,A.J. | Ari | 26 | 150 | 562 | 154 | 37 | 4 | 9 | 80 | 56 | 74 | 4.64 | 41 | 87 | 20 | 7 | .74 | .274 | .325 | .402 | .727 |
| Posey,Buster | SF | 27 | 136 | 503 | 159 | 33 | 1 | 19 | 68 | 83 | 98 | 7.39 | 60 | 69 | 2 | 1 | .67 | .316 | .394 | .499 | .893 |
| Prado,Martin | Ari | 30 | 158 | 602 | 176 | 39 | 2 | 13 | 79 | 71 | 88 | 5.32 | 48 | 62 | 5 | 4 | .56 | .292 | .347 | .429 | .775 |
| Presley,Alex | Min | 28 | 66 | 229 | 65 | 10 | 3 | 5 | 31 | 22 | 32 | 4.95 | 19 | 39 | 8 | 4 | .67 | .284 | .341 | .419 | .761 |
| Profar,Jurickson | Tex | 21 | 153 | 551 | 140 | 27 | 3 | 14 | 73 | 60 | 71 | 4.43 | 61 | 99 | 13 | 6 | .68 | .254 | .332 | .390 | .722 |
| Puig,Yasiel | LAD | 23 | 150 | 553 | 181 | 37 | 4 | 32 | 103 | 87 | 123 | 8.28 | 56 | 122 | 26 | 14 | .65 | .327 | .401 | .582 | .983 |
| Pujols,Albert | LAA | 34 | 152 | 572 | 166 | 37 | 0 | 33 | 91 | 105 | 113 | 7.20 | 76 | 74 | 5 | 2 | .71 | .290 | .378 | .528 | .906 |
| Punto,Nick | LAD | 36 | 115 | 294 | 68 | 13 | 1 | 1 | 35 | 22 | 28 | 3.19 | 37 | 66 | 5 | 2 | .71 | .231 | .317 | .293 | .610 |
| Quentin,Carlos | SD | 31 | 118 | 428 | 112 | 29 | 1 | 23 | 67 | 76 | 70 | 5.74 | 46 | 80 | 1 | 1 | .50 | .262 | .354 | .495 | .849 |
| Quintero,Humberto | Sea | 34 | 45 | 134 | 32 | 7 | 0 | 2 | 11 | 13 | 12 | 3.06 | 5 | 26 | 0 | 0 | .00 | .239 | .277 | .336 | .612 |
| Raburn,Ryan | Cle | 33 | 92 | 251 | 62 | 16 | 1 | 11 | 35 | 39 | 35 | 4.79 | 23 | 70 | 1 | 1 | .50 | .247 | .318 | .450 | .768 |
| Ramirez,Alexei | CWS | 32 | 159 | 615 | 169 | 30 | 2 | 11 | 70 | 67 | 73 | 4.17 | 32 | 75 | 20 | 9 | .69 | .275 | .314 | .384 | .698 |
| Ramirez,Aramis | Mil | 36 | 137 | 516 | 145 | 33 | 1 | 23 | 72 | 90 | 85 | 5.94 | 47 | 84 | 2 | 1 | .67 | .281 | .350 | .483 | .833 |
| Ramirez,Hanley | LAD | 30 | 151 | 588 | 174 | 38 | 2 | 27 | 102 | 86 | 108 | 6.62 | 62 | 113 | 23 | 10 | .70 | .296 | .368 | .505 | .873 |
| Ramos,Wilson | Was | 26 | 118 | 410 | 112 | 21 | 0 | 18 | 48 | 65 | 60 | 5.23 | 28 | 61 | 0 | 0 | .00 | .273 | .320 | .456 | .776 |
| Ransom,Cody | ChC | 38 | 70 | 173 | 39 | 10 | 0 | 8 | 23 | 25 | 22 | 4.24 | 19 | 54 | 1 | 1 | .50 | .225 | .306 | .422 | .728 |
| Rasmus,Colby | Tor | 27 | 134 | 464 | 113 | 26 | 2 | 20 | 69 | 61 | 63 | 4.64 | 47 | 133 | 3 | 2 | .60 | .244 | .317 | .438 | .755 |
| Recker,Anthony | NYM | 30 | 72 | 217 | 51 | 11 | 1 | 8 | 26 | 27 | 27 | 4.20 | 22 | 63 | 1 | 1 | .50 | .235 | .305 | .406 | .711 |
| Reddick,Josh | Oak | 27 | 144 | 576 | 139 | 32 | 4 | 25 | 85 | 82 | 79 | 4.65 | 59 | 118 | 11 | 5 | .69 | .241 | .313 | .441 | .754 |
| Reimold,Nolan | Bal | 30 | 71 | 226 | 56 | 11 | 1 | 9 | 29 | 30 | 31 | 4.71 | 24 | 54 | 3 | 1 | .75 | .248 | .323 | .425 | .747 |
| Rendon,Anthony | Was | 24 | 148 | 522 | 140 | 38 | 4 | 16 | 70 | 63 | 83 | 5.63 | 70 | 99 | 2 | 1 | .67 | .268 | .358 | .448 | .806 |
| Revere,Ben | Phi | 26 | 133 | 548 | 161 | 14 | 5 | 0 | 68 | 34 | 64 | 4.15 | 32 | 52 | 40 | 14 | .74 | .294 | .334 | .338 | .671 |
| Reyes,Jose | Tor | 31 | 137 | 559 | 166 | 31 | 7 | 11 | 88 | 52 | 88 | 5.68 | 50 | 59 | 28 | 10 | .74 | .297 | .356 | .436 | .792 |
| Reynolds,Mark | NYY | 30 | 115 | 339 | 78 | 16 | 1 | 19 | 50 | 55 | 49 | 4.84 | 46 | 123 | 3 | 2 | .60 | .230 | .332 | .451 | .784 |

# 2014 Hitter Projections

| PLAYER | | | BATTING | | | | | | | | | | | | BASERUNNING | | | AVERAGES | | | |
|---|---|---|---|---|---|---|---|---|---|---|---|---|---|---|---|---|---|---|---|---|---|
| Hitter | Team | Age | G | AB | H | 2B | 3B | HR | R | RBI | RC | RC27 | BB | SO | SB | CS | SB% | Avg | OBP | Slg | OPS |
| Rios,Alex | Tex | 33 | 147 | 534 | 145 | 30 | 3 | 17 | 73 | 69 | 74 | 4.85 | 34 | 91 | 25 | 8 | .76 | .272 | .319 | .434 | .753 |
| Rizzo,Anthony | ChC | 24 | 160 | 612 | 163 | 42 | 2 | 30 | 83 | 101 | 101 | 5.80 | 68 | 123 | 7 | 4 | .64 | .266 | .344 | .489 | .832 |
| Roberts,Brian | Bal | 36 | 120 | 418 | 107 | 27 | 1 | 9 | 57 | 43 | 54 | 4.46 | 46 | 73 | 10 | 4 | .71 | .256 | .330 | .390 | .720 |
| Roberts,Ryan | TB | 33 | 104 | 298 | 69 | 15 | 1 | 8 | 36 | 33 | 34 | 3.81 | 33 | 70 | 5 | 3 | .62 | .232 | .310 | .369 | .679 |
| Robinson,Derrick | Cin | 26 | 113 | 323 | 78 | 11 | 2 | 1 | 38 | 18 | 30 | 3.08 | 29 | 69 | 19 | 8 | .70 | .241 | .304 | .297 | .601 |
| Robinson,Shane | StL | 29 | 86 | 144 | 37 | 6 | 1 | 2 | 20 | 15 | 17 | 4.06 | 15 | 19 | 4 | 2 | .67 | .257 | .327 | .354 | .681 |
| Rodriguez,Alex | NYY | 38 | 112 | 429 | 112 | 19 | 0 | 22 | 69 | 75 | 69 | 5.61 | 58 | 109 | 8 | 3 | .73 | .261 | .357 | .459 | .816 |
| Rodriguez,Sean | TB | 29 | 88 | 189 | 44 | 10 | 1 | 6 | 25 | 23 | 22 | 3.89 | 18 | 52 | 3 | 2 | .60 | .233 | .319 | .392 | .711 |
| Rollins,Jimmy | Phi | 35 | 158 | 622 | 155 | 34 | 3 | 14 | 83 | 59 | 75 | 4.11 | 58 | 91 | 22 | 7 | .76 | .249 | .315 | .381 | .696 |
| Romine,Andrew | LAA | 28 | 81 | 290 | 72 | 9 | 2 | 2 | 35 | 23 | 28 | 3.26 | 24 | 54 | 12 | 5 | .71 | .248 | .306 | .314 | .620 |
| Romine,Austin | NYY | 25 | 54 | 120 | 29 | 6 | 0 | 2 | 14 | 14 | 12 | 3.43 | 9 | 26 | 1 | 0 | 1.00 | .242 | .295 | .342 | .636 |
| Rosario,Wilin | Col | 25 | 117 | 421 | 118 | 20 | 1 | 25 | 63 | 72 | 67 | 5.71 | 20 | 95 | 3 | 2 | .60 | .280 | .314 | .511 | .825 |
| Ross,Cody | Ari | 33 | 124 | 419 | 110 | 26 | 1 | 15 | 53 | 60 | 58 | 4.85 | 36 | 92 | 3 | 2 | .60 | .263 | .327 | .437 | .764 |
| Ross,David | Bos | 37 | 76 | 222 | 49 | 12 | 0 | 8 | 22 | 28 | 26 | 3.89 | 27 | 82 | 1 | 1 | .50 | .221 | .308 | .383 | .691 |
| Ruf,Darin | Phi | 27 | 66 | 240 | 65 | 15 | 0 | 12 | 35 | 37 | 40 | 5.94 | 28 | 67 | 1 | 0 | 1.00 | .271 | .359 | .483 | .842 |
| Ruggiano,Justin | Mia | 32 | 117 | 361 | 98 | 22 | 1 | 14 | 50 | 52 | 55 | 5.30 | 35 | 92 | 15 | 7 | .68 | .271 | .339 | .454 | .793 |
| Ruiz,Carlos | Phi | 35 | 122 | 421 | 116 | 27 | 0 | 9 | 48 | 56 | 58 | 4.93 | 41 | 56 | 2 | 1 | .67 | .276 | .351 | .404 | .755 |
| Rutledge,Josh | Col | 25 | 148 | 530 | 151 | 34 | 4 | 17 | 82 | 55 | 80 | 5.42 | 31 | 97 | 16 | 5 | .76 | .285 | .328 | .460 | .788 |
| Ryan,Brendan | NYY | 32 | 102 | 274 | 60 | 12 | 1 | 2 | 31 | 20 | 22 | 2.64 | 22 | 59 | 5 | 3 | .62 | .219 | .287 | .292 | .579 |
| Saltalamacchia,Jarrod | Bos | 29 | 129 | 464 | 112 | 32 | 1 | 19 | 65 | 66 | 63 | 4.64 | 47 | 151 | 3 | 1 | .75 | .241 | .313 | .438 | .750 |
| Sanchez,Gaby | Pit | 30 | 67 | 199 | 51 | 13 | 0 | 6 | 24 | 27 | 28 | 4.89 | 26 | 37 | 1 | 1 | .50 | .256 | .351 | .412 | .763 |
| Sanchez,Hector | SF | 24 | 80 | 213 | 55 | 11 | 0 | 4 | 18 | 30 | 23 | 3.78 | 13 | 41 | 0 | 0 | .00 | .258 | .307 | .366 | .673 |
| Sanchez,Tony | Pit | 26 | 62 | 203 | 51 | 14 | 0 | 6 | 25 | 25 | 27 | 4.62 | 20 | 44 | 1 | 0 | 1.00 | .251 | .321 | .409 | .730 |
| Sandoval,Pablo | SF | 27 | 140 | 528 | 154 | 34 | 2 | 18 | 65 | 81 | 86 | 5.96 | 48 | 78 | 1 | 1 | .50 | .292 | .354 | .466 | .820 |
| Santana,Carlos | Cle | 28 | 148 | 541 | 144 | 38 | 1 | 23 | 83 | 87 | 97 | 6.32 | 102 | 103 | 4 | 2 | .67 | .266 | .384 | .468 | .852 |
| Santiago,Ramon | Det | 34 | 80 | 173 | 41 | 6 | 1 | 2 | 19 | 15 | 16 | 3.15 | 14 | 30 | 0 | 0 | .00 | .237 | .305 | .318 | .623 |
| Satin,Josh | NYM | 29 | 76 | 202 | 57 | 14 | 0 | 5 | 28 | 23 | 32 | 5.70 | 28 | 50 | 1 | 1 | .50 | .282 | .370 | .426 | .795 |
| Saunders,Michael | Sea | 27 | 126 | 398 | 96 | 21 | 2 | 12 | 56 | 42 | 51 | 4.32 | 46 | 103 | 13 | 5 | .72 | .241 | .321 | .394 | .716 |
| Schafer,Jordan | Atl | 27 | 105 | 327 | 76 | 13 | 2 | 4 | 42 | 27 | 34 | 3.40 | 37 | 85 | 24 | 9 | .73 | .232 | .312 | .321 | .633 |
| Schafer,Logan | Mil | 27 | 67 | 112 | 28 | 6 | 1 | 2 | 15 | 11 | 13 | 3.98 | 9 | 18 | 3 | 1 | .75 | .250 | .311 | .375 | .686 |
| Schierholtz,Nate | ChC | 30 | 135 | 470 | 122 | 30 | 4 | 16 | 56 | 58 | 63 | 4.65 | 30 | 92 | 6 | 4 | .60 | .260 | .308 | .443 | .751 |
| Schoop,Jonathan | Bal | 22 | 145 | 553 | 131 | 24 | 1 | 15 | 65 | 58 | 57 | 3.50 | 37 | 112 | 3 | 2 | .60 | .237 | .285 | .365 | .650 |
| Schumaker,Skip | LAD | 34 | 129 | 375 | 101 | 19 | 1 | 3 | 44 | 32 | 43 | 4.05 | 33 | 61 | 2 | 2 | .50 | .269 | .332 | .349 | .681 |
| Scott,Luke | TB | 36 | 83 | 209 | 51 | 12 | 1 | 9 | 25 | 31 | 29 | 4.74 | 24 | 53 | 1 | 1 | .50 | .244 | .331 | .440 | .771 |
| Scutaro,Marco | SF | 38 | 145 | 558 | 159 | 28 | 1 | 6 | 75 | 54 | 72 | 4.67 | 52 | 50 | 4 | 2 | .67 | .285 | .348 | .371 | .719 |
| Seager,Kyle | Sea | 26 | 156 | 598 | 162 | 38 | 2 | 21 | 76 | 77 | 90 | 5.32 | 60 | 104 | 10 | 4 | .71 | .271 | .343 | .446 | .790 |
| Segura,Jean | Mil | 24 | 155 | 606 | 180 | 22 | 9 | 11 | 82 | 58 | 87 | 5.13 | 33 | 81 | 48 | 15 | .76 | .297 | .336 | .417 | .754 |
| Semien,Marcus | CWS | 23 | 134 | 514 | 139 | 32 | 4 | 18 | 92 | 59 | 88 | 5.99 | 80 | 97 | 24 | 7 | .77 | .270 | .369 | .453 | .822 |
| Shoppach,Kelly | Cle | 34 | 71 | 177 | 37 | 9 | 0 | 6 | 19 | 20 | 18 | 3.34 | 17 | 70 | 0 | 0 | .00 | .209 | .300 | .362 | .662 |
| Shuck,J.B. | LAA | 27 | 133 | 451 | 127 | 17 | 3 | 1 | 59 | 36 | 52 | 4.08 | 42 | 46 | 12 | 7 | .63 | .282 | .343 | .339 | .682 |
| Sierra,Moises | Tor | 25 | 55 | 145 | 37 | 7 | 1 | 4 | 19 | 18 | 17 | 4.02 | 10 | 37 | 4 | 2 | .67 | .255 | .308 | .400 | .708 |
| Simmons,Andrelton | Atl | 24 | 160 | 614 | 162 | 29 | 6 | 18 | 82 | 67 | 80 | 4.55 | 46 | 54 | 8 | 5 | .62 | .264 | .317 | .419 | .736 |
| Singleton,Jonathan | Hou | 22 | 138 | 482 | 115 | 25 | 2 | 16 | 68 | 64 | 63 | 4.44 | 66 | 161 | 4 | 2 | .67 | .239 | .330 | .398 | .729 |
| Sizemore,Scott | Oak | 29 | 72 | 246 | 67 | 17 | 1 | 7 | 37 | 31 | 38 | 5.46 | 31 | 60 | 5 | 2 | .71 | .272 | .354 | .435 | .789 |
| Smith,Seth | Oak | 31 | 111 | 312 | 79 | 20 | 2 | 9 | 42 | 39 | 42 | 4.67 | 34 | 74 | 2 | 1 | .67 | .253 | .332 | .417 | .749 |
| Smoak,Justin | Sea | 27 | 150 | 520 | 123 | 25 | 0 | 20 | 59 | 63 | 69 | 4.52 | 72 | 119 | 0 | 0 | .00 | .237 | .332 | .400 | .732 |
| Snider,Travis | Pit | 26 | 85 | 206 | 55 | 13 | 1 | 7 | 29 | 30 | 30 | 5.10 | 20 | 51 | 3 | 2 | .60 | .267 | .335 | .442 | .777 |
| Snyder,Chris | Bal | 33 | 75 | 216 | 46 | 9 | 0 | 8 | 22 | 30 | 24 | 3.67 | 28 | 64 | 0 | 0 | .00 | .213 | .309 | .366 | .675 |
| Sogard,Eric | Oak | 28 | 103 | 296 | 77 | 16 | 2 | 3 | 37 | 28 | 34 | 3.96 | 27 | 37 | 9 | 4 | .69 | .260 | .326 | .358 | .684 |
| Solano,Donovan | Mia | 26 | 102 | 321 | 83 | 15 | 1 | 3 | 31 | 29 | 33 | 3.59 | 20 | 50 | 3 | 1 | .75 | .259 | .308 | .340 | .648 |
| Soriano,Alfonso | NYY | 38 | 147 | 521 | 127 | 30 | 1 | 27 | 66 | 79 | 70 | 4.56 | 37 | 143 | 10 | 5 | .67 | .244 | .300 | .461 | .761 |
| Soto,Geovany | Tex | 31 | 97 | 308 | 72 | 19 | 0 | 13 | 37 | 44 | 41 | 4.50 | 38 | 90 | 1 | 1 | .50 | .234 | .322 | .422 | .744 |
| Span,Denard | Was | 30 | 154 | 614 | 172 | 29 | 7 | 5 | 83 | 54 | 78 | 4.50 | 54 | 81 | 20 | 9 | .69 | .280 | .340 | .375 | .715 |
| Springer,George | Hou | 24 | 144 | 520 | 139 | 27 | 2 | 26 | 79 | 62 | 92 | 6.16 | 72 | 171 | 34 | 7 | .83 | .267 | .356 | .477 | .833 |
| Stanton,Giancarlo | Mia | 24 | 139 | 513 | 142 | 33 | 2 | 38 | 86 | 97 | 108 | 7.53 | 75 | 152 | 3 | 2 | .60 | .277 | .374 | .571 | .946 |
| Stewart,Chris | NYY | 32 | 77 | 170 | 38 | 7 | 0 | 2 | 18 | 15 | 15 | 2.93 | 16 | 24 | 2 | 1 | .67 | .224 | .298 | .300 | .598 |
| Stubbs,Drew | Cle | 29 | 140 | 451 | 106 | 19 | 2 | 12 | 66 | 43 | 52 | 3.85 | 46 | 149 | 21 | 6 | .78 | .235 | .310 | .366 | .676 |
| Suzuki,Ichiro | NYY | 40 | 140 | 475 | 131 | 16 | 2 | 5 | 53 | 31 | 53 | 3.95 | 25 | 55 | 18 | 5 | .78 | .276 | .315 | .349 | .664 |
| Suzuki,Kurt | Oak | 30 | 105 | 322 | 79 | 17 | 0 | 7 | 34 | 38 | 35 | 3.73 | 23 | 45 | 2 | 1 | .67 | .245 | .308 | .363 | .671 |
| Sweeney,Ryan | ChC | 29 | 100 | 287 | 79 | 17 | 2 | 6 | 35 | 32 | 40 | 4.98 | 26 | 50 | 2 | 1 | .67 | .275 | .338 | .411 | .749 |
| Swisher,Nick | Cle | 33 | 144 | 501 | 125 | 28 | 1 | 22 | 72 | 73 | 77 | 5.31 | 78 | 132 | 1 | 1 | .50 | .250 | .356 | .441 | .797 |
| Tabata,Jose | Pit | 25 | 110 | 337 | 94 | 20 | 2 | 4 | 47 | 29 | 44 | 4.61 | 29 | 49 | 9 | 5 | .64 | .279 | .343 | .386 | .729 |
| Taveras,Oscar | StL | 22 | 145 | 520 | 145 | 30 | 4 | 19 | 77 | 92 | 76 | 5.20 | 28 | 61 | 14 | 5 | .74 | .279 | .316 | .462 | .777 |
| Teixeira,Mark | NYY | 34 | 133 | 504 | 128 | 30 | 1 | 29 | 77 | 94 | 85 | 5.86 | 71 | 106 | 1 | 1 | .50 | .254 | .353 | .490 | .843 |
| Tejada,Ruben | NYM | 24 | 50 | 198 | 52 | 10 | 0 | 1 | 22 | 15 | 20 | 3.54 | 14 | 26 | 2 | 1 | .67 | .263 | .324 | .328 | .652 |
| Terdoslavich,Joey | Atl | 25 | 150 | 552 | 151 | 36 | 3 | 18 | 74 | 79 | 81 | 5.20 | 48 | 121 | 6 | 4 | .60 | .274 | .332 | .447 | .779 |
| Thole,Josh | Tor | 27 | 90 | 261 | 67 | 14 | 1 | 4 | 22 | 27 | 31 | 4.15 | 26 | 39 | 0 | 0 | .00 | .257 | .326 | .364 | .690 |
| Torrealba,Yorvit | Col | 35 | 65 | 190 | 48 | 10 | 0 | 3 | 17 | 20 | 20 | 3.64 | 14 | 33 | 1 | 1 | .50 | .253 | .311 | .353 | .663 |
| Torres,Andres | SF | 36 | 111 | 351 | 84 | 20 | 4 | 5 | 47 | 30 | 40 | 3.84 | 37 | 91 | 10 | 4 | .71 | .239 | .314 | .362 | .675 |
| Trout,Mike | LAA | 22 | 159 | 598 | 198 | 36 | 11 | 30 | 134 | 96 | 151 | 9.62 | 96 | 128 | 39 | 8 | .83 | .331 | .429 | .579 | 1.008 |

# 2014 Hitter Projections

| PLAYER | | | BATTING | | | | | | | | | | | | BASERUNNING | | | AVERAGES | | | |
|---|---|---|---|---|---|---|---|---|---|---|---|---|---|---|---|---|---|---|---|---|---|
| Hitter | Team | Age | G | AB | H | 2B | 3B | HR | R | RBI | RC | RC27 | BB | SO | SB | CS | SB% | Avg | OBP | Slg | OPS |
| Trumbo,Mark | LAA | 28 | 155 | 603 | 155 | 32 | 2 | 34 | 79 | 105 | 90 | 5.19 | 46 | 153 | 5 | 3 | .62 | .257 | .312 | .486 | .798 |
| Tuiasosopo,Matt | Det | 28 | 56 | 102 | 23 | 5 | 0 | 3 | 13 | 13 | 12 | 3.95 | 13 | 30 | 1 | 0 | 1.00 | .225 | .319 | .363 | .682 |
| Tulowitzki,Troy | Col | 29 | 126 | 477 | 142 | 29 | 2 | 24 | 78 | 83 | 92 | 7.10 | 56 | 84 | 4 | 2 | .67 | .298 | .376 | .518 | .894 |
| Turner,Justin | NYM | 29 | 82 | 185 | 51 | 13 | 0 | 2 | 20 | 19 | 22 | 4.24 | 13 | 25 | 1 | 1 | .50 | .276 | .333 | .378 | .712 |
| Uggla,Dan | Atl | 34 | 143 | 479 | 102 | 22 | 1 | 23 | 71 | 66 | 62 | 4.26 | 72 | 163 | 2 | 1 | .67 | .213 | .326 | .407 | .733 |
| Upton,B.J. | Atl | 29 | 146 | 530 | 121 | 29 | 2 | 17 | 69 | 60 | 64 | 3.98 | 61 | 174 | 24 | 9 | .73 | .228 | .311 | .387 | .698 |
| Upton,Justin | Atl | 26 | 155 | 588 | 162 | 33 | 4 | 27 | 104 | 83 | 102 | 6.15 | 75 | 153 | 12 | 5 | .71 | .276 | .363 | .483 | .846 |
| Uribe,Juan | LAD | 35 | 125 | 371 | 89 | 19 | 1 | 11 | 39 | 47 | 41 | 3.75 | 26 | 81 | 3 | 2 | .60 | .240 | .295 | .385 | .680 |
| Utley,Chase | Phi | 35 | 131 | 496 | 135 | 27 | 3 | 19 | 78 | 71 | 78 | 5.57 | 55 | 83 | 10 | 3 | .77 | .272 | .360 | .454 | .814 |
| Valbuena,Luis | ChC | 28 | 103 | 298 | 74 | 17 | 1 | 9 | 38 | 35 | 40 | 4.62 | 38 | 57 | 2 | 1 | .67 | .248 | .337 | .403 | .740 |
| Valencia,Danny | Bal | 29 | 71 | 199 | 52 | 13 | 1 | 6 | 23 | 27 | 26 | 4.57 | 12 | 35 | 1 | 1 | .50 | .261 | .303 | .427 | .730 |
| Van Slyke,Scott | LAD | 27 | 83 | 262 | 73 | 20 | 1 | 11 | 39 | 41 | 46 | 6.23 | 35 | 64 | 5 | 3 | .62 | .279 | .364 | .489 | .852 |
| Venable,Will | SD | 31 | 147 | 463 | 121 | 21 | 4 | 17 | 67 | 55 | 64 | 4.77 | 38 | 116 | 21 | 7 | .75 | .261 | .321 | .434 | .756 |
| Viciedo,Dayan | CWS | 25 | 145 | 501 | 136 | 24 | 1 | 20 | 60 | 71 | 69 | 4.92 | 29 | 102 | 1 | 0 | 1.00 | .271 | .315 | .443 | .758 |
| Victorino,Shane | Bos | 33 | 148 | 549 | 148 | 28 | 5 | 14 | 83 | 58 | 75 | 4.78 | 44 | 81 | 23 | 7 | .77 | .270 | .336 | .415 | .751 |
| Villar,Jonathan | Hou | 23 | 147 | 525 | 130 | 21 | 5 | 10 | 68 | 46 | 62 | 3.93 | 49 | 151 | 50 | 15 | .77 | .248 | .312 | .364 | .676 |
| Vogt,Stephen | Oak | 29 | 72 | 233 | 62 | 14 | 1 | 7 | 29 | 33 | 32 | 4.87 | 20 | 38 | 0 | 0 | .00 | .266 | .324 | .425 | .749 |
| Votto,Joey | Cin | 30 | 152 | 558 | 173 | 40 | 2 | 25 | 92 | 89 | 124 | 8.29 | 111 | 130 | 7 | 4 | .64 | .310 | .428 | .523 | .951 |
| Walker,Neil | Pit | 28 | 146 | 549 | 146 | 35 | 3 | 16 | 71 | 76 | 77 | 4.93 | 54 | 105 | 4 | 3 | .57 | .266 | .338 | .428 | .766 |
| Wallace,Brett | Hou | 27 | 91 | 262 | 68 | 15 | 0 | 10 | 32 | 32 | 35 | 4.67 | 21 | 78 | 1 | 1 | .50 | .260 | .324 | .431 | .755 |
| Weeks,Rickie | Mil | 31 | 129 | 448 | 106 | 23 | 2 | 16 | 69 | 44 | 58 | 4.36 | 55 | 129 | 10 | 4 | .71 | .237 | .336 | .404 | .740 |
| Wells,Vernon | NYY | 35 | 81 | 208 | 50 | 10 | 1 | 7 | 25 | 26 | 24 | 3.92 | 14 | 35 | 3 | 1 | .75 | .240 | .291 | .399 | .691 |
| Werth,Jayson | Was | 35 | 148 | 550 | 154 | 30 | 1 | 23 | 86 | 81 | 94 | 6.11 | 76 | 136 | 11 | 4 | .73 | .280 | .372 | .464 | .836 |
| Wheeler,Ryan | Col | 25 | 121 | 370 | 102 | 23 | 1 | 9 | 43 | 59 | 48 | 4.62 | 22 | 77 | 3 | 2 | .60 | .276 | .316 | .416 | .733 |
| Wieters,Matt | Bal | 28 | 145 | 525 | 133 | 30 | 1 | 22 | 64 | 80 | 74 | 4.90 | 53 | 105 | 2 | 1 | .67 | .253 | .323 | .440 | .763 |
| Willingham,Josh | Min | 35 | 124 | 406 | 94 | 22 | 1 | 19 | 53 | 62 | 58 | 4.82 | 59 | 125 | 2 | 1 | .67 | .232 | .347 | .431 | .778 |
| Wong,Kolten | StL | 23 | 133 | 476 | 129 | 23 | 6 | 8 | 68 | 43 | 63 | 4.64 | 39 | 68 | 24 | 6 | .80 | .271 | .326 | .395 | .721 |
| Wright,David | NYM | 31 | 140 | 536 | 160 | 35 | 2 | 21 | 84 | 87 | 101 | 6.86 | 73 | 111 | 18 | 7 | .72 | .299 | .387 | .489 | .875 |
| Yelich,Christian | Mia | 22 | 148 | 573 | 167 | 35 | 8 | 15 | 92 | 62 | 100 | 6.28 | 78 | 146 | 21 | 8 | .72 | .291 | .377 | .459 | .836 |
| Youkilis,Kevin | NYY | 35 | 105 | 385 | 99 | 25 | 1 | 15 | 61 | 59 | 59 | 5.34 | 52 | 97 | 2 | 1 | .67 | .257 | .362 | .444 | .806 |
| Young,Chris | Oak | 30 | 117 | 372 | 85 | 24 | 1 | 15 | 52 | 47 | 48 | 4.27 | 44 | 98 | 12 | 5 | .71 | .228 | .315 | .419 | .734 |
| Young,Delmon | TB | 28 | 123 | 470 | 128 | 26 | 1 | 14 | 52 | 65 | 60 | 4.55 | 22 | 97 | 2 | 1 | .67 | .272 | .312 | .421 | .733 |
| Young,Eric | NYM | 29 | 139 | 448 | 119 | 21 | 4 | 3 | 69 | 29 | 55 | 4.21 | 44 | 77 | 39 | 11 | .78 | .266 | .334 | .350 | .684 |
| Young,Michael | LAD | 37 | 131 | 442 | 126 | 24 | 1 | 8 | 54 | 52 | 59 | 4.84 | 33 | 68 | 2 | 1 | .67 | .285 | .336 | .398 | .734 |
| Zimmerman,Ryan | Was | 29 | 146 | 545 | 152 | 33 | 1 | 23 | 82 | 82 | 89 | 5.86 | 58 | 117 | 4 | 2 | .67 | .279 | .350 | .470 | .820 |
| Zobrist,Ben | TB | 33 | 159 | 603 | 162 | 37 | 3 | 17 | 87 | 78 | 93 | 5.42 | 87 | 107 | 12 | 5 | .71 | .269 | .365 | .425 | .789 |
| Zunino,Mike | Sea | 23 | 118 | 336 | 75 | 16 | 2 | 13 | 45 | 43 | 38 | 3.79 | 28 | 96 | 1 | 0 | 1.00 | .223 | .287 | .399 | .686 |

# 2014 Pitcher Projections

**Bill James**

In reviewing our projections from 2013, pitchers can be sorted into three groups:

a) Those who did better than we expected them to do,
b) Those who didn't do as well as we expected, and
c) Those who did about the same.

In the first category, the most obvious name is Matt Harvey. We had projected Matt Harvey to pitch 192 innings—about accurate, as it turned out-to strike out 196 batters, and to win 11 games. That was all pretty accurate, but we had expected him to walk 88 batters in those 192 innings. In fact, he walked only 31 batters in 178 innings, and because of that, with the high strikeout rate we had expected, his ERA was a run and a half lower than we thought it would be, 2.27 vs. 3.70.

Adam Wainwright, we had projected at 14-8, 3.33 ERA. . .a nice season. He had a BIG season, 19-9, 2.94 ERA, struck out 45 batters more than we expected and walked 18 less. Julio Teheran of Atlanta, we had penciled in for 7-9, 4.23 ERA, strikeout to walk ratio of 119 to 55. His actual numbers were 14-8, 3.20 ERA, strikeout to walk of 170/45. That's better, I think. Koji Uehara, we had expected to pitch very well, 3-1 with a 2.20 ERA, but only 43 games, 40 innings, 4 saves. He pitched twice as much as we expected (74 innings vs. 40), twice as well as we expected (1.09 ERA vs. 2.20), and in a bigger role (21 saves actual vs. 4 projected.)

Corey Kluber, Max Scherzer, Greg Holland, Francisco Liriano, Ubaldo Jimenez, and Chris Archer all pitched much better than we had expected them to pitch. Rick Porcello, Yu Darvish and Dillon Gee pitched somewhat better than we had expected. This chart summarizes all of those pleasant surprises, and some others:

| Pitcher | Label | G | GS | IP | H | BB | SO | W | L | Pct | Sv | ERA |
|---|---|---|---|---|---|---|---|---|---|---|---|---|
| Perkins, Glen | Actual | 61 | 0 | 63 | 43 | 15 | 77 | 2 | 0 | 1.000 | 36 | 2.30 |
| | Projected | 67 | 0 | 72 | 80 | 19 | 56 | 3 | 5 | .375 | 27 | 4.38 |
| Chatwood, Tyler | Actual | 20 | 20 | 111 | 118 | 41 | 66 | 8 | 5 | .615 | 0 | 3.15 |
| | Projected | 23 | 23 | 128 | 150 | 62 | 78 | 5 | 9 | .357 | 0 | 5.34 |
| Sanchez, Anibal | Actual | 29 | 29 | 182 | 156 | 54 | 202 | 14 | 8 | .636 | 0 | 2.57 |
| | Projected | 31 | 31 | 201 | 200 | 56 | 175 | 12 | 10 | .545 | 0 | 3.72 |
| Hunter, Tommy | Actual | 68 | 0 | 86 | 71 | 14 | 68 | 6 | 5 | .545 | 4 | 2.81 |
| | Projected | 48 | 0 | 50 | 56 | 10 | 29 | 2 | 3 | .400 | 0 | 4.50 |
| Hawkins, LaTroy | Actual | 72 | 0 | 71 | 71 | 10 | 55 | 3 | 2 | .600 | 13 | 2.93 |
| | Projected | 49 | 0 | 45 | 45 | 13 | 29 | 3 | 2 | .600 | 0 | 3.60 |
| Tillman, Chris | Actual | 33 | 33 | 206 | 184 | 68 | 179 | 16 | 7 | .696 | 0 | 3.71 |
| | Projected | 31 | 31 | 188 | 191 | 72 | 155 | 9 | 12 | .429 | 0 | 4.31 |
| Minor, Mike | Actual | 32 | 32 | 205 | 177 | 46 | 181 | 13 | 9 | .591 | 0 | 3.21 |
| | Projected | 30 | 30 | 189 | 178 | 61 | 177 | 11 | 10 | .524 | 0 | 3.76 |
| Melancon, Mark | Actual | 72 | 0 | 71 | 60 | 8 | 70 | 3 | 2 | .600 | 16 | 1.39 |
| | Projected | 47 | 0 | 57 | 54 | 17 | 54 | 3 | 3 | .500 | 0 | 3.47 |
| Hochevar, Luke | Actual | 58 | 0 | 70 | 41 | 17 | 82 | 5 | 2 | .714 | 2 | 1.92 |
| | Projected | 31 | 31 | 192 | 204 | 62 | 137 | 9 | 13 | .409 | 0 | 4.45 |
| Parra, Manny | Actual | 57 | 0 | 46 | 40 | 15 | 56 | 2 | 3 | .400 | 0 | 3.33 |
| | Projected | 57 | 0 | 51 | 56 | 29 | 47 | 2 | 4 | .333 | 0 | 5.29 |
| Burnett, A.J. | Actual | 30 | 30 | 191 | 165 | 67 | 209 | 10 | 11 | .476 | 0 | 3.30 |
| | Projected | 32 | 32 | 209 | 203 | 76 | 190 | 11 | 13 | .458 | 0 | 4.05 |
| Masterson, Justin | Actual | 32 | 29 | 193 | 156 | 76 | 195 | 14 | 10 | .583 | 0 | 3.45 |
| | Projected | 34 | 34 | 204 | 206 | 79 | 160 | 10 | 12 | .455 | 0 | 4.01 |
| Torres, Carlos | Actual | 33 | 9 | 86 | 79 | 17 | 75 | 4 | 6 | .400 | 0 | 3.44 |
| | Projected | 44 | 0 | 49 | 48 | 22 | 43 | 3 | 3 | .500 | 0 | 4.04 |
| Gee, Dillon | Actual | 32 | 32 | 199 | 208 | 47 | 142 | 12 | 11 | .522 | 0 | 3.62 |
| | Projected | 8 | 8 | 55 | 55 | 19 | 43 | 3 | 3 | .500 | 0 | 4.09 |
| Darvish, Yu | Actual | 32 | 32 | 210 | 145 | 80 | 277 | 13 | 9 | .591 | 0 | 2.83 |
| | Projected | 32 | 32 | 214 | 176 | 88 | 247 | 14 | 9 | .609 | 0 | 3.45 |
| Porcello, Rick | Actual | 32 | 29 | 177 | 185 | 42 | 142 | 13 | 8 | .619 | 0 | 4.32 |
| | Projected | 31 | 31 | 178 | 207 | 45 | 102 | 9 | 11 | .450 | 0 | 4.50 |
| Archer, Chris | Actual | 23 | 23 | 129 | 107 | 38 | 101 | 9 | 7 | .563 | 0 | 3.22 |
| | Projected | 26 | 26 | 161 | 142 | 90 | 159 | 8 | 10 | .444 | 0 | 3.91 |
| Jimenez, Ubaldo | Actual | 32 | 32 | 183 | 163 | 80 | 194 | 13 | 9 | .591 | 0 | 3.30 |
| | Projected | 29 | 29 | 170 | 158 | 82 | 151 | 9 | 10 | .474 | 0 | 3.97 |
| Liriano, Francisco | Actual | 26 | 26 | 161 | 134 | 63 | 163 | 16 | 8 | .667 | 0 | 3.02 |
| | Projected | 32 | 28 | 154 | 144 | 81 | 152 | 7 | 10 | .412 | 0 | 4.21 |
| Holland, Greg | Actual | 68 | 0 | 67 | 40 | 18 | 103 | 2 | 1 | .667 | .47 | 1.21 |
| | Projected | 70 | 0 | 74 | 61 | 34 | 88 | 5 | 3 | .625 | 31 | 3.04 |
| Scherzer, Max | Actual | 32 | 32 | 214 | 152 | 56 | 240 | 21 | 3 | .875 | 0 | 2.90 |
| | Projected | 31 | 31 | 191 | 180 | 60 | 198 | 12 | 9 | .571 | 0 | 3.72 |
| Kluber, Corey | Actual | 26 | 24 | 147 | 153 | 33 | 136 | 11 | 5 | .688 | 0 | 3.85 |
| | Projected | 27 | 27 | 159 | 172 | 65 | 149 | 7 | 11 | .389 | 0 | 4.75 |
| Uehara, Koji | Actual | 73 | 0 | 74 | 33 | 9 | 101 | 4 | 1 | .800 | 21 | 1.09 |
| | Projected | 43 | 0 | 40 | 34 | 6 | 39 | 3 | 1 | .750 | 4 | 2.25 |
| Teheran, Julio | Actual | 30 | 30 | 186 | 173 | 45 | 170 | 14 | 8 | .636 | 0 | 3.20 |
| | Projected | 25 | 25 | 149 | 151 | 55 | 119 | 7 | 9 | .438 | 0 | 4.23 |

| Pitcher | Label | G | GS | IP | H | BB | SO | W | L | Pct | Sv | ERA |
|---|---|---|---|---|---|---|---|---|---|---|---|---|
| Wainwright, Adam | Actual | 34 | 34 | 242 | 223 | 35 | 219 | 19 | 9 | .679 | 0 | 2.94 |
| | Projected | 31 | 31 | 203 | 191 | 53 | 174 | 14 | 8 | .636 | 0 | 3.33 |
| Harvey, Matt | Actual | 26 | 26 | 178 | 135 | 31 | 191 | 9 | 5 | .643 | 0 | 2.27 |
| | Projected | 30 | 30 | 192 | 172 | 88 | 196 | 11 | 10 | .524 | 0 | 3.70 |

As to pitchers who did not pitch as well as we had projected that they would, start with Roy Halladay. Due to the injury, Halladay pitched less than half as much as we thought he would—62 innings rather than 230-with twice the ERA, 6.82 rather than 3.21. Other under-achievers included Mike Fiers, Ian Kennedy, Lucas Harrell, Sabathia, Brandon Morrow, Phil Hughes, Matt Cain, Shaun Marcum and Brett Anderson. Of course, the guys whose seasons were wiped out by injuries. . .Clayton Richard, Octavio Dotel, Jaime Garcia, Josh Beckett, Ricky Romero. . .none of them were able to meet expectations.

Jorge de la Rosa pitched about the number of innings we had projected (168 vs. 151), struck out substantially less than expected (112 vs. 136) and walked more than expected (62 vs. 58), but nonetheless got terrific results (16-6 with a 3.49 ERA, whereas we had projected 8-9, 4.23). Hard to figure that one.

And in the third category. . .there are lots of relievers who have kind of predictable seasons, among them:

| Pitcher | Label | G | GS | IP | H | BB | SO | W | L | Pct | Sv | ERA |
|---|---|---|---|---|---|---|---|---|---|---|---|---|
| Neshek, Pat | Actual | 45 | 0 | 40 | 40 | 15 | 29 | 2 | 1 | .667 | 0 | 3.35 |
| | Projected | 46 | 0 | 39 | 34 | 14 | 38 | 2 | 2 | .500 | 0 | 3.23 |
| Badenhop, Burke | Actual | 63 | 0 | 62 | 62 | 12 | 42 | 2 | 3 | .400 | 1 | 3.47 |
| | Projected | 58 | 0 | 56 | 56 | 16 | 40 | 3 | 3 | .500 | 0 | 3.54 |
| Gearrin, Cory | Actual | 37 | 0 | 31 | 30 | 16 | 23 | 2 | 1 | .667 | 1 | 3.77 |
| | Projected | 38 | 0 | 34 | 30 | 14 | 35 | 2 | 2 | .500 | 0 | 3.44 |
| Rivera, Mariano | Actual | 64 | 0 | 64 | 58 | 9 | 54 | 6 | 2 | .750 | 44 | 2.11 |
| | Projected | 64 | 0 | 62 | 47 | 10 | 59 | 6 | 1 | .857 | 46 | 1.89 |
| O'Day, Darren | Actual | 68 | 0 | 62 | 47 | 15 | 59 | 5 | 3 | .625 | 2 | 2.18 |
| | Projected | 71 | 0 | 73 | 61 | 16 | 66 | 5 | 3 | .625 | 0 | 2.71 |
| Wright, Wesley | Actual | 70 | 0 | 54 | 54 | 19 | 55 | 0 | 4 | .000 | 0 | 3.69 |
| | Projected | 75 | 0 | 58 | 55 | 21 | 52 | 3 | 4 | .429 | 0 | 3.88 |
| Cook, Ryan | Actual | 71 | 0 | 67 | 62 | 25 | 67 | 6 | 4 | .600 | 2 | 2.54 |
| | Projected | 73 | 0 | 80 | 59 | 32 | 81 | 6 | 3 | .667 | 0 | 2.48 |
| Ambriz, Hector | Actual | 43 | 0 | 36 | 50 | 14 | 27 | 2 | 4 | .333 | 2 | 5.70 |
| | Projected | 35 | 0 | 39 | 44 | 19 | 31 | 1 | 3 | .250 | 0 | 5.31 |
| Smith, Joe | Actual | 70 | 0 | 63 | 54 | 23 | 54 | 6 | 2 | .750 | 3 | 2.29 |
| | Projected | 74 | 0 | 68 | 58 | 25 | 55 | 5 | 3 | .625 | 0 | 2.91 |
| Thayer, Dale | Actual | 69 | 0 | 65 | 59 | 22 | 64 | 3 | 5 | .375 | 1 | 3.32 |
| | Projected | 71 | 0 | 62 | 60 | 14 | 52 | 4 | 3 | .571 | 0 | 3.19 |

And some starters as well:

| Pitcher | Label | G | GS | IP | H | BB | SO | W | L | Pct | Sv | ERA |
|---|---|---|---|---|---|---|---|---|---|---|---|---|
| Latos, Mat | Actual | 32 | 32 | 211 | 197 | 58 | 187 | 14 | 7 | .667 | 0 | 3.16 |
| | Projected | 33 | 33 | 208 | 177 | 64 | 194 | 15 | 8 | .652 | 0 | 3.16 |
| Fister, Doug | Actual | 33 | 32 | 209 | 229 | 44 | 159 | 14 | 9 | .609 | 0 | 3.67 |
| | Projected | 32 | 32 | 212 | 221 | 43 | 147 | 13 | 10 | .565 | 0 | 3.69 |
| Miley, Wade | Actual | 33 | 33 | 203 | 201 | 66 | 147 | 10 | 10 | .500 | 0 | 3.55 |
| | Projected | 30 | 30 | 199 | 200 | 50 | 150 | 12 | 10 | .545 | 0 | 3.57 |
| Arroyo, Bronson | Actual | 32 | 32 | 202 | 199 | 34 | 124 | 14 | 12 | .538 | 0 | 3.79 |
| | Projected | 33 | 33 | 218 | 222 | 43 | 136 | 12 | 12 | .500 | 0 | 3.88 |
| Norris, Bud | Actual | 32 | 30 | 177 | 196 | 67 | 147 | 10 | 12 | .455 | 0 | 4.18 |
| | Projected | 29 | 29 | 173 | 171 | 69 | 168 | 7 | 12 | .368 | 0 | 4.27 |
| Gonzalez, Miguel | Actual | 30 | 28 | 171 | 157 | 53 | 120 | 11 | 8 | .579 | 0 | 3.78 |
| | Projected | 27 | 27 | 174 | 161 | 56 | 138 | 10 | 9 | .526 | 0 | 3.67 |
| Gonzalez, Gio | Actual | 32 | 32 | 196 | 169 | 76 | 192 | 11 | 8 | .579 | 0 | 3.36 |
| | Projected | 32 | 32 | 202 | 172 | 83 | 204 | 14 | 8 | .636 | 0 | 3.21 |
| Lohse, Kyle | Actual | 32 | 32 | 199 | 196 | 36 | 125 | 11 | 10 | .524 | 0 | 3.35 |
| | Projected | 32 | 32 | 208 | 215 | 42 | 130 | 13 | 10 | .565 | 0 | 3.63 |
| Correia, Kevin | Actual | 31 | 31 | 185 | 218 | 45 | 101 | 9 | 13 | .409 | 0 | 4.18 |
| | Projected | 29 | 27 | 176 | 185 | 49 | 112 | 9 | 11 | .450 | 0 | 4.09 |
| Bailey, Homer | Actual | 32 | 32 | 209 | 181 | 54 | 199 | 11 | 12 | .478 | 0 | 3.49 |
| | Projected | 33 | 33 | 210 | 215 | 54 | 172 | 12 | 12 | .500 | 0 | 3.86 |
| Guthrie, Jeremy | Actual | 33 | 33 | 212 | 236 | 59 | 111 | 15 | 12 | .556 | 0 | 4.04 |
| | Projected | 33 | 33 | 197 | 203 | 56 | 118 | 10 | 12 | .455 | 0 | 4.20 |
| Bumgarner, Madison | Actual | 31 | 31 | 201 | 146 | 62 | 199 | 13 | 9 | .591 | 0 | 2.77 |
| | Projected | 32 | 32 | 203 | 194 | 48 | 174 | 13 | 9 | .591 | 0 | 3.37 |
| Hernandez, Felix | Actual | 31 | 31 | 204 | 185 | 46 | 216 | 12 | 10 | .545 | 0 | 3.04 |
| | Projected | 33 | 33 | 232 | 208 | 60 | 216 | 14 | 11 | .560 | 0 | 3.18 |

Bumgarner was the only pitcher with more than five wins whose won-lost record we had projected exactly correct. We nailed the strikeout totals for King Felix (216-216), Ervin Santana (161-161), and a bunch of relievers. Mat Latos was the only pitcher whose ERA we hit right on the nose.

I used to be very skeptical of projections for pitchers, didn't think it could be done accurately. In retrospect, it may have been my own ignorance that I was afraid of. I used to try to project future won-lost records based on past won-lost records, and future ERAs based on past ERAs. That worked for Warren Spahn, but not so well for anybody else. We understand now that to project pitchers accurately, you have to focus on lower performance indicators. . . strikeouts, walks and innings, rather than wins, losses and ERA. How the strikeouts, walks and innings will aggregate themselves into wins and losses is kind of a random process, but if you stay focused on the elements, you won't usually miss by too much on the outcomes.

# 2014 Pitcher Projections

| PLAYER | | | HOW MUCH | | | WHAT HE WILL GIVE UP | | | | | THE RESULTS | | | | | |
|---|---|---|---|---|---|---|---|---|---|---|---|---|---|---|---|---|
| Pitcher | Team | Age | G | GS | IP | H | HR | BB | SO | HB | W | L | Pct | Sv | BR/9 | ERA |
| Aardsma,David | NYM | 32 | 51 | 0 | 45 | 39 | 6 | 25 | 46 | 2 | 2 | 3 | .400 | 0 | 13.2 | 4.20 |
| Abad,Fernando | Was | 28 | 52 | 0 | 51 | 56 | 6 | 14 | 43 | 1 | 3 | 3 | .500 | 0 | 12.5 | 4.24 |
| Aceves,Alfredo | Bos | 31 | 45 | 0 | 70 | 65 | 9 | 30 | 53 | 5 | 4 | 4 | .500 | 0 | 12.9 | 4.24 |
| Adams,Mike | Phi | 35 | 61 | 0 | 51 | 42 | 4 | 18 | 50 | 1 | 3 | 2 | .600 | 0 | 10.8 | 2.82 |
| Affeldt,Jeremy | SF | 35 | 65 | 0 | 60 | 54 | 4 | 26 | 49 | 4 | 4 | 3 | .571 | 0 | 12.6 | 3.45 |
| Albers,Andrew | Min | 28 | 14 | 14 | 80 | 88 | 8 | 16 | 58 | 2 | 4 | 5 | .444 | 0 | 11.9 | 3.94 |
| Albers,Matt | Cle | 31 | 60 | 0 | 67 | 65 | 6 | 25 | 48 | 3 | 3 | 4 | .429 | 0 | 12.5 | 3.90 |
| Alburquerque,Al | Det | 28 | 59 | 0 | 54 | 41 | 3 | 39 | 76 | 3 | 3 | 3 | .500 | 0 | 13.8 | 3.67 |
| Allen,Cody | Cle | 25 | 75 | 0 | 69 | 59 | 7 | 25 | 79 | 1 | 4 | 3 | .571 | 3 | 11.1 | 3.13 |
| Alvarez,Henderson | Mia | 24 | 30 | 30 | 188 | 192 | 19 | 47 | 104 | 7 | 9 | 11 | .450 | 0 | 11.8 | 3.78 |
| Alvarez,Jose | Det | 25 | 30 | 15 | 97 | 105 | 11 | 25 | 69 | 3 | 5 | 6 | .455 | 0 | 12.3 | 4.18 |
| Anderson,Brett | Oak | 26 | 24 | 14 | 97 | 99 | 9 | 40 | 79 | 4 | 5 | 6 | .455 | 0 | 13.3 | 4.18 |
| Archer,Chris | TB | 25 | 29 | 29 | 172 | 156 | 15 | 73 | 160 | 10 | 9 | 10 | .474 | 0 | 12.5 | 3.77 |
| Arrieta,Jake | ChC | 28 | 20 | 20 | 117 | 114 | 14 | 53 | 99 | 6 | 5 | 8 | .385 | 0 | 13.3 | 4.31 |
| Arroyo,Bronson | Cin | 37 | 32 | 32 | 202 | 205 | 32 | 35 | 127 | 6 | 11 | 11 | .500 | 0 | 11 | 3.83 |
| Atchison,Scott | NYM | 38 | 62 | 0 | 56 | 53 | 4 | 12 | 44 | 1 | 4 | 2 | .667 | 0 | 10.6 | 3.05 |
| Aumont,Phillippe | Phi | 25 | 55 | 0 | 56 | 52 | 2 | 50 | 64 | 6 | 2 | 4 | .333 | 0 | 17.4 | 5.30 |
| Avilan,Luis | Atl | 24 | 74 | 0 | 66 | 59 | 5 | 26 | 49 | 3 | 4 | 3 | .571 | 0 | 12 | 3.41 |
| Axelrod,Dylan | CWS | 28 | 38 | 8 | 74 | 80 | 8 | 26 | 56 | 3 | 3 | 5 | .375 | 0 | 13.3 | 4.50 |
| Axford,John | StL | 31 | 70 | 0 | 64 | 57 | 6 | 28 | 75 | 1 | 4 | 3 | .571 | 0 | 12.1 | 3.66 |
| Ayala,Luis | Atl | 36 | 54 | 0 | 44 | 47 | 4 | 14 | 30 | 3 | 2 | 3 | .400 | 0 | 13.1 | 4.09 |
| Badenhop,Burke | Mil | 31 | 64 | 0 | 62 | 63 | 4 | 13 | 44 | 2 | 4 | 3 | .571 | 0 | 11.3 | 3.34 |
| Bailey,Homer | Cin | 28 | 32 | 32 | 208 | 205 | 23 | 53 | 175 | 8 | 12 | 11 | .522 | 0 | 11.5 | 3.68 |
| Baker,Scott | ChC | 32 | 6 | 6 | 30 | 30 | 4 | 7 | 24 | 1 | 2 | 2 | .500 | 0 | 11.4 | 3.60 |
| Balfour,Grant | Oak | 36 | 68 | 0 | 67 | 47 | 6 | 27 | 73 | 0 | 5 | 2 | .714 | 18 | 9.9 | 2.42 |
| Bass,Anthony | SD | 26 | 33 | 0 | 64 | 69 | 6 | 21 | 49 | 1 | 3 | 4 | .429 | 0 | 12.8 | 4.22 |
| Bastardo,Antonio | Phi | 28 | 65 | 0 | 56 | 43 | 6 | 27 | 67 | 2 | 3 | 3 | .500 | 0 | 11.6 | 3.21 |
| Bauer,Trevor | Cle | 23 | 12 | 12 | 70 | 66 | 8 | 46 | 72 | 5 | 3 | 5 | .375 | 0 | 15 | 4.89 |
| Beachy,Brandon | Atl | 27 | 23 | 23 | 139 | 114 | 14 | 51 | 142 | 3 | 9 | 6 | .600 | 0 | 10.9 | 3.24 |
| Beckett,Josh | LAD | 34 | 25 | 25 | 153 | 146 | 19 | 47 | 135 | 6 | 9 | 8 | .529 | 0 | 11.7 | 3.82 |
| Bedard,Erik | Hou | 35 | 25 | 25 | 148 | 140 | 16 | 70 | 142 | 4 | 6 | 10 | .375 | 0 | 13 | 4.14 |
| Belisario,Ronald | LAD | 31 | 71 | 0 | 64 | 59 | 4 | 27 | 51 | 4 | 4 | 3 | .571 | 0 | 12.7 | 3.52 |
| Belisle,Matt | Col | 34 | 68 | 0 | 68 | 74 | 6 | 14 | 54 | 2 | 4 | 4 | .500 | 0 | 11.9 | 3.84 |
| Bell,Heath | Ari | 36 | 68 | 0 | 68 | 63 | 6 | 21 | 70 | 2 | 4 | 3 | .571 | 0 | 11.4 | 3.31 |
| Benoit,Joaquin | Det | 36 | 65 | 0 | 70 | 54 | 8 | 22 | 78 | 1 | 4 | 3 | .571 | 28 | 9.9 | 2.70 |
| Billingsley,Chad | LAD | 29 | 28 | 28 | 168 | 160 | 12 | 59 | 146 | 6 | 10 | 8 | .556 | 0 | 12.1 | 3.64 |
| Black,Vic | NYM | 26 | 60 | 0 | 59 | 45 | 3 | 28 | 74 | 3 | 4 | 2 | .667 | 0 | 11.6 | 2.75 |
| Blackley,Travis | Tex | 31 | 52 | 0 | 60 | 59 | 8 | 21 | 44 | 2 | 3 | 4 | .429 | 0 | 12.3 | 4.05 |
| Blanton,Joe | LAA | 33 | 33 | 15 | 108 | 126 | 17 | 24 | 81 | 3 | 5 | 7 | .417 | 0 | 12.8 | 4.75 |
| Blazek,Michael | Mil | 25 | 56 | 0 | 63 | 56 | 9 | 35 | 61 | 3 | 3 | 4 | .429 | 0 | 13.4 | 4.43 |
| Blevins,Jerry | Oak | 30 | 65 | 0 | 58 | 50 | 6 | 19 | 54 | 3 | 4 | 3 | .571 | 0 | 11.2 | 3.10 |
| Bonderman,Jeremy | Det | 31 | 25 | 3 | 52 | 57 | 7 | 19 | 35 | 2 | 2 | 3 | .400 | 0 | 13.5 | 4.67 |
| Boshers,Buddy | LAA | 26 | 48 | 0 | 31 | 28 | 2 | 15 | 35 | 1 | 2 | 2 | .500 | 0 | 12.8 | 3.77 |
| Bowden,Michael | ChC | 27 | 37 | 0 | 38 | 34 | 4 | 15 | 32 | 1 | 2 | 2 | .500 | 0 | 11.8 | 3.55 |
| Boxberger,Brad | SD | 26 | 62 | 0 | 60 | 47 | 4 | 27 | 82 | 1 | 4 | 2 | .667 | 0 | 11.2 | 2.85 |
| Brach,Brad | SD | 28 | 55 | 0 | 54 | 49 | 5 | 23 | 58 | 2 | 3 | 3 | .500 | 0 | 12.3 | 3.67 |
| Breslow,Craig | Bos | 33 | 64 | 0 | 61 | 54 | 5 | 21 | 51 | 2 | 4 | 3 | .571 | 0 | 11.4 | 3.10 |
| Britton,Zach | Bal | 26 | 12 | 10 | 62 | 67 | 5 | 29 | 44 | 2 | 3 | 4 | .429 | 0 | 14.2 | 4.65 |
| Brothers,Rex | Col | 26 | 71 | 0 | 69 | 57 | 5 | 37 | 88 | 0 | 4 | 3 | .571 | 29 | 12.3 | 3.39 |
| Broxton,Jonathan | Cin | 30 | 56 | 0 | 54 | 46 | 4 | 19 | 60 | 2 | 4 | 2 | .667 | 0 | 11.2 | 3.00 |
| Buchholz,Clay | Bos | 29 | 29 | 29 | 190 | 169 | 18 | 64 | 153 | 6 | 12 | 9 | .571 | 0 | 11.3 | 3.46 |
| Buehrle,Mark | Tor | 35 | 32 | 32 | 204 | 220 | 23 | 47 | 116 | 5 | 10 | 12 | .455 | 0 | 12 | 3.97 |
| Bumgarner,Madison | SF | 24 | 32 | 32 | 205 | 183 | 17 | 57 | 184 | 6 | 14 | 9 | .609 | 0 | 10.8 | 3.25 |
| Burnett,A.J. | Pit | 37 | 31 | 31 | 202 | 191 | 22 | 71 | 191 | 11 | 11 | 12 | .478 | 0 | 12.2 | 3.83 |
| Burnett,Sean | LAA | 31 | 65 | 0 | 51 | 51 | 5 | 15 | 37 | 2 | 3 | 3 | .500 | 0 | 12 | 3.71 |
| Burton,Jared | Min | 33 | 66 | 0 | 63 | 56 | 6 | 20 | 54 | 4 | 4 | 3 | .571 | 0 | 11.4 | 3.29 |
| Byrdak,Tim | NYM | 40 | 60 | 0 | 33 | 28 | 4 | 19 | 33 | 1 | 2 | 2 | .500 | 0 | 13.1 | 3.82 |
| Cahill,Trevor | Ari | 26 | 31 | 31 | 195 | 187 | 19 | 82 | 134 | 8 | 10 | 12 | .455 | 0 | 12.8 | 3.97 |
| Cain,Matt | SF | 29 | 32 | 32 | 210 | 177 | 19 | 58 | 174 | 6 | 15 | 9 | .625 | 0 | 10.3 | 3.09 |
| Capps,Carter | Sea | 23 | 55 | 0 | 65 | 62 | 7 | 24 | 77 | 3 | 3 | 4 | .429 | 0 | 12.3 | 3.88 |
| Capuano,Chris | LAD | 35 | 20 | 20 | 110 | 114 | 14 | 28 | 90 | 2 | 6 | 6 | .500 | 0 | 11.8 | 3.93 |
| Carpenter,Chris | StL | 39 | 12 | 12 | 73 | 71 | 5 | 20 | 56 | 3 | 5 | 3 | .625 | 0 | 11.6 | 3.45 |
| Carpenter,David | Atl | 28 | 71 | 0 | 74 | 68 | 7 | 24 | 75 | 5 | 4 | 4 | .500 | 0 | 11.8 | 3.53 |
| Carrasco,Carlos | Cle | 27 | 20 | 5 | 50 | 52 | 6 | 18 | 42 | 2 | 2 | 3 | .400 | 0 | 13 | 4.32 |
| Cashner,Andrew | SD | 27 | 30 | 30 | 192 | 171 | 14 | 54 | 165 | 6 | 14 | 8 | .636 | 0 | 10.8 | 3.19 |
| Casilla,Santiago | SF | 33 | 71 | 0 | 64 | 55 | 5 | 28 | 56 | 3 | 4 | 3 | .571 | 2 | 12.1 | 3.38 |
| Cecil,Brett | Tor | 27 | 61 | 0 | 61 | 62 | 7 | 21 | 49 | 2 | 3 | 4 | .429 | 0 | 12.5 | 4.13 |
| Chacin,Jhoulys | Col | 26 | 31 | 31 | 204 | 191 | 18 | 70 | 154 | 6 | 13 | 10 | .565 | 0 | 11.8 | 3.62 |
| Chamberlain,Joba | NYY | 28 | 67 | 0 | 65 | 64 | 8 | 33 | 66 | 3 | 3 | 5 | .375 | 0 | 13.8 | 4.71 |

# 2014 Pitcher Projections

| PLAYER | | | HOW MUCH | | | WHAT HE WILL GIVE UP | | | | | THE RESULTS | | | | | |
|---|---|---|---|---|---|---|---|---|---|---|---|---|---|---|---|---|
| Pitcher | Team | Age | G | GS | IP | H | HR | BB | SO | HB | W | L | Pct | Sv | BR/9 | ERA |
| Chapman,Aroldis | Cin | 26 | 63 | 0 | 64 | 40 | 5 | 28 | 99 | 3 | 4 | 3 | .571 | 42 | 10 | 2.25 |
| Chapman,Kevin | Hou | 26 | 48 | 0 | 41 | 36 | 2 | 27 | 43 | 1 | 2 | 3 | .400 | 0 | 14 | 3.95 |
| Chatwood,Tyler | Col | 24 | 29 | 29 | 168 | 188 | 13 | 65 | 107 | 6 | 8 | 11 | .421 | 0 | 13.9 | 4.55 |
| Chavez,Jesse | Oak | 30 | 36 | 0 | 59 | 61 | 7 | 16 | 52 | 1 | 3 | 4 | .429 | 0 | 11.9 | 3.97 |
| Chen,Bruce | KC | 37 | 30 | 30 | 170 | 172 | 24 | 47 | 118 | 6 | 8 | 11 | .421 | 0 | 11.9 | 4.02 |
| Chen,Wei-Yin | Bal | 28 | 27 | 27 | 161 | 160 | 22 | 46 | 124 | 3 | 8 | 10 | .444 | 0 | 11.7 | 3.91 |
| Choate,Randy | StL | 38 | 66 | 0 | 36 | 30 | 2 | 14 | 32 | 2 | 3 | 1 | .750 | 0 | 11.5 | 3.00 |
| Cingrani,Tony | Cin | 24 | 29 | 29 | 175 | 159 | 19 | 76 | 213 | 3 | 13 | 7 | .650 | 0 | 12.2 | 3.03 |
| Cishek,Steve | Mia | 28 | 68 | 0 | 66 | 55 | 2 | 24 | 67 | 4 | 4 | 3 | .571 | 45 | 11.3 | 2.73 |
| Claiborne,Preston | NYY | 26 | 61 | 0 | 60 | 59 | 5 | 21 | 54 | 1 | 3 | 3 | .500 | 0 | 12.2 | 3.60 |
| Clippard,Tyler | Was | 29 | 71 | 0 | 72 | 54 | 9 | 25 | 75 | 2 | 5 | 3 | .625 | 3 | 10.1 | 2.75 |
| Cloyd,Tyler | Phi | 27 | 13 | 13 | 72 | 75 | 9 | 22 | 56 | 2 | 3 | 5 | .375 | 0 | 12.4 | 4.13 |
| Cobb,Alex | TB | 26 | 30 | 30 | 195 | 185 | 15 | 63 | 177 | 7 | 11 | 10 | .524 | 0 | 11.8 | 3.55 |
| Coke,Phil | Det | 31 | 58 | 0 | 46 | 49 | 3 | 19 | 38 | 1 | 2 | 3 | .400 | 0 | 13.5 | 4.30 |
| Cole,Gerrit | Pit | 23 | 29 | 29 | 188 | 168 | 12 | 64 | 160 | 7 | 12 | 9 | .571 | 0 | 11.4 | 3.30 |
| Coleman,Louis | KC | 28 | 53 | 0 | 64 | 49 | 6 | 24 | 73 | 2 | 4 | 3 | .571 | 0 | 10.5 | 2.81 |
| Collins,Tim | KC | 24 | 69 | 0 | 58 | 46 | 5 | 31 | 68 | 1 | 3 | 3 | .500 | 0 | 12.1 | 3.26 |
| Collmenter,Josh | Ari | 28 | 51 | 0 | 96 | 89 | 10 | 29 | 76 | 2 | 6 | 5 | .545 | 0 | 11.2 | 3.38 |
| Colome,Alex | TB | 25 | 12 | 12 | 71 | 66 | 5 | 35 | 62 | 4 | 4 | 4 | .500 | 0 | 13.3 | 3.93 |
| Colon,Bartolo | Oak | 41 | 30 | 30 | 187 | 196 | 21 | 30 | 122 | 2 | 11 | 10 | .524 | 0 | 11 | 3.61 |
| Cook,Ryan | Oak | 27 | 71 | 0 | 64 | 50 | 3 | 24 | 64 | 4 | 5 | 2 | .714 | 0 | 11 | 2.67 |
| Corbin,Patrick | Ari | 24 | 31 | 31 | 200 | 198 | 19 | 52 | 175 | 10 | 11 | 11 | .500 | 0 | 11.7 | 3.69 |
| Corpas,Manny | Col | 31 | 38 | 0 | 44 | 45 | 5 | 15 | 31 | 2 | 2 | 3 | .400 | 0 | 12.7 | 4.30 |
| Correia,Kevin | Min | 33 | 29 | 29 | 184 | 200 | 23 | 46 | 112 | 3 | 9 | 12 | .429 | 0 | 12.2 | 4.16 |
| Cosart,Jarred | Hou | 24 | 26 | 26 | 156 | 143 | 8 | 84 | 120 | 6 | 8 | 10 | .444 | 0 | 13.4 | 3.87 |
| Cotts,Neal | Tex | 34 | 69 | 0 | 65 | 53 | 5 | 21 | 75 | 1 | 5 | 3 | .625 | 0 | 10.4 | 2.63 |
| Crain,Jesse | CWS | 32 | 48 | 0 | 46 | 37 | 3 | 17 | 47 | 1 | 3 | 2 | .600 | 0 | 10.8 | 2.74 |
| Crow,Aaron | KC | 27 | 60 | 0 | 52 | 50 | 6 | 22 | 47 | 1 | 2 | 3 | .400 | 0 | 12.6 | 3.98 |
| Cueto,Johnny | Cin | 28 | 30 | 30 | 195 | 180 | 18 | 51 | 153 | 11 | 12 | 9 | .571 | 0 | 11.2 | 3.42 |
| Danks,John | CWS | 29 | 28 | 28 | 178 | 180 | 24 | 50 | 131 | 5 | 9 | 11 | .450 | 0 | 11.9 | 3.94 |
| Darvish,Yu | Tex | 27 | 33 | 33 | 222 | 167 | 22 | 91 | 277 | 10 | 15 | 10 | .600 | 0 | 10.9 | 3.16 |
| Davis,Wade | KC | 28 | 31 | 17 | 114 | 116 | 13 | 47 | 90 | 4 | 5 | 8 | .385 | 0 | 13.2 | 4.34 |
| De Fratus,Justin | Phi | 26 | 63 | 0 | 56 | 50 | 4 | 24 | 58 | 4 | 3 | 3 | .500 | 0 | 12.5 | 3.54 |
| de la Rosa,Dane | LAA | 31 | 74 | 0 | 69 | 59 | 5 | 33 | 72 | 2 | 4 | 3 | .571 | 0 | 12.3 | 3.39 |
| de la Rosa,Jorge | Col | 33 | 26 | 26 | 146 | 146 | 15 | 54 | 121 | 5 | 8 | 8 | .500 | 0 | 12.6 | 4.01 |
| de la Rosa,Rubby | Bos | 25 | 27 | 15 | 118 | 106 | 11 | 69 | 110 | 7 | 6 | 7 | .462 | 0 | 13.9 | 4.27 |
| Deduno,Samuel | Min | 30 | 20 | 20 | 121 | 109 | 8 | 60 | 97 | 9 | 6 | 7 | .462 | 0 | 13.2 | 3.87 |
| Delabar,Steve | Tor | 30 | 60 | 0 | 63 | 50 | 6 | 32 | 81 | 4 | 4 | 3 | .571 | 0 | 12.3 | 3.43 |
| Delgado,Randall | Ari | 24 | 25 | 25 | 152 | 150 | 21 | 55 | 127 | 5 | 7 | 10 | .412 | 0 | 12.4 | 4.20 |
| Dempster,Ryan | Bos | 37 | 29 | 29 | 168 | 161 | 20 | 68 | 152 | 5 | 9 | 10 | .474 | 0 | 12.5 | 4.02 |
| Detwiler,Ross | Was | 28 | 25 | 25 | 150 | 162 | 12 | 41 | 98 | 5 | 8 | 8 | .500 | 0 | 12.5 | 3.96 |
| DeVries,Cole | Min | 29 | 8 | 4 | 30 | 36 | 5 | 8 | 21 | 1 | 1 | 2 | .333 | 0 | 13.5 | 5.10 |
| Diamond,Scott | Min | 27 | 25 | 25 | 148 | 175 | 15 | 36 | 88 | 2 | 6 | 10 | .375 | 0 | 13 | 4.50 |
| Dickey,R.A. | Tor | 39 | 32 | 32 | 219 | 211 | 25 | 62 | 159 | 9 | 12 | 12 | .500 | 0 | 11.6 | 3.70 |
| Diekman,Jake | Phi | 27 | 55 | 0 | 52 | 45 | 2 | 33 | 63 | 3 | 3 | 3 | .500 | 0 | 14 | 3.81 |
| Doolittle,Sean | Oak | 27 | 64 | 0 | 66 | 51 | 4 | 14 | 72 | 2 | 6 | 2 | .750 | 0 | 9.1 | 1.91 |
| Doubront,Felix | Bos | 26 | 29 | 29 | 160 | 161 | 18 | 70 | 145 | 6 | 8 | 10 | .444 | 0 | 13.3 | 4.39 |
| Downs,Scott | Atl | 38 | 68 | 0 | 41 | 36 | 2 | 16 | 32 | 1 | 3 | 2 | .600 | 0 | 11.6 | 3.07 |
| Drabek,Kyle | Tor | 26 | 25 | 25 | 145 | 150 | 18 | 74 | 102 | 3 | 6 | 10 | .375 | 0 | 14.1 | 4.84 |
| Duensing,Brian | Min | 31 | 70 | 0 | 62 | 70 | 6 | 19 | 41 | 1 | 3 | 4 | .429 | 0 | 13.1 | 4.50 |
| Duffy,Danny | KC | 25 | 28 | 28 | 160 | 157 | 17 | 81 | 162 | 8 | 7 | 11 | .389 | 0 | 13.8 | 4.50 |
| Duke,Zach | Cin | 31 | 33 | 0 | 32 | 38 | 4 | 9 | 17 | 1 | 1 | 2 | .333 | 0 | 13.5 | 4.78 |
| Dunn,Mike | Mia | 29 | 70 | 0 | 66 | 57 | 5 | 31 | 76 | 1 | 4 | 4 | .500 | 0 | 12.1 | 3.41 |
| Dunning,Jake | SF | 25 | 54 | 0 | 56 | 59 | 3 | 20 | 43 | 5 | 3 | 4 | .429 | 0 | 13.5 | 4.18 |
| Eovaldi,Nathan | Mia | 24 | 30 | 30 | 190 | 180 | 11 | 75 | 145 | 5 | 10 | 11 | .476 | 0 | 12.3 | 3.60 |
| Erlin,Robbie | SD | 23 | 26 | 26 | 141 | 153 | 17 | 42 | 131 | 3 | 7 | 9 | .438 | 0 | 12.6 | 4.28 |
| Escalona,Edgmer | Col | 27 | 25 | 0 | 30 | 28 | 4 | 10 | 26 | 1 | 2 | 2 | .500 | 0 | 11.7 | 3.90 |
| Estrada,Marco | Mil | 30 | 24 | 24 | 146 | 138 | 17 | 35 | 131 | 2 | 9 | 7 | .563 | 0 | 10.8 | 3.45 |
| Familia,Jeurys | NYM | 24 | 62 | 0 | 60 | 61 | 5 | 34 | 56 | 3 | 3 | 4 | .429 | 0 | 14.7 | 4.65 |
| Farnsworth,Kyle | Pit | 38 | 62 | 0 | 58 | 54 | 6 | 19 | 53 | 2 | 3 | 3 | .500 | 8 | 11.6 | 3.57 |
| Farquhar,Danny | Sea | 27 | 64 | 0 | 62 | 53 | 4 | 21 | 68 | 4 | 4 | 3 | .571 | 35 | 11.3 | 3.05 |
| Feldman,Scott | Bal | 31 | 28 | 25 | 162 | 166 | 18 | 48 | 104 | 7 | 8 | 10 | .444 | 0 | 12.3 | 3.94 |
| Feliciano,Pedro | NYM | 37 | 65 | 0 | 58 | 52 | 4 | 19 | 53 | 4 | 4 | 3 | .571 | 0 | 11.6 | 3.10 |
| Feliz,Neftali | Tex | 26 | 65 | 0 | 63 | 47 | 4 | 30 | 62 | 3 | 4 | 3 | .571 | 8 | 11.4 | 2.86 |
| Fernandez,Jose | Mia | 21 | 32 | 32 | 212 | 183 | 12 | 71 | 236 | 6 | 17 | 6 | .739 | 0 | 11 | 2.55 |
| Fields,Josh | Hou | 28 | 50 | 0 | 50 | 41 | 5 | 21 | 54 | 2 | 3 | 3 | .500 | 29 | 11.5 | 3.24 |
| Fien,Casey | Min | 30 | 69 | 0 | 57 | 53 | 8 | 14 | 55 | 1 | 3 | 3 | .500 | 0 | 10.7 | 3.47 |
| Fiers,Mike | Mil | 29 | 24 | 24 | 145 | 128 | 17 | 48 | 140 | 4 | 9 | 7 | .563 | 0 | 11.2 | 3.54 |
| Fife,Stephen | LAD | 27 | 12 | 8 | 48 | 52 | 4 | 18 | 33 | 3 | 2 | 3 | .400 | 0 | 13.7 | 4.50 |
| Figaro,Alfredo | Mil | 29 | 63 | 0 | 60 | 64 | 8 | 17 | 47 | 1 | 3 | 4 | .429 | 0 | 12.3 | 4.35 |

# 2014 Pitcher Projections

| PLAYER | | | HOW MUCH | | | WHAT HE WILL GIVE UP | | | | | THE RESULTS | | | | | |
|---|---|---|---|---|---|---|---|---|---|---|---|---|---|---|---|---|
| Pitcher | Team | Age | G | GS | IP | H | HR | BB | SO | HB | W | L | Pct | Sv | BR/9 | ERA |
| Fister,Doug | Det | 30 | 32 | 32 | 215 | 226 | 17 | 45 | 152 | 12 | 13 | 11 | .542 | 0 | 11.8 | 3.73 |
| Floyd,Gavin | CWS | 31 | 10 | 10 | 58 | 58 | 7 | 21 | 46 | 3 | 3 | 4 | .429 | 0 | 12.7 | 4.19 |
| Flynn,Brian | Mia | 24 | 25 | 25 | 152 | 156 | 14 | 52 | 131 | 6 | 7 | 10 | .412 | 0 | 12.7 | 4.03 |
| Francis,Jeff | Col | 33 | 27 | 7 | 59 | 70 | 7 | 15 | 40 | 2 | 3 | 4 | .429 | 0 | 13.3 | 4.73 |
| Francisco,Frank | NYM | 34 | 55 | 0 | 52 | 47 | 5 | 23 | 57 | 1 | 3 | 3 | .500 | 5 | 12.3 | 3.81 |
| Frasor,Jason | Tex | 36 | 60 | 0 | 50 | 44 | 5 | 22 | 51 | 2 | 3 | 3 | .500 | 0 | 12.2 | 3.60 |
| Frieri,Ernesto | LAA | 28 | 64 | 0 | 70 | 53 | 8 | 32 | 85 | 5 | 4 | 4 | .500 | 43 | 11.6 | 3.21 |
| Furbush,Charlie | Sea | 28 | 69 | 0 | 66 | 59 | 9 | 26 | 67 | 3 | 3 | 4 | .429 | 0 | 12 | 3.82 |
| Gallardo,Yovani | Mil | 28 | 31 | 31 | 182 | 169 | 20 | 67 | 178 | 2 | 11 | 9 | .550 | 0 | 11.8 | 3.66 |
| Garcia,Freddy | Atl | 37 | 17 | 11 | 81 | 85 | 13 | 21 | 54 | 1 | 4 | 5 | .444 | 0 | 11.9 | 4.22 |
| Garcia,Jaime | StL | 27 | 26 | 26 | 154 | 157 | 13 | 39 | 128 | 2 | 10 | 8 | .556 | 0 | 11.6 | 3.62 |
| Garland,Jon | Col | 34 | 6 | 6 | 34 | 37 | 4 | 12 | 18 | 1 | 2 | 2 | .500 | 0 | 13.2 | 4.50 |
| Garza,Matt | Tex | 30 | 31 | 31 | 200 | 188 | 22 | 57 | 173 | 7 | 12 | 11 | .522 | 0 | 11.3 | 3.60 |
| Gaudin,Chad | SF | 31 | 40 | 0 | 66 | 67 | 6 | 27 | 55 | 3 | 3 | 4 | .429 | 0 | 13.2 | 4.23 |
| Gee,Dillon | NYM | 28 | 31 | 31 | 192 | 193 | 23 | 50 | 149 | 11 | 10 | 11 | .476 | 0 | 11.9 | 3.89 |
| Germen,Gonzalez | NYM | 26 | 66 | 0 | 66 | 68 | 6 | 21 | 58 | 2 | 4 | 4 | .500 | 0 | 12.4 | 3.95 |
| Gibson,Kyle | Min | 26 | 28 | 28 | 182 | 198 | 18 | 64 | 146 | 5 | 8 | 12 | .400 | 0 | 13.2 | 4.40 |
| Gomez,Jeanmar | Pit | 26 | 38 | 7 | 85 | 88 | 9 | 30 | 58 | 3 | 4 | 5 | .444 | 0 | 12.8 | 4.13 |
| Gonzalez,Gio | Was | 28 | 31 | 31 | 191 | 164 | 16 | 75 | 190 | 5 | 13 | 8 | .619 | 0 | 11.5 | 3.39 |
| Gonzalez,Michael | Mil | 36 | 67 | 0 | 42 | 38 | 5 | 20 | 48 | 2 | 2 | 2 | .500 | 0 | 12.9 | 4.07 |
| Gonzalez,Miguel | Bal | 30 | 28 | 28 | 169 | 157 | 21 | 53 | 127 | 7 | 9 | 9 | .500 | 0 | 11.6 | 3.67 |
| Gorzelanny,Tom | Mil | 31 | 55 | 0 | 55 | 54 | 6 | 20 | 46 | 2 | 3 | 3 | .500 | 0 | 12.4 | 3.93 |
| Gray,Sonny | Oak | 24 | 28 | 28 | 177 | 173 | 9 | 63 | 156 | 2 | 10 | 9 | .526 | 0 | 12.1 | 3.56 |
| Gregerson,Luke | SD | 30 | 73 | 0 | 68 | 58 | 5 | 19 | 67 | 3 | 5 | 2 | .714 | 5 | 10.6 | 2.65 |
| Gregg,Kevin | ChC | 36 | 60 | 0 | 62 | 57 | 7 | 33 | 57 | 2 | 3 | 4 | .429 | 35 | 13.4 | 4.21 |
| Greinke,Zack | LAD | 30 | 31 | 31 | 214 | 200 | 18 | 55 | 200 | 5 | 15 | 9 | .625 | 0 | 10.9 | 3.32 |
| Griffin,A.J. | Oak | 26 | 30 | 30 | 189 | 167 | 27 | 47 | 158 | 5 | 12 | 9 | .571 | 0 | 10.4 | 3.43 |
| Grilli,Jason | Pit | 37 | 59 | 0 | 57 | 49 | 4 | 18 | 67 | 2 | 4 | 3 | .571 | 43 | 10.9 | 3.00 |
| Grimm,Justin | ChC | 25 | 20 | 20 | 118 | 125 | 10 | 39 | 94 | 3 | 6 | 8 | .429 | 0 | 12.7 | 4.04 |
| Guerrier,Matt | ChC | 35 | 45 | 0 | 39 | 35 | 4 | 16 | 27 | 1 | 2 | 2 | .500 | 0 | 12 | 3.69 |
| Guthrie,Jeremy | KC | 35 | 32 | 32 | 205 | 216 | 29 | 58 | 118 | 10 | 9 | 14 | .391 | 0 | 12.5 | 4.30 |
| Gutierrez,J.C. | LAA | 30 | 60 | 0 | 61 | 66 | 8 | 22 | 49 | 2 | 3 | 4 | .429 | 0 | 13.3 | 4.57 |
| Halladay,Roy | Phi | 37 | 27 | 27 | 167 | 159 | 15 | 56 | 138 | 6 | 9 | 9 | .500 | 0 | 11.9 | 3.66 |
| Hamels,Cole | Phi | 30 | 32 | 32 | 218 | 195 | 23 | 50 | 204 | 6 | 14 | 10 | .583 | 0 | 10.4 | 3.22 |
| Hammel,Jason | Bal | 31 | 25 | 25 | 150 | 159 | 17 | 53 | 111 | 6 | 7 | 10 | .412 | 5 | 13.1 | 4.38 |
| Hand,Brad | Mia | 24 | 36 | 12 | 94 | 85 | 12 | 54 | 78 | 1 | 4 | 6 | .400 | 0 | 13.4 | 4.31 |
| Hand,Donovan | Mil | 28 | 61 | 0 | 58 | 67 | 7 | 17 | 36 | 2 | 3 | 4 | .429 | 0 | 13.3 | 4.66 |
| Hanrahan,Joel | Bos | 32 | 45 | 0 | 43 | 38 | 5 | 24 | 44 | 1 | 2 | 2 | .500 | 3 | 13.2 | 3.98 |
| Hanson,Tommy | LAA | 27 | 13 | 13 | 75 | 70 | 9 | 29 | 71 | 3 | 4 | 4 | .500 | 0 | 12.2 | 3.96 |
| Happ,J.A. | Tor | 31 | 23 | 23 | 133 | 132 | 16 | 63 | 117 | 2 | 6 | 9 | .400 | 0 | 13.3 | 4.40 |
| Harang,Aaron | NYM | 36 | 26 | 26 | 143 | 149 | 19 | 50 | 114 | 4 | 7 | 9 | .438 | 0 | 12.8 | 4.34 |
| Haren,Dan | Was | 33 | 30 | 30 | 182 | 179 | 23 | 34 | 157 | 4 | 12 | 9 | .571 | 0 | 10.7 | 3.56 |
| Harrell,Lucas | Hou | 29 | 35 | 14 | 127 | 135 | 11 | 64 | 82 | 3 | 5 | 9 | .357 | 0 | 14.3 | 4.68 |
| Harris,Will | Ari | 29 | 70 | 0 | 62 | 55 | 5 | 20 | 71 | 2 | 4 | 3 | .571 | 0 | 11.2 | 3.05 |
| Harrison,Matt | Tex | 28 | 27 | 27 | 163 | 170 | 16 | 52 | 104 | 1 | 8 | 10 | .444 | 0 | 12.3 | 3.98 |
| Hawkins,LaTroy | NYM | 41 | 71 | 0 | 71 | 72 | 6 | 13 | 47 | 1 | 5 | 3 | .625 | 2 | 10.9 | 3.17 |
| Hellickson,Jeremy | TB | 27 | 30 | 28 | 148 | 135 | 18 | 46 | 118 | 5 | 8 | 8 | .500 | 0 | 11.3 | 3.59 |
| Hellweg,John | Mil | 25 | 15 | 15 | 85 | 84 | 6 | 60 | 58 | 11 | 3 | 6 | .333 | 0 | 16.4 | 5.19 |
| Henderson,Jim | Mil | 31 | 68 | 0 | 69 | 57 | 8 | 30 | 76 | 3 | 4 | 3 | .571 | 38 | 11.7 | 3.39 |
| Hendriks,Liam | Min | 25 | 42 | 14 | 103 | 115 | 11 | 25 | 71 | 3 | 5 | 7 | .417 | 0 | 12.5 | 4.19 |
| Hernandez,David | Ari | 29 | 70 | 0 | 67 | 56 | 8 | 26 | 72 | 3 | 4 | 3 | .571 | 2 | 11.4 | 3.36 |
| Hernandez,Felix | Sea | 28 | 33 | 33 | 222 | 204 | 16 | 53 | 209 | 7 | 15 | 10 | .600 | 0 | 10.7 | 3.20 |
| Hernandez,Pedro | Min | 25 | 14 | 13 | 57 | 69 | 8 | 18 | 36 | 0 | 2 | 4 | .333 | 0 | 13.7 | 5.05 |
| Hernandez,Roberto | TB | 33 | 30 | 25 | 154 | 164 | 18 | 40 | 96 | 10 | 7 | 10 | .412 | 5 | 12.5 | 4.21 |
| Herrera,Kelvin | KC | 24 | 62 | 0 | 64 | 51 | 6 | 20 | 70 | 2 | 4 | 3 | .571 | 0 | 10.3 | 2.67 |
| Hill,Rich | Cle | 34 | 59 | 0 | 35 | 30 | 3 | 23 | 36 | 3 | 2 | 2 | .500 | 0 | 14.4 | 4.37 |
| Hochevar,Luke | KC | 30 | 63 | 0 | 79 | 79 | 10 | 23 | 60 | 4 | 4 | 5 | .444 | 0 | 12.1 | 3.99 |
| Holland,Derek | Tex | 27 | 32 | 32 | 206 | 202 | 27 | 62 | 174 | 5 | 11 | 12 | .478 | 0 | 11.8 | 3.84 |
| Holland,Greg | KC | 28 | 71 | 0 | 72 | 55 | 4 | 25 | 91 | 0 | 4 | 4 | .500 | 43 | 10 | 2.25 |
| Hoover,J.J. | Cin | 26 | 71 | 0 | 65 | 45 | 4 | 25 | 73 | 2 | 5 | 2 | .714 | 0 | 10 | 2.22 |
| Howell,J.P. | LAD | 31 | 67 | 0 | 59 | 50 | 6 | 24 | 56 | 3 | 4 | 3 | .571 | 0 | 11.7 | 3.36 |
| Hudson,Daniel | Ari | 27 | 13 | 3 | 30 | 29 | 3 | 7 | 26 | 1 | 2 | 2 | .500 | 0 | 11.1 | 3.30 |
| Hudson,Tim | Atl | 38 | 26 | 26 | 171 | 158 | 12 | 47 | 110 | 7 | 11 | 8 | .579 | 0 | 11.2 | 3.32 |
| Huff,David | NYY | 29 | 55 | 0 | 56 | 63 | 8 | 15 | 39 | 1 | 2 | 4 | .333 | 0 | 12.7 | 4.66 |
| Hughes,Jared | Pit | 28 | 56 | 0 | 60 | 62 | 4 | 23 | 44 | 5 | 3 | 4 | .429 | 0 | 13.5 | 4.20 |
| Hughes,Phil | NYY | 28 | 29 | 29 | 170 | 174 | 25 | 47 | 146 | 5 | 8 | 11 | .421 | 0 | 12 | 4.13 |
| Humber,Philip | Hou | 31 | 20 | 3 | 56 | 62 | 9 | 21 | 41 | 3 | 2 | 4 | .333 | 0 | 13.8 | 5.14 |
| Hunter,Tommy | Bal | 27 | 72 | 0 | 89 | 96 | 14 | 16 | 54 | 3 | 4 | 6 | .400 | 0 | 11.6 | 4.15 |
| Iwakuma,Hisashi | Sea | 33 | 32 | 32 | 214 | 193 | 26 | 48 | 176 | 3 | 14 | 10 | .583 | 0 | 10.3 | 3.28 |
| Jackson,Edwin | ChC | 30 | 31 | 31 | 190 | 199 | 20 | 62 | 148 | 4 | 9 | 12 | .429 | 0 | 12.6 | 4.07 |

# 2014 Pitcher Projections

| PLAYER | | | HOW MUCH | | | WHAT HE WILL GIVE UP | | | | | THE RESULTS | | | | | |
|---|---|---|---|---|---|---|---|---|---|---|---|---|---|---|---|---|
| Pitcher | Team | Age | G | GS | IP | H | HR | BB | SO | HB | W | L | Pct | Sv | BR/9 | ERA |
| Jansen,Kenley | LAD | 26 | 68 | 0 | 72 | 41 | 5 | 20 | 113 | 3 | 6 | 2 | .750 | 40 | 8 | 1.50 |
| Janssen,Casey | Tor | 32 | 55 | 0 | 54 | 49 | 4 | 12 | 46 | 2 | 4 | 2 | .667 | 35 | 10.5 | 2.83 |
| Jenkins,Chad | Tor | 26 | 30 | 3 | 49 | 58 | 7 | 12 | 27 | 1 | 2 | 3 | .400 | 0 | 13 | 4.96 |
| Jennings,Dan | Mia | 27 | 61 | 0 | 59 | 57 | 3 | 25 | 52 | 1 | 3 | 3 | .500 | 0 | 12.7 | 3.51 |
| Jepsen,Kevin | LAA | 29 | 47 | 0 | 40 | 40 | 3 | 15 | 38 | 1 | 2 | 2 | .500 | 0 | 12.6 | 3.83 |
| Jimenez,Cesar | Phi | 29 | 57 | 0 | 54 | 55 | 3 | 25 | 48 | 1 | 3 | 3 | .500 | 0 | 13.5 | 4.17 |
| Jimenez,Ubaldo | Cle | 30 | 31 | 31 | 185 | 173 | 16 | 86 | 171 | 7 | 9 | 11 | .450 | 0 | 12.9 | 3.94 |
| Johnson,Jim | Bal | 31 | 72 | 0 | 69 | 68 | 5 | 17 | 47 | 4 | 4 | 4 | .500 | 43 | 11.6 | 3.39 |
| Johnson,Josh | Tor | 30 | 20 | 20 | 131 | 126 | 10 | 47 | 119 | 4 | 7 | 7 | .500 | 0 | 12.2 | 3.71 |
| Jones,Nate | CWS | 28 | 71 | 0 | 76 | 71 | 5 | 29 | 78 | 1 | 4 | 4 | .500 | 0 | 12 | 3.32 |
| Kazmir,Scott | Cle | 30 | 29 | 29 | 158 | 158 | 19 | 48 | 148 | 8 | 8 | 10 | .444 | 0 | 12.2 | 3.99 |
| Kelley,Shawn | NYY | 30 | 57 | 0 | 54 | 46 | 6 | 20 | 58 | 1 | 3 | 3 | .500 | 0 | 11.2 | 3.33 |
| Kelly,Casey | SD | 24 | 20 | 20 | 121 | 136 | 11 | 33 | 100 | 6 | 6 | 7 | .462 | 0 | 13 | 4.24 |
| Kelly,Joe | StL | 26 | 35 | 14 | 118 | 124 | 9 | 41 | 81 | 6 | 6 | 7 | .462 | 0 | 13 | 4.12 |
| Kendrick,Kyle | Phi | 29 | 27 | 27 | 172 | 186 | 20 | 47 | 94 | 8 | 8 | 11 | .421 | 0 | 12.6 | 4.24 |
| Kennedy,Ian | SD | 29 | 30 | 30 | 177 | 171 | 22 | 60 | 158 | 10 | 10 | 10 | .500 | 0 | 12.3 | 3.97 |
| Kershaw,Clayton | LAD | 26 | 33 | 33 | 230 | 172 | 14 | 55 | 234 | 4 | 20 | 5 | .800 | 0 | 9 | 2.50 |
| Keuchel,Dallas | Hou | 26 | 29 | 22 | 153 | 169 | 16 | 49 | 96 | 3 | 6 | 11 | .353 | 0 | 13 | 4.41 |
| Kickham,Mike | SF | 25 | 42 | 0 | 40 | 40 | 4 | 20 | 34 | 0 | 2 | 3 | .400 | 0 | 13.5 | 4.28 |
| Kimbrel,Craig | Atl | 26 | 72 | 0 | 74 | 41 | 4 | 22 | 120 | 3 | 6 | 2 | .750 | 50 | 8 | 1.34 |
| Kintzler,Brandon | Mil | 29 | 75 | 0 | 82 | 77 | 4 | 21 | 65 | 2 | 6 | 3 | .667 | 0 | 11 | 2.96 |
| Kluber,Corey | Cle | 28 | 27 | 27 | 163 | 175 | 18 | 49 | 151 | 8 | 7 | 11 | .389 | 0 | 12.8 | 4.25 |
| Koehler,Tom | Mia | 28 | 27 | 27 | 164 | 162 | 19 | 69 | 127 | 6 | 7 | 11 | .389 | 0 | 13 | 4.23 |
| Kohn,Michael | LAA | 28 | 68 | 0 | 56 | 48 | 7 | 27 | 61 | 3 | 3 | 3 | .500 | 0 | 12.5 | 3.86 |
| Kontos,George | SF | 29 | 66 | 0 | 64 | 60 | 8 | 17 | 59 | 1 | 4 | 3 | .571 | 0 | 11 | 3.38 |
| Kuroda,Hiroki | NYY | 39 | 32 | 32 | 201 | 195 | 22 | 45 | 145 | 5 | 12 | 11 | .522 | 0 | 11 | 3.49 |
| Lackey,John | Bos | 35 | 29 | 29 | 199 | 207 | 23 | 46 | 155 | 12 | 11 | 11 | .500 | 0 | 12 | 3.93 |
| Lannan,John | Phi | 29 | 16 | 16 | 93 | 104 | 9 | 35 | 50 | 4 | 4 | 6 | .400 | 0 | 13.8 | 4.65 |
| Latos,Mat | Cin | 26 | 32 | 32 | 213 | 185 | 19 | 61 | 196 | 5 | 15 | 9 | .625 | 0 | 10.6 | 3.17 |
| League,Brandon | LAD | 31 | 66 | 0 | 64 | 64 | 5 | 21 | 47 | 3 | 4 | 3 | .571 | 0 | 12.4 | 3.66 |
| Leake,Mike | Cin | 26 | 30 | 30 | 185 | 192 | 25 | 45 | 122 | 5 | 10 | 11 | .476 | 0 | 11.8 | 3.94 |
| LeBlanc,Wade | Hou | 29 | 20 | 8 | 63 | 66 | 8 | 19 | 49 | 1 | 3 | 4 | .429 | 0 | 12.3 | 4.14 |
| LeCure,Sam | Cin | 30 | 62 | 0 | 60 | 57 | 6 | 23 | 55 | 3 | 3 | 3 | .500 | 0 | 12.4 | 3.75 |
| Lee,Cliff | Phi | 35 | 32 | 32 | 228 | 215 | 21 | 33 | 205 | 4 | 16 | 10 | .615 | 0 | 9.9 | 3.12 |
| Lester,Jon | Bos | 30 | 32 | 32 | 218 | 208 | 21 | 71 | 193 | 8 | 14 | 9 | .609 | 0 | 11.8 | 3.67 |
| Lewis,Colby | Tex | 34 | 22 | 22 | 138 | 133 | 21 | 32 | 119 | 5 | 8 | 8 | .500 | 0 | 11.1 | 3.72 |
| Lilly,Ted | LAD | 38 | 16 | 12 | 68 | 60 | 10 | 23 | 56 | 2 | 4 | 3 | .571 | 0 | 11.2 | 3.71 |
| Lincecum,Tim | SF | 30 | 31 | 31 | 194 | 170 | 17 | 80 | 203 | 5 | 12 | 10 | .545 | 0 | 11.8 | 3.53 |
| Lincoln,Brad | Tor | 29 | 54 | 0 | 52 | 54 | 6 | 20 | 42 | 3 | 2 | 3 | .400 | 0 | 13.3 | 4.33 |
| Lindstrom,Matt | CWS | 34 | 71 | 0 | 60 | 62 | 3 | 21 | 48 | 3 | 3 | 4 | .429 | 0 | 12.9 | 3.90 |
| Liriano,Francisco | Pit | 30 | 29 | 29 | 178 | 163 | 16 | 78 | 175 | 6 | 10 | 10 | .500 | 0 | 12.5 | 3.79 |
| Locke,Jeff | Pit | 26 | 30 | 30 | 165 | 159 | 14 | 74 | 137 | 8 | 8 | 10 | .444 | 0 | 13.1 | 4.04 |
| Logan,Boone | NYY | 29 | 63 | 0 | 41 | 39 | 5 | 16 | 44 | 2 | 2 | 3 | .400 | 0 | 12.5 | 4.17 |
| Lohse,Kyle | Mil | 35 | 30 | 30 | 196 | 197 | 21 | 36 | 124 | 4 | 12 | 9 | .571 | 0 | 10.9 | 3.49 |
| Lopez,Javier | SF | 36 | 68 | 0 | 41 | 38 | 1 | 14 | 30 | 1 | 3 | 2 | .600 | 0 | 11.6 | 3.07 |
| Lopez,Wilton | Col | 30 | 68 | 0 | 72 | 80 | 6 | 15 | 49 | 2 | 4 | 4 | .500 | 0 | 12.1 | 3.88 |
| Loup,Aaron | Tor | 26 | 60 | 0 | 59 | 59 | 4 | 12 | 46 | 5 | 4 | 3 | .571 | 0 | 11.6 | 3.36 |
| Luebke,Cory | SD | 29 | 12 | 12 | 69 | 60 | 6 | 20 | 62 | 1 | 5 | 3 | .625 | 0 | 10.6 | 3.13 |
| Luetge,Lucas | Sea | 27 | 42 | 0 | 44 | 44 | 3 | 21 | 43 | 1 | 2 | 3 | .400 | 0 | 13.5 | 4.09 |
| Lyles,Jordan | Hou | 23 | 25 | 25 | 141 | 161 | 16 | 44 | 101 | 9 | 5 | 11 | .313 | 0 | 13.7 | 4.79 |
| Lynn,Lance | StL | 27 | 32 | 32 | 201 | 193 | 16 | 75 | 190 | 10 | 12 | 10 | .545 | 0 | 12.4 | 3.76 |
| Lyons,Tyler | StL | 26 | 61 | 0 | 60 | 58 | 6 | 15 | 53 | 2 | 4 | 3 | .571 | 0 | 11.2 | 3.45 |
| Machi,Jean | SF | 32 | 54 | 0 | 55 | 54 | 5 | 13 | 45 | 2 | 3 | 3 | .500 | 0 | 11.3 | 3.27 |
| Maholm,Paul | Atl | 32 | 21 | 21 | 128 | 135 | 12 | 38 | 82 | 7 | 6 | 8 | .429 | 0 | 12.7 | 4.08 |
| Maness,Seth | StL | 25 | 75 | 0 | 70 | 74 | 7 | 10 | 44 | 3 | 4 | 3 | .571 | 0 | 11.2 | 3.47 |
| Manship,Jeff | Col | 29 | 12 | 2 | 31 | 36 | 3 | 11 | 21 | 1 | 1 | 2 | .333 | 0 | 13.9 | 4.94 |
| Marcum,Shaun | NYM | 32 | 22 | 22 | 130 | 122 | 16 | 38 | 106 | 3 | 8 | 7 | .533 | 0 | 11.3 | 3.60 |
| Marmol,Carlos | LAD | 31 | 53 | 0 | 52 | 36 | 4 | 41 | 67 | 5 | 3 | 3 | .500 | 0 | 14.2 | 3.81 |
| Marshall,Sean | Cin | 31 | 68 | 0 | 60 | 55 | 4 | 14 | 56 | 2 | 4 | 2 | .667 | 0 | 10.6 | 2.85 |
| Martin,Ethan | Phi | 25 | 27 | 27 | 157 | 139 | 15 | 98 | 152 | 6 | 7 | 10 | .412 | 0 | 13.9 | 4.30 |
| Masterson,Justin | Cle | 29 | 30 | 30 | 198 | 190 | 14 | 78 | 165 | 13 | 10 | 12 | .455 | 0 | 12.8 | 3.82 |
| Matsuzaka,Daisuke | NYM | 33 | 14 | 14 | 77 | 73 | 10 | 33 | 68 | 4 | 4 | 5 | .444 | 0 | 12.9 | 4.21 |
| Mattheus,Ryan | Was | 30 | 47 | 0 | 43 | 43 | 3 | 15 | 29 | 2 | 2 | 2 | .500 | 0 | 12.6 | 3.77 |
| Matusz,Brian | Bal | 27 | 60 | 0 | 43 | 46 | 6 | 16 | 35 | 1 | 2 | 3 | .400 | 0 | 13.2 | 4.60 |
| Maurer,Brandon | Sea | 23 | 40 | 8 | 82 | 93 | 8 | 33 | 69 | 5 | 3 | 6 | .333 | 0 | 14.4 | 4.94 |
| Mazzaro,Vin | Pit | 27 | 57 | 0 | 73 | 78 | 6 | 25 | 54 | 4 | 3 | 5 | .375 | 0 | 13.2 | 4.19 |
| McAllister,Zach | Cle | 26 | 28 | 28 | 165 | 178 | 18 | 55 | 129 | 6 | 7 | 11 | .389 | 0 | 13 | 4.36 |
| McCarthy,Brandon | Ari | 30 | 21 | 21 | 132 | 139 | 13 | 23 | 87 | 4 | 8 | 7 | .533 | 0 | 11.3 | 3.68 |
| McFarland,T.J. | Bal | 25 | 37 | 0 | 67 | 77 | 5 | 24 | 46 | 2 | 3 | 5 | .375 | 0 | 13.8 | 4.57 |
| McGee,Jake | TB | 27 | 69 | 0 | 65 | 54 | 6 | 20 | 73 | 1 | 4 | 3 | .571 | 0 | 10.4 | 2.77 |

# 2014 Pitcher Projections

| PLAYER | | | HOW MUCH | | | WHAT HE WILL GIVE UP | | | | | THE RESULTS | | | | | |
|---|---|---|---|---|---|---|---|---|---|---|---|---|---|---|---|---|
| Pitcher | Team | Age | G | GS | IP | H | HR | BB | SO | HB | W | L | Pct | Sv | BR/9 | ERA |
| Medina,Yoervis | Sea | 25 | 65 | 0 | 73 | 66 | 8 | 43 | 73 | 5 | 3 | 5 | .375 | 0 | 14.1 | 4.44 |
| Medlen,Kris | Atl | 28 | 31 | 31 | 206 | 190 | 16 | 46 | 176 | 6 | 14 | 9 | .609 | 0 | 10.6 | 3.19 |
| Mejia,Jenrry | NYM | 24 | 23 | 23 | 141 | 141 | 10 | 46 | 104 | 4 | 8 | 8 | .500 | 0 | 12.2 | 3.70 |
| Melancon,Mark | Pit | 29 | 69 | 0 | 70 | 63 | 5 | 12 | 67 | 3 | 5 | 3 | .625 | 2 | 10 | 2.57 |
| Mendoza,Luis | KC | 30 | 30 | 10 | 95 | 105 | 8 | 39 | 54 | 6 | 4 | 7 | .364 | 0 | 14.2 | 4.64 |
| Mijares,Jose | SF | 29 | 63 | 0 | 52 | 53 | 4 | 22 | 48 | 3 | 2 | 3 | .400 | 0 | 13.5 | 4.15 |
| Miley,Wade | Ari | 27 | 32 | 32 | 203 | 202 | 18 | 59 | 151 | 3 | 12 | 11 | .522 | 0 | 11.7 | 3.68 |
| Miller,Andrew | Bos | 29 | 55 | 0 | 42 | 42 | 4 | 26 | 49 | 2 | 2 | 3 | .400 | 0 | 15 | 4.50 |
| Miller,Shelby | StL | 23 | 31 | 31 | 172 | 153 | 21 | 59 | 181 | 9 | 11 | 9 | .550 | 0 | 11.6 | 3.66 |
| Milone,Tommy | Oak | 27 | 28 | 28 | 168 | 175 | 19 | 36 | 143 | 3 | 9 | 10 | .474 | 0 | 11.5 | 3.80 |
| Miner,Zach | Phi | 32 | 60 | 0 | 58 | 62 | 6 | 26 | 36 | 2 | 2 | 4 | .333 | 0 | 14 | 4.66 |
| Minor,Mike | Atl | 26 | 30 | 30 | 193 | 177 | 23 | 50 | 177 | 3 | 12 | 9 | .571 | 0 | 10.7 | 3.40 |
| Moore,Matt | TB | 25 | 30 | 30 | 177 | 145 | 16 | 83 | 189 | 6 | 10 | 9 | .526 | 0 | 11.9 | 3.51 |
| Morales,Franklin | Bos | 28 | 30 | 0 | 32 | 29 | 4 | 14 | 28 | 2 | 2 | 2 | .500 | 0 | 12.7 | 3.94 |
| Morris,Bryan | Pit | 27 | 57 | 0 | 62 | 60 | 6 | 22 | 50 | 2 | 3 | 4 | .429 | 0 | 12.2 | 3.77 |
| Morrow,Brandon | Tor | 29 | 26 | 26 | 145 | 130 | 17 | 49 | 144 | 5 | 8 | 8 | .500 | 0 | 11.4 | 3.60 |
| Morton,Charlie | Pit | 30 | 27 | 27 | 168 | 174 | 11 | 57 | 115 | 13 | 8 | 10 | .444 | 0 | 13.1 | 4.02 |
| Moscoso,Guillermo | SF | 30 | 24 | 4 | 56 | 55 | 7 | 25 | 48 | 1 | 3 | 4 | .429 | 0 | 13 | 4.34 |
| Motte,Jason | StL | 32 | 46 | 0 | 42 | 33 | 4 | 10 | 47 | 2 | 3 | 1 | .750 | 2 | 9.6 | 2.36 |
| Mujica,Edward | StL | 30 | 67 | 0 | 67 | 63 | 9 | 8 | 54 | 1 | 5 | 3 | .625 | 34 | 9.7 | 2.96 |
| Myers,Brett | Cle | 33 | 58 | 1 | 55 | 55 | 8 | 15 | 43 | 1 | 3 | 3 | .500 | 0 | 11.6 | 3.93 |
| Nathan,Joe | Tex | 39 | 67 | 0 | 64 | 46 | 5 | 19 | 74 | 2 | 4 | 3 | .571 | 42 | 9.4 | 2.25 |
| Neshek,Pat | Oak | 33 | 55 | 0 | 53 | 47 | 7 | 18 | 48 | 1 | 3 | 3 | .500 | 0 | 11.2 | 3.40 |
| Nicasio,Juan | Col | 27 | 31 | 31 | 159 | 166 | 16 | 59 | 133 | 3 | 8 | 9 | .471 | 0 | 12.9 | 4.19 |
| Niemann,Jeff | TB | 31 | 18 | 18 | 105 | 103 | 12 | 30 | 83 | 5 | 6 | 6 | .500 | 0 | 11.8 | 3.86 |
| Niese,Jon | NYM | 27 | 28 | 28 | 177 | 186 | 17 | 54 | 145 | 5 | 9 | 10 | .474 | 0 | 12.5 | 4.02 |
| Noesi,Hector | Sea | 27 | 35 | 6 | 61 | 69 | 8 | 20 | 46 | 2 | 2 | 4 | .333 | 0 | 13.4 | 4.87 |
| Nolasco,Ricky | LAD | 31 | 32 | 32 | 196 | 207 | 21 | 46 | 157 | 6 | 11 | 11 | .500 | 0 | 11.9 | 3.90 |
| Norris,Bud | Bal | 29 | 30 | 30 | 177 | 179 | 21 | 68 | 165 | 6 | 8 | 12 | .400 | 0 | 12.9 | 4.27 |
| Nova,Ivan | NYY | 27 | 27 | 27 | 180 | 189 | 18 | 57 | 139 | 9 | 8 | 12 | .400 | 0 | 12.8 | 4.20 |
| Oberholtzer,Brett | Hou | 24 | 27 | 27 | 152 | 156 | 17 | 40 | 117 | 3 | 7 | 9 | .438 | 0 | 11.8 | 3.85 |
| ODay,Darren' | Bal | 31 | 62 | 0 | 56 | 46 | 6 | 13 | 51 | 4 | 4 | 2 | .667 | 0 | 10.1 | 2.89 |
| Odorizzi,Jake | TB | 24 | 15 | 15 | 88 | 81 | 11 | 31 | 78 | 1 | 5 | 5 | .500 | 0 | 11.6 | 3.78 |
| OFlaherty,Eric' | Atl | 29 | 45 | 0 | 40 | 35 | 2 | 12 | 32 | 2 | 3 | 2 | .600 | 0 | 11 | 2.70 |
| Ogando,Alexi | Tex | 30 | 61 | 0 | 57 | 48 | 6 | 19 | 45 | 2 | 4 | 3 | .571 | 0 | 10.9 | 3.16 |
| Ohlendorf,Ross | Was | 31 | 15 | 8 | 55 | 60 | 7 | 19 | 41 | 3 | 3 | 4 | .429 | 0 | 13.4 | 4.58 |
| Ondrusek,Logan | Cin | 29 | 56 | 0 | 61 | 56 | 7 | 23 | 46 | 2 | 3 | 3 | .500 | 0 | 12 | 3.69 |
| Ortiz,Joe | Tex | 23 | 49 | 0 | 58 | 57 | 7 | 13 | 47 | 0 | 3 | 3 | .500 | 0 | 10.9 | 3.41 |
| Oswalt,Roy | Col | 36 | 12 | 12 | 68 | 71 | 7 | 17 | 54 | 2 | 4 | 4 | .500 | 0 | 11.9 | 3.84 |
| Otero,Dan | Oak | 29 | 61 | 0 | 59 | 59 | 2 | 7 | 46 | 2 | 4 | 2 | .667 | 0 | 10.4 | 2.75 |
| Ottavino,Adam | Col | 28 | 54 | 0 | 76 | 81 | 8 | 32 | 67 | 4 | 4 | 5 | .444 | 0 | 13.9 | 4.62 |
| Outman,Josh | Col | 29 | 61 | 0 | 48 | 49 | 4 | 22 | 42 | 1 | 2 | 3 | .400 | 0 | 13.5 | 4.31 |
| Papelbon,Jonathan | Phi | 33 | 65 | 0 | 66 | 55 | 6 | 13 | 77 | 3 | 4 | 3 | .571 | 29 | 9.7 | 2.45 |
| Parker,Blake | ChC | 29 | 58 | 0 | 55 | 44 | 6 | 23 | 60 | 2 | 3 | 3 | .500 | 0 | 11.3 | 3.11 |
| Parker,Jarrod | Oak | 25 | 31 | 31 | 192 | 179 | 16 | 64 | 146 | 8 | 11 | 10 | .524 | 0 | 11.8 | 3.56 |
| Parnell,Bobby | NYM | 29 | 45 | 0 | 46 | 46 | 3 | 13 | 40 | 1 | 3 | 2 | .600 | 38 | 11.7 | 3.52 |
| Parra,Manny | Cin | 31 | 64 | 0 | 52 | 54 | 5 | 22 | 50 | 1 | 2 | 3 | .400 | 0 | 13.3 | 4.33 |
| Patton,Troy | Bal | 28 | 55 | 0 | 55 | 57 | 7 | 14 | 38 | 3 | 3 | 3 | .500 | 0 | 12.1 | 4.09 |
| Paxton,James | Sea | 25 | 29 | 29 | 182 | 184 | 13 | 80 | 172 | 3 | 9 | 11 | .450 | 0 | 13.2 | 4.05 |
| Peacock,Brad | Hou | 26 | 28 | 28 | 163 | 150 | 20 | 66 | 161 | 4 | 8 | 10 | .444 | 0 | 12.1 | 3.87 |
| Peavy,Jake | Bos | 33 | 25 | 25 | 163 | 147 | 18 | 39 | 150 | 5 | 11 | 7 | .611 | 0 | 10.5 | 3.31 |
| Pelfrey,Mike | Min | 30 | 29 | 29 | 158 | 179 | 13 | 53 | 94 | 7 | 7 | 11 | .389 | 0 | 13.6 | 4.50 |
| Peralta,Joel | TB | 38 | 78 | 0 | 74 | 58 | 8 | 29 | 72 | 1 | 5 | 3 | .625 | 0 | 10.7 | 2.92 |
| Peralta,Wily | Mil | 25 | 29 | 29 | 172 | 176 | 15 | 78 | 147 | 8 | 8 | 11 | .421 | 0 | 13.7 | 4.34 |
| Perez,Chris | Cle | 28 | 57 | 0 | 58 | 49 | 8 | 21 | 58 | 4 | 3 | 3 | .500 | 21 | 11.5 | 3.41 |
| Perez,Martin | Tex | 23 | 28 | 28 | 184 | 199 | 18 | 64 | 134 | 4 | 8 | 12 | .400 | 0 | 13.1 | 4.35 |
| Perez,Oliver | Sea | 32 | 57 | 0 | 48 | 48 | 7 | 23 | 47 | 2 | 2 | 3 | .400 | 0 | 13.7 | 4.69 |
| Perkins,Glen | Min | 31 | 68 | 0 | 70 | 72 | 8 | 17 | 59 | 3 | 4 | 4 | .500 | 35 | 11.8 | 3.86 |
| Pestano,Vinnie | Cle | 29 | 62 | 0 | 58 | 49 | 5 | 26 | 66 | 3 | 3 | 3 | .500 | 8 | 12.1 | 3.41 |
| Petit,Yusmeiro | SF | 29 | 26 | 26 | 162 | 169 | 22 | 32 | 137 | 1 | 9 | 9 | .500 | 0 | 11.2 | 3.83 |
| Pettibone,Jonathan | Phi | 23 | 28 | 28 | 162 | 174 | 12 | 58 | 110 | 7 | 8 | 10 | .444 | 0 | 13.3 | 4.17 |
| Phelps,David | NYY | 27 | 34 | 13 | 126 | 123 | 13 | 50 | 117 | 5 | 6 | 8 | .429 | 0 | 12.7 | 4.07 |
| Pineda,Michael | Sea | 25 | 27 | 27 | 164 | 142 | 20 | 58 | 159 | 7 | 10 | 8 | .556 | 0 | 11.4 | 3.68 |
| Pomeranz,Drew | Col | 25 | 26 | 26 | 148 | 145 | 15 | 66 | 139 | 5 | 8 | 9 | .471 | 0 | 13.1 | 4.14 |
| Porcello,Rick | Det | 25 | 30 | 30 | 186 | 211 | 19 | 45 | 117 | 6 | 9 | 11 | .450 | 0 | 12.7 | 4.31 |
| Price,David | TB | 28 | 31 | 31 | 218 | 192 | 20 | 44 | 195 | 6 | 15 | 9 | .625 | 0 | 10 | 3.01 |
| Pryor,Stephen | Sea | 24 | 57 | 0 | 54 | 42 | 3 | 24 | 60 | 1 | 4 | 2 | .667 | 0 | 11.2 | 2.67 |
| Purcey,David | CWS | 32 | 33 | 0 | 39 | 38 | 3 | 21 | 35 | 2 | 2 | 3 | .400 | 0 | 14.1 | 4.38 |
| Putkonen,Luke | Det | 28 | 60 | 0 | 60 | 66 | 5 | 23 | 46 | 1 | 3 | 4 | .429 | 0 | 13.5 | 4.50 |
| Putz,J.J. | Ari | 37 | 58 | 0 | 54 | 42 | 4 | 20 | 60 | 1 | 4 | 2 | .667 | 23 | 10.5 | 2.67 |

# 2014 Pitcher Projections

| PLAYER | | | HOW MUCH | | | WHAT HE WILL GIVE UP | | | | | THE RESULTS | | | | | |
|---|---|---|---|---|---|---|---|---|---|---|---|---|---|---|---|---|
| Pitcher | Team | Age | G | GS | IP | H | HR | BB | SO | HB | W | L | Pct | Sv | BR/9 | ERA |
| Qualls,Chad | Mia | 35 | 64 | 0 | 59 | 61 | 6 | 17 | 44 | 1 | 3 | 4 | .429 | 0 | 12.1 | 3.81 |
| Quintana,Jose | CWS | 25 | 32 | 32 | 202 | 199 | 20 | 58 | 150 | 4 | 11 | 12 | .478 | 0 | 11.6 | 3.70 |
| Ramirez,Erasmo | Sea | 24 | 25 | 18 | 111 | 118 | 12 | 33 | 86 | 6 | 5 | 7 | .417 | 0 | 12.7 | 4.22 |
| Ramos,A.J. | Mia | 27 | 68 | 0 | 77 | 55 | 5 | 37 | 89 | 1 | 5 | 3 | .625 | 0 | 10.9 | 2.57 |
| Ramos,Cesar | TB | 30 | 46 | 0 | 70 | 73 | 8 | 23 | 48 | 2 | 3 | 4 | .429 | 0 | 12.6 | 4.11 |
| Rasmus,Cory | LAA | 26 | 32 | 0 | 33 | 28 | 3 | 21 | 35 | 1 | 2 | 2 | .500 | 0 | 13.6 | 4.09 |
| Redmond,Todd | Tor | 29 | 14 | 10 | 63 | 66 | 9 | 18 | 53 | 2 | 3 | 4 | .429 | 0 | 12.3 | 4.29 |
| Reed,Addison | CWS | 25 | 68 | 0 | 74 | 62 | 6 | 23 | 82 | 2 | 5 | 3 | .625 | 46 | 10.6 | 2.92 |
| Rice,Scott | NYM | 32 | 63 | 0 | 44 | 40 | 2 | 20 | 32 | 2 | 3 | 2 | .600 | 0 | 12.7 | 3.48 |
| Richards,Garrett | LAA | 26 | 26 | 26 | 151 | 158 | 13 | 53 | 108 | 6 | 8 | 9 | .471 | 0 | 12.9 | 4.11 |
| Rienzo,Andre | CWS | 26 | 25 | 25 | 142 | 135 | 12 | 66 | 126 | 4 | 7 | 9 | .438 | 0 | 13 | 3.99 |
| Roark,Tanner | Was | 27 | 28 | 28 | 166 | 171 | 14 | 43 | 131 | 6 | 10 | 9 | .526 | 0 | 11.9 | 3.80 |
| Robertson,David | NYY | 29 | 67 | 0 | 66 | 51 | 4 | 20 | 86 | 2 | 4 | 3 | .571 | 36 | 10 | 2.32 |
| Rodney,Fernando | TB | 37 | 70 | 0 | 68 | 55 | 4 | 30 | 67 | 3 | 4 | 3 | .571 | 32 | 11.6 | 2.91 |
| Rodriguez,Francisco | Bal | 32 | 52 | 0 | 52 | 44 | 5 | 19 | 58 | 1 | 3 | 2 | .600 | 2 | 11.1 | 3.12 |
| Rodriguez,Paco | LAD | 23 | 73 | 0 | 54 | 36 | 4 | 20 | 65 | 2 | 5 | 1 | .833 | 0 | 9.7 | 2.17 |
| Rodriguez,Wandy | Pit | 35 | 24 | 24 | 138 | 133 | 16 | 36 | 113 | 4 | 8 | 7 | .533 | 0 | 11.3 | 3.65 |
| Roe,Chaz | Ari | 27 | 35 | 0 | 38 | 41 | 4 | 14 | 28 | 2 | 2 | 3 | .400 | 0 | 13.5 | 4.50 |
| Roenicke,Josh | Min | 31 | 61 | 0 | 60 | 59 | 5 | 32 | 48 | 2 | 3 | 4 | .429 | 0 | 14 | 4.35 |
| Rogers,Esmil | Tor | 28 | 48 | 12 | 121 | 138 | 14 | 42 | 97 | 7 | 5 | 9 | .357 | 0 | 13.9 | 4.91 |
| Romo,Sergio | SF | 31 | 63 | 0 | 62 | 48 | 5 | 12 | 69 | 2 | 4 | 3 | .571 | 41 | 9 | 2.03 |
| Rondon,Bruce | Det | 23 | 62 | 0 | 60 | 48 | 3 | 28 | 70 | 4 | 4 | 3 | .571 | 8 | 12 | 3.00 |
| Rondon,Hector | ChC | 26 | 46 | 0 | 60 | 62 | 8 | 27 | 53 | 3 | 2 | 4 | .333 | 0 | 13.8 | 4.80 |
| Rosario,Sandy | SF | 28 | 62 | 0 | 61 | 61 | 3 | 22 | 51 | 0 | 4 | 3 | .571 | 0 | 12.2 | 3.54 |
| Rosenberg,B.J. | Phi | 28 | 62 | 0 | 60 | 62 | 6 | 27 | 56 | 4 | 3 | 4 | .429 | 0 | 14 | 4.65 |
| Rosenthal,Trevor | StL | 24 | 72 | 0 | 74 | 57 | 5 | 24 | 87 | 4 | 5 | 3 | .625 | 25 | 10.3 | 2.55 |
| Ross,Robbie | Tex | 25 | 57 | 0 | 55 | 52 | 4 | 17 | 47 | 2 | 3 | 3 | .500 | 0 | 11.6 | 3.27 |
| Ross,Tyson | SD | 27 | 28 | 28 | 176 | 177 | 13 | 70 | 145 | 8 | 10 | 10 | .500 | 0 | 13 | 3.99 |
| Rusin,Chris | ChC | 27 | 18 | 18 | 92 | 95 | 9 | 29 | 57 | 4 | 4 | 6 | .400 | 0 | 12.5 | 4.11 |
| Russell,James | ChC | 28 | 66 | 0 | 48 | 51 | 7 | 15 | 34 | 1 | 2 | 3 | .400 | 0 | 12.6 | 4.50 |
| Ryu,Hyun-Jin | LAD | 27 | 29 | 29 | 190 | 180 | 15 | 48 | 152 | 1 | 13 | 8 | .619 | 0 | 10.8 | 3.32 |
| Rzepczynski,Marc | Cle | 28 | 57 | 0 | 46 | 45 | 4 | 18 | 41 | 2 | 2 | 3 | .400 | 0 | 12.7 | 3.91 |
| Sabathia,CC | NYY | 33 | 32 | 32 | 220 | 211 | 21 | 61 | 197 | 7 | 13 | 12 | .520 | 0 | 11.4 | 3.56 |
| Salas,Fernando | StL | 29 | 52 | 0 | 54 | 46 | 6 | 16 | 54 | 2 | 4 | 2 | .667 | 0 | 10.7 | 3.00 |
| Sale,Chris | CWS | 25 | 31 | 31 | 223 | 189 | 23 | 53 | 237 | 10 | 15 | 10 | .600 | 0 | 10.2 | 3.07 |
| Samardzija,Jeff | ChC | 29 | 32 | 32 | 211 | 198 | 24 | 76 | 194 | 7 | 11 | 13 | .458 | 0 | 12 | 3.80 |
| Sanchez,Anibal | Det | 30 | 30 | 30 | 198 | 191 | 16 | 56 | 183 | 5 | 13 | 9 | .591 | 0 | 11.5 | 3.50 |
| Santana,Ervin | KC | 31 | 31 | 31 | 204 | 193 | 29 | 56 | 159 | 9 | 10 | 12 | .455 | 0 | 11.4 | 3.79 |
| Santana,Johan | NYM | 35 | 21 | 21 | 130 | 119 | 15 | 43 | 116 | 1 | 8 | 7 | .533 | 0 | 11.3 | 3.60 |
| Santiago,Hector | CWS | 26 | 29 | 29 | 175 | 156 | 18 | 88 | 165 | 15 | 8 | 11 | .421 | 0 | 13.3 | 4.06 |
| Santos,Sergio | Tor | 30 | 60 | 0 | 57 | 46 | 4 | 16 | 67 | 2 | 4 | 2 | .667 | 2 | 10.1 | 2.53 |
| Saunders,Joe | Sea | 33 | 25 | 25 | 147 | 164 | 19 | 44 | 85 | 3 | 6 | 10 | .375 | 0 | 12.9 | 4.53 |
| Scahill,Rob | Col | 27 | 26 | 0 | 38 | 40 | 3 | 14 | 31 | 2 | 2 | 2 | .500 | 0 | 13.3 | 4.03 |
| Scheppers,Tanner | Tex | 27 | 76 | 0 | 79 | 76 | 7 | 23 | 73 | 7 | 4 | 4 | .500 | 0 | 12.1 | 3.65 |
| Scherzer,Max | Det | 29 | 32 | 32 | 213 | 190 | 23 | 60 | 225 | 7 | 14 | 9 | .609 | 0 | 10.9 | 3.38 |
| Shaw,Bryan | Cle | 26 | 73 | 0 | 82 | 78 | 5 | 30 | 67 | 5 | 5 | 5 | .500 | 0 | 12.4 | 3.62 |
| Shields,James | KC | 32 | 34 | 34 | 234 | 223 | 26 | 66 | 203 | 8 | 13 | 13 | .500 | 0 | 11.4 | 3.65 |
| Simon,Alfredo | Cin | 33 | 64 | 0 | 93 | 95 | 11 | 30 | 68 | 6 | 5 | 6 | .455 | 0 | 12.7 | 4.16 |
| Sipp,Tony | Ari | 30 | 60 | 0 | 51 | 41 | 8 | 25 | 54 | 1 | 3 | 3 | .500 | 0 | 11.8 | 3.71 |
| Skaggs,Tyler | Ari | 22 | 15 | 15 | 92 | 86 | 9 | 33 | 91 | 4 | 5 | 5 | .500 | 0 | 12 | 3.72 |
| Slowey,Kevin | Mia | 30 | 16 | 16 | 97 | 109 | 14 | 20 | 72 | 4 | 4 | 7 | .364 | 0 | 12.3 | 4.36 |
| Smith,Joe | Cle | 30 | 71 | 0 | 68 | 58 | 4 | 25 | 55 | 3 | 5 | 3 | .625 | 0 | 11.4 | 2.91 |
| Smith,Will | KC | 24 | 45 | 0 | 70 | 77 | 8 | 21 | 58 | 2 | 3 | 5 | .375 | 0 | 12.9 | 4.24 |
| Smyly,Drew | Det | 25 | 64 | 0 | 60 | 54 | 5 | 17 | 63 | 1 | 4 | 2 | .667 | 0 | 10.8 | 3.00 |
| Soria,Joakim | Tex | 30 | 63 | 0 | 67 | 54 | 6 | 28 | 73 | 3 | 4 | 3 | .571 | 0 | 11.4 | 3.09 |
| Soriano,Rafael | Was | 34 | 66 | 0 | 67 | 54 | 7 | 20 | 65 | 1 | 4 | 3 | .571 | 46 | 10.1 | 2.69 |
| Stammen,Craig | Was | 30 | 54 | 0 | 78 | 82 | 8 | 27 | 61 | 1 | 4 | 5 | .444 | 0 | 12.7 | 4.15 |
| Stauffer,Tim | SD | 32 | 48 | 0 | 78 | 80 | 7 | 24 | 56 | 3 | 4 | 4 | .500 | 0 | 12.3 | 3.92 |
| Storen,Drew | Was | 26 | 68 | 0 | 63 | 56 | 6 | 18 | 60 | 2 | 4 | 3 | .571 | 3 | 10.9 | 3.00 |
| Straily,Dan | Oak | 25 | 28 | 28 | 161 | 132 | 16 | 55 | 158 | 6 | 11 | 7 | .611 | 0 | 10.8 | 3.24 |
| Strasburg,Stephen | Was | 25 | 31 | 31 | 195 | 151 | 15 | 58 | 222 | 8 | 15 | 6 | .714 | 0 | 10 | 2.86 |
| Street,Huston | SD | 30 | 60 | 0 | 60 | 49 | 8 | 15 | 60 | 1 | 4 | 2 | .667 | 41 | 9.8 | 2.85 |
| Strop,Pedro | ChC | 29 | 67 | 0 | 65 | 56 | 3 | 32 | 68 | 4 | 4 | 4 | .500 | 8 | 12.7 | 3.46 |
| Stults,Eric | SD | 34 | 30 | 30 | 190 | 204 | 18 | 43 | 135 | 3 | 11 | 10 | .524 | 0 | 11.8 | 3.84 |
| Swarzak,Anthony | Min | 28 | 48 | 0 | 95 | 105 | 11 | 25 | 61 | 3 | 4 | 6 | .400 | 0 | 12.6 | 4.26 |
| Tazawa,Junichi | Bos | 28 | 68 | 0 | 67 | 64 | 6 | 15 | 67 | 2 | 5 | 3 | .625 | 0 | 10.9 | 3.09 |
| Teheran,Julio | Atl | 23 | 31 | 31 | 193 | 190 | 21 | 55 | 163 | 13 | 10 | 11 | .476 | 0 | 12 | 3.87 |
| Thatcher,Joe | Ari | 32 | 67 | 0 | 34 | 31 | 2 | 11 | 37 | 2 | 2 | 2 | .500 | 0 | 11.6 | 3.18 |
| Thayer,Dale | SD | 33 | 66 | 0 | 62 | 61 | 5 | 18 | 53 | 2 | 4 | 3 | .571 | 0 | 11.8 | 3.48 |
| Thielbar,Caleb | Min | 27 | 62 | 0 | 61 | 55 | 5 | 19 | 57 | 1 | 4 | 3 | .571 | 0 | 11.1 | 3.10 |

# 2014 Pitcher Projections

| PLAYER | | | HOW MUCH | | | WHAT HE WILL GIVE UP | | | | | THE RESULTS | | | | | |
|---|---|---|---|---|---|---|---|---|---|---|---|---|---|---|---|---|
| Pitcher | Team | Age | G | GS | IP | H | HR | BB | SO | HB | W | L | Pct | Sv | BR/9 | ERA |
| Thornburg,Tyler | Mil | 25 | 25 | 25 | 160 | 153 | 16 | 61 | 149 | 7 | 9 | 9 | .500 | 0 | 12.4 | 3.88 |
| Thornton,Matt | Bos | 37 | 46 | 0 | 35 | 32 | 2 | 11 | 35 | 1 | 2 | 2 | .500 | 0 | 11.3 | 3.09 |
| Tillman,Chris | Bal | 26 | 33 | 33 | 203 | 200 | 28 | 70 | 5 | 5 | 14 | 8 | .636 | 0 | 12.2 | 3.90 |
| Torres,Alex | TB | 26 | 46 | 0 | 66 | 60 | 4 | 38 | 72 | 3 | 3 | 4 | .429 | 0 | 13.8 | 3.95 |
| Torres,Carlos | NYM | 31 | 62 | 0 | 60 | 56 | 6 | 17 | 53 | 2 | 4 | 3 | .571 | 0 | 11.2 | 3.30 |
| Troncoso,Ramon | CWS | 31 | 27 | 0 | 31 | 33 | 3 | 13 | 21 | 1 | 1 | 2 | .333 | 0 | 13.6 | 4.65 |
| Turner,Jacob | Mia | 23 | 30 | 30 | 85 | 84 | 9 | 33 | 58 | 3 | 4 | 6 | .400 | 0 | 12.7 | 4.02 |
| Uehara,Koji | Bos | 39 | 69 | 0 | 75 | 55 | 8 | 9 | 82 | 0 | 6 | 2 | .750 | 23 | 7.7 | 1.80 |
| Vargas,Jason | LAA | 31 | 31 | 31 | 191 | 195 | 25 | 56 | 127 | 4 | 10 | 11 | .476 | 0 | 12 | 4.01 |
| Varvaro,Anthony | Atl | 29 | 57 | 0 | 74 | 62 | 4 | 32 | 68 | 3 | 5 | 3 | .625 | 0 | 11.8 | 3.04 |
| Veal,Donnie | CWS | 29 | 62 | 0 | 37 | 35 | 3 | 20 | 36 | 2 | 2 | 2 | .500 | 0 | 13.9 | 4.38 |
| Venters,Jonny | Atl | 29 | 45 | 0 | 45 | 40 | 2 | 21 | 43 | 3 | 3 | 2 | .600 | 0 | 12.8 | 3.60 |
| Veras,Jose | Det | 33 | 67 | 0 | 59 | 49 | 6 | 26 | 63 | 3 | 4 | 3 | .571 | 5 | 11.9 | 3.36 |
| Verlander,Justin | Det | 31 | 32 | 32 | 221 | 192 | 19 | 67 | 213 | 6 | 16 | 9 | .640 | 0 | 10.8 | 3.22 |
| Villanueva,Carlos | ChC | 30 | 40 | 14 | 125 | 116 | 17 | 41 | 107 | 4 | 6 | 7 | .462 | 0 | 11.6 | 3.74 |
| Vincent,Nick | SD | 27 | 57 | 0 | 59 | 49 | 4 | 18 | 62 | 3 | 4 | 2 | .667 | 0 | 10.7 | 2.75 |
| Vogelsong,Ryan | SF | 36 | 30 | 30 | 182 | 181 | 18 | 62 | 146 | 8 | 9 | 11 | .450 | 0 | 12.4 | 3.91 |
| Volquez,Edinson | LAD | 30 | 25 | 25 | 136 | 127 | 14 | 67 | 127 | 6 | 7 | 8 | .467 | 0 | 13.2 | 4.10 |
| Wagner,Neil | Tor | 30 | 61 | 0 | 63 | 62 | 3 | 24 | 66 | 2 | 4 | 3 | .571 | 0 | 12.6 | 3.57 |
| Wainwright,Adam | StL | 32 | 32 | 32 | 230 | 216 | 16 | 41 | 201 | 6 | 17 | 9 | .654 | 0 | 10.3 | 3.09 |
| Walden,Jordan | Atl | 26 | 55 | 0 | 52 | 47 | 3 | 18 | 57 | 1 | 3 | 2 | .600 | 0 | 11.4 | 3.12 |
| Walker,Taijuan | Sea | 21 | 27 | 27 | 175 | 168 | 19 | 78 | 178 | 12 | 8 | 11 | .421 | 0 | 13.3 | 4.32 |
| Warren,Adam | NYY | 26 | 26 | 15 | 108 | 120 | 11 | 40 | 82 | 4 | 4 | 8 | .333 | 0 | 13.7 | 4.67 |
| Watson,Tony | Pit | 29 | 64 | 0 | 67 | 53 | 6 | 17 | 59 | 3 | 5 | 3 | .625 | 0 | 9.8 | 2.55 |
| Weaver,Jered | LAA | 31 | 31 | 31 | 196 | 169 | 20 | 47 | 163 | 4 | 14 | 7 | .667 | 0 | 10.1 | 3.12 |
| Webb,Ryan | Mia | 28 | 65 | 0 | 89 | 93 | 5 | 30 | 63 | 3 | 4 | 6 | .400 | 0 | 12.7 | 3.84 |
| Westbrook,Jake | StL | 36 | 21 | 21 | 125 | 137 | 10 | 46 | 69 | 5 | 6 | 8 | .429 | 0 | 13.5 | 4.39 |
| Wheeler,Zack | NYM | 24 | 27 | 27 | 174 | 151 | 13 | 74 | 164 | 10 | 11 | 9 | .550 | 0 | 12.2 | 3.52 |
| White,Alex | Col | 25 | 20 | 20 | 112 | 109 | 14 | 51 | 88 | 5 | 5 | 7 | .417 | 0 | 13.3 | 4.18 |
| Wilhelmsen,Tom | Sea | 30 | 62 | 0 | 64 | 60 | 5 | 30 | 57 | 4 | 3 | 4 | .429 | 12 | 13.2 | 4.08 |
| Williams,Jerome | LAA | 32 | 37 | 22 | 162 | 178 | 22 | 48 | 105 | 6 | 8 | 10 | .444 | 0 | 12.9 | 4.56 |
| Wilson,Brian | LAD | 32 | 65 | 0 | 68 | 58 | 3 | 25 | 72 | 2 | 5 | 3 | .625 | 41 | 11.2 | 2.78 |
| Wilson,C.J. | LAA | 33 | 32 | 32 | 215 | 192 | 16 | 88 | 191 | 9 | 13 | 10 | .565 | 0 | 12.1 | 3.56 |
| Wilson,Justin | Pit | 26 | 53 | 0 | 63 | 53 | 5 | 30 | 54 | 3 | 4 | 3 | .571 | 0 | 12.3 | 3.43 |
| Withrow,Chris | LAD | 25 | 62 | 0 | 61 | 56 | 5 | 32 | 62 | 2 | 3 | 3 | .500 | 0 | 13.3 | 3.98 |
| Wolf,Ross | Tex | 31 | 57 | 0 | 72 | 77 | 6 | 22 | 50 | 2 | 4 | 4 | .500 | 0 | 12.6 | 4.00 |
| Wood,Travis | ChC | 27 | 31 | 31 | 197 | 183 | 21 | 66 | 155 | 9 | 10 | 11 | .476 | 0 | 11.8 | 3.70 |
| Wooten,Rob | Mil | 28 | 46 | 0 | 47 | 44 | 4 | 14 | 41 | 3 | 3 | 2 | .600 | 0 | 11.7 | 3.26 |
| Worley,Vance | Min | 26 | 18 | 18 | 105 | 117 | 10 | 35 | 79 | 4 | 5 | 7 | .417 | 0 | 13.4 | 4.46 |
| Wright,Jamey | TB | 39 | 62 | 0 | 63 | 63 | 4 | 24 | 45 | 4 | 3 | 4 | .429 | 0 | 13 | 3.86 |
| Wright,Wesley | TB | 29 | 65 | 0 | 48 | 44 | 5 | 17 | 44 | 3 | 3 | 3 | .500 | 0 | 12 | 3.75 |
| Zeid,Josh | Hou | 27 | 47 | 0 | 54 | 53 | 7 | 28 | 55 | 2 | 2 | 4 | .333 | 10 | 13.8 | 4.67 |
| Ziegler,Brad | Ari | 34 | 72 | 0 | 74 | 68 | 3 | 23 | 48 | 2 | 5 | 3 | .625 | 12 | 11.3 | 2.80 |
| Zimmermann,Jordan | Was | 28 | 31 | 31 | 205 | 191 | 19 | 40 | 162 | 8 | 14 | 9 | .609 | 0 | 10.5 | 3.25 |
| Zito,Barry | SF | 36 | 19 | 19 | 109 | 112 | 13 | 43 | 74 | 3 | 5 | 7 | .417 | 0 | 13 | 4.38 |

# Career Targets

This section is designed to give probabilities on players achieving important career milestones. The method (formerly under the name of "The Favorite Toy") was developed by Bill James and takes into account a player's age and performance level in predicting the probability that he will accumulate certain career stats. A detailed explanation of how the system works can be found in the glossary.

We are thinking about renaming the section Miguel Cabrera's Career Targets since he is at or near the top of almost every list. His consecutive 44-homer seasons have pushed Cabrera up to a 13-percent chance of breaking the home run record. He is also the only player with a reasonable chance of setting the RBI and hits records, although rival MVP candidate Mike Trout has joined him with a two percent chance of setting the runs record.

Alex Rodriguez is less than 100 hits shy of 3,000 and less than 100 RBI shy of 2,000, but his potential suspension throws those eventualities into considerable doubt. Albert Pujols is eight home runs away from 500. Manny Machado leaps to second with a seven percent chance of setting the doubles record following his 51 doubles this season. And Yu Darvish has clearly separated himself from the field with a 43 percent chance of throwing a no-hitter in his career. Darvish allowed only one hit in 8-plus innings twice in 2013. His 11.2 career rate of strikeouts per nine innings will help him avoid the unlucky bounces on balls in play.

**3,000 Hits**

| % chance to reach milestone | |
|---|---|
| Jeter,Derek | done |
| Rodriguez,Alex | 98% |
| Beltre,Adrian | 81% |
| Cabrera,Miguel | 68% |
| Pujols,Albert | 44% |
| Suzuki,Ichiro | 42% |
| Cano,Robinson | 35% |
| Young,Michael | 29% |
| Rollins,Jimmy | 24% |
| Castro,Starlin | 23% |
| Butler,Billy | 21% |
| Andrus,Elvis | 20% |
| Fielder,Prince | 19% |
| Jones,Adam | 18% |
| Pedroia,Dustin | 17% |
| McCutchen,Andrew | 17% |
| Gonzalez,Adrian | 16% |
| Trout,Mike | 15% |
| Reyes,Jose | 13% |
| Markakis,Nick | 13% |
| Upton,Justin | 12% |
| Zimmerman,Ryan | 11% |
| Beltran,Carlos | 11% |
| Freeman,Freddie | 11% |
| Hosmer,Eric | 10% |
| Wright,David | 9% |
| Rios,Alex | 7% |
| Pence,Hunter | 7% |
| Altuve,Jose | 6% |
| Machado,Manny | 6% |
| Bruce,Jay | 5% |
| Gordon,Alex | 5% |
| Holliday,Matt | 4% |
| Prado,Martin | 4% |
| Votto,Joey | 2% |
| Jackson,Austin | 2% |
| Hunter,Torii | 2% |
| Phillips,Brandon | 1% |
| Escobar,Alcides | 1% |
| Murphy,Daniel | < 1% |
| Desmond,Ian | < 1% |

# Career Targets

### 762 Home Runs
% chance to break record

| | |
|---|---|
| Cabrera,Miguel | 13% |

### 2,298 RBI
% chance to break record

| | |
|---|---|
| Cabrera,Miguel | 26% |

### 2,296 Runs Scored
% chance to break record

| | |
|---|---|
| Trout,Mike | 2% |
| Cabrera,Miguel | 2% |

### 4,257 Hits
% chance to break record

| | |
|---|---|
| Cabrera,Miguel | 2% |

### 900 Home Runs
% chance to reach milestone

### 2,000 RBI
% chance to reach milestone

| | |
|---|---|
| Rodriguez,Alex | 98% |
| Cabrera,Miguel | 57% |
| Pujols,Albert | 25% |
| Fielder,Prince | 13% |
| Beltre,Adrian | 6% |
| Bruce,Jay | 5% |
| Freeman,Freddie | 4% |
| Cano,Robinson | 3% |
| Gonzalez,Adrian | < 1% |

### 6,857 Total Bases
% chance to break record

| | |
|---|---|
| Cabrera,Miguel | 15% |

### 4,000 Hits
% chance to reach milestone

| | |
|---|---|
| Cabrera,Miguel | 9% |
| Castro,Starlin | < 1% |

### 800 Home Runs
% chance to reach milestone

| | |
|---|---|
| Cabrera,Miguel | 7% |

### 600 Home Runs
% chance to reach milestone

| | |
|---|---|
| Rodriguez,Alex | done |
| Cabrera,Miguel | 56% |
| Pujols,Albert | 53% |
| Dunn,Adam | 41% |
| Davis,Chris | 13% |
| Fielder,Prince | 9% |
| Stanton,Giancarlo | 9% |
| Bruce,Jay | 8% |
| Beltre,Adrian | 8% |
| Encarnacion,Edwin | 2% |

### 793 Doubles
% chance to break record

| | |
|---|---|
| Cano,Robinson | 13% |
| Machado,Manny | 7% |
| Cabrera,Miguel | 4% |
| Pujols,Albert | 2% |
| Pedroia,Dustin | 2% |

### Most Likely No-Hitter
% chance to reach milestone

| | |
|---|---|
| Darvish,Yu | 43% |
| Scherzer,Max | 21% |
| Fernandez,Jose | 20% |
| Strasburg,Stephen | 18% |
| Hernandez,Felix | 16% |
| Kershaw,Clayton | 16% |
| Harvey,Matt | 16% |
| Cingrani,Tony | 16% |
| Sale,Chris | 16% |
| Bumgarner,Madison | 15% |

### 700 Home Runs
% chance to reach milestone

| | |
|---|---|
| Cabrera,Miguel | 25% |
| Rodriguez,Alex | 16% |
| Dunn,Adam | 6% |
| Pujols,Albert | 3% |
| Davis,Chris | 2% |

### 500 Home Runs
% chance to reach milestone

| | |
|---|---|
| Rodriguez,Alex | done |
| Pujols,Albert | 99% |
| Dunn,Adam | 95% |
| Cabrera,Miguel | 91% |
| Beltre,Adrian | 54% |
| Ortiz,David | 50% |
| Fielder,Prince | 37% |
| Soriano,Alfonso | 35% |
| Davis,Chris | 31% |
| Bruce,Jay | 25% |

### 1,000 Stolen Bases
% chance to reach milestone

# Pitchers on Course for 300 Wins

**Bill James**

Since I became a baseball fan in 1960/1961—not that I am old or anything—but since I became a baseball fan, the field of potential 300-game winners has never been weaker than it is now. It is likely that one or two pitchers now active will win 300 games, however

a) Having one or two active pitchers who will go on to win 300 games is less than the historical norm, and

b) It isn't really clear who those one or two pitchers will be. No one pitcher now active is in a particularly strong position to make a run at 300, with Verlander being the best candidate, with a 30% chance of winning 300.

In the chart below "EWL" stands for Established Win Level, and "Momentum" is a measurement of how strongly the pitcher is moving toward 300 wins. The Established Win Level is mostly based, obviously, on the number of games the pitcher has won in recent years, but that number also looks at the pitcher's innings, ERA and strikeouts, just in case the won-lost records are hinky. The "momentum" is based on

a) age

b) health record, and

c) strikeout rate.

If a pitcher is old, hasn't been consistently healthy and doesn't strike people out—Bartolo Colon—his "momentum" number will be low. If he is young, pitches 200 innings every year and strikes people out—Justin Verlander—then his "momentum" number will be high. If his momentum number is high, his chance of sustaining progress toward 300 wins is better.

Why isn't Zack Greinke on the list, you will want to know? Doesn't qualify. You qualify for the list if your career wins, plus your 2013 innings pitched, total up to at least 300. Greinke's at 284. Scherzer's at 287. Until you reach the point at which your career wins plus your innings pitched total up to 300, you're too far away from 300 to be taken seriously.

As to the chance of winning 300 games now compared to a generation ago, not a lot has changed in the last 25 years. The DH rule and the transition to the five-man starting rotation both happened more than 30 years ago, and, while bullpens continue to evolve, starting pitchers get just as many decisions (and as many wins) now as they did 25 years ago. The only things in the last 25 years that have changed the odds of getting a 300-game winner are

1) The 1990s expansions, and

2) The banning of steroids.

But the absence of strong 300-win candidates at the moment is probably just a cyclical thing, and in five years I would expect that good candidates will have re-emerged.

## Pitchers on Course For 300 Wins

| Name | 2013 Age | R/L | W | L | EWL | Momentum | Chance |
|---|---|---|---|---|---|---|---|
| Verlander, Justin | 30 | R | 137 | 77 | 14.4 | .898 | 30% |
| Sabathia, CC | 32 | L | 205 | 115 | 13.7 | .799 | 21% |
| Kershaw, Clayton | 25 | L | 77 | 46 | 15.3 | .895 | 20% |
| Hernandez, Felix | 27 | R | 110 | 86 | 12.7 | .883 | 16% |
| Lee, Cliff | 34 | L | 139 | 86 | 12.9 | .839 | 11% |
| Pettitte, Andy | 41 | L | 256 | 153 | 8.7 | .640 | 10% |
| Shields, James | 31 | R | 100 | 82 | 13.1 | .858 | 10% |
| Wainwright, Adam | 31 | R | 99 | 57 | 15.8 | .802 | 6% |
| Buehrle, Mark | 34 | L | 186 | 142 | 11.1 | .732 | 4% |
| Burnett, A.J. | 36 | R | 147 | 132 | 11.8 | .775 | 4% |
| Hamels, Cole | 29 | L | 99 | 74 | 11.2 | .825 | 3% |
| Hudson, Tim | 37 | R | 205 | 111 | 9.2 | .701 | 3% |
| Colon, Bartolo | 40 | R | 189 | 128 | 12.2 | .650 | 2% |
| Lester, Jon | 29 | L | 100 | 56 | 13.1 | .757 | 1% |
| Arroyo, Bronson | 36 | R | 138 | 127 | 11.6 | .724 | 1% |
| Santana, Ervin | 30 | R | 105 | 90 | 9.8 | .788 | 1% |
| Lohse, Kyle | 34 | R | 129 | 119 | 10.5 | .705 | <1% |
| Lackey, John | 34 | R | 138 | 107 | 8.9 | .697 | <1% |
| Dempster, Ryan | 36 | R | 132 | 133 | 9.5 | .685 | <1% |

EWL: Established Win Level

# Baseball Glossary

**% Inherited Scored**
The percentage of inherited baserunners a relief pitcher allows to score.

**% Pitches Taken**
The percentage of pitches that a batter does not swing at out of the total number of pitches thrown to him.

**1st Batter Average**
The Batting Average that a relief pitcher allows to the first batter he faces when he enters a game.

**1st Batter OBP**
The On-Base Percentage that a relief pitcher allows to the first batter he faces when he enters a game.

**1st to 3rd (Baserunning)**
"Moved" is the number of times a runner goes from 1st base to 3rd base on a SINGLE. "Chances" are the number of times a runner is on 1st base and a batter is credited with a SINGLE.

**1st to Home (Baserunning)**
"Moved" is the number of times a runner goes from 1st base to home on a DOUBLE. "Chances" are the number of times a runner is on 1st base and a batter is credited with a DOUBLE.

**2nd to Home (Baserunning)**
"Moved" is the number of times a runner goes from 2nd base to home on a SINGLE. "Chances" are the number of times a runner is on 2nd base and a batter is credited with a SINGLE.

**Active Career Batting Leaders**
A list of batting leaders among active (appearing in the most recent season) players. An active player is eligible when he meets the minimum requirements for the following categories:

1,000 At Bats—Batting Average, On-Base Percentage, Slugging Average, At Bats Per HR, At Bats Per GDP, At Bats Per RBI, Strikeout to Walk Ratio
100 Stolen Base Attempts—Stolen Base Success Percentage

**Active Career Pitching Leaders**
A list of pitching leaders among active (appearing in the most recent season) players. An active player is eligible when he meets the minimum requirements for the following categories:

750 Innings Pitched—Earned Run Average, Opponent Batting Average, all "Per 9 Innings" categories, Strikeout to Walk Ratio
250 Games Started—Complete Game Frequency
100 Decisions—Win-Loss Percentage

**AVG Allowed ScPos**
The Batting Average allowed by a pitcher while pitching with runners in scoring position.

**AVG Bases Loaded**
The Batting Average of a hitter while batting with the bases loaded.

**Base Taken**
A player is credited with a Base Taken whenever he moves up a base on a Wild Pitch, Passed Ball, Balk, Sacrifice Fly, or Defensive Indifference.

**Batting Average**
Hits divided by at bats.

**Blown Save**
When a relief pitcher enters a game in a Save Situation (see definition for Save Situation) and allows the other team to score the tying or go-ahead run.

**Bomb (Intentional Walk)**
An Intentional Walk is counted as a "Bomb" if
1) The next batter, after the IBB, does not ground into a double play, and
2) Multiple runs are scored in the inning, after the intentional walk.

**BR Gain (Baserunning)**
BR Gain (or Loss if a negative number) is the total of all the types of extra baserunning advances minus the (triple) penalty for all the BR Outs compared with what would be expected based on the MLB averages.

**BR Outs (Baserunning)**
BR Outs include the sum of Outs Advancing, Doubled Offs, and when a runner is tagged out on the bases when another runner moves up on a Wild Pitch, Passed Ball, or scores on a Sacrifice Fly.

**BS Win**
A Blown Save Win is a "win" credited to a reliever who has blown a save opportunity.

**Career Targets**
This method, once called the Favorite Toy, is a way to estimate the probability that a player will achieve a specific career goal. In this example, 3,000 hits will be used. The four components of the formula are Needed Hits, Years Remaining, Established Hit Level and Projected Remaining Hits.

Needed Hits. This is the number of Hits (or any statistic) that a player needs to reach a desired goal.

Years Remaining. This is the estimated number of years remaining in the player's career. It is determined using the player's age (on June 30th of the previous year; use 2013 when making the calculation after the 2013 season is complete). The formula is (42 - age) divided by two. This means a player who is 20 years old will have 11 remaining seasons, a player who is 25 years old will have 8.5 remaining seasons and a player who is 35 years old will have 3.5 remaining seasons. If the player is a catcher, then multiply his remaining seasons by .7. The only stipulation is that years remaining must always be greater than or equal to 1.5.

Established Hit Level. The Established Hit Level is a weighted average of the player's hits over the past three seasons. To calculate the Established Hit Level after the 2013 season is complete, add 2011 Hits, (2012 Hits multiplied by two) and (2013 Hits multiplied by three), then divide by six. If the Established Hit

Level is less than 75% of the most recent performance (2013 Hits in this case), then the Established Hit Level is equal to .75 times the most recent performance.

Projected Remaining Hits. This is calculated by multiplying Years Remaining by the Established Hit Level.

The probability of achieving the specified goal is found by dividing Projected Remaining Hits by Needed Hits, then subtracting .5. The maximum that any player has of achieving a goal is .97 raised to the power of (Need Hits / Established Hit Level). This prevents the possibility of a player reaching a goal from being higher than 100 percent, which is impossible.

**Catcher's ERA**
The ERA for a catcher is equal to the ERA of pitchers pitching while the catcher is playing behind the plate. It is calculated exactly like ERA for pitchers. Take the number of earned runs allowed while the catcher is playing, multiply it by 9 and then divide it by the total number of defensive innings that the catcher was behind the plate.

**Cheap Win**
A starting pitcher who wins the game with a game score under 50 gets credit for a cheap win. See Game Score.

**Clean Outing**
A Clean Outing is a game in which the reliever is not charged with a run (earned or otherwise) AND does not allow an inherited runner to score.

**Cleanup Slugging Average**
The Slugging Average of a batter when he bats in the cleanup spot, or fourth, in the batting order.

**Close and Late**
A situation in a game that is very similar to a Save Situation. The following requirements are necessary for a Close and Late game:

1. The game is in the seventh inning or later AND
2. The batting team is either leading by one run or tied OR
3. The tying run is on base, at bat, or on deck.

**Component ERA (ERC)**
A statistic that estimates what a pitcher's ERA should have been, based on his pitching performance. The ERC formula is calculated as follows:

1. Subtract the pitcher's Home Runs Allowed from his Hits Allowed.
2. Multiply Step 1 by 1.255.
3. Multiply his Home Runs Allowed by four.
4. Add Steps 2 and 3 together.
5. Multiply Step 4 by .89.
6. Add his Walks and Hit Batsmen.
7. Multiply Step 6 by .475.
8. Add Steps 5 and 7 together.

This yields the pitcher's total base estimate (PTB), which is:

$$PTB = 0.89 \times (1.255 \times (H - HR) + 4 \times HR) + 0.475 \times (BB + HB)$$

For those pitchers for whom there is intentional walk data, use this formula instead:

$$PTB = 0.89 \times (1.255 \times (H - HR) + 4 \times HR) + 0.56 \times (BB + HB - IBB)$$

9.Add Hits and Walks and Hit Batsmen.
10.Multiply Step 9 by PTB.
11.Divide Step 10 by Batters Facing Pitcher. If BFP data is unavailable, approximate it by multiplying Innings Pitched by 2.9, then adding Step 9.
12.Multiply Step 11 by 9.
13.Divide Step 12 by Innings Pitched.
14.Subtract .56 from Step 13.

This is the pitcher's ERC, which is:

$$\frac{(H + BB + HB) \times PTB}{BFP \times IP} \times 9 - 0.56$$

If the result after Step 13 is less than 2.24, adjust the formula as follows:

$$\frac{(H + BB + HB) \times PTB}{BFP \times IP} \times 9 \times 0.75$$

**Consecutive Days**
A count of how many times the pitcher was used after having pitched on the previous day or (in a few cases) in an earlier game on the same day.

**Defensive Runs Saved** (Runs Saved, for short) is the innovative metric introduced by John Dewan in *The Fielding Bible—Volume II* and modified in *The Fielding Bible—Volume III*. The Runs Saved value indicates how many runs a player saved or cost his team in the field compared to the average player at his position. A player of zero Runs Saved is about average; a positive number of runs saved indicates above-average defense, below-average fielders post negative Runs Saved totals. There are seven components of Runs Saved:

Plus Minus Runs Saved (all positions except Catcher)
Adjusted Earned Runs Saved (Catchers)
Stolen Base Runs Saved (Catchers, Pitchers)
Bunt Runs Saved (Corner Infielders, Pitchers, Catchers)
Double Play Runs Saved (Infielders)
Outfield Arm Runs Saved (Outfielders)
Good Play/Misplay Runs Saved (All Positions)

**Double Play %**
Successful Double Plays divided by the number of Double Play opportunities. This statistic includes both the fielder who started the play and the pivot man.

**Double Play Opportunity**
A fielder is considered to have a double play opportunity when a ground ball is hit with a runner on first base and less than 2 outs and that fielder is involved in the play. This is used to calculate Double Play % and Pivot %.

**Doubled Off**
A runner is Doubled Off when he is out for failing to get back to his base before he, or the base, is tagged after a ball hit in the air is caught.

**Early Entry**
A count of the number of times the reliever entered the game in the sixth inning or earlier.

**Earned Run Average**
The number of earned runs that a pitcher surrenders per nine innings that he pitches. It is calculated by multiplying the total earned runs allowed by nine and dividing by the total number of innings pitched.

**Easy Save**
This label is used to separate Saves by difficulty level (Easy or Tough). A Save is considered Easy if the relief pitcher enters the game, pitches one inning or less, and the first batter he faces does not at least represent the tying run.

**Fielding Percentage**
The percentage of plays a player makes in the field without making an error out of the total number of opportunities. It is calculated by adding (Putouts plus Assists) and dividing by (Putouts plus Assists plus Errors).

**Games Finished**
The relief pitcher who is in the game for each team when the game ends is credited with a Game Finished.

**Game Score**
To determine the starting pitcher's Game Score:
Start with 50.
Add 1 point for each out recorded by the starting pitcher.
Add 2 points for each inning the pitcher completes after the fourth inning.
Add 1 point for each strikeout.
Subtract 2 points for each hit allowed.
Subtract 4 points for each earned run allowed.
Subtract 2 points for an unearned run.
Subtract 1 point for each walk.

**GDP**
Grounded into Double Play

**GDP Opportunity**
This is a situation where the batter has a chance to ground into a double play. It occurs with at least a runner on first base and less than two outs.

**Ground / Fly Ratio (Grd/Fly, GB/FB)**
Calculated for both batters and pitchers. For batters, it is the number of groundballs hit divided by the number of flyballs hit. For pitchers, it is exactly the same but uses the number of groundballs and flyballs allowed. Every fair batted ball is included except for bunts and line drives.

**Hold**
A relief pitcher is given a Hold anytime he enters the game in a Save Situation (see definition for Save Situation), records one out or more, and exits the game without giving up the lead. If the pitcher finishes the game, then he will only earn credit for a Save. He cannot receive credit for both a Hold and a Save.

**Holds Adjusted Save Percentage (same as Save/Hold Percentage)**
Holds plus Saves divided by Holds plus Saves Opportunities.

**Inherited Runner**
When a relief pitcher enters the game, any runner who was on base at the time is considered an Inherited Runner.

**Isolated Power**
Slugging Average minus Batting Average.

**K/BB Ratio**
Strikeouts divided by Walks.

**Leadoff On-Base Percentage**
The On-Base Percentage of a batter when he bats leadoff, or first, in the batting order.

**Leverage Index**
Leverage is the amount of swing in the possible change in win probability, compared to the average swing in all situations. The average swing value, by definition, is indexed to 1.00.

If the score of the game is 12-0 or 14-1 the possible changes in win probability will be very close to negligible. Whether the pitcher gives up a home run or gets a double play ball doesn't really change the outcome of the game. There won't be much swing in either direction for the probability of the win. But in the late innings of a close game, the change in win probability among the various events will have rather wild swings. With a runner on first, two outs, down by one, and in the bottom of the ninth, the game can hinge on one swing of that bat. A home run and an out will both end the game, but with different outcomes for the teams involved. The Leverage Index we use (LI) was developed at the website Tangotiger.net, and compiled at the website Fangraphs.com.

**Long Outing**
A Long Outing is one in which the starting pitcher throws more than 110 pitches. Prior to 2002, we used 120 pitches as the cutoff in the Manager's Record section.

**Long Save**
A Long Save is when the pitcher credited with a save pitches more than one inning.

**Manufactured Runs**

1) A run that scores without a hit, or a run on which the only hit(s) is/are infield hits, is always scored as a Manufactured Run.
2) A run which is driven in by a home run is never scored a Manufactured Run, under any circumstance.
3) A run which is driven in by a double or a triple is scored as a Manufactured Run only if ***two*** of the four bases result from advancing on one of these four acts: a sacrifice bunt, a stolen base, a hit and run, or a bunt single.
4) Otherwise, a run is considered to be a Manufactured Run if two of the four bases do not result from the runner being forced along by a walk, a hit batsman, or a safe hit reaching the outfield.
5) A forceout or fielder's choice which does not improve the position of the base runners should not be counted as contributing toward a Manufactured Run. Advancing on a forceout or a fielder's choice DOES count toward a manufactured run, if the play is one which improves the position of the baserunners.
6) A base "gained" on a double play does not count as a contribution to a Manufactured Run. A run scored on a double play is a Manufactured Run only if two of the OTHER bases are not attributable to forced advancement.

**Not Good Outcome (Intentional Walk)**

A Not Good Outcome (NG) for an Intentional Walk occurs when one run scored in the inning after the intentional walk (and the next batter after the intentional walk did not ground into a double play).

**Offensive Winning Percentage (OWP)**

A player's Offensive Winning Percentage is the winning percentage of a hypothetical team which has an offense consisting of nine of that player, and pitching and defense which is average for the player's league. It is calculated by taking the square of RC/27 (see the definition for Runs Created per 27 Outs), dividing it by the sum of the square of RC/27 and the square of the average runs scored per game in the league.

**On-Base Percentage**

(Hits plus Walks plus Hit by Pitcher) divided by (At Bats plus Walks plus Hit by Pitcher plus Sacrifice Flies).

$$\frac{H + BB + HBP}{AB + BB + HBP + SF}$$

**Opponent Batting Average**

Hits Allowed divided by (Batters Faced minus Walks minus Hit Batsmen minus Sacrifice Hits minus Sacrifice Flies minus Catcher's Interference).

$$\frac{H}{BFP - BB - HBP - SH - SF - CI}$$

**Opposition OPS**

The OPS of the hitters facing the pitcher.

**Out Advancing**

A runner is out advancing when he is tagged out attempting to score from 2nd base on a single or from 1st base on a double, or attempting to go from 1st base to 3rd base on a single.

**PA***

Used in the denominator for the calculation of On-Base Percentage. It is calculated by subtracting (Sacrifice Hits plus Times Reached Base on Defensive Interference) from Plate Appearances (see definition for Plate Appearances).

**Park Index**

To calculate the park index for home runs in a given ballpark, we take the total home runs of both the home team and its opponents at the ballpark and compare it to the total home runs of the home team and its opponents in other games. We then divide each of those totals by the at-bats in the equivalent situations, so that if there are more at-bats in either situation the index is not skewed. The result is then multiplied by 100 to yield the familiar form.

The park indices for doubles, triples, walks, strikeouts and home runs by lefties and righties are determined like home runs above—relative to at-bats. Indices of at-bats, runs, hits, errors and infield fielding errors (E-Infield) are calculated relative to games. The three batting average indices are calculated as is, since these are already relative to at-bats.

**PCS (Pitchers' Caught Stealing)**

The number of runners officially scored as Caught Stealing where the pitcher initiated the play. The normal Caught Stealing is when a runner is out attempting to steal a base but the play was initiated by the catcher. PCS plays are often referred to as pickoffs, but differ when the runner breaks towards the next base as opposed to returning to the base he was currently on. Pickoffs occur when the pitcher throws to a base that a runner is leading from, and the runner is out attempting to return to that base. Pickoffs are not an official statistic.

**Pitches per PA**

The total number of pitches a hitter sees divided by his total Plate Appearances.

**Pivot %**

Successful Double Plays turned by pivot man divided by the number of Double Play opportunities with that pivot man involved.

**Plate Appearances**

At Bats plus Total Walks plus Hit By Pitcher plus Sacrifice Hits plus Sacrifice Flies plus Times Reached on Defensive Interference.

**Platoon Advantage %**

Platoon Advantage % is the percentage of players in the starting lineup who have the platoon advantage (i.e. bats right against a left-handed pitcher or bats left against a right-hander) against the starting pitcher; e.g. if the opposing starting pitcher is right handed and the batting team has six left-handed batters in its lineup, the platoon advantage for that game would be 67%.

**Plus/Minus System**

The Plus/Minus System is a method for evaluating defensive play on batted balls. It is made possible by a game scoring system in which each batted ball is rated for type (line drive, grounder, etc.), velocity within its type (hard, medium or soft), and location on the field. A player gets credit (a "plus" number) if he makes a play that at least one other player at his position missed during the season and he loses credit (a "minus" number") if he misses a play that at least one player made. The size of the credits are proportional to the percentage of times all players make the play. All plays for each player at his position are summed to get his total plus/minus for the season. A total of zero would be average and any other number would approximate how many plays more or less the player made than the average player at the position for the number of chances the player had to field batted balls.

**Power/Speed Number**
A single number that reflects a combination of power and speed. To achieve a high Power/Speed Number, a player must score high in both power and speed. To calculate the Power/Speed Number, multiply Home Runs by Stolen Bases by two, and divide by the sum of Home Runs and Stolen Bases.

$$\frac{2 \times HR \times SB}{HR + SB}$$

**PPO (Pitcher Pickoff)**
The number of baserunners thrown out when a pitcher throws to a base with a leading baserunner, and the runner is tagged out attempting to return to the base. PPO is not an official statistic and does not count toward Caught Stealing totals.

**Productive Out**
An out made by the batter which moves at least one baserunner up at least one base. See also Unproductive Out.

**Quality Start**
A game where the starting pitcher pitches for at least six innings and allows no more than three earned runs.

**Quality Start Percentage**
Quality Starts divided by Games Started (see the definition for Quality Start).

**Quick Hooks**
Used in the Manager's Record. For Quick Hooks and Slow Hooks a score is calculated for each game that is the sum of the number of Pitches plus 10 times the number of Runs Allowed. The bottom 25% of scores in the league are considered to be Quick Hooks.

**Range Factor**
The number of Successful Chances (Putouts plus Assists) times nine divided by the number of Defensive Innings Played. The average for a player at each position in 2013:

Second Base: 4.68
Third Base: 2.55
Shortstop: 4.27
Left Field: 1.90
Center Field: 2.57
Right Field: 2.08

**RBI %**
The percentage of all potential runs driven in by a certain hitter. Simply put, it's RBIs divided by RBI Opportunities. RBI Opportunities are a weighted total for baserunners available to be driven in by the batter. They are defined like so:

1.00 for each runner on third base with less than 2 outs, plus
.70 for each runner on third base with 2 out, plus
.70 for each runner on second base, plus
.40 for each runner on first base, plus
.10 for each bases-empty plate appearance.

**Regular Saves**
Any save which does not meet the definition either of an Easy Save or a Tough Save is a "Regular" Save.

**Run Support Per 9 IP**
The total number of runs scored by a pitcher's team while he is in the game multiplied by nine and divided by total Innings Pitched.

**Runs Created**
"Runs Created" is an estimate of the number of a team's runs which are created by each individual hitter. The Cincinnati Reds scored 820 runs last year, let us say. How many of those were created by Joey Votto? How many by Brandon Phillips? How many by Jay Bruce?

There are many different formulas for estimating runs created. . .did you want the one that involves swinging a dead cat in the cemetery under a full moon? Yeah, I don't blame you. . .worm-eaten persimmons are so hard to find in the modern world.

This is the one we use now; it is complicated enough. First, there is an "A" Factor in the formula, a "B" Factor, and a "C" factor. The "A" Factor, which represents the number of times the hitter is on base, is Hits, Plus Walks, Plus Hit Batsmen, Minus Caught Stealing, Minus Grounded Into Double Play. The "B" Factor, which represents the hitter's ability to advance other runners, is 1.125 times the player's Singles, plus 1.69 times his Doubles, plus 3.02 times his Triples, plus 3.73 times his Home Runs, plus .29 times his Walks and Hit Batsmen, not counting intentional walks, plus .492 times Sacrifice Hits, Sacrifice Flies and Stolen Bases, minus .04 times Strikeouts. The "C" Factor, which represents opportunities, is At Bats, Plus Walks, Plus Hit By Pitch, Plus Sacrifice Hits, Plus Sacrifice Flies.

Having made these initial calculations of the A, B and C factors, we then change the "A" factor to "A plus 2.4 times C".

We change the "B" factor to "B plus 3 times C".

We change the "C" factor to "9 times C".

Multiply A times B, divide by the new C ("9 times C"), and subtract .90 times by the original C.

This is our first, temporary estimate of the player's runs created. What we have done here is to ask these questions:

1. How many runs would a team probably score that consisted of eight "ordinary" type of hitters, plus this particular hitter?
2. How many of those runs would be created by the eight ordinary type of hitters?
3. What is the difference and thus, how many runs did our player create?

To estimate this, we have placed our player in the context of eight hitters with a .300 on base percentage (2.4 divided by 8) and a .375 advancement percentage (3 divided by 8). For each trip through the batting order, the eight ordinary-type hitters would produce 9/10 of a run (2.4 times 3, divided by 8). The "9" in the denominator is eight ordinary hitters plus our man. The "-.9" being subtracted at the end is the runs created by the "ordinary" hitters. In essence, we have placed the hitter in a neutral solution, measured the neutral solution without our hitter, measured it with our hitter, and then estimated the contribution of this hitter as being the difference between the two.

We're not quite done. After that, we adjust the player's runs created estimate for his performance in two "run-sensitive" situations. Suppose that a player whose overall batting average is .250 has batted 100 times with runners in scoring position, and has gone 30-for-100. That's five hits better than expected, 30 hits where we would have expected 25. His team will score an extra five runs because he has done that, and so we increase the player's runs created estimate by five runs. If the player has hit poorly with runners in scoring position, we decrease it by the shortfall in the same way.

Suppose that a player has batted 250 times with runners on base, 250 times with the bases empty, and that he has hit 20 home runs overall. We would expect him to have hit 10 with men on base, 10 with the bases empty, right?

Suppose that he didn't. Suppose that he hit 12 with the bases empty, 8 with men on base. His team would score two runs less than expected because he did this, and we would thus penalize him two runs for the shortfall.

This is our second runs created estimate the player's runs created, adjusted for his batting performance in run sensitive situations.

Suppose, however, that we figure the runs created for all of the individuals on a team, and we add them up, and it doesn't match the runs actually scored by the team? What if the formulas say that the team should have scored 800 runs, but they actually scored 820?

Then obviously, the formulas missed. We're trying to measure the runs ACTUALLY created by each hitter as best we can, in the real world, not the theoretical impact of some combination of singles, doubles, triples and walks. If the actual number is different than the estimates, we have to adjust the estimates to fit the facts. In this case—820 runs scored with only 800 runs created— we would multiply each runs created estimate by 820/800, or 1.025. Then we round it off to an integer, and that's the player's estimated runs created.

Let go of that cat, Arthur. Heck, the moon isn't full for three weeks, anyway.

**Runs Created per 27 Outs (RC/27)**
This statistic estimates the number of runs per game that a team made up of nine of the same player would score. To calculate RC/27, multiply Runs Created by league outs per team game, divide the result by outs made by the player (the sum of at bats plus sacrifice hits plus sacrifice flies plus caught stealing plus grounded into double plays, minus hits).

The formula written out is:

$$\frac{\frac{RC \times 3 \times LgIP}{2 \times LgG}}{AB - H + SH + SF + CS + GDP}$$

**Runs Saved**
See Defensive Runs Saved.

**Save Opportunities**
The sum of Saves and Blown Saves (see Save Situation).

**Save/Hold Percentage (same as Holds Adjusted Saves Percentage)**
The sum of Saves and Holds, divided by the sum of Saves, Holds, and Blown Saves.
For several years we figured "Save Percentage", which is simply Saves divided by Save Opportunities, and this stat had some currency in the game. But the Save Percentage severely discriminates against middle relievers, who have no real chance to be credited with the Save, since they will be taken out of the game and replaced by the Closer even if they throw 110 miles an hour and strike out everybody they see. Middle relievers typically have Save Percentages of zero, even if they pitch well. The Save/Hold Percentage is a much more realistic evaluation of a pitcher's success in Save situations.

**Save Percentage**
A pitcher's Saves divided by the total number of Save Situations he faces (see definition for Save Situation).

**Save Situation**
A relief pitcher is in a Save Situation when he enters the game with his team in the lead, has the opportunity to finish the game, is not the winning pitcher of record at the time, and meets any one of the three following conditions:

1. The pitcher's team is leading by no more than three runs and the pitcher has the chance to pitch for at least one inning,

   OR

2. The pitcher enters the game with the potential tying run on base, at bat, or on deck,

   OR

3. The pitcher pitches three or more effective innings regardless of the lead. The determination of a save in this situation is made by the official scorer.

It is not possible to have more than one save credited to a single team in a game.

**SB Gain (Baserunning)**
Stolen Base attempts must be successful greater than about two thirds of the time to have a positive result on the number of runs scored. SB gain is therefore the number of bases stolen minus two times the number of caught stealing (SB Gain = SB - 2CS). For example, a runner steals 30 bases and is caught stealing 7 times. His SB Gain would be 30 - 2*7 = +16. Another runner steals 10 bases and is caught stealing 6 times. His SB Gain (actually a loss) would be 10 - 2*6 = -2.

**SB Success Percentage**
Stolen Bases divided by the number of Stolen Base attempts (Stolen Bases plus Caught Stealing).

$$\frac{SB}{SB + CS}$$

**Secondary Average**
A number meant to reflect everything else except for batting average. A player will have a high Secondary Average if he hits for power, takes walks and steals bases. It is calculated with the following formula:

$$\frac{TB - H + BB + SB}{AB}$$

**Similarity Score**
A number which reflects the similarity between two different statistical lines, either for a player or for a team. A score of 1,000 means that the statistical lines are identical.

**Slow Hooks**
Used in the Manager's Record. For Quick Hooks and Slow Hooks a score is calculated for each game that is the sum of the number of Pitches plus 10 times the number of Runs Allowed. The top 25% of scores in the league are considered to be Slow Hooks.

**Slugging Average**
Total Bases divided by At Bats.

$$\frac{TB}{AB}$$

**Speed Score**
Speed score is an estimate of a player's running speed, based on six indicators of running speed found in his batting and fielding records. Those six indicators are stolen base success rate, the frequency of stolen base attempts, triples, grounding into double plays, runs scored as a percentage of times on base, and defensive position and range.

The full process of estimating Speed Scores is long and complex, and can be found on Bill James Online or by contacting Baseball Info Solutions.

**Total Bases**
Hits plus Doubles plus (2 times Triples) plus (3 times Home Runs).

$$H + 2B + (2 \times 3B) + (3 \times HR)$$

**Tough Loss**
A starting pitcher who loses the game with a game score over 50 gets credit for a tough loss. See Game Score.

**Tough Save**
This label is used to separate Saves by difficulty level (Easy or Tough). A Save is considered Tough if the relief pitcher enters the game with the tying run on base.

**Unproductive Out**
An out made by the batter which is not the third out of an inning, but comes with runners on base which fails to advance any baserunner, or results in a weaker baserunner configuration than before the out. See also Productive Out.

**Win Probability**
The probability of a team winning the game determined at any time during the game based on the score, inning, outs and base situation.

**Winning Percentage**
Wins divided by (Wins plus Losses).

ATLANTIC LEAGUE (INDEPENDENT)
BRIDGEPORT BLUEFISH
PETE ROSE WILL ~~MANAGE~~ MANAGE (1 DAY) 16 JUNE 14

# Minor League Abbreviation Key

| Abbreviation | Team | Level | League | MLB Affiliate | First Year | Last Year |
|---|---|---|---|---|---|---|
| Abrdn | Aberdeen IronBirds | A- | New York-Penn League | Baltimore Orioles | 2002 | 2013 |
| Akron | Akron Aeros | AA | Eastern League | Cleveland Indians | 1997 | 2013 |
| Albq | Albuquerque Isotopes | AAA | Pacific Coast League | Miami Marlins | 2003 | 2008 |
| Albq | Albuquerque Isotopes | AAA | Pacific Coast League | Los Angeles Dodgers | 2009 | 2013 |
| Altna | Altoona Curve | AA | Eastern League | Pittsburgh Pirates | 1999 | 2013 |
| Angels | AZL Angels | R | Arizona League | Los Angeles Angels | 2001 | 2013 |
| Ark | Arkansas Travelers | AA | Texas League | Los Angeles Angels | 2001 | 2013 |
| As | AZL Athletics | R | Arizona League | Oakland Athletics | 1988 | 2013 |
| Ashvll | Asheville Tourists | A | South Atlantic League | Colorado Rockies | 1994 | 2013 |
| Astros | GCL Astros | R | Gulf Coast League | Houston Astros | 2009 | 2013 |
| Auburn | Auburn Doubledays | A- | New York-Penn League | Toronto Blue Jays | 2001 | 2010 |
| Auburn | Auburn Doubledays | A- | New York-Penn League | Washington Nationals | 2011 | 2013 |
| Augsta | Augusta GreenJackets | A | South Atlantic League | San Francisco Giants | 2005 | 2013 |
| Augsta | Augusta Greenjackets | A | South Atlantic League | Boston Red Sox | 1999 | 2004 |
| B Jays | GCL Blue Jays | R | Gulf Coast League | Toronto Blue Jays | 2007 | 2013 |
| Batvia | Batavia Muckdogs | A- | New York-Penn League | Miami Marlins | 2013 | 2013 |
| Batvia | Batavia Muckdogs | A- | New York-Penn League | Philadelphia Phillies | 1998 | 2006 |
| Batvia | Batavia Muckdogs | A- | New York-Penn League | St Louis Cardinals | 2007 | 2012 |
| Beloit | Beloit Snappers | A | Midwest League | Oakland Athletics | 2013 | 2013 |
| Beloit | Beloit Snappers | A | Midwest League | Minnesota Twins | 2005 | 2012 |
| Beloit | Beloit Snappers | A | Midwest League | Milwaukee Brewers | 1995 | 2004 |
| BG | Bowling Green Hot Rods | A | Midwest League | Tampa Bay Rays | 2010 | 2013 |
| BG | Bowling Green Hot Rods | A | South Atlantic League | Tampa Bay Rays | 2009 | 2009 |
| Billings | Billings Mustangs | R+ | Pioneer League | Cincinnati Reds | 1974 | 2013 |
| Bklyn | Brooklyn Cyclones | A- | New York-Penn League | New York Mets | 2001 | 2013 |
| Bkrsfld | Bakersfield Blaze | A+ | California League | Cincinnati Reds | 2011 | 2013 |
| Bkrsfld | Bakersfield Blaze | A+ | California League | Tampa Bay Rays | 2001 | 2004 |
| Bkrsfld | Bakersfield Blaze | A+ | California League | Texas Rangers | 2005 | 2010 |
| Bluefld | Bluefield Orioles | R+ | Appalachian League | Baltimore Orioles | 1963 | 2010 |
| Bluefld | Bluefield Blue Jays | R+ | Appalachian League | Toronto Blue Jays | 2011 | 2013 |
| Bnghtn | Binghamton Mets | AA | Eastern League | New York Mets | 1992 | 2013 |
| Boise | Boise Hawks | A- | Northwest League | Chicago Cubs | 2001 | 2013 |
| Bowie | Bowie Baysox | AA | Eastern League | Baltimore Orioles | 1993 | 2013 |
| Bradtn | Bradenton Marauders | A+ | Florida State League | Pittsburgh Pirates | 2010 | 2013 |
| Braves | GCL Braves | R | Gulf Coast League | Atlanta Braves | 1976 | 2013 |
| Brewrs | AZL Brewers | R | Arizona League | Milwaukee Brewers | 2001 | 2013 |
| Brham | Birmingham Barons | AA | Southern League | Chicago White Sox | 1986 | 2013 |
| Bristol | Bristol White Sox | R+ | Appalachian League | Chicago White Sox | 1995 | 2013 |
| BrvdCt | Brevard County Manatees | A+ | Florida State League | Milwaukee Brewers | 2005 | 2013 |
| BrvdCt | Brevard County Manatees | A+ | Florida State League | Washington Nationals | 2002 | 2004 |
| Btl Crk | Battle Creek Yankees | A | Midwest League | New York Yankees | 2003 | 2004 |
| Buffalo | Buffalo Bisons | AAA | International League | Cleveland Indians | 1995 | 2008 |
| Buffalo | Buffalo Bisons | AAA | International League | New York Mets | 2009 | 2012 |
| Buffalo | Buffalo Bisons | AAA | International League | Toronto Blue Jays | 2013 | 2013 |
| Burlgtn | Burlington Bees | A | Midwest League | Los Angeles Angels | 2013 | 2013 |
| Burlgtn | Burlington Bees | A | Midwest League | Kansas City Royals | 2001 | 2010 |
| Burlgtn | Burlington Royals | R+ | Appalachian League | Kansas City Royals | 2007 | 2013 |
| Burlgtn | Burlington Bees | A | Midwest League | Oakland Athletics | 2011 | 2012 |
| CapeF | Cape Fear Crocs | A | South Atlantic League | Washington Nationals | 1997 | 2000 |
| Cards | GCL Cardinals | R | Gulf Coast League | St Louis Cardinals | 2007 | 2013 |
| Carlina | Carolina Mudcats | AA | Southern League | Miami Marlins | 2003 | 2008 |
| Carlina | Carolina Mudcats | AA | Southern League | Cincinnati Reds | 2009 | 2011 |
| Carlina | Carolina Mudcats | AA | Southern League | Colorado Rockies | 1999 | 2002 |
| Carlina | Carolina Mudcats | A+ | Carolina League | Cleveland Indians | 2012 | 2013 |
| Casper | Casper Rockies | R+ | Pioneer League | Colorado Rockies | 2001 | 2007 |
| Casper | Casper Ghosts | R+ | Pioneer League | Colorado Rockies | 2008 | 2011 |
| Charltt | Charlotte Knights | AAA | International League | Chicago White Sox | 1999 | 2013 |
| Charltt | Charlotte Stone Crabs | A+ | Florida State League | Tampa Bay Rays | 2009 | 2013 |
| Chatt | Chattanooga Lookouts | AA | Southern League | Cincinnati Reds | 1988 | 2008 |
| Chatt | Chattanooga Lookouts | AA | Southern League | Los Angeles Dodgers | 2009 | 2013 |
| Chiba | Chiba Lotte Marines | Jap | Pacific League | Japan | 1992 | 2013 |
| Chnchi | Chunichi Dragons | Jap | Central League | Japan | 1954 | 2013 |

# Minor League Abbreviation Key

| Abbreviation | Team | Level | League | MLB Affiliate | First Year | Last Year |
|---|---|---|---|---|---|---|
| Clinton | Clinton LumberKings | A | Midwest League | Texas Rangers | 2003 | 2008 |
| Clinton | Clinton LumberKings | A | Midwest League | Seattle Mariners | 2009 | 2013 |
| Clmbs | Columbus Catfish | A | South Atlantic League | Tampa Bay Rays | 2007 | 2008 |
| Clmbs | Columbus Catfish | A | South Atlantic League | Los Angeles Dodgers | 2004 | 2006 |
| Clmbs | Columbus Clippers | AAA | International League | New York Yankees | 1979 | 2006 |
| Clmbs | Columbus Clippers | AAA | International League | Cleveland Indians | 2009 | 2013 |
| Clrwtr | Clearwater Threshers | A+ | Florida State League | Philadelphia Phillies | 2004 | 2013 |
| ColSpr | Colorado Springs Sky Sox | AAA | Pacific Coast League | Colorado Rockies | 1993 | 2013 |
| Conn | Connecticut Tigers | A- | New York-Penn League | Detroit Tigers | 2010 | 2013 |
| Conn | Connecticut Defenders | AA | Eastern League | San Francisco Giants | 2006 | 2009 |
| CpChr | Corpus Christi Hooks | AA | Texas League | Houston Astros | 2005 | 2013 |
| CRpds | Cedar Rapids Kernels | A | Midwest League | Los Angeles Angels | 1993 | 2012 |
| CRpds | Cedar Rapids Kernels | A | Midwest League | Minnesota Twins | 2013 | 2013 |
| CtnSC | Charleston - SC RiverDogs | A | South Atlantic League | Tampa Bay Rays | 1997 | 2004 |
| CtnSC | Charleston RiverDogs | A | South Atlantic League | New York Yankees | 2005 | 2013 |
| CtnWV | Charleston - WV Alley Cats | A | South Atlantic League | Toronto Blue Jays | 2001 | 2004 |
| Cubs | AZL Cubs | R | Arizona League | Chicago Cubs | 1993 | 2013 |
| Danvle | Danville Braves | R+ | Appalachian League | Atlanta Braves | 1993 | 2013 |
| Dayton | Dayton Dragons | A | Midwest League | Cincinnati Reds | 2000 | 2013 |
| DBcks | AZL Diamondbacks | R | Arizona League | Arizona Diamondbacks | 2011 | 2013 |
| Ddgrs | GCL Dodgers | R | Gulf Coast League | Los Angeles Dodgers | 2001 | 2008 |
| Ddgrs | AZL Dodgers | R | Arizona League | Los Angeles Dodgers | 2009 | 2013 |
| Dlmrva | Delmarva Shorebirds | A | South Atlantic League | Baltimore Orioles | 1997 | 2013 |
| Dnedin | Dunedin Blue Jays | A+ | Florida State League | Toronto Blue Jays | 1990 | 2013 |
| Drham | Durham Bulls | AAA | International League | Tampa Bay Rays | 1998 | 2013 |
| Dytona | Daytona Cubs | A+ | Florida State League | Chicago Cubs | 1993 | 2013 |
| Edmtn | Edmonton Trappers | AAA | Pacific Coast League | Washington Nationals | 2003 | 2004 |
| Edmtn | Edmonton Trappers | AAA | Pacific Coast League | Minnesota Twins | 2001 | 2002 |
| Elizab | Elizabethton Twins | R+ | Appalachian League | Minnesota Twins | 1974 | 2013 |
| ElPaso | El Paso Diablos | AA | Texas League | Arizona Diamondbacks | 1999 | 2004 |
| Erie | Erie SeaWolves | AA | Eastern League | Detroit Tigers | 2001 | 2013 |
| Eugene | Eugene Emeralds | A- | Northwest League | San Diego Padres | 2001 | 2013 |
| Everett | Everett AquaSox | A- | Northwest League | Seattle Mariners | 1995 | 2013 |
| Expos | GCL Expos | R | Gulf Coast League | Washington Nationals | 1986 | 2004 |
| Fkuoka | Fukuoka Daiei Hawks | Jap | Pacific League | Japan | 1989 | 2004 |
| Fkuoka | Fukuoka SoftBank Hawks | Jap | Pacific League | Japan | 2005 | 2013 |
| Frdrck | Frederick Keys | A+ | Carolina League | Baltimore Orioles | 1990 | 2013 |
| Fresno | Fresno Grizzlies | AAA | Pacific Coast League | San Francisco Giants | 1998 | 2013 |
| Frisco | Frisco RoughRiders | AA | Texas League | Texas Rangers | 2003 | 2013 |
| FtMyrs | Fort Myers Miracle | A+ | Florida State League | Minnesota Twins | 1993 | 2013 |
| FtWyn | Fort Wayne Wizards | A | Midwest League | San Diego Padres | 1999 | 2008 |
| FtWyn | Fort Wayne TinCaps | A | Midwest League | San Diego Padres | 2009 | 2013 |
| GdJunc | Grand Junction Rockies | R+ | Pioneer League | Colorado Rockies | 2012 | 2013 |
| Giants | AZL Giants | R | Arizona League | San Francisco Giants | 2000 | 2013 |
| Gr Falls | Great Falls White Sox | R+ | Pioneer League | Chicago White Sox | 2003 | 2007 |
| Gr Falls | Great Falls Voyagers | R+ | Pioneer League | Chicago White Sox | 2008 | 2013 |
| Grnsbr | Greensboro Grasshoppers | A | South Atlantic League | Miami Marlins | 2005 | 2013 |
| Grnville | Greenville Bombers | A | South Atlantic League | Boston Red Sox | 2005 | 2005 |
| Grnville | Greenville Braves | AA | Southern League | Atlanta Braves | 1984 | 2004 |
| Grnvlle | Greenville Drive | A | South Atlantic League | Boston Red Sox | 2006 | 2013 |
| Grnvlle | Greeneville Astros | R+ | Appalachian League | Houston Astros | 2004 | 2013 |
| Gt Lks | Great Lakes Loons | A | Midwest League | Los Angeles Dodgers | 2007 | 2013 |
| Gwnntt | Gwinnett Braves | AAA | International League | Atlanta Braves | 2009 | 2013 |
| Helena | Helena Brewers | R+ | Pioneer League | Milwaukee Brewers | 2003 | 2013 |
| Hgrstn | Hagerstown Suns | A | South Atlantic League | Washington Nationals | 2007 | 2013 |
| Hgrstn | Hagerstown Suns | A | South Atlantic League | San Francisco Giants | 2001 | 2004 |
| Hi Dsrt | High Desert Mavericks | A+ | California League | Seattle Mariners | 2007 | 2013 |
| Hi Dsrt | High Desert Mavericks | A+ | California League | Milwaukee Brewers | 2001 | 2004 |
| Hkry | Hickory Crawdads | A | South Atlantic League | Pittsburgh Pirates | 1999 | 2008 |
| Hkry | Hickory Crawdads | A | South Atlantic League | Texas Rangers | 2009 | 2013 |
| Hlsboro | Hillsboro Hops | A- | Northwest League | Arizona Diamondbacks | 2013 | 2013 |
| Hnshn | Hanshin Tigers | Jap | Central League | Japan | 1961 | 2013 |
| Hntsvl | Huntsville Stars | AA | Southern League | Milwaukee Brewers | 1999 | 2013 |
| Hokado | Hokkaido Nippon-Ham Fighters | Jap | Pacific League | Japan | 2004 | 2013 |

# Minor League Abbreviation Key

| Abbreviation | Team | Level | League | MLB Affiliate | First Year | Last Year |
|---|---|---|---|---|---|---|
| Hrsbrg | Harrisburg Senators | AA | Eastern League | Washington Nationals | 1991 | 2013 |
| Hrshma | Hiroshima Toyo Carp | Jap | Central League | Japan | 1968 | 2013 |
| HudVal | Hudson Valley Renegades | A- | New York-Penn League | Tampa Bay Rays | 1997 | 2013 |
| Idaho | Idaho Falls Padres | R+ | Pioneer League | San Diego Padres | 1995 | 2003 |
| Idaho | Idaho Falls Chukars | R+ | Pioneer League | Kansas City Royals | 2004 | 2013 |
| Indns | GCL Indians | R | Gulf Coast League | Cleveland Indians | 2006 | 2008 |
| Indns | AZL Indians | R | Arizona League | Cleveland Indians | 2009 | 2013 |
| Indy | Indianapolis Indians | AAA | International League | Pittsburgh Pirates | 2005 | 2013 |
| InldEm | Inland Empire 66ers | A+ | California League | Los Angeles Dodgers | 2007 | 2010 |
| InldEm | Inland Empire 66ers | A+ | California League | Seattle Mariners | 2003 | 2006 |
| InldEm | Inland Empire 66ers | A+ | California League | Los Angeles Angels | 2011 | 2013 |
| Iowa | Iowa Cubs | AAA | Pacific Coast League | Chicago Cubs | 1982 | 2013 |
| Jacksn | Jackson Generals | AA | Southern League | Seattle Mariners | 2011 | 2013 |
| Jaxnvl | Jacksonville Suns | AA | Southern League | Los Angeles Dodgers | 2001 | 2008 |
| Jaxnvl | Jacksonville Suns | AA | Southern League | Miami Marlins | 2009 | 2013 |
| JhsCty | Johnson City Cardinals | R+ | Appalachian League | St Louis Cardinals | 1975 | 2013 |
| Jmstwn | Jamestown Jammers | A- | New York-Penn League | Pittsburgh Pirates | 2013 | 2013 |
| Jmstwn | Jamestown Jammers | A- | New York-Penn League | Miami Marlins | 2002 | 2012 |
| Jupiter | Jupiter Hammerheads | A+ | Florida State League | Miami Marlins | 2002 | 2013 |
| Kane | Kane County Cougars | A | Midwest League | Chicago Cubs | 2013 | 2013 |
| Kane | Kane County Cougars | A | Midwest League | Oakland Athletics | 2003 | 2010 |
| Kane | Kane County Cougars | A | Midwest League | Kansas City Royals | 2011 | 2012 |
| Knapol | Kannapolis Intimidators | A | South Atlantic League | Chicago White Sox | 2001 | 2013 |
| Kngspt | Kingsport Mets | R+ | Appalachian League | New York Mets | 1984 | 2013 |
| Knstn | Kinston Indians | A+ | Carolina League | Cleveland Indians | 1990 | 2011 |
| Lakwd | Lakewood BlueClaws | A | South Atlantic League | Philadelphia Phillies | 2001 | 2013 |
| Lancst | Lancaster JetHawks | A+ | California League | Houston Astros | 2009 | 2013 |
| Lancst | Lancaster Jethawks | A+ | California League | Arizona Diamondbacks | 2001 | 2006 |
| Lansng | Lansing Lugnuts | A | Midwest League | Chicago Cubs | 1999 | 2004 |
| Lk Cty | Lake County Captains | A | South Atlantic League | Cleveland Indians | 2003 | 2009 |
| Lk Cty | Lake County Captains | A | Midwest League | Cleveland Indians | 2010 | 2013 |
| Lk Els | Lake Elsinore Storm | A+ | California League | San Diego Padres | 2001 | 2013 |
| Lkland | Lakeland Flying Tigers | A+ | Florida State League | Detroit Tigers | 2007 | 2013 |
| Lkland | Lakeland Tigers | A+ | Florida State League | Detroit Tigers | 1990 | 2006 |
| Lng Isl | Long Island Ducks | IND | Atlantic League | Independent | 2000 | 2013 |
| Lnsng | Lansing Lugnuts | A | Midwest League | Toronto Blue Jays | 2005 | 2013 |
| Lowell | Lowell Spinners | A- | New York-Penn League | Boston Red Sox | 1996 | 2013 |
| LsVgs | Las Vegas 51s | AAA | Pacific Coast League | Los Angeles Dodgers | 2001 | 2008 |
| LsVgs | Las Vegas 51s | AAA | Pacific Coast League | New York Mets | 2013 | 2013 |
| LsVgs | Las Vegas 51s | AAA | Pacific Coast League | Toronto Blue Jays | 2009 | 2012 |
| Lsvlle | Louisville Bats | AAA | International League | Cincinnati Reds | 2000 | 2013 |
| LV | Lehigh Valley IronPigs | AAA | International League | Philadelphia Phillies | 2008 | 2013 |
| Lxngtn | Lexington Legends | A | South Atlantic League | Kansas City Royals | 2013 | 2013 |
| Lxngtn | Lexington Legends | A | South Atlantic League | Houston Astros | 2001 | 2012 |
| Lynbrg | Lynchburg Hillcats | A+ | Carolina League | Cincinnati Reds | 2010 | 2010 |
| Lynbrg | Lynchburg Hillcats | A+ | Carolina League | Atlanta Braves | 2011 | 2013 |
| Lynbrg | Lynchburg Hillcats | A+ | Carolina League | Pittsburgh Pirates | 1995 | 2009 |
| Macon | Macon Braves | A | South Atlantic League | Atlanta Braves | 1991 | 2002 |
| Mdest | Modesto Nuts | A+ | California League | Colorado Rockies | 2005 | 2013 |
| Mdest | Modesto As' | A+ | California League | Oakland Athletics | 1990 | 2004 |
| MdHat | Medicine Hat Blue Jays | R+ | Pioneer League | Toronto Blue Jays | 1978 | 2002 |
| MdInd | Midland RockHounds | AA | Texas League | Oakland Athletics | 1999 | 2013 |
| Memp | Memphis Redbirds | AAA | Pacific Coast League | St Louis Cardinals | 1998 | 2013 |
| Mets | GCL Mets | R | Gulf Coast League | New York Mets | 2013 | 2013 |
| Mets | GCL Mets | R | Gulf Coast League | New York Mets | 2004 | 2011 |
| MhVlly | Mahoning Valley Scrappers | A- | New York-Penn League | Cleveland Indians | 1999 | 2013 |
| Mich | Michigan Battle Cats | A | Midwest League | Houston Astros | 1999 | 2002 |
| Missi | Mississippi Braves | AA | Southern League | Atlanta Braves | 2005 | 2013 |
| Mobile | Mobile BayBears | AA | Southern League | Arizona Diamondbacks | 2007 | 2013 |
| Mont | Montgomery Biscuits | AA | Southern League | Tampa Bay Rays | 2004 | 2013 |
| Mrlns | GCL Marlins | R | Gulf Coast League | Miami Marlins | 1992 | 2013 |
| MrtlBh | Myrtle Beach Pelicans | A+ | Carolina League | Atlanta Braves | 1999 | 2010 |
| MrtlBh | Myrtle Beach Pelicans | A+ | Carolina League | Texas Rangers | 2011 | 2013 |
| Ms | AZL Mariners | R | Arizona League | Seattle Mariners | 1989 | 2013 |

# Minor League Abbreviation Key

| Abbreviation | Team | Level | League | MLB Affiliate | First Year | Last Year |
|---|---|---|---|---|---|---|
| Msoula | Missoula Osprey | R+ | Pioneer League | Arizona Diamondbacks | 1999 | 2013 |
| Nashv | Nashville Sounds | AAA | Pacific Coast League | Milwaukee Brewers | 2005 | 2013 |
| Nats | GCL Nationals | R | Gulf Coast League | Washington Nationals | 2005 | 2013 |
| NewOr | New Orleans Zephyrs | AAA | Pacific Coast League | New York Mets | 2007 | 2008 |
| NewOr | New Orleans Zephyrs | AAA | Pacific Coast League | Houston Astros | 1997 | 2004 |
| NewOr | New Orleans Zephyrs | AAA | Pacific Coast League | Miami Marlins | 2009 | 2013 |
| NHam | New Hampshire Fisher Cats | AA | Eastern League | Toronto Blue Jays | 2004 | 2013 |
| Norfolk | Norfolk Tides | AAA | International League | New York Mets | 1993 | 2006 |
| Norfolk | Norfolk Tides | AAA | International League | Baltimore Orioles | 2007 | 2013 |
| Nrwich | Norwich Navigators | AA | Eastern League | San Francisco Giants | 2003 | 2005 |
| NWArk | Northwest Arkansas Naturals | AA | Texas League | Kansas City Royals | 2008 | 2013 |
| NwBrit | New Britain Rock Cats | AA | Eastern League | Minnesota Twins | 1997 | 2013 |
| NwHav | New Haven Ravens | AA | Eastern League | Toronto Blue Jays | 2003 | 2003 |
| Ogden | Ogden Raptors | R+ | Pioneer League | Los Angeles Dodgers | 2003 | 2013 |
| OKCity | Oklahoma City RedHawks | AAA | Pacific Coast League | Texas Rangers | 2009 | 2010 |
| OKCity | Oklahoma City RedHawks | AAA | Pacific Coast League | Houston Astros | 2011 | 2013 |
| Okla | Oklahoma RedHawks | AAA | Pacific Coast League | Texas Rangers | 1998 | 2008 |
| Omha | Omaha Royals | AAA | Pacific Coast League | Kansas City Royals | 1969 | 2010 |
| Omha | Omaha Storm Chasers | AAA | Pacific Coast League | Kansas City Royals | 2011 | 2013 |
| Oneont | Oneonta Tigers | A- | New York-Penn League | Detroit Tigers | 1999 | 2009 |
| Orem | Orem Owlz | R+ | Pioneer League | Los Angeles Angels | 2005 | 2013 |
| Orioles | GCL Orioles | R | Gulf Coast League | Baltimore Orioles | 2007 | 2013 |
| Orix | Orix Buffaloes | Jap | Pacific League | Japan | 2005 | 2013 |
| Osaka | Osaka Kintetsu Buffaloes | Jap | Pacific League | Japan | 1999 | 2004 |
| Padres | AZL Padres | R | Arizona League | San Diego Padres | 2004 | 2013 |
| Peoria | Peoria Chiefs | A | Midwest League | St Louis Cardinals | 1995 | 2004 |
| Peoria | Peoria Chiefs | A | Midwest League | St Louis Cardinals | 2013 | 2013 |
| Peoria | Peoria Chiefs | A | Midwest League | Chicago Cubs | 2005 | 2012 |
| Phillies | GCL Phillies | R | Gulf Coast League | Philadelphia Phillies | 1999 | 2013 |
| Pirates | GCL Pirates | R | Gulf Coast League | Pittsburgh Pirates | 1968 | 2013 |
| PlmBh | Palm Beach Cardinals | A+ | Florida State League | St Louis Cardinals | 2003 | 2013 |
| Pnscla | Pensacola Blue Wahoos | AA | Southern League | Cincinnati Reds | 2012 | 2013 |
| Portlnd | Portland Sea Dogs | AA | Eastern League | Boston Red Sox | 2003 | 2013 |
| Portlnd | Portland Beavers | AAA | Pacific Coast League | San Diego Padres | 2001 | 2010 |
| Princtn | Princeton Devil Rays | R+ | Appalachian League | Tampa Bay Rays | 1997 | 2007 |
| Princtn | Princeton Rays | R+ | Appalachian League | Tampa Bay Rays | 2008 | 2013 |
| Provo | Provo Angels | R+ | Pioneer League | Los Angeles Angels | 2001 | 2004 |
| Ptomc | Potomac Cannons | A+ | Carolina League | Cincinnati Reds | 2003 | 2004 |
| Ptomc | Potomac Nationals | A+ | Carolina League | Washington Nationals | 2005 | 2013 |
| Pulaski | Pulaski Blue Jays | R+ | Appalachian League | Toronto Blue Jays | 2003 | 2006 |
| Pulaski | Pulaski Mariners | R+ | Appalachian League | Seattle Mariners | 2008 | 2013 |
| Pwtckt | Pawtucket Red Sox | AAA | International League | Boston Red Sox | 1977 | 2013 |
| QuadC | Quad City Swing | A | Midwest League | St Louis Cardinals | 2005 | 2007 |
| QuadC | Quad Cities River Bandits | A | Midwest League | St Louis Cardinals | 2008 | 2012 |
| QuadC | Quad Cities River Bandits | A | Midwest League | Houston Astros | 2013 | 2013 |
| QuadC | Quad City Swing | A | Midwest League | Minnesota Twins | 2004 | 2004 |
| Rays | GCL Rays | R | Gulf Coast League | Tampa Bay Rays | 2009 | 2013 |
| Rchmd | Richmond Flying Squirrels | AA | Eastern League | San Francisco Giants | 2010 | 2013 |
| Rchmd | Richmond Braves | AAA | International League | Atlanta Braves | 1966 | 2008 |
| RCuca | Rancho Cucamonga Quakes | A+ | California League | Los Angeles Angels | 2001 | 2010 |
| RCuca | Rancho Cucamonga Quakes | A+ | California League | Los Angeles Dodgers | 2011 | 2013 |
| Rdng | Reading Phillies | AA | Eastern League | Philadelphia Phillies | 1967 | 2013 |
| RdRck | Round Rock Express | AAA | Pacific Coast League | Houston Astros | 2005 | 2010 |
| RdRck | Round Rock Express | AA | Texas League | Houston Astros | 2000 | 2004 |
| RdRck | Round Rock Express | AAA | Pacific Coast League | Texas Rangers | 2011 | 2013 |
| Reds | GCL Reds | R | Gulf Coast League | Cincinnati Reds | 1999 | 2009 |
| Reds | AZL Reds | R | Arizona League | Cincinnati Reds | 2010 | 2013 |
| RedSx | GCL Red Sox | R | Gulf Coast League | Boston Red Sox | 1989 | 2013 |
| Reno | Reno Aces | AAA | Pacific Coast League | Arizona Diamondbacks | 2009 | 2013 |
| Rngrs | AZL Rangers | R | Arizona League | Texas Rangers | 2003 | 2013 |
| Roch | Rochester Red Wings | AAA | International League | Minnesota Twins | 2003 | 2013 |
| Rome | Rome Braves | A | South Atlantic League | Atlanta Braves | 2003 | 2013 |
| Royals | AZL Royals | R | Arizona League | Kansas City Royals | 2004 | 2013 |
| S-WB | Scranton/Wikes-Barre Yankees | AAA | International League | New York Yankees | 2007 | 2012 |

# Minor League Abbreviation Key

| Abbreviation | Team | Level | League | MLB Affiliate | First Year | Last Year |
|---|---|---|---|---|---|---|
| S-WB | Scranton/Wikes-Barre Red Barons | AAA | International League | Philadelphia Phillies | 1989 | 2006 |
| S-WB | Scranton/Wikes-Barre RailRiders | AAA | International League | New York Yankees | 2013 | 2013 |
| Salem | Salem Red Sox | A+ | Carolina League | Boston Red Sox | 2009 | 2013 |
| Salem | Salem Avalanche | A+ | Carolina League | Houston Astros | 2003 | 2008 |
| Salt Lk | Salt Lake Stingers | AAA | Pacific Coast League | Los Angeles Angels | 2001 | 2005 |
| Salt Lk | Salt Lake Bees | AAA | Pacific Coast League | Los Angeles Angels | 2006 | 2013 |
| Savann | Savannah Sand Gnats | A | South Atlantic League | New York Mets | 2007 | 2013 |
| Savann | Savannah Sand Gnats | A | South Atlantic League | Washington Nationals | 2003 | 2006 |
| Sbend | South Bend Silver Hawks | A | Midwest League | Arizona Diamondbacks | 1997 | 2013 |
| Scrmto | Sacramento River Cats | AAA | Pacific Coast League | Oakland Athletics | 2000 | 2013 |
| Seibu | Seibu Lions | Jap | Pacific League | Japan | 1979 | 2007 |
| SlmKzr | Salem-Keizer Volcanoes | A- | Northwest League | San Francisco Giants | 1997 | 2013 |
| SnAnt | San Antonio Missions | AA | Texas League | San Diego Padres | 2007 | 2013 |
| SnAnt | San Antonio Missions | AA | Texas League | Seattle Mariners | 2006 | 2006 |
| SnJos | San Jose Giants | A+ | California League | San Francisco Giants | 1990 | 2013 |
| Spkane | Spokane Indians | A- | Northwest League | Texas Rangers | 2003 | 2013 |
| Sprgfld | Springfield Cardinals | AA | Texas League | St Louis Cardinals | 2005 | 2013 |
| Srsota | Sarasota Red Sox | A+ | Florida State League | Boston Red Sox | 1995 | 2004 |
| Srsota | Sarasota Reds | A+ | Florida State League | Cincinnati Reds | 2005 | 2009 |
| Stcktn | Stockton Ports | A+ | California League | Texas Rangers | 2003 | 2004 |
| Stcktn | Stockton Ports | A+ | California League | Oakland Athletics | 2005 | 2013 |
| StCol | State College Spikes | A- | New York-Penn League | St Louis Cardinals | 2013 | 2013 |
| StCol | State College Spikes | A- | New York-Penn League | Pittsburgh Pirates | 2007 | 2012 |
| StIsInd | Staten Island Yankees | A- | New York-Penn League | New York Yankees | 1999 | 2013 |
| StLuci | St. Lucie Mets | A+ | Florida State League | New York Mets | 1990 | 2013 |
| SWMch | Southwest Michigan Devil Rays | A | Midwest League | Tampa Bay Rays | 2005 | 2006 |
| Syrcse | Syracuse SkyChiefs | AAA | International League | Toronto Blue Jays | 1978 | 2006 |
| Syrcse | Syracuse Chiefs | AAA | International League | Toronto Blue Jays | 2007 | 2008 |
| Syrcse | Syracuse Chiefs | AAA | International League | Washington Nationals | 2009 | 2013 |
| Tacom | Tacoma Rainiers | AAA | Pacific Coast League | Seattle Mariners | 1995 | 2013 |
| Tampa | Tampa Yankees | A+ | Florida State League | New York Yankees | 1994 | 2013 |
| Tenn | Tennessee Smokies | AA | Southern League | Chicago Cubs | 2007 | 2013 |
| Tigers | GCL Tigers | R | Gulf Coast League | Detroit Tigers | 1995 | 2013 |
| Tohoku | Tohoku Rakuten Golden Eagles | Jap | Pacific League | Japan | 2005 | 2013 |
| Toledo | Toledo Mud Hens | AAA | International League | Detroit Tigers | 1987 | 2013 |
| TriCity | Tri-City Dust Devils | A- | Northwest League | Colorado Rockies | 2001 | 2013 |
| TriCity | Tri-City ValleyCats | A- | New York-Penn League | Houston Astros | 2002 | 2013 |
| Trntn | Trenton Thunder | AA | Eastern League | Boston Red Sox | 1995 | 2002 |
| Trntn | Trenton Thunder | AA | Eastern League | New York Yankees | 2003 | 2013 |
| Tucsn | Tucson Sidewinders | AAA | Pacific Coast League | Arizona Diamondbacks | 1998 | 2008 |
| Tucsn | Tucson Padres | AAA | Pacific Coast League | San Diego Padres | 2011 | 2013 |
| Tulsa | Tulsa Drillers | AA | Texas League | Colorado Rockies | 2003 | 2013 |
| Twins | GCL Twins | R | Gulf Coast League | Minnesota Twins | 1989 | 2013 |
| Vancvr | Vancouver Canadians | A- | Northwest League | Oakland Athletics | 1999 | 2010 |
| Vancvr | Vancouver Canadians | A- | Northwest League | Toronto Blue Jays | 2011 | 2013 |
| VeroB | Vero Beach Dodgers | A+ | Florida State League | Los Angeles Dodgers | 1990 | 2006 |
| VeroB | Vero Beach Devil Rays | A+ | Florida State League | Tampa Bay Rays | 2007 | 2008 |
| Visalia | Visalia Oaks | A+ | California League | Colorado Rockies | 2003 | 2004 |
| Visalia | Visalia Rawhide | A+ | California League | Arizona Diamondbacks | 2007 | 2013 |
| Vrmnt | Vermont Expos | A- | New York-Penn League | Washington Nationals | 1994 | 2005 |
| Vrmnt | Vermont Lake Monsters | A- | New York-Penn League | Washington Nationals | 2006 | 2010 |
| Vrmnt | Vermont Lake Monsters | A- | New York-Penn League | Oakland Athletics | 2011 | 2013 |
| Wilmg | Wilmington Blue Rocks | A+ | Carolina League | Kansas City Royals | 2007 | 2013 |
| WinSa | Winston-Salem Warthogs | A+ | Carolina League | Chicago White Sox | 1997 | 2008 |
| WinSa | Winston-Salem Dash | A+ | Carolina League | Chicago White Sox | 2009 | 2013 |
| Wisc | Wisconsin Timber Rattlers | A | Midwest League | Seattle Mariners | 1995 | 2008 |
| Wisc | Wisconsin Timber Rattlers | A | Midwest League | Milwaukee Brewers | 2009 | 2013 |
| WMich | West Michigan Whitecaps | A | Midwest League | Detroit Tigers | 1997 | 2013 |
| Wmspt | Williamsport Crosscutters | A- | New York-Penn League | Pittsburgh Pirates | 1999 | 2006 |
| Wmspt | Williamsport Crosscutters | A- | New York-Penn League | Philadelphia Phillies | 2007 | 2013 |
| Wrcstr | Worcester Tornadoes | IND | Can-Am League | Independent | 2000 | 2012 |
| WTenn | West Tenn Diamond Jaxx | AA | Southern League | Seattle Mariners | 2007 | 2010 |
| WTenn | West Tenn Diamond Jaxx | AA | Southern League | Chicago Cubs | 1998 | 2006 |
| WV | West Virginia Power | A | South Atlantic League | Milwaukee Brewers | 2005 | 2008 |

# Minor League Abbreviation Key

| Abbreviation | Team | Level | League | MLB Affiliate | First Year | Last Year |
|---|---|---|---|---|---|---|
| WV | West Virginia Power | A | South Atlantic League | Pittsburgh Pirates | 2009 | 2013 |
| Yakima | Yakima Bears | A- | Northwest League | Arizona Diamondbacks | 2001 | 2012 |
| Yanks | GCL Yankees | R | Gulf Coast League | New York Yankees | 1984 | 2013 |
| Yanks | GCL Yankees2 | R | Gulf Coast League | New York Yankees | 2013 | 2013 |
| Ykhma | Yokohama BayStars | Jap | Central League | Japan | 1993 | 2011 |
| Ykult | Yakult Swallows | Jap | Central League | Japan | 1974 | 2005 |
| Ykult | Tokyo Yakult Swallows | Jap | Central League | Japan | 2006 | 2013 |
| Ymuri | Yomiuri Giants | Jap | Central League | Japan | 1947 | 2013 |

# Baseball Info Solutions

Baseball Info Solutions has been supplying top notch, timely, and in-depth baseball data and analytics to its customers since 2002. BIS collects a statistical snapshot of every important moment of every Major League Baseball game with the most advanced technology, resulting in a database that includes traditional data, pitch-by-pitch data, and defensive positioning data. The company also has the highest quality pitch charting data available anywhere, including pitch type, location, and velocity.

BIS provides data and/or analysis to about half of the 30 Major League Baseball teams as well as media companies, websites, fantasy services, game companies, and private individuals. No request is too big or too small, and every inquiry is answered in a timely and personal manner. We provide the personal touch to meet any customized needs.

Baseball Info Solutions continues to break new ground in data collection and analysis, providing its clients with the latest and greatest baseball information available anywhere. Over the past decade, BIS has specialized in innovative defensive data and analytics that have shifted the landscape of the sabermetric industry.

John Dewan, the principal owner and president of BIS, has been on the cutting edge of baseball analysis for over 25 years. His experience goes all the way back to his days as Executive Director of Project Scoresheet, the Bill James-led effort that pioneered the new wave of baseball statistics that are now common terminology.

The rest of the BIS team includes former scouts and collegiate baseball players as well as research, programming and database management experts. Additionally, BIS recruits and trains the best video scouting talent from across the country, and BIS internships have been the starting point for many successful baseball operations executives.

For data inquiries, job openings, or other information, please contact BIS at:

Baseball Info Solutions
41 S. 2nd Street
Coplay, PA 18037
610-261-2370
www.baseballinfosolutions.com

# Acknowledgments

With only a couple of weeks between the end of the regular season and the submission deadline in order to get you the book by November 1, The Bill James Handbook requires a lot of work by a lot of very dedicated people. We want to take a moment to thank everyone involved.

Most of all, thank you to Bill James. Of course Bill is the genesis of the Handbook, which is a continuation of many of the ideas that date back to his first Baseball Abstract in 1977. Bill remains intimately involved in the production of the Handbook, from the design of new sections like the Hitter Analysis and Scouting Report to minutia like the projected statistics for players most baseball fans have never heard of.

John Dewan is the President of Baseball Info Solutions, and he and his wife Sue Dewan are its majority owners. John never fails to work from cover to cover of the Handbook despite the numerous demands on his time.

Jeff Spoljaric coordinated many of the pieces that went into this year's Handbook. In addition to this role, Jeff serves as Vice President of Information Technology. He, Patrick Coyle, and Greg Thomas make the rest of our work possible in the IT department. Patrick took over Handbook production responsibilities from Andrew Gibson, who was busy helping the Pirates to their first postseason berth in two decades. Patrick handled the job gracefully despite its many challenges.

Jon Vrecsics, Handbook Stat-Checker Extraordinaire, and Jim Swavely handle the minor league side of our operations while Dan Casey, Mike Piekarski, Todd Radcliffe, and Andy Johnson coordinate the major league side. In addition to leading our small army of video scouts, they are the guys who double and triple-check every last number in the Handbook to ensure its accuracy. Other sources may disagree with a handful of our published numbers, but our operations team has put in the time to conclude that our numbers are the correct ones.

Ben Jedlovec is the Vice President of Product Development & Sales, which includes oversight of the Research & Development department of Joe Rosales and Scott Spratt. Glenn DuPaul and Dan Lependorf provided valuable contributions as R&D Interns in the past year. The department analyzes all of the innovative data BIS collects and uses it to build the next generation of cutting-edge research.

Then Ben and Jim Capuano take that a step further. As our Director of Business Development, Jim forges partnerships to bring our latest insights and analysis to our clients and the public.

Our video scouts were tremendous yet again this season. They included Josh Babbitt, Isaac Braun, Nick Brugh, Alex Burritt, David Creatura, Andrew Flores, Matt Gutkes, Ben Horrow, Travis Ice, Spencer Jackman, Doug Kopf, Tim Kwilos, Rod Larson, Josh Lipman, Eric Longenhagen, Mark Nader, Dylan Nagy, Eric Nehs, Nick Siefken, Lee Tackett, and Ken Woolums.

Our partners at ACTA Publications include President and Co-Publisher Greg Pierce, as well as Amanda Modelski, Tom Wright, Donna Ryding, Mary Eggert, and Isz.

Thank you to our friends in the baseball industry who have helped us over the years. They include Greg Ambrosius, Andy Andres, David Appelman, Jim Callis, Dave Cameron, Sean Forman, Peter Gammons, Vince Genarro, Jason Grey, Eric Karabell, Brian Kenny, Peter Kreutzer, Michael Lehrer, Ed Macedo, Gene McCaffrey, Bob Meyerhoff, Mike Murphy, Rob Neyer, Alex Patton, Mike Phillips, David Pinto, Joe Posnanski, Adam Richman, Hal Richman, Peter Schoenke, Ron Shandler, Joe Sheehan, John Sickels, Mark Simon, Dave Studenmund, Tom Tango, Mark Watson, Rick Wilton, and Don Zminda. Thank you Steve Ruskowski for your assistance in stat-checking.

Thanks to everyone we haven't had space to mention by name. And, finally, thank you for reading the book we all put so much time into.